P9-DIF-753

The College Blue Book®

34th Edition

Tabular Data

MACMILLAN REFERENCE USA
An imprint of Thomson Gale, a part of The Thomson Corporation

THOMSON
GALE™

Detroit • New York • San Francisco • New Haven, Conn. • Waterville, Maine • London

The College Blue Book, 34th Edition
Volume 2

Project Editors
Bohdan Romaniuk, Verne Thompson

Editorial
Jessica Boguslawski, Kim Hunt-Lowrance, Amanda Sams, Kristy Swartout

Editorial Support Services
Wayne Fong

Imaging and Multimedia
Randy Bassett, Lezlie Light, Mike Logusz, Dan Newell

Rights and Acquisitions
Dean Dauphinais

Composition and Electronic Prepress
Gary Leach, Evi Seoud

Manufacturing
Rhonda Dover

Product Manager
Jennifer F. Bernardelli

For more information, contact
Thomson Gale
27500 Drake Rd.
Farmington Hills, MI 48331-3535
Or you can visit our Internet site at
http://www.gale.com

ISBN-13:
978-0-02-866006-6 (set)
978-0-02-866008-0 (vol. 2)

ISBN-10:
0-02-866006-4 (set)
0-02-866008-0 (vol. 2)

ISSN 1082-7056

This book is also available as an e-book
ISBN 13: 978-0-02-866084-4 (set) ISBN 10: 0-02-866084-6 (set)
Contact your Thomson Gale sales representative for ordering information.

Printed in the United States of America
10 9 8 7 6 5 4 3 2 1

Contents

The College Blue Book has been a standard, professional reference on higher education since it was first published in 1923. New features have been added during the intervening years to keep pace with the changing needs for information about our educational facilities. The information, especially in the areas of tuition, room and board, enrollment figures, library holdings, is constantly changing. It is difficult to maintain up-to-date figures in these areas, as many schools change tuition and related costs on an ongoing basis. We therefore urge our readers to check directly with the schools for the most current cost information.

Contents of Each Volume

Volume 1: Narrative Descriptions

More than 4,100 colleges in the United States and Canada are fully described. Entrance requirements are detailed and campus facilities and costs are described. A map of each U.S. state and Canadian province is included and each college has a grid index fore easy location. Web sites are also listed.

Volume 2: Tabular Data

Colleges are listed alphabetically by state or province. Information about costs, accreditation, enrollment figures, faculty, and names of the chief administrative officers are given for each school.

Volume 3: Degrees Offered by College and Subject

In Part I, the name of each college is listed alphabetically by state or province, with a list of the subject areas for which degrees are offered. Part II includes an alphabetical listing of subject areas for which degrees are granted by one or more institutions of higher education.

Volume 4: Occupational Education

More than 5,600 schools in the United States that provide occupational or technical training are fully described, offering such information as tuition costs, enrollment figures, and entrance requirements. Two indexes are provided: an alphabetical listing of schools in the "Index of Occupational Education Schools," in addition to the "Curricula and Areas of Instruction" index.

Volume 5: Scholarships, Fellowships, Grants, and Loans

This volume provides a listing of almost 3,500 different sources of financial aid for students wishing to further their education. Split alphabetically into eight broad subject areas (each containing several more specialized concentrations of study), as well as a general section, each listing provides basic information about a specific award, including eligibility requirements, amount of award, and application deadlines.

Volume 6: Distance Learning Programs

Responding to this rapidly growing trend in post-secondary education, this volume features comprehensive profiles of nearly 900 institutions offering distance learning programs within the United States and Canada, providing both basic information as well as in-depth descriptions of certain institutions.

For More Information

We are always open to suggestions and recommendations for improvement of *The College Blue Book* from our readers and from the educational professions. Please write or call:

Editor, *The College Blue Book*

Macmillan Reference USA

27500 Drake Rd.

Farmington Hills, MI 48331-3535

Phone: (248)699-4253

Toll-free: 800-347-GALE

Fax: (248)699-8075

Email: blue.book@thomson.com

Web site: www.gale.com

The decision to continue education beyond high school years, the selection of a collegiate institution, and the area of study to be pursued are some of the essential experiences necessary for students to determine their futures. Alternatives of choice institutions, work selection, job opportunities, professional training, or even discontinuing any further education are all selective decisions open to the students.

Nearly all students today have opportunities to continue education beyond high school. There are more schools accepting wider ranges of student ability and interest than ever before. This means more effort, more planning, and more personal study in making the college choice.

Self Appraisal

The best place to begin is with oneself. An appraisal with objective, honest answers is necessary. What are the personal potentials as a student? Where has the best performance been? What are the probabilities for improvement? What are the reasons for really wanting to go to college; is it for intellectual development, vocational preparation, or simply to satisfy a desire for status? What are the personal ideas of college? What is expected from the college experience? Have career plans been made? Where are the academic abilities? What subjects are preferred? What is the quality of performance in the preferred areas of study? What is the overall grade average? What is the class rank in high school? In what subject areas is there the greatest interest? What is the quality of work in these areas? Are interests and performance generally consistent? Are the expressed and recorded interests truly and accurately reflecting the inward wishes? What was liked best about the high school experience? Has the college preparatory program been followed in high school? What were the social and cultural experiences during high school years that were most meaningful? What was considered, if anything, to be lacking?

Well-thought-out answers to these and similar questions are helpful. Discussions of such topics with counselors, parents, and teachers increases the probability of success in college selection, attendance, and completion.

The counselor today is an extremely valued resource person available to assist the student. When an effective working team of counselor-student-parent actually exists, the probabilities for the student making selective choices that prove to be the "right" ones are unquestionably the greatest. The better the student and the counselor know one another, the more effective the guidance and counseling program will be. For this to occur, the opportunity for face-to-face student-counselor discussion needs to start in the latter elementary school years and continue through high school and college.

College Appraisals

Research is continuing in the areas of college admissions and student success. The identification and understanding of causes of success and failure need professional study. However, one thing is apparent: the more careful the preparations and planning by the student, the better the chances of college admission and success.

Systemized planning should begin early. The more self-understanding and knowledge about available colleges one has, the better one can plan with corresponding success. Certainly, early in the high school career, students should be reviewing detailed information on colleges and universities with the counselor, noting academic requirements such as scholastic performance, course requirements, costs and other particular qualities of individual collegiate institutions. There is no single one-and- only college for the student. Colleges have personalities just as the students do. There are always several colleges with academic and social climates compatible and acceptable to each student.

Entrance requirements, courses available, costs, size of student body, academic pressure, special programs, geographical location, and specialty schools are some of the considerations of every student in appraising available colleges.

The College Blue Book is dedicated to providing detailed information regarding collegiate institutions throughout the United States and Canada. Students and counselors should browse through *The College Blue Book* and become familiar with the colleges of our country and neighboring Canada. As interest sharpens and narrows, a more selective and in-depth study of institutions should be made.

Where feasible, students should plan visits to college campuses. Campus visiting may begin during the summer between the sophomore and junior years of high school. The best time to be on a college campus, however, is during the regular term with a carefully planned visit in the spring semester of the junior year. Preparatory plans should be made with the high school counselor, reviewing discussions of earlier personal conferences. Advance arrangements should be made with admission officers of the colleges the student expects to visit. The admission officer's name and telephone number will be found in most instances in *The College Blue Book* volume entitled *Tabular Data*. The admissions officer in many cases will want to know whether the student has actually applied for admission and probably the areas the student may plan to major in or other special interests the student has in the particular institution. The student should have prepared a summary of personal data. If possible, high school students should also talk to students of the colleges they wish to attend.

The growth of community colleges has opened up another avenue for students, especially those of limited finances or those who have not decided on their ultimate educational goals. Students will find many of these community colleges offer an excellent opportunity to gain a solid college background. Then one can choose a four-year institution to complete an undergraduate degree.

Any regular high school graduate can find a school that will accept him. Many students need to be encouraged to consider the smaller, private and public colleges of good standing.

Students entering professional training such as engineering or law might consider small schools that have cooperative programs with major universities. A knowledgeable student, through planning and guidance, can avoid unnecessary disappointment. A college career can be quite beneficial to the student who spends three to four years on a small campus and one, two, or three additional years of graduate work on another, larger campus.

Costs

Costs are continuing to rise. Tuition charges as listed herein should be only be used as a guide. It would be wise to check with the institution of interest to be sure of having the most up-to- date information available.

Should the need for financial aid be a factor in selecting a college, a college-bound student should be aware that the best single source of financial assistance and information is the financial aid officer or admission director at the college. It is most important for the student to contact the finance office as early as possible during the student's senior year in high school. A principal source of financial assistance is the major federal undergraduate aid programs. Applications can be obtained from the college. Most colleges and universities also offer financial assistance in several forms including academic and general scholarships, grants-in-aid, student loans, and part-time work. For more information, see volume 5 of *The College Blue Book*: *Scholarships, Fellowships, Grants, and Loans.*

Two-Year Colleges

Two-year colleges, referred to as junior colleges or community colleges, both public and private, offer programs that prepare students for technical and semiprofessional careers in business and technology fields, and for transfer to senior colleges. There are hundreds of two-year colleges providing comprehensive programs meeting the lower division requirements of virtually all four-year colleges and universities.

There are decided advantages for some students to enroll in a two-year college. Some of these are: less cost, home residence, availability of highly specialized programs, opportunity for the student to mature, a smaller student body, and generally a closer relationship to the faculty. The development of two-year colleges across the nation is one of the most vital forces in education today. The two-year college is neither an extension of high school, nor a little senior college. It has its own identity, sphere of service, and contribution to make to American education. The comprehensive community college is considered one of the best means of accommodating the demands of higher education, embracing the increasing variety of abilities of students graduating from high schools, preparing students in the technological and semiprofessional occupations, and all in an economical manner.

One very important caution needs to be heeded by students enrolling in two-year colleges who are planning to continue their work through a bachelor's program. Students expecting to transfer should very carefully study the requirements of the institution they ultimately plan to attend. In conference with the junior college counselor, a careful review of the planned program should be made to be sure the contemplated courses at the junior college will satisfy the requirements of the senior institution. Students who depart from prescribed courses stated by the senior institution or fail in any of these courses may experience difficulty with admission or normal progress toward the bachelor degree.

Liberal Arts Colleges

The liberal arts colleges offer four years of college and award the Bachelor of Arts and the Bachelor of Science degrees. The curriculum for the first two years is usually broad with an emphasis in the humanities, natural sciences, and cultural history of our society. The last two years may provide a concentration of specific programs such as premedicine or pre-law leading to graduate professional training.

Students considering professional training at the graduate level should keep this in mind as they plan their work at the liberal arts college. Graduate schools in some cases have strict preparatory requirements. Familiarity with these requirements can greatly assist in making the transfer to graduate level without loss of credit or time.

Specialized Institutions

Four-year institutions of technology are examples of the more specialized schools where concentration in a specialty is intensively pursued throughout the college career. Most of these institutions are quite selective in admission practice and may require more high school mathematics and science than most other schools for entrance. These programs lead to engineering degrees in many fields emphasizing technology and science. Recently there has been a broadening of the program of the first two years, but, in general, such a program is not nearly as comprehensive and varied as the liberal arts college. The demand for engineers and scientists with specially developed skills creates great competition for entrance into schools of technology.

There are other specialized institutions such as conservatories of music, seminaries, medical and law schools, institutions specializing in teacher training, or schools of the fine arts, most of which require specialized preparation for entrance.

Universities

The university is generally composed of a number of degree- granting colleges and schools where both bachelor and graduate degrees are grouped under one administrative head. Bachelor degrees at the university may be earned in liberal arts or one of the professions such as engineering or the physical sciences. The university, to some extent, combines what is available at the liberal arts college with the specialized institution. Complete professional training in such areas as law, medicine, and science is available on the university campus.

As a rule, universities have much larger student bodies than colleges. In order to meet the demand, most state universities have established several campuses. Many state universities are very selective in admitting students. This is particularly true for a student who is applying for admission from out-of-state.

Entrance Examinations

There are more applicants than there is room for students on many campuses. As this demand increases, colleges and universities attempt to identify those applicants who are most likely to succeed on their campuses. A quality scholastic record has more influence on acceptance and admission than any other single factor. High school grades predict with better accuracy than any other single measurement what college grades and success will be. The more selective colleges and universities may choose students who come out highest on quantitative criteria, that is, high school scholastic averages combined with test scores. Some institutions have far more applicants (whose scholastic records and test scores are of a maximum quality) than they can accept. In such cases, applicants are sometimes screened and accepted on the basis of categories according to residence in the state or region, special talents, minority groups, or relationship to alumni. Such procedures are used in an attempt to influence the makeup of the enrollment.

When investigating several schools, one of the most accurate ways for evaluation of an institution is to consider test scores and the high school rank order of the students actually on campus. In many instances this is more informative than the announced admission policies.

College testing is required by many colleges and universities for entering students; some have developed their own tests and over the years have established norms for such tests. Most institutions requiring tests for entrance, however, now use either the test of the American College Testing Program (ACT) or the examinations of the College Entrance Examination Board. The College Entrance Examination Board offers the Preliminary Scholastic Assessment Test/National Merit Scholarship Qualifying Test (PSAT/ NMSQT), the Scholastic Assessment Test I: Reasoning Test (Verbal and Math), and the SAT II: Subject Tests.

Coaching, tutoring, drill, and memorization of facts can do little to improve the scores of the standardized examinations. It is recommended that students not invest time and money in cramming in hopes of improving test scores. Students can do their best preparation in general reading, completing their school assignments, and arriving on the proper day of the test rested and refreshed.

American College Testing Assessment (ACT)

The ACT Assessment provided by the American College Testing Program covers four subject areas: English, mathematics, reading, and science reasoning. The ACT test is scored on a range of 1 to 36. The ACT is administered at various test sites in the United States and other countries on specified dates throughout the year. Many colleges and universities recommend that prospective students take the examination early in the senior year.

The tests provide estimates of the students' current level of educational development in knowledge skill areas often required in college work. The ACT college testing program was founded in 1959. It is a nonprofit educational service offering programs in testing and financial need analysis.

Scholastic Assessment Tests (SAT)

The SAT I: Reasoning Test is an examination to measure the verbal and mathematics abilities students have developed both in and out of school. The SAT II: Subject Tests, which some colleges require for admission or placement purposes, consist of 22 separate tests that cover subjects such as literature, history, math, languages, chemistry, biology, and physics. Unlike the SAT I, which measures more general abilities, the SAT II tests measure the students' knowledge of a particular subject and their ability to apply that knowledge. Because of this, students should try to take a SAT II Test as soon as possible after completion of their last course in that subject.

The SAT I and II tests are given on certain dates throughout the year at various test centers in the United States and foreign countries. The combination of the student's academic record and the SAT scores, along with other pertinent secondary information enables admissions officers to estimate how well the student will perform on a particular college campus. The SAT is scored on a scale of 200 minimum to 800 maximum.

Admission Policies

One of the most important considerations in planning is to note when colleges and universities request applications, and to be sure that the applications are complete and forwarded during the appropriate periods. Failure in any way in this procedure will usually automatically disqualify a student from acceptance.

Counselors can provide students with freshman profiles on many of the institutions. Studying *The College Blue Book*, particularly the volume *Tabular Data*, provides a great amount of information on the kind of student bodies found on the campuses of American institutions. There are four general classifications of admission policies. An understanding of these provides valuable guidelines in identifying colleges for consideration.

Most Selective: Many more students apply who meet the announced admission requirements than the college could possibly accept. In addition to requiring outstanding academic records, personal recommendations are required from the high school, and identification of any special qualities of the student should be made known. In this regard, the high school recommendation made to the collegiate institution requires special attention.

Many times, particularly at selective institutions, the high school recommendation actually provides the necessary edge for admission. The recommendation should be on time, carefully providing all information called for, and finally, be precise and detailed in citing personal qualities of the applicant.

All these qualities, however, do not guarantee acceptance. It is strongly recommended that qualified students apply to more than one institution of this type, and that not all applicants should be made to the same type of institution.

Very Selective: Colleges having a very selective procedure in accepting students require ACT scores of 23 or over, or an SAT I score of 600 or more. Students should rank in the top 10 to 12 percent of their high school graduating classes. In addition, strong recommendations stressing particular talents and achievements are necessary. Applications should be made to several institutions of this type.

Selective: An ACT of 20 or over, or an SAT I score of 550 or more is generally necessary. Applications for admission to selective colleges and universities are usually called for in the spring prior to fall entry. In many situations, applications may be submitted in the fall of the senior year with final confirmation to be made after all grades are recorded and confirmed upon graduation from high school.

Least Selective: The fourth classification represents those institutions that will accept students with a C average on their high school work. In certain unusual instances, and under special situations, even the selective institutions may accept students who are in this category, particularly if the scores on the ACT are in the mid-20's or are in excess of 500 on the SAT I. Generally, for acceptance in the less selective schools, students should have an ACT composite score of 17 or a SAT I score of 450.

Entrance examinations may or may not be required. Occasionally, if examinations are required, the results are used for student placement rather than admission. Most high school graduates can meet the requirements for entry and will be accepted. It should be pointed out, however, that in some cases an institution may be liberal in acceptance but carefully screens candidates for graduation. In such an institution, a high attrition rate may occur.

Open Enrollment Policy: This is becoming more common, particularly with the public community colleges. Many students will find this privilege most helpful in continuing their formal education beyond high school. Such a policy enables those students to have a second chance who have failed to perform up to their ability during their high school years. Enrollment and attendance may enable the student to complete a most rewarding vocational program or to later transfer and complete the Bachelor degree, which otherwise might not have been possible because of the deficiency in the high school scholastic record.

A number of colleges and universities, particularly the publicly supported ones, have adopted the open enrollment policy. In response to a feeling of community responsibility, they accept any student who has a diploma (or G.E.D. equivalency certificate) from an accredited high school. This procedure allows students from disadvantaged and minority backgrounds, who might otherwise be denied such an opportunity, to acquire a college education and prepare for a meaningful occupation. These institutions have not lowered their graduation requirements; they have, instead, created opportunities for more students to satisfy these requirements.

Do not assume the erroneous generality that the tougher it is to get into an institution, the better the quality; or the easier to enter, the poorer the school. In fact, there is research evidence available indicating that it may be wise to re-examine some of our traditional notions and attitudes regarding admissions. Not all degree programs on any particular campus are equally outstanding. Every institution has its particular strengths in programs available. Certain institutions are excellent places for some kinds of students in some kinds of programs, but no institution is the one most suited for everyone.

More than 4,100 educational institutions of the United States and Canada are presented in this volume. The information presented has been collected by questionnaires submitted to these institutions. In addition the most recent college catalogs were often consulted.

Organization

All institutions are arranged in alpha-geographic order. Beginning with the state of Alabama, each institution is listed in alphabetical order within each state. The states are followed by schools in Canada listed by province.

For easier, more comprehensive use this volume is in a ready- reference format that gives statistical data available on each institution. Another use for this volume is to provide easy comparisons of schools as to enrollment, tuition, and other data. Additional information may be obtained from consulting the individual school listing in the *Narrative Descriptions* volume.

Use

Most of the data in this volume are self-explanatory. A few elements, however, need some clarification:

Costs Per Year

Tuition charges are constantly changing and information reported here is as correct as possible. However, it is recommended that the institutions be contacted for the most current information on charges for tuition, room and board, and miscellaneous fees. Many schools will have several tuitions: in- district, instate, nonresident. See *Narrative Descriptions* volume for a more complete breakdown.

Athletics

An Index on Intercollegiate Athletics listed alphabetically by sport and then by school follows the main section of this volume.

Professional Accreditations

Due to space constraints, acronyms have been used. A list of these acronyms follows this section. An Index of Professional Accreditations follows the athletics index in this volume.

Admission Plans

Early admission: Exceptionally able students are admitted before high school graduation. *Early action plan:* Students apply and are notified of admission early; if accepted, the candidate is not committed to enroll. *Early decision:* The school accepts well-qualified students who are notified earlier than usual, generally by mid-December. *Rolling admission:* An admission decision will be given as soon as possible after all application materials are received. *Deferred admission:* A student who wants to work, travel, study abroad, etc., for one year, will be accepted for the following year. *Open admission:* Students are admitted without the usual record for standard qualifications. Almost all students with a high school diploma or equivalent are admitted.

Acronyms for Professional Accreditations

AABB	American Association of Blood Banks
AABC	Accrediting Association of Bible Colleges
AACN	American Association of Colleges of Nursing
AACSB	AACSB International-The Association to Advance Collegiate Schools of Business
AAFCS	American Association of Family and Consumer Sciences
AALE	American Academy for Liberal Education
AALS	Association of American Law Schools
AAMAE	American Association of Medical Assistants Endowment
AAMFT	American Association for Marriage and Family Therapy
AANA	American Association of Nurse Anesthetists
AARTS	Association of Advanced Rabbinical and Talmudic Schools
ABA	American Bar Association
ABET	Accreditation Board for Engineering and Technology, Inc.
ABFSE	American Board of Funeral Service Education
ABHE	Association for Biblical Higher Education
ABHES	Accrediting Bureau of Health Education Schools
ACA	American Counseling Association
ACAOM	Accrediting Commission for Acupuncture and Oriental Medicine
ACBSP	Association of Collegiate Business Schools and Programs
ACCE	American Council for Construction Education
ACCSCT	Accrediting Commission of Career Schools and Colleges of Technology
ACEHSA	Accrediting Commission on Education for Health Services Administration
ACEJMC	Accrediting Council on Education in Journalism and Mass Communications
ACF	American Culinary Federation, Inc.
ACICS	Accrediting Council for Independent Colleges and Schools
ACIPE	Association for Clinical Pastoral Education, Inc.
ACNM	American College of Nurse-Midwives
ACPE	Accreditation Committee for Perfusion Education
ACPhE	American Council on Pharmaceutical Education
ACSP	American Institute of Certified Planners/Association of Collegiate Schools of Planning
ADA	American Dental Association
ADtA	American Dietetic Association
AHIMA	American Health Information Management Association
ALA	American Library Association
AOA	American Optometric Association
AOsA	American Osteopathic Association
AOTA	American Occupational Therapy Association
APA	American Psychological Association
APMA	American Podiatric Medical Association
APTA	American Physical Therapy Association
ARCAA	Accreditation Review Commission on Education for the Anesthesiologist Assistant
ARCEST	Accreditation Review Committee on Education in Surgical Technology
ARCMI	Accreditation Review Committee for the Medical Illustrator
ASC	American Society of Cytopathology
ASLA	American Society of Landscape Architects
ASLHA	American Speech-Language-Hearing Association
ATS	Association of Theological Schools in the United States and Canada
AVMA	American Veterinary Medical Association
CAA	Council on Aviation Accreditation
CAEPK	Committee on Accreditation of Education Programs in Kinesiotherapy
CARC	Committee on Accreditation for Respiratory Care
CCE	Council on Chiropractic Education
CEPH	Council on Education for Public Health
COE	Council on Occupational Education
COpTA	Commission on Opticianry Accreditation
CORE	Council on Rehabilitation Education
CSAB	Computer Science Accreditation Board
CSWE	Council on Social Work Education
DETC	Distance Education and Training Council
FIDER	Foundation for Interior Design Education Research
JCAHPO	Joint Commission on Allied Health Personnel in Ophthalmology
JRCECT	Joint Review Committee on Education in Cardiovascular Technology
JRCEDMS	Joint Review Committee on Education in Diagnostic Medical Sonography
JRCEET	Joint Review Committee on Education in Electroneurodiagnostic Technology
JRCEMT	Joint Review Committee on Educational Programs for the EMT-Paramedic
JRCEPAT	Joint Review Committee on Educational Programs in Athletic Training
JRCERT	Joint Review Committee on Education in Radiological Technology
JRCNMT	Joint Review Committee on Educational Programs in Nuclear Medicine Technology
LCMEAMA	Liaison Committee on Medical Education/American Medical Association
MACTE	Montessori Accreditation Council for Teacher Education
MEAC	Midwifery Education Accreditation Council

NAACLS	National Accrediting Agency for Clinical Laboratory Sciences
NACSCAOM	National Accreditation Commission for Schools and Colleges of Acupuncture and Oriental Medicine
NAIT	National Association of Industrial Technology
NANPWH	National Association of Nurse Practitioners in Women's Health
NASAD	National Association of Schools of Art and Design
NASD	National Association of Schools of Dance
NASM	National Association of Schools of Music
NASPAA	National Association of Schools of Public Affairs and Administration
NAST	National Association of Schools of Theatre
NCATE	National Council for Accreditation of Teacher Education
NCCU	Northwest Commission on Colleges and Universities
NCOPE	National Commission on Orthotic and Prosthetic Education
NLN	National League for Nursing
NRPA	National Recreation and Park Association
NYSBR	New York State Board of Regents
SAF	Society of American Foresters
TACCS	Transnational Association of Christian Colleges and Schools
TEAC	Teacher Education Accreditation Council

Abbreviations

ACT	American College Testing Program
FT	Full-time
GED	General Education Development
Grad	Graduate level
M	Math (SAT); Men
PT	Part-time
SAT I	Scholastic Assessment Test: Reasoning Test
SAT II	Scholastic Assessment Test: Subject Tests
V	Verbal
W	Women

ALABAMA AGRICULTURAL AND MECHANICAL UNIVERSITY
4900 Meridian St.
Huntsville, AL 35811
Tel: (256)372-5000
Free: 800-553-0816
Admissions: (256)372-5245
Fax: (256)372-5881
E-mail: aboyle@asnaam.aamu.edu
Web Site: http://www.aamu.edu/
President/CEO: Dr. John T. Gibson
Registrar: Dr. Shirley Houzer
Admissions: Antonio Boyle
Financial Aid: Carlos Clark
Type: University **Sex:** Coed **Scores:** 39% ACT 18-23; 5% ACT 24-29 **Admission Plans:** Deferred Admission **Application Fee:** $10.00 **H.S. Requirements:** High school diploma required; GED accepted **Costs Per Year:** Application fee: $10. State resident tuition: $4420 full-time. Mandatory fees: $520 full-time. **Scholarships:** Available **Calendar System:** Semester, Summer Session Available **Enrollment:** FT 4,724, PT 367, Grad 1,232 **Faculty:** FT 299, PT 85 **Student-Faculty Ratio:** 16:1 **Exams:** ACT **% Receiving Financial Aid:** 48 **% Residing in College-Owned, -Operated, or -Affiliated Housing:** 45 **Library Holdings:** 507,500 **Regional Accreditation:** Southern Association of Colleges and Schools **Credit Hours For Degree:** 128 semester hours, Bachelors **ROTC:** Army **Professional Accreditation:** ABET, AAFCS, ACSP, ASLHA, CORE, CSWE, NCATE, SAF **Intercollegiate Athletics:** Baseball M; Basketball M & W; Cross-Country Running M & W; Football M; Golf M; Soccer M; Tennis M & W; Track and Field M & W; Volleyball W

ALABAMA SOUTHERN COMMUNITY COLLEGE
PO Box 2000
Monroeville, AL 36461
Tel: (251)575-3156
E-mail: jhorton@ascc.edu
Web Site: http://www.ascc.edu/
President/CEO: Dr. John A. Johnson
Registrar: Jana Horton
Admissions: Jana S. Horton
Financial Aid: Ann Clanton
Type: Two-Year College **Sex:** Coed **Affiliation:** Alabama College System **Admission Plans:** Open Admission; Preferred Admission; Early Admission **Application Fee:** $0.00 **H.S. Requirements:** High school diploma required; GED accepted **Scholarships:** Available **Calendar System:** Semester, Summer Session Available **Faculty:** FT 41, PT 66 **Exams:** ACT, Other **Library Holdings:** 43,000 **Regional Accreditation:** Southern Association of Colleges and Schools **Credit Hours For Degree:** 64 semester hours, Associates **Intercollegiate Athletics:** Baseball M; Basketball M & W; Softball W

ALABAMA STATE UNIVERSITY
915 South Jackson St.
Montgomery, AL 36101-0271
Tel: (334)229-4100
Free: 800-253-5037
Admissions: (334)229-4291
Fax: (334)229-4984
E-mail: mpettway@alasu.edu
Web Site: http://www.alasu.edu/
President/CEO: Dr. Joe A. Lee
Registrar: Ruby Wooding
Admissions: Dr. Martha Pettway
Financial Aid: Dorenda Adams
Type: Comprehensive **Sex:** Coed **Affiliation:** Alabama Commission on Higher Education **Scores:** 45.7% SAT V 400+; 45.6% SAT M 400+; 25.6% ACT 18-23; 2.7% ACT 24-29 **% Accepted:** 67 **Admission Plans:** Early Admission; Deferred Admission **Application Deadline:** July 30 **Application Fee:** $0.00 **H.S. Requirements:** High school diploma required; GED accepted **Costs Per Year:** Application fee: $0. State resident tuition: $4008 full-time, $167 per credit hour part-time. Nonresident tuition: $8016 full-time, $334 per credit hour part-time. Full-time tuition varies according to course load. Part-time tuition varies according to course load. College room and board: $3700. College room only: $1980. Room and board charges vary according to board plan and housing facility. **Scholarships:** Available **Calendar System:** Semester, Summer Session Available **Enrollment:** FT 3,958, PT 527, Grad 984 **Faculty:** FT 234, PT 180 **Student-Faculty Ratio:** 15:1 **Exams:** SAT I or ACT **% Receiving Financial Aid:** 86 **% Residing in College-Owned, -Operated, or -Affiliated Housing:** 43 **Library Holdings:** 396,871 **Regional Accreditation:** Southern Association of Colleges and Schools **Credit Hours For Degree:** 129 credit hours, Bachelors **ROTC:** Army, Navy **Professional Accreditation:** AOTA, APTA, ACBSP, CSWE, NASM, NCATE **Intercollegiate Athletics:** Baseball M; Basketball M & W; Bowling W; Cross-Country Running M & W; Football M; Golf M; Softball W; Tennis M & W; Track and Field M & W; Volleyball W

AMERICAN COLLEGE OF COMPUTER & INFORMATION SCIENCES
2101 Magnolia Ave., Ste. 200
Birmingham, AL 35205
Tel: (205)323-6191
Free: 800-767-2427
Fax: (205)328-2229
Web Site: http://www.accis.edu/
President/CEO: Betty J. Howell
Registrar: Kelly Blair
Admissions: David Lenhart
Type: Comprehensive **Sex:** Coed **Admission Plans:** Open Admission **Application Deadline:** Rolling **Application Fee:** $40.00 **H.S. Requirements:** High school diploma required; GED accepted **Costs Per Year:** Application fee: $40. Tuition: $155 per credit hour part-time. Mandatory fees: $60 per year part-time. **Calendar System:** Continuous **Faculty:** FT 5, PT 29 **Credit Hours For Degree:** 123 credit hours, Bachelors **Professional Accreditation:** DETC

ANDREW JACKSON UNIVERSITY
10 Old Montgomery Hwy.
Birmingham, AL 35209
Tel: (205)871-9288
Fax: (205)871-9294
E-mail: admissions@aju.edu
Web Site: http://www.aju.edu/
President/CEO: Robert McKim Norris, Jr.
Admissions: Bell Woods
Type: Comprehensive **Sex:** Coed **Admission Plans:** Open Admission **Application Fee:** $75.00 **H.S. Requirements:** High school diploma required;

GED accepted **Costs Per Year:** Application fee: $75. Tuition: $3900 full-time, $375 per course part-time. **Enrollment:** , PT 200, Grad 300 **Faculty:** FT 0, PT 50 **Student-Faculty Ratio:** 11:1 **Professional Accreditation:** DETC

ATHENS STATE UNIVERSITY
300 North Beaty St.
Athens, AL 35611
Tel: (256)233-8100
Free: 800-522-0272
Admissions: (256)233-8217
Fax: (256)233-8164
Web Site: http://www.athens.edu/
President/CEO: Dr. Jerry F. Bartlett
Registrar: Teresa Suit
Admissions: Necedah Henderson
Financial Aid: Sarah Crawford-McAbee
Type: Two-Year Upper Division **Sex:** Coed **Affiliation:** The Alabama College System **Admission Plans:** Open Admission; Deferred Admission **Application Deadline:** Rolling **Application Fee:** $30.00 **H.S. Requirements:** High school diploma required; GED accepted **Costs Per Year:** Application fee: $30. State resident tuition: $3330 full-time, $111 per semester hour part-time. Nonresident tuition: $6660 full-time, $222 per semester hour part-time. Mandatory fees: $540 full-time, $18 per semester hour part-time. College room only: $900. **Scholarships:** Available **Calendar System:** Semester, Summer Session Available **Enrollment:** FT 1,141, PT 1,502 **Faculty:** FT 75, PT 102 **Student-Faculty Ratio:** 23:1 **% Receiving Financial Aid:** 45 **Library Holdings:** 137,233 **Regional Accreditation:** Southern Association of Colleges and Schools **Credit Hours For Degree:** 124 credit hours, Bachelors **Professional Accreditation:** ACBSP, NCATE

AUBURN UNIVERSITY
Auburn University, AL 36849
Tel: (334)844-4000
Admissions: (334)844-6444
E-mail: bickecd@auburn.edu
Web Site: http://www.auburn.edu/
President/CEO: Dr. Edward R. Richardson
Registrar: Doyle Bickers
Admissions: Doyle Bickers
Financial Aid: Mike Reynolds
Type: University **Sex:** Coed **Scores:** 99.08% SAT V 400+; 99.15% SAT M 400+; 45.23% ACT 18-23; 41.83% ACT 24-29 **% Accepted:** 82 **Admission Plans:** Early Admission **Application Deadline:** August 01 **Application Fee:** $25.00 **H.S. Requirements:** High school diploma required; GED accepted **Costs Per Year:** Application fee: $25. State resident tuition: $5278 full-time. Nonresident tuition: $14,878 full-time. Mandatory fees: $238 full-time. College room and board: $7232. College room only: $3060. **Scholarships:** Available **Calendar System:** Semester, Summer Session Available **Enrollment:** FT 17,778, PT 1,476, Grad 3,169 **Faculty:** FT 1,176, PT 155 **Student-Faculty Ratio:** 17:1 **Exams:** SAT I and SAT II or ACT **% Receiving Financial Aid:** 35 **% Residing in College-Owned, -Operated, or -Affiliated Housing:** 15 **Library Holdings:** 2,591,255 **Regional Accreditation:** Southern Association of Colleges and Schools **Credit Hours For Degree:** 180 quarter hours, Bachelors **ROTC:** Army, Navy, Air Force **Professional Accreditation:** AACSB, ABET, ACEJMC, AAMFT, AAFCS, ACCE, ACPhE, ACA, ACSP, APA, ASLA, ASLHA, AVMA, CAA, CORE, CSWE, FIDER, NASAD, NASM, NASPAA NAST, NCATE, NLN, SAF **Intercollegiate Athletics:** Baseball M; Basketball M & W; Cross-Country Running M & W; Equestrian Sports W; Football M; Golf M & W; Gymnastics W; Soccer W; Softball W; Swimming and Diving M & W; Tennis M & W; Track and Field M & W; Volleyball W

AUBURN UNIVERSITY MONTGOMERY
PO Box 244023
Montgomery, AL 36124-4023
Tel: (334)244-3000
Admissions: (334)244-3667
Fax: (334)244-3795
Web Site: http://www.aum.edu/
President/CEO: Dr. Guin A. Nance
Registrar: George A. Hill
Admissions: Lynn Bacon
Financial Aid: Dan Miller
Type: Comprehensive **Sex:** Coed **Affiliation:** Auburn University **Scores:** 58% ACT 18-23; 19% ACT 24-29 **% Accepted:** 98 **Admission Plans:** Deferred Admission **Application Deadline:** Rolling **Application Fee:** $25.00 **H.S. Requirements:** High school diploma required; GED accepted **Costs Per Year:** Application fee: $25. State resident tuition: $4410 full-time, $147 per semester hour part-time. Nonresident tuition: $13,230 full-time, $441 per semester hour part-time. Mandatory fees: $230 full-time, $5 per semester hour part-time, $40 per term part-time. Full-time tuition and fees vary according to course load. College room and board: $4890. College room only: $2400. Room and board charges vary according to housing facility. **Scholarships:** Available **Calendar System:** Semester, Summer Session Available **Enrollment:** FT 2,702, PT 1,598, Grad 828 **Faculty:** FT 186, PT 119 **Student-Faculty Ratio:** 16:1 **Exams:** SAT I or ACT **% Receiving Financial Aid:** 52 **% Residing in College-Owned, -Operated, or -Affiliated Housing:** 12 **Library Holdings:** 312,110 **Regional Accreditation:** Southern Association of Colleges and Schools **Credit Hours For Degree:** 120 semester hours, Bachelors **ROTC:** Army, Air Force **Professional Accreditation:** AACSB, AACN, NAACLS, NASPAA, NCATE **Intercollegiate Athletics:** Baseball M; Basketball M & W; Soccer M & W; Tennis M & W

BEVILL STATE COMMUNITY COLLEGE
PO Box 800
Sumiton, AL 35148
Tel: (205)648-3271
Admissions: (205)932-3221
Web Site: http://www.bscc.edu/
President/CEO: Dr. Harold Wade
Registrar: Nelda Oswalt
Admissions: Melissa Stowe
Financial Aid: Suzanne Bush
Type: Two-Year College **Sex:** Coed **Affiliation:** Alabama College System **Admission Plans:** Open Admission; Early Admission; Deferred Admission **Application Fee:** $0.00 **H.S. Requirements:** High school diploma required; GED accepted **Scholarships:** Available **Calendar System:** Semester, Summer Session Available **Enrollment:** FT 2,465, PT 1,862 **Faculty:** FT 119, PT 216 **Student-Faculty Ratio:** 16:1 **Exams:** ACT, Other **Library Holdings:** 31,690 **Regional Accreditation:** Southern Association of Colleges and Schools **Professional Accreditation:** NAACLS, NLN **Intercollegiate Athletics:** Baseball M; Basketball M & W; Softball W; Volleyball W

BIRMINGHAM-SOUTHERN COLLEGE
900 Arkadelphia Rd.
Birmingham, AL 35254
Tel: (205)226-4600
Free: 800-523-5793
Admissions: (205)226-4696
Fax: (205)226-3074
E-mail: admissions@bsc.edu
Web Site: http://www.bsc.edu/
President/CEO: Dr. G. David Pollick
Registrar: Danny Brooks
Admissions: Sheri E. Salmon
Financial Aid: Ron Day
Type: Comprehensive **Sex:** Coed **Affiliation:** Methodist **Scores:** 100% SAT V 400+; 98.1% SAT M 400+; 29.25% ACT 18-23; 52% ACT 24-29 **% Accepted:** 63 **Admission Plans:** Early Admission; Early Action; Deferred Admission **Application Deadline:** Rolling **Application Fee:** $25.00 **H.S. Requirements:** High school diploma required; GED accepted **Costs Per Year:** Application fee: $25. Comprehensive fee: $28,135 includes full-time tuition ($20,425), mandatory fees ($630), and college room and board ($7080). College room only: $5000. Part-time tuition: $867 per credit hour. **Scholarships:** Available **Calendar System:** 4-1-4, Summer Session Available **Enrollment:** FT 1,294, PT 30, Grad 87 **Faculty:** FT 100, PT 37 **Student-Faculty Ratio:** 12:1 **Exams:** SAT I or ACT **% Receiving Financial Aid:** 41 **% Residing in College-Owned, -Operated, or -Affiliated Housing:** 79 **Library Holdings:** 232,330 **Regional Accreditation:** Southern Association of Colleges and Schools **Credit Hours For Degree:** 36 courses, Bachelors **ROTC:** Army, Air Force **Professional Accreditation:** AACSB, NASM, NCATE **Intercollegiate Athletics:** Baseball M; Basketball M & W; Cross-Country Running M & W; Golf M & W; Riflery W; Soccer M & W; Softball W; Tennis M & W; Volleyball W

BISHOP STATE COMMUNITY COLLEGE
351 North Broad St.
Mobile, AL 36603-5898

Tel: (251)690-6801
Admissions: (251)690-6419
Fax: (251)438-5403
Web Site: http://www.bscc.cc.al.us/
President/CEO: Dr. Yvonne Kennedy
Registrar: Wanda Daniels
Admissions: Dr. Terry Hazzard
Financial Aid: Charles Holloway
Type: Two-Year College **Sex:** Coed **Affiliation:** Alabama College System **% Accepted:** 100 **Admission Plans:** Open Admission; Early Admission; Deferred Admission **Application Deadline:** Rolling **Application Fee:** $0.00 **H.S. Requirements:** High school diploma required; GED accepted **Costs Per Year:** Application fee: $0. State resident tuition: $1728 full-time, $72 per credit hour part-time. Nonresident tuition: $3456 full-time, $144 per credit hour part-time. Mandatory fees: $432 full-time, $18 per credit hour part-time. **Scholarships:** Available **Calendar System:** Semester, Summer Session Available **Enrollment:** FT 2,381, PT 2,502 **Faculty:** FT 113, PT 76 **Student-Faculty Ratio:** 14:1 **Library Holdings:** 56,687 **Regional Accreditation:** Southern Association of Colleges and Schools **Credit Hours For Degree:** 96 credit hours, Associates **Professional Accreditation:** ABFSE, ACF, AHIMA, APTA, ACBSP, NLN **Intercollegiate Athletics:** Baseball M; Basketball M & W; Softball W

CALHOUN COMMUNITY COLLEGE
PO Box 2216
Decatur, AL 35609-2216
Tel: (256)306-2500
Admissions: (256)306-2595
Fax: (256)306-2877
Web Site: http://www.calhoun.edu/
President/CEO: Dr. Marilyn C. Beck
Registrar: Dr. Wayne Tosh
Admissions: Dr. Wayne Tosh
Financial Aid: Deborah Byrd
Type: Two-Year College **Sex:** Coed **Affiliation:** Alabama College System **Scores:** 67% SAT V 400+; 61% SAT M 400+; 51% ACT 18-23; 11% ACT 24-29 **Admission Plans:** Open Admission **Application Fee:** $0.00 **H.S. Requirements:** High school diploma required; GED accepted **Costs Per Year:** Application fee: $0. State resident tuition: $3040 full-time, $71 per semester hour part-time. Nonresident tuition: $5312 full-time, $142 per semester hour part-time. Mandatory fees: $768 full-time, $24 per semester hour part-time. **Scholarships:** Available **Calendar System:** Semester, Summer Session Available **Faculty:** FT 117, PT 307 **Student-Faculty Ratio:** 21:1 **Exams:** SAT I or ACT **Library Holdings:** 36,699 **Regional Accreditation:** Southern Association of Colleges and Schools **Credit Hours For Degree:** 64 semester hours, Associates **Professional Accreditation:** ADA, NLN

CENTRAL ALABAMA COMMUNITY COLLEGE
PO Box 699
Alexander City, AL 35011-0699
Tel: (256)234-6346
Fax: (256)234-0384
Web Site: http://www.cacc.cc.al.us/
President/CEO: Dr. James H. Cornell
Admissions: Betty Carol Graham
Financial Aid: Lynn Spraggins
Type: Two-Year College **Sex:** Coed **Affiliation:** Alabama College System **Admission Plans:** Open Admission; Early Admission **Application Fee:** $0.00 **H.S. Requirements:** High school diploma required; GED accepted **Scholarships:** Available **Calendar System:** Semester, Summer Session Available **Faculty:** FT 52, PT 141 **Student-Faculty Ratio:** 15:1 **Exams:** SAT I or ACT **Library Holdings:** 35,000 **Regional Accreditation:** Southern Association of Colleges and Schools **Professional Accreditation:** NLN **Intercollegiate Athletics:** Baseball M; Golf M; Softball W; Tennis M & W; Volleyball W

CHATTAHOOCHEE VALLEY COMMUNITY COLLEGE
2602 College Dr.
Phenix City, AL 36869-7928
Tel: (334)291-4900
Fax: (334)291-4994
Web Site: http://www.cv.edu/
President/CEO: Dr. Laurel Blackwell
Financial Aid: Joan Waters
Type: Two-Year College **Sex:** Coed **Admission Plans:** Open Admission; Preferred Admission; Early Admission **Application Deadline:** Rolling **Application Fee:** $0.00 **H.S. Requirements:** High school diploma required; GED accepted **Scholarships:** Available **Calendar System:** Semester, Summer Session Available **Enrollment:** FT 972, PT 1,062 **Faculty:** FT 28, PT 60 **Library Holdings:** 54,129 **Regional Accreditation:** Southern Association of Colleges and Schools **Professional Accreditation:** NLN **Intercollegiate Athletics:** Baseball M; Softball W

COLUMBIA SOUTHERN UNIVERSITY
24847 Commercial Ave.
PO Box 3110
Orange Beach, AL 36561
Tel: (251)981-3771
Free: 800-977-8449
Fax: (251)981-3815
Web Site: http://www.colsouth.edu/
President/CEO: Dr. Bob Mayes
Registrar: Thomas Cooley
Admissions: Thomas Cooley
Type: Comprehensive **Sex:** Coed **Admission Plans:** Open Admission **Application Fee:** $25.00 **H.S. Requirements:** High school diploma required; GED accepted **Calendar System:** Miscellaneous, Summer Session Not available **Faculty:** FT 1, PT 44 **Credit Hours For Degree:** 120 credit hours, Bachelors **Professional Accreditation:** DETC

COMMUNITY COLLEGE OF THE AIR FORCE
130 West Maxwell Blvd.
Maxwell Air Force Base, AL 36112-6613
Tel: (334)953-2223
Admissions: (334)953-6436
Fax: (334)953-8211
E-mail: bobby.mcalexander@maxwell.af.mil
Web Site: http://www.au.af.mil/au/ccaf/
President/CEO: Col. Eric A. Ash
Registrar: C.M. Sgt. Bobby McAlexander
Admissions: C.M. Sgt. Robert McAlexander
Type: Two-Year College **Sex:** Coed **% Accepted:** 100 **Admission Plans:** Open Admission **Application Deadline:** Rolling **Application Fee:** $0.00 **H.S. Requirements:** High school diploma or equivalent not required **Costs Per Year:** Application fee: $0. **Calendar System:** Continuous, Summer Session Not available **Enrollment:** FT 351,715 **Faculty:** FT 6,720, PT 0 **Student-Faculty Ratio:** 28:1 **Exams:** Other **Library Holdings:** 5,000,000 **Regional Accreditation:** Southern Association of Colleges and Schools **Credit Hours For Degree:** 64 semester hours, Associates **Professional Accreditation:** APTA

CONCORDIA COLLEGE
1804 Green St., PO Box 1329
Selma, AL 36701
Tel: (334)874-5700
Fax: (334)874-3728
Web Site: http://www.concordiaselma.edu/
President/CEO: Dr. Julius Jenkins
Registrar: Chinester Grayson
Admissions: Evelyn Pickens
Financial Aid: Tharsteen E. Bridges
Type: Four-Year College **Sex:** Coed **Affiliation:** Lutheran; Concordia University System **Scores:** 78.94% ACT 18-23 **Admission Plans:** Open Admission; Deferred Admission **Application Fee:** $10.00 **H.S. Requirements:** High school diploma required; GED accepted **Costs Per Year:** Application fee: $10. Comprehensive fee: $9814 includes full-time tuition ($6000), mandatory fees ($214), and college room and board ($3600). College room only: $1600. Full-time tuition and fees vary according to course load. Room and board charges vary according to housing facility. Part-time tuition: $235 per credit hour. Part-time mandatory fees: $114 per term. Part-time tuition and fees vary according to course load. **Scholarships:** Available **Calendar System:** Semester, Summer Session Not available **Enrollment:** FT 731, PT 171 **Faculty:** FT 17, PT 32 **Student-Faculty Ratio:** 18:1 **Exams:** ACT **% Receiving Financial Aid:** 79 **% Residing in College-Owned, -Operated, or -Affiliated Housing:** 34 **Library Holdings:** 60,000 **Regional Accreditation:** Southern Association of Colleges and Schools **Credit Hours For Degree:** 64 credits, Associates; 130 credits, Bachelors **Intercollegiate Athletics:** Baseball M; Basketball M & W; Cheerleading W; Soccer M; Softball W

ENTERPRISE-OZARK COMMUNITY COLLEGE
PO Box 1300
Enterprise, AL 36331-1300
Tel: (334)347-2623
E-mail: gdeas@eocc.edu
Web Site: http://www.eocc.edu/
President/CEO: Dr. Stafford L. Thompson
Registrar: Gary Deas
Admissions: Gary Deas
Financial Aid: Dr. Chip Quisenberry
Type: Two-Year College **Sex:** Coed **Affiliation:** Alabama College System **Admission Plans:** Open Admission; Early Admission; Deferred Admission **Application Fee:** $0.00 **H.S. Requirements:** High school diploma required; GED accepted **Scholarships:** Available **Calendar System:** Semester, Summer Session Available **Enrollment:** FT 866, PT 724 **Faculty:** FT 38, PT 59 **Exams:** SAT I or ACT **Library Holdings:** 45,076 **Regional Accreditation:** Southern Association of Colleges and Schools **Intercollegiate Athletics:** Baseball M; Basketball M & W; Cheerleading M & W; Softball W

FAULKNER UNIVERSITY
5345 Atlanta Hwy.
Montgomery, AL 36109-3398
Tel: (334)386-7324
Free: 800-879-9816
Admissions: (334)386-7200
Fax: (334)386-7268
Web Site: http://www.faulkner.edu/
President/CEO: Dr. Billy D. Hilyer
Registrar: Wiley J. Cutts
Admissions: Keith Mock
Financial Aid: William G. Jackson, II
Type: Comprehensive **Sex:** Coed **Affiliation:** Church of Christ **Scores:** 92% SAT V 400+; 91% SAT M 400+; 62% ACT 18-23; 19% ACT 24-29 **% Accepted:** 60 **Admission Plans:** Early Admission; Deferred Admission **Application Deadline:** Rolling **Application Fee:** $10.00 **H.S. Requirements:** High school diploma required; GED accepted **Costs Per Year:** Application fee: $10. Comprehensive fee: $16,825 includes full-time tuition ($11,400), mandatory fees ($25), and college room and board ($5400). College room only: $2500. Part-time tuition: $395 per semester hour. **Scholarships:** Available **Calendar System:** Semester, Summer Session Available **Enrollment:** FT 1,598, PT 627, Grad 100 **Faculty:** FT 88, PT 50 **Student-Faculty Ratio:** 19:1 **Exams:** SAT I or ACT **% Receiving Financial Aid:** 72 **% Residing in College-Owned, -Operated, or -Affiliated Housing:** 59 **Library Holdings:** 143,906 **Regional Accreditation:** Southern Association of Colleges and Schools **Credit Hours For Degree:** 64 semester hours, Associates; 128 semester hours, Bachelors **ROTC:** Army, Air Force **Intercollegiate Athletics:** Baseball M; Basketball M; Cross-Country Running M & W; Golf M; Soccer M & W; Softball W; Volleyball W

GADSDEN STATE COMMUNITY COLLEGE
PO Box 227
Gadsden, AL 35902-0227
Tel: (256)549-8200
Free: 800-226-5563
Admissions: (256)549-8263
Fax: (256)549-8444
E-mail: info@gadsdenstate.edu
Web Site: http://www.gadsdenstate.edu/
President/CEO: Dr. Renee D. Culverhouse
Registrar: Dr. Teresa Rhea
Admissions: Dr. Teresa Rhea
Financial Aid: Kimberly Carter
Type: Two-Year College **Sex:** Coed **Affiliation:** Alabama College System **% Accepted:** 100 **Admission Plans:** Open Admission; Early Admission; Deferred Admission **Application Deadline:** Rolling **Application Fee:** $0.00 **H.S. Requirements:** High school diploma required; GED accepted. For auto body and mechanic, cosmetology, small engine repair, upholstery, welding, cabinet-making, plumbing: High school diploma or equivalent not required **Costs Per Year:** Application fee: $0. State resident tuition: $90 per credit hour part-time. Nonresident tuition: $161 per credit hour part-time. **Scholarships:** Available **Calendar System:** Semester, Summer Session Available **Enrollment:** FT 2,964, PT 2,462 **Faculty:** FT 141, PT 154 **Library Holdings:** 72,915 **Regional Accreditation:** Southern Association of Colleges and Schools **Professional Accreditation:** ACBSP, JRCERT, JRCEMT, NAACLS, NLN **Intercollegiate Athletics:** Baseball M; Basketball M & W; Cross-Country Running W; Golf M; Softball W; Tennis M; Volleyball W

GADSDEN STATE COMMUNITY COLLEGE-AYERS CAMPUS
PO Box 1647
Anniston, AL 36202-1647
Tel: (256)835-5400
Fax: (256)835-5479
Web Site: http://www.gadsdenstate.edu/
President/CEO: Dr. Edward Meadows
Registrar: Michele Conger
Admissions: Michele Conger
Financial Aid: Carol Tidwell
Type: Two-Year College **Sex:** Coed **Admission Plans:** Open Admission; Deferred Admission **Application Fee:** $0.00 **H.S. Requirements:** High school diploma required; GED accepted **Scholarships:** Available **Calendar System:** Semester, Summer Session Not available **Enrollment:** FT 686, PT 451 **Faculty:** FT 27, PT 67 **Student-Faculty Ratio:** 18:1 **Exams:** Other **Library Holdings:** 4,645 **Regional Accreditation:** Southern Association of Colleges and Schools

GEORGE C. WALLACE COMMUNITY COLLEGE
1141 Wallace Dr.
Dothan, AL 36303-9234
Tel: (334)983-3521
Free: 800-543-2426
Fax: (334)983-3600
E-mail: bbarnes@wallace.edu
Web Site: http://www.wallace.edu/
President/CEO: Dr. Linda C. Young
Registrar: Dr. Brenda Barnes
Admissions: Dr. Brenda Barnes
Financial Aid: Erma Perry
Type: Two-Year College **Sex:** Coed **Admission Plans:** Open Admission; Early Admission **Application Deadline:** Rolling **Application Fee:** $0.00 **H.S. Requirements:** High school diploma required; GED accepted. For various technical programs: High school diploma or equivalent not required **Costs Per Year:** Application fee: $0. State resident tuition: $2160 full-time, $72 per credit hour part-time. Nonresident tuition: $4320 full-time, $144 per credit hour part-time. Mandatory fees: $540 full-time, $18 per credit hour part-time. **Scholarships:** Available **Calendar System:** Semester, Summer Session Available **Enrollment:** FT 1,919, PT 1,581 **Faculty:** FT 126, PT 115 **Student-Faculty Ratio:** 7:1 **Library Holdings:** 45,353 **Regional Accreditation:** Southern Association of Colleges and Schools **Professional Accreditation:** AAMAE, APTA, CARC, JRCERT, JRCEMT, NLN **Intercollegiate Athletics:** Basketball M & W; Tennis M & W

GEORGE CORLEY WALLACE STATE COMMUNITY COLLEGE
PO Box 2530
Selma, AL 36702-2530
Tel: (334)876-9227
Admissions: (334)876-9305
Fax: (334)876-9250
Web Site: http://www.wccs.edu/
President/CEO: James M. Mitchell
Registrar: Dr. Gail May
Admissions: Sunette Newman
Financial Aid: Corey Bowie
Type: Two-Year College **Sex:** Coed **Affiliation:** Alabama College System **Admission Plans:** Open Admission; Early Admission; Deferred Admission **Application Fee:** $0.00 **H.S. Requirements:** High school diploma required; GED accepted **Costs Per Year:** Application fee: $0. State resident tuition: $2160 full-time, $90 per credit hour part-time. Nonresident tuition: $4320 full-time, $180 per credit hour part-time. **Scholarships:** Available **Calendar System:** Semester, Summer Session Available **Faculty:** FT 45, PT 50 **Student-Faculty Ratio:** 17:1 **Exams:** Other **Library Holdings:** 16,598 **Regional Accreditation:** Southern Association of Colleges and Schools **Credit Hours For Degree:** 64 semester hours, Associates **Professional Accreditation:** NLN **Intercollegiate Athletics:** Baseball M; Basketball M; Softball W; Tennis M & W

H. COUNCILL TRENHOLM STATE TECHNICAL COLLEGE
1225 Air Base Blvd.
Montgomery, AL 36116-2699
Tel: (334)420-4200
Admissions: (334)420-4306

Fax: (334)420-4201
Web Site: http://www.trenholmtech.cc.al.us/
President/CEO: Dr. Anthony L. Molina
Registrar: Tennie McBryde
Admissions: Tennie McBryde
Financial Aid: David Jones
Type: Two-Year College **Sex:** Coed **Affiliation:** Alabama Department of Post Secondary Education **% Accepted:** 42 **Admission Plans:** Open Admission; Early Admission **Application Deadline:** Rolling **Application Fee:** $0.00 **H.S. Requirements:** High school diploma required; GED accepted **Costs Per Year:** Application fee: $0. One-time mandatory fee: $35. State resident tuition: $2160 full-time, $71 per hour part-time. Nonresident tuition: $4320 full-time, $142 per hour part-time. Mandatory fees: $540 full-time, $19 per hour part-time. **Scholarships:** Available **Calendar System:** Semester, Summer Session Available **Enrollment:** FT 711, PT 692 **Faculty:** FT 64, PT 47 **Student-Faculty Ratio:** 10:1 **Library Holdings:** 2,945 **Credit Hours For Degree:** 64 credit hours, Associates **Professional Accreditation:** COE

HERITAGE CHRISTIAN UNIVERSITY

PO Box HCU
Florence, AL 35630
Tel: (256)766-6610
Free: 800-367-3565
Fax: (256)760-0981
E-mail: tharmon@hcu.edu
Web Site: http://www.hcu.edu/
President/CEO: Dennis Jones
Registrar: Sara Goldman
Admissions: Travis Harmon
Financial Aid: Bryan Collins
Type: Comprehensive **Sex:** Coed **Affiliation:** Church of Christ **Admission Plans:** Open Admission; Preferred Admission; Early Admission; Deferred Admission **Application Fee:** $25.00 **H.S. Requirements:** High school diploma required; GED accepted **Costs Per Year:** Application fee: $25. Tuition: $7784 full-time, $278 per hour part-time. Mandatory fees: $480 full-time, $20 per hour part-time. College room only: $1650. **Scholarships:** Available **Calendar System:** Semester, Summer Session Available **Enrollment:** FT 46, PT 63, Grad 14 **Faculty:** FT 10, PT 11 **Student-Faculty Ratio:** 9:1 **% Receiving Financial Aid:** 62 **Library Holdings:** 51,000 **Credit Hours For Degree:** 65 semester hours, Associates; 128 semester hours, Bachelors **Professional Accreditation:** AABC

HERZING COLLEGE

280 West Valley Ave.
Birmingham, AL 35209
Tel: (205)916-2800
Fax: (205)916-2807
E-mail: admiss@bhm.herzing.edu
Web Site: http://www.herzing.edu/birmingham/
President/CEO: Donald E. Lewis
Registrar: Mike Cates
Admissions: Tess Anderson
Financial Aid: Kentray Sims
Type: Two-Year College **Sex:** Coed **Affiliation:** Herzing Institutes, Inc **Admission Plans:** Early Admission; Deferred Admission **Application Fee:** $0.00 **H.S. Requirements:** High school diploma required; GED accepted **Scholarships:** Available **Calendar System:** Semester, Summer Session Available **Enrollment:** FT 398, PT 202 **Faculty:** FT 9, PT 18 **Student-Faculty Ratio:** 20:1 **Exams:** Other **Professional Accreditation:** ACCSCT

HUNTINGDON COLLEGE

1500 East Fairview Ave.
Montgomery, AL 36106-2148
Tel: (334)833-4222
Free: 800-763-0313
Admissions: (334)833-4497
Fax: (334)833-4347
E-mail: admiss@huntingdon.edu
Web Site: http://www.huntingdon.edu/
President/CEO: Rev. J. Cameron West
Registrar: Dr. Sidney J. Stubbs
Admissions: Christy C. Mehaffey
Financial Aid: Belinda M. Goris
Type: Four-Year College **Sex:** Coed **Affiliation:** United Methodist **Scores:** 95% SAT V 400+; 93% SAT M 400+; 53% ACT 18-23; 34% ACT 24-29 **Admission Plans:** Early Admission; Deferred Admission **Application Fee:** $25.00 **H.S. Requirements:** High school diploma required; GED accepted **Costs Per Year:** Application fee: $25. Comprehensive fee: $22,050 includes full-time tuition ($15,250), mandatory fees ($700), and college room and board ($6100). Full-time tuition and fees vary according to class time, reciprocity agreements, and student level. Room and board charges vary according to housing facility. Tuition guaranteed not to increase for student's term of enrollment. **Scholarships:** Available **Calendar System:** Semester, Summer Session Available **Enrollment:** FT 669, PT 62 **Faculty:** FT 32, PT 29 **Student-Faculty Ratio:** 15:1 **Exams:** SAT I or ACT **% Receiving Financial Aid:** 78 **% Residing in College-Owned, -Operated, or -Affiliated Housing:** 72 **Library Holdings:** 97,436 **Regional Accreditation:** Southern Association of Colleges and Schools **Credit Hours For Degree:** 66 semester hours, Associates; 124 semester hours, Bachelors **ROTC:** Army, Air Force **Professional Accreditation:** NASM **Intercollegiate Athletics:** Baseball M; Basketball M & W; Crew M & W; Cross-Country Running M & W; Football M; Golf M; Sailing M & W; Soccer M & W; Softball W; Tennis W; Volleyball W

ITT TECHNICAL INSTITUTE

500 Riverhills Business Park
Birmingham, AL 35242
Tel: (205)991-5410
Admissions: (205)497-5700
Fax: (205)991-5025
Web Site: http://www.itt-tech.edu/
President/CEO: Allen E. Rice
Registrar: Tiffany Youngblood
Admissions: Allen Rice
Financial Aid: Steve Meeks
Type: Two-Year College **Sex:** Coed **Affiliation:** ITT Educational Services, Inc **Admission Plans:** Deferred Admission **Application Deadline:** Rolling **Application Fee:** $100.00 **H.S. Requirements:** High school diploma required; GED accepted **Costs Per Year:** Application fee: $100. **Scholarships:** Available **Calendar System:** Quarter, Summer Session Not available **Exams:** Other **Credit Hours For Degree:** 96 credit hours, Associates; 180 credit hours, Bachelors **Professional Accreditation:** ACICS

J. F. DRAKE STATE TECHNICAL COLLEGE

3421 Meridian St. North
Huntsville, AL 35811-1584
Tel: (256)539-8161; 888-413-7253
Admissions: (256)551-3109
E-mail: clemons@drakestate.edu
Web Site: http://www.drakestate.edu/
President/CEO: Dr. Helen McAlpine
Registrar: Shirley Clemons
Admissions: Shirley Clemons
Financial Aid: Joylyn Trotman
Type: Two-Year College **Sex:** Coed **Affiliation:** State of Alabama Department of Postsecondary Education **% Accepted:** 60 **Admission Plans:** Open Admission; Deferred Admission **Application Deadline:** Rolling **Application Fee:** $0.00 **Costs Per Year:** Application fee: $0. State resident tuition: $2700 full-time, $72 per semester hour part-time. Nonresident tuition: $5400 full-time, $144 per semester hour part-time. Mandatory fees: $540 full-time, $18 per semester hour part-time. **Calendar System:** Semester, Summer Session Not available **Enrollment:** FT 454, PT 310 **Faculty:** FT 25, PT 42 **Student-Faculty Ratio:** 21:1 **Credit Hours For Degree:** 72 semester hours, Associates **Professional Accreditation:** COE

JACKSONVILLE STATE UNIVERSITY

700 Pelham Rd. North
Jacksonville, AL 36265-1602
Tel: (256)782-5781
Free: 800-231-5291
Admissions: (256)782-5363
Fax: (256)782-5291
E-mail: mmitchel@jsu.edu
Web Site: http://www.jsu.edu/
President/CEO: Dr. William Meehan
Registrar: Kathy Campbell
Admissions: Martha Mitchell

Financial Aid: Vickie Adams
Type: Comprehensive **Sex:** Coed **Scores:** 85.4% SAT V 400+; 82.8% SAT M 400+; 49.9% ACT 18-23; 17.7% ACT 24-29 **% Accepted:** 88 **Admission Plans:** Early Admission; Deferred Admission **Application Deadline:** Rolling **Application Fee:** $20.00 **H.S. Requirements:** High school diploma required; GED accepted **Costs Per Year:** Application fee: $20. State resident tuition: $4040 full-time, $169 per credit hour part-time. Nonresident tuition: $8080 full-time, $338 per credit hour part-time. College room and board: $3258. College room only: $1680. Room and board charges vary according to board plan and housing facility. **Scholarships:** Available **Calendar System:** Semester, Summer Session Available **Enrollment:** FT 5,813, PT 1,472, Grad 1,825 **Faculty:** FT 305, PT 129 **Student-Faculty Ratio:** 21:1 **Exams:** SAT I or ACT **% Receiving Financial Aid:** 78 **% Residing in College-Owned, -Operated, or -Affiliated Housing:** 20 **Library Holdings:** 685,991 **Regional Accreditation:** Southern Association of Colleges and Schools **Credit Hours For Degree:** 128 semester hours, Bachelors **ROTC:** Army **Professional Accreditation:** AACSB, AACN, AAFCS, CSWE, NAIT, NASAD, NASM, NAST, NCATE **Intercollegiate Athletics:** Baseball M; Basketball M & W; Cross-Country Running M & W; Football M; Golf M & W; Riflery M & W; Softball W; Tennis M & W; Volleyball W

JAMES H. FAULKNER STATE COMMUNITY COLLEGE
1900 Hwy. 31 South
Bay Minette, AL 36507
Tel: (251)580-2100
Free: 800-231-3752
Admissions: (251)580-2152
Fax: (251)580-2285
E-mail: pduck@faulknerstate.edu
Web Site: http://www.faulknerstate.edu/
Registrar: Felisha Pugh
Admissions: Peggy Duck
Financial Aid: Dr. Sam Chuks
Type: Two-Year College **Sex:** Coed **Affiliation:** Alabama College System **Admission Plans:** Open Admission; Early Admission; Deferred Admission **Application Deadline:** Rolling **Application Fee:** $0.00 **H.S. Requirements:** High school diploma required; GED accepted **Costs Per Year:** Application fee: $0. State resident tuition: $2790 full-time, $93 per credit hour part-time. Nonresident tuition: $4920 full-time, $164 per credit hour part-time. College room and board: $2931. **Scholarships:** Available **Calendar System:** Semester, Summer Session Not available **Enrollment:** FT 1,925, PT 1,142 **Faculty:** FT 62, PT 96 **Student-Faculty Ratio:** 15:1 **% Residing in College-Owned, -Operated, or -Affiliated Housing:** 9 **Library Holdings:** 53,100 **Regional Accreditation:** Southern Association of Colleges and Schools **Credit Hours For Degree:** 60 semester hours, Associates **Professional Accreditation:** ARCEST, ACF, ADA **Intercollegiate Athletics:** Baseball M; Basketball M & W; Golf M; Softball W; Tennis M & W; Volleyball W

JEFFERSON DAVIS COMMUNITY COLLEGE
PO Box 958
Brewton, AL 36427-0958
Tel: (251)867-4832
Fax: (251)809-0178
Web Site: http://www.jdcc.edu/
President/CEO: Dr. Susan A. McBride
Registrar: Robin Sessions
Admissions: Robin Sessions
Financial Aid: Vanessa Kyles
Type: Two-Year College **Sex:** Coed **Admission Plans:** Open Admission; Early Admission **Application Fee:** $0.00 **H.S. Requirements:** High school diploma required; GED accepted **Scholarships:** Available **Calendar System:** Semester, Summer Session Available **Enrollment:** FT 908, PT 534 **Faculty:** FT 46, PT 76 **Student-Faculty Ratio:** 11:1 **Exams:** Other **Library Holdings:** 926 **Regional Accreditation:** Southern Association of Colleges and Schools **Credit Hours For Degree:** 60 credit hours, Associates **Professional Accreditation:** NLN

JEFFERSON STATE COMMUNITY COLLEGE
2601 Carson Rd.
Birmingham, AL 35215-3098
Tel: (205)853-1200
Fax: (205)856-8547
Web Site: http://www.jeffstateonline.com
President/CEO: Dr. Judy M. Merritt
Registrar: Michael Hobbs
Admissions: Michael Hobbs
Financial Aid: Tracy Adams
Type: Two-Year College **Sex:** Coed **Affiliation:** Alabama College System **Admission Plans:** Open Admission; Early Admission; Deferred Admission **Application Deadline:** Rolling **Application Fee:** $0.00 **H.S. Requirements:** High school diploma required; GED accepted **Costs Per Year:** Application fee: $0. State resident tuition: $2130 full-time, $71 per semester hour part-time. Nonresident tuition: $4260 full-time, $143 per semester hour part-time. Mandatory fees: $930 full-time, $31 per semester hour part-time. **Scholarships:** Available **Calendar System:** Semester, Summer Session Available **Enrollment:** FT 3,129, PT 4,044 **Faculty:** FT 122, PT 275 **Student-Faculty Ratio:** 21:1 **Library Holdings:** 77,015 **Regional Accreditation:** Southern Association of Colleges and Schools **Credit Hours For Degree:** 60 semester hours, Associates **ROTC:** Army, Air Force **Professional Accreditation:** ABFSE, ACCE, ACF, APTA, ACBSP, JRCERT, NAACLS, NLN **Intercollegiate Athletics:** Baseball M; Softball W

JUDSON COLLEGE
302 Bibb St.
PO Box 120
Marion, AL 36756
Tel: (334)683-5100
Free: 800-447-9472
Admissions: (334)683-5110
Fax: (334)683-5158
E-mail: mscotto@judson.edu
Web Site: http://www.judson.edu/
President/CEO: Dr. David E. Potts
Registrar: Eleanor C. Drake
Admissions: Michael Scotto
Financial Aid: Doris A. Wilson
Type: Four-Year College **Sex:** Women **Affiliation:** Baptist **Scores:** 100% SAT V 400+; 100% SAT M 400+; 51% ACT 18-23; 29% ACT 24-29 **% Accepted:** 76 **Admission Plans:** Early Admission; Deferred Admission **Application Deadline:** Rolling **Application Fee:** $30.00 **H.S. Requirements:** High school diploma required; GED accepted **Costs Per Year:** Application fee: $30. Comprehensive fee: $17,090 includes full-time tuition ($9900) and college room and board ($7190). Part-time tuition: $322 per semester hour. **Scholarships:** Available **Calendar System:** Semester, Summer Session Available **Enrollment:** FT 257, PT 74 **Faculty:** FT 28, PT 6 **Student-Faculty Ratio:** 9:1 **Exams:** SAT I or ACT **% Receiving Financial Aid:** 78 **% Residing in College-Owned, -Operated, or -Affiliated Housing:** 60 **Library Holdings:** 57,783 **Regional Accreditation:** Southern Association of Colleges and Schools **Credit Hours For Degree:** 128 semester hours, Bachelors **ROTC:** Army **Professional Accreditation:** NASM **Intercollegiate Athletics:** Basketball W; Equestrian Sports W; Softball W; Tennis W; Volleyball W

LAWSON STATE COMMUNITY COLLEGE
3060 Wilson Rd., SW
Birmingham, AL 35221-1798
Tel: (205)925-2515
Admissions: (205)929-6361
Fax: (205)929-6316
Web Site: http://www.lawsonstate.edu/
President/CEO: Dr. Perry W. Ward
Registrar: Darren Allen
Admissions: Darren C. Allen
Financial Aid: Cassandra Matthews
Type: Two-Year College **Sex:** Coed **Affiliation:** Alabama College System **% Accepted:** 50 **Admission Plans:** Open Admission; Early Admission; Deferred Admission **Application Deadline:** Rolling **Application Fee:** $0.00 **H.S. Requirements:** High school diploma required; GED accepted **Costs Per Year:** Application fee: $0. State resident tuition: $2160 full-time, $72 per credit part-time. Nonresident tuition: $4320 full-time, $144 per credit part-time. Mandatory fees: $540 full-time. **Scholarships:** Available **Calendar System:** Semester, Summer Session Available **Enrollment:** FT 1,740, PT 1,631 **Faculty:** FT 98, PT 121 **Student-Faculty Ratio:** 16:1 **Library Holdings:** 31,998 **Regional Accreditation:** Southern Association of Colleges and Schools **Credit Hours For Degree:** 60 credit hours, Associates **Professional Accreditation:** ACBSP, NLN **Intercollegiate Athletics:** Baseball W; Basketball M & W; Cross-Country Running M; Equestrian Sports M; Volleyball W

LURLEEN B. WALLACE COMMUNITY COLLEGE
PO Box 1418
Andalusia, AL 36420-1418
Tel: (334)222-6591
Web Site: http://www.lbwcc.edu/
President/CEO: Dr. James D. Krudop
Registrar: Jackie Curry
Admissions: Judy Hall
Financial Aid: Judy Hall
Type: Two-Year College **Sex:** Coed **Affiliation:** Alabama College System **Admission Plans:** Open Admission; Early Admission; Deferred Admission **Application Fee:** $0.00 **H.S. Requirements:** High school diploma required; GED accepted **Scholarships:** Available **Calendar System:** Semester, Summer Session Available **Faculty:** FT 109, PT 56 **Exams:** ACT **Library Holdings:** 35,278 **Regional Accreditation:** Southern Association of Colleges and Schools **Professional Accreditation:** JRCEMT **Intercollegiate Athletics:** Baseball M; Basketball M & W; Cross-Country Running M & W; Softball W

MARION MILITARY INSTITUTE
1101 Washington St.
Marion, AL 36756
Tel: (334)683-2306
Admissions: 800-664-1842
Fax: (334)683-2380
Web Site: http://www.marionmilitary.org/
President/CEO: Lt. Gen. Robert F. Foley
Registrar: Evelyn Vetzel
Admissions: Dan Sumlin
Financial Aid: M. Sgt. Ric Wood
Type: Two-Year College **Sex:** Coed **Admission Plans:** Deferred Admission **Application Fee:** $35.00 **H.S. Requirements:** High school diploma required; GED accepted **Scholarships:** Available **Calendar System:** Semester, Summer Session Not available **Faculty:** FT 40, PT 4 **Student-Faculty Ratio:** 6:1 **Exams:** SAT I or ACT **% Residing in College-Owned, -Operated, or -Affiliated Housing:** 97 **Library Holdings:** 36,000 **Regional Accreditation:** Southern Association of Colleges and Schools **Credit Hours For Degree:** 64 credit hours, Associates **ROTC:** Army, Air Force **Intercollegiate Athletics:** Golf M & W; Soccer M & W; Tennis M & W

MILES COLLEGE
PO Box 3800
Birmingham, AL 35208
Tel: (205)929-1000
Free: 800-445-0708
Admissions: (205)929-1657
E-mail: admissions@miles.edu
Web Site: http://www.miles.edu/
President/CEO: Dr. Albert J. H. Sloan, II
Registrar: Norma J. Kindall
Admissions: Christopher Robertson
Financial Aid: P. N. Lanier
Type: Four-Year College **Sex:** Coed **Affiliation:** Christian Methodist Episcopal **Scores:** 10% ACT 18-23; 1% ACT 24-29 **% Accepted:** 54 **Admission Plans:** Open Admission **Application Deadline:** August 23 **H.S. Requirements:** High school diploma required; GED accepted **Costs Per Year:** Comprehensive fee: $10,962 includes full-time tuition ($5408), mandatory fees ($418), and college room and board ($5136). College room only: $3000. Full-time tuition and fees vary according to course load, location, and program. Room and board charges vary according to housing facility and location. Part-time tuition: $227 per credit. Part-time mandatory fees: $209 per term. **Scholarships:** Available **Calendar System:** Semester, Summer Session Available **Enrollment:** FT 1,628, PT 88 **Faculty:** FT 93, PT 36 **Student-Faculty Ratio:** 20:1 **Exams:** ACT, Other **% Receiving Financial Aid:** 99 **% Residing in College-Owned, -Operated, or -Affiliated Housing:** 36 **Library Holdings:** 180,000 **Regional Accreditation:** Southern Association of Colleges and Schools **Credit Hours For Degree:** 124 semester hours, Bachelors **ROTC:** Army, Air Force **Professional Accreditation:** CSWE **Intercollegiate Athletics:** Baseball M; Basketball M & W; Cheerleading W; Cross-Country Running M; Football M; Softball W; Track and Field M

NORTHEAST ALABAMA COMMUNITY COLLEGE
PO Box 159
Rainsville, AL 35986-0159
Tel: (256)228-6001
Web Site: http://www.nacc.edu/
President/CEO: Dr. David Campbell
Registrar: Larry D. Guffey
Admissions: Dr. Joe Burke
Financial Aid: Harold Brookshire
Type: Two-Year College **Sex:** Coed **Affiliation:** Alabama College System **Admission Plans:** Open Admission; Early Admission; Deferred Admission **Application Fee:** $0.00 **H.S. Requirements:** High school diploma required; GED accepted **Costs Per Year:** Application fee: $0. State resident tuition: $2700 full-time, $90 per credit hour part-time. Nonresident tuition: $4860 full-time, $161 per credit hour part-time. Part-time tuition varies according to location. **Calendar System:** Quarter, Summer Session Available **Enrollment:** FT 978, PT 1,037 **Faculty:** FT 30, PT 106 **Student-Faculty Ratio:** 32:1 **Exams:** Other **Library Holdings:** 45,000 **Regional Accreditation:** Southern Association of Colleges and Schools **Credit Hours For Degree:** 96 quarter hours, Associates **Professional Accreditation:** JRCEMT, NLN

NORTHWEST-SHOALS COMMUNITY COLLEGE
PO Box 2545
Muscle Shoals, AL 35662
Tel: (256)331-5200
Admissions: (256)331-5261
Fax: (256)331-5366
Web Site: http://www.nwscc.edu/
President/CEO: Dr. Humphrey Lee
Registrar: Sheila Williams
Admissions: Dr. Karen Berryhill
Financial Aid: Joel Parris
Type: Two-Year College **Sex:** Coed **Affiliation:** State of Alabama Department of Postsecondary Education **% Accepted:** 69 **Admission Plans:** Open Admission **Application Deadline:** Rolling **Application Fee:** $0.00 **H.S. Requirements:** High school diploma required; GED accepted **Costs Per Year:** Application fee: $0. State resident tuition: $2130 full-time, $71 per credit hour part-time. Nonresident tuition: $4260 full-time, $142 per credit hour part-time. Mandatory fees: $750 full-time, $25 per credit hour part-time. College room only: $1675. **Scholarships:** Available **Calendar System:** Semester, Summer Session Available **Enrollment:** FT 2,132, PT 1,248 **Faculty:** FT 77, PT 177 **Student-Faculty Ratio:** 19:1 **% Residing in College-Owned, -Operated, or -Affiliated Housing:** 2 **Library Holdings:** 57,827 **Regional Accreditation:** Southern Association of Colleges and Schools **Credit Hours For Degree:** 64 credit hours, Associates **ROTC:** Army **Professional Accreditation:** NLN **Intercollegiate Athletics:** Baseball M; Basketball M & W; Cheerleading M & W; Cross-Country Running M; Golf M; Softball W; Tennis W; Volleyball W

OAKWOOD COLLEGE
7000 Adventist Blvd.
Huntsville, AL 35896
Tel: (256)726-7000
Admissions: (256)726-7354
Fax: (256)726-7404
E-mail: jmccracken@oakwood.edu
Web Site: http://www.oakwood.edu/
President/CEO: Dr. Delbert W. Baker
Registrar: Shirley Scott
Admissions: Jason McCracken
Financial Aid: Fred Stennis
Type: Four-Year College **Sex:** Coed **Affiliation:** Seventh-day Adventist **Scores:** 82% SAT V 400+; 65% SAT M 400+; 49% ACT 18-23; 9% ACT 24-29 **% Accepted:** 60 **Admission Plans:** Early Action; Deferred Admission **Application Deadline:** Rolling **Application Fee:** $20.00 **H.S. Requirements:** High school diploma required; GED accepted **Costs Per Year:** Application fee: $20. Comprehensive fee: $18,894 includes full-time tuition ($11,374), mandatory fees ($692), and college room and board ($6828). College room only: $2884. Part-time tuition: $490 per hour. **Scholarships:** Available **Calendar System:** Semester, Summer Session Not available **Enrollment:** FT 1,559, PT 192 **Faculty:** FT 103, PT 67 **Student-Faculty Ratio:** 13:1 **Exams:** SAT I or ACT **% Receiving Financial Aid:** 90 **% Residing in College-Owned, -Operated, or -Affiliated Housing:** 68 **Library Holdings:** 128,000 **Regional Accreditation:** Southern Association of Col-

leges and Schools **Credit Hours For Degree:** 64 semester hours, Associates; 128 semester hours, Bachelors **Professional Accreditation:** ADtA, ACBSP, CSWE, NCATE

PRINCE INSTITUTE OF PROFESSIONAL STUDIES
7735 Atlanta Hwy.
Montgomery, AL 36117-4231
Tel: (334)271-1670
Fax: (334)271-1671
E-mail: admissions@princeinstitute.edu
Web Site: http://www.princeinstitute.edu/
President/CEO: Patricia L. Hill
Admissions: Sherry Hill
Financial Aid: Tracie Campbell
Type: Two-Year College **Sex:** Coed **% Accepted:** 100 **Application Deadline:** October 01 **Application Fee:** $90.00 **H.S. Requirements:** High school diploma required; GED accepted **Costs Per Year:** Application fee: $90. Tuition: $8448 full-time. Mandatory fees: $340 full-time. **Scholarships:** Available **Calendar System:** Quarter **Enrollment:** FT 56, PT 38 **Faculty:** FT 5, PT 2 **Student-Faculty Ratio:** 15:1 **Professional Accreditation:** ACICS

REID STATE TECHNICAL COLLEGE
PO Box 588
Evergreen, AL 36401-0588
Tel: (251)578-1313
Fax: (251)578-5355
Web Site: http://www.rstc.cc.al.us/
President/CEO: Dr. Douglas M. Littles
Registrar: Diannah Rowser
Admissions: F. Diannah Rowser
Financial Aid: Linda Brantley
Type: Two-Year College **Sex:** Coed **Affiliation:** Alabama College System **Admission Plans:** Open Admission; Early Admission **Application Fee:** $0.00 **H.S. Requirements:** High school diploma or equivalent not required. For industrial electricity/electronics, administration programs: High school diploma required; GED accepted **Scholarships:** Available **Calendar System:** Semester, Summer Session Available **Enrollment:** FT 390, PT 230 **Faculty:** FT 24, PT 20 **Student-Faculty Ratio:** 16:1 **Exams:** Other **Credit Hours For Degree:** 114 credit hours, Associates **Professional Accreditation:** ACBSP, COE

REMINGTON COLLEGE-MOBILE CAMPUS
828 Downtowner Loop West
Mobile, AL 36609-5404
Tel: (251)343-8200
Free: 800-866-0850
Fax: (251)343-0577
Web Site: http://www.remingtoncollege.edu/
President/CEO: Mary G. White
Admissions: Chris Jones
Financial Aid: Linda Calvanese
Type: Two-Year College **Sex:** Coed **Affiliation:** Education America **% Accepted:** 96 **Application Fee:** $50.00 **H.S. Requirements:** High school diploma required; GED accepted **Costs Per Year:** Application fee: $50. Tuition: $34,200 full-time. Mandatory fees: $50 full-time. **Scholarships:** Available **Calendar System:** Quarter, Summer Session Not available **Enrollment:** FT 433 **Faculty:** FT 30, PT 11 **Student-Faculty Ratio:** 16:1 **Exams:** Other **Professional Accreditation:** ACCSCT

SAMFORD UNIVERSITY
800 Lakeshore Dr.
Birmingham, AL 35229-0002
Tel: (205)726-2011
Free: 800-888-7218
Admissions: (205)726-3673
Fax: (205)726-2171
E-mail: ppkimrey@samford.edu
Web Site: http://www.samford.edu/
President/CEO: Dr. Thomas E. Corts
Registrar: Paul Aucoin
Admissions: Dr. Phil Kimrey
Financial Aid: Ann P. Campbell
Type: University **Sex:** Coed **Affiliation:** Baptist **Scores:** 100% SAT V 400+; 100% SAT M 400+; 36% ACT 18-23; 53% ACT 24-29 **% Accepted:** 88 **Admission Plans:** Early Admission; Deferred Admission **Application Deadline:** December 15 **Application Fee:** $35.00 **H.S. Requirements:** High school diploma required; GED accepted **Costs Per Year:** Application fee: $35. Comprehensive fee: $20,258 includes full-time tuition ($14,642) and college room and board ($5616). College room only: $2860. Full-time tuition varies according to course load. Room and board charges vary according to board plan and housing facility. Part-time tuition: $486 per semester hour. Part-time tuition varies according to course load. **Scholarships:** Available **Calendar System:** 4-1-4, Summer Session Available **Enrollment:** FT 2,742, PT 199, Grad 400 **Faculty:** FT 278, PT 147 **Student-Faculty Ratio:** 12:1 **Exams:** SAT I or ACT **% Receiving Financial Aid:** 43 **% Residing in College-Owned, -Operated, or -Affiliated Housing:** 65 **Library Holdings:** 439,760 **Regional Accreditation:** Southern Association of Colleges and Schools **Credit Hours For Degree:** 64 semester hours, Associates; 128 semester hours, Bachelors **ROTC:** Army, Air Force **Professional Accreditation:** AACSB, AACN, AAFCS, AANA, ABA, ACPhE, AALS, ATS, FIDER, JRCEPAT, NASM, NCATE **Intercollegiate Athletics:** Baseball M; Basketball M & W; Cross-Country Running M & W; Football M; Golf M & W; Soccer M & W; Softball W; Tennis M & W; Track and Field M & W; Volleyball W

SHELTON STATE COMMUNITY COLLEGE
9500 Old Greensboro Rd.
Tuscaloosa, AL 35405-8522
Tel: (205)391-2211
Admissions: (205)391-2236
Fax: (205)391-2426
Web Site: http://www.sheltonstate.edu/
President/CEO: Dr. J. Richard Rogers
Registrar: Diane Layton
Admissions: Loretta Jones
Financial Aid: JoAnn Cousette
Type: Two-Year College **Sex:** Coed **Affiliation:** Alabama College System **% Accepted:** 100 **Admission Plans:** Open Admission **Application Deadline:** Rolling **Application Fee:** $0.00 **H.S. Requirements:** High school diploma required; GED accepted **Costs Per Year:** Application fee: $0. State resident tuition: $2130 full-time, $71 per credit hour part-time. Nonresident tuition: $4290 full-time, $143 per credit hour part-time. Mandatory fees: $570 full-time, $18 per credit hour part-time. **Scholarships:** Available **Calendar System:** Semester, Summer Session Available **Enrollment:** FT 3,363, PT 2,391 **Faculty:** FT 82, PT 117 **Student-Faculty Ratio:** 30:1 **Library Holdings:** 50,123 **Regional Accreditation:** Southern Association of Colleges and Schools **Credit Hours For Degree:** 64 semester hours, Associates **ROTC:** Army, Air Force **Professional Accreditation:** CARC, NLN **Intercollegiate Athletics:** Baseball M; Basketball M & W; Cheerleading M & W; Soccer W; Softball W

SNEAD STATE COMMUNITY COLLEGE
220 N Walnut St., PO Box 734
Boaz, AL 35957-0734
Tel: (256)593-5120
Fax: (256)593-7180
E-mail: mbucahanan@snead.edu
Web Site: http://www.snead.edu/
President/CEO: Dr. Devin Stephenson
Registrar: Martha Buchanan
Admissions: Martha Buchanan
Financial Aid: Helen Marks
Type: Two-Year College **Sex:** Coed **Affiliation:** Alabama College System **Admission Plans:** Open Admission; Early Admission; Deferred Admission **Application Deadline:** August 24 **Application Fee:** $0.00 **H.S. Requirements:** High school diploma required; GED accepted **Costs Per Year:** Application fee: $0. State resident tuition: $2304 full-time, $72 per semester hour part-time. Nonresident tuition: $4608 full-time, $144 per semester hour part-time. Mandatory fees: $704 full-time, $22 per semester hour part-time. **Scholarships:** Available **Calendar System:** Semester, Summer Session Available **% Residing in College-Owned, -Operated, or -Affiliated Housing:** 2 **Library Holdings:** 40,690 **Regional Accreditation:** Southern Association of Colleges and Schools **Credit Hours For Degree:** 64 semester hours, Associates **Intercollegiate Athletics:** Baseball M; Basketball M & W; Softball W; Tennis W

SOUTH UNIVERSITY
5355 Vaughn Rd.
Montgomery, AL 36116-1120
Tel: (334)395-8800

Fax: (334)395-8859
Web Site: http://www.southuniversity.edu/
President/CEO: Victor K. Biebighauser
Admissions: Anna Pearson
Financial Aid: James D. Berry
Type: Comprehensive **Sex:** Coed **Application Deadline:** Rolling **Application Fee:** $25.00 **H.S. Requirements:** High school diploma required; GED accepted **Costs Per Year:** Application fee: $25. Tuition: $11,475 full-time, $2995 per term part-time. **Scholarships:** Available **Calendar System:** Quarter, Summer Session Available **Enrollment:** FT 256, PT 155, Grad 9 **Faculty:** FT 14, PT 23 **Student-Faculty Ratio:** 13:1 **Exams:** SAT I or ACT **% Receiving Financial Aid:** 95 **Library Holdings:** 17,270 **Credit Hours For Degree:** 90 quarter hours, Associates; 184 quarter hours, Bachelors **Professional Accreditation:** AAMAE, APTA

SOUTHEASTERN BIBLE COLLEGE
2545 Valleydale Rd.
Birmingham, AL 35244-2083
Tel: (205)970-9200
Admissions: (205)970-9218
Fax: (205)970-9207
E-mail: jdunn@sebc.edu
Web Site: http://www.sebc.edu/
President/CEO: Dr. Don Hawkins
Registrar: Barbara Phillips
Admissions: Joel Dunn
Financial Aid: Joanne Belin
Type: Four-Year College **Sex:** Coed **Affiliation:** nondenominational **Scores:** 100% SAT V 400+; 100% SAT M 400+; 60% ACT 18-23; 23% ACT 24-29 **Admission Plans:** Early Admission; Deferred Admission **Application Deadline:** August 01 **Application Fee:** $20.00 **H.S. Requirements:** High school diploma required; GED accepted **Costs Per Year:** Application fee: $20. Tuition: $295 per semester hour part-time. **Scholarships:** Available **Calendar System:** Semester, Summer Session Available **Enrollment:** FT 174, PT 58 **Faculty:** FT 10, PT 15 **Student-Faculty Ratio:** 7:1 **Exams:** SAT I or ACT **% Receiving Financial Aid:** 79 **% Residing in College-Owned, -Operated, or -Affiliated Housing:** 19 **Library Holdings:** 44,539 **Credit Hours For Degree:** 65 semester hours, Associates; 128 semester hours, Bachelors **Professional Accreditation:** AABC

SOUTHERN CHRISTIAN UNIVERSITY
1200 Taylor Rd.
Montgomery, AL 36117
Tel: (334)387-3877
Free: 800-351-4040
Fax: (334)387-3878
E-mail: rickjohnson@southernchristian.edu
Web Site: http://www.southernchristian.edu/
President/CEO: Dr. Rex Turner, Jr.
Registrar: Elaine Tarence
Admissions: Rick Johnson
Financial Aid: Phillip Sampley
Type: University **Sex:** Coed **Affiliation:** Church of Christ **Admission Plans:** Open Admission **Application Deadline:** Rolling **Application Fee:** $50.00 **H.S. Requirements:** High school diploma required; GED accepted **Costs Per Year:** Application fee: $50. Tuition: $6000 full-time, $250 per semester hour part-time. **Scholarships:** Available **Calendar System:** Semester, Summer Session Available **Enrollment:** FT 310, PT 61, Grad 288 **Faculty:** FT 63, PT 15 **Student-Faculty Ratio:** 11:1 **% Receiving Financial Aid:** 81 **Library Holdings:** 80,000 **Regional Accreditation:** Southern Association of Colleges and Schools **Credit Hours For Degree:** 128 semester hours, Bachelors **Professional Accreditation:** ATS

SOUTHERN UNION STATE COMMUNITY COLLEGE
PO Box 1000, Roberts St.
Wadley, AL 36276
Tel: (256)395-2211
Fax: (256)395-2215
Web Site: http://www.suscc.cc.al.us/
President/CEO: Dr. Roy W. Johnson
Registrar: Pat Salatto, Jr.
Admissions: Susan Salatto
Financial Aid: Dorothy Wilkinson
Type: Two-Year College **Sex:** Coed **Affiliation:** Alabama College System **Admission Plans:** Open Admission; Early Admission; Deferred Admission **Application Fee:** $0.00 **H.S. Requirements:** High school diploma required; GED accepted **Scholarships:** Available **Calendar System:** Quarter, Summer Session Available **Faculty:** FT 81, PT 136 **Student-Faculty Ratio:** 19:1 **% Residing in College-Owned, -Operated, or -Affiliated Housing:** 6 **Library Holdings:** 90,791 **Regional Accreditation:** Southern Association of Colleges and Schools **Credit Hours For Degree:** 96 quarter hours, Associates **ROTC:** Air Force **Professional Accreditation:** JRCERT, JRCEMT, NLN **Intercollegiate Athletics:** Baseball M; Basketball M & W; Cross-Country Running M & W; Softball W; Volleyball W

SPRING HILL COLLEGE
4000 Dauphin St.
Mobile, AL 36608-1791
Tel: (251)380-4000
Free: 800-SHC-6704
Admissions: (251)380-3030
Fax: (251)460-2186
E-mail: admit@shc.edu
Web Site: http://www.shc.edu/
President/CEO: Rev. Gregory F. Lucey, SJ
Registrar: Stuart Moore
Admissions: Florence W. Hines
Financial Aid: Art Weeden
Type: Comprehensive **Sex:** Coed **Affiliation:** Roman Catholic (Jesuit) **Scores:** 98% SAT V 400+; 98% SAT M 400+; 56% ACT 18-23; 40% ACT 24-29 **% Accepted:** 80 **Admission Plans:** Early Admission; Deferred Admission **Application Deadline:** July 15 **Application Fee:** $25.00 **H.S. Requirements:** High school diploma required; GED accepted **Costs Per Year:** Application fee: $25. Comprehensive fee: $28,678 includes full-time tuition ($19,658), mandatory fees ($1290), and college room and board ($7730). College room only: $4000. Room and board charges vary according to board plan and housing facility. Part-time tuition: $736 per semester hour. Part-time mandatory fees: $42 per semester hour. **Scholarships:** Available **Calendar System:** Semester, Summer Session Available **Enrollment:** FT 1,174, PT 125, Grad 198 **Faculty:** FT 72, PT 66 **Student-Faculty Ratio:** 14:1 **Exams:** SAT I or ACT **% Receiving Financial Aid:** 66 **% Residing in College-Owned, -Operated, or -Affiliated Housing:** 78 **Library Holdings:** 180,404 **Regional Accreditation:** Southern Association of Colleges and Schools **Credit Hours For Degree:** 66 semester hours, Associates; 128 semester hours, Bachelors **ROTC:** Army, Air Force **Professional Accreditation:** AACN, ACBSP **Intercollegiate Athletics:** Baseball M; Basketball M & W; Cross-Country Running M & W; Golf M & W; Soccer M & W; Softball W; Swimming and Diving M & W; Tennis M & W; Volleyball W

STILLMAN COLLEGE
PO Drawer 1430, 3600 Stillman Blvd.
Tuscaloosa, AL 35403-9990
Tel: (205)349-4240
Free: 800-841-5722
Admissions: (205)366-8817
Fax: (205)366-8996
E-mail: mbonner@stillman.edu
Web Site: http://www.stillman.edu/
President/CEO: Dr. Ernest McNealey
Registrar: Barbara Smith
Admissions: Mason Bonner
Financial Aid: Jacqueline Morris
Type: Four-Year College **Sex:** Coed **Affiliation:** Presbyterian Church (U.S.A.) **Scores:** 33% ACT 18-23; 4% ACT 24-29 **Admission Plans:** Early Admission; Deferred Admission **Application Fee:** $15.00 **H.S. Requirements:** High school diploma required; GED accepted **Scholarships:** Available **Calendar System:** Semester, Summer Session Available **Faculty:** FT 52, PT 34 **Student-Faculty Ratio:** 17:1 **Exams:** SAT I or ACT **% Residing in College-Owned, -Operated, or -Affiliated Housing:** 75 **Regional Accreditation:** Southern Association of Colleges and Schools **Credit Hours For Degree:** 124 semester hours, Bachelors **ROTC:** Army **Professional Accreditation:** NCATE **Intercollegiate Athletics:** Basketball M & W; Cross-Country Running M; Football M; Tennis M & W; Track and Field M & W; Volleyball W

TALLADEGA COLLEGE
627 West Battle St.
Talladega, AL 35160-2354
Tel: (256)362-0206
Free: 800-633-2440

Admissions: (256)761-6219
Fax: (256)362-2268
E-mail: mthornton@talladega.edu
Web Site: http://www.talladega.edu/
Registrar: Floretta James Dortch
Admissions: Monroe Thornton
Financial Aid: Michael Francois
Type: Four-Year College **Sex:** Coed **Scores:** 37.5% SAT V 400+; 37.5% SAT M 400+; 36% ACT 18-23 **% Accepted:** 38 **Admission Plans:** Early Admission; Deferred Admission **Application Deadline:** Rolling **Application Fee:** $25.00 **H.S. Requirements:** High school diploma required; GED not accepted **Costs Per Year:** Application fee: $25. One-time mandatory fee: $150. Comprehensive fee: $11,548 includes full-time tuition ($6720), mandatory fees ($408), and college room and board ($4420). College room only: $1600. Part-time tuition: $280 per credit hour. Part-time mandatory fees: $204 per term. Part-time tuition and fees vary according to course load. **Scholarships:** Available **Calendar System:** Semester, Summer Session Not available **Enrollment:** FT 339, PT 29 **Faculty:** FT 35, PT 9 **Student-Faculty Ratio:** 9:1 **Exams:** SAT I and SAT II or ACT **% Receiving Financial Aid:** 92 **% Residing in College-Owned, -Operated, or -Affiliated Housing:** 76 **Library Holdings:** 121,303 **Regional Accreditation:** Southern Association of Colleges and Schools **Credit Hours For Degree:** 124 credit hours, Bachelors **ROTC:** Army **Professional Accreditation:** CSWE **Intercollegiate Athletics:** Table Tennis M & W; Tennis M & W

TROY UNIVERSITY
University Ave.
Troy, AL 36082
Tel: (334)670-3000
Free: 800-551-9716
Admissions: (334)670-3243
Fax: (334)670-3815
Web Site: http://www.troy.edu/
President/CEO: Dr. Jack Hawkins, Jr.
Registrar: Vickie Miles
Admissions: Buddy Starling
Financial Aid: Fred Carter
Type: Comprehensive **Sex:** Coed **Affiliation:** Troy University System **Admission Plans:** Deferred Admission **Application Deadline:** Rolling **Application Fee:** $20.00 **H.S. Requirements:** High school diploma required; GED accepted **Costs Per Year:** Application fee: $20. State resident tuition: $4004 full-time, $170 per credit hour part-time. Nonresident tuition: $8008 full-time, $340 per credit hour part-time. Mandatory fees: $674 full-time, $9 per credit hour part-time, $50 per term part-time. College room and board: $4964. College room only: $2300. Room and board charges vary according to board plan and housing facility. **Scholarships:** Available **Calendar System:** Semester, Summer Session Available **Enrollment:** FT 8,395, PT 10,383, Grad 8,102 **Faculty:** FT 456, PT 949 **Student-Faculty Ratio:** 21:1 **% Receiving Financial Aid:** 52 **% Residing in College-Owned, -Operated, or -Affiliated Housing:** 29 **Library Holdings:** 443,415 **Regional Accreditation:** Southern Association of Colleges and Schools **Credit Hours For Degree:** 62 credit hours, Associates; 120 credit hours, Bachelors **ROTC:** Army, Air Force **Professional Accreditation:** ACA, ACBSP, CORE, CSWE, JRCEPAT, NASM, NCATE, NLN **Intercollegiate Athletics:** Baseball M; Basketball M & W; Cross-Country Running M & W; Football M; Soccer W; Softball W; Tennis M & W; Track and Field M; Volleyball W

TUSKEGEE UNIVERSITY
Tuskegee, AL 36088
Tel: (334)727-8011
Free: 800-622-6531
Admissions: (334)727-8500
Web Site: http://www.tuskegee.edu/
President/CEO: Dr. Benjamin F. Payton
Registrar: Edrice Leftwich
Admissions: Robert Laney, Jr.
Financial Aid: Barbara Tucker Chisholm
Type: Comprehensive **Sex:** Coed **Scores:** 95% SAT V 400+; 95% SAT M 400+; 48% ACT 18-23; 9% ACT 24-29 **% Accepted:** 81 **Admission Plans:** Early Admission **Application Deadline:** April 15 **Application Fee:** $25.00 **H.S. Requirements:** High school diploma required; GED accepted **Costs Per Year:** Application fee: $25. Comprehensive fee: $20,587 includes full-time tuition ($12,400), mandatory fees ($300), and college room and board ($7887). Part-time tuition: $490 per credit hour. **Scholarships:** Available **Calendar System:** Semester, Summer Session Available **Enrollment:** FT 2,391, PT 119, Grad 148 **Faculty:** FT 223, PT 42 **Student-Faculty Ratio:** 12:1 **Exams:** SAT I or ACT **% Receiving Financial Aid:** 72 **% Residing in College-Owned, -Operated, or -Affiliated Housing:** 63 **Library Holdings:** 623,824 **Regional Accreditation:** Southern Association of Colleges and Schools **Credit Hours For Degree:** 124 credit hours, Bachelors **ROTC:** Army, Air Force **Professional Accreditation:** AACSB, ABET, AAFCS, AOTA, AVMA, CSWE, NAACLS, NCATE, NLN **Intercollegiate Athletics:** Baseball M; Basketball M & W; Cross-Country Running M & W; Football M; Golf M; Riflery M & W; Soccer M; Tennis M & W; Track and Field M & W; Volleyball W

THE UNIVERSITY OF ALABAMA
Tuscaloosa, AL 35487
Tel: (205)348-6010
Free: 800-933-BAMA
Admissions: (205)348-8197
Fax: (205)348-9046
E-mail: admissions@ua.edu
Web Site: http://www.ua.edu/
President/CEO: Dr. Robert E. Witt
Admissions: Mary K. Spiegel
Financial Aid: Jeanetta Allen
Type: University **Sex:** Coed **Affiliation:** The University of Alabama System **Scores:** 98% SAT V 400+; 97% SAT M 400+; 52% ACT 18-23; 36% ACT 24-29 **% Accepted:** 74 **Admission Plans:** Early Admission; Deferred Admission **Application Fee:** $30.00 **H.S. Requirements:** High school diploma required; GED accepted **Costs Per Year:** Application fee: $30. State resident tuition: $4864 full-time. Nonresident tuition: $13,516 full-time. Full-time tuition varies according to course load. College room and board: $5024. College room only: $3120. Room and board charges vary according to board plan and housing facility. **Scholarships:** Available **Calendar System:** Semester, Summer Session Available **Enrollment:** FT 15,832, PT 1,721, Grad 3,687 **Faculty:** FT 922, PT 226 **Student-Faculty Ratio:** 9:1 **Exams:** SAT I or ACT **% Receiving Financial Aid:** 39 **% Residing in College-Owned, -Operated, or -Affiliated Housing:** 22 **Library Holdings:** 2,465,217 **Regional Accreditation:** Southern Association of Colleges and Schools **Credit Hours For Degree:** 120 semester hours, Bachelors **ROTC:** Army, Air Force **Professional Accreditation:** AACSB, ABET, ACEJMC, AACN, AAFCS, ABA, ACA, ADtA, ALA, APA, ASLHA, AALS, CORE, CSWE, FIDER, JRCEPAT, NASAD, NASD, NASM, NAST NCATE **Intercollegiate Athletics:** Baseball M; Basketball M & W; Cheerleading M & W; Crew W; Cross-Country Running M & W; Football M; Golf M & W; Gymnastics W; Soccer W; Softball W; Swimming and Diving M & W; Tennis M & W; Track and Field M & W; Volleyball W

THE UNIVERSITY OF ALABAMA AT BIRMINGHAM
1530 3rd Ave. South
Birmingham, AL 35294
Tel: (205)934-4011
Free: 800-421-8743
Admissions: (205)934-8221
Fax: (205)975-7114
E-mail: uabadmit@uabdpo.dpo.uab.edu
Web Site: http://main.uab.edu/
President/CEO: Dr. Carol Z. Garrison
Registrar: Stella Cocoris
Admissions: Chenise Ryan
Financial Aid: Janet May
Type: University **Sex:** Coed **Affiliation:** University of Alabama System **Scores:** 57% ACT 18-23; 29% ACT 24-29 **% Accepted:** 88 **Admission Plans:** Early Admission; Deferred Admission **Application Deadline:** March 01 **Application Fee:** $30.00 **H.S. Requirements:** High school diploma required; GED accepted **Costs Per Year:** Application fee: $30. State resident tuition: $3960 full-time, $132 per credit hour part-time. Nonresident tuition: $9900 full-time, $330 per credit hour part-time. Mandatory fees: $832 full-time. Full-time tuition and fees vary according to program. Part-time tuition varies according to program. College room only: $3390. Room charges vary according to housing facility and student level. **Scholarships:** Available **Calendar System:** Semester, Summer Session Available **Enrollment:** FT 8,059, PT 3,411, Grad 4,135 **Faculty:** FT 777, PT 103 **Student-Faculty Ratio:** 18:1 **Exams:** SAT I or ACT **% Receiving Financial Aid:** 53 **% Residing in College-Owned, -Operated, or -Affiliated Housing:** 11 **Library Holdings:** 853,445 **Regional Accreditation:** Southern Association of Colleges and Schools **Credit Hours For Degree:** 120 hours, Bachelors **ROTC:** Army, Air Force **Professional Accreditation:** AACSB, ABET,

ACEHSA, AACN, AANA, ADA, ADtA, AHIMA, AOTA, AOA, APTA, APA, ASC, ACIPE, CARC, CEPH, CORE, CSWE, JRCERT, JRCEMT JRCNMT, LCMEAMA, NAACLS, NASAD, NASM, NASPAA, NCATE **Intercollegiate Athletics:** Baseball M; Basketball M & W; Cross-Country Running W; Football M; Golf M & W; Riflery M & W; Soccer M & W; Softball W; Swimming and Diving W; Tennis M & W; Track and Field W; Volleyball W

THE UNIVERSITY OF ALABAMA IN HUNTSVILLE
301 Sparkman Dr.
Huntsville, AL 35899
Tel: (256)824-1000
Free: 800-UAH-CALL
Admissions: (256)824-6070
Fax: (256)824-6073
E-mail: admitme@email.uah.edu
Web Site: http://www.uah.edu/
President/CEO: Dr. Frank Franz
Registrar: Scott Verzyl
Admissions: John Maxon
Financial Aid: Andy Weaver
Type: University **Sex:** Coed **Affiliation:** University of Alabama System **Scores:** 99% SAT V 400+; 98% SAT M 400+; 37% ACT 18-23; 49% ACT 24-29 **% Accepted:** 87 **Admission Plans:** Early Admission; Deferred Admission **Application Deadline:** August 15 **Application Fee:** $30.00 **H.S. Requirements:** High school diploma required; GED accepted **Costs Per Year:** Application fee: $30. State resident tuition: $4688 full-time. Nonresident tuition: $9886 full-time. Full-time tuition varies according to course load. College room and board: $5320. College room only: $3720. Room and board charges vary according to board plan and housing facility. **Scholarships:** Available **Calendar System:** Semester, Summer Session Available **Enrollment:** FT 4,101, PT 1,589, Grad 1,394 **Faculty:** FT 280, PT 188 **Student-Faculty Ratio:** 16:1 **Exams:** SAT I or ACT **% Receiving Financial Aid:** 40 **% Residing in College-Owned, -Operated, or -Affiliated Housing:** 16 **Library Holdings:** 327,663 **Regional Accreditation:** Southern Association of Colleges and Schools **Credit Hours For Degree:** 128 semester hours, Bachelors **ROTC:** Army **Professional Accreditation:** AACSB, ABET, AACN, NASM, NLN **Intercollegiate Athletics:** Archery M & W; Badminton M & W; Baseball M; Basketball M & W; Bowling M & W; Cheerleading M & W; Crew M & W; Cross-Country Running M & W; Ice Hockey M; Soccer M & W; Softball W; Tennis M & W; Track and Field M & W; Volleyball W

UNIVERSITY OF MOBILE
5735 College Parkway
Mobile, AL 36613
Tel: (251)442-2773
Free: 800-946-7267
Admissions: (251)442-2287
Fax: (251)442-2498
E-mail: adminfo@umobile.edu
Web Site: http://www.umobile.edu/
President/CEO: Dr. Mark R. Foley
Registrar: Dr. Don Berry
Admissions: Kris Nelson
Financial Aid: Lydia Houck
Type: Comprehensive **Sex:** Coed **Affiliation:** Southern Baptist **Scores:** 53% ACT 18-23; 21% ACT 24-29 **Admission Plans:** Early Admission; Deferred Admission **Application Deadline:** Rolling **Application Fee:** $30.00 **H.S. Requirements:** High school diploma required; GED accepted **Costs Per Year:** Application fee: $30. Comprehensive fee: $16,950 includes full-time tuition ($10,230), mandatory fees ($330), and college room and board ($6390). College room only: $2680. Full-time tuition and fees vary according to course load. Room and board charges vary according to housing facility. Part-time tuition: $341 per semester hour. Part-time tuition varies according to course load. **Scholarships:** Available **Calendar System:** Semester, Summer Session Available **Enrollment:** FT 1,273, PT 276, Grad 209 **Faculty:** FT 88, PT 68 **Student-Faculty Ratio:** 13:1 **Exams:** SAT I or ACT **% Receiving Financial Aid:** 61 **% Residing in College-Owned, -Operated, or -Affiliated Housing:** 20 **Library Holdings:** 100,250 **Regional Accreditation:** Southern Association of Colleges and Schools **Credit Hours For Degree:** 64 semester hours, Associates; 128 semester hours, Bachelors **ROTC:** Army, Air Force **Professional Accreditation:** APTA, ACBSP, NASM, NLN **Intercollegiate Athletics:** Baseball M; Basketball M & W; Cross-Country Running M & W; Golf M & W; Soccer M & W; Softball W; Tennis W; Track and Field M & W

UNIVERSITY OF MONTEVALLO
Station 6001
Montevallo, AL 35115
Tel: (205)665-6000
Free: 800-292-4349
Admissions: (205)665-6030
E-mail: admissions@um.montevallo.edu
Web Site: http://www.montevallo.edu/
President/CEO: Dr. Robert M. McChesney
Registrar: Katherine Hoefker
Admissions: Lynn Gurganus
Type: Comprehensive **Sex:** Coed **Scores:** 65% ACT 18-23; 29% ACT 24-29 **% Accepted:** 76 **Admission Plans:** Early Admission; Deferred Admission **Application Deadline:** August 01 **Application Fee:** $25.00 **H.S. Requirements:** High school diploma required; GED accepted **Costs Per Year:** Application fee: $25. State resident tuition: $5460 full-time, $182 per credit hour part-time. Nonresident tuition: $10,920 full-time, $364 per credit hour part-time. Mandatory fees: $204 full-time. Full-time tuition and fees vary according to course load. Part-time tuition varies according to course load. College room and board: $3966. Room and board charges vary according to board plan and housing facility. **Scholarships:** Available **Calendar System:** Semester, Summer Session Available **Enrollment:** FT 2,357, PT 259, Grad 383 **Faculty:** FT 140, PT 60 **Student-Faculty Ratio:** 17:1 **Exams:** ACT, SAT I or ACT **% Receiving Financial Aid:** 60 **% Residing in College-Owned, -Operated, or -Affiliated Housing:** 35 **Library Holdings:** 258,122 **Regional Accreditation:** Southern Association of Colleges and Schools **Credit Hours For Degree:** 130 semester hours, Bachelors **ROTC:** Army, Air Force **Professional Accreditation:** AACSB, AAFCS, ACA, ASLHA, CSWE, NASAD, NASM, NCATE **Intercollegiate Athletics:** Baseball M; Basketball M & W; Golf M & W; Soccer M & W; Tennis W; Volleyball W

UNIVERSITY OF NORTH ALABAMA
One Harrison Plaza
Florence, AL 35632-0001
Tel: (256)765-4100
Free: 800-TAL-KUNA
Admissions: (256)765-4316
Fax: (256)765-4329
E-mail: admissions@una.edu
Web Site: http://www.una.edu/
President/CEO: Dr. G. Garry Warren
Registrar: Dr. Sue Wilson
Admissions: Dr. Sue Wilson
Financial Aid: Ben Baker
Type: Comprehensive **Sex:** Coed **Affiliation:** Alabama Commission on Higher Education **Scores:** 75% SAT V 400+; 96% SAT M 400+; 56% ACT 18-23; 20% ACT 24-29 **% Accepted:** 80 **Admission Plans:** Early Admission; Deferred Admission **Application Deadline:** Rolling **Application Fee:** $25.00 **H.S. Requirements:** High school diploma required; GED accepted **Costs Per Year:** Application fee: $25. State resident tuition: $3648 full-time, $143 per credit hour part-time. Nonresident tuition: $7296 full-time, $286 per credit hour part-time. Mandatory fees: $718 full-time. Part-time tuition varies according to course load. College room and board: $4170. College room only: $1960. Room and board charges vary according to board plan and housing facility. **Scholarships:** Available **Calendar System:** Semester, Summer Session Available **Enrollment:** FT 4,444, PT 973, Grad 998 **Faculty:** FT 209, PT 113 **Student-Faculty Ratio:** 20:1 **Exams:** SAT I or ACT **% Receiving Financial Aid:** 57 **% Residing in College-Owned, -Operated, or -Affiliated Housing:** 19 **Library Holdings:** 358,393 **Regional Accreditation:** Southern Association of Colleges and Schools **Credit Hours For Degree:** 128 semester hours, Bachelors **ROTC:** Army **Professional Accreditation:** ABET, AAFCS, ACBSP, CSWE, NASAD, NASM, NCATE, NLN **Intercollegiate Athletics:** Baseball M; Basketball M & W; Cross-Country Running M & W; Football M; Golf M; Soccer W; Softball W; Tennis M & W; Volleyball W

UNIVERSITY OF SOUTH ALABAMA
307 University Blvd.
Mobile, AL 36688-0002
Tel: (251)460-6101
Free: 800-872-5247
Admissions: (251)460-6141
Fax: (251)460-7025
Web Site: http://www.usouthal.edu/
President/CEO: V. Gordon Moulton

Registrar: Melissa Wold
Admissions: Melissa Haab
Financial Aid: Emily Johnston
Type: University **Sex:** Coed **Scores:** 57% ACT 18-23; 29% ACT 24-29 **% Accepted:** 87 **Admission Plans:** Preferred Admission; Early Admission **Application Deadline:** July 15 **Application Fee:** $25.00 **H.S. Requirements:** High school diploma required; GED accepted **Costs Per Year:** Application fee: $25. State resident tuition: $3810 full-time, $127 per credit hour part-time. Nonresident tuition: $7620 full-time, $254 per credit hour part-time. Mandatory fees: $692 full-time, $256 per term part-time. College room and board: $4428. College room only: $2468. Room and board charges vary according to board plan, housing facility, and location. **Scholarships:** Available **Calendar System:** Semester, Summer Session Available **Enrollment:** FT 7,495, PT 2,649, Grad 2,715 **Faculty:** FT 720, PT 250 **Student-Faculty Ratio:** 18:1 **Exams:** SAT I or ACT **% Receiving Financial Aid:** 60 **% Residing in College-Owned, -Operated, or -Affiliated Housing:** 19 **Library Holdings:** 1,044,788 **Regional Accreditation:** Southern Association of Colleges and Schools **Credit Hours For Degree:** 128 semester hours, Bachelors **ROTC:** Army, Air Force **Professional Accreditation:** AACSB, ABET, AACN, AOTA, APTA, ASLHA, CARC, JRCEMT, LCMEAMA, NAACLS, NASAD, NASM, NCATE **Intercollegiate Athletics:** Baseball M; Basketball M & W; Cross-Country Running M & W; Fencing M & W; Football M; Golf M & W; Soccer W; Tennis M & W; Track and Field M & W; Volleyball W

THE UNIVERSITY OF WEST ALABAMA
Livingston, AL 35470
Tel: (205)652-3400
Free: 800-621-8044
Web Site: http://www.uwa.edu/
President/CEO: Dr. Richard D. Holland
Registrar: Clarence W. Egbert
Admissions: Richard Hester
Financial Aid: Patsy Reedy
Type: Comprehensive **Sex:** Coed **Scores:** 50.4% ACT 18-23; 12.4% ACT 24-29 **Admission Plans:** Early Admission; Deferred Admission **Application Fee:** $20.00 **H.S. Requirements:** High school diploma required; GED accepted **Costs Per Year:** Application fee: $20. State resident tuition: $3838 full-time, $162 per semester hour part-time. Nonresident tuition: $7676 full-time, $324 per semester hour part-time. Mandatory fees: $488 full-time, $235 per term part-time. Part-time tuition and fees vary according to course level. College room and board: $3285. College room only: $1746. Room and board charges vary according to board plan and housing facility. **Scholarships:** Available **Calendar System:** Semester, Summer Session Available **Enrollment:** FT 1,450, PT 187, Grad 1,030 **Faculty:** FT 88, PT 4 **Student-Faculty Ratio:** 23:1 **Exams:** SAT I or ACT **% Receiving Financial Aid:** 58 **% Residing in College-Owned, -Operated, or -Affiliated Housing:** 35 **Library Holdings:** 151,991 **Regional Accreditation:** Southern Association of Colleges and Schools **Credit Hours For Degree:** 60 quarter hours, Associates; 120 quarter hours, Bachelors **ROTC:** Army, Air Force **Professional Accreditation:** ACBSP, JRCEPAT, NCATE, NLN **Intercollegiate Athletics:** Baseball M; Basketball M & W; Cross-Country Running M & W; Football M; Softball W; Volleyball W

VC TECH
2790 Pelham Parkway
Pelham, AL 35124
Tel: (205)943-2100; 877-5-VCTECH
Web Site: http://www.vctechnical.com/
President/CEO: Dick Daigle
Type: Two-Year College **Sex:** Coed **Professional Accreditation:** ACICS

VIRGINIA COLLEGE AT BIRMINGHAM
65 Bagby Dr.
Birmingham, AL 35209
Tel: (205)802-1200
Fax: (205)802-1597
Web Site: http://www.vc.edu/
President/CEO: Dr. Kenneth C. Horne
Registrar: Angela Payne
Admissions: Bibbie J. McLaughlin
Financial Aid: Larry Moore
Type: Comprehensive **Sex:** Coed **H.S. Requirements:** High school diploma required; GED accepted **Costs Per Year:** Tuition: $10,800 full-time, $300 per credit part-time. Mandatory fees: $150 full-time. Full-time tuition and fees vary according to program. Part-time tuition varies according to program. Tuition guaranteed not to increase for student's term of enrollment. **Scholarships:** Available **Calendar System:** Quarter **Enrollment:** FT 2,407 **Faculty:** FT 138, PT 63 **Student-Faculty Ratio:** 14:1 **Exams:** Other **Library Holdings:** 3,900 **Credit Hours For Degree:** 96 quarter hours, Associates **Professional Accreditation:** ACICS, ACF

VIRGINIA COLLEGE AT HUNTSVILLE
2800-A Bob Wallace Ave.
Huntsville, AL 35805
Tel: (256)533-7387
Admissions: (205)533-7387
Fax: (256)533-7785
Web Site: http://www.vc.edu/
President/CEO: Dr. Kenneth C. Horne
Registrar: Bridget McConnell
Admissions: Pat Foster
Financial Aid: Dave Hall
Type: Two-Year College **Sex:** Coed **H.S. Requirements:** High school diploma required; GED accepted **Costs Per Year:** Tuition: $9900 full-time, $255 per credit hour part-time. Full-time tuition varies according to course load, degree level, and program. Part-time tuition varies according to course load, degree level, and program. **Scholarships:** Available **Calendar System:** Quarter **Faculty:** FT 5, PT 16 **Exams:** Other **Credit Hours For Degree:** 90 quarter hours, Associates **Professional Accreditation:** ACICS

WALLACE STATE COMMUNITY COLLEGE
PO Box 2000
Hanceville, AL 35077-2000
Tel: (256)352-8000
Admissions: (256)352-8278
Fax: (256)352-8228
Web Site: http://www.wallacestate.edu/
President/CEO: Dr. Vicki Hawsey
Registrar: Linda Sperling
Admissions: Linda Sperling
Financial Aid: Allison Rice
Type: Two-Year College **Sex:** Coed **Scores:** 58% ACT 18-23; 13% ACT 24-29 **Admission Plans:** Open Admission; Early Admission; Deferred Admission **Application Fee:** $0.00 **H.S. Requirements:** High school diploma required; GED accepted **Scholarships:** Available **Calendar System:** Semester, Summer Session Available **Faculty:** FT 225, PT 387 **Student-Faculty Ratio:** 30:1 **Exams:** ACT, Other **% Residing in College-Owned, -Operated, or -Affiliated Housing:** 3 **Library Holdings:** 41,500 **Regional Accreditation:** Southern Association of Colleges and Schools **Credit Hours For Degree:** 60 semester hours, Associates **Professional Accreditation:** AAMAE, ADA, AHIMA, AOTA, APTA, CARC, JRCEDMS, JRCERT, JRCEMT, NAACLS, NLN **Intercollegiate Athletics:** Baseball M; Basketball M & W; Cross-Country Running M & W; Golf M; Soccer M & W; Softball W; Tennis M & W; Track and Field M & W; Volleyball W

ALASKA BIBLE COLLEGE
Box 289
Glennallen, AK 99588-0289
Tel: (907)822-3201
Free: 800-478-7884
Fax: (907)822-5027
E-mail: info@akbible.edu
Web Site: http://www.akbible.edu/
President/CEO: Steven J. Hostetter
Registrar: Carol C. Ridley
Admissions: Carol C. Ridley
Financial Aid: James A. Folsom
Type: Four-Year College **Sex:** Coed **Affiliation:** nondenominational **% Accepted:** 92 **Admission Plans:** Deferred Admission **Application Deadline:** July 01 **Application Fee:** $35.00 **H.S. Requirements:** High school diploma required; GED accepted **Costs Per Year:** Application fee: $35. Comprehensive fee: $10,700 includes full-time tuition ($5950) and college room and board ($4750). Part-time tuition: $260 per credit hour. **Scholarships:** Available **Calendar System:** Semester, Summer Session Not available **Enrollment:** FT 37, PT 11 **Faculty:** FT 3, PT 8 **Student-Faculty Ratio:** 7:1 **Exams:** SAT I or ACT **% Receiving Financial Aid:** 87 **% Residing in College-Owned, -Operated, or -Affiliated Housing:** 82 **Library Holdings:** 29,888 **Credit Hours For Degree:** 61 credits, Associates; 120 credits, Bachelors **Professional Accreditation:** AABC

ALASKA PACIFIC UNIVERSITY
4101 University Dr.
Anchorage, AK 99508-4672
Tel: (907)561-1266
Free: 800-252-7528
Admissions: (907)564-8248
Fax: (907)564-8317
E-mail: mwarner@alaskapacific.edu
Web Site: http://www.alaskapacific.edu/
President/CEO: Dr. Douglas M. North
Registrar: Jeanette D. Brooks
Admissions: Michael Warner
Financial Aid: Peter Miller
Type: Comprehensive **Sex:** Coed **Scores:** 96% SAT V 400+; 92% SAT M 400+; 50% ACT 18-23; 39% ACT 24-29 **% Accepted:** 44 **Admission Plans:** Early Decision Plan; Deferred Admission **Application Deadline:** February 01 **Application Fee:** $25.00 **H.S. Requirements:** High school diploma required; GED accepted **Costs Per Year:** Application fee: $25. Comprehensive fee: $26,410 includes full-time tuition ($19,500), mandatory fees ($110), and college room and board ($6800). Part-time tuition: $812 per semester hour. Part-time mandatory fees: $55 per term. **Scholarships:** Available **Calendar System:** Semester, Summer Session Available **Enrollment:** FT 336, PT 244, Grad 220 **Faculty:** FT 40, PT 40 **Student-Faculty Ratio:** 8:1 **Exams:** SAT I or ACT **% Receiving Financial Aid:** 72 **% Residing in College-Owned, -Operated, or -Affiliated Housing:** 22 **Library Holdings:** 788,708 **Credit Hours For Degree:** 64 semester hours, Associates; 128 semester hours, Bachelors **Professional Accreditation:** NCATE, NCCU

CHARTER COLLEGE
2221 East Northern Lights Blvd., Ste. 120
Anchorage, AK 99508-4140
Tel: (907)277-1000
Fax: (907)274-3342
Web Site: http://www.chartercollege.org/
President/CEO: Dr. Milton Byrd
Admissions: Lily Sirianni
Financial Aid: Janell McIntyre
Type: Two-Year College **Sex:** Coed **Admission Plans:** Open Admission **Application Fee:** $20.00 **H.S. Requirements:** High school diploma required; GED accepted **Scholarships:** Available **Calendar System:** Quarter, Summer Session Available **Faculty:** FT 10, PT 33 **Student-Faculty Ratio:** 15:1 **Library Holdings:** 1,000 **Credit Hours For Degree:** 90 credit hours, Associates **Professional Accreditation:** ACICS

ILISAGVIK COLLEGE
UIC/Narl
Barrow, AK 99723
Tel: (907)852-3333
Admissions: (907)852-1820
Fax: (907)852-2729
Web Site: http://www.ilisagvik.cc/
President/CEO: Dr. Edna Ahgeak MacLean
Admissions: Beverly Patkotak Grinage
Type: Two-Year College **Sex:** Coed **% Accepted:** 100 **Application Deadline:** August 01 **Application Fee:** $0.00 **Costs Per Year:** Application fee: $0. Area resident tuition: $1440 full-time, $60 per credit hour part-time. State resident tuition: $2880 full-time, $120 per credit hour part-time. Nonresident tuition: $2880 full-time, $120 per credit hour part-time. Mandatory fees: $100 full-time, $50 per term part-time. College room only: $4000. **Calendar System:** Semester **Enrollment:** FT 49, PT 214 **Faculty:** FT 12, PT 0 **Student-Faculty Ratio:** 10:1 **Exams:** Other **Professional Accreditation:** NCCU

SHELDON JACKSON COLLEGE
801 Lincoln St.
Sitka, AK 99835-7699
Tel: (907)747-5222
Free: 800-478-4556
Admissions: (907)747-5208
Fax: (907)747-5212
E-mail: admissions@sj-alaska.edu
Web Site: http://www.sj-alaska.edu/
President/CEO: Dr. Arthur Cleveland
Registrar: Kathy Newman
Admissions: Andrew R. Lee
Financial Aid: Brian Chamberlain
Type: Four-Year College **Sex:** Coed **Affiliation:** Presbyterian Church (U.S.A.) **Admission Plans:** Open Admission; Preferred Admission; Deferred Admission **Application Fee:** $25.00 **H.S. Requirements:** High school diploma required; GED accepted **Costs Per Year:** Application fee: $25. Comprehensive fee: $18,500 includes full-time tuition ($10,600), mandatory fees ($600), and college room and board ($7300). College room only: $3700. Room and board charges vary according to board plan and housing facility. Part-time tuition: $355 per credit. Part-time mandatory fees: $355 per credit. Part-time tuition and fees vary according to course load and degree level. **Scholarships:** Available **Calendar System:** Semester, Summer Session Not available **Enrollment:** FT 135, PT 139 **Faculty:** FT 20, PT 18

Student-Faculty Ratio: 7:1 **% Receiving Financial Aid:** 90 **% Residing in College-Owned, -Operated, or -Affiliated Housing:** 80 **Library Holdings:** 46,000 **Credit Hours For Degree:** 60 credits, Associates; 120 credits, Bachelors **Professional Accreditation:** NCCU

UNIVERSITY OF ALASKA ANCHORAGE
3211 Providence Dr.
Anchorage, AK 99508-8060
Tel: (907)786-1800
Admissions: (907)786-1558
Fax: (907)786-4888
Web Site: http://www.uaa.alaska.edu/
President/CEO: Dr. Elaine P. Maimon
Registrar: Jean Stanley
Admissions: Cecile Mitchell
Financial Aid: Ted Malone
Type: Comprehensive **Sex:** Coed **Affiliation:** University of Alaska System **Scores:** 88% SAT V 400+; 89% SAT M 400+; 52% ACT 18-23; 24% ACT 24-29 **Admission Plans:** Deferred Admission **Application Fee:** $40.00 **H.S. Requirements:** High school diploma required; GED accepted. For applicants to associate degree programs, 18 or over, provided they complete Advisement/Assessment Program: High school diploma or equivalent not required **Costs Per Year:** Application fee: $40. State resident tuition: $2952 full-time, $116 per credit hour part-time. Nonresident tuition: $9048 full-time, $370 per credit hour part-time. Mandatory fees: $513 full-time. Full-time tuition and fees vary according to course level. Part-time tuition varies according to course level. College room and board: $7810. College room only: $4710. Room and board charges vary according to board plan and housing facility. **Scholarships:** Available **Calendar System:** Semester, Summer Session Available **Enrollment:** FT 6,906, PT 8,575, Grad 780 **Faculty:** FT 530, PT 672 **Student-Faculty Ratio:** 18:1 **Exams:** SAT I or ACT **% Receiving Financial Aid:** 38 **% Residing in College-Owned, -Operated, or -Affiliated Housing:** 6 **Library Holdings:** 894,080 **Credit Hours For Degree:** 60 semester credits, Associates; 120 semester credits, Bachelors **ROTC:** Air Force **Professional Accreditation:** AACSB, ABET, ACEJMC, AAMAE, ADA, ADtA, CSWE, NAACLS, NASAD, NASM, NLN, NCCU **Intercollegiate Athletics:** Basketball M & W; Cross-Country Running M; Gymnastics W; Ice Hockey M; Skiing (Cross-Country) M & W; Skiing (Downhill) M & W; Swimming and Diving M; Volleyball W

UNIVERSITY OF ALASKA ANCHORAGE, KENAI PENINSULA COLLEGE
34820 College Dr.
Soldotna, AK 99669-9798
Tel: (907)262-0300
Fax: (907)262-0322
Web Site: http://www.kpc.alaska.edu/
President/CEO: Gary Turner
Admissions: Shelly Love
Financial Aid: Carrie Burford
Type: Two-Year College **Sex:** Coed **Affiliation:** University of Alaska System **Admission Plans:** Open Admission **Application Fee:** $40.00 **H.S. Requirements:** High school diploma required; GED accepted **Scholarships:** Available **Calendar System:** Semester, Summer Session Not available **Faculty:** FT 30, PT 120 **Student-Faculty Ratio:** 15:1 **Exams:** Other **Library Holdings:** 25,000 **Credit Hours For Degree:** 60 credits, Associates **Professional Accreditation:** NCCU

UNIVERSITY OF ALASKA ANCHORAGE, KODIAK COLLEGE
117 Benny Benson Dr.
Kodiak, AK 99615-6643
Tel: (907)486-4161
Admissions: (907)486-1235
Fax: (907)486-1257
Web Site: http://www.koc.alaska.edu/
President/CEO: Dr. Douglas E. Hammer
Registrar: Karen Hamer
Admissions: Karen Hamer
Financial Aid: Christine Jamin
Type: Two-Year College **Sex:** Coed **Affiliation:** University of Alaska System **Admission Plans:** Open Admission **Application Fee:** $35.00 **H.S. Requirements:** High school diploma required; GED accepted **Scholarships:** Available **Calendar System:** Semester, Summer Session Not available **Faculty:** FT 10, PT 30 **Student-Faculty Ratio:** 19:1 **Exams:** Other **Library Holdings:** 21,000 **Credit Hours For Degree:** 60 credits, Associates **Professional Accreditation:** NCCU

UNIVERSITY OF ALASKA ANCHORAGE, MATANUSKA-SUSITNA COLLEGE
PO Box 2889
Palmer, AK 99645-2889
Tel: (907)745-9774
Admissions: (907)745-9712
Fax: (907)745-9747
Web Site: http://www.matsu.alaska.edu/
President/CEO: Dr. Paul Dauphinais
Registrar: Sandra Gravley
Admissions: Sandra Gravley
Financial Aid: Connie Cannon
Type: Two-Year College **Sex:** Coed **Affiliation:** University of Alaska System **Admission Plans:** Open Admission **Application Deadline:** November 01 **Application Fee:** $40.00 **H.S. Requirements:** High school diploma required; GED accepted **Costs Per Year:** Application fee: $40. State resident tuition: $2880 full-time. Nonresident tuition: $9576 full-time. Mandatory fees: $250 full-time. **Scholarships:** Available **Calendar System:** Semester, Summer Session Available **Enrollment:** FT 384, PT 942 **Faculty:** FT 21, PT 75 **Student-Faculty Ratio:** 14:1 **Library Holdings:** 50,000 **Credit Hours For Degree:** 60 credits, Associates **Professional Accreditation:** NCCU

UNIVERSITY OF ALASKA FAIRBANKS
PO Box 757500
Fairbanks, AK 99775-7520
Tel: (907)474-7211
Free: 800-478-1823
Admissions: (907)474-7500
Fax: (907)474-5379
E-mail: fyapply@uaf.edu
Web Site: http://www.uaf.edu/
President/CEO: Steve B. Jones
Registrar: Tim Stickel
Admissions: Nancy Dix
Financial Aid: Tamara M. Hornbuckle
Type: University **Sex:** Coed **Affiliation:** University of Alaska System **Scores:** 92% SAT V 400+; 90% SAT M 400+; 43% ACT 18-23; 26% ACT 24-29 **% Accepted:** 78 **Admission Plans:** Early Admission; Deferred Admission **Application Deadline:** August 01 **Application Fee:** $40.00 **H.S. Requirements:** High school diploma required; GED accepted **Costs Per Year:** Application fee: $40. State resident tuition: $3825 full-time, $128 per credit part-time. Nonresident tuition: $12,195 full-time, $407 per credit part-time. Mandatory fees: $693 full-time. College room and board: $5580. College room only: $2990. **Scholarships:** Available **Calendar System:** Semester, Summer Session Available **Enrollment:** FT 3,462, PT 3,674, Grad 1,094 **Faculty:** FT 288, PT 7 **Student-Faculty Ratio:** 16:1 **Exams:** SAT I or ACT **% Receiving Financial Aid:** 40 **% Residing in College-Owned, -Operated, or -Affiliated Housing:** 41 **Library Holdings:** 616,456 **Credit Hours For Degree:** 60 credits, Associates; 120 credits, Bachelors **ROTC:** Army **Professional Accreditation:** AACSB, ABET, ACEJMC, AAMAE, CSWE, NASM, NCATE, NCCU, SAF **Intercollegiate Athletics:** Basketball M & W; Cross-Country Running M & W; Ice Hockey M; Riflery M & W; Skiing (Cross-Country) M & W; Swimming and Diving W; Volleyball W

UNIVERSITY OF ALASKA, PRINCE WILLIAM SOUND COMMUNITY COLLEGE
PO Box 97
Valdez, AK 99686-0097
Tel: (907)834-1600
Admissions: (907)834-1632
Fax: (907)834-1661
E-mail: sfoster@pwscc.edu
Web Site: http://www.pwscc.edu/
President/CEO: Dr. JoAnne C. McDowell
Registrar: Shannon Foster
Admissions: Shannon Foster
Financial Aid: Angela Coccoran
Type: Two-Year College **Sex:** Coed **Affiliation:** University of Alaska System **Admission Plans:** Open Admission; Early Admission **Application Fee:** $10.00 **Scholarships:** Available **Calendar System:** Semester, Summer Session Available **Faculty:** FT 6, PT 46 **Exams:** Other **% Residing in College-Owned, -Operated, or -Affiliated Housing:** 2 **Library Holdings:** 40,870 **Credit Hours For Degree:** 60 credits, Associates **Professional Accreditation:** NCCU

UNIVERSITY OF ALASKA SOUTHEAST
11120 Glacier Hwy.
Juneau, AK 99801
Tel: (907)796-6457; 877-796-4827
Admissions: (907)796-6294
Fax: (907)796-6365
E-mail: admissions@uas.alaska.edu
Web Site: http://www.uas.alaska.edu/
President/CEO: John Pugh
Registrar: Barbara Hegel
Admissions: Barbara Hegel
Financial Aid: Barbara C. Burnett
Type: Comprehensive **Sex:** Coed **Affiliation:** University of Alaska System **Scores:** 89.3% SAT V 400+; 86.9% SAT M 400+; 44.1% ACT 18-23; 41.2% ACT 24-29 **% Accepted:** 63 **Admission Plans:** Open Admission; Early Admission; Deferred Admission **Application Deadline:** Rolling **Application Fee:** $40.00 **H.S. Requirements:** High school diploma required; GED accepted **Costs Per Year:** Application fee: $40. State resident tuition: $3060 full-time, $135 per credit hour part-time. Nonresident tuition: $9756 full-time, $414 per credit hour part-time. Mandatory fees: $796 full-time. College room and board: $6714. College room only: $4177. **Scholarships:** Available **Calendar System:** Semester, Summer Session Available **Enrollment:** FT 866, PT 2,048, Grad 212 **Faculty:** FT 101, PT 128 **Student-Faculty Ratio:** 12:1 **Exams:** SAT I or ACT **% Receiving Financial Aid:** 45 **Library Holdings:** 176,312 **Credit Hours For Degree:** 60 credits, Associates; 120 credits, Bachelors **Professional Accreditation:** NCATE, NCCU **Intercollegiate Athletics:** Riflery M & W

UNIVERSITY OF ALASKA SOUTHEAST, KETCHIKAN CAMPUS
2600 7th Ave.
Ketchikan, AK 99901-5798
Tel: (907)225-6177
Admissions: (907)228-4508
Fax: (907)225-3624
E-mail: knblj@acad1.alaska.edu
Web Site: http://www.ketch.alaska.edu/
President/CEO: Karen Polley
Registrar: Brenda Hurley
Admissions: Gail Klein
Financial Aid: Gail Klein
Type: Two-Year College **Sex:** Coed **Affiliation:** University of Alaska System **Admission Plans:** Open Admission; Early Admission **Application Fee:** $35.00 **H.S. Requirements:** High school diploma required; GED accepted **Costs Per Year:** Application fee: $35. State resident tuition: $2784 full-time. Mandatory fees: $796 full-time. Full-time tuition and fees vary according to course level and course load. College room and board: $6714. College room only: $4177. **Scholarships:** Available **Calendar System:** Semester, Summer Session Not available **Faculty:** FT 12, PT 0 **Student-Faculty Ratio:** 15:1 **Exams:** Other, SAT I or ACT **Library Holdings:** 54,000 **Credit Hours For Degree:** 60 credits, Associates **Professional Accreditation:** NCCU

UNIVERSITY OF ALASKA SOUTHEAST, SITKA CAMPUS
1332 Seward Ave.
Sitka, AK 99835-9418
Tel: (907)747-6653
Admissions: (907)747-7703
Fax: (907)747-7747
Web Site: http://www.uas.alaska.edu/
President/CEO: Dr. John W. Carnegie
Registrar: Marie Wickman
Admissions: Tim Schroeder
Financial Aid: Timothy Schroeder
Type: Two-Year College **Sex:** Coed **Affiliation:** University of Alaska System **Admission Plans:** Open Admission; Early Admission **Application Fee:** $35.00 **H.S. Requirements:** High school diploma required; GED accepted **Calendar System:** Semester, Summer Session Available **Student-Faculty Ratio:** 13:1 **Library Holdings:** 80,050 **Credit Hours For Degree:** 60 credits, Associates **Professional Accreditation:** AHIMA, NCCU

AMERICAN INDIAN COLLEGE OF THE ASSEMBLIES OF GOD, INC.
10020 North Fifteenth Ave.
Phoenix, AZ 85021-2199
Tel: (602)944-3335
Free: 800-933-3828
E-mail: sticeahkie@aicag.edu
Web Site: http://www.aicag.edu/
President/CEO: Jim H. Lopez
Registrar: Donald Keeter
Admissions: Sandy Ticeahkie
Financial Aid: Nadine Waldrop
Type: Four-Year College **Sex:** Coed **Affiliation:** Assemblies of God **Admission Plans:** Preferred Admission **Application Fee:** $0.00 **H.S. Requirements:** High school diploma required; GED accepted **Scholarships:** Available **Calendar System:** Semester, Summer Session Not available **Enrollment:** FT 60, PT 13 **Faculty:** FT 5, PT 15 **Student-Faculty Ratio:** 8:1 **Exams:** SAT I or ACT **Library Holdings:** 19,899 **Regional Accreditation:** North Central Association of Colleges and Schools **Credit Hours For Degree:** 73 semester hours, Associates; 128 semester hours, Bachelors

APOLLO COLLEGE-PHOENIX, INC.
8503 North 27th Ave.
Phoenix, AZ 85051
Tel: (602)864-1571
Fax: (602)864-8207
E-mail: rutley@apollocollege.com
Web Site: http://www.apollocollege.com/
President/CEO: Margaret Carlson
Registrar: Karen Rotarius
Admissions: Randy Utley
Financial Aid: Carol Deman
Type: Two-Year College **Sex:** Coed **Affiliation:** Apollo Colleges, Inc **Admission Plans:** Open Admission **Application Fee:** $75.00 **H.S. Requirements:** High school diploma required; GED accepted **Scholarships:** Available **Calendar System:** Continuous, Summer Session Not available **Enrollment:** FT 603 **Faculty:** FT 30, PT 8 **Credit Hours For Degree:** 66 credit hours, Associates **Professional Accreditation:** ABHES, CARC

APOLLO COLLEGE-TRI-CITY, INC.
630 West Southern Ave.
Mesa, AZ 85210-5004
Tel: (480)831-6585
Free: 800-36-TRAIN
Fax: (480)827-0022
E-mail: jmiller@apollocollege.com
Web Site: http://www.apollocollege.com/
President/CEO: Margaret Carlson
Registrar: Cynthia Gamingaso
Admissions: James Norris Miller
Financial Aid: Emma Rutherford
Type: Two-Year College **Sex:** Coed **Affiliation:** Apollo Colleges, Inc **Admission Plans:** Open Admission **Application Fee:** $75.00 **Scholarships:** Available **Calendar System:** Semester **Faculty:** FT 12, PT 5 **Exams:** Other **Credit Hours For Degree:** 66 credit hours, Associates **Professional Accreditation:** ABHES, CARC

APOLLO COLLEGE-TUCSON, INC.
3870 North Oracle Rd.
Tucson, AZ 85705-3227
Tel: (520)888-5885
Free: 800-36-TRAIN
E-mail: jmckinney@apollocollege.com
Web Site: http://www.apollocollege.com/
President/CEO: Margaret Carlson
Registrar: Darlene Lewis
Admissions: Jenell McKinney
Financial Aid: Barbra Disney
Type: Two-Year College **Sex:** Coed **Affiliation:** Apollo Colleges, Inc **Application Fee:** $75.00 **Calendar System:** Semester **Credit Hours For Degree:** 67 credits, Associates **Professional Accreditation:** ABHES

APOLLO COLLEGE-WESTSIDE, INC.
2701 West Bethany Home Rd.
Phoenix, AZ 85017
Tel: (602)433-1333
Free: 800-36-TRAIN
Admissions: (602)433-1222
E-mail: cnestor@apollocollege.com
Web Site: http://www.apollocollege.com/
President/CEO: Margaret Carlson
Admissions: Cindy Nestor
Financial Aid: Suellen Boyer
Type: Two-Year College **Sex:** Coed **Affiliation:** Apollo Colleges, Inc **Admission Plans:** Open Admission **Application Fee:** $75.00 **Scholarships:** Available **Calendar System:** Semester **Faculty:** FT 11, PT 2 **Exams:** Other **Credit Hours For Degree:** 66 credit hours, Associates **Professional Accreditation:** ABHES

ARGOSY UNIVERSITY/PHOENIX
2301 West Dunlap Ave., Ste. 211
Phoenix, AZ 85021
Tel: (602)216-2600; (866)216-2777
Fax: (602)216-2601
E-mail: ahughes@argosyu.edu
Web Site: http://www.argosyu.edu/
President/CEO: Mike Robinson
Admissions: Andy Hughes
Type: Two-Year Upper Division **Sex:** Coed **Affiliation:** Argosy University **Costs Per Year:** Tuition: $14,400 full-time. Mandatory fees: $25 full-time. **Scholarships:** Available **Calendar System:** Semester **Enrollment:** FT 36, Grad 358 **Faculty:** FT 16, PT 10 **Student-Faculty Ratio:** 13:1 **% Receiving Financial Aid:** 100 **Regional Accreditation:** North Central Association of Colleges and Schools **Professional Accreditation:** APA

ARIZONA AUTOMOTIVE INSTITUTE
6829 North 46th Ave.
Glendale, AZ 85301-3597
Tel: (602)934-7273

Admissions: (623)934-7273
Fax: (602)937-5000
Web Site: http://www.azautoinst.com/
President/CEO: Alan Klager
Admissions: Mark LaCara
Type: Two-Year College **Faculty:** FT 13, PT 2 **Professional Accreditation:** ACCSCT

ARIZONA COLLEGE OF ALLIED HEALTH
4425 West Olive Ave., Ste. 300
Glendale, AZ 85302-3843
Tel: (602)222-9300
Fax: (602)200-8726
Web Site: http://www.arizonacollege.edu/
President/CEO: C. Larkin Hicks
Financial Aid: Carline Harbour
Type: Two-Year College **Sex:** Coed **Calendar System:** Quarter **Professional Accreditation:** ABHES

ARIZONA STATE UNIVERSITY
Tempe, AZ 85287
Tel: (480)965-9011
Admissions: (480)965-7788
E-mail: ugradadm@asuvm.inre.asu.edu
Web Site: http://www.asu.edu/
President/CEO: Dr. Michael M. Crow
Registrar: Lou Ann Denny
Admissions: Martha Byrd
Financial Aid: Craig Fennell
Type: University **Sex:** Coed **Affiliation:** Arizona State University **Scores:** 96.8% SAT V 400+; 96.7% SAT M 400+; 44.7% ACT 18-23; 40.1% ACT 24-29 **% Accepted:** 91 **Admission Plans:** Early Action **Application Deadline:** Rolling **Application Fee:** $25.00 **H.S. Requirements:** High school diploma required; GED accepted **Costs Per Year:** Application fee: $25, $50 for nonresidents. State resident tuition: $4311 full-time, $225 per credit part-time. Nonresident tuition: $15,000 full-time, $625 per credit part-time. Mandatory fees: $95 full-time, $24 per term part-time. Full-time tuition and fees vary according to program. Part-time tuition and fees vary according to program. College room and board: $6768. College room only: $4275. Room and board charges vary according to board plan and housing facility. **Scholarships:** Available **Calendar System:** Semester, Summer Session Available **Enrollment:** FT 32,865, PT 8,391, Grad 9,719 **Faculty:** FT 1,878, PT 404 **Student-Faculty Ratio:** 22:1 **Exams:** SAT I or ACT **% Receiving Financial Aid:** 42 **% Residing in College-Owned, -Operated, or -Affiliated Housing:** 18 **Library Holdings:** 2,380,457 **Regional Accreditation:** North Central Association of Colleges and Schools **Credit Hours For Degree:** 120 credits, Bachelors **ROTC:** Army, Air Force **Professional Accreditation:** AACSB, ABET, ACEHSA, ACEJMC, AACN, ABA, ACCE, ACA, ACSP, APA, ASLA, ASLHA, AALS, CEPH, CSWE, FIDER, NAACLS, NASAD, NASM, NASPAA NLN, NRPA **Intercollegiate Athletics:** Baseball M; Basketball M & W; Cross-Country Running M & W; Football M; Golf M & W; Gymnastics W; Soccer W; Softball W; Swimming and Diving M & W; Tennis M & W; Track and Field M & W; Volleyball W; Water Polo W; Wrestling M

ARIZONA STATE UNIVERSITY AT THE POLYTECHNIC CAMPUS
7001 East Williams Field Rd.
Mesa, AZ 85212
Tel: (480)727-3278
Admissions: (480)727-1041
Fax: (480)727-1008
E-mail: gary.mcgrath@asu.edu
Web Site: http://www.poly.asu.edu/
President/CEO: Dr. Charles Backus
Admissions: Dr. Gary McGrath
Type: Comprehensive **Sex:** Coed **Affiliation:** Arizona State University **Scores:** 93% SAT V 400+; 97% SAT M 400+; 54% ACT 18-23; 28% ACT 24-29 **% Accepted:** 86 **Admission Plans:** Early Action **Application Deadline:** Rolling **Application Fee:** $50.00 **H.S. Requirements:** High school diploma required; GED accepted **Costs Per Year:** Application fee: $50. State resident tuition: $4301 full-time, $221 per credit hour part-time. Nonresident tuition: $13,918 full-time, $580 per credit hour part-time. Mandatory fees: $45 full-time. Full-time tuition and fees vary according to degree level, location, and program. Part-time tuition varies according to course load, degree level, location, and program. College room and board: $5155. College room only: $2655. Room and board charges vary according to board plan, housing facility, and student level. **Scholarships:** Available **Calendar System:** Semester, Summer Session Available **Enrollment:** FT 1,244, PT 2,839, Grad 782 **Faculty:** FT 130, PT 9 **Student-Faculty Ratio:** 28:1 **Exams:** SAT I or ACT **% Receiving Financial Aid:** 52 **Regional Accreditation:** North Central Association of Colleges and Schools **Credit Hours For Degree:** 120 semester hours, Bachelors **ROTC:** Army, Air Force **Professional Accreditation:** ABET, ADtA, CAA, NAIT

ARIZONA STATE UNIVERSITY WEST
PO Box 37100, 4701 W Thunderbird Rd
Phoenix, AZ 85069-7100
Tel: (602)543-5500
Admissions: (602)543-8134
E-mail: cabot@asu.edu
Web Site: http://www.west.asu.edu/
President/CEO: Dr. Michael M. Crow
Registrar: Thomas Cabot
Admissions: Thomas Cabot
Financial Aid: Leah Samudio
Type: Comprehensive **Sex:** Coed **Affiliation:** Arizona State University **Scores:** 91% SAT V 400+; 93% SAT M 400+; 58% ACT 18-23; 31% ACT 24-29 **% Accepted:** 63 **Application Deadline:** Rolling **Application Fee:** $50.00 **H.S. Requirements:** High school diploma required; GED accepted **Costs Per Year:** Application fee: $50. State resident tuition: $4251 full-time, $221 per credit hour part-time. Nonresident tuition: $15,000 full-time, $625 per credit hour part-time. Mandatory fees: $95 full-time. Part-time tuition varies according to course load. College room only: $5836. **Scholarships:** Available **Calendar System:** Semester, Summer Session Available **Enrollment:** FT 4,843, PT 1,777, Grad 1,114 **Faculty:** FT 233, PT 155 **Student-Faculty Ratio:** 19:1 **Exams:** SAT I or ACT **% Receiving Financial Aid:** 55 **% Residing in College-Owned, -Operated, or -Affiliated Housing:** 2 **Library Holdings:** 397,987 **Regional Accreditation:** North Central Association of Colleges and Schools **Credit Hours For Degree:** 120 credit hours, Bachelors **Professional Accreditation:** AACSB, CSWE, NRPA

ARIZONA WESTERN COLLEGE
PO Box 929
Yuma, AZ 85366-0929
Tel: (928)317-6000; 888-293-0392
Admissions: (928)317-7617
Fax: (928)344-7730
E-mail: bryan.doak@azwestern.edu
Web Site: http://www.azwestern.edu/
President/CEO: Dr. Don Schoening
Admissions: Bryan Doak
Financial Aid: Luis Barajas
Type: Two-Year College **Sex:** Coed **Affiliation:** Arizona State Community College System **Admission Plans:** Open Admission; Early Admission; Deferred Admission **Application Deadline:** Rolling **Application Fee:** $0.00 **H.S. Requirements:** High school diploma required; GED accepted. For applicants 18 or over: High school diploma or equivalent not required **Costs Per Year:** Application fee: $0. State resident tuition: $1200 full-time, $40 per credit hour part-time. Nonresident tuition: $5760 full-time, $46 per credit hour part-time. College room and board: $4468. College room only: $1790. **Scholarships:** Available **Calendar System:** Semester, Summer Session Available **Enrollment:** FT 1,849, PT 4,882 **Faculty:** FT 109, PT 235 **Student-Faculty Ratio:** 16:1 **% Residing in College-Owned, -Operated, or -Affiliated Housing:** 6 **Regional Accreditation:** North Central Association of Colleges and Schools **Credit Hours For Degree:** 64 credit hours, Associates **Professional Accreditation:** NLN **Intercollegiate Athletics:** Baseball M; Basketball M; Football M; Soccer M; Softball W; Volleyball W

THE ART CENTER DESIGN COLLEGE
2525 North Country Club Rd.
Tucson, AZ 85716-2505
Tel: (520)325-0123
Free: 800-825-8753
Fax: (520)325-5535
E-mail: cgf@theartcenter.edu
Web Site: http://www.theartcenter.edu/
President/CEO: Sharmon Woods
Registrar: Amy Woods
Admissions: Colleen Gimbel-Froebe
Type: Four-Year College **Sex:** Coed **Application Deadline:** Rolling **Application Fee:** $25.00 **H.S. Requirements:** High school diploma required;

GED accepted. For non-degree programs: High school diploma or equivalent not required **Costs Per Year:** Application fee: $25. Tuition: $11,376 full-time, $474 per credit hour part-time. **Scholarships:** Available **Calendar System:** Miscellaneous **Exams:** Other **Credit Hours For Degree:** 156 quarter hours, Associates **Professional Accreditation:** ACCSCT, FIDER

THE ART INSTITUTE OF PHOENIX

2233 West Dunlap Ave.
Phoenix, AZ 85021-2859
Tel: (602)331-7500
Free: 800-474-2479
Fax: (602)331-5301
Web Site: http://www.aipx.artinstitutes.edu/
President/CEO: Karyn A. Bryant
Registrar: Stephanie Schroeder
Admissions: Jerry Driskill
Financial Aid: Paula Cady
Type: Four-Year College **Sex:** Coed **Affiliation:** Education Management Corporation **Application Deadline:** Rolling **Application Fee:** $50.00 **H.S. Requirements:** High school diploma required; GED accepted **Costs Per Year:** Application fee: $50. One-time mandatory fee: $100. Tuition: $18,144 full-time, $378 per credit hour part-time. Full-time tuition varies according to course load. Part-time tuition varies according to course load. College room only: $5217. Tuition guaranteed not to increase for student's term of enrollment. **Scholarships:** Available **Calendar System:** Quarter, Summer Session Not available **Enrollment:** FT 866, PT 248 **Faculty:** FT 45, PT 64 **Student-Faculty Ratio:** 16:1 **% Residing in College-Owned, -Operated, or -Affiliated Housing:** 10 **Library Holdings:** 13,463 **Credit Hours For Degree:** 96 credits, Associates; 186 credits, Bachelors **Professional Accreditation:** ACICS

THE BRYMAN SCHOOL

2250 W. Peoria Ave.
Phoenix, AZ 85029
Tel: (602)274-4300
Free: 800-729-4819
Fax: (602)248-9087
Web Site: http://www.brymanschool.edu/
President/CEO: Cathy Brauff
Admissions: Vicki Maurer
Financial Aid: Tim Kulesha
Type: Two-Year College **Sex:** Coed **H.S. Requirements:** High school diploma required; GED accepted **Scholarships:** Available **Calendar System:** Continuous, Summer Session Not available **Faculty:** FT 59, PT 0 **Student-Faculty Ratio:** 18:1 **Exams:** Other **Professional Accreditation:** ABHES, ACCSCT, AAMAE

CENTRAL ARIZONA COLLEGE

8470 North Overfield Rd.
Coolidge, AZ 85228-9779
Tel: (520)426-4444
Admissions: (520)426-4406
Fax: (520)426-4234
Web Site: http://www.cac.cc.az.us/
President/CEO: Dr. Terry Calaway
Admissions: Doris Helmich
Type: Two-Year College **Sex:** Coed **% Accepted:** 73 **Admission Plans:** Open Admission; Early Admission; Deferred Admission **Application Deadline:** Rolling **H.S. Requirements:** High school diploma or equivalent not required **Costs Per Year:** State resident tuition: $1316 full-time, $47 per credit part-time. Nonresident tuition: $6356 full-time, $94 per credit part-time. Mandatory fees: $16 full-time, $8 per term part-time. Part-time tuition and fees vary according to course level. College room and board: $4160. Room and board charges vary according to housing facility. **Scholarships:** Available **Calendar System:** Semester, Summer Session Available **Enrollment:** FT 1,928, PT 4,460 **Faculty:** FT 94, PT 236 **Student-Faculty Ratio:** 17:1 **% Residing in College-Owned, -Operated, or -Affiliated Housing:** 17 **Library Holdings:** 99,480 **Regional Accreditation:** North Central Association of Colleges and Schools **Credit Hours For Degree:** 64 credits, Associates **Professional Accreditation:** NLN **Intercollegiate Athletics:** Baseball M; Basketball M & W; Cross-Country Running M & W; Equestrian Sports M & W; Golf M; Softball W; Track and Field M & W

CHANDLER-GILBERT COMMUNITY COLLEGE

2626 East Pecos Rd.
Chandler, AZ 85225-2479
Tel: (480)732-7000
Admissions: (480)732-7307
Web Site: http://www.cgc.maricopa.edu/
President/CEO: Maria L. Hesse
Registrar: Lois Bartholomew
Admissions: Irene Pearl
Financial Aid: Doug Bullock
Type: Two-Year College **Sex:** Coed **Affiliation:** Maricopa County Community College District System **Admission Plans:** Open Admission **Application Fee:** $0.00 **H.S. Requirements:** High school diploma or equivalent not required **Calendar System:** Semester, Summer Session Available **Faculty:** FT 92, PT 320 **Student-Faculty Ratio:** 19:1 **Exams:** Other **Library Holdings:** 26,060 **Regional Accreditation:** North Central Association of Colleges and Schools **Credit Hours For Degree:** 64 credits, Associates

CHAPARRAL COLLEGE

4585 East Speedway, No 204
Tucson, AZ 85712
Tel: (520)327-6866
Fax: (520)325-0108
Web Site: http://www.chap-col.edu/
President/CEO: Scott Rhude
Admissions: Becki Rossini
Financial Aid: Kris Johnson
Type: Two-Year College **Sex:** Coed **Admission Plans:** Open Admission **Application Fee:** $35.00 **H.S. Requirements:** High school diploma required; GED accepted **Scholarships:** Available **Calendar System:** Miscellaneous, Summer Session Available **Faculty:** FT 14, PT 24 **Student-Faculty Ratio:** 20:1 **Exams:** Other **Library Holdings:** 6,000 **Credit Hours For Degree:** 90 credit hours, Associates; 183 credit hours, Bachelors **Professional Accreditation:** ACICS

COCHISE COLLEGE (DOUGLAS)

4190 West Hwy. 80
Douglas, AZ 85607-9724
Tel: (520)364-7943
Free: 800-966-7946
Admissions: (520)417-4050
Fax: (520)364-0236
E-mail: info@tron.cochise.cc.az.us
Web Site: http://www.cochise.edu/
President/CEO: Dr. Karen Nicodemus
Registrar: Catherine Knapp
Admissions: Dr. Bo Hall
Financial Aid: Phillip Schroeder
Type: Two-Year College **Sex:** Coed **Affiliation:** Cochise College **% Accepted:** 100 **Admission Plans:** Open Admission; Early Admission; Deferred Admission **Application Deadline:** Rolling **H.S. Requirements:** High school diploma or equivalent not required. For applicants under 18, nursing program: High school diploma required; GED accepted **Costs Per Year:** State resident tuition: $1350 full-time, $45 per credit hour part-time. Nonresident tuition: $6300 full-time, $65 per credit hour part-time. Mandatory fees: $60 full-time, $30 per term part-time. College room and board: $3562. **Scholarships:** Available **Calendar System:** Semester, Summer Session Available **Enrollment:** FT 1,440, PT 3,170 **Faculty:** FT 91, PT 277 **Student-Faculty Ratio:** 13:1 **% Residing in College-Owned, -Operated, or -Affiliated Housing:** 17 **Library Holdings:** 42,876 **Regional Accreditation:** North Central Association of Colleges and Schools **Credit Hours For Degree:** 64 credit hours, Associates **Professional Accreditation:** NLN **Intercollegiate Athletics:** Baseball M; Basketball M & W; Soccer W

COCHISE COLLEGE (SIERRA VISTA)

901 North Columbo
Sierra Vista, AZ 85635-2317
Tel: (520)515-0500
Free: 800-593-9567
Admissions: (520)515-4770

Fax: (520)364-0206
Web Site: http://www.cochise.cc.az.us/
President/CEO: Dr. Karen A. Nicodemus
Admissions: Dr. James (Bo) Hall
Financial Aid: Dartle Atherton
Type: Two-Year College **Sex:** Coed **Affiliation:** Cochise College **Admission Plans:** Open Admission; Early Admission; Deferred Admission **H.S. Requirements:** High school diploma or equivalent not required. For applicants under 18, nursing program: High school diploma required; GED accepted **Scholarships:** Available **Calendar System:** Semester, Summer Session Available **Enrollment:** FT 1,257, PT 3,189 **Faculty:** FT 91, PT 303 **Student-Faculty Ratio:** 14:1 **Exams:** ACT, Other, SAT I or ACT, SAT I and SAT II or ACT, SAT I, SAT II **Library Holdings:** 67,317 **Regional Accreditation:** North Central Association of Colleges and Schools **Credit Hours For Degree:** 64 credit hours, Associates **Intercollegiate Athletics:** Baseball M; Basketball M & W; Equestrian Sports M & W; Soccer W

COCONINO COMMUNITY COLLEGE
2800 South Lonetree Rd.
Flagstaff, AZ 86001
Tel: (928)527-1222
Free: 800-350-7122
Fax: (928)526-1821
E-mail: smiller@coco.cc.az.us
Web Site: http://www.coconino.edu/
President/CEO: Dr. Thomas Jordan
Registrar: Steve Miller
Admissions: Steve Miller
Financial Aid: Patricia Sprengeler
Type: Two-Year College **Sex:** Coed **Admission Plans:** Open Admission **Application Fee:** $10.00 **H.S. Requirements:** High school diploma required; GED accepted **Costs Per Year:** Application fee: $10. State resident tuition: $1344 full-time, $56 per credit hour part-time. Nonresident tuition: $5376 full-time, $224 per credit hour part-time. **Scholarships:** Available **Calendar System:** Semester, Summer Session Available **Faculty:** FT 25, PT 180 **Regional Accreditation:** North Central Association of Colleges and Schools **Credit Hours For Degree:** 60 credit hours, Associates

COLLEGE OF THE HUMANITIES AND SCIENCES, HARRISON MIDDLETON UNIVERSITY
1105 East Broadway
Tempe, AZ 85282
Tel: (480)317-5955; 877-248-6724
Fax: (480)829-4999
Web Site: http://www.chumsci.edu/
President/CEO: Dr. David W. Curd
Type: Comprehensive **Sex:** Coed **Calendar System:** Continuous **Professional Accreditation:** DETC

COLLEGEAMERICA-FLAGSTAFF
5200 East Cortland Blvd., Ste. A-19
Flagstaff, AZ 86004
Tel: (928)526-0763
Admissions: 800-977-5455
Fax: (928)526-3468
E-mail: pberlioux@collegeamerica.edu
Web Site: http://www.collegeamerica.com/
President/CEO: Pescal Berlioux
Admissions: Pescal Berlioux
Type: Two-Year College **Sex:** Coed **Professional Accreditation:** ABHES, ACCSCT

COLLINS COLLEGE: A SCHOOL OF DESIGN AND TECHNOLOGY
1140 South Priest Dr.
Tempe, AZ 85281-5206
Tel: (480)966-3000
Free: 800-876-7070
Fax: (480)966-2599
E-mail: toby@collinscollege.edu
Web Site: http://www.collinscollege.edu/
President/CEO: John Calman
Admissions: Toby Craver
Type: Four-Year College **Sex:** Coed **Affiliation:** Career Education Corporation **% Accepted:** 37 **Admission Plans:** Open Admission; Early Admission; Deferred Admission **Application Deadline:** Rolling **Application Fee:** $50.00 **H.S. Requirements:** High school diploma required; GED accepted **Costs Per Year:** Application fee: $50. Tuition: $13,875 full-time. Full-time tuition varies according to class time, course level, course load, degree level, location, program, reciprocity agreements, and student level. College room only: $2970. Tuition guaranteed not to increase for student's term of enrollment. **Scholarships:** Available **Calendar System:** Trimester **Enrollment:** FT 1,828 **Faculty:** FT 101, PT 0 **Student-Faculty Ratio:** 30:1 **Exams:** SAT I or ACT **% Receiving Financial Aid:** 69 **Library Holdings:** 1,000 **Professional Accreditation:** ACCSCT

DEVRY UNIVERSITY (MESA)
1201 South Alma School Rd.
Mesa, AZ 85210-2011
Tel: (480)827-1511
Fax: (480)827-2552
Web Site: http://www.devry.edu/ **Type:** Comprehensive **Sex:** Coed **Costs Per Year:** One-time mandatory fee: $40. Tuition: $11,790 full-time, $440 per credit part-time. Mandatory fees: $60 full-time, $30 per year part-time. **Calendar System:** Semester **Regional Accreditation:** North Central Association of Colleges and Schools

DEVRY UNIVERSITY (PHOENIX)
2149 West Dunlap Ave.
Phoenix, AZ 85021-2995
Tel: (602)870-9222; (866)338-7934
Web Site: http://www.devry.edu/
President/CEO: Jim Dugan
Registrar: Pam Nadeau-Morrison
Financial Aid: Kathy Wyse
Type: Comprehensive **Sex:** Coed **Affiliation:** DeVry University **Admission Plans:** Deferred Admission **Application Deadline:** Rolling **Application Fee:** $50.00 **H.S. Requirements:** High school diploma required; GED accepted **Costs Per Year:** Application fee: $50. One-time mandatory fee: $40. Tuition: $11,790 full-time, $440 per credit part-time. Mandatory fees: $270 full-time, $160 per year part-time. Full-time tuition and fees vary according to course load. Part-time tuition and fees vary according to course load. **Scholarships:** Available **Calendar System:** Semester, Summer Session Available **Enrollment:** FT 774, PT 390, Grad 216 **Faculty:** FT 39, PT 48 **Student-Faculty Ratio:** 20:1 **% Receiving Financial Aid:** 75 **Library Holdings:** 22,500 **Regional Accreditation:** North Central Association of Colleges and Schools **Credit Hours For Degree:** 86 credit hours, Associates; 122 credit hours, Bachelors **ROTC:** Air Force **Professional Accreditation:** ABET

DINE COLLEGE
PO Box 98
Tsaile, AZ 86556
Tel: (520)724-6600
Admissions: (928)724-6633
Fax: (520)724-3349
E-mail: louise@dinecollege.edu
Web Site: http://www.dinecollege.edu/
President/CEO: Cassandra Manuelito-Kerkvliet
Registrar: Louise Litzin
Admissions: Louise Litzin
Financial Aid: Grace Nakaidinae
Type: Two-Year College **Sex:** Coed **Admission Plans:** Open Admission; Preferred Admission; Early Admission **Application Deadline:** Rolling **Application Fee:** $0.00 **H.S. Requirements:** High school diploma required; GED accepted **Costs Per Year:** Application fee: $0. State resident tuition: $720 full-time, $30 per hour part-time. Nonresident tuition: $720 full-time, $30 per hour part-time. College room and board: $3764. College room only: $1180. **Scholarships:** Available **Calendar System:** Semester, Summer Session Available **Enrollment:** FT 843, PT 982 **Faculty:** FT 65, PT 91 **% Residing in College-Owned, -Operated, or -Affiliated Housing:** 8 **Library Holdings:** 50,000 **Regional Accreditation:** North Central Association of Colleges and Schools **Credit Hours For Degree:** 64 credit hours, Associates **Intercollegiate Athletics:** Archery M & W; Cross-Country Running M & W

EASTERN ARIZONA COLLEGE
PO Box 769
Thatcher, AZ 85552-0769
Tel: (520)428-8322
Admissions: (928)428-8247
Fax; (520)428-8462

E-mail: admissions@eac.edu
Web Site: http://www.eac.edu/
President/CEO: Gherald L. Hoopes, Jr.
Registrar: Ralph Orr
Admissions: Jeff Savage
Financial Aid: Melvin Jones
Type: Two-Year College **Sex:** Coed **Affiliation:** Arizona State Community College System **% Accepted:** 100 **Admission Plans:** Open Admission; Early Admission; Deferred Admission **Application Deadline:** Rolling **Application Fee:** $0.00 **H.S. Requirements:** High school diploma or equivalent not required **Costs Per Year:** Application fee: $0. State resident tuition: $1220 full-time, $50 per credit part-time. Nonresident tuition: $6460 full-time, $100 per credit part-time. College room and board: $4320. **Scholarships:** Available **Calendar System:** Semester, Summer Session Available **Enrollment:** FT 1,413, PT 3,826 **Faculty:** FT 88, PT 210 **Student-Faculty Ratio:** 17:1 **% Residing in College-Owned, -Operated, or -Affiliated Housing:** 5 **Regional Accreditation:** North Central Association of Colleges and Schools **Credit Hours For Degree:** 64 semester hours, Associates **Intercollegiate Athletics:** Baseball M; Basketball M & W; Football M; Golf M & W; Softball W; Volleyball W

EMBRY-RIDDLE AERONAUTICAL UNIVERSITY
3700 Willow Creek Rd.
Prescott, AZ 86301-3720
Tel: (928)777-3728
Free: 800-888-3728
Admissions: (928)777-6600
Fax: (928)777-3740
E-mail: pradmit@erau.edu
Web Site: http://www.embryriddle.edu/
President/CEO: Daniel Carrell
Registrar: Mary Lahann
Admissions: Bill Thompson
Financial Aid: Dan Lupin
Type: Comprehensive **Sex:** Coed **Scores:** 97% SAT V 400+; 98% SAT M 400+; 38% ACT 18-23; 45% ACT 24-29 **% Accepted:** 89 **Admission Plans:** Early Admission; Early Decision Plan; Deferred Admission **Application Deadline:** March 01 **Application Fee:** $50.00 **H.S. Requirements:** High school diploma required; GED accepted **Costs Per Year:** Application fee: $50. Comprehensive fee: $30,006 includes full-time tuition ($22,820), mandatory fees ($670), and college room and board ($6516). College room only: $3580. Part-time tuition: $955 per credit hour. **Scholarships:** Available **Calendar System:** Semester, Summer Session Available **Enrollment:** FT 1,466, PT 187, Grad 32 **Faculty:** FT 96, PT 18 **Student-Faculty Ratio:** 15:1 **Exams:** SAT I or ACT **% Receiving Financial Aid:** 63 **% Residing in College-Owned, -Operated, or -Affiliated Housing:** 49 **Library Holdings:** 28,264 **Regional Accreditation:** Southern Association of Colleges and Schools **Credit Hours For Degree:** 120 credit hours, Bachelors **ROTC:** Army, Air Force **Professional Accreditation:** ABET, CAA **Intercollegiate Athletics:** Volleyball W; Wrestling M

ESTRELLA MOUNTAIN COMMUNITY COLLEGE
3000 North Dysart Rd.
Avondale, AZ 85323-1000
Tel: (623)935-8000
Admissions: (623)935-8808
Web Site: http://www.emc.maricopa.edu/
President/CEO: Dr. Homero Lopez
Registrar: Joe Ochap
Admissions: Dr. Ernesto Laura
Financial Aid: Lauren Shellenbarger
Type: Two-Year College **Sex:** Coed **Affiliation:** Maricopa County Community College District System **Admission Plans:** Open Admission **Scholarships:** Available **Calendar System:** Semester **Enrollment:** FT 1,372, PT 4,575 **Faculty:** FT 55, PT 230 **Student-Faculty Ratio:** 20:1 **Regional Accreditation:** North Central Association of Colleges and Schools

EVEREST COLLEGE
10400 North 25th Ave.
Ste. 190
Phoenix, AZ 85021
Tel: (602)942-4141
Fax: (602)943-0960
E-mail: magee@cci.edu
Web Site: http://www.everest-college.com/
President/CEO: Donna L. Green
Registrar: Maud Chesnutt
Admissions: Melissa Agee
Type: Two-Year College **Sex:** Coed **% Accepted:** 73 **Admission Plans:** Deferred Admission **Application Deadline:** Rolling **Application Fee:** $0.00 **H.S. Requirements:** High school diploma required; GED accepted **Costs Per Year:** Application fee: $0. Tuition: $13,111 full-time, $259 per quarter hour part-time. Mandatory fees: $100 full-time, $25 per term part-time. **Scholarships:** Available **Calendar System:** Miscellaneous, Summer Session Available **Enrollment:** FT 378, PT 426 **Faculty:** FT 7, PT 27 **Student-Faculty Ratio:** 24:1 **Regional Accreditation:** North Central Association of Colleges and Schools **Credit Hours For Degree:** 60 credits, Associates **Professional Accreditation:** ACICS

GATEWAY COMMUNITY COLLEGE
108 North 40th St.
Phoenix, AZ 85034-1795
Tel: (602)286-8000
Admissions: (602)286-8052
Fax: (602)286-8003
E-mail: cathy.gibson@gwmail.maricopa.edu
Web Site: http://www.gwc.maricopa.edu/
President/CEO: Eugene Giovannini
Registrar: Cathy Gibson
Admissions: Cathy Gibson
Financial Aid: Bradley Honious
Type: Two-Year College **Sex:** Coed **Affiliation:** Maricopa County Community College District System **Admission Plans:** Open Admission; Early Admission; Deferred Admission **Application Deadline:** Rolling **Application Fee:** $0.00 **H.S. Requirements:** High school diploma or equivalent not required. For health science, nursing programs: High school diploma required; GED accepted **Costs Per Year:** Application fee: $0. Area resident tuition: $1560 full-time, $65 per credit part-time. State resident tuition: $6720 full-time, $85 per credit part-time. Nonresident tuition: $6720 full-time, $85 per credit part-time. Mandatory fees: $30 full-time. **Scholarships:** Available **Calendar System:** Semester, Summer Session Available **Enrollment:** FT 976, PT 8,401 **Faculty:** FT 70, PT 189 **Student-Faculty Ratio:** 25:1 **Library Holdings:** 50,000 **Regional Accreditation:** North Central Association of Colleges and Schools **Credit Hours For Degree:** 60 credit hours, Associates **ROTC:** Army, Air Force **Professional Accreditation:** APTA, CARC, JRCERT, NLN **Intercollegiate Athletics:** Cross-Country Running M & W; Golf M & W; Tennis M & W

GLENDALE COMMUNITY COLLEGE
6000 West Olive Ave.
Glendale, AZ 85302-3090
Tel: (623)845-3000
Admissions: (623)435-3305
Fax: (623)845-3329
E-mail: info@gc.maricopa.edu
Web Site: http://www.gc.maricopa.edu/
President/CEO: Dr. Phil D. Randolph
Registrar: Mary Lou Massal
Admissions: Mary Lou Massal
Financial Aid: Ellen Neel
Type: Two-Year College **Sex:** Coed **Affiliation:** Maricopa County Community College District System **Admission Plans:** Open Admission **Application Deadline:** August 23 **Application Fee:** $0.00 **H.S. Requirements:** High school diploma or equivalent not required **Costs Per Year:** Application fee: $0. Area resident tuition: $1560 full-time, $65 per credit hour part-time. State resident tuition: $6720 full-time, $280 per credit hour part-time. Nonresident tuition: $6720 full-time, $280 per credit hour part-time. Mandatory fees: $30 full-time, $15 per term part-time. **Scholarships:** Available **Calendar System:** Semester, Summer Session Available **Enrollment:** FT 6,108, PT 13,962 **Faculty:** FT 277, PT 635 **Student-Faculty Ratio:** 22:1 **Library Holdings:** 79,006 **Regional Accreditation:** North Central Association of Colleges and Schools **Credit Hours For Degree:** 60 credit hours, Associates **ROTC:** Army, Air Force **Professional Accreditation:** NLN **Intercollegiate Athletics:** Baseball M; Basketball M & W; Cross-Country Running M & W; Football M; Golf M; Soccer M & W; Softball W; Tennis M & W; Track and Field M & W; Volleyball W

GRAND CANYON UNIVERSITY
3300 W Camelback Rd., PO Box 11097
Phoenix, AZ 85017-1097

Tel: (602)249-3300
Fax: (602)589-2580
Web Site: http://www.gcu.edu/
President/CEO: Dr. Gil Stafford
Registrar: April Chapman
Financial Aid: Rosanna Short
Type: Comprehensive **Sex:** Coed **Affiliation:** Southern Baptist **Scores:** 53% ACT 18-23; 22% ACT 24-29 **% Accepted:** 69 **Application Deadline:** Rolling **Application Fee:** $50.00 **H.S. Requirements:** High school diploma required; GED accepted **Costs Per Year:** Application fee: $50. State resident tuition: $4875 full-time. Nonresident tuition: $6000 full-time. College room and board: $7130. **Scholarships:** Available **Calendar System:** Semester, Summer Session Available **Enrollment:** FT 1,327, PT 282, Grad 2,504 **Faculty:** FT 97, PT 177 **Student-Faculty Ratio:** 16:1 **Exams:** SAT I or ACT **% Receiving Financial Aid:** 66 **% Residing in College-Owned, -Operated, or -Affiliated Housing:** 30 **Library Holdings:** 75,905 **Regional Accreditation:** North Central Association of Colleges and Schools **Credit Hours For Degree:** 128 semester hours, Bachelors **ROTC:** Army, Air Force **Professional Accreditation:** AACN, ACBSP, NLN **Intercollegiate Athletics:** Baseball M; Basketball M & W; Golf M; Soccer M & W; Tennis W; Volleyball W

HIGH-TECH INSTITUTE
1515 East Indian School Rd.
Phoenix, AZ 85014-4901
Tel: (602)279-9700
Fax: (602)279-2999
E-mail: rcraven@hightechschools.com
Web Site: http://www.high-techinstitute.com/
President/CEO: David Wyckoff
Registrar: Patt Meisler
Admissions: Rich Craven
Type: Two-Year College **Sex:** Coed **Admission Plans:** Open Admission **H.S. Requirements:** High school diploma required; GED accepted **Scholarships:** Available **Calendar System:** Semester **Enrollment:** FT 1,544 **Faculty:** FT 55, PT 5 **Student-Faculty Ratio:** 27:1 **Credit Hours For Degree:** 75 credit hours, Associates **Professional Accreditation:** ACCSCT

INTERNATIONAL BAPTIST COLLEGE
2150 East Southern Ave.
Tempe, AZ 85282
Tel: (480)838-7070
Free: 800-422-4858
E-mail: registrar@ibconline.edu
Web Site: http://www.tri-citybaptist.org/ibc/
President/CEO: Dr. Jerry Tetreau
Registrar: Dr. Stan Bushey
Admissions: Rebecca M. Stertzbach
Financial Aid: Norm Fisher
Type: Comprehensive **Sex:** Coed **Affiliation:** Baptist **Admission Plans:** Open Admission; Early Admission **Application Deadline:** August 20 **Application Fee:** $35.00 **H.S. Requirements:** High school diploma or equivalent not required **Costs Per Year:** Application fee: $35. Comprehensive fee: $10,870 includes full-time tuition ($6000), mandatory fees ($570), and college room and board ($4300). Part-time tuition: $250 per credit. Part-time mandatory fees: $9 per credit. **Scholarships:** Available **Calendar System:** 4-1-4 **Enrollment:** FT 47, PT 28, Grad 1 **Faculty:** FT 3, PT 10 **Student-Faculty Ratio:** 12:1 **Credit Hours For Degree:** 67 semester hours, Associates; 133 semester hours, Bachelors **Professional Accreditation:** TACCS

INTERNATIONAL IMPORT-EXPORT INSTITUTE
2432 West Peoria Ave., Ste. 1026
Phoenix, AZ 85029
Tel: (602)648-5750
Free: 800-474-8013
Fax: (602)648-5755
E-mail: director@expandglobal.com
Web Site: http://www.iiei.edu/
President/CEO: Ted Nicholson
Admissions: Dr. Donald N. Burton
Type: Two-Year Upper Division **Sex:** Coed **Application Fee:** $0.00 **Costs Per Year:** Application fee: $0. **Calendar System:** Miscellaneous **Student-Faculty Ratio:** 15:1 **Professional Accreditation:** DETC

INTERNATIONAL INSTITUTE OF THE AMERICAS (MESA)
925 South Gilbert Rd., Ste. 201
Mesa, AZ 85204-4448
Tel: (480)545-8755; 888-886-2428
Fax: (480)926-1371
E-mail: mkiljan@iia.edu
Web Site: http://www.aibtonline.com/
President/CEO: Meredith D. Jenson
Admissions: Meredith Kiljan
Type: Two-Year College **Sex:** Coed **Application Deadline:** Rolling **Costs Per Year:** One-time mandatory fee: $200. Tuition: $9850 full-time. Mandatory fees: $350 full-time. **Calendar System:** Semester **Enrollment:** FT 174 **Faculty:** FT 7, PT 18 **Student-Faculty Ratio:** 13:1 **Professional Accreditation:** ACICS

INTERNATIONAL INSTITUTE OF THE AMERICAS (PHOENIX)
6049 North 43rd Ave.
Phoenix, AZ 85019-1600
Tel: (602)242-6265
Free: 800-793-2428
Fax: (602)973-2572
E-mail: lmcconnell@iia.edu
Web Site: http://www.aibtonline.com/
President/CEO: Dr. Logan P. Bauer
Admissions: Lynn McConnell
Type: Two-Year College **Sex:** Coed **Admission Plans:** Open Admission; Early Admission; Deferred Admission **Application Deadline:** Rolling **H.S. Requirements:** High school diploma required; GED accepted **Costs Per Year:** One-time mandatory fee: $200. Tuition: $9850 full-time. Mandatory fees: $350 full-time. **Calendar System:** Semester, Summer Session Available **Enrollment:** FT 240 **Faculty:** FT 14, PT 12 **Student-Faculty Ratio:** 13:1 **Library Holdings:** 1,974 **Credit Hours For Degree:** 60 credits, Associates **Professional Accreditation:** ACICS

INTERNATIONAL INSTITUTE OF THE AMERICAS (TUCSON)
5441 East 22nd St., Ste. 125
Tucson, AZ 85711-5444
Tel: (520)748-9799; 888-292-2428
Fax: (520)748-9355
E-mail: lpechota@iia.edu
Web Site: http://www.aibtonline.com/
President/CEO: Leigh Pechota
Admissions: Leigh Anne Pechota
Type: Two-Year College **Sex:** Coed **Application Deadline:** Rolling **Calendar System:** Semester **Enrollment:** FT 298 **Faculty:** FT 20, PT 3 **Student-Faculty Ratio:** 14:1 **Professional Accreditation:** ACICS

INTERNATIONAL INSTITUTE OF THE AMERICAS (WEST VALLEY)
4136 North 75th Ave., Ste. 211
Phoenix, AZ 85033-3196
Tel: (623)849-8208; 888-884-2428
Fax: (623)849-0110
E-mail: lebert@iia.edu
Web Site: http://www.aibtonline.com/
Admissions: Dr. Lori Ebert
Type: Two-Year College **Sex:** Coed **Application Deadline:** Rolling **Costs Per Year:** One-time mandatory fee: $200. Tuition: $9850 full-time. Mandatory fees: $350 full-time. **Calendar System:** Semester **Enrollment:** FT 205 **Faculty:** FT 10, PT 10 **Student-Faculty Ratio:** 15:1 **Professional Accreditation:** ACICS

ITT TECHNICAL INSTITUTE (PHOENIX)
4837 East McDowell Rd.
Phoenix, AZ 85008-4292
Tel: (602)252-2331
Free: 800-879-4881
Fax: (602)267-8727
Web Site: http://www.itt-tech.edu/
President/CEO: Michael M. Henry
Registrar: Michael Valletta

Admissions: Chuck Wilson
Financial Aid: Laurie Robbins
Type: Two-Year College **Sex:** Coed **Affiliation:** ITT Educational Services, Inc **Admission Plans:** Deferred Admission **Application Fee:** $100.00 **H.S. Requirements:** High school diploma required; GED accepted **Scholarships:** Available **Calendar System:** Quarter, Summer Session Not available **Exams:** Other **Credit Hours For Degree:** 90 credit hours, Associates; 180 credit hours, Bachelors **Professional Accreditation:** ACICS

ITT TECHNICAL INSTITUTE (TEMPE)
5005 S. Wendler Dr.
Tempe, AZ 85282
Tel: (602)437-7500
Free: 800-879-4881
Web Site: http://www.itt-tech.edu/
President/CEO: Charles R. Wilson
Registrar: Glenda Kelsey
Admissions: Chuck Wilson
Type: Four-Year College **Application Deadline:** Rolling **Application Fee:** $100.00 **Costs Per Year:** Application fee: $100. **Exams:** Other

ITT TECHNICAL INSTITUTE (TUCSON)
1455 West River Rd.
Tucson, AZ 85704
Tel: (520)408-7488
Free: 800-870-9730
Fax: (520)292-9899
Web Site: http://www.itt-tech.edu/
President/CEO: Timothy Riordan
Admissions: Timothy Riordan
Financial Aid: Betty Marchant
Type: Two-Year College **Sex:** Coed **Affiliation:** ITT Educational Services, Inc **Admission Plans:** Deferred Admission **Application Deadline:** Rolling **Application Fee:** $100.00 **H.S. Requirements:** High school diploma required; GED accepted **Costs Per Year:** Application fee: $100. **Scholarships:** Available **Calendar System:** Quarter, Summer Session Not available **Exams:** Other **Credit Hours For Degree:** 96 credit hours, Associates; 180 credit hours, Bachelors **Professional Accreditation:** ACICS

LAMSON COLLEGE
1126 North Scottsdale Rd., Ste. 17
Tempe, AZ 85281
Tel: (480)898-7000
Free: 800-898-7017
Fax: (480)967-6645
Web Site: http://www.lamsoncollege.com/
President/CEO: Ralph Bilbao, EdD
Registrar: Harry Merritt
Admissions: Chico Chavez
Financial Aid: Brian Whitney
Type: Two-Year College **Sex:** Coed **Affiliation:** National Career Education, Inc **Application Fee:** $25.00 **H.S. Requirements:** High school diploma required; GED accepted **Scholarships:** Available **Calendar System:** Quarter, Summer Session Available **Faculty:** FT 4, PT 7 **Exams:** Other **Library Holdings:** 4,400 **Credit Hours For Degree:** 92 quarter hours, Associates **Professional Accreditation:** ACICS

LONG TECHNICAL COLLEGE
13450 North Black Canyon Hwy., Ste. 104
Phoenix, AZ 85029
Tel: (602)548-1955; 877-548-1955
Fax: (602)548-1956
E-mail: msavely@longtechnicalcollege.com
Web Site: http://www.longtechnicalcollege.com/
President/CEO: Michael Savely
Admissions: Michael S. Savely
Type: Two-Year College **Sex:** Coed **Calendar System:** Continuous **Professional Accreditation:** ACCSCT, ACICS, CARC

MESA COMMUNITY COLLEGE
1833 West Southern Ave.
Mesa, AZ 85202-4866
Tel: (480)461-7000
Admissions: (480)461-7478
Fax: (480)461-7805
E-mail: admissions@mc.maricopa.edu
Web Site: http://www.mc.maricopa.edu/
President/CEO: Dr. Larry K. Christiansen
Registrar: Gordon Benson
Admissions: Carol Petersen
Financial Aid: Joan Grover
Type: Two-Year College **Sex:** Coed **Affiliation:** Maricopa County Community College District System **Admission Plans:** Open Admission; Early Admission; Deferred Admission **Application Fee:** $0.00 **H.S. Requirements:** High school diploma or equivalent not required **Scholarships:** Available **Calendar System:** Semester, Summer Session Available **Faculty:** FT 265, PT 800 **Exams:** Other **Library Holdings:** 56,224 **Regional Accreditation:** North Central Association of Colleges and Schools **Credit Hours For Degree:** 60 credit hours, Associates **ROTC:** Army, Air Force **Professional Accreditation:** ABFSE, NLN **Intercollegiate Athletics:** Baseball M; Basketball M & W; Cross-Country Running M; Football M; Golf M & W; Soccer M & W; Softball W; Tennis M & W; Track and Field M & W; Volleyball W; Wrestling M

METROPOLITAN COLLEGE OF COURT REPORTING
4640 East Elwood St., Ste. 12
Phoenix, AZ 85040
Tel: (602)955-5900
Admissions: (480)955-5900
Fax: (480)894-8999
Web Site: http://www.metropolitancollege.edu/
President/CEO: Terry Smith
Registrar: Tom Kildow
Admissions: Shannon Buchanan
Financial Aid: Michelle C. Lawrence
Type: Four-Year College **Sex:** Coed **Admission Plans:** Open Admission; Early Admission; Deferred Admission **Application Fee:** $50.00 **H.S. Requirements:** High school diploma required; GED accepted **Scholarships:** Available **Calendar System:** Trimester, Summer Session Available **Enrollment:** FT 118 **Faculty:** FT 4, PT 7 **Student-Faculty Ratio:** 12:1 **Credit Hours For Degree:** 90 credit hours, Associates; 123 credits hours, Bachelors **Professional Accreditation:** ACCSCT

MIDWESTERN UNIVERSITY, GLENDALE CAMPUS
19555 North 59th Ave.
Glendale, AZ 85308
Tel: (623)572-3200; 888-247-9271
Admissions: (623)572-3340
Web Site: http://www.midwestern.edu/
President/CEO: Dr. Kathleen Goeppinger
Admissions: James Walters
Type: Two-Year Upper Division **Sex:** Coed **% Accepted:** 80 **Application Deadline:** August 06 **Application Fee:** $0.00 **Costs Per Year:** Application fee: $0. Comprehensive fee: $24,341 includes full-time tuition ($15,306), mandatory fees ($250), and college room and board ($8785). College room only: $5670. **Scholarships:** Available **Calendar System:** Quarter **Enrollment:** FT 20 **Student-Faculty Ratio:** 20:1 **% Receiving Financial Aid:** 91 **Regional Accreditation:** North Central Association of Colleges and Schools **Professional Accreditation:** AANA, ACPhE, AOTA, AOsA, APTA

MOHAVE COMMUNITY COLLEGE
1971 Jagerson Ave.
Kingman, AZ 86401
Tel: (928)757-4331; 888-664-2832
Admissions: (928)757-0847
Fax: (928)757-0808
Web Site: http://www.mohave.edu/
President/CEO: Dr. Thomas C. Henry
Registrar: John Wilson
Admissions: John Wilson
Type: Two-Year College **Sex:** Coed **Admission Plans:** Open Admission; Early Admission; Deferred Admission **H.S. Requirements:** High school diploma or equivalent not required **Costs Per Year:** State resident tuition: $1104 full-time, $46 per credit hour part-time. Nonresident tuition: $3312 full-time, $138 per credit hour part-time. Part-time tuition varies according to course load. **Scholarships:** Available **Calendar System:** Semester, Summer Session Available **Enrollment:** FT 1,208, PT 4,979 **Faculty:** FT 58, PT 531 **Student-Faculty Ratio:** 13:1 **Library Holdings:** 45,849 **Regional Accreditation:** North Central Association of Colleges and Schools **Credit**

Hours For Degree: 60 semester hours, Associates

NORTHCENTRAL UNIVERSITY

505 West Whipple St.
Prescott, AZ 86301-1747
Tel: (928)541-7777; 888-327-2877
Admissions: (866)776-0331
Fax: (928)541-7817
E-mail: enrol@ncu.edu
Web Site: http://www.ncu.edu/
President/CEO: Dr. Donald Hecht
Registrar: Cathy Righter
Admissions: Melissa Bowers
Financial Aid: Jane Hersh
Type: Comprehensive **Sex:** Coed **Application Fee:** $100.00 **H.S. Requirements:** High school diploma required; GED accepted **Costs Per Year:** Application fee: $100. Tuition: $9000 full-time, $375 per credit part-time. **Calendar System:** Continuous, Summer Session Available **Enrollment:** FT 10, PT 156, Grad 1,235 **Faculty:** FT 3, PT 135 **Regional Accreditation:** North Central Association of Colleges and Schools **Credit Hours For Degree:** 120 semester hour, Bachelors

NORTHERN ARIZONA UNIVERSITY

South San Francisco St.
Flagstaff, AZ 86011
Tel: (928)523-9011; 888-MORE-NAU
Admissions: (928)523-6053
Fax: (928)523-0226
E-mail: Christopher.Lynch@nau.edu
Web Site: http://www.nau.edu/
President/CEO: John Denis Haeger
Registrar: Patrick F. Martin
Admissions: Chris Lynch
Financial Aid: Jane Kuhn
Type: University **Sex:** Coed **Affiliation:** Arizona University System **Scores:** 95% SAT V 400+; 95% SAT M 400+; 50% ACT 18-23; 34% ACT 24-29 **% Accepted:** 86 **Admission Plans:** Deferred Admission **Application Deadline:** Rolling **Application Fee:** $25.00 **H.S. Requirements:** High school diploma required; GED accepted **Costs Per Year:** Application fee: $25. State resident tuition: $4223 full-time, $221 per credit part-time. Nonresident tuition: $12,853 full-time, $536 per credit part-time. Mandatory fees: $170 full-time, $85 per term part-time. Full-time tuition and fees vary according to program. Part-time tuition and fees vary according to program. College room and board: $5960. College room only: $3256. Room and board charges vary according to board plan and housing facility. **Scholarships:** Available **Calendar System:** Semester, Summer Session Available **Enrollment:** FT 11,261, PT 1,991, Grad 5,405 **Faculty:** FT 723, PT 651 **Student-Faculty Ratio:** 16:1 **Exams:** SAT I or ACT **% Receiving Financial Aid:** 54 **% Residing in College-Owned, -Operated, or -Affiliated Housing:** 38 **Library Holdings:** 633,417 **Regional Accreditation:** North Central Association of Colleges and Schools **Credit Hours For Degree:** 120 semester hours, Bachelors **ROTC:** Army, Air Force **Professional Accreditation:** AACSB, ABET, AACN, ACCE, ACA, ADA, APTA, ASLHA, CEPH, CSWE, NASM, NRPA, SAF **Intercollegiate Athletics:** Basketball M & W; Cross-Country Running M & W; Football M; Golf W; Soccer W; Swimming and Diving W; Tennis M & W; Track and Field M & W; Volleyball W

NORTHLAND PIONEER COLLEGE

PO Box 610
Holbrook, AZ 86025-0610
Tel: (928)524-7600
Free: 800-266-7845
Admissions: (928)536-6257
Fax: (928)524-7612
Web Site: http://www.npc.edu/
President/CEO: Dr. Richard B. Fleming
Registrar: A. Daniel Simper
Admissions: Dawn Edgmon
Financial Aid: Beaulah Bob Pennypacker
Type: Two-Year College **Sex:** Coed **Affiliation:** Arizona State Community College System **Admission Plans:** Open Admission; Early Admission **Application Fee:** $0.00 **H.S. Requirements:** High school diploma or equivalent not required **Scholarships:** Available **Calendar System:** Semester, Summer Session Available **Enrollment:** FT 971, PT 3,957 **Faculty:** FT 64, PT 299 **Student-Faculty Ratio:** 14:1 **% Residing in College-Owned, -Operated, or -Affiliated Housing:** 1 **Library Holdings:** 60,000 **Regional Accreditation:** North Central Association of Colleges and Schools **Credit Hours For Degree:** 64 semester hours, Associates

PARADISE VALLEY COMMUNITY COLLEGE

18401 North 32nd St.
Phoenix, AZ 85032-1200
Tel: (602)787-6500
Admissions: (602)787-7020
Fax: (602)787-6625
Web Site: http://www.pvc.maricopa.edu/
President/CEO: Dr. Mary Kathryn Kickels
Registrar: Dr. Shirley Green
Admissions: Dr. Shirley Green
Financial Aid: Joann Caufield
Type: Two-Year College **Sex:** Coed **Affiliation:** Maricopa County Community College District System **Admission Plans:** Open Admission; Early Admission **Application Fee:** $0.00 **H.S. Requirements:** High school diploma or equivalent not required **Scholarships:** Available **Calendar System:** Semester, Summer Session Available **Enrollment:** FT 2,118, PT 6,119 **Faculty:** FT 84, PT 260 **Regional Accreditation:** North Central Association of Colleges and Schools **Credit Hours For Degree:** 60 credit hours, Associates **Intercollegiate Athletics:** Cross-Country Running M & W; Golf M & W; Soccer M & W; Softball W; Tennis M & W; Track and Field M & W

THE PARALEGAL INSTITUTE, INC.

2933 West Indian School Rd.
Phoenix, AZ 85017
Tel: (602)212-0501
Free: 800-354-1254
Web Site: http://www.theparalegalinstitute.com/
President/CEO: John Morrison
Admissions: John W. Morrison
Type: Two-Year College **% Accepted:** 25 **Faculty:** FT 1, PT 3 **Credit Hours For Degree:** 60 credits, Associates **Professional Accreditation:** DETC

PHOENIX COLLEGE

1202 West Thomas Rd.
Phoenix, AZ 85013-4234
Tel: (602)285-7500
Admissions: (602)285-7503
Fax: (602)285-7813
Web Site: http://www.pc.maricopa.edu/
President/CEO: Dr. Corina Gardea
Admissions: Mary Blackwell
Financial Aid: Genevieve Watson
Type: Two-Year College **Sex:** Coed **Affiliation:** Maricopa County Community College District System **Admission Plans:** Open Admission; Early Admission; Deferred Admission **Application Deadline:** Rolling **Application Fee:** $0.00 **H.S. Requirements:** High school diploma or equivalent not required **Costs Per Year:** Application fee: $0. State resident tuition: $1560 full-time, $65 per credit hour part-time. Nonresident tuition: $6720 full-time, $280 per credit hour part-time. Mandatory fees: $30 full-time, $15 per term part-time. **Scholarships:** Available **Calendar System:** Semester, Summer Session Available **Faculty:** FT 104, PT 0 **Library Holdings:** 83,000 **Regional Accreditation:** North Central Association of Colleges and Schools **Credit Hours For Degree:** 64 credit hours, Associates **ROTC:** Army, Air Force **Professional Accreditation:** ADA, AHIMA, NLN **Intercollegiate Athletics:** Baseball M; Basketball M & W; Cross-Country Running M & W; Football M; Golf M & W; Soccer M & W; Softball W; Tennis M & W; Track and Field M & W; Volleyball W

PIMA COMMUNITY COLLEGE

4905 East Broadway
Tucson, AZ 85709-1010
Tel: (520)206-4666
Admissions: (520)206-4640
Fax: (520)884-6728
E-mail: wendy.kilgore@pima.edu
Web Site: http://www.pima.edu/
President/CEO: Dr. Robert Jensen
Registrar: Nancee Sorenson
Admissions: Dr. Wendy Kilgore

Financial Aid: Lupita Murphy
Type: Two-Year College **Sex:** Coed **Scores:** 38% ACT 18-23; 12% ACT 24-29 **% Accepted:** 100 **Admission Plans:** Open Admission; Early Admission **Application Deadline:** Rolling **Application Fee:** $5.00 **H.S. Requirements:** High school diploma or equivalent not required **Costs Per Year:** Application fee: $5. State resident tuition: $1104 full-time, $46 per credit part-time. Nonresident tuition: $5544 full-time, $78 per credit part-time. Mandatory fees: $80 full-time, $2.50 per credit part-time, $10 per term part-time. **Scholarships:** Available **Calendar System:** Semester, Summer Session Available **Enrollment:** FT 9,187, PT 21,697 **Faculty:** FT 318, PT 1,057 **Student-Faculty Ratio:** 21:1 **Library Holdings:** 217,049 **Regional Accreditation:** North Central Association of Colleges and Schools **Credit Hours For Degree:** 60 credit hours, Associates **ROTC:** Army, Navy, Air Force **Professional Accreditation:** ADA, CARC, JRCERT, NLN **Intercollegiate Athletics:** Baseball M; Basketball M & W; Cheerleading W; Cross-Country Running M & W; Football M; Golf M & W; Soccer M & W; Softball W; Tennis M & W; Track and Field M & W; Volleyball W

PIMA MEDICAL INSTITUTE (MESA)
957 South Dobson Rd.
Mesa, AZ 85202
Tel: (480)644-0267; 888-898-9048
Fax: (480)649-5249
E-mail: lipima@aol.com
Web Site: http://www.pimamedical.com/
President/CEO: Janis Stiewing
Admissions: Lisa LaTourette
Financial Aid: William Ellis
Type: Two-Year College **Sex:** Coed **Affiliation:** Vocational Training Institutes, Inc **Calendar System:** Miscellaneous **Student-Faculty Ratio:** 15:1 **Exams:** Other **Professional Accreditation:** ABHES, ACCSCT, CARC, JRCERT

PIMA MEDICAL INSTITUTE (TUCSON)
3350 East Grant Rd.
Tucson, AZ 85716-2800
Tel: (520)326-1600; 888-898-9048
Fax: (520)326-4125
Web Site: http://www.pmi.edu
President/CEO: Stan Bodzioney
Admissions: Carlos Flores
Financial Aid: Mike Nigl
Type: Two-Year College **Sex:** Coed **Affiliation:** Vocational Training Institutes, Inc **Admission Plans:** Early Admission **Application Fee:** $150.00 **H.S. Requirements:** High school diploma required; GED accepted **Costs Per Year:** Application fee: $150. **Calendar System:** Miscellaneous, Summer Session Not available **Faculty:** FT 6, PT 30 **Student-Faculty Ratio:** 13:1 **Exams:** Other **Credit Hours For Degree:** 66 credits, Associates **Professional Accreditation:** ABHES, CARC, JRCERT

PRESCOTT COLLEGE
220 Grove Ave.
Prescott, AZ 86301
Tel: (928)778-2090
Free: 800-628-6364
Fax: (928)776-5157
Web Site: http://www.prescott.edu/
President/CEO: Dr. Daniel Garvey
Registrar: Mary Trevor
Admissions: Timothy Robison
Financial Aid: Heather Lester
Type: Comprehensive **Sex:** Coed **Scores:** 98% SAT V 400+; 95% SAT M 400+; 35% ACT 18-23; 56% ACT 24-29 **% Accepted:** 88 **Admission Plans:** Deferred Admission **Application Deadline:** August 15 **Application Fee:** $25.00 **H.S. Requirements:** High school diploma required; GED accepted **Costs Per Year:** Application fee: $25. Tuition: $18,576 full-time, $516 per credit hour part-time. Mandatory fees: $935 full-time. **Scholarships:** Available **Calendar System:** Quarter, Summer Session Available **Enrollment:** FT 723, PT 70, Grad 251 **Faculty:** FT 50, PT 37 **Student-Faculty Ratio:** 7:1 **Exams:** SAT I or ACT **% Receiving Financial Aid:** 54 **Library Holdings:** 23,899 **Regional Accreditation:** North Central Association of Colleges and Schools **Credit Hours For Degree:** 32 courses, Bachelors

THE REFRIGERATION SCHOOL
4210 East Washington St.
Phoenix, AZ 85034-1816
Tel: (602)275-7133
Web Site: http://www.refrigerationschool.com/
President/CEO: Elizabeth Loney-Cline
Registrar: Anne-Marie O'Rourke
Admissions: Mary Simmons
Financial Aid: Anne-Marie O'Rourke
Type: Two-Year College **Sex:** Coed **Scholarships:** Available **Calendar System:** Continuous **Faculty:** FT 10, PT 9 **Student-Faculty Ratio:** 38:1 **Professional Accreditation:** ACCSCT

REMINGTON COLLEGE-TEMPE CAMPUS
875 West Elliot Rd., Ste. 216
Tempe, AZ 85284
Tel: (480)834-1000
Free: 800-395-4322
Fax: (480)491-2970
E-mail: jdrennen@edamerica.com
Web Site: http://www.remingtoncollege.edu/
President/CEO: Joe Drennen
Admissions: Joe Drennen
Type: Four-Year College **Sex:** Coed **Professional Accreditation:** ACICS

RIO SALADO COLLEGE
2323 West 14th St.
Tempe, AZ 85281-6950
Tel: (480)517-8000
Free: 800-729-1197
Admissions: (480)517-8151
Fax: (480)517-8199
Web Site: http://www.rio.maricopa.edu/
President/CEO: Dr. Linda Thor
Registrar: Ruby Miller
Admissions: Barbara Poe
Financial Aid: Linda Ross
Type: Two-Year College **Sex:** Coed **Affiliation:** Maricopa County Community College District System **Admission Plans:** Open Admission; Early Admission; Deferred Admission **Application Fee:** $0.00 **H.S. Requirements:** High school diploma or equivalent not required **Scholarships:** Available **Calendar System:** Semester, Summer Session Available **Faculty:** FT 15, PT 989 **Student-Faculty Ratio:** 25:1 **Exams:** Other **Library Holdings:** 16,000 **Regional Accreditation:** North Central Association of Colleges and Schools **Credit Hours For Degree:** 64 credit hours, Associates **Professional Accreditation:** ADA

SCOTTSDALE COMMUNITY COLLEGE
9000 East Chaparral Rd.
Scottsdale, AZ 85256-2626
Tel: (480)423-6000
Admissions: (602)423-6133
Fax: (480)423-6200
E-mail: fran.watkins@sccmail.maricopa.edu
Web Site: http://www.sc.maricopa.edu/
President/CEO: Dr. Arthur W. DeCabooter
Admissions: Fran Watkins
Financial Aid: Dolores Shipley
Type: Two-Year College **Sex:** Coed **Affiliation:** Maricopa County Community College District System **% Accepted:** 100 **Admission Plans:** Open Admission; Early Admission **Application Deadline:** Rolling **Application Fee:** $0.00 **H.S. Requirements:** High school diploma or equivalent not required **Costs Per Year:** Application fee: $0. Area resident tuition: $1980 full-time, $65 per credit hour part-time. State resident tuition: $8430 full-time, $90 per credit hour part-time. Nonresident tuition: $8430 full-time, $90 per credit hour part-time. Mandatory fees: $15 full-time. **Scholarships:** Available **Calendar System:** Semester, Summer Session Available **Enrollment:** FT 3,342, PT 7,919 **Faculty:** FT 167, PT 477 **Student-Faculty Ratio:** 18:1 **Regional Accreditation:** North Central Association of Colleges and Schools **Credit Hours For Degree:** 64 credit hours, Associates **Professional Accreditation:** NLN **Intercollegiate Athletics:** Baseball M; Basketball M & W; Cross-Country Running M & W; Football M; Golf M & W; Soccer M & W; Softball W; Tennis M & W; Track and Field M & W; Volleyball W

SCOTTSDALE CULINARY INSTITUTE
8100 East Camelback Rd., Ste. 1001
Scottsdale, AZ 85251-3940
Tel: (480)990-3773

Free: 800-848-2433
Fax: (480)990-0351
Web Site: http://www.scichefs.com/
President/CEO: Jacalyn Lynn
Registrar: Andrea Hendricks
Admissions: Jon Alberts
Financial Aid: Ida Hernandez
Type: Two-Year College **Sex:** Coed **Scholarships:** Available **Calendar System:** Semester **Faculty:** FT 67, PT 8 **Student-Faculty Ratio:** 16:1 **Professional Accreditation:** ACCSCT, ACF

SOUTH MOUNTAIN COMMUNITY COLLEGE

7050 South Twenty-fourth St.
Phoenix, AZ 85040
Tel: (602)243-8000
Admissions: (602)243-8120
Fax: (602)243-8329
Web Site: http://www.smc.maricopa.edu/
President/CEO: Dr. Ken Atwater
Registrar: Tony Bracamonte
Admissions: Tony Bracamonte
Financial Aid: Inez Weinert-Moreno
Type: Two-Year College **Sex:** Coed **Affiliation:** Maricopa County Community College District System **Admission Plans:** Open Admission **Application Fee:** $0.00 **Costs Per Year:** Application fee: $0. Area resident tuition: $1440 full-time. State resident tuition: $6192 full-time. Nonresident tuition: $6192 full-time. Mandatory fees: $10 full-time. **Scholarships:** Available **Calendar System:** Semester, Summer Session Available **Faculty:** FT 49, PT 146 **Exams:** Other **Library Holdings:** 35,591 **Regional Accreditation:** North Central Association of Colleges and Schools **Credit Hours For Degree:** 62 credit hours, Associates **ROTC:** Air Force **Intercollegiate Athletics:** Baseball M; Basketball M & W; Cross-Country Running M & W; Soccer M; Softball W; Tennis M & W; Track and Field M & W; Volleyball W

SOUTHWEST INSTITUTE OF HEALING ARTS

1100 East Apache Blvd.
Tempe, AZ 85281
Tel: (480)994-9244; 888-504-9106
Fax: (480)994-3228
E-mail: joannl@swiha.net
Web Site: http://www.swiha.org/
President/CEO: K. C. Miller
Admissions: Katie Yearous
Type: Two-Year College **Sex:** Coed **Calendar System:** Quarter **Professional Accreditation:** ACCSCT

SOUTHWESTERN COLLEGE

2625 East Cactus Rd.
Phoenix, AZ 85032-7042
Tel: (602)992-6101
Free: 800-247-2697
Web Site: http://www.swcaz.edu/
President/CEO: Dr. Brent D. Garrison
Registrar: Judy Cross
Admissions: Pete Leonard
Financial Aid: Pete Leonard
Type: Four-Year College **Sex:** Coed **Affiliation:** Conservative Baptist **Admission Plans:** Deferred Admission **Application Fee:** $25.00 **H.S. Requirements:** High school diploma required; GED accepted **Costs Per Year:** Application fee: $25. Comprehensive fee: $15,930 includes full-time tuition ($11,130), mandatory fees ($440), and college room and board ($4360). College room only: $3360. Full-time tuition and fees vary according to course load and program. Room and board charges vary according to housing facility. Part-time tuition: $464 per credit hour. Part-time mandatory fees: $220 per term. Part-time tuition and fees vary according to course load and program. **Scholarships:** Available **Calendar System:** Miscellaneous, Summer Session Available **Enrollment:** FT 237, PT 30 **Faculty:** FT 9, PT 24 **Student-Faculty Ratio:** 17:1 **Exams:** SAT I and SAT II or ACT **% Receiving Financial Aid:** 75 **% Residing in College-Owned, -Operated, or -Affiliated Housing:** 40 **Library Holdings:** 29,948 **Regional Accreditation:** North Central Association of Colleges and Schools **Credit Hours For Degree:** 62 semester hours, Associates; 128 semester hours, Bachelors **ROTC:** Air Force **Intercollegiate Athletics:** Basketball M & W; Volleyball W

TOHONO O'ODHAM COMMUNITY COLLEGE

PO Box 3129
Sells, AZ 85634
Tel: (520)383-8401
Fax: (520)383-8403
Web Site: http://www.tocc.cc.az.us/
President/CEO: Olivia Vanegas-Funcheon
Type: Two-Year College **Sex:** Coed **Calendar System:** Semester **Regional Accreditation:** North Central Association of Colleges and Schools

UNIVERSAL TECHNICAL INSTITUTE

10695 W. Pierce St.
Avondale, AZ 85323-7946
Tel: (602)264-4164
Free: 800-859-1202
Fax: (602)264-6412
Web Site: http://www.uticorp.com/
President/CEO: Robert D. Hartman
Type: Two-Year College **H.S. Requirements:** High school diploma required; GED accepted **Scholarships:** Available **Faculty:** FT 107 **Student-Faculty Ratio:** 30:1 **Professional Accreditation:** ACCSCT

UNIVERSITY OF ADVANCING TECHNOLOGY

2625 West Baseline Rd.
Tempe, AZ 85283-1042
Tel: (602)383-8228
Free: 800-658-5744
Fax: (602)383-8222
E-mail: admissions@uact.edu
Web Site: http://www.uat.edu/
President/CEO: Dominic Pistillo
Registrar: Judith Drayer
Admissions: Jason Pistillo
Type: Comprehensive **Sex:** Coed **Application Fee:** $0.00 **H.S. Requirements:** High school diploma required; GED accepted **Costs Per Year:** Application fee: $0. Tuition: $14,600 full-time. **Scholarships:** Available **Calendar System:** Semester, Summer Session Available **Enrollment:** FT 983, Grad 21 **Faculty:** FT 28, PT 15 **Student-Faculty Ratio:** 13:1 **Exams:** ACT, SAT I or ACT, SAT II **Library Holdings:** 19,211 **Credit Hours For Degree:** 60 credits, Associates; 120 credits, Bachelors **Professional Accreditation:** ACICS

THE UNIVERSITY OF ARIZONA

Tucson, AZ 85721
Tel: (520)621-2211
Admissions: (520)621-3237
Fax: (520)621-9799
E-mail: appinfo@arizona.edu
Web Site: http://www.arizona.edu/
President/CEO: Dr. Peter Likins
Registrar: Gary Wagner
Admissions: Lori Goldman
Financial Aid: Magdalena Vargas
Type: University **Sex:** Coed **Affiliation:** Arizona Board of Regents **Scores:** 96.8% SAT V 400+; 96.7% SAT M 400+; 41.9% ACT 18-23; 41.6% ACT 24-29 **% Accepted:** 83 **Admission Plans:** Preferred Admission; Early Admission **Application Deadline:** April 01 **Application Fee:** $25.00 **H.S. Requirements:** High school diploma required; GED accepted **Costs Per Year:** Application fee: $25. State resident tuition: $4394 full-time, $246 per credit hour part-time. Nonresident tuition: $13,578 full-time, $582 per credit hour part-time. Mandatory fees: $104 full-time, $83 per year part-time. Full-time tuition and fees vary according to course load. Part-time tuition and fees vary according to course load. College room and board: $7460. College room only: $4100. Room and board charges vary according to board plan and housing facility. **Scholarships:** Available **Calendar System:** Semester, Summer Session Available **Enrollment:** FT 24,725, PT 3,737, Grad 7,361 **Faculty:** FT 1,378, PT 46 **Student-Faculty Ratio:** 19:1 **Exams:** SAT I or ACT **% Receiving Financial Aid:** 39 **% Residing in College-Owned, -Operated, or -Affiliated Housing:** 18 **Library Holdings:** 4,359,195 **Regional Accreditation:** North Central Association of Colleges and Schools **Credit Hours For Degree:** 125 semester hours, Bachelors **ROTC:** Army, Navy, Air Force **Professional Accreditation:** AACSB, ABET, ACEJMC,

AACN, AAFCS, ABA, ACPhE, ADtA, ACSP, ALA, APA, ASLA, ASLHA, AALS, CEPH, CORE, LCMEAMA, NAACLS, NASAD, NASD NASM, NASPAA, NAST, NLN **Intercollegiate Athletics:** Baseball M; Basketball M & W; Cross-Country Running M & W; Football M; Golf M & W; Gymnastics W; Ice Hockey M; Lacrosse M & W; Rugby M & W; Soccer M & W; Softball W; Swimming and Diving M & W; Tennis M & W; Track and Field M & W; Volleyball M & W; Wrestling M

UNIVERSITY OF PHOENIX ONLINE CAMPUS
3157 East Elwood St.
Phoenix, AZ 85034-7209
Tel: (602)387-7000
Free: 800-228-7240
Admissions: (480)557-1712
Web Site: http://www.uopxonline.com/
Admissions: Nina Omelchanko
Type: Comprehensive **Sex:** Coed **Admission Plans:** Open Admission; Deferred Admission **Application Deadline:** Rolling **Application Fee:** $110.00 **H.S. Requirements:** High school diploma required; GED accepted **Costs Per Year:** Application fee: $110. Tuition: $13,320 full-time, $444 per credit part-time. Mandatory fees: $560 full-time. Full-time tuition and fees vary according to program. **Scholarships:** Available **Calendar System:** Continuous, Summer Session Not available **Enrollment:** FT 70,820, Grad 46,439 **Faculty:** FT 16, PT 5,958 **Student-Faculty Ratio:** 16:1 **Library Holdings:** 444 **Regional Accreditation:** North Central Association of Colleges and Schools **Credit Hours For Degree:** 60 credits, Associates; 120 credits, Bachelors **Professional Accreditation:** NLN

UNIVERSITY OF PHOENIX-PHOENIX CAMPUS
4635 East Elwood St.
Phoenix, AZ 85040-1958
Tel: (480)804-7600
Free: 800-228-7240
Admissions: (480)557-1712
E-mail: babarill@phoenix.edu
Web Site: http://www.phoenix.edu/
President/CEO: Dr. Laura Palmer Noone
Registrar: Tandy Elisala
Admissions: Nina Omelchanko
Financial Aid: Robert Collins
Type: Comprehensive **Sex:** Coed **Admission Plans:** Open Admission; Deferred Admission **Application Deadline:** Rolling **Application Fee:** $110.00 **H.S. Requirements:** High school diploma required; GED accepted **Costs Per Year:** Application fee: $110. Tuition: $9765 full-time, $323 per credit part-time. Mandatory fees: $560 full-time, $70 per course part-time. **Scholarships:** Available **Calendar System:** Continuous, Summer Session Not available **Enrollment:** FT 5,898, Grad 3,510 **Faculty:** FT 19, PT 765 **Student-Faculty Ratio:** 10:1 **Library Holdings:** 442 **Regional Accreditation:** North Central Association of Colleges and Schools **Credit Hours For Degree:** 60 credits, Associates; 120 credits, Bachelors **Professional Accreditation:** ACA, NLN

UNIVERSITY OF PHOENIX-SOUTHERN ARIZONA CAMPUS
5099 East Grant Rd.
Tucson, AZ 85712-2732
Tel: (520)881-6512
Free: 800-228-7240
Admissions: (480)557-1712
Fax: (520)795-6177
Web Site: http://www.phoenix.edu/
President/CEO: Dr. Laura Palmer Noone
Registrar: Tandy Elisala
Admissions: Nina Omelchanko
Financial Aid: Robert Collins
Type: Comprehensive **Sex:** Coed **Admission Plans:** Open Admission; Deferred Admission **Application Deadline:** Rolling **Application Fee:** $110.00 **H.S. Requirements:** High school diploma required; GED accepted **Costs Per Year:** Application fee: $110. Tuition: $9675 full-time, $322.50 per credit part-time. Mandatory fees: $560 full-time, $70 per course part-time. **Scholarships:** Available **Calendar System:** Continuous, Summer Session Not available **Enrollment:** FT 2,431, Grad 961 **Faculty:** FT 4, PT 376 **Student-Faculty Ratio:** 8:1 **Library Holdings:** 444 **Regional Accreditation:** North Central Association of Colleges and Schools **Credit Hours For Degree:** 60 credits, Associates; 120 credits, Bachelors **Professional Accreditation:** ACA, NLN

WESTERN INTERNATIONAL UNIVERSITY
9215 North Black Canyon Hwy.
Phoenix, AZ 85021-2718
Tel: (602)943-2311
Web Site: http://www.wintu.edu/
President/CEO: Michael J. Siedien
Registrar: Hue Haslim
Admissions: Jo Arney
Type: Comprehensive **Sex:** Coed **Affiliation:** Apollo Group, Inc **Admission Plans:** Deferred Admission **Application Fee:** $85.00 **H.S. Requirements:** High school diploma required; GED accepted **Calendar System:** Continuous, Summer Session Available **Enrollment:** FT 2,856, Grad 895 **Faculty:** PT 243 **Student-Faculty Ratio:** 10:1 **Library Holdings:** 7,500 **Regional Accreditation:** North Central Association of Colleges and Schools **Credit Hours For Degree:** 60 credit hours, Associates; 126 credit hours, Bachelors

YAVAPAI COLLEGE
1100 East Sheldon St.
Prescott, AZ 86301-3297
Tel: (928)445-7300
Free: 800-922-6787
Admissions: (928)776-2188
Fax: (928)776-2151
Web Site: http://www2.yc.edu/
President/CEO: Dr. Doreen Dailey
Admissions: David Vanness
Financial Aid: Vikki Gill
Type: Two-Year College **Sex:** Coed **Affiliation:** Arizona State Community College System **Admission Plans:** Open Admission; Early Admission; Deferred Admission **Application Deadline:** Rolling **H.S. Requirements:** High school diploma required; GED accepted **Costs Per Year:** State resident tuition: $1080 full-time, $45 per credit part-time. Nonresident tuition: $6880 full-time, $56 per credit part-time. **Scholarships:** Available **Calendar System:** Semester, Summer Session Available **Enrollment:** FT 1,322, PT 6,100 **Faculty:** FT 107, PT 265 **Student-Faculty Ratio:** 15:1 **% Residing in College-Owned, -Operated, or -Affiliated Housing:** 5 **Library Holdings:** 81,144 **Regional Accreditation:** North Central Association of Colleges and Schools **Credit Hours For Degree:** 64 credits, Associates **ROTC:** Army, Air Force **Professional Accreditation:** NLN **Intercollegiate Athletics:** Baseball M; Basketball M & W; Cross-Country Running W; Soccer M; Volleyball W

ARKANSAS BAPTIST COLLEGE
1600 Bishop St.
Little Rock, AR 72202-6067
Tel: (501)374-7856
Web Site: http://www.arbaptcol.edu/
President/CEO: Dr. Israel R. Dunn, Jr.
Registrar: Annie A. Hightower
Admissions: Freddie M. Fox
Financial Aid: Evelyn Jones
Type: Four-Year College **Sex:** Coed **Affiliation:** Baptist **Admission Plans:** Open Admission; Deferred Admission **H.S. Requirements:** High school diploma required; GED accepted **Scholarships:** Available **Calendar System:** Semester, Summer Session Available **Enrollment:** FT 258, PT 117 **Faculty:** FT 17, PT 14 **Student-Faculty Ratio:** 9:1 **Regional Accreditation:** North Central Association of Colleges and Schools **Credit Hours For Degree:** 124 semester hours, Bachelors **Intercollegiate Athletics:** Basketball M & W; Volleyball M & W

ARKANSAS NORTHEASTERN COLLEGE
PO Box 1109
Blytheville, AR 72316-1109
Tel: (870)762-1020
Fax: (870)763-3704
Web Site: http://www.anc.edu/
President/CEO: Dr. John P. Sullins
Registrar: June Walters
Admissions: June Walters
Financial Aid: June Walters
Type: Two-Year College **Sex:** Coed **% Accepted:** 100 **Admission Plans:** Open Admission; Deferred Admission **Application Deadline:** Rolling **Application Fee:** $0.00 **H.S. Requirements:** High school diploma required; GED accepted **Costs Per Year:** Application fee: $0. Area resident tuition: $1410 full-time, $47 per semester hour part-time. State resident tuition: $1710 full-time, $57 per semester hour part-time. Nonresident tuition: $3210 full-time, $107 per semester hour part-time. Mandatory fees: $220 full-time, $6 per semester hour part-time, $20 per term part-time. **Scholarships:** Available **Calendar System:** Semester, Summer Session Available **Enrollment:** FT 962, PT 868 **Faculty:** FT 73, PT 100 **Student-Faculty Ratio:** 18:1 **Library Holdings:** 15,493 **Regional Accreditation:** North Central Association of Colleges and Schools **Credit Hours For Degree:** 62 semester hours, Associates **Professional Accreditation:** ACBSP, NLN

ARKANSAS STATE UNIVERSITY
PO Box 10
State University, AR 72467
Tel: (870)972-2100
Admissions: (870)972-3024
Fax: (870)972-2090
E-mail: admissions@astate.edu
Web Site: http://www.astate.edu/
President/CEO: Dr. Leslie Wyatt
Registrar: Tracy Finch
Admissions: Tammy Fowler
Financial Aid: Gregory Thornburg
Type: Comprehensive **Sex:** Coed **Affiliation:** Arkansas State University System **Scores:** 47.6% ACT 18-23; 29.6% ACT 24-29 **% Accepted:** 65 **Admission Plans:** Early Admission; Deferred Admission **Application Deadline:** Rolling **Application Fee:** $15.00 **H.S. Requirements:** High school diploma required; GED accepted **Costs Per Year:** Application fee: $15. State resident tuition: $4260 full-time, $142 per credit hour part-time. Nonresident tuition: $10,965 full-time, $365.50 per credit hour part-time. Mandatory fees: $1180 full-time, $37 per credit hour part-time, $25 per term part-time. Full-time tuition and fees vary according to course load, location, and program. Part-time tuition and fees vary according to course load, location, and program. College room and board: $4190. Room and board charges vary according to board plan and housing facility. **Scholarships:** Available **Calendar System:** Semester, Summer Session Available **Enrollment:** FT 7,194, PT 1,944, Grad 1,276 **Faculty:** FT 447, PT 159 **Student-Faculty Ratio:** 17:1 **Exams:** ACT, Other, SAT I or ACT **% Receiving Financial Aid:** 74 **% Residing in College-Owned, -Operated, or -Affiliated Housing:** 18 **Library Holdings:** 586,176 **Regional Accreditation:** North Central Association of Colleges and Schools **Credit Hours For Degree:** 62 credit hours, Associates; 124 credit hours, Bachelors **ROTC:** Army **Professional Accreditation:** AACSB, ABET, ACEJMC, AANA, ACA, APTA, ASLHA, CORE, CSWE, JRCERT, JRCEPAT, NAACLS, NASAD, NASM, NASPAA, NCATE, NLN **Intercollegiate Athletics:** Baseball M; Basketball M & W; Bowling W; Cross-Country Running M & W; Football M; Golf M & W; Soccer W; Tennis W; Track and Field M & W; Volleyball W

ARKANSAS STATE UNIVERSITY-BEEBE
PO Box 1000
Beebe, AR 72012-1000
Tel: (501)882-3600
Admissions: (501)882-8280
Fax: (501)882-8370
Web Site: http://www.asub.edu/
President/CEO: Dr. Eugene McKay
Registrar: James Washburn
Admissions: James Washburn
Financial Aid: Dena Prior
Type: Two-Year College **Sex:** Coed **Affiliation:** Arkansas State University System **Admission Plans:** Open Admission; Deferred Admission **Application Deadline:** Rolling **Application Fee:** $0.00 **H.S. Requirements:** High school diploma required; GED accepted **Costs Per Year:** Application fee: $0. State resident tuition: $1824 full-time. Nonresident tuition: $3000 full-time. College room and board: $2480. **Scholarships:** Available **Calendar System:** Semester, Summer Session Available **Enrollment:** FT 2,124, PT 1,852 **Faculty:** FT 63, PT 34 **Student-Faculty Ratio:** 30:1 **Exams:** ACT **% Residing in College-Owned, -Operated, or -Affiliated Housing:** 12 **Library Holdings:** 90,000 **Regional Accreditation:** North Central Association of Colleges and Schools **Credit Hours For Degree:** 62 credit hours, Associates **Professional Accreditation:** ABET, NAACLS

ARKANSAS STATE UNIVERSITY-MOUNTAIN HOME
1600 South College St.
Mountain Home, AR 72653
Tel: (870)508-6100
Admissions: (870)508-6104
E-mail: rblagg@asumh.edu
Web Site: http://www.asumh.edu/
President/CEO: Ed Coulter
Admissions: Rosalyn Blagg

Type: Two-Year College **Sex:** Coed **Affiliation:** Arkansas State University **Scores:** 60% ACT 18-23; 24% ACT 24-29 **% Accepted:** 52 **Admission Plans:** Open Admission **Application Fee:** $0.00 **H.S. Requirements:** High school diploma required; GED accepted **Costs Per Year:** Application fee: $0. State resident tuition: $2130 full-time, $71 per credit part-time. Nonresident tuition: $3660 full-time, $122 per credit part-time. Mandatory fees: $240 full-time, $8 per credit part-time. **Scholarships:** Available **Calendar System:** Semester, Summer Session Available **Enrollment:** FT 625, PT 406 **Faculty:** FT 38, PT 24 **Student-Faculty Ratio:** 20:1 **Exams:** ACT, Other, SAT II **Library Holdings:** 30,682 **Regional Accreditation:** North Central Association of Colleges and Schools **Credit Hours For Degree:** 60 credits, Associates **Professional Accreditation:** ABFSE

ARKANSAS STATE UNIVERSITY-NEWPORT
7648 Victory Blvd.
Newport, AR 72112
Tel: (870)512-7800
Free: 800-976-1676
Web Site: http://www.asun.edu/
President/CEO: Larry Williams
Admissions: Tara Byrd
Type: Two-Year College **Sex:** Coed **Affiliation:** Arkansas State University **Admission Plans:** Open Admission **H.S. Requirements:** High school diploma required; GED accepted **Scholarships:** Available **Calendar System:** Semester **Faculty:** FT 23, PT 27 **Student-Faculty Ratio:** 12:1 **Exams:** ACT, Other **Regional Accreditation:** North Central Association of Colleges and Schools **Credit Hours For Degree:** 62 credits, Associates

ARKANSAS TECH UNIVERSITY
Russellville, AR 72801
Tel: (479)968-0389
Free: 800-582-6953
Admissions: (479)968-0343
Fax: (479)964-0522
E-mail: shauna.donnell@atu.edu
Web Site: http://www.atu.edu/
President/CEO: Dr. Robert C. Brown
Registrar: Tammy Rhodes
Admissions: Shauna Donnell
Financial Aid: Shirley M. Goines
Type: Comprehensive **Sex:** Coed **Scores:** 100% SAT V 400+; 100% SAT M 400+; 45.61% ACT 18-23; 34.98% ACT 24-29 **% Accepted:** 48 **Admission Plans:** Deferred Admission **Application Fee:** $0.00 **H.S. Requirements:** High school diploma required; GED accepted **Costs Per Year:** Application fee: $0. State resident tuition: $4290 full-time, $143 per credit hour part-time. Nonresident tuition: $8580 full-time, $286 per credit hour part-time. Mandatory fees: $410 full-time, $4 per credit hour part-time, $145 per term part-time. Full-time tuition and fees vary according to course load and location. Part-time tuition and fees vary according to course load and location. College room and board: $4290. College room only: $2290. Room and board charges vary according to board plan and housing facility. **Scholarships:** Available **Calendar System:** Semester, Summer Session Available **Enrollment:** FT 5,365, PT 963, Grad 514 **Faculty:** FT 252, PT 146 **Student-Faculty Ratio:** 19:1 **Exams:** SAT I or ACT **% Receiving Financial Aid:** 63 **% Residing in College-Owned, -Operated, or -Affiliated Housing:** 30 **Library Holdings:** 259,372 **Regional Accreditation:** North Central Association of Colleges and Schools **Credit Hours For Degree:** 62 semester hours, Associates; 124 semester hours, Bachelors **ROTC:** Army **Professional Accreditation:** AACSB, ABET, AAMAE, AHIMA, NASM, NCATE, NLN, NRPA **Intercollegiate Athletics:** Baseball M; Basketball M & W; Cheerleading M & W; Cross-Country Running W; Football M; Golf M; Tennis W; Volleyball W

BLACK RIVER TECHNICAL COLLEGE
1410 Hwy. 304 East
Pocahontas, AR 72455
Tel: (870)248-4000
Free: 800-919-3086
Admissions: (870)892-4565
Fax: (870)248-4100
Web Site: http://www.blackrivertech.edu/
President/CEO: Richard Gaines
Registrar: Margaret Snapp
Admissions: Jim Ulmer
Financial Aid: Carolyn Collins
Type: Two-Year College **Sex:** Coed **Scores:** 15% ACT 18-23; 10% ACT 24-29 **Admission Plans:** Open Admission **Application Fee:** $0.00 **H.S. Requirements:** High school diploma required; GED accepted **Scholarships:** Available **Calendar System:** Semester, Summer Session Available **Enrollment:** FT 652, PT 591 **Faculty:** FT 30, PT 40 **Student-Faculty Ratio:** 16:1 **Exams:** Other **Library Holdings:** 10,000 **Regional Accreditation:** North Central Association of Colleges and Schools **Credit Hours For Degree:** 62 credit hours, Associates **Professional Accreditation:** CARC

CENTRAL BAPTIST COLLEGE
1501 College Ave.
Conway, AR 72034-6470
Tel: (501)329-6872
Free: 800-205-6872
E-mail: ccalhoun@cbc.edu
Web Site: http://www.cbc.edu/
President/CEO: Charles Attebery
Registrar: Phylis Hoffmann
Admissions: Cory Calhoun
Financial Aid: Christi Bell
Type: Four-Year College **Sex:** Coed **Affiliation:** Baptist **% Accepted:** 68 **Admission Plans:** Early Admission **Application Deadline:** August 15 **Application Fee:** $25.00 **H.S. Requirements:** High school diploma required; GED accepted **Costs Per Year:** Application fee: $25. Comprehensive fee: $13,110 includes full-time tuition ($7950), mandatory fees ($500), and college room and board ($4660). **Scholarships:** Available **Calendar System:** Semester, Summer Session Available **Enrollment:** FT 328, PT 67 **Faculty:** FT 17, PT 33 **Student-Faculty Ratio:** 11:1 **Exams:** ACT **% Residing in College-Owned, -Operated, or -Affiliated Housing:** 40 **Library Holdings:** 50,448 **Regional Accreditation:** North Central Association of Colleges and Schools **Credit Hours For Degree:** 64 credit hours, Associates; 127 credit hours, Bachelors **ROTC:** Army **Intercollegiate Athletics:** Baseball M & W; Basketball M & W; Softball W; Volleyball W

COSSATOT COMMUNITY COLLEGE OF THE UNIVERSITY OF ARKANSAS
PO Box 960
De Queen, AR 71832
Tel: (870)584-4471
Free: 800-844-4471
Web Site: http://www.cccua.edu/
President/CEO: Frank G. Adams
Registrar: Brenda Morris
Admissions: Kay Cobb
Financial Aid: Denise Hammond
Type: Two-Year College **Sex:** Coed **Affiliation:** University of Arkansas System **% Accepted:** 83 **Admission Plans:** Open Admission **H.S. Requirements:** High school diploma required; GED accepted **Costs Per Year:** Area resident tuition: $1350 full-time, $45 per credit hour part-time. State resident tuition: $1650 full-time, $55 per credit hour part-time. Nonresident tuition: $4950 full-time, $165 per credit hour part-time. Mandatory fees: $250 full-time, $15 per course part-time, $53 per term part-time. Full-time tuition and fees vary according to course load and program. Part-time tuition and fees vary according to course load and program. **Scholarships:** Available **Calendar System:** Semester, Summer Session Available **Faculty:** FT 34, PT 40 **Student-Faculty Ratio:** 12:1 **Regional Accreditation:** North Central Association of Colleges and Schools **Credit Hours For Degree:** 60 credit hours, Associates **Professional Accreditation:** ACBSP

CROWLEY'S RIDGE COLLEGE
100 College Dr.
Paragould, AR 72450-9731
Tel: (870)236-6901
Free: 800-264-1096
Fax: (870)236-7748
E-mail: njoneshi@crowleysridgecollege.edu
Web Site: http://www.crowleysridgecollege.edu/
President/CEO: Ken Hoppe
Registrar: Paul McFadden
Admissions: Nancy Joneshill
Financial Aid: David Goff
Type: Two-Year College **Sex:** Coed **Affiliation:** Church of Christ **Admission Plans:** Open Admission **Application Fee:** $0.00 **H.S. Requirements:** High school diploma required; GED accepted **Scholarships:** Available **Calendar System:** Semester, Summer Session Available **Faculty:** FT 6, PT 10

Student-Faculty Ratio: 16:1 **Exams:** Other **Regional Accreditation:** North Central Association of Colleges and Schools **Credit Hours For Degree:** 64 credit hours, Associates **Intercollegiate Athletics:** Baseball M; Basketball M & W; Volleyball W

EAST ARKANSAS COMMUNITY COLLEGE
1700 Newcastle Rd.
Forrest City, AR 72335-2204
Tel: (870)633-4480; 877-797-3222
Fax: (870)633-7222
E-mail: dadams@eacc.edu
Web Site: http://www.eacc.edu/
President/CEO: Dr. Coy Grace
Registrar: Sarah Buford
Admissions: DeAnna Adams
Financial Aid: Alvin Coleman
Type: Two-Year College **Sex:** Coed **Scores:** 48% ACT 18-23; 4% ACT 24-29 **Admission Plans:** Open Admission; Early Admission; Deferred Admission **Application Deadline:** Rolling **Application Fee:** $0.00 **H.S. Requirements:** High school diploma required; GED accepted. For applicants 18 or over who demonstrate ability to benefit from college: High school diploma or equivalent not required **Costs Per Year:** Application fee: $0. Area resident tuition: $1470 full-time, $49 per credit hour part-time. State resident tuition: $1710 full-time, $57 per credit hour part-time. Nonresident tuition: $2070 full-time, $69 per credit hour part-time. Mandatory fees: $150 full-time, $5 per credit hour part-time. **Scholarships:** Available **Calendar System:** Semester, Summer Session Available **Enrollment:** FT 745, PT 732 **Faculty:** FT 38, PT 53 **Student-Faculty Ratio:** 17:1 **Library Holdings:** 21,908 **Regional Accreditation:** North Central Association of Colleges and Schools **Credit Hours For Degree:** 64 credits, Associates **Professional Accreditation:** ACBSP, NLN

HARDING UNIVERSITY
900 East Center
Searcy, AR 72149-0001
Tel: (501)279-4000
Free: 800-477-4407
Admissions: (501)279-4407
Fax: (501)279-4865
E-mail: admissions@harding.edu
Web Site: http://www.harding.edu/
President/CEO: Dr. David B. Burks
Registrar: Ron Finley
Admissions: Glenn Dillard
Financial Aid: Dr. Jon Roberts
Type: Comprehensive **Sex:** Coed **Affiliation:** Church of Christ **Scores:** 97% SAT V 400+; 96% SAT M 400+; 41% ACT 18-23; 39% ACT 24-29 **% Accepted:** 62 **Admission Plans:** Early Admission; Deferred Admission **Application Deadline:** June 01 **Application Fee:** $35.00 **H.S. Requirements:** High school diploma required; GED accepted **Costs Per Year:** Application fee: $35. Comprehensive fee: $16,512 includes full-time tuition ($10,800), mandatory fees ($400), and college room and board ($5312). College room only: $2636. Full-time tuition and fees vary according to course load. Room and board charges vary according to board plan and housing facility. Part-time tuition: $360 per semester hour. Part-time mandatory fees: $20 per semester hour. Part-time tuition and fees vary according to course load. **Scholarships:** Available **Calendar System:** Semester, Summer Session Available **Enrollment:** FT 3,879, PT 213, Grad 1,652 **Faculty:** FT 226, PT 106 **Student-Faculty Ratio:** 18:1 **Exams:** SAT I or ACT **% Receiving Financial Aid:** 56 **% Residing in College-Owned, -Operated, or -Affiliated Housing:** 73 **Library Holdings:** 253,436 **Regional Accreditation:** North Central Association of Colleges and Schools **Credit Hours For Degree:** 128 semester hours, Bachelors **ROTC:** Army **Professional Accreditation:** AAMFT, AAFCS, ACBSP, CSWE, NASM, NCATE, NLN **Intercollegiate Athletics:** Baseball M; Basketball M & W; Cheerleading M & W; Cross-Country Running M & W; Football M; Golf M; Lacrosse M; Soccer M & W; Tennis M & W; Track and Field M & W; Ultimate Frisbee M & W; Volleyball W

HENDERSON STATE UNIVERSITY
1100 Henderson St.
Arkadelphia, AR 71999-0001
Tel: (870)230-5000
Free: 800-228-7333
Admissions: (870)230-5028
Fax: (870)230-5144
E-mail: hardwrv@hsu.edu
Web Site: http://www.hsu.edu
President/CEO: Dr. Charles D. Dunn
Registrar: Tom Gattin
Admissions: Vikita Hardwrick
Financial Aid: Jo Holland
Type: Comprehensive **Sex:** Coed **Scores:** 97% SAT V 400+; 97% SAT M 400+; 55% ACT 18-23; 32% ACT 24-29 **% Accepted:** 58 **Admission Plans:** Deferred Admission **Application Deadline:** July 15 **Application Fee:** $0.00 **H.S. Requirements:** High school diploma required; GED accepted **Costs Per Year:** Application fee: $0. State resident tuition: $4050 full-time, $135 per credit hour part-time. Nonresident tuition: $8100 full-time, $270 per credit hour part-time. Mandatory fees: $575 full-time. Full-time tuition and fees vary according to course load and program. Part-time tuition varies according to course load and program. College room and board: $3888. Room and board charges vary according to board plan and housing facility. **Scholarships:** Available **Calendar System:** Semester, Summer Session Available **Enrollment:** FT 2,713, PT 376, Grad 495 **Faculty:** FT 161, PT 68 **Student-Faculty Ratio:** 14:1 **Exams:** ACT, SAT I or ACT **% Receiving Financial Aid:** 56 **Library Holdings:** 262,572 **Regional Accreditation:** North Central Association of Colleges and Schools **Credit Hours For Degree:** 60 semester hours, Associates; 124 semester hours, Bachelors **Professional Accreditation:** AACSB, AAFCS, NASM, NCATE, NLN **Intercollegiate Athletics:** Baseball M; Basketball M & W; Cross-Country Running W; Football M; Golf M & W; Softball W; Swimming and Diving M & W; Tennis M & W; Volleyball W

HENDRIX COLLEGE
1600 Washington Ave.
Conway, AR 72032-3080
Tel: (501)329-6811
Free: 800-277-9017
Admissions: (501)450-1362
Fax: (501)450-3843
E-mail: foust@hendrix.edu
Web Site: http://www.hendrix.edu/
President/CEO: Dr. J. Timothy Cloyd
Registrar: Xinying Wang
Admissions: Karen R. Foust
Financial Aid: Tammy Gillis
Type: Comprehensive **Sex:** Coed **Affiliation:** United Methodist **Scores:** 100% SAT V 400+; 100% SAT M 400+; 12% ACT 18-23; 54% ACT 24-29 **% Accepted:** 83 **Admission Plans:** Early Admission; Deferred Admission **Application Deadline:** August 01 **Application Fee:** $40.00 **H.S. Requirements:** High school diploma required; GED accepted **Costs Per Year:** Application fee: $40. Comprehensive fee: $27,946 includes full-time tuition ($21,336), mandatory fees ($300), and college room and board ($6310). College room only: $2760. Full-time tuition and fees vary according to course load. Room and board charges vary according to board plan and housing facility. Part-time tuition: $2248 per course. Part-time mandatory fees: $40 per year. Part-time tuition and fees vary according to course load. **Scholarships:** Available **Calendar System:** Semester, Summer Session Not available **Enrollment:** FT 1,001, PT 21, Grad 9 **Faculty:** FT 85, PT 22 **Student-Faculty Ratio:** 11:1 **Exams:** SAT I or ACT **% Receiving Financial Aid:** 56 **% Residing in College-Owned, -Operated, or -Affiliated Housing:** 97 **Library Holdings:** 216,172 **Regional Accreditation:** North Central Association of Colleges and Schools **Credit Hours For Degree:** 32 courses, Bachelors **ROTC:** Army **Professional Accreditation:** NASM, NCATE **Intercollegiate Athletics:** Baseball M; Basketball M & W; Cross-Country Running M & W; Golf M & W; Rugby M; Soccer M & W; Softball W; Swimming and Diving M & W; Tennis M & W; Track and Field M & W; Volleyball W

ITT TECHNICAL INSTITUTE
4520 South University
Little Rock, AR 72204
Tel: (501)565-5550
Web Site: http://www.itt-tech.edu/
Registrar: Dr. Pat Hunnicutt
Admissions: Tom Crawford
Financial Aid: Tresa Smith
Type: Two-Year College **Sex:** Coed **Affiliation:** ITT Educational Services, Inc **Admission Plans:** Deferred Admission **Application Deadline:** Rolling **Application Fee:** $100.00 **H.S. Requirements:** High school diploma required; GED accepted **Costs Per Year:** Application fee: $100. **Scholar-**

ships: Available **Calendar System:** Quarter, Summer Session Not available **Exams:** Other **Credit Hours For Degree:** 96 credit hours, Associates **Professional Accreditation:** ACICS

JOHN BROWN UNIVERSITY
2000 West University St.
Siloam Springs, AR 72761-2121
Tel: (479)524-9500; 877-JBU-INFO
Admissions: (479)524-7150
Fax: (479)524-9548
E-mail: jbuinfo@acc.jbu.edu
Web Site: http://www.jbu.edu/
President/CEO: Dr. Charles Pollard
Registrar: Dr. Paul Hines
Admissions: Don Crandall
Financial Aid: Kim Eldridge
Type: Comprehensive **Sex:** Coed **Affiliation:** interdenominational **Scores:** 99.06% SAT V 400+; 98.12% SAT M 400+; 37.31% ACT 18-23; 45.77% ACT 24-29 **% Accepted:** 62 **Admission Plans:** Deferred Admission **Application Deadline:** Rolling **Application Fee:** $25.00 **H.S. Requirements:** High school diploma required; GED accepted **Costs Per Year:** Application fee: $25. Comprehensive fee: $20,910 includes full-time tuition ($14,544), mandatory fees ($736), and college room and board ($5630). Full-time tuition and fees vary according to program. Room and board charges vary according to board plan and housing facility. Part-time tuition: $600 per semester hour. Part-time tuition varies according to course load and program. **Scholarships:** Available **Calendar System:** Semester, Summer Session Not available **Enrollment:** FT 1,581, PT 78, Grad 245 **Faculty:** FT 83, PT 65 **Student-Faculty Ratio:** 12:1 **Exams:** SAT I or ACT **% Receiving Financial Aid:** 63 **% Residing in College-Owned, -Operated, or -Affiliated Housing:** 76 **Library Holdings:** 114,799 **Regional Accreditation:** North Central Association of Colleges and Schools **Credit Hours For Degree:** 62 semester hours, Associates; 124 semester hours, Bachelors **ROTC:** Army, Air Force **Professional Accreditation:** ABET, ACCE, NCATE **Intercollegiate Athletics:** Basketball M & W; Soccer M & W; Swimming and Diving M & W; Tennis M & W; Volleyball W

LYON COLLEGE
PO Box 2317
Batesville, AR 72503-2317
Tel: (870)793-9813
Free: 800-423-2542
Admissions: (870)698-4250
Fax: (870)698-4622
E-mail: admissions@lyon.edu
Web Site: http://www.lyon.edu/
President/CEO: Dr. Walter B. Roettger
Registrar: Janelle Elliott
Admissions: Denny Bardos
Type: Four-Year College **Sex:** Coed **Affiliation:** Presbyterian **Scores:** 95% SAT V 400+; 100% SAT M 400+; 28% ACT 18-23; 56% ACT 24-29 **% Accepted:** 72 **Admission Plans:** Early Admission; Deferred Admission **Application Deadline:** Rolling **Application Fee:** $25.00 **H.S. Requirements:** High school diploma required; GED accepted **Costs Per Year:** Application fee: $25. Comprehensive fee: $21,130 includes full-time tuition ($14,420), mandatory fees ($440), and college room and board ($6270). College room only: $2580. Part-time tuition: $600 per credit hour. **Scholarships:** Available **Calendar System:** Semester, Summer Session Available **Enrollment:** FT 458, PT 30 **Faculty:** FT 44, PT 15 **Student-Faculty Ratio:** 10:1 **Exams:** SAT I or ACT **% Receiving Financial Aid:** 70 **% Residing in College-Owned, -Operated, or -Affiliated Housing:** 75 **Library Holdings:** 181,789 **Regional Accreditation:** North Central Association of Colleges and Schools **Credit Hours For Degree:** 120 credits, Bachelors **Professional Accreditation:** NCATE **Intercollegiate Athletics:** Baseball M; Basketball M & W; Cross-Country Running M & W; Golf M & W; Soccer M & W; Tennis M & W; Volleyball W

MID-SOUTH COMMUNITY COLLEGE
2000 West Broadway
West Memphis, AR 72301
Tel: (870)733-6722
Admissions: (870)733-6732
Fax: (870)733-6719
Web Site: http://www.midsouthcc.edu/
President/CEO: Dr. Glen F. Fenter
Registrar: Leslie Anderson
Admissions: Leslie Anderson
Financial Aid: Jackie Brubaker
Type: Two-Year College **Sex:** Coed **Scores:** 51% ACT 18-23; 9% ACT 24-29 **% Accepted:** 100 **Admission Plans:** Open Admission; Early Admission **Application Deadline:** Rolling **Application Fee:** $0.00 **H.S. Requirements:** High school diploma required; GED accepted. For adults who demonstrate ability to benefit from college: High school diploma or equivalent not required **Costs Per Year:** Application fee: $0. Area resident tuition: $1410 full-time, $47 per credit part-time. State resident tuition: $1740 full-time, $58 per credit part-time. Nonresident tuition: $3150 full-time, $105 per credit part-time. Mandatory fees: $210 full-time, $7 per credit part-time. Full-time tuition and fees vary according to course load and reciprocity agreements. Part-time tuition and fees vary according to course load and reciprocity agreements. **Scholarships:** Available **Calendar System:** Semester, Summer Session Available **Enrollment:** FT 457, PT 1,010 **Faculty:** FT 34, PT 65 **Student-Faculty Ratio:** 15:1 **Exams:** ACT, Other **Library Holdings:** 14,672 **Regional Accreditation:** North Central Association of Colleges and Schools **Credit Hours For Degree:** 64 credit hours, Associates

NATIONAL PARK COMMUNITY COLLEGE
101 College Dr.
Hot Springs, AR 71913
Tel: (501)760-4222
Fax: (501)760-4100
E-mail: bmoody@npcc.edu
Web Site: http://www.npcc.edu/
President/CEO: Dr. Tom Spencer
Registrar: Dr. Allen Bradley Moody
Admissions: Dr. Allen B. Moody
Financial Aid: Lisa Hopper
Type: Two-Year College **Sex:** Coed **Affiliation:** Arkansas Department of Higher Education **Admission Plans:** Open Admission; Early Admission; Deferred Admission **Application Fee:** $0.00 **H.S. Requirements:** High school diploma required; GED accepted **Scholarships:** Available **Calendar System:** Semester, Summer Session Available **Enrollment:** FT 1,237, PT 1,759 **Faculty:** FT 64, PT 83 **Student-Faculty Ratio:** 21:1 **Exams:** Other, SAT I and SAT II or ACT **Library Holdings:** 17,800 **Regional Accreditation:** North Central Association of Colleges and Schools **Credit Hours For Degree:** 60 semester hours, Associates **Professional Accreditation:** AHIMA, ACBSP, JRCERT, NAACLS, NLN

NORTH ARKANSAS COLLEGE
1515 Pioneer Dr.
Harrison, AR 72601
Tel: (870)743-3000
Free: 800-679-6622
Admissions: (870)391-3221
Fax: (870)391-3339
E-mail: charlam@northark.edu
Web Site: http://www.northark.edu/
President/CEO: Dr. Jeffrey Olson
Registrar: Jane Brown
Admissions: Charla McDonald Jennings
Financial Aid: Nancy Fountain
Type: Two-Year College **Sex:** Coed **Scores:** 61.93% ACT 18-23; 11.47% ACT 24-29 **% Accepted:** 100 **Admission Plans:** Open Admission; Deferred Admission **Application Deadline:** Rolling **Application Fee:** $0.00 **H.S. Requirements:** High school diploma required; GED accepted **Costs Per Year:** Application fee: $0. Area resident tuition: $1590 full-time, $53 per credit hour part-time. State resident tuition: $2130 full-time, $71 per credit hour part-time. Nonresident tuition: $4110 full-time, $137 per credit hour part-time. Mandatory fees: $150 full-time. **Scholarships:** Available **Calendar System:** Semester, Summer Session Available **Enrollment:** FT 1,138, PT 1,049 **Faculty:** FT 66, PT 90 **Student-Faculty Ratio:** 16:1 **Library Holdings:** 29,969 **Regional Accreditation:** North Central Association of Colleges and Schools **Credit Hours For Degree:** 62 credit hours, Associates **Professional Accreditation:** ARCEST, JRCERT, NAACLS, NLN **Intercollegiate Athletics:** Baseball M; Basketball M & W; Softball W

NORTHWEST ARKANSAS COMMUNITY COLLEGE
One College Dr.
Bentonville, AR 72712
Tel: (479)636-9222

Free: 800-995-6922
Fax: (479)619-4116
Web Site: http://www.nwacc.edu/
President/CEO: Dr. Becky Paneitz
Admissions: Dr. Charles Mullins
Financial Aid: Diana Johnson
Type: Two-Year College **Sex:** Coed **Admission Plans:** Open Admission **Application Fee:** $10.00 **H.S. Requirements:** High school diploma required; GED accepted **Scholarships:** Available **Calendar System:** Semester, Summer Session Available **Faculty:** FT 66, PT 169 **Exams:** Other, SAT I or ACT **Library Holdings:** 15,500 **Regional Accreditation:** North Central Association of Colleges and Schools **Credit Hours For Degree:** 62 credits, Associates **Professional Accreditation:** CARC, JRCEMT

OUACHITA BAPTIST UNIVERSITY
410 Ouachita St.
Arkadelphia, AR 71998-0001
Tel: (870)245-5000
Admissions: (870)245-5578
Fax: (870)245-5500
E-mail: jonesj@sigma.obu.edu
Web Site: http://www.obu.edu/
President/CEO: Dr. Andrew Westmoreland
Registrar: Judy Jones
Admissions: Judy Jones
Financial Aid: Lane Smith
Type: Four-Year College **Sex:** Coed **Affiliation:** Baptist **Scores:** 97% SAT V 400+; 96% SAT M 400+; 41% ACT 18-23; 39% ACT 24-29 **% Accepted:** 58 **Admission Plans:** Early Admission; Deferred Admission **Application Deadline:** August 15 **Application Fee:** $50.00 **H.S. Requirements:** High school diploma required; GED accepted **Costs Per Year:** Application fee: $50. Comprehensive fee: $21,990 includes full-time tuition ($16,650), mandatory fees ($340), and college room and board ($5000). Part-time tuition: $460 per semester hour. **Scholarships:** Available **Calendar System:** Semester, Summer Session Available **Enrollment:** FT 1,399, PT 100 **Faculty:** FT 114, PT 28 **Student-Faculty Ratio:** 12:1 **Exams:** SAT I or ACT **% Receiving Financial Aid:** 48 **% Residing in College-Owned, -Operated, or -Affiliated Housing:** 86 **Library Holdings:** 139,278 **Regional Accreditation:** North Central Association of Colleges and Schools **Credit Hours For Degree:** 64 semester hours, Associates; 128 semester hours, Bachelors **ROTC:** Army **Professional Accreditation:** AACSB, AAFCS, NASM, NCATE **Intercollegiate Athletics:** Baseball M; Basketball M & W; Cross-Country Running W; Football M; Golf M; Soccer M & W; Softball W; Swimming and Diving M & W; Tennis M & W; Volleyball W

OUACHITA TECHNICAL COLLEGE
One College Circle
Malvern, AR 72104
Tel: (501)337-5000
Fax: (501)337-9382
E-mail: lindaj@otcweb.edu
Web Site: http://www.otcweb.edu/
President/CEO: Dr. Barry Ballard
Registrar: Linda Johnson
Admissions: Linda Johnson
Financial Aid: Teresa Avery
Type: Two-Year College **Sex:** Coed **Scores:** 53% ACT 18-23; 9% ACT 24-29 **% Accepted:** 100 **Admission Plans:** Open Admission; Early Admission; Deferred Admission **Application Deadline:** Rolling **H.S. Requirements:** High school diploma required; GED accepted **Costs Per Year:** One-time mandatory fee: $35. State resident tuition: $1560 full-time, $52 per credit hour part-time. Nonresident tuition: $3120 full-time, $104 per credit hour part-time. Mandatory fees: $420 full-time, $14 per credit hour part-time. **Scholarships:** Available **Calendar System:** Semester, Summer Session Available **Enrollment:** FT 556, PT 1,034 **Faculty:** FT 33, PT 66 **Student-Faculty Ratio:** 16:1 **Exams:** Other, SAT I or ACT **Library Holdings:** 8,000 **Regional Accreditation:** North Central Association of Colleges and Schools **Credit Hours For Degree:** 60 credit hours, Associates

OZARKA COLLEGE
PO Box 10
Melbourne, AR 72556
Tel: (870)368-7371
Free: 800-821-4335
Fax: (870)368-4733
Web Site: http://www.ozarka.edu/
President/CEO: Douglas Rush
Registrar: Ron Helm
Admissions: Randy Scaggs
Financial Aid: Gayle Cooper
Type: Two-Year College **Sex:** Coed **Admission Plans:** Open Admission; Deferred Admission **Application Fee:** $0.00 **H.S. Requirements:** High school diploma required; GED accepted **Costs Per Year:** Application fee: $0. State resident tuition: $1950 full-time, $65 per credit hour part-time. Nonresident tuition: $5040 full-time, $168 per credit hour part-time. Mandatory fees: $330 full-time, $10 per credit hour part-time, $30 per term part-time. Full-time tuition and fees vary according to course load. Part-time tuition and fees vary according to course load. **Scholarships:** Available **Calendar System:** Semester, Summer Session Available **Enrollment:** FT 569, PT 187 **Faculty:** FT 31, PT 40 **Student-Faculty Ratio:** 20:1 **Exams:** ACT, Other **Library Holdings:** 10,500 **Regional Accreditation:** North Central Association of Colleges and Schools **Credit Hours For Degree:** 62 credit hours, Associates

PHILANDER SMITH COLLEGE
812 West 13th St.
Little Rock, AR 72202-3799
Tel: (501)375-9845
Free: 800-446-6772
Admissions: (501)370-5310
Fax: (501)370-5225
Web Site: http://www.philander.edu/
President/CEO: Dr. Julius S. Scott, Jr.
Registrar: Delores Voliber
Admissions: Arnella Hayes
Financial Aid: Linda Bell
Type: Four-Year College **Sex:** Coed **Affiliation:** United Methodist **Scores:** 41% SAT V 400+; 39% SAT M 400+; 21% ACT 18-23 **Admission Plans:** Open Admission; Deferred Admission **Application Fee:** $10.00 **H.S. Requirements:** High school diploma required; GED accepted **Costs Per Year:** Application fee: $10. Comprehensive fee: $13,515 includes full-time tuition ($6950), mandatory fees ($1415), and college room and board ($5150). College room only: $3330. Full-time tuition and fees vary according to class time, course load, and program. Room and board charges vary according to housing facility. Part-time tuition: $290 per credit hour. Part-time mandatory fees: $21 per credit hour, $200 per term. Part-time tuition and fees vary according to class time, course load, and program. **Scholarships:** Available **Calendar System:** Semester, Summer Session Available **Enrollment:** FT 781, PT 168 **Faculty:** FT 40, PT 46 **Student-Faculty Ratio:** 15:1 **Exams:** SAT I or ACT **% Residing in College-Owned, -Operated, or -Affiliated Housing:** 26 **Library Holdings:** 60,000 **Regional Accreditation:** North Central Association of Colleges and Schools **Credit Hours For Degree:** 124 semester hours, Bachelors **ROTC:** Army **Professional Accreditation:** ACBSP, CSWE, NCATE **Intercollegiate Athletics:** Basketball M & W; Volleyball W

PHILLIPS COMMUNITY COLLEGE OF THE UNIVERSITY OF ARKANSAS
PO Box 785
Helena, AR 72342-0785
Tel: (870)338-6474
Fax: (870)338-7542
Web Site: http://www.pccua.edu/
President/CEO: Dr. Steven W. Jones
Registrar: James Brasel
Admissions: Lynn Boone
Financial Aid: Barbra Stevenson
Type: Two-Year College **Sex:** Coed **Affiliation:** University of Arkansas System **Admission Plans:** Open Admission; Early Admission **H.S. Requirements:** High school diploma required; GED accepted **Costs Per Year:** Area resident tuition: $750 full-time, $50 per semester hour part-time. State resident tuition: $885 full-time, $59 per semester hour part-time. Nonresident tuition: $1455 full-time, $97 per semester hour part-time. **Scholarships:** Available **Calendar System:** Semester, Summer Session Available **Faculty:** FT 60, PT 10 **Exams:** ACT, Other **Library Holdings:** 39,000 **Regional Ac-**

creditation: North Central Association of Colleges and Schools **Credit Hours For Degree:** 64 semester hours, Associates **Professional Accreditation:** ACBSP, NAACLS, NLN

PULASKI TECHNICAL COLLEGE
3000 West Scenic Dr.
North Little Rock, AR 72118
Tel: (501)812-2200
Admissions: (501)812-2734
Fax: (501)812-2316
E-mail: catkins@pulaskitech.edu
Web Site: http://www.pulaskitech.edu/
President/CEO: Dr. Dan Bakke
Admissions: Clark Atkins
Financial Aid: Kris Burford
Type: Two-Year College **Sex:** Coed **% Accepted:** 100 **Admission Plans:** Open Admission **Application Deadline:** Rolling **Application Fee:** $0.00 **H.S. Requirements:** High school diploma required; GED accepted **Costs Per Year:** Application fee: $0. State resident tuition: $2161 full-time, $72 per credit hour part-time. Nonresident tuition: $3570 full-time, $119 per credit hour part-time. Mandatory fees: $255 full-time, $8 per credit hour part-time, $15. **Scholarships:** Available **Calendar System:** Semester, Summer Session Available **Enrollment:** FT 3,953, PT 3,732 **Faculty:** FT 111, PT 344 **Student-Faculty Ratio:** 25:1 **Library Holdings:** 16,378 **Regional Accreditation:** North Central Association of Colleges and Schools **Credit Hours For Degree:** 62 semester hours, Associates **Professional Accreditation:** ADA, CARC

REMINGTON COLLEGE-LITTLE ROCK CAMPUS
8901 Kanis Rd.
Little Rock, AR 72205
Tel: (501)312-0007
Fax: (501)225-3819
E-mail: david.caldwell@remingtoncollege.edu
Web Site: http://www.remingtoncollege.edu/
President/CEO: David Caldwell
Admissions: David Caldwell
Type: Two-Year College **Sex:** Coed **Professional Accreditation:** ACCSCT

RICH MOUNTAIN COMMUNITY COLLEGE
1100 College Dr.
Mena, AR 71953
Tel: (479)394-7622
Fax: (479)394-2628
Web Site: http://www.rmcc.edu/
President/CEO: Dr. Janet Smith
Admissions: Dr. Steve Rook
Financial Aid: Mary Standerfer
Type: Two-Year College **Sex:** Coed **Admission Plans:** Open Admission; Early Admission **Application Fee:** $0.00 **H.S. Requirements:** High school diploma required; GED accepted **Costs Per Year:** Application fee: $0. Area resident tuition: $960 full-time, $40 per semester hour part-time. State resident tuition: $1200 full-time, $50 per semester hour part-time. Nonresident tuition: $3600 full-time, $150 per semester hour part-time. Mandatory fees: $72 full-time, $3 per semester hour part-time. **Scholarships:** Available **Calendar System:** Semester, Summer Session Available **Enrollment:** FT 348, PT 625 **Faculty:** FT 19, PT 36 **Student-Faculty Ratio:** 18:1 **Library Holdings:** 13,299 **Regional Accreditation:** North Central Association of Colleges and Schools **Credit Hours For Degree:** 60 credits, Associates

SOUTH ARKANSAS COMMUNITY COLLEGE
PO Box 7010
El Dorado, AR 71731-7010
Tel: (870)862-8131
Free: 800-955-2289
Admissions: (870)864-7142
Fax: (870)864-7122
E-mail: dinman@southark.edu
Web Site: http://www.southark.edu/
President/CEO: Dr. Kathy Matlock
Registrar: Dean Inman
Admissions: Dean Inman
Financial Aid: John Jefferson
Type: Two-Year College **Sex:** Coed **Affiliation:** Arkansas Department of Higher Education **Admission Plans:** Open Admission; Early Admission; Deferred Admission **Application Deadline:** August 25 **H.S. Requirements:** High school diploma or equivalent not required **Costs Per Year:** Area resident tuition: $1710 full-time. State resident tuition: $1950 full-time. Nonresident tuition: $3600 full-time. **Scholarships:** Available **Calendar System:** Semester, Summer Session Available **Enrollment:** FT 612, PT 756 **Student-Faculty Ratio:** 13:1 **Exams:** Other, SAT I or ACT **Library Holdings:** 22,652 **Regional Accreditation:** North Central Association of Colleges and Schools **Credit Hours For Degree:** 60 semester hours, Associates **Professional Accreditation:** AOTA, APTA, JRCERT, NAACLS

SOUTHEAST ARKANSAS COLLEGE
1900 Hazel St.
Pine Bluff, AR 71603
Tel: (870)543-5900
Admissions: (870)543-5957
E-mail: main@seark.edu
Web Site: http://www.seark.edu/
President/CEO: Dr. Philip E. Shirley
Admissions: Barbara Dunn
Financial Aid: Donna Cox
Type: Two-Year College **Sex:** Coed **Admission Plans:** Open Admission; Early Admission **H.S. Requirements:** High school diploma required; GED accepted **Scholarships:** Available **Calendar System:** Semester, Summer Session Available **Enrollment:** FT 1,017, PT 1,180 **Faculty:** FT 49, PT 80 **Student-Faculty Ratio:** 18:1 **Exams:** Other, SAT I or ACT **Library Holdings:** 5,000 **Regional Accreditation:** North Central Association of Colleges and Schools **Credit Hours For Degree:** 62 credits, Associates **Professional Accreditation:** ARCEST, JRCERT, NLN

SOUTHERN ARKANSAS UNIVERSITY-MAGNOLIA
100 East University
Magnolia, AR 71753
Tel: (870)235-4000
Admissions: (870)235-4040
Fax: (870)235-5005
E-mail: addanna@saumag.edu
Web Site: http://www.saumag.edu/
President/CEO: Dr. David Rankin
Registrar: Dr. G. Edward Nipper
Admissions: Sarah Jennings
Financial Aid: Bronwyn Sneed
Type: Comprehensive **Sex:** Coed **Affiliation:** Southern Arkansas University System **Scores:** 56% ACT 18-23; 20% ACT 24-29 **Admission Plans:** Early Admission; Deferred Admission **H.S. Requirements:** High school diploma required; GED accepted **Costs Per Year:** State resident tuition: $3900 full-time, $130 per credit hour part-time. Nonresident tuition: $5910 full-time, $197 per credit hour part-time. Mandatory fees: $390 full-time, $390 per year part-time. Full-time tuition and fees vary according to course load. Part-time tuition and fees vary according to course load. College room and board: $3790. College room only: $1960. **Scholarships:** Available **Calendar System:** Semester, Summer Session Available **Enrollment:** FT 2,398, PT 405, Grad 254 **Faculty:** FT 141, PT 43 **Student-Faculty Ratio:** 15:1 **Exams:** ACT, SAT I or ACT **% Receiving Financial Aid:** 54 **% Residing in College-Owned, -Operated, or -Affiliated Housing:** 36 **Library Holdings:** 151,166 **Regional Accreditation:** North Central Association of Colleges and Schools **Credit Hours For Degree:** 65 semester hours, Associates; 124 semester hours, Bachelors **Professional Accreditation:** CSWE, NASM, NCATE, NLN **Intercollegiate Athletics:** Baseball M; Basketball M & W; Cross-Country Running M & W; Football M; Golf M; Softball W; Tennis W; Track and Field M & W; Volleyball W

SOUTHERN ARKANSAS UNIVERSITY TECH
100 Carr Rd.
PO Box 3499
Camden, AR 71711
Tel: (870)574-4500
Admissions: (870)574-4492
E-mail: psindle@sautech.edu
Web Site: http://www.sautech.edu/
President/CEO: Dr. Roger L. Worsley
Registrar: Wayne Banks
Admissions: Dr. Reginald Cooper

Financial Aid: Vicki Taylor
Type: Two-Year College **Sex:** Coed **Affiliation:** Arkansas Department of Higher Education **Scores:** 64% ACT 18-23; 8% ACT 24-29 **% Accepted:** 100 **Admission Plans:** Open Admission; Deferred Admission **Application Deadline:** August 15 **Application Fee:** $0.00 **H.S. Requirements:** High school diploma required; GED accepted **Costs Per Year:** Application fee: $0. State resident tuition: $1638 full-time, $63 per hour part-time. Nonresident tuition: $2184 full-time, $84 per hour part-time. Mandatory fees: $574 full-time, $21 per credit hour part-time. College room and board: $3413. College room only: $2100. **Scholarships:** Available **Calendar System:** Semester, Summer Session Available **Enrollment:** FT 554, PT 1,213 **Faculty:** FT 38, PT 43 **Student-Faculty Ratio:** 21:1 **Library Holdings:** 17,389 **Regional Accreditation:** North Central Association of Colleges and Schools **Credit Hours For Degree:** 62 semester hours, Associates

UNIVERSITY OF ARKANSAS
800 Hotz Hall
Fayetteville, AR 72701-1201
Tel: (479)575-2000
Free: 800-377-8632
Admissions: (479)575-5346
Fax: (479)575-7515
E-mail: uafadmis@comp.uark.edu
Web Site: http://www.uark.edu/
President/CEO: Dr. John A. White
Registrar: Alice Lacey
Admissions: Dawn Medley
Financial Aid: Ed Schroeder
Type: University **Sex:** Coed **Affiliation:** University of Arkansas System **Scores:** 98% SAT V 400+; 98.9% SAT M 400+; 35.5% ACT 18-23; 46.4% ACT 24-29 **% Accepted:** 87 **Admission Plans:** Early Admission; Early Action; Deferred Admission **Application Deadline:** August 15 **Application Fee:** $40.00 **H.S. Requirements:** High school diploma required; GED accepted **Costs Per Year:** Application fee: $40. State resident tuition: $4361 full-time, $145.38 per credit hour part-time. Nonresident tuition: $12,089 full time, $402.96 per credit hour part-time. Mandatory fees: $1133 full-time. College room and board: $6365. College room only: $3782. Room and board charges vary according to board plan and housing facility. **Scholarships:** Available **Calendar System:** Semester, Summer Session Available **Enrollment:** FT 11,743, PT 2,538, Grad 3,095 **Faculty:** FT 787, PT 37 **Student-Faculty Ratio:** 18:1 **Exams:** SAT I or ACT **% Receiving Financial Aid:** 39 **% Residing in College-Owned, -Operated, or -Affiliated Housing:** 28 **Library Holdings:** 1,714,085 **Regional Accreditation:** North Central Association of Colleges and Schools **Credit Hours For Degree:** 124 credit hours, Bachelors **ROTC:** Army, Air Force **Professional Accreditation:** AACSB, ABET, ACEJMC, AACN, AAFCS, ABA, ACA, APA, ASLA, ASLHA, AALS, CORE, CSWE, FIDER, NASM, NCATE, NLN, NRPA **Intercollegiate Athletics:** Baseball M; Basketball M & W; Cross-Country Running M & W; Football M; Golf M & W; Gymnastics W; Soccer W; Softball W; Swimming and Diving W; Tennis M & W; Track and Field M & W; Volleyball W

UNIVERSITY OF ARKANSAS COMMUNITY COLLEGE AT BATESVILLE
PO Box 3350
Batesville, AR 72503
Tel: (870)793-7581
Admissions: (870)612-2010
Fax: (870)793-4988
Web Site: http://www.uaccb.edu/
President/CEO: Dr. Anthony G. Kinkel
Admissions: Andy Thomas
Financial Aid: Kristen Cross
Type: Two-Year College **Sex:** Coed **Affiliation:** University of Arkansas System **Admission Plans:** Open Admission **Application Fee:** $0.00 **H.S. Requirements:** High school diploma required; GED accepted **Scholarships:** Available **Calendar System:** Semester, Summer Session Available **Enrollment:** FT 784, PT 533 **Faculty:** FT 38, PT 58 **Student-Faculty Ratio:** 13:1 **Exams:** SAT I and SAT II or ACT **Library Holdings:** 8,000 **Regional Accreditation:** North Central Association of Colleges and Schools **Credit Hours For Degree:** 60 credits, Associates **Professional Accreditation:** NLN

UNIVERSITY OF ARKANSAS COMMUNITY COLLEGE AT HOPE
PO Box 140
Hope, AR 71802-0140
Tel: (870)777-5722
Fax: (870)722-5957
Web Site: http://www.uacch.edu/
President/CEO: Dr. James L. Taylor
Registrar: Danita Ormand
Admissions: Danita Ormand
Financial Aid: Judy Anderson
Type: Two-Year College **Sex:** Coed **Affiliation:** University of Arkansas System **Admission Plans:** Open Admission; Early Admission **Application Fee:** $0.00 **H.S. Requirements:** High school diploma or equivalent not required **Scholarships:** Available **Calendar System:** Semester, Summer Session Available **Enrollment:** FT 676, PT 537 **Faculty:** FT 37, PT 25 **Student-Faculty Ratio:** 19:1 **Exams:** ACT, Other **Library Holdings:** 8,023 **Regional Accreditation:** North Central Association of Colleges and Schools **Credit Hours For Degree:** 60 credits, Associates **Professional Accreditation:** ABFSE, CARC

UNIVERSITY OF ARKANSAS COMMUNITY COLLEGE AT MORRILTON
One Bruce St.
Morrilton, AR 72110
Tel: (501)354-2465
Admissions: (501)977-2014
Fax: (501)354-9948
Web Site: http://www.uaccm.edu/
President/CEO: Nathan Crook
Registrar: Wanda Hensley
Admissions: Dr. Gary Gaston
Financial Aid: Teresa Cash
Type: Two-Year College **Sex:** Coed **Affiliation:** University of Arkansas System **Scores:** 50% ACT 18-23; 15% ACT 24-29 **Admission Plans:** Open Admission; Early Admission; Deferred Admission **Application Fee:** $0.00 **H.S. Requirements:** High school diploma required; GED accepted **Costs Per Year:** Application fee: $0. Area resident tuition: $1920 full-time, $64 per credit hour part-time. State resident tuition: $2100 full-time, $70 per credit hour part-time. Nonresident tuition: $3060 full-time, $102 per credit hour part-time. Mandatory fees: $210 full-time, $7. Full-time tuition and fees vary according to course load. Part-time tuition and fees vary according to course load. **Scholarships:** Available **Calendar System:** Semester, Summer Session Available **Faculty:** FT 40, PT 40 **Student-Faculty Ratio:** 19:1 **Exams:** ACT, Other **Library Holdings:** 6,600 **Regional Accreditation:** North Central Association of Colleges and Schools **Credit Hours For Degree:** 63 credit hours, Associates

UNIVERSITY OF ARKANSAS AT FORT SMITH
PO Box 3649
Fort Smith, AR 72913-3649
Tel: (479)788-7000; 888-512-5466
Admissions: (479)788-7038
Fax: (479)788-7003
E-mail: information@uafortsmith.edu
Web Site: http://www.uafortsmith.edu/
President/CEO: Joel R. Stubblefield
Registrar: Penny Pendleton
Admissions: Marion M. Dunagan
Financial Aid: Mary Cogbill
Type: Four-Year College **Sex:** Coed **Affiliation:** University of Arkansas System **Scores:** 56% ACT 18-23; 24% ACT 24-29 **% Accepted:** 63 **Admission Plans:** Open Admission; Early Admission; Deferred Admission **Application Deadline:** Rolling **Application Fee:** $0.00 **H.S. Requirements:** High school diploma required; GED accepted **Costs Per Year:** Application fee: $0. State resident tuition: $2160 full-time, $72 per credit hour part-time. Nonresident tuition: $7050 full-time, $235 per credit hour part-time. Mandatory fees: $670 full-time, $21 per credit hour part-time, $20 per term part-time. College room and board: $5400. **Scholarships:** Available **Calendar System:** Semester, Summer Session Available **Enrollment:** FT 3,838, PT 2,949 **Faculty:** FT 186, PT 185 **Student-Faculty Ratio:** 23:1 **% Receiving Financial Aid:** 57 **Library Holdings:** 82,000 **Regional Accreditation:** North Central Association of Colleges and Schools **Credit Hours For Degree:** 60 credit hours, Associates; 124 credit hours, Bachelors **ROTC:** Air Force **Professional Accreditation:** ARCEST, ADA, JRCERT, NLN **Intercollegiate Athletics:** Baseball M; Basketball M & W; Volleyball W

UNIVERSITY OF ARKANSAS AT LITTLE ROCK
2801 South University Ave.
Little Rock, AR 72204-1099

Tel: (501)569-3000
Admissions: (501)569-3127
Fax: (501)569-8915
Web Site: http://www.ualr.edu/
President/CEO: Dr. Joel E. Anderson
Registrar: Dr. Sam Howell
Admissions: John Noah
Financial Aid: John Noah

Type: University **Sex:** Coed **Affiliation:** University of Arkansas System **Scores:** 43.9% ACT 18-23; 16.9% ACT 24-29 **Admission Plans:** Early Admission; Deferred Admission **Application Fee:** $0.00 **H.S. Requirements:** High school diploma required; GED accepted **Costs Per Year:** Application fee: $0. State resident tuition: $4230 full-time, $141 per credit hour part-time. Nonresident tuition: $11,100 full-time, $370 per credit hour part-time. Mandatory fees: $982 full-time, $32.75 per credit hour part-time. College room only: $2950. **Scholarships:** Available **Calendar System:** Semester, Summer Session Available **Enrollment:** FT 5,733, PT 3,597, Grad 1,984 **Faculty:** FT 429, PT 320 **Student-Faculty Ratio:** 16:1 **Exams:** SAT I or ACT **% Residing in College-Owned, -Operated, or -Affiliated Housing:** 3 **Regional Accreditation:** North Central Association of Colleges and Schools **Credit Hours For Degree:** 65 credit hours, Associates; 124 credit hours, Bachelors **ROTC:** Army **Professional Accreditation:** AACSB, ABET, ACEHSA, ABA, ACCE, ASLHA, AALS, CORE, CSWE, NASAD, NASM, NASPAA, NAST, NCATE, NLN **Intercollegiate Athletics:** Baseball M; Basketball M; Cross-Country Running M & W; Golf M & W; Soccer W; Swimming and Diving W; Tennis M & W; Track and Field M & W; Volleyball W

UNIVERSITY OF ARKANSAS FOR MEDICAL SCIENCES
4301 West Markham
Little Rock, AR 72205-7199
Tel: (501)686-5000
Admissions: (501)686-5730
Web Site: http://www.uams.edu/
President/CEO: I. Dodd Wilson
Registrar: Dwana McKay
Admissions: Mona Stiles
Financial Aid: Paul Carter

Type: Two-Year Upper Division **Sex:** Coed **Affiliation:** University of Arkansas System **H.S. Requirements:** High school diploma required; GED accepted **Scholarships:** Available **Calendar System:** Semester, Summer Session Not available **Enrollment:** FT 506, PT 177, Grad 447 **% Receiving Financial Aid:** 51 **Library Holdings:** 183,975 **Regional Accreditation:** North Central Association of Colleges and Schools **ROTC:** Army **Professional Accreditation:** ARCEST, ACPhE, ADA, ADtA, APA, ASC, ACIPE, CARC, CEPH, JRCERT, JRCEMT, JRCNMT, LCMEAMA, NAACLS, NLN

UNIVERSITY OF ARKANSAS AT MONTICELLO
Monticello, AR 71656
Tel: (870)367-6811
Admissions: (870)460-1026
Fax: (870)460-1321
Web Site: http://www.uamont.edu/
President/CEO: Dr. Jack Lassiter
Registrar: Dr. Debbie Bryant
Admissions: Mary Whiting
Financial Aid: Susan Brewer

Type: Comprehensive **Sex:** Coed **Affiliation:** University of Arkansas System **Admission Plans:** Open Admission; Early Admission; Deferred Admission **Application Fee:** $0.00 **H.S. Requirements:** High school diploma required; GED accepted **Scholarships:** Available **Calendar System:** Semester, Summer Session Available **Enrollment:** FT 2,253, PT 441, Grad 181 **Faculty:** FT 157, PT 90 **Student-Faculty Ratio:** 18:1 **Exams:** ACT, SAT I or ACT **% Residing in College-Owned, -Operated, or -Affiliated Housing:** 25 **Library Holdings:** 126,229 **Regional Accreditation:** North Central Association of Colleges and Schools **Credit Hours For Degree:** 62 hours, Associates; 124 hours, Bachelors **Professional Accreditation:** CSWE, NASM, NCATE, NLN, SAF **Intercollegiate Athletics:** Baseball M; Basketball M & W; Cross-Country Running W; Football M; Golf M; Softball W; Tennis W

UNIVERSITY OF ARKANSAS AT PINE BLUFF
1200 North University Dr.
Pine Bluff, AR 71601-2799
Tel: (870)543-8000
Free: 800-264-6585
Admissions: (870)575-8487
Fax: (870)543-2021
Web Site: http://www.uapb.edu/
President/CEO: Dr. Lawrence A. Davis, Jr.
Registrar: Erica Fulton
Admissions: Erica W. Fulton
Financial Aid: Carolyn Iverson

Type: Comprehensive **Sex:** Coed **Affiliation:** University of Arkansas System **Scores:** 61.6% SAT V 400+; 52.6% SAT M 400+; 30.2% ACT 18-23; 2.5% ACT 24-29 **Admission Plans:** Early Admission; Deferred Admission **H.S. Requirements:** High school diploma required; GED accepted **Scholarships:** Available **Calendar System:** Semester, Summer Session Available **Enrollment:** FT 2,897, PT 303, Grad 103 **Faculty:** FT 168, PT 68 **Student-Faculty Ratio:** 16:1 **Exams:** SAT I or ACT **% Receiving Financial Aid:** 96 **% Residing in College-Owned, -Operated, or -Affiliated Housing:** 43 **Library Holdings:** 287,857 **Regional Accreditation:** North Central Association of Colleges and Schools **Credit Hours For Degree:** 62 semester hours, Associates; 124 semester hours, Bachelors **ROTC:** Army **Professional Accreditation:** AAFCS, CSWE, NAIT, NASAD, NASM, NCATE, NLN **Intercollegiate Athletics:** Baseball M; Basketball M & W; Cross-Country Running M & W; Football M; Golf M; Track and Field M & W; Volleyball W

UNIVERSITY OF CENTRAL ARKANSAS
201 Donaghey Ave.
Conway, AR 72035-0001
Tel: (501)450-5000
Admissions: (501)450-5145
Fax: (501)450-5228
E-mail: admissons@uca.edu
Web Site: http://www.uca.edu/
President/CEO: Dr. Lu Hardin
Registrar: Anthony D. Sitz
Admissions: Penny Hatfield
Financial Aid: Cheryl Lyons

Type: Comprehensive **Sex:** Coed **Scores:** 95.2% SAT V 400+; 100% SAT M 400+; 40% ACT 18-23; 39.7% ACT 24-29 **% Accepted:** 68 **Admission Plans:** Early Admission; Deferred Admission **Application Deadline:** Rolling **Application Fee:** $0.00 **H.S. Requirements:** High school diploma required; GED accepted **Costs Per Year:** Application fee: $0. State resident tuition: $4500 full-time, $150 per credit hour part-time. Nonresident tuition: $9000 full-time, $300 per credit hour part-time. Mandatory fees: $1164 full-time, $35 per credit hour part-time, $61 per term part-time. Part-time tuition and fees vary according to course load. College room and board: $4320. College room only: $1940. Room and board charges vary according to board plan and housing facility. **Scholarships:** Available **Calendar System:** Semester, Summer Session Available **Enrollment:** FT 9,127, PT 842, Grad 1,406 **Faculty:** FT 478, PT 129 **Student-Faculty Ratio:** 20:1 **Exams:** SAT I or ACT **% Residing in College-Owned, -Operated, or -Affiliated Housing:** 42 **Library Holdings:** 505,000 **Regional Accreditation:** North Central Association of Colleges and Schools **Credit Hours For Degree:** 60 credit hours, Associates; 124 credit hours, Bachelors **ROTC:** Army **Professional Accreditation:** AACSB, AACN, AAFCS, ADtA, AOTA, APTA, ASLHA, NASAD, NASM, NAST, NCATE, NLN **Intercollegiate Athletics:** Baseball M; Basketball M & W; Cheerleading M & W; Cross-Country Running W; Football M; Golf M & W; Soccer M & W; Softball W; Tennis W; Track and Field W; Volleyball W

UNIVERSITY OF THE OZARKS
415 North College Ave.
Clarksville, AR 72830-2880
Tel: (479)979-1000
Free: 800-264-8636
Admissions: (479)979-1421
Fax: (479)979-1355
E-mail: admiss@ozarks.edu
Web Site: http://www.ozarks.edu/
President/CEO: Dr. Rick Niece
Registrar: Wilma Harris
Admissions: James D. Decker
Financial Aid: Jana Hart

Type: Four-Year College **Sex:** Coed **Affiliation:** Presbyterian **Scores:** 96% SAT V 400+; 88% SAT M 400+; 63% ACT 18-23; 24% ACT 24-29 **% Accepted:** 93 **Admission Plans:** Deferred Admission **Application Deadline:** Rolling **H.S. Requirements:** High school diploma required; GED accepted **Costs Per Year:** Comprehensive fee: $20,210 includes full-time tuition

($14,470), mandatory fees ($480), and college room and board ($5260). Part-time tuition: $605 per credit hour. **Scholarships:** Available **Calendar System:** Semester, Summer Session Available **Enrollment:** FT 588, PT 40 **Faculty:** FT 44, PT 17 **Student-Faculty Ratio:** 12:1 **Exams:** SAT I or ACT **% Receiving Financial Aid:** 52 **% Residing in College-Owned, -Operated, or -Affiliated Housing:** 66 **Library Holdings:** 105,000 **Regional Accreditation:** North Central Association of Colleges and Schools **Credit Hours For Degree:** 124 semester hours, Bachelors **Professional Accreditation:** NCATE **Intercollegiate Athletics:** Baseball M; Basketball M & W; Cheerleading M & W; Cross-Country Running M & W; Soccer M & W; Softball W; Tennis M & W

UNIVERSITY OF PHOENIX-LITTLE ROCK CAMPUS
10800 Financial Center Parkway
Little Rock, AR 72211
Tel: (501)225-9337
Free: 800-228-7240
Admissions: (480)557-1712
Web Site: http://www.phoenix.edu/
Admissions: Nina Omelchanko
Type: Comprehensive **Sex:** Coed **Admission Plans:** Open Admission; Deferred Admission **Application Deadline:** Rolling **Application Fee:** $110.00 **H.S. Requirements:** High school diploma required; GED accepted **Costs Per Year:** Application fee: $110. Tuition: $9540 full-time, $318 per credit part-time. Mandatory fees: $560 full-time, $70 per course part-time. **Scholarships:** Available **Calendar System:** Continuous, Summer Session Not available **Enrollment:** FT 327, Grad 172 **Faculty:** FT 2, PT 67 **Student-Faculty Ratio:** 7:1 **Library Holdings:** 442 **Regional Accreditation:** North Central Association of Colleges and Schools **Credit Hours For Degree:** 60 credits, Associates; 120 credits, Bachelors

WILLIAMS BAPTIST COLLEGE
60 West Fulbright Ave.
Walnut Ridge, AR 72476
Tel: (870)886-6741
Free: 800-722-4434
Admissions: (870)759-4117
E-mail: admissions@wbclab.wbcoll.edu
Web Site: http://www.wbcoll.edu/
President/CEO: Dr. Jerol B. Swaim
Registrar: Tonya Bolton
Admissions: Angela Flippo
Financial Aid: Barbara Turner
Type: Four-Year College **Sex:** Coed **Affiliation:** Southern Baptist **Application Fee:** $20.00 **H.S. Requirements:** High school diploma required; GED accepted **Scholarships:** Available **Calendar System:** Semester, Summer Session Available **Enrollment:** FT 511, PT 142 **Faculty:** FT 27, PT 10 **Student-Faculty Ratio:** 13:1 **Exams:** SAT I or ACT **% Receiving Financial Aid:** 75 **% Residing in College-Owned, -Operated, or -Affiliated Housing:** 62 **Library Holdings:** 57,321 **Regional Accreditation:** North Central Association of Colleges and Schools **Credit Hours For Degree:** 60 hours, Associates; 128 hours, Bachelors **ROTC:** Army **Professional Accreditation:** NCATE **Intercollegiate Athletics:** Baseball M; Basketball M & W; Golf M; Soccer M & W; Softball W; Volleyball W

ACADEMY OF ART UNIVERSITY
79 New Montgomery St.
San Francisco, CA 94105-3410
Tel: (415)274-2200
Free: 800-544-ARTS
Admissions: (415)263-5518
Fax: (415)263-4130
Web Site: http://www.academyart.edu/
President/CEO: Dr. Elisa Stephens
Registrar: Olivia Cortez-Figueroa
Admissions: John Meurer
Financial Aid: Joe Vollaro
Type: Comprehensive **Sex:** Coed **Admission Plans:** Open Admission; Early Admission; Deferred Admission **Application Deadline:** Rolling **Application Fee:** $100.00 **H.S. Requirements:** High school diploma required; GED accepted **Costs Per Year:** Application fee: $100. Comprehensive fee: $26,480 includes full-time tuition ($14,400), mandatory fees ($80), and college room and board ($12,000). College room only: $8400. **Scholarships:** Available **Calendar System:** Semester, Summer Session Available **Enrollment:** FT 4,111, PT 2,575, Grad 1,584 **Faculty:** FT 135, PT 540 **Student-Faculty Ratio:** 15:1 **% Receiving Financial Aid:** 37 **% Residing in College-Owned, -Operated, or -Affiliated Housing:** 10 **Library Holdings:** 37,342 **Credit Hours For Degree:** 132 units, Bachelors **Professional Accreditation:** ACICS, FIDER, NASAD

ALLAN HANCOCK COLLEGE
800 South College Dr.
Santa Maria, CA 93454-6399
Tel: (805)922-6966; (866)342-5242
Fax: (805)922-3477
Web Site: http://www.hancockcollege.edu/
President/CEO: Dr. Ann Foxworthy
Registrar: Norma Razo
Admissions: Marian Quaid Maltagliati
Financial Aid: Robert Parisi
Type: Two-Year College **Sex:** Coed **Admission Plans:** Open Admission; Early Admission **Application Deadline:** Rolling **Application Fee:** $0.00 **H.S. Requirements:** High school diploma required; GED accepted. For applicants 18 or over: High school diploma or equivalent not required **Costs Per Year:** Application fee: $0. State resident tuition: $0 full-time. Nonresident tuition: $4956 full-time, $177 per unit part-time. Mandatory fees: $792 full-time, $27 per unit part-time. **Scholarships:** Available **Calendar System:** Semester, Summer Session Available **Enrollment:** FT 2,996, PT 7,391 **Faculty:** FT 152, PT 442 **Student-Faculty Ratio:** 17:1 **Library Holdings:** 47,370 **Regional Accreditation:** Western Association of Schools and Colleges **Credit Hours For Degree:** 60 units, Associates **Intercollegiate Athletics:** Baseball M; Basketball M & W; Cross-Country Running M & W; Football M; Golf M; Soccer M & W; Softball W; Tennis M & W; Track and Field M & W; Volleyball W

ALLIANT INTERNATIONAL UNIVERSITY
10455 Pomerado Rd.
San Diego, CA 92131-1799
Tel: (858)271-4300; (866)825-5426
Admissions: (858)635-4772
Fax: (858)635-4739
E-mail: stopham@alliant.edu
Web Site: http://www.alliant.edu/
President/CEO: Dr. Geoffrey Cox
Registrar: Nancy Stevens
Admissions: Susan Topham
Financial Aid: Karen P. Nelson
Type: University **Sex:** Coed **Affiliation:** Alliant International University **Admission Plans:** Deferred Admission **Application Deadline:** Rolling **Application Fee:** $45.00 **H.S. Requirements:** High school diploma required; GED accepted **Costs Per Year:** Application fee: $45. Comprehensive fee: $22,170 includes full-time tuition ($14,000), mandatory fees ($370), and college room and board ($7800). Part-time tuition: $515 per unit. **Scholarships:** Available **Calendar System:** Semester, Summer Session Available **Enrollment:** FT 226, PT 28, Grad 3,233 **Faculty:** FT 131, PT 157 **Student-Faculty Ratio:** 15:1 **% Receiving Financial Aid:** 62 **% Residing in College-Owned, -Operated, or -Affiliated Housing:** 41 **Library Holdings:** 212,394 **Regional Accreditation:** Western Association of Schools and Colleges **Credit Hours For Degree:** 120 semester units, Bachelors **ROTC:** Army **Professional Accreditation:** AAMFT **Intercollegiate Athletics:** Cross-Country Running M & W; Soccer M & W; Tennis M & W; Track and Field M & W; Volleyball W

AMERICAN ACADEMY OF DRAMATIC ARTS/HOLLYWOOD
1336 North La Brea Ave.
Hollywood, CA 90028
Tel: (323)464-2777
Free: 800-222-2867
Fax: (323)464-1250
Web Site: http://www.aada.org/
President/CEO: Roger Croucher
Registrar: Steve Martinez
Admissions: Dan Justin
Financial Aid: George Ramirez
Type: Two-Year College **Sex:** Coed **Admission Plans:** Deferred Admission **Application Fee:** $50.00 **H.S. Requirements:** High school diploma required; GED accepted **Costs Per Year:** Application fee: $50. Tuition: $16,000 full-time. Mandatory fees: $500 full-time. **Scholarships:** Available **Calendar System:** Continuous, Summer Session Not available **Enrollment:** FT 308 **Faculty:** FT 0, PT 27 **Student-Faculty Ratio:** 16:1 **Library Holdings:** 7,700 **Regional Accreditation:** Western Association of Schools and Colleges **Credit Hours For Degree:** 70 units, Associates **Professional Accreditation:** NAST

AMERICAN INTERCONTINENTAL UNIVERSITY
12655 West Jefferson Blvd.
Los Angeles, CA 90066
Tel: (310)302-2000
Free: 800-333-2652
Fax: (310)302-2001
Web Site: http://www.aiuniv.edu/
President/CEO: Steven E. Tartaglini
Registrar: Vicki Pasek
Admissions: Amadou Tall
Financial Aid: Hugo Aguilar
Type: Comprehensive **Sex:** Coed **Admission Plans:** Open Admission; Early Admission; Deferred Admission **Application Fee:** $50.00 **H.S.**

Requirements: High school diploma required; GED accepted **Scholarships:** Available **Calendar System:** Miscellaneous, Summer Session Available **Enrollment:** FT 827, PT 477, Grad 101 **Faculty:** FT 24, PT 109 **Student-Faculty Ratio:** 24:1 **% Residing in College-Owned, -Operated, or -Affiliated Housing:** 10 **Library Holdings:** 20,000 **Regional Accreditation:** Southern Association of Colleges and Schools **Credit Hours For Degree:** 120 credit hours, Associates; 190 credit hours, Bachelors **Professional Accreditation:** FIDER

AMERICAN RIVER COLLEGE
4700 College Oak Dr.
Sacramento, CA 95841-4286
Tel: (916)484-8011
Admissions: (916)484-8171
E-mail: esposic@arc.losrios.cc.ca.us
Web Site: http://www.arc.losrios.edu/
President/CEO: Dr. Marie B. Smith
Registrar: Celia Esposito
Admissions: Robin Neal
Financial Aid: Robin Neal
Type: Two-Year College **Sex:** Coed **Affiliation:** Los Rios Community College District System **Admission Plans:** Open Admission; Early Admission; Deferred Admission **Application Fee:** $0.00 **H.S. Requirements:** High school diploma or equivalent not required. For nursing, respiratory therapy programs, applicants under 18: High school diploma required; GED accepted **Costs Per Year:** Application fee: $0. Nonresident tuition: $4248 full-time, $177 per unit part-time. Mandatory fees: $639 full-time, $26 per unit part-time. **Scholarships:** Available **Calendar System:** Semester, Summer Session Available **Student-Faculty Ratio:** 34:1 **Exams:** Other, SAT I or ACT **Library Holdings:** 78,400 **Regional Accreditation:** Western Association of Schools and Colleges **Credit Hours For Degree:** 60 units, Associates **Professional Accreditation:** ABFSE, CARC **Intercollegiate Athletics:** Basketball M & W; Cross-Country Running M & W; Football M; Golf M & W; Soccer M & W; Swimming and Diving M & W; Tennis M & W; Track and Field M & W; Volleyball M & W

ANTELOPE VALLEY COLLEGE
3041 West Ave. K
Lancaster, CA 93536-5426
Tel: (661)722-6300
Fax: (661)943-5573
Web Site: http://www.avc.edu/
President/CEO: Dr. Jackie Fisher
Financial Aid: Sherrie Padilla
Type: Two-Year College **Sex:** Coed **Affiliation:** California Community College System **Admission Plans:** Open Admission; Early Admission **Application Fee:** $0.00 **H.S. Requirements:** High school diploma or equivalent not required. For applicants under 18: High school diploma required; GED accepted **Scholarships:** Available **Calendar System:** Semester, Summer Session Available **Faculty:** FT 124, PT 200 **Library Holdings:** 43,000 **Regional Accreditation:** Western Association of Schools and Colleges **Credit Hours For Degree:** 60 units, Associates **ROTC:** Air Force **Intercollegiate Athletics:** Baseball M; Basketball M & W; Cross-Country Running M & W; Football M; Soccer W; Softball W; Tennis W; Track and Field M & W; Volleyball W

ANTIOCH UNIVERSITY LOS ANGELES
400 Corporate Pointe
Culver City, CA 90230
Tel: (310)578-1080
Free: 800-7ANTIOCH
Fax: (310)827-4742
Web Site: http://www.antiochla.edu/
President/CEO: Dr. Lucy Ann Geiselman
Registrar: Allan Scott
Admissions: Kathie Rawding
Financial Aid: Kathie Rawding
Type: Two-Year Upper Division **Sex:** Coed **Affiliation:** Antioch University **% Accepted:** 88 **Admission Plans:** Deferred Admission **Application Fee:** $60.00 **H.S. Requirements:** High school diploma required; GED accepted **Costs Per Year:** Application fee: $60. Tuition: $13,500 full-time, $2700 per term part-time. **Calendar System:** Quarter, Summer Session Available **Enrollment:** FT 81, PT 107, Grad 462 **Faculty:** FT 21, PT 151 **Student-Faculty Ratio:** 14:1 **Regional Accreditation:** North Central Association of Colleges and Schools **Credit Hours For Degree:** 180 units, Bachelors

ANTIOCH UNIVERSITY SANTA BARBARA
801 Garden St.
Santa Barbara, CA 93101-1581
Tel: (805)962-8179
Fax: (805)962-4786
E-mail: amcpherson@antiochsb.edu
Web Site: http://www.antiochsb.edu/
President/CEO: Dr. Lucy Ann Geiselman
Registrar: MaryAnn Marwitz
Admissions: Ankara M. McPherson
Financial Aid: Cecilia Schneider
Type: Two-Year Upper Division **Sex:** Coed **Affiliation:** Antioch University **Admission Plans:** Deferred Admission **Application Fee:** $60.00 **H.S. Requirements:** High school diploma required; GED accepted **Costs Per Year:** Application fee: $60. Tuition: $13,140 full-time, $440 per unit part-time. Mandatory fees: $16 full-time. **Scholarships:** Available **Calendar System:** Quarter, Summer Session Available **Enrollment:** FT 39, PT 56, Grad 210 **Faculty:** FT 14, PT 52 **Student-Faculty Ratio:** 15:1 **Regional Accreditation:** North Central Association of Colleges and Schools **Credit Hours For Degree:** 180 quarter hours, Bachelors

ARGOSY UNIVERSITY/ORANGE COUNTY
3501 West Sunflower Ave., Ste. 110
Santa Ana, CA 92704
Tel: (714)338-6200
Free: 800-716-9598
Web Site: http://www.argosyu.edu/
President/CEO: Dr. Mark Rocha
Type: Two-Year College **Sex:** Coed **Admission Plans:** Early Admission; Deferred Admission **Application Fee:** $50.00 **H.S. Requirements:** High school diploma required; GED accepted **Scholarships:** Available **Calendar System:** Semester **Enrollment:** FT 66, PT 15, Grad 565 **Faculty:** FT 11, PT 70 **Student-Faculty Ratio:** 22:1 **Library Holdings:** 1,200 **Regional Accreditation:** North Central Association of Colleges and Schools **Credit Hours For Degree:** 120 credit hours, Bachelors

ARGOSY UNIVERSITY/SAN DIEGO
7650 Mission Valley Rd.
San Diego, CA 92108
; (866)505-0333
Web Site: http://www.argosyu.edu/sandiego/ **Type:** Two-Year College **Sex:** Coed

ARGOSY UNIVERSITY/SAN FRANCISCO BAY AREA
999A Canal Blvd.
Point Richmond, CA 94804-3547
Tel: (510)215-0277; (866)215-2777
Admissions: (510)837-3709
Fax: (510)215-0299
E-mail: jstofan@argosyu.edu
Web Site: http://www.argosyu.edu/
Admissions: John Stofan
Type: Two-Year Upper Division **Sex:** Coed **Affiliation:** Education Management Corporation **% Accepted:** 92 **Application Fee:** $50.00 **Costs Per Year:** Application fee: $50. Tuition: $400 full-time, $400 per credit part-time. Mandatory fees: $10 per credit part-time, $50 per year part-time. **Scholarships:** Available **Calendar System:** Semester **Enrollment:** FT 22, PT 26 **Faculty:** FT 1, PT 10 **Student-Faculty Ratio:** 10:1 **% Receiving Financial Aid:** 94 **Regional Accreditation:** North Central Association of Colleges and Schools **Professional Accreditation:** APA

ARGOSY UNIVERSITY/SANTA MONICA
2950 31st St.
Santa Monica, CA 90405
; (866)505-0332
Web Site: http://www.argosyu.edu/santamonica/ **Type:** Comprehensive **Sex:** Coed

ART CENTER COLLEGE OF DESIGN
1700 Lida St.
Pasadena, CA 91103-1999
Tel: (626)396-2200
Admissions: (626)396-2373
Fax: (626)795-0578

E-mail: admissions@artcenter.edu
Web Site: http://www.artcenter.edu/
President/CEO: Richard Koshalek
Admissions: Kit Baron
Financial Aid: Clema McKenzie
Type: Comprehensive **Sex:** Coed **% Accepted:** 74 **Admission Plans:** Deferred Admission **Application Deadline:** Rolling **Application Fee:** $45.00 **H.S. Requirements:** High school diploma required; GED accepted **Costs Per Year:** Application fee: $45. Tuition: $27,800 full-time. Mandatory fees: $200 full-time. **Scholarships:** Available **Calendar System:** Trimester, Summer Session Available **Enrollment:** FT 1,304, PT 208, Grad 130 **Faculty:** FT 66, PT 341 **Student-Faculty Ratio:** 12:1 **Exams:** SAT I or ACT **% Receiving Financial Aid:** 82 **Library Holdings:** 93,038 **Regional Accreditation:** Western Association of Schools and Colleges **Credit Hours For Degree:** 135 credits, Bachelors **Professional Accreditation:** NASAD

THE ART INSTITUTE OF CALIFORNIA-INLAND EMPIRE
630 East Brier Dr.
San Bernardino, CA 92408
Tel: (909)915-2100
Free: 800-353-0812
E-mail: mjeffs@aii.edu
Web Site: http://www.artinstitutes.edu/inlandempire/
Admissions: Monica Jeffs
Type: Four-Year College **Sex:** Coed **Application Fee:** $150.00 **Costs Per Year:** Application fee: $150. Tuition: $18,911 full-time, $392 per credit part-time. Mandatory fees: $1200 full-time.

THE ART INSTITUTE OF CALIFORNIA-LOS ANGELES
2900 31st St.
Santa Monica, CA 90405-3035
Tel: (310)752-4700; 888-646-4610
Fax: (310)752-4708
E-mail: ailaadm@aii.edu
Web Site: http://www.aicala.artinstitutes.edu/
President/CEO: Laura Soloff
Admissions: Andrea Sylvester
Type: Four-Year College **Sex:** Coed **Affiliation:** Education Management Corporation **% Accepted:** 77 **Admission Plans:** Open Admission; Deferred Admission **Application Deadline:** Rolling **Application Fee:** $50.00 **H.S. Requirements:** High school diploma required; GED accepted. For Game Art and Design: minimum 2.5 HS GPA: High school diploma required; GED accepted **Costs Per Year:** Application fee: $50. Tuition: $19,824 full-time. College room only: $7920. **Calendar System:** Quarter **Enrollment:** FT 2,102 **Student-Faculty Ratio:** 20:1 **% Residing in College-Owned, -Operated, or -Affiliated Housing:** 15 **Library Holdings:** 20,000 **Professional Accreditation:** ACICS

THE ART INSTITUTE OF CALIFORNIA-ORANGE COUNTY
3601 West Sunflower Ave.
Santa Ana, CA 92704-9888
Tel: (714)830-0200; 888-549-3055
E-mail: vdavid@aii.edu
Web Site: http://www.aicaoc.artinstitutes.edu/
President/CEO: George Sebolt
Admissions: Vincent David
Type: Four-Year College **Sex:** Coed **Affiliation:** Education Management Corporation **% Accepted:** 68 **Admission Plans:** Early Admission; Early Decision Plan; Deferred Admission **Application Deadline:** Rolling **H.S. Requirements:** High school diploma required; GED accepted **Costs Per Year:** Tuition: $403 per quarter hour part-time. Mandatory fees: $15 per quarter hour part-time. College room only: $9800. Tuition guaranteed not to increase for student's term of enrollment. **Scholarships:** Available **Calendar System:** Quarter **Enrollment:** FT 1,485, PT 272 **Faculty:** FT 63, PT 51 **Student-Faculty Ratio:** 20:1 **Exams:** SAT I and SAT II or ACT **% Residing in College-Owned, -Operated, or -Affiliated Housing:** 9 **Credit Hours For Degree:** 112 credits, Associates; 192 credits, Bachelors **Professional Accreditation:** ACICS

THE ART INSTITUTE OF CALIFORNIA-SAN DIEGO
10025 Mesa Rim Rd.
San Diego, CA 92121
Tel: (858)546-0602
Admissions: (858)598-1399
Web Site: http://www.aica.artinstitutes.edu/
President/CEO: Daniel Levinson
Admissions: Jo-Ann White
Financial Aid: Kathy Smith
Type: Four-Year College **Sex:** Coed **Affiliation:** Education Management Corporation **Admission Plans:** Early Admission; Deferred Admission **Application Deadline:** Rolling **Application Fee:** $50.00 **H.S. Requirements:** High school diploma required; GED accepted **Costs Per Year:** Application fee: $50. Tuition: $19,344 full-time, $403 per credit part-time. Mandatory fees: $784 full-time. Full-time tuition and fees vary according to program. College room only: $9480. **Scholarships:** Available **Calendar System:** Quarter, Summer Session Available **Enrollment:** FT 1,600, PT 312 **Faculty:** FT 55, PT 64 **Student-Faculty Ratio:** 22:1 **Exams:** Other **% Residing in College-Owned, -Operated, or -Affiliated Housing:** 12 **Library Holdings:** 7,197 **Credit Hours For Degree:** 112 credits, Associates; 192 credits, Bachelors **Professional Accreditation:** ACCSCT

THE ART INSTITUTE OF CALIFORNIA-SAN FRANCISCO
1170 Market St.
San Francisco, CA 94102-4908
Tel: (415)865-0198; 888-493-3261
Fax: (415)863-6344
Web Site: http://www.aicasf.artinstitutes.edu/
President/CEO: Bill Tsatsoulis
Registrar: Cindy Shelton
Admissions: Daniel Cardenas
Financial Aid: Roger Gomez
Type: Four-Year College **Sex:** Coed **Affiliation:** Education Management Corporation **Admission Plans:** Deferred Admission **Application Fee:** $50.00 **H.S. Requirements:** High school diploma required; GED accepted **Scholarships:** Available **Calendar System:** Quarter, Summer Session Available **Faculty:** FT 22, PT 86 **Student-Faculty Ratio:** 16:1 **Credit Hours For Degree:** 112 credits, Associates; 192 credits, Bachelors **Professional Accreditation:** ACICS

AVIATION & ELECTRONIC SCHOOLS OF AMERICA
210 South Railroad St.
PO Box 1810
Colfax, CA 95713-1810
Tel: (530)346-6792
Free: 800-345-2742
Fax: (530)346-8466
Web Site: http://www.aesa.com/
President/CEO: James P. Doyle
Type: Two-Year College **Sex:** Coed **Calendar System:** Continuous **Professional Accreditation:** COE

AZUSA PACIFIC UNIVERSITY
901 East Alosta Ave., PO Box 7000
Azusa, CA 91702-7000
Tel: (626)969-3434
Free: 800-TALK-APU
Admissions: (626)812-3016
E-mail: admissions@apu.edu
Web Site: http://www.apu.edu/
President/CEO: Dr. Jon R. Wallace
Registrar: Todd Ross
Admissions: Dave Burke
Type: Comprehensive **Sex:** Coed **Affiliation:** nondenominational **Scores:** 99% SAT V 400+; 99% SAT M 400+; 49% ACT 18-23; 42% ACT 24-29 **% Accepted:** 73 **Admission Plans:** Early Admission; Early Action; Deferred Admission **Application Deadline:** June 01 **Application Fee:** $45.00 **H.S. Requirements:** High school diploma required; GED accepted **Costs Per Year:** Application fee: $45. Comprehensive fee: $28,526 includes full-time tuition ($21,500), mandatory fees ($660), and college room and board ($6366). College room only: $3510. Full-time tuition and fees vary according to course load. Room and board charges vary according to board plan, housing facility, and student level. Part-time tuition: $900 per unit. Part-time tuition varies according to course load. **Scholarships:** Available **Calendar System:** Semester, Summer Session Available **Enrollment:** FT 3,770, PT 671, Grad 3,558 **Faculty:** FT 344, PT 12 **Student-Faculty Ratio:** 15:1 **Exams:** SAT I or ACT **% Receiving Financial Aid:** 63 **% Residing in College-Owned, -Operated, or -Affiliated Housing:** 69 **Library Holdings:** 185,708 **Regional Accreditation:** Western Association of Schools and Colleges **Credit Hours For Degree:** 126 units, Bachelors **ROTC:** Army **Professional Accreditation:** AACN, APTA, APA, ATS, CSWE, JRCEPAT, NCATE,

NLN **Intercollegiate Athletics:** Baseball M; Basketball M & W; Cross-Country Running M & W; Football M; Golf M; Soccer M & W; Softball W; Tennis M; Track and Field M & W; Volleyball M & W

BAKERSFIELD COLLEGE
1801 Panorama Dr.
Bakersfield, CA 93305-1299
Tel: (661)395-4011
Admissions: (661)395-4301
Fax: (661)395-4230
E-mail: svaughn@bc.cc.ca.us
Web Site: http://www.bakersfieldcollege.edu/
President/CEO: Sandra Serrano
Admissions: Sue Vaughn
Financial Aid: Joan Wegner
Type: Two-Year College **Sex:** Coed **Affiliation:** California Community College System **Admission Plans:** Open Admission; Preferred Admission **Application Fee:** $0.00 **H.S. Requirements:** High school diploma or equivalent not required. For applicants under 18: High school diploma required; GED accepted **Scholarships:** Available **Calendar System:** Semester, Summer Session Available **Library Holdings:** 93,500 **Regional Accreditation:** Western Association of Schools and Colleges **Credit Hours For Degree:** 60 units, Associates **Professional Accreditation:** JRCERT **Intercollegiate Athletics:** Baseball M; Basketball M & W; Cross-Country Running M & W; Football M; Golf M; Soccer W; Softball W; Tennis M & W; Track and Field M & W; Volleyball W; Wrestling M

BARSTOW COLLEGE
2700 Barstow Rd.
Barstow, CA 92311-6699
Tel: (760)252-2411
Fax: (760)252-1875
Web Site: http://www.barstow.edu/
President/CEO: Dr. James M. Meznek
Registrar: Mary Marble
Admissions: Don Low
Financial Aid: Katherine Lister
Type: Two-Year College **Sex:** Coed **Affiliation:** California Community College System **Admission Plans:** Open Admission; Early Admission; Deferred Admission **H.S. Requirements:** High school diploma or equivalent not required. For applicants under 18: High school diploma required; GED accepted **Scholarships:** Available **Calendar System:** Semester, Summer Session Available **Faculty:** FT 36, PT 91 **Student-Faculty Ratio:** 20:1 **Exams:** Other **Library Holdings:** 38,000 **Regional Accreditation:** Western Association of Schools and Colleges **Credit Hours For Degree:** 60 units, Associates **Intercollegiate Athletics:** Baseball M; Basketball M; Volleyball W

BERKELEY CITY COLLEGE
2050 Center St.
Berkeley, CA 94704-5102
Tel: (510)981-2800
Admissions: (510)466-7363
Fax: (510)841-7333
E-mail: hperdue@peralta.edu
Web Site: http://www.peralta.cc.ca.us/
President/CEO: Dr. John Garmon
Registrar: Howard Perdue
Admissions: Howard Perdue
Financial Aid: Hermia Yam
Type: Two-Year College **Sex:** Coed **Admission Plans:** Open Admission; Preferred Admission; Early Admission; Deferred Admission **Application Deadline:** Rolling **Application Fee:** $0.00 **H.S. Requirements:** High school diploma or equivalent not required. For applicants under 18: High school diploma required; GED accepted **Costs Per Year:** Application fee: $0. Nonresident tuition: $172 per unit part-time. Mandatory fees: $26 per unit part-time. **Scholarships:** Available **Calendar System:** Semester, Summer Session Available **Faculty:** FT 34, PT 130 **Student-Faculty Ratio:** 25:1 **Regional Accreditation:** Western Association of Schools and Colleges **Credit Hours For Degree:** 60 semester hours, Associates

BETHANY UNIVERSITY
800 Bethany Dr.
Scotts Valley, CA 95066-2820
Tel: (831)438-3800
Free: 800-843-9410
Fax: (831)438-4517
E-mail: info@bethany.edu
Web Site: http://www.bethany.edu/
President/CEO: Dr. Everett Wilson
Registrar: Wes Wick
Admissions: Charles Riley
Financial Aid: Debbie Snow
Type: Comprehensive **Sex:** Coed **Affiliation:** Assemblies of God **Scores:** 82% SAT V 400+; 77% SAT M 400+ **% Accepted:** 56 **Admission Plans:** Preferred Admission; Early Admission; Deferred Admission **Application Deadline:** July 01 **Application Fee:** $35.00 **H.S. Requirements:** High school diploma required; GED accepted **Costs Per Year:** Application fee: $35. One-time mandatory fee: $135. Comprehensive fee: $22,765 includes full-time tuition ($15,500), mandatory fees ($765), and college room and board ($6500). College room only: $3300. Part-time tuition: $650 per unit. Part-time mandatory fees: $245 per term. **Scholarships:** Available **Calendar System:** Semester, Summer Session Available **Enrollment:** FT 391, PT 78, Grad 80 **Faculty:** FT 27, PT 45 **Student-Faculty Ratio:** 11:1 **Exams:** SAT I or ACT **% Receiving Financial Aid:** 85 **% Residing in College-Owned, -Operated, or -Affiliated Housing:** 80 **Library Holdings:** 59,453 **Regional Accreditation:** Western Association of Schools and Colleges **Credit Hours For Degree:** 66 credit hours, Associates; 124 credit hours, Bachelors **Intercollegiate Athletics:** Baseball M; Basketball M & W; Golf M & W; Soccer M & W; Softball W; Volleyball M & W

BETHESDA CHRISTIAN UNIVERSITY
730 North Euclid St.
Anaheim, CA 92801
Tel: (714)517-1945
Fax: (714)517-1948
E-mail: admission@bcu.edu
Web Site: http://www.bcu.edu/
President/CEO: John Stetz
Admissions: Samuel C. Jung
Financial Aid: Mung Ha Huang
Type: Comprehensive **Sex:** Coed **Affiliation:** Full Gospel World Mission **Admission Plans:** Open Admission; Early Admission **Application Fee:** $35.00 **H.S. Requirements:** High school diploma required; GED accepted **Costs Per Year:** Application fee: $35. Tuition: $6300 full-time. Mandatory fees: $120 full-time. **Scholarships:** Available **Calendar System:** Semester, Summer Session Available **Enrollment:** FT 129, PT 35, Grad 1 **Faculty:** FT 6, PT 19 **Student-Faculty Ratio:** 15:1 **% Receiving Financial Aid:** 100 **% Residing in College-Owned, -Operated, or -Affiliated Housing:** 0 **Library Holdings:** 27,763 **Credit Hours For Degree:** 125 units, Bachelors **Professional Accreditation:** AABC, TACCS

BIOLA UNIVERSITY
13800 Biola Ave.
La Mirada, CA 90639-0001
Tel: (562)903-6000
Free: 800-652-4652
Admissions: (562)903-4752
Fax: (562)903-4709
E-mail: admissions@biola.edu
Web Site: http://www.biola.edu/
President/CEO: Dr. Clyde Cook
Registrar: Wayne Chute
Admissions: Greg Vaughan
Financial Aid: Les Butler
Type: University **Sex:** Coed **Affiliation:** interdenominational **Scores:** 99.4% SAT V 400+; 98.8% SAT M 400+; 5.3% ACT 18-23 **% Accepted:** 82 **Admission Plans:** Early Admission; Early Action; Deferred Admission **Application Deadline:** March 01 **Application Fee:** $45.00 **H.S. Requirements:** High school diploma required; GED accepted **Costs Per Year:** Application fee: $45. Comprehensive fee: $30,998 includes full-time tuition ($23,782), mandatory fees ($100), and college room and board ($7116). College room only: $3756. Part-time tuition: $942 per unit. **Scholarships:** Available **Calendar System:** 4-1-4, Summer Session Available **Enrollment:** FT 3,138, PT 108, Grad 1,715 **Faculty:** FT 191, PT 204 **Student-Faculty Ratio:** 16:1 **Exams:** SAT I or ACT **% Receiving Financial Aid:** 65 **% Residing in College-Owned, -Operated, or -Affiliated Housing:** 65 **Library Holdings:** 279,560 **Regional Accreditation:** Western Association of Schools and Colleges **Credit Hours For Degree:** 130 units, Bachelors **ROTC:** Army, Air Force **Professional Accreditation:** APA, ACBSP, ATS,

NASAD, NASM, NLN **Intercollegiate Athletics:** Baseball M; Basketball M & W; Cross-Country Running M & W; Soccer M & W; Softball W; Swimming and Diving M & W; Tennis W; Track and Field M & W; Volleyball W

BROOKS COLLEGE (LONG BEACH)
4825 East Pacific Coast Hwy.
Long Beach, CA 90804-3291
Tel: (562)498-2441
Free: 800-421-3775
Fax: (562)597-7412
Web Site: http://www.brookscollege.edu/
President/CEO: Tom Azim
Registrar: Todd Pheifer
Admissions: Christina Varon
Financial Aid: Gary Buyers
Type: Two-Year College **Sex:** Coed **Admission Plans:** Deferred Admission **Application Deadline:** Rolling **Application Fee:** $50.00 **H.S. Requirements:** High school diploma required; GED accepted **Calendar System:** Quarter, Summer Session Available **Enrollment:** FT 757, PT 69 **% Residing in College-Owned, -Operated, or -Affiliated Housing:** 60 **Library Holdings:** 15,000 **Regional Accreditation:** Western Association of Schools and Colleges **Credit Hours For Degree:** 88 credit hours, Associates **Professional Accreditation:** ACICS

BROOKS COLLEGE (SUNNYVALE)
1120 Kifer Rd.
Sunnyvale, CA 94086
Tel: (408)719-9209
Fax: (408)719-0722
Web Site: http://www.brookssv.com/ **Type:** Two-Year College **Sex:** Coed **Calendar System:** Quarter **Professional Accreditation:** ACICS

BROOKS INSTITUTE OF PHOTOGRAPHY
801 Alston Rd.
Santa Barbara, CA 93108-2399
Tel: (805)966-3888; 888-304-3456
Fax: (805)564-1475
E-mail: admissions@brooks.edu
Web Site: http://www.brooks.edu/
President/CEO: John P. Calman
Registrar: Cam VanWingerden
Admissions: Inge B. Kautzmann
Financial Aid: Robert Peters
Type: Comprehensive **Sex:** Coed **Admission Plans:** Deferred Admission **Application Fee:** $35.00 **H.S. Requirements:** High school diploma required; GED accepted **Scholarships:** Available **Calendar System:** Trimester, Summer Session Not available **Enrollment:** FT 1,425, Grad 82 **Faculty:** FT 19, PT 20 **Student-Faculty Ratio:** 12:1 **Library Holdings:** 6,500 **Credit Hours For Degree:** 153 credits, Bachelors **Professional Accreditation:** ACICS

BROWN MACKIE COLLEGE-ORANGE COUNTY
3601 West Sunflower Ave.
Santa Ana, CA 92704
; (866)505-0334
Web Site: http://www.brownmackie.edu/locations.asp?locid=15 **Type:** Two-Year College **Sex:** Coed

BRYMAN COLLEGE (CITY OF INDUSTRY)
12801 Crossroads Parkway South
City of Industry, CA 91746
Tel: (562)908-2500
Fax: (562)908-7656
Web Site: http://bryman-college.com/ **Type:** Two-Year College **Sex:** Coed **Calendar System:** Quarter

BRYMAN COLLEGE (ONTARIO)
1460 South Milliken Ave.
Ontario, CA 91761
Tel: (909)984-5027
Fax: (909)988-9339
Web Site: http://bryman-college.com/ **Type:** Two-Year College **Sex:** Coed **Calendar System:** Quarter **Professional Accreditation:** ACCSCT

BUTTE COLLEGE
3536 Butte Campus Dr.
Oroville, CA 95965-8399
Tel: (530)895-2511
Admissions: (530)895-2366
Fax: (530)895-2345
Web Site: http://www.butte.edu/
President/CEO: Dr. Diana Van Der Ploeg
Registrar: Nancy Jenson
Admissions: Dr. Don Grey
Financial Aid: Karen Micalizio
Type: Two-Year College **Sex:** Coed **Affiliation:** California Community College System **Admission Plans:** Open Admission; Early Admission; Deferred Admission **Application Fee:** $0.00 **H.S. Requirements:** High school diploma or equivalent not required. For applicants under 18: High school diploma required; GED accepted **Scholarships:** Available **Calendar System:** Semester, Summer Session Available **Faculty:** FT 175, PT 450 **Student-Faculty Ratio:** 24:1 **Library Holdings:** 50,000 **Regional Accreditation:** Western Association of Schools and Colleges **Credit Hours For Degree:** 60 semester hours, Associates **Professional Accreditation:** CARC **Intercollegiate Athletics:** Baseball M; Basketball M & W; Cross-Country Running M & W; Football M; Golf M & W; Soccer W; Softball W; Tennis M & W; Track and Field M & W; Volleyball W

CABRILLO COLLEGE
6500 Soquel Dr.
Aptos, CA 95003-3194
Tel: (831)479-6100
Admissions: (831)479-6201
Fax: (831)479-6425
Web Site: http://www.cabrillo.edu/
President/CEO: John D. Hurd
Registrar: Gloria Garing
Admissions: Gloria Garing
Financial Aid: Debbie Soria
Type: Two-Year College **Sex:** Coed **Affiliation:** California Community College System **Admission Plans:** Open Admission; Early Admission **Application Fee:** $0.00 **H.S. Requirements:** High school diploma or equivalent not required. For applicants under 18: High school diploma required; GED accepted **Scholarships:** Available **Calendar System:** Semester, Summer Session Available **Enrollment:** FT 4,041, PT 9,864 **Faculty:** FT 116, PT 535 **Library Holdings:** 60,000 **Regional Accreditation:** Western Association of Schools and Colleges **Credit Hours For Degree:** 60 semester hours, Associates **Professional Accreditation:** AAMAE, ADA, JRCERT **Intercollegiate Athletics:** Baseball M; Basketball M & W; Cross-Country Running M & W; Football M; Golf M & W; Soccer M & W; Softball W; Swimming and Diving M & W; Tennis M & W; Track and Field M & W; Volleyball M & W; Water Polo M & W; Wrestling M

CALIFORNIA BAPTIST UNIVERSITY
8432 Magnolia Ave.
Riverside, CA 92504-3206
Tel: (909)689-5771; 877-228-8866
Admissions: (951)343-5037
Fax: (909)351-1808
E-mail: admissions@calbaptist.edu
Web Site: http://www.calbaptist.edu/
President/CEO: Dr. Ronald L. Ellis
Registrar: Shawnn Koning
Admissions: Doug Wible
Financial Aid: Eileen Terry
Type: Comprehensive **Sex:** Coed **Affiliation:** Southern Baptist **Scores:** 95% SAT V 400+; 94% SAT M 400+; 62% ACT 18-23; 20% ACT 24-29 **% Accepted:** 71 **Admission Plans:** Early Admission; Early Action; Deferred Admission **Application Deadline:** Rolling **Application Fee:** $45.00 **H.S. Requirements:** High school diploma required; GED accepted **Costs Per Year:** Application fee: $45. Comprehensive fee: $23,780 includes full-time tuition ($16,250), mandatory fees ($1220), and college room and board ($6310). College room only: $2640. Full-time tuition and fees vary according to class time and program. Room and board charges vary according to board plan and housing facility. Part-time tuition: $625 per semester hour. Part-time tuition varies according to class time and program. **Scholarships:** Available **Calendar System:** Miscellaneous, Summer Session Available **Enrollment:** FT 1,976, PT 439, Grad 690 **Faculty:** FT 96, PT 130 **Student-Faculty Ratio:** 16:1 **Exams:** SAT I or ACT **% Receiving Financial Aid:** 96 **% Residing in College-Owned, -Operated, or -Affiliated Housing:** 57 **Library Holdings:** 100,230 **Regional Accreditation:** Western Association of Schools and Colleges **Credit Hours For Degree:** 124 units, Bachelors

ROTC: Army, Air Force **Professional Accreditation:** ACBSP, NASM **Intercollegiate Athletics:** Baseball M; Basketball M & W; Golf W; Soccer M & W; Softball W; Swimming and Diving M & W; Tennis W; Volleyball M & W; Water Polo M & W

CALIFORNIA CHRISTIAN COLLEGE
4881 East University Ave.
Fresno, CA 93703-3533
Tel: (559)251-4215
Web Site: http://www.calchristiancollege.org/
President/CEO: Wendell Walley
Registrar: Brian C. Henderer
Admissions: Brian Henderer
Financial Aid: Melinda Scroggins
Type: Four-Year College **Sex:** Coed **Admission Plans:** Open Admission **Application Fee:** $40.00 **H.S. Requirements:** High school diploma required; GED accepted **Scholarships:** Available **Calendar System:** Semester, Summer Session Available **Enrollment:** FT 45, PT 7 **Faculty:** FT 7, PT 11 **Student-Faculty Ratio:** 8:1 **Exams:** Other, SAT I or ACT **% Receiving Financial Aid:** 80 **% Residing in College-Owned, -Operated, or -Affiliated Housing:** 21 **Library Holdings:** 13,154 **Credit Hours For Degree:** 64 units, Associates; 128 units, Bachelors **Professional Accreditation:** TACCS **Intercollegiate Athletics:** Basketball M; Volleyball W

CALIFORNIA COAST UNIVERSITY
700 North Main St.
Santa Ana, CA 92701
Tel: (714)547-9625; 888-CCU-UNIV
Web Site: http://www.calcoast.edu/
Admissions: Dr. William L. Barcroft
Type: Comprehensive **Sex:** Coed **Costs Per Year:** Tuition: $85 per unit part-time.

CALIFORNIA COLLEGE OF THE ARTS
1111 Eighth St.
San Francisco, CA 94107
Tel: (415)703-9500
Free: 800-447-1ART
Admissions: (415)703-9523
Fax: (415)703-9539
E-mail: enroll@cca.edu
Web Site: http://www.cca.edu/
President/CEO: Dr. Michael Roth
Registrar: Jerry Allen
Admissions: Sheri Sivin McKenzie
Financial Aid: Don Crewell
Type: Comprehensive **Sex:** Coed **Scores:** 97% SAT V 400+; 95% SAT M 400+; 65% ACT 18-23; 25% ACT 24-29 **% Accepted:** 78 **Admission Plans:** Deferred Admission **Application Deadline:** February 01 **Application Fee:** $50.00 **H.S. Requirements:** High school diploma required; GED accepted **Costs Per Year:** Application fee: $50. Comprehensive fee: $34,530 includes full-time tuition ($25,810), mandatory fees ($290), and college room and board ($8430). Full-time tuition and fees vary according to course load. Room and board charges vary according to housing facility. Part-time tuition: $1075 per unit. Part-time tuition varies according to course load. **Scholarships:** Available **Calendar System:** Semester, Summer Session Available **Enrollment:** FT 1,227, PT 85, Grad 304 **Faculty:** FT 42, PT 328 **Student-Faculty Ratio:** 14:1 **Exams:** SAT I or ACT **% Receiving Financial Aid:** 72 **% Residing in College-Owned, -Operated, or -Affiliated Housing:** 12 **Library Holdings:** 39,000 **Regional Accreditation:** Western Association of Schools and Colleges **Credit Hours For Degree:** 126 units, Bachelors **Professional Accreditation:** FIDER, NASAD

CALIFORNIA CULINARY ACADEMY
625 Polk St.
San Francisco, CA 94102-3368
Tel: (415)771-3500
Free: 800-BAY-CHEF
Admissions: 800-229-2433
Fax: (415)771-2194
Web Site: http://www.baychef.com/
President/CEO: Barry Gordon
Admissions: Nancy Seyfert
Type: Two-Year College **Sex:** Coed **Application Fee:** $65.00 **H.S. Requirements:** High school diploma required; GED accepted **Scholarships:** Available **Calendar System:** Continuous, Summer Session Not available **Enrollment:** FT 822 **Faculty:** FT 70, PT 2 **Student-Faculty Ratio:** 16:1 **% Residing in College-Owned, -Operated, or -Affiliated Housing:** 38 **Library Holdings:** 3,000 **Credit Hours For Degree:** 78 credit hours, Associates **Professional Accreditation:** ACCSCT, ACF

CALIFORNIA DESIGN COLLEGE
3440 Wilshire Blvd., Tenth Floor
Los Angeles, CA 90010
Tel: (213)251-3636; 877-468-6232
Fax: (213)385-3545
Web Site: http://www.cdc.edu/
President/CEO: Liz Erickson
Registrar: Danica Suzuki
Admissions: Joshua S. Pond
Financial Aid: Adis Ceballos
Type: Four-Year College **Sex:** Coed **Affiliation:** Education Management Corporation, The Art Institutes **Admission Plans:** Deferred Admission **Application Fee:** $0.00 **H.S. Requirements:** High school diploma required; GED accepted **Scholarships:** Available **Calendar System:** Quarter, Summer Session Not available **Enrollment:** FT 338, PT 15 **Faculty:** FT 3, PT 33 **Student-Faculty Ratio:** 27:1 **Library Holdings:** 3,200 **Credit Hours For Degree:** 112 credits, Associates; 192 credits, Bachelors **Professional Accreditation:** ACICS

CALIFORNIA INSTITUTE OF THE ARTS
24700 McBean Parkway
Valencia, CA 91355-2340
Tel: (661)255-1050
Free: 800-545-2787
E-mail: admiss@muse.calarts.edu
Web Site: http://www.calarts.edu/
President/CEO: Dr. Steven D. Lavine
Registrar: Nancy Whittemore
Admissions: Carol Kim
Type: Comprehensive **Sex:** Coed **% Accepted:** 31 **Application Deadline:** January 05 **Application Fee:** $65.00 **H.S. Requirements:** High school diploma required; GED accepted **Costs Per Year:** Application fee: $65. Comprehensive fee: $35,422 includes full-time tuition ($27,260), mandatory fees ($465), and college room and board ($7697). College room only: $4095. Full-time tuition and fees vary according to course load. Room and board charges vary according to board plan, housing facility, and location. **Scholarships:** Available **Calendar System:** Semester, Summer Session Not available **Enrollment:** FT 812, PT 9, Grad 203 **Faculty:** FT 147, PT 140 **Student-Faculty Ratio:** 7:1 **% Receiving Financial Aid:** 66 **% Residing in College-Owned, -Operated, or -Affiliated Housing:** 40 **Library Holdings:** 98,415 **Regional Accreditation:** Western Association of Schools and Colleges **Credit Hours For Degree:** 120 units, Bachelors **Professional Accreditation:** NASAD, NASD, NASM, NAST

CALIFORNIA INSTITUTE OF INTEGRAL STUDIES
1453 Mission St.
San Francisco, CA 94103
Tel: (415)575-6100
Admissions: (415)575-6156
Fax: (415)575-1264
E-mail: admissions@ciis.edu
Web Site: http://www.ciis.edu/
President/CEO: Dr. Joseph L. Subbiondo
Registrar: Nancy Hager
Admissions: Michael Fosler
Financial Aid: Michael Szkotak
Type: Two-Year Upper Division **Sex:** Coed **Admission Plans:** Deferred Admission **Application Fee:** $65.00 **Costs Per Year:** Application fee: $65. Tuition: $610 per unit part-time. **Scholarships:** Available **Calendar System:** Semester, Summer Session Not available **Student-Faculty Ratio:** 19:1 **Library Holdings:** 4,000 **Regional Accreditation:** Western Association of Schools and Colleges **Credit Hours For Degree:** 120 credits, Bachelors **Professional Accreditation:** APA

CALIFORNIA INSTITUTE OF TECHNOLOGY
1200 East California Blvd.
Pasadena, CA 91125-0001
Tel: (626)395-6811
Admissions: (626)395-6341

Fax: (626)683-3026
E-mail: ugadmissions@caltech.edu
Web Site: http://www.caltech.edu/
President/CEO: Dr. David Baltimore
Registrar: Mary Morley
Admissions: Rick T. Bischoff
Financial Aid: David S. Levy
Type: University **Sex:** Coed **Scores:** 99% SAT V 400+; 100% SAT M 400+ **Admission Plans:** Early Admission; Early Action; Deferred Admission **Application Fee:** $50.00 **H.S. Requirements:** High school diploma or equivalent not required **Costs Per Year:** Application fee: $50. Comprehensive fee: $36,123 includes full-time tuition ($27,309) and college room and board ($8814). **Scholarships:** Available **Calendar System:** Miscellaneous, Summer Session Not available **Enrollment:** FT 891, Grad 1,281 **Faculty:** FT 292, PT 32 **Student-Faculty Ratio:** 3:1 **Exams:** Other, SAT I or ACT **% Receiving Financial Aid:** 54 **% Residing in College-Owned, -Operated, or -Affiliated Housing:** 90 **Library Holdings:** 3,165,000 **Regional Accreditation:** Western Association of Schools and Colleges **ROTC:** Army, Air Force **Professional Accreditation:** ABET **Intercollegiate Athletics:** Baseball M; Basketball M & W; Cross-Country Running M & W; Fencing M & W; Golf M; Ice Hockey M; Rugby M; Soccer M & W; Swimming and Diving M & W; Tennis M & W; Track and Field M & W; Volleyball M & W; Water Polo M & W

CALIFORNIA LUTHERAN UNIVERSITY
60 West Olsen Rd.
Thousand Oaks, CA 91360-2787
Tel: (805)492-2411; 877-258-3678
Admissions: (805)493-3135
Fax: (805)493-3114
E-mail: cluadm@clunet.edu
Web Site: http://www.clunet.edu/
President/CEO: Dr. Luther S. Luedtke
Registrar: Maria Kohnke
Admissions: Matthew Ward
Financial Aid: Della Greenlee
Type: Comprehensive **Sex:** Coed **Affiliation:** Lutheran **Scores:** 99.71% SAT V 400+; 99.43% SAT M 400+; 54.7% ACT 18-23; 38.1% ACT 24-29 **% Accepted:** 69 **Admission Plans:** Deferred Admission **Application Fee:** $45.00 **H.S. Requirements:** High school diploma required; GED accepted **Costs Per Year:** Application fee: $45. Comprehensive fee: $31,690 includes full-time tuition ($23,170), mandatory fees ($200), and college room and board ($8320). College room only: $4330. Room and board charges vary according to board plan. Part-time tuition: $750 per unit. Part-time mandatory fees: $200 per year. **Scholarships:** Available **Calendar System:** Semester, Summer Session Available **Enrollment:** FT 1,884, PT 211, Grad 1,117 **Faculty:** FT 130, PT 130 **Student-Faculty Ratio:** 15:1 **Exams:** SAT I or ACT **% Receiving Financial Aid:** 64 **% Residing in College-Owned, -Operated, or -Affiliated Housing:** 65 **Library Holdings:** 132,744 **Regional Accreditation:** Western Association of Schools and Colleges **Credit Hours For Degree:** 124 units, Bachelors **ROTC:** Army, Air Force **Professional Accreditation:** NCATE **Intercollegiate Athletics:** Baseball M; Basketball M & W; Cheerleading M & W; Cross-Country Running M & W; Football M; Golf M; Soccer M & W; Softball W; Swimming and Diving M & W; Tennis M & W; Track and Field M & W; Volleyball W; Water Polo M & W

CALIFORNIA MARITIME ACADEMY
200 Maritime Academy Dr.
Vallejo, CA 94590
Tel: (707)654-1000
Free: 800-561-1945
Admissions: (707)654-1331
Fax: (707)648-4204
Web Site: http://www.csum.edu/
President/CEO: Dr. William Eisenhardt
Registrar: Deborah Fischer
Admissions: Chris Krzak
Financial Aid: Karen Neal
Type: Four-Year College **Sex:** Coed **Affiliation:** California State University System **% Accepted:** 56 **Admission Plans:** Preferred Admission **Application Fee:** $55.00 **H.S. Requirements:** High school diploma required; GED accepted **Costs Per Year:** Application fee: $55. State resident tuition: $0 full-time. Nonresident tuition: $12,690 full-time. Mandatory fees: $5884 full-time. Full-time tuition and fees vary according to program and student level. College room and board: $7270. College room only: $3390. Room and board charges vary according to board plan and housing facility. **Scholarships:** Available **Calendar System:** Semester, Summer Session Available **Enrollment:** FT 702 **Student-Faculty Ratio:** 22:1 **Exams:** SAT I or ACT **% Residing in College-Owned, -Operated, or -Affiliated Housing:** 65 **Library Holdings:** 28,377 **Regional Accreditation:** Western Association of Schools and Colleges **Credit Hours For Degree:** 126 units, Bachelors **Professional Accreditation:** ABET **Intercollegiate Athletics:** Basketball M & W; Crew M & W; Golf M & W; Rugby M; Sailing M & W; Soccer M; Volleyball W; Water Polo M & W

CALIFORNIA NATIONAL UNIVERSITY FOR ADVANCED STUDIES
8550 Balboa Blvd., Ste. 210
Northridge, CA 91325-3576
Tel: (818)830-2411
Free: 800-782-2422
Fax: (818)830-2418
E-mail: smmith@mail.cauas.edu
Web Site: http://www.cnuas.edu/
President/CEO: Dr. Lolly Horn
Registrar: Stephanie M. Smith
Admissions: Stephanie M. Smith
Type: Comprehensive **Sex:** Coed **Admission Plans:** Open Admission; Deferred Admission **Application Deadline:** Rolling **Application Fee:** $75.00 **H.S. Requirements:** High school diploma required; GED accepted **Costs Per Year:** Application fee: $75. Tuition: $4860 full-time, $270 per unit part-time. **Calendar System:** Trimester **Faculty:** FT 0, PT 98 **Student-Faculty Ratio:** 10:1 **Credit Hours For Degree:** 120 per semester hour, Bachelors **Professional Accreditation:** DETC

CALIFORNIA POLYTECHNIC STATE UNIVERSITY, SAN LUIS OBISPO
1 Grand Ave.
San Luis Obispo, CA 93407
Tel: (805)756-1111
Admissions: (805)756-2311
E-mail: dp141@oasis.calpoly.edu
Web Site: http://www.calpoly.edu/
President/CEO: Dr. Warren J. Baker
Registrar: Tom Zuur
Admissions: James Maraviglia
Financial Aid: Mary Spady
Type: Comprehensive **Sex:** Coed **Affiliation:** California State University System **Scores:** 100% SAT V 400+; 100% SAT M 400+; 27% ACT 18-23; 61% ACT 24-29 **% Accepted:** 45 **Admission Plans:** Early Admission; Early Decision Plan **Application Deadline:** November 30 **Application Fee:** $55.00 **H.S. Requirements:** High school diploma required; GED accepted **Costs Per Year:** Application fee: $55. State resident tuition: $0 full-time. Nonresident tuition: $10,170 full-time, $226 per unit part-time. Mandatory fees: $4245 full-time, $2853 per year part-time. Full-time tuition and fees vary according to course load and program. Part-time tuition and fees vary according to course load and program. College room and board: $8145. College room only: $4583. Room and board charges vary according to board plan and housing facility. **Scholarships:** Available **Calendar System:** Quarter, Summer Session Available **Enrollment:** FT 16,591, PT 897, Grad 987 **Faculty:** FT 726, PT 520 **Student-Faculty Ratio:** 20:1 **Exams:** SAT I or ACT **% Receiving Financial Aid:** 34 **% Residing in College-Owned, -Operated, or -Affiliated Housing:** 22 **Library Holdings:** 763,651 **Regional Accreditation:** Western Association of Schools and Colleges **Credit Hours For Degree:** 186 units, Bachelors **ROTC:** Army **Professional Accreditation:** AACSB, ABET, ACCE, ACA, ACSP, ASLA, NAIT, NASAD, NASM, NRPA, SAF **Intercollegiate Athletics:** Baseball M; Basketball M & W; Cross-Country Running M & W; Equestrian Sports M & W; Football M; Golf M; Gymnastics W; Soccer M & W; Softball W; Swimming and Diving M & W; Tennis M & W; Track and Field M & W; Volleyball W; Wrestling M

CALIFORNIA SCHOOL OF CULINARY ARTS
521 East Green St.
Pasadena, CA 91101
Web Site: http://calchef.com **Type:** Two-Year College **Sex:** Coed

CALIFORNIA STATE POLYTECHNIC UNIVERSITY, POMONA
3801 West Temple Ave.
Pomona, CA 91768-2557
Tel: (909)869-7659

Admissions: (909)869-3427
Fax: (909)869-4529
Web Site: http://www.csupomona.edu/
President/CEO: Dr. J. Michael Ortiz
Registrar: Rose Beardsley Kukla
Admissions: Dr. George R. Bradshaw
Financial Aid: Melanie S. Saracco
Type: Comprehensive **Sex:** Coed **Affiliation:** California State University System **Scores:** 89.54% SAT V 400+; 94.92% SAT M 400+; 54.28% ACT 18-23; 23.8% ACT 24-29 **% Accepted:** 24 **Application Deadline:** November 30 **Application Fee:** $55.00 **H.S. Requirements:** High school diploma required; GED accepted. For applicants out of high school 5 years or more: High school diploma or equivalent not required **Costs Per Year:** Application fee: $55. State resident tuition: $0 full-time. Nonresident tuition: $10,170 full-time, $226 per unit part-time. Mandatory fees: $3015 full-time. College room and board: $7908. **Scholarships:** Available **Calendar System:** Quarter, Summer Session Available **Enrollment:** FT 14,982, PT 2,992, Grad 1,911 **Faculty:** FT 659, PT 622 **Student-Faculty Ratio:** 23:1 **Exams:** SAT I or ACT **% Receiving Financial Aid:** 50 **% Residing in College-Owned, -Operated, or -Affiliated Housing:** 9 **Library Holdings:** 758,700 **Regional Accreditation:** Western Association of Schools and Colleges **Credit Hours For Degree:** 180 units, Bachelors **ROTC:** Army, Air Force **Professional Accreditation:** AACSB, ABET, ADtA, ACSP, ASLA, NASAD **Intercollegiate Athletics:** Baseball M; Basketball M & W; Cross-Country Running M & W; Soccer M & W; Tennis M & W; Track and Field M & W; Volleyball W

CALIFORNIA STATE UNIVERSITY, BAKERSFIELD
9001 Stockdale Hwy.
Bakersfield, CA 93311-1022
Tel: (661)664-2011
Admissions: (661)654-3036
Fax: (661)664-3188
E-mail: kmagnuson@csub.edu
Web Site: http://www.csubak.edu/
President/CEO: Dr. Horace Mitchell
Registrar: Dr. Kendyl Magnuson
Admissions: Dr. Kendyl Magnuson
Financial Aid: Dr. M. Steven Herndon
Type: Comprehensive **Sex:** Coed **Affiliation:** California State University System **Scores:** 36% ACT 18-23; 13% ACT 24-29 **Admission Plans:** Preferred Admission; Early Admission; Deferred Admission **Application Deadline:** September 23 **Application Fee:** $55.00 **H.S. Requirements:** High school diploma required; GED accepted **Costs Per Year:** Application fee: $55. State resident tuition: $0 full-time. Nonresident tuition: $6780 full-time, $226 per unit part-time. Mandatory fees: $2959 full-time, $579 per term part-time. College room and board: $5946. **Scholarships:** Available **Calendar System:** Quarter, Summer Session Available **Enrollment:** FT 4,881, PT 1,079, Grad 1,589 **Faculty:** FT 332, PT 183 **Student-Faculty Ratio:** 17:1 **Exams:** SAT I or ACT, SAT II **% Receiving Financial Aid:** 60 **% Residing in College-Owned, -Operated, or -Affiliated Housing:** 4 **Library Holdings:** 354,016 **Regional Accreditation:** Western Association of Schools and Colleges **Credit Hours For Degree:** 186 quarter units, Bachelors **Professional Accreditation:** AACSB, AACN, CSWE, NASPAA, NCATE, NLN **Intercollegiate Athletics:** Basketball M; Golf M; Soccer M; Softball W; Swimming and Diving M & W; Tennis W; Track and Field M & W; Volleyball W; Water Polo W; Wrestling M

CALIFORNIA STATE UNIVERSITY CHANNEL ISLANDS
One University Dr.
Camarillo, CA 93012
Tel: (805)437-8979
Admissions: (805)437-8500
Fax: (805)437-8951
E-mail: admissionsandrecords@csuci.edu
Web Site: http://www.csuci.edu/
Admissions: Jane Sweetland
Type: Four-Year College **Sex:** Coed **Scores:** 94.6% SAT V 400+; 94.9% SAT M 400+; 54.9% ACT 18-23; 26.8% ACT 24-29 **% Accepted:** 43 **Application Fee:** $50.00 **Costs Per Year:** Application fee: $50. Nonresident tuition: $10,170 full-time, $339 per unit part-time. Mandatory fees: $2980 full-time. College room and board: $8800. **Enrollment:** FT 1,805, PT 555 **Faculty:** FT 84, PT 143 **Student-Faculty Ratio:** 16:1 **Exams:** SAT I and SAT II or ACT **Regional Accreditation:** Western Association of Schools and Colleges

CALIFORNIA STATE UNIVERSITY, CHICO
400 West First St.
Chico, CA 95929-0722
Tel: (530)898-6116
Free: 800-542-4426
Admissions: (530)898-4428
Fax: (530)898-6456
E-mail: info@csuchico.edu
Web Site: http://www.csuchico.edu/
President/CEO: Paul J. Zingg
Registrar: Dr. Bruce Rowen
Admissions: Dr. John F. Swiney
Financial Aid: Meredith Kelley
Type: Comprehensive **Sex:** Coed **Affiliation:** California State University System **Scores:** 93% SAT V 400+; 95% SAT M 400+; 59% ACT 18-23; 24% ACT 24-29 **% Accepted:** 85 **Admission Plans:** Deferred Admission **Application Deadline:** November 30 **Application Fee:** $55.00 **H.S. Requirements:** High school diploma required; GED accepted **Costs Per Year:** Application fee: $55. State resident tuition: $0 full-time. Nonresident tuition: $12,690 full-time, $339 per unit part-time. Mandatory fees: $3370 full-time, $425 per term part-time. Part-time tuition and fees vary according to course load. College room and board: $7993. College room only: $5550. Room and board charges vary according to board plan and housing facility. **Scholarships:** Available **Calendar System:** Semester, Summer Session Available **Enrollment:** FT 13,079, PT 1,447, Grad 1,393 **Faculty:** FT 499, PT 414 **Student-Faculty Ratio:** 21:1 **Exams:** SAT I or ACT **% Receiving Financial Aid:** 52 **% Residing in College-Owned, -Operated, or -Affiliated Housing:** 12 **Library Holdings:** 957,181 **Regional Accreditation:** Western Association of Schools and Colleges **Credit Hours For Degree:** 120 units, Bachelors **Professional Accreditation:** AACSB, ABET, ACEJMC, AACN, ACCE, ADtA, ASLHA, CSWE, NAIT, NASAD, NASM, NASPAA, NLN, NRPA **Intercollegiate Athletics:** Badminton M & W; Baseball M; Basketball M & W; Bowling M & W; Cheerleading M & W; Cross-Country Running M & W; Field Hockey M & W; Golf M & W; Lacrosse M & W; Rock Climbing M & W; Rugby M & W; Soccer M & W; Softball W; Track and Field M & W; Ultimate Frisbee M & W; Volleyball M & W; Water Polo M & W

CALIFORNIA STATE UNIVERSITY, DOMINGUEZ HILLS
1000 East Victoria St.
Carson, CA 90747-0001
Tel: (310)243-3300
Admissions: (310)243-3600
Web Site: http://www.csudh.edu/
President/CEO: Dr. James E. Lyons, Sr.
Registrar: Gayle Ball
Admissions: James Woods
Financial Aid: Delores Lee
Type: Comprehensive **Sex:** Coed **Affiliation:** California State University System **Scores:** 59% SAT V 400+; 60% SAT M 400+; 28% ACT 18-23; 6% ACT 24-29 **% Accepted:** 45 **Admission Plans:** Preferred Admission; Early Admission **Application Deadline:** Rolling **Application Fee:** $55.00 **H.S. Requirements:** High school diploma required; GED accepted **Costs Per Year:** Application fee: $55. State resident tuition: $0 full-time. Nonresident tuition: $339 per unit part-time. Mandatory fees: $3618 full-time. College room only: $5850. **Scholarships:** Available **Calendar System:** Semester, Summer Session Available **Enrollment:** FT 5,322, PT 3,621, Grad 3,414 **Faculty:** FT 252, PT 426 **Student-Faculty Ratio:** 22:1 **Exams:** SAT I or ACT **% Receiving Financial Aid:** 82 **Library Holdings:** 440,181 **Regional Accreditation:** Western Association of Schools and Colleges **Credit Hours For Degree:** 124 semester units, Bachelors **ROTC:** Army, Air Force **Professional Accreditation:** ABET, AACN, AOTA, ACBSP, NAACLS, NASM, NASPAA, NAST, NCOPE, NCATE, NLN **Intercollegiate Athletics:** Badminton M & W; Basketball M & W; Soccer M & W; Volleyball W

CALIFORNIA STATE UNIVERSITY, EAST BAY
25800 Carlos Bee Blvd.
Hayward, CA 94542-3000
Tel: (510)885-3000
Admissions: (510)885-7002
Fax: (510)885-3816
E-mail: adminfo@csuhayward.edu
Web Site: http://www.csueastbay.edu/
President/CEO: Dr. Norma Rees

Registrar: Bruce Purcell
Admissions: Dr. Ray Wallace
Financial Aid: Jeff Cook
Type: Comprehensive **Sex:** Coed **Affiliation:** California State University System **Scores:** 73.6% SAT V 400+; 82.2% SAT M 400+; 55.4% ACT 18-23; 8.4% ACT 24-29 **% Accepted:** 10 **Admission Plans:** Deferred Admission **Application Deadline:** August 31 **Application Fee:** $55.00 **H.S. Requirements:** High school diploma required; GED accepted **Costs Per Year:** Application fee: $55. State resident tuition: $0 full-time. Nonresident tuition: $10,170 full-time. Mandatory fees: $2916 full-time. College room only: $6759. **Scholarships:** Available **Calendar System:** Quarter, Summer Session Available **Enrollment:** FT 7,262, PT 1,867, Grad 3,406 **Faculty:** FT 324, PT 417 **Student-Faculty Ratio:** 17:1 **Exams:** SAT I or ACT **% Receiving Financial Aid:** 44 **% Residing in College-Owned, -Operated, or -Affiliated Housing:** 4 **Library Holdings:** 908,577 **Regional Accreditation:** Western Association of Schools and Colleges **Credit Hours For Degree:** 180 units, Bachelors **Professional Accreditation:** AACSB, ASLHA, NASAD, NASM, NASPAA, NCATE, NLN **Intercollegiate Athletics:** Baseball M; Basketball M & W; Cross-Country Running M & W; Soccer M & W; Softball W; Swimming and Diving W; Volleyball W; Water Polo W

CALIFORNIA STATE UNIVERSITY, FRESNO

5241 North Maple Ave.
Fresno, CA 93740-8027
Tel: (559)278-4240
Admissions: (559)278-2261
Fax: (559)278-4715
E-mail: vivian_franco@csufresno.edu
Web Site: http://www.csufresno.edu/
President/CEO: John Welty
Registrar: Tina Beddall
Admissions: Vivian Franco
Financial Aid: Maria Hernandez
Type: Comprehensive **Sex:** Coed **Affiliation:** California State University System **Scores:** 76% SAT V 400+; 83% SAT M 400+; 45% ACT 18-23; 13% ACT 24-29 **% Accepted:** 65 **Admission Plans:** Preferred Admission **Application Deadline:** April 01 **Application Fee:** $55.00 **H.S. Requirements:** High school diploma required; GED accepted **Costs Per Year:** Application fee: $55. State resident tuition: $0 full-time. Nonresident tuition: $13,207 full-time, $339 per unit part-time. Mandatory fees: $3037 full-time, $990 per term part-time. College room and board: $7344. **Scholarships:** Available **Calendar System:** Semester, Summer Session Available **Enrollment:** FT 14,786, PT 2,642, Grad 2,943 **Faculty:** FT 754, PT 513 **Student-Faculty Ratio:** 20:1 **Exams:** SAT I or ACT **% Receiving Financial Aid:** 61 **% Residing in College-Owned, -Operated, or -Affiliated Housing:** 5 **Regional Accreditation:** Western Association of Schools and Colleges **Credit Hours For Degree:** 124 units, Bachelors **ROTC:** Army, Air Force **Professional Accreditation:** AACSB, ABET, AAFCS, ACCE, ACA, ADtA, APTA, ASLHA, CEPH, CORE, CSWE, FIDER, JRCEPAT, NASM, NASPAA, NAST, NCATE, NLN, NRPA **Intercollegiate Athletics:** Baseball M; Basketball M & W; Cross-Country Running M & W; Equestrian Sports W; Football M; Golf M; Soccer M & W; Softball W; Swimming and Diving W; Tennis M & W; Track and Field M & W; Volleyball W; Wrestling M

CALIFORNIA STATE UNIVERSITY, FULLERTON

PO Box 34080
Fullerton, CA 92834-9480
Tel: (714)278-2011
Admissions: (714)278-2350
Web Site: http://www.fullerton.edu/
President/CEO: Dr. Milton A. Gordon
Registrar: Melissa Whatley
Admissions: Nancy J. Dority
Financial Aid: Deborah S. McCracken
Type: Comprehensive **Sex:** Coed **Affiliation:** California State University System **Scores:** 88% SAT V 400+; 91% SAT M 400+; 54% ACT 18-23; 16% ACT 24-29 **% Accepted:** 69 **Admission Plans:** Preferred Admission **Application Deadline:** November 30 **Application Fee:** $55.00 **H.S. Requirements:** High school diploma required; GED not accepted **Costs Per Year:** Application fee: $55. State resident tuition: $0 full-time. Nonresident tuition: $10,170 full-time, $339 per unit part-time. Mandatory fees: $2990 full-time, $967 per term part-time. Full-time tuition and fees vary according to course load. Part-time tuition and fees vary according to course load. College room only: $4504. **Scholarships:** Available **Calendar System:** Semester, Summer Session Available **Enrollment:** FT 21,187, PT 8,275, Grad 5,578 **Faculty:** FT 719, PT 1,216 **Student-Faculty Ratio:** 23:1 **Exams:** SAT I or ACT **% Receiving Financial Aid:** 26 **% Residing in College-Owned, -Operated, or -Affiliated Housing:** 2 **Library Holdings:** 1,169,030 **Regional Accreditation:** Western Association of Schools and Colleges **Credit Hours For Degree:** 120 semester units, Bachelors **ROTC:** Army **Professional Accreditation:** AACSB, ABET, ACEJMC, AACN, AANA, ACNM, ASLHA, JRCEPAT, NASAD, NASD, NASM, NASPAA, NAST, NCATE, NLN **Intercollegiate Athletics:** Baseball M; Basketball M & W; Bowling M & W; Cross-Country Running M & W; Fencing M & W; Gymnastics W; Rugby M; Soccer M & W; Softball W; Tennis W; Track and Field M & W; Volleyball W; Wrestling M

CALIFORNIA STATE UNIVERSITY, LONG BEACH

1250 Bellflower Blvd.
Long Beach, CA 90840
Tel: (562)985-4111
Admissions: (562)985-4641
Web Site: http://www.csulb.edu/
President/CEO: Dr. Robert C. Maxson
Registrar: Nancy Cohn
Admissions: Thomas Enders
Financial Aid: Dr. Gloria Kapp
Type: Comprehensive **Sex:** Coed **Affiliation:** California State University System **Scores:** 90.52% SAT V 400+; 93.51% SAT M 400+; 52.74% ACT 18-23; 20.93% ACT 24-29 **% Accepted:** 55 **Admission Plans:** Preferred Admission **Application Deadline:** November 30 **Application Fee:** $55.00 **H.S. Requirements:** High school diploma required; GED accepted **Costs Per Year:** Application fee: $55. State resident tuition: $0 full-time. Nonresident tuition: $10,170 full-time. Mandatory fees: $2864 full-time. College room and board: $6648. **Scholarships:** Available **Calendar System:** Semester, Summer Session Available **Enrollment:** FT 22,525, PT 5,989, Grad 6,033 **Faculty:** FT 966, PT 1,108 **Student-Faculty Ratio:** 20:1 **Exams:** SAT I or ACT **% Receiving Financial Aid:** 45 **% Residing in College-Owned, -Operated, or -Affiliated Housing:** 7 **Library Holdings:** 1,472,080 **Regional Accreditation:** Western Association of Schools and Colleges **Credit Hours For Degree:** 124 units, Bachelors **ROTC:** Army **Professional Accreditation:** AACSB, ABET, ACEHSA, AACN, AAFCS, ADtA, APTA, APA, ASLHA, CAEPK, CEPH, CSWE, JRCERT, NASAD, NASD, NASM, NASPAA, NAST, NCATE, NRPA **Intercollegiate Athletics:** Archery M & W; Badminton M & W; Basketball M & W; Bowling M & W; Crew M & W; Cross-Country Running M & W; Fencing M & W; Golf M & W; Rugby M; Sailing M & W; Skiing (Downhill) M & W; Soccer M & W; Softball W; Table Tennis M; Tennis W; Track and Field M & W; Volleyball M & W; Water Polo M & W

CALIFORNIA STATE UNIVERSITY, LOS ANGELES

5151 State University Dr.
Los Angeles, CA 90032-8530
Tel: (323)343-3000
Admissions: (323)343-3940
Fax: (323)343-2670
E-mail: jwoosley@csianet.calstatela.edu
Web Site: http://www.calstatela.edu/
President/CEO: Dr. James M. Rosser
Registrar: Mary Kulich
Admissions: Joan Woosley
Financial Aid: Nancy Kudo-Hombo
Type: Comprehensive **Sex:** Coed **Affiliation:** California State University System **Scores:** 69.1% SAT V 400+; 77.1% SAT M 400+; 39.6% ACT 18-23; 10.4% ACT 24-29 **% Accepted:** 62 **Admission Plans:** Early Admission **Application Deadline:** June 15 **Application Fee:** $55.00 **H.S. Requirements:** High school diploma required; GED accepted **Costs Per Year:** Application fee: $55. State resident tuition: $0 full-time. Nonresident tuition: $11,171 full-time, $226 per unit part-time. Mandatory fees: $3035 full-time, $658.75 per term part-time. Full-time tuition and fees vary according to course level. Part-time tuition and fees vary according to course level. College room and board: $7353. **Scholarships:** Available **Calendar System:** Quarter, Summer Session Available **Enrollment:** FT 10,872, PT 4,083, Grad 5,059 **Faculty:** FT 581, PT 560 **Student-Faculty Ratio:** 16:1 **Exams:** SAT I or ACT **% Receiving Financial Aid:** 65 **Library Holdings:** 1,736,107 **Regional Accreditation:** Western Association of Schools and Colleges **Credit Hours For Degree:** 186 quarter units, Bachelors **ROTC:** Army, Air Force **Professional Accreditation:** AACSB, ABET, ACA, ADtA, ASLHA, CORE, CSWE, NASAD, NASM, NASPAA, NCATE, NLN **Intercollegiate Athletics:** Baseball M; Basketball M & W; Cross-Country Running W; Soc-

cer M & W; Tennis W; Track and Field M & W; Volleyball W

CALIFORNIA STATE UNIVERSITY, MONTEREY BAY
100 Campus Center
Seaside, CA 93955-8001
Tel: (831)582-3000
Admissions: (831)582-3544
Fax: (831)582-3540
Web Site: http://csumb.edu/
President/CEO: Dr. Peter Smith
Registrar: Dr. Valarie Brown
Admissions: Dennis L. Geyer
Financial Aid: Bonnie Brown
Type: Comprehensive **Sex:** Coed **Affiliation:** California State University **Admission Plans:** Deferred Admission **Application Fee:** $55.00 **H.S. Requirements:** High school diploma required; GED accepted **Costs Per Year:** Application fee: $55. State resident tuition: $0 full-time. Nonresident tuition: $10,848 full-time, $339 per credit part-time. Mandatory fees: $2947 full-time, $945.50 per term part-time. College room and board: $6900. College room only: $4400. **Scholarships:** Available **Calendar System:** Semester **Enrollment:** FT 2,673, PT 80, Grad 267 **Faculty:** FT 114, PT 166 **Student-Faculty Ratio:** 20:1 **Exams:** SAT I or ACT **% Residing in College-Owned, -Operated, or -Affiliated Housing:** 65 **Regional Accreditation:** Western Association of Schools and Colleges **Credit Hours For Degree:** 124 units, Bachelors **Intercollegiate Athletics:** Basketball M & W; Cross-Country Running M & W; Golf M & W; Soccer M & W; Volleyball W

CALIFORNIA STATE UNIVERSITY, NORTHRIDGE
18111 Nordhoff St.
Northridge, CA 91330
Tel: (818)677-1200
Admissions: (818)677-3700
Fax: (818)677-3766
Web Site: http://www.csun.edu/
President/CEO: Dr. Jolene Koester
Registrar: Eric Forbes
Admissions: Mary E. Baxton
Financial Aid: Kathryn Anderson
Type: Comprehensive **Sex:** Coed **Affiliation:** California State University System **Scores:** 78.6% SAT V 400+; 81.3% SAT M 400+ **% Accepted:** 75 **Admission Plans:** Preferred Admission; Early Admission; Early Action **Application Deadline:** November 30 **Application Fee:** $55.00 **H.S. Requirements:** High school diploma required; GED accepted **Costs Per Year:** Application fee: $55. State resident tuition: $0 full-time. Nonresident tuition: $10,170 full-time, $339 per unit part-time. Mandatory fees: $3036 full-time, $1464 per term part-time. College room and board: $7616. College room only: $4766. Room and board charges vary according to housing facility. **Scholarships:** Available **Calendar System:** Semester, Summer Session Available **Enrollment:** FT 20,638, PT 6,216, Grad 6,389 **Faculty:** FT 803, PT 1,019 **Student-Faculty Ratio:** 23:1 **Exams:** SAT I or ACT **% Receiving Financial Aid:** 63 **Library Holdings:** 1,207,345 **Regional Accreditation:** Western Association of Schools and Colleges **Credit Hours For Degree:** 124 units, Bachelors **ROTC:** Army, Air Force **Professional Accreditation:** ABET, ACEJMC, AACN, AAFCS, ACA, ADtA, APTA, ASLHA, CEPH, CSWE, FIDER, JRCERT, JRCEPAT, NASAD, NASM, NAST, NCATE, NRPA **Intercollegiate Athletics:** Baseball M; Basketball M & W; Cross-Country Running M & W; Football M; Golf M; Soccer M; Softball W; Swimming and Diving M & W; Tennis W; Track and Field M & W; Volleyball M & W

CALIFORNIA STATE UNIVERSITY, SACRAMENTO
6000 J St.
Sacramento, CA 95819-6048
Tel: (916)278-6011
Admissions: (916)278-7362
Web Site: http://www.csus.edu/
President/CEO: Alexander Gonzalez
Registrar: Larry Glasmire
Admissions: Emiliano Diaz
Financial Aid: Linda Clemons
Type: Comprehensive **Sex:** Coed **Affiliation:** California State University System **Scores:** 83% SAT V 400+; 88% SAT M 400+; 53% ACT 18-23; 12% ACT 24-29 **% Accepted:** 47 **Admission Plans:** Early Action; Deferred Admission **Application Deadline:** August 01 **Application Fee:** $55.00 **H.S. Requirements:** High school diploma required; GED accepted **Costs Per Year:** Application fee: $55. Nonresident tuition: $13,242 full-time, $339 per unit part-time. Mandatory fees: $3624 full-time, $276 per term part-time. College room and board: $7458. **Scholarships:** Available **Calendar System:** Semester, Summer Session Available **Enrollment:** FT 17,864, PT 5,164, Grad 4,904 **Faculty:** FT 812, PT 718 **Student-Faculty Ratio:** 22:1 **Exams:** SAT I or ACT **% Receiving Financial Aid:** 48 **% Residing in College-Owned, -Operated, or -Affiliated Housing:** 5 **Library Holdings:** 1,309,619 **Regional Accreditation:** Western Association of Schools and Colleges **Credit Hours For Degree:** 124 units, Bachelors **ROTC:** Army, Air Force **Professional Accreditation:** AACSB, ABET, AACN, ACCE, ADtA, APTA, ASLHA, CORE, CSWE, FIDER, JRCEPAT, NASAD, NASM, NAST, NRPA **Intercollegiate Athletics:** Baseball M; Basketball M & W; Bowling M & W; Cheerleading M & W; Crew M & W; Cross-Country Running M & W; Football M; Golf M & W; Gymnastics W; Ice Hockey M; Lacrosse M & W; Racquetball M & W; Rugby M; Skiing (Downhill) M & W; Soccer M & W; Softball W; Tennis M & W; Track and Field M & W; Volleyball M & W

CALIFORNIA STATE UNIVERSITY, SAN BERNARDINO
5500 University Parkway
San Bernardino, CA 92407-2397
Tel: (909)537-5000
Admissions: (909)537-5188
E-mail: orosas@csusb.edu
Web Site: http://www.csusb.edu/
President/CEO: Dr. Albert K. Karnig
Registrar: Dr. Lydia Ortega
Admissions: Olivia Rosas
Financial Aid: Lois E. Madsen
Type: Comprehensive **Sex:** Coed **Affiliation:** California State University System **Scores:** 76% SAT V 400+; 82% SAT M 400+; 49% ACT 18-23; 10% ACT 24-29 **% Accepted:** 25 **Admission Plans:** Early Admission **Application Deadline:** Rolling **Application Fee:** $55.00 **H.S. Requirements:** High school diploma required; GED accepted **Costs Per Year:** Application fee: $55. State resident tuition: $0 full-time. Nonresident tuition: $8136 full-time, $226 per unit part-time. Mandatory fees: $3398 full-time. Part-time tuition varies according to course load. College room and board: $5886. College room only: $4376. Room and board charges vary according to board plan and housing facility. **Scholarships:** Available **Calendar System:** Quarter, Summer Session Available **Enrollment:** FT 10,375, PT 2,089, Grad 3,967 **Faculty:** FT 363, PT 84 **Student-Faculty Ratio:** 22:1 **Exams:** Other **% Receiving Financial Aid:** 60 **% Residing in College-Owned, -Operated, or -Affiliated Housing:** 11 **Library Holdings:** 731,259 **Regional Accreditation:** Western Association of Schools and Colleges **Credit Hours For Degree:** 186 units, Bachelors **ROTC:** Army, Air Force **Professional Accreditation:** AACSB, ABET, AACN, CORE, CSWE, NASAD, NASM, NASPAA, NAST, NCATE, NLN **Intercollegiate Athletics:** Baseball M; Basketball M & W; Golf M; Soccer M & W; Softball W; Swimming and Diving M & W; Volleyball W

CALIFORNIA STATE UNIVERSITY, SAN MARCOS
333 South Twin Oaks Valley Rd.
San Marcos, CA 92096-0001
Tel: (760)750-4000
Admissions: (760)750-4848
Fax: (760)750-4030
E-mail: apply@csusm.edu
Web Site: http://www.csusm.edu/
President/CEO: Dr. Karen S. Haynes
Registrar: Dr. Karl Beeler
Admissions: Cherine Heckman
Financial Aid: Addalou Davis
Type: Comprehensive **Sex:** Coed **Affiliation:** California State University System **Scores:** 88.5% SAT V 400+; 89.7% SAT M 400+ **% Accepted:** 44 **Application Deadline:** November 30 **Application Fee:** $55.00 **H.S. Requirements:** High school diploma required; GED accepted **Costs Per Year:** Application fee: $55. State resident tuition: $0 full-time. Nonresident tuition: $8136 full-time, $339 per credit hour part-time. Mandatory fees: $3062 full-time. Part-time tuition varies according to course load. College room only: $7470. Room charges vary according to housing facility. **Scholarships:** Available **Calendar System:** Semester, Summer Session Available **Enrollment:** FT 4,658, PT 1,669, Grad 629 **Exams:** SAT I or ACT **% Receiving Financial Aid:** 40 **% Residing in College-Owned, -Operated, or -Affiliated Housing:** 7 **Library Holdings:** 233,445 **Regional Accreditation:** Western Association of Schools and Colleges **Credit Hours For Degree:** 124 units, Bachelors **ROTC:** Army, Navy, Air Force **Professional Accreditation:** NCATE **Intercollegiate Athletics:** Cross-Country Running

M & W; Golf M & W; Track and Field M & W

CALIFORNIA STATE UNIVERSITY, STANISLAUS
801 West Monte Vista Ave.
Turlock, CA 95382
Tel: (209)667-3122
Admissions: (209)667-3152
Fax: (209)667-3333
E-mail: outreach_help_desk@csustan.edu
Web Site: http://www.csustan.edu/
President/CEO: Dr. Marvalene Hughes
Admissions: Lisa Bernardo
Financial Aid: David Gomes
Type: Comprehensive **Sex:** Coed **Affiliation:** California State University System **Scores:** 100% SAT V 400+; 100% SAT M 400+; 48.5% ACT 18-23; 15.5% ACT 24-29 **% Accepted:** 65 **Admission Plans:** Early Decision Plan **Application Deadline:** July 01 **Application Fee:** $55.00 **H.S. Requirements:** High school diploma required; GED accepted **Costs Per Year:** Application fee: $55. State resident tuition: $0 full-time. Nonresident tuition: $10,170 full-time, $339 per unit part-time. Mandatory fees: $3030 full-time, $855.50 per term part-time. College room and board: $8253. College room only: $5612. Room and board charges vary according to board plan and housing facility. **Scholarships:** Available **Calendar System:** 4-1-4, Summer Session Available **Enrollment:** FT 4,500, PT 1,983, Grad 1,654 **Faculty:** FT 285, PT 210 **Student-Faculty Ratio:** 17:1 **Exams:** Other, SAT I or ACT **% Receiving Financial Aid:** 53 **% Residing in College-Owned, -Operated, or -Affiliated Housing:** 8 **Library Holdings:** 365,870 **Regional Accreditation:** Western Association of Schools and Colleges **Credit Hours For Degree:** 120 units, Bachelors **Professional Accreditation:** AACSB, AACN, CSWE, NASAD, NASM, NASPAA, NAST, NCATE, NLN **Intercollegiate Athletics:** Baseball M; Basketball M & W; Cross-Country Running M & W; Golf M; Soccer M & W; Softball W; Track and Field M & W; Volleyball W

CAÑADA COLLEGE
4200 Farm Hill Blvd.
Redwood City, CA 94061-1099
Tel: (650)306-3100
Admissions: (650)306-3125
Fax: (650)306-3457
Web Site: http://www.canadacollege.net/
President/CEO: Rosa G. Perez
Admissions: Denise Swett
Financial Aid: Margie Carrington
Type: Two-Year College **Sex:** Coed **Affiliation:** San Mateo County Community College District System **Admission Plans:** Open Admission; Early Admission **Application Fee:** $0.00 **H.S. Requirements:** High school diploma required; GED accepted **Scholarships:** Available **Calendar System:** Semester, Summer Session Available **Library Holdings:** 53,417 **Regional Accreditation:** Western Association of Schools and Colleges **Credit Hours For Degree:** 60 credits, Associates **Professional Accreditation:** JRCERT **Intercollegiate Athletics:** Baseball M

CERRITOS COLLEGE
11110 Alondra Blvd.
Norwalk, CA 90650-6298
Tel: (562)860-2451
E-mail: smurguia@cerritos.edu
Web Site: http://www.cerritos.edu/
President/CEO: John A. Grindel
Registrar: Stephanie Murguia
Admissions: Stephanie Murguia
Financial Aid: Dr. Erlinda Martinez
Type: Two-Year College **Sex:** Coed **Affiliation:** California Community College System **Admission Plans:** Open Admission; Early Admission; Deferred Admission **Application Fee:** $0.00 **H.S. Requirements:** High school diploma or equivalent not required. For applicants under 18: High school diploma required; GED accepted **Scholarships:** Available **Calendar System:** Semester, Summer Session Available **Faculty:** FT 250, PT 440 **Exams:** Other **Library Holdings:** 74,502 **Regional Accreditation:** Western Association of Schools and Colleges **Credit Hours For Degree:** 64 units, Associates **Professional Accreditation:** ADA, APTA, NLN **Intercollegiate Athletics:** Baseball M; Basketball M & W; Cross-Country Running M & W; Football M; Golf M; Soccer M; Softball W; Swimming and Diving M & W; Tennis M & W; Track and Field M & W; Volleyball W; Water Polo M; Wrestling M

CERRO COSO COMMUNITY COLLEGE
3000 College Heights Blvd.
Ridgecrest, CA 93555-9571
Tel: (760)384-6100
Admissions: (760)384-6291
Fax: (760)375-4776
Web Site: http://www.cerrocoso.edu/
President/CEO: Dr. Sharon K. Dyer
Registrar: Jill Board
Admissions: Robert Weisenthal
Financial Aid: Robert Weisenthal
Type: Two-Year College **Sex:** Coed **Affiliation:** Kern Community College District System **Admission Plans:** Open Admission; Early Admission **Application Fee:** $0.00 **H.S. Requirements:** High school diploma or equivalent not required. For nursing program: High school diploma required; GED accepted **Costs Per Year:** Application fee: $0. State resident tuition: $0 full-time. Nonresident tuition: $5010 full-time, $162 per unit part-time. Mandatory fees: $780 full-time, $26 per unit part-time. **Scholarships:** Available **Calendar System:** Semester, Summer Session Available **Enrollment:** FT 1,218, PT 3,802 **Faculty:** FT 59, PT 155 **Student-Faculty Ratio:** 14:1 **Exams:** Other **Library Holdings:** 25,000 **Regional Accreditation:** Western Association of Schools and Colleges **Credit Hours For Degree:** 60 semester hours, Associates **Intercollegiate Athletics:** Baseball M; Basketball W

CHABOT COLLEGE
25555 Hesperian Blvd.
Hayward, CA 94545-5001
Tel: (510)723-6600
Admissions: (510)723-6700
Web Site: http://www.chabotcollege.edu/
President/CEO: Dr. Robert E. Carlson
Registrar: Carlo E. Vecchiarelli
Admissions: Judy Young
Financial Aid: Kathryn Linzmeyer
Type: Two-Year College **Sex:** Coed **Affiliation:** California Community College System **Admission Plans:** Open Admission; Preferred Admission **Application Fee:** $0.00 **H.S. Requirements:** High school diploma required; GED accepted **Scholarships:** Available **Calendar System:** Semester, Summer Session Available **Faculty:** FT 182, PT 330 **Student-Faculty Ratio:** 24:1 **Library Holdings:** 100,000 **Regional Accreditation:** Western Association of Schools and Colleges **Credit Hours For Degree:** 60 semester hours, Associates **ROTC:** Army, Air Force **Professional Accreditation:** AAMAE, ADA, AHIMA **Intercollegiate Athletics:** Baseball M; Basketball M & W; Cross-Country Running M & W; Football M; Golf M; Soccer M & W; Softball W; Swimming and Diving M & W; Tennis M & W; Track and Field M & W; Wrestling M

CHAFFEY COLLEGE
5885 Haven Ave.
Rancho Cucamonga, CA 91737-3002
Tel: (909)987-1737
Admissions: (909)941-2631
Fax: (909)941-2783
Web Site: http://www.chaffey.edu/
President/CEO: Cid Pinedo
Registrar: Cecilia Carrera
Admissions: Cecilia Carerra
Financial Aid: Karen Sanders
Type: Two-Year College **Sex:** Coed **Affiliation:** California Community College System **Admission Plans:** Open Admission; Early Admission **Application Fee:** $0.00 **H.S. Requirements:** High school diploma or equivalent not required. For applicants under 18: High school diploma required; GED accepted **Scholarships:** Available **Calendar System:** Semester, Summer Session Available **Faculty:** FT 182, PT 501 **Library Holdings:** 72,000 **Regional Accreditation:** Western Association of Schools and Colleges **Credit Hours For Degree:** 60 units, Associates **ROTC:** Army **Professional Accreditation:** ADA, JRCERT, NLN **Intercollegiate Athletics:** Baseball M; Basketball M & W; Football M; Soccer M & W; Softball W; Swimming and Diving M & W; Tennis M & W; Track and Field M & W; Volleyball W; Water Polo M & W

CHAPMAN UNIVERSITY
One University Dr.
Orange, CA 92866

Tel: (714)997-6815; 888-CUAPPLY
Admissions: (714)997-6711
Fax: (714)997-6713
E-mail: low@chapman.edu
Web Site: http://www.chapman.edu/
President/CEO: Dr. James Doti
Registrar: John Snodgrass
Admissions: Michael O. Drummy
Financial Aid: Greg Ball
Type: Comprehensive **Sex:** Coed **Affiliation:** Christian Church (Disciples of Christ) **Scores:** 100% SAT V 400+; 100% SAT M 400+; 32% ACT 18-23; 60% ACT 24-29 **% Accepted:** 53 **Admission Plans:** Early Admission; Early Action **Application Deadline:** January 31 **Application Fee:** $55.00 **H.S. Requirements:** High school diploma required; GED accepted **Costs Per Year:** Application fee: $55. Comprehensive fee: $41,248 includes full-time tuition ($29,900), mandatory fees ($848), and college room and board ($10,500). Part-time tuition: $920 per credit. **Scholarships:** Available **Calendar System:** 4-1-4, Summer Session Available **Enrollment:** FT 3,661, PT 203, Grad 1,303 **Faculty:** FT 264, PT 317 **Student-Faculty Ratio:** 14:1 **Exams:** SAT I or ACT, SAT II **% Receiving Financial Aid:** 62 **% Residing in College-Owned, -Operated, or -Affiliated Housing:** 38 **Library Holdings:** 182,169 **Regional Accreditation:** Western Association of Schools and Colleges **Credit Hours For Degree:** 124 credits, Bachelors **ROTC:** Army, Air Force **Professional Accreditation:** AACSB, ABA, APTA, NASM **Intercollegiate Athletics:** Baseball M; Basketball M & W; Crew W; Cross-Country Running M & W; Football M; Golf M & W; Soccer M & W; Softball W; Swimming and Diving M & W; Tennis M & W; Track and Field W; Volleyball W; Water Polo M & W

CHARLES R. DREW UNIVERSITY OF MEDICINE AND SCIENCE
1731 East 120th St.
Los Angeles, CA 90059
Tel: (323)563-4800
Admissions: (323)563-5849
E-mail: mavalero@cdrewu.edu
Web Site: http://www.cdrewu.edu/
President/CEO: Dr. Harry E. Douglas, III
Registrar: Marla Sharma
Admissions: Mayella Valero
Financial Aid: Marla Sharma
Type: Comprehensive **Sex:** Coed **% Accepted:** 55 **Application Deadline:** April 30 **Application Fee:** $35.00 **H.S. Requirements:** High school diploma required; GED accepted **Costs Per Year:** Application fee: $35. Tuition: $10,000 full-time, $250 per unit part-time. Mandatory fees: $100 full-time, $100 per year part-time. **Scholarships:** Available **Calendar System:** Trimester **Enrollment:** FT 250 **Student-Faculty Ratio:** 7:1 **Exams:** SAT I or ACT **Regional Accreditation:** Western Association of Schools and Colleges **Professional Accreditation:** AAMAE, ACNM, AHIMA, JRCERT

CITRUS COLLEGE
1000 West Foothill Blvd.
Glendora, CA 91741-1899
Tel: (626)963-0323
Web Site: http://www.citruscollege.edu/
President/CEO: Dr. Michael J. Viera
Financial Aid: Jannice Szymanski
Type: Two-Year College **Sex:** Coed **Affiliation:** California Community College System **Admission Plans:** Open Admission **Application Fee:** $0.00 **H.S. Requirements:** High school diploma required; GED accepted **Costs Per Year:** Application fee: $0. State resident tuition: $0 full-time. Nonresident tuition: $4954 full-time, $150 per unit part-time. Mandatory fees: $754 full-time, $26 per unit part-time. Full-time tuition and fees vary according to course load. Part-time tuition and fees vary according to course load. **Scholarships:** Available **Calendar System:** Semester, Summer Session Available **Faculty:** FT 136, PT 257 **Student-Faculty Ratio:** 29:1 **Library Holdings:** 45,091 **Regional Accreditation:** Western Association of Schools and Colleges **Credit Hours For Degree:** 60 units, Associates **Professional Accreditation:** ADA **Intercollegiate Athletics:** Baseball M; Basketball M & W; Cross-Country Running M & W; Football M; Golf M & W; Soccer M & W; Softball W; Swimming and Diving M & W; Tennis M & W; Track and Field M & W; Volleyball W; Water Polo M & W

CITY COLLEGE OF SAN FRANCISCO
50 Phelan Ave.
San Francisco, CA 94112-1821
Tel: (415)239-3000
Admissions: (415)239-3291
Fax: (415)239-3936
Web Site: http://www.ccsf.edu/
President/CEO: Dr. Philip Day, Jr.
Registrar: Robert Balestreri
Admissions: Robert Balesteri
Financial Aid: Jorge Bell
Type: Two-Year College **Sex:** Coed **Affiliation:** California Community College System **Admission Plans:** Open Admission; Early Admission **H.S. Requirements:** High school diploma or equivalent not required. For applicants under 18: High school diploma required; GED accepted **Scholarships:** Available **Calendar System:** Semester, Summer Session Available **Faculty:** FT 770, PT 1,547 **Library Holdings:** 93,518 **Regional Accreditation:** Western Association of Schools and Colleges **Credit Hours For Degree:** 60 units, Associates **ROTC:** Army **Professional Accreditation:** AAMAE, ACF, ADA, AHIMA, JRCERT **Intercollegiate Athletics:** Archery W; Basketball M; Cross-Country Running M & W; Fencing W; Football M; Golf M; Gymnastics W; Soccer M; Swimming and Diving M; Tennis M & W; Track and Field M & W; Volleyball M & W; Water Polo M

CLAREMONT MCKENNA COLLEGE
500 East 9th St.
Claremont, CA 91711
Tel: (909)621-8000
Admissions: (909)621-8088
E-mail: admission@claremontmckenna.edu
Web Site: http://www.claremontmckenna.edu/
President/CEO: Pamela Brooks Gann
Registrar: Elizabeth Morgan
Admissions: Richard C. Vos
Financial Aid: Georgette DeVeres
Type: Four-Year College **Sex:** Coed **Affiliation:** The Claremont Colleges Consortium **Scores:** 100% SAT V 400+; 100% SAT M 400+; 2% ACT 18-23; 45% ACT 24-29 **% Accepted:** 21 **Admission Plans:** Early Admission; Early Decision Plan; Deferred Admission **Application Deadline:** January 02 **Application Fee:** $60.00 **H.S. Requirements:** High school diploma required; GED accepted **Costs Per Year:** Application fee: $60. Comprehensive fee: $42,920 includes full-time tuition ($30,800), mandatory fees ($1850), and college room and board ($10,270). College room only: $5160. Full-time tuition and fees vary according to reciprocity agreements. Room and board charges vary according to board plan and housing facility. Part-time tuition: $5100 per course. **Scholarships:** Available **Calendar System:** Semester, Summer Session Not available **Enrollment:** FT 1,139 **Faculty:** FT 116, PT 18 **Student-Faculty Ratio:** 9:1 **Exams:** SAT I or ACT, SAT II **% Receiving Financial Aid:** 50 **% Residing in College-Owned, -Operated, or -Affiliated Housing:** 96 **Library Holdings:** 2,028,793 **Regional Accreditation:** Western Association of Schools and Colleges **Credit Hours For Degree:** 32 courses, Bachelors **ROTC:** Army, Air Force **Intercollegiate Athletics:** Badminton M & W; Baseball M; Basketball M & W; Cheerleading M & W; Cross-Country Running M & W; Football M; Golf M; Lacrosse M & W; Rugby M & W; Skiing (Downhill) M & W; Soccer M & W; Softball W; Swimming and Diving M & W; Tennis M & W; Track and Field M & W; Volleyball M & W; Water Polo M & W

CLEVELAND CHIROPRACTIC COLLEGE-LOS ANGELES CAMPUS
590 North Vermont Ave.
Los Angeles, CA 90004-2196
Tel: (323)660-6166
Free: 800-446-CCLA
Admissions: (323)906-2031
Fax: (323)660-5387
Web Site: http://www.clevelandchiropractic.edu/
President/CEO: Dr. Carl S. Cleveland, III
Registrar: Gilda Ceniza
Admissions: Theresa Moon
Financial Aid: Gilda Ceniza
Type: Two-Year Upper Division **Sex:** Coed **Affiliation:** Cleveland Chiropractic College-Kansas City **Admission Plans:** Open Admission **Application Deadline:** August 29 **Application Fee:** $35.00 **H.S. Requirements:** High school diploma required; GED accepted **Costs Per Year:** Application fee: $35. Tuition: $5242 full-time, $219 per credit part-time. Mandatory fees: $200 full-time, $200 per year part-time. **Calendar System:** Trimester, Summer Session Available **Enrollment:** FT 92, PT 31 **Faculty:** FT 22, PT 17 **Student-Faculty Ratio:** 6:1 **Library Holdings:** 23,618 **Credit Hours For**

Degree: 60 credits, Associates; 123 credits, Bachelors **Professional Accreditation:** CCE

COASTLINE COMMUNITY COLLEGE
11460 Warner Ave.
Fountain Valley, CA 92708-2597
Tel: (714)546-7600
Admissions: (714)241-6160
Fax: (714)241-6288
Web Site: http://coastline.cccd.edu/
President/CEO: Dr. Ding-Jo Currie
Admissions: John Breihan
Financial Aid: Cynthia Pienkowski
Type: Two-Year College **Sex:** Coed **Affiliation:** Coast Community College District System **Admission Plans:** Open Admission; Early Admission **Application Fee:** $0.00 **H.S. Requirements:** High school diploma or equivalent not required. For applicants under 18: High school diploma required; GED accepted **Scholarships:** Available **Calendar System:** Semester, Summer Session Available **Enrollment:** FT 493, PT 8,066 **Faculty:** FT 49, PT 300 **Student-Faculty Ratio:** 24:1 **Regional Accreditation:** Western Association of Schools and Colleges **Credit Hours For Degree:** 60 units, Associates

COGSWELL POLYTECHNICAL COLLEGE
1175 Bordeaux Dr.
Sunnyvale, CA 94089-1299
Tel: (408)541-0100
Free: 800-264-7955
Fax: (408)747-0764
E-mail: info@cogswell.edu
Web Site: http://www.cogswell.edu/
President/CEO: Dr. Chester D. Haskell
Registrar: Lisa Willet
Admissions: Dr. Valarie Brown
Financial Aid: Matt Clemons
Type: Four-Year College **Sex:** Coed **Affiliation:** Foundation for Educational Achievement, San Diego **% Accepted:** 98 **Admission Plans:** Deferred Admission **Application Deadline:** June 01 **Application Fee:** $55.00 **H.S. Requirements:** High school diploma required; GED accepted **Costs Per Year:** Application fee: $55. Tuition: $13,680 full-time, $570 per credit part-time. Full-time tuition varies according to course load. Part-time tuition varies according to course load. College room only: $3000. Room charges vary according to housing facility. **Scholarships:** Available **Calendar System:** Semester, Summer Session Available **Enrollment:** FT 133, PT 149 **Faculty:** FT 14, PT 27 **Student-Faculty Ratio:** 8:1 **% Receiving Financial Aid:** 88 **% Residing in College-Owned, -Operated, or -Affiliated Housing:** 9 **Library Holdings:** 11,257 **Regional Accreditation:** Western Association of Schools and Colleges **Credit Hours For Degree:** 120 semester hours, Bachelors

THE COLBURN SCHOOL CONSERVATORY OF MUSIC
200 South Grand Ave.
Los Angeles, CA 90012
Tel: (213)621-2200
Fax: (213)621-2110
E-mail: ktesar@colburnschool.edu
Web Site: http://www.colburnschool.edu/
President/CEO: Joseph J. Thayer
Admissions: Kathleen Tesar
Type: Four-Year College **Sex:** Coed **Application Fee:** $100.00 **Costs Per Year:** Application fee: $100. Tuition: $0 full-time. Mandatory fees: $1200 full-time. **Calendar System:** Semester **Enrollment:** FT 17 **Exams:** SAT I or ACT **Professional Accreditation:** NASM

COLEMAN COLLEGE (LA MESA)
7380 Parkway Dr.
La Mesa, CA 91942-1532
Tel: (619)465-3990
Fax: (619)465-0162
Web Site: http://www.coleman.edu/
President/CEO: Pritpal Panesar
Registrar: William Fall
Admissions: Stephen Collins
Financial Aid: Elizabeth Salas
Type: Comprehensive **Sex:** Coed **Admission Plans:** Deferred Admission **Application Fee:** $100.00 **H.S. Requirements:** High school diploma required; GED accepted **Costs Per Year:** Application fee: $100. Tuition: $20,580 full-time, $245 per unit part-time. Mandatory fees: $100 full-time. Tuition guaranteed not to increase for student's term of enrollment. **Scholarships:** Available **Calendar System:** Quarter, Summer Session Available **Enrollment:** FT 444, Grad 24 **Faculty:** FT 62, PT 31 **Library Holdings:** 66,800 **Credit Hours For Degree:** 108 quarter hours, Associates; 180 quarter hours, Bachelors **Professional Accreditation:** ACICS

COLEMAN COLLEGE (SAN MARCOS)
1284 West San Marcos Blvd.
San Marcos, CA 92069
Tel: (760)747-3990
Fax: (760)752-9808
Web Site: http://www.coleman.edu/
President/CEO: Darlene Ankton
Admissions: James Warner
Type: Two-Year College **Sex:** Coed **Calendar System:** Quarter **Enrollment:** FT 203 **Professional Accreditation:** ACICS

COLLEGE OF ALAMEDA
555 Atlantic Ave.
Alameda, CA 94501-2109
Tel: (510)522-7221
Admissions: (510)466-7365
E-mail: hperdue@peralta.cc.ca.us
Web Site: http://www.peralta.cc.ca.us/
President/CEO: Dr. Cecilia Cervantes
Admissions: Howard Perdue
Financial Aid: Dr. Kerry Compton
Type: Two-Year College **Sex:** Coed **Affiliation:** Peralta Community College District System **Admission Plans:** Open Admission **Application Fee:** $0.00 **H.S. Requirements:** High school diploma required; GED accepted. For applicants 18 or over: High school diploma or equivalent not required **Scholarships:** Available **Calendar System:** Semester, Summer Session Available **Faculty:** FT 80, PT 86 **Exams:** SAT I or ACT **Library Holdings:** 40,000 **Regional Accreditation:** Western Association of Schools and Colleges **Credit Hours For Degree:** 60 semester hours, Associates **Professional Accreditation:** ADA **Intercollegiate Athletics:** Basketball M & W; Bowling M & W

COLLEGE OF THE CANYONS
26455 Rockwell Canyon Rd.
Santa Clarita, CA 91355-1803
Tel: (661)259-7800; 888-206-7827
Admissions: (661)362-3280
Fax: (661)362-5300
Web Site: http://www.canyons.edu/
President/CEO: Dr. Dianne G. Van Hook
Registrar: Deborah Rio
Admissions: Deborah Rio
Financial Aid: Beth Asmus
Type: Two-Year College **Sex:** Coed **Affiliation:** California Community College System **Admission Plans:** Open Admission; Early Admission **Application Deadline:** August 22 **Application Fee:** $0.00 **H.S. Requirements:** High school diploma or equivalent not required **Costs Per Year:** Application fee: $0. State resident tuition: $0 full-time. Nonresident tuition: $5168 full-time, $171 per unit part-time. Mandatory fees: $818 full-time, $26 per unit part-time. **Scholarships:** Available **Calendar System:** Semester, Summer Session Available **Enrollment:** FT 12,679, PT 3,825 **Faculty:** FT 173, PT 418 **Student-Faculty Ratio:** 27:1 **Library Holdings:** 40,646 **Regional Accreditation:** Western Association of Schools and Colleges **Credit Hours For Degree:** 60 units, Associates **Professional Accreditation:** NLN **Intercollegiate Athletics:** Baseball M; Basketball M & W; Cross-Country Running M & W; Football M; Golf M; Soccer W; Softball W; Swimming and Diving M & W; Track and Field M & W; Volleyball W; Water Polo M

COLLEGE OF THE DESERT
43-500 Monterey Ave.
Palm Desert, CA 92260-9305
Tel: (760)346-8041
Admissions: (760)773-7516
Web Site: http://desert.cc.ca.us/
President/CEO: Dr. Maria C. Sheehan
Registrar: Kathie Westerfield

Admissions: Carlene Gibson
Financial Aid: Kathie Westerfield
Type: Two-Year College **Sex:** Coed **Affiliation:** California Community College System **Admission Plans:** Open Admission; Preferred Admission; Early Admission **Application Fee:** $0.00 **H.S. Requirements:** High school diploma required; GED accepted. For applicants 18 or over: High school diploma or equivalent not required **Scholarships:** Available **Calendar System:** Semester, Summer Session Available **Faculty:** FT 103, PT 235 **Library Holdings:** 58,000 **Regional Accreditation:** Western Association of Schools and Colleges **Credit Hours For Degree:** 60 units, Associates **Professional Accreditation:** NLN **Intercollegiate Athletics:** Baseball M; Basketball M & W; Cross-Country Running M & W; Football M; Golf M & W; Soccer M; Softball W; Tennis M & W; Track and Field M & W; Volleyball W

COLLEGE OF MARIN
835 College Ave.
Kentfield, CA 94904
Tel: (415)457-8811
Admissions: (415)485-9417
Fax: (415)883-2632
Web Site: http://www.marin.cc.ca.us/
President/CEO: Dr. James E. Middleton
Registrar: Pamela J. Mize
Admissions: Gina Longo
Financial Aid: David Cook
Type: Two-Year College **Sex:** Coed **Affiliation:** California Community College System **Admission Plans:** Open Admission; Early Admission **H.S. Requirements:** High school diploma or equivalent not required **Scholarships:** Available **Calendar System:** Semester, Summer Session Available **Faculty:** FT 145, PT 344 **Library Holdings:** 85,000 **Regional Accreditation:** Western Association of Schools and Colleges **Credit Hours For Degree:** 60 units, Associates **Professional Accreditation:** ADA, NLN **Intercollegiate Athletics:** Basketball M & W; Cross-Country Running M & W; Football M & W; Golf M & W; Soccer M & W; Swimming and Diving M & W; Tennis M & W; Track and Field M & W; Volleyball M & W; Water Polo M & W

COLLEGE OF THE REDWOODS
7351 Tompkins Hill Rd.
Eureka, CA 95501-9300
Tel: (707)476-4100
Admissions: (707)476-4177
Web Site: http://www.redwoods.edu/
President/CEO: Dr. Kathleen E. Crabill
Registrar: Sue Bailey
Admissions: Leslie Lawson
Financial Aid: Karen Johnson
Type: Two-Year College **Sex:** Coed **Affiliation:** California Community College System **Admission Plans:** Open Admission; Early Admission **Application Fee:** $0.00 **H.S. Requirements:** High school diploma required; GED accepted. For applicants 18 or over: High school diploma or equivalent not required **Scholarships:** Available **Calendar System:** Semester, Summer Session Available **Faculty:** FT 104, PT 310 **Student-Faculty Ratio:** 21:1 **% Residing in College-Owned, -Operated, or -Affiliated Housing:** 2 **Library Holdings:** 50,266 **Regional Accreditation:** Western Association of Schools and Colleges **Credit Hours For Degree:** 60 units, Associates **Professional Accreditation:** ADA, NAIT **Intercollegiate Athletics:** Baseball M; Basketball M & W; Cross-Country Running M & W; Football M; Golf M; Soccer W; Softball W; Track and Field M & W; Volleyball W

COLLEGE OF SAN MATEO
1700 West Hillsdale Blvd.
San Mateo, CA 94402-3784
Tel: (650)574-6161
Admissions: (650)574-6594
E-mail: csmadmission@smcccd.cc.ca.us
Web Site: http://www.collegeofsanmateo.edu/
President/CEO: Dr. Shirley Kelly
Registrar: Henry Villareal
Admissions: Henry Villareal
Financial Aid: Steven Myrow
Type: Two-Year College **Sex:** Coed **Affiliation:** California Community College System **Admission Plans:** Open Admission; Early Admission **Application Fee:** $0.00 **H.S. Requirements:** High school diploma or equivalent not required. For applicants under 18: High school diploma required; GED accepted **Calendar System:** Semester, Summer Session Available **Faculty:** FT 184, PT 292 **Student-Faculty Ratio:** 15:1 **Library Holdings:** 85,085 **Regional Accreditation:** Western Association of Schools and Colleges **Credit Hours For Degree:** 60 semester hours, Associates **ROTC:** Army, Navy, Air Force **Professional Accreditation:** ADA **Intercollegiate Athletics:** Basketball M & W; Cross-Country Running M & W; Football M; Golf M; Soccer W; Tennis W; Track and Field M & W

COLLEGE OF THE SEQUOIAS
915 South Mooney Blvd.
Visalia, CA 93277-2234
Tel: (559)730-3700
Admissions: (559)737-4844
Web Site: http://www.cos.edu/
President/CEO: Dr. Kamiran S. Badrkhan
Registrar: Don Mast
Admissions: Don Mast
Financial Aid: Ron Hays
Type: Two-Year College **Sex:** Coed **Affiliation:** California Community College System **Admission Plans:** Open Admission; Early Admission **Application Fee:** $0.00 **H.S. Requirements:** High school diploma or equivalent not required. For applicants under 18: High school diploma required; GED accepted **Scholarships:** Available **Calendar System:** Semester, Summer Session Available **Enrollment:** FT 4,427, PT 6,742 **Faculty:** FT 174 **Student-Faculty Ratio:** 26:1 **Library Holdings:** 73,557 **Regional Accreditation:** Western Association of Schools and Colleges **Credit Hours For Degree:** 60 units, Associates **ROTC:** Air Force **Intercollegiate Athletics:** Baseball M; Basketball M & W; Cross-Country Running M & W; Football M; Golf M; Soccer W; Softball W; Swimming and Diving M & W; Tennis M & W; Track and Field M & W; Volleyball W; Water Polo M

COLLEGE OF THE SISKIYOUS
800 College Ave.
Weed, CA 96094-2899
Tel: (530)938-5555
Admissions: (530)938-5374
Fax: (530)938-5227
E-mail: richards@siskiyous.edu
Web Site: http://www.siskiyous.edu/
President/CEO: Dr. W. Pelham
Registrar: Teresa Winkleman
Admissions: Robin Richards
Financial Aid: Vicki Wrobel
Type: Two-Year College **Sex:** Coed **Affiliation:** California Community College System **% Accepted:** 100 **Admission Plans:** Open Admission; Early Admission; Deferred Admission **Application Deadline:** Rolling **H.S. Requirements:** High school diploma or equivalent not required. For applicants under 18: High school diploma required; GED accepted **Costs Per Year:** Nonresident tuition: $174 per unit part-time. Mandatory fees: $26 per unit part-time, $12 per term part-time. **Scholarships:** Available **Calendar System:** Semester, Summer Session Available **Faculty:** FT 49, PT 102 **Student-Faculty Ratio:** 21:1 **% Residing in College-Owned, -Operated, or -Affiliated Housing:** 10 **Library Holdings:** 34,708 **Regional Accreditation:** Western Association of Schools and Colleges **Credit Hours For Degree:** 60 units, Associates **Intercollegiate Athletics:** Baseball M; Basketball M & W; Cross-Country Running M & W; Football M; Softball W; Track and Field M & W; Volleyball W

COLUMBIA COLLEGE
11600 Columbia College Dr.
Sonora, CA 95370
Tel: (209)588-5100
Admissions: (209)588-5107
E-mail: gervind@yosemite.edu
Web Site: http://www.gocolumbia.org/
President/CEO: Dr. Jim Riggs
Registrar: Kathy Smith
Admissions: Dr. Dennis Gervine
Financial Aid: Cass Larkin
Type: Two-Year College **Sex:** Coed **Affiliation:** Yosemite Community College District System **% Accepted:** 100 **Admission Plans:** Open Admission; Preferred Admission; Early Admission **Application Deadline:** Rolling **Application Fee:** $0.00 **H.S. Requirements:** High school diploma required; GED accepted. For applicants 18 or over: High school diploma or equivalent not required **Costs Per Year:** Application fee: $0. State resident tuition: $0

full-time. Nonresident tuition: $4286 full-time, $177 per unit part-time. Mandatory fees: $662 full-time, $26 per unit part-time, $24 per term part-time. College room and board: $6115. **Scholarships:** Available **Calendar System:** Semester, Summer Session Available **Enrollment:** FT 940, PT 1,751 **Faculty:** FT 57, PT 110 **Student-Faculty Ratio:** 16:1 **Library Holdings:** 34,892 **Regional Accreditation:** Western Association of Schools and Colleges **Credit Hours For Degree:** 60 units, Associates **Professional Accreditation:** ACF, JRCEMT **Intercollegiate Athletics:** Basketball M; Cross-Country Running M & W; Tennis M & W; Volleyball W

COLUMBIA COLLEGE HOLLYWOOD
18618 Oxnard St.
Tarzana, CA 91356
Tel: (818)345-8414
Fax: (818)345-9053
Web Site: http://www.columbiacollege.edu/
President/CEO: Paul Lo
Registrar: Lois Becker
Admissions: Carmen Munoz
Financial Aid: Chris Freeman
Type: Four-Year College **Sex:** Coed **Admission Plans:** Deferred Admission **Application Fee:** $50.00 **H.S. Requirements:** High school diploma required; GED accepted **Costs Per Year:** Application fee: $50. Comprehensive fee: $18,350 includes full-time tuition ($11,400), mandatory fees ($1100), and college room and board ($5850). Part-time tuition: $325 per unit. **Scholarships:** Available **Calendar System:** Quarter, Summer Session Available **Enrollment:** FT 177 **Faculty:** FT 0, PT 36 **Student-Faculty Ratio:** 15:1 **Exams:** SAT I **% Receiving Financial Aid:** 68 **Library Holdings:** 5,500 **Credit Hours For Degree:** 96 units, Associates; 192 units, Bachelors **Professional Accreditation:** ACCSCT

COMPTON COMMUNITY COLLEGE
1111 East Artesia Blvd.
Compton, CA 90221-5393
Tel: (310)900-1600
Fax: (310)900-1692
Web Site: http://www.compton.edu/
President/CEO: Ulis C. Williams
Registrar: Dr. Essie French-Preston
Admissions: Phillip Glezer
Financial Aid: Henry Ross
Type: Two-Year College **Sex:** Coed **Affiliation:** California Community College System **Admission Plans:** Open Admission; Early Admission **H.S. Requirements:** High school diploma or equivalent not required **Scholarships:** Available **Calendar System:** Semester, Summer Session Available **Faculty:** FT 100, PT 247 **Library Holdings:** 45,000 **Regional Accreditation:** Western Association of Schools and Colleges **Credit Hours For Degree:** 60 units, Associates **Intercollegiate Athletics:** Baseball M; Basketball M & W; Cross-Country Running M & W; Football M; Golf M; Track and Field M & W

CONCORDE CAREER INSTITUTE
12412 Victory Blvd.
North Hollywood, CA 91606
Tel: (818)766-8151
Fax: (818)766-1587
Web Site: http://www.concordecareercolleges.com/
President/CEO: Michael Kerwin
Type: Two-Year College **Sex:** Coed **Professional Accreditation:** ACCSCT, CARC

CONCORDIA UNIVERSITY
1530 Concordia West
Irvine, CA 92612-3299
Tel: (949)854-8002
Free: 800-229-1200
Fax: (949)854-6894
E-mail: admission@cui.edu
Web Site: http://www.cui.edu/
President/CEO: Dr. Jacob A. O. Preus, III
Registrar: Kenneth Clavir
Admissions: Gary R. McDaniel
Financial Aid: Lori McDonald
Type: Comprehensive **Sex:** Coed **Affiliation:** Lutheran Church–Missouri Synod;The Ten-campus Concordia University System **Scores:** 96% SAT V 400+; 97% SAT M 400+; 61% ACT 18-23; 33% ACT 24-29 **% Accepted:** 68 **Admission Plans:** Deferred Admission **Application Deadline:** Rolling **Application Fee:** $50.00 **H.S. Requirements:** High school diploma required; GED accepted **Costs Per Year:** Application fee: $50. Comprehensive fee: $28,190 includes full-time tuition ($21,130) and college room and board ($7060). College room only: $4380. Part-time tuition: $600 per unit. **Scholarships:** Available **Calendar System:** Semester, Summer Session Available **Enrollment:** FT 1,370, PT 75, Grad 647 **Faculty:** FT 77, PT 131 **Student-Faculty Ratio:** 15:1 **Exams:** SAT I or ACT **% Receiving Financial Aid:** 66 **% Residing in College-Owned, -Operated, or -Affiliated Housing:** 73 **Library Holdings:** 85,432 **Regional Accreditation:** Western Association of Schools and Colleges **Credit Hours For Degree:** 128 semester hours, Bachelors **Intercollegiate Athletics:** Baseball M; Basketball M & W; Cross-Country Running M & W; Soccer M & W; Softball W; Track and Field M & W; Volleyball W

CONTRA COSTA COLLEGE
2600 Mission Bell Dr.
San Pablo, CA 94806-3195
Tel: (510)235-7800
Web Site: http://www.contracosta.edu/
President/CEO: Dr. Helen Carr
Admissions: Frank Hernandez
Financial Aid: Dr. Mickey Mathews
Type: Two-Year College **Sex:** Coed **Affiliation:** Contra Costa Community College District and California Community College System **Admission Plans:** Open Admission; Early Admission **Application Fee:** $0.00 **H.S. Requirements:** High school diploma or equivalent not required. For dental assisting, nursing programs: High school diploma required; GED accepted **Scholarships:** Available **Calendar System:** Semester, Summer Session Available **Enrollment:** FT 3,973, PT 4,861 **Faculty:** FT 115, PT 300 **Exams:** SAT I or ACT **Library Holdings:** 57,017 **Regional Accreditation:** Western Association of Schools and Colleges **Credit Hours For Degree:** 60 units, Associates **ROTC:** Army, Air Force **Professional Accreditation:** ADA, MACTE **Intercollegiate Athletics:** Baseball M; Basketball M & W; Cross-Country Running M & W; Football M; Softball W; Track and Field M & W; Volleyball W

COPPER MOUNTAIN COLLEGE
6162 Rotary Way
Joshua Tree, CA 92252
Tel: (760)366-3791
Admissions: (760)366-5290
Web Site: http://www.cmccd.cc.ca.us/
President/CEO: Greg Gilbert
Admissions: Dr. Laraine Turk
Type: Two-Year College **Sex:** Coed **Calendar System:** Semester

COSUMNES RIVER COLLEGE (SACRAMENTO)
8401 Center Parkway
Sacramento, CA 95823-5799
Tel: (916)691-7451
Admissions: (916)688-7410
Fax: (916)691-7375
Web Site: http://www.crc.losrios.edu/
President/CEO: Francisco C. Rodriguez
Admissions: Richard Andrews
Type: Two-Year College **Sex:** Coed **Affiliation:** Los Rios Community College District System **Admission Plans:** Open Admission; Early Admission **Application Fee:** $0.00 **H.S. Requirements:** High school diploma required; GED accepted. For applicants 18 or over: High school diploma or equivalent not required **Scholarships:** Available **Calendar System:** Semester, Summer Session Available **Faculty:** FT 150, PT 400 **Exams:** SAT I or ACT **Library Holdings:** 55,447 **Regional Accreditation:** Western Association of Schools and Colleges **Credit Hours For Degree:** 60 units, Associates **Professional Accreditation:** AAMAE, AHIMA **Intercollegiate Athletics:** Baseball M & W; Basketball M & W; Soccer M & W; Softball W; Swimming and Diving M & W; Tennis M & W; Track and Field M & W; Volleyball W; Water Polo M & W

CRAFTON HILLS COLLEGE
11711 Sand Canyon Rd.
Yucaipa, CA 92399-1799
Tel: (909)794-2161
Admissions: (909)389-3355

Fax: (909)389-9141
Web Site: http://www.craftonhills.edu/
President/CEO: Gloria M. Harrison
Registrar: Marco Cota
Admissions: Marco Cota
Financial Aid: John Muskavitch
Type: Two-Year College **Sex:** Coed **Affiliation:** California Community College System **Admission Plans:** Open Admission; Preferred Admission; Early Admission; Deferred Admission **Application Fee:** $0.00 **H.S. Requirements:** High school diploma required; GED accepted **Scholarships:** Available **Calendar System:** Semester, Summer Session Available **Faculty:** FT 77, PT 131 **Exams:** Other **Library Holdings:** 65,731 **Regional Accreditation:** Western Association of Schools and Colleges **Credit Hours For Degree:** 60 credits, Associates **Professional Accreditation:** CARC, JRCEMT

CUESTA COLLEGE
PO Box 8106
San Luis Obispo, CA 93403-8106
Tel: (805)546-3100
Admissions: (805)546-3130
Web Site: http://www.cuesta.edu/
President/CEO: Dr. Marie E. Rosenwasser
Admissions: Joy Gadbois
Financial Aid: Robin Crawford
Type: Two-Year College **Sex:** Coed **Admission Plans:** Open Admission; Preferred Admission; Early Admission; Deferred Admission **Application Fee:** $0.00 **H.S. Requirements:** High school diploma or equivalent not required **Scholarships:** Available **Calendar System:** Semester, Summer Session Available **Faculty:** FT 134, PT 283 **Exams:** Other **Library Holdings:** 64,814 **Regional Accreditation:** Western Association of Schools and Colleges **Credit Hours For Degree:** 60 units, Associates **ROTC:** Army **Intercollegiate Athletics:** Baseball M; Basketball M & W; Cross-Country Running M & W; Soccer W; Softball W; Swimming and Diving M & W; Tennis W; Track and Field M & W; Volleyball W; Water Polo M & W; Wrestling M

CUYAMACA COLLEGE
900 Rancho San Diego Parkway
El Cajon, CA 92019-4304
Tel: (619)660-4000
Admissions: (619)660-4302
Web Site: http://www.cuyamaca.net/
President/CEO: Geraldine M. Perri
Registrar: David Agosto
Admissions: Dr. Beth Appenzeller
Financial Aid: Carmen Solom
Type: Two-Year College **Sex:** Coed **Affiliation:** Grossmont-Cuyamaca Community College District **Admission Plans:** Open Admission; Early Admission **Application Fee:** $0.00 **H.S. Requirements:** High school diploma required; GED accepted. For applicants 18 or over: High school diploma or equivalent not required **Scholarships:** Available **Calendar System:** Semester, Summer Session Available **Faculty:** FT 66, PT 214 **Exams:** Other **Library Holdings:** 32,129 **Regional Accreditation:** Western Association of Schools and Colleges **Credit Hours For Degree:** 60 units, Associates **ROTC:** Army, Air Force **Intercollegiate Athletics:** Basketball M & W; Cross-Country Running M & W; Soccer M & W; Tennis W; Track and Field M & W; Volleyball W

CYPRESS COLLEGE
9200 Valley View
Cypress, CA 90630-5897
Tel: (714)484-7000
Admissions: (714)484-7435
Fax: (714)761-3934
E-mail: dwassenaar@cypresscollege.edu
Web Site: http://www.cypress.cc.ca.us/
President/CEO: Dr. Marjorie Lewis
Registrar: Regina Ford
Admissions: David Wassenaar
Financial Aid: Marlene Miranda
Type: Two-Year College **Sex:** Coed **Affiliation:** California Community College System **Admission Plans:** Open Admission **Application Fee:** $0.00 **H.S. Requirements:** High school diploma or equivalent not required **Scholarships:** Available **Calendar System:** Semester, Summer Session Available **Faculty:** FT 230, PT 360 **Library Holdings:** 76,696 **Regional Accreditation:** Western Association of Schools and Colleges **Credit Hours For Degree:** 60 units, Associates **Professional Accreditation:** ABFSE, ADA, AHIMA, JRCERT, NLN **Intercollegiate Athletics:** Baseball M; Basketball M & W; Golf M & W; Soccer M & W; Softball W; Swimming and Diving M & W; Tennis M & W; Volleyball W; Water Polo M & W; Wrestling M

DE ANZA COLLEGE
21250 Stevens Creek Blvd.
Cupertino, CA 95014-5793
Tel: (408)864-5678
Admissions: (408)864-8292
Fax: (408)864-8329
E-mail: webregda@mercury.fhda.edu
Web Site: http://www.deanza.fhda.edu/
President/CEO: Dr. M. Brian Murphy
Registrar: Kathleen Kyne
Admissions: Kathleen Kayne
Financial Aid: Cindy Castillo
Type: Two-Year College **Sex:** Coed **Affiliation:** California Community College System **Admission Plans:** Open Admission; Early Admission **Application Fee:** $22.00 **H.S. Requirements:** High school diploma required; GED accepted **Costs Per Year:** Application fee: $22. State resident tuition: $0 full-time. Nonresident tuition: $3636 full-time, $101 per unit part-time. Mandatory fees: $818 full-time, $17 per unit part-time. **Scholarships:** Available **Calendar System:** Quarter, Summer Session Available **Enrollment:** FT 8,860, PT 14,484 **Faculty:** FT 512, PT 300 **Exams:** Other, SAT I **Library Holdings:** 80,000 **Regional Accreditation:** Western Association of Schools and Colleges **Credit Hours For Degree:** 90 units, Associates **ROTC:** Army, Air Force **Professional Accreditation:** AAMAE, APTA **Intercollegiate Athletics:** Baseball M; Basketball M & W; Cross-Country Running M & W; Football M; Golf M & W; Soccer M & W; Softball W; Swimming and Diving M & W; Tennis M & W; Track and Field M & W; Volleyball M & W; Water Polo M

DESIGN INSTITUTE OF SAN DIEGO
8555 Commerce Ave.
San Diego, CA 92121-2685
Tel: (858)566-1200
Free: 800-619-4337
Fax: (858)566-2711
E-mail: admisssions@disd.edu
Web Site: http://www.disd.edu/
President/CEO: Arthur Rosenstein
Registrar: Tracy Gulino
Admissions: Paula Parrish
Financial Aid: Jackie Brewer
Type: Four-Year College **Sex:** Coed **Application Fee:** $25.00 **H.S. Requirements:** High school diploma required; GED accepted **Scholarships:** Available **Calendar System:** Semester, Summer Session Not available **Library Holdings:** 5,000 **Professional Accreditation:** ACICS, FIDER

DEVRY UNIVERSITY (ELK GROVE)
Sacramento Center
2218 Kausen Dr.
Elk Grove, CA 95758
Tel: (916)478-2847; (866)573-3879
Fax: (916)478-2849
Web Site: http://www.devry.edu/ **Type:** Comprehensive **Sex:** Coed **Costs Per Year:** One-time mandatory fee: $40. Tuition: $11,790 full-time, $440 per credit part-time. Mandatory fees: $60 full-time, $30 per year part-time. Full-time tuition and fees vary according to course load. Part-time tuition and fees vary according to course load. **Calendar System:** Semester **Regional Accreditation:** North Central Association of Colleges and Schools

DEVRY UNIVERSITY (FREMONT)
6600 Dumbarton Circle
Fremont, CA 94555
Tel: (510)574-1100; 888-393-3879
Fax: (510)742-0868
Web Site: http://www.devry.edu/
President/CEO: Dr. James W. Kho
Registrar: Deborah Crittendon
Financial Aid: Toi Kawaii
Type: Comprehensive **Sex:** Coed **Affiliation:** DeVry University **Admission Plans:** Deferred Admission **Application Deadline:** Rolling **Application Fee:** $50.00 **H.S. Requirements:** High school diploma required; GED accepted

Costs Per Year: Application fee: $50. One-time mandatory fee: $40. Tuition: $13,060 full-time, $475 per credit part-time. Mandatory fees: $270 full-time, $160 per year part-time. Full-time tuition and fees vary according to course load. Part-time tuition and fees vary according to course load. **Scholarships:** Available **Calendar System:** Semester, Summer Session Available **Enrollment:** FT 942, PT 506, Grad 132 **Faculty:** FT 46, PT 32 **Student-Faculty Ratio:** 21:1 **% Receiving Financial Aid:** 80 **Library Holdings:** 40,000 **Regional Accreditation:** North Central Association of Colleges and Schools **Credit Hours For Degree:** 67 credit hours, Associates; 122 credit hours, Bachelors **Professional Accreditation:** ABET

DEVRY UNIVERSITY (IRVINE)
3333 Michelson Dr., Ste. 420
Irvine, CA 92612-1682
Tel: (949)752-5631
Fax: (949)752-5637
Web Site: http://www.devry.edu/ **Type:** Comprehensive **Sex:** Coed **Costs Per Year:** One-time mandatory fee: $40. Tuition: $12,450 full-time, $460 per credit part-time. Mandatory fees: $60 full-time, $30 per year part-time. **Calendar System:** Semester **Regional Accreditation:** North Central Association of Colleges and Schools

DEVRY UNIVERSITY (LONG BEACH)
3880 Kilroy Airport Way
Long Beach, CA 90806
Tel: (562)427-0861
Free: 800-597-0444
Web Site: http://www.devry.edu/
President/CEO: Fardad Fateri
Registrar: Deborah Nelson
Financial Aid: Brenda Woods
Type: Comprehensive **Sex:** Coed **Affiliation:** DeVry University **Admission Plans:** Deferred Admission **Application Deadline:** Rolling **Application Fee:** $50.00 **H.S. Requirements:** High school diploma required; GED accepted **Costs Per Year:** Application fee: $50. One-time mandatory fee: $40. Tuition: $12,450 full-time, $460 per credit part-time. Mandatory fees: $270 full-time, $160 per year part-time. Full-time tuition and fees vary according to course load. Part-time tuition and fees vary according to course load. **Scholarships:** Available **Calendar System:** Semester, Summer Session Available **Enrollment:** FT 614, PT 409, Grad 178 **Faculty:** FT 27, PT 124 **Student-Faculty Ratio:** 12:1 **% Receiving Financial Aid:** 73 **Library Holdings:** 15,500 **Regional Accreditation:** North Central Association of Colleges and Schools **Credit Hours For Degree:** 66 credit hours, Associates; 122 credit hours, Bachelors **Professional Accreditation:** ABET

DEVRY UNIVERSITY (POMONA)
901 Corporate Center Dr.
Pomona, CA 91768-2642
Tel: (909)622-8866; (866)338-7934
Fax: (909)623-5666
Web Site: http://www.devry.edu/
President/CEO: Fardad Fatari
Registrar: Robert Boggs
Financial Aid: Kathy Odom
Type: Comprehensive **Sex:** Coed **Affiliation:** DeVry University **Admission Plans:** Deferred Admission **Application Deadline:** Rolling **Application Fee:** $50.00 **H.S. Requirements:** High school diploma required; GED accepted **Costs Per Year:** Application fee: $50. One-time mandatory fee: $40. Tuition: $12,450 full-time, $460 per credit part-time. Mandatory fees: $270 full-time, $160 per year part-time. Full-time tuition and fees vary according to course load. Part-time tuition and fees vary according to course load. **Scholarships:** Available **Calendar System:** Semester, Summer Session Available **Enrollment:** FT 956, PT 765, Grad 178 **Faculty:** FT 38, PT 42 **Student-Faculty Ratio:** 25:1 **% Receiving Financial Aid:** 76 **Library Holdings:** 17,000 **Regional Accreditation:** North Central Association of Colleges and Schools **Credit Hours For Degree:** 66 credit hours, Associates; 122 credit hours, Bachelors **Professional Accreditation:** ABET

DEVRY UNIVERSITY (SAN DIEGO)
2655 Camino Del Rio North, Ste. 201
San Diego, CA 92108-1633
Tel: (619)683-2446
Fax: (619)683-2448
Web Site: http://www.devry.edu/ **Type:** Comprehensive **Sex:** Coed **Costs Per Year:** One-time mandatory fee: $40. Tuition: $12,450 full-time, $460 per credit part-time. Mandatory fees: $60 full-time, $30 per year part-time. Full-time tuition and fees vary according to course load. Part-time tuition and fees vary according to course load. **Calendar System:** Semester **Regional Accreditation:** North Central Association of Colleges and Schools

DEVRY UNIVERSITY (SAN FRANCISCO)
455 Market St., Ste. 1650
San Francisco, CA 94105-2472
Tel: (415)243-8787
Fax: (415)243-8686
Web Site: http://www.devry.edu/ **Type:** Comprehensive **Sex:** Coed **Costs Per Year:** One-time mandatory fee: $40. Tuition: $13,060 full-time, $475 per credit part-time. Mandatory fees: $60 full-time, $30 per year part-time. Full-time tuition and fees vary according to course load. Part-time tuition and fees vary according to course load. **Calendar System:** Semester **Regional Accreditation:** North Central Association of Colleges and Schools

DEVRY UNIVERSITY (WEST HILLS)
22801 West Roscoe Blvd.
West Hills, CA 91304
Tel: (818)932-3001; 888-610-0800
Fax: (818)932-3091
Web Site: http://www.devry.edu/
President/CEO: Fardad Fateri
Registrar: Kimberly Duncan
Financial Aid: Ann Logan
Type: Comprehensive **Sex:** Coed **Affiliation:** DeVry University **Admission Plans:** Deferred Admission **Application Deadline:** Rolling **Application Fee:** $50.00 **H.S. Requirements:** High school diploma required; GED accepted **Costs Per Year:** Application fee: $50. One-time mandatory fee: $40. Tuition: $12,450 full-time, $460 per credit part-time. Mandatory fees: $270 full-time, $160 per year part-time. Full-time tuition and fees vary according to course load. Part-time tuition and fees vary according to course load. **Scholarships:** Available **Calendar System:** Semester, Summer Session Available **Enrollment:** FT 329, PT 342, Grad 98 **Faculty:** FT 17, PT 44 **Student-Faculty Ratio:** 16:1 **% Receiving Financial Aid:** 74 **Library Holdings:** 16,177 **Regional Accreditation:** North Central Association of Colleges and Schools **Credit Hours For Degree:** 66 credit hours, Associates; 122 credit hours, Bachelors **Professional Accreditation:** ABET

DIABLO VALLEY COLLEGE
321 Golf Club Rd.
Pleasant Hill, CA 94523-1544
Tel: (925)685-1230
Fax: (925)685-1551
Web Site: http://www.dvc.edu/
President/CEO: Dr. Mark Edelstein
Registrar: Catherine Fites-Chavis
Admissions: Judith Watkins
Financial Aid: Brenda Jerez
Type: Two-Year College **Sex:** Coed **Affiliation:** Contra Costa Community College District, part of California Community Colleges **Admission Plans:** Open Admission; Early Admission **Application Deadline:** August 15 **Application Fee:** $0.00 **H.S. Requirements:** High school diploma or equivalent not required. For applicants under 18: High school diploma required; GED accepted **Costs Per Year:** Application fee: $0. State resident tuition: $0 full-time. Nonresident tuition: $5190 full-time, $173 per unit part-time. Mandatory fees: $799 full-time, $26 per unit part-time, $19 per term part-time. **Scholarships:** Available **Calendar System:** Semester, Summer Session Available **Enrollment:** FT 6,848, PT 13,840 **Faculty:** FT 261, PT 570 **Student-Faculty Ratio:** 15:1 **Library Holdings:** 88,286 **Regional Accreditation:** Western Association of Schools and Colleges **Credit Hours For Degree:** 60 units, Associates **ROTC:** Air Force **Professional Accreditation:** ACF, ADA **Intercollegiate Athletics:** Basketball M & W; Cross-Country Running M & W; Football M; Soccer W; Softball W; Swimming and Diving M & W; Tennis M & W; Track and Field M & W; Volleyball W; Water Polo M & W

DOMINICAN SCHOOL OF PHILOSOPHY AND THEOLOGY
2301 Vine St.
Berkeley, CA 94708
Tel: (510)849-2030
Admissions: (510)883-2073

Web Site: http://www.dspt.edu/
President/CEO: Rev. Gregory Rocca, OP
Registrar: R. Scott Connolly
Admissions: Susan McGinnis Hardie
Financial Aid: R. Scott Connolly
Type: Two-Year Upper Division **Sex:** Coed **Affiliation:** Roman Catholic **Admission Plans:** Early Admission; Deferred Admission **Application Fee:** $30.00 **H.S. Requirements:** High school diploma required; GED accepted **Costs Per Year:** Application fee: $30. Tuition: $10,560 full-time, $440 per credit part-time. Mandatory fees: $50 full-time, $50 per year part-time. **Calendar System:** Semester, Summer Session Not available **Enrollment:** FT 11, PT 4, Grad 72 **Faculty:** FT 11, PT 9 **Student-Faculty Ratio:** 5:1 **% Residing in College-Owned, -Operated, or -Affiliated Housing:** 17 **Library Holdings:** 409,592 **Regional Accreditation:** Western Association of Schools and Colleges **Credit Hours For Degree:** 120 credits, Bachelors **Professional Accreditation:** ATS

DOMINICAN UNIVERSITY OF CALIFORNIA
50 Acacia Ave.
San Rafael, CA 94901-2298
Tel: (415)457-4440; 888-323-6763
Admissions: (415)485-3204
Fax: (415)485-3214
E-mail: enroll@dominican.edu
Web Site: http://www.dominican.edu/
President/CEO: Dr. Joseph R. Fink
Registrar: Marianne Stickel
Admissions: Art Criss
Financial Aid: Audrey Tanner
Type: Comprehensive **Sex:** Coed **Affiliation:** Roman Catholic Church **Scores:** 96.6% SAT V 400+; 94.8% SAT M 400+; 61.5% ACT 18-23; 23% ACT 24-29 **% Accepted:** 53 **Admission Plans:** Early Admission; Deferred Admission **Application Deadline:** August 01 **Application Fee:** $40.00 **H.S. Requirements:** High school diploma required; GED accepted **Costs Per Year:** Application fee: $40. Comprehensive fee: $39,370 includes full-time tuition ($27,770), mandatory fees ($300), and college room and board ($11,300). College room only: $6580. Part-time tuition: $1160 per unit. Part-time mandatory fees: $150 per term. **Scholarships:** Available **Calendar System:** Semester, Summer Session Available **Enrollment:** FT 1,058, PT 119, Grad 454 **Faculty:** FT 71, PT 216 **Student-Faculty Ratio:** 10:1 **Exams:** SAT I or ACT, SAT II **% Receiving Financial Aid:** 76 **% Residing in College-Owned, -Operated, or -Affiliated Housing:** 42 **Library Holdings:** 95,000 **Regional Accreditation:** Western Association of Schools and Colleges **Credit Hours For Degree:** 124 units, Bachelors **Professional Accreditation:** AACN, AOTA, NLN **Intercollegiate Athletics:** Basketball M & W; Cheerleading W; Soccer M & W; Softball W; Tennis M & W; Volleyball W

DON BOSCO TECHNICAL INSTITUTE
1151 San Gabriel Blvd.
Rosemead, CA 91770-4299
Tel: (626)940-2000
Fax: (626)940-2001
Web Site: http://www.boscotech.edu/
President/CEO: Rev. Carmine Vairo
Registrar: Bill Rice
Financial Aid: Bill Rice
Type: Two-Year College **Sex:** Coed **Affiliation:** Roman Catholic Church **Application Fee:** $25.00 **H.S. Requirements:** High school diploma required; GED accepted **Scholarships:** Available **Calendar System:** Semester, Summer Session Not available **Exams:** SAT I or ACT **Library Holdings:** 16,400 **Regional Accreditation:** Western Association of Schools and Colleges **Credit Hours For Degree:** 60 units, Associates

EAST LOS ANGELES COLLEGE
1301 Avenida Cesar Chavez
Monterey Park, CA 91754-6099
Tel: (323)265-8650
Admissions: (323)265-8801
Fax: (323)265-8763
Web Site: http://www.elac.edu/
President/CEO: Ernest H. Moreno
Registrar: Jeremy Allred
Admissions: Jeremy Allred
Financial Aid: Gene Willis
Type: Two-Year College **Sex:** Coed **Affiliation:** Los Angeles Community College District **Admission Plans:** Early Admission **Application Fee:** $0.00 **H.S. Requirements:** High school diploma or equivalent not required. For applicants under 18: High school diploma required; GED accepted **Scholarships:** Available **Calendar System:** Semester, Summer Session Not available **Enrollment:** FT 5,773, PT 18,242 **Faculty:** FT 245, PT 374 **Student-Faculty Ratio:** 34:1 **Library Holdings:** 102,000 **Regional Accreditation:** Western Association of Schools and Colleges **Credit Hours For Degree:** 60 units, Associates **Professional Accreditation:** AHIMA, CARC **Intercollegiate Athletics:** Baseball M; Basketball M; Football M; Golf M; Soccer M; Softball W; Swimming and Diving W; Track and Field M & W; Wrestling M

EL CAMINO COLLEGE
16007 Crenshaw Blvd.
Torrance, CA 90506-0001
Tel: (310)532-3670; (866)ELCAMINO
Admissions: (310)660-3418
Fax: (310)660-3818
Web Site: http://www.elcamino.edu/
President/CEO: Dr. Thomas Fallo
Registrar: William Mulrooney
Admissions: William Robinson
Financial Aid: Hortense Cooper
Type: Two-Year College **Sex:** Coed **Affiliation:** California Community College System **Admission Plans:** Open Admission; Early Admission **H.S. Requirements:** High school diploma or equivalent not required. For applicants under 18: High school diploma required; GED accepted **Calendar System:** Semester, Summer Session Available **Faculty:** FT 330, PT 203 **Library Holdings:** 116,051 **Regional Accreditation:** Western Association of Schools and Colleges **Credit Hours For Degree:** 60 units, Associates **Professional Accreditation:** CARC, JRCERT, NLN **Intercollegiate Athletics:** Baseball M; Basketball M & W; Cross-Country Running M & W; Football M; Golf M; Gymnastics W; Soccer M; Swimming and Diving M & W; Tennis M & W; Track and Field M & W; Volleyball M & W; Water Polo M; Wrestling M

EMMANUEL BIBLE COLLEGE
1605 East Elizabeth St.
Pasadena, CA 91104
Tel: (626)791-2575
Fax: (626)398-2424
Web Site: http://www.emmanuelbiblecollege.edu/
President/CEO: Dr. Yeghia Babikian
Admissions: Yeghia Babikian
Type: Four-Year College **Affiliation:** Church of the Nazarene **Admission Plans:** Open Admission; Early Admission **Application Fee:** $25.00 **Calendar System:** Quarter, Summer Session Not available **Enrollment:** FT 6, PT 14 **Faculty:** FT 1, PT 5 **Student-Faculty Ratio:** 10:1 **Library Holdings:** 15,000 **Credit Hours For Degree:** 96 credits, Associates; 192 credits, Bachelors **Professional Accreditation:** AABC

EMPIRE COLLEGE
3035 Cleveland Ave.
Santa Rosa, CA 95403
Tel: (707)546-4000
Fax: (707)546-4058
Web Site: http://www.empcol.com/
President/CEO: Roy O. Hurd
Registrar: Margareta Campbell
Admissions: Dahnja Barker
Financial Aid: Carol Worden
Type: Two-Year College **Sex:** Coed **Application Fee:** $75.00 **H.S. Requirements:** High school diploma required; GED accepted **Scholarships:** Available **Calendar System:** Continuous, Summer Session Not available **Enrollment:** FT 834 **Faculty:** FT 29, PT 17 **Student-Faculty Ratio:** 20:1 **Exams:** Other **Credit Hours For Degree:** 105 units, Associates **Professional Accreditation:** ACICS

EVEREST COLLEGE
9616 Archibald Ave., Ste. 100
Rancho Cucamonga, CA 91730
Tel: (909)484-4311
Web Site: http://www.everest-college.com/ **Type:** Two-Year College **Sex:**

Coed **Calendar System:** Miscellaneous **Professional Accreditation:** ACICS

EVERGREEN VALLEY COLLEGE
3095 Yerba Buena Rd.
San Jose, CA 95135-1598
Tel: (408)274-7900
Admissions: (408)270-6423
Fax: (408)223-9351
Web Site: http://www.evc.edu/
President/CEO: H. Clay Whitlow
Admissions: Kathleen Moberg
Financial Aid: Patricia Salazar-Robbins
Type: Two-Year College **Sex:** Coed **Affiliation:** California Community College System **% Accepted:** 100 **Admission Plans:** Open Admission; Early Admission **Application Deadline:** Rolling **H.S. Requirements:** High school diploma or equivalent not required. For applicants under 18: High school diploma required; GED accepted **Costs Per Year:** State resident tuition: $0 full-time. Nonresident tuition: $4872 full-time, $177 per unit part-time. Mandatory fees: $664 full-time, $26 per unit part-time. **Scholarships:** Available **Calendar System:** Semester, Summer Session Available **Enrollment:** FT 11,751 **Faculty:** FT 125, PT 176 **Library Holdings:** 42,782 **Regional Accreditation:** Western Association of Schools and Colleges **Credit Hours For Degree:** 60 units, Associates **ROTC:** Army **Professional Accreditation:** NLN **Intercollegiate Athletics:** Soccer M

FASHION CAREERS COLLEGE
1923 Morena Blvd.
San Diego, CA 92110
Tel: (619)275-4700; 888-FCCC999
Fax: (619)275-0635
E-mail: judy@fashioncareerscollege.com
Web Site: http://www.fashioncollege.com/
President/CEO: Patricia O'Connor
Registrar: Alesha Ballón
Admissions: Judith Thacker
Financial Aid: Tom Cutler
Type: Two-Year College **Sex:** Coed **% Accepted:** 100 **Application Deadline:** Rolling **Application Fee:** $25.00 **H.S. Requirements:** High school diploma required; GED accepted **Costs Per Year:** Application fee: $25. Tuition: $15,900 full-time, $400 per credit part-time. Mandatory fees: $325 full-time. **Scholarships:** Available **Calendar System:** Quarter, Summer Session Not available **Enrollment:** FT 101 **Faculty:** FT 0, PT 9 **Student-Faculty Ratio:** 32:1 **Exams:** Other **Library Holdings:** 800 **Credit Hours For Degree:** 90 credits, Associates **Professional Accreditation:** ACICS

FEATHER RIVER COLLEGE
570 Golden Eagle Ave.
Quincy, CA 95971-9124
Tel: (530)283-0202
Free: 800-442-9799
Fax: (530)283-3757
E-mail: info@frc.edu
Web Site: http://www.frc.edu/
President/CEO: Dr. Susan Carroll
Registrar: Connie West
Admissions: Karen Hayden
Financial Aid: Virginia Cokor
Type: Two-Year College **Sex:** Coed **Affiliation:** California Community College System **Admission Plans:** Open Admission **Application Fee:** $0.00 **H.S. Requirements:** High school diploma or equivalent not required **Costs Per Year:** Application fee: $0. State resident tuition: $0 full-time. Nonresident tuition: $5250 full-time, $175 per unit part-time. Mandatory fees: $806 full-time, $27 per unit part-time, $13 per term part-time. College room only: $3865. Room charges vary according to housing facility. **Scholarships:** Available **Calendar System:** Semester, Summer Session Available **Enrollment:** FT 732, PT 982 **Faculty:** FT 27, PT 66 **Student-Faculty Ratio:** 18:1 **% Residing in College-Owned, -Operated, or -Affiliated Housing:** 24 **Library Holdings:** 20,782 **Regional Accreditation:** Western Association of Schools and Colleges **Credit Hours For Degree:** 60 units, Associates **Intercollegiate Athletics:** Baseball M; Basketball M & W; Equestrian Sports M & W; Football M; Soccer M & W; Softball W

FIDM/THE FASHION INSTITUTE OF DESIGN & MERCHANDISING, LOS ANGELES CAMPUS
919 South Grand Ave.
Los Angeles, CA 90015-1421
Tel: (213)624-1200
Free: 800-624-1200
Fax: (213)624-4799
E-mail: info@fidm.com
Web Site: http://www.fidm.edu/
President/CEO: Tonian Hohberg
Registrar: Michael Gilbert
Admissions: Vivien Lowy
Financial Aid: Norinne Fuller
Type: Two-Year College **Sex:** Coed **Affiliation:** Fashion Institute of Design and Merchandising **Admission Plans:** Deferred Admission **Application Deadline:** Rolling **Application Fee:** $225.00 **H.S. Requirements:** High school diploma required; GED accepted **Costs Per Year:** Application fee: $225. Tuition: $17,415 full-time, $387 per unit part-time. Mandatory fees: $500 full-time. **Scholarships:** Available **Calendar System:** Quarter, Summer Session Available **Enrollment:** FT 2,778, PT 744 **Faculty:** FT 55, PT 158 **Student-Faculty Ratio:** 26:1 **Exams:** Other **Library Holdings:** 19,099 **Regional Accreditation:** Western Association of Schools and Colleges **Credit Hours For Degree:** 90 quarter hours, Associates **Professional Accreditation:** NASAD

FIDM/THE FASHION INSTITUTE OF DESIGN & MERCHANDISING, ORANGE COUNTY CAMPUS
17590 Gillette Ave.
Irvine, CA 92614-5610
Tel: (949)851-6200
Fax: (949)851-6808
Web Site: http://www.fidm.com/
Registrar: Michael Gilbert
Admissions: Michael Mirabella
Financial Aid: Norine Fuller
Type: Two-Year College **Sex:** Coed **Calendar System:** Quarter **Enrollment:** FT 320 **Student-Faculty Ratio:** 20:1 **Regional Accreditation:** Western Association of Schools and Colleges **Professional Accreditation:** NASAD

FIDM/THE FASHION INSTITUTE OF DESIGN & MERCHANDISING, SAN DIEGO CAMPUS
1010 Second Ave., Ste. 200
San Diego, CA 92101-4903
Tel: (619)235-2049
Free: 800-243-3436
Fax: (619)232-4322
E-mail: dbaca@fidm.com
Web Site: http://www.fidm.com/
Registrar: Mike Gilbert
Admissions: Denise Baca
Financial Aid: Matt Holland
Type: Two-Year College **Sex:** Coed **Affiliation:** Fashion Institute of Design and Merchandising **Admission Plans:** Deferred Admission **Application Deadline:** Rolling **Application Fee:** $225.00 **H.S. Requirements:** High school diploma required; GED accepted **Costs Per Year:** Application fee: $225. Tuition: $17,415 full-time, $387 per unit part-time. Mandatory fees: $500 full-time. **Calendar System:** Quarter, Summer Session Available **Enrollment:** FT 235, PT 37 **Faculty:** FT 3, PT 26 **Student-Faculty Ratio:** 20:1 **Library Holdings:** 2,642 **Regional Accreditation:** Western Association of Schools and Colleges **Credit Hours For Degree:** 90 units, Associates **Professional Accreditation:** NASAD

FIDM/THE FASHION INSTITUTE OF DESIGN & MERCHANDISING, SAN FRANCISCO CAMPUS
55 Stockton St.
San Francisco, CA 94108-5829
Tel: (415)675-5200
Free: 800-711-7175
Admissions: (415)433-6691
Fax: (415)296-7299

E-mail: info@fidm.com
Web Site: http://www.fidm.edu/
Registrar: Derek Seitz
Admissions: Sheryl Badalamente
Financial Aid: Ida Dilanchian
Type: Two-Year College **Sex:** Coed **Affiliation:** Fashion Institute of Design and Merchandising **Admission Plans:** Deferred Admission **Application Deadline:** Rolling **Application Fee:** $225.00 **H.S. Requirements:** High school diploma required; GED accepted **Costs Per Year:** Application fee: $225. Tuition: $17,415 full-time, $387 per unit part-time. **Calendar System:** Quarter, Summer Session Available **Enrollment:** FT 747, PT 189 **Faculty:** FT 14, PT 57 **Exams:** Other **Library Holdings:** 5,073 **Regional Accreditation:** Western Association of Schools and Colleges **Credit Hours For Degree:** 90 quarter hours, Associates **Professional Accreditation:** NASAD

FOLSOM LAKE COLLEGE
100 Scholar Way
Folsom, CA 95630
Tel: (916)608-6500
Web Site: http://www.flc.losrios.edu/ **Type:** Two-Year College **Sex:** Coed **Affiliation:** Los Rios Community College District **Faculty:** FT 74, PT 179

FOOTHILL COLLEGE
12345 El Monte Rd.
Los Altos Hills, CA 94022-4599
Tel: (650)949-7777
Admissions: (650)949-7326
Web Site: http://www.foothill.edu/
President/CEO: Dr. Bernadine Chuck Fong
Registrar: Penelope Johnson
Admissions: Penny Johnson
Financial Aid: Francis Gusman
Type: Two-Year College **Sex:** Coed **Affiliation:** Foothill-DeAnza Community College District **% Accepted:** 100 **Admission Plans:** Open Admission **Application Deadline:** September 15 **H.S. Requirements:** High school diploma or equivalent not required **Costs Per Year:** Nonresident tuition: $4500 full-time, $100 per unit part-time. Mandatory fees: $780 full-time, $17 per unit part-time, $28.50 per term part-time. **Scholarships:** Available **Calendar System:** Quarter, Summer Session Available **Faculty:** FT 196, PT 420 **Student-Faculty Ratio:** 28:1 **Library Holdings:** 70,000 **Regional Accreditation:** Western Association of Schools and Colleges **Credit Hours For Degree:** 90 quarter hours, Associates **ROTC:** Army, Air Force **Professional Accreditation:** ADA, CARC, JRCERT **Intercollegiate Athletics:** Basketball M & W; Football M; Golf M & W; Soccer M & W; Softball W; Swimming and Diving M & W; Tennis M; Volleyball W; Water Polo M & W

FOUNDATION COLLEGE
5353 Mission Center Rd., Ste. 100
San Diego, CA 92108-1306
Tel: (619)683-3273; 888-707-3273
Fax: (619)683-3224
Web Site: http://www.foundationcollege.org/
President/CEO: James L. Durbin, Jr.
Admissions: Peggy Aplin
Financial Aid: Patricia McKee
Type: Two-Year College **Sex:** Coed **H.S. Requirements:** High school diploma required; GED accepted **Costs Per Year:** Tuition: $17,940 full-time, $260 per credit part-time. Mandatory fees: $1200 full-time, $120 per course part-time. **Calendar System:** Continuous **Enrollment:** FT 106 **Faculty:** FT 10, PT 3 **Student-Faculty Ratio:** 8:1 **Professional Accreditation:** ACCSCT

FRESNO CITY COLLEGE
1101 East University Ave.
Fresno, CA 93741-0002
Tel: (559)442-4600
Admissions: (559)442-8217
Web Site: http://www.fresnocitycollege.com/
President/CEO: Dr. Ned Doffoney
Registrar: Doris Griffin
Admissions: John H. Cummings
Type: Two-Year College **Sex:** Coed **Affiliation:** California Community College System **Admission Plans:** Open Admission; Early Admission; Deferred Admission **Application Fee:** $0.00 **H.S. Requirements:** High school diploma or equivalent not required. For applicants under 18: High school diploma required; GED accepted **Scholarships:** Available **Calendar System:** Semester, Summer Session Available **Faculty:** FT 276, PT 1,200 **Student-Faculty Ratio:** 16:1 **Exams:** Other **Library Holdings:** 67,500 **Regional Accreditation:** Western Association of Schools and Colleges **Credit Hours For Degree:** 60 units, Associates **ROTC:** Army, Air Force **Professional Accreditation:** ADA, AHIMA, CARC, JRCERT **Intercollegiate Athletics:** Baseball M; Basketball M & W; Cross-Country Running M & W; Football M; Golf M & W; Soccer M & W; Softball W; Tennis M & W; Track and Field M & W; Volleyball W; Wrestling M

FRESNO PACIFIC UNIVERSITY
1717 South Chestnut Ave.
Fresno, CA 93702-4709
Tel: (559)453-2000
Admissions: (559)453-2030
Fax: (559)453-2007
E-mail: cwtemple@fresno.edu
Web Site: http://www.fresno.edu/
President/CEO: Dr. D. Merrill Ewert
Registrar: Dr. Norman Rempel
Admissions: Cary Templeton
Financial Aid: Korey Compaan
Type: Comprehensive **Sex:** Coed **Affiliation:** Mennonite Brethren Church **Scores:** 90.3% SAT V 400+; 90.1% SAT M 400+; 49.5% ACT 18-23; 20.7% ACT 24-29 **% Accepted:** 68 **Admission Plans:** Early Admission; Deferred Admission **Application Deadline:** Rolling **Application Fee:** $40.00 **H.S. Requirements:** High school diploma required; GED accepted **Costs Per Year:** Application fee: $40. Comprehensive fee: $26,780 includes full-time tuition ($20,550), mandatory fees ($240), and college room and board ($5990). Part-time tuition: $735 per unit. **Scholarships:** Available **Calendar System:** Semester, Summer Session Available **Enrollment:** FT 1,319, PT 173, Grad 879 **Faculty:** FT 81, PT 117 **Student-Faculty Ratio:** 16:1 **Exams:** SAT I and SAT II or ACT **% Receiving Financial Aid:** 80 **% Residing in College-Owned, -Operated, or -Affiliated Housing:** 53 **Library Holdings:** 181,020 **Regional Accreditation:** Western Association of Schools and Colleges **Credit Hours For Degree:** 60 units, Associates; 124 units, Bachelors **Intercollegiate Athletics:** Baseball M; Basketball M & W; Cross-Country Running M & W; Soccer M & W; Tennis M & W; Track and Field M & W; Volleyball M & W

FULLERTON COLLEGE
321 East Chapman Ave.
Fullerton, CA 92832-2095
Tel: (714)992-7000
Admissions: (714)992-7582
Web Site: http://www.fullcoll.edu/
President/CEO: Sam Schauerman
Registrar: Kristeen Burns
Admissions: Peter Fong
Financial Aid: Robert Miranda
Type: Two-Year College **Sex:** Coed **Affiliation:** California Community College System **Admission Plans:** Open Admission; Early Admission **H.S. Requirements:** High school diploma or equivalent not required **Scholarships:** Available **Calendar System:** Semester, Summer Session Available **Faculty:** FT 324, PT 511 **Library Holdings:** 113,236 **Regional Accreditation:** Western Association of Schools and Colleges **Credit Hours For Degree:** 60 semester hours, Associates **ROTC:** Army, Navy, Air Force **Intercollegiate Athletics:** Basketball M & W; Cross-Country Running M & W; Football M; Golf M & W; Soccer M; Swimming and Diving M & W; Tennis M & W; Track and Field M & W; Volleyball W; Water Polo M

GAVILAN COLLEGE
5055 Santa Teresa Blvd.
Gilroy, CA 95020-9599
Tel: (408)847-1400
Admissions: (408)848-4735
Fax: (408)848-4801
E-mail: jparker@gavilan.edu
Web Site: http://www.gavilan.edu/
President/CEO: Dr. Rose Marie Joyce
Registrar: Joy Parker
Admissions: Joy Parker
Financial Aid: Audrea Morris

Type: Two-Year College **Sex:** Coed **Affiliation:** California Community College System **Admission Plans:** Open Admission **Application Deadline:** Rolling **Application Fee:** $0.00 **H.S. Requirements:** High school diploma required; GED accepted. For applicants 18 or over: High school diploma or equivalent not required **Costs Per Year:** Application fee: $0. State resident tuition: $0 full-time. Nonresident tuition: $4800 full-time. Mandatory fees: $676 full-time, $26. **Scholarships:** Available **Calendar System:** Semester, Summer Session Available **Enrollment:** FT 1,212, PT 4,852 **Faculty:** FT 74, PT 90 **Library Holdings:** 55,440 **Regional Accreditation:** Western Association of Schools and Colleges **Credit Hours For Degree:** 60 units, Associates **Intercollegiate Athletics:** Baseball W; Basketball M & W; Football M; Golf M; Soccer M & W; Softball W; Tennis M; Volleyball W

GLENDALE COMMUNITY COLLEGE
1500 North Verdugo Rd.
Glendale, CA 91208-2894
Tel: (818)240-1000
Admissions: (818)551-5115
Fax: (818)549-9436
Web Site: http://www.glendale.edu/
President/CEO: Dr. John A. Davitt
Registrar: Michelle Mora
Admissions: Sharon Combs
Financial Aid: Patricia Hurley
Type: Two-Year College **Sex:** Coed **Affiliation:** California Community College System **% Accepted:** 52 **Admission Plans:** Open Admission; Early Admission; Deferred Admission **Application Deadline:** Rolling **Application Fee:** $0.00 **H.S. Requirements:** High school diploma required; GED accepted. For applicants 18 or older: High school diploma or equivalent not required **Costs Per Year:** Application fee: $0. State resident tuition: $0 full-time. Nonresident tuition: $4280 full-time, $150 per unit part-time. Mandatory fees: $680 full-time, $26 per unit part-time, $170 per term part-time. **Scholarships:** Available **Calendar System:** Semester, Summer Session Available **Enrollment:** FT 4,730, PT 9,535 **Faculty:** FT 249, PT 605 **Exams:** Other **Library Holdings:** 91,371 **Regional Accreditation:** Western Association of Schools and Colleges **Credit Hours For Degree:** 60 units, Associates **Intercollegiate Athletics:** Baseball M; Basketball M & W; Cross-Country Running M & W; Football M; Soccer M & W; Softball W; Tennis M & W; Track and Field M & W; Volleyball W

GOLDEN GATE UNIVERSITY
536 Mission St.
San Francisco, CA 94105-2968
Tel: (415)442-7000
Free: 800-448-4968
Admissions: (415)442-7800
Fax: (415)442-7807
E-mail: info@ggu.edu
Web Site: http://www.ggu.edu/
President/CEO: Dr. Philip Friedman
Admissions: Cherron Hoppes
Financial Aid: Jerra Chang
Type: University **Sex:** Coed **Admission Plans:** Deferred Admission **Application Deadline:** Rolling **Application Fee:** $55.00 **H.S. Requirements:** High school diploma required; GED accepted **Costs Per Year:** Application fee: $55. Tuition: $11,520 full-time, $1440 per course part-time. **Scholarships:** Available **Calendar System:** Trimester, Summer Session Available **Enrollment:** FT 135, PT 432, Grad 2,291 **Faculty:** FT 30, PT 459 **Student-Faculty Ratio:** 16:1 **% Receiving Financial Aid:** 66 **Library Holdings:** 79,204 **Regional Accreditation:** Western Association of Schools and Colleges **Credit Hours For Degree:** 123 units, Bachelors **Professional Accreditation:** ABA, AALS

GOLDEN WEST COLLEGE
PO Box 2748, 15744 Golden West St.
Huntington Beach, CA 92647-2748
Tel: (714)892-7711
Web Site: http://www.gwc.cccd.edu/
President/CEO: Dr. Kenneth D. Yglesias
Registrar: Connie Olson
Admissions: Shirley Donnelly
Financial Aid: Juan Cepeda
Type: Two-Year College **Sex:** Coed **Affiliation:** Coast Community College District System **Admission Plans:** Open Admission; Early Admission **Application Fee:** $0.00 **H.S. Requirements:** High school diploma required; GED accepted. For applicants 18 or over: High school diploma or equivalent not required **Costs Per Year:** Application fee: $0. State resident tuition: $0 full-time. Nonresident tuition: $5034 full-time, $152 per unit part-time. Mandatory fees: $778 full-time, $26 per unit part-time. **Scholarships:** Available **Calendar System:** Semester, Summer Session Available **Enrollment:** FT 4,244, PT 8,847 **Faculty:** FT 194, PT 246 **Student-Faculty Ratio:** 32:1 **Exams:** Other **Library Holdings:** 95,000 **Regional Accreditation:** Western Association of Schools and Colleges **Credit Hours For Degree:** 60 units, Associates **ROTC:** Air Force **Professional Accreditation:** NLN **Intercollegiate Athletics:** Baseball M; Basketball M & W; Cross-Country Running M & W; Football M; Golf M & W; Soccer M & W; Softball W; Swimming and Diving M & W; Tennis M & W; Track and Field M & W; Volleyball M & W; Water Polo M & W; Wrestling M

GROSSMONT COLLEGE
8800 Grossmont College Dr.
El Cajon, CA 92020-1799
Tel: (619)644-7000
Admissions: (619)644-7188
Fax: (619)644-7922
Web Site: http://www.grossmont.edu/
President/CEO: Dr. Ted Martinez, Jr.
Registrar: Brad Tiffany
Admissions: Brad Tiffany
Financial Aid: Susan Lipsmeyer
Type: Two-Year College **Sex:** Coed **Affiliation:** California Community College System **Admission Plans:** Open Admission; Early Admission **Application Fee:** $0.00 **H.S. Requirements:** High school diploma or equivalent not required. For applicants under 18: High school diploma required; GED accepted **Scholarships:** Available **Calendar System:** Semester, Summer Session Available **Faculty:** FT 220, PT 574 **Student-Faculty Ratio:** 17:1 **Exams:** Other **Library Holdings:** 105,000 **Regional Accreditation:** Western Association of Schools and Colleges **Credit Hours For Degree:** 60 units, Associates **ROTC:** Army, Air Force **Professional Accreditation:** AOTA, CARC, JRCECT, NLN **Intercollegiate Athletics:** Baseball M; Basketball M & W; Cross-Country Running M; Football M; Golf M; Soccer W; Softball W; Swimming and Diving M & W; Tennis M & W; Track and Field M; Volleyball M & W; Water Polo M & W

HARTNELL COLLEGE
156 Homestead Ave.
Salinas, CA 93901-1697
Tel: (831)755-6700
Admissions: (831)755-6711
Web Site: http://www.hartnell.edu/
President/CEO: Dr. Edward J. Valeau
Registrar: Dr. Celia Barberena
Admissions: Mary Dominguez
Financial Aid: MaryHelen Dorado
Type: Two-Year College **Sex:** Coed **Affiliation:** California Community College System **Admission Plans:** Open Admission; Early Admission; Deferred Admission **Application Fee:** $0.00 **H.S. Requirements:** High school diploma required; GED accepted **Scholarships:** Available **Calendar System:** Semester, Summer Session Available **Faculty:** FT 105, PT 273 **Library Holdings:** 70,000 **Regional Accreditation:** Western Association of Schools and Colleges **Credit Hours For Degree:** 60 semester hours, Associates **Professional Accreditation:** NAACLS **Intercollegiate Athletics:** Baseball M; Basketball M & W; Cross-Country Running M & W; Football M; Golf M; Soccer M & W; Softball W; Swimming and Diving M & W; Tennis M & W; Track and Field M & W; Volleyball W; Water Polo M

HARVEY MUDD COLLEGE
301 East 12th St.
Claremont, CA 91711-5994
Tel: (909)621-8000
Admissions: (909)621-8011
Fax: (909)621-8360
E-mail: admission@hmc.edu
Web Site: http://www.hmc.edu/
President/CEO: Dr. Jon C. Strauss
Registrar: Michael Hearon
Admissions: Youlonda Copeland-Morgan
Financial Aid: Youlonda Copeland-Morgan
Type: Four-Year College **Sex:** Coed **Affiliation:** The Claremont Colleges Consortium **Scores:** 100% SAT V 400+; 100% SAT M 400+ **% Accepted:**

36 **Admission Plans:** Early Decision Plan; Deferred Admission **Application Deadline:** January 15 **Application Fee:** $50.00 **H.S. Requirements:** High school diploma required; GED accepted **Costs Per Year:** Application fee: $50. Comprehensive fee: $42,352 includes full-time tuition ($31,738), mandatory fees ($202), and college room and board ($10,412). College room only: $5282. Room and board charges vary according to board plan. **Scholarships:** Available **Calendar System:** Semester, Summer Session Not available **Enrollment:** FT 743 **Faculty:** FT 79, PT 14 **Student-Faculty Ratio:** 8:1 **Exams:** Other, SAT I and SAT II **% Receiving Financial Aid:** 53 **% Residing in College-Owned, -Operated, or -Affiliated Housing:** 97 **Library Holdings:** 3,203,500 **Regional Accreditation:** Western Association of Schools and Colleges **Credit Hours For Degree:** 128 credit hours, Bachelors **ROTC:** Army, Air Force **Professional Accreditation:** ABET **Intercollegiate Athletics:** Baseball M; Basketball M & W; Cross-Country Running M & W; Football M; Golf M; Lacrosse W; Soccer M & W; Softball W; Swimming and Diving M & W; Tennis M & W; Track and Field M & W; Volleyball W; Water Polo M & W

HEALD COLLEGE-CONCORD
5130 Commercial Circle
Concord, CA 94520
Tel: (925)288-5800
Fax: (925)288-5896
Web Site: http://www.heald.edu/
President/CEO: Doug Cole
Registrar: Cheryl Brandt
Financial Aid: Kathleen Haugh
Type: Two-Year College **Sex:** Coed **Admission Plans:** Open Admission; Early Admission; Deferred Admission **Application Deadline:** Rolling **Application Fee:** $40.00 **H.S. Requirements:** High school diploma required; GED accepted **Calendar System:** Quarter, Summer Session Available **Enrollment:** FT 524, PT 115 **Faculty:** FT 25, PT 19 **Student-Faculty Ratio:** 18:1 **Exams:** Other **Regional Accreditation:** Western Association of Schools and Colleges

HEALD COLLEGE-FRESNO
255 West Bullard Ave.
Fresno, CA 93704-1706
Tel: (559)438-4222
Web Site: http://www.heald.edu/
President/CEO: Carolyn Kovalski
Registrar: Sylvia Garza
Financial Aid: Theresa Costa
Type: Two-Year College **Sex:** Coed **Admission Plans:** Open Admission; Early Admission; Deferred Admission **Application Deadline:** Rolling **Application Fee:** $40.00 **H.S. Requirements:** High school diploma required; GED accepted **Scholarships:** Available **Calendar System:** Quarter, Summer Session Available **Enrollment:** FT 547, PT 182 **Faculty:** FT 26, PT 12 **Student-Faculty Ratio:** 20:1 **Exams:** Other **Regional Accreditation:** Western Association of Schools and Colleges

HEALD COLLEGE-HAYWARD
25500 Industrial Blvd.
Hayward, CA 94545
Tel: (510)783-2100
Fax: (510)783-3287
Web Site: http://www.heald.edu/
President/CEO: Barbara Gordon
Registrar: Jan Jones
Financial Aid: Belinda Bauer
Type: Two-Year College **Sex:** Coed **Admission Plans:** Open Admission; Early Admission; Deferred Admission **Application Deadline:** Rolling **Application Fee:** $40.00 **H.S. Requirements:** High school diploma required; GED accepted **Scholarships:** Available **Calendar System:** Quarter, Summer Session Available **Enrollment:** FT 637, PT 227 **Faculty:** FT 23, PT 13 **Student-Faculty Ratio:** 26:1 **Exams:** Other **Regional Accreditation:** Western Association of Schools and Colleges

HEALD COLLEGE-RANCHO CORDOVA
2910 Prospect Park Dr.
Rancho Cordova, CA 95670-6005
Tel: (916)638-1616
Fax: (916)853-8282
Web Site: http://www.heald.edu/
President/CEO: Donald E. Hardenbrook
Registrar: Tricia Mahon
Financial Aid: Rhonda Shaw
Type: Two-Year College **Sex:** Coed **Admission Plans:** Open Admission; Early Admission; Deferred Admission **Application Deadline:** Rolling **Application Fee:** $40.00 **H.S. Requirements:** High school diploma required; GED accepted **Scholarships:** Available **Calendar System:** Quarter, Summer Session Available **Enrollment:** FT 349, PT 122 **Faculty:** FT 19, PT 3 **Student-Faculty Ratio:** 20:1 **Exams:** Other **Regional Accreditation:** Western Association of Schools and Colleges

HEALD COLLEGE-ROSEVILLE
Seven Sierra Gate Plaza
Roseville, CA 95678
Tel: (916)789-8600
Web Site: http://www.heald.edu/
President/CEO: Donald E. Hardenbrook
Financial Aid: Rhonda Shaw
Type: Two-Year College **Sex:** Coed **Admission Plans:** Early Admission; Deferred Admission **Application Fee:** $40.00 **H.S. Requirements:** High school diploma required; GED accepted **Scholarships:** Available **Calendar System:** Quarter, Summer Session Available **Enrollment:** FT 376, PT 152 **Faculty:** FT 21, PT 2 **Student-Faculty Ratio:** 19:1 **Exams:** Other **Regional Accreditation:** Western Association of Schools and Colleges

HEALD COLLEGE-SALINAS
1450 North Main St.
Salinas, CA 93906
Tel: (831)443-1700
Fax: (831)443-1050
Web Site: http://www.heald.edu/
President/CEO: Michael Burton
Type: Two-Year College **Sex:** Coed **Admission Plans:** Open Admission; Early Admission; Deferred Admission **Application Deadline:** Rolling **Application Fee:** $40.00 **H.S. Requirements:** High school diploma required; GED accepted **Calendar System:** Quarter, Summer Session Available **Enrollment:** FT 329, PT 85 **Faculty:** FT 14, PT 4 **Student-Faculty Ratio:** 24:1 **Exams:** Other **Regional Accreditation:** Western Association of Schools and Colleges

HEALD COLLEGE-SAN FRANCISCO
350 Mission St.
San Francisco, CA 94105-2206
Tel: (415)808-3000
Fax: (415)808-3003
Web Site: http://www.heald.edu/
President/CEO: Ada Gerard
Financial Aid: Cihl Loggins
Type: Two-Year College **Sex:** Coed **Admission Plans:** Open Admission; Early Admission; Deferred Admission **Application Deadline:** Rolling **Application Fee:** $40.00 **H.S. Requirements:** High school diploma required; GED accepted **Calendar System:** Quarter, Summer Session Available **Enrollment:** FT 273, PT 116 **Faculty:** FT 18, PT 6 **Student-Faculty Ratio:** 16:1 **Exams:** Other **Regional Accreditation:** Western Association of Schools and Colleges

HEALD COLLEGE-SAN JOSE
341 Great Mall Parkway
Milpitas, CA 95035
Tel: (408)934-4900
Fax: (408)934-7777
Web Site: http://www.heald.edu/
President/CEO: John Luotto
Registrar: Cathy Souza
Financial Aid: Diane Setlock
Type: Two-Year College **Sex:** Coed **Admission Plans:** Open Admission; Early Admission; Deferred Admission **Application Deadline:** Rolling **Application Fee:** $40.00 **H.S. Requirements:** High school diploma required; GED accepted **Scholarships:** Available **Calendar System:** Quarter, Summer Session Available **Enrollment:** FT 502, PT 137 **Faculty:** FT 25, PT 7 **Student-Faculty Ratio:** 20:1 **Exams:** Other **Regional Accreditation:** Western Association of Schools and Colleges

HEALD COLLEGE-STOCKTON
1605 East March Ln.
Stockton, CA 95210

Tel: (209)473-5200
Fax: (209)477-2739
Web Site: http://www.heald.edu/
President/CEO: Michael Mallory
Financial Aid: Jim Cordero
Type: Two-Year College **Sex:** Coed **Admission Plans:** Open Admission; Early Admission; Deferred Admission **Application Deadline:** Rolling **Application Fee:** $40.00 **H.S. Requirements:** High school diploma required; GED accepted **Calendar System:** Quarter, Summer Session Available **Enrollment:** FT 398, PT 132 **Faculty:** FT 20, PT 17 **Student-Faculty Ratio:** 17:1 **Exams:** Other **Regional Accreditation:** Western Association of Schools and Colleges

HIGH-TECH INSTITUTE

1111 Howe Ave., No. 250
Sacramento, CA 95825
Tel: (916)929-9700
Free: 800-987-0110
Fax: (916)929-9703
E-mail: rdyer@hightechschools.com
Web Site: http://www.high-techinstitute.com/
President/CEO: Gordon Kent
Admissions: Richard Dyer
Type: Two-Year College **Sex:** Coed **Professional Accreditation:** ACCSCT

HOLY NAMES UNIVERSITY

3500 Mountain Blvd.
Oakland, CA 94619-1699
Tel: (510)436-1000
Free: 800-430-1321
Admissions: (510)436-1351
Fax: (510)436-1325
E-mail: admissions@hnu.edu
Web Site: http://www.hnu.edu/
President/CEO: Dr. Rosemarie T. Nassif
Registrar: Jeanette Calixto
Admissions: Lonnie R. Morris, Jr.
Financial Aid: Loretta Williams
Type: Comprehensive **Sex:** Coed **Affiliation:** Roman Catholic **Scores:** 100% SAT V 400+; 96% SAT M 400+; 78% ACT 18-23; 11% ACT 24-29 **% Accepted:** 64 **Admission Plans:** Deferred Admission **Application Deadline:** August 01 **Application Fee:** $50.00 **H.S. Requirements:** High school diploma required; GED accepted **Costs Per Year:** Application fee: $50. Tuition: $22,470 full-time. Mandatory fees: $240 full-time. **Scholarships:** Available **Calendar System:** Semester, Summer Session Available **Enrollment:** FT 465, PT 221, Grad 407 **Faculty:** FT 34, PT 106 **Student-Faculty Ratio:** 13:1 **Exams:** SAT I or ACT **% Receiving Financial Aid:** 82 **% Residing in College-Owned, -Operated, or -Affiliated Housing:** 30 **Library Holdings:** 111,243 **Regional Accreditation:** Western Association of Schools and Colleges **Credit Hours For Degree:** 120 units, Bachelors **ROTC:** Army, Air Force **Professional Accreditation:** AACN, NLN **Intercollegiate Athletics:** Basketball M & W; Cross-Country Running M & W; Golf M; Soccer M & W; Volleyball M & W

HOPE INTERNATIONAL UNIVERSITY

2500 East Nutwood Ave.
Fullerton, CA 92831-3138
Tel: (714)879-3901
Free: 800-762-1294
Fax: (714)526-0231
Web Site: http://www.hiu.edu/
President/CEO: John Derry
Registrar: Michael Boon
Admissions: Butch Ellis
Financial Aid: Mai Bui
Type: Comprehensive **Sex:** Coed **Affiliation:** Christian Churches and Churches of Christ **Admission Plans:** Early Admission; Deferred Admission **Application Deadline:** June 01 **Application Fee:** $40.00 **H.S. Requirements:** High school diploma required; GED accepted **Costs Per Year:** Application fee: $40. Comprehensive fee: $24,000 includes full-time tuition ($17,700), mandatory fees ($300), and college room and board ($6000). College room only: $3300. Full-time tuition and fees vary according to program. Room and board charges vary according to board plan. Part-time tuition: $655 per unit. Part-time tuition varies according to program. **Scholarships:** Available **Calendar System:** 4-1-4, Summer Session Available **Enrollment:** FT 646, PT 211, Grad 279 **Faculty:** FT 27, PT 184 **Student-Faculty Ratio:** 10:1 **Exams:** SAT I or ACT, SAT I **% Receiving Financial Aid:** 84 **% Residing in College-Owned, -Operated, or -Affiliated Housing:** 75 **Library Holdings:** 100,000 **Regional Accreditation:** Western Association of Schools and Colleges **Credit Hours For Degree:** 62 units, Associates; 124 units, Bachelors **Intercollegiate Athletics:** Basketball M & W; Cheerleading M & W; Soccer M & W; Softball W; Tennis M & W; Volleyball M & W

HUMBOLDT STATE UNIVERSITY

1 Harpst St.
Arcata, CA 95521-8299
Tel: (707)826-3011
Admissions: (707)826-6220
Fax: (707)826-6194
E-mail: hsuinfo@humboldt.edu
Web Site: http://www.humboldt.edu/
President/CEO: Dr. Rollin C. Richmond
Registrar: Linda Phillips
Admissions: Linda Phillips
Type: Comprehensive **Sex:** Coed **Affiliation:** California State University System **Scores:** 91.5% SAT V 400+; 93.2% SAT M 400+; 48.2% ACT 18-23; 32.1% ACT 24-29 **Admission Plans:** Preferred Admission **Application Fee:** $55.00 **H.S. Requirements:** High school diploma required; GED accepted **Scholarships:** Available **Calendar System:** Semester, Summer Session Available **Enrollment:** FT 5,899, PT 630, Grad 1,021 **Faculty:** FT 287, PT 203 **Student-Faculty Ratio:** 18:1 **Exams:** SAT I or ACT **% Receiving Financial Aid:** 54 **% Residing in College-Owned, -Operated, or -Affiliated Housing:** 20 **Library Holdings:** 585,386 **Regional Accreditation:** Western Association of Schools and Colleges **Credit Hours For Degree:** 124 semester units, Bachelors **Professional Accreditation:** ABET, AACN, CSWE, NASAD, NASM, NAST, SAF **Intercollegiate Athletics:** Basketball M & W; Crew M & W; Cross-Country Running M & W; Football M; Lacrosse M & W; Rugby M & W; Soccer M & W; Softball W; Track and Field M & W; Volleyball M & W

HUMPHREYS COLLEGE

6650 Inglewood Ave.
Stockton, CA 95207-3896
Tel: (209)478-0800
Fax: (209)478-8721
Web Site: http://www.humphreys.edu/
President/CEO: Dr. Robert G. Humphreys
Registrar: Maria Garcia
Admissions: Wilma Okamoto Vaughn
Financial Aid: Judi Johnston
Type: Comprehensive **Sex:** Coed **Admission Plans:** Open Admission; Early Admission; Deferred Admission **Application Fee:** $20.00 **H.S. Requirements:** High school diploma required; GED accepted **Scholarships:** Available **Calendar System:** Quarter, Summer Session Available **Faculty:** FT 22, PT 48 **Exams:** SAT I and SAT II or ACT **% Receiving Financial Aid:** 89 **% Residing in College-Owned, -Operated, or -Affiliated Housing:** 6 **Library Holdings:** 20,500 **Regional Accreditation:** Western Association of Schools and Colleges **Credit Hours For Degree:** 90 units, Associates; 180 units, Bachelors

IMPERIAL VALLEY COLLEGE

380 East Aten Rd.
PO Box 158
Imperial, CA 92251-0158
Tel: (760)352-8320
Web Site: http://www.imperial.cc.ca.us/
President/CEO: Dr. Paul Pai
Registrar: Kathie Westerfield
Admissions: Sandra Standiford
Financial Aid: Jan Magno
Type: Two-Year College **Sex:** Coed **Affiliation:** California Community College System **Admission Plans:** Open Admission **Application Fee:** $0.00 **H.S. Requirements:** High school diploma or equivalent not required **Scholarships:** Available **Calendar System:** Semester, Summer Session Available **Library Holdings:** 55,875 **Regional Accreditation:** Western As-

sociation of Schools and Colleges **Credit Hours For Degree:** 60 units, Associates **Intercollegiate Athletics:** Baseball M; Basketball M & W; Soccer M & W; Softball W; Tennis M & W

INSTITUTE OF COMPUTER TECHNOLOGY
3200 Wilshire Blvd., No. 400
Los Angeles, CA 90010-1308
Tel: (213)381-3333
Fax: (213)383-9369
Web Site: http://www.ictcollege.edu/
President/CEO: Dr. K. C. You, PhD
Admissions: Randy Taylor
Financial Aid: Janice Hu
Type: Four-Year College **Sex:** Coed **Admission Plans:** Open Admission **Application Fee:** $75.00 **H.S. Requirements:** High school diploma required; GED accepted **Scholarships:** Available **Calendar System:** Quarter, Summer Session Not available **Enrollment:** FT 286 **Faculty:** PT 25 **Student-Faculty Ratio:** 21:1 **Exams:** Other **Library Holdings:** 2,000 **Professional Accreditation:** ACICS

INTERIOR DESIGNERS INSTITUTE
1061 Camelback Rd.
Newport Beach, CA 92660
Tel: (949)675-4451
Fax: (949)759-0667
Web Site: http://www.idi.edu/
President/CEO: Judy Deaton
Financial Aid: Sharon Deaton
Type: Four-Year College **Professional Accreditation:** ACCSCT, FIDER

INTERNATIONAL TECHNOLOGICAL UNIVERSITY
1650 Warburton Ave.
Santa Clara, CA 95050
Tel: (408)556-9010
Admissions: (408)556-9027
Fax: (408)556-9016
Web Site: http://www.itu.edu/
President/CEO: Shu-Park Chan
Registrar: Gordon Turner
Admissions: Chun Mou Peng
Type: Two-Year Upper Division **Sex:** Coed **Admission Plans:** Open Admission **H.S. Requirements:** High school diploma required; GED accepted **Calendar System:** Trimester **Enrollment:** FT 28, PT 12, Grad 120 **Faculty:** FT 5, PT 35 **Student-Faculty Ratio:** 6:1 **Library Holdings:** 1,200 **Credit Hours For Degree:** 60 per semester, Bachelors **Professional Accreditation:** ACICS

IRVINE VALLEY COLLEGE
5500 Irvine Center Dr.
Irvine, CA 92618
Tel: (949)451-5100
Admissions: (949)451-5416
Fax: (949)559-3443
Web Site: http://www.ivc.edu/
President/CEO: Dr. Glenn Roquemore
Registrar: Jess Craig
Admissions: John Edwards
Financial Aid: Darryl Cox
Type: Two-Year College **Sex:** Coed **Affiliation:** Saddleback Community College District **Admission Plans:** Open Admission; Early Admission **Application Fee:** $0.00 **H.S. Requirements:** High school diploma or equivalent not required **Scholarships:** Available **Calendar System:** Semester, Summer Session Available **Faculty:** FT 94, PT 250 **Library Holdings:** 24,000 **Regional Accreditation:** Western Association of Schools and Colleges **Credit Hours For Degree:** 60 units, Associates **Intercollegiate Athletics:** Basketball M & W; Cross-Country Running M & W; Soccer M & W; Tennis M & W; Volleyball M

ITT TECHNICAL INSTITUTE (ANAHEIM)
525 North Muller St.
Anaheim, CA 92801-9938
Tel: (714)535-3700
Web Site: http://www.itt-tech.edu/
President/CEO: Louis E. Osborn
Registrar: Timothy J. Mayo
Admissions: Louis Osborn
Financial Aid: Janice Richards
Type: Two-Year College **Sex:** Coed **Affiliation:** ITT Educational Services, Inc **Admission Plans:** Deferred Admission **Application Deadline:** Rolling **Application Fee:** $100.00 **H.S. Requirements:** High school diploma required; GED accepted **Costs Per Year:** Application fee: $100. **Scholarships:** Available **Calendar System:** Quarter, Summer Session Not available **Exams:** Other **Credit Hours For Degree:** 96 credit hours, Associates; 180 credit hours, Bachelors **Professional Accreditation:** ACICS

ITT TECHNICAL INSTITUTE (LATHROP)
16916 South Harlan Rd.
Lathrop, CA 95330
Tel: (209)858-0077
Web Site: http://www.itt-tech.edu/
President/CEO: David Parker
Admissions: Don Fraser
Type: Two-Year College **Sex:** Coed **Affiliation:** ITT Educational Services **Admission Plans:** Deferred Admission **Application Deadline:** Rolling **Application Fee:** $100.00 **H.S. Requirements:** High school diploma required; GED accepted **Costs Per Year:** Application fee: $100. **Scholarships:** Available **Calendar System:** Quarter, Summer Session Not available **Exams:** Other **Credit Hours For Degree:** 96 credit hours, Associates; 180 credit hours, Bachelors **Professional Accreditation:** ACICS

ITT TECHNICAL INSTITUTE (OXNARD)
2051 Solar Dr., Ste. 150
Oxnard, CA 93036
Tel: (805)988-0143
Fax: (805)988-1813
Web Site: http://www.itt-tech.edu/
President/CEO: Lorraine Bunt
Registrar: Adele Mavillo
Admissions: Lorraine Bunt
Financial Aid: Anna Barcenas
Type: Two-Year College **Sex:** Coed **Affiliation:** ITT Educational Services, Inc **Admission Plans:** Deferred Admission **Application Deadline:** Rolling **Application Fee:** $100.00 **H.S. Requirements:** High school diploma required; GED accepted **Costs Per Year:** Application fee: $100. **Scholarships:** Available **Calendar System:** Quarter, Summer Session Not available **Exams:** Other **Credit Hours For Degree:** 96 credit hours, Associates; 180 credit hours, Bachelors **Professional Accreditation:** ACICS

ITT TECHNICAL INSTITUTE (RANCHO CORDOVA)
10863 Gold Center Dr.
Rancho Cordova, CA 95670-6034
Tel: (916)851-3900
Free: 800-488-8466
Fax: (916)366-9225
Web Site: http://www.itt-tech.edu/
President/CEO: Jeffrey S. Ortega
Registrar: Robert J. Johanneson
Admissions: Richard Flann
Financial Aid: Kathy Henson
Type: Two-Year College **Sex:** Coed **Affiliation:** ITT Educational Services, Inc **Admission Plans:** Deferred Admission **Application Deadline:** Rolling **Application Fee:** $100.00 **H.S. Requirements:** High school diploma required; GED accepted **Costs Per Year:** Application fee: $100. **Scholarships:** Available **Calendar System:** Quarter, Summer Session Not available **Exams:** Other **Credit Hours For Degree:** 96 credit hours, Associates; 180 credit hours, Bachelors **Professional Accreditation:** ACICS

ITT TECHNICAL INSTITUTE (SAN BERNARDINO)
630 East Brier Dr., Ste. 150
San Bernardino, CA 92408-2800
Tel: (909)889-3800
Admissions: (909)806-4600
Fax: (909)888-6970
Web Site: http://www.itt-tech.edu/
President/CEO: Terry Lorenz
Registrar: Luka M'Bewe
Admissions: Terry Lorenz
Financial Aid: Sherry La Bleu

Type: Two-Year College **Sex:** Coed **Affiliation:** ITT Educational Services, Inc **Admission Plans:** Deferred Admission **Application Deadline:** Rolling **Application Fee:** $100.00 **H.S. Requirements:** High school diploma required; GED accepted **Costs Per Year:** Application fee: $100. **Scholarships:** Available **Calendar System:** Quarter, Summer Session Not available **Exams:** Other **Credit Hours For Degree:** 96 credit hours, Associates; 180 credit hours, Bachelors **Professional Accreditation:** ACICS

ITT TECHNICAL INSTITUTE (SAN DIEGO)
9680 Granite Ridge Dr., Ste. 100
San Diego, CA 92123
Tel: (858)571-8500
Fax: (858)571-1277
Web Site: http://www.itt-tech.edu/
President/CEO: David B. Parker
Registrar: Ginger Davis
Admissions: Jackie Parma
Financial Aid: Kurt Johnson
Type: Two-Year College **Sex:** Coed **Affiliation:** ITT Educational Services, Inc **Admission Plans:** Deferred Admission **Application Deadline:** Rolling **Application Fee:** $100.00 **H.S. Requirements:** High school diploma required; GED accepted **Costs Per Year:** Application fee: $100. **Scholarships:** Available **Calendar System:** Quarter, Summer Session Not available **Exams:** Other **Credit Hours For Degree:** 96 credit hours, Associates; 180 credit hours, Bachelors **Professional Accreditation:** ACICS

ITT TECHNICAL INSTITUTE (SYLMAR)
12669 Encinitas Ave.
Sylmar, CA 91342-3664
Tel: (818)364-5151
Web Site: http://www.itt-tech.edu/
President/CEO: Nader Mojtabai
Registrar: Abe Atarodi
Financial Aid: Willetta Collins
Type: Two-Year College **Sex:** Coed **Affiliation:** ITT Educational Services, Inc **Admission Plans:** Deferred Admission **Application Deadline:** Rolling **Application Fee:** $100.00 **H.S. Requirements:** High school diploma required; GED accepted **Costs Per Year:** Application fee: $100. **Scholarships:** Available **Calendar System:** Quarter, Summer Session Not available **Exams:** Other **Credit Hours For Degree:** 96 credit hours, Associates; 180 credit hours, Bachelors **Professional Accreditation:** ACICS

ITT TECHNICAL INSTITUTE (TORRANCE)
20050 South Vermont Ave.
Torrance, CA 90502
Tel: (310)380-1555
Fax: (310)380-1557
Web Site: http://www.itt-tech.edu/
President/CEO: Ann Marie Koerin
Registrar: Annie Vellpradit
Admissions: Arnulfo Runas
Financial Aid: Wylodin Banez
Type: Two-Year College **Sex:** Coed **Affiliation:** ITT Educational Services, Inc **Admission Plans:** Deferred Admission **Application Deadline:** Rolling **Application Fee:** $100.00 **H.S. Requirements:** High school diploma required; GED accepted **Costs Per Year:** Application fee: $100. **Scholarships:** Available **Calendar System:** Quarter, Summer Session Not available **Exams:** Other **Credit Hours For Degree:** 96 credit hours, Associates; 180 credit hours, Bachelors **Professional Accreditation:** ACICS

ITT TECHNICAL INSTITUTE (WEST COVINA)
1530 West Cameron Ave.
West Covina, CA 91790-2711
Tel: (626)960-8681
Fax: (626)960-8681
Web Site: http://www.itt-tech.edu/
President/CEO: Maria Alamat
Registrar: Raquel Belongie
Admissions: Maria S. Alamat
Financial Aid: Judith DeGuzman
Type: Two-Year College **Sex:** Coed **Affiliation:** ITT Educational Services, Inc **Admission Plans:** Deferred Admission **Application Deadline:** Rolling **Application Fee:** $100.00 **H.S. Requirements:** High school diploma required; GED accepted **Costs Per Year:** Application fee: $100. **Scholarships:** Available **Calendar System:** Quarter, Summer Session Not available **Exams:** Other **Credit Hours For Degree:** 96 credit hours, Associates; 180 credit hours, Bachelors **Professional Accreditation:** ACICS

JOHN F. KENNEDY UNIVERSITY
100 Ellinwood Way
Pleasant Hill, CA 94523-4817
Tel: (925)969-3300
Free: 800-696-JFKU
Admissions: (925)969-3330
Fax: (925)254-6964
Web Site: http://www.jfku.edu/
President/CEO: Dr. Steven Stargardter
Registrar: Gwen D. Swenson
Admissions: Michael Raine
Financial Aid: Mindy Bergeron
Type: Comprehensive **Sex:** Coed **Admission Plans:** Open Admission; Deferred Admission **Application Fee:** $50.00 **H.S. Requirements:** High school diploma required; GED accepted **Scholarships:** Available **Calendar System:** Quarter, Summer Session Available **Enrollment:** FT 37, PT 160, Grad 1,273 **Faculty:** FT 55, PT 673 **Student-Faculty Ratio:** 12:1 **% Receiving Financial Aid:** 44 **Library Holdings:** 96,366 **Regional Accreditation:** Western Association of Schools and Colleges **Credit Hours For Degree:** 180 quarter hours, Bachelors **Professional Accreditation:** APA

THE KING'S COLLEGE AND SEMINARY
14800 Sherman Way
Van Nuys, CA 91405-8040
Tel: (818)779-8040
Fax: (818)779-8241
Web Site: http://www.kingscollege.edu/
President/CEO: Dr. Gregor A. Campbell
Admissions: Marilyn J. Chappell
Type: Four-Year College **Sex:** Coed **Affiliation:** International Church of the Foursquare Gospel **Costs Per Year:** Tuition: $7200 full-time, $160 per quarter hour part-time. Mandatory fees: $285 full-time, $35. **Calendar System:** Quarter **Professional Accreditation:** AABC, TACCS

LA SIERRA UNIVERSITY
45 Riverwalk Parkway
Riverside, CA 92515
Tel: (951)785-2000
Free: 800-874-5587
Admissions: (909)785-2176
Fax: (951)785-2901
E-mail: ivy@lasierra.edu
Web Site: http://www.lasierra.edu/
President/CEO: Dr. Lawrence T. Geraty
Registrar: Faye Swayze
Admissions: Bobby Brown
Financial Aid: Dr. William Chunestudy
Type: Comprehensive **Sex:** Coed **Affiliation:** Seventh-day Adventist **Scores:** 85% SAT V 400+; 84% SAT M 400+; 47% ACT 18-23; 14% ACT 24-29 **% Accepted:** 38 **Admission Plans:** Preferred Admission **Application Deadline:** Rolling **Application Fee:** $30.00 **H.S. Requirements:** High school diploma required; GED accepted **Costs Per Year:** Application fee: $30. Comprehensive fee: $26,507 includes full-time tuition ($19,908), mandatory fees ($726), and college room and board ($5873). Part-time tuition: $553 per unit. **Scholarships:** Available **Calendar System:** Quarter, Summer Session Available **Enrollment:** FT 1,454, PT 184, Grad 289 **Faculty:** FT 88, PT 76 **Student-Faculty Ratio:** 15:1 **Exams:** SAT I or ACT **% Receiving Financial Aid:** 71 **Library Holdings:** 251,632 **Regional Accreditation:** Western Association of Schools and Colleges **Credit Hours For Degree:** 190 units, Bachelors **Professional Accreditation:** ATS, CSWE, NASM **Intercollegiate Athletics:** Basketball M & W; Soccer M; Volleyball M & W

LAGUNA COLLEGE OF ART & DESIGN
2222 Laguna Canyon Rd.
Laguna Beach, CA 92651-1136
Tel: (949)376-6000
Free: 800-255-0762
Fax: (949)376-6009
Web Site: http://www.lagunacollege.edu/
President/CEO: Alan Barkley

Registrar: Laura Wolf
Admissions: Anthony Padilla
Financial Aid: Christopher Brown
Type: Four-Year College **Sex:** Coed **Scores:** 98% SAT V 400+; 100% SAT M 400+; 20% ACT 18-23; 70% ACT 24-29 **Admission Plans:** Deferred Admission **Application Fee:** $45.00 **H.S. Requirements:** High school diploma required; GED accepted **Scholarships:** Available **Calendar System:** Semester, Summer Session Available **Enrollment:** FT 310 **Faculty:** FT 10, PT 62 **Student-Faculty Ratio:** 10:1 **Exams:** SAT I or ACT **% Receiving Financial Aid:** 88 **Library Holdings:** 16,000 **Regional Accreditation:** Western Association of Schools and Colleges **Credit Hours For Degree:** 122 units, Bachelors **Professional Accreditation:** NASAD

LAKE TAHOE COMMUNITY COLLEGE
One College Dr.
South Lake Tahoe, CA 96150-4524
Tel: (530)541-4660
Fax: (530)541-7852
Web Site: http://www.ltcc.edu/
President/CEO: Dr. Guy F. Lease
Registrar: Linda Stevenson
Admissions: Linda M. Stevenson
Financial Aid: Lynn Thieson
Type: Two-Year College **Sex:** Coed **Affiliation:** California Community College System **Admission Plans:** Open Admission; Early Admission **H.S. Requirements:** High school diploma or equivalent not required. For applicants under 18: High school diploma required; GED accepted **Scholarships:** Available **Calendar System:** Quarter, Summer Session Available **Faculty:** FT 50, PT 150 **Library Holdings:** 38,950 **Regional Accreditation:** Western Association of Schools and Colleges **Credit Hours For Degree:** 90 units, Associates **Intercollegiate Athletics:** Skiing (Cross-Country) M & W; Volleyball W

LANEY COLLEGE
900 Fallon St.
Oakland, CA 94607-4893
Tel: (510)834-5740
Admissions: (510)466-7365
Web Site: http://www.peralta.cc.ca.us/
President/CEO: Dr. Deborah G. Blue
Admissions: Howard Perdue
Financial Aid: Milton Shimabukuro
Type: Two-Year College **Sex:** Coed **Affiliation:** Peralta Community College District System **Admission Plans:** Open Admission; Early Admission **Application Fee:** $0.00 **H.S. Requirements:** High school diploma required; GED accepted. For applicants 18 or over: High school diploma or equivalent not required **Scholarships:** Available **Calendar System:** Semester, Summer Session Available **Enrollment:** FT 2,424, PT 11,039 **Faculty:** FT 118, PT 333 **Library Holdings:** 78,054 **Regional Accreditation:** Western Association of Schools and Colleges **Credit Hours For Degree:** 60 semester hours, Associates **Intercollegiate Athletics:** Baseball M; Football M; Golf M; Softball W; Volleyball W

LAS POSITAS COLLEGE
3033 Collier Canyon Rd.
Livermore, CA 94551-7650
Tel: (925)373-5800
Admissions: (925)373-4942
Fax: (925)443-0742
Web Site: http://www.clpccd.cc.ca.us/lpc/
President/CEO: Karen Halliday
Registrar: Sylvia Rodriguez
Admissions: Sylvia R. Rodriguez
Type: Two-Year College **Sex:** Coed **Affiliation:** California Community College System **Admission Plans:** Open Admission **Application Fee:** $0.00 **H.S. Requirements:** High school diploma required; GED accepted **Scholarships:** Available **Calendar System:** Semester, Summer Session Available **Regional Accreditation:** Western Association of Schools and Colleges **Credit Hours For Degree:** 60 units, Associates **Intercollegiate Athletics:** Cross-Country Running M & W; Soccer M & W

LASSEN COMMUNITY COLLEGE DISTRICT
Hwy. 139
PO Box 3000
Susanville, CA 96130
Tel: (530)257-6181
Fax: (530)257-8964
Web Site: http://www.lassencollege.edu/
President/CEO: Kenneth B. Cerreta
Registrar: Chris J. Alberico
Admissions: Chris J. Alberico
Financial Aid: Connie K. Burden
Type: Two-Year College **Sex:** Coed **Affiliation:** California Community College System **Admission Plans:** Open Admission; Early Admission **H.S. Requirements:** High school diploma or equivalent not required. For applicants under 18: High school diploma required; GED accepted **Scholarships:** Available **Calendar System:** Semester, Summer Session Available **Faculty:** FT 44, PT 160 **Exams:** ACT **Library Holdings:** 15,000 **Regional Accreditation:** Western Association of Schools and Colleges **Credit Hours For Degree:** 60 units, Associates **Intercollegiate Athletics:** Basketball M & W; Cross-Country Running M & W; Golf M & W; Riflery M & W; Softball W; Track and Field M & W; Volleyball W; Wrestling M

LIFE PACIFIC COLLEGE
1100 Covina Blvd.
San Dimas, CA 91773-3298
Tel: (909)599-5433; 877-886-5433
Fax: (909)599-6690
E-mail: adm@lifepacific.edu
Web Site: http://www.lifepacific.edu/
President/CEO: Dr. Dan Stewart
Registrar: Bruce Primrose
Admissions: Gina Nicodemus
Financial Aid: Becky Huyck
Type: Four-Year College **Sex:** Coed **Affiliation:** International Church of the Foursquare Gospel **Scores:** 88% SAT V 400+; 79% SAT M 400+; 36% ACT 18-23; 14% ACT 24-29 **% Accepted:** 87 **Admission Plans:** Deferred Admission **Application Deadline:** June 01 **Application Fee:** $35.00 **H.S. Requirements:** High school diploma required; GED accepted **Costs Per Year:** Application fee: $35. Comprehensive fee: $15,100 includes full-time tuition ($9750), mandatory fees ($350), and college room and board ($5000). Part-time tuition: $325 per credit hour. Part-time tuition varies according to course load. **Scholarships:** Available **Calendar System:** Semester, Summer Session Available **Enrollment:** FT 403, PT 125 **Faculty:** FT 12, PT 27 **Student-Faculty Ratio:** 18:1 **Exams:** SAT I or ACT **% Receiving Financial Aid:** 74 **% Residing in College-Owned, -Operated, or -Affiliated Housing:** 50 **Library Holdings:** 40,022 **Regional Accreditation:** Western Association of Schools and Colleges **Credit Hours For Degree:** 64 semester hours, Associates; 128 semester hours, Bachelors **Professional Accreditation:** AABC **Intercollegiate Athletics:** Basketball M; Volleyball W

LINCOLN UNIVERSITY
401 15th St.
Oakland, CA 94612
Tel: (510)628-8010
Fax: (510)628-8026
E-mail: admissions@lincolnuca.edu
Web Site: http://www.lincolnuca.edu/
President/CEO: Dr. Mikhail Brodsky
Registrar: Peggy Au
Admissions: Dr. Pete Bogue
Financial Aid: James E. Peterson
Type: Comprehensive **Sex:** Coed **Admission Plans:** Deferred Admission **Application Fee:** $75.00 **H.S. Requirements:** High school diploma required; GED accepted **Costs Per Year:** Application fee: $75. Tuition: $7320 full-time, $305 per unit part-time. Mandatory fees: $400 full-time. Full-time tuition and fees vary according to program. **Calendar System:** Semester, Summer Session Available **Enrollment:** FT 30, PT 21, Grad 96 **Faculty:** FT 8, PT 27 **Student-Faculty Ratio:** 14:1 **Library Holdings:** 17,532 **Credit Hours For Degree:** 124 units, Bachelors **Professional Accreditation:** ACICS

LOMA LINDA UNIVERSITY
Loma Linda, CA 92350
Tel: (909)558-1000
Fax: (909)558-4577
Web Site: http://www.llu.edu/
President/CEO: Dr. Richard Hart
Registrar: Janelle Pyke
Financial Aid: Verdell C. Schaefer

Type: Two-Year Upper Division **Sex:** Coed **Affiliation:** Seventh-day Adventist **Application Deadline:** April 15 **Application Fee:** $60.00 **Costs Per Year:** Application fee: $60. Tuition: $23,280 full-time, $485 per unit part-time. Mandatory fees: $1290 full-time, $430 per term part-time. College room only: $2370. **Scholarships:** Available **Calendar System:** Quarter, Summer Session Not available **Enrollment:** FT 798, PT 321, Grad 1,490 **Faculty:** FT 106, PT 44 **Student-Faculty Ratio:** 8:1 **% Receiving Financial Aid:** 77 **% Residing in College-Owned, -Operated, or -Affiliated Housing:** 25 **Library Holdings:** 322,657 **Regional Accreditation:** Western Association of Schools and Colleges **Professional Accreditation:** ARCEST, AAMFT, AACN, ACPhE, ADA, ADtA, AHIMA, AOTA, APTA, APA, ASC, ASLHA, ACIPE, CARC, CEPH, CSWE, JRCERT, LCMEAMA, NAACLS

LONG BEACH CITY COLLEGE

4901 East Carson St.
Long Beach, CA 90808-1780
Tel: (562)938-4353
Admissions: (562)938-4130
Web Site: http://www.lbcc.edu/
President/CEO: Dr. E. Jan Kehoe
Registrar: Lynda Luuga
Admissions: Ross Miyashiro
Financial Aid: Toni Du Bois

Type: Two-Year College **Sex:** Coed **Affiliation:** California Community College System **Admission Plans:** Open Admission; Early Admission **Application Deadline:** Rolling **Application Fee:** $0.00 **H.S. Requirements:** High school diploma or equivalent not required. For applicants under 18, international students: High school diploma required; GED accepted **Costs Per Year:** Application fee: $0. State resident tuition: $0 full-time. Nonresident tuition: $3840 full-time, $160 per unit part-time. Mandatory fees: $692 full-time, $26 per unit part-time, $34 per term part-time. **Scholarships:** Available **Calendar System:** Semester, Summer Session Available **Enrollment:** FT 9,580, PT 16,716 **Faculty:** FT 356, PT 777 **Student-Faculty Ratio:** 24:1 **Library Holdings:** 151,367 **Regional Accreditation:** Western Association of Schools and Colleges **Credit Hours For Degree:** 60 units, Associates **Professional Accreditation:** JRCERT, NLN **Intercollegiate Athletics:** Badminton M & W; Baseball M; Basketball M & W; Cross-Country Running M & W; Football M; Golf M & W; Soccer M & W; Softball W; Swimming and Diving M & W; Tennis M & W; Track and Field M & W; Volleyball M & W; Water Polo M & W

LOS ANGELES CITY COLLEGE

855 North Vermont Ave.
Los Angeles, CA 90029-3590
Tel: (323)953-4000
Fax: (323)953-4294
Web Site: http://www.lacc.cc.ca.us/
President/CEO: Dr. Mary Spangler
Registrar: Lawrence Bradford
Admissions: Lawrence Bradford
Financial Aid: Jeremy Villar

Type: Two-Year College **Sex:** Coed **Affiliation:** Los Angeles Community College District System **Admission Plans:** Open Admission **Application Fee:** $0.00 **H.S. Requirements:** High school diploma or equivalent not required **Calendar System:** Semester, Summer Session Available **Faculty:** FT 249, PT 323 **Library Holdings:** 150,000 **Regional Accreditation:** Western Association of Schools and Colleges **Credit Hours For Degree:** 60 units, Associates **ROTC:** Army, Air Force **Professional Accreditation:** ADA, JRCERT **Intercollegiate Athletics:** Basketball M; Cross-Country Running M; Football M; Gymnastics M; Track and Field M & W; Volleyball M & W

LOS ANGELES COUNTY COLLEGE OF NURSING AND ALLIED HEALTH

1237 North Mission Rd.
Los Angeles, CA 90033
Tel: (323)226-4911
Fax: (323)226-6427
Web Site: http://www.ladhs.org/lacusc/lacnah/
President/CEO: Maria Elena Sanchez, RN
Admissions: Maria Caballero

Type: Two-Year College **Sex:** Coed **Scholarships:** Available **Calendar System:** Semester **Regional Accreditation:** Western Association of Schools and Colleges

LOS ANGELES HARBOR COLLEGE

1111 Figueroa Place
Wilmington, CA 90744-2397
Tel: (310)233-4000
Admissions: (310)233-4091
Fax: (310)233-4223
Web Site: http://www.lahc.edu/
President/CEO: Dr. Linda M. Spink
Registrar: David M. Ching
Admissions: David Ching
Financial Aid: Dr. Charlie Bossler

Type: Two-Year College **Sex:** Coed **Affiliation:** Los Angeles Community College District System **Admission Plans:** Open Admission; Early Admission; Deferred Admission **Application Fee:** $0.00 **H.S. Requirements:** High school diploma or equivalent not required. For applicants under 18: High school diploma required; GED not accepted **Scholarships:** Available **Calendar System:** Semester, Summer Session Available **Enrollment:** FT 2,311, PT 7,158 **Faculty:** FT 110, PT 160 **Student-Faculty Ratio:** 40:1 **Library Holdings:** 82,790 **Regional Accreditation:** Western Association of Schools and Colleges **Credit Hours For Degree:** 60 units, Associates **Professional Accreditation:** NLN **Intercollegiate Athletics:** Baseball M; Basketball M & W; Football M; Golf M; Soccer M; Tennis W; Volleyball W

LOS ANGELES MISSION COLLEGE

13356 Eldridge Ave.
Sylmar, CA 91342-3245
Tel: (818)364-7600
Admissions: (818)364-7766
Web Site: http://www.lamission.cc.ca.us/
President/CEO: Dr. Adriana D. Barrera
Registrar: Carlos Nava
Admissions: Carlos Nava
Financial Aid: Carlos Nava

Type: Two-Year College **Sex:** Coed **Affiliation:** Los Angeles Community College District System **Admission Plans:** Open Admission; Early Admission **H.S. Requirements:** High school diploma or equivalent not required. For applicants under 18: High school diploma required; GED accepted **Scholarships:** Available **Calendar System:** Semester, Summer Session Available **Faculty:** FT 85, PT 185 **Student-Faculty Ratio:** 33:1 **Library Holdings:** 40,000 **Regional Accreditation:** Western Association of Schools and Colleges **Credit Hours For Degree:** 60 credits, Associates

LOS ANGELES PIERCE COLLEGE

6201 Winnetka Ave.
Woodland Hills, CA 91371-0001
Tel: (818)710-4123
Admissions: (818)719-6448
Fax: (818)710-9844
Web Site: http://www.lapc.cc.ca.us/
President/CEO: Darroch Young
Registrar: Shelley Gerstl
Admissions: Shelley L. Gerstl
Financial Aid: Phyllis Braxton

Type: Two-Year College **Sex:** Coed **Affiliation:** Los Angeles Community College District System **Admission Plans:** Open Admission; Early Admission **Application Fee:** $0.00 **H.S. Requirements:** High school diploma or equivalent not required. For applicants under 18, nursing program: High school diploma required; GED accepted **Scholarships:** Available **Calendar System:** Semester, Summer Session Available **Library Holdings:** 106,122 **Regional Accreditation:** Western Association of Schools and Colleges **Credit Hours For Degree:** 60 credits, Associates **Professional Accreditation:** NLN **Intercollegiate Athletics:** Baseball M; Basketball W; Football M; Softball W; Swimming and Diving M & W; Tennis M & W; Volleyball M & W; Water Polo M

LOS ANGELES SOUTHWEST COLLEGE

1600 West Imperial Hwy.
Los Angeles, CA 90047-4810
Tel: (323)241-5225
Admissions: (323)241-5279
Web Site: http://www.lasc.cc.ca.us/

President/CEO: Dr. Mary E. Lee
Admissions: Dr. Lawrence Jarmon
Financial Aid: Kathleen Stiger
Type: Two-Year College **Sex:** Coed **Affiliation:** Los Angeles Community College District System **Admission Plans:** Open Admission; Early Admission **H.S. Requirements:** High school diploma or equivalent not required. For applicants under 18: High school diploma required; GED accepted **Scholarships:** Available **Calendar System:** Semester, Summer Session Available **Faculty:** FT 75, PT 148 **Library Holdings:** 60,000 **Regional Accreditation:** Western Association of Schools and Colleges **Credit Hours For Degree:** 60 units, Associates **Intercollegiate Athletics:** Basketball M & W; Cross-Country Running M & W; Football M; Track and Field M & W

LOS ANGELES TRADE-TECHNICAL COLLEGE
400 West Washington Blvd.
Los Angeles, CA 90015-4108
Tel: (213)744-9500
Admissions: (213)763-5301
Fax: (213)748-7334
Web Site: http://www.lattc.edu/
President/CEO: Dr. Daniel A. Castro
Registrar: Dr. Robert K. Richards
Admissions: Rosemary Royal
Financial Aid: Dr. Theda Douglas
Type: Two-Year College **Sex:** Coed **Affiliation:** Los Angeles Community College District System **Admission Plans:** Open Admission; Early Admission; Deferred Admission **Application Fee:** $0.00 **H.S. Requirements:** High school diploma or equivalent not required. For nursing program: High school diploma required; GED accepted **Scholarships:** Available **Calendar System:** Semester, Summer Session Available **Enrollment:** FT 4,160, PT 9,034 **Faculty:** FT 200, PT 243 **Library Holdings:** 98,000 **Regional Accreditation:** Western Association of Schools and Colleges **Credit Hours For Degree:** 60 units, Associates **Professional Accreditation:** ACF, NLN **Intercollegiate Athletics:** Basketball M & W; Cross-Country Running M & W; Tennis M; Track and Field M & W

LOS ANGELES VALLEY COLLEGE
5800 Fulton Ave.
Van Nuys, CA 91401-4096
Tel: (818)947-2600
Admissions: (818)947-2353
Fax: (818)947-2610
E-mail: manzanf@lavc.edu
Web Site: http://www.lavc.cc.ca.us/
President/CEO: Dr. Tyree Wieder
Admissions: Florentino Manzano
Financial Aid: Barbara Ralston
Type: Two-Year College **Sex:** Coed **Affiliation:** Los Angeles Community College District System **Admission Plans:** Open Admission; Early Admission **Application Fee:** $0.00 **H.S. Requirements:** High school diploma or equivalent not required **Scholarships:** Available **Calendar System:** Semester, Summer Session Available **Enrollment:** FT 5,021, PT 13,740 **Faculty:** FT 236, PT 289 **Exams:** ACT **Library Holdings:** 124,000 **Regional Accreditation:** Western Association of Schools and Colleges **Credit Hours For Degree:** 60 units, Associates **Professional Accreditation:** CARC, NLN **Intercollegiate Athletics:** Basketball M & W; Cross-Country Running M & W; Fencing M & W; Football M; Gymnastics M & W; Swimming and Diving M & W; Tennis M & W; Track and Field M & W; Volleyball M & W; Water Polo M; Wrestling M

LOS MEDANOS COLLEGE
2700 East Leland Rd.
Pittsburg, CA 94565-5197
Tel: (925)439-2181
Fax: (925)439-8797
Web Site: http://www.losmedanos.net/
President/CEO: Peter Garcia
Registrar: Gail Newman
Admissions: Gail Newman
Financial Aid: Felipe Torres
Type: Two-Year College **Sex:** Coed **Affiliation:** California Community College System **Admission Plans:** Open Admission **Application Fee:** $0.00 **H.S. Requirements:** High school diploma required; GED accepted. For applicants 18 or over: High school diploma or equivalent not required **Scholarships:** Available **Calendar System:** Semester, Summer Session Available **Faculty:** FT 104, PT 140 **Exams:** Other **Library Holdings:** 15,439 **Regional Accreditation:** Western Association of Schools and Colleges **Credit Hours For Degree:** 60 units, Associates **Intercollegiate Athletics:** Baseball M; Basketball M & W; Football M; Soccer M; Softball W; Volleyball W

LOYOLA MARYMOUNT UNIVERSITY
One LMU Dr.
Los Angeles, CA 90045-2659
Tel: (310)338-2700
Free: 800-LMU-INFO
Admissions: (310)338-2750
Fax: (310)338-2797
E-mail: admissions@lmu.edu
Web Site: http://www.lmu.edu/
President/CEO: Rev. Robert B. Lawton, SJ
Registrar: Rosenia St. Onge
Admissions: Matthew X. Fissinger
Financial Aid: Catherine Kasakoff
Type: Comprehensive **Sex:** Coed **Affiliation:** Roman Catholic **Scores:** 99% SAT V 400+; 100% SAT M 400+ **Admission Plans:** Early Admission; Deferred Admission **Application Fee:** $50.00 **H.S. Requirements:** High school diploma required; GED accepted **Costs Per Year:** Application fee: $50. Comprehensive fee: $38,212 includes full-time tuition ($27,710) and college room and board ($10,502). Room and board charges vary according to board plan and housing facility. **Scholarships:** Available **Calendar System:** Semester, Summer Session Available **Enrollment:** FT 5,375, PT 346, Grad 1,673 **Faculty:** FT 431, PT 437 **Student-Faculty Ratio:** 13:1 **Exams:** SAT I or ACT **% Receiving Financial Aid:** 61 **% Residing in College-Owned, -Operated, or -Affiliated Housing:** 49 **Library Holdings:** 495,920 **Regional Accreditation:** Western Association of Schools and Colleges **Credit Hours For Degree:** 120 units, Bachelors **ROTC:** Army, Air Force **Professional Accreditation:** AACSB, ABET, ABA, AALS, ATS, NASAD, NASD, NASM, NAST, NCATE **Intercollegiate Athletics:** Baseball M; Basketball M & W; Crew M & W; Cross-Country Running M & W; Golf M; Lacrosse M & W; Rugby M; Soccer M & W; Swimming and Diving W; Tennis M & W; Volleyball M & W; Water Polo M & W

MARIC COLLEGE (ANAHEIM)
1360 South Anaheim Blvd.
Anaheim, CA 92805
Tel: (714)758-1500
Free: 800-206-0095
Fax: (714)758-1220
Web Site: http://www.mariccollege.edu/
President/CEO: Mustapha Belayachi
Type: Two-Year College **Sex:** Coed **Professional Accreditation:** ACICS

MARIC COLLEGE (NORTH HOLLYWOOD)
6180 Laurel Canyon Blvd., Ste. 101
North Hollywood, CA 91606
Tel: (818)763-2563
Free: 800-404-9729
Fax: (818)763-1623
E-mail: mark@moderntec.com
Web Site: http://www.mariccollege.edu/
President/CEO: Mark Newman
Admissions: Mark Newman
Type: Two-Year College **Sex:** Coed **Calendar System:** Quarter **Professional Accreditation:** ACCSCT

MARIC COLLEGE (PANORAMA CITY)
14355 Roscoe Blvd.
Panorama City, CA 91402
Tel: (818)672-8907
Free: 800-206-0095
Fax: (818)672-8919
Web Site: http://www.mariccollege.edu/
President/CEO: Sharon Ahearn
Type: Two-Year College **Sex:** Coed **Professional Accreditation:** ACICS

MARIC COLLEGE (SACRAMENTO)
4330 Watt Ave.,Ste. 400
Sacramento, CA 95821
Tel: (916)649-8168

Free: 800-955-8168
Fax: (916)649-8344
Web Site: http://www.californiacollege.com/
President/CEO: Tapas Ghosh
Admissions: Charles Reese
Financial Aid: Clarita Cortez
Type: Two-Year College **Calendar System:** Semester **Exams:** Other **Professional Accreditation:** ACICS

MARIC COLLEGE (SALIDA)
5172 Kiernan Ct.
Salida, CA 95368
Tel: (209)571-8777
Admissions: (209)543-7000
Fax: (209)571-9836
Web Site: http://www.mariccollege.edu/
President/CEO: MaryAnn Crone
Admissions: Linda Stovall
Type: Two-Year College **Sex:** Coed **Calendar System:** Semester **Enrollment:** FT 289 **Faculty:** FT 1, PT 4 **Student-Faculty Ratio:** 8:1

MARIC COLLEGE (SAN DIEGO)
3666 Kearny Villa Rd., Ste. 100
San Diego, CA 92123-1995
Tel: (858)279-4000
Free: 800-400-8232
Admissions: (858)654-3624
Fax: (858)279-4885
Web Site: http://www.mariccollege.edu/
President/CEO: John Hanson
Registrar: Martha Ann Haney
Admissions: Angela Robertson
Financial Aid: Jean Winchell
Type: Two-Year College **Sex:** Coed **H.S. Requirements:** High school diploma required; GED accepted. For certificate programs: High school diploma or equivalent not required **Calendar System:** Semester, Summer Session Available **Enrollment:** FT 298 **Faculty:** FT 45, PT 20 **Credit Hours For Degree:** 42 credits, Associates **Professional Accreditation:** ACCSCT

MARYMOUNT COLLEGE, PALOS VERDES, CALIFORNIA
30800 Palos Verdes Dr. East
Rancho Palos Verdes, CA 90275-6299
Tel: (310)377-5501
Fax: (310)377-6223
E-mail: admission@marymountpv.edu
Web Site: http://www.marymountpv.edu/
President/CEO: Dr. Thomas M. McFadden
Registrar: Lynn Elliott
Admissions: Nina Lococo
Financial Aid: David Carnevale
Type: Two-Year College **Sex:** Coed **Affiliation:** Roman Catholic **Scores:** 65% SAT V 400+; 75% SAT M 400+ **Admission Plans:** Early Admission **Application Fee:** $35.00 **H.S. Requirements:** High school diploma required; GED accepted **Scholarships:** Available **Calendar System:** Semester, Summer Session Available **Enrollment:** FT 683, PT 107 **Faculty:** FT 42, PT 49 **Student-Faculty Ratio:** 16:1 **Exams:** SAT I or ACT **% Residing in College-Owned, -Operated, or -Affiliated Housing:** 48 **Library Holdings:** 42,104 **Regional Accreditation:** Western Association of Schools and Colleges **Credit Hours For Degree:** 60 units, Associates **Intercollegiate Athletics:** Golf M & W; Tennis M & W

THE MASTER'S COLLEGE AND SEMINARY
21726 Placerita Canyon Rd.
Santa Clarita, CA 91321-1200
Tel: (661)259-3540
Free: 800-568-6248
E-mail: admissions@masters.edu
Web Site: http://www.masters.edu/
President/CEO: Dr. John MacArthur
Registrar: Don Gilmore
Admissions: Hollie Gorsh
Financial Aid: Karen Smith
Type: Comprehensive **Sex:** Coed **Affiliation:** nondenominational **Scores:** 98% SAT V 400+; 97% SAT M 400+; 33% ACT 18-23; 41% ACT 24-29 **% Accepted:** 29 **Admission Plans:** Early Admission; Early Action; Deferred Admission **Application Fee:** $55.00 **H.S. Requirements:** High school diploma required; GED accepted **Costs Per Year:** Application fee: $55. Comprehensive fee: $25,850 includes full-time tuition ($19,230) and college room and board ($6620). College room only: $3660. Full-time tuition varies according to course load, degree level, and program. Room and board charges vary according to board plan. Part-time tuition: $805 per credit hour. Part-time tuition varies according to course load, degree level, and program. **Scholarships:** Available **Calendar System:** Semester, Summer Session Available **Enrollment:** FT 957, PT 182, Grad 99 **Faculty:** FT 76, PT 83 **Student-Faculty Ratio:** 12:1 **Exams:** SAT I or ACT **% Receiving Financial Aid:** 71 **% Residing in College-Owned, -Operated, or -Affiliated Housing:** 75 **Library Holdings:** 215,649 **Regional Accreditation:** Western Association of Schools and Colleges **Credit Hours For Degree:** 122 units, Bachelors **Professional Accreditation:** AAFCS **Intercollegiate Athletics:** Baseball M; Basketball M & W; Cross-Country Running M & W; Golf M; Soccer M & W; Softball W; Volleyball W

MENDOCINO COLLEGE
1000 Hensley Creek Rd.
Ukiah, CA 95482-0300
Tel: (707)468-3000
Admissions: (707)468-3103
Fax: (707)468-3430
E-mail: ktaylor@mendocino.cc.ca.us
Web Site: http://www.mendocino.cc.ca.us/
Registrar: Kristie Anderson
Admissions: Kristie A. Taylor
Type: Two-Year College **Sex:** Coed **Affiliation:** California Community College System **Admission Plans:** Open Admission; Preferred Admission; Early Admission; Deferred Admission **Application Fee:** $0.00 **H.S. Requirements:** High school diploma or equivalent not required **Scholarships:** Available **Calendar System:** Semester, Summer Session Available **Faculty:** FT 53, PT 187 **Student-Faculty Ratio:** 12:1 **Exams:** Other, SAT I or ACT **Library Holdings:** 27,441 **Regional Accreditation:** Western Association of Schools and Colleges **Credit Hours For Degree:** 60 units, Associates **Intercollegiate Athletics:** Baseball M; Basketball M & W; Football M; Golf M; Track and Field M & W; Volleyball W

MENLO COLLEGE
1000 El Camino Real
Atherton, CA 94027-4301
Tel: (650)688-3753
Free: 800-556-3656
Admissions: (650)543-3910
Fax: (650)617-2395
E-mail: admissions@menlo.edu
Web Site: http://www.menlo.edu/
President/CEO: Dr. Carlos Lopez
Registrar: Cathy McDermott
Admissions: Dr. Greg Smith
Financial Aid: Elinore Burkhardt
Type: Four-Year College **Sex:** Coed **Scores:** 81% SAT V 400+; 84% SAT M 400+; 51% ACT 18-23; 11% ACT 24-29 **% Accepted:** 69 **Admission Plans:** Early Admission; Early Action; Deferred Admission **Application Deadline:** Rolling **Application Fee:** $40.00 **H.S. Requirements:** High school diploma required; GED accepted **Costs Per Year:** Application fee: $40. Comprehensive fee: $34,050 includes full-time tuition ($24,300), mandatory fees ($150), and college room and board ($9600). Full-time tuition and fees vary according to program. Room and board charges vary according to housing facility. Part-time tuition: $1000 per unit. Part-time mandatory fees: $75. Part-time tuition and fees vary according to course load and program. **Scholarships:** Available **Calendar System:** Semester, Summer Session Available **Enrollment:** FT 669, PT 100 **Faculty:** FT 23, PT 50 **Student-Faculty Ratio:** 18:1 **Exams:** SAT I or ACT **% Receiving Financial Aid:** 62 **% Residing in College-Owned, -Operated, or -Affiliated Housing:** 66 **Library Holdings:** 64,700 **Regional Accreditation:** Western Association of Schools and Colleges **Credit Hours For Degree:** 124 units, Bachelors **ROTC:** Army **Intercollegiate Athletics:** Baseball M; Basketball M & W; Cross-Country Running M & W; Football M; Golf M & W; Soccer M & W; Softball W; Volleyball W; Wrestling M & W

MERCED COLLEGE
3600 M St.
Merced, CA 95348-2898
Tel: (209)384-6000

Admissions: (209)384-6188
Fax: (209)384-6339
Web Site: http://www.mccd.edu/
President/CEO: Dr. Benjamin T. Duran
Registrar: Sharon Reinhardt
Admissions: Sharon Reinhardt
Type: Two-Year College **Sex:** Coed **Affiliation:** California Community College System **Admission Plans:** Open Admission; Early Admission **H.S. Requirements:** High school diploma or equivalent not required. For applicants under 18: High school diploma required; GED accepted **Scholarships:** Available **Calendar System:** Semester, Summer Session Available **Faculty:** FT 145, PT 276 **Exams:** SAT I or ACT **Library Holdings:** 35,000 **Regional Accreditation:** Western Association of Schools and Colleges **Credit Hours For Degree:** 60 units, Associates **ROTC:** Army **Professional Accreditation:** JRCERT **Intercollegiate Athletics:** Baseball M; Basketball M & W; Bowling M & W; Cross-Country Running M; Equestrian Sports M & W; Football M; Golf M & W; Soccer M; Softball W; Swimming and Diving M & W; Tennis M & W; Track and Field M & W; Volleyball W; Water Polo M

MERRITT COLLEGE
12500 Campus Dr.
Oakland, CA 94619-3196
Tel: (510)531-4911
Admissions: (510)466-7365
E-mail: hperdue@peralta.cc.ca.us
Web Site: http://www.merritt.edu/
President/CEO: Dr. Evelyn Wesley
Admissions: Howard Perdue
Financial Aid: Judy Adams
Type: Two-Year College **Sex:** Coed **Affiliation:** Peralta Community College District System **Admission Plans:** Open Admission; Early Admission; Deferred Admission **H.S. Requirements:** High school diploma required; GED accepted. For applicants 18 or over: High school diploma or equivalent not required **Calendar System:** Semester, Summer Session Available **Enrollment:** FT 1,195, PT 6,789 **Faculty:** FT 94, PT 107 **Exams:** SAT I or ACT **Library Holdings:** 80,000 **Regional Accreditation:** Western Association of Schools and Colleges **Credit Hours For Degree:** 60 semester hours, Associates **Professional Accreditation:** JRCERT **Intercollegiate Athletics:** Basketball M; Cross-Country Running M; Fencing M; Gymnastics M & W; Soccer M; Tennis M & W; Track and Field M

MILLS COLLEGE
5000 MacArthur Blvd.
Oakland, CA 94613-1000
Tel: (510)430-2255
Free: 800-87-MILLS
Admissions: (510)430-2135
Fax: (510)430-3314
E-mail: admission@mills.edu
Web Site: http://www.mills.edu/
President/CEO: Dr. Janet L. Holmgren
Registrar: Alice Knudsen
Admissions: Julie Richardson
Financial Aid: David Gin
Type: Comprehensive **Scores:** 97% SAT V 400+; 98% SAT M 400+; 57% ACT 18-23; 29% ACT 24-29 **% Accepted:** 77 **Admission Plans:** Early Action; Deferred Admission **Application Deadline:** February 01 **Application Fee:** $40.00 **H.S. Requirements:** High school diploma required; GED accepted **Costs Per Year:** Application fee: $40. Comprehensive fee: $39,870 includes full-time tuition ($27,750), mandatory fees ($2240), and college room and board ($9880). College room only: $5150. Room and board charges vary according to board plan and housing facility. Part-time tuition: $4630 per course. Part-time tuition varies according to course load. **Scholarships:** Available **Calendar System:** Semester, Summer Session Not available **Enrollment:** FT 849, PT 32, Grad 491 **Faculty:** FT 90, PT 94 **Student-Faculty Ratio:** 11:1 **Exams:** SAT I or ACT, SAT II **% Receiving Financial Aid:** 90 **% Residing in College-Owned, -Operated, or -Affiliated Housing:** 54 **Library Holdings:** 254,351 **Regional Accreditation:** Western Association of Schools and Colleges **Credit Hours For Degree:** 34 courses, Bachelors **Intercollegiate Athletics:** Crew W; Cross-Country Running W; Soccer W; Swimming and Diving W; Tennis W; Volleyball W

MIRACOSTA COLLEGE
One Barnard Dr.
Oceanside, CA 92056-3899
Tel: (760)757-2121; 888-201-8480
Admissions: (760)795-6627
Fax: (760)795-6609
Web Site: http://www.miracosta.edu/
President/CEO: Dr. Victoria Munoz Richart
Registrar: Alicia Terry
Admissions: Alicia Terry
Financial Aid: JoAnn Bernard
Type: Two-Year College **Sex:** Coed **Affiliation:** California Community College System **Admission Plans:** Open Admission; Early Admission; Deferred Admission **Application Deadline:** Rolling **Application Fee:** $0.00 **H.S. Requirements:** High school diploma or equivalent not required **Costs Per Year:** Application fee: $0. State resident tuition: $0 full-time. Nonresident tuition: $4800 full-time, $160 per unit part-time. Mandatory fees: $804 full-time, $26 per unit part-time. **Scholarships:** Available **Calendar System:** Semester, Summer Session Available **Faculty:** FT 135, PT 394 **Student-Faculty Ratio:** 23:1 **Library Holdings:** 113,810 **Regional Accreditation:** Western Association of Schools and Colleges **Credit Hours For Degree:** 60 units, Associates **Intercollegiate Athletics:** Basketball M; Cross-Country Running M & W; Soccer W; Track and Field W

MISSION COLLEGE
3000 Mission College Blvd.
Santa Clara, CA 95054-1897
Tel: (408)988-2200
Admissions: (408)855-5195
Web Site: http://www.missioncollege.org/
President/CEO: Dr. Frank Chong
Admissions: Dr. Sam Bersolo
Financial Aid: Donna Stewart
Type: Two-Year College **Sex:** Coed **Affiliation:** California Community College System **Admission Plans:** Open Admission; Preferred Admission; Early Admission **H.S. Requirements:** High school diploma or equivalent not required. For applicants under 18, nursing program: High school diploma required; GED accepted **Scholarships:** Available **Calendar System:** Semester, Summer Session Available **Enrollment:** FT 4,000, PT 6,500 **Faculty:** FT 180, PT 210 **Student-Faculty Ratio:** 26:1 **Exams:** SAT I **Library Holdings:** 43,456 **Regional Accreditation:** Western Association of Schools and Colleges **Credit Hours For Degree:** 60 semester hours, Associates **ROTC:** Army, Air Force **Intercollegiate Athletics:** Badminton M & W; Baseball M; Basketball W; Soccer M & W; Softball W; Tennis M & W

MODESTO JUNIOR COLLEGE
435 College Ave.
Modesto, CA 95350-5800
Tel: (209)575-6498
Admissions: (209)575-6470
Web Site: http://www.mjc.edu/
President/CEO: Dr. James Williams
Admissions: Susie Agostini
Financial Aid: Myra E. Rush
Type: Two-Year College **Sex:** Coed **Affiliation:** Yosemite Community College District System **% Accepted:** 100 **Admission Plans:** Open Admission **Application Deadline:** Rolling **Application Fee:** $0.00 **H.S. Requirements:** High school diploma or equivalent not required. For applicants under 18: High school diploma required; GED accepted **Costs Per Year:** Application fee: $0. State resident tuition: $0 full-time. Nonresident tuition: $3840 full-time, $160 per unit part-time. Mandatory fees: $664 full-time, $26 per unit part-time, $40 per year part-time. **Scholarships:** Available **Calendar System:** Semester, Summer Session Available **Faculty:** FT 283, PT 251 **Student-Faculty Ratio:** 40:1 **Library Holdings:** 69,865 **Regional Accreditation:** Western Association of Schools and Colleges **Credit Hours For Degree:** 62 units, Associates **Professional Accreditation:** AAMAE, ADA, CARC **Intercollegiate Athletics:** Baseball M; Basketball M & W; Cross-Country Running M & W; Football M; Golf M; Gymnastics W; Soccer M & W; Softball W; Swimming and Diving M & W; Tennis M & W; Track and Field M & W; Volleyball W; Water Polo M & W; Wrestling M

MONTEREY PENINSULA COLLEGE
980 Fremont St.
Monterey, CA 93940-4799
Tel: (831)646-4000
Admissions: (831)646-4007
Fax: (831)655-2627
E-mail: vcoleman@mpc.edu

Web Site: http://www.mpc.edu/
President/CEO: Dr. Kirk Avery
Registrar: Vera Coleman
Admissions: Vera Coleman
Type: Two-Year College **Sex:** Coed **Affiliation:** California Community College System **Admission Plans:** Open Admission; Early Admission **Application Fee:** $0.00 **H.S. Requirements:** High school diploma or equivalent not required. For international students: High school diploma required; GED accepted **Scholarships:** Available **Calendar System:** Semester, Summer Session Available **Faculty:** FT 136, PT 181 **Library Holdings:** 52,000 **Regional Accreditation:** Western Association of Schools and Colleges **Credit Hours For Degree:** 60 credits, Associates **Professional Accreditation:** ADA, NLN **Intercollegiate Athletics:** Baseball M; Basketball M; Cross-Country Running M & W; Football M; Golf M & W; Softball W; Swimming and Diving M & W; Tennis M & W; Track and Field M & W; Volleyball W

MOORPARK COLLEGE
7075 Campus Rd.
Moorpark, CA 93021-1695
Tel: (805)378-1400
Admissions: (805)378-1406
Web Site: http://www.moorpark.cc.ca.us/
President/CEO: Dr. Eva Conrad
Registrar: Kathy Colborn
Admissions: Dr. Judith Gerhart
Type: Two-Year College **Sex:** Coed **Affiliation:** Ventura County Community College District System **Admission Plans:** Open Admission; Early Admission; Deferred Admission **Application Fee:** $0.00 **H.S. Requirements:** High school diploma required; GED accepted. For nursing program: High school diploma required; GED not accepted **Scholarships:** Available **Calendar System:** Semester, Summer Session Available **Enrollment:** FT 6,183, PT 9,083 **Faculty:** FT 170, PT 420 **Student-Faculty Ratio:** 30:1 **Library Holdings:** 50,000 **Regional Accreditation:** Western Association of Schools and Colleges **Credit Hours For Degree:** 60 units, Associates **Professional Accreditation:** JRCERT, NLN **Intercollegiate Athletics:** Baseball M; Basketball M & W; Cross-Country Running M & W; Football M; Golf M & W; Soccer M & W; Softball W; Track and Field M & W; Volleyball M & W; Wrestling M

MOUNT ST. MARY'S COLLEGE
12001 Chalon Rd.
Los Angeles, CA 90049-1599
Tel: (310)954-4000
Free: 800-999-9893
Admissions: (310)954-4252
E-mail: admissions@msmc.la.edu
Web Site: http://www.msmc.la.edu/
President/CEO: Dr. Jacqueline P. Doud
Registrar: Rocio DeLeon
Admissions: Dean Kilgour
Financial Aid: La Royce Dodd
Type: Comprehensive **Sex:** Coed **Affiliation:** Roman Catholic **Scores:** 98% SAT V 400+; 96% SAT M 400+ **% Accepted:** 85 **Admission Plans:** Early Action; Deferred Admission **Application Deadline:** February 15 **Application Fee:** $40.00 **H.S. Requirements:** High school diploma required; GED accepted **Costs Per Year:** Application fee: $40. Comprehensive fee: $32,897 includes full-time tuition ($23,380), mandatory fees ($770), and college room and board ($8747). Part-time tuition: $900 per unit. **Scholarships:** Available **Calendar System:** Semester, Summer Session Available **Enrollment:** FT 1,470, PT 510, Grad 500 **Faculty:** FT 74, PT 225 **Student-Faculty Ratio:** 13:1 **Exams:** SAT I or ACT, SAT I **% Receiving Financial Aid:** 90 **% Residing in College-Owned, -Operated, or -Affiliated Housing:** 59 **Library Holdings:** 140,000 **Regional Accreditation:** Western Association of Schools and Colleges **Credit Hours For Degree:** 60 units, Associates; 129 units, Bachelors **Professional Accreditation:** AACN, APTA, NASM

MT. SAN ANTONIO COLLEGE
1100 North Grand Ave.
Walnut, CA 91789-1399
Tel: (909)594-5611
Free: 800-672-2463
Web Site: http://www.mtsac.edu/
President/CEO: Dr. Christopher C. O'Hearn
Registrar: Patricia Montoya
Admissions: James Ocampo
Financial Aid: Susan Jones
Type: Two-Year College **Sex:** Coed **Affiliation:** California Community College System **Admission Plans:** Open Admission; Early Admission; Deferred Admission **H.S. Requirements:** High school diploma or equivalent not required **Costs Per Year:** State resident tuition: $0 full-time. Nonresident tuition: $4248 full-time, $177 per term part-time. Mandatory fees: $672 full-time, $26 per unit part-time, $24 per term part-time. **Scholarships:** Available **Calendar System:** Semester, Summer Session Available **Enrollment:** FT 8,567, PT 18,628 **Faculty:** FT 362, PT 860 **Library Holdings:** 64,291 **Regional Accreditation:** Western Association of Schools and Colleges **Credit Hours For Degree:** 60 units, Associates **Professional Accreditation:** CARC, JRCERT, NAACLS **Intercollegiate Athletics:** Badminton W; Baseball M; Basketball M & W; Cross-Country Running M & W; Football M; Golf M & W; Soccer M & W; Softball W; Swimming and Diving M & W; Tennis M & W; Track and Field M & W; Volleyball M & W; Water Polo M & W; Wrestling M

MT. SAN JACINTO COLLEGE
1499 North State St.
San Jacinto, CA 92583-2399
Tel: (909)487-6752
Fax: (909)654-6738
E-mail: egonzale@msjc.edu
Web Site: http://www.msjc.edu/
President/CEO: Dr. Richard J. Giese
Registrar: Elida Gonzales
Admissions: Elida Gonzales
Financial Aid: Mary Ellen Muehring
Type: Two-Year College **Sex:** Coed **Affiliation:** California Community College System **Admission Plans:** Open Admission; Early Admission **Application Fee:** $0.00 **H.S. Requirements:** High school diploma or equivalent not required **Scholarships:** Available **Calendar System:** Semester, Summer Session Available **Enrollment:** FT 3,506, PT 9,086 **Faculty:** FT 105, PT 316 **Student-Faculty Ratio:** 24:1 **Exams:** Other **Library Holdings:** 28,000 **Regional Accreditation:** Western Association of Schools and Colleges **Credit Hours For Degree:** 60 units, Associates **Intercollegiate Athletics:** Baseball M; Basketball M & W; Football M; Golf M; Soccer W; Tennis M & W; Volleyball W

MT. SIERRA COLLEGE
101 East Huntington Dr.
Monrovia, CA 91016
Tel: (626)873-2144; 888-828-8800.
Admissions: (626)873-2100
Fax: (626)359-5528
Web Site: http://www.mtsierra.edu/
President/CEO: Vaughn Hartunian
Registrar: Jeanette Anderson
Admissions: Al Desrosiors
Financial Aid: Adel Moini
Type: Four-Year College **Sex:** Coed **Admission Plans:** Open Admission **Application Fee:** $95.00 **H.S. Requirements:** High school diploma required; GED accepted **Calendar System:** Quarter, Summer Session Available **Enrollment:** FT 1,085, PT 15 **Faculty:** FT 22, PT 28 **Student-Faculty Ratio:** 15:1 **Library Holdings:** 6,000 **Credit Hours For Degree:** 199 credits, Bachelors **Professional Accreditation:** ACCSCT

MTI COLLEGE OF BUSINESS AND TECHNOLOGY
5221 Madison Ave.
Sacramento, CA 95841
Tel: (916)339-1500
Fax: (916)339-0305
E-mail: mmiller@mticollege.edu
Web Site: http://www.mticollege.com/
President/CEO: John Zimmerman
Admissions: Marije Miller
Financial Aid: Fran Belisle
Type: Two-Year College **Sex:** Coed **Application Fee:** $75.00 **Scholarships:** Available **Calendar System:** Continuous **Exams:** Other **Regional Accreditation:** Western Association of Schools and Colleges

MUSICIANS INSTITUTE
1655 North McCadden Place
Hollywood, CA 90028

Tel: (323)462-1384
Free: 800-255-PLAY
Fax: (323)462-6978
E-mail: admissions@mi.edu
Web Site: http://www.mi.edu/
Admissions: Steve Lunn
Financial Aid: Melissa Cuesta
Type: Four-Year College **Sex:** Coed **Application Fee:** $100.00 **H.S. Requirements:** High school diploma required; GED accepted **Costs Per Year:** Application fee: $100. Tuition: $16,800 full-time, $280 per credit part-time. Mandatory fees: $400 full-time, $100 per term part-time. Full-time tuition and fees vary according to degree level and program. Part-time tuition and fees vary according to course load. **Scholarships:** Available **Calendar System:** Quarter **% Receiving Financial Aid:** 61 **Professional Accreditation:** NASM

NAPA VALLEY COLLEGE
2277 Napa-Vallejo Hwy.
Napa, CA 94558-6236
Tel: (707)253-3000
Fax: (707)253-3064
E-mail: eshenk@napavalley.edu
Web Site: http://www.napavalley.edu/
President/CEO: Dr. Chris McCarthy
Admissions: Dr. Edward Shenk
Financial Aid: Jill Schrutz
Type: Two-Year College **Sex:** Coed **Affiliation:** California Community College System **Admission Plans:** Open Admission **Application Fee:** $0.00 **H.S. Requirements:** High school diploma or equivalent not required. For allied health programs: High school diploma required; GED accepted **Costs Per Year:** Application fee: $0. State resident tuition: $0 full-time. Nonresident tuition: $3624 full-time, $151 per unit part-time. Mandatory fees: $648 full-time, $26 per unit part-time, $12 per term part-time. Full-time tuition and fees vary according to course load. Part-time tuition and fees vary according to course load. **Scholarships:** Available **Calendar System:** Semester, Summer Session Available **Enrollment:** FT 1,909, PT 4,999 **Faculty:** FT 99, PT 212 **Student-Faculty Ratio:** 22:1 **Exams:** SAT I or ACT **Library Holdings:** 42,000 **Regional Accreditation:** Western Association of Schools and Colleges **Credit Hours For Degree:** 60 units, Associates **Professional Accreditation:** CARC **Intercollegiate Athletics:** Baseball M; Basketball M & W; Cross-Country Running M & W; Soccer M; Softball W; Swimming and Diving M & W; Tennis M & W; Volleyball W; Wrestling M

THE NATIONAL HISPANIC UNIVERSITY
14271 Story Rd.
San Jose, CA 95127-3823
Tel: (408)254-6900
Web Site: http://www.nhu.edu/
President/CEO: Dr. B. Roberto Cruz, II
Registrar: David Chacon
Admissions: Pamela Bustillo
Financial Aid: Takeo Kubo
Type: Four-Year College **Sex:** Coed **Application Fee:** $50.00 **H.S. Requirements:** High school diploma required; GED accepted **Scholarships:** Available **Calendar System:** Semester, Summer Session Available **Enrollment:** FT 176, PT 117 **Faculty:** FT 17, PT 35 **Student-Faculty Ratio:** 14:1 **Exams:** SAT I and SAT II or ACT **% Receiving Financial Aid:** 64 **Library Holdings:** 10,000 **Regional Accreditation:** Western Association of Schools and Colleges **Credit Hours For Degree:** 64 units, Associates; 124 units, Bachelors **Professional Accreditation:** ACICS

NATIONAL POLYTECHNIC COLLEGE OF ENGINEERING AND OCEANEERING
272 South Fries Ave.
Wilmington, CA 90744-6399
Tel: (310)834-2501
Free: 800-432-DIVE
Fax: (310)834-7132
Web Site: http://www.coo.edu/
President/CEO: Kevin B. Casey
Registrar: Carol Valiene
Admissions: Deborah Montgomery
Financial Aid: Lida Castillo
Type: Two-Year College **Sex:** Coed **Admission Plans:** Deferred Admission **Application Fee:** $50.00 **H.S. Requirements:** High school diploma required; GED accepted. For applicants sponsored by foreign governments: High school diploma or equivalent not required **Scholarships:** Available **Calendar System:** Continuous, Summer Session Not available **Faculty:** FT 14, PT 0 **Student-Faculty Ratio:** 15:1 **Regional Accreditation:** Western Association of Schools and Colleges **Credit Hours For Degree:** 90 quarter hours, Associates

NATIONAL UNIVERSITY
11255 North Torrey Pines Rd.
La Jolla, CA 92037-1011
Tel: (619)563-7100
Free: 800-NAT-UNIV
Admissions: (858)628-8648
Fax: (619)563-7299
E-mail: mmagee@nu.edu
Web Site: http://www.nu.edu/
President/CEO: Dr. Jerry C. Lee
Registrar: Dr. Douglas Slawson
Admissions: Megan Magee
Financial Aid: Mathew Levine
Type: Comprehensive **Sex:** Coed **Admission Plans:** Open Admission; Deferred Admission **Application Deadline:** Rolling **Application Fee:** $60.00 **H.S. Requirements:** High school diploma required; GED accepted **Costs Per Year:** Application fee: $60. Tuition: $8352 full-time, $1044 per course part-time. Full-time tuition varies according to course load. Part-time tuition varies according to course load. **Scholarships:** Available **Calendar System:** Quarter, Summer Session Available **Enrollment:** FT 1,631, PT 4,890, Grad 19,514 **Faculty:** FT 199, PT 2,502 **Student-Faculty Ratio:** 14:1 **% Receiving Financial Aid:** 63 **Library Holdings:** 226,049 **Regional Accreditation:** Western Association of Schools and Colleges **Credit Hours For Degree:** 90 quarter hours, Associates; 180 quarter hours, Bachelors **ROTC:** Army, Air Force **Professional Accreditation:** AACN

NEW COLLEGE OF CALIFORNIA
50 Fell St.
San Francisco, CA 94102-5206
Tel: (415)437-3460; 888-437-3460
Fax: (415)626-5171
Web Site: http://www.newcollege.edu/
President/CEO: Martin Hamilton
Registrar: Mary Elizabeth Kransberger
Admissions: Sarah Starpoli
Financial Aid: Mary Elizabeth Kransberger
Type: Comprehensive **Sex:** Coed **Admission Plans:** Open Admission; Deferred Admission **Application Fee:** $50.00 **H.S. Requirements:** High school diploma required; GED accepted **Costs Per Year:** Application fee: $50. Tuition: $12,642 full-time, $550 per unit part-time. Mandatory fees: $200 full-time, $100 per term part-time. **Calendar System:** Semester, Summer Session Not available **Enrollment:** FT 611, PT 7, Grad 70 **Faculty:** FT 122, PT 70 **Student-Faculty Ratio:** 15:1 **Library Holdings:** 24,000 **Regional Accreditation:** Western Association of Schools and Colleges **Credit Hours For Degree:** 120 semester credits, Bachelors

NEWSCHOOL OF ARCHITECTURE & DESIGN
1249 F St.
San Diego, CA 92101-6634
Tel: (619)235-4100
E-mail: nsa1249@aol.com
Web Site: http://www.newschoolarch.edu/
President/CEO: Gilbert D. Cooke
Admissions: Victor Parga
Financial Aid: Cara Baker
Type: Comprehensive **Sex:** Coed **Admission Plans:** Early Decision Plan **H.S. Requirements:** High school diploma required; GED accepted **Scholarships:** Available **Calendar System:** Quarter, Summer Session Available **Enrollment:** FT 4, Grad 98 **Faculty:** FT 7, PT 29 **Student-Faculty Ratio:** 15:1 **% Residing in College-Owned, -Operated, or -Affiliated Housing:** 10 **Library Holdings:** 7,500 **Credit Hours For Degree:** 100 quarter hours, Associates; 235 quarter hours, Bachelors **Professional Accreditation:** ACICS

NORTHROP RICE AVIATION INSTITUTE OF TECHNOLOGY
1155 West Arbor Vitae St., Ste. 115
Inglewood, CA 90301-2904
Tel: (310)568-8541

Fax: (310)568-8542
E-mail: info@nrait.edu
Web Site: http://www.nrait.edu/
President/CEO: James Michael Rice
Admissions: James Michael Rice
Type: Two-Year College **Sex:** Coed **Calendar System:** Quarter **Professional Accreditation:** ACCSCT

NORTHWESTERN POLYTECHNIC UNIVERSITY
117 Fourier Ave.
Fremont, CA 94539-7482
Tel: (510)657-5913
Admissions: (510)657-0256
Fax: (510)657-8975
Web Site: http://www.npu.edu/
President/CEO: Dr. George Hsieh
Registrar: Li Sun
Admissions: Alice Ye
Type: Comprehensive **Sex:** Coed **Application Fee:** $75.00 **H.S. Requirements:** High school diploma required; GED accepted **Costs Per Year:** Application fee: $75. Tuition: $6600 full-time, $275 per unit part-time. Mandatory fees: $140 full-time, $70 per term part-time. Full-time tuition and fees vary according to course load. Part-time tuition and fees vary according to course load. **Calendar System:** Trimester, Summer Session Available **Enrollment:** FT 62, PT 55, Grad 234 **Faculty:** FT 6, PT 50 **Student-Faculty Ratio:** 12:1 **% Residing in College-Owned, -Operated, or -Affiliated Housing:** 12 **Library Holdings:** 12,000 **Professional Accreditation:** ACICS **Intercollegiate Athletics:** Table Tennis M

NORTHWESTERN TECHNICAL COLLEGE
1825 Bell St., No. 100
Sacramento, CA 95825
Tel: (916)649-2400; (866)649-2400
Fax: (916)649-8649
E-mail: rnaylor@ntcollege.com
Web Site: http://www.ntcollege.com/
Admissions: Robert Naylor
Type: Two-Year College **Sex:** Coed **Scholarships:** Available **Professional Accreditation:** ACCSCT

NOTRE DAME DE NAMUR UNIVERSITY
1500 Ralston Ave.
Belmont, CA 94002-1908
Tel: (650)508-3500
Free: 800-263-0545
Admissions: (650)508-3600
Fax: (650)508-3660
E-mail: admissions@ndnu.edu
Web Site: http://www.ndnu.edu
President/CEO: Dr. John B. Oblak
Registrar: Sandy Lee
Admissions: Katy Murphy
Type: Comprehensive **Sex:** Coed **Affiliation:** Roman Catholic **Scores:** 89% SAT V 400+; 88% SAT M 400+; 33% ACT 18-23; 27% ACT 24-29 **% Accepted:** 96 **Admission Plans:** Early Action; Deferred Admission **Application Deadline:** Rolling **Application Fee:** $40.00 **H.S. Requirements:** High school diploma required; GED accepted **Costs Per Year:** Application fee: $40. Comprehensive fee: $34,230 includes full-time tuition ($23,650), mandatory fees ($200), and college room and board ($10,380). College room only: $7000. Part-time tuition: $545 per unit. Part-time mandatory fees: $30 per term. **Scholarships:** Available **Calendar System:** Semester, Summer Session Available **Enrollment:** FT 631, PT 259, Grad 698 **Faculty:** FT 50, PT 93 **Student-Faculty Ratio:** 13:1 **Exams:** SAT I or ACT **% Residing in College-Owned, -Operated, or -Affiliated Housing:** 36 **Regional Accreditation:** Western Association of Schools and Colleges **Credit Hours For Degree:** 124 credit hours, Bachelors **ROTC:** Air Force **Professional Accreditation:** NASM **Intercollegiate Athletics:** Basketball M & W; Cross-Country Running M & W; Golf M & W; Lacrosse M; Soccer M & W; Softball W; Volleyball W

OCCIDENTAL COLLEGE
1600 Campus Rd.
Los Angeles, CA 90041-3314
Tel: (323)259-2500
Free: 800-825-5262
Admissions: (323)259-2700
Fax: (323)341-4875
E-mail: admission@oxy.edu
Web Site: http://www.oxy.edu/
President/CEO: Theodore R. Mitchell
Registrar: Victor Egitto
Admissions: Vince Cuseo
Financial Aid: William D. Tingley
Type: Comprehensive **Sex:** Coed **Scores:** 98.2% SAT M 400+ **% Accepted:** 41 **Admission Plans:** Early Admission; Early Decision Plan; Deferred Admission **Application Deadline:** January 10 **Application Fee:** $50.00 **H.S. Requirements:** High school diploma required; GED accepted **Costs Per Year:** Application fee: $50. Comprehensive fee: $42,686 includes full-time tuition ($32,800), mandatory fees ($844), and college room and board ($9042). College room only: $4972. Part-time tuition: $1387 per credit. **Scholarships:** Available **Calendar System:** Semester, Summer Session Available **Enrollment:** FT 1,794, PT 25, Grad 20 **Faculty:** FT 148, PT 67 **Student-Faculty Ratio:** 10:1 **Exams:** SAT I or ACT, SAT II **% Receiving Financial Aid:** 55 **% Residing in College-Owned, -Operated, or -Affiliated Housing:** 70 **Library Holdings:** 497,161 **Regional Accreditation:** Western Association of Schools and Colleges **Credit Hours For Degree:** 128 units, Bachelors **ROTC:** Army, Navy, Air Force **Intercollegiate Athletics:** Baseball M; Basketball M & W; Cheerleading W; Crew W; Cross-Country Running M & W; Football M; Golf M & W; Lacrosse M & W; Rugby M & W; Soccer M & W; Softball W; Swimming and Diving M & W; Tennis M & W; Track and Field M & W; Ultimate Frisbee M & W; Volleyball M & W; Water Polo M & W

OHLONE COLLEGE
43600 Mission Blvd.
Fremont, CA 94539-5884
Tel: (510)659-6000
Admissions: (510)659-6108
Web Site: http://www.ohlone.edu/
President/CEO: Dr. Douglas Treadway
Registrar: Ron Travenick
Admissions: Allison Hill
Type: Two-Year College **Sex:** Coed **Affiliation:** California Community College System **Admission Plans:** Open Admission; Early Admission **Application Fee:** $0.00 **H.S. Requirements:** High school diploma required; GED accepted. For part-time programs: High school diploma or equivalent not required **Scholarships:** Available **Calendar System:** Semester, Summer Session Available **Faculty:** FT 134, PT 300 **Exams:** Other **Library Holdings:** 65,000 **Regional Accreditation:** Western Association of Schools and Colleges **Credit Hours For Degree:** 60 units, Associates **ROTC:** Army, Air Force **Professional Accreditation:** APTA, CARC, NLN **Intercollegiate Athletics:** Baseball M; Basketball M & W; Soccer M & W; Softball W; Swimming and Diving M & W; Track and Field M & W; Volleyball M & W; Water Polo M

ORANGE COAST COLLEGE
2701 Fairview Rd., PO Box 5005
Costa Mesa, CA 92628-5005
Tel: (714)432-0202
Admissions: (714)432-5788
Fax: (714)432-5072
Web Site: http://www.orangecoastcollege.com/
President/CEO: Gene Farrell
Registrar: Jess Craig
Admissions: Nancy Kidder
Financial Aid: Melissa Moser
Type: Two-Year College **Sex:** Coed **Affiliation:** Coast Community College District System **Admission Plans:** Open Admission **Application Deadline:** Rolling **Application Fee:** $0.00 **H.S. Requirements:** High school diploma or equivalent not required **Costs Per Year:** Application fee: $0. Nonresident tuition: $152 per unit part-time. Mandatory fees: $26 per unit part-time, $28 per term part-time. **Scholarships:** Available **Calendar System:** Semester, Summer Session Available **Enrollment:** FT 10,671, PT 13,679 **Faculty:** FT 298, PT 642 **Student-Faculty Ratio:** 20:1 **Library Holdings:** 84,447 **Regional Accreditation:** Western Association of Schools and Colleges **Credit Hours For Degree:** 60 units, Associates **ROTC:** Army, Air Force **Professional Accreditation:** ACF, ADA, CARC, JRCECT, JRCEDMS, JRCEET, JRCERT **Intercollegiate Athletics:** Baseball M; Basketball M & W; Bowling M & W; Crew M & W; Cross-Country Running M & W; Football M; Golf M & W; Soccer M & W; Softball W; Swimming and Diving M & W;

Tennis M & W; Track and Field M & W; Volleyball M & W; Water Polo M & W

OTIS COLLEGE OF ART AND DESIGN

9045 Lincoln Blvd.
Los Angeles, CA 90045-9785
Tel: (310)665-6800
Free: 800-527-OTIS
Admissions: (310)665-6820
Fax: (310)665-6805
E-mail: otisinfo@otisart.edu
Web Site: http://www.otis.edu/
President/CEO: Samuel Hoi
Registrar: River Montijo
Admissions: Marc D. Meredith
Financial Aid: Robin Bailey-Chen

Type: Comprehensive **Sex:** Coed **Scores:** 81% SAT V 400+; 93% SAT M 400+; 75% ACT 18-23 **% Accepted:** 62 **Admission Plans:** Early Admission **Application Deadline:** Rolling **Application Fee:** $50.00 **H.S. Requirements:** High school diploma required; GED accepted **Costs Per Year:** Application fee: $50. Tuition: $26,996 full-time, $900 per credit part-time. Mandatory fees: $550 full-time. **Scholarships:** Available **Calendar System:** Semester, Summer Session Available **Enrollment:** FT 1,020, PT 20, Grad 58 **Faculty:** FT 51, PT 226 **Student-Faculty Ratio:** 9:1 **Exams:** SAT I or ACT **% Receiving Financial Aid:** 75 **Library Holdings:** 42,000 **Regional Accreditation:** Western Association of Schools and Colleges **Credit Hours For Degree:** 134 credits, Bachelors **Professional Accreditation:** NASAD

OXNARD COLLEGE

4000 South Rose Ave.
Oxnard, CA 93033-6699
Tel: (805)986-5800
Admissions: (805)986-5843
Fax: (805)986-5806
Web Site: http://www.oxnard.cc.ca.us/
President/CEO: Dr. Lydia Ledesma-Reese
Registrar: Susan Brent
Admissions: Susan O. Brent
Financial Aid: Joe Ramirez

Type: Two-Year College **Sex:** Coed **Affiliation:** Ventura County Community College District System **Admission Plans:** Open Admission; Early Admission **H.S. Requirements:** High school diploma required; GED accepted. For applicants 18 or over: High school diploma or equivalent not required **Scholarships:** Available **Calendar System:** Semester, Summer Session Available **Faculty:** FT 90, PT 279 **Student-Faculty Ratio:** 25:1 **Library Holdings:** 31,500 **Regional Accreditation:** Western Association of Schools and Colleges **Credit Hours For Degree:** 60 units, Associates **Professional Accreditation:** ADA **Intercollegiate Athletics:** Baseball M; Basketball M & W; Cross-Country Running M & W; Soccer M & W; Track and Field M & W; Volleyball W

PACIFIC OAKS COLLEGE

5 Westmoreland Place
Pasadena, CA 91103
Tel: (626)397-1300
Free: 800-684-0900
Admissions: (626)397-4945
Fax: (626)397-1317
Web Site: http://www.pacificoaks.edu/
President/CEO: Dr. Carolyn H. Denham
Registrar: Tracie Matthews
Admissions: Teresa Cook
Financial Aid: Tracie Matthews

Type: Two-Year Upper Division **Sex:** Coed **Admission Plans:** Deferred Admission **Application Fee:** $55.00 **H.S. Requirements:** High school diploma required; GED accepted **Costs Per Year:** Application fee: $55. Tuition: $16,320 full-time, $680 per unit part-time. Mandatory fees: $60 full-time, $30 per term part-time. **Scholarships:** Available **Calendar System:** Semester, Summer Session Available **Enrollment:** FT 14, PT 194, Grad 655 **Faculty:** FT 24, PT 39 **Student-Faculty Ratio:** 11:1 **Library Holdings:** 32,580 **Regional Accreditation:** Western Association of Schools and Colleges **Credit Hours For Degree:** 124 units, Bachelors

PACIFIC STATES UNIVERSITY

1516 South Western Ave.
Los Angeles, CA 90006
Tel: (323)731-2383; 888-200-0383
Fax: (323)731-7276
Web Site: http://www.psuca.edu/
President/CEO: Dr. Jae Duk Kim
Registrar: Mai Diep
Financial Aid: Mai Diep

Type: Comprehensive **Sex:** Coed **% Accepted:** 100 **Admission Plans:** Open Admission; Early Admission; Deferred Admission **Application Deadline:** September 21 **Application Fee:** $100.00 **H.S. Requirements:** High school diploma required; GED accepted **Costs Per Year:** Application fee: $100. Tuition: $8400 full-time, $195 per unit part-time. Mandatory fees: $480 full-time. Full-time tuition and fees vary according to course load. Part-time tuition varies according to course load. **Calendar System:** Quarter, Summer Session Available **Enrollment:** FT 44 **Faculty:** FT 4, PT 12 **Student-Faculty Ratio:** 20:1 **Library Holdings:** 15,000 **Credit Hours For Degree:** 180 units, Bachelors **Professional Accreditation:** ACICS

PACIFIC UNION COLLEGE

One Angwin Ave.
Angwin, CA 94508-9707
Tel: (707)965-6311
Free: 800-862-7080
Admissions: (707)965-6425
Fax: (707)965-6390
E-mail: enroll@puc.edu
Web Site: http://www.puc.edu/
President/CEO: Dr. Richard C. Osborn
Registrar: Susi Mundy
Admissions: Sean Kootsey
Financial Aid: Glen Bobst

Type: Comprehensive **Sex:** Coed **Affiliation:** Seventh-day Adventist **Scores:** 91% SAT V 400+; 87% SAT M 400+; 47% ACT 18-23; 28% ACT 24-29 **% Accepted:** 29 **Admission Plans:** Deferred Admission **Application Deadline:** Rolling **Application Fee:** $30.00 **H.S. Requirements:** High school diploma required; GED accepted **Costs Per Year:** Application fee: $30. Comprehensive fee: $24,555 includes full-time tuition ($18,990), mandatory fees ($135), and college room and board ($5430). College room only: $3312. Full-time tuition and fees vary according to course load. Part-time tuition: $550 per quarter hour. Part-time mandatory fees: $45 per term. Part-time tuition and fees vary according to course load. Tuition guaranteed not to increase for student's term of enrollment. **Scholarships:** Available **Calendar System:** Quarter, Summer Session Available **Enrollment:** FT 1,370, PT 146, Grad 2 **Faculty:** FT 80, PT 19 **Student-Faculty Ratio:** 15:1 **Exams:** ACT, SAT I or ACT, SAT I and SAT II or ACT **% Receiving Financial Aid:** 62 **% Residing in College-Owned, -Operated, or -Affiliated Housing:** 70 **Library Holdings:** 173,839 **Regional Accreditation:** Western Association of Schools and Colleges **Credit Hours For Degree:** 90 quarter hours, Associates; 192 quarter hours, Bachelors **Professional Accreditation:** CSWE, NASM, NLN **Intercollegiate Athletics:** Basketball M & W; Cross-Country Running M & W; Volleyball M & W

PALO VERDE COLLEGE

One College Dr.
Blythe, CA 92225-9561
Tel: (760)921-5500
Admissions: (760)921-5409
Fax: (760)921-5590
Web Site: http://www.paloverde.edu/
President/CEO: Dr. James W. Hottois
Registrar: Melinda Walnoha
Admissions: Pat Koester
Financial Aid: Linda Pratt

Type: Two-Year College **Sex:** Coed **Affiliation:** California Community College System **% Accepted:** 100 **Admission Plans:** Open Admission; Early Admission **Application Deadline:** Rolling **Application Fee:** $0.00 **H.S. Requirements:** High school diploma or equivalent not required **Costs Per Year:** Application fee: $0. Nonresident tuition: $4248 full-time, $177 per unit part-time. Mandatory fees: $624 full-time, $26 per unit part-time. **Scholarships:** Available **Calendar System:** Semester, Summer Session Available **Enrollment:** FT 3,648 **Faculty:** FT 33, PT 128 **Library Holdings:** 21,457 **Regional Accreditation:** Western Association of Schools and Colleges **Credit Hours For Degree:** 60 units, Associates

PALOMAR COLLEGE

1140 West Mission Rd.
San Marcos, CA 92069-1487

Tel: (760)744-1150
Fax: (760)744-2932
E-mail: hlee@palomar.edu
Web Site: http://www.palomar.edu/
President/CEO: Dr. Sherrill L. Amador
Registrar: Herman Lee
Admissions: Herman Lee
Financial Aid: Mary San Agustin
Type: Two-Year College **Sex:** Coed **Affiliation:** California Community College System **Admission Plans:** Open Admission **Application Fee:** $0.00 **H.S. Requirements:** High school diploma or equivalent not required **Scholarships:** Available **Calendar System:** Semester, Summer Session Available **Enrollment:** FT 7,499, PT 21,098 **Faculty:** FT 267, PT 822 **Student-Faculty Ratio:** 24:1 **Exams:** Other **Library Holdings:** 108,000 **Regional Accreditation:** Western Association of Schools and Colleges **Credit Hours For Degree:** 60 units, Associates **Professional Accreditation:** ADA, NLN **Intercollegiate Athletics:** Basketball M & W; Football M; Soccer M; Swimming and Diving M & W; Tennis M & W; Volleyball W; Water Polo M; Wrestling M

PASADENA CITY COLLEGE
1570 East Colorado Blvd.
Pasadena, CA 91106-2041
Tel: (626)585-7123
Admissions: (626)585-7805
Fax: (626)585-7915
E-mail: mbramey@pasadena.edu
Web Site: http://www.pasadena.edu/
President/CEO: Dr. James P. Kossler
Admissions: Margaret B. Ramey
Financial Aid: Kim Miles
Type: Two-Year College **Sex:** Coed **Affiliation:** California Community College System **Admission Plans:** Open Admission; Early Admission; Deferred Admission **Application Deadline:** Rolling **H.S. Requirements:** High school diploma or equivalent not required. For applicants under 18: High school diploma required; GED accepted **Costs Per Year:** State resident tuition: $0 full-time. Nonresident tuition: $5000 full-time, $160 per unit part-time. Mandatory fees: $780 full-time, $26 per unit part-time. **Calendar System:** Semester, Summer Session Available **Enrollment:** FT 29,189 **Faculty:** FT 400, PT 925 **Student-Faculty Ratio:** 20:1 **Library Holdings:** 120,000 **Regional Accreditation:** Western Association of Schools and Colleges **Credit Hours For Degree:** 60 units, Associates **Professional Accreditation:** ADA, JRCERT, NLN **Intercollegiate Athletics:** Baseball M; Basketball M & W; Cross-Country Running M & W; Football M; Soccer M & W; Softball W; Swimming and Diving M & W; Tennis M & W; Track and Field M & W; Volleyball W; Water Polo M

PATTEN UNIVERSITY
2433 Coolidge Ave.
Oakland, CA 94601-2699
Tel: (510)261-8500
Fax: (510)534-8564
Web Site: http://www.patten.edu/
President/CEO: Dr. Gary Moncher
Registrar: Melanie Duchesne
Admissions: Inez Bailey
Financial Aid: Dennis Clark
Type: Comprehensive **Sex:** Coed **Affiliation:** interdenominational **Admission Plans:** Open Admission; Early Admission; Deferred Admission **Application Fee:** $30.00 **H.S. Requirements:** High school diploma required; GED accepted **Scholarships:** Available **Calendar System:** Semester, Summer Session Available **Enrollment:** FT 207, PT 239 **Faculty:** FT 16, PT 42 **Student-Faculty Ratio:** 14:1 **Exams:** SAT I or ACT **% Residing in College-Owned, -Operated, or -Affiliated Housing:** 15 **Library Holdings:** 35,000 **Regional Accreditation:** Western Association of Schools and Colleges **Credit Hours For Degree:** 63 units, Associates; 125 units, Bachelors **Intercollegiate Athletics:** Basketball M & W; Cross-Country Running M & W; Golf M; Soccer M & W; Softball W

PEPPERDINE UNIVERSITY
24255 Pacific Coast Hwy.
Malibu, CA 90263
Tel: (310)506-4000
Admissions: (310)506-4392
Fax: (310)506-4861
E-mail: admission-seaver@pepperdine.edu
Web Site: http://www.pepperdine.edu/
President/CEO: Dr. Andrew K. Benton
Admissions: Paul A. Long
Financial Aid: Edna Powell
Type: University **Sex:** Coed **Affiliation:** Church of Christ **Scores:** 99.7% SAT V 400+; 99.6% SAT M 400+; 23.1% ACT 18-23; 56.5% ACT 24-29 **% Accepted:** 28 **Application Deadline:** January 15 **Application Fee:** $65.00 **H.S. Requirements:** High school diploma required; GED accepted **Costs Per Year:** Application fee: $65. Comprehensive fee: $42,240 includes full-time tuition ($32,620), mandatory fees ($120), and college room and board ($9500). Part-time tuition: $1010 per unit. **Scholarships:** Available **Calendar System:** Semester, Summer Session Available **Enrollment:** FT 2,740, PT 458, Grad 3,762 **Faculty:** FT 400, PT 326 **Student-Faculty Ratio:** 12:1 **Exams:** SAT I or ACT **% Receiving Financial Aid:** 49 **% Residing in College-Owned, -Operated, or -Affiliated Housing:** 62 **Library Holdings:** 315,078 **Regional Accreditation:** Western Association of Schools and Colleges **Credit Hours For Degree:** 128 units, Bachelors **ROTC:** Army, Air Force **Professional Accreditation:** AACSB, ABA, AALS, NASM **Intercollegiate Athletics:** Baseball M; Basketball M & W; Cheerleading M & W; Crew M & W; Cross-Country Running M & W; Field Hockey W; Golf M & W; Lacrosse M; Rugby M; Sailing M & W; Soccer M & W; Swimming and Diving W; Tennis M & W; Volleyball M & W; Water Polo M & W

PIMA MEDICAL INSTITUTE
780 Bay Blvd., Ste. 101
Chula Vista, CA 91910
Tel: (619)425-3200; 888-898-9048
Fax: (619)425-3450
Web Site: http://www.pmi.edu
Admissions: Marie DeFede
Type: Two-Year College **Sex:** Coed **Affiliation:** Vocational Training Institutes, Inc **Application Fee:** $100.00 **H.S. Requirements:** High school diploma required; GED accepted **Costs Per Year:** Application fee: $100. Tuition guaranteed not to increase for student's term of enrollment. **Faculty:** FT 6, PT 1 **Student-Faculty Ratio:** 14:1 **Exams:** Other **Credit Hours For Degree:** 88 credits, Associates **Professional Accreditation:** ABHES

PITZER COLLEGE
1050 North Mills Ave.
Claremont, CA 91711-6101
Tel: (909)621-8000
Free: 800-748-9371
Admissions: (909)621-8129
Fax: (909)621-8770
E-mail: admission@email.pitzer.edu
Web Site: http://www.pitzer.edu/
President/CEO: Laura Skandera Trombley
Registrar: Cheryl Morales
Admissions: Dr. Arnaldo Rodriguez
Financial Aid: Dr. Arnaldo Rodriguez
Type: Four-Year College **Sex:** Coed **Affiliation:** The Claremont Colleges Consortium **Scores:** 100% SAT V 400+; 100% SAT M 400+ **% Accepted:** 39 **Admission Plans:** Early Admission; Early Action; Deferred Admission **Application Deadline:** January 01 **Application Fee:** $50.00 **H.S. Requirements:** High school diploma required; GED accepted **Costs Per Year:** Application fee: $50. Comprehensive fee: $41,644 includes full-time tuition ($29,520), mandatory fees ($3492), and college room and board ($8632). College room only: $5402. Full-time tuition and fees vary according to course load. Room and board charges vary according to board plan. Part-time tuition: $3690 per course. Part-time tuition varies according to course load. **Scholarships:** Available **Calendar System:** Semester, Summer Session Available **Enrollment:** FT 911, PT 52 **Faculty:** FT 68, PT 24 **Student-Faculty Ratio:** 11:1 **Exams:** SAT I or ACT **% Receiving Financial Aid:** 40 **% Residing in College-Owned, -Operated, or -Affiliated Housing:** 73 **Library Holdings:** 2,000,000 **Regional Accreditation:** Western Association of Schools and Colleges **Credit Hours For Degree:** 32 courses, Bachelors **ROTC:** Army, Air Force **Intercollegiate Athletics:** Baseball M; Basketball M & W; Cross-Country Running M & W; Football M; Golf M; Soccer M & W; Softball W; Swimming and Diving M & W; Tennis M & W; Track and Field M & W; Volleyball W; Water Polo M & W; Wrestling M

PLATT COLLEGE (CERRITOS)
10900 East 183rd St., Ste. 290
Cerritos, CA 90703-5342

Tel: (562)809-5100
Free: 800-807-5288
Fax: (562)809-7100
Web Site: http://www.platt.edu/
President/CEO: Margaret Simons
Registrar: Leslie Paramo
Admissions: Bob Cios
Financial Aid: Garnett McKinney
Type: Two-Year College **Sex:** Coed **H.S. Requirements:** High school diploma required; GED accepted **Scholarships:** Available **Calendar System:** Continuous **Faculty:** PT 30 **Student-Faculty Ratio:** 12:1 **Exams:** Other **Professional Accreditation:** ACCSCT

PLATT COLLEGE-LOS ANGELES, INC
1000 South Fremont A9W
Alhambra, CA 91803
Tel: (323)258-8050
Fax: (323)258-8532
Web Site: http://www.plattcollege.edu/
President/CEO: Gina Marinello
Registrar: Joyce Boylan
Admissions: Detroit Whiteside
Financial Aid: Tracey Karp
Type: Two-Year College **Sex:** Coed **Application Fee:** $75.00 **H.S. Requirements:** High school diploma required; GED accepted **Calendar System:** Continuous, Summer Session Available **Enrollment:** FT 179 **Faculty:** FT 1, PT 11 **Exams:** Other **Library Holdings:** 808 **Credit Hours For Degree:** 96 credits, Associates **Professional Accreditation:** ACCSCT

PLATT COLLEGE (NEWPORT BEACH)
3901 MacArthur Blvd.
Newport Beach, CA 92660
Tel: (949)833-2300; 888-866-6697
Web Site: http://www.plattcollege.edu/
President/CEO: Lisa Rhodes
Registrar: Mary Brouwer
Admissions: Lisa Rhodes
Financial Aid: Jennifer Olevson
Type: Two-Year College **Sex:** Coed **Application Fee:** $75.00 **H.S. Requirements:** High school diploma required; GED accepted **Calendar System:** Continuous, Summer Session Available **Enrollment:** FT 270 **Faculty:** FT 8, PT 16 **Student-Faculty Ratio:** 16:1 **Exams:** Other **Library Holdings:** 1,100 **Credit Hours For Degree:** 96 credits, Associates **Professional Accreditation:** ACCSCT

PLATT COLLEGE (ONTARIO)
3700 Inland Empire Blvd., Ste. 400
Ontario, CA 91764
Tel: (909)941-9410; 888-866-6697
Fax: (909)989-8974
Web Site: http://www.plattcollege.edu/
President/CEO: Alan Purvis
Registrar: Sherry Henderson
Admissions: Jennifer Abandonato
Financial Aid: Donna Wickers
Type: Two-Year College **Sex:** Coed **Application Fee:** $75.00 **H.S. Requirements:** High school diploma required; GED accepted **Calendar System:** Continuous, Summer Session Available **Enrollment:** FT 385 **Faculty:** FT 6, PT 23 **Exams:** Other **Library Holdings:** 2,800 **Credit Hours For Degree:** 96 credit hours, Associates **Professional Accreditation:** ACCSCT

PLATT COLLEGE SAN DIEGO
6250 El Cajon Blvd.
San Diego, CA 92115-3919
Tel: (619)265-0107; (866)752-8826
Fax: (619)265-8655
E-mail: mleiker@platt.edu
Web Site: http://www.platt.edu/
President/CEO: Robert Leiker
Registrar: Marita Gubbe
Admissions: Margaret Leiker
Financial Aid: Opel Oliver
Type: Two-Year College **Sex:** Coed **Application Fee:** $110.00 **H.S. Requirements:** High school diploma required; GED accepted **Costs Per Year:** Application fee: $110. Tuition: $17,226 full-time. Mandatory fees: $110 full-time. **Calendar System:** Continuous **Enrollment:** FT 253 **Faculty:** FT 5, PT 25 **Student-Faculty Ratio:** 20:1 **Professional Accreditation:** ACCSCT

POINT LOMA NAZARENE UNIVERSITY
3900 Lomaland Dr.
San Diego, CA 92106-2899
Tel: (619)849-2200
Free: 800-733-7770
Admissions: (619)849-2273
Fax: (619)849-2579
Web Site: http://www.ptloma.edu/
President/CEO: Dr. Bob Brower
Registrar: Cheryl Gaughan
Admissions: Scott Shoemaker
Financial Aid: Mary Jane Towne-Denton
Type: Comprehensive **Sex:** Coed **Affiliation:** Nazarene **Scores:** 100% SAT V 400+; 98% SAT M 400+; 36% ACT 18-23; 51% ACT 24-29 **% Accepted:** 65 **Admission Plans:** Early Action; Deferred Admission **Application Deadline:** March 01 **Application Fee:** $50.00 **H.S. Requirements:** High school diploma required; GED accepted **Costs Per Year:** Application fee: $50. Comprehensive fee: $29,310 includes full-time tuition ($21,620), mandatory fees ($530), and college room and board ($7160). **Scholarships:** Available **Calendar System:** Semester, Summer Session Available **Enrollment:** FT 2,282, PT 78, Grad 1,085 **Faculty:** FT 139, PT 199 **Student-Faculty Ratio:** 11:1 **Exams:** SAT I or ACT, SAT I **% Receiving Financial Aid:** 54 **% Residing in College-Owned, -Operated, or -Affiliated Housing:** 68 **Library Holdings:** 152,377 **Regional Accreditation:** Western Association of Schools and Colleges **Credit Hours For Degree:** 128 semester units, Bachelors **ROTC:** Army, Navy, Air Force **Professional Accreditation:** AACN, AAFCS, ACBSP, NASM, NLN **Intercollegiate Athletics:** Baseball M; Basketball M & W; Cross-Country Running M & W; Golf M; Soccer M & W; Softball W; Tennis M & W; Track and Field M & W; Volleyball W

POMONA COLLEGE
333 North College Way
Claremont, CA 91711
Tel: (909)621-8000
Admissions: (909)621-8134
Fax: (909)621-8403
E-mail: admissions@pomona.edu
Web Site: http://www.pomona.edu/
President/CEO: Dr. David W. Oxtoby
Registrar: Margaret Adorno
Admissions: Bruce Poch
Financial Aid: Patricia A. Coye
Type: Four-Year College **Sex:** Coed **Affiliation:** The Claremont Colleges Consortium **Scores:** 100% SAT V 400+; 100% SAT M 400+; 7% ACT 18-23; 18% ACT 24-29 **% Accepted:** 19 **Admission Plans:** Early Admission; Early Decision Plan; Deferred Admission **Application Deadline:** January 02 **Application Fee:** $60.00 **H.S. Requirements:** High school diploma or equivalent not required **Costs Per Year:** Application fee: $60. Comprehensive fee: $40,774 includes full-time tuition ($29,650), mandatory fees ($273), and college room and board ($10,851). Room and board charges vary according to board plan. **Scholarships:** Available **Calendar System:** Semester, Summer Session Not available **Enrollment:** FT 1,532 **Faculty:** FT 172, PT 34 **Student-Faculty Ratio:** 8:1 **Exams:** SAT II **% Receiving Financial Aid:** 53 **% Residing in College-Owned, -Operated, or -Affiliated Housing:** 97 **Regional Accreditation:** Western Association of Schools and Colleges **Credit Hours For Degree:** 32 courses, Bachelors **Intercollegiate Athletics:** Baseball M; Basketball M & W; Cross-Country Running M & W; Football M; Golf M & W; Soccer M & W; Softball W; Swimming and Diving M & W; Tennis M & W; Track and Field M & W; Ultimate Frisbee M & W; Volleyball W; Water Polo M & W

PORTERVILLE COLLEGE
100 East College Ave.
Porterville, CA 93257-6058
Tel: (559)791-2200
Admissions: (559)791-2222
Fax: (559)791-2349
Web Site: http://www.pc.cc.ca.us/
President/CEO: Dr. William M. Andrews
Registrar: Virginia Gurrola
Admissions: Judy Pope

Financial Aid: Steven Schultz
Type: Two-Year College **Sex:** Coed **Affiliation:** Kern Community College District System **Admission Plans:** Open Admission; Early Admission **Application Fee:** $0.00 **H.S. Requirements:** High school diploma or equivalent not required. For licensed vocational nursing program: High school diploma required; GED accepted **Calendar System:** Semester, Summer Session Available **Faculty:** FT 60, PT 80 **Library Holdings:** 31,557 **Regional Accreditation:** Western Association of Schools and Colleges **Credit Hours For Degree:** 60 units, Associates **Intercollegiate Athletics:** Baseball M; Basketball M & W; Soccer M & W; Softball W; Tennis M & W; Volleyball W

PROFESSIONAL GOLFERS CAREER COLLEGE
PO Box 892319
Temecula, CA 92589
Tel: (909)693-2963
Free: 800-877-4380
Admissions: (951)693-2963
Fax: (909)693-2863
Web Site: http://www.golfcollege.edu/
President/CEO: Dr. Tim Somerville
Admissions: David Ober
Financial Aid: Ann Arnold
Type: Two-Year College **Sex:** Coed **Admission Plans:** Early Admission; Deferred Admission **Application Fee:** $75.00 **H.S. Requirements:** High school diploma required; GED accepted **Costs Per Year:** Application fee: $75. Tuition: $14,370 full-time. Mandatory fees: $475 full-time. Full-time tuition and fees vary according to student level. College room only: $2525. Room charges vary according to location. **Calendar System:** Semester **Enrollment:** FT 318 **Faculty:** FT 5, PT 18 **Student-Faculty Ratio:** 15:1 **Library Holdings:** 2,291 **Credit Hours For Degree:** 66 credits, Associates **Professional Accreditation:** ACICS

QUEEN OF THE HOLY ROSARY COLLEGE
PO Box 3908
Mission San Jose, CA 94539-0391
Tel: (510)657-2468
Fax: (510)657-1734
Web Site: http://www.msjdominicans.org/college.html
President/CEO: Sr. Rose Marie Hennessy
Registrar: Sr. Mary Martin Bush
Admissions: Sr. Mary Paul Mehegan
Type: Two-Year College **Sex:** Coed **Affiliation:** Roman Catholic **Admission Plans:** Open Admission **Application Fee:** $15.00 **H.S. Requirements:** High school diploma required; GED accepted **Calendar System:** Semester, Summer Session Available **Enrollment:** FT 5, PT 190 **Faculty:** FT 0, PT 17 **Student-Faculty Ratio:** 5:1 **Exams:** SAT I **Library Holdings:** 24,937 **Regional Accreditation:** Western Association of Schools and Colleges **Credit Hours For Degree:** 70 credits, Associates

REEDLEY COLLEGE
995 North Reed Ave.
Reedley, CA 93654-2099
Tel: (559)638-3641
Admissions: (559)638-0323
Web Site: http://www.reedleycollege.com/
President/CEO: Dr. Thomas A. Crow
Registrar: Leticia Alvarez
Admissions: Leticia Alvarez
Financial Aid: Christina Cortes
Type: Two-Year College **Sex:** Coed **Affiliation:** State Center Community College District System **Admission Plans:** Open Admission **Application Fee:** $0.00 **H.S. Requirements:** High school diploma required; GED accepted **Scholarships:** Available **Calendar System:** Semester, Summer Session Available **Enrollment:** FT 4,556, PT 6,749 **Faculty:** FT 150, PT 392 **Student-Faculty Ratio:** 14:1 **Exams:** Other **Library Holdings:** 36,000 **Regional Accreditation:** Western Association of Schools and Colleges **Credit Hours For Degree:** 60 units, Associates **ROTC:** Air Force **Intercollegiate Athletics:** Baseball M; Basketball M & W; Football M; Golf M; Softball W; Tennis M & W; Track and Field M & W; Volleyball W

REMINGTON COLLEGE-SAN DIEGO CAMPUS
123 Camino de la Reina
North Bldg., Ste. 100
San Diego, CA 92108
Tel: (619)686-8600
Free: 800-214-7001
Fax: (619)686-8684
E-mail: jose.cisneros@remingtoncollege.edu
Web Site: http://www.remingtoncollege.edu/
President/CEO: Jose Cisneros
Admissions: Jose Cisneros
Type: Comprehensive **Sex:** Coed **Faculty:** FT 15, PT 8 **Professional Accreditation:** ACICS

RIO HONDO COLLEGE
3600 Workman Mill Rd.
Whittier, CA 90601-1699
Tel: (562)692-0921
Fax: (562)692-9318
Web Site: http://www.rh.cc.ca.us/
President/CEO: Rose Marie Joyce, PhD
Registrar: Dr. Frank O'Kelley
Admissions: Judy G. Pearson
Financial Aid: Maria-Graceli Romero
Type: Two-Year College **Sex:** Coed **Affiliation:** California Community College System **Admission Plans:** Open Admission; Early Admission **Application Fee:** $0.00 **H.S. Requirements:** High school diploma or equivalent not required **Scholarships:** Available **Calendar System:** Semester, Summer Session Available **Faculty:** FT 210, PT 500 **Library Holdings:** 94,143 **Regional Accreditation:** Western Association of Schools and Colleges **Credit Hours For Degree:** 62 units, Associates **ROTC:** Army, Navy, Air Force **Intercollegiate Athletics:** Baseball M; Basketball M & W; Cross-Country Running M & W; Softball W; Swimming and Diving M & W; Tennis M & W; Volleyball W; Water Polo M & W; Wrestling M

RIVERSIDE COMMUNITY COLLEGE DISTRICT
4800 Magnolia Ave.
Riverside, CA 92506-1299
Tel: (909)222-8000
Admissions: (951)222-8600
Fax: (909)222-8037
E-mail: admissions@rcc.edu
Web Site: http://www.rcc.edu/
President/CEO: Dr. Salvatore Rotella
Registrar: Lorraine Shoaf
Admissions: Lorraine Anderson
Financial Aid: Eugenia Vincent
Type: Two-Year College **Sex:** Coed **Affiliation:** California Community College System **% Accepted:** 100 **Admission Plans:** Open Admission **Application Deadline:** Rolling **Application Fee:** $0.00 **H.S. Requirements:** High school diploma or equivalent not required. For registered nursing program: High school diploma required; GED not accepted **Costs Per Year:** Application fee: $0. State resident tuition: $0 full-time. Nonresident tuition: $6090 full-time, $203 per unit part-time. Mandatory fees: $820 full-time, $26 per unit part-time, $20 per term part-time. **Scholarships:** Available **Calendar System:** Semester, Summer Session Available **Enrollment:** FT 8,701, PT 21,689 **Faculty:** FT 322, PT 1,054 **Student-Faculty Ratio:** 22:1 **Library Holdings:** 101,243 **Regional Accreditation:** Western Association of Schools and Colleges **Credit Hours For Degree:** 60 units, Associates **ROTC:** Army, Air Force **Professional Accreditation:** ADA, NLN **Intercollegiate Athletics:** Baseball M; Basketball M & W; Cross-Country Running M & W; Football M; Golf M; Soccer M & W; Softball W; Swimming and Diving M & W; Tennis M & W; Track and Field M & W; Volleyball W; Water Polo M & W

SACRAMENTO CITY COLLEGE
3835 Freeport Blvd.
Sacramento, CA 95822-1386
Tel: (916)558-2111
Admissions: (916)558-2438
Fax: (916)558-2190
Web Site: http://www.scc.losrios.edu/
President/CEO: Robert Harris, PhD
Admissions: Sam T. Sandusky
Financial Aid: Pat Maga
Type: Two-Year College **Sex:** Coed **Affiliation:** California Community College System **Admission Plans:** Open Admission **Application Fee:** $0.00 **H.S. Requirements:** High school diploma or equivalent not required **Scholarships:** Available **Calendar System:** Semester, Summer Session Available **Student-Faculty Ratio:** 30:1 **Library Holdings:** 68,462 **Regional**

Accreditation: Western Association of Schools and Colleges **Credit Hours For Degree:** 60 units, Associates **Professional Accreditation:** ADA, AOTA, APTA **Intercollegiate Athletics:** Baseball M; Basketball M & W; Cross-Country Running M & W; Football M; Golf M & W; Soccer W; Softball W; Swimming and Diving M & W; Tennis M & W; Track and Field M & W; Volleyball W; Water Polo W; Wrestling M

SADDLEBACK COLLEGE
28000 Marguerite Parkway
Mission Viejo, CA 92692-3635
Tel: (949)582-4500
Admissions: (949)582-4340
Fax: (949)347-8315
E-mail: jrosenkrans@saddleback.edu
Web Site: http://www.saddleback.cc.ca.us/
President/CEO: Dixie Bullock
Registrar: Joyce Semanik
Admissions: Jane Rosenkrans
Financial Aid: Wendy Baker
Type: Two-Year College **Sex:** Coed **Admission Plans:** Open Admission; Early Admission **Application Deadline:** Rolling **H.S. Requirements:** High school diploma or equivalent not required **Costs Per Year:** Nonresident tuition: $178 per unit part-time. Mandatory fees: $26 per unit part-time, $14 per term part-time. **Scholarships:** Available **Calendar System:** Semester, Summer Session Available **Enrollment:** FT 6,337, PT 12,014 **Faculty:** FT 215, PT 539 **Library Holdings:** 109,000 **Regional Accreditation:** Western Association of Schools and Colleges **Credit Hours For Degree:** 64 units, Associates **Professional Accreditation:** NLN **Intercollegiate Athletics:** Baseball M; Basketball M & W; Cross-Country Running M & W; Football M; Golf M & W; Softball W; Swimming and Diving M & W; Tennis M & W; Track and Field M & W; Volleyball W; Water Polo M & W

SAGE COLLEGE
12125 Day St., Bldg. L
Moreno Valley, CA 92557-6720
Tel: (951)781-2727
Fax: (951)781-0570
Web Site: http://www.sagecollege.edu/
President/CEO: Lauren Somma
Type: Two-Year College **Sex:** Coed **Calendar System:** Quarter **Professional Accreditation:** ACICS

SAINT MARY'S COLLEGE OF CALIFORNIA
1928 Saint Mary's Rd.
Moraga, CA 94575
Tel: (925)631-4000
Free: 800-800-4SMC
Admissions: (925)631-4224
Fax: (925)376-7193
E-mail: smcadmit@stmarys-ca.edu
Web Site: http://www.stmarys-ca.edu/
President/CEO: Br. Craig J. Franz, PhD
Registrar: Julia Odom
Admissions: Dorothy Jones
Financial Aid: Billie Jones
Type: Comprehensive **Sex:** Coed **Affiliation:** Roman Catholic **Scores:** 99.6% SAT V 400+; 99.5% SAT M 400+ **% Accepted:** 85 **Admission Plans:** Early Action; Deferred Admission **Application Deadline:** February 01 **Application Fee:** $55.00 **H.S. Requirements:** High school diploma required; GED accepted **Costs Per Year:** Application fee: $55. Comprehensive fee: $37,290 includes full-time tuition ($27,130), mandatory fees ($150), and college room and board ($10,010). College room only: $5590. Full-time tuition and fees vary according to course load. Room and board charges vary according to board plan and housing facility. Part-time tuition: $3392 per course. Part-time tuition varies according to course load. **Scholarships:** Available **Calendar System:** 4-1-4, Summer Session Not available **Enrollment:** FT 2,514, PT 777, Grad 1,141 **Faculty:** FT 213, PT 334 **Student-Faculty Ratio:** 12:1 **Exams:** SAT I or ACT **% Receiving Financial Aid:** 63 **% Residing in College-Owned, -Operated, or -Affiliated Housing:** 63 **Library Holdings:** 111,068 **Regional Accreditation:** Western Association of Schools and Colleges **Credit Hours For Degree:** 36 courses, Bachelors **ROTC:** Army, Air Force **Professional Accreditation:** AACN, MACTE **Intercollegiate Athletics:** Baseball M; Basketball M & W; Crew M & W; Cross-Country Running M & W; Golf M; Lacrosse M & W; Rugby M & W; Soccer M & W; Softball W; Tennis M & W; Volleyball M & W; Water Polo M & W

THE SALVATION ARMY COLLEGE FOR OFFICER TRAINING AT CRESTMONT
30840 Hawthorne Blvd.
Rancho Palos Verdes, CA 90275
Tel: (310)377-0481
Admissions: (310)544-6442
Fax: (310)265-6565
E-mail: kevin_jackson@usw.salvationarmy.org
Web Site: http://www.crestmont.edu/
President/CEO: Lt. Col. Raymond Peacock
Registrar: Maj. Donna Ames
Admissions: Capt. Kevin Jackson
Type: Two-Year College **Sex:** Coed **Affiliation:** The Salvation Army **% Accepted:** 67 **Admission Plans:** Preferred Admission **Application Deadline:** June 01 **Application Fee:** $15.00 **H.S. Requirements:** High school diploma required; GED accepted **Costs Per Year:** Application fee: $15. Comprehensive fee: $10,600 includes full-time tuition ($1500), mandatory fees ($850), and college room and board ($8250). **Calendar System:** Quarter, Summer Session Not available **Enrollment:** FT 27 **Faculty:** FT 13, PT 22 **Student-Faculty Ratio:** 1:1 **% Residing in College-Owned, -Operated, or -Affiliated Housing:** 100 **Library Holdings:** 35,700 **Regional Accreditation:** Western Association of Schools and Colleges **Credit Hours For Degree:** 90 quarter units, Associates

SAMUEL MERRITT COLLEGE
370 Hawthorne Ave.
Oakland, CA 94609-3108
Tel: (510)869-6511
Free: 800-607-MERRITT
Admissions: (510)869-6610
Fax: (510)869-6525
E-mail: admission@samuelmerritt.edu
Web Site: http://www.samuelmerritt.edu/
President/CEO: Dr. Sharon Diaz
Registrar: Gilbert Rocha
Admissions: Anne Seed
Financial Aid: Mary Robinson
Type: Comprehensive **Sex:** Coed **Admission Plans:** Deferred Admission **Application Fee:** $35.00 **H.S. Requirements:** High school diploma required; GED accepted **Costs Per Year:** Application fee: $35. Tuition: $29,220 full-time, $1214 per unit part-time. Mandatory fees: $356 full-time, $356 per year part-time. College room only: $5903. **Scholarships:** Available **Calendar System:** 4-1-4, Summer Session Available **Enrollment:** FT 304, PT 59, Grad 591 **Faculty:** FT 64, PT 93 **Student-Faculty Ratio:** 10:1 **% Receiving Financial Aid:** 91 **% Residing in College-Owned, -Operated, or -Affiliated Housing:** 6 **Library Holdings:** 33,000 **Regional Accreditation:** Western Association of Schools and Colleges **Credit Hours For Degree:** 128 units, Bachelors **ROTC:** Army, Air Force **Professional Accreditation:** AACN, AANA, AOTA, APTA

SAN BERNARDINO VALLEY COLLEGE
701 South Mt Vernon Ave.
San Bernardino, CA 92410-2748
Tel: (909)384-4400
Admissions: (909)384-4401
Web Site: http://www.valleycollege.edu/
President/CEO: Denise Whittaker
Registrar: Jessie Gates
Admissions: Helena Johnson
Financial Aid: Maureen Martinez
Type: Two-Year College **Sex:** Coed **Affiliation:** San Bernardino Community College District System **Admission Plans:** Open Admission **H.S. Requirements:** High school diploma required; GED accepted **Scholarships:** Available **Calendar System:** Semester, Summer Session Available **Faculty:** FT 175, PT 200 **Exams:** Other **Library Holdings:** 122,802 **Regional Accreditation:** Western Association of Schools and Colleges **Credit Hours For Degree:** 60 semester hours, Associates **Professional Accreditation:** NLN **Intercollegiate Athletics:** Basketball M & W; Cross-Country Running M & W; Football M; Golf M; Soccer M & W; Tennis M & W; Track and Field M & W; Volleyball W; Wrestling M

SAN DIEGO CHRISTIAN COLLEGE
2100 Greenfield Dr.
El Cajon, CA 92019-1157
Tel: (619)441-2200

Free: 800-676-2242
Fax: (619)440-0209
Web Site: http://www.sdcc.edu/
President/CEO: Dr. David Jeremiah
Registrar: Susie M. Parks
Financial Aid: Nancy DeMars
Type: Four-Year College **Sex:** Coed **Affiliation:** nondenominational **Scores:** 90% SAT V 400+; 81% SAT M 400+; 64% ACT 18-23; 18% ACT 24-29 **% Accepted:** 72 **Admission Plans:** Deferred Admission **Application Deadline:** July 01 **Application Fee:** $25.00 **H.S. Requirements:** High school diploma required; GED accepted **Costs Per Year:** Application fee: $25. Comprehensive fee: $24,522 includes full-time tuition ($16,476), mandatory fees ($866), and college room and board ($7180). Part-time tuition: $570 per credit. **Scholarships:** Available **Calendar System:** Semester, Summer Session Available **Enrollment:** FT 457, PT 54, Grad 42 **Faculty:** FT 29, PT 38 **Student-Faculty Ratio:** 12:1 **Exams:** SAT I or ACT **% Receiving Financial Aid:** 84 **% Residing in College-Owned, -Operated, or -Affiliated Housing:** 43 **Library Holdings:** 75,001 **Regional Accreditation:** Western Association of Schools and Colleges **Credit Hours For Degree:** 124 semester credits, Bachelors **ROTC:** Army, Air Force **Professional Accreditation:** TACCS **Intercollegiate Athletics:** Basketball M & W; Cross-Country Running M & W; Soccer M & W; Volleyball W

SAN DIEGO CITY COLLEGE
1313 Park Blvd.
San Diego, CA 92101-4787
Tel: (619)388-3400
Admissions: (619)388-3474
Fax: (619)388-3063
E-mail: lhumphri@sdccd.edu
Web Site: http://www.sdcity.edu/
President/CEO: Terrence Burgess
Registrar: Lou Humphries
Admissions: Lou Humphries
Financial Aid: Mario Chacon
Type: Two-Year College **Sex:** Coed **Affiliation:** San Diego Community College District System **Admission Plans:** Open Admission **Application Deadline:** Rolling **Application Fee:** $0.00 **H.S. Requirements:** High school diploma or equivalent not required. For applicants under 18: High school diploma required; GED accepted **Costs Per Year:** Application fee: $0. State resident tuition: $0 full-time. Nonresident tuition: $4800 full-time, $186 per unit part-time. Mandatory fees: $806 full-time, $26 per unit part-time, $13 per term part-time. **Scholarships:** Available **Calendar System:** Semester, Summer Session Available **Faculty:** FT 160, PT 325 **Student-Faculty Ratio:** 35:1 **Library Holdings:** 73,000 **Regional Accreditation:** Western Association of Schools and Colleges **Credit Hours For Degree:** 60 semester hours, Associates **ROTC:** Air Force **Professional Accreditation:** NLN **Intercollegiate Athletics:** Baseball M; Basketball M & W; Cross-Country Running M & W; Football M; Golf M & W; Soccer M & W; Softball W; Tennis M & W; Track and Field M & W; Volleyball M & W

SAN DIEGO GOLF ACADEMY
1910 Shadowridge Dr., Ste. 111
Vista, CA 92083
Tel: (760)734-1208
Free: 800-342-7342
Admissions: (760)414-1501
Fax: (760)734-1642
E-mail: sdga@sdgagolf.com
Web Site: http://www.sdgagolf.com/
President/CEO: Tim Eberlein
Registrar: Patti Luna
Admissions: Deborah Wells
Financial Aid: Patti Luna
Type: Two-Year College **Application Fee:** $50.00 **H.S. Requirements:** High school diploma required; GED accepted **Scholarships:** Available **Calendar System:** Semester **Credit Hours For Degree:** 66 credits, Associates **Professional Accreditation:** ACICS

SAN DIEGO MESA COLLEGE
7250 Mesa College Dr.
San Diego, CA 92111-4998
Tel: (619)388-2600
Admissions: (619)388-2689
Fax: (619)388-2968
E-mail: ialvarez@sdccd.edu
Web Site: http://www.sandiegomesacollege.net/
President/CEO: Dr. Rita Cepeda
Registrar: Ivonne Alvarez
Admissions: Ivonne Alvarez
Financial Aid: Judy Permetti
Type: Two-Year College **Sex:** Coed **Affiliation:** San Diego Community College District System **% Accepted:** 100 **Admission Plans:** Open Admission; Early Admission **Application Deadline:** Rolling **Application Fee:** $0.00 **H.S. Requirements:** High school diploma or equivalent not required **Scholarships:** Available **Calendar System:** Semester, Summer Session Available **Enrollment:** FT 21,198 **Faculty:** FT 287, PT 553 **Library Holdings:** 84,353 **Regional Accreditation:** Western Association of Schools and Colleges **Credit Hours For Degree:** 60 semester hours, Associates **Professional Accreditation:** AAMAE, ADA, AHIMA, APTA **Intercollegiate Athletics:** Baseball M; Basketball M & W; Cross-Country Running M & W; Football M; Soccer M & W; Softball W; Swimming and Diving M & W; Tennis M & W; Track and Field M & W; Volleyball M & W; Water Polo M & W

SAN DIEGO MIRAMAR COLLEGE
10440 Black Mountain Rd.
San Diego, CA 92126-2999
Tel: (619)388-7800
Admissions: (619)388-7844
Fax: (619)388-7801
E-mail: dandras@sdccd.net
Web Site: http://www.miramar.sdccd.cc.ca.us/
President/CEO: Ron Manzoni
Registrar: Dana Andras
Admissions: Dana Andras
Financial Aid: Judy Permetti
Type: Two-Year College **Sex:** Coed **Affiliation:** San Diego Community College District System **Admission Plans:** Open Admission **Application Fee:** $0.00 **H.S. Requirements:** High school diploma or equivalent not required **Costs Per Year:** Application fee: $0. State resident tuition: $0 full-time. Nonresident tuition: $4492 full-time, $186 per unit part-time. Mandatory fees: $652 full-time, $26 per unit part-time. **Scholarships:** Available **Calendar System:** Semester, Summer Session Available **Faculty:** FT 70, PT 214 **Library Holdings:** 19,301 **Regional Accreditation:** Western Association of Schools and Colleges **Credit Hours For Degree:** 60 credits, Associates **Intercollegiate Athletics:** Water Polo M & W

SAN DIEGO STATE UNIVERSITY
5500 Campanile Dr.
San Diego, CA 92182
Tel: (619)594-5200
Admissions: (619)594-6336
Web Site: http://www.sdsu.edu/
President/CEO: Dr. Stephen L. Weber
Admissions: Beverly Arata
Financial Aid: Chrys Dutton
Type: University **Sex:** Coed **Affiliation:** California State University System **Scores:** 96.29% SAT V 400+; 97.87% SAT M 400+; 52.35% ACT 18-23; 36.33% ACT 24-29 **% Accepted:** 47 **Application Deadline:** November 30 **Application Fee:** $55.00 **H.S. Requirements:** High school diploma required; GED accepted **Costs Per Year:** Application fee: $55. State resident tuition: $0 full-time. Nonresident tuition: $10,170 full-time, $339 per unit part-time. Mandatory fees: $3155 full-time, $1033 per term part-time. Full-time tuition and fees vary according to degree level. Part-time tuition and fees vary according to course load and degree level. College room and board: $9849. Room and board charges vary according to board plan and housing facility. **Scholarships:** Available **Calendar System:** Semester, Summer Session Available **Enrollment:** FT 21,630, PT 5,223, Grad 6,083 **Faculty:** FT 915, PT 703 **Student-Faculty Ratio:** 24:1 **Exams:** SAT I or ACT **% Receiving Financial Aid:** 48 **% Residing in College-Owned, -Operated, or -Affiliated Housing:** 11 **Library Holdings:** 1,342,735 **Regional Accreditation:** Western Association of Schools and Colleges **Credit Hours For Degree:** 120 units, Bachelors **ROTC:** Army, Navy, Air Force **Professional Accreditation:** AACSB, ABET, ACEHSA, AACN, ACNM, ADtA, APA, ASLHA, CAEPK, CEPH, CORE, CSWE, JRCEPAT, NASAD, NASPAA, NAST, NCATE, NRPA **Intercollegiate Athletics:** Baseball M; Basketball M & W; Cross-Country Running W; Football M; Golf

M & W; Soccer M & W; Softball W; Swimming and Diving W; Tennis M & W; Track and Field W; Volleyball M & W; Water Polo W

SAN FRANCISCO ART INSTITUTE
800 Chestnut St.
San Francisco, CA 94133
Tel: (415)771-7020
Free: 800-345-SFAI
Admissions: (415)749-4580
Web Site: http://www.sfai.edu/
President/CEO: Larry Thomas
Registrar: Herbert Tobey
Admissions: Victoria Valle
Financial Aid: Dennis Tominaga
Type: Comprehensive **Sex:** Coed **Scores:** 96.8% SAT V 400+; 93.5% SAT M 400+; 37.5% ACT 18-23; 25% ACT 24-29 **% Accepted:** 88 **Admission Plans:** Early Admission; Deferred Admission **Application Deadline:** Rolling **Application Fee:** $65.00 **H.S. Requirements:** High school diploma required; GED accepted **Costs Per Year:** Application fee: $65. Tuition: $27,400 full-time, $1175 per unit part-time. Mandatory fees: $15. College room only: $6540. **Scholarships:** Available **Calendar System:** Semester, Summer Session Available **Enrollment:** FT 319, PT 65, Grad 19 **Faculty:** FT 14, PT 132 **Student-Faculty Ratio:** 4:1 **Exams:** SAT I or ACT **Library Holdings:** 35,500 **Regional Accreditation:** Western Association of Schools and Colleges **Credit Hours For Degree:** 120 units, Bachelors **Professional Accreditation:** NASAD

SAN FRANCISCO CONSERVATORY OF MUSIC
1201 Ortega St.
San Francisco, CA 94122-4411
Tel: (415)564-8086
Admissions: (415)759-3431
Fax: (415)759-3499
Web Site: http://www.sfcm.edu/
President/CEO: Colin Murdoch
Registrar: Ruby Pleasure
Admissions: Susan Dean
Financial Aid: Doris Howard
Type: Comprehensive **Sex:** Coed **Scores:** 100% SAT V 400+; 93% SAT M 400+ **Admission Plans:** Early Admission **Application Fee:** $70.00 **H.S. Requirements:** High school diploma required; GED accepted **Scholarships:** Available **Calendar System:** Semester, Summer Session Not available **Faculty:** FT 24, PT 70 **Student-Faculty Ratio:** 6:1 **Exams:** SAT I or ACT, SAT I **% Receiving Financial Aid:** 83 **Library Holdings:** 36,821 **Regional Accreditation:** Western Association of Schools and Colleges **Credit Hours For Degree:** 130 semester hours, Bachelors **Professional Accreditation:** AOTA, NASM

SAN FRANCISCO STATE UNIVERSITY
1600 Holloway Ave.
San Francisco, CA 94132-1722
Tel: (415)338-1100
Web Site: http://www.sfsu.edu/
President/CEO: Dr. Robert A. Corrigan
Registrar: Suzanne Dmytrenko
Financial Aid: Barbara Hubler
Type: Comprehensive **Sex:** Coed **Affiliation:** California State University System **Scores:** 87.4% SAT V 400+; 91.7% SAT M 400+; 51.7% ACT 18-23; 18.6% ACT 24-29 **% Accepted:** 67 **Application Deadline:** Rolling **Application Fee:** $55.00 **H.S. Requirements:** High school diploma required; GED accepted **Costs Per Year:** Application fee: $55. State resident tuition: $0 full-time. Nonresident tuition: $13,540 full-time, $339 per unit part-time. Mandatory fees: $3370 full-time. College room and board: $9124. College room only: $5900. **Scholarships:** Available **Calendar System:** Semester, Summer Session Available **Enrollment:** FT 17,917, PT 5,157, Grad 5,876 **Faculty:** FT 865, PT 860 **Student-Faculty Ratio:** 21:1 **Exams:** SAT I or ACT **% Receiving Financial Aid:** 49 **% Residing in College-Owned, -Operated, or -Affiliated Housing:** 10 **Library Holdings:** 780,230 **Regional Accreditation:** Western Association of Schools and Colleges **Credit Hours For Degree:** 124 units, Bachelors **ROTC:** Army, Navy, Air Force **Professional Accreditation:** AACSB, ABET, ACEJMC, AACN, AAFCS, ACA, ADtA, APTA, ASLHA, CEPH, CORE, CSWE, NAACLS, NASAD, NASM, NASPAA, NAST, NCATE, NLN, NRPA **Intercollegiate Athletics:** Baseball M & W; Basketball M & W; Cross-Country Running M & W; Soccer M & W; Softball W; Swimming and Diving M & W; Track and Field M & W; Volleyball W; Wrestling M

SAN JOAQUIN DELTA COLLEGE
5151 Pacific Ave.
Stockton, CA 95207-6370
Tel: (209)954-5151
Admissions: (209)954-5635
Fax: (209)954-5600
Web Site: http://www.deltacollege.edu/
President/CEO: Raúl Rodriguez
Registrar: Catherine Mooney
Admissions: Catherine Mooney
Financial Aid: Ena S. Hull
Type: Two-Year College **Sex:** Coed **Affiliation:** California Community College System **% Accepted:** 100 **Admission Plans:** Open Admission; Early Admission **Application Deadline:** Rolling **Application Fee:** $0.00 **H.S. Requirements:** High school diploma or equivalent not required. For applicants under 18: High school diploma required; GED not accepted **Costs Per Year:** Application fee: $0. State resident tuition: $0 full-time. Nonresident tuition: $5250 full-time, $175 per unit part-time. Mandatory fees: $780 full-time, $26 per unit part-time. **Scholarships:** Available **Calendar System:** Semester, Summer Session Available **Faculty:** FT 208, PT 407 **Student-Faculty Ratio:** 33:1 **Library Holdings:** 92,398 **Regional Accreditation:** Western Association of Schools and Colleges **Credit Hours For Degree:** 60 units, Associates **Professional Accreditation:** ACF, NLN **Intercollegiate Athletics:** Baseball M; Basketball M & W; Cross-Country Running M & W; Fencing M & W; Football M; Golf M & W; Soccer M & W; Softball W; Swimming and Diving M & W; Tennis M & W; Track and Field M & W; Volleyball W; Water Polo M & W; Wrestling M

SAN JOAQUIN VALLEY COLLEGE
8400 West Mineral King Ave.
Visalia, CA 93291
Tel: (559)651-2500
E-mail: josephh@sjvc.edu
Web Site: http://www.sjvc.edu
President/CEO: Mark Perry
Registrar: Annette Valdez
Admissions: Joseph Holt
Financial Aid: Kevin Robinson
Type: Two-Year College **Sex:** Coed **% Accepted:** 97 **Admission Plans:** Open Admission **Application Deadline:** Rolling **H.S. Requirements:** High school diploma required; GED accepted **Costs Per Year:** Tuition: $11,475 full-time, $348 per unit part-time. **Scholarships:** Available **Calendar System:** Semester, Summer Session Not available **Enrollment:** FT 3,351, PT 1 **Faculty:** FT 275, PT 237 **Student-Faculty Ratio:** 10:1 **Library Holdings:** 4,720 **Regional Accreditation:** Western Association of Schools and Colleges **Credit Hours For Degree:** 60 credits, Associates **Professional Accreditation:** ARCEST, ADA, CARC

SAN JOSE CITY COLLEGE
2100 Moorpark Ave.
San Jose, CA 95128-2799
Tel: (408)298-2181
Admissions: (408)288-3707
Web Site: http://www.sjcc.edu/
President/CEO: Dr. Chui L. Tsang
Admissions: Carlo Santos
Financial Aid: Patricia Burke
Type: Two-Year College **Sex:** Coed **Affiliation:** San Jose/Evergreen Community College District System **Admission Plans:** Open Admission; Preferred Admission; Early Admission; Deferred Admission **Application Fee:** $0.00 **H.S. Requirements:** High school diploma or equivalent not required. For applicants under 18: High school diploma required; GED accepted **Scholarships:** Available **Calendar System:** Semester, Summer Session Available **Enrollment:** FT 7,578, PT 2,241 **Faculty:** FT 123, PT 215 **Library Holdings:** 54,075 **Regional Accreditation:** Western Association of Schools and Colleges **Credit Hours For Degree:** 60 units, Associates **ROTC:** Army, Air Force **Professional Accreditation:** ADA **Intercollegiate Athletics:** Baseball M; Basketball M & W; Cross-Country Running M & W; Football M; Golf M; Softball W; Track and Field M & W; Volleyball W

SAN JOSE STATE UNIVERSITY
One Washington Square
San Jose, CA 95192-0001
Tel: (408)924-1000
Admissions: (408)283-7500

Fax: (408)924-2050
E-mail: contact@sjsu.edu
Web Site: http://www.sjsu.edu/
President/CEO: Don Kassing
Registrar: Frank Wada
Admissions: Susan Hoagland
Financial Aid: Colleen Brown
Type: Comprehensive **Sex:** Coed **Affiliation:** California State University System **Scores:** 84.57% SAT V 400+; 91.04% SAT M 400+; 49.01% ACT 18-23; 19.06% ACT 24-29 **% Accepted:** 65 **Admission Plans:** Preferred Admission **Application Deadline:** November 30 **Application Fee:** $55.00 **H.S. Requirements:** High school diploma required; GED accepted **Costs Per Year:** Application fee: $55. Nonresident tuition: $10,170 full-time, $339 per unit part-time. Mandatory fees: $3292 full-time. Full-time tuition and fees vary according to course load. Part-time tuition varies according to course load. College room and board: $8718. College room only: $5412. Room and board charges vary according to board plan and housing facility. **Scholarships:** Available **Calendar System:** Semester, Summer Session Available **Enrollment:** FT 16,950, PT 5,783, Grad 7,242 **Exams:** SAT I or ACT **% Receiving Financial Aid:** 43 **Regional Accreditation:** Western Association of Schools and Colleges **Credit Hours For Degree:** 120 units, Bachelors **ROTC:** Army, Air Force **Professional Accreditation:** AACSB, ABET, ACEJMC, AACN, ADtA, ACSP, ALA, AOTA, ASLHA, CEPH, CSWE, JRCEPAT, NAIT, NASAD, NASD, NASM, NASPAA, NAST, NCATE, NRPA **Intercollegiate Athletics:** Badminton M & W; Baseball M; Basketball M & W; Bowling M & W; Cheerleading M & W; Cross-Country Running M & W; Football M; Golf M & W; Gymnastics W; Ice Hockey M & W; Rugby M; Sailing M & W; Soccer M & W; Softball W; Swimming and Diving W; Tennis W; Volleyball M & W; Water Polo W; Wrestling M & W

SANTA ANA COLLEGE
1530 West 17th St.
Santa Ana, CA 92706-3398
Tel: (714)564-6000
Web Site: http://www.sac.edu/
President/CEO: Dr. Edward Hernandez, Jr.
Registrar: Linda Miskovic
Financial Aid: Dr. Audrey Noji
Type: Two-Year College **Sex:** Coed **Affiliation:** California Community College System **Admission Plans:** Open Admission; Early Admission **H.S. Requirements:** High school diploma required; GED accepted **Scholarships:** Available **Calendar System:** Semester, Summer Session Available **Faculty:** FT 249, PT 1,047 **Student-Faculty Ratio:** 20:1 **Library Holdings:** 99,473 **Regional Accreditation:** Western Association of Schools and Colleges **Credit Hours For Degree:** 60 credits, Associates **ROTC:** Air Force **Professional Accreditation:** AOTA, NLN **Intercollegiate Athletics:** Baseball M; Basketball M & W; Cross-Country Running M & W; Football M; Golf M; Soccer M; Softball W; Swimming and Diving M; Tennis M & W; Track and Field M & W; Volleyball W; Water Polo M; Wrestling M

SANTA BARBARA CITY COLLEGE
721 Cliff Dr.
Santa Barbara, CA 93109-2394
Tel: (805)965-0581
Fax: (805)963-SBCC
E-mail: admissions@sbcc.edu
Web Site: http://www.sbcc.edu/
President/CEO: John B. Romo
Registrar: Jane Craven
Admissions: Allison Curtis
Financial Aid: Marsha Wright
Type: Two-Year College **Sex:** Coed **Affiliation:** California Community College System **% Accepted:** 100 **Admission Plans:** Open Admission; Early Admission **Application Deadline:** August 26 **Application Fee:** $0.00 **H.S. Requirements:** High school diploma required; GED accepted. For applicants 18 or over: High school diploma or equivalent not required **Costs Per Year:** Application fee: $0. State resident tuition: $0 full-time. Nonresident tuition: $5310 full-time, $151 per unit part-time. Mandatory fees: $831 full-time, $26 per unit part-time, $51 per year part-time. Full-time tuition and fees vary according to course load. Part-time tuition and fees vary according to course load. **Scholarships:** Available **Calendar System:** Semester, Summer Session Available **Enrollment:** FT 6,488, PT 9,252 **Faculty:** FT 259, PT 479 **Student-Faculty Ratio:** 29:1 **Library Holdings:** 121,622 **Regional Accreditation:** Western Association of Schools and Colleges **Credit Hours For Degree:** 60 units, Associates **ROTC:** Army **Professional Accreditation:** ACF, AHIMA, JRCERT, NLN **Intercollegiate Athletics:** Baseball M; Basketball M & W; Cross-Country Running M & W; Football M; Golf M & W; Soccer M & W; Softball W; Tennis M & W; Track and Field M & W; Volleyball M & W

SANTA CLARA UNIVERSITY
500 El Camino Real
Santa Clara, CA 95053
Tel: (408)554-4000
Admissions: (408)554-4700
Fax: (408)554-5255
E-mail: ugadmissions@scu.edu
Web Site: http://www.scu.edu/
President/CEO: Rev. Paul L. Locatelli, SJ
Registrar: Carol Lamoreaux
Admissions: Sandra Hayes
Financial Aid: Charles Nolan
Type: University **Sex:** Coed **Affiliation:** Roman Catholic (Jesuit) **Scores:** 99.5% SAT V 400+; 100% SAT M 400+; 21.4% ACT 18-23; 63.3% ACT 24-29 **% Accepted:** 61 **Admission Plans:** Early Action; Deferred Admission **Application Deadline:** January 15 **Application Fee:** $55.00 **H.S. Requirements:** High school diploma required; GED not accepted **Costs Per Year:** Application fee: $55. Comprehensive fee: $38,931 includes full-time tuition ($28,899) and college room and board ($10,032). Room and board charges vary according to board plan, housing facility, and student level. Part-time tuition: $925 per unit. Part-time tuition varies according to course load. **Scholarships:** Available **Calendar System:** Quarter, Summer Session Available **Enrollment:** FT 4,525, PT 113, Grad 2,485 **Faculty:** FT 447, PT 299 **Student-Faculty Ratio:** 12:1 **Exams:** SAT I or ACT **% Receiving Financial Aid:** 42 **% Residing in College-Owned, -Operated, or -Affiliated Housing:** 44 **Library Holdings:** 1,160,342 **Regional Accreditation:** Western Association of Schools and Colleges **Credit Hours For Degree:** 175 units, Bachelors **ROTC:** Army, Air Force **Professional Accreditation:** AACSB, ABET, ABA, AALS **Intercollegiate Athletics:** Baseball M; Basketball M & W; Crew M & W; Cross-Country Running M & W; Golf M & W; Lacrosse M & W; Rugby M & W; Soccer M & W; Softball W; Tennis M & W; Track and Field M & W; Volleyball M & W; Water Polo M & W

SANTA MONICA COLLEGE
1900 Pico Blvd.
Santa Monica, CA 90405-1628
Tel: (310)434-4000
Admissions: (310)434-4880
Web Site: http://www.smc.edu/
President/CEO: Dr. Piedad F. Robertson
Registrar: Brenda Simmons
Admissions: Teresita Rodriguez
Financial Aid: Heidi Granger
Type: Two-Year College **Sex:** Coed **Affiliation:** California Community College System **Admission Plans:** Open Admission; Early Admission **Application Fee:** $0.00 **H.S. Requirements:** High school diploma required; GED accepted. For international students: High school diploma required; GED not accepted **Costs Per Year:** Application fee: $0. Nonresident tuition: $171 per unit part-time. Mandatory fees: $26 per unit part-time, $27 per term part-time. **Scholarships:** Available **Calendar System:** Miscellaneous, Summer Session Available **Enrollment:** FT 8,902, PT 15,595 **Faculty:** FT 337, PT 901 **Student-Faculty Ratio:** 26:1 **Exams:** Other **Library Holdings:** 101,317 **Regional Accreditation:** Western Association of Schools and Colleges **Credit Hours For Degree:** 60 units, Associates **ROTC:** Army **Professional Accreditation:** CARC, NLN **Intercollegiate Athletics:** Basketball M & W; Cross-Country Running M & W; Football M; Soccer W; Softball W; Swimming and Diving M & W; Tennis W; Track and Field M & W; Volleyball M & W; Water Polo M & W

SANTA ROSA JUNIOR COLLEGE
1501 Mendocino Ave.
Santa Rosa, CA 95401-4395
Tel: (707)527-4011
Admissions: (707)527-4510
E-mail: rlopilato@santarosa.edu
Web Site: http://www.santarosa.edu/
President/CEO: Dr. Robert F. Agrella
Registrar: Renee LoPilato
Admissions: Ricardo Navarette

Financial Aid: Kris Shear
Type: Two-Year College **Sex:** Coed **Affiliation:** California Community College System **% Accepted:** 100 **Admission Plans:** Open Admission; Early Admission **Application Deadline:** Rolling **Application Fee:** $0.00 **H.S. Requirements:** High school diploma or equivalent not required. For applicants under 18, allied health programs: High school diploma required; GED accepted **Costs Per Year:** Application fee: $0. State resident tuition: $0 full-time. Nonresident tuition: $5630 full-time. Mandatory fees: $746 full-time, $26 per unit part-time. **Scholarships:** Available **Calendar System:** Semester, Summer Session Available **Faculty:** FT 305, PT 1,261 **Student-Faculty Ratio:** 19:1 **Library Holdings:** 119,803 **Regional Accreditation:** Western Association of Schools and Colleges **Credit Hours For Degree:** 60 units, Associates **ROTC:** Army **Professional Accreditation:** ADA, JRCERT **Intercollegiate Athletics:** Baseball M; Basketball M & W; Cross-Country Running M & W; Football M; Golf M; Ice Hockey M; Rugby M; Soccer M & W; Softball W; Swimming and Diving M & W; Tennis M & W; Track and Field M & W; Volleyball W; Water Polo M & W; Wrestling M

SANTIAGO CANYON COLLEGE

8045 East Chapman Ave.
Orange, CA 92869
Tel: (714)564-4000
Fax: (714)564-4379
Web Site: http://www.sccollege.edu/ **Type:** Two-Year College **Sex:** Coed **Affiliation:** California Community College System **Admission Plans:** Open Admission; Early Admission **H.S. Requirements:** High school diploma required; GED accepted **Calendar System:** Semester, Summer Session Available **Faculty:** FT 92, PT 325 **Student-Faculty Ratio:** 23:1 **Library Holdings:** 31,000 **Regional Accreditation:** Western Association of Schools and Colleges **Credit Hours For Degree:** 60 credits, Associates

SCRIPPS COLLEGE

1030 Columbia Ave.
Claremont, CA 91711-3948
Tel: (909)621-8000
Free: 800-770-1333
Admissions: (909)621-8149
Fax: (909)621-8323
E-mail: admission@scrippscollege.edu
Web Site: http://www.scrippscollege.edu
President/CEO: Nancy Y. Bekavac
Registrar: Carol Entler
Admissions: Patricia F. Goldsmith
Financial Aid: Sean Smith
Type: Four-Year College **Sex:** Women **Affiliation:** The Claremont Colleges Consortium **Scores:** 100% SAT V 400+; 100% SAT M 400+; 4% ACT 18-23; 60% ACT 24-29 **% Accepted:** 46 **Admission Plans:** Early Decision Plan; Deferred Admission **Application Deadline:** January 15 **Application Fee:** $50.00 **H.S. Requirements:** High school diploma required; GED accepted **Costs Per Year:** Application fee: $50. Comprehensive fee: $41,000 includes full-time tuition ($31,332), mandatory fees ($168), and college room and board ($9500). College room only: $5100. Full-time tuition and fees vary according to program. Room and board charges vary according to board plan. **Scholarships:** Available **Calendar System:** Semester, Summer Session Not available **Enrollment:** FT 879, PT 8, Grad 21 **Faculty:** FT 66, PT 34 **Student-Faculty Ratio:** 11:1 **Exams:** SAT I or ACT **% Receiving Financial Aid:** 43 **% Residing in College-Owned, -Operated, or -Affiliated Housing:** 92 **Library Holdings:** 998,823 **Regional Accreditation:** Western Association of Schools and Colleges **Credit Hours For Degree:** 32 courses, Bachelors **ROTC:** Army, Air Force **Intercollegiate Athletics:** Basketball W; Cross-Country Running W; Fencing W; Golf W; Lacrosse W; Rugby W; Skiing (Downhill) W; Soccer W; Softball W; Swimming and Diving W; Tennis W; Track and Field W; Volleyball W; Water Polo W

SHASTA BIBLE COLLEGE

2951 Goodwater Ave.
Redding, CA 96002
Tel: (530)221-4275
Free: 800-800-6929
Web Site: http://www.shasta.edu/
President/CEO: Dr. David R. Nicholas
Registrar: Mark A. Mueller
Admissions: George Gunn
Financial Aid: Jeff Hage
Type: Comprehensive **Sex:** Coed **Affiliation:** nondenominational **Admission Plans:** Open Admission; Early Admission **Application Fee:** $35.00 **H.S. Requirements:** High school diploma required; GED accepted **Costs Per Year:** Application fee: $35. Tuition: $6400 full-time, $200 per unit part-time. Mandatory fees: $350 full-time, $350 per year part-time. College room only: $1650. **Scholarships:** Available **Calendar System:** Semester, Summer Session Available **Enrollment:** FT 57, PT 33, Grad 33 **Faculty:** FT 7, PT 18 **Student-Faculty Ratio:** 9:1 **% Receiving Financial Aid:** 82 **% Residing in College-Owned, -Operated, or -Affiliated Housing:** 39 **Library Holdings:** 30,321 **Credit Hours For Degree:** 64 credit hours, Associates; 128 credit hours, Bachelors **Professional Accreditation:** TACCS

SHASTA COLLEGE

PO Box 496006
Redding, CA 96049-6006
Tel: (530)225-4600
Admissions: (530)225-4841
Web Site: http://www.shastacollege.edu/
Registrar: Cassandra Ryan
Admissions: Cassandra Ryan
Financial Aid: Benna Starrett
Type: Two-Year College **Sex:** Coed **Affiliation:** California Community College System **Admission Plans:** Open Admission; Early Admission **Application Fee:** $0.00 **H.S. Requirements:** High school diploma or equivalent not required **Scholarships:** Available **Calendar System:** Semester, Summer Session Available **Enrollment:** FT 4,336, PT 5,904 **Faculty:** FT 146, PT 345 **Exams:** Other, SAT I or ACT **Library Holdings:** 67,500 **Regional Accreditation:** Western Association of Schools and Colleges **Credit Hours For Degree:** 60 semester hours, Associates **Professional Accreditation:** ADA **Intercollegiate Athletics:** Baseball M; Basketball M & W; Cross-Country Running M & W; Football M; Golf M & W; Soccer M & W; Softball W; Swimming and Diving M & W; Tennis M & W; Track and Field M & W; Volleyball W

SIERRA COLLEGE

5000 Rocklin Rd.
Rocklin, CA 95677-3397
Tel: (916)624-3333
Admissions: (916)789-2939
Web Site: http://www.sierracollege.edu/
President/CEO: Dr. Kevin M. Ramirez
Registrar: Carla Epting-Davis
Admissions: Carla Epting-Davis
Financial Aid: Craig Yamamoto
Type: Two-Year College **Sex:** Coed **Affiliation:** California Community College System **Admission Plans:** Open Admission; Early Admission **Application Fee:** $0.00 **H.S. Requirements:** High school diploma or equivalent not required. For applicants 18 or over: High school diploma required; GED accepted **Costs Per Year:** Application fee: $0. State resident tuition: $0 full-time. Nonresident tuition: $4470 full-time, $149 per unit part-time. Mandatory fees: $780 full-time, $26 per unit part-time. **Scholarships:** Available **Calendar System:** Semester, Summer Session Available **Enrollment:** FT 5,355, PT 14,061 **Faculty:** FT 158, PT 712 **Student-Faculty Ratio:** 25:1 **Exams:** ACT, Other **% Residing in College-Owned, -Operated, or -Affiliated Housing:** 1 **Library Holdings:** 69,879 **Regional Accreditation:** Western Association of Schools and Colleges **Credit Hours For Degree:** 60 units, Associates **Intercollegiate Athletics:** Baseball M; Basketball M & W; Cross-Country Running M & W; Football M; Golf M & W; Skiing (Cross-Country) M & W; Skiing (Downhill) M & W; Softball W; Swimming and Diving M & W; Tennis M & W; Track and Field M & W; Volleyball W; Water Polo M & W; Wrestling M

SILICON VALLEY UNIVERSITY

3590 North First St., Ste. 320
San Jose, CA 95134
Tel: (408)435-8989
Fax: (408)435-8989
Web Site: http://www.svuca.edu/
President/CEO: Dr. Jerry Shiao

Type: Comprehensive **Sex:** Coed **Calendar System:** Trimester **Professional Accreditation:** ACICS

SIMPSON UNIVERSITY
2211 College View Dr.
Redding, CA 96003-8606
Tel: (530)226-4606
Free: 800-598-2493
Admissions: (530)226-5600
Fax: (530)226-4861
E-mail: admissions@simpsonuniversity.edu
Web Site: http://www.simpsonuniversity.edu/
President/CEO: Dr. James M. Grant
Registrar: Danny Posada
Admissions: Ronald G. Cushman
Financial Aid: James A. Herberger
Type: Comprehensive **Sex:** Coed **Affiliation:** The Christian and Missionary Alliance **Scores:** 89% SAT V 400+; 86% SAT M 400+; 45% ACT 18-23; 32% ACT 24-29 **% Accepted:** 54 **Admission Plans:** Deferred Admission **Application Deadline:** Rolling **Application Fee:** $20.00 **H.S. Requirements:** High school diploma required; GED accepted **Costs Per Year:** Application fee: $20. Comprehensive fee: $24,000 includes full-time tuition ($17,800) and college room and board ($6200). Part-time tuition: $750 per credit hour. **Scholarships:** Available **Calendar System:** Semester, Summer Session Available **Enrollment:** FT 899, PT 24, Grad 164 **Faculty:** FT 40, PT 67 **Student-Faculty Ratio:** 17:1 **Exams:** SAT I or ACT **% Receiving Financial Aid:** 85 **% Residing in College-Owned, -Operated, or -Affiliated Housing:** 67 **Library Holdings:** 87,203 **Regional Accreditation:** Western Association of Schools and Colleges **Credit Hours For Degree:** 62 credits, Associates; 124 credits, Bachelors **Intercollegiate Athletics:** Baseball M; Basketball M & W; Cheerleading W; Cross-Country Running M & W; Soccer M & W; Volleyball W

SKYLINE COLLEGE
3300 College Dr.
San Bruno, CA 94066-1698
Tel: (650)738-4100
Web Site: http://skylinecollege.net/
President/CEO: Dr. Frances L. White
Registrar: Sherri Hancock
Financial Aid: Sherri Hancock
Type: Two-Year College **Sex:** Coed **Affiliation:** San Mateo County Community College District System **Admission Plans:** Open Admission **Application Deadline:** Rolling **Application Fee:** $0.00 **H.S. Requirements:** High school diploma or equivalent not required. For applicants under 18, international students: High school diploma required; GED accepted **Costs Per Year:** Application fee: $0. **Scholarships:** Available **Calendar System:** Semester, Summer Session Available **Faculty:** FT 88, PT 212 **Student-Faculty Ratio:** 27:1 **Library Holdings:** 50,000 **Regional Accreditation:** Western Association of Schools and Colleges **Credit Hours For Degree:** 60 credits, Associates **Professional Accreditation:** ARCEST, CARC **Intercollegiate Athletics:** Baseball M; Basketball M; Cross-Country Running M & W; Soccer M; Softball W; Track and Field M & W; Volleyball W; Wrestling M

SOKA UNIVERSITY OF AMERICA
1 University Dr.
Aliso Viejo, CA 92656
Tel: (949)480-4000; 888-600-SOKA
Admissions: (949)480-4007
Fax: (949)480-4001
E-mail: hauber@soka.edu
Web Site: http://www.soka.edu/
President/CEO: Dr. Daniel Y. Habuki
Registrar: Wayne W. Van Ellis
Admissions: Dr. Eric Hauber
Financial Aid: Nirmala Sharma
Type: Four-Year College **Sex:** Coed **Scores:** 87% SAT V 400+; 100% SAT M 400+; 46% ACT 18-23; 38% ACT 24-29 **% Accepted:** 42 **Admission Plans:** Early Admission; Deferred Admission **Application Deadline:** January 06 **Application Fee:** $45.00 **H.S. Requirements:** High school diploma required; GED accepted **Costs Per Year:** Application fee: $45. Comprehensive fee: $29,256 includes full-time tuition ($20,856) and college room and board ($8400). **Calendar System:** Semester **Enrollment:** FT 360, Grad 20 **Faculty:** FT 37, PT 33 **Student-Faculty Ratio:** 8:1 **Exams:** Other, SAT I or ACT, SAT II **% Residing in College-Owned, -Operated, or -Affiliated Housing:** 99 **Library Holdings:** 63,806 **Credit Hours For Degree:** 120 units, Bachelors **Professional Accreditation:** AALE **Intercollegiate Athletics:** Cross-Country Running M & W; Swimming and Diving M & W; Track and Field M & W; Water Polo M & W

SOLANO COMMUNITY COLLEGE
4000 Suisun Valley Rd.
Suisun City, CA 94534-3197
Tel: (707)864-7000
Admissions: (707)864-7113
Fax: (707)864-7175
E-mail: admissions@solano.cc.ca.us
Web Site: http://www.solano.edu/
President/CEO: Armond Phillips
Registrar: Gerald Fisher
Admissions: Gerald Fisher
Financial Aid: Salvador Alcala
Type: Two-Year College **Sex:** Coed **Affiliation:** California Community College System **Admission Plans:** Open Admission; Early Admission; Deferred Admission **Application Fee:** $0.00 **H.S. Requirements:** High school diploma required; GED accepted **Scholarships:** Available **Calendar System:** Semester, Summer Session Available **Faculty:** FT 147, PT 227 **Student-Faculty Ratio:** 27:1 **Exams:** SAT I and SAT II or ACT **Library Holdings:** 32,000 **Regional Accreditation:** Western Association of Schools and Colleges **Credit Hours For Degree:** 60 credits, Associates **Intercollegiate Athletics:** Baseball M; Basketball M & W; Football M; Softball W; Swimming and Diving M & W; Volleyball W; Water Polo M & W

SONOMA COLLEGE (PETALUMA)
1304 South Point Blvd., Ste. 280
Petaluma, CA 94954
Tel: (707)283-0800
Free: 800-437-9474
Admissions: (707)664-9267
Web Site: http://www.sonomacollege.com/
President/CEO: Edward Schwartz
Registrar: Jo Ann Sotelo
Admissions: Delores Ford
Type: Two-Year College **Sex:** Coed **Admission Plans:** Open Admission **Application Fee:** $100.00 **H.S. Requirements:** High school diploma required; GED accepted **Scholarships:** Available **Calendar System:** Semester **Faculty:** FT 2, PT 20 **Student-Faculty Ratio:** 8:1 **Credit Hours For Degree:** 71 credits, Associates **Professional Accreditation:** ABHES, APTA

SONOMA COLLEGE (SAN FRANCISCO)
78 First St.
San Francisco, CA 94105
Tel: (415)543-1833; 888-649-7801
Fax: (415)543-1833
Web Site: http://www.sonomacollege.com/
President/CEO: John Stalcup
Type: Two-Year College **Sex:** Coed **Calendar System:** Semester **Professional Accreditation:** ABHES

SONOMA STATE UNIVERSITY
1801 East Cotati Ave.
Rohnert Park, CA 94928-3609
Tel: (707)664-2880
Admissions: (707)664-2846
Web Site: http://www.sonoma.edu/
President/CEO: Dr. Ruben Armiñana
Registrar: Lisa Noto
Admissions: Dr. Katharyn Crabbe
Financial Aid: Susan Gutierrez
Type: Comprehensive **Sex:** Coed **Affiliation:** California State University System **Scores:** 94.5% SAT V 400+; 95.3% SAT M 400+ **% Accepted:** 66 **Admission Plans:** Early Admission **Application Deadline:** Rolling **Application Fee:** $55.00 **H.S. Requirements:** High school diploma required; GED accepted **Costs Per Year:** Application fee: $55. State resident tuition: $0 full-time. Nonresident tuition: $10,170 full-time. Mandatory fees: $3616 full-time. Full-time tuition and fees vary according to course load. College room and board: $8890. College room only: $6052. Room and board charges vary according to board plan and housing facility. **Scholarships:** Available **Calendar System:** Semester, Summer Session Available **Enrollment:** FT 5,653, PT 946, Grad 1,150 **Student-Faculty Ratio:** 23:1 **Exams:** SAT I or

ACT **% Receiving Financial Aid:** 34 **% Residing in College-Owned, -Operated, or -Affiliated Housing:** 35 **Library Holdings:** 636,613 **Regional Accreditation:** Western Association of Schools and Colleges **Credit Hours For Degree:** 124 units, Bachelors **ROTC:** Army, Air Force **Professional Accreditation:** ACA, NASAD, NASM, NCATE, NLN **Intercollegiate Athletics:** Baseball M; Basketball M & W; Cross-Country Running W; Golf M; Soccer M & W; Softball W; Tennis M & W; Track and Field W; Volleyball W; Water Polo W

SOUTH COAST COLLEGE
2011 West Chapman Ave.
Orange, CA 92868
Tel: (714)867-5009
Free: 800-337-8366
Fax: (714)867-5026
Web Site: http://www.southcoastcollege.com/ **Type:** Two-Year College **Sex:** Coed **Professional Accreditation:** ACICS

SOUTHERN CALIFORNIA INSTITUTE OF ARCHITECTURE
960 East Third St.
Los Angeles, CA 90013
Tel: (213)613-2200
Free: 800-774-7242
Fax: (213)613-0524
E-mail: admissions@sciarc.edu
Web Site: http://www.sciarc.edu/
President/CEO: Eric O. Moss
Registrar: Lisa Russo
Admissions: Wenona Colinco
Financial Aid: Odessa Mathis
Type: Comprehensive **Sex:** Coed **Scores:** 100% SAT V 400+; 100% SAT M 400+; 100% ACT 18-23 **Admission Plans:** Deferred Admission **Application Fee:** $60.00 **H.S. Requirements:** High school diploma required; GED accepted **Scholarships:** Available **Calendar System:** Semester, Summer Session Available **Enrollment:** FT 183, Grad 25 **Student-Faculty Ratio:** 15:1 **Exams:** SAT I or ACT **% Receiving Financial Aid:** 72 **Library Holdings:** 10,000 **Regional Accreditation:** Western Association of Schools and Colleges **Credit Hours For Degree:** 150 units, Bachelors

SOUTHERN CALIFORNIA INSTITUTE OF TECHNOLOGY
1900 West Crescent Ave., Bldg. B
Anaheim, CA 92801
Tel: (714)520-5552
Web Site: http://www.scitcollege.com/ **Type:** Two-Year College **Scholarships:** Available **Enrollment:** FT 664, Grad 14 **Faculty:** FT 8, PT 12 **Student-Faculty Ratio:** 24:1 **Professional Accreditation:** ACCSCT

SOUTHERN CALIFORNIA SEMINARY
2075 East Madison Ave.
El Cajon, CA 92019
Tel: (619)442-9841
Fax: (619)442-4510
E-mail: coombsd@scbs.edu
Web Site: http://www.socalsem.edu/
President/CEO: Dr. Gary F. Combs
Registrar: Dr. Gary Woods
Admissions: Donna Coombs
Type: Comprehensive **Affiliation:** interdenominational **Professional Accreditation:** TACCS

SOUTHWESTERN COLLEGE
900 Otay Lakes Rd.
Chula Vista, CA 91910-7299
Tel: (619)421-6700
Admissions: (619)482-6550
Web Site: http://www.swc.cc.ca.us/
President/CEO: Norma L. Hernandez
Registrar: Georgia A. Copeland
Admissions: Georgia A. Copeland
Financial Aid: Virginia Hansen, PhD
Type: Two-Year College **Sex:** Coed **Affiliation:** California Community College System **Admission Plans:** Open Admission; Early Admission **Application Fee:** $0.00 **H.S. Requirements:** High school diploma or equivalent not required. For applicants under 18: High school diploma required; GED accepted **Scholarships:** Available **Calendar System:** Semester, Summer Session Available **Enrollment:** FT 5,609, PT 13,190 **Faculty:** FT 197, PT 609 **Student-Faculty Ratio:** 22:1 **Library Holdings:** 85,003 **Regional Accreditation:** Western Association of Schools and Colleges **Credit Hours For Degree:** 60 units, Associates **Professional Accreditation:** ARCEST, ADA, NLN **Intercollegiate Athletics:** Baseball M; Basketball M & W; Cross-Country Running M & W; Football M; Golf M; Soccer M; Softball W; Swimming and Diving M & W; Tennis M & W; Track and Field M & W

STANFORD UNIVERSITY
Stanford, CA 94305-9991
Tel: (650)723-2300
Admissions: (650)723-2091
Fax: (650)725-2846
E-mail: admission@stanford.edu
Web Site: http://www.stanford.edu/
President/CEO: John Hennessy
Registrar: Roger Printup
Admissions: Rick Shaw
Financial Aid: Robin G. Mamlet
Type: University **Sex:** Coed **Scores:** 100% SAT V 400+; 100% SAT M 400+; 2% ACT 18-23; 27% ACT 24-29 **% Accepted:** 12 **Admission Plans:** Early Action; Deferred Admission **Application Deadline:** December 15 **Application Fee:** $75.00 **H.S. Requirements:** High school diploma required; GED accepted **Costs Per Year:** Application fee: $75. One-time mandatory fee: $425. Comprehensive fee: $41,132 includes full-time tuition ($31,200) and college room and board ($9932). College room only: $5275. Room and board charges vary according to board plan. **Scholarships:** Available **Calendar System:** Quarter, Summer Session Available **Enrollment:** FT 6,515, PT 61, Grad 11,421 **Faculty:** FT 1,010, PT 21 **Student-Faculty Ratio:** 6:1 **Exams:** SAT I or ACT, SAT II **% Receiving Financial Aid:** 46 **% Residing in College-Owned, -Operated, or -Affiliated Housing:** 94 **Library Holdings:** 8,000,000 **Regional Accreditation:** Western Association of Schools and Colleges **Credit Hours For Degree:** 180 quarter hours, Bachelors **ROTC:** Army, Navy, Air Force **Professional Accreditation:** AACSB, ABET, ABA, APA, ACIPE, AALS, LCMEAMA, NCATE **Intercollegiate Athletics:** Baseball M; Basketball M & W; Crew M & W; Cross-Country Running M & W; Equestrian Sports M & W; Fencing M & W; Field Hockey M & W; Football M; Golf M & W; Gymnastics M & W; Ice Hockey M; Lacrosse M & W; Racquetball M & W; Rugby M & W; Sailing M & W; Skiing (Cross-Country) M & W; Skiing (Downhill) M & W; Soccer M & W; Softball W; Squash M & W; Swimming and Diving M & W; Tennis M & W; Track and Field M & W; Ultimate Frisbee M & W; Volleyball M & W; Water Polo M & W; Wrestling M

TAFT COLLEGE
29 Emmons Park Dr.
Taft, CA 93268-2317
Tel: (661)763-7700
Admissions: (661)763-7763
Fax: (661)763-7705
Web Site: http://www.taftcollege.edu/
President/CEO: Dr. D. Roe Darnell
Registrar: Denise Earl
Admissions: Gayle Roberts
Type: Two-Year College **Sex:** Coed **Affiliation:** California Community College System **Admission Plans:** Open Admission **Application Fee:** $0.00 **H.S. Requirements:** High school diploma or equivalent not required. For applicants under 18: High school diploma required; GED accepted **Costs Per Year:** Application fee: $0. State resident tuition: $0 full-time. Nonresident tuition: $4530 full-time, $151 per unit part-time. Mandatory fees: $780 full-time, $26 per unit part-time. Full-time tuition and fees vary according to course load. Part-time tuition and fees vary according to course load. College room and board: $3146. College room only: $1294. **Scholarships:** Available **Calendar System:** Semester, Summer Session Available **Enrollment:** FT 561, PT 6,463 **Faculty:** FT 37, PT 54 **Student-Faculty Ratio:** 18:1 **% Residing in College-Owned, -Operated, or -Affiliated Housing:** 6 **Library Holdings:** 28,500 **Regional Accreditation:** Western Association of Schools and Colleges **Credit Hours For Degree:** 60 units, Associates **Professional Accreditation:** ADA **Intercollegiate Athletics:** Baseball M; Basketball W; Soccer M; Softball W; Volleyball W

THOMAS AQUINAS COLLEGE
10000 North Ojai Rd.
Santa Paula, CA 93060-9980
Tel: (805)525-4417

Free: 800-634-9797
Fax: (805)525-9342
E-mail: jpdaly@thomasaquinas.edu
Web Site: http://www.thomasaquinas.edu/
President/CEO: Dr. Thomas E. Dillon
Registrar: Dr. Paul J. O'Reilly
Admissions: Jonathan P. Daly
Financial Aid: Gregory J. Becher
Type: Four-Year College **Sex:** Coed **Affiliation:** Roman Catholic **Scores:** 100% SAT V 400+; 100% SAT M 400+; 25% ACT 18-23; 50% ACT 24-29 **% Accepted:** 81 **Admission Plans:** Early Admission; Deferred Admission **Application Deadline:** Rolling **Application Fee:** $0.00 **H.S. Requirements:** High school diploma required; GED accepted **Costs Per Year:** Application fee: $0. Comprehensive fee: $25,300 includes full-time tuition ($19,300) and college room and board ($6000). **Scholarships:** Available **Calendar System:** Semester, Summer Session Not available **Enrollment:** FT 359 **Faculty:** FT 29, PT 5 **Student-Faculty Ratio:** 12:1 **Exams:** SAT I or ACT **% Receiving Financial Aid:** 67 **% Residing in College-Owned, -Operated, or -Affiliated Housing:** 99 **Library Holdings:** 58,000 **Regional Accreditation:** Western Association of Schools and Colleges **Credit Hours For Degree:** 146 hours, Bachelors **Professional Accreditation:** AALE

TOURO UNIVERSITY INTERNATIONAL
5665 Plaza Dr., 3rd Floor
Cypress, CA 90630
Tel: (714)816-0366
Fax: (714)816-0367
Web Site: http://www.tourou.edu/
President/CEO: Dr. Bernard Lander
Admissions: Wei Ren
Type: University **Sex:** Coed **Affiliation:** Touro College **% Accepted:** 71 **Admission Plans:** Open Admission **Application Deadline:** Rolling **Application Fee:** $75.00 **H.S. Requirements:** High school diploma required; GED accepted **Costs Per Year:** Application fee: $75. Tuition: $8000 full-time, $250 per credit part-time. Part-time tuition varies according to degree level. **Calendar System:** Miscellaneous, Summer Session Available **Enrollment:** FT 1,795, PT 712 **Faculty:** FT 41, PT 153 **Student-Faculty Ratio:** 18:1 **Library Holdings:** 30,692 **Credit Hours For Degree:** 120 credits, Bachelors

TRINITY LIFE BIBLE COLLEGE
5225 Hillsdale Blvd.
Sacramento, CA 95842
Tel: (916)348-4689
Fax: (916)334-2315
E-mail: kathyc@tlbc.org
Web Site: http://www.tlbc.edu/
President/CEO: Dr. Ron Harden
Registrar: Rev. Cherilyn Dean
Admissions: Kathy Clarke
Type: Four-Year College **Sex:** Coed **Affiliation:** nondenominational **Calendar System:** Quarter **Professional Accreditation:** TACCS

UNIVERSITY OF CALIFORNIA, BERKELEY
Berkeley, CA 94720-1500
Tel: (510)642-6000
Admissions: (510)642-2316
Fax: (510)642-7333
E-mail: ouars@uclink.berkeley.edu
Web Site: http://www.berkeley.edu/
President/CEO: Dr. Robert J. Birgeneau
Registrar: Susie Castillo-Robson
Admissions: Walter Robinson
Financial Aid: Dr. Richard W. Black
Type: University **Sex:** Coed **Affiliation:** University of California System **Scores:** 99% SAT V 400+; 100% SAT M 400+ **% Accepted:** 27 **Admission Plans:** Preferred Admission **Application Deadline:** November 30 **Application Fee:** $60.00 **H.S. Requirements:** High school diploma required; GED accepted **Costs Per Year:** Application fee: $60. State resident tuition: $0 full-time. Nonresident tuition: $18,684 full-time. Mandatory fees: $6558 full-time. College room and board: $13,074. **Scholarships:** Available **Calendar System:** Semester, Summer Session Available **Enrollment:** FT 22,295, PT 1,187, Grad 9,000 **Faculty:** FT 1,543, PT 483 **Student-Faculty Ratio:** 15:1 **Exams:** SAT I or ACT, SAT II **% Receiving Financial Aid:** 49 **% Residing in College-Owned, -Operated, or -Affiliated Housing:** 35 **Library Holdings:** 13,915,488 **Regional Accreditation:** Western Association of Schools and Colleges **Credit Hours For Degree:** 120 credits, Bachelors **ROTC:** Army, Navy, Air Force **Professional Accreditation:** AACSB, ABET, ACEHSA, ACEJMC, ABA, ADtA, ACSP, AOA, APA, ASLA, AALS, CEPH, CSWE, FIDER, SAF **Intercollegiate Athletics:** Baseball M; Basketball M & W; Crew M & W; Cross-Country Running M & W; Field Hockey W; Football M; Golf M & W; Gymnastics M & W; Lacrosse W; Rugby M; Soccer M & W; Softball W; Swimming and Diving M & W; Tennis M & W; Track and Field M; Volleyball W

UNIVERSITY OF CALIFORNIA, DAVIS
One Shields Ave.
Davis, CA 95616
Tel: (530)752-1011
Admissions: (530)752-3018
Fax: (530)752-6363
E-mail: plburnett@ucdavis.edu
Web Site: http://www.ucdavis.edu/
President/CEO: Dr. Larry N. Vanderhoef
Registrar: Dr. Jack Farrell
Admissions: Pamela Burnett
Financial Aid: Patricia Gutierrez
Type: University **Sex:** Coed **Affiliation:** University of California System **Scores:** 95% SAT V 400+; 100% SAT M 400+; 33% ACT 18-23; 49% ACT 24-29 **% Accepted:** 61 **Admission Plans:** Preferred Admission **Application Deadline:** November 30 **Application Fee:** $60.00 **H.S. Requirements:** High school diploma required; GED accepted **Costs Per Year:** Application fee: $60. State resident tuition: $0 full-time. Nonresident tuition: $18,168 full-time. Mandatory fees: $7593 full-time. College room and board: $11,239. **Scholarships:** Available **Calendar System:** Quarter, Summer Session Available **Enrollment:** FT 22,445, PT 290, Grad 4,051 **Faculty:** FT 1,610, PT 273 **Student-Faculty Ratio:** 19:1 **Exams:** SAT I or ACT, SAT II **% Receiving Financial Aid:** 48 **% Residing in College-Owned, -Operated, or -Affiliated Housing:** 25 **Library Holdings:** 4,447,563 **Regional Accreditation:** Western Association of Schools and Colleges **Credit Hours For Degree:** 180 units, Bachelors **ROTC:** Army, Navy, Air Force **Professional Accreditation:** AACSB, ABET, ABA, ADtA, APA, ASLA, AVMA, ACIPE, AALS, LCMEAMA, NAACLS **Intercollegiate Athletics:** Baseball M; Basketball M & W; Cross-Country Running M & W; Football M; Golf M & W; Gymnastics W; Lacrosse M & W; Soccer M & W; Softball W; Swimming and Diving M & W; Tennis M & W; Track and Field M & W; Volleyball M & W; Water Polo M & W; Wrestling M

UNIVERSITY OF CALIFORNIA, IRVINE
Irvine, CA 92697
Tel: (949)824-5011
Admissions: (949)824-6703
Web Site: http://www.uci.edu/
President/CEO: Dr. Ralph Cicerone
Registrar: Charlene Bradley
Admissions: Marguerite Bonous-Hammarth
Financial Aid: Brent W. Yunek
Type: University **Sex:** Coed **Affiliation:** University of California System **Scores:** 99% SAT V 400+; 100% SAT M 400+ **% Accepted:** 60 **Application Deadline:** November 30 **Application Fee:** $60.00 **H.S. Requirements:** High school diploma required; GED accepted **Costs Per Year:** Application fee: $60. State resident tuition: $0 full-time. Nonresident tuition: $17,820 full-time. Mandatory fees: $6141 full-time. College room and board: $9875. **Scholarships:** Available **Calendar System:** Quarter, Summer Session Available **Enrollment:** FT 19,333, PT 597, Grad 4,065 **Faculty:** FT 992, PT 298 **Student-Faculty Ratio:** 19:1 **Exams:** SAT I and SAT II or ACT, SAT II **% Receiving Financial Aid:** 47 **% Residing in College-Owned, -Operated, or -Affiliated Housing:** 26 **Library Holdings:** 2,617,561 **Regional Accreditation:** Western Association of Schools and Colleges **Credit Hours For Degree:** 180 units, Bachelors **ROTC:** Army, Air Force **Professional Accreditation:** AACSB, ABET, ACSP, APA, LCMEAMA, NAACLS **Intercollegiate Athletics:** Badminton M & W; Baseball M; Basketball M & W; Crew M & W; Cross-Country Running M & W; Fencing M & W; Golf M & W; Lacrosse M & W; Racquetball M & W; Rugby M; Sailing M & W; Soccer M & W; Softball M & W; Swimming and Diving M & W; Table Tennis M & W; Tennis M & W; Track and Field M & W; Volleyball M & W; Water Polo M & W; Weight Lifting M & W

UNIVERSITY OF CALIFORNIA, LOS ANGELES
405 Hilgard Ave.
Los Angeles, CA 90095

Tel: (310)825-4321
Admissions: (310)825-3101
E-mail: ugadm@saonet.ucla.edu
Web Site: http://www.ucla.edu/
President/CEO: Dr. Albert Carnesale
Registrar: Dr. Thomas E. Lifka
Admissions: Dr. Vu T. Tran
Financial Aid: Ronald W. Johnson
Type: University **Sex:** Coed **Affiliation:** University of California System **Scores:** 99.8% SAT V 400+; 99.8% SAT M 400+; 23.4% ACT 18-23; 46.5% ACT 24-29 **% Accepted:** 27 **Application Deadline:** November 30 **Application Fee:** $60.00 **H.S. Requirements:** High school diploma required; GED accepted **Costs Per Year:** Application fee: $60. State resident tuition: $0 full-time. Nonresident tuition: $17,457 full-time. Mandatory fees: $6504 full-time. College room and board: $11,928. Room and board charges vary according to board plan and housing facility. **Scholarships:** Available **Calendar System:** Quarter, Summer Session Available **Enrollment:** FT 23,850, PT 961, Grad 10,492 **Faculty:** FT 1,859, PT 601 **Student-Faculty Ratio:** 18:1 **Exams:** SAT I or ACT, SAT II **% Receiving Financial Aid:** 53 **% Residing in College-Owned, -Operated, or -Affiliated Housing:** 35 **Library Holdings:** 7,616,016 **Regional Accreditation:** Western Association of Schools and Colleges **Credit Hours For Degree:** 180 quarter credits, Bachelors **ROTC:** Army, Navy, Air Force **Professional Accreditation:** AACSB, ABET, ACEHSA, AACN, ABA, ADA, ADtA, ACSP, ALA, APA, ASC, ACIPE, AALS, CEPH, CSWE, FIDER, LCMEAMA, NAST, NLN **Intercollegiate Athletics:** Baseball M; Basketball M & W; Crew W; Cross-Country Running M & W; Football M; Golf M & W; Gymnastics W; Soccer M & W; Softball W; Swimming and Diving W; Tennis M & W; Track and Field M & W; Volleyball M & W; Water Polo M & W

UNIVERSITY OF CALIFORNIA, RIVERSIDE
900 University Ave.
Riverside, CA 92521-0102
Tel: (951)827-1012
Admissions: (951)827-3411
Fax: (951)827-6344
E-mail: discover@ucr.edu
Web Site: http://www.ucr.edu/
President/CEO: France A. Cordova
Registrar: Elizabeth Bennett
Admissions: LaRae Lundgren
Financial Aid: James Sandoval
Type: University **Sex:** Coed **Affiliation:** University of California System **Scores:** 93% SAT V 400+; 97% SAT M 400+; 58% ACT 18-23; 21% ACT 24-29 **% Accepted:** 76 **Admission Plans:** Early Admission **Application Deadline:** November 30 **Application Fee:** $60.00 **H.S. Requirements:** High school diploma required; GED accepted **Costs Per Year:** Application fee: $60. State resident tuition: $0 full-time. Nonresident tuition: $17,820 full-time. Mandatory fees: $7250 full-time. College room and board: $10,200. Room and board charges vary according to board plan and housing facility. **Scholarships:** Available **Calendar System:** Quarter, Summer Session Available **Enrollment:** FT 14,128, PT 443, Grad 2,002 **Faculty:** FT 709, PT 140 **Student-Faculty Ratio:** 18:1 **Exams:** SAT I or ACT **% Receiving Financial Aid:** 60 **% Residing in College-Owned, -Operated, or -Affiliated Housing:** 28 **Library Holdings:** 2,081,146 **Regional Accreditation:** Western Association of Schools and Colleges **Credit Hours For Degree:** 180 quarter hours, Bachelors **ROTC:** Army, Air Force **Professional Accreditation:** AACSB, ABET **Intercollegiate Athletics:** Baseball M; Basketball M & W; Cross-Country Running M & W; Softball W; Tennis M & W; Track and Field M & W; Volleyball W

UNIVERSITY OF CALIFORNIA, SAN DIEGO
9500 Gilman Dr.
La Jolla, CA 92093
Tel: (858)534-2230
Admissions: (858)534-4831
E-mail: admissionsinfo@ucsd.edu
Web Site: http://www.ucsd.edu/
President/CEO: Dr. Marye Anne Fox
Registrar: Mae Brown
Admissions: Mae Brown
Financial Aid: Vincent DeAnda
Type: University **Sex:** Coed **Affiliation:** University of California System **Scores:** 99% SAT V 400+; 100% SAT M 400+; 25% ACT 18-23; 53% ACT 24-29 **% Accepted:** 42 **Admission Plans:** Preferred Admission **Application Deadline:** November 30 **Application Fee:** $60.00 **H.S. Requirements:** High school diploma required; GED accepted **Costs Per Year:** Application fee: $60. State resident tuition: $0 full-time. Nonresident tuition: $17,820 full-time. Mandatory fees: $6,681 full-time. Full-time tuition and fees vary according to location. College room and board: $9421. Room and board charges vary according to board plan and location. **Scholarships:** Available **Calendar System:** Quarter, Summer Session Available **Enrollment:** FT 20,048, PT 291, Grad 3,511 **Faculty:** FT 965, PT 184 **Student-Faculty Ratio:** 19:1 **Exams:** Other, SAT I or ACT, SAT II **% Receiving Financial Aid:** 51 **% Residing in College-Owned, -Operated, or -Affiliated Housing:** 33 **Library Holdings:** 3,086,871 **Regional Accreditation:** Western Association of Schools and Colleges **Credit Hours For Degree:** 180 credit hours, Bachelors **ROTC:** Army **Professional Accreditation:** ABET, ACPhE, APA, ASLHA, LCMEAMA **Intercollegiate Athletics:** Baseball M; Basketball M & W; Cheerleading M & W; Crew M & W; Cross-Country Running M & W; Fencing M & W; Golf M; Soccer M & W; Softball W; Swimming and Diving M & W; Tennis M & W; Track and Field M & W; Volleyball M & W; Water Polo M & W

UNIVERSITY OF CALIFORNIA, SANTA BARBARA
Santa Barbara, CA 93106
Tel: (805)893-8000
Admissions: (805)893-2485
Web Site: http://www.ucsb.edu/
President/CEO: Dr. Henry T. Yang
Registrar: Beverly Q. Lewis
Admissions: Christine Van Gieson
Financial Aid: Ron Andrade
Type: University **Sex:** Coed **Affiliation:** University of California System **Scores:** 99% SAT V 400+; 100% SAT M 400+ **% Accepted:** 53 **Application Deadline:** November 30 **Application Fee:** $40.00 **H.S. Requirements:** High school diploma required; GED accepted **Costs Per Year:** Application fee: $40. State resident tuition: $0 full-time. Nonresident tuition: $17,820 full-time. Mandatory fees: $6993 full-time. College room and board: $10,577. College room only: $8110. **Scholarships:** Available **Calendar System:** Quarter, Summer Session Available **Enrollment:** FT 17,432, PT 645, Grad 2,939 **Faculty:** FT 919, PT 135 **Student-Faculty Ratio:** 17:1 **Exams:** SAT I or ACT, SAT II **% Receiving Financial Aid:** 45 **% Residing in College-Owned, -Operated, or -Affiliated Housing:** 26 **Library Holdings:** 3,228,557 **Regional Accreditation:** Western Association of Schools and Colleges **Credit Hours For Degree:** 180 quarter units, Bachelors **ROTC:** Army **Professional Accreditation:** ABET, APA, NASD **Intercollegiate Athletics:** Baseball M; Basketball M & W; Bowling M & W; Crew M & W; Cross-Country Running M & W; Equestrian Sports M & W; Fencing M & W; Field Hockey W; Golf M & W; Gymnastics M & W; Lacrosse M & W; Rugby M; Sailing M & W; Skiing (Downhill) M & W; Soccer M & W; Softball W; Swimming and Diving M & W; Tennis M & W; Track and Field M & W; Ultimate Frisbee M & W; Volleyball M & W; Water Polo M & W

UNIVERSITY OF CALIFORNIA, SANTA CRUZ
1156 High St.
Santa Cruz, CA 95064
Tel: (831)459-0111
Admissions: (831)459-5779
Fax: (831)459-4452
E-mail: admissions@ucsc.edu
Web Site: http://www.ucsc.edu/
President/CEO: Dr. Martin M. Chemers
Registrar: Pamela Hunt-Carter
Admissions: Kevin M. Browne
Financial Aid: Esperanza Nee
Type: University **Sex:** Coed **Affiliation:** University of California System **Scores:** 97.15% SAT V 400+; 98.54% SAT M 400+; 38.2% ACT 18-23; 48.42% ACT 24-29 **% Accepted:** 75 **Admission Plans:** Preferred Admission **Application Deadline:** November 30 **Application Fee:** $65.00 **H.S. Requirements:** High school diploma required; GED accepted **Costs Per Year:** Application fee: $65. State resident tuition: $0 full-time. Nonresident tuition: $17,820 full-time. Mandatory fees: $7603 full-time. College room and board: $11,571. Room and board charges vary according to board plan and housing facility. **Scholarships:** Available **Calendar System:** Quarter, Summer Session Available **Enrollment:** FT 13,139, PT 486, Grad 1,387 **Faculty:** FT 537, PT 205 **Student-Faculty Ratio:** 19:1 **Exams:** Other, SAT I or ACT **% Receiving Financial Aid:** 46 **% Residing in College-Owned, -Operated, or -Affiliated Housing:** 45 **Library Holdings:** 1,535,118 **Regional Accreditation:** Western Association of Schools and Colleges **Credit Hours**

For Degree: 180 credits, Bachelors **ROTC:** Army, Navy, Air Force **Professional Accreditation:** ABET, APA **Intercollegiate Athletics:** Basketball M & W; Cross-Country Running M & W; Equestrian Sports M & W; Fencing M & W; Golf W; Lacrosse M & W; Rugby M & W; Sailing M & W; Soccer M & W; Softball W; Swimming and Diving M & W; Table Tennis M & W; Tennis M & W; Track and Field M & W; Ultimate Frisbee M & W; Volleyball M & W; Water Polo M & W

UNIVERSITY OF JUDAISM
15600 Mulholland Dr.
Bel Air, CA 90077-1599
Tel: (310)476-9777; 888-853-6763
Fax: (310)471-3657
E-mail: bpisetsky@uj.edu
Web Site: http://www.uj.edu/
President/CEO: Dr. Robert Wexler
Registrar: Jill Lasker
Admissions: Bryan Pisetsky
Financial Aid: Catherine Nelson
Type: Comprehensive **Sex:** Coed **Affiliation:** Jewish **Scores:** 100% SAT V 400+; 100% SAT M 400+; 75% ACT 18-23; 25% ACT 24-29 **% Accepted:** 79 **Admission Plans:** Early Admission; Early Decision Plan; Deferred Admission **Application Deadline:** January 31 **Application Fee:** $35.00 **H.S. Requirements:** High school diploma required; GED accepted **Costs Per Year:** Application fee: $35. Comprehensive fee: $32,376 includes full-time tuition ($18,480), mandatory fees ($850), and college room and board ($13,046). College room only: $7964. Room and board charges vary according to board plan. Part-time tuition: $770 per credit. **Scholarships:** Available **Calendar System:** Semester, Summer Session Not available **Faculty:** FT 19, PT 72 **Student-Faculty Ratio:** 7:1 **Exams:** SAT I or ACT **% Receiving Financial Aid:** 90 **% Residing in College-Owned, -Operated, or -Affiliated Housing:** 60 **Library Holdings:** 105,000 **Regional Accreditation:** Western Association of Schools and Colleges **Credit Hours For Degree:** 124 units, Bachelors

UNIVERSITY OF LA VERNE
1950 Third St.
La Verne, CA 91750-4443
Tel: (909)593-3511
Free: 800-876-4858
Fax: (909)593-0965
E-mail: laup@ulavacs.ulaverne.edu
Web Site: http://www.ulv.edu/
President/CEO: Dr. Stephen Morgan
Registrar: Marilyn Davies
Admissions: Ana Liza V. Zell
Financial Aid: Pat Coleman
Type: University **Sex:** Coed **Scores:** 98% SAT V 400+; 97% SAT M 400+; 60% ACT 18-23; 24% ACT 24-29 **% Accepted:** 62 **Admission Plans:** Deferred Admission **Application Deadline:** February 01 **Application Fee:** $50.00 **H.S. Requirements:** High school diploma required; GED accepted **Costs Per Year:** Application fee: $50. Comprehensive fee: $33,470 includes full-time tuition ($24,260) and college room and board ($9210). College room only: $4780. Part-time tuition: $685 per unit. **Scholarships:** Available **Calendar System:** 4-1-4, Summer Session Available **Enrollment:** FT 1,583, PT 102, Grad 2,060 **Faculty:** FT 187, PT 211 **Student-Faculty Ratio:** 12:1 **Exams:** SAT I or ACT **% Receiving Financial Aid:** 82 **% Residing in College-Owned, -Operated, or -Affiliated Housing:** 32 **Library Holdings:** 215,000 **Regional Accreditation:** Western Association of Schools and Colleges **Credit Hours For Degree:** 128 semester hours, Bachelors **Professional Accreditation:** APA, NASPAA **Intercollegiate Athletics:** Baseball M; Basketball M & W; Cross-Country Running M & W; Football M; Golf M; Soccer M & W; Softball W; Swimming and Diving M & W; Tennis M & W; Track and Field M & W; Volleyball W; Water Polo M & W

UNIVERSITY OF THE PACIFIC
3601 Pacific Ave.
Stockton, CA 95211-0197
Tel: (209)946-2344
Free: 800-959-2867
Admissions: (209)946-2211
Fax: (209)946-2413
E-mail: admissions@pacific.edu
Web Site: http://www.pacific.edu/
President/CEO: Dr. Donald V. DeRosa
Registrar: Cecilia Rodriguez
Admissions: Marc McGee
Financial Aid: Lynn Fox
Type: University **Sex:** Coed **Scores:** 99.2% SAT V 400+; 99.4% SAT M 400+; 32.1% ACT 18-23; 53.1% ACT 24-29 **% Accepted:** 56 **Admission Plans:** Early Action **Application Deadline:** January 15 **Application Fee:** $60.00 **H.S. Requirements:** High school diploma required; GED accepted **Costs Per Year:** Application fee: $60. Comprehensive fee: $34,566 includes full-time tuition ($25,658), mandatory fees ($430), and college room and board ($8478). College room only: $5760. Room and board charges vary according to board plan and housing facility. Part-time tuition: $886 per unit. Part-time tuition varies according to course load. **Scholarships:** Available **Calendar System:** Semester, Summer Session Available **Enrollment:** FT 3,357, PT 100, Grad 592 **Faculty:** FT 401, PT 255 **Student-Faculty Ratio:** 14:1 **Exams:** SAT I or ACT **% Receiving Financial Aid:** 67 **% Residing in College-Owned, -Operated, or -Affiliated Housing:** 58 **Library Holdings:** 282,313 **Regional Accreditation:** Western Association of Schools and Colleges **Credit Hours For Degree:** 124 units, Bachelors **Professional Accreditation:** AACSB, ABET, ABA, ACPhE, ADA, APTA, ASLHA, AALS, NASAD, NASM, NCATE **Intercollegiate Athletics:** Baseball M; Basketball M & W; Cross-Country Running W; Field Hockey W; Golf M; Soccer W; Softball W; Swimming and Diving M & W; Tennis M & W; Volleyball M & W; Water Polo M & W

UNIVERSITY OF PHOENIX-BAY AREA CAMPUS
7901 Stoneridge Dr., Ste. 100
Pleasanton, CA 94588-3677
Tel: (925)416-4100; 877-4-STUDENT
Admissions: (480)557-1712
Web Site: http://www.phoenix.edu/
President/CEO: Daniel Waterman
Admissions: Nina Omelchanko
Type: Comprehensive **Sex:** Coed **Admission Plans:** Open Admission; Deferred Admission **Application Deadline:** Rolling **Application Fee:** $110.00 **H.S. Requirements:** High school diploma required; GED accepted **Costs Per Year:** Application fee: $110. Tuition: $12,990 full-time, $444 per credit part-time. Mandatory fees: $560 full-time, $70 per course part-time. **Scholarships:** Available **Calendar System:** Continuous, Summer Session Not available **Enrollment:** FT 2,581, Grad 1,100 **Faculty:** FT 8, PT 739 **Student-Faculty Ratio:** 7:1 **Library Holdings:** 444 **Regional Accreditation:** North Central Association of Colleges and Schools **Credit Hours For Degree:** 60 credits, Associates; 120 credits, Bachelors **Professional Accreditation:** NLN

UNIVERSITY OF PHOENIX-CENTRAL VALLEY CAMPUS
8355 N. Fresno St., Ste. 200
Fresno, CA 93720
; 888-228-7240
Admissions: (480)557-1712
Web Site: http://phoenix.edu/
Admissions: Nina Omelchanko
Type: Comprehensive **Sex:** Coed **Admission Plans:** Open Admission; Deferred Admission **Application Deadline:** Rolling **Application Fee:** $110.00 **H.S. Requirements:** High school diploma required; GED accepted **Costs Per Year:** Application fee: $110. Tuition: $11,775 full-time, $392.50 per credit part-time. Mandatory fees: $560 full-time, $70 per course part-time. Full-time tuition and fees vary according to program. **Scholarships:** Available **Enrollment:** FT 1,606, Grad 281 **Faculty:** FT 11, PT 647 **Student-Faculty Ratio:** 9:1 **Library Holdings:** 444 **Credit Hours For Degree:** 60 credits, Associates; 120 credits, Bachelors

UNIVERSITY OF PHOENIX-SACRAMENTO VALLEY CAMPUS
1760 Creekside Oaks Dr., Ste. 100
Sacramento, CA 95833-3632
Tel: (916)923-2107
Free: 800-228-7240
Admissions: (480)557-1712
Fax: (916)923-3914
Web Site: http://www.phoenix.edu/
President/CEO: Jo Hoffmeier
Admissions: Nina Omelchanko
Type: Comprehensive **Sex:** Coed **Admission Plans:** Open Admission; Deferred Admission **Application Deadline:** Rolling **Application Fee:** $110.00 **H.S. Requirements:** High school diploma required; GED accepted

Costs Per Year: Application fee: $110. Tuition: $12,225 full-time, $407.50 per credit part-time. Mandatory fees: $560 full-time, $70 per course part-time. **Scholarships:** Available **Calendar System:** Continuous, Summer Session Not available **Enrollment:** FT 3,506, Grad 1,123 **Faculty:** FT 12, PT 535 **Student-Faculty Ratio:** 8:1 **Library Holdings:** 444 **Regional Accreditation:** North Central Association of Colleges and Schools **Credit Hours For Degree:** 60 credits, Associates; 120 credits, Bachelors **Professional Accreditation:** NLN

UNIVERSITY OF PHOENIX-SAN DIEGO CAMPUS
3870 Murphy Canyon Rd., Ste. 210
San Diego, CA 92123
Tel: 800-473-4346; 888-228-7240
Admissions: (480)557-1712
Fax: (858)576-0032
Web Site: http://www.phoenix.edu/
President/CEO: Bruce Williams
Admissions: Nina Omelchanko
Type: Comprehensive **Sex:** Coed **Admission Plans:** Open Admission; Deferred Admission **Application Deadline:** Rolling **Application Fee:** $110.00 **H.S. Requirements:** High school diploma required; GED accepted **Costs Per Year:** Application fee: $110. Tuition: $11,940 full-time, $398 per credit part-time. Mandatory fees: $560 full-time, $70 per course part-time. **Scholarships:** Available **Calendar System:** Continuous, Summer Session Not available **Enrollment:** FT 3,459, Grad 1,104 **Faculty:** FT 15, PT 461 **Student-Faculty Ratio:** 9:1 **Library Holdings:** 444 **Regional Accreditation:** North Central Association of Colleges and Schools **Credit Hours For Degree:** 60 credits, Associates; 120 credits, Bachelors **Professional Accreditation:** NLN

UNIVERSITY OF PHOENIX-SOUTHERN CALIFORNIA CAMPUS
3150 Bristol St., Ste. 340
Costa Mesa, CA 92626
Tel: 800-GO-TO-UOP
Free: 800-228-7240
Admissions: (480)557-1712
Web Site: http://www.phoenix.edu/
President/CEO: Jennifer Cisna
Admissions: Nina Omelchanko
Type: Comprehensive **Sex:** Coed **Admission Plans:** Open Admission; Deferred Admission **Application Deadline:** Rolling **Application Fee:** $110.00 **H.S. Requirements:** High school diploma required; GED accepted **Costs Per Year:** Application fee: $110. Tuition: $13,125 full-time, $437.50 per credit part-time. Mandatory fees: $560 full-time, $70 per course part-time. **Scholarships:** Available **Calendar System:** Continuous, Summer Session Not available **Enrollment:** FT 12,476, Grad 3,658 **Faculty:** FT 14, PT 1,283 **Student-Faculty Ratio:** 12:1 **Library Holdings:** 444 **Regional Accreditation:** North Central Association of Colleges and Schools **Credit Hours For Degree:** 60 credits, Associates; 120 credits, Bachelors **Professional Accreditation:** NLN

UNIVERSITY OF REDLANDS
1200 East Colton Ave.
PO Box 3080
Redlands, CA 92373-0999
Tel: (909)793-2121
Free: 800-455-5064
Admissions: (909)335-4074
Fax: (909)335-4089
Web Site: http://www.redlands.edu/
President/CEO: Dr. James R. Appleton
Registrar: Charlotte M. Lucey
Admissions: Paul Driscoll
Financial Aid: Bethann S. Corey
Type: Comprehensive **Sex:** Coed **Scores:** 96% SAT V 400+; 98% SAT M 400+; 43% ACT 18-23; 42% ACT 24-29 **% Accepted:** 66 **Admission Plans:** Deferred Admission **Application Deadline:** March 01 **Application Fee:** $45.00 **H.S. Requirements:** High school diploma required; GED accepted **Costs Per Year:** Application fee: $45. Comprehensive fee: $36,164 includes full-time tuition ($26,864), mandatory fees ($300), and college room and board ($9000). College room only: $5020. Room and board charges vary according to board plan and housing facility. Part-time tuition: $840 per credit. Part-time mandatory fees: $150 per term. Part-time tuition and fees vary according to course load. **Scholarships:** Available **Calendar System:** Miscellaneous, Summer Session Not available **Enrollment:** FT 2,338, PT 24, Grad 92 **Faculty:** FT 165, PT 151 **Student-Faculty Ratio:** 12:1 **Exams:** SAT I or ACT **% Receiving Financial Aid:** 69 **% Residing in College-Owned, -Operated, or -Affiliated Housing:** 73 **Library Holdings:** 262,893 **Regional Accreditation:** Western Association of Schools and Colleges **Credit Hours For Degree:** 132 units, Bachelors **Professional Accreditation:** ASLHA, NASM **Intercollegiate Athletics:** Baseball M; Basketball M & W; Cross-Country Running M & W; Football M; Golf M & W; Lacrosse W; Soccer M & W; Softball W; Swimming and Diving M & W; Tennis M & W; Track and Field M & W; Volleyball W; Water Polo M & W

UNIVERSITY OF SAN DIEGO
5998 Alcala Park
San Diego, CA 92110-2492
Tel: (619)260-4600
Free: 800-248-4873
Admissions: (619)260-4506
E-mail: admissions@sandiego.edu
Web Site: http://www.sandiego.edu/
President/CEO: Dr. Mary Lyons
Registrar: Nicholas M. De Turi
Admissions: Stephen Pultz
Financial Aid: Judith Lewis Logue
Type: University **Sex:** Coed **Affiliation:** Roman Catholic **Scores:** 99% SAT V 400+; 100% SAT M 400+; 25% ACT 18-23; 64% ACT 24-29 **% Accepted:** 60 **Admission Plans:** Early Admission; Early Action; Deferred Admission **Application Deadline:** January 05 **Application Fee:** $55.00 **H.S. Requirements:** High school diploma required; GED accepted **Costs Per Year:** Application fee: $55. Comprehensive fee: $41,664 includes full-time tuition ($30,480), mandatory fees ($224), and college room and board ($10,960). Part-time tuition: $1050 per unit. Part-time mandatory fees: $38. **Scholarships:** Available **Calendar System:** 4-1-4, Summer Session Available **Enrollment:** FT 4,801, PT 169, Grad 1,504 **Faculty:** FT 359, PT 363 **Student-Faculty Ratio:** 15:1 **Exams:** SAT I or ACT **% Receiving Financial Aid:** 47 **% Residing in College-Owned, -Operated, or -Affiliated Housing:** 50 **Library Holdings:** 714,082 **Regional Accreditation:** Western Association of Schools and Colleges **Credit Hours For Degree:** 124 units, Bachelors **ROTC:** Army, Navy, Air Force **Professional Accreditation:** AACSB, ABET, AAMFT, AACN, ABA, APA, AALS, NCATE **Intercollegiate Athletics:** Baseball M; Basketball M & W; Crew M & W; Cross-Country Running M & W; Equestrian Sports W; Football M; Golf M; Ice Hockey M; Lacrosse M & W; Rugby M; Soccer M & W; Softball W; Swimming and Diving W; Tennis M & W; Volleyball M & W

UNIVERSITY OF SAN FRANCISCO
2130 Fulton St.
San Francisco, CA 94117-1080
Tel: (415)422-6886
Free: 800-CALL USF
Admissions: (415)422-6563
Fax: (415)422-2217
E-mail: admissions@usfca.edu
Web Site: http://www.usfca.edu/
President/CEO: Rev. Stephen A. Privett, SJ
Registrar: Archie Porter
Admissions: Michael Hughes
Financial Aid: Susan Murphy
Type: University **Sex:** Coed **Affiliation:** Roman Catholic (Jesuit) **Scores:** 99% SAT V 400+; 99% SAT M 400+; 51% ACT 18-23; 35% ACT 24-29 **% Accepted:** 72 **Admission Plans:** Early Action; Deferred Admission **Application Deadline:** February 01 **Application Fee:** $55.00 **H.S. Requirements:** High school diploma required; GED accepted **Costs Per Year:** Application fee: $55. Comprehensive fee: $39,160 includes full-time tuition ($28,420), mandatory fees ($160), and college room and board ($10,580). College room only: $7230. Part-time tuition: $1015 per credit. Part-time mandatory fees: $160 per year. **Scholarships:** Available **Calendar System:** 4-1-4, Summer Session Available **Enrollment:** FT 4,981, PT 231, Grad 2,511 **Faculty:** FT 348, PT 513 **Student-Faculty Ratio:** 14:1 **Exams:** SAT I or ACT **% Receiving Financial Aid:** 59 **% Residing in College-Owned, -Operated, or -Affiliated Housing:** 48 **Library Holdings:** 1,148,737 **Regional Accreditation:** Western Association of Schools and Colleges **Credit Hours For Degree:** 128 units, Bachelors **ROTC:** Army, Air Force **Professional Accreditation:** AACSB, AACN, ABA, AALS, NLN **Intercollegiate Athletics:** Baseball M; Basketball M & W; Cross-Country Running M & W; Golf M & W; Riflery M & W; Soccer M & W; Softball M & W; Tennis M & W; Track and Field W; Volleyball M & W

UNIVERSITY OF SOUTHERN CALIFORNIA
University Park Campus
Los Angeles, CA 90089
Tel: (213)740-2311
Admissions: (213)740-1111
Fax: (213)740-6364
E-mail: admitusc@usc.edu
Web Site: http://www.usc.edu/
President/CEO: Dr. Steven B. Sample
Registrar: Dr. Kenneth L. Servis
Admissions: Katharine L. Harrington
Financial Aid: Catherine Thomas
Type: University **Sex:** Coed **Scores:** 99.95% SAT V 400+; 100% SAT M 400+; 3.28% ACT 18-23; 44.3% ACT 24-29 **% Accepted:** 27 **Application Deadline:** January 10 **Application Fee:** $65.00 **H.S. Requirements:** High school diploma required; GED not accepted **Costs Per Year:** Application fee: $65. Comprehensive fee: $41,618 includes full-time tuition ($31,458), mandatory fees ($550), and college room and board ($9610). College room only: $5260. Full-time tuition and fees vary according to program. Room and board charges vary according to board plan and housing facility. Part-time tuition: $1059 per credit hour. Part-time mandatory fees: $685 per year. Part-time tuition and fees vary according to course load and program. **Scholarships:** Available **Calendar System:** Semester, Summer Session Available **Enrollment:** FT 16,072, PT 825, Grad 13,238 **Faculty:** FT 1,495, PT 984 **Student-Faculty Ratio:** 10:1 **Exams:** SAT I **% Receiving Financial Aid:** 45 **% Residing in College-Owned, -Operated, or -Affiliated Housing:** 36 **Library Holdings:** 3,865,914 **Regional Accreditation:** Western Association of Schools and Colleges **Credit Hours For Degree:** 128 units, Bachelors **ROTC:** Army, Air Force **Professional Accreditation:** AACSB, ABET, ACEHSA, ACEJMC, AACN, AANA, ABA, ACPhE, ADA, ADtA, ACSP, AOTA, APTA, APA, AALS, CEPH, CSWE, LCMEAMA, NASM, NASPAA **Intercollegiate Athletics:** Baseball M; Basketball M & W; Crew W; Cross-Country Running M & W; Football M; Golf M & W; Soccer W; Swimming and Diving M & W; Tennis M & W; Track and Field M & W; Volleyball M & W; Water Polo M & W

UNIVERSITY OF THE WEST
1409 North Walnut Grove Ave.
Rosemead, CA 91770
Tel: (626)571-8811
Fax: (626)571-1413
Web Site: http://www.uwest.edu/
President/CEO: Naichen Chen
Registrar: Grace Hsiao
Admissions: Grace Hsiao
Type: Comprehensive **Sex:** Coed **Application Fee:** $50.00 **Scholarships:** Available **Calendar System:** Semester **% Receiving Financial Aid:** 25 **Regional Accreditation:** Western Association of Schools and Colleges

UNIVERSITY OF WEST LOS ANGELES
1155 West Arbor Vitae St.
Inglewood, CA 90301-2902
Tel: (310)342-5200
Admissions: (310)342-5287
Fax: (310)313-2124
Web Site: http://www.uwla.edu/
President/CEO: Robert Brown
Registrar: Cynthia Moj
Admissions: Yvonne Alwag
Financial Aid: Edward Mervine
Type: Two-Year Upper Division **Sex:** Coed **Admission Plans:** Deferred Admission **Application Fee:** $55.00 **H.S. Requirements:** High school diploma or equivalent not required **Costs Per Year:** Application fee: $55. Tuition: $9150 full-time, $305 per unit part-time. Mandatory fees: $360 full-time, $120 per term part-time. **Scholarships:** Available **Calendar System:** Trimester, Summer Session Not available **Enrollment:** FT 19, PT 44 **Faculty:** FT 1, PT 20 **Student-Faculty Ratio:** 10:1 **% Receiving Financial Aid:** 72 **Library Holdings:** 33,000 **Regional Accreditation:** Western Association of Schools and Colleges **Credit Hours For Degree:** 120 units, Bachelors

VANGUARD UNIVERSITY OF SOUTHERN CALIFORNIA
55 Fair Dr.
Costa Mesa, CA 92626-9601
Tel: (714)556-3610
Free: 800-722-6279
Fax: (714)966-5460
E-mail: admissions@vanguard.edu
Web Site: http://www.vanguard.edu/
President/CEO: Dr. Murray Dempster
Registrar: Judy Hamilton
Admissions: Jessica Mireles
Financial Aid: Robyn Fournier
Type: Comprehensive **Sex:** Coed **Affiliation:** Assemblies of God **Scores:** 95% SAT V 400+; 90% SAT M 400+ **% Accepted:** 86 **Admission Plans:** Preferred Admission; Early Admission; Deferred Admission **Application Deadline:** December 01 **Application Fee:** $45.00 **H.S. Requirements:** High school diploma required; GED accepted **Costs Per Year:** Application fee: $45. Comprehensive fee: $27,071 includes full-time tuition ($19,900), mandatory fees ($415), and college room and board ($6756). College room only: $3366. Room and board charges vary according to board plan and housing facility. Part-time tuition: $829 per credit hour. Part-time mandatory fees: $25 per term. **Scholarships:** Available **Calendar System:** Semester, Summer Session Available **Enrollment:** FT 1,493, PT 407, Grad 346 **Faculty:** FT 66, PT 131 **Student-Faculty Ratio:** 14:1 **Exams:** SAT I or ACT **% Receiving Financial Aid:** 87 **% Residing in College-Owned, -Operated, or -Affiliated Housing:** 70 **Library Holdings:** 142,893 **Regional Accreditation:** Western Association of Schools and Colleges **Credit Hours For Degree:** 124 credits, Bachelors **ROTC:** Air Force **Professional Accreditation:** JRCEPAT **Intercollegiate Athletics:** Baseball M; Basketball M & W; Cross-Country Running M & W; Soccer M & W; Softball W; Tennis M & W; Track and Field M & W; Volleyball W

VENTURA COLLEGE
4667 Telegraph Rd.
Ventura, CA 93003-3899
Tel: (805)654-6400
Admissions: (805)654-6456
Fax: (805)654-6466
E-mail: sbricker@vcccd.net
Web Site: http://www.venturacollege.edu/
President/CEO: Michael Gregoryk
Registrar: Susan Bricker
Admissions: Susan Bricker
Financial Aid: Dora Washington
Type: Two-Year College **Sex:** Coed **Affiliation:** California Community College System **Admission Plans:** Open Admission **Application Fee:** $0.00 **H.S. Requirements:** High school diploma required; GED accepted **Costs Per Year:** Application fee: $0. State resident tuition: $0 full-time. Nonresident tuition: $4650 full-time. Mandatory fees: $850 full-time. **Scholarships:** Available **Calendar System:** Semester, Summer Session Available **Enrollment:** FT 4,112, PT 7,984 **Faculty:** FT 133, PT 386 **Student-Faculty Ratio:** 22:1 **Library Holdings:** 63,529 **Regional Accreditation:** Western Association of Schools and Colleges **Credit Hours For Degree:** 60 semester hours, Associates **Intercollegiate Athletics:** Baseball M; Basketball M & W; Cross-Country Running M & W; Football M; Golf M; Soccer M & W; Softball W; Swimming and Diving M & W; Tennis M & W; Track and Field M & W; Volleyball W; Water Polo M & W

VICTOR VALLEY COLLEGE
18422 Bear Valley Rd.
Victorville, CA 92392-5849
Tel: (760)245-4271
Fax: (760)245-9745
Web Site: http://www.vvc.edu/
President/CEO: Dr. Patricia Spencer
Registrar: Leonard Crawford
Admissions: Becky Millen
Financial Aid: Mary Pringle
Type: Two-Year College **Sex:** Coed **Affiliation:** California Community College System **Admission Plans:** Open Admission; Early Admission **Application Fee:** $0.00 **H.S. Requirements:** High school diploma or equivalent not required. For applicants under 18: High school diploma required; GED accepted **Costs Per Year:** Application fee: $0. State resident tuition: $0 full-time. Nonresident tuition: $3768 full-time, $157 per unit part-time. Mandatory fees: $624 full-time, $26 per unit part-time. **Scholarships:** Available **Calendar System:** Semester, Summer Session Available **Enrollment:** FT 3,663, PT 6,917 **Faculty:** FT 136, PT 324 **Exams:** Other **Library Holdings:** 41,789 **Regional Accreditation:** Western Association of Schools and Colleges **Credit Hours For Degree:** 60 units, Associates **Professional Ac-**

creditation: CARC **Intercollegiate Athletics:** Baseball M; Basketball M & W; Cross-Country Running M & W; Football M; Golf M; Soccer M & W; Softball W; Tennis M & W; Track and Field M & W; Volleyball W; Wrestling M

WEST HILLS COMMUNITY COLLEGE
300 Cherry Ln.
Coalinga, CA 93210-1399
Tel: (559)934-2000
Free: 800-266-1114
Admissions: (559)934-3204
Fax: (559)934-1511
E-mail: darlenegeorgatos@westhillcollege.com
Web Site: http://www.westhillscollege.com/
President/CEO: Dr. Frank P. Gornick
Admissions: Darlene Georgatos
Financial Aid: Jill Stearns
Type: Two-Year College **Sex:** Coed **Affiliation:** California Community College System **Admission Plans:** Open Admission; Preferred Admission; Early Admission **Application Fee:** $0.00 **H.S. Requirements:** High school diploma or equivalent not required **Scholarships:** Available **Calendar System:** Semester, Summer Session Available **Enrollment:** FT 1,828, PT 2,516 **Faculty:** FT 80, PT 100 **Student-Faculty Ratio:** 20:1 **Exams:** SAT I or ACT **Library Holdings:** 32,000 **Regional Accreditation:** Western Association of Schools and Colleges **Credit Hours For Degree:** 60 units, Associates **Intercollegiate Athletics:** Baseball M; Basketball M; Equestrian Sports M & W; Football M; Softball W; Tennis W; Volleyball W

WEST LOS ANGELES COLLEGE
4800 Freshman Dr.
Culver City, CA 90230-3519
Tel: (310)287-4200
Admissions: (310)287-4255
Fax: (310)841-0396
Web Site: http://www.wlac.cc.ca.us/
President/CEO: Frank Quiambao
Registrar: Len Isaksen
Admissions: Len Isaksen
Financial Aid: Glenn Schenk
Type: Two-Year College **Sex:** Coed **Affiliation:** Los Angeles Community College District System **Admission Plans:** Open Admission; Early Admission **H.S. Requirements:** High school diploma or equivalent not required **Scholarships:** Available **Calendar System:** Semester, Summer Session Available **Faculty:** FT 120, PT 200 **Library Holdings:** 51,000 **Regional Accreditation:** Western Association of Schools and Colleges **Credit Hours For Degree:** 60 units, Associates **ROTC:** Army, Air Force **Professional Accreditation:** ADA **Intercollegiate Athletics:** Basketball M; Football M; Golf M; Track and Field M & W; Volleyball W

WEST VALLEY COLLEGE
14000 Fruitvale Ave.
Saratoga, CA 95070-5698
Tel: (408)867-2200
Admissions: (408)741-2454
Fax: (408)867-5033
Web Site: http://www.westvalley.edu/
President/CEO: Dr. Phillip Hartley
Admissions: Paula Pritchett
Financial Aid: Maureen Kent
Type: Two-Year College **Sex:** Coed **Affiliation:** California Community College System **Admission Plans:** Open Admission; Preferred Admission; Early Admission **Application Fee:** $0.00 **H.S. Requirements:** High school diploma or equivalent not required **Scholarships:** Available **Calendar System:** Semester, Summer Session Available **Faculty:** FT 210, PT 350 **Library Holdings:** 82,959 **Regional Accreditation:** Western Association of Schools and Colleges **Credit Hours For Degree:** 60 units, Associates **ROTC:** Army, Air Force **Professional Accreditation:** AAMAE, FIDER **Intercollegiate Athletics:** Basketball M & W; Cross-Country Running M & W; Football M; Golf M; Soccer M; Swimming and Diving M & W; Tennis M & W; Track and Field M; Volleyball M & W; Water Polo M; Wrestling M

WESTERN CAREER COLLEGE (EMERYVILLE)
1400 65th St., Ste. 200
Emeryville, CA 94608
Tel: (510)601-0133
Fax: (510)601-0793
Web Site: http://www.westerncollege.edu/
President/CEO: Elvie Engstrom
Admissions: Marianne Dulay
Type: Two-Year College **Sex:** Coed **Admission Plans:** Open Admission **Application Fee:** $125.00 **H.S. Requirements:** High school diploma required; GED accepted **Calendar System:** Semester, Summer Session Not available **Enrollment:** FT 375 **Faculty:** FT 9, PT 8 **Student-Faculty Ratio:** 18:1 **Exams:** ACT **Library Holdings:** 1,000 **Professional Accreditation:** ACCSCT

WESTERN CAREER COLLEGE (FREMONT)
41350 Christy St.
Fremont, CA 94538
Tel: (510)623-9966
Fax: (510)623-9822
Web Site: http://www.westerncollege.edu/
President/CEO: Darryl Lindsay
Registrar: Elvie Engstrom
Admissions: Anton Croos
Financial Aid: Carol Corrie
Type: Two-Year College **Sex:** Coed **Admission Plans:** Open Admission **Application Fee:** $125.00 **H.S. Requirements:** High school diploma required; GED accepted **Calendar System:** Semester, Summer Session Not available **Faculty:** FT 22, PT 4 **Student-Faculty Ratio:** 18:1 **Exams:** ACT **Library Holdings:** 1,000 **Professional Accreditation:** ACCSCT

WESTERN CAREER COLLEGE (PLEASANT HILL)
380 Civic Dr.
Pleasant Hill, CA 94523
Tel: (925)609-6650
Free: 800-584-4520
Fax: (925)609-6666
Web Site: http://www.westerncollege.edu/
President/CEO: Bill Grady
Type: Two-Year College **Sex:** Coed **Calendar System:** Semester **Regional Accreditation:** Western Association of Schools and Colleges **Professional Accreditation:** AAMAE

WESTERN CAREER COLLEGE (SACRAMENTO)
8909 Folsom Blvd.
Sacramento, CA 95826
Tel: (916)361-1660
Free: 800-321-2386
Fax: (916)361-6666
Web Site: http://www.westerncollege.edu/
President/CEO: Sue Fleming
Type: Two-Year College **Sex:** Coed **Calendar System:** Semester **Regional Accreditation:** Western Association of Schools and Colleges **Professional Accreditation:** AAMAE

WESTERN CAREER COLLEGE (SAN JOSE)
6201 San Ignacio Blvd.
San Jose, CA 95119
Tel: (408)360-0840
Fax: (408)360-0840
Web Site: http://www.westerncollege.edu/
President/CEO: Steve Ashab
Admissions: Patricia Fraser
Type: Two-Year College **Sex:** Coed **Admission Plans:** Open Admission **Application Fee:** $125.00 **H.S. Requirements:** High school diploma required; GED accepted **Calendar System:** Semester, Summer Session Not available **Enrollment:** FT 478 **Faculty:** FT 18, PT 6 **Student-Faculty Ratio:** 20:1 **Exams:** ACT **Library Holdings:** 1,000 **Professional Accreditation:** ACCSCT

WESTERN CAREER COLLEGE (SAN LEANDRO)
170 Bay Fair Mall
San Leandro, CA 94578
Tel: (510)276-3888
Free: 800-584-4553
Fax: (510)276-3854
Web Site: http://www.westerncollege.edu/
President/CEO: Dawn Matthews
Type: Two-Year College **Sex:** Coed **Calendar System:** Semester **Regional Accreditation:** Western Association of Schools and Colleges **Professional Accreditation:** AAMAE, AOTA

WESTERN CAREER COLLEGE (WALNUT CREEK)
2800 Mitchell Dr.
Walnut Creek, CA 94598
Tel: (925)280-0235
Web Site: http://www.westerncollege.edu/campus_locations/antioch_campus.html
President/CEO: Mark Millen
Admissions: Mark Millen
Type: Two-Year College **Sex:** Coed **Application Fee:** $125.00 **Calendar System:** Continuous, Summer Session Not available **Enrollment:** FT 472 **Faculty:** FT 12, PT 5 **Exams:** Other **Library Holdings:** 1,000 **Professional Accreditation:** ACCSCT

WESTMONT COLLEGE
955 La Paz Rd.
Santa Barbara, CA 93108-1099
Tel: (805)565-6000
Free: 800-777-9011
Admissions: (805)565-6200
Fax: (805)565-6234
E-mail: admissions@westmont.edu
Web Site: http://www.westmont.edu/
President/CEO: Dr. Stan Gaede
Registrar: Bob Kuntz
Admissions: Joyce Luy
Financial Aid: Diane Horvath
Type: Four-Year College **Sex:** Coed **Affiliation:** nondenominational **Scores:** 100% SAT V 400+; 100% SAT M 400+; 18% ACT 18-23; 55% ACT 24-29 **% Accepted:** 68 **Admission Plans:** Early Action **Application Deadline:** February 15 **Application Fee:** $50.00 **H.S. Requirements:** High school diploma required; GED accepted **Costs Per Year:** Application fee: $50. Comprehensive fee: $36,672 includes full-time tuition ($27,076), mandatory fees ($730), and college room and board ($8866). College room only: $5376. Room and board charges vary according to board plan. **Scholarships:** Available **Calendar System:** Semester, Summer Session Available **Faculty:** FT 91, PT 42 **Student-Faculty Ratio:** 12:1 **Exams:** SAT I or ACT **% Receiving Financial Aid:** 55 **% Residing in College-Owned, -Operated, or -Affiliated Housing:** 80 **Library Holdings:** 150,385 **Regional Accreditation:** Western Association of Schools and Colleges **Credit Hours For Degree:** 124 units, Bachelors **ROTC:** Army, Air Force **Intercollegiate Athletics:** Baseball M; Basketball M & W; Cross-Country Running M & W; Lacrosse W; Rugby M; Soccer M & W; Tennis M & W; Track and Field M & W; Volleyball M & W

WESTWOOD COLLEGE-ANAHEIM
2461 West La Palma Ave.
Anaheim, CA 92801
Tel: (714)226-9990
Fax: (714)826-7398
Web Site: http://www.westwood.edu/
Admissions: Paul Sallenbach
Type: Two-Year College **Sex:** Coed **% Accepted:** 37 **Scholarships:** Available **Calendar System:** Continuous **Enrollment:** FT 570, PT 104 **Professional Accreditation:** ACCSCT

WESTWOOD COLLEGE-INLAND EMPIRE
20 West 7th St.
Upland, CA 91786
Tel: (909)931-7550
Fax: (909)931-9195
Web Site: http://www.westwood.edu/
Admissions: Lyle Seavers
Type: Two-Year College **Sex:** Coed **Scholarships:** Available **Calendar System:** Continuous **Enrollment:** FT 647, PT 156 **Professional Accreditation:** ACCSCT

WESTWOOD COLLEGE-LONG BEACH
3901 Via Oro Ave.
Long Beach, CA 90801
Tel: (310)522-2088; 888-403-3308
Fax: (310)522-4318
Web Site: http://www.westwood.edu
President/CEO: Vicki Bowles
Admissions: Jesse Kamekona
Type: Two-Year College **Sex:** Coed **Affiliation:** AITU Colleges **% Accepted:** 50 **Admission Plans:** Open Admission **Application Deadline:** August 02 **Application Fee:** $100.00 **H.S. Requirements:** High school diploma required; GED accepted **Scholarships:** Available **Calendar System:** Continuous **Enrollment:** FT 265 **Faculty:** FT 2, PT 17 **Student-Faculty Ratio:** 15:1 **Exams:** Other, SAT I or ACT **Credit Hours For Degree:** 114 credits, Associates; 202.5 credits, Bachelors **Professional Accreditation:** ACCSCT

WESTWOOD COLLEGE-LOS ANGELES
3460 Wilshire Blvd., Ste. 700
Los Angeles, CA 90010
Tel: (213)739-9999
Fax: (213)382-2468
Web Site: http://www.westwood.edu/
Admissions: Ron Milman
Type: Two-Year College **Sex:** Coed **Application Fee:** $100.00 **Scholarships:** Available **Calendar System:** Continuous **Enrollment:** FT 577, PT 102 **Professional Accreditation:** ACICS

WHITTIER COLLEGE
13406 E Philadelphia St.
Whittier, CA 90608-0634
Tel: (562)907-4200
Admissions: (562)907-4238
Fax: (562)907-4870
E-mail: admission@whittier.edu
Web Site: http://www.whittier.edu/
President/CEO: Dr. Katherine Haley Will
Registrar: Wayne Van Ellis
Admissions: Lisa Meyer
Financial Aid: Nina Martinez
Type: Comprehensive **Sex:** Coed **Scores:** 98% SAT V 400+; 99% SAT M 400+; 55% ACT 18-23; 31% ACT 24-29 **Admission Plans:** Early Action; Deferred Admission **Application Fee:** $50.00 **H.S. Requirements:** High school diploma required; GED not accepted. For transfer students with at least 30 units: High school diploma required; GED accepted **Costs Per Year:** Application fee: $50. Comprehensive fee: $34,066 includes full-time tuition ($25,838), mandatory fees ($300), and college room and board ($7928). **Scholarships:** Available **Calendar System:** 4-1-4, Summer Session Available **Enrollment:** FT 1,293, PT 14 **Faculty:** FT 85, PT 42 **Student-Faculty Ratio:** 13:1 **Exams:** SAT I or ACT, SAT II **% Receiving Financial Aid:** 69 **% Residing in College-Owned, -Operated, or -Affiliated Housing:** 68 **Library Holdings:** 225,337 **Regional Accreditation:** Western Association of Schools and Colleges **Credit Hours For Degree:** 120 credits, Bachelors **ROTC:** Army, Air Force **Professional Accreditation:** ABA, AALS, CSWE **Intercollegiate Athletics:** Baseball M; Basketball M & W; Cross-Country Running M & W; Football M; Golf M; Lacrosse M & W; Soccer M & W; Softball W; Swimming and Diving M & W; Tennis M & W; Track and Field M & W; Volleyball W; Water Polo M & W

WILLIAM JESSUP UNIVERSITY
333 Sunset Blvd.
Rocklin, CA 95765
Tel: (916)577-1800
Free: 800-355-7522
Admissions: (916)577-2222
Fax: (916)577-1813
E-mail: vpascua@jessup.edu
Web Site: http://www.jessup.edu/
President/CEO: Dr. Bryce Jessup
Admissions: Vance Pascua
Financial Aid: Kristi Kindberg
Type: Four-Year College **Sex:** Coed **Affiliation:** nondenominational **Scores:** 96% SAT V 400+; 83% SAT M 400+; 53% ACT 18-23; 27% ACT 24-29 **% Accepted:** 66 **Admission Plans:** Early Action; Deferred Admission **Application Deadline:** August 01 **Application Fee:** $35.00 **H.S. Requirements:** High school diploma required; GED accepted **Costs Per Year:** Application fee: $35. Comprehensive fee: $22,174 includes full-time tuition ($15,814) and college room and board ($6360). Part-time tuition: $670 per semester hour. **Scholarships:** Available **Calendar System:** Semester, Summer Session Available **Enrollment:** FT 388, PT 133, Grad 11 **Faculty:** FT 24, PT 50 **Student-Faculty Ratio:** 11:1 **Exams:** SAT I or ACT **% Receiving Financial Aid:** 81 **% Residing in College-Owned, -Operated, or -Affiliated Housing:** 36 **Library Holdings:** 58,114 **Regional Accreditation:** Western As-

sociation of Schools and Colleges **Credit Hours For Degree:** 96 semester hours, Associates; 192 semester hours, Bachelors **Professional Accreditation:** AABC **Intercollegiate Athletics:** Basketball M & W; Soccer M & W; Volleyball W

WOODBURY UNIVERSITY
7500 Glenoaks Blvd.
Burbank, CA 91504-1099
Tel: (818)767-0888
Free: 800-784-WOOD
Fax: (818)504-9320
E-mail: mauro.diaz@woodbury.edu
Web Site: http://www.woodbury.edu/
President/CEO: Dr. Kenneth R. Nielsen
Registrar: Jan Leath
Admissions: Mauro Diaz
Financial Aid: Celeastia Williams
Type: Comprehensive **Sex:** Coed **Scores:** 75% SAT V 400+; 83% SAT M 400+ **% Accepted:** 80 **Admission Plans:** Deferred Admission **Application Deadline:** Rolling **Application Fee:** $35.00 **H.S. Requirements:** High school diploma required; GED accepted **Costs Per Year:** Application fee: $35. Comprehensive fee: $31,672 includes full-time tuition ($23,234), mandatory fees ($240), and college room and board ($8198). College room only: $5000. Part-time tuition: $758 per unit. **Scholarships:** Available **Calendar System:** Semester, Summer Session Available **Enrollment:** FT 1,027, PT 240, Grad 169 **Faculty:** FT 44, PT 186 **Student-Faculty Ratio:** 12:1 **Exams:** SAT I or ACT **% Receiving Financial Aid:** 73 **% Residing in College-Owned, -Operated, or -Affiliated Housing:** 16 **Library Holdings:** 66,157 **Regional Accreditation:** Western Association of Schools and Colleges **Credit Hours For Degree:** 120 units, Bachelors **Professional Accreditation:** ACBSP, FIDER

WYOTECH (FREMONT)
200 Whitney Place
Fremont, CA 94539-7663
Tel: (510)490-6900
Free: 800-248-8585
Admissions: (510)580-3507
Fax: (510)490-8599
Web Site: http://www.wyotech.com/
President/CEO: Jeanette Prickett
Admissions: Corey Faria
Financial Aid: David Caldwell
Type: Two-Year College **Sex:** Coed **% Accepted:** 81 **Costs Per Year:** Tuition: $24,525 full-time. Mandatory fees: $50 full-time. **Calendar System:** Continuous **Enrollment:** FT 1,364 **Faculty:** FT 59, PT 0 **Student-Faculty Ratio:** 23:1 **Exams:** Other **Professional Accreditation:** ACCSCT

WYOTECH (WEST SACRAMENTO)
980 Riverside Parkway
West Sacramento, CA 95605-1507
Tel: (916)376-8888
Web Site: http://www.wyotech.com/
President/CEO: Jeanette Prickett
Type: Two-Year College **Sex:** Coed **Calendar System:** Miscellaneous **Professional Accreditation:** ACCSCT

YESHIVA OHR ELCHONON CHABAD/WEST COAST TALMUDICAL SEMINARY
7215 Waring Ave.
Los Angeles, CA 90046-7660
Tel: (213)937-3763
President/CEO: Rabbi Ezra Schochet
Registrar: Rabbi Chaim Citron
Admissions: Rabbi Ezra Binyomin Schochet
Financial Aid: Hendy Tauber
Type: Four-Year College **Sex:** Men **Affiliation:** Jewish **Admission Plans:** Preferred Admission; Early Admission; Deferred Admission **Application Fee:** $0.00 **H.S. Requirements:** High school diploma required; GED accepted **Calendar System:** Semester, Summer Session Available **Enrollment:** FT 62 **Faculty:** FT 5, PT 0 **% Residing in College-Owned, -Operated, or -Affiliated Housing:** 100 **Library Holdings:** 12,000 **Credit Hours For Degree:** 120 credits, Bachelors **Professional Accreditation:** AARTS

YUBA COLLEGE
2088 North Beale Rd.
Marysville, CA 95901-7699
Tel: (530)741-6700
Admissions: (530)741-6705
Fax: (530)741-3541
Web Site: http://www.yccd.edu/
President/CEO: Dr. Stephen Epler
Registrar: Connie Elder
Admissions: Dr. David Farrell
Financial Aid: Dr. Marisela Arce
Type: Two-Year College **Sex:** Coed **Affiliation:** California Community College System **% Accepted:** 100 **Admission Plans:** Open Admission **Application Deadline:** Rolling **Application Fee:** $0.00 **H.S. Requirements:** High school diploma required; GED accepted. For applicants 18 or over: High school diploma required; GED accepted **Costs Per Year:** Application fee: $0. State resident tuition: $0 full-time. Mandatory fees: $780 full-time, $26 per unit part-time. **Scholarships:** Available **Calendar System:** Semester, Summer Session Available **Enrollment:** FT 6,294, PT 4,163 **Faculty:** FT 135, PT 375 **Library Holdings:** 65,000 **Regional Accreditation:** Western Association of Schools and Colleges **Credit Hours For Degree:** 60 units, Associates **Professional Accreditation:** JRCERT **Intercollegiate Athletics:** Baseball M; Basketball M & W; Cross-Country Running M & W; Football M; Soccer M & W; Softball W; Tennis M & W; Track and Field M & W; Volleyball W

ADAMS STATE COLLEGE
208 Edgemont Blvd.
Alamosa, CO 81102
Tel: (719)587-7011
Free: 800-824-6494
Admissions: (719)587-7712
Fax: (719)587-7522
E-mail: ecarpio@adams.edu
Web Site: http://www.adams.edu/
President/CEO: Dr. Lee A. Halgren
Registrar: Belen Maestas
Admissions: Eric Carpio
Financial Aid: Philip Schroeder
Type: Comprehensive **Sex:** Coed **Scores:** 82.75% SAT V 400+; 82.75% SAT M 400+; 48.76% ACT 18-23; 12.81% ACT 24-29 **% Accepted:** 60 **Admission Plans:** Early Admission; Deferred Admission **Application Deadline:** August 01 **Application Fee:** $20.00 **H.S. Requirements:** High school diploma required; GED accepted **Costs Per Year:** Application fee: $20. Area resident tuition: $90 per credit hour part-time. State resident tuition: $1980 full-time. Nonresident tuition: $8250 full-time, $344 per credit hour part-time. Mandatory fees: $874 full-time. College room and board: $5760. **Scholarships:** Available **Calendar System:** Semester, Summer Session Available **Enrollment:** FT 1,876, PT 562, Grad 3,140 **Faculty:** FT 104, PT 81 **Student-Faculty Ratio:** 18:1 **Exams:** SAT I or ACT **% Receiving Financial Aid:** 91 **% Residing in College-Owned, -Operated, or -Affiliated Housing:** 40 **Library Holdings:** 493,581 **Regional Accreditation:** North Central Association of Colleges and Schools **Credit Hours For Degree:** 60 semester hours, Associates; 120 semester hours, Bachelors **Professional Accreditation:** ACA, NASM **Intercollegiate Athletics:** Basketball M & W; Cross-Country Running M & W; Football M; Golf M; Softball W; Track and Field M & W; Volleyball W; Wrestling M

AIMS COMMUNITY COLLEGE
Box 69
Greeley, CO 80632-0069
Tel: (970)330-8008
E-mail: stuart.thomas@aims.edu
Web Site: http://www.aims.edu/
President/CEO: Dr. Marilynn Liddell
Registrar: Stuart Thomas
Admissions: Stuart Thomas
Financial Aid: Lynne Suppes
Type: Two-Year College **Sex:** Coed **Admission Plans:** Open Admission; Early Admission; Deferred Admission **H.S. Requirements:** High school diploma or equivalent not required **Scholarships:** Available **Calendar System:** Semester, Summer Session Available **Enrollment:** FT 2,252, PT 2,846 **Faculty:** FT 102, PT 219 **Student-Faculty Ratio:** 16:1 **Exams:** Other **Library Holdings:** 39,129 **Regional Accreditation:** North Central Association of Colleges and Schools **Credit Hours For Degree:** 96 quarter hours, Associates **ROTC:** Air Force **Professional Accreditation:** JRCERT

ARAPAHOE COMMUNITY COLLEGE
5900 South Santa Fe Dr., PO Box 9002
Littleton, CO 80160-9002
Tel: (303)797-4222
Admissions: (303)797-5623
Fax: (303)797-5970
Web Site: http://www.arapahoe.edu/
President/CEO: Dr. Berton Glandon
Registrar: Matt Jamison
Admissions: Matt Jamison
Financial Aid: James Contreras
Type: Two-Year College **Sex:** Coed **Affiliation:** Community Colleges of Colorado **% Accepted:** 100 **Admission Plans:** Open Admission; Early Admission; Deferred Admission **Application Deadline:** Rolling **Application Fee:** $0.00 **H.S. Requirements:** High school diploma or equivalent not required. For medical laboratory technology, medical assistant technology, nursing, medical records technology, police & fire science academy, mortuary science: High school diploma required; GED accepted **Costs Per Year:** Application fee: $0. State resident tuition: $1619 full-time, $89.90 per credit hour part-time. Nonresident tuition: $8000 full-time, $369.30 per credit hour part-time. Mandatory fees: $81 full-time. **Scholarships:** Available **Calendar System:** Semester, Summer Session Available **Enrollment:** FT 2,312, PT 5,248 **Faculty:** FT 114, PT 300 **Student-Faculty Ratio:** 19:1 **Library Holdings:** 45,000 **Regional Accreditation:** North Central Association of Colleges and Schools **Credit Hours For Degree:** 61 credit hours, Associates **ROTC:** Army, Air Force **Professional Accreditation:** ABFSE, AHIMA, APTA, NAACLS

ARGOSY UNIVERSITY/DENVER
1200 Lincoln St.
Denver, CO 80203
Tel: (303)248-2700; (866)431-5981
Web Site: http://www.argosyu.edu/ **Type:** Two-Year College **Sex:** Coed

THE ART INSTITUTE OF COLORADO
1200 Lincoln St.
Denver, CO 80203
Tel: (303)837-0825
Free: 800-275-2420
Fax: (303)860-8520
E-mail: baparker@aii.edu
Web Site: http://www.aic.artinstitutes.edu/
President/CEO: David C. Zorn
Registrar: Bonnie Gronenthal
Admissions: Brian Parker
Financial Aid: Shannon May
Type: Four-Year College **Sex:** Coed **Affiliation:** Education Management Corporation **Admission Plans:** Early Admission; Deferred Admission **Application Deadline:** Rolling **Application Fee:** $0.00 **H.S. Requirements:** High school diploma required; GED accepted **Costs Per Year:** Application fee: $0. Tuition: $25,088 full-time, $392 per credit part-time. College room only: $7980. **Scholarships:** Available **Calendar System:** Quarter, Summer Session Not available **Enrollment:** FT 2,137, PT 749 **Faculty:** FT 68, PT 54 **Student-Faculty Ratio:** 18:1 **% Receiving Financial Aid:** 82 **% Residing in College-Owned, -Operated, or -Affiliated Housing:** 9 **Library Holdings:** 13,100 **Credit Hours For Degree:** 105 credit hours, Associates; 192 credit hours, Bachelors **Professional Accreditation:** ACICS, ACF

ASPEN UNIVERSITY
501 South Cherry St., Ste. 350
Denver, CO 80246

Tel: (303)333-4224
Fax: (303)336-1144
Web Site: http://www.aspen.edu/
President/CEO: Ron Boehm
Registrar: Kris Larson
Type: Two-Year Upper Division **Sex:** Coed **Application Fee:** $50.00 **Calendar System:** Miscellaneous **Professional Accreditation:** DETC

BEL-REA INSTITUTE OF ANIMAL TECHNOLOGY
1681 South Dayton St.
Denver, CO 80247
Tel: (303)751-8700
Free: 800-950-8001
Fax: (303)751-9969
Web Site: http://www.bel-rea.com/
President/CEO: Marc Schapiro
Admissions: Paulette Kaufman
Financial Aid: Staci Bottinelli
Type: Two-Year College **Sex:** Coed **Application Fee:** $100.00 **H.S. Requirements:** High school diploma required; GED accepted **Scholarships:** Available **Calendar System:** Quarter, Summer Session Not available **Faculty:** FT 19, PT 5 **Student-Faculty Ratio:** 25:1 **Library Holdings:** 1,800 **Credit Hours For Degree:** 125 credits, Associates **Professional Accreditation:** ACCSCT

BLAIR COLLEGE
1815 Jet Wing Dr.
Colorado Springs, CO 80916
Tel: (719)638-6580; 888-741-4271
Admissions: (719)630-6580
Fax: (719)638-6818
E-mail: dcollins@cci.edu
Web Site: http://blair-college.com/
President/CEO: Tom Andron
Registrar: Robert Johnston
Admissions: Dawn Collins
Financial Aid: Jami Moore
Type: Two-Year College **Sex:** Coed **Affiliation:** Corinthian Colleges, Inc **Admission Plans:** Open Admission **Application Fee:** $25.00 **H.S. Requirements:** High school diploma required; GED accepted **Scholarships:** Available **Calendar System:** Quarter, Summer Session Not available **Faculty:** FT 12, PT 16 **Student-Faculty Ratio:** 13:1 **Exams:** Other **Credit Hours For Degree:** 96 credit hours, Associates **Professional Accreditation:** ACICS, AAMAE

BOULDER COLLEGE OF MASSAGE THERAPY
6255 Longbow Dr.
Boulder, CO 80301
Tel: (303)530-2100
Free: 800-442-5131
Fax: (303)530-2204
Web Site: http://www.bcmt.org/
President/CEO: Dr. Suzanne Miller
Type: Two-Year College **Sex:** Coed **Calendar System:** Quarter **Professional Accreditation:** ACCSCT

CAMBRIDGE COLLEGE
12500 East Iliff Ave., No. 100
Aurora, CO 80014
Tel: (303)338-9700
Fax: (303)338-9701
Web Site: http://www.cambridgecollege.com/
President/CEO: Sandi Parks
Financial Aid: Richard Semakula
Type: Two-Year College **Professional Accreditation:** ABHES, ACCSCT

COLLEGEAMERICA-COLORADO SPRINGS
3645 Citadel Dr. South
Colorado Springs, CO 80909
Tel: (719)637-0600
Fax: (719)637-0806
Web Site: http://www.collegeamerica.com/ **Type:** Two-Year College **Sex:** Coed **Professional Accreditation:** ACCSCT

COLLEGEAMERICA-DENVER
1385 South Colorado Blvd.
Denver, CO 80222-1912
Tel: (303)691-9756
Fax: (303)692-9156
E-mail: collegeamerica@aol.com
Web Site: http://www.collegeamerica.com/
President/CEO: Barbara W. Thomas
Registrar: Mary Acker
Admissions: Barbara W. Thomas
Financial Aid: Marty Doyscher
Type: Two-Year College **Sex:** Coed **Scholarships:** Available **Professional Accreditation:** ACCSCT

COLLEGEAMERICA-FORT COLLINS
4601 South Mason St.
Fort Collins, CO 80525-3740
Tel: (970)223-6060
Fax: (970)223-6060
Web Site: http://www.collegeamerica.edu/
President/CEO: Anna DiTorrice-Mull
Admissions: Anna DiTorrice-Mull
Type: Two-Year College **Sex:** Coed **Admission Plans:** Open Admission **Application Fee:** $0.00 **H.S. Requirements:** High school diploma required; GED accepted **Calendar System:** Continuous, Summer Session Not available **Faculty:** FT 11, PT 22 **Student-Faculty Ratio:** 22:1 **Professional Accreditation:** ACCSCT

COLORADO CHRISTIAN UNIVERSITY
8787 West Alameda
Lakewood, CO 80226
Tel: (303)202-0100
Free: 800-44-FAITH
Admissions: (303)963-3163
Fax: (303)238-2191
E-mail: admission@ccu.edu
Web Site: http://www.ccu.edu/
President/CEO: Dr. Larry Donnithorne
Registrar: Wendy Wibbens
Admissions: Ronald Rex
Financial Aid: Steve Woodburn
Type: Comprehensive **Sex:** Coed **Affiliation:** interdenominational **Scores:** 100% SAT V 400+; 92% SAT M 400+; 46% ACT 18-23; 37% ACT 24-29 **% Accepted:** 77 **Admission Plans:** Deferred Admission **Application Deadline:** August 21 **Application Fee:** $50.00 **H.S. Requirements:** High school diploma required; GED accepted **Costs Per Year:** Application fee: $50. Comprehensive fee: $23,422 includes full-time tuition ($16,590), mandatory fees ($150), and college room and board ($6682). College room only: $3930. Part-time tuition: $700 per credit hour. **Scholarships:** Available **Calendar System:** Semester, Summer Session Available **Enrollment:** FT 1,075, PT 751, Grad 316 **Faculty:** FT 43, PT 3 **Student-Faculty Ratio:** 21:1 **Exams:** SAT I or ACT **% Receiving Financial Aid:** 67 **% Residing in College-Owned, -Operated, or -Affiliated Housing:** 65 **Library Holdings:** 71,565 **Regional Accreditation:** North Central Association of Colleges and Schools **Credit Hours For Degree:** 64 semester hours, Associates; 128 semester hours, Bachelors **ROTC:** Army **Intercollegiate Athletics:** Basketball M & W; Cross-Country Running M & W; Golf M; Soccer M & W; Tennis M & W; Volleyball W

THE COLORADO COLLEGE
14 East Cache La Poudre
Colorado Springs, CO 80903-3294
Tel: (719)389-6000
Free: 800-542-7214
Admissions: (719)389-6344
Fax: (719)389-6282
E-mail: admission@cc.colorado.edu
Web Site: http://www.coloradocollege.edu/
President/CEO: Dr. Richard F. Celeste
Admissions: Mark Hatch
Financial Aid: James M. Swanson
Type: Comprehensive **Sex:** Coed **Scores:** 100% SAT V 400+; 99.66% SAT M 400+; 8.74% ACT 18-23; 52.46% ACT 24-29 **% Accepted:** 38 **Admission Plans:** Early Action; Deferred Admission **Application Deadline:** January 15 **Application Fee:** $50.00 **H.S. Requirements:** High school diploma or equivalent not required **Costs Per Year:** Application fee: $50. Comprehensive fee: $37,668 includes full-time tuition ($30,048) and college room and board ($7620). College room only: $4116. Room and board charges

vary according to board plan. Part-time tuition: $948.38 per credit hour. **Scholarships:** Available **Calendar System:** Miscellaneous, Summer Session Available **Enrollment:** FT 1,928, PT 49, Grad 39 **Faculty:** FT 176, PT 30 **Student-Faculty Ratio:** 9:1 **Exams:** SAT I or ACT **% Receiving Financial Aid:** 45 **% Residing in College-Owned, -Operated, or -Affiliated Housing:** 73 **Regional Accreditation:** North Central Association of Colleges and Schools **Credit Hours For Degree:** 128 semester hours, Bachelors **ROTC:** Army **Intercollegiate Athletics:** Basketball M & W; Cross-Country Running M & W; Equestrian Sports M & W; Field Hockey M & W; Football M; Ice Hockey M & W; Lacrosse M & W; Rugby M & W; Skiing (Downhill) M & W; Soccer M & W; Softball W; Swimming and Diving M & W; Tennis M & W; Track and Field M & W; Ultimate Frisbee M & W; Volleyball M & W; Water Polo M & W

COLORADO MOUNTAIN COLLEGE
831 Grand Ave.
Glenwood Springs, CO 81601
Tel: (970)945-7481
Free: 800-621-8559
Admissions: (970)947-8328
E-mail: joinus@coloradomtn.edu
Web Site: http://www.coloradomtn.edu/
President/CEO: Dr. Cynthia M. Heelan
Registrar: Mearl Kerns
Admissions: Bill Sommers
Financial Aid: Gary Lewis
Type: Two-Year College **Sex:** Coed **Affiliation:** Colorado Mountain College District System **% Accepted:** 100 **Admission Plans:** Open Admission; Early Admission; Deferred Admission **Application Deadline:** Rolling **Application Fee:** $0.00 **H.S. Requirements:** High school diploma required; GED accepted. For some adult applicants: High school diploma or equivalent not required **Costs Per Year:** Application fee: $0. Area resident tuition: $1290 full-time, $43 per credit part-time. State resident tuition: $2160 full-time, $72 per credit part-time. Nonresident tuition: $6930 full-time, $231 per credit part-time. Mandatory fees: $180 full-time. College room and board: $6600. College room only: $3400. **Scholarships:** Available **Calendar System:** Semester, Summer Session Available **Faculty:** FT 22 **Student-Faculty Ratio:** 17:1 **Exams:** SAT I or ACT **% Residing in College-Owned, -Operated, or -Affiliated Housing:** 44 **Library Holdings:** 36,000 **Regional Accreditation:** North Central Association of Colleges and Schools **Credit Hours For Degree:** 62 credits, Associates **Intercollegiate Athletics:** Soccer M & W

COLORADO MOUNTAIN COLLEGE, ALPINE CAMPUS
1330 Bob Adams Dr.
Steamboat Springs, CO 80487
Tel: (970)870-4444
Free: 800-621-8559
Admissions: (970)945-8691
E-mail: joinus@coloradomtn.edu
Web Site: http://www.coloradomtn.edu/
President/CEO: Dr. Robert Ritschel
Registrar: Merle Kearns
Admissions: Bill Sommers
Financial Aid: Mary Edwards
Type: Two-Year College **Sex:** Coed **Affiliation:** Colorado Mountain College District System **% Accepted:** 100 **Admission Plans:** Open Admission; Early Admission; Deferred Admission **Application Deadline:** Rolling **Application Fee:** $0.00 **H.S. Requirements:** High school diploma required; GED accepted **Costs Per Year:** Application fee: $0. Area resident tuition: $1290 full-time, $43 per credit part-time. State resident tuition: $2160 full-time, $72 per credit part-time. Nonresident tuition: $6930 full-time, $231 per credit part-time. Mandatory fees: $180 full-time. College room and board: $6600. College room only: $3400. **Scholarships:** Available **Calendar System:** Semester, Summer Session Available **Enrollment:** FT 454, PT 650 **Faculty:** FT 19 **Exams:** SAT I or ACT **% Residing in College-Owned, -Operated, or -Affiliated Housing:** 44 **Library Holdings:** 17,000 **Regional Accreditation:** North Central Association of Colleges and Schools **Credit Hours For Degree:** 62 credits, Associates **Intercollegiate Athletics:** Skiing (Downhill) M & W

COLORADO MOUNTAIN COLLEGE, TIMBERLINE CAMPUS
901 South Hwy. 24
Leadville, CO 80461
Tel: (719)486-2015
Free: 800-621-8559
Admissions: (970)945-8691
E-mail: joinus@coloradomtn.edu
Web Site: http://www.coloradomtn.edu/
President/CEO: Gary Smith, PhD
Registrar: Mearl Kerns
Admissions: Bill Sommers
Type: Two-Year College **Sex:** Coed **Affiliation:** Colorado Mountain College District System **% Accepted:** 100 **Admission Plans:** Open Admission; Early Admission; Deferred Admission **Application Deadline:** Rolling **Application Fee:** $0.00 **H.S. Requirements:** High school diploma required; GED accepted **Costs Per Year:** Application fee: $0. Area resident tuition: $1290 full-time, $43 per credit part-time. State resident tuition: $2160 full-time, $72 per credit part-time. Nonresident tuition: $6930 full-time, $231 per credit part-time. Mandatory fees: $180 full-time. College room and board: $6600. College room only: $3400. **Scholarships:** Available **Calendar System:** Semester, Summer Session Available **Faculty:** FT 14 **% Residing in College-Owned, -Operated, or -Affiliated Housing:** 30 **Library Holdings:** 25,000 **Regional Accreditation:** North Central Association of Colleges and Schools **Credit Hours For Degree:** 62 credits, Associates

COLORADO NORTHWESTERN COMMUNITY COLLEGE
500 Kennedy Dr.
Rangely, CO 81648-3598
Tel: (970)675-2261
Free: 800-562-1105
Admissions: (970)824-1103
Fax: (970)675-3343
E-mail: gene.bilodeau@cncc.edu
Web Site: http://www.cncc.edu/
President/CEO: Peter Angstadt
Registrar: Gene Bilodeau
Admissions: Gene Bilodeau
Financial Aid: Tresa England
Type: Two-Year College **Sex:** Coed **Affiliation:** Colorado Community College and Occupational Education System **Admission Plans:** Open Admission; Early Admission; Deferred Admission **Application Fee:** $0.00 **H.S. Requirements:** High school diploma required; GED accepted. For except dental hygiene program: High school diploma required; GED accepted **Scholarships:** Available **Calendar System:** Semester, Summer Session Available **Enrollment:** FT 499, PT 1,743 **Faculty:** FT 41, PT 236 **Student-Faculty Ratio:** 9:1 **% Residing in College-Owned, -Operated, or -Affiliated Housing:** 62 **Library Holdings:** 20,063 **Regional Accreditation:** North Central Association of Colleges and Schools **Credit Hours For Degree:** 60 semester hours, Associates **Professional Accreditation:** ADA **Intercollegiate Athletics:** Baseball M; Basketball M & W; Cross-Country Running W; Softball W

COLORADO SCHOOL OF HEALING ARTS
7655 West Mississippi Ave., Ste. 100
Lakewood, CO 80226
Tel: (303)986-2320
Free: 800-233-7114
Fax: (303)980-6594
Web Site: http://www.csha.net/
President/CEO: Dennis Simpson
Admissions: Victoria Steere
Type: Two-Year College **Sex:** Coed **% Accepted:** 100 **Application Deadline:** October 01 **Application Fee:** $50.00 **Costs Per Year:** Application fee: $50. Tuition: $8925 full-time. Mandatory fees: $1236 full-time. **Calendar System:** Quarter **Enrollment:** FT 149, PT 91 **Faculty:** FT 4, PT 31 **Student-Faculty Ratio:** 13:1 **Professional Accreditation:** ACCSCT

COLORADO SCHOOL OF MINES
1500 Illinois St.
Golden, CO 80401-1887
Tel: (303)273-3000
Free: 800-446-9488
Admissions: (303)273-3227
Fax: (303)273-3509
E-mail: admit@mines.edu
Web Site: http://www.mines.edu/
President/CEO: Dr. John U. Trefny
Registrar: Lara Medley

Admissions: Bill Young
Financial Aid: Roger A. Koester
Type: University **Sex:** Coed **Scores:** 100% SAT V 400+; 100% SAT M 400+; 13% ACT 18-23; 64% ACT 24-29 **% Accepted:** 80 **Admission Plans:** Deferred Admission **Application Deadline:** June 01 **Application Fee:** $45.00 **H.S. Requirements:** High school diploma required; GED accepted **Costs Per Year:** Application fee: $45. State resident tuition: $7248 full-time, $382 per semester hour part-time. Nonresident tuition: $19,830 full-time, $661 per semester hour part-time. Mandatory fees: $895 full-time, $60 per semester hour part-time. Part-time tuition and fees vary according to course load. College room and board: $6750. College room only: $3550. Room and board charges vary according to board plan and housing facility. **Scholarships:** Available **Calendar System:** Semester, Summer Session Available **Enrollment:** FT 2,909, PT 189, Grad 817 **Faculty:** FT 193, PT 106 **Student-Faculty Ratio:** 14:1 **Exams:** SAT I or ACT **% Receiving Financial Aid:** 68 **% Residing in College-Owned, -Operated, or -Affiliated Housing:** 25 **Library Holdings:** 150,000 **Regional Accreditation:** North Central Association of Colleges and Schools **Credit Hours For Degree:** 137 semester hours, Bachelors **ROTC:** Army **Professional Accreditation:** ABET **Intercollegiate Athletics:** Baseball M; Basketball M & W; Cross-Country Running M & W; Football M; Golf M; Skiing (Downhill) M; Soccer M; Softball W; Swimming and Diving M & W; Tennis M & W; Track and Field M & W; Volleyball W; Wrestling M

COLORADO SCHOOL OF TRADES
1575 Hoyt St.
Lakewood, CO 80215-2996
Tel: (303)233-4697
Free: 800-234-4594
Fax: (303)233-4723
Web Site: http://www.schooloftrades.com/
President/CEO: Robert Martin
Admissions: Robert Martin
Type: Two-Year College **Sex:** Coed **% Accepted:** 87 **Application Fee:** $25.00 **Costs Per Year:** Application fee: $25. Tuition: $16,200 full-time. Mandatory fees: $154 full-time. **Scholarships:** Available **Enrollment:** FT 125 **Faculty:** FT 10 **Student-Faculty Ratio:** 12:1 **Professional Accreditation:** ACCSCT

COLORADO STATE UNIVERSITY
Fort Collins, CO 80523-0015
Tel: (970)491-1101
Admissions: (970)491-6909
Fax: (970)491-7799
E-mail: admissions@vines.colostate.edu
Web Site: http://www.colostate.edu/
President/CEO: Dr. Larry E. Penley
Registrar: G. Kay Jacks
Admissions: Mary Ontiveros
Financial Aid: Sandy Calhoun
Type: University **Sex:** Coed **Affiliation:** Colorado State University System **Scores:** 98% SAT V 400+; 99% SAT M 400+; 46% ACT 18-23; 45% ACT 24-29 **% Accepted:** 88 **Admission Plans:** Deferred Admission **Application Deadline:** July 01 **Application Fee:** $50.00 **H.S. Requirements:** High school diploma required; GED accepted **Costs Per Year:** Application fee: $50. State resident tuition: $3381 full-time, $188 per credit part-time. Nonresident tuition: $14,343 full-time, $797 per credit part-time. Mandatory fees: $1181 full-time. Part-time tuition varies according to course load. College room and board: $6316. College room only: $2852. Room and board charges vary according to board plan and housing facility. **Scholarships:** Available **Calendar System:** Semester, Summer Session Available **Enrollment:** FT 18,995, PT 2,511, Grad 5,090 **Faculty:** FT 851, PT 30 **Student-Faculty Ratio:** 18:1 **Exams:** SAT I or ACT **% Receiving Financial Aid:** 39 **% Residing in College-Owned, -Operated, or -Affiliated Housing:** 23 **Library Holdings:** 1,863,052 **Regional Accreditation:** North Central Association of Colleges and Schools **Credit Hours For Degree:** 120 credits, Bachelors **ROTC:** Army, Air Force **Professional Accreditation:** AACSB, ABET, ACEJMC, AAMFT, AAFCS, ACCE, ACA, ADtA, AOTA, APA, ASLA, AVMA, CSWE, FIDER, NASM, NCATE, NRPA, SAF **Intercollegiate Athletics:** Basketball M & W; Cross-Country Running M & W; Football M; Golf M & W; Softball W; Swimming and Diving W; Tennis W; Track and Field M & W; Volleyball W; Water Polo W

COLORADO STATE UNIVERSITY-PUEBLO
2200 Bonforte Blvd.
Pueblo, CO 81001-4901
Tel: (719)549-2100
Admissions: (719)549-2461
Fax: (719)549-2419
Web Site: http://www.colostate-pueblo.edu/
President/CEO: Dr. Ronald Applbaum
Registrar: Joe Marshall
Admissions: Joe Marshall
Financial Aid: Ofelia Morales
Type: Comprehensive **Sex:** Coed **Affiliation:** Colorado State University System **Scores:** 80% SAT V 400+; 82% SAT M 400+; 62% ACT 18-23; 12% ACT 24-29 **Admission Plans:** Deferred Admission **Application Fee:** $25.00 **H.S. Requirements:** High school diploma required; GED accepted **Costs Per Year:** Application fee: $25. State resident tuition: $2902 full-time, $120.92 per credit part-time. Nonresident tuition: $13,542 full-time, $564.25 per credit part-time. Mandatory fees: $964 full-time, $40.17 per credit part-time. Full-time tuition and fees vary according to course load and reciprocity agreements. Part-time tuition and fees vary according to reciprocity agreements. College room and board: $6088. College room only: $2960. Room and board charges vary according to board plan and housing facility. **Scholarships:** Available **Calendar System:** Semester, Summer Session Available **Enrollment:** FT 3,367, PT 2,050, Grad 418 **Faculty:** FT 149, PT 163 **Student-Faculty Ratio:** 17:1 **Exams:** SAT I or ACT **% Receiving Financial Aid:** 65 **% Residing in College-Owned, -Operated, or -Affiliated Housing:** 18 **Library Holdings:** 270,761 **Regional Accreditation:** North Central Association of Colleges and Schools **Credit Hours For Degree:** 120 semester hours, Bachelors **ROTC:** Army **Professional Accreditation:** AACSB, ABET, CSWE, NASM, NLN **Intercollegiate Athletics:** Baseball M; Basketball M & W; Cross-Country Running W; Golf M & W; Soccer M & W; Softball W; Tennis M & W; Volleyball W

COLORADO TECHNICAL UNIVERSITY
4435 North Chestnut St.
Colorado Springs, CO 80907-3896
Tel: (719)598-0200
E-mail: tjohnson@cos.coloradotech.edu
Web Site: http://www.coloradotech.edu
President/CEO: David D. O'Donnell
Registrar: Bob Golightly
Admissions: Ron Begora
Financial Aid: Pat Hollenbeck
Type: Comprehensive **Sex:** Coed **Affiliation:** Whitman Education Group **Admission Plans:** Deferred Admission **Application Fee:** $50.00 **H.S. Requirements:** High school diploma required; GED accepted **Scholarships:** Available **Calendar System:** Quarter, Summer Session Available **Enrollment:** FT 305, PT 910, Grad 469 **Faculty:** FT 35, PT 102 **Student-Faculty Ratio:** 20:1 **Exams:** Other, SAT I or ACT **Library Holdings:** 29,819 **Regional Accreditation:** North Central Association of Colleges and Schools **Credit Hours For Degree:** 90 quarter hours, Associates; 178 quarter hours, Bachelors **ROTC:** Army **Professional Accreditation:** ABET

COLORADO TECHNICAL UNIVERSITY DENVER CAMPUS
5775 Denver Tech Center Blvd.
Greenwood Village, CO 80111
Tel: (303)694-6600
Fax: (303)694-6673
Web Site: http://www.coloradotech.edu/
President/CEO: Robert Golightly
Admissions: Suzanne Hyman
Type: Comprehensive **Sex:** Coed **Affiliation:** Whitman Education Group **Admission Plans:** Deferred Admission **Application Fee:** $50.00 **H.S. Requirements:** High school diploma required; GED accepted **Scholarships:** Available **Calendar System:** Quarter, Summer Session Available **Enrollment:** FT 41, PT 151, Grad 106 **Faculty:** FT 5, PT 46 **Student-Faculty Ratio:** 14:1 **Exams:** Other, SAT I or ACT **Library Holdings:** 12,715 **Regional Accreditation:** North Central Association of Colleges and Schools **Credit Hours For Degree:** 90 credit hours, Associates; 178 credit hours, Bachelors

COMMUNITY COLLEGE OF AURORA
16000 East Centre Tech Parkway
Aurora, CO 80011-9036
Tel: (303)360-4700
E-mail: kristen.cusak@ccaurora.edu
Web Site: http://www.ccaurora.edu/
President/CEO: Dr. Linda S. Bowman

Registrar: Connie Simpson
Admissions: Kristen Cusak
Financial Aid: Terry Campbell-Caron
Type: Two-Year College **Sex:** Coed **% Accepted:** 100 **Admission Plans:** Open Admission; Early Admission **Application Deadline:** Rolling **Application Fee:** $0.00 **H.S. Requirements:** High school diploma or equivalent not required **Costs Per Year:** Application fee: $0. State resident tuition: $2236 full-time, $74.55 per credit hour part-time. Nonresident tuition: $10,354 full-time, $345.15 per credit hour part-time. Mandatory fees: $126 full-time, $3 per credit hour part-time, $20.75. **Scholarships:** Available **Calendar System:** Semester, Summer Session Available **Enrollment:** FT 1,412, PT 4,065 **Faculty:** FT 27, PT 320 **Student-Faculty Ratio:** 21:1 **Library Holdings:** 7,440 **Regional Accreditation:** North Central Association of Colleges and Schools **Credit Hours For Degree:** 60 semester hours, Associates **Professional Accreditation:** CARC

COMMUNITY COLLEGE OF DENVER
PO Box 173363
Denver, CO 80217-3363
Tel: (303)556-2600
Admissions: (303)556-6325
Web Site: http://www.ccd.edu/
President/CEO: Dr. Christine Johnson
Registrar: Emita Samuels
Admissions: Emita Samuels
Financial Aid: Carol Linsley
Type: Two-Year College **Sex:** Coed **Affiliation:** Community Colleges of Colorado **Scores:** 68.75% SAT V 400+; 81.25% SAT M 400+; 38.16% ACT 18-23; 6% ACT 24-29 **Admission Plans:** Open Admission; Early Admission; Deferred Admission **Application Deadline:** Rolling **Application Fee:** $0.00 **H.S. Requirements:** High school diploma or equivalent not required **Costs Per Year:** Application fee: $0. State resident tuition: $2237 full-time, $74.55 per credit part-time. Nonresident tuition: $10,355 full-time, $345.15 per credit part-time. Mandatory fees: $612 full-time. **Scholarships:** Available **Calendar System:** Semester, Summer Session Available **Enrollment:** FT 2,041, PT 6,868 **Faculty:** FT 64, PT 377 **Student-Faculty Ratio:** 23:1 **Library Holdings:** 683,045 **Regional Accreditation:** North Central Association of Colleges and Schools **Credit Hours For Degree:** 60 credit hours, Associates **ROTC:** Army **Professional Accreditation:** ARCEST, ADA, JRCERT

DENVER ACADEMY OF COURT REPORTING
9051 Harlan St., Unit 20
Westminster, CO 80030
Tel: (303)427-5292
Free: 800-574-2087
Fax: (303)427-5383
Web Site: http://www.dacr.org/
President/CEO: Charles W. Jarstfer
Registrar: Eva Gomez
Admissions: Howard Brookner
Financial Aid: Maureen Connors
Type: Two-Year College **Sex:** Coed **Admission Plans:** Open Admission **Application Fee:** $75.00 **H.S. Requirements:** High school diploma required; GED accepted **Scholarships:** Available **Calendar System:** Quarter **Faculty:** FT 8, PT 4 **Credit Hours For Degree:** 99 credits, Associates **Professional Accreditation:** ACICS

DENVER AUTOMOTIVE AND DIESEL COLLEGE
460 South Lipan St.
Denver, CO 80223-2025
Tel: (303)722-5724
Free: 800-347-3232
Fax: (303)778-8264
Web Site: http://www.dadc.com/
President/CEO: Joe Chalupa
Registrar: Roseanne Kosovich
Admissions: John Chalupa
Financial Aid: Sonja Aceves
Type: Two-Year College **Sex:** Coed **Application Fee:** $150.00 **H.S. Requirements:** High school diploma required; GED accepted **Scholarships:** Available **Calendar System:** Miscellaneous, Summer Session Available **Enrollment:** FT 368 **Faculty:** FT 21 **Library Holdings:** 1,050 **Credit Hours For Degree:** 108 credit hours, Associates **Professional Accreditation:** ACCSCT

DENVER CAREER COLLEGE
500 East 84th Ave., Ste. W-200
Thornton, CO 80229
Tel: (303)295-0550
Web Site: http://www.denvercareercollege.com/
President/CEO: William P. Murtagh, Jr.
Registrar: Betsy Covington
Type: Two-Year College **Sex:** Coed **Calendar System:** Continuous **Professional Accreditation:** ACCSCT

DEVRY UNIVERSITY (BROOMFIELD)
12202 Airport Way, Ste. 190
Broomfield, CO 80021-2588
Tel: (303)469-9220
Admissions: (303)329-3340
Fax: (303)469-9224
Web Site: http://www.devry.edu/
President/CEO: Timothy Campagna
Registrar: Lisa Barry
Admissions: Rick Rodman
Financial Aid: Terry Bargas
Type: Comprehensive **Sex:** Coed **Affiliation:** DeVry University **Admission Plans:** Deferred Admission **H.S. Requirements:** High school diploma required; GED accepted **Scholarships:** Available **Calendar System:** Semester **Enrollment:** FT 307, PT 153 **Faculty:** FT 19, PT 43 **Student-Faculty Ratio:** 7:1 **Exams:** Other, SAT I or ACT **% Receiving Financial Aid:** 87 **Library Holdings:** 5,037 **Regional Accreditation:** North Central Association of Colleges and Schools **Credit Hours For Degree:** 67 credit hours, Associates; 128 credit hours, Bachelors

DEVRY UNIVERSITY (COLORADO SPRINGS)
225 South Union Blvd.
Colorado Springs, CO 80910
Tel: (719)632-3000; (866)338-7934
Web Site: http://www.devry.edu/
President/CEO: Timothy Campagna
Registrar: Sam Pedregon
Financial Aid: Terry Bargas
Type: Comprehensive **Sex:** Coed **Affiliation:** DeVry University **Admission Plans:** Deferred Admission **Application Deadline:** Rolling **Application Fee:** $50.00 **H.S. Requirements:** High school diploma required; GED accepted **Costs Per Year:** Application fee: $50. One-time mandatory fee: $40. Tuition: $12,450 full-time, $460 per credit part-time. Mandatory fees: $270 full-time, $30 per year part-time. Full-time tuition and fees vary according to course load. Part-time tuition and fees vary according to course load. **Scholarships:** Available **Calendar System:** Semester, Summer Session Available **Enrollment:** FT 89, PT 127, Grad 59 **Faculty:** FT 1, PT 41 **Student-Faculty Ratio:** 9:1 **% Receiving Financial Aid:** 73 **Regional Accreditation:** North Central Association of Colleges and Schools **Credit Hours For Degree:** 67 credit hours, Associates; 122 credit hours, Bachelors

DEVRY UNIVERSITY (WESTMINSTER)
1870 West 122nd Ave.
Westminster, CO 80234-2010
Tel: (303)280-7400; (866)338-7934
Web Site: http://www.devry.edu/
President/CEO: Timothy N. Campagna
Registrar: Lisa Barry
Financial Aid: Carey Brown
Type: Four-Year College **Sex:** Coed **Affiliation:** DeVry, Inc **Admission Plans:** Open Admission **Application Deadline:** Rolling **Application Fee:** $50.00 **H.S. Requirements:** High school diploma required; GED accepted **Costs Per Year:** Application fee: $50. One-time mandatory fee: $40. Tuition: $12,450 full-time, $460 per term part-time. Mandatory fees: $270 full-time, $160 per year part-time. Full-time tuition and fees vary according to course load. Part-time tuition and fees vary according to course load. **Scholarships:** Available **Calendar System:** Semester, Summer Session Available **Enrollment:** FT 407, PT 216, Grad 122 **Faculty:** FT 14, PT 59 **Student-Faculty Ratio:** 17:1 **% Receiving Financial Aid:** 67 **Library Holdings:** 500,000 **Regional Accreditation:** North Central Association of Colleges and Schools

FORT LEWIS COLLEGE
1000 Rim Dr.
Durango, CO 81301-3999

Tel: (970)247-7010
Admissions: (970)247-7184
Fax: (970)247-7179
Web Site: http://www.fortlewis.edu/
President/CEO: Dr. Brad Bartel
Registrar: Sherri Waggoner
Admissions: Gretchen Foster
Financial Aid: Elaine S. Redwine
Type: Four-Year College **Sex:** Coed **Scores:** 93% SAT V 400+; 94% SAT M 400+; 59% ACT 18-23; 20% ACT 24-29 **% Accepted:** 74 **Application Deadline:** August 01 **Application Fee:** $30.00 **H.S. Requirements:** High school diploma required; GED accepted **Costs Per Year:** Application fee: $30. State resident tuition: $4862 full-time, $121 per credit hour part-time. Nonresident tuition: $12,870 full-time, $643 per credit hour part-time. Mandatory fees: $830 full-time, $45.75 per credit hour part-time. Full-time tuition and fees vary according to reciprocity agreements. Part-time tuition and fees vary according to course load and reciprocity agreements. College room and board: $6160. College room only: $3258. Room and board charges vary according to board plan and housing facility. **Scholarships:** Available **Calendar System:** Miscellaneous, Summer Session Available **Enrollment:** FT 3,637, PT 309 **Faculty:** FT 177, PT 64 **Student-Faculty Ratio:** 18:1 **Exams:** SAT I or ACT **% Receiving Financial Aid:** 49 **% Residing in College-Owned, -Operated, or -Affiliated Housing:** 32 **Library Holdings:** 184,860 **Regional Accreditation:** North Central Association of Colleges and Schools **Credit Hours For Degree:** 120 credit hours, Bachelors **Professional Accreditation:** AACSB, JRCEPAT, NASM **Intercollegiate Athletics:** Baseball M; Basketball M & W; Cheerleading M & W; Cross-Country Running M & W; Fencing M & W; Football M; Golf M; Ice Hockey M & W; Lacrosse M; Rock Climbing M & W; Skiing (Cross-Country) M & W; Skiing (Downhill) M & W; Soccer M & W; Softball W; Track and Field M & W; Ultimate Frisbee M & W; Volleyball W; Wrestling M & W

FRONT RANGE COMMUNITY COLLEGE
3645 West 112th Ave.
Westminster, CO 80031-2105
Tel: (303)466-8811
Admissions: (303)404-5000
Web Site: http://frcc.cc.co.us/
President/CEO: Dr. Thomas Gonzales
Registrar: Dr. Phyllis Abt
Admissions: Yolanda Espinoza
Financial Aid: Elaine Redwine
Type: Two-Year College **Sex:** Coed **Affiliation:** Community Colleges of Colorado System **% Accepted:** 100 **Admission Plans:** Open Admission; Early Admission; Deferred Admission **Application Deadline:** Rolling **Application Fee:** $0.00 **H.S. Requirements:** High school diploma or equivalent not required **Costs Per Year:** Application fee: $0. State resident tuition: $1746 full-time, $72 per credit part-time. Nonresident tuition: $8284 full-time, $345 per credit part-time. Mandatory fees: $223 full-time, $4.05 per credit part-time, $40.40 per term part-time. **Scholarships:** Available **Calendar System:** Semester, Summer Session Available **Enrollment:** FT 5,149, PT 9,808 **Faculty:** FT 175, PT 826 **Student-Faculty Ratio:** 16:1 **Regional Accreditation:** North Central Association of Colleges and Schools **Credit Hours For Degree:** 60 credit hours, Associates **ROTC:** Army, Air Force **Professional Accreditation:** ADA, CARC

HERITAGE COLLEGE
12 Lakeside Ln.
Denver, CO 80212-7413
Tel: (303)477-7240
Fax: (303)477-7276
Web Site: http://www.heritage-education.com/
President/CEO: Dr. Roy Sutton
Type: Two-Year College **Sex:** Coed **Professional Accreditation:** ACCSCT

INSTITUTE OF BUSINESS & MEDICAL CAREERS
1609 Oakridge Dr., Ste. 102
Fort Collins, CO 80525
Tel: (970)223-2669
Web Site: http://www.ibmcedu.com/
President/CEO: Richard Laub
Registrar: Karla Alpers
Admissions: Steve Steele
Financial Aid: Bill Bush
Type: Two-Year College **Sex:** Coed **Application Fee:** $75.00 **Costs Per Year:** Application fee: $75. Tuition: $13,800 full-time. Mandatory fees: $75 full-time. Tuition guaranteed not to increase for student's term of enrollment. **Scholarships:** Available **Calendar System:** Continuous **Enrollment:** FT 302 **Faculty:** FT 11, PT 23 **Student-Faculty Ratio:** 14:1 **% Residing in College-Owned, -Operated, or -Affiliated Housing:** 0 **Professional Accreditation:** ACICS

INTELLITEC COLLEGE (COLORADO SPRINGS)
2315 East Pikes Peak Ave.
Colorado Springs, CO 80909-6030
Tel: (719)632-7626
Free: 800-748-2282
Fax: (719)632-7451
Web Site: http://www.intelliteccollege.edu/
President/CEO: Dave Bean
Registrar: Rhonda Motte
Admissions: Ellen Pitrone
Financial Aid: Kristy Schaeffer
Type: Two-Year College **Sex:** Coed **Affiliation:** Technical Trades Institute, Inc **Admission Plans:** Open Admission **Application Fee:** $0.00 **H.S. Requirements:** High school diploma required; GED accepted **Scholarships:** Available **Calendar System:** Miscellaneous **Enrollment:** FT 427 **Faculty:** FT 13, PT 15 **Student-Faculty Ratio:** 18:1 **Library Holdings:** 274 **Credit Hours For Degree:** 90 credit hours, Associates **Professional Accreditation:** ACCSCT

INTELLITEC COLLEGE (GRAND JUNCTION)
772 Horizon Dr.
Grand Junction, CO 81506
Tel: (970)245-8101
Fax: (970)243-8074
Web Site: http://www.intelliteccollege.edu/
President/CEO: Rich Counts
Registrar: Vanessa Rhodes
Financial Aid: Sherry Martin
Type: Two-Year College **Sex:** Coed **% Accepted:** 100 **Application Fee:** $0.00 **Costs Per Year:** Application fee: $0. Tuition: $5940 full-time. **Scholarships:** Available **Calendar System:** Continuous **Enrollment:** FT 486 **Faculty:** FT 26, PT 20 **Professional Accreditation:** ACCSCT

INTELLITEC MEDICAL INSTITUTE
2345 North Academy Blvd.
Colorado Springs, CO 80909
Tel: (719)596-7400
Fax: (719)596-2464
Web Site: http://www.intelliteccollege.edu/
President/CEO: Tom Andron
Admissions: Michelle Squibb
Financial Aid: Paula M. Rizzi
Type: Two-Year College **Sex:** Coed **Admission Plans:** Open Admission **Application Fee:** $0.00 **H.S. Requirements:** High school diploma required; GED accepted **Scholarships:** Available **Calendar System:** Miscellaneous, Summer Session Not available **Enrollment:** FT 361 **Faculty:** FT 3, PT 17 **Student-Faculty Ratio:** 14:1 **Credit Hours For Degree:** 99 credit hours, Associates **Professional Accreditation:** ABHES

ITT TECHNICAL INSTITUTE
500 East 84th Ave., Ste. B12
Thornton, CO 80229
Tel: (303)288-4488
Free: 800-395-4488
Fax: (303)288-8166
Web Site: http://www.itt-tech.edu/
President/CEO: Richard F. Hanson
Registrar: Dr. Gloria Griswold
Admissions: Fred Hansen
Financial Aid: Brad Hettich
Type: Two-Year College **Sex:** Coed **Affiliation:** ITT Educational Services, Inc **Admission Plans:** Deferred Admission **Application Deadline:** Rolling **Application Fee:** $100.00 **H.S. Requirements:** High school diploma required; GED accepted **Costs Per Year:** Application fee: $100. **Scholarships:** Available **Calendar System:** Quarter, Summer Session Not available **Exams:** Other **Credit Hours For Degree:** 96 credit hours, Associates; 180 credit hours, Bachelors **Professional Accreditation:** ACICS

JOHNSON & WALES UNIVERSITY
7150 Montview Blvd.
Denver, CO 80220
Tel: (303)256-9300; 877-598-3368
Fax: (303)256-9333
E-mail: den.admissions@jwu.edu
Web Site: http://www.jwu.edu/
President/CEO: Mark Burke
Admissions: Kim Ostrowski
Type: Four-Year College **Sex:** Coed **Affiliation:** Johnson & Wales University (RI) **% Accepted:** 84 **Admission Plans:** Early Admission; Deferred Admission **Application Deadline:** Rolling **Application Fee:** $0.00 **H.S. Requirements:** High school diploma required; GED accepted **Costs Per Year:** Application fee: $0. Comprehensive fee: $29,326 includes full-time tuition ($19,875), mandatory fees ($951), and college room and board ($8500). Part-time tuition: $368 per quarter hour. **Scholarships:** Available **Calendar System:** Miscellaneous, Summer Session Available **Enrollment:** FT 1,521, PT 23 **Faculty:** FT 47, PT 35 **Student-Faculty Ratio:** 27:1 **Exams:** SAT I or ACT **% Receiving Financial Aid:** 73 **Library Holdings:** 26,000 **Regional Accreditation:** New England Association of Schools and Colleges **Credit Hours For Degree:** 90 credits, Associates; 180 credits, Bachelors **Intercollegiate Athletics:** Baseball M; Basketball M & W; Cheerleading M & W; Golf M; Soccer M; Tennis M & W

JONES INTERNATIONAL UNIVERSITY
9697 East Mineral Ave.
Centennial, CO 80112
Tel: (303)784-8904
Free: 800-811-5663
Fax: (303)784-8547
Web Site: http://www.jonesinternational.edu/
President/CEO: Dr. Pamela S. Pease
Admissions: Candice Morrissey
Type: Comprehensive **Sex:** Coed **% Accepted:** 57 **Admission Plans:** Open Admission; Deferred Admission **Application Deadline:** Rolling **Application Fee:** $50.00 **H.S. Requirements:** High school diploma required; GED accepted **Costs Per Year:** Application fee: $50. Tuition: $9720 full-time, $1215 per course part-time. Mandatory fees: $480 full-time, $60 per course part-time. **Scholarships:** Available **Calendar System:** Semester, Summer Session Available **Enrollment:** , PT 255, Grad 1,156 **Faculty:** FT 0, PT 60 **Student-Faculty Ratio:** 23:1 **Regional Accreditation:** North Central Association of Colleges and Schools **Credit Hours For Degree:** 120 semester hour, Bachelors

LAMAR COMMUNITY COLLEGE
2401 South Main St.
Lamar, CO 81052-3999
Tel: (719)336-2248
Free: 800-968-6920
Fax: (719)336-2448
E-mail: a_woodward@mash.colorado.edu
Web Site: http://www.lamarcc.edu/
President/CEO: Bette Matkowski
Registrar: Gary Hammer
Admissions: Angela Woodward
Financial Aid: Gary Hammer
Type: Two-Year College **Sex:** Coed **Affiliation:** Colorado Community College and Occupational Education System **Admission Plans:** Open Admission; Preferred Admission; Early Admission **Application Fee:** $0.00 **H.S. Requirements:** High school diploma required; GED accepted **Scholarships:** Available **Calendar System:** Semester, Summer Session Available **Faculty:** FT 24, PT 24 **Exams:** SAT I or ACT **Library Holdings:** 27,729 **Regional Accreditation:** North Central Association of Colleges and Schools **Credit Hours For Degree:** 64 semester hours, Associates **Intercollegiate Athletics:** Baseball M; Basketball M; Cross-Country Running W; Equestrian Sports M & W; Golf M; Softball W; Volleyball W

MESA STATE COLLEGE
1100 North Ave.
Grand Junction, CO 81501-3122
Tel: (970)248-1020
Free: 800-982-MESA
Admissions: (970)248-1875
Fax: (970)248-1973
E-mail: tbush@mesastate.edu
Web Site: http://www.mesastate.edu/
President/CEO: Tim Foster
Registrar: Patrick Hampton
Admissions: Tyre Bush
Financial Aid: Curt Martin
Type: Comprehensive **Sex:** Coed **Affiliation:** State Colleges in Colorado **Scores:** 85.2% SAT V 400+; 86.2% SAT M 400+; 55.6% ACT 18-23; 16.5% ACT 24-29 **% Accepted:** 82 **Admission Plans:** Open Admission; Early Admission; Deferred Admission **Application Deadline:** Rolling **Application Fee:** $30.00 **H.S. Requirements:** High school diploma required; GED accepted **Costs Per Year:** Application fee: $30. State resident tuition: $3442 full-time, $132.40 per hour part-time. Nonresident tuition: $10,660 full-time, $410 per hour part-time. **Scholarships:** Available **Calendar System:** Semester, Summer Session Available **Enrollment:** FT 4,521, PT 1,513, Grad 28 **Faculty:** FT 206, PT 190 **Student-Faculty Ratio:** 19:1 **Exams:** SAT I or ACT **% Receiving Financial Aid:** 58 **% Residing in College-Owned, -Operated, or -Affiliated Housing:** 18 **Library Holdings:** 247,338 **Regional Accreditation:** North Central Association of Colleges and Schools **Credit Hours For Degree:** 60 credit hours, Associates; 123 credit hours, Bachelors **Professional Accreditation:** AACN, JRCERT **Intercollegiate Athletics:** Baseball M; Basketball M & W; Cross-Country Running W; Football M; Golf W; Soccer W; Softball W; Tennis M & W; Volleyball W

METROPOLITAN STATE COLLEGE OF DENVER
PO Box 173362
Denver, CO 80217-3362
Tel: (303)556-2400
Admissions: (303)556-3058
Fax: (303)556-6345
Web Site: http://www.mscd.edu/
President/CEO: Dr. Raymond N. Kieft
Registrar: Tom Gray
Admissions: William Hathaway-Clark
Financial Aid: Cindy Hejl
Type: Four-Year College **Sex:** Coed **Scores:** 92.3% SAT V 400+; 88% SAT M 400+; 58.3% ACT 18-23; 14.4% ACT 24-29 **Admission Plans:** Deferred Admission **Application Fee:** $25.00 **H.S. Requirements:** High school diploma required; GED accepted. For 20 or over or at least 30 college credits: High school diploma or equivalent not required **Costs Per Year:** Application fee: $25. State resident tuition: $2283 full-time. Nonresident tuition: $9366 full-time. Mandatory fees: $576 full-time. Full-time tuition and fees vary according to course load and location. **Scholarships:** Available **Calendar System:** Semester, Summer Session Available **Enrollment:** FT 12,397, PT 8,364 **Faculty:** FT 395, PT 746 **Student-Faculty Ratio:** 23:1 **Exams:** SAT I or ACT **% Receiving Financial Aid:** 45 **Library Holdings:** 607,971 **Regional Accreditation:** North Central Association of Colleges and Schools **Credit Hours For Degree:** 120 semester hours, Bachelors **ROTC:** Army, Air Force **Professional Accreditation:** ABET, APA, CSWE, NASAD, NASM, NCATE, NLN, NRPA **Intercollegiate Athletics:** Baseball M; Basketball M & W; Cheerleading M & W; Soccer M & W; Swimming and Diving M & W; Tennis M & W; Volleyball W

MORGAN COMMUNITY COLLEGE
17800 County Rd. 20
Fort Morgan, CO 80701-4399
Tel: (970)542-3100
Free: 800-622-0216
Admissions: (970)542-3156
Web Site: http://www.morgancc.edu/
President/CEO: Dr. Michele Haney
Registrar: Kent Bauer
Admissions: Randall Watson
Financial Aid: Kent Bauer
Type: Two-Year College **Sex:** Coed **Affiliation:** Colorado Community College and Occupational Education System **Admission Plans:** Open Admission; Early Admission; Deferred Admission **H.S. Requirements:** High school diploma or equivalent not required **Scholarships:** Available **Calendar System:** Semester, Summer Session Available **Enrollment:** FT 351, PT 1,213 **Faculty:** FT 36, PT 185 **Student-Faculty Ratio:** 10:1 **Exams:** ACT **Library Holdings:** 13,800 **Regional Accreditation:** North Central Association of Colleges and Schools **Credit Hours For Degree:** 62 credit hours, Associates **Professional Accreditation:** APTA

NAROPA UNIVERSITY
2130 Arapahoe Ave.
Boulder, CO 80302-6697

Tel: (303)444-0202
Free: 800-772-0410
Admissions: (303)546-3572
Fax: (303)444-0410
E-mail: admissions@naropa.edu
Web Site: http://www.naropa.edu/
President/CEO: Dr. Thomas B. Coburn
Registrar: Jamie Peta
Admissions: Susan Boyle
Financial Aid: Cheryl Barbour
Type: Comprehensive **Sex:** Coed **Scores:** 100% SAT V 400+; 100% SAT M 400+; 57% ACT 18-23; 29% ACT 24-29 **% Accepted:** 84 **Admission Plans:** Deferred Admission **Application Deadline:** January 15 **Application Fee:** $50.00 **H.S. Requirements:** High school diploma required; GED accepted **Costs Per Year:** Application fee: $50. Comprehensive fee: $25,736 includes full-time tuition ($18,500) and college room and board ($7236). College room only: $4437. Full-time tuition varies according to course load. Room and board charges vary according to board plan. Part-time tuition: $600 per semester hour. Part-time mandatory fees: $250 per term. Part-time tuition and fees vary according to course load. **Scholarships:** Available **Calendar System:** Semester, Summer Session Available **Enrollment:** FT 404, PT 75, Grad 709 **Faculty:** FT 55, PT 169 **Student-Faculty Ratio:** 10:1 **Exams:** SAT I or ACT **% Receiving Financial Aid:** 69 **% Residing in College-Owned, -Operated, or -Affiliated Housing:** 6 **Library Holdings:** 27,500 **Regional Accreditation:** North Central Association of Colleges and Schools **Credit Hours For Degree:** 120 semester hours, Bachelors

NATIONAL AMERICAN UNIVERSITY (COLORADO SPRINGS)

5125 North Academy Blvd.
Colorado Springs, CO 80918
Tel: (719)277-0588
Fax: (719)277-0589
Web Site: http://www.national.edu/
President/CEO: Jeanne Liepe
Admissions: Markita McKamie
Financial Aid: Teresa Thomas
Type: Four-Year College **Sex:** Coed **Admission Plans:** Open Admission; Deferred Admission **Application Fee:** $25.00 **H.S. Requirements:** High school diploma required; GED accepted **Costs Per Year:** Application fee: $25. Tuition: $11,650 full-time, $235 per credit hour part-time. Mandatory fees: $200 full-time. **Scholarships:** Available **Calendar System:** Quarter, Summer Session Available **Faculty:** FT 10, PT 35 **Student-Faculty Ratio:** 15:1 **Library Holdings:** 15,000 **Regional Accreditation:** North Central Association of Colleges and Schools **Credit Hours For Degree:** 96 quarter hours, Associates; 193 quarter hours, Bachelors

NATIONAL AMERICAN UNIVERSITY (DENVER)

1325 South Colorado Blvd, Ste. 100
Denver, CO 80222
Tel: (303)758-6700
Fax: (303)758-6810
Web Site: http://www.national.edu/
President/CEO: Nathan Larson
Admissions: Casey Crist
Financial Aid: Tina Black
Type: Four-Year College **Sex:** Coed **Admission Plans:** Open Admission; Early Admission; Deferred Admission **Application Fee:** $25.00 **H.S. Requirements:** High school diploma required; GED accepted **Costs Per Year:** Application fee: $25. Tuition: $8820 full-time. Full-time tuition varies according to course load, location, and program. **Scholarships:** Available **Calendar System:** Quarter, Summer Session Available **Faculty:** PT 35 **Student-Faculty Ratio:** 10:1 **Exams:** SAT I or ACT **Library Holdings:** 400 **Regional Accreditation:** North Central Association of Colleges and Schools **Credit Hours For Degree:** 97 quarter credits, Associates; 193 quarter credits, Bachelors

NAZARENE BIBLE COLLEGE

1111 Academy Park Loop
Colorado Springs, CO 80910-3704
Tel: (719)884-5000
Free: 800-873-3873
Admissions: (719)884-5061
Fax: (719)884-5199
Web Site: http://www.nbc.edu/
President/CEO: Dr. Hiram E. Sanders
Registrar: Dr. Mike Worrell
Admissions: Dr. Laurel Matson
Financial Aid: Malcolm Britton
Type: Four-Year College **Sex:** Coed **Affiliation:** Church of the Nazarene **% Accepted:** 44 **Admission Plans:** Open Admission; Deferred Admission **Application Deadline:** August 31 **Application Fee:** $35.00 **H.S. Requirements:** High school diploma required; GED accepted **Costs Per Year:** Application fee: $35. Tuition: $8460 full-time, $235 per semester hour part-time. Mandatory fees: $225 full-time. **Scholarships:** Available **Calendar System:** Quarter, Summer Session Available **Enrollment:** FT 181, PT 351 **Faculty:** FT 14, PT 38 **Student-Faculty Ratio:** 13:1 **% Receiving Financial Aid:** 89 **Library Holdings:** 75,842 **Credit Hours For Degree:** 64 semester hours, Associates; 128 semester hours, Bachelors **Professional Accreditation:** AABC

NORTHEASTERN JUNIOR COLLEGE

100 College Ave.
Sterling, CO 80751-2399
Tel: (970)521-6600
Admissions: (970)521-7000
Fax: (970)522-4945
Web Site: http://www.njc.edu/
President/CEO: Dr. Bruce C. Perryman
Registrar: Karen Munson
Admissions: Tina Joyce
Financial Aid: Carolee Goldsmith
Type: Two-Year College **Sex:** Coed **Affiliation:** Colorado Community College and Occupational Education System **Admission Plans:** Open Admission; Preferred Admission; Early Admission; Deferred Admission **Application Fee:** $0.00 **H.S. Requirements:** High school diploma required; GED accepted **Scholarships:** Available **Calendar System:** Semester, Summer Session Available **Enrollment:** FT 910, PT 2,723 **Faculty:** FT 57, PT 229 **Student-Faculty Ratio:** 4:1 **Exams:** ACT, SAT I or ACT **Library Holdings:** 45,260 **Regional Accreditation:** North Central Association of Colleges and Schools **Credit Hours For Degree:** 62 credit hours, Associates **Intercollegiate Athletics:** Baseball M; Basketball M & W; Equestrian Sports M & W; Softball W; Volleyball W

OTERO JUNIOR COLLEGE

1802 Colorado Ave.
La Junta, CO 81050-3415
Tel: (719)384-6831
Admissions: (719)384-6833
Fax: (719)384-6880
E-mail: j_schiro@ojc.axp.cccoes.edu
Web Site: http://www.ojc.edu/
President/CEO: Jim Rizzuto
Registrar: Brad Franz
Admissions: Brad Franz
Financial Aid: Jeff Paolucci
Type: Two-Year College **Sex:** Coed **Affiliation:** Colorado Community College and Occupational Education System **Admission Plans:** Open Admission; Early Admission **Application Deadline:** August 30 **Application Fee:** $0.00 **H.S. Requirements:** High school diploma required; GED accepted **Costs Per Year:** Application fee: $0. State resident tuition: $1788 full-time, $74.50 per credit part-time. Nonresident tuition: $6626 full-time, $276.10 per credit part-time. Mandatory fees: $184 full-time. College room and board: $4512. **Scholarships:** Available **Calendar System:** Semester, Summer Session Available **Enrollment:** FT 771, PT 865 **Faculty:** FT 36, PT 42 **% Residing in College-Owned, -Operated, or -Affiliated Housing:** 14 **Library Holdings:** 36,701 **Regional Accreditation:** North Central Association of Colleges and Schools **Credit Hours For Degree:** 60 semester hours, Associates **Professional Accreditation:** NLN **Intercollegiate Athletics:** Baseball M; Basketball M & W; Golf M & W; Softball W; Volleyball W

PARKS COLLEGE (AURORA)

14280 East Jewell Ave., Ste. 100
Aurora, CO 80014
Tel: (303)745-6244
E-mail: rharding@cci.edu
Web Site: http://www.parks-college.com/
Admissions: Rick Harding
Type: Two-Year College **Sex:** Coed **Calendar System:** Quarter **Professional Accreditation:** ACICS

PARKS COLLEGE (DENVER)
9065 Grant St.
Denver, CO 80229-4339
Tel: (303)457-2757
E-mail: jqnira@cci.edu
Web Site: http://www.parks-college.com/
President/CEO: Jan Schoonmaker
Registrar: Erin L. Maloney
Admissions: JoAnn Q. Navarro
Financial Aid: Joyce Sitton
Type: Two-Year College **Sex:** Coed **Admission Plans:** Deferred Admission **Application Fee:** $50.00 **H.S. Requirements:** High school diploma required; GED accepted **Scholarships:** Available **Calendar System:** Quarter, Summer Session Available **Faculty:** FT 29, PT 44 **Exams:** Other **Library Holdings:** 2,000 **Credit Hours For Degree:** 96 credits, Associates **Professional Accreditation:** ACICS, AAMAE

PIKES PEAK COMMUNITY COLLEGE
5675 South Academy Blvd.
Colorado Springs, CO 80906-5498
Tel: (719)576-7711; (866)411-7722
Admissions: (719)540-7041
Fax: (719)540-7614
Web Site: http://www.ppcc.edu/
President/CEO: Joseph A. Garcia
Registrar: Nicole Striegel
Admissions: Troy Nelson
Financial Aid: Sherri McCullough
Type: Two-Year College **Sex:** Coed **Affiliation:** Colorado Community College System **Scores:** 75% SAT V 400+; 100% SAT M 400+; 48% ACT 18-23; 10% ACT 24-29 **Admission Plans:** Open Admission **H.S. Requirements:** High school diploma or equivalent not required **Costs Per Year:** State resident tuition: $2183 full-time, $72.75 per credit hour part-time. Nonresident tuition: $10,355 full-time, $345.15 per credit hour part-time. Mandatory fees: $156 full-time. Full-time tuition and fees vary according to course load and reciprocity agreements. Part-time tuition varies according to course load and reciprocity agreements. **Scholarships:** Available **Calendar System:** Semester, Summer Session Available **Enrollment:** FT 3,944, PT 6,973 **Faculty:** FT 150, PT 523 **Student-Faculty Ratio:** 18:1 **Library Holdings:** 34,332 **Regional Accreditation:** North Central Association of Colleges and Schools **Credit Hours For Degree:** 60 credit hours, Associates **ROTC:** Army **Professional Accreditation:** ADA **Intercollegiate Athletics:** Basketball M; Soccer M; Volleyball W

PIMA MEDICAL INSTITUTE
1701 West 72nd Ave., Ste. 130
Denver, CO 80221
Tel: (303)426-1800; 888-898-9048
Fax: (303)412-8752
E-mail: denverpima@aol.com
Web Site: http://www.pmi.edu
President/CEO: Susan J. Anderson
Registrar: Melody Pozerl
Admissions: Susan J. Anderson
Financial Aid: Casey Frei
Type: Two-Year College **Sex:** Coed **Affiliation:** Vocational Training Institutes, Inc **Scholarships:** Available **Calendar System:** Miscellaneous, Summer Session Not available **Student-Faculty Ratio:** 15:1 **Exams:** Other **Credit Hours For Degree:** 76 credits, Associates **Professional Accreditation:** ABHES, CARC, JRCERT

PLATT COLLEGE
3100 South Parker Rd., Ste. 200
Aurora, CO 80014-3141
Tel: (303)369-5151
Web Site: http://www.plattcolorado.edu/
President/CEO: Jerald B. Sirbu
Registrar: Cherri Lamarr
Admissions: Jerald Sirbu
Financial Aid: Margaret Rose
Type: Two-Year College **Sex:** Coed **Admission Plans:** Open Admission **Application Fee:** $75.00 **H.S. Requirements:** High school diploma required; GED accepted **Scholarships:** Available **Calendar System:** Continuous **Enrollment:** FT 215 **Faculty:** FT 14, PT 8 **Student-Faculty Ratio:** 14:1 **Credit Hours For Degree:** 96 quarter hours, Associates; 200 quarter hours, Bachelors **Professional Accreditation:** ACCSCT

PUEBLO COMMUNITY COLLEGE
900 West Orman Ave.
Pueblo, CO 81004-1499
Tel: (719)549-3200
Admissions: (719)549-3010
Fax: (719)549-3012
Web Site: http://www.pueblocc.edu/
President/CEO: Mike Davis
Admissions: Mary Santoro
Financial Aid: Audrey Osswald
Type: Two-Year College **Sex:** Coed **Affiliation:** Colorado Community College and Occupational Education System **Scores:** 45.7% ACT 18-23; 6.9% ACT 24-29 **Admission Plans:** Open Admission; Early Admission; Deferred Admission **Application Fee:** $0.00 **H.S. Requirements:** High school diploma required; GED accepted **Scholarships:** Available **Calendar System:** Semester, Summer Session Available **Enrollment:** FT 2,208, PT 3,539 **Faculty:** FT 83, PT 285 **Student-Faculty Ratio:** 19:1 **Exams:** ACT **Library Holdings:** 23,755 **Regional Accreditation:** North Central Association of Colleges and Schools **Credit Hours For Degree:** 60 credits, Associates **Professional Accreditation:** ACF, ADA, AOTA, APTA, CARC, JCAHPO, JRCEMT, NLN

RED ROCKS COMMUNITY COLLEGE
13300 West 6th Ave.
Lakewood, CO 80228-1255
Tel: (303)914-6600
Fax: (303)914-6666
Web Site: http://www.rrcc.edu/
President/CEO: Dr. Eric Reno
Registrar: Jennifer Hughes
Financial Aid: Diane DeReyes
Type: Two-Year College **Sex:** Coed **Affiliation:** Colorado Community College and Occupational Education System **Admission Plans:** Open Admission; Early Admission **Application Fee:** $0.00 **H.S. Requirements:** High school diploma or equivalent not required **Scholarships:** Available **Calendar System:** Semester, Summer Session Available **Enrollment:** FT 2,264, PT 5,429 **Faculty:** FT 74, PT 350 **Student-Faculty Ratio:** 9:1 **Library Holdings:** 55,188 **Regional Accreditation:** North Central Association of Colleges and Schools **Credit Hours For Degree:** 60 credit hours, Associates **ROTC:** Army **Professional Accreditation:** AAMAE

REGIS UNIVERSITY
3333 Regis Blvd.
Denver, CO 80221-1099
Tel: (303)458-4100
Free: 800-388-2366
Admissions: (303)458-4905
Fax: (303)964-5534
E-mail: regisadm@regis.edu
Web Site: http://www.regis.edu/
President/CEO: Rev. Michael J. Sheeran, SJ
Registrar: Patsy Young
Admissions: Vic Davolt
Financial Aid: Lydia MacMillan
Type: Comprehensive **Sex:** Coed **Affiliation:** Roman Catholic (Jesuit) **Scores:** 97.12% SAT V 400+; 95.67% SAT M 400+; 51.23% ACT 18-23; 36.49% ACT 24-29 **Application Fee:** $40.00 **H.S. Requirements:** High school diploma required; GED accepted **Costs Per Year:** Application fee: $40. Comprehensive fee: $31,890 includes full-time tuition ($23,500), mandatory fees ($200), and college room and board ($8190). College room only: $4700. Full-time tuition and fees vary according to program. Room and board charges vary according to board plan and housing facility. Part-time tuition: $734 per hour. Part-time mandatory fees: $140 per year. Part-time tuition and fees vary according to program. **Scholarships:** Available **Calendar System:** Semester, Summer Session Available **Enrollment:** FT 2,261, PT 5,898, Grad 7,978 **Faculty:** FT 240, PT 2,139 **Student-Faculty Ratio:** 10:1 **Exams:** SAT I or ACT, SAT II **% Receiving Financial Aid:** 59 % **Residing in College-Owned, -Operated, or -Affiliated Housing:** 8 **Library Holdings:** 350,000 **Regional Accreditation:** North Central Association of Colleges and Schools **Credit Hours For Degree:** 128 semester hours, Bachelors **ROTC:** Army, Air Force **Professional Accreditation:** AACN, AHIMA, APTA, NLN **Intercollegiate Athletics:** Baseball M; Basketball M & W; Golf M & W; Lacrosse W; Soccer M & W; Softball W; Volleyball W

REMINGTON COLLEGE-COLORADO SPRINGS CAMPUS
6050 Erin Park Dr., No. 250
Colorado Springs, CO 80918
Tel: (719)532-1234
Admissions: (719)532-1234
Fax: (719)264-1234
Web Site: http://www.remingtoncollege.edu/
Admissions: Shibu Thomas
Type: Four-Year College **Sex:** Coed **Costs Per Year:** Tuition: $15,745 full-time. Tuition guaranteed not to increase for student's term of enrollment. **Calendar System:** Quarter **Enrollment:** FT 282 **Faculty:** FT 7, PT 23 **Student-Faculty Ratio:** 17:1 **Professional Accreditation:** ACICS

REMINGTON COLLEGE-DENVER CAMPUS
11011 West 6th Ave.
Lakewood, CO 80215-0090
Tel: (303)445-0500
Free: 800-999-5181
Fax: (303)445-0090
E-mail: jim.ploskonka@remingtoncollege.edu
Web Site: http://www.remingtoncollege.edu/
President/CEO: Shibu Thomas
Registrar: Wayne Sell
Admissions: Jim Ploskonka
Financial Aid: Jamie Weisberg
Type: Four-Year College **Sex:** Coed **Affiliation:** Education America Inc **Admission Plans:** Open Admission; Early Admission; Deferred Admission **Application Fee:** $50.00 **H.S. Requirements:** High school diploma required; GED accepted **Scholarships:** Available **Calendar System:** Quarter, Summer Session Available **Faculty:** FT 3, PT 28 **% Receiving Financial Aid:** 98 **Library Holdings:** 5,000 **Professional Accreditation:** ACICS

ROCKY MOUNTAIN COLLEGE OF ART & DESIGN
1600 Pierce St.
Lakewood, CO 80214
Tel: (303)753-6046
Free: 800-888-ARTS
Fax: (303)759-4970
Web Site: http://www.rmcad.edu/
President/CEO: Steven Sumner
Registrar: Cathy Hehr
Admissions: Marianna Bagge
Financial Aid: Julia Alexander
Type: Four-Year College **Sex:** Coed **% Accepted:** 100 **Admission Plans:** Deferred Admission **Application Deadline:** Rolling **Application Fee:** $35.00 **H.S. Requirements:** High school diploma required; GED accepted **Costs Per Year:** Application fee: $35. Tuition: $17,880 full-time, $745 per credit part-time. College room only: $3840. **Scholarships:** Available **Calendar System:** Trimester, Summer Session Available **Enrollment:** FT 365, PT 83 **Faculty:** FT 25, PT 40 **Student-Faculty Ratio:** 10:1 **% Receiving Financial Aid:** 85 **% Residing in College-Owned, -Operated, or -Affiliated Housing:** 18 **Library Holdings:** 6,287 **Regional Accreditation:** North Central Association of Colleges and Schools **Credit Hours For Degree:** 126 credits, Bachelors **Professional Accreditation:** FIDER, NASAD

TEIKYO LORETTO HEIGHTS UNIVERSITY
3001 South Federal Blvd.
Denver, CO 80236-2711
Tel: (303)937-4200
Web Site: http://www.tlhu.edu/
President/CEO: Dr. Shigeho Morita
Registrar: Kohtaro Miyazawa
Type: Four-Year College **Affiliation:** Teikyo University Group **Application Fee:** $65.00 **Scholarships:** Available **Professional Accreditation:** ACICS

TRINIDAD STATE JUNIOR COLLEGE
600 Prospect
Trinidad, CO 81082-2396
Tel: (719)846-5011
Free: 800-621-8752
Admissions: (719)846-5545
Fax: (719)846-5667
E-mail: alex.borja@trinidadstate.edu
Web Site: http://www.trinidadstate.edu/
President/CEO: Dr. Frank Armijo
Registrar: Gloria Coke
Admissions: Alex Borja
Financial Aid: Gary Fresquez
Type: Two-Year College **Sex:** Coed **Affiliation:** Colorado Community College and Occupational Education System **% Accepted:** 100 **Admission Plans:** Open Admission; Deferred Admission **Application Deadline:** Rolling **Application Fee:** $0.00 **H.S. Requirements:** High school diploma required; GED accepted **Costs Per Year:** Application fee: $0. State resident tuition: $2,182 full-time, $72.75 per credit part-time. Nonresident tuition: $8280 full-time, $276 per credit part-time. Mandatory fees: $528 full-time, $14.35 per credit part-time. College room and board: $4298. College room only: $1048. Room and board charges vary according to board plan. **Scholarships:** Available **Calendar System:** Semester, Summer Session Available **Enrollment:** FT 775, PT 1,056 **Faculty:** FT 40, PT 100 **Student-Faculty Ratio:** 16:1 **% Residing in College-Owned, -Operated, or -Affiliated Housing:** 30 **Library Holdings:** 54,255 **Regional Accreditation:** North Central Association of Colleges and Schools **Credit Hours For Degree:** 60 semester hours, Associates **Professional Accreditation:** ABET **Intercollegiate Athletics:** Baseball M; Basketball M; Softball W; Volleyball W

UNITED STATES AIR FORCE ACADEMY
HQ USAFA/XPR
2304 Cadet Dr., Ste. 200
USAF Academy, CO 80840-5025
Tel: (719)333-1818
Free: 800-443-9266
Admissions: (719)333-2520
Fax: (719)333-3012
E-mail: wilsoncm.rr@usafa.af.mil
Web Site: http://www.usafa.edu/
President/CEO: Lt. Gen. John W. Rosa, Jr.
Registrar: Dr. Dean H. Wilson
Admissions: Col. William Carpenter
Type: Four-Year College **Sex:** Coed **% Accepted:** 15 **Application Deadline:** January 31 **Application Fee:** $0.00 **H.S. Requirements:** High school diploma or equivalent not required **Costs Per Year:** Application fee: $0. **Calendar System:** Semester, Summer Session Available **Enrollment:** FT 4,365 **Faculty:** FT 559, PT 0 **Student-Faculty Ratio:** 8:1 **Exams:** SAT I or ACT **% Residing in College-Owned, -Operated, or -Affiliated Housing:** 100 **Library Holdings:** 445,379 **Regional Accreditation:** North Central Association of Colleges and Schools **Credit Hours For Degree:** 145 semester hours, Bachelors **Professional Accreditation:** AACSB, ABET **Intercollegiate Athletics:** Baseball M; Basketball M & W; Cheerleading M & W; Cross-Country Running M & W; Fencing M & W; Football M; Golf M; Gymnastics M & W; Ice Hockey M; Lacrosse M; Riflery M & W; Rugby W; Skiing (Cross-Country) M & W; Skiing (Downhill) M & W; Soccer M & W; Softball W; Swimming and Diving M & W; Tennis M & W; Track and Field M & W; Volleyball W; Water Polo M; Weight Lifting M & W; Wrestling M

UNIVERSITY OF COLORADO AT BOULDER
Boulder, CO 80309
Tel: (303)492-1411
Admissions: (303)492-6301
Fax: (303)492-7115
Web Site: http://www.colorado.edu/
President/CEO: Dr. Richard Byyny
Admissions: Kevin MacLennan
Type: University **Sex:** Coed **Affiliation:** University of Colorado System **Scores:** 99% SAT V 400+; 99% SAT M 400+; 30% ACT 18-23; 56% ACT 24-29 **% Accepted:** 88 **Admission Plans:** Preferred Admission; Deferred Admission **Application Deadline:** January 15 **Application Fee:** $50.00 **H.S. Requirements:** High school diploma required; GED accepted **Costs Per Year:** Application fee: $50. One-time mandatory fee: $108. State resident tuition: $4446 full-time. Nonresident tuition: $21,900 full-time. Mandatory fees: $926 full-time. Full-time tuition and fees vary according to program. College room and board: $7980. Room and board charges vary according to board plan, location, and student level. **Scholarships:** Available **Calendar System:** Semester, Summer Session Available **Enrollment:** FT 23,539, PT 2,303, Grad 4,732 **Faculty:** FT 1,227, PT 559 **Student-Faculty Ratio:** 16:1 **Exams:** SAT I or ACT **% Receiving Financial Aid:** 32 **% Residing in College-Owned, -Operated, or -Affiliated Housing:** 22 **Library Holdings:** 3,484,982 **Regional Accreditation:** North Central Association of Colleges and Schools **Credit Hours For Degree:** 120 semester hours, Bachelors

ROTC: Army, Navy, Air Force **Professional Accreditation:** AACSB, ABET, ACEJMC, ABA, APA, ASLHA, AALS, NASM, NCATE **Intercollegiate Athletics:** Baseball M; Basketball M & W; Bowling M & W; Crew M & W; Cross-Country Running M & W; Equestrian Sports M & W; Fencing M & W; Field Hockey M & W; Football M; Golf M & W; Ice Hockey M & W; Lacrosse M & W; Racquetball M & W; Rugby M & W; Skiing (Cross-Country) M & W; Skiing (Downhill) M & W; Soccer M & W; Softball W; Squash M & W; Swimming and Diving M & W; Tennis M & W; Track and Field M & W; Ultimate Frisbee M & W; Volleyball M & W; Water Polo M & W; Wrestling M

UNIVERSITY OF COLORADO AT COLORADO SPRINGS
1420 Austin Bluffs Parkway
PO Box 7150
Colorado Springs, CO 80933-7150
Tel: (719)262-3000
Free: 800-990-8227
Admissions: (719)262-3375
E-mail: admrec@mail.uccs.edu
Web Site: http://www.uccs.edu/
President/CEO: Dr. Pamela Shockley
Admissions: Steve Ellis
Financial Aid: Lee Ingalls Noble
Type: Comprehensive **Sex:** Coed **Scores:** 96.04% SAT V 400+; 96.04% SAT M 400+; 55.24% ACT 18-23; 38.24% ACT 24-29 **% Accepted:** 76 **Admission Plans:** Preferred Admission; Deferred Admission **Application Deadline:** July 01 **Application Fee:** $50.00 **H.S. Requirements:** High school diploma required; GED accepted **Costs Per Year:** Application fee: $50. State resident tuition: $3966 full-time, $178 per credit hour part-time. Nonresident tuition: $15,260 full-time, $763 per credit hour part-time. Mandatory fees: $922 full-time. College room and board: $6418. College room only: $4878. **Scholarships:** Available **Calendar System:** Semester, Summer Session Available **Enrollment:** FT 4,827, PT 1,444, Grad 2,166 **Faculty:** FT 200, PT 356 **Student-Faculty Ratio:** 18:1 **Exams:** SAT I or ACT **% Receiving Financial Aid:** 50 **% Residing in College-Owned, -Operated, or -Affiliated Housing:** 10 **Library Holdings:** 391,638 **Regional Accreditation:** North Central Association of Colleges and Schools **Credit Hours For Degree:** 120 credit hours, Bachelors **ROTC:** Army **Professional Accreditation:** AACSB, ABET, AACN, ACA, NASPAA, NCATE, NLN **Intercollegiate Athletics:** Baseball M; Basketball M & W; Cross-Country Running M & W; Golf M; Soccer M & W; Softball W; Tennis M & W; Track and Field M & W; Volleyball M & W

UNIVERSITY OF COLORADO AT DENVER AND HEALTH SCIENCES CENTER - DOWNTOWN DENVER CAMPUS
PO Box 173364
Denver, CO 80217-3364
Tel: (303)556-2400
Admissions: (303)556-3287
Fax: (303)556-2398
E-mail: admissions@cudenver.edu
Web Site: http://www.cudenver.edu/
President/CEO: James Shore
Registrar: Cheryl Apodaca
Admissions: Barbara Edwards
Financial Aid: Ellie Miller
Type: University **Sex:** Coed **Affiliation:** University of Colorado System **Scores:** 93.8% SAT V 400+; 97.7% SAT M 400+; 55.2% ACT 18-23; 33.4% ACT 24-29 **% Accepted:** 69 **Admission Plans:** Deferred Admission **Application Deadline:** July 22 **Application Fee:** $50.00 **H.S. Requirements:** High school diploma required; GED accepted **Costs Per Year:** Application fee: $50. State resident tuition: $4224 full-time, $210 per semester hour part-time. Nonresident tuition: $15,394 full-time, $924 per semester hour part-time. Mandatory fees: $797 full-time, $14 per semester hour part-time, $377. **Scholarships:** Available **Calendar System:** Semester, Summer Session Available **Enrollment:** FT 5,763, PT 4,479, Grad 8,111 **Faculty:** FT 579, PT 783 **Student-Faculty Ratio:** 15:1 **Exams:** SAT I or ACT **% Receiving Financial Aid:** 47 **Library Holdings:** 588,582 **Regional Accreditation:** North Central Association of Colleges and Schools **Credit Hours For Degree:** 120 semester hours, Bachelors **ROTC:** Army, Air Force **Professional Accreditation:** AACSB, ABET, ACEHSA, ACA, ACSP, ASLA, NASM, NASPAA, NCATE

UNIVERSITY OF DENVER
University Park
2199 South University Park
Denver, CO 80208
Tel: (303)871-2000
Free: 800-525-9495
Admissions: (303)871-3383
Fax: (303)871-3301
E-mail: admission@du.edu
Web Site: http://www.du.edu/
President/CEO: Daniel Ritchie
Registrar: Dennis Becker
Admissions: Thomas F. Willoughby
Financial Aid: Craig Johnson
Type: University **Sex:** Coed **Scores:** 98% SAT V 400+; 99% SAT M 400+; 28% ACT 18-23; 55% ACT 24-29 **% Accepted:** 82 **Admission Plans:** Early Admission; Early Action; Deferred Admission **Application Deadline:** January 15 **Application Fee:** $50.00 **H.S. Requirements:** High school diploma required; GED accepted **Costs Per Year:** Application fee: $50. Comprehensive fee: $37,159 includes full-time tuition ($27,756), mandatory fees ($654), and college room and board ($8749). College room only: $5355. Full-time tuition and fees vary according to class time, course load, and program. Room and board charges vary according to board plan and housing facility. Part-time tuition: $771 per quarter hour. Part-time tuition varies according to class time, course load, and program. **Scholarships:** Available **Calendar System:** Quarter, Summer Session Available **Enrollment:** FT 4,431, PT 446, Grad 4,315 **Faculty:** FT 484, PT 566 **Student-Faculty Ratio:** 11:1 **Exams:** SAT I or ACT **% Receiving Financial Aid:** 43 **% Residing in College-Owned, -Operated, or -Affiliated Housing:** 49 **Library Holdings:** 1,212,392 **Regional Accreditation:** North Central Association of Colleges and Schools **Credit Hours For Degree:** 183 quarter hours, Bachelors **ROTC:** Army, Air Force **Professional Accreditation:** AACSB, ABET, ABA, ALA, APA, AALS, CSWE, NASAD, NASM **Intercollegiate Athletics:** Basketball M & W; Golf M & W; Gymnastics W; Ice Hockey M; Lacrosse M & W; Skiing (Cross-Country) M & W; Skiing (Downhill) M & W; Soccer M & W; Swimming and Diving M & W; Tennis M & W; Volleyball M & W

UNIVERSITY OF NORTHERN COLORADO
Greeley, CO 80639
Tel: (970)351-1890
Admissions: (970)351-2881
E-mail: admissions.help@unco.edu
Web Site: http://www.unco.edu/
President/CEO: Kay Norton
Registrar: Rebecca Barnes
Admissions: Gary Gullickson
Financial Aid: Donni Clark
Type: University **Sex:** Coed **Scores:** 96% SAT V 400+; 95% SAT M 400+; 61% ACT 18-23; 31% ACT 24-29 **% Accepted:** 82 **Admission Plans:** Deferred Admission **Application Deadline:** August 01 **Application Fee:** $40.00 **H.S. Requirements:** High school diploma required; GED accepted **Costs Per Year:** Application fee: $40. State resident tuition: $3192 full-time, $133 per credit hour part-time. Nonresident tuition: $11,736 full-time, $489 per credit hour part-time. Mandatory fees: $645 full-time, $32.25 per credit hour part-time. College room and board: $6412. College room only: $3150. Room and board charges vary according to board plan and housing facility. **Scholarships:** Available **Calendar System:** Semester, Summer Session Available **Enrollment:** FT 9,685, PT 1,126, Grad 2,345 **Faculty:** FT 400, PT 201 **Student-Faculty Ratio:** 24:1 **Exams:** SAT I or ACT **% Receiving Financial Aid:** 45 **% Residing in College-Owned, -Operated, or -Affiliated Housing:** 31 **Library Holdings:** 1,046,197 **Regional Accreditation:** North Central Association of Colleges and Schools **Credit Hours For Degree:** 120 semester hours, Bachelors **ROTC:** Army, Air Force **Professional Accreditation:** AACSB, AACN, ACA, ADtA, APA, ASLHA, CEPH, CORE, JRCEPAT, NASM, NCATE, NLN **Intercollegiate Athletics:** Baseball M; Basketball M & W; Cross-Country Running W; Football M; Golf M & W; Lacrosse M; Rugby M & W; Soccer M & W; Softball W; Swimming and Diving W; Tennis M & W; Track and Field M & W; Volleyball W; Wrestling M

UNIVERSITY OF PHOENIX-DENVER CAMPUS
10004 Park Meadows Dr.
Lone Tree, CO 80124-5453
Tel: (303)694-9093
Free: 800-228-7240
Admissions: (480)557-1712
Web Site: http://www.phoenix.edu/
President/CEO: Dr. Laura Palmer Noone
Registrar: Tandy Elisala

Admissions: Nina Omelchanko
Financial Aid: Robert Collins
Type: Comprehensive **Sex:** Coed **Admission Plans:** Open Admission; Deferred Admission **Application Deadline:** Rolling **Application Fee:** $110.00 **H.S. Requirements:** High school diploma required; GED accepted **Costs Per Year:** Application fee: $110. Tuition: $9480 full-time, $316 per credit part-time. Mandatory fees: $560 full-time, $70 per course part-time. **Scholarships:** Available **Calendar System:** Continuous, Summer Session Not available **Enrollment:** FT 2,010, Grad 1,410 **Faculty:** FT 5, PT 373 **Student-Faculty Ratio:** 9:1 **Library Holdings:** 444 **Regional Accreditation:** North Central Association of Colleges and Schools **Credit Hours For Degree:** 60 credits, Associates; 120 credits, Bachelors **Professional Accreditation:** NLN

UNIVERSITY OF PHOENIX-SOUTHERN COLORADO CAMPUS
5475 Tech Center, Ste. 130
Colorado Springs, CO 80919-2335
Tel: (719)599-5282
Free: 800-228-7240
Admissions: (480)557-1712
Web Site: http://www.phoenix.edu/
President/CEO: Dr. Laura Palmer Noone
Registrar: Tandy Elisala
Admissions: Nina Omelchanko
Financial Aid: Robert Collins
Type: Comprehensive **Sex:** Coed **Admission Plans:** Open Admission; Deferred Admission **Application Deadline:** Rolling **Application Fee:** $110.00 **H.S. Requirements:** High school diploma required; GED accepted **Costs Per Year:** Application fee: $110. Tuition: $9489 full-time, $316 per credit part-time. Mandatory fees: $560 full-time, $70 per course part-time. **Scholarships:** Available **Calendar System:** Continuous, Summer Session Not available **Enrollment:** FT 775, Grad 519 **Faculty:** FT 2, PT 173 **Student-Faculty Ratio:** 7:1 **Library Holdings:** 444 **Regional Accreditation:** North Central Association of Colleges and Schools **Credit Hours For Degree:** 60 credits, Associates; 120 credits, Bachelors **Professional Accreditation:** NLN

WESTERN STATE COLLEGE OF COLORADO
600 North Adams St.
Gunnison, CO 81231
Tel: (970)943-0120
Free: 800-876-5309
Admissions: (970)943-2119
Fax: (970)943-7069
E-mail: talbers@western.edu
Web Site: http://www.western.edu/
President/CEO: Dr. Jay W. Helman
Registrar: Maryette Rogers
Admissions: Timothy Albers
Financial Aid: Marty Somero
Type: Four-Year College **Sex:** Coed **Scores:** 93% SAT V 400+; 92% SAT M 400+; 60% ACT 18-23; 23% ACT 24-29 **% Accepted:** 83 **Admission Plans:** Deferred Admission **Application Deadline:** August 01 **Application Fee:** $30.00 **H.S. Requirements:** High school diploma required; GED accepted **Costs Per Year:** Application fee: $30. State resident tuition: $2,411 full-time, $100.45 per credit hour part-time. Nonresident tuition: $10,968 full-time, $457 per credit hour part-time. Mandatory fees: $796 full-time, $26.05 per credit hour part-time. College room and board: $6976. College room only: $3794. **Scholarships:** Available **Calendar System:** Semester, Summer Session Available **Enrollment:** FT 2,034, PT 143 **Faculty:** FT 104, PT 31 **Student-Faculty Ratio:** 18:1 **Exams:** SAT I or ACT **% Receiving Financial Aid:** 37 **% Residing in College-Owned, -Operated, or -Affiliated Housing:** 41 **Library Holdings:** 158,698 **Regional Accreditation:** North Central Association of Colleges and Schools **Credit Hours For Degree:** 120 credits, Bachelors **Professional Accreditation:** NASM **Intercollegiate Athletics:** Baseball M; Basketball M & W; Cheerleading W; Cross-Country Running M & W; Football M; Ice Hockey M; Lacrosse M & W; Rugby M & W; Skiing (Cross-Country) M & W; Skiing (Downhill) M & W; Soccer M & W; Track and Field M & W; Volleyball M & W; Wrestling M & W

WESTWOOD COLLEGE-DENVER NORTH
7350 North Broadway
Denver, CO 80221-3653
Tel: (303)650-5050
Free: 800-992-5050
Fax: (303)426-0702
Web Site: http://www.westwood.edu/
President/CEO: Jamie Turner
Registrar: Martin Easters
Admissions: Ben Simms
Financial Aid: Lisa Engelking
Type: Two-Year College **Sex:** Coed **% Accepted:** 45 **Admission Plans:** Deferred Admission **Application Deadline:** Rolling **Application Fee:** $100.00 **H.S. Requirements:** High school diploma required; GED accepted **Costs Per Year:** Application fee: $100. Tuition: $2796 per term part-time. Mandatory fees: $425 per credit part-time, $120 per term part-time. Part-time tuition and fees vary according to course load and program. **Scholarships:** Available **Calendar System:** Miscellaneous, Summer Session Available **Enrollment:** FT 1,086, PT 337 **Faculty:** FT 34, PT 63 **Student-Faculty Ratio:** 13:1 **Exams:** Other, SAT I or ACT, SAT I and SAT II or ACT **Library Holdings:** 2,000 **Credit Hours For Degree:** 128 credit hours, Bachelors **Professional Accreditation:** ACCSCT, AAMAE

WESTWOOD COLLEGE-DENVER SOUTH
3150 South Sheridan Blvd.
Denver, CO 80227
Tel: (303)934-2790
Free: 800-281-2978
Fax: (303)934-2583
Web Site: http://www.westwood.edu/
Admissions: Ron DeJong
Type: Two-Year College **Sex:** Coed **% Accepted:** 58 **Scholarships:** Available **Calendar System:** Continuous **Enrollment:** FT 294, PT 135 **Professional Accreditation:** ACCSCT

YESHIVA TORAS CHAIM TALMUDICAL SEMINARY
1400 Quitman St.
Denver, CO 80204-1415
Tel: (303)629-8200
Fax: (303)623-5949
President/CEO: Zvi Gelt
Admissions: Rabbi Israel Kagan
Type: Comprehensive **Sex:** Men **Affiliation:** Jewish **Admission Plans:** Early Admission **H.S. Requirements:** High school diploma required; GED accepted **Calendar System:** Trimester **Credit Hours For Degree:** 168 credits, Bachelors **Professional Accreditation:** AARTS

ALBERTUS MAGNUS COLLEGE
700 Prospect St.
New Haven, CT 06511-1189
Tel: (203)773-8550
Free: 800-578-9160
Admissions: (203)773-8501
Fax: (203)785-8652
Web Site: http://www.albertus.edu/
President/CEO: Dr. Julia M. McNamara
Registrar: Eileen Perrillo
Admissions: Richard Lolatte
Financial Aid: Maureen Morrison
Type: Comprehensive **Sex:** Coed **Affiliation:** Roman Catholic **Scores:** 74.7% SAT V 400+; 72% SAT M 400+ **% Accepted:** 36 **Admission Plans:** Deferred Admission **Application Deadline:** August 20 **Application Fee:** $35.00 **H.S. Requirements:** High school diploma required; GED accepted **Costs Per Year:** Application fee: $35. Comprehensive fee: $24,860 includes full-time tuition ($16,600), mandatory fees ($710), and college room and board ($7550). Full-time tuition and fees vary according to class time and program. Part-time tuition: $1726 per course. Part-time tuition varies according to class time and program. **Scholarships:** Available **Calendar System:** Semester, Summer Session Available **Enrollment:** FT 1,695, PT 87, Grad 448 **Faculty:** FT 34, PT 133 **Student-Faculty Ratio:** 15:1 **Exams:** SAT I or ACT, SAT II **% Receiving Financial Aid:** 89 **% Residing in College-Owned, -Operated, or -Affiliated Housing:** 60 **Regional Accreditation:** New England Association of Schools and Colleges **Credit Hours For Degree:** 60 credits, Associates; 120 credits, Bachelors **Intercollegiate Athletics:** Baseball M; Basketball M & W; Cross-Country Running M & W; Soccer M & W; Softball W; Tennis M & W; Volleyball W

ASNUNTUCK COMMUNITY COLLEGE
170 Elm St.
Enfield, CT 06082-3800
Tel: (860)253-3000
Free: 800-501-3967
Admissions: (860)253-3018
Fax: (860)253-9310
E-mail: dshaw@acc.commnet.edu
Web Site: http://www.acc.commnet.edu/
President/CEO: Dr. Harvey S. Irlen
Registrar: Rita Moriarty
Admissions: Donna Shaw
Financial Aid: Donna Jones-Searle
Type: Two-Year College **Sex:** Coed **Affiliation:** Connecticut Community College System **% Accepted:** 100 **Admission Plans:** Open Admission; Deferred Admission **Application Deadline:** Rolling **Application Fee:** $20.00 **H.S. Requirements:** High school diploma required; GED accepted **Costs Per Year:** Application fee: $20. State resident tuition: $2352 full-time, $98 per credit part-time. Nonresident tuition: $7976 full-time, $294 per credit part-time. Mandatory fees: $320 full-time, $58 per credit part-time. **Scholarships:** Available **Calendar System:** Semester, Summer Session Available **Enrollment:** FT 526, PT 957 **Faculty:** FT 25, PT 90 **Student-Faculty Ratio:** 16:1 **Library Holdings:** 31,700 **Regional Accreditation:** New England Association of Schools and Colleges **Credit Hours For Degree:** 60 credits, Associates

BETH BENJAMIN ACADEMY OF CONNECTICUT
132 Prospect St.
Stamford, CT 06901-1202
Tel: (203)325-4351
President/CEO: Rabbi S. Schustal
Registrar: Rabbi M. Bender
Admissions: Rabbi David Mayer
Financial Aid: Rabbi M. Hershkowitz
Type: Comprehensive **Sex:** Men **Affiliation:** Jewish **H.S. Requirements:** High school diploma required; GED accepted **Calendar System:** Trimester **Professional Accreditation:** AARTS

BRIARWOOD COLLEGE
2279 Mount Vernon Rd.
Southington, CT 06489-1057
Tel: (860)628-4751
Fax: (860)628-6444
E-mail: yamanisd@briarwood.edu
Web Site: http://www.briarwood.edu/
President/CEO: Lynn Alan Brooks
Registrar: Stephanie Crombie
Admissions: Donna Yamanis
Financial Aid: Deborah Flinn
Type: Two-Year College **Sex:** Coed **Scores:** 58% SAT V 400+; 32% SAT M 400+ **% Accepted:** 73 **Application Deadline:** Rolling **Application Fee:** $25.00 **H.S. Requirements:** High school diploma required; GED accepted **Costs Per Year:** Application fee: $25. Tuition: $15,200 full-time, $500 per credit part-time. Mandatory fees: $220 full-time, $125 per term part-time. Full-time tuition and fees vary according to program. Part-time tuition and fees vary according to course load and program. College room only: $3320. Tuition guaranteed not to increase for student's term of enrollment. **Scholarships:** Available **Calendar System:** Semester, Summer Session Available **Enrollment:** FT 389, PT 258 **Faculty:** FT 29, PT 66 **Student-Faculty Ratio:** 10:1 **% Residing in College-Owned, -Operated, or -Affiliated Housing:** 21 **Library Holdings:** 11,500 **Regional Accreditation:** New England Association of Schools and Colleges **Credit Hours For Degree:** 60 credit hours, Associates **Professional Accreditation:** AAMAE, ABFSE, ADA, AHIMA, AOTA

CAPITAL COMMUNITY COLLEGE
950 Main St.
Hartford, CT 06103
Tel: (860)906-5000
Admissions: (860)906-5127
E-mail: mbell-davis@ccc.commnet.edu
Web Site: http://www.ccc.commnet.edu/
President/CEO: Dr. Ira Rubenzahl
Registrar: Lynn Davis
Admissions: Marsha Ball-Davis
Financial Aid: Margaret Wolf
Type: Two-Year College **Sex:** Coed **Affiliation:** Connecticut Community College System **Admission Plans:** Open Admission **Application Deadline:**

Rolling **Application Fee:** $20.00 **H.S. Requirements:** High school diploma required; GED accepted. For students with baccalaureate degrees: High school diploma or equivalent not required **Costs Per Year:** Application fee: $20. State resident tuition: $2352 full-time, $98 per credit hour part-time. Nonresident tuition: $7056 full-time, $294 per credit hour part-time. Mandatory fees: $320 full-time. **Scholarships:** Available **Calendar System:** Semester, Summer Session Available **Enrollment:** FT 927, PT 2,646 **Faculty:** FT 63 **Library Holdings:** 46,760 **Regional Accreditation:** New England Association of Schools and Colleges **Credit Hours For Degree:** 60 credit hours, Associates **Professional Accreditation:** AAMAE, APTA, JRCERT, JRCEMT, NLN

CENTRAL CONNECTICUT STATE UNIVERSITY
1615 Stanley St.
New Britain, CT 06050-4010
Tel: (860)832-3200
Admissions: (860)832-2285
Fax: (860)832-2522
E-mail: admissions@ccsu.edu
Web Site: http://www.ccsu.edu/
President/CEO: Dr. Richard L. Judd
Registrar: Susan Petrosino
Admissions: Richard Bishop
Financial Aid: Richard Bishop
Type: Comprehensive **Sex:** Coed **Affiliation:** Connecticut State University System **Scores:** 94% SAT V 400+; 95% SAT M 400+ **% Accepted:** 62 **Application Deadline:** June 01 **Application Fee:** $50.00 **H.S. Requirements:** High school diploma required; GED accepted **Costs Per Year:** Application fee: $50. State resident tuition: $3034 full-time, $290 per credit part-time. Nonresident tuition: $9820 full-time, $290 per credit part-time. Mandatory fees: $3130 full-time, $55 per term part-time. Full-time tuition and fees vary according to course level, course load, and reciprocity agreements. Part-time tuition and fees vary according to course level and course load. College room and board: $7456. College room only: $4250. Room and board charges vary according to board plan. **Scholarships:** Available **Calendar System:** Semester, Summer Session Available **Enrollment:** FT 7,445, PT 2,233, Grad 2,637 **Faculty:** FT 416, PT 434 **Student-Faculty Ratio:** 19:1 **Exams:** SAT I **% Receiving Financial Aid:** 58 **% Residing in College-Owned, -Operated, or -Affiliated Housing:** 21 **Library Holdings:** 639,257 **Regional Accreditation:** New England Association of Schools and Colleges **Credit Hours For Degree:** 122 credit hours, Bachelors **ROTC:** Army, Air Force **Professional Accreditation:** ABET, AAMFT, AACN, AANA, ACCE, CSWE, JRCEPAT, NAIT, NASM, NCATE **Intercollegiate Athletics:** Baseball M; Basketball M & W; Cross-Country Running M & W; Fencing M & W; Football M; Golf M & W; Lacrosse M & W; Soccer M & W; Softball W; Swimming and Diving W; Track and Field M & W; Volleyball W

CHARTER OAK STATE COLLEGE
55 Paul Manafort Dr.
New Britain, CT 06053-2142
Tel: (860)832-3800
Admissions: (860)832-3858
Fax: (860)832-3999
E-mail: pmorganti@commnet.edu
Web Site: http://www.charteroak.edu/
President/CEO: Dr. Merle W. Harris
Registrar: Patricia Derech
Admissions: Lori Pendleton
Financial Aid: Velma Walters
Type: Four-Year College **Sex:** Coed **Admission Plans:** Open Admission; Deferred Admission **Application Fee:** $60.00 **H.S. Requirements:** High school diploma or equivalent not required. For all applicants must have successfully completed a minimum of 9 college credits: High school diploma or equivalent not required **Costs Per Year:** Application fee: $60. State resident tuition: $165 per credit part-time. Nonresident tuition: $235 per credit part-time. **Scholarships:** Available **Calendar System:** Continuous, Summer Session Available **Enrollment:** , PT 1,902 **Faculty:** PT 85 **Student-Faculty Ratio:** 12:1 **% Receiving Financial Aid:** 14 **Regional Accreditation:** New England Association of Schools and Colleges **Credit Hours For Degree:** 60 credits, Associates; 120 credits, Bachelors

CONNECTICUT COLLEGE
270 Mohegan Ave.
New London, CT 06320-4196
Tel: (860)447-1911
Admissions: (860)439-2200
Fax: (860)439-4301
E-mail: admissions@conncoll.edu
Web Site: http://www.connecticutcollege.edu/
President/CEO: Norman Fainstein, PhD
Registrar: Aileen Burdick
Admissions: Martha Merrill
Financial Aid: Elaine Solinga
Type: Comprehensive **Sex:** Coed **Scores:** 100% SAT V 400+; 100% SAT M 400+; 15% ACT 18-23; 67% ACT 24-29 **% Accepted:** 35 **Admission Plans:** Early Decision Plan; Deferred Admission **Application Deadline:** January 01 **Application Fee:** $60.00 **H.S. Requirements:** High school diploma required; GED accepted **Costs Per Year:** Application fee: $60. Comprehensive fee: $41,975. Part-time tuition: $975 per credit hour. Part-time tuition varies according to program. Tuition: $975 per credit hour part-time. Part-time tuition varies according to program. **Scholarships:** Available **Calendar System:** Semester, Summer Session Available **Enrollment:** FT 1,808, PT 79, Grad 11 **Faculty:** FT 162, PT 80 **Student-Faculty Ratio:** 10:1 **Exams:** ACT, Other, SAT I **% Receiving Financial Aid:** 42 **% Residing in College-Owned, -Operated, or -Affiliated Housing:** 99 **Library Holdings:** 496,817 **Regional Accreditation:** New England Association of Schools and Colleges **Credit Hours For Degree:** 128 semester hours, Bachelors **Intercollegiate Athletics:** Baseball M; Basketball M & W; Crew M & W; Cross-Country Running M & W; Equestrian Sports M & W; Field Hockey W; Ice Hockey M & W; Lacrosse M & W; Rugby W; Sailing M & W; Skiing (Cross-Country) M & W; Skiing (Downhill) M & W; Soccer M & W; Squash M & W; Swimming and Diving M & W; Tennis M & W; Track and Field M & W; Ultimate Frisbee M & W; Volleyball M & W; Water Polo M & W

EASTERN CONNECTICUT STATE UNIVERSITY
83 Windham St.
Willimantic, CT 06226-2295
Tel: (860)465-5000; 877-353-3278
Admissions: (860)465-5286
E-mail: admissions@ecsu.ctstateu.edu
Web Site: http://www.easternct.edu
President/CEO: Dr. David G. Carter
Registrar: Kathleen Fabian
Admissions: Kimberly Crone
Financial Aid: Richard A. Savage
Type: Comprehensive **Sex:** Coed **Affiliation:** Connecticut State University System **% Accepted:** 69 **Admission Plans:** Early Admission; Deferred Admission **Application Deadline:** May 01 **Application Fee:** $50.00 **H.S. Requirements:** High school diploma required; GED accepted **Costs Per Year:** Application fee: $50. State resident tuition: $3034 full-time, $277 per credit part-time. Nonresident tuition: $9820 full-time, $277 per credit part-time. Mandatory fees: $2930 full-time, $35 per term part-time. Full-time tuition and fees vary according to degree level. Part-time tuition and fees vary according to course load, degree level, and reciprocity agreements. College room and board: $7300. College room only: $4230. Room and board charges vary according to board plan and housing facility. **Scholarships:** Available **Calendar System:** Semester, Summer Session Available **Enrollment:** FT 3,751, PT 994, Grad 368 **Faculty:** FT 188, PT 209 **Exams:** SAT I or ACT **Library Holdings:** 239,218 **Regional Accreditation:** New England Association of Schools and Colleges **Credit Hours For Degree:** 60 credit hours, Associates; 120 credit hours, Bachelors **ROTC:** Army, Air Force **Professional Accreditation:** CSWE, NCATE **Intercollegiate Athletics:** Baseball M; Basketball M & W; Cheerleading W; Cross-Country Running M & W; Field Hockey W; Lacrosse M & W; Soccer M & W; Softball W; Swimming and Diving W; Track and Field M & W; Volleyball W

FAIRFIELD UNIVERSITY
1073 North Benson Rd.
Fairfield, CT 06824-5195
Tel: (203)254-4000
Admissions: (203)254-4100
Fax: (203)254-4199
E-mail: admis@mail.fairfield.edu
Web Site: http://www.fairfield.edu/
President/CEO: Rev. Jeffrey P. von Arx, SJ
Registrar: Robert C. Russo
Admissions: Karen Pellegrino
Financial Aid: Erin Chiaro
Type: Comprehensive **Sex:** Coed **Affiliation:** Roman Catholic (Jesuit) **Scores:** 100% SAT V 400+; 100% SAT M 400+ **% Accepted:** 74 **Admis-**

sion Plans: Early Admission; Early Decision Plan; Deferred Admission **Application Deadline:** January 15 **Application Fee:** $55.00 **H.S. Requirements:** High school diploma required; GED not accepted **Costs Per Year:** Application fee: $55. Comprehensive fee: $39,855 includes full-time tuition ($29,750), mandatory fees ($505), and college room and board ($9600). College room only: $5560. Full-time tuition and fees vary according to student level. Room and board charges vary according to board plan and housing facility. Part-time tuition: $395 per credit. Part-time mandatory fees: $60 per term. Part-time tuition and fees vary according to course load and program. **Scholarships:** Available **Calendar System:** Semester, Summer Session Available **Enrollment:** FT 3,485, PT 588, Grad 1,100 **Faculty:** FT 226, PT 197 **Student-Faculty Ratio:** 13:1 **Exams:** SAT I or ACT **% Receiving Financial Aid:** 47 **% Residing in College-Owned, -Operated, or -Affiliated Housing:** 80 **Library Holdings:** 325,166 **Regional Accreditation:** New England Association of Schools and Colleges **Credit Hours For Degree:** 120 credits, Bachelors **ROTC:** Army **Professional Accreditation:** AACSB, ABET, AAMFT, AACN, ACA, NLN **Intercollegiate Athletics:** Baseball M; Basketball M & W; Cheerleading M & W; Crew M & W; Cross-Country Running M & W; Equestrian Sports M & W; Field Hockey W; Golf M & W; Lacrosse M & W; Soccer M & W; Softball W; Swimming and Diving M & W; Tennis M & W; Volleyball W

GATEWAY COMMUNITY COLLEGE
60 Sargent Dr.
New Haven, CT 06511-5918
Tel: (203)285-2000
Free: 800-390-7723
Admissions: (203)789-7043
Fax: (203)285-2018
Web Site: http://www.gwcc.commnet.edu/
President/CEO: Dr. Dorsey L. Kendrick
Registrar: David M. Swirsky
Admissions: Catherine Surface
Financial Aid: Cheryl A. Pegues
Type: Two-Year College **Sex:** Coed **Affiliation:** Connecticut Community College System **% Accepted:** 94 **Admission Plans:** Open Admission; Early Admission; Deferred Admission **Application Deadline:** September 01 **Application Fee:** $20.00 **H.S. Requirements:** High school diploma required; GED accepted **Costs Per Year:** Application fee: $20. State resident tuition: $2352 full-time, $98 per credit part-time. Nonresident tuition: $7056 full-time, $294 per credit part-time. Mandatory fees: $320 full-time. **Scholarships:** Available **Calendar System:** Semester, Summer Session Available **Enrollment:** FT 1,809, PT 3,930 **Faculty:** FT 72, PT 231 **Student-Faculty Ratio:** 21:1 **Library Holdings:** 54,802 **Regional Accreditation:** New England Association of Schools and Colleges **Credit Hours For Degree:** 60 credit hours, Associates **Professional Accreditation:** ABET, JRCERT, JRCNMT **Intercollegiate Athletics:** Baseball M; Basketball M & W; Soccer M; Softball W

GIBBS COLLEGE
142 East Ave.
Norwalk, CT 06851-5754
Tel: (203)838-4173
Free: 800-845-5333
Admissions: (203)633-2311
Fax: (203)853-6402
Web Site: http://www.gibbscollege.com/
President/CEO: Lorren West
Registrar: Ashanti Lyons
Admissions: Ted Havelka
Financial Aid: Marie Chevres
Type: Two-Year College **Sex:** Coed **Affiliation:** Career Education Corporation **Admission Plans:** Deferred Admission **Application Fee:** $50.00 **H.S. Requirements:** High school diploma required; GED accepted **Scholarships:** Available **Calendar System:** Quarter, Summer Session Not available **Enrollment:** FT 770 **Faculty:** FT 18, PT 47 **Student-Faculty Ratio:** 20:1 **Library Holdings:** 10,000 **Credit Hours For Degree:** 90 credits, Associates **Professional Accreditation:** ACICS

GOODWIN COLLEGE
745 Burnside Ave.
East Hartford, CT 06108
Tel: (860)528-4111
Fax: (860)291-9550
E-mail: dnoonan@goodwincollege.edu
Web Site: http://www.goodwin.edu/
President/CEO: Mark Scheinberg
Admissions: Daniel P. Noonan
Type: Two-Year College **Sex:** Coed **% Accepted:** 90 **Admission Plans:** Open Admission; Deferred Admission **Application Fee:** $50.00 **H.S. Requirements:** High school diploma required; GED accepted **Costs Per Year:** Application fee: $50. Tuition: $13,570 full-time, $425 per credit part-time. Mandatory fees: $300 full-time. **Scholarships:** Available **Calendar System:** Semester, Summer Session Available **Enrollment:** FT 132, PT 1,087 **Faculty:** FT 22, PT 76 **Student-Faculty Ratio:** 10:1 **Library Holdings:** 6,000 **Regional Accreditation:** New England Association of Schools and Colleges **Credit Hours For Degree:** 62 semester hours, Associates **Professional Accreditation:** ACICS, AAMAE

HOLY APOSTLES COLLEGE AND SEMINARY
33 Prospect Hill Rd.
Cromwell, CT 06416-2005
Tel: (860)632-3010
Free: 800-330-7272
Fax: (860)632-3030
Web Site: http://www.holyapostles.edu/
President/CEO: Very Rev. Douglas L. Mosey, CSB
Admissions: Very Rev. Douglas Mosey, CSB
Financial Aid: Henry Miller
Type: Comprehensive **Sex:** Coed **Affiliation:** Roman Catholic **% Accepted:** 100 **Admission Plans:** Open Admission; Deferred Admission **Application Deadline:** Rolling **Application Fee:** $25.00 **H.S. Requirements:** High school diploma required; GED accepted **Costs Per Year:** Application fee: $25. Tuition: $5520 full-time, $230 per credit part-time. Mandatory fees: $25 full-time. **Scholarships:** Available **Calendar System:** Semester **Enrollment:** FT 9, PT 32, Grad 213 **Faculty:** FT 14, PT 10 **Student-Faculty Ratio:** 7:1 **Exams:** SAT I **% Residing in College-Owned, -Operated, or -Affiliated Housing:** 80 **Library Holdings:** 84,584 **Regional Accreditation:** New England Association of Schools and Colleges **Credit Hours For Degree:** 60 credit hours, Associates; 120 credit hours, Bachelors

HOUSATONIC COMMUNITY COLLEGE
900 Lafayette Blvd.
Bridgeport, CT 06604-4704
Tel: (203)332-5000
Admissions: (203)332-5102
Web Site: http://www.hctc.commnet.edu/
President/CEO: Dr. Janis M. Hadley
Registrar: Edward Sylvia
Admissions: Delores Y. Curtis
Financial Aid: Paul Marchelli
Type: Two-Year College **Sex:** Coed **Affiliation:** Connecticut Community-Technical College System **Admission Plans:** Open Admission; Deferred Admission **Application Fee:** $20.00 **H.S. Requirements:** High school diploma required; GED accepted **Scholarships:** Available **Calendar System:** Semester, Summer Session Available **Faculty:** FT 66, PT 177 **Student-Faculty Ratio:** 17:1 **Exams:** Other **Library Holdings:** 30,000 **Regional Accreditation:** New England Association of Schools and Colleges **Credit Hours For Degree:** 60 credits, Associates **ROTC:** Army **Professional Accreditation:** AOTA, APTA, NAACLS

INTERNATIONAL COLLEGE OF HOSPITALITY MANAGEMENT
101 Wykeham Rd.
Suffield, CT 06078
Tel: (860)868-9555
Free: 800-955-0809
Admissions: (860)668-3515
Fax: (860)868-2114
E-mail: admissions@ichm.edu
Web Site: http://www.ichm.edu/
President/CEO: Tad L. Graham-Handley
Registrar: Karen Jackson
Admissions: Tina Merullo
Type: Two-Year College **Sex:** Coed **% Accepted:** 77 **Admission Plans:** Deferred Admission **Application Deadline:** Rolling **Application Fee:** $100.00 **H.S. Requirements:** High school diploma required; GED accepted **Costs Per Year:** Application fee: $100. Comprehensive fee: $20,878 includes full-time tuition ($15,900) and college room and board ($4978). Room and board charges vary according to board plan. **Scholarships:** Available **Calendar System:** Continuous, Summer Session Not available

Enrollment: FT 116 **Faculty:** FT 7, PT 6 **Exams:** SAT I **% Residing in College-Owned, -Operated, or -Affiliated Housing:** 90 **Library Holdings:** 10,000 **Regional Accreditation:** New England Association of Schools and Colleges **Credit Hours For Degree:** 66 credits, Associates

LYME ACADEMY COLLEGE OF FINE ARTS
84 Lyme St.
Old Lyme, CT 06371
Tel: (860)434-5232
Fax: (860)434-8725
Web Site: http://www.lymeacademy.edu/
President/CEO: Frederick S. Osborne
Registrar: James Falconer
Admissions: John D. Werenko
Financial Aid: James Falconer
Type: Four-Year College **Sex:** Coed **Scores:** 100% SAT V 400+; 92% SAT M 400+ **Admission Plans:** Deferred Admission **Application Fee:** $35.00 **H.S. Requirements:** High school diploma required; GED accepted **Costs Per Year:** Application fee: $35. Tuition: $16,416 full-time. Mandatory fees: $500 full-time. **Scholarships:** Available **Calendar System:** Semester, Summer Session Available **Enrollment:** FT 71, PT 89 **Faculty:** FT 10, PT 12 **Student-Faculty Ratio:** 7:1 **Exams:** SAT I or ACT **Library Holdings:** 8,686 **Regional Accreditation:** New England Association of Schools and Colleges **Credit Hours For Degree:** 132 credits, Bachelors **Professional Accreditation:** NASAD

MANCHESTER COMMUNITY COLLEGE
PO Box 1046
Manchester, CT 06045-1046
Tel: (860)512-3000
Admissions: (860)512-3210
Fax: (860)647-6238
Web Site: http://www.mcc.commnet.edu/
President/CEO: Dr. Jonathan M. Daube
Registrar: Lourdes Cruz
Admissions: Peter Harris
Financial Aid: Ivette Rivera-Dreyer
Type: Two-Year College **Sex:** Coed **Affiliation:** Connecticut Community College System **% Accepted:** 100 **Admission Plans:** Open Admission; Deferred Admission **Application Deadline:** Rolling **Application Fee:** $20.00 **H.S. Requirements:** High school diploma required; GED accepted **Costs Per Year:** Application fee: $20. State resident tuition: $2232 full-time, $93 per credit hour part-time. Nonresident tuition: $6696 full-time, $279 per credit hour part-time. **Scholarships:** Available **Calendar System:** Semester, Summer Session Available **Enrollment:** FT 2,713, PT 3,422 **Faculty:** FT 95, PT 258 **Student-Faculty Ratio:** 21:1 **Library Holdings:** 45,265 **Regional Accreditation:** New England Association of Schools and Colleges **Credit Hours For Degree:** 60 credit hours, Associates **Professional Accreditation:** ARCEST, ACF, AOTA, APTA, CARC, NAACLS **Intercollegiate Athletics:** Baseball M; Basketball M & W; Soccer M & W; Softball W

MIDDLESEX COMMUNITY COLLEGE
100 Training Hill Rd.
Middletown, CT 06457-4889
Tel: (860)343-5800
Admissions: (860)343-5742
Fax: (860)344-7488
E-mail: mshabazz@mxcc.commnet.edu
Web Site: http://www.mxcc.commnet.edu/
President/CEO: Dr. Wilfredo Nieves
Registrar: Susan Salowitz
Admissions: Mensimah Shabazz
Financial Aid: Gladys Colon
Type: Two-Year College **Sex:** Coed **Affiliation:** Connecticut Community College System **% Accepted:** 100 **Admission Plans:** Open Admission; Early Admission; Deferred Admission **Application Deadline:** Rolling **Application Fee:** $20.00 **H.S. Requirements:** High school diploma required; GED accepted **Costs Per Year:** Application fee: $20. State resident tuition: $2232 full-time, $93 per credit part-time. Nonresident tuition: $6696 full-time, $279 per credit part-time. Mandatory fees: $304 full-time, $2.50 per credit part-time, $53 per term part-time. **Scholarships:** Available **Calendar System:** Semester, Summer Session Available **Enrollment:** FT 876, PT 1,410 **Faculty:** FT 39, PT 86 **Student-Faculty Ratio:** 18:1 **Library Holdings:** 45,000 **Regional Accreditation:** New England Association of Schools and Colleges **Credit Hours For Degree:** 60 credits, Associates **ROTC:** Army **Professional Accreditation:** COptA, JRCERT

MITCHELL COLLEGE
437 Pequot Ave.
New London, CT 06320-4498
Tel: (860)701-5000
Free: 800-443-2811
Admissions: (860)701-5038
Fax: (860)444-1209
Web Site: http://www.mitchell.edu/
President/CEO: Mary Ellen Jukoski
Registrar: Donald Dykes
Admissions: Kimberly Hodges
Financial Aid: Kevin M. R. Mayne
Type: Four-Year College **Sex:** Coed **Scores:** 60% SAT V 400+; 61% SAT M 400+; 43% ACT 18-23; 14% ACT 24-29 **% Accepted:** 58 **Admission Plans:** Early Admission; Early Decision Plan; Deferred Admission **Application Deadline:** Rolling **Application Fee:** $30.00 **H.S. Requirements:** High school diploma required; GED accepted **Costs Per Year:** Application fee: $30. Comprehensive fee: $28,735 includes full-time tuition ($19,405) and college room and board ($9330). College room only: $4850. Part-time tuition: $275 per credit hour. Part-time mandatory fees: $35 per term. **Scholarships:** Available **Calendar System:** Semester, Summer Session Available **Enrollment:** FT 644, PT 83 **Faculty:** FT 26, PT 45 **Student-Faculty Ratio:** 12:1 **Exams:** SAT I or ACT **% Residing in College-Owned, -Operated, or -Affiliated Housing:** 80 **Library Holdings:** 80,000 **Regional Accreditation:** New England Association of Schools and Colleges **Credit Hours For Degree:** 60 credit hours, Associates; 120 credit hours, Bachelors **Intercollegiate Athletics:** Baseball M; Basketball M & W; Cheerleading M & W; Cross-Country Running M & W; Golf M; Lacrosse M; Sailing M & W; Soccer M & W; Softball W; Volleyball W

NAUGATUCK VALLEY COMMUNITY COLLEGE
750 Chase Parkway
Waterbury, CT 06708-3000
Tel: (203)575-8040
Admissions: (203)575-8016
Fax: (203)596-8766
E-mail: lsveda@nvcc.commnet.edu
Web Site: http://www.nvcc.commnet.edu/
President/CEO: Dr. Richard L. Sanders
Registrar: Joan Arbusto
Admissions: Lucretia Sveda
Financial Aid: Rodney Butler
Type: Two-Year College **Sex:** Coed **Affiliation:** Connecticut Community–Technical College System **% Accepted:** 42 **Admission Plans:** Open Admission; Deferred Admission **Application Deadline:** Rolling **Application Fee:** $20.00 **H.S. Requirements:** High school diploma required; GED accepted **Costs Per Year:** Application fee: $20. State resident tuition: $2672 full-time. Nonresident tuition: $7976 full-time. **Scholarships:** Available **Calendar System:** Semester, Summer Session Available **Enrollment:** FT 2,215, PT 3,456 **Student-Faculty Ratio:** 5:1 **Exams:** Other **Library Holdings:** 35,000 **Regional Accreditation:** New England Association of Schools and Colleges **Credit Hours For Degree:** 60 credits, Associates **Professional Accreditation:** ABET, APTA, CARC, JRCERT, NLN

NORTHWESTERN CONNECTICUT COMMUNITY COLLEGE
Park Place East
Winsted, CT 06098-1798
Tel: (860)738-6300
Admissions: (860)738-6329
Fax: (860)379-4465
Web Site: http://www.nwctc.commnet.edu/
President/CEO: Dr. R. Eileen Baccus
Registrar: Debra Reynolds
Admissions: Beverly Chrzan
Financial Aid: Louis Bristol
Type: Two-Year College **Sex:** Coed **Affiliation:** Connecticut Community–Technical College System **% Accepted:** 100 **Admission Plans:** Open Admission; Deferred Admission **Application Deadline:** Rolling **Application Fee:** $20.00 **H.S. Requirements:** High school diploma required; GED accepted **Costs Per Year:** Application fee: $20. State resident tuition: $2672 full-time, $156 per semester hour part-time. Nonresident tuition: $7976 full-time, $458 per semester hour part-time. **Scholarships:** Available **Calendar System:** Semester, Summer Session Available **Enrollment:** FT

527, PT 1,042 **Faculty:** FT 27, PT 86 **Student-Faculty Ratio:** 16:1 **Library Holdings:** 37,666 **Regional Accreditation:** New England Association of Schools and Colleges **Credit Hours For Degree:** 62 credits, Associates **Professional Accreditation:** AAMAE, APTA

NORWALK COMMUNITY COLLEGE
188 Richards Ave.
Norwalk, CT 06854-1655
Tel: (203)857-7000
Admissions: (203)857-7060
Fax: (203)857-3335
Web Site: http://www.ncc.commnet.edu/
President/CEO: Dr. David L. Levinson
Registrar: Erika Vogel
Admissions: Kimberlee Csapo-Ebert
Financial Aid: Norma McNerney
Type: Two-Year College **Sex:** Coed **Affiliation:** Connecticut Community College System **Admission Plans:** Open Admission; Deferred Admission **Application Deadline:** Rolling **Application Fee:** $20.00 **H.S. Requirements:** High school diploma required; GED accepted **Costs Per Year:** Application fee: $20. State resident tuition: $2352 full-time, $98 per credit part-time. Nonresident tuition: $7056 full-time, $294 per credit part-time. Mandatory fees: $320 full-time, $20 per credit part-time, $160 per term part-time. **Scholarships:** Available **Calendar System:** Semester, Summer Session Available **Enrollment:** FT 2,016, PT 4,020 **Faculty:** FT 89, PT 260 **Student-Faculty Ratio:** 20:1 **Library Holdings:** 66,080 **Regional Accreditation:** New England Association of Schools and Colleges **Credit Hours For Degree:** 60 credits, Associates **Professional Accreditation:** CARC, NLN

PAIER COLLEGE OF ART, INC.
20 Gorham Ave.
Hamden, CT 06514-3902
Tel: (203)287-3030
Admissions: (203)287-3031
Web Site: http://www.paiercollegeofart.edu/
President/CEO: Jonathan E. Paier
Registrar: Maureen Derose
Admissions: Daniel Paier
Financial Aid: John DeRose
Type: Four-Year College **Sex:** Coed **Scores:** 77% SAT V 400+; 72% SAT M 400+ **% Accepted:** 91 **Admission Plans:** Deferred Admission **Application Deadline:** Rolling **Application Fee:** $25.00 **H.S. Requirements:** High school diploma required; GED accepted **Costs Per Year:** Application fee: $25. Tuition: $12,000 full-time, $380 per credit part-time. Mandatory fees: $320 full-time. **Scholarships:** Available **Calendar System:** Semester, Summer Session Available **Enrollment:** FT 191, PT 86 **Faculty:** FT 9, PT 36 **Student-Faculty Ratio:** 7:1 **Exams:** SAT I or ACT **% Receiving Financial Aid:** 88 **Library Holdings:** 11,515 **Credit Hours For Degree:** 64 semester hours, Associates; 130 semester hours, Bachelors **Professional Accreditation:** ACCSCT

POST UNIVERSITY
800 Country Club Rd.
Waterbury, CT 06723-2540
Tel: (203)596-4500
Free: 800-345-2562
Admissions: (203)596-4630
Fax: (203)756-5810
E-mail: _dmiciotta@post.edu
Web Site: http://www.post.edu
President/CEO: Dr. Jon Jay DeTemple
Registrar: Donna B. Campbell
Admissions: Dominick Miciotta
Financial Aid: Patricia DelBuono
Type: Four-Year College **Sex:** Coed **Scores:** 85% SAT V 400+; 88% SAT M 400+; 33% ACT 18-23; 17% ACT 24-29 **% Accepted:** 62 **Admission Plans:** Deferred Admission **Application Deadline:** Rolling **Application Fee:** $40.00 **H.S. Requirements:** High school diploma required; GED accepted **Costs Per Year:** Application fee: $40. Comprehensive fee: $29,900 includes full-time tuition ($20,750), mandatory fees ($750), and college room and board ($8400). Part-time tuition: $690 per credit. **Scholarships:** Available **Calendar System:** Semester, Summer Session Available **Enrollment:** FT 664, PT 437 **Faculty:** FT 30, PT 92 **Student-Faculty Ratio:** 13:1 **Exams:** SAT I or ACT **% Receiving Financial Aid:** 79 **% Residing in College-Owned, -Operated, or -Affiliated Housing:** 54 **Library Holdings:** 85,000 **Regional Accreditation:** New England Association of Schools and Colleges **Credit Hours For Degree:** 60 credits, Associates; 120 credits, Bachelors **Intercollegiate Athletics:** Baseball M; Basketball M & W; Cross-Country Running M & W; Equestrian Sports M & W; Golf M; Soccer M & W; Softball W; Volleyball W

QUINEBAUG VALLEY COMMUNITY COLLEGE
742 Upper Maple St.
Danielson, CT 06239-1440
Tel: (860)774-1130
Fax: (860)774-7768
E-mail: tmoumouris@qvcc.commnet.edu
Web Site: http://www.qvcc.commnet.edu/
President/CEO: Dianne E. Williams
Registrar: Antonio Veloso
Admissions: Dr. Toni Moumouris
Financial Aid: Alfred Williams
Type: Two-Year College **Sex:** Coed **Affiliation:** Connecticut Community College System **% Accepted:** 98 **Admission Plans:** Open Admission; Early Admission; Deferred Admission **Application Deadline:** September 01 **Application Fee:** $20.00 **H.S. Requirements:** High school diploma required; GED accepted **Costs Per Year:** Application fee: $20. State resident tuition: $2112 full-time. Nonresident tuition: $6336 full-time. Mandatory fees: $294 full-time. Full-time tuition and fees vary according to reciprocity agreements. **Scholarships:** Available **Calendar System:** Semester, Summer Session Available **Enrollment:** FT 643, PT 1,071 **Faculty:** FT 21, PT 101 **Student-Faculty Ratio:** 18:1 **Library Holdings:** 31,000 **Regional Accreditation:** New England Association of Schools and Colleges **Credit Hours For Degree:** 60 credit hours, Associates **Professional Accreditation:** AAMAE

QUINNIPIAC UNIVERSITY
275 Mount Carmel Ave.
Hamden, CT 06518-1940
Tel: (203)582-8200
Free: 800-462-1944
Admissions: (203)582-8600
Fax: (203)582-6347
E-mail: admissions@quinnipiac.edu
Web Site: http://www.quinnipiac.edu/
President/CEO: Dr. John L. Lahey
Registrar: Dorothy Lauria
Admissions: Joan Isaac Mohr
Financial Aid: Heather Hamilton
Type: Comprehensive **Sex:** Coed **Scores:** 100% SAT V 400+; 100% SAT M 400+; 40% ACT 18-23; 51% ACT 24-29 **% Accepted:** 53 **Admission Plans:** Deferred Admission **Application Deadline:** February 01 **Application Fee:** $45.00 **H.S. Requirements:** High school diploma required; GED accepted **Costs Per Year:** Application fee: $45. Comprehensive fee: $36,980 includes full-time tuition ($25,240), mandatory fees ($1040), and college room and board ($10,700). Part-time tuition: $625 per credit. Part-time mandatory fees: $30 per credit. **Scholarships:** Available **Calendar System:** Semester, Summer Session Available **Enrollment:** FT 5,286, PT 420, Grad 1,043 **Faculty:** FT 280, PT 500 **Student-Faculty Ratio:** 15:1 **Exams:** SAT I or ACT **% Receiving Financial Aid:** 57 **% Residing in College-Owned, -Operated, or -Affiliated Housing:** 70 **Library Holdings:** 285,000 **Regional Accreditation:** New England Association of Schools and Colleges **Credit Hours For Degree:** 120 semester hours, Bachelors **ROTC:** Army, Air Force **Professional Accreditation:** AACSB, ABA, AOTA, APTA, AALS, CARC, JRCERT, NAACLS, NLN **Intercollegiate Athletics:** Baseball M; Basketball M & W; Cross-Country Running M & W; Field Hockey W; Golf M; Ice Hockey M & W; Lacrosse M & W; Soccer M & W; Softball W; Tennis M & W; Track and Field M & W; Volleyball W

SACRED HEART UNIVERSITY
5151 Park Ave.
Fairfield, CT 06825-1000
Tel: (203)371-7999
Admissions: (203)365-4763
Fax: (203)371-7889
E-mail: enroll@sacredheart.edu
Web Site: http://www.sacredheart.edu/
President/CEO: Dr. Anthony J. Cernera
Registrar: Douglas J. Bohn
Admissions: James Barquinero

Financial Aid: Julie Savino
Type: Comprehensive **Sex:** Coed **Affiliation:** Roman Catholic **Scores:** 99% SAT V 400+; 99% SAT M 400+ **% Accepted:** 64 **Admission Plans:** Early Admission; Early Decision Plan; Deferred Admission **Application Fee:** $50.00 **H.S. Requirements:** High school diploma required; GED accepted **Costs Per Year:** Application fee: $50. Comprehensive fee: $33,404 includes full-time tuition ($23,750) and college room and board ($9654). College room only: $7078. Full-time tuition varies according to program. Room and board charges vary according to board plan and housing facility. Part-time tuition: $390 per credit. Part-time mandatory fees: $76 per term. Part-time tuition and fees vary according to program. **Scholarships:** Available **Calendar System:** Semester, Summer Session Available **Enrollment:** FT 3,244, PT 860, Grad 1,456 **Faculty:** FT 186, PT 286 **Student-Faculty Ratio:** 13:1 **Exams:** SAT I or ACT **% Receiving Financial Aid:** 67 **% Residing in College-Owned, -Operated, or -Affiliated Housing:** 68 **Regional Accreditation:** New England Association of Schools and Colleges **Credit Hours For Degree:** 60 credits, Associates; 120 credits, Bachelors **ROTC:** Army **Professional Accreditation:** AACN, AOTA, APTA, CSWE, JRCEPAT, NLN **Intercollegiate Athletics:** Baseball M; Basketball M & W; Bowling M & W; Cheerleading W; Crew W; Cross-Country Running M & W; Equestrian Sports W; Fencing M & W; Field Hockey W; Football M; Golf M & W; Ice Hockey M & W; Lacrosse M & W; Soccer M & W; Softball W; Swimming and Diving W; Tennis M & W; Track and Field M & W; Volleyball M & W; Wrestling M

SAINT JOSEPH COLLEGE

1678 Asylum Ave.
West Hartford, CT 06117-2700
Tel: (860)232-4571; (866)442-8752
Admissions: (860)231-5216
Fax: (860)233-5695
E-mail: admissions@sjc.edu
Web Site: http://www.sjc.edu/
President/CEO: Dr. Evelyn C. Lynch
Registrar: Brenda Sebastianelli
Admissions: Alan Chesterton
Financial Aid: Philip Malinoski
Type: Comprehensive **Affiliation:** Roman Catholic **Scores:** 93% SAT V 400+; 91% SAT M 400+ **% Accepted:** 72 **Admission Plans:** Early Admission; Early Action; Deferred Admission **Application Deadline:** Rolling **Application Fee:** $35.00 **H.S. Requirements:** High school diploma required; GED accepted **Costs Per Year:** Application fee: $35. Comprehensive fee: $33,250 includes full-time tuition ($22,890), mandatory fees ($600), and college room and board ($9760). College room only: $4780. Part-time tuition: $530 per credit. Part-time mandatory fees: $25 per credit. **Scholarships:** Available **Calendar System:** Semester, Summer Session Available **Enrollment:** FT 871, PT 288, Grad 699 **Faculty:** FT 77, PT 11 **Student-Faculty Ratio:** 11:1 **Exams:** SAT I or ACT **% Receiving Financial Aid:** 83 **Library Holdings:** 120,094 **Regional Accreditation:** New England Association of Schools and Colleges **Credit Hours For Degree:** 120 credits, Bachelors **Professional Accreditation:** AAMFT, AACN, AAFCS, ADtA, CSWE, NLN **Intercollegiate Athletics:** Basketball W; Cross-Country Running W; Lacrosse W; Soccer W; Softball W; Swimming and Diving W; Tennis W; Volleyball W

ST. VINCENT'S COLLEGE

2800 Main St.
Bridgeport, CT 06606-4292
Tel: (203)576-5235
Admissions: (203)576-5515
E-mail: jmarrone@stvincentscollege.edu
Web Site: http://www.stvincentscollege.edu/
President/CEO: Anne T. Avallone
Registrar: Joseph Macionus
Admissions: Joseph Marrone
Financial Aid: Mary L. Rich
Type: Two-Year College **Sex:** Coed **Affiliation:** Roman Catholic Church **Admission Plans:** Deferred Admission **Application Fee:** $30.00 **H.S. Requirements:** High school diploma required; GED accepted **Scholarships:** Available **Calendar System:** Semester, Summer Session Available **Faculty:** FT 10, PT 9 **Student-Faculty Ratio:** 23:1 **Exams:** SAT I or ACT **Library Holdings:** 9,428 **Regional Accreditation:** New England Association of Schools and Colleges **Credit Hours For Degree:** 72 credits, Associates **Professional Accreditation:** AAMAE, NLN

SOUTHERN CONNECTICUT STATE UNIVERSITY

501 Crescent St.
New Haven, CT 06515-1355
Tel: (203)392-5200
Admissions: (203)392-5656
Fax: (203)392-5727
Web Site: http://www.southernct.edu/
President/CEO: Dr. Cheryl Norton
Registrar: Lynn Kohrn
Admissions: Sharon Brennan
Financial Aid: Avon Dennis
Type: Comprehensive **Sex:** Coed **Affiliation:** Connecticut State University System **Scores:** 89% SAT V 400+; 86% SAT M 400+ **% Accepted:** 54 **Admission Plans:** Deferred Admission **Application Deadline:** July 01 **Application Fee:** $50.00 **H.S. Requirements:** High school diploma required; GED accepted **Costs Per Year:** Application fee: $50. State resident tuition: $3187 full-time, $322 per credit part-time. Nonresident tuition: $10,315 full-time, $322 per credit part-time. Mandatory fees: $3255 full-time, $8 per credit part-time, $55 per term part-time. College room and board: $8031. College room only: $4446. **Scholarships:** Available **Calendar System:** Semester, Summer Session Available **Enrollment:** FT 6,697, PT 1,612, Grad 3,849 **Faculty:** FT 403, PT 555 **Student-Faculty Ratio:** 17:1 **Exams:** SAT I or ACT **% Receiving Financial Aid:** 46 **% Residing in College-Owned, -Operated, or -Affiliated Housing:** 33 **Library Holdings:** 495,660 **Regional Accreditation:** New England Association of Schools and Colleges **Credit Hours For Degree:** 120 semester hours, Bachelors **ROTC:** Army, Air Force **Professional Accreditation:** ABET, AAMFT, AACN, AANA, ACA, ALA, ASLHA, CEPH, CSWE, JRCEPAT, NLN **Intercollegiate Athletics:** Baseball M; Basketball M & W; Cross-Country Running M & W; Field Hockey W; Football M; Golf M; Gymnastics M & W; Soccer M & W; Softball W; Swimming and Diving M & W; Track and Field M & W; Volleyball W; Wrestling M

THREE RIVERS COMMUNITY COLLEGE

7 Mahan Dr.
Norwich, CT 06360
Tel: (860)886-0177
Admissions: (860)892-5762
Fax: (860)886-0691
E-mail: info3rivers@trcc.commnet.edu
Web Site: http://www.trcc.commnet.edu/
President/CEO: Dr. Grace Sawyer-Jones
Registrar: Karen Aubin
Admissions: Karin Edwards
Financial Aid: Daniel Zaneski
Type: Two-Year College **Sex:** Coed **Affiliation:** Connecticut Community–Technical College System **Admission Plans:** Open Admission; Early Admission; Deferred Admission **Application Fee:** $20.00 **H.S. Requirements:** High school diploma required; GED accepted. For adults who demonstrate ability to benefit from college: High school diploma or equivalent not required **Costs Per Year:** Application fee: $20. State resident tuition: $2232 full-time, $93 per semester hour part-time. Nonresident tuition: $7264 full-time, $279 per semester hour part-time. Mandatory fees: $304 full-time. **Scholarships:** Available **Calendar System:** Semester, Summer Session Available **Faculty:** FT 72, PT 150 **Exams:** Other **Library Holdings:** 53,768 **Regional Accreditation:** New England Association of Schools and Colleges **Credit Hours For Degree:** 60 credits, Associates **Professional Accreditation:** ABET, ACBSP, MACTE, NLN

TRINITY COLLEGE

300 Summit St.
Hartford, CT 06106-3100
Tel: (860)297-2000
Admissions: (860)297-2180
Fax: (860)297-2287
E-mail: admissions.office@mail.trincoll.edu
Web Site: http://www.trincoll.edu/
President/CEO: James F. Jones, Jr.
Registrar: Patricia McGregor
Admissions: Larry Dow
Financial Aid: Kelly L. O'Brien

Type: Comprehensive **Sex:** Coed **Scores:** 100% SAT V 400+; 100% SAT M 400+; 6.84% ACT 18-23; 68.38% ACT 24-29 **% Accepted:** 39 **Admission Plans:** Early Admission; Early Decision Plan; Deferred Admission **Application Deadline:** January 01 **Application Fee:** $60.00 **H.S. Requirements:** High school diploma required; GED accepted **Costs Per Year:** Application fee: $60. Comprehensive fee: $42,220 includes full-time tuition ($32,000), mandatory fees ($1630), and college room and board ($8590). College room only: $5550. Full-time tuition and fees vary according to program. Room and board charges vary according to board plan. Part-time tuition: $1185 per credit hour. Part-time tuition varies according to program. **Scholarships:** Available **Calendar System:** Semester, Summer Session Available **Enrollment:** FT 2,165, PT 178, Grad 183 **Faculty:** FT 183, PT 75 **Student-Faculty Ratio:** 10:1 **Exams:** Other **% Receiving Financial Aid:** 46 **% Residing in College-Owned, -Operated, or -Affiliated Housing:** 96 **Library Holdings:** 988,536 **Regional Accreditation:** New England Association of Schools and Colleges **Credit Hours For Degree:** 36 courses, Bachelors **ROTC:** Army **Professional Accreditation:** ABET **Intercollegiate Athletics:** Baseball M; Basketball M & W; Crew M & W; Cross-Country Running M & W; Equestrian Sports M & W; Fencing M & W; Field Hockey W; Football M; Golf M; Ice Hockey M & W; Lacrosse M & W; Riflery M & W; Rugby M & W; Sailing M & W; Skiing (Downhill) M & W; Soccer M & W; Softball W; Squash M & W; Swimming and Diving M & W; Tennis M & W; Track and Field M & W; Ultimate Frisbee M & W; Volleyball M & W; Water Polo M & W; Wrestling M

TUNXIS COMMUNITY COLLEGE
271 Scott Swamp Rd.
Farmington, CT 06032-3026
Tel: (860)677-7701
Admissions: (860)255-3350
E-mail: pmccluskey@txcc.commnet.edu
Web Site: http://www.tunxis.commnet.edu/
President/CEO: Dr. Cathryn Addy
Registrar: Susan Juba
Admissions: Peter McCloskey
Financial Aid: David Welsh
Type: Two-Year College **Sex:** Coed **Affiliation:** Connecticut Community College System **Admission Plans:** Open Admission; Preferred Admission; Deferred Admission **Application Deadline:** Rolling **Application Fee:** $20.00 **H.S. Requirements:** High school diploma required; GED accepted **Costs Per Year:** Application fee: $20. Area resident tuition: $98 per credit hour part-time. State resident tuition: $2352 full-time. Nonresident tuition: $7056 full-time, $294 per credit hour part-time. Mandatory fees: $320 full-time, $178 per term part-time. **Calendar System:** Semester, Summer Session Available **Enrollment:** FT 1,488, PT 2,406 **Faculty:** FT 62, PT 172 **Student-Faculty Ratio:** 19:1 **Library Holdings:** 33,866 **Regional Accreditation:** New England Association of Schools and Colleges **Credit Hours For Degree:** 60 credits, Associates **Professional Accreditation:** ADA, APTA

UNITED STATES COAST GUARD ACADEMY
15 Mohegan Ave.
New London, CT 06320-8100
Tel: (860)444-8444
Free: 800-883-8724
Admissions: (860)444-8500
Fax: (860)444-8289
E-mail: admissions@cga.uscg.mil
Web Site: http://www.cga.edu/
President/CEO: Rear Adm. Robert C. Olsen, Jr.
Registrar: G. Phillip Boeding
Admissions: Capt. Susan D. Bibeau
Type: Four-Year College **Sex:** Coed **Scores:** 100% SAT V 400+; 100% SAT M 400+; 14% ACT 18-23; 62% ACT 24-29 **% Accepted:** 26 **Admission Plans:** Early Action **Application Deadline:** March 01 **Application Fee:** $0.00 **H.S. Requirements:** High school diploma required; GED accepted. For home schooled applicants: High school diploma or equivalent not required **Costs Per Year:** Application fee: $0. **Calendar System:** Semester, Summer Session Available **Enrollment:** FT 1,012 **Faculty:** FT 100, PT 18 **Student-Faculty Ratio:** 9:1 **Exams:** SAT I or ACT **% Residing in College-Owned, -Operated, or -Affiliated Housing:** 100 **Regional Accreditation:** New England Association of Schools and Colleges **Credit Hours For Degree:** 126 credit hours, Bachelors **Professional Accreditation:** ABET **Intercollegiate Athletics:** Baseball M; Basketball M & W; Bowling M & W; Crew M & W; Cross-Country Running M & W; Football M; Golf M & W; Ice Hockey M; Lacrosse M & W; Riflery M & W; Rugby M & W; Sailing M & W; Soccer M & W; Softball W; Swimming and Diving M & W; Tennis M & W; Track and Field M & W; Volleyball W; Water Polo M; Wrestling M

UNIVERSITY OF BRIDGEPORT
126 Park Ave.
Bridgeport, CT 06604
Tel: (203)576-4000
Free: 800-243-9496
Admissions: (203)576-4552
Fax: (203)576-4941
E-mail: admit@bridgeport.edu
Web Site: http://www.bridgeport.edu/
President/CEO: Neil Albert Salonen
Registrar: Valerie E. Powell Baldwin
Admissions: Audrey Sikton-Savage
Financial Aid: Robbie deLevr
Type: Comprehensive **Sex:** Coed **Scores:** 67% SAT V 400+; 72% SAT M 400+; 40% ACT 18-23; 12% ACT 24-29 **% Accepted:** 74 **Admission Plans:** Early Admission; Early Action; Deferred Admission **Application Deadline:** Rolling **Application Fee:** $25.00 **H.S. Requirements:** High school diploma required; GED accepted **Costs Per Year:** Application fee: $25. Comprehensive fee: $29,595 includes full-time tuition ($19,200), mandatory fees ($1395), and college room and board ($9000). College room only: $4600. Full-time tuition and fees vary according to program. Room and board charges vary according to board plan and student level. Part-time tuition: $640 per credit. Part-time mandatory fees: $60 per term. Part-time tuition and fees vary according to program. **Scholarships:** Available **Calendar System:** Semester, Summer Session Available **Enrollment:** FT 1,247, PT 429, Grad 1,749 **Faculty:** FT 89, PT 260 **Student-Faculty Ratio:** 12:1 **Exams:** SAT I or ACT, SAT II **% Residing in College-Owned, -Operated, or -Affiliated Housing:** 45 **Library Holdings:** 272,430 **Regional Accreditation:** New England Association of Schools and Colleges **Credit Hours For Degree:** 60 credits, Associates; 120 credits, Bachelors **ROTC:** Army **Professional Accreditation:** ABET, ADA, ACBSP, NACSCAO, NASAD, CCE **Intercollegiate Athletics:** Baseball M; Basketball M & W; Cross-Country Running M & W; Gymnastics W; Soccer M & W; Softball W; Swimming and Diving W; Volleyball W

UNIVERSITY OF CONNECTICUT
Storrs, CT 06269
Tel: (860)486-2000
Admissions: (860)486-3137
Fax: (860)486-1476
E-mail: beahusky@uconn.edu
Web Site: http://www.uconn.edu/
President/CEO: Dr. Philip E. Austin
Registrar: Dr. Jeffrey von Munkwitz-Smith
Admissions: Lee Melvin
Financial Aid: Jean Main
Type: University **Sex:** Coed **Scores:** 99% SAT V 400+; 100% SAT M 400+; 29% ACT 18-23; 56% ACT 24-29 **% Accepted:** 51 **Admission Plans:** Early Admission; Early Action; Deferred Admission **Application Deadline:** February 01 **Application Fee:** $70.00 **H.S. Requirements:** High school diploma required; GED accepted **Costs Per Year:** Application fee: $70. State resident tuition: $6456 full-time, $269 per credit part-time. Nonresident tuition: $19,656 full-time, $819 per credit part-time. Mandatory fees: $1906 full-time, $635 per term part-time. College room and board: $8266. College room only: $4350. **Scholarships:** Available **Calendar System:** Semester, Summer Session Available **Enrollment:** FT 15,296, PT 816, Grad 6,180 **Faculty:** FT 975, PT 290 **Student-Faculty Ratio:** 17:1 **Exams:** SAT I or ACT **% Receiving Financial Aid:** 47 **% Residing in College-Owned, -Operated, or -Affiliated Housing:** 72 **Library Holdings:** 2,987,772 **Regional Accreditation:** New England Association of Schools and Colleges **Credit Hours For Degree:** 120 credits, Bachelors **ROTC:** Army, Air Force **Professional Accreditation:** AACSB, ABET, ACEJMC, AAMFT, ABA, ACPhE, ADtA, APTA, APA, ASLA, ASLHA, AALS, CSWE, NAACLS, NASAD, NASM, NASPAA, NAST, NCATE, NLN **Intercollegiate Athletics:** Baseball M; Basketball M & W; Crew W; Cross-Country Running M & W; Field Hockey W; Football M; Golf M; Ice Hockey M & W; Lacrosse W; Soccer M & W; Softball W; Swimming and Diving M & W; Tennis M & W; Track and Field M & W; Volleyball W

UNIVERSITY OF HARTFORD
200 Bloomfield Ave.
West Hartford, CT 06117-1599

Tel: (860)768-4100
Free: 800-947-4303
Admissions: (860)768-4296
Fax: (860)768-4961
E-mail: admission@hartford.edu
Web Site: http://www.hartford.edu/
President/CEO: Dr. Walter Harrison
Registrar: Doreen Lay
Admissions: Richard Zeiser
Financial Aid: Suzanne E. Peters
Type: Comprehensive **Sex:** Coed **Scores:** 99% SAT V 400+; 100% SAT M 400+; 47% ACT 18-23; 42% ACT 24-29 **% Accepted:** 66 **Admission Plans:** Early Admission; Deferred Admission **Application Deadline:** Rolling **Application Fee:** $35.00 **H.S. Requirements:** High school diploma required; GED accepted **Costs Per Year:** Application fee: $35. Comprehensive fee: $35,688 includes full-time tuition ($24,576), mandatory fees ($1190), and college room and board ($9922). College room only: $6118. Part-time tuition: $360 per credit. **Scholarships:** Available **Calendar System:** Semester, Summer Session Available **Enrollment:** FT 4,657, PT 935, Grad 1,668 **Faculty:** FT 325, PT 428 **Student-Faculty Ratio:** 14:1 **Exams:** SAT I or ACT **% Receiving Financial Aid:** 64 **% Residing in College-Owned, -Operated, or -Affiliated Housing:** 74 **Library Holdings:** 468,780 **Regional Accreditation:** New England Association of Schools and Colleges **Credit Hours For Degree:** 60 credits, Associates; 120 credits, Bachelors **ROTC:** Army, Air Force **Professional Accreditation:** AACSB, ABET, AOTA, APTA, APA, CARC, JRCERT, NAACLS, NASAD, NASD, NASM, NCATE, NLN **Intercollegiate Athletics:** Badminton M & W; Baseball M; Basketball M & W; Cross-Country Running M & W; Golf M & W; Lacrosse M; Racquetball M & W; Rugby M & W; Soccer M & W; Softball W; Squash M & W; Tennis M & W; Track and Field M & W; Volleyball M & W

UNIVERSITY OF NEW HAVEN
300 Orange Ave.
West Haven, CT 06516-1916
Tel: (203)932-7000
Free: 800-DIAL-UNH
Admissions: (203)932-7319
Fax: (203)937-0756
Web Site: http://www.newhaven.edu/
President/CEO: Dr. Steven Kaplan
Registrar: Virginia Klump
Admissions: Jane C. Sangeloty
Financial Aid: Karen Flynn
Type: Comprehensive **Sex:** Coed **Scores:** 95% SAT V 400+; 93.5% SAT M 400+ **% Accepted:** 73 **Application Deadline:** Rolling **Application Fee:** $50.00 **H.S. Requirements:** High school diploma required; GED accepted **Costs Per Year:** Application fee: $50. Comprehensive fee: $32,532 includes full-time tuition ($22,380), mandatory fees ($602), and college room and board ($9550). College room only: $5796. Full-time tuition and fees vary according to course load and program. Room and board charges vary according to board plan and housing facility. Part-time tuition: $746 per credit hour. Part-time tuition varies according to class time, course load, location, and program. **Scholarships:** Available **Calendar System:** 4-1-4, Summer Session Available **Enrollment:** FT 2,301, PT 487, Grad 1,678 **Faculty:** FT 162, PT 309 **Student-Faculty Ratio:** 14:1 **Exams:** SAT I or ACT, SAT I **% Receiving Financial Aid:** 74 **% Residing in College-Owned, -Operated, or -Affiliated Housing:** 64 **Regional Accreditation:** New England Association of Schools and Colleges **Credit Hours For Degree:** 60 credit hours, Associates; 120 credit hours, Bachelors **Professional Accreditation:** ABET, ADA **Intercollegiate Athletics:** Baseball M; Basketball M & W; Cheerleading M & W; Cross-Country Running M & W; Golf M; Lacrosse W; Soccer M & W; Softball W; Tennis W; Track and Field M & W; Volleyball M & W

WESLEYAN UNIVERSITY
Middletown, CT 06459-0260
Tel: (860)685-2000
Admissions: (860)685-3000
Fax: (860)685-3001
E-mail: admissions@wesleyan.edu
Web Site: http://www.wesleyan.edu/
President/CEO: Dr. Douglas J. Bennet, Jr.
Registrar: Anna Van der Burg
Admissions: Nancy Hargrave Meislahn
Financial Aid: Elizabeth McCormick
Type: University **Sex:** Coed **Scores:** 100% SAT V 400+; 100% SAT M 400+; 3% ACT 18-23; 31% ACT 24-29 **% Accepted:** 28 **Admission Plans:** Early Admission; Early Decision Plan; Deferred Admission **Application Deadline:** January 01 **Application Fee:** $55.00 **H.S. Requirements:** High school diploma required; GED accepted **Costs Per Year:** Application fee: $55. Comprehensive fee: $44,770 includes full-time tuition ($34,930), mandatory fees ($300), and college room and board ($9540). College room only: $5808. **Scholarships:** Available **Calendar System:** Semester, Summer Session Available **Enrollment:** FT 2,750, PT 14, Grad 443 **Faculty:** FT 325, PT 43 **Student-Faculty Ratio:** 9:1 **Exams:** SAT I and SAT II or ACT **% Receiving Financial Aid:** 48 **% Residing in College-Owned, -Operated, or -Affiliated Housing:** 94 **Library Holdings:** 1,301,176 **Regional Accreditation:** New England Association of Schools and Colleges **Credit Hours For Degree:** 32 courses, Bachelors **ROTC:** Air Force **Intercollegiate Athletics:** Baseball M; Basketball M & W; Crew M & W; Cross-Country Running M & W; Equestrian Sports M & W; Field Hockey W; Football M; Golf M; Ice Hockey M & W; Lacrosse M & W; Rugby M & W; Sailing M & W; Skiing (Downhill) M & W; Soccer M & W; Softball W; Squash M & W; Swimming and Diving M & W; Tennis M & W; Track and Field M & W; Volleyball M & W; Water Polo M; Wrestling M

WESTERN CONNECTICUT STATE UNIVERSITY
181 White St.
Danbury, CT 06810-6885
Tel: (203)837-8200; 877-837-9278
Admissions: (203)837-9000
Fax: (203)837-8320
E-mail: _hawkinsw@wcsu.edu
Web Site: http://www.wcsu.edu/
President/CEO: Dr. James W. Schmotter
Registrar: Irene Duffy
Admissions: William Hawkins
Financial Aid: Nancy Barton
Type: Comprehensive **Sex:** Coed **Affiliation:** Connecticut State University System **Scores:** 95% SAT V 400+; 93% SAT M 400+ **% Accepted:** 58 **Admission Plans:** Preferred Admission; Early Admission; Deferred Admission **Application Deadline:** May 01 **Application Fee:** $40.00 **H.S. Requirements:** High school diploma required; GED accepted **Costs Per Year:** Application fee: $40. State resident tuition: $3187 full-time, $304 per semester hour part-time. Nonresident tuition: $10,315 full-time, $304 per semester hour part-time. Mandatory fees: $2919 full-time, $60 per term part-time. College room and board: $7784. College room only: $4516. **Scholarships:** Available **Calendar System:** Semester, Summer Session Available **Enrollment:** FT 4,002, PT 1,193, Grad 712 **Faculty:** FT 197, PT 288 **Student-Faculty Ratio:** 16:1 **Exams:** SAT I or ACT **% Receiving Financial Aid:** 39 **% Residing in College-Owned, -Operated, or -Affiliated Housing:** 33 **Library Holdings:** 182,915 **Regional Accreditation:** New England Association of Schools and Colleges **Credit Hours For Degree:** 62 semester hours, Associates; 122 semester hours, Bachelors **ROTC:** Army, Air Force **Professional Accreditation:** AACN, ACA, CSWE, NASM, NLN **Intercollegiate Athletics:** Baseball M; Basketball M & W; Football M; Lacrosse W; Soccer M & W; Softball W; Swimming and Diving W; Tennis M & W; Volleyball W

YALE UNIVERSITY
New Haven, CT 06520
Tel: (203)432-4771
Admissions: (203)432-9316
Fax: (203)432-9392
E-mail: undergraduate.admissions@yale.edu
Web Site: http://www.yale.edu/
President/CEO: Richard C. Levin
Registrar: Barry Kane
Admissions: Richard H. Shaw, Jr.
Financial Aid: Myra B. Smith
Type: University **Sex:** Coed **Scores:** 100% SAT V 400+; 100% SAT M 400+ **% Accepted:** 10 **Admission Plans:** Early Admission; Early Action; Deferred Admission **Application Deadline:** December 31 **Application Fee:** $75.00 **H.S. Requirements:** High school diploma or equivalent not required **Costs Per Year:** Application fee: $75. Comprehensive fee: $41,000 includes full-time tuition ($31,460) and college room and board ($9540). **Scholarships:** Available **Calendar System:** Semester, Summer Session Available **Enrollment:** FT 5,350, PT 59, Grad 4,828 **Faculty:** FT 1,054, PT 376 **Student-Faculty Ratio:** 6:1 **Exams:** SAT I and SAT II or ACT **% Receiving Financial Aid:** 42 **% Residing in College-Owned, -Operated, or

-**Affiliated Housing:** 87 **Library Holdings:** 11,100,000 **Regional Accreditation:** New England Association of Schools and Colleges **Credit Hours For Degree:** 36 courses, Bachelors **ROTC:** Army, Air Force **Professional Accreditation:** AACSB, ABET, ACEHSA, AACN, ABA, ACNM, ADtA, APA, ACIPE, AALS, ATS, CEPH, LCMEAMA, NASM, NLN, SAF **Intercollegiate Athletics:** Baseball M; Basketball M & W; Crew M & W; Cross-Country Running M & W; Fencing M & W; Field Hockey W; Football M; Golf M & W; Gymnastics W; Ice Hockey M & W; Lacrosse M & W; Soccer M & W; Softball W; Squash M & W; Swimming and Diving M & W; Table Tennis M; Tennis M & W; Track and Field M & W; Volleyball M & W

DELAWARE COLLEGE OF ART AND DESIGN
600 North Market St.
Wilmington, DE 19801
Tel: (302)622-8000
Fax: (302)622-8870
E-mail: thaman@dcad.edu
Web Site: http://www.dcad.edu/
President/CEO: James P. Lecky
Admissions: Lynda Schmid
Type: Two-Year College **Sex:** Coed **Affiliation:** Corcoran College of Art and Design **% Accepted:** 58 **Admission Plans:** Deferred Admission **Application Deadline:** Rolling **Application Fee:** $25.00 **H.S. Requirements:** High school diploma required; GED accepted **Costs Per Year:** Application fee: $25. Tuition: $14,070 full-time, $595 per credit part-time. Mandatory fees: $200 per term part-time. College room only: $5490. **Calendar System:** Semester, Summer Session Available **Enrollment:** FT 148, PT 46 **Faculty:** FT 5, PT 15 **Student-Faculty Ratio:** 5:1 **% Residing in College-Owned, -Operated, or -Affiliated Housing:** 50 **Library Holdings:** 8,000 **Regional Accreditation:** Middle State Association of Colleges and Schools **Credit Hours For Degree:** 68 semester hours, Associates

DELAWARE STATE UNIVERSITY
1200 North DuPont Hwy.
Dover, DE 19901-2277
Tel: (302)857-6290
Free: 800-845-2544
Admissions: (302)857-6103
Fax: (302)857-6352
E-mail: cheatha@desu.edu
Web Site: http://www.desu.edu/
President/CEO: Allen L. Sessoms
Registrar: Cornelia Caballero
Admissions: Lawita Cheatham
Financial Aid: Carylin C. Brinkley
Type: Comprehensive **Sex:** Coed **Affiliation:** Delaware Higher Education Commission **Scores:** 60% SAT V 400+; 55% SAT M 400+; 17% ACT 18-23; 2% ACT 24-29 **% Accepted:** 63 **Admission Plans:** Preferred Admission; Early Admission **Application Deadline:** April 01 **Application Fee:** $25.00 **H.S. Requirements:** High school diploma required; GED accepted **Costs Per Year:** Application fee: $25. State resident tuition: $5480 full-time, $213 per credit hour part-time. Nonresident tuition: $11,704 full-time, $472 per credit hour part-time. Mandatory fees: $370 full-time, $105 per term part-time. College room and board: $8298. College room only: $5502. **Scholarships:** Available **Calendar System:** Semester, Summer Session Available **Enrollment:** FT 2,946, PT 494, Grad 282 **Faculty:** FT 182 **Exams:** SAT I or ACT **% Receiving Financial Aid:** 79 **% Residing in College-Owned, -Operated, or -Affiliated Housing:** 46 **Library Holdings:** 204,127 **Regional Accreditation:** Middle State Association of Colleges and Schools **Credit Hours For Degree:** 121 credit hours, Bachelors **ROTC:** Army, Air Force **Professional Accreditation:** AACN, CSWE, NCATE, NLN **Intercollegiate Athletics:** Baseball M; Basketball M & W; Bowling W; Cross-Country Running M & W; Football M; Softball W; Tennis M & W; Track and Field M & W; Volleyball W; Wrestling M

DELAWARE TECHNICAL & COMMUNITY COLLEGE, JACK F. OWENS CAMPUS
PO Box 610
Georgetown, DE 19947
Tel: (302)856-5400
Fax: (302)856-9461
Web Site: http://www.dtcc.edu/
President/CEO: Dr. Ileana M. Smith
Registrar: Walton Johnson
Admissions: Claire McDonald
Type: Two-Year College **Sex:** Coed **Affiliation:** Delaware Technical and Community College System **% Accepted:** 73 **Admission Plans:** Open Admission; Preferred Admission; Early Admission **Application Deadline:** Rolling **Application Fee:** $10.00 **H.S. Requirements:** High school diploma or equivalent not required. For nursing program: High school diploma required; GED not accepted **Costs Per Year:** Application fee: $10. State resident tuition: $1956 full-time, $81.50 per credit hour part-time. Nonresident tuition: $4890 full-time, $203.75 per credit hour part-time. Mandatory fees: $204 full-time, $6 per credit hour part-time, $21 per term part-time. **Scholarships:** Available **Calendar System:** Semester, Summer Session Available **Enrollment:** FT 1,600, PT 2,336 **Faculty:** FT 103, PT 177 **Student-Faculty Ratio:** 15:1 **Library Holdings:** 72,657 **Regional Accreditation:** Middle State Association of Colleges and Schools **Credit Hours For Degree:** 70 credits, Associates **Professional Accreditation:** AOTA, APTA, ACBSP, CARC, JRCERT, NAACLS, NLN **Intercollegiate Athletics:** Baseball M; Softball W

DELAWARE TECHNICAL & COMMUNITY COLLEGE, STANTON/ WILMINGTON CAMPUS
400 Stanton-Christiana Rd.
Newark, DE 19713
Tel: (302)454-3900
Admissions: (302)571-5366
Fax: (302)577-2548
Web Site: http://www.dtcc.edu/
President/CEO: Lawrence H. Miller
Registrar: Evelyn M. Barnes
Admissions: Rebecca Bailey
Financial Aid: Larry DiGregorio
Type: Two-Year College **Sex:** Coed **Affiliation:** Delaware Technical and Community College System **% Accepted:** 74 **Admission Plans:** Open Admission; Preferred Admission; Early Admission **Application Deadline:** Rolling **Application Fee:** $10.00 **H.S. Requirements:** High school diploma or equivalent not required **Costs Per Year:** Application fee: $10. State resident tuition: $1956 full-time, $81.50 per credit hour part-time. Nonresident tuition: $4890 full-time, $203.75 per credit hour part-time. Mandatory fees: $204 full-time, $6 per credit hour part-time, $21 per term part-time. **Scholarships:** Available **Calendar System:** Semester, Summer Session Available **Enrollment:** FT 2,767, PT 4,706 **Faculty:** FT 162, PT 363 **Student-Faculty Ratio:** 15:1 **Library Holdings:** 60,066 **Regional Accreditation:** Middle State Association of Colleges and Schools **Credit Hours For Degree:** 70 credits, Associates **Professional Accreditation:**

ABET, AAMAE, ADA, AOTA, APTA, ACBSP, CARC, JRCEDMS, JRCERT, JRCNMT, NAACLS, NLN **Intercollegiate Athletics:** Basketball M; Soccer M; Softball W; Tennis M & W; Volleyball M & W

DELAWARE TECHNICAL & COMMUNITY COLLEGE, TERRY CAMPUS

100 Campus Dr.
Dover, DE 19904-1383
Tel: (302)857-1000
Admissions: (302)857-1020
Fax: (302)857-1296
E-mail: mharris@outland.dtcc.edu
Web Site: http://www.dtcc.edu/terry/
President/CEO: Dr. Marguerite M. Johnson
Registrar: Nauleen Perry
Admissions: Maria Harris
Financial Aid: Jennifer Grunden

Type: Two-Year College **Sex:** Coed **Affiliation:** Delaware Technical and Community College System **% Accepted:** 80 **Admission Plans:** Open Admission; Preferred Admission; Early Admission **Application Deadline:** Rolling **Application Fee:** $10.00 **H.S. Requirements:** High school diploma or equivalent not required. For nursing program: High school diploma required; GED not accepted **Costs Per Year:** Application fee: $10. State resident tuition: $1956 full-time, $81.50 per credit hour part-time. Nonresident tuition: $4890 full-time, $203.75 per credit hour part-time. Mandatory fees: $204 full-time, $6 per credit hour part-time, $21 per term part-time. **Scholarships:** Available **Calendar System:** Semester, Summer Session Available **Enrollment:** FT 875, PT 1,694 **Faculty:** FT 64, PT 120 **Student-Faculty Ratio:** 14:1 **Library Holdings:** 9,663 **Regional Accreditation:** Middle State Association of Colleges and Schools **Credit Hours For Degree:** 70 credits, Associates **Professional Accreditation:** ACBSP, JRCEMT, NLN

GOLDEY-BEACOM COLLEGE

4701 Limestone Rd.
Wilmington, DE 19808-1999
Tel: (302)998-8814
Free: 800-833-4877
Fax: (302)996-5408
Web Site: http://goldey.gbc.edu/
President/CEO: Dr. Mohammad Ilyas
Registrar: Jane H. Lysle
Admissions: Stacey Schwartz
Financial Aid: Jane H. Lysle

Type: Comprehensive **Sex:** Coed **Scores:** 86% SAT V 400+; 75% SAT M 400+ **Admission Plans:** Early Admission; Deferred Admission **Application Fee:** $30.00 **H.S. Requirements:** High school diploma required; GED accepted **Costs Per Year:** Application fee: $30. Tuition: $13,430 full-time. Mandatory fees: $306 full-time. College room only: $4240. **Scholarships:** Available **Calendar System:** Semester, Summer Session Available **Enrollment:** FT 1,028, PT 21, Grad 275 **Faculty:** FT 25, PT 24 **Student-Faculty Ratio:** 28:1 **Exams:** Other, SAT I **% Receiving Financial Aid:** 49 **% Residing in College-Owned, -Operated, or -Affiliated Housing:** 16 **Library Holdings:** 29,700 **Regional Accreditation:** Middle State Association of Colleges and Schools **Credit Hours For Degree:** 66 credits, Associates; 133 credits, Bachelors **Professional Accreditation:** ACBSP **Intercollegiate Athletics:** Basketball M & W; Field Hockey W; Soccer M & W; Softball W; Tennis M & W; Volleyball W

UNIVERSITY OF DELAWARE

Newark, DE 19716
Tel: (302)831-2000
Admissions: (302)831-8123
Fax: (302)831-6905
E-mail: admissions@udel.edu
Web Site: http://www.udel.edu/
President/CEO: Dr. David P. Roselle
Registrar: Joseph V. DiMartile
Admissions: Lou Hirsh
Financial Aid: Johnie A. Burton

Type: University **Sex:** Coed **Scores:** 99% SAT V 400+; 99% SAT M 400+; 23% ACT 18-23; 59% ACT 24-29 **% Accepted:** 47 **Admission Plans:** Preferred Admission; Early Decision Plan; Deferred Admission **Application Deadline:** January 15 **Application Fee:** $60.00 **H.S. Requirements:** High school diploma required; GED accepted **Costs Per Year:** Application fee: $60. State resident tuition: $6614 full-time, $276 per credit part-time. Nonresident tuition: $16,770 full-time, $699 per credit part-time. Mandatory fees: $704 full-time, $25 per term part-time. College room and board: $6824. College room only: $3924. Room and board charges vary according to housing facility. **Scholarships:** Available **Calendar System:** 4-1-4, Summer Session Available **Enrollment:** FT 14,899, PT 2,040, Grad 3,434 **Faculty:** FT 1,126, PT 244 **Student-Faculty Ratio:** 13:1 **Exams:** SAT I or ACT, SAT II **% Receiving Financial Aid:** 38 **% Residing in College-Owned, -Operated, or -Affiliated Housing:** 45 **Library Holdings:** 2,623,554 **Regional Accreditation:** Middle State Association of Colleges and Schools **Credit Hours For Degree:** 60 credit hours, Associates; 120 credit hours, Bachelors **ROTC:** Army, Air Force **Professional Accreditation:** AACSB, ABET, ADtA, APTA, APA, JRCEPAT, NAACLS, NASM, NASPAA, NCATE, NLN **Intercollegiate Athletics:** Baseball M; Basketball M & W; Bowling M & W; Cheerleading M & W; Crew M & W; Cross-Country Running M & W; Equestrian Sports M & W; Field Hockey W; Football M; Golf M; Ice Hockey M; Lacrosse M & W; Rugby W; Sailing M & W; Soccer M & W; Softball W; Swimming and Diving M & W; Tennis M & W; Track and Field M & W; Volleyball W; Wrestling M

WESLEY COLLEGE

120 North State St.
Dover, DE 19901-3875
Tel: (302)736-2300
Free: 800-937-5398
Admissions: (302)736-2400
Fax: (302)736-2301
E-mail: admissions@wesley.edu
Web Site: http://www.wesley.edu/
President/CEO: Dr. Scott D. Miller
Registrar: Peter Medwick
Admissions: Arthur Jacobs
Financial Aid: James Marks

Type: Comprehensive **Sex:** Coed **Affiliation:** United Methodist **Scores:** 96% SAT V 400+; 95% SAT M 400+ **% Accepted:** 60 **Admission Plans:** Early Admission; Early Decision Plan; Deferred Admission **Application Deadline:** Rolling **Application Fee:** $25.00 **H.S. Requirements:** High school diploma required; GED accepted **Costs Per Year:** Application fee: $25. Comprehensive fee: $21,560 includes full-time tuition ($14,600) and college room and board ($6960). Full-time tuition varies according to class time. Room and board charges vary according to board plan and housing facility. **Scholarships:** Available **Calendar System:** Semester, Summer Session Available **Enrollment:** FT 1,745, PT 371, Grad 166 **Faculty:** FT 63, PT 74 **Student-Faculty Ratio:** 20:1 **% Receiving Financial Aid:** 88 **% Residing in College-Owned, -Operated, or -Affiliated Housing:** 65 **Library Holdings:** 102,528 **Regional Accreditation:** Middle State Association of Colleges and Schools **Credit Hours For Degree:** 64 credit hours, Associates; 124 credit hours, Bachelors **ROTC:** Army **Professional Accreditation:** NCATE, NLN **Intercollegiate Athletics:** Baseball M; Basketball M & W; Field Hockey W; Football M; Golf M & W; Lacrosse M & W; Soccer M & W; Softball W; Tennis M & W

WILMINGTON COLLEGE

320 North DuPont Hwy.
New Castle, DE 19720-6491
Tel: (302)328-9401; 877-967-5464
Admissions: (302)328-9407
Fax: (302)328-5902
Web Site: http://www.wilmcoll.edu/
President/CEO: Dr. Audrey K. Doberstein
Registrar: Erin DiMarco
Admissions: Christopher Ferguson
Financial Aid: Lynn Iocono

Type: Comprehensive **Sex:** Coed **% Accepted:** 100 **Admission Plans:** Open Admission; Early Admission; Deferred Admission **Application Deadline:** Rolling **Application Fee:** $25.00 **H.S. Requirements:** High school diploma required; GED accepted **Costs Per Year:** Application fee: $25. Tuition: $7620 full-time, $254 per credit part-time. Mandatory fees: $50 full-time, $25 per term part-time. Full-time tuition and fees vary according to course load, degree level, and location. Part-time tuition and fees vary according to course load, degree level, and location. **Scholarships:** Available **Calendar System:** Semester, Summer Session Available **Enrollment:** FT 2,148, PT 2,422, Grad 2,941 **Faculty:** FT 90, PT 552 **Student-Faculty Ratio:** 17:1 **% Receiving Financial Aid:** 40 **Library Holdings:** 98,713 **Regional Accreditation:** Middle State Association of Colleges and Schools

Credit Hours For Degree: 60 credit hours, Associates; 120 credit hours, Bachelors **ROTC:** Army, Air Force **Professional Accreditation:** AACN, ACA, NLN **Intercollegiate Athletics:** Baseball M; Basketball M & W; Cross-Country Running M & W; Softball W; Volleyball W

AMERICAN UNIVERSITY
4400 Massachusetts Ave., NW
Washington, DC 20016-8001
Tel: (202)885-1000
Admissions: (202)885-6000
Fax: (202)885-6014
E-mail: afa@american.edu
Web Site: http://www.american.edu/
President/CEO: Dr. Benjamin Ladner
Registrar: Linda Bolden-Pitcher
Admissions: Dr. Sharon Alston
Financial Aid: Brian Lee-Sang
Type: University **Sex:** Coed **Affiliation:** Methodist **Scores:** 100% SAT V 400+; 100% SAT M 400+; 8.9% ACT 18-23; 62% ACT 24-29 **% Accepted:** 51 **Admission Plans:** Early Decision Plan; Deferred Admission **Application Deadline:** January 15 **Application Fee:** $45.00 **H.S. Requirements:** High school diploma required; GED accepted **Costs Per Year:** Application fee: $45. Comprehensive fee: $41,043 includes full-time tuition ($29,205), mandatory fees ($496), and college room and board ($11,342). College room only: $7197. Part-time tuition: $973 per semester hour. Part-time mandatory fees: $159 per year. **Scholarships:** Available **Calendar System:** Semester, Summer Session Available **Enrollment:** FT 5,624, PT 297, Grad 3,693 **Faculty:** FT 513, PT 428 **Student-Faculty Ratio:** 15:1 **Exams:** SAT I or ACT, SAT II **% Receiving Financial Aid:** 47 **% Residing in College-Owned, -Operated, or -Affiliated Housing:** 68 **Library Holdings:** 796,000 **Regional Accreditation:** Middle State Association of Colleges and Schools **Credit Hours For Degree:** 60 semester hours, Associates; 120 semester hours, Bachelors **ROTC:** Army, Air Force **Professional Accreditation:** AACSB, ACEJMC, ABA, APA, AALS, NASM, NASPAA, NCATE **Intercollegiate Athletics:** Basketball M & W; Cross-Country Running M & W; Field Hockey W; Golf M; Lacrosse W; Soccer M & W; Swimming and Diving M & W; Tennis M & W; Track and Field M & W; Volleyball W; Wrestling M

THE CATHOLIC UNIVERSITY OF AMERICA
Cardinal Station
Washington, DC 20064
Tel: (202)319-5000
Free: 800-673-2772
Admissions: (202)319-5305
Fax: (202)319-6533
E-mail: cua-admissions@cua.edu
Web Site: http://www.cua.edu/
President/CEO: Very Rev. David M. O'Connell, CM,JCD
Registrar: Mary Ellen Flaherty, JD
Admissions: Christine Mica
Financial Aid: Doris Torosian, BA
Type: University **Sex:** Coed **Affiliation:** Roman Catholic Church **Scores:** 99% SAT V 400+; 99% SAT M 400+; 38% ACT 18-23; 51% ACT 24-29 **% Accepted:** 81 **Admission Plans:** Early Admission; Early Decision Plan; Deferred Admission **Application Deadline:** February 01 **Application Fee:** $55.00 **H.S. Requirements:** High school diploma required; GED accepted **Costs Per Year:** Application fee: $55. One-time mandatory fee: $365. Comprehensive fee: $35,838 includes full-time tuition ($24,800), mandatory fees ($1200), and college room and board ($9838). College room only: $5646. Full-time tuition and fees vary according to program. Room and board charges vary according to board plan and housing facility. Part-time tuition: $940 per credit. Part-time mandatory fees: $605 per year. Part-time tuition and fees vary according to course load. **Scholarships:** Available **Calendar System:** Semester, Summer Session Available **Enrollment:** FT 2,802, PT 251, Grad 2,070 **Faculty:** FT 344, PT 370 **Student-Faculty Ratio:** 9:1 **Exams:** SAT I or ACT, SAT II **% Receiving Financial Aid:** 52 **% Residing in College-Owned, -Operated, or -Affiliated Housing:** 66 **Library Holdings:** 1,580,282 **Regional Accreditation:** Middle State Association of Colleges and Schools **Credit Hours For Degree:** 120 credits, Bachelors **ROTC:** Army, Navy, Air Force **Professional Accreditation:** ABET, ABA, ALA, APA, AALS, ATS, CSWE, NASM, NCATE, NLN **Intercollegiate Athletics:** Baseball M; Basketball M & W; Cross-Country Running M & W; Field Hockey W; Football M; Lacrosse M & W; Soccer M & W; Softball W; Swimming and Diving M & W; Tennis M & W; Track and Field M & W; Volleyball W

CORCORAN COLLEGE OF ART AND DESIGN
500 17th St. NW
Washington, DC 20006-4804
Tel: (202)639-1800; 888-CORCORAN
Admissions: (202)639-1814
E-mail: admissions@corcoran.org
Web Site: http://www.corcoran.edu/
President/CEO: Christina DePaul
Registrar: Glenn Parker
Admissions: Anne E. Boerner
Financial Aid: Diane Morris
Type: Comprehensive **Sex:** Coed **Scores:** 94% SAT V 400+; 96% SAT M 400+; 50% ACT 18-23; 13% ACT 24-29 **% Accepted:** 61 **Admission Plans:** Early Admission; Deferred Admission **Application Deadline:** Rolling **Application Fee:** $40.00 **H.S. Requirements:** High school diploma required; GED accepted **Costs Per Year:** Application fee: $40. Comprehensive fee: $32,850 includes full-time tuition ($22,700), mandatory fees ($100), and college room and board ($10,050). College room only: $8150. Full-time tuition and fees vary according to degree level. Part-time tuition: $630 per credit. Part-time mandatory fees: $100. Part-time tuition and fees vary according to degree level. **Scholarships:** Available **Calendar System:** Semester, Summer Session Available **Enrollment:** FT 348, PT 172, Grad 70 **Faculty:** FT 34, PT 187 **Student-Faculty Ratio:** 4:1 **Exams:** SAT I or ACT **% Receiving Financial Aid:** 77 **% Residing in College-Owned, -Operated, or -Affiliated Housing:** 17 **Library Holdings:** 29,413 **Regional Accreditation:** Middle State Association of Colleges and Schools **Credit Hours For Degree:** 66 credits, Associates; 126 credits, Bachelors **Professional Accreditation:** NASAD

GALLAUDET UNIVERSITY
800 Florida Ave., NE
Washington, DC 20002-3625
Tel: (202)651-5000
Free: 800-995-0550
Admissions: (202)651-5750
Fax: (202)651-5774
E-mail: admissions@gallua.gallaudet.edu
Web Site: http://www.gallaudet.edu/
President/CEO: Dr. I. King Jordan
Registrar: Nancy Carroll
Admissions: Charity Reedy-Hines

Financial Aid: Nancy Goodman
Type: University **Sex:** Coed **Admission Plans:** Early Admission; Deferred Admission **Application Fee:** $50.00 **H.S. Requirements:** High school diploma required; GED accepted **Costs Per Year:** Application fee: $50. Comprehensive fee: $18,750 includes full-time tuition ($9920), mandatory fees ($330), and college room and board ($8500). College room only: $4850. Room and board charges vary according to board plan. Part-time tuition: $481.50 per credit. **Scholarships:** Available **Calendar System:** Semester, Summer Session Available **Enrollment:** FT 1,098, PT 109, Grad 627 **Faculty:** FT 230, PT 0 **Student-Faculty Ratio:** 7:1 **Exams:** SAT I or ACT **% Receiving Financial Aid:** 67 **% Residing in College-Owned, -Operated, or -Affiliated Housing:** 70 **Library Holdings:** 242,543 **Regional Accreditation:** Middle State Association of Colleges and Schools **Credit Hours For Degree:** 124 credit hours, Bachelors **Professional Accreditation:** ACA, APA, ASLHA, ACBSP, CSWE, NCATE, NRPA **Intercollegiate Athletics:** Baseball M; Basketball M & W; Cross-Country Running M & W; Football M; Soccer M & W; Softball W; Swimming and Diving M & W; Tennis M; Track and Field M & W; Volleyball W; Wrestling M

THE GEORGE WASHINGTON UNIVERSITY
2121 Eye St., NW
Washington, DC 20052
Tel: (202)994-1000
Free: 800-447-3765
Admissions: (202)994-6040
E-mail: gwadm@gwis2.circ.gwu.edu
Web Site: http://www.gwu.edu/
President/CEO: Stephen J. Trachtenberg
Registrar: Dennis L. Geyer
Admissions: Dr. Kathryn M. Napper
Financial Aid: Geri Rypkema
Type: University **Sex:** Coed **Scores:** 100% SAT V 400+; 100% SAT M 400+; 11% ACT 18-23; 65% ACT 24-29 **% Accepted:** 37 **Admission Plans:** Early Admission; Early Decision Plan; Deferred Admission **Application Deadline:** January 15 **Application Fee:** $70.00 **H.S. Requirements:** High school diploma required; GED not accepted **Costs Per Year:** Application fee: $70. Comprehensive fee: $48,820 includes full-time tuition ($37,790), mandatory fees ($30), and college room and board ($11,000). College room only: $8000. Part-time tuition: $1050 per credit hour. **Scholarships:** Available **Calendar System:** Semester, Summer Session Available **Enrollment:** FT 9,741, PT 1,020, Grad 11,022 **Faculty:** FT 826, PT 1,210 **Student-Faculty Ratio:** 14:1 **Exams:** SAT I or ACT, SAT I and SAT II **% Receiving Financial Aid:** 39 **% Residing in College-Owned, -Operated, or -Affiliated Housing:** 62 **Library Holdings:** 1,984,094 **Regional Accreditation:** Middle State Association of Colleges and Schools **Credit Hours For Degree:** 60 semester hours, Associates; 120 semester hours, Bachelors **ROTC:** Army, Navy, Air Force **Professional Accreditation:** AACSB, ABET, ACEHSA, AABB, ABA, ACA, APTA, APA, ASLHA, AALS, CEPH, CORE, FIDER, JRCEDMS, JRCEPAT, LCMEAMA, NAACLS, NASM, NASPAA, NCATE **Intercollegiate Athletics:** Baseball M; Basketball M & W; Crew M & W; Cross-Country Running M & W; Golf M; Gymnastics W; Soccer M & W; Swimming and Diving M & W; Tennis M & W; Volleyball W; Water Polo M

GEORGETOWN UNIVERSITY
37th and O Sts., NW
Washington, DC 20057
Tel: (202)687-5055
Admissions: (202)687-3600
Fax: (202)687-6660
Web Site: http://www.georgetown.edu/
President/CEO: Dr. John J. "Jack" DeGioia
Registrar: John Q. Pierce, IV
Admissions: Charles A. Deacon
Financial Aid: Patricia A. McWade
Type: University **Sex:** Coed **Affiliation:** Roman Catholic (Jesuit) **Scores:** 100% SAT V 400+; 100% SAT M 400+; 11.4% ACT 18-23; 30.5% ACT 24-29 **% Accepted:** 21 **Admission Plans:** Early Action; Deferred Admission **Application Deadline:** January 10 **Application Fee:** $60.00 **H.S. Requirements:** High school diploma required; GED accepted **Costs Per Year:** Application fee: $60. Comprehensive fee: $43,183 includes full-time tuition ($31,656), mandatory fees ($368), and college room and board ($11,159). College room only: $7410. Room and board charges vary according to board plan and housing facility. Part-time tuition: $1319 per credit hour. Part-time tuition varies according to course level. **Scholarships:** Available **Calendar System:** Semester, Summer Session Available **Enrollment:** FT 6,504, PT 215, Grad 4,193 **Faculty:** FT 752, PT 506 **Student-Faculty Ratio:** 11:1 **Exams:** SAT I or ACT, SAT II **% Receiving Financial Aid:** 42 **% Residing in College-Owned, -Operated, or -Affiliated Housing:** 78 **Library Holdings:** 2,405,461 **Regional Accreditation:** Middle State Association of Colleges and Schools **Credit Hours For Degree:** 120 credit hours, Bachelors **ROTC:** Army, Navy, Air Force **Professional Accreditation:** AACSB, AACN, AANA, ABA, ACNM, ACIPE, AALS, LCMEAMA, NLN **Intercollegiate Athletics:** Baseball M; Basketball M & W; Crew M & W; Cross-Country Running M & W; Field Hockey W; Football M; Golf M; Ice Hockey M; Lacrosse M & W; Rugby M & W; Sailing M & W; Soccer M & W; Softball W; Swimming and Diving M & W; Tennis M & W; Track and Field M & W; Ultimate Frisbee M & W; Volleyball M & W; Water Polo M

HOWARD UNIVERSITY
2400 Sixth St., NW
Washington, DC 20059-0002
Tel: (202)806-6100
Free: 800-HOWARD-U
Web Site: http://www.howard.edu/
President/CEO: H. Patrick Swygert, Esq
Financial Aid: Linda Sanders-Hawkins
Type: University **Sex:** Coed **Scores:** 99% SAT V 400+; 99% SAT M 400+; 61% ACT 18-23; 31% ACT 24-29 **Admission Plans:** Early Admission; Early Action; Deferred Admission **Application Fee:** $45.00 **H.S. Requirements:** High school diploma required; GED accepted **Costs Per Year:** Application fee: $45. Comprehensive fee: $18,481 includes full-time tuition ($11,490), mandatory fees ($805), and college room and board ($6186). College room only: $3736. Room and board charges vary according to board plan and housing facility. Part-time tuition: $479 per credit hour. **Scholarships:** Available **Calendar System:** Semester, Summer Session Available **Enrollment:** FT 6,730, PT 382, Grad 1,766 **Faculty:** FT 1,126, PT 450 **Student-Faculty Ratio:** 8:1 **Exams:** SAT I or ACT **% Receiving Financial Aid:** 63 **% Residing in College-Owned, -Operated, or -Affiliated Housing:** 56 **Library Holdings:** 2,465,162 **Regional Accreditation:** Middle State Association of Colleges and Schools **Credit Hours For Degree:** 127 credit hours, Bachelors **ROTC:** Army, Air Force **Professional Accreditation:** AACSB, ABET, ACEJMC, ABA, ACPhE, ADA, ADtA, AOTA, APTA, APA, ASLHA, ACIPE, AALS, ATS, CSWE, JRCERT, LCMEAMA, NASAD, NASM, NASPAA NAST, NCATE, NLN **Intercollegiate Athletics:** Baseball M & W; Basketball M & W; Bowling W; Cross-Country Running M & W; Football M; Lacrosse W; Soccer M; Swimming and Diving M & W; Tennis M & W; Track and Field M & W; Volleyball W

POTOMAC COLLEGE
4000 Chesapeake St., NW
Washington, DC 20016
Tel: (202)686-0876; 888-686-0876
Admissions: (202)274-2305
Fax: (202)686-0818
E-mail: cparker@potomac.edu
Web Site: http://www.potomac.edu/
President/CEO: Florence S. Tate
Registrar: Greta Bonaparte
Admissions: Ron Parker
Type: Four-Year College **Sex:** Coed **% Accepted:** 76 **Admission Plans:** Open Admission **Application Deadline:** Rolling **Application Fee:** $15.00 **H.S. Requirements:** High school diploma required; GED accepted **Costs Per Year:** Application fee: $15. Tuition: $17,220 full-time. Mandatory fees: $90 full-time. Full-time tuition and fees vary according to course load and program. **Scholarships:** Available **Calendar System:** Miscellaneous, Summer Session Available **Enrollment:** FT 87, PT 311 **Faculty:** FT 14, PT 33 **Student-Faculty Ratio:** 15:1 **Library Holdings:** 5,565 **Regional Accreditation:** Middle State Association of Colleges and Schools **Credit Hours For Degree:** 123 semester credits, Bachelors **Professional Accreditation:** ACICS

SOUTHEASTERN UNIVERSITY
501 I St., SW
Washington, DC 20024-2788
Tel: (202)478-8200
Fax: (202)488-8162
Web Site: http://www.seu.edu/
President/CEO: Dr. Charlene Drew Jarvis
Registrar: Otello Jean

Admissions: Ron Burleson
Financial Aid: Willis Parker
Type: Comprehensive **Sex:** Coed **Admission Plans:** Open Admission; Deferred Admission **Application Fee:** $45.00 **H.S. Requirements:** High school diploma required; GED accepted **Scholarships:** Available **Calendar System:** Miscellaneous, Summer Session Available **Enrollment:** FT 212, PT 453, Grad 270 **Faculty:** FT 15, PT 95 **Student-Faculty Ratio:** 13:1 **Library Holdings:** 32,000 **Regional Accreditation:** Middle State Association of Colleges and Schools **Credit Hours For Degree:** 60 credit hours, Associates; 120 credit hours, Bachelors

STRAYER UNIVERSITY
1025 15th St., NW
Washington, DC 20005-2603
Tel: (202)408-2400; 888-4-STRAYER
Admissions: (202)419-4190
Fax: (202)289-1831
Web Site: http://www.strayer.edu/
President/CEO: Dr. J. Chris Toe
Registrar: Cyndi Wastler
Admissions: Melvin Menns
Financial Aid: Marjorie Arrington
Type: Comprehensive **Sex:** Coed **Affiliation:** Strayer Education, Inc. **Admission Plans:** Open Admission; Early Admission; Deferred Admission **Application Fee:** $70.00 **H.S. Requirements:** High school diploma required; GED accepted **Scholarships:** Available **Calendar System:** Quarter, Summer Session Available **Enrollment:** FT 2,867, PT 13,105, Grad 4,166 **Faculty:** FT 144, PT 737 **Student-Faculty Ratio:** 20:1 **Library Holdings:** 34,000 **Regional Accreditation:** Middle State Association of Colleges and Schools **Credit Hours For Degree:** 90 quarter hours, Associates; 180 quarter hours, Bachelors

TRINITY (WASHINGTON) UNIVERSITY
125 Michigan Ave., NE
Washington, DC 20017-1094
Tel: (202)884-9000
Free: 800-IWA-NTTC
Admissions: 800-492-6882
Fax: (202)884-9229
E-mail: admissions@trinitydc.edu
Web Site: http://www.trinitydc.edu/
President/CEO: Patricia A. McGuire
Registrar: Marueen Fittig
Admissions: Marien Noblitt
Financial Aid: Jessica Findley
Type: Comprehensive **Affiliation:** Roman Catholic **Scores:** 58% SAT V 400+; 49% SAT M 400+; 44% ACT 18-23; 4% ACT 24-29 **Admission Plans:** Early Action; Deferred Admission **Application Fee:** $35.00 **H.S. Requirements:** High school diploma required; GED accepted **Costs Per Year:** Application fee: $35. Comprehensive fee: $24,934 includes full-time tuition ($17,200), mandatory fees ($160), and college room and board ($7574). College room only: $3350. Full-time tuition and fees vary according to class time. Room and board charges vary according to board plan and housing facility. Part-time tuition: $555 per credit hour. Part-time tuition varies according to class time. **Scholarships:** Available **Calendar System:** Semester, Summer Session Available **Enrollment:** FT 549, PT 419, Grad 704 **Faculty:** FT 61, PT 97 **Student-Faculty Ratio:** 11:1 **Exams:** SAT I or ACT **% Receiving Financial Aid:** 87 **% Residing in College-Owned, -Operated, or -Affiliated Housing:** 30 **Library Holdings:** 207,000 **Regional Accreditation:** Middle State Association of Colleges and Schools **Credit Hours For Degree:** 128 credit hours, Bachelors **ROTC:** Army **Professional Accreditation:** NCATE **Intercollegiate Athletics:** Basketball W; Field Hockey W; Lacrosse W; Soccer W; Softball W; Swimming and Diving W; Tennis W; Volleyball W

UNIVERSITY OF THE DISTRICT OF COLUMBIA
4200 Connecticut Ave., NW
Washington, DC 20008-1175
Tel: (202)274-5000
Admissions: (202)274-6110
Web Site: http://www.udc.edu/
President/CEO: Dr. William L. Pollard
Registrar: La Hugh Bankston
Admissions: Laverne Hill-Flannigan
Financial Aid: Alice Dais
Type: Comprehensive **Sex:** Coed **% Accepted:** 82 **Admission Plans:** Open Admission; Preferred Admission; Deferred Admission **Application Deadline:** August 01 **Application Fee:** $20.00 **H.S. Requirements:** High school diploma required; GED accepted **Costs Per Year:** Application fee: $20. Area resident tuition: $1800 full-time, $75 per credit part-time. Nonresident tuition: $4440 full-time, $185 per credit part-time. Mandatory fees: $270 full-time, $135 per term part-time. Part-time tuition and fees vary according to course load. **Scholarships:** Available **Calendar System:** Semester, Summer Session Available **Enrollment:** FT 1,966, PT 3,204, Grad 123 **Faculty:** FT 242, PT 236 **Student-Faculty Ratio:** 13:1 **Exams:** SAT I **% Receiving Financial Aid:** 63 **Library Holdings:** 544,412 **Regional Accreditation:** Middle State Association of Colleges and Schools **Credit Hours For Degree:** 60 semester hours, Associates; 120 semester hours, Bachelors **ROTC:** Army, Air Force **Professional Accreditation:** ABET, ABA, ABFSE, ASLHA, ACBSP, CARC, CSWE, JRCERT, NCATE, NLN **Intercollegiate Athletics:** Golf M; Soccer M; Tennis M & W; Track and Field M & W; Volleyball W

AMERICAN INTERCONTINENTAL UNIVERSITY
2250 North Commerce Parkway, Ste. 100
Weston, FL 33326
Tel: (954)446-6100; (866)248-4723
Fax: (954)835-1020
Web Site: http://www.aiufl.edu/
President/CEO: Vernon Czelusnial, PhD
Registrar: John Kramer
Admissions: Kris George
Financial Aid: Derek Philips
Type: Comprehensive **Sex:** Coed **Affiliation:** Career Education Corporation **Admission Plans:** Open Admission **Application Deadline:** Rolling **Application Fee:** $50.00 **H.S. Requirements:** High school diploma required; GED accepted **Costs Per Year:** Application fee: $50. Tuition: $55,000 full-time, $398 per credit part-time. Mandatory fees: $3500 full-time, $3500 per year part-time. Full-time tuition and fees vary according to course load and program. Part-time tuition and fees vary according to course load and program. **Calendar System:** Miscellaneous **Enrollment:** FT 1,114, PT 91, Grad 113 **Faculty:** FT 38, PT 41 **Student-Faculty Ratio:** 22:1 **Exams:** Other **Library Holdings:** 3,256 **Regional Accreditation:** Southern Association of Colleges and Schools **Credit Hours For Degree:** 100 quarter hours, Associates; 200 quarter hours, Bachelors

ANGLEY COLLEGE
230 N. Woodland Blvd., Ste. 310
Deland, FL 32720
Tel: (386)740-1215
Web Site: http://www.angley.edu **Type:** Two-Year College **Calendar System:** Continuous

ARGOSY UNIVERSITY/SARASOTA
5250 17th St.
Sarasota, FL 34235-8246
Tel: (941)379-0404
Free: 800-331-5995
Fax: (941)379-9464
Web Site: http://www.sarasota.edu/
President/CEO: Dr. Nivine Megahed
Registrar: Jackie Reece
Admissions: Linda Volz
Financial Aid: Deborah Kerris
Type: Two-Year Upper Division **Sex:** Coed **Affiliation:** Education Management Corporation **Application Fee:** $50.00 **H.S. Requirements:** High school diploma required; GED accepted **Scholarships:** Available **Calendar System:** Semester **Enrollment:** FT 14, PT 26 **Faculty:** FT 1, PT 7 **% Receiving Financial Aid:** 55 **Library Holdings:** 10,000 **Regional Accreditation:** North Central Association of Colleges and Schools

ARGOSY UNIVERSITY/TAMPA
4401 North Himes Ave., Ste. 150
Tampa, FL 33614
Tel: (813)246-4419
Free: 800-850-6488
Admissions: (813)393-5260
Fax: (813)246-4045
Web Site: http://www.argosyu.edu/
President/CEO: Dr. Melanie Storms
Registrar: Marcia Kuchelema
Admissions: Jean Graham
Financial Aid: Sharon Brechue
Type: Two-Year Upper Division **Sex:** Coed **Affiliation:** Education Management Corporation **Application Fee:** $50.00 **Scholarships:** Available **Calendar System:** Semester **Enrollment:** FT 26, PT 23, Grad 360 **Faculty:** PT 9 **Student-Faculty Ratio:** 9:1 **% Receiving Financial Aid:** 79 **Regional Accreditation:** North Central Association of Colleges and Schools **Professional Accreditation:** APA

THE ART INSTITUTE OF FORT LAUDERDALE
1799 Southeast 17th St. Causeway
Fort Lauderdale, FL 33316-3000
Tel: (954)527-1799
Free: 800-275-7603
Fax: (954)728-8637
Web Site: http://www.aifl.edu/
President/CEO: William S. Kalaboke
Registrar: Laura Johnston
Admissions: Eileen L. Northrop
Financial Aid: Melissa Ziselman
Type: Four-Year College **Sex:** Coed **Affiliation:** The Art Institutes; Education Management Corporation **Application Fee:** $50.00 **H.S. Requirements:** High school diploma required; GED accepted **Scholarships:** Available **Calendar System:** Quarter, Summer Session Available **Student-Faculty Ratio:** 20:1 **% Residing in College-Owned, -Operated, or -Affiliated Housing:** 13 **Library Holdings:** 19,614 **Credit Hours For Degree:** 96 credits, Associates; 180 credits, Bachelors **Professional Accreditation:** ACICS, ACF

THE ART INSTITUTE OF TAMPA
4401 North Himes Ave., Ste. 150
Tampa, FL 33614
Tel: (866)703-3277; (866)703-3277
Admissions: (813)873-2112
Fax: (813)873-2171
E-mail: johanneg@aii.edu
Web Site: http://www.aita.artinstitutes.edu/
Admissions: Glenn Johannesen
Type: Four-Year College **Sex:** Coed **Affiliation:** Education Management Corporation **% Accepted:** 65 **Application Deadline:** October 11 **Application Fee:** $50.00 **H.S. Requirements:** High school diploma required; GED accepted **Costs Per Year:** Application fee: $50. Tuition: $15,405 full-time. College room only: $3500. **Calendar System:** Quarter, Summer Session Available **Enrollment:** FT 450, PT 40 **Faculty:** FT 9, PT 38 **Student-Faculty Ratio:** 10:1 **Exams:** SAT I and SAT II or ACT **% Residing in College-Owned, -Operated, or -Affiliated Housing:** 18 **Library Holdings:** 2,039 **Credit Hours For Degree:** 112 credits, Associates; 192 credits, Bachelors

ATI CAREER TRAINING CENTER (FORT LAUDERDALE)
2880 NW 62nd St.
Fort Lauderdale, FL 33309-9731
Tel: (954)973-4760
Fax: (954)973-6422
Web Site: http://www.aticareertraining.com/

President/CEO: Connie Bailius
Registrar: Vicki Brady
Admissions: Wendy Hopkins Goffinet
Financial Aid: Terrie Owens
Type: Two-Year College **Sex:** Coed **H.S. Requirements:** High school diploma required; GED accepted **Scholarships:** Available **Calendar System:** Quarter **Professional Accreditation:** ACCSCT

ATI CAREER TRAINING CENTER (MIAMI)
1 NE 19th St.
Miami, FL 33132
Tel: (305)573-1600
Web Site: http://www.aticareertraining.com/
President/CEO: Errol Stephenson
Admissions: Mary Fernandez
Type: Two-Year College **Professional Accreditation:** ACCSCT, CARC

ATI CAREER TRAINING CENTER (OAKLAND PARK)
3501 NW 9th Ave.
Oakland Park, FL 33309-9612
Tel: (954)563-5899
Web Site: http://www.aticareertraining.com/
President/CEO: Cindy Gordon
Financial Aid: Daisy Debs
Type: Two-Year College **Professional Accreditation:** ACCSCT

ATI HEALTH EDUCATION CENTER
1395 NW 167th St., Ste. 200
Miami, FL 33169-5742
Tel: (305)628-1000
E-mail: bwoolsey@atienterprises.edu
Web Site: http://www.aticareertraining.com/
President/CEO: Barbara Woosley
Registrar: Fred Adkins
Admissions: Barbara Woosley
Financial Aid: Aida Diaz
Type: Two-Year College **Sex:** Coed **Affiliation:** ATI Enterprises Inc. of Florida **Application Fee:** $100.00 **H.S. Requirements:** High school diploma required; GED accepted **Scholarships:** Available **Calendar System:** Semester, Summer Session Not available **Faculty:** FT 7, PT 12 **Exams:** Other **Credit Hours For Degree:** 86 semester hours, Associates **Professional Accreditation:** ACCSCT, CARC

AVE MARIA UNIVERSITY
1025 Commons Circle
Naples, FL 34119
Tel: (239)280-2554; 877-AVE-UNIV
Fax: (239)352-2392
E-mail: dan.murphy@avemaria.edu
Web Site: http://www.avemaria.edu/
Admissions: Richard Dittus
Type: Comprehensive **Sex:** Coed **Affiliation:** Roman Catholic **Scores:** 100% SAT V 400+; 99% SAT M 400+; 40% ACT 18-23; 47% ACT 24-29 **Application Fee:** $50.00 **H.S. Requirements:** High school diploma required; GED accepted **Calendar System:** Semester, Summer Session Available **Enrollment:** FT 307, PT 9 **Faculty:** FT 42, PT 2 **Student-Faculty Ratio:** 7:1 **Exams:** ACT **% Residing in College-Owned, -Operated, or -Affiliated Housing:** 98 **Credit Hours For Degree:** 128 credit hours, Bachelors **Professional Accreditation:** AALE

THE BAPTIST COLLEGE OF FLORIDA
5400 College Dr.
Graceville, FL 32440-1898
Tel: (850)263-3261
Free: 800-328-2660
Fax: (850)263-7506
E-mail: cmbishop@baptistcollege.edu
Web Site: http://www.baptistcollege.edu/
President/CEO: Dr. Thomas A. Kinchen
Registrar: Sue Diehl
Admissions: Christopher Bishop
Financial Aid: Angela Rathel
Type: Four-Year College **Sex:** Coed **Affiliation:** Southern Baptist **Scores:** 89% SAT V 400+; 67% SAT M 400+; 68% ACT 18-23 **% Accepted:** 78 **Admission Plans:** Open Admission; Preferred Admission; Early Admission; Deferred Admission **Application Deadline:** Rolling **Application Fee:** $20.00 **H.S. Requirements:** High school diploma required; GED accepted **Costs Per Year:** Application fee: $20. Comprehensive fee: $10,820 includes full-time tuition ($6900), mandatory fees ($350), and college room and board ($3570). Full-time tuition and fees vary according to course load. Room and board charges vary according to board plan and housing facility. Part-time tuition: $230 per semester hour. Part-time mandatory fees: $175 per term. Part-time tuition and fees vary according to course load. **Scholarships:** Available **Calendar System:** Miscellaneous, Summer Session Available **Enrollment:** FT 429, PT 194 **Faculty:** FT 26, PT 43 **Student-Faculty Ratio:** 12:1 **Exams:** ACT **% Receiving Financial Aid:** 84 **% Residing in College-Owned, -Operated, or -Affiliated Housing:** 34 **Library Holdings:** 72,211 **Regional Accreditation:** Southern Association of Colleges and Schools **Credit Hours For Degree:** 66 semester hours, Associates; 130 semester hours, Bachelors **Professional Accreditation:** NASM

BARRY UNIVERSITY
11300 Northeast Second Ave.
Miami Shores, FL 33161-6695
Tel: (305)899-3000
Free: 800-695-2279
Admissions: (305)899-3138
Fax: (305)899-2971
E-mail: admissions@mail.barry.edu
Web Site: http://www.barry.edu/
President/CEO: Sr. Linda Bevilacqua, OP,PhD
Registrar: Debra Weyman
Admissions: Helen L. Corpuz
Financial Aid: Dart Humeston
Type: University **Sex:** Coed **Affiliation:** Roman Catholic **Scores:** 91% SAT V 400+; 90% SAT M 400+; 63% ACT 18-23; 9% ACT 24-29 **Admission Plans:** Early Admission; Deferred Admission **Application Fee:** $30.00 **H.S. Requirements:** High school diploma required; GED accepted **Costs Per Year:** Application fee: $30. Comprehensive fee: $30,050 includes full-time tuition ($22,430) and college room and board ($7620). Room and board charges vary according to board plan. **Scholarships:** Available **Calendar System:** Semester, Summer Session Available **Enrollment:** FT 4,427, PT 1,515, Grad 2,533 **Faculty:** FT 346, PT 564 **Student-Faculty Ratio:** 14:1 **Exams:** SAT I or ACT **% Receiving Financial Aid:** 77 **% Residing in College-Owned, -Operated, or -Affiliated Housing:** 17 **Library Holdings:** 233,938 **Regional Accreditation:** Southern Association of Colleges and Schools **Credit Hours For Degree:** 120 credits, Bachelors **ROTC:** Air Force **Professional Accreditation:** AACSB, ACPE, AACN, AANA, ABA, ACA, AOTA, APMA, ATS, CSWE, JRCEPAT, MACTE **Intercollegiate Athletics:** Baseball M; Basketball M & W; Crew W; Golf M & W; Soccer M & W; Softball W; Tennis M & W; Volleyball W

BEACON COLLEGE
105 East Main St.
Leesburg, FL 34748
Tel: (352)787-7660
Admissions: (352)315-9269
Fax: (352)787-0721
E-mail: cscott@beaconcollege.edu
Web Site: http://www.beaconcollege.edu/
President/CEO: Deborah Brodbeck
Admissions: Carolyn Scott
Type: Four-Year College **Sex:** Coed **% Accepted:** 55 **Admission Plans:** Early Admission; Deferred Admission **Application Fee:** $50.00 **H.S. Requirements:** High school diploma required; GED accepted **Costs Per Year:** Application fee: $50. Comprehensive fee: $31,100 includes full-time tuition ($23,900) and college room and board ($7200). College room only: $4400. **Calendar System:** Semester **Enrollment:** FT 101 **Faculty:** FT 10, PT 7 **Student-Faculty Ratio:** 7:1 **% Residing in College-Owned, -Operated, or -Affiliated Housing:** 99 **Library Holdings:** 56,979 **Regional Accreditation:** Southern Association of Colleges and Schools **Credit Hours For Degree:** 60 credits, Associates; 120 credits, Bachelors

BETHUNE-COOKMAN COLLEGE
640 Dr Mary McLeod Bethune Blvd
Daytona Beach, FL 32114-3099
Tel: (386)481-2000
Free: 800-448-0228
Admissions: (386)481-2600
Fax: (386)481-2010

Web Site: http://www.bethune.cookman.edu/
President/CEO: Dr. Trudie K. Reed
Registrar: Ann Thomas
Admissions: Les Ferrier
Financial Aid: Joseph L. Coleman
Type: Four-Year College **Sex:** Coed **Affiliation:** Methodist **Scores:** 57% SAT V 400+; 55% SAT M 400+; 25% ACT 18-23; 1% ACT 24-29 **% Accepted:** 74 **Admission Plans:** Early Admission; Deferred Admission **Application Deadline:** June 30 **Application Fee:** $25.00 **H.S. Requirements:** High school diploma required; GED accepted **Costs Per Year:** Application fee: $25. Comprehensive fee: $17,922 includes full-time tuition ($11,140), mandatory fees ($90), and college room and board ($6692). Part-time tuition: $464 per credit hour. **Scholarships:** Available **Calendar System:** Semester, Summer Session Available **Enrollment:** FT 2,795, PT 295 **Faculty:** FT 147, PT 56 **Student-Faculty Ratio:** 17:1 **Exams:** SAT I or ACT **% Receiving Financial Aid:** 87 **% Residing in College-Owned, -Operated, or -Affiliated Housing:** 57 **Library Holdings:** 173,193 **Regional Accreditation:** Southern Association of Colleges and Schools **Credit Hours For Degree:** 124 credit hours, Bachelors **ROTC:** Army, Air Force **Professional Accreditation:** NCATE, NLN **Intercollegiate Athletics:** Baseball M; Basketball M & W; Bowling W; Cross-Country Running M & W; Football M; Golf M & W; Softball W; Tennis M & W; Track and Field M & W; Volleyball W

BREVARD COMMUNITY COLLEGE
1519 Clearlake Rd.
Cocoa, FL 32922-6597
Tel: (321)632-1111
Admissions: (321)433-7056
Fax: (321)633-4565
E-mail: cocoaadmissions@brevardcc.edu
Web Site: http://www.brevardcc.edu/
President/CEO: Dr. Thomas E. Gamble
Admissions: Dr. Brenda Fettrow
Financial Aid: Joan Buchanan
Type: Two-Year College **Sex:** Coed **Affiliation:** Florida Community College System **% Accepted:** 100 **Admission Plans:** Open Admission **Application Deadline:** Rolling **Application Fee:** $30.00 **H.S. Requirements:** High school diploma required; GED accepted **Costs Per Year:** Application fee: $30. State resident tuition: $1542 full-time, $64.25 per credit hour part-time. Nonresident tuition: $5664 full-time, $236 per credit hour part-time. **Scholarships:** Available **Calendar System:** Semester, Summer Session Available **Enrollment:** FT 5,129, PT 8,910 **Faculty:** FT 193, PT 849 **Student-Faculty Ratio:** 18:1 **Library Holdings:** 213,873 **Regional Accreditation:** Southern Association of Colleges and Schools **Credit Hours For Degree:** 60 credit hours, Associates **ROTC:** Army, Air Force **Professional Accreditation:** ADA, CARC, JRCERT, JRCEMT, MACTE, NAACLS **Intercollegiate Athletics:** Baseball M; Basketball M & W; Golf M; Softball W; Volleyball W

BROWARD COMMUNITY COLLEGE
225 East Las Olas Blvd.
Fort Lauderdale, FL 33301-2298
Tel: (954)761-7450
Admissions: (954)761-7465
Fax: (954)761-7484
E-mail: bbryan@broward.edu
Web Site: http://www.broward.edu/
President/CEO: Dr. Willis N. Holcombe
Registrar: Barbara Bryan, PhD
Admissions: Barbara Bryan, PhD
Financial Aid: Marcia Conliffe
Type: Two-Year College **Sex:** Coed **Affiliation:** Florida Community College System **Scores:** 73% SAT V 400+; 74% SAT M 400+ **% Accepted:** 100 **Admission Plans:** Open Admission; Preferred Admission; Early Admission; Deferred Admission **Application Fee:** $35.00 **H.S. Requirements:** High school diploma required; GED accepted **Costs Per Year:** Application fee: $35. State resident tuition: $1,574 full-time, $63.05 per credit hour part-time. Nonresident tuition: $6294 full-time, $228.55 per credit hour part-time. Mandatory fees: $318 full-time. **Scholarships:** Available **Calendar System:** Trimester, Summer Session Available **Enrollment:** FT 10,044, PT 21,997 **Faculty:** FT 441, PT 1,120 **Exams:** SAT I and SAT II or ACT **Library Holdings:** 200,000 **Regional Accreditation:** Southern Association of Colleges and Schools **Credit Hours For Degree:** 60 semester hours, Associates **ROTC:** Army **Professional Accreditation:** ADA, AHIMA, APTA, CARC, JRCEDMS, JRCEMT, JRCNMT, NASM, NLN **Intercollegiate Athletics:** Baseball M; Basketball M & W; Soccer W; Softball W; Swimming and Diving M & W; Tennis W; Volleyball W; Wrestling M

BROWN MACKIE COLLEGE-MIAMI
1501 Biscayne Blvd.
Miami, FL 33132
Tel: (305)341-6600; (866)505-0335
Admissions: (305)341-6601
Web Site: http://www.brownmackie.edu/locations.asp?locid=25
Admissions: Julia Denniston
Type: Two-Year College **Sex:** Coed **% Accepted:** 53 **Application Deadline:** Rolling **Application Fee:** $0.00 **Costs Per Year:** Application fee: $0. Comprehensive fee: $19,272 includes full-time tuition ($10,992), mandatory fees ($480), and college room and board ($7800). **Enrollment:** FT 136 **Faculty:** FT 0, PT 9

CARLOS ALBIZU UNIVERSITY, MIAMI CAMPUS
2173 NW 99th Ave.
Miami, FL 33172-2209
Tel: (305)593-1223
Free: 800-672-3246
Fax: (305)592-7930
E-mail: galvarado@albizu.edu
Web Site: http://www.mia.albizu.edu/
President/CEO: Dr. Salvador Santiago Negron
Registrar: Fina Campa
Admissions: Gerardo Alvarado
Financial Aid: Carmen Freire
Type: Comprehensive **Sex:** Coed **Affiliation:** Carlos Albizu University **% Accepted:** 73 **Admission Plans:** Open Admission **Application Deadline:** September 10 **Application Fee:** $25.00 **H.S. Requirements:** High school diploma required; GED accepted **Costs Per Year:** Application fee: $25. Tuition: $10,440 full-time, $290 per credit part-time. Mandatory fees: $669 full-time, $223 per term part-time. **Scholarships:** Available **Calendar System:** Trimester, Summer Session Available **Enrollment:** FT 202, PT 251, Grad 623 **Faculty:** FT 8, PT 42 **Student-Faculty Ratio:** 13:1 **% Receiving Financial Aid:** 94 **Library Holdings:** 26,027 **Regional Accreditation:** Middle State Association of Colleges and Schools **Credit Hours For Degree:** 120 credits, Bachelors **Professional Accreditation:** APA

CENTRAL FLORIDA COLLEGE
1573 West Fairbanks Ave., Ste. 1-A
Winter Park, FL 32789
Tel: (407)843-3984
Fax: (407)843-9828 **Type:** Two-Year College **Sex:** Coed **Professional Accreditation:** ACCSCT

CENTRAL FLORIDA COMMUNITY COLLEGE
PO Box 1388
Ocala, FL 34478-1388
Tel: (352)854-2322
Admissions: (352)237-2111
Fax: (352)237-3747
E-mail: jonesch@cf.edu
Web Site: http://www.cf.edu/
President/CEO: Dr. Charles Dassance
Registrar: Sheryl Graham
Admissions: Christy Jones
Financial Aid: Sheryl Graham
Type: Two-Year College **Sex:** Coed **Affiliation:** Florida Community College System **Admission Plans:** Open Admission; Early Admission **Application Deadline:** Rolling **Application Fee:** $20.00 **H.S. Requirements:** High school diploma required; GED accepted **Costs Per Year:** Application fee: $20. State resident tuition: $1961 full-time, $65.37 per credit hour part-time. Nonresident tuition: $7177 full-time, $239.24 per credit hour part-time. College room and board: $5562. **Scholarships:** Available **Calendar System:** Semester, Summer Session Available **Enrollment:** FT 2,476, PT 3,502 **Faculty:** FT 118, PT 487 **Student-Faculty Ratio:** 13:1 **Library Holdings:** 54,491 **Regional Accreditation:** Southern Association of Colleges and Schools **Credit Hours For Degree:** 60 credit hours, Associates **Professional Accreditation:** APTA, JRCEMT, NLN **Intercollegiate Athletics:** Baseball M; Basketball M & W; Softball W; Tennis W

CENTRAL FLORIDA INSTITUTE
60522 US Hwy. 19 North, Ste. 200
Palm Harbor, FL 34684

Tel: (727)786-4707
Fax: (727)781-9421
Web Site: http://www.cfinstitute.com/
President/CEO: Al McCloy
Admissions: Carol Bruno
Type: Two-Year College **Sex:** Coed **Calendar System:** Continuous **Enrollment:** FT 346 **Faculty:** FT 22, PT 1 **Student-Faculty Ratio:** 7:1 **Professional Accreditation:** ARCEST, ABHES

CHIPOLA COLLEGE
3094 Indian Circle
Marianna, FL 32446-3065
Tel: (850)526-2761
Admissions: (850)718-2209
Fax: (850)718-2388
E-mail: robertsj@chipola.edu
Web Site: http://www.chipola.edu/
President/CEO: Dr. H. Dale O'Daniel
Registrar: Annette Widner
Admissions: Dr. Jayne Roberts
Financial Aid: Sybil Cloud
Type: Two-Year College **Sex:** Coed **Scores:** 76% SAT V 400+; 72% SAT M 400+; 56% ACT 18-23; 22% ACT 24-29 **Admission Plans:** Open Admission; Early Admission **Application Fee:** $0.00 **H.S. Requirements:** High school diploma required; GED accepted **Scholarships:** Available **Calendar System:** Semester, Summer Session Available **Enrollment:** FT 1,030, PT 1,219 **Faculty:** FT 54, PT 15 **Student-Faculty Ratio:** 24:1 **Exams:** SAT I or ACT **Library Holdings:** 37,740 **Regional Accreditation:** Southern Association of Colleges and Schools **Credit Hours For Degree:** 60 semester hours, Associates; 120 semester hours, Bachelors **Intercollegiate Athletics:** Baseball M; Basketball M & W; Softball W

CITY COLLEGE (CASSELBERRY)
853 Semoran Blvd., Ste. 200
Casselberry, FL 32707-5342
Tel: (407)831-8466
Admissions: (407)831-9816
Fax: (407)831-1147
E-mail: yhunter@citycollege.edu
Web Site: http://www.citycollege.edu/
President/CEO: Ron Roundtree
Admissions: Yvonne C. Hunter
Type: Two-Year College **Sex:** Coed **Calendar System:** Semester **Professional Accreditation:** ACICS

CITY COLLEGE (FORT LAUDERDALE)
1401 West Cypress Creek Rd.
Fort Lauderdale, FL 33309
Tel: (954)492-5353
Fax: (954)491-1965
Web Site: http://www.citycollege.edu/
President/CEO: C. M. Fike, II
Registrar: Marjorie Ward
Admissions: Michael Beauregard
Financial Aid: Ginger Ruback
Type: Two-Year College **Sex:** Coed **Scholarships:** Available **Calendar System:** Semester **Faculty:** FT 14, PT 47 **Professional Accreditation:** ACICS

CITY COLLEGE (GAINESVILLE)
2400 Southwest 13th St.
Gainesville, FL 32608
Tel: (352)335-4000
Fax: (352)335-4303
Web Site: http://www.citycollege.edu/
President/CEO: Walter Wilfong
Type: Two-Year College **Sex:** Coed **Calendar System:** Semester **Professional Accreditation:** ACICS

CITY COLLEGE (MIAMI)
9300 South Dadeland Blvd.
Miami, FL 33156
Tel: (305)666-9242
Fax: (305)666-9243
Web Site: http://www.citycollege.edu/
President/CEO: Tom Kretschmer
Type: Two-Year College **Sex:** Coed **Calendar System:** Semester **Professional Accreditation:** ACICS

CLEARWATER CHRISTIAN COLLEGE
3400 Gulf-to-Bay Blvd.
Clearwater, FL 33759-4595
Tel: (727)726-1153
Free: 800-348-4463
Fax: (727)726-8597
Web Site: http://www.clearwater.edu/
President/CEO: Dr. Richard Stratton
Registrar: Dr. Roger Bradley
Admissions: Dr. Keith Hutchison
Financial Aid: Ruth Strum
Type: Four-Year College **Sex:** Coed **Affiliation:** nondenominational **Scores:** 97% SAT V 400+; 89% SAT M 400+; 53% ACT 18-23; 28% ACT 24-29 **% Accepted:** 86 **Admission Plans:** Early Admission; Deferred Admission **Application Deadline:** Rolling **Application Fee:** $35.00 **H.S. Requirements:** High school diploma required; GED accepted **Costs Per Year:** Application fee: $35. Comprehensive fee: $17,830 includes full-time tuition ($11,860), mandatory fees ($640), and college room and board ($5330). Part-time tuition: $460 per hour. **Scholarships:** Available **Calendar System:** Semester, Summer Session Available **Enrollment:** FT 548, PT 34 **Faculty:** FT 36, PT 17 **Student-Faculty Ratio:** 15:1 **Exams:** SAT I or ACT **% Receiving Financial Aid:** 95 **% Residing in College-Owned, -Operated, or -Affiliated Housing:** 70 **Library Holdings:** 106,000 **Regional Accreditation:** Southern Association of Colleges and Schools **Credit Hours For Degree:** 64 credit hours, Associates; 128 credit hours, Bachelors **ROTC:** Army, Air Force **Intercollegiate Athletics:** Baseball M; Basketball M & W; Golf M & W; Soccer M; Softball W; Volleyball W

COLLEGE OF BUSINESS AND TECHNOLOGY
8991 SW 107th Ave., Ste. 200
Miami, FL 33176
Tel: (305)273-4499
Fax: (305)273-5216
E-mail: carlos@cbt.edu
Web Site: http://www.cbt.edu/
Admissions: Carlos Rentas
Type: Two-Year College **Sex:** Coed **% Accepted:** 71 **Admission Plans:** Open Admission **Application Deadline:** June 15 **Application Fee:** $100.00 **H.S. Requirements:** High school diploma required; GED accepted **Costs Per Year:** Application fee: $100. Tuition: $10,500 full-time, $278 per semester hour part-time. Mandatory fees: $200 full-time. College room only: $6000. **Calendar System:** Semester, Summer Session Available **Faculty:** FT 10, PT 5 **Student-Faculty Ratio:** 10:1 **Library Holdings:** 700,000 **Credit Hours For Degree:** 68 credits, Associates **Professional Accreditation:** COE

DAYTONA BEACH COMMUNITY COLLEGE
PO Box 2811
Daytona Beach, FL 32120-2811
Tel: (386)255-8131
Admissions: (386)506-3732
Fax: (386)254-4458
Web Site: http://www.dbcc.edu/
President/CEO: Dr. D. Kent Sharples
Registrar: Kristy Presswood
Admissions: Thomas LoBasso
Financial Aid: Elly Will
Type: Two-Year College **Sex:** Coed **Affiliation:** Florida Community College System **Admission Plans:** Open Admission; Early Admission; Deferred Admission **H.S. Requirements:** High school diploma required; GED accepted **Scholarships:** Available **Calendar System:** Semester, Summer Session Available **Enrollment:** FT 4,776, PT 7,169 **Faculty:** FT 254, PT 521 **Student-Faculty Ratio:** 17:1 **Exams:** Other, SAT I and SAT II or ACT **Library Holdings:** 66,312 **Regional Accreditation:** Southern Association of Colleges and Schools **Credit Hours For Degree:** 60 semester hours, As-

sociates **ROTC:** Army, Air Force **Professional Accreditation:** ADA, AHIMA, AOTA, APTA, CARC, JRCEMT, NLN **Intercollegiate Athletics:** Basketball M; Softball W

DEVRY UNIVERSITY (MIAMI)
200 South Biscayne Blvd., Ste. 500
Miami, FL 33131-5351
Tel: (786)425-1113
Fax: (786)425-1136
Web Site: http://www.devry.edu/ **Type:** Comprehensive **Sex:** Coed **Costs Per Year:** One-time mandatory fee: $40. Tuition: $12,450 full-time. Mandatory fees: $60 full-time. **Calendar System:** Semester **Regional Accreditation:** North Central Association of Colleges and Schools

DEVRY UNIVERSITY (MIRAMAR)
2300 Southwest 145th Ave.
Miramar, FL 33027-4150
Tel: (954)499-9700; (866)338-7934
Web Site: http://www.devry.edu/
President/CEO: Julio Torres
Registrar: Mitch Hecht
Type: Comprehensive **Sex:** Coed **Affiliation:** DeVry University **Application Deadline:** Rolling **Application Fee:** $50.00 **H.S. Requirements:** High school diploma required; GED accepted **Costs Per Year:** Application fee: $50. One-time mandatory fee: $40. Tuition: $12,450 full-time, $460 per credit part-time. Mandatory fees: $270 full-time, $160 per year part-time. Full-time tuition and fees vary according to course load. Part-time tuition and fees vary according to course load. **Scholarships:** Available **Calendar System:** Semester **Enrollment:** FT 647, PT 322, Grad 99 **Faculty:** FT 34, PT 22 **Student-Faculty Ratio:** 20:1 **% Receiving Financial Aid:** 69 **Library Holdings:** 1,700 **Regional Accreditation:** North Central Association of Colleges and Schools **Credit Hours For Degree:** 66 credit hours, Associates; 122 credit hours, Bachelors

DEVRY UNIVERSITY (ORLANDO)
4000 Millenia Blvd.
Orlando, FL 32839
Tel: (407)370-3131; (866)338-7934
Web Site: http://www.devry.edu/
President/CEO: Steve Brown
Registrar: Sheila Dial
Financial Aid: Estrella Velazquez-Domenech
Type: Comprehensive **Sex:** Coed **Affiliation:** DeVry University **Admission Plans:** Deferred Admission **Application Deadline:** Rolling **Application Fee:** $50.00 **H.S. Requirements:** High school diploma required; GED accepted **Costs Per Year:** Application fee: $50. One-time mandatory fee: $40. Tuition: $12,450 full-time. Mandatory fees: $270 full-time. Full-time tuition and fees vary according to course load. **Scholarships:** Available **Calendar System:** Semester, Summer Session Available **Enrollment:** FT 703, PT 345, Grad 133 **Faculty:** FT 37, PT 54 **Student-Faculty Ratio:** 16:1 **% Receiving Financial Aid:** 79 **Library Holdings:** 11,000 **Regional Accreditation:** North Central Association of Colleges and Schools **Credit Hours For Degree:** 67 credit hours, Associates; 122 credit hours, Bachelors

DEVRY UNIVERSITY (TAMPA)
3030 North Rocky Point Dr. West, Ste. 100
Tampa, FL 33607-5901
Tel: (813)288-8994
Fax: (813)288-8980
Web Site: http://www.devry.edu/ **Type:** Comprehensive **Sex:** Coed **Costs Per Year:** One-time mandatory fee: $40. Tuition: $12,450 full-time. Mandatory fees: $60 full-time. **Calendar System:** Semester **Regional Accreditation:** North Central Association of Colleges and Schools

ECKERD COLLEGE
4200 54th Ave. South
St. Petersburg, FL 33711
Tel: (727)867-1166
Free: 800-456-9009
Admissions: (727)864-8331
Fax: (727)866-2304
E-mail: admissions@eckerd.edu
Web Site: http://www.eckerd.edu/
President/CEO: Dr. Donald R. Eastman III
Registrar: Linda Swindall
Admissions: Laura Martin
Financial Aid: Laura Schlack
Type: Four-Year College **Sex:** Coed **Affiliation:** Presbyterian **Scores:** 99% SAT V 400+; 99% SAT M 400+; 36% ACT 18-23; 54% ACT 24-29 **% Accepted:** 72 **Admission Plans:** Early Admission; Deferred Admission **Application Deadline:** Rolling **Application Fee:** $35.00 **H.S. Requirements:** High school diploma required; GED accepted **Costs Per Year:** Application fee: $35. Comprehensive fee: $35,486 includes full-time tuition ($27,352), mandatory fees ($266), and college room and board ($7868). College room only: $4072. Part-time tuition: $3300 per course. **Scholarships:** Available **Calendar System:** 4-1-4, Summer Session Available **Enrollment:** FT 1,755, PT 24 **Faculty:** FT 107, PT 53 **Student-Faculty Ratio:** 13:1 **Exams:** SAT I or ACT, SAT II **% Receiving Financial Aid:** 56 **% Residing in College-Owned, -Operated, or -Affiliated Housing:** 79 **Library Holdings:** 165,085 **Regional Accreditation:** Southern Association of Colleges and Schools **Credit Hours For Degree:** 36 courses, Bachelors **ROTC:** Army, Air Force **Intercollegiate Athletics:** Baseball M; Basketball M & W; Cross-Country Running W; Golf M; Sailing M & W; Soccer M & W; Softball W; Swimming and Diving M & W; Tennis M & W; Volleyball M & W

EDISON COLLEGE
PO Box 60210
Fort Myers, FL 33906-6210
Tel: (239)489-9300
Free: 800-749-2ECC
Admissions: (941)489-9349
Fax: (239)489-9399
E-mail: llugo@edison.edu
Web Site: http://www.edison.edu/
President/CEO: Dr. Kenneth Walker
Registrar: Lester Lugo
Admissions: Lester Lugo
Financial Aid: Lucinda Lewis
Type: Two-Year College **Sex:** Coed **Affiliation:** Florida Community College System **Admission Plans:** Open Admission; Early Admission; Deferred Admission **Application Fee:** $20.00 **H.S. Requirements:** High school diploma required; GED accepted **Scholarships:** Available **Calendar System:** Semester, Summer Session Available **Faculty:** FT 92, PT 325 **Exams:** Other **Library Holdings:** 181,085 **Regional Accreditation:** Southern Association of Colleges and Schools **Credit Hours For Degree:** 60 credits, Associates **Professional Accreditation:** ADA, CARC, JRCECT, JRCERT, JRCEMT, NLN

EDWARD WATERS COLLEGE
1658 Kings Rd.
Jacksonville, FL 32209-6199
Tel: (904)470-8000; 888-898-3191
Admissions: (904)366-2715
Fax: (904)470-8039
Web Site: http://www.ewc.edu/
President/CEO: Dr. Jimmy R. Jenkins, Sr.
Registrar: Dr. Deborah Jones
Admissions: Sadie Milliner-Smith
Financial Aid: Jacquelyn Heggs
Type: Four-Year College **Sex:** Coed **Affiliation:** African Methodist Episcopal **Admission Plans:** Open Admission **Application Fee:** $25.00 **H.S. Requirements:** High school diploma required; GED accepted **Scholarships:** Available **Calendar System:** Semester, Summer Session Available **Enrollment:** FT 1,284, PT 36 **Faculty:** FT 33, PT 16 **Exams:** Other, SAT I or ACT **% Receiving Financial Aid:** 91 **Library Holdings:** 120,000 **Regional Accreditation:** Southern Association of Colleges and Schools **Credit Hours For Degree:** 120 semester hours, Bachelors **ROTC:** Army **Intercollegiate Athletics:** Basketball M & W; Tennis M & W; Track and Field M & W

EMBRY-RIDDLE AERONAUTICAL UNIVERSITY
600 South Clyde Morris Blvd.
Daytona Beach, FL 32114-3900
Tel: (386)226-6000
Free: 800-862-2416
Admissions: (386)226-6100
Fax: (386)226-7070
E-mail: dbadmit@erau.edu

Web Site: http://www.embryriddle.edu/
President/CEO: Dr. George H. Ebbs
Registrar: Val Kruse
Admissions: Richard Clarke
Financial Aid: Maria Shaulis
Type: Comprehensive **Sex:** Coed **Scores:** 96% SAT V 400+; 98% SAT M 400+; 45% ACT 18-23; 43% ACT 24-29 **% Accepted:** 84 **Admission Plans:** Early Admission; Early Decision Plan; Deferred Admission **Application Deadline:** Rolling **Application Fee:** $50.00 **H.S. Requirements:** High school diploma required; GED accepted **Costs Per Year:** Application fee: $50. Comprehensive fee: $30,436 includes full-time tuition ($22,820), mandatory fees ($680), and college room and board ($6936). College room only: $2800. Part-time tuition: $855 per credit hour. **Scholarships:** Available **Calendar System:** Semester, Summer Session Available **Enrollment:** FT 4,093, PT 289, Grad 394 **Faculty:** FT 227, PT 87 **Student-Faculty Ratio:** 16:1 **Exams:** SAT I or ACT **% Receiving Financial Aid:** 60 **% Residing in College-Owned, -Operated, or -Affiliated Housing:** 41 **Library Holdings:** 138,327 **Regional Accreditation:** Southern Association of Colleges and Schools **Credit Hours For Degree:** 63 credit hours, Associates; 120 credit hours, Bachelors **ROTC:** Army, Navy, Air Force **Professional Accreditation:** ABET, ACBSP, CAA **Intercollegiate Athletics:** Baseball M; Basketball M; Cheerleading M & W; Cross-Country Running M & W; Golf M & W; Soccer M & W; Tennis M & W; Volleyball W

EMBRY-RIDDLE AERONAUTICAL UNIVERSITY, EXTENDED CAMPUS

600 South Clyde Morris Blvd.
Daytona Beach, FL 32114-3900
Tel: (386)226-6910
Free: 800-522-6787
Admissions: (386)226-7610
Fax: (386)226-6984
E-mail: ecinfo@erau.edu
Web Site: http://www.embryriddle.edu/
President/CEO: Robert Myers, PhD
Admissions: Pam Thomas
Type: Comprehensive **Sex:** Coed **Admission Plans:** Deferred Admission **Application Deadline:** Rolling **Application Fee:** $50.00 **H.S. Requirements:** High school diploma required; GED accepted **Costs Per Year:** Application fee: $50. Tuition: $4224 full-time. **Scholarships:** Available **Calendar System:** Miscellaneous, Summer Session Not available **Enrollment:** FT 2,192, PT 10,368, Grad 3,695 **Faculty:** FT 137, PT 1,967 **Student-Faculty Ratio:** 28:1 **% Receiving Financial Aid:** 22 **Library Holdings:** 138,237 **Regional Accreditation:** Southern Association of Colleges and Schools **Credit Hours For Degree:** 60 credit hours, Associates; 120 credit hours, Bachelors **Professional Accreditation:** ACBSP

EVERGLADES UNIVERSITY (BOCA RATON)

T-Rex Corporate Center
5002 T-Rex Ave., Ste. 100
Boca Raton, FL 33431
Tel: (561)912-1211; 888-772-6077
Fax: (561)912-1191
E-mail: jgraham@evergladesuniversity.edu
Web Site: http://www.evergladesuniversity.edu/
President/CEO: Kristi Mollis
Registrar: Leslie Lauer
Admissions: Jean Graham
Financial Aid: Seeta Singh
Type: Comprehensive **Sex:** Coed **Admission Plans:** Open Admission **Application Fee:** $50.00 **H.S. Requirements:** High school diploma required; GED accepted **Costs Per Year:** Application fee: $50. Tuition: $9744 full-time. Mandatory fees: $400 full-time. **Scholarships:** Available **Calendar System:** Continuous, Summer Session Available **Faculty:** FT 24, PT 93 **Exams:** Other, SAT I or ACT **% Receiving Financial Aid:** 100 **Regional Accreditation:** Southern Association of Colleges and Schools **Professional Accreditation:** ACCSCT

EVERGLADES UNIVERSITY (SARASOTA)

6151 Lake Osprey Dr.
Sarasota, FL 34240
Tel: (941)907-2262; (866)907-2262
Fax: (941)907-6634
E-mail: bbrewer@evergladesuniversity.edu
Web Site: http://www.evergladesuniversity.edu/
President/CEO: Kristi Mollis
Registrar: Sherry Waters
Admissions: Brad Brewer
Type: Four-Year College **Sex:** Coed **Costs Per Year:** Tuition: $406 per credit hour part-time. **Calendar System:** Continuous **Professional Accreditation:** ACCSCT

FLAGLER COLLEGE

74 King St.
PO Box 1027
St. Augustine, FL 32085-1027
Tel: (904)829-6481
Free: 800-304-4208
Admissions: (904)819-6220
Fax: (904)826-0094
E-mail: admiss@flagler.edu
Web Site: http://www.flagler.edu/
President/CEO: Dr. William L. Proctor
Registrar: Darwin L. White
Admissions: Marc Williar
Financial Aid: Robert Sterling
Type: Four-Year College **Sex:** Coed **Scores:** 100% SAT V 400+; 99% SAT M 400+; 47% ACT 18-23; 49% ACT 24-29 **% Accepted:** 25 **Admission Plans:** Early Admission; Early Decision Plan **Application Deadline:** March 01 **Application Fee:** $30.00 **H.S. Requirements:** High school diploma required; GED accepted **Costs Per Year:** Application fee: $30. Comprehensive fee: $13,790 includes full-time tuition ($8600) and college room and board ($5190). College room only: $2130. Part-time tuition: $295 per credit hour. **Scholarships:** Available **Calendar System:** Semester, Summer Session Available **Enrollment:** FT 2,089, PT 68 **Faculty:** FT 74, PT 91 **Student-Faculty Ratio:** 20:1 **Exams:** SAT I or ACT **% Receiving Financial Aid:** 46 **% Residing in College-Owned, -Operated, or -Affiliated Housing:** 36 **Library Holdings:** 130,201 **Regional Accreditation:** Southern Association of Colleges and Schools **Credit Hours For Degree:** 120 credit hours, Bachelors **Intercollegiate Athletics:** Baseball M; Basketball M & W; Cross-Country Running M & W; Golf M & W; Lacrosse M; Soccer M & W; Tennis M & W; Volleyball M & W

FLORIDA AGRICULTURAL AND MECHANICAL UNIVERSITY

Tallahassee, FL 32307-3200
Tel: (850)599-3000
Admissions: (850)599-3796
Fax: (850)561-2428
Web Site: http://www.famu.edu/
President/CEO: Dr. Fred Gainous
Registrar: Michael James
Admissions: Dr. Kimberly Davis
Financial Aid: Freda Donald
Type: University **Sex:** Coed **Affiliation:** State University System of Florida **Scores:** 87.1% SAT V 400+; 85.62% SAT M 400+; 59.96% ACT 18-23; 13.73% ACT 24-29 **Admission Plans:** Preferred Admission; Early Admission; Deferred Admission **Application Fee:** $20.00 **H.S. Requirements:** High school diploma required; GED accepted **Costs Per Year:** Application fee: $20. State resident tuition: $3318 full-time, $110.60 per credit hour part-time. Nonresident tuition: $16,662 full-time, $555.40 per credit hour part-time. Full-time tuition varies according to course load. Part-time tuition varies according to course load. College room and board: $5766. College room only: $3476. Room and board charges vary according to board plan and housing facility. **Scholarships:** Available **Calendar System:** Semester, Summer Session Available **Enrollment:** FT 9,349, PT 1,227, Grad 1,010 **Faculty:** FT 621 **Student-Faculty Ratio:** 21:1 **Exams:** SAT I or ACT **% Receiving Financial Aid:** 78 **Library Holdings:** 484,801 **Regional Accreditation:** Southern Association of Colleges and Schools **Credit Hours For Degree:** 60 semester hours, Associates; 120 semester hours, Bachelors **ROTC:** Army, Navy, Air Force **Professional Accreditation:** ABET, ACEJMC, ABA, ACPhE, AHIMA, AOTA, APTA, CARC, CEPH, CSWE, NCATE, NLN **Intercollegiate Athletics:** Baseball M; Basketball M & W; Cross-Country Running M & W; Football M; Golf M & W; Softball W; Swimming and Diving M & W; Tennis M & W; Track and Field M & W; Volleyball W

FLORIDA ATLANTIC UNIVERSITY

777 Glades Rd., PO Box 3091
Boca Raton, FL 33431-0991
Tel: (561)297-3000
Free: 800-299-4FAU

Admissions: (561)297-3040
E-mail: pletcher!@fau.edu
Web Site: http://www.fau.edu/
President/CEO: Frank T. Brogan
Registrar: Harry DeMik
Admissions: Barbara Pletcher
Financial Aid: Carole Pfeilsticker
Type: University **Sex:** Coed **Affiliation:** State University System of Florida **Scores:** 99% SAT V 400+; 99% SAT M 400+; 58% ACT 18-23; 17% ACT 24-29 **% Accepted:** 56 **Admission Plans:** Early Admission; Deferred Admission **Application Deadline:** June 01 **Application Fee:** $30.00 **H.S. Requirements:** High school diploma required; GED accepted **Costs Per Year:** Application fee: $30. State resident tuition: $2147 full-time, $108.64 per credit hour part-time. Nonresident tuition: $14,653 full-time, $546.36 per credit hour part-time. Mandatory fees: $1112 full-time. Full-time tuition and fees vary according to course load. Part-time tuition varies according to course load. College room and board: $7962. Room and board charges vary according to board plan and housing facility. **Scholarships:** Available **Calendar System:** Semester, Summer Session Available **Enrollment:** FT 11,810, PT 9,695, Grad 4,199 **Faculty:** FT 767, PT 619 **Student-Faculty Ratio:** 18:1 **Exams:** SAT I and SAT II or ACT **% Receiving Financial Aid:** 46 **% Residing in College-Owned, -Operated, or -Affiliated Housing:** 9 **Library Holdings:** 1,352,118 **Regional Accreditation:** Southern Association of Colleges and Schools **Credit Hours For Degree:** 60 semester hours, Associates; 120 semester hours, Bachelors **ROTC:** Army, Air Force **Professional Accreditation:** AACSB, ABET, AACN, ACSP, ASLHA, CSWE, NASM, NASPAA, NCATE, NLN **Intercollegiate Athletics:** Baseball M; Basketball M & W; Cheerleading W; Cross-Country Running M & W; Football M; Golf M & W; Soccer M & W; Softball W; Swimming and Diving M & W; Tennis M & W; Track and Field W; Volleyball W

FLORIDA ATLANTIC UNIVERSITY, JUPITER CAMPUS
5353 Parkside Dr.
Jupiter, FL 33458
Tel: (561)799-8500
Web Site: http://www.fau.edu/jupiter/ **Type:** Comprehensive **Sex:** Coed **Calendar System:** Semester

FLORIDA CAREER COLLEGE
1321 Southwest 107 Ave., Ste. 201B
Miami, FL 33174
Tel: (305)553-6065
Fax: (305)225-0128
Web Site: http://www.careercollege.edu/
President/CEO: David Knobel
Admissions: David Knobel
Type: Two-Year College **Sex:** Coed **Admission Plans:** Open Admission; Deferred Admission **Application Fee:** $100.00 **H.S. Requirements:** High school diploma required; GED accepted **Scholarships:** Available **Calendar System:** Quarter, Summer Session Available **Enrollment:** FT 1,717, PT 414 **Faculty:** FT 43, PT 39 **Student-Faculty Ratio:** 15:1 **Library Holdings:** 1,200 **Credit Hours For Degree:** 90 credits, Associates **Professional Accreditation:** ACICS

FLORIDA CHRISTIAN COLLEGE
1011 Bill Beck Blvd.
Kissimmee, FL 34744-5301
Tel: (407)847-8966
Fax: (407)847-3925
Web Site: http://www.fcc.edu/
President/CEO: Harold Armstrong
Registrar: Brian Smith
Admissions: Terry Davis
Financial Aid: Sandi Peppard
Type: Four-Year College **Sex:** Coed **Affiliation:** Christian Churches and Churches of Christ **Admission Plans:** Early Admission; Deferred Admission **Application Fee:** $25.00 **H.S. Requirements:** High school diploma required; GED accepted **Costs Per Year:** Application fee: $25. Tuition: $9280 full-time, $290 per credit part-time. Mandatory fees: $440 full-time. Full-time tuition and fees vary according to course load. Part-time tuition varies according to course load. College room only: $2200. Tuition guaranteed not to increase for student's term of enrollment. **Scholarships:** Available **Calendar System:** Semester, Summer Session Available **Enrollment:** FT 236, PT 23 **Faculty:** FT 10, PT 17 **Student-Faculty Ratio:** 12:1 **Exams:** ACT **% Receiving Financial Aid:** 100 **% Residing in College-Owned, -Operated, or -Affiliated Housing:** 65 **Library Holdings:** 31,000 **Regional Accreditation:** Southern Association of Colleges and Schools **Credit Hours For Degree:** 65 credits, Associates; 135 credits, Bachelors **Professional Accreditation:** AABC **Intercollegiate Athletics:** Basketball M & W; Volleyball W

FLORIDA COLLEGE
119 North Glen Arven Ave.
Temple Terrace, FL 33617
Tel: (813)988-5131
Free: 800-326-7655
Fax: (813)899-6772
E-mail: admissions@flcoll.edu
Web Site: http://www.floridacollege.edu/
President/CEO: Dr. Charles G. Caldwell, III
Registrar: Beth Grant
Admissions: Matthew Qualls
Financial Aid: Karla Nicholas
Type: Four-Year College **Sex:** Coed **% Accepted:** 72 **Application Deadline:** August 01 **Application Fee:** $25.00 **H.S. Requirements:** High school diploma required; GED accepted **Costs Per Year:** Application fee: $25. Comprehensive fee: $15,930 includes full-time tuition ($10,180), mandatory fees ($550), and college room and board ($5200). Room and board charges vary according to board plan and housing facility. Part-time tuition: $410 per semester hour. Part-time mandatory fees: $200 per term. **Scholarships:** Available **Calendar System:** Semester, Summer Session Not available **Enrollment:** FT 438, PT 18 **Faculty:** FT 31, PT 6 **Student-Faculty Ratio:** 15:1 **Exams:** SAT I or ACT **% Receiving Financial Aid:** 50 **% Residing in College-Owned, -Operated, or -Affiliated Housing:** 83 **Library Holdings:** 114,938 **Regional Accreditation:** Southern Association of Colleges and Schools **Credit Hours For Degree:** 64 semester hours, Associates; 124 semester hours, Bachelors **ROTC:** Army, Air Force **Intercollegiate Athletics:** Baseball M; Basketball M; Volleyball W

FLORIDA COLLEGE OF NATURAL HEALTH (BRADENTON)
616 67th St. Circle East
Bradenton, FL 34208
Tel: (941)954-8999
Free: 800-966-7117
Fax: (941)954-8991
E-mail: sarasota@fcnh.com
Web Site: http://www.fcnh.com/
President/CEO: Wayne Dawson
Admissions: Karen Curry
Type: Two-Year College **Sex:** Coed **Professional Accreditation:** ACCSCT

FLORIDA COLLEGE OF NATURAL HEALTH (MAITLAND)
2600 Lake Lucien Dr., Ste. 140
Maitland, FL 32751
Tel: (407)261-0319
Free: 800-393-7337
Fax: (407)261-0342
E-mail: orlando@fcnh.com
Web Site: http://www.fcnh.com/
President/CEO: Steve Richards
Admissions: Steve Richards
Type: Two-Year College **Sex:** Coed **Professional Accreditation:** ACCSCT

FLORIDA COLLEGE OF NATURAL HEALTH (MIAMI)
7925 Northwest 12th St.
Ste. 201
Miami, FL 33126
Tel: (305)597-9599
Free: 800-599-9599
Fax: (305)597-9110
E-mail: miami@fcnh.com
Web Site: http://www.fcnh.com/
President/CEO: Debra Starr-Cohen
Admissions: Lissette Vidal
Type: Two-Year College **Sex:** Coed **Professional Accreditation:** ACCSCT

FLORIDA COLLEGE OF NATURAL HEALTH (POMPANO BEACH)
2001 West Sample Rd., Ste. 100
Pompano Beach, FL 33064
Tel: (954)975-6400

Free: 800-541-9299
Fax: (954)975-9633
E-mail: adrener@fcnh.com
Web Site: http://www.fcnh.com/
President/CEO: Darren Teigue
Admissions: Peter Hogaboom
Type: Two-Year College **Sex:** Coed **Professional Accreditation:** ACCSCT

FLORIDA COMMUNITY COLLEGE AT JACKSONVILLE

501 West State St.
Jacksonville, FL 32202-4030
Tel: (904)632-3000
Admissions: (904)632-3131
Fax: (904)632-3393
Web Site: http://www.fccj.edu/
President/CEO: Dr. Steven R. Wallace
Registrar: Peter Biegel
Admissions: Peter J. Biegel
Financial Aid: Joel A. Friedman
Type: Two-Year College **Sex:** Coed **Affiliation:** Florida Community College System **Scores:** 94.94% SAT V 400+; 78.15% SAT M 400+; 33.95% ACT 18-23; 5.86% ACT 24-29 **% Accepted:** 100 **Admission Plans:** Open Admission; Early Admission; Deferred Admission **Application Deadline:** Rolling **Application Fee:** $15.00 **H.S. Requirements:** High school diploma required; GED accepted **Costs Per Year:** Application fee: $15. State resident tuition: $1518 full-time, $63.25 per credit part-time. Nonresident tuition: $5742 full-time, $239.25 per credit part-time. **Calendar System:** Semester, Summer Session Available **Enrollment:** FT 7,462, PT 22,369 **Faculty:** FT 365, PT 769 **Student-Faculty Ratio:** 21:1 **Library Holdings:** 412,856 **Regional Accreditation:** Southern Association of Colleges and Schools **Credit Hours For Degree:** 60 semester hours, Associates **ROTC:** Navy **Professional Accreditation:** ABFSE, ACF, ADA, AHIMA, APTA, ACBSP, CARC, JRCEMT, NAACLS, NLN **Intercollegiate Athletics:** Baseball M; Basketball M & W; Softball W; Tennis W; Volleyball W

FLORIDA CULINARY INSTITUTE

2400 Metrocenter Blvd.
West Palm Beach, FL 33407
Tel: (561)688-2001
Admissions: (561)842-8324
E-mail: info@floridaculinary.com
Web Site: http://www.floridaculinary.com/
Admissions: David Conway
Type: Two-Year College **Scholarships:** Available **Enrollment:** FT 600 **Professional Accreditation:** ACF, COE

FLORIDA GULF COAST UNIVERSITY

10501 FGCU Blvd. South
Fort Myers, FL 33965-6565
Tel: (239)590-1000; 888-889-1095
Admissions: (239)590-7878
Fax: (239)590-7894
Web Site: http://www.fgcu.edu/
President/CEO: Dr. William Merwin
Registrar: Marsha Bankston
Admissions: Marc Laviolette
Type: Comprehensive **Sex:** Coed **Affiliation:** State University System of Florida **Scores:** 98% SAT V 400+; 98% SAT M 400+; 69% ACT 18-23; 22% ACT 24-29 **% Accepted:** 76 **Admission Plans:** Deferred Admission **Application Deadline:** August 01 **Application Fee:** $30.00 **H.S. Requirements:** High school diploma required; GED accepted **Costs Per Year:** Application fee: $30. State resident tuition: $3260 full-time, $108.67 per credit part-time. Nonresident tuition: $15,249 full-time, $508.31 per credit part-time. Mandatory fees: $160 full-time, $2 per credit part-time, $100 per year part-time. Full-time tuition and fees vary according to course load. Part-time tuition and fees vary according to course load. College room and board: $7460. College room only: $3620. Room and board charges vary according to board plan. **Scholarships:** Available **Calendar System:** Semester, Summer Session Available **Enrollment:** FT 4,601, PT 1,537, Grad 1,111 **Faculty:** FT 253, PT 188 **Student-Faculty Ratio:** 18:1 **Exams:** SAT I or ACT **% Receiving Financial Aid:** 40 **% Residing in College-Owned, -Operated, or -Affiliated Housing:** 32 **Library Holdings:** 282,557 **Regional Accreditation:** Southern Association of Colleges and Schools **Credit Hours For Degree:** 60 credits, Associates; 120 credits, Bachelors **Professional Accreditation:** AACSB, AACN, AANA, AOTA, APTA, CSWE, NAACLS, NLN **Intercollegiate Athletics:** Baseball M; Basketball M & W; Cheerleading W; Cross-Country Running M & W; Golf M & W; Softball W; Tennis M & W; Volleyball W

FLORIDA HOSPITAL COLLEGE OF HEALTH SCIENCES

800 Lake Estelle Dr.
Orlando, FL 32803
Tel: (407)303-7747
Free: 800-500-7747
Admissions: (407)303-9798
Web Site: http://www.fhchs.edu/
President/CEO: Dr. David E. Greenlaw
Registrar: Debbie Gray
Admissions: Fiona Ghosn
Financial Aid: Starr Bender
Type: Two-Year College **Sex:** Coed **Scores:** 56% ACT 18-23; 12% ACT 24-29 **Admission Plans:** Open Admission **Application Fee:** $20.00 **H.S. Requirements:** High school diploma required; GED accepted **Costs Per Year:** Application fee: $20. Tuition: $8060 full-time, $230 per credit part-time. Mandatory fees: $570 full-time. College room only: $1760. **Scholarships:** Available **Calendar System:** Semester, Summer Session Not available **Enrollment:** FT 609, PT 794 **Faculty:** FT 44, PT 40 **Exams:** SAT I or ACT **% Residing in College-Owned, -Operated, or -Affiliated Housing:** 8 **Library Holdings:** 74,581 **Regional Accreditation:** Southern Association of Colleges and Schools **Credit Hours For Degree:** 60 credits, Associates; 120 credits, Bachelors **ROTC:** Air Force **Professional Accreditation:** AOTA, JRCEDMS, JRCERT, JRCNMT, NLN

FLORIDA INSTITUTE OF TECHNOLOGY

150 West University Blvd.
Melbourne, FL 32901-6975
Tel: (321)674-8000
Free: 800-888-4348
Admissions: (321)674-8030
Fax: (321)723-9468
E-mail: admissions@fit.edu
Web Site: http://www.fit.edu/
President/CEO: Dr. Anthony J. Catanese
Admissions: Judith Marino
Financial Aid: John Lally
Type: University **Sex:** Coed **Scores:** 98% SAT V 400+; 100% SAT M 400+; 23% ACT 18-23; 38% ACT 24-29 **% Accepted:** 83 **Admission Plans:** Early Admission; Deferred Admission **Application Deadline:** Rolling **Application Fee:** $50.00 **H.S. Requirements:** High school diploma required; GED accepted **Costs Per Year:** Application fee: $50. Comprehensive fee: $31,950 includes full-time tuition ($25,150) and college room and board ($6800). College room only: $4000. Full-time tuition varies according to course load and program. Room and board charges vary according to board plan and housing facility. Part-time tuition: $765 per credit hour. Part-time tuition varies according to course load and program. **Scholarships:** Available **Calendar System:** Semester, Summer Session Available **Enrollment:** FT 2,264, PT 94, Grad 2,387 **Faculty:** FT 215, PT 193 **Student-Faculty Ratio:** 13:1 **Exams:** SAT I or ACT **% Receiving Financial Aid:** 64 **% Residing in College-Owned, -Operated, or -Affiliated Housing:** 52 **Library Holdings:** 281,809 **Regional Accreditation:** Southern Association of Colleges and Schools **Credit Hours For Degree:** 120 credits, Bachelors **ROTC:** Army **Professional Accreditation:** ABET, APA, CAA **Intercollegiate Athletics:** Baseball M; Basketball M & W; Crew M & W; Cross-Country Running M & W; Golf M & W; Soccer M & W; Softball W; Tennis M & W; Volleyball W

FLORIDA INTERNATIONAL UNIVERSITY

11200 S.W. 8th St.
Miami, FL 33199
Tel: (305)348-2000
Admissions: (305)348-3675
Fax: (305)348-3648
E-mail: admiss@servms.fiu.edu
Web Site: http://www.fiu.edu/
President/CEO: Dr. Modesto A. Maidique
Registrar: Lynette Housty
Admissions: Carmen Brown
Financial Aid: Ana Sarasti
Type: University **Sex:** Coed **Affiliation:** State University System of Florida **Scores:** 99% SAT V 400+; 100% SAT M 400+; 50% ACT 18-23; 33% ACT 24-29 **% Accepted:** 47 **Admission Plans:** Early Admission; Deferred

Admission **Application Deadline:** Rolling **Application Fee:** $25.00 **H.S. Requirements:** High school diploma required; GED accepted **Costs Per Year:** Application fee: $25. State resident tuition: $3062 full-time, $102.08 per credit hour part-time. Nonresident tuition: $15,461 full-time, $515.38 per credit hour part-time. Mandatory fees: $252 full-time, $126 per term part-time. Full-time tuition and fees vary according to course load. Part-time tuition and fees vary according to course load. College room and board: $9102. College room only: $5518. Room and board charges vary according to housing facility. **Scholarships:** Available **Calendar System:** Semester, Summer Session Available **Enrollment:** FT 18,697, PT 11,987, Grad 5,890 **Faculty:** FT 757, PT 672 **Student-Faculty Ratio:** 17:1 **Exams:** SAT I or ACT **% Receiving Financial Aid:** 37 **% Residing in College-Owned, -Operated, or -Affiliated Housing:** 7 **Library Holdings:** 1,837,534 **Regional Accreditation:** Southern Association of Colleges and Schools **Credit Hours For Degree:** 120 credit hours, Bachelors **ROTC:** Army, Air Force **Professional Accreditation:** AACSB, ABET, ACEHSA, ACEJMC, AANA, ABA, ACCE, ADtA, AHIMA, AOTA, APTA, ASLA, ASLHA, CEPH, CSWE, NASAD, NASM, NASPAA, NAST, NCATE NLN, NRPA **Intercollegiate Athletics:** Baseball M; Basketball M & W; Cross-Country Running M & W; Football M; Golf W; Soccer M & W; Softball W; Tennis W; Track and Field M & W; Volleyball W

FLORIDA KEYS COMMUNITY COLLEGE
5901 College Rd.
Key West, FL 33040-4397
Tel: (305)296-9081
Web Site: http://www.fkcc.edu/
President/CEO: Dr. William A. Seeker
Registrar: Cheryl A. Malsheimer
Admissions: Cheryl A. Malsheimer
Financial Aid: Jean Warren
Type: Two-Year College **Sex:** Coed **Affiliation:** Florida Community College System **Admission Plans:** Open Admission; Early Admission; Deferred Admission **Application Fee:** $20.00 **H.S. Requirements:** High school diploma required; GED accepted **Scholarships:** Available **Calendar System:** Trimester, Summer Session Available **Faculty:** FT 33, PT 105 **Student-Faculty Ratio:** 11:1 **Exams:** SAT I or ACT **Library Holdings:** 29,402 **Regional Accreditation:** Southern Association of Colleges and Schools **Credit Hours For Degree:** 60 credits, Associates

FLORIDA MEMORIAL COLLEGE
15800 NW 42nd Ave.
Miami, FL 33054
Tel: (305)626-3600
Free: 800-822-1362
Admissions: (305)626-3147
Web Site: http://www.fmuniv.edu/
President/CEO: Dr. Albert E. Smith
Registrar: Lourdes Silva Pagan
Admissions: Peggy Murray Martin
Financial Aid: Brian Phillip
Type: Four-Year College **Sex:** Coed **Affiliation:** Baptist Church **Admission Plans:** Open Admission **Application Fee:** $15.00 **H.S. Requirements:** High school diploma required; GED accepted **Scholarships:** Available **Calendar System:** Semester, Summer Session Available **Faculty:** FT 114 **Exams:** SAT I or ACT **% Receiving Financial Aid:** 82 **Library Holdings:** 122,919 **Regional Accreditation:** Southern Association of Colleges and Schools **Credit Hours For Degree:** 124 credit hours, Bachelors **ROTC:** Army, Air Force **Professional Accreditation:** ACBSP, NCATE **Intercollegiate Athletics:** Baseball M; Basketball M & W; Cross-Country Running M & W; Track and Field M & W; Volleyball W

FLORIDA METROPOLITAN UNIVERSITY-BRANDON CAMPUS
3924 Coconut Palm Dr.
Tampa, FL 33619
Tel: (813)621-0041; 877-338-0068
E-mail: spointer@cci.edu
Web Site: http://www.fmu.edu/
President/CEO: Steve Backman
Registrar: Ingrid Zekan
Admissions: Shandretta Pointer
Financial Aid: Lori Lacey
Type: Comprehensive **Sex:** Coed **Affiliation:** Corinthian Colleges, Inc **Admission Plans:** Early Admission; Deferred Admission **Application Deadline:** Rolling **Application Fee:** $25.00 **H.S. Requirements:** High school diploma required; GED accepted. For ATB (Ability to Benefit) students must pass entrance evaluation, diploma/GED not required: High school diploma required; GED accepted **Costs Per Year:** Application fee: $25. Tuition: $13,200 full-time, $275 per quarter hour part-time. Mandatory fees: $240 full-time, $60 per term part-time. Full-time tuition and fees vary according to program. Part-time tuition and fees vary according to program. **Scholarships:** Available **Calendar System:** Quarter, Summer Session Available **Faculty:** FT 12, PT 56 **Student-Faculty Ratio:** 17:1 **Exams:** Other, SAT I or ACT **% Receiving Financial Aid:** 75 **Library Holdings:** 1,000 **Credit Hours For Degree:** 96 quarter hours, Associates; 192 quarter hours, Bachelors **Professional Accreditation:** ACICS, AAMAE

FLORIDA METROPOLITAN UNIVERSITY-JACKSONVILLE CAMPUS
8226 Phillips Hwy.
Jacksonville, FL 32256
Tel: (904)731-4949; 888-741-4271
Fax: (904)731-0599
Web Site: http://www.fmu.edu/
Admissions: Donna Wilhelm
Type: Comprehensive **Sex:** Coed **Calendar System:** Quarter **Faculty:** FT 7, PT 30 **Professional Accreditation:** ACICS

FLORIDA METROPOLITAN UNIVERSITY-LAKELAND CAMPUS
995 East Memorial Blvd., Ste. 110
Lakeland, FL 33801
Tel: (863)686-1444
Fax: (863)688-9881
Web Site: http://www.fmu.edu/
President/CEO: Diane Walton
Registrar: Marie McCosky
Admissions: Diane Y. Walton
Financial Aid: Linda Wagner
Type: Comprehensive **Sex:** Coed **Affiliation:** Corinthian Colleges, Inc **Admission Plans:** Early Admission **Application Fee:** $25.00 **H.S. Requirements:** High school diploma required; GED accepted **Scholarships:** Available **Calendar System:** Quarter, Summer Session Available **Enrollment:** FT 506, PT 206, Grad 40 **Faculty:** FT 10, PT 39 **Student-Faculty Ratio:** 15:1 **Exams:** ACT, Other, SAT I **% Receiving Financial Aid:** 86 **Library Holdings:** 5,000 **Credit Hours For Degree:** 96 quarter hours, Associates; 192 quarter hours, Bachelors **Professional Accreditation:** ACICS, AAMAE

FLORIDA METROPOLITAN UNIVERSITY-MELBOURNE CAMPUS
2401 North Harbor City Blvd.
Melbourne, FL 32935-6657
Tel: (321)253-2929
Fax: (321)255-2017
Web Site: http://www.fmu.edu/
Registrar: Leslie Savoie
Admissions: Timothy Alexander
Financial Aid: Rhonda Landolfi
Type: Comprehensive **Sex:** Coed **Affiliation:** Corinthian Colleges, Inc **Admission Plans:** Deferred Admission **Application Fee:** $25.00 **H.S. Requirements:** High school diploma required; GED accepted **Scholarships:** Available **Calendar System:** Quarter, Summer Session Available **Enrollment:** FT 718, PT 100, Grad 62 **Faculty:** FT 16, PT 33 **Student-Faculty Ratio:** 18:1 **Exams:** Other **Library Holdings:** 5,000 **Credit Hours For Degree:** 96 quarter hours, Associates; 192 quarter hours, Bachelors **Professional Accreditation:** ACICS, AAMAE

FLORIDA METROPOLITAN UNIVERSITY-NORTH ORLANDO CAMPUS
5421 Diplomat Circle
Orlando, FL 32810-5674
Tel: (407)628-5870
Free: 800-628-5870
Fax: (407)628-2616
Web Site: http://www.cci.edu/
President/CEO: Ouida B. Kirby
Registrar: Heather Calvart
Admissions: David Ritchie
Financial Aid: Linda Kaisrlik
Type: Comprehensive **Sex:** Coed **Affiliation:** Corinthian Colleges, Inc **Admission Plans:** Deferred Admission **Application Fee:** $0.00 **H.S. Requirements:** High school diploma required; GED accepted **Costs Per Year:** Application fee: $0. Tuition: $9720 full-time, $270 per quarter hour

part-time. Mandatory fees: $180 full-time, $60 per term part-time. Full-time tuition and fees vary according to program. Part-time tuition and fees vary according to program. **Scholarships:** Available **Calendar System:** Quarter, Summer Session Available **Enrollment:** FT 790, PT 601, Grad 107 **Faculty:** FT 10, PT 86 **Student-Faculty Ratio:** 15:1 **Library Holdings:** 18,000 **Credit Hours For Degree:** 96 credit hours, Associates; 192 credit hours, Bachelors **Professional Accreditation:** ACICS

FLORIDA METROPOLITAN UNIVERSITY-ORANGE PARK CAMPUS
805 Wells Rd.
Orange Park, FL 32073
Tel: (904)264-9122
Fax: (904)264-9952
Web Site: http://www.fmu.edu/
President/CEO: Dr. Roxanne Jordan
Type: Two-Year College **Sex:** Coed **Calendar System:** Quarter **Professional Accreditation:** ACICS

FLORIDA METROPOLITAN UNIVERSITY-PINELLAS CAMPUS
2471 McMullen Booth Rd.
Clearwater, FL 33759
Tel: (727)725-2688
Free: 800-353-FMUS
Fax: (727)796-3722
E-mail: tcpinellas2@juno.com
Web Site: http://www.fmu.edu/
President/CEO: Dr. Jack R. Jones
Registrar: Maja Pursae
Admissions: Gary Gaetano
Type: Comprehensive **Sex:** Coed **Affiliation:** Corinthian Colleges, Inc **Admission Plans:** Early Admission; Deferred Admission **Application Fee:** $25.00 **H.S. Requirements:** High school diploma required; GED accepted **Scholarships:** Available **Calendar System:** Quarter, Summer Session Available **Enrollment:** FT 428, PT 629, Grad 144 **Faculty:** FT 13, PT 31 **Student-Faculty Ratio:** 24:1 **Exams:** Other, SAT I or ACT **% Receiving Financial Aid:** 69 **Library Holdings:** 6,721 **Credit Hours For Degree:** 96 quarter hours, Associates; 192 quarter hours, Bachelors **Professional Accreditation:** ACICS, AAMAE

FLORIDA METROPOLITAN UNIVERSITY-POMPANO BEACH CAMPUS
225 North Federal Hwy.
Pompano Beach, FL 33062
Tel: (954)783-7339
Free: 800-468-0168
Fax: (954)568-2008
Web Site: http://www.fmu.edu/
President/CEO: John V. Peterson
Registrar: Orlando Restrepo
Admissions: Fran Heaston
Type: Comprehensive **Sex:** Coed **Affiliation:** Corinthian Colleges, Inc **Admission Plans:** Deferred Admission **Application Fee:** $25.00 **H.S. Requirements:** High school diploma required; GED accepted **Scholarships:** Available **Calendar System:** Quarter, Summer Session Available **Enrollment:** FT 941, PT 581, Grad 90 **Faculty:** FT 24, PT 46 **Student-Faculty Ratio:** 17:1 **Exams:** Other, SAT I or ACT **Library Holdings:** 14,500 **Credit Hours For Degree:** 96 quarter hours, Associates; 192 quarter hours, Bachelors **Professional Accreditation:** ACICS

FLORIDA METROPOLITAN UNIVERSITY-SOUTH ORLANDO CAMPUS
9200 South Park Center Loop
Orlando, FL 32819
Tel: (407)851-2525; 888-471-4270
Fax: (407)851-1477
Web Site: http://www.fmu.edu/
President/CEO: Barbara A. Huybers
Registrar: Terrie Baker
Admissions: Annette Cloin
Financial Aid: Sherri Williams
Type: Comprehensive **Sex:** Coed **Scores:** 19% ACT 18-23; 26% ACT 24-29 **Application Fee:** $50.00 **H.S. Requirements:** High school diploma required; GED accepted **Costs Per Year:** Application fee: $50. Tuition: $9900 full-time. Full-time tuition varies according to program. **Scholarships:** Available **Calendar System:** Quarter, Summer Session Not available **Enrollment:** FT 1,142, PT 746, Grad 76 **Faculty:** FT 10, PT 67 **Student-Faculty Ratio:** 20:1 **Exams:** ACT, SAT II **Library Holdings:** 5,113 **Credit Hours For Degree:** 96 quarter hours, Associates; 192 quarter hours, Bachelors **Professional Accreditation:** ACICS, AAMAE

FLORIDA METROPOLITAN UNIVERSITY-TAMPA CAMPUS
3319 West Hillsborough Ave.
Tampa, FL 33614-5899
Tel: (813)879-6000
Fax: (813)871-2483
Web Site: http://fmu.edu/
President/CEO: Kathryn J. Knox
Registrar: Dr. Diane Owens
Admissions: Donnie Broughton
Financial Aid: Rod Kirkwood
Type: Comprehensive **Sex:** Coed **Affiliation:** Corinthian Colleges, Inc **Admission Plans:** Deferred Admission **Application Fee:** $25.00 **H.S. Requirements:** High school diploma required; GED accepted **Costs Per Year:** Application fee: $25. Tuition: $9720 full-time, $270 per quarter hour part-time. Mandatory fees: $180 full-time, $60 per term part-time. Full-time tuition and fees vary according to program. Part-time tuition and fees vary according to program. **Scholarships:** Available **Calendar System:** Quarter, Summer Session Available **Enrollment:** FT 798, PT 483, Grad 109 **Faculty:** FT 13, PT 70 **Student-Faculty Ratio:** 20:1 **Exams:** ACT, Other, SAT I **% Receiving Financial Aid:** 85 **Library Holdings:** 4,000 **Credit Hours For Degree:** 96 quarter hours, Associates; 192 quarter hours, Bachelors **Professional Accreditation:** ACICS, AAMAE

FLORIDA NATIONAL COLLEGE
4425 West 20th Ave.
Hialeah, FL 33012
Tel: (305)821-3333
Fax: (305)362-0595
Web Site: http://www.fnc.edu/
President/CEO: Jose Regueiro
Registrar: Gustavo Zapata
Admissions: Maria C. Reguerio
Financial Aid: Omar Sanchez
Type: Two-Year College **Sex:** Coed **% Accepted:** 72 **Admission Plans:** Open Admission; Deferred Admission **Application Deadline:** Rolling **H.S. Requirements:** High school diploma required; GED accepted **Costs Per Year:** Tuition: $10,200 full-time, $340 per credit part-time. Mandatory fees: $760 full-time. **Scholarships:** Available **Calendar System:** Semester, Summer Session Available **Enrollment:** FT 1,723, PT 148 **Faculty:** FT 43, PT 33 **Student-Faculty Ratio:** 24:1 **Library Holdings:** 23,507 **Regional Accreditation:** Southern Association of Colleges and Schools **Credit Hours For Degree:** 60 credits, Associates

THE FLORIDA SCHOOL OF MIDWIFERY
PO Box 5505
Gainesville, FL 32601
Tel: (352)338-0766
Fax: (352)338-2013
Web Site: http://www.midwiferyschool.org/
President/CEO: Jana Borino
Admissions: Gloria Huffman
Type: Two-Year College **Sex:** Women **Calendar System:** Quarter **Faculty:** PT 40 **Student-Faculty Ratio:** 10:1 **Professional Accreditation:** MEAC

FLORIDA SOUTHERN COLLEGE
111 Lake Hollingsworth Dr.
Lakeland, FL 33801-5698
Tel: (863)680-4111
Free: 800-274-4131
Admissions: (863)680-3905
Fax: (863)680-4120
E-mail: fscadm@flsouthern.edu
Web Site: http://www.flsouthern.edu/
President/CEO: Dr. Anne B. Kerr
Registrar: Sally L. Thissen
Admissions: Bill C. Langston
Financial Aid: David M. Bodwell
Type: Comprehensive **Sex:** Coed **Affiliation:** United Methodist Church **Scores:** 98% SAT V 400+; 98% SAT M 400+; 52% ACT 18-23; 38% ACT 24-29 **% Accepted:** 73 **Admission Plans:** Early Admission; Early Decision

Plan; Deferred Admission **Application Deadline:** April 01 **Application Fee:** $30.00 **H.S. Requirements:** High school diploma required; GED accepted **Costs Per Year:** Application fee: $30. Comprehensive fee: $25,965 includes full-time tuition ($18,765), mandatory fees ($400), and college room and board ($6800). College room only: $3750. Full-time tuition and fees vary according to student level. Room and board charges vary according to board plan and housing facility. Part-time tuition: $500 per credit hour. Part-time mandatory fees: $400 per year. **Scholarships:** Available **Calendar System:** Semester, Summer Session Available **Enrollment:** FT 1,759, PT 57, Grad 105 **Faculty:** FT 107, PT 59 **Student-Faculty Ratio:** 14:1 **Exams:** SAT I or ACT **% Receiving Financial Aid:** 72 **% Residing in College-Owned, -Operated, or -Affiliated Housing:** 67 **Library Holdings:** 172,803 **Regional Accreditation:** Southern Association of Colleges and Schools **Credit Hours For Degree:** 124 semester hours, Bachelors **ROTC:** Army, Air Force **Professional Accreditation:** AACN, JRCEPAT **Intercollegiate Athletics:** Baseball M; Basketball M & W; Cross-Country Running M & W; Golf M & W; Soccer M & W; Softball W; Swimming and Diving M & W; Tennis M & W; Volleyball M & W

FLORIDA STATE UNIVERSITY
Tallahassee, FL 32306
Tel: (850)644-2525
Admissions: (850)644-6200
Fax: (850)644-0197
E-mail: admissions@admin.fsu.edu
Web Site: http://www.fsu.edu/
President/CEO: Dr. T. K. Wetherell
Registrar: Tim Martin
Admissions: Janice V. Finney
Financial Aid: Darryl Marshall
Type: University **Sex:** Coed **Affiliation:** State University System of Florida **Scores:** 100% SAT V 400+; 100% SAT M 400+; 35% ACT 18-23; 58% ACT 24-29 **% Accepted:** 62 **Admission Plans:** Early Admission **Application Deadline:** March 01 **Application Fee:** $30.00 **H.S. Requirements:** High school diploma required; GED accepted **Costs Per Year:** Application fee: $30. State resident tuition: $3208 full-time, $106.93 per credit hour part-time. Nonresident tuition: $16,340 full-time, $544.67 per credit hour part-time. Full-time tuition varies according to location. Part-time tuition varies according to location. College room and board: $6778. College room only: $3600. Room and board charges vary according to board plan and housing facility. **Scholarships:** Available **Calendar System:** Semester, Summer Session Available **Enrollment:** FT 27,203, PT 3,582, Grad 7,378 **Faculty:** FT 1,265, PT 327 **Student-Faculty Ratio:** 22:1 **Exams:** SAT I or ACT **% Receiving Financial Aid:** 32 **% Residing in College-Owned, -Operated, or -Affiliated Housing:** 14 **Library Holdings:** 2,738,777 **Regional Accreditation:** Southern Association of Colleges and Schools **Credit Hours For Degree:** 60 semester hours, Associates; 120 semester hours, Bachelors **ROTC:** Army, Navy, Air Force **Professional Accreditation:** AACSB, ABET, AAMFT, AACN, AAFCS, ABA, ACA, ADtA, ACSP, ALA, APA, ASLHA, AALS, CORE, CSWE, FIDER, LCMEAMA, NASAD, NASD, NASM NASPAA, NAST, NCATE, NLN, NRPA **Intercollegiate Athletics:** Baseball M; Basketball M & W; Bowling M & W; Cheerleading M & W; Cross-Country Running M & W; Football M; Golf M & W; Rugby M & W; Soccer M & W; Softball W; Swimming and Diving M & W; Table Tennis M & W; Tennis M & W; Track and Field M & W; Volleyball M & W; Wrestling M & W

FLORIDA TECHNICAL COLLEGE (AUBURNDALE)
298 Havendale Blvd.
Auburndale, FL 33823
Tel: (863)967-8822
Fax: (863)967-4972
Web Site: http://www.flatech.edu/
President/CEO: Rodney Amadori
Admissions: Charles Owens
Type: Two-Year College **Sex:** Coed **Scholarships:** Available **Calendar System:** Quarter **Faculty:** FT 5, PT 3 **Professional Accreditation:** ACICS

FLORIDA TECHNICAL COLLEGE (DELAND)
1450 South Woodland Blvd., 3rd Floor
DeLand, FL 32720
Tel: (904)734-3303
Admissions: (386)734-3303
Fax: (904)734-5150
E-mail: batkinson@flatech.edu
Web Site: http://www.flatech.edu/
President/CEO: Bill Atkinson
Admissions: Bill Atkinson
Type: Two-Year College **Sex:** Coed **Application Fee:** $25.00 **Calendar System:** Quarter **Enrollment:** FT 260 **Faculty:** FT 11, PT 2 **Student-Faculty Ratio:** 22:1 **Professional Accreditation:** ACICS

FLORIDA TECHNICAL COLLEGE (JACKSONVILLE)
8711 Lone Star Rd.
Jacksonville, FL 32211
Tel: (904)724-2229
Admissions: (407)678-5600
Fax: (904)720-0920
Web Site: http://www.flatech.edu/
President/CEO: Dr. James Powell
Registrar: Cheryl Quaintance
Admissions: Bryan Gulebiam
Financial Aid: Vivan Woods
Type: Two-Year College **Sex:** Coed **Admission Plans:** Open Admission **Scholarships:** Available **Calendar System:** Quarter **Faculty:** FT 9, PT 2 **Student-Faculty Ratio:** 19:1 **Professional Accreditation:** ACICS

FLORIDA TECHNICAL COLLEGE (ORLANDO)
1819 North Semoran Blvd.
Orlando, FL 32807-3546
Tel: (407)678-5600
Fax: (407)678-1149
Web Site: http://www.flatech.edu/
President/CEO: Don Slayter
Registrar: Pat Sharp
Admissions: Jeanette E. Muschlitz
Financial Aid: Lynn Borges
Type: Two-Year College **Sex:** Coed **Affiliation:** Forefront Education **H.S. Requirements:** High school diploma required; GED accepted **Scholarships:** Available **Calendar System:** Quarter, Summer Session Not available **Enrollment:** FT 231 **Faculty:** FT 11, PT 0 **Credit Hours For Degree:** 90 quarter hours, Associates **Professional Accreditation:** ACICS

FULL SAIL REAL WORLD EDUCATION
3300 University Blvd.
Winter Park, FL 32792-7437
Tel: (407)679-6333
Free: 800-226-7625
Admissions: (407)679-0100
Fax: (407)678-0070
E-mail: admissions@fullsail.com
Web Site: http://www.fullsail.com/
President/CEO: E. Haddock
Registrar: Vivian Blanford
Admissions: Marybeth Plank
Financial Aid: Sharon Griffith
Type: Two-Year College **Sex:** Coed **% Accepted:** 69 **Admission Plans:** Open Admission **Application Deadline:** Rolling **Application Fee:** $150.00 **H.S. Requirements:** High school diploma required; GED accepted **Scholarships:** Available **Calendar System:** Miscellaneous, Summer Session Available **Enrollment:** FT 5,219 **Faculty:** FT 482 **Student-Faculty Ratio:** 10:1 **Library Holdings:** 2,531 **Credit Hours For Degree:** 74 - 94 credit hours, Associates; 127 - 154 credit hours, Bachelors **Professional Accreditation:** ACCSCT

GULF COAST COLLEGE
3910 US Hwy. 301 North, Ste. 200
Tampa, FL 33619-1259
Tel: (813)620-1446; 888-729-7247
Web Site: http://gulfcoastcollege.com/
President/CEO: Fran Haddaway
Admissions: Todd A. Matthews, Sr.
Type: Two-Year College **Sex:** Coed **Admission Plans:** Open Admission **H.S. Requirements:** High school diploma required; GED accepted **Scholarships:** Available **Calendar System:** Quarter **Student-Faculty Ratio:** 12:1 **Library Holdings:** 2,063 **Credit Hours For Degree:** 90 quarter hours, Associates **Professional Accreditation:** ACICS

GULF COAST COMMUNITY COLLEGE
5230 West Hwy. 98
Panama City, FL 32401-1058

Tel: (850)769-1551
Free: 800-311-3628
Admissions: (850)872-3891
Fax: (850)913-3308
Web Site: http://www.gulfcoast.edu/
President/CEO: Dr. Robert L. McSpadden
Registrar: Sharon Todd
Admissions: Dr. Sheri L. Rowland
Financial Aid: Judy L. Mitchell
Type: Two-Year College **Sex:** Coed **Admission Plans:** Open Admission; Early Admission; Deferred Admission **Application Fee:** $0.00 **H.S. Requirements:** High school diploma required; GED accepted **Costs Per Year:** Application fee: $0. State resident tuition: $1446 full-time, $48.20 per credit part-time. Nonresident tuition: $6232 full-time, $207.74 per credit part-time. Mandatory fees: $309 full-time, $10.30 per credit part-time. Full-time tuition and fees vary according to course load. Part-time tuition and fees vary according to course load. **Scholarships:** Available **Calendar System:** Semester, Summer Session Available **Enrollment:** FT 2,248, PT 3,810 **Faculty:** FT 122, PT 372 **Student-Faculty Ratio:** 14:1 **Exams:** Other, SAT I and SAT II or ACT **Library Holdings:** 80,000 **Regional Accreditation:** Southern Association of Colleges and Schools **Credit Hours For Degree:** 60 credit hours, Associates **Professional Accreditation:** ACF, ADA, APTA, CARC, JRCERT, JRCEMT, NLN **Intercollegiate Athletics:** Baseball M; Basketball M & W; Cheerleading M & W; Softball W; Volleyball W

HERZING COLLEGE
1595 South Semoran Blvd., Ste. 1501
Winter Park, FL 32792-5509
Tel: (407)380-6315
Admissions: (407)478-0500
Fax: (407)380-0269
Web Site: http://www.herzing.edu/
President/CEO: Randy Atwater
Admissions: Karen Mohamad
Type: Two-Year College **Sex:** Coed **Scholarships:** Available **Calendar System:** Semester **Enrollment:** FT 243, PT 64 **Faculty:** FT 8, PT 6 **Student-Faculty Ratio:** 21:1 **Professional Accreditation:** ACICS

HIGH-TECH INSTITUTE
1000 Woodcock Rd.
Orlando, FL 32803
Tel: (407)895-1985
Free: 800-987-0110
Fax: (407)657-9778
Web Site: http://www.high-techinstitute.com/ **Type:** Two-Year College **Sex:** Coed **Professional Accreditation:** ACCSCT

HILLSBOROUGH COMMUNITY COLLEGE
PO Box 31127
Tampa, FL 33631-3127
Tel: (813)253-7000
Admissions: (813)253-7027
Fax: (813)253-7196
Web Site: http://www.hccfl.edu/
President/CEO: Dr. Gwendolyn W. Stephenson
Registrar: Kathy Cecil
Admissions: Kathy G. Cecil
Financial Aid: Charlotte Johns
Type: Two-Year College **Sex:** Coed **Affiliation:** Florida Community College System **Admission Plans:** Open Admission; Early Admission **Application Fee:** $20.00 **H.S. Requirements:** High school diploma required; GED accepted **Scholarships:** Available **Calendar System:** Semester, Summer Session Available **Enrollment:** FT 7,009, PT 15,140 **Faculty:** FT 233, PT 541 **Student-Faculty Ratio:** 28:1 **Exams:** Other **Library Holdings:** 170,615 **Regional Accreditation:** Southern Association of Colleges and Schools **Credit Hours For Degree:** 60 credit hours, Associates **ROTC:** Army, Air Force **Professional Accreditation:** ACF, ADA, COptA, CARC, JRCEDMS, JRCERT, JRCEMT, JRCNMT, NLN **Intercollegiate Athletics:** Baseball M; Basketball M & W; Softball W; Tennis W; Volleyball W

HOBE SOUND BIBLE COLLEGE
PO Box 1065
Hobe Sound, FL 33475-1065
Tel: (561)546-5534
Free: 800-881-5534
Admissions: (772)546-5534
Fax: (561)545-1422
E-mail: hsbcuwin@aol.com
Web Site: http://www.hsbc.edu/
President/CEO: P. Daniel Stetler
Registrar: Lynda Lee
Admissions: Ann French
Financial Aid: Rev. Philip Gray
Type: Four-Year College **Sex:** Coed **Affiliation:** nondenominational **Scores:** 75% SAT V 400+; 100% SAT M 400+; 70% ACT 18-23; 20% ACT 24-29 % **Accepted:** 92 **Admission Plans:** Open Admission; Preferred Admission; Early Admission **Application Deadline:** Rolling **Application Fee:** $25.00 **H.S. Requirements:** High school diploma required; GED accepted **Costs Per Year:** Application fee: $25. Comprehensive fee: $7360 includes full-time tuition ($4020), mandatory fees ($100), and college room and board ($3240). **Scholarships:** Available **Calendar System:** Semester, Summer Session Available **Faculty:** FT 10, PT 11 **Student-Faculty Ratio:** 7:1 **Exams:** SAT I or ACT **% Residing in College-Owned, -Operated, or -Affiliated Housing:** 75 **Library Holdings:** 35,468 **Credit Hours For Degree:** 70 semester hours, Associates; 128 semester hours, Bachelors **Professional Accreditation:** AABC

INDIAN RIVER COMMUNITY COLLEGE
3209 Virginia Ave.
Fort Pierce, FL 34981-5596
Tel: (772)462-4700
Admissions: (772)462-4740
Fax: (772)462-4796
Web Site: http://www.ircc.edu/
President/CEO: Dr. Edwin R. Massey
Registrar: Steven Payne
Admissions: Linda Hays
Financial Aid: Mary Lewis
Type: Two-Year College **Sex:** Coed **Affiliation:** Florida Community College System **Scores:** 84% SAT V 400+; 90% SAT M 400+ **Admission Plans:** Open Admission; Early Admission; Deferred Admission **Application Fee:** $0.00 **H.S. Requirements:** High school diploma required; GED accepted **Scholarships:** Available **Calendar System:** Semester, Summer Session Available **Faculty:** FT 162, PT 1,400 **Exams:** Other **Library Holdings:** 58,657 **Regional Accreditation:** Southern Association of Colleges and Schools **Credit Hours For Degree:** 60 semester hours, Associates **Professional Accreditation:** AAMAE, ADA, AHIMA, APTA, CARC, JRCERT, JRCEMT, NAACLS, NLN **Intercollegiate Athletics:** Baseball M; Basketball M & W; Softball W; Swimming and Diving M & W; Volleyball W

INTERNATIONAL ACADEMY OF DESIGN & TECHNOLOGY
5225 Memorial Hwy.
Tampa, FL 33634-7350
Tel: (813)881-0007
Free: 800-ACA-DEMY
Fax: (813)881-0008
E-mail: admissions@academy.edu
Web Site: http://www.academy.edu/
President/CEO: Mark A. Page
Registrar: Joan Foreman
Admissions: Richard Costa
Financial Aid: Robin Hall
Type: Four-Year College **Sex:** Coed **Affiliation:** Career Education Corporation **% Accepted:** 46 **Admission Plans:** Early Admission; Deferred Admission **Application Deadline:** Rolling **Application Fee:** $50.00 **H.S. Requirements:** High school diploma required; GED accepted **Costs Per Year:** Application fee: $50. Tuition: $385 per credit hour part-time. Mandatory fees: $100 per term part-time. **Scholarships:** Available **Calendar System:** Quarter, Summer Session Available **Enrollment:** FT 1,702, PT 703 **Faculty:** FT 20, PT 147 **Student-Faculty Ratio:** 16:1 **Library Holdings:** 6,000 **Credit Hours For Degree:** 90 quarter hours, Associates; 180 quarter hours, Bachelors **Professional Accreditation:** ACICS, FIDER

INTERNATIONAL COLLEGE
2655 Northbrooke Dr.
Naples, FL 34119
Tel: (239)513-1122
Free: 800-466-8017
Fax: (239)513-9071
E-mail: admit@international.edu

Web Site: http://www.internationalcollege.edu/
President/CEO: Dr. Terry McMahan
Registrar: Carol Morrison
Admissions: Rita Lampus
Financial Aid: Joe Gilchrist
Type: Comprehensive **Sex:** Coed **Admission Plans:** Deferred Admission **Application Fee:** $20.00 **H.S. Requirements:** High school diploma required; GED accepted **Costs Per Year:** Application fee: $20. Tuition: $9120 full-time, $380 per credit part-time. Mandatory fees: $380 full-time, $190 per term part-time. **Scholarships:** Available **Calendar System:** Trimester, Summer Session Available **Enrollment:** FT 947, PT 395, Grad 202 **Faculty:** FT 57, PT 52 **Student-Faculty Ratio:** 16:1 **Exams:** ACT, Other, SAT I **% Receiving Financial Aid:** 85 **Library Holdings:** 29,711 **Regional Accreditation:** Southern Association of Colleges and Schools **Credit Hours For Degree:** 60 semester hour credits, Associates; 120 semester hour credits, Bachelors **Professional Accreditation:** AAMAE, AHIMA

ITT TECHNICAL INSTITUTE (FORT LAUDERDALE)
3401 South University Dr.
Fort Lauderdale, FL 33328-2021
Tel: (954)476-9300
Fax: (954)476-6889
Web Site: http://www.itt-tech.edu/
President/CEO: Nan Lough
Registrar: Tina Daley
Admissions: Nan Lough
Type: Two-Year College **Sex:** Coed **Affiliation:** ITT Educational Services, Inc **Admission Plans:** Deferred Admission **Application Deadline:** Rolling **Application Fee:** $100.00 **H.S. Requirements:** High school diploma required; GED accepted **Costs Per Year:** Application fee: $100. **Scholarships:** Available **Calendar System:** Quarter, Summer Session Not available **Exams:** Other **Credit Hours For Degree:** 96 credit hours, Associates; 180 credit hours, Bachelors **Professional Accreditation:** ACICS

ITT TECHNICAL INSTITUTE (JACKSONVILLE)
6600-10 Youngerman Circle
Jacksonville, FL 32244-6630
Tel: (904)573-9100
Web Site: http://www.itt-tech.edu/
President/CEO: John Peterson
Admissions: Brian Quirk
Financial Aid: Roberta Wilson
Type: Two-Year College **Sex:** Coed **Affiliation:** ITT Educational Services, Inc **Admission Plans:** Deferred Admission **Application Deadline:** Rolling **Application Fee:** $100.00 **H.S. Requirements:** High school diploma required; GED accepted **Costs Per Year:** Application fee: $100. **Scholarships:** Available **Calendar System:** Quarter, Summer Session Not available **Exams:** Other **Credit Hours For Degree:** 96 credit hours, Associates; 180 credit hours, Bachelors **Professional Accreditation:** ACICS

ITT TECHNICAL INSTITUTE (LAKE MARY)
1400 South International Parkway
Lake Mary, FL 32746
Tel: (407)660-2900
Web Site: http://www.itt-tech.edu/
President/CEO: Gary P. Cosgrove
Registrar: Gary Cosgrove
Admissions: Gary Cosgrove
Financial Aid: Rebecca Lydic
Type: Two-Year College **Sex:** Coed **Affiliation:** ITT Educational Services, Inc **Admission Plans:** Deferred Admission **Application Deadline:** Rolling **Application Fee:** $100.00 **H.S. Requirements:** High school diploma required; GED accepted **Costs Per Year:** Application fee: $100. **Scholarships:** Available **Calendar System:** Quarter, Summer Session Not available **Exams:** Other **Credit Hours For Degree:** 96 credit hours, Associates; 180 credit hours, Bachelors **Professional Accreditation:** ACICS

ITT TECHNICAL INSTITUTE (MIAMI)
7955 NW 12th St.
Miami, FL 33126
Tel: (305)477-3080
Web Site: http://www.itt-tech.edu/
President/CEO: Robert T. Hayward
Admissions: Robert Hayward
Financial Aid: Carlos Alayon
Type: Two-Year College **Sex:** Coed **Affiliation:** ITT Educational Services, Inc **Admission Plans:** Deferred Admission **Application Deadline:** Rolling **Application Fee:** $100.00 **H.S. Requirements:** High school diploma required; GED accepted **Costs Per Year:** Application fee: $100. **Scholarships:** Available **Calendar System:** Quarter, Summer Session Not available **Exams:** Other **Credit Hours For Degree:** 96 credit hours, Associates; 180 credit hours, Bachelors **Professional Accreditation:** ACICS

ITT TECHNICAL INSTITUTE (TAMPA)
4809 Memorial Hwy.
Tampa, FL 33634-7151
Tel: (813)885-2244
Fax: (813)888-6078
Web Site: http://www.itt-tech.edu/
President/CEO: Dennis W. Alspaugh
Admissions: Denny Alspaugh
Financial Aid: Julie Cummings
Type: Two-Year College **Sex:** Coed **Affiliation:** ITT Educational Services, Inc **Admission Plans:** Deferred Admission **Application Deadline:** Rolling **Application Fee:** $100.00 **H.S. Requirements:** High school diploma required; GED accepted **Costs Per Year:** Application fee: $100. **Scholarships:** Available **Calendar System:** Quarter, Summer Session Not available **Exams:** Other **Credit Hours For Degree:** 96 credit hours, Associates; 180 credit hours, Bachelors **Professional Accreditation:** ACICS

JACKSONVILLE UNIVERSITY
2800 University Blvd. North
Jacksonville, FL 32211-3394
Tel: (904)256-8000
Free: 800-225-2027
Admissions: (904)256-7000
Fax: (904)256-7086
E-mail: admissions@junix.ju.edu
Web Site: http://www.ju.edu/
President/CEO: Dr. Kerry D. Romesburg
Registrar: Carolyn A. Barnett
Admissions: Yvonne D. Martel
Financial Aid: Catherine N. Huntress
Type: Comprehensive **Sex:** Coed **Scores:** 95% SAT V 400+; 95% SAT M 400+; 58% ACT 18-23; 29% ACT 24-29 **% Accepted:** 72 **Admission Plans:** Early Admission; Deferred Admission **Application Deadline:** Rolling **Application Fee:** $30.00 **H.S. Requirements:** High school diploma required; GED accepted **Costs Per Year:** Application fee: $30. Comprehensive fee: $26,430 includes full-time tuition ($19,970) and college room and board ($6460). College room only: $3030. Part-time tuition: $666 per credit hour. **Scholarships:** Available **Calendar System:** Semester, Summer Session Available **Enrollment:** FT 1,877, PT 684, Grad 28 **Faculty:** FT 121, PT 41 **Student-Faculty Ratio:** 15:1 **Exams:** SAT I or ACT **% Receiving Financial Aid:** 71 **% Residing in College-Owned, -Operated, or -Affiliated Housing:** 58 **Library Holdings:** 374,016 **Regional Accreditation:** Southern Association of Colleges and Schools **Credit Hours For Degree:** 128 credit hours, Bachelors **ROTC:** Navy **Professional Accreditation:** AACN, ADA, NASD, NASM, NLN **Intercollegiate Athletics:** Baseball M; Basketball M & W; Crew M & W; Cross-Country Running M & W; Football M; Golf M & W; Soccer M & W; Softball W; Tennis M & W; Track and Field W; Volleyball W

JOHNSON & WALES UNIVERSITY
1701 Northeast 127th St.
North Miami, FL 33181
Tel: (305)892-7000
Free: 800-232-2433
Admissions: (305)892-7002
Fax: (305)892-7030
E-mail: admissions.mia@jwu.edu
Web Site: http://www.jwu.edu/
President/CEO: Dr. Donald McGregor
Registrar: Maheen Caroll
Admissions: Jeff Greenip
Financial Aid: Chris Magnan
Type: Four-Year College **Sex:** Coed **Affiliation:** Johnson & Wales University (RI) **% Accepted:** 73 **Admission Plans:** Early Admission; Deferred Admission **Application Deadline:** Rolling **Application Fee:** $0.00 **H.S. Requirements:** High school diploma required; GED accepted **Costs Per Year:** Ap-

plication fee: $0. Comprehensive fee: $30,126 includes full-time tuition ($19,875), mandatory fees ($951), and college room and board ($9300). Part-time tuition: $368 per quarter hour. **Calendar System:** Quarter, Summer Session Available **Enrollment:** FT 2,317, PT 135 **Faculty:** FT 59, PT 17 **Student-Faculty Ratio:** 36:1 **Exams:** SAT I or ACT **% Receiving Financial Aid:** 80 **Library Holdings:** 11,642 **Regional Accreditation:** New England Association of Schools and Colleges **Credit Hours For Degree:** 90 quarter credit hours, Associates; 180 quarter credit hours, Bachelors

JONES COLLEGE (JACKSONVILLE)
5353 Arlington Expressway
Jacksonville, FL 32211
Tel: (904)743-1122
E-mail: jmccaffe@jones.edu
Web Site: http://www.jones.edu/
President/CEO: Dr. David V. Swann
Admissions: Frank McCafferty
Financial Aid: Becky Davis
Type: Four-Year College **Sex:** Coed **% Accepted:** 72 **Admission Plans:** Open Admission; Early Admission; Deferred Admission **Application Deadline:** Rolling **Application Fee:** $0.00 **H.S. Requirements:** High school diploma required; GED accepted **Costs Per Year:** Application fee: $0. Tuition: $6600 full-time, $275 per credit hour part-time. Mandatory fees: $90 full-time. **Scholarships:** Available **Calendar System:** Trimester, Summer Session Available **Enrollment:** FT 183, PT 440 **Faculty:** FT 4, PT 57 **Student-Faculty Ratio:** 14:1 **Library Holdings:** 34,000 **Credit Hours For Degree:** 60 credit hours, Associates; 120 credit hours, Bachelors **Professional Accreditation:** ACICS

JONES COLLEGE (MIAMI)
11430 North Kendall Dr., Ste. 200
Miami, FL 33176
Tel: (305)275-9996
Admissions: (904)743-1122
Fax: (305)275-9571
Web Site: http://www.jones.edu/
President/CEO: Barclay Charles
Admissions: LeAnne Osburne
Type: Four-Year College **Sex:** Coed **Calendar System:** Trimester **Enrollment:** , PT 837 **Faculty:** FT 182, PT 64 **Professional Accreditation:** ACICS

KEISER COLLEGE (DAYTONA BEACH)
1800 Business Park Blvd.
Daytona Beach, FL 32114
Tel: (904)274-5060
Free: 800-749-4456
Admissions: (386)274-5060
Fax: (904)274-2725
Web Site: http://www.keisercollege.edu/
President/CEO: Peter F. Crocitto, Jr.
Registrar: Glenn LaMarque
Admissions: Heather Armstrong
Financial Aid: Kim Dunkin
Type: Two-Year College **Sex:** Coed **Application Fee:** $50.00 **H.S. Requirements:** High school diploma required; GED accepted **Scholarships:** Available **Calendar System:** Miscellaneous, Summer Session Not available **Exams:** Other **Library Holdings:** 5,000 **Regional Accreditation:** Southern Association of Colleges and Schools **Credit Hours For Degree:** 60 semester hours, Associates **Professional Accreditation:** AAMAE, JRCEDMS

KEISER COLLEGE (FORT LAUDERDALE)
1500 Northwest 49th St.
Fort Lauderdale, FL 33309
Tel: (954)776-4456
Free: 800-749-4456
Admissions: (954)776-4476
E-mail: admissions@keisercollege.edu
Web Site: http://www.keisercollege.edu
President/CEO: Peter F. Crocitto
Registrar: Connie Haynie
Admissions: Brian Woods
Financial Aid: Gloria Wright
Type: Two-Year College **Sex:** Coed **Admission Plans:** Deferred Admission **Application Fee:** $55.00 **H.S. Requirements:** High school diploma required; GED accepted **Costs Per Year:** Application fee: $55. **Scholarships:** Available **Calendar System:** Miscellaneous **Enrollment:** FT 5,043, PT 1,078 **Faculty:** FT 178, PT 317 **Exams:** Other **Regional Accreditation:** Southern Association of Colleges and Schools **Credit Hours For Degree:** 60 semester hours, Associates; 120 semester hours, Bachelors **Professional Accreditation:** ABHES, AOTA, APTA, JRCEDMS, JRCERT, NAACLS

KEISER COLLEGE (LAKELAND)
3515 Aviation Dr.
Lakeland, FL 33811
Tel: (863)701-7789
Fax: (863)701-8758
Web Site: http://www.keisercollege.edu/
Admissions: Walter Bequette
Type: Two-Year College **Sex:** Coed **Calendar System:** Miscellaneous **Regional Accreditation:** Southern Association of Colleges and Schools

KEISER COLLEGE (MELBOURNE)
900 South Babcock St.
Melbourne, FL 32901-1461
Tel: (321)255-2255
Admissions: (954)776-4456
Web Site: http://www.keisercollege.edu/
President/CEO: Peter F. Crocitto, Jr.
Registrar: Susan Lockman
Admissions: Susan Zeigelhofer
Financial Aid: Patti Robertson
Type: Two-Year College **Scholarships:** Available **Calendar System:** Miscellaneous **Faculty:** FT 94, PT 102 **Exams:** Other **Regional Accreditation:** Southern Association of Colleges and Schools **Credit Hours For Degree:** 60 semester hours, Associates **Professional Accreditation:** ABHES, ACF, AOTA

KEISER COLLEGE (MIAMI)
8505 Mills Dr.
Miami, FL 33183
Tel: (305)596-2226
Fax: (305)596-7077
Web Site: http://www.keisercollege.edu/
Admissions: Ted Weiner
Type: Two-Year College **Sex:** Coed **Application Fee:** $55.00 **Costs Per Year:** Application fee: $55. Tuition: $11,032 full-time. Mandatory fees: $400 full-time. **Calendar System:** Miscellaneous **Enrollment:** FT 739 **Faculty:** FT 40, PT 7 **Student-Faculty Ratio:** 18:1 **Exams:** SAT I or ACT **Regional Accreditation:** Southern Association of Colleges and Schools

KEISER COLLEGE (ORLANDO)
5600 Lake Underhill Rd.
Orlando, FL 32807
Tel: (407)273-5800
Web Site: http://www.keisercollege.edu/ **Type:** Two-Year College **Sex:** Coed **Calendar System:** Miscellaneous **Regional Accreditation:** Southern Association of Colleges and Schools

KEISER COLLEGE (PEMBROKE PINES)
12520 Pines Blvd.
Pembroke Pines, FL 33027
Tel: (954)431-4300
Fax: (954)431-2929
Web Site: http://www.keisercollege.edu **Type:** Two-Year College **Sex:** Coed **Calendar System:** Semester **Professional Accreditation:** ABHES, COE

KEISER COLLEGE (PORT ST. LUCIE)
9468 South US Hwy. 1
Port St. Lucie, FL 34952
Tel: (772)398-9990
Fax: (772)335-9619
Web Site: http://www.keisercollege.edu **Type:** Two-Year College **Sex:** Coed **Calendar System:** Semester **Professional Accreditation:** ABHES, COE

KEISER COLLEGE (SARASOTA)
6151 Lake Osprey Dr.
Sarasota, FL 34240

Tel: (941)954-0954; (866)KEI-SER2
Admissions: (941)907-3900
Web Site: http://www.keisercollege.edu/
President/CEO: Peter F. Crocitto, Jr.
Registrar: Robin Vickers
Admissions: Brandon Barnhill
Financial Aid: Fred Pfeffer
Type: Two-Year College **Sex:** Coed **Application Fee:** $50.00 **H.S. Requirements:** High school diploma required; GED accepted **Scholarships:** Available **Calendar System:** Miscellaneous, Summer Session Not available **Faculty:** FT 11, PT 6 **Exams:** Other **Regional Accreditation:** Southern Association of Colleges and Schools **Credit Hours For Degree:** 60 semester hours, Associates **Professional Accreditation:** ABHES

KEISER COLLEGE (TALLAHASSEE)
1700 Halstead Blvd.
Tallahassee, FL 32308
Tel: (850)906-9494
Fax: (850)906-9497
Web Site: http://www.keisercollege.edu/
President/CEO: Peter F. Crocitto, Jr.
Registrar: Beth Lewis
Admissions: Phil Hooks
Financial Aid: Fred Pfeffer
Type: Two-Year College **Sex:** Coed **H.S. Requirements:** High school diploma required; GED accepted **Scholarships:** Available **Calendar System:** Miscellaneous, Summer Session Not available **Faculty:** FT 16, PT 11 **Exams:** Other **Regional Accreditation:** Southern Association of Colleges and Schools **Credit Hours For Degree:** 60 semester hours, Associates **Professional Accreditation:** ABHES, ACF

KEISER COLLEGE (WEST PALM BEACH)
2085 Vista Parkway
West Palm Beach, FL 33411
Tel: (561)471-6000
Fax: (561)547-6609
Web Site: http://www.keisercollege.edu **Type:** Two-Year College **Sex:** Coed **Calendar System:** Semester **Professional Accreditation:** COE

KEY COLLEGE
5225 West Broward Blvd.
Fort Lauderdale, FL 33317
Tel: (954)581-2223
Free: 800-581-8292
Fax: (954)583-9458
Web Site: http://www.keycollege.edu/
President/CEO: Ronald H. Dooley
Admissions: Ronald H. Dooley
Financial Aid: Chris Miller
Type: Two-Year College **Sex:** Coed **Admission Plans:** Deferred Admission **Application Fee:** $95.00 **H.S. Requirements:** High school diploma required; GED accepted **Scholarships:** Available **Calendar System:** Quarter, Summer Session Not available **Enrollment:** FT 147 **Faculty:** FT 9, PT 3 **Student-Faculty Ratio:** 12:1 **Exams:** Other **Credit Hours For Degree:** 90 credits, Associates **Professional Accreditation:** ACICS

LAKE CITY COMMUNITY COLLEGE
Route 19, Box 1030
Lake City, FL 32025-8703
Tel: (386)752-1822
Admissions: (386)754-4288
Fax: (386)755-1521
E-mail: admissions@mail.lakecity.cc.fl.us
Web Site: http://www.lakecity.cc.fl.us/
President/CEO: Dr. Charles W. Hall
Registrar: Robert Ray Carver
Admissions: Vince Rice
Financial Aid: Debberin Tunsil
Type: Two-Year College **Sex:** Coed **Affiliation:** Florida Community College System **% Accepted:** 57 **Admission Plans:** Open Admission; Early Admission; Deferred Admission **Application Deadline:** Rolling **Application Fee:** $15.00 **H.S. Requirements:** High school diploma required; GED accepted **Costs Per Year:** Application fee: $15. State resident tuition: $2037 full-time. Nonresident tuition: $7290 full-time. College room and board: $4535. **Scholarships:** Available **Calendar System:** Semester, Summer Session Available **Enrollment:** FT 1,084, PT 1,652 **Faculty:** FT 55, PT 110 **Student-Faculty Ratio:** 18:1 **% Residing in College-Owned, -Operated, or -Affiliated Housing:** 2 **Library Holdings:** 42,000 **Regional Accreditation:** Southern Association of Colleges and Schools **Credit Hours For Degree:** 60 semester hours, Associates **Professional Accreditation:** APTA, JRCEMT, NAACLS, NLN **Intercollegiate Athletics:** Baseball M; Golf W; Softball W

LAKE-SUMTER COMMUNITY COLLEGE
9501 US Hwy. 441
Leesburg, FL 34788-8751
Tel: (352)787-3747
Admissions: (352)323-3677
Web Site: http://www.lscc.edu/
President/CEO: Dr. Charles Mojock
Registrar: Tabitha Richards
Admissions: Tabitha Richards
Financial Aid: Audrey Maxwell
Type: Two-Year College **Sex:** Coed **Affiliation:** Florida Department of Education **% Accepted:** 100 **Admission Plans:** Open Admission **Application Deadline:** Rolling **Application Fee:** $25.00 **H.S. Requirements:** High school diploma required; GED accepted **Costs Per Year:** Application fee: $25. State resident tuition: $1932 full-time, $64.40 per credit hour part-time. Nonresident tuition: $7108 full-time, $236.95 per credit hour part-time. Mandatory fees: $30 full-time, $1 per credit hour part-time. Full-time tuition and fees vary according to course load. Part-time tuition and fees vary according to course load. **Scholarships:** Available **Calendar System:** Semester, Summer Session Available **Enrollment:** FT 1,208, PT 2,201 **Faculty:** FT 48, PT 120 **Student-Faculty Ratio:** 20:1 **Library Holdings:** 69,465 **Regional Accreditation:** Southern Association of Colleges and Schools **Credit Hours For Degree:** 60 semester hours, Associates **Professional Accreditation:** AHIMA **Intercollegiate Athletics:** Baseball M; Softball W; Volleyball W

LYNN UNIVERSITY
3601 North Military Trail
Boca Raton, FL 33431-5598
Tel: (561)237-7000
Free: 800-888-5966
Admissions: (561)237-7900
Fax: (561)241-3552
E-mail: admission@lynn.edu
Web Site: http://www.lynn.edu/
President/CEO: Dr. Donald E. Ross
Admissions: Melanie Glines
Financial Aid: Evelyn Nelson
Type: Comprehensive **Sex:** Coed **Affiliation:** American College Dublin **Scores:** 76% SAT V 400+; 74% SAT M 400+; 54% ACT 18-23; 7% ACT 24-29 **% Accepted:** 80 **Admission Plans:** Early Admission; Deferred Admission **Application Deadline:** Rolling **Application Fee:** $35.00 **H.S. Requirements:** High school diploma required; GED accepted **Costs Per Year:** Application fee: $35. Comprehensive fee: $37,000 includes full-time tuition ($26,200), mandatory fees ($1150), and college room and board ($9650). Part-time tuition: $760 per credit hour. **Scholarships:** Available **Calendar System:** Semester, Summer Session Available **Enrollment:** FT 1,951, PT 332, Grad 464 **Faculty:** FT 93, PT 178 **Student-Faculty Ratio:** 17:1 **Exams:** SAT I or ACT **% Receiving Financial Aid:** 36 **% Residing in College-Owned, -Operated, or -Affiliated Housing:** 45 **Library Holdings:** 235,000 **Regional Accreditation:** Southern Association of Colleges and Schools **Credit Hours For Degree:** 120 credit hours, Bachelors **ROTC:** Air Force **Professional Accreditation:** NASM **Intercollegiate Athletics:** Baseball M; Basketball M & W; Cross-Country Running M & W; Golf M & W; Soccer M & W; Softball W; Tennis M & W; Volleyball W

MANATEE COMMUNITY COLLEGE
5840 26th St. West, PO Box 1849
Bradenton, FL 34206-7046
Tel: (941)752-5000
Admissions: (941)752-5031
Fax: (941)727-6177
Web Site: http://www.mccfl.edu/
President/CEO: Dr. Sarah H. Pappas
Registrar: Mari Lynn Paro
Admissions: MariLynn Paro

Financial Aid: Anders Nilsen
Type: Two-Year College **Sex:** Coed **Affiliation:** Florida Community College System **Scores:** 82.58% SAT V 400+; 80.1% SAT M 400+; 52.9% ACT 18-23; 10.3% ACT 24-29 **Admission Plans:** Open Admission; Early Admission **Application Deadline:** August 20 **Application Fee:** $40.00 **H.S. Requirements:** High school diploma required; GED accepted **Costs Per Year:** Application fee: $40. State resident tuition: $1,983 full-time, $66.11 per credit part-time. Nonresident tuition: $7,352 full-time, $245.05 per credit part-time. **Scholarships:** Available **Calendar System:** Semester, Summer Session Available **Enrollment:** FT 3,855, PT 5,912 **Faculty:** FT 126, PT 337 **Student-Faculty Ratio:** 23:1 **Library Holdings:** 65,386 **Regional Accreditation:** Southern Association of Colleges and Schools **Credit Hours For Degree:** 60 credit hours, Associates **Professional Accreditation:** ADA, AOTA, APTA, CARC, JRCERT, NLN **Intercollegiate Athletics:** Baseball M; Basketball M; Softball W; Volleyball W

MEDVANCE INSTITUTE
170 JFK Dr.
Atlantis, FL 33462
Tel: (561)304-3466; 888-86-GO-MED
Fax: (561)304-3471
E-mail: bcortez@medvance.org
Web Site: http://www.medvance.org/
President/CEO: Brenda Cortez
Admissions: Brenda Cortez
Type: Two-Year College **Sex:** Coed **Calendar System:** Quarter **Professional Accreditation:** ABHES, COE

MIAMI DADE COLLEGE
300 Northeast Second Ave.
Miami, FL 33132-2296
Tel: (305)237-3131
Admissions: (305)237-0633
Fax: (305)237-3761
E-mail: skelly@mdc.edu
Web Site: http://www.mdc.edu/
President/CEO: Dr. Eduardo J. Padrón
Admissions: Steven Kelly
Financial Aid: James McMillan
Type: Two-Year College **Sex:** Coed **Affiliation:** Florida Community College System **Scores:** 67% SAT V 400+; 62% SAT M 400+; 30% ACT 18-23; 2% ACT 24-29 **% Accepted:** 100 **Admission Plans:** Open Admission; Early Admission **Application Deadline:** Rolling **Application Fee:** $20.00 **H.S. Requirements:** High school diploma required; GED accepted **Costs Per Year:** Application fee: $20. State resident tuition: $1620 full-time, $54 per credit part-time. Nonresident tuition: $5997 full-time, $199.90 per credit part-time. Mandatory fees: $302 full-time. **Scholarships:** Available **Calendar System:** Miscellaneous, Summer Session Available **Enrollment:** FT 18,836, PT 35,333 **Faculty:** FT 722, PT 1,381 **Student-Faculty Ratio:** 26:1 **Library Holdings:** 327,417 **Regional Accreditation:** Southern Association of Colleges and Schools **Credit Hours For Degree:** 60 credit hours, Associates; 120 credit hours, Bachelors **ROTC:** Army, Air Force **Professional Accreditation:** ABFSE, ADA, AHIMA, APTA, COptA, CARC, JRCEDMS, JRCERT, JRCEMT, MEAC, NAACLS, NLN **Intercollegiate Athletics:** Baseball M; Basketball M & W; Softball W; Volleyball W

MIAMI INTERNATIONAL UNIVERSITY OF ART & DESIGN
1501 Biscayne Blvd., Ste. 100
Miami, FL 33132-1418
Tel: (305)428-5700
Free: 800-225-9023
Fax: (305)374-7946
Web Site: http://www.aimiu.aii.edu/
President/CEO: Erika Fleming
Registrar: Monica Reina-Fernandez
Admissions: Carmen Topper
Financial Aid: Mitzie Forrest
Type: Comprehensive **Sex:** Coed **Affiliation:** Education Management Corporation **% Accepted:** 32 **Admission Plans:** Deferred Admission **Application Deadline:** Rolling **Application Fee:** $50.00 **H.S. Requirements:** High school diploma required; GED accepted **Costs Per Year:** Application fee: $50. Tuition: $18,960 full-time. College room only: $6150. **Scholarships:** Available **Calendar System:** Quarter, Summer Session Available **Enrollment:** FT 1,328, Grad 78 **Faculty:** FT 45, PT 65 **Student-Faculty Ratio:** 20:1 **Exams:** SAT I and SAT II or ACT **% Residing in College-Owned, -Operated, or -Affiliated Housing:** 40 **Library Holdings:** 22,000 **Regional Accreditation:** Southern Association of Colleges and Schools **Credit Hours For Degree:** 112 quarter credits, Associates; 192 quarter credits, Bachelors

NATIONAL SCHOOL OF TECHNOLOGY, INC. (FORT LAUDERDALE)
1040 Bayview Dr.
Fort Lauderdale, FL 33304
Tel: (954)630-0066
Fax: (954)630-0076
E-mail: amiller@cci.edu
Web Site: http://www.nst.cc/
Admissions: Ashly Miller
Type: Two-Year College **Sex:** Coed **Calendar System:** Continuous **Professional Accreditation:** ABHES

NATIONAL SCHOOL OF TECHNOLOGY, INC. (HIALEAH)
4410 West 16th Ave., Ste. 52
Hialeah, FL 33012
Tel: (305)558-9500
Fax: (305)558-4419
E-mail: dalonso@cci.edu
Web Site: http://www.nst.cc/
President/CEO: Gilbert Delgado
Admissions: Daniel Alonso
Type: Two-Year College **Sex:** Coed **Calendar System:** Continuous **Professional Accreditation:** ARCEST, ABHES

NATIONAL SCHOOL OF TECHNOLOGY, INC. (MIAMI)
111 Northwest 183rd St., 2nd Floor
Miami, FL 33169
Tel: (305)386-9900
Fax: (305)388-1740
Web Site: http://www.nst.cc/
Admissions: Amber Stenbeck
Type: Two-Year College **Sex:** Coed **Calendar System:** Continuous **Faculty:** FT 30, PT 10 **Student-Faculty Ratio:** 20:1 **Professional Accreditation:** ABHES

NATIONAL SCHOOL OF TECHNOLOGY, INC. (NORTH MIAMI BEACH)
16150 Northeast 17th Ave.
North Miami Beach, FL 33162-4744
Tel: (305)949-9500
Fax: (305)956-5758
Web Site: http://www.nst.cc/
President/CEO: Mario Miro
Admissions: Walter McQuade
Type: Two-Year College **Sex:** Coed **Calendar System:** Continuous **Enrollment:** FT 608 **Faculty:** FT 35, PT 15 **Student-Faculty Ratio:** 12:1 **Professional Accreditation:** ARCEST, ABHES

NEW COLLEGE OF FLORIDA
5700 North Tamiami Trail
Sarasota, FL 34243-2197
Tel: (941)359-4700
Admissions: (941)359-4269
Fax: (941)359-4435
E-mail: ncadmissions@virtu.sar.usf.edu
Web Site: http://www.ncf.edu/
President/CEO: Dr. Gordon E. Michalson, Jr.
Registrar: Adrian Cornelius
Admissions: Kathleen M. Killian
Financial Aid: Monica Mattscheck
Type: Four-Year College **Sex:** Coed **Affiliation:** State University System of Florida **Scores:** 100% SAT V 400+; 100% SAT M 400+; 15% ACT 18-23; 61% ACT 24-29 **% Accepted:** 60 **Admission Plans:** Early Admission; Deferred Admission **Application Deadline:** May 01 **Application Fee:** $30.00 **H.S. Requirements:** High school diploma required; GED accepted **Costs Per Year:** Application fee: $30. State resident tuition: $3797 full-time. Nonresident tuition: $20,345 full-time. College room and board: $6750. College room only: $4170. **Scholarships:** Available **Calendar System:** 4-1-4, Summer Session Not available **Enrollment:** FT 761 **Faculty:** FT 68, PT 9 **Student-Faculty Ratio:** 10:1 **Exams:** SAT I or ACT **% Receiving Financial Aid:** 36 **% Residing in College-Owned, -Operated, or -Affiliated Hous-**

ing: 68 **Library Holdings:** 256,581 **Regional Accreditation:** Southern Association of Colleges and Schools **Credit Hours For Degree:** 7 semester-long contracts and 3 independent study projects, senior thesis

NEW ENGLAND INSTITUTE OF TECHNOLOGY AT PALM BEACH
2410 Metro Centre Blvd.
West Palm Beach, FL 33407
Tel: (561)842-8324
Free: 800-826-9986
Fax: (561)842-9503
Web Site: http://newenglandtech.com/
President/CEO: Charles Halliday
Registrar: Kathy Patterson
Admissions: Kevin Cassidy
Financial Aid: Elizabeth Layton
Type: Two-Year College **Sex:** Coed **Admission Plans:** Open Admission; Early Admission **Application Fee:** $150.00 **H.S. Requirements:** High school diploma required; GED accepted **Scholarships:** Available **Calendar System:** Quarter, Summer Session Not available **Faculty:** FT 46 **Student-Faculty Ratio:** 25:1 **Credit Hours For Degree:** 90 quarter hours, Associates **Professional Accreditation:** AAMAE, COE

NEW WORLD SCHOOL OF THE ARTS
300 NE 2nd Ave.
Miami, FL 33132
Tel: (305)237-3135
Admissions: (305)237-3472
Fax: (305)237-3794
E-mail: nwsaadm@mdc.edu
Web Site: http://www.mdc.edu/nwsa
President/CEO: John Otis
Admissions: Lourdes Werner
Type: Four-Year College **Sex:** Coed **Affiliation:** Miami Dade College and University of Florida **% Accepted:** 47 **Application Deadline:** Rolling **Application Fee:** $0.00 **H.S. Requirements:** High school diploma required; GED accepted **Costs Per Year:** Application fee: $0. State resident tuition: $12,000 full-time, $65.05 per credit part-time. Nonresident tuition: $17,000 full-time, $216.15 per credit part-time. **Calendar System:** Semester, Summer Session Available **Enrollment:** FT 371 **Faculty:** FT 23, PT 50 **Student-Faculty Ratio:** 5:1 **Credit Hours For Degree:** 72 credit hours, Associates; 136 credit hours, Bachelors **Professional Accreditation:** NASAD, NASD, NASM, NAST

NORTH FLORIDA COMMUNITY COLLEGE
1000 Turner Davis Dr.
Madison, FL 32340-1602
Tel: (850)973-2288
Admissions: (850)973-1622
Fax: (850)973-1696
Web Site: http://www.nfcc.edu/
President/CEO: Morris G. Steen, Jr.
Registrar: Mary Anne Wheeler
Admissions: Carolyn Blount
Type: Two-Year College **Sex:** Coed **Scores:** 86% SAT V 400+; 83% SAT M 400+; 28% ACT 18-23; 9% ACT 24-29 **Admission Plans:** Open Admission; Early Admission **Application Fee:** $20.00 **H.S. Requirements:** High school diploma required; GED accepted **Scholarships:** Available **Calendar System:** Semester, Summer Session Available **Enrollment:** FT 593, PT 704 **Faculty:** FT 25, PT 19 **Student-Faculty Ratio:** 18:1 **Exams:** SAT I or ACT **Library Holdings:** 30,137 **Regional Accreditation:** Southern Association of Colleges and Schools **Credit Hours For Degree:** 60 semester hours, Associates **Intercollegiate Athletics:** Baseball M; Basketball W; Softball W

NORTHWOOD UNIVERSITY, FLORIDA CAMPUS
2600 North Military Trail
West Palm Beach, FL 33409-2911
Tel: (561)478-5500
Free: 800-458-8325
Admissions: (989)837-4367
Fax: (561)640-3328
E-mail: admissions@northwood.edu
Web Site: http://www.northwood.edu/
President/CEO: John H. Haynie
Registrar: Michelle Webb
Admissions: Dr. David D. Long
Financial Aid: Teresa Palmer
Type: Four-Year College **Sex:** Coed **Scores:** 80% SAT V 400+; 89% SAT M 400+; 56% ACT 18-23; 18% ACT 24-29 **% Accepted:** 60 **Admission Plans:** Early Admission; Deferred Admission **Application Deadline:** Rolling **Application Fee:** $25.00 **H.S. Requirements:** High school diploma required; GED accepted **Costs Per Year:** Application fee: $25. Comprehensive fee: $23,316 includes full-time tuition ($15,216), mandatory fees ($585), and college room and board ($7515). College room only: $3870. Part-time tuition: $317 per credit hour. **Scholarships:** Available **Calendar System:** Quarter, Summer Session Available **Enrollment:** FT 794, PT 129 **Faculty:** FT 19, PT 31 **Student-Faculty Ratio:** 25:1 **Exams:** SAT I or ACT **% Receiving Financial Aid:** 45 **% Residing in College-Owned, -Operated, or -Affiliated Housing:** 46 **Library Holdings:** 25,362 **Regional Accreditation:** North Central Association of Colleges and Schools **Credit Hours For Degree:** 90 credit hours, Associates; 180 credit hours, Bachelors **Intercollegiate Athletics:** Baseball M; Basketball M & W; Golf M & W; Soccer M & W; Softball W; Tennis M & W; Volleyball W

NOVA SOUTHEASTERN UNIVERSITY
3301 College Ave.
Fort Lauderdale, FL 33314-7796
Tel: (954)262-7300
Free: 800-541-NOVA
Admissions: (954)262-8000
Fax: (954)262-3967
E-mail: nsuinfo@nova.edu
Web Site: http://www.nova.edu/
President/CEO: Ray Ferrero, Jr.
Registrar: G. Elaine Poff
Admissions: Maria Dillard
Financial Aid: Peggy Loewy-Wellisch
Type: University **Sex:** Coed **Scores:** 98% SAT V 400+; 97% SAT M 400+ **% Accepted:** 54 **Admission Plans:** Early Admission; Deferred Admission **Application Deadline:** Rolling **Application Fee:** $50.00 **H.S. Requirements:** High school diploma required; GED accepted **Costs Per Year:** Application fee: $50. Comprehensive fee: $24,320 includes full-time tuition ($17,250), mandatory fees ($550), and college room and board ($6520). College room only: $4120. Full-time tuition and fees vary according to class time and program. Room and board charges vary according to board plan and housing facility. Part-time tuition: $575 per credit hour. Part-time tuition varies according to class time, course load, and program. **Scholarships:** Available **Calendar System:** Trimester, Summer Session Available **Enrollment:** FT 3,379, PT 2,074, Grad 17,548 **Faculty:** FT 582, PT 1,033 **Student-Faculty Ratio:** 18:1 **Exams:** SAT I or ACT **% Receiving Financial Aid:** 51 **% Residing in College-Owned, -Operated, or -Affiliated Housing:** 9 **Library Holdings:** 668,738 **Regional Accreditation:** Southern Association of Colleges and Schools **Credit Hours For Degree:** 60 credits, Associates; 120 credits, Bachelors **Professional Accreditation:** AAMFT, ABA, ACPhE, ADA, AOTA, AOA, AOsA, APTA, APA, ASLHA, AALS, CEPH **Intercollegiate Athletics:** Baseball M; Basketball M & W; Cheerleading W; Crew W; Cross-Country Running M & W; Golf M & W; Soccer M & W; Softball W; Tennis W; Volleyball W

OKALOOSA-WALTON COLLEGE
100 College Blvd.
Niceville, FL 32578-1295
Tel: (850)678-5111
Admissions: (850)729-5373
E-mail: registrar@owc.edu
Web Site: http://www.owc.edu/
President/CEO: Dr. James R. Richburg
Registrar: Christine C. Bishop
Admissions: Christine Bishop
Financial Aid: Patricia Bennett
Type: Two-Year College **Sex:** Coed **Affiliation:** Florida Community College System **Admission Plans:** Open Admission; Preferred Admission; Early Admission; Deferred Admission **Application Deadline:** Rolling **Application Fee:** $0.00 **H.S. Requirements:** High school diploma or equivalent not required. For associate of arts degree programs: High school diploma required; GED accepted **Costs Per Year:** Application fee: $0. State resident tuition: $1774 full-time, $55.45 per credit part-time. Nonresident tuition: $6661 full-time, $208.15 per credit part-time. **Scholarships:** Available **Calendar System:** Semester, Summer Session Available **Faculty:** FT 83, PT 160 **Student-Faculty Ratio:** 20:1 **Exams:** Other **Library Holdings:**

84,991 **Regional Accreditation:** Southern Association of Colleges and Schools **Credit Hours For Degree:** 60 semester hours, Associates **ROTC:** Army **Professional Accreditation:** ADA **Intercollegiate Athletics:** Baseball M; Basketball M & W; Softball W

ORLANDO CULINARY ACADEMY
8511 Commodity Circle, Ste. 100
Orlando, FL 32819
Tel: (407)888-4000; (866)OCA-CHEF
Fax: (407)888-4019
Web Site: http://www.orlandoculinary.com/ **Type:** Two-Year College **Sex:** Coed **Professional Accreditation:** ACICS

PALM BEACH ATLANTIC UNIVERSITY
901 South Flagler Dr, PO Box 24708
West Palm Beach, FL 33416-4708
Tel: (561)803-2000
Free: 800-238-3998
E-mail: admit@pbac.edu
Web Site: http://www.pba.edu/
President/CEO: Dr. David W. Clark
Registrar: Carolanne Brown
Admissions: Buck James
Financial Aid: Margherite Powell
Type: Comprehensive **Sex:** Coed **Affiliation:** nondenominational **Scores:** 99.49% SAT V 400+; 97.9% SAT M 400+; 45.52% ACT 18-23; 35.18% ACT 24-29 **% Accepted:** 44 **Admission Plans:** Early Admission; Early Action; Deferred Admission **Application Deadline:** Rolling **Application Fee:** $25.00 **H.S. Requirements:** High school diploma required; GED accepted **Costs Per Year:** Application fee: $25. Comprehensive fee: $24,030 includes full-time tuition ($17,130), mandatory fees ($220), and college room and board ($6680). College room only: $3350. Full-time tuition and fees vary according to course load, degree level, program, and reciprocity agreements. Room and board charges vary according to board plan and housing facility. Part-time tuition: $420 per credit. Part-time mandatory fees: $85 per term. Part-time tuition and fees vary according to course load, degree level, program, and reciprocity agreements. **Scholarships:** Available **Calendar System:** Semester, Summer Session Available **Enrollment:** FT 2,285, PT 201, Grad 394 **Faculty:** FT 138, PT 130 **Student-Faculty Ratio:** 13:1 **Exams:** SAT I or ACT **% Receiving Financial Aid:** 23 **% Residing in College-Owned, -Operated, or -Affiliated Housing:** 45 **Library Holdings:** 140,714 **Regional Accreditation:** Southern Association of Colleges and Schools **Credit Hours For Degree:** 60 credit hours, Associates; 120 credit hours, Bachelors **Professional Accreditation:** ACPhE, NASM **Intercollegiate Athletics:** Baseball M; Basketball M & W; Cross-Country Running M & W; Golf M; Soccer M & W; Softball W; Tennis M & W; Volleyball M & W

PALM BEACH COMMUNITY COLLEGE
4200 Congress Ave.
Lake Worth, FL 33461-4796
Tel: (561)967-7222
Admissions: (561)868-3032
Web Site: http://www.pbcc.edu/
President/CEO: Dr. Dennis P. Gallon
Registrar: Annaleah Morrow
Admissions: Annaleah Morrow
Financial Aid: Michele Bowles
Type: Two-Year College **Sex:** Coed **Affiliation:** Florida Community College System **% Accepted:** 100 **Admission Plans:** Open Admission; Preferred Admission; Early Admission; Deferred Admission **Application Deadline:** August 20 **Application Fee:** $20.00 **H.S. Requirements:** High school diploma required; GED accepted **Costs Per Year:** Application fee: $20. Area resident tuition: $63 per hour part-time. State resident tuition: $1890 full-time, $63 per hour part-time. Nonresident tuition: $6892 full-time, $229.75 per hour part-time. Mandatory fees: $10 full-time. **Scholarships:** Available **Calendar System:** Semester, Summer Session Available **Enrollment:** FT 6,917, PT 15,749 **Faculty:** FT 231, PT 793 **Student-Faculty Ratio:** 22:1 **Library Holdings:** 151,000 **Regional Accreditation:** Southern Association of Colleges and Schools **Credit Hours For Degree:** 60 semester hours, Associates **Professional Accreditation:** ADA, CARC, JRCERT, JRCEMT, MACTE, NLN **Intercollegiate Athletics:** Baseball M; Basketball M & W; Softball W; Volleyball M & W

PASCO-HERNANDO COMMUNITY COLLEGE
10230 Ridge Rd.
New Port Richey, FL 34654-5199
Tel: (727)847-2727
Admissions: (727)816-3261
Fax: (727)816-3450
E-mail: bullard@phcc.edu
Web Site: http://www.phcc.edu/
President/CEO: Dr. Robert W. Judson, Jr.
Registrar: Michael Malizia
Admissions: Debra Bullard
Financial Aid: S. Rebecca Shanafelt
Type: Two-Year College **Sex:** Coed **Affiliation:** Florida Community College System **Admission Plans:** Open Admission **Application Deadline:** Rolling **Application Fee:** $20.00 **H.S. Requirements:** High school diploma required; GED accepted **Costs Per Year:** Application fee: $20. State resident tuition: $1872 full-time, $62 per credit part-time. Nonresident tuition: $7222 full-time, $241 per credit part-time. **Scholarships:** Available **Calendar System:** Semester, Summer Session Available **Enrollment:** FT 2,670, PT 4,676 **Faculty:** FT 98, PT 217 **Student-Faculty Ratio:** 25:1 **Library Holdings:** 67,852 **Regional Accreditation:** Southern Association of Colleges and Schools **Credit Hours For Degree:** 60 semester hours, Associates **ROTC:** Army **Professional Accreditation:** ADA, JRCEMT, NLN **Intercollegiate Athletics:** Baseball M; Basketball M; Softball W; Tennis W; Volleyball W

PENSACOLA JUNIOR COLLEGE
1000 College Blvd.
Pensacola, FL 32504-8998
Tel: (850)484-1000
Admissions: (850)484-1600
Fax: (850)484-1826
Web Site: http://www.pjc.edu/
President/CEO: Dr. G. Thomas Delaino, Jr.
Admissions: Martha Caughey
Financial Aid: Karen Kessler
Type: Two-Year College **Sex:** Coed **Affiliation:** Florida Community College System **Admission Plans:** Open Admission; Early Admission **Application Fee:** $30.00 **H.S. Requirements:** High school diploma required; GED accepted **Costs Per Year:** Application fee: $30. State resident tuition: $1755 full-time. Nonresident tuition: $6540 full-time. Mandatory fees: $300 full-time. **Scholarships:** Available **Calendar System:** Semester, Summer Session Available **Faculty:** FT 212, PT 535 **Regional Accreditation:** Southern Association of Colleges and Schools **Credit Hours For Degree:** 60 semester hours, Associates **ROTC:** Army **Professional Accreditation:** ACF, ADA, AHIMA, APTA, CARC, JRCERT, JRCEMT **Intercollegiate Athletics:** Baseball M; Basketball M & W; Softball W

POLK COMMUNITY COLLEGE
999 Ave. H, NE
Winter Haven, FL 33881-4299
Tel: (863)297-1000
Admissions: (863)297-1010
Fax: (863)297-1060
E-mail: clyle@polk.edu and rwebb@polk.edu
Web Site: http://www.polk.edu/
President/CEO: Dr. J. Larry Durrence
Registrar: Barbara Guthrie
Admissions: Charles Lyle III and Reggie Webb
Type: Two-Year College **Sex:** Coed **Affiliation:** Florida Community College System **% Accepted:** 100 **Admission Plans:** Open Admission; Early Admission; Deferred Admission **Application Deadline:** Rolling **Application Fee:** $20.00 **H.S. Requirements:** High school diploma required; GED accepted **Costs Per Year:** Application fee: $20. State resident tuition: $1901 full-time, $63.38 per credit hour part-time. Nonresident tuition: $7044 full-time, $234.79 per credit hour part-time. **Scholarships:** Available **Calendar System:** Semester, Summer Session Available **Enrollment:** FT 2,037, PT 5,045 **Faculty:** FT 122, PT 324 **Student-Faculty Ratio:** 16:1 **Library Holdings:** 181,000 **Regional Accreditation:** Southern Association of Colleges and Schools **Credit Hours For Degree:** 60 credit hours, Associates **ROTC:** Army **Professional Accreditation:** AHIMA, AOTA, APTA, JRCERT, JRCEMT, NLN **Intercollegiate Athletics:** Baseball M; Basketball M; Soccer W; Softball W; Volleyball W

REMINGTON COLLEGE-JACKSONVILLE CAMPUS
7011 A.C. Skinner Parkway
Jacksonville, FL 32256
Tel: (904)296-3435

Fax: (904)296-9097
E-mail: tony.galang@remingtoncollege.edu
Web Site: http://www.remingtoncollege.edu/
President/CEO: Tony Galang
Admissions: Tony Galang
Type: Two-Year College **Sex:** Coed **Faculty:** FT 14, PT 10 **Student-Faculty Ratio:** 15:1 **Professional Accreditation:** ACCSCT

REMINGTON COLLEGE-PINELLAS CAMPUS
8550 Ulmerton Rd.
Largo, FL 33771
Tel: (727)532-1999; 888-900-2343
Fax: (727)530-7710
Web Site: http://www.remingtoncollege.edu/
Admissions: Edna Higgins
Type: Two-Year College **Sex:** Coed **Calendar System:** Continuous **Professional Accreditation:** ACCSCT

REMINGTON COLLEGE-TAMPA CAMPUS
2410 East Busch Blvd.
Tampa, FL 33612-8410
Tel: (813)932-0701
Admissions: (813)935-5700
Fax: (813)935-7415
Web Site: http://www.remingtoncollege.edu/
President/CEO: William D. Polmear
Registrar: Carol-Ann J. Mendoza
Admissions: James Royster
Financial Aid: Chris Schilling
Type: Two-Year College **Sex:** Coed **Admission Plans:** Open Admission; Deferred Admission **Application Deadline:** Rolling **Application Fee:** $50.00 **H.S. Requirements:** High school diploma required; GED accepted **Costs Per Year:** Application fee: $50. **Scholarships:** Available **Calendar System:** Quarter, Summer Session Not available **Enrollment:** FT 685 **Faculty:** FT 18, PT 8 **Student-Faculty Ratio:** 15:1 **Exams:** Other **Library Holdings:** 4,100 **Credit Hours For Degree:** 99 quarter hours, Associates; 90 quarter hours, Bachelors **Professional Accreditation:** ACCSCT

RINGLING SCHOOL OF ART AND DESIGN
2700 North Tamiami Trail
Sarasota, FL 34234-5895
Tel: (941)351-5100
Free: 800-255-7695
Fax: (941)359-7517
E-mail: admissions@rsad.edu
Web Site: http://www.ringling.edu/
President/CEO: Dr. Larry R. Thompson
Registrar: Donna Anderson
Admissions: James Dean
Financial Aid: Kurt Wolf
Type: Four-Year College **Sex:** Coed **% Accepted:** 27 **Admission Plans:** Deferred Admission **Application Deadline:** Rolling **Application Fee:** $35.00 **H.S. Requirements:** High school diploma required; GED accepted **Costs Per Year:** Application fee: $35. Comprehensive fee: $30,565 includes full-time tuition ($21,200), mandatory fees ($200), and college room and board ($9165). College room only: $4917. Full-time tuition and fees vary according to course load, program, and student level. Room and board charges vary according to board plan and housing facility. Part-time tuition: $1000 per credit hour. Part-time tuition varies according to course load, program, and student level. **Scholarships:** Available **Calendar System:** Semester, Summer Session Not available **Enrollment:** FT 1,050, PT 38 **Faculty:** FT 60, PT 59 **Student-Faculty Ratio:** 13:1 **% Receiving Financial Aid:** 63 **% Residing in College-Owned, -Operated, or -Affiliated Housing:** 47 **Library Holdings:** 46,802 **Regional Accreditation:** Southern Association of Colleges and Schools **Credit Hours For Degree:** 123 semester hours, Bachelors **Professional Accreditation:** FIDER, NASAD

ROLLINS COLLEGE
1000 Holt Ave.
Winter Park, FL 32789-4499
Tel: (407)646-2000
Admissions: (407)646-2161
Fax: (407)646-2600
E-mail: admission@rollins.edu
Web Site: http://www.rollins.edu/
President/CEO: Dr. Lewis Duncan
Admissions: David Erdmann
Financial Aid: Phil Asbury
Type: Comprehensive **Sex:** Coed **Scores:** 100% SAT V 400+; 100% SAT M 400+; 39% ACT 18-23; 46% ACT 24-29 **% Accepted:** 53 **Admission Plans:** Early Admission; Early Decision Plan; Deferred Admission **Application Deadline:** February 15 **Application Fee:** $40.00 **H.S. Requirements:** High school diploma required; GED accepted **Costs Per Year:** Application fee: $40. Comprehensive fee: $38,366 includes full-time tuition ($28,390), mandatory fees ($834), and college room and board ($9142). College room only: $5376. **Scholarships:** Available **Calendar System:** Semester, Summer Session Not available **Enrollment:** FT 1,719, Grad 774 **Faculty:** FT 185, PT 32 **Student-Faculty Ratio:** 11:1 **Exams:** SAT I or ACT **% Receiving Financial Aid:** 42 **% Residing in College-Owned, -Operated, or -Affiliated Housing:** 66 **Library Holdings:** 288,323 **Regional Accreditation:** Southern Association of Colleges and Schools **Credit Hours For Degree:** 35 courses equaling at least 35 course units, Bachelors **Professional Accreditation:** AACSB, ACA, NASM **Intercollegiate Athletics:** Baseball M; Basketball M & W; Cheerleading M & W; Crew M & W; Cross-Country Running M & W; Golf M & W; Sailing M & W; Soccer M & W; Softball W; Swimming and Diving M & W; Tennis M & W; Volleyball W

ST. JOHN VIANNEY COLLEGE SEMINARY
2900 Southwest 87th Ave.
Miami, FL 33165-3244
Tel: (305)223-4561
E-mail: noonan@sjvcs.edu
Web Site: http://www.sjvcs.edu/
President/CEO: Rev. John Noonan
Registrar: Dr. Zoila Diaz
Admissions: Msgr. John Noonan
Type: Four-Year College **Sex:** Coed **Affiliation:** Roman Catholic **Scores:** 75% SAT V 400+; 65% SAT M 400+; 100% ACT 18-23 **Admission Plans:** Preferred Admission **Application Fee:** $0.00 **H.S. Requirements:** High school diploma required; GED accepted **Scholarships:** Available **Calendar System:** Semester, Summer Session Not available **Enrollment:** FT 47 **Faculty:** FT 6, PT 13 **Exams:** SAT I or ACT **% Residing in College-Owned, -Operated, or -Affiliated Housing:** 98 **Library Holdings:** 54,000 **Regional Accreditation:** Southern Association of Colleges and Schools **Credit Hours For Degree:** 128 semester hours, Bachelors

ST. JOHNS RIVER COMMUNITY COLLEGE
5001 Saint Johns Ave.
Palatka, FL 32177-3897
Tel: (386)312-4200
Admissions: (386)312-4032
Fax: (386)312-4292
Web Site: http://www.sjrcc.cc.fl.us/
President/CEO: Dr. R. L. McLendon, Jr.
Registrar: Wayne Bodiford
Admissions: O'Neal Williams
Financial Aid: Wayne Bodiford
Type: Two-Year College **Sex:** Coed **Admission Plans:** Open Admission; Early Admission **H.S. Requirements:** High school diploma required; GED accepted **Costs Per Year:** State resident tuition: $1732 full-time, $66.88 per semester hour part-time. Nonresident tuition: $6348 full-time, $251.14 per semester hour part-time. **Scholarships:** Available **Calendar System:** Semester, Summer Session Available **Faculty:** FT 61, PT 96 **Exams:** SAT I and SAT II or ACT **Library Holdings:** 56,925 **Regional Accreditation:** Southern Association of Colleges and Schools **Credit Hours For Degree:** 60 credit hours, Associates **Intercollegiate Athletics:** Baseball M; Basketball M; Softball W; Volleyball W

SAINT LEO UNIVERSITY
PO Box 6665
St. Leo, FL 33574-6665
Tel: (352)588-8200
Free: 800-334-5532
Admissions: (352)588-8283
Fax: (352)588-8257
E-mail: admissions@saintleo.edu
Web Site: http://www.saintleo.edu/
President/CEO: Dr. Arthur F. Kirk, Jr.

Registrar: Karen Hatfield
Admissions: Gary Bracken
Financial Aid: James Wingate
Type: Comprehensive **Sex:** Coed **Affiliation:** Roman Catholic **Scores:** 97% SAT V 400+; 97% SAT M 400+; 72% ACT 18-23; 25% ACT 24-29 **% Accepted:** 43 **Admission Plans:** Early Admission; Deferred Admission **Application Deadline:** August 15 **Application Fee:** $35.00 **H.S. Requirements:** High school diploma required; GED accepted **Costs Per Year:** Application fee: $35. Comprehensive fee: $22,140 includes full-time tuition ($14,250), mandatory fees ($430), and college room and board ($7460). College room only: $3920. Full-time tuition and fees vary according to location. Room and board charges vary according to board plan and housing facility. **Scholarships:** Available **Calendar System:** Semester, Summer Session Available **Enrollment:** FT 1,335, PT 49, Grad 879 **Faculty:** FT 66, PT 56 **Student-Faculty Ratio:** 16:1 **Exams:** SAT I or ACT **% Receiving Financial Aid:** 68 **% Residing in College-Owned, -Operated, or -Affiliated Housing:** 68 **Library Holdings:** 141,521 **Regional Accreditation:** Southern Association of Colleges and Schools **Credit Hours For Degree:** 62 semester hours, Associates; 122 semester hours, Bachelors **ROTC:** Army, Air Force **Professional Accreditation:** CSWE **Intercollegiate Athletics:** Baseball M; Basketball M & W; Crew M & W; Cross-Country Running M & W; Golf M & W; Lacrosse M; Soccer M & W; Softball W; Swimming and Diving M & W; Tennis M & W; Volleyball W

ST. PETERSBURG COLLEGE
PO Box 13489
St. Petersburg, FL 33733-3489
Tel: (727)341-3600
Admissions: (727)712-5892
Fax: (727)341-3150
Web Site: http://www.spjc.edu/
President/CEO: Dr. Carl M. Kuttler, Jr.
Registrar: Martyn Clay
Admissions: Martyn Clay
Financial Aid: Theresa Furnas
Type: Two-Year College **Sex:** Coed **% Accepted:** 100 **Admission Plans:** Open Admission; Early Admission; Deferred Admission **Application Deadline:** Rolling **Application Fee:** $35.00 **H.S. Requirements:** High school diploma required; GED accepted **Costs Per Year:** Application fee: $35. State resident tuition: $1646 full-time, $54.88 per credit part-time. Nonresident tuition: $6587 full-time, $219.11 per credit part-time. Mandatory fees: $337 full-time, $25.17 per credit part-time. Full-time tuition and fees vary according to degree level and program. Part-time tuition and fees vary according to degree level and program. **Scholarships:** Available **Calendar System:** Semester, Summer Session Available **Enrollment:** FT 8,012, PT 16,090 **Faculty:** FT 313, PT 1,599 **Library Holdings:** 222,990 **Regional Accreditation:** Southern Association of Colleges and Schools **Credit Hours For Degree:** 60 credit hours, Associates; 120 credit hours, Bachelors **Professional Accreditation:** ABFSE, ADA, AHIMA, APTA, CARC, JRCEMT, NAACLS, NLN **Intercollegiate Athletics:** Baseball M; Basketball M & W; Softball W; Volleyball W

ST. PETERSBURG THEOLOGICAL SEMINARY
10830 Navajo Dr.
St. Petersburg, FL 33708
Tel: (727)399-0276
Fax: (727)347-3695
E-mail: sptseminary@tampabay.rr.com
Web Site: http://www.sptseminary.edu/
President/CEO: Dr. Myron M. Miller
Admissions: Jane Cargile
Type: Two-Year Upper Division **Sex:** Coed **Affiliation:** interdenominational **H.S. Requirements:** High school diploma required; GED accepted **Costs Per Year:** Tuition: $3600 full-time, $120 per credit hour part-time. Mandatory fees: $30 full-time, $15 per term part-time. Full-time tuition and fees vary according to course level and degree level. Part-time tuition and fees vary according to course level and degree level. **Calendar System:** Semester, Summer Session Available **Enrollment:** FT 4, PT 25, Grad 41 **Faculty:** FT 12, PT 16 **Student-Faculty Ratio:** 2:1 **Library Holdings:** 25,146 **Credit Hours For Degree:** 120 credits, Bachelors **Professional Accreditation:** TACCS

ST. THOMAS UNIVERSITY
16401 Northwest 37th Ave.
Miami Gardens, FL 33054-6459
Tel: (305)625-6000
Free: 800-367-9010
Admissions: (305)628-6546
Fax: (305)628-6591
Web Site: http://www.stu.edu/
President/CEO: Rev. Msgr. Franklyn M. Casale
Registrar: Dr. Kenneth C. Johnson
Admissions: Patricia Bisciotti
Financial Aid: Anh Do
Type: Comprehensive **Sex:** Coed **Affiliation:** Roman Catholic **Scores:** 78% SAT V 400+; 66% SAT M 400+; 36.4% ACT 18-23; 9.1% ACT 24-29 **% Accepted:** 91 **Admission Plans:** Early Admission; Deferred Admission **Application Deadline:** Rolling **Application Fee:** $40.00 **H.S. Requirements:** High school diploma required; GED accepted **Costs Per Year:** Application fee: $40. Comprehensive fee: $23,490 includes full-time tuition ($17,860) and college room and board ($5630). Room and board charges vary according to board plan and housing facility. Part-time tuition: $595 per credit. **Scholarships:** Available **Calendar System:** Semester, Summer Session Available **Enrollment:** FT 1,096, PT 62, Grad 730 **Faculty:** FT 95, PT 155 **Student-Faculty Ratio:** 17:1 **Exams:** SAT I or ACT **% Receiving Financial Aid:** 69 **% Residing in College-Owned, -Operated, or -Affiliated Housing:** 10 **Library Holdings:** 154,017 **Regional Accreditation:** Southern Association of Colleges and Schools **Credit Hours For Degree:** 120 credits, Bachelors **ROTC:** Army, Air Force **Professional Accreditation:** ABA, AALS **Intercollegiate Athletics:** Baseball M; Cross-Country Running M & W; Golf M & W; Soccer M & W; Softball W; Tennis M & W; Volleyball W

SANFORD-BROWN INSTITUTE (JACKSONVILLE)
10255 Fortune Parkway, Ste. 501
Jacksonville, FL 32256
Tel: (904)363-6221
Fax: (904)363-6824
Web Site: http://www.sbjacksonville.com/
President/CEO: Wyman Dickey
Type: Two-Year College **Sex:** Coed **Professional Accreditation:** ABHES, ACICS

SANFORD-BROWN INSTITUTE (LAUDERDALE LAKES)
4780 N. State Rd., 7 Bldg. E, Ste. 100
Lauderdale Lakes, FL 33309
Tel: (954)733-8900
Fax: (954)733-8994
Web Site: http://www.sbftlauderdale.com/
President/CEO: Jay Asher
Type: Two-Year College **Sex:** Coed

SANFORD-BROWN INSTITUTE (TAMPA)
5701 E. Hillsborough Ave.
Tampa, FL 33610
Tel: (813)621-0072
Fax: (813)626-0392
Web Site: http://www.sbtampa.com/
President/CEO: Pamela Bowman
Type: Two-Year College **Sex:** Coed **Professional Accreditation:** ACICS

SANTA FE COMMUNITY COLLEGE
3000 Northwest 83rd St.
Gainesville, FL 32606-6200
Tel: (352)395-5000
Admissions: (352)395-5857
Fax: (352)395-5581
E-mail: information@santafe.cc.fl.us
Web Site: http://www.sfcc.edu/
President/CEO: Dr. Jackson N. Sasser
Registrar: Margaret Karrh
Admissions: Margaret Karrh
Financial Aid: Steven H. Fisher
Type: Two-Year College **Sex:** Coed **Affiliation:** Florida Community College System **Admission Plans:** Open Admission; Early Admission **Application Fee:** $30.00 **H.S. Requirements:** High school diploma required; GED accepted **Costs Per Year:** Application fee: $30. State resident tuition: $1755 full-time, $58.50 per credit hour part-time. Nonresident tuition: $6540 full-time, $218 per credit hour part-time. **Scholarships:** Available **Calendar System:** Semester, Summer Session Available **Enrollment:** FT 6,560, PT 7,246 **Faculty:** FT 311, PT 471 **Exams:** Other **Library Holdings:** 81,832

Regional Accreditation: Southern Association of Colleges and Schools **Credit Hours For Degree:** 60 semester hours, Associates **ROTC:** Army, Air Force **Professional Accreditation:** ACCE, ADA, AHIMA, CARC, JRCERT, JRCEMT, JRCNMT, NLN **Intercollegiate Athletics:** Baseball M; Basketball M & W; Softball W

SCHILLER INTERNATIONAL UNIVERSITY
453 Edgewater Dr.
Dunedin, FL 34698-7532
Tel: (727)736-5082
Free: 800-336-4133
Fax: (727)734-0359
E-mail: admissions@schiller.edu
Web Site: http://www.schiller.edu/
President/CEO: Dr. Walter W. Leibrecht
Admissions: Kamala Dontamsetti
Financial Aid: Terry Reeves
Type: Comprehensive **Sex:** Coed **Affiliation:** Schiller International University **Admission Plans:** Deferred Admission **Application Deadline:** Rolling **Application Fee:** $35.00 **H.S. Requirements:** High school diploma required; GED accepted **Costs Per Year:** Application fee: $35. Comprehensive fee: $24,480 includes full-time tuition ($16,880) and college room and board ($7600). Part-time tuition: $470 per credit. **Calendar System:** Semester, Summer Session Available **Enrollment:** FT 103, PT 5, Grad 69 **Faculty:** FT 4, PT 30 **Student-Faculty Ratio:** 5:1 **Library Holdings:** 1,918 **Credit Hours For Degree:** 62 credits, Associates; 124 credits, Bachelors **Professional Accreditation:** ACICS

SEMINOLE COMMUNITY COLLEGE
100 Weldon Blvd.
Sanford, FL 32773-6199
Tel: (407)328-4722
Admissions: (407)708-2380
Fax: (407)328-2395
Web Site: http://www.scc-fl.edu/
President/CEO: Dr. E. Ann McGee
Registrar: Dr. Travis Spaulding
Admissions: Pamela Mennechey
Financial Aid: Robert Lynn
Type: Two-Year College **Sex:** Coed **Admission Plans:** Open Admission; Early Admission; Deferred Admission **Application Deadline:** Rolling **Application Fee:** $0.00 **H.S. Requirements:** High school diploma required; GED accepted **Costs Per Year:** Application fee: $0. State resident tuition: $1592 full-time, $53.08 per credit hour part-time. Nonresident tuition: $6125 full-time, $214.18 per credit hour part-time. Mandatory fees: $488 full-time, $16.28 per credit hour part-time. **Scholarships:** Available **Calendar System:** Semester, Summer Session Available **Enrollment:** FT 4,079, PT 7,603 **Faculty:** FT 200, PT 609 **Student-Faculty Ratio:** 11:1 **Library Holdings:** 102,744 **Regional Accreditation:** Southern Association of Colleges and Schools **Credit Hours For Degree:** 60 credit hours, Associates **ROTC:** Army **Professional Accreditation:** APTA, CARC, JRCEMT, NLN **Intercollegiate Athletics:** Baseball M; Basketball M & W; Softball W

SOUTH FLORIDA COMMUNITY COLLEGE
600 West College Dr.
Avon Park, FL 33825-9356
Tel: (863)453-6661
Fax: (863)453-0165
Web Site: http://www.sfcc.cc.fl.us/
President/CEO: Dr. Norman L. Stephens, Jr.
Registrar: Dr. Deborah Fuschetti
Admissions: Annie Alexander-Harvey
Financial Aid: Susie Johnson
Type: Two-Year College **Sex:** Coed **Affiliation:** Florida Community College System **Admission Plans:** Open Admission; Early Admission; Deferred Admission **Application Fee:** $0.00 **H.S. Requirements:** High school diploma required; GED accepted **Scholarships:** Available **Calendar System:** Semester, Summer Session Available **Enrollment:** FT 813, PT 1,263 **Faculty:** FT 46, PT 157 **Student-Faculty Ratio:** 15:1 **Exams:** Other **Library Holdings:** 42,000 **Regional Accreditation:** Southern Association of Colleges and Schools **Credit Hours For Degree:** 60 semester hours, Associates **Professional Accreditation:** ADA **Intercollegiate Athletics:** Baseball M; Tennis W; Volleyball W

SOUTH UNIVERSITY (TAMPA)
4401 N. Himes Ave.
Tampa, FL 33614
Tel: (813)393-3800
Web Site: http://www.southuniversity.edu **Type:** Four-Year College **Sex:** Coed **Costs Per Year:** Tuition: $11,475 full-time, $2995 per term part-time. **Exams:** SAT I or ACT, SAT I and SAT II

SOUTH UNIVERSITY (WEST PALM BEACH)
1760 North Congress Ave.
West Palm Beach, FL 33409
Tel: (561)697-9200; (866)629-9200
Admissions: (866)629-2902
Fax: (561)697-9944
E-mail: jrogalski@southuniversity.edu
Web Site: http://www.southuniversity.edu/
President/CEO: John T. South, III
Registrar: Stephanie Tinsley
Admissions: Joe Rogalski
Financial Aid: Amy Hart
Type: Two-Year College **Sex:** Coed **Affiliation:** Education Management Corporation **Admission Plans:** Early Admission; Deferred Admission **Application Deadline:** Rolling **Application Fee:** $25.00 **H.S. Requirements:** High school diploma required; GED accepted **Costs Per Year:** Application fee: $25. Tuition: $11,475 full-time, $2995 per term part-time. **Scholarships:** Available **Calendar System:** Quarter **Enrollment:** FT 347, PT 155 **Faculty:** FT 18, PT 40 **Student-Faculty Ratio:** 13:1 **Exams:** SAT I or ACT **Library Holdings:** 8,400 **Credit Hours For Degree:** 106 quarter hours, Associates; 180 quarter hours, Bachelors **Professional Accreditation:** AAMAE, APTA

SOUTHEASTERN UNIVERSITY
1000 Longfellow Blvd.
Lakeland, FL 33801-6099
Tel: (863)667-5000
Free: 800-500-8760
Fax: (863)667-5200
Web Site: http://www.seuniversity.edu/
President/CEO: Dr. Mark Rutland
Registrar: Kathy Bucklew
Admissions: Omar Rashed
Financial Aid: Carol Bradley
Type: Four-Year College **Sex:** Coed **Affiliation:** Assemblies of God **Admission Plans:** Early Admission; Deferred Admission **Application Fee:** $40.00 **H.S. Requirements:** High school diploma required; GED accepted **Costs Per Year:** Application fee: $40. Comprehensive fee: $17,178 includes full-time tuition ($11,040), mandatory fees ($460), and college room and board ($5678). Full-time tuition and fees vary according to degree level, program, and reciprocity agreements. Room and board charges vary according to board plan and housing facility. Part-time tuition: $460 per credit. Part-time tuition varies according to course load, degree level, program, and reciprocity agreements. **Scholarships:** Available **Calendar System:** Semester, Summer Session Available **Enrollment:** FT 1,851, PT 113 **Faculty:** FT 48, PT 68 **Student-Faculty Ratio:** 21:1 **Exams:** SAT I or ACT **% Receiving Financial Aid:** 69 **% Residing in College-Owned, -Operated, or -Affiliated Housing:** 60 **Library Holdings:** 96,000 **Regional Accreditation:** Southern Association of Colleges and Schools **Credit Hours For Degree:** 125 credits, Bachelors **ROTC:** Army, Air Force **Intercollegiate Athletics:** Baseball M; Basketball M & W; Golf M; Soccer M & W; Volleyball W

SOUTHWEST FLORIDA COLLEGE (FORT MYERS)
1685 Medical Ln.
Fort Myers, FL 33907
Tel: (239)939-4766; (866)SWFC-NOW
Fax: (239)936-4040
Web Site: http://www.swfc.edu/
President/CEO: Gregory H. Jones
Registrar: Shannon Woostey
Financial Aid: Keith Thomas
Type: Two-Year College **Sex:** Coed **Admission Plans:** Open Admission **Application Deadline:** Rolling **H.S. Requirements:** High school diploma required; GED accepted **Scholarships:** Available **Calendar System:**

Quarter **Library Holdings:** 1,000 **Credit Hours For Degree:** 96 quarter hours, Associates **Professional Accreditation:** ACICS

SOUTHWEST FLORIDA COLLEGE (TAMPA)
3910 Riga Blvd.
Tampa, FL 33619
Tel: (813)630-4401; 877-907-2456
Web Site: http://www.swfc.edu/ **Type:** Two-Year College **Sex:** Coed **Calendar System:** Quarter

STETSON UNIVERSITY
421 North Woodland Blvd.
DeLand, FL 32723
Tel: (386)822-7000
Free: 800-688-0101
Admissions: (386)822-7100
Fax: (386)822-8832
E-mail: admissions@stetson.edu
Web Site: http://www.stetson.edu/
President/CEO: Dr. H. Douglas Lee
Registrar: Dr. John M. Tichenor
Admissions: Deborah Thompson
Financial Aid: Terry Whittum
Type: Comprehensive **Sex:** Coed **Scores:** 100% SAT V 400+; 100% SAT M 400+; 42% ACT 18-23; 50% ACT 24-29 **% Accepted:** 69 **Admission Plans:** Early Admission; Early Decision Plan; Deferred Admission **Application Deadline:** March 15 **Application Fee:** $40.00 **H.S. Requirements:** High school diploma required; GED accepted. For adult students, transfer students: High school diploma required; GED accepted **Costs Per Year:** Application fee: $40. Comprehensive fee: $32,725 includes full-time tuition ($23,975), mandatory fees ($1475), and college room and board ($7275). College room only: $4075. Full-time tuition and fees vary according to course load and student level. Room and board charges vary according to board plan and housing facility. Part-time tuition: $760 per credit hour. Part-time tuition varies according to course load. **Scholarships:** Available **Calendar System:** Semester, Summer Session Available **Enrollment:** FT 2,160, PT 74, Grad 415 **Faculty:** FT 186, PT 82 **Student-Faculty Ratio:** 10:1 **Exams:** SAT I or ACT **% Receiving Financial Aid:** 54 **% Residing in College-Owned, -Operated, or -Affiliated Housing:** 67 **Library Holdings:** 382,154 **Regional Accreditation:** Southern Association of Colleges and Schools **Credit Hours For Degree:** 120 hours, Bachelors **ROTC:** Army **Professional Accreditation:** AACSB, ABA, ACA, AALS, JRCEPAT, NASM, NCATE **Intercollegiate Athletics:** Baseball M; Basketball M & W; Crew M & W; Cross-Country Running M & W; Golf M & W; Soccer M & W; Softball W; Tennis M & W; Volleyball W

TALLAHASSEE COMMUNITY COLLEGE
444 Appleyard Dr.
Tallahassee, FL 32304-2895
Tel: (850)201-6200
Web Site: http://www.tcc.fl.edu/
President/CEO: Dr. William D. Law, Jr.
Registrar: Sharon Jefferson
Financial Aid: William Spiers
Type: Two-Year College **Sex:** Coed **Affiliation:** Florida Community College System **Admission Plans:** Open Admission; Early Admission; Deferred Admission **Application Fee:** $0.00 **H.S. Requirements:** High school diploma required; GED accepted **Scholarships:** Available **Calendar System:** Semester, Summer Session Available **Enrollment:** FT 5,533, PT 6,433 **Faculty:** FT 145, PT 342 **Student-Faculty Ratio:** 30:1 **Exams:** Other, SAT I or ACT **Library Holdings:** 84,415 **Regional Accreditation:** Southern Association of Colleges and Schools **Credit Hours For Degree:** 60 semester hours, Associates **ROTC:** Army, Air Force **Professional Accreditation:** ADA, CARC, JRCEMT **Intercollegiate Athletics:** Baseball M; Basketball M & W; Softball W

TALMUDIC COLLEGE OF FLORIDA
1910 Alton Rd.
Miami Beach, FL 33139
Tel: (305)534-7050; 888-825-6834
Fax: (305)534-8444
Web Site: http://www.talmudicu.edu/
President/CEO: Rabbi Yochanan Zweig
Registrar: Rabbi Moshe Mendel Simon
Admissions: Rabbi Ira Hill
Financial Aid: Rabbi Yitzchak Zweig
Type: Comprehensive **Sex:** Men **Affiliation:** Jewish **Admission Plans:** Early Admission; Deferred Admission **Application Fee:** $250.00 **H.S. Requirements:** High school diploma required; GED accepted **Costs Per Year:** Application fee: $250. Comprehensive fee: $12,500 includes full-time tuition ($7250), mandatory fees ($250), and college room and board ($5000). College room only: $2500. Tuition guaranteed not to increase for student's term of enrollment. **Scholarships:** Available **Calendar System:** Semester, Summer Session Available **Enrollment:** FT 15, Grad 15 **Faculty:** FT 6 **Student-Faculty Ratio:** 5:1 **% Receiving Financial Aid:** 70 **% Residing in College-Owned, -Operated, or -Affiliated Housing:** 99 **Library Holdings:** 25,000 **Credit Hours For Degree:** 120 credits, Bachelors **Professional Accreditation:** AARTS

TRINITY BAPTIST COLLEGE
800 Hammond Blvd.
Jacksonville, FL 32221
Tel: (904)596-2400
Free: 800-786-2206
Admissions: (904)596-2538
Fax: (904)596-2531
E-mail: trinity@tbc.edu
Web Site: http://www.tbc.edu/
President/CEO: Dr. Thomas Messer
Registrar: John Cash
Admissions: Larry Appleby
Financial Aid: Ben Brochie
Type: Comprehensive **Sex:** Coed **Affiliation:** Baptist **Scores:** 97.62% SAT V 400+; 95.12% SAT M 400+; 64.52% ACT 18-23; 16.13% ACT 24-29 **% Accepted:** 100 **Application Deadline:** Rolling **Application Fee:** $30.00 **H.S. Requirements:** High school diploma required; GED accepted **Costs Per Year:** Application fee: $30. Comprehensive fee: $10,600. Part-time tuition: $245 per semester hour. Tuition: $245 per semester hour part-time. **Scholarships:** Available **Calendar System:** Semester, Summer Session Available **Enrollment:** FT 294, PT 128, Grad 43 **Faculty:** FT 12, PT 38 **Student-Faculty Ratio:** 15:1 **Exams:** SAT I or ACT **% Receiving Financial Aid:** 48 **% Residing in College-Owned, -Operated, or -Affiliated Housing:** 57 **Library Holdings:** 35,070 **Credit Hours For Degree:** 64 semester hours, Associates; 130 semester hours, Bachelors **Professional Accreditation:** TACCS **Intercollegiate Athletics:** Basketball M & W; Track and Field M

TRINITY COLLEGE OF FLORIDA
2430 Welbilt Blvd.
New Port Richey, FL 34655
Tel: (727)376-6911
Free: 800-388-0869
Fax: (727)376-0781
Web Site: http://www.trinitycollege.edu/
President/CEO: Dr. Bill W. Lanpher
Registrar: Mark Sawyer
Admissions: Dr. David Colburn
Financial Aid: Sue Wayne
Type: Four-Year College **Sex:** Coed **Affiliation:** nondenominational **Scores:** 90% SAT V 400+; 47% SAT M 400+; 28% ACT 18-23; 36% ACT 24-29 **Admission Plans:** Early Admission; Deferred Admission **Application Fee:** $25.00 **H.S. Requirements:** High school diploma required; GED accepted **Scholarships:** Available **Calendar System:** Semester, Summer Session Available **Enrollment:** FT 138, PT 65 **Faculty:** FT 6, PT 20 **Student-Faculty Ratio:** 13:1 **Exams:** SAT I or ACT **% Receiving Financial Aid:** 95 **% Residing in College-Owned, -Operated, or -Affiliated Housing:** 54 **Library Holdings:** 40,523 **Credit Hours For Degree:** 60 credit hours, Associates; 123 credit hours, Bachelors **Professional Accreditation:** AABC

UNIVERSIDAD FLET
14540 SW 136th St., Ste. 200
Miami, FL 33186
Tel: (305)232-5880; 888-376-3538
Admissions: (305)378-8700
Fax: (305)232-3592
Web Site: http://www.flet.edu/
President/CEO: Dr. Larry Mccullough
Admissions: Lourdes Ramirez

Type: Comprehensive **Sex:** Coed **Costs Per Year:** Tuition: $30 per credit part-time. Mandatory fees: $700 full-time. **Enrollment:** FT 75, PT 707, Grad 84 **Faculty:** FT 4, PT 16 **Student-Faculty Ratio:** 36:1 **Professional Accreditation:** DETC

UNIVERSITY OF CENTRAL FLORIDA
4000 Central Florida Blvd.
Orlando, FL 32816
Tel: (407)823-2000
Admissions: (407)823-3000
Fax: (407)823-3419
E-mail: admission@mail.ucf.edu
Web Site: http://www.ucf.edu/
President/CEO: Dr. John C. Hitt
Registrar: Dr. Dennis Dulniak
Admissions: Dr. Gordon Chavis, Jr.
Financial Aid: Mary McKinney
Type: University **Sex:** Coed **Affiliation:** State University System of Florida **Scores:** 99.7% SAT V 400+; 99.9% SAT M 400+; 47.3% ACT 18-23; 47.7% ACT 24-29 **% Accepted:** 62 **Admission Plans:** Preferred Admission; Early Admission **Application Deadline:** March 01 **Application Fee:** $30.00 **H.S. Requirements:** High school diploma required; GED accepted **Costs Per Year:** Application fee: $30. State resident tuition: $3141 full-time, $105 per credit part-time. Nonresident tuition: $16,272 full-time, $542 per credit part-time. Mandatory fees: $198 full-time, $6.60 per credit part-time. Full-time tuition and fees vary according to course load. Part-time tuition and fees vary according to course load. College room and board: $7400. College room only: $4300. Room and board charges vary according to board plan and housing facility. **Scholarships:** Available **Calendar System:** Semester, Summer Session Available **Enrollment:** FT 28,584, PT 9,212, Grad 7,157 **Faculty:** FT 1,192, PT 445 **Student-Faculty Ratio:** 27:1 **Exams:** SAT I or ACT **% Receiving Financial Aid:** 56 **% Residing in College-Owned, -Operated, or -Affiliated Housing:** 20 **Library Holdings:** 1,152,653 **Regional Accreditation:** Southern Association of Colleges and Schools **Credit Hours For Degree:** 60 semester hours, Associates; 120 semester hours, Bachelors **ROTC:** Army, Air Force **Professional Accreditation:** AACSB, ABET, ACEHSA, AACN, ACA, AHIMA, APTA, APA, ASLHA, CARC, CSWE, JRCERT, JRCEPAT, NAACLS, NASM, NASPAA, NCATE, NLN **Intercollegiate Athletics:** Baseball M; Basketball M & W; Cheerleading M & W; Crew W; Cross-Country Running M & W; Football M; Golf M & W; Soccer M & W; Tennis M & W; Track and Field W; Volleyball W

UNIVERSITY OF FLORIDA
Gainesville, FL 32611
Tel: (352)392-3261
Admissions: (352)392-1365
Web Site: http://www.ufl.edu/
President/CEO: Bernard J. Machen
Registrar: Stephen J. Pritz
Admissions: Patrick C. Herring
Financial Aid: Karen L. Fooks
Type: University **Sex:** Coed **Affiliation:** Board of Trustees **Scores:** 100% SAT V 400+; 100% SAT M 400+; 16% ACT 18-23; 60% ACT 24-29 **% Accepted:** 52 **Admission Plans:** Preferred Admission; Early Admission; Early Decision Plan **Application Deadline:** January 17 **Application Fee:** $30.00 **H.S. Requirements:** High school diploma required; GED accepted **Costs Per Year:** Application fee: $30. State resident tuition: $3,094 full-time, $103.12 per credit hour part-time. Nonresident tuition: $17,222 full-time, $574.08 per credit hour part-time. College room and board: $6260. College room only: $3940. Room and board charges vary according to board plan and housing facility. **Scholarships:** Available **Calendar System:** Semester, Summer Session Available **Enrollment:** FT 32,006, PT 2,662, Grad 10,957 **Faculty:** FT 2,229, PT 82 **Student-Faculty Ratio:** 21:1 **Exams:** SAT I or ACT **% Receiving Financial Aid:** 39 **% Residing in College-Owned, -Operated, or -Affiliated Housing:** 21 **Library Holdings:** 5,024,637 **Regional Accreditation:** Southern Association of Colleges and Schools **Credit Hours For Degree:** 120 semester hours, Bachelors **ROTC:** Army, Air Force **Professional Accreditation:** AACSB, ABET, ACEHSA, ACEJMC, AACN, AAFCS, ABA, ACNM, ACCE, ACPhE, ACA, ADA, ADtA, ACSP, AOTA, APTA, APA, ASLA, ASLHA, AVMA AALS, CORE, FIDER, JRCEPAT, LCMEAMA, NASAD, NASM, NAST, NCATE, NRPA, SAF **Intercollegiate Athletics:** Baseball M; Basketball M & W; Cross-Country Running M & W; Football M; Golf M & W; Gymnastics W; Soccer W; Softball W; Swimming and Diving M & W; Tennis M & W; Track and Field M & W; Volleyball W

UNIVERSITY OF MIAMI
University of Miami Branch
Coral Gables, FL 33124
Tel: (305)284-2211
Admissions: (305)284-4323
Fax: (305)284-2507
Web Site: http://www.miami.edu/
President/CEO: Dr. Donna E. Shalala
Registrar: Dr. Scott Ingold
Admissions: Edward M. Gillis
Financial Aid: James Bauer
Type: University **Sex:** Coed **Scores:** 99% SAT V 400+; 100% SAT M 400+; 14% ACT 18-23; 54% ACT 24-29 **% Accepted:** 46 **Admission Plans:** Early Admission; Early Action; Early Decision Plan; Deferred Admission **Application Deadline:** February 01 **Application Fee:** $65.00 **H.S. Requirements:** High school diploma required; GED accepted **Costs Per Year:** Application fee: $65. Comprehensive fee: $37,926 includes full-time tuition ($29,020) and college room and board ($8906). College room only: $5224. Full-time tuition varies according to course load, location, and program. Room and board charges vary according to board plan and housing facility. Part-time tuition: $1208 per credit. Part-time tuition varies according to course load, location, and program. Tuition guaranteed not to increase for student's term of enrollment. **Scholarships:** Available **Calendar System:** Semester, Summer Session Available **Enrollment:** FT 9,766, PT 771, Grad 3,219 **Faculty:** FT 892, PT 383 **Student-Faculty Ratio:** 13:1 **Exams:** SAT I or ACT, SAT I and SAT II, SAT II **% Receiving Financial Aid:** 52 **% Residing in College-Owned, -Operated, or -Affiliated Housing:** 42 **Library Holdings:** 1,415,781 **Regional Accreditation:** Southern Association of Colleges and Schools **Credit Hours For Degree:** 120 credits, Bachelors **ROTC:** Army, Air Force **Professional Accreditation:** AACSB, ABET, ACEHSA, ACEJMC, ABA, ACNM, APTA, APA, AALS, CEPH, LCMEAMA, NASM, NCATE, NLN **Intercollegiate Athletics:** Badminton M & W; Baseball M; Basketball M & W; Cheerleading M & W; Crew W; Cross-Country Running M & W; Football M; Golf W; Racquetball M & W; Soccer W; Softball W; Squash M & W; Swimming and Diving W; Tennis M & W; Track and Field M & W; Volleyball M & W; Water Polo M & W

UNIVERSITY OF NORTH FLORIDA
4567 St. Johns Bluff Rd. South
Jacksonville, FL 32224-2645
Tel: (904)620-1000
Admissions: (904)620-2624
Fax: (904)620-1040
E-mail: osprey@unfivm.unf.edu
Web Site: http://www.unf.edu/
President/CEO: John A. Delaney
Registrar: Kimberly Luther
Admissions: John Yancey
Financial Aid: Janice Nowak
Type: Comprehensive **Sex:** Coed **Affiliation:** State University System of Florida **Scores:** 100% SAT V 400+; 100% SAT M 400+; 79% ACT 18-23; 18% ACT 24-29 **% Accepted:** 62 **Admission Plans:** Early Admission; Early Action; Deferred Admission **Application Deadline:** July 02 **Application Fee:** $30.00 **H.S. Requirements:** High school diploma required; GED accepted **Costs Per Year:** Application fee: $30. State resident tuition: $3269 full-time, $108.95 per semester hour part-time. Nonresident tuition: $14,911 full-time, $497.02 per semester hour part-time. College room and board: $6640. College room only: $3810. Room and board charges vary according to board plan and housing facility. **Scholarships:** Available **Calendar System:** Semester, Summer Session Available **Enrollment:** FT 9,540, PT 3,870, Grad 1,824 **Faculty:** FT 448, PT 252 **Student-Faculty Ratio:** 22:1 **Exams:** SAT I or ACT **% Receiving Financial Aid:** 15 **% Residing in College-Owned, -Operated, or -Affiliated Housing:** 17 **Library Holdings:** 746,604 **Regional Accreditation:** Southern Association of Colleges and Schools **Credit Hours For Degree:** 60 semester hours, Associates; 120 semester hours, Bachelors **ROTC:** Navy **Professional Accreditation:** AACSB, ABET, ACCE, ACA, ADtA, APTA, CORE, JRCEPAT, NASM, NASPAA, NCATE, NLN **Intercollegiate Athletics:** Baseball M; Basketball M

& W; Cheerleading M & W; Cross-Country Running M & W; Golf M; Soccer M & W; Softball W; Swimming and Diving W; Tennis M & W; Track and Field M & W; Volleyball W

UNIVERSITY OF PHOENIX-CENTRAL FLORIDA CAMPUS
2290 Lucien Way, Ste. 400
Maitland, FL 32751-7057
Tel: (407)667-0555
Free: 800-228-7240
Admissions: (480)557-1712
Web Site: http://www.phoenix.edu/
President/CEO: Dr. Laura Palmer Noone
Admissions: Nina Omelchanko
Financial Aid: Robert Collins
Type: Comprehensive **Sex:** Coed **Admission Plans:** Open Admission; Deferred Admission **Application Deadline:** Rolling **Application Fee:** $110.00 **H.S. Requirements:** High school diploma required; GED accepted **Costs Per Year:** Application fee: $110. Tuition: $9960 full-time, $332 per credit part-time. Mandatory fees: $560 full-time, $70 per course part-time. Full-time tuition and fees vary according to program. **Scholarships:** Available **Calendar System:** Continuous, Summer Session Not available **Enrollment:** FT 1,654, Grad 613 **Faculty:** FT 17, PT 226 **Student-Faculty Ratio:** 10:1 **Library Holdings:** 444 **Regional Accreditation:** North Central Association of Colleges and Schools **Credit Hours For Degree:** 60 credits, Associates; 120 credits, Bachelors **Professional Accreditation:** NLN

UNIVERSITY OF PHOENIX-NORTH FLORIDA CAMPUS
4500 Salisbury Rd.
Jacksonville, FL 32216-0959
Tel: (904)636-6645
Free: 800-894-1758
Admissions: (480)557-1712
Web Site: http://www.phoenix.edu/
President/CEO: Steve Flatt
Admissions: Nina Omelchanko
Type: Comprehensive **Sex:** Coed **Admission Plans:** Open Admission; Deferred Admission **Application Deadline:** Rolling **Application Fee:** $110.00 **H.S. Requirements:** High school diploma required; GED accepted **Costs Per Year:** Application fee: $110. Tuition: $9960 full-time, $332 per credit part-time. Mandatory fees: $560 full-time, $70 per course part-time. **Scholarships:** Available **Calendar System:** Continuous, Summer Session Not available **Enrollment:** FT 1,784, Grad 596 **Faculty:** FT 9, PT 246 **Student-Faculty Ratio:** 10:1 **Library Holdings:** 444 **Regional Accreditation:** North Central Association of Colleges and Schools **Credit Hours For Degree:** 60 credits, Associates; 120 credits, Bachelors **Professional Accreditation:** NLN

UNIVERSITY OF PHOENIX-SOUTH FLORIDA CAMPUS
600 North Pine Island Rd., Ste. 500
Fort Lauderdale, FL 33324-1393
Tel: (954)382-5303
Free: 800-228-7240
Admissions: (480)557-1712
Web Site: http://www.phoenix.edu/
President/CEO: Dr. Laura Palmer Noone
Registrar: Tandy Elisala
Admissions: Nina Omelchanko
Financial Aid: Robert Collins
Type: Comprehensive **Sex:** Coed **Admission Plans:** Open Admission; Deferred Admission **Application Deadline:** Rolling **Application Fee:** $110.00 **H.S. Requirements:** High school diploma required; GED accepted **Costs Per Year:** Application fee: $110. Tuition: $9960 full-time, $332 per credit part-time. Mandatory fees: $560 full-time, $70 per course part-time. **Scholarships:** Available **Calendar System:** Continuous, Summer Session Not available **Enrollment:** FT 2,043, Grad 748 **Faculty:** FT 10, PT 254 **Student-Faculty Ratio:** 10:1 **Regional Accreditation:** North Central Association of Colleges and Schools **Credit Hours For Degree:** 60 credits, Associates; 120 credits, Bachelors **Professional Accreditation:** NLN

UNIVERSITY OF PHOENIX-WEST FLORIDA CAMPUS
12802 Tampa Oaks Blvd., Ste. 200
Temple Terrace, FL 33637
Tel: (813)626-7911
Free: 800-228-7240
Admissions: (480)557-1712
Fax: (813)977-1449
Web Site: http://www.phoenix.edu/
President/CEO: Dr. Laura Palmer Noone
Registrar: Tandy Elisala
Admissions: Nina Omelchanko
Financial Aid: Robert Collins
Type: Comprehensive **Sex:** Coed **Admission Plans:** Open Admission; Deferred Admission **Application Deadline:** Rolling **Application Fee:** $110.00 **H.S. Requirements:** High school diploma required; GED accepted **Costs Per Year:** Application fee: $110. Tuition: $9960 full-time, $332 per credit part-time. Mandatory fees: $560 full-time, $70 per course part-time. **Scholarships:** Available **Calendar System:** Continuous, Summer Session Not available **Enrollment:** FT 2,064, Grad 691 **Faculty:** FT 18, PT 216 **Student-Faculty Ratio:** 10:1 **Library Holdings:** 444 **Regional Accreditation:** North Central Association of Colleges and Schools **Credit Hours For Degree:** 60 credits, Associates; 120 credits, Bachelors **Professional Accreditation:** NLN

UNIVERSITY OF SOUTH FLORIDA
4202 East Fowler Ave.
Tampa, FL 33620-9951
Tel: (813)974-2011; 877-USF-BULLS
Admissions: (813)974-3350
Fax: (813)974-9689
E-mail: bullseye@admin.usf.edu
Web Site: http://www.usf.edu
President/CEO: Dr. Judy Genshaft
Registrar: Angela Debose
Admissions: J. Robert Spatig
Financial Aid: Leonard E. Gude
Type: University **Sex:** Coed **Affiliation:** State University System of Florida **Scores:** 99.7% SAT V 400+; 99.6% SAT M 400+; 50.5% ACT 18-23; 42.4% ACT 24-29 **% Accepted:** 58 **Admission Plans:** Early Admission **Application Deadline:** April 15 **Application Fee:** $30.00 **H.S. Requirements:** High school diploma required; GED accepted **Costs Per Year:** Application fee: $30. State resident tuition: $3310 full-time, $108 per credit hour part-time. Nonresident tuition: $16,076 full-time, $533 per credit hour part-time. Mandatory fees: $74 full-time, $37 per term part-time. Full-time tuition and fees vary according to course level, course load, and location. Part-time tuition and fees vary according to course level, course load, and location. College room and board: $6900. College room only: $3563. Room and board charges vary according to board plan, housing facility, and location. **Scholarships:** Available **Calendar System:** Semester, Summer Session Available **Enrollment:** FT 23,945, PT 9,758, Grad 8,520 **Faculty:** FT 1,727, PT 702 **Exams:** SAT I or ACT **% Receiving Financial Aid:** 44 **% Residing in College-Owned, -Operated, or -Affiliated Housing:** 13 **Library Holdings:** 1,970,283 **Regional Accreditation:** Southern Association of Colleges and Schools **Credit Hours For Degree:** 60 semester hours, Associates; 120 semester hours, Bachelors **ROTC:** Army, Navy, Air Force **Professional Accreditation:** AACSB, ABET, ACEJMC, AACN, ALA, APTA, APA, ASLHA, CEPH, CORE, CSWE, LCMEAMA, NASAD, NASM, NASPAA, NAST, NCATE, NLN **Intercollegiate Athletics:** Baseball M; Basketball M & W; Cross-Country Running M & W; Football M; Golf M & W; Soccer M & W; Softball W; Tennis M & W; Track and Field M & W; Volleyball W

THE UNIVERSITY OF TAMPA
401 West Kennedy Blvd.
Tampa, FL 33606-1490
Tel: (813)253-3333; 888-MINARET
Admissions: (813)253-6211
Fax: (813)254-4955
E-mail: bstrickler@alpha.utampa.edu
Web Site: http://www.utampa.edu/
President/CEO: Dr. Ronald L. Vaughn
Registrar: Leslie Sutton-Smith
Admissions: Barbara P. Strickler
Financial Aid: John Marsh
Type: Comprehensive **Sex:** Coed **Scores:** 99.7% SAT V 400+; 99.5% SAT M 400+; 57.5% ACT 18-23; 36.2% ACT 24-29 **% Accepted:** 50 **Admission Plans:** Early Admission; Deferred Admission **Application Deadline:** Rolling **Application Fee:** $35.00 **H.S. Requirements:** High school diploma required; GED accepted **Costs Per Year:** Application fee: $35. Comprehensive fee: $25,784 includes full-time tuition ($17,906), mandatory fees ($942), and college room and board ($6936). College room only: $3710. Full-time tuition and fees vary according to class time. Room and board charges vary

according to board plan and housing facility. Part-time tuition: $380 per hour. Part-time mandatory fees: $35 per term. Part-time tuition and fees vary according to class time. **Scholarships:** Available **Calendar System:** Semester, Summer Session Available **Enrollment:** FT 4,169, PT 467, Grad 566 **Faculty:** FT 208, PT 217 **Student-Faculty Ratio:** 17:1 **Exams:** SAT I or ACT **% Receiving Financial Aid:** 55 **% Residing in College-Owned, -Operated, or -Affiliated Housing:** 59 **Library Holdings:** 252,147 **Regional Accreditation:** Southern Association of Colleges and Schools **Credit Hours For Degree:** 62 semester hours, Associates; 124 semester hours, Bachelors **ROTC:** Army, Air Force **Professional Accreditation:** AACSB, NASM, NLN **Intercollegiate Athletics:** Baseball M; Basketball M & W; Crew M & W; Cross-Country Running M & W; Golf M; Soccer M & W; Softball W; Swimming and Diving M & W; Tennis W; Volleyball W

UNIVERSITY OF WEST FLORIDA

11000 University Parkway
Pensacola, FL 32514-5750
Tel: (850)474-2000
Free: 800-263-1074
Admissions: (850)474-2230
Fax: (850)474-2096
E-mail: admissions@uwf.edu
Web Site: http://uwf.edu/
President/CEO: Dr. John C. Cavanaugh
Registrar: Ann Dziadon
Admissions: Dr. Richard A. Barth
Financial Aid: Cathy Brown

Type: Comprehensive **Sex:** Coed **Affiliation:** State University System of Florida **Scores:** 100% SAT V 400+; 98% SAT M 400+; 54% ACT 18-23; 41% ACT 24-29 **% Accepted:** 68 **Admission Plans:** Preferred Admission; Early Admission; Deferred Admission **Application Deadline:** June 30 **Application Fee:** $30.00 **H.S. Requirements:** High school diploma required; GED accepted **Costs Per Year:** Application fee: $30. State resident tuition: $2147 full-time, $106.59 per semester hour part-time. Nonresident tuition: $14,654 full-time, $523.48 per semester hour part-time. Mandatory fees: $1050 full-time. Full-time tuition and fees vary according to location. Part-time tuition varies according to location. College room and board: $6600. Room and board charges vary according to housing facility. **Scholarships:** Available **Calendar System:** Semester, Summer Session Available **Enrollment:** FT 5,771, PT 2,397, Grad 1,464 **Faculty:** FT 308, PT 219 **Student-Faculty Ratio:** 19:1 **Exams:** SAT I or ACT **% Residing in College-Owned, -Operated, or -Affiliated Housing:** 18 **Library Holdings:** 414,418 **Regional Accreditation:** Southern Association of Colleges and Schools **Credit Hours For Degree:** 60 semester hours, Associates; 120 semester hours, Bachelors **ROTC:** Army, Air Force **Professional Accreditation:** AACSB, AACN, CSWE, NAACLS, NASM, NASPAA, NCATE, NLN **Intercollegiate Athletics:** Baseball M; Basketball M & W; Cross-Country Running M & W; Golf M; Soccer M & W; Softball W; Tennis M & W; Track and Field W; Volleyball W

VALENCIA COMMUNITY COLLEGE

PO Box 3028
Orlando, FL 32802-3028
Tel: (407)299-5000
Admissions: (407)582-1511
Web Site: http://www.valencia.cc.fl.us/
President/CEO: Dr. Sanford C. Shugart
Registrar: Dr. Renee K. Simpson
Admissions: Dr. Renee Simpson
Financial Aid: Linda Downing

Type: Two-Year College **Sex:** Coed **Affiliation:** Florida Community College System **Scores:** 97% SAT V 400+; 93% SAT M 400+ **Admission Plans:** Open Admission; Preferred Admission; Early Admission **Application Deadline:** August 12 **Application Fee:** $25.00 **H.S. Requirements:** High school diploma required; GED accepted **Costs Per Year:** Application fee: $25. State resident tuition: $1673 full-time, $66.11 per credit hour part-time. Nonresident tuition: $6287 full-time, $248.05 per credit hour part-time. **Scholarships:** Available **Calendar System:** Semester, Summer Session Available **Faculty:** FT 396, PT 794 **Student-Faculty Ratio:** 21:1 **Library Holdings:** 101,000 **Regional Accreditation:** Southern Association of Colleges and Schools **Credit Hours For Degree:** 60 semester hours, Associates **ROTC:** Army **Professional Accreditation:** ADA, CARC, JRCEDMS, JRCERT, JRCEMT, NLN

WARNER SOUTHERN COLLEGE

13895 US Hwy. 27
Lake Wales, FL 33859
Tel: (863)638-1426
Admissions: (863)638-7212
Web Site: http://www.warner.edu/
President/CEO: Dr. Gregory V. Hall
Registrar: Sara Fasel
Admissions: Jason Roe
Financial Aid: Lorrie White

Type: Comprehensive **Sex:** Coed **Affiliation:** Church of God **Scores:** 76% SAT V 400+; 75% SAT M 400+; 48% ACT 18-23; 6% ACT 24-29 **% Accepted:** 58 **Admission Plans:** Deferred Admission **Application Deadline:** Rolling **Application Fee:** $20.00 **H.S. Requirements:** High school diploma required; GED accepted. For a portfolio on standardized tests for home schoolers: High school diploma required; GED accepted **Costs Per Year:** Application fee: $20. Comprehensive fee: $18,466 includes full-time tuition ($12,440), mandatory fees ($150), and college room and board ($5876). College room only: $2890. Full-time tuition and fees vary according to program. Room and board charges vary according to board plan. Part-time tuition: $320 per hour. Part-time mandatory fees: $25 per term. Part-time tuition and fees vary according to program. **Scholarships:** Available **Calendar System:** Semester, Summer Session Available **Enrollment:** FT 778, PT 143, Grad 49 **Faculty:** FT 35, PT 64 **Student-Faculty Ratio:** 16:1 **Exams:** SAT I or ACT **% Receiving Financial Aid:** 66 **% Residing in College-Owned, -Operated, or -Affiliated Housing:** 41 **Library Holdings:** 56,419 **Regional Accreditation:** Southern Association of Colleges and Schools **Credit Hours For Degree:** 64 credit hours, Associates; 128 credit hours, Bachelors **Intercollegiate Athletics:** Baseball M; Basketball M & W; Cheerleading M & W; Cross-Country Running M & W; Golf M & W; Soccer M & W; Softball W; Tennis M & W; Track and Field M & W; Volleyball W

WEBBER INTERNATIONAL UNIVERSITY

PO Box 96, 1200 North Scenic Hwy.
Babson Park, FL 33827-0096
Tel: (863)638-1431
Free: 800-741-1844
Admissions: (863)638-2910
Fax: (863)638-2823
E-mail: admissions@webber.edu
Web Site: http://www.webber.edu/
President/CEO: Rex R. Yentes
Registrar: Kathy Wilson
Admissions: Julie Ragans
Financial Aid: Kathy Wilson

Type: Comprehensive **Sex:** Coed **Scores:** 79.6% SAT V 400+; 80.58% SAT M 400+; 50% ACT 18-23; 1.72% ACT 24-29 **% Accepted:** 66 **Admission Plans:** Early Action **Application Deadline:** August 01 **Application Fee:** $35.00 **H.S. Requirements:** High school diploma required; GED accepted **Costs Per Year:** Application fee: $35. Comprehensive fee: $19,090 includes full-time tuition ($14,390) and college room and board ($4700). **Scholarships:** Available **Calendar System:** Semester, Summer Session Available **Enrollment:** FT 506, PT 51, Grad 59 **Faculty:** FT 25, PT 20 **Student-Faculty Ratio:** 17:1 **Exams:** SAT I or ACT **% Receiving Financial Aid:** 59 **% Residing in College-Owned, -Operated, or -Affiliated Housing:** 37 **Library Holdings:** 25,000 **Regional Accreditation:** Southern Association of Colleges and Schools **Credit Hours For Degree:** 60 credit hours, Associates; 120 credit hours, Bachelors **Intercollegiate Athletics:** Baseball M; Basketball M & W; Cross-Country Running M & W; Football M; Golf M & W; Soccer M & W; Softball W; Tennis M & W; Track and Field M & W; Volleyball M & W

WEBSTER COLLEGE (HOLIDAY)

2127 Grand Blvd.
Holiday, FL 34690
Tel: (727)942-0069; 888-729-7247
Fax: (727)938-5709
Web Site: http://www.webstercollege.com/
President/CEO: Claire L. Walker
Admissions: Claire L. Walker

Financial Aid: Tina Fisher
Type: Two-Year College **Scholarships:** Available **Faculty:** FT 6, PT 12 **Student-Faculty Ratio:** 12:1 **Exams:** Other **Professional Accreditation:** ACICS

WEBSTER COLLEGE (OCALA)
1530 SW Third Ave.
Ocala, FL 34474
Tel: (352)629-1941
Fax: (352)629-0926
Web Site: http://www.webstercollege.com/
President/CEO: Todd Matthews
Registrar: Doreen Crandall
Admissions: Todd Matthews
Financial Aid: Susan Van House
Type: Two-Year College **Sex:** Coed **Admission Plans:** Open Admission; Deferred Admission **Application Fee:** $20.00 **H.S. Requirements:** High school diploma required; GED accepted **Scholarships:** Available **Calendar System:** Quarter, Summer Session Available **Faculty:** FT 12, PT 24 **Library Holdings:** 2,400 **Credit Hours For Degree:** 90 credits, Associates **Professional Accreditation:** ACICS

YESHIVA GEDOLAH RABBINICAL COLLEGE
1140 Alton Rd.
Miami Beach, FL 33139
Tel: (305)673-5664
Fax: (305)532-9820 **Type:** Four-Year College **Affiliation:** Jewish **Professional Accreditation:** AARTS

ABRAHAM BALDWIN AGRICULTURAL COLLEGE
2802 Moore Hwy.
Tifton, GA 31793
Tel: (229)386-3236
Free: 800-733-3653
Admissions: (229)391-5001
Fax: (229)386-7006
E-mail: esaxon@abac.edu
Web Site: http://www.abac.edu/
President/CEO: Michael Vollmer
Registrar: Beth Saxon
Admissions: Beth Saxon
Financial Aid: Jenelle Handcox
Type: Two-Year College **Sex:** Coed **Affiliation:** University System of Georgia **% Accepted:** 60 **Admission Plans:** Open Admission; Early Admission; Deferred Admission **Application Deadline:** September 24 **Application Fee:** $20.00 **H.S. Requirements:** High school diploma required; GED accepted **Costs Per Year:** Application fee: $20. State resident tuition: $1542 full-time, $65 per credit hour part-time. Nonresident tuition: $6166 full-time, $257 per credit hour part-time. Mandatory fees: $232 full-time, $52 per term part-time. College room and board: $5040. **Scholarships:** Available **Calendar System:** Semester, Summer Session Available **Enrollment:** FT 2,237, PT 1,186 **Faculty:** FT 100, PT 54 **Student-Faculty Ratio:** 22:1 **% Residing in College-Owned, -Operated, or -Affiliated Housing:** 28 **Library Holdings:** 69,986 **Regional Accreditation:** Southern Association of Colleges and Schools **Professional Accreditation:** NLN **Intercollegiate Athletics:** Baseball M; Basketball M; Golf M; Soccer W; Softball W; Tennis M & W

AGNES SCOTT COLLEGE
141 East College Ave.
Decatur, GA 30030-3797
Tel: (404)471-6000
Free: 800-868-8602
Admissions: (404)471-6285
Fax: (404)471-6414
E-mail: admission@agnesscott.edu
Web Site: http://www.agnesscott.edu/
President/CEO: Dr. Mary Brown Bullock
Registrar: Nancy Albert
Admissions: Stephanie Balmer
Financial Aid: Karen Smith
Type: Comprehensive **Affiliation:** Presbyterian Church (U.S.A.) **Scores:** 99.1% SAT V 400+; 100% SAT M 400+; 20.4% ACT 18-23; 59.2% ACT 24-29 **% Accepted:** 53 **Admission Plans:** Early Admission; Early Decision Plan; Deferred Admission **Application Deadline:** March 01 **Application Fee:** $35.00 **H.S. Requirements:** High school diploma required; GED accepted **Costs Per Year:** Application fee: $35. Comprehensive fee: $32,070 includes full-time tuition ($23,260), mandatory fees ($310), and college room and board ($8500). College room only: $4250. Room and board charges vary according to board plan and housing facility. Part-time tuition: $970 per credit hour. Part-time mandatory fees: $310 per year. Part-time tuition and fees vary according to course load. **Scholarships:** Available **Calendar System:** Semester, Summer Session Available **Enrollment:** FT 879, PT 124, Grad 13 **Faculty:** FT 81, PT 29 **Student-Faculty Ratio:** 10:1 **Exams:** SAT I or ACT, SAT II **% Receiving Financial Aid:** 63 **% Residing in College-Owned, -Operated, or -Affiliated Housing:** 86 **Library Holdings:** 220,041 **Regional Accreditation:** Southern Association of Colleges and Schools **Credit Hours For Degree:** 130 semester hours, Bachelors **ROTC:** Air Force **Intercollegiate Athletics:** Basketball W; Cross-Country Running W; Soccer W; Softball W; Swimming and Diving W; Tennis W; Volleyball W

ALBANY STATE UNIVERSITY
504 College Dr.
Albany, GA 31705-2717
Tel: (229)430-4600
Admissions: (229)430-4646
Fax: (229)430-3936
Web Site: http://www.asurams.edu/
President/CEO: Dr. Portia Shields
Registrar: Arna Albritten
Admissions: Robin McDermott
Financial Aid: Kathleen Caldwell
Type: Comprehensive **Sex:** Coed **Affiliation:** University System of Georgia **Scores:** 94.1% SAT V 400+; 93.93% SAT M 400+; 2.74% ACT 18-23 **Admission Plans:** Early Admission; Deferred Admission **Application Fee:** $20.00 **H.S. Requirements:** High school diploma required; GED accepted **Scholarships:** Available **Calendar System:** Semester, Summer Session Available **Enrollment:** FT 2,658, PT 554, Grad 456 **Faculty:** FT 142, PT 69 **Student-Faculty Ratio:** 16:1 **Exams:** SAT I or ACT **% Receiving Financial Aid:** 82 **% Residing in College-Owned, -Operated, or -Affiliated Housing:** 35 **Library Holdings:** 338,744 **Regional Accreditation:** Southern Association of Colleges and Schools **Credit Hours For Degree:** 120 credits, Bachelors **ROTC:** Army **Professional Accreditation:** ACBSP, CSWE, NASPAA, NCATE, NLN **Intercollegiate Athletics:** Baseball M; Basketball M & W; Cross-Country Running M & W; Football M; Softball W; Tennis M; Track and Field M & W; Volleyball W

ALBANY TECHNICAL COLLEGE
1704 South Slappey Blvd.
Albany, GA 31701-3514
Tel: (229)430-3500
Admissions: (229)430-3520
Fax: (229)430-5155
E-mail: lcheevers@albanytech.edu
Web Site: http://www.albanytech.edu/
President/CEO: Dr. Anthony O. Parker
Admissions: Lynderia S. Cheevers
Financial Aid: Kenneth Wilson
Type: Two-Year College **Sex:** Coed **Admission Plans:** Open Admission; Deferred Admission **Application Fee:** $15.00 **H.S. Requirements:** High school diploma or equivalent not required **Costs Per Year:** Application fee: $15. State resident tuition: $1116 full-time, $31 per credit hour part-time. Nonresident tuition: $2232 full-time, $62 per credit hour part-time. **Calendar System:** Quarter **Enrollment:** FT 1,390, PT 1,397 **Faculty:** FT 91, PT 0 **Exams:** Other **Library Holdings:** 42,000 **Regional Accreditation:** Southern Association of Colleges and Schools **Credit Hours For Degree:** 90 credits, Associates **Professional Accreditation:** ADA, COE, JRCERT

ALTAMAHA TECHNICAL COLLEGE
1777 West Cherry St.
Jesup, GA 31545

Tel: (912)427-5800
Admissions: (912)427-5817
Fax: (912)427-5823
E-mail: lburns@altamahatech.edu
Web Site: http://www.altamahatech.edu/
President/CEO: Dr. C. Paul Scott
Admissions: Lillian Burns
Type: Two-Year College **Sex:** Coed **Admission Plans:** Open Admission; Deferred Admission **Application Fee:** $15.00 **H.S. Requirements:** High school diploma or equivalent not required **Costs Per Year:** Application fee: $15. State resident tuition: $1116 full-time, $31 per credit hour part-time. Nonresident tuition: $2232 full-time, $62 per credit hour part-time. **Calendar System:** Quarter **Enrollment:** FT 342, PT 517 **Faculty:** FT 41, PT 65 **Exams:** Other **Library Holdings:** 4,435 **Professional Accreditation:** COE

AMERICAN INTERCONTINENTAL UNIVERSITY (ATLANTA)
3330 Peachtree Rd., NE
Atlanta, GA 30326-1016
Tel: (404)231-9000; 888-999-4248
Admissions: (404)965-5772
Fax: (404)231-1062
E-mail: david.naylor@buckhead.aiuniv.edu
Web Site: http://www.aiuniv.edu/
President/CEO: Rafael Lago
Registrar: Kirk Morrison
Admissions: David Naylor
Financial Aid: Sherry Rizzi
Type: Four-Year College **Sex:** Coed **Affiliation:** Career Education Corporation **Admission Plans:** Open Admission; Early Admission; Deferred Admission **Application Fee:** $50.00 **H.S. Requirements:** High school diploma required; GED accepted **Costs Per Year:** Application fee: $50. Tuition: $16,386 full-time, $430 per credit part-time. Full-time tuition varies according to course load and program. Part-time tuition varies according to course load and program. College room only: $5400. Tuition guaranteed not to increase for student's term of enrollment. **Scholarships:** Available **Calendar System:** Miscellaneous, Summer Session Available **Enrollment:** FT 1,319, PT 378, Grad 35 **Faculty:** FT 27, PT 84 **Student-Faculty Ratio:** 15:1 **Exams:** SAT I or ACT, SAT II **% Residing in College-Owned, -Operated, or -Affiliated Housing:** 14 **Library Holdings:** 29,672 **Regional Accreditation:** Southern Association of Colleges and Schools **Credit Hours For Degree:** 90 credit hours, Associates; 180 credit hours, Bachelors **Professional Accreditation:** FIDER

AMERICAN INTERCONTINENTAL UNIVERSITY (DUNWOODY CAMPUS)
6600 Peachtree-Dunwoody Rd.
500 Embassy Row
Atlanta, GA 30328
Tel: (404)965-6500
Free: 800-255-6839
Admissions: (404)965-8050
Fax: (404)965-6501
Web Site: http://www.aiudunwoody.com/
President/CEO: Dr. Richard Farmer
Admissions: Jeff Bostick
Type: Comprehensive **Sex:** Coed **Affiliation:** AIU is owned by Career Education Corporation **Scores:** 100% SAT V 400+; 100% SAT M 400+; 22% ACT 18-23; 59% ACT 24-29 **Application Fee:** $50.00 **Calendar System:** Miscellaneous **Enrollment:** FT 924, PT 183, Grad 43 **Faculty:** FT 39, PT 80 **Student-Faculty Ratio:** 18:1 **Exams:** Other, SAT I or ACT **Regional Accreditation:** Southern Association of Colleges and Schools

ANDREW COLLEGE
413 College St.
Cuthbert, GA 39840-1313
Tel: (229)732-2171
Free: 800-664-9250
Admissions: (229)732-5934
Fax: (229)732-2176
E-mail: admissions@andrewcollege.edu
Web Site: http://www.andrewcollege.edu/
President/CEO: Dr. David A. Palmer
Registrar: C. Larry Brown
Admissions: Janna Powell
Financial Aid: Amy Thompson
Type: Two-Year College **Sex:** Coed **Affiliation:** United Methodist **Admission Plans:** Early Admission; Deferred Admission **Application Fee:** $20.00 **H.S. Requirements:** High school diploma required; GED accepted **Costs Per Year:** Application fee: $20. Comprehensive fee: $15,980 includes full-time tuition ($9814) and college room and board ($6166). **Scholarships:** Available **Calendar System:** Semester, Summer Session Available **Enrollment:** FT 328, PT 3 **Faculty:** FT 35, PT 6 **Student-Faculty Ratio:** 12:1 **Exams:** SAT I or ACT **% Residing in College-Owned, -Operated, or -Affiliated Housing:** 90 **Library Holdings:** 40,000 **Regional Accreditation:** Southern Association of Colleges and Schools **Credit Hours For Degree:** 64 credit hours, Associates **Intercollegiate Athletics:** Baseball M; Golf M; Soccer M & W; Softball W

APPALACHIAN TECHNICAL COLLEGE
100 Campus Dr.
Jasper, GA 30143
Tel: (706)253-4500
Admissions: (706)253-4537
Fax: (706)253-4510
E-mail: nfaix@appalachiantech.edu
Web Site: http://www.appalachiantech.edu/
President/CEO: Dr. Sanford Chandler
Admissions: Nina Faix
Type: Two-Year College **Sex:** Coed **Admission Plans:** Open Admission; Deferred Admission **Application Fee:** $15.00 **H.S. Requirements:** High school diploma or equivalent not required **Costs Per Year:** Application fee: $15. State resident tuition: $1116 full-time, $31 per credit hour part-time. Nonresident tuition: $2232 full-time, $62 per credit hour part-time. **Calendar System:** Quarter **Enrollment:** FT 414, PT 633 **Faculty:** FT 31, PT 46 **Exams:** Other **Professional Accreditation:** COE

ARGOSY UNIVERSITY/ATLANTA
990 Hammond Dr., 11th Floor
Atlanta, GA 30328-5505
Tel: (770)671-1200; 888-671-4777
Fax: (770)671-0476
Web Site: http://www.argosyu.edu/
President/CEO: Dr. Harry O'Donnell
Registrar: Sheri E. Jones
Admissions: Andrew Horn
Financial Aid: Anna Mendez
Type: Two-Year Upper Division **Sex:** Coed **Affiliation:** Education Management Corporation **Application Fee:** $50.00 **Scholarships:** Available **Calendar System:** Semester **Enrollment:** FT 4, PT 9 **Faculty:** FT 1, PT 12 **% Receiving Financial Aid:** 67 **Regional Accreditation:** North Central Association of Colleges and Schools **Professional Accreditation:** APA

ARMSTRONG ATLANTIC STATE UNIVERSITY
11935 Abercorn St.
Savannah, GA 31419-1997
Tel: (912)927-5211
Free: 800-633-2349
Admissions: (912)927-5275
Fax: (912)921-5462
E-mail: westkim@mail.armstrong.edu
Web Site: http://www.armstrong.edu/
President/CEO: Dr. Thomas Z. Jones
Registrar: Kim West
Admissions: Kim West
Financial Aid: Lee Ann Kirkland
Type: Comprehensive **Sex:** Coed **Affiliation:** University System of Georgia **Scores:** 99% SAT V 400+; 98% SAT M 400+; 67% ACT 18-23; 16% ACT 24-29 **% Accepted:** 100 **Admission Plans:** Early Admission; Deferred Admission **Application Deadline:** July 01 **Application Fee:** $20.00 **H.S. Requirements:** High school diploma required; GED accepted **Costs Per Year:** Application fee: $20. State resident tuition: $2894 full-time, $102 per hour part-time. Nonresident tuition: $10,210 full-time, $407 per hour part-time. Mandatory fees: $456 full-time, $213 per term part-time. Full-time tuition and fees vary according to program. Part-time tuition and fees vary according to course load and program. College room only: $4980. Room charges vary according to housing facility. **Scholarships:** Available **Calendar System:** Semester, Summer Session Available **Enrollment:** FT 3,677, PT 2,238, Grad 795 **Faculty:** FT 224, PT 200 **Student-Faculty Ratio:** 17:1 **Exams:** SAT I or ACT, SAT II **% Receiving Financial Aid:** 55 %

Residing in College-Owned, -Operated, or -Affiliated Housing: 10 **Library Holdings:** 223,412 **Regional Accreditation:** Southern Association of Colleges and Schools **Credit Hours For Degree:** 60 semester hours, Associates; 123 semester hours, Bachelors **ROTC:** Army, Navy **Professional Accreditation:** ABET, AACN, ADA, APTA, CARC, CEPH, JRCERT, NAACLS, NASM, NCATE, NLN **Intercollegiate Athletics:** Baseball M; Basketball M & W; Golf M; Softball W; Tennis M & W; Volleyball W

THE ART INSTITUTE OF ATLANTA
6600 Peachtree Dunwoody Rd., 100 Embassy Row
Atlanta, GA 30328
Tel: (770)394-8300
Free: 800-275-4242
Fax: (770)394-0008
Web Site: http://www.aia.artinstitutes.edu/
President/CEO: Janet S. Day
Registrar: Martha Richardson
Admissions: Donna Scott
Financial Aid: Rena Marroquin
Type: Four-Year College **Sex:** Coed **Affiliation:** Education Management Corporation **Admission Plans:** Deferred Admission **Application Fee:** $50.00 **H.S. Requirements:** High school diploma required; GED accepted **Costs Per Year:** Application fee: $50. Tuition: $18,000 full-time, $375 per credit part-time. Full-time tuition varies according to course load. Part-time tuition varies according to course load. College room only: $7311. Room charges vary according to housing facility. Tuition guaranteed not to increase for student's term of enrollment. **Scholarships:** Available **Calendar System:** Quarter, Summer Session Available **Enrollment:** FT 2,322, PT 329 **Faculty:** FT 91, PT 74 **Student-Faculty Ratio:** 21:1 **% Receiving Financial Aid:** 88 **% Residing in College-Owned, -Operated, or -Affiliated Housing:** 13 **Library Holdings:** 40,799 **Regional Accreditation:** Southern Association of Colleges and Schools **Credit Hours For Degree:** 96 credits, Associates; 192 credits, Bachelors **Professional Accreditation:** ACF, FIDER

ASHWORTH COLLEGE
430 Technology Parkway
Norcross, GA 30092
Tel: (770)729-8400
Free: 800-223-4542
Fax: (770)729-9296
Web Site: http://www.ashworthcollege.com/
President/CEO: Dr. F. Milton Miller
Admissions: John Graves
Type: Two-Year College **Sex:** Coed **Affiliation:** Professional Career Development, LLC **H.S. Requirements:** High school diploma required; GED accepted **Calendar System:** Semester, Summer Session Available **Faculty:** FT 2, PT 53 **Credit Hours For Degree:** 20 courses, Associates **Professional Accreditation:** DETC

ATHENS TECHNICAL COLLEGE
800 US Hwy. 29 North
Athens, GA 30601-1500
Tel: (706)355-5000
Admissions: (706)355-5124
Fax: (706)369-5753
E-mail: lreid@athenstech.org
Web Site: http://www.athenstech.edu/
President/CEO: Dr. Coy Hodges
Registrar: Andrea Daniel
Admissions: Lenzy Reid
Financial Aid: Wanda Hicks
Type: Two-Year College **Sex:** Coed **Affiliation:** Georgia Department of Technical and Adult Education **Admission Plans:** Open Admission; Deferred Admission **Application Fee:** $15.00 **H.S. Requirements:** High school diploma or equivalent not required **Costs Per Year:** Application fee: $15. State resident tuition: $1116 full-time, $31 per credit hour part-time. Nonresident tuition: $2232 full-time, $62 per credit hour part-time. **Scholarships:** Available **Calendar System:** Quarter, Summer Session Available **Enrollment:** FT 1,436, PT 2,369 **Faculty:** FT 81, PT 208 **Exams:** Other **Library Holdings:** 33,891 **Regional Accreditation:** Southern Association of Colleges and Schools **Credit Hours For Degree:** 120 credit hours, Associates **Professional Accreditation:** ADA, APTA, ACBSP, CARC, JRCERT, NLN

ATLANTA CHRISTIAN COLLEGE
2605 Ben Hill Rd.
East Point, GA 30344-1999
Tel: (404)761-8861
Free: 800-776-1ACC
Web Site: http://www.acc.edu/
President/CEO: Dr. R. Edwin Groover
Registrar: Kathy David
Admissions: Keith Wagner
Financial Aid: Blair Walker
Type: Four-Year College **Sex:** Coed **Affiliation:** Christian **Admission Plans:** Early Admission; Early Decision Plan; Deferred Admission **Application Fee:** $25.00 **H.S. Requirements:** High school diploma required; GED accepted **Costs Per Year:** Application fee: $25. Comprehensive fee: $17,180 includes full-time tuition ($11,800), mandatory fees ($580), and college room and board ($4800). Full-time tuition and fees vary according to course level. Part-time tuition: $495 per hour. Part-time tuition varies according to course level and student level. **Scholarships:** Available **Calendar System:** Semester, Summer Session Available **Enrollment:** FT 370, PT 73 **Student-Faculty Ratio:** 16:1 **Exams:** SAT I or ACT **% Residing in College-Owned, -Operated, or -Affiliated Housing:** 60 **Library Holdings:** 50,000 **Regional Accreditation:** Southern Association of Colleges and Schools **Credit Hours For Degree:** 64 semester hours, Associates; 128 semester hours, Bachelors **Professional Accreditation:** NCATE **Intercollegiate Athletics:** Baseball M; Basketball M & W; Golf M; Soccer M & W; Softball W; Volleyball W

ATLANTA METROPOLITAN COLLEGE
1630 Metropolitan Parkway, SW
Atlanta, GA 30310-4498
Tel: (404)756-4000
Admissions: (404)756-4004
E-mail: admissions@atlm.edu
Web Site: http://www.atlm.edu/
President/CEO: Dr. Harold E. Wade
Registrar: John Brown
Admissions: Audrey Reid
Financial Aid: Vera Brooks
Type: Two-Year College **Sex:** Coed **Affiliation:** University System of Georgia **% Accepted:** 57 **Application Deadline:** July 15 **Application Fee:** $20.00 **H.S. Requirements:** High school diploma required; GED accepted **Costs Per Year:** Application fee: $20. State resident tuition: $1560 full-time, $65 per credit hour part-time. Nonresident tuition: $6168 full-time, $257 per credit hour part-time. Mandatory fees: $230 full-time, $115 per term part-time. **Scholarships:** Available **Calendar System:** Semester, Summer Session Available **Enrollment:** FT 860, PT 888 **Faculty:** FT 44, PT 28 **Student-Faculty Ratio:** 23:1 **Library Holdings:** 48,719 **Regional Accreditation:** Southern Association of Colleges and Schools **Credit Hours For Degree:** 60 credit hours, Associates **Professional Accreditation:** ACBSP **Intercollegiate Athletics:** Basketball M & W; Cheerleading M & W

ATLANTA TECHNICAL COLLEGE
1560 Metropolitan Parkway
Atlanta, GA 30310
Tel: (404)756-3700
Admissions: (404)225-4446
Fax: (404)752-0809
E-mail: jtriplet@atlantatech.edu
Web Site: http://www.atlantatech.org/
President/CEO: Dr. Brenda Watts Jones
Admissions: Jill Triplett
Type: Two-Year College **Sex:** Coed **Admission Plans:** Open Admission; Deferred Admission **Application Fee:** $15.00 **H.S. Requirements:** High school diploma or equivalent not required **Costs Per Year:** Application fee: $15. State resident tuition: $1116 full-time, $31 per credit hour part-time. Nonresident tuition: $2232 full-time, $62 per credit hour part-time. **Calendar System:** Quarter **Enrollment:** FT 1,535, PT 1,988 **Faculty:** FT 86, PT 102 **Exams:** Other **Professional Accreditation:** ADA, COE

AUGUSTA STATE UNIVERSITY
2500 Walton Way
Augusta, GA 30904-2200

Tel: (706)737-1400
Free: 800-341-4373
Admissions: (706)737-1632
Fax: (706)737-1774
E-mail: admissions@ac.edu
Web Site: http://www.aug.edu/
President/CEO: Dr. William A. Bloodworth, Jr.
Registrar: Katherine Sweeney
Admissions: Katherine Sweeney
Financial Aid: Willene C. Holmes
Type: Comprehensive **Sex:** Coed **Affiliation:** University System of Georgia **Scores:** 88.7% SAT V 400+; 86.6% SAT M 400+; 53.5% ACT 18-23; 8.1% ACT 24-29 **% Accepted:** 63 **Admission Plans:** Early Admission; Deferred Admission **Application Deadline:** July 21 **Application Fee:** $20.00 **H.S. Requirements:** High school diploma required; GED accepted **Costs Per Year:** Application fee: $20. State resident tuition: $2438 full-time, $102 per hour part-time. Nonresident tuition: $9754 full-time, $407 per hour part-time. Mandatory fees: $482 full-time, $241 per term part-time. College room only: $4920. **Scholarships:** Available **Calendar System:** Semester, Summer Session Available **Enrollment:** FT 3,686, PT 1,775, Grad 851 **Faculty:** FT 215, PT 115 **Student-Faculty Ratio:** 19:1 **Exams:** SAT I or ACT **% Receiving Financial Aid:** 51 **Library Holdings:** 454,590 **Regional Accreditation:** Southern Association of Colleges and Schools **Credit Hours For Degree:** 60 credits, Associates; 120 credits, Bachelors **ROTC:** Army **Professional Accreditation:** AACSB, NASAD, NASM, NCATE, NLN **Intercollegiate Athletics:** Baseball M; Basketball M & W; Cross-Country Running M & W; Softball W; Tennis M & W; Volleyball W

AUGUSTA TECHNICAL COLLEGE
3200 Augusta Tech Dr.
Augusta, GA 30906
Tel: (706)771-4000
Admissions: (706)771-4027
Fax: (706)771-4016
E-mail: bcrobert@augustatech.edu
Web Site: http://www.augustatech.edu/
President/CEO: Terry Elam
Registrar: Denise Anderson
Admissions: Brian Roberts
Financial Aid: Beverly Smyre
Type: Two-Year College **Sex:** Coed **Affiliation:** Georgia Department of Technical and Adult Education **Admission Plans:** Open Admission; Preferred Admission; Deferred Admission **Application Fee:** $15.00 **H.S. Requirements:** High school diploma or equivalent not required **Costs Per Year:** Application fee: $15. State resident tuition: $1116 full-time, $31 per credit hour part-time. Nonresident tuition: $2232 full-time, $62 per credit hour part-time. **Scholarships:** Available **Calendar System:** Quarter, Summer Session Available **Enrollment:** FT 1,986, PT 2,185 **Faculty:** FT 136, PT 240 **Exams:** Other **Library Holdings:** 70,816 **Regional Accreditation:** Southern Association of Colleges and Schools **Credit Hours For Degree:** 101 quarter hours, Associates **Professional Accreditation:** ABET, ARCEST, ADA, AOTA, CARC, JRCECT

BAINBRIDGE COLLEGE
2500 East Shotwell St.
Bainbridge, GA 39819
Tel: (229)248-2500
Admissions: (229)248-2504
Fax: (229)248-2525
Web Site: http://www.bainbridge.edu/
President/CEO: Dr. Clifford M. Brock
Registrar: Connie Snyder
Admissions: Connie Snyder
Type: Two-Year College **Sex:** Coed **Affiliation:** University System of Georgia **% Accepted:** 78 **Admission Plans:** Early Admission **Application Deadline:** August 01 **Application Fee:** $0.00 **H.S. Requirements:** High school diploma required; GED accepted **Costs Per Year:** Application fee: $0. State resident tuition: $1542 full-time, $65 per credit hour part-time. Nonresident tuition: $6166 full-time, $257 per credit hour part-time. Mandatory fees: $124 full-time. **Scholarships:** Available **Calendar System:** Semester, Summer Session Available **Enrollment:** FT 954, PT 1,521 **Faculty:** FT 62, PT 68 **Exams:** Other, SAT I or ACT **Library Holdings:** 37,387 **Regional Accreditation:** Southern Association of Colleges and Schools **Credit Hours For Degree:** 60 semester hours, Associates

BAUDER COLLEGE
Phipps Plaza, 3500 Peachtree Rd, NE
Atlanta, GA 30326
Tel: (404)237-7573
Free: 800-241-3797
Fax: (404)237-1642
Web Site: http://www.bauder.edu/
President/CEO: Jo Ann Wilson
Registrar: Brantley Taylor
Admissions: Lyn Diaz
Financial Aid: Rhonda Staines
Type: Two-Year College **Sex:** Coed **Application Fee:** $0.00 **H.S. Requirements:** High school diploma required; GED accepted **Scholarships:** Available **Calendar System:** Quarter, Summer Session Available **Faculty:** FT 52, PT 23 **Library Holdings:** 4,000 **Regional Accreditation:** Southern Association of Colleges and Schools **Credit Hours For Degree:** 90 credit hours, Associates

BEACON UNIVERSITY
6003 Veterans Parkway
Columbus, GA 31909
Tel: (706)323-5364
Fax: (706)323-3236
E-mail: registrar@beacon.edu
Web Site: http://www.beacon.edu/
President/CEO: Dr. Ronald E. Cottle
Admissions: Rita Roberts
Type: Comprehensive **Sex:** Coed **Admission Plans:** Early Admission **Application Fee:** $25.00 **H.S. Requirements:** High school diploma required; GED accepted **Scholarships:** Available **Calendar System:** Semester, Summer Session Available **Student-Faculty Ratio:** 5:1 **Exams:** Other, SAT I or ACT **% Receiving Financial Aid:** 100 **Library Holdings:** 25,000 **Credit Hours For Degree:** 66 semester hours, Associates; 126 semester hours, Bachelors **Professional Accreditation:** TACCS

BERRY COLLEGE
PO Box 490159
Mount Berry, GA 30149-0159
Tel: (706)232-5374
Free: 800-237-7942
Admissions: (706)236-2215
Fax: (706)236-2248
E-mail: admissions@berry.edu
Web Site: http://www.berry.edu/
President/CEO: Dr. John Scott Colley
Registrar: Linda Tennant
Admissions: Richard D. Paul
Financial Aid: William G. Fron
Type: Comprehensive **Sex:** Coed **Affiliation:** interdenominational **Scores:** 99.2% SAT V 400+; 99.7% SAT M 400+; 33% ACT 18-23; 53.6% ACT 24-29 **% Accepted:** 83 **Admission Plans:** Early Admission; Deferred Admission **Application Deadline:** July 21 **Application Fee:** $50.00 **H.S. Requirements:** High school diploma required; GED accepted **Costs Per Year:** Application fee: $50. Comprehensive fee: $26,114 includes full-time tuition ($18,950) and college room and board ($7164). College room only: $4024. **Scholarships:** Available **Calendar System:** Semester, Summer Session Available **Enrollment:** FT 1,829, PT 34, Grad 107 **Faculty:** FT 134, PT 62 **Student-Faculty Ratio:** 13:1 **Exams:** SAT I or ACT **% Receiving Financial Aid:** 57 **% Residing in College-Owned, -Operated, or -Affiliated Housing:** 72 **Library Holdings:** 321,335 **Regional Accreditation:** Southern Association of Colleges and Schools **Credit Hours For Degree:** 124 semester hours, Bachelors **Professional Accreditation:** AAFCS, NASM, NCATE **Intercollegiate Athletics:** Baseball M; Basketball M & W; Cheerleading M & W; Crew M & W; Cross-Country Running M & W; Equestrian Sports M & W; Golf M & W; Lacrosse M & W; Soccer M & W; Tennis M & W; Track and Field M & W; Volleyball W

BEULAH HEIGHTS BIBLE COLLEGE
892 Berne St., SE, PO Box 18145
Atlanta, GA 30316
Tel: (404)627-2681; 888-777-BHBC
Fax: (404)627-0702

Web Site: http://www.beulah.org/
President/CEO: Dr. Benson M. Karanja
Registrar: Jackie Armstrong
Admissions: Jacquelyn B. Armstrong
Financial Aid: Patricia Banks
Type: Four-Year College **Sex:** Coed **Affiliation:** Pentecostal **Admission Plans:** Open Admission; Early Admission **Application Fee:** $20.00 **H.S. Requirements:** High school diploma required; GED accepted **Scholarships:** Available **Calendar System:** Semester, Summer Session Available **Enrollment:** FT 256, PT 364 **Faculty:** FT 18, PT 21 **Student-Faculty Ratio:** 17:1 **Exams:** SAT I or ACT **% Receiving Financial Aid:** 60 **% Residing in College-Owned, -Operated, or -Affiliated Housing:** 10 **Library Holdings:** 40,000 **Credit Hours For Degree:** 66 semester hours, Associates; 129 semester hours, Bachelors **Professional Accreditation:** AABC, TACCS

BRENAU UNIVERSITY
500 Washington St. SE
Gainesville, GA 30501
Tel: (770)534-6299
Free: 800-252-5119
Admissions: (770)718-5320
Fax: (770)534-6114
Web Site: http://www.brenau.edu/
President/CEO: Dr. John S. Burd
Registrar: Laura Ledford
Admissions: Christina White
Financial Aid: Pam Barrett
Type: Comprehensive **Scores:** 94.86% SAT V 400+; 92.96% SAT M 400+ **% Accepted:** 38 **Admission Plans:** Early Admission; Deferred Admission **Application Deadline:** Rolling **Application Fee:** $35.00 **H.S. Requirements:** High school diploma required; GED accepted **Costs Per Year:** Application fee: $35. Comprehensive fee: $24,990 includes full-time tuition ($16,440) and college room and board ($8550). Full-time tuition varies according to class time, location, and program. Room and board charges vary according to housing facility. Part-time tuition: $548 per semester hour. Part-time mandatory fees: $75 per term. Part-time tuition and fees vary according to class time, location, and program. **Scholarships:** Available **Calendar System:** Semester, Summer Session Available **Enrollment:** FT 670, PT 41, Grad 32 **Faculty:** FT 72, PT 33 **Student-Faculty Ratio:** 9:1 **Exams:** SAT I or ACT **% Receiving Financial Aid:** 73 **% Residing in College-Owned, -Operated, or -Affiliated Housing:** 55 **Library Holdings:** 61,059 **Regional Accreditation:** Southern Association of Colleges and Schools **Credit Hours For Degree:** 120 semester hours, Bachelors **Professional Accreditation:** AOTA, FIDER, NCATE, NLN **Intercollegiate Athletics:** Crew W; Cross-Country Running W; Soccer W; Softball W; Tennis W; Volleyball W

BREWTON-PARKER COLLEGE
Hwy. 280
Mt. Vernon, GA 30445-0197
Tel: (912)583-2241
Free: 800-342-1087
Admissions: (912)583-3265
Fax: (912)583-4498
Web Site: http://www.bpc.edu/
President/CEO: Dr. David R. Smith
Admissions: Brad Kissell
Financial Aid: Ione Maze
Type: Four-Year College **Sex:** Coed **Affiliation:** Southern Baptist **Scores:** 88% SAT V 400+; 82% SAT M 400+; 42% ACT 18-23; 8% ACT 24-29 **% Accepted:** 97 **Admission Plans:** Early Admission **Application Deadline:** Rolling **Application Fee:** $25.00 **H.S. Requirements:** High school diploma required; GED accepted **Costs Per Year:** Application fee: $25. Comprehensive fee: $17,504 includes full-time tuition ($11,584), mandatory fees ($1100), and college room and board ($4820). College room only: $2150. Room and board charges vary according to board plan and housing facility. Part-time tuition: $362 per credit hour. Part-time mandatory fees: $275 per term. **Scholarships:** Available **Calendar System:** Semester, Summer Session Available **Enrollment:** FT 846, PT 248 **Faculty:** FT 50, PT 87 **Student-Faculty Ratio:** 13:1 **Exams:** SAT I or ACT **% Receiving Financial Aid:** 90 **% Residing in College-Owned, -Operated, or -Affiliated Housing:** 34 **Library Holdings:** 74,331 **Regional Accreditation:** Southern Association of Colleges and Schools **Credit Hours For Degree:** 61 semesters, Associates; 121 semesters, Bachelors **Professional Accreditation:** NASM **Intercollegiate Athletics:** Baseball M; Basketball M & W; Cheerleading M & W; Soccer M & W; Softball W; Volleyball W

BROWN MACKIE COLLEGE-ATLANTA
4975 Jimmy Carter Blvd., Ste. 600
Norcross, GA 30093
Tel: (770)638-0121
Admissions: (770)510-2312
Fax: (770)638-0479
E-mail: rlcampbell@brownmackie.edu
Web Site: http://www.brownmackie.edu/locations.asp?locid=3
President/CEO: Darrell Woodrum
Admissions: Robert L. Campbell
Type: Two-Year College **Sex:** Coed **Application Deadline:** Rolling **Application Fee:** $0.00 **Costs Per Year:** Application fee: $0. Tuition: $6084 full-time, $169 per credit hour part-time. Mandatory fees: $360 full-time, $10 per credit hour part-time. **Scholarships:** Available **Enrollment:** FT 150 **Faculty:** FT 4, PT 4 **Student-Faculty Ratio:** 19:1 **Professional Accreditation:** COE

CARVER BIBLE COLLEGE
437 Nelson St.
Atlanta, GA 30313
Tel: (404)527-4520
Fax: (404)527-4526
Web Site: http://www.carver.edu/
President/CEO: Robert W. Crummie, Sr.
Admissions: Patsy S. Singh
Type: Four-Year College **Sex:** Coed **Affiliation:** nondenominational **Admission Plans:** Open Admission **H.S. Requirements:** High school diploma required; GED accepted **Calendar System:** Semester, Summer Session Available **Enrollment:** FT 47, PT 103 **Faculty:** FT 3, PT 18 **Student-Faculty Ratio:** 10:1 **Credit Hours For Degree:** 65 hours, Associates; 130 hours, Bachelors **Professional Accreditation:** AABC **Intercollegiate Athletics:** Basketball M

CENTRAL GEORGIA TECHNICAL COLLEGE
3300 Macon Tech Dr.
Macon, GA 31206-3628
Tel: (478)757-3400
Admissions: (478)757-3408
Fax: (478)757-3454
E-mail: amymc@cgtcollege.edu
Web Site: http://www.cgtcollege.org/
President/CEO: Dr. Melton Palmer, Jr.
Registrar: Rosemary Culverhouse
Admissions: Amy McDonald
Financial Aid: Pennie Strong
Type: Two-Year College **Sex:** Coed **Affiliation:** Georgia Department of Technical and Adult Education **Admission Plans:** Open Admission; Deferred Admission **Application Fee:** $15.00 **H.S. Requirements:** High school diploma or equivalent not required **Costs Per Year:** Application fee: $15. State resident tuition: $1116 full-time, $61 per credit hour part-time. Nonresident tuition: $2232 full-time, $62 per credit hour part-time. **Scholarships:** Available **Calendar System:** Quarter, Summer Session Not available **Enrollment:** FT 3,057, PT 2,990 **Faculty:** FT 109, PT 375 **Exams:** Other **Library Holdings:** 16,500 **Regional Accreditation:** Southern Association of Colleges and Schools **Credit Hours For Degree:** 90 quarter hours, Associates **Professional Accreditation:** ADA, COE, NAACLS

CHATTAHOOCHEE TECHNICAL COLLEGE
980 South Cobb Dr.
Marietta, GA 30060
Tel: (770)528-4500
Fax: (770)528-4578
Web Site: http://www.chattcollege.com
President/CEO: Dr. Harlon Crimm
Registrar: Nancy Beaver
Financial Aid: Lori Burnett
Type: Two-Year College **Sex:** Coed **Affiliation:** Georgia Department of Technical and Adult Education **Admission Plans:** Open Admission; Deferred Admission **Application Fee:** $15.00 **H.S. Requirements:** High school diploma or equivalent not required **Costs Per Year:** Application fee: $15. State resident tuition: $1116 full-time, $31 per credit hour part-time. Nonresident tuition: $2232 full-time, $62 per credit hour part-time. **Scholarships:** Available **Calendar System:** Quarter, Summer Session Not available **Enrollment:** FT 2,260, PT 3,983 **Faculty:** FT 66, PT 234 **Exams:** Other **Library Holdings:** 22,127 **Regional Accreditation:** Southern Association of Colleges and Schools **Credit Hours For Degree:** 90 credit hours, Associ-

ates **Professional Accreditation:** ABET, ACF, ACBSP

CLARK ATLANTA UNIVERSITY
223 James P. Brawley Dr., SW
Atlanta, GA 30314
Tel: (404)880-8000
Free: 800-688-3228
Fax: (404)880-6174
Web Site: http://www.cau.edu/
President/CEO: Dr. Walter D. Broadnax
Registrar: Amy Graham
Admissions: Julius Dodds
Financial Aid: Dolores S. Davis
Type: University **Sex:** Coed **Affiliation:** United Methodist **Admission Plans:** Early Admission; Deferred Admission **Application Fee:** $35.00 **H.S. Requirements:** High school diploma required; GED accepted **Costs Per Year:** Application fee: $35. Comprehensive fee: $21,338 includes full-time tuition ($14,522) and college room and board ($6816). Room and board charges vary according to board plan and housing facility. **Scholarships:** Available **Calendar System:** Semester, Summer Session Available **Enrollment:** FT 3,557, PT 144, Grad 897 **Faculty:** FT 260, PT 4 **Student-Faculty Ratio:** 13:1 **Exams:** SAT I or ACT **% Receiving Financial Aid:** 90 **% Residing in College-Owned, -Operated, or -Affiliated Housing:** 37 **Library Holdings:** 520,727 **Regional Accreditation:** Southern Association of Colleges and Schools **Credit Hours For Degree:** 122 credits, Bachelors **ROTC:** Army, Air Force **Professional Accreditation:** AACSB, AHIMA, ALA, CSWE, NASPAA, NCATE **Intercollegiate Athletics:** Basketball M & W; Cheerleading W; Cross-Country Running M & W; Football M; Golf M; Softball W; Tennis M & W; Track and Field M & W; Volleyball W

CLAYTON STATE UNIVERSITY
5900 North Lee St.
Morrow, GA 30260-0285
Tel: (678)466-4000
Admissions: (678)466-4115
E-mail: csc-info@ce.clayton.peachnet.edu
Web Site: http://www.clayton.edu/
President/CEO: Dr. Thomas K. Harden
Registrar: Rebecca Gmeiner
Admissions: Anne Meservey
Financial Aid: Melissa Belle
Type: Four-Year College **Sex:** Coed **Affiliation:** University System of Georgia **Scores:** 97.5% SAT V 400+; 96.9% SAT M 400+; 67% ACT 18-23; 9.7% ACT 24-29 **% Accepted:** 55 **Admission Plans:** Early Admission; Deferred Admission. **Application Deadline:** July 17 **Application Fee:** $40.00 **H.S. Requirements:** High school diploma required; GED not accepted **Costs Per Year:** Application fee: $40. State resident tuition: $2802 full-time, $102 per credit hour part-time. Nonresident tuition: $9770 full-time, $407 per credit hour part-time. Mandatory fees: $488 full-time, $244 per term part-time. **Scholarships:** Available **Calendar System:** Semester, Summer Session Available **Enrollment:** FT 3,291, PT 2,861 **Faculty:** FT 197, PT 170 **Student-Faculty Ratio:** 20:1 **Exams:** SAT I or ACT, SAT II **% Receiving Financial Aid:** 60 **Library Holdings:** 77,043 **Regional Accreditation:** Southern Association of Colleges and Schools **Credit Hours For Degree:** 60 credit hours, Associates; 120 credit hours, Bachelors **ROTC:** Army, Navy, Air Force **Professional Accreditation:** ADA, NCATE, NLN **Intercollegiate Athletics:** Basketball M & W; Cheerleading W; Cross-Country Running M & W; Golf M; Soccer M & W; Tennis W; Track and Field M & W

COASTAL GEORGIA COMMUNITY COLLEGE
3700 Altama Ave.
Brunswick, GA 31520
Tel: (912)264-7235
Free: 800-675-7235
Admissions: (912)264-7253
Fax: (912)262-3072
Web Site: http://www.cgcc.edu/
President/CEO: Dr. Dorothy L. Lord
Admissions: Lisa Lessig
Financial Aid: Betty Coen
Type: Two-Year College **Sex:** Coed **Affiliation:** University System of Georgia **% Accepted:** 54 **Admission Plans:** Deferred Admission **Application Deadline:** August 15 **Application Fee:** $20.00 **H.S. Requirements:** High school diploma required; GED accepted. For technical and industrial programs: High school diploma or equivalent not required **Costs Per Year:** Application fee: $20. State resident tuition: $1468 full-time, $62 per credit hour part-time. Nonresident tuition: $245 per credit hour part-time. Mandatory fees: $212 full-time, $52 per term part-time. **Scholarships:** Available **Calendar System:** Semester, Summer Session Available **Enrollment:** FT 1,002, PT 2,060 **Faculty:** FT 73, PT 67 **Student-Faculty Ratio:** 18:1 **Regional Accreditation:** Southern Association of Colleges and Schools **Credit Hours For Degree:** 60 semester hours, Associates **Professional Accreditation:** JRCERT, NAACLS, NLN **Intercollegiate Athletics:** Basketball M; Softball W

COLUMBUS STATE UNIVERSITY
4225 University Ave.
Columbus, GA 31907-5645
Tel: (706)568-2001; (866)264-2035
Admissions: (706)568-2035
Fax: (706)568-2123
Web Site: http://www.colstate.edu/
President/CEO: Dr. Frank D. Brown
Registrar: Beverly Johnson
Admissions: Susan Lovell
Financial Aid: Janis Bowles
Type: Comprehensive **Sex:** Coed **Affiliation:** University System of Georgia **Scores:** 92.96% SAT V 400+; 92.06% SAT M 400+; 57.83% ACT 18-23; 11.36% ACT 24-29 **% Accepted:** 64 **Admission Plans:** Early Admission; Deferred Admission **Application Deadline:** July 01 **Application Fee:** $25.00 **H.S. Requirements:** High school diploma required; GED not accepted **Costs Per Year:** Application fee: $25. State resident tuition: $2438 full-time, $102 per semester hour part-time. Nonresident tuition: $9754 full-time, $407 per semester hour part-time. Mandatory fees: $506 full-time. College room and board: $5720. College room only: $3510. Room and board charges vary according to board plan and location. **Scholarships:** Available **Calendar System:** Semester, Summer Session Available **Enrollment:** FT 4,414, PT 2,210, Grad 851 **Faculty:** FT 216, PT 195 **Student-Faculty Ratio:** 20:1 **Exams:** SAT I or ACT, SAT II **% Receiving Financial Aid:** 47 **% Residing in College-Owned, -Operated, or -Affiliated Housing:** 13 **Library Holdings:** 250,000 **Regional Accreditation:** Southern Association of Colleges and Schools **Credit Hours For Degree:** 63 credits, Associates; 123 credits, Bachelors **ROTC:** Army **Professional Accreditation:** AACSB, ACA, NASAD, NASM, NAST, NCATE, NLN **Intercollegiate Athletics:** Baseball M; Basketball M & W; Cross-Country Running M & W; Golf M; Soccer W; Softball W; Tennis M & W

COLUMBUS TECHNICAL COLLEGE
928 Manchester Expressway
Columbus, GA 31904-6572
Tel: (706)649-1800
Admissions: (706)649-1174
Fax: (706)649-1937
E-mail: nkennedy@columbustech.edu
Web Site: http://www.columbustech.edu
President/CEO: Robert Jones
Registrar: Dr. Pamela Robinson
Admissions: Nichole Kennedy
Financial Aid: Debbie Henshaw
Type: Two-Year College **Sex:** Coed **Affiliation:** Georgia Department of Technical and Adult Education **Admission Plans:** Open Admission; Deferred Admission **Application Fee:** $15.00 **H.S. Requirements:** High school diploma or equivalent not required **Costs Per Year:** Application fee: $15. State resident tuition: $1116 full-time, $31 per credit hour part-time. Nonresident tuition: $2232 full-time, $62 per credit hour part-time. **Scholarships:** Available **Calendar System:** Quarter **Enrollment:** FT 1,536, PT 1,994 **Faculty:** FT 77, PT 153 **Exams:** Other **Library Holdings:** 26,072 **Regional Accreditation:** Southern Association of Colleges and Schools **Credit Hours For Degree:** 100 credits, Associates **Professional Accreditation:** ARCEST, ADA

COOSA VALLEY TECHNICAL COLLEGE
One Maurice Culberson Dr.
Rome, GA 30161
Tel: (706)295-6963
Admissions: (706)624-1117
Fax: (706)295-6944
E-mail: sphillip@coosavalleytech.edu
Web Site: http://www.coosavalleytech.edu/

President/CEO: Craig McDaniel
Admissions: Stuart Phillips
Type: Two-Year College **Sex:** Coed **Admission Plans:** Open Admission; Deferred Admission **Application Fee:** $15.00 **H.S. Requirements:** High school diploma or equivalent not required **Costs Per Year:** Application fee: $15. State resident tuition: $1116 full-time, $31 per credit hour part-time. Nonresident tuition: $2232 full-time, $62 per credit hour part-time. **Calendar System:** Quarter **Enrollment:** FT 1,219, PT 1,674 **Faculty:** FT 73, PT 118 **Exams:** Other **Professional Accreditation:** COE

COVENANT COLLEGE
14049 Scenic Hwy.
Lookout Mountain, GA 30750
Tel: (706)820-1560; 888-451-2683
Admissions: (706)419-1127
E-mail: admissions@covenant.edu
Web Site: http://www.covenant.edu/
President/CEO: Neil B. Nielson
Registrar: Rodney Miller
Admissions: Wallace Anderson
Financial Aid: Brenda Rapier
Type: Comprehensive **Sex:** Coed **Affiliation:** Presbyterian Church in America **Scores:** 99% SAT V 400+; 98% SAT M 400+; 40% ACT 18-23; 49% ACT 24-29 **% Accepted:** 33 **Admission Plans:** Early Admission; Deferred Admission **Application Deadline:** Rolling **Application Fee:** $35.00 **H.S. Requirements:** High school diploma required; GED accepted **Costs Per Year:** Application fee: $35. Comprehensive fee: $28,030 includes full-time tuition ($21,100), mandatory fees ($750), and college room and board ($6180). Part-time tuition: $880 per credit hour. **Scholarships:** Available **Calendar System:** Semester, Summer Session Available **Enrollment:** FT 898 **Faculty:** FT 58, PT 19 **Student-Faculty Ratio:** 15:1 **Exams:** ACT, SAT I or ACT **% Receiving Financial Aid:** 68 **% Residing in College-Owned, -Operated, or -Affiliated Housing:** 86 **Library Holdings:** 85,000 **Regional Accreditation:** Southern Association of Colleges and Schools **Credit Hours For Degree:** 62 units, Associates; 126 units, Bachelors **Intercollegiate Athletics:** Baseball M; Basketball M & W; Cross-Country Running M & W; Golf M; Soccer M & W; Softball W; Tennis M & W; Volleyball W

DALTON STATE COLLEGE
213 North College Dr.
Dalton, GA 30720-3797
Tel: (706)272-4436
Free: 800-829-4436
Fax: (706)272-2530
Web Site: http://www.daltonstate.edu/
President/CEO: Dr. James A. Burran
Registrar: Jodi Johnson
Admissions: Jodi Johnson
Financial Aid: Dianne Cox
Type: Four-Year College **Sex:** Coed **Affiliation:** University System of Georgia **% Accepted:** 69 **Admission Plans:** Open Admission; Early Admission **Application Deadline:** Rolling **Application Fee:** $25.00 **H.S. Requirements:** High school diploma required; GED accepted **Costs Per Year:** Application fee: $25. Area resident tuition: $66.75 per credit hour part-time. State resident tuition: $1592 full-time. Nonresident tuition: $5996 full-time. **Scholarships:** Available **Calendar System:** Semester, Summer Session Available **Enrollment:** FT 1,914, PT 2,353 **Faculty:** FT 125, PT 62 **Student-Faculty Ratio:** 23:1 **% Receiving Financial Aid:** 61 **Library Holdings:** 119,515 **Regional Accreditation:** Southern Association of Colleges and Schools **Credit Hours For Degree:** 60 semester hours, Associates; 120 semester hours, Bachelors **Professional Accreditation:** AAMAE, NAACLS, NLN **Intercollegiate Athletics:** Basketball M & W; Golf W; Softball M & W; Table Tennis M & W; Tennis M & W; Volleyball M & W

DARTON COLLEGE
2400 Gillionville Rd.
Albany, GA 31707-3098
Tel: (229)430-6000
Admissions: (229)430-6740
Fax: (229)430-2926
E-mail: darton@cavalier.dartnet.peachnet.edu
Web Site: http://www.darton.edu/
President/CEO: Dr. Peter J. Sireno
Registrar: Holly Basko
Admissions: Terri Carroll
Financial Aid: Martha Whittle
Type: Two-Year College **Sex:** Coed **Affiliation:** University System of Georgia **Scores:** 71% SAT V 400+; 66% SAT M 400+; 28% ACT 18-23; 1% ACT 24-29 **Admission Plans:** Early Admission **Application Fee:** $20.00 **H.S. Requirements:** High school diploma required; GED accepted **Costs Per Year:** Application fee: $20. State resident tuition: $1542 full-time, $65 per credit hour part-time. Nonresident tuition: $6166 full-time, $257 per credit hour part-time. Mandatory fees: $300 full-time, $150 per term part-time. Full-time tuition and fees vary according to course load. Part-time tuition and fees vary according to course load. **Scholarships:** Available **Calendar System:** Semester, Summer Session Available **Enrollment:** FT 1,904, PT 2,222 **Faculty:** FT 88, PT 129 **Student-Faculty Ratio:** 20:1 **Exams:** SAT I or ACT, SAT II **Library Holdings:** 67,507 **Regional Accreditation:** Southern Association of Colleges and Schools **Credit Hours For Degree:** 60 semester hours, Associates **ROTC:** Army **Professional Accreditation:** ADA, AHIMA, AOTA, APTA, CARC, NAACLS, NLN **Intercollegiate Athletics:** Baseball M; Basketball W; Golf M; Soccer M & W; Softball W; Swimming and Diving M & W

DEKALB TECHNICAL COLLEGE
495 North Indian Creek Dr.
Clarkston, GA 30021-2397
Tel: (404)297-9522
Fax: (404)294-4234
E-mail: richardt@dekalbtech.org
Web Site: http://www.dekalbtech.edu/
President/CEO: Dr. Robin W. Hoffman
Registrar: Karen Sills
Admissions: Terry Richardson
Financial Aid: John Gottardy
Type: Two-Year College **Sex:** Coed **Affiliation:** Georgia Department of Technical and Adult Education **Admission Plans:** Open Admission; Deferred Admission **Application Fee:** $15.00 **H.S. Requirements:** High school diploma or equivalent not required **Costs Per Year:** Application fee: $15. State resident tuition: $1116 full-time, $31 per credit hour part-time. Nonresident tuition: $2232 full-time, $62 per credit hour part-time. **Scholarships:** Available **Calendar System:** Quarter, Summer Session Available **Enrollment:** FT 1,535, PT 2,548 **Faculty:** FT 96, PT 363 **Student-Faculty Ratio:** 15:1 **Exams:** Other **Regional Accreditation:** Southern Association of Colleges and Schools **Credit Hours For Degree:** 100 credit hours, Associates **Professional Accreditation:** ABET, COptA, NAACLS

DEVRY UNIVERSITY (ALPHARETTA)
2555 Northwinds Parkway
Alpharetta, GA 30004
Tel: (770)521-4900; (866)338-7934
Web Site: http://www.devry.edu/
President/CEO: Dr. Donna Loraine
Registrar: Marie Brown
Financial Aid: David Pickett
Type: Comprehensive **Sex:** Coed **Affiliation:** DeVry University **Admission Plans:** Deferred Admission **Application Deadline:** Rolling **Application Fee:** $50.00 **H.S. Requirements:** High school diploma required; GED accepted **Costs Per Year:** Application fee: $50. One-time mandatory fee: $40. Tuition: $11,790 full-time, $440 per credit part-time. Mandatory fees: $270 full-time, $160 per year part-time. Full-time tuition and fees vary according to course load. Part-time tuition and fees vary according to course load. **Scholarships:** Available **Calendar System:** Semester, Summer Session Available **Enrollment:** FT 452, PT 399, Grad 193 **Faculty:** FT 36, PT 40 **Student-Faculty Ratio:** 14:1 **% Receiving Financial Aid:** 71 **Library Holdings:** 7,659 **Regional Accreditation:** North Central Association of Colleges and Schools **Credit Hours For Degree:** 66 credit hours, Associates; 122 credit hours, Bachelors **Professional Accreditation:** ABET

DEVRY UNIVERSITY (ATLANTA)
Fifteen Piedmont Center, Plaza Level 100
Atlanta, GA 30305-1543
Tel: (404)296-7400
Fax: (404)240-0227
Web Site: http://www.devry.edu/ **Type:** Comprehensive **Sex:** Coed **Costs Per Year:** One-time mandatory fee: $40. Tuition: $11,790 full-time, $440 per credit part-time. Mandatory fees: $60 full-time, $60 per year part-time. Full-time tuition and fees vary according to course load. Part-time tuition and fees vary according to course load. **Calendar**

System: Semester **Regional Accreditation:** North Central Association of Colleges and Schools

DEVRY UNIVERSITY (DECATUR)
250 North Arcadia Ave.
Decatur, GA 30030-2198
Tel: (404)292-7900; (866)338-7934
Fax: (404)292-2321
Web Site: http://www.devry.edu/
President/CEO: Donna Loraine
Registrar: Marie Brown
Financial Aid: Beverly Love
Type: Comprehensive **Sex:** Coed **Affiliation:** DeVry University **Admission Plans:** Deferred Admission **Application Deadline:** Rolling **Application Fee:** $50.00 **H.S. Requirements:** High school diploma required; GED accepted **Costs Per Year:** Application fee: $50. One-time mandatory fee: $40. Tuition: $11,790 full-time, $440 per credit part-time. Mandatory fees: $270 full-time, $160 per year part-time. Full-time tuition and fees vary according to course load. Part-time tuition and fees vary according to course load. **Scholarships:** Available **Calendar System:** Semester, Summer Session Available **Enrollment:** FT 977, PT 891, Grad 329 **Faculty:** FT 53, PT 80 **Student-Faculty Ratio:** 18:1 **% Receiving Financial Aid:** 85 **Library Holdings:** 18,849 **Regional Accreditation:** North Central Association of Colleges and Schools **Credit Hours For Degree:** 66 credit hours, Associates; 122 credit hours, Bachelors **Professional Accreditation:** ABET

DEVRY UNIVERSITY (DULUTH)
3505 Koger Blvd., Ste. 170
Duluth, GA 30096-7671
Tel: (678)380-9780
Fax: (678)924-0958
Web Site: http://www.devry.edu/ **Type:** Comprehensive **Sex:** Coed **Costs Per Year:** One-time mandatory fee: $40. Tuition: $11,790 full-time, $440 per credit part-time. Mandatory fees: $60 full-time, $30 per year part-time. Full-time tuition and fees vary according to course load. Part-time tuition and fees vary according to course load. **Calendar System:** Semester **Regional Accreditation:** North Central Association of Colleges and Schools

EAST CENTRAL TECHNICAL COLLEGE
667 Perry House Rd.
Fitzgerald, GA 31750
Tel: (229)468-2000
Admissions: (229)468-2033
Fax: (229)468-2110
E-mail: ccoffey@ectcollege.org
Web Site: http://www.eastcentraltech.edu/
President/CEO: Dr. Diane Harper
Admissions: Connie Coffey
Type: Two-Year College **Sex:** Coed **Admission Plans:** Open Admission; Deferred Admission **Application Fee:** $15.00 **H.S. Requirements:** High school diploma or equivalent not required **Costs Per Year:** Application fee: $15. State resident tuition: $1116 full-time, $31 per credit hour part-time. Nonresident tuition: $2232 full-time, $62 per credit hour part-time. **Calendar System:** Quarter **Enrollment:** FT 561, PT 677 **Faculty:** FT 47, PT 43 **Exams:** Other **Professional Accreditation:** COE

EAST GEORGIA COLLEGE
131 College Circle
Swainsboro, GA 30401-2699
Tel: (478)289-2000
Admissions: (478)289-2009
Fax: (478)289-2038
Web Site: http://www.ega.edu/
President/CEO: Dr. Jeremiah J. Ashcroft
Registrar: Donald D. Avery
Admissions: Donald D. Avery
Financial Aid: Barbara Green
Type: Two-Year College **Sex:** Coed **Affiliation:** University System of Georgia **Scores:** 70% SAT V 400+; 61% SAT M 400+ **Admission Plans:** Early Admission; Deferred Admission **Application Fee:** $20.00 **H.S. Requirements:** High school diploma required; GED accepted **Costs Per Year:** Application fee: $20. State resident tuition: $1560 full-time, $65 per credit hour part-time. Nonresident tuition: $6168 full-time, $257 per credit hour part-time. Mandatory fees: $38 per term part-time. Full-time tuition varies according to course load and location. Part-time tuition and fees vary according to course load and location. **Scholarships:** Available **Calendar System:** Semester, Summer Session Available **Enrollment:** FT 887, PT 431 **Faculty:** FT 33, PT 28 **Student-Faculty Ratio:** 23:1 **Library Holdings:** 43,780 **Regional Accreditation:** Southern Association of Colleges and Schools **Credit Hours For Degree:** 64 semester hours, Associates

EMMANUEL COLLEGE
PO Box 129
181 Springs St.
Franklin Springs, GA 30639-0129
Tel: (706)245-7226
E-mail: admissions@emmanuel-college.edu
Web Site: http://www.emmanuelcollege.edu/
President/CEO: Dr. David Hopkins
Registrar: Debra F. Grizzle
Admissions: Kirk McConnell
Financial Aid: Donna Quick
Type: Four-Year College **Sex:** Coed **Affiliation:** Pentecostal Holiness Church **% Accepted:** 38 **Admission Plans:** Early Admission; Deferred Admission **Application Deadline:** August 01 **Application Fee:** $25.00 **H.S. Requirements:** High school diploma required; GED accepted **Costs Per Year:** Application fee: $25. Comprehensive fee: $14,850 includes full-time tuition ($9800), mandatory fees ($350), and college room and board ($4700). College room only: $2150. Room and board charges vary according to board plan. Part-time tuition: $408 per hour. **Scholarships:** Available **Calendar System:** Semester, Summer Session Available **Enrollment:** FT 594, PT 113 **Faculty:** FT 44, PT 24 **Student-Faculty Ratio:** 12:1 **Exams:** SAT I or ACT **% Receiving Financial Aid:** 73 **% Residing in College-Owned, -Operated, or -Affiliated Housing:** 44 **Library Holdings:** 74,735 **Regional Accreditation:** Southern Association of Colleges and Schools **Credit Hours For Degree:** 64 semester hours, Associates; 124 semester hours, Bachelors **Intercollegiate Athletics:** Baseball M; Basketball M & W; Soccer M & W; Softball W; Tennis M & W

EMORY UNIVERSITY
1380 South Oxford Rd.
Atlanta, GA 30322-1100
Tel: (404)727-6123
Free: 800-727-6036
Admissions: (404)727-6036
E-mail: admiss@unix.cc.emory.edu
Web Site: http://www.emory.edu/
President/CEO: Dr. James W. Wagner
Registrar: Charles R. Nicolaysen
Admissions: Daniel C. Walls
Financial Aid: Julia Perreault
Type: University **Sex:** Coed **Affiliation:** Methodist **Scores:** 100% SAT V 400+; 100% SAT M 400+; 4.2% ACT 18-23; 49.2% ACT 24-29 **% Accepted:** 37 **Admission Plans:** Early Admission; Early Decision Plan; Deferred Admission **Application Deadline:** January 15 **Application Fee:** $50.00 **H.S. Requirements:** High school diploma required; GED not accepted. For transfer students with a full year of college credit: High school diploma or equivalent not required **Costs Per Year:** Application fee: $50. Comprehensive fee: $40,546 includes full-time tuition ($30,400), mandatory fees ($394), and college room and board ($9752). College room only: $6112. Room and board charges vary according to board plan, housing facility, and student level. Part-time tuition: $1267 per credit. **Scholarships:** Available **Calendar System:** Semester, Summer Session Available **Enrollment:** FT 6,421, PT 89, Grad 3,980 **Faculty:** FT 1,236, PT 199 **Student-Faculty Ratio:** 7:1 **Exams:** SAT I or ACT, SAT II **% Receiving Financial Aid:** 38 **% Residing in College-Owned, -Operated, or -Affiliated Housing:** 70 **Library Holdings:** 2,500,000 **Regional Accreditation:** Southern Association of Colleges and Schools **Credit Hours For Degree:** 132 semester hours, Bachelors **ROTC:** Air Force **Professional Accreditation:** AACSB, ARCAA, AACN, ABA, ACNM, ADtA, APTA, APA, ACIPE, AALS, ATS, CEPH, JCAHPO, JRCERT, LCMEAMA, NANPWH, NASM, NCATE **Intercollegiate Athletics:** Badminton M & W; Baseball M; Basketball M & W; Bowling M & W; Crew M & W; Cross-Country Running M & W; Equestrian Sports M & W; Fencing M & W; Field Hockey W; Golf M; Gymnastics M & W; Lacrosse M & W; Racquetball M & W; Rugby M; Sailing M & W; Soccer M & W; Softball W;

Swimming and Diving M & W; Table Tennis M & W; Tennis M & W; Track and Field M & W; Ultimate Frisbee M & W; Volleyball M & W; Water Polo M & W; Wrestling M

EMORY UNIVERSITY, OXFORD COLLEGE
100 Hamill St., PO Box 1328
Oxford, GA 30054
Tel: (770)784-8888
Free: 800-723-8328
Admissions: (770)784-8328
Fax: (770)784-8359
Web Site: http://www.emory.edu/OXFORD/
President/CEO: Dr. Dana Greene
Admissions: Jennifer B. Taylor
Financial Aid: Jennifer B. Taylor
Type: Two-Year College **Sex:** Coed **Affiliation:** Methodist; Emory University **Scores:** 100% SAT V 400+; 100% SAT M 400+; 24.4% ACT 18-23; 61.8% ACT 24-29 **Admission Plans:** Early Admission; Early Action; Deferred Admission **Application Fee:** $40.00 **H.S. Requirements:** High school diploma required; GED accepted **Scholarships:** Available **Calendar System:** Semester, Summer Session Available **Enrollment:** FT 554 **Faculty:** FT 43, PT 11 **Student-Faculty Ratio:** 10:1 **Exams:** SAT I or ACT, SAT II **% Residing in College-Owned, -Operated, or -Affiliated Housing:** 95 **Library Holdings:** 80,099 **Regional Accreditation:** Southern Association of Colleges and Schools **Credit Hours For Degree:** 67 semester hours, Associates **Intercollegiate Athletics:** Basketball M; Soccer W; Tennis M & W

FLINT RIVER TECHNICAL COLLEGE
1533 US Hwy. 19 South
Thomaston, GA 30286
Tel: (706)646-6148
Free: 800-752-9681
Fax: (706)646-6163
E-mail: gwilliams@flintrivertech.edu
Web Site: http://www.flintrivertech.edu/
President/CEO: Kathy S. Love
Admissions: Gary Williams
Type: Two-Year College **Sex:** Coed **Admission Plans:** Open Admission; Deferred Admission **Application Fee:** $15.00 **H.S. Requirements:** High school diploma or equivalent not required **Costs Per Year:** Application fee: $15. State resident tuition: $1116 full-time, $31 per credit hour part-time. Nonresident tuition: $2232 full-time, $62 per credit hour part-time. **Calendar System:** Quarter **Enrollment:** FT 425, PT 380 **Faculty:** FT 29, PT 59 **Exams:** Other **Library Holdings:** 2,653 **Professional Accreditation:** COE

FORT VALLEY STATE UNIVERSITY
1005 State University Dr.
Fort Valley, GA 31030-4313
Tel: (478)825-6211
Free: 800-248-7343
Admissions: (478)825-6307
Fax: (478)825-6394
Web Site: http://www.fvsu.edu/
President/CEO: Dr. Kofi Lomotey
Registrar: Sharee Lawrence
Admissions: Debra McGhee
Financial Aid: Russelle Keese
Type: Comprehensive **Sex:** Coed **Affiliation:** University System of Georgia **Scores:** 65.82% SAT V 400+; 64.12% SAT M 400+ **% Accepted:** 36 **Admission Plans:** Early Admission; Deferred Admission **Application Deadline:** August 01 **Application Fee:** $20.00 **H.S. Requirements:** High school diploma required; GED accepted **Costs Per Year:** Application fee: $20. State resident tuition: $3044 full-time, $102 per credit part-time. Nonresident tuition: $10,360 full-time, $407 per credit part-time. Mandatory fees: $606 full-time, $303 per term part-time. Full-time tuition and fees vary according to course load. Part-time tuition and fees vary according to course load. College room and board: $4496. College room only: $2200. Room and board charges vary according to board plan. **Scholarships:** Available **Calendar System:** Semester, Summer Session Available **Enrollment:** FT 1,723, PT 274, Grad 177 **Faculty:** FT 105, PT 16 **Student-Faculty Ratio:** 22:1 **Exams:** SAT I or ACT **% Residing in College-Owned, -Operated, or -Affiliated Housing:** 59 **Library Holdings:** 186,365 **Regional Accreditation:** Southern Association of Colleges and Schools **Credit Hours For Degree:** 60 hours, Associates; 120 hours, Bachelors **ROTC:** Army **Professional Accreditation:** ABET, AAFCS, CORE, MACTE, NCATE **Intercollegiate Athletics:** Basketball M & W; Football M; Golf M; Tennis M & W; Track and Field M & W; Volleyball W

GAINESVILLE COLLEGE
PO Box 1358
Gainesville, GA 30503-1358
Tel: (770)718-3639
Admissions: (770)718-3641
Fax: (770)718-3859
E-mail: mpalmour@gsc.edu
Web Site: http://www.gc.peachnet.edu/
President/CEO: Dr. Martha T. Nesbitt
Registrar: Janice Hartsoe
Admissions: W. Palmour
Financial Aid: Susan A. Smith
Type: Two-Year College **Sex:** Coed **Affiliation:** University System of Georgia **Scores:** 91% SAT V 400+; 88.5% SAT M 400+ **% Accepted:** 84 **Admission Plans:** Early Admission **Application Deadline:** July 01 **Application Fee:** $35.00 **H.S. Requirements:** High school diploma required; GED accepted **Costs Per Year:** Application fee: $35. State resident tuition: $1542 full-time, $65 per credit hour part-time. Nonresident tuition: $6166 full-time, $257 per credit hour part-time. Mandatory fees: $164 full-time. **Scholarships:** Available **Calendar System:** Semester, Summer Session Available **Enrollment:** FT 3,550, PT 2,435 **Student-Faculty Ratio:** 24:1 **Exams:** SAT I or ACT **Library Holdings:** 70,000 **Regional Accreditation:** Southern Association of Colleges and Schools **Credit Hours For Degree:** 60 semester hours, Associates **Professional Accreditation:** ADA, ACBSP

GEORGIA AVIATION & TECHNICAL COLLEGE
71 Airport Rd., Heart of Georgia Regional Airport
Eastman, GA 31023
Tel: (478)374-6980
Fax: (478)374-6809
E-mail: tspires@gaaviationtech.edu
Web Site: http://www.gavtc.org/
President/CEO: Andy Lundell
Admissions: Teresa Spires
Type: Two-Year College **Sex:** Coed **Admission Plans:** Open Admission; Deferred Admission **Application Fee:** $15.00 **H.S. Requirements:** High school diploma or equivalent not required **Costs Per Year:** Application fee: $15. State resident tuition: $1116 full-time, $31 per credit hour part-time. Nonresident tuition: $2232 full-time, $62 per credit hour part-time. **Calendar System:** Quarter **Enrollment:** FT 158, PT 94 **Faculty:** FT 23, PT 0 **Exams:** Other **Professional Accreditation:** COE

GEORGIA COLLEGE & STATE UNIVERSITY
Hancock St.
Milledgeville, GA 31061
Tel: (478)445-5004
Admissions: (478)445-1283
Fax: (478)445-6795
E-mail: paul.jones@gcsu.edu
Web Site: http://www.gcsu.edu/
President/CEO: Dr. Dorothy Leland
Registrar: Sarah L. Scott
Admissions: Dr. Paul Jones
Financial Aid: Suzanne Buttram
Type: Comprehensive **Sex:** Coed **Affiliation:** University System of Georgia **Scores:** 100% SAT V 400+; 100% SAT M 400+; 60% ACT 18-23; 34% ACT 24-29 **% Accepted:** 60 **Admission Plans:** Early Admission; Early Action; Deferred Admission **Application Deadline:** April 01 **Application Fee:** $25.00 **H.S. Requirements:** High school diploma required; GED accepted **Costs Per Year:** Application fee: $25. State resident tuition: $3404 full-time, $142 per semester hour part-time. Nonresident tuition: $13,616 full-time, $568 per semester hour part-time. Mandatory fees: $738 full-time, $369 per term part-time. Full-time tuition and fees vary according to location. Part-time tuition and fees vary according to course load and location. College room and board: $6878. College room only: $3690. Room and board charges vary according to board plan and housing facility. **Scholarships:** Available **Calendar System:** Semester, Summer Session Available **Enrollment:** FT 4,243, PT 555, Grad 861 **Faculty:** FT 268, PT 134 **Student-Faculty Ratio:** 15:1 **Exams:** SAT I or ACT, SAT II **% Receiving Financial Aid:** 40 **% Residing in College-Owned, -Operated, or -Affiliated Housing:** 36 **Library Holdings:** 169,735 **Regional Accreditation:** Southern Association of Col-

leges and Schools **Credit Hours For Degree:** 120 semester hours, Bachelors **ROTC:** Army **Professional Accreditation:** AACSB, NASM, NASPAA, NCATE, NLN **Intercollegiate Athletics:** Baseball M; Basketball M & W; Cross-Country Running M & W; Fencing M & W; Golf M; Soccer W; Softball W; Tennis M & W

GEORGIA HIGHLANDS COLLEGE

3175 Cedartown Hwy., SE
PO Box 1864
Rome, GA 30162-1864
Tel: (706)802-5000
Free: 800-332-2406
Admissions: (706)295-6339
Fax: (706)295-6610
E-mail: tjones@highlands.edu
Web Site: http://www.highlands.edu/
President/CEO: Dr. J. Randolph Pierce
Registrar: Sandie Davis
Admissions: Todd Jones
Financial Aid: Wendy Shapiro

Type: Two-Year College **Sex:** Coed **Affiliation:** University System of Georgia **% Accepted:** 84 **Admission Plans:** Early Admission; Deferred Admission **Application Deadline:** Rolling **Application Fee:** $20.00 **H.S. Requirements:** High school diploma required; GED accepted **Costs Per Year:** Application fee: $20. State resident tuition: $1542 full-time, $65 per hour part-time. Nonresident tuition: $6168 full-time, $257 per hour part-time. Mandatory fees: $198 full-time, $99 per term part-time. Part-time tuition and fees vary according to course load. **Scholarships:** Available **Calendar System:** Semester, Summer Session Available **Enrollment:** FT 2,059, PT 1,758 **Faculty:** FT 89, PT 165 **Student-Faculty Ratio:** 40:1 **Exams:** SAT I or ACT **Library Holdings:** 65,090 **Regional Accreditation:** Southern Association of Colleges and Schools **Credit Hours For Degree:** 60 semester hours, Associates **Professional Accreditation:** ADA, NLN

GEORGIA INSTITUTE OF TECHNOLOGY

225 North Ave., NW
Atlanta, GA 30332-0001
Tel: (404)894-2000
Admissions: (404)894-4154
Fax: (404)853-9163
E-mail: admission@gatech.edu
Web Site: http://www.gatech.edu/
President/CEO: Dr. G. Wayne Clough
Registrar: M. Jo McIver
Admissions: Ingrid Hayes

Type: University **Sex:** Coed **Affiliation:** University System of Georgia **Scores:** 100% SAT V 400+; 100% SAT M 400+; 7% ACT 18-23; 61% ACT 24-29 **% Accepted:** 67 **Admission Plans:** Preferred Admission; Early Admission **Application Deadline:** January 15 **Application Fee:** $50.00 **H.S. Requirements:** High school diploma required; GED accepted **Costs Per Year:** Application fee: $50. State resident tuition: $3638 full-time, $152 per hour part-time. Nonresident tuition: $17,980 full-time, $750 per hour part-time. Mandatory fees: $1010 full-time, $505 per term part-time. Part-time tuition and fees vary according to course load. College room and board: $6802. College room only: $3992. Room and board charges vary according to board plan and housing facility. **Scholarships:** Available **Calendar System:** Semester, Summer Session Available **Enrollment:** FT 10,992, PT 849, Grad 5,294 **Faculty:** FT 810, PT 27 **Student-Faculty Ratio:** 14:1 **Exams:** SAT I or ACT **% Receiving Financial Aid:** 30 **% Residing in College-Owned, -Operated, or -Affiliated Housing:** 53 **Library Holdings:** 213,128 **Regional Accreditation:** Southern Association of Colleges and Schools **Credit Hours For Degree:** 122 semester hours, Bachelors **ROTC:** Army, Navy, Air Force **Professional Accreditation:** AACSB, ABET, ACCE, ACSP **Intercollegiate Athletics:** Baseball M; Basketball M & W; Cross-Country Running M & W; Equestrian Sports M & W; Football M; Golf M; Ice Hockey M; Lacrosse M & W; Rugby M; Softball W; Swimming and Diving M & W; Tennis M & W; Track and Field M & W; Volleyball W; Wrestling M

GEORGIA MEDICAL INSTITUTE-DEKALB

1706 Northeast Expressway
Atlanta, GA 30329
Tel: (404)327-8787
Fax: (404)327-8980
Web Site: http://www.georgia-med.com/
President/CEO: John England
Admissions: Trish Sherwood

Type: Two-Year College **Sex:** Coed **Calendar System:** Continuous **Faculty:** FT 19, PT 2 **Student-Faculty Ratio:** 18:1 **Professional Accreditation:** ACCSCT

GEORGIA MILITARY COLLEGE

201 East Greene St.
Milledgeville, GA 31061-3398
Tel: (478)445-2700
Free: 800-342-0413
Admissions: (478)445-2751
Fax: (478)445-2688
Web Site: http://www.gmc.cc.ga.us/
President/CEO: Maj. Gen. Peter J. Boylan, Jr.
Registrar: Patricia Smith
Admissions: Donna W. Findley
Financial Aid: Cindy Allard

Type: Two-Year College **Sex:** Coed **Admission Plans:** Early Admission; Deferred Admission **Application Fee:** $25.00 **H.S. Requirements:** High school diploma required; GED accepted **Scholarships:** Available **Calendar System:** Quarter, Summer Session Available **Enrollment:** FT 2,471, PT 1,591 **Faculty:** FT 82, PT 149 **Student-Faculty Ratio:** 20:1 **Exams:** SAT I or ACT **Library Holdings:** 20,000 **Regional Accreditation:** Southern Association of Colleges and Schools **Credit Hours For Degree:** 90 quarter hours, Associates **ROTC:** Army **Intercollegiate Athletics:** Football M; Riflery M & W

GEORGIA PERIMETER COLLEGE

3251 Panthersville Rd.
Decatur, GA 30034-3897
Tel: (404)244-5090; 888-696-2780
Admissions: (404)299-4551
Fax: (404)244-2996
Web Site: http://www.gpc.edu/
President/CEO: Dr. Jacquelyn Belcher
Admissions: Erin Hart
Financial Aid: Mary Knellman

Type: Two-Year College **Sex:** Coed **Affiliation:** University System of Georgia **Admission Plans:** Early Admission **Application Fee:** $20.00 **H.S. Requirements:** High school diploma required; GED not accepted **Scholarships:** Available **Calendar System:** Semester, Summer Session Available **Enrollment:** FT 8,548, PT 10,438 **Faculty:** FT 336, PT 1,317 **Student-Faculty Ratio:** 21:1 **Exams:** SAT I or ACT **Library Holdings:** 369,969 **Regional Accreditation:** Southern Association of Colleges and Schools **Credit Hours For Degree:** 62 semester hours, Associates **ROTC:** Army **Professional Accreditation:** ADA, NLN **Intercollegiate Athletics:** Baseball M; Basketball M & W; Soccer M & W; Softball W; Tennis M & W

GEORGIA SOUTHERN UNIVERSITY

PO Box 8055
Statesboro, GA 30460
Tel: (912)681-5611
Admissions: (912)681-5391
Fax: (912)681-5635
E-mail: admissions@gasou.edu
Web Site: http://www.georgiasouthern.edu/
President/CEO: Dr. Bruce Grube
Registrar: Michael Deal
Admissions: Susan Davies
Financial Aid: Connie Murphey

Type: Comprehensive **Sex:** Coed **Affiliation:** University System of Georgia **Scores:** 100% SAT V 400+; 100% SAT M 400+; 72% ACT 18-23; 21% ACT 24-29 **% Accepted:** 55 **Admission Plans:** Early Admission; Deferred Admission **Application Deadline:** May 01 **Application Fee:** $50.00 **H.S. Requirements:** High school diploma required; GED not accepted. For applicants out of high school at least 5 years: High school diploma required; GED accepted **Costs Per Year:** Application fee: $50. State resident tuition: $2438 full-time, $102 per semester hour part-time. Nonresident tuition: $9754 full-time, $407 per semester hour part-time. Mandatory fees: $1024 full-time, $512 per term part-time. Full-time tuition and fees vary according to degree level and location. Part-time tuition and fees vary according to course load, degree level, and location. College room and board: $6300. College room only: $3968. Room and board charges vary according to board plan and housing facility. **Scholarships:** Available **Calendar System:** Semester, Summer Session Available **Enrollment:** FT 13,119, PT 1,531, Grad 1,996

Faculty: FT 660, PT 53 **Student-Faculty Ratio:** 20:1 **Exams:** SAT I or ACT **% Receiving Financial Aid:** 52 **% Residing in College-Owned, -Operated, or -Affiliated Housing:** 23 **Library Holdings:** 568,551 **Regional Accreditation:** Southern Association of Colleges and Schools **Credit Hours For Degree:** 125 semester hours, Bachelors **ROTC:** Army **Professional Accreditation:** AACSB, ABET, AACN, AAFCS, ACCE, FIDER, JRCEPAT, NAIT, NASAD, NASM, NASPAA, NCATE, NLN, NRPA **Intercollegiate Athletics:** Baseball M; Basketball M & W; Bowling M & W; Cheerleading M & W; Cross-Country Running W; Equestrian Sports M & W; Fencing M & W; Football M; Golf M; Lacrosse M; Rugby M & W; Soccer M & W; Softball W; Swimming and Diving W; Tennis M & W; Track and Field W; Ultimate Frisbee M & W; Volleyball W; Wrestling M & W

GEORGIA SOUTHWESTERN STATE UNIVERSITY
800 Wheatley St.
Americus, GA 31709-4693
Tel: (229)928-1273
Free: 800-338-0082
Fax: (229)931-2983
E-mail: ghayes@gsw.edu
Web Site: http://www.gsw.edu/
President/CEO: Dr. Michael L. Hanes
Registrar: Lori Urbani
Admissions: Gaye S. Hayes
Financial Aid: Freida Jones
Type: Comprehensive **Sex:** Coed **Affiliation:** University System of Georgia **Scores:** 99% SAT V 400+; 97% SAT M 400+; 61% ACT 18-23; 8% ACT 24-29 **% Accepted:** 74 **Admission Plans:** Early Admission; Early Decision Plan **Application Deadline:** July 21 **Application Fee:** $25.00 **H.S. Requirements:** High school diploma required; GED not accepted. For students out of high school 5 years or more: High school diploma required; GED accepted **Costs Per Year:** Application fee: $25. State resident tuition: $2438 full-time, $102 per semester hour part-time. Nonresident tuition: $9754 full-time, $407 per semester hour part-time. Mandatory fees: $596 full-time, $289 per term part-time. Part-time tuition and fees vary according to course load. College room and board: $4810. College room only: $2620. Room and board charges vary according to board plan and housing facility. **Scholarships:** Available **Calendar System:** Semester, Summer Session Available **Enrollment:** FT 1,699, PT 539, Grad 189 **Faculty:** FT 96, PT 55 **Student-Faculty Ratio:** 17:1 **Exams:** SAT I or ACT **% Receiving Financial Aid:** 62 **% Residing in College-Owned, -Operated, or -Affiliated Housing:** 27 **Library Holdings:** 428,197 **Regional Accreditation:** Southern Association of Colleges and Schools **Credit Hours For Degree:** 60 semester hours, Associates; 120 semester hours, Bachelors **Professional Accreditation:** NCATE, NLN **Intercollegiate Athletics:** Baseball M; Basketball M & W; Golf M & W; Soccer M & W; Softball W; Tennis M & W; Volleyball W

GEORGIA STATE UNIVERSITY
Atlanta, GA 30303-3083
Tel: (404)651-2000
Admissions: (404)651-2365
E-mail: admdmw@langate.gsu.edu
Web Site: http://www.gsu.edu/
President/CEO: Dr. Carl V. Patton
Admissions: Diane Weber
Financial Aid: David R. Bledsoe
Type: University **Sex:** Coed **Affiliation:** University System of Georgia **Scores:** 99% SAT V 400+; 99% SAT M 400+; 65% ACT 18-23; 25% ACT 24-29 **% Accepted:** 50 **Admission Plans:** Deferred Admission **Application Deadline:** March 01 **Application Fee:** $50.00 **H.S. Requirements:** High school diploma required; GED not accepted **Costs Per Year:** Application fee: $50. State resident tuition: $3638 full-time, $152 per semester hour part-time. Nonresident tuition: $14,552 full-time, $607 per semester hour part-time. Mandatory fees: $826 full-time, $413 per term part-time. Full-time tuition and fees vary according to course load, degree level, and program. Part-time tuition and fees vary according to course load, degree level, and program. College room and board: $6980. College room only: $5380. Room and board charges vary according to board plan and housing facility. **Scholarships:** Available **Calendar System:** Semester, Summer Session Available **Enrollment:** FT 13,752, PT 5,208, Grad 6,308 **Faculty:** FT 1,054, PT 376 **Student-Faculty Ratio:** 20:1 **Exams:** SAT I or ACT, SAT II **% Receiving Financial Aid:** 66 **% Residing in College-Owned, -Operated, or -Affiliated Housing:** 10 **Library Holdings:** 2,204,853 **Regional Accreditation:** Southern Association of Colleges and Schools **Credit Hours For Degree:** 120 semester hours, Bachelors **ROTC:** Army, Navy, Air Force **Professional Accreditation:** AACSB, ACEHSA, AACN, ABA, ACA, ADtA, APTA, APA, ASLHA, AALS, CARC, CORE, CSWE, NASAD, NASM, NASPAA, NCATE, NLN **Intercollegiate Athletics:** Baseball M; Basketball M & W; Cross-Country Running M & W; Golf M & W; Soccer M & W; Softball W; Tennis M & W; Track and Field M & W; Volleyball W

GORDON COLLEGE
419 College Dr.
Barnesville, GA 30204-1762
Tel: (770)358-5000
Admissions: (770)358-5354
Fax: (770)358-3031
Web Site: http://www.gdn.edu/
President/CEO: Dr. Lawrence V. Weill
Registrar: Janet Adams Barras
Admissions: Dr. Patricia Lemmons
Financial Aid: Larry Mitcham
Type: Two-Year College **Sex:** Coed **Affiliation:** University System of Georgia **Scores:** 75% SAT V 400+; 73% SAT M 400+ **Admission Plans:** Open Admission; Early Admission; Deferred Admission **Application Fee:** $20.00 **H.S. Requirements:** High school diploma required; GED accepted **Scholarships:** Available **Calendar System:** Semester, Summer Session Available **Enrollment:** FT 2,297, PT 1,152 **Faculty:** FT 84, PT 60 **Student-Faculty Ratio:** 25:1 **Exams:** SAT I or ACT **% Residing in College-Owned, -Operated, or -Affiliated Housing:** 20 **Library Holdings:** 118,000 **Regional Accreditation:** Southern Association of Colleges and Schools **Credit Hours For Degree:** 64 semester hours, Associates **Professional Accreditation:** NLN **Intercollegiate Athletics:** Baseball M; Soccer M & W; Softball W; Tennis W

GRIFFIN TECHNICAL COLLEGE
501 Varsity Rd.
Griffin, GA 30223
Tel: (770)228-7348
Admissions: (770)228-7371
Fax: (770)229-3227
E-mail: cbrown@griftec.org
Web Site: http://www.griffintech.edu
President/CEO: Dr. Robert H. Arnold
Registrar: Karen Williams
Admissions: Christine James-Brown
Financial Aid: Debbie Bowles
Type: Two-Year College **Sex:** Coed **Affiliation:** Georgia Department of Technical and Adult Education **Admission Plans:** Open Admission; Deferred Admission **Application Fee:** $15.00 **H.S. Requirements:** High school diploma or equivalent not required **Costs Per Year:** Application fee: $15. State resident tuition: $1116 full-time, $31 per credit hour part-time. Nonresident tuition: $2232 full-time, $62 per credit hour part-time. **Scholarships:** Available **Calendar System:** Quarter, Summer Session Not available **Enrollment:** FT 1,494, PT 1,913 **Faculty:** FT 68, PT 172 **Exams:** Other **Library Holdings:** 12,493 **Regional Accreditation:** Southern Association of Colleges and Schools **Credit Hours For Degree:** 100 credit hours, Associates **Professional Accreditation:** ARCEST, COE

GUPTON-JONES COLLEGE OF FUNERAL SERVICE
5141 Snapfinger Woods Dr.
Decatur, GA 30035-4022
Tel: (770)593-2257
Free: 800-848-5352
Fax: (770)593-1891
Web Site: http://www.gupton-jones.edu/
President/CEO: Patty Hutcheson
Registrar: Beverly A. Wheaton
Admissions: Patty S. Hutcheson
Financial Aid: Jacqueline B. Houze
Type: Two-Year College **Sex:** Coed **Affiliation:** Pierce Mortuary Colleges, Inc **Admission Plans:** Open Admission **Application Fee:** $25.00 **H.S. Requirements:** High school diploma required; GED accepted **Scholarships:** Available **Calendar System:** Quarter, Summer Session Available **Enrollment:** FT 198 **Faculty:** FT 9, PT 0 **Student-Faculty Ratio:** 25:1 **Library Holdings:** 3,500 **Credit Hours For Degree:** 107 quarter hours, Associates **Professional Accreditation:** ABFSE

GWINNETT TECHNICAL COLLEGE
PO Box 1505
Lawrenceville, GA 30046-1505

Tel: (770)962-7580
E-mail: mmcintire@gwinnett.tec.ga.us
Web Site: http://www.gwinnetttech.edu/
President/CEO: Sharon J. Rigsby
Registrar: Sandra Causey
Admissions: Michelle McIntire
Financial Aid: Vincent Walters
Type: Two-Year College **Sex:** Coed **Admission Plans:** Open Admission; Deferred Admission **Application Fee:** $20.00 **H.S. Requirements:** High school diploma or equivalent not required **Costs Per Year:** Application fee: $20. State resident tuition: $1116 full-time, $31 per credit hour part-time. Nonresident tuition: $2232 full-time, $62 per credit hour part-time. **Scholarships:** Available **Calendar System:** Quarter, Summer Session Available **Enrollment:** FT 1,617, PT 2,587 **Faculty:** FT 71, PT 135 **Exams:** Other **Library Holdings:** 19,547 **Regional Accreditation:** Southern Association of Colleges and Schools **Credit Hours For Degree:** 98 quarter hours, Associates **Professional Accreditation:** ADA, APTA, CARC, JRCERT

HEART OF GEORGIA TECHNICAL COLLEGE

560 Pinehill Rd.
Dublin, GA 31021
Tel: (478)275-6589
Admissions: (478)274-7837
Fax: (478)275-6642
E-mail: lisak@hgtc.org
Web Site: http://www.hgtc.org/
President/CEO: Randall Peters
Admissions: Lisa Kelly
Financial Aid: Ramona Wooten
Type: Two-Year College **Sex:** Coed **Admission Plans:** Open Admission; Deferred Admission **Application Fee:** $15.00 **H.S. Requirements:** High school diploma or equivalent not required **Costs Per Year:** Application fee: $15. State resident tuition: $1116 full-time, $31 per credit hour part-time. Nonresident tuition: $2232 full-time, $62 per credit hour part-time. **Calendar System:** Quarter **Enrollment:** FT 576, PT 1,179 **Faculty:** FT 64, PT 122 **Exams:** Other **Regional Accreditation:** Southern Association of Colleges and Schools **Professional Accreditation:** COE

HERZING COLLEGE

3355 Lenox Rd., Ste. 100
Atlanta, GA 30326
Tel: (404)816-4533
Free: 800-573-4533
Fax: (404)816-5576
E-mail: rwhite@ath.lerzing.edu
Web Site: http://www.herzing.edu/atlanta/
President/CEO: Dr. Robert Spicer
Registrar: Doreen McNemar
Admissions: Rose White
Financial Aid: Latasha Watkins
Type: Two-Year College **Sex:** Coed **Affiliation:** Herzing Institutes, Inc **% Accepted:** 75 **Application Deadline:** Rolling **Application Fee:** $25.00 **H.S. Requirements:** High school diploma required; GED accepted **Costs Per Year:** Application fee: $25. Tuition: $11,200 full-time, $350 per credit hour part-time. Mandatory fees: $125 full-time, $30 per credit hour part-time, $25 per term part-time. **Scholarships:** Available **Calendar System:** Semester **Enrollment:** FT 161, PT 115 **Faculty:** FT 10, PT 15 **Student-Faculty Ratio:** 8:1 **Exams:** Other **Library Holdings:** 6,000 **Credit Hours For Degree:** 80 credit hours, Associates **Professional Accreditation:** ACICS

HIGH-TECH INSTITUTE

1090 Northchase Parkway, Ste. 150
Marietta, GA 30067
Tel: (770)988-9877
Free: 800-987-0110
Fax: (770)988-8824
E-mail: ckusema@hightechschools.com
Web Site: http://www.high-techinstitute.com/
President/CEO: Frank Webster
Admissions: Frank Webster
Type: Two-Year College **Sex:** Coed **Calendar System:** Semester **Professional Accreditation:** ACCSCT

INTERACTIVE COLLEGE OF TECHNOLOGY

5303 New Peachtree Rd.
Chamblee, GA 30341
Tel: (770)216-2960
Free: 800-550-3475
Fax: (770)216-2989
Web Site: http://www.ict-ils.edu/
President/CEO: Elmer R. Smith
Admissions: Nicole Caruso
Type: Two-Year College **Sex:** Coed **Affiliation:** Interactive Learning Systems **Admission Plans:** Open Admission **Application Deadline:** Rolling **Application Fee:** $50.00 **H.S. Requirements:** High school diploma required; GED accepted **Costs Per Year:** Application fee: $50. Tuition: $6480 full-time. **Enrollment:** FT 1,063, PT 6 **Faculty:** FT 18, PT 44 **Student-Faculty Ratio:** 18:1 **Library Holdings:** 1,600 **Professional Accreditation:** COE

ITT TECHNICAL INSTITUTE (DULUTH)

10700 Abbotts Bridge Rd., Ste. 190
Duluth, GA 30097
Tel: (678)957-8510; (866)489-8818
Web Site: http://www.itt-tech.edu/
President/CEO: Sue Schmith
Admissions: Nick Karimi
Type: Two-Year College **Sex:** Coed **Affiliation:** ITT Educational Services, Inc **Admission Plans:** Deferred Admission **Application Deadline:** Rolling **Application Fee:** $100.00 **H.S. Requirements:** High school diploma required; GED accepted **Costs Per Year:** Application fee: $100. **Scholarships:** Available **Calendar System:** Quarter, Summer Session Not available **Exams:** Other **Credit Hours For Degree:** 96 credit hours, Associates; 180 credit hours, Bachelors **Professional Accreditation:** ACICS

ITT TECHNICAL INSTITUTE (KENNESAW)

1000 Cobb Place Blvd., NW
Kennesaw, GA 30144-3605
Admissions: (770)426-2300
Web Site: http://www.itt-tech.edu/
Admissions: Jerry L. Causey
Type: Two-Year College **Sex:** Coed **Application Deadline:** Rolling **Application Fee:** $100.00 **Costs Per Year:** Application fee: $100. **Calendar System:** Quarter **Exams:** Other

KENNESAW STATE UNIVERSITY

1000 Chastain Rd.
Kennesaw, GA 30144-5591
Tel: (770)423-6000
Admissions: (770)423-6300
Fax: (770)423-6541
E-mail: ksuadmit@ksumail.kennesaw.edu
Web Site: http://www.kennesaw.edu/
President/CEO: Dr. Betty L. Siegel
Registrar: William L. Hamrick
Admissions: Joe Head
Financial Aid: Dr. Terry L. Faust
Type: Comprehensive **Sex:** Coed **Affiliation:** University System of Georgia **Scores:** 99% SAT V 400+; 99% SAT M 400+; 72% ACT 18-23; 25% ACT 24-29 **% Accepted:** 62 **Admission Plans:** Deferred Admission **Application Deadline:** May 19 **Application Fee:** $40.00 **H.S. Requirements:** High school diploma required; GED not accepted **Costs Per Year:** Application fee: $40. State resident tuition: $2438 full-time, $102 per credit hour part-time. Nonresident tuition: $9754 full-time, $407 per credit hour part-time. Mandatory fees: $606 full-time, $303 per term part-time. Part-time tuition and fees vary according to course load. College room only: $5880. Room charges vary according to housing facility. **Scholarships:** Available **Calendar System:** Semester, Summer Session Available **Enrollment:** FT 11,411, PT 5,328, Grad 1,817 **Faculty:** FT 586, PT 329 **Student-Faculty Ratio:** 20:1 **Exams:** SAT I or ACT, SAT II **% Receiving Financial Aid:** 38 **% Residing in College-Owned, -Operated, or -Affiliated Housing:** 9 **Library Holdings:** 608,342 **Regional Accreditation:** Southern Association of Colleges and Schools **Credit Hours For Degree:** 123 semester hours, Bachelors **ROTC:** Army, Air Force **Professional Accreditation:** AACSB, AACN, NASAD, NASM, NAST, NCATE, NLN **Intercollegiate Athletics:** Baseball M; Basketball M & W; Cheerleading W; Cross-Country Running M & W; Golf M; Softball W; Tennis W

LAGRANGE COLLEGE

601 Broad St.
LaGrange, GA 30240-2999

Tel: (706)880-8000
Free: 800-593-2885
Admissions: (706)880-8253
Fax: (706)880-8040
Web Site: http://www.lagrange.edu/
President/CEO: Dr. F. Stuart Gulley
Registrar: Jimmy G. Herring
Admissions: Wells Shepard
Financial Aid: Sylvia Smith
Type: Comprehensive **Sex:** Coed **Affiliation:** United Methodist **Scores:** 98% SAT V 400+; 97% SAT M 400+; 56% ACT 18-23; 30% ACT 24-29 **% Accepted:** 48 **Admission Plans:** Early Admission; Deferred Admission **Application Deadline:** August 30 **Application Fee:** $20.00 **H.S. Requirements:** High school diploma required; GED accepted **Costs Per Year:** Application fee: $20. Comprehensive fee: $22,874 includes full-time tuition ($16,200) and college room and board ($6674). Full-time tuition varies according to class time, degree level, location, and program. Room and board charges vary according to housing facility. Part-time tuition: $668 per hour. Part-time tuition varies according to class time, degree level, location, and program. **Scholarships:** Available **Calendar System:** 4-1-4, Summer Session Available **Enrollment:** FT 898, PT 88, Grad 60 **Faculty:** FT 65, PT 53 **Student-Faculty Ratio:** 10:1 **Exams:** SAT I or ACT **% Receiving Financial Aid:** 73 **% Residing in College-Owned, -Operated, or -Affiliated Housing:** 61 **Library Holdings:** 108,389 **Regional Accreditation:** Southern Association of Colleges and Schools **Credit Hours For Degree:** 90 quarter hours, Associates; 108 semester hours, Bachelors **Professional Accreditation:** ACBSP, NLN **Intercollegiate Athletics:** Baseball M; Basketball M & W; Cross-Country Running M & W; Golf M; Soccer M & W; Softball W; Swimming and Diving M & W; Tennis M & W; Volleyball W

LANIER TECHNICAL COLLEGE
2990 Landrun Education Dr.
PO Box 58
Oakwood, GA 30566
Tel: (770)531-6300
Admissions: (770)531-6332
Fax: (770)531-6328
E-mail: mike@laniertech.edu
Web Site: http://www.laniertech.edu/
President/CEO: Michael D. Moye
Admissions: Mike Marlowe
Financial Aid: Patsy Griffin
Type: Two-Year College **Sex:** Coed **Admission Plans:** Open Admission; Deferred Admission **Application Fee:** $15.00 **H.S. Requirements:** High school diploma or equivalent not required **Costs Per Year:** Application fee: $15. State resident tuition: $1116 full-time, $31 per credit hour part-time. Nonresident tuition: $2232 full-time, $62 per credit hour part-time. **Calendar System:** Quarter **Enrollment:** FT 1,248, PT 1,948 **Faculty:** FT 72, PT 190 **Exams:** Other **Library Holdings:** 7,096 **Professional Accreditation:** ADA, COE, NAACLS

LE CORDON BLEU COLLEGE OF CULINARY ARTS, ATLANTA
1957 Lakeside Parkway, Ste. 515
Tucker, GA 30084
Web Site: http://www.atlantaculinary.com/ **Type:** Two-Year College **Sex:** Coed

LIFE UNIVERSITY
1269 Barclay Circle
Marietta, GA 30060-2903
Tel: (770)426-2600
Admissions: (770)426-2884
E-mail: drdeb@life.edu
Web Site: http://www.life.edu/
President/CEO: Dr. Guy Riekeman
Registrar: Brian Sheres
Admissions: Dr. Deb Hearilston
Financial Aid: Julie Lacour
Type: Comprehensive **Sex:** Coed **Scores:** 91.31% SAT V 400+; 85.19% SAT M 400+; 54.55% ACT 18-23 **% Accepted:** 100 **Admission Plans:** Open Admission **Application Deadline:** September 01 **Application Fee:** $50.00 **H.S. Requirements:** High school diploma required; GED accepted **Costs Per Year:** Application fee: $50. Comprehensive fee: $18,045 includes full-time tuition ($6750), mandatory fees ($315), and college room and board ($10,980). Full-time tuition and fees vary according to course load. Part-time tuition: $148 per hour. Part-time mandatory fees: $105 per term. Part-time tuition and fees vary according to course load. **Scholarships:** Available **Calendar System:** Quarter, Summer Session Available **Faculty:** FT 93, PT 15 **Student-Faculty Ratio:** 12:1 **Exams:** SAT I or ACT **% Receiving Financial Aid:** 68 **Library Holdings:** 53,619 **Regional Accreditation:** Southern Association of Colleges and Schools **Credit Hours For Degree:** 185 hours, Associates; 95 hours, Bachelors **Professional Accreditation:** ADtA, CCE

LUTHER RICE UNIVERSITY
3038 Evans Mill Rd.
Lithonia, GA 30038-2454
Tel: (770)484-1204
Free: 800-442-1577
Web Site: http://www.lrs.edu/
President/CEO: Dr. James Flanagan
Registrar: Dr. Bruce Kreutzer
Admissions: Russ Sorrow
Type: Comprehensive **Sex:** Coed **Affiliation:** Baptist **Admission Plans:** Open Admission; Early Admission **Application Fee:** $50.00 **H.S. Requirements:** High school diploma required; GED accepted **Costs Per Year:** Application fee: $50. Tuition: $4128 full-time, $516 per course part-time. Mandatory fees: $100 full-time, $50 per term part-time. **Scholarships:** Available **Calendar System:** Semester **Enrollment:** FT 60, PT 595, Grad 853 **Faculty:** FT 10, PT 23 **Exams:** Other **% Receiving Financial Aid:** 9 **Library Holdings:** 45,200 **Credit Hours For Degree:** 126 semester hours, Bachelors **Professional Accreditation:** TACCS

MACON STATE COLLEGE
100 College Station Dr.
Macon, GA 31206
Tel: (478)471-2800
Free: 800-272-7619
Fax: (478)471-2846
E-mail: mscinfo@mail.maconstate.edu
Web Site: http://www.maconstate.edu/
President/CEO: Dr. David A. Bell
Registrar: Thomas Waugh
Admissions: Bruce Applewhite
Financial Aid: Pat Simmons
Type: Four-Year College **Sex:** Coed **Affiliation:** University System of Georgia **Admission Plans:** Early Admission **Application Deadline:** Rolling **Application Fee:** $20.00 **H.S. Requirements:** High school diploma required; GED accepted **Costs Per Year:** Application fee: $20. One-time mandatory fee: $25. State resident tuition: $1542 full-time, $65 per credit hour part-time. Nonresident tuition: $6166 full-time, $257 per credit hour part-time. Mandatory fees: $188 full-time, $94 per term part-time. **Scholarships:** Available **Calendar System:** Semester, Summer Session Available **Enrollment:** FT 2,786, PT 3,364 **Faculty:** FT 163, PT 77 **Student-Faculty Ratio:** 21:1 **Exams:** SAT I or ACT, SAT II **% Receiving Financial Aid:** 55 **Library Holdings:** 80,000 **Regional Accreditation:** Southern Association of Colleges and Schools **Credit Hours For Degree:** 64 semester hours, Associates; 124 semester hours, Bachelors **Professional Accreditation:** AHIMA, CARC, NLN

MEDICAL COLLEGE OF GEORGIA
1120 Fifteenth St.
Augusta, GA 30912
Tel: (706)721-0211
Admissions: (706)721-2725
Fax: (706)721-3461
E-mail: underadm@mail.mcg.edu
Web Site: http://www.mcg.edu/
President/CEO: Dr. Daniel W. Rahn
Registrar: Dr. Michael H. Miller
Admissions: Carol S. Nobles
Financial Aid: Cynthia Parks
Type: Two-Year Upper Division **Sex:** Coed **Affiliation:** University System of Georgia **Admission Plans:** Preferred Admission **H.S. Requirements:** High school diploma required; GED accepted **Costs Per Year:** State resident tuition: $3638 full-time, $152 per hour part-time. Nonresident tuition: $14,552 full-time, $607 per hour part-time. Mandatory fees: $418 full-time, $209 per term part-time. Full-time tuition and fees vary according to location. Part-time tuition and fees vary according to course load and location. College room only: $2334. Room charges vary according to housing facility. **Scholar-**

ships: Available **Calendar System:** Semester, Summer Session Available **Enrollment:** FT 637, PT 88, Grad 445 **Faculty:** FT 646, PT 118 **Student-Faculty Ratio:** 3:1 **% Receiving Financial Aid:** 74 **% Residing in College-Owned, -Operated, or -Affiliated Housing:** 9 **Library Holdings:** 164,154 **Regional Accreditation:** Southern Association of Colleges and Schools **Professional Accreditation:** ARCMI, AANA, ADA, AHIMA, AOTA, APTA, APA, CARC, JRCEDMS, JRCERT, JRCNMT, LCMEAMA, NAACLS, NLN

MERCER UNIVERSITY
1400 Coleman Ave.
Macon, GA 31207-0003
Tel: (478)301-2700
Free: 800-840-8577
Admissions: (478)301-2650
Fax: (478)301-2828
E-mail: admissions@mercer.edu
Web Site: http://www.mercer.edu/
President/CEO: Dr. R. Kirby Godsey
Registrar: Paul Schnepf
Admissions: John Cole
Financial Aid: Carol K. Williams
Type: Comprehensive **Sex:** Coed **Affiliation:** Baptist **Scores:** 100% SAT V 400+; 100% SAT M 400+; 43% ACT 18-23; 44% ACT 24-29 **% Accepted:** 80 **Admission Plans:** Early Admission; Early Action; Deferred Admission **Application Deadline:** July 01 **Application Fee:** $50.00 **H.S. Requirements:** High school diploma required; GED accepted **Costs Per Year:** Application fee: $50. Comprehensive fee: $30,873 includes full-time tuition ($23,460) and college room and board ($7413). College room only: $3570. Full-time tuition varies according to class time, course load, and location. Room and board charges vary according to board plan, housing facility, and location. Part-time tuition: $782 per credit hour. Part-time tuition varies according to class time, course load, and location. **Scholarships:** Available **Calendar System:** Semester, Summer Session Available **Enrollment:** FT 3,796, PT 702, Grad 1,221 **Faculty:** FT 345, PT 269 **Student-Faculty Ratio:** 13:1 **Exams:** SAT I or ACT **% Receiving Financial Aid:** 64 **% Residing in College-Owned, -Operated, or -Affiliated Housing:** 65 **Library Holdings:** 692,225 **Regional Accreditation:** Southern Association of Colleges and Schools **Credit Hours For Degree:** 128 semester hours, Bachelors **ROTC:** Army **Professional Accreditation:** AACSB, ABET, AAMFT, AACN, ABA, ACPhE, AALS, ATS, LCMEAMA, NASM **Intercollegiate Athletics:** Baseball M; Basketball M & W; Cross-Country Running M & W; Golf M & W; Riflery M & W; Soccer M & W; Softball W; Tennis M & W; Volleyball W

MIDDLE GEORGIA COLLEGE
1100 Second St., SE
Cochran, GA 31014-1599
Tel: (478)934-6221
Admissions: (478)934-3138
Fax: (478)934-3199
Web Site: http://www.mgc.edu/
President/CEO: Dr. Richard J. Federinko
Registrar: Dianne Barlow
Admissions: Jennifer Brannon
Financial Aid: Charlene Morgan
Type: Two-Year College **Sex:** Coed **Affiliation:** University System of Georgia **Scores:** 80% SAT V 400+; 79% SAT M 400+; 26% ACT 18-23; 5% ACT 24-29 **% Accepted:** 91 **Admission Plans:** Early Admission; Deferred Admission **Application Deadline:** Rolling **Application Fee:** $20.00 **H.S. Requirements:** High school diploma required; GED accepted. For Georgia Academy of Mathematics, Engineering, and Science Program: High school diploma or equivalent not required **Costs Per Year:** Application fee: $20. State resident tuition: $1542 full-time, $65 per credit hour part-time. Nonresident tuition: $6166 full-time, $257 per credit hour part-time. Mandatory fees: $424 full-time. Full-time tuition and fees vary according to location. Part-time tuition varies according to location. College room and board: $4200. College room only: $1950. Room and board charges vary according to board plan and housing facility. **Scholarships:** Available **Calendar System:** Semester, Summer Session Available **Enrollment:** FT 1,808, PT 869 **Faculty:** FT 77, PT 52 **Student-Faculty Ratio:** 22:1 **% Residing in College-Owned, -Operated, or -Affiliated Housing:** 32 **Library Holdings:** 110,000 **Regional Accreditation:** Southern Association of Colleges and Schools **Credit Hours For Degree:** 60 semester hours, Associates **Professional Accreditation:** AOTA, NLN **Intercollegiate Athletics:** Baseball M; Basketball M & W; Soccer M & W; Softball W

MIDDLE GEORGIA TECHNICAL COLLEGE
80 Cohen Walker Dr.
Warner Robins, GA 31088
Tel: (912)988-6800
Free: 800-474-1031
Admissions: (478)988-6843
Fax: (912)988-6813
E-mail: cjackson@middlegatech.edu
Web Site: http://www.middlegatech.edu/
President/CEO: Billy G. Edenfield
Admissions: Craig B. Jackson
Type: Two-Year College **Sex:** Coed **Admission Plans:** Open Admission; Deferred Admission **Application Fee:** $15.00 **H.S. Requirements:** High school diploma or equivalent not required **Costs Per Year:** Application fee: $15. State resident tuition: $1116 full-time, $31 per credit hour part-time. Nonresident tuition: $2232 full-time, $62 per credit hour part-time. **Scholarships:** Available **Calendar System:** Quarter **Enrollment:** FT 1,078, PT 1,273 **Faculty:** FT 110, PT 125 **Exams:** Other **Library Holdings:** 2,124 **Regional Accreditation:** Southern Association of Colleges and Schools **Professional Accreditation:** ADA, COE

MOREHOUSE COLLEGE
830 Westview Dr., SW
Atlanta, GA 30314
Tel: (404)681-2800
Free: 800-851-1254
Admissions: (404)215-2632
Fax: (404)659-6536
Web Site: http://www.morehouse.edu/
President/CEO: Dr. Walter E. Massey
Admissions: Terrance Dixon
Financial Aid: James Stotts
Type: Four-Year College **Sex:** Men **Scores:** 96% SAT V 400+; 96% SAT M 400+; 54% ACT 18-23; 28% ACT 24-29 **% Accepted:** 53 **Admission Plans:** Early Admission; Early Decision Plan; Deferred Admission **Application Deadline:** February 15 **Application Fee:** $45.00 **H.S. Requirements:** High school diploma required; GED accepted **Costs Per Year:** Application fee: $45. Comprehensive fee: $26,284 includes full-time tuition ($15,284), mandatory fees ($1546), and college room and board ($9454). College room only: $5388. **Scholarships:** Available **Calendar System:** Semester, Summer Session Available **Enrollment:** FT 2,857, PT 172 **Faculty:** FT 167, PT 56 **Student-Faculty Ratio:** 16:1 **Exams:** SAT I or ACT, SAT II **% Receiving Financial Aid:** 89 **% Residing in College-Owned, -Operated, or -Affiliated Housing:** 40 **Library Holdings:** 560,000 **Regional Accreditation:** Southern Association of Colleges and Schools **Credit Hours For Degree:** 120 semester hours, Bachelors **ROTC:** Army, Navy, Air Force **Professional Accreditation:** AACSB **Intercollegiate Athletics:** Basketball M; Cross-Country Running M; Football M; Tennis M; Track and Field M

MOULTRIE TECHNICAL COLLEGE
361 Industrial Dr.
Moultrie, GA 31768
Tel: (229)891-7000
Admissions: (229)891-4144
Fax: (229)891-7010
E-mail: lwallace@moultrietech.edu
Web Site: http://www.moultrietech.edu/
President/CEO: Dr. Tina K. Anderson
Admissions: Leigh Wallace
Type: Two-Year College **Sex:** Coed **Admission Plans:** Open Admission; Deferred Admission **Application Fee:** $15.00 **H.S. Requirements:** High school diploma or equivalent not required **Costs Per Year:** Application fee: $15. State resident tuition: $1116 full-time, $31 per credit hour part-time. Nonresident tuition: $2232 full-time, $62 per credit hour part-time. **Calendar System:** Quarter **Enrollment:** FT 831, PT 1,120 **Faculty:** FT 47, PT 49 **Exams:** Other **Professional Accreditation:** COE

NORTH GEORGIA COLLEGE & STATE UNIVERSITY
82 College Circle
Dahlonega, GA 30597
Tel: (706)864-1400
Free: 800-498-9581
Admissions: (706)864-2885
Fax: (706)864-1478
Web Site: http://www.ngcsu.edu/

President/CEO: Dr. Nathaniel Hansford
Registrar: Jason Pruitt
Admissions: Robert J. LaVerriere
Financial Aid: Deborah Barbone
Type: Comprehensive **Sex:** Coed **Affiliation:** University System of Georgia **Scores:** 99.8% SAT V 400+; 99.79% SAT M 400+; 59.88% ACT 18-23; 30.25% ACT 24-29 **% Accepted:** 68 **Admission Plans:** Early Admission **Application Deadline:** July 01 **Application Fee:** $25.00 **H.S. Requirements:** High school diploma required; GED not accepted **Costs Per Year:** Application fee: $25. State resident tuition: $2438 full-time, $102 per semester hour part-time. Nonresident tuition: $9754 full-time, $407 per semester hour part-time. Mandatory fees: $630 full-time. Part-time tuition varies according to course load. College room and board: $4596. College room only: $2292. Room and board charges vary according to board plan and housing facility. **Scholarships:** Available **Calendar System:** Semester, Summer Session Available **Enrollment:** FT 3,353, PT 837, Grad 575 **Faculty:** FT 191, PT 123 **Student-Faculty Ratio:** 16:1 **Exams:** SAT I or ACT **% Receiving Financial Aid:** 30 **% Residing in College-Owned, -Operated, or -Affiliated Housing:** 37 **Library Holdings:** 146,888 **Regional Accreditation:** Southern Association of Colleges and Schools **Credit Hours For Degree:** 60 semester hours, Associates; 120 semester hours, Bachelors **ROTC:** Army **Professional Accreditation:** APTA, ACBSP, NCATE, NLN **Intercollegiate Athletics:** Baseball M; Basketball M & W; Cheerleading W; Cross-Country Running M & W; Equestrian Sports M & W; Riflery M & W; Soccer M & W; Softball W; Tennis M & W; Track and Field M & W

NORTH GEORGIA TECHNICAL COLLEGE

Georgia Hwy. 197, North
PO Box 65
Clarkesville, GA 30523
Tel: (706)754-7700
Admissions: (706)754-7724
Fax: (706)754-7777
E-mail: gtaylor@northgatech.edu
Web Site: http://www.northgatech.edu/
President/CEO: Dr. Ruth R. Nichols
Admissions: Gail Taylor
Type: Two-Year College **Sex:** Coed **Admission Plans:** Open Admission; Deferred Admission **Application Fee:** $15.00 **H.S. Requirements:** High school diploma or equivalent not required **Costs Per Year:** Application fee: $15. State resident tuition: $1116 full-time, $31 per credit hour part-time. Nonresident tuition: $2232 full-time, $62 per credit hour part-time. **Calendar System:** Quarter **Enrollment:** FT 974, PT 838 **Faculty:** FT 68, PT 121 **Exams:** Other **Library Holdings:** 15,684 **Professional Accreditation:** COE, NAACLS

NORTH METRO TECHNICAL COLLEGE

5198 Ross Rd.
Acworth, GA 30102
Tel: (770)975-4000
Admissions: (770)975-4079
Fax: (770)975-4044
E-mail: mcusack@northmetrotech.edu
Web Site: http://www.northmetrotech.edu/
President/CEO: Steve Dougherty
Admissions: Missy Cusack
Type: Two-Year College **Sex:** Coed **Admission Plans:** Open Admission; Deferred Admission **Application Fee:** $15.00 **H.S. Requirements:** High school diploma or equivalent not required **Costs Per Year:** Application fee: $15. State resident tuition: $1116 full-time, $31 per credit hour part-time. Nonresident tuition: $2232 full-time, $62 per credit hour part-time. **Calendar System:** Quarter **Enrollment:** FT 790, PT 1,113 **Faculty:** FT 34, PT 76 **Exams:** Other **Professional Accreditation:** COE

NORTHWESTERN TECHNICAL COLLEGE

PO Box 569, 265 Bicentennial Trail
Rock Spring, GA 30739
Tel: (706)764-3510
Free: 800-735-5726
Admissions: (706)764-3511
E-mail: csolmon@northwesterntech.edu
Web Site: http://www.northwesterntech.edu/
President/CEO: Dr. Ray Brooks
Registrar: Selena Magnusson
Admissions: Carolyn Solmon
Financial Aid: Sarah Twiggs
Type: Two-Year College **Sex:** Coed **Affiliation:** Georgia Department of Technical and Adult Education **Admission Plans:** Open Admission; Deferred Admission **Application Fee:** $15.00 **H.S. Requirements:** High school diploma or equivalent not required **Costs Per Year:** Application fee: $15. State resident tuition: $1116 full-time, $31 per credit hour part-time. Nonresident tuition: $2232 full-time, $62 per credit hour part-time. **Scholarships:** Available **Calendar System:** Quarter, Summer Session Available **Enrollment:** FT 891, PT 1,412 **Faculty:** FT 49, PT 61 **Exams:** Other **Library Holdings:** 350,000 **Regional Accreditation:** Southern Association of Colleges and Schools **Credit Hours For Degree:** 110 quarter hours, Associates **Professional Accreditation:** ARCEST, AAMAE, AOTA, COE

OGEECHEE TECHNICAL COLLEGE

One Joe Kennedy Blvd.
Statesboro, GA 30458
Tel: (912)681-5500
Free: 800-646-1316
Admissions: (912)871-1600
E-mail: rfoley@ogeecheetech.edu
Web Site: http://www.ogeecheetech.edu
Admissions: Ryan Foley
Type: Two-Year College **Sex:** Coed **Affiliation:** Georgia Department of Technical and Adult Education **Admission Plans:** Open Admission; Deferred Admission **Application Fee:** $15.00 **H.S. Requirements:** High school diploma or equivalent not required **Costs Per Year:** Application fee: $15. State resident tuition: $31 per credit hour part-time. Nonresident tuition: $62 per credit hour part-time. **Calendar System:** Quarter **Enrollment:** FT 1,008, PT 942 **Faculty:** FT 73, PT 69 **Exams:** Other **Library Holdings:** 2,477 **Professional Accreditation:** ABFSE, ADA, COptA, COE

OGLETHORPE UNIVERSITY

4484 Peachtree Rd., NE
Atlanta, GA 30319-2797
Tel: (404)261-1441
Free: 800-428-4484
Admissions: (404)364-8307
Fax: (404)364-8500
E-mail: admission@oglethorpe.edu
Web Site: http://www.oglethorpe.edu/
President/CEO: Dr. Larry D. Large
Registrar: Susan Bacher
Admissions: David Rhodes
Financial Aid: Patrick Bonones
Type: Comprehensive **Sex:** Coed **Scores:** 98% SAT V 400+; 97% SAT M 400+; 42% ACT 18-23; 46% ACT 24-29 **% Accepted:** 64 **Admission Plans:** Early Action; Deferred Admission **Application Deadline:** Rolling **Application Fee:** $35.00 **H.S. Requirements:** High school diploma required; GED accepted **Costs Per Year:** Application fee: $35. Comprehensive fee: $30,300 includes full-time tuition ($22,200), mandatory fees ($100), and college room and board ($8000). Room and board charges vary according to board plan and housing facility. Part-time tuition: $925 per credit hour. Part-time tuition varies according to program. **Scholarships:** Available **Calendar System:** Semester, Summer Session Available **Enrollment:** FT 886, PT 132, Grad 65 **Faculty:** FT 56, PT 59 **Student-Faculty Ratio:** 13:1 **Exams:** SAT I and SAT II or ACT **% Receiving Financial Aid:** 58 **% Residing in College-Owned, -Operated, or -Affiliated Housing:** 58 **Library Holdings:** 150,000 **Regional Accreditation:** Southern Association of Colleges and Schools **Credit Hours For Degree:** 120 semester hours, Bachelors **Intercollegiate Athletics:** Baseball M; Basketball M & W; Cross-Country Running M & W; Golf M & W; Soccer M & W; Tennis M & W; Track and Field M & W; Volleyball W

OKEFENOKEE TECHNICAL COLLEGE

1701 Carswell Ave.
Waycross, GA 31503
Tel: (912)287-6584
Admissions: (912)287-5806
Fax: (912)287-4865
E-mail: reba@okefenokeetech.org
Web Site: http://www.okefenokeetech.org/
President/CEO: John Pike

Admissions: Reba Smith
Financial Aid: Angie Wilson
Type: Two-Year College **Sex:** Coed **Admission Plans:** Open Admission; Deferred Admission **Application Fee:** $15.00 **H.S. Requirements:** High school diploma or equivalent not required **Costs Per Year:** Application fee: $15. State resident tuition: $1116 full-time, $31 per credit hour part-time. Nonresident tuition: $2232 full-time, $62 per credit hour part-time. **Calendar System:** Quarter **Enrollment:** FT 595, PT 1,136 **Faculty:** FT 48, PT 65 **Exams:** Other **Library Holdings:** 1,714 **Professional Accreditation:** COE, NAACLS

PAINE COLLEGE
1235 15th St.
Augusta, GA 30901-3182
Tel: (706)821-8200
Free: 800-476-7703
Admissions: (706)821-8320
Fax: (706)821-8293
E-mail: tinsleyi@mail.paine.edu
Web Site: http://www.paine.edu/
President/CEO: Dr. Shirley A. R. Lewis
Registrar: Carolyn Martin
Admissions: Joseph Tinsley
Financial Aid: Gerri Bogan
Type: Four-Year College **Sex:** Coed **Affiliation:** Methodist **Scores:** 60.5% SAT V 400+; 55% SAT M 400+; 16.2% ACT 18-23; 1.5% ACT 24-29 **% Accepted:** 29 **Admission Plans:** Early Admission; Deferred Admission **Application Deadline:** August 01 **Application Fee:** $20.00 **H.S. Requirements:** High school diploma required; GED accepted **Costs Per Year:** Application fee: $20. Comprehensive fee: $14,418 includes full-time tuition ($8952), mandatory fees ($738), and college room and board ($4728). Full-time tuition and fees vary according to course load and reciprocity agreements. Room and board charges vary according to housing facility. Part-time tuition: $373 per credit hour. Part-time mandatory fees: $369 per term. Part-time tuition and fees vary according to course load, location, and reciprocity agreements. **Scholarships:** Available **Calendar System:** Semester, Summer Session Available **Enrollment:** FT 760, PT 68 **Faculty:** FT 74, PT 17 **Student-Faculty Ratio:** 10:1 **Exams:** SAT I or ACT **% Residing in College-Owned, -Operated, or -Affiliated Housing:** 58 **Library Holdings:** 88,809 **Regional Accreditation:** Southern Association of Colleges and Schools **Credit Hours For Degree:** 124 semester hours, Bachelors **ROTC:** Army **Professional Accreditation:** ACBSP **Intercollegiate Athletics:** Baseball M; Basketball M & W; Cross-Country Running M & W; Golf M; Softball W; Track and Field M & W; Volleyball W

PIEDMONT COLLEGE
PO Box 10
165 Central Ave.
Demorest, GA 30535-0010
Tel: (706)778-3000
Free: 800-277-7020
Admissions: (706)776-0103
Fax: (706)776-6635
E-mail: cpeterson@piedmont.edu
Web Site: http://www.piedmont.edu/
President/CEO: Dr. W. Ray Cleere
Registrar: Linda Wofford
Admissions: Cynthia L. Peterson
Financial Aid: Kimberly C. Lovell
Type: Comprehensive **Sex:** Coed **Affiliation:** United Church of Christ **Scores:** 98% SAT V 400+; 94% SAT M 400+; 55% ACT 18-23; 28% ACT 24-29 **% Accepted:** 66 **Admission Plans:** Early Admission; Deferred Admission **Application Deadline:** July 01 **Application Fee:** $0.00 **H.S. Requirements:** High school diploma required; GED accepted. For home schooled students can submit a portfolio in lieu of transcripts: High school diploma or equivalent not required **Costs Per Year:** Application fee: $0. Comprehensive fee: $20,500 includes full-time tuition ($15,500) and college room and board ($5000). College room only: $2600. Full-time tuition varies according to course load and program. Room and board charges vary according to housing facility. Part-time tuition: $646 per semester hour. Part-time tuition varies according to course load and program. **Scholarships:** Available **Calendar System:** Semester, Summer Session Available **Enrollment:** FT 845, PT 94, Grad 999 **Faculty:** FT 98, PT 102 **Student-Faculty Ratio:** 13:1 **Exams:** SAT I or ACT **% Receiving Financial Aid:** 80 **% Residing in College-Owned, -Operated, or -Affiliated Housing:** 16 **Library Holdings:** 118,750 **Regional Accreditation:** Southern Association of Colleges and Schools **Credit Hours For Degree:** 120 semester hours, Bachelors **Intercollegiate Athletics:** Baseball M; Basketball M & W; Cross-Country Running M & W; Golf M & W; Soccer M & W; Softball W; Tennis M & W; Volleyball W

REINHARDT COLLEGE
7300 Reinhardt College Circle
Waleska, GA 30183-2981
Tel: (770)720-5600; (87R)EINHARDT
Admissions: (770)720-5526
Fax: (770)720-5602
E-mail: admissions@reinhardt.edu
Web Site: http://www.reinhardt.edu/
President/CEO: Dr. J. Thomas Isherwood
Admissions: Julie Fleming
Financial Aid: Robert K. Gregory
Type: Four-Year College **Sex:** Coed **Affiliation:** United Methodist Church **Scores:** 86.3% SAT V 400+; 86.1% SAT M 400+; 61% ACT 18-23; 7% ACT 24-29 **% Accepted:** 52 **Admission Plans:** Early Admission; Deferred Admission **Application Deadline:** Rolling **Application Fee:** $25.00 **H.S. Requirements:** High school diploma required; GED accepted **Costs Per Year:** Application fee: $25. Comprehensive fee: $20,020 includes full-time tuition ($13,020), mandatory fees ($200), and college room and board ($6800). Part-time tuition: $435 per hour. **Scholarships:** Available **Calendar System:** Semester, Summer Session Available **Enrollment:** FT 881, PT 129 **Faculty:** FT 52, PT 60 **Student-Faculty Ratio:** 13:1 **Exams:** SAT I or ACT **% Residing in College-Owned, -Operated, or -Affiliated Housing:** 39 **Library Holdings:** 48,614 **Regional Accreditation:** Southern Association of Colleges and Schools **Credit Hours For Degree:** 60 credit hours, Associates; 120 credit hours, Bachelors **Intercollegiate Athletics:** Baseball M; Basketball M & W; Cross-Country Running M & W; Golf M; Soccer M & W; Softball W; Tennis M & W

SANDERSVILLE TECHNICAL COLLEGE
1189 Deepstep Rd.
Sandersville, GA 31082
Tel: (478)553-2050
Admissions: (478)553-2065
Fax: (478)553-2118
E-mail: pwilson@sandervilletech.edu
Web Site: http://www.sandersvilletech.org/
President/CEO: John H. Sterrett
Admissions: Patrick Wilson
Financial Aid: Vivian Spivey
Type: Two-Year College **Sex:** Coed **Admission Plans:** Open Admission; Deferred Admission **Application Fee:** $15.00 **H.S. Requirements:** High school diploma or equivalent not required **Costs Per Year:** Application fee: $15. State resident tuition: $1116 full-time, $31 per credit hour part-time. Nonresident tuition: $2232 full-time, $62 per credit hour part-time. **Calendar System:** Quarter **Enrollment:** FT 237, PT 528 **Faculty:** FT 30, PT 70 **Exams:** Other **Professional Accreditation:** COE

SAVANNAH COLLEGE OF ART AND DESIGN
342 Bull St., PO Box 3146
Savannah, GA 31402-3146
Tel: (912)525-5000
Free: 800-869-7223
Admissions: (912)525-5100
Fax: (912)238-2436
E-mail: admission@scad.edu
Web Site: http://www.scad.edu/
President/CEO: Paula S. Wallace
Registrar: Margo McLeod
Admissions: Pamela Rhame
Financial Aid: Cindy Bradley
Type: Comprehensive **Sex:** Coed **Scores:** 96% SAT V 400+; 94% SAT M 400+; 40% ACT 18-23; 39% ACT 24-29 **% Accepted:** 68 **Admission Plans:** Early Admission **Application Deadline:** Rolling **Application Fee:** $50.00 **H.S. Requirements:** High school diploma required; GED accepted **Costs Per Year:** Application fee: $50. Comprehensive fee: $33,045 includes full-time tuition ($22,950), mandatory fees ($500), and college room and board ($9595). College room only: $6250. Part-time tuition: $2550 per course. **Scholarships:** Available **Calendar System:** Quarter, Summer Session Available **Enrollment:** FT 5,528, PT 608, Grad 1,220 **Faculty:** FT 366, PT

53 **Student-Faculty Ratio:** 18:1 **Exams:** SAT I or ACT **% Receiving Financial Aid:** 51 **% Residing in College-Owned, -Operated, or -Affiliated Housing:** 33 **Library Holdings:** 126,680 **Regional Accreditation:** Southern Association of Colleges and Schools **Credit Hours For Degree:** 180 quarter credit hours, Bachelors **Intercollegiate Athletics:** Baseball M; Basketball M & W; Cheerleading W; Crew M & W; Cross-Country Running M & W; Equestrian Sports M & W; Fencing M & W; Golf M & W; Sailing M & W; Soccer M & W; Softball W; Swimming and Diving M & W; Tennis M & W; Volleyball W

SAVANNAH RIVER COLLEGE
2528 Center West Parkway
Augusta, GA 30909
Tel: (706)738-5046
Web Site: http://www.savannahrivercollege.edu/ **Type:** Two-Year College **Sex:** Coed

SAVANNAH STATE UNIVERSITY
3219 College Ave.
Savannah, GA 31404
Tel: (912)356-2186
Free: 800-788-0478
Admissions: (912)356-2181
Fax: (912)356-2529
E-mail: mooreg@savstate.edu
Web Site: http://www.savstate.edu/
President/CEO: Dr. Carlton E. Brown
Registrar: Matthew Latson
Admissions: Gwendolyn J. Moore
Financial Aid: Mark Adkins
Type: Comprehensive **Sex:** Coed **Affiliation:** University System of Georgia **Scores:** 86.7% SAT V 400+; 83.2% SAT M 400+; 45.6% ACT 18-23; 1.9% ACT 24-29 **% Accepted:** 50 **Admission Plans:** Preferred Admission; Early Admission; Deferred Admission **Application Deadline:** June 01 **Application Fee:** $20.00 **H.S. Requirements:** High school diploma required; GED accepted **Costs Per Year:** Application fee: $20. State resident tuition: $3056 full-time. Nonresident tuition: $10,372 full-time. College room and board: $4716. College room only: $2136. **Scholarships:** Available **Calendar System:** Semester, Summer Session Available **Enrollment:** FT 2,365, PT 574, Grad 116 **Faculty:** FT 123, PT 44 **Student-Faculty Ratio:** 19:1 **Exams:** SAT I or ACT, SAT I, SAT II **% Residing in College-Owned, -Operated, or -Affiliated Housing:** 45 **Library Holdings:** 187,916 **Regional Accreditation:** Southern Association of Colleges and Schools **Credit Hours For Degree:** 120 semester hours, Bachelors **ROTC:** Army, Navy **Professional Accreditation:** ABET, CSWE, NASPAA **Intercollegiate Athletics:** Baseball M; Basketball M & W; Cross-Country Running W; Football M; Tennis W; Track and Field M & W; Volleyball W

SAVANNAH TECHNICAL COLLEGE
5717 White Bluff Rd.
Savannah, GA 31405
Tel: (912)351-6362
Admissions: (912)303-1772
Fax: (912)352-4362
E-mail: asoutherland@savannahtech.edu
Web Site: http://www.savannahtech.edu/
President/CEO: Dr. C. B. Rathburn, III
Registrar: Verlene Lampley
Admissions: Angela Southerland
Financial Aid: Timothy Cranford
Type: Two-Year College **Sex:** Coed **Affiliation:** Georgia Department of Technical and Adult Education **Admission Plans:** Open Admission; Deferred Admission **Application Fee:** $15.00 **H.S. Requirements:** High school diploma or equivalent not required **Costs Per Year:** Application fee: $15. State resident tuition: $1116 full-time, $31 per credit hour part-time. Nonresident tuition: $2232 full-time, $62 per credit hour part-time. **Scholarships:** Available **Calendar System:** Quarter, Summer Session Available **Enrollment:** FT 1,577, PT 2,209 **Faculty:** FT 61, PT 229 **Exams:** Other **Library Holdings:** 20,804 **Regional Accreditation:** Southern Association of Colleges and Schools **Credit Hours For Degree:** 104 credits, Associates **Professional Accreditation:** ABET, ACF, ADA

SHORTER COLLEGE
315 Shorter Ave.
Rome, GA 30165
Tel: (706)291-2121
Free: 800-868-6980
Admissions: (706)233-7342
Fax: (706)236-1515
E-mail: admissions@shorter.edu
Web Site: http://www.shorter.edu/
President/CEO: Dr. Ed L. Schrader
Registrar: Katharine Lovvorn
Admissions: John Head
Financial Aid: Philip Hawkins
Type: Four-Year College **Sex:** Coed **Affiliation:** Baptist **Scores:** 97% SAT V 400+; 94% SAT M 400+; 51% ACT 18-23; 24% ACT 24-29 **% Accepted:** 75 **Admission Plans:** Early Admission; Deferred Admission **Application Deadline:** August 25 **Application Fee:** $25.00 **H.S. Requirements:** High school diploma required; GED accepted **Costs Per Year:** Application fee: $25. Comprehensive fee: $19,700 includes full-time tuition ($13,200), mandatory fees ($300), and college room and board ($6200). College room only: $3400. Full-time tuition and fees vary according to course load. Room and board charges vary according to board plan and housing facility. Part-time tuition: $285 per semester hour. **Scholarships:** Available **Calendar System:** Semester, Summer Session Available **Enrollment:** FT 929, PT 38 **Faculty:** FT 65, PT 55 **Student-Faculty Ratio:** 11:1 **Exams:** SAT I or ACT **% Receiving Financial Aid:** 68 **% Residing in College-Owned, -Operated, or -Affiliated Housing:** 63 **Library Holdings:** 134,201 **Regional Accreditation:** Southern Association of Colleges and Schools **Credit Hours For Degree:** 126 semester hours, Bachelors **Professional Accreditation:** NASM **Intercollegiate Athletics:** Baseball M; Basketball M & W; Cheerleading M & W; Cross-Country Running M & W; Golf M & W; Soccer M & W; Tennis M & W; Track and Field M & W; Volleyball W

SOUTH GEORGIA COLLEGE
100 West College Park Dr.
Douglas, GA 31533-5098
Tel: (912)389-4510
Admissions: (912)389-4200
Fax: (912)389-4392
E-mail: rbraswell@sga.edu
Web Site: http://www.sga.edu/
President/CEO: Dr. Edward D. Jackson, Jr.
Registrar: Dr. Randy Braswell
Admissions: Dr. Randy L. Braswell
Financial Aid: Robin Fowler
Type: Two-Year College **Sex:** Coed **Affiliation:** University System of Georgia **Scores:** 40% SAT V 400+; 53% SAT M 400+ **Admission Plans:** Early Admission; Deferred Admission **H.S. Requirements:** High school diploma required; GED accepted **Scholarships:** Available **Calendar System:** Semester, Summer Session Available **Faculty:** FT 45, PT 10 **Student-Faculty Ratio:** 24:1 **Exams:** SAT I or ACT, SAT II **% Residing in College-Owned, -Operated, or -Affiliated Housing:** 11 **Library Holdings:** 79,190 **Regional Accreditation:** Southern Association of Colleges and Schools **Credit Hours For Degree:** 64 semester hours, Associates **Professional Accreditation:** NLN **Intercollegiate Athletics:** Baseball M; Soccer M; Softball W

SOUTH GEORGIA TECHNICAL COLLEGE
1583 Southerfield Rd.
Americus, GA 31709
Tel: (229)931-2394
Admissions: (229)931-2299
Fax: (229)931-2459
E-mail: kwerling@southgatech.edu
Web Site: http://www.southgatech.edu/
Admissions: Karen Werling
Type: Two-Year College **Sex:** Coed **Admission Plans:** Open Admission; Deferred Admission **Application Fee:** $15.00 **H.S. Requirements:** High school diploma or equivalent not required **Costs Per Year:** Application fee: $15. State resident tuition: $1116 full-time, $31 per credit hour part-time. Nonresident tuition: $2232 full-time, $62 per credit hour part-time. **Calendar System:** Quarter **Enrollment:** FT 886, PT 783 **Faculty:** FT 69, PT 74 **Exams:** Other **Professional Accreditation:** COE **Intercollegiate Athletics:** Basketball M & W

SOUTH UNIVERSITY
709 Mall Blvd.
Savannah, GA 31406-4805

Tel: (912)201-8000; (866)629-2901
Fax: (912)201-8070
E-mail: mmills@southuniversity.edu
Web Site: http://www.southuniversity.edu/
President/CEO: David P. Higley
Registrar: Bryan Logie
Admissions: Matthew Mills
Financial Aid: Anne Rader
Type: Comprehensive **Sex:** Coed **Admission Plans:** Deferred Admission **Application Deadline:** Rolling **Application Fee:** $25.00 **H.S. Requirements:** High school diploma required; GED accepted **Costs Per Year:** Application fee: $25. Tuition: $11,475 full-time, $2995 per term part-time. **Scholarships:** Available **Calendar System:** Quarter, Summer Session Available **Faculty:** FT 41, PT 50 **Student-Faculty Ratio:** 13:1 **Exams:** SAT I and SAT II, SAT I and SAT II or ACT **% Receiving Financial Aid:** 72 **Library Holdings:** 22,240 **Regional Accreditation:** Southern Association of Colleges and Schools **Credit Hours For Degree:** 120 quarter hours, Associates; 180 quarter hours, Bachelors **Professional Accreditation:** AAMAE, ACPhE, APTA

SOUTHEASTERN TECHNICAL COLLEGE
3001 East First St.
Vidalia, GA 30474
Tel: (912)538-3100
Admissions: (912)538-3121
Fax: (912)538-3156
E-mail: ccarroll@southeasterntech.edu
Web Site: http://www.southeasterntech.edu/
President/CEO: Dr. Cathryn T. Meehan
Admissions: Christopher P. Carroll
Type: Two-Year College **Sex:** Coed **Admission Plans:** Open Admission; Deferred Admission **Application Fee:** $15.00 **H.S. Requirements:** High school diploma or equivalent not required **Costs Per Year:** Application fee: $15. State resident tuition: $1116 full-time, $31 per credit hour part-time. Nonresident tuition: $2232 full-time, $62 per credit hour part-time. **Calendar System:** Quarter **Enrollment:** FT 447, PT 535 **Faculty:** FT 40, PT 62 **Exams:** Other **Professional Accreditation:** COE

SOUTHERN POLYTECHNIC STATE UNIVERSITY
1100 South Marietta Parkway
Marietta, GA 30060-2896
Tel: (678)915-7778
Free: 800-635-3204
Admissions: (678)915-4188
E-mail: vhead@sct.edu
Web Site: http://www.spsu.edu/
President/CEO: Dr. Lisa A. Rossbacher
Admissions: Virginia Head
Financial Aid: Helen Spivak
Type: Comprehensive **Sex:** Coed **Affiliation:** University System of Georgia **Scores:** 100% SAT V 400+; 100% SAT M 400+; 62% ACT 18-23; 28% ACT 24-29 **% Accepted:** 66 **Admission Plans:** Early Admission **Application Deadline:** August 01 **Application Fee:** $20.00 **H.S. Requirements:** High school diploma required; GED not accepted **Costs Per Year:** Application fee: $20. State resident tuition: $2622 full-time, $110 per credit hour part-time. Nonresident tuition: $10,486 full-time, $437 per credit hour part-time. Mandatory fees: $552 full-time. College room and board: $5490. College room only: $3210. **Scholarships:** Available **Calendar System:** Semester, Summer Session Available **Enrollment:** FT 2,193, PT 1,137, Grad 476 **Faculty:** FT 135, PT 91 **Student-Faculty Ratio:** 17:1 **Exams:** SAT I or ACT **% Receiving Financial Aid:** 44 **% Residing in College-Owned, -Operated, or -Affiliated Housing:** 12 **Library Holdings:** 117,963 **Regional Accreditation:** Southern Association of Colleges and Schools **Credit Hours For Degree:** 60 semester hours, Associates; 120 semester hours, Bachelors **ROTC:** Army, Navy, Air Force **Professional Accreditation:** ABET, ACCE, ACBSP **Intercollegiate Athletics:** Baseball M; Basketball M & W; Soccer M

SOUTHWEST GEORGIA TECHNICAL COLLEGE
15689 US 19 North
Thomasville, GA 31792
Tel: (229)225-4096
Admissions: (229)225-5077
Fax: (229)225-4330
E-mail: lhoover@southwestgatech.edu
Web Site: http://www.southwestgatech.edu/
President/CEO: Dr. Freida Hill
Registrar: Sabine Herring
Admissions: Lorette Hoover
Financial Aid: Mike Rayburn
Type: Two-Year College **Sex:** Coed **Affiliation:** Georgia Department of Technical and Adult Education **Admission Plans:** Open Admission; Deferred Admission **Application Fee:** $20.00 **H.S. Requirements:** High school diploma or equivalent not required. For welding certificate: High school diploma or equivalent not required **Costs Per Year:** Application fee: $20. State resident tuition: $1116 full-time, $31 per credit hour part-time. Nonresident tuition: $2232 full-time, $62 per credit hour part-time. **Scholarships:** Available **Calendar System:** Quarter, Summer Session Available **Enrollment:** FT 588, PT 903 **Faculty:** FT 62, PT 0 **Exams:** Other **Library Holdings:** 19,767 **Regional Accreditation:** Southern Association of Colleges and Schools **Credit Hours For Degree:** 142 credit hours, Associates **Professional Accreditation:** APTA, CARC, COE, NAACLS

SPELMAN COLLEGE
350 Spelman Ln., SW
Atlanta, GA 30314-4399
Tel: (404)681-3643
Free: 800-982-2411
Fax: (404)215-7788
E-mail: admiss@spelman.edu
Web Site: http://www.spelman.edu/
President/CEO: Dr. Beverly Daniel Tatum
Registrar: Dr. Fred Buddy
Admissions: Arlene Cash
Financial Aid: Lenora Jackson
Type: Four-Year College **Sex:** Women **Scores:** 100% SAT V 400+; 99% SAT M 400+; 65% ACT 18-23; 32% ACT 24-29 **% Accepted:** 39 **Admission Plans:** Early Admission; Early Action; Deferred Admission **Application Deadline:** February 01 **Application Fee:** $35.00 **H.S. Requirements:** High school diploma required; GED accepted **Costs Per Year:** Application fee: $35. Comprehensive fee: $24,250 includes full-time tuition ($13,525), mandatory fees ($2270), and college room and board ($8455). Part-time tuition: $565 per credit hour. **Scholarships:** Available **Calendar System:** Semester, Summer Session Not available **Enrollment:** FT 2,226, PT 92 **Faculty:** FT 169, PT 76 **Student-Faculty Ratio:** 12:1 **Exams:** SAT I or ACT **% Receiving Financial Aid:** 85 **% Residing in College-Owned, -Operated, or -Affiliated Housing:** 53 **Library Holdings:** 727,767 **Regional Accreditation:** Southern Association of Colleges and Schools **Credit Hours For Degree:** 124 hours, Bachelors **ROTC:** Army, Air Force **Professional Accreditation:** NASM, NCATE **Intercollegiate Athletics:** Basketball W; Cross-Country Running W; Golf W; Soccer W; Tennis W; Track and Field W; Volleyball W

SWAINSBORO TECHNICAL COLLEGE
346 Kite Rd.
Swainsboro, GA 30401
Tel: (478)289-2200
Admissions: (478)289-2259
Fax: (478)289-2263
E-mail: mfagler@swainsborotech.edu
Web Site: http://www.swainsborotech.edu/
President/CEO: Dr. Glenn Deibert
Admissions: Mitchell Fagler
Financial Aid: Diane Claxton
Type: Two-Year College **Sex:** Coed **Admission Plans:** Open Admission; Deferred Admission **Application Fee:** $15.00 **H.S. Requirements:** High school diploma or equivalent not required **Costs Per Year:** Application fee: $15. State resident tuition: $1116 full-time, $31 per credit hour part-time. Nonresident tuition: $2232 full-time, $62 per credit hour part-time. **Calendar System:** Quarter **Enrollment:** FT 286, PT 398 **Faculty:** FT 41, PT 38 **Exams:** Other **Professional Accreditation:** COE

THOMAS UNIVERSITY
1501 Millpond Rd.
Thomasville, GA 31792-7499
Tel: (229)226-1621
Free: 800-538-9784
E-mail: hmueller@thomasu.edu
Web Site: http://www.thomasu.edu/
President/CEO: Dr. John M. Hutchinson

Admissions: Heather Mueller
Financial Aid: Debbie White
Type: Comprehensive **Sex:** Coed **% Accepted:** 68 **Admission Plans:** Open Admission; Early Admission; Deferred Admission **Application Deadline:** Rolling **Application Fee:** $25.00 **H.S. Requirements:** High school diploma required; GED accepted **Costs Per Year:** Application fee: $25. Tuition: $10,050 full-time, $395 per semester hour part-time. Mandatory fees: $520 full-time, $130 per term part-time. College room only: $2500. **Scholarships:** Available **Calendar System:** Semester, Summer Session Available **Enrollment:** FT 445, PT 190, Grad 104 **Faculty:** FT 46, PT 33 **Student-Faculty Ratio:** 10:1 **% Receiving Financial Aid:** 86 **% Residing in College-Owned, -Operated, or -Affiliated Housing:** 9 **Library Holdings:** 61,096 **Regional Accreditation:** Southern Association of Colleges and Schools **Credit Hours For Degree:** 60 semester hours, Associates; 120 semester hours, Bachelors **Professional Accreditation:** CORE **Intercollegiate Athletics:** Baseball M; Golf M & W; Soccer M & W; Softball W

TOCCOA FALLS COLLEGE
325 Chapel Dr.
Toccoa Falls, GA 30598
Tel: (706)886-6831
Fax: (706)282-6012
E-mail: admissions@tfc.edu
Web Site: http://www.tfc.edu/
Registrar: Kelly Vickers
Admissions: Christy Meadows
Financial Aid: Vince Welch
Type: Four-Year College **Sex:** Coed **Affiliation:** interdenominational **Scores:** 91% SAT V 400+; 86% SAT M 400+; 43% ACT 18-23; 34% ACT 24-29 **% Accepted:** 61 **Admission Plans:** Early Admission; Deferred Admission **Application Deadline:** Rolling **Application Fee:** $20.00 **H.S. Requirements:** High school diploma required; GED accepted **Costs Per Year:** Application fee: $20. One-time mandatory fee: $475. Comprehensive fee: $16,650 includes full-time tuition ($12,050) and college room and board ($4600). Full-time tuition varies according to course load. Room and board charges vary according to board plan. Part-time tuition: $502 per credit hour. Part-time tuition varies according to course load. **Scholarships:** Available **Calendar System:** Semester, Summer Session Available **Enrollment:** FT 863, PT 59 **Faculty:** FT 45, PT 38 **Student-Faculty Ratio:** 16:1 **Exams:** SAT I or ACT **% Receiving Financial Aid:** 78 **% Residing in College-Owned, -Operated, or -Affiliated Housing:** 63 **Library Holdings:** 139,082 **Regional Accreditation:** Southern Association of Colleges and Schools **Credit Hours For Degree:** 54 credit hours, Associates; 126 credit hours, Bachelors **Professional Accreditation:** AABC, NASM **Intercollegiate Athletics:** Baseball M; Basketball M & W; Cross-Country Running M & W; Soccer M & W; Volleyball W

TRUETT-MCCONNELL COLLEGE
100 Alumni Dr.
Cleveland, GA 30528
Tel: (706)865-2134
Fax: (706)219-3339
E-mail: ploggins@truett.edu
Web Site: http://www.truett.edu/
President/CEO: Dr. T. Clark Bryan
Registrar: Carol Parker
Admissions: Penny Loggins
Financial Aid: Robert Gregory
Type: Two-Year College **Sex:** Coed **Affiliation:** Baptist **Scores:** 85% SAT V 400+; 81% SAT M 400+; 46% ACT 18-23; 1% ACT 24-29 **% Accepted:** 42 **Admission Plans:** Early Admission; Deferred Admission **Application Deadline:** August 01 **Application Fee:** $25.00 **H.S. Requirements:** High school diploma required; GED accepted **Costs Per Year:** Application fee: $25. Comprehensive fee: $17,450 includes full-time tuition ($11,950), mandatory fees ($500), and college room and board ($5000). College room only: $2300. Part-time tuition: $398 per credit hour. Part-time mandatory fees: $250 per term. **Scholarships:** Available **Calendar System:** Semester, Summer Session Available **Enrollment:** FT 340, PT 35 **Faculty:** FT 25, PT 19 **Student-Faculty Ratio:** 11:1 **Exams:** SAT I or ACT **% Residing in College-Owned, -Operated, or -Affiliated Housing:** 73 **Library Holdings:** 30,779 **Regional Accreditation:** Southern Association of Colleges and Schools **Credit Hours For Degree:** 61 semester hours, Associates; 120 semester hours, Bachelors **Professional Accreditation:** NASM **Intercollegiate Athletics:** Baseball M; Basketball M & W; Cross-Country Running M & W; Golf M; Soccer M & W; Softball W

UNIVERSITY OF GEORGIA
Athens, GA 30602
Tel: (706)542-3000
Admissions: (706)542-8776
E-mail: adm-info@uga.edu
Web Site: http://www.uga.edu/
President/CEO: Dr. Michael F. Adams
Registrar: Rebecca L. Macon
Admissions: Nancy McDuff
Financial Aid: Susan D. Little
Type: University **Sex:** Coed **Affiliation:** University System of Georgia **Scores:** 99.77% SAT V 400+; 99.9% SAT M 400+; 19.2% ACT 18-23; 66% ACT 24-29 **% Accepted:** 65 **Admission Plans:** Early Admission; Early Action; Deferred Admission **Application Deadline:** January 15 **Application Fee:** $50.00 **H.S. Requirements:** High school diploma required; GED accepted **Costs Per Year:** Application fee: $50. State resident tuition: $3638 full-time, $152 per credit part-time. Nonresident tuition: $15,858 full-time, $661 per credit part-time. Mandatory fees: $990 full-time, $495 per term part-time. Full-time tuition and fees vary according to course load, location, program, and reciprocity agreements. Part-time tuition and fees vary according to course load, location, program, and reciprocity agreements. College room and board: $6376. College room only: $3436. Room and board charges vary according to board plan and housing facility. **Scholarships:** Available **Calendar System:** Semester, Summer Session Available **Enrollment:** FT 22,730, PT 2,474, Grad 6,835 **Faculty:** FT 1,661, PT 450 **Student-Faculty Ratio:** 18:1 **Exams:** Other, SAT I or ACT, SAT II **% Receiving Financial Aid:** 25 **% Residing in College-Owned, -Operated, or -Affiliated Housing:** 27 **Library Holdings:** 3,955,004 **Regional Accreditation:** Southern Association of Colleges and Schools **Credit Hours For Degree:** 65 semester hours, Associates; 120 semester hours, Bachelors **ROTC:** Army, Air Force **Professional Accreditation:** AACSB, ABET, ACEJMC, AAMFT, AAFCS, ABA, ACPhE, ACA, ADtA, APA, ASLA, ASLHA, AVMA, AALS, CSWE, FIDER, JRCEPAT, NASAD, NASM, NASPAA NAST, NCATE, NRPA, SAF **Intercollegiate Athletics:** Baseball M; Basketball M & W; Cheerleading M & W; Cross-Country Running M & W; Equestrian Sports M & W; Football M; Golf M & W; Gymnastics W; Soccer M & W; Softball W; Swimming and Diving M & W; Tennis M & W; Track and Field M & W; Volleyball M & W

UNIVERSITY OF PHOENIX-ATLANTA CAMPUS
8200 Roberts Dr., Ste. 300
Atlanta, GA 30350-4153
Tel: (678)731-0555
Free: 800-228-7240
Admissions: (480)557-1712
Fax: (770)821-5399
Web Site: http://www.phoenix.edu/
President/CEO: Shane Clem
Admissions: Nina Omelchanko
Type: Comprehensive **Sex:** Coed **Admission Plans:** Open Admission; Deferred Admission **Application Deadline:** Rolling **Application Fee:** $110.00 **H.S. Requirements:** High school diploma required; GED accepted **Costs Per Year:** Application fee: $110. Tuition: $10,590 full-time, $353 per credit part-time. Mandatory fees: $560 full-time, $70 per course part-time. **Scholarships:** Available **Calendar System:** Continuous, Summer Session Not available **Enrollment:** FT 1,741, Grad 754 **Faculty:** FT 9, PT 208 **Student-Faculty Ratio:** 9:1 **Library Holdings:** 444 **Regional Accreditation:** North Central Association of Colleges and Schools **Credit Hours For Degree:** 60 credits, Associates; 120 credits, Bachelors **Professional Accreditation:** NLN

UNIVERSITY OF PHOENIX-COLUMBUS GEORGIA CAMPUS
4747 Hamilton Rd., Ste. E
Columbus, GA 31904
Tel: (706)320-1262
Free: 800-228-7240
Admissions: (480)557-1712
Web Site: http://www.phoenix.edu/
Admissions: Nina Omelchanko
Type: Comprehensive **Sex:** Coed **Admission Plans:** Open Admission; Deferred Admission **Application Deadline:** Rolling **Application Fee:** $110.00 **H.S. Requirements:** High school diploma required; GED accepted **Costs Per Year:** Application fee: $110. Tuition: $10,320 full-time, $344 per credit part-time. Mandatory fees: $560 full-time, $70 per course part-time. **Scholarships:** Available **Calendar System:** Continuous, Summer Session

Not available **Enrollment:** FT 581, Grad 95 **Faculty:** FT 9, PT 73 **Student-Faculty Ratio:** 8:1 **Library Holdings:** 444 **Regional Accreditation:** North Central Association of Colleges and Schools **Credit Hours For Degree:** 60 credits, Associates; 120 credits, Bachelors

UNIVERSITY OF WEST GEORGIA
1601 Maple St.
Carrollton, GA 30118
Tel: (678)839-5000
Admissions: (678)839-4000
E-mail: admiss@westga.edu
Web Site: http://www.westga.edu/
President/CEO: Dr. Beheruz N. Sethna
Registrar: Bonita Stevens
Admissions: Dr. Robert Johnson
Financial Aid: Kimberly Jordan
Type: Comprehensive **Sex:** Coed **Affiliation:** University System of Georgia **Scores:** 100% SAT V 400+; 100% SAT M 400+; 74% ACT 18-23; 15% ACT 24-29 **% Accepted:** 55 **Admission Plans:** Early Admission **Application Deadline:** July 01 **Application Fee:** $20.00 **H.S. Requirements:** High school diploma required; GED not accepted. For nontraditional students: High school diploma required; GED accepted **Costs Per Year:** Application fee: $20. State resident tuition: $2438 full-time, $102 per semester hour part-time. Nonresident tuition: $9754 full-time, $407 per semester hour part-time. Mandatory fees: $832 full-time, $25.17 per semester hour part-time, $114 per term part-time. Full-time tuition and fees vary according to course load. Part-time tuition and fees vary according to course load. College room and board: $5568. College room only: $3540. Room and board charges vary according to board plan and housing facility. **Scholarships:** Available **Calendar System:** Semester, Summer Session Available **Enrollment:** FT 6,921, PT 1,425, Grad 1,809 **Faculty:** FT 383, PT 135 **Student-Faculty Ratio:** 19:1 **Exams:** SAT I or ACT **% Receiving Financial Aid:** 49 **% Residing in College-Owned, -Operated, or -Affiliated Housing:** 30 **Library Holdings:** 391,330 **Regional Accreditation:** Southern Association of Colleges and Schools **Credit Hours For Degree:** 120 semester hours, Bachelors **ROTC:** Army **Professional Accreditation:** AACSB, ABET, AACN, ACA, NASAD, NASM, NASPAA, NAST, NCATE, NLN **Intercollegiate Athletics:** Baseball M; Basketball M & W; Cheerleading M & W; Cross-Country Running M & W; Football M; Golf M & W; Soccer W; Softball W; Volleyball W

VALDOSTA STATE UNIVERSITY
1500 North Patterson St.
Valdosta, GA 31698
Tel: (229)333-5800
Free: 800-618-1878
Admissions: (229)333-5791
Fax: (229)333-5482
E-mail: wpeacock@valdosta.edu
Web Site: http://www.valdosta.edu/
President/CEO: Ronald M. Zaccari
Registrar: Gerald Wright
Admissions: Walter Peacock
Financial Aid: Douglas Tanner
Type: University **Sex:** Coed **Affiliation:** University System of Georgia **Scores:** 100% SAT V 400+; 100% SAT M 400+; 78% ACT 18-23; 12% ACT 24-29 **% Accepted:** 63 **Admission Plans:** Early Admission **Application Deadline:** July 01 **Application Fee:** $20.00 **H.S. Requirements:** High school diploma required; GED not accepted **Costs Per Year:** Application fee: $20. State resident tuition: $2438 full-time, $102 per semester hour part-time. Nonresident tuition: $9754 full-time, $407 per semester hour part-time. Mandatory fees: $840 full-time, $38. Part-time tuition and fees vary according to course load. College room and board: $5524. College room only: $2904. Room and board charges vary according to board plan and housing facility. **Scholarships:** Available **Calendar System:** Semester, Summer Session Available **Enrollment:** FT 7,557, PT 1,536, Grad 1,410 **Faculty:** FT 435, PT 110 **Student-Faculty Ratio:** 20:1 **Exams:** SAT I or ACT, SAT I and SAT II or ACT, SAT II **% Receiving Financial Aid:** 51 **% Residing in College-Owned, -Operated, or -Affiliated Housing:** 17 **Library Holdings:** 467,560 **Regional Accreditation:** Southern Association of Colleges and Schools **Credit Hours For Degree:** 60 semester hours, Associates; 120 semester hours, Bachelors **ROTC:** Air Force **Professional Accreditation:** AACSB, AAMFT, AACN, ADA, ASLHA, CSWE, JRCEPAT, NASAD, NASM, NASPAA, NAST, NCATE, NLN **Intercollegiate Athletics:** Baseball M; Basketball M & W; Cross-Country Running M & W; Football M; Golf M; Softball W; Tennis M & W; Volleyball W

VALDOSTA TECHNICAL COLLEGE
4089 Val Tech Rd.
PO Box 928
Valdosta, GA 31603-0928
Tel: (229)333-2100
Admissions: (229)333-1394
Fax: (229)333-2129
E-mail: aleavy@valdostatech.edu
Web Site: http://www.valdostatech.edu/
President/CEO: James Bridges
Admissions: Amanda Leavy
Type: Two-Year College **Sex:** Coed **Affiliation:** Georgia Department of Technical and Adult Education **Admission Plans:** Open Admission; Deferred Admission **Application Fee:** $15.00 **H.S. Requirements:** High school diploma or equivalent not required **Costs Per Year:** Application fee: $15. State resident tuition: $1116 full-time, $31 per credit hour part-time. Nonresident tuition: $2232 full-time, $62 per credit hour part-time. **Calendar System:** Quarter **Enrollment:** FT 992, PT 1,452 **Faculty:** FT 67, PT 119 **Exams:** Other **Library Holdings:** 3,373 **Professional Accreditation:** ADA, COE, JRCERT, NAACLS

WAYCROSS COLLEGE
2001 South Georgia Parkway
Waycross, GA 31503-9248
Tel: (912)285-6133
Fax: (912)287-4909
E-mail: jporter@mail.way.peachnet.edu
Web Site: http://www.waycross.edu/
President/CEO: Dr. Barbara P. Losty
Registrar: Dr. Robert T. Stewart
Admissions: J. Porter
Financial Aid: William E. Deason
Type: Two-Year College **Sex:** Coed **Affiliation:** University System of Georgia **Admission Plans:** Early Admission; Deferred Admission **Application Fee:** $20.00 **H.S. Requirements:** High school diploma required; GED accepted **Scholarships:** Available **Calendar System:** Semester, Summer Session Available **Enrollment:** FT 326, PT 700 **Faculty:** FT 20, PT 27 **Student-Faculty Ratio:** 22:1 **Exams:** SAT I or ACT **Library Holdings:** 32,461 **Regional Accreditation:** Southern Association of Colleges and Schools **Credit Hours For Degree:** 60 semester hours, Associates

WESLEYAN COLLEGE
4760 Forsyth Rd.
Macon, GA 31210-4462
Tel: (478)477-1110
Free: 800-447-6610
Admissions: (478)757-5206
Fax: (478)757-4030
E-mail: admissions@wesleyancollege.edu
Web Site: http://www.wesleyancollege.edu/
President/CEO: Ruth A. Knox
Registrar: Patricia Hardeman
Admissions: Patricia Gibbs
Financial Aid: Sylvia Jones
Type: Comprehensive **Affiliation:** United Methodist **Scores:** 100% SAT V 400+; 100% SAT M 400+; 63% ACT 18-23; 25% ACT 24-29 **% Accepted:** 55 **Admission Plans:** Early Admission; Early Action; Early Decision Plan; Deferred Admission **Application Deadline:** April 01 **Application Fee:** $30.00 **H.S. Requirements:** High school diploma required; GED accepted **Costs Per Year:** Application fee: $30. Comprehensive fee: $19,560 includes full-time tuition ($11,260), mandatory fees ($850), and college room and board ($7450). Full-time tuition and fees vary according to class time, course load, and program. Room and board charges vary according to board plan and housing facility. Part-time tuition: $355 per semester hour. Part-time tuition varies according to class time, course load, and program. **Scholarships:** Available **Calendar System:** Semester, Summer Session Available **Enrollment:** FT 400, PT 151, Grad 89 **Faculty:** FT 47, PT 33 **Student-Faculty Ratio:** 8:1 **Exams:** SAT I or ACT **% Receiving Financial Aid:** 62 **% Residing in College-Owned, -Operated, or -Affiliated Housing:** 63 **Library Holdings:** 141,818 **Regional Accreditation:** Southern Association of Colleges and Schools **Credit Hours For Degree:** 120 semester hours, Bachelors **Professional Accreditation:** NASM **Intercollegiate Athletics:** Basketball W; Equestrian Sports W; Soccer W; Softball W; Tennis W; Volleyball W

WEST CENTRAL TECHNICAL COLLEGE
176 Murphy Campus Blvd.
Waco, GA 30182
Tel: (770)537-6000
Admissions: (770)537-5712
Fax: (770)836-4719
E-mail: malderhold@westcentral.edu
Web Site: http://www.westcentraltech.edu/
President/CEO: Janet B. Ayers
Admissions: Mary Alderhold
Financial Aid: Judy Akers
Type: Two-Year College **Sex:** Coed **Affiliation:** Georgia Department of Technical and Adult Education **Admission Plans:** Open Admission; Deferred Admission **Application Fee:** $25.00 **H.S. Requirements:** High school diploma or equivalent not required **Costs Per Year:** Application fee: $25. State resident tuition: $1116 full-time, $31 per credit hour part-time. Nonresident tuition: $2232 full-time, $62 per credit hour part-time. **Scholarships:** Available **Calendar System:** Quarter **Enrollment:** FT 877, PT 2,011 **Faculty:** FT 83, PT 227 **Exams:** Other **Library Holdings:** 18,462 **Regional Accreditation:** Southern Association of Colleges and Schools **Credit Hours For Degree:** 120 credit hours, Associates **Professional Accreditation:** ADA, COE, NAACLS

WEST GEORGIA TECHNICAL COLLEGE
303 Fort Dr.
LaGrange, GA 30240
Tel: (706)845-4323
Admissions: (706)837-4244
Fax: (706)845-4339
E-mail: lbasham@westgatech.edu
Web Site: http://www.westgatech.edu/
President/CEO: Daryl Gilley
Admissions: Lori Basham
Type: Two-Year College **Sex:** Coed **Affiliation:** Georgia Department of Technical and Adult Education **Admission Plans:** Open Admission; Deferred Admission **Application Fee:** $15.00 **H.S. Requirements:** High school diploma or equivalent not required **Costs Per Year:** Application fee: $15. State resident tuition: $1116 full-time, $31 per credit hour part-time. Nonresident tuition: $2232 full-time, $62 per credit hour part-time. **Scholarships:** Available **Calendar System:** Quarter **Enrollment:** FT 843, PT 1,015 **Faculty:** FT 46, PT 96 **Exams:** Other **Library Holdings:** 19,683 **Professional Accreditation:** COE

WESTWOOD COLLEGE-ATLANTA MIDTOWN
1100 Spring St.
Atlanta, GA 30309
Tel: (404)745-9096
Admissions: (404)870-8982
Fax: (404)892-7253
Web Site: http://www.westwood.edu/
President/CEO: Bill Armour
Admissions: Rory Laney
Type: Two-Year College **Sex:** Coed **Application Fee:** $100.00 **Calendar System:** Continuous **Professional Accreditation:** ACCSCT

WESTWOOD COLLEGE-ATLANTA NORTHLAKE
2220 Parklake Dr.
Ste. 175
Atlanta, GA 30345
Tel: (404)962-2999
Web Site: http://www.westwood.edu/ **Type:** Four-Year College **Sex:** Coed **Application Fee:** $0.00 **Student-Faculty Ratio:** 12:1

YOUNG HARRIS COLLEGE
PO Box 98
Young Harris, GA 30582-0098
Tel: (706)379-3111
Fax: (706)379-4306
E-mail: admissions@yhc.edu
Web Site: http://www.yhc.edu/
President/CEO: Dr. Thomas S. Yow, III
Registrar: Pat Strickland
Admissions: Clinton G. Hobbs
Financial Aid: Linda Adams
Type: Two-Year College **Sex:** Coed **Affiliation:** United Methodist **Scores:** 96% SAT V 400+; 95% SAT M 400+; 51% ACT 18-23; 28% ACT 24-29 **% Accepted:** 58 **Admission Plans:** Early Admission; Deferred Admission **Application Deadline:** Rolling **Application Fee:** $30.00 **H.S. Requirements:** High school diploma required; GED accepted **Costs Per Year:** Application fee: $30. Comprehensive fee: $19,510 includes full-time tuition ($14,730) and college room and board ($4780). College room only: $1970. Part-time tuition: $500 per hour. **Scholarships:** Available **Calendar System:** Semester, Summer Session Available **Enrollment:** FT 508, PT 25 **Faculty:** FT 50, PT 4 **Student-Faculty Ratio:** 14:1 **Exams:** SAT I or ACT **% Residing in College-Owned, -Operated, or -Affiliated Housing:** 90 **Library Holdings:** 55,201 **Regional Accreditation:** Southern Association of Colleges and Schools **Credit Hours For Degree:** 62 semester hours, Associates **Professional Accreditation:** NASM **Intercollegiate Athletics:** Baseball M; Soccer M & W; Softball W; Tennis W

GUAM COMMUNITY COLLEGE
PO Box 23069 Guam Main Facility
Barrigada, GU 96921-3069
Tel: (671)735-4422
Admissions: (671)735-5531
Fax: (671)734-5238
Web Site: http://www.guamcc.net/
President/CEO: John T. Cruz
Registrar: Deborah D. Leon Guerrero
Admissions: Patrick L. Clymer
Financial Aid: Micki Lonsdale
Type: Two-Year College **Sex:** Coed **Admission Plans:** Open Admission; Early Admission **Application Deadline:** Rolling **Application Fee:** $0.00 **H.S. Requirements:** High school diploma required; GED accepted. For some adult applicants: High school diploma or equivalent not required **Costs Per Year:** Application fee: $0. Area resident tuition: $2100 full-time. Nonresident tuition: $2850 full-time. Mandatory fees: $244 full-time. **Scholarships:** Available **Calendar System:** Semester, Summer Session Available **Enrollment:** FT 504, PT 2,337 **Faculty:** FT 74, PT 46 **Library Holdings:** 15,806 **Regional Accreditation:** Western Association of Schools and Colleges **Credit Hours For Degree:** 60 semester hours, Associates **ROTC:** Army **Professional Accreditation:** AAMAE

PACIFIC ISLANDS BIBLE COLLEGE
PO Box 22619
Guam Main Facility, GU 96921-2619
Tel: (671)734-1812
Fax: (671)734-1813
E-mail: guamcampus@pibc.edu
Web Site: http://www.pibc-edu.org/
President/CEO: Dr. William P. Wood
Admissions: Karin Schulz
Type: Four-Year College **Sex:** Coed **Affiliation:** interdenominational **Application Deadline:** August 25 **Application Fee:** $25.00 **Costs Per Year:** Application fee: $25. Comprehensive fee: $8530 includes full-time tuition ($5400), mandatory fees ($270), and college room and board ($2860). Part-time tuition: $675 per course. Part-time mandatory fees: $85. **Calendar System:** Semester **Enrollment:** FT 132, PT 56 **Faculty:** FT 12, PT 10 **Student-Faculty Ratio:** 7:1 **Exams:** Other **Professional Accreditation:** TACCS

UNIVERSITY OF GUAM
UOG Station
Mangilao, GU 96923
Tel: (671)735-2350
Admissions: (671)735-2207
Fax: (671)734-6005
E-mail: admitme@uog9.uog.edu
Web Site: http://www.uog.edu/
President/CEO: Harold L. Allen
Registrar: Deborah Guerrero
Admissions: Deborah Guerrero
Type: Comprehensive **Sex:** Coed **% Accepted:** 99 **Admission Plans:** Open Admission; Early Admission; Deferred Admission **Application Deadline:** June 01 **Application Fee:** $49.00 **H.S. Requirements:** High school diploma required; GED accepted. For applicants 18 or over admitted as special students: High school diploma or equivalent not required **Costs Per Year:** Application fee: $49. Territory resident tuition: $3900 full-time, $130 per credit part-time. Nonresident tuition: $11,580 full-time, $386 per credit part-time. Mandatory fees: $450 full-time, $225 per term part-time. College room and board: $6918. College room only: $1555. **Scholarships:** Available **Calendar System:** Semester, Summer Session Available **Enrollment:** FT 2,042, PT 778, Grad 214 **Faculty:** FT 176, PT 78 **Student-Faculty Ratio:** 11:1 **Library Holdings:** 327,925 **Regional Accreditation:** Western Association of Schools and Colleges **Credit Hours For Degree:** 124 credits, Bachelors **ROTC:** Army **Professional Accreditation:** CSWE, NCATE, NLN **Intercollegiate Athletics:** Basketball M & W; Football M; Golf M; Soccer M; Volleyball M & W

ARGOSY UNIVERSITY/HAWAII
400 ASBTower, 1001 Bishop St.
Honolulu, HI 96813
Tel: (808)536-5555
Fax: (808)536-5505
Web Site: http://www.argosyu.edu/honolulu/
President/CEO: Jim Otten, PhD
Registrar: Heidi Ross
Financial Aid: Heidi Ross
Type: Two-Year Upper Division **Sex:** Coed **Scholarships:** Available **Calendar System:** Semester **% Receiving Financial Aid:** 43 **Regional Accreditation:** North Central Association of Colleges and Schools **Professional Accreditation:** APA

BRIGHAM YOUNG UNIVERSITY-HAWAII
55-220 Kulanui St.
Laie, HI 96762-1294
Tel: (808)293-3211
Admissions: (808)293-3731
Web Site: http://www.byuh.edu/
President/CEO: Dr. Eric B. Shumway
Registrar: Vernelle Lakatani
Admissions: Jeffrey N. Bunker
Financial Aid: Wes Duke
Type: Four-Year College **Sex:** Coed **Affiliation:** Latter-day Saints; Brigham Young University **Scores:** 85.72% SAT V 400+; 96.43% SAT M 400+; 59. 21% ACT 18-23; 28.95% ACT 24-29 **Admission Plans:** Preferred Admission; Early Admission; Deferred Admission **Application Fee:** $30.00 **H.S. Requirements:** High school diploma required; GED not accepted **Costs Per Year:** Application fee: $30. Comprehensive fee: $7740 includes full-time tuition ($2760) and college room and board ($4980). Full-time tuition varies according to course load. Room and board charges vary according to board plan and housing facility. Part-time tuition: $187 per credit. **Scholarships:** Available **Calendar System:** Miscellaneous, Summer Session Available **Enrollment:** FT 2,190, PT 296 **Faculty:** FT 111, PT 113 **Student-Faculty Ratio:** 15:1 **Exams:** ACT, SAT I or ACT **% Receiving Financial Aid:** 71 **% Residing in College-Owned, -Operated, or -Affiliated Housing:** 52 **Library Holdings:** 321,400 **Regional Accreditation:** Western Association of Schools and Colleges **Credit Hours For Degree:** 60 credits, Associates; 120 credits, Bachelors **ROTC:** Army, Navy, Air Force **Professional Accreditation:** CSWE **Intercollegiate Athletics:** Basketball M; Cross-Country Running M & W; Softball W; Tennis M & W; Volleyball W; Water Polo M

CHAMINADE UNIVERSITY OF HONOLULU
3140 Waialae Ave.
Honolulu, HI 96816-1578
Tel: (808)735-4711
Free: 800-735-3733
Admissions: (808)735-4735
Fax: (808)739-4647
E-mail: admissions@chaminade.edu
Web Site: http://www.chaminade.edu/
President/CEO: Dr. Mary Wesselkamper
Registrar: Marlene Baker
Admissions: Dr. Joy Bouey
Financial Aid: Joy Bouey
Type: Comprehensive **Sex:** Coed **Affiliation:** Roman Catholic **Scores:** 90% SAT V 400+; 85% SAT M 400+; 61% ACT 18-23; 22% ACT 24-29 **% Accepted:** 96 **Admission Plans:** Deferred Admission **Application Deadline:** Rolling **Application Fee:** $50.00 **H.S. Requirements:** High school diploma required; GED accepted **Costs Per Year:** Application fee: $50. Comprehensive fee: $24,340 includes full-time tuition ($14,820), mandatory fees ($140), and college room and board ($9380). College room only: $4980. Part-time tuition: $494 per credit. **Scholarships:** Available **Calendar System:** Semester, Summer Session Available **Enrollment:** FT 1,058, PT 48, Grad 704 **Faculty:** FT 82, PT 49 **Student-Faculty Ratio:** 11:1 **Exams:** SAT I or ACT **% Receiving Financial Aid:** 74 **Library Holdings:** 78,000 **Regional Accreditation:** Western Association of Schools and Colleges **Credit Hours For Degree:** 60 credit hours, Associates; 124 credit hours, Bachelors **ROTC:** Army, Air Force **Professional Accreditation:** MACTE **Intercollegiate Athletics:** Basketball M; Cross-Country Running M & W; Golf M & W; Softball W; Tennis M & W; Volleyball W; Water Polo M

HAWAII BUSINESS COLLEGE
33 South King St., Fourth Floor
Honolulu, HI 96813-4316
Tel: (808)524-4014
Fax: (808)524-0284
Web Site: http://www.hbc.edu/
President/CEO: Anne Omori
Registrar: Scot Perry
Admissions: Seira Puletasi
Type: Two-Year College **Sex:** Coed **Admission Plans:** Open Admission; Deferred Admission **Application Fee:** $30.00 **H.S. Requirements:** High school diploma required; GED accepted **Scholarships:** Available **Calendar System:** Quarter, Summer Session Available **Enrollment:** FT 279, PT 24 **Student-Faculty Ratio:** 15:1 **Exams:** Other **Library Holdings:** 1,000 **Credit Hours For Degree:** 90 credits, Associates **Professional Accreditation:** ACICS

HAWAII COMMUNITY COLLEGE
200 West Kawili St.
Hilo, HI 96720-4091
Tel: (808)974-7611
Admissions: (808)974-7661
Fax: (808)974-7692
Web Site: http://www.hawcc.hawaii.edu/
President/CEO: Sandra Sakaguchi
Registrar: David Loeding
Admissions: Tammy M. Tanaka
Financial Aid: Sheryl Lundberg-Sprague
Type: Two-Year College **Sex:** Coed **Affiliation:** University of Hawaii System **Admission Plans:** Open Admission; Early Admission **H.S. Requirements:** High school diploma or equivalent not required. For nursing program: High school diploma required; GED accepted **Calendar System:** Semester, Summer Session Available **Enrollment:** FT 1,025, PT 1,384 **Faculty:** FT 130, PT 130 **Regional Accreditation:** Western Association of Schools and Colleges **Credit Hours For Degree:** 60 credit hours, Associates **Professional Accreditation:** NLN

HAWAII PACIFIC UNIVERSITY
1166 Fort St.
Honolulu, HI 96813-2785

Tel: (808)544-0200; (866)225-5478
Admissions: (808)544-0238
Fax: (808)544-1136
E-mail: admissions@hpu.edu
Web Site: http://www.hpu.edu/
President/CEO: Chatt Wright
Registrar: Kelly Nashiro-Yoshida
Admissions: Scott Stensrud
Financial Aid: Catherine Ganung
Type: Comprehensive **Sex:** Coed **Scores:** 87% SAT V 400+; 89% SAT M 400+; 48% ACT 18-23; 30% ACT 24-29 **% Accepted:** 82 **Admission Plans:** Early Admission; Deferred Admission **Application Deadline:** Rolling **Application Fee:** $50.00 **H.S. Requirements:** High school diploma required; GED accepted **Costs Per Year:** Application fee: $50. Comprehensive fee: $21,080 includes full-time tuition ($11,550), mandatory fees ($80), and college room and board ($9450). Full-time tuition and fees vary according to course load, program, and student level. Room and board charges vary according to housing facility. Part-time tuition: $225 per credit. Part-time tuition varies according to course load. **Scholarships:** Available **Calendar System:** Semester, Summer Session Available **Enrollment:** FT 4,240, PT 2,671, Grad 1,135 **Faculty:** FT 238, PT 374 **Student-Faculty Ratio:** 16:1 **Exams:** SAT I or ACT **% Receiving Financial Aid:** 36 **% Residing in College-Owned, -Operated, or -Affiliated Housing:** 10 **Library Holdings:** 162,000 **Regional Accreditation:** Western Association of Schools and Colleges **Credit Hours For Degree:** 60 credits, Associates; 124 credits, Bachelors **ROTC:** Army, Air Force **Professional Accreditation:** CSWE, NLN **Intercollegiate Athletics:** Baseball M; Basketball M; Cheerleading M & W; Cross-Country Running M & W; Golf M & W; Soccer M & W; Softball W; Tennis M & W; Volleyball W

HAWAII THEOLOGICAL SEMINARY

20 Dowsett Ave.
Honolulu, HI 96817
Tel: (808)595-4247
Fax: (808)595-4779
E-mail: icgs@hawaii.rr.com
Web Site: http://www.icgshawaii.org/
President/CEO: Dr. Bong Rin Ro
Registrar: Carol White
Admissions: Jon Rawlings
Type: Two-Year Upper Division **Sex:** Coed **Affiliation:** interdenominational **Admission Plans:** Open Admission; Deferred Admission **Application Fee:** $50.00 **H.S. Requirements:** High school diploma required; GED accepted **Costs Per Year:** Application fee: $50. Tuition: $6150 full-time, $615 per course part-time. Mandatory fees: $200 full-time, $100 per term part-time. Full-time tuition and fees vary according to course load. Part-time tuition and fees vary according to course load. **Scholarships:** Available **Calendar System:** Semester, Summer Session Available **Enrollment:** FT 8, PT 14, Grad 32 **Faculty:** FT 3, PT 6 **Student-Faculty Ratio:** 8:1 **% Receiving Financial Aid:** 69 **Library Holdings:** 21,182 **Credit Hours For Degree:** 127 semester hours, Bachelors **Professional Accreditation:** TACCS

HAWAII TOKAI INTERNATIONAL COLLEGE

2241 Kapiolani Blvd.
Honolulu, HI 96826-4310
Tel: (808)983-4000
Admissions: (808)983-4154
Fax: (808)983-4107
E-mail: htic@tokai.edu
Web Site: http://www.tokai.edu/
President/CEO: Prof. Nobuyoshi Tanaka
Registrar: Richard Crandall
Admissions: Derrick Kerr
Type: Two-Year College **Sex:** Coed **Affiliation:** Tokai University Educational System (Japan) **% Accepted:** 100 **Admission Plans:** Deferred Admission **Application Deadline:** September 01 **Application Fee:** $50.00 **H.S. Requirements:** High school diploma required; GED accepted **Costs Per Year:** Application fee: $50. Tuition: $375 per credit part-time. **Scholarships:** Available **Calendar System:** Quarter, Summer Session Available **Enrollment:** FT 54 **Faculty:** FT 10, PT 14 **Student-Faculty Ratio:** 4:1 **% Residing in College-Owned, -Operated, or -Affiliated Housing:** 60 **Library Holdings:** 7,000 **Regional Accreditation:** Western Association of Schools and Colleges **Credit Hours For Degree:** 60 credits, Associates

HEALD COLLEGE-HONOLULU

1500 Kapiolani Blvd.
Honolulu, HI 96814-3797
Tel: (808)955-1500
Fax: (808)955-6964
Web Site: http://www.heald.edu/
President/CEO: Evelyn A. Schemmel
Registrar: Phyllis Miyamura
Type: Two-Year College **Sex:** Coed **Admission Plans:** Open Admission; Early Admission; Deferred Admission **Application Deadline:** Rolling **Application Fee:** $40.00 **H.S. Requirements:** High school diploma required; GED accepted **Scholarships:** Available **Calendar System:** Quarter, Summer Session Available **Enrollment:** FT 591, PT 216 **Faculty:** FT 30, PT 31 **Student-Faculty Ratio:** 17:1 **Exams:** Other **Regional Accreditation:** Western Association of Schools and Colleges **Professional Accreditation:** AAMAE

HONOLULU COMMUNITY COLLEGE

874 Dillingham Blvd.
Honolulu, HI 96817-4598
Tel: (808)845-9211
Admissions: (808)845-9129
E-mail: admission@hccadb.hcc.hawaii.edu
Web Site: http://www.honolulu.hawaii.edu/
President/CEO: Ramsey Pedersen
Registrar: Geri Imai
Admissions: Charles Anderson
Financial Aid: Jannine Oyama
Type: Two-Year College **Sex:** Coed **Affiliation:** University of Hawaii System **Admission Plans:** Open Admission; Preferred Admission; Early Admission **Application Fee:** $0.00 **H.S. Requirements:** High school diploma or equivalent not required. For cosmetology program: High school diploma required; GED accepted **Scholarships:** Available **Calendar System:** Semester, Summer Session Available **Enrollment:** FT 1,672, PT 2,566 **Faculty:** FT 112, PT 71 **Student-Faculty Ratio:** 23:1 **Library Holdings:** 54,902 **Regional Accreditation:** Western Association of Schools and Colleges **Credit Hours For Degree:** 60 semester hours, Associates **ROTC:** Army, Air Force

KAPIOLANI COMMUNITY COLLEGE

4303 Diamond Head Rd.
Honolulu, HI 96816-4421
Tel: (808)734-9111
Admissions: (808)734-9897
Web Site: http://www.kcc.hawaii.edu/
President/CEO: Dr. John Morton
Admissions: Cynthia Suzuki
Financial Aid: Coleen Araki
Type: Two-Year College **Sex:** Coed **Affiliation:** University of Hawaii System **% Accepted:** 92 **Admission Plans:** Open Admission; Preferred Admission; Early Admission **Application Deadline:** July 01 **H.S. Requirements:** High school diploma or equivalent not required. For nursing, health sciences, paralegal programs: High school diploma required; GED accepted **Costs Per Year:** State resident tuition: $1344 full-time, $56 per credit hour part-time. Nonresident tuition: $5976 full-time, $249 per credit hour part-time. Mandatory fees: $60 full-time, $2 per credit hour part-time, $10 per term part-time. **Scholarships:** Available **Calendar System:** Semester, Summer Session Available **Enrollment:** FT 2,833, PT 4,341 **Faculty:** FT 200, PT 144 **Library Holdings:** 50,000 **Regional Accreditation:** Western Association of Schools and Colleges **Credit Hours For Degree:** 60 credits, Associates **ROTC:** Army, Air Force **Professional Accreditation:** AAMAE, ACF, AOTA, APTA, CARC, JRCERT, NAACLS, NLN

KAUAI COMMUNITY COLLEGE

3-1901 Kaumualii Hwy.
Lihue, HI 96766
Tel: (808)245-8311
Admissions: (808)245-8225
Fax: (808)245-8297
E-mail: leighton@hawaii.edu
Web Site: http://kauai.hawaii.edu/

President/CEO: Peggy Cha
Registrar: Leighton Oride
Admissions: Leighton Oride
Financial Aid: Frances Dinnan
Type: Two-Year College **Sex:** Coed **Affiliation:** University of Hawaii System **Admission Plans:** Open Admission; Preferred Admission; Early Admission **Application Deadline:** August 01 **Application Fee:** $0.00 **H.S. Requirements:** High school diploma or equivalent not required. For nursing program: High school diploma required; GED accepted **Costs Per Year:** Application fee: $0. State resident tuition: $1176 full-time, $49 per credit part-time. Nonresident tuition: $5808 full-time, $242 per credit part-time. Mandatory fees: $15 full-time, $1.25 per credit part-time. Full-time tuition and fees vary according to course load. Part-time tuition and fees vary according to course load. **Scholarships:** Available **Calendar System:** Semester, Summer Session Available **Library Holdings:** 51,875 **Regional Accreditation:** Western Association of Schools and Colleges **Credit Hours For Degree:** 60 credits, Associates **Professional Accreditation:** NLN

LEEWARD COMMUNITY COLLEGE
96-045 Ala Ike
Pearl City, HI 96782-3393
Tel: (808)455-0011
Admissions: (808)455-0219
Fax: (808)455-0471
Web Site: http://www.lcc.hawaii.edu/
President/CEO: Sharon Narimatsu
Registrar: Warren Mau
Admissions: Warren Mau
Financial Aid: Valerie Chun
Type: Two-Year College **Sex:** Coed **Affiliation:** University of Hawaii System **Admission Plans:** Open Admission; Preferred Admission; Early Admission **Application Fee:** $25.00 **H.S. Requirements:** High school diploma required; GED accepted. For applicants 18 or over: High school diploma or equivalent not required **Scholarships:** Available **Calendar System:** Semester, Summer Session Available **Faculty:** FT 179, PT 57 **Library Holdings:** 62,000 **Regional Accreditation:** Western Association of Schools and Colleges **Credit Hours For Degree:** 60 credits, Associates **ROTC:** Army, Air Force **Professional Accreditation:** ACF

MAUI COMMUNITY COLLEGE
310 Kaahumanu Ave.
Kahului, HI 96732
Tel: (808)984-3500
Free: 800-479-6692
Admissions: (808)984-3267
Fax: (808)242-9618
E-mail: kameda@hawaii.edu
Web Site: http://mauicc.hawaii.edu/
President/CEO: Dr. Clyde Sakamoto
Registrar: Stephen Kameda
Admissions: Stephen Kameda
Financial Aid: Paula Purdy
Type: Two-Year College **Sex:** Coed **Affiliation:** University of Hawaii System **Admission Plans:** Open Admission; Early Admission **Application Fee:** $25.00 **H.S. Requirements:** High school diploma or equivalent not required **Scholarships:** Available **Calendar System:** Semester, Summer Session Available **Enrollment:** FT 978, PT 1,679 **Faculty:** FT 89, PT 5 **Exams:** Other **% Residing in College-Owned, -Operated, or -Affiliated Housing:** 75 **Library Holdings:** 49,812 **Regional Accreditation:** Western Association of Schools and Colleges **Credit Hours For Degree:** 60 credits, Associates **Professional Accreditation:** ACF, ADA, NLN

REMINGTON COLLEGE-HONOLULU CAMPUS
1111 Bishop St., Ste. 400
Honolulu, HI 96813
Tel: (808)942-1000
Fax: (808)533-3064
E-mail: ken.heinemann@remingtoncollege.edu
Web Site: http://www.remingtoncollege.edu/
President/CEO: Kenneth Heinemann
Admissions: Kenneth G. Heinemann
Type: Four-Year College **Sex:** Coed **Professional Accreditation:** ACICS

TRANSPACIFIC HAWAII COLLEGE
5257 Kalanianaole Hwy.
Honolulu, HI 96821-1884
Tel: (808)377-5402
Fax: (808)373-4754
E-mail: jnorris@transpacific.org
Web Site: http://www.transpacific.org/
President/CEO: Dr. John Norris
Registrar: Rachel Enomoto
Admissions: Dr. John Norris
Type: Two-Year College **Sex:** Coed **% Accepted:** 89 **Admission Plans:** Open Admission; Preferred Admission; Early Admission; Deferred Admission **Application Deadline:** August 05 **Application Fee:** $50.00 **H.S. Requirements:** High school diploma required; GED accepted **Costs Per Year:** Application fee: $50. Tuition: $16,250 full-time. **Calendar System:** Quarter, Summer Session Not available **Enrollment:** FT 240 **Faculty:** FT 16, PT 29 **Student-Faculty Ratio:** 5:1 **Library Holdings:** 606 **Regional Accreditation:** Western Association of Schools and Colleges

UNIVERSITY OF HAWAII AT HILO
200 West Kawili St.
Hilo, HI 96720-4091
Tel: (808)974-7311
Free: 800-897-4456
Admissions: (808)974-7414
Fax: (808)933-0861
E-mail: uhhao@uhhadc.uhh.hawaii.edu
Web Site: http://www.uhh.hawaii.edu/
President/CEO: Dr. Rose Y. Tseng
Registrar: Cathy Zenz
Admissions: James Cromwell
Financial Aid: Jeff R. Scofield
Type: Comprehensive **Sex:** Coed **Affiliation:** University of Hawaii System **Scores:** 90% SAT V 400+; 94% SAT M 400+ **Admission Plans:** Deferred Admission **Application Fee:** $40.00 **H.S. Requirements:** High school diploma required; GED accepted **Costs Per Year:** Application fee: $40. State resident tuition: $2472 full-time, $103 per credit hour part-time. Nonresident tuition: $8040 full-time, $335 per credit hour part-time. Mandatory fees: $132 full-time. College room and board: $5374. College room only: $2774. **Scholarships:** Available **Calendar System:** Semester, Summer Session Available **Faculty:** FT 171, PT 93 **Student-Faculty Ratio:** 14:1 **Exams:** SAT I or ACT **% Receiving Financial Aid:** 69 **% Residing in College-Owned, -Operated, or -Affiliated Housing:** 29 **Library Holdings:** 250,000 **Regional Accreditation:** Western Association of Schools and Colleges **Credit Hours For Degree:** 120 semester hours, Bachelors **Professional Accreditation:** NLN **Intercollegiate Athletics:** Baseball M; Basketball M; Cross-Country Running M & W; Golf M; Softball W; Tennis M & W; Volleyball W

UNIVERSITY OF HAWAII AT MANOA
2500 Campus Rd.
Honolulu, HI 96822
Tel: (808)956-8111
Free: 800-823-9771
Admissions: (808)956-8975
E-mail: ar-info@hawaii.edu
Web Site: http://www.uhm.hawaii.edu/
President/CEO: Dr. Peter Englert
Registrar: Stuart Lau
Admissions: Janice Heu
Financial Aid: Gail C. Koki
Type: University **Sex:** Coed **Scores:** 97.4% SAT V 400+; 99.9% SAT M 400+; 50% ACT 18-23; 40.8% ACT 24-29 **% Accepted:** 68 **Admission Plans:** Preferred Admission **Application Deadline:** May 01 **Application Fee:** $50.00 **H.S. Requirements:** High school diploma required; GED accepted **Costs Per Year:** Application fee: $50. State resident tuition: $4320 full-time, $180 per credit hour part-time. Nonresident tuition: $12,942 full-time, $508 per credit hour part-time. Mandatory fees: $193 full-time. Full-time tuition and fees vary according to class time, course load, program, and reciprocity agreements. Part-time tuition varies according to class time, course load, program, and reciprocity agreements. College room and board: $6690. College room only: $4232. Room and board charges vary according to board plan and housing facility. **Scholarships:** Available **Calendar System:** Semester, Summer Session Available **Enrollment:** FT 11,857, PT 2,494, Grad 5,653 **Faculty:** FT 1,086, PT 83 **Student-Faculty Ratio:** 12:1 **Exams:** SAT I or ACT **% Receiving Financial Aid:** 32 **% Residing in College-Owned, -Operated, or -Affiliated Housing:** 13 **Library Holdings:** 3,234,881 **Regional Accreditation:** Western Association of Schools and

Colleges **Credit Hours For Degree:** 124 semester hours, Bachelors **ROTC:** Army, Air Force **Professional Accreditation:** AACSB, ABET, ACEJMC, AACN, ABA, ACA, ADA, ACSP, ALA, APA, ASLHA, AALS, CEPH, CORE, CSWE, LCMEAMA, NAACLS, NASM, NCATE, NLN **Intercollegiate Athletics:** Baseball M; Basketball M & W; Cross-Country Running W; Football M; Golf M & W; Rugby M; Sailing M & W; Soccer W; Softball W; Swimming and Diving M & W; Tennis M & W; Track and Field W; Volleyball M & W; Water Polo W

UNIVERSITY OF HAWAII-WEST OAHU
96-129 Ala Ike
Pearl City, HI 96782-3366
Tel: (808)454-4700
Admissions: (808)453-4700
E-mail: robyno@hawaii.edu
Web Site: http://www.uhwo.hawaii.edu/
President/CEO: Dr. William A. Pearman
Registrar: Dan Cormony
Admissions: Robyn Oshiro
Financial Aid: Jennifer Bradley
Type: Two-Year Upper Division **Sex:** Coed **Affiliation:** University of Hawaii System **% Accepted:** 86 **Admission Plans:** Preferred Admission **Application Fee:** $50.00 **H.S. Requirements:** High school diploma or equivalent not required **Costs Per Year:** Application fee: $50. State resident tuition: $2736 full-time, $114 per credit part-time. Nonresident tuition: $8784 full-time, $366 per credit part-time. Mandatory fees: $10 full-time, $5 per term part-time. **Scholarships:** Available **Calendar System:** Semester, Summer Session Available **Enrollment:** FT 284, PT 568 **Faculty:** FT 28, PT 20 **Student-Faculty Ratio:** 13:1 **% Receiving Financial Aid:** 44 **Library Holdings:** 25,000 **Regional Accreditation:** Western Association of Schools and Colleges **Credit Hours For Degree:** 120 credits, Bachelors **ROTC:** Army, Air Force

UNIVERSITY OF PHOENIX-HAWAII CAMPUS
827 Fort St.
Honolulu, HI 96813-4317
Tel: (808)536-2686
Free: 800-228-7240
Admissions: (480)557-1712
Web Site: http://www.phoenix.edu/
President/CEO: Dr. Laura Palmer Noone
Registrar: Tandy Elisala
Admissions: Nina Omelchanko
Financial Aid: Robert Collins
Type: Comprehensive **Sex:** Coed **Admission Plans:** Open Admission; Deferred Admission **Application Deadline:** Rolling **Application Fee:** $110.00 **H.S. Requirements:** High school diploma required; GED accepted **Costs Per Year:** Application fee: $110. Tuition: $11,550 full-time, $385 per credit part-time. Mandatory fees: $560 full-time, $70 per course part-time. **Scholarships:** Available **Calendar System:** Continuous, Summer Session Not available **Enrollment:** FT 907, Grad 441 **Faculty:** FT 4, PT 202 **Student-Faculty Ratio:** 6:1 **Regional Accreditation:** North Central Association of Colleges and Schools **Credit Hours For Degree:** 60 credits, Associates; 120 credits, Bachelors **Professional Accreditation:** NLN

WINDWARD COMMUNITY COLLEGE
45-720 Keaahala Rd.
Kaneohe, HI 96744-3528
Tel: (808)235-7400
Web Site: http://www.wcc.hawaii.edu/
President/CEO: Dr. Angela Meixell
Registrar: Russell Chan
Admissions: Russell Chan
Financial Aid: Steven Chigawa
Type: Two-Year College **Sex:** Coed **Affiliation:** University of Hawaii System **Admission Plans:** Open Admission; Preferred Admission; Early Admission **Application Fee:** $25.00 **H.S. Requirements:** High school diploma or equivalent not required **Costs Per Year:** Application fee: $25. State resident tuition: $1176 full-time, $49 per credit part-time. Nonresident tuition: $5808 full-time, $242 per credit part-time. Mandatory fees: $40 full-time. **Scholarships:** Available **Calendar System:** Semester, Summer Session Available **Regional Accreditation:** Western Association of Schools and Colleges **Credit Hours For Degree:** 60 credits, Associates **ROTC:** Army, Air Force

ALBERTSON COLLEGE OF IDAHO

2112 Cleveland Blvd.
Caldwell, ID 83605-4494
Tel: (208)459-5011
Free: 800-244-3246
Admissions: (208)459-5689
Fax: (208)454-2077
E-mail: admission@albertson.edu
Web Site: http://www.albertson.edu/
President/CEO: Dr. Robert Hoover
Registrar: E. Ann Kuck
Admissions: Charlene Brown
Financial Aid: Juanitta Pearson

Type: Comprehensive **Sex:** Coed **Scores:** 100% SAT V 400+; 98.4% SAT M 400+; 29.4% ACT 18-23; 55.2% ACT 24-29 **% Accepted:** 84 **Admission Plans:** Early Admission; Early Action; Deferred Admission **Application Deadline:** June 01 **Application Fee:** $50.00 **H.S. Requirements:** High school diploma required; GED accepted **Costs Per Year:** Application fee: $50. Comprehensive fee: $22,191 includes full-time tuition ($16,000) and college room and board ($6191). College room only: $2700. Part-time tuition: $670 per credit. **Scholarships:** Available **Calendar System:** Semester, Summer Session Not available **Enrollment:** FT 761, PT 39, Grad 18 **Faculty:** FT 66, PT 5 **Student-Faculty Ratio:** 11:1 **Exams:** SAT I or ACT **% Receiving Financial Aid:** 64 **% Residing in College-Owned, -Operated, or -Affiliated Housing:** 52 **Library Holdings:** 183,308 **Credit Hours For Degree:** 124 credits, Bachelors **ROTC:** Army **Professional Accreditation:** NCCU **Intercollegiate Athletics:** Baseball M; Basketball M & W; Golf M & W; Skiing (Cross-Country) M & W; Skiing (Downhill) M & W; Soccer M & W; Softball W; Tennis M & W; Volleyball W

APOLLO COLLEGE

1200 North Liberty Rd.
Boise, ID 83704
Tel: (208)377-8080
Free: 800-473-4365
Fax: (208)322-7658
Web Site: http://www.apolloboise.com/
President/CEO: Judy Groothuis
Admissions: Kevin Price

Type: Two-Year College **Sex:** Coed **Affiliation:** U.S. Education Corporation **Admission Plans:** Open Admission **Application Fee:** $0.00 **H.S. Requirements:** High school diploma required; GED accepted **Scholarships:** Available **Calendar System:** Semester, Summer Session Not available **Enrollment:** FT 444, PT 25 **Faculty:** FT 19, PT 30 **Student-Faculty Ratio:** 10:1 **Exams:** Other **Library Holdings:** 20,000 **Professional Accreditation:** ABHES, ADA

BOISE BIBLE COLLEGE

8695 West Marigold St.
Boise, ID 83714-1220
Tel: (208)376-7731
Free: 800-893-7755
Fax: (208)376-7743
Web Site: http://www.boisebible.edu/
President/CEO: Dr. Charles A. Crane
Registrar: Ross Knudsen
Admissions: Ross Knudsen
Financial Aid: Joyce Anderson

Type: Four-Year College **Sex:** Coed **Affiliation:** nondenominational **Scores:** 75% SAT V 400+; 63% SAT M 400+; 38% ACT 18-23; 16% ACT 24-29 **Admission Plans:** Deferred Admission **Application Fee:** $25.00 **H.S. Requirements:** High school diploma required; GED accepted **Scholarships:** Available **Calendar System:** Semester, Summer Session Not available **Faculty:** FT 6, PT 7 **Student-Faculty Ratio:** 13:1 **Exams:** SAT I or ACT **% Receiving Financial Aid:** 81 **Library Holdings:** 29,431 **Credit Hours For Degree:** 64 semester hours, Associates; 128 semester hours, Bachelors **Professional Accreditation:** AABC

BOISE STATE UNIVERSITY

1910 University Dr.
Boise, ID 83725-0399
Tel: (208)426-1011
Free: 800-824-7017
Admissions: (208)426-1177
E-mail: bfortin@boisestate.edu
Web Site: http://www.boisestate.edu/
President/CEO: Dr. Robert Kustra
Registrar: Tim Ebner
Admissions: Barbara Fortin
Financial Aid: David Tolman

Type: Comprehensive **Sex:** Coed **Affiliation:** Idaho System of Higher Education **Scores:** 94% SAT V 400+; 94% SAT M 400+; 48% ACT 18-23; 26% ACT 24-29 **% Accepted:** 90 **Application Deadline:** July 12 **Application Fee:** $30.00 **H.S. Requirements:** High school diploma required; GED accepted **Costs Per Year:** Application fee: $30. State resident tuition: $2568 full-time, $138 per credit part-time. Nonresident tuition: $9976 full-time, $138 per credit part-time. Mandatory fees: $1304 full-time, $57 per credit part-time. Full-time tuition and fees vary according to reciprocity agreements. Part-time tuition and fees vary according to course load. College room and board: $5566. Room and board charges vary according to board plan and housing facility. **Scholarships:** Available **Calendar System:** Semester, Summer Session Available **Enrollment:** FT 10,840, PT 6,085, Grad 1,661 **Faculty:** FT 578, PT 549 **Student-Faculty Ratio:** 18:1 **Exams:** SAT I or ACT **% Receiving Financial Aid:** 49 **% Residing in College-Owned, -Operated, or -Affiliated Housing:** 8 **Library Holdings:** 675,000 **Credit Hours For Degree:** 64 semester hours, Associates; 128 semester hours, Bachelors **ROTC:** Army **Professional Accreditation:** AACSB, ABET, ACCE, ACA, ACF, ADA, AHIMA, CARC, CSWE, JRCEDMS, JRCERT, JRCEPAT, NASAD, NASM, NASPAA, NAST, NCATE, NLN, NCCU **Intercollegiate Athletics:** Basketball M & W; Cross-Country Running M & W; Football M; Golf M & W; Gymnastics W; Skiing (Downhill) W; Soccer W; Tennis M & W; Track and Field M & W; Volleyball W; Wrestling M

BRIGHAM YOUNG UNIVERSITY -IDAHO

Rexburg, ID 83460-1650
Tel: (208)496-2011
Admissions: (208)496-1026
Fax: (208)496-1220
E-mail: westenskowg@byui.edu
Web Site: http://www.byui.edu/
President/CEO: Dr. David Bednar
Registrar: Kevin Miyasaki

Admissions: Gordon Westenskow
Financial Aid: Dan Gulbransen
Type: Two-Year College **Sex:** Coed **Affiliation:** The Church of Jesus Christ of Latter-day Saints **Scores:** 49.4% ACT 18-23; 41.4% ACT 24-29 **Admission Plans:** Preferred Admission **Application Fee:** $30.00 **H.S. Requirements:** High school diploma required; GED accepted **Scholarships:** Available **Calendar System:** Semester, Summer Session Available **Student-Faculty Ratio:** 25:1 **Exams:** SAT I or ACT **% Residing in College-Owned, -Operated, or -Affiliated Housing:** 20 **Library Holdings:** 134,423 **Credit Hours For Degree:** 64 semester hours, Associates **ROTC:** Army **Professional Accreditation:** ABET, FIDER, NASM, NLN, NCCU

COLLEGE OF SOUTHERN IDAHO
PO Box 1238
Twin Falls, ID 83303-1238
Tel: (208)733-9554
Admissions: (208)732-6232
Fax: (208)736-3014
Web Site: http://www.csi.edu/
President/CEO: Gerald R. Meyerhoeffer
Registrar: Dr. John S. Martin
Admissions: Dr. John S. Martin
Financial Aid: Colin Randolph
Type: Two-Year College **Sex:** Coed **Admission Plans:** Open Admission **H.S. Requirements:** High school diploma required; GED accepted **Costs Per Year:** State resident tuition: $1900 full-time, $95 per credit part-time. Nonresident tuition: $5300 full-time, $265 per credit part-time. College room and board: $3870. Room and board charges vary according to board plan. **Scholarships:** Available **Calendar System:** Semester, Summer Session Available **Enrollment:** FT 3,175, PT 3,930 **Faculty:** FT 160, PT 45 **Student-Faculty Ratio:** 26:1 **Exams:** ACT, Other **% Residing in College-Owned, -Operated, or -Affiliated Housing:** 10 **Library Holdings:** 62,556 **Credit Hours For Degree:** 64 credits, Associates **Professional Accreditation:** AAMAE, NLN, NCCU **Intercollegiate Athletics:** Baseball M & W; Basketball M & W; Cheerleading M & W; Equestrian Sports M & W; Volleyball M & W

EASTERN IDAHO TECHNICAL COLLEGE
1600 South 25th East
Idaho Falls, ID 83404-5788
Tel: (208)524-3000
Free: 800-662-0261
Fax: (208)524-3007
E-mail: salbisto@eite.edu
Web Site: http://www.eitc.edu/
President/CEO: William A. Robertson
Registrar: Suzanne Robison
Admissions: Dr. Steve Albiston
Financial Aid: Tony Siebers
Type: Two-Year College **Sex:** Coed **% Accepted:** 42 **Admission Plans:** Open Admission; Deferred Admission **Application Deadline:** August 21 **Application Fee:** $10.00 **H.S. Requirements:** High school diploma required; GED accepted **Costs Per Year:** Application fee: $10. State resident tuition: $1578 full-time, $79 per credit part-time. Nonresident tuition: $5784 full-time, $158 per credit part-time. Mandatory fees: $124 full-time, $15 per term part-time. **Scholarships:** Available **Calendar System:** Semester, Summer Session Available **Enrollment:** FT 229, PT 526 **Faculty:** FT 41, PT 70 **Student-Faculty Ratio:** 12:1 **Library Holdings:** 18,000 **Credit Hours For Degree:** 60 credits, Associates **Professional Accreditation:** ARCEST, AAMAE, NCCU

IDAHO STATE UNIVERSITY
921 South 8th Ave.
Pocatello, ID 83209
Tel: (208)282-0211
Admissions: (208)282-2578
Web Site: http://www.isu.edu/
President/CEO: Dr. Richard Bowen
Registrar: Nathan Peterson
Admissions: Alan Frantz, PhD
Financial Aid: Douglas Severs
Type: University **Sex:** Coed **Scores:** 88% SAT V 400+; 92% SAT M 400+; 53% ACT 18-23; 22% ACT 24-29 **% Accepted:** 77 **Admission Plans:** Open Admission; Early Admission; Deferred Admission **Application Deadline:** August 01 **Application Fee:** $40.00 **H.S. Requirements:** High school diploma required; GED accepted **Costs Per Year:** Application fee: $40. One-time mandatory fee: $660. Nonresident tuition: $7700 full-time. Mandatory fees: $4000 full-time. College room and board: $5030. College room only: $2100. **Scholarships:** Available **Calendar System:** Semester, Summer Session Available **Enrollment:** FT 7,745, PT 3,907, Grad 2,078 **Faculty:** FT 651, PT 257 **Student-Faculty Ratio:** 15:1 **Exams:** ACT, SAT I or ACT **% Receiving Financial Aid:** 71 **% Residing in College-Owned, -Operated, or -Affiliated Housing:** 4 **Library Holdings:** 712,041 **Credit Hours For Degree:** 64 credits, Associates; 128 credits, Bachelors **ROTC:** Army **Professional Accreditation:** AACSB, ABET, AACN, AAMAE, ACPhE, ACA, ACF, ADA, ADtA, AHIMA, AOTA, APTA, APA, ASLHA, CEPH, CSWE, NAACLS, NASM, NCATE, NCCU **Intercollegiate Athletics:** Basketball M & W; Cross-Country Running M & W; Football M; Golf M & W; Skiing (Downhill) M & W; Tennis M & W; Track and Field M & W; Volleyball W

ITT TECHNICAL INSTITUTE
12302 West Explorer Dr.
Boise, ID 83713
Tel: (208)322-8844
Fax: (208)322-0173
Web Site: http://www.itt-tech.edu/
President/CEO: Jennifer Kandler
Admissions: Jennifer Kandler
Financial Aid: Larry Hallam
Type: Two-Year College **Sex:** Coed **Affiliation:** ITT Educational Services, Inc **Admission Plans:** Deferred Admission **Application Deadline:** Rolling **Application Fee:** $100.00 **H.S. Requirements:** High school diploma required; GED accepted **Costs Per Year:** Application fee: $100. **Scholarships:** Available **Calendar System:** Quarter, Summer Session Not available **Exams:** Other **Credit Hours For Degree:** 96 credit hours, Associates; 180 credit hours, Bachelors **Professional Accreditation:** ACICS

LEWIS-CLARK STATE COLLEGE
500 Eighth Ave.
Lewiston, ID 83501-2698
Tel: (208)792-5272
Free: 800-933-LCSC
Admissions: (208)792-2210
Fax: (208)799-2063
E-mail: sbussoli@lcsc.edu
Web Site: http://www.lcsc.edu/
President/CEO: Dr. Dene K. Thomas
Registrar: Diane Johnson
Admissions: Steve Bussolini
Financial Aid: Laura Hughes
Type: Four-Year College **Sex:** Coed **Scores:** 84% SAT V 400+; 87% SAT M 400+; 54% ACT 18-23; 15% ACT 24-29 **Admission Plans:** Deferred Admission **Application Deadline:** Rolling **Application Fee:** $35.00 **H.S. Requirements:** High school diploma required; GED accepted **Costs Per Year:** Application fee: $35. Area resident tuition: $185 per credit part-time. State resident tuition: $3714 full-time, $185 per credit part-time. Nonresident tuition: $10,266 full-time. Mandatory fees: $11 per credit part-time. Full-time tuition varies according to course load and reciprocity agreements. College room and board: $4500. College room only: $1900. Room and board charges vary according to board plan and housing facility. **Scholarships:** Available **Calendar System:** Semester, Summer Session Available **Enrollment:** FT 2,281, PT 1,170 **Faculty:** FT 158, PT 71 **Student-Faculty Ratio:** 15:1 **Exams:** Other, SAT I or ACT **% Receiving Financial Aid:** 70 **% Residing in College-Owned, -Operated, or -Affiliated Housing:** 8 **Library Holdings:** 139,499 **Credit Hours For Degree:** 64 credit hours, Associates; 128 credit hours, Bachelors **ROTC:** Army, Air Force **Professional Accreditation:** AACN, CSWE, NCCU **Intercollegiate Athletics:** Baseball M; Basketball M & W; Cross-Country Running M & W; Golf M & W; Tennis M & W; Volleyball W

NEW SAINT ANDREWS COLLEGE
PO Box 9025
Moscow, ID 83843
Tel: (208)882-1566
Fax: (208)882-4293
Web Site: http://www.nsa.edu/
President/CEO: Dr. Roy Alden Atwood
Registrar: Beverlee Atwood

Type: Four-Year College **Sex:** Coed **Calendar System:** Miscellaneous **Professional Accreditation:** TACCS

NORTH IDAHO COLLEGE

1000 West Garden Ave.
Coeur d'Alene, ID 83814-2199
Tel: (208)769-3300; 877-404-4536
Admissions: (208)769-3303
Fax: (208)769-3273
E-mail: maxine_gish@nic.edu
Web Site: http://www.nic.edu/
President/CEO: Dr. Michael Burke
Registrar: Richard Bevans
Admissions: Maxine Gish
Type: Two-Year College **Sex:** Coed **% Accepted:** 59 **Admission Plans:** Early Admission; Deferred Admission **Application Deadline:** August 20 **Application Fee:** $25.00 **H.S. Requirements:** High school diploma required; GED accepted **Costs Per Year:** Application fee: $25. Area resident tuition: $1068 full-time, $67 per credit part-time. State resident tuition: $2068 full-time, $129 per credit part-time. Nonresident tuition: $5620 full-time, $351 per credit part-time. Mandatory fees: $820 full-time, $60 per credit part-time. Full-time tuition and fees vary according to course load, program, and reciprocity agreements. College room and board: $5010. College room only: $3210. Room and board charges vary according to board plan and housing facility. **Scholarships:** Available **Calendar System:** Semester, Summer Session Available **Enrollment:** FT 2,492, PT 1,607 **Faculty:** FT 155, PT 142 **Student-Faculty Ratio:** 14:1 **Library Holdings:** 60,893 **Credit Hours For Degree:** 64 credit hours, Associates **Professional Accreditation:** NLN, NCCU **Intercollegiate Athletics:** Basketball M & W; Cheerleading M & W; Soccer M & W; Softball W; Volleyball W; Wrestling M

NORTHWEST NAZARENE UNIVERSITY

623 Holly St.
Nampa, ID 83686-5897
Tel: (208)467-8011; 877-668-4968
Admissions: (208)467-8000
Fax: (208)467-8645
E-mail: slberggren@nnu.edu
Web Site: http://www.nnu.edu/
President/CEO: Dr. Richard A. Hagood
Registrar: Merilyn Thompson
Admissions: Stacey Berggren
Financial Aid: Randy Dalzell
Type: Comprehensive **Sex:** Coed **Affiliation:** Church of the Nazarene **Scores:** 51% ACT 18-23; 31% ACT 24-29 **% Accepted:** 52 **Admission Plans:** Early Action; Deferred Admission **Application Deadline:** August 08 **Application Fee:** $25.00 **H.S. Requirements:** High school diploma required; GED accepted **Costs Per Year:** Application fee: $25. Comprehensive fee: $23,780 includes full-time tuition ($18,430), mandatory fees ($340), and college room and board ($5010). Part-time tuition: $798 per credit. **Scholarships:** Available **Calendar System:** Semester, Summer Session Available **Enrollment:** FT 1,073, PT 91, Grad 461 **Faculty:** FT 95, PT 5 **Student-Faculty Ratio:** 12:1 **Exams:** SAT I or ACT **% Receiving Financial Aid:** 72 **% Residing in College-Owned, -Operated, or -Affiliated Housing:** 70 **Library Holdings:** 100,966 **Credit Hours For Degree:** 124 semester credits, Bachelors **ROTC:** Army **Professional Accreditation:** AACN, ACA, ACBSP, CSWE, NASM, NCATE, NCCU **Intercollegiate Athletics:** Baseball M; Basketball M & W; Cross-Country Running M & W; Golf M; Soccer W; Softball W; Track and Field M & W; Volleyball M & W

UNIVERSITY OF IDAHO

875 Perimeter Dr., PO Box 442282
Moscow, ID 83844-2282
Tel: (208)885-6111; 888-884-3246
Admissions: (208)885-6326
Fax: (208)885-6911
E-mail: admappl@uidaho.edu
Web Site: http://www.uidaho.edu/
President/CEO: Gary Michael
Registrar: Reta W. Pikowsky
Admissions: Dan Davenport
Financial Aid: Dr. Daniel Davenport
Type: University **Sex:** Coed **Scores:** 97% SAT V 400+; 95.8% SAT M 400+; 46.34% ACT 18-23; 35.36% ACT 24-29 **% Accepted:** 82 **Admission Plans:** Deferred Admission **Application Deadline:** August 01 **Application Fee:** $40.00 **H.S. Requirements:** High school diploma required; GED accepted **Costs Per Year:** Application fee: $40. State resident tuition: $0 full-time. Nonresident tuition: $8770 full-time, $130 per credit part-time. Mandatory fees: $3968 full-time, $190 per credit part-time. Full-time tuition and fees vary according to degree level and program. Part-time tuition and fees vary according to course load, degree level, and program. College room and board: $5342. Room and board charges vary according to board plan and housing facility. **Scholarships:** Available **Calendar System:** Semester, Summer Session Available **Enrollment:** FT 8,380, PT 1,123, Grad 2,657 **Faculty:** FT 564, PT 22 **Student-Faculty Ratio:** 20:1 **Exams:** SAT I or ACT, SAT I **% Receiving Financial Aid:** 59 **% Residing in College-Owned, -Operated, or -Affiliated Housing:** 55 **Library Holdings:** 1,355,911 **Credit Hours For Degree:** 128 credits, Bachelors **ROTC:** Army, Navy, Air Force **Professional Accreditation:** AACSB, ABET, AAFCS, ABA, ACA, ADtA, ASLA, AALS, CORE, NASAD, NASM, NCATE, NRPA, NCCU, SAF **Intercollegiate Athletics:** Baseball M; Basketball M & W; Cross-Country Running M & W; Football M; Golf M & W; Ice Hockey M; Riflery M & W; Rugby M & W; Skiing (Cross-Country) M & W; Skiing (Downhill) M & W; Soccer M & W; Tennis M & W; Track and Field M & W; Volleyball W

UNIVERSITY OF PHOENIX-IDAHO CAMPUS

3080 Gentry Way, Ste. 150
Meridian, ID 83642-3014
Tel: (208)888-1505
Free: 800-228-7240
Admissions: (480)557-1712
Fax: (208)888-4775
Web Site: http://www.phoenix.edu/
President/CEO: Julie Johnson
Admissions: Nina Omelchanko
Type: Comprehensive **Sex:** Coed **Admission Plans:** Open Admission; Deferred Admission **Application Deadline:** Rolling **Application Fee:** $110.00 **H.S. Requirements:** High school diploma required; GED accepted **Costs Per Year:** Application fee: $110. Tuition: $9900 full-time, $330 per credit part-time. Mandatory fees: $560 full-time, $70 per course part-time. **Scholarships:** Available **Calendar System:** Continuous, Summer Session Not available **Enrollment:** FT 656, Grad 111 **Faculty:** FT 2, PT 114 **Student-Faculty Ratio:** 6:1 **Regional Accreditation:** North Central Association of Colleges and Schools **Credit Hours For Degree:** 60 credits, Associates; 120 credits, Bachelors

AMERICAN ACADEMY OF ART
332 South Michigan Ave, Ste. 300
Chicago, IL 60604-4302
Tel: (312)461-0600
E-mail: srosenbloom@aaart.edu
Web Site: http://www.aaart.edu/
President/CEO: Richard Otto
Registrar: Marcia Thomas
Admissions: Stuart Rosenbloom
Financial Aid: Ione Fitzgerald
Type: Comprehensive **Sex:** Coed **Application Deadline:** Rolling **Application Fee:** $25.00 **H.S. Requirements:** High school diploma required; GED accepted **Costs Per Year:** Application fee: $25. Tuition: $20,680 full-time. Mandatory fees: $250 full-time. **Scholarships:** Available **Calendar System:** Semester, Summer Session Available **Enrollment:** FT 338, PT 58, Grad 14 **Faculty:** FT 25, PT 10 **Student-Faculty Ratio:** 10:1 **Library Holdings:** 1,730 **Credit Hours For Degree:** 133 semester hours, Bachelors **Professional Accreditation:** ACCSCT

AMERICAN INTERCONTINENTAL UNIVERSITY ONLINE
5550 Prairie Stone Parkway, Ste. 400
Hoffman Estates, IL 60192
Tel: (847)851-5000; 877-701-3800
Fax: (847)851-6002
Web Site: http://www.aiuonline.edu/
President/CEO: Nick Fluge
Admissions: Steve Fireng
Financial Aid: John Morton
Type: Comprehensive **Sex:** Coed **Affiliation:** American InterContinental University **Application Fee:** $50.00 **Calendar System:** Miscellaneous **Regional Accreditation:** Southern Association of Colleges and Schools

ARGOSY UNIVERSITY/CHICAGO
20 South Clark St., Ste. 300
Chicago, IL 60603
Tel: (312)201-0200
Admissions: 800-626-4123
Fax: (312)201-1907
E-mail: adelaney@argosyu.edu
Web Site: http://www.argosyu.edu/
President/CEO: Dr. David Harpool, JD,PhD
Registrar: Keith Werosh
Admissions: Ashley Delaney
Financial Aid: Ardith Elgersma
Type: Two-Year Upper Division **Sex:** Coed **Admission Plans:** Early Admission; Early Decision Plan; Deferred Admission **Application Fee:** $50.00 **H.S. Requirements:** High school diploma required; GED accepted **Scholarships:** Available **Calendar System:** Semester, Summer Session Available **Enrollment:** FT 8, PT 29, Grad 853 **Faculty:** PT 5 **% Receiving Financial Aid:** 60 **Library Holdings:** 20,000 **Regional Accreditation:** North Central Association of Colleges and Schools **Credit Hours For Degree:** 120 credit hours, Bachelors **Professional Accreditation:** APA

ARGOSY UNIVERSITY/SCHAUMBURG
1000 North Plaza Dr., Ste. 100
Schaumburg, IL 60173
Tel: (847)290-7400; (866)290-2777
Fax: (847)598-6191
Web Site: http://www.argosyu.edu/
President/CEO: Dr. Roger Widmer
Registrar: Pete Zaragoza
Financial Aid: Virginia Carlin
Type: Two-Year Upper Division **Sex:** Coed **Application Fee:** $50.00 **Scholarships:** Available **Calendar System:** Semester **% Receiving Financial Aid:** 88 **Regional Accreditation:** North Central Association of Colleges and Schools **Professional Accreditation:** APA

AUGUSTANA COLLEGE
639 38th St.
Rock Island, IL 61201-2296
Tel: (309)794-7000
Free: 800-798-8100
Admissions: (309)794-7341
Fax: (309)794-7431
E-mail: admissions@augustana.edu
Web Site: http://www.augustana.edu/
President/CEO: Steven C. Bahls
Registrar: Leisl Fowler
Admissions: Martin Sauer
Financial Aid: Susan B. Standley
Type: Four-Year College **Sex:** Coed **Affiliation:** Evangelical Lutheran Church in America **Scores:** 30% ACT 18-23; 57% ACT 24-29 **% Accepted:** 84 **Admission Plans:** Deferred Admission **Application Deadline:** Rolling **Application Fee:** $25.00 **H.S. Requirements:** High school diploma required; GED accepted **Costs Per Year:** Application fee: $25. Comprehensive fee: $29,862 includes full-time tuition ($22,971), mandatory fees ($486), and college room and board ($6405). College room only: $3243. Full-time tuition and fees vary according to course load. Room and board charges vary according to board plan and housing facility. Part-time tuition: $960 per credit hour. **Scholarships:** Available **Calendar System:** Quarter, Summer Session Available **Enrollment:** FT 2,363, PT 23 **Faculty:** FT 149, PT 86 **Student-Faculty Ratio:** 12:1 **Exams:** SAT I or ACT **% Receiving Financial Aid:** 67 **% Residing in College-Owned, -Operated, or -Affiliated Housing:** 72 **Library Holdings:** 190,641 **Regional Accreditation:** North Central Association of Colleges and Schools **Credit Hours For Degree:** 123 credits, Bachelors **Professional Accreditation:** NASM, NCATE **Intercollegiate Athletics:** Baseball M; Basketball M & W; Cheerleading M & W; Cross-Country Running M & W; Football M; Golf M & W; Lacrosse M; Soccer M & W; Softball W; Swimming and Diving M & W; Tennis M & W; Track and Field M & W; Ultimate Frisbee M & W; Volleyball M & W; Wrestling M

AURORA UNIVERSITY
347 South Gladstone Ave.
Aurora, IL 60506-4892
Tel: (630)892-6431
Free: 800-742-5281
Admissions: (630)844-5533
Fax: (630)844-5535
E-mail: admissions@aurora.edu
Web Site: http://www.aurora.edu/
President/CEO: Dr. Rebecca L. Sherrick
Registrar: Ellen J. Goldberg

Admissions: Dr. Carol Dunn
Financial Aid: Heather Gutierrez
Type: Comprehensive **Sex:** Coed **Scores:** 100% SAT V 400+; 100% SAT M 400+; 75% ACT 18-23; 22% ACT 24-29 **% Accepted:** 74 **Admission Plans:** Deferred Admission **Application Deadline:** Rolling **Application Fee:** $25.00 **H.S. Requirements:** High school diploma required; GED accepted **Costs Per Year:** Application fee: $25. Comprehensive fee: $22,770 includes full-time tuition ($16,080), mandatory fees ($100), and college room and board ($6590). College room only: $2994. Part-time tuition: $495 per semester hour. **Scholarships:** Available **Calendar System:** Trimester, Summer Session Available **Enrollment:** FT 1,686, PT 221, Grad 1,649 **Faculty:** FT 95, PT 176 **Student-Faculty Ratio:** 17:1 **% Receiving Financial Aid:** 76 **% Residing in College-Owned, -Operated, or -Affiliated Housing:** 30 **Library Holdings:** 115,642 **Regional Accreditation:** North Central Association of Colleges and Schools **Credit Hours For Degree:** 30 semester hours, Bachelors **Professional Accreditation:** AACN, ACBSP, CSWE, NRPA **Intercollegiate Athletics:** Baseball M; Basketball M & W; Football M; Golf M; Soccer M & W; Softball W; Tennis M & W; Volleyball W

BENEDICTINE UNIVERSITY
5700 College Rd.
Lisle, IL 60532-0900
Tel: (630)829-6000; 888-829-6363
Admissions: (630)829-6306
Fax: (630)960-1126
Web Site: http://www.ben.edu/
President/CEO: Dr. William J. Carroll
Registrar: David Striker
Admissions: Kari Gibbons
Type: Comprehensive **Sex:** Coed **Affiliation:** Roman Catholic **Scores:** 55% ACT 18-23; 34% ACT 24-29 **% Accepted:** 82 **Admission Plans:** Deferred Admission **Application Deadline:** Rolling **Application Fee:** $40.00 **H.S. Requirements:** High school diploma required; GED accepted **Costs Per Year:** Application fee: $40. Comprehensive fee: $25,810 includes full-time tuition ($18,700), mandatory fees ($510), and college room and board ($6600). Full-time tuition and fees vary according to class time, degree level, and location. Room and board charges vary according to board plan and housing facility. Part-time tuition: $630 per credit hour. Part-time mandatory fees: $15 per credit hour. Part-time tuition and fees vary according to class time and degree level. **Scholarships:** Available **Calendar System:** Semester, Summer Session Available **Enrollment:** FT 1,518, PT 802, Grad 1,080 **Faculty:** FT 87, PT 266 **Student-Faculty Ratio:** 12:1 **Exams:** ACT **% Receiving Financial Aid:** 73 **% Residing in College-Owned, -Operated, or -Affiliated Housing:** 24 **Regional Accreditation:** North Central Association of Colleges and Schools **Credit Hours For Degree:** 60 semester hours, Associates; 120 semester hours, Bachelors **ROTC:** Army **Professional Accreditation:** ADtA, NLN **Intercollegiate Athletics:** Baseball M; Basketball M & W; Cross-Country Running M & W; Football M; Golf M; Soccer M & W; Softball W; Swimming and Diving M & W; Tennis W; Track and Field M & W; Volleyball W

BLACK HAWK COLLEGE
6600 34th Ave.
Moline, IL 61265-5899
Tel: (309)796-5000
Admissions: (309)796-5043
Web Site: http://www.bhc.edu/
President/CEO: Dr. Keith Miller
Registrar: Dr. Rose Campbell
Admissions: Dr. Rose Campbell
Financial Aid: Robert C. Bopp
Type: Two-Year College **Sex:** Coed **Affiliation:** Black Hawk College District System **Scores:** 48.5% ACT 18-23; 14% ACT 24-29 **Admission Plans:** Open Admission; Early Admission; Deferred Admission **Application Fee:** $0.00 **H.S. Requirements:** High school diploma or equivalent not required **Costs Per Year:** Application fee: $0. Area resident tuition: $1860 full-time, $62 per credit hour part-time. State resident tuition: $4200 full-time, $140 per credit hour part-time. Nonresident tuition: $7770 full-time, $259 per credit hour part-time. Mandatory fees: $210 full-time, $7 per credit hour part-time. Full-time tuition and fees vary according to program and reciprocity agreements. Part-time tuition and fees vary according to program and reciprocity agreements. **Scholarships:** Available **Calendar System:** Semester, Summer Session Available **Enrollment:** FT 3,138, PT 3,462 **Faculty:** FT 137, PT 227 **Student-Faculty Ratio:** 18:1 **Exams:** ACT, Other **Library Holdings:** 59,840 **Regional Accreditation:** North Central Association of Colleges and Schools **Credit Hours For Degree:** 64 semester hours, Associates **Professional Accreditation:** APTA, NLN **Intercollegiate Athletics:** Baseball M; Basketball M & W; Golf M; Softball W; Volleyball W

BLACKBURN COLLEGE
700 College Ave.
Carlinville, IL 62626-1498
Tel: (217)854-3231
Free: 800-233-3550
Fax: (217)854-3713
E-mail: jmali@mail.blackburn.edu
Web Site: http://www.blackburn.edu/
President/CEO: Dr. Miriam R. Pride
Registrar: Dianna Ruyle
Admissions: John Malin
Financial Aid: Jane Kelsey
Type: Four-Year College **Sex:** Coed **Affiliation:** Presbyterian **Scores:** 56% ACT 18-23; 28% ACT 24-29 **Admission Plans:** Deferred Admission **Application Fee:** $0.00 **H.S. Requirements:** High school diploma required; GED accepted **Costs Per Year:** Application fee: $0. Comprehensive fee: $16,628 includes full-time tuition ($12,733) and college room and board ($3895). College room only: $1795. Full-time tuition varies according to program. Room and board charges vary according to board plan. Part-time tuition: $501 per semester hour. **Scholarships:** Available **Calendar System:** Semester, Summer Session Not available **Enrollment:** FT 580, PT 10 **Faculty:** FT 35, PT 16 **Student-Faculty Ratio:** 16:1 **Exams:** SAT I or ACT **% Receiving Financial Aid:** 88 **Library Holdings:** 61,586 **Regional Accreditation:** North Central Association of Colleges and Schools **Credit Hours For Degree:** 122 semester hours, Bachelors **Intercollegiate Athletics:** Baseball M; Basketball M & W; Cheerleading M & W; Cross-Country Running M & W; Football M; Golf M & W; Soccer M & W; Softball W; Tennis W; Volleyball W

BLESSING-RIEMAN COLLEGE OF NURSING
Broadway at 11th St., POB 7005
Quincy, IL 62305-7005
Tel: (217)228-5520
Free: 800-877-9140
Fax: (217)223-6400
E-mail: aosullivan@brcn.edu
Web Site: http://www.brcn.edu/
President/CEO: Dr. Pamela Brown
Registrar: Ann O'Sullivan
Admissions: Ann O'Sullivan
Financial Aid: Sara Brehm
Type: Four-Year College **Sex:** Coed **Scores:** 33% ACT 18-23; 67% ACT 24-29 **% Accepted:** 63 **Admission Plans:** Deferred Admission **Application Deadline:** Rolling **Application Fee:** $0.00 **H.S. Requirements:** High school diploma required; GED accepted **Costs Per Year:** Application fee: $0. Comprehensive fee: $20,025 includes full-time tuition ($13,900), mandatory fees ($350), and college room and board ($5775). Full-time tuition and fees vary according to course load, location, and student level. Room and board charges vary according to location. **Scholarships:** Available **Calendar System:** Semester, Summer Session Available **Enrollment:** FT 193, PT 18 **Faculty:** FT 16, PT 0 **Student-Faculty Ratio:** 13:1 **Exams:** SAT I or ACT **% Receiving Financial Aid:** 100 **% Residing in College-Owned, -Operated, or -Affiliated Housing:** 82 **Library Holdings:** 4,282 **Regional Accreditation:** North Central Association of Colleges and Schools **Credit Hours For Degree:** 124 semester hours, Bachelors **Professional Accreditation:** AACN, NLN **Intercollegiate Athletics:** Baseball M & W; Basketball M & W; Football M; Soccer M & W; Volleyball M & W

BRADLEY UNIVERSITY
1501 West Bradley Ave.
Peoria, IL 61625-0002
Tel: (309)676-7611
Free: 800-447-6460
Admissions: (309)677-3144
E-mail: admissions@bradley.edu
Web Site: http://www.bradley.edu/
President/CEO: Dr. David C. Broski
Registrar: Katherine M. Beaty
Admissions: Nicki Roberson
Financial Aid: David Pardieck

Type: Comprehensive **Sex:** Coed **Scores:** 96% SAT V 400+; 99% SAT M 400+; 37% ACT 18-23; 53% ACT 24-29 **% Accepted:** 91 **Admission Plans:** Early Admission; Deferred Admission **Application Deadline:** Rolling **Application Fee:** $35.00 **H.S. Requirements:** High school diploma required; GED accepted **Costs Per Year:** Application fee: $35. Comprehensive fee: $25,280 includes full-time tuition ($18,700), mandatory fees ($130), and college room and board ($6450). College room only: $3700. Full-time tuition and fees vary according to program. Room and board charges vary according to board plan. Part-time tuition: $510 per credit. Part-time tuition varies according to course load. **Scholarships:** Available **Calendar System:** Semester, Summer Session Available **Enrollment:** FT 5,055, PT 314, Grad 785 **Faculty:** FT 326, PT 224 **Student-Faculty Ratio:** 14:1 **Exams:** SAT I or ACT **% Receiving Financial Aid:** 72 **% Residing in College-Owned, -Operated, or -Affiliated Housing:** 42 **Library Holdings:** 435,394 **Regional Accreditation:** North Central Association of Colleges and Schools **Credit Hours For Degree:** 124 credits, Bachelors **ROTC:** Army **Professional Accreditation:** AACSB, ABET, AAFCS, AANA, ACCE, ACA, APTA, CSWE, NASAD, NASM, NAST, NCATE, NLN **Intercollegiate Athletics:** Baseball M; Basketball M & W; Cheerleading M & W; Cross-Country Running M & W; Fencing M & W; Golf M & W; Ice Hockey M; Soccer M & W; Softball W; Table Tennis M & W; Tennis M & W; Track and Field W; Volleyball W

CAREER COLLEGES OF CHICAGO
11 East Adams St., 2nd Floor
Chicago, IL 60603-6301
Tel: (312)895-6300
Admissions: (312)895-6217
Fax: (312)895-6301
Web Site: http://www.careerchi.com/
President/CEO: Rev. Mark S. Pranaitis, CM
Registrar: Edward C. Young, III
Admissions: Michael Nulf
Financial Aid: Dr. William J. Kakish
Type: Two-Year College **Sex:** Coed **Admission Plans:** Open Admission; Deferred Admission **Application Fee:** $40.00 **H.S. Requirements:** High school diploma required; GED accepted **Scholarships:** Available **Calendar System:** Quarter, Summer Session Available **Enrollment:** FT 35, PT 109 **Faculty:** FT 0, PT 19 **Student-Faculty Ratio:** 11:1 **Exams:** ACT **Library Holdings:** 1,000 **Credit Hours For Degree:** 90 credits, Associates **Professional Accreditation:** ACICS

CARL SANDBURG COLLEGE
2400 Tom L. Wilson Blvd.
Galesburg, IL 61401-9576
Tel: (309)344-2518
Admissions: (309)341-5234
Fax: (309)344-1395
Web Site: http://www.sandburg.edu/
Registrar: Carol A. Kreider
Admissions: Carol Kreider
Financial Aid: Lisa A. Hanson
Type: Two-Year College **Sex:** Coed **Affiliation:** Illinois Community College Board **Admission Plans:** Open Admission; Early Admission; Deferred Admission **Application Fee:** $0.00 **H.S. Requirements:** High school diploma or equivalent not required. For allied health programs: High school diploma required; GED accepted **Scholarships:** Available **Calendar System:** Semester, Summer Session Available **Faculty:** FT 58, PT 150 **Student-Faculty Ratio:** 17:1 **Exams:** Other **Library Holdings:** 39,900 **Regional Accreditation:** North Central Association of Colleges and Schools **Credit Hours For Degree:** 64 semester hours, Associates **ROTC:** Army **Professional Accreditation:** ABFSE, ADA, JRCERT, NLN **Intercollegiate Athletics:** Baseball M; Basketball M & W; Volleyball W

CHICAGO STATE UNIVERSITY
9501 South King Dr.
Chicago, IL 60628
Tel: (773)995-2000
Admissions: (773)995-2513
Web Site: http://www.csu.edu/
President/CEO: Dr. Elnora D. Daniel
Registrar: Lois Davis
Admissions: Addie Epps
Financial Aid: Brenda J. Hooker
Type: Comprehensive **Sex:** Coed **Scores:** 64% ACT 18-23; 3% ACT 24-29 **% Accepted:** 51 **Application Fee:** $25.00 **H.S. Requirements:** High school diploma required; GED accepted **Costs Per Year:** Application fee: $25. State resident tuition: $5670 full-time, $189 per credit hour part-time. Nonresident tuition: $11,280 full-time, $376 per credit hour part-time. Mandatory fees: $1468 full-time, $227 per term part-time. College room and board: $6492. **Scholarships:** Available **Calendar System:** Semester, Summer Session Available **Enrollment:** FT 3,456, PT 1,704, Grad 1,971 **Faculty:** FT 307, PT 155 **Student-Faculty Ratio:** 14:1 **Exams:** SAT I or ACT, SAT I and SAT II or ACT **% Residing in College-Owned, -Operated, or -Affiliated Housing:** 7 **Library Holdings:** 320,000 **Regional Accreditation:** North Central Association of Colleges and Schools **Credit Hours For Degree:** 120 credit hours, Bachelors **ROTC:** Army, Navy, Air Force **Professional Accreditation:** ACA, AHIMA, AOTA, CSWE, NASM, NCATE, NLN **Intercollegiate Athletics:** Baseball M; Basketball M & W; Cross-Country Running M & W; Golf M & W; Tennis M & W; Track and Field M & W; Volleyball W

CHRISTIAN LIFE COLLEGE
400 East Gregory St.
Mount Prospect, IL 60056
Tel: (847)259-1840
E-mail: jspenner@christianlifecollege.edu
Web Site: http://www.christianlifecollege.edu/
President/CEO: Harry Schmidt
Registrar: JeAnna Brown
Admissions: Jim Spenner
Financial Aid: Roger Stevens
Type: Four-Year College **Sex:** Coed **Scholarships:** Available **Enrollment:** FT 47, PT 33 **Faculty:** FT 6, PT 9 **Student-Faculty Ratio:** 10:1 **% Receiving Financial Aid:** 60 **Professional Accreditation:** TACCS

CITY COLLEGES OF CHICAGO, HAROLD WASHINGTON COLLEGE
30 East Lake St.
Chicago, IL 60601-2449
Tel: (312)553-5600
Admissions: (312)553-6006
Fax: (312)553-6077
Web Site: http://hwashington.ccc.edu/
President/CEO: Nancy DeSombre
Registrar: Robert Brown
Admissions: Terry Pendleton
Financial Aid: Francois Hajduk
Type: Two-Year College **Sex:** Coed **Affiliation:** City Colleges of Chicago **Admission Plans:** Open Admission; Early Admission; Deferred Admission **Application Fee:** $0.00 **H.S. Requirements:** High school diploma required; GED accepted **Scholarships:** Available **Calendar System:** Semester, Summer Session Available **Enrollment:** FT 2,608, PT 5,826 **Faculty:** FT 117, PT 114 **Student-Faculty Ratio:** 23:1 **Exams:** Other **Library Holdings:** 65,926 **Regional Accreditation:** North Central Association of Colleges and Schools **Credit Hours For Degree:** 60 credit hours, Associates **Professional Accreditation:** ACBSP

CITY COLLEGES OF CHICAGO, HARRY S. TRUMAN COLLEGE
1145 West Wilson Ave.
Chicago, IL 60640-5616
Tel: (773)907-4000
Admissions: (773)907-4720
Fax: (773)907-4464
Web Site: http://www.trumancollege.cc/
President/CEO: Dr. Phoebe K. Helm
Registrar: Michael E. D. Kritikos
Admissions: Kelly O'Malley
Financial Aid: Mark Latuszek
Type: Two-Year College **Sex:** Coed **Affiliation:** City Colleges of Chicago **Admission Plans:** Open Admission; Early Admission; Deferred Admission **Application Fee:** $0.00 **H.S. Requirements:** High school diploma required; GED accepted **Scholarships:** Available **Calendar System:** Semester, Summer Session Available **Faculty:** FT 116, PT 387 **Student-Faculty Ratio:** 61:1 **Exams:** ACT **Library Holdings:** 59,750 **Regional Accreditation:** North Central Association of Colleges and Schools **Credit Hours For**

Degree: 60 semester hours, Associates **Professional Accreditation:** NLN **Intercollegiate Athletics:** Baseball M; Basketball M & W; Tennis M & W; Wrestling M

CITY COLLEGES OF CHICAGO, KENNEDY-KING COLLEGE
6800 South Wentworth Ave.
Chicago, IL 60621-3733
Tel: (773)602-5000
Admissions: (773)602-5080
Web Site: http://kennedyking.ccc.edu/
President/CEO: Wellington Wilson
Registrar: Iver Watson
Admissions: Welton Murphy
Financial Aid: Paul H. Simon
Type: Two-Year College **Sex:** Coed **Affiliation:** City Colleges of Chicago **Admission Plans:** Open Admission; Preferred Admission **Application Fee:** $0.00 **H.S. Requirements:** High school diploma or equivalent not required **Scholarships:** Available **Calendar System:** Semester, Summer Session Available **Faculty:** FT 61, PT 86 **Exams:** SAT I or ACT **Library Holdings:** 45,000 **Regional Accreditation:** North Central Association of Colleges and Schools **Credit Hours For Degree:** 90 quarter credits, Associates **Professional Accreditation:** ADA, NLN **Intercollegiate Athletics:** Basketball M & W; Soccer M; Track and Field M & W; Wrestling M

CITY COLLEGES OF CHICAGO, MALCOLM X COLLEGE
1900 West Van Buren St.
Chicago, IL 60612-3145
Tel: (312)850-7000
Admissions: (312)850-7120
Fax: (312)850-7092
Web Site: http://malcolmx.ccc.edu/
President/CEO: Zerrie D. Campbell
Registrar: Mary Marsh
Admissions: Ghingo Brooks
Financial Aid: Patricia Burke
Type: Two-Year College **Sex:** Coed **Affiliation:** City Colleges of Chicago **Admission Plans:** Open Admission; Preferred Admission; Early Admission; Deferred Admission **Application Fee:** $0.00 **H.S. Requirements:** High school diploma required; GED accepted **Scholarships:** Available **Calendar System:** Semester, Summer Session Available **Enrollment:** FT 4,069, PT 3,955 **Faculty:** FT 58, PT 136 **Student-Faculty Ratio:** 22:1 **Exams:** SAT I and SAT II or ACT **Library Holdings:** 50,000 **Regional Accreditation:** North Central Association of Colleges and Schools **Credit Hours For Degree:** 60 credit hours, Associates **Professional Accreditation:** ARCEST, ABFSE, JRCERT, NLN **Intercollegiate Athletics:** Basketball M & W; Cross-Country Running M

CITY COLLEGES OF CHICAGO, OLIVE-HARVEY COLLEGE
10001 South Woodlawn Ave.
Chicago, IL 60628-1645
Tel: (773)291-6100
Admissions: (773)291-6349
Fax: (773)291-6304
E-mail: madams@ccc.edu
Web Site: http://oliveharvey.ccc.edu/
President/CEO: Dr. Lawrence M. Cox
Registrar: Ruby Howard
Admissions: Michelle Adams
Type: Two-Year College **Sex:** Coed **Affiliation:** City Colleges of Chicago **Admission Plans:** Open Admission; Preferred Admission; Early Admission; Deferred Admission **Application Deadline:** Rolling **Application Fee:** $0.00 **H.S. Requirements:** High school diploma required; GED accepted **Costs Per Year:** Application fee: $0. Area resident tuition: $72 per credit part-time. State resident tuition: $180.83 per credit part-time. Nonresident tuition: $291.61 per credit part-time. Mandatory fees: $250 per year part-time. **Scholarships:** Available **Calendar System:** Semester, Summer Session Available **Enrollment:** FT 1,002, PT 695 **Faculty:** FT 80, PT 50 **Library Holdings:** 56,318 **Regional Accreditation:** North Central Association of Colleges and Schools **Credit Hours For Degree:** 60 credit hours, Associates **ROTC:** Air Force **Intercollegiate Athletics:** Baseball M; Basketball M; Volleyball W

CITY COLLEGES OF CHICAGO, RICHARD J. DALEY COLLEGE
7500 South Pulaski Rd.
Chicago, IL 60652-1242
Tel: (773)838-7500
Fax: (773)838-7524
Web Site: http://daley.ccc.edu/
President/CEO: Dr. Silvia Ramos
Registrar: Saundra Listenbee
Admissions: Saundra Listenbee
Financial Aid: Christine Lopez
Type: Two-Year College **Sex:** Coed **Affiliation:** City Colleges of Chicago **Admission Plans:** Open Admission; Preferred Admission; Early Admission; Deferred Admission **Application Fee:** $0.00 **H.S. Requirements:** High school diploma required; GED accepted. For special student category: High school diploma or equivalent not required **Scholarships:** Available **Calendar System:** Semester, Summer Session Available **Enrollment:** FT 3,545, PT 7,109 **Exams:** ACT **Library Holdings:** 53,201 **Regional Accreditation:** North Central Association of Colleges and Schools **Credit Hours For Degree:** 60 credit hours, Associates **ROTC:** Air Force **Professional Accreditation:** NLN

CITY COLLEGES OF CHICAGO, WILBUR WRIGHT COLLEGE
4300 North Narragansett Ave.
Chicago, IL 60634-1591
Tel: (773)777-7900
Admissions: (773)481-8207
Web Site: http://wright.ccc.edu/
President/CEO: Dr. Charles Guengerich
Registrar: Dr. Michael P. Langley
Admissions: Amy Aiello
Financial Aid: Marco Sepulveda
Type: Two-Year College **Sex:** Coed **Affiliation:** City Colleges of Chicago **% Accepted:** 100 **Admission Plans:** Open Admission; Preferred Admission; Early Admission; Deferred Admission **Application Deadline:** Rolling **Application Fee:** $0.00 **H.S. Requirements:** High school diploma required; GED accepted. For applicants 18 or over: High school diploma or equivalent not required **Costs Per Year:** Application fee: $0. Area resident tuition: $2304 full-time, $72 per credit hour part-time. State resident tuition: $5787 full-time, $181 per credit hour part-time. Nonresident tuition: $9332 full-time, $292 per credit hour part-time. Mandatory fees: $250 full-time, $75 per term part-time. **Scholarships:** Available **Calendar System:** Semester, Summer Session Available **Enrollment:** FT 2,211, PT 5,154 **Faculty:** FT 107, PT 150 **Student-Faculty Ratio:** 22:1 **Library Holdings:** 60,000 **Regional Accreditation:** North Central Association of Colleges and Schools **Credit Hours For Degree:** 64 credit hours, Associates **Professional Accreditation:** AOTA, ACBSP, JRCERT **Intercollegiate Athletics:** Basketball M & W; Wrestling M

COLLEGE OF DUPAGE
425 Fawell Blvd.
Glen Ellyn, IL 60137-6599
Tel: (630)942-2800
Admissions: (630)942-2442
Fax: (630)790-2686
E-mail: protis@cdnet.cod.edu
Web Site: http://www.cod.edu/
President/CEO: Dr. Sunil Chand
Registrar: Suzanne Blasi
Admissions: Christine A. Legner
Financial Aid: Marilyn A. Comer
Type: Two-Year College **Sex:** Coed **Affiliation:** Illinois Community College Board **Admission Plans:** Open Admission; Early Admission; Deferred Admission **Application Deadline:** Rolling **Application Fee:** $10.00 **H.S. Requirements:** High school diploma or equivalent not required **Costs Per Year:** Application fee: $10. Area resident tuition: $2850 full-time, $96 per semester hour part-time. State resident tuition: $6690 full-time, $223 per semester hour part-time. Nonresident tuition: $8400 full-time, $280 per semester hour part-time. Mandatory fees: $634 full-time. **Scholarships:** Available **Calendar System:** Quarter, Summer Session Available **Enrollment:** FT 8,784, PT 18,333 **Faculty:** FT 303, PT 994 **Student-Faculty Ratio:** 21:1 **Library Holdings:** 203,300 **Regional Accreditation:** North Central Association of Colleges and Schools **Credit Hours For Degree:** 96 quarter hours, Associates **Professional Accreditation:** ACF, ADA, AHIMA, APTA, CARC, JRCERT, NLN **Intercollegiate Athletics:** Baseball M; Basketball M & W; Cheerleading M & W; Cross-Country Running M & W;

Football M; Golf M; Soccer M & W; Softball W; Swimming and Diving M & W; Tennis M & W; Track and Field M & W; Volleyball W

COLLEGE OF LAKE COUNTY
19351 West Washington St.
Grayslake, IL 60030-1198
Tel: (847)543-2000
Admissions: (847)543-2384
Fax: (847)223-1017
Web Site: http://www.clcillinois.edu/
President/CEO: Dr. Gretchen J. Naff
Admissions: Karen Hlavin
Financial Aid: Verna Wilson-Gross
Type: Two-Year College **Sex:** Coed **Affiliation:** Illinois Community College Board **% Accepted:** 100 **Admission Plans:** Open Admission; Preferred Admission; Early Admission; Deferred Admission **Application Deadline:** Rolling **Application Fee:** $0.00 **H.S. Requirements:** High school diploma or equivalent not required. For health programs: High school diploma required; GED accepted **Costs Per Year:** Application fee: $0. Area resident tuition: $2130 full-time, $71 per credit hour part-time. State resident tuition: $5880 full-time, $196 per credit hour part-time. Nonresident tuition: $8010 full-time, $267 per credit hour part-time. Mandatory fees: $270 full-time, $9 per credit hour part-time. **Scholarships:** Available **Calendar System:** Semester, Summer Session Available **Enrollment:** FT 4,514, PT 11,231 **Faculty:** FT 178, PT 616 **Student-Faculty Ratio:** 20:1 **Library Holdings:** 106,842 **Regional Accreditation:** North Central Association of Colleges and Schools **Credit Hours For Degree:** 60 credits, Associates **Professional Accreditation:** ADA, AHIMA, JRCERT, NLN **Intercollegiate Athletics:** Baseball M; Basketball M & W; Cross-Country Running M & W; Golf M; Soccer M & W; Softball W; Tennis M & W; Volleyball W

THE COLLEGE OF OFFICE TECHNOLOGY
1514-20 West Division St., Second Floor
Chicago, IL 60622
Tel: (773)278-0042
Fax: (773)278-0143
E-mail: bbolton@cotedu.com
Web Site: http://www.cotedu.com/
President/CEO: Pedro Galva
Registrar: Patricia Campos
Admissions: William Bolton
Financial Aid: Paula Terronez
Type: Two-Year College **Scholarships:** Available **Professional Accreditation:** ACICS

COLUMBIA COLLEGE CHICAGO
600 South Michigan Ave.
Chicago, IL 60605-1996
Tel: (312)663-1600
Admissions: (312)344-7133
E-mail: admissions@colum.edu
Web Site: http://www.colum.edu/
President/CEO: Dr. Warrick L. Carter
Registrar: Marvin Cohen
Admissions: Murphy Monroe
Financial Aid: Timothy Bauhs
Type: Comprehensive **Sex:** Coed **Scores:** 48% ACT 18-23; 26% ACT 24-29 **% Accepted:** 91 **Admission Plans:** Open Admission; Deferred Admission **Application Deadline:** June 15 **Application Fee:** $35.00 **H.S. Requirements:** High school diploma required; GED accepted **Costs Per Year:** Application fee: $35. Comprehensive fee: $26,553 includes full-time tuition ($16,328), mandatory fees ($460), and college room and board ($9765). College room only: $8265. Part-time tuition: $565 per credit hour. **Scholarships:** Available **Calendar System:** Semester, Summer Session Available **Enrollment:** FT 8,728, PT 1,416, Grad 698 **Faculty:** FT 299, PT 1,327 **Student-Faculty Ratio:** 14:1 **Exams:** SAT I or ACT **Library Holdings:** 219,952 **Regional Accreditation:** North Central Association of Colleges and Schools **Credit Hours For Degree:** 124 semester hours, Bachelors

CONCORDIA UNIVERSITY
7400 Augusta St.
River Forest, IL 60305-1499
Tel: (708)771-8300
Free: 800-285-2668
Admissions: (708)209-3100
Fax: (708)209-3176
E-mail: crfadmis@curf.edu
Web Site: http://www.curf.edu/
President/CEO: Dr. Manfred B. Boos
Registrar: Dr. Gary Wenzel
Admissions: Dr. Evelyn Burdick
Financial Aid: Deborah Ness
Type: Comprehensive **Sex:** Coed **Affiliation:** Lutheran Church–Missouri Synod; Concordia University System **Scores:** 47.7% ACT 18-23; 32.8% ACT 24-29 **% Accepted:** 62 **Admission Plans:** Deferred Admission **Application Deadline:** Rolling **H.S. Requirements:** High school diploma required; GED accepted **Costs Per Year:** Comprehensive fee: $26,300 includes full-time tuition ($19,500), mandatory fees ($500), and college room and board ($6300). Full-time tuition and fees vary according to program. Part-time tuition: $585 per semester hour. Part-time mandatory fees: $10 per semester hour, $100 per year. Part-time tuition and fees vary according to program. **Scholarships:** Available **Calendar System:** Semester, Summer Session Available **Enrollment:** FT 961, PT 71, Grad 1,751 **Faculty:** FT 80 **Student-Faculty Ratio:** 11:1 **Exams:** SAT I or ACT **% Receiving Financial Aid:** 69 **% Residing in College-Owned, -Operated, or -Affiliated Housing:** 40 **Library Holdings:** 163,711 **Regional Accreditation:** North Central Association of Colleges and Schools **Credit Hours For Degree:** 128 semester hours, Bachelors **Professional Accreditation:** ACA, NASM, NCATE, NLN **Intercollegiate Athletics:** Baseball M; Basketball M & W; Cheerleading M & W; Cross-Country Running M & W; Football M; Golf M; Soccer M & W; Softball W; Tennis M & W; Track and Field M & W; Volleyball W

THE COOKING AND HOSPITALITY INSTITUTE OF CHICAGO
361 West Chestnut
Chicago, IL 60610-3050
Tel: (312)944-0882
Admissions: (312)873-2064
Fax: (312)944-8557
Web Site: http://www.chicnet.org/
President/CEO: James Simpson
Registrar: Sharon Walker
Admissions: Alan Schultz
Financial Aid: Maria Calafiore
Type: Two-Year College **Sex:** Coed **Affiliation:** Career Education Corporation **Scores:** 60% ACT 18-23; 15% ACT 24-29 **Admission Plans:** Open Admission; Deferred Admission **Application Fee:** $150.00 **H.S. Requirements:** High school diploma required; GED accepted **Scholarships:** Available **Calendar System:** Continuous, Summer Session Available **Enrollment:** FT 950 **Student-Faculty Ratio:** 16:1 **Exams:** SAT I or ACT **Library Holdings:** 5,000 **Regional Accreditation:** North Central Association of Colleges and Schools **Credit Hours For Degree:** 69 credits, Associates **Professional Accreditation:** ACCSCT, ACF

DANVILLE AREA COMMUNITY COLLEGE
2000 East Main St.
Danville, IL 61832-5199
Tel: (217)443-3222
Admissions: (217)443-8800
Fax: (217)443-8560
Web Site: http://www.dacc.cc.il.us/
President/CEO: Dr. Alice Marie Jacobs
Registrar: Stacy Ehmen
Admissions: Stacy L. Ehmen
Financial Aid: Janet Ingargiola
Type: Two-Year College **Sex:** Coed **Affiliation:** Illinois Community College Board **Admission Plans:** Open Admission; Early Admission; Deferred Admission **Application Fee:** $0.00 **H.S. Requirements:** High school diploma required; GED accepted **Costs Per Year:** Application fee: $0. State resident tuition: $1392 full-time, $58 per credit hour part-time. Nonresident tuition: $3600 full-time, $150 per credit hour part-time. Mandatory fees: $144 full-time, $6 per credit hour part-time. **Scholarships:** Available **Calendar System:** Semester, Summer Session Available **Faculty:** FT 50, PT 71 **Student-Faculty Ratio:** 20:1 **Exams:** Other **Library Holdings:** 50,000 **Regional Accreditation:** North Central Association of Colleges and Schools **Credit Hours For Degree:** 62 semester hours, Associates **Intercollegiate Athletics:** Baseball M; Basketball M & W; Cross-Country Running M; Softball W; Track and Field M & W; Volleyball W

DEPAUL UNIVERSITY
1 East Jackson Blvd.
Chicago, IL 60604-2287

Tel: (312)362-8000
Admissions: (312)362-8650
Fax: (312)362-3322
E-mail: admitdpu@depaul.edu
Web Site: http://www.depaul.edu/
President/CEO: Rev. Dennis H. Holtschneider, CM
Registrar: Susan Leigh
Admissions: Dr. David Kalsbeek
Financial Aid: John Schoultz
Type: University **Sex:** Coed **Affiliation:** Roman Catholic **Scores:** 99.41% SAT V 400+; 98% SAT M 400+; 46.2% ACT 18-23; 46.2% ACT 24-29 **% Accepted:** 71 **Admission Plans:** Early Admission; Early Action; Early Decision Plan; Deferred Admission **Application Deadline:** Rolling **Application Fee:** $40.00 **H.S. Requirements:** High school diploma required; GED accepted **Costs Per Year:** Application fee: $40. Comprehensive fee: $29,905 includes full-time tuition ($20,900), mandatory fees ($140), and college room and board ($8865). College room only: $6507. Full-time tuition and fees vary according to program. Room and board charges vary according to board plan, housing facility, and location. Part-time tuition: $384 per quarter hour. Part-time tuition varies according to program. **Scholarships:** Available **Calendar System:** Quarter, Summer Session Available **Enrollment:** FT 11,381, PT 3,359, Grad 7,229 **Faculty:** FT 834, PT 643 **Student-Faculty Ratio:** 17:1 **Exams:** SAT I or ACT **% Receiving Financial Aid:** 59 **% Residing in College-Owned, -Operated, or -Affiliated Housing:** 17 **Library Holdings:** 896,864 **Regional Accreditation:** North Central Association of Colleges and Schools **Credit Hours For Degree:** 192 quarter hours, Bachelors **ROTC:** Army **Professional Accreditation:** AACSB, AACN, AANA, ABA, APA, AALS, NASM, NASPAA, NCATE **Intercollegiate Athletics:** Basketball M & W; Cross-Country Running M & W; Golf M & W; Soccer M & W; Softball W; Tennis M & W; Track and Field M & W; Volleyball W

DEVRY UNIVERSITY (ADDISON)
1221 North Swift Rd.
Addison, IL 60101-6106
Tel: (630)953-1300
Free: 800-346-5420
Fax: (630)953-1236
Web Site: http://www.devry.edu/
President/CEO: Susan L. Friedberg
Registrar: Janet Sabri
Financial Aid: Sejal Amin
Type: Four-Year College **Sex:** Coed **Affiliation:** DeVry University **Admission Plans:** Deferred Admission **Application Deadline:** Rolling **Application Fee:** $50.00 **H.S. Requirements:** High school diploma required; GED accepted **Costs Per Year:** Application fee: $50. One-time mandatory fee: $40. Tuition: $11,890 full-time, $445 per credit part-time. Mandatory fees: $270 full-time, $160 per year part-time. Full-time tuition and fees vary according to course load. Part-time tuition and fees vary according to course load. **Scholarships:** Available **Calendar System:** Semester, Summer Session Available **Enrollment:** FT 1,142, PT 435 **Faculty:** FT 51, PT 61 **Student-Faculty Ratio:** 18:1 **% Receiving Financial Aid:** 49 **Library Holdings:** 18,500 **Regional Accreditation:** North Central Association of Colleges and Schools **Credit Hours For Degree:** 67 credit hours, Associates; 122 credit hours, Bachelors **Professional Accreditation:** ABET

DEVRY UNIVERSITY (CHICAGO)
3300 North Campbell Ave.
Chicago, IL 60618-5994
Tel: (773)929-8500
Free: 800-383-3879
Web Site: http://www.devry.edu/
President/CEO: Dr. Eugene Hallongren
Registrar: Gilbert Martinez
Financial Aid: Milena Dobrina
Type: Comprehensive **Sex:** Coed **Affiliation:** DeVry University **Admission Plans:** Deferred Admission **Application Deadline:** Rolling **Application Fee:** $50.00 **H.S. Requirements:** High school diploma required; GED accepted **Costs Per Year:** Application fee: $50. One-time mandatory fee: $40. Tuition: $11,890 full-time, $445 per credit part-time. Mandatory fees: $270 full-time, $160 per year part-time. Full-time tuition and fees vary according to course load. Part-time tuition and fees vary according to course load. **Scholarships:** Available **Calendar System:** Semester, Summer Session Available **Enrollment:** FT 1,343, PT 823 **Faculty:** FT 53, PT 60 **Student-Faculty Ratio:** 22:1 **% Receiving Financial Aid:** 64 **Library Holdings:** 16,573 **Regional Accreditation:** North Central Association of Colleges and Schools **Credit Hours For Degree:** 67 credit hours, Associates; 122 credit hours, Bachelors **Professional Accreditation:** ABET

DEVRY UNIVERSITY (ELGIN)
385 Airport Rd.
Elgin, IL 60123-9341
Tel: (847)622-1135
Fax: (847)622-1246
Web Site: http://www.devry.edu/ **Type:** Comprehensive **Sex:** Coed **Calendar System:** Semester **Regional Accreditation:** North Central Association of Colleges and Schools

DEVRY UNIVERSITY (GURNEE)
1075 Tri-State Parkway, Ste. 800
Gurnee, IL 60031-9126
Tel: (847)855-2649; (866)563-3879
Fax: (847)855-5932
Web Site: http://www.devry.edu/ **Type:** Comprehensive **Sex:** Coed **Costs Per Year:** One-time mandatory fee: $40. Tuition: $11,890 full-time, $445 per credit part-time. Mandatory fees: $60 full-time, $30 per year part-time. Full-time tuition and fees vary according to course load. Part-time tuition and fees vary according to course load. **Calendar System:** Semester **Regional Accreditation:** North Central Association of Colleges and Schools

DEVRY UNIVERSITY (NAPERVILLE)
2056 Westings Ave., Ste. 40
Naperville, IL 60563-2361
Tel: (630)428-9086
Fax: (630)428-4721
Web Site: http://www.devry.edu/ **Type:** Comprehensive **Sex:** Coed **Costs Per Year:** One-time mandatory fee: $40. Tuition: $11,890 full-time, $445 per credit part-time. Mandatory fees: $60 full-time, $30 per year part-time. Full-time tuition and fees vary according to course load. Part-time tuition and fees vary according to course load. **Calendar System:** Semester **Regional Accreditation:** North Central Association of Colleges and Schools

DEVRY UNIVERSITY (OAKBROOK TERRACE)
One Tower Ln.
Oakbrook Terrace, IL 60181
Tel: (630)574-1960
Web Site: http://www.devry.edu/
President/CEO: Cecil Horst
Financial Aid: Mike Alexander
Type: Comprehensive **Sex:** Coed **Costs Per Year:** One-time mandatory fee: $40. Tuition: $11,890 full-time, $445 per credit part-time. Mandatory fees: $60 full-time, $30 per year part-time. Full-time tuition and fees vary according to course load. Part-time tuition and fees vary according to course load. **Calendar System:** Semester **Regional Accreditation:** North Central Association of Colleges and Schools

DEVRY UNIVERSITY ONLINE
One Tower Ln., Ste. 1000
Oakbrook Terrace, IL 60181
Tel: (630)574-1960; (866)338-7934
Fax: (630)574-1969
Web Site: http://online.devry.edu/ **Type:** Comprehensive **Sex:** Coed **Application Deadline:** Rolling **Application Fee:** $50.00 **Costs Per Year:** Application fee: $50. One-time mandatory fee: $40. Tuition: $13,060 full-time. Mandatory fees: $30 full-time. **Calendar System:** Semester **Enrollment:** FT 2,146, PT 2,281, Grad 2,142 **Faculty:** FT 0, PT 791 **Student-Faculty Ratio:** 16:1 **Regional Accreditation:** North Central Association of Colleges and Schools

DEVRY UNIVERSITY (TINLEY PARK)
18624 West Creek Dr.
Tinley Park, IL 60477
Tel: (708)342-3300; (866)338-7934
Web Site: http://www.devry.edu/
President/CEO: Susan Friedberg
Registrar: Carol Cortilet
Financial Aid: Connie Alabi
Type: Comprehensive **Sex:** Coed **Affiliation:** DeVry University **Admission Plans:** Deferred Admission **Application Deadline:** Rolling **Application Fee:**

$50.00 **H.S. Requirements:** High school diploma required; GED accepted **Costs Per Year:** Application fee: $50. One-time mandatory fee: $40. Tuition: $11,890 full-time, $445 per credit part-time. Mandatory fees: $270 full-time, $160 per year part-time. Full-time tuition and fees vary according to course load. Part-time tuition and fees vary according to course load. **Scholarships:** Available **Calendar System:** Semester, Summer Session Available **Enrollment:** FT 701, PT 348, Grad 236 **Faculty:** FT 33, PT 41 **Student-Faculty Ratio:** 20:1 **% Receiving Financial Aid:** 45 **Library Holdings:** 17,500 **Regional Accreditation:** North Central Association of Colleges and Schools **Credit Hours For Degree:** 67 credit hours, Associates; 122 credit hours, Bachelors

DOMINICAN UNIVERSITY
7900 West Division St.
River Forest, IL 60305-1099
Tel: (708)366-2490
Free: 800-828-8475
Admissions: (708)524-6800
Fax: (708)366-5360
E-mail: domadmis@dom.edu
Web Site: http://www.dom.edu/
President/CEO: Dr. Donna M. Carroll
Registrar: Marilyn Benakis
Admissions: Pamela Johnson
Financial Aid: Michael Shields
Type: Comprehensive **Sex:** Coed **Affiliation:** Roman Catholic **Scores:** 59% ACT 18-23; 33% ACT 24-29 **% Accepted:** 81 **Admission Plans:** Deferred Admission **Application Deadline:** Rolling **Application Fee:** $25.00 **H.S. Requirements:** High school diploma required; GED accepted **Costs Per Year:** Application fee: $25. Comprehensive fee: $26,370 includes full-time tuition ($19,950), mandatory fees ($100), and college room and board ($6320). Full-time tuition and fees vary according to program. Room and board charges vary according to board plan and housing facility. Part-time tuition: $665 per semester hour. Part-time mandatory fees: $10 per course. Part-time tuition and fees vary according to location and program. **Scholarships:** Available **Calendar System:** Semester, Summer Session Available **Enrollment:** FT 1,146, PT 191, Grad 1,913 **Faculty:** FT 109, PT 200 **Student-Faculty Ratio:** 11:1 **Exams:** SAT I or ACT **% Receiving Financial Aid:** 81 **% Residing in College-Owned, -Operated, or -Affiliated Housing:** 35 **Library Holdings:** 255,840 **Regional Accreditation:** North Central Association of Colleges and Schools **Credit Hours For Degree:** 124 credit hours, Bachelors **Professional Accreditation:** ALA, ACBSP, CSWE **Intercollegiate Athletics:** Baseball M; Basketball M & W; Cross-Country Running M & W; Golf M & W; Soccer M & W; Softball W; Tennis M & W; Volleyball W

EAST-WEST UNIVERSITY
816 South Michigan Ave.
Chicago, IL 60605-2103
Tel: (312)939-0111
Fax: (312)939-0083
Web Site: http://www.eastwest.edu/
President/CEO: Dr. M. Wasiullah Khan
Registrar: Amal Matari
Admissions: William Link
Financial Aid: Elizabeth V. Guzman
Type: Four-Year College **Sex:** Coed **Scores:** 30% ACT 18-23; 1% ACT 24-29 **Admission Plans:** Early Decision Plan **Application Fee:** $50.00 **H.S. Requirements:** High school diploma required; GED accepted **Costs Per Year:** Application fee: $50. Tuition: $10,950 full-time, $365 per credit hour part-time. Mandatory fees: $495 full-time. Full-time tuition and fees vary according to course level. **Scholarships:** Available **Calendar System:** Quarter, Summer Session Available **Enrollment:** FT 1,031, PT 9 **Faculty:** FT 15, PT 55 **Student-Faculty Ratio:** 17:1 **Exams:** ACT **% Receiving Financial Aid:** 100 **Library Holdings:** 32,000 **Regional Accreditation:** North Central Association of Colleges and Schools **Credit Hours For Degree:** 96 quarter hours, Associates; 192 quarter hours, Bachelors **Intercollegiate Athletics:** Basketball M

EASTERN ILLINOIS UNIVERSITY
600 Lincoln Ave.
Charleston, IL 61920-3099
Tel: (217)581-5000
Free: 800-252-5711
Admissions: (217)581-2223
Fax: (217)581-7060
E-mail: bmajor@eiu.edu
Web Site: http://www.eiu.edu/
President/CEO: Louis V. Hencken
Registrar: G. Sue Harvey
Admissions: Brenda Major
Financial Aid: Jone Zieren
Type: Comprehensive **Sex:** Coed **Scores:** 63% ACT 18-23; 26% ACT 24-29 **% Accepted:** 78 **Application Deadline:** Rolling **Application Fee:** $30.00 **H.S. Requirements:** High school diploma required; GED accepted **Costs Per Year:** Application fee: $30. State resident tuition: $4629 full-time, $154 per credit hour part-time. Nonresident tuition: $13,887 full-time, $463 per credit hour part-time. Mandatory fees: $1744 full-time, $63 per credit hour part-time. Full-time tuition and fees vary according to course load. Part-time tuition and fees vary according to course load. College room and board: $6196. Room and board charges vary according to board plan and housing facility. **Scholarships:** Available **Calendar System:** Semester, Summer Session Available **Enrollment:** FT 9,293, PT 1,082, Grad 1,754 **Faculty:** FT 610, PT 145 **Student-Faculty Ratio:** 16:1 **Exams:** SAT I or ACT **% Receiving Financial Aid:** 47 **% Residing in College-Owned, -Operated, or -Affiliated Housing:** 44 **Library Holdings:** 1,013,336 **Regional Accreditation:** North Central Association of Colleges and Schools **Credit Hours For Degree:** 120 semester hours, Bachelors **ROTC:** Army **Professional Accreditation:** AACSB, ACEJMC, AAFCS, ACA, ADtA, ASLHA, JRCEPAT, NAIT, NASAD, NASM, NCATE, NRPA **Intercollegiate Athletics:** Baseball M; Basketball M & W; Cross-Country Running M & W; Football M; Golf M & W; Rugby M & W; Soccer M & W; Softball W; Swimming and Diving M & W; Tennis M & W; Track and Field M & W; Volleyball W; Wrestling M

ELGIN COMMUNITY COLLEGE
1700 Spartan Dr.
Elgin, IL 60123-7193
Tel: (847)697-1000
Admissions: (847)214-7414
Web Site: http://www.elgin.edu/
President/CEO: Dr. Michael Shirley
Registrar: Roberta Haskins
Admissions: Kelly Sinclair
Financial Aid: Robert Laws
Type: Two-Year College **Sex:** Coed **Affiliation:** Illinois Community College Board **Admission Plans:** Open Admission; Early Admission **Application Fee:** $15.00 **H.S. Requirements:** High school diploma or equivalent not required. For nursing, selected health programs: High school diploma required; GED accepted **Costs Per Year:** Application fee: $15. Area resident tuition: $2250 full-time, $75 per credit hour part-time. State resident tuition: $7666 full-time, $255.54 per credit hour part-time. Nonresident tuition: $9947 full-time, $331.59 per credit hour part-time. Mandatory fees: $10 full-time, $5 per term part-time. **Calendar System:** Semester, Summer Session Available **Enrollment:** FT 3,348, PT 7,503 **Faculty:** FT 123, PT 389 **Student-Faculty Ratio:** 23:1 **Exams:** ACT **Library Holdings:** 58,413 **Regional Accreditation:** North Central Association of Colleges and Schools **Credit Hours For Degree:** 60 credit hours, Associates **Professional Accreditation:** ACF, ADA, NAACLS, NLN **Intercollegiate Athletics:** Baseball M & W; Basketball M & W; Cross-Country Running M & W; Golf M; Softball W; Tennis W; Volleyball W

ELMHURST COLLEGE
190 Prospect Ave.
Elmhurst, IL 60126-3296
Tel: (630)617-3500
Free: 800-697-1871
Admissions: (630)617-3400
Fax: (630)617-5501
E-mail: admit@elmhurst.edu
Web Site: http://www.elmhurst.edu/
President/CEO: Dr. Bryant L. Cureton
Registrar: Elizabeth Smith
Admissions: Gary Rold
Financial Aid: Ruth Pusich
Type: Comprehensive **Sex:** Coed **Affiliation:** United Church of Christ **Scores:** 43% ACT 18-23; 40% ACT 24-29 **Admission Plans:** Deferred Admission **Application Fee:** $25.00 **H.S. Requirements:** High school diploma required; GED accepted **Costs Per Year:** Application fee: $25. Comprehensive fee: $28,506 includes full-time tuition ($21,600) and college room and board ($6906). College room only: $3816. Room and board

charges vary according to board plan and housing facility. Part-time tuition: $614 per semester hour. **Scholarships:** Available **Calendar System:** 4-1-4, Summer Session Available **Enrollment:** FT 2,129, PT 355, Grad 186 **Faculty:** FT 110, PT 168 **Student-Faculty Ratio:** 13:1 **Exams:** SAT I or ACT **% Receiving Financial Aid:** 70 **% Residing in College-Owned, -Operated, or -Affiliated Housing:** 40 **Library Holdings:** 222,441 **Regional Accreditation:** North Central Association of Colleges and Schools **Credit Hours For Degree:** 32 courses, Bachelors **ROTC:** Army, Air Force **Professional Accreditation:** AACN, NCATE **Intercollegiate Athletics:** Baseball M; Basketball M & W; Cross-Country Running M & W; Football M; Golf M & W; Soccer W; Softball W; Tennis M & W; Track and Field M & W; Volleyball W; Wrestling M

EUREKA COLLEGE
300 East College Ave.
Eureka, IL 61530-1500
Tel: (309)467-3721; 888-4-EUREKA
Admissions: (309)467-6350
Fax: (309)467-6576
E-mail: admissions@eureka.edu
Web Site: http://www.eureka.edu/
President/CEO: Paul R. Lister
Registrar: Scott Wignall
Admissions: Dr. Brian Sajko
Financial Aid: Ellen Rigsby
Type: Four-Year College **Sex:** Coed **Affiliation:** Christian Church (Disciples of Christ) **Scores:** 40% ACT 18-23; 37% ACT 24-29 **Admission Plans:** Deferred Admission **Application Fee:** $0.00 **H.S. Requirements:** High school diploma required; GED accepted **Costs Per Year:** Application fee: $0. Comprehensive fee: $19,280 includes full-time tuition ($13,000), mandatory fees ($400), and college room and board ($5880). College room only: $2820. Full-time tuition and fees vary according to course load and program. Room and board charges vary according to board plan and housing facility. Part-time tuition: $375 per semester hour. Part-time tuition varies according to course load and program. **Scholarships:** Available **Calendar System:** Miscellaneous, Summer Session Available **Enrollment:** FT 505, PT 11 **Faculty:** FT 42, PT 27 **Student-Faculty Ratio:** 13:1 **Exams:** SAT I or ACT **% Receiving Financial Aid:** 78 **% Residing in College-Owned, -Operated, or -Affiliated Housing:** 84 **Library Holdings:** 75,000 **Regional Accreditation:** North Central Association of Colleges and Schools **Credit Hours For Degree:** 124 semester hours, Bachelors **Intercollegiate Athletics:** Baseball M; Basketball M & W; Football M; Golf M & W; Softball W; Swimming and Diving M & W; Tennis M & W; Volleyball W

FOX COLLEGE
4201 West 93rd St.
Oak Lawn, IL 60453
Tel: (708)636-7700; (866)636-7711
Fax: (708)636-8078
E-mail: sszala@foxcollege.edu
Web Site: http://www.foxcollege.com/
Admissions: Susan Szala
Type: Two-Year College **Sex:** Coed **Costs Per Year:** Tuition: $12,720 full-time. **Enrollment:** FT 251 **Professional Accreditation:** ACICS

GEM CITY COLLEGE
PO Box 179
Quincy, IL 62301
Tel: (217)222-0391
Fax: (217)222-1557
Web Site: http://www.gemcitycollege.com/
President/CEO: Russell H. Hagenah
Registrar: Ruth Nesbit
Financial Aid: Joan Mast
Type: Two-Year College **Sex:** Coed **Admission Plans:** Open Admission; Early Admission; Deferred Admission **Application Fee:** $25.00 **H.S. Requirements:** High school diploma required; GED accepted **Scholarships:** Available **Calendar System:** Quarter, Summer Session Available **Faculty:** FT 5, PT 2 **Library Holdings:** 2,700 **Professional Accreditation:** ACICS

GOVERNORS STATE UNIVERSITY
One University Parkway
University Park, IL 60466-0975
Tel: (708)534-5000
Admissions: (708)534-4490
Fax: (708)534-1640
Web Site: http://www.govst.edu/
President/CEO: Dr. Stuart I. Fagan
Registrar: Dora Smith
Admissions: Randall Tumblin
Financial Aid: Frieda Comer
Type: Two-Year Upper Division **Sex:** Coed **Admission Plans:** Deferred Admission **Application Fee:** $0.00 **Costs Per Year:** Application fee: $0. State resident tuition: $3720 full-time, $155 per credit part-time. Nonresident tuition: $11,160 full-time, $465 per credit part-time. Mandatory fees: $580 full-time, $170 per term part-time. **Scholarships:** Available **Calendar System:** Trimester, Summer Session Available **Enrollment:** FT 856, PT 1,776, Grad 2,773 **Faculty:** FT 185, PT 27 **Student-Faculty Ratio:** 16:1 **Library Holdings:** 260,000 **Regional Accreditation:** North Central Association of Colleges and Schools **Credit Hours For Degree:** 120 credit hours, Bachelors **ROTC:** Army, Air Force **Professional Accreditation:** ACEHSA, ACA, AOTA, APTA, ASLHA, ACBSP, CSWE, NASPAA, NCATE, NLN

GREENVILLE COLLEGE
315 East College, PO Box 159
Greenville, IL 62246-0159
Tel: (618)664-2800
Free: 800-345-4440
Admissions: (618)664-7100
Fax: (618)664-9841
E-mail: admissions@greenville.edu
Web Site: http://www.greenville.edu/
President/CEO: Dr. V. James Mannoia, Jr.
Registrar: Dr. Kay Paulsen
Admissions: Dr. R. Pepper Dill
Financial Aid: Karl Somerville
Type: Comprehensive **Sex:** Coed **Affiliation:** Free Methodist **Scores:** 87% SAT V 400+; 84% SAT M 400+; 47% ACT 18-23; 31% ACT 24-29 **% Accepted:** 90 **Admission Plans:** Early Admission; Deferred Admission **Application Deadline:** August 01 **Application Fee:** $25.00 **H.S. Requirements:** High school diploma required; GED accepted **Costs Per Year:** Application fee: $25. Comprehensive fee: $23,146 includes full-time tuition ($17,142), mandatory fees ($100), and college room and board ($5904). College room only: $2794. Room and board charges vary according to housing facility. Part-time tuition: $361 per credit hour. Part-time tuition varies according to course load. **Scholarships:** Available **Calendar System:** 4-1-4, Summer Session Available **Enrollment:** FT 1,175, PT 40, Grad 135 **Faculty:** FT 59, PT 65 **Student-Faculty Ratio:** 15:1 **Exams:** SAT I or ACT **% Receiving Financial Aid:** 85 **% Residing in College-Owned, -Operated, or -Affiliated Housing:** 62 **Library Holdings:** 126,210 **Regional Accreditation:** North Central Association of Colleges and Schools **Credit Hours For Degree:** 126 credits, Bachelors **Intercollegiate Athletics:** Baseball M; Basketball M & W; Cross-Country Running M & W; Football M; Soccer M & W; Softball W; Tennis M & W; Track and Field M & W; Volleyball W

HARRINGTON COLLEGE OF DESIGN
200 West Madison St.
Chicago, IL 60606
Tel: (312)939-4975; 877-939-4975
Fax: (312)939-8005
Web Site: http://www.interiordesign.edu/
President/CEO: Patrick W. Comstock
Registrar: Sam Delarosa
Admissions: Wendi Franczyk
Financial Aid: Renee Darosky
Type: Four-Year College **Sex:** Coed **Affiliation:** Career Education Corporation **Admission Plans:** Deferred Admission **Application Deadline:** Rolling **Application Fee:** $60.00 **H.S. Requirements:** High school diploma required; GED accepted **Costs Per Year:** Application fee: $60. Tuition: $6930 full-time, $550 per credit hour part-time. Mandatory fees: $580 full-time. Full-time tuition and fees vary according to course load and program. Part-time tuition varies according to course load and program. College room only: $5000. Room charges vary according to housing facility. **Scholarships:** Available **Calendar System:** Semester, Summer Session Not available **Enrollment:** FT 747, PT 816 **Faculty:** FT 17, PT 125 **Student-Faculty Ratio:** 12:1 **% Residing in College-Owned, -Operated, or -Affiliated Housing:** 6 **Library Holdings:** 19,672 **Credit Hours For Degree:** 67.5 credit hours, Associates; 129.5 credit hours, Bachelors **Professional Accreditation:** FIDER, NASAD

HEARTLAND COMMUNITY COLLEGE
1500 West Raab Rd.
Normal, IL 61761
Tel: (309)268-8000
Fax: (309)268-7999
Web Site: http://www.heartland.edu/
President/CEO: Dr. Jonathan Astroth
Registrar: Dr. Fred Peterson
Admissions: Christine Riley
Financial Aid: Cheryl Schaffer
Type: Two-Year College **Sex:** Coed **Affiliation:** Illinois Community College Board **Admission Plans:** Open Admission **Application Deadline:** Rolling **Application Fee:** $0.00 **H.S. Requirements:** High school diploma required; GED accepted **Costs Per Year:** Application fee: $0. Area resident tuition: $2010 full-time, $67 per semester hour part-time. State resident tuition: $4020 full-time, $134 per semester hour part-time. Nonresident tuition: $6030 full-time, $201 per semester hour part-time. Mandatory fees: $90 full-time, $3 per semester hour part-time. **Scholarships:** Available **Calendar System:** Semester, Summer Session Available **Faculty:** FT 70, PT 183 **Student-Faculty Ratio:** 19:1 **Exams:** ACT, Other, SAT I **Library Holdings:** 5,000 **Regional Accreditation:** North Central Association of Colleges and Schools **Credit Hours For Degree:** 60 semester hours, Associates **ROTC:** Army **Professional Accreditation:** NLN

HEBREW THEOLOGICAL COLLEGE
7135 North Carpenter Rd.
Skokie, IL 60077-3263
Tel: (847)982-2500
Web Site: http://www.htcnet.edu/
President/CEO: Rabbi Dr. Jerold Isenberg
Registrar: Adele Feldman
Admissions: Rabbi Berish Cardash
Financial Aid: Rabbi Shmuel Schuman
Type: Comprehensive **Sex:** Men **Affiliation:** Jewish **Application Fee:** $50.00 **H.S. Requirements:** High school diploma required; GED accepted **Calendar System:** Semester, Summer Session Available **Exams:** SAT I or ACT **Library Holdings:** 63,000 **Regional Accreditation:** North Central Association of Colleges and Schools **Credit Hours For Degree:** 120 credit hours, Bachelors

HIGHLAND COMMUNITY COLLEGE
2998 West Pearl City Rd.
Freeport, IL 61032-9341
Tel: (815)235-6121
Fax: (815)235-6130
Web Site: http://www.highland.edu/
President/CEO: Dr. Ronald J. Field
Registrar: Karl Richards
Admissions: Karl Richards
Financial Aid: Phil Gordon
Type: Two-Year College **Sex:** Coed **Affiliation:** Illinois Community College Board **Scores:** 47% ACT 18-23; 22% ACT 24-29 **% Accepted:** 100 **Admission Plans:** Open Admission; Preferred Admission; Early Admission; Deferred Admission **Application Deadline:** Rolling **Application Fee:** $0.00 **H.S. Requirements:** High school diploma required; GED accepted **Costs Per Year:** Application fee: $0. Area resident tuition: $1608 full-time, $67 per credit part-time. State resident tuition: $2880 full-time, $120 per credit part-time. Nonresident tuition: $2880 full-time, $120 per credit part-time. Mandatory fees: $120 full-time, $5 per credit part-time. **Scholarships:** Available **Calendar System:** Semester, Summer Session Available **Enrollment:** FT 1,134; PT 1,272 **Faculty:** FT 48, PT 142 **Student-Faculty Ratio:** 16:1 **Library Holdings:** 47,000 **Regional Accreditation:** North Central Association of Colleges and Schools **Credit Hours For Degree:** 62 credit hours, Associates **Intercollegiate Athletics:** Baseball M & W; Basketball M & W; Golf M & W; Softball W; Volleyball W

ILLINOIS CENTRAL COLLEGE
One College Dr.
East Peoria, IL 61635-0001
Tel: (309)694-5011
Admissions: (309)694-5784
Fax: (309)694-5450
Web Site: http://www.icc.edu/
President/CEO: Dr. John S. Erwin
Registrar: Guy Goodman
Admissions: John Avendano
Type: Two-Year College **Sex:** Coed **Affiliation:** Illinois Community College Board **Admission Plans:** Open Admission; Early Admission **Application Deadline:** Rolling **Application Fee:** $0.00 **H.S. Requirements:** High school diploma or equivalent not required **Costs Per Year:** Application fee: $0. Area resident tuition: $2240 full-time, $70 per semester hour part-time. State resident tuition: $4960 full-time, $155 per semester hour part-time. Nonresident tuition: $4960 full-time, $155 per semester hour part-time. College room only: $3978. **Scholarships:** Available **Calendar System:** Semester, Summer Session Available **Enrollment:** FT 4,907, PT 7,436 **Faculty:** FT 172, PT 486 **Library Holdings:** 82,492 **Regional Accreditation:** North Central Association of Colleges and Schools **Credit Hours For Degree:** 64 semester hours, Associates **Professional Accreditation:** ADA, AOTA, APTA, CARC, JRCERT, NAACLS, NASM, NLN **Intercollegiate Athletics:** Baseball M; Basketball M & W; Golf M & W; Soccer M & W; Softball W; Volleyball W

ILLINOIS COLLEGE
1101 West College Ave.
Jacksonville, IL 62650-2299
Tel: (217)245-3000; (866)464-5265
Admissions: (217)245-3030
Fax: (217)245-3034
E-mail: admissions@ic.edu
Web Site: http://www.ic.edu/
President/CEO: Dr. Axel D. Steuer
Registrar: Dr. Glen W. Clatterbuck
Admissions: Scott Belobrajdic
Financial Aid: Katherine Taylor
Type: Four-Year College **Sex:** Coed **Affiliation:** interdenominational **Scores:** 95.3% SAT V 400+; 100% SAT M 400+; 42.3% ACT 18-23; 48.5% ACT 24-29 **% Accepted:** 64 **Application Deadline:** July 01 **Application Fee:** $25.00 **H.S. Requirements:** High school diploma required; GED accepted **Costs Per Year:** Application fee: $25. Comprehensive fee: $23,600 includes full-time tuition ($17,100) and college room and board ($6500). Part-time tuition: $712 per credit hour. **Scholarships:** Available **Calendar System:** Semester, Summer Session Available **Enrollment:** FT 1,009, PT 21 **Faculty:** FT 71, PT 38 **Student-Faculty Ratio:** 12:1 **Exams:** SAT I or ACT **% Receiving Financial Aid:** 75 **% Residing in College-Owned, -Operated, or -Affiliated Housing:** 75 **Library Holdings:** 163,810 **Regional Accreditation:** North Central Association of Colleges and Schools **Credit Hours For Degree:** 120 credits, Bachelors **Intercollegiate Athletics:** Baseball M; Cheerleading W; Cross-Country Running M & W; Football M; Golf M & W; Soccer M & W; Softball W; Tennis M & W; Track and Field M & W; Volleyball W; Wrestling M

ILLINOIS EASTERN COMMUNITY COLLEGES, FRONTIER COMMUNITY COLLEGE
Frontier Dr.
Fairfield, IL 62837-2601
Tel: (618)842-3711
Fax: (618)842-6340
Web Site: http://www.iecc.edu/fcc/
President/CEO: Dr. Michael Dreith
Registrar: Suzanne Brooks
Admissions: Suzanne Brooks
Financial Aid: Carroll Hilliard
Type: Two-Year College **Sex:** Coed **Affiliation:** Illinois Eastern Community College System **Admission Plans:** Open Admission; Preferred Admission; Early Admission; Deferred Admission **Application Deadline:** Rolling **Application Fee:** $10.00 **H.S. Requirements:** High school diploma required; GED accepted **Costs Per Year:** Application fee: $10. Area resident tuition: $1696 full-time, $53 per credit hour part-time. State resident tuition: $5908 full-time, $184.63 per credit hour part-time. Nonresident tuition: $7314 full-time, $228.55 per credit hour part-time. Mandatory fees: $106 full-time, $3 per credit hour part-time. **Scholarships:** Available **Calendar System:** Semester, Summer Session Available **Enrollment:** FT 249, PT 1,915 **Faculty:** FT 5, PT 230 **Library Holdings:** 19,088 **Regional Accreditation:** North Central Association of Colleges and Schools **Credit Hours For Degree:** 64 credit hours, Associates **Professional Accreditation:** NLN

ILLINOIS EASTERN COMMUNITY COLLEGES, LINCOLN TRAIL COLLEGE
11220 State Hwy. 1
Robinson, IL 62454

Tel: (618)544-8657
Fax: (618)544-7423
Web Site: http://www.iecc.edu/ltc/
President/CEO: Dr. Carl Heilman
Registrar: Becky Mikeworth
Admissions: Becky Mikeworth
Financial Aid: Deborah Kull
Type: Two-Year College **Sex:** Coed **Affiliation:** Illinois Eastern Community College System **Admission Plans:** Open Admission; Preferred Admission; Early Admission; Deferred Admission **Application Deadline:** Rolling **Application Fee:** $10.00 **H.S. Requirements:** High school diploma required; GED accepted **Costs Per Year:** Application fee: $10. Area resident tuition: $1696 full-time, $53 per credit hour part-time. State resident tuition: $5908 full-time, $184.63 per credit hour part-time. Nonresident tuition: $7314 full-time, $228.55 per credit hour part-time. Mandatory fees: $106 full-time, $3 per credit hour part-time. **Scholarships:** Available **Calendar System:** Semester, Summer Session Available **Enrollment:** FT 505, PT 1,027 **Faculty:** FT 26, PT 60 **Library Holdings:** 16,654 **Regional Accreditation:** North Central Association of Colleges and Schools **Credit Hours For Degree:** 64 credit hours, Associates **Professional Accreditation:** NLN **Intercollegiate Athletics:** Baseball M; Basketball M & W; Softball W; Volleyball W

ILLINOIS EASTERN COMMUNITY COLLEGES, OLNEY CENTRAL COLLEGE
305 North West St.
Olney, IL 62450
Tel: (618)395-7777
Fax: (618)392-5212
Web Site: http://www.iecc.edu/occ/
President/CEO: Dr. Jackie L. Davis
Registrar: Chris Webber
Admissions: Chris Webber
Financial Aid: Vicky Stuckey
Type: Two-Year College **Sex:** Coed **Affiliation:** Illinois Eastern Community College System **Admission Plans:** Open Admission; Preferred Admission; Early Admission; Deferred Admission **Application Deadline:** Rolling **Application Fee:** $10.00 **H.S. Requirements:** High school diploma required; GED accepted **Costs Per Year:** Application fee: $10. Area resident tuition: $1696 full-time, $53 per credit hour part-time. State resident tuition: $5908 full-time, $184.63 per credit hour part-time. Nonresident tuition: $7314 full-time, $228.55 per credit hour part-time. Mandatory fees: $106 full-time, $3 per credit hour part-time. **Scholarships:** Available **Calendar System:** Semester, Summer Session Available **Enrollment:** FT 758, PT 943 **Faculty:** FT 48, PT 70 **Library Holdings:** 22,976 **Regional Accreditation:** North Central Association of Colleges and Schools **Credit Hours For Degree:** 64 credit hours, Associates **Professional Accreditation:** JRCERT, NLN **Intercollegiate Athletics:** Baseball M; Basketball M & W; Softball W; Volleyball W

ILLINOIS EASTERN COMMUNITY COLLEGES, WABASH VALLEY COLLEGE
2200 College Dr.
Mount Carmel, IL 62863-2657
Tel: (618)262-8641
Fax: (618)262-8641
Web Site: http://www.iecc.edu/wvc/
President/CEO: Dr. Harry K. Benson
Registrar: Diana Spear
Admissions: Diana Spear
Type: Two-Year College **Sex:** Coed **Affiliation:** Illinois Eastern Community College System **Admission Plans:** Open Admission; Preferred Admission; Early Admission; Deferred Admission **Application Deadline:** Rolling **Application Fee:** $10.00 **H.S. Requirements:** High school diploma required; GED accepted **Costs Per Year:** Application fee: $10. Area resident tuition: $1696 full-time, $53 per credit hour part-time. State resident tuition: $5908 full-time, $184.63 per credit hour part-time. Nonresident tuition: $7314 full-time, $228.55 per credit hour part-time. Mandatory fees: $106 full-time, $3 per credit hour part-time. **Scholarships:** Available **Calendar System:** Semester, Summer Session Available **Enrollment:** FT 631, PT 2,524 **Faculty:** FT 38, PT 148 **Library Holdings:** 34,589 **Regional Accreditation:** North Central Association of Colleges and Schools **Credit Hours For Degree:** 64 credit hours, Associates **Professional Accreditation:** NLN **Intercollegiate Athletics:** Baseball M; Basketball M & W; Softball W; Tennis M; Volleyball W

THE ILLINOIS INSTITUTE OF ART-CHICAGO
350 North Orleans
Chicago, IL 60654
Tel: (312)280-3500
Free: 800-351-3450
Fax: (312)280-3528
Web Site: http://www.ilic.artinstitutes.edu/
President/CEO: Saundra Van Dyke
Registrar: Veronica Morrison
Admissions: Janis Anton
Financial Aid: Anna Mendez
Type: Four-Year College **Sex:** Coed **Affiliation:** Education Management Corporation **Scores:** 91% SAT V 400+; 75% SAT M 400+; 50% ACT 18-23; 14% ACT 24-29 **% Accepted:** 48 **Admission Plans:** Early Admission; Deferred Admission **Application Deadline:** Rolling **Application Fee:** $150.00 **H.S. Requirements:** High school diploma required; GED accepted **Costs Per Year:** Application fee: $150. Tuition: $18,720 full-time, $390 per credit part-time. Mandatory fees: $300 full-time. College room only: $8070. **Scholarships:** Available **Calendar System:** Quarter, Summer Session Available **Enrollment:** FT 1,932, PT 656 **Faculty:** FT 73, PT 102 **Student-Faculty Ratio:** 24:1 **Exams:** ACT, Other, SAT I and SAT II or ACT **Library Holdings:** 11,324 **Professional Accreditation:** ACCSCT, ACF, FIDER

THE ILLINOIS INSTITUTE OF ART-SCHAUMBURG
1000 Plaza Dr.
Schaumburg, IL 60173
Tel: (847)619-3450
Free: 800-314-3450
Fax: (847)619-3064
Web Site: http://www.ilis.artinstitutes.edu/
President/CEO: Dr. John Becker
Admissions: Ron McKinney
Type: Four-Year College **Sex:** Coed **Affiliation:** Education Management Corporation **Scores:** 100% SAT V 400+; 100% SAT M 400+; 52% ACT 18-23; 27% ACT 24-29 **% Accepted:** 74 **Application Deadline:** Rolling **Application Fee:** $0.00 **H.S. Requirements:** High school diploma required; GED accepted **Costs Per Year:** Application fee: $0. Tuition: $16,605 full-time, $369 per credit hour part-time. Tuition guaranteed not to increase for student's term of enrollment. **Scholarships:** Available **Calendar System:** Quarter, Summer Session Available **Enrollment:** FT 911, PT 276 **Faculty:** FT 39, PT 34 **Student-Faculty Ratio:** 19:1 **Credit Hours For Degree:** 96 credits, Associates; 180 credits, Bachelors **Professional Accreditation:** ACCSCT, FIDER

ILLINOIS INSTITUTE OF TECHNOLOGY
3300 South Federal St.
Chicago, IL 60616-3793
Tel: (312)567-3000
Free: 800-448-2329
Admissions: (312)567-3025
Fax: (312)567-6939
E-mail: admission@vax1.ais.iit.edu
Web Site: http://www.iit.edu/
President/CEO: Lewis Collens
Admissions: Brent Benner
Financial Aid: Virginia Foster
Type: University **Sex:** Coed **Scores:** 100% SAT V 400+; 100% SAT M 400+; 7% ACT 18-23; 61% ACT 24-29 **Admission Plans:** Deferred Admission **Application Fee:** $30.00 **H.S. Requirements:** High school diploma required; GED not accepted **Costs Per Year:** Application fee: $30. Comprehensive fee: $30,520 includes full-time tuition ($22,218), mandatory fees ($784), and college room and board ($7518). College room only: $3900. Room and board charges vary according to board plan and housing facility. Part-time tuition: $692 per credit hour. Part-time mandatory fees: $7 per credit hour. Part-time tuition and fees vary according to course load. **Scholarships:** Available **Calendar System:** Semester, Summer Session Available **Enrollment:** FT 1,825, PT 264, Grad 3,116 **Faculty:** FT 303, PT 277 **Student-Faculty Ratio:** 13:1 **Exams:** SAT I or ACT **% Receiving Financial Aid:** 57 **% Residing in College-Owned, -Operated, or -Affiliated Housing:** 56 **Library Holdings:** 877,581 **Regional Accreditation:** North Central Association of Colleges and Schools **Credit Hours For Degree:** 126 semester hours, Bachelors **ROTC:** Army, Navy, Air Force **Professional Accreditation:** AACSB, ABET, ABA, APA, AALS, CORE **Intercollegiate Athletics:** Baseball M; Basketball M & W; Cross-Country Running M & W; Soccer M & W; Swimming and Diving M & W; Volleyball W

ILLINOIS STATE UNIVERSITY
Normal, IL 61790-2200
Tel: (309)438-2111
Admissions: (309)438-2181
Fax: (309)438-3932
E-mail: pawutz@ilstu.edu
Web Site: http://www.ilstu.edu/
President/CEO: Dr. C. Alvin Bowman
Registrar: Dr. Carolyn Bartlett
Admissions: Molly Arnold
Financial Aid: Dr. Charles Boudreau
Type: University **Sex:** Coed **Scores:** 45.25% ACT 18-23; 48.75% ACT 24-29 **% Accepted:** 77 **Application Deadline:** March 01 **Application Fee:** $30.00 **H.S. Requirements:** High school diploma required; GED accepted **Costs Per Year:** Application fee: $30. State resident tuition: $5400 full-time, $180 per credit hour part-time. Nonresident tuition: $11,280 full-time, $376 per credit hour part-time. Mandatory fees: $1691 full-time, $46.70 per credit hour part-time, $700.50 per term part-time. Full-time tuition and fees vary according to course load. Part-time tuition and fees vary according to course load. College room and board: $5748. College room only: $3010. Room and board charges vary according to board plan. Tuition guaranteed not to increase for student's term of enrollment. **Scholarships:** Available **Calendar System:** Semester, Summer Session Available **Enrollment:** FT 16,635, PT 1,223, Grad 2,795 **Faculty:** FT 829, PT 274 **Student-Faculty Ratio:** 19:1 **Exams:** SAT I or ACT **% Receiving Financial Aid:** 44 **% Residing in College-Owned, -Operated, or -Affiliated Housing:** 35 **Library Holdings:** 1,604,061 **Regional Accreditation:** North Central Association of Colleges and Schools **Credit Hours For Degree:** 120 credits, Bachelors **ROTC:** Army **Professional Accreditation:** AACSB, ABET, AACN, AAFCS, ACA, ADtA, AHIMA, APA, ASLHA, CSWE, FIDER, JRCEPAT, NAACLS, NAIT, NASAD, NASM, NAST, NCATE, NLN, NRPA **Intercollegiate Athletics:** Baseball M; Basketball M & W; Cross-Country Running M & W; Football M; Golf M & W; Gymnastics W; Soccer W; Softball W; Swimming and Diving W; Tennis M & W; Track and Field M & W; Volleyball W

ILLINOIS VALLEY COMMUNITY COLLEGE
815 North Orlando Smith Ave.
Oglesby, IL 61348-9692
Tel: (815)224-2720
Admissions: (815)224-0437
Fax: (815)224-3033
Web Site: http://www.ivcc.edu/
President/CEO: Dr. Jean Goodnow
Admissions: Tracy Morris
Financial Aid: Steve Crick
Type: Two-Year College **Sex:** Coed **Affiliation:** Illinois Community College Board **Admission Plans:** Open Admission; Early Admission; Deferred Admission **Application Deadline:** Rolling **H.S. Requirements:** High school diploma or equivalent not required **Costs Per Year:** Area resident tuition: $63.25 per credit hour part-time. State resident tuition: $214.02 per credit hour part-time. Nonresident tuition: $246.71 per credit hour part-time. **Scholarships:** Available **Calendar System:** Semester, Summer Session Available **Faculty:** FT 68, PT 121 **Exams:** ACT **Library Holdings:** 58,250 **Regional Accreditation:** North Central Association of Colleges and Schools **Credit Hours For Degree:** 64 semester hours, Associates **Professional Accreditation:** ADA, NLN **Intercollegiate Athletics:** Basketball M & W; Golf M; Tennis M & W

ILLINOIS WESLEYAN UNIVERSITY
PO Box 2900
Bloomington, IL 61702-2900
Tel: (309)556-1000
Free: 800-332-2498
Admissions: (309)556-3031
Fax: (309)556-3411
E-mail: iwuadmit@iwu.edu
Web Site: http://www.iwu.edu/
President/CEO: Dr. Richard F. Wilson
Registrar: Dr. Jack Fields
Admissions: Tony Bankston
Financial Aid: Lynn O. Nichelson
Type: Four-Year College **Sex:** Coed **Scores:** 100% SAT V 400+; 100% SAT M 400+; 6% ACT 18-23; 54% ACT 24-29 **% Accepted:** 57 **Admission Plans:** Early Admission; Deferred Admission **Application Fee:** $0.00 **H.S. Requirements:** High school diploma required; GED accepted **Costs Per Year:** Application fee: $0. Comprehensive fee: $35,790 includes full-time tuition ($28,926), mandatory fees ($150), and college room and board ($6714). College room only: $4104. Part-time tuition: $3619 per course. **Scholarships:** Available **Calendar System:** Miscellaneous, Summer Session Not available **Enrollment:** FT 2,140, PT 6 **Faculty:** FT 161, PT 61 **Student-Faculty Ratio:** 12:1 **Exams:** SAT I or ACT **% Receiving Financial Aid:** 54 **% Residing in College-Owned, -Operated, or -Affiliated Housing:** 81 **Library Holdings:** 314,894 **Regional Accreditation:** North Central Association of Colleges and Schools **Credit Hours For Degree:** 32 courses, Bachelors **ROTC:** Army **Professional Accreditation:** AACN, NASM **Intercollegiate Athletics:** Baseball M; Basketball M & W; Cheerleading M & W; Cross-Country Running M & W; Football M; Golf M & W; Lacrosse M; Soccer M & W; Softball W; Swimming and Diving M & W; Tennis M & W; Track and Field M & W; Ultimate Frisbee M & W; Volleyball M & W; Water Polo M

INTERNATIONAL ACADEMY OF DESIGN & TECHNOLOGY
One North State St., Ste. 400
Chicago, IL 60602-9736
Tel: (312)980-9200; 877-ACADEMY
Fax: (312)828-9405
E-mail: dlochbaum@iadtchicago.com
Web Site: http://www.iadtchicago.edu/
Registrar: Thomas Timmons
Admissions: Doug Lochbaum
Financial Aid: Barbara Williams
Type: Four-Year College **Sex:** Coed **Affiliation:** Career Education Corporation **% Accepted:** 99 **Admission Plans:** Early Admission **Application Deadline:** Rolling **Application Fee:** $50.00 **H.S. Requirements:** High school diploma required; GED accepted **Costs Per Year:** Application fee: $50. Tuition: $22,400 full-time, $2200 per course part-time. Mandatory fees: $600 full-time, $150 per term part-time. **Scholarships:** Available **Calendar System:** Quarter, Summer Session Available **Enrollment:** FT 2,409, PT 359 **Faculty:** FT 26, PT 158 **Student-Faculty Ratio:** 15:1 **Library Holdings:** 6,500 **Credit Hours For Degree:** 90 quarter hours, Associates; 180 quarter hours, Bachelors **Professional Accreditation:** ACICS, FIDER

ITT TECHNICAL INSTITUTE (BURR RIDGE)
7040 High Grove Blvd.
Burr Ridge, IL 60527
Tel: (630)455-6470
Web Site: http://www.itt-tech.edu/
President/CEO: Joan Malatesta
Admissions: Alida Carpenter
Type: Two-Year College **Sex:** Coed **Affiliation:** ITT Educational Services, Inc **Admission Plans:** Deferred Admission **Application Deadline:** Rolling **Application Fee:** $100.00 **H.S. Requirements:** High school diploma required; GED accepted **Costs Per Year:** Application fee: $100. **Scholarships:** Available **Calendar System:** Quarter, Summer Session Not available **Exams:** Other **Credit Hours For Degree:** 96 credit hours, Associates **Professional Accreditation:** ACICS

ITT TECHNICAL INSTITUTE (MATTESON)
600 Holiday Plaza Dr.
Matteson, IL 60443
Tel: (708)747-2571
Web Site: http://www.itt-tech.edu/
President/CEO: Lillian Williams-McClain
Registrar: Lisa Breitenberg
Admissions: Lillian Williams-McClain
Financial Aid: Ines Ornelas
Type: Two-Year College **Sex:** Coed **Affiliation:** ITT Educational Services, Inc **Admission Plans:** Deferred Admission **Application Deadline:** Rolling **Application Fee:** $100.00 **H.S. Requirements:** High school diploma required; GED accepted **Costs Per Year:** Application fee: $100. **Scholarships:** Available **Calendar System:** Quarter, Summer Session Not available **Exams:** Other **Credit Hours For Degree:** 96 credit hours, Associates **Professional Accreditation:** ACICS

ITT TECHNICAL INSTITUTE (MOUNT PROSPECT)
1401 Feehanville Dr.
Mount Prospect, IL 60056
Tel: (847)375-8800
Web Site: http://www.itt-tech.edu/
President/CEO: Elvis Parker

Registrar: Brenda Hickey
Admissions: Elvis Parker
Financial Aid: Jose Navarro
Type: Two-Year College **Sex:** Coed **Affiliation:** ITT Educational Services, Inc **Admission Plans:** Deferred Admission **Application Deadline:** Rolling **Application Fee:** $100.00 **H.S. Requirements:** High school diploma required; GED accepted **Costs Per Year:** Application fee: $100. **Scholarships:** Available **Calendar System:** Quarter, Summer Session Not available **Exams:** Other **Credit Hours For Degree:** 96 credit hours, Associates; 180 credit hours, Bachelors **Professional Accreditation:** ACICS

JOHN A. LOGAN COLLEGE
700 Logan College Rd.
Carterville, IL 62918-9900
Tel: (618)985-3741
Fax: (618)985-2248
E-mail: terry.crain@jalc.edu
Web Site: http://www.jalc.edu/
President/CEO: Dr. Robert Mees
Registrar: Dr. Larry Chapman
Admissions: Terry Crain
Financial Aid: Stacy Holloway
Type: Two-Year College **Sex:** Coed **Affiliation:** Illinois Community College Board **Admission Plans:** Open Admission; Early Admission **Application Fee:** $0.00 **H.S. Requirements:** High school diploma required; GED accepted **Costs Per Year:** Application fee: $0. Area resident tuition: $1900 full-time, $61 per credit hour part-time. State resident tuition: $6000 full-time, $169.24 per credit hour part-time. Nonresident tuition: $9000 full-time, $254.89 per credit hour part-time. **Scholarships:** Available **Calendar System:** Semester, Summer Session Available **Faculty:** FT 23, PT 20 **Exams:** Other, SAT I or ACT **Library Holdings:** 33,306 **Regional Accreditation:** North Central Association of Colleges and Schools **Credit Hours For Degree:** 62 semester hours, Associates **ROTC:** Army, Air Force **Professional Accreditation:** ACCE, ADA, AHIMA, AOTA, NAACLS **Intercollegiate Athletics:** Baseball M; Basketball M & W; Golf M & W; Softball W; Volleyball W

JOHN WOOD COMMUNITY COLLEGE
1301 South 48th St.
Quincy, IL 62305-8736
Tel: (217)224-6500
Admissions: (217)641-4339
Fax: (217)224-4208
E-mail: admissions@jwcc.edu
Web Site: http://www.jwcc.edu/
President/CEO: Dr. William Simpson
Registrar: Bertie Rose
Admissions: Mark C. McNett
Financial Aid: D. Denny
Type: Two-Year College **Sex:** Coed **Affiliation:** Illinois Community College Board **Scores:** 52% ACT 18-23; 13% ACT 24-29 **% Accepted:** 100 **Admission Plans:** Open Admission; Preferred Admission; Early Admission **Application Deadline:** Rolling **H.S. Requirements:** High school diploma required; GED accepted **Costs Per Year:** Area resident tuition: $2280 full-time, $76 per credit hour part-time. State resident tuition: $5280 full-time, $176 per credit hour part-time. Mandatory fees: $150 full-time, $5 per credit hour part-time. **Scholarships:** Available **Calendar System:** Semester, Summer Session Available **Enrollment:** FT 1,197, PT 1,333 **Faculty:** FT 51, PT 139 **Student-Faculty Ratio:** 15:1 **Exams:** ACT **Library Holdings:** 18,000 **Regional Accreditation:** North Central Association of Colleges and Schools **Credit Hours For Degree:** 64 credit hours, Associates **Intercollegiate Athletics:** Baseball M; Basketball M & W; Golf M; Softball W; Volleyball W

JOLIET JUNIOR COLLEGE
1215 Houbolt Rd.
Joliet, IL 60431-8938
Tel: (815)729-9020
Admissions: (815)280-2493
E-mail: admission@jjc.edu
Web Site: http://www.jjc.edu/
President/CEO: J. D. Ross
Registrar: Keith Tillman
Admissions: Jennifer Kloberdanz
Financial Aid: John Rdzak
Type: Two-Year College **Sex:** Coed **Affiliation:** Illinois Community College Board **% Accepted:** 100 **Admission Plans:** Open Admission; Preferred Admission; Early Admission; Deferred Admission **Application Deadline:** Rolling **Application Fee:** $0.00 **H.S. Requirements:** High school diploma or equivalent not required. For nursing program, veterinary technician: High school diploma required; GED accepted **Costs Per Year:** Application fee: $0. Area resident tuition: $1800 full-time, $60 per hour part-time. State resident tuition: $6248 full-time, $208 per hour part-time. Nonresident tuition: $7149 full-time, $238 per hour part-time. Mandatory fees: $390 full-time, $13 per hour part-time. **Scholarships:** Available **Calendar System:** Semester, Summer Session Available **Enrollment:** FT 4,895, PT 8,127 **Faculty:** FT 187, PT 375 **Student-Faculty Ratio:** 24:1 **Library Holdings:** 60,364 **Regional Accreditation:** North Central Association of Colleges and Schools **Credit Hours For Degree:** 64 credits, Associates **Professional Accreditation:** ACF, ACBSP, NASM, NLN **Intercollegiate Athletics:** Basketball M & W; Football M; Golf M; Softball W; Tennis M & W; Volleyball W

JUDSON COLLEGE
1151 North State St.
Elgin, IL 60123-1498
Tel: (847)628-2500
Free: 800-879-5376
Admissions: (847)695-2500
Fax: (847)695-0712
E-mail: pguth@judsoncollege.edu
Web Site: http://www.judsoncollege.edu/
President/CEO: Dr. Jerry B. Cain
Registrar: Virginia Guth
Admissions: Philip G. Guth
Type: Comprehensive **Sex:** Coed **Affiliation:** Baptist **Scores:** 90% SAT V 400+; 97% SAT M 400+; 51% ACT 18-23; 43% ACT 24-29 **% Accepted:** 76 **Admission Plans:** Early Admission; Deferred Admission **Application Deadline:** Rolling **Application Fee:** $35.00 **H.S. Requirements:** High school diploma required; GED accepted **Costs Per Year:** Application fee: $35. Comprehensive fee: $26,350 includes full-time tuition ($19,150), mandatory fees ($300), and college room and board ($6900). **Scholarships:** Available **Calendar System:** Semester, Summer Session Not available **Enrollment:** FT 915, PT 278, Grad 48 **Faculty:** FT 55, PT 56 **Student-Faculty Ratio:** 14:1 **Exams:** SAT I and SAT II or ACT **% Residing in College-Owned, -Operated, or -Affiliated Housing:** 64 **Library Holdings:** 104,331 **Regional Accreditation:** North Central Association of Colleges and Schools **Credit Hours For Degree:** 126 semester hours, Bachelors **Intercollegiate Athletics:** Baseball M; Basketball M & W; Cross-Country Running M & W; Soccer M & W; Softball W; Tennis M & W; Volleyball W

KANKAKEE COMMUNITY COLLEGE
PO Box 888
Kankakee, IL 60901-0888
Tel: (815)933-0345
Admissions: (815)802-8520
Fax: (815)933-0217
Web Site: http://www.kcc.cc.il.us/
President/CEO: Dr. Larry D. Huffman
Registrar: Tom Dolliger
Admissions: Michelle Driscoll
Financial Aid: Al Widhalm
Type: Two-Year College **Sex:** Coed **Affiliation:** Illinois Community College Board **Admission Plans:** Open Admission; Preferred Admission; Early Admission **Application Fee:** $0.00 **H.S. Requirements:** High school diploma required; GED accepted **Scholarships:** Available **Calendar System:** Semester, Summer Session Available **Enrollment:** FT 1,027, PT 2,448 **Faculty:** FT 49, PT 122 **Exams:** ACT, Other **Library Holdings:** 48,239 **Regional Accreditation:** North Central Association of Colleges and Schools **Credit Hours For Degree:** 64 semester hours, Associates **Professional Accreditation:** CARC, NAACLS **Intercollegiate Athletics:** Baseball M; Basketball M & W; Softball W; Volleyball W

KASKASKIA COLLEGE
27210 College Rd.
Centralia, IL 62801-7878
Tel: (618)545-3000
Admissions: (618)545-3066
Fax: (618)532-1135
Web Site: http://www.kaskaskia.edu/
President/CEO: Dr. James Underwood

Registrar: Janice Ripperda
Admissions: Daniel Herbst
Financial Aid: Sherry Summary
Type: Two-Year College **Sex:** Coed **Affiliation:** Illinois Community College Board **% Accepted:** 100 **Admission Plans:** Open Admission; Preferred Admission; Early Admission; Deferred Admission **Application Deadline:** Rolling **Application Fee:** $0.00 **H.S. Requirements:** High school diploma required; GED accepted **Costs Per Year:** Application fee: $0. Area resident tuition: $1590 full-time, $53 per credit hour part-time. State resident tuition: $3030 full-time, $101 per credit hour part-time. Nonresident tuition: $7038 full-time, $234.60 per credit hour part-time. Mandatory fees: $210 full-time, $7 per credit hour part-time. Full-time tuition and fees vary according to location. Part-time tuition and fees vary according to location. **Scholarships:** Available **Calendar System:** Semester, Summer Session Available **Enrollment:** FT 1,908, PT 2,834 **Faculty:** FT 72, PT 174 **Student-Faculty Ratio:** 22:1 **Exams:** ACT, Other **Library Holdings:** 23,685 **Regional Accreditation:** North Central Association of Colleges and Schools **Credit Hours For Degree:** 64 semester hours, Associates **Professional Accreditation:** ADA, APTA, CARC, JRCERT, NLN **Intercollegiate Athletics:** Baseball M; Basketball M & W; Cheerleading M & W; Golf M; Softball W; Volleyball W

KENDALL COLLEGE

900 North Branch St.
Chicago, IL 60622
Tel: (847)448-2000; 877-588-8860
Admissions: (312)752-2160
Fax: (847)448-2556
E-mail: tfitzgibbons@kendall.edu
Web Site: http://www.kendall.edu/
President/CEO: Howard A. Tullman, JD
Registrar: Brad Bergeron
Admissions: Tom Fitzgibbon
Financial Aid: Denise Coleman
Type: Four-Year College **Sex:** Coed **Affiliation:** United Methodist **% Accepted:** 30 **Admission Plans:** Deferred Admission **Application Deadline:** Rolling **Application Fee:** $75.00 **H.S. Requirements:** High school diploma required; GED accepted **Costs Per Year:** Application fee: $75. Comprehensive fee: $30,750 includes full-time tuition ($20,100), mandatory fees ($450), and college room and board ($10,200). **Scholarships:** Available **Calendar System:** Quarter, Summer Session Available **Enrollment:** FT 497, PT 283 **Faculty:** FT 37, PT 43 **Student-Faculty Ratio:** 19:1 **Exams:** SAT I or ACT **% Receiving Financial Aid:** 79 **% Residing in College-Owned, -Operated, or -Affiliated Housing:** 20 **Library Holdings:** 37,000 **Regional Accreditation:** North Central Association of Colleges and Schools **Credit Hours For Degree:** 96 quarter hours, Associates; 192 quarter hours, Bachelors **Professional Accreditation:** ACF

KISHWAUKEE COLLEGE

21193 Malta Rd.
Malta, IL 60150-9699
Tel: (815)825-2086
Fax: (815)825-2306
Web Site: http://www.kishwaukeecollege.edu/
President/CEO: Dr. David Louis
Registrar: Lea Houdek
Admissions: Lea Houdek
Financial Aid: Pamela Wagener
Type: Two-Year College **Sex:** Coed **Affiliation:** Illinois Community College Board **Admission Plans:** Open Admission; Early Admission; Deferred Admission **Application Fee:** $0.00 **H.S. Requirements:** High school diploma required; GED accepted. For nursing, radiological technology programs: High school diploma required; GED accepted **Scholarships:** Available **Calendar System:** Semester, Summer Session Available **Enrollment:** FT 577, PT 3,499 **Faculty:** FT 80, PT 151 **Student-Faculty Ratio:** 15:1 **Exams:** Other **Library Holdings:** 52,075 **Regional Accreditation:** North Central Association of Colleges and Schools **Credit Hours For Degree:** 64 semester hours, Associates **Professional Accreditation:** JRCERT **Intercollegiate Athletics:** Baseball M; Basketball M & W; Golf M; Soccer M; Softball W; Tennis W; Volleyball W

KNOX COLLEGE

2 East South St.
Galesburg, IL 61401
Tel: (309)341-7000
Free: 800-678-KNOX
Admissions: (309)341-7100
Fax: (309)341-7070
E-mail: admission@knox.edu
Web Site: http://www.knox.edu/
President/CEO: Roger L. Taylor
Registrar: Kevin Hastings
Admissions: Paul Steenis
Financial Aid: Teresa Jackson
Type: Four-Year College **Sex:** Coed **Scores:** 99% SAT V 400+; 100% SAT M 400+; 17% ACT 18-23; 49% ACT 24-29 **% Accepted:** 76 **Admission Plans:** Early Admission; Early Action; Deferred Admission **Application Deadline:** February 01 **Application Fee:** $40.00 **H.S. Requirements:** High school diploma required; GED accepted **Costs Per Year:** Application fee: $40. Comprehensive fee: $32,385 includes full-time tuition ($25,815), mandatory fees ($285), and college room and board ($6285). College room only: $2784. Room and board charges vary according to board plan. Part-time tuition: $870 per credit. Part-time tuition varies according to course load. **Scholarships:** Available **Calendar System:** Miscellaneous, Summer Session Not available **Enrollment:** FT 1,218, PT 27 **Faculty:** FT 95, PT 22 **Student-Faculty Ratio:** 12:1 **Exams:** SAT I and SAT II or ACT **% Receiving Financial Aid:** 67 **% Residing in College-Owned, -Operated, or -Affiliated Housing:** 95 **Library Holdings:** 308,614 **Regional Accreditation:** North Central Association of Colleges and Schools **Credit Hours For Degree:** 36 credits, Bachelors **Intercollegiate Athletics:** Baseball M; Basketball M & W; Cross-Country Running M & W; Football M; Golf M & W; Soccer M & W; Softball W; Swimming and Diving M & W; Tennis M & W; Track and Field M & W; Volleyball W; Wrestling M

LAKE FOREST COLLEGE

555 North Sheridan Rd.
Lake Forest, IL 60045-2399
Tel: (847)234-3100
Free: 800-828-4751
Admissions: (847)735-5000
Fax: (847)735-6271
E-mail: motzer@lfc.edu
Web Site: http://www.lakeforest.edu/
President/CEO: Stephen D. Schutt
Registrar: Ruthane I. Bopp
Admissions: William G. Motzer, Jr.
Financial Aid: Gerard J. Cebrzynski
Type: Comprehensive **Sex:** Coed **Scores:** 100% SAT V 400+; 100% SAT M 400+; 33% ACT 18-23; 54% ACT 24-29 **% Accepted:** 65 **Admission Plans:** Early Admission; Early Action; Early Decision Plan; Deferred Admission **Application Deadline:** February 15 **Application Fee:** $40.00 **H.S. Requirements:** High school diploma required; GED accepted **Costs Per Year:** Application fee: $40. Comprehensive fee: $33,860 includes full-time tuition ($27,000), mandatory fees ($334), and college room and board ($6526). College room only: $3456. Room and board charges vary according to housing facility. Part-time tuition: $3375 per course. **Scholarships:** Available **Calendar System:** Semester, Summer Session Available **Enrollment:** FT 1,398, PT 20, Grad 17 **Faculty:** FT 89, PT 69 **Student-Faculty Ratio:** 12:1 **Exams:** SAT I or ACT **% Receiving Financial Aid:** 78 **% Residing in College-Owned, -Operated, or -Affiliated Housing:** 80 **Library Holdings:** 259,977 **Regional Accreditation:** North Central Association of Colleges and Schools **Credit Hours For Degree:** 32 courses, Bachelors **Intercollegiate Athletics:** Basketball M & W; Cheerleading M & W; Cross-Country Running M & W; Fencing M & W; Football M; Golf M & W; Ice Hockey M & W; Lacrosse M & W; Rugby M & W; Sailing M & W; Soccer M & W; Softball W; Swimming and Diving M & W; Tennis M & W; Track and Field M & W; Ultimate Frisbee M & W; Volleyball M & W; Water Polo M & W; Wrestling M & W

LAKE LAND COLLEGE

5001 Lake Land Blvd.
Mattoon, IL 61938-9366
Tel: (217)234-5253
Admissions: (217)234-5378
Web Site: http://www.lakelandcollege.edu/
President/CEO: Dr. Robert K. Luther
Registrar: Eva Blair
Admissions: Jon VanDyke
Financial Aid: Tynia Kessler
Type: Two-Year College **Sex:** Coed **Affiliation:** Illinois Community College Board **% Accepted:** 100 **Admission Plans:** Open Admission; Early Admis-

sion **Application Deadline:** Rolling **Application Fee:** $0.00 **Costs Per Year:** Application fee: $0. Area resident tuition: $1545 full-time, $51.50 per credit hour part-time. State resident tuition: $3595 full-time, $119.86 per credit hour part-time. Nonresident tuition: $7568 full-time, $252.27 per credit hour part-time. Mandatory fees: $358 full-time, $11.95 per credit hour part-time. **Scholarships:** Available **Calendar System:** Semester, Summer Session Available **Enrollment:** FT 3,108, PT 3,930 **Faculty:** FT 116, PT 75 **Student-Faculty Ratio:** 21:1 **Library Holdings:** 36,912 **Regional Accreditation:** North Central Association of Colleges and Schools **Credit Hours For Degree:** 64 semester hours, Associates **Professional Accreditation:** ADA, APTA, NLN **Intercollegiate Athletics:** Baseball M; Basketball M & W; Cheerleading W; Softball W; Tennis M & W; Volleyball W

LAKEVIEW COLLEGE OF NURSING
903 North Logan Ave.
Danville, IL 61832
Tel: (217)443-5238
Fax: (217)431-4015
E-mail: kholden@lakeviewcol.edu
Web Site: http://www.lakeviewcol.edu/
President/CEO: Sarah Rich Wheeler, DNS
Registrar: Kelly Holden
Admissions: Kelly M. Holden
Financial Aid: Janet Ingargiola
Type: Two-Year Upper Division **Sex:** Coed **Affiliation:** Danville Area Community College **Admission Plans:** Deferred Admission **Application Fee:** $50.00 **H.S. Requirements:** High school diploma required; GED accepted **Scholarships:** Available **Calendar System:** Semester, Summer Session Available **Enrollment:** FT 41, PT 42 **Faculty:** FT 3, PT 10 **Student-Faculty Ratio:** 8:1 **Library Holdings:** 1,500 **Regional Accreditation:** North Central Association of Colleges and Schools **Credit Hours For Degree:** 124 credit hours, Bachelors **Professional Accreditation:** AACN, NLN

LEWIS AND CLARK COMMUNITY COLLEGE
5800 Godfrey Rd.
Godfrey, IL 62035-2466
Tel: (618)466-7000
Admissions: (618)468-5100
Fax: (618)466-2798
Web Site: http://www.lc.edu/
President/CEO: Dr. Dale T. Chapman
Registrar: Peter Basola, Jr.
Admissions: Peggy Hudson
Financial Aid: Angela Weaver
Type: Two-Year College **Sex:** Coed **Affiliation:** Illinois Community College Board **Admission Plans:** Open Admission; Early Admission; Deferred Admission **Application Fee:** $0.00 **H.S. Requirements:** High school diploma or equivalent not required. For nursing, dental assisting, dental hygiene, occupational therapy programs: High school diploma required; GED accepted **Scholarships:** Available **Calendar System:** Semester, Summer Session Available **Enrollment:** FT 2,377, PT 5,069 **Faculty:** FT 86, PT 223 **Library Holdings:** 47,000 **Regional Accreditation:** North Central Association of Colleges and Schools **Credit Hours For Degree:** 60 credit hours, Associates **ROTC:** Army **Professional Accreditation:** ADA, AOTA, NLN **Intercollegiate Athletics:** Baseball M; Basketball M & W; Golf M; Soccer M & W; Softball W; Tennis M & W; Volleyball W

LEWIS UNIVERSITY
One University Parkway
Romeoville, IL 60446
Tel: (815)838-0500
Free: 800-897-9000
Fax: (815)838-9456
Web Site: http://www.lewisu.edu/
President/CEO: Br. James Gaffney, FSC
Registrar: Robert J. Kempiak
Admissions: Andrew Sison
Financial Aid: Janeen Decharinte
Type: Comprehensive **Sex:** Coed **Affiliation:** Roman Catholic Church **Scores:** 100% SAT V 400+; 100% SAT M 400+; 61% ACT 18-23; 29% ACT 24-29 **% Accepted:** 69 **Admission Plans:** Deferred Admission **Application Deadline:** August 01 **Application Fee:** $40.00 **H.S. Requirements:** High school diploma required; GED accepted **Costs Per Year:** Application fee: $40. Comprehensive fee: $26,800 includes full-time tuition ($19,200) and college room and board ($7600). College room only: $5100. Part-time tuition: $605 per credit hour. **Scholarships:** Available **Calendar System:** Semester, Summer Session Available **Enrollment:** FT 2,662, PT 931, Grad 1,472 **Faculty:** FT 164, PT 308 **Student-Faculty Ratio:** 13:1 **Exams:** SAT I or ACT **% Receiving Financial Aid:** 71 **% Residing in College-Owned, -Operated, or -Affiliated Housing:** 27 **Library Holdings:** 149,870 **Regional Accreditation:** North Central Association of Colleges and Schools **Credit Hours For Degree:** 77 credit hours, Associates; 128 credit hours, Bachelors **ROTC:** Army, Air Force **Professional Accreditation:** AACN, NCATE, NLN **Intercollegiate Athletics:** Baseball M; Basketball M & W; Cheerleading M & W; Cross-Country Running M & W; Golf M & W; Soccer M & W; Softball W; Swimming and Diving M & W; Tennis M & W; Track and Field M & W; Volleyball M & W

LEXINGTON COLLEGE
310 South Peoria St., Ste. 512
Chicago, IL 60607-3534
Tel: (312)226-6294
Fax: (312)226-6405
E-mail: pr@lexingtoncollege.edu
Web Site: http://lexingtoncollege.edu/general-education.htm
President/CEO: Susan E. Mangels
Registrar: Regina Ready
Admissions: Tammy Schofield
Type: Four-Year College **Sex:** Women **Scores:** 36% ACT 18-23 **% Accepted:** 51 **Admission Plans:** Open Admission **Application Deadline:** Rolling **Application Fee:** $30.00 **H.S. Requirements:** High school diploma required; GED accepted **Costs Per Year:** Application fee: $30. Tuition: $16,100 full-time, $530 per credit hour part-time. Mandatory fees: $940 full-time, $200 per term part-time. **Scholarships:** Available **Calendar System:** Semester, Summer Session Not available **Enrollment:** FT 45, PT 11 **Faculty:** FT 4, PT 13 **Student-Faculty Ratio:** 6:1 **Exams:** SAT I or ACT **% Receiving Financial Aid:** 100 **Library Holdings:** 3,000 **Regional Accreditation:** North Central Association of Colleges and Schools **Credit Hours For Degree:** 66 credits, Associates; 129 credits, Bachelors

LINCOLN CHRISTIAN COLLEGE
100 Campus View Dr.
Lincoln, IL 62656-2167
Tel: (217)732-3168; 888-522-5228
Fax: (217)732-5914
E-mail: coladmis@iccs.edu
Web Site: http://www.lccs.edu/
President/CEO: Dr. Keith H. Ray
Registrar: Alan W. Kline
Admissions: Greg Taylor
Financial Aid: Jack Getchel
Type: Four-Year College **Sex:** Coed **Affiliation:** Christian Churches and Churches of Christ; Lincoln Christian Seminary **Scores:** 59% ACT 18-23; 22% ACT 24-29 **% Accepted:** 78 **Admission Plans:** Preferred Admission; Deferred Admission **Application Deadline:** Rolling **Application Fee:** $20.00 **H.S. Requirements:** High school diploma required; GED accepted **Costs Per Year:** Application fee: $20. Comprehensive fee: $15,100 includes full-time tuition ($10,200) and college room and board ($4900). Part-time tuition: $340 per semester hour. **Scholarships:** Available **Calendar System:** Semester, Summer Session Available **Enrollment:** FT 610, PT 98 **Faculty:** FT 29, PT 30 **Student-Faculty Ratio:** 13:1 **Exams:** SAT I or ACT **% Receiving Financial Aid:** 80 **% Residing in College-Owned, -Operated, or -Affiliated Housing:** 50 **Library Holdings:** 127,000 **Regional Accreditation:** North Central Association of Colleges and Schools **Credit Hours For Degree:** 65 semester hours, Associates; 130 semester hours, Bachelors **Professional Accreditation:** AABC **Intercollegiate Athletics:** Baseball M; Basketball M & W; Cheerleading M & W; Cross-Country Running M & W; Golf M & W; Soccer M & W; Softball M & W; Volleyball W

LINCOLN COLLEGE
300 Keokuk St.
Lincoln, IL 62656-1699
Tel: (217)732-3155
Free: 800-569-0556
Fax: (217)732-8859
Web Site: http://www.lincolncollege.edu/
President/CEO: Dr. Jack D. Nutt
Registrar: Deb Harmon
Admissions: Tony Schilling

Financial Aid: Kevin Stephens
Type: Two-Year College **Sex:** Coed **Scores:** 40% ACT 18-23; 8% ACT 24-29 **% Accepted:** 65 **Admission Plans:** Early Admission; Deferred Admission **Application Deadline:** Rolling **Application Fee:** $25.00 **H.S. Requirements:** High school diploma required; GED accepted **Costs Per Year:** Application fee: $25. Comprehensive fee: $21,370 includes full-time tuition ($15,000), mandatory fees ($570), and college room and board ($5800). College room only: $2200. Part-time tuition: $500 per credit. Part-time mandatory fees: $19 per credit. **Scholarships:** Available **Calendar System:** Semester, Summer Session Available **Enrollment:** FT 700, PT 58 **Faculty:** FT 34, PT 19 **Student-Faculty Ratio:** 16:1 **Exams:** SAT I or ACT **% Residing in College-Owned, -Operated, or -Affiliated Housing:** 90 **Library Holdings:** 42,500 **Regional Accreditation:** North Central Association of Colleges and Schools **Credit Hours For Degree:** 64 semester hours, Associates **Intercollegiate Athletics:** Baseball M; Basketball M & W; Golf M & W; Soccer M & W; Softball W; Swimming and Diving M & W; Tennis M & W; Volleyball W; Wrestling M

LINCOLN COLLEGE-NORMAL
715 West Raab Rd.
Normal, IL 61761
Tel: (309)452-0500
Free: 800-569-0558
Fax: (309)454-5652
E-mail: admissions@lincolncollege.edu
Web Site: http://www.lincolncollege.edu/normal/
President/CEO: Dr. Jack Nutt
Admissions: Joe Hendrix
Type: Two-Year College **Sex:** Coed **Scores:** 65% ACT 18-23; 15% ACT 24-29 **Admission Plans:** Deferred Admission **Application Deadline:** Rolling **Application Fee:** $25.00 **H.S. Requirements:** High school diploma required; GED accepted **Costs Per Year:** Application fee: $25. Tuition: $1500 full-time, $413 per credit hour part-time. Mandatory fees: $810 full-time, $8 per credit hour part-time, $35 per term part-time. College room only: $3200. **Scholarships:** Available **Calendar System:** Semester, Summer Session Available **Enrollment:** FT 350, PT 170 **Faculty:** FT 9, PT 41 **Student-Faculty Ratio:** 14:1 **Exams:** SAT I or ACT **% Residing in College-Owned, -Operated, or -Affiliated Housing:** 40 **Library Holdings:** 1,800,000 **Regional Accreditation:** North Central Association of Colleges and Schools **Credit Hours For Degree:** 63 credit hours, Associates; 123 credit hours, Bachelors **Intercollegiate Athletics:** Baseball M; Basketball M & W; Golf M & W; Soccer M & W; Softball W; Swimming and Diving M & W; Volleyball W; Wrestling M

LINCOLN LAND COMMUNITY COLLEGE
5250 Shepherd Rd.
PO Box 19256
Springfield, IL 62794-9256
Tel: (217)786-2200
Admissions: (217)786-2243
Fax: (217)786-2492
Web Site: http://www.llcc.edu/
President/CEO: Dr. Jack E. Daniels, III
Admissions: Ron Gregoire
Financial Aid: Lee Bursi
Type: Two-Year College **Sex:** Coed **Affiliation:** Illinois Community College Board **Scores:** 100% SAT V 400+; 46.5% ACT 18-23; 15.5% ACT 24-29 **% Accepted:** 100 **Admission Plans:** Open Admission; Early Admission; Deferred Admission **Application Deadline:** Rolling **Application Fee:** $0.00 **H.S. Requirements:** High school diploma or equivalent not required. For allied health programs: High school diploma required; GED accepted **Costs Per Year:** Application fee: $0. Area resident tuition: $1890 full-time, $63 per credit hour part-time. State resident tuition: $7980 full-time, $266 per credit hour part-time. Nonresident tuition: $9510 full-time, $317 per credit hour part-time. Mandatory fees: $165 full-time, $5.50 per credit hour part-time. Full-time tuition and fees vary according to course load. Part-time tuition and fees vary according to course load. **Scholarships:** Available **Calendar System:** Semester, Summer Session Available **Enrollment:** FT 2,700, PT 4,147 **Faculty:** FT 125, PT 263 **Student-Faculty Ratio:** 19:1 **Library Holdings:** 65,000 **Regional Accreditation:** North Central Association of Colleges and Schools **Credit Hours For Degree:** 60 credit hours, Associates **Professional Accreditation:** AOTA, CARC, JRCERT, NLN **Intercollegiate Athletics:** Baseball M; Basketball M & W; Soccer M; Softball W; Volleyball W

LOYOLA UNIVERSITY CHICAGO
820 North Michigan Ave.
Chicago, IL 60611-2196
Tel: (773)274-3000
Free: 800-262-2373
Admissions: (773)508-3080
Fax: (773)915-6414
E-mail: admission@luc.edu
Web Site: http://www.luc.edu/
President/CEO: Rev. Michael Garanzini, SJ
Registrar: Clare Korinek
Admissions: April Hansen
Financial Aid: Eric Weems
Type: University **Sex:** Coed **Affiliation:** Roman Catholic (Jesuit) **Scores:** 99.1% SAT V 400+; 99.2% SAT M 400+; 34.7% ACT 18-23; 51.8% ACT 24-29 **% Accepted:** 81 **Admission Plans:** Deferred Admission **Application Deadline:** April 01 **Application Fee:** $25.00 **H.S. Requirements:** High school diploma required; GED accepted **Costs Per Year:** Application fee: $25. Comprehensive fee: $36,520 includes full-time tuition ($26,150), mandatory fees ($756), and college room and board ($9614). College room only: $6490. Part-time tuition: $530 per semester hour. Part-time mandatory fees: $75. **Scholarships:** Available **Calendar System:** Semester, Summer Session Available **Enrollment:** FT 8,318, PT 922, Grad 4,131 **Faculty:** FT 523, PT 583 **Student-Faculty Ratio:** 14:1 **Exams:** SAT I or ACT **% Receiving Financial Aid:** 70 **% Residing in College-Owned, -Operated, or -Affiliated Housing:** 29 **Library Holdings:** 1,108,157 **Regional Accreditation:** North Central Association of Colleges and Schools **Credit Hours For Degree:** 128 semester hours, Bachelors **ROTC:** Army, Navy **Professional Accreditation:** AACSB, AACN, ABA, ADtA, APA, ACIPE, AALS, ATS, CSWE, LCMEAMA, NAST, NCATE, NLN **Intercollegiate Athletics:** Basketball M & W; Cross-Country Running M & W; Golf M & W; Soccer M & W; Softball W; Track and Field M & W; Volleyball M & W

MACCORMAC COLLEGE
506 South Wabash Ave.
Chicago, IL 60605-1667
Tel: (312)922-1884
Fax: (312)922-3196
Web Site: http://www.maccormac.edu/
President/CEO: Dr. Edward J. Kies
Registrar: Patricia Dopp
Admissions: Rosa Medina
Financial Aid: Judith Byrd
Type: Two-Year College **Sex:** Coed **Admission Plans:** Deferred Admission **Application Fee:** $20.00 **H.S. Requirements:** High school diploma required; GED accepted **Scholarships:** Available **Calendar System:** Semester, Summer Session Available **Enrollment:** FT 159, PT 218 **Faculty:** FT 4, PT 30 **Student-Faculty Ratio:** 15:1 **Exams:** ACT, SAT I **Library Holdings:** 11,000 **Regional Accreditation:** North Central Association of Colleges and Schools **Credit Hours For Degree:** 96 quarter hours, Associates

MACMURRAY COLLEGE
447 East College Ave.
Jacksonville, IL 62650
Tel: (217)479-7000
Admissions: (217)479-7056
Fax: (217)245-0405
E-mail: admiss@mac.edu
Web Site: http://www.mac.edu/
President/CEO: Dr. Lawrence D. Bryan
Registrar: Allan Metcalf
Admissions: Rhonda Cors
Financial Aid: Julie Speers
Type: Four-Year College **Sex:** Coed **Affiliation:** United Methodist **Scores:** 69% SAT V 400+; 92% SAT M 400+; 53% ACT 18-23; 23% ACT 24-29 **% Accepted:** 57 **Admission Plans:** Early Admission **Application Deadline:** Rolling **Application Fee:** $0.00 **H.S. Requirements:** High school diploma required; GED accepted **Costs Per Year:** Application fee: $0. Comprehensive fee: $21,748 includes full-time tuition ($15,500), mandatory fees ($250), and college room and board ($5998). College room only: $2732. Part-time tuition: $250 per credit hour. Part-time mandatory fees: $35 per term.

Scholarships: Available **Calendar System:** 4-1-4, Summer Session Available **Enrollment:** FT 646, PT 57 **Faculty:** FT 38, PT 41 **Student-Faculty Ratio:** 13:1 **Exams:** SAT I or ACT **% Receiving Financial Aid:** 90 **% Residing in College-Owned, -Operated, or -Affiliated Housing:** 50 **Library Holdings:** 1,813,620 **Regional Accreditation:** North Central Association of Colleges and Schools **Credit Hours For Degree:** 60 semester hours, Associates; 120 semester hours, Bachelors **Professional Accreditation:** AACN, CSWE **Intercollegiate Athletics:** Baseball M; Basketball M & W; Cheerleading M & W; Cross-Country Running M & W; Football M; Golf M & W; Soccer M & W; Softball W; Swimming and Diving M & W; Tennis M & W; Volleyball W; Wrestling M & W

MCHENRY COUNTY COLLEGE
8900 US Hwy. 14
Crystal Lake, IL 60012-2761
Tel: (815)455-3700
Admissions: (815)479-7620
Web Site: http://www.mchenry.edu/
President/CEO: Dr. Walter J. Packard
Admissions: Marilyn Weniger
Financial Aid: Marianne Devenny
Type: Two-Year College **Sex:** Coed **Affiliation:** Illinois Community College Board **Scores:** 50.4% ACT 18-23; 19.4% ACT 24-29 **Admission Plans:** Open Admission; Early Admission; Deferred Admission **Application Fee:** $0.00 **H.S. Requirements:** High school diploma or equivalent not required **Scholarships:** Available **Calendar System:** Semester, Summer Session Available **Enrollment:** FT 2,048, PT 3,892 **Faculty:** FT 88, PT 207 **Student-Faculty Ratio:** 20:1 **Exams:** ACT **Library Holdings:** 40,000 **Regional Accreditation:** North Central Association of Colleges and Schools **Credit Hours For Degree:** 60 semester hours, Associates **Professional Accreditation:** ACBSP **Intercollegiate Athletics:** Baseball M; Basketball M & W; Soccer M; Softball W; Tennis M & W; Volleyball W

MCKENDREE COLLEGE
701 College Rd.
Lebanon, IL 62254-1299
Tel: (618)537-4481
Free: 800-232-7228
Fax: (618)537-6259
Web Site: http://www.mckendree.edu/
President/CEO: Dr. James M. Dennis
Registrar: Gretchen Fricke
Admissions: Chris Hall
Financial Aid: Debra Hintz
Type: Comprehensive **Sex:** Coed **Affiliation:** United Methodist Church **Scores:** 91% SAT V 400+; 83% SAT M 400+; 56% ACT 18-23; 31% ACT 24-29 **% Accepted:** 66 **Admission Plans:** Deferred Admission **Application Deadline:** Rolling **Application Fee:** $40.00 **H.S. Requirements:** High school diploma required; GED accepted **Costs Per Year:** Application fee: $40. Comprehensive fee: $26,280 includes full-time tuition ($18,300), mandatory fees ($600), and college room and board ($7380). College room only: $3900. Part-time tuition: $615 per hour. **Scholarships:** Available **Calendar System:** Semester, Summer Session Available **Enrollment:** FT 1,617, PT 640, Grad 328 **Faculty:** FT 74, PT 140 **Student-Faculty Ratio:** 21:1 **Exams:** SAT I or ACT **% Receiving Financial Aid:** 78 **% Residing in College-Owned, -Operated, or -Affiliated Housing:** 54 **Library Holdings:** 105,000 **Regional Accreditation:** North Central Association of Colleges and Schools **Credit Hours For Degree:** 128 credit hours, Bachelors **ROTC:** Army, Air Force **Professional Accreditation:** NLN **Intercollegiate Athletics:** Baseball M; Basketball M & W; Bowling M & W; Cheerleading M & W; Cross-Country Running M & W; Football M; Golf M & W; Ice Hockey M; Soccer M & W; Softball W; Tennis M & W; Track and Field M & W; Volleyball W; Wrestling M

MIDSTATE COLLEGE
411 West Northmoor Rd.
Peoria, IL 61614
Tel: (309)692-4092
Fax: (309)692-3893
Web Site: http://www.midstate.edu/
President/CEO: R. Dale Bunch
Registrar: Gail Piscaglia
Admissions: Jessica Auer
Financial Aid: Irene Bimrose
Type: Four-Year College **Sex:** Coed **Admission Plans:** Early Admission; Deferred Admission **Application Fee:** $25.00 **H.S. Requirements:** High school diploma required; GED accepted **Scholarships:** Available **Calendar System:** Quarter, Summer Session Available **Enrollment:** FT 244, PT 234 **Faculty:** FT 10, PT 35 **Student-Faculty Ratio:** 13:1 **Exams:** Other **Library Holdings:** 8,724 **Regional Accreditation:** North Central Association of Colleges and Schools **Credit Hours For Degree:** 92 quarter hours, Associates **Professional Accreditation:** AAMAE

MILLIKIN UNIVERSITY
1184 West Main St.
Decatur, IL 62522-2084
Tel: (217)424-6211
Free: 800-373-7733
Admissions: (217)424-6210
Fax: (217)425-4669
E-mail: phughes@millikin.edu
Web Site: http://www.millikin.edu/
President/CEO: Douglas E. Zemke
Registrar: Walter Wessel
Admissions: Patrick Hughes
Financial Aid: Stacey Hubbard
Type: Comprehensive **Sex:** Coed **Affiliation:** Presbyterian Church (U.S.A.) **Scores:** 86% SAT V 400+; 91% SAT M 400+; 50% ACT 18-23; 40% ACT 24-29 **% Accepted:** 70 **Admission Plans:** Deferred Admission **Application Deadline:** Rolling **Application Fee:** $0.00 **H.S. Requirements:** High school diploma required; GED accepted **Costs Per Year:** Application fee: $0. One-time mandatory fee: $75. Comprehensive fee: $27,834 includes full-time tuition ($20,696), mandatory fees ($425), and college room and board ($6713). College room only: $3763. Full-time tuition and fees vary according to course load. Room and board charges vary according to board plan and housing facility. Part-time tuition: $717 per credit hour. **Scholarships:** Available **Calendar System:** Semester, Summer Session Available **Enrollment:** FT 2,438, PT 178, Grad 25 **Faculty:** FT 145, PT 137 **Student-Faculty Ratio:** 13:1 **Exams:** SAT I or ACT **% Receiving Financial Aid:** 67 **% Residing in College-Owned, -Operated, or -Affiliated Housing:** 70 **Library Holdings:** 199,660 **Regional Accreditation:** North Central Association of Colleges and Schools **Credit Hours For Degree:** 124 credits, Bachelors **Professional Accreditation:** AACN, ACBSP, NASM, NLN **Intercollegiate Athletics:** Baseball M; Basketball M & W; Cross-Country Running M & W; Football M; Golf M & W; Soccer M & W; Softball W; Swimming and Diving M & W; Tennis W; Track and Field M & W; Volleyball W; Wrestling M

MONMOUTH COLLEGE
700 East Broadway
Monmouth, IL 61462-1998
Tel: (309)457-2311
Free: 800-747-2687
Admissions: (309)457-2131
Fax: (309)457-2141
Web Site: http://www.monm.edu/
President/CEO: Dr. Mauri Ditzler
Registrar: Sue Dagit
Admissions: John Klockentager
Financial Aid: Jayne Whiteside
Type: Four-Year College **Sex:** Coed **Affiliation:** Presbyterian Church **Scores:** 100% SAT V 400+; 100% SAT M 400+; 58% ACT 18-23; 34% ACT 24-29 **% Accepted:** 79 **Admission Plans:** Deferred Admission **Application Deadline:** Rolling **Application Fee:** $0.00 **H.S. Requirements:** High school diploma required; GED accepted **Costs Per Year:** Application fee: $0. Comprehensive fee: $25,950 includes full-time tuition ($20,200) and college room and board ($5750). College room only: $3240. **Scholarships:** Available **Calendar System:** Semester, Summer Session Not available **Enrollment:** FT 1,329, PT 16 **Faculty:** FT 109, PT 46 **Student-Faculty Ratio:** 15:1 **Exams:** SAT I or ACT **% Receiving Financial Aid:** 86 **% Residing in College-Owned, -Operated, or -Affiliated Housing:** 94 **Library Holdings:** 176,470 **Regional Accreditation:** North Central Association of Colleges and Schools **Credit Hours For Degree:** 124 semester hours, Bachelors **ROTC:** Army **Intercollegiate Athletics:** Baseball M; Basketball M & W; Cheerleading M & W; Cross-Country Running M & W; Football M; Golf M & W; Soccer M & W; Softball W; Swimming and Diving M & W; Tennis M & W; Track and Field M & W; Volleyball W

MOODY BIBLE INSTITUTE
820 North LaSalle Blvd.
Chicago, IL 60610-3284

Tel: (312)329-4000
Free: 800-967-4MBI
Admissions: (312)329-4267
Fax: (312)329-8987
E-mail: admissions@moody.edu
Web Site: http://www.moody.edu/
President/CEO: Dr. Joseph M. Stowell, III
Registrar: Timothy Wiegert
Admissions: Annette Moy
Financial Aid: Daniel Ward
Type: Comprehensive **Sex:** Coed **Affiliation:** nondenominational **Scores:** 36% ACT 18-23; 53% ACT 24-29 **Admission Plans:** Early Admission; Early Decision Plan **Application Fee:** $35.00 **H.S. Requirements:** High school diploma required; GED accepted **Costs Per Year:** Application fee: $35. Comprehensive fee: $13,880 includes full-time tuition ($0), mandatory fees ($1400), and college room and board ($12,480). College room only: $4300. Room and board charges vary according to housing facility. All students are awarded full-tuition scholarships. **Scholarships:** Available **Calendar System:** Semester, Summer Session Available **Enrollment:** FT 1,458, PT 944, Grad 184 **Faculty:** FT 84, PT 16 **Student-Faculty Ratio:** 20:1 **Exams:** SAT I and SAT II or ACT **% Receiving Financial Aid:** 21 **% Residing in College-Owned, -Operated, or -Affiliated Housing:** 90 **Library Holdings:** 135,000 **Regional Accreditation:** North Central Association of Colleges and Schools **Credit Hours For Degree:** 130 semester hours, Bachelors **Professional Accreditation:** AABC, NASM **Intercollegiate Athletics:** Basketball M & W; Soccer M; Volleyball M & W

MORAINE VALLEY COMMUNITY COLLEGE
10900 South 88th Ave.
Palos Hills, IL 60465-0937
Tel: (708)974-4300
Admissions: (708)974-5346
Fax: (708)974-0681
E-mail: manser@morainevalley.edu
Web Site: http://www.morainevalley.edu/
President/CEO: Dr. Vernon O. Crawley
Admissions: Wendy Manser
Financial Aid: Laurie Anema
Type: Two-Year College **Sex:** Coed **Affiliation:** Illinois Community College Board **Scores:** 51.1% ACT 18-23; 11.9% ACT 24-29 **% Accepted:** 100 **Admission Plans:** Open Admission; Preferred Admission; Early Admission; Deferred Admission **Application Deadline:** Rolling **Application Fee:** $0.00 **H.S. Requirements:** High school diploma required; GED accepted **Costs Per Year:** Application fee: $0. Area resident tuition: $1920 full-time, $64 per credit hour part-time. State resident tuition: $5970 full-time, $199 per credit hour part-time. Nonresident tuition: $7260 full-time, $242 per credit hour part-time. Mandatory fees: $152 full-time, $5 per credit hour part-time, $1 per term part-time. **Scholarships:** Available **Calendar System:** Semester, Summer Session Available **Enrollment:** FT 6,654, PT 9,275 **Faculty:** FT 165, PT 596 **Student-Faculty Ratio:** 36:1 **Library Holdings:** 77,164 **Regional Accreditation:** North Central Association of Colleges and Schools **Credit Hours For Degree:** 62 semester hours, Associates **Professional Accreditation:** AHIMA, CARC, JRCERT, NLN **Intercollegiate Athletics:** Baseball M; Basketball M & W; Cross-Country Running M & W; Golf M; Soccer M & W; Softball W; Tennis M & W; Volleyball W

MORRISON INSTITUTE OF TECHNOLOGY
701 Portland Ave.
Morrison, IL 61270-0410
Tel: (815)772-7218
Fax: (815)772-7584
E-mail: mit@essexl.com
Web Site: http://www.morrison.tec.il.us/
President/CEO: Richard C. Parkinson
Registrar: Judy Turney
Admissions: Carl J. Rhodes
Financial Aid: Julie Damhoff
Type: Two-Year College **Sex:** Coed **Scores:** 62% ACT 18-23; 8% ACT 24-29 **Admission Plans:** Open Admission; Deferred Admission **Application Deadline:** Rolling **Application Fee:** $100.00 **H.S. Requirements:** High school diploma required; GED accepted **Costs Per Year:** Application fee: $100. Tuition: $12,100 full-time, $504.60 per credit part-time. Mandatory fees: $560 full-time, $125 per term part-time. College room only: $2600. **Scholarships:** Available **Calendar System:** Semester, Summer Session Not available **Faculty:** FT 10, PT 1 **Student-Faculty Ratio:** 12:1 **Exams:** SAT I or ACT **% Residing in College-Owned, -Operated, or -Affiliated Housing:** 55 **Library Holdings:** 7,946 **Credit Hours For Degree:** 67 semester hours, Associates **Professional Accreditation:** ABET, COE

MORTON COLLEGE
3801 South Central Ave.
Cicero, IL 60804-4398
Tel: (708)656-8000
Fax: (708)656-9592
Web Site: http://www.morton.edu/
President/CEO: Dr. W. Patrick Leonard
Registrar: Scott D. Heck
Admissions: Jill Caccamo-Beer
Financial Aid: Nicole Smith
Type: Two-Year College **Sex:** Coed **Affiliation:** Illinois Community College Board **Admission Plans:** Open Admission; Preferred Admission **Application Fee:** $10.00 **H.S. Requirements:** High school diploma required; GED accepted **Scholarships:** Available **Calendar System:** Semester, Summer Session Available **Enrollment:** FT 5,244 **Faculty:** FT 48, PT 143 **Library Holdings:** 40,972 **Regional Accreditation:** North Central Association of Colleges and Schools **Credit Hours For Degree:** 62 semester hours, Associates **Professional Accreditation:** APTA **Intercollegiate Athletics:** Baseball M; Basketball M & W; Cross-Country Running M & W; Soccer M; Softball W; Volleyball W

NATIONAL-LOUIS UNIVERSITY
122 South Michigan Ave.
Chicago, IL 60603
Tel: (312)621-9650
Free: 800-443-5522
Admissions: 888-NLU-TODAY
Fax: (312)261-3057
Web Site: http://www.nl.edu/
President/CEO: Dr. Curtis L. McCray
Admissions: Pat Petillo
Type: University **Sex:** Coed **Admission Plans:** Deferred Admission **Application Deadline:** Rolling **Application Fee:** $25.00 **H.S. Requirements:** High school diploma required; GED accepted **Costs Per Year:** Application fee: $25. Tuition: $17,640 full-time, $393 per quarter hour part-time. Mandatory fees: $120 full-time, $40 per term part-time. **Scholarships:** Available **Calendar System:** Quarter, Summer Session Available **Enrollment:** FT 1,588, PT 572, Grad 5,185 **Faculty:** FT 284, PT 0 **Student-Faculty Ratio:** 16:1 **Exams:** SAT I or ACT **% Residing in College-Owned, -Operated, or -Affiliated Housing:** 5 **Regional Accreditation:** North Central Association of Colleges and Schools **Credit Hours For Degree:** 180 quarter hours, Bachelors **Professional Accreditation:** CARC, JRCERT, NCATE

NORTH CENTRAL COLLEGE
30 North Brainard St., PO Box 3063
Naperville, IL 60566-7063
Tel: (630)637-5100
Free: 800-411-1861
Admissions: (630)637-5802
E-mail: admissions@noctrl.edu
Web Site: http://www.noctrl.edu/
President/CEO: Dr. Harold R. Wilde
Registrar: Jonathan Pickering
Admissions: Martin Sauer
Financial Aid: Katherine Edmunds
Type: Comprehensive **Sex:** Coed **Affiliation:** United Methodist **Scores:** 98% SAT V 400+; 100% SAT M 400+; 43% ACT 18-23; 44% ACT 24-29 **% Accepted:** 70 **Admission Plans:** Early Admission; Deferred Admission **Application Deadline:** Rolling **Application Fee:** $25.00 **H.S. Requirements:** High school diploma required; GED accepted **Costs Per Year:** Application fee: $25. Comprehensive fee: $28,926 includes full-time tuition ($21,528), mandatory fees ($405), and college room and board ($6993). Room and board charges vary according to housing facility. Part-time tuition: $540 per semester hour. Part-time mandatory fees: $20 per term. **Scholarships:** Available **Calendar System:** Quarter, Summer Session Available **Enrollment:** FT 1,910, PT 223, Grad 339 **Faculty:** FT 111, PT 92 **Student-Faculty Ratio:** 15:1 **Exams:** ACT, SAT I or ACT **% Receiving Financial Aid:** 68 **% Residing in College-Owned, -Operated, or -Affiliated Housing:** 58 **Library Holdings:** 149,181 **Regional Accreditation:** North Central Association of Colleges and Schools **Credit Hours For Degree:** 120 semester hours, Bachelors **ROTC:** Army, Air Force **Intercollegiate Athletics:**

Baseball M; Basketball M & W; Cheerleading W; Cross-Country Running M & W; Football M; Golf M & W; Soccer M & W; Softball W; Swimming and Diving M & W; Tennis M & W; Track and Field M & W; Volleyball W; Wrestling M

NORTH PARK UNIVERSITY
3225 West Foster Ave.
Chicago, IL 60625-4895
Tel: (773)244-6200
Free: 800-888-NPC8
Admissions: (773)244-5500
Fax: (773)583-0858
E-mail: afao@northpark.edu
Web Site: http://www.northpark.edu/
President/CEO: Dr. David G. Horner
Registrar: Aaron Schoof
Admissions: Mark Olson
Financial Aid: Mark Olson
Type: Comprehensive **Sex:** Coed **Affiliation:** Evangelical Covenant Church **Scores:** 100% SAT V 400+; 96% SAT M 400+; 47% ACT 18-23; 33% ACT 24-29 **Admission Plans:** Early Admission **Application Fee:** $20.00 **H.S. Requirements:** High school diploma required; GED accepted **Costs Per Year:** Application fee: $20. Comprehensive fee: $21,240 includes full-time tuition ($13,900), mandatory fees ($60), and college room and board ($7280). College room only: $3800. Full-time tuition and fees vary according to program. Room and board charges vary according to board plan, housing facility, and student level. Part-time tuition: $650 per credit. Part-time tuition varies according to program. **Scholarships:** Available **Calendar System:** Semester, Summer Session Available **Enrollment:** FT 1,252, PT 321, Grad 516 **Faculty:** FT 88, PT 33 **Student-Faculty Ratio:** 16:1 **Exams:** SAT I or ACT **Library Holdings:** 260,685 **Regional Accreditation:** North Central Association of Colleges and Schools **Credit Hours For Degree:** 120 semester hours, Bachelors **Professional Accreditation:** AACN, NASM **Intercollegiate Athletics:** Baseball M; Basketball M & W; Cross-Country Running M & W; Football M; Golf M; Soccer M & W; Softball W; Tennis W; Track and Field M & W; Volleyball M & W

NORTHEASTERN ILLINOIS UNIVERSITY
5500 North St Louis Ave.
Chicago, IL 60625-4699
Tel: (773)583-4050
Admissions: (773)442-4000
Fax: (773)794-6243
Web Site: http://www.neiu.edu/
President/CEO: Dr. Salme Harju Steinberg
Registrar: Alice Medenwald
Admissions: Dr. Janice Harring-Hendon
Financial Aid: Marshall Jennings
Type: Comprehensive **Sex:** Coed **Scores:** 49% ACT 18-23; 9% ACT 24-29 **% Accepted:** 75 **Admission Plans:** Deferred Admission **Application Deadline:** July 01 **Application Fee:** $25.00 **H.S. Requirements:** High school diploma required; GED accepted **Costs Per Year:** Application fee: $25. State resident tuition: $4800 full-time, $160 per credit hour part-time. Nonresident tuition: $9600 full-time, $320 per credit hour part-time. Mandatory fees: $846 full-time. Full-time tuition and fees vary according to student level. **Scholarships:** Available **Calendar System:** Semester, Summer Session Available **Enrollment:** FT 5,207, PT 4,211, Grad 2,809 **Faculty:** FT 415, PT 265 **Student-Faculty Ratio:** 16:1 **Exams:** ACT, SAT I or ACT **% Receiving Financial Aid:** 49 **Library Holdings:** 713,076 **Regional Accreditation:** North Central Association of Colleges and Schools **Credit Hours For Degree:** 120 credit hours, Bachelors **ROTC:** Army, Air Force **Professional Accreditation:** ACA, CSWE, NCATE

NORTHERN ILLINOIS UNIVERSITY
DeKalb, IL 60115-2854
Tel: (815)753-1000
Admissions: (815)753-0446
E-mail: admission-info@niu.edu
Web Site: http://www.niu.edu/
President/CEO: Dr. John G. Peters
Registrar: Donald R. Larson
Admissions: Dr. Robert Burk
Financial Aid: Kathleen Brunson
Type: University **Sex:** Coed **Scores:** 57% ACT 18-23; 31% ACT 24-29 **% Accepted:** 66 **Application Deadline:** August 01 **H.S. Requirements:** High school diploma required; GED accepted **Costs Per Year:** State resident tuition: $5061 full-time, $169 per credit hour part-time. Nonresident tuition: $10,123 full-time, $338 per credit hour part-time. Mandatory fees: $1378 full-time, $58 per credit hour part-time. Full-time tuition and fees vary according to course load. Part-time tuition and fees vary according to course load. College room and board: $5950. Room and board charges vary according to board plan and housing facility. **Scholarships:** Available **Calendar System:** Semester, Summer Session Available **Enrollment:** FT 16,609, PT 1,858, Grad 6,408 **Faculty:** FT 894, PT 299 **Student-Faculty Ratio:** 17:1 **Exams:** SAT I or ACT **% Receiving Financial Aid:** 52 **% Residing in College-Owned, -Operated, or -Affiliated Housing:** 33 **Library Holdings:** 3,119,829 **Regional Accreditation:** North Central Association of Colleges and Schools **Credit Hours For Degree:** 124 credit hours, Bachelors **ROTC:** Army, Air Force **Professional Accreditation:** AACSB, ABET, AAMFT, AACN, AAFCS, ABA, ACA, ADtA, APTA, APA, ASLHA, AALS, CEPH, CORE, JRCEPAT, NAACLS, NAIT, NASAD, NASM, NASPAA NAST, NCATE, NLN **Intercollegiate Athletics:** Baseball M; Basketball M & W; Cross-Country Running W; Football M; Golf M & W; Gymnastics W; Soccer M & W; Softball W; Swimming and Diving M & W; Tennis M & W; Volleyball W; Wrestling M

NORTHWESTERN BUSINESS COLLEGE
4829 North Lipps Ave.
Chicago, IL 60630-2298
Tel: (773)777-4220
Free: 800-396-5613
Admissions: (773)481-3730
Web Site: http://www.northwesternbc.edu/
President/CEO: Lawrence Schumacher
Registrar: Gertrude Domke
Admissions: Mark Sliz
Financial Aid: Harold Burtley
Type: Two-Year College **Sex:** Coed **Application Fee:** $25.00 **H.S. Requirements:** High school diploma required; GED accepted **Scholarships:** Available **Calendar System:** Quarter, Summer Session Available **Student-Faculty Ratio:** 18:1 **Exams:** SAT I or ACT **Library Holdings:** 2,000 **Regional Accreditation:** North Central Association of Colleges and Schools **Credit Hours For Degree:** 100 quarter hours, Associates **Professional Accreditation:** AAMAE, AHIMA, ACBSP

NORTHWESTERN UNIVERSITY
Evanston, IL 60208
Tel: (847)491-3741
Admissions: (847)491-7271
E-mail: ug-admission@nwu.edu
Web Site: http://www.northwestern.edu/
President/CEO: Dr. Henry S. Bienen
Registrar: Suzanne M. Anderson
Admissions: Carol Lunkenheimer
Financial Aid: Carolyn V. Lindley
Type: University **Sex:** Coed **Scores:** 100% SAT V 400+; 100% SAT M 400+; 4% ACT 18-23; 27% ACT 24-29 **% Accepted:** 30 **Admission Plans:** Early Admission; Early Decision Plan; Deferred Admission **Application Deadline:** January 01 **Application Fee:** $65.00 **H.S. Requirements:** High school diploma or equivalent not required **Costs Per Year:** Application fee: $65. Comprehensive fee: $43,825 includes full-time tuition ($33,408), mandatory fees ($151), and college room and board ($10,266). College room only: $5835. Part-time tuition: $3963 per course. **Scholarships:** Available **Calendar System:** Quarter, Summer Session Available **Enrollment:** FT 7,872, PT 151, Grad 7,531 **Faculty:** FT 938, PT 207 **Student-Faculty Ratio:** 7:1 **Exams:** SAT I or ACT, SAT II **% Receiving Financial Aid:** 43 **% Residing in College-Owned, -Operated, or -Affiliated Housing:** 65 **Library Holdings:** 4,408,830 **Regional Accreditation:** North Central Association of Colleges and Schools **Credit Hours For Degree:** 45 courses, Bachelors **ROTC:** Army, Navy, Air Force **Professional Accreditation:** AACSB, ABET, ACEHSA, ACEJMC, AAMFT, ABA, APTA, APA, ASLHA, AALS, CEPH, LCMEAMA, NASM, NAST **Intercollegiate Athletics:** Baseball M; Basketball M & W; Cheerleading M & W; Cross-Country Running W; Fencing W; Field Hockey W; Football M; Golf M & W; Lacrosse W; Soccer M & W; Softball W; Swimming and Diving M & W; Tennis M & W; Volleyball W; Wrestling M

OAKTON COMMUNITY COLLEGE
1600 East Golf Rd.
Des Plaines, IL 60016-1268
Tel: (847)635-1600

Admissions: (847)635-1629
Fax: (847)635-1706
E-mail: dcohen@oakton.edu
Web Site: http://www.oakton.edu/
President/CEO: Dr. Margaret B. Lee
Registrar: Bruce Oates
Admissions: Michele Brown
Financial Aid: Cheryl Warmann
Type: Two-Year College **Sex:** Coed **Affiliation:** Illinois Community College Board **Admission Plans:** Open Admission **Application Fee:** $25.00 **H.S. Requirements:** High school diploma required; GED accepted **Scholarships:** Available **Calendar System:** Semester, Summer Session Available **Faculty:** FT 154, PT 508 **Student-Faculty Ratio:** 25:1 **Library Holdings:** 92,000 **Regional Accreditation:** North Central Association of Colleges and Schools **Credit Hours For Degree:** 60 semester hours, Associates **Professional Accreditation:** AHIMA, APTA, NAACLS, NLN **Intercollegiate Athletics:** Baseball M; Basketball M & W; Cross-Country Running M & W; Golf M; Soccer M & W; Softball W; Tennis M & W; Track and Field M & W; Volleyball W

OLIVET NAZARENE UNIVERSITY
One University Ave.
Bourbonnais, IL 60914-2271
Tel: (815)939-5011
Free: 800-648-1463
Admissions: (815)939-5203
E-mail: admissions@olivet.edu
Web Site: http://www.olivet.edu/
President/CEO: Dr. John C. Bowling
Registrar: Dr. Jim D. Knight
Admissions: Brian Parker
Financial Aid: Greg Bruner
Type: Comprehensive **Sex:** Coed **Affiliation:** Church of the Nazarene **Scores:** 46% ACT 18-23; 36% ACT 24-29 **Admission Plans:** Deferred Admission **Application Fee:** $0.00 **H.S. Requirements:** High school diploma required; GED accepted **Costs Per Year:** Application fee: $0. Comprehensive fee: $22,590 includes full-time tuition ($15,650), mandatory fees ($840), and college room and board ($6100). College room only: $3050. Full-time tuition and fees vary according to course load. Room and board charges vary according to board plan. Part-time tuition: $652 per hour. Part-time mandatory fees: $10 per term. Part-time tuition and fees vary according to course load. **Scholarships:** Available **Calendar System:** Semester, Summer Session Available **Enrollment:** FT 2,352, PT 281, Grad 1,731 **Faculty:** FT 86, PT 37 **Student-Faculty Ratio:** 21:1 **Exams:** ACT **% Receiving Financial Aid:** 70 **% Residing in College-Owned, -Operated, or -Affiliated Housing:** 79 **Library Holdings:** 160,039 **Regional Accreditation:** North Central Association of Colleges and Schools **Credit Hours For Degree:** 64 semester hours, Associates; 128 semester hours, Bachelors **ROTC:** Army **Professional Accreditation:** ABET, AACN, AAFCS, CSWE, NASM, NCATE **Intercollegiate Athletics:** Baseball M; Basketball M & W; Cheerleading M & W; Cross-Country Running M & W; Football M; Golf M; Soccer M & W; Softball W; Tennis M & W; Track and Field M & W; Volleyball W

PARKLAND COLLEGE
2400 West Bradley Ave.
Champaign, IL 61821-1899
Tel: (217)351-2200
Admissions: (217)351-2558
Fax: (217)351-7640
Web Site: http://www.parkland.edu/
President/CEO: Dr. Zelema M. Harris
Registrar: Micheal Henry
Admissions: Michael D. Henry
Financial Aid: John K. Lyons
Type: Two-Year College **Sex:** Coed **Affiliation:** Illinois Community College Board **Scores:** 45.17% ACT 18-23; 15.68% ACT 24-29 **% Accepted:** 52 **Admission Plans:** Open Admission; Deferred Admission **Application Deadline:** Rolling **Application Fee:** $0.00 **H.S. Requirements:** High school diploma required; GED accepted **Costs Per Year:** Application fee: $0. Area resident tuition: $2220 full-time, $72 per credit hour part-time. State resident tuition: $6360 full-time, $212 per credit hour part-time. Nonresident tuition: $9450 full-time, $315 per credit hour part-time. **Scholarships:** Available **Calendar System:** Semester, Summer Session Available **Enrollment:** FT 4,536, PT 5,216 **Faculty:** FT 164, PT 371 **Student-Faculty Ratio:** 17:1 **Exams:** ACT **Library Holdings:** 122,676 **Regional Accreditation:** North Central Association of Colleges and Schools **Credit Hours For Degree:** 60 semester hours, Associates **ROTC:** Army, Navy, Air Force **Professional Accreditation:** ARCEST, ADA, AOTA, CARC, JRCERT, NLN **Intercollegiate Athletics:** Baseball M; Basketball M & W; Golf M; Soccer M & W; Softball W; Volleyball W

PRAIRIE STATE COLLEGE
202 South Halsted St.
Chicago Heights, IL 60411-8226
Tel: (708)709-3500; (708)709-3516
Admissions: (708)709-3542
Web Site: http://www.prairiestate.edu/
President/CEO: Dr. Paul J. McCarthy
Registrar: Mary Welsh
Admissions: Dr. Linda Uzureau
Financial Aid: Alice Garcia
Type: Two-Year College **Sex:** Coed **Affiliation:** Illinois Community College Board **% Accepted:** 100 **Admission Plans:** Open Admission; Deferred Admission **Application Deadline:** Rolling **Application Fee:** $10.00 **H.S. Requirements:** High school diploma or equivalent not required. For transfer associate programs: High school diploma or equivalent not required **Costs Per Year:** Application fee: $10. Area resident tuition: $1824 full-time, $67 per credit hour part-time. State resident tuition: $5280 full-time, $211 per credit hour part-time. Nonresident tuition: $7200 full-time, $291 per credit hour part-time. Mandatory fees: $236 full-time, $9 per credit hour part-time, $10 per term part-time. Full-time tuition and fees vary according to course load. Part-time tuition and fees vary according to course load. College room and board: $4500. Room and board charges vary according to location. **Scholarships:** Available **Calendar System:** Semester, Summer Session Available **Enrollment:** FT 1,714, PT 3,369 **Faculty:** FT 80, PT 283 **Student-Faculty Ratio:** 16:1 **Library Holdings:** 45,000 **Regional Accreditation:** North Central Association of Colleges and Schools **Credit Hours For Degree:** 62 credit hours, Associates **Professional Accreditation:** ADA, NLN **Intercollegiate Athletics:** Baseball M; Basketball M & W; Football M; Golf M & W; Soccer M & W; Softball M & W; Tennis W

PRINCIPIA COLLEGE
One Maybeck Place
Elsah, IL 62028-9799
Tel: (618)374-2131
Free: 800-277-4648 Ext. 2802
Admissions: (618)374-5180
Fax: (618)374-4000
E-mail: collegeadmissions@prin.edu
Web Site: http://www.prin.edu/college/
President/CEO: Dr. George D. Moffett
Registrar: Patricia Langton
Admissions: Martha Green Quirk
Financial Aid: Ruth Schock
Type: Four-Year College **Sex:** Coed **Affiliation:** Christian Science **Scores:** 98.1% SAT V 400+; 100% SAT M 400+; 26.3% ACT 18-23; 42.1% ACT 24-29 **% Accepted:** 89 **Admission Plans:** Early Action; Deferred Admission **Application Deadline:** March 01 **Application Fee:** $0.00 **H.S. Requirements:** High school diploma required; GED accepted **Costs Per Year:** Application fee: $0. Comprehensive fee: $29,346 includes full-time tuition ($21,150), mandatory fees ($300), and college room and board ($7896). College room only: $3831. Part-time tuition: $470 per quarter hour. **Scholarships:** Available **Calendar System:** Quarter, Summer Session Not available **Enrollment:** FT 536, PT 6 **Faculty:** FT 55, PT 11 **Student-Faculty Ratio:** 8:1 **Exams:** SAT I or ACT, SAT I and SAT II or ACT, SAT II **% Receiving Financial Aid:** 58 **% Residing in College-Owned, -Operated, or -Affiliated Housing:** 100 **Library Holdings:** 211,460 **Regional Accreditation:** North Central Association of Colleges and Schools **Credit Hours For Degree:** 180 quarter hours, Bachelors **Intercollegiate Athletics:** Baseball M; Basketball M & W; Cross-Country Running M & W; Football M; Golf M; Soccer M & W; Swimming and Diving M & W; Tennis M & W; Track and Field M & W; Volleyball W

QUINCY UNIVERSITY
1800 College Ave.
Quincy, IL 62301-2699
Tel: (217)222-8020
Free: 800-688-4295
Admissions: (217)228-5210

Fax: (217)228-5479
E-mail: clynes@quincy.edu
Web Site: http://www.quincy.edu/
President/CEO: Margaret Feldner, OSF
Admissions: Mark P. Clynes
Financial Aid: Shann Doerr
Type: Comprehensive **Sex:** Coed **Affiliation:** Roman Catholic **Scores:** 100% SAT V 400+; 100% SAT M 400+; 64% ACT 18-23; 27% ACT 24-29 **% Accepted:** 94 **Admission Plans:** Early Admission; Deferred Admission **Application Deadline:** Rolling **Application Fee:** $25.00 **H.S. Requirements:** High school diploma required; GED accepted **Costs Per Year:** Application fee: $25. Comprehensive fee: $25,970 includes full-time tuition ($18,450), mandatory fees ($560), and college room and board ($6960). College room only: $3740. Part-time tuition: $465 per credit hour. Part-time mandatory fees: $15 per credit hour. **Scholarships:** Available **Calendar System:** Semester, Summer Session Available **Enrollment:** FT 927, PT 148, Grad 284 **Faculty:** FT 54, PT 73 **Student-Faculty Ratio:** 13:1 **Exams:** SAT I or ACT **% Receiving Financial Aid:** 74 **% Residing in College-Owned, -Operated, or -Affiliated Housing:** 77 **Library Holdings:** 239,983 **Regional Accreditation:** North Central Association of Colleges and Schools **Credit Hours For Degree:** 64 credit hours, Associates; 124 credit hours, Bachelors **Professional Accreditation:** NASM **Intercollegiate Athletics:** Baseball M; Basketball M & W; Football M; Golf M & W; Soccer M & W; Softball W; Tennis M & W; Volleyball M & W

REND LAKE COLLEGE
468 North Ken Gray Parkway
Ina, IL 62846-9801
Tel: (618)437-5321
Fax: (618)437-5677
E-mail: mitchelp@rlc.cc.il.us
Web Site: http://www.rlc.edu/
President/CEO: Mark S. Kern
Admissions: Kimberly M. Harvey
Financial Aid: Doug Carlson
Type: Two-Year College **Sex:** Coed **Affiliation:** Illinois Community College Board **Admission Plans:** Open Admission; Deferred Admission **Application Fee:** $0.00 **H.S. Requirements:** High school diploma required; GED accepted **Scholarships:** Available **Calendar System:** Semester, Summer Session Available **Enrollment:** FT 1,499, PT 3,643 **Faculty:** FT 61, PT 163 **Exams:** Other, SAT I or ACT **Library Holdings:** 35,426 **Regional Accreditation:** North Central Association of Colleges and Schools **Credit Hours For Degree:** 64 semester hours, Associates **Professional Accreditation:** AHIMA, AOTA, NAACLS **Intercollegiate Athletics:** Baseball M; Basketball M & W; Cross-Country Running M; Golf M & W; Softball W; Tennis W; Volleyball W

RICHLAND COMMUNITY COLLEGE
One College Park
Decatur, IL 62521-8513
Tel: (217)875-7200
Fax: (217)875-6991
E-mail: sblahnik@richland.edu
Web Site: http://www.richland.edu/
President/CEO: Dr. Gayle Saunders
Registrar: JoAnn Wireg
Admissions: Sheryl Blahnik
Financial Aid: Karen Zalkin
Type: Two-Year College **Sex:** Coed **Affiliation:** Illinois Community College Board **Scores:** 52% ACT 18-23; 20% ACT 24-29 **% Accepted:** 100 **Admission Plans:** Open Admission; Early Admission **Application Deadline:** Rolling **Application Fee:** $0.00 **H.S. Requirements:** High school diploma required; GED accepted **Costs Per Year:** Application fee: $0. Area resident tuition: $1785 full-time, $59.50 per credit hour part-time. State resident tuition: $7566 full-time, $258.20 per credit hour part-time. Nonresident tuition: $11,490 full-time, $383 per credit hour part-time. Mandatory fees: $155 full-time, $4.50 per credit hour part-time, $10 per term part-time. **Scholarships:** Available **Calendar System:** Semester, Summer Session Available **Enrollment:** FT 1,048, PT 1,986 **Faculty:** FT 68, PT 149 **Student-Faculty Ratio:** 14:1 **Exams:** ACT **Library Holdings:** 39,452 **Regional Accreditation:** North Central Association of Colleges and Schools **Credit Hours For Degree:** 60 semester hours, Associates **Professional Accreditation:** ARCEST, NLN

ROBERT MORRIS COLLEGE
401 South State St.
Chicago, IL 60605
Tel: (312)935-6800
Free: 800-RMC-5960
Admissions: (312)935-6640
Fax: (312)836-4599
E-mail: enroll@rmcil.edu
Web Site: http://www.robertmorris.edu/
President/CEO: Michael P. Viollt
Registrar: Nancy Smith-Irons
Admissions: Candace Goodwin
Financial Aid: Karen Leveque
Type: Four-Year College **Sex:** Coed **% Accepted:** 80 **Admission Plans:** Deferred Admission **Application Deadline:** Rolling **Application Fee:** $30.00 **H.S. Requirements:** High school diploma required; GED accepted **Costs Per Year:** Application fee: $30. Tuition: $15,900 full-time. **Scholarships:** Available **Calendar System:** Miscellaneous, Summer Session Available **Enrollment:** FT 4,706, PT 712 **Faculty:** FT 134, PT 234 **Student-Faculty Ratio:** 26:1 **% Receiving Financial Aid:** 92 **% Residing in College-Owned, -Operated, or -Affiliated Housing:** 2 **Library Holdings:** 121,737 **Regional Accreditation:** North Central Association of Colleges and Schools **Credit Hours For Degree:** 92 quarter hours, Associates; 188 quarter hours, Bachelors **ROTC:** Army **Professional Accreditation:** AAMAE **Intercollegiate Athletics:** Baseball M; Basketball M & W; Bowling M; Cross-Country Running M & W; Golf M & W; Soccer M & W; Softball W; Tennis W; Volleyball W

ROCK VALLEY COLLEGE
3301 North Mulford Rd.
Rockford, IL 61114-5699
Tel: (815)921-7821
Free: 800-973-7821
Admissions: (815)921-4088
Fax: (815)654-5568
Web Site: http://www.rockvalleycollege.edu/
President/CEO: Dr. Roland Chapdelaine
Registrar: Lisa Allman
Admissions: Steve Ullrick
Financial Aid: Sue Ullrick
Type: Two-Year College **Sex:** Coed **Affiliation:** Illinois Community College Board **Admission Plans:** Open Admission **Application Deadline:** August 29 **Application Fee:** $0.00 **H.S. Requirements:** High school diploma or equivalent not required. For nursing, respiratory therapy programs: High school diploma required; GED accepted **Costs Per Year:** Application fee: $0. Area resident tuition: $1830 full-time, $61 per credit part-time. State resident tuition: $7350 full-time, $245 per credit part-time. Nonresident tuition: $12,030 full-time, $401 per credit part-time. **Scholarships:** Available **Calendar System:** Semester, Summer Session Available **Enrollment:** FT 3,508, PT 4,637 **Faculty:** FT 139, PT 152 **Student-Faculty Ratio:** 21:1 **Library Holdings:** 67,168 **Regional Accreditation:** North Central Association of Colleges and Schools **Credit Hours For Degree:** 64 semester hours, Associates **Professional Accreditation:** ADA, CARC **Intercollegiate Athletics:** Baseball M; Basketball M & W; Football M; Golf M; Softball W; Tennis M & W; Volleyball W

ROCKFORD BUSINESS COLLEGE
730 North Church St.
Rockford, IL 61103
Tel: (815)965-8616
Fax: (815)965-0360
Web Site: http://www.rbcsuccess.com/
President/CEO: Susan A. Swank
Registrar: Jack E. Martin
Admissions: Barbara Holliman
Financial Aid: Chad Wick
Type: Two-Year College **Sex:** Coed **Admission Plans:** Open Admission; Early Admission **Application Fee:** $50.00 **H.S. Requirements:** High school diploma required; GED accepted **Scholarships:** Available **Calendar System:** Quarter, Summer Session Available **Enrollment:** FT 243, PT 185 **Faculty:** FT 8, PT 18 **Student-Faculty Ratio:** 15:1 **Library Holdings:** 1,823

Credit Hours For Degree: 100 credits, Associates **Professional Accreditation:** ACICS, AAMAE

ROCKFORD COLLEGE
5050 East State St.
Rockford, IL 61108-2393
Tel: (815)226-4000
Free: 800-892-2984
Admissions: (815)226-4050
Fax: (815)226-4119
E-mail: mplocinski@rockford.edu
Web Site: http://www.rockford.edu/
President/CEO: Paul C. Pribbenow
Registrar: Bernie Lalor
Admissions: Michael Plocinski
Financial Aid: Todd Free
Type: Comprehensive **Sex:** Coed **Scores:** 91% SAT V 400+; 95% SAT M 400+; 47% ACT 18-23; 28% ACT 24-29 **% Accepted:** 59 **Admission Plans:** Early Admission; Deferred Admission **Application Deadline:** August 01 **Application Fee:** $35.00 **H.S. Requirements:** High school diploma required; GED accepted **Costs Per Year:** Application fee: $35. Comprehensive fee: $29,681 includes full-time tuition ($22,460) and college room and board ($7221). College room only: $4441. Part-time tuition: $595 per credit. **Scholarships:** Available **Calendar System:** Semester, Summer Session Available **Enrollment:** FT 731, PT 141, Grad 504 **Faculty:** FT 68 **Student-Faculty Ratio:** 11:1 **Exams:** SAT I or ACT **% Receiving Financial Aid:** 93 **% Residing in College-Owned, -Operated, or -Affiliated Housing:** 36 **Library Holdings:** 140,000 **Regional Accreditation:** North Central Association of Colleges and Schools **Credit Hours For Degree:** 124 credits, Bachelors **ROTC:** Army **Professional Accreditation:** NLN **Intercollegiate Athletics:** Baseball M; Basketball M & W; Football M; Golf M; Soccer M & W; Softball W; Tennis M & W; Volleyball M & W

ROOSEVELT UNIVERSITY
430 South Michigan Ave.
Chicago, IL 60605-1394
Tel: (312)341-3500; 877-APPLYRU
E-mail: dessimm@admvsbk.roosevelt.edu
Web Site: http://www.roosevelt.edu/
President/CEO: Dr. Charles Middleton
Registrar: Michael Ford
Admissions: Gwen Kanelos
Financial Aid: Walter O'Neill
Type: Comprehensive **Sex:** Coed **Scores:** 94.6% SAT V 400+; 87.4% SAT M 400+; 50% ACT 18-23; 38.8% ACT 24-29 **% Accepted:** 60 **Admission Plans:** Deferred Admission **Application Deadline:** September 01 **Application Fee:** $25.00 **H.S. Requirements:** High school diploma required; GED accepted **Costs Per Year:** Application fee: $25. Comprehensive fee: $22,420 includes full-time tuition ($14,180), mandatory fees ($250), and college room and board ($7990). College room only: $5800. Full-time tuition and fees vary according to course load and program. Room and board charges vary according to board plan, housing facility, and location. Part-time tuition: $575 per hour. Part-time mandatory fees: $125 per term. Part-time tuition and fees vary according to course load and program. **Scholarships:** Available **Calendar System:** Semester, Summer Session Available **Enrollment:** FT 2,041, PT 2,032, Grad 3,161 **Faculty:** FT 212, PT 432 **Student-Faculty Ratio:** 12:1 **Exams:** SAT I or ACT **% Receiving Financial Aid:** 66 **% Residing in College-Owned, -Operated, or -Affiliated Housing:** 9 **Library Holdings:** 186,944 **Regional Accreditation:** North Central Association of Colleges and Schools **Credit Hours For Degree:** 120 semester hours, Bachelors **Professional Accreditation:** ACA, APA, ACBSP, NASM, NCATE

RUSH UNIVERSITY
600 South Paulina
Chicago, IL 60612-3832
Tel: (312)942-5000
Admissions: (312)942-7100
Fax: (312)942-2100
Web Site: http://www.rushu.rush.edu/
President/CEO: Dr. Larry J. Goodman
Registrar: William F. Karnoscak
Admissions: Hicela Castruita Woods
Financial Aid: Robert Dame
Type: Two-Year Upper Division **Sex:** Coed **Admission Plans:** Preferred Admission **Application Fee:** $40.00 **Costs Per Year:** Application fee: $40. Tuition: $18,195 full-time, $475 per quarter hour part-time. Full-time tuition varies according to course load, degree level, and program. Part-time tuition varies according to course load, degree level, and program. College room only: $5715. Room charges vary according to housing facility. **Scholarships:** Available **Calendar System:** Quarter, Summer Session Not available **Enrollment:** FT 195, PT 17, Grad 641 **Faculty:** FT 796, PT 0 **Student-Faculty Ratio:** 8:1 **% Receiving Financial Aid:** 76 **% Residing in College-Owned, -Operated, or -Affiliated Housing:** 27 **Library Holdings:** 120,042 **Regional Accreditation:** North Central Association of Colleges and Schools **Credit Hours For Degree:** 180 quarter hours, Bachelors **Professional Accreditation:** ACPE, ACEHSA, AACN, AANA, ADtA, AOTA, ASLHA, ACIPE, LCMEAMA, NAACLS, NLN

SAINT ANTHONY COLLEGE OF NURSING
5658 East State St.
Rockford, IL 61108-2468
Tel: (815)395-5091
Admissions: (815)395-5100
Web Site: http://www.sacn.edu/
President/CEO: Dr. Terese Burch
Registrar: Nancy Sanders
Admissions: Nancy Sanders
Financial Aid: Lisa Ruch
Type: Two-Year Upper Division **Sex:** Coed **Affiliation:** Roman Catholic **Admission Plans:** Deferred Admission **Application Fee:** $50.00 **H.S. Requirements:** High school diploma or equivalent not required **Costs Per Year:** Application fee: $50. Tuition: $16,192 full-time, $506 per credit part-time. Mandatory fees: $116 full-time. **Scholarships:** Available **Calendar System:** Semester, Summer Session Available **Enrollment:** FT 108, PT 17 **Faculty:** FT 12, PT 3 **Student-Faculty Ratio:** 9:1 **% Receiving Financial Aid:** 95 **Library Holdings:** 1,394 **Regional Accreditation:** North Central Association of Colleges and Schools **Credit Hours For Degree:** 128 credits, Bachelors **Professional Accreditation:** AACN, NLN

ST. AUGUSTINE COLLEGE
1333-1345 West Argyle
Chicago, IL 60640-3501
Tel: (773)878-8756
Admissions: (773)878-3256
Web Site: http://www.staugustinecollege.edu/
President/CEO: Dr. Z. Clara Brennan
Admissions: Gloria Quiroz
Financial Aid: Maria Zambonino
Type: Four-Year College **Sex:** Coed **Admission Plans:** Open Admission; Deferred Admission **Application Fee:** $0.00 **H.S. Requirements:** High school diploma or equivalent not required. For international students: High school diploma required; GED not accepted **Costs Per Year:** Application fee: $0. Tuition: $7128 full-time, $297 per credit part-time. **Scholarships:** Available **Calendar System:** Semester, Summer Session Available **Enrollment:** FT 1,279, PT 303 **Faculty:** FT 27, PT 108 **Student-Faculty Ratio:** 13:1 **Exams:** Other **% Receiving Financial Aid:** 83 **Library Holdings:** 21,000 **Regional Accreditation:** North Central Association of Colleges and Schools **Credit Hours For Degree:** 60 semester hours, Associates; 128 semester hours, Bachelors **Professional Accreditation:** CARC

SAINT FRANCIS MEDICAL CENTER COLLEGE OF NURSING
511 NE Greenleaf St.
Peoria, IL 61603-3783
Tel: (309)655-2201
Admissions: (309)624-8980
Web Site: http://www.sfmccon.edu/
President/CEO: Sr. Mary Ludgera, OSF,RN
Registrar: Janice Farquharson
Admissions: Janice Farquharson
Financial Aid: Kathy Casey
Type: Two-Year Upper Division **Sex:** Coed **Affiliation:** Roman Catholic **Admission Plans:** Deferred Admission **Application Fee:** $50.00 **H.S. Requirements:** High school diploma required; GED accepted **Costs Per Year:** Application fee: $50. Tuition: $10,200 full-time, $425 per semester hour part-time. Mandatory fees: $450 full-time, $225 per term part-time. Full-time tuition and fees vary according to course load. Part-time tuition and fees vary according to course load. College room only: $1880. **Scholarships:** Available **Calendar System:** Semester, Summer Session Available **Enroll-**

ment: FT 182, PT 38, Grad 52 **Faculty:** FT 19 **Student-Faculty Ratio:** 8:1 **% Receiving Financial Aid:** 73 **% Residing in College-Owned, -Operated, or -Affiliated Housing:** 28 **Library Holdings:** 6,215 **Regional Accreditation:** North Central Association of Colleges and Schools **Credit Hours For Degree:** 124 semester hours, Bachelors **Professional Accreditation:** NLN

ST. JOHN'S COLLEGE
421 North Ninth St.
Springfield, IL 62702-5317
Tel: (217)525-5628
Web Site: http://www.st-johns.org/education/schools/nursing/
President/CEO: Dr. Jane Schachtsiek
Registrar: Linda Quigley
Admissions: Beth Beasley
Type: Two-Year Upper Division **Sex:** Coed **Affiliation:** Roman Catholic **Admission Plans:** Early Action **Application Fee:** $35.00 **H.S. Requirements:** High school diploma required; GED accepted **Costs Per Year:** Application fee: $35. Tuition: $9980 full-time, $416 per credit hour part-time. Mandatory fees: $380 full-time. Full-time tuition and fees vary according to course load. Part-time tuition varies according to course load. **Scholarships:** Available **Calendar System:** Semester, Summer Session Not available **Enrollment:** FT 79, PT 3 **Faculty:** FT 14, PT 1 **Student-Faculty Ratio:** 4:1 **% Receiving Financial Aid:** 72 **Library Holdings:** 7,715 **Regional Accreditation:** North Central Association of Colleges and Schools **Credit Hours For Degree:** 125 semester hours, Bachelors **Professional Accreditation:** NLN

SAINT XAVIER UNIVERSITY
3700 West 103rd St.
Chicago, IL 60655-3105
Tel: (773)298-3000
Free: 800-462-9288
Admissions: (773)298-3063
Fax: (773)298-3076
E-mail: admissions@sxu.edu
Web Site: http://www.sxu.edu/
President/CEO: Dr. Judith Dwyer
Registrar: Mary Lou Griffin
Admissions: Elizabeth A. Gierach
Financial Aid: Susan Swisher
Type: Comprehensive **Sex:** Coed **Affiliation:** Roman Catholic **Scores:** 96% SAT V 400+; 96% SAT M 400+; 69% ACT 18-23; 27% ACT 24-29 **% Accepted:** 69 **Admission Plans:** Deferred Admission **Application Deadline:** Rolling **Application Fee:** $25.00 **H.S. Requirements:** High school diploma required; GED accepted **Costs Per Year:** Application fee: $25. Comprehensive fee: $25,598 includes full-time tuition ($18,350), mandatory fees ($170), and college room and board ($7078). College room only: $4428. Full-time tuition and fees vary according to course load. Room and board charges vary according to board plan and housing facility. Part-time tuition: $611 per credit hour. Part-time mandatory fees: $110 per year. Part-time tuition and fees vary according to course load. **Scholarships:** Available **Calendar System:** Semester, Summer Session Available **Enrollment:** FT 2,391, PT 791, Grad 2,523 **Faculty:** FT 168, PT 258 **Student-Faculty Ratio:** 15:1 **Exams:** SAT I or ACT **% Receiving Financial Aid:** 80 **% Residing in College-Owned, -Operated, or -Affiliated Housing:** 20 **Library Holdings:** 170,753 **Regional Accreditation:** North Central Association of Colleges and Schools **Credit Hours For Degree:** 120 semester hours, Bachelors **ROTC:** Air Force **Professional Accreditation:** AACN, ASLHA, ACBSP, NASM, NCATE, NLN **Intercollegiate Athletics:** Baseball M; Basketball M; Cross-Country Running W; Football M; Golf M; Soccer M & W; Softball W; Volleyball W

SAUK VALLEY COMMUNITY COLLEGE
173 Illinois Route 2
Dixon, IL 61021
Tel: (815)288-5511
E-mail: clodfep@svcc.edu
Web Site: http://www.svcc.edu/
President/CEO: Dr. Richard L. Behrendt
Admissions: Pamela Clodfelter
Financial Aid: Marcia Wells
Type: Two-Year College **Sex:** Coed **Affiliation:** Illinois Community College Board **Scores:** 57% ACT 18-23; 18% ACT 24-29 **% Accepted:** 100 **Admission Plans:** Open Admission; Early Admission; Deferred Admission **Application Deadline:** Rolling **Application Fee:** $0.00 **H.S. Requirements:** High school diploma or equivalent not required **Costs Per Year:** Application fee: $0. Area resident tuition: $2418 full-time, $74 per credit hour part-time. State resident tuition: $9065 full-time, $259 per credit hour part-time. Nonresident tuition: $9375 full-time, $293 per credit hour part-time. **Scholarships:** Available **Calendar System:** Semester **Enrollment:** FT 1,154, PT 1,591 **Faculty:** FT 52, PT 105 **Student-Faculty Ratio:** 19:1 **Exams:** ACT **Library Holdings:** 55,000 **Regional Accreditation:** North Central Association of Colleges and Schools **Credit Hours For Degree:** 64 semester hours, Associates **Professional Accreditation:** JRCERT **Intercollegiate Athletics:** Baseball M; Basketball M & W; Cross-Country Running M & W; Softball W; Tennis M & W

SCHOOL OF THE ART INSTITUTE OF CHICAGO
37 South Wabash
Chicago, IL 60603-3103
Tel: (312)899-5100
Free: 800-232-SAIC
Admissions: (312)899-5219
Fax: (312)263-0141
E-mail: admiss@artic.edu
Web Site: http://www.artic.edu/saic/
President/CEO: Anthony Jones
Registrar: Brad Erz
Admissions: Scott Ramon
Financial Aid: Patrick James
Type: Comprehensive **Sex:** Coed **% Accepted:** 84 **Admission Plans:** Deferred Admission **Application Deadline:** Rolling **Application Fee:** $65.00 **H.S. Requirements:** High school diploma required; GED accepted **Costs Per Year:** Application fee: $65. Tuition: $28,950 full-time, $965 per credit hour part-time. Mandatory fees: $250 full-time. College room only: $8600. **Scholarships:** Available **Calendar System:** Semester, Summer Session Available **Enrollment:** FT 1,889, PT 210, Grad 580 **Faculty:** FT 124, PT 344 **Student-Faculty Ratio:** 11:1 **Exams:** SAT I or ACT **% Receiving Financial Aid:** 59 **% Residing in College-Owned, -Operated, or -Affiliated Housing:** 35 **Library Holdings:** 72,490 **Regional Accreditation:** North Central Association of Colleges and Schools **Credit Hours For Degree:** 132 semester hours, Bachelors **Professional Accreditation:** NASAD

SHAWNEE COMMUNITY COLLEGE
8364 Shawnee College Rd.
Ullin, IL 62992-2206
Tel: (618)634-3200
Fax: (618)634-3300
Web Site: http://www.shawneecc.edu/
President/CEO: Dr. Larry D. Choate
Registrar: Mindy Gordon
Admissions: Dee Blakely
Financial Aid: Tammy Capps
Type: Two-Year College **Sex:** Coed **Affiliation:** Illinois Community College Board **Admission Plans:** Open Admission; Preferred Admission; Early Admission; Deferred Admission **Application Fee:** $0.00 **H.S. Requirements:** High school diploma required; GED accepted **Scholarships:** Available **Calendar System:** Semester, Summer Session Available **Enrollment:** FT 943, PT 2,248 **Faculty:** FT 40, PT 140 **Exams:** ACT, Other **Library Holdings:** 38,000 **Regional Accreditation:** North Central Association of Colleges and Schools **Credit Hours For Degree:** 64 semester hours, Associates **Professional Accreditation:** AHIMA, AOTA, NAACLS **Intercollegiate Athletics:** Baseball M; Basketball M & W; Softball W; Tennis M; Volleyball W

SHIMER COLLEGE
PO Box 500
Waukegan, IL 60079-0500
Tel: (847)623-8400
Free: 800-215-7173
Admissions: (847)249-7174
Fax: (847)249-7171
Web Site: http://www.shimer.edu/
President/CEO: Dr. William C. Rice
Registrar: Barbara Bogart
Admissions: Bill Paterson
Financial Aid: Chris Miller
Type: Four-Year College **Sex:** Coed **Scores:** 100% SAT V 400+; 100% SAT M 400+; 23% ACT 18-23; 47% ACT 24-29 **Admission Plans:** Open Admission; Early Admission; Deferred Admission **Application Fee:** $25.00 **H.S.**

Requirements: High school diploma required; GED accepted **Scholarships:** Available **Calendar System:** Semester, Summer Session Available **Enrollment:** FT 114, PT 12, Grad 12 **Faculty:** FT 13, PT 2 **Student-Faculty Ratio:** 8:1 **Exams:** SAT I or ACT **% Receiving Financial Aid:** 85 **% Residing in College-Owned, -Operated, or -Affiliated Housing:** 50 **Library Holdings:** 200,000 **Regional Accreditation:** North Central Association of Colleges and Schools **Credit Hours For Degree:** 125 credit hours, Bachelors

SOUTH SUBURBAN COLLEGE
15800 South State St.
South Holland, IL 60473-1270
Tel: (708)596-2000
Web Site: http://www.southsuburbancollege.edu/
President/CEO: George Dammer
Registrar: Jane Stocker
Admissions: Jazaer Farrar
Financial Aid: John Semple
Type: Two-Year College **Sex:** Coed **Affiliation:** Illinois Community College Board **Admission Plans:** Open Admission; Preferred Admission; Early Admission; Deferred Admission **Application Fee:** $20.00 **H.S. Requirements:** High school diploma required; GED accepted **Scholarships:** Available **Calendar System:** Semester, Summer Session Available **Faculty:** FT 126, PT 228 **Student-Faculty Ratio:** 18:1 **Exams:** Other **Library Holdings:** 38,845 **Regional Accreditation:** North Central Association of Colleges and Schools **Credit Hours For Degree:** 60 semester hours, Associates **Professional Accreditation:** AOTA, ACBSP, JRCERT, NASM, NLN **Intercollegiate Athletics:** Baseball M; Basketball M & W; Cross-Country Running M & W; Softball W; Volleyball W

SOUTHEASTERN ILLINOIS COLLEGE
3575 College Rd.
Harrisburg, IL 62946-4925
Tel: (618)252-5400; (866)338-2742
Web Site: http://www.sic.edu/
President/CEO: Dr. Mary Jo Oldham
Financial Aid: Brad McCormick
Type: Two-Year College **Sex:** Coed **Affiliation:** Illinois Community College Board **Scores:** 39% ACT 18-23; 22% ACT 24-29 **% Accepted:** 100 **Admission Plans:** Open Admission; Preferred Admission; Early Admission; Deferred Admission **Application Deadline:** September 01 **Application Fee:** $0.00 **H.S. Requirements:** High school diploma required; GED accepted **Costs Per Year:** Application fee: $0. Area resident tuition: $1920 full-time, $64 per hour part-time. State resident tuition: $2790 full-time, $93 per hour part-time. Nonresident tuition: $3210 full-time, $107 per hour part-time. Mandatory fees: $60 full-time, $2 per hour part-time, $2. College room and board: $3655. **Scholarships:** Available **Calendar System:** Semester, Summer Session Available **Enrollment:** FT 795, PT 1,764 **Faculty:** FT 53, PT 200 **Student-Faculty Ratio:** 12:1 **Library Holdings:** 58,030 **Regional Accreditation:** North Central Association of Colleges and Schools **Credit Hours For Degree:** 62 semester hours, Associates **Professional Accreditation:** AHIMA, AOTA, NAACLS **Intercollegiate Athletics:** Baseball M; Basketball M & W; Softball W

SOUTHERN ILLINOIS UNIVERSITY CARBONDALE
Carbondale, IL 62901-4701
Tel: (618)453-2121
Admissions: (618)453-2908
Fax: (618)453-3250
E-mail: admrec@siu.edu
Web Site: http://www.siu.edu/siuc/
President/CEO: Dr. Walter V. Wendler
Admissions: Dr. Anne DeLuca
Financial Aid: Dan Mann
Type: University **Sex:** Coed **Affiliation:** Southern Illinois University **Scores:** 93% SAT V 400+; 98% SAT M 400+; 58% ACT 18-23; 28% ACT 24-29 **% Accepted:** 77 **Admission Plans:** Deferred Admission **Application Deadline:** August 22 **Application Fee:** $30.00 **H.S. Requirements:** High school diploma required; GED accepted **Costs Per Year:** Application fee: $30. State resident tuition: $5310 full-time, $177 per semester hour part-time. Nonresident tuition: $13,275 full-time, $442.50 per semester hour part-time. Mandatory fees: $1521 full-time, $654 per term part-time. Full-time tuition and fees vary according to course load and student level. Part-time tuition and fees vary according to course load and student level. College room and board: $5560. College room only: $3058. Room and board charges vary according to board plan and housing facility. Tuition guaranteed not to increase for student's term of enrollment. **Scholarships:** Available **Calendar System:** Semester, Summer Session Available **Enrollment:** FT 14,962, PT 1,735, Grad 4,071 **Faculty:** FT 901, PT 180 **Student-Faculty Ratio:** 17:1 **Exams:** SAT I or ACT **% Receiving Financial Aid:** 56 **% Residing in College-Owned, -Operated, or -Affiliated Housing:** 27 **Library Holdings:** 4,165,239 **Regional Accreditation:** North Central Association of Colleges and Schools **Credit Hours For Degree:** 60 semester hours, Associates; 120 semester hours, Bachelors **ROTC:** Army, Air Force **Professional Accreditation:** AACSB, ABET, ACEJMC, ABA, ABFSE, ACA, ADA, ADtA, APTA, APA, ASLHA, AALS, CARC, CORE, CSWE, FIDER, JRCEPAT, LCMEAMA, NAACLS, NAIT NASAD, NASM, NASPAA, NAST, NCATE, NRPA, SAF **Intercollegiate Athletics:** Baseball M; Basketball M & W; Cheerleading M & W; Cross-Country Running M & W; Football M; Golf M & W; Softball W; Swimming and Diving M & W; Tennis M & W; Track and Field M & W; Volleyball W

SOUTHERN ILLINOIS UNIVERSITY EDWARDSVILLE
Edwardsville, IL 62026-0001
Tel: (618)650-2000
Free: 800-447-SIUE
Admissions: (618)650-2298
Fax: (618)692-2081
E-mail: admissions@siue.edu
Web Site: http://www.siue.edu/
President/CEO: Dr. Vaughn Vandegrift
Registrar: Laura Strom
Admissions: Boyd Bradshaw
Financial Aid: Sharon Berry
Type: Comprehensive **Sex:** Coed **Affiliation:** Southern Illinois University **Scores:** 57.5% ACT 18-23; 33% ACT 24-29 **% Accepted:** 71 **Admission Plans:** Early Admission; Deferred Admission **Application Deadline:** May 01 **Application Fee:** $50.00 **H.S. Requirements:** High school diploma required; GED accepted **Costs Per Year:** Application fee: $50. State resident tuition: $4320 full-time, $144 per semester hour part-time. Nonresident tuition: $10,800 full-time, $360 per semester hour part-time. Mandatory fees: $859 full-time, $366.50 per term part-time. Full-time tuition and fees vary according to course load. Part-time tuition and fees vary according to course load. College room and board: $5819. College room only: $3389. Room and board charges vary according to board plan and housing facility. **Scholarships:** Available **Calendar System:** Semester, Summer Session Available **Enrollment:** FT 9,232, PT 1,713, Grad 2,232 **Faculty:** FT 556, PT 263 **Student-Faculty Ratio:** 17:1 **Exams:** SAT I or ACT **% Receiving Financial Aid:** 50 **% Residing in College-Owned, -Operated, or -Affiliated Housing:** 28 **Library Holdings:** 788,003 **Regional Accreditation:** North Central Association of Colleges and Schools **Credit Hours For Degree:** 124 semester hours, Bachelors **ROTC:** Army, Air Force **Professional Accreditation:** AACSB, ABET, AACN, AANA, ACCE, ACPhE, ADA, ASLHA, CSWE, NAACLS, NASM, NASPAA, NCATE, NLN **Intercollegiate Athletics:** Baseball M; Basketball M & W; Cross-Country Running M & W; Golf M & W; Soccer M & W; Softball W; Tennis M & W; Track and Field M & W; Volleyball W; Wrestling M

SOUTHWESTERN ILLINOIS COLLEGE
2500 Carlyle Rd.
Belleville, IL 62221-5899
Tel: (618)235-2700
Fax: (618)235-1578
E-mail: michelle.birk@swic.edu
Web Site: http://www.southwestern.cc.il.us/
President/CEO: Dr. Elmer Kirchoff
Registrar: Sherri Patterson
Admissions: Mike Leiker
Financial Aid: Bob Clement
Type: Two-Year College **Sex:** Coed **Affiliation:** Illinois Community College Board **Admission Plans:** Open Admission; Early Admission; Deferred Admission **Application Deadline:** Rolling **Application Fee:** $10.00 **H.S. Requirements:** High school diploma required; GED accepted **Costs Per Year:** Application fee: $10. Area resident tuition: $1890 full-time, $63 per credit hour part-time. State resident tuition: $5220 full-time, $174 per credit hour part-time. Nonresident tuition: $8070 full-time, $269 per credit hour part-time. **Scholarships:** Available **Calendar System:** Semester, Summer Session Available **Enrollment:** FT 5,296, PT 9,183 **Faculty:** FT 125, PT 704 **Student-Faculty Ratio:** 17:1 **Exams:** Other **Library Holdings:** 82,537 **Regional Accreditation:** North Central Association of Colleges and Schools

Credit Hours For Degree: 64 credit hours, Associates **ROTC:** Army, Air Force **Professional Accreditation:** AAMAE, ACF, AHIMA, APTA, ACBSP, CARC, JRCERT, NAACLS, NLN **Intercollegiate Athletics:** Baseball M; Basketball M & W; Soccer M; Softball W; Tennis M & W; Volleyball W

SPOON RIVER COLLEGE
23235 North County 22
Canton, IL 61520-9801
Tel: (309)647-4645
Admissions: (309)649-6305
Fax: (309)649-6235
Web Site: http://www.spoonrivercollege.net/
President/CEO: Tom Hines
Registrar: Sue Freeman
Admissions: Dr. Sharon Wrenn
Financial Aid: Louise White
Type: Two-Year College **Sex:** Coed **Affiliation:** Illinois Community College Board **Scores:** 52% ACT 18-23; 12% ACT 24-29 **Admission Plans:** Open Admission; Early Admission **Application Deadline:** Rolling **Application Fee:** $0.00 **H.S. Requirements:** High school diploma required; GED accepted **Costs Per Year:** Application fee: $0. Area resident tuition: $1845 full-time, $61.50 per credit hour part-time. State resident tuition: $3465 full-time, $115.50 per credit hour part-time. Nonresident tuition: $4545 full-time, $151.50 per credit hour part-time. Mandatory fees: $255 full-time, $8.50 per credit hour part-time. Full-time tuition and fees vary according to course load. Part-time tuition and fees vary according to course load. **Scholarships:** Available **Calendar System:** Semester, Summer Session Available **Enrollment:** FT 1,053, PT 1,280 **Faculty:** FT 41, PT 101 **Student-Faculty Ratio:** 20:1 **Library Holdings:** 34,799 **Regional Accreditation:** North Central Association of Colleges and Schools **Credit Hours For Degree:** 64 semester hours, Associates **ROTC:** Army **Intercollegiate Athletics:** Baseball M; Basketball M & W; Softball W; Track and Field M & W; Volleyball W

SPRINGFIELD COLLEGE IN ILLINOIS
1500 North Fifth St.
Springfield, IL 62702-2694
Tel: (217)525-1420
Free: 800-635-7289
Fax: (217)789-1698
Web Site: http://www.sci.edu/
President/CEO: Dr. William J. Carroll
Admissions: Kim Fontana
Financial Aid: Josie Negro
Type: Two-Year College **Sex:** Coed **Affiliation:** Roman Catholic Church **Scores:** 47.7% ACT 18-23; 18% ACT 24-29 **% Accepted:** 86 **Application Deadline:** Rolling **Application Fee:** $20.00 **H.S. Requirements:** High school diploma required; GED accepted **Costs Per Year:** Application fee: $20. Comprehensive fee: $15,400 includes full-time tuition ($7490), mandatory fees ($1990), and college room and board ($5920). Part-time tuition: $312 per hour. **Scholarships:** Available **Calendar System:** Semester, Summer Session Available **Enrollment:** FT 271, PT 281 **Faculty:** FT 21, PT 50 **Student-Faculty Ratio:** 12:1 **Exams:** SAT I and SAT II or ACT **Library Holdings:** 19,951 **Regional Accreditation:** North Central Association of Colleges and Schools **Credit Hours For Degree:** 60 semester hours, Associates **Intercollegiate Athletics:** Baseball M; Golf M; Soccer M & W; Softball W; Volleyball W

TAYLOR BUSINESS INSTITUTE
200 North Michigan Ave., Ste. 301
Chicago, IL 60601
Tel: (312)236-6400
Fax: (312)658-0867
President/CEO: Janice C. Parker
Admissions: Rashed Jahangir
Type: Two-Year College **Sex:** Coed **Professional Accreditation:** ACICS

TELSHE YESHIVA-CHICAGO
3535 West Foster Ave.
Chicago, IL 60625-5598
Tel: (773)463-7738
Registrar: Rabbi Samuel Adler
Financial Aid: Rabbi Samuel Adler
Type: Comprehensive **Sex:** Men **Affiliation:** Jewish **H.S. Requirements:** High school diploma required; GED not accepted **Calendar System:** Semester, Summer Session Available **Credit Hours For Degree:** 150 credits, Bachelors **Professional Accreditation:** AARTS

TRINITY CHRISTIAN COLLEGE
6601 West College Dr.
Palos Heights, IL 60463-0929
Tel: (708)597-3000
Free: 800-748-0085
Admissions: (708)239-4708
Fax: (708)239-3995
E-mail: admissions@trnty.edu
Web Site: http://www.trnty.edu/
President/CEO: Dr. Steven Timmermans
Registrar: Dean Ellens
Admissions: Josh Lenarz
Financial Aid: Denise Coleman
Type: Four-Year College **Sex:** Coed **Affiliation:** Christian Reformed **Scores:** 92% SAT V 400+; 87% SAT M 400+; 49.5% ACT 18-23; 30% ACT 24-29 **% Accepted:** 89 **Admission Plans:** Deferred Admission **Application Deadline:** Rolling **Application Fee:** $20.00 **H.S. Requirements:** High school diploma required; GED accepted **Costs Per Year:** Application fee: $20. Comprehensive fee: $23,735 includes full-time tuition ($16,985), mandatory fees ($150), and college room and board ($6600). College room only: $3400. Room and board charges vary according to board plan. Part-time tuition: $570 per semester hour. Part-time tuition varies according to course load. **Scholarships:** Available **Calendar System:** Semester, Summer Session Not available **Enrollment:** FT 1,049, PT 231 **Faculty:** FT 76, PT 51 **Student-Faculty Ratio:** 12:1 **Exams:** ACT, SAT I or ACT **% Receiving Financial Aid:** 75 **% Residing in College-Owned, -Operated, or -Affiliated Housing:** 67 **Library Holdings:** 77,833 **Regional Accreditation:** North Central Association of Colleges and Schools **Credit Hours For Degree:** 125 credit hours, Bachelors **Professional Accreditation:** AACN, ACBSP, NLN **Intercollegiate Athletics:** Baseball M; Basketball M & W; Cross-Country Running M & W; Soccer M & W; Softball W; Track and Field M & W; Volleyball W

TRINITY COLLEGE OF NURSING AND HEALTH SCIENCES
2122-25th Ave.
Rock Island, IL 91201
Tel: (309)779-7700
Admissions: (309)779-7812
Fax: (309)779-7796
Web Site: http://www.trinitycollegeqc.edu/
President/CEO: Carol Dwyer
Admissions: Barbara Kimpe
Financial Aid: Joanne Cunningham
Type: Four-Year College **Sex:** Coed **Affiliation:** Trinity Medical Center **Scores:** 90% ACT 18-23 **Admission Plans:** Preferred Admission **Application Fee:** $50.00 **H.S. Requirements:** High school diploma required; GED accepted **Scholarships:** Available **Calendar System:** Semester, Summer Session Available **Enrollment:** FT 109, PT 56 **Faculty:** FT 12, PT 2 **Student-Faculty Ratio:** 10:1 **Exams:** SAT I or ACT **% Receiving Financial Aid:** 40 **Regional Accreditation:** North Central Association of Colleges and Schools **Credit Hours For Degree:** 70 credits, Associates; 122 credits, Bachelors

TRINITY INTERNATIONAL UNIVERSITY
2065 Half Day Rd.
Deerfield, IL 60015-1284
Tel: (847)945-8800
Free: 800-822-3225
Admissions: (847)317-7000
Fax: (847)317-7081
E-mail: tcadmissions@tiu.edu
Web Site: http://www.tiu.edu/
President/CEO: Dr. Gregory Waybright
Registrar: Robert Bosanac
Admissions: Matt Yoder
Financial Aid: Ron Anderson
Type: University **Sex:** Coed **Affiliation:** Evangelical Free Church of America; Evangelical Free Church of America **Scores:** 92% SAT V 400+; 100% SAT M 400+; 56.62% ACT 18-23; 29.41% ACT 24-29 **% Accepted:** 82 **Admission Plans:** Early Admission; Deferred Admission **Application Deadline:** Rolling **Application Fee:** $25.00 **H.S. Requirements:** High school diploma required; GED accepted **Costs Per Year:** Application fee:

$25. Comprehensive fee: $25,686 includes full-time tuition ($19,080), mandatory fees ($286), and college room and board ($6320). College room only: $3430. Full-time tuition and fees vary according to location. Room and board charges vary according to board plan. Part-time tuition: $796 per hour. Part-time mandatory fees: $143 per term. Part-time tuition and fees vary according to location. **Scholarships:** Available **Calendar System:** Semester, Summer Session Not available **Enrollment:** FT 1,090, PT 173, Grad 1,061 **Faculty:** FT 86, PT 274 **Student-Faculty Ratio:** 13:1 **Exams:** SAT I or ACT **% Receiving Financial Aid:** 68 **% Residing in College-Owned, -Operated, or -Affiliated Housing:** 80 **Library Holdings:** 206,404 **Regional Accreditation:** North Central Association of Colleges and Schools **Credit Hours For Degree:** 126 hours, Bachelors **Professional Accreditation:** ATS **Intercollegiate Athletics:** Baseball M; Basketball M & W; Football M; Soccer M & W; Softball W; Track and Field M & W; Volleyball W

TRITON COLLEGE
2000 5th Ave.
River Grove, IL 60171-1995
Tel: (708)456-0300
Free: 800-942-7404
Fax: (708)583-3121
E-mail: dolson@triton.edu
Web Site: http://www.triton.cc.il.us/
President/CEO: Patricia Granados
Admissions: Doug Olson
Financial Aid: Patricia Williamson
Type: Two-Year College **Sex:** Coed **Affiliation:** Illinois Community College Board **% Accepted:** 100 **Admission Plans:** Open Admission; Preferred Admission; Deferred Admission **Application Deadline:** Rolling **Application Fee:** $0.00 **H.S. Requirements:** High school diploma required; GED accepted **Costs Per Year:** Application fee: $0. Area resident tuition: $1680 full-time, $56 per semester hour part-time. State resident tuition: $5244 full-time, $174.80 per semester hour part-time. Nonresident tuition: $6670 full-time, $222.32 per semester hour part-time. Mandatory fees: $250 full-time, $5 per credit hour part-time, $30 per term part-time. **Scholarships:** Available **Calendar System:** Semester, Summer Session Available **Enrollment:** FT 3,831, PT 7,190 **Faculty:** FT 126, PT 471 **Student-Faculty Ratio:** 22:1 **Library Holdings:** 70,859 **Regional Accreditation:** North Central Association of Colleges and Schools **Credit Hours For Degree:** 64 credit hours, Associates **Professional Accreditation:** CARC, JCAHPO, JRCEDMS, JRCERT, JRCNMT, NLN **Intercollegiate Athletics:** Baseball M; Basketball M & W; Soccer M; Softball W; Swimming and Diving W; Volleyball W; Wrestling M

UNIVERSITY OF CHICAGO
5801 Ellis Ave.
Chicago, IL 60637-1513
Tel: (773)702-1234
Admissions: (773)702-8650
Fax: (773)702-4199
E-mail: toneill@uchicago.edu
Web Site: http://www.uchicago.edu/
President/CEO: Don M. Randel
Registrar: Thomas Black
Admissions: Theodore O'Neill
Financial Aid: Alicia Reyes
Type: University **Sex:** Coed **Scores:** 100% SAT V 400+; 100% SAT M 400+; 26% ACT 24-29 **% Accepted:** 40 **Admission Plans:** Early Admission; Early Action; Deferred Admission **Application Deadline:** January 01 **Application Fee:** $60.00 **H.S. Requirements:** High school diploma or equivalent not required **Costs Per Year:** Application fee: $60. Comprehensive fee: $42,369 includes full-time tuition ($31,629), mandatory fees ($636), and college room and board ($10,104). Room and board charges vary according to board plan and housing facility. **Scholarships:** Available **Calendar System:** Quarter, Summer Session Available **Enrollment:** FT 4,614, PT 57, Grad 8,407 **Faculty:** FT 1,057, PT 530 **Student-Faculty Ratio:** 4:1 **Exams:** SAT I or ACT **% Residing in College-Owned, -Operated, or -Affiliated Housing:** 67 **Library Holdings:** 7,000,000 **Regional Accreditation:** North Central Association of Colleges and Schools **Credit Hours For Degree:** 42 courses, Bachelors **ROTC:** Army, Air Force **Professional Accreditation:** AACSB, ABA, APA, ACIPE, AALS, ATS, CSWE, LCMEAMA **Intercollegiate Athletics:** Baseball M; Basketball M & W; Cross-Country Running M & W; Football M; Soccer M & W; Softball W; Swimming and Diving M & W; Tennis M & W; Track and Field M & W; Volleyball W; Wrestling M

UNIVERSITY OF ILLINOIS AT CHICAGO
601 South Morgan St.
Chicago, IL 60607-7128
Tel: (312)996-7000
Admissions: (312)996-4350
E-mail: uic.admit@uic.edu
Web Site: http://www.uic.edu/
President/CEO: Dr. Sylvia Manning
Registrar: Robert Dixon
Admissions: Thomas E. Glenn
Financial Aid: Marsha S. Weiss
Type: University **Sex:** Coed **Affiliation:** University of Illinois System **Scores:** 52.7% ACT 18-23; 36.8% ACT 24-29 **% Accepted:** 58 **Application Deadline:** January 15 **Application Fee:** $40.00 **H.S. Requirements:** High school diploma required; GED accepted **Costs Per Year:** Application fee: $40. State resident tuition: $6194 full-time. Nonresident tuition: $18,584 full-time. Mandatory fees: $2108 full-time. College room and board: $7954. **Scholarships:** Available **Calendar System:** Semester, Summer Session Available **Enrollment:** FT 13,733, PT 1,417, Grad 7,404 **Faculty:** FT 1,193, PT 263 **Student-Faculty Ratio:** 16:1 **Exams:** SAT I or ACT **% Receiving Financial Aid:** 53 **% Residing in College-Owned, -Operated, or -Affiliated Housing:** 11 **Library Holdings:** 2,998,147 **Regional Accreditation:** North Central Association of Colleges and Schools **Credit Hours For Degree:** 120 semester hours, Bachelors **ROTC:** Army, Navy, Air Force **Professional Accreditation:** AACSB, ABET, ARCMI, AABB, AACN, ACNM, ACPhE, ADA, ADtA, AHIMA, ACSP, AOTA, APTA, APA, CEPH, CSWE, LCMEAMA, NASAD, NASPAA **Intercollegiate Athletics:** Baseball M; Basketball M & W; Cross-Country Running M & W; Gymnastics M & W; Soccer M; Softball W; Swimming and Diving M & W; Tennis M & W; Track and Field M & W; Volleyball W

UNIVERSITY OF ILLINOIS AT SPRINGFIELD
One University Plaza
Springfield, IL 62703-5407
Tel: (217)206-6600; 888-977-4847
Fax: (217)206-7279
Web Site: http://www.uis.edu/
President/CEO: Dr. Richard D. Ringeisen
Registrar: Brian Clevenger
Financial Aid: Gerard Joseph
Type: Comprehensive **Sex:** Coed **Affiliation:** University of Illinois **Scores:** 39.9% ACT 18-23; 50.7% ACT 24-29 **% Accepted:** 63 **Application Deadline:** Rolling **Application Fee:** $40.00 **H.S. Requirements:** High school diploma required; GED accepted **Costs Per Year:** Application fee: $40. State resident tuition: $3953 full-time, $132 per credit hour part-time. Nonresident tuition: $11,858 full-time, $396 per credit hour part-time. Mandatory fees: $1382 full-time, $586 per term part-time. Full-time tuition and fees vary according to program. College room and board: $7110. College room only: $3270. Room and board charges vary according to housing facility. Tuition guaranteed not to increase for student's term of enrollment. **Scholarships:** Available **Calendar System:** Semester, Summer Session Available **Enrollment:** FT 1,558, PT 1,076, Grad 1,883 **Faculty:** FT 179, PT 152 **Student-Faculty Ratio:** 12:1 **Exams:** SAT I or ACT **% Receiving Financial Aid:** 59 **Regional Accreditation:** North Central Association of Colleges and Schools **Credit Hours For Degree:** 120 semester hours, Bachelors **Professional Accreditation:** ACA, CSWE, NAACLS, NASPAA **Intercollegiate Athletics:** Basketball M & W; Soccer M; Softball W; Tennis M & W; Volleyball W

UNIVERSITY OF ILLINOIS AT URBANA-CHAMPAIGN
601 East John St.
Champaign, IL 61820
Tel: (217)333-1000
Admissions: (217)333-0302
Fax: (217)244-7278
E-mail: admssion@uiuc.edu
Web Site: http://www.uiuc.edu/
President/CEO: Dr. Richard Herman
Registrar: Alice Poehls
Admissions: Dr. Keith Marshall
Financial Aid: Dr. Orlo B. Austin
Type: University **Sex:** Coed **Affiliation:** University of Illinois System **Scores:** 98.48% SAT V 400+; 99.56% SAT M 400+; 10.09% ACT 18-23; 55.89% ACT 24-29 **% Accepted:** 76 **Admission Plans:** Deferred Admission **Application Deadline:** December 15 **Application Fee:** $40.00 **H.S. Require-**

ments: High school diploma required; GED accepted **Costs Per Year:** Application fee: $40. State resident tuition: $7042 full-time. Nonresident tuition: $21,128 full-time. Mandatory fees: $1582 full-time. Full-time tuition and fees vary according to course load, program, and student level. College room and board: $7176. College room only: $2970. Room and board charges vary according to board plan and housing facility. Tuition guaranteed not to increase for student's term of enrollment. **Scholarships:** Available **Calendar System:** Semester, Summer Session Available **Enrollment:** FT 29,912, PT 997, Grad 10,000 **Faculty:** FT 2,271, PT 430 **Student-Faculty Ratio:** 14:1 **Exams:** SAT I or ACT **% Receiving Financial Aid:** 39 **% Residing in College-Owned, -Operated, or -Affiliated Housing:** 39 **Library Holdings:** 10,189,657 **Regional Accreditation:** North Central Association of Colleges and Schools **Credit Hours For Degree:** 120 semester hours, Bachelors **ROTC:** Army, Navy, Air Force **Professional Accreditation:** AACSB, ABET, ACEJMC, ABA, ADtA, ACSP, ALA, APA, ASLA, ASLHA, AVMA, AALS, CORE, CSWE, JRCEPAT, NASAD, NASD, NASM, NAST, NRPA SAF **Intercollegiate Athletics:** Baseball M; Basketball M & W; Cheerleading M & W; Cross-Country Running M & W; Football M; Golf M & W; Gymnastics M & W; Soccer W; Swimming and Diving W; Tennis M & W; Track and Field M & W; Volleyball W; Wrestling M

UNIVERSITY OF PHOENIX-CHICAGO CAMPUS
1500 McConner Parkway, Ste. 700
Schaumburg, IL 60173-4399
Tel: (847)413-1922
Free: 800-228-7240
Admissions: (480)557-1712
Fax: (847)413-8706
Web Site: http://www.phoenix.edu/
President/CEO: Mark Pyszkowski
Admissions: Nina Omelchanko
Type: Comprehensive **Sex:** Coed **Admission Plans:** Open Admission; Deferred Admission **Application Deadline:** Rolling **Application Fee:** $110.00 **H.S. Requirements:** High school diploma required; GED accepted **Costs Per Year:** Application fee: $110. Tuition: $11,145 full-time, $371.50 per credit part-time. Mandatory fees: $560 full-time, $70 per course part-time. **Scholarships:** Available **Calendar System:** Continuous, Summer Session Not available **Enrollment:** FT 1,279, Grad 323 **Faculty:** FT 12, PT 195 **Student-Faculty Ratio:** 8:1 **Library Holdings:** 444 **Regional Accreditation:** North Central Association of Colleges and Schools **Credit Hours For Degree:** 60 credits, Associates; 120 credits, Bachelors

UNIVERSITY OF ST. FRANCIS
500 Wilcox St.
Joliet, IL 60435-6169
Tel: (815)740-3400
Free: 800-735-3500
Admissions: 800-735-7500
Fax: (815)740-4285
E-mail: cbeutel@stfrancis.edu
Web Site: http://www.stfrancis.edu/
President/CEO: Dr. Michael J. Vinciguerra
Registrar: Chuck Beutel
Admissions: Chuck Beutel
Financial Aid: Mary Shaw
Type: Comprehensive **Sex:** Coed **Affiliation:** Roman Catholic **Scores:** 63% ACT 18-23; 29% ACT 24-29 **% Accepted:** 57 **Admission Plans:** Deferred Admission **Application Deadline:** August 01 **Application Fee:** $30.00 **H.S. Requirements:** High school diploma required; GED accepted **Costs Per Year:** Application fee: $30. Comprehensive fee: $26,430 includes full-time tuition ($19,150) and college room and board ($7280). Part-time tuition: $625 per credit hour. **Scholarships:** Available **Calendar System:** Semester, Summer Session Available **Enrollment:** FT 1,138, PT 138, Grad 786 **Faculty:** FT 74, PT 145 **Student-Faculty Ratio:** 12:1 **Exams:** SAT I or ACT **% Receiving Financial Aid:** 71 **% Residing in College-Owned, -Operated, or -Affiliated Housing:** 22 **Library Holdings:** 106,346 **Regional Accreditation:** North Central Association of Colleges and Schools **Credit Hours For Degree:** 128 credits, Bachelors **Professional Accreditation:** CSWE, NLN, NRPA **Intercollegiate Athletics:** Baseball M; Basketball M & W; Cheerleading W; Cross-Country Running W; Football M; Golf M & W; Soccer M & W; Softball W; Tennis M & W; Track and Field W; Volleyball W

VANDERCOOK COLLEGE OF MUSIC
3140 South Federal St.
Chicago, IL 60616-3731
Tel: (312)225-6288
Free: 800-448-2655
Fax: (312)225-5211
E-mail: vcmusic@mcs.com
Web Site: http://www.vandercook.edu/
President/CEO: Dr. Roseanne Rosenthal
Registrar: Carolyn Berghoff
Admissions: Tamara V. Trutwin
Financial Aid: Susan Frost
Type: Comprehensive **Sex:** Coed **Scores:** 100% SAT V 400+; 100% SAT M 400+; 55% ACT 18-23; 35% ACT 24-29 **% Accepted:** 95 **Application Deadline:** Rolling **Application Fee:** $35.00 **H.S. Requirements:** High school diploma required; GED accepted **Costs Per Year:** Application fee: $35. Comprehensive fee: $25,940 includes full-time tuition ($17,120), mandatory fees ($770), and college room and board ($8050). Part-time tuition: $590 per credit hour. **Scholarships:** Available **Calendar System:** Semester, Summer Session Not available **Enrollment:** FT 105, PT 45, Grad 77 **Exams:** SAT I or ACT **Regional Accreditation:** North Central Association of Colleges and Schools **Credit Hours For Degree:** 140.5 semester hours, Bachelors **Professional Accreditation:** NASM

WAUBONSEE COMMUNITY COLLEGE
Route 47 at Waubonsee Dr.
Sugar Grove, IL 60554-9799
Tel: (630)466-7900
Fax: (630)466-4964
E-mail: recruitment@waubonsee.edu
Web Site: http://www.waubonsee.edu/
President/CEO: Dr. Christine J. Sobek
Registrar: Dr. Douglas McCoy
Admissions: Dr. Douglas R. McCoy
Financial Aid: Dr. Douglas McCoy
Type: Two-Year College **Sex:** Coed **Affiliation:** Illinois Community College Board **% Accepted:** 100 **Admission Plans:** Open Admission; Preferred Admission **Application Deadline:** Rolling **Application Fee:** $0.00 **H.S. Requirements:** High school diploma or equivalent not required. For financial aid recipients: High school diploma required; GED accepted **Costs Per Year:** Application fee: $0. Area resident tuition: $2010 full-time, $67 per semester hour part-time. State resident tuition: $6300 full-time, $210 per semester hour part-time. Nonresident tuition: $7110 full-time, $237 per semester hour part-time. Mandatory fees: $90 full-time, $3 per semester hour part-time. **Scholarships:** Available **Calendar System:** Semester, Summer Session Available **Enrollment:** FT 2,624, PT 6,210 **Faculty:** FT 92, PT 785 **Student-Faculty Ratio:** 17:1 **Library Holdings:** 53,679 **Regional Accreditation:** North Central Association of Colleges and Schools **Credit Hours For Degree:** 64 semester hours, Associates **ROTC:** Army **Intercollegiate Athletics:** Baseball M; Basketball M & W; Cross-Country Running M & W; Golf M; Soccer M; Softball W; Tennis M & W; Volleyball W; Wrestling M

WEST SUBURBAN COLLEGE OF NURSING
3 Erie Ct.
Oak Park, IL 60302
Tel: (708)763-6530
Fax: (708)763-1531
Web Site: http://www.wscn.edu/
President/CEO: Dr. Rebecca Jones
Registrar: Cynthia Valdez
Admissions: Cindy Valdez
Financial Aid: Thomas Lambert
Type: Two-Year Upper Division **Sex:** Coed **Scores:** 56% ACT 18-23; 33% ACT 24-29 **Admission Plans:** Deferred Admission **Application Fee:** $0.00 **H.S. Requirements:** High school diploma required; GED accepted **Calendar System:** Semester, Summer Session Available **Enrollment:** FT 90, PT 15 **Faculty:** FT 10, PT 4 **Student-Faculty Ratio:** 14:1 **% Residing in College-Owned, -Operated, or -Affiliated Housing:** 50 **Regional Accreditation:** North Central Association of Colleges and Schools **Credit Hours For Degree:** 124 semester hours, Bachelors **Professional Accreditation:** AACN, NLN

WESTERN ILLINOIS UNIVERSITY
1 University Circle
Macomb, IL 61455-1390
Tel: (309)298-1414; 877-742-5948
Admissions: (309)298-3157
Fax: (309)298-3111

E-mail: karen_helmers@uniu.edu
Web Site: http://www.wiu.edu/
President/CEO: Dr. Alvin Goldfarb
Registrar: Alan DeRoos
Admissions: Karen Helmers
Financial Aid: William Bushaw
Type: Comprehensive **Sex:** Coed **Scores:** 67% ACT 18-23; 21% ACT 24-29 **% Accepted:** 72 **Admission Plans:** Deferred Admission **Application Deadline:** May 15 **Application Fee:** $30.00 **H.S. Requirements:** High school diploma required; GED accepted **Costs Per Year:** Application fee: $30. State resident tuition: $4968 full-time, $213.69 per semester hour part-time. Nonresident tuition: $7452 full-time, $296.49 per semester hour part-time. Mandatory fees: $1931 full-time, $48.09 per semester hour part-time. Full-time tuition and fees vary according to location and student level. Part-time tuition and fees vary according to location and student level. College room and board: $6143. College room only: $3693. Room and board charges vary according to housing facility and student level. Tuition guaranteed not to increase for student's term of enrollment. **Scholarships:** Available **Calendar System:** Semester, Summer Session Available **Enrollment:** FT 10,317, PT 967, Grad 2,120 **Faculty:** FT 649, PT 82 **Student-Faculty Ratio:** 17:1 **Exams:** SAT I or ACT **% Receiving Financial Aid:** 54 **% Residing in College-Owned, -Operated, or -Affiliated Housing:** 51 **Library Holdings:** 998,041 **Regional Accreditation:** North Central Association of Colleges and Schools **Credit Hours For Degree:** 120 credit hours, Bachelors **ROTC:** Army **Professional Accreditation:** AACSB, AAFCS, ACA, ASLHA, CSWE, JRCEPAT, NASM, NCATE, NRPA **Intercollegiate Athletics:** Baseball M; Basketball M & W; Cross-Country Running M & W; Football M; Golf M & W; Soccer M & W; Softball W; Swimming and Diving M & W; Tennis M & W; Track and Field M & W; Volleyball W

WESTWOOD COLLEGE-CHICAGO DU PAGE
7155 Janes Ave.
Woodridge, IL 60517
Tel: (630)434-8244
Fax: (630)434-8255
Web Site: http://www.westwood.edu/
Admissions: Scott Kawall
Type: Two-Year College **Sex:** Coed **Scholarships:** Available **Calendar System:** Continuous **Enrollment:** FT 420, PT 50 **Professional Accreditation:** ACICS

WESTWOOD COLLEGE-CHICAGO LOOP CAMPUS
17 North State St., Ste. 1500
Chicago, IL 60602
Tel: (312)739-0850
Fax: (312)739-1004
Web Site: http://www.westwood.edu/
President/CEO: Tamara Rozhon
Admissions: Gus Pyrolis
Type: Two-Year College **Sex:** Coed **Enrollment:** FT 105, PT 1 **Professional Accreditation:** ACICS

WESTWOOD COLLEGE-CHICAGO O'HARE AIRPORT
4825 North Scott St., Ste. 100
Schiller Park, IL 60176
Tel: (847)928-0200
Fax: (847)928-2120
Web Site: http://www.westwood.edu/
Admissions: David Traub
Type: Two-Year College **Sex:** Coed **Scholarships:** Available **Calendar System:** Continuous **Enrollment:** FT 315, PT 110 **Professional Accreditation:** ACCSCT, ACICS

WESTWOOD COLLEGE-CHICAGO RIVER OAKS
80 River Oaks Dr., Ste. D-49
Calumet City, IL 60409
Tel: (708)832-1988
Fax: (708)832-9617
Web Site: http://www.westwood.edu/
Admissions: Tash Uray
Type: Two-Year College **Sex:** Coed **Scholarships:** Available **Calendar System:** Continuous **Enrollment:** FT 592, PT 58 **Professional Accreditation:** ACICS

WHEATON COLLEGE
501 East College Ave.
Wheaton, IL 60187-5593
Tel: (630)752-5000
Free: 800-222-2419
Admissions: (630)752-5011
Fax: (630)752-5285
E-mail: admissions@wheaton.edu
Web Site: http://www.wheaton.edu/
President/CEO: Dr. Duane Litfin
Registrar: Paul Johnson
Admissions: Shawn Leftwich
Financial Aid: Donna J. Peltz
Type: Comprehensive **Sex:** Coed **Affiliation:** nondenominational **Scores:** 100% SAT V 400+; 100% SAT M 400+; 6.4% ACT 18-23; 47% ACT 24-29 **% Accepted:** 51 **Admission Plans:** Preferred Admission; Early Action **Application Deadline:** January 15 **Application Fee:** $50.00 **H.S. Requirements:** High school diploma required; GED accepted **Costs Per Year:** Application fee: $50. Comprehensive fee: $27,700 includes full-time tuition ($21,100) and college room and board ($6600). College room only: $3900. Room and board charges vary according to board plan and housing facility. Part-time tuition: $586 per credit hour. Part-time tuition varies according to course load. **Scholarships:** Available **Calendar System:** Semester, Summer Session Available **Enrollment:** FT 2,342, PT 75, Grad 515 **Faculty:** FT 191, PT 96 **Student-Faculty Ratio:** 12:1 **Exams:** Other, SAT I or ACT **% Receiving Financial Aid:** 50 **% Residing in College-Owned, -Operated, or -Affiliated Housing:** 89 **Library Holdings:** 450,620 **Regional Accreditation:** North Central Association of Colleges and Schools **Credit Hours For Degree:** 124 hours, Bachelors **ROTC:** Army, Air Force **Professional Accreditation:** APA, NASM, NCATE **Intercollegiate Athletics:** Baseball M; Basketball M & W; Cheerleading W; Crew M & W; Cross-Country Running M & W; Football M; Golf M & W; Ice Hockey M; Lacrosse M & W; Soccer M & W; Softball W; Swimming and Diving M & W; Tennis M & W; Track and Field M & W; Volleyball M & W; Water Polo W; Wrestling M

WILLIAM RAINEY HARPER COLLEGE
1200 West Algonquin Rd.
Palatine, IL 60067-7398
Tel: (847)925-6000
Fax: (847)925-6044
Web Site: http://www.harpercollege.edu/
President/CEO: Dr. Robert L. Breuder
Registrar: Steven J. Catlin
Financial Aid: Maria Moten
Type: Two-Year College **Sex:** Coed **Affiliation:** Illinois Community College Board **% Accepted:** 100 **Admission Plans:** Open Admission; Preferred Admission; Early Admission; Deferred Admission **Application Deadline:** Rolling **Application Fee:** $25.00 **H.S. Requirements:** High school diploma required; GED accepted **Costs Per Year:** Application fee: $25. Area resident tuition: $1800 full-time, $75 per credit hour part-time. State resident tuition: $6600 full-time, $275 per credit hour part-time. Nonresident tuition: $8256 full-time, $344 per credit hour part-time. Mandatory fees: $450 full-time. **Scholarships:** Available **Calendar System:** Semester, Summer Session Available **Enrollment:** FT 6,174, PT 8,852 **Faculty:** FT 195, PT 635 **Student-Faculty Ratio:** 22:1 **Library Holdings:** 143,817 **Regional Accreditation:** North Central Association of Colleges and Schools **Credit Hours For Degree:** 60 semester hours, Associates **Professional Accreditation:** AAMAE, ADA, ACBSP, NASM, NLN **Intercollegiate Athletics:** Baseball M; Basketball M & W; Cross-Country Running M & W; Football M; Soccer M & W; Softball W; Track and Field M & W; Volleyball W; Wrestling M

WORSHAM COLLEGE OF MORTUARY SCIENCE
495 Northgate Parkway
Wheeling, IL 60090-2646
Tel: (847)808-8444
Fax: (847)808-8493
Web Site: http://www.worshamcollege.com/
President/CEO: Stephanie J. Kann
Admissions: Stephanie Kann
Type: Two-Year College **Sex:** Coed **Scholarships:** Available **Calendar System:** Quarter **Faculty:** PT 12 **Student-Faculty Ratio:** 10:1 **Professional Accreditation:** ABFSE

AMERICAN TRANS AIR AVIATION TRAINING ACADEMY
7251 West McCarty St.
Indianapolis, IN 46241
Tel: (317)243-4519
Free: 800-241-9699
Fax: (317)243-4569
Web Site: http://www.aviationtraining.net/
President/CEO: Steve Genco
Type: Two-Year College **Sex:** Coed **Calendar System:** Semester **Professional Accreditation:** ACCSCT

ANCILLA COLLEGE
Union Rd., PO Box 1
Donaldson, IN 46513
Tel: (574)936-8898
Fax: (574)935-1773
Web Site: http://www.ancilla.edu/
President/CEO: Dr. Robert M. Abene
Registrar: Sharon Blubaugh
Admissions: Erin Wittmeyer
Financial Aid: Michael Schmaltz
Type: Two-Year College **Sex:** Coed **Affiliation:** Roman Catholic **Scores:** 60% SAT V 400+; 66% SAT M 400+; 40% ACT 18-23; 1% ACT 24-29 **% Accepted:** 95 **Admission Plans:** Open Admission **Application Deadline:** Rolling **Application Fee:** $25.00 **H.S. Requirements:** High school diploma required; GED accepted **Costs Per Year:** Application fee: $25. Tuition: $10,800 full-time, $360 per credit hour part-time. Mandatory fees: $230 full-time, $55 per term part-time. **Scholarships:** Available **Calendar System:** Semester, Summer Session Available **Enrollment:** FT 397, PT 227 **Faculty:** FT 22, PT 28 **Student-Faculty Ratio:** 15:1 **Exams:** SAT I or ACT, SAT I and SAT II or ACT, SAT I **Library Holdings:** 27,859 **Regional Accreditation:** North Central Association of Colleges and Schools **Credit Hours For Degree:** 64 semester hours, Associates **Intercollegiate Athletics:** Baseball M; Basketball M & W; Softball W; Volleyball W

ANDERSON UNIVERSITY
1100 East Fifth St.
Anderson, IN 46012-3495
Tel: (765)649-9071
Free: 800-428-6414
Admissions: (765)641-4080
Fax: (765)641-3851
E-mail: info@anderson.edu
Web Site: http://www.anderson.edu/
President/CEO: Dr. James L. Edwards
Registrar: Dr. Michael Collette
Admissions: Jim King
Financial Aid: Kenneth Nieman
Type: Comprehensive **Sex:** Coed **Affiliation:** Church of God **Scores:** 97% SAT V 400+; 97% SAT M 400+; 47% ACT 18-23; 39% ACT 24-29 **% Accepted:** 90 **Admission Plans:** Deferred Admission **Application Deadline:** July 01 **Application Fee:** $20.00 **H.S. Requirements:** High school diploma required; GED accepted **Costs Per Year:** Application fee: $20. Comprehensive fee: $26,450 includes full-time tuition ($19,990) and college room and board ($6460). College room only: $3940. Part-time tuition: $850 per semester hour. **Scholarships:** Available **Calendar System:** Semester, Summer Session Available **Enrollment:** FT 2,149, PT 188, Grad 406 **Faculty:** FT 137, PT 117 **Student-Faculty Ratio:** 14:1 **Exams:** SAT I or ACT **% Receiving Financial Aid:** 76 **% Residing in College-Owned, -Operated, or -Affiliated Housing:** 60 **Library Holdings:** 245,019 **Regional Accreditation:** North Central Association of Colleges and Schools **Credit Hours For Degree:** 62 semester hours, Associates; 124 semester hours, Bachelors **Professional Accreditation:** ACIPE, ACBSP, ATS, CSWE, JRCEPAT, NASM, NCATE, NLN **Intercollegiate Athletics:** Baseball M; Basketball M & W; Cross-Country Running M & W; Football M; Golf M & W; Soccer M & W; Softball W; Tennis M & W; Track and Field M & W; Volleyball W

THE ART INSTITUTE OF INDIANAPOLIS
3500 Depauw Blvd.
Indianapolis, IN 46268
Tel: (866)441-9031
Web Site: http://www.artinstitutes.edu/indianapolis/ **Type:** Four-Year College **Sex:** Coed **Application Deadline:** Rolling

AVIATION INSTITUTE OF MAINTENANCE-INDIANAPOLIS
7251 W. McCarty St.
Indianapolis, IN 46241
Tel: (317)243-4519; 888-349-5387
Fax: (317)243-4569
E-mail: directorami@aviationmaintenance.edu
Web Site: http://www.aviationmaintenance.edu/aviation-indianapolis.asp
Admissions: Andrew Duncan
Type: Two-Year College **Application Fee:** $25.00 **Costs Per Year:** Application fee: $25. **Calendar System:** Quarter

BALL STATE UNIVERSITY
2000 University Ave.
Muncie, IN 47306-1099
Tel: (765)289-1241
Free: 800-482-4BSU
Admissions: (765)285-8300
Fax: (765)285-1632
E-mail: askus@wp.bsu.edu
Web Site: http://www.bsu.edu/
Admissions: Dr. Lawrence Waters
Financial Aid: Dr. Robert Zellers
Type: University **Sex:** Coed **Scores:** 96% SAT V 400+; 97% SAT M 400+; 60% ACT 18-23; 24% ACT 24-29 **% Accepted:** 80 **Admission Plans:** Deferred Admission **Application Deadline:** Rolling **Application Fee:** $25.00 **H.S. Requirements:** High school diploma required; GED accepted **Costs Per Year:** Application fee: $25. State resident tuition: $6030 full-time, $221 per credit hour part-time. Nonresident tuition: $15,790 full-time, $569 per credit hour part-time. Mandatory fees: $428 full-time. College room and board: $6680. **Scholarships:** Available **Calendar System:** Semester, Summer Session Available **Enrollment:** FT 16,063, PT 1,363, Grad 2,925 **Faculty:** FT 910, PT 239 **Student-Faculty Ratio:** 17:1 **Exams:** SAT I or ACT **% Receiving Financial Aid:** 55 **% Residing in College-Owned, -Operated, or -Affiliated Housing:** 41 **Library Holdings:** 1,146,899 **Regional Accreditation:** North Central Association of Colleges and Schools **Credit Hours For Degree:** 63 credit hours, Associates; 126 credit hours, Bachelors **ROTC:** Army **Professional Accreditation:** AACSB, ABET,

ACEJMC, AAFCS, ACA, ADtA, ACSP, APA, ASLA, ASLHA, CORE, CSWE, JRCERT, JRCEPAT, NASAD, NASM, NAST, NCATE, NLN **Intercollegiate Athletics:** Baseball M; Basketball M & W; Cross-Country Running M & W; Equestrian Sports M & W; Field Hockey W; Football M; Golf M; Gymnastics W; Ice Hockey M; Rugby M & W; Sailing M & W; Soccer M & W; Softball W; Swimming and Diving M & W; Tennis M & W; Track and Field M & W; Volleyball M & W; Water Polo M; Wrestling M

BETHEL COLLEGE
1001 West McKinley Ave.
Mishawaka, IN 46545-5591
Tel: (574)259-8511
Free: 800-422-4101
Admissions: (574)257-3319
Fax: (574)257-3326
Web Site: http://www.bethelcollege.edu
President/CEO: Dr. Steven Cramer
Registrar: Steve Matteson
Admissions: Randy Beachy
Financial Aid: Guy Fisher
Type: Comprehensive **Sex:** Coed **Affiliation:** Missionary Church **Scores:** 96.8% SAT V 400+; 95.7% SAT M 400+; 39.4% ACT 18-23; 35% ACT 24-29 **% Accepted:** 75 **Admission Plans:** Early Admission; Deferred Admission **Application Deadline:** August 06 **Application Fee:** $25.00 **H.S. Requirements:** High school diploma required; GED accepted **Costs Per Year:** Application fee: $25. One-time mandatory fee: $600. Comprehensive fee: $22,830 includes full-time tuition ($17,450) and college room and board ($5380). Part-time tuition: $350 per hour. **Scholarships:** Available **Calendar System:** Semester, Summer Session Available **Enrollment:** FT 1,338, PT 596, Grad 159 **Faculty:** FT 90, PT 94 **Student-Faculty Ratio:** 13:1 **Exams:** SAT I or ACT **% Receiving Financial Aid:** 80 **% Residing in College-Owned, -Operated, or -Affiliated Housing:** 49 **Library Holdings:** 106,584 **Regional Accreditation:** North Central Association of Colleges and Schools **Credit Hours For Degree:** 62 semester hours, Associates; 124 semester hours, Bachelors **ROTC:** Army, Air Force **Professional Accreditation:** NCATE, NLN **Intercollegiate Athletics:** Baseball M; Basketball M & W; Cheerleading M & W; Cross-Country Running M & W; Golf M & W; Soccer M & W; Softball W; Tennis M & W; Track and Field M & W; Volleyball W; Wrestling M

BROWN MACKIE COLLEGE-FORT WAYNE
4422 East State Blvd.
Fort Wayne, IN 46815
Tel: (219)484-4400
Admissions: (260)481-5038
Fax: (219)484-2678
E-mail: ktaboh@brownmackie.edu
Web Site: http://www.brownmackie.edu/locations.asp?locid=1
President/CEO: Daniel Summer
Admissions: Ken Taboh
Type: Two-Year College **Sex:** Coed **% Accepted:** 65 **Admission Plans:** Open Admission **Application Deadline:** Rolling **Application Fee:** $0.00 **H.S. Requirements:** High school diploma required; GED accepted **Costs Per Year:** Application fee: $0. Tuition: $8592 full-time, $179 per credit hour part-time. Mandatory fees: $480 full-time, $10 per credit hour part-time. **Scholarships:** Available **Calendar System:** Quarter **Enrollment:** FT 706 **Faculty:** FT 19, PT 28 **Student-Faculty Ratio:** 13:1 **Professional Accreditation:** ACICS, AOTA

BROWN MACKIE COLLEGE-MERRILLVILLE
1000 East 80th Place, Ste. 101, N
Merrillville, IN 46410
Tel: (219)769-3321
Fax: (219)258-3321
E-mail: admissions@brownmackie.edu
Web Site: http://www.brownmackie.edu/locations.asp?locid=19
President/CEO: Antonio Rios
Registrar: Marion Fowdi
Admissions: Don Richardson
Financial Aid: Lorie Williams
Type: Two-Year College **Sex:** Coed **Affiliation:** American Education Centers **Admission Plans:** Open Admission; Early Admission; Deferred Admission **Application Deadline:** Rolling **Application Fee:** $0.00 **H.S. Requirements:** High school diploma required; GED accepted **Costs Per Year:** Application fee: $0. Tuition: $8592 full-time, $179 per credit hour part-time. **Scholarships:** Available **Calendar System:** Quarter, Summer Session Available **Enrollment:** FT 585 **Faculty:** FT 26, PT 37 **Student-Faculty Ratio:** 15:1 **Credit Hours For Degree:** 96 credits, Associates **Professional Accreditation:** ABHES, ACICS

BROWN MACKIE COLLEGE-MICHIGAN CITY
325 East US Hwy. 20
Michigan City, IN 46360
Tel: (219)877-3100
Free: 800-519-2416
Fax: (219)877-3110
E-mail: selston@brownmackie.edu
Web Site: http://www.brownmackie.edu/locations.asp?locid=20
President/CEO: J. Williams Brooks
Registrar: Susan Pedue
Admissions: Sheryl Elston
Financial Aid: Kim Sornson
Type: Two-Year College **Sex:** Coed **Affiliation:** Commonwealth Business College, Inc **% Accepted:** 100 **Admission Plans:** Early Admission; Deferred Admission **Application Deadline:** Rolling **Application Fee:** $0.00 **H.S. Requirements:** High school diploma required; GED accepted **Costs Per Year:** Application fee: $0. Tuition: $6444 full-time, $179 per credit hour part-time. Mandatory fees: $960 full-time. **Scholarships:** Available **Calendar System:** Quarter, Summer Session Available **Enrollment:** FT 461 **Faculty:** FT 3, PT 12 **Student-Faculty Ratio:** 13:1 **Credit Hours For Degree:** 85 credits, Associates **Professional Accreditation:** ABHES, ACICS

BROWN MACKIE COLLEGE-SOUTH BEND
1030 East Jefferson Blvd.
South Bend, IN 46617-3123
Tel: (574)237-0774
Free: 800-743-2447
Fax: (219)237-3585
Web Site: http://www.brownmackie.edu/locations.asp?locid=2
Admissions: Laurie Oliver
Type: Two-Year College **Sex:** Coed **Affiliation:** American Education Centers **% Accepted:** 100 **Admission Plans:** Deferred Admission **Application Deadline:** Rolling **Application Fee:** $0.00 **H.S. Requirements:** High school diploma required; GED accepted **Costs Per Year:** Application fee: $0. Comprehensive fee: $12,402 includes full-time tuition ($6444), mandatory fees ($360), and college room and board ($5598). College room only: $3618. Part-time tuition: $179 per credit hour. Part-time mandatory fees: $10 per credit hour. **Scholarships:** Available **Calendar System:** Quarter, Summer Session Available **Enrollment:** FT 619 **Faculty:** FT 18, PT 34 **Student-Faculty Ratio:** 12:1 **Library Holdings:** 1,409 **Credit Hours For Degree:** 96 credit hours, Associates **Professional Accreditation:** ACICS, AAMAE, AOTA, APTA

BUTLER UNIVERSITY
4600 Sunset Ave.
Indianapolis, IN 46208-3485
Tel: (317)940-8000; 888-940-8100
Admissions: (317)940-8100
Fax: (317)940-8150
E-mail: admission@butler.edu
Web Site: http://www.butler.edu/
President/CEO: Dr. Bobby Fong
Registrar: Sondra Ozolins
Admissions: Scott McIntyre
Financial Aid: Richard Bellows
Type: Comprehensive **Sex:** Coed **Scores:** 99.9% SAT V 400+; 99.9% SAT M 400+; 27.4% ACT 18-23; 56% ACT 24-29 **% Accepted:** 72 **Admission Plans:** Early Action; Deferred Admission **Application Deadline:** Rolling **Application Fee:** $35.00 **H.S. Requirements:** High school diploma required; GED accepted **Costs Per Year:** Application fee: $35. Comprehensive fee: $31,944 includes full-time tuition ($23,530), mandatory fees ($244), and college room and board ($8170). College room only: $3980. Full-time tuition and fees vary according to program. Room and board charges vary according to housing facility. Part-time tuition: $980 per credit. Part-time tuition varies according to program. **Scholarships:** Available **Calendar System:** Semester, Summer Session Available **Enrollment:** FT 3,576, PT 75, Grad 505 **Faculty:** FT 279, PT 155 **Student-Faculty Ratio:** 12:1 **Exams:** SAT I or ACT **% Receiving Financial Aid:** 60 **% Residing in College-Owned, -Operated, or -Affiliated Housing:** 57 **Library Holdings:** 311,429 **Regional Accreditation:** North Central Association of Colleges and Schools

Credit Hours For Degree: 63 semester hours, Associates; 126 semester hours, Bachelors **ROTC:** Army, Air Force **Professional Accreditation:** AACSB, ACPhE, ACA, APA, NASD, NASM, NAST, NCATE **Intercollegiate Athletics:** Baseball M; Basketball M & W; Crew M & W; Cross-Country Running M & W; Football M; Golf M & W; Ice Hockey M; Lacrosse M; Rugby M; Soccer M & W; Softball W; Swimming and Diving M & W; Tennis M & W; Track and Field M & W; Volleyball W

CALUMET COLLEGE OF SAINT JOSEPH

2400 New York Ave.
Whiting, IN 46394-2195
Tel: (219)473-7770; 877-700-9100
Admissions: (219)473-4215
Fax: (219)473-4259
Web Site: http://www.ccsj.edu/
President/CEO: Dr. Dennis C. Rittenmeyer
Registrar: Diana Francis
Admissions: Chuck Walz
Financial Aid: Richard D. Miller
Type: Comprehensive **Sex:** Coed **Affiliation:** Roman Catholic **Scores:** 75% SAT V 400+; 67% SAT M 400+; 53% ACT 18-23 **% Accepted:** 27 **Admission Plans:** Deferred Admission **Application Deadline:** Rolling **Application Fee:** $0.00 **H.S. Requirements:** High school diploma required; GED accepted **Costs Per Year:** Application fee: $0. Tuition: $9900 full-time, $330 per credit hour part-time. **Scholarships:** Available **Calendar System:** Semester, Summer Session Available **Enrollment:** FT 475, PT 707, Grad 83 **Faculty:** FT 32, PT 99 **Student-Faculty Ratio:** 22:1 **Exams:** Other, SAT I or ACT **% Receiving Financial Aid:** 60 **Library Holdings:** 93,067 **Regional Accreditation:** North Central Association of Colleges and Schools **Credit Hours For Degree:** 60 credit hours, Associates; 124 credit hours, Bachelors **Intercollegiate Athletics:** Baseball M; Basketball M & W; Cheerleading W; Cross-Country Running M & W; Golf M & W; Soccer M & W; Softball W; Volleyball M & W

COLLEGE OF COURT REPORTING

111 West Tenth St., Ste. 111
Hobart, IN 46342
Tel: (219)942-1459
Fax: (219)942-1631
E-mail: sdrohoskie@ccvedu.com
Web Site: http://www.ccredu.com/
President/CEO: Kay Moody
Admissions: Stacy Drohosky
Financial Aid: Jeff Moody
Type: Two-Year College **Sex:** Coed **Costs Per Year:** Tuition: $8100 full-time, $225 per credit hour part-time. Mandatory fees: $50 full-time. Tuition guaranteed not to increase for student's term of enrollment. **Enrollment:** FT 89, PT 67 **Faculty:** FT 8, PT 8 **Student-Faculty Ratio:** 8:1 **Professional Accreditation:** ACICS

CROSSROADS BIBLE COLLEGE

601 North Shortridge Rd.
Indianapolis, IN 46219
Tel: (317)352-8736
Free: 800-273-2224
Fax: (317)352-9145
E-mail: bholdcroft@crossroads.edu
Web Site: http://www.crossroads.edu/
President/CEO: Dr. A. Charles Ware
Registrar: Phyllis Dodson
Admissions: Bethanie Holdcroft
Financial Aid: Phyllis Dodson
Type: Four-Year College **Sex:** Coed **Affiliation:** Baptist **Scores:** 100% SAT V 400+; 100% SAT M 400+; 80% ACT 18-23; 20% ACT 24-29 **Admission Plans:** Open Admission; Deferred Admission **Application Fee:** $10.00 **H.S. Requirements:** High school diploma required; GED accepted **Costs Per Year:** Application fee: $10. Tuition: $6600 full-time, $210 per credit hour part-time. Mandatory fees: $140 full-time, $140 per term part-time. College room only: $3000. **Scholarships:** Available **Calendar System:** Semester, Summer Session Available **Enrollment:** FT 88, PT 156 **Faculty:** FT 5, PT 20 **Student-Faculty Ratio:** 16:1 **Exams:** SAT I and SAT II or ACT **% Receiving Financial Aid:** 20 **% Residing in College-Owned, -Operated, or -Affiliated Housing:** 10 **Credit Hours For Degree:** 69 credit hours, Associates; 129 credit hours, Bachelors **Professional Accreditation:** AABC

DAVENPORT UNIVERSITY (GRANGER)

7121 Grape Rd.
Granger, IN 46530
Tel: (574)277-8447
Free: 800-632-9569
Fax: (574)272-2967
Web Site: http://www.davenport.edu/ **Type:** Two-Year College **Sex:** Coed **Affiliation:** Davenport Educational System **Admission Plans:** Open Admission; Deferred Admission **Application Fee:** $25.00 **H.S. Requirements:** High school diploma required; GED accepted **Scholarships:** Available **Calendar System:** Semester **Student-Faculty Ratio:** 16:1 **Regional Accreditation:** North Central Association of Colleges and Schools **Professional Accreditation:** ABHES

DAVENPORT UNIVERSITY (HAMMOND)

5727 Solh Ave.
Hammond, IN 46320
Tel: (219)937-6236
Free: 800-632-9569
Fax: (219)937-6265
Web Site: http://www.davenport.edu/ **Type:** Two-Year College **Sex:** Coed **Affiliation:** Davenport Educational System **Admission Plans:** Open Admission; Deferred Admission **Application Fee:** $25.00 **H.S. Requirements:** High school diploma required; GED accepted **Costs Per Year:** Application fee: $25. Tuition: $7080 full-time, $295 per credit hour part-time. Mandatory fees: $120 full-time. **Scholarships:** Available **Calendar System:** Semester **Student-Faculty Ratio:** 16:1 **Regional Accreditation:** North Central Association of Colleges and Schools

DAVENPORT UNIVERSITY (MERRILLVILLE)

8200 Georgia St.
Merrillville, IN 46410
Tel: (219)769-5556
Free: 800-632-9569
Fax: (219)756-8911
Web Site: http://www.davenport.edu/ **Type:** Two-Year College **Sex:** Coed **Affiliation:** Davenport Educational System **Admission Plans:** Open Admission; Deferred Admission **Application Fee:** $25.00 **H.S. Requirements:** High school diploma required; GED accepted **Costs Per Year:** Application fee: $25. Tuition: $7080 full-time, $295 per credit hour part-time. Mandatory fees: $120 full-time. **Scholarships:** Available **Calendar System:** Semester **Student-Faculty Ratio:** 16:1 **Regional Accreditation:** North Central Association of Colleges and Schools **Professional Accreditation:** ABHES

DEPAUW UNIVERSITY

313 South Locust St.
Greencastle, IN 46135-0037
Tel: (765)658-4800
Free: 800-447-2495
Admissions: (765)658-4006
Fax: (765)658-4007
E-mail: admission@depauw.edu
Web Site: http://www.depauw.edu/
President/CEO: Dr. Robert G. Bottoms
Registrar: Dr. Eleanor S. Ypma
Admissions: Stefanie Niles
Financial Aid: Anna Sinnet
Type: Four-Year College **Sex:** Coed **Affiliation:** United Methodist Church **Scores:** 99.9% SAT V 400+; 99.8% SAT M 400+; 17.9% ACT 18-23; 61.6% ACT 24-29 **% Accepted:** 66 **Admission Plans:** Early Admission; Early Action; Early Decision Plan; Deferred Admission **Application Deadline:** February 01 **Application Fee:** $40.00 **H.S. Requirements:** High school diploma required; GED accepted **Costs Per Year:** Application fee: $40. Comprehensive fee: $35,580 includes full-time tuition ($27,400), mandatory fees ($380), and college room and board ($7800). College room only: $4100. Part-time tuition: $856.25 per semester hour. **Scholarships:** Available **Calendar System:** 4-1-4, Summer Session Not available **Enrollment:** FT 2,351, PT 46 **Faculty:** FT 212, PT 41 **Student-Faculty Ratio:** 10:1 **Exams:** SAT I or ACT **% Receiving Financial Aid:** 46 **% Residing in College-Owned, -Operated, or -Affiliated Housing:** 95 **Library Holdings:** 545,736 **Regional Accreditation:** North Central Association of Colleges and Schools

Credit Hours For Degree: 31 courses, Bachelors **ROTC:** Army, Air Force **Professional Accreditation:** JRCEPAT, NASM, NCATE **Intercollegiate Athletics:** Baseball M; Basketball M & W; Cheerleading M & W; Crew M & W; Cross-Country Running M & W; Field Hockey W; Football M; Golf M & W; Rugby M; Soccer M & W; Softball W; Swimming and Diving M & W; Tennis M & W; Track and Field M & W; Volleyball W

DEVRY UNIVERSITY (INDIANAPOLIS)
9100 Keystone Crossing, Ste. 350
Indianapolis, IN 46240-2158
Tel: (317)581-8854; (866)513-3879
Web Site: http://www.devry.edu/ **Type:** Comprehensive **Sex:** Coed **Affiliation:** DeVry University **Admission Plans:** Deferred Admission **Application Deadline:** Rolling **Application Fee:** $50.00 **H.S. Requirements:** High school diploma required; GED accepted **Costs Per Year:** Application fee: $50. One-time mandatory fee: $40. Tuition: $11,790 full-time, $440 per credit part-time. Mandatory fees: $30 full-time, $30 per year part-time. Full-time tuition and fees vary according to course load. Part-time tuition and fees vary according to course load. **Calendar System:** Semester, Summer Session Available **Enrollment:** FT 21, PT 51, Grad 71 **Faculty:** FT 0, PT 27 **Student-Faculty Ratio:** 4:1 **Regional Accreditation:** North Central Association of Colleges and Schools **Credit Hours For Degree:** 122 credit hours, Bachelors

DEVRY UNIVERSITY (MERRILLVILLE)
Twin Towers
1000 East 80th Place, Ste. 222 Mall
Merrillville, IN 46410-5673
Tel: (219)736-7440
Fax: (219)736-7874
Web Site: http://www.devry.edu/ **Type:** Comprehensive **Sex:** Coed **Costs Per Year:** One-time mandatory fee: $40. Tuition: $11,890 full-time, $445 per credit part-time. Mandatory fees: $60 full-time, $30 per year part-time. Full-time tuition and fees vary according to course load. Part-time tuition and fees vary according to course load. **Calendar System:** Semester **Regional Accreditation:** North Central Association of Colleges and Schools

EARLHAM COLLEGE
801 National Rd. West
Richmond, IN 47374-4095
Tel: (765)983-1200
Free: 800-327-5426
Admissions: (765)983-1600
Fax: (765)983-1560
E-mail: admission@earlham.edu
Web Site: http://www.earlham.edu/
President/CEO: Douglas Bennett
Registrar: Bonita Washington-Lacey
Admissions: Jeff Rickey
Financial Aid: Robert Arnold
Type: Comprehensive **Sex:** Coed **Affiliation:** Society of Friends **Scores:** 99% SAT V 400+; 99% SAT M 400+; 18% ACT 18-23; 62% ACT 24-29 **% Accepted:** 70 **Admission Plans:** Preferred Admission; Early Admission; Early Action; Early Decision Plan; Deferred Admission **Application Deadline:** February 15 **Application Fee:** $30.00 **H.S. Requirements:** High school diploma required; GED accepted. For home schooled students: High school diploma or equivalent not required **Costs Per Year:** Application fee: $30. Comprehensive fee: $33,604 includes full-time tuition ($26,984), mandatory fees ($700), and college room and board ($5920). College room only: $2900. Room and board charges vary according to board plan. Part-time tuition: $899 per credit hour. Part-time mandatory fees: $700 per year. **Scholarships:** Available **Calendar System:** Semester, Summer Session Not available **Enrollment:** FT 1,201, PT 25, Grad 81 **Faculty:** FT 93, PT 15 **Student-Faculty Ratio:** 12:1 **Exams:** SAT I or ACT **% Receiving Financial Aid:** 65 **% Residing in College-Owned, -Operated, or -Affiliated Housing:** 88 **Library Holdings:** 392,100 **Regional Accreditation:** North Central Association of Colleges and Schools **Credit Hours For Degree:** 120 semester hours, Bachelors **Intercollegiate Athletics:** Baseball M; Basketball M & W; Cheerleading M & W; Cross-Country Running M & W; Equestrian Sports M & W; Field Hockey W; Football M; Lacrosse M & W; Rugby M & W; Soccer M & W; Tennis M & W; Track and Field M & W; Ultimate Frisbee M & W; Volleyball M & W

FRANKLIN COLLEGE
101 Branigin Blvd.
Franklin, IN 46131-2623
Tel: (317)738-8000
Free: 800-852-0232
Admissions: (317)738-8062
Fax: (317)738-8274
E-mail: admissions@franklincoll.edu
Web Site: http://www.franklincollege.edu/
President/CEO: Dr. James Moseley
Registrar: Lois Coy
Admissions: Jacqueline Acosta
Financial Aid: Richard Nash
Type: Four-Year College **Sex:** Coed **Affiliation:** American Baptist Churches in the U.S.A. **Scores:** 95.6% SAT V 400+; 94% SAT M 400+; 60% ACT 18-23; 34% ACT 24-29 **% Accepted:** 80 **Admission Plans:** Deferred Admission **Application Fee:** $30.00 **H.S. Requirements:** High school diploma required; GED accepted **Costs Per Year:** Application fee: $30. Comprehensive fee: $25,005 includes full-time tuition ($19,100), mandatory fees ($175), and college room and board ($5730). College room only: $3340. Room and board charges vary according to board plan and housing facility. Part-time tuition: $265 per credit hour. Part-time tuition varies according to course load. **Scholarships:** Available **Calendar System:** 4-1-4, Summer Session Available **Enrollment:** FT 946, PT 57 **Faculty:** FT 65, PT 45 **Student-Faculty Ratio:** 12:1 **Exams:** SAT I or ACT **% Receiving Financial Aid:** 82 **% Residing in College-Owned, -Operated, or -Affiliated Housing:** 72 **Library Holdings:** 126,345 **Regional Accreditation:** North Central Association of Colleges and Schools **Credit Hours For Degree:** 128 semester hours, Bachelors **ROTC:** Army **Professional Accreditation:** NCATE **Intercollegiate Athletics:** Baseball M; Basketball M & W; Cross-Country Running M & W; Football M; Golf M & W; Soccer M & W; Softball W; Tennis M & W; Track and Field M & W; Volleyball W

GOSHEN COLLEGE
1700 South Main St.
Goshen, IN 46526-4794
Tel: (574)535-7000
Free: 800-348-7422
Admissions: (574)535-7535
Fax: (574)535-7060
E-mail: admissions@goshen.edu
Web Site: http://www.goshen.edu/
President/CEO: Dr. Shirley H. Showalter
Registrar: Stanley Miller
Admissions: Galen Graber
Financial Aid: Galen Graber
Type: Four-Year College **Sex:** Coed **Affiliation:** Mennonite **Scores:** 98% SAT V 400+; 97% SAT M 400+; 33% ACT 18-23; 49% ACT 24-29 **% Accepted:** 76 **Admission Plans:** Early Action; Deferred Admission **Application Deadline:** August 15 **Application Fee:** $25.00 **H.S. Requirements:** High school diploma required; GED accepted **Costs Per Year:** Application fee: $25. Comprehensive fee: $27,000 includes full-time tuition ($20,300) and college room and board ($6700). College room only: $3600. Part-time tuition: $800 per credit hour. **Scholarships:** Available **Calendar System:** Semester, Summer Session Available **Enrollment:** FT 831, PT 91 **Faculty:** FT 72, PT 32 **Student-Faculty Ratio:** 10:1 **Exams:** SAT I or ACT **% Receiving Financial Aid:** 78 **% Residing in College-Owned, -Operated, or -Affiliated Housing:** 67 **Library Holdings:** 127,028 **Regional Accreditation:** North Central Association of Colleges and Schools **Credit Hours For Degree:** 120 credit hours, Bachelors **Professional Accreditation:** AACN, CSWE, NCATE, NLN **Intercollegiate Athletics:** Baseball M; Basketball M & W; Cross-Country Running M & W; Golf M; Soccer M & W; Softball W; Tennis M & W; Track and Field M & W; Volleyball W

GRACE COLLEGE
200 Seminary Dr.
Winona Lake, IN 46590-1294
Tel: (574)372-5100
Free: 800-54 GRACE
Fax: (574)372-5139
E-mail: millerar@grace.edu
Web Site: http://www.grace.edu/

President/CEO: Dr. Ronald E. Manahan
Registrar: Anecia Miller
Admissions: Anecia Miller
Financial Aid: Shelly Johnson
Type: Comprehensive **Sex:** Coed **Affiliation:** Fellowship of Grace Brethren Churches; Grace Theological Seminary **Scores:** 97.98% SAT V 400+; 94. 59% SAT M 400+; 46.72% ACT 18-23; 41.8% ACT 24-29 **% Accepted:** 73 **Admission Plans:** Early Admission; Deferred Admission **Application Deadline:** August 01 **Application Fee:** $20.00 **H.S. Requirements:** High school diploma required; GED accepted **Costs Per Year:** Application fee: $20. Comprehensive fee: $22,170 includes full-time tuition ($15,620), mandatory fees ($400), and college room and board ($6150). College room only: $3070. Room and board charges vary according to board plan and housing facility. Part-time tuition: $295 per credit. Part-time mandatory fees: $280 per year. Part-time tuition and fees vary according to course load. **Scholarships:** Available **Calendar System:** Semester, Summer Session Available **Enrollment:** FT 980, PT 148, Grad 125 **Faculty:** FT 43, PT 78 **Student-Faculty Ratio:** 16:1 **Exams:** SAT I or ACT **% Receiving Financial Aid:** 76 **% Residing in College-Owned, -Operated, or -Affiliated Housing:** 36 **Library Holdings:** 142,865 **Regional Accreditation:** North Central Association of Colleges and Schools **Credit Hours For Degree:** 73 semester hours, Associates; 124 semester hours, Bachelors **Professional Accreditation:** CSWE, NASM, NCATE **Intercollegiate Athletics:** Baseball M; Basketball M & W; Cheerleading M & W; Cross-Country Running M & W; Golf M; Soccer M & W; Softball W; Tennis M & W; Track and Field M & W; Volleyball W

HANOVER COLLEGE
PO Box 108
Hanover, IN 47243-0108
Tel: (812)866-7000
Free: 800-213-2178
Admissions: (812)866-7021
Fax: (812)866-7098
E-mail: admissions@hanover.edu
Web Site: http://www.hanover.edu/
President/CEO: Dr. Russell L. Nichols
Registrar: Dr. Kenneth P. Prince
Admissions: Kenneth Moyer
Financial Aid: Jon Riester
Type: Four-Year College **Sex:** Coed **Affiliation:** Presbyterian **Scores:** 99% SAT V 400+; 100% SAT M 400+; 27% ACT 18-23; 50% ACT 24-29 **% Accepted:** 70 **Admission Plans:** Early Admission; Early Action; Deferred Admission **Application Deadline:** March 01 **Application Fee:** $35.00 **H.S. Requirements:** High school diploma required; GED not accepted **Costs Per Year:** Application fee: $35. Comprehensive fee: $28,150 includes full-time tuition ($21,150), mandatory fees ($500), and college room and board ($6500). College room only: $3100. Full-time tuition and fees vary according to reciprocity agreements. Room and board charges vary according to housing facility and location. Part-time tuition: $2350 per unit. Part-time tuition varies according to course load and reciprocity agreements. **Scholarships:** Available **Calendar System:** Miscellaneous, Summer Session Not available **Enrollment:** FT 1,004, PT 4 **Faculty:** FT 95, PT 8 **Student-Faculty Ratio:** 10:1 **Exams:** SAT I or ACT **% Receiving Financial Aid:** 73 **% Residing in College-Owned, -Operated, or -Affiliated Housing:** 96 **Library Holdings:** 224,478 **Regional Accreditation:** North Central Association of Colleges and Schools **Credit Hours For Degree:** 37 units, Bachelors **Professional Accreditation:** NCATE **Intercollegiate Athletics:** Baseball M; Basketball M & W; Cross-Country Running M & W; Football M; Golf M & W; Soccer M & W; Softball W; Tennis M & W; Track and Field M & W; Volleyball W

HOLY CROSS COLLEGE
PO Box 308, 54515 State Rd. 933 North
Notre Dame, IN 46556-0308
Tel: (574)239-8400
Fax: (574)239-8323
E-mail: vduke@hcc-nd.edu
Web Site: http://www.hcc-nd.edu/
President/CEO: Br. Richard Gilman, CSC
Registrar: Richard Sullivan
Admissions: Vincent M. Duke
Financial Aid: Joce Arvisais
Type: Two-Year College **Sex:** Coed **Affiliation:** Roman Catholic **Admission Plans:** Deferred Admission **Application Deadline:** Rolling **Application Fee:** $50.00 **H.S. Requirements:** High school diploma required; GED accepted **Costs Per Year:** Application fee: $50. Comprehensive fee: $23,500 includes full-time tuition ($14,500), mandatory fees ($1000), and college room and board ($8000). Part-time tuition: $365 per semester hour. **Scholarships:** Available **Calendar System:** Semester, Summer Session Available **Enrollment:** FT 328, PT 41 **Faculty:** FT 26, PT 12 **Student-Faculty Ratio:** 12:1 **Exams:** SAT I or ACT **% Residing in College-Owned, -Operated, or -Affiliated Housing:** 54 **Library Holdings:** 15,000 **Regional Accreditation:** North Central Association of Colleges and Schools **Credit Hours For Degree:** 61 semester hours, Associates; 122 semester hours, Bachelors **ROTC:** Army, Air Force **Intercollegiate Athletics:** Basketball M; Crew M & W; Cross-Country Running M & W; Lacrosse M; Soccer M & W

HUNTINGTON UNIVERSITY
2303 College Ave.
Huntington, IN 46750-1299
Tel: (260)356-6000
Free: 800-642-6493
Fax: (260)356-9448
E-mail: jberggren@huntington.edu
Web Site: http://www.huntington.edu/
President/CEO: Dr. G. Blair Dowden
Registrar: Sarah Harvey
Admissions: Jeff Berggren
Financial Aid: Sharon Woods
Type: Comprehensive **Sex:** Coed **Affiliation:** Church of the United Brethren in Christ **Scores:** 98% SAT V 400+; 94% SAT M 400+; 50% ACT 18-23; 37% ACT 24-29 **% Accepted:** 93 **Admission Plans:** Deferred Admission **Application Deadline:** August 01 **Application Fee:** $20.00 **H.S. Requirements:** High school diploma required; GED accepted **Costs Per Year:** Application fee: $20. Comprehensive fee: $25,390 includes full-time tuition ($18,420), mandatory fees ($440), and college room and board ($6530). Part-time tuition: $530 per semester hour. **Scholarships:** Available **Calendar System:** 4-1-4, Summer Session Available **Enrollment:** FT 830, PT 119, Grad 70 **Faculty:** FT 59, PT 63 **Student-Faculty Ratio:** 11:1 **Exams:** SAT I or ACT **% Receiving Financial Aid:** 73 **% Residing in College-Owned, -Operated, or -Affiliated Housing:** 70 **Library Holdings:** 91,709 **Regional Accreditation:** North Central Association of Colleges and Schools **Credit Hours For Degree:** 128 semester hours, Bachelors **Professional Accreditation:** NASM, NCATE **Intercollegiate Athletics:** Baseball M; Basketball M & W; Cross-Country Running M & W; Golf M; Soccer M & W; Softball W; Tennis M & W; Track and Field M & W; Volleyball W

INDIANA BUSINESS COLLEGE (ANDERSON)
140 East 53rd St.
Anderson, IN 46013
Tel: (765)644-7514
Web Site: http://www.ibcschools.edu/
Financial Aid: Nicole Pierson
Type: Two-Year College **Sex:** Coed **Admission Plans:** Early Admission **Application Deadline:** Rolling **Application Fee:** $50.00 **H.S. Requirements:** High school diploma required; GED accepted **Costs Per Year:** Application fee: $50. **Calendar System:** Quarter **Student-Faculty Ratio:** 20:1 **Exams:** Other **Professional Accreditation:** ACICS

INDIANA BUSINESS COLLEGE (COLUMBUS)
2222 Poshard Dr.
Columbus, IN 47203-1843
Tel: (812)379-9000
Web Site: http://www.ibcschools.edu/
Financial Aid: Kathy England
Type: Two-Year College **Sex:** Coed **Application Deadline:** Rolling **Application Fee:** $50.00 **H.S. Requirements:** High school diploma required; GED accepted **Costs Per Year:** Application fee: $50. **Scholarships:** Available **Calendar System:** Quarter **Student-Faculty Ratio:** 20:1 **Exams:** Other **Professional Accreditation:** ACICS

INDIANA BUSINESS COLLEGE (EVANSVILLE)
4601 Theatre Dr.
Evansville, IN 47715-4601
Tel: (812)476-6000
Web Site: http://www.ibcschools.edu/
Financial Aid: Crystal Thomas
Type: Two-Year College **Sex:** Coed **Application Deadline:** Rolling **Application Fee:** $50.00 **Costs Per Year:** Application fee: $50. **Scholarships:** Available **Calendar System:** Quarter **Student-Faculty Ratio:** 20:1 **Exams:**

Other **Professional Accreditation:** ACICS, AAMAE

INDIANA BUSINESS COLLEGE (FORT WAYNE)
6413 North Clinton St.
Fort Wayne, IN 46825
Tel: (260)471-7667
Web Site: http://www.ibcschools.edu/
Financial Aid: Jennifer Littler
Type: Two-Year College **Sex:** Coed **Application Deadline:** Rolling **Application Fee:** $50.00 **H.S. Requirements:** High school diploma required; GED accepted **Costs Per Year:** Application fee: $50. **Scholarships:** Available **Calendar System:** Quarter **Student-Faculty Ratio:** 20:1 **Exams:** Other **Professional Accreditation:** ACICS

INDIANA BUSINESS COLLEGE (INDIANAPOLIS)
6300 Technology Center Dr.
Indianapolis, IN 46278
Tel: (317)873-6500
Web Site: http://www.ibcschools.edu/Campuses/northwest.asp **Type:** Two-Year College **Sex:** Coed **Application Deadline:** Rolling **Application Fee:** $50.00 **Costs Per Year:** Application fee: $50. **Calendar System:** Quarter **Exams:** Other

INDIANA BUSINESS COLLEGE (INDIANAPOLIS)
550 East Washington St.
Indianapolis, IN 46204
Tel: (317)264-5656
Fax: (317)264-5650
Web Site: http://www.ibcschools.edu/
President/CEO: Kenneth J. Konesco
Financial Aid: Vikki Goeke
Type: Two-Year College **Sex:** Coed **Application Deadline:** Rolling **Application Fee:** $50.00 **H.S. Requirements:** High school diploma required; GED accepted **Costs Per Year:** Application fee: $50. **Scholarships:** Available **Calendar System:** Quarter, Summer Session Available **Student-Faculty Ratio:** 20:1 **Exams:** Other **Professional Accreditation:** ACICS

INDIANA BUSINESS COLLEGE (INDIANAPOLIS-NORTHWEST CAMPUS)
6300 Technology Center Dr.
Indianapolis, IN 46278
Tel: (317)873-6500
Web Site: http://www.ibcschools.edu/campuses/northwest.asp **Type:** Two-Year College **Sex:** Coed **Application Deadline:** Rolling **Application Fee:** $50.00 **Costs Per Year:** Application fee: $50. **Calendar System:** Quarter **Student-Faculty Ratio:** 20:1 **Exams:** Other

INDIANA BUSINESS COLLEGE (LAFAYETTE)
2 Executive Dr.
Lafayette, IN 47905
Tel: (765)447-9550
Web Site: http://www.ibcschools.edu/
Financial Aid: Mary Robinson
Type: Two-Year College **Sex:** Coed **Application Deadline:** Rolling **Application Fee:** $50.00 **H.S. Requirements:** High school diploma required; GED accepted **Costs Per Year:** Application fee: $50. **Scholarships:** Available **Calendar System:** Quarter **Student-Faculty Ratio:** 20:1 **Exams:** Other **Professional Accreditation:** ACICS

INDIANA BUSINESS COLLEGE (MARION)
830 North Miller Ave.
Marion, IN 46952-2338
Tel: (765)662-7497
Web Site: http://www.ibcschools.edu/
Financial Aid: Bradley Roe
Type: Two-Year College **Sex:** Coed **Application Deadline:** Rolling **Application Fee:** $50.00 **H.S. Requirements:** High school diploma required; GED accepted **Costs Per Year:** Application fee: $50. **Calendar System:** Quarter **Student-Faculty Ratio:** 20:1 **Exams:** Other **Professional Accreditation:** ACICS

INDIANA BUSINESS COLLEGE-MEDICAL
8150 Brookville Rd.
Indianapolis, IN 46239
Tel: (317)375-8000
Fax: (317)351-1871
Web Site: http://www.ibcschools.edu/
Financial Aid: Michael Hess
Type: Two-Year College **Sex:** Coed **Application Deadline:** Rolling **Application Fee:** $50.00 **H.S. Requirements:** High school diploma required; GED accepted **Costs Per Year:** Application fee: $50. **Calendar System:** Quarter **Student-Faculty Ratio:** 20:1 **Exams:** Other **Professional Accreditation:** ACICS

INDIANA BUSINESS COLLEGE (MUNCIE)
411 West Riggin Rd.
Muncie, IN 47303
Tel: (765)288-8681
Fax: (765)288-8797
Web Site: http://www.ibcschools.edu/
Financial Aid: Clay Bainter
Type: Two-Year College **Sex:** Coed **Application Deadline:** Rolling **Application Fee:** $50.00 **H.S. Requirements:** High school diploma required; GED accepted **Costs Per Year:** Application fee: $50. **Scholarships:** Available **Calendar System:** Quarter **Student-Faculty Ratio:** 20:1 **Exams:** Other **Professional Accreditation:** ACICS

INDIANA BUSINESS COLLEGE (TERRE HAUTE)
3175 South Third Place
Terre Haute, IN 47802
Tel: (812)232-4458
Web Site: http://www.ibcschools.edu/
Financial Aid: David Marshall
Type: Two-Year College **Sex:** Coed **Application Deadline:** Rolling **Application Fee:** $50.00 **H.S. Requirements:** High school diploma required; GED accepted **Costs Per Year:** Application fee: $50. **Calendar System:** Quarter **Student-Faculty Ratio:** 20:1 **Exams:** Other **Professional Accreditation:** ACICS

INDIANA STATE UNIVERSITY
210 North Seventh St.
Terre Haute, IN 47809-1401
Tel: (812)237-6311
Free: 800-742-0891
Admissions: (812)237-2121
Fax: (812)237-8023
Web Site: http://web.indstate.edu/
President/CEO: Dr. Lloyd W. Benjamin
Registrar: Stacey J. Thomas
Admissions: Richard Toomey
Financial Aid: Thomas M. Ratliff
Type: University **Sex:** Coed **Scores:** 85.41% SAT V 400+; 85.19% SAT M 400+; 46.13% ACT 18-23; 21.07% ACT 24-29 **% Accepted:** 80 **Admission Plans:** Deferred Admission **Application Deadline:** August 15 **Application Fee:** $25.00 **H.S. Requirements:** High school diploma required; GED accepted **Costs Per Year:** Application fee: $25. State resident tuition: $5756 full-time, $208 per credit hour part-time. Nonresident tuition: $12,752 full-time, $450 per credit hour part-time. Mandatory fees: $108 full-time, $54 per term part-time. Full-time tuition and fees vary according to course load. College room and board: $5938. College room only: $3150. Room and board charges vary according to board plan, housing facility, and student level. **Scholarships:** Available **Calendar System:** Semester, Summer Session Available **Enrollment:** FT 7,628, PT 1,042, Grad 1,979 **Faculty:** FT 489, PT 173 **Student-Faculty Ratio:** 17:1 **Exams:** SAT I or ACT **% Receiving Financial Aid:** 60 **% Residing in College-Owned, -Operated, or -Affiliated Housing:** 36 **Library Holdings:** 2,458,424 **Regional Accreditation:** North Central Association of Colleges and Schools **Credit Hours For Degree:** 62 credit hours, Associates; 124 credit hours, Bachelors **ROTC:** Army, Air Force **Professional Accreditation:** AACSB, AAMFT, AAFCS, ACCE, ADtA, APA, ASLHA, CSWE, JRCEPAT, NAIT, NASAD, NASM, NCATE, NLN, NRPA **Intercollegiate Athletics:** Baseball M; Basketball M & W; Cross-Country Running M & W; Football M; Soccer W; Softball W; Tennis M & W; Track and Field M & W; Volleyball W

INDIANA TECH
1600 East Washington Blvd.
Fort Wayne, IN 46803-1297
Tel: (260)422-5561; 888-666-TECH
Fax: (260)422-7696

E-mail: agcarnahan@indianatech.edu
Web Site: http://www.indianatech.edu
President/CEO: Dr. Arthur E. Snyder
Registrar: Lori Brubaker
Admissions: Allison Carnahan
Financial Aid: Teresa M. Vasquez
Type: Comprehensive **Sex:** Coed **Scores:** 75% SAT V 400+; 81.26% SAT M 400+; 47.31% ACT 18-23; 10.75% ACT 24-29 **% Accepted:** 54 **Admission Plans:** Early Admission; Deferred Admission **Application Fee:** $50.00 **H.S. Requirements:** High school diploma required; GED accepted **Costs Per Year:** Application fee: $50. Comprehensive fee: $24,600 includes full-time tuition ($17,600), mandatory fees ($250), and college room and board ($6750). Part-time tuition: $586 per credit hour. **Scholarships:** Available **Calendar System:** Semester, Summer Session Available **Enrollment:** FT 1,579, PT 1,278, Grad 372 **Faculty:** FT 35, PT 210 **Student-Faculty Ratio:** 20:1 **Exams:** SAT I or ACT **% Residing in College-Owned, -Operated, or -Affiliated Housing:** 49 **Library Holdings:** 32,000 **Regional Accreditation:** North Central Association of Colleges and Schools **Credit Hours For Degree:** 60 credit hours, Associates; 127 credit hours, Bachelors **Professional Accreditation:** ABET **Intercollegiate Athletics:** Baseball M; Basketball M & W; Cheerleading M & W; Soccer M & W; Softball W; Volleyball W

INDIANA UNIVERSITY BLOOMINGTON
107 S. Indiana Ave.
Bloomington, IN 47405-7000
Tel: (812)855-4848
Admissions: (812)855-0661
Fax: (812)855-1871
E-mail: iuadmit@indiana.edu
Web Site: http://www.iub.edu/
President/CEO: Dr. Kenneth Gros Louis
Registrar: Roland Cote
Admissions: Mary Ellen Anderson
Financial Aid: Dr. Susan Pugh
Type: University **Sex:** Coed **Affiliation:** Indiana University System **Scores:** 96.7% SAT V 400+; 97.8% SAT M 400+; 37.6% ACT 18-23; 47.5% ACT 24-29 **% Accepted:** 85 **Admission Plans:** Preferred Admission; Deferred Admission **Application Deadline:** Rolling **Application Fee:** $50.00 **H.S. Requirements:** High school diploma required; GED accepted **Costs Per Year:** Application fee: $50. State resident tuition: $6291 full-time, $196.40 per credit hour part-time. Nonresident tuition: $18,687 full-time, $584.05 per credit hour part-time. Mandatory fees: $821 full-time. Full-time tuition and fees vary according to location, program, and student level. Part-time tuition varies according to course load, location, program, and student level. College room and board: $6240. College room only: $3760. Room and board charges vary according to board plan and housing facility. **Scholarships:** Available **Calendar System:** Semester, Summer Session Available **Enrollment:** FT 27,974, PT 1,588, Grad 7,442 **Faculty:** FT 1,589 **Student-Faculty Ratio:** 18:1 **Exams:** SAT I or ACT, SAT II **% Receiving Financial Aid:** 54 **% Residing in College-Owned, -Operated, or -Affiliated Housing:** 42 **Library Holdings:** 6,512,090 **Regional Accreditation:** North Central Association of Colleges and Schools **Credit Hours For Degree:** 60 credit hours, Associates; 122 credit hours, Bachelors **ROTC:** Army, Air Force **Professional Accreditation:** AACSB, ACEJMC, ACA, ALA, AOA, APA, ASLHA, COptA, CEPH, CSWE, FIDER, JRCEPAT, NASAD, NASM, NASPAA, NAST, NCATE, NLN, NRPA **Intercollegiate Athletics:** Baseball M; Basketball M & W; Crew W; Cross-Country Running M & W; Field Hockey W; Football M; Golf M & W; Soccer M & W; Softball W; Swimming and Diving M & W; Tennis M & W; Track and Field M & W; Volleyball W; Water Polo W; Wrestling M

INDIANA UNIVERSITY EAST
2325 Chester Blvd.
Richmond, IN 47374-1289
Tel: (765)973-8200
Free: 800-959-EAST
Admissions: (765)973-8208
Fax: (765)973-8288
E-mail: musmith@indiana.edu
Web Site: http://www.iu.edu/
President/CEO: Dr. David J. Fulton
Registrar: Dennis Hicks
Admissions: James Bland
Financial Aid: James Bland
Type: Four-Year College **Sex:** Coed **Affiliation:** Indiana University System **Scores:** 79.2% SAT V 400+; 75% SAT M 400+; 50.7% ACT 18-23; 8.7% ACT 24-29 **% Accepted:** 88 **Admission Plans:** Early Admission; Deferred Admission **Application Deadline:** Rolling **Application Fee:** $25.00 **H.S. Requirements:** High school diploma required; GED accepted **Costs Per Year:** Application fee: $25. State resident tuition: $4475 full-time, $149.15 per credit hour part-time. Nonresident tuition: $11,153 full-time, $371.75 per credit hour part-time. Mandatory fees: $331 full-time. Full-time tuition and fees vary according to course load and reciprocity agreements. Part-time tuition varies according to course load and reciprocity agreements. **Scholarships:** Available **Calendar System:** Semester, Summer Session Available **Enrollment:** FT 1,292, PT 1,100, Grad 67 **Faculty:** FT 83 **Student-Faculty Ratio:** 13:1 **Exams:** SAT I or ACT **% Receiving Financial Aid:** 70 **Library Holdings:** 67,036 **Regional Accreditation:** North Central Association of Colleges and Schools **Credit Hours For Degree:** 60 credit hours, Associates; 120 credit hours, Bachelors **Professional Accreditation:** ACBSP, CSWE, NCATE, NLN

INDIANA UNIVERSITY KOKOMO
PO Box 9003
Kokomo, IN 46904-9003
Tel: (765)453-2000; 888-875-4485
Admissions: (765)455-9216
Fax: (765)455-9537
E-mail: iuadmis@iuk.edu
Web Site: http://www.iuk.edu/
President/CEO: Dr. Ruth J. Person
Registrar: Holly Hamilton
Admissions: Jackie Kennedy-Fletcher
Type: Comprehensive **Sex:** Coed **Affiliation:** Indiana University System **Scores:** 90.3% SAT V 400+; 87.6% SAT M 400+; 59.5% ACT 18-23; 12.6% ACT 24-29 **% Accepted:** 82 **Admission Plans:** Early Admission; Deferred Admission **Application Deadline:** Rolling **Application Fee:** $30.00 **H.S. Requirements:** High school diploma required; GED accepted **Costs Per Year:** Application fee: $30. State resident tuition: $4475 full-time, $149.15 per credit hour part-time. Nonresident tuition: $11,153 full-time, $371.75 per credit hour part-time. Mandatory fees: $360 full-time. Full-time tuition and fees vary according to course load. Part-time tuition varies according to course load. **Scholarships:** Available **Calendar System:** Semester, Summer Session Available **Enrollment:** FT 1,423, PT 1,314, Grad 158 **Faculty:** FT 85 **Student-Faculty Ratio:** 16:1 **Exams:** SAT I or ACT **% Receiving Financial Aid:** 52 **Library Holdings:** 132,424 **Regional Accreditation:** North Central Association of Colleges and Schools **Credit Hours For Degree:** 60 credit hours, Associates; 120 credit hours, Bachelors **ROTC:** Army **Professional Accreditation:** AACSB, AACN, NCATE, NLN

INDIANA UNIVERSITY NORTHWEST
3400 Broadway
Gary, IN 46408-1197
Tel: (219)980-6500
Free: 800-968-7486
Admissions: (219)980-6767
Fax: (219)981-4219
E-mail: wlee@unhaw1.iun.indiana.edu
Web Site: http://www.iun.edu/
President/CEO: Dr. Bruce Bergland
Registrar: Peter Kesheimer
Admissions: Dr. Linda B. Templeton
Financial Aid: Charles R. Carothers
Type: Comprehensive **Sex:** Coed **Affiliation:** Indiana University System **Scores:** 76.1% SAT V 400+; 74.4% SAT M 400+; 45.5% ACT 18-23; 12.1% ACT 24-29 **% Accepted:** 75 **Admission Plans:** Early Admission; Deferred Admission **Application Deadline:** Rolling **Application Fee:** $35.00 **H.S. Requirements:** High school diploma required; GED accepted **Costs Per Year:** Application fee: $35. State resident tuition: $4475 full-time, $149.15 per credit hour part-time. Nonresident tuition: $11,153 full-time, $371.75 per credit hour part-time. Mandatory fees: $427 full-time. Full-time tuition and fees vary according to course load. Part-time tuition varies according to course load. **Scholarships:** Available **Calendar System:** Semester, Summer Session Available **Enrollment:** FT 2,469, PT 1,918, Grad 600 **Faculty:** FT 163 **Student-Faculty Ratio:** 13:1 **Exams:** SAT I or ACT **% Receiving Financial Aid:** 62 **Library Holdings:** 251,508 **Regional Accreditation:** North Central Association of Colleges and Schools **Credit Hours For Degree:** 60 credits, Associates; 120 credits, Bachelors **ROTC:** Army **Profes-**

sional Accreditation: AACSB, AACN, ADA, AHIMA, CARC, CSWE, JRCERT, NAACLS, NASPAA, NCATE, NLN **Intercollegiate Athletics:** Baseball M; Basketball M; Golf M & W; Softball W; Volleyball W

INDIANA UNIVERSITY-PURDUE UNIVERSITY FORT WAYNE

2101 East Coliseum Blvd.
Fort Wayne, IN 46805-1499
Tel: (260)481-6100
Admissions: (260)481-6812
E-mail: ipfwadmns@ppfw.edu
Web Site: http://www.ipfw.edu/
President/CEO: Dr. Michael A. Wartell
Registrar: Patrick A. McLaughlin
Admissions: Carol Isaacs
Financial Aid: Mark Franke

Type: Comprehensive **Sex:** Coed **Affiliation:** Indiana University System and Purdue University System **Scores:** 86.6% SAT V 400+; 89.3% SAT M 400+; 53% ACT 18-23; 24.8% ACT 24-29 **% Accepted:** 96 **Admission Plans:** Early Admission; Deferred Admission **Application Deadline:** August 01 **Application Fee:** $30.00 **H.S. Requirements:** High school diploma required; GED accepted **Costs Per Year:** Application fee: $30. State resident tuition: $4523 full-time, $168 per semester hour part-time. Nonresident tuition: $11,142 full-time, $413 per semester hour part-time. Mandatory fees: $544 full-time, $20 per semester hour part-time. Full-time tuition and fees vary according to course load, location, and student level. Part-time tuition and fees vary according to course load, location, and student level. College room only: $4750. Room charges vary according to housing facility. **Scholarships:** Available **Calendar System:** Semester, Summer Session Available **Enrollment:** FT 6,813, PT 4,215, Grad 767 **Faculty:** FT 372, PT 394 **Student-Faculty Ratio:** 17:1 **Exams:** SAT I or ACT **% Receiving Financial Aid:** 58 **% Residing in College-Owned, -Operated, or -Affiliated Housing:** 6 **Library Holdings:** 479,992 **Regional Accreditation:** North Central Association of Colleges and Schools **Credit Hours For Degree:** 60 semester hours, Associates; 120 semester hours, Bachelors **Professional Accreditation:** AACSB, ABET, ADA, AHIMA, NASM, NASPAA, NCATE, NLN **Intercollegiate Athletics:** Baseball M; Basketball M & W; Cross-Country Running M & W; Soccer M & W; Softball W; Tennis M & W; Track and Field W; Volleyball M & W

INDIANA UNIVERSITY-PURDUE UNIVERSITY INDIANAPOLIS

355 North Lansing
Indianapolis, IN 46202-2896
Tel: (317)274-5555
Admissions: (317)274-4591
Fax: (317)278-1862
E-mail: apply@ses.iupui.edu
Web Site: http://www.iupui.edu/
President/CEO: Dr. Charles R. Bantz
Admissions: Michael Donahue
Financial Aid: Kathy Purvis

Type: University **Sex:** Coed **Affiliation:** Indiana University System **Scores:** 90% SAT V 400+; 91.4% SAT M 400+; 54.3% ACT 18-23; 19.2% ACT 24-29 **% Accepted:** 74 **Admission Plans:** Early Admission; Deferred Admission **Application Deadline:** June 01 **Application Fee:** $50.00 **H.S. Requirements:** High school diploma required; GED accepted **Costs Per Year:** Application fee: $50. State resident tuition: $5625 full-time, $188 per credit hour part-time. Nonresident tuition: $15,953 full-time, $532 per credit hour part-time. Mandatory fees: $594 full-time. Full-time tuition and fees vary according to course load and program. Part-time tuition varies according to course load and program. College room and board: $4740. College room only: $2340. Room and board charges vary according to board plan and housing facility. **Scholarships:** Available **Calendar System:** Semester, Summer Session Available **Enrollment:** FT 13,736, PT 7,702, Grad 5,945 **Faculty:** FT 875 **Student-Faculty Ratio:** 17:1 **Exams:** SAT I or ACT **% Receiving Financial Aid:** 60 **% Residing in College-Owned, -Operated, or -Affiliated Housing:** 2 **Library Holdings:** 1,481,216 **Regional Accreditation:** North Central Association of Colleges and Schools **Credit Hours For Degree:** 60 credit hours, Associates; 120 credit hours, Bachelors **ROTC:** Army, Navy, Air Force **Professional Accreditation:** AACSB, ABET, ACEHSA, AACN, ADA, ADtA, AHIMA, APTA, APA, ASC, ACIPE, CARC, CEPH, CSWE, JRCERT, JRCNMT, LCMEAMA, NAACLS, NASAD, NASPAA NLN **Intercollegiate Athletics:** Basketball M & W; Cross-Country Running M & W; Golf M & W; Soccer M & W; Softball W; Swimming and Diving M & W; Tennis M & W; Volleyball W

INDIANA UNIVERSITY SOUTH BEND

1700 Mishawaka Ave., PO Box 7111
South Bend, IN 46634-7111
Tel: (574)520-4872; 877-GO-2-IUSB
Admissions: (574)237-4480
Fax: (574)520-4834
Web Site: http://www.iusb.edu/
President/CEO: Dr. Una Mae Reck
Registrar: Michael Carroll
Admissions: Jeff Johnston
Financial Aid: Beverly Cooper

Type: Comprehensive **Sex:** Coed **Affiliation:** Indiana University System **Scores:** 87.85% SAT V 400+; 85.85% SAT M 400+; 57.9% ACT 18-23; 20% ACT 24-29 **% Accepted:** 88 **Admission Plans:** Deferred Admission **Application Deadline:** Rolling **Application Fee:** $43.00 **H.S. Requirements:** High school diploma required; GED accepted **Costs Per Year:** Application fee: $43. State resident tuition: $4583 full-time, $152.75 per credit hour part-time. Nonresident tuition: $12,002 full-time, $400.05 per credit hour part-time. Mandatory fees: $406 full-time. Full-time tuition and fees vary according to course load. Part-time tuition varies according to course load. **Scholarships:** Available **Calendar System:** Semester, Summer Session Available **Enrollment:** FT 3,636, PT 2,688, Grad 1,135 **Faculty:** FT 232 **Student-Faculty Ratio:** 14:1 **Exams:** SAT I or ACT **% Receiving Financial Aid:** 58 **Library Holdings:** 300,202 **Regional Accreditation:** North Central Association of Colleges and Schools **Credit Hours For Degree:** 60 credit hours, Associates; 120 credit hours, Bachelors **ROTC:** Army, Navy, Air Force **Professional Accreditation:** AACSB, AACN, ADA, CSWE, JRCERT, MACTE, NASPAA, NCATE, NLN **Intercollegiate Athletics:** Basketball M & W

INDIANA UNIVERSITY SOUTHEAST

4201 Grant Line Rd.
New Albany, IN 47150-6405
Tel: (812)941-2000
Admissions: (812)941-2212
E-mail: admissions@ius.indiana.edu
Web Site: http://www.ius.edu/
President/CEO: Dr. Sandra R. Patterson-Randles
Registrar: Janice E. Williamson
Admissions: Anne Skuce

Type: Comprehensive **Sex:** Coed **Affiliation:** Indiana University System **Scores:** 85.4% SAT V 400+; 84.8% SAT M 400+; 56.6% ACT 18-23; 14% ACT 24-29 **% Accepted:** 89 **Admission Plans:** Early Admission; Deferred Admission **Application Deadline:** Rolling **Application Fee:** $30.00 **H.S. Requirements:** High school diploma required; GED accepted **Costs Per Year:** Application fee: $30. State resident tuition: $4475 full-time, $149.15 per credit hour part-time. Nonresident tuition: $11,153 full-time, $371.75 per credit hour part-time. Mandatory fees: $405 full-time. Full-time tuition and fees vary according to course load and reciprocity agreements. Part-time tuition varies according to course load and reciprocity agreements. **Scholarships:** Available **Calendar System:** Semester, Summer Session Available **Enrollment:** FT 3,220, PT 2,080, Grad 864 **Faculty:** FT 172 **Student-Faculty Ratio:** 16:1 **Exams:** SAT I or ACT **% Receiving Financial Aid:** 58 **Library Holdings:** 215,429 **Regional Accreditation:** North Central Association of Colleges and Schools **Credit Hours For Degree:** 63 credit hours, Associates; 120 credit hours, Bachelors **ROTC:** Army, Air Force **Professional Accreditation:** AACSB, AACN, NCATE **Intercollegiate Athletics:** Baseball M; Basketball M & W; Tennis M & W; Volleyball W

INDIANA WESLEYAN UNIVERSITY

4201 South Washington St.
Marion, IN 46953-4974
Tel: (765)674-6901
Free: 800-332-6901
Admissions: (765)677-2138
Fax: (765)677-2333
E-mail: daniel.solms@indwes.edu
Web Site: http://www.indwes.edu/
President/CEO: Dr. James Barnes
Registrar: Karen Roorbach

Admissions: Daniel Solms
Financial Aid: Lois Kelly
Type: Comprehensive **Sex:** Coed **Affiliation:** Wesleyan **Scores:** 100% SAT V 400+; 97% SAT M 400+; 33% ACT 18-23; 54.1% ACT 24-29 **Admission Plans:** Deferred Admission **Application Fee:** $25.00 **H.S. Requirements:** High school diploma required; GED accepted **Costs Per Year:** Application fee: $25. Comprehensive fee: $22,074 includes full-time tuition ($16,184) and college room and board ($5890). College room only: $2800. Room and board charges vary according to board plan. Part-time tuition: $344 per credit hour. Part-time tuition varies according to course load. **Scholarships:** Available **Calendar System:** Miscellaneous, Summer Session Available **Enrollment:** FT 6,908, PT 701, Grad 3,411 **Faculty:** FT 148 **Exams:** SAT I or ACT **Library Holdings:** 110,000 **Regional Accreditation:** North Central Association of Colleges and Schools **Credit Hours For Degree:** 62 semester hours, Associates; 124 semester hours, Bachelors **Professional Accreditation:** AACN, ACA, CSWE, NASM, NCATE **Intercollegiate Athletics:** Baseball M; Basketball M & W; Cheerleading M & W; Cross-Country Running M & W; Golf M; Soccer M & W; Softball W; Tennis M & W; Track and Field M & W; Volleyball W

INTERNATIONAL BUSINESS COLLEGE (FORT WAYNE)
5699 Covington Ln.
Fort Wayne, IN 46804
Tel: (219)459-4500
Free: 800-589-6363
Admissions: (219)459-4513
Fax: (219)436-1896
Web Site: http://www.ibcfortwayne.edu/
President/CEO: Jim C. Zillman
Registrar: Cindy Rohlfing
Admissions: Steve Kinzer
Financial Aid: Roxanna Shull
Type: Two-Year College **Sex:** Coed **Affiliation:** Bradford Schools, Inc **Admission Plans:** Deferred Admission **Application Fee:** $50.00 **H.S. Requirements:** High school diploma required; GED accepted **Scholarships:** Available **Calendar System:** Semester, Summer Session Not available **Enrollment:** FT 690, PT 110 **Faculty:** FT 12, PT 36 **Student-Faculty Ratio:** 24:1 **Library Holdings:** 2,100 **Credit Hours For Degree:** 69 semester credits, Associates; 127 semester credits, Bachelors **Professional Accreditation:** ACICS, AAMAE

INTERNATIONAL BUSINESS COLLEGE (INDIANAPOLIS)
7205 Shadeland Station
Indianapolis, IN 46256
Tel: (317)841-6400
Admissions: (317)213-2320
Fax: (317)841-6419
Web Site: http://www.intlbusinesscollege.com/
President/CEO: Kathy Chiudioni
Registrar: Devon Wade
Admissions: Kathy Chiudioni
Financial Aid: Molly Pope
Type: Two-Year College **Sex:** Coed **Affiliation:** Bradford Schools, Charlotte, NC **% Accepted:** 94 **Admission Plans:** Open Admission **Application Deadline:** Rolling **Application Fee:** $50.00 **H.S. Requirements:** High school diploma required; GED accepted **Costs Per Year:** Application fee: $50. Tuition: $11,960 full-time. College room only: $6100. **Scholarships:** Available **Calendar System:** Semester **Enrollment:** FT 289 **Faculty:** FT 6, PT 9 **Student-Faculty Ratio:** 20:1 **Professional Accreditation:** ACICS

ITT TECHNICAL INSTITUTE (FORT WAYNE)
4919 Coldwater Rd.
Fort Wayne, IN 46825-5532
Tel: (219)484-4107
Free: 800-866-4488
Admissions: (260)497-6200
Web Site: http://www.itt-tech.edu/
President/CEO: Jack B. Cozad
Registrar: Willie Vaughn
Admissions: Alois Johnson
Financial Aid: Alois Johnson
Type: Two-Year College **Sex:** Coed **Affiliation:** ITT Educational Services, Inc **Admission Plans:** Deferred Admission **Application Deadline:** Rolling **Application Fee:** $100.00 **H.S. Requirements:** High school diploma required; GED accepted **Costs Per Year:** Application fee: $100. **Scholarships:** Available **Calendar System:** Quarter, Summer Session Not available **Exams:** Other **Credit Hours For Degree:** 96 credit hours, Associates; 180 credit hours, Bachelors **Professional Accreditation:** ACICS

ITT TECHNICAL INSTITUTE (INDIANAPOLIS)
9511 Angola Ct.
Indianapolis, IN 46268-1119
Tel: (317)875-8640
Free: 800-937-4488
Fax: (317)875-8641
Web Site: http://www.itt-tech.edu/
President/CEO: James Horner
Admissions: Melinda Catron
Financial Aid: Michele Hurst
Type: Two-Year College **Sex:** Coed **Affiliation:** ITT Educational Services, Inc **Admission Plans:** Deferred Admission **Application Deadline:** Rolling **Application Fee:** $100.00 **H.S. Requirements:** High school diploma required; GED accepted **Costs Per Year:** Application fee: $100. **Scholarships:** Available **Calendar System:** Quarter, Summer Session Not available **Exams:** Other **Credit Hours For Degree:** 96 credit hours, Associates; 180 credit hours, Bachelors **Professional Accreditation:** ACICS

ITT TECHNICAL INSTITUTE (NEWBURGH)
10999 Stahl Rd.
Newburgh, IN 47630-7430
Tel: (812)858-1600
Web Site: http://www.itt-tech.edu/
President/CEO: Kenneth E. Butler
Registrar: Diana Hamer
Admissions: Kenneth Butler
Financial Aid: Cathy Lynn
Type: Two-Year College **Sex:** Coed **Affiliation:** ITT Educational Services, Inc **Admission Plans:** Deferred Admission **Application Deadline:** Rolling **Application Fee:** $100.00 **H.S. Requirements:** High school diploma required; GED accepted **Costs Per Year:** Application fee: $100. **Scholarships:** Available **Calendar System:** Quarter, Summer Session Not available **Exams:** Other **Credit Hours For Degree:** 96 credit hours, Associates; 180 credit hours, Bachelors **Professional Accreditation:** ACICS

IVY TECH COMMUNITY COLLEGE-BLOOMINGTON
3116 Canterbury Ct.
Bloomington, IN 47404
Tel: (812)332-1559
Admissions: (812)330-6026
Fax: (812)332-8147
E-mail: nfrederi@ivytech.edu
Web Site: http://www.ivytech.edu/
Admissions: Neil Frederick
Type: Two-Year College **Sex:** Coed **Affiliation:** Ivy Tech State College System **% Accepted:** 100 **Admission Plans:** Open Admission; Preferred Admission; Deferred Admission **Application Deadline:** Rolling **Application Fee:** $0.00 **Costs Per Year:** Application fee: $0. State resident tuition: $2520 full-time, $83.95 per credit part-time. Nonresident tuition: $5108 full-time, $170.25 per credit part-time. Mandatory fees: $70 full-time, $35 per term part-time. **Scholarships:** Available **Calendar System:** Semester, Summer Session Available **Enrollment:** FT 1,639, PT 1,926 **Faculty:** FT 48, PT 227 **Library Holdings:** 5,516 **Regional Accreditation:** North Central Association of Colleges and Schools **Credit Hours For Degree:** 60 credits, Associates **Professional Accreditation:** ACBSP, NLN

IVY TECH COMMUNITY COLLEGE-CENTRAL INDIANA
50 W. Fall Creek Parkway North Dr.
Indianapolis, IN 46208
Tel: (317)921-4800; 888-IVYLINE
Admissions: (317)921-4371
E-mail: tfunk@ivytech.edu
Web Site: http://www.ivytech.edu/
President/CEO: Dr. Meredith L. Carter
Registrar: Jane Paterson-Smith
Admissions: Tracy Funk
Financial Aid: Mildred Williamson
Type: Two-Year College **Sex:** Coed **% Accepted:** 100 **Admission Plans:** Open Admission; Preferred Admission; Early Admission; Deferred Admission **Application Deadline:** Rolling **Application Fee:** $0.00 **H.S. Requirements:** High school diploma or equivalent not required. For allied health programs-

high school diploma or GED required: High school diploma required; GED accepted **Costs Per Year:** Application fee: $0. State resident tuition: $2520 full-time, $83.95 per credit part-time. Nonresident tuition: $5108 full-time, $170.25 per credit part-time. Mandatory fees: $70 full-time, $35 per term part-time. **Scholarships:** Available **Calendar System:** Semester, Summer Session Available **Enrollment:** FT 3,581, PT 8,009 **Faculty:** FT 137, PT 525 **Library Holdings:** 20,247 **Regional Accreditation:** North Central Association of Colleges and Schools **Credit Hours For Degree:** 60 credits, Associates **Professional Accreditation:** ARCEST, AAMAE, ACF, ACBSP, CARC, JRCERT, NAIT, NLN

IVY TECH COMMUNITY COLLEGE-COLUMBUS
4475 Central Ave.
Columbus, IN 47203-1868
Tel: (812)372-9925
Free: 800-922-4838
Fax: (812)372-0311
E-mail: nbagadio@ivytech.edu
Web Site: http://www.ivytech.edu/
President/CEO: Dr. John A. Hogan, PhD
Registrar: Kathleen G. Adams
Admissions: Neil Bagadiong
Financial Aid: Douglas Hess
Type: Two-Year College **Sex:** Coed **Affiliation:** Ivy Tech State College System **% Accepted:** 100 **Admission Plans:** Open Admission; Preferred Admission; Early Admission; Deferred Admission **Application Deadline:** Rolling **Application Fee:** $0.00 **H.S. Requirements:** High school diploma or equivalent not required. For allied health programs: High school diploma required; GED accepted **Costs Per Year:** Application fee: $0. State resident tuition: $2520 full-time, $83.95 per credit part-time. Nonresident tuition: $5108 full-time, $170.25 per credit part-time. Mandatory fees: $70 full-time, $35 per term part-time. **Scholarships:** Available **Calendar System:** Semester, Summer Session Available **Enrollment:** FT 777, PT 1,439 **Faculty:** FT 39, PT 154 **Library Holdings:** 7,855 **Regional Accreditation:** North Central Association of Colleges and Schools **Credit Hours For Degree:** 60 credits, Associates **Professional Accreditation:** ARCEST, AAMAE, ADA, ACBSP

IVY TECH COMMUNITY COLLEGE-EAST CENTRAL
4301 South Cowan Rd., PO Box 3100
Muncie, IN 47302-9448
Tel: (765)289-2291
E-mail: mlewelle@ivytech.edu
Web Site: http://www.ivytech.edu/
President/CEO: Dr. J. Robert Jeffs
Registrar: Mary Lewellen
Admissions: Mary Lewellen
Financial Aid: Sylvia Bogle
Type: Two-Year College **Sex:** Coed **Affiliation:** Ivy Tech State College System **% Accepted:** 100 **Admission Plans:** Open Admission; Preferred Admission; Early Admission; Deferred Admission **Application Deadline:** Rolling **Application Fee:** $0.00 **H.S. Requirements:** High school diploma or equivalent not required. For allied health programs: High school diploma required; GED accepted **Costs Per Year:** Application fee: $0. State resident tuition: $2520 full-time, $83.95 per credit part-time. Nonresident tuition: $5108 full-time, $170.25 per credit part-time. Mandatory fees: $70 full-time, $35 per term part-time. **Scholarships:** Available **Calendar System:** Semester, Summer Session Not available **Enrollment:** FT 2,551, PT 3,392 **Faculty:** FT 87, PT 358 **Library Holdings:** 5,779 **Regional Accreditation:** North Central Association of Colleges and Schools **Credit Hours For Degree:** 60 credits, Associates **Professional Accreditation:** ARCEST, AAMAE, APTA, ACBSP

IVY TECH COMMUNITY COLLEGE-KOKOMO
1815 East Morgan St, PO Box 1373
Kokomo, IN 46903-1373
Tel: (765)459-0561
E-mail: acook@ivytech.edu
Web Site: http://www.ivytech.edu/
President/CEO: Stephen J. Daily
Registrar: Patricia Dzierla
Admissions: Alayne Cook
Financial Aid: Julie Ward
Type: Two-Year College **Sex:** Coed **Affiliation:** Ivy Tech State College System **% Accepted:** 100 **Admission Plans:** Open Admission; Preferred Admission; Early Admission **Application Deadline:** Rolling **Application Fee:** $0.00 **H.S. Requirements:** High school diploma or equivalent not required. For allied health programs: High school diploma required; GED accepted **Costs Per Year:** Application fee: $0. State resident tuition: $2520 full-time, $83.95 per credit part-time. Nonresident tuition: $5108 full-time, $170.25 per credit part-time. Mandatory fees: $70 full-time, $35 per term part-time. **Scholarships:** Available **Calendar System:** Semester, Summer Session Available **Enrollment:** FT 1,031, PT 2,217 **Faculty:** FT 58, PT 197 **Library Holdings:** 5,177 **Regional Accreditation:** North Central Association of Colleges and Schools **Credit Hours For Degree:** 60 credits, Associates **Professional Accreditation:** AAMAE, ACBSP

IVY TECH COMMUNITY COLLEGE-LAFAYETTE
3101 South Creasy Ln.
Lafayette, IN 47905-5266
Tel: (765)772-9100
Admissions: (765)772-9116
E-mail: jdoppelf@ivytech.edu
Web Site: http://www.ivytech.edu/
President/CEO: Dr. Elizabeth J. Doversberger
Registrar: Ron Israel
Admissions: Judy Dopplefeld
Financial Aid: Kirsten Reynolds
Type: Two-Year College **Sex:** Coed **Affiliation:** Ivy Tech State College System **% Accepted:** 100 **Admission Plans:** Open Admission; Preferred Admission **Application Deadline:** Rolling **Application Fee:** $0.00 **H.S. Requirements:** High school diploma or equivalent not required. For allied health programs: High school diploma required; GED accepted **Costs Per Year:** Application fee: $0. State resident tuition: $2520 full-time, $83.95 per credit part-time. Nonresident tuition: $5108 full-time, $170.25 per credit part-time. Mandatory fees: $70 full-time, $35 per term part-time. **Scholarships:** Available **Calendar System:** Semester, Summer Session Available **Enrollment:** FT 2,374, PT 3,596 **Faculty:** FT 64, PT 261 **Library Holdings:** 8,043 **Regional Accreditation:** North Central Association of Colleges and Schools **Credit Hours For Degree:** 60 credits, Associates **Professional Accreditation:** ARCEST, AAMAE, ADA, ACBSP, CARC, NAIT, NLN

IVY TECH COMMUNITY COLLEGE-NORTH CENTRAL
220 Dean Johnson Blvd.
South Bend, IN 46601
Tel: (574)289-7001
Fax: (574)236-7181
E-mail: pdecker@ivytech.edu
Web Site: http://www.ivytech.edu/
President/CEO: Dr. Virginia B. Calvin
Registrar: Ed Grams
Admissions: Pam Decker
Financial Aid: Jeff Fisher
Type: Two-Year College **Sex:** Coed **Affiliation:** Ivy Tech State College System **% Accepted:** 100 **Admission Plans:** Open Admission; Preferred Admission; Early Admission; Deferred Admission **Application Deadline:** Rolling **Application Fee:** $0.00 **H.S. Requirements:** High school diploma or equivalent not required. For allied health programs: High school diploma required; GED accepted **Costs Per Year:** Application fee: $0. State resident tuition: $2520 full-time, $83.95 per credit part-time. Nonresident tuition: $5108 full-time, $170.25 per credit part-time. Mandatory fees: $70 full-time, $35 per term part-time. **Scholarships:** Available **Calendar System:** Semester, Summer Session Available **Enrollment:** FT 1,225, PT 4,003 **Faculty:** FT 72, PT 239 **Library Holdings:** 6,246 **Regional Accreditation:** North Central Association of Colleges and Schools **Credit Hours For Degree:** 60 credits, Associates **Professional Accreditation:** AAMAE, ACF, ACBSP, NAACLS, NLN

IVY TECH COMMUNITY COLLEGE-NORTHEAST
3800 North Anthony Blvd.
Fort Wayne, IN 46805-1430
Tel: (260)482-9171
Free: 800-859-4882
Admissions: (260)480-4221
Fax: (260)480-4177
E-mail: sscheer@ivytech.edu
Web Site: http://www.ivytech.edu/
President/CEO: Jon L. Rupright
Registrar: Suzanne Ashton

Admissions: Steve Scheer
Financial Aid: Tom Liggett
Type: Two-Year College **Sex:** Coed **Affiliation:** Ivy Tech State College System **% Accepted:** 100 **Admission Plans:** Open Admission; Preferred Admission; Early Admission **Application Deadline:** Rolling **Application Fee:** $0.00 **H.S. Requirements:** High school diploma or equivalent not required. For allied health programs: High school diploma required; GED accepted **Costs Per Year:** Application fee: $0. State resident tuition: $2520 full-time, $83.95 per credit part-time. Nonresident tuition: $5108 full-time, $170.25 per credit part-time. Mandatory fees: $70 full-time, $35 per term part-time. **Scholarships:** Available **Calendar System:** Semester, Summer Session Available **Enrollment:** FT 2,120, PT 3,962 **Faculty:** FT 87, PT 348 **Library Holdings:** 18,389 **Regional Accreditation:** North Central Association of Colleges and Schools **Credit Hours For Degree:** 60 credits, Associates **Professional Accreditation:** AAMAE, ACF, ACBSP, CARC, NAIT

IVY TECH COMMUNITY COLLEGE-NORTHWEST
1440 East 35th Ave.
Gary, IN 46409-1499
Tel: (219)981-1111
E-mail: tlewis@ivytech.edu
Web Site: http://www.ivytech.edu/
President/CEO: J. Guadalupe Valtierra
Registrar: Carol Bowron
Admissions: Twilla Lewis
Financial Aid: Barbara Jerzyk
Type: Two-Year College **Sex:** Coed **Affiliation:** Ivy Tech State College System **% Accepted:** 100 **Admission Plans:** Open Admission; Preferred Admission; Deferred Admission **Application Deadline:** Rolling **Application Fee:** $0.00 **H.S. Requirements:** High school diploma or equivalent not required. For allied health programs: High school diploma required; GED accepted **Costs Per Year:** Application fee: $0. State resident tuition: $2520 full-time, $83.95 per credit part-time. Nonresident tuition: $5108 full-time, $170.25 per credit part-time. Mandatory fees: $70 full-time, $35 per term part-time. **Scholarships:** Available **Calendar System:** Semester, Summer Session Available **Enrollment:** FT 1,395, PT 3,420 **Faculty:** FT 91, PT 328 **Library Holdings:** 13,805 **Regional Accreditation:** North Central Association of Colleges and Schools **Credit Hours For Degree:** 60 credits, Associates **Professional Accreditation:** ARCEST, AAMAE, ACF, APTA, ACBSP, CARC

IVY TECH COMMUNITY COLLEGE-SOUTHEAST
590 Ivy Tech Dr., PO Box 209
Madison, IN 47250-1883
Tel: (812)265-4028
Admissions: (812)265-2580
E-mail: chutcher@ivytech.edu
Web Site: http://www.ivytech.edu/
President/CEO: Homer B. Smith
Registrar: Kevin Bradley
Admissions: Cindy Hutcherson
Financial Aid: Richard Hill
Type: Two-Year College **Sex:** Coed **Affiliation:** Ivy Tech State College System **% Accepted:** 100 **Admission Plans:** Open Admission; Preferred Admission **Application Deadline:** Rolling **Application Fee:** $0.00 **H.S. Requirements:** High school diploma or equivalent not required. For allied health programs-high school diploma or GED required: High school diploma required; GED accepted **Costs Per Year:** Application fee: $0. State resident tuition: $2520 full-time, $83.95 per credit part-time. Nonresident tuition: $5108 full-time, $170.25 per credit part-time. Mandatory fees: $70 full-time, $35 per term part-time. **Scholarships:** Available **Calendar System:** Semester, Summer Session Available **Enrollment:** FT 630, PT 1,136 **Faculty:** FT 35, PT 113 **Library Holdings:** 9,027 **Regional Accreditation:** North Central Association of Colleges and Schools **Credit Hours For Degree:** 60 credits, Associates **Professional Accreditation:** ACBSP

IVY TECH COMMUNITY COLLEGE-SOUTHERN INDIANA
8204 Hwy. 311
Sellersburg, IN 47172-1829
Tel: (812)246-3301
E-mail: msteinba@ivytech.edu
Web Site: http://www.ivytech.edu/
President/CEO: Ty Handy
Registrar: Vicki L. Stoffregen
Admissions: Mindy Steinberg
Financial Aid: Gary L. Cottrill
Type: Two-Year College **Sex:** Coed **Affiliation:** Ivy Tech State College System **% Accepted:** 100 **Admission Plans:** Open Admission; Preferred Admission; Early Admission; Deferred Admission **Application Deadline:** Rolling **Application Fee:** $0.00 **H.S. Requirements:** High school diploma or equivalent not required. For allied health programs-high school diploma or GED required: High school diploma required; GED accepted **Costs Per Year:** Application fee: $0. State resident tuition: $2520 full-time, $83.95 per credit part-time. Nonresident tuition: $5108 full-time, $170.25 per credit part-time. Mandatory fees: $70 full-time, $35 per term part-time. **Scholarships:** Available **Calendar System:** Semester, Summer Session Available **Enrollment:** FT 904, PT 2,208 **Faculty:** FT 47, PT 126 **Library Holdings:** 7,634 **Regional Accreditation:** North Central Association of Colleges and Schools **Credit Hours For Degree:** 60 credits, Associates **Professional Accreditation:** AAMAE, ACBSP, NAIT

IVY TECH COMMUNITY COLLEGE-SOUTHWEST
3501 First Ave.
Evansville, IN 47710-3398
Tel: (812)426-2865
Admissions: (812)429-1430
E-mail: ajohnson@ivytech.edu
Web Site: http://www.ivytech.edu/
President/CEO: Dr. Daniel L. Schenk
Registrar: Helen Finke
Admissions: Denise Johnson-Kincaid
Financial Aid: Lois Rini
Type: Two-Year College **Sex:** Coed **Affiliation:** Ivy Tech State College System **% Accepted:** 100 **Admission Plans:** Open Admission; Preferred Admission; Early Admission; Deferred Admission **Application Deadline:** Rolling **Application Fee:** $0.00 **H.S. Requirements:** High school diploma or equivalent not required. For allied health programs-high school diploma or GED required: High school diploma required; GED accepted **Costs Per Year:** Application fee: $0. State resident tuition: $2520 full-time, $83.95 per credit part-time. Nonresident tuition: $5108 full-time, $170.25 per credit part-time. Mandatory fees: $70 full-time, $35 per term part-time. **Scholarships:** Available **Calendar System:** Semester, Summer Session Available **Enrollment:** FT 1,526, PT 3,332 **Faculty:** FT 71, PT 237 **Library Holdings:** 7,082 **Regional Accreditation:** North Central Association of Colleges and Schools **Credit Hours For Degree:** 60 credits, Associates **Professional Accreditation:** ARCEST, AAMAE, ACBSP, JRCEMT, NAIT, NLN

IVY TECH COMMUNITY COLLEGE-WABASH VALLEY
7999 US Hwy. 41, South
Terre Haute, IN 47802
Tel: (812)299-1121
Admissions: (812)298-2300
E-mail: mfisher@ivytech.edu
Web Site: http://www.ivytech.edu/
President/CEO: Jeff Pittman
Registrar: Leslie King
Admissions: Michael Fisher
Financial Aid: Julie Wonderlin
Type: Two-Year College **Sex:** Coed **Affiliation:** Ivy Tech State College System **% Accepted:** 100 **Admission Plans:** Open Admission; Preferred Admission; Early Admission; Deferred Admission **Application Deadline:** Rolling **Application Fee:** $0.00 **H.S. Requirements:** High school diploma or equivalent not required. For allied health programs: High school diploma required; GED accepted **Costs Per Year:** Application fee: $0. State resident tuition: $2520 full-time, $83.95 per credit part-time. Nonresident tuition: $5180 full-time, $170.25 per credit part-time. Mandatory fees: $70 full-time, $35 per term part-time. **Scholarships:** Available **Calendar System:** Semester, Summer Session Available **Enrollment:** FT 2,169, PT 2,823 **Faculty:** FT 78, PT 235 **Library Holdings:** 4,403 **Regional Accreditation:** North Central Association of Colleges and Schools **Credit Hours For Degree:** 60 credits, Associates **Professional Accreditation:** ARCEST, AAMAE, ACBSP, JRCERT, NAACLS, NAIT

IVY TECH COMMUNITY COLLEGE-WHITEWATER
2325 Chester Blvd.
Richmond, IN 47374-1220
Tel: (765)966-2656
E-mail: jplaster@ivytech.edu
Web Site: http://www.ivytech.edu/

President/CEO: James Steck
Registrar: Valerie Ray
Admissions: Jeff Plasterer
Financial Aid: Ann Franzen-Roha
Type: Two-Year College **Sex:** Coed **Affiliation:** Ivy Tech State College System **% Accepted:** 100 **Admission Plans:** Open Admission; Preferred Admission; Early Admission **Application Deadline:** Rolling **Application Fee:** $0.00 **H.S. Requirements:** High school diploma or equivalent not required. For allied health programs-high school diploma or GED required: High school diploma required; GED accepted **Costs Per Year:** Application fee: $0. State resident tuition: $2520 full-time, $83.95 per credit part-time. Nonresident tuition: $15,108 full-time, $170.25 per credit part-time. Mandatory fees: $70 full-time, $35 per term part-time. **Scholarships:** Available **Calendar System:** Semester, Summer Session Available **Enrollment:** FT 570, PT 1,262 **Faculty:** FT 29, PT 146 **Regional Accreditation:** North Central Association of Colleges and Schools **Credit Hours For Degree:** 60 credits, Associates **Professional Accreditation:** AAMAE, ACBSP, NAIT, NLN

LINCOLN TECHNICAL INSTITUTE
1201 Stadium Dr.
Indianapolis, IN 46202-2194
Tel: (317)632-5553
Free: 800-554-4465
Web Site: http://www.lincolntech.com/
President/CEO: Carlos Llarena
Registrar: Stephanie Miller
Admissions: Cindy Ryan
Financial Aid: Mary Funke
Type: Two-Year College **Sex:** Coed **Affiliation:** Lincoln Technical Institute, Inc **H.S. Requirements:** High school diploma required; GED accepted **Scholarships:** Available **Calendar System:** Miscellaneous, Summer Session Available **Faculty:** FT 18, PT 2 **Library Holdings:** 800 **Credit Hours For Degree:** 59 credits, Associates **Professional Accreditation:** ACCSCT

MANCHESTER COLLEGE
604 East College Ave.
North Manchester, IN 46962-1225
Tel: (260)982-5000
Free: 800-852-3648
Admissions: (260)982-5055
Fax: (260)982-5043
E-mail: admitinfo@manchester.edu
Web Site: http://www.manchester.edu/
President/CEO: Dr. Parker G. Marden
Registrar: Lila D. Hammer
Admissions: Jolane Rohr
Financial Aid: Gina Voelz
Type: Comprehensive **Sex:** Coed **Affiliation:** Church of the Brethren **Scores:** 94.12% SAT V 400+; 94.12% SAT M 400+; 47.06% ACT 18-23; 30.25% ACT 24-29 **% Accepted:** 73 **Admission Plans:** Deferred Admission **Application Deadline:** Rolling **Application Fee:** $25.00 **H.S. Requirements:** High school diploma required; GED accepted **Costs Per Year:** Application fee: $25. Tuition: $19,800 full-time, $670 per credit hour part-time. Mandatory fees: $700 full-time. College room only: $4500. **Scholarships:** Available **Calendar System:** 4-1-4, Summer Session Available **Enrollment:** FT 1,056, PT 38, Grad 10 **Faculty:** FT 68, PT 21 **Student-Faculty Ratio:** 14:1 **Exams:** SAT I or ACT **% Receiving Financial Aid:** 85 **% Residing in College-Owned, -Operated, or -Affiliated Housing:** 74 **Regional Accreditation:** North Central Association of Colleges and Schools **Credit Hours For Degree:** 64 semester hours, Associates; 128 semester hours, Bachelors **Professional Accreditation:** CSWE, JRCEPAT, NCATE **Intercollegiate Athletics:** Baseball M; Basketball M & W; Cheerleading M & W; Cross-Country Running M & W; Football M; Golf M & W; Soccer M & W; Softball W; Tennis M & W; Track and Field M & W; Volleyball W; Wrestling M

MARIAN COLLEGE
3200 Cold Spring Rd.
Indianapolis, IN 46222-1997
Tel: (317)955-6000
Admissions: (317)955-6300
Web Site: http://www.marian.edu/
President/CEO: Daniel J. Elsener
Registrar: John A. Hill
Admissions: Steve Bushouse
Financial Aid: John E. Shelton
Type: Comprehensive **Sex:** Coed **Affiliation:** Roman Catholic **Scores:** 94% SAT V 400+; 95% SAT M 400+; 66% ACT 18-23; 24% ACT 24-29 **Admission Plans:** Early Admission; Deferred Admission **Application Fee:** $20.00 **H.S. Requirements:** High school diploma required; GED accepted **Costs Per Year:** Application fee: $20. Comprehensive fee: $25,360 includes full-time tuition ($18,400), mandatory fees ($660), and college room and board ($6300). Full-time tuition and fees vary according to class time and course load. Room and board charges vary according to board plan and housing facility. Part-time tuition: $780 per credit hour. Part-time tuition varies according to class time and course load. **Scholarships:** Available **Calendar System:** Semester, Summer Session Available **Enrollment:** FT 1,091, PT 575, Grad 19 **Faculty:** FT 70, PT 75 **Student-Faculty Ratio:** 13:1 **Exams:** SAT I or ACT **% Receiving Financial Aid:** 79 **% Residing in College-Owned, -Operated, or -Affiliated Housing:** 40 **Library Holdings:** 132,000 **Regional Accreditation:** North Central Association of Colleges and Schools **Credit Hours For Degree:** 64 credit hours, Associates; 128 credit hours, Bachelors **ROTC:** Army **Professional Accreditation:** NCATE, NLN **Intercollegiate Athletics:** Baseball M; Basketball M & W; Cheerleading M & W; Cross-Country Running M & W; Golf M & W; Soccer M & W; Softball W; Tennis M & W; Track and Field M & W; Volleyball W

MARTIN UNIVERSITY
2171 Avondale Place, PO Box 18567
Indianapolis, IN 46218-3867
Tel: (317)543-3235
Admissions: (317)543-3237
Fax: (317)543-3257
Web Site: http://www.martin.edu/
President/CEO: Rev. Fr. Boniface Hardin
Registrar: Bobbi Smith
Admissions: Brenda Shaheed
Financial Aid: Mason Morton
Type: Comprehensive **Sex:** Coed **Admission Plans:** Open Admission; Early Admission; Deferred Admission **Application Fee:** $25.00 **H.S. Requirements:** High school diploma required; GED accepted **Costs Per Year:** Application fee: $25. Tuition: $11,100 full-time, $370 per credit part-time. Mandatory fees: $320 full-time, $160 per term part-time. **Scholarships:** Available **Calendar System:** Semester, Summer Session Available **Enrollment:** FT 219, PT 246, Grad 106 **Faculty:** FT 32, PT 6 **Student-Faculty Ratio:** 20:1 **Exams:** Other **% Receiving Financial Aid:** 83 **Regional Accreditation:** North Central Association of Colleges and Schools **Credit Hours For Degree:** 134 credits, Bachelors

MID-AMERICA COLLEGE OF FUNERAL SERVICE
3111 Hamburg Pike
Jeffersonville, IN 47130-9630
Tel: (812)288-8878
Free: 800-221-6158
Web Site: http://www.mid-america.edu/
President/CEO: John R. Braboy
Registrar: Nancy Merriwether
Admissions: Kimberly Kendall
Financial Aid: Richard Nelson
Type: Two-Year College **Sex:** Coed **Admission Plans:** Open Admission; Deferred Admission **Application Fee:** $25.00 **H.S. Requirements:** High school diploma required; GED accepted **Scholarships:** Available **Calendar System:** Quarter, Summer Session Not available **Enrollment:** FT 120 **Faculty:** FT 6, PT 1 **Student-Faculty Ratio:** 13:1 **Library Holdings:** 1,500 **Credit Hours For Degree:** 133 quarter hours, Associates **Professional Accreditation:** ABFSE **Intercollegiate Athletics:** Softball M & W

OAKLAND CITY UNIVERSITY
138 North Lucretia St.
Oakland City, IN 47660-1099
Tel: (812)749-4781
Free: 800-737-5125
Admissions: (812)749-1222
Fax: (812)749-1233
Web Site: http://www.oak.edu/
President/CEO: Dr. James W. Murray
Registrar: Betty Burns
Admissions: Brian Baker

Financial Aid: Caren K. Richeson
Type: Comprehensive **Sex:** Coed **Affiliation:** General Baptist **Scores:** 83% SAT V 400+; 92.5% SAT M 400+; 52% ACT 18-23; 10% ACT 24-29 **Admission Plans:** Early Admission; Deferred Admission **Application Deadline:** Rolling **Application Fee:** $35.00 **H.S. Requirements:** High school diploma required; GED accepted **Costs Per Year:** Application fee: $35. Comprehensive fee: $19,620 includes full-time tuition ($13,860), mandatory fees ($360), and college room and board ($5400). College room only: $1760. Part-time tuition: $462 per hour. Part-time mandatory fees: $15 per hour. **Scholarships:** Available **Calendar System:** Semester, Summer Session Available **Enrollment:** FT 1,275, PT 291, Grad 319 **Faculty:** FT 19, PT 164 **Student-Faculty Ratio:** 14:1 **Exams:** SAT I or ACT **% Residing in College-Owned, -Operated, or -Affiliated Housing:** 49 **Library Holdings:** 87,724 **Regional Accreditation:** North Central Association of Colleges and Schools **Credit Hours For Degree:** 64 semester hours, Associates; 128 semester hours, Bachelors **Professional Accreditation:** ATS, NCATE **Intercollegiate Athletics:** Baseball M; Basketball M & W; Cross-Country Running M & W; Golf M & W; Soccer M & W; Softball W; Tennis M & W; Volleyball W

PROFESSIONAL CAREERS INSTITUTE

7302 Woodland Dr.
Indianapolis, IN 46278
Tel: (317)299-6001
Web Site: http://www.pcicareers.com/
President/CEO: Richard Weiss
Registrar: Phyllis A. Robbins
Admissions: Paulette M. Clay
Financial Aid: Sonya Derf
Type: Two-Year College **Sex:** Coed **Application Fee:** $100.00 **H.S. Requirements:** High school diploma required; GED accepted **Scholarships:** Available **Enrollment:** FT 469 **Faculty:** FT 29, PT 10 **Student-Faculty Ratio:** 12:1 **Professional Accreditation:** ACCSCT, ADA

PURDUE UNIVERSITY

West Lafayette, IN 47907
Tel: (765)494-4600
Admissions: (765)494-1776
Fax: (765)494-0544
E-mail: admissions@adms.purdue.edu
Web Site: http://www.purdue.edu/
President/CEO: Dr. Martin C. Jischke
Registrar: Debra Kay Sheets
Admissions: Dr. Douglas Christiansen
Financial Aid: Joyce Hall
Type: University **Sex:** Coed **Affiliation:** Purdue University System **Scores:** 98% SAT V 400+; 99% SAT M 400+; 32% ACT 18-23; 52% ACT 24-29 **% Accepted:** 85 **Admission Plans:** Early Admission; Deferred Admission **Application Deadline:** March 01 **Application Fee:** $30.00 **H.S. Requirements:** High school diploma required; GED accepted **Costs Per Year:** Application fee: $30. State resident tuition: $7096 full-time, $254.15 per credit part-time. Nonresident tuition: $21,266 full-time, $706.25 per credit part-time. **Scholarships:** Available **Calendar System:** Semester, Summer Session Available **Enrollment:** FT 29,196, PT 1,679, Grad 6,932 **Faculty:** FT 1,960, PT 333 **Student-Faculty Ratio:** 14:1 **Exams:** SAT I or ACT **% Receiving Financial Aid:** 41 **% Residing in College-Owned, -Operated, or -Affiliated Housing:** 34 **Library Holdings:** 2,430,566 **Regional Accreditation:** North Central Association of Colleges and Schools **Credit Hours For Degree:** 63 semester hours, Associates; 126 semester hours, Bachelors **ROTC:** Army, Navy, Air Force **Professional Accreditation:** AACSB, ABET, AAMFT, AACN, AAFCS, ACCE, ACPhE, ACA, ADtA, APA, ASLA, ASLHA, AVMA, CAA, FIDER, JRCEPAT, NAIT, NAST, NCATE, NLN SAF **Intercollegiate Athletics:** Baseball M; Basketball M & W; Cross-Country Running M & W; Football M; Golf M & W; Soccer W; Softball W; Swimming and Diving M & W; Tennis M & W; Track and Field M & W; Volleyball W; Wrestling M

PURDUE UNIVERSITY CALUMET

2200 169th St.
Hammond, IN 46323-2094
Tel: (219)989-2400
Admissions: (219)989-2213
Fax: (219)989-2775
E-mail: mcguinn@calumet.purdue.edu
Web Site: http://www.calumet.purdue.edu/
President/CEO: Dr. Howard Cohen
Admissions: Paul McGuinness
Financial Aid: Mary Ann Bishel
Type: Comprehensive **Sex:** Coed **Scores:** 74.8% SAT V 400+; 74.07% SAT M 400+ **% Accepted:** 80 **Admission Plans:** Early Admission **Application Deadline:** Rolling **Application Fee:** $0.00 **H.S. Requirements:** High school diploma required; GED accepted **Costs Per Year:** Application fee: $0. State resident tuition: $4368 full-time, $156 per credit hour part-time. Nonresident tuition: $10,260 full-time, $366 per credit hour part-time. Mandatory fees: $346 full-time, $14.80 per credit hour part-time. Full-time tuition and fees vary according to program. Part-time tuition and fees vary according to course load and program. College room only: $3990. Room charges vary according to housing facility. **Scholarships:** Available **Calendar System:** Semester, Summer Session Available **Enrollment:** FT 5,029, PT 3,330, Grad 943 **Faculty:** FT 270, PT 201 **Student-Faculty Ratio:** 19:1 **Exams:** SAT I or ACT **% Receiving Financial Aid:** 47 **% Residing in College-Owned, -Operated, or -Affiliated Housing:** 0 **Library Holdings:** 269,648 **Regional Accreditation:** North Central Association of Colleges and Schools **Credit Hours For Degree:** 61 credit hours, Associates; 120 credit hours, Bachelors **ROTC:** Army **Professional Accreditation:** ABET, AAMFT, NCATE, NLN **Intercollegiate Athletics:** Basketball M & W

PURDUE UNIVERSITY NORTH CENTRAL

1401 South US Hwy. 421
Westville, IN 46391-9542
Tel: (219)785-5200
Admissions: (219)785-5283
Fax: (219)785-5538
Web Site: http://www.pnc.edu/
President/CEO: James B. Dworkin
Registrar: George M. Royster
Admissions: Cathy Buckman
Financial Aid: Gerald L. Lewis
Type: Comprehensive **Sex:** Coed **Affiliation:** Purdue University System **Scores:** 89% SAT V 400+; 84% SAT M 400+; 57% ACT 18-23; 18% ACT 24-29 **% Accepted:** 96 **Admission Plans:** Early Admission **Application Deadline:** August 06 **H.S. Requirements:** High school diploma required; GED accepted **Costs Per Year:** State resident tuition: $5195 full-time, $173 per credit hour part-time. Nonresident tuition: $11,817 full-time, $407 per credit hour part-time. Mandatory fees: $388 full-time, $8.30 per credit hour part-time. **Scholarships:** Available **Calendar System:** Semester, Summer Session Available **Enrollment:** FT 2,053, PT 1,434, Grad 32 **Faculty:** FT 103, PT 150 **Student-Faculty Ratio:** 17:1 **Exams:** ACT, SAT I or ACT, SAT I **% Receiving Financial Aid:** 53 **Library Holdings:** 87,675 **Regional Accreditation:** North Central Association of Colleges and Schools **Credit Hours For Degree:** 60 credit hours, Associates; 123 credit hours, Bachelors **Professional Accreditation:** ABET, ACBSP, NLN **Intercollegiate Athletics:** Cheerleading M & W; Softball W

ROSE-HULMAN INSTITUTE OF TECHNOLOGY

5500 Wabash Ave.
Terre Haute, IN 47803-3999
Tel: (812)877-1511
Free: 800-248-7448
Admissions: (812)877-8213
Fax: (812)877-8941
E-mail: admis.ofc@rose-hulman.edu
Web Site: http://www.rose-hulman.edu/
President/CEO: Dr. John J. Midgley
Registrar: Timothy J. Prickel
Admissions: James Goecker
Financial Aid: Melinda L. Middleton
Type: Comprehensive **Sex:** Coed **Scores:** 100% SAT V 400+; 100% SAT M 400+; 7.2% ACT 18-23; 46% ACT 24-29 **% Accepted:** 69 **Admission Plans:** Deferred Admission **Application Deadline:** March 01 **Application Fee:** $40.00 **H.S. Requirements:** High school diploma required; GED not accepted **Costs Per Year:** Application fee: $40. Comprehensive fee: $34,557 includes full-time tuition ($26,688), mandatory fees ($450), and college room and board ($7419). College room only: $4236. Full-time tuition and fees vary according to course load. Room and board charges vary according to board plan. Part-time tuition: $768 per credit. Part-time tuition varies according to course load. **Scholarships:** Available **Calendar System:** Quarter, Summer Session Available **Enrollment:** FT 1,766, PT 9, Grad 112 **Faculty:** FT 148, PT 9 **Student-Faculty Ratio:** 12:1 **Exams:** SAT I or ACT **% Receiving Financial Aid:** 69 **% Residing in College-Owned, -Operated, or -Affiliated Housing:** 57 **Library Holdings:** 77,839 **Regional Accredita-**

tion: North Central Association of Colleges and Schools **Credit Hours For Degree:** 188 quarter hours, Bachelors **ROTC:** Army, Air Force **Professional Accreditation:** ABET **Intercollegiate Athletics:** Baseball M; Basketball M & W; Cheerleading M & W; Cross-Country Running M & W; Football M; Golf M & W; Riflery M & W; Soccer M & W; Softball W; Swimming and Diving M & W; Tennis M & W; Track and Field M & W; Volleyball W; Wrestling M

SAINT JOSEPH'S COLLEGE
U.S. Hwy. 231, PO Box 890
Rensselaer, IN 47978
Tel: (219)866-6000
Free: 800-447-8781
Admissions: (219)866-6170
Fax: (219)866-6122
E-mail: admissions@saintjoe.edu
Web Site: http://www.saintjoe.edu/
President/CEO: Dr. Ernest Mills, III
Registrar: Maureen Healey
Admissions: Karen Raftus
Financial Aid: Dianne Mickey
Type: Comprehensive **Sex:** Coed **Affiliation:** Roman Catholic **Scores:** 90% SAT V 400+; 91% SAT M 400+; 61% ACT 18-23; 28% ACT 24-29 **% Accepted:** 78 **Admission Plans:** Deferred Admission **Application Deadline:** Rolling **Application Fee:** $25.00 **H.S. Requirements:** High school diploma required; GED accepted **Costs Per Year:** Application fee: $25. Comprehensive fee: $26,240 includes full-time tuition ($19,600), mandatory fees ($160), and college room and board ($6480). Full-time tuition and fees vary according to reciprocity agreements. Room and board charges vary according to housing facility. Part-time tuition: $670 per credit. Part-time tuition varies according to course load and reciprocity agreements. **Scholarships:** Available **Calendar System:** Semester, Summer Session Available **Enrollment:** FT 886, PT 117 **Faculty:** FT 56, PT 21 **Student-Faculty Ratio:** 15:1 **Exams:** SAT I or ACT **% Receiving Financial Aid:** 72 **% Residing in College-Owned, -Operated, or -Affiliated Housing:** 66 **Library Holdings:** 157,021 **Regional Accreditation:** North Central Association of Colleges and Schools **Credit Hours For Degree:** 60 credits, Associates; 120 credits, Bachelors **Professional Accreditation:** NCATE **Intercollegiate Athletics:** Baseball M; Basketball M & W; Cheerleading M & W; Cross-Country Running M & W; Football M; Golf M & W; Soccer M & W; Softball W; Tennis M & W; Track and Field M & W; Volleyball W

SAINT MARY-OF-THE-WOODS COLLEGE
St. Mary-of-the-Woods, IN 47876
Tel: (812)535-5151
Free: 800-926-SMWC
Admissions: (812)535-5106
Fax: (812)535-5215
E-mail: adms@woods.smwc.edu
Web Site: http://www.smwc.edu/
President/CEO: Dr. Joan Lescinski, CSJ
Registrar: Susan Meier
Admissions: Theresa Denton
Financial Aid: Jan Benton
Type: Comprehensive **Affiliation:** Roman Catholic **Scores:** 92% SAT V 400+; 93% SAT M 400+; 56% ACT 18-23; 29% ACT 24-29 **Admission Plans:** Early Admission; Deferred Admission **Application Deadline:** August 15 **Application Fee:** $30.00 **H.S. Requirements:** High school diploma required; GED accepted **Costs Per Year:** Application fee: $30. Comprehensive fee: $25,480 includes full-time tuition ($18,060), mandatory fees ($600), and college room and board ($6820). College room only: $2660. Full-time tuition and fees vary according to program. Part-time tuition: $342 per hour. Part-time mandatory fees: $70 per year. Part-time tuition and fees vary according to course load and program. **Scholarships:** Available **Calendar System:** Semester, Summer Session Available **Enrollment:** FT 510, PT 1,116, Grad 131 **Faculty:** FT 64, PT 3 **Student-Faculty Ratio:** 14:1 **Exams:** SAT I or ACT **% Residing in College-Owned, -Operated, or -Affiliated Housing:** 74 **Library Holdings:** 155,771 **Regional Accreditation:** North Central Association of Colleges and Schools **Credit Hours For Degree:** 62 credit hours, Associates; 125 credit hours, Bachelors **ROTC:** Army, Air Force **Professional Accreditation:** NASM, NCATE **Intercollegiate Athletics:** Basketball W; Equestrian Sports W; Soccer W; Softball W

SAINT MARY'S COLLEGE
Notre Dame, IN 46556
Tel: (574)284-4000
Free: 800-551-7621
Admissions: (574)284-4587
Fax: (574)284-4713
E-mail: admission@saintmarys.edu
Web Site: http://www.saintmarys.edu/
President/CEO: Carol Ann Mooney
Registrar: Lorraine Kitchner
Admissions: Mona Bowe
Financial Aid: Mary Nucciarone
Type: Four-Year College **Sex:** Women **Affiliation:** Roman Catholic **Scores:** 99% SAT V 400+; 99% SAT M 400+; 35% ACT 18-23; 57% ACT 24-29 **% Accepted:** 81 **Admission Plans:** Early Admission; Early Decision Plan; Deferred Admission **Application Deadline:** March 01 **Application Fee:** $30.00 **H.S. Requirements:** High school diploma required; GED not accepted **Costs Per Year:** Application fee: $30. Comprehensive fee: $34,005 includes full-time tuition ($25,030), mandatory fees ($550), and college room and board ($8425). College room only: $5190. Part-time tuition: $989 per semester hour. **Scholarships:** Available **Calendar System:** Semester, Summer Session Available **Enrollment:** FT 1,366, PT 31 **Faculty:** FT 125, PT 73 **Student-Faculty Ratio:** 10:1 **Exams:** SAT I or ACT **% Receiving Financial Aid:** 70 **% Residing in College-Owned, -Operated, or -Affiliated Housing:** 81 **Library Holdings:** 215,616 **Regional Accreditation:** North Central Association of Colleges and Schools **Credit Hours For Degree:** 128 semester hours, Bachelors **ROTC:** Army, Navy, Air Force **Professional Accreditation:** CSWE, NASAD, NASM, NCATE, NLN **Intercollegiate Athletics:** Basketball W; Crew W; Cross-Country Running W; Equestrian Sports W; Field Hockey W; Gymnastics W; Sailing W; Skiing (Downhill) W; Soccer W; Softball W; Swimming and Diving W; Tennis W; Ultimate Frisbee W; Volleyball W; Water Polo W

SAWYER COLLEGE (HAMMOND)
6040 Hohman Ave.
Hammond, IN 46320
Tel: (219)931-0436
Fax: (219)933-1239
Web Site: http://www.sawyercollege.edu/
President/CEO: Christopher Artim
Type: Two-Year College **Sex:** Coed **Scholarships:** Available **Calendar System:** Quarter **Exams:** Other **Professional Accreditation:** ACICS

SAWYER COLLEGE (MERRILLVILLE)
3803 East Lincoln Hwy.
Merrillville, IN 46410
Tel: (219)736-0436
Fax: (219)942-3762
Web Site: http://www.sawyercollege.edu/
President/CEO: Mary Dixon
Type: Two-Year College **Sex:** Coed **Exams:** Other **Professional Accreditation:** ACICS

TAYLOR UNIVERSITY
236 West Reade Ave.
Upland, IN 46989-1001
Tel: (765)998-2751
Free: 800-882-3456
Admissions: (765)998-5206
Fax: (765)998-4925
E-mail: stmortland@tayloru.edu
Web Site: http://www.taylor.edu/
President/CEO: Dr. David J. Gyertson
Registrar: LaGatha Adkison
Admissions: Stephen R. Mortland
Financial Aid: Timothy A. Nace
Type: Comprehensive **Sex:** Coed **Affiliation:** interdenominational **Scores:** 99% SAT V 400+; 98% SAT M 400+; 25% ACT 18-23; 58% ACT 24-29 **% Accepted:** 82 **Admission Plans:** Preferred Admission; Early Action; Deferred Admission **Application Fee:** $25.00 **H.S. Requirements:** High school diploma required; GED accepted **Costs Per Year:** Application fee: $25. Comprehensive fee: $26,376 includes full-time tuition ($20,520), mandatory fees ($226), and college room and board ($5630). College room only: $2732. Full-time tuition and fees vary according to course load. Room and board charges vary according to housing facility. Part-time tuition: $696 per credit. Part-time mandatory fees: $64 per year. Part-time tuition and fees vary according to course load. **Scholarships:** Available **Calendar System:** 4-1-4, Summer Session Available **Enrollment:** FT 1,794, PT 57, Grad 14

Faculty: FT 128, PT 59 **Student-Faculty Ratio:** 13:1 **Exams:** SAT I or ACT **% Receiving Financial Aid:** 57 **% Residing in College-Owned, -Operated, or -Affiliated Housing:** 91 **Library Holdings:** 189,007 **Regional Accreditation:** North Central Association of Colleges and Schools **Credit Hours For Degree:** 64 credit hours, Associates; 128 credit hours, Bachelors **Professional Accreditation:** CSWE, NASM, NCATE **Intercollegiate Athletics:** Baseball M; Basketball M & W; Cross-Country Running M & W; Equestrian Sports M & W; Football M; Golf M; Lacrosse M & W; Soccer M & W; Softball W; Tennis M & W; Track and Field M & W; Volleyball M & W

TAYLOR UNIVERSITY FORT WAYNE
1025 West Rudisill Blvd.
Fort Wayne, IN 46807-2197
Tel: (260)744-8600
Free: 800-233-3922
Admissions: (260)744-8689
Fax: (260)744-8660
E-mail: admissions@fw.taylor.edu
Web Site: http://www.tayloru.edu/
President/CEO: Dr. David J. Gyertson
Registrar: Gladys Smith
Admissions: Leo Gonot
Financial Aid: Paul Johnston
Type: Comprehensive **Sex:** Coed **Affiliation:** interdenominational; Taylor University **Scores:** 94% SAT V 400+; 87% SAT M 400+; 43% ACT 18-23; 33% ACT 24-29 **% Accepted:** 83 **Admission Plans:** Deferred Admission **Application Deadline:** Rolling **Application Fee:** $20.00 **H.S. Requirements:** High school diploma required; GED accepted **Costs Per Year:** Application fee: $20. Comprehensive fee: $22,674 includes full-time tuition ($17,600), mandatory fees ($114), and college room and board ($4960). College room only: $2160. Room and board charges vary according to board plan. Part-time tuition: $250 per credit hour. Part-time mandatory fees: $52 per year. Part-time tuition and fees vary according to course load. **Scholarships:** Available **Calendar System:** 4-1-4, Summer Session Available **Enrollment:** FT 337, PT 207, Grad 51 **Faculty:** FT 26, PT 29 **Student-Faculty Ratio:** 12:1 **Exams:** SAT I or ACT **% Receiving Financial Aid:** 82 **% Residing in College-Owned, -Operated, or -Affiliated Housing:** 47 **Library Holdings:** 78,955 **Regional Accreditation:** North Central Association of Colleges and Schools **Credit Hours For Degree:** 64 semester hours, Associates; 128 semester hours, Bachelors **Intercollegiate Athletics:** Basketball M & W; Cheerleading M & W; Soccer M; Softball W; Volleyball W

TRI-STATE UNIVERSITY
1 University Ave.
Angola, IN 46703-1764
Tel: (260)665-4100
Free: 800-347-4TSU
Admissions: (260)665-4365
Fax: (260)665-4292
E-mail: admit@alpha.tristate.edu
Web Site: http://www.tristate.edu/
President/CEO: Dr. Earl D. Brooks, II
Registrar: Debbie Helmsing
Admissions: Scott Goplin
Type: Comprehensive **Sex:** Coed **Scores:** 96% SAT V 400+; 95% SAT M 400+; 57% ACT 18-23; 31% ACT 24-29 **% Accepted:** 75 **Application Deadline:** August 01 **Application Fee:** $20.00 **H.S. Requirements:** High school diploma required; GED accepted **Costs Per Year:** Application fee: $20. Comprehensive fee: $27,450 includes full-time tuition ($21,210) and college room and board ($6240). Part-time tuition: $663 per credit hour. **Scholarships:** Available **Calendar System:** Semester, Summer Session Available **Enrollment:** FT 1,000, PT 168, Grad 4 **Faculty:** FT 69, PT 30 **Student-Faculty Ratio:** 13:1 **Exams:** SAT I or ACT **% Receiving Financial Aid:** 73 **% Residing in College-Owned, -Operated, or -Affiliated Housing:** 48 **Library Holdings:** 73,859 **Regional Accreditation:** North Central Association of Colleges and Schools **Credit Hours For Degree:** 61 semester hours, Associates; 120 semester hours, Bachelors **Professional Accreditation:** ABET **Intercollegiate Athletics:** Baseball M; Basketball M & W; Cross-Country Running M & W; Football M; Golf M & W; Soccer M & W; Softball W; Tennis M & W; Track and Field M & W; Volleyball W; Wrestling M

UNIVERSITY OF EVANSVILLE
1800 Lincoln Ave.
Evansville, IN 47722
Tel: (812)488-2000
Free: 800-423-8633
Admissions: (812)488-2468
Fax: (812)474-4076
E-mail: dv9@evansville.edu
Web Site: http://www.evansville.edu/
President/CEO: Dr. Stephen G. Jennings
Registrar: Keith Kutzler
Admissions: Don Vos
Financial Aid: JoAnn Laugel
Type: Comprehensive **Sex:** Coed **Affiliation:** United Methodist Church **Scores:** 98% SAT V 400+; 99% SAT M 400+; 34% ACT 18-23; 45% ACT 24-29 **% Accepted:** 91 **Admission Plans:** Early Action; Deferred Admission **Application Deadline:** February 01 **Application Fee:** $35.00 **H.S. Requirements:** High school diploma required; GED accepted **Costs Per Year:** Application fee: $35. Comprehensive fee: $28,320 includes full-time tuition ($21,120), mandatory fees ($540), and college room and board ($6660). College room only: $3280. Room and board charges vary according to board plan and housing facility. Part-time tuition: $580 per hour. Part-time mandatory fees: $35 per term. Part-time tuition and fees vary according to course load. **Scholarships:** Available **Calendar System:** Semester, Summer Session Available **Enrollment:** FT 2,432, PT 335, Grad 69 **Faculty:** FT 175, PT 59 **Student-Faculty Ratio:** 13:1 **Exams:** SAT I or ACT **% Receiving Financial Aid:** 71 **% Residing in College-Owned, -Operated, or -Affiliated Housing:** 67 **Library Holdings:** 281,729 **Regional Accreditation:** North Central Association of Colleges and Schools **Credit Hours For Degree:** 69 semester hours, Associates; 120 semester hours, Bachelors **Professional Accreditation:** ABET, APTA, NASM, NCATE, NLN **Intercollegiate Athletics:** Baseball M; Basketball M & W; Cross-Country Running M & W; Golf M; Soccer M & W; Softball W; Swimming and Diving M & W; Tennis W; Volleyball W

UNIVERSITY OF INDIANAPOLIS
1400 East Hanna Ave.
Indianapolis, IN 46227-3697
Tel: (317)788-3368
Free: 800-232-8634
Admissions: (317)788-3216
Fax: (317)788-3300
E-mail: admissions@uindy.edu
Web Site: http://www.uindy.edu/
President/CEO: Dr. Jerry Israel
Registrar: Mary Beth Bagg
Admissions: Ronald Wilks
Financial Aid: Linda B. Handy
Type: Comprehensive **Sex:** Coed **Affiliation:** United Methodist Church **Scores:** 93% SAT V 400+; 94% SAT M 400+; 55% ACT 18-23; 30% ACT 24-29 **% Accepted:** 76 **Admission Plans:** Deferred Admission **Application Deadline:** Rolling **Application Fee:** $20.00 **H.S. Requirements:** High school diploma required; GED accepted **Costs Per Year:** Application fee: $20. Comprehensive fee: $24,990 includes full-time tuition ($17,980) and college room and board ($7010). Full-time tuition varies according to program. Room and board charges vary according to board plan and housing facility. Part-time tuition: $750 per hour. Part-time tuition varies according to class time. **Scholarships:** Available **Calendar System:** Miscellaneous, Summer Session Available **Enrollment:** FT 2,389, PT 972, Grad 1,101 **Faculty:** FT 166, PT 250 **Student-Faculty Ratio:** 12:1 **Exams:** SAT I or ACT **% Receiving Financial Aid:** 75 **% Residing in College-Owned, -Operated, or -Affiliated Housing:** 31 **Library Holdings:** 173,363 **Regional Accreditation:** North Central Association of Colleges and Schools **Credit Hours For Degree:** 62 credit hours, Associates; 124 credit hours, Bachelors **ROTC:** Army **Professional Accreditation:** AACN, ACNM, AOTA, APTA, APA, ACBSP, CSWE, JRCEPAT, NASM, NCATE, NLN **Intercollegiate Athletics:** Baseball M; Basketball M & W; Cross-Country Running M & W; Football M; Golf M & W; Soccer M & W; Softball W; Swimming and Diving M & W; Tennis M & W; Track and Field M & W; Volleyball W; Wrestling M

UNIVERSITY OF NOTRE DAME
Notre Dame, IN 46556
Tel: (574)631-5000
Admissions: (574)631-7505
Fax: (574)631-8865
E-mail: admissions@nd.edu
Web Site: http://www.nd.edu/
President/CEO: Rev. Edward A. Malloy, PhD

Registrar: Dr. Harold L. Pace
Admissions: Daniel J. Saracino
Financial Aid: Joseph Russo
Type: University **Sex:** Coed **Affiliation:** Roman Catholic **Scores:** 100% SAT V 400+; 100% SAT M 400+; 2% ACT 18-23; 18% ACT 24-29 **% Accepted:** 32 **Admission Plans:** Early Action; Deferred Admission **Application Deadline:** December 31 **Application Fee:** $50.00 **H.S. Requirements:** High school diploma required; GED not accepted **Costs Per Year:** Application fee: $50. Comprehensive fee: $42,172 includes full-time tuition ($32,900), mandatory fees ($542), and college room and board ($8730). Part-time tuition: $1371 per credit. **Scholarships:** Available **Calendar System:** Semester, Summer Session Available **Enrollment:** FT 8,260, PT 15, Grad 2,569 **Faculty:** FT 877 **Student-Faculty Ratio:** 12:1 **Exams:** SAT I or ACT **% Receiving Financial Aid:** 48 **% Residing in College-Owned, -Operated, or -Affiliated Housing:** 76 **Library Holdings:** 2,797,065 **Regional Accreditation:** North Central Association of Colleges and Schools **Credit Hours For Degree:** 120 credit hours, Bachelors **ROTC:** Army, Navy, Air Force **Professional Accreditation:** AACSB, ABET, ABA, APA, ACIPE, AALS, ATS, NASAD **Intercollegiate Athletics:** Baseball M; Basketball M & W; Crew W; Cross-Country Running M & W; Fencing M & W; Football M; Golf M & W; Ice Hockey M; Lacrosse M & W; Soccer M & W; Softball W; Swimming and Diving M & W; Tennis M & W; Track and Field M & W; Volleyball W

UNIVERSITY OF PHOENIX-INDIANAPOLIS CAMPUS
7999 Knue Rd. Dr., Ste. 150
Indianapolis, IN 46250
Tel: (317)585-8610
Free: 800-228-7240
Admissions: (480)557-1712
Web Site: http://www.phoenix.edu/
Admissions: Nina Omelchanko
Type: Comprehensive **Sex:** Coed **Admission Plans:** Open Admission; Deferred Admission **Application Deadline:** Rolling **Application Fee:** $110.00 **H.S. Requirements:** High school diploma required; GED accepted **Costs Per Year:** Application fee: $110. Tuition: $9780 full-time, $326 per credit part-time. Mandatory fees: $560 full-time, $70 per course part-time. **Scholarships:** Available **Calendar System:** Continuous, Summer Session Not available **Enrollment:** FT 474, Grad 142 **Faculty:** FT 4, PT 78 **Student-Faculty Ratio:** 8:1 **Library Holdings:** 444 **Regional Accreditation:** North Central Association of Colleges and Schools **Credit Hours For Degree:** 60 credits, Associates; 120 credits, Bachelors

UNIVERSITY OF SAINT FRANCIS
2701 Spring St.
Fort Wayne, IN 46808-3994
Tel: (260)434-3100
Free: 800-729-4732
Admissions: (260)434-3279
E-mail: admiss@sfc.edu
Web Site: http://www.sf.edu/
President/CEO: Sr. M. Elise Kriss
Registrar: Frank Connor
Admissions: Ron Schumacher
Financial Aid: Sherri Shockey
Type: Comprehensive **Sex:** Coed **Affiliation:** Roman Catholic **Scores:** 90% SAT V 400+; 91% SAT M 400+; 57% ACT 18-23; 20% ACT 24-29 **% Accepted:** 59 **Admission Plans:** Deferred Admission **Application Deadline:** Rolling **Application Fee:** $20.00 **H.S. Requirements:** High school diploma required; GED accepted **Costs Per Year:** Application fee: $20. Comprehensive fee: $24,312 includes full-time tuition ($17,760), mandatory fees ($718), and college room and board ($5834). Part-time tuition: $560 per hour. Part-time mandatory fees: $17 per hour. **Scholarships:** Available **Calendar System:** Semester, Summer Session Available **Enrollment:** FT 1,343, PT 425, Grad 235 **Faculty:** FT 108, PT 121 **Student-Faculty Ratio:** 11:1 **Exams:** SAT I or ACT **% Receiving Financial Aid:** 86 **% Residing in College-Owned, -Operated, or -Affiliated Housing:** 16 **Library Holdings:** 50,186 **Regional Accreditation:** North Central Association of Colleges and Schools **Credit Hours For Degree:** 64 semester hours, Associates; 128 semester hours, Bachelors **Professional Accreditation:** ARCEST, AACN, AOTA, APTA, CSWE, JRCERT, NASAD, NCATE, NLN **Intercollegiate Athletics:** Baseball M; Basketball M & W; Cheerleading M & W; Cross-Country Running M & W; Football M; Golf M & W; Soccer M & W; Softball W; Tennis M & W; Track and Field M & W; Volleyball W

UNIVERSITY OF SOUTHERN INDIANA
8600 University Blvd.
Evansville, IN 47712-3590
Tel: (812)464-8600
Free: 800-467-1965
Admissions: (812)464-1765
Fax: (812)465-7154
Web Site: http://www.usi.edu/
President/CEO: Dr. H. Ray Hoops
Registrar: Sandy K. Farmer
Admissions: Eric Otto
Financial Aid: James M. Patton
Type: Comprehensive **Sex:** Coed **Affiliation:** Indiana Commission for Higher Education **Scores:** 84.9% SAT V 400+; 87.06% SAT M 400+; 56.52% ACT 18-23; 18.84% ACT 24-29 **% Accepted:** 91 **Application Deadline:** August 15 **Application Fee:** $25.00 **H.S. Requirements:** High school diploma required; GED accepted **Costs Per Year:** Application fee: $25. State resident tuition: $4244 full-time, $141.45 per credit hour part-time. Nonresident tuition: $10,118 full-time, $337.25 per credit hour part-time. Mandatory fees: $60 full-time, $22.75 per term part-time. College room and board: $6368. College room only: $3170. **Scholarships:** Available **Calendar System:** Semester, Summer Session Available **Enrollment:** FT 7,477, PT 1,775, Grad 752 **Faculty:** FT 303, PT 316 **Student-Faculty Ratio:** 18:1 **Exams:** SAT I or ACT **% Receiving Financial Aid:** 52 **% Residing in College-Owned, -Operated, or -Affiliated Housing:** 31 **Library Holdings:** 247,329 **Regional Accreditation:** North Central Association of Colleges and Schools **Credit Hours For Degree:** 62 semester hours, Associates; 124 semester hours, Bachelors **ROTC:** Army **Professional Accreditation:** AACSB, ABET, AACN, ADA, AOTA, CARC, CSWE, JRCERT, NCATE **Intercollegiate Athletics:** Baseball M; Basketball M & W; Cheerleading M & W; Cross-Country Running M & W; Golf M & W; Ice Hockey M; Rugby M; Soccer M & W; Softball W; Tennis M & W; Ultimate Frisbee M & W; Volleyball W

VALPARAISO UNIVERSITY
1700 Chapel Dr.
Valparaiso, IN 46383
Tel: (219)464-5000; 888-GO-VALPO
Admissions: (219)464-5011
Fax: (219)464-6898
E-mail: undergrad_admissions@valpo.edu
Web Site: http://www.valpo.edu/
President/CEO: Dr. Alan F. Harre
Registrar: Ann Trost
Admissions: Katharine E. Wehling
Financial Aid: Katharine E. Wehling
Type: Comprehensive **Sex:** Coed **Affiliation:** Lutheran Church **Scores:** 99% SAT V 400+; 99% SAT M 400+; 27% ACT 18-23; 55% ACT 24-29 **% Accepted:** 83 **Admission Plans:** Early Admission; Early Action; Deferred Admission **Application Deadline:** August 15 **Application Fee:** $30.00 **H.S. Requirements:** High school diploma required; GED accepted **Costs Per Year:** Application fee: $30. Comprehensive fee: $28,970 includes full-time tuition ($22,000), mandatory fees ($750), and college room and board ($6220). College room only: $3910. Room and board charges vary according to housing facility and student level. Part-time tuition: $1000 per credit hour. Part-time mandatory fees: $20 per credit hour. Part-time tuition and fees vary according to course load. **Scholarships:** Available **Calendar System:** Semester, Summer Session Available **Enrollment:** FT 2,825, PT 139, Grad 371 **Faculty:** FT 243, PT 119 **Student-Faculty Ratio:** 13:1 **Exams:** SAT I or ACT **% Receiving Financial Aid:** 68 **% Residing in College-Owned, -Operated, or -Affiliated Housing:** 65 **Library Holdings:** 1,148,993 **Regional Accreditation:** North Central Association of Colleges and Schools **Credit Hours For Degree:** 60 credits, Associates; 124 credits, Bachelors **ROTC:** Air Force **Professional Accreditation:** AACSB, ABET, AACN, ABA, AALS, CSWE, NASM, NCATE **Intercollegiate Athletics:** Baseball M; Basketball M & W; Cross-Country Running M & W; Football M; Soccer M & W; Softball W; Swimming and Diving M & W; Tennis M & W; Track and Field M & W; Volleyball W

VINCENNES UNIVERSITY
1002 North First St.
Vincennes, IN 47591-5202

Tel: (812)888-8888
Admissions: (812)888-4313
Fax: (812)888-5868
Web Site: http://www.vinu.edu/
President/CEO: Dr. Richard E. Helton
Registrar: Donna Jo Weaver
Admissions: Chris M. Crews
Financial Aid: Stan Werne
Type: Two-Year College **Sex:** Coed **Scores:** 70% SAT V 400+; 70% SAT M 400+; 40% ACT 18-23; 15% ACT 24-29 **Admission Plans:** Open Admission; Early Admission; Deferred Admission **Application Fee:** $20.00 **H.S. Requirements:** High school diploma required; GED accepted **Scholarships:** Available **Calendar System:** Semester, Summer Session Available **Enrollment:** FT 4,467, PT 708 **Faculty:** FT 290, PT 522 **Student-Faculty Ratio:** 15:1 **Exams:** SAT I or ACT **% Residing in College-Owned, -Operated, or -Affiliated Housing:** 50 **Library Holdings:** 103,000 **Regional Accreditation:** North Central Association of Colleges and Schools **Credit Hours For Degree:** 64 credits, Associates **ROTC:** Army, Air Force **Professional Accreditation:** ARCEST, ABFSE, AHIMA, APTA, ACBSP, CARC, NASAD, NAST, NLN **Intercollegiate Athletics:** Baseball M; Basketball M & W; Bowling M & W; Cheerleading M & W; Cross-Country Running M & W; Golf M; Soccer M & W; Swimming and Diving M & W; Tennis M; Track and Field M & W; Volleyball W

VINCENNES UNIVERSITY JASPER CAMPUS
850 College Ave.
Jasper, IN 47546-9393
Tel: (812)482-3030
Free: 800-809-VUJC
Fax: (812)481-5960
E-mail: lgilbert@indian.vinu.edu
Web Site: http://vujc.vinu.edu/
President/CEO: Dr. Christopher Ezell
Registrar: Virginia Eichmiller
Admissions: LouAnn Gilbert
Financial Aid: Virginia Eichmiller
Type: Two-Year College **Sex:** Coed **Affiliation:** Vincennes University **Admission Plans:** Open Admission **Application Fee:** $20.00 **H.S. Requirements:** High school diploma required; GED accepted **Scholarships:** Available **Calendar System:** Semester, Summer Session Available **Enrollment:** FT 339, PT 496 **Faculty:** FT 20, PT 31 **Student-Faculty Ratio:** 16:1 **Exams:** SAT I or ACT **Library Holdings:** 14,000 **Regional Accreditation:** North Central Association of Colleges and Schools **Credit Hours For Degree:** 62 credit hours, Associates

WABASH COLLEGE
PO Box 352
Crawfordsville, IN 47933-0352
Tel: (765)361-6100
Free: 800-345-5385
Admissions: (765)361-6225
Fax: (765)361-6437
E-mail: admissions@wabash.edu
Web Site: http://www.wabash.edu/
President/CEO: Dr. Andrew T. Ford
Registrar: Dr. Julie Olsen
Admissions: Steve Klein
Financial Aid: Clinton Gasaway
Type: Four-Year College **Sex:** Men **Scores:** 99% SAT V 400+; 99% SAT M 400+; 25% ACT 18-23; 58% ACT 24-29 **% Accepted:** 51 **Admission Plans:** Early Admission; Early Action; Early Decision Plan; Deferred Admission **Application Deadline:** March 15 **Application Fee:** $30.00 **H.S. Requirements:** High school diploma required; GED accepted **Costs Per Year:** Application fee: $30. Comprehensive fee: $30,116 includes full-time tuition ($22,964), mandatory fees ($424), and college room and board ($6728). College room only: $2740. Room and board charges vary according to board plan and housing facility. Part-time tuition: $3827 per course. Part-time tuition varies according to course load. **Scholarships:** Available **Calendar System:** Semester, Summer Session Not available **Enrollment:** FT 871, PT 6 **Faculty:** FT 87, PT 2 **Student-Faculty Ratio:** 10:1 **Exams:** SAT I or ACT **% Receiving Financial Aid:** 70 **% Residing in College-Owned, -Operated, or -Affiliated Housing:** 87 **Library Holdings:** 434,460 **Regional Accreditation:** North Central Association of Colleges and Schools **Credit Hours For Degree:** 34 courses, Bachelors **ROTC:** Army **Professional Accreditation:** NCATE **Intercollegiate Athletics:** Baseball M; Basketball M; Crew M; Cross-Country Running M; Football M; Golf M; Lacrosse M; Rugby M; Sailing M; Soccer M; Swimming and Diving M; Tennis M; Track and Field M; Water Polo M; Wrestling M

AIB COLLEGE OF BUSINESS
2500 Fleur Dr.
Des Moines, IA 50321-1799
Tel: (515)244-4221
Free: 800-444-1921
Fax: (515)244-6773
E-mail: clineg@aib.edu
Web Site: http://www.aib.edu/
President/CEO: Nancy Williams
Registrar: Judy Wilderman
Admissions: Gail Cline
Financial Aid: Connie Jensen
Type: Two-Year College **Sex:** Coed **Scores:** 57% ACT 18-23; 20% ACT 24-29 **Application Fee:** $25.00 **H.S. Requirements:** High school diploma required; GED accepted **Costs Per Year:** Application fee: $25. Comprehensive fee: $15,837 includes full-time tuition ($11,880) and college room and board ($3957). College room only: $2895. Part-time tuition: $330 per credit hour. **Scholarships:** Available **Calendar System:** Continuous, Summer Session Available **Enrollment:** FT 750, PT 188 **Faculty:** FT 26, PT 41 **Student-Faculty Ratio:** 21:1 **Exams:** ACT **% Residing in College-Owned, -Operated, or -Affiliated Housing:** 48 **Library Holdings:** 5,400 **Regional Accreditation:** North Central Association of Colleges and Schools **Credit Hours For Degree:** 96 credits, Associates

ALLEN COLLEGE
1825 Logan Ave.
Waterloo, IA 50703
Tel: (319)226-2000
Admissions: (319)226-2002
Fax: (319)226-2020
Web Site: http://www.allencollege.edu/
President/CEO: Dr. Jane Hasek
Registrar: Joanna Ramsden-Meier
Admissions: Holly Risetter
Financial Aid: Kathie Walters
Type: Comprehensive **Sex:** Coed **Affiliation:** Allen Health System/Iowa Health System **Scores:** 83% ACT 18-23; 11% ACT 24-29 **% Accepted:** 73 **Application Deadline:** July 01 **Application Fee:** $50.00 **H.S. Requirements:** High school diploma required; GED accepted **Costs Per Year:** Application fee: $50. Comprehensive fee: $19,184 includes full-time tuition ($11,958), mandatory fees ($1514), and college room and board ($5712). College room only: $2666. Part-time tuition: $415 per credit hour. Part-time mandatory fees: $37 per credit hour, $170 per term. **Scholarships:** Available **Calendar System:** Semester, Summer Session Not available **Enrollment:** FT 318, PT 56, Grad 30 **Faculty:** FT 19, PT 12 **Student-Faculty Ratio:** 13:1 **Exams:** ACT **% Receiving Financial Aid:** 79 **% Residing in College-Owned, -Operated, or -Affiliated Housing:** 15 **Library Holdings:** 2,797 **Regional Accreditation:** North Central Association of Colleges and Schools **Credit Hours For Degree:** 73 credit hours, Associates; 125 credit hours, Bachelors **ROTC:** Army **Professional Accreditation:** JRCERT, NLN

ASHFORD UNIVERSITY
400 North Bluff Blvd., PO Box 2967
Clinton, IA 52733-2967
Tel: (563)242-4023
Free: 800-242-4153
Fax: (563)242-2003
E-mail: admissns@tfu.edu
Web Site: http://www.ashford.edu/
President/CEO: Dr. Michael E. Kaelke
Registrar: Mary Lou Mallicoat
Admissions: Waunita M. Sullivan
Financial Aid: Lisa Kramer
Type: Four-Year College **Sex:** Coed **Scores:** 59% ACT 18-23; 16% ACT 24-29 **Admission Plans:** Early Admission; Deferred Admission **Application Fee:** $20.00 **H.S. Requirements:** High school diploma required; GED accepted **Scholarships:** Available **Calendar System:** Semester, Summer Session Available **Enrollment:** FT 342, PT 49, Grad 68 **Faculty:** FT 27, PT 25 **Student-Faculty Ratio:** 12:1 **Exams:** SAT I or ACT **% Receiving Financial Aid:** 87 **% Residing in College-Owned, -Operated, or -Affiliated Housing:** 29 **Library Holdings:** 98,974 **Regional Accreditation:** North Central Association of Colleges and Schools **Credit Hours For Degree:** 62 credit hours, Associates; 122 credit hours, Bachelors **Intercollegiate Athletics:** Baseball M; Basketball M & W; Cross-Country Running M & W; Golf M & W; Soccer M & W; Softball W; Track and Field M & W; Volleyball W

BRIAR CLIFF UNIVERSITY
3303 Rebecca St.
Sioux City, IA 51104-0100
Tel: (712)279-5321
Free: 800-662-3303
Admissions: (712)279-5200
Fax: (712)279-5410
E-mail: admissions@briar-cliff.edu
Web Site: http://www.briarcliff.edu/
President/CEO: Beverly Wharton
Registrar: Deidre Engel
Admissions: Sharisue Wilcoxon
Financial Aid: Robert Piechota
Type: Comprehensive **Sex:** Coed **Affiliation:** Roman Catholic **Scores:** 89% SAT V 400+; 67% SAT M 400+; 66% ACT 18-23; 26% ACT 24-29 **% Accepted:** 76 **Admission Plans:** Early Admission; Deferred Admission **Application Deadline:** Rolling **Application Fee:** $20.00 **H.S. Requirements:** High school diploma required; GED accepted **Costs Per Year:** Application fee: $20. Comprehensive fee: $23,550 includes full-time tuition ($17,490), mandatory fees ($495), and college room and board ($5565). College room only: $2760. Room and board charges vary according to board plan and housing facility. Part-time tuition: $583 per hour. Part-time mandatory fees: $16.50 per hour. Part-time tuition and fees vary according to class time and course load. **Scholarships:** Available **Calendar System:** Miscellaneous, Summer Session Available **Enrollment:** FT 970, PT 126, Grad 26 **Faculty:** FT 56, PT 42 **Student-Faculty Ratio:** 13:1 **Exams:** SAT I or ACT **% Receiving Financial Aid:** 73 **% Residing in College-Owned, -Operated, or -Affiliated Housing:** 0 **Library Holdings:** 84,411 **Regional Accreditation:** North Central Association of Colleges and Schools **Credit Hours For Degree:** 60 credit hours, Associates; 120 credit hours, Bachelors **Professional Accreditation:** CSWE, NLN **Intercollegiate Athletics:** Baseball M;

Basketball M & W; Cross-Country Running M & W; Football M; Golf M & W; Soccer M & W; Softball W; Tennis W; Track and Field M & W; Volleyball W; Wrestling M

BUENA VISTA UNIVERSITY
610 West Fourth St.
Storm Lake, IA 50588
Tel: (712)749-2351
Free: 800-383-9600
Admissions: (712)749-2235
Fax: (712)749-2037
E-mail: admissions@bvu.edu
Web Site: http://www.bvu.edu/
President/CEO: Dr. Frederick V. Moore
Registrar: Nancy Penna
Admissions: Chris Coons
Financial Aid: Leanne Valentine
Type: Comprehensive **Sex:** Coed **Affiliation:** Presbyterian Church (U.S.A.) **Scores:** 54% ACT 18-23; 31% ACT 24-29 **% Accepted:** 83 **Admission Plans:** Deferred Admission **Application Fee:** $25.00 **H.S. Requirements:** High school diploma required; GED accepted **Costs Per Year:** Application fee: $25. Comprehensive fee: $27,742 includes full-time tuition ($21,688) and college room and board ($6054). Part-time tuition: $729 per semester hour. **Scholarships:** Available **Calendar System:** 4-1-4, Summer Session Available **Enrollment:** FT 1,198, PT 16, Grad 69 **Faculty:** FT 81, PT 35 **Student-Faculty Ratio:** 13:1 **Exams:** SAT I or ACT **% Receiving Financial Aid:** 92 **% Residing in College-Owned, -Operated, or -Affiliated Housing:** 89 **Library Holdings:** 145,085 **Regional Accreditation:** North Central Association of Colleges and Schools **Credit Hours For Degree:** 128 semester hours, Bachelors **Professional Accreditation:** CSWE **Intercollegiate Athletics:** Baseball M; Basketball M & W; Cross-Country Running M & W; Football M; Golf M & W; Soccer M & W; Softball W; Tennis M & W; Track and Field M & W; Volleyball W; Wrestling M

CENTRAL COLLEGE
812 University St.
Pella, IA 50219-1999
Tel: (641)628-9000; 877-462-3689
Admissions: (641)628-7600
Fax: (641)628-5316
E-mail: admissions@central.edu
Web Site: http://www.central.edu/
President/CEO: Dr. David Roe
Registrar: Steven J. Sanchez
Admissions: Carol Williamson
Financial Aid: Jean Vander Wert
Type: Four-Year College **Sex:** Coed **Affiliation:** Reformed Church in America **Scores:** 48% ACT 18-23; 43% ACT 24-29 **% Accepted:** 84 **Admission Plans:** Deferred Admission **Application Deadline:** Rolling **Application Fee:** $25.00 **H.S. Requirements:** High school diploma required; GED accepted **Costs Per Year:** Application fee: $25. Comprehensive fee: $28,196 includes full-time tuition ($20,972) and college room and board ($7224). College room only: $3542. Part-time tuition: $728 per semester hour. **Scholarships:** Available **Calendar System:** Semester, Summer Session Available **Enrollment:** FT 1,601, PT 34 **Faculty:** FT 94, PT 45 **Student-Faculty Ratio:** 13:1 **Exams:** SAT I or ACT **% Receiving Financial Aid:** 81 **% Residing in College-Owned, -Operated, or -Affiliated Housing:** 86 **Library Holdings:** 220,526 **Regional Accreditation:** North Central Association of Colleges and Schools **Credit Hours For Degree:** 120 semester hours, Bachelors **Professional Accreditation:** NASM **Intercollegiate Athletics:** Baseball M; Basketball M & W; Cross-Country Running M & W; Football M; Golf M & W; Soccer M & W; Softball W; Tennis M & W; Track and Field M & W; Volleyball W; Wrestling M

CLARKE COLLEGE
1550 Clarke Dr.
Dubuque, IA 52001-3198
Tel: (563)588-6300
Free: 800-383-2345
Admissions: (563)588-6316
Fax: (563)588-6789
E-mail: admissions@clarke.edu
Web Site: http://www.clarke.edu/
President/CEO: Dr. Catherine Dunn, BVM
Registrar: Kristi Droessler
Admissions: Andy Shroeder
Financial Aid: Michael Pope
Type: Comprehensive **Sex:** Coed **Affiliation:** Roman Catholic **Scores:** 90% SAT V 400+; 90% SAT M 400+; 60% ACT 18-23; 28% ACT 24-29 **% Accepted:** 61 **Admission Plans:** Deferred Admission **Application Deadline:** Rolling **Application Fee:** $25.00 **H.S. Requirements:** High school diploma required; GED accepted **Costs Per Year:** Application fee: $25. Comprehensive fee: $25,390 includes full-time tuition ($18,360), mandatory fees ($585), and college room and board ($6445). College room only: $3135. Full-time tuition and fees vary according to class time. Room and board charges vary according to board plan and housing facility. Part-time tuition: $465 per credit hour. Part-time tuition varies according to class time. **Scholarships:** Available **Calendar System:** Semester, Summer Session Available **Enrollment:** FT 857, PT 164, Grad 225 **Faculty:** FT 83, PT 47 **Student-Faculty Ratio:** 11:1 **Exams:** SAT I or ACT **% Receiving Financial Aid:** 86 **% Residing in College-Owned, -Operated, or -Affiliated Housing:** 47 **Library Holdings:** 157,576 **Regional Accreditation:** North Central Association of Colleges and Schools **Credit Hours For Degree:** 62 credits, Associates; 124 credits, Bachelors **Professional Accreditation:** AACN, APTA, CSWE, NASM, NLN **Intercollegiate Athletics:** Baseball M; Basketball M & W; Cross-Country Running M & W; Golf M & W; Soccer M & W; Softball W; Tennis M & W; Volleyball M & W

CLINTON COMMUNITY COLLEGE
1000 Lincoln Blvd.
Clinton, IA 52732-6299
Tel: (563)244-7001
Admissions: (563)244-7007
Fax: (563)244-7107
Web Site: http://www.eicc.edu/ccc/
President/CEO: Karen Vickers
Registrar: Sue Carmody
Admissions: Neil Mandsager
Financial Aid: Teresa Thiede
Type: Two-Year College **Sex:** Coed **Affiliation:** Eastern Iowa Community College District **Admission Plans:** Open Admission; Early Admission; Deferred Admission **Application Fee:** $0.00 **H.S. Requirements:** High school diploma or equivalent not required **Scholarships:** Available **Calendar System:** Semester, Summer Session Available **Enrollment:** FT 590, PT 708 **Faculty:** FT 31, PT 44 **Library Holdings:** 18,701 **Regional Accreditation:** North Central Association of Colleges and Schools **Credit Hours For Degree:** 62 semester hours, Associates **Intercollegiate Athletics:** Basketball M; Cheerleading M & W; Soccer M & W; Softball W; Volleyball W

COE COLLEGE
1220 1st Ave., NE
Cedar Rapids, IA 52402-5092
Tel: (319)399-8000; 877-225-5263
Admissions: (319)399-8500
Fax: (319)399-8816
E-mail: admission@coe.edu
Web Site: http://www.coe.edu/
President/CEO: Dr. James R. Phifer
Registrar: Dr. Evelyn Moore
Admissions: John Grundig
Financial Aid: Barbara Hoffman
Type: Four-Year College **Sex:** Coed **Affiliation:** Presbyterian Church **Scores:** 100% SAT V 400+; 100% SAT M 400+; 33% ACT 18-23; 52% ACT 24-29 **% Accepted:** 72 **Admission Plans:** Early Admission; Early Action; Deferred Admission **Application Deadline:** March 01 **Application Fee:** $30.00 **H.S. Requirements:** High school diploma required; GED accepted **Costs Per Year:** Application fee: $30. Comprehensive fee: $31,670 includes full-time tuition ($24,830), mandatory fees ($290), and college room and board ($6550). College room only: $2990. Part-time tuition: $3200 per course. **Scholarships:** Available **Calendar System:** Miscellaneous, Summer Session Available **Enrollment:** FT 1,245, PT 86, Grad 24 **Faculty:** FT 76, PT 49 **Student-Faculty Ratio:** 12:1 **Exams:** SAT I or ACT **% Receiving Financial Aid:** 77 **% Residing in College-Owned, -Operated, or -Affiliated Housing:** 84 **Library Holdings:** 218,881 **Regional Accreditation:** North Central Association of Colleges and Schools **Credit Hours For Degree:** 32 courses, Bachelors **ROTC:** Army, Air Force **Professional Accreditation:** AACN, NASM **Intercollegiate Athletics:** Baseball M; Basketball M & W; Cheerleading W; Cross-Country Running M & W; Football

M; Golf M & W; Soccer M & W; Softball W; Swimming and Diving M & W; Tennis M & W; Track and Field M & W; Volleyball W; Wrestling M

CORNELL COLLEGE
600 First St. West
Mount Vernon, IA 52314-1098
Tel: (319)895-4000
Free: 800-747-1112
Admissions: (319)895-4477
Fax: (319)895-4492
E-mail: admissions@cornellcollege.edu
Web Site: http://www.cornellcollege.edu/
President/CEO: Dr. Leslie H. Garner, Jr.
Registrar: Dr. James Brown
Admissions: Jonathan Stroud
Financial Aid: Cindi Reints
Type: Four-Year College **Sex:** Coed **Affiliation:** Methodist **Scores:** 100% SAT V 400+; 100% SAT M 400+; 25% ACT 18-23; 55% ACT 24-29 **% Accepted:** 66 **Admission Plans:** Deferred Admission **Application Deadline:** March 01 **Application Fee:** $30.00 **H.S. Requirements:** High school diploma required; GED accepted **Costs Per Year:** Application fee: $30. Comprehensive fee: $30,110 includes full-time tuition ($23,500), mandatory fees ($180), and college room and board ($6430). College room only: $3010. Full-time tuition and fees vary according to reciprocity agreements. Room and board charges vary according to board plan. Part-time tuition: $734 per credit. Part-time mandatory fees: $180 per year. Part-time tuition and fees vary according to course load. **Scholarships:** Available **Calendar System:** Miscellaneous, Summer Session Not available **Enrollment:** FT 1,166, PT 13 **Faculty:** FT 94, PT 18 **Student-Faculty Ratio:** 11:1 **Exams:** SAT I or ACT, SAT II **% Receiving Financial Aid:** 80 **% Residing in College-Owned, -Operated, or -Affiliated Housing:** 88 **Library Holdings:** 186,318 **Regional Accreditation:** North Central Association of Colleges and Schools **Credit Hours For Degree:** 128 semester hours, Bachelors **Intercollegiate Athletics:** Baseball M; Basketball M & W; Cross-Country Running M & W; Football M; Golf M & W; Soccer M & W; Softball W; Tennis M & W; Track and Field M & W; Volleyball M & W; Wrestling M

DES MOINES AREA COMMUNITY COLLEGE
2006 South Ankeny Blvd.
Ankeny, IA 50021-8995
Tel: (515)964-6200
Admissions: (515)964-6216
Web Site: http://www.dmacc.edu/
President/CEO: Dr. Joseph A. Borgen
Registrar: Kim Kirschman
Admissions: Keith Knowles
Financial Aid: Delores Hawkins
Type: Two-Year College **Sex:** Coed **Affiliation:** Iowa Area Community Colleges System **Scores:** 58.4% ACT 18-23; 16.2% ACT 24-29 **Admission Plans:** Open Admission; Early Admission; Deferred Admission **Application Fee:** $0.00 **H.S. Requirements:** High school diploma required; GED accepted **Costs Per Year:** Application fee: $0. State resident tuition: $2850 full-time, $95 per credit hour part-time. Nonresident tuition: $5700 full-time, $190 per credit hour part-time. Full-time tuition varies according to course load. Part-time tuition varies according to course load. **Scholarships:** Available **Calendar System:** Semester, Summer Session Available **Enrollment:** FT 6,002, PT 7,717 **Faculty:** FT 266, PT 6 **Student-Faculty Ratio:** 50:1 **Exams:** ACT, Other **Library Holdings:** 62,986 **Regional Accreditation:** North Central Association of Colleges and Schools **Credit Hours For Degree:** 64 semester hours, Associates **Professional Accreditation:** ACF, ADA, CARC, NAACLS, NLN **Intercollegiate Athletics:** Basketball M & W; Golf M & W; Softball W

DIVINE WORD COLLEGE
102 Jacoby Dr. SW
Epworth, IA 52045-0380
Tel: (563)876-3353
Free: 800-553-3321
Fax: (563)876-3407
Web Site: http://www.dwci.edu/
President/CEO: Rev. Michael Hutchins
Registrar: Deborah Hirsch
Financial Aid: Linda Weidemann
Type: Four-Year College **Sex:** Coed **Affiliation:** Roman Catholic **Admission Plans:** Early Admission **Application Fee:** $25.00 **H.S. Requirements:** High school diploma required; GED accepted **Calendar System:** Semester, Summer Session Not available **Enrollment:** FT 110, PT 1 **Faculty:** FT 23, PT 3 **Exams:** SAT I or ACT **% Residing in College-Owned, -Operated, or -Affiliated Housing:** 98 **Library Holdings:** 94,583 **Regional Accreditation:** North Central Association of Colleges and Schools **Credit Hours For Degree:** 60 semester hours, Associates; 128 semester hours, Bachelors

DORDT COLLEGE
498 4th Ave., NE
Sioux Center, IA 51250-1697
Tel: (712)722-6000
Free: 800-343-6738
Admissions: (712)722-6080
Fax: (712)722-1967
E-mail: admissions@dordt.edu
Web Site: http://www.dordt.edu/
President/CEO: Dr. Carl E. Zylstra
Registrar: James Bos
Admissions: Quentin Van Essen
Financial Aid: Michael Epema
Type: Comprehensive **Sex:** Coed **Affiliation:** Christian Reformed **Scores:** 100% SAT V 400+; 100% SAT M 400+; 40% ACT 18-23; 42% ACT 24-29 **% Accepted:** 92 **Admission Plans:** Deferred Admission **Application Fee:** $25.00 **H.S. Requirements:** High school diploma required; GED accepted **Costs Per Year:** Application fee: $25. Comprehensive fee: $22,540 includes full-time tuition ($17,400), mandatory fees ($240), and college room and board ($4900). College room only: $2580. Room and board charges vary according to board plan and housing facility. Part-time tuition: $690 per credit hour. Part-time mandatory fees: $120 per term. **Scholarships:** Available **Calendar System:** Semester, Summer Session Not available **Enrollment:** FT 1,192, PT 62, Grad 73 **Faculty:** FT 73, PT 32 **Student-Faculty Ratio:** 15:1 **Exams:** SAT I or ACT **% Receiving Financial Aid:** 76 **% Residing in College-Owned, -Operated, or -Affiliated Housing:** 90 **Library Holdings:** 160,000 **Regional Accreditation:** North Central Association of Colleges and Schools **Credit Hours For Degree:** 63 credits, Associates; 126 credits, Bachelors **Professional Accreditation:** ABET, CSWE **Intercollegiate Athletics:** Baseball M; Basketball M & W; Cross-Country Running M & W; Golf M; Ice Hockey M; Lacrosse M; Soccer M & W; Softball W; Tennis M & W; Track and Field M & W; Volleyball W

DRAKE UNIVERSITY
2507 University Ave.
Des Moines, IA 50311-4516
Tel: (515)271-2011
Free: 800-44D-RAKE
Admissions: (515)271-3181
Fax: (515)271-2831
E-mail: laura.linn@drake.edu
Web Site: http://www.drake.edu/
President/CEO: Dr. David Maxwell
Registrar: Dr. Wanda E. Everage
Admissions: Laura Linn
Financial Aid: Susan Ladd
Type: University **Sex:** Coed **Scores:** 98% SAT V 400+; 98% SAT M 400+; 22% ACT 18-23; 61% ACT 24-29 **% Accepted:** 82 **Admission Plans:** Early Admission; Deferred Admission **Application Deadline:** March 01 **Application Fee:** $25.00 **H.S. Requirements:** High school diploma required; GED accepted **Costs Per Year:** Application fee: $25. Comprehensive fee: $27,632 includes full-time tuition ($21,100), mandatory fees ($362), and college room and board ($6170). College room only: $3000. Full-time tuition and fees vary according to class time, course load, and student level. Room and board charges vary according to board plan. Part-time tuition: $430 per hour. Part-time mandatory fees: $8 per hour. Part-time tuition and fees vary according to class time. **Scholarships:** Available **Calendar System:** Semester, Summer Session Available **Enrollment:** FT 2,913, PT 228, Grad 1,160 **Faculty:** FT 246, PT 142 **Student-Faculty Ratio:** 14:1 **Exams:** Other, SAT I or ACT **% Receiving Financial Aid:** 62 **% Residing in College-Owned, -Operated, or -Affiliated Housing:** 57 **Library Holdings:** 488,659 **Regional Accreditation:** North Central Association of Colleges and Schools **Credit Hours For Degree:** 124 semester hours, Bachelors **ROTC:** Army, Air Force **Professional Accreditation:** AACSB, ACEJMC, ABA, ACPhE, AALS, CORE, NASAD, NASM, NLN **Intercollegiate Athletics:** Basketball M & W; Cheerleading M & W; Crew W; Cross-Country Running M & W; Football M; Golf M & W; Soccer M & W; Softball W; Tennis M & W; Track and Field M & W; Volleyball W

ELLSWORTH COMMUNITY COLLEGE
1100 College Ave.
Iowa Falls, IA 50126-1199
Tel: (641)648-4611
Free: 800-ECC-9235
Fax: (641)648-3128
Web Site: http://www.iavalley.cc.ia.us/ecc/
President/CEO: Dr. Max Friddell
Registrar: Barb Brady
Admissions: Nancy Walters
Financial Aid: Barbara Brady
Type: Two-Year College **Sex:** Coed **Affiliation:** Iowa Valley Community College District System **Scores:** 51% ACT 18-23; 13% ACT 24-29 **Admission Plans:** Open Admission; Early Admission; Deferred Admission **H.S. Requirements:** High school diploma required; GED accepted **Scholarships:** Available **Calendar System:** Semester, Summer Session Available **Enrollment:** FT 627, PT 303 **Faculty:** FT 33, PT 30 **Student-Faculty Ratio:** 17:1 **Exams:** ACT, Other **% Residing in College-Owned, -Operated, or -Affiliated Housing:** 38 **Library Holdings:** 25,500 **Regional Accreditation:** North Central Association of Colleges and Schools **Credit Hours For Degree:** 64 semester hours, Associates **Intercollegiate Athletics:** Baseball M; Basketball M & W; Football M; Golf M & W; Softball W; Volleyball W; Wrestling M

EMMAUS BIBLE COLLEGE
2570 Asbury Rd.
Dubuque, IA 52001-3097
Tel: (319)588-8000
Free: 800-397-2425
Admissions: (563)588-8000
Fax: (319)588-1216
Web Site: http://www.emmaus.edu/
President/CEO: Dr. Daniel H. Smith
Registrar: Mark Stevenson
Admissions: Steve Schimpf
Financial Aid: Phil Gardner
Type: Four-Year College **Sex:** Coed **Affiliation:** nondenominational **Admission Plans:** Open Admission; Deferred Admission **Application Fee:** $25.00 **H.S. Requirements:** High school diploma required; GED accepted **Costs Per Year:** Application fee: $25. Comprehensive fee: $12,372 includes full-time tuition ($7700), mandatory fees ($510), and college room and board ($4162). Full-time tuition and fees vary according to course load. Part-time tuition: $342 per credit hour. Part-time tuition varies according to course load. **Scholarships:** Available **Calendar System:** Semester, Summer Session Not available **Enrollment:** FT 270, PT 26 **Faculty:** FT 14, PT 13 **Student-Faculty Ratio:** 12:1 **Exams:** SAT I or ACT **% Receiving Financial Aid:** 47 **% Residing in College-Owned, -Operated, or -Affiliated Housing:** 79 **Library Holdings:** 86,000 **Credit Hours For Degree:** 101 semester hours, Associates; 132 semester hours, Bachelors **Professional Accreditation:** AABC **Intercollegiate Athletics:** Basketball M & W

FAITH BAPTIST BIBLE COLLEGE AND THEOLOGICAL SEMINARY
1900 Northwest 4th St.
Ankeny, IA 50021
Tel: (515)964-0601; 888-FAITH 4U
Fax: (515)964-1638
E-mail: fbblenroll@aol.com
Web Site: http://www.faith.edu/
President/CEO: Dr. Richard Houg
Registrar: David Stout
Admissions: Tim Nilius
Financial Aid: Breck Appell
Type: Comprehensive **Sex:** Coed **Affiliation:** General Association of Regular Baptist Churches **Scores:** 86% SAT V 400+; 100% SAT M 400+; 52% ACT 18-23; 25% ACT 24-29 **% Accepted:** 65 **Admission Plans:** Deferred Admission **Application Deadline:** August 01 **Application Fee:** $25.00 **H.S. Requirements:** High school diploma required; GED accepted **Costs Per Year:** Application fee: $25. Comprehensive fee: $15,520 includes full-time tuition ($10,804), mandatory fees ($400), and college room and board ($4316). College room only: $2010. Full-time tuition and fees vary according to course load. Room and board charges vary according to board plan. Part-time tuition: $395 per semester hour. Part-time mandatory fees: $95 per term. **Scholarships:** Available **Calendar System:** Semester, Summer Session Available **Enrollment:** FT 289, PT 39, Grad 114 **Faculty:** FT 21, PT 16 **Student-Faculty Ratio:** 12:1 **Exams:** SAT I or ACT **% Receiving Financial Aid:** 91 **% Residing in College-Owned, -Operated, or -Affiliated Housing:** 81 **Library Holdings:** 67,040 **Regional Accreditation:** North Central Association of Colleges and Schools **Credit Hours For Degree:** 64 semester hours, Associates; 126 semester hours, Bachelors **Professional Accreditation:** AABC **Intercollegiate Athletics:** Basketball M & W; Soccer M & W; Volleyball W

GRACELAND UNIVERSITY
1 University Place
Lamoni, IA 50140
Tel: (641)784-5000; (866)GRACELAND
Admissions: (641)784-5118
Fax: (641)784-5480
E-mail: admissions@graceland.edu
Web Site: http://www.graceland.edu/
President/CEO: Ambassador John K. Menzies
Registrar: M. Joyce Lighthill
Admissions: James R. Simpson
Financial Aid: Dr. Sherry Mesle Morain
Type: Comprehensive **Sex:** Coed **Affiliation:** Community of Christ **Scores:** 79% SAT V 400+; 83% SAT M 400+; 45% ACT 18-23; 26% ACT 24-29 **Admission Plans:** Early Admission; Deferred Admission **Application Fee:** $50.00 **H.S. Requirements:** High school diploma required; GED accepted **Costs Per Year:** Application fee: $50. Comprehensive fee: $21,550 includes full-time tuition ($16,000), mandatory fees ($150), and college room and board ($5400). Full-time tuition and fees vary according to course load and location. Room and board charges vary according to board plan, housing facility, and location. Part-time tuition: $500 per semester hour. Part-time tuition varies according to location. **Scholarships:** Available **Calendar System:** 4-1-4, Summer Session Available **Enrollment:** FT 1,398, PT 547, Grad 406 **Faculty:** FT 93, PT 21 **Student-Faculty Ratio:** 14:1 **Exams:** SAT I or ACT **% Receiving Financial Aid:** 62 **% Residing in College-Owned, -Operated, or -Affiliated Housing:** 66 **Library Holdings:** 193,109 **Regional Accreditation:** North Central Association of Colleges and Schools **Credit Hours For Degree:** 128 semester hours, Bachelors **Professional Accreditation:** AACN, NCATE, NLN **Intercollegiate Athletics:** Baseball M; Basketball M & W; Cross-Country Running M & W; Football M; Golf M & W; Soccer M & W; Softball W; Tennis M & W; Track and Field M & W; Volleyball M & W

GRAND VIEW COLLEGE
1200 Grandview Ave.
Des Moines, IA 50316-1599
Tel: (515)263-2800
Free: 800-444-6083
Admissions: (515)263-2810
Fax: (515)263-2974
E-mail: admissions@gvc.edu
Web Site: http://www.gvc.edu/
President/CEO: Kent Henning
Registrar: Dr. Ellen Strachota
Admissions: Diane Schaefer
Financial Aid: Deb Barger
Type: Four-Year College **Sex:** Coed **Affiliation:** Evangelical Lutheran Church in America **Scores:** 89% SAT V 400+; 100% SAT M 400+; 61% ACT 18-23; 15% ACT 24-29 **% Accepted:** 95 **Application Deadline:** August 15 **Application Fee:** $35.00 **H.S. Requirements:** High school diploma required; GED accepted **Costs Per Year:** Application fee: $35. Comprehensive fee: $21,774 includes full-time tuition ($15,750), mandatory fees ($360), and college room and board ($5664). Full-time tuition and fees vary according to class time. Room and board charges vary according to board plan and housing facility. Part-time tuition: $425 per hour. Part-time tuition varies according to class time. **Scholarships:** Available **Calendar System:** Semester, Summer Session Available **Enrollment:** FT 1,372, PT 389 **Faculty:** FT 86, PT 116 **Student-Faculty Ratio:** 12:1 **Exams:** SAT I or ACT **% Receiving Financial Aid:** 80 **% Residing in College-Owned, -Operated, or -Affiliated Housing:** 32 **Library Holdings:** 104,225 **Regional Accreditation:** North Central Association of Colleges and Schools **Credit Hours For Degree:** 62 semester hours, Associates; 124 semester hours, Bachelors **ROTC:** Army, Air Force **Professional Accreditation:** AACN **Intercollegiate Athletics:** Baseball M; Basketball M & W; Cross-Country Running M & W; Golf M & W; Soccer M & W; Softball W; Track and Field M & W; Volleyball W

GRINNELL COLLEGE
1121 Park St.
Grinnell, IA 50112-1690

Tel: (641)269-4000
Free: 800-247-0113
Admissions: (641)269-3600
Fax: (641)269-3408
E-mail: askgrin@admin.grin.edu
Web Site: http://www.grinnell.edu/
President/CEO: Russell K. Osgood
Registrar: Gerald S. Adams
Admissions: James Sumner
Financial Aid: Arnold A. Woods, Jr.
Type: Four-Year College **Sex:** Coed **Scores:** 99.6% SAT V 400+; 100% SAT M 400+; 6.9% ACT 18-23; 27.6% ACT 24-29 **% Accepted:** 45 **Admission Plans:** Early Admission; Early Decision Plan; Deferred Admission **Application Deadline:** January 20 **Application Fee:** $30.00 **H.S. Requirements:** High school diploma required; GED accepted **Costs Per Year:** Application fee: $30. Comprehensive fee: $34,814 includes full-time tuition ($27,060), mandatory fees ($444), and college room and board ($7310). College room only: $3424. Room and board charges vary according to board plan and housing facility. Part-time tuition: $846 per credit hour. **Scholarships:** Available **Calendar System:** Semester, Summer Session Not available **Enrollment:** FT 1,546, PT 31 **Faculty:** FT 156, PT 43 **Student-Faculty Ratio:** 9:1 **Exams:** SAT I or ACT **% Receiving Financial Aid:** 50 **% Residing in College-Owned, -Operated, or -Affiliated Housing:** 75 **Library Holdings:** 1,063,390 **Regional Accreditation:** North Central Association of Colleges and Schools **Credit Hours For Degree:** 124 credits, Bachelors **Intercollegiate Athletics:** Baseball M; Basketball M & W; Cross-Country Running M & W; Football M; Golf M & W; Soccer M & W; Softball W; Swimming and Diving M & W; Tennis M & W; Track and Field M & W; Volleyball W

HAMILTON COLLEGE (CEDAR FALLS)
7009 Nordic Dr.
Cedar Falls, IA 50613
Tel: (319)277-0220
Free: 800-728-1220
E-mail: jilines@hamiltoncf.com
Web Site: http://www.hamiltoncf.com/
Admissions: Jill Lines
Type: Two-Year College **Application Deadline:** Rolling **Application Fee:** $20.00 **Costs Per Year:** Application fee: $20. **Calendar System:** Quarter **Enrollment:** FT 541, PT 154 **Faculty:** FT 17, PT 20 **Student-Faculty Ratio:** 25:1 **Exams:** Other

HAMILTON COLLEGE (CEDAR RAPIDS)
3165 Edgewood Parkway, SW
Cedar Rapids, IA 52404
Tel: (319)363-0481
Free: 800-728-0481
Fax: (319)363-3812
Web Site: http://www.hamiltonia.edu/
President/CEO: Gary Kerber
Admissions: Niki Donahue
Type: Two-Year College **Sex:** Coed **Admission Plans:** Early Admission; Deferred Admission **Application Deadline:** Rolling **Application Fee:** $50.00 **H.S. Requirements:** High school diploma or equivalent not required **Costs Per Year:** Application fee: $50. Tuition: $17,040 full-time, $355 per credit hour part-time. **Scholarships:** Available **Calendar System:** Quarter, Summer Session Not available **Enrollment:** FT 440, PT 71 **Faculty:** FT 7, PT 33 **Student-Faculty Ratio:** 25:1 **Exams:** Other **Library Holdings:** 5,500 **Regional Accreditation:** North Central Association of Colleges and Schools **Credit Hours For Degree:** 92 credit hours, Associates **Professional Accreditation:** AAMAE

HAMILTON COLLEGE (COUNCIL BLUFFS)
1751 Madison Ave.
Council Bluffs, IA 51503
Free: 800-518-4212
Web Site: http://www.hamiltoncb.com/ **Type:** Two-Year College

HAMILTON TECHNICAL COLLEGE
1011 East 53rd St.
Davenport, IA 52807-2653
Tel: (319)386-3570
Admissions: (563)386-3570
Fax: (319)386-6756
Web Site: http://www.hamiltontechcollege.com/
President/CEO: Maryanne Hamilton
Registrar: Brian Beert
Admissions: Chad Nelson
Financial Aid: Lisa Boyd
Type: Four-Year College **Sex:** Coed **Admission Plans:** Open Admission; Deferred Admission **Application Fee:** $25.00 **H.S. Requirements:** High school diploma required; GED accepted **Costs Per Year:** Application fee: $25. Tuition: $6900 full-time, $230 per credit part-time. Tuition guaranteed not to increase for student's term of enrollment. **Scholarships:** Available **Calendar System:** Continuous, Summer Session Not available **Student-Faculty Ratio:** 20:1 **Library Holdings:** 4,500 **Credit Hours For Degree:** 75 credit hours, Associates; 120 credit hours, Bachelors **Professional Accreditation:** ACCSCT

HAWKEYE COMMUNITY COLLEGE
PO Box 8015
Waterloo, IA 50704-8015
Tel: (319)296-2320
Free: 800-670-4769
Admissions: (319)296-4204
Fax: (319)296-2874
E-mail: dball@hawkeyecollege.edu
Web Site: http://www.hawkeyecollege.edu/
President/CEO: Dr. Bettsey Barhorst
Registrar: Pat Yuska
Admissions: Dave Ball
Financial Aid: Brian Will
Type: Two-Year College **Sex:** Coed **Admission Plans:** Open Admission; Deferred Admission **Application Deadline:** Rolling **Application Fee:** $0.00 **H.S. Requirements:** High school diploma required; GED accepted **Costs Per Year:** Application fee: $0. State resident tuition: $2940 full-time, $98 per credit part-time. Nonresident tuition: $5880 full-time, $196 per credit part-time. Mandatory fees: $300 full-time, $10 per credit part-time. **Scholarships:** Available **Calendar System:** Semester, Summer Session Available **Enrollment:** FT 2,751, PT 2,521 **Faculty:** FT 114, PT 243 **Student-Faculty Ratio:** 16:1 **Exams:** ACT **Library Holdings:** 37,155 **Regional Accreditation:** North Central Association of Colleges and Schools **Credit Hours For Degree:** 62 credits, Associates **ROTC:** Army **Professional Accreditation:** ADA, CARC, NAACLS

INDIAN HILLS COMMUNITY COLLEGE
525 Grandview Ave., Bldg. No. 1
Ottumwa, IA 52501-1398
Tel: (641)683-5111
Free: 800-726-2585
Admissions: (641)683-5151
Web Site: http://www.ihcc.cc.ia.us/
President/CEO: Dr. Jim Lindenmayer
Registrar: Gail Lockridge
Admissions: Gail Lockridge
Type: Two-Year College **Sex:** Coed **Affiliation:** Iowa Area Community Colleges System **Admission Plans:** Open Admission; Early Admission **Application Fee:** $0.00 **H.S. Requirements:** High school diploma required; GED accepted **Scholarships:** Available **Calendar System:** Quarter, Summer Session Available **Enrollment:** FT 2,046, PT 821 **Faculty:** FT 127, PT 21 **Exams:** ACT, Other **% Residing in College-Owned, -Operated, or -Affiliated Housing:** 15 **Library Holdings:** 53,073 **Regional Accreditation:** North Central Association of Colleges and Schools **Credit Hours For Degree:** 61 credit hours, Associates **Professional Accreditation:** ACF, AHIMA, APTA, JRCERT **Intercollegiate Athletics:** Baseball M; Basketball M; Golf M; Softball W; Volleyball W

IOWA CENTRAL COMMUNITY COLLEGE
330 Ave. M
Fort Dodge, IA 50501-5798
Tel: (515)576-7201
Admissions: (515)576-0099
Fax: (515)576-7724
Web Site: http://www.iccc.cc.ia.us/
President/CEO: Dr. Robert A. Paxton
Registrar: Mary Kay Matisheck
Admissions: Brian K. Dioguardi
Financial Aid: Angela Martin

Type: Two-Year College **Sex:** Coed **Affiliation:** Iowa Department of Education Division of Community Colleges **Admission Plans:** Open Admission; Early Admission; Deferred Admission **Application Fee:** $0.00 **H.S. Requirements:** High school diploma required; GED accepted **Costs Per Year:** Application fee: $0. State resident tuition: $2790 full-time, $93 per credit part-time. Nonresident tuition: $4135 full-time, $139.50 per credit part-time. Mandatory fees: $300 full-time, $10 per credit part-time. **Scholarships:** Available **Calendar System:** Semester, Summer Session Available **Faculty:** FT 73, PT 207 **Student-Faculty Ratio:** 18:1 **Exams:** Other, SAT I or ACT **% Residing in College-Owned, -Operated, or -Affiliated Housing:** 22 **Library Holdings:** 55,000 **Regional Accreditation:** North Central Association of Colleges and Schools **Credit Hours For Degree:** 60 semester hours, Associates **Professional Accreditation:** JRCERT, NAACLS, NLN **Intercollegiate Athletics:** Baseball M; Basketball M & W; Cross-Country Running M & W; Football M; Golf M & W; Soccer M & W; Softball W; Volleyball W; Wrestling M

IOWA LAKES COMMUNITY COLLEGE

19 South 7th St.
Estherville, IA 51334-2295
Tel: (712)362-2604
Free: 800-521-5054
E-mail: info@iowalakes.edu
Web Site: http://www.iowalakes.edu/
President/CEO: Dr. Michael Hupfer
Registrar: Thomas Spalding
Admissions: Julie Carlson
Financial Aid: John Beneke

Type: Two-Year College **Sex:** Coed **Affiliation:** Iowa Area Community Colleges System **Scores:** 55% ACT 18-23; 11% ACT 24-29 **Admission Plans:** Open Admission; Deferred Admission **Application Fee:** $0.00 **H.S. Requirements:** High school diploma required; GED accepted **Costs Per Year:** Application fee: $0. State resident tuition: $3296 full-time. Nonresident tuition: $3360 full-time. Mandatory fees: $452 full-time. Full-time tuition and fees vary according to course load and program. College room and board: $4120. Room and board charges vary according to board plan. **Scholarships:** Available **Calendar System:** Semester, Summer Session Available **Enrollment:** FT 1,371, PT 1,622 **Faculty:** FT 81, PT 72 **Student-Faculty Ratio:** 19:1 **Exams:** ACT, Other **% Residing in College-Owned, -Operated, or -Affiliated Housing:** 24 **Library Holdings:** 36,881 **Regional Accreditation:** North Central Association of Colleges and Schools **Credit Hours For Degree:** 64 credit hours, Associates **Professional Accreditation:** AAMAE **Intercollegiate Athletics:** Baseball M; Basketball M & W; Cross-Country Running M & W; Golf M & W; Softball W; Volleyball W; Weight Lifting M & W

IOWA STATE UNIVERSITY OF SCIENCE AND TECHNOLOGY

Ames, IA 50011
Tel: (515)294-4111
Free: 800-262-3810
Admissions: (515)294-0815
Fax: (515)294-2592
E-mail: admissions@iastate.edu
Web Site: http://www.iastate.edu/
President/CEO: Dr. Gregory L. Geoffroy
Registrar: Kathleen Jones
Admissions: Marc L. Harding
Financial Aid: Roberta Johnson

Type: University **Sex:** Coed **Scores:** 97% SAT V 400+; 99% SAT M 400+; 39% ACT 18-23; 47% ACT 24-29 **% Accepted:** 90 **Admission Plans:** Early Admission; Deferred Admission **Application Deadline:** July 01 **Application Fee:** $30.00 **H.S. Requirements:** High school diploma required; GED accepted **Costs Per Year:** Application fee: $30. State resident tuition: $4890 full-time, $204 per semester hour part-time. Nonresident tuition: $14,980 full-time, $625 per semester hour part-time. Mandatory fees: $744 full-time. Full-time tuition and fees vary according to class time, degree level, and program. Part-time tuition varies according to class time, course load, degree level, and program. College room and board: $6197. College room only: $3295. Room and board charges vary according to board plan and housing facility. **Scholarships:** Available **Calendar System:** Semester, Summer Session Available **Enrollment:** FT 19,433, PT 1,299, Grad 4,578 **Faculty:** FT 1,419, PT 217 **Student-Faculty Ratio:** 15:1 **Exams:** SAT I or ACT **% Receiving Financial Aid:** 57 **% Residing in College-Owned, -Operated, or -Affiliated Housing:** 31 **Library Holdings:** 2,416,670 **Regional Accreditation:** North Central Association of Colleges and Schools **Credit Hours For Degree:** 120.5 semester hours, Bachelors **ROTC:** Army, Navy, Air Force **Professional Accreditation:** AACSB, ABET, ACEJMC, AAMFT, AAFCS, ADtA, ACSP, APA, ASLA, AVMA, FIDER, JRCEPAT, NAIT, NASM, NASPAA, SAF **Intercollegiate Athletics:** Basketball M & W; Cross-Country Running M & W; Football M; Golf M & W; Gymnastics W; Soccer W; Softball W; Swimming and Diving M & W; Tennis W; Track and Field M & W; Volleyball W; Wrestling M

IOWA WESLEYAN COLLEGE

601 North Main St.
Mount Pleasant, IA 52641-1398
Tel: (319)385-8021
Free: 800-582-2383
Admissions: (319)385-6230
Fax: (319)385-6296
E-mail: admitrwl@iwc.edu
Web Site: http://www.iwc.edu/
President/CEO: Dr. William N. Johnston
Registrar: Edward L. Kropa
Admissions: Cary A. Owens
Financial Aid: Crystal Filer-Ogden

Type: Four-Year College **Sex:** Coed **Affiliation:** United Methodist **Scores:** 54% ACT 18-23; 23% ACT 24-29 **% Accepted:** 59 **Admission Plans:** Early Admission; Deferred Admission **Application Deadline:** August 15 **H.S. Requirements:** High school diploma required; GED accepted **Costs Per Year:** Comprehensive fee: $23,330 includes full-time tuition ($17,800) and college room and board ($5530). College room only: $2280. Part-time tuition: $439 per credit hour. **Scholarships:** Available **Calendar System:** Semester, Summer Session Available **Faculty:** FT 54, PT 40 **Student-Faculty Ratio:** 14:1 **Exams:** SAT I or ACT **% Receiving Financial Aid:** 92 **% Residing in College-Owned, -Operated, or -Affiliated Housing:** 57 **Library Holdings:** 107,227 **Regional Accreditation:** North Central Association of Colleges and Schools **Credit Hours For Degree:** 124 credit hours, Bachelors **Professional Accreditation:** NLN **Intercollegiate Athletics:** Baseball M; Basketball M & W; Football M; Golf M & W; Soccer M & W; Softball W; Track and Field M & W; Volleyball W

IOWA WESTERN COMMUNITY COLLEGE

2700 College Rd., Box 4-C
Council Bluffs, IA 51502
Tel: (712)325-3200
Free: 800-432-5852
Admissions: (712)388-6878
Fax: (712)325-3720
Web Site: http://www.iwcc.edu/
President/CEO: Dr. Dan Kinney
Registrar: Jeanine Larsen
Admissions: Christopher LaFerla
Financial Aid: Blaine Dustermars

Type: Two-Year College **Sex:** Coed **Affiliation:** Iowa Department of Education Division of Community Colleges **Admission Plans:** Open Admission; Early Admission; Deferred Admission **H.S. Requirements:** High school diploma required; GED accepted **Costs Per Year:** State resident tuition: $3200 full-time, $100 per credit part-time. Nonresident tuition: $4800 full-time, $150 per credit part-time. Mandatory fees: $320 full-time, $10 per credit part-time. College room and board: $4350. Room and board charges vary according to board plan and housing facility. **Scholarships:** Available **Calendar System:** Semester, Summer Session Available **Enrollment:** FT 2,152, PT 2,147 **Faculty:** FT 114, PT 108 **Exams:** Other, SAT I or ACT **% Residing in College-Owned, -Operated, or -Affiliated Housing:** 19 **Library Holdings:** 59,200 **Regional Accreditation:** North Central Association of Colleges and Schools **Credit Hours For Degree:** 64 credit hours, Associates **ROTC:** Army, Air Force **Professional Accreditation:** ABET, ACF, ADA **Intercollegiate Athletics:** Baseball M; Basketball M & W; Softball W; Volleyball W

KAPLAN UNIVERSITY

1801 East Kimberly Rd., Ste. 1
Davenport, IA 52807-2095
Tel: (563)355-3500
Admissions: (563)441-2496
Web Site: http://www.kaplancollegeia.com/
President/CEO: Dr. Ed DeJaegher
Registrar: Janet Gehrls
Admissions: Robert Hoffmann

Financial Aid: Sue McCabe
Type: Two-Year College **Sex:** Coed **Affiliation:** Kaplan Higher Education **Admission Plans:** Early Admission; Deferred Admission **Application Fee:** $25.00 **H.S. Requirements:** High school diploma required; GED accepted **Scholarships:** Available **Calendar System:** Quarter, Summer Session Available **Enrollment:** FT 1,648, PT 7,546 **Faculty:** FT 56, PT 355 **Student-Faculty Ratio:** 11:1 **Library Holdings:** 7,000 **Regional Accreditation:** North Central Association of Colleges and Schools **Credit Hours For Degree:** 90 credits, Associates; 180 credits, Bachelors **Professional Accreditation:** AAMAE

KIRKWOOD COMMUNITY COLLEGE
PO Box 2068
Cedar Rapids, IA 52406-2068
Tel: (319)398-5411
Free: 800-332-2055
Admissions: (319)398-5517
Fax: (319)398-1244
E-mail: dbannon@kirkwood.cc.ia.us
Web Site: http://www.kirkwood.cc.ia.us/
President/CEO: Dr. Norm Nielsen
Admissions: Doug Bannon
Financial Aid: Peg Julius
Type: Two-Year College **Sex:** Coed **Affiliation:** Iowa Department of Education Division of Community Colleges **Scores:** 55% ACT 18-23; 15% ACT 24-29 **Admission Plans:** Open Admission; Early Admission **Application Fee:** $0.00 **H.S. Requirements:** High school diploma required; GED accepted **Scholarships:** Available **Calendar System:** Semester, Summer Session Available **Enrollment:** FT 8,319, PT 6,713 **Faculty:** FT 257, PT 480 **Student-Faculty Ratio:** 23:1 **Exams:** ACT, Other **Library Holdings:** 60,622 **Regional Accreditation:** North Central Association of Colleges and Schools **Credit Hours For Degree:** 62 semester hours, Associates **Professional Accreditation:** ARCEST, AAMAE, ACF, ADA, AHIMA, AOTA, APTA, CARC, JRCEET **Intercollegiate Athletics:** Baseball M; Basketball M & W; Golf M; Soccer M & W; Softball W; Volleyball W

LORAS COLLEGE
1450 Alta Vista
Dubuque, IA 52004-0178
Tel: (563)588-7100
Free: 800-245-6727
Admissions: (563)588-7829
Fax: (563)588-7964
E-mail: adms@loras.edu
Web Site: http://www.loras.edu/
President/CEO: James E. Collins
Registrar: Dr. Mary K. Weck
Admissions: Sharon Lyons
Financial Aid: Julie A. Dunn
Type: Comprehensive **Sex:** Coed **Affiliation:** Roman Catholic **Scores:** 88.89% SAT V 400+; 100% SAT M 400+; 60.92% ACT 18-23; 30.46% ACT 24-29 **% Accepted:** 82 **Admission Plans:** Deferred Admission **Application Deadline:** Rolling **Application Fee:** $25.00 **H.S. Requirements:** High school diploma required; GED accepted **Costs Per Year:** Application fee: $25. Comprehensive fee: $27,193 includes full-time tuition ($19,990), mandatory fees ($1108), and college room and board ($6095). College room only: $3100. Full-time tuition and fees vary according to course load and degree level. Room and board charges vary according to board plan and housing facility. Part-time tuition: $400 per credit. **Scholarships:** Available **Calendar System:** Semester, Summer Session Available **Enrollment:** FT 1,512, PT 82, Grad 89 **Faculty:** FT 112, PT 30 **Student-Faculty Ratio:** 13:1 **Exams:** SAT I or ACT **% Receiving Financial Aid:** 76 **% Residing in College-Owned, -Operated, or -Affiliated Housing:** 63 **Library Holdings:** 224,971 **Regional Accreditation:** North Central Association of Colleges and Schools **Credit Hours For Degree:** 60 credits, Associates; 120 credits, Bachelors **Professional Accreditation:** CSWE **Intercollegiate Athletics:** Baseball M; Basketball M & W; Cross-Country Running M & W; Football M; Golf M & W; Ice Hockey M; Rugby M; Skiing (Downhill) M; Soccer M & W; Softball W; Swimming and Diving M & W; Tennis M & W; Track and Field M & W; Volleyball M & W; Wrestling M

LUTHER COLLEGE
700 College Dr.
Decorah, IA 52101-1045
Tel: (563)387-2000
Free: 800-458-8437
Admissions: (563)387-1430
Fax: (563)387-2159
E-mail: admissions@luther.edu
Web Site: http://www.luther.edu/
President/CEO: Dr. Richard L. Torgerson
Registrar: Dr. Liang Chee Wee
Admissions: Jon Lund
Financial Aid: Janice Cordell
Type: Four-Year College **Sex:** Coed **Affiliation:** Evangelical Lutheran Church in America **Scores:** 100% SAT V 400+; 99% SAT M 400+; 31.9% ACT 18-23; 50.9% ACT 24-29 **% Accepted:** 75 **Admission Plans:** Deferred Admission **Application Fee:** $25.00 **H.S. Requirements:** High school diploma required; GED accepted **Costs Per Year:** Application fee: $25. Comprehensive fee: $30,670 includes full-time tuition ($26,380) and college room and board ($4290). College room only: $2100. Part-time tuition: $924 per semester hour. **Scholarships:** Available **Calendar System:** 4-1-4, Summer Session Available **Enrollment:** FT 2,476, PT 69 **Faculty:** FT 179, PT 60 **Student-Faculty Ratio:** 13:1 **Exams:** SAT I or ACT **% Receiving Financial Aid:** 71 **% Residing in College-Owned, -Operated, or -Affiliated Housing:** 82 **Library Holdings:** 339,173 **Regional Accreditation:** North Central Association of Colleges and Schools **Credit Hours For Degree:** 128 semester hours, Bachelors **Professional Accreditation:** AACN, CSWE, NASM, NCATE **Intercollegiate Athletics:** Baseball M; Basketball M & W; Cross-Country Running M & W; Football M; Golf M & W; Soccer M & W; Softball W; Swimming and Diving M & W; Tennis M & W; Track and Field M & W; Volleyball W; Wrestling M

MAHARISHI UNIVERSITY OF MANAGEMENT
1000 North 4th St.
Fairfield, IA 52557
Tel: (641)472-7000
Free: 800-369-6480
Admissions: (641)472-1110
Fax: (641)472-1189
E-mail: admissions@miu.edu
Web Site: http://www.mum.edu/
President/CEO: Dr. Bevan Morris
Registrar: Arla Rabalais
Admissions: Richard Neate
Financial Aid: Tom Rowe
Type: University **Sex:** Coed **% Accepted:** 66 **Admission Plans:** Preferred Admission; Early Admission; Deferred Admission **Application Deadline:** August 01 **Application Fee:** $15.00 **H.S. Requirements:** High school diploma required; GED accepted **Costs Per Year:** Application fee: $15. Comprehensive fee: $30,430 includes full-time tuition ($24,000), mandatory fees ($430), and college room and board ($6000). **Scholarships:** Available **Calendar System:** Semester, Summer Session Not available **Enrollment:** FT 206, PT 12, Grad 523 **Faculty:** FT 39, PT 8 **Student-Faculty Ratio:** 16:1 **Exams:** SAT I or ACT **% Receiving Financial Aid:** 92 **% Residing in College-Owned, -Operated, or -Affiliated Housing:** 46 **Library Holdings:** 137,775 **Regional Accreditation:** North Central Association of Colleges and Schools **Credit Hours For Degree:** 166 units, Bachelors **Intercollegiate Athletics:** Golf M & W; Soccer M & W

MARSHALLTOWN COMMUNITY COLLEGE
3700 South Center St.
Marshalltown, IA 50158-4760
Tel: (641)752-7106; (866)622-4748
Fax: (641)752-8149
E-mail: dtrawny@iavalley.cc.ia.us
Web Site: http://www.marshalltowncommunitycollege.com/
President/CEO: Dr. Barbara Burrows
Registrar: Sylvia Grandgeorge
Admissions: Deana Trawny
Financial Aid: Larry Pfantz
Type: Two-Year College **Sex:** Coed **Affiliation:** Iowa Valley Community College District System **Admission Plans:** Open Admission; Early Admission **Application Fee:** $0.00 **H.S. Requirements:** High school diploma required; GED accepted **Scholarships:** Available **Calendar System:** Semester, Summer Session Available **Enrollment:** FT 903, PT 518 **Faculty:** FT 41, PT 68 **Student-Faculty Ratio:** 29:1 **Exams:** ACT, Other **% Residing in College-Owned, -Operated, or -Affiliated Housing:** 8 **Library Holdings:** 39,348 **Regional Accreditation:** North Central Association of Colleges and Schools **Credit Hours For Degree:** 64 credits, Associates **ROTC:** Air Force **Profes-**

sional **Accreditation:** ADA **Intercollegiate Athletics:** Baseball M; Basketball M & W; Cheerleading M & W; Golf M & W; Soccer M & W; Softball W; Volleyball W

MERCY COLLEGE OF HEALTH SCIENCES
928 Sixth Ave.
Des Moines, IA 50309-1239
Tel: (515)643-3180
Free: 800-637-2994
Fax: (515)643-6698
Web Site: http://www.mchs.edu/
President/CEO: Deanne M. Remer, PhD
Registrar: Susan Rhoades
Admissions: Susan Rhoades
Financial Aid: Lisa Croat
Type: Four-Year College **Sex:** Coed **Affiliation:** Roman Catholic Church **Admission Plans:** Open Admission **Application Fee:** $25.00 **H.S. Requirements:** High school diploma required; GED accepted **Costs Per Year:** Application fee: $25. Tuition: $11,700 full-time, $395 per semester hour part-time. Mandatory fees: $25 full-time. Full-time tuition and fees vary according to program. Part-time tuition varies according to course load and program. **Scholarships:** Available **Calendar System:** Semester **Enrollment:** FT 411, PT 249 **Faculty:** FT 30, PT 28 **Student-Faculty Ratio:** 12:1 **Exams:** ACT **% Receiving Financial Aid:** 84 **Regional Accreditation:** North Central Association of Colleges and Schools **Professional Accreditation:** ARCEST, AACN, JRCEDMS, NLN

MORNINGSIDE COLLEGE
1501 Morningside Ave.
Sioux City, IA 51106
Tel: (712)274-5000
Free: 800-831-0806
Admissions: (712)274-5111
E-mail: mscadm@alpha.morningside.edu
Web Site: http://www.morningside.edu/
President/CEO: John C. Reynders
Registrar: Mary Peshek
Admissions: Joel Weyand
Financial Aid: Karen Gagnon
Type: Comprehensive **Sex:** Coed **Affiliation:** United Methodist Church **Scores:** 56.3% ACT 18-23; 29.6% ACT 24-29 **% Accepted:** 74 **Admission Plans:** Deferred Admission **Application Deadline:** Rolling **Application Fee:** $25.00 **H.S. Requirements:** High school diploma required; GED accepted **Costs Per Year:** Application fee: $25. Comprehensive fee: $23,704 includes full-time tuition ($17,170), mandatory fees ($910), and college room and board ($5624). College room only: $2940. Full-time tuition and fees vary according to program. Room and board charges vary according to housing facility. Part-time tuition: $530 per semester hour. Part-time tuition varies according to course load. **Scholarships:** Available **Calendar System:** Semester, Summer Session Available **Enrollment:** FT 1,066, PT 83, Grad 291 **Faculty:** FT 66, PT 66 **Student-Faculty Ratio:** 16:1 **Exams:** SAT I or ACT **% Receiving Financial Aid:** 87 **% Residing in College-Owned, -Operated, or -Affiliated Housing:** 70 **Library Holdings:** 113,169 **Regional Accreditation:** North Central Association of Colleges and Schools **Credit Hours For Degree:** 124 semester hours, Bachelors **ROTC:** Army **Professional Accreditation:** NASM, NCATE, NLN **Intercollegiate Athletics:** Baseball M; Basketball M & W; Cross-Country Running M & W; Football M; Golf M & W; Soccer M & W; Softball W; Swimming and Diving M & W; Tennis M & W; Track and Field M & W; Volleyball W; Wrestling M

MOUNT MERCY COLLEGE
1330 Elmhurst Dr., NE
Cedar Rapids, IA 52402-4797
Tel: (319)363-8213
Free: 800-248-4504
Admissions: (319)368-6460
Fax: (319)368-6492
E-mail: admission@mtmercy.edu
Web Site: http://www.mtmercy.edu/
President/CEO: Dr. Robert W. Pearce
Registrar: Lori Heying
Admissions: Jim Krystofiak
Financial Aid: Lois Mulbrook
Type: Four-Year College **Sex:** Coed **Affiliation:** Roman Catholic **Scores:** 73% ACT 18-23; 25% ACT 24-29 **% Accepted:** 79 **Admission Plans:** Early Admission; Deferred Admission **Application Deadline:** August 25 **Application Fee:** $20.00 **H.S. Requirements:** High school diploma required; GED accepted **Costs Per Year:** Application fee: $20. Comprehensive fee: $23,710 includes full-time tuition ($18,030) and college room and board ($5680). Full-time tuition varies according to course load. Room and board charges vary according to board plan and housing facility. Part-time tuition: $500 per credit hour. Part-time tuition varies according to course load. **Scholarships:** Available **Calendar System:** 4-1-4, Summer Session Available **Enrollment:** FT 1,019, PT 471 **Faculty:** FT 73, PT 78 **Student-Faculty Ratio:** 12:1 **Exams:** SAT I and SAT II or ACT **% Receiving Financial Aid:** 84 **% Residing in College-Owned, -Operated, or -Affiliated Housing:** 28 **Library Holdings:** 118,000 **Regional Accreditation:** North Central Association of Colleges and Schools **Credit Hours For Degree:** 123 credit hours, Bachelors **Professional Accreditation:** AACN, CSWE **Intercollegiate Athletics:** Baseball M; Basketball M & W; Cheerleading W; Cross-Country Running M & W; Golf M & W; Soccer M & W; Softball W; Track and Field M & W; Volleyball W

MUSCATINE COMMUNITY COLLEGE
152 Colorado St.
Muscatine, IA 52761-5396
Tel: (563)288-6001
Admissions: (563)288-6012
Fax: (563)288-6074
Web Site: http://www.eicc.edu/
President/CEO: Dr. Victor G. McAvoy
Registrar: Linda Keldgord
Admissions: Neil Mandsager
Financial Aid: Deb Beatty
Type: Two-Year College **Sex:** Coed **Affiliation:** Eastern Iowa Community College District **Scores:** 56% ACT 18-23; 23% ACT 24-29 **Admission Plans:** Open Admission; Early Admission; Deferred Admission **H.S. Requirements:** High school diploma or equivalent not required **Scholarships:** Available **Calendar System:** Semester, Summer Session Available **Enrollment:** FT 552, PT 728 **Faculty:** FT 36, PT 59 **Exams:** Other **Library Holdings:** 19,588 **Regional Accreditation:** North Central Association of Colleges and Schools **Credit Hours For Degree:** 62 credits, Associates **Intercollegiate Athletics:** Baseball M; Softball W

NORTH IOWA AREA COMMUNITY COLLEGE
500 College Dr.
Mason City, IA 50401-7299
Tel: (641)423-1264; 888-GO NIACC
Admissions: (641)422-4104
Fax: (641)423-1711
Web Site: http://www.niacc.edu/
President/CEO: Dr. Michael Morrison
Admissions: Rachel McGuire
Financial Aid: Mary Bloomingdale
Type: Two-Year College **Sex:** Coed **Affiliation:** Iowa Community Colleges System **Scores:** 51.9% ACT 18-23; 15.8% ACT 24-29 **Admission Plans:** Open Admission **Application Deadline:** Rolling **Application Fee:** $0.00 **H.S. Requirements:** High school diploma required; GED accepted **Costs Per Year:** Application fee: $0. State resident tuition: $2790 full-time, $93 per credit part-time. Nonresident tuition: $4184 full-time, $139.50 per credit part-time. Mandatory fees: $174 full-time, $11 per credit part-time. College room and board: $3920. **Scholarships:** Available **Calendar System:** Semester, Summer Session Available **Enrollment:** FT 1,698, PT 1,435 **Faculty:** FT 84, PT 111 **Student-Faculty Ratio:** 13:1 **% Residing in College-Owned, -Operated, or -Affiliated Housing:** 15 **Library Holdings:** 29,540 **Regional Accreditation:** North Central Association of Colleges and Schools **Credit Hours For Degree:** 60 semester hours, Associates **Professional Accreditation:** APTA, NLN **Intercollegiate Athletics:** Baseball M; Basketball M & W; Cross-Country Running W; Football M; Golf M & W; Soccer M & W; Softball W; Track and Field M & W; Volleyball W

NORTHEAST IOWA COMMUNITY COLLEGE
Box 400
Calmar, IA 52132-0480
Tel: (563)562-3263
Free: 800-728-CALMAR
Fax: (563)562-3719
E-mail: keunem@nicc.edu
Web Site: http://www.nicc.edu/

President/CEO: Robert J. Denson
Registrar: Karla Winter
Admissions: Martha Keune
Type: Two-Year College **Sex:** Coed **Affiliation:** Iowa Area Community Colleges System **% Accepted:** 66 **Admission Plans:** Open Admission **Application Deadline:** Rolling **Application Fee:** $0.00 **H.S. Requirements:** High school diploma required; GED accepted **Costs Per Year:** Application fee: $0. State resident tuition: $3590 full-time, $105 per credit part-time. Nonresident tuition: $3590 full-time, $105 per credit part-time. Mandatory fees: $442 full-time, $13 per credit part-time. **Scholarships:** Available **Calendar System:** Semester, Summer Session Available **Enrollment:** FT 2,140, PT 2,693 **Faculty:** FT 113, PT 67 **Student-Faculty Ratio:** 15:1 **Library Holdings:** 18,634 **Regional Accreditation:** North Central Association of Colleges and Schools **Credit Hours For Degree:** 64 credit hours, Associates **Professional Accreditation:** AHIMA, CARC

NORTHWEST IOWA COMMUNITY COLLEGE
603 West Park St.
Sheldon, IA 51201-1046
Tel: (712)324-5061
Free: 800-352-4907
Fax: (712)324-4136
Web Site: http://www.nwicc.edu/
President/CEO: Dr. Andrew Matonak
Registrar: Gene McDaniel
Admissions: Lisa Story
Financial Aid: Karna Hofmeyer
Type: Two-Year College **Sex:** Coed **Affiliation:** Iowa Department of Education Division of Community Colleges **Admission Plans:** Open Admission **Application Fee:** $10.00 **H.S. Requirements:** High school diploma required; GED accepted **Scholarships:** Available **Calendar System:** Semester, Summer Session Available **Enrollment:** FT 533, PT 546 **Faculty:** FT 38, PT 42 **Student-Faculty Ratio:** 15:1 **Exams:** Other **% Residing in College-Owned, -Operated, or -Affiliated Housing:** 5 **Library Holdings:** 12,500 **Regional Accreditation:** North Central Association of Colleges and Schools **Credit Hours For Degree:** 60 credit hours, Associates **Professional Accreditation:** AHIMA

NORTHWESTERN COLLEGE
101 Seventh St., SW
Orange City, IA 51041-1996
Tel: (712)707-7000
Free: 800-747-4757
Admissions: (712)737-7130
Fax: (712)707-7247
E-mail: markb@nwciowa.edu
Web Site: http://www.nwciowa.edu/
President/CEO: Dr. Bruce G. Murphy
Registrar: Charles D. Couch
Admissions: Mark Bloemendaal
Financial Aid: Gerry Korver
Type: Four-Year College **Sex:** Coed **Affiliation:** Reformed Church in America **Scores:** 41% ACT 18-23; 44% ACT 24-29 **% Accepted:** 93 **Admission Plans:** Early Admission; Deferred Admission **Application Deadline:** Rolling **Application Fee:** $25.00 **H.S. Requirements:** High school diploma required; GED accepted **Costs Per Year:** Application fee: $25. Comprehensive fee: $22,174 includes full-time tuition ($17,260) and college room and board ($4914). College room only: $2090. Room and board charges vary according to housing facility. **Scholarships:** Available **Calendar System:** Semester, Summer Session Available **Enrollment:** FT 1,226, PT 47 **Faculty:** FT 78, PT 50 **Student-Faculty Ratio:** 15:1 **Exams:** SAT I and SAT II or ACT **% Receiving Financial Aid:** 80 **% Residing in College-Owned, -Operated, or -Affiliated Housing:** 89 **Library Holdings:** 125,000 **Regional Accreditation:** North Central Association of Colleges and Schools **Credit Hours For Degree:** 62 credit hours, Associates; 124 credit hours, Bachelors **Professional Accreditation:** CSWE, NCATE **Intercollegiate Athletics:** Baseball M; Basketball M & W; Cross-Country Running M & W; Football M; Golf M & W; Soccer M & W; Softball W; Track and Field M & W; Volleyball W; Wrestling M

PALMER COLLEGE OF CHIROPRACTIC
1000 Brady St.
Davenport, IA 52803-5287
Tel: (563)884-5000
Free: 800-722-3648
Admissions: (563)884-5656
Fax: (563)884-5897
E-mail: pcadmit@palmer.edu
Web Site: http://www.palmer.edu/
President/CEO: Dr. Guy F. Riekeman
Registrar: Mindy Leahy
Admissions: Karen Eden
Financial Aid: Brenda Gran
Type: Comprehensive **Sex:** Coed **Admission Plans:** Preferred Admission; Deferred Admission **Application Deadline:** Rolling **Application Fee:** $50.00 **H.S. Requirements:** High school diploma required; GED accepted **Costs Per Year:** Application fee: $50. Tuition: $5775 full-time, $145 per credit part-time. Mandatory fees: $255 full-time, $100 per term part-time. **Scholarships:** Available **Calendar System:** Trimester, Summer Session Available **Enrollment:** FT 81, PT 15, Grad 13 **Faculty:** FT 136, PT 0 **Student-Faculty Ratio:** 16:1 **Library Holdings:** 55,278 **Regional Accreditation:** North Central Association of Colleges and Schools **Credit Hours For Degree:** 60 credit hours, Associates; 120 credit hours, Bachelors **Professional Accreditation:** CCE

ST. AMBROSE UNIVERSITY
518 West Locust St.
Davenport, IA 52803-2898
Tel: (563)333-6000
Free: 800-383-2627
Admissions: (563)333-6300
Fax: (563)383-8791
E-mail: higginsmegf@sau.edu
Web Site: http://www.sau.edu/
President/CEO: Dr. Edward J. Rogalski
Registrar: Dan Zeimet
Admissions: Meg Halligan
Financial Aid: Julie Haack
Type: Comprehensive **Sex:** Coed **Affiliation:** Roman Catholic **Scores:** 62% ACT 18-23; 27% ACT 24-29 **% Accepted:** 84 **Admission Plans:** Deferred Admission **Application Deadline:** Rolling **Application Fee:** $25.00 **H.S. Requirements:** High school diploma required; GED accepted **Costs Per Year:** Application fee: $25. Comprehensive fee: $26,700 includes full-time tuition ($19,460) and college room and board ($7240). College room only: $3690. Part-time tuition: $605 per semester hour. **Scholarships:** Available **Calendar System:** 4-1-4, Summer Session Available **Enrollment:** FT 2,200, PT 498, Grad 925 **Faculty:** FT 160, PT 130 **Student-Faculty Ratio:** 15:1 **Exams:** ACT, SAT I or ACT **% Receiving Financial Aid:** 75 **% Residing in College-Owned, -Operated, or -Affiliated Housing:** 52 **Library Holdings:** 143,634 **Regional Accreditation:** North Central Association of Colleges and Schools **Credit Hours For Degree:** 120 credit hours, Bachelors **Professional Accreditation:** ABET, AACN, AOTA, APTA, ACBSP, CSWE **Intercollegiate Athletics:** Baseball M; Basketball M & W; Cheerleading W; Cross-Country Running M & W; Football M; Golf M & W; Soccer M & W; Softball W; Tennis M & W; Track and Field M & W; Volleyball M & W

ST. LUKE'S COLLEGE
2720 Stone Park Blvd.
Sioux City, IA 51104
Tel: (712)279-3149
Free: 800-352-4660
Fax: (712)233-8017
E-mail: mccartsj@stlukes.org
Web Site: http://stlukescollege.edu/
President/CEO: Michael D. Stiles
Registrar: Danelle Johannsen
Admissions: Sherry McCarthy
Financial Aid: Danelle Johannsen
Type: Two-Year College **Sex:** Coed **Affiliation:** St. Luke's Regional Medical Center **Scores:** 50% ACT 18-23; 50% ACT 24-29 **Admission Plans:** Early Admission; Early Action **Application Deadline:** August 01 **Application Fee:** $25.00 **H.S. Requirements:** High school diploma required; GED accepted **Costs Per Year:** Application fee: $25. Tuition: $11,900 full-time, $340 per credit part-time. Mandatory fees: $600 full-time. **Scholarships:** Available **Calendar System:** Semester, Summer Session Available **Enrollment:** FT 128, PT 27 **Faculty:** FT 10, PT 6 **Student-Faculty Ratio:** 11:1 **Exams:** ACT **% Residing in College-Owned, -Operated, or -Affiliated Housing:** 15 **Library Holdings:** 2,038 **Regional Accreditation:** North Central Association of Colleges and Schools **Credit Hours For Degree:** 71 credit hours, Associates

SCOTT COMMUNITY COLLEGE
500 Belmont Rd.
Bettendorf, IA 52722-6804
Tel: (563)441-4001
Admissions: (563)441-4007
Fax: (563)441-4066
Web Site: http://www.eicc.edu/scc/
President/CEO: Dr. David A. Claeys
Registrar: Linda Turner
Admissions: Neil Mandsager
Financial Aid: Jane Havgland
Type: Two-Year College **Sex:** Coed **Affiliation:** Eastern Iowa Community College District **Admission Plans:** Open Admission; Early Admission; Deferred Admission **H.S. Requirements:** High school diploma or equivalent not required **Scholarships:** Available **Calendar System:** Semester, Summer Session Available **Enrollment:** FT 2,212, PT 2,485 **Faculty:** FT 82, PT 240 **Student-Faculty Ratio:** 20:1 **Exams:** ACT, Other **Library Holdings:** 22,700 **Regional Accreditation:** North Central Association of Colleges and Schools **Credit Hours For Degree:** 62 credits, Associates **Professional Accreditation:** ADA, JRCEET, JRCERT **Intercollegiate Athletics:** Golf M & W; Soccer M & W

SIMPSON COLLEGE
701 North C St.
Indianola, IA 50125-1297
Tel: (515)961-6251
Free: 800-362-2454
Admissions: (515)961-1624
Fax: (515)961-1498
E-mail: admiss@simpson.edu
Web Site: http://www.simpson.edu/
President/CEO: Dr. Kevin La Gree
Registrar: Dr. John Bolen
Admissions: Deborah Tierney
Financial Aid: Tracie Pavon
Type: Four-Year College **Sex:** Coed **Affiliation:** United Methodist **Scores:** 38% ACT 18-23; 52% ACT 24-29 **% Accepted:** 87 **Admission Plans:** Early Admission; Deferred Admission **Application Deadline:** August 15 **Application Fee:** $0.00 **H.S. Requirements:** High school diploma required; GED accepted **Costs Per Year:** Application fee: $0. Comprehensive fee: $26,833 includes full-time tuition ($20,693), mandatory fees ($218), and college room and board ($5922). College room only: $2842. Room and board charges vary according to board plan and housing facility. **Scholarships:** Available **Calendar System:** Miscellaneous, Summer Session Available **Enrollment:** FT 1,485, PT 525, Grad 25 **Faculty:** FT 87, PT 83 **Student-Faculty Ratio:** 14:1 **Exams:** SAT I or ACT **% Receiving Financial Aid:** 87 **% Residing in College-Owned, -Operated, or -Affiliated Housing:** 82 **Library Holdings:** 157,713 **Regional Accreditation:** North Central Association of Colleges and Schools **Credit Hours For Degree:** 128 credit hours, Bachelors **Professional Accreditation:** NASM **Intercollegiate Athletics:** Baseball M; Basketball M & W; Cheerleading M & W; Cross-Country Running M & W; Football M; Golf M & W; Soccer M & W; Softball W; Swimming and Diving M & W; Tennis M & W; Track and Field M & W; Volleyball W; Wrestling M

SOUTHEASTERN COMMUNITY COLLEGE, NORTH CAMPUS
1500 West Agency St.
PO Box 180
West Burlington, IA 52655-0180
Tel: (319)752-2731
Fax: (319)752-4957
Web Site: http://www.secc.cc.ia.us/
President/CEO: Jim Richardson
Registrar: Tim Gray
Admissions: Dana Chrisman
Financial Aid: Gwen Scholer
Type: Two-Year College **Sex:** Coed **Affiliation:** Iowa Department of Education Division of Community Colleges **Admission Plans:** Open Admission; Early Admission; Deferred Admission **Application Fee:** $0.00 **H.S. Requirements:** High school diploma required; GED accepted **Scholarships:** Available **Calendar System:** Semester, Summer Session Available **Faculty:** FT 12, PT 82 **Exams:** ACT, Other **% Residing in College-Owned, -Operated, or -Affiliated Housing:** 3 **Library Holdings:** 39,304 **Regional Accreditation:** North Central Association of Colleges and Schools **Credit Hours For Degree:** 62 credit hours, Associates **Professional Accreditation:** AAMAE **Intercollegiate Athletics:** Baseball M; Basketball M; Softball W; Volleyball W

SOUTHEASTERN COMMUNITY COLLEGE, SOUTH CAMPUS
335 Messenger Rd., PO Box 6007
Keokuk, IA 52632-6007
Tel: (319)524-3221
Admissions: (319)752-2731
Fax: (319)524-8621
Web Site: http://www.secc.cc.ia.us/
President/CEO: Jim Richardson
Registrar: Ginny Dusanek
Admissions: Kari Bevans
Financial Aid: James C. Bowles
Type: Two-Year College **Sex:** Coed **Affiliation:** Iowa Department of Education Division of Community Colleges **Admission Plans:** Open Admission; Early Admission; Deferred Admission **Application Fee:** $0.00 **H.S. Requirements:** High school diploma or equivalent not required **Scholarships:** Available **Calendar System:** Semester, Summer Session Available **Faculty:** FT 18, PT 7 **Library Holdings:** 10,000 **Regional Accreditation:** North Central Association of Colleges and Schools **Credit Hours For Degree:** 62 credit hours, Associates

SOUTHWESTERN COMMUNITY COLLEGE
1501 West Townline St.
Creston, IA 50801
Tel: (641)782-7081
Free: 800-247-4023
Fax: (641)782-3312
E-mail: carstens@swcc.cc.ia.us
Web Site: http://www.swcc.cc.ia.us/
President/CEO: Dr. Barbara J. Crittenden
Registrar: Bill Taylor
Admissions: Lisa Carstens
Type: Two-Year College **Sex:** Coed **Affiliation:** Iowa Department of Education Division of Community Colleges **Admission Plans:** Open Admission; Early Admission **Application Fee:** $0.00 **H.S. Requirements:** High school diploma required; GED accepted **Costs Per Year:** Application fee: $0. State resident tuition: $3104 full-time, $97 per credit hour part-time. Nonresident tuition: $4560 full-time, $142.50 per credit hour part-time. Mandatory fees: $384 full-time, $13 per credit hour part-time. College room and board: $3700. **Scholarships:** Available **Calendar System:** Semester, Summer Session Available **Enrollment:** FT 666, PT 588 **Faculty:** FT 46, PT 50 **Student-Faculty Ratio:** 14:1 **Exams:** Other, SAT I or ACT **% Residing in College-Owned, -Operated, or -Affiliated Housing:** 5 **Library Holdings:** 14,742 **Regional Accreditation:** North Central Association of Colleges and Schools **Credit Hours For Degree:** 62 credit hours, Associates **Intercollegiate Athletics:** Baseball M; Basketball M & W; Golf M; Softball W; Volleyball W

UNIVERSITY OF DUBUQUE
2000 University Ave.
Dubuque, IA 52001-5099
Tel: (563)589-3000
Admissions: (563)589-3214
Fax: (563)589-3690
Web Site: http://www.dbq.edu/
President/CEO: Dr. Jeffrey F. Bullock
Registrar: Paul Johnson
Admissions: Jesse James
Financial Aid: Timothy Kremer
Type: Comprehensive **Sex:** Coed **Affiliation:** Presbyterian **Scores:** 77% SAT V 400+; 87% SAT M 400+; 61% ACT 18-23 **% Accepted:** 77 **Application Deadline:** Rolling **Application Fee:** $25.00 **H.S. Requirements:** High school diploma required; GED accepted **Costs Per Year:** Application fee: $25. Comprehensive fee: $23,420 includes full-time tuition ($17,250), mandatory fees ($220), and college room and board ($5950). College room only: $3100. Part-time tuition: $390 per credit. **Scholarships:** Available **Calendar System:** Semester, Summer Session Available **Enrollment:** FT 1,127, PT 52, Grad 102 **Faculty:** FT 70, PT 88 **Student-Faculty Ratio:** 13:1 **Exams:** SAT I or ACT **% Receiving Financial Aid:** 90 **% Residing in College-Owned, -Operated, or -Affiliated Housing:** 70 **Library Holdings:** 168,579 **Regional Accreditation:** North Central Association of Colleges and Schools **Credit Hours For Degree:** 120 semester hours, Bachelors **ROTC:**

Army **Professional Accreditation:** ACIPE, ATS **Intercollegiate Athletics:** Baseball M; Basketball M & W; Cross-Country Running M & W; Football M; Golf M & W; Soccer M & W; Softball W; Tennis M & W; Track and Field M & W; Volleyball W; Wrestling M

THE UNIVERSITY OF IOWA
Iowa City, IA 52242-1316
Tel: (319)335-3500
Free: 800-553-4692
Admissions: (319)335-3847
Fax: (319)335-1535
E-mail: admissions@uiowa.edu
Web Site: http://www.uiowa.edu/
President/CEO: Dr. David J. Skorton
Registrar: Dr. Larry Lockwood
Admissions: Michael Barron
Financial Aid: Mark S. Warner
Type: University **Sex:** Coed **Scores:** 98% SAT V 400+; 99% SAT M 400+; 37% ACT 18-23; 52% ACT 24-29 **% Accepted:** 84 **Admission Plans:** Early Admission; Deferred Admission **Application Deadline:** April 01 **Application Fee:** $40.00 **H.S. Requirements:** High school diploma required; GED accepted **Costs Per Year:** Application fee: $40. State resident tuition: $5110 full-time, $213 per semester hour part-time. Nonresident tuition: $17,334 full-time, $757 per semester hour part-time. Mandatory fees: $825 full-time, $413 per term part-time. College room and board: $6912. **Scholarships:** Available **Calendar System:** Semester, Summer Session Available **Enrollment:** FT 18,194, PT 2,106, Grad 6,085 **Faculty:** FT 1,595, PT 98 **Student-Faculty Ratio:** 15:1 **Exams:** SAT I or ACT **% Receiving Financial Aid:** 51 **% Residing in College-Owned, -Operated, or -Affiliated Housing:** 28 **Library Holdings:** 4,027,546 **Regional Accreditation:** North Central Association of Colleges and Schools **Credit Hours For Degree:** 120 semester hours, Bachelors **ROTC:** Army, Air Force **Professional Accreditation:** AACSB, ABET, ACEHSA, ACEJMC, AACN, AANA, ABA, ACPhE, ACA, ADA, ADtA, ACSP, ALA, APTA, APA, ASLHA, ACIPE, AALS, CEPH, CORE CSWE, JRCEPAT, JRCNMT, LCMEAMA, NAACLS, NASM, NAST, NRPA **Intercollegiate Athletics:** Baseball M; Basketball M & W; Crew M & W; Cross-Country Running M & W; Field Hockey W; Football M; Golf M & W; Gymnastics M & W; Ice Hockey M; Lacrosse M & W; Rugby M & W; Sailing M & W; Soccer M & W; Softball W; Swimming and Diving M & W; Table Tennis M & W; Tennis M & W; Track and Field M & W; Ultimate Frisbee M & W; Volleyball M & W; Wrestling M

UNIVERSITY OF NORTHERN IOWA
1227 West 27th St.
Cedar Falls, IA 50614
Tel: (319)273-2311
Free: 800-772-2037
Admissions: (319)273-2701
Fax: (319)273-2885
E-mail: admissions@uni.edu
Web Site: http://www.uni.edu/
President/CEO: Dr. Robert D. Koob
Registrar: Philip Patton
Admissions: Roland Carrillo
Financial Aid: Roland Carrillo
Type: Comprehensive **Sex:** Coed **Affiliation:** Board of Regents, State of Iowa **Scores:** 93.6% SAT V 400+; 96.1% SAT M 400+; 53.5% ACT 18-23; 37.1% ACT 24-29 **% Accepted:** 78 **Admission Plans:** Deferred Admission **Application Deadline:** August 15 **Application Fee:** $30.00 **H.S. Requirements:** High school diploma required; GED accepted **Costs Per Year:** Application fee: $30. State resident tuition: $4890 full-time, $204 per hour part-time. Nonresident tuition: $12,502 full-time, $521 per hour part-time. Mandatory fees: $712 full-time, $313.75 per term part-time. Full-time tuition and fees vary according to course load. Part-time tuition and fees vary according to course load. College room and board: $5531. College room only: $2588. Room and board charges vary according to board plan and housing facility. **Scholarships:** Available **Calendar System:** Semester, Summer Session Available **Enrollment:** FT 9,753, PT 1,241, Grad 1,628 **Faculty:** FT 641, PT 188 **Student-Faculty Ratio:** 16:1 **Exams:** SAT I or ACT **% Receiving Financial Aid:** 55 **% Residing in College-Owned, -Operated, or -Affiliated Housing:** 34 **Library Holdings:** 1,201,459 **Regional Accreditation:** North Central Association of Colleges and Schools **Credit Hours For Degree:** 120 semester hours, Bachelors **ROTC:** Army **Professional Accreditation:** AACSB, AAFCS, ACA, ASLHA, CSWE, JRCEPAT, NAIT, NASAD, NASM, NRPA **Intercollegiate Athletics:** Baseball M; Basketball M & W; Cross-Country Running M & W; Football M; Golf M & W; Soccer W; Softball W; Swimming and Diving W; Tennis M & W; Track and Field M & W; Volleyball W; Wrestling M

UPPER IOWA UNIVERSITY
605 Washington St., Box 1857
Fayette, IA 52142-1857
Tel: (563)425-5200
Free: 800-553-4150
Admissions: (563)425-5281
Fax: (563)425-5277
E-mail: admission@uiu.edu
Web Site: http://www.uiu.edu/
President/CEO: Dr. Alan G. Walker
Registrar: Holly Streeter
Admissions: Linda Hoopes
Financial Aid: Jobyna Johnston
Type: Comprehensive **Sex:** Coed **Scores:** 48% ACT 18-23; 25% ACT 24-29 **Admission Plans:** Early Admission; Deferred Admission **Application Fee:** $15.00 **H.S. Requirements:** High school diploma required; GED accepted **Costs Per Year:** Application fee: $15. Comprehensive fee: $23,596 includes full-time tuition ($18,056) and college room and board ($5540). College room only: $2300. Full-time tuition varies according to course load. Room and board charges vary according to board plan and housing facility. Part-time tuition: $600 per credit hour. **Scholarships:** Available **Calendar System:** Miscellaneous, Summer Session Available **Enrollment:** FT 678, PT 47, Grad 162 **Faculty:** FT 57, PT 8 **Student-Faculty Ratio:** 14:1 **Exams:** SAT I or ACT **% Residing in College-Owned, -Operated, or -Affiliated Housing:** 70 **Library Holdings:** 64,043 **Regional Accreditation:** North Central Association of Colleges and Schools **Credit Hours For Degree:** 60 semester hours, Associates; 120 semester hours, Bachelors **Intercollegiate Athletics:** Baseball M; Basketball M & W; Football M; Golf M & W; Soccer M & W; Softball W; Tennis M & W; Track and Field M & W; Volleyball M & W; Wrestling M

VATTEROTT COLLEGE
6100 Thornton Ave., Ste. 290
Des Moines, IA 50321
Tel: (515)309-9000
Free: 800-353-7264
Fax: (515)309-0366
Web Site: http://www.vatterott-college.edu/
President/CEO: Henry Franken
Admissions: Henry Franken
Type: Two-Year College **Sex:** Coed **Calendar System:** Miscellaneous **Faculty:** FT 8, PT 6 **Student-Faculty Ratio:** 15:1 **Professional Accreditation:** ACCSCT

VENNARD COLLEGE
PO Box 29
University Park, IA 52595
Tel: (515)673-8391
Free: 800-686-8391
Admissions: (641)673-8391
Fax: (515)673-8365
Web Site: http://www.vennard.edu/
President/CEO: Bruce Moyer
Registrar: DeAnne Doll
Admissions: Robyn Chrisman
Financial Aid: Kevin Klucas
Type: Four-Year College **Sex:** Coed **Affiliation:** interdenominational **Scores:** 100% SAT V 400+; 100% SAT M 400+; 38.2% ACT 18-23; 12.5% ACT 24-29 **Admission Plans:** Early Admission **Application Fee:** $20.00 **H.S. Requirements:** High school diploma required; GED accepted **Scholarships:** Available **Calendar System:** Semester, Summer Session Available **Enrollment:** FT 58, PT 14 **Faculty:** FT 4, PT 10 **Student-Faculty Ratio:** 9:1 **Exams:** SAT I or ACT, SAT I and SAT II or ACT **Library Holdings:** 19,619 **Credit Hours For Degree:** 64 semester hours, Associates; 128 semester hours, Bachelors **Professional Accreditation:** AABC **Intercollegiate Athletics:** Basketball M & W; Soccer M; Volleyball W

WALDORF COLLEGE
106 South 6th St.
Forest City, IA 50436-1713
Tel: (641)585-2450

Free: 800-292-1903
Admissions: (641)585-8112
Fax: (641)585-8194
E-mail: admissions@waldorf.edu
Web Site: http://www.waldorf.edu/
President/CEO: Rev. Thomas L. Jolivette
Registrar: Twylah Kragel
Admissions: Steve Lovik
Financial Aid: Duane Polsdofer
Type: Four-Year College **Sex:** Coed **Affiliation:** Lutheran **Scores:** 58% ACT 18-23; 16% ACT 24-29 **Admission Plans:** Early Admission **Application Fee:** $0.00 **H.S. Requirements:** High school diploma required; GED accepted **Costs Per Year:** Application fee: $0. Comprehensive fee: $20,140 includes full-time tuition ($14,785), mandatory fees ($735), and college room and board ($4620). College room only: $2150. Full-time tuition and fees vary according to class time, course load, and program. Room and board charges vary according to board plan and housing facility. Part-time tuition: $180 per credit. Part-time mandatory fees: $200 per credit. **Scholarships:** Available **Calendar System:** Semester, Summer Session Available **Enrollment:** FT 546, PT 83 **Faculty:** FT 36, PT 17 **Student-Faculty Ratio:** 17:1 **Exams:** SAT I or ACT **% Receiving Financial Aid:** 82 **% Residing in College-Owned, -Operated, or -Affiliated Housing:** 93 **Library Holdings:** 33,422 **Regional Accreditation:** North Central Association of Colleges and Schools **Credit Hours For Degree:** 64 semester hours, Associates; 124 semester hours, Bachelors **Intercollegiate Athletics:** Baseball M; Basketball M & W; Football M; Golf M & W; Soccer M & W; Softball W; Volleyball W; Wrestling M

WARTBURG COLLEGE
100 Wartburg Blvd., PO Box 1003
Waverly, IA 50677-0903
Tel: (319)352-8200
Free: 800-772-2085
Admissions: (319)352-8264
Fax: (319)352-8279
E-mail: admissions@wartburg.edu
Web Site: http://www.wartburg.edu/
President/CEO: Dr. Jack R. Ohle
Registrar: Sheree Covert
Admissions: Brent Matthias
Financial Aid: Jennifer Sassman
Type: Four-Year College **Sex:** Coed **Affiliation:** Lutheran **Scores:** 97% SAT V 400+; 100% SAT M 400+; 47% ACT 18-23; 43% ACT 24-29 **% Accepted:** 88 **Admission Plans:** Early Action; Deferred Admission **Application Fee:** $20.00 **H.S. Requirements:** High school diploma required; GED accepted **Costs Per Year:** Application fee: $20. Comprehensive fee: $26,895 includes full-time tuition ($20,500), mandatory fees ($630), and college room and board ($5765). College room only: $2815. Room and board charges vary according to board plan and housing facility. Part-time tuition: $760 per credit. Part-time mandatory fees: $50 per term. Part-time tuition and fees vary according to course load. **Scholarships:** Available **Calendar System:** Miscellaneous, Summer Session Available **Enrollment:** FT 1,732, PT 79 **Faculty:** FT 106, PT 73 **Student-Faculty Ratio:** 12:1 **Exams:** SAT I or ACT **% Receiving Financial Aid:** 78 **% Residing in College-Owned, -Operated, or -Affiliated Housing:** 79 **Library Holdings:** 186,089 **Regional Accreditation:** North Central Association of Colleges and Schools **Credit Hours For Degree:** 126 semester hours, Bachelors **Professional Accreditation:** CSWE, NASM, NCATE **Intercollegiate Athletics:** Baseball M; Basketball M & W; Cheerleading W; Cross-Country Running M & W; Football M; Golf M & W; Soccer M & W; Softball W; Tennis M & W; Track and Field M & W; Volleyball W; Wrestling M

WESTERN IOWA TECH COMMUNITY COLLEGE
4647 Stone Ave., PO Box 5199
Sioux City, IA 51102-5199
Tel: (712)274-6400
Fax: (712)274-6412
Web Site: http://www.witcc.edu/
President/CEO: Dr. Robert E. Dunker
Admissions: Lora Vanderzwaag
Financial Aid: Don Duzik
Type: Two-Year College **Sex:** Coed **Affiliation:** Iowa Department of Education Division of Community Colleges **Scores:** 46.4% ACT 18-23; 8.2% ACT 24-29 **% Accepted:** 100 **Admission Plans:** Open Admission; Early Admission; Deferred Admission **Application Deadline:** Rolling **Application Fee:** $20.00 **H.S. Requirements:** High school diploma required; GED accepted **Costs Per Year:** Application fee: $20. State resident tuition: $93 per credit hour part-time. Nonresident tuition: $133 per credit hour part-time. Mandatory fees: $15 per credit hour part-time. **Scholarships:** Available **Calendar System:** Semester, Summer Session Available **Enrollment:** FT 2,086, PT 3,248 **Faculty:** FT 88, PT 218 **Student-Faculty Ratio:** 20:1 **% Residing in College-Owned, -Operated, or -Affiliated Housing:** 2 **Library Holdings:** 25,696 **Regional Accreditation:** North Central Association of Colleges and Schools **Credit Hours For Degree:** 64 semester hours, Associates **Professional Accreditation:** ADA, APTA, NLN

WILLIAM PENN UNIVERSITY
201 Trueblood Ave.
Oskaloosa, IA 52577-1799
Tel: (641)673-1001
Free: 800-779-7366
Admissions: (641)673-1012
Fax: (641)673-1396
E-mail: admissions@wmpenn.edu
Web Site: http://www.wmpenn.edu/
President/CEO: Dr. Richard E. Sours
Registrar: Patrick McAdams
Admissions: John Ottosson
Financial Aid: Cyndi Peiffer
Type: Four-Year College **Sex:** Coed **Affiliation:** Society of Friends **Scores:** 63% ACT 18-23; 14% ACT 24-29 **Admission Plans:** Deferred Admission **Application Fee:** $20.00 **H.S. Requirements:** High school diploma required; GED accepted **Costs Per Year:** Application fee: $20. Comprehensive fee: $20,927 includes full-time tuition ($15,575), mandatory fees ($370), and college room and board ($4982). **Scholarships:** Available **Calendar System:** Semester, Summer Session Available **Enrollment:** FT 1,804, PT 88 **Faculty:** FT 35, PT 17 **Student-Faculty Ratio:** 15:1 **Exams:** SAT I or ACT **% Receiving Financial Aid:** 94 **% Residing in College-Owned, -Operated, or -Affiliated Housing:** 40 **Library Holdings:** 72,907 **Regional Accreditation:** North Central Association of Colleges and Schools **Credit Hours For Degree:** 64 credit hours, Associates; 124 credit hours, Bachelors **Intercollegiate Athletics:** Baseball M; Basketball M & W; Cheerleading M & W; Cross-Country Running M & W; Football M; Golf M; Soccer M & W; Softball W; Track and Field M & W; Volleyball W; Wrestling M

ALLEN COUNTY COMMUNITY COLLEGE
1801 North Cottonwood St.
Iola, KS 66749-1607
Tel: (620)365-5116
Fax: (620)365-7406
Web Site: http://www.allencc.net/
President/CEO: John Masterson
Registrar: Barbara Leavitt
Admissions: Randall Weber
Financial Aid: Barbara Leavitt
Type: Two-Year College **Sex:** Coed **Affiliation:** Kansas State Board of Regents **Scores:** 50% ACT 18-23; 12% ACT 24-29 **% Accepted:** 100 **Admission Plans:** Open Admission; Early Admission; Deferred Admission **Application Deadline:** August 24 **Application Fee:** $0.00 **H.S. Requirements:** High school diploma required; GED accepted **Costs Per Year:** Application fee: $0. Area resident tuition: $1184 full-time, $37 per hour part-time. State resident tuition: $1280 full-time, $40 per hour part-time. Nonresident tuition: $1280 full-time, $40 per part-time. Mandatory fees: $512 full-time, $16 per hour part-time. College room and board: $3600. College room only: $2600. **Scholarships:** Available **Calendar System:** Semester, Summer Session Available **Enrollment:** FT 824, PT 1,432 **Student-Faculty Ratio:** 17:1 **% Residing in College-Owned, -Operated, or -Affiliated Housing:** 10 **Library Holdings:** 49,416 **Regional Accreditation:** North Central Association of Colleges and Schools **Credit Hours For Degree:** 64 credit hours, Associates **Intercollegiate Athletics:** Baseball M; Basketball M & W; Cross-Country Running M & W; Golf M; Soccer M & W; Softball W; Track and Field M & W; Volleyball W

BAKER UNIVERSITY
Box 65
Baldwin City, KS 66006-0065
Tel: (785)594-6451
Free: 800-873-4282
Admissions: (785)594-8307
Fax: (785)594-6721
E-mail: daniel.mckinney@bakeru.edu
Web Site: http://www.bakeru.edu/
President/CEO: Dr. Daniel M. Lambert
Registrar: Lisa Johnston
Admissions: Daniel McKinney
Financial Aid: Jeanne Mott
Type: Comprehensive **Sex:** Coed **Affiliation:** United Methodist **Scores:** 48% ACT 18-23; 40.2% ACT 24-29 **% Accepted:** 63 **Admission Plans:** Deferred Admission **Application Deadline:** Rolling **Application Fee:** $0.00 **H.S. Requirements:** High school diploma required; GED accepted **Costs Per Year:** Application fee: $0. Comprehensive fee: $22,190 includes full-time tuition ($16,100), mandatory fees ($460), and college room and board ($5630). College room only: $2580. Full-time tuition and fees vary according to location and program. Room and board charges vary according to board plan and housing facility. Part-time tuition: $485 per credit hour. Part-time mandatory fees: $45. Part-time tuition and fees vary according to course load. **Scholarships:** Available **Calendar System:** Miscellaneous, Summer Session Available **Enrollment:** FT 860, PT 56 **Faculty:** FT 73, PT 38 **Student-Faculty Ratio:** 10:1 **Exams:** SAT I or ACT **% Residing in College-Owned, -Operated, or -Affiliated Housing:** 82 **Library Holdings:** 98,258 **Regional Accreditation:** North Central Association of Colleges and Schools **Credit Hours For Degree:** 132 credit hours, Bachelors **ROTC:** Army, Air Force **Professional Accreditation:** AACN, ACBSP, NASM, NCATE, NLN **Intercollegiate Athletics:** Baseball M; Basketball M & W; Cheerleading M & W; Cross-Country Running M & W; Football M; Golf M & W; Soccer M & W; Softball W; Tennis M & W; Track and Field M & W; Volleyball W

BARCLAY COLLEGE
607 North Kingman
Haviland, KS 67059-0288
Tel: (620)862-5252
Free: 800-862-0226
Fax: (620)862-5403
E-mail: frahe@barclaycollege.edu
Web Site: http://www.barclaycollege.edu/
President/CEO: Dr. David Hietala
Registrar: Dr. Glenn W. Leppert
Admissions: Herb Frazier
Financial Aid: Richard Sandstrom
Type: Four-Year College **Sex:** Coed **Affiliation:** Society of Friends **Scores:** 100% SAT V 400+; 100% SAT M 400+; 41% ACT 18-23; 32% ACT 24-29 **% Accepted:** 58 **Admission Plans:** Early Admission; Deferred Admission **Application Deadline:** September 01 **Application Fee:** $15.00 **H.S. Requirements:** High school diploma required; GED accepted **Costs Per Year:** Application fee: $15. Comprehensive fee: $17,830 includes full-time tuition ($12,730) and college room and board ($5100). College room only: $2000. Part-time tuition: $390 per hour. **Scholarships:** Available **Calendar System:** Semester, Summer Session Not available **Enrollment:** FT 90, PT 41 **Faculty:** FT 6, PT 23 **Student-Faculty Ratio:** 7:1 **Exams:** SAT I or ACT **% Receiving Financial Aid:** 97 **Library Holdings:** 63,759 **Regional Accreditation:** North Central Association of Colleges and Schools **Credit Hours For Degree:** 65 credit hours, Associates; 128 credit hours, Bachelors **Professional Accreditation:** AABC **Intercollegiate Athletics:** Baseball M; Basketball M & W; Cheerleading M & W; Soccer M; Tennis M & W; Volleyball W

BARTON COUNTY COMMUNITY COLLEGE
245 Northeast 30th Rd.
Great Bend, KS 67530-9283
Tel: (620)792-2701
Free: 800-722-6842
Admissions: (620)792-9241
Fax: (620)792-3238
Web Site: http://www.bartonccc.edu/
President/CEO: Dr. Veldon L. Law
Registrar: Lori Crowther
Admissions: Todd Moore
Financial Aid: Mryna Perkins
Type: Two-Year College **Sex:** Coed **Affiliation:** Kansas Board of Regents **Scores:** 75% SAT V 400+; 75% SAT M 400+; 51.04% ACT 18-23; 14.58% ACT 24-29 **Admission Plans:** Open Admission; Early Admission **Application Deadline:** Rolling **Application Fee:** $0.00 **H.S. Requirements:** High school diploma required; GED accepted **Costs Per Year:** Application fee: $0. State resident tuition: $1568 full-time, $49 per credit hour part-time. Nonresident tuition: $2176 full-time, $68 per credit hour part-time. Mandatory fees: $576 full-time, $18 per credit hour part-time. College room and board: $3854. **Scholarships:** Available **Calendar System:** Semester, Summer

Session Available **Enrollment:** FT 943, PT 2,878 **Faculty:** FT 72, PT 108 **Student-Faculty Ratio:** 18:1 **% Residing in College-Owned, -Operated, or -Affiliated Housing:** 4 **Library Holdings:** 26,322 **Regional Accreditation:** North Central Association of Colleges and Schools **Credit Hours For Degree:** 64 credit hours, Associates **Professional Accreditation:** NAACLS, NLN **Intercollegiate Athletics:** Baseball M; Basketball M & W; Cheerleading M & W; Cross-Country Running M & W; Golf M; Soccer M & W; Softball W; Tennis M & W; Track and Field M & W; Volleyball W

BENEDICTINE COLLEGE
1020 North 2nd St.
Atchison, KS 66002-1499
Tel: (913)367-5340
Free: 800-467-5340
Fax: (913)367-3673
E-mail: mail@benedictine.edu
Web Site: http://www.benedictine.edu/
President/CEO: Daniel J. Carey, PhD
Registrar: Beverly McConaughey
Admissions: Kelly Vowels
Financial Aid: Keith Jaloma
Type: Comprehensive **Sex:** Coed **Affiliation:** Roman Catholic **Scores:** 96.2% SAT V 400+; 96.1% SAT M 400+; 48.8% ACT 18-23; 35.4% ACT 24-29 **% Accepted:** 90 **Admission Plans:** Deferred Admission **Application Fee:** $25.00 **H.S. Requirements:** High school diploma required; GED accepted **Costs Per Year:** Application fee: $25. Comprehensive fee: $22,968 includes full-time tuition ($15,110), mandatory fees ($650), and college room and board ($7208). College room only: $2730. Full-time tuition and fees vary according to course load and degree level. Room and board charges vary according to board plan and housing facility. Part-time tuition: $450 per credit hour. Part-time tuition varies according to course load and degree level. **Scholarships:** Available **Calendar System:** Semester, Summer Session Available **Enrollment:** FT 1,176, PT 280, Grad 52 **Faculty:** FT 68, PT 46 **Student-Faculty Ratio:** 16:1 **Exams:** SAT I or ACT **% Receiving Financial Aid:** 77 **% Residing in College-Owned, -Operated, or -Affiliated Housing:** 69 **Library Holdings:** 368,558 **Regional Accreditation:** North Central Association of Colleges and Schools **Credit Hours For Degree:** 65 credit hours, Associates; 128 credit hours, Bachelors **ROTC:** Army **Professional Accreditation:** NASM, NCATE **Intercollegiate Athletics:** Baseball M; Basketball M & W; Cheerleading M & W; Cross-Country Running M & W; Football M; Golf M & W; Soccer M & W; Softball W; Tennis M & W; Track and Field M & W; Volleyball W

BETHANY COLLEGE
421 North First St.
Lindsborg, KS 67456-1897
Tel: (785)227-3311
Free: 800-826-2281
Fax: (785)227-2860
E-mail: admissions@bethanylb.edu
Web Site: http://www.bethanylb.edu/
President/CEO: Dr. Paul K. Formo
Registrar: Sharon Bruce
Admissions: Thandabantu Maceo
Financial Aid: Brenda Meagher
Type: Four-Year College **Sex:** Coed **Affiliation:** Lutheran **Scores:** 67% SAT V 400+; 78% SAT M 400+; 55% ACT 18-23; 28% ACT 24-29 **% Accepted:** 63 **Admission Plans:** Deferred Admission **Application Deadline:** Rolling **Application Fee:** $20.00 **H.S. Requirements:** High school diploma required; GED accepted **Costs Per Year:** Application fee: $20. Comprehensive fee: $21,480 includes full-time tuition ($16,000), mandatory fees ($210), and college room and board ($5270). College room only: $2850. Part-time tuition: $300 per credit hour. **Scholarships:** Available **Calendar System:** 4-1-4, Summer Session Available **Enrollment:** FT 552, PT 36 **Faculty:** FT 40, PT 30 **Student-Faculty Ratio:** 11:1 **Exams:** SAT I or ACT **% Receiving Financial Aid:** 82 **% Residing in College-Owned, -Operated, or -Affiliated Housing:** 68 **Library Holdings:** 84,730 **Regional Accreditation:** North Central Association of Colleges and Schools **Credit Hours For Degree:** 128 semester hours, Bachelors **Professional Accreditation:** CSWE, NASM, NCATE **Intercollegiate Athletics:** Baseball M; Basketball M & W; Cross-Country Running M & W; Football M; Golf M; Soccer M & W; Softball W; Tennis M & W; Track and Field M & W; Volleyball W

BETHEL COLLEGE
300 East 27th St.
North Newton, KS 67117
Tel: (316)283-2500
Free: 800-522-1887
Admissions: (316)284-5230
Fax: (316)284-5286
E-mail: admissions@bethelks.edu
Web Site: http://www.bethelks.edu/
President/CEO: E. LaVerne Epp
Registrar: Dr. Rodney Frey
Admissions: Allan Bartel
Financial Aid: Tony Graber
Type: Four-Year College **Sex:** Coed **Affiliation:** Mennonite Church USA **Scores:** 89% SAT V 400+; 100% SAT M 400+; 52% ACT 18-23; 32% ACT 24-29 **% Accepted:** 72 **Admission Plans:** Deferred Admission **Application Deadline:** Rolling **Application Fee:** $20.00 **H.S. Requirements:** High school diploma required; GED accepted **Costs Per Year:** Application fee: $20. Comprehensive fee: $21,650 includes full-time tuition ($15,550) and college room and board ($6100). College room only: $3200. Full-time tuition varies according to course load. Room and board charges vary according to board plan and housing facility. Part-time tuition: $550 per credit hour. Part-time tuition varies according to course load. **Scholarships:** Available **Calendar System:** 4-1-4, Summer Session Available **Enrollment:** FT 476, PT 38 **Faculty:** FT 47, PT 19 **Student-Faculty Ratio:** 9:1 **Exams:** SAT I or ACT **% Receiving Financial Aid:** 85 **% Residing in College-Owned, -Operated, or -Affiliated Housing:** 68 **Library Holdings:** 137,130 **Regional Accreditation:** North Central Association of Colleges and Schools **Credit Hours For Degree:** 124 credit hours, Bachelors **Professional Accreditation:** AACN, CSWE **Intercollegiate Athletics:** Basketball M & W; Cross-Country Running M & W; Football M; Golf M & W; Soccer M & W; Tennis M & W; Track and Field M & W; Volleyball W

BROWN MACKIE COLLEGE-KANSAS CITY
9705 Lenexa Dr.
Lenexa, KS 66215
Tel: (913)768-1900
Free: 800-635-9101
Fax: (913)823-7448
E-mail: dewhite@brownmackie.edu
Web Site: http://www.bmcaec.com/
President/CEO: Richard M. Thome
Registrar: Mary Lou Whitton
Admissions: Dorie E. White
Financial Aid: Cheryl Hanerhoff
Type: Two-Year College **Sex:** Coed **Affiliation:** The Brown Mackie College **Admission Plans:** Open Admission; Deferred Admission **Application Deadline:** Rolling **H.S. Requirements:** High school diploma required; GED accepted **Costs Per Year:** Tuition: $7164 full-time. Mandatory fees: $432 full-time. **Scholarships:** Available **Calendar System:** Quarter, Summer Session Available **Enrollment:** FT 370 **Faculty:** FT 8, PT 13 **Regional Accreditation:** North Central Association of Colleges and Schools **Credit Hours For Degree:** 96 credit hours, Associates

BROWN MACKIE COLLEGE-SALINA
2106 South 9th St.
Salina, KS 67401-2810
Tel: (785)825-5422
Free: 800-365-0433
Fax: (785)827-7623
Web Site: http://www.brownmackie.edu/locations.asp?locid=13
President/CEO: Richard M. Thome
Registrar: Lisa Graves
Admissions: Diann Heath
Financial Aid: Betty Charles
Type: Two-Year College **Sex:** Coed **% Accepted:** 96 **Admission Plans:** Open Admission; Deferred Admission **Application Deadline:** Rolling **H.S. Requirements:** High school diploma required; GED accepted **Costs Per Year:** Tuition: $9072 full-time. Mandatory fees: $576 full-time. **Scholarships:** Available **Calendar System:** Miscellaneous, Summer Session Available **Enrollment:** FT 367 **Faculty:** FT 6, PT 10 **Student-Faculty Ratio:** 15:1 **Library Holdings:** 14,788 **Regional Accreditation:** North Central Association of Colleges and Schools **Credit Hours For Degree:** 64 semester hours, Associates **Intercollegiate Athletics:** Baseball M; Basketball M & W; Softball W

BUTLER COMMUNITY COLLEGE
901 South Haverhill Rd.
El Dorado, KS 67042-3280

Tel: (316)321-2222
Fax: (316)322-3109
Web Site: http://www.butlercc.edu/
President/CEO: Dr. Jacqueline Vietti
Registrar: Connie Craft
Admissions: Paul Kyle
Financial Aid: G. Susie Edwards
Type: Two-Year College **Sex:** Coed **Affiliation:** Kansas Board of Regents **Scores:** 52% ACT 18-23; 22% ACT 24-29 **Admission Plans:** Open Admission; Early Admission; Deferred Admission **Application Deadline:** August 19 **Application Fee:** $0.00 **H.S. Requirements:** High school diploma required; GED accepted **Costs Per Year:** Application fee: $0. State resident tuition: $1756 full-time, $55 per credit hour part-time. Nonresident tuition: $3164 full-time, $99 per credit hour part-time. Mandatory fees: $448 full-time, $14 per credit hour part-time. College room and board: $4335. Room and board charges vary according to housing facility. **Scholarships:** Available **Calendar System:** Semester, Summer Session Available **Enrollment:** FT 3,658, PT 5,205 **Faculty:** FT 140, PT 473 **Student-Faculty Ratio:** 18:1 **% Residing in College-Owned, -Operated, or -Affiliated Housing:** 4 **Library Holdings:** 38,000 **Regional Accreditation:** North Central Association of Colleges and Schools **Credit Hours For Degree:** 62 credit hours, Associates **Professional Accreditation:** NLN **Intercollegiate Athletics:** Baseball M; Basketball M & W; Cross-Country Running M & W; Football M; Soccer W; Softball W; Tennis M & W; Track and Field M & W; Volleyball W

CENTRAL CHRISTIAN COLLEGE OF KANSAS
1200 South Main
PO Box 1403
McPherson, KS 67460-5799
Tel: (620)241-0723
Free: 800-835-0078
Fax: (620)241-6032
E-mail: david.ferrell@centralchristian.edu
Web Site: http://www.centralchristian.edu/
President/CEO: Dr. Donald L. Mason
Registrar: Marie Alexander
Admissions: Dr. David Ferrell
Type: Four-Year College **Sex:** Coed **Affiliation:** Free Methodist **Scores:** 47% ACT 18-23; 29% ACT 24-29 **% Accepted:** 98 **Admission Plans:** Deferred Admission **Application Deadline:** Rolling **Application Fee:** $20.00 **H.S. Requirements:** High school diploma required; GED accepted **Costs Per Year:** Application fee: $20. Comprehensive fee: $19,500 includes full-time tuition ($14,000), mandatory fees ($500), and college room and board ($5000). College room only: $2400. Part-time tuition: $405 per credit hour. **Scholarships:** Available **Calendar System:** 4-1-4, Summer Session Not available **Enrollment:** FT 314, PT 22 **Faculty:** FT 18, PT 20 **Student-Faculty Ratio:** 16:1 **Exams:** SAT I or ACT **% Receiving Financial Aid:** 84 **% Residing in College-Owned, -Operated, or -Affiliated Housing:** 81 **Library Holdings:** 35,156 **Regional Accreditation:** North Central Association of Colleges and Schools **Credit Hours For Degree:** 64 credit hours, Associates; 128 credit hours, Bachelors **Intercollegiate Athletics:** Baseball M; Basketball M & W; Cheerleading M & W; Cross-Country Running M & W; Golf M & W; Soccer M & W; Softball W; Tennis M & W; Volleyball W

CLOUD COUNTY COMMUNITY COLLEGE
2221 Campus Dr., PO Box 1002
Concordia, KS 66901-1002
Tel: (785)243-1435
Free: 800-729-5101
Fax: (785)243-1043
Web Site: http://www.cloud.edu/
President/CEO: Dr. George C. Knox
Registrar: Linda Peterson
Admissions: Chris Burlew
Financial Aid: Sherry Campbell
Type: Two-Year College **Sex:** Coed **Affiliation:** Kansas Community College System **Admission Plans:** Open Admission; Early Admission; Deferred Admission **Application Fee:** $0.00 **H.S. Requirements:** High school diploma required; GED accepted **Costs Per Year:** Application fee: $0. State resident tuition: $1560 full-time, $52 per credit hour part-time. Nonresident tuition: $2220 full-time, $74 per credit hour part-time. Mandatory fees: $540 full-time, $18 per credit hour part-time. College room and board: $3780. **Scholarships:** Available **Calendar System:** Semester, Summer Session Available **Faculty:** FT 38, PT 180 **Exams:** ACT, Other **Library Holdings:** 18,010 **Regional Accreditation:** North Central Association of Colleges and Schools **Credit Hours For Degree:** 64 credit hours, Associates **Professional Accreditation:** NLN **Intercollegiate Athletics:** Baseball M; Basketball M & W; Cross-Country Running M & W; Soccer M & W; Softball W; Tennis M & W; Track and Field M & W; Volleyball W

COFFEYVILLE COMMUNITY COLLEGE
400 West 11th St.
Coffeyville, KS 67337-5063
Tel: (620)251-7700
Fax: (620)252-7098
Web Site: http://www.coffeyville.edu/
President/CEO: Dr. Don A. Woodburn
Registrar: Deborah Oestmann
Admissions: Marlon Thornburg
Financial Aid: Rhonda Baker
Type: Two-Year College **Sex:** Coed **Affiliation:** Kansas Board of Regents **Scores:** 41% ACT 18-23; 12% ACT 24-29 **Admission Plans:** Open Admission; Early Admission; Deferred Admission **Application Fee:** $0.00 **H.S. Requirements:** High school diploma or equivalent not required **Costs Per Year:** Application fee: $0. State resident tuition: $896 full-time, $28 per credit hour part-time. Nonresident tuition: $2176 full-time, $68 per credit hour part-time. Mandatory fees: $704 full-time, $22 per credit hour part-time. College room and board: $3380. **Scholarships:** Available **Calendar System:** Semester, Summer Session Available **Enrollment:** FT 665, PT 1,101 **Faculty:** FT 51, PT 34 **Student-Faculty Ratio:** 20:1 **Exams:** ACT, Other **% Residing in College-Owned, -Operated, or -Affiliated Housing:** 27 **Library Holdings:** 27,482 **Regional Accreditation:** North Central Association of Colleges and Schools **Credit Hours For Degree:** 64 credit hours, Associates **Intercollegiate Athletics:** Baseball M; Basketball M & W; Cross-Country Running M & W; Football M; Golf M; Softball W; Track and Field M & W; Volleyball W

COLBY COMMUNITY COLLEGE
1255 South Range
Colby, KS 67701-4099
Tel: (785)462-3984
Fax: (785)462-4600
Web Site: http://www.colbycc.edu/
President/CEO: Dr. Mikel Ary
Registrar: Betty Kruse
Admissions: Nikol Nolan
Financial Aid: Jonathan Wilson
Type: Two-Year College **Sex:** Coed **Affiliation:** Kansas Board of Regents **% Accepted:** 100 **Admission Plans:** Open Admission; Early Admission; Deferred Admission **Application Deadline:** Rolling **H.S. Requirements:** High school diploma required; GED accepted **Costs Per Year:** State resident tuition: $1536 full-time, $48 per credit hour part-time. Nonresident tuition: $2784 full-time, $87 per credit hour part-time. Mandatory fees: $768 full-time, $24 per credit hour part-time. College room and board: $3632. **Scholarships:** Available **Calendar System:** Semester, Summer Session Available **Faculty:** FT 60, PT 0 **Student-Faculty Ratio:** 19:1 **% Residing in College-Owned, -Operated, or -Affiliated Housing:** 30 **Library Holdings:** 32,000 **Regional Accreditation:** North Central Association of Colleges and Schools **Credit Hours For Degree:** 62 semester hours, Associates **Professional Accreditation:** APTA, NLN **Intercollegiate Athletics:** Baseball M; Basketball M & W; Cheerleading W; Cross-Country Running M & W; Equestrian Sports M & W; Golf M & W; Softball W; Track and Field M & W; Volleyball W; Wrestling M

COWLEY COUNTY COMMUNITY COLLEGE AND AREA VOCATIONAL-TECHNICAL SCHOOL
125 South Second, PO Box 1147
Arkansas City, KS 67005-1147
Tel: (620)442-0430
Free: 800-593-CCCC
Admissions: (620)441-5245
Fax: (620)441-5350
E-mail: admissions@paws.cowley.cc.ks.us
Web Site: http://www.cowley.cc.ks.us/
President/CEO: Dr. Patrick J. McAtee
Registrar: Forest Smith
Admissions: Sue Saia
Financial Aid: Sally Palmer
Type: Two-Year College **Sex:** Coed **Affiliation:** Kansas State Board of Education **Scores:** 58.3% ACT 18-23; 11.8% ACT 24-29 **% Accepted:** 100

Admission Plans: Open Admission; Early Admission; Deferred Admission **Application Deadline:** Rolling **Application Fee:** $0.00 **H.S. Requirements:** High school diploma required; GED accepted **Costs Per Year:** Application fee: $0. Area resident tuition: $1290 full-time, $43 per credit hour part-time. State resident tuition: $1440 full-time, $48 per credit hour part-time. Nonresident tuition: $3000 full-time, $100 per credit hour part-time. Mandatory fees: $570 full-time, $19 per credit hour part-time. College room and board: $3530. **Scholarships:** Available **Calendar System:** Semester, Summer Session Available **Enrollment:** FT 2,386, PT 2,293 **Faculty:** FT 46, PT 170 **Student-Faculty Ratio:** 31:1 **Exams:** ACT **% Residing in College-Owned, -Operated, or -Affiliated Housing:** 7 **Library Holdings:** 26,000 **Regional Accreditation:** North Central Association of Colleges and Schools **Credit Hours For Degree:** 62 credit hours, Associates **Intercollegiate Athletics:** Baseball M; Basketball M & W; Golf M; Softball W; Tennis M & W; Volleyball W

DODGE CITY COMMUNITY COLLEGE
2501 North 14th Ave.
Dodge City, KS 67801-2399
Tel: (620)225-1321
Admissions: (316)225-1321
Fax: (620)225-0918
E-mail: admin@dccc.dodge-city.cc.ks.us
Web Site: http://www.dccc.cc.ks.us/
President/CEO: Dr. Richard Burke
Registrar: Marcus Garstecki
Admissions: Corbin Strobel
Type: Two-Year College **Sex:** Coed **Affiliation:** Kansas State Board of Education **Admission Plans:** Open Admission; Early Admission; Deferred Admission **Application Fee:** $0.00 **H.S. Requirements:** High school diploma or equivalent not required **Costs Per Year:** Application fee: $0. State resident tuition: $1120 full-time, $35 per credit hour part-time. Nonresident tuition: $1344 full-time, $42 per credit hour part-time. Mandatory fees: $806 full-time, $23 per credit hour part-time, $35 per term part-time. Full-time tuition and fees vary according to course load. Part-time tuition and fees vary according to course load. College room and board: $4060. **Scholarships:** Available **Calendar System:** Semester, Summer Session Available **Faculty:** FT 55, PT 108 **Exams:** Other, SAT I and SAT II or ACT **% Residing in College-Owned, -Operated, or -Affiliated Housing:** 20 **Library Holdings:** 30,000 **Regional Accreditation:** North Central Association of Colleges and Schools **Credit Hours For Degree:** 62 credit hours, Associates **Professional Accreditation:** NLN **Intercollegiate Athletics:** Baseball M; Basketball M & W; Cross-Country Running M & W; Equestrian Sports M & W; Football M; Golf M; Softball W; Volleyball W

DONNELLY COLLEGE
608 North 18th St.
Kansas City, KS 66102-4298
Tel: (913)621-6070
Admissions: (913)621-8769
Fax: (913)621-0354
Web Site: http://www.donnelly.edu/
President/CEO: Dr. Kenneth Gibson
Registrar: Sr. Fran Cross
Admissions: Kevin Kelley
Financial Aid: Dora Clark
Type: Two-Year College **Sex:** Coed **Affiliation:** Roman Catholic **Admission Plans:** Open Admission; Early Admission; Deferred Admission **Application Fee:** $0.00 **H.S. Requirements:** High school diploma required; GED accepted **Scholarships:** Available **Calendar System:** Semester, Summer Session Available **Enrollment:** FT 198, PT 200 **Faculty:** FT 13, PT 33 **Student-Faculty Ratio:** 10:1 **Library Holdings:** 33,752 **Regional Accreditation:** North Central Association of Colleges and Schools **Credit Hours For Degree:** 64 credit hours, Associates

EMPORIA STATE UNIVERSITY
1200 Commercial St.
Emporia, KS 66801-5087
Tel: (620)341-1200; 877-468-6378
Admissions: (620)341-5465
E-mail: go2esu@emporia.edu
Web Site: http://www.emporia.edu/
President/CEO: Dr. Kay Schallenkamp
Registrar: Dr. L. F. Robinson
Admissions: Laura Eddy
Financial Aid: Elaine Henrie
Type: Comprehensive **Sex:** Coed **Affiliation:** Kansas Board of Regents **Scores:** 51% ACT 18-23; 32% ACT 24-29 **% Accepted:** 78 **Admission Plans:** Early Admission; Deferred Admission **Application Deadline:** Rolling **Application Fee:** $30.00 **H.S. Requirements:** High school diploma required; GED accepted **Costs Per Year:** Application fee: $30. State resident tuition: $2638 full-time, $88 per credit hour part-time. Nonresident tuition: $9990 full-time, $333 per credit hour part-time. Mandatory fees: $668 full-time, $41 per credit hour part-time. Full-time tuition and fees vary according to degree level. Part-time tuition and fees vary according to degree level. College room and board: $4787. College room only: $2363. Room and board charges vary according to board plan and housing facility. **Scholarships:** Available **Calendar System:** Semester, Summer Session Available **Enrollment:** FT 3,797, PT 554, Grad 1,937 **Faculty:** FT 252, PT 30 **Student-Faculty Ratio:** 18:1 **Exams:** SAT I or ACT **% Receiving Financial Aid:** 59 **% Residing in College-Owned, -Operated, or -Affiliated Housing:** 25 **Library Holdings:** 2,364,320 **Regional Accreditation:** North Central Association of Colleges and Schools **Credit Hours For Degree:** 124 credit hours, Bachelors **Professional Accreditation:** AACSB, ACA, ALA, CORE, JRCEPAT, NASAD, NASM, NCATE, NLN **Intercollegiate Athletics:** Baseball M; Basketball M & W; Cheerleading M & W; Cross-Country Running M & W; Football M; Soccer W; Softball W; Tennis M & W; Track and Field M & W; Volleyball W

FLINT HILLS TECHNICAL COLLEGE
3301 West 18th Ave.
Emporia, KS 66801
Tel: (620)341-2300
Free: 800-711-6947
Fax: (620)343-7252
Web Site: http://www.fhtc.net/
President/CEO: Dr. Lee V. Alderman
Type: Two-Year College **Sex:** Coed **Calendar System:** Semester **Regional Accreditation:** North Central Association of Colleges and Schools **Professional Accreditation:** ADA, COE

FORT HAYS STATE UNIVERSITY
600 Park St.
Hays, KS 67601-4099
Tel: (785)628-4000
Free: 800-628-FHSU
Admissions: (785)628-5666
Fax: (785)628-4014
E-mail: tigers@fhsuvm.fhsu.edu
Web Site: http://www.fhsu.edu/
President/CEO: Dr. Edward H. Hammond
Registrar: Joey Linn
Admissions: Roger Schieferecke
Financial Aid: Craig Karlin
Type: Comprehensive **Sex:** Coed **Affiliation:** Kansas Board of Regents **Scores:** 55.41% ACT 18-23; 28.85% ACT 24-29 **Application Fee:** $30.00 **H.S. Requirements:** High school diploma required; GED accepted. For applicants 25 or over: High school diploma or equivalent not required **Costs Per Year:** Application fee: $30. State resident tuition: $1886 full-time, $101.75 per credit hour part-time. Nonresident tuition: $7104 full-time, $319.17 per credit hour part-time. Mandatory fees: $556 full-time. Full-time tuition and fees vary according to course load, location, and reciprocity agreements. Part-time tuition varies according to course load and location. College room and board: $6190. College room only: $3577. Room and board charges vary according to board plan, housing facility, and student level. **Scholarships:** Available **Calendar System:** Semester, Summer Session Available **Enrollment:** FT 4,126, PT 1,794, Grad 1,483 **Faculty:** FT 253, PT 38 **Student-Faculty Ratio:** 17:1 **Exams:** ACT, SAT I or ACT **% Receiving Financial Aid:** 68 **% Residing in College-Owned, -Operated, or -Affiliated Housing:** 20 **Library Holdings:** 624,637 **Regional Accreditation:** North Central Association of Colleges and Schools **Credit Hours For Degree:** 62 credit hours, Associates; 124 credit hours, Bachelors **Professional Accreditation:** AACN, ASLHA, CSWE, JRCERT, NASM, NCATE **Intercollegiate Athletics:** Baseball M; Basketball M & W; Cross-Country Running M & W; Football M; Golf M; Softball W; Tennis W; Track and Field M & W; Volleyball W; Wrestling M

FORT SCOTT COMMUNITY COLLEGE
2108 South Horton
Fort Scott, KS 66701

Tel: (316)223-2700
Free: 800-874-3722
Fax: (316)223-4927
Web Site: http://www.fortscott.edu/
President/CEO: Richard Hedges
Registrar: William Meyer
Admissions: Mert Barrows
Financial Aid: Steve Armstrong
Type: Two-Year College **Sex:** Coed **Admission Plans:** Open Admission; Early Admission; Deferred Admission **Application Fee:** $0.00 **H.S. Requirements:** High school diploma required; GED accepted **Scholarships:** Available **Calendar System:** Semester, Summer Session Available **Faculty:** FT 35, PT 70 **Student-Faculty Ratio:** 26:1 **Exams:** ACT, Other **% Residing in College-Owned, -Operated, or -Affiliated Housing:** 9 **Library Holdings:** 25,308 **Regional Accreditation:** North Central Association of Colleges and Schools **Credit Hours For Degree:** 60 semester hours, Associates **ROTC:** Army **Professional Accreditation:** NLN **Intercollegiate Athletics:** Baseball M; Basketball M & W; Football M; Softball W; Volleyball W

FRIENDS UNIVERSITY
2100 West University St.
Wichita, KS 67213
Tel: (316)295-5000
Free: 800-577-2233
Admissions: (316)295-5100
Fax: (316)262-5027
E-mail: tmyers@friends.edu
Web Site: http://www.friends.edu/
President/CEO: Dr. Biff Green
Registrar: Marcia Morton
Admissions: Tony Myers
Financial Aid: Myra Pfannenstiel
Type: Comprehensive **Sex:** Coed **Admission Plans:** Early Admission **Application Fee:** $15.00 **H.S. Requirements:** High school diploma required; GED accepted **Scholarships:** Available **Calendar System:** Semester, Summer Session Available **Faculty:** FT 75, PT 150 **Exams:** SAT I or ACT **% Receiving Financial Aid:** 85 **% Residing in College-Owned, -Operated, or -Affiliated Housing:** 18 **Library Holdings:** 105,989 **Regional Accreditation:** North Central Association of Colleges and Schools **Credit Hours For Degree:** 62 semester hours, Associates; 124 semester hours, Bachelors **Professional Accreditation:** AAMFT, NASM, NCATE **Intercollegiate Athletics:** Baseball M; Basketball M & W; Cross-Country Running M & W; Football M; Golf M; Soccer M & W; Softball W; Tennis M & W; Track and Field M & W; Volleyball W

GARDEN CITY COMMUNITY COLLEGE
801 Campus Dr.
Garden City, KS 67846-6399
Tel: (316)276-7611
Admissions: (620)276-7611
Web Site: http://www.gcccks.edu/
President/CEO: Carol E. Ballantyne, PhD
Registrar: Nancy Unruh
Admissions: Nikki Geier
Financial Aid: Beth Tedrow
Type: Two-Year College **Sex:** Coed **Affiliation:** Kansas Board of Regents **Scores:** 52% ACT 18-23; 12% ACT 24-29 **Admission Plans:** Open Admission **Application Fee:** $0.00 **H.S. Requirements:** High school diploma required; GED accepted **Costs Per Year:** Application fee: $0. State resident tuition: $1248 full-time, $39 per credit hour part-time. Nonresident tuition: $2080 full-time, $65 per credit hour part-time. Mandatory fees: $672 full-time, $21 per credit hour part-time. Full-time tuition and fees vary according to course load and location. Part-time tuition and fees vary according to course load and location. College room and board: $4500. Room and board charges vary according to housing facility. **Scholarships:** Available **Calendar System:** Semester, Summer Session Available **Enrollment:** FT 925, PT 1,249 **Faculty:** FT 71, PT 113 **Student-Faculty Ratio:** 17:1 **Exams:** Other **% Residing in College-Owned, -Operated, or -Affiliated Housing:** 12 **Library Holdings:** 42,080 **Regional Accreditation:** North Central Association of Colleges and Schools **Credit Hours For Degree:** 64 credit hours, Associates **Professional Accreditation:** NLN **Intercollegiate Athletics:** Baseball M; Basketball M & W; Cheerleading M & W; Cross-Country Running M & W; Football M; Soccer M & W; Softball W; Track and Field M & W; Volleyball W

HASKELL INDIAN NATIONS UNIVERSITY
155 Indian Ave., No. 5031
Lawrence, KS 66046-4800
Tel: (785)749-8404
Admissions: (785)749-8454
Fax: (785)749-8429
Web Site: http://www.haskell.edu/
President/CEO: Dr. Karen Gayton Swisher
Registrar: Ellen Allen
Admissions: Ellen Allen
Financial Aid: Reta Beaver
Type: Four-Year College **Sex:** Coed **Admission Plans:** Preferred Admission **Application Fee:** $10.00 **H.S. Requirements:** High school diploma required; GED accepted **Costs Per Year:** Application fee: $10. State resident tuition: $0 full-time. Nonresident tuition: $0 full-time. Mandatory fees: $420 full-time, $70 per term part-time. **Scholarships:** Available **Calendar System:** Semester, Summer Session Available **Enrollment:** FT 922, PT 106 **Faculty:** FT 48, PT 0 **Student-Faculty Ratio:** 15:1 **Exams:** ACT **Library Holdings:** 50,000 **Regional Accreditation:** North Central Association of Colleges and Schools **Credit Hours For Degree:** 61 credit hours, Associates; 128 credit hours, Bachelors **ROTC:** Air Force **Intercollegiate Athletics:** Basketball M & W; Cheerleading M & W; Cross-Country Running M & W; Football M; Golf M; Softball W; Track and Field M & W; Volleyball W

HESSTON COLLEGE
Box 3000
Hesston, KS 67062-2093
Tel: (620)327-4221
Free: 800-995-2757
Admissions: (620)327-8222
Fax: (620)327-8300
E-mail: admissions@hesston.edu
Web Site: http://www.hesston.edu/
President/CEO: Rev. Peter Wiebe
Registrar: Gerry Selzer
Admissions: Clark Roth
Financial Aid: Marcia Mendez
Type: Two-Year College **Sex:** Coed **Affiliation:** Mennonite **Scores:** 86% SAT V 400+; 77% SAT M 400+; 46% ACT 18-23; 30% ACT 24-29 **% Accepted:** 83 **Admission Plans:** Open Admission; Early Admission; Deferred Admission **Application Deadline:** Rolling **Application Fee:** $15.00 **H.S. Requirements:** High school diploma required; GED accepted **Costs Per Year:** Application fee: $15. Comprehensive fee: $22,354 includes full-time tuition ($16,246), mandatory fees ($250), and college room and board ($5858). Part-time tuition: $676 per hour. Part-time mandatory fees: $60 per term. **Scholarships:** Available **Calendar System:** Semester, Summer Session Available **Enrollment:** FT 414, PT 63 **Faculty:** FT 19, PT 25 **Exams:** SAT I or ACT **% Residing in College-Owned, -Operated, or -Affiliated Housing:** 74 **Library Holdings:** 35,000 **Regional Accreditation:** North Central Association of Colleges and Schools **Credit Hours For Degree:** 60 credit hours, Associates **Professional Accreditation:** NLN **Intercollegiate Athletics:** Baseball M; Basketball M & W; Soccer M; Softball W; Tennis M & W; Volleyball W

HIGHLAND COMMUNITY COLLEGE
606 West Main St.
Highland, KS 66035
Tel: (785)442-6000
Admissions: (785)442-6020
Fax: (785)442-6100
Web Site: http://www.highlandcc.edu/
President/CEO: David Reist
Registrar: Alice Hamilton
Admissions: Cheryl Rasmussen
Financial Aid: Kelly Twombly
Type: Two-Year College **Sex:** Coed **Affiliation:** Kansas Community College System **Admission Plans:** Open Admission; Preferred Admission; Early Admission **Application Fee:** $0.00 **H.S. Requirements:** High school diploma required; GED accepted **Costs Per Year:** Application fee: $0. Area resident tuition: $888 full-time, $37 per credit hour part-time. State resident

tuition: $1080 full-time, $45 per credit hour part-time. Nonresident tuition: $2280 full-time, $95 per credit hour part-time. Mandatory fees: $1056 full-time, $44 per credit hour part-time. College room and board: $3872. College room only: $2242. **Scholarships:** Available **Calendar System:** Semester, Summer Session Available **Faculty:** FT 34, PT 192 **Exams:** ACT, Other **Library Holdings:** 30,000 **Regional Accreditation:** North Central Association of Colleges and Schools **Credit Hours For Degree:** 62 credit hours, Associates **ROTC:** Army **Intercollegiate Athletics:** Baseball M & W; Basketball M & W; Cross-Country Running M & W; Football M; Golf M; Track and Field M & W; Volleyball W

HUTCHINSON COMMUNITY COLLEGE AND AREA VOCATIONAL SCHOOL

1300 North Plum St.
Hutchinson, KS 67501-5894
Tel: (620)665-3500
Free: 800-289-3501
Admissions: (620)665-3536
Fax: (620)665-3310
E-mail: strobelc@hutchcc.edu
Web Site: http://www.hutchcc.edu/
President/CEO: Dr. Edward E. Berger
Registrar: Kathie Tyrell
Admissions: Corbin Strobel
Financial Aid: Ron Menefee

Type: Two-Year College **Sex:** Coed **Affiliation:** Kansas Board of Regents **Scores:** 56% ACT 18-23; 18% ACT 24-29 **% Accepted:** 100 **Admission Plans:** Open Admission; Early Admission; Deferred Admission **Application Deadline:** Rolling **Application Fee:** $0.00 **H.S. Requirements:** High school diploma required; GED accepted. For continuing education program: High school diploma or equivalent not required **Costs Per Year:** Application fee: $0. Area resident tuition: $50 per hour part-time. State resident tuition: $1600 full-time, $50 per hour part-time. Nonresident tuition: $2816 full-time, $88 per hour part-time. Mandatory fees: $480 full-time, $15 per hour part-time. College room and board: $4060. Room and board charges vary according to board plan. **Scholarships:** Available **Calendar System:** Semester, Summer Session Available **Enrollment:** FT 1,956, PT 2,913 **Faculty:** FT 113, PT 220 **Student-Faculty Ratio:** 16:1 **% Residing in College-Owned, -Operated, or -Affiliated Housing:** 11 **Library Holdings:** 41,812 **Regional Accreditation:** North Central Association of Colleges and Schools **Credit Hours For Degree:** 64 credit hours, Associates **ROTC:** Army **Professional Accreditation:** AHIMA, JRCERT, NLN **Intercollegiate Athletics:** Baseball M; Basketball M & W; Cheerleading M & W; Cross-Country Running M & W; Football M; Golf M; Soccer W; Softball W; Tennis M & W; Track and Field M & W; Volleyball W

INDEPENDENCE COMMUNITY COLLEGE

Brookside Dr. and College Ave.
PO Box 708
Independence, KS 67301-0708
Tel: (620)331-4100
Free: 800-842-6063
Admissions: (620)332-5400
Fax: (620)331-5344
E-mail: sciufulescu@indycc.edu
Web Site: http://www.indycc.edu/
President/CEO: Dr. Judith M.L. Hansen
Registrar: Sonja Conley
Admissions: Sally A. Ciufulescu
Financial Aid: Sheila Smither

Type: Two-Year College **Sex:** Coed **Affiliation:** Kansas State Board of Education **Admission Plans:** Open Admission; Early Admission **Application Deadline:** Rolling **Application Fee:** $0.00 **H.S. Requirements:** High school diploma required; GED accepted **Costs Per Year:** Application fee: $0. Area resident tuition: $800 full-time. State resident tuition: $800 full-time, $25 per credit hour part-time. Nonresident tuition: $2080 full-time, $65 per credit hour part-time. Mandatory fees: $800 full-time. College room and board: $4100. **Scholarships:** Available **Calendar System:** Semester, Summer Session Available **Enrollment:** FT 478, PT 428 **Faculty:** FT 29, PT 65 **Student-Faculty Ratio:** 17:1 **Exams:** SAT I or ACT **% Residing in College-Owned, -Operated, or -Affiliated Housing:** 10 **Library Holdings:** 32,408 **Regional Accreditation:** North Central Association of Colleges and Schools **Credit Hours For Degree:** 64 semester hours, Associates **Intercollegiate Athletics:** Baseball M; Basketball M & W; Cheerleading M & W; Football M; Softball W; Tennis M & W; Track and Field M & W; Volleyball W

JOHNSON COUNTY COMMUNITY COLLEGE

12345 College Blvd.
Overland Park, KS 66210-1299
Tel: (913)469-8500
Web Site: http://www.johnco.cc.ks.us/
President/CEO: Dr. Charles J. Carlsen
Registrar: Marge Shelley
Admissions: Dr. Charles J. Carlsen
Financial Aid: Julie Cooper

Type: Two-Year College **Sex:** Coed **Affiliation:** Kansas State Board of Education **Admission Plans:** Open Admission; Early Admission **Application Fee:** $10.00 **H.S. Requirements:** High school diploma required; GED accepted **Costs Per Year:** Application fee: $10. Area resident tuition: $1920 full-time, $64 per credit hour part-time. State resident tuition: $2370 full-time, $79 per credit hour part-time. Nonresident tuition: $4350 full-time, $145 per credit hour part-time. Full-time tuition varies according to course load. Part-time tuition varies according to course load. **Scholarships:** Available **Calendar System:** Semester, Summer Session Available **Enrollment:** FT 6,378, PT 12,234 **Faculty:** FT 302, PT 535 **Student-Faculty Ratio:** 21:1 **Exams:** ACT, Other **Library Holdings:** 89,400 **Regional Accreditation:** North Central Association of Colleges and Schools **Credit Hours For Degree:** 64 credit hours, Associates **Professional Accreditation:** ACF, ADA, ACBSP, CARC, JRCEMT, NLN **Intercollegiate Athletics:** Baseball M; Basketball M & W; Cross-Country Running M & W; Soccer M; Softball W; Tennis M & W; Track and Field M & W; Volleyball W

KANSAS CITY KANSAS COMMUNITY COLLEGE

7250 State Ave.
Kansas City, KS 66112-3003
Tel: (913)334-1100
Admissions: (913)288-7694
Fax: (913)696-9646
Web Site: http://www.kckcc.edu/
President/CEO: Dr. Thomas R. Burke
Registrar: Dr. Denise McDowell
Admissions: Dr. Denise McDowell
Financial Aid: Mary Dorr

Type: Two-Year College **Sex:** Coed **Admission Plans:** Open Admission **Application Deadline:** Rolling **Application Fee:** $0.00 **H.S. Requirements:** High school diploma required; GED accepted. For partnership and dual enrollment: High school diploma or equivalent not required **Costs Per Year:** Application fee: $0. State resident tuition: $1470 full-time, $49 per credit hour part-time. Nonresident tuition: $4410 full-time, $147 per credit hour part-time. Mandatory fees: $300 full-time, $10 per credit hour part-time. Full-time tuition and fees vary according to course load. Part-time tuition and fees vary according to course load. **Scholarships:** Available **Calendar System:** Semester, Summer Session Available **Enrollment:** FT 1,925, PT 3,494 **Faculty:** FT 108, PT 244 **Student-Faculty Ratio:** 14:1 **Library Holdings:** 65,000 **Regional Accreditation:** North Central Association of Colleges and Schools **Credit Hours For Degree:** 60 credit hours, Associates **Professional Accreditation:** ABFSE, APTA, ACBSP, CARC, NLN **Intercollegiate Athletics:** Baseball M; Basketball M & W; Cross-Country Running M & W; Golf M; Soccer M; Softball W; Track and Field M & W; Volleyball W

KANSAS STATE UNIVERSITY

Manhattan, KS 66506
Tel: (785)532-6011
Admissions: (785)532-6250
Fax: (785)532-6393
E-mail: kstate@ksu.edu
Web Site: http://www.ksu.edu/
President/CEO: Dr. Jon Wefald
Registrar: Jackie Dean
Admissions: Dr. Larry Moeder
Financial Aid: Lawrence Moeder

Type: University **Sex:** Coed **Affiliation:** Kansas Board of Regents **Scores:** 44.9% ACT 18-23; 39% ACT 24-29 **% Accepted:** 59 **Application Deadline:** Rolling **Application Fee:** $30.00 **H.S. Requirements:** High school diploma required; GED accepted **Costs Per Year:** Application fee: $30. State resident tuition: $4560 full-time, $152 per credit hour part-time. Nonresident tuition: $13,890 full-time, $463 per credit hour part-time. Mandatory fees: $564 full-time. College room and board: $5772. Room and board charges vary according to board plan. **Scholarships:** Available **Calendar System:** Semester, Summer Session Available **Enrollment:** FT 16,519, PT 2,319, Grad 3,916 **Faculty:** FT 714, PT 78 **Student-Faculty Ratio:** 21:1 **Exams:**

SAT I or ACT **% Receiving Financial Aid:** 54 **% Residing in College-Owned, -Operated, or -Affiliated Housing:** 36 **Library Holdings:** 1,573,645 **Regional Accreditation:** North Central Association of Colleges and Schools **Credit Hours For Degree:** 60 semester hours, Associates; 120 semester hours, Bachelors **ROTC:** Army, Air Force **Professional Accreditation:** AACSB, ABET, ACEJMC, AAMFT, AAFCS, ACCE, ACA, ADtA, ACSP, APA, ASLA, ASLHA, AVMA, CSWE, FIDER, JRCEPAT, NASAD, NASM, NASPAA, NAST NCATE, NRPA **Intercollegiate Athletics:** Baseball M; Basketball M & W; Crew W; Cross-Country Running M & W; Football M; Golf M & W; Tennis W; Track and Field M & W; Volleyball W

KANSAS WESLEYAN UNIVERSITY
100 East Claflin Ave.
Salina, KS 67401-6196
Tel: (785)827-5541
Free: 800-874-1154
Admissions: (785)829-5541
Fax: (785)827-0927
E-mail: jallen@kwu.edu
Web Site: http://www.kwu.edu/
President/CEO: Dr. Philip P. Kerstetter
Registrar: Glenna Alexander
Admissions: Jim Allen
Financial Aid: Glenna Alexander
Type: Comprehensive **Sex:** Coed **Affiliation:** United Methodist **Scores:** 66% ACT 18-23; 24% ACT 24-29 **Admission Plans:** Deferred Admission **Application Fee:** $20.00 **H.S. Requirements:** High school diploma required; GED accepted **Costs Per Year:** Application fee: $20. Comprehensive fee: $21,400 includes full-time tuition ($15,800) and college room and board ($5600). College room only: $2400. Part-time tuition: $200 per credit hour. Part-time tuition varies according to course load. **Scholarships:** Available **Calendar System:** Miscellaneous, Summer Session Available **Enrollment:** FT 597, PT 171, Grad 37 **Faculty:** FT 42, PT 17 **Student-Faculty Ratio:** 18:1 **Exams:** ACT, SAT I or ACT, SAT I **% Receiving Financial Aid:** 90 **% Residing in College-Owned, -Operated, or -Affiliated Housing:** 65 **Regional Accreditation:** North Central Association of Colleges and Schools **Credit Hours For Degree:** 63 credit hours, Associates; 126 credit hours, Bachelors **Professional Accreditation:** NCATE, NLN **Intercollegiate Athletics:** Baseball M; Basketball M & W; Cheerleading M & W; Cross-Country Running M & W; Football M; Golf M & W; Soccer M & W; Softball W; Tennis M & W; Track and Field M & W; Volleyball W

LABETTE COMMUNITY COLLEGE
200 South 14th St.
Parsons, KS 67357-4299
Tel: (620)421-6700
Web Site: http://www.labette.edu/
President/CEO: Ronald Fundis
Registrar: Kathy Johnston
Admissions: Dr. Wayne Hatcher
Financial Aid: Dr. Janet Eads
Type: Two-Year College **Sex:** Coed **Affiliation:** Kansas State Board of Education **Admission Plans:** Open Admission; Early Admission **Application Fee:** $0.00 **H.S. Requirements:** High school diploma required; GED accepted **Scholarships:** Available **Calendar System:** Semester, Summer Session Available **Enrollment:** FT 466, PT 935 **Faculty:** FT 31, PT 177 **Exams:** ACT, Other **Library Holdings:** 26,000 **Regional Accreditation:** North Central Association of Colleges and Schools **Credit Hours For Degree:** 62 credit hours, Associates **ROTC:** Army **Professional Accreditation:** CARC, JRCERT, NLN **Intercollegiate Athletics:** Baseball M; Basketball M & W; Cheerleading W; Softball W; Tennis W; Volleyball W; Wrestling M

MANHATTAN AREA TECHNICAL COLLEGE
3136 Dickens Ave.
Manhattan, KS 66503-2499
Tel: (913)587-2800
Free: 800-352-7575
Admissions: (785)587-2800
Fax: (913)587-2804
Web Site: http://www.matc.net/
President/CEO: Dr. Duane M. Dunn
Admissions: Rick Smith
Type: Two-Year College **Sex:** Coed **Application Fee:** $40.00 **H.S. Requirements:** High school diploma required; GED accepted **Costs Per Year:** Application fee: $40. State resident tuition: $2035 full-time, $55 per credit hour part-time. Mandatory fees: $400 full-time, $10 per credit hour part-time. **Calendar System:** Semester **Enrollment:** FT 324, PT 77 **Faculty:** FT 27, PT 8 **Student-Faculty Ratio:** 11:1 **Regional Accreditation:** North Central Association of Colleges and Schools **Credit Hours For Degree:** 62 credit hours, Associates **Professional Accreditation:** NLN

MANHATTAN CHRISTIAN COLLEGE
1415 Anderson Ave.
Manhattan, KS 66502-4081
Tel: (785)539-3571; 877-246-4622
Fax: (785)539-0832
Web Site: http://www.mccks.edu/
President/CEO: Kenneth Cable
Admissions: Pam Schmidt
Financial Aid: Margaret Carlisle
Type: Four-Year College **Sex:** Coed **Affiliation:** Christian Churches and Churches of Christ **Scores:** 78% SAT V 400+; 78% SAT M 400+; 50% ACT 18-23; 35% ACT 24-29 **Application Fee:** $25.00 **H.S. Requirements:** High school diploma required; GED accepted **Costs Per Year:** Application fee: $25. Comprehensive fee: $15,228 includes full-time tuition ($9444), mandatory fees ($194), and college room and board ($5590). Room and board charges vary according to board plan. Part-time tuition: $389 per hour. Part-time tuition varies according to course load. **Scholarships:** Available **Calendar System:** Semester, Summer Session Available **Enrollment:** FT 262, PT 69 **Faculty:** FT 10, PT 22 **Student-Faculty Ratio:** 15:1 **Exams:** SAT I or ACT **% Receiving Financial Aid:** 66 **% Residing in College-Owned, -Operated, or -Affiliated Housing:** 65 **Library Holdings:** 3,300 **Regional Accreditation:** North Central Association of Colleges and Schools **Credit Hours For Degree:** 62 credit hours, Associates; 120 credit hours, Bachelors **ROTC:** Army, Air Force **Professional Accreditation:** AABC **Intercollegiate Athletics:** Baseball M; Basketball M & W; Soccer M & W; Volleyball W

MCPHERSON COLLEGE
1600 East Euclid, PO Box 1402
McPherson, KS 67460-1402
Tel: (620)241-0731
Free: 800-365-7402
Fax: (620)241-8443
Web Site: http://www.mcpherson.edu/
President/CEO: Ron Hovis
Registrar: Karlene Tyler
Admissions: Carol L. Williams
Financial Aid: Carol Williams
Type: Four-Year College **Sex:** Coed **Affiliation:** Church of the Brethren **Scores:** 95% SAT V 400+; 90% SAT M 400+; 68% ACT 18-23; 20% ACT 24-29 **Admission Plans:** Deferred Admission **Application Fee:** $25.00 **H.S. Requirements:** High school diploma required; GED accepted **Costs Per Year:** Application fee: $25. Comprehensive fee: $21,010 includes full-time tuition ($14,900), mandatory fees ($260), and college room and board ($5850). College room only: $2400. Part-time tuition: $450 per credit hour. Part-time mandatory fees: $280 per credit hour, $1580 per term. Part-time tuition and fees vary according to course load. **Scholarships:** Available **Calendar System:** 4-1-4, Summer Session Available **Enrollment:** FT 443, PT 21 **Faculty:** FT 39, PT 13 **Student-Faculty Ratio:** 11:1 **Exams:** ACT, SAT I or ACT **% Receiving Financial Aid:** 83 **% Residing in College-Owned, -Operated, or -Affiliated Housing:** 70 **Library Holdings:** 89,946 **Regional Accreditation:** North Central Association of Colleges and Schools **Credit Hours For Degree:** 65 credit hours, Associates; 124 credit hours, Bachelors **Professional Accreditation:** NCATE **Intercollegiate Athletics:** Basketball M & W; Cross-Country Running M & W; Football M; Softball W; Track and Field M & W; Volleyball W

MIDAMERICA NAZARENE UNIVERSITY
2030 East College Way
Olathe, KS 66062-1899
Tel: (913)782-3750
Free: 800-800-8887
Admissions: (913)791-3380
Fax: (913)791-3481
E-mail: admissions@mnu.edu
Web Site: http://www.mnu.edu/
President/CEO: Dr. Richard Spindle

Registrar: Patricia Walsh
Admissions: Dennis Troyer
Financial Aid: Rhonda Cole
Type: Comprehensive **Sex:** Coed **Affiliation:** Church of the Nazarene **Scores:** 82% SAT V 400+; 82% SAT M 400+; 49% ACT 18-23; 30% ACT 24-29 **% Accepted:** 69 **Admission Plans:** Early Admission; Deferred Admission **Application Deadline:** August 01 **Application Fee:** $25.00 **H.S. Requirements:** High school diploma required; GED accepted **Costs Per Year:** Application fee: $25. Comprehensive fee: $21,798 includes full-time tuition ($14,968), mandatory fees ($1000), and college room and board ($5830). Part-time tuition: $500 per semester hour. Part-time mandatory fees: $500 per term. **Scholarships:** Available **Calendar System:** Semester, Summer Session Available **Enrollment:** FT 1,198, PT 159, Grad 422 **Faculty:** FT 71, PT 102 **Student-Faculty Ratio:** 18:1 **Exams:** SAT I or ACT **% Receiving Financial Aid:** 70 **% Residing in College-Owned, -Operated, or -Affiliated Housing:** 62 **Library Holdings:** 132,991 **Regional Accreditation:** North Central Association of Colleges and Schools **Credit Hours For Degree:** 63 semester hours, Associates; 126 semester hours, Bachelors **ROTC:** Army, Air Force **Professional Accreditation:** AACN, NASM, NLN **Intercollegiate Athletics:** Baseball M; Basketball M & W; Cheerleading M & W; Cross-Country Running M & W; Football M; Soccer M & W; Softball W; Track and Field M & W; Volleyball W

NATIONAL AMERICAN UNIVERSITY
10310 Mastin
Overland Park, KS 66212
Tel: (913)217-2900
Web Site: http://www.national.edu/ **Type:** Two-Year College **Sex:** Coed

NEOSHO COUNTY COMMUNITY COLLEGE
800 West 14th St.
Chanute, KS 66720-2699
Tel: (620)431-2820
Free: 800-729-6222
Fax: (620)431-6222
E-mail: llast@neosho.edu
Web Site: http://www.neosho.edu/
President/CEO: Vicky R. Smith
Admissions: Lisa Last
Financial Aid: Sheldon Woolery
Type: Two-Year College **Sex:** Coed **Affiliation:** Kansas State Board of Education **Admission Plans:** Open Admission; Early Admission **Application Fee:** $0.00 **H.S. Requirements:** High school diploma required; GED accepted **Scholarships:** Available **Calendar System:** Semester, Summer Session Available **Enrollment:** FT 615, PT 1,211 **Faculty:** FT 40, PT 86 **Exams:** ACT **% Residing in College-Owned, -Operated, or -Affiliated Housing:** 5 **Library Holdings:** 33,000 **Regional Accreditation:** North Central Association of Colleges and Schools **Credit Hours For Degree:** 62 semester hours, Associates **Professional Accreditation:** NLN **Intercollegiate Athletics:** Baseball M; Basketball M & W; Cross-Country Running M & W; Softball W; Track and Field M; Volleyball W

NEWMAN UNIVERSITY
3100 McCormick Ave.
Wichita, KS 67213-2097
Tel: (316)942-4291; 877-NEWMANU
Fax: (316)942-4483
E-mail: admissions@newmanu.edu
Web Site: http://www.newmanu.edu/
President/CEO: Dr. Aidan O. Dunleavy
Registrar: Shirley Rueb
Admissions: Todd Lucas
Financial Aid: Kelli Hartman
Type: Comprehensive **Sex:** Coed **Affiliation:** Roman Catholic **Scores:** 89.6% SAT V 400+; 89.7% SAT M 400+; 54.3% ACT 18-23; 31.8% ACT 24-29 **% Accepted:** 85 **Admission Plans:** Early Admission; Deferred Admission **Application Deadline:** Rolling **Application Fee:** $20.00 **H.S. Requirements:** High school diploma required; GED accepted. For international students: High school diploma required; GED not accepted **Costs Per Year:** Application fee: $20. Comprehensive fee: $22,680 includes full-time tuition ($17,008), mandatory fees ($300), and college room and board ($5372). Part-time tuition: $567 per credit hour. Part-time mandatory fees: $10 per credit hour. **Scholarships:** Available **Calendar System:** Semester, Summer Session Available **Enrollment:** FT 1,123, PT 609, Grad 371 **Faculty:** FT 85, PT 68 **Student-Faculty Ratio:** 17:1 **Exams:** SAT I or ACT **% Receiving Financial Aid:** 72 **% Residing in College-Owned, -Operated, or -Affiliated Housing:** 21 **Library Holdings:** 107,057 **Regional Accreditation:** North Central Association of Colleges and Schools **Credit Hours For Degree:** 62 semester hours, Associates; 124 semester hours, Bachelors **Professional Accreditation:** AACN, AANA, CARC, CSWE, JRCERT **Intercollegiate Athletics:** Baseball M; Basketball M & W; Bowling M & W; Cheerleading M & W; Cross-Country Running M & W; Golf M & W; Lacrosse M; Soccer M & W; Softball W; Tennis M & W; Volleyball M & W; Wrestling M

NORTH CENTRAL KANSAS TECHNICAL COLLEGE
PO Box 507
Beloit, KS 67420
Tel: (913)738-2276
Free: 800-658-4655
E-mail: jheidrick@ncktc.tec.ks.us
Web Site: http://www.ncktc.tec.ks.us/
President/CEO: Dr. George Mihel
Registrar: Judy Heidrick
Admissions: Judy Heidrick
Type: Two-Year College **Sex:** Coed **Calendar System:** Semester **Regional Accreditation:** North Central Association of Colleges and Schools

NORTHEAST KANSAS TECHNICAL COLLEGE
1501 West Riley St.
Atchison, KS 66002
Tel: (913)367-6204
Free: 800-567-4890
Fax: (913)367-3107
Web Site: http://www.nektc.net/ **Type:** Two-Year College **Sex:** Coed **Calendar System:** Semester **Professional Accreditation:** COE

NORTHWEST KANSAS TECHNICAL COLLEGE
PO Box 668
1209 Harrison St.
Goodland, KS 67735
Tel: (785)899-3641
Free: 800-316-4127
Fax: (785)899-5711
Web Site: http://www.nwktc.org/
President/CEO: Ken Clouse
Financial Aid: Jackie Schmidt
Type: Two-Year College **Sex:** Coed **Calendar System:** Semester **Professional Accreditation:** COE

OTTAWA UNIVERSITY
1001 South Cedar
Ottawa, KS 66067-3399
Tel: (785)242-5200
Free: 800-755-5200
Fax: (785)242-7429
E-mail: admiss@ottawa.edu
Web Site: http://www.ottawa.edu/
President/CEO: Dr. John Neal
Registrar: Karen Adams
Admissions: Fola Akande
Financial Aid: Howard Fischer
Type: Comprehensive **Sex:** Coed **Affiliation:** American Baptist Churches in the USA **Scores:** 64% ACT 18-23; 25% ACT 24-29 **% Accepted:** 71 **Application Deadline:** Rolling **Application Fee:** $15.00 **H.S. Requirements:** High school diploma required; GED accepted **Costs Per Year:** Application fee: $15. Comprehensive fee: $20,042 includes full-time tuition ($14,500) and college room and board ($5542). College room only: $2400. Full-time tuition varies according to course load. Room and board charges vary according to board plan and housing facility. **Scholarships:** Available **Calendar System:** Semester, Summer Session Available **Enrollment:** FT 401, PT 39 **Faculty:** FT 18, PT 39 **Student-Faculty Ratio:** 16:1 **Exams:** SAT I or ACT **Library Holdings:** 80,500 **Regional Accreditation:** North Central Association of Colleges and Schools **Credit Hours For Degree:** 124 credit hours, Bachelors **Professional Accreditation:** NCATE **Intercollegiate Athletics:** Baseball M; Basketball M & W; Cross-Country Running M & W; Football M; Golf M; Soccer M & W; Softball W; Track and Field M & W; Volleyball W

PITTSBURG STATE UNIVERSITY
1701 South Broadway
Pittsburg, KS 66762

Tel: (620)231-7000
Free: 800-854-7488
Fax: (620)235-4080
Web Site: http://www.pittstate.edu/
President/CEO: Dr. Tom W. Bryant
Registrar: Dr. Lee Christensen
Financial Aid: Marilyn Haverly
Type: Comprehensive **Sex:** Coed **Affiliation:** Kansas Board of Regents **Scores:** 53% ACT 18-23; 28% ACT 24-29 **% Accepted:** 90 **Admission Plans:** Open Admission; Early Admission; Deferred Admission **Application Deadline:** Rolling **Application Fee:** $30.00 **H.S. Requirements:** High school diploma required; GED accepted **Costs Per Year:** Application fee: $30. State resident tuition: $2850 full-time, $95 per credit hour part-time. Nonresident tuition: $9732 full-time, $324 per credit hour part-time. Mandatory fees: $712 full-time, $32 per credit hour part-time. College room and board: $4550. Room and board charges vary according to board plan and housing facility. **Scholarships:** Available **Calendar System:** Semester, Summer Session Available **Enrollment:** FT 5,126, PT 417, Grad 1,085 **Faculty:** FT 291, PT 82 **Student-Faculty Ratio:** 18:1 **Exams:** ACT **% Receiving Financial Aid:** 57 **% Residing in College-Owned, -Operated, or -Affiliated Housing:** 14 **Library Holdings:** 639,136 **Regional Accreditation:** North Central Association of Colleges and Schools **Credit Hours For Degree:** 60 semester hours, Associates; 124 semester hours, Bachelors **ROTC:** Army **Professional Accreditation:** AACSB, ABET, AACN, AAFCS, ACA, CSWE, NASM, NCATE, NLN **Intercollegiate Athletics:** Baseball M; Basketball M & W; Cross-Country Running M & W; Football M; Golf M; Softball W; Track and Field M & W; Volleyball W

PRATT COMMUNITY COLLEGE
348 NE State Rd. 61
Pratt, KS 67124-8317
Tel: (620)672-9800
Admissions: (620)450-2222
Fax: (620)672-5288
E-mail: lynnp@prattcc.edu
Web Site: http://www.prattcc.edu/
President/CEO: Dr. William Wojciechowski
Registrar: Randy Thode
Admissions: Lynn Perez
Financial Aid: Debbie Boley
Type: Two-Year College **Sex:** Coed **Affiliation:** Kansas Board of Regents **% Accepted:** 100 **Admission Plans:** Open Admission; Early Admission **Application Deadline:** Rolling **Application Fee:** $0.00 **H.S. Requirements:** High school diploma required; GED accepted **Costs Per Year:** Application fee: $0. State resident tuition: $42 per credit hour part-time. Nonresident tuition: $1344 full-time, $42 per credit hour part-time. Mandatory fees: $928 full-time, $29 per credit hour part-time. College room and board: $3768. **Scholarships:** Available **Calendar System:** Semester, Summer Session Available **Enrollment:** FT 625, PT 921 **Faculty:** FT 41, PT 79 **Student-Faculty Ratio:** 14:1 **Exams:** Other **% Residing in College-Owned, -Operated, or -Affiliated Housing:** 21 **Library Holdings:** 33,000 **Regional Accreditation:** North Central Association of Colleges and Schools **Credit Hours For Degree:** 64 credit hours, Associates **Professional Accreditation:** ACBSP, NLN **Intercollegiate Athletics:** Baseball M; Basketball M & W; Cheerleading W; Cross-Country Running M & W; Golf M & W; Softball W; Track and Field M & W; Volleyball W

SEWARD COUNTY COMMUNITY COLLEGE
PO Box 1137
Liberal, KS 67905-1137
Tel: (620)624-1951
Free: 800-373-9951
Fax: (620)629-2725
Web Site: http://www.sccc.edu/
President/CEO: Dr. Duane M. Dunn
Registrar: Donetta Dreitz
Admissions: Dr. Gerald Harris
Financial Aid: Bea Rosales
Type: Two-Year College **Sex:** Coed **Affiliation:** Kansas State Board of Regents **Admission Plans:** Open Admission; Early Admission; Deferred Admission **Application Fee:** $0.00 **H.S. Requirements:** High school diploma required; GED accepted **Scholarships:** Available **Calendar System:** Semester, Summer Session Available **Enrollment:** FT 538, PT 1,787 **Student-Faculty Ratio:** 18:1 **Exams:** SAT I or ACT **% Residing in College-Owned, -Operated, or -Affiliated Housing:** 21 **Library Holdings:** 32,926 **Regional Accreditation:** North Central Association of Colleges and Schools **Credit Hours For Degree:** 64 semester hours, Associates **Professional Accreditation:** ARCEST, CARC, NAACLS, NLN **Intercollegiate Athletics:** Baseball M; Basketball M & W; Tennis M & W; Volleyball W

SOUTHWESTERN COLLEGE
100 College St.
Winfield, KS 67156-2499
Tel: (620)229-6000
Free: 800-846-1543
Admissions: (620)229-6236
Fax: (620)229-6224
E-mail: scadmit@jinx.sckans.edu
Web Site: http://www.sckans.edu/
President/CEO: Dr. W. Richard Merriman, Jr.
Registrar: Jill L. Megredy
Admissions: Todd Moore
Financial Aid: Brenda D. Hicks
Type: Comprehensive **Sex:** Coed **Affiliation:** United Methodist **Scores:** 84.21% SAT V 400+; 89.48% SAT M 400+; 48.39% ACT 18-23; 37.9% ACT 24-29 **% Accepted:** 28 **Admission Plans:** Deferred Admission **Application Deadline:** August 01 **Application Fee:** $20.00 **H.S. Requirements:** High school diploma required; GED accepted **Costs Per Year:** Application fee: $20. One-time mandatory fee: $100. Comprehensive fee: $22,238 includes full-time tuition ($16,800) and college room and board ($5438). College room only: $2428. Part-time tuition: $700 per semester hour. **Scholarships:** Available **Calendar System:** Semester, Summer Session Available **Enrollment:** FT 569, PT 694, Grad 153 **Faculty:** FT 46, PT 98 **Student-Faculty Ratio:** 10:1 **Exams:** SAT I or ACT **% Receiving Financial Aid:** 81 **% Residing in College-Owned, -Operated, or -Affiliated Housing:** 63 **Library Holdings:** 77,000 **Regional Accreditation:** North Central Association of Colleges and Schools **Credit Hours For Degree:** 124 semester hours, Bachelors **Professional Accreditation:** AACN, NASM, NCATE, NLN **Intercollegiate Athletics:** Basketball M & W; Cheerleading M & W; Cross-Country Running M & W; Football M; Golf M & W; Soccer M & W; Softball W; Tennis M & W; Track and Field M & W; Volleyball W

STERLING COLLEGE
PO Box 98
Sterling, KS 67579-0098
Tel: (620)278-2173
Free: 800-346-1017
Admissions: (620)278-4364
Fax: (620)278-3690
Web Site: http://www.sterling.edu/
President/CEO: Dr. Albert Anderson
Registrar: Janet E. Caywood
Admissions: Dennis Dutton
Type: Four-Year College **Sex:** Coed **Affiliation:** Presbyterian **Scores:** 95% SAT V 400+; 95% SAT M 400+; 56% ACT 18-23; 25% ACT 24-29 **% Accepted:** 56 **Admission Plans:** Early Action; Deferred Admission **Application Deadline:** July 15 **Application Fee:** $25.00 **H.S. Requirements:** High school diploma required; GED accepted **Costs Per Year:** Application fee: $25. Comprehensive fee: $20,486 includes full-time tuition ($14,300), mandatory fees ($100), and college room and board ($6086). **Scholarships:** Available **Calendar System:** 4-1-4, Summer Session Not available **Enrollment:** FT 433, PT 61, Grad 22 **Faculty:** FT 40, PT 21 **Student-Faculty Ratio:** 10:1 **Exams:** SAT I or ACT **% Receiving Financial Aid:** 81 **% Residing in College-Owned, -Operated, or -Affiliated Housing:** 83 **Library Holdings:** 76,637 **Regional Accreditation:** North Central Association of Colleges and Schools **Credit Hours For Degree:** 124 credit hours, Bachelors **Intercollegiate Athletics:** Baseball M; Basketball M & W; Cheerleading W; Cross-Country Running M & W; Football M; Soccer M & W; Softball W; Track and Field M & W; Volleyball W

TABOR COLLEGE
400 South Jefferson
Hillsboro, KS 67063
Tel: (620)947-3121
Free: 800-822-6799
Fax: (620)947-2607
Web Site: http://www.tabor.edu/
President/CEO: Larry Nikkel
Registrar: Deanne Duerksen

Admissions: Rusty Allen
Financial Aid: Bruce Jost
Type: Comprehensive **Sex:** Coed **Affiliation:** Mennonite Brethren **Scores:** 55% ACT 18-23; 32% ACT 24-29 **Admission Plans:** Early Decision Plan **Application Fee:** $20.00 **H.S. Requirements:** High school diploma required; GED accepted **Costs Per Year:** Application fee: $20. Comprehensive fee: $21,604 includes full-time tuition ($15,574), mandatory fees ($360), and college room and board ($5670). College room only: $2215. Full-time tuition and fees vary according to course load. Room and board charges vary according to board plan, housing facility, and location. **Scholarships:** Available **Calendar System:** 4-1-4, Summer Session Not available **Enrollment:** FT 463, PT 123, Grad 20 **Faculty:** FT 36, PT 19 **Student-Faculty Ratio:** 11:1 **Exams:** SAT I or ACT **% Receiving Financial Aid:** 74 **% Residing in College-Owned, -Operated, or -Affiliated Housing:** 80 **Library Holdings:** 80,099 **Regional Accreditation:** North Central Association of Colleges and Schools **Credit Hours For Degree:** 64 credit hours, Associates; 124 credit hours, Bachelors **Professional Accreditation:** AACN, NASM **Intercollegiate Athletics:** Baseball M; Basketball M & W; Cheerleading M & W; Cross-Country Running M & W; Football M; Golf M & W; Rugby M; Soccer M & W; Softball W; Tennis M & W; Track and Field M & W; Volleyball W

UNIVERSITY OF KANSAS

Lawrence, KS 66045
Tel: (785)864-2700
Admissions: (785)864-3911
Fax: (785)864-5006
E-mail: be.a.jayhawk@st37.eds.ukans.edu
Web Site: http://www.ku.edu
President/CEO: Dr. Robert E. Hemenway
Registrar: Cindy Derritt
Admissions: Lisa Pinamonti Kress
Financial Aid: Dr. Brenda Maigaard
Type: University **Sex:** Coed **Scores:** 39% ACT 18-23; 46% ACT 24-29 **% Accepted:** 69 **Admission Plans:** Deferred Admission **Application Deadline:** April 01 **Application Fee:** $30.00 **H.S. Requirements:** High school diploma required; GED accepted **Costs Per Year:** Application fee: $30. State resident tuition: $4824 full-time, $160.80 per credit hour part-time. Nonresident tuition: $13,277 full-time, $442.55 per credit hour part-time. Mandatory fees: $589 full-time, $49.08 per credit hour part-time. Full-time tuition and fees vary according to program and reciprocity agreements. Part-time tuition and fees vary according to program and reciprocity agreements. College room and board: $5502. College room only: $2752. Room and board charges vary according to board plan and housing facility. **Scholarships:** Available **Calendar System:** Semester, Summer Session Available **Enrollment:** FT 18,888, PT 2,503, Grad 6,052 **Faculty:** FT 1,185, PT 127 **Student-Faculty Ratio:** 20:1 **Exams:** SAT I or ACT **% Receiving Financial Aid:** 36 **% Residing in College-Owned, -Operated, or -Affiliated Housing:** 23 **Library Holdings:** 4,768,862 **Regional Accreditation:** North Central Association of Colleges and Schools **Credit Hours For Degree:** 124 credit hours, Bachelors **ROTC:** Army, Navy, Air Force **Professional Accreditation:** AACSB, ABET, ACEHSA, ACEJMC, AACN, AANA, ABA, ACNM, ACPhE, ADtA, AHIMA, ACSP, AOTA, APTA, APA, ASC, ASLHA, AALS, CARC, CEPH CSWE, LCMEAMA, NAACLS, NASAD, NASM, NASPAA, NCATE **Intercollegiate Athletics:** Baseball M; Basketball M & W; Crew M & W; Cross-Country Running M & W; Fencing M & W; Football M; Golf M & W; Rugby M & W; Soccer W; Softball W; Swimming and Diving W; Tennis W; Track and Field M & W; Volleyball W

UNIVERSITY OF PHOENIX-WICHITA CAMPUS

3020 North Cypress Dr., Ste. 150
Wichita, KS 67226
Tel: (316)630-8121
Free: 800-228-7240
Admissions: (480)557-1712
Web Site: http://www.phoenix.edu/
Admissions: Nina Omelchanko
Type: Comprehensive **Sex:** Coed **Admission Plans:** Open Admission; Deferred Admission **Application Deadline:** Rolling **Application Fee:** $110.00 **H.S. Requirements:** High school diploma required; GED accepted **Costs Per Year:** Application fee: $110. Tuition: $10,440 full-time, $348 per credit part-time. Mandatory fees: $560 full-time, $70 per course part-time. **Scholarships:** Available **Calendar System:** Continuous, Summer Session Not available **Enrollment:** FT 331, Grad 69 **Faculty:** FT 2, PT 74 **Student-Faculty Ratio:** 5:1 **Library Holdings:** 444 **Regional Accreditation:** North Central Association of Colleges and Schools **Credit Hours For Degree:** 60 credits, Associates; 120 credits, Bachelors

UNIVERSITY OF SAINT MARY

4100 South Fourth St. Trafficway
Leavenworth, KS 66048-5082
Tel: (913)682-5151
Free: 800-752-7043
Fax: (913)758-6140
E-mail: admiss@stmary.edu
Web Site: http://www.stmary.edu/
President/CEO: Dr. Diane Steele
Registrar: Wanda Owen
Admissions: Jessica Goffinet
Financial Aid: Judy Wiedower
Type: Comprehensive **Sex:** Coed **Affiliation:** Roman Catholic **Scores:** 57% SAT V 400+; 71% SAT M 400+; 52% ACT 18-23; 21% ACT 24-29 **% Accepted:** 45 **Application Deadline:** Rolling **Application Fee:** $25.00 **H.S. Requirements:** High school diploma required; GED accepted **Costs Per Year:** Application fee: $25. Comprehensive fee: $22,510 includes full-time tuition ($16,100), mandatory fees ($310), and college room and board ($6100). College room only: $2600. Part-time tuition: $310 per credit. Part-time mandatory fees: $108 per term. **Scholarships:** Available **Calendar System:** Semester, Summer Session Available **Enrollment:** FT 376, PT 152, Grad 289 **Faculty:** FT 39, PT 50 **Student-Faculty Ratio:** 10:1 **Exams:** SAT I or ACT **% Residing in College-Owned, -Operated, or -Affiliated Housing:** 42 **Library Holdings:** 118,195 **Regional Accreditation:** North Central Association of Colleges and Schools **Credit Hours For Degree:** 64 semester hours, Associates; 128 semester hours, Bachelors **ROTC:** Army, Air Force **Professional Accreditation:** NCATE **Intercollegiate Athletics:** Baseball M; Basketball M & W; Football M; Soccer M & W; Softball W; Volleyball W

WASHBURN UNIVERSITY

1700 SW College Ave.
Topeka, KS 66621
Tel: (785)670-1010
Admissions: (785)670-1812
Fax: (785)231-1089
E-mail: al.dickes@washburn.edu
Web Site: http://www.washburn.edu/
President/CEO: Dr. Jerry Farley
Registrar: Dr. Carla Rasch
Admissions: Al Dickes
Financial Aid: Annita Huff
Type: Comprehensive **Sex:** Coed **Scores:** 54% ACT 18-23; 28% ACT 24-29 **% Accepted:** 99 **Admission Plans:** Open Admission; Early Admission **Application Deadline:** August 01 **Application Fee:** $20.00 **H.S. Requirements:** High school diploma required; GED accepted **Costs Per Year:** Application fee: $20. State resident tuition: $4920 full-time, $164 per credit hour part-time. Nonresident tuition: $11,130 full-time, $371 per credit hour part-time. Mandatory fees: $62 full-time, $15 per term part-time. College room and board: $4752. College room only: $2772. **Scholarships:** Available **Calendar System:** Semester, Summer Session Available **Enrollment:** FT 4,151, PT 2,273, Grad 382 **Faculty:** FT 258, PT 252 **Student-Faculty Ratio:** 16:1 **Exams:** ACT **% Receiving Financial Aid:** 30 **% Residing in College-Owned, -Operated, or -Affiliated Housing:** 13 **Library Holdings:** 1,500,000 **Regional Accreditation:** North Central Association of Colleges and Schools **Credit Hours For Degree:** 62 credit hours, Associates; 124 credit hours, Bachelors **ROTC:** Army, Navy, Air Force **Professional Accreditation:** AACN, ABA, AHIMA, APTA, AALS, CARC, CSWE, JRCERT, NASAD, NASM, NCATE **Intercollegiate Athletics:** Baseball M; Basketball M & W; Cheerleading M & W; Crew M & W; Football M; Golf M; Soccer W; Softball W; Tennis M & W; Volleyball W

WICHITA AREA TECHNICAL COLLEGE

301 South Grove St.
Wichita, KS 67211
Tel: (316)677-9282
Admissions: (316)677-9400
E-mail: info@watc.edu
Web Site: http://www.wichitatech.com/
President/CEO: Camille Kluge
Admissions: Jessica Ross

Type: Two-Year College **Sex:** Coed **% Accepted:** 49 **Application Deadline:** Rolling **Application Fee:** $16.00 **Costs Per Year:** Application fee: $16. State resident tuition: $2970 full-time, $99 per credit part-time. Nonresident tuition: $11,730 full-time, $345 per credit part-time. Mandatory fees: $236 full-time, $118 per term part-time. **Calendar System:** Semester **Enrollment:** FT 313, PT 731 **Faculty:** FT 36, PT 15 **Student-Faculty Ratio:** 14:1 **Exams:** Other **Professional Accreditation:** ARCEST, ADA, COE, NAACLS

WICHITA STATE UNIVERSITY
1845 North Fairmount
Wichita, KS 67260
Tel: (316)978-3456
Free: 800-362-2594
Admissions: (316)978-3085
Fax: (316)978-3795
E-mail: crabtree@witchita.edu
Web Site: http://www.wichita.edu/
President/CEO: Dr. Donald L. Beggs
Registrar: William E. Wynne
Admissions: Gina Crabtree
Financial Aid: Deborah D. Byers
Type: University **Sex:** Coed **Affiliation:** Kansas Board of Regents **Scores:** 97% SAT V 400+; 96% SAT M 400+; 48% ACT 18-23; 39% ACT 24-29 **% Accepted:** 84 **Admission Plans:** Open Admission; Deferred Admission **Application Deadline:** Rolling **Application Fee:** $30.00 **H.S. Requirements:** High school diploma required; GED accepted **Costs Per Year:** Application fee: $30. State resident tuition: $3434 full-time, $114.45 per credit hour part-time. Nonresident tuition: $10,887 full-time, $362.90 per credit hour part-time. Mandatory fees: $797 full-time, $25.45 per credit hour part-time, $17 per term part-time. Full-time tuition and fees vary according to course load. Part-time tuition and fees vary according to course load. College room and board: $5070. Room and board charges vary according to board plan and housing facility. **Scholarships:** Available **Calendar System:** Semester, Summer Session Available **Enrollment:** FT 7,198, PT 3,777, Grad 3,101 **Faculty:** FT 467, PT 48 **Student-Faculty Ratio:** 18:1 **Exams:** SAT I and SAT II or ACT **% Receiving Financial Aid:** 62 **% Residing in College-Owned, -Operated, or -Affiliated Housing:** 7 **Library Holdings:** 1,590,705 **Regional Accreditation:** North Central Association of Colleges and Schools **Credit Hours For Degree:** 62 credit hours, Associates; 124 credit hours, Bachelors **Professional Accreditation:** AACSB, ABET, AACN, ADA, APTA, APA, ASLHA, CEPH, CSWE, NAACLS, NASD, NASM, NASPAA, NCATE **Intercollegiate Athletics:** Baseball M; Basketball M & W; Bowling M & W; Cheerleading M & W; Crew M & W; Cross-Country Running M & W; Golf M & W; Ice Hockey M & W; Racquetball M & W; Rugby M; Soccer M & W; Softball W; Swimming and Diving M & W; Tennis M & W; Track and Field M & W; Volleyball M & W; Wrestling M

ALICE LLOYD COLLEGE
100 Purpose Rd.
Pippa Passes, KY 41844
Tel: (606)368-2101
Admissions: (606)368-6134
Fax: (606)368-2125
Web Site: http://www.alc.edu/
President/CEO: Dr. Joe A. Stepp
Registrar: Thelmarie Thornsberry
Admissions: Sean Damron
Financial Aid: Nancy Melton
Type: Four-Year College **Sex:** Coed **Scores:** 100% SAT V 400+; 100% SAT M 400+; 73% ACT 18-23; 13% ACT 24-29 **% Accepted:** 59 **Admission Plans:** Deferred Admission **Application Deadline:** Rolling **Application Fee:** $0.00 **H.S. Requirements:** High school diploma required; GED accepted **Costs Per Year:** Application fee: $0. Comprehensive fee: $4900 includes full-time tuition ($0), mandatory fees ($1150), and college room and board ($3750). College room only: $1730. Part-time tuition: $212 per credit hour. Full-time students in the 108-county service area are granted guaranteed tuition. **Scholarships:** Available **Calendar System:** Semester, Summer Session Not available **Enrollment:** FT 575, PT 18 **Faculty:** FT 28, PT 12 **Student-Faculty Ratio:** 18:1 **Exams:** SAT I or ACT **% Receiving Financial Aid:** 54 **% Residing in College-Owned, -Operated, or -Affiliated Housing:** 74 **Library Holdings:** 74,216 **Regional Accreditation:** Southern Association of Colleges and Schools **Credit Hours For Degree:** 128 credit hours, Bachelors **Intercollegiate Athletics:** Baseball M; Basketball M & W; Cheerleading M & W; Golf M & W; Softball W; Tennis M & W

ASBURY COLLEGE
1 Macklem Dr.
Wilmore, KY 40390-1198
Tel: (859)858-3511
Free: 800-888-1818
Fax: (859)858-3921
E-mail: admissions@asbury.edu
Web Site: http://www.asbury.edu/
President/CEO: Dr. Paul A. Rader
Registrar: Dr. Timothy L. Thomas
Admissions: Ronald Anderson
Financial Aid: Patricia Kelly
Type: Comprehensive **Sex:** Coed **Affiliation:** nondenominational **Scores:** 97% SAT V 400+; 96% SAT M 400+; 45% ACT 18-23; 40% ACT 24-29 **% Accepted:** 74 **Admission Plans:** Early Admission; Deferred Admission **Application Deadline:** Rolling **Application Fee:** $30.00 **H.S. Requirements:** High school diploma required; GED accepted **Costs Per Year:** Application fee: $30. Comprehensive fee: $23,762 includes full-time tuition ($18,808), mandatory fees ($148), and college room and board ($4806). College room only: $2810. Full-time tuition and fees vary according to course load. Room and board charges vary according to board plan, housing facility, and location. Part-time tuition: $723 per semester hour. Part-time tuition varies according to course load. **Scholarships:** Available **Calendar System:** Semester, Summer Session Available **Enrollment:** FT 1,124, PT 105, Grad 64 **Faculty:** FT 86, PT 65 **Student-Faculty Ratio:** 11:1 **Exams:** SAT I or ACT **% Receiving Financial Aid:** 71 **% Residing in College-Owned, -Operated, or -Affiliated Housing:** 87 **Library Holdings:** 145,424 **Regional Accreditation:** Southern Association of Colleges and Schools **Credit Hours For Degree:** 124 semester hours, Bachelors **ROTC:** Army, Air Force **Professional Accreditation:** NASM, NCATE **Intercollegiate Athletics:** Basketball M & W; Cross-Country Running M & W; Soccer M & W; Swimming and Diving M & W; Tennis M & W; Volleyball W

ASHLAND COMMUNITY AND TECHNICAL COLLEGE
1400 College Dr.
Ashland, KY 41101-3683
Tel: (606)329-2999
Free: 800-370-7191
Admissions: (606)326-2114
Fax: (606)325-8124
E-mail: steve.flouhouse@kctcs.edu
Web Site: http://www.ashland.kctcs.edu/
President/CEO: Dr. Greg D. Adkins
Registrar: Willie G. McCullough
Admissions: Steven D. Flouhouse
Financial Aid: Martha J. Persinger
Type: Two-Year College **Sex:** Coed **Affiliation:** Kentucky Community and Technical College System **Scores:** 46% ACT 18-23; 7% ACT 24-29 **Admission Plans:** Open Admission; Early Admission; Deferred Admission **Application Fee:** $0.00 **H.S. Requirements:** High school diploma required; GED accepted **Costs Per Year:** Application fee: $0. State resident tuition: $2940 full-time, $98 per credit hour part-time. Nonresident tuition: $8820 full-time, $294 per credit hour part-time. Full-time tuition varies according to reciprocity agreements. Part-time tuition varies according to reciprocity agreements. **Scholarships:** Available **Calendar System:** Semester, Summer Session Available **Faculty:** FT 64, PT 68 **Student-Faculty Ratio:** 19:1 **Exams:** ACT, Other **Library Holdings:** 41,379 **Regional Accreditation:** Southern Association of Colleges and Schools **Credit Hours For Degree:** 60 credit hours, Associates **Professional Accreditation:** ARCEST, ACBSP, CARC, COE, NLN

BECKFIELD COLLEGE
16 Spiral Dr.
Florence, KY 41042
Tel: (859)371-9393
Fax: (859)371-5096
E-mail: kleeds@beckfield.org
Web Site: http://www.beckfield.edu/
President/CEO: Harry L. Beck
Registrar: Cindy Griggs
Admissions: Ken Leeds
Type: Two-Year College **Sex:** Coed **Admission Plans:** Open Admission **H.S. Requirements:** High school diploma required; GED accepted **Scholarships:** Available **Calendar System:** Quarter **Enrollment:** FT 480 **Faculty:** FT 4, PT 22 **Student-Faculty Ratio:** 17:1 **Professional Accreditation:** ACICS

BELLARMINE UNIVERSITY
2001 Newburg Rd.
Louisville, KY 40205-0671
Tel: (502)452-8000
Free: 800-274-4723
Admissions: (502)452-8131
Fax: (502)452-8002

Web Site: http://www.bellarmine.edu/
President/CEO: Dr. Joseph J. McGowan
Registrar: Beverly Gradisek
Admissions: Timothy A. Sturgeon
Financial Aid: David Wuinee
Type: Comprehensive **Sex:** Coed **Affiliation:** Roman Catholic **Scores:** 99% SAT V 400+; 99% SAT M 400+; 46% ACT 18-23; 47% ACT 24-29 **% Accepted:** 71 **Admission Plans:** Early Admission; Early Action; Deferred Admission **Application Deadline:** February 01 **Application Fee:** $25.00 **H.S. Requirements:** High school diploma required; GED accepted **Costs Per Year:** Application fee: $25. Comprehensive fee: $31,030 includes full-time tuition ($23,300), mandatory fees ($850), and college room and board ($6880). College room only: $3860. Part-time tuition: $550 per credit. Part-time mandatory fees: $35 per course. **Scholarships:** Available **Calendar System:** Semester, Summer Session Available **Enrollment:** FT 1,737, PT 522, Grad 541 **Faculty:** FT 115, PT 136 **Student-Faculty Ratio:** 13:1 **Exams:** SAT I or ACT **% Residing in College-Owned, -Operated, or -Affiliated Housing:** 37 **Library Holdings:** 97,737 **Regional Accreditation:** Southern Association of Colleges and Schools **Credit Hours For Degree:** 126 credits, Bachelors **ROTC:** Army, Air Force **Professional Accreditation:** AACSB, AACN, APTA, ASC, CARC, NAACLS, NCATE, NLN **Intercollegiate Athletics:** Baseball M; Basketball M & W; Cross-Country Running M & W; Field Hockey W; Golf M & W; Lacrosse M; Soccer M & W; Softball W; Tennis M & W; Track and Field M & W; Volleyball W

BEREA COLLEGE
Berea, KY 40404
Tel: (859)985-3000
Free: 800-326-5948
Admissions: (859)985-3500
E-mail: admissions@berea.edu
Web Site: http://www.berea.edu/
President/CEO: Dr. Larry D. Shinn
Admissions: Jamie Ealy
Financial Aid: Bryan Erslan
Type: Four-Year College **Sex:** Coed **Scores:** 100% SAT V 400+; 99% SAT M 400+; 55% ACT 18-23; 40% ACT 24-29 **% Accepted:** 27 **Admission Plans:** Preferred Admission **Application Deadline:** April 30 **Application Fee:** $0.00 **H.S. Requirements:** High school diploma required; GED accepted **Costs Per Year:** Application fee: $0. Comprehensive fee: $5496 includes full-time tuition ($0), mandatory fees ($516), and college room and board ($4980). Financial aid is provided to all students for tuition costs. **Scholarships:** Available **Calendar System:** 4-1-4, Summer Session Available **Enrollment:** FT 1,529, PT 66 **Faculty:** FT 130, PT 29 **Student-Faculty Ratio:** 11:1 **Exams:** SAT I or ACT **% Receiving Financial Aid:** 100 **% Residing in College-Owned, -Operated, or -Affiliated Housing:** 84 **Library Holdings:** 358,556 **Regional Accreditation:** Southern Association of Colleges and Schools **Credit Hours For Degree:** 33 courses, Bachelors **Professional Accreditation:** AACN, AAFCS, NCATE, NLN **Intercollegiate Athletics:** Baseball M; Basketball M & W; Cross-Country Running M & W; Golf M; Soccer M & W; Softball W; Swimming and Diving M & W; Tennis M & W; Track and Field M & W; Volleyball W

BIG SANDY COMMUNITY AND TECHNICAL COLLEGE
One Bert T. Combs Dr.
Prestonsburg, KY 41653-1815
Tel: (606)886-3863; 888-641-4132
Fax: (606)886-6943
E-mail: ccsprerg@kctcs.edu
Web Site: http://www.bigsandy.kctcs.edu/
President/CEO: Dr. George D. Edwards
Admissions: Jim Glover
Financial Aid: Denese S. Atkinson
Type: Two-Year College **Sex:** Coed **Affiliation:** Kentucky Community and Technical College System **Admission Plans:** Open Admission; Early Admission; Deferred Admission **Application Fee:** $0.00 **H.S. Requirements:** High school diploma required; GED accepted **Costs Per Year:** Application fee: $0. Area resident tuition: $2940 full-time, $98 per credit hour part-time. State resident tuition: $3540 full-time, $118 per credit hour part-time. Nonresident tuition: $8820 full-time, $294 per credit hour part-time. **Scholarships:** Available **Calendar System:** Semester, Summer Session Available **Faculty:** FT 69, PT 45 **Exams:** ACT, Other **Library Holdings:** 34,668 **Regional Accreditation:** Southern Association of Colleges and Schools **Credit Hours For Degree:** 60 credit hours, Associates **Professional Accreditation:** ADA, COE

BOWLING GREEN TECHNICAL COLLEGE
1845 Loop Dr.
Bowling Green, KY 42101
Tel: (270)901-1000
Fax: (270)746-7466
Web Site: http://www.bowlinggreen.kctcs.edu/
President/CEO: Dr. Jack Thomas
Financial Aid: Rick Wilson
Type: Two-Year College **Sex:** Coed **Calendar System:** Semester **Professional Accreditation:** CARC, COE

BRESCIA UNIVERSITY
717 Frederica St.
Owensboro, KY 42301-3023
Tel: (270)685-3131; 877-273-7242
Admissions: (270)686-4241
Fax: (270)686-6422
Web Site: http://www.brescia.edu/
President/CEO: Sr. Vivian Bowles, OSU
Registrar: Sr. Helena Fischer
Admissions: Sr. Mary Austin Blank
Financial Aid: Martie Ruxer-Bovken
Type: Comprehensive **Sex:** Coed **Affiliation:** Roman Catholic **Scores:** 63% ACT 18-23; 34% ACT 24-29 **Admission Plans:** Deferred Admission **Application Fee:** $25.00 **H.S. Requirements:** High school diploma required; GED accepted **Costs Per Year:** Application fee: $25. Comprehensive fee: $15,330 includes full-time tuition ($12,400), mandatory fees ($220), and college room and board ($2710). College room only: $1560. Full-time tuition and fees vary according to class time. Room and board charges vary according to board plan and housing facility. Part-time tuition: $395 per credit hour. Part-time mandatory fees: $10 per credit hour, $100 per term. **Scholarships:** Available **Calendar System:** Semester, Summer Session Available **Enrollment:** FT 477, PT 192, Grad 40 **Faculty:** FT 43, PT 32 **Student-Faculty Ratio:** 13:1 **Exams:** SAT I or ACT **% Receiving Financial Aid:** 74 **% Residing in College-Owned, -Operated, or -Affiliated Housing:** 26 **Regional Accreditation:** Southern Association of Colleges and Schools **Credit Hours For Degree:** 63 credit hours, Associates; 128 credit hours, Bachelors **Professional Accreditation:** CSWE **Intercollegiate Athletics:** Baseball M; Basketball M & W; Golf M & W; Soccer M & W; Softball W; Tennis W; Volleyball W

BROWN MACKIE COLLEGE-HOPKINSVILLE
4001 Ft. Cambell Blvd.
Hopkinsville, KY 42240
Tel: (270)886-1302
Free: 800-359-4753
Fax: (270)886-3544
E-mail: bcortez@borwnmackie.edu
Web Site: http://www.brownmackie.edu/locations.asp?locid=17
President/CEO: Elizabeth Ashy
Admissions: Brenda Cortez
Type: Two-Year College **Sex:** Coed **% Accepted:** 100 **Application Deadline:** Rolling **Costs Per Year:** Tuition: $8592 full-time, $179 per credit hour part-time. Mandatory fees: $480 full-time, $10 per credit hour part-time. **Scholarships:** Available **Calendar System:** Quarter **Enrollment:** FT 146 **Faculty:** FT 3, PT 7 **Student-Faculty Ratio:** 15:1 **Professional Accreditation:** ACCSCT, ACICS

BROWN MACKIE COLLEGE-LOUISVILLE
300 High Rise Dr.
Louisville, KY 40213
Tel: (502)968-7191
Free: 800-999-7387
Fax: (502)968-1727
E-mail: kbelanger@brownmackie.edu
Web Site: http://www.brownmackie.edu/locations.asp?locid=18
President/CEO: Terry Queeno
Admissions: Kathleen Belanger
Financial Aid: Beverly Sensenbrenner
Type: Two-Year College **Sex:** Coed **% Accepted:** 72 **Admission Plans:** Early Admission; Deferred Admission **Application Deadline:** Rolling **Application Fee:** $0.00 **H.S. Requirements:** High school diploma required; GED accepted **Costs Per Year:** Application fee: $0. Tuition: $8592 full-time. Mandatory fees: $480 full-time. **Scholarships:** Available **Calendar System:** Quarter **Enrollment:** FT 315 **Faculty:** FT 7, PT 10 **Student-Faculty Ratio:**

18:1 **Library Holdings:** 1,210 **Credit Hours For Degree:** 90 quarter hours, Associates **Professional Accreditation:** ACCSCT, ACICS

BROWN MACKIE COLLEGE-NORTHERN KENTUCKY
309 Buttermilk Pike
Fort Mitchell, KY 41017-2191
Tel: (859)341-5627
Free: 800-888-1445
Fax: (859)341-6483
E-mail: jdellefield@brownmackie.edu
Web Site: http://www.brownmackie.edu
President/CEO: Dr. G. Edward Hughs
Registrar: Diana Wagner
Admissions: Joanne Dellefield
Financial Aid: Pamela Wright
Type: Two-Year College **Sex:** Coed **Affiliation:** American Education Centers, Inc **Admission Plans:** Open Admission **Application Deadline:** Rolling **Application Fee:** $0.00 **H.S. Requirements:** High school diploma required; GED accepted **Scholarships:** Available **Calendar System:** Quarter, Summer Session Available **Enrollment:** FT 465 **Student-Faculty Ratio:** 14:1 **Library Holdings:** 1,500 **Credit Hours For Degree:** 102 quarter hours, Associates **Professional Accreditation:** ACICS

CAMPBELLSVILLE UNIVERSITY
1 University Dr.
Campbellsville, KY 42718-2799
Tel: (270)789-5000
Free: 800-264-6014
Admissions: (270)789-5220
Fax: (270)789-5071
Web Site: http://www.campbellsville.edu/
President/CEO: Dr. Michael V. Carter
Registrar: Rita L. Creason
Admissions: David Walters
Financial Aid: Chris Tolson
Type: Comprehensive **Sex:** Coed **Affiliation:** Kentucky Baptist Convention **Scores:** 87% SAT V 400+; 88% SAT M 400+; 57% ACT 18-23; 15% ACT 24-29 **% Accepted:** 73 **Admission Plans:** Deferred Admission **Application Deadline:** Rolling **Application Fee:** $20.00 **H.S. Requirements:** High school diploma required; GED accepted **Costs Per Year:** Application fee: $20. Comprehensive fee: $22,272 includes full-time tuition ($15,960), mandatory fees ($380), and college room and board ($5932). **Scholarships:** Available **Calendar System:** Semester, Summer Session Available **Enrollment:** FT 1,266, PT 570, Grad 450 **Faculty:** FT 86, PT 131 **Student-Faculty Ratio:** 12:1 **Exams:** SAT I or ACT **% Receiving Financial Aid:** 77 **% Residing in College-Owned, -Operated, or -Affiliated Housing:** 55 **Library Holdings:** 172,000 **Regional Accreditation:** Southern Association of Colleges and Schools **Credit Hours For Degree:** 64 credits, Associates; 128 credits, Bachelors **Professional Accreditation:** CSWE, NASM **Intercollegiate Athletics:** Baseball M; Basketball M & W; Cheerleading M & W; Cross-Country Running M & W; Football M; Golf M & W; Soccer M & W; Softball W; Tennis M & W; Track and Field M & W; Volleyball W; Wrestling M

CENTRE COLLEGE
600 West Walnut St.
Danville, KY 40422-1394
Tel: (859)238-5200
Free: 800-423-6236
Admissions: (859)238-5350
Fax: (859)238-5456
E-mail: admission@centre.edu
Web Site: http://www.centre.edu/
President/CEO: Dr. John A. Roush
Registrar: Timothy Culhan
Admissions: J. Carey Thompson
Financial Aid: Elaine Larson
Type: Four-Year College **Sex:** Coed **Affiliation:** Presbyterian Church (U.S.A.) **Scores:** 100% SAT V 400+; 100% SAT M 400+; 13% ACT 18-23; 63% ACT 24-29 **% Accepted:** 63 **Admission Plans:** Early Admission; Early Action; Deferred Admission **Application Deadline:** February 01 **Application Fee:** $40.00 **H.S. Requirements:** High school diploma or equivalent not required **Costs Per Year:** Application fee: $40. Comprehensive fee: $30,810 includes full-time tuition ($23,110) and college room and board ($7700). College room only: $3900. Room and board charges vary according to board plan. Part-time tuition: $830 per credit hour. Part-time tuition varies according to course load. **Scholarships:** Available **Calendar System:** 4-1-4, Summer Session Not available **Enrollment:** FT 1,127, PT 3 **Faculty:** FT 96, PT 27 **Student-Faculty Ratio:** 11:1 **Exams:** SAT I or ACT **% Receiving Financial Aid:** 61 **% Residing in College-Owned, -Operated, or -Affiliated Housing:** 95 **Library Holdings:** 217,751 **Regional Accreditation:** Southern Association of Colleges and Schools **Credit Hours For Degree:** 111 semester hours, Bachelors **ROTC:** Army, Air Force **Intercollegiate Athletics:** Baseball M; Basketball M & W; Cheerleading W; Cross-Country Running M & W; Field Hockey W; Football M; Golf M & W; Soccer M & W; Softball W; Swimming and Diving M & W; Tennis M & W; Track and Field M & W; Volleyball W

CLEAR CREEK BAPTIST BIBLE COLLEGE
300 Clear Creek Rd.
Pineville, KY 40977-9754
Tel: (606)337-3196
Web Site: http://www.ccbbc.edu/
President/CEO: Dr. Bill D. Whittaker
Registrar: Brenda Hester
Admissions: Billy Howell
Financial Aid: Sam Risner
Type: Four-Year College **Sex:** Coed **Affiliation:** Southern Baptist **Admission Plans:** Open Admission; Deferred Admission **Application Fee:** $40.00 **H.S. Requirements:** High school diploma or equivalent not required. For bachelor's degree program: High school diploma required; GED accepted **Costs Per Year:** Application fee: $40. Comprehensive fee: $7830 includes full-time tuition ($4520) and college room and board ($3310). College room only: $1870. Part-time tuition: $205 per semester hour. **Scholarships:** Available **Calendar System:** Semester, Summer Session Available **Enrollment:** FT 154, PT 58 **Faculty:** FT 8, PT 8 **% Receiving Financial Aid:** 67 **Library Holdings:** 38,000 **Regional Accreditation:** Southern Association of Colleges and Schools **Credit Hours For Degree:** 66 semester hours, Associates; 128 semester hours, Bachelors **Professional Accreditation:** AABC

DAYMAR COLLEGE (LOUISVILLE)
4400 Breckenridge Ln., Ste. 415
Louisville, KY 40218
Tel: (502)495-1040
Web Site: http://www.daymarcollege.edu/
Admissions: Patrick Carney
Type: Two-Year College **Sex:** Coed **Calendar System:** Quarter **Professional Accreditation:** ACICS

DAYMAR COLLEGE (OWENSBORO)
3361 Buckland Square
Owensboro, KY 42301
Tel: (270)926-4040
Free: 800-960-4090
Fax: (270)685-4090
E-mail: mdowney@ojcb.com
Web Site: http://www.daymarcollege.edu/
President/CEO: Mark Gabis
Registrar: Debi Sweeden
Admissions: Vickie McDougal
Financial Aid: Tricia Dukes
Type: Two-Year College **Sex:** Coed **Admission Plans:** Deferred Admission **Application Fee:** $20.00 **H.S. Requirements:** High school diploma required; GED accepted **Scholarships:** Available **Calendar System:** Quarter, Summer Session Available **Enrollment:** FT 334, PT 112 **Faculty:** FT 9, PT 21 **Student-Faculty Ratio:** 9:1 **Exams:** Other, SAT I or ACT **Library Holdings:** 3,215 **Credit Hours For Degree:** 96 quarter hours, Associates **Professional Accreditation:** ACICS

DRAUGHONS JUNIOR COLLEGE
2421 Fitzgerald Industrial Dr.
Bowling Green, KY 42101
Tel: (270)843-6750
Fax: (270)843-6976
Web Site: http://www.draughons.edu/
President/CEO: Melva Hale
Registrar: Sarah Hunley
Admissions: Melva Hale
Financial Aid: Mary Hood
Type: Two-Year College **Sex:** Coed **Affiliation:** Draughons Junior College, Inc **Admission Plans:** Open Admission **Application Fee:** $20.00 **H.S.**

Requirements: High school diploma required; GED accepted **Costs Per Year:** Application fee: $20. Tuition: $300 per credit part-time. Mandatory fees: $1000 full-time. Full-time fees vary according to course load and program. Part-time tuition varies according to course load and program. Tuition guaranteed not to increase for student's term of enrollment. **Scholarships:** Available **Calendar System:** Semester **Enrollment:** FT 172, PT 196 **Faculty:** FT 10, PT 17 **Student-Faculty Ratio:** 13:1 **Exams:** SAT I or ACT **Library Holdings:** 5,000 **Credit Hours For Degree:** 63 credit hours, Associates **Professional Accreditation:** ACICS

EASTERN KENTUCKY UNIVERSITY
521 Lancaster Ave.
Richmond, KY 40475-3102
Tel: (859)622-1000
Admissions: (859)622-2106
Fax: (859)622-1020
Web Site: http://www.eku.edu/
President/CEO: Joanne Glasser, Esq
Registrar: Jill Allgier
Admissions: Stephen Byrn
Financial Aid: Shelley Park
Type: Comprehensive **Sex:** Coed **Affiliation:** Kentucky Council on Post Secondary Education **% Accepted:** 75 **Admission Plans:** Open Admission; Deferred Admission **Application Deadline:** August 01 **Application Fee:** $30.00 **H.S. Requirements:** High school diploma required; GED accepted **Costs Per Year:** Application fee: $30. State resident tuition: $4660 full-time, $194 per credit hour part-time. Nonresident tuition: $13,070 full-time, $545 per credit hour part-time. Mandatory fees: $460 full-time. Part-time tuition varies according to course load. College room and board: $4088. College room only: $2208. Room and board charges vary according to board plan and housing facility. **Scholarships:** Available **Calendar System:** Semester, Summer Session Available **Enrollment:** FT 10,919, PT 3,023, Grad 2,277 **Faculty:** FT 556, PT 454 **Student-Faculty Ratio:** 17:1 **Exams:** ACT **% Receiving Financial Aid:** 54 **% Residing in College-Owned, -Operated, or -Affiliated Housing:** 33 **Library Holdings:** 768,300 **Regional Accreditation:** Southern Association of Colleges and Schools **Credit Hours For Degree:** 64 semester hours, Associates; 128 semester hours, Bachelors **ROTC:** Army, Air Force **Professional Accreditation:** AACSB, ABET, AACN, AAFCS, AAMAE, ACCE, ACA, ADtA, AHIMA, AOTA, ASC, ASLHA, CSWE, JRCEMT, JRCEPAT, NAACLS, NAIT, NASM, NASPAA, NCATE NLN, NRPA **Intercollegiate Athletics:** Baseball M; Basketball M & W; Cheerleading M & W; Cross-Country Running M & W; Football M; Golf M & W; Softball W; Tennis M & W; Track and Field M & W; Volleyball W

ELIZABETHTOWN COMMUNITY AND TECHNICAL COLLEGE
600 College St. Rd.
Elizabethtown, KY 42701-3081
Tel: (270)769-2371; 877-246-2322
Fax: (270)769-1632
Web Site: http://www.elizabethtown.kctcs.edu/
President/CEO: Dr. Thelma White
Registrar: Peggy Hoskinson
Admissions: Dr. Dale Buckles
Financial Aid: Sharon Hodges
Type: Two-Year College **Sex:** Coed **Affiliation:** Kentucky Community and Technical College System **Admission Plans:** Open Admission; Early Admission **Application Fee:** $0.00 **H.S. Requirements:** High school diploma required; GED accepted **Costs Per Year:** Application fee: $0. State resident tuition: $2352 full-time, $98 per credit hour part-time. Nonresident tuition: $7056 full-time, $294 per credit hour part-time. Full-time tuition varies according to course load. Part-time tuition varies according to course load. **Scholarships:** Available **Calendar System:** Semester, Summer Session Available **Enrollment:** FT 1,645, PT 1,970 **Exams:** ACT **Library Holdings:** 35,175 **Regional Accreditation:** Southern Association of Colleges and Schools **Credit Hours For Degree:** 60 credits, Associates **Professional Accreditation:** JRCERT, NLN

GATEWAY COMMUNITY AND TECHNICAL COLLEGE
1025 Amsterdam Rd.
Covington, KY 41011
Tel: (859)441-4500
Fax: (859)292-6415
Web Site: http://www.gateway.kctcs.edu/
President/CEO: G. Edward Hughes
Admissions: Paul Brinkman
Type: Two-Year College **Sex:** Coed **H.S. Requirements:** High school diploma required; GED accepted **Costs Per Year:** State resident tuition: $2940 full-time, $98 per credit hour part-time. Nonresident tuition: $8820 full-time, $294 per credit hour part-time. **Calendar System:** Semester **Exams:** Other **Professional Accreditation:** COE

GEORGETOWN COLLEGE
400 East College St.
Georgetown, KY 40324-1696
Tel: (502)863-8000
Free: 800-788-9985
Admissions: (502)863-8009
Fax: (502)868-8891
Web Site: http://www.georgetowncollege.edu/
President/CEO: Dr. William H. Crouch, Jr.
Registrar: Winnie Bratcher
Admissions: Johnnie Johnson
Financial Aid: Rhyan Conyers
Type: Comprehensive **Sex:** Coed **Affiliation:** Baptist Church **Scores:** 99% SAT V 400+; 98% SAT M 400+; 51% ACT 18-23; 40% ACT 24-29 **% Accepted:** 95 **Admission Plans:** Deferred Admission **Application Deadline:** July 01 **Application Fee:** $30.00 **H.S. Requirements:** High school diploma required; GED accepted **Costs Per Year:** Application fee: $30. Comprehensive fee: $26,770 includes full-time tuition ($20,700) and college room and board ($6070). College room only: $2940. Part-time tuition: $860 per hour. **Scholarships:** Available **Calendar System:** Semester, Summer Session Available **Enrollment:** FT 1,310, PT 55, Grad 539 **Faculty:** FT 101, PT 66 **Student-Faculty Ratio:** 11:1 **Exams:** ACT, SAT I or ACT **% Receiving Financial Aid:** 66 **% Residing in College-Owned, -Operated, or -Affiliated Housing:** 88 **Library Holdings:** 160,862 **Regional Accreditation:** Southern Association of Colleges and Schools **Credit Hours For Degree:** 120 semester hours, Bachelors **ROTC:** Army, Air Force **Intercollegiate Athletics:** Baseball M; Basketball M & W; Cheerleading W; Cross-Country Running M & W; Football M; Golf M & W; Soccer M & W; Softball W; Tennis M & W; Track and Field M & W; Volleyball W

HAZARD COMMUNITY AND TECHNICAL COLLEGE
1 Community College Dr.
Hazard, KY 41701-2403
Tel: (606)436-5721
Free: 800-246-7521
Fax: (606)439-2988
Web Site: http://www.hazard.kctcs.edu/
President/CEO: Jay Box
Registrar: Elizabeth Roberts
Admissions: Germain Shaffer
Financial Aid: Charles Anderson
Type: Two-Year College **Sex:** Coed **Affiliation:** Kentucky Community and Technical College System **Admission Plans:** Open Admission; Early Admission **Application Fee:** $0.00 **H.S. Requirements:** High school diploma required; GED accepted **Calendar System:** Semester, Summer Session Available **Faculty:** FT 100, PT 60 **Exams:** ACT **Library Holdings:** 36,550 **Regional Accreditation:** Southern Association of Colleges and Schools **Credit Hours For Degree:** 60 credit hours, Associates **Professional Accreditation:** APTA, JRCERT, NAACLS

HENDERSON COMMUNITY COLLEGE
2660 South Green St.
Henderson, KY 42420-4623
Tel: (270)827-1867
E-mail: patty.mitchell@kctcs.edu
Web Site: http://www.henderson.kctcs.edu/
President/CEO: Dr. Patrick R. Lake
Registrar: Patricia Mitchell
Admissions: Patty Mitchell
Type: Two-Year College **Sex:** Coed **Affiliation:** Kentucky Community and Technical College System **Admission Plans:** Open Admission **H.S. Requirements:** High school diploma required; GED accepted **Costs Per Year:** State resident tuition: $2490 full-time, $98 per credit hour part-time. Nonresident tuition: $8820 full-time, $294 per credit hour part-time. Full-time tuition varies according to course load. Part-time tuition varies according to course load. **Scholarships:** Available **Calendar System:** Semester, Summer Session Available **Enrollment:** FT 690, PT 1,551 **Faculty:** FT 48, PT 53 **Student-Faculty Ratio:** 13:1 **Exams:** ACT, Other **Library Holdings:** 30,206 **Regional Accreditation:** Southern Association of Colleges and Schools

Credit Hours For Degree: 60 credit hours, Associates **Professional Accreditation:** ADA, NAACLS, NLN

HOPKINSVILLE COMMUNITY COLLEGE
PO Box 2100
Hopkinsville, KY 42241-2100
Tel: (270)886-3921
Fax: (270)886-0237
Web Site: http://www.hopcc.kctcs.edu/
President/CEO: Dr. Bonnie L. Rogers
Registrar: Ruth Ann Rettie
Admissions: Ruth Ann Rettie
Financial Aid: Vincent Shykes
Type: Two-Year College **Sex:** Coed **Affiliation:** Kentucky Community and Technical College System **Scores:** 48.78% ACT 18-23; 14.53% ACT 24-29 **Admission Plans:** Open Admission; Early Admission; Deferred Admission **Application Fee:** $0.00 **H.S. Requirements:** High school diploma required; GED accepted **Costs Per Year:** Application fee: $0. State resident tuition: $2940 full-time, $98 per credit hour part-time. Nonresident tuition: $8820 full-time, $294 per credit hour part-time. Full-time tuition varies according to location and reciprocity agreements. Part-time tuition varies according to location and reciprocity agreements. **Scholarships:** Available **Calendar System:** Semester, Summer Session Available **Enrollment:** FT 1,413, PT 1,691 **Faculty:** FT 68, PT 101 **Student-Faculty Ratio:** 23:1 **Exams:** ACT, Other **Library Holdings:** 45,674 **Regional Accreditation:** Southern Association of Colleges and Schools **Credit Hours For Degree:** 60 credit hours, Associates **Professional Accreditation:** NLN

ITT TECHNICAL INSTITUTE (LEXINGTON)
2473 Fortune Dr., Ste. 180
Lexington, KY 40509
Tel: (859)246-3300
Web Site: http://www.itt-tech.edu/ **Type:** Four-Year College **Sex:** Coed **Application Fee:** $100.00 **Exams:** Other

ITT TECHNICAL INSTITUTE (LOUISVILLE)
10509 Timberwood Circle, Ste. 100
Louisville, KY 40223-5392
Tel: (502)327-7424
Web Site: http://www.itt-tech.edu/
President/CEO: Alan S. Crews
Admissions: Steve Allen
Type: Two-Year College **Sex:** Coed **Affiliation:** ITT Educational Services, Inc **Admission Plans:** Deferred Admission **Application Deadline:** Rolling **Application Fee:** $100.00 **H.S. Requirements:** High school diploma required; GED accepted **Costs Per Year:** Application fee: $100. **Scholarships:** Available **Calendar System:** Quarter, Summer Session Not available **Exams:** Other **Credit Hours For Degree:** 96 credit hours, Associates; 180 credit hours, Bachelors **Professional Accreditation:** ACICS

JEFFERSON COMMUNITY AND TECHNICAL COLLEGE
109 East Broadway
Louisville, KY 40202-2005
Tel: (502)213-5333
Admissions: (502)213-2183
Fax: (502)213-2115
Web Site: http://www.jctc.kctcs.edu/
President/CEO: Dr. Anthony Newberry
Registrar: Vivian Thomas
Admissions: Melanie Vaughan-Cooke
Financial Aid: Angela Johnson
Type: Two-Year College **Sex:** Coed **Affiliation:** Kentucky Community and Technical College System **Admission Plans:** Open Admission; Early Admission **Application Deadline:** Rolling **Application Fee:** $0.00 **H.S. Requirements:** High school diploma or equivalent not required. For certain academic programs (Allied Health): High school diploma required; GED accepted **Costs Per Year:** Application fee: $0. State resident tuition: $3270 full-time, $109 per credit hour part-time. Nonresident tuition: $9810 full-time, $327 per credit hour part-time. Mandatory fees: $50 full-time, $25 per term part-time. **Scholarships:** Available **Calendar System:** Semester, Summer Session Available **Enrollment:** FT 4,941, PT 9,299 **Faculty:** FT 304, PT 357 **Student-Faculty Ratio:** 19:1 **Library Holdings:** 76,578 **Regional Accreditation:** Southern Association of Colleges and Schools **Credit Hours For Degree:** 60 credits, Associates **ROTC:** Army **Professional Accreditation:** ACF, AOTA, APTA, CARC, NLN

KENTUCKY CHRISTIAN UNIVERSITY
100 Academic Parkway
Grayson, KY 41143-2205
Tel: (606)474-3000
Free: 800-522-3181
Admissions: (606)474-3266
Fax: (606)474-3155
E-mail: sdeakins@email.kcc.edu
Web Site: http://www.kcu.edu/
President/CEO: Dr. Keith P. Keeran
Registrar: George Waggoner
Admissions: Sandra Deakins
Financial Aid: Jennie Bender
Type: Comprehensive **Sex:** Coed **Affiliation:** Christian Churches and Churches of Christ **Scores:** 82.35% SAT V 400+; 85.19% SAT M 400+; 50% ACT 18-23; 27.08% ACT 24-29 **Admission Plans:** Early Action; Deferred Admission **Application Fee:** $25.00 **H.S. Requirements:** High school diploma required; GED accepted **Scholarships:** Available **Calendar System:** Semester, Summer Session Available **Enrollment:** FT 530, PT 14, Grad 15 **Faculty:** FT 42, PT 16 **Student-Faculty Ratio:** 16:1 **Exams:** SAT I and SAT II or ACT **% Receiving Financial Aid:** 81 **% Residing in College-Owned, -Operated, or -Affiliated Housing:** 88 **Library Holdings:** 103,323 **Regional Accreditation:** Southern Association of Colleges and Schools **Credit Hours For Degree:** 66 credit hours, Associates; 132 credit hours, Bachelors **Professional Accreditation:** CSWE **Intercollegiate Athletics:** Basketball M & W; Cross-Country Running M & W; Soccer M & W; Volleyball W

KENTUCKY MOUNTAIN BIBLE COLLEGE
PO Box 10
Vancleve, KY 41385-0010
Tel: (606)693-5000
Free: 800-879-KMBC
Fax: (606)693-7744
Web Site: http://www.kmbc.edu/
President/CEO: Dr. Philip Speas
Registrar: Catherine Nelson
Admissions: Jay Wisler
Financial Aid: Jewel MacGregor
Type: Four-Year College **Sex:** Coed **Affiliation:** interdenominational **Scores:** 47.6% ACT 18-23; 9.5% ACT 24-29 **% Accepted:** 46 **Admission Plans:** Preferred Admission; Deferred Admission **Application Deadline:** Rolling **Application Fee:** $25.00 **H.S. Requirements:** High school diploma required; GED accepted **Costs Per Year:** Application fee: $25. Comprehensive fee: $8460 includes full-time tuition ($4800), mandatory fees ($460), and college room and board ($3200). College room only: $1000. Full-time tuition and fees vary according to course load. Room and board charges vary according to housing facility. Part-time tuition: $160 per credit hour. Part-time mandatory fees: $30 per term. Part-time tuition and fees vary according to course load. **Scholarships:** Available **Calendar System:** Semester, Summer Session Not available **Faculty:** FT 8, PT 7 **Student-Faculty Ratio:** 6:1 **Exams:** ACT **% Receiving Financial Aid:** 75 **% Residing in College-Owned, -Operated, or -Affiliated Housing:** 91 **Library Holdings:** 23,520 **Credit Hours For Degree:** 65 credit hours, Associates; 130 credit hours, Bachelors **Professional Accreditation:** AABC

KENTUCKY STATE UNIVERSITY
400 East Main St.
Frankfort, KY 40601
Tel: (502)597-6000
Free: 800-325-1716
Admissions: (502)597-6322
Fax: (502)597-6239
Web Site: http://www.kysu.edu/
President/CEO: Dr. Mary Evans Sias
Registrar: John Martin
Admissions: James Burrell
Financial Aid: Carmella Conner
Type: Comprehensive **Sex:** Coed **% Accepted:** 28 **Admission Plans:** Early Admission **Application Deadline:** Rolling **Application Fee:** $22.00 **H.S. Requirements:** High school diploma required; GED accepted **Costs Per Year:** Application fee: $22. State resident tuition: $3550 full-time, $148 per credit part-time. Nonresident tuition: $9992 full-time, $419 per credit part-time. Mandatory fees: $918 full-time, $20 per credit part-time, $49 per term part-time. Full-time tuition and fees vary according to class time, course

level, course load, location, program, reciprocity agreements, and student level. Part-time tuition and fees vary according to class time, course level, course load, location, program, reciprocity agreements, and student level. College room and board: $5620. College room only: $2592. Room and board charges vary according to board plan, housing facility, location, and student level. **Scholarships:** Available **Calendar System:** Semester, Summer Session Available **Enrollment:** FT 1,619, PT 609, Grad 158 **Faculty:** FT 152, PT 8 **Student-Faculty Ratio:** 15:1 **Exams:** ACT, SAT I or ACT **% Receiving Financial Aid:** 47 **% Residing in College-Owned, -Operated, or -Affiliated Housing:** 26 **Library Holdings:** 296,631 **Regional Accreditation:** Southern Association of Colleges and Schools **Credit Hours For Degree:** 64 credit hours, Associates; 128 credit hours, Bachelors **ROTC:** Air Force **Professional Accreditation:** ACBSP, CSWE, NASM, NASPAA, NCATE, NLN **Intercollegiate Athletics:** Baseball M; Basketball M & W; Cross-Country Running M & W; Football M; Golf M; Softball W; Tennis M & W; Track and Field M & W; Volleyball W

KENTUCKY WESLEYAN COLLEGE
3000 Frederica St., PO Box 1039
Owensboro, KY 42302-1039
Tel: (270)926-3111
Free: 800-990-0592
Admissions: (270)852-3120
Fax: (270)926-3196
E-mail: admission@kwc.edu
Web Site: http://www.kwc.edu/
President/CEO: Dr. Anne C. Federlein
Registrar: Donald C. Schmied
Admissions: Claude Bacon
Financial Aid: Vivian J. Rinaldo
Type: Four-Year College **Sex:** Coed **Affiliation:** Methodist **Scores:** 78% SAT V 400+; 90% SAT M 400+; 54% ACT 18-23; 30% ACT 24-29 **% Accepted:** 77 **Admission Plans:** Early Admission; Deferred Admission **Application Deadline:** September 01 **Application Fee:** $0.00 **H.S. Requirements:** High school diploma required; GED accepted **Costs Per Year:** Application fee: $0. Comprehensive fee: $19,350 includes full-time tuition ($13,200), mandatory fees ($400), and college room and board ($5750). College room only: $2600. Part-time tuition: $400 per credit hour. **Scholarships:** Available **Calendar System:** Semester, Summer Session Available **Enrollment:** FT 717, PT 38 **Faculty:** FT 34, PT 34 **Student-Faculty Ratio:** 16:1 **Exams:** SAT I or ACT **% Receiving Financial Aid:** 84 **% Residing in College-Owned, -Operated, or -Affiliated Housing:** 45 **Regional Accreditation:** Southern Association of Colleges and Schools **Credit Hours For Degree:** 128 semester hours, Bachelors **Intercollegiate Athletics:** Baseball M; Basketball M & W; Cheerleading M & W; Football M; Golf M & W; Soccer M & W; Softball W; Tennis W; Volleyball W

LEXINGTON COMMUNITY COLLEGE
Cooper Dr.
Lexington, KY 40506-0235
Tel: (859)257-4872
E-mail: shugl00@uky.edu
Web Site: http://www.uky.edu/lcc/
President/CEO: Dr. James Kerley
Registrar: Becky Harp
Admissions: Shelbie Hugle
Financial Aid: Runan Pendergrast
Type: Two-Year College **Sex:** Coed **Affiliation:** Kentucky Community and Technical College System **Scores:** 50% ACT 18-23; 9% ACT 24-29 **Admission Plans:** Open Admission; Preferred Admission; Early Admission **Application Fee:** $20.00 **H.S. Requirements:** High school diploma required; GED accepted **Scholarships:** Available **Calendar System:** Semester, Summer Session Available **Enrollment:** FT 5,354, PT 3,285 **Faculty:** FT 155, PT 291 **Student-Faculty Ratio:** 19:1 **% Residing in College-Owned, -Operated, or -Affiliated Housing:** 5 **Library Holdings:** 27,000 **Regional Accreditation:** Southern Association of Colleges and Schools **Credit Hours For Degree:** 60 credit hours, Associates **ROTC:** Army, Air Force **Professional Accreditation:** ADA, CARC, NLN

LINDSEY WILSON COLLEGE
210 Lindsey Wilson St.
Columbia, KY 42728-1298
Tel: (270)384-2126
Free: 800-264-0138
Admissions: (270)384-8100
Fax: (270)384-8200
E-mail: poolert@lindsey.edu
Web Site: http://www.lindsey.edu/
President/CEO: Dr. William T. Luckey, Jr.
Registrar: Sue Coomer
Admissions: Traci Pooler
Financial Aid: Denise Fudge
Type: Comprehensive **Sex:** Coed **Affiliation:** United Methodist **Scores:** 52% ACT 18-23; 15.9% ACT 24-29 **Admission Plans:** Open Admission **Application Deadline:** Rolling **Application Fee:** $0.00 **H.S. Requirements:** High school diploma required; GED accepted **Costs Per Year:** Application fee: $0. Comprehensive fee: $20,601 includes full-time tuition ($14,208), mandatory fees ($230), and college room and board ($6163). Part-time tuition: $592 per credit hour. **Scholarships:** Available **Calendar System:** Semester, Summer Session Available **Enrollment:** FT 1,457, PT 165, Grad 280 **Faculty:** FT 70, PT 41 **Student-Faculty Ratio:** 23:1 **Exams:** SAT I or ACT **% Receiving Financial Aid:** 91 **% Residing in College-Owned, -Operated, or -Affiliated Housing:** 47 **Library Holdings:** 80,000 **Regional Accreditation:** Southern Association of Colleges and Schools **Credit Hours For Degree:** 64 semester hours, Associates; 128 semester hours, Bachelors **ROTC:** Army **Professional Accreditation:** ACA **Intercollegiate Athletics:** Baseball M; Basketball M & W; Bowling M & W; Cheerleading M & W; Cross-Country Running M & W; Golf M & W; Soccer M & W; Softball W; Tennis M & W; Track and Field M & W; Volleyball W

LOUISVILLE TECHNICAL INSTITUTE
3901 Atkinson Square Dr.
Louisville, KY 40218-4528
Tel: (502)456-6509
Free: 800-884-6528
Fax: (502)456-2341
Web Site: http://www.louisvilletech.com/
President/CEO: Dr. A.R. Sullivan
Registrar: Cathy Druin
Admissions: David Ritz
Financial Aid: Lisa Wright
Type: Two-Year College **Sex:** Coed **Affiliation:** Sullivan University System **Admission Plans:** Deferred Admission **Application Fee:** $90.00 **H.S. Requirements:** High school diploma required; GED accepted **Costs Per Year:** Application fee: $90. One-time mandatory fee: $90. Tuition: $13,110 full-time, $270 per credit hour part-time. Mandatory fees: $435 full-time, $30 per course part-time. Full-time tuition and fees vary according to class time and program. Part-time tuition and fees vary according to program. College room only: $3960. Tuition guaranteed not to increase for student's term of enrollment. **Scholarships:** Available **Calendar System:** Quarter, Summer Session Available **Enrollment:** FT 626, PT 41 **Faculty:** FT 30, PT 29 **Student-Faculty Ratio:** 9:1 **Exams:** Other **% Residing in College-Owned, -Operated, or -Affiliated Housing:** 6 **Library Holdings:** 3,463 **Credit Hours For Degree:** 97 quarter hours, Associates **Professional Accreditation:** ACICS

MADISONVILLE COMMUNITY COLLEGE
2000 College Dr.
Madisonville, KY 42431-9185
Tel: (270)821-2250
Fax: (270)821-1555
Web Site: http://www.madcc.kctcs.edu/
President/CEO: Dr. Judith L. Rhoads
Registrar: Jay Parrent
Admissions: Jay Parent
Financial Aid: Caroline Clayton
Type: Two-Year College **Sex:** Coed **Affiliation:** Kentucky Community and Technical College System **Admission Plans:** Open Admission; Early Admission; Deferred Admission **Application Fee:** $0.00 **H.S. Requirements:** High school diploma required; GED accepted **Scholarships:** Available **Calendar System:** Semester, Summer Session Available **Faculty:** FT 95, PT 89 **Exams:** ACT, Other **Library Holdings:** 26,793 **Regional Accreditation:** Southern Association of Colleges and Schools **Credit Hours For Degree:** 60 credit hours, Associates **Professional Accreditation:** AOTA, APTA, CARC, NLN

MAYSVILLE COMMUNITY AND TECHNICAL COLLEGE
1755 US 68
Maysville, KY 41056
Tel: (606)759-7141

E-mail: ccsmayrg@ukcc.uky.edu
Web Site: http://www.maycc.kctcs.net/
President/CEO: Augusta Julian
Registrar: Patricia K. Massie
Admissions: Patee Massie
Financial Aid: Jerome Greiner
Type: Two-Year College **Sex:** Coed **Affiliation:** Kentucky Community and Technical College System **Admission Plans:** Open Admission; Early Admission **Application Fee:** $0.00 **H.S. Requirements:** High school diploma required; GED accepted **Scholarships:** Available **Calendar System:** Semester, Summer Session Available **Enrollment:** FT 776, PT 1,141 **Faculty:** FT 53, PT 68 **Exams:** ACT **Library Holdings:** 36,600 **Regional Accreditation:** Southern Association of Colleges and Schools **Credit Hours For Degree:** 60 credit hours, Associates **Professional Accreditation:** CARC

MID-CONTINENT UNIVERSITY
99 Powell Rd. East
Mayfield, KY 42066-9007
Tel: (270)247-8521
Fax: (270)247-3115
E-mail: admissions@midcontinent.edu
Web Site: http://www.midcontinent.edu/
President/CEO: Dr. Robert Imhoff
Registrar: Yvonne Yates
Admissions: Dr. Dutch Booth
Financial Aid: Kent Youngblood
Type: Four-Year College **Sex:** Coed **Affiliation:** Southern Baptist **Scores:** 44% ACT 18-23; 12% ACT 24-29 **Admission Plans:** Early Admission **Application Deadline:** Rolling **Application Fee:** $20.00 **H.S. Requirements:** High school diploma required; GED accepted **Costs Per Year:** Application fee: $20. Comprehensive fee: $15,800 includes full-time tuition ($8850), mandatory fees ($1250), and college room and board ($5700). Full-time tuition and fees vary according to course load and program. Room and board charges vary according to board plan and housing facility. Part-time tuition: $295 per credit hour. Part-time tuition varies according to course load and program. **Scholarships:** Available **Calendar System:** Semester, Summer Session Available **Enrollment:** FT 587, PT 62 **Faculty:** FT 20, PT 36 **Student-Faculty Ratio:** 15:1 **Exams:** SAT I or ACT **% Receiving Financial Aid:** 74 **% Residing in College-Owned, -Operated, or -Affiliated Housing:** 33 **Library Holdings:** 32,697 **Regional Accreditation:** Southern Association of Colleges and Schools **Credit Hours For Degree:** 60 semester hours, Associates; 128 semester hours, Bachelors **Intercollegiate Athletics:** Baseball M; Cross-Country Running M & W; Soccer M; Softball W; Volleyball W

MIDWAY COLLEGE
512 East Stephens St.
Midway, KY 40347-1120
Tel: (859)846-4421
Free: 800-755-0031
Admissions: (859)846-5799
Fax: (859)846-5823
Web Site: http://www.midway.edu/
President/CEO: Dr. William B. Drake, Jr.
Registrar: P. Edward Presler
Admissions: Dr. Jim Wombles
Financial Aid: Karen Britt Statler
Type: Four-Year College **Sex:** Women **Affiliation:** Christian Church (Disciples of Christ) **Scores:** 100% SAT V 400+; 82% SAT M 400+; 57% ACT 18-23; 15% ACT 24-29 **% Accepted:** 75 **Admission Plans:** Early Admission; Deferred Admission **Application Deadline:** Rolling **Application Fee:** $25.00 **H.S. Requirements:** High school diploma required; GED accepted **Costs Per Year:** Application fee: $25. Comprehensive fee: $20,150 includes full-time tuition ($13,800), mandatory fees ($150), and college room and board ($6200). College room only: $3000. Full-time tuition and fees vary according to class time, location, and program. Room and board charges vary according to board plan and housing facility. Part-time tuition: $460 per semester hour. Part-time tuition varies according to class time, location, and program. **Scholarships:** Available **Calendar System:** Semester, Summer Session Available **Enrollment:** FT 876, PT 403 **Faculty:** FT 50, PT 99 **Student-Faculty Ratio:** 12:1 **Exams:** SAT I or ACT **% Receiving Financial Aid:** 81 **% Residing in College-Owned, -Operated, or -Affiliated Housing:** 23 **Library Holdings:** 96,236 **Regional Accreditation:** Southern Association of Colleges and Schools **Credit Hours For Degree:** 65 semester hours, Associates; 130 semester hours, Bachelors **ROTC:** Army **Professional Accreditation:** NLN **Intercollegiate Athletics:** Basketball W; Equestrian Sports W; Soccer W; Softball W; Tennis W

MOREHEAD STATE UNIVERSITY
University Blvd.
Morehead, KY 40351
Tel: (606)783-2221
Free: 800-585-6781
Admissions: (606)783-2000
Fax: (606)783-5038
Web Site: http://www.moreheadstate.edu/
President/CEO: Dr. Ronald Eaglin
Registrar: Loretta Lykins
Admissions: Joel Pace
Financial Aid: Carol Becker
Type: Comprehensive **Sex:** Coed **Scores:** 56% ACT 18-23; 18% ACT 24-29 **% Accepted:** 69 **Admission Plans:** Early Admission; Deferred Admission **Application Deadline:** Rolling **Application Fee:** $0.00 **H.S. Requirements:** High school diploma required; GED accepted **Costs Per Year:** Application fee: $0. State resident tuition: $4320 full-time, $180 per credit hour part-time. Nonresident tuition: $11,480 full-time, $480 per credit hour part-time. Full-time tuition varies according to course load and reciprocity agreements. College room and board: $4830. Room and board charges vary according to board plan and housing facility. **Scholarships:** Available **Calendar System:** Semester, Summer Session Available **Enrollment:** FT 5,964, PT 1,580, Grad 1,518 **Faculty:** FT 378, PT 156 **Student-Faculty Ratio:** 17:1 **Exams:** ACT, SAT I or ACT **% Receiving Financial Aid:** 67 **% Residing in College-Owned, -Operated, or -Affiliated Housing:** 33 **Library Holdings:** 333,518 **Regional Accreditation:** Southern Association of Colleges and Schools **Credit Hours For Degree:** 64 credit hours, Associates; 128 credit hours, Bachelors **ROTC:** Army **Professional Accreditation:** AACSB, AAFCS, ADtA, ACBSP, CARC, CSWE, JRCERT, NAIT, NASM, NCATE, NLN **Intercollegiate Athletics:** Baseball M; Basketball M & W; Bowling M & W; Cross-Country Running M & W; Equestrian Sports M & W; Football M; Golf M; Riflery M & W; Soccer W; Softball W; Tennis M & W; Track and Field M & W; Volleyball W

MURRAY STATE UNIVERSITY
PO Box 9
Murray, KY 42071-0009
Tel: (270)762-3011
Free: 800-272-4678
Admissions: (270)762-3592
Fax: (270)762-3413
E-mail: jim.vaughan@murraystate.edu
Web Site: http://www.murraystate.edu/
President/CEO: Dr. F. King Alexander
Registrar: Donna Harris
Admissions: Jim Vaughn
Financial Aid: Charles Vinson
Type: Comprehensive **Sex:** Coed **Affiliation:** Kentucky Council on Postsecondary Education **Scores:** 57% ACT 18-23; 37% ACT 24-29 **% Accepted:** 64 **Application Fee:** $30.00 **H.S. Requirements:** High school diploma required; GED accepted **Costs Per Year:** Application fee: $30. State resident tuition: $3792 full-time, $185 per hour part-time. Nonresident tuition: $5464 full-time, $240 per hour part-time. Mandatory fees: $636 full-time, $23 per hour part-time. Full-time tuition and fees vary according to reciprocity agreements. Part-time tuition and fees vary according to reciprocity agreements. College room and board: $4472. College room only: $2366. Room and board charges vary according to board plan. **Scholarships:** Available **Calendar System:** Semester, Summer Session Available **Enrollment:** FT 7,155, PT 1,422, Grad 1,689 **Faculty:** FT 386, PT 151 **Student-Faculty Ratio:** 17:1 **Exams:** ACT **% Receiving Financial Aid:** 44 **% Residing in College-Owned, -Operated, or -Affiliated Housing:** 40 **Library Holdings:** 400,000 **Regional Accreditation:** Southern Association of Colleges and Schools **Credit Hours For Degree:** 64 credit hours, Associates; 128 credit hours, Bachelors **ROTC:** Army **Professional Accreditation:** AACSB, ABET, ACEJMC, AACN, AAFCS, AANA, ACA, ADtA, AOTA, ASLHA, CSWE, NASAD, NASM, NCATE, NLN **Intercollegiate Athletics:** Baseball M; Basketball M & W; Bowling M & W; Cheerleading M & W; Crew M & W;

Cross-Country Running M & W; Equestrian Sports M & W; Football M; Golf M & W; Riflery M & W; Soccer W; Tennis M & W; Track and Field M & W; Volleyball W

NATIONAL COLLEGE OF BUSINESS & TECHNOLOGY (DANVILLE)
115 East Lexington Ave.
Danville, KY 40422
Tel: (859)236-6991
Free: 800-664-1886
Web Site: http://www.ncbt.edu/
Admissions: Stacie Catlett
Financial Aid: Pamela Cotton
Type: Two-Year College **Sex:** Coed **Affiliation:** National College of Business and Technology **Admission Plans:** Open Admission **Application Fee:** $30.00 **H.S. Requirements:** High school diploma required; GED accepted **Costs Per Year:** Application fee: $30. Tuition: $6408 full-time, $178 per credit hour part-time. Mandatory fees: $75 full-time, $15 per term part-time. **Scholarships:** Available **Calendar System:** Quarter, Summer Session Available **Faculty:** FT 1, PT 29 **Student-Faculty Ratio:** 10:1 **Credit Hours For Degree:** 96 credit hours, Associates **Professional Accreditation:** ACICS, AAMAE

NATIONAL COLLEGE OF BUSINESS & TECHNOLOGY (FLORENCE)
7627 Ewing Blvd.
Florence, KY 41042
Tel: (859)525-6510
Free: 800-664-1886
Fax: (859)525-8961
Web Site: http://www.ncbt.edu/
President/CEO: Frank Longaker
Admissions: Ron Thomas
Financial Aid: Pamela Cotton
Type: Two-Year College **Sex:** Coed **Affiliation:** National College of Business and Technology **Admission Plans:** Open Admission **Application Fee:** $30.00 **H.S. Requirements:** High school diploma required; GED accepted **Costs Per Year:** Application fee: $30. Tuition: $6408 full-time, $178 per credit hour part-time. Mandatory fees: $75 full-time, $15 per term part-time. **Scholarships:** Available **Calendar System:** Quarter, Summer Session Available **Faculty:** FT 2, PT 21 **Student-Faculty Ratio:** 12:1 **Credit Hours For Degree:** 96 credit hours, Associates **Professional Accreditation:** ACICS, AAMAE

NATIONAL COLLEGE OF BUSINESS & TECHNOLOGY (LEXINGTON)
628 East Main St.
Lexington, KY 40508-2312
Tel: (859)253-0621
Free: 800-664-1886
Admissions: (859)266-0401
Web Site: http://www.ncbt.edu/
President/CEO: Frank Longaker
Registrar: Martha Arthur
Admissions: Kim Thomasson
Financial Aid: Pam Cotton
Type: Two-Year College **Sex:** Coed **Affiliation:** National College of Business and Technology **Admission Plans:** Open Admission **Application Fee:** $30.00 **H.S. Requirements:** High school diploma required; GED accepted **Costs Per Year:** Application fee: $30. Tuition: $6408 full-time, $178 per credit hour part-time. Mandatory fees: $75 full-time, $15 per term part-time. **Scholarships:** Available **Calendar System:** Quarter, Summer Session Available **Faculty:** FT 4, PT 41 **Student-Faculty Ratio:** 12:1 **Credit Hours For Degree:** 96 credit hours, Associates **Professional Accreditation:** ACICS, AAMAE

NATIONAL COLLEGE OF BUSINESS & TECHNOLOGY (LOUISVILLE)
3950 Dixie Hwy.
Louisville, KY 40216
Tel: (502)447-7634
Free: 800-664-1886
Web Site: http://www.ncbt.edu/
President/CEO: Bob Boutell
Admissions: Mike Fiore
Financial Aid: Marsha Tucker
Type: Two-Year College **Sex:** Coed **Affiliation:** National College of Business and Technology **Admission Plans:** Open Admission **Application Fee:** $30.00 **H.S. Requirements:** High school diploma required; GED accepted **Costs Per Year:** Application fee: $30. Tuition: $6408 full-time, $178 per credit hour part-time. Mandatory fees: $75 full-time, $15 per term part-time. Full-time tuition and fees vary according to course load. Part-time tuition and fees vary according to course load. **Scholarships:** Available **Calendar System:** Quarter, Summer Session Available **Faculty:** FT 2, PT 34 **Student-Faculty Ratio:** 10:1 **Credit Hours For Degree:** 96 credit hours, Associates **Professional Accreditation:** ACICS, AAMAE, AHIMA

NATIONAL COLLEGE OF BUSINESS & TECHNOLOGY (PIKEVILLE)
288 South Mayo Trail, Ste. 2
Pikeville, KY 41501
Tel: (606)432-5477
Free: 800-664-1886
Fax: (606)437-4952
Web Site: http://www.ncbt.edu/
President/CEO: Tina Adkins
Admissions: Jerry Lafferty
Financial Aid: Rita Chaney
Type: Two-Year College **Sex:** Coed **Affiliation:** National College of Business and Technology **Admission Plans:** Open Admission **Application Fee:** $30.00 **H.S. Requirements:** High school diploma required; GED accepted **Costs Per Year:** Application fee: $30. Tuition: $6408 full-time, $178 per credit hour part-time. Mandatory fees: $75 full-time, $15 per term part-time. **Scholarships:** Available **Calendar System:** Quarter, Summer Session Available **Faculty:** FT 2, PT 13 **Student-Faculty Ratio:** 10:1 **Credit Hours For Degree:** 96 credit hours, Associates **Professional Accreditation:** ACICS, AAMAE

NATIONAL COLLEGE OF BUSINESS & TECHNOLOGY (RICHMOND)
139 South Killarney Ln.
Richmond, KY 40475
Tel: (859)623-8956
Free: 800-664-1886
Fax: (859)624-5544
Web Site: http://www.ncbt.edu/
President/CEO: Keeley Gadd
Admissions: Keeley Gadd
Type: Two-Year College **Sex:** Coed **Affiliation:** National College of Business and Technology **Admission Plans:** Open Admission **Application Fee:** $30.00 **H.S. Requirements:** High school diploma required; GED accepted **Costs Per Year:** Application fee: $30. Tuition: $6408 full-time, $178 per credit hour part-time. Mandatory fees: $75 full-time, $15 per term part-time. **Scholarships:** Available **Calendar System:** Quarter, Summer Session Available **Faculty:** FT 1, PT 27 **Student-Faculty Ratio:** 12:1 **Credit Hours For Degree:** 96 credit hours, Associates **Professional Accreditation:** ACICS, AAMAE

NORTHERN KENTUCKY UNIVERSITY
Louie B Nunn Dr.
Highland Heights, KY 41099
Tel: (859)572-5100
Free: 800-637-9948
Admissions: (859)572-5220
E-mail: admitnku@nku.edu
Web Site: http://www.nku.edu/
President/CEO: Dr. James C. Votruba
Registrar: Kimberly Taylor
Admissions: Melissa Gorbandt
Financial Aid: Robert Sprague
Type: Comprehensive **Sex:** Coed **Scores:** 82.7% SAT V 400+; 82% SAT M 400+; 56% ACT 18-23; 18% ACT 24-29 **% Accepted:** 81 **Admission Plans:** Open Admission; Early Admission; Early Action; Deferred Admission **Application Deadline:** August 01 **Application Fee:** $30.00 **H.S. Requirements:** High school diploma required; GED accepted **Costs Per Year:** Application fee: $30. State resident tuition: $4968 full-time, $207 per credit hour part-time. Nonresident tuition: $9696 full-time, $404 per credit hour part-time. Full-time tuition varies according to location. Part-time tuition varies according to location. College room and board: $4660. College room only: $2580. Room and board charges vary according to board plan, housing facility, and location. **Scholarships:** Available **Calendar System:** Semester, Summer Session Available **Enrollment:** FT 8,989, PT 3,068, Grad 1,272 **Faculty:** FT 487, PT 301 **Student-Faculty Ratio:** 18:1 **Exams:** ACT, SAT I or ACT **% Receiving Financial Aid:** 60 **% Residing in College-Owned, -Operated, or -Affiliated Housing:** 9 **Library Holdings:** 325,721 **Regional Accredita-**

tion: Southern Association of Colleges and Schools **Credit Hours For Degree:** 64 semester hours, Associates; 128 semester hours, Bachelors **ROTC:** Army, Air Force **Professional Accreditation:** AACSB, ABET, ABA, ACCE, AALS, CARC, CSWE, JRCERT, NASM, NCATE, NLN **Intercollegiate Athletics:** Baseball M; Basketball M & W; Cheerleading M & W; Cross-Country Running M & W; Golf M & W; Soccer M & W; Softball W; Tennis M & W; Volleyball W

OWENSBORO COMMUNITY AND TECHNICAL COLLEGE
4800 New Hartford Rd.
Owensboro, KY 42303-1899
Tel: (270)686-4400; (866)755-6282
Admissions: (270)686-4527
Fax: (270)686-4496
Web Site: http://www.octc.kctcs.edu/
President/CEO: Dr. Jacqueline Addington
Registrar: Sandy Carden
Admissions: Barbara Tipmore
Financial Aid: Bernice Ayer
Type: Two-Year College **Sex:** Coed **Affiliation:** Kentucky Community and Technical College System **Scores:** 55% ACT 18-23; 16% ACT 24-29 **Admission Plans:** Open Admission **Application Fee:** $0.00 **H.S. Requirements:** High school diploma required; GED accepted **Scholarships:** Available **Calendar System:** Semester, Summer Session Available **Enrollment:** FT 1,848, PT 1,816 **Faculty:** FT 95, PT 108 **Student-Faculty Ratio:** 21:1 **Exams:** ACT, Other **Library Holdings:** 18,200 **Regional Accreditation:** Southern Association of Colleges and Schools **Credit Hours For Degree:** 60 semester hours, Associates **Professional Accreditation:** COE, JRCERT

PADUCAH TECHNICAL COLLEGE
509 South 30th St., PO Box 8252
Paducah, KY 42001
Tel: (270)444-9676
Admissions: (502)444-9676
Fax: (270)441-7202
Web Site: http://www.ptc-ky.com/
President/CEO: Jesse Adkison
Admissions: Arnold Harris
Financial Aid: Carolyn Watson
Type: Two-Year College **Sex:** Coed **Admission Plans:** Open Admission; Deferred Admission **H.S. Requirements:** High school diploma required; GED accepted **Scholarships:** Available **Calendar System:** Trimester, Summer Session Available **Faculty:** FT 8, PT 4 **Student-Faculty Ratio:** 20:1 **Credit Hours For Degree:** 72 semester hours, Associates **Professional Accreditation:** ACCSCT

PIKEVILLE COLLEGE
147 Sycamore St.
Pikeville, KY 41501
Tel: (606)218-5250; (866)232-7700
Admissions: (606)218-5251
Fax: (606)218-5269
Web Site: http://www.pc.edu/
President/CEO: Harold H. Smith
Registrar: Natalie Stewart
Admissions: Melinda Lynch
Financial Aid: Judy Vance Bradley
Type: Comprehensive **Sex:** Coed **Affiliation:** Presbyterian Church (U.S.A.) **Scores:** 54% ACT 18-23; 15% ACT 24-29 **% Accepted:** 100 **Admission Plans:** Open Admission; Deferred Admission **Application Deadline:** August 16 **Application Fee:** $0.00 **H.S. Requirements:** High school diploma required; GED accepted. For some part-time and nontraditional students: High school diploma or equivalent not required **Costs Per Year:** Application fee: $0. Comprehensive fee: $16,500 includes full-time tuition ($11,500) and college room and board ($5000). Full-time tuition varies according to course load. Part-time tuition: $479 per credit hour. **Scholarships:** Available **Calendar System:** Semester, Summer Session Available **Enrollment:** FT 778, PT 66 **Faculty:** FT 54, PT 7 **Student-Faculty Ratio:** 14:1 **Exams:** SAT I or ACT **% Receiving Financial Aid:** 96 **% Residing in College-Owned, -Operated, or -Affiliated Housing:** 41 **Library Holdings:** 72,673 **Regional Accreditation:** Southern Association of Colleges and Schools **Credit Hours For Degree:** 64 semester hours, Associates; 128 semester hours, Bachelors **Professional Accreditation:** AOsA, NAACLS **Intercollegiate Athletics:** Baseball M; Basketball M & W; Bowling M & W; Cheerleading M & W; Cross-Country Running M & W; Football M; Golf M & W; Soccer M & W; Softball W; Tennis M & W; Volleyball W

ROWAN TECHNICAL COLLEGE
609 Viking Dr.
Morehead, KY 40351
Tel: (606)783-1538
Admissions: (606)759-7141
Fax: (606)784-9876
Web Site: http://www.rowtc.kctcs.edu/
Admissions: Patee Massie
Financial Aid: Jo McCarty
Type: Two-Year College **Sex:** Coed **Calendar System:** Semester **Enrollment:** FT 294, PT 548 **Faculty:** FT 22, PT 6 **Professional Accreditation:** CARC, COE

ST. CATHARINE COLLEGE
2735 Bardstown Rd.
St. Catharine, KY 40061-9499
Tel: (859)336-5082
Fax: (859)336-5031
Web Site: http://www.sccky.edu/
President/CEO: William D. Huston
Registrar: Anita Foster
Admissions: Amy C. Carrico
Financial Aid: Jane Moore
Type: Two-Year College **Sex:** Coed **Affiliation:** Roman Catholic **Admission Plans:** Early Admission **Application Fee:** $15.00 **H.S. Requirements:** High school diploma required; GED accepted **Scholarships:** Available **Calendar System:** Semester, Summer Session Available **Faculty:** FT 35, PT 14 **Student-Faculty Ratio:** 15:1 **Exams:** ACT **% Residing in College-Owned, -Operated, or -Affiliated Housing:** 19 **Library Holdings:** 25,000 **Regional Accreditation:** Southern Association of Colleges and Schools **Credit Hours For Degree:** 66 semester hours, Associates **Intercollegiate Athletics:** Baseball M & W; Basketball M & W; Softball W

SOMERSET COMMUNITY COLLEGE
808 Monticello St.
Somerset, KY 42501-2973
Tel: (606)679-8501
Web Site: http://www.somerset.kctcs.edu/
President/CEO: Dr. Jo Marshall
Registrar: Paula Guffey
Admissions: Tracy Casada
Financial Aid: Shawn Anderson
Type: Two-Year College **Sex:** Coed **Affiliation:** Kentucky Community and Technical College System **Scores:** 51.82% ACT 18-23; 8.18% ACT 24-29 **Admission Plans:** Open Admission; Early Admission **Application Fee:** $0.00 **H.S. Requirements:** High school diploma required; GED accepted **Scholarships:** Available **Calendar System:** Semester, Summer Session Available **Faculty:** FT 148, PT 161 **Student-Faculty Ratio:** 19:1 **Exams:** ACT, Other **Library Holdings:** 58,918 **Regional Accreditation:** Southern Association of Colleges and Schools **Credit Hours For Degree:** 60 credit hours, Associates **Professional Accreditation:** APTA, COE, NAACLS, NLN

SOUTHEAST KENTUCKY COMMUNITY AND TECHNICAL COLLEGE
700 College Rd.
Cumberland, KY 40823-1099
Tel: (606)589-2145; 888-274-SECC
Fax: (606)589-5423
Web Site: http://www.soucc.kctcs.net/
President/CEO: Dr. W. Bruce Ayers
Registrar: Karin Gibson
Admissions: Cookie Baker
Financial Aid: Rebecca P. Robbins
Type: Two-Year College **Sex:** Coed **Affiliation:** Kentucky Community and Technical College System **Admission Plans:** Open Admission **Application Fee:** $0.00 **H.S. Requirements:** High school diploma required; GED accepted **Costs Per Year:** Application fee: $0. State resident tuition: $2352 full-time, $98 per credit hour part-time. Nonresident tuition: $7056 full-time, $294 per credit hour part-time. Mandatory fees: $164 full-time. **Scholarships:** Available **Calendar System:** Semester, Summer Session Available **Enrollment:** FT 1,939, PT 2,580 **Faculty:** FT 114, PT 64 **Student-Faculty Ratio:** 20:1 **Library Holdings:** 25,921 **Regional Accreditation:** Southern

Association of Colleges and Schools **Credit Hours For Degree:** 60 credit hours, Associates **Professional Accreditation:** APTA, CARC, NAACLS, NLN

SOUTHERN BAPTIST THEOLOGICAL SEMINARY
2825 Lexington Rd.
Louisville, KY 40280-0004
Tel: (502)897-4011
Web Site: http://www.sbts.edu/
President/CEO: Dr. R. Albert Mohler, Jr.
Registrar: Kim Atchley
Admissions: Scott Davis
Financial Aid: Dr. Daniel Hatfield
Type: Comprehensive **Sex:** Coed **Affiliation:** Southern Baptist **Scholarships:** Available **% Receiving Financial Aid:** 17 **Regional Accreditation:** Southern Association of Colleges and Schools **Professional Accreditation:** ACIPE, ATS, NASM

SOUTHWESTERN COLLEGE OF BUSINESS
8095 Connector Dr.
Florence, KY 41042
Tel: (859)282-9999
Admissions: (859)341-6633
E-mail: bbudesheim@swcollege.net
Web Site: http://www.swcollege.net/
President/CEO: Gary Wright
Admissions: Bruce Budesheim
Financial Aid: Kay Boone
Type: Two-Year College **Sex:** Coed **Admission Plans:** Open Admission; Early Admission **Scholarships:** Available **Calendar System:** Quarter **Faculty:** FT 1, PT 7 **Student-Faculty Ratio:** 30:1 **Professional Accreditation:** ACICS

SPALDING UNIVERSITY
851 South Fourth St.
Louisville, KY 40203-2188
Tel: (502)585-9911
Free: 800-896-8941
Fax: (502)585-7158
E-mail: admissions@spalding.edu
Web Site: http://www.spalding.edu/
President/CEO: Jo Ann Rooney
Registrar: Jennifer Gohmann
Admissions: Vicki Prince
Financial Aid: Gina Kuzuoka
Type: Comprehensive **Sex:** Coed **Affiliation:** Roman Catholic Church **Scores:** 85.3% SAT V 400+; 83% SAT M 400+; 2.3% ACT 18-23; 1.1% ACT 24-29 **% Accepted:** 67 **Admission Plans:** Deferred Admission **Application Deadline:** Rolling **Application Fee:** $20.00 **H.S. Requirements:** High school diploma required; GED accepted **Costs Per Year:** Application fee: $20. Comprehensive fee: $19,572 includes full-time tuition ($15,300), mandatory fees ($600), and college room and board ($3672). College room only: $2100. Part-time tuition: $510 per hour. Part-time mandatory fees: $20 per hour. **Scholarships:** Available **Calendar System:** Semester, Summer Session Available **Enrollment:** FT 645, PT 255, Grad 741 **Faculty:** FT 76, PT 98 **Student-Faculty Ratio:** 12:1 **Exams:** SAT I or ACT **% Residing in College-Owned, -Operated, or -Affiliated Housing:** 13 **Library Holdings:** 160,954 **Regional Accreditation:** Southern Association of Colleges and Schools **Credit Hours For Degree:** 64 semester hours, Associates; 125 semester hours, Bachelors **ROTC:** Army, Air Force **Professional Accreditation:** AACN, AOTA, APA, CSWE, NCATE, NLN **Intercollegiate Athletics:** Baseball M; Basketball M & W; Soccer M & W; Softball W; Volleyball W

SPENCERIAN COLLEGE
4627 Dixie Hwy.
Louisville, KY 40216
Tel: (502)447-1000
Free: 800-264-1799
Fax: (502)447-4574
Web Site: http://www.spencerian.edu/
President/CEO: Dr. A. R. Sullivan
Registrar: Cheryl Eaton
Admissions: Terri D. Thomas
Financial Aid: Jill Schuler
Type: Two-Year College **Sex:** Coed **Affiliation:** The Sullivan University System **Admission Plans:** Open Admission; Preferred Admission **Application Fee:** $90.00 **H.S. Requirements:** High school diploma required; GED accepted **Costs Per Year:** Application fee: $90. Tuition: $12,120 full-time, $202 per credit hour part-time. Mandatory fees: $575 full-time, $30. College room only: $3960. **Scholarships:** Available **Calendar System:** Quarter **Enrollment:** FT 1,326 **Faculty:** FT 48, PT 39 **Student-Faculty Ratio:** 14:1 **Exams:** SAT I or ACT **% Residing in College-Owned, -Operated, or -Affiliated Housing:** 0 **Credit Hours For Degree:** 103 quarter credits, Associates **Professional Accreditation:** ACICS

SPENCERIAN COLLEGE-LEXINGTON
2355 Harrodsburg Rd.
Lexington, KY 40504
Tel: (859)223-9608
Admissions: 800-456-3253
Fax: (859)224-7744
Web Site: http://www.spencerian.edu/
President/CEO: Ernest G. Clark
Registrar: Chris Douglas
Admissions: Victor Adcock, II
Financial Aid: Brian Highley
Type: Two-Year College **Sex:** Coed **Affiliation:** Sullivan Colleges System **Application Fee:** $90.00 **H.S. Requirements:** High school diploma required; GED accepted **Scholarships:** Available **Calendar System:** Quarter, Summer Session Available **Enrollment:** FT 306, PT 70 **Faculty:** FT 17, PT 23 **Student-Faculty Ratio:** 9:1 **Exams:** Other **% Residing in College-Owned, -Operated, or -Affiliated Housing:** 13 **Library Holdings:** 450 **Credit Hours For Degree:** 96 credit hours, Associates **Professional Accreditation:** ACICS

SULLIVAN UNIVERSITY
3101 Bardstown Rd.
Louisville, KY 40205
Tel: (502)456-6504
Free: 800-844-1354
Admissions: (502)456-6505
Fax: (502)456-0040
E-mail: gcawthon@sullivan.edu
Web Site: http://www.sullivan.edu/
President/CEO: Dr. A.R. Sullivan
Registrar: Kim Mitchell
Admissions: Greg Cawthon
Financial Aid: Charlene Geiser
Type: Comprehensive **Sex:** Coed **Affiliation:** Sullivan Colleges System **Application Deadline:** Rolling **Application Fee:** $90.00 **H.S. Requirements:** High school diploma required; GED accepted **Costs Per Year:** Application fee: $90. Tuition: $12,900 full-time, $215 per credit part-time. Mandatory fees: $435 full-time, $30 per course part-time. Full-time tuition and fees vary according to program. Part-time tuition and fees vary according to program. College room only: $3960. Tuition guaranteed not to increase for student's term of enrollment. **Scholarships:** Available **Calendar System:** Quarter, Summer Session Available **Faculty:** FT 93, PT 120 **Student-Faculty Ratio:** 20:1 **Exams:** Other **% Receiving Financial Aid:** 71 **% Residing in College-Owned, -Operated, or -Affiliated Housing:** 9 **Library Holdings:** 22,500 **Regional Accreditation:** Southern Association of Colleges and Schools **Credit Hours For Degree:** 95 quarter hours, Associates; 180 quarter hours, Bachelors **ROTC:** Army **Professional Accreditation:** AAMAE, ACF

THOMAS MORE COLLEGE
333 Thomas More Parkway
Crestview Hills, KY 41017-3495
Tel: (859)341-5800
Free: 800-825-4557
Admissions: (859)344-3332
Fax: (859)344-3638
E-mail: admissions@thomasmore.edu
Web Site: http://www.thomasmore.edu/
President/CEO: Sr. Margaret Stallmeyer, CDP
Registrar: Patsy Kenner
Admissions: Angela Griffin-Jones
Financial Aid: Linda Hayes
Type: Comprehensive **Sex:** Coed **Affiliation:** Roman Catholic **Scores:** 97% SAT V 400+; 94% SAT M 400+; 59% ACT 18-23; 23% ACT 24-29 **% Accepted:** 63 **Admission Plans:** Deferred Admission **Application Deadline:**

August 15 **Application Fee:** $25.00 **H.S. Requirements:** High school diploma required; GED accepted **Costs Per Year:** Application fee: $25. Comprehensive fee: $24,470 includes full-time tuition ($17,600), mandatory fees ($720), and college room and board ($6150). College room only: $2900. Full-time tuition and fees vary according to program. Room and board charges vary according to board plan and housing facility. Part-time tuition: $450 per credit hour. Part-time mandatory fees: $30 per credit hour, $15 per term. Part-time tuition and fees vary according to course load and program. **Scholarships:** Available **Calendar System:** Semester, Summer Session Available **Enrollment:** FT 1,128, PT 215, Grad 91 **Faculty:** FT 71, PT 63 **Student-Faculty Ratio:** 14:1 **Exams:** SAT I or ACT **% Receiving Financial Aid:** 73 **% Residing in College-Owned, -Operated, or -Affiliated Housing:** 20 **Library Holdings:** 127,429 **Regional Accreditation:** Southern Association of Colleges and Schools **Credit Hours For Degree:** 64 credit hours, Associates; 128 credit hours, Bachelors **ROTC:** Army, Air Force **Professional Accreditation:** NLN **Intercollegiate Athletics:** Baseball M; Basketball M & W; Football M; Golf M & W; Soccer M & W; Softball W; Tennis M & W; Volleyball W

TRANSYLVANIA UNIVERSITY
300 North Broadway
Lexington, KY 40508-1797
Tel: (859)233-8300
Free: 800-872-6798
Admissions: (859)233-8242
Fax: (859)233-8797
E-mail: dison@transi/.edu
Web Site: http://www.transy.edu/
President/CEO: Dr. Charles L. Shearer
Registrar: James M. Mills
Admissions: Deana Ison
Financial Aid: David Cecil
Type: Four-Year College **Sex:** Coed **Affiliation:** Christian Church (Disciples of Christ) **Scores:** 100% SAT V 400+; 100% SAT M 400+; 24% ACT 18-23; 57% ACT 24-29 **% Accepted:** 84 **Admission Plans:** Early Admission; Early Action; Deferred Admission **Application Deadline:** February 01 **Application Fee:** $30.00 **H.S. Requirements:** High school diploma required; GED accepted **Costs Per Year:** Application fee: $30. Comprehensive fee: $26,240 includes full-time tuition ($19,650) and college room and board ($6590). Room and board charges vary according to board plan and location. Part-time tuition: $2100 per course. Part-time mandatory fees: $84 per course. **Scholarships:** Available **Calendar System:** Miscellaneous, Summer Session Available **Enrollment:** FT 1,135, PT 16 **Faculty:** FT 81, PT 15 **Student-Faculty Ratio:** 13:1 **Exams:** SAT I or ACT **% Receiving Financial Aid:** 60 **% Residing in College-Owned, -Operated, or -Affiliated Housing:** 80 **Library Holdings:** 124,000 **Regional Accreditation:** Southern Association of Colleges and Schools **Credit Hours For Degree:** 36 units, Bachelors **ROTC:** Army, Air Force **Professional Accreditation:** NCATE **Intercollegiate Athletics:** Baseball M; Basketball M & W; Cheerleading M & W; Cross-Country Running M & W; Field Hockey W; Golf M & W; Soccer M & W; Softball W; Swimming and Diving M & W; Tennis M & W; Volleyball W

UNION COLLEGE
310 College St.
Barbourville, KY 40906-1499
Tel: (606)546-4151
Free: 800-489-8646
Admissions: (606)546-1222
Fax: (606)546-1667
E-mail: enroll@unionky.edu
Web Site: http://www.unionky.edu/
President/CEO: Edward de Rosset
Registrar: Kathy Webb
Admissions: Jerry Jackson
Financial Aid: Andre Washington
Type: Comprehensive **Sex:** Coed **Affiliation:** United Methodist **% Accepted:** 64 **Admission Plans:** Early Admission; Deferred Admission **Application Deadline:** August 01 **Application Fee:** $20.00 **H.S. Requirements:** High school diploma required; GED accepted **Costs Per Year:** Application fee: $20. One-time mandatory fee: $800. Comprehensive fee: $19,890 includes full-time tuition ($14,950), mandatory fees ($340), and college room and board ($4600). College room only: $1700. Part-time tuition: $260 per hour. Part-time mandatory fees: $15 per semester hour. **Scholarships:** Available **Calendar System:** Semester, Summer Session Available **Enrollment:** FT 555, PT 56, Grad 613 **Faculty:** FT 46, PT 25 **Student-Faculty Ratio:** 14:1 **Exams:** SAT I and SAT II or ACT **% Receiving Financial Aid:** 97 **% Residing in College-Owned, -Operated, or -Affiliated Housing:** 45 **Library Holdings:** 142,667 **Regional Accreditation:** Southern Association of Colleges and Schools **Credit Hours For Degree:** 64 credit hours, Associates; 128 credit hours, Bachelors **ROTC:** Army **Professional Accreditation:** NCATE **Intercollegiate Athletics:** Baseball M; Basketball M & W; Cheerleading M & W; Cross-Country Running M & W; Football M; Golf M & W; Soccer M & W; Softball W; Swimming and Diving M & W; Tennis M & W; Track and Field M & W; Volleyball W

UNIVERSITY OF THE CUMBERLANDS
6178 College Station Dr.
Williamsburg, KY 40769-1372
Tel: (606)549-2200
Free: 800-343-1609
Admissions: (606)539-4201
Fax: (606)539-4303
E-mail: swake@ucumberlands.edu
Web Site: http://www.cumberlandcollege.edu/
President/CEO: Dr. James Taylor
Registrar: Emily Meadors
Admissions: Sue Wake
Financial Aid: Steve Allen
Type: Comprehensive **Sex:** Coed **Affiliation:** Kentucky Baptist **Scores:** 96% SAT V 400+; 97% SAT M 400+; 70% ACT 18-23; 25% ACT 24-29 **% Accepted:** 83 **Application Deadline:** Rolling **Application Fee:** $30.00 **H.S. Requirements:** High school diploma required; GED accepted **Costs Per Year:** Application fee: $30. Comprehensive fee: $19,984 includes full-time tuition ($13,298), mandatory fees ($360), and college room and board ($6326). Part-time tuition: $410 per hour. Part-time mandatory fees: $48.75 per term. **Scholarships:** Available **Calendar System:** Semester, Summer Session Available **Enrollment:** FT 1,411, PT 222, Grad 210 **Faculty:** FT 86, PT 26 **Student-Faculty Ratio:** 15:1 **Exams:** SAT I or ACT **% Receiving Financial Aid:** 83 **% Residing in College-Owned, -Operated, or -Affiliated Housing:** 53 **Regional Accreditation:** Southern Association of Colleges and Schools **Credit Hours For Degree:** 128 credit hours, Bachelors **ROTC:** Army **Intercollegiate Athletics:** Baseball M; Basketball M & W; Cheerleading M & W; Cross-Country Running M & W; Football M; Golf M & W; Soccer M & W; Softball W; Swimming and Diving M & W; Tennis M & W; Track and Field M & W; Volleyball W; Wrestling M & W

UNIVERSITY OF KENTUCKY
Lexington, KY 40506-0032
Tel: (859)257-9000
Admissions: (859)257-2000
Fax: (859)257-4000
Web Site: http://www.uky.edu/
President/CEO: Dr. Lee T. Todd, Jr.
Admissions: Don Witt
Financial Aid: Lynda S. George
Type: University **Sex:** Coed **Scores:** 98.4% SAT V 400+; 99.23% SAT M 400+; 43.09% ACT 18-23; 46.83% ACT 24-29 **% Accepted:** 82 **Admission Plans:** Preferred Admission; Early Admission **Application Deadline:** February 15 **Application Fee:** $40.00 **H.S. Requirements:** High school diploma required; GED accepted **Costs Per Year:** Application fee: $40. State resident tuition: $5162 full-time, $216 per credit hour part-time. Nonresident tuition: $12,148 full-time, $507 per credit hour part-time. Mandatory fees: $650 full-time, $16.25 per credit hour part-time. Full-time tuition and fees vary according to degree level, program, reciprocity agreements, and student level. Part-time tuition and fees vary according to degree level, program, reciprocity agreements, and student level. College room and board: $5129. College room only: $3363. Room and board charges vary according to board plan and housing facility. **Scholarships:** Available **Calendar System:** Semester, Summer Session Available **Enrollment:** FT 17,050, PT 1,652, Grad 5,485 **Faculty:** FT 1,211, PT 513 **Student-Faculty Ratio:** 17:1 **Exams:** SAT I or ACT **% Receiving Financial Aid:** 38 **% Residing in College-Owned, -Operated, or -Affiliated Housing:** 31 **Library Holdings:** 3,092,616 **Regional Accreditation:** Southern Association of Colleges and Schools **Credit Hours For Degree:** 120 semester hours, Bachelors **ROTC:** Army, Air Force **Professional Accreditation:** AACSB, ABET, ACEHSA, ACEJMC, AAMFT, AACN, AAFCS, ABA, ACPhE, ADA, ADtA, ALA, AOTA, APTA, APA, ASLA, ASLHA, ACIPE, AALS, CORE CSWE, FIDER, LCMEAMA, NAACLS, NASM, NASPAA, NCATE, NLN, SAF **Intercollegiate Athletics:** Baseball M; Basketball M & W; Cross-Country Running M & W; Football M; Golf M & W; Gymnastics W; Riflery M & W;

Soccer M & W; Softball W; Swimming and Diving M & W; Tennis M & W; Track and Field M & W; Volleyball W

UNIVERSITY OF LOUISVILLE
2301 South Third St.
Louisville, KY 40292-0001
Tel: (502)852-5555
Free: 800-334-8635
Admissions: (502)852-6531
Fax: (502)852-4776
E-mail: admitme@ulkyvm.louisville.edu
Web Site: http://www.louisville.edu/
President/CEO: James R. Ramsey
Registrar: Kathy L. Otto
Admissions: Jenny Sawyer
Financial Aid: Patricia O. Arauz
Type: University **Sex:** Coed **Scores:** 97% SAT V 400+; 98% SAT M 400+; 49% ACT 18-23; 41% ACT 24-29 **% Accepted:** 79 **Admission Plans:** Early Admission; Deferred Admission **Application Deadline:** Rolling **Application Fee:** $30.00 **H.S. Requirements:** High school diploma required; GED accepted **Costs Per Year:** Application fee: $30. State resident tuition: $5532 full-time, $231 per hour part-time. Nonresident tuition: $15,092 full-time, $629 per hour part-time. Full-time tuition varies according to reciprocity agreements. Part-time tuition varies according to course load and reciprocity agreements. College room and board: $6036. College room only: $4490. Room and board charges vary according to board plan and housing facility. **Scholarships:** Available **Calendar System:** Semester, Summer Session Available **Enrollment:** FT 11,441, PT 3,492, Grad 4,472 **Faculty:** FT 802, PT 511 **Student-Faculty Ratio:** 17:1 **Exams:** SAT I or ACT **% Receiving Financial Aid:** 51 **% Residing in College-Owned, -Operated, or -Affiliated Housing:** 14 **Library Holdings:** 1,983,162 **Regional Accreditation:** Southern Association of Colleges and Schools **Credit Hours For Degree:** 62 credit hours, Associates; 122 credit hours, Bachelors **ROTC:** Army, Air Force **Professional Accreditation:** AACSB, ABET, AAMFT, AACN, ABA, ADA, APTA, APA, ASLHA, ACIPE, AALS, CSWE, FIDER, JRCERT, LCMEAMA, NASM, NASPAA, NAST, NCATE **Intercollegiate Athletics:** Baseball M; Basketball M & W; Cheerleading M & W; Crew W; Cross-Country Running M & W; Field Hockey W; Football M; Golf M & W; Soccer M & W; Softball W; Swimming and Diving M & W; Tennis M & W; Track and Field M & W; Volleyball W

WEST KENTUCKY COMMUNITY AND TECHNICAL COLLEGE
4810 Alben Barkley Dr.
PO Box 7380
Paducah, KY 42002-7380
Tel: (270)554-9200
Fax: (270)554-6217
Web Site: http://www.westkentucky.kctcs.edu/
President/CEO: Dr. Barbara Veazey
Registrar: Sherry Cope
Admissions: Anton Reece
Financial Aid: Betsy Irby
Type: Two-Year College **Sex:** Coed **Affiliation:** University of Kentucky Community College System **Admission Plans:** Open Admission; Early Admission **H.S. Requirements:** High school diploma required; GED accepted **Costs Per Year:** Area resident tuition: $98 per credit hour part-time. State resident tuition: $118 per credit hour part-time. Nonresident tuition: $294 per credit hour part-time. **Scholarships:** Available **Calendar System:** Semester, Summer Session Available **Enrollment:** FT 1,455, PT 2,090 **Faculty:** FT 76, PT 77 **Student-Faculty Ratio:** 15:1 **Exams:** ACT **Library Holdings:** 31,339 **Regional Accreditation:** Southern Association of Colleges and Schools **Credit Hours For Degree:** 60 credit hours, Associates **Professional Accreditation:** ADA, APTA, COE, NLN

WESTERN KENTUCKY UNIVERSITY
1 Big Red Way
Bowling Green, KY 42101-3576
Tel: (270)745-0111
Admissions: (270)745-2551
Fax: (270)745-6133
E-mail: admission@wku.edu
Web Site: http://www.wku.edu/
President/CEO: Dr. Gary A. Ransdell
Registrar: Freida K. Eggleton
Admissions: Dr. Dean R. Kahler
Financial Aid: Cindy Burnette
Type: Comprehensive **Sex:** Coed **Scores:** 92.8% SAT V 400+; 90.09% SAT M 400+; 52.91% ACT 18-23; 22.22% ACT 24-29 **% Accepted:** 92 **Admission Plans:** Open Admission **Application Deadline:** August 01 **Application Fee:** $35.00 **H.S. Requirements:** High school diploma required; GED accepted **Costs Per Year:** Application fee: $35. State resident tuition: $5316 full-time, $228 per hour part-time. Nonresident tuition: $12,732 full-time, $537 per hour part-time. Full-time tuition varies according to course load, location, program, and reciprocity agreements. Part-time tuition varies according to course load, location, program, and reciprocity agreements. College room and board: $4876. College room only: $2800. Room and board charges vary according to board plan and housing facility. **Scholarships:** Available **Calendar System:** Semester, Summer Session Available **Enrollment:** FT 13,053, PT 2,914, Grad 2,667 **Faculty:** FT 694, PT 413 **Student-Faculty Ratio:** 19:1 **Exams:** SAT I or ACT **% Receiving Financial Aid:** 54 **% Residing in College-Owned, -Operated, or -Affiliated Housing:** 30 **Regional Accreditation:** Southern Association of Colleges and Schools **Credit Hours For Degree:** 64 semester hours, Associates; 128 semester hours, Bachelors **ROTC:** Army, Air Force **Professional Accreditation:** AACSB, ABET, ACEJMC, AACN, AAFCS, ADA, AHIMA, AOTA, ASLHA, CEPH, CSWE, NAIT, NASAD, NASM, NCATE, NLN, NRPA **Intercollegiate Athletics:** Baseball M; Basketball M & W; Cheerleading M & W; Cross-Country Running M & W; Football M; Golf M & W; Riflery M & W; Soccer M; Softball W; Swimming and Diving M & W; Tennis M & W; Track and Field M & W; Volleyball W

BATON ROUGE COMMUNITY COLLEGE
5310 Florida Blvd.
Baton Rouge, LA 70806
Tel: (225)216-8000
Free: 800-601-4558
Admissions: (225)216-8700
Fax: (225)216-8100
Web Site: http://www.brcc.cc.la.us/
President/CEO: Dr. Myrtle E.B. Dorsey
Admissions: Michelle L. Hill
Type: Two-Year College **Sex:** Coed **Costs Per Year:** State resident tuition: $1656 full-time. Nonresident tuition; $4464 full-time. Mandatory fees: $432 full-time. Full-time tuition and fees vary according to course load. **Calendar System:** Semester **Regional Accreditation:** Southern Association of Colleges and Schools

BATON ROUGE SCHOOL OF COMPUTERS
10425 Plaza Americana
Baton Rouge, LA 70816
Tel: (504)923-2525
Fax: (504)923-2979
Web Site: http://www.brsc.net/
President/CEO: Betty Truxillo
Type: Two-Year College **Sex:** Coed **Professional Accreditation:** ACCSCT

BLUE CLIFF COLLEGE-LAFAYETTE
100 Asma Blvd., Ste. 350
Lafayette, LA 70508-3862
Tel: (504)456-3141
Web Site: http://www.bluecliffcollege.com **Type:** Two-Year College **Sex:** Coed

BLUE CLIFF COLLEGE-SHREVEPORT
200 N. Thomas Dr., Ste. A
Shreveport, LA 71107-6520
Tel: (504)456-3141
Web Site: http://www.bluecliffcollege.com **Type:** Two-Year College **Sex:** Coed

BOSSIER PARISH COMMUNITY COLLEGE
2719 Airline Dr. North
Bossier City, LA 71111-5801
Tel: (318)746-9851
Admissions: (318)678-6166
Fax: (318)742-8664
Web Site: http://www.bpcc.edu/
President/CEO: Thomas N. Carleton
Registrar: Patty Stewart
Admissions: Ann Jempole
Financial Aid: Vicki Temple
Type: Two-Year College **Sex:** Coed **Affiliation:** University of Louisiana System **Admission Plans:** Open Admission; Early Admission **Application Fee:** $15.00 **H.S. Requirements:** High school diploma required; GED accepted **Costs Per Year:** Application fee: $15. State resident tuition: $1720 full-time, $254 per credit part-time. Nonresident tuition: $3860 full-time, $414 per credit part-time. Mandatory fees: $448 full-time, $19 per credit part-time, $55 per term part-time. **Scholarships:** Available **Calendar System:** Semester, Summer Session Available **Faculty:** FT 120, PT 100 **Exams:** ACT **Library Holdings:** 29,600 **Regional Accreditation:** Southern Association of Colleges and Schools **Credit Hours For Degree:** 66 semester hours, Associates **Professional Accreditation:** AAMAE, ACF, APTA, CARC **Intercollegiate Athletics:** Baseball M; Basketball M; Soccer M; Softball W

BRYMAN COLLEGE
1201 Elmwood Park Blvd., Ste. 600
New Orleans, LA 70123
Tel: (504)733-7117
Fax: (504)734-1217
Web Site: http://bryman-college.com/ **Type:** Two-Year College **Sex:** Coed

CAMELOT COLLEGE
2618 Wooddale Blvd., Ste. A
Baton Rouge, LA 70805
Tel: (225)928-3005
Free: 800-470-3320
Fax: (225)927-3794
E-mail: home@camelotcollege.com
Web Site: http://www.camelotcollege.com/
President/CEO: Rev. Ronny L. Williams
Registrar: Constance Williams
Admissions: Rev. Ronny L. Williams
Financial Aid: Constance Williams
Type: Two-Year College **Sex:** Coed **Scholarships:** Available **Professional Accreditation:** ACICS

CAMERON COLLEGE
2740 Canal St.
New Orleans, LA 70119
Tel: (504)821-5881
Web Site: http://www.cameroncollege.com/
President/CEO: Eleanor Camerson Skov
Type: Two-Year College **Professional Accreditation:** COE

CAREER TECHNICAL COLLEGE
2319 Louisville Ave.
Monroe, LA 71201
Tel: (318)323-2889
Free: 800-234-6766
Fax: (318)324-9883
Web Site: http://www.careertc.com/ **Type:** Two-Year College **Sex:** Coed **Calendar System:** Quarter **Professional Accreditation:** ARCEST, COE

CENTENARY COLLEGE OF LOUISIANA
2911 Centenary Blvd, PO Box 41188
Shreveport, LA 71104
Tel: (318)869-5011
Free: 800-234-4448
Admissions: (318)869-5104
Fax: (318)869-5005
E-mail: dcolson@centenary.edu

Web Site: http://www.centenary.edu/
President/CEO: Dr. Kenneth L. Schwab
Registrar: Gary Young, PhD
Admissions: Dr. Darrel D. Colson
Financial Aid: Mary Sue Rix
Type: Comprehensive **Sex:** Coed **Affiliation:** United Methodist **Scores:** 100% SAT V 400+; 99.1% SAT M 400+; 33.5% ACT 18-23; 49% ACT 24-29 **% Accepted:** 64 **Admission Plans:** Early Admission; Early Action; Early Decision Plan; Deferred Admission **Application Deadline:** August 01 **Application Fee:** $30.00 **H.S. Requirements:** High school diploma required; GED accepted **Costs Per Year:** Application fee: $30. Comprehensive fee: $25,680 includes full-time tuition ($18,900) and college room and board ($6780). College room only: $3310. Part-time tuition: $630 per semester hour. Part-time mandatory fees: $50 per term. **Scholarships:** Available **Calendar System:** Miscellaneous, Summer Session Available **Enrollment:** FT 882, PT 22, Grad 140 **Faculty:** FT 72, PT 50 **Student-Faculty Ratio:** 10:1 **Exams:** SAT I or ACT **% Receiving Financial Aid:** 60 **% Residing in College-Owned, -Operated, or -Affiliated Housing:** 68 **Library Holdings:** 186,564 **Regional Accreditation:** Southern Association of Colleges and Schools **Credit Hours For Degree:** 124 semester hours, Bachelors **Professional Accreditation:** NASM **Intercollegiate Athletics:** Baseball M; Basketball M & W; Crew M & W; Cross-Country Running M & W; Golf M & W; Gymnastics W; Soccer M & W; Softball W; Swimming and Diving M & W; Tennis M & W; Volleyball W

DELGADO COMMUNITY COLLEGE
501 City Park Ave.
New Orleans, LA 70119-4399
Tel: (504)483-4400
Admissions: (504)483-4004
Fax: (504)483-1986
E-mail: jbolde@dcc.edu
Web Site: http://www.dcc.edu/
President/CEO: Dr. J. Terence Kelly
Admissions: Gwen Boute
Financial Aid: Diane Jackson
Type: Two-Year College **Sex:** Coed **Affiliation:** Louisiana Community and Technical College System **Admission Plans:** Open Admission **Application Deadline:** Rolling **Application Fee:** $15.00 **H.S. Requirements:** High school diploma required; GED accepted **Costs Per Year:** Application fee: $15. State resident tuition: $1482 full-time, $420 per term part-time. Nonresident tuition: $4462 full-time, $1275 per term part-time. Mandatory fees: $362 full-time, $5 per credit part-time, $10 per term part-time. Part-time tuition and fees vary according to course load. **Scholarships:** Available **Calendar System:** Semester, Summer Session Available **Enrollment:** FT 7,376, PT 9,125 **Faculty:** FT 356, PT 477 **Student-Faculty Ratio:** 20:1 **Exams:** ACT **Library Holdings:** 110,000 **Regional Accreditation:** Southern Association of Colleges and Schools **Credit Hours For Degree:** 66 semester hours, Associates **ROTC:** Army, Air Force **Professional Accreditation:** ABET, ABFSE, ACF, AHIMA, AOTA, APTA, ACBSP, CARC, JRCERT, JRCEMT, NAACLS, NAIT, NLN **Intercollegiate Athletics:** Baseball M; Basketball M & W; Track and Field W

DELTA COLLEGE OF ARTS AND TECHNOLOGY
7380 Exchange Place
Baton Rouge, LA 70806-3851
Tel: (504)928-7770
Admissions: (225)928-7770
Fax: (504)927-9096
Web Site: http://www.deltacollege.com/
President/CEO: Billy L. Clark
Admissions: Beulah Laverghe-Brown
Type: Two-Year College **Sex:** Coed **Application Fee:** $100.00 **Calendar System:** Continuous **Faculty:** FT 30, PT 5 **Professional Accreditation:** ACCSCT

DELTA SCHOOL OF BUSINESS & TECHNOLOGY
517 Broad St.
Lake Charles, LA 70601
Tel: (337)439-5765
Fax: (337)436-5151
E-mail: gholt@deltatech.edu
Web Site: http://www.deltatech.edu/
President/CEO: Gary J. Holt
Admissions: Gary J. Holt
Type: Two-Year College **Scholarships:** Available **Calendar System:** Quarter **Professional Accreditation:** ACICS

DILLARD UNIVERSITY
2601 Gentilly Blvd.
New Orleans, LA 70122-3097
Tel: (504)283-8822
Free: 800-216-6637
Admissions: (504)816-4356
Fax: (504)286-4895
Web Site: http://www.dillard.edu/
President/CEO: Dr. Michael L. Lomax
Admissions: Darrin Q. Rankin
Financial Aid: Cynthia Thornon
Type: Four-Year College **Sex:** Coed **Affiliation:** interdenominational **Scores:** 79% SAT V 400+; 75% SAT M 400+; 82% ACT 18-23; 9% ACT 24-29 **Application Fee:** $20.00 **H.S. Requirements:** High school diploma required; GED accepted **Scholarships:** Available **Calendar System:** Semester, Summer Session Available **Enrollment:** FT 1,920, PT 235 **Faculty:** FT 145, PT 56 **Student-Faculty Ratio:** 12:1 **Exams:** SAT I or ACT **% Receiving Financial Aid:** 89 **% Residing in College-Owned, -Operated, or -Affiliated Housing:** 50 **Regional Accreditation:** Southern Association of Colleges and Schools **Credit Hours For Degree:** 126 credit hours, Bachelors **ROTC:** Army, Air Force **Professional Accreditation:** NCATE, NLN **Intercollegiate Athletics:** Basketball M & W; Cross-Country Running M & W; Tennis M & W; Volleyball W

ELAINE P. NUNEZ COMMUNITY COLLEGE
3710 Paris Rd.
Chalmette, LA 70043-1249
Tel: (504)680-2240
Admissions: (504)680-2457
Fax: (504)680-2243
Web Site: http://www.nunez.edu/
President/CEO: Dr. Thomas R. Warner
Registrar: Tanya Crump
Admissions: Donna Clark
Financial Aid: John Whisnant
Type: Two-Year College **Sex:** Coed **Affiliation:** Louisiana Community and Technical Colleges System **Admission Plans:** Open Admission; Deferred Admission **Application Fee:** $10.00 **H.S. Requirements:** High school diploma or equivalent not required. For practical nursing and EMT programs: High school diploma required; GED accepted **Scholarships:** Available **Calendar System:** Semester, Summer Session Available **Enrollment:** FT 1,213, PT 1,150 **Faculty:** FT 58, PT 97 **Student-Faculty Ratio:** 18:1 **Exams:** ACT, Other **Library Holdings:** 37,626 **Regional Accreditation:** Southern Association of Colleges and Schools **Credit Hours For Degree:** 60 semester hours, Associates **Professional Accreditation:** NAIT

GRAMBLING STATE UNIVERSITY
PO Box 607
Grambling, LA 71245
Tel: (318)247-3811
Admissions: (318)274-6183
Fax: (318)274-6172
Web Site: http://www.gram.edu/
President/CEO: Dr. Horace Judson
Registrar: Karen C. Lewis
Admissions: Norma Taylor
Financial Aid: Alvina C. Thomas
Type: University **Sex:** Coed **Affiliation:** University of Louisiana System Board of Supervisors **Scores:** 71.74% SAT V 400+; 70.66% SAT M 400+; 33.98% ACT 18-23; 1.29% ACT 24-29 **Admission Plans:** Open Admission; Early Admission; Early Decision Plan; Deferred Admission **Application Fee:** $20.00 **H.S. Requirements:** High school diploma required; GED accepted **Costs Per Year:** Application fee: $20. State resident tuition: $2232 full-time, $558 per term part-time. Nonresident tuition: $7582 full-time, $558 per term part-time. Mandatory fees: $1274 full-time. Part-time tuition varies according to course load. College room and board: $4034. College room only: $2138. Room and board charges vary according to housing facility. **Scholarships:** Available **Calendar System:** Semester, Summer Session Available **Enrollment:** FT 4,088, PT 352, Grad 599 **Faculty:** FT 244, PT 3 **Student-Faculty Ratio:** 20:1 **Exams:** SAT I or ACT **% Receiving Financial Aid:** 83 **Library Holdings:** 208,935 **Regional Accreditation:** Southern Association of Col-

leges and Schools **Credit Hours For Degree:** 62 semester hours, Associates; 124 semester hours, Bachelors **ROTC:** Army, Air Force **Professional Accreditation:** AACSB, ABET, ACEJMC, CSWE, NASM, NASPAA, NAST, NCATE, NLN, NRPA **Intercollegiate Athletics:** Baseball M; Basketball M & W; Bowling W; Cross-Country Running M & W; Football M; Golf M & W; Tennis M & W; Track and Field M & W; Volleyball W

GRETNA CAREER COLLEGE
1415 Whitney Ave.
Gretna, LA 70053-5835
Tel: (504)366-5409
Fax: (504)365-1004
Web Site: http://www.gretnacareercollege.com/
President/CEO: Nicholas Randazzo
Type: Two-Year College **Sex:** Coed **Professional Accreditation:** ACCSCT

HERZING COLLEGE
2400 Veterans Blvd.
Kenner, LA 70062
Tel: (504)733-0074
Fax: (504)733-0020
Web Site: http://www.herzing.edu/
President/CEO: Darla Chin
Admissions: Genny Bordelon
Type: Two-Year College **Sex:** Coed **Calendar System:** Semester **Enrollment:** FT 153, PT 67 **Faculty:** FT 5, PT 15 **Student-Faculty Ratio:** 17:1 **Professional Accreditation:** ACICS

ITI TECHNICAL COLLEGE
13944 Airline Hwy.
Baton Rouge, LA 70817
Tel: (225)752-4233
Free: 800-467-4484
Admissions: (225)752-4230
Fax: (225)756-0903
E-mail: jmartin@iticollege.edu
Web Site: http://www.iticollege.edu/
President/CEO: Joe Martin
Admissions: Joe Martin
Type: Two-Year College **Sex:** Coed **% Accepted:** 85 **Application Fee:** $0.00 **Costs Per Year:** Application fee: $0. **Calendar System:** Continuous **Enrollment:** FT 226, PT 125 **Faculty:** FT 22, PT 22 **Student-Faculty Ratio:** 10:1 **Professional Accreditation:** ACCSCT

ITT TECHNICAL INSTITUTE
140 James Dr. E
St. Rose, LA 70087
Tel: (504)463-0338
Web Site: http://www.itt-tech.edu/
President/CEO: Brenda Nash
Admissions: Heather E. Alleman
Type: Two-Year College **Sex:** Coed **Affiliation:** ITT Educational Services, Inc **Admission Plans:** Deferred Admission **Application Deadline:** Rolling **Application Fee:** $100.00 **H.S. Requirements:** High school diploma required; GED accepted **Costs Per Year:** Application fee: $100. **Scholarships:** Available **Calendar System:** Quarter, Summer Session Not available **Exams:** Other **Credit Hours For Degree:** 96 credit hours, Associates; 180 credit hours, Bachelors **Professional Accreditation:** ACICS

LOUISIANA COLLEGE
1140 College Dr.
Pineville, LA 71359-0001
Tel: (318)487-7011
Free: 800-487-1906
Admissions: (318)487-7439
Fax: (318)487-7550
E-mail: admissions@lacollege.edu
Web Site: http://www.lacollege.edu/
President/CEO: Dr. Malcolm Yarnell
Registrar: Alan Mobley
Admissions: Byron McGee
Financial Aid: Shelley Jinks
Type: Four-Year College **Sex:** Coed **Affiliation:** Southern Baptist **Scores:** 94.1% SAT V 400+; 94.1% SAT M 400+; 51.1% ACT 18-23; 35.6% ACT 24-29 **Admission Plans:** Early Admission **Application Fee:** $25.00 **H.S. Requirements:** High school diploma required; GED accepted **Scholarships:** Available **Calendar System:** Semester, Summer Session Available **Enrollment:** FT 920, PT 165 **Faculty:** FT 64, PT 28 **Student-Faculty Ratio:** 13:1 **Exams:** SAT I or ACT **% Receiving Financial Aid:** 59 **% Residing in College-Owned, -Operated, or -Affiliated Housing:** 55 **Library Holdings:** 135,566 **Regional Accreditation:** Southern Association of Colleges and Schools **Credit Hours For Degree:** 127 credit hours, Bachelors **ROTC:** Army **Professional Accreditation:** AACN, ACBSP, CSWE, NLN **Intercollegiate Athletics:** Baseball M; Basketball M & W; Cheerleading M & W; Cross-Country Running W; Football M; Golf M; Soccer M & W; Softball W; Tennis W

LOUISIANA STATE UNIVERSITY AND AGRICULTURAL AND MECHANICAL COLLEGE
Baton Rouge, LA 70803
Tel: (225)578-3202
Admissions: (225)578-1175
Fax: (225)578-4433
E-mail: admissions@lsu.edu
Web Site: http://www.lsu.edu/
President/CEO: Sean O'Keefe
Registrar: Robert K. Doolos
Admissions: Cleve Brooks
Financial Aid: Mary G. Parker
Type: University **Sex:** Coed **Affiliation:** Louisiana State University System **Scores:** 98.9% SAT V 400+; 99.4% SAT M 400+; 38% ACT 18-23; 52.2% ACT 24-29 **% Accepted:** 73 **Admission Plans:** Early Admission; Deferred Admission **Application Deadline:** April 15 **Application Fee:** $40.00 **H.S. Requirements:** High school diploma required; GED accepted **Costs Per Year:** Application fee: $40. State resident tuition: $2981 full-time. Nonresident tuition: $11,281 full-time. Mandatory fees: $1438 full-time. College room and board: $6330. College room only: $3930. Room and board charges vary according to board plan and housing facility. **Scholarships:** Available **Calendar System:** Semester, Summer Session Available **Enrollment:** FT 23,766, PT 1,939, Grad 4,507 **Faculty:** FT 1,277, PT 190 **Student-Faculty Ratio:** 22:1 **Exams:** SAT I or ACT **% Receiving Financial Aid:** 35 **% Residing in College-Owned, -Operated, or -Affiliated Housing:** 23 **Library Holdings:** 1,369,607 **Regional Accreditation:** Southern Association of Colleges and Schools **Credit Hours For Degree:** 119 semester hours, Bachelors **ROTC:** Army, Navy, Air Force **Professional Accreditation:** AACSB, ABET, ACEJMC, AAFCS, ABA, ACCE, ACA, ADtA, ALA, APA, ASLA, ASLHA, AVMA, AALS, CSWE, FIDER, NASAD, NASM, NCATE, SAF **Intercollegiate Athletics:** Baseball M; Basketball M & W; Cheerleading M & W; Cross-Country Running M & W; Football M; Golf M & W; Gymnastics W; Soccer W; Softball W; Swimming and Diving M & W; Tennis M & W; Track and Field M & W; Volleyball W

LOUISIANA STATE UNIVERSITY AT ALEXANDRIA
8100 Hwy. 71 South
Alexandria, LA 71302-9121
Tel: (318)445-3672; 888-473-6417
Admissions: (318)473-6542
Fax: (318)473-6418
Web Site: http://www.lsua.edu/
President/CEO: Dr. Robert Cavanaugh
Registrar: Leslie Quinn
Admissions: Leslie Quinn
Financial Aid: Kenn Posey
Type: Two-Year College **Sex:** Coed **Affiliation:** Louisiana State University System **Scores:** 49.7% ACT 18-23; 11.3% ACT 24-29 **% Accepted:** 77 **Admission Plans:** Open Admission; Early Admission **Application Deadline:** Rolling **Application Fee:** $20.00 **H.S. Requirements:** High school diploma required; GED accepted **Costs Per Year:** Application fee: $20. Area resident tuition: $3092 full-time. State resident tuition: $128 per credit hour part-time. Nonresident tuition: $5552 full-time, $231 per credit hour part-time. **Scholarships:** Available **Calendar System:** Semester, Summer Session Available **Enrollment:** FT 1,572, PT 1,416 **Faculty:** FT 105, PT 75 **Student-Faculty Ratio:** 16:1 **Exams:** ACT **Library Holdings:** 154,935 **Regional Accreditation:** Southern Association of Colleges and Schools **ROTC:** Army **Professional Accreditation:** NAACLS, NLN

LOUISIANA STATE UNIVERSITY AT EUNICE
PO Box 1129
Eunice, LA 70535-1129
Tel: (337)457-7311

Admissions: (337)550-1302
Fax: (337)457-7311
Web Site: http://www.lsue.edu/
President/CEO: Dr. William J. Nunez, III
Admissions: Brenda Williams
Financial Aid: Jacqueline Lachapelle
Type: Two-Year College **Sex:** Coed **Affiliation:** Louisiana State University System **Scores:** 54% ACT 18-23; 20% ACT 24-29 **Admission Plans:** Open Admission; Early Admission **Application Fee:** $25.00 **H.S. Requirements:** High school diploma required; GED accepted **Scholarships:** Available **Calendar System:** Semester, Summer Session Available **Exams:** ACT **Library Holdings:** 100,000 **Regional Accreditation:** Southern Association of Colleges and Schools **Credit Hours For Degree:** 66 credit hours, Associates **Professional Accreditation:** CARC, JRCERT, NLN **Intercollegiate Athletics:** Baseball M; Basketball W

LOUISIANA STATE UNIVERSITY HEALTH SCIENCES CENTER
433 Bolivar St.
New Orleans, LA 70112-2223
Tel: (504)568-4808
Admissions: (504)568-4829
Web Site: http://www.lsuhsc.edu/no/
President/CEO: Dr. John A. Rock
Registrar: W. Bryant Faust
Admissions: W. Bryant Faust, IV
Financial Aid: Patrick Gorman
Type: University **Sex:** Coed **Affiliation:** Louisiana State University System **Application Fee:** $50.00 **H.S. Requirements:** High school diploma or equivalent not required **Scholarships:** Available **Calendar System:** Semester, Summer Session Available **Enrollment:** FT 585, PT 57, Grad 666 **Faculty:** FT 1,242, PT 138 **% Residing in College-Owned, -Operated, or -Affiliated Housing:** 11 **Library Holdings:** 232,617 **Regional Accreditation:** Southern Association of Colleges and Schools **Professional Accreditation:** AACN, AANA, ADA, AOTA, APTA, APA, ASLHA, CARC, CEPH, CORE, JCAHPO, LCMEAMA, NAACLS

LOUISIANA STATE UNIVERSITY IN SHREVEPORT
1 University Place
Shreveport, LA 71115-2399
Tel: (318)797-5000
Admissions: (318)797-5063
Fax: (318)797-5286
E-mail: admissions@pilot.lsus.edu
Web Site: http://www.lsus.edu/
President/CEO: Dr. Vincent J. Marsala
Registrar: Jennifer K. Carter
Admissions: Jennifer Carter
Financial Aid: Betty McCrary
Type: Comprehensive **Sex:** Coed **Affiliation:** Louisiana State University System **Scores:** 57% ACT 18-23; 18% ACT 24-29 **Admission Plans:** Open Admission; Early Admission; Deferred Admission **Application Fee:** $10.00 **H.S. Requirements:** High school diploma required; GED accepted **Scholarships:** Available **Calendar System:** Semester, Summer Session Available **Enrollment:** FT 2,648, PT 1,105, Grad 648 **Faculty:** FT 155, PT 99 **Student-Faculty Ratio:** 16:1 **Exams:** ACT, SAT I or ACT, SAT II **% Residing in College-Owned, -Operated, or -Affiliated Housing:** 5 **Library Holdings:** 279,821 **Regional Accreditation:** Southern Association of Colleges and Schools **Credit Hours For Degree:** 128 semester hours, Bachelors **ROTC:** Army **Professional Accreditation:** AACSB, ABET, APTA, LCMEAMA, NCATE **Intercollegiate Athletics:** Baseball M; Basketball M & W

LOUISIANA TECH UNIVERSITY
PO Box 3168
Ruston, LA 71272
Tel: (318)257-0211
Free: 800-528-3241
Admissions: (318)257-3036
E-mail: usjba@latech.edu
Web Site: http://www.latech.edu/
President/CEO: Dr. Daniel D. Reneau
Registrar: Robert D. Vento, Jr.
Admissions: Jan B. Albritton
Financial Aid: Roger Vick
Type: University **Sex:** Coed **Affiliation:** University of Louisiana System **Scores:** 52.5% ACT 18-23; 33.2% ACT 24-29 **Admission Plans:** Early Admission **Application Fee:** $20.00 **H.S. Requirements:** High school diploma required; GED accepted **Costs Per Year:** Application fee: $20. State resident tuition: $3914 full-time. Nonresident tuition: $8819 full-time. Mandatory fees: $461 full-time. College room and board: $4035. College room only: $2130. **Scholarships:** Available **Calendar System:** Quarter, Summer Session Available **Enrollment:** FT 7,553, PT 1,765, Grad 2,373 **Faculty:** FT 394, PT 105 **Student-Faculty Ratio:** 23:1 **Exams:** ACT, SAT I or ACT **% Receiving Financial Aid:** 53 **% Residing in College-Owned, -Operated, or -Affiliated Housing:** 30 **Library Holdings:** 3,319 **Regional Accreditation:** Southern Association of Colleges and Schools **Credit Hours For Degree:** 60 credit hours, Associates; 126 credit hours, Bachelors **ROTC:** Army, Navy **Professional Accreditation:** AACSB, ABET, AAFCS, ADtA, AHIMA, APA, ASLHA, CAA, FIDER, NASAD, NASM, NCATE, NLN, SAF **Intercollegiate Athletics:** Baseball M; Basketball M & W; Cross-Country Running M & W; Football M; Golf M; Softball W; Tennis W; Track and Field M & W; Volleyball W; Weight Lifting M & W

LOUISIANA TECHNICAL COLLEGE
150 3rd St.
Baton Rouge, LA 70801
Free: 800-351-7611
Web Site: http://www.ltc.edu/
Admissions: Janice M. Bolden
Type: Two-Year College **Sex:** Coed **% Accepted:** 100 **Application Fee:** $5.00 **Costs Per Year:** Application fee: $5. State resident tuition: $552 full-time, $23 per credit hour part-time. Nonresident tuition: $1104 full-time, $46 per credit hour part-time. Mandatory fees: $214 full-time, $9 per credit hour part-time, $5 per term part-time. **Enrollment:** FT 7,264, PT 6,150 **Faculty:** FT 780, PT 573 **Student-Faculty Ratio:** 10:1

LOYOLA UNIVERSITY NEW ORLEANS
6363 Saint Charles Ave.
New Orleans, LA 70118-6195
Tel: (504)865-2011
Free: 800-4-LOYOLA
Admissions: (504)865-3240
Fax: (504)865-3383
Web Site: http://www.loyno.edu/
President/CEO: Rev. Kevin Wildes, SJ
Registrar: Kathy R. Gros
Admissions: Deborah C. Stieffel
Financial Aid: Cathy Simoneaux
Type: Comprehensive **Sex:** Coed **Affiliation:** Roman Catholic (Jesuit) **Scores:** 100% SAT V 400+; 100% SAT M 400+; 15.7% ACT 18-23; 73% ACT 24-29 **% Accepted:** 68 **Admission Plans:** Early Admission; Deferred Admission **Application Deadline:** January 15 **Application Fee:** $20.00 **H.S. Requirements:** High school diploma required; GED accepted. For home schooled students are required to provide proof of high school graduation or its equivalent: High school diploma required; GED accepted **Costs Per Year:** Application fee: $20. Comprehensive fee: $33,558 includes full-time tuition ($24,410), mandatory fees ($836), and college room and board ($8312). College room only: $5166. Room and board charges vary according to board plan and housing facility. Part-time tuition: $696 per credit hour. **Scholarships:** Available **Calendar System:** Semester, Summer Session Available **Enrollment:** FT 3,220, PT 468, Grad 931 **Faculty:** FT 306, PT 177 **Student-Faculty Ratio:** 11:1 **Exams:** Other, SAT I or ACT **% Receiving Financial Aid:** 52 **% Residing in College-Owned, -Operated, or -Affiliated Housing:** 40 **Library Holdings:** 401,548 **Regional Accreditation:** Southern Association of Colleges and Schools **Credit Hours For Degree:** 120 credit hours, Bachelors **ROTC:** Army, Navy, Air Force **Professional Accreditation:** AACSB, ABA, ACA, AALS, NASM, NCATE, NLN **Intercollegiate Athletics:** Baseball M; Basketball M & W; Bowling M & W; Cheerleading M & W; Crew M & W; Cross-Country Running M & W; Golf M & W; Rugby M; Soccer M & W; Swimming and Diving M & W; Tennis M & W; Track and Field M & W; Ultimate Frisbee M & W; Volleyball W; Wrestling M

MCNEESE STATE UNIVERSITY
4205 Ryan St.
Lake Charles, LA 70609
Tel: (337)475-5000
Free: 800-622-3352
Admissions: (337)475-5148
Web Site: http://www.mcneese.edu/
President/CEO: Dr. Robert D. Hebert

Registrar: Stephanie B. Tarver
Admissions: Tammie Pettis
Financial Aid: Taina Savoit
Type: Comprehensive **Sex:** Coed **Affiliation:** University of Louisiana System **Scores:** 60% ACT 18-23; 16% ACT 24-29 **Admission Plans:** Early Admission **Application Fee:** $20.00 **H.S. Requirements:** High school diploma required; GED accepted **Costs Per Year:** Application fee: $20. State resident tuition: $2226 full-time, $571.50 per term part-time. Nonresident tuition: $8292 full-time, $571.50 per term part-time. Mandatory fees: $933 full-time, $292.50 per term part-time. College room and board: $4637. **Scholarships:** Available **Calendar System:** Semester, Summer Session Available **Enrollment:** FT 6,399, PT 1,327, Grad 1,059 **Faculty:** FT 300, PT 113 **Student-Faculty Ratio:** 22:1 **Exams:** SAT I or ACT **% Residing in College-Owned, -Operated, or -Affiliated Housing:** 12 **Library Holdings:** 351,708 **Regional Accreditation:** Southern Association of Colleges and Schools **Credit Hours For Degree:** 60 semester hours, Associates; 120 semester hours, Bachelors **Professional Accreditation:** AACSB, ABET, AAFCS, ADtA, JRCERT, NAACLS, NASM, NCATE, NLN **Intercollegiate Athletics:** Baseball M; Basketball M & W; Cross-Country Running M & W; Football M; Golf M & W; Riflery M & W; Soccer W; Softball W; Tennis W; Track and Field M & W; Volleyball W; Weight Lifting M & W

MEDVANCE INSTITUTE
9255 Interline Ave.
Baton Rouge, LA 70809
Tel: (225)248-1015
Fax: (225)248-9571
Web Site: http://www.medvance.org/
President/CEO: Debbie Schwarzberg
Registrar: Michael Floyd
Admissions: Sheri Kirley
Financial Aid: Cindy Hill
Type: Two-Year College **Sex:** Coed **Application Fee:** $100.00 **H.S. Requirements:** High school diploma required; GED accepted **Scholarships:** Available **Calendar System:** Quarter, Summer Session Not available **Enrollment:** FT 294 **Faculty:** FT 10, PT 0 **Student-Faculty Ratio:** 11:1 **Exams:** Other **Credit Hours For Degree:** 96 quarter hours, Associates **Professional Accreditation:** COE, NAACLS

METROPOLITAN COMMUNITY COLLEGE
2550 Belle Chasse Hwy.
Gretna, LA 70053
Tel: (504)366-4613
Fax: (504)366-4614
Web Site: http://www.metrocc.us/
President/CEO: Jim Claudet
Type: Two-Year College **Sex:** Coed **Professional Accreditation:** COE

NEW ORLEANS BAPTIST THEOLOGICAL SEMINARY
3939 Gentilly Blvd.
New Orleans, LA 70126-4858
Tel: (504)282-4455
Free: 800-662-8701
Web Site: http://www.nobts.edu/
President/CEO: Dr. Charles S. Kelley, Jr.
Registrar: Tate Cockrell
Admissions: Dr. Paul E. Gregoire, Jr.
Type: Comprehensive **Sex:** Coed **Affiliation:** Southern Baptist **Admission Plans:** Deferred Admission **Application Fee:** $25.00 **H.S. Requirements:** High school diploma required; GED accepted **Scholarships:** Available **Calendar System:** Semester, Summer Session Available **Enrollment:** FT 316, PT 747, Grad 1,380 **Faculty:** FT 10, PT 74 **% Receiving Financial Aid:** 73 **Library Holdings:** 206,321 **Regional Accreditation:** Southern Association of Colleges and Schools **Credit Hours For Degree:** 69 hours, Associates; 126 hours, Bachelors **Professional Accreditation:** ACIPE, ATS, NASM

NICHOLLS STATE UNIVERSITY
906 East First St.
Thibodaux, LA 70310
Tel: (985)446-8111; 877-NICHOLLS
Admissions: (985)448-4507
Fax: (985)448-4929
E-mail: nicholls@nich-nsunet.nich.edu
Web Site: http://www.nicholls.edu
President/CEO: Dr. Stephen T. Hulbert
Registrar: Kelly Rodrigue
Admissions: Becky L. Durocher
Financial Aid: Colette Lagarde
Type: Comprehensive **Sex:** Coed **Affiliation:** University of Louisiana System **Scores:** 63% ACT 18-23; 17% ACT 24-29 **% Accepted:** 67 **Admission Plans:** Early Admission; Deferred Admission **Application Deadline:** Rolling **Application Fee:** $20.00 **H.S. Requirements:** High school diploma required; GED accepted **Costs Per Year:** Application fee: $20. State resident tuition: $2230 full-time. Nonresident tuition: $7679 full-time. Mandatory fees: $1159 full-time. College room and board: $3720. College room only: $1900. **Scholarships:** Available **Calendar System:** Semester, Summer Session Available **Enrollment:** FT 5,501, PT 1,385, Grad 639 **Faculty:** FT 289, PT 1 **Student-Faculty Ratio:** 21:1 **Exams:** SAT I or ACT **% Receiving Financial Aid:** 53 **% Residing in College-Owned, -Operated, or -Affiliated Housing:** 18 **Library Holdings:** 303,962 **Regional Accreditation:** Southern Association of Colleges and Schools **Credit Hours For Degree:** 60 semester hours, Associates; 120 semester hours, Bachelors **Professional Accreditation:** AACSB, ABET, ACEJMC, AACN, AAFCS, ADtA, ASC, CARC, JRCEMT, NASAD, NASM, NCATE, NLN **Intercollegiate Athletics:** Baseball M; Basketball M & W; Cross-Country Running M & W; Football M; Golf M & W; Soccer W; Softball W; Tennis M & W; Track and Field M & W; Volleyball W

NORTHWESTERN STATE UNIVERSITY OF LOUISIANA
350 Sam Sibley Dr.
Natchitoches, LA 71497
Tel: (318)357-6361
Free: 800-327-1903
Admissions: (318)357-4078
E-mail: admissions@nsula.edu
Web Site: http://www.nsula.edu/
President/CEO: Dr. Randall Webb
Registrar: Lillie Bell
Admissions: Yvette Williams
Financial Aid: Misti Adams
Type: Comprehensive **Sex:** Coed **Affiliation:** University of Louisiana System **Scores:** 89.36% SAT V 400+; 87.24% SAT M 400+; 55.16% ACT 18-23; 16.63% ACT 24-29 **% Accepted:** 77 **Admission Plans:** Early Action; Deferred Admission **Application Deadline:** July 06 **Application Fee:** $20.00 **H.S. Requirements:** High school diploma required; GED accepted **Costs Per Year:** Application fee: $20. State resident tuition: $2240 full-time, $240 per credit part-time. Nonresident tuition: $8318 full-time, $493 per credit part-time. Mandatory fees: $1153 full-time. Full-time tuition and fees vary according to course load. Part-time tuition varies according to course load. College room and board: $3626. College room only: $2050. Room and board charges vary according to board plan, housing facility, and location. **Scholarships:** Available **Calendar System:** Semester, Summer Session Available **Enrollment:** FT 6,460, PT 2,328, Grad 1,059 **Faculty:** FT 309, PT 237 **Student-Faculty Ratio:** 18:1 **Exams:** SAT I or ACT **% Receiving Financial Aid:** 59 **% Residing in College-Owned, -Operated, or -Affiliated Housing:** 20 **Library Holdings:** 325,829 **Regional Accreditation:** Southern Association of Colleges and Schools **Credit Hours For Degree:** 63 credit hours, Associates; 120 credit hours, Bachelors **ROTC:** Army **Professional Accreditation:** AACSB, ABET, ACEJMC, AACN, AAFCS, ACA, CSWE, JRCERT, NASAD, NASM, NAST, NCATE, NLN **Intercollegiate Athletics:** Baseball M; Basketball M & W; Cross-Country Running M & W; Football M; Soccer W; Softball W; Tennis W; Track and Field M & W; Volleyball W

OUR LADY OF HOLY CROSS COLLEGE
4123 Woodland Dr.
New Orleans, LA 70131-7399
Tel: (504)394-7744
Free: 800-259-7744
Fax: (504)391-2421
Web Site: http://www.olhcc.edu/
President/CEO: Dr. Paul T. Ceasar
Registrar: Michael Ferguson
Admissions: Kristine Hatfield Kopecky
Financial Aid: Johnell Armer
Type: Comprehensive **Sex:** Coed **Affiliation:** Roman Catholic **Scores:** 67% ACT 18-23; 4% ACT 24-29 **Admission Plans:** Deferred Admission **Application Fee:** $15.00 **H.S. Requirements:** High school diploma required; GED

accepted **Scholarships:** Available **Calendar System:** Semester, Summer Session Available **Enrollment:** FT 831, PT 485, Grad 130 **Faculty:** FT 39, PT 84 **Student-Faculty Ratio:** 22:1 **Exams:** ACT, SAT I or ACT **% Receiving Financial Aid:** 40 **Library Holdings:** 83,631 **Regional Accreditation:** Southern Association of Colleges and Schools **Credit Hours For Degree:** 60 semester hours, Associates; 125 semester hours, Bachelors **ROTC:** Army, Air Force **Professional Accreditation:** ACA, CARC, NCATE, NLN

OUR LADY OF THE LAKE COLLEGE
7434 Perkins Rd.
Baton Rouge, LA 70808
Tel: (225)768-1700; 877-242-3509
Fax: (225)768-1726
Web Site: http://www.ololcollege.edu/
President/CEO: Dr. Michael Smith
Registrar: Melodie Leggett
Financial Aid: Sharon Butler
Type: Four-Year College **Sex:** Coed **Affiliation:** Roman Catholic **Scores:** 75.6% ACT 18-23; 7.4% ACT 24-29 **Admission Plans:** Open Admission **Application Fee:** $35.00 **H.S. Requirements:** High school diploma required; GED accepted **Costs Per Year:** Application fee: $35. Tuition: $6780 full-time, $226 per credit hour part-time. Mandatory fees: $500 full-time, $75 per term part-time. **Scholarships:** Available **Calendar System:** Semester, Summer Session Available **Faculty:** FT 65, PT 69 **Student-Faculty Ratio:** 18:1 **Exams:** ACT, Other **Library Holdings:** 12,409 **Regional Accreditation:** Southern Association of Colleges and Schools **Credit Hours For Degree:** 63 credit hours, Associates; 129 credit hours, Bachelors **ROTC:** Army, Air Force **Professional Accreditation:** ARCEST, APTA, JRCERT, NAACLS, NLN

REMINGTON COLLEGE-BATON ROUGE CAMPUS
1900 North Lobdell
Baton Rouge, LA 70806
Tel: (225)922-3990
Fax: (225)922-9569
E-mail: gregg.falcon@remingtoncollege.edu
Web Site: http://www.remingtoncollege.edu/
President/CEO: Midge Jacobson
Registrar: Carolyn DeLoch
Admissions: Gregg Falcon
Financial Aid: Eddie Callier
Type: Two-Year College **Sex:** Coed **Calendar System:** Continuous **Professional Accreditation:** ACICS

REMINGTON COLLEGE-LAFAYETTE CAMPUS
303 Rue Louis XIV
Lafayette, LA 70508
Tel: (337)981-4010
Admissions: (337)981-9010
Fax: (337)983-7130
Web Site: http://www.remingtoncollege.edu/
President/CEO: Dr. Rosalie Lampone
Registrar: Tamie Coontz
Admissions: Gary Schwartz
Financial Aid: Jo Ann Boudreaux
Type: Two-Year College **Sex:** Coed **Affiliation:** Education America Inc **% Accepted:** 100 **Admission Plans:** Early Admission; Deferred Admission **Application Fee:** $50.00 **H.S. Requirements:** High school diploma required; GED accepted **Costs Per Year:** Application fee: $50. Tuition: $12,825 full-time. **Scholarships:** Available **Calendar System:** Continuous, Summer Session Not available **Enrollment:** FT 367 **Faculty:** FT 16, PT 12 **Student-Faculty Ratio:** 18:1 **Library Holdings:** 15,435 **Professional Accreditation:** ACICS

REMINGTON COLLEGE-NEW ORLEANS CAMPUS
321 Veterans Memorial Blvd.
Metairie, LA 70005
Tel: (504)831-8889
Fax: (504)831-6803
Web Site: http://www.remingtoncollege.edu/
President/CEO: Gregg Falcon
Admissions: Roy Kimble
Financial Aid: Toni Bannon
Type: Two-Year College **Sex:** Coed **Application Fee:** $50.00 **H.S. Requirements:** High school diploma required; GED accepted **Calendar System:** Quarter **Credit Hours For Degree:** 100 hours, Associates **Professional Accreditation:** ACCSCT

RIVER PARISHES COMMUNITY COLLEGE
PO Box 310
Sorrento, LA 70778
Tel: (225)675-8270
Fax: (225)675-5478
E-mail: adauzat@rpcc.cc.la.us
Web Site: http://rpcc.cc.la.us/
President/CEO: Dr. Joe Ben Welch
Admissions: Allison Dauzat
Financial Aid: Kim Dudley
Type: Two-Year College **Sex:** Coed **Application Fee:** $10.00 **Costs Per Year:** Application fee: $10. State resident tuition: $1458 full-time, $66 per credit hour part-time. Nonresident tuition: $4174 full-time, $66 per credit hour part-time. Mandatory fees: $310 full-time, $40 per term part-time. **Calendar System:** Semester **Faculty:** FT 16, PT 17 **Regional Accreditation:** Southern Association of Colleges and Schools **Credit Hours For Degree:** 61 credits, Associates

SAINT JOSEPH SEMINARY COLLEGE
St. Benedict, LA 70457
Tel: (504)892-1800
Admissions: (985)867-2225
Web Site: http://www.sjasc.edu/
President/CEO: Very Rev. Gregory Boquet, OSB
Admissions: Dr. Russ Pottle
Financial Aid: Les Lavergne
Type: Four-Year College **Sex:** Men **Affiliation:** Roman Catholic **Scores:** 33% ACT 18-23; 22% ACT 24-29 **Admission Plans:** Preferred Admission; Early Admission; Deferred Admission **Application Fee:** $10.00 **H.S. Requirements:** High school diploma required; GED accepted **Scholarships:** Available **Calendar System:** Semester, Summer Session Not available **Enrollment:** FT 77, PT 90 **Faculty:** FT 14, PT 22 **Student-Faculty Ratio:** 3:1 **Exams:** ACT **% Receiving Financial Aid:** 26 **% Residing in College-Owned, -Operated, or -Affiliated Housing:** 100 **Library Holdings:** 70,000 **Regional Accreditation:** Southern Association of Colleges and Schools **Credit Hours For Degree:** 124 semester hours, Bachelors

SCHOOL OF URBAN MISSIONS-NEW ORLEANS
PO Box 53344
New Orleans, LA 70153
Tel: (504)362-6364
Free: 800-385-6364
Fax: (504)362-4895
Web Site: http://www.sumonline.org/
President/CEO: Rev. Anthony Freeman
Type: Two-Year College **Sex:** Coed **Affiliation:** interdenominational **Calendar System:** Quarter **Professional Accreditation:** AABC

SOUTHEASTERN LOUISIANA UNIVERSITY
Hammond, LA 70402
Tel: (985)549-2000
Free: 800-222-7358
Admissions: (985)549-2066
Fax: (985)549-5095
E-mail: Richard.Beaugh@selu.edu
Web Site: http://www.selu.edu/
President/CEO: Dr. M. Randy Moffett
Registrar: Paulette Poche
Admissions: Richard Beaugh
Financial Aid: Richard Beaugh
Type: Comprehensive **Sex:** Coed **Affiliation:** University of Louisiana System **Scores:** 21.7% ACT 18-23 **% Accepted:** 94 **Admission Plans:** Early Admission; Deferred Admission **Application Deadline:** August 16 **Application Fee:** $20.00 **H.S. Requirements:** High school diploma required; GED accepted **Costs Per Year:** Application fee: $20. State resident tuition: $3341 full-time, $139 per credit hour part-time. Nonresident tuition: $8669 full-time, $361 per credit hour part-time. Full-time tuition varies according to course load. Part-time tuition varies according to course load. College room and board: $5180. College room only: $3150. Room and board charges vary according to board plan and housing facility. **Scholarships:** Available **Calendar System:** Semester, Summer Session Available **Enrollment:** FT 11,157, PT 2,507, Grad 1,808 **Faculty:** FT 497, PT 233 **Student-Faculty**

Ratio: 27:1 **Exams:** SAT I or ACT, SAT II **% Receiving Financial Aid:** 56 **% Residing in College-Owned, -Operated, or -Affiliated Housing:** 11 **Library Holdings:** 572,563 **Regional Accreditation:** Southern Association of Colleges and Schools **Credit Hours For Degree:** 61 semester hours, Associates; 120 semester hours, Bachelors **ROTC:** Army **Professional Accreditation:** AACSB, ABET, ACA, ASLHA, CSWE, NAIT, NASM, NCATE, NLN **Intercollegiate Athletics:** Baseball M; Basketball M & W; Cheerleading M & W; Cross-Country Running M & W; Football M; Golf M; Soccer W; Softball W; Tennis M & W; Track and Field M & W; Volleyball W

SOUTHERN UNIVERSITY AND AGRICULTURAL AND MECHANICAL COLLEGE
Baton Rouge, LA 70813
Tel: (225)771-4500
Free: 800-256-1531
Admissions: (225)771-2430
Web Site: http://www.subr.edu/
President/CEO: Dr. Edward R. Jackson
Registrar: Brenda Williams
Admissions: Tracie Abraham
Financial Aid: Philip Rogers
Type: Comprehensive **Sex:** Coed **Affiliation:** Southern University System **Scores:** 69% SAT V 400+; 74% SAT M 400+; 43% ACT 18-23; 2% ACT 24-29 **% Accepted:** 53 **Admission Plans:** Early Admission **Application Deadline:** July 01 **Application Fee:** $20.00 **H.S. Requirements:** High school diploma required; GED accepted **Costs Per Year:** Application fee: $20. State resident tuition: $3592 full-time. Nonresident tuition: $9384 full-time. Full-time tuition varies according to course load and location. College room and board: $4646. College room only: $2816. Room and board charges vary according to board plan and housing facility. **Scholarships:** Available **Calendar System:** Semester, Summer Session Available **Enrollment:** FT 7,729, PT 847, Grad 1,365 **Faculty:** FT 406, PT 167 **Student-Faculty Ratio:** 18:1 **Exams:** SAT I or ACT **% Receiving Financial Aid:** 79 **% Residing in College-Owned, -Operated, or -Affiliated Housing:** 35 **Library Holdings:** 808,365 **Regional Accreditation:** Southern Association of Colleges and Schools **Credit Hours For Degree:** 65 credits, Associates; 124 credits, Bachelors **ROTC:** Army, Navy, Air Force **Professional Accreditation:** AACSB, ABET, ACEJMC, AACN, AAFCS, ABA, ADtA, ASLHA, CORE, CSWE, NASM, NASPAA, NCATE, NLN **Intercollegiate Athletics:** Baseball M; Basketball M & W; Bowling W; Cross-Country Running M; Football M; Golf M & W; Softball W; Tennis M & W; Track and Field M & W; Volleyball W

SOUTHERN UNIVERSITY AT NEW ORLEANS
6400 Press Dr.
New Orleans, LA 70126-1009
Tel: (504)286-5000
Admissions: (504)286-5314
E-mail: tbailey@suno.edu
Web Site: http://www.suno.edu/
President/CEO: Dr. Press Robinson
Admissions: Timeotea Bailey
Financial Aid: Ursula Shorty
Type: Comprehensive **Sex:** Coed **Affiliation:** Southern University System **Admission Plans:** Open Admission; Early Admission; Deferred Admission **Costs Per Year:** State resident tuition: $2990 full-time. Nonresident tuition: $6728 full-time. **Scholarships:** Available **Calendar System:** Semester **Exams:** SAT I or ACT **Regional Accreditation:** Southern Association of Colleges and Schools **Credit Hours For Degree:** 62 semester hours, Associates; 124 semester hours, Bachelors **ROTC:** Army, Air Force **Professional Accreditation:** CSWE, NCATE **Intercollegiate Athletics:** Basketball M; Cross-Country Running M & W; Track and Field M & W

SOUTHERN UNIVERSITY AT SHREVEPORT
3050 Martin Luther King, Jr. Dr.
Shreveport, LA 71107
Tel: (318)674-3300
Admissions: (318)674-3426
Fax: (318)674-3489
E-mail: tscott@susla.edu
Web Site: http://www.susla.edu/
President/CEO: Dr. Ray L. Belton
Registrar: Mahailer Broom
Admissions: Ted Scott
Financial Aid: Linda Hines
Type: Two-Year College **Sex:** Coed **Affiliation:** Southern University System **Scores:** 7.7% ACT 18-23 **Admission Plans:** Open Admission; Early Admission **Application Fee:** $5.00 **H.S. Requirements:** High school diploma required; GED accepted **Scholarships:** Available **Calendar System:** Semester, Summer Session Available **Enrollment:** FT 921, PT 403 **Faculty:** FT 49, PT 49 **Student-Faculty Ratio:** 16:1 **Exams:** ACT **Regional Accreditation:** Southern Association of Colleges and Schools **Credit Hours For Degree:** 68 credits, Associates **Professional Accreditation:** ARCEST, ADA, AHIMA, CARC, JRCERT, NAACLS, NAIT **Intercollegiate Athletics:** Basketball M & W

TULANE UNIVERSITY
6823 St Charles Ave.
New Orleans, LA 70118-5669
Tel: (504)865-5000
Free: 800-873-9283
Admissions: (504)865-5731
Fax: (504)862-8715
E-mail: undergrad.admission@tulane.edu
Web Site: http://www.tulane.edu/
President/CEO: Dr. Scott S. Cowen
Registrar: Earl Retif
Admissions: Richard Whiteside
Financial Aid: Elaine L. Rivera
Type: University **Sex:** Coed **Scores:** 99.5% SAT V 400+; 100% SAT M 400+ **% Accepted:** 45 **Admission Plans:** Early Admission; Early Action; Early Decision Plan; Deferred Admission **Application Deadline:** January 15 **Application Fee:** $55.00 **H.S. Requirements:** High school diploma required; GED accepted **Costs Per Year:** Application fee: $55. Comprehensive fee: $41,357 includes full-time tuition ($30,350), mandatory fees ($2596), and college room and board ($8411). College room only: $4841. Part-time tuition: $1340 per credit hour. Part-time mandatory fees: $20. **Scholarships:** Available **Calendar System:** Semester, Summer Session Available **Enrollment:** FT 6,151, PT 1,825, Grad 3,098 **Faculty:** FT 1,099, PT 272 **Student-Faculty Ratio:** 13:1 **Exams:** SAT I or ACT **% Receiving Financial Aid:** 47 **% Residing in College-Owned, -Operated, or -Affiliated Housing:** 65 **Library Holdings:** 2,331,250 **Regional Accreditation:** Southern Association of Colleges and Schools **Credit Hours For Degree:** 120 credit hours, Bachelors **ROTC:** Army, Navy, Air Force **Professional Accreditation:** AACSB, ABET, ACEHSA, ABA, ADtA, APA, AALS, CEPH, CSWE, LCMEAMA **Intercollegiate Athletics:** Baseball M; Basketball M & W; Crew M & W; Cross-Country Running M & W; Football M; Golf M & W; Gymnastics M & W; Ice Hockey M & W; Lacrosse M & W; Rugby M; Sailing M & W; Soccer M & W; Swimming and Diving M & W; Tennis M & W; Track and Field M & W; Volleyball M & W; Water Polo M & W

UNIVERSITY OF LOUISIANA AT LAFAYETTE
104 University Circle
PO Drawer 41008
Lafayette, LA 70504
Tel: (337)482-1000
Admissions: (337)482-6553
Fax: (337)482-6195
E-mail: dan@louisiana.edu
Web Site: http://www.louisiana.edu/
President/CEO: Dr. Ray P. Authement
Registrar: Dewayne Bowie
Admissions: Dan Rosenfield
Financial Aid: Cynthia Shows-Perez
Type: University **Sex:** Coed **Affiliation:** University of Louisiana System **Scores:** 62.14% ACT 18-23; 27.43% ACT 24-29 **% Accepted:** 76 **Admission Plans:** Early Admission; Deferred Admission **Application Deadline:** Rolling **Application Fee:** $25.00 **H.S. Requirements:** High school diploma required; GED accepted. For applicants 21 or over: High school diploma or equivalent not required **Costs Per Year:** Application fee: $25. State resident tuition: $3324 full-time, $92.75 per credit hour part-time. Nonresident tuition: $9504 full-time, $350.25 per credit hour part-time. Full-time tuition varies according to course load. Part-time tuition varies according to course load. College room and board: $3478. Room and board charges vary according to board plan and housing facility. **Scholarships:** Available **Calendar System:** Semester, Summer Session Available **Enrollment:** FT 12,926, PT 2,638, Grad 1,511 **Faculty:** FT 548, PT 171 **Student-Faculty Ratio:** 22:1 **Exams:** SAT I or ACT **% Receiving Financial Aid:** 53 **% Residing in College-Owned, -Operated, or -Affiliated Housing:** 11 **Library Holdings:** 986,000

Regional Accreditation: Southern Association of Colleges and Schools **Credit Hours For Degree:** 124 semester hours, Bachelors **ROTC:** Army **Professional Accreditation:** AACSB, ABET, ACEJMC, AAFCS, ADtA, AHIMA, ASLHA, FIDER, NAIT, NASAD, NASM, NCATE, NLN **Intercollegiate Athletics:** Baseball M; Basketball M & W; Cross-Country Running M & W; Football M; Golf M; Soccer W; Softball W; Tennis M & W; Track and Field M & W; Volleyball W

UNIVERSITY OF LOUISIANA AT MONROE
700 University Ave.
Monroe, LA 71209-0001
Tel: (318)342-1000
Free: 800-372-5127
Admissions: (318)342-5272
Fax: (318)342-1049
E-mail: lmiller@ulm.edu
Web Site: http://www.ulm.edu/
President/CEO: Dr. James E. Cofer, Sr.
Registrar: Dr. James Robertson, Jr.
Admissions: Lisa Miller
Financial Aid: Ralph Perri
Type: University **Sex:** Coed **Scores:** 87% SAT V 400+; 90% SAT M 400+; 58% ACT 18-23; 19% ACT 24-29 **% Accepted:** 87 **Admission Plans:** Early Admission; Deferred Admission **Application Deadline:** Rolling **Application Fee:** $20.00 **H.S. Requirements:** High school diploma required; GED accepted **Costs Per Year:** Application fee: $20. State resident tuition: $2334 full-time, $93 per credit hour part-time. Nonresident tuition: $8284 full-time. Mandatory fees: $1068 full-time, $64 per credit hour part-time. Full-time tuition and fees vary according to course load and program. Part-time tuition and fees vary according to course load and program. College room and board: $4120. College room only: $2230. Room and board charges vary according to board plan and housing facility. **Scholarships:** Available **Calendar System:** Semester, Summer Session Available **Enrollment:** FT 6,251, PT 1,496, Grad 886 **Faculty:** FT 373, PT 82 **Exams:** ACT **% Residing in College-Owned, -Operated, or -Affiliated Housing:** 15 **Library Holdings:** 642,582 **Regional Accreditation:** Southern Association of Colleges and Schools **Credit Hours For Degree:** 60 credit hours, Associates; 128 credit hours, Bachelors **ROTC:** Army **Professional Accreditation:** AACSB, ABET, ACEJMC, AAMFT, AACN, AAFCS, ACCE, ACPhE, ACA, ADA, AOTA, ASLHA, CSWE, JRCERT, NASM, NCATE **Intercollegiate Athletics:** Baseball M; Basketball M & W; Cheerleading M & W; Cross-Country Running M & W; Football M; Golf M & W; Soccer W; Softball W; Swimming and Diving M & W; Tennis M & W; Track and Field M & W; Volleyball W

UNIVERSITY OF NEW ORLEANS
Lake Front
New Orleans, LA 70148
Tel: (504)280-6000
Free: 800-256-5866
Admissions: (504)280-7013
Fax: (504)280-5522
Web Site: http://www.uno.edu/
President/CEO: Dr. Timothy P. Ryan
Registrar: Kathleen G. Plante
Admissions: Roslyn S. Sheley
Financial Aid: Emily London Jones
Type: University **Sex:** Coed **Affiliation:** Louisiana State University System **Scores:** 90% SAT V 400+; 93% SAT M 400+; 59% ACT 18-23; 19% ACT 24-29 **% Accepted:** 63 **Admission Plans:** Early Admission; Deferred Admission **Application Deadline:** Rolling **Application Fee:** $20.00 **H.S. Requirements:** High school diploma required; GED accepted **Costs Per Year:** Application fee: $20. State resident tuition: $3292 full-time, $133 per hour part-time. Nonresident tuition: $10,336 full-time, $426 per hour part-time. Mandatory fees: $518 full-time. Part-time tuition varies according to course load. College room only: $4590. Room charges vary according to housing facility. **Scholarships:** Available **Calendar System:** Semester, Summer Session Available **Enrollment:** FT 9,551, PT 3,674, Grad 4,125 **Faculty:** FT 556, PT 229 **Student-Faculty Ratio:** 25:1 **Exams:** SAT I or ACT **% Receiving Financial Aid:** 59 **% Residing in College-Owned, -Operated, or -Affiliated Housing:** 9 **Library Holdings:** 896,000 **Regional Accreditation:** Southern Association of Colleges and Schools **Credit Hours For Degree:** 128 semester hours, Bachelors **ROTC:** Army, Navy, Air Force **Professional Accreditation:** AACSB, ABET, ACA, ACSP, NASAD, NASM, NAST, NCATE **Intercollegiate Athletics:** Baseball M; Basketball M & W; Cross-Country Running M & W; Golf M & W; Tennis M & W; Track and Field M & W; Volleyball W

UNIVERSITY OF PHOENIX-LOUISIANA CAMPUS
1 Galleria Blvd., Ste. 725
Metairie, LA 70001-2082
Tel: (504)461-8852
Free: 800-228-7240
Admissions: (480)557-1712
Web Site: http://www.phoenix.edu/
President/CEO: Brent Fitch
Admissions: Nina Omelchanko
Type: Comprehensive **Sex:** Coed **Admission Plans:** Open Admission; Deferred Admission **Application Deadline:** Rolling **Application Fee:** $110.00 **H.S. Requirements:** High school diploma required; GED accepted **Costs Per Year:** Application fee: $110. Tuition: $9120 full-time, $304 per credit part-time. Mandatory fees: $560 full-time, $70 per course part-time. Full-time tuition and fees vary according to program. **Scholarships:** Available **Calendar System:** Continuous, Summer Session Not available **Enrollment:** FT 2,085, Grad 662 **Faculty:** FT 2, PT 302 **Student-Faculty Ratio:** 6:1 **Library Holdings:** 444 **Regional Accreditation:** North Central Association of Colleges and Schools **Credit Hours For Degree:** 60 credits, Associates; 120 credits, Bachelors **Professional Accreditation:** NLN

XAVIER UNIVERSITY OF LOUISIANA
1 Drexel Dr.
New Orleans, LA 70125-1098
Tel: (504)486-7411; 877-XAVIERU
Admissions: (504)520-7388
E-mail: apply@xula.edu
Web Site: http://www.xula.edu/
President/CEO: Dr. Norman C. Francis
Registrar: JoAnn Taylor
Admissions: Winston Brown
Financial Aid: Mildred Higgins
Type: Comprehensive **Sex:** Coed **Affiliation:** Roman Catholic **Scores:** 91% SAT V 400+; 89% SAT M 400+; 57% ACT 18-23; 25% ACT 24-29 **% Accepted:** 83 **Admission Plans:** Early Action **Application Deadline:** March 01 **Application Fee:** $25.00 **H.S. Requirements:** High school diploma required; GED accepted **Costs Per Year:** Application fee: $25. Comprehensive fee: $20,200 includes full-time tuition ($12,100), mandatory fees ($1000), and college room and board ($7100). Room and board charges vary according to location. Part-time tuition: $500 per credit hour. **Scholarships:** Available **Calendar System:** Semester, Summer Session Available **Enrollment:** FT 3,143, PT 147, Grad 242 **Faculty:** FT 241, PT 48 **Student-Faculty Ratio:** 16:1 **Exams:** SAT I or ACT **% Receiving Financial Aid:** 77 **% Residing in College-Owned, -Operated, or -Affiliated Housing:** 30 **Library Holdings:** 238,455 **Regional Accreditation:** Southern Association of Colleges and Schools **Credit Hours For Degree:** 128 semester hours, Bachelors **ROTC:** Army, Navy, Air Force **Professional Accreditation:** AANA, ACPhE, ACBSP, NASM, NCATE **Intercollegiate Athletics:** Basketball M & W; Cross-Country Running M & W; Tennis M & W

ANDOVER COLLEGE
901 Washington Ave.
Portland, ME 04103-2791
Tel: (207)774-6126
Free: 800-639-3110
Fax: (207)774-1715
Web Site: http://www.andovercollege.com/
President/CEO: Mark E. Jenkins
Registrar: Celia Dobson
Admissions: David Blessing
Financial Aid: Adrienne Amari
Type: Two-Year College **Sex:** Coed **Admission Plans:** Open Admission; Early Admission; Deferred Admission **Application Fee:** $25.00 **H.S. Requirements:** High school diploma required; GED accepted **Scholarships:** Available **Calendar System:** Miscellaneous, Summer Session Available **Enrollment:** FT 490, PT 12 **Faculty:** FT 12, PT 24 **Student-Faculty Ratio:** 19:1 **Library Holdings:** 6,500 **Regional Accreditation:** New England Association of Schools and Colleges **Credit Hours For Degree:** 60 credit hours, Associates

BATES COLLEGE
Andrews Rd.
Lewiston, ME 04240-6028
Tel: (207)786-6255
Admissions: (207)786-6000
Fax: (207)786-6025
E-mail: admissions@bates.edu
Web Site: http://www.bates.edu/
President/CEO: Dr. Donald W. Harward
Registrar: Meredith H. Braz
Admissions: Wylie L. Mitchell
Financial Aid: Leigh P. Campbell
Type: Four-Year College **Sex:** Coed **Scores:** 100% SAT V 400+; 100% SAT M 400+ **% Accepted:** 29 **Admission Plans:** Early Admission; Early Decision Plan; Deferred Admission **Application Deadline:** January 01 **Application Fee:** $60.00 **H.S. Requirements:** High school diploma required; GED not accepted **Costs Per Year:** Application fee: $60. Comprehensive fee: $42,100. **Scholarships:** Available **Calendar System:** Miscellaneous, Summer Session Not available **Enrollment:** FT 1,699, PT 31 **Faculty:** FT 164, PT 23 **Student-Faculty Ratio:** 10:1 **% Receiving Financial Aid:** 40 **% Residing in College-Owned, -Operated, or -Affiliated Housing:** 90 **Library Holdings:** 588,211 **Regional Accreditation:** New England Association of Schools and Colleges **Credit Hours For Degree:** 32 courses and 2 short terms, Bachelors **Intercollegiate Athletics:** Badminton M & W; Baseball M; Basketball M & W; Crew M & W; Cross-Country Running M & W; Equestrian Sports M & W; Fencing M & W; Field Hockey W; Football M; Golf M & W; Ice Hockey M & W; Lacrosse M & W; Rugby M & W; Sailing M & W; Skiing (Cross-Country) M & W; Skiing (Downhill) M & W; Soccer M & W; Softball W; Squash M & W; Swimming and Diving M & W; Tennis M & W; Track and Field M & W; Ultimate Frisbee M & W; Volleyball M & W; Water Polo M & W

BEAL COLLEGE
629 Main St.
Bangor, ME 04401-6896
Tel: (207)947-4591
Web Site: http://www.bealcollege.edu/
President/CEO: Allen T. Stehle
Registrar: Darin Pridham
Admissions: Catherine Haskell
Financial Aid: Diane Willett
Type: Two-Year College **Sex:** Coed **Admission Plans:** Open Admission; Deferred Admission **Application Deadline:** Rolling **Application Fee:** $25.00 **H.S. Requirements:** High school diploma required; GED accepted **Scholarships:** Available **Calendar System:** Miscellaneous, Summer Session Available **Enrollment:** FT 239, PT 134 **Faculty:** FT 6, PT 10 **Student-Faculty Ratio:** 16:1 **Library Holdings:** 7,275 **Credit Hours For Degree:** 72 credit hours, Associates **Professional Accreditation:** ACICS, AAMAE

BOWDOIN COLLEGE
5000 College Station
Brunswick, ME 04011
Tel: (207)725-3000
Admissions: (207)725-3958
Fax: (207)725-3003
E-mail: admissions@bowdoin.edu
Web Site: http://www.bowdoin.edu/
President/CEO: Dr. Barry Mills
Registrar: Dr. Christine A. Brooks Cote
Admissions: Richard Steele
Financial Aid: Stephen H. Joyce
Type: Four-Year College **Sex:** Coed **Scores:** 100% SAT V 400+; 100% SAT M 400+ **% Accepted:** 25 **Admission Plans:** Early Decision Plan; Deferred Admission **Application Deadline:** January 01 **Application Fee:** $60.00 **H.S. Requirements:** High school diploma required; GED not accepted **Costs Per Year:** Application fee: $60. Comprehensive fee: $41,660 includes full-time tuition ($32,650), mandatory fees ($340), and college room and board ($8670). College room only: $3900. Room and board charges vary according to board plan. **Scholarships:** Available **Calendar System:** Semester, Summer Session Not available **Enrollment:** FT 1,661, PT 5 **Faculty:** FT 157, PT 37 **Student-Faculty Ratio:** 10:1 **% Receiving Financial Aid:** 49 **% Residing in College-Owned, -Operated, or -Affiliated Housing:** 93 **Library Holdings:** 981,074 **Regional Accreditation:** New England Association of Schools and Colleges **Credit Hours For Degree:** 32 courses, Bachelors **Intercollegiate Athletics:** Baseball M; Basketball M & W; Crew M & W; Cross-Country Running M & W; Field Hockey W; Football M; Golf M & W; Ice Hockey M & W; Lacrosse M & W; Rugby M & W; Sailing M & W; Skiing (Cross-Country) M & W; Soccer M & W; Softball W; Squash M & W; Swimming and Diving M & W; Tennis M & W; Track and Field M & W; Ultimate Frisbee M & W; Volleyball W; Water Polo M & W

CENTRAL MAINE COMMUNITY COLLEGE
1250 Turner St.
Auburn, ME 04210-6498
Tel: (207)755-5100
Free: 800-891-2002
Admissions: (207)755-5334
Fax: (207)755-5491
E-mail: admissions@cmtc.mtcs.tec.me.us
Web Site: http://www.cmcc.edu/
President/CEO: Dr. Scott E. Knapp
Registrar: Ronald Bolstridge

Admissions: Elizabeth Oken
Financial Aid: Michael Roy
Type: Two-Year College **Sex:** Coed **Affiliation:** Maine Technical College System **Scores:** 69% SAT V 400+; 73% SAT M 400+ **Admission Plans:** Deferred Admission **Application Fee:** $20.00 **H.S. Requirements:** High school diploma required; GED accepted **Scholarships:** Available **Calendar System:** Semester, Summer Session Available **Faculty:** FT 53, PT 82 **Student-Faculty Ratio:** 15:1 **Exams:** Other, SAT I **% Residing in College-Owned, -Operated, or -Affiliated Housing:** 11 **Library Holdings:** 15,000 **Regional Accreditation:** New England Association of Schools and Colleges **Credit Hours For Degree:** 66 credits, Associates **Professional Accreditation:** ABET, ACBSP, NAACLS, NLN **Intercollegiate Athletics:** Baseball M; Basketball M & W; Soccer M & W; Softball W

CENTRAL MAINE MEDICAL CENTER SCHOOL OF NURSING
70 Middle St.
Lewiston, ME 04240-0305
Tel: (207)795-2840
Admissions: (207)795-2868
Fax: (207)795-2849
Web Site: http://www.cmmcson.edu/
President/CEO: Sharon Kuhrt
Registrar: Kathleen C. Jacques
Admissions: Lucille Webber
Financial Aid: Keith Bourgault
Type: Two-Year College **Sex:** Coed **Scores:** 100% SAT V 400+; 100% SAT M 400+ **Application Fee:** $40.00 **H.S. Requirements:** High school diploma required; GED accepted **Costs Per Year:** Application fee: $40. Tuition: $2898 full-time, $138 per credit part-time. Mandatory fees: $1205 full-time, $20 per term part-time. College room only: $1500. **Scholarships:** Available **Calendar System:** Semester, Summer Session Not available **Enrollment:** FT 22, PT 92 **Faculty:** FT 9, PT 3 **Student-Faculty Ratio:** 5:1 **Exams:** SAT I **% Residing in College-Owned, -Operated, or -Affiliated Housing:** 2 **Library Holdings:** 1,975 **Regional Accreditation:** New England Association of Schools and Colleges **Credit Hours For Degree:** 69 credits, Associates **Professional Accreditation:** NLN

COLBY COLLEGE
Mayflower Hill
Waterville, ME 04901-8840
Tel: (207)872-3000
Free: 800-723-3032
Admissions: (207)859-4802
Fax: (207)872-3474
E-mail: admissions@colby.edu
Web Site: http://www.colby.edu/
President/CEO: William D. Adams
Registrar: George L. Coleman, II
Admissions: Parker Beverage
Financial Aid: Lucia Whittelsey
Type: Four-Year College **Sex:** Coed **Scores:** 100% SAT V 400+; 100% SAT M 400+; 2% ACT 18-23; 57% ACT 24-29 **% Accepted:** 38 **Admission Plans:** Early Admission; Early Decision Plan; Deferred Admission **Application Deadline:** January 01 **Application Fee:** $0.00 **H.S. Requirements:** High school diploma or equivalent not required **Costs Per Year:** Application fee: $0. Comprehensive fee: $41,770. **Scholarships:** Available **Calendar System:** 4-1-4, Summer Session Not available **Enrollment:** FT 1,871 **Faculty:** FT 161, PT 64 **Student-Faculty Ratio:** 10:1 **Exams:** SAT I or ACT **% Receiving Financial Aid:** 38 **% Residing in College-Owned, -Operated, or -Affiliated Housing:** 93 **Library Holdings:** 350,000 **Regional Accreditation:** New England Association of Schools and Colleges **Credit Hours For Degree:** 128 semester hours, Bachelors **ROTC:** Army **Intercollegiate Athletics:** Badminton M & W; Baseball M; Basketball M & W; Crew M & W; Cross-Country Running M & W; Equestrian Sports M & W; Fencing M & W; Field Hockey W; Football M; Golf M & W; Ice Hockey M & W; Lacrosse M & W; Rugby M & W; Sailing M & W; Skiing (Cross-Country) M & W; Skiing (Downhill) M & W; Soccer M & W; Softball W; Squash M & W; Swimming and Diving M & W; Tennis M & W; Track and Field M & W; Ultimate Frisbee M & W; Volleyball M & W; Water Polo M & W

COLLEGE OF THE ATLANTIC
105 Eden St.
Bar Harbor, ME 04609-1198
Tel: (207)288-5015
Free: 800-528-0025
Fax: (207)288-4126
E-mail: inquiry@coa.edu
Web Site: http://www.coa.edu/
President/CEO: Dr. Steven K. Katona
Registrar: David Baldwin
Admissions: Sarah G. Baker
Financial Aid: Sarah Baker
Type: Comprehensive **Sex:** Coed **Scores:** 100% SAT V 400+; 96% SAT M 400+; 27% ACT 18-23; 59% ACT 24-29 **% Accepted:** 66 **Admission Plans:** Early Admission; Early Decision Plan; Deferred Admission **Application Deadline:** February 15 **Application Fee:** $45.00 **H.S. Requirements:** High school diploma required; GED accepted **Costs Per Year:** Application fee: $45. Comprehensive fee: $35,675 includes full-time tuition ($27,700), mandatory fees ($375), and college room and board ($7600). College room only: $4700. Part-time tuition: $9234 per term. Part-time mandatory fees: $125 per term. **Scholarships:** Available **Calendar System:** Miscellaneous, Summer Session Not available **Enrollment:** FT 296, PT 14, Grad 8 **Faculty:** FT 19, PT 11 **Student-Faculty Ratio:** 9:1 **Exams:** SAT I or ACT **% Receiving Financial Aid:** 93 **% Residing in College-Owned, -Operated, or -Affiliated Housing:** 40 **Library Holdings:** 50,000 **Regional Accreditation:** New England Association of Schools and Colleges **Credit Hours For Degree:** 36 credits, Bachelors **Intercollegiate Athletics:** Soccer M & W

EASTERN MAINE COMMUNITY COLLEGE
354 Hogan Rd.
Bangor, ME 04401-4206
Tel: (207)974-4600
Admissions: (207)974-4680
Fax: (207)974-4683
Web Site: http://www.emcc.edu/
President/CEO: Dr. Joyce B. Hedlund
Registrar: Candace Ward
Admissions: Veronica Delcort
Financial Aid: Candace Ward
Type: Two-Year College **Sex:** Coed **Affiliation:** Maine Community College System **Admission Plans:** Preferred Admission; Deferred Admission **Application Fee:** $20.00 **H.S. Requirements:** High school diploma required; GED accepted **Scholarships:** Available **Calendar System:** Semester, Summer Session Available **Enrollment:** FT 744, PT 1,046 **Faculty:** FT 54, PT 88 **Student-Faculty Ratio:** 11:1 **Exams:** Other, SAT I **% Residing in College-Owned, -Operated, or -Affiliated Housing:** 20 **Library Holdings:** 17,554 **Regional Accreditation:** New England Association of Schools and Colleges **Credit Hours For Degree:** 62 credit hours, Associates **Professional Accreditation:** JRCERT, NLN **Intercollegiate Athletics:** Basketball M; Soccer M & W

HUSSON COLLEGE
One College Circle
Bangor, ME 04401-2999
Tel: (207)941-7000
Free: 800-4-HUSSON
Admissions: (207)941-7100
Fax: (207)941-7935
E-mail: admit@husson.husson.edu
Web Site: http://www.husson.edu/
President/CEO: Dr. William H. Beardsley
Registrar: Donna Townsend
Admissions: Jane Goodwin
Financial Aid: Linda Conant
Type: Comprehensive **Sex:** Coed **Scores:** 84.5% SAT V 400+; 83.5% SAT M 400+; 38% ACT 18-23 **% Accepted:** 95 **Admission Plans:** Early Admission; Early Action; Deferred Admission **Application Deadline:** September 01 **Application Fee:** $25.00 **H.S. Requirements:** High school diploma required; GED accepted **Costs Per Year:** Application fee: $25. Comprehensive fee: $17,410 includes full-time tuition ($11,130), mandatory fees ($250), and college room and board ($6030). Full-time tuition and fees vary according to class time. Part-time tuition: $371 per credit hour. Part-time tuition varies according to class time and course load. **Scholarships:** Available **Calendar System:** Semester, Summer Session Available **Enrollment:** FT 1,605, PT 372, Grad 268 **Faculty:** FT 50, PT 4 **Student-Faculty Ratio:** 19:1 **Exams:** SAT I or ACT **% Receiving Financial Aid:** 65 **% Residing in College-Owned, -Operated, or -Affiliated Housing:** 56 **Library Holdings:** 37,871 **Regional Accreditation:** New England Association of Schools and Colleges **Credit Hours For Degree:** 60 semester hours, Associates; 120 semester hours, Bachelors **ROTC:** Army, Navy **Professional Accreditation:**

AACN, AOTA, APTA, NLN **Intercollegiate Athletics:** Baseball M; Basketball M & W; Field Hockey W; Football M; Golf M & W; Soccer M & W; Softball W; Swimming and Diving W; Volleyball W

KENNEBEC VALLEY COMMUNITY COLLEGE
92 Western Ave.
Fairfield, ME 04937-1367
Tel: (207)453-5000
Admissions: (207)453-5033
Web Site: http://www.kvcc.me.edu/
President/CEO: Dr. Barbara Woodlee
Registrar: Lisa York-Lemelin
Admissions: Jim Bourgoin
Financial Aid: Ann Connors
Type: Two-Year College **Sex:** Coed **Affiliation:** Maine Community College System **% Accepted:** 71 **Admission Plans:** Open Admission; Deferred Admission **Application Deadline:** Rolling **Application Fee:** $20.00 **H.S. Requirements:** High school diploma required; GED accepted **Costs Per Year:** Application fee: $20. State resident tuition: $2220 full-time, $74 per credit part-time. Nonresident tuition: $4650 full-time, $155 per credit part-time. Mandatory fees: $600 full-time. **Scholarships:** Available **Calendar System:** Semester, Summer Session Available **Enrollment:** FT 523, PT 1,259 **Faculty:** FT 40, PT 176 **Student-Faculty Ratio:** 22:1 **Exams:** Other, SAT I or ACT **Library Holdings:** 19,629 **Regional Accreditation:** New England Association of Schools and Colleges **Credit Hours For Degree:** 61 credits, Associates **Professional Accreditation:** AHIMA, AOTA, APTA, ACBSP, CARC, NLN

MAINE COLLEGE OF ART
97 Spring St.
Portland, ME 04101-3987
Tel: (207)775-3052
Free: 800-639-4808
Admissions: (207)775-5157
Fax: (207)772-5069
E-mail: admissions@meca.edu
Web Site: http://www.meca.edu/
President/CEO: Christine J. Vincent
Registrar: Anne Dennison
Admissions: Karen Townsend
Financial Aid: Michelle A. Leclerc
Type: Comprehensive **Sex:** Coed **Scores:** 95.3% SAT V 400+; 88.6% SAT M 400+; 25% ACT 18-23; 25% ACT 24-29 **% Accepted:** 69 **Admission Plans:** Early Admission; Deferred Admission **Application Deadline:** Rolling **Application Fee:** $40.00 **H.S. Requirements:** High school diploma required; GED accepted **Costs Per Year:** Application fee: $40. Comprehensive fee: $34,590 includes full-time tuition ($24,670), mandatory fees ($650), and college room and board ($9270). **Scholarships:** Available **Calendar System:** Semester, Summer Session Not available **Enrollment:** FT 435, PT 23, Grad 32 **Faculty:** FT 32, PT 37 **Student-Faculty Ratio:** 10:1 **Exams:** SAT I or ACT **% Receiving Financial Aid:** 80 **% Residing in College-Owned, -Operated, or -Affiliated Housing:** 25 **Library Holdings:** 24,609 **Regional Accreditation:** New England Association of Schools and Colleges **Credit Hours For Degree:** 120 credits, Bachelors **Professional Accreditation:** NASAD

MAINE MARITIME ACADEMY
Castine, ME 04420
Tel: (207)326-4311
Free: 800-227-8465
Admissions: (207)326-2215
Fax: (207)326-2515
Web Site: http://www.mainemaritime.edu/
President/CEO: Leonard H. Tyler, Jr.
Registrar: Tom Sawyer
Admissions: Jeffrey C. Wright
Financial Aid: Deidra Davis
Type: Comprehensive **Sex:** Coed **% Accepted:** 67 **Admission Plans:** Early Admission; Early Decision Plan; Deferred Admission **Application Deadline:** July 01 **Application Fee:** $15.00 **H.S. Requirements:** High school diploma required; GED accepted **Costs Per Year:** Application fee: $15. State resident tuition: $6380 full-time, $230 per credit hour part-time. Nonresident tuition: $9570 full-time, $410 per credit hour part-time. Mandatory fees: $1240 full-time. Full-time tuition and fees vary according to program. Part-time tuition varies according to program. College room and board: $6720. College room only: $2420. Room and board charges vary according to board plan. **Scholarships:** Available **Calendar System:** Semester, Summer Session Not available **Enrollment:** FT 747, PT 99, Grad 15 **Faculty:** FT 50, PT 16 **Student-Faculty Ratio:** 12:1 **Exams:** SAT I or ACT **% Receiving Financial Aid:** 69 **% Residing in College-Owned, -Operated, or -Affiliated Housing:** 80 **Library Holdings:** 177,800 **Regional Accreditation:** New England Association of Schools and Colleges **Credit Hours For Degree:** 78 credit hours, Associates; 140 credit hours, Bachelors **ROTC:** Army, Navy **Professional Accreditation:** ABET **Intercollegiate Athletics:** Basketball M & W; Cross-Country Running M & W; Football M; Lacrosse M; Sailing M & W; Soccer M & W; Softball W; Volleyball W

NEW ENGLAND SCHOOL OF COMMUNICATIONS
1 College Circle
Bangor, ME 04401-2999
Tel: (207)941-7176; 888-877-1876
Fax: (207)947-3987
E-mail: grantl@nescom.edu
Web Site: http://www.nescom.edu/
President/CEO: George E. Wildey
Registrar: Kim Nason
Admissions: Louise G. Grant
Financial Aid: Nicole Rediker
Type: Four-Year College **Sex:** Coed **% Accepted:** 69 **Admission Plans:** Open Admission; Early Admission; Deferred Admission **Application Deadline:** Rolling **Application Fee:** $15.00 **H.S. Requirements:** High school diploma required; GED accepted **Costs Per Year:** Application fee: $15. Comprehensive fee: $15,620 includes full-time tuition ($8890), mandatory fees ($700), and college room and board ($6030). Part-time tuition: $275 per credit. **Scholarships:** Available **Calendar System:** Semester, Summer Session Available **Enrollment:** FT 295, PT 10 **Faculty:** FT 7, PT 30 **Student-Faculty Ratio:** 18:1 **Exams:** Other, SAT I or ACT **% Receiving Financial Aid:** 80 **% Residing in College-Owned, -Operated, or -Affiliated Housing:** 54 **Credit Hours For Degree:** 60 credits, Associates; 120 credits, Bachelors **Professional Accreditation:** ACCSCT

NORTHERN MAINE COMMUNITY COLLEGE
33 Edgemont Dr.
Presque Isle, ME 04769-2016
Tel: (207)768-2700
Admissions: (207)768-2786
Fax: (207)768-2831
E-mail: ncasavant@nmcc.edu
Web Site: http://www.nmcc.edu/
President/CEO: Timothy Crowley
Registrar: Betsy Harris
Admissions: William G. Casavant
Type: Two-Year College **Sex:** Coed **Affiliation:** Maine Technical College System **% Accepted:** 52 **Admission Plans:** Open Admission; Early Admission **Application Deadline:** Rolling **Application Fee:** $20.00 **H.S. Requirements:** High school diploma required; GED accepted **Costs Per Year:** Application fee: $20. Area resident tuition: $2390 full-time, $78 per credit hour part-time. State resident tuition: $115 per credit hour part-time. Nonresident tuition: $4770 full-time, $159 per credit hour part-time. College room and board: $4930. **Scholarships:** Available **Calendar System:** Semester, Summer Session Available **Enrollment:** FT 605, PT 316 **Faculty:** FT 44, PT 43 **Exams:** Other **% Residing in College-Owned, -Operated, or -Affiliated Housing:** 28 **Library Holdings:** 11,200 **Regional Accreditation:** New England Association of Schools and Colleges **Credit Hours For Degree:** 64 credit hours, Associates **Professional Accreditation:** ACBSP, NLN **Intercollegiate Athletics:** Basketball M & W; Cross-Country Running M & W; Golf M & W; Ice Hockey M & W; Soccer M & W

SAINT JOSEPH'S COLLEGE OF MAINE
278 Whites Bridge Rd.
Standish, ME 04084-5263
Tel: (207)892-6766
Free: 800-338-7057
Admissions: (207)893-7746
Fax: (207)893-7862
E-mail: vkloskow@sjcme.edu
Web Site: http://www.sjcme.edu/
President/CEO: Dr. David House
Admissions: Vincent J. Kloskowski

Financial Aid: Andrea Cross
Type: Comprehensive **Sex:** Coed **Affiliation:** Roman Catholic Church **Scores:** 96% SAT V 400+; 97% SAT M 400+; 50% ACT 18-23; 6% ACT 24-29 **% Accepted:** 77 **Admission Plans:** Early Action; Deferred Admission **Application Deadline:** Rolling **Application Fee:** $40.00 **H.S. Requirements:** High school diploma required; GED accepted **Costs Per Year:** Application fee: $40. Comprehensive fee: $29,185 includes full-time tuition ($19,890), mandatory fees ($715), and college room and board ($8580). Full-time tuition and fees vary according to program. Part-time tuition: $350 per credit. Part-time mandatory fees: $125 per year. Part-time tuition and fees vary according to course load and program. **Scholarships:** Available **Calendar System:** Semester, Summer Session Available **Enrollment:** FT 925, PT 30 **Faculty:** FT 64, PT 44 **Student-Faculty Ratio:** 15:1 **Exams:** SAT I or ACT **% Receiving Financial Aid:** 81 **% Residing in College-Owned, -Operated, or -Affiliated Housing:** 83 **Library Holdings:** 98,626 **Regional Accreditation:** New England Association of Schools and Colleges **Credit Hours For Degree:** 128 credit hours, Bachelors **ROTC:** Army **Professional Accreditation:** AACN **Intercollegiate Athletics:** Baseball M; Basketball M & W; Cheerleading M & W; Cross-Country Running M & W; Field Hockey W; Golf M; Ice Hockey M & W; Soccer M & W; Softball W; Volleyball W

SOUTHERN MAINE COMMUNITY COLLEGE
2 Fort Rd.
South Portland, ME 04106
Tel: (207)741-5500
Admissions: (207)741-5664
Fax: (207)741-5751
Web Site: http://www.smccme.edu/
President/CEO: Dr. James O. Ortiz
Registrar: Lisa Dolan
Admissions: David Tracy
Financial Aid: Scott MacDonald
Type: Two-Year College **Sex:** Coed **Affiliation:** Maine Community College System **Admission Plans:** Preferred Admission **Application Fee:** $20.00 **H.S. Requirements:** High school diploma required; GED accepted **Costs Per Year:** Application fee: $20. State resident tuition: $2220 full-time. Nonresident tuition: $4650 full-time. College room and board: $5824. College room only: $2678. **Scholarships:** Available **Calendar System:** Semester, Summer Session Available **Enrollment:** FT 2,135, PT 1,968 **Faculty:** FT 89, PT 170 **Student-Faculty Ratio:** 18:1 **Exams:** Other, SAT I **% Residing in College-Owned, -Operated, or -Affiliated Housing:** 10 **Library Holdings:** 15,000 **Regional Accreditation:** New England Association of Schools and Colleges **Credit Hours For Degree:** 60 credit hours, Associates **Professional Accreditation:** CARC, JRCERT, NLN **Intercollegiate Athletics:** Baseball M; Basketball M; Golf M & W; Soccer M & W; Softball W; Volleyball M & W

THOMAS COLLEGE
180 West River Rd.
Waterville, ME 04901-5097
Tel: (207)859-1111
Free: 800-339-7001
Admissions: (207)859-1101
Fax: (207)859-1114
E-mail: admiss@thomas.edu
Web Site: http://www.thomas.edu/
President/CEO: Dr. George R. Spann
Registrar: Valerie Sirois
Admissions: Wendy Martin
Financial Aid: Angela Dostie
Type: Comprehensive **Sex:** Coed **Scores:** 80% SAT V 400+; 83% SAT M 400+; 12.5% ACT 18-23; 12.5% ACT 24-29 **% Accepted:** 73 **Admission Plans:** Early Action; Deferred Admission **Application Deadline:** Rolling **Application Fee:** $50.00 **H.S. Requirements:** High school diploma required; GED accepted **Costs Per Year:** Application fee: $50. Comprehensive fee: $25,160 includes full-time tuition ($17,280), mandatory fees ($450), and college room and board ($7430). Part-time tuition: $720 per credit hour. **Scholarships:** Available **Calendar System:** Semester, Summer Session Available **Enrollment:** FT 598, PT 133, Grad 144 **Faculty:** FT 23, PT 55 **Student-Faculty Ratio:** 17:1 **Exams:** SAT I or ACT **% Receiving Financial Aid:** 90 **% Residing in College-Owned, -Operated, or -Affiliated Housing:** 65 **Library Holdings:** 20,000 **Regional Accreditation:** New England Association of Schools and Colleges **Credit Hours For Degree:** 60 credits, Associates; 120 credits, Bachelors **Intercollegiate Athletics:** Baseball M; Basketball M & W; Field Hockey W; Golf M; Lacrosse M & W; Soccer M & W; Softball W; Tennis M; Volleyball W

UNITY COLLEGE
90 Quaker Hill Rd.
Unity, ME 04988
Tel: (207)948-3131
Fax: (207)948-6277
Web Site: http://www.unity.edu/
President/CEO: Dr. David C. Glenn-Lewin
Registrar: Holly Hein
Admissions: Kay Fiedler
Financial Aid: Rand Newell
Type: Four-Year College **Sex:** Coed **Scores:** 88% SAT V 400+; 85.95% SAT M 400+ **Admission Plans:** Early Admission; Early Action; Deferred Admission **Application Fee:** $25.00 **H.S. Requirements:** High school diploma required; GED accepted **Costs Per Year:** Application fee: $25. Comprehensive fee: $24,310 includes full-time tuition ($16,740), mandatory fees ($940), and college room and board ($6630). Room and board charges vary according to board plan. Part-time tuition: $630 per credit hour. Part-time tuition varies according to course load. **Scholarships:** Available **Calendar System:** Semester, Summer Session Available **Enrollment:** FT 515, PT 6 **Faculty:** FT 32, PT 10 **Student-Faculty Ratio:** 13:1 **Exams:** SAT I or ACT **% Receiving Financial Aid:** 71 **% Residing in College-Owned, -Operated, or -Affiliated Housing:** 66 **Library Holdings:** 46,000 **Regional Accreditation:** New England Association of Schools and Colleges **Credit Hours For Degree:** 120 semester hours, Bachelors **ROTC:** Army **Intercollegiate Athletics:** Basketball M; Cross-Country Running M & W; Soccer M; Volleyball W

UNIVERSITY OF MAINE
Orono, ME 04469
Tel: (207)581-1110; 877-486-2364
Admissions: (207)581-1561
Fax: (207)581-1213
E-mail: um-admit@maine.edu
Web Site: http://www.umaine.edu/
President/CEO: Dr. Peter Hoff
Registrar: Peter Reid
Admissions: Sharon Oliver
Financial Aid: Peggy L. Crawford
Type: University **Sex:** Coed **Affiliation:** University of Maine System **Scores:** 99% SAT V 400+; 98% SAT M 400+; 43% ACT 18-23; 37% ACT 24-29 **% Accepted:** 80 **Admission Plans:** Early Admission; Deferred Admission **Application Deadline:** Rolling **Application Fee:** $40.00 **H.S. Requirements:** High school diploma required; GED accepted **Costs Per Year:** Application fee: $40. State resident tuition: $5520 full-time, $184 per credit hour part-time. Nonresident tuition: $15,660 full-time, $522 per credit hour part-time. Mandatory fees: $1390 full-time. Full-time tuition and fees vary according to reciprocity agreements. Part-time tuition varies according to reciprocity agreements. College room and board: $6732. College room only: $3390. Room and board charges vary according to board plan and housing facility. **Scholarships:** Available **Calendar System:** Semester, Summer Session Available **Enrollment:** FT 7,617, PT 1,562, Grad 2,256 **Faculty:** FT 496, PT 327 **Student-Faculty Ratio:** 16:1 **Exams:** SAT I or ACT **% Receiving Financial Aid:** 71 **% Residing in College-Owned, -Operated, or -Affiliated Housing:** 30 **Library Holdings:** 1,034,248 **Regional Accreditation:** New England Association of Schools and Colleges **Credit Hours For Degree:** 120 credit hours, Bachelors **ROTC:** Army, Navy **Professional Accreditation:** AACSB, ABET, AACN, ADtA, AHIMA, APA, ASLHA, AALS, CSWE, NASM, NASPAA, NCATE, SAF **Intercollegiate Athletics:** Baseball M; Basketball M & W; Cross-Country Running M & W; Field Hockey W; Football M; Ice Hockey M & W; Soccer M & W; Softball W; Swimming and Diving M & W; Track and Field M & W; Volleyball W

THE UNIVERSITY OF MAINE AT AUGUSTA
46 University Dr.
Augusta, ME 04330-9410
Tel: (207)621-3000
Admissions: (207)621-3390
Fax: (207)621-3116
E-mail: umaar@maine.edu
Web Site: http://www.uma.maine.edu/
President/CEO: Dr. Charles M. Lyons

Registrar: Ann Corbett
Admissions: Sheri Cranston Fraser
Financial Aid: Lisa Bongiovanni
Type: Four-Year College **Sex:** Coed **Affiliation:** University of Maine System **% Accepted:** 52 **Admission Plans:** Early Admission; Deferred Admission **Application Deadline:** August 31 **Application Fee:** $40.00 **H.S. Requirements:** High school diploma required; GED accepted **Costs Per Year:** Application fee: $40. State resident tuition: $4290 full-time, $143 per credit hour part-time. Nonresident tuition: $10,380 full-time, $346 per credit hour part-time. Mandatory fees: $735 full-time, $24.50 per credit hour part-time. Full-time tuition and fees vary according to reciprocity agreements. Part-time tuition and fees vary according to reciprocity agreements. **Scholarships:** Available **Calendar System:** Semester, Summer Session Available **Enrollment:** FT 1,544, PT 3,950 **Faculty:** FT 95, PT 229 **Student-Faculty Ratio:** 19:1 **% Receiving Financial Aid:** 89 **Library Holdings:** 83,766 **Regional Accreditation:** New England Association of Schools and Colleges **Credit Hours For Degree:** 60 credits, Associates; 120 credits, Bachelors **Professional Accreditation:** ADA, NAACLS, NLN **Intercollegiate Athletics:** Basketball M & W; Soccer W

UNIVERSITY OF MAINE AT FARMINGTON

224 Main St.
Farmington, ME 04938-1990
Tel: (207)778-7000
Admissions: (207)778-7087
Fax: (207)778-8182
E-mail: umfadmit@maine.edu
Web Site: http://www.umf.maine.edu/
President/CEO: Dr. Theodora J. Kalikow
Registrar: Hazel Doak
Admissions: Dr. William W. Geller
Financial Aid: Ronald Milliken
Type: Four-Year College **Sex:** Coed **Affiliation:** University of Maine System **Scores:** 91% SAT V 400+; 90% SAT M 400+ **% Accepted:** 74 **Admission Plans:** Early Admission; Early Action; Deferred Admission **Application Deadline:** Rolling **Application Fee:** $40.00 **H.S. Requirements:** High school diploma required; GED accepted **Costs Per Year:** Application fee: $40. State resident tuition: $5010 full-time, $167 per credit hour part-time. Nonresident tuition: $12,240 full-time, $408 per credit hour part-time. Mandatory fees: $621 full-time, $75 per term part-time. Full-time tuition and fees vary according to course load, reciprocity agreements, and student level. Part-time tuition and fees vary according to course load, reciprocity agreements, and student level. College room and board: $5984. College room only: $3200. Room and board charges vary according to board plan and housing facility. **Scholarships:** Available **Calendar System:** Semester, Summer Session Available **Enrollment:** FT 2,123, PT 329 **Faculty:** FT 118, PT 57 **Student-Faculty Ratio:** 16:1 **Exams:** SAT I or ACT **% Receiving Financial Aid:** 67 **% Residing in College-Owned, -Operated, or -Affiliated Housing:** 44 **Library Holdings:** 98,248 **Regional Accreditation:** New England Association of Schools and Colleges **Credit Hours For Degree:** 120 credit hours, Bachelors **Professional Accreditation:** NCATE **Intercollegiate Athletics:** Baseball M; Basketball M & W; Cross-Country Running M & W; Field Hockey W; Golf M & W; Ice Hockey M; Lacrosse M; Soccer M & W; Softball W; Volleyball W

UNIVERSITY OF MAINE AT FORT KENT

23 University Dr.
Fort Kent, ME 04743-1292
Tel: (207)834-7500; 888-TRY-UMFK
Admissions: (207)834-7600
Fax: (207)834-7609
E-mail: dbarley@maine.edu
Web Site: http://www.umfk.maine.edu/
President/CEO: Dr. Richard Cost
Registrar: Donald M. Raymond
Admissions: Douglas Barley
Financial Aid: Lisa Lipe
Type: Four-Year College **Sex:** Coed **Affiliation:** University of Maine System **Scores:** 72% SAT V 400+; 74% SAT M 400+ **Admission Plans:** Early Admission; Early Decision Plan; Deferred Admission **Application Fee:** $40.00 **H.S. Requirements:** High school diploma required; GED accepted **Scholarships:** Available **Calendar System:** Semester, Summer Session Available **Enrollment:** FT 786, PT 290 **Faculty:** FT 35, PT 37 **Student-Faculty Ratio:** 25:1 **Exams:** SAT I and SAT II or ACT, SAT I **% Receiving Financial Aid:** 44 **% Residing in College-Owned, -Operated, or -Affiliated Housing:** 30 **Library Holdings:** 69,189 **Regional Accreditation:** New England Association of Schools and Colleges **Credit Hours For Degree:** 60 credit hours, Associates; 120 credit hours, Bachelors **Professional Accreditation:** AACN, NLN **Intercollegiate Athletics:** Basketball M & W; Cross-Country Running M & W; Golf M & W; Skiing (Cross-Country) M & W; Skiing (Downhill) M & W; Soccer M & W

UNIVERSITY OF MAINE AT MACHIAS

9 O'Brien Ave.
Machias, ME 04654-1321
Tel: (207)255-1200; 888-GOTOUMM
Admissions: (207)255-1318
Fax: (207)255-1363
E-mail: ummadmissions@maine.edu
Web Site: http://www.umm.maine.edu/
President/CEO: Dr. Sue Ann Huseman
Registrar: Mary Stover
Admissions: Stewart Bennett
Financial Aid: Stephanie D. Larrabee
Type: Four-Year College **Sex:** Coed **Affiliation:** University of Maine System **Scores:** 90.7% SAT V 400+; 77.9% SAT M 400+; 35.7% ACT 18-23; 35.7% ACT 24-29 **% Accepted:** 83 **Admission Plans:** Early Admission; Early Action; Deferred Admission **Application Deadline:** August 15 **Application Fee:** $40.00 **H.S. Requirements:** High school diploma required; GED accepted **Costs Per Year:** Application fee: $40. State resident tuition: $4290 full-time, $143 per credit hour part-time. Nonresident tuition: $11,640 full-time, $388 per credit hour part-time. Mandatory fees: $555 full-time, $17.50 per credit hour part-time, $45 per term part-time. College room and board: $5678. College room only: $2858. Room and board charges vary according to housing facility. **Scholarships:** Available **Calendar System:** Semester, Summer Session Available **Enrollment:** FT 462, PT 687 **Faculty:** FT 30, PT 58 **Student-Faculty Ratio:** 14:1 **Exams:** SAT I or ACT **% Receiving Financial Aid:** 77 **% Residing in College-Owned, -Operated, or -Affiliated Housing:** 42 **Library Holdings:** 82,664 **Regional Accreditation:** New England Association of Schools and Colleges **Credit Hours For Degree:** 60 credits, Associates; 120 credits, Bachelors **Professional Accreditation:** NRPA **Intercollegiate Athletics:** Basketball M & W; Cross-Country Running M & W; Lacrosse M & W; Soccer M & W; Volleyball W

UNIVERSITY OF MAINE AT PRESQUE ISLE

181 Main St.
Presque Isle, ME 04769-2888
Tel: (207)768-9400
Admissions: (207)768-9453
Fax: (207)768-9608
E-mail: benson@umpi.maine.edu
Web Site: http://www.umpi.maine.edu/
President/CEO: Dr. William A. Shields
Registrar: Sharon E. Roix
Admissions: Erin V. Benson
Financial Aid: Barbara J. Bridges
Type: Four-Year College **Sex:** Coed **Affiliation:** University of Maine System **Scores:** 73% SAT V 400+; 74% SAT M 400+ **% Accepted:** 87 **Admission Plans:** Early Admission; Early Action; Deferred Admission **Application Deadline:** Rolling **Application Fee:** $40.00 **H.S. Requirements:** High school diploma required; GED accepted **Costs Per Year:** Application fee: $40. State resident tuition: $4290 full-time, $143 per credit hour part-time. Nonresident tuition: $10,680 full-time, $356 per credit hour part-time. Mandatory fees: $530 full-time, $19 per credit hour part-time. Full-time tuition and fees vary according to course load and reciprocity agreements. Part-time tuition and fees vary according to course load and reciprocity agreements. College room and board: $5246. College room only: $3000. Room and board charges vary according to board plan. **Scholarships:** Available **Calendar System:** Semester, Summer Session Available **Enrollment:** FT 1,112, PT 436 **Faculty:** FT 54, PT 62 **Student-Faculty Ratio:** 16:1 **% Receiving Financial Aid:** 57 **% Residing in College-Owned, -Operated, or -Affiliated Housing:** 28 **Library Holdings:** 455,372 **Regional Accreditation:** New England Association of Schools and Colleges **Credit Hours For Degree:** 61 credit hours, Associates; 120 credit hours, Bachelors **Professional Accreditation:** CSWE, NAACLS, NRPA **Intercollegiate Athletics:** Baseball M; Basketball M & W; Cross-Country Running M & W; Golf M; Soccer M & W; Softball W; Volleyball W

UNIVERSITY OF NEW ENGLAND

Hills Beach Rd.
Biddeford, ME 04005-9526

Tel: (207)283-0171
Free: 800-477-4UNE
Admissions: (207)283-0170
E-mail: admissions@une.edu
Web Site: http://www.une.edu/
President/CEO: Dr. Sandra Featherman
Registrar: Mark Osborn
Admissions: Alan Liebrecht
Financial Aid: John Bowie

Type: Comprehensive **Sex:** Coed **Scores:** 97% SAT V 400+; 97% SAT M 400+ **% Accepted:** 92 **Admission Plans:** Deferred Admission **Application Deadline:** Rolling **Application Fee:** $40.00 **H.S. Requirements:** High school diploma required; GED accepted **Costs Per Year:** Application fee: $40. Comprehensive fee: $31,005 includes full-time tuition ($21,540), mandatory fees ($735), and college room and board ($8730). Room and board charges vary according to housing facility. Part-time tuition: $775 per credit. **Scholarships:** Available **Calendar System:** Semester, Summer Session Available **Enrollment:** FT 1,519, PT 217, Grad 1,077 **Faculty:** FT 137, PT 104 **Student-Faculty Ratio:** 11:1 **Exams:** Other **% Receiving Financial Aid:** 83 **% Residing in College-Owned, -Operated, or -Affiliated Housing:** 60 **Library Holdings:** 142,181 **Regional Accreditation:** New England Association of Schools and Colleges **Credit Hours For Degree:** 68 credits, Associates; 120 credits, Bachelors **ROTC:** Army **Professional Accreditation:** AANA, ADA, AOTA, AOsA, APTA, CSWE, NLN **Intercollegiate Athletics:** Basketball M & W; Cross-Country Running M & W; Field Hockey W; Golf M; Lacrosse M & W; Soccer M & W; Softball W; Swimming and Diving W; Volleyball W

UNIVERSITY OF SOUTHERN MAINE

96 Falmouth St., PO Box 9300
Portland, ME 04104-9300
Tel: (207)780-4141
Free: 800-800-4USM
Admissions: (207)780-5670
Fax: (207)780-5640
E-mail: usmadm@usm.maine.edu
Web Site: http://www.usm.maine.edu/
President/CEO: Dr. Richard L. Pattenaude
Registrar: Steven Rand
Admissions: Dee Gardner
Financial Aid: Keith DuBois

Type: Comprehensive **Sex:** Coed **Affiliation:** University of Maine System **Scores:** 92% SAT V 400+; 95% SAT M 400+; 55% ACT 18-23; 21% ACT 24-29 **% Accepted:** 79 **Admission Plans:** Early Admission; Deferred Admission **Application Deadline:** February 15 **Application Fee:** $40.00 **H.S. Requirements:** High school diploma required; GED accepted **Costs Per Year:** Application fee: $40. State resident tuition: $4980 full-time, $166 per credit hour part-time. Nonresident tuition: $13,800 full-time, $460 per credit hour part-time. Mandatory fees: $926 full-time. Full-time tuition and fees vary according to course load, degree level, and reciprocity agreements. Part-time tuition varies according to course load, degree level, and reciprocity agreements. College room and board: $6755. College room only: $3586. Room and board charges vary according to board plan, housing facility, and location. **Scholarships:** Available **Calendar System:** Semester, Summer Session Available **Enrollment:** FT 4,788, PT 3,834, Grad 2,063 **Faculty:** FT 402, PT 302 **Student-Faculty Ratio:** 13:1 **Exams:** SAT I or ACT **% Receiving Financial Aid:** 65 **% Residing in College-Owned, -Operated, or -Affiliated Housing:** 40 **Library Holdings:** 545,246 **Regional Accreditation:** New England Association of Schools and Colleges **Credit Hours For Degree:** 60 credit hours, Associates; 120 credit hours, Bachelors **ROTC:** Army, Air Force **Professional Accreditation:** AACSB, ABET, ACEHSA, ABA, ACA, AOTA, CORE, CSWE, JRCEPAT, NAIT, NASAD, NASM, NASPAA, NCATE, NLN **Intercollegiate Athletics:** Baseball M; Basketball M & W; Cheerleading M & W; Cross-Country Running M & W; Field Hockey W; Golf M & W; Ice Hockey M & W; Lacrosse M & W; Sailing M & W; Soccer M & W; Softball W; Tennis M & W; Track and Field M & W; Volleyball W; Wrestling M

WASHINGTON COUNTY COMMUNITY COLLEGE

RR No. 1, Box 22C River Rd.
Calais, ME 04619
Tel: (207)454-1000
Fax: (207)454-1026
Web Site: http://www.wccc.me.edu/
President/CEO: Dr. William Flahive
Registrar: Cindy Thompson
Admissions: Kent Lyons
Financial Aid: Joyce Maker

Type: Two-Year College **Sex:** Coed **Affiliation:** Maine Technical College System **Admission Plans:** Open Admission; Deferred Admission **Application Fee:** $20.00 **H.S. Requirements:** High school diploma required; GED accepted **Scholarships:** Available **Calendar System:** Semester **Faculty:** FT 29, PT 10 **Student-Faculty Ratio:** 9:1 **Exams:** Other **% Residing in College-Owned, -Operated, or -Affiliated Housing:** 22 **Library Holdings:** 26,370 **Regional Accreditation:** New England Association of Schools and Colleges **Credit Hours For Degree:** 64 credits, Associates

YORK COUNTY COMMUNITY COLLEGE

112 College Dr.
Wells, ME 04090
Tel: (207)646-9282
Free: 800-580-3820
Fax: (207)641-0837
E-mail: admissions@yctc.net
Web Site: http://www.yccc.edu/
President/CEO: Dr. Patricia Ryan
Registrar: Doreen Rogan
Admissions: Leisa Collins
Financial Aid: David Daigle

Type: Two-Year College **Sex:** Coed **Affiliation:** Maine Technical College System **Admission Plans:** Open Admission **Application Fee:** $20.00 **H.S. Requirements:** High school diploma required; GED accepted **Scholarships:** Available **Calendar System:** Semester, Summer Session Available **Faculty:** FT 7, PT 60 **Student-Faculty Ratio:** 13:1 **Exams:** SAT I **Library Holdings:** 4,000 **Regional Accreditation:** New England Association of Schools and Colleges **Credit Hours For Degree:** 63 credit hours, Associates

ALLEGANY COLLEGE OF MARYLAND
12401 Willowbrook Rd., SE
Cumberland, MD 21502-2596
Tel: (301)784-5000
Fax: (301)784-5024
E-mail: cnolan@allegany.edu
Web Site: http://www.allegany.edu/
President/CEO: Dr. Donald L. Alexander
Registrar: Gloria Brooks-Broadwater
Admissions: Cathy Nolan
Financial Aid: Cindy Harbel
Type: Two-Year College **Sex:** Coed **Affiliation:** Maryland State Community Colleges System **Scores:** 68% SAT V 400+; 65% SAT M 400+; 62% ACT 18-23; 6% ACT 24-29 **% Accepted:** 100 **Admission Plans:** Open Admission; Early Admission **Application Deadline:** Rolling **Application Fee:** $0.00 **H.S. Requirements:** High school diploma required; GED accepted. For Dislocated Workers Program: High school diploma or equivalent not required **Costs Per Year:** Application fee: $0. Area resident tuition: $2700 full-time, $90 per credit part-time. State resident tuition: $5160 full-time, $172 per credit part-time. Nonresident tuition: $6060 full-time, $202 per credit part-time. Mandatory fees: $194 full-time, $8.30 per credit part-time, $41 per term part-time. Full-time tuition and fees vary according to course load and location. Part-time tuition and fees vary according to course load and location. **Scholarships:** Available **Calendar System:** Semester, Summer Session Available **Enrollment:** FT 2,073, PT 1,593 **Faculty:** FT 111, PT 119 **Student-Faculty Ratio:** 17:1 **Exams:** ACT **Library Holdings:** 86,636 **Regional Accreditation:** Middle State Association of Colleges and Schools **Credit Hours For Degree:** 60 credits, Associates **ROTC:** Army **Professional Accreditation:** ADA, AOTA, APTA, CARC, JRCERT, NAACLS, NLN **Intercollegiate Athletics:** Baseball M; Basketball M & W; Soccer M & W; Softball W; Tennis M & W; Volleyball W

ANNE ARUNDEL COMMUNITY COLLEGE
101 College Parkway
Arnold, MD 21012-1895
Tel: (410)647-7100
Admissions: (410)777-2240
Fax: (410)541-2245
Web Site: http://www.aacc.edu/
President/CEO: Dr. Martha A. Smith
Registrar: Judith A. Coughlin
Admissions: Thomas McGinn
Financial Aid: Richard Heath
Type: Two-Year College **Sex:** Coed **Admission Plans:** Open Admission; Early Admission; Deferred Admission **Application Fee:** $0.00 **H.S. Requirements:** High school diploma or equivalent not required. For except for certain allied health programs: High school diploma required; GED accepted **Costs Per Year:** Application fee: $0. Area resident tuition: $1992 full-time, $83 per credit hour part-time. State resident tuition: $3816 full-time, $159 per credit hour part-time. Nonresident tuition: $6768 full-time, $282 per credit hour part-time. Mandatory fees: $232 full-time, $8 per credit hour part-time, $20 per term part-time. Full-time tuition and fees vary according to course load. Part-time tuition and fees vary according to course load. **Scholarships:** Available **Calendar System:** Semester, Summer Session Available **Enrollment:** FT 4,780, PT 9,510 **Faculty:** FT 236, PT 591 **Student-Faculty Ratio:** 18:1 **Exams:** SAT I or ACT **Library Holdings:** 144,694 **Regional Accreditation:** Middle State Association of Colleges and Schools **Credit Hours For Degree:** 60 credit hours, Associates **ROTC:** Army, Air Force **Professional Accreditation:** ACF, APTA, JRCERT, NLN **Intercollegiate Athletics:** Baseball M; Basketball M & W; Cross-Country Running M & W; Golf M; Lacrosse M; Soccer M & W; Softball W; Volleyball W

BALTIMORE CITY COMMUNITY COLLEGE
2901 Liberty Heights Ave.
Baltimore, MD 21215-7893
Tel: (410)462-8300
Fax: (410)462-7677
Web Site: http://www.bccc.state.md.us/
Registrar: Kathy Styles
Admissions: Scheherazade Forman
Financial Aid: Ronald H. Smith
Type: Two-Year College **Sex:** Coed **Admission Plans:** Open Admission; Early Admission; Deferred Admission **Application Fee:** $10.00 **H.S. Requirements:** High school diploma required; GED accepted **Scholarships:** Available **Calendar System:** Semester, Summer Session Available **Faculty:** FT 121, PT 315 **Student-Faculty Ratio:** 17:1 **Exams:** SAT I and SAT II or ACT, SAT II **Library Holdings:** 72,413 **Regional Accreditation:** Middle State Association of Colleges and Schools **Credit Hours For Degree:** 62 credits, Associates **Professional Accreditation:** ARCEST, ADA, AHIMA, APTA, ACBSP, CARC, NLN **Intercollegiate Athletics:** Basketball M & W; Cross-Country Running M & W; Track and Field M & W

BALTIMORE HEBREW UNIVERSITY
5800 Park Heights Ave.
Baltimore, MD 21215-3996
Tel: (410)578-6900; 888-248-7420
Admissions: (410)578-6967
Fax: (410)578-6940
E-mail: bhu@bhu.edu
Web Site: http://www.bhu.edu/
President/CEO: Diane Kempler
Registrar: Zelda Rachbach
Admissions: Essie Keyser
Financial Aid: Yelena Feldman
Type: Comprehensive **Sex:** Coed **Admission Plans:** Early Admission; Deferred Admission **Application Fee:** $20.00 **H.S. Requirements:** High school diploma required; GED accepted **Scholarships:** Available **Calendar System:** Semester, Summer Session Available **Enrollment:** FT 43, PT 53, Grad 65 **Faculty:** FT 10, PT 20 **Student-Faculty Ratio:** 4:1 **% Receiving Financial Aid:** 93 **Library Holdings:** 70,000 **Regional Accreditation:** Middle State Association of Colleges and Schools **Credit Hours For Degree:** 60 credits, Associates; 120 credits, Bachelors

BALTIMORE INTERNATIONAL COLLEGE
Commerce Exchange
17 Commerce St.
Baltimore, MD 21202-3230
Tel: (410)752-4710
Free: 800-624-9926
Fax: (410)752-3730
Web Site: http://www.bic.edu/
President/CEO: Dr. Roger Chylinski

Registrar: Elizabeth Rogers
Admissions: Marti Hackett
Financial Aid: Lesley Otterbein
Type: Two-Year College **Sex:** Coed **Admission Plans:** Early Action; Deferred Admission **Application Deadline:** Rolling **Application Fee:** $35.00 **H.S. Requirements:** High school diploma required; GED accepted **Costs Per Year:** Application fee: $35. Comprehensive fee: $20,313 includes full-time tuition ($14,751), mandatory fees ($107), and college room and board ($5455). College room only: $3255. Room and board charges vary according to housing facility. **Scholarships:** Available **Calendar System:** Semester, Summer Session Not available **Enrollment:** FT 486, PT 30 **Faculty:** FT 14, PT 18 **Exams:** Other, SAT I or ACT **% Residing in College-Owned, -Operated, or -Affiliated Housing:** 24 **Library Holdings:** 13,000 **Regional Accreditation:** Middle State Association of Colleges and Schools **Credit Hours For Degree:** 60 credits, Associates; 120 credits, Bachelors

BOWIE STATE UNIVERSITY
14000 Jericho Park Rd.
Bowie, MD 20715-9465
Tel: (301)860-4000; 877-772-6943
Admissions: (301)860-3427
Fax: (301)860-3510
E-mail: dkiah@bowiestate.edu
Web Site: http://www.bowiestate.edu/
President/CEO: Dr. Calvin W. Lowe
Registrar: Carlene Wilson
Admissions: Don Kiah
Financial Aid: Veronica Pickett
Type: Comprehensive **Sex:** Coed **Affiliation:** University System of Maryland **Scores:** 81% SAT V 400+; 78% SAT M 400+ **Admission Plans:** Preferred Admission **Application Fee:** $40.00 **H.S. Requirements:** High school diploma required; GED accepted **Costs Per Year:** Application fee: $40. State resident tuition: $5096 full-time. Nonresident tuition: $13,088 full-time. Mandatory fees: $1750 full-time. College room and board: $5219. College room only: $3859. Room and board charges vary according to board plan and housing facility. **Scholarships:** Available **Calendar System:** Semester, Summer Session Available **Enrollment:** FT 3,216, PT 811, Grad 1,388 **Faculty:** FT 191, PT 160 **Student-Faculty Ratio:** 20:1 **Exams:** SAT I or ACT **% Receiving Financial Aid:** 55 **% Residing in College-Owned, -Operated, or -Affiliated Housing:** 33 **Library Holdings:** 331,640 **Regional Accreditation:** Middle State Association of Colleges and Schools **Credit Hours For Degree:** 120 credits, Bachelors **ROTC:** Army **Professional Accreditation:** ABET, ACBSP, CSWE, NCATE, NLN **Intercollegiate Athletics:** Basketball M & W; Bowling W; Cross-Country Running M & W; Football M; Softball W; Tennis W; Track and Field M & W; Volleyball W

CAPITOL COLLEGE
11301 Springfield Rd.
Laurel, MD 20708-9759
Tel: (301)369-2800
Free: 800-950-1992
Admissions: (301)953-3200
E-mail: admissions@capitol-college.edu
Web Site: http://www.capitol-college.edu/
President/CEO: Dr. Michael T. Wood
Registrar: Sallie McKevitt
Admissions: Darnell Edwards
Financial Aid: Suzanne Thompson
Type: Comprehensive **Sex:** Coed **Scores:** 81% SAT V 400+; 88% SAT M 400+ **Admission Plans:** Deferred Admission **Application Fee:** $25.00 **H.S. Requirements:** High school diploma required; GED accepted **Costs Per Year:** Application fee: $25. Tuition: $17,688 full-time. College room only: $3869. Room charges vary according to housing facility. **Scholarships:** Available **Calendar System:** Semester, Summer Session Available **Enrollment:** FT 319, PT 311, Grad 171 **Faculty:** FT 15, PT 39 **Student-Faculty Ratio:** 12:1 **Exams:** SAT I or ACT **% Receiving Financial Aid:** 76 **% Residing in College-Owned, -Operated, or -Affiliated Housing:** 17 **Library Holdings:** 10,000 **Regional Accreditation:** Middle State Association of Colleges and Schools **Credit Hours For Degree:** 62 semester hours, Associates; 122 semester hours, Bachelors **ROTC:** Army **Professional Accreditation:** ABET

CARROLL COMMUNITY COLLEGE
1601 Washington Rd.
Westminster, MD 21157
Tel: (410)386-8000
Admissions: (410)386-8430
Fax: (410)876-8855
E-mail: cedwards@carrollcc.edu
Web Site: http://www.carrollcc.edu/
President/CEO: Dr. Faye Pappalardo
Registrar: Robert Koermer
Admissions: Candace Edwards
Financial Aid: Robert Koermer
Type: Two-Year College **Sex:** Coed **Affiliation:** Maryland Higher Education Commission **% Accepted:** 100 **Admission Plans:** Open Admission; Early Admission **Application Deadline:** Rolling **Application Fee:** $0.00 **H.S. Requirements:** High school diploma or equivalent not required **Costs Per Year:** Application fee: $0. Area resident tuition: $3234 full-time, $92 per credit part-time. State resident tuition: $4476 full-time, $128 per credit part-time. Nonresident tuition: $6788 full-time, $195 per credit part-time. **Scholarships:** Available **Calendar System:** Semester, Summer Session Available **Enrollment:** FT 1,327, PT 1,788 **Faculty:** FT 60, PT 150 **Student-Faculty Ratio:** 17:1 **Library Holdings:** 39,187 **Regional Accreditation:** Middle State Association of Colleges and Schools **Credit Hours For Degree:** 62 credits, Associates **Professional Accreditation:** APTA

CECIL COMMUNITY COLLEGE
One Seahawk Dr.
North East, MD 21901-1999
Tel: (410)287-6060
Admissions: (410)287-1002
Fax: (410)287-1026
E-mail: dlane@cecilcc.edu
Web Site: http://www.cecilcc.edu/
President/CEO: Dr. Stephen Pannill
Registrar: Sandra Rajaski
Admissions: Dr. Diane Lane
Financial Aid: Kate Lockhart
Type: Two-Year College **Sex:** Coed **% Accepted:** 100 **Admission Plans:** Open Admission; Early Admission; Deferred Admission **Application Deadline:** Rolling **H.S. Requirements:** High school diploma required; GED accepted **Costs Per Year:** Area resident tuition: $2550 full-time, $85 per credit hour part-time. State resident tuition: $5250 full-time, $175 per credit hour part-time. Nonresident tuition: $6600 full-time, $220 per credit hour part-time. **Scholarships:** Available **Calendar System:** Semester, Summer Session Available **Enrollment:** FT 687, PT 1,229 **Faculty:** FT 41, PT 151 **Library Holdings:** 35,575 **Regional Accreditation:** Middle State Association of Colleges and Schools **Credit Hours For Degree:** 60 credits, Associates **Professional Accreditation:** NLN **Intercollegiate Athletics:** Baseball M; Basketball M & W; Cheerleading W; Softball W; Volleyball W

CHESAPEAKE COLLEGE
PO Box 8
Wye Mills, MD 21679-0008
Tel: (410)822-5400
Fax: (410)827-9466
Web Site: http://www.chesapeake.edu/
President/CEO: Dr. Stuart M. Bounds
Registrar: Claudia Jewell
Admissions: Kathy Petrichenko
Financial Aid: Dr. Richard Midcap
Type: Two-Year College **Sex:** Coed **Admission Plans:** Open Admission; Early Admission; Deferred Admission **Application Fee:** $0.00 **H.S. Requirements:** High school diploma required; GED accepted **Scholarships:** Available **Calendar System:** Semester, Summer Session Available **Enrollment:** FT 724, PT 1,630 **Faculty:** FT 47, PT 90 **Student-Faculty Ratio:** 16:1 **Library Holdings:** 44,049 **Regional Accreditation:** Middle State Association of Colleges and Schools **Credit Hours For Degree:** 63 credit hours, Associates **Professional Accreditation:** APTA, JRCERT **Intercollegiate Athletics:** Baseball M; Basketball M & W; Soccer M & W; Softball W; Tennis M & W; Volleyball W

COLLEGE OF NOTRE DAME OF MARYLAND
4701 North Charles St.
Baltimore, MD 21210-2476
Tel: (410)435-0100
Free: 800-435-0300
Admissions: (410)532-5330
Fax: (410)532-6287

E-mail: admiss@ndm.edu
Web Site: http://www.ndm.edu/
President/CEO: Dr. Mary Pat Seurkamp
Registrar: Sharon Bogdan
Admissions: Dr. Jennifer Blair
Financial Aid: James Otterbein
Type: Comprehensive **Affiliation:** Roman Catholic **Scores:** 100% SAT V 400+; 95% SAT M 400+ **Admission Plans:** Early Admission; Early Action; Deferred Admission **Application Fee:** $25.00 **H.S. Requirements:** High school diploma required; GED accepted **Costs Per Year:** Application fee: $25. Comprehensive fee: $29,600 includes full-time tuition ($21,100), mandatory fees ($500), and college room and board ($8000). Part-time tuition: $345 per credit. Part-time mandatory fees: $60 per term. **Scholarships:** Available **Calendar System:** 4-1-4, Summer Session Available **Enrollment:** FT 607, PT 1,079, Grad 1,621 **Faculty:** FT 79, PT 9 **Student-Faculty Ratio:** 13:1 **Exams:** SAT I or ACT **% Receiving Financial Aid:** 74 **% Residing in College-Owned, -Operated, or -Affiliated Housing:** 57 **Library Holdings:** 400,000 **Regional Accreditation:** Middle State Association of Colleges and Schools **Credit Hours For Degree:** 120 credits, Bachelors **ROTC:** Army **Professional Accreditation:** NCATE, NLN **Intercollegiate Athletics:** Basketball W; Field Hockey W; Lacrosse W; Soccer W; Swimming and Diving W; Tennis W; Volleyball W

COLLEGE OF SOUTHERN MARYLAND
8730 Mitchell Rd., PO Box 910
La Plata, MD 20646-0910
Tel: (301)934-2251
Free: 800-933-9177
Admissions: (301)934-7520
Fax: (301)934-5255
E-mail: juliap@csmd.edu
Web Site: http://www.csmd.edu/
President/CEO: Dr. Elaine Ryan
Registrar: Carol Harrison
Admissions: Julia Pitman
Financial Aid: Chad Norcross
Type: Two-Year College **Sex:** Coed **% Accepted:** 55 **Admission Plans:** Open Admission; Early Admission; Deferred Admission **Application Deadline:** Rolling **Application Fee:** $0.00 **H.S. Requirements:** High school diploma or equivalent not required. For nursing program: High school diploma required; GED accepted **Costs Per Year:** Application fee: $0. Area resident tuition: $2650 full-time, $110 per credit part-time. State resident tuition: $4608 full-time, $192 per credit part-time. Nonresident tuition: $5789 full-time, $241 per credit part-time. Mandatory fees: $552 full-time. Full-time tuition and fees vary according to course load. Part-time tuition varies according to course load. **Scholarships:** Available **Calendar System:** Semester, Summer Session Available **Enrollment:** FT 2,599, PT 4,947 **Faculty:** FT 122, PT 311 **Student-Faculty Ratio:** 9:1 **Library Holdings:** 44,896 **Regional Accreditation:** Middle State Association of Colleges and Schools **Credit Hours For Degree:** 62 credits, Associates **Professional Accreditation:** APTA, ACBSP, NLN **Intercollegiate Athletics:** Baseball M; Basketball M & W; Golf M & W; Soccer M & W; Softball W; Tennis M & W; Volleyball W

COLUMBIA UNION COLLEGE
7600 Flower Ave.
Takoma Park, MD 20912-7796
Tel: (301)891-4000
Free: 800-835-4212
Admissions: (301)891-4502
Fax: (301)891-4230
Web Site: http://www.cuc.edu/
President/CEO: Dr. Randal Wisbey
Registrar: Dr. Anthony Futcher
Admissions: Emil John
Financial Aid: Elaine Oliver
Type: Comprehensive **Sex:** Coed **Affiliation:** Seventh-day Adventist **Scores:** 66.9% SAT V 400+; 61.7% SAT M 400+; 52.7% ACT 18-23; 10.5% ACT 24-29 **% Accepted:** 35 **Admission Plans:** Early Admission; Deferred Admission **Application Deadline:** August 01 **Application Fee:** $25.00 **H.S. Requirements:** High school diploma required; GED accepted **Costs Per Year:** Application fee: $25. Comprehensive fee: $23,536 includes full-time tuition ($16,514), mandatory fees ($1072), and college room and board ($5950). Part-time tuition: $688 per semester hour. Part-time mandatory fees: $670 per term. Part-time tuition and fees vary according to class time. **Scholarships:** Available **Calendar System:** Semester, Summer Session Available **Enrollment:** FT 730, PT 288, Grad 29 **Faculty:** FT 53, PT 3 **Student-Faculty Ratio:** 12:1 **Exams:** SAT I or ACT **% Residing in College-Owned, -Operated, or -Affiliated Housing:** 50 **Library Holdings:** 141,534 **Regional Accreditation:** Middle State Association of Colleges and Schools **Credit Hours For Degree:** 64 semester hours, Associates; 128 semester hours, Bachelors **Professional Accreditation:** CARC, NLN **Intercollegiate Athletics:** Baseball M; Basketball M & W; Cross-Country Running M & W; Soccer M & W; Softball W; Track and Field M & W

THE COMMUNITY COLLEGE OF BALTIMORE COUNTY
800 South Rolling Rd.
Baltimore, MD 21228-5381
Tel: (410)455-6050
Admissions: (410)455-4392
Fax: (410)719-6546
Web Site: http://www.ccbcmd.edu/
President/CEO: Dr. Irving Pressley McPhail
Admissions: Diane Drake
Financial Aid: M. Pat Mohr
Type: Two-Year College **Sex:** Coed **Costs Per Year:** Area resident tuition: $2610 full-time, $87 per hour part-time. State resident tuition: $4500 full-time, $150 per hour part-time. Nonresident tuition: $6150 full-time, $205 per hour part-time. Mandatory fees: $316 full-time, $316 per term part-time. **Calendar System:** Semester **Enrollment:** FT 7,049, PT 12,573 **Faculty:** FT 355, PT 731 **Student-Faculty Ratio:** 20:1 **Regional Accreditation:** Middle State Association of Colleges and Schools **Professional Accreditation:** ABFSE, AOTA, CARC, JRCERT, NASM, NAST, NLN

COPPIN STATE UNIVERSITY
2500 West North Ave.
Baltimore, MD 21216-3698
Tel: (410)951-3000
Free: 800-635-3674
Admissions: (410)951-3600
Fax: (410)523-7238
Web Site: http://www.coppin.edu/
President/CEO: Dr. Stanley F. Battle
Registrar: Margaret Turner
Admissions: Michelle Gross
Financial Aid: Lady Jenkins
Type: Comprehensive **Sex:** Coed **Affiliation:** University System of Maryland **Admission Plans:** Early Admission; Deferred Admission **Application Fee:** $35.00 **H.S. Requirements:** High school diploma required; GED accepted **Costs Per Year:** Application fee: $35. State resident tuition: $3527 full-time, $151 per credit hour part-time. Nonresident tuition: $10,048 full-time, $347 per credit hour part-time. Mandatory fees: $1352 full-time, $22 per credit hour part-time, $150 per term part-time. College room and board: $6239. College room only: $3881. **Scholarships:** Available **Calendar System:** Semester, Summer Session Available **Faculty:** FT 110, PT 92 **Student-Faculty Ratio:** 17:1 **Exams:** SAT I or ACT **% Receiving Financial Aid:** 78 **% Residing in College-Owned, -Operated, or -Affiliated Housing:** 10 **Library Holdings:** 134,983 **Regional Accreditation:** Middle State Association of Colleges and Schools **Credit Hours For Degree:** 120 credit hours, Bachelors **ROTC:** Army **Professional Accreditation:** CORE, CSWE, NCATE, NLN **Intercollegiate Athletics:** Baseball M; Basketball M & W; Bowling M & W; Cross-Country Running M & W; Rugby M; Softball W; Tennis M & W; Track and Field M & W; Volleyball W; Weight Lifting M & W; Wrestling M

DEVRY UNIVERSITY
4550 Montgomery Ave.. Ste. 100 North
Bethesda, MD 20814-3304
Tel: (301)652-8477; (866)338-7934
Fax: (301)652-8577
Web Site: http://www.devry.edu/ **Type:** Comprehensive **Sex:** Coed **Affiliation:** DeVry University **Admission Plans:** Deferred Admission **Application Deadline:** Rolling **Application Fee:** $50.00 **H.S. Requirements:** High school diploma required; GED accepted **Costs Per Year:** Application fee: $50. One-time mandatory fee: $40. Tuition: $13,060 full-time, $475 per credit part-time. Mandatory fees: $30 full-time, $30 per year part-time. Full-time tuition and fees vary according to course load. Part-time tuition and fees vary according to course load. **Calendar System:** Semester, Summer Session Available **Enrollment:** FT 9, PT 23, Grad 64 **Faculty:** FT 2, PT 13 **Student-Faculty Ratio:** 3:1 **Regional Ac-**

creditation: North Central Association of Colleges and Schools **Credit Hours For Degree:** 122 credits, Bachelors

FREDERICK COMMUNITY COLLEGE
7932 Opossumtown Pike
Frederick, MD 21702-2097
Tel: (301)846-2400
Admissions: (301)846-2432
Web Site: http://www.frederick.edu/
President/CEO: Dr. Patricia Stanley
Registrar: Kathy Frawley
Admissions: Kathy Frawley
Financial Aid: Brenda Dayhoff
Type: Two-Year College **Sex:** Coed **Admission Plans:** Open Admission; Early Admission; Deferred Admission **Application Deadline:** September 01 **Application Fee:** $0.00 **H.S. Requirements:** High school diploma or equivalent not required **Costs Per Year:** Application fee: $0. Area resident tuition: $2088 full-time, $87 per credit hour part-time. State resident tuition: $4560 full-time, $190 per credit hour part-time. Nonresident tuition: $6216 full-time, $259 per credit hour part-time. Mandatory fees: $300 full-time, $10.95 per credit hour part-time, $37 per year part-time. **Scholarships:** Available **Calendar System:** Semester, Summer Session Available **Enrollment:** FT 1,855, PT 2,967 **Faculty:** FT 79, PT 299 **Library Holdings:** 40,000 **Regional Accreditation:** Middle State Association of Colleges and Schools **Credit Hours For Degree:** 60 credit hours, Associates **ROTC:** Army **Professional Accreditation:** ARCEST, CARC **Intercollegiate Athletics:** Baseball M; Basketball M & W; Golf M & W; Soccer M & W; Softball W; Volleyball W

FROSTBURG STATE UNIVERSITY
101 Braddock Rd.
Frostburg, MD 21532-1099
Tel: (301)687-4000
Admissions: (301)687-4201
Fax: (301)687-7074
Web Site: http://www.frostburg.edu/
President/CEO: Dr. Catherine R. Gira
Registrar: Morris Willey
Admissions: Trish Gregory
Financial Aid: Angela Hovatter
Type: Comprehensive **Sex:** Coed **Affiliation:** University System of Maryland **Scores:** 93% SAT V 400+; 84% SAT M 400+; 51% ACT 18-23; 17% ACT 24-29 **% Accepted:** 76 **Admission Plans:** Early Admission **Application Deadline:** Rolling **Application Fee:** $30.00 **H.S. Requirements:** High school diploma required; GED accepted **Costs Per Year:** Application fee: $30. State resident tuition: $5224 full-time, $216 per credit hour part-time. Nonresident tuition: $14,050 full-time, $396 per credit hour part-time. Mandatory fees: $1392 full-time, $67 per credit hour part-time, $9 per term part-time. College room and board: $6442. College room only: $3132. **Scholarships:** Available **Calendar System:** Semester, Summer Session Available **Enrollment:** FT 4,053, PT 268, Grad 720 **Faculty:** FT 233, PT 118 **Student-Faculty Ratio:** 17:1 **Exams:** SAT I or ACT **% Receiving Financial Aid:** 48 **% Residing in College-Owned, -Operated, or -Affiliated Housing:** 35 **Library Holdings:** 261,712 **Regional Accreditation:** Middle State Association of Colleges and Schools **Credit Hours For Degree:** 120 credit hours, Bachelors **Professional Accreditation:** CSWE, NCATE, NRPA **Intercollegiate Athletics:** Baseball M; Basketball M & W; Cross-Country Running M & W; Field Hockey W; Football M; Golf M; Lacrosse W; Soccer M & W; Softball W; Swimming and Diving M & W; Tennis M & W; Track and Field M & W; Volleyball W

GARRETT COLLEGE
687 Mosser Rd.
McHenry, MD 21541
Tel: (301)387-3000
Admissions: (301)387-3046
Fax: (301)387-3055
E-mail: admission@garrett.ncin.com
Web Site: http://www.garrettcollege.edu/
President/CEO: Dr. Stephen J. Herman
Registrar: Kimberly DeGiovanni
Admissions: Dr. Nancy Priselac
Type: Two-Year College **Sex:** Coed **Admission Plans:** Open Admission; Early Admission; Deferred Admission **Application Fee:** $0.00 **H.S. Requirements:** High school diploma or equivalent not required **Costs Per Year:** Application fee: $0. Area resident tuition: $2340 full-time, $78 per credit hour part-time. State resident tuition: $5460 full-time, $182 per credit hour part-time. Nonresident tuition: $6540 full-time, $218 per credit hour part-time. Mandatory fees: $570 full-time, $18 per credit hour part-time, $15. College room and board: $4970. College room only: $2550. **Scholarships:** Available **Calendar System:** Semester, Summer Session Available **Enrollment:** FT 360, PT 253 **Faculty:** FT 18, PT 31 **Student-Faculty Ratio:** 13:1 **Exams:** SAT I or ACT **% Residing in College-Owned, -Operated, or -Affiliated Housing:** 8 **Library Holdings:** 24,230 **Regional Accreditation:** Middle State Association of Colleges and Schools **Credit Hours For Degree:** 64 credit hours, Associates **Intercollegiate Athletics:** Baseball M; Basketball M & W; Golf M; Skiing (Downhill) M & W; Volleyball W

GEORGE MEANY CENTER FOR LABOR STUDIES-THE NATIONAL LABOR COLLEGE
10000 New Hampshire Ave.
Silver Spring, MD 20903
Tel: (301)431-6400
Free: 800-GMC-4CDP
Admissions: (301)431-5404
Fax: (301)431-5411
E-mail: cspruill@georgemeany.org
Web Site: http://www.georgemeany.org/
President/CEO: Dr. Susan J. Schurman
Registrar: Eve Dauer
Admissions: Carrie Spruill
Financial Aid: Carrie Spruill
Type: Comprehensive **Sex:** Coed **Calendar System:** Quarter **Regional Accreditation:** Middle State Association of Colleges and Schools

GOUCHER COLLEGE
1021 Dulaney Valley Rd.
Baltimore, MD 21204-2794
Tel: (410)337-6000
Free: 800-468-2437
Admissions: (410)337-6100
Fax: (410)337-6236
E-mail: admissions@goucher.edu
Web Site: http://www.goucher.edu/
President/CEO: Sanford J. Ungar
Registrar: Patricia Kelly
Admissions: Carlton E. Surbeck, III
Financial Aid: Sharon Hassan
Type: Comprehensive **Sex:** Coed **Scores:** 100% SAT V 400+; 100% SAT M 400+; 36% ACT 18-23; 51% ACT 24-29 **% Accepted:** 67 **Admission Plans:** Early Admission; Early Action; Deferred Admission **Application Deadline:** February 01 **Application Fee:** $40.00 **H.S. Requirements:** High school diploma required; GED accepted **Costs Per Year:** Application fee: $40. Comprehensive fee: $37,000 includes full-time tuition ($27,100), mandatory fees ($425), and college room and board ($9475). College room only: $5625. Room and board charges vary according to board plan and housing facility. Part-time tuition: $950 per credit hour. **Scholarships:** Available **Calendar System:** Semester, Summer Session Not available **Enrollment:** FT 1,306, PT 40, Grad 887 **Faculty:** FT 112, PT 78 **Student-Faculty Ratio:** 10:1 **Exams:** SAT I or ACT **% Receiving Financial Aid:** 60 **% Residing in College-Owned, -Operated, or -Affiliated Housing:** 80 **Library Holdings:** 303,000 **Regional Accreditation:** Middle State Association of Colleges and Schools **Credit Hours For Degree:** 120 semester hours, Bachelors **ROTC:** Army **Intercollegiate Athletics:** Basketball M & W; Cross-Country Running M & W; Equestrian Sports M & W; Field Hockey W; Lacrosse M & W; Soccer M & W; Swimming and Diving M & W; Tennis M & W; Track and Field M & W; Volleyball W

GRIGGS UNIVERSITY
PO Box 4437, 12501 Old Columbia Pk
Silver Spring, MD 20914-4437
Tel: (301)680-6570
Admissions: (301)680-6579
Fax: (301)680-6577
E-mail: 74617.74@compuserve.com
Web Site: http://www.griggs.edu/
President/CEO: Dr. Joseph E. Gurubatham
Registrar: Anita L. Jacobs
Admissions: Anita L. Jacobs

Type: Four-Year College **Sex:** Coed **Affiliation:** Seventh-day Adventist; Seventh-day Adventist Parochial School System **Admission Plans:** Early Admission; Deferred Admission **Application Fee:** $50.00 **H.S. Requirements:** High school diploma required; GED accepted **Costs Per Year:** Application fee: $50. Tuition: $7350 full-time, $245 per semester hour part-time. Mandatory fees: $70 full-time, $70 per year part-time. Full-time tuition and fees vary according to course load. Part-time tuition and fees vary according to course load. **Calendar System:** Continuous, Summer Session Available **Faculty:** PT 38 **Credit Hours For Degree:** 60 semester hours, Associates; 120 semester hours, Bachelors **Professional Accreditation:** DETC

HAGERSTOWN BUSINESS COLLEGE
18618 Crestwood Dr.
Hagerstown, MD 21742-2797
Tel: (301)739-2670
Free: 800-422-2670
Fax: (301)791-7661
E-mail: jklein@hagerstownbusinesscol.org
Web Site: http://www.hagerstownbusinesscol.org/
President/CEO: W. Chrisopher Motz
Registrar: Lisa Copenhaver
Admissions: Jim Klein
Financial Aid: John Huffman
Type: Two-Year College **Sex:** Coed **Affiliation:** Kaplan Higher Education Corporation **Admission Plans:** Open Admission; Early Admission; Deferred Admission **Application Deadline:** Rolling **H.S. Requirements:** High school diploma required; GED accepted **Scholarships:** Available **Calendar System:** Quarter, Summer Session Available **Enrollment:** FT 770, PT 162 **Faculty:** FT 20, PT 45 **Student-Faculty Ratio:** 18:1 **% Residing in College-Owned, -Operated, or -Affiliated Housing:** 3 **Library Holdings:** 8,000 **Professional Accreditation:** ACICS, AHIMA

HAGERSTOWN COMMUNITY COLLEGE
11400 Robinwood Dr.
Hagerstown, MD 21742-6590
Tel: (301)790-2800
Fax: (301)739-0737
E-mail: fisherj@hagerstowncc.edu
Web Site: http://www.hagerstowncc.edu/
President/CEO: Dr. Guy Altieri
Registrar: Jacqueline L. Baldwin
Admissions: Jennifer Fisher
Financial Aid: Carolyn S. Cox
Type: Two-Year College **Sex:** Coed **% Accepted:** 100 **Admission Plans:** Open Admission; Early Admission; Deferred Admission **Application Deadline:** Rolling **Application Fee:** $0.00 **H.S. Requirements:** High school diploma or equivalent not required **Costs Per Year:** Application fee: $0. Area resident tuition: $2670 full-time, $89 per credit hour part-time. State resident tuition: $4260 full-time, $142 per credit hour part-time. Nonresident tuition: $5580 full-time, $186 per credit hour part-time. Mandatory fees: $280 full-time, $8 per credit hour part-time, $20. Full-time tuition and fees vary according to course load. Part-time tuition and fees vary according to course load. **Scholarships:** Available **Calendar System:** Semester, Summer Session Available **Enrollment:** FT 1,204, PT 2,317 **Faculty:** FT 69, PT 158 **Student-Faculty Ratio:** 14:1 **Library Holdings:** 45,705 **Regional Accreditation:** Middle State Association of Colleges and Schools **Credit Hours For Degree:** 64 credit hours, Associates **Professional Accreditation:** JRCERT **Intercollegiate Athletics:** Baseball M; Basketball M & W; Cross-Country Running M & W; Golf M & W; Soccer M & W; Softball W; Track and Field M & W; Volleyball W

HARFORD COMMUNITY COLLEGE
401 Thomas Run Rd.
Bel Air, MD 21015-1698
Tel: (410)836-4000
Admissions: (410)836-4379
Fax: (410)836-4197
Web Site: http://www.harford.edu/
President/CEO: Dr. Claudia E. Chiesi
Registrar: Lynne LaCalle
Admissions: Nanette Reckart
Financial Aid: Lynn Lee
Type: Two-Year College **Sex:** Coed **Admission Plans:** Open Admission **Application Fee:** $0.00 **H.S. Requirements:** High school diploma or equivalent not required **Costs Per Year:** Application fee: $0. Area resident tuition: $2250 full-time, $75 per credit part-time. State resident tuition: $4500 full-time, $150 per credit part-time. Nonresident tuition: $6750 full-time, $225 per credit part-time. Mandatory fees: $225 full-time, $7.50 per credit part-time. Full-time tuition and fees vary according to course load. Part-time tuition and fees vary according to course load. **Scholarships:** Available **Calendar System:** Semester, Summer Session Available **Enrollment:** FT 2,157, PT 3,335 **Faculty:** FT 99, PT 194 **Student-Faculty Ratio:** 20:1 **Exams:** Other **Library Holdings:** 74,731 **Regional Accreditation:** Middle State Association of Colleges and Schools **Credit Hours For Degree:** 62 credit hours, Associates **Professional Accreditation:** NAACLS, NLN **Intercollegiate Athletics:** Baseball M; Basketball M & W; Field Hockey W; Golf M; Lacrosse M & W; Soccer M & W; Softball W; Tennis M & W

HOOD COLLEGE
401 Rosemont Ave.
Frederick, MD 21701-8575
Tel: (301)663-3131
Free: 800-922-1599
Admissions: (301)696-3400
E-mail: admissions@nimue.hood.edu
Web Site: http://www.hood.edu/
President/CEO: Dr. Ronald J. Volpe
Registrar: Nanette Markey
Admissions: Glen Thomas
Type: Comprehensive **Sex:** Coed **Scores:** 99% SAT V 400+; 99% SAT M 400+; 53% ACT 18-23; 29% ACT 24-29 **% Accepted:** 51 **Admission Plans:** Early Action; Deferred Admission **Application Deadline:** February 15 **Application Fee:** $35.00 **H.S. Requirements:** High school diploma required; GED accepted **Costs Per Year:** Application fee: $35. Comprehensive fee: $30,085 includes full-time tuition ($22,000), mandatory fees ($335), and college room and board ($7750). College room only: $4050. Full-time tuition and fees vary according to course load. Room and board charges vary according to board plan. Part-time tuition: $635 per credit. Part-time mandatory fees: $105 per term. Part-time tuition and fees vary according to course load. **Scholarships:** Available **Calendar System:** Semester, Summer Session Available **Enrollment:** FT 1,007, PT 176, Grad 934 **Faculty:** FT 81, PT 121 **Student-Faculty Ratio:** 12:1 **Exams:** SAT I or ACT **% Receiving Financial Aid:** 77 **% Residing in College-Owned, -Operated, or -Affiliated Housing:** 53 **Library Holdings:** 182,786 **Regional Accreditation:** Middle State Association of Colleges and Schools **Credit Hours For Degree:** 124 credits, Bachelors **ROTC:** Army **Professional Accreditation:** CSWE **Intercollegiate Athletics:** Basketball M & W; Cross-Country Running M & W; Equestrian Sports M & W; Field Hockey W; Golf M & W; Lacrosse M & W; Soccer M & W; Softball W; Swimming and Diving M & W; Tennis M & W; Track and Field M & W; Volleyball W

HOWARD COMMUNITY COLLEGE
10901 Little Patuxent Parkway
Columbia, MD 21044-3197
Tel: (410)772-4800
Admissions: (410)772-4856
Fax: (410)772-4589
E-mail: hsinfo@howardcc.edu
Web Site: http://www.howardcc.edu/
President/CEO: Dr. Mary Ellen Duncan
Registrar: Judith C. Bulliner
Admissions: Barbara Greenfeld
Financial Aid: Stephanie Pina
Type: Two-Year College **Sex:** Coed **Admission Plans:** Open Admission; Early Admission; Deferred Admission **Application Deadline:** Rolling **Application Fee:** $25.00 **H.S. Requirements:** High school diploma or equivalent not required **Costs Per Year:** Application fee: $25. Area resident tuition: $3300 full-time, $110 per credit part-time. State resident tuition: $5790 full-time, $193 per credit part-time. Nonresident tuition: $7140 full-time, $238 per credit part-time. Mandatory fees: $553 full-time, $18.43 per credit part-time. **Scholarships:** Available **Calendar System:** Semester, Summer Session Available **Enrollment:** FT 2,636, PT 4,206 **Faculty:** FT 115, PT 372 **Student-Faculty Ratio:** 18:1 **Exams:** SAT I or ACT **Library Holdings:** 40,380 **Regional Accreditation:** Middle State Association of Colleges and Schools **Credit Hours For Degree:** 60 credit hours, Associates **Professional Accreditation:** NLN **Intercollegiate Athletics:** Basketball M

& W; Cross-Country Running M & W; Lacrosse M; Soccer M & W; Tennis M & W; Track and Field M & W; Volleyball W

ITT TECHNICAL INSTITUTE
11301 Red Run Blvd.
Owings Mills, MD 21117
Admissions: (443)394-7115
Web Site: http://www.itt-tech.edu/
Admissions: Shaher Shanti
Type: Two-Year College **Sex:** Coed **Application Deadline:** Rolling **Application Fee:** $100.00 **Costs Per Year:** Application fee: $100. **Calendar System:** Quarter **Exams:** Other

THE JOHNS HOPKINS UNIVERSITY
3400 North Charles St.
Baltimore, MD 21218-2699
Tel: (410)516-8000
Admissions: (410)516-8341
Fax: (410)516-6025
E-mail: gotojhu@jhu.edu
Web Site: http://www.jhu.edu/
President/CEO: Dr. William R. Brody
Registrar: Hedy Schaedel
Admissions: John Latting
Financial Aid: Ellen Frishberg
Type: University **Sex:** Coed **Scores:** 100% SAT V 400+; 100% SAT M 400+; 5% ACT 18-23; 36% ACT 24-29 **% Accepted:** 35 **Admission Plans:** Early Admission; Early Decision Plan; Deferred Admission **Application Deadline:** January 01 **Application Fee:** $60.00 **H.S. Requirements:** High school diploma required; GED accepted **Costs Per Year:** Application fee: $60. Comprehensive fee: $45,022 includes full-time tuition ($33,900), mandatory fees ($500), and college room and board ($10,622). College room only: $6096. Part-time tuition: $1130 per credit. **Scholarships:** Available **Calendar System:** 4-1-4, Summer Session Available **Enrollment:** FT 4,351, PT 66, Grad 1,608 **Faculty:** FT 451, PT 74 **Student-Faculty Ratio:** 9:1 **Exams:** SAT I or ACT, SAT I and SAT II or ACT **% Receiving Financial Aid:** 49 **% Residing in College-Owned, -Operated, or -Affiliated Housing:** 50 **Library Holdings:** 3,509,413 **Regional Accreditation:** Middle State Association of Colleges and Schools **Credit Hours For Degree:** 120 credits, Bachelors **ROTC:** Army, Air Force **Professional Accreditation:** ABET, ARCMI, ACEHSA, AACN, ADtA, APA, ACIPE, CEPH, LCMEAMA, NASM, NCATE, NLN **Intercollegiate Athletics:** Baseball M; Basketball M & W; Crew M & W; Cross-Country Running M & W; Fencing M & W; Field Hockey W; Football M; Lacrosse M & W; Soccer M & W; Swimming and Diving M & W; Tennis M & W; Track and Field M & W; Volleyball W; Water Polo M; Wrestling M

LOYOLA COLLEGE IN MARYLAND
4501 North Charles St.
Baltimore, MD 21210-2699
Tel: (410)617-2000
Fax: (410)323-2768
Web Site: http://www.loyola.edu/
President/CEO: Rev. Harold Ridley, SJ
Registrar: Rita Steiner
Admissions: William Bossemeyer
Financial Aid: Mark Lindenmeyer
Type: Comprehensive **Sex:** Coed **Affiliation:** Roman Catholic (Jesuit) **Scores:** 100% SAT V 400+; 100% SAT M 400+; 23% ACT 18-23; 66% ACT 24-29 **% Accepted:** 47 **Admission Plans:** Early Admission; Deferred Admission **Application Deadline:** January 15 **Application Fee:** $50.00 **H.S. Requirements:** High school diploma required; GED accepted **Costs Per Year:** Application fee: $50. Comprehensive fee: $38,898 includes full-time tuition ($28,683), mandatory fees ($1000), and college room and board ($9215). College room only: $7215. Full-time tuition and fees vary according to student level. Room and board charges vary according to board plan. Part-time tuition: $486 per credit. Part-time mandatory fees: $25 per term. **Scholarships:** Available **Calendar System:** Semester, Summer Session Available **Enrollment:** FT 3,501, PT 55, Grad 2,631 **Faculty:** FT 305, PT 232 **Student-Faculty Ratio:** 12:1 **Exams:** SAT I or ACT **% Receiving Financial Aid:** 44 **% Residing in College-Owned, -Operated, or -Affiliated Housing:** 79 **Library Holdings:** 293,639 **Regional Accreditation:** Middle State Association of Colleges and Schools **Credit Hours For Degree:** 120 credits, Bachelors **ROTC:** Army, Air Force **Professional Accreditation:** AACSB, ABET, ACA, APA, ASLHA, NCATE **Intercollegiate Athletics:** Basketball M & W; Crew M & W; Cross-Country Running M & W; Golf M; Lacrosse M & W; Soccer M & W; Swimming and Diving M & W; Tennis M & W; Volleyball W

MAPLE SPRINGS BAPTIST BIBLE COLLEGE AND SEMINARY
4130 Belt Rd.
Capitol Heights, MD 20743
Tel: (301)736-3631
Fax: (301)735-6507
E-mail: percy.coker@msbbcs.edu
Web Site: http://www.msbbcs.edu/
President/CEO: Dr. Larry W. Jordan
Admissions: Rev. Percy Coker
Type: Comprehensive **Sex:** Coed **Affiliation:** Baptist **Admission Plans:** Open Admission; Deferred Admission **Application Fee:** $25.00 **H.S. Requirements:** High school diploma required; GED accepted **Scholarships:** Available **Calendar System:** Semester **Enrollment:** FT 7, PT 82, Grad 62 **Faculty:** FT 5, PT 25 **Exams:** Other **Library Holdings:** 1,781 **Credit Hours For Degree:** 66 credit hours, Associates; 132 credit hours, Bachelors **Professional Accreditation:** TACCS

MARYLAND INSTITUTE COLLEGE OF ART
1300 Mount Royal Ave.
Baltimore, MD 21217
Tel: (410)669-9200
Admissions: (410)225-2222
Fax: (410)225-2337
E-mail: admissions@mica.edu
Web Site: http://www.mica.edu/
President/CEO: Fred Lazarus, IV
Registrar: Christine Peterson
Admissions: Theresa Lynch Bedoya
Financial Aid: Diane Prengaman
Type: Comprehensive **Sex:** Coed **Scores:** 100% SAT V 400+; 99% SAT M 400+ **% Accepted:** 45 **Admission Plans:** Early Admission; Early Action; Early Decision Plan; Deferred Admission **Application Deadline:** February 15 **Application Fee:** $50.00 **H.S. Requirements:** High school diploma required; GED accepted **Costs Per Year:** Application fee: $50. Comprehensive fee: $34,450 includes full-time tuition ($26,140), mandatory fees ($780), and college room and board ($7530). College room only: $5500. Room and board charges vary according to board plan and housing facility. Part-time tuition: $1090 per credit. Part-time mandatory fees: $390 per term. **Scholarships:** Available **Calendar System:** Semester, Summer Session Available **Enrollment:** FT 1,478, PT 19, Grad 220 **Faculty:** FT 118, PT 149 **Student-Faculty Ratio:** 10:1 **Exams:** SAT I or ACT **% Residing in College-Owned, -Operated, or -Affiliated Housing:** 88 **Library Holdings:** 55,000 **Regional Accreditation:** Middle State Association of Colleges and Schools **Credit Hours For Degree:** 126 credits, Bachelors **ROTC:** Army **Professional Accreditation:** NASAD

MCDANIEL COLLEGE
2 College Hill
Westminster, MD 21157-4390
Tel: (410)848-7000
Free: 800-638-5005
Admissions: (410)857-2230
Fax: (410)857-2729
E-mail: admissions@mcdaniel.edu
Web Site: http://www.mcdaniel.edu/
President/CEO: Dr. Joan Develin Coley
Registrar: Jan Kiphart
Admissions: M. O'Connell
Financial Aid: Patricia M. Williams
Type: Comprehensive **Sex:** Coed **Scores:** 98% SAT V 400+; 98% SAT M 400+ **% Accepted:** 79 **Admission Plans:** Early Admission; Early Action; Deferred Admission **Application Deadline:** February 01 **Application Fee:** $50.00 **H.S. Requirements:** High school diploma required; GED accepted **Costs Per Year:** Application fee: $50. Comprehensive fee: $33,180 includes full-time tuition ($26,980), mandatory fees ($300), and college room and board ($5900). College room only: $3200. Part-time tuition: $843 per credit. Part-time mandatory fees: $150 per term. **Scholarships:** Available **Calendar System:** 4-1-4, Summer Session Available **Enrollment:** FT 1,643, PT 52, Grad 1,829 **Faculty:** FT 129, PT 61 **Student-Faculty Ratio:** 13:1 **Exams:** SAT I or ACT, SAT II **% Receiving Financial Aid:** 62 **% Residing in College-Owned, -Operated, or -Affiliated Housing:** 80 **Library Holdings:**

629,965 **Regional Accreditation:** Middle State Association of Colleges and Schools **Credit Hours For Degree:** 128 semester hours, Bachelors **ROTC:** Army **Professional Accreditation:** CSWE, NCATE **Intercollegiate Athletics:** Baseball M; Basketball M & W; Cross-Country Running M & W; Field Hockey W; Football M; Golf M & W; Lacrosse M & W; Soccer M & W; Softball W; Swimming and Diving M & W; Tennis M & W; Track and Field M & W; Volleyball W; Wrestling M

MONTGOMERY COLLEGE
900 Hungerford Dr.
Rockville, MD 20850
Tel: (301)279-5000
Admissions: (301)279-5034
Web Site: http://www.montgomerycollege.org/
President/CEO: Dr. Charlene Nunley
Admissions: Sherman Helberg
Financial Aid: Judith M. Taylor
Type: Two-Year College **Sex:** Coed **Application Fee:** $25.00 **Scholarships:** Available **Calendar System:** Semester **Enrollment:** FT 7,748, PT 14,057 **Faculty:** FT 435, PT 873 **Student-Faculty Ratio:** 20:1 **Regional Accreditation:** Middle State Association of Colleges and Schools **Professional Accreditation:** ARCEST, AHIMA, APTA, NASM **Intercollegiate Athletics:** Baseball M & W; Basketball M & W; Cross-Country Running M & W; Golf M; Soccer M & W; Swimming and Diving M & W; Tennis M & W; Track and Field M & W; Volleyball W

MORGAN STATE UNIVERSITY
1700 East Cold Spring Ln.
Baltimore, MD 21251
Tel: (443)885-3333
Free: 800-332-6674
Admissions: (443)885-3000
E-mail: ejohnson@moac.morgan.edu
Web Site: http://www.morgan.edu/
President/CEO: Dr. Earl Richardson
Registrar: Dr. D. Jason De Sousa
Admissions: Edwin T. Johnson
Type: University **Sex:** Coed **Scores:** 85% SAT V 400+; 81% SAT M 400+; 12% ACT 18-23; 9% ACT 24-29 **Admission Plans:** Preferred Admission; Early Admission; Deferred Admission **Application Fee:** $25.00 **H.S. Requirements:** High school diploma required; GED accepted **Costs Per Year:** Application fee: $25. State resident tuition: $4280 full-time, $194 per credit part-time. Nonresident tuition: $11,690 full-time, $445 per credit part-time. Mandatory fees: $1830 full-time, $55 per credit part-time. College room and board: $6990. College room only: $4430. Room and board charges vary according to board plan and housing facility. **Scholarships:** Available **Calendar System:** Semester, Summer Session Available **Enrollment:** FT 5,328, PT 677, Grad 616 **Faculty:** FT 364, PT 94 **Student-Faculty Ratio:** 15:1 **Exams:** SAT I or ACT **% Residing in College-Owned, -Operated, or -Affiliated Housing:** 30 **Library Holdings:** 333,101 **Regional Accreditation:** Middle State Association of Colleges and Schools **Credit Hours For Degree:** 120 semester hours, Bachelors **ROTC:** Army **Professional Accreditation:** AACSB, ABET, ACSP, ASLA, CEPH, CSWE, NAACLS, NASM, NCATE **Intercollegiate Athletics:** Basketball M & W; Bowling W; Cheerleading W; Cross-Country Running M & W; Football M; Softball W; Tennis M & W; Track and Field M & W; Volleyball W

MOUNT ST. MARY'S UNIVERSITY
16300 Old Emmitsburg Rd.
Emmitsburg, MD 21727-7799
Tel: (301)447-6122
Free: 800-448-4347
Admissions: (301)447-5214
E-mail: admissions@msmary.edu
Web Site: http://www.msmary.edu/
President/CEO: Thomas H. Powell, EdD
Registrar: John Gill
Admissions: Stephen Neitz
Financial Aid: David C. Reeder
Type: Comprehensive **Sex:** Coed **Affiliation:** Roman Catholic **Scores:** 100% SAT V 400+; 99% SAT M 400+ **% Accepted:** 84 **Admission Plans:** Early Action; Deferred Admission **Application Deadline:** Rolling **Application Fee:** $35.00 **H.S. Requirements:** High school diploma required; GED accepted **Costs Per Year:** Application fee: $35. Comprehensive fee: $32,720 includes full-time tuition ($23,630), mandatory fees ($400), and college room and board ($8690). College room only: $4380. Part-time tuition: $790 per credit hour. Part-time mandatory fees: $12 per credit hour. **Scholarships:** Available **Calendar System:** Semester, Summer Session Available **Enrollment:** FT 1,485, PT 171, Grad 405 **Faculty:** FT 105, PT 100 **Student-Faculty Ratio:** 13:1 **Exams:** SAT I or ACT **% Receiving Financial Aid:** 61 **% Residing in College-Owned, -Operated, or -Affiliated Housing:** 80 **Library Holdings:** 210,359 **Regional Accreditation:** Middle State Association of Colleges and Schools **Credit Hours For Degree:** 120 credits, Bachelors **ROTC:** Army **Professional Accreditation:** ATS **Intercollegiate Athletics:** Baseball M; Basketball M & W; Cross-Country Running M & W; Equestrian Sports M & W; Golf M & W; Ice Hockey M; Lacrosse M & W; Rugby M & W; Soccer M & W; Softball W; Tennis M & W; Track and Field M & W

NER ISRAEL RABBINICAL COLLEGE
400 Mount Wilson Ln.
Baltimore, MD 21208
Tel: (410)484-7200
Fax: (410)484-3060
President/CEO: Rabbi Herman Neuberger
Registrar: Rabbi C. D. Lapidus
Admissions: Rabbi Berel Weisbord
Financial Aid: Moshe Pelberg
Type: Comprehensive **Sex:** Men **Affiliation:** Jewish **Admission Plans:** Early Admission; Deferred Admission **H.S. Requirements:** High school diploma required; GED accepted **Calendar System:** Semester, Summer Session Available **Enrollment:** FT 353, Grad 210 **Faculty:** FT 22, PT 0 **Credit Hours For Degree:** 120 credits, Bachelors **Professional Accreditation:** AARTS

PEABODY CONSERVATORY OF MUSIC OF THE JOHNS HOPKINS UNIVERSITY
1 East Mount Vernon Place
Baltimore, MD 21202-2397
Tel: (410)659-8150
Free: 800-368-2521
Admissions: (410)659-8110
Web Site: http://www.peabody.jhu.edu/
Admissions: David Lane
Type: Comprehensive **Sex:** Coed **Affiliation:** Johns Hopkins University **Scores:** 95.59% SAT V 400+; 95.59% SAT M 400+ **% Accepted:** 43 **Application Deadline:** December 01 **Application Fee:** $60.00 **H.S. Requirements:** High school diploma required; GED accepted **Costs Per Year:** Application fee: $60. Comprehensive fee: $39,490 includes full-time tuition ($29,630), mandatory fees ($360), and college room and board ($9500). Part-time tuition: $840 per semester hour. **Scholarships:** Available **Calendar System:** Semester, Summer Session Not available **Enrollment:** FT 311, PT 12, Grad 324 **Student-Faculty Ratio:** 4:1 **Exams:** SAT I or ACT **% Receiving Financial Aid:** 55 **Library Holdings:** 90,706 **Regional Accreditation:** Middle State Association of Colleges and Schools **Credit Hours For Degree:** 149 semester hours, Bachelors **Professional Accreditation:** NASM

PRINCE GEORGE'S COMMUNITY COLLEGE
301 Largo Rd.
Largo, MD 20774-2199
Tel: (301)336-6000
Admissions: (301)322-0801
Web Site: http://www.pgcc.edu/
President/CEO: Ronald A. Williams
Registrar: Vera Bagley
Admissions: Vera Bagley
Financial Aid: Nancy Pat Weaver
Type: Two-Year College **Sex:** Coed **Admission Plans:** Open Admission; Early Admission **Application Fee:** $25.00 **H.S. Requirements:** High school diploma or equivalent not required. For nursing, allied health programs: High school diploma required; GED accepted **Scholarships:** Available **Calendar System:** Semester, Summer Session Available **Enrollment:** FT 3,352, PT 9,212 **Faculty:** FT 249, PT 390 **Student-Faculty Ratio:** 18:1 **Exams:** Other **Library Holdings:** 242,519 **Regional Accreditation:** Middle State Association of Colleges and Schools **Credit Hours For Degree:** 62 credits, Associates **ROTC:** Army **Professional Accreditation:** ABET, AHIMA, CARC, JRCERT, JRCNMT, NLN **Intercollegiate Athletics:** Baseball M; Basketball M & W; Bowling M & W; Golf M; Soccer M & W; Softball W; Tennis M & W; Volleyball W

ST. JOHN'S COLLEGE
PO Box 2800
Annapolis, MD 21404
Tel: (410)263-2371
Free: 800-727-9238
Admissions: (410)626-2522
E-mail: admissions@sjca.edu
Web Site: http://www.stjohnscollege.edu/
President/CEO: Christopher B. Nelson
Registrar: Noreen Craven
Admissions: John Christensen
Financial Aid: Caroline Christensen
Type: Comprehensive **Sex:** Coed **Scores:** 100% SAT V 400+; 99% SAT M 400+ **% Accepted:** 76 **Admission Plans:** Early Admission; Deferred Admission **Application Deadline:** Rolling **Application Fee:** $0.00 **H.S. Requirements:** High school diploma required; GED accepted **Costs Per Year:** Application fee: $0. Comprehensive fee: $40,451 includes full-time tuition ($32,375), mandatory fees ($200), and college room and board ($7876). Room and board charges vary according to board plan. **Scholarships:** Available **Calendar System:** Semester, Summer Session Not available **Enrollment:** FT 472, PT 2, Grad 92 **Faculty:** FT 71, PT 7 **Student-Faculty Ratio:** 8:1 **Exams:** SAT I or ACT **% Receiving Financial Aid:** 56 **% Residing in College-Owned, -Operated, or -Affiliated Housing:** 87 **Library Holdings:** 102,400 **Regional Accreditation:** Middle State Association of Colleges and Schools **Credit Hours For Degree:** 132 credits, Bachelors **Intercollegiate Athletics:** Crew M & W; Fencing M & W

ST. MARY'S COLLEGE OF MARYLAND
18952 East Fisher Rd.
St. Mary's City, MD 20686-3001
Tel: (240)895-2000
Free: 800-492-7181
Admissions: (240)895-5000
Fax: (240)895-5001
E-mail: admissions@smcm.edu
Web Site: http://www.smcm.edu/
President/CEO: Dr. Jane Margaret O'Brien
Registrar: Mark W. Heidrich
Admissions: Dr. Wesley P. Jordan
Financial Aid: Timothy A. Wolfe
Type: Four-Year College **Sex:** Coed **Affiliation:** Maryland State Colleges and Universities System **Scores:** 99% SAT V 400+; 99% SAT M 400+ **% Accepted:** 68 **Admission Plans:** Early Admission; Early Decision Plan **Application Deadline:** January 15 **Application Fee:** $40.00 **H.S. Requirements:** High school diploma required; GED accepted **Costs Per Year:** Application fee: $40. State resident tuition: $9770 full-time, $160 per credit part-time. Nonresident tuition: $19,340 full-time, $160 per credit part-time. Mandatory fees: $1940 full-time. College room and board: $8505. College room only: $4820. **Scholarships:** Available **Calendar System:** Semester, Summer Session Available **Enrollment:** FT 1,849, PT 115 **Faculty:** FT 128, PT 81 **Student-Faculty Ratio:** 12:1 **Exams:** SAT I or ACT **% Receiving Financial Aid:** 46 **% Residing in College-Owned, -Operated, or -Affiliated Housing:** 84 **Library Holdings:** 157,077 **Regional Accreditation:** Middle State Association of Colleges and Schools **Credit Hours For Degree:** 128 credits, Bachelors **Intercollegiate Athletics:** Baseball M; Basketball M & W; Crew M & W; Fencing M & W; Field Hockey W; Golf M & W; Lacrosse M & W; Rugby M & W; Sailing M & W; Soccer M & W; Swimming and Diving M & W; Tennis M & W; Ultimate Frisbee M & W; Volleyball M & W

SALISBURY UNIVERSITY
1101 Camden Ave.
Salisbury, MD 21801-6837
Tel: (410)543-6000; 888-543-0148
Admissions: (410)543-6161
Fax: (410)548-2587
E-mail: admissions@salisbury.edu
Web Site: http://www.ssu.edu/
President/CEO: Dr. Janet Dudley-Eshbach
Registrar: Jacqueline Maisel
Admissions: Jane Dane
Financial Aid: Beverly A. Horner
Type: Comprehensive **Sex:** Coed **Affiliation:** University System of Maryland **Scores:** 98% SAT V 400+; 99% SAT M 400+ **% Accepted:** 57 **Admission Plans:** Early Admission; Early Action **Application Deadline:** January 15 **Application Fee:** $45.00 **H.S. Requirements:** High school diploma required; GED accepted **Costs Per Year:** Application fee: $45. State resident tuition: $4814 full-time, $200 per credit hour part-time. Nonresident tuition: $12,492 full-time, $520 per credit hour part-time. Mandatory fees: $1562 full-time, $50 per credit hour part-time. College room and board: $6932. College room only: $3554. Room and board charges vary according to board plan and housing facility. **Scholarships:** Available **Calendar System:** 4-1-4, Summer Session Available **Enrollment:** FT 5,798, PT 639, Grad 572 **Faculty:** FT 323, PT 171 **Student-Faculty Ratio:** 16:1 **Exams:** SAT I or ACT **% Receiving Financial Aid:** 42 **% Residing in College-Owned, -Operated, or -Affiliated Housing:** 46 **Library Holdings:** 254,151 **Regional Accreditation:** Middle State Association of Colleges and Schools **Credit Hours For Degree:** 120 semester hours, Bachelors **ROTC:** Army **Professional Accreditation:** AACSB, AACN, CARC, CSWE, JRCEPAT, NAACLS, NCATE, NLN **Intercollegiate Athletics:** Baseball M; Basketball M & W; Cross-Country Running M & W; Field Hockey W; Football M; Lacrosse M & W; Soccer M & W; Softball W; Swimming and Diving M & W; Tennis M & W; Track and Field M & W; Volleyball W

SOJOURNER-DOUGLASS COLLEGE
500 North Caroline St.
Baltimore, MD 21205-1814
Tel: (410)276-0306
Fax: (410)675-1810
Web Site: http://sdc.edu/
President/CEO: Dr. Charles W. Simmons
Registrar: Inetta McNeill
Admissions: Diana Samuels
Financial Aid: Rebecca Chalk
Type: Comprehensive **Sex:** Coed **Admission Plans:** Deferred Admission **H.S. Requirements:** High school diploma required; GED accepted **Costs Per Year:** Tuition: $6540 full-time, $363 per credit part-time. Mandatory fees: $208 full-time, $104 per term part-time. Part-time tuition and fees vary according to course load. **Scholarships:** Available **Calendar System:** Trimester, Summer Session Available **Enrollment:** FT 714, PT 346, Grad 64 **Faculty:** FT 35, PT 101 **Student-Faculty Ratio:** 10:1 **% Receiving Financial Aid:** 64 **Library Holdings:** 10,000 **Regional Accreditation:** Middle State Association of Colleges and Schools **Credit Hours For Degree:** 132 credits, Bachelors

TESST COLLEGE OF TECHNOLOGY (BALTIMORE)
1520 South Caton Ave.
Baltimore, MD 21227-1063
Tel: (410)644-6400
Fax: (410)644-6481
E-mail: ssherwood@tesst.com
Web Site: http://www.tesst.com/
President/CEO: Sue Sherwood
Admissions: Susan Sherwood
Type: Two-Year College **Sex:** Coed **Calendar System:** Quarter **Professional Accreditation:** ACCSCT

TESST COLLEGE OF TECHNOLOGY (BELTSVILLE)
4600 Powder Mill Rd.
Beltsville, MD 20705
Tel: (301)937-8448
Fax: (301)937-5327
E-mail: mcolling@tesst.com
Web Site: http://www.tesst.com/
President/CEO: Reginald Morton
Admissions: Mary Colling
Type: Two-Year College **Sex:** Coed **Calendar System:** Quarter **Professional Accreditation:** ACCSCT

TESST COLLEGE OF TECHNOLOGY (TOWSON)
803 Glen Eagles Ct.
Towson, MD 21286-2201
Tel: (410)296-5350
Free: 800-48-TESST
Fax: (410)296-5356
E-mail: dmcrae@tesst.com
Web Site: http://www.tesst.com/
President/CEO: Ray Joll
Admissions: Diane McRae

Type: Two-Year College **Sex:** Coed **Calendar System:** Quarter **Professional Accreditation:** ACCSCT

TOWSON UNIVERSITY
8000 York Rd.
Towson, MD 21252-0001
Tel: (410)704-2000; 888-4TOWSON
Admissions: (410)704-2113
Fax: (410)704-3030
E-mail: lshulack@towson.edu
Web Site: http://www.towson.edu/
President/CEO: Dr. Robert Caret
Admissions: Louise Shulack
Financial Aid: Vincent Pecora
Type: University **Sex:** Coed **Affiliation:** University System of Maryland **Scores:** 96.6% SAT V 400+; 97.1% SAT M 400+; 60.98% ACT 18-23; 32.2% ACT 24-29 **% Accepted:** 64 **Admission Plans:** Deferred Admission **Application Deadline:** February 15 **Application Fee:** $45.00 **H.S. Requirements:** High school diploma required; GED accepted **Costs Per Year:** Application fee: $45. State resident tuition: $5180 full-time, $225 per credit part-time. Nonresident tuition: $14,114 full-time, $528 per credit part-time. Mandatory fees: $1916 full-time, $74 per credit part-time. Full-time tuition and fees vary according to course load. College room and board: $6828. College room only: $3968. Room and board charges vary according to board plan and housing facility. **Scholarships:** Available **Calendar System:** Semester, Summer Session Available **Enrollment:** FT 12,812, PT 1,683, Grad 3,516 **Faculty:** FT 663, PT 582 **Student-Faculty Ratio:** 17:1 **Exams:** SAT I or ACT **% Receiving Financial Aid:** 30 **% Residing in College-Owned, -Operated, or -Affiliated Housing:** 23 **Library Holdings:** 574,096 **Regional Accreditation:** Middle State Association of Colleges and Schools **Credit Hours For Degree:** 120 credit hours, Bachelors **ROTC:** Army, Air Force **Professional Accreditation:** AACSB, ABET, AACN, AOTA, APA, ASLHA, JRCEPAT, NASD, NASM, NAST, NCATE **Intercollegiate Athletics:** Baseball M; Basketball M & W; Cheerleading M & W; Cross-Country Running M & W; Field Hockey W; Football M; Golf M; Gymnastics W; Lacrosse M & W; Soccer M & W; Softball W; Swimming and Diving M & W; Tennis M & W; Track and Field M & W; Volleyball M & W

UNITED STATES NAVAL ACADEMY
121 Blake Rd.
Annapolis, MD 21402-5000
Tel: (410)293-1000
Admissions: (410)293-4361
Fax: (410)293-4348
Web Site: http://www.usna.edu/
President/CEO: Vice Adm. Rodney P. Rempt
Registrar: Dr. Richard L. Davis
Admissions: Col. David Vetter
Type: Four-Year College **Sex:** Coed **Scores:** 100% SAT V 400+; 100% SAT M 400+ **% Accepted:** 13 **Application Deadline:** January 31 **Application Fee:** $0.00 **H.S. Requirements:** High school diploma or equivalent not required **Costs Per Year:** Application fee: $0. **Calendar System:** Semester, Summer Session Available **Enrollment:** FT 4,422 **Faculty:** FT 530, PT 56 **Student-Faculty Ratio:** 7:1 **Exams:** SAT I or ACT **% Residing in College-Owned, -Operated, or -Affiliated Housing:** 100 **Library Holdings:** 800,000 **Regional Accreditation:** Middle State Association of Colleges and Schools **Credit Hours For Degree:** 139 semester hours, Bachelors **Professional Accreditation:** ABET **Intercollegiate Athletics:** Baseball M; Basketball M & W; Cheerleading M & W; Crew M & W; Cross-Country Running M & W; Football M; Golf M; Gymnastics M & W; Ice Hockey M; Lacrosse M & W; Riflery M & W; Rugby M & W; Sailing M & W; Skiing (Downhill) M & W; Soccer M & W; Softball W; Squash M; Swimming and Diving M & W; Tennis M & W; Track and Field M & W; Volleyball M & W; Water Polo M; Weight Lifting M & W; Wrestling M

UNIVERSITY OF BALTIMORE
1420 North Charles St.
Baltimore, MD 21201-5779
Tel: (410)837-4200; 877-APPLYUB
Admissions: (410)837-4777
Fax: (410)837-4793
E-mail: admissions@ubmail.ubalt.edu
Web Site: http://www.ubalt.edu/
President/CEO: Robert Bogemolny
Admissions: Dawn Griffith
Financial Aid: Barbara Miller
Type: Two-Year Upper Division **Sex:** Coed **Affiliation:** University System of Maryland **Admission Plans:** Open Admission **Application Fee:** $35.00 **Costs Per Year:** Application fee: $35. State resident tuition: $5324 full-time, $243 per credit part-time. Nonresident tuition: $16,904 full-time, $704 per credit part-time. Mandatory fees: $1469 full-time, $27 per credit part-time. Full-time tuition and fees vary according to class time, course load, and degree level. Part-time tuition and fees vary according to class time, course load, and degree level. **Scholarships:** Available **Calendar System:** Semester, Summer Session Available **Enrollment:** FT 1,051, PT 1,066, Grad 1,793 **Faculty:** FT 159, PT 172 **Student-Faculty Ratio:** 15:1 **% Receiving Financial Aid:** 64 **Library Holdings:** 258,747 **Regional Accreditation:** Middle State Association of Colleges and Schools **Credit Hours For Degree:** 120 semester hours, Bachelors **ROTC:** Army, Air Force **Professional Accreditation:** AACSB, ABA, AALS, NASPAA

UNIVERSITY OF MARYLAND, BALTIMORE COUNTY
1000 Hilltop Circle
Baltimore, MD 21250
Tel: (410)455-1000
Free: 800-862-2402
Admissions: (410)455-2291
Fax: (410)455-1210
E-mail: admissions@umbc.edu
Web Site: http://www.umbc.edu/
President/CEO: Dr. Freeman A. Hrabowski
Registrar: Dave Hollander
Admissions: Dale Bittinger
Type: University **Sex:** Coed **Affiliation:** University System of Maryland **Scores:** 100% SAT V 400+; 100% SAT M 400+; 30.9% ACT 18-23; 52.4% ACT 24-29 **% Accepted:** 71 **Admission Plans:** Early Admission; Early Action; Deferred Admission **Application Deadline:** February 01 **Application Fee:** $50.00 **H.S. Requirements:** High school diploma required; GED accepted **Costs Per Year:** Application fee: $50. State resident tuition: $6484 full-time, $270 per credit hour part-time. Nonresident tuition: $14,560 full-time, $606 per credit hour part-time. Mandatory fees: $2036 full-time, $5 per credit hour part-time. College room and board: $8090. College room only: $4930. **Scholarships:** Available **Calendar System:** 4-1-4, Summer Session Available **Enrollment:** FT 7,980, PT 1,426, Grad 2,244 **Faculty:** FT 458, PT 295 **Student-Faculty Ratio:** 17:1 **Exams:** SAT I or ACT **% Receiving Financial Aid:** 46 **% Residing in College-Owned, -Operated, or -Affiliated Housing:** 33 **Library Holdings:** 766,261 **Regional Accreditation:** Middle State Association of Colleges and Schools **Credit Hours For Degree:** 120 credit hours, Bachelors **ROTC:** Army **Professional Accreditation:** ABET, APA, CSWE, JRCEMT, NASPAA, NCATE **Intercollegiate Athletics:** Baseball M; Basketball M & W; Bowling M & W; Crew M & W; Cross-Country Running M & W; Fencing M & W; Field Hockey W; Ice Hockey M; Lacrosse M & W; Rugby M & W; Sailing M & W; Skiing (Downhill) M & W; Soccer M & W; Softball W; Swimming and Diving M & W; Tennis M & W; Track and Field M & W; Ultimate Frisbee M & W; Volleyball M & W; Wrestling M

UNIVERSITY OF MARYLAND, COLLEGE PARK
College Park, MD 20742
Tel: (301)405-1000
Free: 800-422-5867
Admissions: (301)314-8385
Fax: (301)314-9693
E-mail: um-admit@uga.umd.edu
Web Site: http://www.maryland.edu/
President/CEO: Dr. C.D. Mote, Jr.
Registrar: David D. Robb
Admissions: Barbara Gill
Financial Aid: William McLean
Type: University **Sex:** Coed **Affiliation:** University System of Maryland **Scores:** 99.49% SAT V 400+; 99.52% SAT M 400+ **% Accepted:** 49 **Admission Plans:** Preferred Admission; Early Admission; Early Action **Application Deadline:** January 20 **Application Fee:** $55.00 **H.S. Requirements:** High school diploma required; GED accepted **Costs Per Year:** Application fee: $55. State resident tuition: $6566 full-time, $273 per credit hour part-time. Nonresident tuition: $18,890 full-time, $787 per credit hour part-time. Mandatory fees: $1255 full-time, $288 per term part-time. Part-time tuition and fees vary according to course load. College room and board: $8075. College room only: $4784. Room and board charges vary according

to board plan. **Scholarships:** Available **Calendar System:** Semester, Summer Session Available **Enrollment:** FT 23,226, PT 2,147, Grad 9,813 **Faculty:** FT 1,508, PT 562 **Student-Faculty Ratio:** 19:1 **Exams:** SAT I or ACT **% Receiving Financial Aid:** 40 **% Residing in College-Owned, -Operated, or -Affiliated Housing:** 39 **Library Holdings:** 3,016,940 **Regional Accreditation:** Middle State Association of Colleges and Schools **Credit Hours For Degree:** 120 semester hours, Bachelors **ROTC:** Army, Navy, Air Force **Professional Accreditation:** AACSB, ABET, ACEJMC, AAMFT, ACA, ADtA, ACSP, ALA, APA, ASLA, ASLHA, AVMA, CEPH, CORE, NASM, NASPAA, NAST, NCATE **Intercollegiate Athletics:** Baseball M; Basketball M & W; Cheerleading W; Cross-Country Running M & W; Field Hockey W; Football M; Golf M & W; Gymnastics W; Lacrosse M & W; Soccer M & W; Softball W; Swimming and Diving M & W; Tennis M & W; Track and Field M & W; Volleyball W; Water Polo W; Wrestling M

UNIVERSITY OF MARYLAND EASTERN SHORE
Princess Anne, MD 21853-1299
Tel: (410)651-2200
Admissions: (410)651-8410
Fax: (410)651-7922
Web Site: http://www.umes.edu/
President/CEO: Thelma B. Thompson
Registrar: Cheryl Holden-Duffy
Admissions: Edwina Morse
Financial Aid: James Kellam
Type: University **Sex:** Coed **Affiliation:** University System of Maryland **Scores:** 66.2% SAT V 400+; 60.2% SAT M 400+; 2.8% ACT 18-23 **Admission Plans:** Preferred Admission; Early Admission; Early Action; Deferred Admission **Application Fee:** $25.00 **H.S. Requirements:** High school diploma required; GED accepted **Costs Per Year:** Application fee: $25. State resident tuition: $4112 full-time, $171 per credit hour part-time. Nonresident tuition: $10,268 full-time, $371 per credit hour part-time. Mandatory fees: $1696 full-time, $40 per term part-time. Full-time tuition and fees vary according to course load. Part-time tuition and fees vary according to course load. College room and board: $6130. College room only: $3430. Room and board charges vary according to board plan and housing facility. **Scholarships:** Available **Calendar System:** Semester, Summer Session Available **Enrollment:** FT 2,902, PT 424, Grad 436 **Faculty:** FT 181, PT 53 **Student-Faculty Ratio:** 17:1 **Exams:** Other, SAT I or ACT **% Receiving Financial Aid:** 65 **% Residing in College-Owned, -Operated, or -Affiliated Housing:** 60 **Library Holdings:** 150,000 **Regional Accreditation:** Middle State Association of Colleges and Schools **Credit Hours For Degree:** 122 credits, Bachelors **Professional Accreditation:** AAFCS, ACCE, ADtA, APTA, CORE, NCATE **Intercollegiate Athletics:** Baseball M; Basketball M & W; Cheerleading M & W; Cross-Country Running M & W; Softball W; Tennis M & W; Track and Field M & W; Volleyball W; Wrestling M

UNIVERSITY OF MARYLAND UNIVERSITY COLLEGE
3501 University Blvd. East
Adelphi, MD 20783
Tel: (301)985-7000
Fax: (301)985-7678
Web Site: http://www.umuc.edu/
President/CEO: Dr. Gerald Heeger
Registrar: J. Matthew Gaglione
Admissions: Anne Rahill
Financial Aid: Dawn Mosisa
Type: Comprehensive **Sex:** Coed **Affiliation:** University System of Maryland **Admission Plans:** Open Admission; Deferred Admission **Application Fee:** $30.00 **H.S. Requirements:** High school diploma required; GED accepted **Costs Per Year:** Application fee: $30. State resident tuition: $5520 full-time, $230 per semester hour part-time. Nonresident tuition: $10,152 full-time, $423 per semester hour part-time. Mandatory fees: $120 full-time, $5 per semester hour part-time. **Scholarships:** Available **Calendar System:** Semester, Summer Session Available **Enrollment:** FT 2,779, PT 17,078, Grad 8,517 **Faculty:** FT 189, PT 1,152 **Student-Faculty Ratio:** 20:1 **% Receiving Financial Aid:** 50 **Library Holdings:** 5,807 **Regional Accreditation:** Middle State Association of Colleges and Schools **Credit Hours For Degree:** 60 semester hours, Associates; 120 semester hours, Bachelors

UNIVERSITY OF PHOENIX-MARYLAND CAMPUS
8830 Stanford Blvd., Ste. 100
Columbia, MD 21045-5424
Tel: (410)872-9001
Free: 800-228-7240
Admissions: (480)557-1712
Web Site: http://www.phoenix.edu/
President/CEO: Tim Moscato
Admissions: Nina Omelchanko
Type: Comprehensive **Sex:** Coed **Admission Plans:** Open Admission; Deferred Admission **Application Deadline:** Rolling **Application Fee:** $110.00 **H.S. Requirements:** High school diploma required; GED accepted **Costs Per Year:** Application fee: $110. Tuition: $11,950 full-time, $398 per credit part-time. Mandatory fees: $560 full-time, $70 per course part-time. Full-time tuition and fees vary according to program. **Scholarships:** Available **Calendar System:** Continuous, Summer Session Not available **Enrollment:** FT 1,586, Grad 442 **Faculty:** FT 9, PT 209 **Student-Faculty Ratio:** 11:1 **Library Holdings:** 444 **Regional Accreditation:** North Central Association of Colleges and Schools **Credit Hours For Degree:** 60 credits, Associates; 120 credits, Bachelors

VILLA JULIE COLLEGE
Green Spring Valley Rd.
Stevenson, MD 21153
Tel: (410)486-7000; 877-468-3852
Admissions: (410)486-7001
E-mail: admissions@mail.vjc.edu
Web Site: http://www.vjc.edu/
President/CEO: Dr. Kevin J. Manning
Registrar: Tracy Bolt
Admissions: Mark Hergan
Financial Aid: Debra Bottomms
Type: Comprehensive **Sex:** Coed **Scores:** 95% SAT V 400+; 96% SAT M 400+ **% Accepted:** 70 **Admission Plans:** Early Admission; Deferred Admission **Application Deadline:** March 01 **Application Fee:** $25.00 **H.S. Requirements:** High school diploma required; GED accepted **Costs Per Year:** Application fee: $25. Comprehensive fee: $25,222 includes full-time tuition ($14,674), mandatory fees ($1000), and college room and board ($9548). College room only: $6550. Room and board charges vary according to board plan and housing facility. Part-time tuition: $415 per credit. Part-time mandatory fees: $75 per term. **Scholarships:** Available **Calendar System:** Semester, Summer Session Available **Enrollment:** FT 2,304, PT 503, Grad 149 **Faculty:** FT 93, PT 256 **Student-Faculty Ratio:** 14:1 **Exams:** SAT I or ACT **% Receiving Financial Aid:** 56 **% Residing in College-Owned, -Operated, or -Affiliated Housing:** 26 **Library Holdings:** 64,930 **Regional Accreditation:** Middle State Association of Colleges and Schools **Credit Hours For Degree:** 60 credits, Associates; 120 credits, Bachelors **ROTC:** Army **Professional Accreditation:** NAACLS, NLN **Intercollegiate Athletics:** Baseball M; Basketball M & W; Cheerleading M & W; Cross-Country Running M & W; Field Hockey W; Golf M & W; Lacrosse M & W; Soccer M & W; Softball W; Tennis M & W; Track and Field M & W; Volleyball W

WASHINGTON BIBLE COLLEGE
6511 Princess Garden Parkway
Lanham, MD 20706-3599
Tel: (301)552-1400; 877-793-7227
Fax: (301)552-2775
E-mail: admissions@bible.edu
Web Site: http://www.bible.edu/
President/CEO: Dr. Homer Heater, Jr.
Registrar: Dr. Neil A. Holliker
Admissions: Mark D. Johnson
Financial Aid: Nancy Minton
Type: Four-Year College **Sex:** Coed **Affiliation:** nondenominational; Capital Bible Seminary **Admission Plans:** Early Admission; Deferred Admission **Application Fee:** $25.00 **H.S. Requirements:** High school diploma required; GED accepted **Costs Per Year:** Application fee: $25. Comprehensive fee: $22,690 includes full-time tuition ($16,000), mandatory fees ($450), and college room and board ($6240). College room only: $3000. Full-time tuition and fees vary according to course load and location. Room and board charges vary according to board plan. Part-time tuition: $350 per credit. Part-time tuition varies according to course load and location. **Scholarships:** Available **Calendar System:** Semester, Summer Session Available **Enrollment:** FT 187, PT 144 **Faculty:** FT 14, PT 0 **Student-Faculty Ratio:** 13:1 **Exams:** SAT I or ACT **% Receiving Financial Aid:** 80 **% Residing in College-Owned, -Operated, or -Affiliated Housing:** 28 **Library Holdings:** 78,000 **Regional Accreditation:** Middle State Association of Colleges and Schools **Credit Hours For Degree:** 64 credit hours, Associates; 120 credit hours, Bachelors **Professional Accreditation:** AABC **Intercollegiate**

Athletics: Basketball M & W; Soccer M & W; Volleyball W

WASHINGTON COLLEGE
300 Washington Ave.
Chestertown, MD 21620-1197
Tel: (410)778-2800
Free: 800-422-1782
Admissions: (410)778-7700
Fax: (410)778-7287
E-mail: admissions_office@washcoll.edu
Web Site: http://www.washcoll.edu/
President/CEO: Dr. Baird Tipson
Registrar: Jen Bershon
Admissions: Kevin Coveney
Financial Aid: Jean M. Narcum
Type: Comprehensive **Sex:** Coed **Scores:** 99% SAT V 400+; 100% SAT M 400+; 47% ACT 18-23; 53% ACT 24-29 **% Accepted:** 59 **Admission Plans:** Early Action; Early Decision Plan; Deferred Admission **Application Deadline:** March 01 **Application Fee:** $45.00 **H.S. Requirements:** High school diploma required; GED accepted **Costs Per Year:** Application fee: $45. Comprehensive fee: $34,990 includes full-time tuition ($28,230), mandatory fees ($560), and college room and board ($6200). College room only: $3000. Full-time tuition and fees vary according to program and reciprocity agreements. Room and board charges vary according to board plan and housing facility. Part-time tuition: $4705 per course. Part-time tuition varies according to course load and program. **Scholarships:** Available **Calendar System:** Semester, Summer Session Not available **Enrollment:** FT 1,312, PT 29, Grad 71 **Faculty:** FT 93, PT 51 **Student-Faculty Ratio:** 12:1 **Exams:** SAT I or ACT **% Receiving Financial Aid:** 44 **% Residing in College-Owned, -Operated, or -Affiliated Housing:** 80 **Library Holdings:** 243,030 **Regional Accreditation:** Middle State Association of Colleges and Schools **Credit Hours For Degree:** 128 credits, Bachelors **Intercollegiate Athletics:** Baseball M; Basketball M & W; Crew M & W; Equestrian Sports M & W; Fencing M & W; Field Hockey W; Ice Hockey M; Lacrosse M & W; Rugby M & W; Sailing M & W; Soccer M & W; Softball W; Swimming and Diving M & W; Table Tennis M & W; Tennis M & W; Ultimate Frisbee M & W; Volleyball W

WOR-WIC COMMUNITY COLLEGE
32000 Campus Dr.
Salisbury, MD 21804
Tel: (410)334-2800
Admissions: (410)334-2895
Web Site: http://www.worwic.edu/
President/CEO: Dr. Murray K. Hoy
Registrar: Amanda Trego
Admissions: Richard Webster
Financial Aid: Deborah E. Jenkins
Type: Two-Year College **Sex:** Coed **Affiliation:** Maryland State Community Colleges System **% Accepted:** 100 **Admission Plans:** Open Admission; Early Admission **Application Deadline:** Rolling **Application Fee:** $0.00 **H.S. Requirements:** High school diploma or equivalent not required **Costs Per Year:** Application fee: $0. Area resident tuition: $2250 full-time, $75 per credit hour part-time. State resident tuition: $5700 full-time, $190 per credit hour part-time. Nonresident tuition: $6630 full-time, $221 per credit hour part-time. Mandatory fees: $86 full-time, $2 per credit hour part-time, $13 per term part-time. **Calendar System:** Semester, Summer Session Available **Enrollment:** FT 970, PT 2,073 **Faculty:** FT 56, PT 112 **Student-Faculty Ratio:** 20:1 **Exams:** ACT **Library Holdings:** 25 **Regional Accreditation:** Middle State Association of Colleges and Schools **Credit Hours For Degree:** 60 credit hours, Associates **Professional Accreditation:** JRCERT

YESHIVA COLLEGE OF THE NATION'S CAPITAL
1216 Arcola Ave.
Silver Spring, MD 20902
Tel: (301)593-2534
Fax: (301)949-7040 **Type:** Four-Year College **Affiliation:** Jewish **Professional Accreditation:** AARTS

AMERICAN INTERNATIONAL COLLEGE
1000 State St.
Springfield, MA 01109-3189
Tel: (413)737-7000
Admissions: (413)205-3201
Fax: (413)737-2803
E-mail: inquiry@acad.aic.edu
Web Site: http://www.aic.edu/
President/CEO: Dr. Harry J. Courniotes
Registrar: Judith E. Syner
Admissions: Peter Miller
Financial Aid: Irene Martin
Type: Comprehensive **Sex:** Coed **Scores:** 96% SAT V 400+; 97% SAT M 400+; 50% ACT 18-23; 2% ACT 24-29 **% Accepted:** 84 **Admission Plans:** Early Admission; Deferred Admission **Application Deadline:** Rolling **Application Fee:** $20.00 **H.S. Requirements:** High school diploma required; GED accepted **Costs Per Year:** Application fee: $20. Comprehensive fee: $30,260 includes full-time tuition ($20,990) and college room and board ($9270). Part-time tuition: $470 per credit. **Scholarships:** Available **Calendar System:** Semester, Summer Session Available **Enrollment:** FT 1,214, PT 184, Grad 417 **Faculty:** FT 72, PT 87 **Student-Faculty Ratio:** 12:1 **Exams:** SAT I or ACT **% Receiving Financial Aid:** 90 **% Residing in College-Owned, -Operated, or -Affiliated Housing:** 55 **Library Holdings:** 118,000 **Regional Accreditation:** New England Association of Schools and Colleges **Credit Hours For Degree:** 60 credits, Associates; 120 credits, Bachelors **ROTC:** Army, Air Force **Professional Accreditation:** AOTA, APTA, NLN **Intercollegiate Athletics:** Baseball M; Basketball M & W; Field Hockey W; Football M; Golf M; Ice Hockey M; Lacrosse M & W; Soccer M & W; Softball W; Tennis M & W; Volleyball W; Wrestling M

AMHERST COLLEGE
PO Box 5000
Amherst, MA 01002-5000
Tel: (413)542-2000
Admissions: (413)542-2328
Fax: (413)542-2040
E-mail: admissions@amherst.edu
Web Site: http://www.amherst.edu/
President/CEO: Dr. Anthony W. Marx
Registrar: Dr. Gerald M. Mager
Admissions: Thomas Parker
Financial Aid: Joe Paul Case
Type: Four-Year College **Sex:** Coed **Scores:** 100% SAT V 400+; 100% SAT M 400+; 29.3% ACT 24-29 **% Accepted:** 19 **Admission Plans:** Early Admission; Early Decision Plan; Deferred Admission **Application Deadline:** January 01 **Application Fee:** $55.00 **H.S. Requirements:** High school diploma or equivalent not required **Costs Per Year:** Application fee: $55. Comprehensive fee: $41,590 includes full-time tuition ($32,395), mandatory fees ($610), and college room and board ($8585). College room only: $4600. **Scholarships:** Available **Calendar System:** Semester, Summer Session Not available **Enrollment:** FT 1,623 **Faculty:** FT 190, PT 28 **Student-Faculty Ratio:** 8:1 **Exams:** SAT I and SAT II or ACT **% Receiving Financial Aid:** 48 **% Residing in College-Owned, -Operated, or -Affiliated Housing:** 98 **Library Holdings:** 1,003,887 **Regional Accreditation:** New England Association of Schools and Colleges **Credit Hours For Degree:** 32 courses, Bachelors **Intercollegiate Athletics:** Baseball M; Basketball M & W; Crew M & W; Cross-Country Running M & W; Equestrian Sports M & W; Fencing M & W; Field Hockey W; Football M; Golf M & W; Ice Hockey M & W; Lacrosse M & W; Rugby M & W; Sailing M & W; Skiing (Downhill) M & W; Soccer M & W; Softball W; Squash M & W; Swimming and Diving M & W; Tennis M & W; Track and Field M & W; Ultimate Frisbee M & W; Volleyball M & W; Water Polo M & W

ANNA MARIA COLLEGE
Sunset Ln.
Paxton, MA 01612
Tel: (508)849-3300
Free: 800-344-4586
Admissions: (508)849-3360
Web Site: http://www.annamaria.edu/
President/CEO: William McGarry
Registrar: Sr. Rollande Quintal
Admissions: Elaine Lapomardo
Financial Aid: Nicole Brennan
Type: Comprehensive **Sex:** Coed **Affiliation:** Roman Catholic **Scores:** 84.41% SAT V 400+; 76.14% SAT M 400+; 61.54% ACT 18-23; 7.69% ACT 24-29 **% Accepted:** 90 **Admission Plans:** Deferred Admission **Application Deadline:** Rolling **Application Fee:** $40.00 **H.S. Requirements:** High school diploma required; GED accepted **Costs Per Year:** Application fee: $40. Comprehensive fee: $29,815 includes full-time tuition ($19,900), mandatory fees ($1980), and college room and board ($7935). Part-time tuition: $663.33 per credit hour. **Scholarships:** Available **Calendar System:** Semester, Summer Session Available **Enrollment:** FT 540, PT 205, Grad 297 **Faculty:** FT 38, PT 132 **Student-Faculty Ratio:** 9:1 **Exams:** SAT I and SAT II or ACT **% Receiving Financial Aid:** 81 **% Residing in College-Owned, -Operated, or -Affiliated Housing:** 60 **Library Holdings:** 79,039 **Regional Accreditation:** New England Association of Schools and Colleges **Credit Hours For Degree:** 60 credit hours, Associates; 120 credit hours, Bachelors **ROTC:** Air Force **Professional Accreditation:** CSWE, NASM, NLN **Intercollegiate Athletics:** Baseball M; Basketball M & W; Cheerleading W; Cross-Country Running M & W; Field Hockey W; Golf M & W; Soccer M & W; Softball W; Volleyball W

THE ART INSTITUTE OF BOSTON AT LESLEY UNIVERSITY
700 Beacon St.
Boston, MA 02215-2598
Tel: (617)585-6600
Admissions: (617)585-6701
Fax: (617)437-1226
E-mail: broth@lesley.edu
Web Site: http://www.aiboston.edu/
President/CEO: Margaret A. McKenna
Registrar: Andy Rademaker
Admissions: Bonnie Roth Galinski
Financial Aid: Paul Henderson
Type: Comprehensive **Sex:** Coed **Affiliation:** Lesley University; Education Management Corporation **Scores:** 97% SAT V 400+; 95% SAT M 400+ **Admission Plans:** Deferred Admission **Application Fee:** $40.00 **H.S. Requirements:** High school diploma required; GED accepted **Costs Per Year:** Application fee: $40. Comprehensive fee: $29,550 includes full-time tuition ($19,600) and college room and board ($9950). College room only: $6100. Full-time tuition varies according to program. Room and board

charges vary according to housing facility. Part-time tuition: $824 per credit. **Scholarships:** Available **Calendar System:** Semester, Summer Session Available **Enrollment:** FT 964, PT 78, Grad 5,479 **Faculty:** FT 54, PT 131 **Student-Faculty Ratio:** 10:1 **Exams:** SAT I or ACT **% Receiving Financial Aid:** 78 **% Residing in College-Owned, -Operated, or -Affiliated Housing:** 66 **Library Holdings:** 100,000 **Regional Accreditation:** New England Association of Schools and Colleges **Credit Hours For Degree:** 128 credits, Bachelors **Professional Accreditation:** NASAD **Intercollegiate Athletics:** Basketball W; Crew W; Soccer M & W; Softball W; Volleyball M & W

ASSUMPTION COLLEGE
500 Salisbury St.
Worcester, MA 01609-1296
Tel: (508)767-7000; 888-882-7786
Admissions: (508)767-7110
Fax: (508)799-4412
Web Site: http://www.assumption.edu/
President/CEO: Dr. Thomas R. Plough
Registrar: David A. Aalto
Admissions: Kathleen Murphy
Financial Aid: Karen Puntillo
Type: Comprehensive **Sex:** Coed **Affiliation:** Roman Catholic **Scores:** 98% SAT V 400+; 99% SAT M 400+; 48% ACT 18-23; 27% ACT 24-29 **% Accepted:** 76 **Admission Plans:** Early Decision Plan; Deferred Admission **Application Deadline:** March 01 **Application Fee:** $50.00 **H.S. Requirements:** High school diploma required; GED accepted **Costs Per Year:** Application fee: $50. Comprehensive fee: $32,085 includes full-time tuition ($25,895), mandatory fees ($415), and college room and board ($5775). College room only: $3395. **Scholarships:** Available **Calendar System:** Semester, Summer Session Available **Enrollment:** FT 2,099, PT 25, Grad 327 **Faculty:** FT 129, PT 87 **Student-Faculty Ratio:** 13:1 **Exams:** SAT I or ACT **% Receiving Financial Aid:** 70 **% Residing in College-Owned, -Operated, or -Affiliated Housing:** 90 **Library Holdings:** 103,467 **Regional Accreditation:** New England Association of Schools and Colleges **Credit Hours For Degree:** 40 courses, Bachelors **ROTC:** Army, Air Force **Professional Accreditation:** CORE **Intercollegiate Athletics:** Baseball M; Basketball M & W; Crew M & W; Cross-Country Running M & W; Field Hockey W; Football M; Golf M; Ice Hockey M; Lacrosse M & W; Soccer M & W; Softball W; Tennis M & W; Track and Field M & W; Volleyball W

ATLANTIC UNION COLLEGE
PO Box 1000
South Lancaster, MA 01561-1000
Tel: (978)368-2000
Free: 800-282-2030
Admissions: (978)368-2239
Fax: (978)368-2015
E-mail: info@atlanticuc.edu
Web Site: http://www.atlanticuc.edu/
President/CEO: Dr. George P. Babcock
Registrar: Dr. Issumael Nzamutuma
Admissions: Rosita Lashley
Financial Aid: Sandra Boucher
Type: Comprehensive **Sex:** Coed **Affiliation:** Seventh-day Adventist **Application Fee:** $25.00 **H.S. Requirements:** High school diploma required; GED accepted **Costs Per Year:** Application fee: $25. Comprehensive fee: $17,600. Part-time tuition: $525 per credit hour. Part-time tuition varies according to class time and program. Tuition: $525 per credit hour part-time. Part-time tuition varies according to class time and program. Tuition guaranteed not to increase for student's term of enrollment. **Scholarships:** Available **Calendar System:** Semester, Summer Session Available **Student-Faculty Ratio:** 13:1 **Exams:** SAT I or ACT, SAT I **% Receiving Financial Aid:** 68 **% Residing in College-Owned, -Operated, or -Affiliated Housing:** 68 **Library Holdings:** 135,694 **Regional Accreditation:** New England Association of Schools and Colleges **Credit Hours For Degree:** 64 hours, Associates; 128 hours, Bachelors **Professional Accreditation:** CSWE, NASM, NLN

BABSON COLLEGE
Babson Park, MA 02457-0310
Tel: (781)235-1200
Free: 800-488-3696
Fax: (781)239-5614
E-mail: ugradadmission@babson.edu
Web Site: http://www.babson.edu/
President/CEO: Brian M. Barefoot
Registrar: Linda Kean
Admissions: R. Alan Kines
Financial Aid: Melissa Shaak
Type: Comprehensive **Sex:** Coed **Scores:** 100% SAT V 400+; 100% SAT M 400+; 83% ACT 24-29 **% Accepted:** 37 **Admission Plans:** Early Action; Early Decision Plan; Deferred Admission **Application Deadline:** January 15 **Application Fee:** $60.00 **H.S. Requirements:** High school diploma required; GED accepted **Costs Per Year:** Application fee: $60. Comprehensive fee: $43,478 includes full-time tuition ($32,256) and college room and board ($11,222). College room only: $7242. **Scholarships:** Available **Calendar System:** Semester, Summer Session Available **Enrollment:** FT 1,725, Grad 1,485 **Faculty:** FT 151, PT 78 **Student-Faculty Ratio:** 14:1 **Exams:** Other, SAT I or ACT **% Receiving Financial Aid:** 41 **% Residing in College-Owned, -Operated, or -Affiliated Housing:** 83 **Library Holdings:** 131,436 **Regional Accreditation:** New England Association of Schools and Colleges **Credit Hours For Degree:** 128 credit hours, Bachelors **ROTC:** Army, Navy, Air Force **Professional Accreditation:** AACSB **Intercollegiate Athletics:** Baseball M; Basketball M & W; Cheerleading W; Cross-Country Running M & W; Field Hockey W; Golf M; Ice Hockey M & W; Lacrosse M & W; Rugby M & W; Skiing (Downhill) M & W; Soccer M & W; Softball W; Swimming and Diving M & W; Tennis M & W; Track and Field M & W; Volleyball W

BAY PATH COLLEGE
588 Longmeadow St.
Longmeadow, MA 01106-2292
Tel: (413)565-1000
Free: 800-782-7284
Fax: (413)567-0501
E-mail: admiss@baypath.edu
Web Site: http://www.baypath.edu/
President/CEO: Dr. Carol A. Leary
Registrar: Charles Bertolino
Admissions: Lisa Casassa
Financial Aid: Stephanie King
Type: Comprehensive **Scores:** 95.4% SAT V 400+; 96.8% SAT M 400+ **% Accepted:** 69 **Admission Plans:** Early Admission; Early Action; Deferred Admission **Application Deadline:** Rolling **Application Fee:** $25.00 **H.S. Requirements:** High school diploma required; GED accepted **Costs Per Year:** Application fee: $25. Comprehensive fee: $30,220 includes full-time tuition ($20,606) and college room and board ($9614). Room and board charges vary according to board plan. Part-time tuition: $440 per credit. **Scholarships:** Available **Calendar System:** Semester, Summer Session Available **Enrollment:** FT 1,109, PT 234, Grad 113 **Faculty:** FT 38, PT 124 **Student-Faculty Ratio:** 17:1 **Exams:** SAT I or ACT **% Receiving Financial Aid:** 87 **% Residing in College-Owned, -Operated, or -Affiliated Housing:** 40 **Library Holdings:** 55,060 **Regional Accreditation:** New England Association of Schools and Colleges **Credit Hours For Degree:** 60 credits, Associates; 120 credits, Bachelors **ROTC:** Army, Air Force **Professional Accreditation:** AOTA **Intercollegiate Athletics:** Basketball W; Cross-Country Running W; Soccer W; Softball W; Tennis W; Volleyball W

BAY STATE COLLEGE
122 Commonwealth Ave.
Boston, MA 02116-2975
Tel: (617)236-8000
Free: 800-81-LEARN
Fax: (617)536-1735
E-mail: admissions@baystate.edu
Web Site: http://www.baystate.edu/
President/CEO: Howard E. Horton, Esq
Registrar: Raymond Barnes
Admissions: Pamela DellaPorta
Financial Aid: Melissa Holster
Type: Two-Year College **Sex:** Coed **% Accepted:** 80 **Admission Plans:** Early Admission **Application Deadline:** Rolling **Application Fee:** $40.00 **H.S. Requirements:** High school diploma required; GED accepted **Costs Per Year:** Application fee: $40. Comprehensive fee: $26,325 includes full-time tuition ($15,900), mandatory fees ($350), and college room and board ($10,075). Part-time tuition: $1530 per course. **Scholarships:** Available **Calendar System:** Semester, Summer Session Not available **Enrollment:** FT 522, PT 235 **Faculty:** FT 19, PT 47 **Student-Faculty Ratio:** 13:1 **% Residing in College-Owned, -Operated, or -Affiliated Housing:** 21 **Library Holdings:** 4,490 **Regional Accreditation:** New England Associa-

tion of Schools and Colleges **Credit Hours For Degree:** 60 credits, Associates **Professional Accreditation:** ABHES, APTA

BECKER COLLEGE
61 Sever St.
Worcester, MA 01609
Tel: (508)791-9241; 877-5BECKER
Fax: (508)831-7505
E-mail: admissions@go.becker.edu
Web Site: http://www.beckercollege.edu/
President/CEO: Dr. Kenneth Zirkle
Registrar: Andrew Baglio
Admissions: Elaine Lapomardo
Financial Aid: Denise Lawrie
Type: Four-Year College **Sex:** Coed **Scores:** 73% SAT V 400+; 71% SAT M 400+; 41% ACT 18-23; 13% ACT 24-29 **Admission Plans:** Deferred Admission **Application Fee:** $30.00 **H.S. Requirements:** High school diploma required; GED accepted **Costs Per Year:** Application fee: $30. Comprehensive fee: $26,425 includes full-time tuition ($18,000), mandatory fees ($425), and college room and board ($8000). Part-time tuition: $750 per credit hour. Part-time tuition varies according to program. **Scholarships:** Available **Calendar System:** Semester, Summer Session Available **Enrollment:** FT 910, PT 750 **Faculty:** FT 39, PT 64 **Student-Faculty Ratio:** 15:1 **Exams:** SAT I or ACT **% Receiving Financial Aid:** 86 **% Residing in College-Owned, -Operated, or -Affiliated Housing:** 40 **Library Holdings:** 75,000 **Regional Accreditation:** New England Association of Schools and Colleges **Credit Hours For Degree:** 60 credits, Associates; 122 credits, Bachelors **ROTC:** Army, Navy, Air Force **Professional Accreditation:** APTA, NLN **Intercollegiate Athletics:** Baseball M; Basketball M & W; Cheerleading M & W; Cross-Country Running M & W; Equestrian Sports M & W; Field Hockey W; Football M; Golf M; Ice Hockey M & W; Lacrosse M; Soccer M & W; Softball W; Tennis M & W; Volleyball W

BENJAMIN FRANKLIN INSTITUTE OF TECHNOLOGY
41 Berkeley St.
Boston, MA 02116-6296
Tel: (617)423-4630
Fax: (617)482-3706
E-mail: nkraft@bfit.edu
Web Site: http://www.bfit.edu/
President/CEO: Dr. Richard K. Fields
Registrar: Kevin M. Sullivan
Admissions: Norman R. Kraft
Financial Aid: Kevin M. Sullivan
Type: Two-Year College **Sex:** Coed **% Accepted:** 91 **Admission Plans:** Open Admission; Deferred Admission **Application Deadline:** August 15 **Application Fee:** $20.00 **H.S. Requirements:** High school diploma required; GED accepted **Costs Per Year:** Application fee: $20. Tuition: $12,750 full-time, $531 per credit part-time. **Calendar System:** Semester, Summer Session Available **Faculty:** FT 22, PT 20 **Student-Faculty Ratio:** 11:1 **Exams:** SAT I or ACT **Library Holdings:** 10,000 **Regional Accreditation:** New England Association of Schools and Colleges **Credit Hours For Degree:** 70 credits, Associates; 134 credits, Bachelors **Professional Accreditation:** ABET

BENTLEY COLLEGE
175 Forest St.
Waltham, MA 02452-4705
Tel: (781)891-2000
Free: 800-523-2354
Admissions: (781)891-2244
Fax: (781)891-3414
E-mail: krinehart@bentley.edu
Web Site: http://www.bentley.edu
President/CEO: Dr. Joseph G. Morone
Registrar: Dr. Barbara H. Palmer
Admissions: Kenton W. Rinehart
Financial Aid: Donna Kendall
Type: Comprehensive **Sex:** Coed **Scores:** 100% SAT V 400+; 100% SAT M 400+ **% Accepted:** 43 **Admission Plans:** Early Admission; Early Action; Early Decision Plan; Deferred Admission **Application Deadline:** February 01 **Application Fee:** $50.00 **H.S. Requirements:** High school diploma required; GED accepted **Costs Per Year:** Application fee: $50. Comprehensive fee: $38,784 includes full-time tuition ($28,390), mandatory fees ($224), and college room and board ($10,170). College room only: $6060. Full-time tuition and fees vary according to student level. Room and board charges vary according to board plan and housing facility. Part-time tuition: $1368 per course. Part-time mandatory fees: $10 per term. Part-time tuition and fees vary according to class time and student level. **Scholarships:** Available **Calendar System:** Semester, Summer Session Available **Enrollment:** FT 3,958, PT 336, Grad 1,271 **Faculty:** FT 270, PT 205 **Student-Faculty Ratio:** 12:1 **Exams:** SAT I or ACT **% Receiving Financial Aid:** 51 **% Residing in College-Owned, -Operated, or -Affiliated Housing:** 79 **Library Holdings:** 136,094 **Regional Accreditation:** New England Association of Schools and Colleges **Credit Hours For Degree:** 122 credits, Bachelors **ROTC:** Army **Professional Accreditation:** AACSB **Intercollegiate Athletics:** Baseball M; Basketball M & W; Cross-Country Running M & W; Field Hockey W; Football M; Golf W; Ice Hockey M; Lacrosse M & W; Soccer M & W; Softball W; Swimming and Diving M & W; Tennis M & W; Track and Field M & W; Volleyball W

BERKLEE COLLEGE OF MUSIC
1140 Boylston St.
Boston, MA 02215-3693
Tel: (617)266-1400
Free: 800-BER-KLEE
Admissions: (617)747-2222
Fax: (617)747-2047
E-mail: admissions@berklee.edu
Web Site: http://www.berklee.edu/
President/CEO: Roger H. Brown
Registrar: Michael Hagarty
Admissions: Damien Bracken
Financial Aid: Pamela Gilligan
Type: Four-Year College **Sex:** Coed **% Accepted:** 57 **Admission Plans:** Early Action; Deferred Admission **Application Deadline:** February 01 **Application Fee:** $100.00 **H.S. Requirements:** High school diploma required; GED accepted **Costs Per Year:** Application fee: $100. Comprehensive fee: $37,997 includes full-time tuition ($21,790), mandatory fees ($4517), and college room and board ($11,690). **Scholarships:** Available **Calendar System:** Semester, Summer Session Available **Enrollment:** FT 4,037 **Faculty:** FT 207, PT 277 **Student-Faculty Ratio:** 13:1 **Exams:** SAT I or ACT **% Receiving Financial Aid:** 44 **% Residing in College-Owned, -Operated, or -Affiliated Housing:** 20 **Library Holdings:** 30,208 **Regional Accreditation:** New England Association of Schools and Colleges **Credit Hours For Degree:** 120 credit hours, Bachelors

BERKSHIRE COMMUNITY COLLEGE
1350 West St.
Pittsfield, MA 01201-5786
Tel: (413)499-4660
Fax: (413)496-9511
E-mail: mbullock@berkshirecc.edu
Web Site: http://www.berkshirecc.edu/
President/CEO: Dr. Bryan K. Blanchard
Registrar: Donald Pfeifer
Admissions: Michael Bullock
Financial Aid: Anne Moore
Type: Two-Year College **Sex:** Coed **Affiliation:** Massachusetts Public Higher Education System **% Accepted:** 100 **Admission Plans:** Open Admission; Deferred Admission **Application Deadline:** Rolling **Application Fee:** $10.00 **H.S. Requirements:** High school diploma required; GED accepted **Costs Per Year:** Application fee: $10. State resident tuition: $780 full-time, $26 per credit part-time. Nonresident tuition: $7800 full-time, $260 per credit part-time. Mandatory fees: $2820 full-time, $94 per credit part-time. **Scholarships:** Available **Calendar System:** Semester, Summer Session Available **Enrollment:** FT 923, PT 1,405 **Faculty:** FT 55, PT 115 **Student-Faculty Ratio:** 14:1 **Library Holdings:** 74,271 **Regional Accreditation:** New England Association of Schools and Colleges **Credit Hours For Degree:** 60 credits, Associates **Professional Accreditation:** APTA, CARC, NLN

BOSTON ARCHITECTURAL COLLEGE
320 Newbury St.
Boston, MA 02115-2795
Tel: (617)262-5000; 877-585-0100
Admissions: (617)585-0256
Fax: (617)585-0111
Web Site: http://www.the-bac.edu/
President/CEO: Dr. Theodore C. Landsmark

Registrar: Valerie Nichols
Admissions: Jeff Cutting
Financial Aid: Maureen Samways
Type: Comprehensive **Sex:** Coed **% Accepted:** 70 **Admission Plans:** Open Admission **Application Deadline:** Rolling **Application Fee:** $50.00 **H.S. Requirements:** High school diploma required; GED accepted **Costs Per Year:** Application fee: $50. Tuition: $8610 full-time, $717 per credit part-time. Mandatory fees: $20 full-time, $150. Full-time tuition and fees vary according to course load, degree level, program, and reciprocity agreements. Part-time tuition and fees vary according to course load, degree level, program, and reciprocity agreements. **Scholarships:** Available **Calendar System:** Semester, Summer Session Available **Enrollment:** FT 466, PT 41, Grad 403 **Faculty:** FT 10, PT 317 **Student-Faculty Ratio:** 12:1 **% Receiving Financial Aid:** 77 **Library Holdings:** 27,000 **Regional Accreditation:** New England Association of Schools and Colleges **Credit Hours For Degree:** 178.50 credit hours, Bachelors **Professional Accreditation:** FIDER

BOSTON BAPTIST COLLEGE

950 Metropolitan Ave.
Boston, MA 02136
Tel: (617)364-3510; 888-235-2014
Fax: (617)364-0723
E-mail: kfox@boston.edu
Web Site: http://www.boston.edu/
President/CEO: Dr. Harry Boyle
Admissions: Karen Fox
Type: Four-Year College **Sex:** Coed **Affiliation:** Baptist **Application Deadline:** Rolling **Application Fee:** $40.00 **H.S. Requirements:** High school diploma required; GED accepted **Costs Per Year:** Application fee: $40. Comprehensive fee: $14,784 includes full-time tuition ($6930), mandatory fees ($1600), and college room and board ($6254). College room only: $3594. Part-time tuition: $290 per hour. Part-time mandatory fees: $900 per term. **Scholarships:** Available **Calendar System:** Semester, Summer Session Available **Enrollment:** FT 120, PT 10 **Faculty:** FT 4, PT 5 **Exams:** SAT I or ACT **% Residing in College-Owned, -Operated, or -Affiliated Housing:** 65 **Credit Hours For Degree:** 64 credit hours, Associates **Professional Accreditation:** TACCS

BOSTON COLLEGE

140 Commonwealth Ave.
Chestnut Hill, MA 02467-3800
Tel: (617)552-8000
Free: 800-360-2522
Admissions: (617)552-3100
Fax: (617)552-0798
E-mail: admissions@bcvms.bc.edu
Web Site: http://www.bc.edu/
President/CEO: Rev. William P. Leahy, SJ
Registrar: Dr. Louise M. Lonabocker
Admissions: John L. Mahoney, Jr.
Financial Aid: Bernard Pekala
Type: University **Sex:** Coed **Affiliation:** Roman Catholic (Jesuit) **Scores:** 100% SAT V 400+; 100% SAT M 400+ **% Accepted:** 31 **Admission Plans:** Early Admission; Early Action; Deferred Admission **Application Deadline:** January 01 **Application Fee:** $70.00 **H.S. Requirements:** High school diploma required; GED not accepted **Costs Per Year:** Application fee: $70. One-time mandatory fee: $355. Comprehensive fee: $42,283 includes full-time tuition ($30,950), mandatory fees ($488), and college room and board ($10,845). College room only: $6945. Room and board charges vary according to housing facility. **Scholarships:** Available **Calendar System:** Semester, Summer Session Available **Enrollment:** FT 9,019, Grad 3,917 **Faculty:** FT 662, PT 623 **Student-Faculty Ratio:** 13:1 **Exams:** SAT I and SAT II or ACT **% Receiving Financial Aid:** 40 **% Residing in College-Owned, -Operated, or -Affiliated Housing:** 78 **Library Holdings:** 2,236,516 **Regional Accreditation:** New England Association of Schools and Colleges **Credit Hours For Degree:** 114 credits, Bachelors **ROTC:** Army, Air Force **Professional Accreditation:** AACSB, AACN, AANA, ABA, APA, AALS, ATS, CSWE, NCATE **Intercollegiate Athletics:** Baseball M; Basketball M & W; Crew M & W; Cross-Country Running M & W; Fencing M & W; Field Hockey W; Football M; Golf M & W; Ice Hockey M & W; Lacrosse M & W; Rugby M & W; Sailing M & W; Skiing (Downhill) M & W; Soccer M & W; Softball W; Swimming and Diving M & W; Tennis M & W; Track and Field M & W; Volleyball W; Water Polo M; Wrestling M

THE BOSTON CONSERVATORY

8 The Fenway
Boston, MA 02215
Tel: (617)536-6340
Admissions: (617)912-9153
Fax: (617)536-3176
Web Site: http://www.bostonconservatory.edu/
President/CEO: Richard Ortner
Registrar: Jacque Wilson
Admissions: Halley Shefler
Financial Aid: James Bynum
Type: Comprehensive **Sex:** Coed **Admission Plans:** Deferred Admission **Application Fee:** $105.00 **H.S. Requirements:** High school diploma required; GED accepted **Costs Per Year:** Application fee: $105. Comprehensive fee: $42,155 includes full-time tuition ($26,400), mandatory fees ($1435), and college room and board ($14,320). **Scholarships:** Available **Calendar System:** Semester, Summer Session Available **Enrollment:** FT 404, PT 3, Grad 130 **Faculty:** FT 44, PT 127 **Student-Faculty Ratio:** 4:1 **Exams:** SAT I or ACT **% Receiving Financial Aid:** 54 **% Residing in College-Owned, -Operated, or -Affiliated Housing:** 29 **Library Holdings:** 40,000 **Regional Accreditation:** New England Association of Schools and Colleges **Credit Hours For Degree:** 125 credits, Bachelors **Professional Accreditation:** NASM

BOSTON UNIVERSITY

Boston, MA 02215
Tel: (617)353-2000
Admissions: (617)353-2300
Fax: (617)353-9695
E-mail: admissions@bu.edu
Web Site: http://www.bu.edu/
President/CEO: Daniel S. Goldin
Registrar: Florence Bergeron
Admissions: Kelly A. Walter
Financial Aid: Christine W. McGuire
Type: University **Sex:** Coed **Scores:** 99% SAT V 400+; 100% SAT M 400+; 10% ACT 18-23; 61% ACT 24-29 **% Accepted:** 57 **Admission Plans:** Early Admission; Early Decision Plan; Deferred Admission **Application Deadline:** January 01 **Application Fee:** $70.00 **H.S. Requirements:** High school diploma required; GED accepted **Costs Per Year:** Application fee: $70. Comprehensive fee: $42,046 includes full-time tuition ($31,530), mandatory fees ($436), and college room and board ($10,080). College room only: $6450. Full-time tuition and fees vary according to class time and degree level. Room and board charges vary according to board plan and housing facility. Part-time tuition: $985 per credit. Part-time mandatory fees: $40. Part-time tuition and fees vary according to class time, course load, and degree level. **Scholarships:** Available **Calendar System:** Semester, Summer Session Available **Enrollment:** FT 17,384, PT 1,310, Grad 10,217 **Faculty:** FT 1,454, PT 984 **Student-Faculty Ratio:** 12:1 **Exams:** SAT I or ACT, SAT II **% Receiving Financial Aid:** 41 **% Residing in College-Owned, -Operated, or -Affiliated Housing:** 74 **Library Holdings:** 2,346,194 **Regional Accreditation:** New England Association of Schools and Colleges **Credit Hours For Degree:** 128 credits, Bachelors **ROTC:** Army, Navy, Air Force **Professional Accreditation:** AACSB, ABET, ACEHSA, ABA, ACNM, ADA, ADtA, AOTA, APTA, APA, ASLHA, ACIPE, AALS, ATS, CEPH, CORE, CSWE, JRCEPAT, LCMEAMA, NASM **Intercollegiate Athletics:** Badminton M & W; Baseball M; Basketball M & W; Cheerleading M & W; Crew M & W; Cross-Country Running M & W; Equestrian Sports M & W; Fencing M & W; Field Hockey W; Golf M & W; Gymnastics M & W; Ice Hockey M & W; Lacrosse M & W; Rugby M & W; Sailing M & W; Skiing (Downhill) M & W; Soccer M & W; Softball W; Swimming and Diving M & W; Tennis M & W; Track and Field M & W; Ultimate Frisbee M & W; Volleyball M & W; Water Polo W; Wrestling M

BRANDEIS UNIVERSITY

415 South St.
Waltham, MA 02454-9110
Tel: (781)736-2000
Free: 800-622-0622
Admissions: (781)736-3500
Fax: (781)736-3536
E-mail: admissions@brandeis.edu

Web Site: http://www.brandeis.edu/
President/CEO: Dr. Jehuda Reinharz
Registrar: Dr. Mark Hewitt
Admissions: Gil J. Villanueva
Financial Aid: Peter Giumette
Type: University **Sex:** Coed **Scores:** 100% SAT V 400+; 100% SAT M 400+; 2% ACT 18-23; 48% ACT 24-29 **% Accepted:** 38 **Admission Plans:** Early Decision Plan; Deferred Admission **Application Deadline:** January 15 **Application Fee:** $55.00 **H.S. Requirements:** High school diploma required; GED accepted **Costs Per Year:** Application fee: $55. Comprehensive fee: $41,551 includes full-time tuition ($31,532), mandatory fees ($969), and college room and board ($9050). College room only: $5083. Room and board charges vary according to board plan and housing facility. Part-time tuition: $986 per credit. Part-time tuition varies according to course load. **Scholarships:** Available **Calendar System:** Semester, Summer Session Available **Enrollment:** FT 3,242, PT 25, Grad 1,922 **Faculty:** FT 343, PT 129 **Student-Faculty Ratio:** 8:1 **Exams:** SAT I and SAT II or ACT **% Receiving Financial Aid:** 47 **% Residing in College-Owned, -Operated, or -Affiliated Housing:** 82 **Library Holdings:** 938,835 **Regional Accreditation:** New England Association of Schools and Colleges **Credit Hours For Degree:** 32 courses, Bachelors **ROTC:** Army, Air Force **Intercollegiate Athletics:** Baseball M; Basketball M & W; Crew M; Cross-Country Running M & W; Fencing M & W; Field Hockey W; Golf M; Lacrosse M & W; Rugby M & W; Sailing M & W; Skiing (Downhill) M & W; Soccer W; Softball W; Squash M; Swimming and Diving M & W; Tennis M & W; Track and Field M & W; Volleyball W

BRIDGEWATER STATE COLLEGE
Bridgewater, MA 02325-0001
Tel: (508)531-1000
Admissions: (508)531-1237
Fax: (508)531-1707
E-mail: admission@bridgew.edu
Web Site: http://www.bridgew.edu/
President/CEO: Dr. Dana Mohler-Faria
Registrar: Irene Checkovich
Admissions: Gregg Meyer
Financial Aid: Janet Gumbris
Type: Comprehensive **Sex:** Coed **Affiliation:** Massachusetts Public Higher Education System **Scores:** 95.15% SAT V 400+; 93.8% SAT M 400+; 63.9% ACT 18-23; 22.2% ACT 24-29 **% Accepted:** 80 **Admission Plans:** Early Admission; Early Action; Deferred Admission **Application Deadline:** February 15 **Application Fee:** $25.00 **H.S. Requirements:** High school diploma required; GED accepted **Costs Per Year:** Application fee: $25. State resident tuition: $910 full-time, $38 per credit hour part-time. Nonresident tuition: $7050 full-time, $294 per credit hour part-time. Mandatory fees: $4596 full-time, $188 per credit hour part-time. College room and board: $6614. College room only: $4114. Room and board charges vary according to board plan and housing facility. **Scholarships:** Available **Calendar System:** Semester, Summer Session Available **Enrollment:** FT 6,435, PT 1,416, Grad 1,798 **Faculty:** FT 261, PT 233 **Student-Faculty Ratio:** 20:1 **Exams:** SAT I or ACT **% Receiving Financial Aid:** 52 **% Residing in College-Owned, -Operated, or -Affiliated Housing:** 31 **Library Holdings:** 326,662 **Regional Accreditation:** New England Association of Schools and Colleges **Credit Hours For Degree:** 120 semester hours, Bachelors **ROTC:** Army, Air Force **Professional Accreditation:** CSWE, JRCEPAT, NCATE **Intercollegiate Athletics:** Baseball M; Basketball M & W; Cross-Country Running M & W; Field Hockey W; Football M; Lacrosse M & W; Soccer M & W; Softball W; Swimming and Diving M & W; Tennis M & W; Track and Field M & W; Volleyball W; Water Polo M & W; Wrestling M

BRISTOL COMMUNITY COLLEGE
777 Elsbree St.
Fall River, MA 02720-7395
Tel: (508)678-2811
Fax: (508)674-8838
E-mail: rclark@bristol.mass.edu
Web Site: http://www.bristol.mass.edu/
President/CEO: John J. Sbrega, PhD
Registrar: Joanne Carroll-Connor
Admissions: Rodney S. Clark
Financial Aid: David Allen
Type: Two-Year College **Sex:** Coed **% Accepted:** 80 **Admission Plans:** Open Admission; Preferred Admission **Application Fee:** $10.00 **H.S. Requirements:** High school diploma required; GED accepted **Costs Per Year:** Application fee: $10. State resident tuition: $576 full-time, $24 per credit part-time. Nonresident tuition: $5520 full-time, $230 per credit part-time. Mandatory fees: $2544 full-time, $99 per credit part-time, $30 per term part-time. **Scholarships:** Available **Calendar System:** Semester, Summer Session Available **Enrollment:** FT 3,097, PT 3,776 **Faculty:** FT 316, PT 476 **Student-Faculty Ratio:** 19:1 **Library Holdings:** 65,000 **Regional Accreditation:** New England Association of Schools and Colleges **Credit Hours For Degree:** 60 credits, Associates **Professional Accreditation:** ADA, AHIMA, AOTA, NAACLS, NLN

BUNKER HILL COMMUNITY COLLEGE
250 New Rutherford Ave.
Boston, MA 02129-2925
Tel: (617)228-2000
Admissions: (617)228-2420
Fax: (617)228-2120
Web Site: http://www.bhcc.mass.edu/
President/CEO: Dr. Mary L. Fifield
Registrar: Debra Boyer
Admissions: Debra Boyer
Financial Aid: Scott Jewel
Type: Two-Year College **Sex:** Coed **% Accepted:** 69 **Admission Plans:** Open Admission; Deferred Admission **Application Deadline:** Rolling **Application Fee:** $10.00 **H.S. Requirements:** High school diploma required; GED accepted **Costs Per Year:** Application fee: $10. State resident tuition: $576 full-time, $24 per credit part-time. Nonresident tuition: $5520 full-time, $230 per credit part-time. Mandatory fees: $1824 full-time, $76 per credit part-time. **Scholarships:** Available **Calendar System:** Semester, Summer Session Available **Enrollment:** FT 2,388, PT 5,449 **Faculty:** FT 123, PT 325 **Student-Faculty Ratio:** 19:1 **Library Holdings:** 65,953 **Regional Accreditation:** New England Association of Schools and Colleges **Credit Hours For Degree:** 60 credits, Associates **Professional Accreditation:** ARCEST, JRCEDMS, JRCERT, NLN **Intercollegiate Athletics:** Baseball M; Basketball M & W; Golf M & W; Soccer M & W; Softball W

CAMBRIDGE COLLEGE
1000 Massachusetts Ave.
Cambridge, MA 02138-5304
Tel: (617)868-1000
Free: 800-877-4723
Fax: (617)349-3545
Web Site: http://www.cambridgecollege.edu/
President/CEO: Mahesh C. Sharma
Registrar: Cecelia Cull
Financial Aid: Dr. Gerri Major
Type: Comprehensive **Sex:** Coed **% Accepted:** 99 **Admission Plans:** Open Admission; Deferred Admission **Application Deadline:** Rolling **Application Fee:** $30.00 **H.S. Requirements:** High school diploma required; GED accepted **Costs Per Year:** Application fee: $30. One-time mandatory fee: $110. Tuition: $8040 full-time, $335 per credit part-time. Mandatory fees: $150 full-time. **Scholarships:** Available **Calendar System:** Trimester, Summer Session Available **Enrollment:** FT 226, PT 685, Grad 3,120 **Faculty:** FT 33, PT 773 **Student-Faculty Ratio:** 10:1 **% Receiving Financial Aid:** 72 **Regional Accreditation:** New England Association of Schools and Colleges **Credit Hours For Degree:** 120 credit hours, Bachelors

CAPE COD COMMUNITY COLLEGE
2240 Iyanough Rd.
West Barnstable, MA 02668-1599
Tel: (508)362-2131
Web Site: http://www.capecod.mass.edu/
President/CEO: Dr. Kathleen Schatzberg
Registrar: Sandra Brito
Admissions: Susan Kline-Symington
Financial Aid: Sherry Andersen
Type: Two-Year College **Sex:** Coed **Affiliation:** Massachusetts Public Higher Education System **Admission Plans:** Open Admission; Preferred Admission; Deferred Admission **Application Fee:** $10.00 **H.S. Requirements:** High school diploma required; GED accepted **Costs Per Year:** Application fee: $10. State resident tuition: $720 full-time, $24 per credit hour part-time. Nonresident tuition: $6900 full-time, $230 per credit hour part-time. Mandatory fees: $2940 full-time, $98 per credit hour part-time. **Scholarships:** Available **Calendar System:** Semester, Summer Session Available **Enrollment:** FT 1,470, PT 2,773 **Faculty:** FT 79, PT 252 **Student-Faculty Ratio:** 18:1 **Library Holdings:** 54,342 **Regional Accreditation:** New

England Association of Schools and Colleges **Credit Hours For Degree:** 60 credit hours, Associates **Professional Accreditation:** ADA, NLN

CLARK UNIVERSITY
950 Main St.
Worcester, MA 01610-1477
Tel: (508)793-7711
Free: 800-GO-CLARK
Admissions: (508)793-7431
Fax: (508)793-8821
E-mail: admissions@clarku.edu
Web Site: http://www.clarku.edu/
President/CEO: Dr. John E. Bassett
Registrar: Jane Reno
Admissions: Harold M. Wingood
Financial Aid: Mary Ellen Severance
Type: University **Sex:** Coed **Scores:** 99% SAT V 400+; 100% SAT M 400+; 23% ACT 18-23; 67% ACT 24-29 **% Accepted:** 62 **Admission Plans:** Early Admission; Early Decision Plan; Deferred Admission **Application Deadline:** January 15 **Application Fee:** $50.00 **H.S. Requirements:** High school diploma required; GED accepted **Costs Per Year:** Application fee: $50. Comprehensive fee: $37,365 includes full-time tuition ($31,200), mandatory fees ($265), and college room and board ($5900). College room only: $3550. Room and board charges vary according to board plan and housing facility. Part-time tuition: $915.63 per credit hour. **Scholarships:** Available **Calendar System:** Semester, Summer Session Available **Enrollment:** FT 2,097, PT 158, Grad 863 **Faculty:** FT 167, PT 96 **Student-Faculty Ratio:** 10:1 **Exams:** SAT I or ACT **% Receiving Financial Aid:** 54 **% Residing in College-Owned, -Operated, or -Affiliated Housing:** 77 **Library Holdings:** 289,658 **Regional Accreditation:** New England Association of Schools and Colleges **Credit Hours For Degree:** 32 courses, Bachelors **ROTC:** Army, Navy, Air Force **Professional Accreditation:** AACSB, APA **Intercollegiate Athletics:** Baseball M; Basketball M & W; Crew M & W; Cross-Country Running M & W; Field Hockey W; Lacrosse M; Soccer M & W; Softball W; Swimming and Diving M & W; Tennis M & W; Volleyball W

COLLEGE OF THE HOLY CROSS
1 College St.
Worcester, MA 01610-2395
Tel: (508)793-2011
Free: 800-442-2421
Admissions: (508)793-2443
Fax: (508)793-3888
E-mail: admissions@holycross.edu
Web Site: http://www.holycross.edu/
President/CEO: Rev. Michael C. McFarland, SJ
Registrar: Elaine J. Rynders
Admissions: Ann Bowe McDermott
Financial Aid: Lynne M. Myers
Type: Four-Year College **Sex:** Coed **Affiliation:** Roman Catholic (Jesuit) **Scores:** 99% SAT V 400+; 100% SAT M 400+ **% Accepted:** 48 **Admission Plans:** Early Admission; Early Decision Plan; Deferred Admission **Application Deadline:** January 15 **Application Fee:** $50.00 **H.S. Requirements:** High school diploma required; GED accepted **Costs Per Year:** Application fee: $50. Comprehensive fee: $40,664 includes full-time tuition ($30,960), mandatory fees ($484), and college room and board ($9220). College room only: $4610. Room and board charges vary according to board plan and housing facility. **Scholarships:** Available **Calendar System:** Semester, Summer Session Not available **Enrollment:** FT 2,788, PT 28 **Faculty:** FT 240, PT 57 **Student-Faculty Ratio:** 11:1 **% Receiving Financial Aid:** 53 **% Residing in College-Owned, -Operated, or -Affiliated Housing:** 88 **Library Holdings:** 606,647 **Regional Accreditation:** New England Association of Schools and Colleges **Credit Hours For Degree:** 32 courses, Bachelors **ROTC:** Army, Navy, Air Force **Professional Accreditation:** NAST **Intercollegiate Athletics:** Baseball M; Basketball M & W; Crew M & W; Cross-Country Running M & W; Field Hockey W; Football M; Golf M & W; Ice Hockey M & W; Lacrosse M & W; Soccer M & W; Softball W; Swimming and Diving M & W; Tennis M & W; Track and Field M & W; Volleyball W

CURRY COLLEGE
1071 Blue Hill Ave.
Milton, MA 02186-9984
Tel: (617)333-0500
Free: 800-669-0686
Admissions: (617)333-2210
Fax: (617)333-6860
E-mail: curryadm@curry.edu
Web Site: http://www.curry.edu/
President/CEO: Kenneth Quigley
Registrar: Sally Buckley
Admissions: Jane P. Fidler
Financial Aid: Anne Downey
Type: Comprehensive **Sex:** Coed **Scores:** 91% SAT V 400+; 83% SAT M 400+ **% Accepted:** 69 **Admission Plans:** Early Admission; Early Decision Plan; Deferred Admission **Application Deadline:** April 01 **Application Fee:** $40.00 **H.S. Requirements:** High school diploma required; GED accepted **Costs Per Year:** Application fee: $40. Comprehensive fee: $33,940 includes full-time tuition ($23,400), mandatory fees ($900), and college room and board ($9640). College room only: $5640. **Scholarships:** Available **Calendar System:** Semester, Summer Session Available **Enrollment:** FT 2,203, PT 752, Grad 75 **Faculty:** FT 102, PT 270 **Student-Faculty Ratio:** 12:1 **Exams:** Other, SAT I or ACT **% Receiving Financial Aid:** 66 **% Residing in College-Owned, -Operated, or -Affiliated Housing:** 65 **Library Holdings:** 90,000 **Regional Accreditation:** New England Association of Schools and Colleges **Credit Hours For Degree:** 120 credit hours, Bachelors **ROTC:** Army **Professional Accreditation:** AACN **Intercollegiate Athletics:** Baseball M; Basketball M & W; Cross-Country Running W; Football M; Ice Hockey M; Lacrosse M & W; Soccer M & W; Softball W; Tennis M & W

DEAN COLLEGE
99 Main St.
Franklin, MA 02038-1994
Tel: (508)541-1900; 877-TRY-DEAN
Admissions: (508)541-1508
Fax: (508)541-8726
E-mail: admissions@dean.edu
Web Site: http://www.dean.edu/
President/CEO: Dr. Paula M. Rooney
Admissions: Jay Leiendecker
Financial Aid: Jamey Cournoyer
Type: Two-Year College **Sex:** Coed **Scores:** 75% SAT V 400+; 72% SAT M 400+; 32% ACT 18-23; 10% ACT 24-29 **% Accepted:** 74 **Admission Plans:** Deferred Admission **Application Deadline:** Rolling **Application Fee:** $35.00 **H.S. Requirements:** High school diploma required; GED accepted **Costs Per Year:** Application fee: $35. One-time mandatory fee: $200. Comprehensive fee: $34,350 includes full-time tuition ($24,000) and college room and board ($10,350). College room only: $6550. Part-time tuition: $690 per course. **Scholarships:** Available **Calendar System:** Semester, Summer Session Available **Enrollment:** FT 925, PT 324 **Faculty:** FT 30, PT 67 **Student-Faculty Ratio:** 19:1 **Exams:** SAT I or ACT **% Residing in College-Owned, -Operated, or -Affiliated Housing:** 90 **Library Holdings:** 46,226 **Regional Accreditation:** New England Association of Schools and Colleges **Credit Hours For Degree:** 63 credits, Associates **Intercollegiate Athletics:** Baseball M; Basketball M & W; Football M; Golf M; Lacrosse M & W; Soccer M & W; Softball W; Volleyball W

EASTERN NAZARENE COLLEGE
23 East Elm Ave.
Quincy, MA 02170-2999
Tel: (617)745-3000
Free: 800-88-ENC88
Admissions: (617)745-3732
Fax: (617)745-3907
E-mail: webbd@enc.edu
Web Site: http://www.enc.edu/
President/CEO: Dr. David McClung
Registrar: Myrna F. Giberson
Admissions: Doris Webb
Financial Aid: Douglas Fish
Type: Comprehensive **Sex:** Coed **Affiliation:** Church of the Nazarene **Scores:** 100% SAT V 400+; 100% SAT M 400+; 53% ACT 18-23; 31% ACT 24-29 **Admission Plans:** Early Admission; Deferred Admission **Application Fee:** $25.00 **H.S. Requirements:** High school diploma required; GED accepted **Costs Per Year:** Application fee: $25. Comprehensive fee: $24,900 includes full-time tuition ($17,700), mandatory fees ($610), and college room and board ($6590). Full-time tuition and fees vary according to course load. Room and board charges vary according to board plan, gender, and housing facility. Part-time tuition: $750 per credit hour. Part-time tuition varies according to course load. **Scholarships:** Available **Calendar System:** 4-1-4, Sum-

mer Session Available **Enrollment:** FT 1,043, PT 26, Grad 143 **Faculty:** FT 44, PT 4 **Student-Faculty Ratio:** 15:1 **Exams:** SAT I or ACT **% Receiving Financial Aid:** 73 **% Residing in College-Owned, -Operated, or -Affiliated Housing:** 82 **Library Holdings:** 117,540 **Regional Accreditation:** New England Association of Schools and Colleges **Credit Hours For Degree:** 65 hours, Associates; 130 hours, Bachelors **ROTC:** Army **Professional Accreditation:** CSWE **Intercollegiate Athletics:** Baseball M; Basketball M & W; Cross-Country Running M & W; Lacrosse M; Soccer M & W; Softball W; Tennis M & W; Volleyball M & W

ELMS COLLEGE
291 Springfield St.
Chicopee, MA 01013-2839
Tel: (413)594-2761
Free: 800-255-ELMS
Admissions: (413)592-3189
Fax: (413)594-2781
Web Site: http://www.elms.edu/
President/CEO: Rev. Mark S. Stelzer
Registrar: Laura Lander
Admissions: Joseph P. Wagner
Financial Aid: Troy Davis
Type: Comprehensive **Sex:** Coed **Affiliation:** Roman Catholic **Scores:** 97% SAT V 400+; 99% SAT M 400+ **% Accepted:** 89 **Admission Plans:** Early Admission; Deferred Admission **Application Deadline:** Rolling **Application Fee:** $30.00 **H.S. Requirements:** High school diploma required; GED accepted **Costs Per Year:** Application fee: $30. Comprehensive fee: $29,920 includes full-time tuition ($21,520) and college room and board ($8400). Part-time tuition: $440 per credit. Part-time mandatory fees: $20 per term. **Scholarships:** Available **Calendar System:** Semester, Summer Session Available **Enrollment:** FT 681, PT 385, Grad 168 **Faculty:** FT 59, PT 87 **Student-Faculty Ratio:** 12:1 **Exams:** SAT I or ACT **% Receiving Financial Aid:** 84 **% Residing in College-Owned, -Operated, or -Affiliated Housing:** 39 **Library Holdings:** 111,379 **Regional Accreditation:** New England Association of Schools and Colleges **Credit Hours For Degree:** 120 credits, Bachelors **ROTC:** Army, Air Force **Professional Accreditation:** AACN, CSWE **Intercollegiate Athletics:** Baseball M; Basketball M & W; Cross-Country Running M & W; Field Hockey W; Golf M; Lacrosse W; Soccer M & W; Softball W; Swimming and Diving M & W; Volleyball M & W

EMERSON COLLEGE
120 Boylston St.
Boston, MA 02116-4624
Tel: (617)824-8500
Admissions: (617)824-8600
Fax: (617)824-8609
E-mail: admission@emerson.edu
Web Site: http://www.emerson.edu/
President/CEO: Dr. Jacqueline W. Liebergott
Registrar: William DeWolf
Admissions: Sara Ramirez
Financial Aid: Daniel Pinch
Type: Comprehensive **Sex:** Coed **Scores:** 100% SAT V 400+; 100% SAT M 400+; 15% ACT 18-23; 68% ACT 24-29 **% Accepted:** 45 **Admission Plans:** Early Admission; Early Action; Deferred Admission **Application Deadline:** January 05 **Application Fee:** $60.00 **H.S. Requirements:** High school diploma required; GED accepted **Costs Per Year:** Application fee: $60. Comprehensive fee: $35,042 includes full-time tuition ($24,064), mandatory fees ($558), and college room and board ($10,420). College room only: $6200. Part-time tuition: $752 per credit hour. **Scholarships:** Available **Calendar System:** Semester, Summer Session Available **Enrollment:** FT 3,092, PT 281, Grad 953 **Faculty:** FT 143, PT 238 **Student-Faculty Ratio:** 14:1 **Exams:** SAT I or ACT **% Receiving Financial Aid:** 52 **% Residing in College-Owned, -Operated, or -Affiliated Housing:** 45 **Library Holdings:** 174,782 **Regional Accreditation:** New England Association of Schools and Colleges **Credit Hours For Degree:** 128 credits, Bachelors **Professional Accreditation:** ASLHA **Intercollegiate Athletics:** Baseball M; Basketball M & W; Cross-Country Running M & W; Lacrosse M & W; Soccer M & W; Softball W; Tennis M & W; Volleyball W

EMMANUEL COLLEGE
400 The Fenway
Boston, MA 02115
Tel: (617)277-9340
Admissions: (617)735-9715
Fax: (617)735-9801
E-mail: enroll@emmanuel.edu
Web Site: http://www.emmanuel.edu/
President/CEO: Sr. Janet Eisner, SND
Registrar: Beth Ross
Admissions: Sandra Robbins
Financial Aid: Jennifer Porter
Type: Comprehensive **Sex:** Coed **Affiliation:** Roman Catholic **Scores:** 99% SAT V 400+; 99% SAT M 400+; 63% ACT 18-23; 18% ACT 24-29 **% Accepted:** 61 **Admission Plans:** Early Admission; Early Decision Plan; Deferred Admission **Application Deadline:** March 01 **Application Fee:** $40.00 **H.S. Requirements:** High school diploma required; GED accepted **Costs Per Year:** Application fee: $40. Comprehensive fee: $32,000 includes full-time tuition ($21,900), mandatory fees ($400), and college room and board ($9700). Full-time tuition and fees vary according to course load, degree level, and program. Room and board charges vary according to housing facility. Part-time tuition: $684 per credit. Part-time tuition varies according to program. **Scholarships:** Available **Calendar System:** Semester, Summer Session Available **Enrollment:** FT 1,503, PT 593, Grad 200 **Faculty:** FT 67, PT 155 **Student-Faculty Ratio:** 16:1 **Exams:** SAT I or ACT **% Receiving Financial Aid:** 78 **% Residing in College-Owned, -Operated, or -Affiliated Housing:** 65 **Library Holdings:** 97,627 **Regional Accreditation:** New England Association of Schools and Colleges **Credit Hours For Degree:** 128 credits, Bachelors **ROTC:** Army **Professional Accreditation:** NLN **Intercollegiate Athletics:** Basketball M & W; Cross-Country Running M & W; Soccer M & W; Softball W; Tennis W; Track and Field M & W; Volleyball M & W

ENDICOTT COLLEGE
376 Hale St.
Beverly, MA 01915-2096
Tel: (978)927-0585
Free: 800-325-1114
Admissions: (978)921-1000
Fax: (978)927-0084
E-mail: admissio@endicott.edu
Web Site: http://www.endicott.edu/
President/CEO: Dr. Richard E. Wylie
Registrar: Anita McFarlane
Admissions: Thomas J. Redman
Financial Aid: Marcia Toomey
Type: Comprehensive **Sex:** Coed **Scores:** 99% SAT V 400+; 99% SAT M 400+; 66% ACT 18-23; 25% ACT 24-29 **% Accepted:** 47 **Admission Plans:** Deferred Admission **Application Deadline:** February 15 **Application Fee:** $40.00 **H.S. Requirements:** High school diploma required; GED accepted **Costs Per Year:** Application fee: $40. Comprehensive fee: $30,156 includes full-time tuition ($19,690), mandatory fees ($700), and college room and board ($9766). College room only: $6846. Full-time tuition and fees vary according to student level. Room and board charges vary according to board plan and housing facility. Part-time tuition: $615 per credit. Part-time mandatory fees: $200 per term. Part-time tuition and fees vary according to student level. **Scholarships:** Available **Calendar System:** Semester, Summer Session Available **Enrollment:** FT 1,860, PT 178, Grad 1,288 **Faculty:** FT 66, PT 80 **Student-Faculty Ratio:** 16:1 **Exams:** SAT I or ACT **% Receiving Financial Aid:** 62 **% Residing in College-Owned, -Operated, or -Affiliated Housing:** 84 **Library Holdings:** 121,000 **Regional Accreditation:** New England Association of Schools and Colleges **Credit Hours For Degree:** 67 credits, Associates; 124 credits, Bachelors **ROTC:** Army **Professional Accreditation:** FIDER, JRCEPAT, NLN **Intercollegiate Athletics:** Baseball M; Basketball M & W; Cross-Country Running M & W; Equestrian Sports M & W; Field Hockey W; Football M; Golf M & W; Lacrosse M & W; Soccer M & W; Softball W; Tennis M & W; Volleyball M & W

FINE MORTUARY COLLEGE, LLC
150 Kerry Place
Norwood, MA 02062
Tel: (781)762-1211
Fax: (781)762-7177
Web Site: http://www.fine-ne.com/
President/CEO: Dr. Louis Misantone
Type: Two-Year College **Sex:** Coed **Calendar System:** Continuous

FISHER COLLEGE
118 Beacon St.
Boston, MA 02116-1500

Tel: (617)236-8800
Free: 800-446-1226
Admissions: (617)236-8822
Fax: (617)236-8858
Web Site: http://www.fisher.edu/
President/CEO: Dr. Charles C. Perkins
Registrar: John Ohotnicky
Admissions: Robert Melaragni
Financial Aid: Frank Lauder
Type: Two-Year College **Sex:** Coed **% Accepted:** 62 **Admission Plans:** Deferred Admission **Application Deadline:** Rolling **Application Fee:** $25.00 **H.S. Requirements:** High school diploma required; GED accepted **Costs Per Year:** Application fee: $25. Comprehensive fee: $30,280 includes full-time tuition ($18,330), mandatory fees ($950), and college room and board ($11,000). **Scholarships:** Available **Calendar System:** Semester, Summer Session Available **Enrollment:** FT 507 **Faculty:** FT 24, PT 24 **Student-Faculty Ratio:** 18:1 **% Residing in College-Owned, -Operated, or -Affiliated Housing:** 50 **Library Holdings:** 30,000 **Regional Accreditation:** New England Association of Schools and Colleges **Credit Hours For Degree:** 60 credits, Associates **Professional Accreditation:** AHIMA **Intercollegiate Athletics:** Baseball M; Basketball M & W; Softball W

FITCHBURG STATE COLLEGE
160 Pearl St.
Fitchburg, MA 01420-2697
Tel: (978)345-2151
Free: 800-705-9692
Fax: (978)665-4540
Web Site: http://www.fsc.edu/
President/CEO: Robert V. Antonucci
Registrar: Marion Karanja
Type: Comprehensive **Sex:** Coed **Affiliation:** Massachusetts Public Higher Education System **Scores:** 96% SAT V 400+; 97% SAT M 400+; 63% ACT 18-23; 17% ACT 24-29 **% Accepted:** 67 **Admission Plans:** Deferred Admission **Application Fee:** $10.00 **H.S. Requirements:** High school diploma required; GED accepted **Costs Per Year:** Application fee: $10. State resident tuition: $970 full-time, $40.42 per credit part-time. Nonresident tuition: $7050 full-time, $293.75 per credit part-time. Mandatory fees: $4032 full-time, $168 per credit part-time. College room and board: $6274. **Scholarships:** Available **Calendar System:** Semester, Summer Session Available **Enrollment:** FT 2,950, PT 703, Grad 1,687 **Faculty:** FT 166, PT 76 **Student-Faculty Ratio:** 16:1 **Exams:** SAT I or ACT **% Receiving Financial Aid:** 49 **% Residing in College-Owned, -Operated, or -Affiliated Housing:** 48 **Library Holdings:** 238,743 **Regional Accreditation:** New England Association of Schools and Colleges **Credit Hours For Degree:** 120 semester hours, Bachelors **ROTC:** Air Force **Professional Accreditation:** AACN, NAACLS, NCATE **Intercollegiate Athletics:** Baseball M; Basketball M & W; Cross-Country Running M & W; Field Hockey W; Football M; Ice Hockey M; Soccer M & W; Softball W; Track and Field M & W

FRAMINGHAM STATE COLLEGE
100 State St., PO Box 9101
Framingham, MA 01701-9101
Tel: (508)620-1220
Admissions: (508)626-4500
Fax: (508)626-4017
E-mail: admiss@frc.mass.edu
Web Site: http://www.framingham.edu/
President/CEO: Dr. Helen L. Heineman
Registrar: Mark Powers
Admissions: Elizabeth J. Canella
Financial Aid: Susan Lanzillo
Type: Comprehensive **Sex:** Coed **Affiliation:** Massachusetts Public Higher Education System **Scores:** 99% SAT V 400+; 99% SAT M 400+ **% Accepted:** 64 **Admission Plans:** Preferred Admission; Early Admission; Early Action; Deferred Admission **Application Deadline:** February 15 **Application Fee:** $25.00 **H.S. Requirements:** High school diploma required; GED accepted **Costs Per Year:** Application fee: $25. State resident tuition: $970 full-time, $41 per credit part-time. Nonresident tuition: $7050 full-time, $294 per credit part-time. Mandatory fees: $4029 full-time, $184 per credit part-time. Full-time tuition and fees vary according to class time. Part-time tuition and fees vary according to class time and course load. College room and board: $6157. Room and board charges vary according to board plan and housing facility. **Scholarships:** Available **Calendar System:** Semester, Summer Session Available **Enrollment:** FT 3,045, PT 727, Grad 2,102 **Faculty:** FT 167, PT 67 **Student-Faculty Ratio:** 15:1 **Exams:** SAT I or ACT **% Receiving Financial Aid:** 47 **% Residing in College-Owned, -Operated, or -Affiliated Housing:** 45 **Library Holdings:** 165,219 **Regional Accreditation:** New England Association of Schools and Colleges **Credit Hours For Degree:** 128 semester hours, Bachelors **ROTC:** Army **Professional Accreditation:** AAFCS, ADtA, NLN **Intercollegiate Athletics:** Baseball M; Basketball M & W; Cross-Country Running M & W; Field Hockey W; Football M; Ice Hockey M; Lacrosse W; Soccer M & W; Softball W; Volleyball W

FRANKLIN W. OLIN COLLEGE OF ENGINEERING
Olin Way
Needham, MA 02492-1200
Tel: (781)292-2300
Admissions: (781)292-2250
E-mail: duncan.murdoch@olin.edu
Web Site: http://www.olin.edu/
Admissions: Duncan C. Murdoch
Type: Four-Year College **Sex:** Coed **Scores:** 100% SAT V 400+; 100% SAT M 400+; 5% ACT 24-29 **% Accepted:** 23 **Admission Plans:** Deferred Admission **Application Deadline:** January 06 **Application Fee:** $60.00 **H.S. Requirements:** High school diploma required; GED accepted **Costs Per Year:** Application fee: $60. **Enrollment:** FT 285 **Faculty:** FT 33, PT 4 **Student-Faculty Ratio:** 9:1 **Exams:** SAT I or ACT, SAT II **% Residing in College-Owned, -Operated, or -Affiliated Housing:** 100

GIBBS COLLEGE
126 Newbury St.
Boston, MA 02116-2904
Tel: (617)578-7100
Free: 800-6SK-ILLS
Admissions: (617)578-7150
Fax: (617)262-2610
Web Site: http://www.katharinegibbs.com/
President/CEO: David J. Waldron
Registrar: Alisa Seraton-Cazeau
Admissions: Robert A. Andriola
Financial Aid: Lisa Sander
Type: Two-Year College **Sex:** Coed **Affiliation:** Career Education Corporation **Application Fee:** $25.00 **H.S. Requirements:** High school diploma required; GED accepted **Scholarships:** Available **Calendar System:** Quarter, Summer Session Available **Faculty:** FT 6, PT 36 **Exams:** Other **Library Holdings:** 3,270 **Regional Accreditation:** New England Association of Schools and Colleges **Credit Hours For Degree:** 96 credits, Associates **Professional Accreditation:** ACICS

GORDON COLLEGE
255 Grapevine Rd.
Wenham, MA 01984-1899
Tel: (978)927-2300; (866)464-6736
Admissions: (978)867-4218
Fax: (978)524-3704
E-mail: admissions@hope.gordonc.edu
Web Site: http://www.gordon.edu/
President/CEO: Dr. R. Judson Carlberg
Registrar: Carol Herrick
Admissions: Nancy Mering
Financial Aid: Barbara R. Layne
Type: Comprehensive **Sex:** Coed **Affiliation:** nondenominational **Scores:** 99.2% SAT V 400+; 99.4% SAT M 400+ **% Accepted:** 84 **Admission Plans:** Early Admission; Early Action; Early Decision Plan; Deferred Admission **Application Deadline:** Rolling **Application Fee:** $50.00 **H.S. Requirements:** High school diploma required; GED accepted. For home schooled students: High school diploma or equivalent not required **Costs Per Year:** Application fee: $50. Comprehensive fee: $29,194 includes full-time tuition ($21,930), mandatory fees ($994), and college room and board ($6270). College room only: $4200. Room and board charges vary according to board plan and housing facility. Part-time mandatory fees: $1550 per credit, $248.50 per term. Part-time fees vary according to course load. **Scholarships:** Available **Calendar System:** Semester, Summer Session Not available **Enrollment:** FT 1,555, PT 34, Grad 61 **Faculty:** FT 93, PT 52 **Student-Faculty Ratio:** 14:1 **Exams:** SAT I or ACT **% Receiving Financial Aid:** 67 **% Residing in College-Owned, -Operated, or -Affiliated Housing:** 88 **Library Holdings:** 142,688 **Regional Accreditation:** New England Association of Schools and Colleges **Credit Hours For Degree:** 124 semester hours, Bachelors **ROTC:** Army, Air Force **Professional Accreditation:**

CSWE, NASM **Intercollegiate Athletics:** Baseball M; Basketball M & W; Cheerleading M & W; Cross-Country Running M & W; Field Hockey W; Golf M & W; Lacrosse M & W; Soccer M & W; Softball W; Swimming and Diving M & W; Tennis M & W; Volleyball W

GREENFIELD COMMUNITY COLLEGE
1 College Dr.
Greenfield, MA 01301-9739
Tel: (413)775-1000
Admissions: (413)775-1806
Fax: (413)773-5129
Web Site: http://www.gcc.mass.edu/
President/CEO: Dr. Robert Pura
Registrar: Heather A. Hoyt
Admissions: Herbert Hentz
Financial Aid: Jane L. Abbott
Type: Two-Year College **Sex:** Coed **% Accepted:** 100 **Admission Plans:** Open Admission; Preferred Admission **Application Deadline:** Rolling **Application Fee:** $10.00 **H.S. Requirements:** High school diploma required; GED accepted **Costs Per Year:** Application fee: $10. State resident tuition: $780 full-time, $26 per credit part-time. Nonresident tuition: $8430 full-time, $281 per credit part-time. Mandatory fees: $3227 full-time, $103.50 per credit part-time, $61. Full-time tuition and fees vary according to class time. Part-time tuition and fees vary according to class time. **Scholarships:** Available **Calendar System:** Semester, Summer Session Available **Enrollment:** FT 994, PT 1,223 **Faculty:** FT 56, PT 143 **Student-Faculty Ratio:** 23:1 **Exams:** Other **Library Holdings:** 52,690 **Regional Accreditation:** New England Association of Schools and Colleges **Credit Hours For Degree:** 60 credits, Associates **Professional Accreditation:** NLN

HAMPSHIRE COLLEGE
893 West St.
Amherst, MA 01002
Tel: (413)549-4600; 877-937-4267
Admissions: (413)559-5471
Fax: (413)582-5631
E-mail: admissions@hampshire.edu
Web Site: http://www.hampshire.edu/
President/CEO: Dr. Gregory S. Prince, Jr.
Registrar: Roberta Stuart
Admissions: Karen S. Parker
Financial Aid: Kathy Methot
Type: Four-Year College **Sex:** Coed **Scores:** 100% SAT V 400+; 100% SAT M 400+; 15% ACT 18-23; 56% ACT 24-29 **% Accepted:** 64 **Admission Plans:** Early Admission; Early Action; Early Decision Plan; Deferred Admission **Application Deadline:** January 15 **Application Fee:** $55.00 **H.S. Requirements:** High school diploma or equivalent not required **Costs Per Year:** Application fee: $55. Comprehensive fee: $41,038 includes full-time tuition ($31,939), mandatory fees ($580), and college room and board ($8519). College room only: $5433. Room and board charges vary according to board plan. **Scholarships:** Available **Calendar System:** 4-1-4, Summer Session Not available **Enrollment:** FT 1,376 **Faculty:** FT 94, PT 43 **Student-Faculty Ratio:** 12:1 **% Receiving Financial Aid:** 56 **% Residing in College-Owned, -Operated, or -Affiliated Housing:** 93 **Library Holdings:** 136,326 **Regional Accreditation:** New England Association of Schools and Colleges **ROTC:** Army **Intercollegiate Athletics:** Basketball M & W; Fencing M & W; Soccer M & W

HARVARD UNIVERSITY
Cambridge, MA 02138
Tel: (617)495-1000
Admissions: (617)495-1551
E-mail: college@harvard.edu
Web Site: http://www.harvard.edu/
President/CEO: Dr. Lawrence H. Summers
Registrar: Arlene Becella
Admissions: Dr. William R. Fitzsimmons
Financial Aid: James S. Miller
Type: University **Sex:** Coed **% Accepted:** 9 **Admission Plans:** Early Action; Deferred Admission **Application Deadline:** January 01 **Application Fee:** $65.00 **H.S. Requirements:** High school diploma or equivalent not required **Costs Per Year:** Application fee: $65. Comprehensive fee: $43,655 includes full-time tuition ($30,275), mandatory fees ($3434), and college room and board ($9946). College room only: $5328. **Scholarships:** Available **Calendar System:** Semester, Summer Session Available **Enrollment:** FT 6,649, Grad 9,960 **Faculty:** FT 1,592, PT 443 **Student-Faculty Ratio:** 7:1 **Exams:** SAT I and SAT II or ACT **% Receiving Financial Aid:** 49 **% Residing in College-Owned, -Operated, or -Affiliated Housing:** 96 **Library Holdings:** 14,000,000 **Regional Accreditation:** New England Association of Schools and Colleges **Credit Hours For Degree:** 16 full-year courses, Bachelors **ROTC:** Army, Air Force **Professional Accreditation:** AACSB, ABET, ABA, ADA, ADtA, ACSP, APA, ASLA, ACIPE, AALS, ATS, CEPH, LCMEAMA, NASPAA **Intercollegiate Athletics:** Baseball M; Basketball M & W; Crew M & W; Cross-Country Running M & W; Fencing M & W; Field Hockey W; Football M; Golf M & W; Ice Hockey M & W; Lacrosse M & W; Sailing M & W; Skiing (Cross-Country) M & W; Skiing (Downhill) M & W; Soccer M & W; Softball W; Squash M & W; Swimming and Diving M & W; Tennis M & W; Track and Field M & W; Volleyball M & W; Water Polo M & W; Wrestling M

HEBREW COLLEGE
160 Herrick Rd.
Newton Centre, MA 02459
Tel: (617)559-8600
Free: 800-866-4814
Admissions: (617)559-8610
Fax: (617)559-8601
Web Site: http://www.hebrewcollege.edu/
President/CEO: Dr. David Gordis
Registrar: Evelyn Herwitz
Admissions: Ina Regosin
Financial Aid: Norma Frankel
Type: Comprehensive **Sex:** Coed **Affiliation:** Jewish **Admission Plans:** Open Admission; Early Admission; Early Decision Plan; Deferred Admission **Application Fee:** $50.00 **H.S. Requirements:** High school diploma required; GED not accepted **Costs Per Year:** Application fee: $50. Tuition: $18,600 full-time, $775 per credit part-time. Mandatory fees: $200 full-time, $100 per semester hour part-time. **Scholarships:** Available **Calendar System:** Semester, Summer Session Available **Enrollment:** FT 5, PT 1 **Faculty:** FT 20, PT 21 **Exams:** SAT I **Library Holdings:** 125,000 **Regional Accreditation:** New England Association of Schools and Colleges **Credit Hours For Degree:** 120 credits, Bachelors

HELLENIC COLLEGE
50 Goddard Ave.
Brookline, MA 02445-7496
Tel: (617)731-3500; (866)424-2338
Fax: (617)232-7819
E-mail: sdaly@hchc.edu
Web Site: http://www.hchc.edu/
Registrar: Dr. Eugen Pentiuc
Admissions: Sonia Daly
Financial Aid: George A. Georgenes
Type: Four-Year College **Sex:** Coed **Affiliation:** Greek Orthodox **% Accepted:** 50 **Admission Plans:** Early Action; Deferred Admission **Application Deadline:** Rolling **Application Fee:** $50.00 **H.S. Requirements:** High school diploma required; GED accepted **Costs Per Year:** Application fee: $50. Comprehensive fee: $25,075 includes full-time tuition ($15,435), mandatory fees ($380), and college room and board ($9260). Part-time tuition: $643 per credit. Part-time mandatory fees: $260 per term. Part-time tuition and fees vary according to course load. **Scholarships:** Available **Calendar System:** Semester, Summer Session Available **Enrollment:** FT 84, Grad 35 **Faculty:** FT 16, PT 16 **Student-Faculty Ratio:** 9:1 **Exams:** SAT I or ACT, SAT II **% Receiving Financial Aid:** 93 **% Residing in College-Owned, -Operated, or -Affiliated Housing:** 90 **Library Holdings:** 115,805 **Regional Accreditation:** New England Association of Schools and Colleges **Credit Hours For Degree:** 128 credits, Bachelors

HOLYOKE COMMUNITY COLLEGE
303 Homestead Ave.
Holyoke, MA 01040-1099
Tel: (413)538-7000; (413)552-2850
Admissions: (413)552-2321
Web Site: http://www.hcc.mass.edu/
President/CEO: Dr. William F. Messner
Registrar: Anthony Sbalbi
Admissions: Marcia Rosbury-Henne
Financial Aid: Karen Derouin
Type: Two-Year College **Sex:** Coed **Affiliation:** Massachusetts Public Higher Education System **Admission Plans:** Open Admission; Early Admis-

sion; Deferred Admission **Application Deadline:** Rolling **Application Fee:** $10.00 **H.S. Requirements:** High school diploma required; GED accepted **Costs Per Year:** Application fee: $10. State resident tuition: $2570 full-time, $103 per credit part-time. Nonresident tuition: $7514 full-time, $309 per credit part-time. **Scholarships:** Available **Calendar System:** Semester, Summer Session Available **Enrollment:** FT 3,075, PT 3,183 **Faculty:** FT 112, PT 315 **Student-Faculty Ratio:** 15:1 **Library Holdings:** 75,222 **Regional Accreditation:** New England Association of Schools and Colleges **Credit Hours For Degree:** 60 credits, Associates **ROTC:** Army, Air Force **Professional Accreditation:** ACBSP, COptA, JRCERT, NASM, NLN **Intercollegiate Athletics:** Baseball M; Basketball M & W; Golf M & W; Skiing (Downhill) M & W; Soccer M & W; Softball W; Tennis M & W; Volleyball W

ITT TECHNICAL INSTITUTE (NORWOOD)
333 Providence Hwy.
Norwood, MA 02062
Tel: (781)278-7200
Free: 800-879-8324
Web Site: http://www.itt-tech.edu/
President/CEO: Steve Bonkowski
Admissions: Dennis Saccoia
Type: Two-Year College **Sex:** Coed **Affiliation:** ITT Educational Services, Inc **Admission Plans:** Deferred Admission **Application Deadline:** Rolling **Application Fee:** $100.00 **H.S. Requirements:** High school diploma required; GED accepted **Costs Per Year:** Application fee: $100. **Scholarships:** Available **Calendar System:** Quarter, Summer Session Not available **Exams:** Other **Credit Hours For Degree:** 96 credit hours, Associates **Professional Accreditation:** ACICS

ITT TECHNICAL INSTITUTE (WOBURN)
10 Forbes Rd.
Woburn, MA 01801
Tel: (781)937-8324
Web Site: http://www.itt-tech.edu/
President/CEO: Jeffrey Abrams
Admissions: Nadine Dowling
Type: Two-Year College **Sex:** Coed **Affiliation:** ITT Educational Services, Inc **Admission Plans:** Open Admission; Deferred Admission **Application Deadline:** Rolling **Application Fee:** $100.00 **H.S. Requirements:** High school diploma required; GED accepted **Costs Per Year:** Application fee: $100. **Scholarships:** Available **Calendar System:** Quarter, Summer Session Not available **Exams:** Other **Credit Hours For Degree:** 96 credit hours, Associates **Professional Accreditation:** ACICS

LABOURÉ COLLEGE
2120 Dorchester Ave.
Boston, MA 02124-5698
Tel: (617)296-8300
Web Site: http://www.laboure.edu/
President/CEO: Joseph W. McNabb, PhD
Registrar: Dr. Ann Belanger
Admissions: Gina M. Morrissette
Financial Aid: Daniel Smith
Type: Two-Year College **Sex:** Coed **Affiliation:** Roman Catholic **Admission Plans:** Deferred Admission **Application Fee:** $25.00 **H.S. Requirements:** High school diploma required; GED accepted **Scholarships:** Available **Calendar System:** Semester, Summer Session Available **Faculty:** FT 25, PT 14 **Student-Faculty Ratio:** 8:1 **Library Holdings:** 10,975 **Regional Accreditation:** New England Association of Schools and Colleges **Credit Hours For Degree:** 60 credits, Associates **Professional Accreditation:** AHIMA, JRCEET, JRCERT, NLN

LASELL COLLEGE
1844 Commonwealth Ave.
Newton, MA 02466-2709
Tel: (617)243-2000; 888-LASELL-4
Admissions: (617)243-2225
Fax: (617)796-4343
E-mail: info@lasell.edu
Web Site: http://www.lasell.edu/
President/CEO: Dr. Thomas E.J. de Witt
Registrar: Dianne Polizzi
Admissions: James Tweed
Financial Aid: Michele Kosboth
Type: Comprehensive **Sex:** Coed **Scores:** 94% SAT V 400+; 95% SAT M 400+ **% Accepted:** 67 **Admission Plans:** Deferred Admission **Application Deadline:** Rolling **Application Fee:** $40.00 **H.S. Requirements:** High school diploma required; GED accepted **Costs Per Year:** Application fee: $40. Comprehensive fee: $30,100 includes full-time tuition ($19,900), mandatory fees ($1000), and college room and board ($9200). Part-time tuition: $660 per credit hour. Part-time mandatory fees: $250. **Scholarships:** Available **Calendar System:** Semester, Summer Session Not available **Enrollment:** FT 1,194, PT 22, Grad 37 **Faculty:** FT 55, PT 107 **Student-Faculty Ratio:** 13:1 **Exams:** SAT I or ACT **% Receiving Financial Aid:** 84 **% Residing in College-Owned, -Operated, or -Affiliated Housing:** 80 **Library Holdings:** 60,250 **Regional Accreditation:** New England Association of Schools and Colleges **Credit Hours For Degree:** 120 semester hours, Bachelors **Professional Accreditation:** JRCEPAT **Intercollegiate Athletics:** Basketball M & W; Cross-Country Running M & W; Field Hockey W; Lacrosse M & W; Soccer M & W; Softball W; Volleyball M & W

LESLEY UNIVERSITY
29 Everett St.
Cambridge, MA 02138-2790
Tel: (617)868-9600
Free: 800-999-1959
Admissions: (617)349-8800
Fax: (617)349-8150
E-mail: lcadmissions@lesley.edu
Web Site: http://www.lesley.edu/
President/CEO: Margaret A. McKenna
Registrar: Scott James
Admissions: Deborah Kocar
Type: Comprehensive **Sex:** Coed **Scores:** 95% SAT V 400+; 94% SAT M 400+ **% Accepted:** 72 **Admission Plans:** Deferred Admission **Application Deadline:** March 01 **Application Fee:** $40.00 **H.S. Requirements:** High school diploma required; GED accepted **Costs Per Year:** Application fee: $40. One-time mandatory fee: $950. Comprehensive fee: $34,950 includes full-time tuition ($24,200), mandatory fees ($250), and college room and board ($10,500). College room only: $6400. Full-time tuition and fees vary according to program. Room and board charges vary according to housing facility. Part-time tuition: $1020 per credit. **Scholarships:** Available **Calendar System:** Semester, Summer Session Available **Enrollment:** FT 1,023, PT 242, Grad 6,033 **Faculty:** FT 53, PT 131 **Student-Faculty Ratio:** 11:1 **Exams:** SAT I or ACT **% Receiving Financial Aid:** 71 **% Residing in College-Owned, -Operated, or -Affiliated Housing:** 66 **Library Holdings:** 118,729 **Regional Accreditation:** New England Association of Schools and Colleges **Credit Hours For Degree:** 128 credits, Bachelors **Intercollegiate Athletics:** Basketball M & W; Crew M & W; Soccer M & W; Softball W; Volleyball M & W

MARIAN COURT COLLEGE
35 Little's Point Rd.
Swampscott, MA 01907-2840
Tel: (781)595-6768
Fax: (781)595-3560
E-mail: lparker@mariancourt.edu
Web Site: http://www.mariancourt.edu/
President/CEO: Sr. Joanne Bibeau
Registrar: Linda Lundstrom
Admissions: Lisa Emerson Parker
Financial Aid: Melissa Foye
Type: Two-Year College **Sex:** Coed **Affiliation:** Roman Catholic **Admission Plans:** Deferred Admission **Application Fee:** $0.00 **H.S. Requirements:** High school diploma required; GED accepted **Scholarships:** Available **Calendar System:** Semester, Summer Session Available **Enrollment:** FT 194, PT 87 **Faculty:** FT 7, PT 18 **Student-Faculty Ratio:** 10:1 **Library Holdings:** 5,006 **Regional Accreditation:** New England Association of Schools and Colleges **Credit Hours For Degree:** 60 credits, Associates

MASSACHUSETTS BAY COMMUNITY COLLEGE
50 Oakland St.
Wellesley Hills, MA 02481
Tel: (781)239-3000
Admissions: (781)239-2501
Fax: (781)239-1047
Web Site: http://www.massbay.edu/
President/CEO: Dr. Lindsay D. Norman

Registrar: Michael Rice
Admissions: Donna Raposa
Financial Aid: Paula L. Ogden
Type: Two-Year College **Sex:** Coed **% Accepted:** 99 **Admission Plans:** Open Admission; Deferred Admission **Application Deadline:** Rolling **Application Fee:** $20.00 **H.S. Requirements:** High school diploma required; GED accepted **Costs Per Year:** Application fee: $20. State resident tuition: $720 full-time. Nonresident tuition: $6900 full-time. **Scholarships:** Available **Calendar System:** Semester, Summer Session Available **Enrollment:** FT 2,145, PT 2,870 **Faculty:** FT 73, PT 263 **Student-Faculty Ratio:** 19:1 **Library Holdings:** 50,333 **Regional Accreditation:** New England Association of Schools and Colleges **Credit Hours For Degree:** 62 credits, Associates **Professional Accreditation:** APTA, CARC, JRCERT, NLN **Intercollegiate Athletics:** Baseball M; Basketball M & W; Cross-Country Running M & W; Golf M & W; Soccer M & W; Softball W; Tennis M & W; Volleyball W

MASSACHUSETTS COLLEGE OF ART
621 Huntington Ave.
Boston, MA 02115-5882
Tel: (617)879-7000
Admissions: (617)879-7225
Fax: (617)879-7250
E-mail: admissions@massart.edu
Web Site: http://www.massart.edu/
President/CEO: Dr. Katherine Sloan
Registrar: Frank Callahan
Admissions: Kay Ransdell
Financial Aid: Ken Berryhill
Type: Comprehensive **Sex:** Coed **Affiliation:** Massachusetts Public Higher Education System **Scores:** 100% SAT V 400+; 96% SAT M 400+; 55% ACT 18-23; 45% ACT 24-29 **% Accepted:** 61 **Admission Plans:** Preferred Admission; Early Admission; Early Action; Deferred Admission **Application Deadline:** February 15 **Application Fee:** $30.00 **H.S. Requirements:** High school diploma required; GED accepted **Costs Per Year:** Application fee: $30. State resident tuition: $6850 full-time. Nonresident tuition: $19,200 full-time. College room and board: $9800. **Scholarships:** Available **Calendar System:** Semester, Summer Session Available **Enrollment:** FT 1,379, PT 615, Grad 136 **Faculty:** FT 86, PT 123 **Student-Faculty Ratio:** 13:1 **Exams:** SAT I or ACT **% Receiving Financial Aid:** 57 **% Residing in College-Owned, -Operated, or -Affiliated Housing:** 26 **Library Holdings:** 231,586 **Regional Accreditation:** New England Association of Schools and Colleges **Credit Hours For Degree:** 120 credits, Bachelors **Professional Accreditation:** NASAD

MASSACHUSETTS COLLEGE OF LIBERAL ARTS
375 Church St.
North Adams, MA 01247-4100
Tel: (413)662-5000
Admissions: (413)662-5410
Fax: (413)662-5179
E-mail: admissions@nasc.mass.edu
Web Site: http://www.mcla.edu/
President/CEO: Dr. Mary K. Grant
Registrar: Andrea Demayo
Admissions: Denise Richardello
Financial Aid: Elizabeth Petri
Type: Comprehensive **Sex:** Coed **Affiliation:** Massachusetts Public Higher Education System **Scores:** 96.2% SAT V 400+; 92.4% SAT M 400+; 100% ACT 24-29 **Admission Plans:** Early Action; Deferred Admission **Application Fee:** $25.00 **H.S. Requirements:** High school diploma required; GED accepted **Scholarships:** Available **Calendar System:** Semester, Summer Session Available **Enrollment:** FT 1,193, PT 265, Grad 353 **Faculty:** FT 80, PT 42 **Student-Faculty Ratio:** 14:1 **Exams:** SAT I or ACT, SAT I **% Receiving Financial Aid:** 68 **% Residing in College-Owned, -Operated, or -Affiliated Housing:** 65 **Regional Accreditation:** New England Association of Schools and Colleges **Credit Hours For Degree:** 120 credits, Bachelors **Intercollegiate Athletics:** Baseball M; Basketball M & W; Cross-Country Running M & W; Golf M; Ice Hockey M & W; Soccer M & W; Softball W; Tennis W

MASSACHUSETTS COLLEGE OF PHARMACY AND HEALTH SCIENCES
179 Longwood Ave.
Boston, MA 02115-5896
Tel: (617)732-2800
Free: 800-225-5506
Admissions: (617)732-2850
Fax: (617)732-2801
E-mail: admissions@mcphs.edu
Web Site: http://www.mcphs.edu/
President/CEO: Charles F. Monahan
Registrar: Marjorie McMahon
Admissions: William Dunpey
Financial Aid: Carrie Glass
Type: University **Sex:** Coed **Scores:** 99% SAT V 400+; 100% SAT M 400+; 62% ACT 18-23; 28% ACT 24-29 **% Accepted:** 76 **Admission Plans:** Early Admission; Early Decision Plan; Deferred Admission **Application Deadline:** February 01 **Application Fee:** $70.00 **H.S. Requirements:** High school diploma required; GED accepted **Costs Per Year:** Application fee: $70. Comprehensive fee: $32,270 includes full-time tuition ($20,400), mandatory fees ($650), and college room and board ($11,220). College room only: $7900. Part-time tuition: $750 per credit. Part-time mandatory fees: $160 per term. **Scholarships:** Available **Calendar System:** Semester, Summer Session Available **Enrollment:** FT 1,764, PT 122, Grad 276 **Faculty:** FT 157, PT 5 **Student-Faculty Ratio:** 17:1 **Exams:** SAT I or ACT **% Receiving Financial Aid:** 85 **% Residing in College-Owned, -Operated, or -Affiliated Housing:** 30 **Library Holdings:** 32,000 **Regional Accreditation:** New England Association of Schools and Colleges **Credit Hours For Degree:** 127 semester hours, Bachelors **ROTC:** Army, Air Force **Professional Accreditation:** ACPhE, ADA, JRCNMT, NLN

MASSACHUSETTS INSTITUTE OF TECHNOLOGY
77 Massachusetts Ave.
Cambridge, MA 02139-4307
Tel: (617)253-1000
Admissions: (617)253-4791
Fax: (617)258-8304
E-mail: admissions@mit.edu
Web Site: http://web.mit.edu/
President/CEO: Dr. Susan Hockfield
Registrar: Mary R. Callahan
Admissions: Marilee Jones
Financial Aid: Elizabeth M. Hicks
Type: University **Sex:** Coed **Scores:** 100% SAT V 400+; 100% SAT M 400+; 12% ACT 24-29 **% Accepted:** 14 **Admission Plans:** Early Action; Deferred Admission **Application Deadline:** January 01 **Application Fee:** $65.00 **H.S. Requirements:** High school diploma or equivalent not required **Costs Per Year:** Application fee: $65. Comprehensive fee: $41,800 includes full-time tuition ($32,100), mandatory fees ($200), and college room and board ($9500). College room only: $5250. Room and board charges vary according to board plan and housing facility. Part-time tuition: $505 per unit. Part-time tuition varies according to course load. **Scholarships:** Available **Calendar System:** 4-1-4, Summer Session Available **Enrollment:** FT 4,014, PT 52, Grad 6,140 **Faculty:** FT 1,177, PT 377 **Student-Faculty Ratio:** 7:1 **Exams:** SAT I or ACT, SAT II **% Receiving Financial Aid:** 64 **% Residing in College-Owned, -Operated, or -Affiliated Housing:** 93 **Library Holdings:** 2,707,849 **Regional Accreditation:** New England Association of Schools and Colleges **Credit Hours For Degree:** 17 General Institute Requirements (GIR) plus 180 units beyond the GIRs, Bachelors **ROTC:** Army, Navy, Air Force **Professional Accreditation:** AACSB, ABET, ACSP **Intercollegiate Athletics:** Baseball M; Basketball M & W; Cheerleading M & W; Crew M & W; Cross-Country Running M & W; Fencing M & W; Field Hockey W; Football M; Golf M; Gymnastics M & W; Ice Hockey M & W; Lacrosse M & W; Riflery M & W; Sailing M & W; Skiing (Cross-Country) M & W; Skiing (Downhill) M & W; Soccer M & W; Softball W; Squash M; Swimming and Diving M & W; Tennis M & W; Track and Field M & W; Volleyball M & W; Water Polo M; Wrestling M

MASSACHUSETTS MARITIME ACADEMY
101 Academy Dr.
Buzzards Bay, MA 02532-1803
Tel: (508)830-5000
Free: 800-544-3411
Admissions: (508)830-6441
Fax: (508)830-5077
Web Site: http://www.maritime.edu/
President/CEO: Rear Adm. Maurice J. Bresnahan, Jr.
Registrar: Capt. Allen R. Hansen
Admissions: Capt. Fran McDonald

Financial Aid: Elizabeth Benway
Type: Comprehensive **Sex:** Coed **Affiliation:** Massachusetts Public Higher Education System **Scores:** 93% SAT V 400+; 99% SAT M 400+; 90% ACT 18-23; 2% ACT 24-29 **% Accepted:** 61 **Admission Plans:** Early Decision Plan; Deferred Admission **Application Deadline:** Rolling **Application Fee:** $50.00 **H.S. Requirements:** High school diploma required; GED accepted **Costs Per Year:** Application fee: $50. Area resident tuition: $1062 full-time. State resident tuition: $1591 full-time. Nonresident tuition: $11,591 full-time. Mandatory fees: $4045 full-time. College room and board: $6464. College room only: $3286. **Scholarships:** Available **Calendar System:** Semester, Summer Session Available **Enrollment:** FT 923, PT 46, Grad 39 **Faculty:** FT 59, PT 11 **Student-Faculty Ratio:** 15:1 **Exams:** SAT I or ACT **% Receiving Financial Aid:** 44 **% Residing in College-Owned, -Operated, or -Affiliated Housing:** 100 **Library Holdings:** 55,000 **Regional Accreditation:** New England Association of Schools and Colleges **Credit Hours For Degree:** 164 semester hours, Bachelors **ROTC:** Army, Navy **Intercollegiate Athletics:** Baseball M; Crew M & W; Cross-Country Running M & W; Football M; Lacrosse M; Riflery M & W; Sailing M & W; Soccer M; Softball W; Volleyball W

MASSASOIT COMMUNITY COLLEGE
1 Massasoit Blvd.
Brockton, MA 02302-3996
Tel: (508)588-9100
Fax: (508)427-1220
Web Site: http://www.massasoit.mass.edu/
President/CEO: Dr. Robert R. Rose
Registrar: Daniel Kimborowicz
Admissions: Michelle Hughes
Financial Aid: Sharon McLaughlin
Type: Two-Year College **Sex:** Coed **Admission Plans:** Open Admission; Preferred Admission **Application Fee:** $0.00 **H.S. Requirements:** High school diploma required; GED accepted **Costs Per Year:** Application fee: $0. State resident tuition: $576 full-time. Nonresident tuition: $5520 full-time. Mandatory fees: $2088 full-time. Full-time tuition and fees vary according to course load. **Scholarships:** Available **Calendar System:** Semester, Summer Session Available **Enrollment:** FT 3,178, PT 3,630 **Faculty:** FT 131, PT 359 **Library Holdings:** 75,000 **Regional Accreditation:** New England Association of Schools and Colleges **Credit Hours For Degree:** 60 credits, Associates **Professional Accreditation:** ADA, CARC, JRCERT, NLN **Intercollegiate Athletics:** Baseball M; Basketball M & W; Soccer M & W; Softball W

MERRIMACK COLLEGE
315 Turnpike St.
North Andover, MA 01845-5800
Tel: (978)837-5000
Fax: (978)837-5222
Web Site: http://www.merrimack.edu/
President/CEO: Richard J. Santagati
Registrar: Martin Grace
Financial Aid: Christine A. Mordach
Type: Comprehensive **Sex:** Coed **Affiliation:** Roman Catholic **Scores:** 100% SAT V 400+; 100% SAT M 400+; 78% ACT 18-23; 19% ACT 24-29 **% Accepted:** 71 **Admission Plans:** Early Admission; Early Action; Deferred Admission **Application Deadline:** February 01 **Application Fee:** $50.00 **H.S. Requirements:** High school diploma required; GED accepted **Costs Per Year:** Application fee: $50. Comprehensive fee: $34,380 includes full-time tuition ($24,200), mandatory fees ($450), and college room and board ($9730). College room only: $5500. Full-time tuition and fees vary according to program and student level. Room and board charges vary according to board plan and housing facility. Part-time tuition: $900 per credit. Part-time mandatory fees: $55 per term. Part-time tuition and fees vary according to class time, course level, course load, and degree level. **Scholarships:** Available **Calendar System:** Semester, Summer Session Available **Enrollment:** FT 1,950, PT 204, Grad 34 **Faculty:** FT 143, PT 80 **Student-Faculty Ratio:** 12:1 **Exams:** SAT I or ACT **% Receiving Financial Aid:** 61 **% Residing in College-Owned, -Operated, or -Affiliated Housing:** 74 **Library Holdings:** 115,639 **Regional Accreditation:** New England Association of Schools and Colleges **Credit Hours For Degree:** 20 courses, Associates; 40 courses, Bachelors **ROTC:** Air Force **Professional Accreditation:** ABET, JRCEPAT **Intercollegiate Athletics:** Baseball M; Basketball M & W; Cross-Country Running M & W; Field Hockey W; Football M; Ice Hockey M; Lacrosse M & W; Soccer M & W; Softball W; Tennis M & W; Track and Field M & W; Volleyball M & W

MIDDLESEX COMMUNITY COLLEGE
Springs Rd.
Bedford, MA 01730-1655
Tel: (781)280-3200
Admissions: (978)656-3207
Fax: (978)656-3322
E-mail: orellanad@middlesex.cc.ma.us
Web Site: http://www.middlesex.mass.edu/
President/CEO: Dr. Carole A. Cowan
Registrar: Audrey Nahabedian
Admissions: Laurie Dimitrov
Financial Aid: Christopher J. Fiori
Type: Two-Year College **Sex:** Coed **Affiliation:** Massachusetts Public Higher Education System **Admission Plans:** Open Admission; Preferred Admission; Early Admission **Application Fee:** $0.00 **H.S. Requirements:** High school diploma required; GED accepted **Scholarships:** Available **Calendar System:** Semester, Summer Session Available **Faculty:** FT 125, PT 343 **Exams:** Other **Library Holdings:** 52,960 **Regional Accreditation:** New England Association of Schools and Colleges **Credit Hours For Degree:** 60 credits, Associates **ROTC:** Air Force **Professional Accreditation:** AAMAE, ADA, JRCEDMS, JRCERT, NLN

MONTSERRAT COLLEGE OF ART
23 Essex St., Box 26
Beverly, MA 01915
Tel: (978)922-8222
Free: 800-836-0487
Admissions: (978)921-4242
Fax: (978)922-4268
E-mail: admiss@montserrat.edu
Web Site: http://www.montserrat.edu/
President/CEO: Stan Trecker
Registrar: Theresa Bonacci
Admissions: Jessica Sarin-Perry
Financial Aid: Creda Camacho
Type: Four-Year College **Sex:** Coed **Scores:** 92% SAT V 400+; 86% SAT M 400+; 83% ACT 18-23 **% Accepted:** 85 **Admission Plans:** Deferred Admission **Application Deadline:** August 01 **Application Fee:** $40.00 **H.S. Requirements:** High school diploma required; GED accepted **Costs Per Year:** Application fee: $40. One-time mandatory fee: $725. Tuition: $19,934 full-time, $831 per credit part-time. Mandatory fees: $745 full-time, $22 per credit part-time. Full-time tuition and fees vary according to course load. Part-time tuition and fees vary according to course load. College room only: $5300. Room charges vary according to housing facility. **Scholarships:** Available **Calendar System:** Semester, Summer Session Not available **Enrollment:** FT 279, PT 29 **Faculty:** FT 26, PT 37 **Student-Faculty Ratio:** 7:1 **Exams:** SAT I or ACT **% Receiving Financial Aid:** 76 **% Residing in College-Owned, -Operated, or -Affiliated Housing:** 53 **Library Holdings:** 12,025 **Regional Accreditation:** New England Association of Schools and Colleges **Credit Hours For Degree:** 120 credits, Bachelors **ROTC:** Air Force **Professional Accreditation:** NASAD

MOUNT HOLYOKE COLLEGE
50 College St.
South Hadley, MA 01075
Tel: (413)538-2000
Admissions: (413)538-2023
Fax: (413)538-2409
E-mail: admission@mtholyoke.edu
Web Site: http://www.mtholyoke.edu/
President/CEO: Dr. Joanne V. Creighton
Registrar: Monica Augustin
Admissions: Diane Anci
Financial Aid: Jill Cashman
Type: Comprehensive **Sex:** Women **Scores:** 100% SAT V 400+; 99.67% SAT M 400+; 57.5% ACT 18-23; 3.75% ACT 24-29 **% Accepted:** 52 **Admission Plans:** Early Admission; Early Decision Plan; Deferred Admission **Application Deadline:** January 15 **Application Fee:** $60.00 **H.S. Requirements:** High school diploma required; GED accepted **Costs Per Year:** Application fee: $60. Comprehensive fee: $42,148 includes full-time tuition ($32,430), mandatory fees ($168), and college room and board ($9550). College room only: $4670. Room and board charges vary according to board plan and housing facility. Part-time tuition: $1015 per credit hour. **Scholarships:** Available **Calendar System:** 4-1-4, Summer Session Not available **Enrollment:** FT 2,052, PT 73, Grad 2 **Faculty:** FT 207, PT 34 **Student-**

Faculty Ratio: 10:1 **Exams:** SAT II **% Receiving Financial Aid:** 63 **% Residing in College-Owned, -Operated, or -Affiliated Housing:** 93 **Library Holdings:** 909,720 **Regional Accreditation:** New England Association of Schools and Colleges **Credit Hours For Degree:** 128 credit hours, Bachelors **ROTC:** Army, Air Force **Intercollegiate Athletics:** Basketball W; Crew W; Cross-Country Running W; Equestrian Sports W; Field Hockey W; Golf W; Lacrosse W; Soccer W; Softball W; Squash W; Swimming and Diving W; Tennis W; Track and Field W; Volleyball W

MOUNT IDA COLLEGE
777 Dedham St.
Newton, MA 02459-3310
Tel: (617)928-4500
Fax: (617)928-4507
Web Site: http://www.mountida.edu/
President/CEO: Dr. Carol J. Matteson
Admissions: Judith Kaufman
Financial Aid: Linda Mularczyk
Type: Four-Year College **Sex:** Coed **Scores:** 73.3% SAT V 400+; 68.3% SAT M 400+ **Admission Plans:** Early Action; Deferred Admission **Application Fee:** $35.00 **H.S. Requirements:** High school diploma required; GED accepted **Costs Per Year:** Application fee: $35. Comprehensive fee: $28,926 includes full-time tuition ($18,500), mandatory fees ($596), and college room and board ($9830). Part-time tuition: $515 per credit hour. Part-time mandatory fees: $15 per credit. **Scholarships:** Available **Calendar System:** Semester, Summer Session Not available **Enrollment:** FT 1,191, PT 106 **Faculty:** FT 60, PT 154 **Student-Faculty Ratio:** 14:1 **Exams:** SAT I or ACT **% Receiving Financial Aid:** 83 **% Residing in College-Owned, -Operated, or -Affiliated Housing:** 38 **Library Holdings:** 100,695 **Regional Accreditation:** New England Association of Schools and Colleges **Credit Hours For Degree:** 60 credit hours, Associates; 120 credit hours, Bachelors **Professional Accreditation:** ABFSE, ADA, FIDER, NASAD **Intercollegiate Athletics:** Basketball M & W; Cross-Country Running W; Equestrian Sports W; Football M; Lacrosse M; Soccer M & W; Softball W; Volleyball M & W

MOUNT WACHUSETT COMMUNITY COLLEGE
444 Green St.
Gardner, MA 01440-1000
Tel: (978)632-6600
Fax: (978)632-8925
Web Site: http://www.mwcc.mass.edu/
President/CEO: Dr. Daniel M. Asquino
Registrar: Glenn Roberts
Admissions: John D. Walsh
Financial Aid: Kelly Morrissey
Type: Two-Year College **Sex:** Coed **Affiliation:** Massachusetts Public Higher Education System **% Accepted:** 98 **Admission Plans:** Open Admission; Preferred Admission; Early Admission **Application Deadline:** Rolling **Application Fee:** $10.00 **H.S. Requirements:** High school diploma required; GED accepted **Costs Per Year:** Application fee: $10. State resident tuition: $750 full-time, $25 per credit part-time. Nonresident tuition: $6900 full-time, $230 per credit part-time. Mandatory fees: $3480 full-time, $111 per credit part-time, $55 per term part-time. **Scholarships:** Available **Calendar System:** Semester, Summer Session Available **Enrollment:** FT 1,958, PT 2,212 **Faculty:** FT 71, PT 150 **Student-Faculty Ratio:** 22:1 **Library Holdings:** 56,344 **Regional Accreditation:** New England Association of Schools and Colleges **Credit Hours For Degree:** 60 credits, Associates **Professional Accreditation:** AAMAE, APTA, NLN

NEW ENGLAND COLLEGE OF FINANCE
10 High St.
Ste. 204
Boston, MA 02111-2645
Tel: (617)951-2350; 888-696-NECF
Fax: (617)951-2533
Web Site: http://www.finance.edu/
President/CEO: Robert A. Regan
Registrar: Robert Nagstaff
Admissions: Robert Wagstaff
Type: Two-Year College **Sex:** Coed **Admission Plans:** Open Admission **Application Deadline:** Rolling **Application Fee:** $0.00 **H.S. Requirements:** High school diploma required; GED accepted **Costs Per Year:** Application fee: $0. Tuition: $242 per semester hour part-time. **Calendar System:** Miscellaneous, Summer Session Available **Enrollment:** , PT 412 **Faculty:** FT 0, PT 216 **Student-Faculty Ratio:** 11:1 **Regional Accreditation:** New England Association of Schools and Colleges **Credit Hours For Degree:** 63 credits, Associates

NEW ENGLAND CONSERVATORY OF MUSIC
290 Huntington Ave.
Boston, MA 02115-5000
Tel: (617)585-1100
Admissions: (617)585-1101
Fax: (617)585-1115
E-mail: tnovak@newenglandconservatory.edu
Web Site: http://www.newenglandconservatory.edu/
President/CEO: Daniel Steiner
Registrar: Robert Winkley
Admissions: Tom Novak
Financial Aid: Ken Ferreira
Type: Comprehensive **Sex:** Coed **% Accepted:** 30 **Admission Plans:** Deferred Admission **Application Deadline:** December 01 **Application Fee:** $100.00 **H.S. Requirements:** High school diploma required; GED accepted **Costs Per Year:** Application fee: $100. Comprehensive fee: $40,389 includes full-time tuition ($29,000), mandatory fees ($300), and college room and board ($11,089). Part-time tuition: $950 per credit. **Scholarships:** Available **Calendar System:** Semester, Summer Session Available **Enrollment:** FT 388, PT 24, Grad 389 **Faculty:** FT 83, PT 127 **Student-Faculty Ratio:** 4:1 **Exams:** SAT I or ACT **% Receiving Financial Aid:** 61 **% Residing in College-Owned, -Operated, or -Affiliated Housing:** 40 **Library Holdings:** 78,853 **Regional Accreditation:** New England Association of Schools and Colleges **Credit Hours For Degree:** 120 credit hours, Bachelors **Professional Accreditation:** NASM

THE NEW ENGLAND INSTITUTE OF ART
10 Brookline Place West
Brookline, MA 02445
Tel: (617)267-7910
Admissions: (617)739-1700
Fax: (617)236-7883
E-mail: aine_admissions@aii.edu
Web Site: http://www.neia.aii.edu/
President/CEO: Stacy Sweeney
Registrar: Adrienne McLaughlin
Admissions: Ken Post
Financial Aid: Deana Coady
Type: Four-Year College **Sex:** Coed **Affiliation:** Education Management Corporation **% Accepted:** 97 **Application Deadline:** Rolling **Application Fee:** $50.00 **H.S. Requirements:** High school diploma required; GED accepted **Costs Per Year:** Application fee: $50. Comprehensive fee: $28,053 includes full-time tuition ($17,850), mandatory fees ($225), and college room and board ($9978). College room only: $7718. Part-time tuition: $595 per credit. **Calendar System:** Semester, Summer Session Not available **Enrollment:** FT 1,004, PT 289 **Faculty:** FT 34, PT 81 **Student-Faculty Ratio:** 18:1 **Library Holdings:** 8,800 **Regional Accreditation:** New England Association of Schools and Colleges **Credit Hours For Degree:** 61 credits, Associates; 120 credits, Bachelors

NEWBURY COLLEGE
129 Fisher Ave.
Brookline, MA 02445
Tel: (617)730-7000
Free: 800-NEW-BURY
Admissions: (617)730-7007
Fax: (617)731-9618
E-mail: info@newbury.edu
Web Site: http://www.newbury.edu/
President/CEO: Dr. David A. Ellis
Registrar: Rachelle Mazza
Admissions: Salvadore Liberto
Financial Aid: Jeannie Gonzales
Type: Four-Year College **Sex:** Coed **Scores:** 67% SAT V 400+; 64% SAT M 400+; 50% ACT 18-23; 25% ACT 24-29 **% Accepted:** 74 **Admission Plans:** Early Admission; Early Action; Deferred Admission **Application Deadline:** Rolling **Application Fee:** $50.00 **H.S. Requirements:** High school diploma required; GED accepted **Costs Per Year:** Application fee: $50. Comprehensive fee: $24,350 includes full-time tuition ($15,500), mandatory fees ($600), and college room and board ($8250). Full-time tuition and fees vary according to class time, course load, and program. Room and board charges vary

according to board plan and housing facility. Part-time tuition: $220 per credit. Part-time tuition varies according to class time, course load, and program. **Scholarships:** Available **Calendar System:** Semester, Summer Session Available **Enrollment:** FT 928, PT 383 **Faculty:** FT 28, PT 65 **Student-Faculty Ratio:** 15:1 **Exams:** SAT I or ACT **% Receiving Financial Aid:** 65 **% Residing in College-Owned, -Operated, or -Affiliated Housing:** 47 **Library Holdings:** 32,500 **Regional Accreditation:** New England Association of Schools and Colleges **Credit Hours For Degree:** 60 credits, Associates; 121 credits, Bachelors **Professional Accreditation:** FIDER **Intercollegiate Athletics:** Basketball M & W; Cross-Country Running M & W; Golf M & W; Soccer M; Softball W; Tennis M & W; Volleyball M & W

NICHOLS COLLEGE
PO Box 5000
Dudley, MA 01571-5000
Tel: (508)213-1560
Free: 800-470-3379
Admissions: (508)213-2203
Fax: (508)213-9885
E-mail: joe.bellavance@nichols.edu
Web Site: http://www.nichols.edu/
President/CEO: Dr. Debra M. Murphy
Registrar: Deana Gleason
Admissions: R. Joseph Bellavance
Financial Aid: Diane Gillespie
Type: Comprehensive **Sex:** Coed **Scores:** 79.9% SAT V 400+; 83.2% SAT M 400+ **Admission Plans:** Early Admission; Deferred Admission **Application Fee:** $25.00 **H.S. Requirements:** High school diploma required; GED accepted **Scholarships:** Available **Calendar System:** Semester, Summer Session Available **Enrollment:** FT 938, PT 494, Grad 360 **Faculty:** FT 38, PT 27 **Student-Faculty Ratio:** 20:1 **Exams:** SAT I or ACT **% Receiving Financial Aid:** 65 **% Residing in College-Owned, -Operated, or -Affiliated Housing:** 80 **Library Holdings:** 43,989 **Regional Accreditation:** New England Association of Schools and Colleges **Credit Hours For Degree:** 122 credit hours, Bachelors **ROTC:** Army **Intercollegiate Athletics:** Baseball M; Basketball M & W; Cheerleading M & W; Field Hockey W; Football M; Golf M & W; Ice Hockey M; Lacrosse M & W; Racquetball M & W; Rugby M & W; Skiing (Downhill) M; Soccer M & W; Softball W; Tennis M & W; Volleyball W

NORTH SHORE COMMUNITY COLLEGE
1 Ferncroft Rd.
Danvers, MA 01923-4093
Tel: (978)762-4000
Fax: (978)762-4021
Web Site: http://www.northshore.edu/
President/CEO: Dr. Wayne Burton
Admissions: Dr. Joanne Light
Financial Aid: Del Brown
Type: Two-Year College **Sex:** Coed **% Accepted:** 90 **Admission Plans:** Open Admission; Preferred Admission; Early Admission **Application Deadline:** Rolling **Application Fee:** $0.00 **H.S. Requirements:** High school diploma required; GED accepted **Costs Per Year:** Application fee: $0. State resident tuition: $600 full-time, $25 per credit part-time. Nonresident tuition: $6168 full-time, $257 per credit part-time. Mandatory fees: $2184 full-time, $91 per credit part-time. **Scholarships:** Available **Calendar System:** Semester, Summer Session Available **Enrollment:** FT 2,764, PT 3,840 **Faculty:** FT 135, PT 269 **Student-Faculty Ratio:** 18:1 **Library Holdings:** 97,818 **Regional Accreditation:** New England Association of Schools and Colleges **Credit Hours For Degree:** 60 credits, Associates **Professional Accreditation:** AOTA, APTA, CARC, CAA, JRCERT, NLN

NORTHEASTERN UNIVERSITY
360 Huntington Ave.
Boston, MA 02115-5096
Tel: (617)373-2000
Admissions: (617)373-2200
Fax: (617)373-8780
E-mail: admissions@neu.edu
Web Site: http://www.northeastern.edu
Registrar: Linda D. Allen
Admissions: Ronne Turner
Financial Aid: Seamus Harreys
Type: University **Sex:** Coed **Scores:** 99% SAT V 400+; 100% SAT M 400+; 14% ACT 18-23; 69% ACT 24-29 **% Accepted:** 47 **Admission Plans:** Early Admission; Deferred Admission **Application Deadline:** January 15 **Application Fee:** $75.00 **H.S. Requirements:** High school diploma required; GED accepted **Costs Per Year:** Application fee: $75. Comprehensive fee: $39,342 includes full-time tuition ($28,400), mandatory fees ($392), and college room and board ($10,550). College room only: $5620. Room and board charges vary according to board plan and housing facility. **Scholarships:** Available **Calendar System:** Semester, Summer Session Available **Enrollment:** FT 14,730, Grad 4,193 **Faculty:** FT 853, PT 404 **Student-Faculty Ratio:** 16:1 **Exams:** SAT I or ACT **% Receiving Financial Aid:** 60 **Library Holdings:** 965,833 **Regional Accreditation:** New England Association of Schools and Colleges **Credit Hours For Degree:** 128 semester hour, Bachelors **ROTC:** Army, Navy, Air Force **Professional Accreditation:** AACSB, ABET, ACPE, AACN, AANA, ABA, ACPhE, AHIMA, APTA, APA, ASLHA, AALS, CARC, CORE, JRCEPAT, NAACLS, NASPAA, NLN **Intercollegiate Athletics:** Baseball M; Basketball M & W; Crew M & W; Cross-Country Running M & W; Field Hockey W; Football M; Ice Hockey M & W; Soccer M & W; Swimming and Diving W; Tennis M; Track and Field M & W; Volleyball W

NORTHERN ESSEX COMMUNITY COLLEGE
100 Elliott St.
Haverhill, MA 01830
Tel: (978)556-3000
Free: 800-NECC-123
Admissions: (978)556-3616
E-mail: nsheridan@necc.mass.edu
Web Site: http://www.necc.mass.edu/
President/CEO: Dr. David F. Hartleb
Registrar: Kevin Stanley
Admissions: Nora Sheridan
Financial Aid: Nancy Sabin
Type: Two-Year College **Sex:** Coed **% Accepted:** 95 **Admission Plans:** Open Admission; Preferred Admission; Early Admission **Application Deadline:** Rolling **Application Fee:** $0.00 **H.S. Requirements:** High school diploma required; GED accepted **Costs Per Year:** Application fee: $0. State resident tuition: $3150 full-time, $105 per credit part-time. Nonresident tuition: $3660 full-time, $346 per credit part-time. Full-time tuition varies according to course load, degree level, program, and reciprocity agreements. Part-time tuition varies according to course load, degree level, program, and reciprocity agreements. **Scholarships:** Available **Calendar System:** Semester, Summer Session Available **Enrollment:** FT 2,300, PT 4,062 **Faculty:** FT 99, PT 398 **Student-Faculty Ratio:** 20:1 **Exams:** Other **Library Holdings:** 61,120 **Regional Accreditation:** New England Association of Schools and Colleges **Credit Hours For Degree:** 60 credits, Associates **ROTC:** Air Force **Professional Accreditation:** ADA, AHIMA, CARC, JRCERT, NLN **Intercollegiate Athletics:** Baseball M; Basketball M & W; Cross-Country Running M & W; Volleyball M & W

PINE MANOR COLLEGE
400 Heath St.
Chestnut Hill, MA 02467
Tel: (617)731-7000
Free: 800-762-1357
Admissions: (617)731-7104
Fax: (617)731-7199
E-mail: admisson@pmc.edu
Web Site: http://www.pmc.edu/
President/CEO: Dr. Gloria Nemerowicz
Registrar: Kerry Boyd
Admissions: Robin Engel
Financial Aid: Nancy Amaral
Type: Four-Year College **Sex:** Women **Scores:** 59% SAT V 400+; 53% SAT M 400+; 56% ACT 18-23 **% Accepted:** 94 **Admission Plans:** Preferred Admission; Deferred Admission **Application Deadline:** Rolling **Application Fee:** $25.00 **H.S. Requirements:** High school diploma required; GED accepted **Costs Per Year:** Application fee: $25. Comprehensive fee: $25,288 includes full-time tuition ($15,538), mandatory fees ($250), and college room and board ($9500). Full-time tuition and fees vary according to course load. Part-time tuition: $460 per credit. Part-time tuition varies according to course load. **Scholarships:** Available **Calendar System:** Semester, Summer Session Available **Enrollment:** FT 448, PT 13 **Faculty:** FT 30, PT 36 **Student-Faculty Ratio:** 10:1 **Exams:** SAT I or ACT **% Receiving Financial Aid:** 77 **% Residing in College-Owned, -Operated, or -Affiliated Housing:** 74 **Library Holdings:** 65,359 **Regional Accreditation:** New England Association of Schools and Colleges **Credit Hours For Degree:** 16 courses, Associ-

ates; 32 courses, Bachelors **Intercollegiate Athletics:** Basketball W; Cross-Country Running W; Lacrosse W; Soccer W; Softball W; Tennis W; Volleyball W

QUINCY COLLEGE
34 Coddington St.
Quincy, MA 02169-4522
Tel: (617)984-1600
Admissions: (617)984-1775
Fax: (617)984-1669
Web Site: http://www.quincycollege.edu/
President/CEO: Sean L. Barry
Admissions: Tom DeSantes
Financial Aid: Rose DeVito
Type: Two-Year College **Sex:** Coed **Admission Plans:** Open Admission; Early Admission; Deferred Admission **Application Fee:** $20.00 **H.S. Requirements:** High school diploma required; GED accepted **Costs Per Year:** Application fee: $20. State resident tuition: $4500 full-time. **Scholarships:** Available **Calendar System:** Semester, Summer Session Available **Faculty:** FT 20, PT 384 **Exams:** Other **Library Holdings:** 32,000 **Regional Accreditation:** New England Association of Schools and Colleges **Credit Hours For Degree:** 60 credits, Associates **Professional Accreditation:** NLN

QUINSIGAMOND COMMUNITY COLLEGE
670 West Boylston St.
Worcester, MA 01606-2092
Tel: (508)853-2300
Admissions: (508)854-4262
Fax: (508)852-6943
E-mail: qccadm@qcc.mass.edu
Web Site: http://www.qcc.mass.edu/
President/CEO: Dr. Sandra Kurtinitis
Registrar: Tara Fitzgerald-Jenkins
Admissions: Ronald Smith
Financial Aid: Maribeth Ford
Type: Two-Year College **Sex:** Coed **% Accepted:** 100 **Admission Plans:** Open Admission **Application Deadline:** Rolling **Application Fee:** $20.00 **H.S. Requirements:** High school diploma required; GED accepted **Costs Per Year:** Application fee: $20. State resident tuition: $576 full-time, $24 per credit part-time. Nonresident tuition: $5520 full-time, $230 per credit part-time. Mandatory fees: $2479 full-time, $96 per credit part-time, $85 per term part-time. **Scholarships:** Available **Calendar System:** Semester, Summer Session Available **Enrollment:** FT 2,761, PT 3,209 **Faculty:** FT 106, PT 292 **Library Holdings:** 54,000 **Regional Accreditation:** New England Association of Schools and Colleges **Credit Hours For Degree:** 60 credits, Associates **ROTC:** Army **Professional Accreditation:** AAMAE, ADA, AOTA, CARC, JRCERT, NLN **Intercollegiate Athletics:** Baseball M; Basketball M & W; Softball W

REGIS COLLEGE
235 Wellesley St.
Weston, MA 02493
Tel: (781)768-7000; (866)438-7344
Admissions: (781)768-7100
Fax: (781)768-8339
Web Site: http://www.regiscollege.edu/
President/CEO: Dr. Mary Jane England
Registrar: Dr. Patricia McDonough, CSJ
Admissions: Emily Keily
Financial Aid: Delores Ludwick
Type: Comprehensive **Affiliation:** Roman Catholic **Scores:** 85.07% SAT V 400+; 80.52% SAT M 400+; 40% ACT 18-23; 20% ACT 24-29 **% Accepted:** 76 **Admission Plans:** Deferred Admission **Application Deadline:** Rolling **Application Fee:** $40.00 **H.S. Requirements:** High school diploma required; GED accepted **Costs Per Year:** Application fee: $40. Comprehensive fee: $31,350 includes full-time tuition ($21,525) and college room and board ($9825). College room only: $4995. **Scholarships:** Available **Calendar System:** Semester, Summer Session Available **Enrollment:** FT 621, PT 222, Grad 460 **Faculty:** FT 55, PT 58 **Student-Faculty Ratio:** 13:1 **Exams:** SAT I or ACT **% Receiving Financial Aid:** 80 **% Residing in College-Owned, -Operated, or -Affiliated Housing:** 46 **Library Holdings:** 137,070 **Regional Accreditation:** New England Association of Schools and Colleges **Credit Hours For Degree:** 72 credits, Associates; 36 courses, Bachelors **ROTC:** Army **Professional Accreditation:** CSWE, NLN **Intercollegiate Athletics:** Basketball W; Cross-Country Running W; Field Hockey W; Lacrosse W; Soccer W; Softball W; Swimming and Diving W; Tennis W; Track and Field W; Volleyball W

ROXBURY COMMUNITY COLLEGE
1234 Columbus Ave.
Roxbury Crossing, MA 02120-3400
Tel: (617)427-0060
Admissions: (617)541-5310
Web Site: http://www.rcc.mass.edu/
President/CEO: Dr. Randolph Bromery
Registrar: Valerie Abrahamsen
Admissions: Milton Samuels
Financial Aid: Raymond O'Rourke
Type: Two-Year College **Sex:** Coed **Affiliation:** Massachusetts Public Higher Education System **Admission Plans:** Open Admission; Preferred Admission; Deferred Admission **Application Fee:** $10.00 **H.S. Requirements:** High school diploma required; GED accepted **Scholarships:** Available **Calendar System:** Semester, Summer Session Available **Enrollment:** FT 1,124, PT 1,258 **Faculty:** FT 65, PT 55 **Student-Faculty Ratio:** 16:1 **Library Holdings:** 12,800 **Regional Accreditation:** New England Association of Schools and Colleges **Credit Hours For Degree:** 60 credits, Associates **Professional Accreditation:** NLN **Intercollegiate Athletics:** Baseball M; Basketball M & W; Soccer M & W; Tennis M & W

SALEM STATE COLLEGE
352 Lafayette St.
Salem, MA 01970-5353
Tel: (978)542-6000
Admissions: (978)542-6200
Fax: (978)542-6126
Web Site: http://www.salemstate.edu/
President/CEO: Dr. Nancy D. Harrington
Registrar: Ali Guvendiren
Admissions: Nate Bryant
Financial Aid: Mary Benda
Type: Comprehensive **Sex:** Coed **Affiliation:** Massachusetts Public Higher Education System **Scores:** 83.6% SAT V 400+; 84.29% SAT M 400+; 68.4% ACT 18-23; 10.5% ACT 24-29 **% Accepted:** 90 **Admission Plans:** Preferred Admission; Early Admission **Application Deadline:** Rolling **Application Fee:** $25.00 **H.S. Requirements:** High school diploma required; GED accepted **Costs Per Year:** Application fee: $25. State resident tuition: $910 full-time, $37.92 per credit part-time. Nonresident tuition: $7050 full-time, $293.75 per credit part-time. Mandatory fees: $4,374 full-time, $182.24 per credit part-time, $13.50 per term part-time. Full-time tuition and fees vary according to class time. Part-time tuition and fees vary according to class time. College room and board: $7350. College room only: $5047. Room and board charges vary according to board plan and housing facility. **Scholarships:** Available **Calendar System:** Semester, Summer Session Available **Enrollment:** FT 5,468, PT 1,828, Grad 2,567 **Faculty:** FT 296, PT 372 **Student-Faculty Ratio:** 17:1 **Exams:** SAT I and SAT II or ACT **% Receiving Financial Aid:** 48 **% Residing in College-Owned, -Operated, or -Affiliated Housing:** 21 **Library Holdings:** 217,842 **Regional Accreditation:** New England Association of Schools and Colleges **Credit Hours For Degree:** 125 semester hours, Bachelors **Professional Accreditation:** AACN, AOTA, CSWE, JRCEPAT, JRCNMT, NASAD, NAST, NCATE, NLN **Intercollegiate Athletics:** Baseball M; Basketball M & W; Cross-Country Running M & W; Field Hockey W; Golf M; Ice Hockey M; Soccer M & W; Softball W; Swimming and Diving M & W; Tennis M & W; Track and Field M & W; Volleyball W

SCHOOL OF THE MUSEUM OF FINE ARTS, BOSTON
230 The Fenway
Boston, MA 02115
Tel: (617)267-6100
Admissions: (617)369-3626
Fax: (617)369-3679
E-mail: info@smfa.edu
Web Site: http://www.smfa.edu/
President/CEO: Deborah Dluhy
Registrar: Cheryl Martin
Admissions: Susan Clain
Financial Aid: Beth Goreham
Type: Comprehensive **Sex:** Coed **Affiliation:** Tufts University; Museum of Fine Arts, Boston **Scores:** 97% SAT V 400+; 95% SAT M 400+; 14% ACT

18-23; 57% ACT 24-29 **% Accepted:** 84 **Admission Plans:** Deferred Admission **Application Deadline:** February 01 **Application Fee:** $65.00 **H.S. Requirements:** High school diploma required; GED accepted **Costs Per Year:** Application fee: $65. Tuition: $23,850 full-time, $1000 per credit hour part-time. Mandatory fees: $910 full-time, $455 per term part-time. Full-time tuition and fees vary according to course load, degree level, and program. Part-time tuition and fees vary according to class time, course load, and program. College room only: $10,795. Room charges vary according to housing facility. **Scholarships:** Available **Calendar System:** Semester, Summer Session Available **Enrollment:** FT 611, PT 66, Grad 96 **Faculty:** FT 51, PT 129 **Student-Faculty Ratio:** 9:1 **Exams:** SAT I or ACT **% Receiving Financial Aid:** 66 **% Residing in College-Owned, -Operated, or -Affiliated Housing:** 9 **Library Holdings:** 280,000 **Credit Hours For Degree:** 162 credits, Bachelors **Professional Accreditation:** NASAD

SIMMONS COLLEGE
300 The Fenway
Boston, MA 02115
Tel: (617)521-2000
Free: 800-345-8468
Admissions: (617)521-2057
Fax: (617)521-3199
E-mail: ugadm@simmons.edu
Web Site: http://www.simmons.edu/
President/CEO: Dr. Daniel Cheever
Registrar: Donna Dolan
Admissions: Catherine Childs-Capolupo
Financial Aid: Barry Paine
Type: University **Scores:** 99% SAT V 400+; 100% SAT M 400+; 55% ACT 18-23; 40% ACT 24-29 **% Accepted:** 64 **Admission Plans:** Early Admission; Early Action; Deferred Admission **Application Deadline:** February 02 **Application Fee:** $35.00 **H.S. Requirements:** High school diploma required; GED accepted **Costs Per Year:** Application fee: $35. Comprehensive fee: $35,640 includes full-time tuition ($24,680), mandatory fees ($760), and college room and board ($10,200). Full-time tuition and fees vary according to course load. Part-time tuition: $770 per semester hour. Part-time tuition varies according to course load. **Scholarships:** Available **Calendar System:** Semester, Summer Session Available **Enrollment:** FT 1,688, PT 277, Grad 2,840 **Faculty:** FT 193, PT 181 **Student-Faculty Ratio:** 12:1 **Exams:** SAT I or ACT **% Receiving Financial Aid:** 70 **% Residing in College-Owned, -Operated, or -Affiliated Housing:** 70 **Library Holdings:** 253,145 **Regional Accreditation:** New England Association of Schools and Colleges **Credit Hours For Degree:** 128 semester hours, Bachelors **ROTC:** Army, Navy, Air Force **Professional Accreditation:** ACEHSA, AACN, ADtA, ALA, APTA, CSWE, NLN **Intercollegiate Athletics:** Basketball W; Crew W; Field Hockey W; Sailing W; Soccer W; Softball W; Swimming and Diving W; Tennis W; Track and Field W; Volleyball W

SIMON'S ROCK COLLEGE OF BARD
84 Alford Rd.
Great Barrington, MA 01230-9702
Tel: (413)528-0771
Free: 800-235-7186
Admissions: (413)528-7245
Fax: (413)528-7334
E-mail: admit@simons-rock.edu
Web Site: http://www.simons-rock.edu/
President/CEO: Dr. Leon Botstein
Registrar: Rochelle Duffy
Admissions: Leslie Davidson
Financial Aid: Kristin Johnson
Type: Four-Year College **Sex:** Coed **Affiliation:** Bard College **Scores:** 98% SAT V 400+; 98% SAT M 400+; 22% ACT 18-23; 45% ACT 24-29 **% Accepted:** 79 **Admission Plans:** Early Admission; Deferred Admission **Application Deadline:** June 15 **Application Fee:** $40.00 **H.S. Requirements:** High school diploma or equivalent not required **Costs Per Year:** Application fee: $40. Comprehensive fee: $41,988 includes full-time tuition ($32,834), mandatory fees ($500), and college room and board ($8654). Full-time tuition and fees vary according to course load and program. Part-time tuition: $285 per credit hour. Part-time mandatory fees: $650. Part-time tuition and fees vary according to course load and program. **Scholarships:** Available **Calendar System:** Semester, Summer Session Not available **Enrollment:** FT 369, PT 17 **Faculty:** FT 38, PT 30 **Student-Faculty Ratio:** 8:1 **Exams:** ACT, Other, SAT I **% Receiving Financial Aid:** 71 **% Residing in College-Owned, -Operated, or -Affiliated Housing:** 81 **Library Holdings:** 73,514 **Regional Accreditation:** New England Association of Schools and Colleges **Credit Hours For Degree:** 60 credit hours, Associates; 120 credit hours, Bachelors **Intercollegiate Athletics:** Basketball M & W; Cheerleading M & W; Cross-Country Running M & W; Fencing M & W; Racquetball M & W; Soccer M & W; Swimming and Diving M & W

SMITH COLLEGE
Northampton, MA 01063
Tel: (413)584-2700
Free: 800-383-3232
Admissions: (413)585-2500
Fax: (413)585-2123
E-mail: admission@smith.edu
Web Site: http://www.smith.edu/
President/CEO: Carol Christ
Registrar: Patricia O'Neil
Admissions: Debra Shaver
Financial Aid: Deborah Leukens
Type: Comprehensive **Scores:** 99.83% SAT V 400+; 100% SAT M 400+; 16.8% ACT 18-23; 53.3% ACT 24-29 **% Accepted:** 52 **Admission Plans:** Early Admission; Early Decision Plan; Deferred Admission **Application Deadline:** January 15 **Application Fee:** $60.00 **H.S. Requirements:** High school diploma or equivalent not required **Costs Per Year:** Application fee: $60. Comprehensive fee: $41,474 includes full-time tuition ($30,520), mandatory fees ($234), and college room and board ($10,720). College room only: $5160. Room and board charges vary according to housing facility. Part-time tuition: $955 per credit hour. **Scholarships:** Available **Calendar System:** Semester, Summer Session Not available **Enrollment:** FT 2,612, PT 30, Grad 451 **Faculty:** FT 288, PT 28 **Student-Faculty Ratio:** 9:1 **Exams:** SAT I or ACT **% Receiving Financial Aid:** 60 **% Residing in College-Owned, -Operated, or -Affiliated Housing:** 90 **Library Holdings:** 1,296,828 **Regional Accreditation:** New England Association of Schools and Colleges **Credit Hours For Degree:** 128 credits, Bachelors **ROTC:** Army **Professional Accreditation:** CSWE **Intercollegiate Athletics:** Basketball W; Crew W; Cross-Country Running W; Equestrian Sports W; Field Hockey W; Lacrosse W; Skiing (Downhill) W; Soccer W; Softball W; Squash W; Swimming and Diving W; Tennis W; Track and Field W; Volleyball W

SPRINGFIELD COLLEGE
263 Alden St.
Springfield, MA 01109-3797
Tel: (413)748-3000
Free: 800-343-1257
Admissions: (413)748-3136
Fax: (413)748-3764
E-mail: admissions@spfldcol.edu
Web Site: http://www.spfldcol.edu/
President/CEO: Dr. Richard B. Flynn
Registrar: Irene Rios
Admissions: Mary N. DeAngelo
Financial Aid: Ed Ciosek
Type: Comprehensive **Sex:** Coed **% Accepted:** 69 **Admission Plans:** Preferred Admission; Early Admission; Early Decision Plan; Deferred Admission **Application Deadline:** April 01 **Application Fee:** $50.00 **H.S. Requirements:** High school diploma required; GED accepted **Costs Per Year:** Application fee: $50. Comprehensive fee: $30,845 includes full-time tuition ($22,390), mandatory fees ($325), and college room and board ($8130). College room only: $4400. Part-time tuition: $679 per credit. **Scholarships:** Available **Calendar System:** Semester, Summer Session Available **Enrollment:** FT 2,172, PT 45, Grad 938 **Faculty:** FT 174, PT 168 **Student-Faculty Ratio:** 12:1 **Exams:** SAT I or ACT **% Receiving Financial Aid:** 77 **% Residing in College-Owned, -Operated, or -Affiliated Housing:** 85 **Library Holdings:** 125,000 **Regional Accreditation:** New England Association of Schools and Colleges **Credit Hours For Degree:** 130 credit hours, Bachelors **ROTC:** Army, Air Force **Professional Accreditation:** AOTA, APTA, CORE, CSWE, JRCEPAT, NRPA **Intercollegiate Athletics:** Baseball M; Basketball M & W; Cross-Country Running M & W; Field Hockey W; Football M; Golf M; Gymnastics M & W; Lacrosse M & W; Soccer M & W; Softball W; Swimming and Diving M & W; Tennis M & W; Track and Field M & W; Volleyball M & W; Wrestling M

SPRINGFIELD TECHNICAL COMMUNITY COLLEGE
1 Armory Square, PO Box 9000
Springfield, MA 01102-9000

Tel: (413)781-7822
Fax: (413)781-5805
E-mail: admissions@stccadm.stcc.mass.edu
Web Site: http://www.stcc.edu/
President/CEO: Dr. Andrew M. Scibelli
Registrar: Jane Alinovi
Admissions: Louisa Davis-Freeman
Type: Two-Year College **Sex:** Coed **% Accepted:** 93 **Admission Plans:** Open Admission **Application Deadline:** Rolling **Application Fee:** $10.00 **H.S. Requirements:** High school diploma required; GED accepted **Costs Per Year:** Application fee: $10. State resident tuition: $750 full-time, $25 per credit hour part-time. Nonresident tuition: $7260 full-time, $242 per credit hour part-time. Mandatory fees: $2604 full-time, $80 per credit hour part-time, $109 per term part-time. Full-time tuition and fees vary according to course load. Part-time tuition and fees vary according to course load. Tuition guaranteed not to increase for student's term of enrollment. **Scholarships:** Available **Calendar System:** Semester, Summer Session Available **Enrollment:** FT 2,658, PT 3,165 **Faculty:** FT 154, PT 281 **Student-Faculty Ratio:** 15:1 **Exams:** SAT I **Library Holdings:** 63,945 **Regional Accreditation:** New England Association of Schools and Colleges **Credit Hours For Degree:** 60 credits, Associates **Professional Accreditation:** ARCEST, AAMAE, ADA, AOTA, APTA, CARC, JRCEDMS, JRCERT, JRCNMT, NAACLS, NLN **Intercollegiate Athletics:** Basketball M & W; Golf M & W; Soccer M & W; Tennis M & W; Wrestling M

STONEHILL COLLEGE

320 Washington St.
Easton, MA 02357-5510
Tel: (508)565-1000
Admissions: (508)565-1373
Fax: (508)565-1500
E-mail: admissions@stonehill.edu
Web Site: http://www.stonehill.edu/
President/CEO: Rev. Mark T. Cregan, CSC
Registrar: Linda I. Sullivan
Admissions: Brian P. Murphy
Financial Aid: Eileen K. O'Leary
Type: Comprehensive **Sex:** Coed **Affiliation:** Roman Catholic **Scores:** 100% SAT V 400+; 100% SAT M 400+; 25% ACT 18-23; 69% ACT 24-29 **% Accepted:** 57 **Admission Plans:** Early Admission; Early Decision Plan; Deferred Admission **Application Deadline:** January 15 **Application Fee:** $50.00 **H.S. Requirements:** High school diploma required; GED accepted **Costs Per Year:** Application fee: $50. Comprehensive fee: $36,104 includes full-time tuition ($25,540) and college room and board ($10,564). Part-time tuition: $840 per course. Part-time mandatory fees: $25 per term. Part-time tuition and fees vary according to course load. **Scholarships:** Available **Calendar System:** Semester, Summer Session Available **Enrollment:** FT 2,260, PT 171, Grad 12 **Faculty:** FT 132, PT 121 **Student-Faculty Ratio:** 13:1 **Exams:** SAT I or ACT **% Receiving Financial Aid:** 64 **% Residing in College-Owned, -Operated, or -Affiliated Housing:** 82 **Library Holdings:** 215,581 **Regional Accreditation:** New England Association of Schools and Colleges **Credit Hours For Degree:** 40 courses, Bachelors **ROTC:** Army **Intercollegiate Athletics:** Baseball M; Basketball M & W; Cheerleading M & W; Cross-Country Running M & W; Equestrian Sports W; Field Hockey W; Football M; Golf M & W; Ice Hockey M; Lacrosse M & W; Rugby M & W; Soccer M & W; Softball W; Tennis M & W; Track and Field M & W; Ultimate Frisbee M & W; Volleyball M & W

SUFFOLK UNIVERSITY

8 Ashburton Place
Boston, MA 02108-2770
Tel: (617)573-8000
Free: 800-6-SUFFOLK
Admissions: (617)573-8749
Fax: (617)742-4291
E-mail: admission@admin.suffolk.edu
Web Site: http://www.suffolk.edu/
President/CEO: David J. Sargent
Registrar: Mary Lally
Admissions: John Hamel
Financial Aid: Christine Perry
Type: Comprehensive **Sex:** Coed **Scores:** 93.1% SAT V 400+; 94.8% SAT M 400+; 61.5% ACT 18-23; 25% ACT 24-29 **% Accepted:** 82 **Admission Plans:** Early Action; Deferred Admission **Application Deadline:** March 15 **Application Fee:** $50.00 **H.S. Requirements:** High school diploma required; GED accepted **Costs Per Year:** Application fee: $50. Comprehensive fee: $33,160 includes full-time tuition ($21,140), mandatory fees ($80), and college room and board ($11,940). College room only: $10,020. Room and board charges vary according to board plan and housing facility. Part-time tuition: $526 per credit. Part-time mandatory fees: $10 per term. **Scholarships:** Available **Calendar System:** Semester, Summer Session Available **Enrollment:** FT 4,075, PT 709, Grad 2,019 **Faculty:** FT 255, PT 524 **Student-Faculty Ratio:** 12:1 **Exams:** SAT I or ACT **% Receiving Financial Aid:** 54 **% Residing in College-Owned, -Operated, or -Affiliated Housing:** 19 **Library Holdings:** 129,562 **Regional Accreditation:** New England Association of Schools and Colleges **Credit Hours For Degree:** 66 semester hours, Associates; 122 semester hours, Bachelors **ROTC:** Army **Professional Accreditation:** AACSB, ABA, APA, AALS, FIDER, NASAD, NASPAA **Intercollegiate Athletics:** Baseball M; Basketball M & W; Cross-Country Running M & W; Golf M; Ice Hockey M; Soccer M; Softball W; Tennis M & W; Volleyball W

TUFTS UNIVERSITY

Medford, MA 02155
Tel: (617)628-5000
Admissions: (617)627-3170
Fax: (617)627-3860
E-mail: admissions.inquiry@ase.tufts.edu
Web Site: http://www.tufts.edu/
President/CEO: Dr. Lawrence S. Bacow
Registrar: JoAnn M. Smith
Admissions: Lee Coffin
Financial Aid: Patricia Reilly
Type: University **Sex:** Coed **Scores:** 100% SAT V 400+; 100% SAT M 400+; 3% ACT 18-23; 33% ACT 24-29 **% Accepted:** 28 **Admission Plans:** Early Admission; Early Decision Plan; Deferred Admission **Application Deadline:** January 01 **Application Fee:** $70.00 **H.S. Requirements:** High school diploma required; GED accepted **Costs Per Year:** Application fee: $70. Comprehensive fee: $42,018 includes full-time tuition ($31,828), mandatory fees ($793), and college room and board ($9397). College room only: $4827. Room and board charges vary according to board plan. **Scholarships:** Available **Calendar System:** Semester, Summer Session Available **Enrollment:** FT 4,971, PT 107, Grad 3,051 **Faculty:** FT 765, PT 429 **Student-Faculty Ratio:** 9:1 **Exams:** SAT I and SAT II or ACT **% Receiving Financial Aid:** 38 **% Residing in College-Owned, -Operated, or -Affiliated Housing:** 75 **Library Holdings:** 1,613,000 **Regional Accreditation:** New England Association of Schools and Colleges **Credit Hours For Degree:** 34 courses, Bachelors **ROTC:** Army, Navy, Air Force **Professional Accreditation:** ABET, ADA, ADtA, ACSP, AOTA, APA, AVMA, CEPH, LCMEAMA **Intercollegiate Athletics:** Baseball M; Basketball M & W; Crew M & W; Cross-Country Running M & W; Fencing W; Field Hockey W; Football M; Golf M; Ice Hockey M; Lacrosse M & W; Sailing M & W; Soccer M & W; Softball W; Squash M & W; Swimming and Diving M & W; Tennis M & W; Track and Field M & W; Volleyball W

UNIVERSITY OF MASSACHUSETTS AMHERST

Amherst, MA 01003
Tel: (413)545-0111
Admissions: (413)545-0222
Fax: (413)545-4312
E-mail: kk@admissions.umass.edu
Web Site: http://www.umass.edu/
President/CEO: Dr. John V. Lombardi
Registrar: Patricia M. Stowell
Admissions: Kevin Kelly
Financial Aid: Kenneth W. Burnham
Type: University **Sex:** Coed **Affiliation:** University of Massachusetts **Scores:** 97.9% SAT V 400+; 99.1% SAT M 400+ **% Accepted:** 80 **Admission Plans:** Early Action **Application Deadline:** January 15 **Application Fee:** $40.00 **H.S. Requirements:** High school diploma required; GED accepted **Costs Per Year:** Application fee: $40. State resident tuition: $2031 full-time. Nonresident tuition: $10,857 full-time. Mandatory fees: $7564 full-time. **Scholarships:** Available **Calendar System:** Semester, Summer Session Available **Enrollment:** FT 18,054, PT 1,340, Grad 5,699 **Faculty:** FT 1,148, PT 190 **Student-Faculty Ratio:** 17:1 **Exams:** SAT I or ACT **% Receiving Financial Aid:** 51 **% Residing in College-Owned, -Operated, or -Affiliated Housing:** 61 **Library Holdings:** 3,158,359 **Regional Accreditation:** New England Association of Schools and Colleges **Credit Hours For Degree:** 60 credits, Associates; 120 credits, Bachelors **ROTC:** Army, Air Force **Professional Accreditation:** AACSB, ABET, AACN,

AAFCS, ADtA, ACSP, APA, ASLA, ASLHA, CEPH, NASM, NCATE, SAF **Intercollegiate Athletics:** Baseball M; Basketball M & W; Cheerleading M & W; Crew W; Cross-Country Running M & W; Field Hockey W; Football M; Ice Hockey M; Lacrosse M & W; Skiing (Downhill) M & W; Soccer M & W; Softball W; Swimming and Diving M & W; Tennis M; Track and Field M & W; Volleyball W

UNIVERSITY OF MASSACHUSETTS BOSTON
100 Morrissey Blvd.
Boston, MA 02125-3393
Tel: (617)287-5000
Admissions: (617)287-6100
E-mail: undergrad@umassp.edu
Web Site: http://www.umb.edu/
President/CEO: Dr. Jo Ann M. Gora
Registrar: David Cesario
Admissions: Liliana Mickle
Financial Aid: Judy Keyes
Type: University **Sex:** Coed **Affiliation:** University of Massachusetts **Scores:** 96% SAT V 400+; 97% SAT M 400+ **% Accepted:** 60 **Admission Plans:** Deferred Admission **Application Deadline:** June 01 **Application Fee:** $40.00 **H.S. Requirements:** High school diploma required; GED accepted **Costs Per Year:** Application fee: $40. State resident tuition: $1714 full-time, $71.50 per credit hour part-time. Nonresident tuition: $9758 full-time, $406.50 per credit hour part-time. Mandatory fees: $6551 full-time, $273 per credit hour part-time. Full-time tuition and fees vary according to class time, course load, program, reciprocity agreements, and student level. Part-time tuition and fees vary according to class time, course load, program, reciprocity agreements, and student level. **Scholarships:** Available **Calendar System:** Semester, Summer Session Available **Enrollment:** FT 5,768, PT 3,190, Grad 2,904 **Faculty:** FT 445, PT 368 **Student-Faculty Ratio:** 14:1 **Exams:** SAT I or ACT **% Receiving Financial Aid:** 64 **Library Holdings:** 584,015 **Regional Accreditation:** New England Association of Schools and Colleges **Credit Hours For Degree:** 120 credits, Bachelors **Professional Accreditation:** AACSB, AAMFT, AACN, APA, CORE, NCATE **Intercollegiate Athletics:** Baseball M; Basketball M & W; Cross-Country Running M & W; Ice Hockey M; Lacrosse M; Soccer M & W; Softball W; Tennis M & W; Track and Field M & W; Volleyball W

UNIVERSITY OF MASSACHUSETTS DARTMOUTH
285 Old Westport Rd.
North Dartmouth, MA 02747-2300
Tel: (508)999-8000
Admissions: (508)999-8605
Fax: (508)999-8755
E-mail: sbriggs@umassd.edu
Web Site: http://www.umassd.edu/
President/CEO: Dr. Jean F. MacCormack
Admissions: Steven Briggs
Financial Aid: Bruce Palmer
Type: University **Sex:** Coed **Affiliation:** University of Massachusetts **Scores:** 96% SAT V 400+; 97% SAT M 400+; 67% ACT 18-23; 22% ACT 24-29 **% Accepted:** 74 **Admission Plans:** Early Admission; Early Decision Plan; Deferred Admission **Application Deadline:** Rolling **Application Fee:** $35.00 **H.S. Requirements:** High school diploma required; GED accepted **Costs Per Year:** Application fee: $35, $55 for nonresidents. State resident tuition: $1417 full-time, $59.04 per credit part-time. Nonresident tuition: $8099 full-time, $454.88 per credit part-time. Mandatory fees: $6619 full-time, $275.79 per credit part-time. Full-time tuition and fees vary according to reciprocity agreements. Part-time tuition and fees vary according to course load and reciprocity agreements. College room and board: $7634. College room only: $4460. Room and board charges vary according to board plan and housing facility. **Scholarships:** Available **Calendar System:** Semester, Summer Session Available **Enrollment:** FT 6,449, PT 1,070, Grad 1,030 **Faculty:** FT 355, PT 216 **Student-Faculty Ratio:** 17:1 **Exams:** SAT I or ACT **% Receiving Financial Aid:** 64 **% Residing in College-Owned, -Operated, or -Affiliated Housing:** 48 **Library Holdings:** 947,000 **Regional Accreditation:** New England Association of Schools and Colleges **Credit Hours For Degree:** 120 credit hours, Bachelors **ROTC:** Army **Professional Accreditation:** AACSB, ABET, NAACLS, NASAD, NLN **Intercollegiate Athletics:** Baseball M; Basketball M & W; Cheerleading W; Cross-Country Running M & W; Equestrian Sports M & W; Field Hockey W; Football M; Golf M & W; Ice Hockey M; Lacrosse M & W; Soccer M & W; Softball W; Swimming and Diving M & W; Tennis M & W; Track and Field M & W; Volleyball W

UNIVERSITY OF MASSACHUSETTS LOWELL
1 University Ave.
Lowell, MA 01854-2881
Tel: (978)934-4000
Free: 800-410-4607
Admissions: (978)934-3944
Fax: (978)934-3000
Web Site: http://www.uml.edu/
President/CEO: Dr. William T. Hogan
Registrar: Janet King
Admissions: Kerri Mead
Financial Aid: Richard Barrett
Type: University **Sex:** Coed **Affiliation:** University of Massachusetts **Scores:** 98% SAT V 400+; 99% SAT M 400+ **% Accepted:** 63 **Admission Plans:** Deferred Admission **Application Deadline:** Rolling **Application Fee:** $20.00 **H.S. Requirements:** High school diploma required; GED accepted **Costs Per Year:** Application fee: $20. State resident tuition: $1454 full-time, $60.58 per credit part-time. Nonresident tuition: $8567 full-time, $356.96 per credit part-time. Mandatory fees: $6712 full-time, $291.33 per credit part-time. College room and board: $6311. College room only: $3810. Room and board charges vary according to board plan and housing facility. **Scholarships:** Available **Calendar System:** Semester, Summer Session Available **Faculty:** FT 383, PT 240 **Student-Faculty Ratio:** 17:1 **Exams:** SAT I or ACT **% Receiving Financial Aid:** 50 **% Residing in College-Owned, -Operated, or -Affiliated Housing:** 40 **Library Holdings:** 549,243 **Regional Accreditation:** New England Association of Schools and Colleges **Credit Hours For Degree:** 60 credits, Associates; 120 credits, Bachelors **ROTC:** Air Force **Professional Accreditation:** AACSB, ABET, AACN, APTA, NAACLS, NASAD, NASM, NCATE **Intercollegiate Athletics:** Basketball M & W; Crew M & W; Cross-Country Running M & W; Field Hockey W; Football M; Golf M; Ice Hockey M; Soccer M; Swimming and Diving M; Tennis M & W; Track and Field M & W; Volleyball W; Wrestling M

UNIVERSITY OF PHOENIX-BOSTON CAMPUS
100 Grossman Dr.
Braintree, MA 02184-4949
Tel: (781)843-0844
Free: 800-228-7240
Admissions: (480)557-1712
Web Site: http://www.phoenix.edu/
President/CEO: Jackie Armitage
Admissions: Nina Omelchanko
Type: Comprehensive **Sex:** Coed **Admission Plans:** Open Admission; Deferred Admission **Application Deadline:** Rolling **Application Fee:** $110.00 **H.S. Requirements:** High school diploma required; GED accepted **Costs Per Year:** Application fee: $110. Tuition: $13,020 full-time, $434 per credit part-time. Mandatory fees: $560 full-time, $70 per course part-time. **Scholarships:** Available **Calendar System:** Continuous, Summer Session Not available **Enrollment:** FT 421, Grad 207 **Faculty:** FT 4, PT 115 **Student-Faculty Ratio:** 5:1 **Library Holdings:** 444 **Regional Accreditation:** North Central Association of Colleges and Schools **Credit Hours For Degree:** 60 credits, Associates; 120 credits, Bachelors

UNIVERSITY OF PHOENIX-CENTRAL MASSACHUSETTS CAMPUS
One Research Dr.
Westborough, MA 01581
Tel: (508)614-4100
Free: 800-228-7240
Admissions: (480)557-1712
Web Site: http://www.phoenix.edu/
Admissions: Nina Omelchanko
Type: Comprehensive **Sex:** Coed **Admission Plans:** Open Admission; Deferred Admission **Application Deadline:** Rolling **Application Fee:** $110.00 **H.S. Requirements:** High school diploma required; GED accepted **Costs Per Year:** Application fee: $110. Tuition: $13,020 full-time, $434 per credit part-time. Mandatory fees: $560 full-time, $70 per course part-time. **Scholarships:** Available **Calendar System:** Continuous, Summer Session Not available **Enrollment:** FT 233, Grad 106 **Faculty:** FT 2, PT 49 **Student-Faculty Ratio:** 4:1 **Library Holdings:** 444 **Regional Accreditation:** North Central Association of Colleges and Schools **Credit Hours For Degree:** 60 credits, Associates; 120 credits, Bachelors

URBAN COLLEGE OF BOSTON
178 Tremont St.
Boston, MA 02111

Tel: (617)292-4723
Fax: (617)423-4758
Web Site: http://www.urbancollegeofboston.org/
President/CEO: Dr. Linda E. Turner
Admissions: Dr. Henry J. Johnson
Financial Aid: Pat Harden
Type: Two-Year College **Sex:** Coed **Application Fee:** $10.00 **H.S. Requirements:** High school diploma required; GED accepted **Scholarships:** Available **Calendar System:** Semester **Enrollment:** FT 12, PT 597 **Faculty:** FT 3, PT 21 **Student-Faculty Ratio:** 20:1 **Regional Accreditation:** New England Association of Schools and Colleges **Credit Hours For Degree:** 65 credits, Associates

WELLESLEY COLLEGE
106 Central St.
Wellesley, MA 02481
Tel: (781)283-1000
Admissions: (781)283-2257
Fax: (781)283-3678
E-mail: admission@wellesley.edu
Web Site: http://www.wellesley.edu/
President/CEO: Dr. Diana Chapman Walsh
Registrar: Ann Hamilton
Admissions: Heather Woodcock Ayres
Financial Aid: Kathryn Osmond
Type: Four-Year College **Sex:** Women **Scores:** 100% SAT V 400+; 100% SAT M 400+; 2% ACT 18-23; 42% ACT 24-29 **% Accepted:** 34 **Admission Plans:** Early Admission; Early Decision Plan; Deferred Admission **Application Deadline:** January 15 **Application Fee:** $50.00 **H.S. Requirements:** High school diploma or equivalent not required **Costs Per Year:** Application fee: $50. Comprehensive fee: $41,030 includes full-time tuition ($30,696), mandatory fees ($652), and college room and board ($9682). College room only: $4906. Room and board charges vary according to board plan. **Scholarships:** Available **Calendar System:** Semester, Summer Session Available **Enrollment:** FT 2,216, PT 115 **Faculty:** FT 227, PT 102 **Student-Faculty Ratio:** 9:1 **Exams:** SAT I and SAT II or ACT **% Receiving Financial Aid:** 60 **% Residing in College-Owned, -Operated, or -Affiliated Housing:** 97 **Library Holdings:** 765,530 **Regional Accreditation:** New England Association of Schools and Colleges **Credit Hours For Degree:** 32 courses, Bachelors **ROTC:** Army, Air Force **Intercollegiate Athletics:** Basketball W; Crew W; Cross-Country Running W; Fencing W; Field Hockey W; Golf W; Lacrosse W; Rugby W; Sailing W; Skiing (Downhill) W; Soccer W; Softball W; Squash W; Swimming and Diving W; Tennis W; Track and Field W; Ultimate Frisbee W; Volleyball W

WENTWORTH INSTITUTE OF TECHNOLOGY
550 Huntington Ave.
Boston, MA 02115-5998
Tel: (617)989-4590
Free: 800-556-0610
Fax: (617)989-4010
Web Site: http://www.wit.edu/
President/CEO: Dr. John F. Van Domelen
Registrar: Kevin Stanley
Financial Aid: Traci Cady
Type: Four-Year College **Sex:** Coed **Scores:** 86% SAT V 400+; 94% SAT M 400+ **% Accepted:** 60 **Admission Plans:** Deferred Admission **Application Deadline:** Rolling **Application Fee:** $30.00 **H.S. Requirements:** High school diploma required; GED accepted **Costs Per Year:** Application fee: $30. Comprehensive fee: $27,500 includes full-time tuition ($18,500) and college room and board ($9000). **Scholarships:** Available **Calendar System:** Miscellaneous, Summer Session Available **Enrollment:** FT 3,141, PT 495 **Faculty:** FT 115, PT 124 **Student-Faculty Ratio:** 24:1 **Exams:** SAT I or ACT **% Receiving Financial Aid:** 42 **% Residing in College-Owned, -Operated, or -Affiliated Housing:** 41 **Library Holdings:** 77,000 **Regional Accreditation:** New England Association of Schools and Colleges **Credit Hours For Degree:** 72 credits, Associates; 128 credits, Bachelors **ROTC:** Army, Air Force **Professional Accreditation:** ABET, ACCE, FIDER **Intercollegiate Athletics:** Baseball M; Basketball M & W; Golf M & W; Ice Hockey M; Lacrosse M; Riflery M & W; Rugby M; Soccer M & W; Softball W; Tennis M & W; Volleyball M & W

WESTERN NEW ENGLAND COLLEGE
1215 Wilbraham Rd.
Springfield, MA 01119
Tel: (413)782-3111
Free: 800-325-1122
Admissions: (413)782-1321
Fax: (413)782-1777
E-mail: ugradmis@wnec.edu
Web Site: http://www.wnec.edu/
President/CEO: Dr. Anthony S. Caprio
Registrar: Rodney W. Pease
Admissions: Dr. Charles R. Pollock
Financial Aid: Kathleen M. Chambers
Type: Comprehensive **Sex:** Coed **Scores:** 99% SAT V 400+; 99% SAT M 400+; 60% ACT 18-23; 30% ACT 24-29 **% Accepted:** 75 **Application Deadline:** Rolling **Application Fee:** $50.00 **H.S. Requirements:** High school diploma required; GED accepted **Costs Per Year:** Application fee: $50. Comprehensive fee: $32,054 includes full-time tuition ($21,600), mandatory fees ($1564), and college room and board ($8890). Full-time tuition and fees vary according to program and student level. Room and board charges vary according to board plan and housing facility. Part-time tuition: $452 per credit hour. Part-time mandatory fees: $21 per term. Part-time tuition and fees vary according to program. **Scholarships:** Available **Calendar System:** Semester, Summer Session Available **Enrollment:** FT 2,363, PT 477, Grad 293 **Faculty:** FT 164, PT 156 **Student-Faculty Ratio:** 15:1 **Exams:** SAT I or ACT **% Receiving Financial Aid:** 71 **% Residing in College-Owned, -Operated, or -Affiliated Housing:** 57 **Library Holdings:** 100,010 **Regional Accreditation:** New England Association of Schools and Colleges **Credit Hours For Degree:** 60 semester hours, Associates; 122 semester hours, Bachelors **ROTC:** Army, Air Force **Professional Accreditation:** AACSB, ABET, ABA, AALS, CSWE **Intercollegiate Athletics:** Baseball M; Basketball M & W; Bowling M & W; Cross-Country Running M & W; Field Hockey W; Football M; Golf M; Ice Hockey M; Lacrosse M & W; Soccer M & W; Softball W; Swimming and Diving W; Tennis M & W; Volleyball W; Wrestling M

WESTFIELD STATE COLLEGE
Western Ave.
Westfield, MA 01086
Tel: (413)572-5300
Admissions: (413)572-5218
E-mail: admission@wsc.mass.edu
Web Site: http://www.wsc.ma.edu/
President/CEO: Dr. Frederick Woodward
Registrar: Cynthia Siegler
Admissions: Michelle Mattie
Financial Aid: Michelle Mattie
Type: Comprehensive **Sex:** Coed **Affiliation:** Massachusetts Public Higher Education System **Scores:** 97.07% SAT V 400+; 97.06% SAT M 400+; 60% ACT 18-23; 33.33% ACT 24-29 **% Accepted:** 74 **Admission Plans:** Deferred Admission **Application Deadline:** March 01 **Application Fee:** $25.00 **H.S. Requirements:** High school diploma required; GED accepted **Costs Per Year:** Application fee: $25. State resident tuition: $970 full-time. Nonresident tuition: $7050 full-time. Mandatory fees: $4687 full-time. College room and board: $6470. **Scholarships:** Available **Calendar System:** Semester, Summer Session Available **Enrollment:** FT 4,112, PT 555, Grad 678 **Faculty:** FT 179, PT 165 **Student-Faculty Ratio:** 18:1 **Exams:** SAT I or ACT, SAT I **% Receiving Financial Aid:** 65 **% Residing in College-Owned, -Operated, or -Affiliated Housing:** 54 **Library Holdings:** 124,363 **Regional Accreditation:** New England Association of Schools and Colleges **Credit Hours For Degree:** 120 credit hours, Bachelors **ROTC:** Army, Air Force **Professional Accreditation:** CSWE, JRCEPAT, NCATE **Intercollegiate Athletics:** Baseball M; Basketball M & W; Cheerleading M & W; Cross-Country Running M & W; Field Hockey W; Football M; Soccer M & W; Softball W; Swimming and Diving W; Track and Field M & W; Volleyball W

WHEATON COLLEGE
East Main St.
Norton, MA 02766
Tel: (508)285-7722
Free: 800-394-6003
Admissions: (508)286-8251
Fax: (508)285-8271
E-mail: admission@wheatonma.edu
Web Site: http://www.wheatoncollege.edu/
President/CEO: Dr. Dale Rogers Marshall
Registrar: Patricia Santilli

Admissions: Gail Berson
Financial Aid: Susan Beard
Type: Four-Year College **Sex:** Coed **Scores:** 100% SAT V 400+; 100% SAT M 400+; 8% ACT 18-23; 65% ACT 24-29 **% Accepted:** 44 **Admission Plans:** Early Admission; Early Decision Plan; Deferred Admission **Application Deadline:** January 15 **Application Fee:** $55.00 **H.S. Requirements:** High school diploma required; GED accepted **Costs Per Year:** Application fee: $55. Comprehensive fee: $40,180 includes full-time tuition ($32,115), mandatory fees ($235), and college room and board ($7830). College room only: $4130. **Scholarships:** Available **Calendar System:** Semester, Summer Session Not available **Enrollment:** FT 1,558, PT 10 **Faculty:** FT 121, PT 40 **Student-Faculty Ratio:** 11:1 **% Receiving Financial Aid:** 49 **% Residing in College-Owned, -Operated, or -Affiliated Housing:** 97 **Library Holdings:** 372,322 **Regional Accreditation:** New England Association of Schools and Colleges **Credit Hours For Degree:** 32 courses, Bachelors **ROTC:** Army **Intercollegiate Athletics:** Baseball M; Basketball M & W; Cross-Country Running M & W; Field Hockey W; Lacrosse W; Soccer M & W; Softball W; Swimming and Diving M & W; Tennis M & W; Track and Field M & W; Volleyball W

WHEELOCK COLLEGE
200 The Riverway
Boston, MA 02215-4176
Tel: (617)879-2000
Free: 800-734-5212
Admissions: (617)879-2209
Fax: (617)566-7531
E-mail: undergrad@wheelock.edu
Web Site: http://www.wheelock.edu/
President/CEO: Dr. Marjorie Bakken
Registrar: David Twombly
Admissions: Lisa Walmsley
Financial Aid: Daniel Forster
Type: Comprehensive **Sex:** Coed **Scores:** 92% SAT V 400+; 87% SAT M 400+; 50% ACT 18-23; 50% ACT 24-29 **% Accepted:** 77 **Admission Plans:** Early Decision Plan; Deferred Admission **Application Deadline:** March 01 **Application Fee:** $35.00 **H.S. Requirements:** High school diploma required; GED accepted **Costs Per Year:** Application fee: $35. Comprehensive fee: $33,075 includes full-time tuition ($23,100), mandatory fees ($525), and college room and board ($9450). Part-time tuition: $722 per credit. **Scholarships:** Available **Calendar System:** Semester, Summer Session Not available **Enrollment:** FT 623, PT 40, Grad 353 **Faculty:** FT 65, PT 30 **Student-Faculty Ratio:** 11:1 **Exams:** SAT I or ACT **% Receiving Financial Aid:** 73 **% Residing in College-Owned, -Operated, or -Affiliated Housing:** 69 **Library Holdings:** 93,534 **Regional Accreditation:** New England Association of Schools and Colleges **Credit Hours For Degree:** 134 credits, Bachelors **Professional Accreditation:** CSWE, NCATE **Intercollegiate Athletics:** Basketball W; Field Hockey W; Soccer W; Softball W; Swimming and Diving W

WILLIAMS COLLEGE
PO Box 687
Williamstown, MA 01267
Tel: (413)597-3131
Admissions: (413)597-2211
Fax: (413)597-4018
E-mail: admission@williams.edu
Web Site: http://www.williams.edu/
President/CEO: Dr. Morton Owen Schapiro
Registrar: Charles R. Toomajian, Jr.
Admissions: Richard L. Nesbitt
Financial Aid: Paul J. Boyer
Type: Comprehensive **Sex:** Coed **Scores:** 100% SAT V 400+; 100% SAT M 400+; 1% ACT 18-23; 29% ACT 24-29 **% Accepted:** 19 **Admission Plans:** Early Admission; Early Decision Plan; Deferred Admission **Application Deadline:** January 01 **Application Fee:** $60.00 **H.S. Requirements:** High school diploma or equivalent not required **Costs Per Year:** Application fee: $60. Comprehensive fee: $40,310 includes full-time tuition ($31,548), mandatory fees ($212), and college room and board ($8550). College room only: $4330. Room and board charges vary according to board plan. **Scholarships:** Available **Calendar System:** 4-1-4, Summer Session Not available **Enrollment:** FT 1,984, PT 33, Grad 53 **Faculty:** FT 257, PT 55 **Student-Faculty Ratio:** 7:1 **Exams:** SAT I and SAT II or ACT **% Receiving Financial Aid:** 42 **% Residing in College-Owned, -Operated, or -Affiliated Housing:** 93 **Library Holdings:** 932,000 **Regional Accreditation:** New England Association of Schools and Colleges **Credit Hours For Degree:** 36 courses, Bachelors **Intercollegiate Athletics:** Baseball M; Basketball M & W; Crew M & W; Cross-Country Running M & W; Equestrian Sports M & W; Field Hockey W; Football M; Golf M & W; Ice Hockey M & W; Lacrosse M & W; Rugby M & W; Sailing M & W; Skiing (Cross-Country) M & W; Skiing (Downhill) M & W; Soccer M & W; Softball W; Squash M & W; Swimming and Diving M & W; Tennis M & W; Track and Field M & W; Volleyball M & W; Water Polo M & W; Wrestling M

WORCESTER POLYTECHNIC INSTITUTE
100 Institute Rd.
Worcester, MA 01609-2280
Tel: (508)831-5000
Admissions: (508)831-5286
Fax: (508)831-5875
E-mail: admissiosn@wpi.edu
Web Site: http://www.wpi.edu/
President/CEO: Dennis D. Berkey
Registrar: Nikki Andrews
Admissions: Edward J. Connor
Financial Aid: Michael J. Curley
Type: University **Sex:** Coed **Scores:** 100% SAT V 400+; 100% SAT M 400+; 16% ACT 18-23; 60% ACT 24-29 **% Accepted:** 71 **Admission Plans:** Early Admission; Early Action; Early Decision Plan; Deferred Admission **Application Deadline:** February 01 **Application Fee:** $60.00 **H.S. Requirements:** High school diploma required; GED accepted **Costs Per Year:** Application fee: $60. Comprehensive fee: $43,110 includes full-time tuition ($32,850), mandatory fees ($420), and college room and board ($9840). College room only: $5720. Part-time tuition: $2738 per unit. **Scholarships:** Available **Calendar System:** Miscellaneous, Summer Session Available **Enrollment:** FT 2,811, PT 81, Grad 1,018 **Faculty:** FT 232, PT 85 **Student-Faculty Ratio:** 13:1 **Exams:** SAT I or ACT, SAT II **% Receiving Financial Aid:** 74 **% Residing in College-Owned, -Operated, or -Affiliated Housing:** 60 **Library Holdings:** 275,299 **Regional Accreditation:** New England Association of Schools and Colleges **Credit Hours For Degree:** 45 courses, Bachelors **ROTC:** Army, Navy, Air Force **Professional Accreditation:** AACSB, ABET **Intercollegiate Athletics:** Baseball M; Basketball M & W; Crew M & W; Cross-Country Running M & W; Field Hockey W; Football M; Soccer M & W; Softball W; Swimming and Diving M & W; Track and Field M & W; Volleyball W; Water Polo M & W; Wrestling M

WORCESTER STATE COLLEGE
486 Chandler St.
Worcester, MA 01602-2597
Tel: (508)929-8000; (866)WSC-CALL
Admissions: (508)929-8825
Fax: (508)929-8131
Web Site: http://www.worcester.edu/
President/CEO: Dr. Janelle C. Ashley
Registrar: Julie Chaffee
Admissions: Jay Tierney
Financial Aid: Jayne McGinn
Type: Comprehensive **Sex:** Coed **Affiliation:** Massachusetts Public Higher Education System **Scores:** 93.3% SAT V 400+; 97.55% SAT M 400+; 57.45% ACT 18-23; 10.64% ACT 24-29 **% Accepted:** 59 **Admission Plans:** Early Admission; Deferred Admission **Application Deadline:** June 01 **Application Fee:** $20.00 **H.S. Requirements:** High school diploma required; GED not accepted **Costs Per Year:** Application fee: $20. State resident tuition: $970 full-time, $40.42 per credit part-time. Nonresident tuition: $7050 full-time, $293.75 per credit part-time. Mandatory fees: $4109 full-time, $167.04 per credit part-time. Full-time tuition and fees vary according to class time, course load, and reciprocity agreements. Part-time tuition and fees vary according to class time, course load, and reciprocity agreements. College room and board: $7420. College room only: $4730. Room and board charges vary according to board plan and housing facility. **Scholarships:** Available **Calendar System:** Semester, Summer Session Available **Enrollment:** FT 3,242, PT 1,356, Grad 873 **Faculty:** FT 167, PT 233 **Student-Faculty Ratio:** 17:1 **Exams:** SAT I or ACT **% Receiving Financial Aid:** 43 **% Residing in College-Owned, -Operated, or -Affiliated Housing:** 34 **Library Holdings:** 150,419 **Regional Accreditation:** New England Association of Schools and Colleges **Credit Hours For Degree:** 120 credits, Bachelors **ROTC:** Army, Navy, Air Force **Professional Accreditation:** AOTA, ASLHA, JRCNMT, NLN **Intercollegiate Athletics:** Baseball M; Basketball M & W; Cheerleading M & W; Crew M & W; Cross-Country Running M & W; Equestrian Sports M & W; Field Hockey W; Football M; Golf M;

Ice Hockey M; Lacrosse W; Soccer M & W; Softball W; Tennis M & W; Track and Field M & W; Volleyball M & W

ADRIAN COLLEGE
110 South Madison St.
Adrian, MI 49221-2575
Tel: (517)265-5161
Free: 800-877-2246
Fax: (517)265-3331
E-mail: admission@adrian.adrian.edu
Web Site: http://www.adrian.edu/
President/CEO: Dr. Stanley P. Caine
Registrar: Michael H. Jacobitz
Admissions: Carolyn Quinlan
Financial Aid: Michael J. Hague
Type: Four-Year College **Sex:** Coed **Affiliation:** United Methodist Church **Scores:** 50% ACT 18-23; 21% ACT 24-29 **Admission Plans:** Deferred Admission **Application Fee:** $20.00 **H.S. Requirements:** High school diploma required; GED accepted **Costs Per Year:** Application fee: $20. Comprehensive fee: $24,900 includes full-time tuition ($18,530), mandatory fees ($100), and college room and board ($6270). College room only: $2880. Room and board charges vary according to board plan. **Scholarships:** Available **Calendar System:** Semester, Summer Session Available **Enrollment:** FT 959, PT 54 **Faculty:** FT 64, PT 40 **Student-Faculty Ratio:** 13:1 **Exams:** ACT, SAT I or ACT **% Receiving Financial Aid:** 78 **% Residing in College-Owned, -Operated, or -Affiliated Housing:** 77 **Library Holdings:** 148,407 **Regional Accreditation:** North Central Association of Colleges and Schools **Credit Hours For Degree:** 62 credit hours, Associates; 124 credit hours, Bachelors **Intercollegiate Athletics:** Baseball M; Basketball M & W; Cross-Country Running M & W; Football M; Golf M & W; Soccer M & W; Softball W; Tennis M & W; Track and Field M & W; Volleyball W

ALBION COLLEGE
611 East Porter St.
Albion, MI 49224-1831
Tel: (517)629-1000
Free: 800-858-6770
Admissions: (517)629-0600
Fax: (517)629-0569
E-mail: admissions@albion.edu
Web Site: http://www.albion.edu/
President/CEO: Dr. Peter T. Mitchell
Registrar: Cherie Hatlem
Admissions: Doug Kellar
Financial Aid: Kristi Maze
Type: Four-Year College **Sex:** Coed **Affiliation:** Methodist **Scores:** 98.68% SAT V 400+; 100% SAT M 400+; 36.13% ACT 18-23; 52.73% ACT 24-29 **% Accepted:** 82 **Admission Plans:** Early Admission; Early Action; Deferred Admission **Application Deadline:** March 01 **Application Fee:** $20.00 **H.S. Requirements:** High school diploma required; GED accepted. For home schooled students: High school diploma or equivalent not required **Costs Per Year:** Application fee: $20. Comprehensive fee: $31,224 includes full-time tuition ($24,012), mandatory fees ($284), and college room and board ($6928). College room only: $3388. Room and board charges vary according to housing facility. Part-time tuition: $1020 per semester hour. **Scholarships:** Available **Calendar System:** Semester, Summer Session Available **Enrollment:** FT 1,941, PT 38 **Faculty:** FT 139, PT 36 **Student-Faculty Ratio:** 13:1 **Exams:** SAT I or ACT **% Receiving Financial Aid:** 60 **% Residing in College-Owned, -Operated, or -Affiliated Housing:** 93 **Library Holdings:** 363,000 **Regional Accreditation:** North Central Association of Colleges and Schools **Credit Hours For Degree:** 32 units, Bachelors **Professional Accreditation:** NASM **Intercollegiate Athletics:** Baseball M; Basketball M & W; Cheerleading M & W; Cross-Country Running M & W; Football M; Golf M & W; Soccer M & W; Softball W; Swimming and Diving M & W; Tennis M & W; Track and Field M & W; Volleyball M & W

ALMA COLLEGE
614 West Superior St.
Alma, MI 48801-1599
Tel: (989)463-7111
Free: 800-321-ALMA
Fax: (989)463-7057
E-mail: admissions@alma.edu
Web Site: http://www.alma.edu/
President/CEO: Dr. Saundra J. Tracy
Registrar: Sue Deel
Admissions: Dr. Karen Klumpp
Financial Aid: Christopher Brown
Type: Four-Year College **Sex:** Coed **Affiliation:** Presbyterian **Scores:** 96% SAT V 400+; 89% SAT M 400+; 40% ACT 18-23; 47% ACT 24-29 **% Accepted:** 81 **Admission Plans:** Early Admission; Early Action; Deferred Admission **Application Deadline:** Rolling **Application Fee:** $25.00 **H.S. Requirements:** High school diploma required; GED accepted **Costs Per Year:** Application fee: $25. Comprehensive fee: $28,544 includes full-time tuition ($20,934), mandatory fees ($200), and college room and board ($7410). College room only: $3650. Room and board charges vary according to board plan and housing facility. Part-time tuition: $810 per credit. Part-time tuition varies according to course load. **Scholarships:** Available **Calendar System:** Miscellaneous, Summer Session Available **Enrollment:** FT 1,242, PT 42 **Faculty:** FT 82, PT 37 **Student-Faculty Ratio:** 13:1 **Exams:** SAT I or ACT **% Receiving Financial Aid:** 75 **% Residing in College-Owned, -Operated, or -Affiliated Housing:** 84 **Library Holdings:** 261,393 **Regional Accreditation:** North Central Association of Colleges and Schools **Credit Hours For Degree:** 136 credits, Bachelors **ROTC:** Army **Professional Accreditation:** NASM **Intercollegiate Athletics:** Baseball M; Basketball M & W; Cross-Country Running M & W; Football M; Golf M & W; Soccer M & W; Softball W; Swimming and Diving M & W; Tennis M & W; Track and Field M & W; Volleyball W

ALPENA COMMUNITY COLLEGE
666 Johnson St.
Alpena, MI 49707-1495
Tel: (989)356-9021
Admissions: (989)358-7339
Fax: (989)358-7553
Web Site: http://www.alpenacc.edu/
President/CEO: Dr. Olin H. Joynton
Registrar: Max P. Lindsay
Admissions: Mike Kollien
Financial Aid: Max P. Lindsay
Type: Two-Year College **Sex:** Coed **Admission Plans:** Open Admission; Early Admission; Deferred Admission **Application Fee:** $0.00 **H.S. Requirements:** High school diploma or equivalent not required. For nursing, utility technician programs: High school diploma required; GED accepted **Costs**

Per Year: Application fee: $0. Area resident tuition: $2532 full-time, $67.75 per contact hour part-time. State resident tuition: $3545 full-time, $101.50 per contact hour part-time. Nonresident tuition: $4550 full-time, $135 per contact hour part-time. Mandatory fees: $500 full-time, $16 per contact hour part-time, $10 per term part-time. College room only: $3000. **Scholarships:** Available **Calendar System:** Semester, Summer Session Available **Enrollment:** FT 984, PT 953 **Faculty:** FT 51, PT 70 **Student-Faculty Ratio:** 17:1 **Exams:** ACT, Other **% Residing in College-Owned, -Operated, or -Affiliated Housing:** 2 **Library Holdings:** 29,000 **Regional Accreditation:** North Central Association of Colleges and Schools **Credit Hours For Degree:** 60 semester hours, Associates **Professional Accreditation:** AAMAE, ACBSP **Intercollegiate Athletics:** Basketball M & W; Golf M; Softball W; Volleyball W

ANDREWS UNIVERSITY
Berrien Springs, MI 49104
Tel: (269)471-7771
Free: 800-253-2874
Fax: (269)471-3228
Web Site: http://www.andrews.edu/
President/CEO: Dr. Niels-Erik Andreasen
Registrar: Dr. Emilio Garcia-Marenko
Admissions: Stephen Payne
Financial Aid: Jerri Gifford
Type: University **Sex:** Coed **Affiliation:** Seventh-day Adventist **Scores:** 95% SAT V 400+; 93% SAT M 400+; 51% ACT 18-23; 34% ACT 24-29 **% Accepted:** 40 **Admission Plans:** Deferred Admission **Application Deadline:** Rolling **Application Fee:** $30.00 **H.S. Requirements:** High school diploma required; GED accepted **Costs Per Year:** Application fee: $30. Comprehensive fee: $21,786 includes full-time tuition ($16,030), mandatory fees ($476), and college room and board ($5280). College room only: $2850. Full-time tuition and fees vary according to course load. Room and board charges vary according to board plan. Part-time tuition: $670 per credit hour. Part-time tuition varies according to course load. **Scholarships:** Available **Calendar System:** Semester, Summer Session Available **Enrollment:** FT 1,489, PT 237, Grad 985 **Faculty:** FT 207, PT 61 **Student-Faculty Ratio:** 10:1 **Exams:** SAT I or ACT **% Receiving Financial Aid:** 64 **% Residing in College-Owned, -Operated, or -Affiliated Housing:** 54 **Library Holdings:** 512,100 **Regional Accreditation:** North Central Association of Colleges and Schools **Credit Hours For Degree:** 62 semester hours, Associates; 124 semester hours, Bachelors **Professional Accreditation:** ACA, ADtA, APTA, ATS, CSWE, NAACLS, NASM, NCATE, NLN

AQUINAS COLLEGE
1607 Robinson Rd., SE
Grand Rapids, MI 49506-1799
Tel: (616)459-8281
Free: 800-678-9593
Admissions: (616)632-2852
Fax: (616)459-2563
E-mail: admissions@aquinas.edu
Web Site: http://www.aquinas.edu/
President/CEO: Dr. Harry J. Knopke
Registrar: Cecelia Mesler
Admissions: Paula Meehan
Financial Aid: David Steffee
Type: Comprehensive **Sex:** Coed **Affiliation:** Roman Catholic **Scores:** 73. 24% ACT 18-23; 11.27% ACT 24-29 **% Accepted:** 86 **Admission Plans:** Early Admission; Deferred Admission **Application Deadline:** Rolling **Application Fee:** $0.00 **H.S. Requirements:** High school diploma required; GED not accepted. For continuing education program: High school diploma required; GED accepted **Costs Per Year:** Application fee: $0. Comprehensive fee: $23,750 includes full-time tuition ($17,926) and college room and board ($5824). College room only: $2690. Full-time tuition varies according to course load. Room and board charges vary according to board plan and housing facility. Part-time tuition: $361 per credit. Part-time tuition varies according to course load. **Scholarships:** Available **Calendar System:** Semester, Summer Session Available **Enrollment:** FT 1,469, PT 313, Grad 411 **Faculty:** FT 94, PT 105 **Student-Faculty Ratio:** 14:1 **Exams:** SAT I or ACT **% Receiving Financial Aid:** 72 **% Residing in College-Owned, -Operated, or -Affiliated Housing:** 75 **Library Holdings:** 112,458 **Regional Accreditation:** North Central Association of Colleges and Schools **Credit Hours For Degree:** 64 credits, Associates; 124 credits, Bachelors **Intercollegiate Athletics:** Baseball M; Basketball M & W; Cross-Country Running M & W; Golf M & W; Soccer M & W; Softball W; Tennis M & W; Track and Field M & W; Volleyball W

AVE MARIA COLLEGE
300 West Forest Ave.
Ypsilanti, MI 48197
Tel: (734)337-4100; (866)866-3030
Admissions: (734)337-4528
Fax: (734)337-4140
Web Site: http://www.avemaria.edu/
President/CEO: Dr. Ronald Muller
Registrar: Maria Herbel
Admissions: Suzanne Abdalla
Financial Aid: Lesa Briggs
Type: Four-Year College **Sex:** Coed **Affiliation:** Roman Catholic **Application Fee:** $25.00 **Scholarships:** Available **Calendar System:** Semester **Faculty:** FT 17, PT 10 **Student-Faculty Ratio:** 15:1 **Exams:** SAT I or ACT **% Receiving Financial Aid:** 61 **% Residing in College-Owned, -Operated, or -Affiliated Housing:** 95 **Regional Accreditation:** North Central Association of Colleges and Schools **Professional Accreditation:** AALE

BAKER COLLEGE OF ALLEN PARK
4500 Enterprise Dr.
Allen Park, MI 48101
Tel: (313)425-3700
Web Site: http://www.baker.edu/
Admissions: Steve Peterson
Type: Four-Year College **Sex:** Coed **Affiliation:** Baker College System **% Accepted:** 100 **Application Deadline:** September 24 **Application Fee:** $0.00 **Costs Per Year:** Application fee: $0. Tuition: $6480 full-time, $180 per quarter hour part-time. **Calendar System:** Quarter **Enrollment:** FT 837, PT 685 **Faculty:** FT 2, PT 86 **Student-Faculty Ratio:** 34:1 **Regional Accreditation:** North Central Association of Colleges and Schools **Credit Hours For Degree:** 90 quarter hours, Associates; 180 quarter hours, Bachelors

BAKER COLLEGE OF AUBURN HILLS
1500 University Dr.
Auburn Hills, MI 48326-1586
Tel: (248)340-0600
E-mail: love_j@auburnhills.baker.edu
Web Site: http://www.baker.edu/
President/CEO: F. James Cummins
Registrar: Timothy M. Yount
Admissions: Jan Bohlen
Financial Aid: Gregory Little
Type: Four-Year College **Sex:** Coed **Affiliation:** Baker College System **% Accepted:** 100 **Admission Plans:** Open Admission; Early Admission; Deferred Admission **Application Deadline:** Rolling **Application Fee:** $20.00 **H.S. Requirements:** High school diploma required; GED accepted **Costs Per Year:** Application fee: $20. Tuition: $6480 full-time, $180 per quarter hour part-time. **Calendar System:** Quarter, Summer Session Available **Enrollment:** FT 1,688, PT 1,829 **Faculty:** FT 11, PT 144 **Student-Faculty Ratio:** 59:1 **Library Holdings:** 5,400 **Regional Accreditation:** North Central Association of Colleges and Schools **Credit Hours For Degree:** 90 quarter hours, Associates; 180 quarter hours, Bachelors **Professional Accreditation:** AAMAE

BAKER COLLEGE OF CADILLAC
9600 East 13th St.
Cadillac, MI 49601
Tel: (231)876-3100
Fax: (231)775-8505
E-mail: mike.tisdale@baker.edu
Web Site: http://www.baker.edu/
President/CEO: Maynard W. Thompson
Registrar: Cliff Redes
Admissions: Mike Tisdale
Financial Aid: Kristin Bonney
Type: Four-Year College **Sex:** Coed **Affiliation:** Baker College System **% Accepted:** 100 **Admission Plans:** Open Admission; Early Admission; Deferred Admission **Application Deadline:** Rolling **Application Fee:** $20.00 **H.S. Requirements:** High school diploma required; GED accepted **Costs Per Year:** Application fee: $20. Tuition: $6480 full-time, $180 per quarter

hour part-time. **Calendar System:** Quarter, Summer Session Available **Enrollment:** FT 873, PT 686 **Faculty:** FT 4, PT 101 **Student-Faculty Ratio:** 42:1 **Exams:** SAT I or ACT **Library Holdings:** 4,000 **Regional Accreditation:** North Central Association of Colleges and Schools **Credit Hours For Degree:** 90 quarter hours, Associates; 180 quarter hours, Bachelors **Professional Accreditation:** ARCEST, AAMAE

BAKER COLLEGE OF CLINTON TOWNSHIP
34950 Little Mack Ave.
Clinton Township, MI 48035-4701
Tel: (586)791-6610; 888-272-2842
Admissions: (586)790-9580
Fax: (586)791-6611
E-mail: annette.looser@baker.edu
Web Site: http://www.baker.edu/
President/CEO: F. James Cummins
Registrar: Nichole Adams
Admissions: Annette Looser
Financial Aid: Lisa Harvener
Type: Four-Year College **Sex:** Coed **Affiliation:** Baker College System **% Accepted:** 100 **Admission Plans:** Open Admission; Early Admission; Deferred Admission **Application Deadline:** Rolling **Application Fee:** $20.00 **H.S. Requirements:** High school diploma required; GED accepted **Costs Per Year:** Application fee: $20. Tuition: $6480 full-time, $180 per quarter hour part-time. **Calendar System:** Quarter, Summer Session Available **Enrollment:** FT 2,807, PT 2,296 **Faculty:** FT 17, PT 191 **Student-Faculty Ratio:** 60:1 **Exams:** SAT I or ACT **Library Holdings:** 8,000 **Regional Accreditation:** North Central Association of Colleges and Schools **Credit Hours For Degree:** 90 quarter hours, Associates; 180 quarter hours, Bachelors **Professional Accreditation:** ARCEST, AAMAE, AHIMA

BAKER COLLEGE OF FLINT
1050 West Bristol Rd.
Flint, MI 48507-5508
Tel: (810)767-7600
Free: 800-964-4299
Admissions: (810)766-4015
Fax: (810)766-4049
Web Site: http://www.baker.edu/
President/CEO: Dr. Julianne T. Princinsky
Registrar: Robert Martin
Admissions: Troy Crowe
Financial Aid: Gerald McCarty, II
Type: Four-Year College **Sex:** Coed **Affiliation:** Baker College System **% Accepted:** 100 **Admission Plans:** Open Admission; Early Admission; Deferred Admission **Application Deadline:** September 20 **Application Fee:** $20.00 **H.S. Requirements:** High school diploma required; GED accepted **Costs Per Year:** Application fee: $20. Tuition: $6480 full-time, $180 per quarter hour part-time. College room only: $2600. **Calendar System:** Quarter, Summer Session Available **Enrollment:** FT 3,457, PT 2,608 **Faculty:** FT 40, PT 275 **Student-Faculty Ratio:** 42:1 **% Residing in College-Owned, -Operated, or -Affiliated Housing:** 2 **Library Holdings:** 168,700 **Regional Accreditation:** North Central Association of Colleges and Schools **Credit Hours For Degree:** 90 quarter hours, Associates; 180 quarter hours, Bachelors **Professional Accreditation:** ARCEST, AAMAE, AHIMA, APTA

BAKER COLLEGE OF JACKSON
2800 Springport Rd.
Jackson, MI 49202
Tel: (517)789-6123; 888-343-3683
Admissions: (517)788-7800
E-mail: heldt_v@jackson.baker.edu
Web Site: http://www.baker.edu/
President/CEO: H. Ronald Griffith
Registrar: Jill Dutton
Admissions: Kelli Stepka
Financial Aid: Janet Zukowski
Type: Four-Year College **Sex:** Coed **Affiliation:** Baker College System **% Accepted:** 100 **Admission Plans:** Open Admission; Early Admission; Deferred Admission **Application Deadline:** September 19 **Application Fee:** $20.00 **H.S. Requirements:** High school diploma required; GED accepted **Costs Per Year:** Application fee: $20. Tuition: $6480 full-time, $180 per quarter hour part-time. **Calendar System:** Quarter, Summer Session Available **Enrollment:** FT 796, PT 829 **Faculty:** FT 5, PT 80 **Student-Faculty Ratio:** 50:1 **Library Holdings:** 7,000 **Regional Accreditation:** North Central Association of Colleges and Schools **Credit Hours For Degree:** 90 quarter hours, Associates; 180 quarter hours, Bachelors **Professional Accreditation:** ARCEST, AAMAE, AHIMA, JRCERT

BAKER COLLEGE OF MUSKEGON
1903 Marquette Ave.
Muskegon, MI 49442-3497
Tel: (231)777-5200
Admissions: (231)777-5207
Fax: (231)777-5201
E-mail: jacobs_k@muskegon.baker.edu
Web Site: http://www.baker.edu/
President/CEO: Rick E. Amidon
Registrar: Christine Fogg
Admissions: Kathy Jacobson
Financial Aid: Jody Zerlaut
Type: Four-Year College **Sex:** Coed **Affiliation:** Baker College System **% Accepted:** 100 **Admission Plans:** Open Admission; Early Admission; Deferred Admission **Application Deadline:** September 24 **Application Fee:** $20.00 **H.S. Requirements:** High school diploma required; GED accepted **Costs Per Year:** Application fee: $20. Tuition: $6480 full-time, $180 per quarter hour part-time. College room only: $2400. **Calendar System:** Quarter, Summer Session Available **Enrollment:** FT 3,036, PT 1,708 **Faculty:** FT 17, PT 160 **Student-Faculty Ratio:** 63:1 **% Residing in College-Owned, -Operated, or -Affiliated Housing:** 11 **Library Holdings:** 32,000 **Regional Accreditation:** North Central Association of Colleges and Schools **Credit Hours For Degree:** 90 quarter hours, Associates; 180 quarter hours, Bachelors **Professional Accreditation:** ARCEST, AAMAE, ACF, AHIMA, AOTA, APTA

BAKER COLLEGE OF OWOSSO
1020 South Washington St.
Owosso, MI 48867-4400
Tel: (989)729-3300
Free: 800-879-3797
Admissions: (989)729-3350
Fax: (989)729-3411
E-mail: mike.konopacke@baker.edu
Web Site: http://www.baker.edu/
President/CEO: Dr. Denise Bannan
Registrar: Traci Gulick
Admissions: Michael Konopacke
Financial Aid: David J. Lewis
Type: Four-Year College **Sex:** Coed **Affiliation:** Baker College System **% Accepted:** 100 **Admission Plans:** Open Admission; Early Admission; Deferred Admission **Application Deadline:** Rolling **Application Fee:** $20.00 **H.S. Requirements:** High school diploma required; GED accepted **Costs Per Year:** Application fee: $20. Tuition: $6480 full-time, $180 per quarter hour part-time. College room only: $2400. **Calendar System:** Quarter, Summer Session Available **Enrollment:** FT 1,722, PT 1,101 **Faculty:** FT 8, PT 136 **Student-Faculty Ratio:** 50:1 **% Residing in College-Owned, -Operated, or -Affiliated Housing:** 15 **Library Holdings:** 35,424 **Regional Accreditation:** North Central Association of Colleges and Schools **Credit Hours For Degree:** 90 quarter hours, Associates; 180 quarter hours, Bachelors **Professional Accreditation:** AAMAE, JRCERT, NAACLS

BAKER COLLEGE OF PORT HURON
3403 Lapeer Rd.
Port Huron, MI 48060-2597
Tel: (810)985-7000; 888-262-2442
Fax: (810)985-7066
Web Site: http://www.baker.edu/
President/CEO: Dr. Gary L. Sullenger
Registrar: Sheila Kautzman
Admissions: Daniel Kenny
Financial Aid: Wendi Hickman
Type: Four-Year College **Sex:** Coed **Affiliation:** Baker College System **% Accepted:** 100 **Admission Plans:** Open Admission; Early Admission; Deferred Admission **Application Deadline:** September 24 **Application Fee:** $20.00 **H.S. Requirements:** High school diploma required; GED accepted **Costs Per Year:** Application fee: $20. Tuition: $6480 full-time, $180 per quarter hour part-time. **Calendar System:** Quarter, Summer Session Available **Enrollment:** FT 900, PT 678 **Faculty:** FT 12, PT 114 **Student-Faculty Ratio:** 28:1 **Library Holdings:** 16,823 **Regional Accreditation:** North

Central Association of Colleges and Schools **Credit Hours For Degree:** 90 quarter hours, Associates; 180 quarter hours, Bachelors **Professional Accreditation:** ARCEST, AAMAE, ADA

BAY MILLS COMMUNITY COLLEGE
12214 West Lakeshore Dr.
Brimley, MI 49715
Tel: (906)248-3354
Free: 800-844-BMCC
Fax: (906)248-3351
Web Site: http://www.bmcc.edu/
President/CEO: Michael Parish
Admissions: Elaine Lehre
Financial Aid: Tina Miller
Type: Two-Year College **Sex:** Coed **Admission Plans:** Open Admission; Early Admission **Application Fee:** $0.00 **H.S. Requirements:** High school diploma required; GED accepted **Costs Per Year:** Application fee: $0. State resident tuition: $2040 full-time, $85 per credit hour part-time. Mandatory fees: $300 full-time, $10 per credit hour part-time, $30 per term part-time. **Scholarships:** Available **Calendar System:** Semester **Faculty:** FT 9, PT 10 **Student-Faculty Ratio:** 10:1 **Exams:** Other **Regional Accreditation:** North Central Association of Colleges and Schools **Credit Hours For Degree:** 63 credits, Associates

BAY DE NOC COMMUNITY COLLEGE
2001 North Lincoln Rd.
Escanaba, MI 49829-2511
Tel: (906)786-5802
Free: 800-221-2001
Fax: (906)786-6555
Web Site: http://www.baydenoc.cc.mi.us/
President/CEO: Dr. Michael T. Allkins
Registrar: Mary Leisner
Admissions: Mary Leisner
Financial Aid: Gloria Seney
Type: Two-Year College **Sex:** Coed **Affiliation:** Michigan Department of Education **Admission Plans:** Open Admission; Early Admission **H.S. Requirements:** High school diploma required; GED accepted **Scholarships:** Available **Calendar System:** Semester, Summer Session Available **Faculty:** FT 42, PT 85 **Exams:** Other **Library Holdings:** 30,000 **Regional Accreditation:** North Central Association of Colleges and Schools **Credit Hours For Degree:** 62 credit hours, Associates

CALVIN COLLEGE
3201 Burton St., SE
Grand Rapids, MI 49546-4388
Tel: (616)526-6000
Free: 800-688-0122
Admissions: (616)526-6106
Fax: (616)526-8551
E-mail: admissions@calvin.edu
Web Site: http://www.calvin.edu/
President/CEO: Dr. Gaylen J. Byker
Registrar: Thomas Steenwyk
Admissions: Dale D. Kuiper
Financial Aid: Edward Kerestly
Type: Comprehensive **Sex:** Coed **Affiliation:** Christian Reformed Church **Scores:** 99.7% SAT V 400+; 99.7% SAT M 400+; 38% ACT 18-23; 43.8% ACT 24-29 **% Accepted:** 98 **Admission Plans:** Deferred Admission **Application Deadline:** August 15 **Application Fee:** $35.00 **H.S. Requirements:** High school diploma required; GED accepted **Costs Per Year:** Application fee: $35. Comprehensive fee: $25,735 includes full-time tuition ($18,925), mandatory fees ($225), and college room and board ($6585). College room only: $3580. Full-time tuition and fees vary according to program. Room and board charges vary according to board plan. Part-time tuition: $460 per credit hour. Part-time tuition varies according to course load. **Scholarships:** Available **Calendar System:** 4-1-4, Summer Session Available **Enrollment:** FT 3,968, PT 157, Grad 52 **Faculty:** FT 309, PT 89 **Student-Faculty Ratio:** 12:1 **Exams:** SAT I and SAT II or ACT **% Receiving Financial Aid:** 61 **% Residing in College-Owned, -Operated, or -Affiliated Housing:** 56 **Library Holdings:** 824,806 **Regional Accreditation:** North Central Association of Colleges and Schools **Credit Hours For Degree:** 124 semester hours, Bachelors **ROTC:** Army **Professional Accreditation:** ABET, CSWE, NASM, NCATE, NLN **Intercollegiate Athletics:** Baseball M; Basketball M & W; Cross-Country Running M & W; Golf M & W; Ice Hockey M; Lacrosse M & W; Soccer M & W; Softball W; Swimming and Diving M & W; Tennis M & W; Track and Field M & W; Volleyball W

CENTRAL MICHIGAN UNIVERSITY
Mount Pleasant, MI 48859
Tel: (989)774-4000; 888-292-5366
Admissions: (989)774-3076
Fax: (989)774-3537
Web Site: http://www.cmich.edu/
President/CEO: Dr. Michael Rao
Registrar: Karen E. Hutslar
Admissions: Betty J. Wagner
Type: University **Sex:** Coed **Scores:** 87.1% SAT V 400+; 89.2% SAT M 400+; 60.2% ACT 18-23; 28.1% ACT 24-29 **% Accepted:** 75 **Admission Plans:** Early Admission; Deferred Admission **Application Deadline:** Rolling **Application Fee:** $35.00 **H.S. Requirements:** High school diploma required; GED accepted **Costs Per Year:** Application fee: $35. State resident tuition: $5868 full-time, $195.60 per credit part-time. Nonresident tuition: $13,632 full-time, $454.40 per credit part-time. Full-time tuition varies according to student level. Part-time tuition varies according to student level. College room and board: $6376. College room only: $3188. Room and board charges vary according to board plan, housing facility, and location. Tuition guaranteed not to increase for student's term of enrollment. **Scholarships:** Available **Calendar System:** Semester, Summer Session Available **Enrollment:** FT 17,620, PT 2,377, Grad 7,224 **Faculty:** FT 704, PT 391 **Student-Faculty Ratio:** 22:1 **Exams:** ACT **% Receiving Financial Aid:** 51 **% Residing in College-Owned, -Operated, or -Affiliated Housing:** 34 **Library Holdings:** 1,009,746 **Regional Accreditation:** North Central Association of Colleges and Schools **Credit Hours For Degree:** 124 credits, Bachelors **ROTC:** Army **Professional Accreditation:** AACSB, ACEJMC, ADtA, APTA, APA, ASLHA, CSWE, JRCEPAT, NASM, NCATE, NRPA **Intercollegiate Athletics:** Baseball M; Basketball M & W; Cross-Country Running M & W; Field Hockey W; Football M; Gymnastics W; Soccer W; Softball W; Track and Field M & W; Volleyball W; Wrestling M

CLEARY UNIVERSITY
3601 Plymouth Rd.
Ann Arbor, MI 48105-2659
Tel: (734)332-4477; 888-5-CLEARY
Admissions: (517)548-3670
Fax: (734)332-4646
Web Site: http://www.cleary.edu/
President/CEO: Thomas P. Sullivan
Registrar: Rose Smith
Admissions: Roy Coons
Financial Aid: Vesta Smith-Campbell
Type: Comprehensive **Sex:** Coed **Scores:** 50% ACT 18-23; 27% ACT 24-29 **Admission Plans:** Early Admission; Deferred Admission **Application Deadline:** August 15 **Application Fee:** $25.00 **H.S. Requirements:** High school diploma required; GED accepted **Costs Per Year:** Application fee: $25. Tuition: $13,680 full-time, $285 per quarter hour part-time. **Scholarships:** Available **Calendar System:** Quarter, Summer Session Available **Enrollment:** FT 396, PT 167, Grad 34 **Faculty:** FT 12, PT 94 **Student-Faculty Ratio:** 10:1 **Exams:** Other, SAT I or ACT, SAT II **% Receiving Financial Aid:** 47 **Library Holdings:** 4,500 **Regional Accreditation:** North Central Association of Colleges and Schools **Credit Hours For Degree:** 90 quarter hours, Associates; 180 quarter hours, Bachelors

COLLEGE FOR CREATIVE STUDIES
201 East Kirby
Detroit, MI 48202-4034
Tel: (313)664-7400
Free: 800-952-ARTS
Fax: (313)872-2739
Web Site: http://www.ccscad.edu/
President/CEO: Richard L. Rogers
Registrar: Nadine Hagoort
Financial Aid: Kristin Moskovitz
Type: Four-Year College **Sex:** Coed **% Accepted:** 60 **Admission Plans:** Deferred Admission **Application Deadline:** Rolling **Application Fee:** $35.00 **H.S. Requirements:** High school diploma required; GED accepted **Costs Per Year:** Application fee: $35. Tuition: $23,490 full-time, $788 per credit hour part-time. Mandatory fees: $1145 full-time, $563 per term part-time. College room only: $3900. **Scholarships:** Available **Calendar System:** Semester, Summer Session Available **Enrollment:** FT 1,067, PT 224

Faculty: FT 47, PT 180 **Student-Faculty Ratio:** 10:1 **Exams:** SAT I or ACT **% Residing in College-Owned, -Operated, or -Affiliated Housing:** 23 **Library Holdings:** 24,000 **Regional Accreditation:** North Central Association of Colleges and Schools **Credit Hours For Degree:** 126 credit hours, Bachelors **Professional Accreditation:** NASAD

CONCORDIA UNIVERSITY
4090 Geddes Rd.
Ann Arbor, MI 48105-2797
Tel: (734)995-7300
Free: 800-253-0680
Admissions: (734)995-7311
Fax: (734)995-4610
E-mail: admissions@ccaa.edu or neumag@cuaa.edu
Web Site: http://www.cuaa.edu/
President/CEO: Dr. Thomas R. Ahlersmeyer
Registrar: Timothy Taylor
Admissions: Gary Neumann
Financial Aid: Sandra Tarbox
Type: Comprehensive **Sex:** Coed **Affiliation:** Lutheran Church–Missouri Synod; Concordia University System **Scores:** 100% SAT V 400+; 92% SAT M 400+; 48% ACT 18-23; 32% ACT 24-29 **% Accepted:** 82 **Admission Plans:** Deferred Admission **Application Deadline:** Rolling **Application Fee:** $25.00 **H.S. Requirements:** High school diploma required; GED accepted **Costs Per Year:** Application fee: $25. One-time mandatory fee: $100. Comprehensive fee: $25,153 includes full-time tuition ($18,035), mandatory fees ($170), and college room and board ($6948). College room only: $5042. Full-time tuition and fees vary according to course load, degree level, and program. Part-time tuition: $590 per credit hour. Part-time tuition varies according to course load, degree level, and program. **Scholarships:** Available **Calendar System:** Semester, Summer Session Available **Enrollment:** FT 506, PT 53, Grad 41 **Faculty:** FT 35, PT 50 **Student-Faculty Ratio:** 11:1 **Exams:** ACT, SAT I or ACT **% Receiving Financial Aid:** 80 **% Residing in College-Owned, -Operated, or -Affiliated Housing:** 56 **Library Holdings:** 120,000 **Regional Accreditation:** North Central Association of Colleges and Schools **Credit Hours For Degree:** 60 semester hours, Associates; 128 semester hours, Bachelors **ROTC:** Army, Air Force **Professional Accreditation:** NCATE **Intercollegiate Athletics:** Baseball M; Basketball M & W; Cross-Country Running M & W; Golf M & W; Soccer M & W; Softball W; Volleyball W

CORNERSTONE UNIVERSITY
1001 East Beltline Ave., NE
Grand Rapids, MI 49525-5897
Tel: (616)949-5300
Free: 800-787-9778
Admissions: (616)222-1426
Fax: (616)222-1540
E-mail: admissions@cornerstone.edu
Web Site: http://www.cornerstone.edu/
President/CEO: Dr. Rex Rogers
Admissions: Brent Rudin
Financial Aid: Geoff Marsh
Type: Comprehensive **Sex:** Coed **Affiliation:** nondenominational **% Accepted:** 76 **Admission Plans:** Deferred Admission **Application Deadline:** Rolling **Application Fee:** $25.00 **H.S. Requirements:** High school diploma required; GED accepted **Costs Per Year:** Application fee: $25. Comprehensive fee: $20,500 includes full-time tuition ($14,700) and college room and board ($5800). College room only: $2650. Room and board charges vary according to board plan. Part-time tuition: $595 per hour. Part-time tuition varies according to course load. **Scholarships:** Available **Calendar System:** Semester, Summer Session Available **Enrollment:** FT 1,653, PT 519, Grad 279 **Faculty:** FT 76, PT 64 **Student-Faculty Ratio:** 15:1 **Exams:** SAT I or ACT **% Receiving Financial Aid:** 76 **% Residing in College-Owned, -Operated, or -Affiliated Housing:** 56 **Library Holdings:** 109,376 **Regional Accreditation:** North Central Association of Colleges and Schools **Credit Hours For Degree:** 64 credit hours, Associates; 120 credit hours, Bachelors **ROTC:** Army **Professional Accreditation:** CSWE, NASM **Intercollegiate Athletics:** Basketball M & W; Cross-Country Running M & W; Golf M; Soccer M & W; Softball W; Track and Field M & W; Volleyball W

DAVENPORT UNIVERSITY (ALMA)
1500 North Pine St.
Alma, MI 48801
Tel: (989)463-8922
Free: 800-632-9569
Fax: (989)463-4540
Web Site: http://www.davenport.edu/ **Type:** Two-Year College **Sex:** Coed **Affiliation:** Davenport Educational System **Admission Plans:** Open Admission; Deferred Admission **Application Fee:** $25.00 **H.S. Requirements:** High school diploma required; GED accepted **Costs Per Year:** Application fee: $25. Tuition: $6216 full-time, $259 per credit hour part-time. Mandatory fees: $120 full-time. **Scholarships:** Available **Calendar System:** Semester **Student-Faculty Ratio:** 16:1 **Regional Accreditation:** North Central Association of Colleges and Schools

DAVENPORT UNIVERSITY (BAD AXE)
150 Nugent Rd.
Bad Axe, MI 48413
Tel: (989)269-9288
Free: 800-632-9569
Fax: (989)269-2772
Web Site: http://www.davenport.edu/ **Type:** Two-Year College **Sex:** Coed **Affiliation:** Davenport Educational System **Admission Plans:** Open Admission; Deferred Admission **Application Fee:** $25.00 **H.S. Requirements:** High school diploma required; GED accepted **Costs Per Year:** Application fee: $25. Tuition: $6600 full-time, $275 per credit hour part-time. Mandatory fees: $120 full-time. **Scholarships:** Available **Calendar System:** Semester **Student-Faculty Ratio:** 16:1 **Regional Accreditation:** North Central Association of Colleges and Schools

DAVENPORT UNIVERSITY (BAY CITY)
3930 Traxler Ct.
Bay City, MI 48706
Tel: (989)686-1572
Free: 800-632-9569
Fax: (989)686-2380
Web Site: http://www.davenport.edu/ **Type:** Two-Year College **Sex:** Coed **Affiliation:** Davenport Educational System **Admission Plans:** Open Admission; Deferred Admission **Application Fee:** $25.00 **H.S. Requirements:** High school diploma required; GED accepted **Costs Per Year:** Application fee: $25. Tuition: $6600 full-time, $275 per credit hour part-time. Mandatory fees: $120 full-time. **Scholarships:** Available **Calendar System:** Semester **Student-Faculty Ratio:** 16:1 **Regional Accreditation:** North Central Association of Colleges and Schools

DAVENPORT UNIVERSITY (CARO)
1231 Cleaver Rd.
Caro, MI 48723
Tel: (989)673-5857
Free: 800-632-9569
Fax: (989)673-7543
Web Site: http://www.davenport.edu/ **Type:** Two-Year College **Sex:** Coed **Affiliation:** Davenport Educational System **Admission Plans:** Open Admission; Deferred Admission **Application Fee:** $25.00 **H.S. Requirements:** High school diploma required; GED accepted **Costs Per Year:** Application fee: $25. Tuition: $6600 full-time, $275 per credit hour part-time. Mandatory fees: $120 full-time. **Scholarships:** Available **Calendar System:** Semester **Student-Faculty Ratio:** 16:1 **Regional Accreditation:** North Central Association of Colleges and Schools

DAVENPORT UNIVERSITY (DEARBORN)
4801 Oakman Blvd.
Dearborn, MI 48126-3799
Tel: (313)581-4400
Free: 800-632-9569
Admissions: (616)451-3511
Fax: (313)581-1853
E-mail: lynnae.selberg@davenport.edu
Web Site: http://www.davenport.edu/
President/CEO: Randolph Flechsig
Registrar: Nickolas Fleezanis
Admissions: Lynnae Selberg
Financial Aid: Susan Crkovski
Type: Comprehensive **Sex:** Coed **Affiliation:** Davenport Educational System **% Accepted:** 100 **Admission Plans:** Open Admission; Deferred Admission **Application Deadline:** Rolling **Application Fee:** $25.00 **H.S. Requirements:** High school diploma required; GED accepted **Costs Per Year:** Application fee: $25. Tuition: $8760 full-time, $365 per credit hour part-time. Mandatory fees: $120 full-time. **Scholarships:** Available **Calendar**

System: Semester, Summer Session Available **Enrollment:** FT 3,104, PT 8,962, Grad 756 **Faculty:** FT 130, PT 966 **Student-Faculty Ratio:** 13:1 **% Receiving Financial Aid:** 81 **Regional Accreditation:** North Central Association of Colleges and Schools **Credit Hours For Degree:** 100 quarter hours, Associates; 196 quarter hours, Bachelors

DAVENPORT UNIVERSITY (MIDLAND)
3555 East Patrick Rd.
Midland, MI 48642
Tel: (989)835-5588
Free: 800-632-9569
Fax: (989)835-8363
Web Site: http://www.davenport.edu/
Registrar: Paul Saft
Financial Aid: Patricia Finerty
Type: Two-Year College **Sex:** Coed **Affiliation:** Davenport Educational System **Admission Plans:** Open Admission; Deferred Admission **Application Fee:** $25.00 **H.S. Requirements:** High school diploma required; GED accepted **Costs Per Year:** Application fee: $25. Tuition: $6600 full-time, $275 per credit hour part-time. Mandatory fees: $120 full-time. **Scholarships:** Available **Calendar System:** Semester, Summer Session Available **Student-Faculty Ratio:** 16:1 **Regional Accreditation:** North Central Association of Colleges and Schools **Credit Hours For Degree:** 60 semester hours, Associates

DAVENPORT UNIVERSITY (ROMEO)
71180 Van Dyke Rd.
Romeo, MI 48065
Tel: (586)752-5229
Free: 800-632-9569
Fax: (586)752-5756
Web Site: http://www.davenport.edu/ **Type:** Two-Year College **Sex:** Coed **Affiliation:** Davenport Educational System **Admission Plans:** Open Admission; Deferred Admission **Application Fee:** $25.00 **H.S. Requirements:** High school diploma required; GED accepted **Costs Per Year:** Application fee: $25. Tuition: $6216 full-time, $259 per credit hour part-time. Mandatory fees: $120 full-time. **Scholarships:** Available **Calendar System:** Semester **Student-Faculty Ratio:** 16:1 **Regional Accreditation:** North Central Association of Colleges and Schools

DAVENPORT UNIVERSITY (SAGINAW)
5300 Bay Rd.
Saginaw, MI 48604
Tel: (989)799-7800
Free: 800-632-9569
Fax: (989)799-9696
Web Site: http://www.davenport.edu/ **Type:** Two-Year College **Sex:** Coed **Affiliation:** Davenport Educational System **Admission Plans:** Open Admission; Deferred Admission **Application Fee:** $25.00 **H.S. Requirements:** High school diploma required; GED accepted **Costs Per Year:** Application fee: $25. Tuition: $6600 full-time, $275 per credit hour part-time. Mandatory fees: $120 full-time. **Scholarships:** Available **Calendar System:** Semester **Student-Faculty Ratio:** 16:1 **Regional Accreditation:** North Central Association of Colleges and Schools

DELTA COLLEGE
1961 Delta Rd.
University Center, MI 48710
Tel: (989)686-9000
Free: 800-285-1705
Admissions: (989)686-9449
Fax: (989)686-8736
Web Site: http://www.delta.edu/
President/CEO: Dr. Peter D. Boyse
Registrar: Duff Zube
Admissions: Duff Zube
Financial Aid: Kim Donat
Type: Two-Year College **Sex:** Coed **% Accepted:** 100 **Admission Plans:** Open Admission; Early Admission; Deferred Admission **Application Deadline:** Rolling **Application Fee:** $20.00 **H.S. Requirements:** High school diploma or equivalent not required. For international students: High school diploma required; GED accepted **Costs Per Year:** Application fee: $20. Area resident tuition: $1740 full-time, $72.50 per credit hour part-time. State resident tuition: $2496 full-time, $104 per credit hour part-time. Nonresident tuition: $3564 full-time, $148.50 per credit hour part-time. Mandatory fees: $192 full-time, $5.50 per credit part-time, $30 per term part-time. **Scholarships:** Available **Calendar System:** Semester, Summer Session Available **Enrollment:** FT 3,938, PT 6,272 **Faculty:** FT 211, PT 300 **Student-Faculty Ratio:** 20:1 **Library Holdings:** 93,167 **Regional Accreditation:** North Central Association of Colleges and Schools **Credit Hours For Degree:** 62 semester hours, Associates **Professional Accreditation:** ABET, ARCEST, ADA, APTA, CARC, JRCEDMS, JRCERT, NLN **Intercollegiate Athletics:** Basketball M & W; Golf M; Soccer M; Softball W; Volleyball W

EASTERN MICHIGAN UNIVERSITY
Ypsilanti, MI 48197
Tel: (734)487-1849
Free: 800-GO TO EMU
Admissions: (734)487-3060
Fax: (734)487-1484
Web Site: http://www.emich.edu/
President/CEO: Dr. Samuel A. Kirkpatrick
Registrar: Joy Garrett
Admissions: Judy Benfield-Tatum
Financial Aid: Bernice Lindke
Type: Comprehensive **Sex:** Coed **Scores:** 91% SAT V 400+; 91% SAT M 400+; 53% ACT 18-23; 24% ACT 24-29 **% Accepted:** 79 **Admission Plans:** Deferred Admission **Application Fee:** $30.00 **H.S. Requirements:** High school diploma required; GED accepted **Costs Per Year:** Application fee: $30. State resident tuition: $5463 full-time, $182.10 per credit hour part-time. Nonresident tuition: $16,818 full-time, $560.60 per credit hour part-time. Mandatory fees: $1078 full-time, $33.25 per credit hour part-time, $40 per term part-time. College room and board: $6356. **Scholarships:** Available **Calendar System:** Semester, Summer Session Available **Enrollment:** FT 12,998, PT 5,580, Grad 4,662 **Faculty:** FT 769, PT 427 **Student-Faculty Ratio:** 19:1 **Exams:** ACT, Other **% Receiving Financial Aid:** 50 **% Residing in College-Owned, -Operated, or -Affiliated Housing:** 20 **Library Holdings:** 658,648 **Regional Accreditation:** North Central Association of Colleges and Schools **Credit Hours For Degree:** 124 semester hours, Bachelors **ROTC:** Army, Navy, Air Force **Professional Accreditation:** AACSB, AACN, ACCE, ACA, ADtA, ACSP, AOTA, ASLHA, CSWE, FIDER, JRCEPAT, NAACLS, NAIT, NASM, NASPAA, NCATE, NRPA **Intercollegiate Athletics:** Baseball M; Basketball M & W; Crew W; Cross-Country Running M & W; Football M; Golf M & W; Gymnastics W; Soccer W; Softball W; Swimming and Diving M & W; Tennis W; Track and Field M & W; Volleyball W; Wrestling M

FERRIS STATE UNIVERSITY
1201 South State St.
Big Rapids, MI 49307
Tel: (231)591-2000
Free: 800-433-7747
Admissions: (231)591-2797
Fax: (231)591-2978
E-mail: admissions@act01.ferris.edu
Web Site: http://www.ferris.edu/
President/CEO: Dr. David Eisler
Registrar: Craig Westman
Admissions: Dr. Craig Westman
Financial Aid: Ronnie Higgs
Type: Comprehensive **Sex:** Coed **Scores:** 53% ACT 18-23; 23% ACT 24-29 **% Accepted:** 47 **Admission Plans:** Open Admission **Application Deadline:** August 04 **Application Fee:** $30.00 **H.S. Requirements:** High school diploma required; GED accepted **Costs Per Year:** Application fee: $30. State resident tuition: $6740 full-time, $265 per credit hour part-time. Nonresident tuition: $13,480 full-time, $530 per credit hour part-time. Mandatory fees: $142 full-time. Full-time tuition and fees vary according to reciprocity agreements. College room and board: $6816. College room only: $3462. Room and board charges vary according to board plan and housing facility. **Scholarships:** Available **Calendar System:** Semester, Summer Session Available **Enrollment:** FT 8,868, PT 2,569, Grad 490 **Faculty:** FT 545, PT 278 **Student-Faculty Ratio:** 17:1 **Exams:** SAT I or ACT **% Receiving Financial Aid:** 66 **% Residing in College-Owned, -Operated, or -Affiliated Housing:** 38 **Library Holdings:** 344,496 **Regional Accreditation:** North Central Association of Colleges and Schools **ROTC:** Army **Professional Accreditation:** ABET, ACCE, ACPhE, ADA, AHIMA, AOA, CARC, CSWE, JRCERT, JRCNMT, NAACLS, NASAD, NLN, NRPA **Intercollegiate Athletics:** Basketball M & W; Cheerleading M & W; Cross-Country Running M & W; Football M; Golf M & W; Ice Hockey M; Softball W; Tennis

M & W; Track and Field M & W; Volleyball W

FINLANDIA UNIVERSITY
601 Quincy St.
Hancock, MI 49930-1882
Tel: (906)482-5300; 877-202-5491
Admissions: (906)487-7311
Fax: (906)487-7300
E-mail: ben.larson@finlandia.edu
Web Site: http://www.finlandia.edu/
President/CEO: Dr. Robert Ubbelohde
Registrar: Evelyn Goke
Admissions: Ben Larson
Financial Aid: Sandra Turnquist
Type: Four-Year College **Sex:** Coed **Affiliation:** Evangelical Lutheran Church in America **Scores:** 49% ACT 18-23; 21% ACT 24-29 **% Accepted:** 95 **Admission Plans:** Early Admission **Application Deadline:** August 15 **Application Fee:** $30.00 **H.S. Requirements:** High school diploma required; GED accepted **Costs Per Year:** Application fee: $30. Comprehensive fee: $20,847 includes full-time tuition ($15,434), mandatory fees ($99), and college room and board ($5314). Full-time tuition and fees vary according to program. Room and board charges vary according to housing facility. Part-time tuition: $520 per credit. Part-time mandatory fees: $99 per year. Part-time tuition and fees vary according to course load, degree level, and program. **Scholarships:** Available **Calendar System:** Semester, Summer Session Available **Enrollment:** FT 469, PT 79 **Faculty:** FT 39, PT 2 **Student-Faculty Ratio:** 11:1 **Exams:** SAT I or ACT **% Receiving Financial Aid:** 96 **% Residing in College-Owned, -Operated, or -Affiliated Housing:** 27 **Library Holdings:** 46,092 **Regional Accreditation:** North Central Association of Colleges and Schools **Credit Hours For Degree:** 60 credits, Associates; 129 credits, Bachelors **ROTC:** Army, Air Force **Professional Accreditation:** APTA **Intercollegiate Athletics:** Baseball M; Basketball M & W; Cross-Country Running M & W; Ice Hockey M & W; Skiing (Cross-Country) M & W; Soccer M & W; Softball W; Volleyball W

GLEN OAKS COMMUNITY COLLEGE
62249 Shimmel Rd.
Centreville, MI 49032-9719
Tel: (616)467-9945; 888-994-7818
Admissions: (269)467-9945
Fax: (616)467-9068
Web Site: http://www.glenoaks.edu/
President/CEO: Dr. Marilynn Liddell
Registrar: Beverly Andrews
Admissions: Janene Breneman
Financial Aid: Dr. Richard Wedemeyer
Type: Two-Year College **Sex:** Coed **Affiliation:** Michigan Department of Career Development **Admission Plans:** Open Admission **Application Fee:** $0.00 **H.S. Requirements:** High school diploma or equivalent not required **Costs Per Year:** Application fee: $0. Area resident tuition: $1800 full-time, $60 per credit hour part-time. State resident tuition: $2670 full-time, $89 per credit hour part-time. Nonresident tuition: $3450 full-time, $114 per credit hour part-time. Mandatory fees: $255 full-time, $7.50 per credit hour part-time, $31 per term part-time. **Scholarships:** Available **Calendar System:** Semester, Summer Session Available **Enrollment:** FT 659, PT 1,051 **Faculty:** FT 29, PT 80 **Student-Faculty Ratio:** 16:1 **Exams:** Other **Library Holdings:** 37,087 **Regional Accreditation:** North Central Association of Colleges and Schools **Credit Hours For Degree:** 62 credit hours, Associates **Intercollegiate Athletics:** Baseball M; Basketball M & W; Golf M; Softball W; Tennis W; Volleyball W

GOGEBIC COMMUNITY COLLEGE
E-4946 Jackson Rd.
Ironwood, MI 49938
Tel: (906)932-4231
Fax: (906)932-5541
Web Site: http://www.gogebic.edu/
President/CEO: Dr. Donald J. Foster
Registrar: Steve Wesselhoft
Admissions: Steven Wesselhoft
Financial Aid: Suzetta Forbes
Type: Two-Year College **Sex:** Coed **Affiliation:** Michigan Department of Education **Admission Plans:** Open Admission; Early Admission; Deferred Admission **Application Fee:** $10.00 **H.S. Requirements:** High school diploma required; GED accepted **Costs Per Year:** Application fee: $10. Area resident tuition: $2294 full-time, $74 per credit part-time. State resident tuition: $2914 full-time, $94 per credit part-time. Nonresident tuition: $3720 full-time, $120 per credit part-time. Mandatory fees: $442 full-time, $5 per credit part-time. Full-time tuition and fees vary according to course load and reciprocity agreements. Part-time tuition and fees vary according to course load and reciprocity agreements. **Scholarships:** Available **Calendar System:** Semester, Summer Session Available **Enrollment:** FT 517, PT 464 **Faculty:** FT 30, PT 60 **Student-Faculty Ratio:** 13:1 **Library Holdings:** 22,000 **Regional Accreditation:** North Central Association of Colleges and Schools **Credit Hours For Degree:** 63 credit hours, Associates **Professional Accreditation:** AHIMA **Intercollegiate Athletics:** Basketball M & W; Cheerleading M & W

GRACE BIBLE COLLEGE
1011 Aldon St. SW
PO Box 910
Grand Rapids, MI 49509-0910
Tel: (616)538-2330
Free: 800-968-1887
Fax: (616)538-0599
Web Site: http://www.gbcol.edu/
President/CEO: Kenneth Kemper
Registrar: Linda K. Siler
Admissions: Kevin Gilliam
Financial Aid: Marlene E. DeVries
Type: Four-Year College **Sex:** Coed **Affiliation:** Grace Gospel Fellowship **Scores:** 100% SAT V 400+; 100% SAT M 400+; 61% ACT 18-23; 13% ACT 24-29 **% Accepted:** 64 **Admission Plans:** Early Admission; Deferred Admission **Application Deadline:** July 15 **Application Fee:** $0.00 **H.S. Requirements:** High school diploma required; GED accepted **Costs Per Year:** Application fee: $0. Comprehensive fee: $17,810 includes full-time tuition ($10,450), mandatory fees ($500), and college room and board ($6860). Room and board charges vary according to housing facility. Part-time tuition: $450 per semester hour. Part-time tuition varies according to course load. **Scholarships:** Available **Calendar System:** Semester, Summer Session Not available **Enrollment:** FT 150, PT 11 **Faculty:** FT 8, PT 25 **Student-Faculty Ratio:** 9:1 **Exams:** SAT I and SAT II or ACT **% Receiving Financial Aid:** 85 **% Residing in College-Owned, -Operated, or -Affiliated Housing:** 53 **Library Holdings:** 39,079 **Regional Accreditation:** North Central Association of Colleges and Schools **Credit Hours For Degree:** 64 semester hours, Associates; 124 semester hours, Bachelors **ROTC:** Army **Professional Accreditation:** AABC **Intercollegiate Athletics:** Basketball M & W; Soccer M; Volleyball W

GRAND RAPIDS COMMUNITY COLLEGE
143 Bostwick Ave., NE
Grand Rapids, MI 49503-3201
Tel: (616)234-4000
Admissions: (616)234-4100
Fax: (616)234-4005
Web Site: http://www.grcc.edu/
President/CEO: Dr. Juan Olivarez
Registrar: Howard Shaken
Admissions: Diane Patrick
Financial Aid: Jill Nutt
Type: Two-Year College **Sex:** Coed **Affiliation:** Michigan Department of Education **% Accepted:** 93 **Admission Plans:** Open Admission; Early Admission; Deferred Admission **Application Deadline:** August 30 **Application Fee:** $20.00 **H.S. Requirements:** High school diploma required; GED accepted **Costs Per Year:** Application fee: $20. Area resident tuition: $2205 full-time, $73.50 per contact hour part-time. State resident tuition: $4260 full-time, $142 per contact hour part-time. Nonresident tuition: $6060 full-time, $202 per contact hour part-time. Mandatory fees: $100 full-time, $70 per term part-time. **Scholarships:** Available **Calendar System:** Semester, Summer Session Available **Enrollment:** FT 6,483, PT 8,315 **Faculty:** FT 224, PT 424 **Student-Faculty Ratio:** 25:1 **Exams:** Other, SAT I or ACT **Library Holdings:** 101,077 **Regional Accreditation:** North Central Association of Colleges and Schools **Credit Hours For Degree:** 62 credits, Associates **Professional Accreditation:** ACF, ADA, AOTA, JRCERT, NASM, NLN **Intercollegiate Athletics:** Baseball M & W; Basketball M & W; Football M; Golf M; Softball W; Swimming and Diving M & W; Tennis M & W; Track and Field M; Volleyball W; Wrestling M

GRAND VALLEY STATE UNIVERSITY
1 Campus Dr.
Allendale, MI 49401-9403

Tel: (616)331-5000
Free: 800-748-0246
Admissions: (616)331-2025
Fax: (616)331-2000
E-mail: go2gvsu@gvsu.edu
Web Site: http://www.gvsu.edu/
President/CEO: Mark Murray
Registrar: Lynn M. Blue
Admissions: Jodi Chycinski
Financial Aid: Kenneth Fridsma
Type: Comprehensive **Sex:** Coed **Scores:** 49% ACT 18-23; 44% ACT 24-29 **% Accepted:** 68 **Application Deadline:** May 01 **Application Fee:** $30.00 **H.S. Requirements:** High school diploma required; GED accepted **Costs Per Year:** Application fee: $30. State resident tuition: $6220 full-time, $271 per credit hour part-time. Nonresident tuition: $12,510 full-time, $532 per credit hour part-time. Full-time tuition varies according to course level, program, and student level. Part-time tuition varies according to course level, course load, program, and student level. College room and board: $6360. Room and board charges vary according to board plan, housing facility, and location. **Scholarships:** Available **Calendar System:** Semester, Summer Session Available **Enrollment:** FT 16,457, PT 2,446, Grad 3,662 **Faculty:** FT 910, PT 460 **Student-Faculty Ratio:** 18:1 **Exams:** SAT I or ACT **% Receiving Financial Aid:** 55 **% Residing in College-Owned, -Operated, or -Affiliated Housing:** 29 **Library Holdings:** 634,000 **Regional Accreditation:** North Central Association of Colleges and Schools **Credit Hours For Degree:** 120 semester hours, Bachelors **Professional Accreditation:** AACSB, ABET, AACN, AOTA, APTA, APA, CSWE, JRCEPAT, NAACLS, NASAD, NASM, NASPAA, NCATE **Intercollegiate Athletics:** Baseball M; Basketball M & W; Cheerleading M & W; Crew M & W; Cross-Country Running M & W; Football M; Golf M & W; Ice Hockey M; Rugby M & W; Sailing M & W; Skiing (Downhill) M & W; Soccer M & W; Softball W; Swimming and Diving M & W; Tennis M & W; Track and Field M & W; Volleyball M & W; Water Polo M & W; Wrestling M

GREAT LAKES CHRISTIAN COLLEGE

6211 West Willow Hwy.
Lansing, MI 48917-1299
Tel: (517)321-0242
Free: 800-YES-GLCC
Fax: (517)321-5902
Web Site: http://www.glcc.edu/
President/CEO: Larry Carter
Registrar: Lloyd Scharer
Admissions: Mike Klauka
Financial Aid: Tedd C. Kees
Type: Four-Year College **Sex:** Coed **Affiliation:** Christian Churches and Churches of Christ **Scores:** 60% ACT 18-23; 17% ACT 24-29 **Admission Plans:** Early Admission; Deferred Admission **Application Fee:** $30.00 **H.S. Requirements:** High school diploma required; GED accepted **Costs Per Year:** Application fee: $30. Comprehensive fee: $14,898 includes full-time tuition ($8448), mandatory fees ($1250), and college room and board ($5200). Full-time tuition and fees vary according to program, reciprocity agreements, and student level. Room and board charges vary according to board plan and housing facility. Part-time tuition: $264 per hour. **Calendar System:** Semester, Summer Session Not available **Faculty:** FT 10, PT 10 **Student-Faculty Ratio:** 14:1 **Exams:** SAT I and SAT II or ACT **% Residing in College-Owned, -Operated, or -Affiliated Housing:** 68 **Library Holdings:** 34,000 **Regional Accreditation:** North Central Association of Colleges and Schools **Credit Hours For Degree:** 64 semester hours, Associates; 128 semester hours, Bachelors **Professional Accreditation:** AABC **Intercollegiate Athletics:** Basketball M & W; Soccer M & W; Volleyball W

HENRY FORD COMMUNITY COLLEGE

5101 Evergreen Rd.
Dearborn, MI 48128-1495
Tel: (313)845-9615
Fax: (313)845-9658
Web Site: http://www.hfcc.edu/
President/CEO: Dr. Andrew A. Mazzara
Registrar: Mark Ulseth
Admissions: Mark Ulseth
Financial Aid: Kevin Culler
Type: Two-Year College **Sex:** Coed **Admission Plans:** Open Admission; Early Admission; Deferred Admission **Application Fee:** $30.00 **H.S. Requirements:** High school diploma required; GED accepted **Scholarships:** Available **Calendar System:** Semester, Summer Session Available **Faculty:** FT 220, PT 550 **Exams:** ACT **Library Holdings:** 80,000 **Regional Accreditation:** North Central Association of Colleges and Schools **Credit Hours For Degree:** 60 credit hours, Associates **Professional Accreditation:** ARCEST, ACF, AHIMA, APTA, ACBSP, CARC, NLN **Intercollegiate Athletics:** Baseball M; Basketball M & W; Golf M; Softball W; Tennis W; Track and Field M; Volleyball W

HILLSDALE COLLEGE

33 East College St.
Hillsdale, MI 49242-1298
Tel: (517)437-7341
Admissions: (517)607-2327
Fax: (517)437-0190
E-mail: jefflantis@hillsdale.edu
Web Site: http://www.hillsdale.edu/
President/CEO: Dr. Larry P. Arnn
Registrar: Lindsay Buchinger
Admissions: Jeffrey S. Lantis
Financial Aid: Connie Bricker
Type: Four-Year College **Sex:** Coed **Scores:** 100% SAT V 400+; 100% SAT M 400+; 20% ACT 18-23; 57% ACT 24-29 **% Accepted:** 82 **Admission Plans:** Early Admission; Deferred Admission **Application Deadline:** February 15 **Application Fee:** $35.00 **H.S. Requirements:** High school diploma required; GED accepted. For home schooled applicants: High school diploma or equivalent not required **Costs Per Year:** Application fee: $35. Comprehensive fee: $24,160 includes full-time tuition ($17,000), mandatory fees ($410), and college room and board ($6750). College room only: $3350. Room and board charges vary according to board plan. Part-time tuition: $670 per semester hour. **Scholarships:** Available **Calendar System:** Semester, Summer Session Available **Enrollment:** FT 1,262, PT 42 **Faculty:** FT 100, PT 36 **Student-Faculty Ratio:** 10:1 **Exams:** SAT I or ACT, SAT II **% Receiving Financial Aid:** 32 **% Residing in College-Owned, -Operated, or -Affiliated Housing:** 83 **Library Holdings:** 240,000 **Regional Accreditation:** North Central Association of Colleges and Schools **Credit Hours For Degree:** 124 semester hours, Bachelors **Intercollegiate Athletics:** Baseball M; Basketball M & W; Equestrian Sports W; Football M; Ice Hockey M; Lacrosse M; Riflery M & W; Soccer W; Softball W; Swimming and Diving W; Track and Field M & W; Volleyball W

HOPE COLLEGE

141 East 12th St., PO Box 9000
Holland, MI 49422-9000
Tel: (616)395-7000
Free: 800-968-7850
Admissions: (616)395-7850
Fax: (616)395-7130
E-mail: admissions@hope.edu
Web Site: http://www.hope.edu/
President/CEO: Dr. James E. Bultman
Registrar: Jon Huisken
Admissions: Dr. James R. Bekkering
Financial Aid: Phyllis Hooyman
Type: Four-Year College **Sex:** Coed **Affiliation:** Reformed Church in America **Scores:** 100% SAT V 400+; 99% SAT M 400+; 30% ACT 18-23; 52% ACT 24-29 **% Accepted:** 77 **Admission Plans:** Early Admission; Deferred Admission **Application Deadline:** Rolling **Application Fee:** $35.00 **H.S. Requirements:** High school diploma required; GED accepted **Costs Per Year:** Application fee: $35. Comprehensive fee: $28,208 includes full-time tuition ($21,420), mandatory fees ($120), and college room and board ($6668). College room only: $3040. Full-time tuition and fees vary according to course load. Room and board charges vary according to board plan. **Scholarships:** Available **Calendar System:** Semester, Summer Session Available **Enrollment:** FT 3,029, PT 112 **Faculty:** FT 215, PT 117 **Student-Faculty Ratio:** 13:1 **Exams:** SAT I or ACT **% Receiving Financial Aid:** 59 **% Residing in College-Owned, -Operated, or -Affiliated Housing:** 79 **Library Holdings:** 358,329 **Regional Accreditation:** North Central Association of Colleges and Schools **Credit Hours For Degree:** 126 credit hours, Bachelors **ROTC:** Army **Professional Accreditation:** ABET, CSWE, JRCEPAT, NASAD, NASD, NASM, NAST, NCATE, NLN **Intercollegiate Athletics:** Baseball M; Basketball M & W; Cheerleading M & W; Cross-

Country Running M & W; Football M; Golf M & W; Ice Hockey M; Lacrosse M; Soccer M & W; Softball W; Swimming and Diving M & W; Tennis M & W; Track and Field M & W; Volleyball W

ITT TECHNICAL INSTITUTE (CANTON)
1905 South Haggerty Rd.
Canton, MI 48188-2025
Tel: (734)397-7800
Free: 800-247-4477
Fax: (734)397-1945
Web Site: http://www.itt-tech.edu/
President/CEO: Nadine Palazzolo
Admissions: Nadine Palazzolo
Type: Two-Year College **Sex:** Coed **Affiliation:** ITT Educational Services, Inc **Admission Plans:** Deferred Admission **Application Deadline:** Rolling **Application Fee:** $100.00 **H.S. Requirements:** High school diploma required; GED accepted **Costs Per Year:** Application fee: $100. **Scholarships:** Available **Calendar System:** Quarter, Summer Session Not available **Exams:** Other **Credit Hours For Degree:** 96 credit hours, Associates **Professional Accreditation:** ACICS

ITT TECHNICAL INSTITUTE (GRAND RAPIDS)
4020 Sparks Dr., SE
Grand Rapids, MI 49546
Tel: (616)956-1060
Web Site: http://www.itt-tech.edu/
President/CEO: Dennis Hormel
Admissions: Dennis Hormel
Financial Aid: Beth Berggren
Type: Two-Year College **Sex:** Coed **Affiliation:** ITT Educational Services, Inc **Admission Plans:** Deferred Admission **Application Deadline:** Rolling **Application Fee:** $100.00 **H.S. Requirements:** High school diploma required; GED accepted **Costs Per Year:** Application fee: $100. **Scholarships:** Available **Calendar System:** Quarter, Summer Session Not available **Exams:** Other **Credit Hours For Degree:** 96 credit hours, Associates **Professional Accreditation:** ACICS

ITT TECHNICAL INSTITUTE (TROY)
1522 East Big Beaver Rd.
Troy, MI 48083-1905
Tel: (248)524-1800
Web Site: http://www.itt-tech.edu/
President/CEO: Dr. Stephen Goddard
Registrar: Julie Angott
Admissions: Richard Zeeman
Financial Aid: Marj McGuire
Type: Two-Year College **Sex:** Coed **Affiliation:** ITT Educational Services, Inc **Admission Plans:** Deferred Admission **Application Deadline:** Rolling **Application Fee:** $100.00 **H.S. Requirements:** High school diploma required; GED accepted **Costs Per Year:** Application fee: $100. **Scholarships:** Available **Calendar System:** Quarter, Summer Session Not available **Exams:** Other **Credit Hours For Degree:** 96 credit hours, Associates **Professional Accreditation:** ACICS

JACKSON COMMUNITY COLLEGE
2111 Emmons Rd.
Jackson, MI 49201-8399
Tel: (517)787-0800; 888-522-7344
Admissions: (517)796-8425
Web Site: http://www.jccmi.edu
President/CEO: Dr. Daniel Phelan
Registrar: Christine Beacco
Admissions: Julie Hand
Type: Two-Year College **Sex:** Coed **Admission Plans:** Open Admission; Early Admission **Application Deadline:** Rolling **Application Fee:** $0.00 **H.S. Requirements:** High school diploma required; GED accepted **Costs Per Year:** Application fee: $0. Area resident tuition: $1776 full-time, $74 per credit hour part-time. State resident tuition: $2496 full-time, $104 per credit hour part-time. Nonresident tuition: $3192 full-time, $133 per credit hour part-time. Mandatory fees: $384 full-time, $4.50 per credit hour part-time, $18 per term part-time. Full-time tuition and fees vary according to location. Part-time tuition and fees vary according to location. **Scholarships:** Available **Calendar System:** Semester, Summer Session Available **Enrollment:** FT 2,108, PT 3,762 **Faculty:** FT 93, PT 239 **Student-Faculty Ratio:** 19:1 **Library Holdings:** 67,000 **Regional Accreditation:** North Central Association of Colleges and Schools **Credit Hours For Degree:** 60 credit hours, Associates **Professional Accreditation:** AAMAE, ACBSP, JRCEDMS

KALAMAZOO COLLEGE
1200 Academy St.
Kalamazoo, MI 49006-3295
Tel: (269)337-7000
Free: 800-253-3602
Admissions: (269)337-7166
Fax: (269)337-7251
E-mail: admissions@kzoo.edu
Web Site: http://www.kzoo.edu/
President/CEO: Bernard S. Palchick
Registrar: Sandra Hudson
Admissions: John Carroll
Financial Aid: Marian Conrad
Type: Four-Year College **Sex:** Coed **Affiliation:** American Baptist Churches in the U.S.A. **Scores:** 100% SAT V 400+; 100% SAT M 400+; 9% ACT 18-23; 60% ACT 24-29 **% Accepted:** 68 **Admission Plans:** Early Action; Early Decision Plan; Deferred Admission **Application Deadline:** February 15 **Application Fee:** $35.00 **H.S. Requirements:** High school diploma required; GED accepted **Costs Per Year:** Application fee: $35. Comprehensive fee: $32,353 includes full-time tuition ($25,644) and college room and board ($6709). College room only: $3273. Room and board charges vary according to board plan. **Scholarships:** Available **Calendar System:** Quarter, Summer Session Not available **Enrollment:** FT 1,263 **Faculty:** FT 100, PT 14 **Student-Faculty Ratio:** 12:1 **Exams:** SAT I or ACT **% Receiving Financial Aid:** 52 **% Residing in College-Owned, -Operated, or -Affiliated Housing:** 75 **Library Holdings:** 342,939 **Regional Accreditation:** North Central Association of Colleges and Schools **Credit Hours For Degree:** 35 courses, Bachelors **ROTC:** Army **Intercollegiate Athletics:** Baseball M; Basketball M & W; Cross-Country Running M & W; Football M; Golf M & W; Soccer M & W; Softball W; Swimming and Diving M & W; Tennis M & W; Volleyball W

KALAMAZOO VALLEY COMMUNITY COLLEGE
PO Box 4070
Kalamazoo, MI 49003-4070
Tel: (269)488-4400
Admissions: (269)488-4207
Fax: (269)448-4555
Web Site: http://www.kvcc.edu/
President/CEO: Dr. Marilyn J. Schlack
Registrar: Michael McCall
Admissions: Michael McCall
Financial Aid: Roger Miller
Type: Two-Year College **Sex:** Coed **Admission Plans:** Open Admission; Early Admission; Deferred Admission **Application Fee:** $0.00 **H.S. Requirements:** High school diploma or equivalent not required **Costs Per Year:** Application fee: $0. Area resident tuition: $1320 full-time, $55 per credit part-time. State resident tuition: $2256 full-time, $94 per credit part-time. Nonresident tuition: $3072 full-time, $128 per credit part-time. **Scholarships:** Available **Calendar System:** Semester, Summer Session Available **Enrollment:** FT 3,959, PT 6,675 **Faculty:** FT 127, PT 337 **Student-Faculty Ratio:** 26:1 **Exams:** ACT **Library Holdings:** 88,791 **Regional Accreditation:** North Central Association of Colleges and Schools **Credit Hours For Degree:** 62 credit hours, Associates **ROTC:** Army **Professional Accreditation:** AAMAE, ADA, CARC **Intercollegiate Athletics:** Baseball M; Basketball M & W; Golf M; Softball W; Tennis M & W; Volleyball W

KELLOGG COMMUNITY COLLEGE
450 North Ave.
Battle Creek, MI 49017-3397
Tel: (616)965-3931
Admissions: (269)965-3931
Fax: (616)965-4133
Web Site: http://www.kellogg.edu/
President/CEO: Dr. G. Edward Haring
Registrar: Kay L. Keck
Admissions: Sedgwick Harris
Financial Aid: Colin McCaleb
Type: Two-Year College **Sex:** Coed **Affiliation:** Michigan Department of Education **% Accepted:** 87 **Admission Plans:** Open Admission; Early Admission; Deferred Admission **Application Deadline:** August 30 **Application Fee:** $0.00 **H.S. Requirements:** High school diploma or equivalent not

required. For allied health programs: High school diploma required; GED accepted **Costs Per Year:** Application fee: $0. Area resident tuition: $1950 full-time, $65 per credit hour part-time. State resident tuition: $3165 full-time, $105.50 per credit hour part-time. Nonresident tuition: $4770 full-time, $159 per credit hour part-time. Mandatory fees: $210 full-time, $7 per credit hour part-time. **Scholarships:** Available **Calendar System:** Semester, Summer Session Available **Enrollment:** FT 1,954, PT 4,246 **Faculty:** FT 91, PT 291 **Student-Faculty Ratio:** 22:1 **Exams:** ACT, SAT I or ACT **Library Holdings:** 42,131 **Regional Accreditation:** North Central Association of Colleges and Schools **Credit Hours For Degree:** 62 credit hours, Associates **Professional Accreditation:** ADA, APTA, JRCERT, NAACLS **Intercollegiate Athletics:** Baseball M; Basketball M & W; Soccer M; Softball W; Volleyball W

KETTERING UNIVERSITY
1700 West Third Ave.
Flint, MI 48504-4898
Tel: (810)762-9500
Free: 800-955-4464
Admissions: (810)762-7865
Fax: (810)762-9837
E-mail: admissions@kettering.edu
Web Site: http://www.kettering.edu/
President/CEO: Dr. James E. A. John
Registrar: Michelle Vyskocil
Admissions: Barbara Sosin
Financial Aid: Diane K. Bice
Type: Comprehensive **Sex:** Coed **Scores:** 100% SAT V 400+; 100% SAT M 400+; 24% ACT 18-23; 62% ACT 24-29 **% Accepted:** 73 **Admission Plans:** Deferred Admission **Application Deadline:** Rolling **Application Fee:** $35.00 **H.S. Requirements:** High school diploma required; GED not accepted **Costs Per Year:** Application fee: $35. Comprehensive fee: $29,188 includes full-time tuition ($23,360), mandatory fees ($388), and college room and board ($5440). College room only: $3432. Room and board charges vary according to student level. Part-time tuition: $730 per credit. **Scholarships:** Available **Calendar System:** Semester, Summer Session Not available **Enrollment:** FT 2,411, Grad 524 **Faculty:** FT 140, PT 17 **Student-Faculty Ratio:** 11:1 **Exams:** SAT I or ACT, SAT II **% Receiving Financial Aid:** 68 **% Residing in College-Owned, -Operated, or -Affiliated Housing:** 48 **Library Holdings:** 122,000 **Regional Accreditation:** North Central Association of Colleges and Schools **Credit Hours For Degree:** 160 credit hours, Bachelors **Professional Accreditation:** ABET, ACBSP **Intercollegiate Athletics:** Ice Hockey M; Lacrosse M; Soccer M; Volleyball M

KIRTLAND COMMUNITY COLLEGE
10775 North St Helen Rd.
Roscommon, MI 48653-9699
Tel: (989)275-5000
Fax: (989)275-8210
Web Site: http://www.kirtland.edu/
President/CEO: Dr. Charles D. Rorie
Registrar: Penny Lund
Financial Aid: Christen Horndt
Type: Two-Year College **Sex:** Coed **Affiliation:** Michigan Department of Education **Admission Plans:** Open Admission; Early Admission; Deferred Admission **Application Fee:** $0.00 **H.S. Requirements:** High school diploma required; GED accepted **Scholarships:** Available **Calendar System:** Semester, Summer Session Available **Enrollment:** FT 609, PT 1,309 **Faculty:** FT 39, PT 56 **Exams:** Other, SAT I or ACT **Library Holdings:** 35,000 **Regional Accreditation:** North Central Association of Colleges and Schools **Credit Hours For Degree:** 60 credit hours, Associates **Professional Accreditation:** AAMAE

KUYPER COLLEGE
3333 East Beltline, NE
Grand Rapids, MI 49525-9749
Tel: (616)222-3000
Free: 800-511-3749
Admissions: (616)988-3695
Fax: (616)222-3045
E-mail: llighthiser@kuyper.edu
Web Site: http://www.kuyper.edu/
President/CEO: Dr. Nicholas V. Kroeze
Registrar: Ben Meyer, EdD
Admissions: Larissa Lynn Lighthiser
Financial Aid: Agnes Russell
Type: Four-Year College **Sex:** Coed **Scores:** 66.66% SAT V 400+; 66.66% SAT M 400+; 45% ACT 18-23; 30% ACT 24-29 **% Accepted:** 61 **Admission Plans:** Deferred Admission **Application Deadline:** Rolling **Application Fee:** $25.00 **H.S. Requirements:** High school diploma required; GED accepted **Costs Per Year:** Application fee: $25. Comprehensive fee: $17,908 includes full-time tuition ($11,700), mandatory fees ($508), and college room and board ($5700). College room only: $2300. Full-time tuition and fees vary according to course load and student level. Room and board charges vary according to board plan, housing facility, and student level. Part-time tuition: $525 per credit hour. Part-time tuition varies according to course load. **Scholarships:** Available **Calendar System:** Semester, Summer Session Available **Enrollment:** FT 220, PT 50, Grad 4 **Faculty:** FT 12, PT 14 **Student-Faculty Ratio:** 15:1 **Exams:** SAT I or ACT **% Receiving Financial Aid:** 76 **% Residing in College-Owned, -Operated, or -Affiliated Housing:** 44 **Library Holdings:** 56,177 **Regional Accreditation:** North Central Association of Colleges and Schools **Credit Hours For Degree:** 63 credits, Associates; 124 credits, Bachelors **Professional Accreditation:** AABC

LAKE MICHIGAN COLLEGE
2755 East Napier
Benton Harbor, MI 49022-1899
Tel: (616)927-8100
Admissions: (269)927-8120
Web Site: http://www.lmc.cc.mi.us/
President/CEO: Dr. Richard Pappas
Registrar: Ann Liska
Admissions: Thomas Hoiles
Financial Aid: Anne Tews
Type: Two-Year College **Sex:** Coed **Affiliation:** Michigan Department of Education **Scores:** 100% SAT V 400+; 100% SAT M 400+; 58% ACT 18-23; 6% ACT 24-29 **% Accepted:** 76 **Admission Plans:** Open Admission; Early Admission; Deferred Admission **Application Deadline:** Rolling **Application Fee:** $0.00 **H.S. Requirements:** High school diploma required; GED accepted **Costs Per Year:** Application fee: $0. Area resident tuition: $2175 full-time, $72.50 per credit hour part-time. State resident tuition: $3060 full-time, $102 per credit hour part-time. Nonresident tuition: $4080 full-time, $136 per credit hour part-time. Mandatory fees: $930 full-time, $31 per credit hour part-time. **Scholarships:** Available **Calendar System:** Semester, Summer Session Available **Enrollment:** FT 1,235, PT 2,808 **Faculty:** FT 60, PT 167 **Student-Faculty Ratio:** 18:1 **Library Holdings:** 79,000 **Regional Accreditation:** North Central Association of Colleges and Schools **Credit Hours For Degree:** 61 credit hours, Associates **Professional Accreditation:** ADA, AOTA, JRCERT, NLN **Intercollegiate Athletics:** Baseball M; Basketball M & W; Softball W; Volleyball W

LAKE SUPERIOR STATE UNIVERSITY
650 W Easterday Ave.
Sault Sainte Marie, MI 49783
Tel: (906)632-6841; 888-800-LSSU
Admissions: (906)635-2231
Fax: (906)635-6669
E-mail: admissions@lssu.edu
Web Site: http://www.lssu.edu/
President/CEO: Dr. Betty J. Youngblood
Registrar: Arlene MacaPherson
Admissions: Susan Camp
Financial Aid: Deborah Faust
Type: Four-Year College **Sex:** Coed **Scores:** 58% ACT 18-23; 21% ACT 24-29 **% Accepted:** 85 **Admission Plans:** Deferred Admission **Application Deadline:** August 15 **Application Fee:** $20.00 **H.S. Requirements:** High school diploma required; GED accepted **Costs Per Year:** Application fee: $20. State resident tuition: $5988 full-time, $249.50 per credit hour part-time. Nonresident tuition: $11,976 full-time, $499 per credit hour part-time. Mandatory fees: $318 full-time, $7 per credit hour part-time, $75 per term part-time. Full-time tuition and fees vary according to reciprocity agreements. Part-time tuition and fees vary according to course load and reciprocity agreements. College room and board: $6536. Room and board charges vary according to board plan and housing facility. **Scholarships:** Available **Calendar System:** Semester, Summer Session Available **Enrollment:** FT 2,315, PT 573 **Faculty:** FT 112, PT 99 **Student-Faculty Ratio:** 17:1 **Exams:** ACT **% Receiving Financial Aid:** 64 **% Residing in College-Owned, -Operated, or -Affiliated Housing:** 29 **Library Holdings:** 200,449 **Regional Accreditation:** North Central Association of Colleges and Schools **Credit Hours For**

Degree: 62 semester hours, Associates; 124 semester hours, Bachelors **Professional Accreditation:** ABET, NLN **Intercollegiate Athletics:** Basketball M & W; Cross-Country Running M & W; Golf M; Ice Hockey M; Softball W; Tennis M & W; Track and Field M & W; Volleyball W

LANSING COMMUNITY COLLEGE
PO Box 40010
Lansing, MI 48901-7210
Tel: (517)483-1957
Free: 800-644-4LCC
Admissions: (517)483-9886
Fax: (517)483-9668
E-mail: grossbt@lcc.edu
Web Site: http://www.lcc.edu/
President/CEO: Paula Cunningham
Registrar: Tom Hoiles
Admissions: Tammy Grossbauer
Financial Aid: Evan Montague
Type: Two-Year College **Sex:** Coed **Affiliation:** Michigan Department of Education **% Accepted:** 100 **Admission Plans:** Open Admission; Preferred Admission; Early Admission; Deferred Admission **Application Deadline:** Rolling **Application Fee:** $0.00 **H.S. Requirements:** High school diploma or equivalent not required. For allied health programs, international students: High school diploma required; GED accepted **Costs Per Year:** Application fee: $0. Area resident tuition: $1975 full-time, $65 per contact hour part-time. State resident tuition: $3175 full-time, $105 per contact hour part-time. Nonresident tuition: $4375 full-time, $145 per contact hour part-time. Mandatory fees: $50 full-time, $25 per term part-time. **Scholarships:** Available **Calendar System:** Semester, Summer Session Available **Enrollment:** FT 6,154, PT 13,903 **Faculty:** FT 227, PT 1,156 **Student-Faculty Ratio:** 14:1 **Library Holdings:** 98,125 **Regional Accreditation:** North Central Association of Colleges and Schools **Credit Hours For Degree:** 60 semester hours, Associates **ROTC:** Army, Air Force **Professional Accreditation:** ADA, JRCERT, JRCEMT, NAACLS, NLN **Intercollegiate Athletics:** Basketball M & W; Cross-Country Running M & W; Golf M; Track and Field M & W; Volleyball W

LAWRENCE TECHNOLOGICAL UNIVERSITY
21000 West Ten Mile Rd.
Southfield, MI 48075-1058
Tel: (248)204-4000
Free: 800-225-5588
Admissions: (248)204-3160
Fax: (248)204-3727
E-mail: admissions@ltu.edu
Web Site: http://www.ltu.edu/
President/CEO: Dr. Charles M. Chambers
Registrar: Holly Diamond
Admissions: Jane Rohrback
Financial Aid: Mark Martin
Type: University **Sex:** Coed **Scores:** 84% SAT V 400+; 90% SAT M 400+; 45% ACT 18-23; 36% ACT 24-29 **% Accepted:** 76 **Application Deadline:** August 15 **Application Fee:** $30.00 **H.S. Requirements:** High school diploma required; GED accepted **Costs Per Year:** Application fee: $30. Comprehensive fee: $26,709 includes full-time tuition ($19,073), mandatory fees ($370), and college room and board ($7266). College room only: $5286. Part-time tuition: $635 per credit hour. Part-time mandatory fees: $185 per term. **Scholarships:** Available **Calendar System:** Semester, Summer Session Available **Enrollment:** FT 1,604, PT 1,264, Grad 1,254 **Faculty:** FT 113, PT 276 **Student-Faculty Ratio:** 12:1 **Exams:** SAT I or ACT, SAT I **% Receiving Financial Aid:** 57 **% Residing in College-Owned, -Operated, or -Affiliated Housing:** 14 **Library Holdings:** 110,250 **Regional Accreditation:** North Central Association of Colleges and Schools **Credit Hours For Degree:** 60 credit hours, Associates; 120 credit hours, Bachelors **ROTC:** Army, Air Force **Professional Accreditation:** ABET, ACBSP, FIDER, NASAD

LEWIS COLLEGE OF BUSINESS
17370 Meyers Rd.
Detroit, MI 48235-1423
Tel: (313)862-6300
Fax: (313)862-1027
Web Site: http://www.lewiscollege.edu/
President/CEO: Dr. Marjorie Harris
Registrar: Sherely Fordum
Admissions: Carl King
Financial Aid: Kamisha Watts
Type: Two-Year College **Sex:** Coed **Admission Plans:** Open Admission; Early Admission; Deferred Admission **Application Fee:** $15.00 **H.S. Requirements:** High school diploma required; GED accepted **Scholarships:** Available **Calendar System:** Semester, Summer Session Available **Faculty:** FT 9, PT 27 **Student-Faculty Ratio:** 15:1 **Library Holdings:** 3,355 **Regional Accreditation:** North Central Association of Colleges and Schools **Credit Hours For Degree:** 67 credit hours, Associates **Intercollegiate Athletics:** Basketball M

MACOMB COMMUNITY COLLEGE
14500 East Twelve Mile Rd.
Warren, MI 48088-3896
Tel: (586)445-7000; (866)622-6624
Admissions: (586)445-7183
Fax: (586)445-7140
E-mail: hughesr@macomb.edu
Web Site: http://www.macomb.edu/
President/CEO: Dr. Albert L. Lorenzo
Registrar: Ronald Hughes
Admissions: Ron Hughes
Financial Aid: Judith Florian
Type: Two-Year College **Sex:** Coed **Admission Plans:** Open Admission; Early Admission; Deferred Admission **Application Deadline:** Rolling **Application Fee:** $0.00 **H.S. Requirements:** High school diploma or equivalent not required **Costs Per Year:** Application fee: $0. Area resident tuition: $2108 full-time, $68 per credit hour part-time. State resident tuition: $3224 full-time, $104 per credit hour part-time. Nonresident tuition: $4185 full-time, $135 per credit hour part-time. Mandatory fees: $40 full-time, $20 per term part-time. **Scholarships:** Available **Calendar System:** Semester, Summer Session Available **Enrollment:** FT 7,520, PT 13,076 **Faculty:** FT 229, PT 803 **Student-Faculty Ratio:** 28:1 **Library Holdings:** 159,226 **Regional Accreditation:** North Central Association of Colleges and Schools **Credit Hours For Degree:** 62 semester hours, Associates **Professional Accreditation:** ARCEST, AAMAE, ACF, AOTA, APTA, CARC, NLN **Intercollegiate Athletics:** Baseball M; Basketball M; Cross-Country Running M & W; Soccer M; Softball W; Track and Field M & W; Volleyball W

MADONNA UNIVERSITY
36600 Schoolcraft Rd.
Livonia, MI 48150-1173
Tel: (734)432-5300
Free: 800-852-4951
Admissions: (734)432-5317
Fax: (734)432-5393
E-mail: muinfo@smtp.munet.edu
Web Site: http://www.madonna.edu
President/CEO: Sr. Rose Marie Kujawa
Registrar: Steven Grenus
Admissions: Frank J. Hribar
Financial Aid: Chris Ziegler
Type: Comprehensive **Sex:** Coed **Affiliation:** Roman Catholic **Scores:** 54% ACT 18-23; 26% ACT 24-29 **% Accepted:** 86 **Admission Plans:** Early Admission; Deferred Admission **Application Deadline:** Rolling **Application Fee:** $25.00 **H.S. Requirements:** High school diploma required; GED accepted **Costs Per Year:** Application fee: $25. Comprehensive fee: $16,168 includes full-time tuition ($10,300), mandatory fees ($100), and college room and board ($5768). College room only: $2318. Room and board charges vary according to board plan. Part-time tuition: $340 per credit hour. Part-time mandatory fees: $50 per term. **Scholarships:** Available **Calendar System:** Semester, Summer Session Available **Enrollment:** FT 1,679, PT 1,697, Grad 932 **Faculty:** FT 127, PT 273 **Student-Faculty Ratio:** 17:1 **Exams:** SAT I or ACT **% Residing in College-Owned, -Operated, or -Affiliated Housing:** 3 **Library Holdings:** 199,144 **Regional Accreditation:** North Central Association of Colleges and Schools **Credit Hours For Degree:** 60 semester hours, Associates; 120 semester hours, Bachelors **Professional Accreditation:** CSWE, NCATE, NLN **Intercollegiate Athletics:** Baseball M; Basketball M & W; Cross-Country Running M & W; Golf M & W; Soccer M & W; Softball W; Volleyball W

MARYGROVE COLLEGE
8425 West McNichols Rd.
Detroit, MI 48221-2599
Tel: (313)927-1200; (866)313-1297

Admissions: (313)927-1236
Fax: (313)927-1345
E-mail: info@marygrove.edu
Web Site: http://www.marygrove.edu/
President/CEO: Dr. Glenda Price
Registrar: Gayle Reynolds
Admissions: John Ambrose
Financial Aid: Patricia Chaplin
Type: Comprehensive **Sex:** Coed **Affiliation:** Roman Catholic **% Accepted:** 42 **Admission Plans:** Early Admission; Deferred Admission **Application Deadline:** August 15 **Application Fee:** $25.00 **H.S. Requirements:** High school diploma required; GED accepted **Costs Per Year:** Application fee: $25. Comprehensive fee: $19,335 includes full-time tuition ($12,800), mandatory fees ($335), and college room and board ($6200). Part-time tuition: $478 per credit. **Calendar System:** Semester, Summer Session Available **Enrollment:** FT 398, PT 334, Grad 2,859 **Faculty:** FT 65, PT 6 **Student-Faculty Ratio:** 51:1 **Exams:** ACT **% Residing in College-Owned, -Operated, or -Affiliated Housing:** 7 **Library Holdings:** 83,483 **Regional Accreditation:** North Central Association of Colleges and Schools **Credit Hours For Degree:** 64 credits, Associates; 128 credits, Bachelors **Professional Accreditation:** AAFCS, CARC, CSWE, JRCERT, NCATE **Intercollegiate Athletics:** Basketball M & W

MICHIGAN JEWISH INSTITUTE
25401 Coolidge Hwy.
Oak Park, MI 48237-1304
Tel: (248)414-6900
Fax: (248)414-6907
E-mail: thgardin@mji.edu
Web Site: http://www.mji.edu/
Admissions: Dr. T. Hershel Gardin
Type: Four-Year College **Sex:** Coed **Admission Plans:** Open Admission; Early Admission; Early Action; Early Decision Plan; Deferred Admission **Application Fee:** $50.00 **H.S. Requirements:** High school diploma required; GED accepted **Costs Per Year:** Application fee: $50. Tuition: $320 full-time, $320 per credit part-time. Mandatory fees: $50 full-time. **Calendar System:** Semester, Summer Session Available **Faculty:** FT 2, PT 34 **Credit Hours For Degree:** 62 credits, Associates; 120 credits, Bachelors **Professional Accreditation:** ACICS

MICHIGAN STATE UNIVERSITY
East Lansing, MI 48824
Tel: (517)355-1855
Admissions: (517)355-8332
E-mail: admis@msu.edu
Web Site: http://www.msu.edu/
President/CEO: M. Peter McPherson
Registrar: Dr. Linda O. Stanford
Admissions: Pamela Horne
Financial Aid: Richard Eddington-Shipman
Type: University **Sex:** Coed **Scores:** 95.2% SAT V 400+; 97.6% SAT M 400+; 36.5% ACT 18-23; 50.3% ACT 24-29 **% Accepted:** 76 **Admission Plans:** Deferred Admission **Application Deadline:** Rolling **Application Fee:** $35.00 **H.S. Requirements:** High school diploma required; GED accepted **Costs Per Year:** Application fee: $35. State resident tuition: $6705 full-time, $223.50 per credit part-time. Nonresident tuition: $18,458 full-time, $615.25 per credit part-time. Mandatory fees: $882 full-time, $882 per year part-time. Full-time tuition and fees vary according to course load, degree level, program, and student level. Part-time tuition and fees vary according to course load, degree level, program, and student level. College room and board: $5744. College room only: $2488. Room and board charges vary according to board plan and housing facility. **Scholarships:** Available **Calendar System:** Semester, Summer Session Available **Enrollment:** FT 32,200, PT 3,478, Grad 7,996 **Faculty:** FT 2,411, PT 351 **Student-Faculty Ratio:** 18:1 **Exams:** SAT I or ACT **% Receiving Financial Aid:** 40 **% Residing in College-Owned, -Operated, or -Affiliated Housing:** 42 **Library Holdings:** 4,420,208 **Regional Accreditation:** North Central Association of Colleges and Schools **Credit Hours For Degree:** 120 semester hours, Bachelors **ROTC:** Army, Air Force **Professional Accreditation:** AACSB, ABET, ACEJMC, AALE, AAMFT, AACN, AAFCS, ACCE, ADtA, ACSP, AOsA, APA, ASLA, ASLHA, AVMA, CORE, CSWE, FIDER, LCMEAMA, NAACLS NASM, NASPAA, NRPA, SAF **Intercollegiate Athletics:** Baseball M; Basketball M & W; Cheerleading M & W; Crew W; Cross-Country Running M & W; Equestrian Sports M & W; Field Hockey W; Football M; Golf M & W; Gymnastics M & W; Ice Hockey M & W; Lacrosse M; Rugby M & W; Sailing M & W; Skiing (Cross-Country) M & W; Skiing (Downhill) M; Soccer M & W; Softball W; Swimming and Diving M & W; Tennis M & W; Track and Field M & W; Volleyball M & W; Water Polo M & W; Wrestling M

MICHIGAN TECHNOLOGICAL UNIVERSITY
1400 Townsend Dr.
Houghton, MI 49931-1295
Tel: (906)487-1885; 888-MTU-1885
Admissions: (906)487-2335
Fax: (906)487-3343
E-mail: mtu4u@mtu.edu
Web Site: http://www.mtu.edu/
President/CEO: Dr. Glenn D. Mroz
Registrar: Sharron Paris
Admissions: Allison Carter
Financial Aid: Timothy T. Malette
Type: University **Sex:** Coed **Scores:** 98% SAT V 400+; 99% SAT M 400+; 33% ACT 18-23; 51% ACT 24-29 **% Accepted:** 85 **Admission Plans:** Deferred Admission **Application Deadline:** Rolling **Application Fee:** $40.00 **H.S. Requirements:** High school diploma required; GED accepted **Costs Per Year:** Application fee: $40. State resident tuition: $7560 full-time, $252 per credit hour part-time. Nonresident tuition: $18,750 full-time, $625 per credit hour part-time. Mandatory fees: $634 full-time, $316.86 per term part-time. Full-time tuition and fees vary according to course load, location, and program. Part-time tuition and fees vary according to course load, location, and program. College room and board: $6375. College room only: $3120. Room and board charges vary according to board plan and housing facility. **Scholarships:** Available **Calendar System:** Semester, Summer Session Available **Enrollment:** FT 5,159, PT 455, Grad 896 **Faculty:** FT 343, PT 46 **Student-Faculty Ratio:** 11:1 **Exams:** SAT I or ACT **% Receiving Financial Aid:** 49 **% Residing in College-Owned, -Operated, or -Affiliated Housing:** 40 **Library Holdings:** 820,414 **Regional Accreditation:** North Central Association of Colleges and Schools **Credit Hours For Degree:** 64 credit hours, Associates; 120 credit hours, Bachelors **ROTC:** Army, Air Force **Professional Accreditation:** AACSB, ABET, SAF **Intercollegiate Athletics:** Basketball M & W; Cross-Country Running M & W; Fencing M & W; Football M; Ice Hockey M & W; Racquetball M & W; Riflery M & W; Skiing (Cross-Country) M & W; Skiing (Downhill) M & W; Soccer M & W; Squash M & W; Swimming and Diving M & W; Table Tennis M & W; Tennis M & W; Track and Field M & W; Volleyball W; Water Polo M & W

MID MICHIGAN COMMUNITY COLLEGE
1375 South Clare Ave.
Harrison, MI 48625-9447
Tel: (989)386-6622
Admissions: (989)386-6660
Fax: (989)386-9088
Web Site: http://www.midmich.cc.mi.us/
President/CEO: Ronald G. Verch
Registrar: Stephen Eaton
Admissions: Kim Barnes
Financial Aid: Jennifer Cooper
Type: Two-Year College **Sex:** Coed **Affiliation:** Michigan Department of Education **Scores:** 60% ACT 18-23; 7% ACT 24-29 **Admission Plans:** Open Admission; Early Admission **Application Fee:** $0.00 **H.S. Requirements:** High school diploma required; GED accepted **Costs Per Year:** Application fee: $0. Area resident tuition: $2000 full-time. State resident tuition: $3500 full-time. Nonresident tuition: $6400 full-time. Mandatory fees: $150 full-time. **Scholarships:** Available **Calendar System:** Semester, Summer Session Available **Enrollment:** FT 1,465, PT 1,767 **Faculty:** FT 58, PT 198 **Student-Faculty Ratio:** 15:1 **Exams:** ACT **Library Holdings:** 29,450 **Regional Accreditation:** North Central Association of Colleges and Schools **Credit Hours For Degree:** 62 credit hours, Associates **Professional Accreditation:** JRCERT

MONROE COUNTY COMMUNITY COLLEGE
1555 South Raisinville Rd.
Monroe, MI 48161-9047
Tel: (734)242-7300
Admissions: (734)384-4261
Fax: (734)242-9711
Web Site: http://www.monroeccc.edu/
President/CEO: Dr. David E. Nixon
Registrar: Paul C. Schmidt

Admissions: Randell W. Daniels
Financial Aid: Tracy Vogt
Type: Two-Year College **Sex:** Coed **Affiliation:** Michigan Department of Education **Admission Plans:** Open Admission; Early Admission; Deferred Admission **Application Fee:** $25.00 **H.S. Requirements:** High school diploma required; GED accepted **Calendar System:** Semester, Summer Session Available **Enrollment:** FT 1,501, PT 2,442 **Faculty:** FT 54, PT 147 **Exams:** ACT, Other **Library Holdings:** 47,352 **Regional Accreditation:** North Central Association of Colleges and Schools **Credit Hours For Degree:** 60 credit hours, Associates **Professional Accreditation:** ACF, CARC, NLN

MONTCALM COMMUNITY COLLEGE
2800 College Dr.
Sidney, MI 48885-9723
Tel: (989)328-2111
Admissions: (989)328-1206
Fax: (989)328-2950
E-mail: admissions@montcalm.cc.mi.us
Web Site: http://www.montcalm.edu/
President/CEO: Dr. Donald C. Burns
Admissions: Tammy Headworth
Financial Aid: Rebecca Powell
Type: Two-Year College **Sex:** Coed **Affiliation:** Michigan Department of Education **Scores:** 59% ACT 18-23; 15% ACT 24-29 **Admission Plans:** Open Admission; Early Admission; Deferred Admission **Application Fee:** $0.00 **H.S. Requirements:** High school diploma required; GED accepted **Costs Per Year:** Application fee: $0. Area resident tuition: $1920 full-time, $64 per credit hour part-time. State resident tuition: $2940 full-time, $98 per credit hour part-time. Nonresident tuition: $3810 full-time, $127 per credit hour part-time. Mandatory fees: $165 full-time, $5.50 per credit hour part-time. Full-time tuition and fees vary according to course load. Part-time tuition and fees vary according to course load. **Scholarships:** Available **Calendar System:** Semester, Summer Session Available **Enrollment:** FT 674, PT 1,406 **Faculty:** FT 25, PT 108 **Student-Faculty Ratio:** 13:1 **Exams:** ACT, Other **Library Holdings:** 29,848 **Regional Accreditation:** North Central Association of Colleges and Schools **Credit Hours For Degree:** 60 credit hours, Associates

MOTT COMMUNITY COLLEGE
1401 East Ct. St.
Flint, MI 48503-2089
Tel: (810)762-0200
Admissions: (810)762-0315
Fax: (810)762-0292
E-mail: marc.payne@mcc.edu
Web Site: http://www.mcc.edu/
President/CEO: Dr. M. Richard Shaink
Admissions: Marc Payne
Financial Aid: Carlos Cisneros
Type: Two-Year College **Sex:** Coed **Affiliation:** Michigan Labor and Economic Growth Department **% Accepted:** 39 **Admission Plans:** Open Admission; Early Admission; Deferred Admission **Application Deadline:** August 31 **Application Fee:** $0.00 **H.S. Requirements:** High school diploma or equivalent not required. For nursing, allied health programs, applicants under 19: High school diploma required; GED accepted **Costs Per Year:** Application fee: $0. Area resident tuition: $2385 full-time, $79.50 per contact hour part-time. State resident tuition: $3572 full-time, $119.05 per contact hour part-time. Nonresident tuition: $4766 full-time, $158.85 per contact hour part-time. Mandatory fees: $107 full-time, $53.50 per term part-time. **Scholarships:** Available **Calendar System:** Semester, Summer Session Available **Enrollment:** FT 3,663, PT 6,636 **Faculty:** FT 147, PT 362 **Student-Faculty Ratio:** 22:1 **Library Holdings:** 112,251 **Regional Accreditation:** North Central Association of Colleges and Schools **Credit Hours For Degree:** 62 credit hours, Associates **Professional Accreditation:** ADA, AOTA, APTA, CARC, NLN **Intercollegiate Athletics:** Baseball M; Basketball M & W; Cross-Country Running M & W; Golf M; Softball W; Volleyball W

MUSKEGON COMMUNITY COLLEGE
221 South Quarterline Rd.
Muskegon, MI 49442-1493
Tel: (231)773-9131
Admissions: (231)777-0261
Fax: (231)777-0255
E-mail: bamfiej@muskegoncc.edu
Web Site: http://www.muskegon.cc.mi.us/
President/CEO: Dr. Frank P. Marczak
Registrar: John Bamfield
Admissions: John Bamfield
Financial Aid: Mary Jo McCann
Type: Two-Year College **Sex:** Coed **Affiliation:** Michigan Department of Education **Admission Plans:** Open Admission; Early Admission; Deferred Admission **H.S. Requirements:** High school diploma required; GED accepted **Scholarships:** Available **Calendar System:** Semester, Summer Session Available **Faculty:** FT 100, PT 50 **Exams:** SAT I or ACT **Library Holdings:** 48,597 **Regional Accreditation:** North Central Association of Colleges and Schools **Credit Hours For Degree:** 62 credit hours, Associates **Professional Accreditation:** CARC **Intercollegiate Athletics:** Baseball M; Basketball M & W; Golf M & W; Softball W; Tennis M & W; Volleyball W; Wrestling M

NORTH CENTRAL MICHIGAN COLLEGE
1515 Howard St.
Petoskey, MI 49770-8717
Tel: (231)348-6600; 888-298-6605
Admissions: (231)439-6511
Web Site: http://www.ncmc.cc.mi.us/
President/CEO: Dr. Cameron Brunet-Koch
Registrar: Naomi DeWinter
Admissions: Julieanne Tobin
Financial Aid: Sharron Hemme
Type: Two-Year College **Sex:** Coed **Affiliation:** Michigan Department of Education **Admission Plans:** Open Admission **Application Fee:** $0.00 **H.S. Requirements:** High school diploma or equivalent not required. For nursing program: High school diploma required; GED accepted **Scholarships:** Available **Calendar System:** Semester, Summer Session Available **Faculty:** FT 31, PT 102 **Student-Faculty Ratio:** 17:1 **Exams:** ACT **% Residing in College-Owned, -Operated, or -Affiliated Housing:** 3 **Library Holdings:** 29,249 **Regional Accreditation:** North Central Association of Colleges and Schools **Credit Hours For Degree:** 60 credit hours, Associates

NORTHERN MICHIGAN UNIVERSITY
1401 Presque Isle Ave.
Marquette, MI 49855-5301
Tel: (906)227-1000
Free: 800-682-9797
Admissions: (906)227-2650
Fax: (906)227-1747
E-mail: admiss@nmu.edu
Web Site: http://www.nmu.edu/
President/CEO: Dr. Leslie E. Wong
Registrar: Dr. Marilyn M. Robbert
Admissions: Gerri Daniels
Financial Aid: Mark J. Delorey
Type: Comprehensive **Sex:** Coed **Scores:** 54% ACT 18-23; 36% ACT 24-29 **% Accepted:** 84 **Admission Plans:** Deferred Admission **Application Deadline:** Rolling **Application Fee:** $30.00 **H.S. Requirements:** High school diploma required; GED accepted **Costs Per Year:** Application fee: $30. One-time mandatory fee: $150. State resident tuition: $5328 full-time, $222 per credit hour part-time. Nonresident tuition: $9072 full-time, $378 per credit hour part-time. Mandatory fees: $630 full-time, $30 per term part-time. Part-time tuition and fees vary according to location. College room and board: $6013. Room and board charges vary according to board plan and housing facility. **Scholarships:** Available **Calendar System:** Semester, Summer Session Available **Enrollment:** FT 7,841, PT 873, Grad 665 **Faculty:** FT 305, PT 117 **Student-Faculty Ratio:** 23:1 **Exams:** SAT I or ACT **% Receiving Financial Aid:** 61 **% Residing in College-Owned, -Operated, or -Affiliated Housing:** 32 **Library Holdings:** 592,689 **Regional Accreditation:** North Central Association of Colleges and Schools **Credit Hours For Degree:** 62 credit hours, Associates; 124 credit hours, Bachelors **ROTC:** Army **Professional Accreditation:** AACSB, AACN, ASLHA, CSWE, NAACLS, NAIT, NASM, NCATE **Intercollegiate Athletics:** Basketball M & W; Cheerleading M & W; Crew M & W; Cross-Country Running W; Equestrian Sports M & W; Football M; Golf M; Ice Hockey M & W;

Lacrosse M; Rugby M & W; Skiing (Cross-Country) M & W; Skiing (Downhill) M & W; Soccer W; Softball W; Swimming and Diving W; Track and Field W; Volleyball W

NORTHWESTERN MICHIGAN COLLEGE
1701 East Front St.
Traverse City, MI 49686-3061
Tel: (231)995-1000
Free: 800-748-0566
Admissions: (231)995-1034
Fax: (231)995-1680
Web Site: http://www.nmc.edu/
President/CEO: Timothy J. Nelson
Registrar: Charles Shreve
Admissions: James Bensley
Financial Aid: Deborah Faas
Type: Two-Year College **Sex:** Coed **Admission Plans:** Open Admission; Early Admission; Deferred Admission **Application Fee:** $15.00 **H.S. Requirements:** High school diploma required; GED accepted **Costs Per Year:** Application fee: $15. Area resident tuition: $2339 full-time, $68.80 per contact hour part-time. State resident tuition: $4077 full-time, $119.92 per contact hour part-time. Nonresident tuition: $5087 full-time, $149 per contact hour part-time. Mandatory fees: $383 full-time, $10.33 per contact hour part-time, $16 per term part-time. Part-time tuition and fees vary according to course load. College room and board: $6285. Room and board charges vary according to board plan and housing facility. **Scholarships:** Available **Calendar System:** Semester, Summer Session Available **Enrollment:** FT 2,011, PT 2,598 **Faculty:** FT 92, PT 215 **Student-Faculty Ratio:** 23:1 **Exams:** Other **% Residing in College-Owned, -Operated, or -Affiliated Housing:** 5 **Library Holdings:** 97,458 **Regional Accreditation:** North Central Association of Colleges and Schools **Credit Hours For Degree:** 64 credits, Associates **Professional Accreditation:** ACF, ADA, ACBSP

NORTHWOOD UNIVERSITY
4000 Whiting Dr.
Midland, MI 48640-2398
Tel: (989)837-4200
Free: 800-457-7878
Admissions: (989)837-4367
Fax: (989)837-4490
E-mail: admissions@northwood.edu
Web Site: http://www.northwood.edu/
President/CEO: Dr. David E. Fry
Registrar: Tina Brisbois
Admissions: Dr. David D. Long
Financial Aid: Terri Mieler
Type: Comprehensive **Sex:** Coed **Scores:** 86% SAT V 400+; 87% SAT M 400+; 62% ACT 18-23; 18% ACT 24-29 **% Accepted:** 85 **Admission Plans:** Early Admission; Deferred Admission **Application Deadline:** Rolling **Application Fee:** $25.00 **H.S. Requirements:** High school diploma required; GED accepted **Costs Per Year:** Application fee: $25. Comprehensive fee: $22,475 includes full-time tuition ($15,216), mandatory fees ($317), and college room and board ($6942). College room only: $3567. Part-time tuition: $317 per credit hour. **Scholarships:** Available **Calendar System:** Quarter, Summer Session Available **Enrollment:** FT 2,587, PT 990, Grad 311 **Faculty:** FT 46, PT 31 **Student-Faculty Ratio:** 34:1 **Exams:** SAT I or ACT **% Receiving Financial Aid:** 58 **% Residing in College-Owned, -Operated, or -Affiliated Housing:** 39 **Library Holdings:** 41,275 **Regional Accreditation:** North Central Association of Colleges and Schools **Credit Hours For Degree:** 90 credit hours, Associates; 180 credit hours, Bachelors **Intercollegiate Athletics:** Baseball M; Basketball M & W; Cheerleading M & W; Cross-Country Running M & W; Football M; Golf M & W; Soccer M & W; Softball W; Tennis M & W; Track and Field M & W; Volleyball W

OAKLAND COMMUNITY COLLEGE
2480 Opdyke Rd.
Bloomfield Hills, MI 48304-2266
Tel: (248)341-2000
Admissions: (248)341-2186
Fax: (248)341-2099
Web Site: http://www.oaklandcc.edu/
President/CEO: Richard T. Thompson
Registrar: Dr. Maurice McCall
Admissions: Dr. Maurice H. McCall
Type: Two-Year College **Sex:** Coed **Affiliation:** Michigan Department of Career Development **% Accepted:** 100 **Admission Plans:** Open Admission; Deferred Admission **Application Deadline:** Rolling **Application Fee:** $0.00 **H.S. Requirements:** High school diploma or equivalent not required. For allied health programs: High school diploma required; GED accepted **Costs Per Year:** Application fee: $0. Area resident tuition: $1704 full-time, $56.80 per credit hour part-time. State resident tuition: $2885 full-time, $96.15 per credit hour part-time. Nonresident tuition: $4045 full-time, $134.83 per credit hour part-time. Mandatory fees: $70 full-time, $35 per term part-time. **Scholarships:** Available **Calendar System:** Semester, Summer Session Available **Enrollment:** FT 7,705, PT 16,582 **Faculty:** FT 275, PT 670 **Student-Faculty Ratio:** 27:1 **Library Holdings:** 243,137 **Regional Accreditation:** North Central Association of Colleges and Schools **Credit Hours For Degree:** 62 credit hours, Associates **Professional Accreditation:** AAMAE, ACF, ADA, CARC, JRCEDMS, JRCERT, NLN **Intercollegiate Athletics:** Basketball M & W; Cross-Country Running M & W; Golf M; Soccer M; Softball W; Tennis W; Volleyball W

OAKLAND UNIVERSITY
Rochester, MI 48309-4401
Tel: (248)370-2100
Free: 800-OAK-UNIV
Admissions: (248)370-4467
Fax: (248)370-4462
E-mail: ouinfo@oakland.edu
Web Site: http://www.oakland.edu/
President/CEO: Dr. Gary D. Russi
Registrar: Steven J. Shablin
Admissions: Eleanor Reynolds
Financial Aid: Cindy Hermsen
Type: University **Sex:** Coed **Scores:** 54.1% ACT 18-23; 28.3% ACT 24-29 **% Accepted:** 82 **Admission Plans:** Early Action; Deferred Admission **Application Deadline:** Rolling **Application Fee:** $40.00 **H.S. Requirements:** High school diploma required; GED accepted **Costs Per Year:** Application fee: $40. State resident tuition: $6443 full-time, $204.75 per credit part-time. Nonresident tuition: $14,869 full-time, $478.50 per credit part-time. Full-time tuition varies according to program and student level. Part-time tuition varies according to program and student level. College room and board: $6080. Room and board charges vary according to housing facility. **Scholarships:** Available **Calendar System:** Semester, Summer Session Available **Enrollment:** FT 9,760, PT 3,688, Grad 3,891 **Faculty:** FT 449, PT 441 **Student-Faculty Ratio:** 23:1 **Exams:** SAT I and SAT II or ACT **% Receiving Financial Aid:** 31 **% Residing in College-Owned, -Operated, or -Affiliated Housing:** 13 **Regional Accreditation:** North Central Association of Colleges and Schools **Credit Hours For Degree:** 124 credits, Bachelors **ROTC:** Air Force **Professional Accreditation:** AACSB, ABET, AACN, AANA, ACA, APTA, ASC, NASD, NASM, NASPAA, NAST, NCATE **Intercollegiate Athletics:** Baseball M; Basketball M & W; Cross-Country Running M & W; Golf M & W; Ice Hockey M & W; Soccer M & W; Softball W; Swimming and Diving M & W; Tennis W; Track and Field M & W; Volleyball W

OLIVET COLLEGE
320 South Main St.
Olivet, MI 49076-9701
Tel: (269)749-7000
Free: 800-456-7189
Fax: (616)749-3821
E-mail: kleonard@olivetcollege.edu
Web Site: http://www.olivetcollege.edu/
President/CEO: Dr. Donald L. Tuski
Registrar: Nicole Baker
Admissions: Tom Shaw
Financial Aid: Douglas Gilbertson
Type: Comprehensive **Sex:** Coed **Affiliation:** Congregational Christian Church **Scores:** 68% ACT 18-23; 16% ACT 24-29 **Admission Plans:** Deferred Admission **Application Fee:** $25.00 **H.S. Requirements:** High school diploma required; GED accepted **Costs Per Year:** Application fee: $25. Comprehensive fee: $21,944 includes full-time tuition ($15,970), mandatory fees ($494), and college room and board ($5480). College room only: $2980. Full-time tuition and fees vary according to reciprocity agreements. Room and board charges vary according to board plan and housing facility. Part-time tuition: $515 per credit. Part-time tuition varies according to course load and reciprocity agreements. **Scholarships:** Available **Calendar System:** Miscellaneous, Summer Session Available **Enrollment:** FT 954, PT 69, Grad 46 **Faculty:** FT 34, PT 33 **Student-Faculty Ratio:** 15:1 **Exams:**

SAT I or ACT **% Receiving Financial Aid:** 87 **% Residing in College-Owned, -Operated, or -Affiliated Housing:** 59 **Library Holdings:** 90,000 **Regional Accreditation:** North Central Association of Colleges and Schools **Credit Hours For Degree:** 120 semester hours, Bachelors **Intercollegiate Athletics:** Baseball M; Basketball M & W; Cross-Country Running M & W; Football M; Golf M & W; Soccer M & W; Softball W; Swimming and Diving M & W; Tennis M & W; Track and Field M & W; Volleyball W; Wrestling M

ROCHESTER COLLEGE
800 West Avon Rd.
Rochester Hills, MI 48307-2764
Tel: (248)218-2000
Free: 800-521-6010
Admissions: (248)218-2032
Fax: (248)218-2005
E-mail: admissions@rc.edu
Web Site: http://www.rc.edu/
President/CEO: Dr. Michael W. Westerfield
Registrar: Cathy MacKenzie
Admissions: Kelvin Brown
Financial Aid: Lee Watson
Type: Four-Year College **Sex:** Coed **Affiliation:** Church of Christ **Scores:** 92% SAT V 400+; 76% SAT M 400+; 51% ACT 18-23; 29% ACT 24-29 **% Accepted:** 87 **Admission Plans:** Early Admission; Deferred Admission **Application Deadline:** Rolling **Application Fee:** $25.00 **H.S. Requirements:** High school diploma required; GED accepted **Costs Per Year:** Application fee: $25. Comprehensive fee: $18,916 includes full-time tuition ($11,120), mandatory fees ($1236), and college room and board ($6560). Room and board charges vary according to board plan and housing facility. Part-time tuition: $360 per credit hour. Part-time mandatory fees: $180 per term. Part-time tuition and fees vary according to course load. **Scholarships:** Available **Calendar System:** Semester, Summer Session Available **Enrollment:** FT 690, PT 357, Grad 8 **Faculty:** FT 45, PT 90 **Student-Faculty Ratio:** 14:1 **% Receiving Financial Aid:** 84 **% Residing in College-Owned, -Operated, or -Affiliated Housing:** 26 **Library Holdings:** 55,000 **Regional Accreditation:** North Central Association of Colleges and Schools **Credit Hours For Degree:** 64 credit hours, Associates; 128 credit hours, Bachelors **Intercollegiate Athletics:** Baseball M; Basketball M & W; Soccer M & W; Softball W; Volleyball W

SACRED HEART MAJOR SEMINARY
2701 Chicago Blvd.
Detroit, MI 48206-1799
Tel: (313)883-8500
Admissions: (313)883-8710
Web Site: http://www.archdioceseofdetroit.org/shms/shms.htm
President/CEO: Very Rev. Steven Boguslawski
Registrar: Janet Galea
Admissions: John Lajiness
Type: Comprehensive **Sex:** Coed **Affiliation:** Roman Catholic **% Accepted:** 100 **Admission Plans:** Preferred Admission; Deferred Admission **Application Deadline:** July 31 **Application Fee:** $30.00 **H.S. Requirements:** High school diploma required; GED accepted **Costs Per Year:** Application fee: $30. Comprehensive fee: $16,671 includes full-time tuition ($10,341), mandatory fees ($80), and college room and board ($6250). Full-time tuition and fees vary according to course load. Part-time tuition: $245 per credit hour. Part-time mandatory fees: $40 per term. Part-time tuition and fees vary according to course load. **Scholarships:** Available **Calendar System:** Semester, Summer Session Not available **Enrollment:** FT 45, PT 254, Grad 110 **Faculty:** FT 27, PT 13 **Student-Faculty Ratio:** 10:1 **Exams:** SAT I or ACT **Library Holdings:** 136,975 **Regional Accreditation:** North Central Association of Colleges and Schools **Credit Hours For Degree:** 64 credits, Associates; 120 credits, Bachelors **Professional Accreditation:** ACIPE, ATS

SAGINAW CHIPPEWA TRIBAL COLLEGE
2274 Enterprise Dr.
Mount Pleasant, MI 48858
Tel: (989)775-4123
Fax: (989)775-4528
E-mail: treed@sagchip.org
Web Site: http://www.sagchip.org/tribalcollege/
President/CEO: Dr. Jeffrey L. Hamley
Admissions: Tracy Reed
Type: Two-Year College **Sex:** Coed **% Accepted:** 100 **Application Fee:** $0.00 **Costs Per Year:** Application fee: $0. Tuition: $1320 full-time, $55 per credit hour part-time. Mandatory fees: $136 full-time, $68 per term part-time. **Calendar System:** Semester **Enrollment:** FT 43, PT 80 **Faculty:** FT 4, PT 13 **Student-Faculty Ratio:** 9:1 **Regional Accreditation:** North Central Association of Colleges and Schools

SAGINAW VALLEY STATE UNIVERSITY
7400 Bay Rd.
University Center, MI 48710
Tel: (989)964-4000
Free: 800-968-9500
Admissions: (989)964-4200
Fax: (989)964-0180
E-mail: admissions@svsu.edu
Web Site: http://www.svsu.edu/
President/CEO: Dr. Eric R. Gilbertson
Registrar: Chris J. Looney
Admissions: James P. Dwyer
Financial Aid: Robert Lemuel
Type: Comprehensive **Sex:** Coed **Scores:** 54.9% ACT 18-23; 24% ACT 24-29 **% Accepted:** 89 **Admission Plans:** Deferred Admission **Application Deadline:** Rolling **Application Fee:** $25.00 **H.S. Requirements:** High school diploma required; GED accepted **Costs Per Year:** Application fee: $25. State resident tuition: $4,876 full-time, $162.55 per credit hour part-time. Nonresident tuition: $11,486 full-time, $382.85 per credit hour part-time. Mandatory fees: $405 full-time, $13.50 per credit hour part-time. Full-time tuition and fees vary according to course level, course load, location, and program. Part-time tuition and fees vary according to course level, course load, location, and program. College room and board: $6150. College room only: $3600. Room and board charges vary according to board plan, housing facility, and student level. **Scholarships:** Available **Calendar System:** Semester, Summer Session Available **Enrollment:** FT 6,044, PT 1,885, Grad 1,640 **Faculty:** FT 260, PT 300 **Student-Faculty Ratio:** 20:1 **Exams:** ACT **% Receiving Financial Aid:** 53 **% Residing in College-Owned, -Operated, or -Affiliated Housing:** 13 **Library Holdings:** 226,952 **Regional Accreditation:** North Central Association of Colleges and Schools **Credit Hours For Degree:** 124 credit hours, Bachelors **Professional Accreditation:** AACSB, ABET, AOTA, CSWE, NCATE, NLN **Intercollegiate Athletics:** Baseball M; Basketball M & W; Bowling M; Cheerleading M & W; Cross-Country Running M & W; Football M; Golf M; Lacrosse W; Soccer M & W; Softball W; Tennis W; Track and Field M & W; Volleyball W

ST. CLAIR COUNTY COMMUNITY COLLEGE
323 Erie St., PO Box 5015
Port Huron, MI 48061-5015
Tel: (810)984-3881
Admissions: (810)989-5500
Fax: (810)984-4730
Web Site: http://www.sc4.edu/
President/CEO: Dr. Rose Bellanca
Registrar: Pete Lacey
Admissions: Pete Lacey
Financial Aid: Josephine Cassar
Type: Two-Year College **Sex:** Coed **Affiliation:** Michigan Department of Education **Admission Plans:** Open Admission; Early Admission **Application Fee:** $0.00 **H.S. Requirements:** High school diploma required; GED accepted. Certain applicants 18 or over camn be admitted as special students without a high school diploma or GED: High school diploma or equivalent not required. **Scholarships:** Available **Calendar System:** Semester, Summer Session Available **Faculty:** FT 79, PT 197 **Exams:** ACT **Library Holdings:** 59,134 **Regional Accreditation:** North Central Association of Colleges and Schools **Credit Hours For Degree:** 62 credits, Associates **Intercollegiate Athletics:** Baseball M; Basketball M & W; Golf M; Softball W; Volleyball W

SCHOOLCRAFT COLLEGE
18600 Haggerty Rd.
Livonia, MI 48152-2696
Tel: (734)462-4400
Admissions: (734)462-4426
Fax: (734)462-4553
Web Site: http://www.schoolcraft.edu/
President/CEO: Dr. Conway Jeffress

Registrar: Mary Beaudoin
Admissions: Cheryl Wright
Financial Aid: Cheryl Wright
Type: Two-Year College **Sex:** Coed **Affiliation:** Michigan Department of Education **Admission Plans:** Open Admission; Early Admission; Deferred Admission **Application Fee:** $0.00 **H.S. Requirements:** High school diploma required; GED accepted **Costs Per Year:** Application fee: $0. Area resident tuition: $1950 full-time, $65 per credit hour part-time. State resident tuition: $2910 full-time, $97 per credit hour part-time. Nonresident tuition: $4290 full-time, $143 per credit hour part-time. Mandatory fees: $130 full-time. **Scholarships:** Available **Calendar System:** Semester, Summer Session Available **Enrollment:** FT 3,377, PT 6,836 **Faculty:** FT 99, PT 336 **Student-Faculty Ratio:** 27:1 **Exams:** ACT, Other **Library Holdings:** 96,216 **Regional Accreditation:** North Central Association of Colleges and Schools **Credit Hours For Degree:** 60 credit hours, Associates **Professional Accreditation:** AHIMA **Intercollegiate Athletics:** Basketball M & W; Cross-Country Running W; Golf M & W; Soccer M & W; Volleyball W

SIENA HEIGHTS UNIVERSITY
1247 East Siena Heights Dr.
Adrian, MI 49221-1796
Tel: (517)263-0731
Free: 800-521-0009
Admissions: (517)264-7180
Fax: (517)264-7745
E-mail: admissions@sienahts.edu
Web Site: http://www.sienahts.edu
President/CEO: Dr. Richard Artman
Registrar: Amy G. Smith
Admissions: Kevin Kucera
Financial Aid: Deborah Schmidt
Type: Comprehensive **Sex:** Coed **Affiliation:** Roman Catholic **Scores:** 63% ACT 18-23; 24% ACT 24-29 **Admission Plans:** Deferred Admission **Application Fee:** $25.00 **H.S. Requirements:** High school diploma required; GED accepted **Scholarships:** Available **Calendar System:** Semester, Summer Session Available **Faculty:** FT 65 **Student-Faculty Ratio:** 14:1 **Exams:** SAT I or ACT **% Residing in College-Owned, -Operated, or -Affiliated Housing:** 33 **Library Holdings:** 120,407 **Regional Accreditation:** North Central Association of Colleges and Schools **Credit Hours For Degree:** 60 semester hours, Associates; 120 semester hours, Bachelors **Professional Accreditation:** NASAD **Intercollegiate Athletics:** Baseball M; Basketball M & W; Cross-Country Running M & W; Golf M; Soccer M & W; Softball W; Track and Field M & W; Volleyball W

SOUTHWESTERN MICHIGAN COLLEGE
58900 Cherry Grove Rd.
Dowagiac, MI 49047-9793
Tel: (269)782-1000
Free: 800-456-8675
Fax: (269)782-8414
E-mail: mhay@swmich.edu
Web Site: http://www.swmich.edu/
President/CEO: Dr. David Mathews
Registrar: Kathy Peterson
Admissions: Dr. Margaret Hay
Type: Two-Year College **Sex:** Coed **Affiliation:** Michigan Department of Education **% Accepted:** 100 **Admission Plans:** Open Admission; Deferred Admission **Application Deadline:** Rolling **Application Fee:** $0.00 **H.S. Requirements:** High school diploma required; GED accepted **Costs Per Year:** Application fee: $0. Area resident tuition: $2101 full-time. State resident tuition: $2659 full-time. Nonresident tuition: $2868 full-time. Mandatory fees: $465 full-time. Full-time tuition and fees vary according to course load. **Scholarships:** Available **Calendar System:** Semester, Summer Session Available **Enrollment:** FT 1,015, PT 1,661 **Faculty:** FT 45, PT 119 **Student-Faculty Ratio:** 19:1 **Library Holdings:** 38,000 **Regional Accreditation:** North Central Association of Colleges and Schools **Credit Hours For Degree:** 62 credit hours, Associates

SPRING ARBOR UNIVERSITY
106 East Main St.
Spring Arbor, MI 49283-9799
Tel: (517)750-1200
Free: 800-968-0011
Fax: (517)750-1604
E-mail: admissions@arbor.edu
Web Site: http://www.arbor.edu/
President/CEO: Dr. Gayle Beebe
Registrar: Darlene Mefford
Admissions: Randy Comfort
Financial Aid: Lois M. Hardy
Type: Comprehensive **Sex:** Coed **Affiliation:** Free Methodist **Scores:** 97% SAT V 400+; 96% SAT M 400+; 48.4% ACT 18-23; 33.2% ACT 24-29 **% Accepted:** 75 **Admission Plans:** Early Admission; Deferred Admission **Application Deadline:** August 01 **Application Fee:** $30.00 **H.S. Requirements:** High school diploma required; GED accepted **Costs Per Year:** Application fee: $30. Comprehensive fee: $22,476 includes full-time tuition ($16,270), mandatory fees ($396), and college room and board ($5810). College room only: $2730. Room and board charges vary according to board plan, housing facility, and location. Part-time tuition: $350 per credit. Part-time mandatory fees: $306 per year. Part-time tuition and fees vary according to course load and reciprocity agreements. **Scholarships:** Available **Calendar System:** 4-1-4, Summer Session Available **Enrollment:** FT 1,913, PT 697, Grad 1,091 **Faculty:** FT 80, PT 58 **Student-Faculty Ratio:** 15:1 **Exams:** ACT, SAT I or ACT **% Receiving Financial Aid:** 72 **% Residing in College-Owned, -Operated, or -Affiliated Housing:** 63 **Library Holdings:** 100,094 **Regional Accreditation:** North Central Association of Colleges and Schools **Credit Hours For Degree:** 62 credits, Associates; 124 credits, Bachelors **ROTC:** Army **Professional Accreditation:** AACN, CSWE, NCATE **Intercollegiate Athletics:** Baseball M; Basketball M & W; Cross-Country Running M & W; Golf M; Soccer M & W; Softball W; Tennis M & W; Track and Field M & W; Volleyball W

UNIVERSITY OF DETROIT MERCY
4001 W McNichols Rd, PO Box 19900
Detroit, MI 48219-0900
Tel: (313)993-1000
Free: 800-635-5020
Admissions: (313)993-1245
Fax: (313)993-3326
Web Site: http://www.udmercy.edu/
President/CEO: Dr. Gerard L. Stockhausen, SJ
Registrar: Diane M. Praet
Admissions: Denise Williams
Financial Aid: Sandra Ross
Type: University **Sex:** Coed **Affiliation:** Roman Catholic (Jesuit) **Scores:** 49% ACT 18-23; 35% ACT 24-29 **Admission Plans:** Deferred Admission **Application Fee:** $25.00 **H.S. Requirements:** High school diploma required; GED accepted **Costs Per Year:** Application fee: $25. Comprehensive fee: $29,798 includes full-time tuition ($21,900), mandatory fees ($570), and college room and board ($7328). College room only: $4288. Part-time tuition: $535 per credit hour. **Scholarships:** Available **Calendar System:** Semester, Summer Session Available **Enrollment:** FT 1,901, PT 1,410, Grad 1,296 **Faculty:** FT 268, PT 440 **Student-Faculty Ratio:** 13:1 **Exams:** SAT I or ACT **% Receiving Financial Aid:** 82 **% Residing in College-Owned, -Operated, or -Affiliated Housing:** 21 **Regional Accreditation:** North Central Association of Colleges and Schools **Credit Hours For Degree:** 63 credit hours, Associates; 126 credit hours, Bachelors **Professional Accreditation:** AACSB, ABET, AANA, ABA, ACA, ADA, APA, AALS, CSWE, NLN **Intercollegiate Athletics:** Baseball M; Basketball M & W; Cross-Country Running M & W; Fencing M & W; Golf M & W; Soccer M & W; Softball W; Tennis W; Track and Field M & W

UNIVERSITY OF MICHIGAN
Ann Arbor, MI 48109
Tel: (734)764-1817
Admissions: (734)764-7433
Fax: (734)936-0740
E-mail: ugadmiss@umich.edu
Web Site: http://www.umich.edu/
President/CEO: Mary Sue Coleman
Registrar: Paul A. Robinson
Admissions: Ted Spencer
Financial Aid: Pamela Fowler
Type: University **Sex:** Coed **Scores:** 99% SAT V 400+; 99% SAT M 400+; 9% ACT 18-23; 56% ACT 24-29 **% Accepted:** 57 **Admission Plans:** Preferred Admission; Deferred Admission **Application Deadline:** February 01 **Application Fee:** $40.00 **H.S. Requirements:** High school diploma required; GED accepted **Costs Per Year:** Application fee: $40. State resident tuition: $9213 full-time, $349 per hour part-time. Nonresident tuition: $27,602 full-time, $1115 per hour part-time. Mandatory fees: $187 full-time,

$94.69 per term part-time. Full-time tuition and fees vary according to course load, degree level, location, program, and student level. Part-time tuition and fees vary according to course load, degree level, location, program, and student level. College room and board: $7374. Room and board charges vary according to board plan and housing facility. **Scholarships:** Available **Calendar System:** Trimester, Summer Session Available **Enrollment:** FT 24,446, PT 1,021, Grad 11,966 **Faculty:** FT 2,347, PT 589 **Student-Faculty Ratio:** 15:1 **Exams:** SAT I or ACT, SAT II **% Receiving Financial Aid:** 45 **% Residing in College-Owned, -Operated, or -Affiliated Housing:** 37 **Library Holdings:** 7,958,145 **Regional Accreditation:** North Central Association of Colleges and Schools **Credit Hours For Degree:** 120 credits, Bachelors **ROTC:** Army, Air Force **Professional Accreditation:** AACSB, ABET, ARCMI, ACEHSA, AACN, ABA, ACNM, ACPhE, ADA, ADtA, ACSP, ALA, APA, ASLA, AALS, CEPH, CSWE, LCMEAMA, NASAD, NASM SAF **Intercollegiate Athletics:** Baseball M; Basketball M & W; Crew W; Cross-Country Running M & W; Field Hockey W; Football M; Golf M & W; Gymnastics M & W; Ice Hockey M; Soccer M & W; Softball W; Swimming and Diving M & W; Tennis M & W; Track and Field M & W; Volleyball W; Water Polo W; Wrestling M

UNIVERSITY OF MICHIGAN-DEARBORN
4901 Evergreen Rd.
Dearborn, MI 48128-1491
Tel: (313)593-5000
Admissions: (313)593-5100
E-mail: cwtrem@umd.umich.edu
Web Site: http://www.umd.umich.edu/
President/CEO: Dr. Daniel Little
Registrar: Dr. Linda Ellis-Brown
Admissions: Christopher Treblay
Financial Aid: John Mason
Type: Comprehensive **Sex:** Coed **Affiliation:** University of Michigan System **Scores:** 92.3% SAT V 400+; 98% SAT M 400+; 48.5% ACT 18-23; 45% ACT 24-29 **% Accepted:** 71 **Admission Plans:** Deferred Admission **Application Deadline:** Rolling **Application Fee:** $30.00 **H.S. Requirements:** High school diploma required; GED accepted **Costs Per Year:** Application fee: $30. State resident tuition: $6718 full-time, $256.10 per credit hour part-time. Nonresident tuition: $14,858 full-time, $581.50 per credit hour part-time. Mandatory fees: $123 full-time, $123.50 per term part-time. Full-time tuition and fees vary according to course level, course load, program, and student level. Part-time tuition and fees vary according to course level, course load, program, and student level. **Scholarships:** Available **Calendar System:** Semester, Summer Session Available **Enrollment:** FT 4,031, PT 2,540, Grad 2,042 **Faculty:** FT 287, PT 225 **Student-Faculty Ratio:** 16:1 **Exams:** ACT, SAT I or ACT **% Receiving Financial Aid:** 46 **Library Holdings:** 340,897 **Regional Accreditation:** North Central Association of Colleges and Schools **Credit Hours For Degree:** 120 credit hours, Bachelors **ROTC:** Army, Navy, Air Force **Professional Accreditation:** AACSB, ABET **Intercollegiate Athletics:** Basketball M & W; Ice Hockey M; Volleyball W

UNIVERSITY OF MICHIGAN-FLINT
303 East Kearsley St.
Flint, MI 48502-1950
Tel: (810)762-3000
Admissions: (810)762-3434
E-mail: maryjoss@umflint.edu
Web Site: http://www.umflint.edu/
President/CEO: Dr. Juan E. Mestas
Registrar: Karen Arnold
Admissions: Dr. Mary Jo Sekelsky
Financial Aid: Lori Vedder
Type: Comprehensive **Sex:** Coed **Affiliation:** University of Michigan System **Scores:** 79% SAT V 400+; 74% SAT M 400+; 51% ACT 18-23; 27% ACT 24-29 **% Accepted:** 85 **Admission Plans:** Deferred Admission **Application Fee:** $30.00 **H.S. Requirements:** High school diploma required; GED accepted **Costs Per Year:** Application fee: $30. State resident tuition: $6082 full-time, $240 per credit part-time. Nonresident tuition: $11,834 full-time, $480 per credit part-time. Mandatory fees: $316 full-time, $124 per term part-time. Full-time tuition and fees vary according to program. Part-time tuition and fees vary according to program. **Scholarships:** Available **Calendar System:** Semester, Summer Session Available **Enrollment:** FT 3,458, PT 2,213, Grad 692 **Faculty:** FT 213, PT 207 **Student-Faculty Ratio:** 15:1 **Exams:** SAT I or ACT **% Receiving Financial Aid:** 57 **Library Holdings:** 253,182 **Regional Accreditation:** North Central Association of Colleges and Schools **Credit Hours For Degree:** 120 credit hours, Bachelors **Professional Accreditation:** AACSB, AACN, AANA, APTA, CSWE, JRCERT, NASM, NLN

UNIVERSITY OF PHOENIX-METRO DETROIT CAMPUS
5480 Corporate Dr., Ste. 240
Troy, MI 48098-2623
Tel: (248)925-4100
Free: 800-228-7240
Admissions: (480)557-1712
Fax: (248)267-0147
Web Site: http://www.phoenix.edu/
President/CEO: Ted Blashak
Admissions: Nina Omelchanko
Type: Comprehensive **Sex:** Coed **Admission Plans:** Open Admission; Deferred Admission **Application Deadline:** Rolling **Application Fee:** $110.00 **H.S. Requirements:** High school diploma required; GED accepted **Costs Per Year:** Application fee: $110. Tuition: $11,340 full-time, $378 per credit part-time. Mandatory fees: $560 full-time, $70 per course part-time. **Scholarships:** Available **Calendar System:** Continuous, Summer Session Not available **Enrollment:** FT 2,970, Grad 1,023 **Faculty:** FT 11, PT 330 **Student-Faculty Ratio:** 11:1 **Library Holdings:** 444 **Regional Accreditation:** North Central Association of Colleges and Schools **Credit Hours For Degree:** 60 credits, Associates; 120 credits, Bachelors **Professional Accreditation:** NLN

UNIVERSITY OF PHOENIX-WEST MICHIGAN CAMPUS
318 River Ridge Dr. NW
Grand Rapids, MI 49544-1683
Tel: (616)647-5100
Free: 800-228-7240
Admissions: (480)557-1712
Web Site: http://www.phoenix.edu/
President/CEO: Simon Lumley
Admissions: Nina Omelchanko
Type: Comprehensive **Sex:** Coed **Admission Plans:** Open Admission; Deferred Admission **Application Deadline:** Rolling **Application Fee:** $110.00 **H.S. Requirements:** High school diploma required; GED accepted **Costs Per Year:** Application fee: $110. Tuition: $11,100 full-time, $370 per credit part-time. Mandatory fees: $560 full-time, $70 per course part-time. **Scholarships:** Available **Calendar System:** Continuous, Summer Session Not available **Enrollment:** FT 959, Grad 197 **Faculty:** FT 8, PT 195 **Student-Faculty Ratio:** 6:1 **Library Holdings:** 444 **Regional Accreditation:** North Central Association of Colleges and Schools **Credit Hours For Degree:** 60 credits, Associates; 120 credits, Bachelors **Professional Accreditation:** NLN

WALSH COLLEGE OF ACCOUNTANCY AND BUSINESS ADMINISTRATION
3838 Livernois Rd., PO Box 7006
Troy, MI 48007-7006
Tel: (248)689-8282
Admissions: (248)823-1209
Fax: (248)524-2520
Web Site: http://www.walshcollege.edu/
President/CEO: Keith Pretty
Registrar: Victoria R. Scavone
Admissions: Victoria R. Scavone
Financial Aid: Howard Thomas
Type: Two-Year Upper Division **Sex:** Coed **Admission Plans:** Open Admission; Deferred Admission **Application Fee:** $25.00 **Costs Per Year:** Application fee: $25. Tuition: $9000 full-time, $250 per credit part-time. Mandatory fees: $230 full-time, $115 per term part-time. **Scholarships:** Available **Calendar System:** Miscellaneous, Summer Session Available **Enrollment:** FT 145, PT 764, Grad 2,196 **Faculty:** FT 14, PT 114 **Student-Faculty Ratio:** 20:1 **% Receiving Financial Aid:** 41 **Library Holdings:** 26,300 **Regional Accreditation:** North Central Association of Colleges and Schools **Credit Hours For Degree:** 127 credit hours, Bachelors

WASHTENAW COMMUNITY COLLEGE
4800 East Huron River Dr., PO Box D-1
Ann Arbor, MI 48106
Tel: (734)973-3300
Admissions: (734)973-3315
Fax: (734)677-5408

Web Site: http://www.wccnet.edu/
President/CEO: Dr. Larry L. Whitworth
Registrar: Linda Blakey
Admissions: Sukanya J. Jett
Financial Aid: Guy Hower
Type: Two-Year College **Sex:** Coed **Admission Plans:** Open Admission; Preferred Admission; Early Admission; Deferred Admission **H.S. Requirements:** High school diploma required; GED accepted. For health occupations programs only, otherwise open enrollment: High school diploma required; GED accepted **Scholarships:** Available **Calendar System:** Semester, Summer Session Available **Enrollment:** FT 3,432, PT 8,638 **Faculty:** FT 162, PT 610 **Student-Faculty Ratio:** 17:1 **Exams:** SAT I or ACT **Library Holdings:** 76,500 **Regional Accreditation:** North Central Association of Colleges and Schools **Credit Hours For Degree:** 60 credit hours, Associates **ROTC:** Army, Navy, Air Force **Professional Accreditation:** ACF, ADA, JRCERT, NLN

WAYNE COUNTY COMMUNITY COLLEGE DISTRICT
801 West Fort St.
Detroit, MI 48226-3010
Tel: (313)496-2600
Admissions: (313)496-2884
Fax: (313)961-2791
E-mail: caafjh@wccc.edu
Web Site: http://www.wcccd.edu/
President/CEO: Dr. Curtis L. Ivery
Admissions: Patricia Hawkins
Financial Aid: Marcus McGrew
Type: Two-Year College **Sex:** Coed **Admission Plans:** Open Admission; Early Admission; Deferred Admission **Application Fee:** $10.00 **H.S. Requirements:** High school diploma or equivalent not required. For applicants under 18, allied health program: High school diploma required; GED accepted **Scholarships:** Available **Calendar System:** Semester, Summer Session Available **Enrollment:** FT 2,912, PT 8,761 **Faculty:** FT 150, PT 250 **Exams:** Other **Library Holdings:** 70,000 **Regional Accreditation:** North Central Association of Colleges and Schools **Credit Hours For Degree:** 60 credits, Associates **Professional Accreditation:** ARCEST, ADA, AOTA, CARC **Intercollegiate Athletics:** Basketball M & W; Golf M & W; Volleyball W

WAYNE STATE UNIVERSITY
656 West Kirby St.
Detroit, MI 48202
Tel: (313)577-2424
Free: 800-WSU-INFO
Admissions: (313)577-3577
Fax: (313)577-7536
E-mail: admissions@wayne.edu
Web Site: http://www.wayne.edu/
President/CEO: Dr. Irvin D. Reid
Registrar: Linda Falkiewicz
Admissions: Susan Zwieg
Financial Aid: Catherine Kay
Type: University **Sex:** Coed **Scores:** 45% ACT 18-23; 21% ACT 24-29 **% Accepted:** 60 **Admission Plans:** Deferred Admission **Application Deadline:** August 01 **Application Fee:** $30.00 **H.S. Requirements:** High school diploma required; GED accepted **Costs Per Year:** Application fee: $30. State resident tuition: $5682 full-time, $189.40 per semester hour part-time. Nonresident tuition: $13,014 full-time, $433.80 per semester hour part-time. Mandatory fees: $757 full-time, $15.80 per semester hour part-time, $141.70 per term part-time. Full-time tuition and fees vary according to student level. Part-time tuition and fees vary according to student level. College room and board: $5350. Room and board charges vary according to housing facility. **Scholarships:** Available **Calendar System:** Semester, Summer Session Available **Enrollment:** FT 11,924, PT 8,813, Grad 9,348 **Faculty:** FT 1,004, PT 913 **Student-Faculty Ratio:** 16:1 **Exams:** SAT I or ACT **% Receiving Financial Aid:** 54 **% Residing in College-Owned, -Operated, or -Affiliated Housing:** 7 **Library Holdings:** 1,883,570 **Regional Accreditation:** North Central Association of Colleges and Schools **Credit Hours For Degree:** 120 credit hours, Bachelors **ROTC:** Air Force **Professional Accreditation:** AACSB, ABET, AACN, AANA, ABA, ABFSE, ACNM, ACPhE, ACA, ADtA, ACSP, ALA, AOTA, APTA, APA, ASC, ASLHA, AALS, CORE, CSWE JRCERT, LCMEAMA, NAACLS, NASD, NASM, NASPAA, NAST, NLN **Intercollegiate Athletics:** Baseball M; Basketball M & W; Cross-Country Running M & W; Fencing M & W; Football M; Golf M; Ice Hockey M & W; Softball W; Swimming and Diving M & W; Tennis M & W; Volleyball W

WEST SHORE COMMUNITY COLLEGE
PO Box 277, 3000 North Stiles Rd.
Scottville, MI 49454-0277
Tel: (231)845-6211
Fax: (231)845-0207
E-mail: admissions@westshore.cc.mi.us
Web Site: http://www.westshore.edu/
President/CEO: Dr. Charles T. Dillon
Registrar: Dr. Denise Ottinger
Admissions: Tom Bell
Financial Aid: Victoria Oddo
Type: Two-Year College **Sex:** Coed **Affiliation:** Michigan Department of Education **Admission Plans:** Open Admission; Early Admission; Deferred Admission **Application Fee:** $10.00 **H.S. Requirements:** High school diploma or equivalent not required. For nursing program: High school diploma required; GED not accepted **Scholarships:** Available **Calendar System:** Semester, Summer Session Available **Faculty:** FT 25, PT 30 **Student-Faculty Ratio:** 25:1 **Exams:** ACT, Other **Library Holdings:** 2,500 **Regional Accreditation:** North Central Association of Colleges and Schools **Credit Hours For Degree:** 60 credits, Associates

WESTERN MICHIGAN UNIVERSITY
1903 West Michigan Ave.
Kalamazoo, MI 49008-5202
Tel: (269)387-1000
Admissions: (269)387-2000
Fax: (269)387-2096
E-mail: ask-wmu@wmich.edu
Web Site: http://www.wmich.edu/
President/CEO: Dr. Judith I. Bailey
Admissions: Pamela Liberacki
Financial Aid: Susan O'Flaherty
Type: University **Sex:** Coed **Scores:** 59% ACT 18-23; 30.1% ACT 24-29 **% Accepted:** 85 **Admission Plans:** Deferred Admission **Application Deadline:** Rolling **Application Fee:** $35.00 **H.S. Requirements:** High school diploma required; GED accepted **Costs Per Year:** Application fee: $35. State resident tuition: $5826 full-time, $194.18 per credit hour part-time. Nonresident tuition: $15,204 full-time, $506.81 per credit hour part-time. Mandatory fees: $652 full-time, $165.75 per term part-time. Full-time tuition and fees vary according to course load, location, and student level. Part-time tuition and fees vary according to course load, location, and student level. College room and board: $6651. College room only: $3518. Room and board charges vary according to board plan. **Scholarships:** Available **Calendar System:** Semester, Summer Session Available **Enrollment:** FT 18,760, PT 2,674, Grad 4,805 **Faculty:** FT 922, PT 538 **Student-Faculty Ratio:** 20:1 **Exams:** SAT I or ACT **% Receiving Financial Aid:** 53 **% Residing in College-Owned, -Operated, or -Affiliated Housing:** 24 **Library Holdings:** 2,040,692 **Regional Accreditation:** North Central Association of Colleges and Schools **Credit Hours For Degree:** 122 credit hours, Bachelors **ROTC:** Army **Professional Accreditation:** AACSB, ABET, AACN, AAFCS, ACA, ADtA, AOTA, APA, ASLHA, CAA, CORE, CSWE, FIDER, NASAD, NASD, NASM, NASPAA, NAST, NCATE, NLN **Intercollegiate Athletics:** Baseball M; Basketball M & W; Cross-Country Running W; Football M; Golf W; Gymnastics W; Ice Hockey M; Soccer M & W; Softball W; Tennis M & W; Track and Field W; Volleyball W

YESHIVA GEDDOLAH OF GREATER DETROIT RABBINICAL COLLEGE
24600 Greenfield
Oak Park, MI 48237-1544
Tel: (810)968-3360
President/CEO: Rabbi P. Rushnawitz
Registrar: Rabbi Y. Bakst
Admissions: Eric Krohner
Financial Aid: Rabbi Y. Blitz
Type: Four-Year College **Sex:** Men **Affiliation:** Jewish **H.S. Requirements:** High school diploma required; GED not accepted **Professional Accreditation:** AARTS

ACADEMY COLLEGE
1101 East 78th St., Ste. 100
Minneapolis, MN 55420
Tel: (952)851-0066
Free: 800-292-9149
Fax: (952)851-0094
Web Site: http://www.academycollege.edu/
President/CEO: Nancy Grazzini-Olson
Admissions: Paul Burhhartzmeyer
Type: Two-Year College **Sex:** Coed **Admission Plans:** Open Admission; Early Admission; Deferred Admission **Application Fee:** $30.00 **H.S. Requirements:** High school diploma required; GED accepted **Scholarships:** Available **Calendar System:** Quarter, Summer Session Available **Faculty:** FT 4, PT 50 **Student-Faculty Ratio:** 8:1 **Library Holdings:** 1,309 **Credit Hours For Degree:** 102 credit hours, Associates; 180 credit hours, Bachelors **Professional Accreditation:** ACICS

ALEXANDRIA TECHNICAL COLLEGE
1601 Jefferson St.
Alexandria, MN 56308-3707
Tel: (320)762-0221; 888-234-1222
Fax: (320)762-4430
E-mail: admissionsrep@alextech.edu
Web Site: http://www.alextech.edu/
President/CEO: Dr. Larry Shellito
Registrar: Gloria Deick
Admissions: Doug Tatge
Financial Aid: Gary McFarland
Type: Two-Year College **Sex:** Coed **Affiliation:** Minnesota State Colleges and Universities System **% Accepted:** 67 **Admission Plans:** Open Admission; Early Admission **Application Deadline:** Rolling **Application Fee:** $20.00 **H.S. Requirements:** High school diploma required; GED accepted **Costs Per Year:** Application fee: $20. State resident tuition: $4318 full-time, $127 per credit part-time. Nonresident tuition: $8636 full-time, $254 per credit part-time. Mandatory fees: $401 full-time, $11.80 per credit part-time. **Scholarships:** Available **Calendar System:** Semester, Summer Session Not available **Enrollment:** FT 1,591, PT 380 **Faculty:** FT 77, PT 12 **Student-Faculty Ratio:** 20:1 **Library Holdings:** 16,636 **Regional Accreditation:** North Central Association of Colleges and Schools **Credit Hours For Degree:** 72 credits, Associates **Professional Accreditation:** NAACLS **Intercollegiate Athletics:** Basketball M; Volleyball W

ANOKA-RAMSEY COMMUNITY COLLEGE
11200 Mississippi Blvd., NW
Coon Rapids, MN 55433-3470
Tel: (763)427-2600
Admissions: (763)422-3420
Fax: (763)576-5944
Web Site: http://www.anokaramsey.edu/
President/CEO: Dr. Patrick M. Johns
Registrar: Rhonda Kern
Admissions: Matthew Crawford
Financial Aid: Karla Seymour
Type: Two-Year College **Sex:** Coed **Affiliation:** Minnesota State Colleges and Universities System **% Accepted:** 99 **Admission Plans:** Open Admission; Early Admission; Deferred Admission **Application Deadline:** Rolling **Application Fee:** $20.00 **H.S. Requirements:** High school diploma required; GED accepted **Costs Per Year:** Application fee: $20. State resident tuition: $3390 full-time, $113 per credit part-time. Nonresident tuition: $6780 full-time, $226 per credit part-time. Mandatory fees: $414 full-time, $13.80 per credit part-time. **Scholarships:** Available **Calendar System:** Semester, Summer Session Available **Enrollment:** FT 2,422, PT 3,371 **Faculty:** FT 95, PT 134 **Student-Faculty Ratio:** 25:1 **Library Holdings:** 40,651 **Regional Accreditation:** North Central Association of Colleges and Schools **Credit Hours For Degree:** 64 semester credits, Associates **ROTC:** Air Force **Professional Accreditation:** APTA, NLN **Intercollegiate Athletics:** Baseball M; Basketball M & W; Volleyball W

ANOKA-RAMSEY COMMUNITY COLLEGE, CAMBRIDGE CAMPUS
300 Polk St. South
Cambridge, MN 55008-5706
Tel: (763)689-7000
Fax: (763)689-7050
Web Site: http://www.anokaramsey.edu/ **Type:** Two-Year College **Sex:** Coed **Affiliation:** Minnesota State Colleges and Universities System **% Accepted:** 100 **Admission Plans:** Open Admission; Early Admission; Deferred Admission **Application Deadline:** Rolling **Application Fee:** $20.00 **H.S. Requirements:** High school diploma required; GED accepted **Costs Per Year:** Application fee: $20. State resident tuition: $3390 full-time, $113 per credit part-time. Nonresident tuition: $6780 full-time, $226 per credit part-time. Mandatory fees: $414 full-time, $13.80 per credit part-time. **Scholarships:** Available **Calendar System:** Semester, Summer Session Available **Enrollment:** FT 514, PT 1,223 **Faculty:** FT 22, PT 38 **Student-Faculty Ratio:** 25:1 **Library Holdings:** 18,927 **Regional Accreditation:** North Central Association of Colleges and Schools **Credit Hours For Degree:** 64 semester credits, Associates **ROTC:** Air Force **Intercollegiate Athletics:** Baseball M; Basketball M & W; Volleyball W

ANOKA TECHNICAL COLLEGE
1355 West Hwy. 10
Anoka, MN 55303
Tel: (612)576-4700
Admissions: (763)576-4746
Web Site: http://www.ank.tec.mn.us/
Admissions: Robert Hoenie
Type: Two-Year College **Sex:** Coed **Affiliation:** Minnesota State Colleges and Universities System **Admission Plans:** Open Admission; Deferred Admission **Application Fee:** $20.00 **H.S. Requirements:** High school diploma required; GED accepted **Costs Per Year:** Application fee: $20. State resident tuition: $3886 full-time, $129.55 per credit part-time. Nonresident tuition: $7772 full-time, $259.10 per credit part-time. Mandatory fees: $421 full-time, $14.05 per credit part-time. Full-time tuition and fees vary according to program and reciprocity agreements. Part-time tuition and fees vary according to program and reciprocity agreements. **Scholarships:** Available **Calendar System:** Semester, Summer Session Not available **Enrollment:** FT 1,058, PT 1,313 **Faculty:** FT 68, PT 42 **Student-Faculty**

Ratio: 16:1 **Regional Accreditation:** North Central Association of Colleges and Schools **Credit Hours For Degree:** 64 credits, Associates **Professional Accreditation:** AOTA

THE ART INSTITUTES INTERNATIONAL MINNESOTA
15 South 9th St.
Minneapolis, MN 55402-3137
Tel: (612)332-3361
Free: 800-777-3643
Fax: (612)332-3934
Web Site: http://www.aim.artinstitutes.edu/
President/CEO: Larry Horn
Registrar: Desiree Boie
Admissions: Russ Gill
Financial Aid: Melanie Lindenmeyer
Type: Four-Year College **Sex:** Coed **Affiliation:** Education Management Corporation **% Accepted:** 100 **Admission Plans:** Deferred Admission **Application Deadline:** Rolling **Application Fee:** $50.00 **H.S. Requirements:** High school diploma required; GED accepted **Costs Per Year:** Application fee: $50. Tuition: $17,904 full-time, $373 per credit part-time. **Scholarships:** Available **Calendar System:** Quarter, Summer Session Available **Enrollment:** FT 885, PT 709 **Faculty:** FT 56, PT 55 **Student-Faculty Ratio:** 20:1 **Exams:** ACT, Other **% Residing in College-Owned, -Operated, or -Affiliated Housing:** 13 **Library Holdings:** 42,752 **Credit Hours For Degree:** 128 credits, Associates; 192 credits, Bachelors **Professional Accreditation:** ACICS, ACF

AUGSBURG COLLEGE
2211 Riverside Ave.
Minneapolis, MN 55454-1351
Tel: (612)330-1000
Free: 800-788-5678
Admissions: (612)330-1001
Fax: (612)330-1649
E-mail: admissions@augsburg.edu
Web Site: http://www.augsburg.edu/
President/CEO: Dr. William Frame
Registrar: Paul Simmons
Admissions: Carrie Carroll
Financial Aid: Herald Johnson
Type: Comprehensive **Sex:** Coed **Affiliation:** Lutheran **Scores:** 100% SAT V 400+; 100% SAT M 400+; 45% ACT 18-23; 44% ACT 24-29 **% Accepted:** 76 **Admission Plans:** Deferred Admission **Application Deadline:** August 15 **Application Fee:** $25.00 **H.S. Requirements:** High school diploma required; GED accepted **Costs Per Year:** Application fee: $25. Comprehensive fee: $30,026 includes full-time tuition ($22,900), mandatory fees ($522), and college room and board ($6604). College room only: $3396. Part-time tuition: $2866 per course. Part-time mandatory fees: $86 per course. **Scholarships:** Available **Calendar System:** Semester, Summer Session Available **Enrollment:** FT 2,269, PT 566, Grad 673 **Faculty:** FT 163, PT 207 **Student-Faculty Ratio:** 15:1 **Exams:** SAT I or ACT **% Receiving Financial Aid:** 70 **% Residing in College-Owned, -Operated, or -Affiliated Housing:** 54 **Library Holdings:** 146,166 **Regional Accreditation:** North Central Association of Colleges and Schools **Credit Hours For Degree:** 32 courses, Bachelors **ROTC:** Army, Navy, Air Force **Professional Accreditation:** AACN, CSWE, NASM, NCATE, NLN **Intercollegiate Athletics:** Baseball M; Basketball M & W; Cross-Country Running M & W; Football M; Golf M & W; Ice Hockey M & W; Soccer M & W; Softball W; Track and Field M & W; Volleyball W; Wrestling M

BEMIDJI STATE UNIVERSITY
1500 Birchmont Dr., NE
Bemidji, MN 56601-2699
Tel: (218)755-2000
Free: 800-652-9747
Admissions: (218)755-2040
Fax: (218)755-2074
E-mail: admissions@bemidjistate.edu
Web Site: http://www.bemidjistate.edu/
President/CEO: Dr. Jon E. Quistgaard
Registrar: David Carlson
Admissions: Russ Kreager
Financial Aid: Paul Lindseth
Type: Comprehensive **Sex:** Coed **Affiliation:** Minnesota State Colleges and Universities System **Scores:** 62% ACT 18-23; 24% ACT 24-29 **% Accepted:** 73 **Admission Plans:** Deferred Admission **Application Deadline:** Rolling **Application Fee:** $20.00 **H.S. Requirements:** High school diploma required; GED accepted **Costs Per Year:** Application fee: $20. State resident tuition: $5246 full-time, $190.50 per credit part-time. Mandatory fees: $768 full-time, $83.89 per credit part-time. Part-time tuition and fees vary according to course load. College room and board: $5014. College room only: $3214. Room and board charges vary according to board plan and housing facility. **Scholarships:** Available **Calendar System:** Semester, Summer Session Available **Enrollment:** FT 3,248, PT 1,208, Grad 437 **Faculty:** FT 246, PT 116 **Student-Faculty Ratio:** 19:1 **Exams:** ACT **% Receiving Financial Aid:** 56 **% Residing in College-Owned, -Operated, or -Affiliated Housing:** 26 **Library Holdings:** 554,087 **Regional Accreditation:** North Central Association of Colleges and Schools **Credit Hours For Degree:** 64 semester credits, Associates; 128 semester credits, Bachelors **Professional Accreditation:** AACN, CSWE, NASM, NCATE, NLN **Intercollegiate Athletics:** Baseball M; Basketball M & W; Cross-Country Running W; Football M; Golf M & W; Ice Hockey M & W; Soccer W; Softball W; Tennis W; Track and Field M & W; Volleyball W

BETHANY LUTHERAN COLLEGE
700 Luther Dr.
Mankato, MN 56001-6163
Tel: (507)344-7000
Free: 800-944-3066
Admissions: (507)344-7320
Fax: (507)344-7376
E-mail: admiss@blc.edu
Web Site: http://www.blc.edu/
President/CEO: Dan R. Bruss, PhD
Registrar: Jean K. Wiechmann
Admissions: Donald Westphal
Financial Aid: Jeffrey Younge
Type: Four-Year College **Sex:** Coed **Affiliation:** Lutheran **Scores:** 50% ACT 18-23; 31% ACT 24-29 **% Accepted:** 84 **Application Deadline:** July 15 **Application Fee:** $0.00 **H.S. Requirements:** High school diploma required; GED accepted **Costs Per Year:** Application fee: $0. One-time mandatory fee: $130. Comprehensive fee: $21,786 includes full-time tuition ($16,248), mandatory fees ($260), and college room and board ($5278). College room only: $1988. Part-time tuition: $690 per credit. Part-time mandatory fees: $130 per term. **Scholarships:** Available **Calendar System:** Semester, Summer Session Not available **Enrollment:** FT 530, PT 36 **Faculty:** FT 40, PT 35 **Student-Faculty Ratio:** 11:1 **Exams:** SAT I or ACT **% Receiving Financial Aid:** 82 **% Residing in College-Owned, -Operated, or -Affiliated Housing:** 77 **Library Holdings:** 72,392 **Regional Accreditation:** North Central Association of Colleges and Schools **Credit Hours For Degree:** 65 credits, Associates; 128 credits, Bachelors **ROTC:** Army **Intercollegiate Athletics:** Baseball M; Basketball M & W; Golf M; Soccer M & W; Softball W; Tennis M & W; Volleyball W

BETHEL UNIVERSITY
3900 Bethel Dr.
St. Paul, MN 55112-6999
Tel: (651)638-6400
Free: 800-255-8706
Admissions: (651)638-6371
Web Site: http://www.bethel.edu/
President/CEO: Dr. George K. Brushaber
Registrar: Chester Duck
Admissions: Dr. James Barnes
Financial Aid: Daniel Nelson
Type: Comprehensive **Sex:** Coed **Affiliation:** Baptist General Conference **Scores:** 100% SAT V 400+; 100% SAT M 400+; 39% ACT 18-23; 50% ACT 24-29 **% Accepted:** 87 **Admission Plans:** Early Admission; Early Action **Application Deadline:** March 01 **Application Fee:** $25.00 **H.S. Requirements:** High school diploma required; GED accepted **Costs Per Year:** Application fee: $25. Comprehensive fee: $29,840 includes full-time tuition ($22,590), mandatory fees ($110), and college room and board ($7140). College room only: $4260. Part-time tuition: $865 per credit. **Scholarships:** Available **Calendar System:** 4-1-4, Summer Session Available **Enrollment:** FT 2,875, PT 322, Grad 660 **Faculty:** FT 175, PT 131 **Student-Faculty Ratio:** 14:1 **Exams:** SAT I or ACT **% Receiving Financial Aid:** 66 **% Residing in College-Owned, -Operated, or -Affiliated Housing:** 72 **Library Holdings:** 194,000 **Regional Accreditation:** North Central Association of Colleges and Schools **Credit Hours For Degree:** 61 credit hours, Associates; 122 credit hours, Bachelors **ROTC:** Army, Air Force **Professional Ac-**

creditation: AACN, CSWE, JRCEPAT, NLN **Intercollegiate Athletics:** Baseball M; Basketball M & W; Cheerleading W; Cross-Country Running M & W; Football M; Golf M; Ice Hockey M & W; Soccer M & W; Softball W; Tennis M & W; Track and Field M & W; Volleyball M & W

BROWN COLLEGE
1440 Northland Dr.
Mendota Heights, MN 55120
Tel: (651)905-3400
Free: 800-6BR-OWN6
Fax: (651)905-3550
Web Site: http://www.browncollege.edu/
President/CEO: Ronald G. Andersen
Admissions: Mark Fredrichs
Financial Aid: Darrell Rhoten
Type: Two-Year College **Sex:** Coed **Affiliation:** Career Education Corporation **% Accepted:** 48 **Admission Plans:** Deferred Admission **Application Deadline:** Rolling **Application Fee:** $50.00 **H.S. Requirements:** High school diploma required; GED accepted **Scholarships:** Available **Calendar System:** Quarter, Summer Session Available **Enrollment:** FT 1,891, PT 163 **Faculty:** FT 78, PT 44 **Student-Faculty Ratio:** 21:1 **Library Holdings:** 768 **Credit Hours For Degree:** 105 credits, Associates **Professional Accreditation:** ACCSCT

CAPELLA UNIVERSITY
225 South 6th St., 9th Floor
Minneapolis, MN 55402
Tel: (612)252-4200; 888-CAPELLA
Admissions: 800-227-3552
Fax: (612)337-5396
Web Site: http://www.capella.edu/
President/CEO: Dr. Michael Offerman
Registrar: Kris Ragozzino
Admissions: Bob Bear
Financial Aid: Tim Lehmann
Type: Two-Year Upper Division **Sex:** Coed **Application Fee:** $75.00 **H.S. Requirements:** High school diploma required; GED accepted **Costs Per Year:** Application fee: $75. **Scholarships:** Available **Calendar System:** Quarter, Summer Session Available **Regional Accreditation:** North Central Association of Colleges and Schools **Professional Accreditation:** ACA

CARLETON COLLEGE
One North College St.
Northfield, MN 55057-4001
Tel: (507)646-4000
Free: 800-995-2275
Admissions: (507)646-4190
Fax: (507)646-4526
E-mail: admissions@acs.carleton.edu
Web Site: http://www.carleton.edu/
President/CEO: Dr. Robert A. Oden, Jr.
Registrar: Roger Lasly
Admissions: Paul Thiboutot
Financial Aid: Rod Oto
Type: Four-Year College **Sex:** Coed **Scores:** 100% SAT V 400+; 100% SAT M 400+; 8% ACT 18-23; 34% ACT 24-29 **% Accepted:** 29 **Admission Plans:** Early Admission; Early Decision Plan; Deferred Admission **Application Deadline:** January 15 **Application Fee:** $30.00 **H.S. Requirements:** High school diploma required; GED accepted **Costs Per Year:** Application fee: $30. Comprehensive fee: $42,864 includes full-time tuition ($34,083), mandatory fees ($189), and college room and board ($8592). College room only: $4299. **Scholarships:** Available **Calendar System:** Miscellaneous, Summer Session Not available **Enrollment:** FT 1,936, PT 23 **Faculty:** FT 198, PT 18 **Student-Faculty Ratio:** 9:1 **Exams:** SAT I or ACT, SAT II **% Receiving Financial Aid:** 60 **% Residing in College-Owned, -Operated, or -Affiliated Housing:** 89 **Library Holdings:** 662,871 **Regional Accreditation:** North Central Association of Colleges and Schools **Credit Hours For Degree:** 210 credits, Bachelors **Intercollegiate Athletics:** Badminton M & W; Baseball M; Basketball M & W; Crew M & W; Cross-Country Running M & W; Equestrian Sports M & W; Fencing M & W; Field Hockey W; Football M; Golf M & W; Gymnastics W; Ice Hockey M & W; Lacrosse M & W; Rugby M & W; Sailing M & W; Skiing (Cross-Country) M & W; Skiing (Downhill) M & W; Soccer M & W; Softball W; Swimming and Diving M & W; Tennis M & W; Track and Field M & W; Ultimate Frisbee M & W; Volleyball M & W; Water Polo M & W

CENTRAL LAKES COLLEGE
501 West College Dr.
Brainerd, MN 56401-3904
Tel: (218)855-8000
Admissions: (218)828-2525
Fax: (218)855-8220
E-mail: cdaniels@clcmn.edu
Web Site: http://www.clcmn.edu/
President/CEO: Dr. Joseph C. Birmingham
Registrar: Sharon Boone
Admissions: Charlotte Daniels
Financial Aid: Mike Barnaby
Type: Two-Year College **Sex:** Coed **Affiliation:** Minnesota State Colleges and Universities System **Admission Plans:** Open Admission; Deferred Admission **Application Deadline:** Rolling **Application Fee:** $20.00 **H.S. Requirements:** High school diploma required; GED accepted **Costs Per Year:** Application fee: $20. Area resident tuition: $3940 full-time. **Scholarships:** Available **Calendar System:** Semester, Summer Session Available **Enrollment:** FT 1,848, PT 920 **Faculty:** FT 93, PT 69 **Student-Faculty Ratio:** 17:1 **Library Holdings:** 16,052 **Regional Accreditation:** North Central Association of Colleges and Schools **Credit Hours For Degree:** 96 credits, Associates **Professional Accreditation:** ADA **Intercollegiate Athletics:** Baseball M; Basketball M & W; Football M; Golf M & W; Soccer M & W; Softball W; Volleyball W

CENTURY COLLEGE
3300 Century Ave. North
White Bear Lake, MN 55110
Tel: (651)779-3200
Free: 800-228-1978
Admissions: (651)779-2619
Fax: (651)779-5810
Web Site: http://www.century.edu/
President/CEO: Dr. Lawrence Litecky
Registrar: Thomas Black
Admissions: Christine Paulos
Financial Aid: Lois Larson
Type: Two-Year College **Sex:** Coed **Affiliation:** Minnesota State Colleges and Universities System **% Accepted:** 100 **Admission Plans:** Open Admission **Application Deadline:** Rolling **Application Fee:** $20.00 **H.S. Requirements:** High school diploma or equivalent not required **Costs Per Year:** Application fee: $20. State resident tuition: $4233 full-time, $141 per credit part-time. Nonresident tuition: $8043 full-time, $254 per credit part-time. Mandatory fees: $423 full-time, $14.11 per credit part-time. **Scholarships:** Available **Calendar System:** Semester, Summer Session Available **Enrollment:** FT 4,042, PT 4,511 **Faculty:** FT 175, PT 191 **Student-Faculty Ratio:** 23:1 **Library Holdings:** 56,867 **Regional Accreditation:** North Central Association of Colleges and Schools **Credit Hours For Degree:** 64 semester credits, Associates **ROTC:** Air Force **Professional Accreditation:** ADA, JRCEMT, NLN **Intercollegiate Athletics:** Golf M & W

COLLEGE OF SAINT BENEDICT
37 South College Ave.
St. Joseph, MN 56374
Tel: (320)363-5011
Free: 800-544-1489
Fax: (320)363-5010
E-mail: admissions@csbsju.edu
Web Site: http://www.csbsju.edu/
President/CEO: Dr. Mary Ann Baenninger
Registrar: Julie Gruska
Admissions: Mary Milbert
Financial Aid: Jane Haugen
Type: Four-Year College **Sex:** Coed **Affiliation:** Roman Catholic **Scores:** 97% SAT V 400+; 97% SAT M 400+; 32% ACT 18-23; 56% ACT 24-29 **% Accepted:** 86 **Admission Plans:** Deferred Admission **Application Deadline:** December 01 **Application Fee:** $0.00 **H.S. Requirements:** High school diploma required; GED accepted. For home schooled students with appropriate documentation of college preparatory curriculum: High school diploma or equivalent not required **Costs Per Year:** Application fee: $0. Comprehensive fee: $30,091 includes full-time tuition ($23,064), mandatory fees ($390), and college room and board ($6637). College room only: $3419. Room and board charges vary according to board plan and housing facility. Part-time tuition: $961 per credit. Part-time mandatory fees: $195 per term. Part-time tuition and fees vary according to course load. **Scholar-**

ships: Available **Calendar System:** Semester, Summer Session Not available **Enrollment:** FT 1,993, PT 52 **Faculty:** FT 148, PT 22 **Student-Faculty Ratio:** 13:1 **Exams:** SAT I or ACT **% Receiving Financial Aid:** 66 **% Residing in College-Owned, -Operated, or -Affiliated Housing:** 84 **Library Holdings:** 805,376 **Regional Accreditation:** North Central Association of Colleges and Schools **Credit Hours For Degree:** 124 credits, Bachelors **ROTC:** Army **Professional Accreditation:** AACN, ADtA, CSWE, NASM, NCATE, NLN **Intercollegiate Athletics:** Basketball W; Crew W; Cross-Country Running W; Golf W; Ice Hockey W; Lacrosse W; Riflery W; Rugby W; Skiing (Cross-Country) W; Soccer W; Softball W; Swimming and Diving W; Tennis W; Track and Field W; Ultimate Frisbee W; Volleyball W

COLLEGE OF ST. CATHERINE
2004 Randolph Ave.
St. Paul, MN 55105-1789
Tel: (651)690-6000
Admissions: (651)690-6505
Fax: (651)690-6042
E-mail: stkate@stkate.edu
Web Site: http://www.stkate.edu/
President/CEO: Dr. Andrea J. Lee, IHM
Registrar: Cynthia Egeness
Admissions: Cal Moseley
Financial Aid: Sandra Sundstrom
Type: Comprehensive **Affiliation:** Roman Catholic **Scores:** 96% SAT V 400+; 98% SAT M 400+; 38% ACT 18-23; 52% ACT 24-29 **% Accepted:** 78 **Admission Plans:** Deferred Admission **Application Deadline:** Rolling **Application Fee:** $0.00 **H.S. Requirements:** High school diploma required; GED accepted **Costs Per Year:** Application fee: $0. Comprehensive fee: $27,505 includes full-time tuition ($21,060), mandatory fees ($325), and college room and board ($6120). College room only: $3420. Full-time tuition and fees vary according to class time. Room and board charges vary according to board plan and housing facility. Part-time tuition: $702 per credit. Part-time tuition varies according to class time. **Scholarships:** Available **Calendar System:** 4-1-4, Summer Session Available **Enrollment:** FT 2,362, PT 1,243, Grad 1,302 **Faculty:** FT 246, PT 237 **Student-Faculty Ratio:** 11:1 **Exams:** SAT I or ACT **% Receiving Financial Aid:** 69 **% Residing in College-Owned, -Operated, or -Affiliated Housing:** 38 **Library Holdings:** 263,495 **Regional Accreditation:** North Central Association of Colleges and Schools **Credit Hours For Degree:** 130 semester credits, Bachelors **ROTC:** Air Force **Professional Accreditation:** AOTA, APTA, CSWE, JRCEDMS, NASM, NLN **Intercollegiate Athletics:** Basketball W; Cross-Country Running W; Ice Hockey W; Soccer W; Softball W; Swimming and Diving W; Tennis W; Track and Field W; Volleyball W

COLLEGE OF ST. CATHERINE-MINNEAPOLIS
601 25th Ave. South
Minneapolis, MN 55454-1494
Tel: (651)690-7700
Free: 800-945-4599
Admissions: (651)690-8600
Fax: (651)690-8107
E-mail: careerinfo@stkate.edu
Web Site: http://www.stkate.edu/
President/CEO: Sr. Andrea J. Lee
Registrar: Tone Blechert
Admissions: Cal Mosley
Financial Aid: Pamela Johnson
Type: Comprehensive **Sex:** Coed **Affiliation:** Roman Catholic; College of St. Catherine **Scores:** 50% ACT 18-23; 42% ACT 24-29 **Admission Plans:** Deferred Admission **Application Fee:** $20.00 **H.S. Requirements:** High school diploma required; GED accepted **Costs Per Year:** Application fee: $20. Comprehensive fee: $20,870 includes full-time tuition ($14,720), mandatory fees ($30), and college room and board ($6120). College room only: $3420. Room and board charges vary according to board plan and housing facility. Part-time tuition: $460 per credit. Part-time mandatory fees: $20 per term. **Scholarships:** Available **Calendar System:** Semester, Summer Session Available **Enrollment:** FT 2,393, PT 1,288, Grad 1,126 **Faculty:** FT 224, PT 295 **Student-Faculty Ratio:** 11:1 **Exams:** ACT **% Residing in College-Owned, -Operated, or -Affiliated Housing:** 9 **Library Holdings:** 267,558 **Regional Accreditation:** North Central Association of Colleges and Schools **Credit Hours For Degree:** 60 semester hours, Associates **Professional Accreditation:** AHIMA, AOTA, APTA, CARC, JRCERT, NLN

THE COLLEGE OF ST. SCHOLASTICA
1200 Kenwood Ave.
Duluth, MN 55811-4199
Tel: (218)723-6000
Free: 800-249-6412
Admissions: (218)723-6053
Fax: (218)723-6290
E-mail: admissions@css1.css.edu
Web Site: http://www.css.edu/
President/CEO: Dr. Larry Goodwin
Registrar: George Beattie
Admissions: Brian Dalton
Financial Aid: Jon Erickson
Type: Comprehensive **Sex:** Coed **Affiliation:** Roman Catholic Church **Scores:** 100% SAT V 400+; 100% SAT M 400+; 48% ACT 18-23; 45% ACT 24-29 **% Accepted:** 87 **Admission Plans:** Early Admission; Deferred Admission **Application Deadline:** Rolling **Application Fee:** $25.00 **H.S. Requirements:** High school diploma required; GED accepted **Costs Per Year:** Application fee: $25. Comprehensive fee: $28,456 includes full-time tuition ($22,110), mandatory fees ($130), and college room and board ($6216). College room only: $3556. Full-time tuition and fees vary according to class time. Room and board charges vary according to board plan and housing facility. Part-time tuition: $688 per credit hour. Part-time tuition varies according to class time and course load. **Scholarships:** Available **Calendar System:** Semester, Summer Session Available **Enrollment:** FT 2,296, PT 317, Grad 567 **Faculty:** FT 142, PT 110 **Student-Faculty Ratio:** 13:1 **Exams:** SAT I or ACT **% Receiving Financial Aid:** 77 **% Residing in College-Owned, -Operated, or -Affiliated Housing:** 44 **Library Holdings:** 127,328 **Regional Accreditation:** North Central Association of Colleges and Schools **Credit Hours For Degree:** 128 credits, Bachelors **ROTC:** Air Force **Professional Accreditation:** AACN, AHIMA, AOTA, APTA, CSWE **Intercollegiate Athletics:** Baseball M; Basketball M & W; Cross-Country Running M & W; Ice Hockey M; Soccer M & W; Softball W; Tennis M & W; Track and Field M & W; Volleyball W

COLLEGE OF VISUAL ARTS
344 Summit Ave.
St. Paul, MN 55102-2124
Tel: (651)224-3416
Free: 800-224-1536
Fax: (651)224-8854
E-mail: jnorhorn@cva.edu
Web Site: http://www.cva.edu/
President/CEO: Joe Culligan
Registrar: Lois Caneday
Admissions: Jane Nordhorn
Financial Aid: Bonnie Clayton
Type: Four-Year College **Sex:** Coed **Scores:** 100% SAT V 400+; 100% SAT M 400+; 50% ACT 18-23; 23% ACT 24-29 **% Accepted:** 64 **Admission Plans:** Deferred Admission **Application Deadline:** Rolling **Application Fee:** $40.00 **H.S. Requirements:** High school diploma required; GED accepted **Costs Per Year:** Application fee: $40. Tuition: $17,510 full-time, $875 per credit part-time. Mandatory fees: $530 full-time, $53 per course part-time. Full-time tuition and fees vary according to course load. Part-time tuition and fees vary according to course load. **Scholarships:** Available **Calendar System:** Semester, Summer Session Available **Enrollment:** FT 171, PT 31 **Faculty:** FT 8, PT 51 **Student-Faculty Ratio:** 8:1 **Exams:** SAT I or ACT **% Receiving Financial Aid:** 75 **Library Holdings:** 7,100 **Regional Accreditation:** North Central Association of Colleges and Schools **Credit Hours For Degree:** 126 credits, Bachelors

CONCORDIA COLLEGE
901 South 8th St.
Moorhead, MN 56562
Tel: (218)299-4000
Free: 800-699-9897
Admissions: (218)299-3004
Fax: (218)299-3947
E-mail: admissions@gloria.cord.edu
Web Site: http://www.concordiacollege.edu/

President/CEO: Dr. Pamela M. Jolicoeur
Registrar: Carole Stalheim
Admissions: Lee Johnson
Financial Aid: Dale Thornton
Type: Four-Year College **Sex:** Coed **Affiliation:** Evangelical Lutheran Church in America **Scores:** 99% SAT V 400+; 96% SAT M 400+; 44% ACT 18-23; 45% ACT 24-29 **% Accepted:** 83 **Admission Plans:** Early Admission; Deferred Admission **Application Deadline:** Rolling **Application Fee:** $20.00 **H.S. Requirements:** High school diploma required; GED accepted **Costs Per Year:** Application fee: $20. Comprehensive fee: $24,664 includes full-time tuition ($19,520), mandatory fees ($154), and college room and board ($4990). College room only: $2300. Room and board charges vary according to board plan and housing facility. Part-time tuition: $3045 per course. Part-time tuition varies according to course load. **Scholarships:** Available **Calendar System:** Semester, Summer Session Available **Enrollment:** FT 2,693, PT 66, Grad 5 **Faculty:** FT 190, PT 62 **Student-Faculty Ratio:** 15:1 **Exams:** SAT I or ACT **% Receiving Financial Aid:** 67 **% Residing in College-Owned, -Operated, or -Affiliated Housing:** 66 **Library Holdings:** 306,644 **Regional Accreditation:** North Central Association of Colleges and Schools **Credit Hours For Degree:** 126 semester hours, Bachelors **ROTC:** Army, Air Force **Professional Accreditation:** AACN, AAFCS, ADtA, CSWE, NASM, NLN **Intercollegiate Athletics:** Baseball M; Basketball M & W; Cheerleading W; Cross-Country Running M & W; Football M; Golf M & W; Ice Hockey M & W; Skiing (Cross-Country) M & W; Soccer M & W; Softball W; Swimming and Diving W; Tennis M & W; Track and Field M & W; Volleyball M & W; Wrestling M

CONCORDIA UNIVERSITY, ST. PAUL
275 Syndicate St. North
St. Paul, MN 55104-5494
Tel: (651)641-8278
Free: 800-333-4705
Admissions: (651)641-8230
Fax: (651)659-0207
E-mail: admiss@csp.edu
Web Site: http://www.csp.edu/
President/CEO: Dr. Robert Holst
Registrar: Jody Ragan
Admissions: Scott Morrell
Financial Aid: Brian Heinemann
Type: Comprehensive **Sex:** Coed **Affiliation:** Lutheran Church–Missouri Synod; Concordia University System **Scores:** 75% SAT V 400+; 84% SAT M 400+; 49% ACT 18-23; 29% ACT 24-29 **% Accepted:** 64 **Admission Plans:** Early Admission; Deferred Admission **Application Deadline:** August 01 **Application Fee:** $30.00 **H.S. Requirements:** High school diploma required; GED accepted **Costs Per Year:** Application fee: $30. Comprehensive fee: $28,974 includes full-time tuition ($22,378) and college room and board ($6596). Part-time tuition: $466 per credit. **Scholarships:** Available **Calendar System:** Semester, Summer Session Available **Enrollment:** FT 1,472, PT 264, Grad 333 **Faculty:** FT 82, PT 356 **Student-Faculty Ratio:** 11:1 **Exams:** ACT **% Receiving Financial Aid:** 66 **% Residing in College-Owned, -Operated, or -Affiliated Housing:** 23 **Library Holdings:** 134,200 **Regional Accreditation:** North Central Association of Colleges and Schools **Credit Hours For Degree:** 64 semester hours, Associates; 128 semester hours, Bachelors **ROTC:** Army, Navy, Air Force **Professional Accreditation:** NCATE **Intercollegiate Athletics:** Baseball M; Basketball M & W; Cross-Country Running M & W; Football M; Golf W; Soccer M & W; Softball W; Track and Field M & W; Volleyball W

CROSSROADS COLLEGE
920 Mayowood Rd., SW
Rochester, MN 55902-2382
Tel: (507)288-4563
Free: 800-456-7651
Fax: (507)288-9046
Web Site: http://www.crossroadscollege.edu/
President/CEO: Dr. Bill Luce
Registrar: Melinda Sargent
Admissions: Scott Klaehn
Financial Aid: Polly Kellogg-Bradley
Type: Four-Year College **Sex:** Coed **Affiliation:** Christian Churches and Churches of Christ **Scores:** 45% ACT 18-23; 16% ACT 24-29 **% Accepted:** 79 **Admission Plans:** Deferred Admission **Application Deadline:** August 15 **Application Fee:** $30.00 **H.S. Requirements:** High school diploma required; GED accepted **Costs Per Year:** Application fee: $30. Tuition: $10,950 full-time, $330 per semester hour part-time. Mandatory fees: $320 full-time, $220 per year part-time. College room only: $3400. **Scholarships:** Available **Calendar System:** Semester, Summer Session Not available **Enrollment:** FT 130, PT 19 **Faculty:** FT 12, PT 13 **Student-Faculty Ratio:** 9:1 **Exams:** SAT I or ACT **% Receiving Financial Aid:** 56 **% Residing in College-Owned, -Operated, or -Affiliated Housing:** 78 **Library Holdings:** 33,697 **Credit Hours For Degree:** 64 semester hours, Associates; 130 semester hours, Bachelors **Professional Accreditation:** AABC **Intercollegiate Athletics:** Baseball M; Basketball M & W; Golf M & W; Softball W; Tennis M & W; Volleyball M & W

CROWN COLLEGE
8700 College View Dr.
St. Bonifacius, MN 55375-9001
Tel: (952)446-4100
Free: 800-68-CROWN
Admissions: (952)446-4144
Fax: (952)446-4149
E-mail: fiskm@crown.edu
Web Site: http://www.crown.edu
President/CEO: Rev. Gary M. Benedict
Registrar: Paul Gedden
Admissions: Mitch Fisk
Financial Aid: Cheryl Fernandez
Type: Comprehensive **Sex:** Coed **Affiliation:** The Christian and Missionary Alliance **Scores:** 95% SAT V 400+; 84% SAT M 400+; 59% ACT 18-23; 24% ACT 24-29 **% Accepted:** 71 **Admission Plans:** Early Admission; Deferred Admission **Application Deadline:** Rolling **Application Fee:** $35.00 **H.S. Requirements:** High school diploma required; GED accepted **Costs Per Year:** Application fee: $35. Comprehensive fee: $24,070 includes full-time tuition ($17,054) and college room and board ($7016). College room only: $3652. Part-time tuition: $713 per credit. **Scholarships:** Available **Calendar System:** Semester, Summer Session Available **Enrollment:** FT 843, PT 345, Grad 116 **Faculty:** FT 39, PT 25 **Student-Faculty Ratio:** 14:1 **Exams:** SAT I or ACT **% Receiving Financial Aid:** 63 **% Residing in College-Owned, -Operated, or -Affiliated Housing:** 70 **Library Holdings:** 79,386 **Regional Accreditation:** North Central Association of Colleges and Schools **Credit Hours For Degree:** 66 credit hours, Associates; 125 credit hours, Bachelors **Professional Accreditation:** AABC **Intercollegiate Athletics:** Baseball M; Basketball M & W; Cross-Country Running M & W; Football M; Golf M & W; Soccer M & W; Softball W; Volleyball W

DAKOTA COUNTY TECHNICAL COLLEGE
1300 East 145th St.
Rosemount, MN 55068
Tel: (651)423-8000; 877-YES-DCTC
Admissions: (651)423-8399
Web Site: http://www.dctc.edu/
Admissions: Patrick Lair
Type: Two-Year College **Sex:** Coed **Affiliation:** Minnesota State Colleges and Universities System **Admission Plans:** Open Admission **Application Fee:** $20.00 **H.S. Requirements:** High school diploma required; GED accepted **Costs Per Year:** Application fee: $20. State resident tuition: $3999 full-time, $124.96 per semester hour part-time. Nonresident tuition: $7997 full-time, $249.92 per semester hour part-time. Mandatory fees: $538 full-time, $16.80 per semester hour part-time. Full-time tuition and fees vary according to reciprocity agreements. Part-time tuition and fees vary according to reciprocity agreements. **Scholarships:** Available **Calendar System:** Semester, Summer Session Available **Enrollment:** FT 2,956, PT 3,113 **Faculty:** FT 85, PT 114 **Student-Faculty Ratio:** 20:1 **Exams:** Other **Library Holdings:** 15,693 **Regional Accreditation:** North Central Association of Colleges and Schools **Credit Hours For Degree:** 72 credits, Associates **Professional Accreditation:** AAMAE, ADA, FIDER **Intercollegiate Athletics:** Baseball M; Soccer M & W; Wrestling M

DEVRY UNIVERSITY
7700 France Ave. South
Ste. 575
Edina, MN 55435
Tel: (952)838-1860
Fax: (952)838-3737
Web Site: http://www.devry.edu/locations/campuses/loc_edina.jsp **Type:** Comprehensive **Sex:** Coed **Application Deadline:** Rolling **Application Fee:** $50.00 **Costs Per Year:** Application fee: $50. One-time mandatory

fee: $40. Tuition: $11,790 full-time. Mandatory fees: $30 full-time. **Enrollment:** FT 16, PT 29, Grad 49 **Faculty:** FT 0, PT 22 **Student-Faculty Ratio:** 4:1

DULUTH BUSINESS UNIVERSITY
4724 Mike Colalillo Dr.
Duluth, MN 55807
Tel: (218)722-4000
Free: 800-777-8406
Web Site: http://www.dbumn.edu/
President/CEO: Bonnie Kupczynski
Admissions: Mark Traux
Type: Two-Year College **Sex:** Coed **Calendar System:** Quarter **Professional Accreditation:** ACICS, AAMAE, ADA

DUNWOODY COLLEGE OF TECHNOLOGY
818 Dunwoody Blvd.
Minneapolis, MN 55403
Tel: (612)374-5800
Free: 800-292-4625
Fax: (612)374-4128
Web Site: http://www.dunwoody.edu/
President/CEO: Frank Starke
Admissions: Raul Galarza
Financial Aid: Art Alexander
Type: Two-Year College **Sex:** Coed **Admission Plans:** Early Admission; Deferred Admission **Application Fee:** $50.00 **H.S. Requirements:** High school diploma required; GED accepted **Scholarships:** Available **Calendar System:** Quarter, Summer Session Available **Enrollment:** FT 1,236, PT 375 **Faculty:** FT 81, PT 24 **Student-Faculty Ratio:** 15:1 **Library Holdings:** 8,000 **Regional Accreditation:** North Central Association of Colleges and Schools

FOND DU LAC TRIBAL AND COMMUNITY COLLEGE
2101 14th St.
Cloquet, MN 55720
Tel: (218)879-0800
Free: 800-657-3712
Admissions: (218)879-0820
Fax: (218)879-0814
E-mail: darla@asab.fdl.cc.mn.us
Web Site: http://www.fdltcc.edu/
President/CEO: Lester Jack Briggs
Admissions: Tom Urbanski
Financial Aid: David Sutherland
Type: Two-Year College **Sex:** Coed **Affiliation:** Minnesota State Colleges and Universities System **Admission Plans:** Open Admission; Early Admission; Deferred Admission **Application Fee:** $20.00 **H.S. Requirements:** High school diploma required; GED accepted **Scholarships:** Available **Calendar System:** Semester, Summer Session Available **Enrollment:** FT 719, PT 1,016 **Faculty:** FT 28, PT 52 **Student-Faculty Ratio:** 21:1 **Exams:** Other **% Residing in College-Owned, -Operated, or -Affiliated Housing:** 10 **Library Holdings:** 3,482 **Regional Accreditation:** North Central Association of Colleges and Schools **Credit Hours For Degree:** 60 credits, Associates

GLOBE COLLEGE
7166 North 10th St.
Oakdale, MN 55128
Tel: (651)730-5100
Admissions: (651)714-7331
Fax: (651)730-5151
Web Site: http://www.globecollege.com/
President/CEO: Mike Hughes
Admissions: Christina Hilipipre
Type: Two-Year College **Sex:** Coed **Admission Plans:** Open Admission **Application Deadline:** October 05 **Application Fee:** $50.00 **H.S. Requirements:** High school diploma required; GED accepted **Costs Per Year:** Application fee: $50. Tuition: $12,600 full-time, $350 per credit part-time. Mandatory fees: $500 full-time. **Scholarships:** Available **Calendar System:** Quarter, Summer Session Available **Enrollment:** FT 533, PT 312 **Student-Faculty Ratio:** 15:1 **Exams:** Other **Library Holdings:** 1,432 **Credit Hours For Degree:** 90 credits, Associates; 180 credits, Bachelors **Professional Accreditation:** ACICS, AAMAE

GUSTAVUS ADOLPHUS COLLEGE
800 West College Ave.
St. Peter, MN 56082-1498
Tel: (507)933-8000
Free: 800-GUSTAVU(S)
Admissions: (507)933-7676
E-mail: admission@gac.edu
Web Site: http://www.gustavus.edu/
President/CEO: Dr. James L. Peterson
Registrar: David L. Wicklund
Admissions: Mark H. Anderson
Financial Aid: Robert Helgeson
Type: Four-Year College **Sex:** Coed **Affiliation:** Evangelical Lutheran Church in America **Scores:** 28% ACT 18-23; 54% ACT 24-29 **% Accepted:** 80 **Admission Plans:** Early Admission; Early Action; Deferred Admission **Application Deadline:** April 01 **Application Fee:** $0.00 **H.S. Requirements:** High school diploma required; GED accepted **Costs Per Year:** Application fee: $0. Comprehensive fee: $30,930 includes full-time tuition ($24,500), mandatory fees ($365), and college room and board ($6065). College room only: $3665. Full-time tuition and fees vary according to student level. Room and board charges vary according to board plan, housing facility, and student level. Part-time tuition: $3000 per course. Tuition guaranteed not to increase for student's term of enrollment. **Scholarships:** Available **Calendar System:** 4-1-4, Summer Session Available **Enrollment:** FT 2,571, PT 32 **Faculty:** FT 187, PT 63 **Student-Faculty Ratio:** 12:1 **Exams:** SAT I or ACT **% Receiving Financial Aid:** 64 **% Residing in College-Owned, -Operated, or -Affiliated Housing:** 85 **Library Holdings:** 288,685 **Regional Accreditation:** North Central Association of Colleges and Schools **Credit Hours For Degree:** 35 courses, Bachelors **ROTC:** Army **Professional Accreditation:** AACN, JRCEPAT, NASM, NCATE, NLN **Intercollegiate Athletics:** Baseball M; Basketball M & W; Cross-Country Running M & W; Football M; Golf M & W; Gymnastics W; Ice Hockey M & W; Lacrosse M; Rugby M & W; Skiing (Cross-Country) M & W; Soccer M & W; Softball W; Swimming and Diving M & W; Tennis M & W; Track and Field M & W; Ultimate Frisbee M & W; Volleyball M & W

HAMLINE UNIVERSITY
1536 Hewitt Ave.
St. Paul, MN 55104-1284
Tel: (651)523-2800
Free: 800-753-9753
Admissions: (651)523-2207
Fax: (651)523-2458
E-mail: cla-admis@hamline.edu
Web Site: http://www.hamline.edu/
President/CEO: Dr. Larry G. Osnes
Registrar: Laurie Herbrand
Admissions: Steven Bjork
Financial Aid: Lynette Wahl
Type: Comprehensive **Sex:** Coed **Affiliation:** United Methodist Church **Scores:** 97.9% SAT V 400+; 97.8% SAT M 400+; 36.4% ACT 18-23; 48.1% ACT 24-29 **% Accepted:** 78 **Admission Plans:** Early Admission; Early Action; Deferred Admission **Application Deadline:** Rolling **Application Fee:** $0.00 **H.S. Requirements:** High school diploma required; GED accepted **Costs Per Year:** Application fee: $0. Comprehensive fee: $30,067 includes full-time tuition ($22,758), mandatory fees ($399), and college room and board ($6910). College room only: $3484. Full-time tuition and fees vary according to student level. Room and board charges vary according to board plan and housing facility. Part-time tuition: $700 per credit. Part-time tuition varies according to course load and student level. **Scholarships:** Available **Calendar System:** 4-1-4, Summer Session Available **Enrollment:** FT 1,945, PT 101, Grad 1,791 **Faculty:** FT 174, PT 326 **Student-Faculty Ratio:** 13:1 **Exams:** SAT I or ACT **% Receiving Financial Aid:** 76 **% Residing in College-Owned, -Operated, or -Affiliated Housing:** 41 **Library Holdings:** 556,450 **Regional Accreditation:** North Central Association of Colleges and Schools **Credit Hours For Degree:** 128 credits, Bachelors **ROTC:** Air Force **Professional Accreditation:** ABA, AALS, NASM, NCATE **Intercollegiate Athletics:** Baseball M; Basketball M & W; Cross-Country Running M & W; Football M; Gymnastics W; Ice Hockey M & W; Soccer M & W; Softball W; Swimming and Diving M & W; Tennis M & W; Track and Field M & W; Volleyball W

HENNEPIN TECHNICAL COLLEGE
9000 Brooklyn Blvd.
Brooklyn Park, MN 55445
Tel: (763)425-3800
Admissions: (763)488-2415
Fax: (763)550-2119
Web Site: http://www.hennepintech.edu/
President/CEO: Dr. Sharon K. Grossbach
Admissions: Joy Bodin
Type: Two-Year College **Sex:** Coed **Affiliation:** Minnesota State Colleges and Universities System **Admission Plans:** Open Admission **Application Fee:** $20.00 **H.S. Requirements:** High school diploma required; GED accepted **Scholarships:** Available **Calendar System:** Semester **Student-Faculty Ratio:** 25:1 **Regional Accreditation:** North Central Association of Colleges and Schools **Professional Accreditation:** ACF, ADA

HERZING COLLEGE
5700 West Broadway
Minneapolis, MN 55428
Tel: (763)535-3000
Free: 800-878-DRAW
Admissions: (763)231-3152
Web Site: http://www.herzing.edu/
President/CEO: Thomas Kosel
Admissions: James Decker
Type: Two-Year College **Sex:** Coed **Affiliation:** Herzing College **Admission Plans:** Open Admission **Application Fee:** $0.00 **H.S. Requirements:** High school diploma required; GED accepted **Costs Per Year:** Application fee: $0. Tuition: $11,029 full-time, $367 per credit part-time. Mandatory fees: $25 full-time. Full-time tuition and fees vary according to course load and program. Part-time tuition varies according to course load and program. **Calendar System:** Semester **Enrollment:** FT 205, PT 141 **Faculty:** FT 21, PT 11 **Student-Faculty Ratio:** 14:1 **Exams:** Other, SAT I and SAT II or ACT **Credit Hours For Degree:** 80 credits, Associates **Professional Accreditation:** ACCSCT

HIBBING COMMUNITY COLLEGE
1515 East 25th St.
Hibbing, MN 55746-3300
Tel: (218)262-7200
Free: 800-224-4HCC
Admissions: (218)262-6713
E-mail: admissions@hibbing.edu
Web Site: http://www.hcc.mnscu.edu/
President/CEO: Dr. Anthony Kuznik
Registrar: Judy Zeiger
Admissions: Holly Bigelow
Financial Aid: Paul Hatch
Type: Two-Year College **Sex:** Coed **Affiliation:** Minnesota State Colleges and Universities System **% Accepted:** 100 **Admission Plans:** Open Admission; Early Admission; Deferred Admission **Application Deadline:** Rolling **Application Fee:** $20.00 **H.S. Requirements:** High school diploma required; GED accepted **Costs Per Year:** Application fee: $20. State resident tuition: $3950 full-time, $116.60 per credit part-time. Nonresident tuition: $145.75 per credit part-time. Mandatory fees: $459 full-time, $15.30 per credit part-time. Full-time tuition and fees vary according to course load and reciprocity agreements. Part-time tuition and fees vary according to course load and reciprocity agreements. College room and board: $4500. College room only: $2900. **Scholarships:** Available **Calendar System:** Semester, Summer Session Available **Faculty:** FT 63, PT 23 **Student-Faculty Ratio:** 14:1 **% Residing in College-Owned, -Operated, or -Affiliated Housing:** 10 **Library Holdings:** 19,536 **Regional Accreditation:** North Central Association of Colleges and Schools **Credit Hours For Degree:** 64 credits, Associates **Professional Accreditation:** ADA, NAACLS **Intercollegiate Athletics:** Baseball M; Basketball M & W; Football M; Golf M & W; Softball W; Volleyball W

HIGH-TECH INSTITUTE
5100 Gamble Dr.
St. Louis Park, MN 55416
Tel: (763)560-9700
Free: 800-987-0110
Fax: (763)560-9777
Web Site: http://www.high-techinstitute.com/
President/CEO: Todd Brown
Type: Two-Year College **Sex:** Coed **Calendar System:** Semester **Professional Accreditation:** ACCSCT

INVER HILLS COMMUNITY COLLEGE
2500 East 80th St.
Inver Grove Heights, MN 55076-3224
Tel: (651)450-8500
Admissions: (651)450-8680
Fax: (651)450-8679
E-mail: lpirius@inverhills.edu
Web Site: http://www.inverhills.edu/
President/CEO: Dr. Cheryl Frank
Registrar: Bruce Lindberg
Admissions: Landon Pirius
Financial Aid: John Pogue
Type: Two-Year College **Sex:** Coed **Affiliation:** Minnesota State Colleges and Universities System **Admission Plans:** Open Admission **Application Fee:** $20.00 **H.S. Requirements:** High school diploma required; GED accepted **Costs Per Year:** Application fee: $20. State resident tuition: $3343 full-time, $125.78 per credit part-time. Nonresident tuition: $6362 full-time, $251.56 per credit part-time. Mandatory fees: $400 full-time, $13.52 per credit part-time. Full-time tuition and fees vary according to program and reciprocity agreements. Part-time tuition and fees vary according to program and reciprocity agreements. **Scholarships:** Available **Calendar System:** Semester, Summer Session Available **Enrollment:** FT 1,566, PT 2,759 **Faculty:** FT 83, PT 127 **Library Holdings:** 42,073 **Regional Accreditation:** North Central Association of Colleges and Schools **Credit Hours For Degree:** 60 credits, Associates **Professional Accreditation:** NLN

ITASCA COMMUNITY COLLEGE
1851 Hwy. 169 East
Grand Rapids, MN 55744
Tel: (218)327-4460
Free: 800-996-6422
Admissions: (218)327-4464
Fax: (218)327-4350
E-mail: iccinfo@itascacc.edu
Web Site: http://www.itascacc.edu/
President/CEO: Dr. Joe Sertich
Registrar: Gwen Litchke
Admissions: Candace Perry
Financial Aid: Patty Holycross
Type: Two-Year College **Sex:** Coed **Affiliation:** Minnesota State Colleges and Universities System **% Accepted:** 100 **Admission Plans:** Open Admission **Application Deadline:** September 06 **Application Fee:** $20.00 **H.S. Requirements:** High school diploma required; GED accepted **Costs Per Year:** Application fee: $20. State resident tuition: $4100 full-time, $128.12 per credit part-time. Nonresident tuition: $5125 full-time, $160.15 per credit part-time. Mandatory fees: $490 full-time, $15.30 per credit part-time. College room and board: $4190. College room only: $3290. **Scholarships:** Available **Calendar System:** Semester, Summer Session Available **Enrollment:** FT 876, PT 261 **Faculty:** FT 42, PT 27 **Student-Faculty Ratio:** 16:1 **Library Holdings:** 28,790 **Regional Accreditation:** North Central Association of Colleges and Schools **Credit Hours For Degree:** 64 credits, Associates **Intercollegiate Athletics:** Baseball M; Basketball M & W; Football M; Softball W; Volleyball W; Wrestling M

ITT TECHNICAL INSTITUTE
8911 Columbine Rd.
Eden Prairie, MN 55347
Tel: (952)914-5300
Web Site: http://www.itt-tech.edu/
President/CEO: Michele F. Ernst
Registrar: Yvonne Rumsey
Admissions: Michele F. Ernst
Type: Two-Year College **Sex:** Coed **Application Deadline:** Rolling **Application Fee:** $100.00 **Costs Per Year:** Application fee: $100. **Calendar System:** Quarter **Exams:** Other **Professional Accreditation:** ACICS

LAKE SUPERIOR COLLEGE
2101 Trinity Rd.
Duluth, MN 55811
Tel: (218)733-7600
Free: 800-432-2884
Admissions: (218)733-5928

Web Site: http://www.lsc.edu/
President/CEO: Dr. Kathleen Nelson
Registrar: Jean Pehl
Admissions: Beth Adams
Financial Aid: Sandy Olin
Type: Two-Year College **Sex:** Coed **Affiliation:** Minnesota State Colleges and Universities System **Admission Plans:** Open Admission; Early Admission; Deferred Admission **Application Deadline:** Rolling **Application Fee:** $20.00 **H.S. Requirements:** High school diploma or equivalent not required **Costs Per Year:** Application fee: $20. State resident tuition: $3450 full-time, $115 per credit part-time. Nonresident tuition: $6900 full-time, $230 per credit part-time. Mandatory fees: $477 full-time, $16 per credit part-time. **Scholarships:** Available **Calendar System:** Semester, Summer Session Available **Enrollment:** FT 2,429, PT 1,771 **Faculty:** FT 97, PT 142 **Student-Faculty Ratio:** 20:1 **Library Holdings:** 2,869 **Regional Accreditation:** North Central Association of Colleges and Schools **Credit Hours For Degree:** 60 credits, Associates **Professional Accreditation:** ADA, APTA, CARC, NAACLS

LEECH LAKE TRIBAL COLLEGE
PO Box 180
Cass Lake, MN 56633-0180
Tel: (218)335-4200; 888-829-4240
Fax: (218)335-4209
Web Site: http://www.lltc.org/
President/CEO: Lenee D. Ross
Type: Two-Year College **Sex:** Coed **Calendar System:** Semester **Regional Accreditation:** North Central Association of Colleges and Schools

MACALESTER COLLEGE
1600 Grand Ave.
St. Paul, MN 55105-1899
Tel: (651)696-6000
Free: 800-231-7974
Admissions: (651)696-6357
Fax: (651)696-6500
E-mail: admissions@macalester.edu
Web Site: http://www.macalester.edu/
President/CEO: Dr. Brian Rosenberg
Registrar: Jayne L. Niemi
Admissions: Lorne T. Robinson
Financial Aid: Brian Lindeman
Type: Four-Year College **Sex:** Coed **Affiliation:** Presbyterian **Scores:** 100% SAT V 400+; 100% SAT M 400+; 3% ACT 18-23; 41% ACT 24-29 **% Accepted:** 44 **Admission Plans:** Early Admission; Early Decision Plan; Deferred Admission **Application Deadline:** January 15 **Application Fee:** $40.00 **H.S. Requirements:** High school diploma or equivalent not required **Costs Per Year:** Application fee: $40. Comprehensive fee: $39,020 includes full-time tuition ($30,870), mandatory fees ($168), and college room and board ($7982). College room only: $4208. Part-time tuition: $965 per semester hour. **Scholarships:** Available **Calendar System:** Semester, Summer Session Not available **Enrollment:** FT 1,827, PT 42 **Faculty:** FT 151, PT 72 **Student-Faculty Ratio:** 11:1 **Exams:** SAT I or ACT **% Receiving Financial Aid:** 69 **% Residing in College-Owned, -Operated, or -Affiliated Housing:** 69 **Library Holdings:** 448,968 **Regional Accreditation:** North Central Association of Colleges and Schools **Credit Hours For Degree:** 128 semester hours, Bachelors **ROTC:** Navy, Air Force **Intercollegiate Athletics:** Baseball M; Basketball M & W; Crew M & W; Cross-Country Running M & W; Fencing M & W; Football M; Golf M & W; Ice Hockey M & W; Rugby M & W; Skiing (Cross-Country) M & W; Soccer M & W; Softball W; Swimming and Diving M & W; Tennis M & W; Track and Field M & W; Ultimate Frisbee W; Volleyball M & W; Water Polo M & W

MARTIN LUTHER COLLEGE
1995 Luther Ct.
New Ulm, MN 56073
Tel: (507)354-8221
Fax: (507)354-8225
E-mail: sebaldja-fac@mlc-wels.edu
Web Site: http://www.mlc-wels.edu/
President/CEO: Rev. Theodore B. Olsen
Admissions: Rev. Theodore B. Olsen
Financial Aid: Gene A. Slettedahl
Type: Four-Year College **Sex:** Coed **Affiliation:** Wisconsin Evangelical Lutheran Synod **Scores:** 43% ACT 18-23; 17% ACT 24-29 **Admission Plans:** Deferred Admission **Application Fee:** $25.00 **H.S. Requirements:** High school diploma required; GED accepted **Costs Per Year:** Application fee: $25. Comprehensive fee: $12,390 includes full-time tuition ($8925) and college room and board ($3465). Part-time tuition: $175 per credit hour. **Scholarships:** Available **Calendar System:** Semester, Summer Session Available **Enrollment:** FT 936, PT 9 **Faculty:** FT 72, PT 12 **Student-Faculty Ratio:** 14:1 **Exams:** ACT **% Receiving Financial Aid:** 63 **% Residing in College-Owned, -Operated, or -Affiliated Housing:** 85 **Library Holdings:** 115,309 **Regional Accreditation:** North Central Association of Colleges and Schools **Credit Hours For Degree:** 134 semester hours, Bachelors **Intercollegiate Athletics:** Baseball M; Basketball M & W; Cross-Country Running M & W; Football M; Golf M; Soccer M & W; Softball W; Tennis M & W; Track and Field M & W; Volleyball W

MCNALLY SMITH COLLEGE OF MUSIC
19 Exchange St. East
St. Paul, MN 55101
Tel: (651)291-0177
Free: 800-594-9500
Fax: (651)291-0366
E-mail: dsandridge@mcnallysmith.edu
Web Site: http://www.mcnallysmith.edu/
President/CEO: John McNally
Registrar: Sara Tomasetti
Admissions: Debbie Sandridge
Financial Aid: Jeffrey R. Aalbers
Type: Two-Year College **Sex:** Coed **% Accepted:** 84 **Admission Plans:** Open Admission **Application Deadline:** August 01 **Application Fee:** $75.00 **H.S. Requirements:** High school diploma required; GED accepted **Costs Per Year:** Application fee: $75. Tuition: $15,240 full-time, $635 per credit part-time. Mandatory fees: $575 full-time, $75 per term part-time. **Calendar System:** Semester, Summer Session Available **Enrollment:** FT 378, PT 93 **Faculty:** FT 33, PT 28 **Student-Faculty Ratio:** 10:1 **Exams:** ACT **Credit Hours For Degree:** 65 credits, Associates **Professional Accreditation:** NASM

MESABI RANGE COMMUNITY AND TECHNICAL COLLEGE
1001 Chestnut St. West
Virginia, MN 55792-3448
Tel: (218)741-3095
Admissions: (218)749-0314
E-mail: b.kochevar@mr.mnscu.edu
Web Site: http://www.mr.mnscu.edu/
President/CEO: Dr. Jill Peterson
Registrar: Shar Anderson
Admissions: Brenda K. Kochevar
Financial Aid: Douglas Furnstahl
Type: Two-Year College **Sex:** Coed **Affiliation:** Minnesota State Colleges and Universities System **Admission Plans:** Open Admission; Early Admission; Deferred Admission **Application Deadline:** Rolling **Application Fee:** $20.00 **H.S. Requirements:** High school diploma required; GED accepted. For Minnesota high school students: High school diploma or equivalent not required **Costs Per Year:** Application fee: $20. State resident tuition: $4252 full-time. Nonresident tuition: $5197 full-time. College room only: $3352. **Scholarships:** Available **Calendar System:** Semester, Summer Session Available **Enrollment:** FT 1,371 **Faculty:** FT 44, PT 29 **Student-Faculty Ratio:** 25:1 **% Residing in College-Owned, -Operated, or -Affiliated Housing:** 10 **Library Holdings:** 23,000 **Regional Accreditation:** North Central Association of Colleges and Schools **Credit Hours For Degree:** 64 credits, Associates **Intercollegiate Athletics:** Baseball M; Basketball M & W; Football M; Softball W; Volleyball W

METROPOLITAN STATE UNIVERSITY
700 East 7th St.
St. Paul, MN 55106-5000
Tel: (651)793-1212
Admissions: (651)793-1303
Fax: (651)772-7632
Web Site: http://www.metrostate.edu
President/CEO: Dr. Wilson Bradshaw
Registrar: Mary Partridge
Admissions: Rosa Rodriguez
Financial Aid: Robert Bode
Type: Comprehensive **Sex:** Coed **Affiliation:** Minnesota State Colleges and Universities System **Scores:** 49% ACT 18-23; 16% ACT 24-29 **Admission**

Plans: Deferred Admission **Application Fee:** $20.00 **H.S. Requirements:** High school diploma or equivalent not required. For non-transfer students: High school diploma required; GED accepted **Costs Per Year:** Application fee: $20. State resident tuition: $4,430 full-time, $147.65 per credit part-time. Nonresident tuition: $8859 full-time, $295.30 per credit part-time. Mandatory fees: $252 full-time, $8.39 per credit part-time. Full-time tuition and fees vary according to program and reciprocity agreements. Part-time tuition and fees vary according to course load, program, and reciprocity agreements. **Scholarships:** Available **Calendar System:** Semester, Summer Session Available **Enrollment:** FT 1,948, PT 3,953, Grad 615 **Faculty:** FT 118, PT 304 **Student-Faculty Ratio:** 15:1 **Exams:** SAT I or ACT **% Receiving Financial Aid:** 49 **Library Holdings:** 29,385 **Regional Accreditation:** North Central Association of Colleges and Schools **Credit Hours For Degree:** 120 credits, Bachelors **Professional Accreditation:** AACN, CSWE, NLN

MINNEAPOLIS BUSINESS COLLEGE
1711 West County Rd. B
Roseville, MN 55113
Tel: (612)636-7406
Free: 800-279-5200
Admissions: (651)604-4118
Fax: (612)636-8185
Web Site: http://www.minneapolisbusinesscollege.edu/
President/CEO: David Whitman
Registrar: Marie Sohomer
Admissions: David Whitman
Financial Aid: Penny Owen
Type: Two-Year College **Sex:** Coed **Affiliation:** The Bradford School **Application Fee:** $50.00 **Costs Per Year:** Application fee: $50. Tuition: $12,240 full-time. College room only: $6360. **Faculty:** FT 9, PT 9 **Student-Faculty Ratio:** 30:1 **Professional Accreditation:** ACICS

MINNEAPOLIS COLLEGE OF ART AND DESIGN
2501 Stevens Ave. South
Minneapolis, MN 55404-4347
Tel: (612)874-3700
Free: 800-874-6223
Admissions: (612)874-3762
Fax: (612)874-3704
E-mail: admissions@mn.mcad.edu
Web Site: http://www.mcad.edu/
President/CEO: T. Michael O'Keefe
Registrar: Jacqueline L. Chestnut
Admissions: William Mullen
Financial Aid: William P. Mullen
Type: Comprehensive **Sex:** Coed **Scores:** 100% SAT V 400+; 95% SAT M 400+; 48% ACT 18-23; 42% ACT 24-29 **% Accepted:** 77 **Admission Plans:** Deferred Admission **Application Deadline:** June 01 **Application Fee:** $35.00 **H.S. Requirements:** High school diploma required; GED accepted **Costs Per Year:** Application fee: $35. Comprehensive fee: $31,010 includes full-time tuition ($24,800), mandatory fees ($240), and college room and board ($5970). College room only: $3770. Room and board charges vary according to housing facility. Part-time tuition: $827 per credit. Part-time mandatory fees: $120 per term. Part-time tuition and fees vary according to course load. **Scholarships:** Available **Calendar System:** Semester, Summer Session Available **Enrollment:** FT 626, PT 49, Grad 47 **Faculty:** FT 38, PT 67 **Student-Faculty Ratio:** 13:1 **Exams:** SAT I or ACT **% Receiving Financial Aid:** 78 **% Residing in College-Owned, -Operated, or -Affiliated Housing:** 45 **Library Holdings:** 47,166 **Regional Accreditation:** North Central Association of Colleges and Schools **Credit Hours For Degree:** 120 credits, Bachelors **Professional Accreditation:** NASAD

MINNEAPOLIS COMMUNITY AND TECHNICAL COLLEGE
1501 Hennepin Ave.
Minneapolis, MN 55403-1779
Tel: (612)659-6000
Admissions: (612)659-6206
Fax: (612)659-6210
Web Site: http://www.mctc.mnscu.edu/
President/CEO: Phillip Davis
Registrar: Lori Kirkeby
Admissions: Dena Russell
Financial Aid: Beth Stevens
Type: Two-Year College **Sex:** Coed **Affiliation:** Minnesota State Colleges and Universities System **Admission Plans:** Open Admission; Early Admission; Deferred Admission **Application Fee:** $20.00 **H.S. Requirements:** High school diploma or equivalent not required. For air traffic control, nursing, law enforcement programs, applicants under 20: High school diploma required; GED accepted **Costs Per Year:** Application fee: $20. State resident tuition: $4028 full-time, $134.25 per credit part-time. Nonresident tuition: $7694 full-time, $256.45 per credit part-time. Full-time tuition varies according to program and reciprocity agreements. Part-time tuition varies according to program and reciprocity agreements. **Scholarships:** Available **Calendar System:** Semester, Summer Session Available **Faculty:** FT 102, PT 265 **Student-Faculty Ratio:** 23:1 **Library Holdings:** 60,352 **Regional Accreditation:** North Central Association of Colleges and Schools **Credit Hours For Degree:** 64 credits, Associates **Professional Accreditation:** ADA, NLN **Intercollegiate Athletics:** Basketball M & W; Golf M & W

MINNESOTA SCHOOL OF BUSINESS
2521 Pennington Dr., NW
Rochester, MN 55901
Tel: (507)536-9500; 888-662-8772
Admissions: (507)586-9500
Fax: (507)535-8011
Web Site: http://www.msbcollege.edu/oncampus/rochester/
Admissions: Shan Pollitt
Type: Four-Year College **Sex:** Coed **Application Fee:** $50.00 **Calendar System:** Quarter **Exams:** Other

MINNESOTA SCHOOL OF BUSINESS-BROOKLYN CENTER
5910 Shingle Creek Parkway
Brooklyn Center, MN 55430
Tel: (763)566-7777
Admissions: (763)585-7777
Fax: (763)566-7030
Web Site: http://www.msbcollege.edu/
President/CEO: Susan Cooke
Admissions: Kristen Swanson
Type: Two-Year College **Sex:** Coed **Admission Plans:** Open Admission **Application Deadline:** October 06 **Application Fee:** $50.00 **H.S. Requirements:** High school diploma required; GED accepted **Costs Per Year:** Application fee: $50. Tuition: $15,750 full-time, $350 per credit hour part-time. **Calendar System:** Quarter **Student-Faculty Ratio:** 13:1 **Exams:** Other **Library Holdings:** 1,534 **Professional Accreditation:** ACICS

MINNESOTA SCHOOL OF BUSINESS-PLYMOUTH
1455 Country Rd. 101 North
Minneapolis, MN 55447
Tel: (763)476-2000
Web Site: http://www.msbcollege.edu/
President/CEO: Jeff Myhre
Type: Two-Year College **Sex:** Coed **Admission Plans:** Open Admission **Application Deadline:** October 06 **Application Fee:** $50.00 **H.S. Requirements:** High school diploma required; GED accepted **Costs Per Year:** Application fee: $50. Tuition: $15,750 full-time, $350 per credit part-time. **Calendar System:** Quarter, Summer Session Available **Student-Faculty Ratio:** 10:1 **Exams:** Other **Library Holdings:** 1,189 **Credit Hours For Degree:** 90 credits, Associates; 180 credits, Bachelors **Professional Accreditation:** ACICS

MINNESOTA SCHOOL OF BUSINESS-RICHFIELD
1401 West 76th St.
Richfield, MN 55423
Tel: (612)861-2000
Fax: (612)861-5548
E-mail: pmurray@msbcollege.edu
Web Site: http://www.msbcollege.edu/
President/CEO: Terry L. Myhre
Registrar: Dorinda Leise
Admissions: Patricia Murray
Financial Aid: Tim Jacobson
Type: Two-Year College **Sex:** Coed **Admission Plans:** Open Admission **Application Deadline:** October 06 **Application Fee:** $50.00 **H.S. Requirements:** High school diploma required; GED accepted **Costs Per Year:** Application fee: $50. Tuition: $15,750 full-time, $350 per credit hour part-time. **Scholarships:** Available **Calendar System:** Quarter, Summer Session Available **Student-Faculty Ratio:** 14:1 **Exams:** Other **Library Holdings:**

2,420 **Credit Hours For Degree:** 90 credits, Associates; 180 credits, Bachelors **Professional Accreditation:** ACICS, AAMAE

MINNESOTA SCHOOL OF BUSINESS-ST. CLOUD

1201 2nd St. South
Waite Park, MN 56387
Tel: (320)257-2000; (866)403-3333
Web Site: http://www.msbcollege.edu/
Admissions: Jim Beck
Type: Two-Year College **Sex:** Coed **Admission Plans:** Open Admission **Application Deadline:** October 06 **Application Fee:** $50.00 **H.S. Requirements:** High school diploma required; GED accepted **Costs Per Year:** Application fee: $50. Tuition: $15,750 full-time, $350 per credit hour part-time. **Calendar System:** Quarter, Summer Session Available **Student-Faculty Ratio:** 13:1 **Exams:** Other **Library Holdings:** 724 **Credit Hours For Degree:** 90 credits, Associates; 180 credits, Bachelors

MINNESOTA SCHOOL OF BUSINESS-SHAKOPEE

1200 Shakopee Town Square
Shakopee, MN 55379
Tel: (952)345-1200; (866)766-1200
Admissions: (952)516-7015
Fax: (952)345-1201
Web Site: http://www.msbcollege.edu/
Admissions: Gretchen Seifert
Type: Two-Year College **Sex:** Coed **Admission Plans:** Open Admission **Application Deadline:** October 06 **Application Fee:** $50.00 **H.S. Requirements:** High school diploma required; GED accepted **Costs Per Year:** Application fee: $50. Tuition: $15,750 full-time, $350 per credit part-time. **Calendar System:** Quarter, Summer Session Available **Student-Faculty Ratio:** 12:1 **Exams:** Other **Library Holdings:** 919 **Credit Hours For Degree:** 90 credits, Associates; 180 credits, Bachelors

MINNESOTA STATE COLLEGE-SOUTHEAST TECHNICAL

1250 Homer Rd., PO Box 409
Winona, MN 55987
Tel: (507)453-2700
Free: 800-372-8164
Fax: (507)453-2715
Web Site: http://www.southeastmn.edu/
President/CEO: James Johnson
Registrar: Mary Johnson
Admissions: Alan DuCett
Financial Aid: Anne Dahlen
Type: Two-Year College **Sex:** Coed **Affiliation:** Minnesota State Colleges and Universities System **Admission Plans:** Open Admission **Application Fee:** $20.00 **H.S. Requirements:** High school diploma required; GED accepted **Costs Per Year:** Application fee: $20. State resident tuition: $124.43 per credit part-time. Nonresident tuition: $248.86 per credit part-time. Mandatory fees: $11.90 per credit part-time. Part-time tuition and fees vary according to reciprocity agreements. **Scholarships:** Available **Calendar System:** Semester, Summer Session Not available **Enrollment:** FT 1,060, PT 757 **Faculty:** FT 55, PT 63 **Library Holdings:** 8,000 **Regional Accreditation:** North Central Association of Colleges and Schools **Credit Hours For Degree:** 72 credits, Associates

MINNESOTA STATE COMMUNITY AND TECHNICAL COLLEGE-FERGUS FALLS

1414 College Way
Fergus Falls, MN 56537-1009
Tel: (218)739-7500; 888-MY-MSCTC
Admissions: (218)736-1528
Fax: (218)739-7475
E-mail: carrie.brimhall@minnesota.edu
Web Site: http://www.minnesota.edu/
President/CEO: Kenneth Peeders
Registrar: Ann Nelson
Admissions: Carrie Brimhall
Financial Aid: Robert Anderson
Type: Two-Year College **Sex:** Coed **Affiliation:** Minnesota State Colleges and Universities System **% Accepted:** 81 **Admission Plans:** Open Admission; Early Admission; Deferred Admission **Application Deadline:** Rolling **Application Fee:** $20.00 **H.S. Requirements:** High school diploma required; GED accepted **Costs Per Year:** Application fee: $20. State resident tuition: $3900 full-time, $133 per credit part-time. Nonresident tuition: $3900 full-time, $133 per credit part-time. Mandatory fees: $569 full-time, $18 per credit part-time. College room only: $3000. **Scholarships:** Available **Calendar System:** Semester, Summer Session Available **Enrollment:** FT 3,587, PT 2,044 **Faculty:** FT 171, PT 181 **Student-Faculty Ratio:** 18:1 **Exams:** ACT **% Residing in College-Owned, -Operated, or -Affiliated Housing:** 22 **Library Holdings:** 30,000 **Regional Accreditation:** North Central Association of Colleges and Schools **Credit Hours For Degree:** 64 semester hours, Associates **Professional Accreditation:** NAACLS **Intercollegiate Athletics:** Baseball M; Basketball M & W; Football M; Golf M & W; Softball W; Volleyball W

MINNESOTA STATE UNIVERSITY MANKATO

228 Wiecking Center
Mankato, MN 56001
Tel: (507)389-2463
Free: 800-722-0544
Admissions: (507)389-6670
E-mail: walter.wolff@mnsu.edu
Web Site: http://www.mnsu.edu/
President/CEO: Richard Davenport
Registrar: David Gjerde
Admissions: Walt Wolff
Financial Aid: Janice Marble
Type: Comprehensive **Sex:** Coed **Affiliation:** Minnesota State Colleges and Universities System **Scores:** 66.7% ACT 18-23; 23.5% ACT 24-29 **% Accepted:** 90 **Admission Plans:** Early Admission; Deferred Admission **Application Deadline:** Rolling **Application Fee:** $20.00 **H.S. Requirements:** High school diploma required; GED accepted **Costs Per Year:** Application fee: $20. State resident tuition: $5104 full-time, $204.10 per credit part-time. Nonresident tuition: $10,932 full-time, $436 per credit part-time. Mandatory fees: $742 full-time, $29.89 per credit part-time. Full-time tuition and fees vary according to course load and reciprocity agreements. Part-time tuition and fees vary according to course load and reciprocity agreements. College room and board: $5083. Room and board charges vary according to board plan. **Scholarships:** Available **Calendar System:** Semester, Summer Session Available **Enrollment:** FT 11,337, PT 1,347, Grad 1,651 **Faculty:** FT 491, PT 226 **Student-Faculty Ratio:** 22:1 **Exams:** ACT **% Receiving Financial Aid:** 50 **% Residing in College-Owned, -Operated, or -Affiliated Housing:** 22 **Library Holdings:** 474,252 **Regional Accreditation:** North Central Association of Colleges and Schools **Credit Hours For Degree:** 64 credits, Associates; 128 credits, Bachelors **ROTC:** Army **Professional Accreditation:** AACSB, ABET, AACN, ACA, ADA, ASLHA, CORE, CSWE, JRCEPAT, NASAD, NASM, NCATE, NLN, NRPA **Intercollegiate Athletics:** Baseball M; Basketball M & W; Cheerleading M & W; Cross-Country Running M & W; Football M; Golf M & W; Ice Hockey M & W; Soccer W; Softball W; Swimming and Diving M & W; Tennis M & W; Track and Field M & W; Volleyball W; Wrestling M

MINNESOTA STATE UNIVERSITY MOORHEAD

1104 7th Ave. South
Moorhead, MN 56563-0002
Tel: (218)236-2011
Free: 800-593-7246
Admissions: (218)477-2161
Fax: (218)236-2168
E-mail: dragon@mastate.edu
Web Site: http://www.mnstate.edu/
President/CEO: Dr. Roland Barden
Registrar: John Tandberg
Admissions: Gina Monson
Financial Aid: Carolyn Zehren
Type: Comprehensive **Sex:** Coed **Affiliation:** Minnesota State Colleges and Universities System **Scores:** 89% SAT V 400+; 93% SAT M 400+; 61% ACT 18-23; 27% ACT 24-29 **% Accepted:** 83 **Admission Plans:** Early Admission; Deferred Admission **Application Deadline:** August 07 **Application Fee:** $20.00 **H.S. Requirements:** High school diploma required; GED accepted **Costs Per Year:** Application fee: $20. State resident tuition: $4464 full-time, $148.80 per credit hour part-time. Nonresident tuition: $4464 full-time, $148.80 per credit hour part-time. Mandatory fees: $761 full-time, $88.85 per credit hour part-time. Full-time tuition and fees vary according to reciprocity agreements. Part-time tuition and fees vary according to reciprocity agreements. College room and board: $4974. College room only: $3044. Room and board charges vary according to board plan and housing facility. **Scholarships:** Available **Calendar System:** Semester, Summer Session Available **Enrollment:** FT 6,198, PT 1,044, Grad 410 **Faculty:** FT 270, PT

33 **Student-Faculty Ratio:** 20:1 **Exams:** SAT I or ACT **% Receiving Financial Aid:** 61 **% Residing in College-Owned, -Operated, or -Affiliated Housing:** 27 **Library Holdings:** 367,334 **Regional Accreditation:** North Central Association of Colleges and Schools **Credit Hours For Degree:** 64 credits, Associates; 128 credits, Bachelors **ROTC:** Army, Air Force **Professional Accreditation:** AACN, ACCE, ACA, ASLHA, CSWE, NAIT, NASAD, NASM, NCATE, NLN **Intercollegiate Athletics:** Basketball M & W; Cross-Country Running M & W; Football M; Golf M & W; Soccer W; Softball W; Swimming and Diving W; Tennis W; Track and Field M & W; Volleyball W; Wrestling M

MINNESOTA WEST COMMUNITY AND TECHNICAL COLLEGE
1314 North Hiawatha Ave.
Pipestone, MN 56164
Tel: (507)825-6800
Free: 800-658-2330
Admissions: (507)825-6804
Fax: (507)825-4656
E-mail: garygillin@mnwest.edu
Web Site: http://www.mnwest.edu/
President/CEO: Paul Dobbs
Registrar: Barbara Benz
Admissions: Gary Gillin
Financial Aid: Janice Pluim
Type: Two-Year College **Sex:** Coed **Affiliation:** Minnesota State Colleges and Universities System **% Accepted:** 81 **Admission Plans:** Open Admission **Application Deadline:** Rolling **Application Fee:** $20.00 **H.S. Requirements:** High school diploma required; GED accepted **Costs Per Year:** Application fee: $20. State resident tuition: $4085 full-time, $136.18 per credit part-time. Nonresident tuition: $8171 full-time, $272.36 per credit part-time. Mandatory fees: $377 full-time, $12.58 per credit part-time. **Scholarships:** Available **Calendar System:** Semester, Summer Session Available **Enrollment:** FT 1,439, PT 1,344 **Faculty:** FT 95, PT 157 **Student-Faculty Ratio:** 13:1 **Library Holdings:** 46,057 **Regional Accreditation:** North Central Association of Colleges and Schools **Credit Hours For Degree:** 64 credits, Associates **Professional Accreditation:** AAMAE, ADA, NAACLS, NLN **Intercollegiate Athletics:** Baseball M; Basketball M & W; Football M; Golf M & W; Softball W; Volleyball W; Wrestling M

NATIONAL AMERICAN UNIVERSITY (BLOOMINGTON)
112 West Market
Bloomington, MN 55425
Tel: (605)394-4800
Web Site: http://www.national.edu/ **Type:** Two-Year College **Sex:** Coed

NATIONAL AMERICAN UNIVERSITY (BROOKLYN CENTER)
6120 Earle Brown Dr.
Ste. 100
Brooklyn Center, MN 55430
Tel: (763)560-8377
Fax: (763)549-9955
Web Site: http://www.national.edu/ **Type:** Two-Year College **Sex:** Coed

NATIONAL AMERICAN UNIVERSITY (ROSEVILLE)
1500 West Hwy. 36
Roseville, MN 55113-4035
Tel: (651)644-1265
Fax: (651)644-0690
Web Site: http://www.national.edu/
Admissions: Steve Grunlan
Type: Four-Year College **Sex:** Coed **Affiliation:** National American University **Application Fee:** $25.00 **Calendar System:** Quarter **Enrollment:** FT 220, PT 226 **Faculty:** FT 5, PT 27 **Student-Faculty Ratio:** 10:1

NORMANDALE COMMUNITY COLLEGE
9700 France Ave. South
Bloomington, MN 55431-4399
Tel: (952)487-8200; (866)880-8740
Admissions: (952)487-8494
Fax: (612)487-8101
Web Site: http://www.normandale.edu/
President/CEO: Dr. Thomas J. Horak
Registrar: Tonya Hanson
Admissions: Russell Kreager
Financial Aid: Catherine Breuer
Type: Two-Year College **Sex:** Coed **Affiliation:** Minnesota State Colleges and Universities System **% Accepted:** 71 **Admission Plans:** Open Admission; Early Admission; Deferred Admission **Application Deadline:** Rolling **Application Fee:** $20.00 **H.S. Requirements:** High school diploma required; GED accepted **Costs Per Year:** Application fee: $20. State resident tuition: $3614 full-time, $133 per credit part-time. Nonresident tuition: $7227 full-time, $253 per credit part-time. Mandatory fees: $362 full-time. **Scholarships:** Available **Calendar System:** Semester, Summer Session Available **Enrollment:** FT 4,139, PT 4,122 **Faculty:** FT 170, PT 60 **Student-Faculty Ratio:** 28:1 **Library Holdings:** 98,141 **Regional Accreditation:** North Central Association of Colleges and Schools **Credit Hours For Degree:** 64 semester hours, Associates **ROTC:** Army, Air Force **Professional Accreditation:** ADA, NASM, NLN

NORTH CENTRAL UNIVERSITY
910 Elliot Ave.
Minneapolis, MN 55404-1322
Tel: (612)332-3491
Free: 800-289-6222
Admissions: (612)343-4460
Fax: (612)343-4778
E-mail: jghubert@northcentral.edu
Web Site: http://www.northcentral.edu/
President/CEO: Dr. Gordon L. Anderson
Registrar: Michael Stalker
Admissions: Jim Hubert
Financial Aid: Donna Jaeger
Type: Four-Year College **Sex:** Coed **Affiliation:** Assemblies of God **Scores:** 100% SAT V 400+; 89% SAT M 400+; 57% ACT 18-23; 23% ACT 24-29 **Admission Plans:** Deferred Admission **Application Fee:** $25.00 **H.S. Requirements:** High school diploma required; GED accepted **Costs Per Year:** Application fee: $25. One-time mandatory fee: $115. Comprehensive fee: $16,646 includes full-time tuition ($11,280), mandatory fees ($886), and college room and board ($4480). College room only: $2050. Room and board charges vary according to board plan and housing facility. Part-time tuition: $376 per credit. Part-time mandatory fees: $35 per credit. **Scholarships:** Available **Calendar System:** Semester, Summer Session Available **Enrollment:** FT 1,143, PT 98 **Faculty:** FT 40, PT 40 **Student-Faculty Ratio:** 19:1 **Exams:** SAT I, or ACT **% Residing in College-Owned, -Operated, or -Affiliated Housing:** 65 **Library Holdings:** 70,041 **Regional Accreditation:** North Central Association of Colleges and Schools **Credit Hours For Degree:** 62 credits, Associates; 127 credits, Bachelors **ROTC:** Army, Air Force **Intercollegiate Athletics:** Basketball M & W; Cross-Country Running M & W; Soccer M & W; Track and Field M & W; Volleyball W

NORTH HENNEPIN COMMUNITY COLLEGE
7411 85th Ave. North
Brooklyn Park, MN 55445-2231
Tel: (763)424-0702
Admissions: (763)424-0713
Fax: (763)424-0929
E-mail: lkirkeby@nhcc.edu
Web Site: http://www.nhcc.edu/
President/CEO: Ann Wynia
Registrar: Tom Wavrin
Admissions: Lori Kirkeby
Financial Aid: Jackie Olsson
Type: Two-Year College **Sex:** Coed **Affiliation:** Minnesota State Colleges and Universities System **% Accepted:** 100 **Admission Plans:** Open Admission; Early Admission; Deferred Admission **Application Deadline:** Rolling **Application Fee:** $20.00 **H.S. Requirements:** High school diploma or equivalent not required. For nursing program: High school diploma required; GED accepted **Costs Per Year:** Application fee: $20. State resident tuition: $3,158 full-time, $131.60 per credit part-time. Mandatory fees: $309 full-time, $10.30 per credit part-time. **Scholarships:** Available **Calendar System:** Semester, Summer Session Available **Faculty:** FT 98, PT 117 **Student-Faculty Ratio:** 29:1 **Library Holdings:** 69,375 **Regional Accreditation:** North Central Association of Colleges and Schools **Credit Hours For Degree:** 64 credits, Associates **Professional Accreditation:** ACBSP, NAACLS, NLN

NORTHLAND COMMUNITY AND TECHNICAL COLLEGE-EAST GRAND FORKS
2022 Central Ave., NW
East Grand Forks, MN 56721-2702

Tel: (218)773-3441
Free: 800-451-3441
Admissions: (218)773-4546
Fax: (218)773-4502
Web Site: http://www.northlandcollege.edu/
Admissions: Rita Lealos
Financial Aid: Rhonda Hettervig
Type: Two-Year College **Sex:** Coed **Application Fee:** $20.00 **Calendar System:** Semester **Student-Faculty Ratio:** 24:1 **Professional Accreditation:** AOTA

NORTHLAND COMMUNITY AND TECHNICAL COLLEGE-THIEF RIVER FALLS

1101 Hwy. One East
Thief River Falls, MN 56701
Tel: (218)681-0701
Free: 800-959-6282
Admissions: (218)681-0862
Fax: (218)681-6405
Web Site: http://www.northlandcollege.edu/
President/CEO: Dr. Orley D. Gunderson
Registrar: Dennis L. Bendickson
Admissions: Eugene Klinke
Financial Aid: Donna Quam
Type: Two-Year College **Sex:** Coed **Affiliation:** Minnesota State Colleges and Universities System **% Accepted:** 100 **Admission Plans:** Open Admission; Early Admission; Deferred Admission **Application Deadline:** September 01 **Application Fee:** $20.00 **H.S. Requirements:** High school diploma required; GED accepted **Costs Per Year:** Application fee: $20. State resident tuition: $4170 full-time, $139 per credit part-time. Mandatory fees: $490 full-time, $16.12 per credit part-time. **Scholarships:** Available **Calendar System:** Semester, Summer Session Available **Enrollment:** FT 2,017, PT 1,635 **Faculty:** FT 61, PT 30 **Student-Faculty Ratio:** 23:1 **Regional Accreditation:** North Central Association of Colleges and Schools **Credit Hours For Degree:** 64 semester hours, Associates **Intercollegiate Athletics:** Baseball M; Basketball M & W; Football M; Golf M & W; Softball W; Volleyball W

NORTHWEST TECHNICAL COLLEGE

905 Grant Ave., SE
Bemidji, MN 56601-4907
Tel: (218)755-4270
Free: 800-942-8324
Admissions: (218)846-7444
Web Site: http://bemidji.ntcmn.edu/
President/CEO: Dr. Ronald Swanson
Registrar: Tom Whelihan
Admissions: Tom Whelihan
Financial Aid: Tom Whelihan
Type: Two-Year College **Sex:** Coed **Affiliation:** Minnesota State Colleges and Universities System **Admission Plans:** Open Admission **Application Fee:** $20.00 **Scholarships:** Available **Calendar System:** Semester, Summer Session Available **Faculty:** FT 300, PT 100 **Exams:** Other **Regional Accreditation:** North Central Association of Colleges and Schools **Professional Accreditation:** ARCEST, AAMAE, ADA, AHIMA, CARC, JRCERT, NAACLS

NORTHWEST TECHNICAL INSTITUTE

11995 Singletree Ln.
Eden Prairie, MN 55344-5351
Tel: (952)944-0080
Free: 800-443-4223
Fax: (952)944-9274
Web Site: http://www.nti.edu/
President/CEO: Norris J. Nelson
Registrar: Carl Storck
Admissions: John Hartman
Financial Aid: Renee Cannon
Type: Two-Year College **Sex:** Coed **Admission Plans:** Open Admission **Application Fee:** $25.00 **H.S. Requirements:** High school diploma required; GED accepted **Scholarships:** Available **Calendar System:** Semester, Summer Session Not available **Enrollment:** FT 108 **Faculty:** FT 8, PT 1 **Student-Faculty Ratio:** 12:1 **Library Holdings:** 565 **Credit Hours For Degree:** 64 credits, Associates **Professional Accreditation:** ACCSCT

NORTHWESTERN COLLEGE

3003 Snelling Ave. North
St. Paul, MN 55113-1598
Tel: (651)631-5100
Free: 800-827-6827
Admissions: (651)631-5111
Fax: (651)631-5680
E-mail: admissions@nwc.edu
Web Site: http://www.nwc.edu/
President/CEO: Dr. Alan S. Cureton
Registrar: Andrew L. Simpson
Admissions: Kenneth K. Faffler
Financial Aid: Richard L. Blatchley
Type: Four-Year College **Sex:** Coed **Affiliation:** nondenominational **Scores:** 44% ACT 18-23; 38% ACT 24-29 **% Accepted:** 98 **Admission Plans:** Early Admission; Deferred Admission **Application Deadline:** July 01 **Application Fee:** $30.00 **H.S. Requirements:** High school diploma required; GED accepted **Costs Per Year:** Application fee: $30. Comprehensive fee: $25,220 includes full-time tuition ($19,100) and college room and board ($6120). College room only: $3400. Full-time tuition varies according to course load. Room and board charges vary according to board plan. Part-time tuition: $810 per credit. Part-time tuition varies according to course load. **Scholarships:** Available **Calendar System:** Semester, Summer Session Available **Enrollment:** FT 1,726, PT 41, Grad 18 **Faculty:** FT 85, PT 80 **Student-Faculty Ratio:** 16:1 **Exams:** SAT I or ACT **% Receiving Financial Aid:** 82 **% Residing in College-Owned, -Operated, or -Affiliated Housing:** 42 **Library Holdings:** 87,877 **Regional Accreditation:** North Central Association of Colleges and Schools **Credit Hours For Degree:** 60 semester hours, Associates; 125 semester hours, Bachelors **ROTC:** Army, Air Force **Professional Accreditation:** ACBSP, NASM **Intercollegiate Athletics:** Baseball M; Basketball M & W; Cheerleading W; Cross-Country Running M & W; Football M; Golf M; Ice Hockey M; Soccer M & W; Softball W; Tennis M & W; Track and Field M & W; Volleyball W

OAK HILLS CHRISTIAN COLLEGE

1600 Oak Hills Rd., SW
Bemidji, MN 56601-8832
Tel: (218)751-8670; 888-751-8670
Fax: (218)751-8825
E-mail: admissions@oakhills.edu
Web Site: http://www.oakhills.edu/
President/CEO: Dr. Daniel Clausen
Registrar: Mary Hannah
Admissions: Dan Hovestol
Financial Aid: Dan Hovestol
Type: Four-Year College **Sex:** Coed **Affiliation:** interdenominational **Scores:** 63% ACT 18-23; 12% ACT 24-29 **% Accepted:** 53 **Admission Plans:** Deferred Admission **Application Deadline:** Rolling **Application Fee:** $25.00 **H.S. Requirements:** High school diploma required; GED accepted **Costs Per Year:** Application fee: $25. Comprehensive fee: $16,390 includes full-time tuition ($11,940) and college room and board ($4450). Part-time tuition: $145 per semester hour. **Scholarships:** Available **Calendar System:** Semester, Summer Session Not available **Enrollment:** FT 152, PT 15 **Faculty:** FT 10, PT 8 **Student-Faculty Ratio:** 14:1 **Exams:** ACT **% Receiving Financial Aid:** 90 **% Residing in College-Owned, -Operated, or -Affiliated Housing:** 80 **Library Holdings:** 24,410 **Credit Hours For Degree:** 64 semester hours, Associates; 124 semester hours, Bachelors **Professional Accreditation:** AABC **Intercollegiate Athletics:** Basketball M & W; Ice Hockey M; Volleyball W

PILLSBURY BAPTIST BIBLE COLLEGE

315 South Grove Ave.
Owatonna, MN 55060-3097
Tel: (507)451-2710
Free: 800-747-4557
Fax: (507)451-6459
Web Site: http://www.pillsbury.edu/
President/CEO: Dr. Robert D. Crane
Registrar: Sherry Segal
Admissions: Steve Seidler
Financial Aid: Thomas D. Lawson

Type: Four-Year College **Sex:** Coed **Affiliation:** Baptist **Scores:** 58% ACT 18-23; 17% ACT 24-29 **Admission Plans:** Open Admission; Deferred Admission **Application Fee:** $25.00 **H.S. Requirements:** High school diploma required; GED accepted **Costs Per Year:** Application fee: $25. Comprehensive fee: $11,522 includes full-time tuition ($6750), mandatory fees ($888), and college room and board ($3884). Full-time tuition and fees vary according to course load. Part-time tuition: $225 per semester hour. Part-time mandatory fees: $21 per semester hour. Part-time tuition and fees vary according to course load. **Scholarships:** Available **Calendar System:** Semester, Summer Session Available **Enrollment:** FT 150, PT 22 **Faculty:** FT 17, PT 11 **Student-Faculty Ratio:** 6:1 **Exams:** ACT **% Residing in College-Owned, -Operated, or -Affiliated Housing:** 83 **Library Holdings:** 53,732 **Credit Hours For Degree:** 60 credit hours, Associates; 128 credit hours, Bachelors **Professional Accreditation:** AABC **Intercollegiate Athletics:** Baseball M; Basketball M & W; Golf M & W; Soccer M; Softball W; Volleyball W

PINE TECHNICAL COLLEGE
900 4th St. SE
Pine City, MN 55063
Tel: (320)629-5100
Free: 800-521-7463
Fax: (320)629-5101
Web Site: http://www.pinetech.edu/
President/CEO: Dr. Robert L. Musgrove
Registrar: Wolfgang Rothen
Admissions: Phil Schroeder
Financial Aid: Susan Pixley
Type: Two-Year College **Sex:** Coed **Affiliation:** Minnesota State Colleges and Universities System **Admission Plans:** Open Admission; Early Admission **Application Fee:** $20.00 **H.S. Requirements:** High school diploma required; GED accepted **Scholarships:** Available **Calendar System:** Semester, Summer Session Available **Enrollment:** FT 258, PT 512 **Faculty:** FT 22, PT 43 **Student-Faculty Ratio:** 16:1 **Exams:** Other **Library Holdings:** 6,000 **Regional Accreditation:** North Central Association of Colleges and Schools **Credit Hours For Degree:** 65 credits, Associates

RAINY RIVER COMMUNITY COLLEGE
1501 Hwy. 71
International Falls, MN 56649
Tel: (218)285-7722
Free: 800-456-3996
Admissions: (218)285-2207
Fax: (218)285-2239
E-mail: admissions@rr.mn.us
Web Site: http://www.rrcc.mnscu.edu/
President/CEO: Dr. Joe Sertich
Registrar: Berta Hagen
Admissions: Berta Hagen
Financial Aid: Scott Riley
Type: Two-Year College **Sex:** Coed **Affiliation:** Minnesota State Colleges and Universities System **Admission Plans:** Open Admission; Early Admission; Deferred Admission **Application Fee:** $20.00 **H.S. Requirements:** High school diploma required; GED accepted. For applicants who demonstrate ability to benefit from college: High school diploma or equivalent not required **Scholarships:** Available **Calendar System:** Semester, Summer Session Available **Enrollment:** FT 265, PT 119 **Faculty:** FT 17, PT 15 **Exams:** ACT, Other **% Residing in College-Owned, -Operated, or -Affiliated Housing:** 10 **Library Holdings:** 20,000 **Regional Accreditation:** North Central Association of Colleges and Schools **Credit Hours For Degree:** 96 credits, Associates **Intercollegiate Athletics:** Basketball M & W; Softball W; Volleyball W

RASMUSSEN COLLEGE EAGAN
3500 Federal Dr.
Eagan, MN 55122-1346
Tel: (651)687-9000
Free: 800-852-6367
Web Site: http://www.rasmussen.edu/
President/CEO: Tawnie Cortez
Registrar: Deborah Glaser
Admissions: Jacinda Miller
Financial Aid: Ken Lettenmaier
Type: Two-Year College **Sex:** Coed **Affiliation:** Rasmussen College System **Application Fee:** $60.00 **H.S. Requirements:** High school diploma required; GED accepted **Scholarships:** Available **Calendar System:** Quarter, Summer Session Not available **Enrollment:** FT 273, PT 67 **Faculty:** FT 10, PT 30 **Student-Faculty Ratio:** 12:1 **Exams:** Other **Credit Hours For Degree:** 113 credits, Associates **Professional Accreditation:** ACICS, AHIMA

RASMUSSEN COLLEGE EDEN PRAIRIE
7905 Golden Triangle Dr., Ste. 100
Eden Prairie, MN 55344
Tel: (952)545-2000
Web Site: http://www.rasmussen.edu/
President/CEO: Kristi Waite
Admissions: Jeff Hagy
Type: Two-Year College **Sex:** Coed **Affiliation:** Rasmussen College System **Admission Plans:** Early Admission; Deferred Admission **Application Deadline:** Rolling **Application Fee:** $60.00 **H.S. Requirements:** High school diploma required; GED accepted **Scholarships:** Available **Calendar System:** Quarter, Summer Session Available **Enrollment:** FT 209, PT 154 **Faculty:** FT 15, PT 17 **Student-Faculty Ratio:** 11:1 **Exams:** Other **Library Holdings:** 3,400 **Regional Accreditation:** North Central Association of Colleges and Schools **Credit Hours For Degree:** 116 credits, Associates **Professional Accreditation:** ACICS, AHIMA

RASMUSSEN COLLEGE MANKATO
501 Holly Ln.
Mankato, MN 56001-6803
Tel: (507)625-6556
Fax: (507)625-6557
E-mail: kathyc@rasmussen.edu
Web Site: http://www.rasmussen.edu/
President/CEO: Douglas Gardner
Admissions: Kathy Clifford
Financial Aid: Toni Hobbs
Type: Two-Year College **Sex:** Coed **Affiliation:** Rasmussen College System **Admission Plans:** Deferred Admission **Application Fee:** $60.00 **H.S. Requirements:** High school diploma required; GED accepted **Costs Per Year:** Application fee: $60. Tuition: $295 per credit part-time. **Scholarships:** Available **Calendar System:** Quarter, Summer Session Available **Enrollment:** FT 463 **Faculty:** FT 13, PT 29 **Student-Faculty Ratio:** 18:1 **Exams:** Other **Library Holdings:** 1,000 **Credit Hours For Degree:** 64 credits, Associates **Professional Accreditation:** ACICS, AHIMA

RASMUSSEN COLLEGE ST. CLOUD
226 Park Ave. South
St. Cloud, MN 56301-3713
Tel: (320)251-5600
Fax: (320)251-3702
Web Site: http://www.rasmussen.edu/
President/CEO: Cathy Wogen
Admissions: Andrea Peters
Financial Aid: Carol Dockendorf
Type: Two-Year College **Sex:** Coed **Affiliation:** Rasmussen College System **Admission Plans:** Early Admission; Deferred Admission **Application Fee:** $60.00 **H.S. Requirements:** High school diploma required; GED accepted **Scholarships:** Available **Calendar System:** Quarter, Summer Session Available **Enrollment:** FT 252, PT 281 **Faculty:** FT 13, PT 15 **Student-Faculty Ratio:** 19:1 **Exams:** Other **Library Holdings:** 689 **Regional Accreditation:** North Central Association of Colleges and Schools **Credit Hours For Degree:** 102 credits, Associates **Professional Accreditation:** ACICS, AHIMA

RIDGEWATER COLLEGE
PO Box 1097
Willmar, MN 56201-1097
Tel: (320)235-5114
Free: 800-722-1151
Admissions: (320)231-2907
Fax: (320)231-6602
E-mail: skerfield@ridgewater.mnscu.edu
Web Site: http://www.ridgewater.mnscu.edu/
President/CEO: Dr. Douglas Allen
Admissions: Sally Kerfeld
Financial Aid: Jim Rice
Type: Two-Year College **Sex:** Coed **Affiliation:** Minnesota State Colleges and Universities System **Admission Plans:** Open Admission; Preferred

Admission; Early Admission; Deferred Admission **Application Fee:** $20.00 **H.S. Requirements:** High school diploma required; GED accepted **Costs Per Year:** Application fee: $20. State resident tuition: $3896 full-time, $129.85 per credit part-time. Nonresident tuition: $3895 full-time. Mandatory fees: $459 full-time, $15.31 per credit part-time. Full-time tuition and fees vary according to program and reciprocity agreements. Part-time tuition and fees vary according to program and reciprocity agreements. **Scholarships:** Available **Calendar System:** Semester, Summer Session Available **Enrollment:** FT 2,419, PT 1,496 **Faculty:** FT 124, PT 108 **Student-Faculty Ratio:** 19:1 **Library Holdings:** 30,000 **Regional Accreditation:** North Central Association of Colleges and Schools **Credit Hours For Degree:** 64 semester hours, Associates **Professional Accreditation:** AHIMA, NLN **Intercollegiate Athletics:** Baseball M; Basketball M & W; Football M; Softball W; Tennis M & W; Volleyball W; Wrestling M

RIVERLAND COMMUNITY COLLEGE
1900 8th Ave., NW
Austin, MN 55912
Tel: (507)433-0600
Free: 800-247-5039
Admissions: (507)433-0517
Fax: (507)433-0515
E-mail: admissions@riverland.edu
Web Site: http://www.riverland.edu/
President/CEO: Dr. Terrence Leas
Registrar: Sue Jech
Admissions: Dani Heiny
Financial Aid: Gary Schindler
Type: Two-Year College **Sex:** Coed **Affiliation:** Minnesota State Colleges and Universities System **Admission Plans:** Open Admission; Early Admission **Application Deadline:** Rolling **Application Fee:** $20.00 **H.S. Requirements:** High school diploma required; GED accepted **Costs Per Year:** Application fee: $20. State resident tuition: $3915 full-time, $130.50 per credit part-time. Nonresident tuition: $3915 full-time, $130.50 per credit part-time. Mandatory fees: $17 per credit part-time. College room only: $2600. **Scholarships:** Available **Calendar System:** Semester, Summer Session Available **Faculty:** FT 101, PT 57 **Student-Faculty Ratio:** 18:1 **% Residing in College-Owned, -Operated, or -Affiliated Housing:** 2 **Library Holdings:** 33,500 **Regional Accreditation:** North Central Association of Colleges and Schools **Credit Hours For Degree:** 64 semester hours, Associates **Professional Accreditation:** JRCERT, NLN **Intercollegiate Athletics:** Baseball M; Basketball M & W; Golf M & W; Softball W; Volleyball W

ROCHESTER COMMUNITY AND TECHNICAL COLLEGE
851 30th Ave., SE
Rochester, MN 55904-4999
Tel: (507)285-7210
Admissions: (507)280-3509
Fax: (507)285-7496
Web Site: http://www.roch.edu/
President/CEO: Donald D. Supalla
Registrar: Nancy Shumaker
Admissions: Troy Tynsky
Financial Aid: Rosemary Hicks
Type: Two-Year College **Sex:** Coed **Affiliation:** Minnesota State Colleges and Universities System **Admission Plans:** Open Admission; Early Admission **Application Fee:** $20.00 **H.S. Requirements:** High school diploma required; GED accepted **Scholarships:** Available **Calendar System:** Semester, Summer Session Available **Faculty:** FT 92, PT 133 **Library Holdings:** 62,000 **Regional Accreditation:** North Central Association of Colleges and Schools **Professional Accreditation:** ARCEST, AAMAE, ADA, AHIMA, CARC, NLN **Intercollegiate Athletics:** Baseball M; Basketball M & W; Football M; Golf M & W; Soccer W; Softball W; Volleyball W; Wrestling M

ST. CLOUD STATE UNIVERSITY
720 4th Ave. South
St. Cloud, MN 56301-4498
Tel: (320)308-0121; 877-654-7278
Admissions: (320)308-2244
E-mail: scsu4u@stcloudstate.edu
Web Site: http://www.stcloudstate.edu/
President/CEO: Dr. Roy H. Saigo
Admissions: Pat Krueger
Financial Aid: Frank Loncorich
Type: Comprehensive **Sex:** Coed **Affiliation:** Minnesota State Colleges and Universities System **Scores:** 61.3% ACT 18-23; 26.8% ACT 24-29 **% Accepted:** 78 **Admission Plans:** Early Admission; Deferred Admission **Application Deadline:** June 01 **Application Fee:** $20.00 **H.S. Requirements:** High school diploma required; GED accepted **Costs Per Year:** Application fee: $20. State resident tuition: $4760 full-time, $159 per credit part-time. Nonresident tuition: $10,332 full-time, $344 per credit part-time. Mandatory fees: $562 full-time, $23 per credit part-time. Full-time tuition and fees vary according to course load and reciprocity agreements. Part-time tuition and fees vary according to course load and reciprocity agreements. College room and board: $4688. College room only: $3340. Room and board charges vary according to board plan and housing facility. **Scholarships:** Available **Calendar System:** Semester, Summer Session Available **Enrollment:** FT 11,611, PT 2,875, Grad 1,478 **Faculty:** FT 650, PT 211 **Student-Faculty Ratio:** 17:1 **Exams:** SAT I or ACT **% Receiving Financial Aid:** 45 **% Residing in College-Owned, -Operated, or -Affiliated Housing:** 21 **Library Holdings:** 897,973 **Regional Accreditation:** North Central Association of Colleges and Schools **Credit Hours For Degree:** 60 credit hours, Associates; 120 credit hours, Bachelors **ROTC:** Army **Professional Accreditation:** AACSB, ABET, ACEJMC, ACA, ASLHA, CAA, CORE, CSWE, NASAD, NASM, NAST, NCATE **Intercollegiate Athletics:** Baseball M; Basketball M & W; Bowling M & W; Cheerleading M & W; Crew M & W; Cross-Country Running M & W; Equestrian Sports M & W; Fencing M & W; Football M; Golf M & W; Ice Hockey M & W; Rugby M & W; Skiing (Cross-Country) M & W; Skiing (Downhill) M & W; Soccer M & W; Softball W; Swimming and Diving M & W; Tennis M & W; Track and Field M & W; Ultimate Frisbee M & W; Volleyball M & W; Wrestling M

ST. CLOUD TECHNICAL COLLEGE
1540 Northway Dr.
St. Cloud, MN 56303-1240
Tel: (320)654-5000
Admissions: (320)308-5089
Fax: (320)654-5981
E-mail: enroll@sctc.edu
Web Site: http://www.sctc.edu/
President/CEO: Dr. Joan B. Barrett-Volkmuth
Registrar: Jodi Elness
Admissions: Jodi Elness
Type: Two-Year College **Sex:** Coed **Affiliation:** Minnesota State Colleges and Universities System **% Accepted:** 62 **Admission Plans:** Open Admission; Early Admission; Deferred Admission **Application Deadline:** Rolling **Application Fee:** $20.00 **H.S. Requirements:** High school diploma required; GED accepted **Costs Per Year:** Application fee: $20. State resident tuition: $3678 full-time, $122.60 per credit part-time. Nonresident tuition: $7356 full-time, $145.20 per credit part-time. Mandatory fees: $302 full-time, $10.06 per credit part-time. **Scholarships:** Available **Calendar System:** Semester, Summer Session Available **Enrollment:** FT 2,188, PT 1,160 **Faculty:** FT 113, PT 139 **Student-Faculty Ratio:** 17:1 **Library Holdings:** 10,000 **Regional Accreditation:** North Central Association of Colleges and Schools **Credit Hours For Degree:** 60 credits, Associates **Professional Accreditation:** ARCEST, ADA **Intercollegiate Athletics:** Baseball M; Basketball M & W; Softball W; Volleyball W

SAINT JOHN'S UNIVERSITY
PO Box 2000
Collegeville, MN 56321
Tel: (320)363-2011
Free: 800-544-1489
Fax: (320)363-3206
E-mail: admissions@csbsju.edu
Web Site: http://www.csbsju.edu/
President/CEO: Br. Dietrich Reinhart, OSB
Registrar: Julie Gruska
Admissions: Mary Milbert
Financial Aid: Stuart Perry
Type: Comprehensive **Sex:** Coed **Affiliation:** Roman Catholic **Scores:** 100% SAT V 400+; 100% SAT M 400+; 33% ACT 18-23; 52% ACT 24-29 **% Accepted:** 87 **Admission Plans:** Deferred Admission **Application Deadline:** December 01 **Application Fee:** $0.00 **H.S. Requirements:** High school diploma required; GED accepted. For home schooled students with appropriate documentation of college preparatory curriculum: High school diploma or equivalent not required **Costs Per Year:** Application fee: $0. Comprehensive fee: $29,749 includes full-time tuition ($23,064), mandatory fees ($410), and college room and board ($6275). College room only:

$3151. Room and board charges vary according to board plan and housing facility. Part-time tuition: $961 per credit. Part-time mandatory fees: $205 per term. Part-time tuition and fees vary according to course load. **Scholarships:** Available **Calendar System:** Semester, Summer Session Not available **Enrollment:** FT 1,845, PT 30, Grad 121 **Faculty:** FT 147, PT 29 **Student-Faculty Ratio:** 12:1 **Exams:** SAT I or ACT **% Receiving Financial Aid:** 60 **% Residing in College-Owned, -Operated, or -Affiliated Housing:** 83 **Library Holdings:** 805,376 **Regional Accreditation:** North Central Association of Colleges and Schools **Credit Hours For Degree:** 124 credits, Bachelors **ROTC:** Army **Professional Accreditation:** AACN, ATS, CSWE, NASM, NCATE, NLN **Intercollegiate Athletics:** Baseball M; Basketball M; Crew M; Cross-Country Running M; Football M; Golf M; Ice Hockey M; Lacrosse M; Riflery M; Rugby M; Skiing (Cross-Country) M; Soccer M; Swimming and Diving M; Tennis M; Track and Field M; Ultimate Frisbee M; Volleyball M; Water Polo M; Wrestling M

SAINT MARY'S UNIVERSITY OF MINNESOTA

700 Terrace Heights
Winona, MN 55987-1399
Tel: (507)452-4430
Free: 800-635-5987
Admissions: (507)457-1700
Fax: (507)457-1722
E-mail: admissions@smumn.edu
Web Site: http://www.smumn.edu/
President/CEO: Br. Louis DeThomasis, FSC
Registrar: Susan K. Edel
Admissions: Anthony M. Piscitiello
Financial Aid: Jayne Wobig

Type: Comprehensive **Sex:** Coed **Affiliation:** Roman Catholic **Scores:** 100% SAT V 400+; 94.74% SAT M 400+; 48.12% ACT 18-23; 33.45% ACT 24-29 **% Accepted:** 83 **Admission Plans:** Early Admission; Deferred Admission **Application Deadline:** May 01 **Application Fee:** $25.00 **H.S. Requirements:** High school diploma required; GED accepted **Costs Per Year:** Application fee: $25. Comprehensive fee: $26,639 includes full-time tuition ($20,294), mandatory fees ($445), and college room and board ($5900). College room only: $3300. **Scholarships:** Available **Calendar System:** Semester, Summer Session Available **Enrollment:** FT 1,286, PT 394, Grad 3,542 **Faculty:** FT 101, PT 460 **Student-Faculty Ratio:** 12:1 **Exams:** SAT I or ACT **% Receiving Financial Aid:** 79 **% Residing in College-Owned, -Operated, or -Affiliated Housing:** 77 **Library Holdings:** 168,923 **Regional Accreditation:** North Central Association of Colleges and Schools **Credit Hours For Degree:** 122 credits, Bachelors **ROTC:** Army **Professional Accreditation:** AANA, JRCNMT **Intercollegiate Athletics:** Baseball M; Basketball M & W; Cross-Country Running M & W; Golf M & W; Ice Hockey M & W; Soccer M & W; Softball W; Swimming and Diving M & W; Tennis M & W; Track and Field M & W; Volleyball W

ST. OLAF COLLEGE

1520 St. Olaf Ave.
Northfield, MN 55057-1098
Tel: (507)646-2222
Free: 800-800-3025
Admissions: (507)646-3025
Fax: (507)646-3832
E-mail: admiss@stolaf.edu
Web Site: http://www.stolaf.edu/
President/CEO: Dr. Christopher Meredith Thomforde
Registrar: Dr. Mary Cisar
Admissions: Jerry Pope
Financial Aid: Katharine Ruby

Type: Four-Year College **Sex:** Coed **Affiliation:** Lutheran **Scores:** 100% SAT V 400+; 100% SAT M 400+; 13.7% ACT 18-23; 56.1% ACT 24-29 **% Accepted:** 73 **Admission Plans:** Early Action; Early Decision Plan; Deferred Admission **Application Deadline:** Rolling **Application Fee:** $35.00 **H.S. Requirements:** High school diploma required; GED accepted **Costs Per Year:** Application fee: $35. Comprehensive fee: $35,600 includes full-time tuition ($28,200) and college room and board ($7400). College room only: $3450. Part-time tuition: $880 per credit hour. **Scholarships:** Available **Calendar System:** 4-1-4, Summer Session Available **Enrollment:** FT 3,005, PT 53 **Faculty:** FT 197, PT 135 **Student-Faculty Ratio:** 12:1 **Exams:** SAT I or ACT **% Receiving Financial Aid:** 62 **% Residing in College-Owned, -Operated, or -Affiliated Housing:** 96 **Library Holdings:** 697,516 **Regional Accreditation:** North Central Association of Colleges and Schools **Credit Hours For Degree:** 35 courses, Bachelors **Professional Accreditation:** AACN, AAFCS, CSWE, NASD, NASM, NAST, NCATE, NLN **Intercollegiate Athletics:** Baseball M; Basketball M & W; Cross-Country Running M & W; Football M; Golf M & W; Ice Hockey M & W; Skiing (Cross-Country) M & W; Skiing (Downhill) M & W; Soccer M & W; Softball W; Swimming and Diving M & W; Tennis M & W; Track and Field M & W; Volleyball W; Wrestling M

SAINT PAUL COLLEGE-A COMMUNITY & TECHNICAL COLLEGE

235 Marshall Ave.
St. Paul, MN 55102-1800
Tel: (651)846-1600
Free: 800-227-6029
Admissions: (651)846-1362
Fax: (651)221-1416
Web Site: http://www.saintpaul.edu/
President/CEO: Dr. Donovan Schwichtenberg
Registrar: Katie Yep
Admissions: Thomas Matos
Financial Aid: Susan Prater

Type: Two-Year College **Sex:** Coed **Affiliation:** Minnesota State Colleges and Universities System **% Accepted:** 89 **Admission Plans:** Open Admission; Early Admission **Application Deadline:** Rolling **Application Fee:** $20.00 **H.S. Requirements:** High school diploma required; GED accepted **Costs Per Year:** Application fee: $20. State resident tuition: $3,068 full-time, $127.85 per credit part-time. Nonresident tuition: $6,137 full-time, $255.70 per credit part-time. Mandatory fees: $232 full-time, $8.90 per credit part-time. **Scholarships:** Available **Calendar System:** Semester, Summer Session Not available **Enrollment:** FT 1,529, PT 3,640 **Faculty:** FT 108, PT 185 **Student-Faculty Ratio:** 16:1 **Exams:** Other **Library Holdings:** 12,000 **Regional Accreditation:** North Central Association of Colleges and Schools **Credit Hours For Degree:** 64 semester credits, Associates **Professional Accreditation:** ACF, CARC, NAACLS, NLN

SOUTH CENTRAL TECHNICAL COLLEGE

1920 Lee Blvd.
North Mankato, MN 56003
Tel: (507)389-7200
Admissions: (507)389-7334
Web Site: http://www.sctc.mnscu.edu/
President/CEO: Keith Stover
Admissions: Beverly Herda

Type: Two-Year College **Sex:** Coed **Affiliation:** Minnesota State Colleges and Universities System **Admission Plans:** Open Admission **Application Fee:** $20.00 **H.S. Requirements:** High school diploma required; GED accepted **Costs Per Year:** Application fee: $20. Area resident tuition: $115 per credit part-time. State resident tuition: $3800 full-time. Mandatory fees: $16 per credit part-time. **Calendar System:** Semester **Enrollment:** FT 2,350 **Faculty:** FT 90, PT 120 **Student-Faculty Ratio:** 18:1 **Regional Accreditation:** North Central Association of Colleges and Schools **Credit Hours For Degree:** 72 credits, Associates **Professional Accreditation:** ADA, NAACLS

SOUTHWEST MINNESOTA STATE UNIVERSITY

1501 State St.
Marshall, MN 56258
Tel: (507)537-7021
Free: 800-642-0684
Admissions: (507)537-6286
Fax: (507)537-7154
E-mail: shearerr@southwest.msus.edu
Web Site: http://www.southwest.msus.edu/
President/CEO: Dr. David C. Danahar
Registrar: Pat Carmody
Admissions: Richard Shearer
Financial Aid: Marcia Hubner

Type: Comprehensive **Sex:** Coed **Affiliation:** Minnesota State Colleges and Universities System **Scores:** 57% ACT 18-23; 25% ACT 24-29 **Admission Plans:** Early Admission; Deferred Admission **Application Fee:** $20.00 **H.S. Requirements:** High school diploma required; GED accepted **Scholarships:** Available **Calendar System:** Semester, Summer Session Available **Enrollment:** FT 2,310, PT 2,857, Grad 469 **Faculty:** FT 122, PT 37 **Student-Faculty Ratio:** 18:1 **Exams:** SAT I or ACT, SAT I and SAT II or ACT **% Receiving Financial Aid:** 60 **% Residing in College-Owned, -Operated, or -Affiliated Housing:** 53 **Library Holdings:** 167,888 **Regional Accreditation:** North Central Association of Colleges and Schools **Credit Hours For Degree:** 64 credit hours, Associates; 128 credit hours, Bachelors **Profes-**

sional Accreditation: CSWE, NASM **Intercollegiate Athletics:** Baseball M; Basketball M & W; Football M; Golf W; Soccer W; Softball W; Tennis W; Volleyball W; Wrestling M

UNIVERSITY OF MINNESOTA, CROOKSTON

2900 University Ave.
Crookston, MN 56716-5001
Tel: (218)281-6510
Free: 800-862-6466
Admissions: (218)281-8569
Fax: (218)281-8050
E-mail: info@crk.umn.edu
Web Site: http://www.crk.umn.edu/
President/CEO: Dr. Velmer S. Burton, Jr.
Admissions: Mary Feller
Financial Aid: Robert B. Nelson
Type: Four-Year College **Sex:** Coed **Affiliation:** University of Minnesota System **Scores:** 62.5% SAT V 400+; 87.5% SAT M 400+; 56% ACT 18-23; 26% ACT 24-29 **% Accepted:** 92 **Admission Plans:** Deferred Admission **Application Deadline:** Rolling **Application Fee:** $30.00 **H.S. Requirements:** High school diploma required; GED accepted **Costs Per Year:** Application fee: $30. State resident tuition: $5865 full-time, $195.50 per credit part-time. Nonresident tuition: $6865 full-time, $195.50 per credit part-time. Mandatory fees: $2254 full-time, $145 per credit part-time. Full-time tuition and fees vary according to reciprocity agreements. Part-time tuition and fees vary according to course load and reciprocity agreements. College room and board: $5038. College room only: $2458. Room and board charges vary according to board plan and housing facility. Tuition guaranteed not to increase for student's term of enrollment. **Scholarships:** Available **Calendar System:** Semester, Summer Session Available **Enrollment:** FT 966, PT 1,168 **Faculty:** FT 53, PT 51 **Student-Faculty Ratio:** 19:1 **Exams:** ACT **% Receiving Financial Aid:** 70 **% Residing in College-Owned, -Operated, or -Affiliated Housing:** 38 **Library Holdings:** 30,000 **Regional Accreditation:** North Central Association of Colleges and Schools **Credit Hours For Degree:** 64 semester hours, Associates; 120 semester hours, Bachelors **ROTC:** Air Force **Intercollegiate Athletics:** Baseball M; Basketball M & W; Cross-Country Running W; Football M; Golf M & W; Ice Hockey M; Soccer W; Softball W; Tennis W; Volleyball W

UNIVERSITY OF MINNESOTA, DULUTH

10 University Dr.
Duluth, MN 55812-2496
Tel: (218)726-8000
Free: 800-232-1339
Admissions: (218)726-7171
Fax: (218)726-6394
E-mail: umdadmis@d.umn.edu
Web Site: http://www.d.umn.edu/
President/CEO: Dr. Kathryn A. Martin
Registrar: Brenda Herzig
Admissions: Beth Esselstrom
Financial Aid: Brenda H. Herzig
Type: Comprehensive **Sex:** Coed **Affiliation:** University of Minnesota System **Scores:** 66% ACT 18-23; 27% ACT 24-29 **% Accepted:** 79 **Application Deadline:** February 01 **Application Fee:** $35.00 **H.S. Requirements:** High school diploma required; GED accepted **Costs Per Year:** Application fee: $35. State resident tuition: $7170 full-time, $239 per credit part-time. Nonresident tuition: $18,270 full-time, $609 per credit part-time. Mandatory fees: $1758 full-time. Full-time tuition and fees vary according to course load, degree level, program, and reciprocity agreements. Part-time tuition varies according to course load, degree level, program, and reciprocity agreements. College room and board: $5546. **Scholarships:** Available **Calendar System:** Semester, Summer Session Available **Enrollment:** FT 8,393, PT 1,145, Grad 696 **Faculty:** FT 407, PT 99 **Student-Faculty Ratio:** 22:1 **Exams:** SAT I or ACT **% Receiving Financial Aid:** 52 **% Residing in College-Owned, -Operated, or -Affiliated Housing:** 30 **Library Holdings:** 709,150 **Regional Accreditation:** North Central Association of Colleges and Schools **Credit Hours For Degree:** 120 credits, Bachelors **ROTC:** Air Force **Professional Accreditation:** AACSB, ABET, ACA, ASLHA, CSWE, LCMEAMA, NASM, NCATE **Intercollegiate Athletics:** Baseball M; Basketball M & W; Bowling M & W; Cheerleading W; Cross-Country Running M & W; Football M; Ice Hockey M & W; Lacrosse M & W; Rugby M & W; Skiing (Downhill) M & W; Soccer M & W; Softball W; Tennis M & W; Track and Field M & W; Volleyball M & W; Weight Lifting M & W

UNIVERSITY OF MINNESOTA, MORRIS

600 East 4th St.
Morris, MN 56267-2134
Tel: (320)589-2211
Free: 800-992-8863
Admissions: (320)539-6035
Fax: (320)589-6399
Web Site: http://www.mrs.umn.edu/
President/CEO: Dr. Samuel Schuman
Registrar: Ruth Thielke
Admissions: Dr. James Morales
Financial Aid: Pam Engebretson
Type: Four-Year College **Sex:** Coed **Affiliation:** University of Minnesota System **Scores:** 100% SAT V 400+; 99% SAT M 400+; 33% ACT 18-23; 51% ACT 24-29 **% Accepted:** 82 **Admission Plans:** Early Admission; Early Action; Deferred Admission **Application Deadline:** March 15 **Application Fee:** $35.00 **H.S. Requirements:** High school diploma required; GED accepted **Costs Per Year:** Application fee: $35. State resident tuition: $8204 full-time, $273.47 per credit part-time. Nonresident tuition: $8204 full-time, $273.47 per credit part-time. Mandatory fees: $1517 full-time. Full-time tuition and fees vary according to reciprocity agreements. Part-time tuition varies according to course load and reciprocity agreements. College room and board: $5750. College room only: $2730. Room and board charges vary according to board plan and housing facility. **Scholarships:** Available **Calendar System:** Semester, Summer Session Available **Enrollment:** FT 1,527, PT 151 **Faculty:** FT 121, PT 55 **Student-Faculty Ratio:** 13:1 **Exams:** SAT I or ACT **% Receiving Financial Aid:** 67 **% Residing in College-Owned, -Operated, or -Affiliated Housing:** 51 **Library Holdings:** 191,469 **Regional Accreditation:** North Central Association of Colleges and Schools **Credit Hours For Degree:** 120 credits, Bachelors **Professional Accreditation:** NCATE **Intercollegiate Athletics;** Baseball M; Basketball M & W; Cross-Country Running W; Football M; Golf M & W; Soccer W; Softball W; Swimming and Diving W; Tennis M & W; Track and Field M & W; Volleyball W

UNIVERSITY OF MINNESOTA, TWIN CITIES CAMPUS

100 Church St., SE
Minneapolis, MN 55455-0213
Tel: (612)625-5000
Free: 800-752-1000
Admissions: (612)625-2008
Fax: (612)626-1693
E-mail: admissions@tc.umn.edu
Web Site: http://www.umn.edu/tc/
President/CEO: Robert H. Bruininks
Registrar: Sue van Voorhis
Admissions: Dr. Wayne Sigler
Financial Aid: Kristine A. Wright
Type: University **Sex:** Coed **Affiliation:** University of Minnesota System **Scores:** 97.3% SAT V 400+; 99.2% SAT M 400+; 28.49% ACT 18-23; 53. 01% ACT 24-29 **% Accepted:** 71 **Admission Plans:** Early Admission; Deferred Admission **Application Deadline:** Rolling **Application Fee:** $45.00 **H.S. Requirements:** High school diploma required; GED accepted **Costs Per Year:** Application fee: $45. State resident tuition: $7140 full-time, $275 per credit part-time. Nonresident tuition: $19,670 full-time, $722 per credit part-time. Mandatory fees: $1482 full-time. Full-time tuition and fees vary according to program and reciprocity agreements. Part-time tuition varies according to course load, program, and reciprocity agreements. College room and board: $6722. College room only: $3886. Room and board charges vary according to board plan, housing facility, and location. Tuition guaranteed not to increase for student's term of enrollment. **Scholarships:** Available **Calendar System:** Semester, Summer Session Available **Enrollment:** FT 26,957, PT 5,860, Grad 14,883 **Faculty:** FT 1,680, PT 253 **Student-Faculty Ratio:** 15:1 **Exams:** SAT I or ACT **% Receiving Financial Aid:** 48 **% Residing in College-Owned, -Operated, or -Affiliated Housing:** 21 **Library Holdings:** 5,700,000 **Regional Accreditation:** North Central Association of Colleges and Schools **Credit Hours For Degree:** 120 semester credits, Bachelors **ROTC:** Army, Air Force **Professional Accreditation:** AACSB, ABET, ACEHSA, ACEJMC, AAMFT, AACN, AANA, ABA, ABFSE, ACNM, ACPhE, ADA, ADtA, ACSP, AOTA, APTA, APA, ASLA, ASLHA, AVMA ACIPE, AALS, CEPH, CSWE, FIDER, LCMEAMA, NAACLS, NASD, NASM, NAST, NCATE, NLN, NRPA, SAF **Intercollegiate Athletics:** Baseball M; Basketball

M & W; Cross-Country Running M & W; Football M; Golf M & W; Gymnastics M & W; Ice Hockey M & W; Soccer W; Softball W; Swimming and Diving M & W; Tennis M & W; Track and Field M & W; Volleyball W; Wrestling M

UNIVERSITY OF ST. THOMAS
2115 Summit Ave.
St. Paul, MN 55105-1096
Tel: (651)962-5000
Free: 800-328-6819
Admissions: (651)962-6150
Fax: (651)962-6160
E-mail: admissions@stthomas.edu
Web Site: http://www.stthomas.edu/
President/CEO: Rev. Dennis Dease
Registrar: Robert McCluskey
Admissions: Marla Friederichs
Financial Aid: Kris Getting
Type: University **Sex:** Coed **Affiliation:** Roman Catholic **Scores:** 99% SAT V 400+; 98% SAT M 400+; 38% ACT 18-23; 51% ACT 24-29 **Admission Plans:** Deferred Admission **Application Fee:** $0.00 **H.S. Requirements:** High school diploma required; GED accepted **Costs Per Year:** Application fee: $0. Comprehensive fee: $30,380. Part-time tuition: $715 per credit hour. Part-time tuition varies according to class time, course load, and program. Tuition: $715 per credit hour part-time. Part-time tuition varies according to class time, course load, and program. **Scholarships:** Available **Calendar System:** 4-1-4, Summer Session Available **Enrollment:** FT 4,788, PT 514, Grad 4,742 **Faculty:** FT 400, PT 417 **Student-Faculty Ratio:** 14:1 **Exams:** ACT, SAT I or ACT **% Receiving Financial Aid:** 46 **% Residing in College-Owned, -Operated, or -Affiliated Housing:** 39 **Library Holdings:** 440,023 **Regional Accreditation:** North Central Association of Colleges and Schools **Credit Hours For Degree:** 132 credits, Bachelors **ROTC:** Army, Air Force **Professional Accreditation:** ABET, ACEHSA, ABA, APA, ACIPE, ATS, CSWE, NASM, NCATE **Intercollegiate Athletics:** Baseball M; Basketball M & W; Crew M & W; Cross-Country Running M & W; Football M; Golf M & W; Ice Hockey M & W; Lacrosse M & W; Skiing (Downhill) M & W; Soccer M & W; Softball W; Swimming and Diving M & W; Tennis M & W; Track and Field M & W; Volleyball W

VERMILION COMMUNITY COLLEGE
1900 East Camp St.
Ely, MN 55731-1996
Tel: (218)365-7200
Free: 800-657-3608
Admissions: (218)365-7224
Web Site: http://www.vcc.edu/
President/CEO: Dr. Sue Collins
Registrar: Nadine Forsman
Admissions: Todd Heiman
Financial Aid: Deb Miller
Type: Two-Year College **Sex:** Coed **Affiliation:** Minnesota State Colleges and Universities System **% Accepted:** 57 **Admission Plans:** Open Admission; Early Admission; Deferred Admission **Application Deadline:** Rolling **Application Fee:** $20.00 **H.S. Requirements:** High school diploma required; GED accepted **Costs Per Year:** Application fee: $20. State resident tuition: $4190 full-time, $140 per credit part-time. Nonresident tuition: $5120 full-time, $171 per credit part-time. College room and board: $4560. College room only: $2900. **Scholarships:** Available **Calendar System:** Semester, Summer Session Available **Enrollment:** FT 533, PT 212 **Faculty:** FT 25, PT 60 **Student-Faculty Ratio:** 13:1 **% Residing in College-Owned, -Operated, or -Affiliated Housing:** 50 **Library Holdings:** 19,500 **Regional Accreditation:** North Central Association of Colleges and Schools **Intercollegiate Athletics:** Baseball M; Basketball M & W; Football M; Softball W; Volleyball W

WALDEN UNIVERSITY
155 Fifth Ave. South
Minneapolis, MN 55401
Tel: (612)338-7224; (866)492-5336
E-mail: request@walden.edu
Web Site: http://www.waldenu.edu/
President/CEO: Dr. Kent Morrison
Registrar: Landon Pirius
Admissions: Seth Saunders
Financial Aid: Michael Rogge
Type: Two-Year Upper Division **Sex:** Coed **Costs Per Year:** Tuition: $8280 full-time, $230 per credit part-time. **Calendar System:** Miscellaneous **Enrollment:** FT 55, PT 1,174, Grad 20,939 **Faculty:** FT 68, PT 1,016 **Student-Faculty Ratio:** 20:1 **Regional Accreditation:** North Central Association of Colleges and Schools

WINONA STATE UNIVERSITY
PO Box 5838
Winona, MN 55987-5838
Tel: (507)457-5000
Free: 800-DIAL WSU
Admissions: (507)457-5100
Fax: (507)457-5620
E-mail: admissions@winona.edu
President/CEO: Dr. Darrell Krueger
Registrar: Glenn Petersen
Admissions: Carl Stange
Financial Aid: Greg Peterson
Type: Comprehensive **Sex:** Coed **Affiliation:** Minnesota State Colleges and Universities System **Scores:** 40% ACT 18-23; 56% ACT 24-29 **% Accepted:** 79 **Admission Plans:** Early Admission; Early Action; Deferred Admission **Application Deadline:** Rolling **Application Fee:** $20.00 **H.S. Requirements:** High school diploma required; GED accepted **Costs Per Year:** Application fee: $20. State resident tuition: $5877 full-time. Nonresident tuition: $10,297 full-time. Mandatory fees: $1850 full-time. College room and board: $5000. Room and board charges vary according to board plan and housing facility. **Scholarships:** Available **Calendar System:** Semester, Summer Session Available **Enrollment:** FT 6,776, PT 793, Grad 452 **Faculty:** FT 315, PT 42 **Student-Faculty Ratio:** 21:1 **Exams:** SAT I or ACT **% Receiving Financial Aid:** 52 **% Residing in College-Owned, -Operated, or -Affiliated Housing:** 28 **Library Holdings:** 243,500 **Regional Accreditation:** North Central Association of Colleges and Schools **Credit Hours For Degree:** 64 semester hours, Associates; 128 semester hours, Bachelors **ROTC:** Army **Professional Accreditation:** ABET, AACN, ACA, CSWE, JRCEPAT, NASM, NAST, NCATE, NLN **Intercollegiate Athletics:** Baseball M; Basketball M & W; Bowling M & W; Cross-Country Running M & W; Fencing M & W; Football M; Golf M & W; Gymnastics W; Ice Hockey M; Rugby M & W; Skiing (Downhill) M & W; Soccer M & W; Softball W; Tennis M & W; Track and Field W; Volleyball M & W; Wrestling M

ALCORN STATE UNIVERSITY
1000 ASU Dr.
Alcorn State, MS 39096-7500
Tel: (601)877-6100
Free: 800-222-6790
Admissions: (601)877-6147
Fax: (601)877-6347
E-mail: ebarnes@alcorn.edu
Web Site: http://www.alcorn.edu/
President/CEO: Dr. Clinton Bristow, Jr.
Registrar: Dr. Alice Davis Gill
Admissions: Emanuel Barnes
Financial Aid: Juanita Russell
Type: Comprehensive **Sex:** Coed **Affiliation:** Mississippi Institutions of Higher Learning **Scores:** 42% ACT 18-23; 7% ACT 24-29 **% Accepted:** 68 **Admission Plans:** Preferred Admission; Early Admission; Deferred Admission **Application Deadline:** Rolling **Application Fee:** $0.00 **H.S. Requirements:** High school diploma required; GED accepted **Costs Per Year:** Application fee: $0. State resident tuition: $3919 full-time, $163 per hour part-time. Nonresident tuition: $8887 full-time, $370 per hour part-time. Mandatory fees: $807 full-time. College room and board: $4272. College room only: $2428. **Scholarships:** Available **Calendar System:** Semester, Summer Session Not available **Enrollment:** FT 2,676, PT 286, Grad 582 **Faculty:** FT 175, PT 34 **Student-Faculty Ratio:** 16:1 **Exams:** SAT I or ACT **% Receiving Financial Aid:** 81 **% Residing in College-Owned, -Operated, or -Affiliated Housing:** 52 **Library Holdings:** 210,036 **Regional Accreditation:** Southern Association of Colleges and Schools **Credit Hours For Degree:** 72 semester hours, Associates; 128 semester hours, Bachelors **ROTC:** Army **Professional Accreditation:** AAFCS, ADtA, NAIT, NASM, NCATE, NLN **Intercollegiate Athletics:** Baseball M; Basketball M & W; Cross-Country Running M & W; Football M; Golf M & W; Soccer W; Softball W; Tennis M & W; Track and Field M & W; Volleyball W

ANTONELLI COLLEGE (HATTIESBURG)
1500 North 31st Ave.
Hattiesburg, MS 39401
Tel: (601)583-4100
Fax: (601)583-0839
Web Site: http://www.antonellic.com/
President/CEO: Karen Selby
Admissions: Karen Gautreau
Type: Two-Year College **Sex:** Coed **Calendar System:** Quarter **Professional Accreditation:** ACCSCT

ANTONELLI COLLEGE (JACKSON)
480 East Woodrow Wilson Dr.
Jackson, MS 39216
Tel: (601)362-9991
Fax: (601)362-2333
Web Site: http://www.antonellic.com/
President/CEO: Karen Gautreau
Admissions: Page McDaniel
Type: Two-Year College **Sex:** Coed **Scholarships:** Available **Calendar System:** Quarter **Professional Accreditation:** ACCSCT

BELHAVEN COLLEGE
1500 Peachtree St.
Jackson, MS 39202-1789
Tel: (601)968-5928
Free: 800-960-5940
Admissions: (601)968-5940
Fax: (601)968-9998
Web Site: http://www.belhaven.edu/
President/CEO: Dr. Roger Parrott
Registrar: Donna Weeks
Admissions: Suzanne T. Sullivan
Financial Aid: Linda Phillips
Type: Comprehensive **Sex:** Coed **Affiliation:** Presbyterian **Scores:** 100% SAT V 400+; 100% SAT M 400+; 39% ACT 18-23; 40% ACT 24-29 **% Accepted:** 57 **Admission Plans:** Early Admission; Deferred Admission **Application Deadline:** Rolling **Application Fee:** $25.00 **H.S. Requirements:** High school diploma required; GED accepted **Costs Per Year:** Application fee: $25. Comprehensive fee: $20,478 includes full-time tuition ($14,124), mandatory fees ($650), and college room and board ($5704). Part-time tuition: $350 per semester hour. **Scholarships:** Available **Calendar System:** Semester, Summer Session Available **Enrollment:** FT 2,166, PT 72, Grad 342 **Faculty:** FT 70, PT 155 **Student-Faculty Ratio:** 21:1 **Exams:** SAT I or ACT **% Receiving Financial Aid:** 86 **% Residing in College-Owned, -Operated, or -Affiliated Housing:** 32 **Library Holdings:** 99,765 **Regional Accreditation:** Southern Association of Colleges and Schools **Credit Hours For Degree:** 62 semester hours, Associates; 124 semester hours, Bachelors **Professional Accreditation:** NASAD, NASM **Intercollegiate Athletics:** Baseball M; Basketball M & W; Cross-Country Running M & W; Football M; Golf M & W; Soccer M & W; Softball W; Tennis M & W; Volleyball W

BLUE MOUNTAIN COLLEGE
PO Box 160
Blue Mountain, MS 38610-9509
Tel: (662)685-4771
Free: 800-235-0136
Admissions: (662)685-4161
Fax: (662)685-4776
E-mail: eteel@bmc.edu
Web Site: http://www.bmc.edu/
President/CEO: Dr. Bettye R. Coward
Registrar: Sheila Freeman
Admissions: Maria Teel
Financial Aid: Angie Gossett
Type: Four-Year College **Sex:** Coed **Affiliation:** Southern Baptist **Scores:** 50% ACT 18-23; 16% ACT 24-29 **% Accepted:** 55 **Admission Plans:** Early Admission **Application Deadline:** September 03 **Application Fee:** $10.00 **H.S. Requirements:** High school diploma required; GED accepted **Costs Per Year:** Application fee: $10. Comprehensive fee: $11,086 includes full-time tuition ($6780), mandatory fees ($540), and college room and board ($3766). College room only: $1400. Full-time tuition and fees vary according to course load. Room and board charges vary according to board plan and gender. Part-time tuition: $230 per hour. Part-time mandatory fees: $80 per

term. Part-time tuition and fees vary according to course load. **Scholarships:** Available **Calendar System:** Semester, Summer Session Available **Enrollment:** FT 283, PT 82 **Faculty:** FT 24, PT 12 **Student-Faculty Ratio:** 11:1 **Exams:** SAT I or ACT **% Receiving Financial Aid:** 72 **% Residing in College-Owned, -Operated, or -Affiliated Housing:** 34 **Library Holdings:** 59,431 **Regional Accreditation:** Southern Association of Colleges and Schools **Credit Hours For Degree:** 120 semester hours, Bachelors **Intercollegiate Athletics:** Basketball W; Tennis W

COAHOMA COMMUNITY COLLEGE
3240 Friars Point Rd.
Clarksdale, MS 38614-9799
Tel: (662)627-2571
Admissions: (662)621-4205
Web Site: http://www.ccc.cc.ms.us/
President/CEO: Dr. Vivian M. Presley
Registrar: Rita Hanfor
Admissions: Wanda Holmes
Financial Aid: Patricia Brooks
Type: Two-Year College **Sex:** Coed **Affiliation:** Mississippi State Board for Community and Junior Colleges **Admission Plans:** Open Admission **Application Deadline:** Rolling **Application Fee:** $0.00 **H.S. Requirements:** High school diploma required; GED accepted **Costs Per Year:** Application fee: $0. Area resident tuition: $1600 full-time, $90 per semester hour part-time. Nonresident tuition: $2900 full-time. Mandatory fees: $140 full-time, $60 per term part-time. College room and board: $2914. **Scholarships:** Available **Calendar System:** Semester **Enrollment:** FT 1,801, PT 145 **Faculty:** FT 73, PT 17 **Student-Faculty Ratio:** 26:1 **Regional Accreditation:** Southern Association of Colleges and Schools **Credit Hours For Degree:** 65 credit hours, Associates **Intercollegiate Athletics:** Baseball M; Basketball M & W; Football M

COPIAH-LINCOLN COMMUNITY COLLEGE
PO Box 649
Wesson, MS 39191-0649
Tel: (601)643-5101
Admissions: (601)643-8307
Fax: (601)643-8212
E-mail: phil.broome@colin.edu
Web Site: http://www.colin.edu/
President/CEO: Dr. Howell C. Garner
Registrar: Dr. Phil Broome
Admissions: Phillip H. Broome
Financial Aid: Leslie Smith
Type: Two-Year College **Sex:** Coed **Affiliation:** Mississippi State Board for Community and Junior Colleges **Admission Plans:** Open Admission; Preferred Admission; Early Admission **Application Deadline:** Rolling **Application Fee:** $0.00 **H.S. Requirements:** High school diploma required; GED accepted **Costs Per Year:** Application fee: $0. State resident tuition: $1700 full-time. Nonresident tuition: $1800 full-time. Mandatory fees: $100 full-time. **Scholarships:** Available **Calendar System:** Semester, Summer Session Available **Faculty:** FT 82, PT 45 **% Residing in College-Owned, -Operated, or -Affiliated Housing:** 30 **Library Holdings:** 38,900 **Regional Accreditation:** Southern Association of Colleges and Schools **Credit Hours For Degree:** 64 semester hours, Associates **Professional Accreditation:** JRCERT, NAACLS, NLN **Intercollegiate Athletics:** Baseball M; Basketball M & W; Football M; Golf M & W; Softball W; Tennis M & W; Track and Field M

COPIAH-LINCOLN COMMUNITY COLLEGE-NATCHEZ CAMPUS
11 Co-Lin Circle
Natchez, MS 39120-8446
Tel: (601)442-9111
Fax: (601)446-9967
Web Site: http://www.colin.edu/
President/CEO: Dr. Howell C. Garner
Registrar: Gwen S. McCalip
Admissions: Gwen S. McCalip
Type: Two-Year College **Sex:** Coed **Affiliation:** Mississippi State Board for Community and Junior Colleges **Admission Plans:** Open Admission; Early Admission **Application Fee:** $0.00 **H.S. Requirements:** High school diploma required; GED accepted. For welding program: High school diploma or equivalent not required **Costs Per Year:** Application fee: $0. State resident tuition: $1600 full-time, $100 per semester hour part-time. Nonresident tuition: $3400 full-time, $175 per semester hour part-time. Mandatory fees: $100 full-time, $5 per semester hour part-time, $10 per year part-time. College room and board: $2600. **Scholarships:** Available **Calendar System:** Semester, Summer Session Available **Enrollment:** FT 554, PT 346 **Faculty:** FT 24, PT 29 **Student-Faculty Ratio:** 20:1 **Exams:** ACT, Other **Library Holdings:** 19,000 **Regional Accreditation:** Southern Association of Colleges and Schools **Credit Hours For Degree:** 64 semester hours, Associates **Professional Accreditation:** CARC

DELTA STATE UNIVERSITY
Hwy. 8 West
Cleveland, MS 38733-0001
Tel: (662)846-3000
Free: 800-468-6378
Admissions: (662)846-4658
Fax: (662)846-4016
E-mail: dheslep@deltastate.edu
Web Site: http://www.deltastate.edu/
President/CEO: Dr. John M. Hilpert
Registrar: Penney Gong
Admissions: Debbie Heslep
Financial Aid: Ann Margaret Mullins
Type: Comprehensive **Sex:** Coed **Affiliation:** Mississippi Institutions of Higher Learning **Scores:** 57% ACT 18-23; 17% ACT 24-29 **Admission Plans:** Deferred Admission **Application Deadline:** August 01 **Application Fee:** $15.00 **H.S. Requirements:** High school diploma required; GED accepted **Costs Per Year:** Application fee: $15. State resident tuition: $3762 full-time, $155 per semester hour part-time. Nonresident tuition: $8950 full-time, $370 per semester hour part-time. Mandatory fees: $490 full-time. College room and board: $4272. Room and board charges vary according to board plan and housing facility. **Scholarships:** Available **Calendar System:** Semester, Summer Session Available **Enrollment:** FT 2,754, PT 504, Grad 740 **Faculty:** FT 165, PT 110 **Student-Faculty Ratio:** 18:1 **Exams:** SAT I and SAT II or ACT **% Residing in College-Owned, -Operated, or -Affiliated Housing:** 35 **Library Holdings:** 345,565 **Regional Accreditation:** Southern Association of Colleges and Schools **Credit Hours For Degree:** 130 semester hours, Bachelors **ROTC:** Air Force **Professional Accreditation:** AACN, AAFCS, ACA, ADtA, ACBSP, CSWE, NASAD, NASM, NCATE, NLN **Intercollegiate Athletics:** Baseball M; Basketball M & W; Cheerleading M & W; Cross-Country Running W; Football M; Golf M; Softball W; Swimming and Diving M & W; Tennis M & W

EAST CENTRAL COMMUNITY COLLEGE
PO Box 129
Decatur, MS 39327-0129
Tel: (601)635-2111; 877-462-3222
Fax: (601)635-2150
Web Site: http://www.eccc.cc.ms.us/
President/CEO: Dr. Phil Sutphin
Registrar: Donna Luke
Admissions: Donna Luke
Financial Aid: Brenda Carson
Type: Two-Year College **Sex:** Coed **Affiliation:** Mississippi State Board for Community and Junior Colleges **Admission Plans:** Open Admission; Early Admission **Application Fee:** $0.00 **H.S. Requirements:** High school diploma required; GED accepted **Scholarships:** Available **Calendar System:** Semester, Summer Session Available **Faculty:** FT 79, PT 65 **Exams:** ACT **% Residing in College-Owned, -Operated, or -Affiliated Housing:** 27 **Regional Accreditation:** Southern Association of Colleges and Schools **Credit Hours For Degree:** 64 semester hours, Associates **Professional Accreditation:** ARCEST, NLN **Intercollegiate Athletics:** Baseball M; Basketball M & W; Football M; Golf M & W; Softball W; Tennis M & W

EAST MISSISSIPPI COMMUNITY COLLEGE
PO Box 158
Scooba, MS 39358-0158
Tel: (662)476-8442
Admissions: (662)476-5041
Web Site: http://www.eastms.edu/
President/CEO: Dr. Rick Young
Registrar: Mary C. Stennis
Admissions: Melinda Sciple
Financial Aid: James Gibson
Type: Two-Year College **Sex:** Coed **Affiliation:** Mississippi State Board for Community and Junior Colleges **Scores:** 34% ACT 18-23; 5% ACT 24-29

Admission Plans: Open Admission; Deferred Admission **Application Fee:** $0.00 **H.S. Requirements:** High school diploma required; GED accepted **Scholarships:** Available **Calendar System:** Semester, Summer Session Available **Enrollment:** FT 2,068, PT 1,349 **Faculty:** FT 91, PT 100 **Student-Faculty Ratio:** 22:1 **Exams:** ACT **% Residing in College-Owned, -Operated, or -Affiliated Housing:** 25 **Library Holdings:** 27,840 **Regional Accreditation:** Southern Association of Colleges and Schools **Credit Hours For Degree:** 64 semester hours, Associates **Professional Accreditation:** ABFSE **Intercollegiate Athletics:** Baseball M; Basketball M & W; Cheerleading W; Football M; Golf M; Soccer M & W; Softball W

HINDS COMMUNITY COLLEGE
PO Box 1100
Raymond, MS 39154-1100
Tel: (601)857-5261
Admissions: (601)857-3280
Web Site: http://www.hindscc.edu/
President/CEO: Dr. Clyde Muse
Admissions: Jay Allen
Financial Aid: Dr. George Barnes
Type: Two-Year College **Sex:** Coed **Affiliation:** Mississippi State Board for Community and Junior Colleges **Scores:** 12.8% ACT 18-23; 2.8% ACT 24-29 **Admission Plans:** Open Admission; Early Admission **Application Fee:** $0.00 **H.S. Requirements:** High school diploma required; GED accepted **Scholarships:** Available **Calendar System:** Semester, Summer Session Available **Enrollment:** FT 7,145, PT 2,816 **Faculty:** FT 351, PT 305 **Student-Faculty Ratio:** 17:1 **Exams:** SAT I and SAT II or ACT **% Residing in College-Owned, -Operated, or -Affiliated Housing:** 15 **Library Holdings:** 165,260 **Regional Accreditation:** Southern Association of Colleges and Schools **Credit Hours For Degree:** 64 semester hours, Associates **ROTC:** Army **Professional Accreditation:** AAMAE, ADA, AHIMA, APTA, CARC, JRCERT, NAACLS, NLN **Intercollegiate Athletics:** Baseball M; Basketball M & W; Cross-Country Running M; Football M; Golf M; Soccer M; Softball W; Tennis M & W; Track and Field M

HOLMES COMMUNITY COLLEGE
PO Box 369
Goodman, MS 39079-0369
Tel: (662)472-2312
Admissions: (601)472-2312
Fax: (662)472-9156
Web Site: http://www.holmescc.edu/
President/CEO: Dr. Starkey A. Morgan, Sr.
Registrar: Dr. Lynn Wright
Admissions: Dr. Lynn Wright
Financial Aid: Wirt Hayes
Type: Two-Year College **Sex:** Coed **Affiliation:** Mississippi State Board for Community and Junior Colleges **Admission Plans:** Open Admission; Early Admission **Application Fee:** $0.00 **H.S. Requirements:** High school diploma required; GED accepted **Costs Per Year:** Application fee: $0. State resident tuition: $1100 full-time, $65 per semester hour part-time. Nonresident tuition: $1750 full-time. Mandatory fees: $330 full-time, $10 per term part-time. Part-time tuition and fees vary according to course load. College room and board: $3330. Room and board charges vary according to housing facility. **Scholarships:** Available **Calendar System:** Semester, Summer Session Available **Enrollment:** FT 3,251, PT 1,243 **Faculty:** FT 128, PT 223 **Student-Faculty Ratio:** 19:1 **Exams:** ACT **% Residing in College-Owned, -Operated, or -Affiliated Housing:** 12 **Library Holdings:** 53,000 **Regional Accreditation:** Southern Association of Colleges and Schools **Credit Hours For Degree:** 64 semester hours, Associates **Professional Accreditation:** ARCEST, AOTA, JRCEMT, NLN **Intercollegiate Athletics:** Baseball M; Basketball M & W; Football M; Golf M & W; Soccer M & W; Softball W; Tennis M & W

ITAWAMBA COMMUNITY COLLEGE
602 West Hill St.
Fulton, MS 38843
Tel: (662)862-8000
Admissions: (662)862-8032
Fax: (662)862-8036
E-mail: hgjefcoat@iccms.edu
Web Site: http://www.icc.cc.ms.us/
President/CEO: Dr. David Cole
Registrar: Mike Eaton
Admissions: Dr. H. Gregory Jefcoat
Financial Aid: Robert Walker
Type: Two-Year College **Sex:** Coed **Affiliation:** Mississippi State Board for Community and Junior Colleges **Admission Plans:** Open Admission; Early Admission **Application Fee:** $0.00 **H.S. Requirements:** High school diploma required; GED accepted **Scholarships:** Available **Calendar System:** Semester, Summer Session Available **Exams:** ACT **Library Holdings:** 36,816 **Regional Accreditation:** Southern Association of Colleges and Schools **Credit Hours For Degree:** 63 semester hours, Associates **ROTC:** Army **Professional Accreditation:** ARCEST, AHIMA, APTA, CARC, JRCERT, NLN **Intercollegiate Athletics:** Basketball M & W; Football M; Golf M; Tennis M & W; Track and Field M

JACKSON STATE UNIVERSITY
1400 John R Lynch St.
Jackson, MS 39217
Tel: (601)979-2121
Free: 800-848-6817
Admissions: (601)979-2100
Fax: (601)979-2358
E-mail: schatman@jsums.edu
Web Site: http://www.jsums.edu/
President/CEO: Ronald Mason, Jr.
Registrar: Alfred Jackson
Admissions: Stephanie Chatman
Financial Aid: Gene Blakley
Type: University **Sex:** Coed **Affiliation:** Mississippi Institutions of Higher Learning **Scores:** 43.3% ACT 18-23; 6% ACT 24-29 **Admission Plans:** Early Admission; Deferred Admission **Application Fee:** $0.00 **H.S. Requirements:** High school diploma required; GED accepted **Costs Per Year:** Application fee: $0. State resident tuition: $3964 full-time, $166 per credit hour part-time. Nonresident tuition: $8872 full-time, $371 per credit hour part-time. College room and board: $5044. College room only: $2998. Room and board charges vary according to board plan. **Scholarships:** Available **Calendar System:** Semester, Summer Session Available **Enrollment:** FT 5,714, PT 891, Grad 1,746 **Faculty:** FT 361, PT 104 **Student-Faculty Ratio:** 18:1 **Exams:** SAT I or ACT **% Residing in College-Owned, -Operated, or -Affiliated Housing:** 34 **Library Holdings:** 236,933 **Regional Accreditation:** Southern Association of Colleges and Schools **Credit Hours For Degree:** 128 credit hours, Bachelors **ROTC:** Army **Professional Accreditation:** AACSB, ABET, ACEJMC, APA, ASLHA, CORE, CSWE, NAIT, NASAD, NASM, NASPAA, NCATE **Intercollegiate Athletics:** Baseball M; Basketball M & W; Bowling W; Cross-Country Running M & W; Football M; Golf M & W; Soccer W; Softball W; Tennis M & W; Track and Field M & W; Volleyball W

JONES COUNTY JUNIOR COLLEGE
900 South Ct. St.
Ellisville, MS 39437-3901
Tel: (601)477-4000
Admissions: (601)477-4025
Fax: (601)477-4212
Web Site: http://www.jcjc.edu/
President/CEO: Dr. Ronald Whitehead
Registrar: Jimmy Temple
Admissions: Dianne Speed
Financial Aid: Joe L. Herrington
Type: Two-Year College **Sex:** Coed **Affiliation:** Mississippi State Board for Community and Junior Colleges **Admission Plans:** Open Admission; Preferred Admission; Early Admission **Application Fee:** $0.00 **H.S. Requirements:** High school diploma required; GED accepted **Scholarships:** Available **Calendar System:** Semester, Summer Session Available **Faculty:** FT 170, PT 5 **Student-Faculty Ratio:** 25:1 **Exams:** SAT I or ACT **% Residing in College-Owned, -Operated, or -Affiliated Housing:** 20 **Library Holdings:** 62,349 **Regional Accreditation:** Southern Association of Colleges and Schools **Credit Hours For Degree:** 64 semester hours, Associates **ROTC:** Army, Air Force **Professional Accreditation:** ACBSP, JRCERT, JRCEMT, NLN **Intercollegiate Athletics:** Baseball M; Basketball M & W; Football M; Golf M; Soccer M & W; Softball W; Tennis M & W; Track and Field M

MAGNOLIA BIBLE COLLEGE
PO Box 1109
Kosciusko, MS 39090-1109
Tel: (601)289-2896

Admissions: (662)289-2896
Web Site: http://www.magnolia.edu/
President/CEO: Dr. Les Ferguson, Sr.
Registrar: John F. Gardner
Admissions: Allen Coker
Financial Aid: Sharon Paseur
Type: Four-Year College **Sex:** Coed **Affiliation:** Church of Christ **% Accepted:** 100 **Admission Plans:** Open Admission; Preferred Admission **Application Deadline:** August 31 **Application Fee:** $0.00 **H.S. Requirements:** High school diploma required; GED accepted **Costs Per Year:** Application fee: $0. Tuition: $4800 full-time, $200 per semester hour part-time. Mandatory fees: $90 full-time, $45 per term part-time. College room only: $1500. **Scholarships:** Available **Calendar System:** Semester, Summer Session Available **Enrollment:** FT 20, PT 21 **Faculty:** FT 1, PT 8 **Student-Faculty Ratio:** 11:1 **% Receiving Financial Aid:** 52 **% Residing in College-Owned, -Operated, or -Affiliated Housing:** 48 **Library Holdings:** 32,589 **Regional Accreditation:** Southern Association of Colleges and Schools **Credit Hours For Degree:** 128 semester hours, Bachelors **Professional Accreditation:** AABC

MERIDIAN COMMUNITY COLLEGE
910 Hwy. 19 North
Meridian, MS 39307
Tel: (601)483-8241
Admissions: (601)484-8895
Web Site: http://www.meridiancc.edu
President/CEO: Dr. Scott D. Elliott
Registrar: Minnie Bryan
Admissions: Dianne Walton
Financial Aid: Soraya Welden
Type: Two-Year College **Sex:** Coed **Affiliation:** Mississippi State Board for Community and Junior Colleges **Admission Plans:** Open Admission; Early Admission **Application Deadline:** Rolling **Application Fee:** $0.00 **H.S. Requirements:** High school diploma required; GED accepted **Costs Per Year:** Application fee: $0. State resident tuition: $1450 full-time, $80 per credit hour part-time. Nonresident tuition: $2740 full-time, $137 per credit hour part-time. Mandatory fees: $4 per credit hour part-time, $5 per term part-time. College room and board: $2600. Room and board charges vary according to board plan. **Scholarships:** Available **Calendar System:** Semester, Summer Session Available **Enrollment:** FT 2,649, PT 923 **Faculty:** FT 144, PT 112 **Exams:** ACT, Other **% Residing in College-Owned, -Operated, or -Affiliated Housing:** 12 **Library Holdings:** 50,000 **Regional Accreditation:** Southern Association of Colleges and Schools **Credit Hours For Degree:** 64 semester hours, Associates **Professional Accreditation:** ADA, AHIMA, APTA, JRCERT, NAACLS, NLN **Intercollegiate Athletics:** Baseball M; Basketball M & W; Cross-Country Running M & W; Golf M; Soccer M; Softball W; Tennis M & W; Track and Field M & W

MILLSAPS COLLEGE
1701 North State St.
Jackson, MS 39210-0001
Tel: (601)974-1000
Free: 800-352-1050
Admissions: (601)974-1050
Fax: (601)974-1059
E-mail: admissions@millsaps.edu
Web Site: http://www.millsaps.edu/
President/CEO: Dr. Frances Lucas
Registrar: Vicki Stuart
Admissions: Mathew Cox
Financial Aid: Patrick G. James
Type: Comprehensive **Sex:** Coed **Affiliation:** United Methodist **Scores:** 99% SAT V 400+; 100% SAT M 400+; 28% ACT 18-23; 45% ACT 24-29 **% Accepted:** 82 **Admission Plans:** Early Admission; Early Action; Deferred Admission **Application Deadline:** June 01 **Application Fee:** $25.00 **H.S. Requirements:** High school diploma required; GED accepted **Costs Per Year:** Application fee: $25. Comprehensive fee: $28,256 includes full-time tuition ($19,490), mandatory fees ($1200), and college room and board ($7566). College room only: $4248. Room and board charges vary according to housing facility. Part-time tuition: $604 per credit hour. Part-time mandatory fees: $30 per credit hour. Part-time tuition and fees vary according to course load. **Scholarships:** Available **Calendar System:** Semester, Summer Session Available **Enrollment:** FT 1,039, PT 46, Grad 69 **Faculty:** FT 92, PT 5 **Student-Faculty Ratio:** 12:1 **Exams:** SAT I or ACT **% Receiving Financial Aid:** 57 **% Residing in College-Owned, -Operated, or -Affiliated Housing:** 82 **Library Holdings:** 190,982 **Regional Accreditation:** Southern Association of Colleges and Schools **Credit Hours For Degree:** 128 semester hours, Bachelors **ROTC:** Army **Professional Accreditation:** AACSB, NCATE **Intercollegiate Athletics:** Baseball M; Basketball M & W; Cheerleading M & W; Cross-Country Running M & W; Football M; Golf M & W; Soccer M & W; Softball W; Tennis M & W; Volleyball W

MISSISSIPPI COLLEGE
200 South Capitol St.
Clinton, MS 39058
Tel: (601)925-3000
Free: 800-738-1236
Admissions: (601)925-3315
Fax: (601)925-3804
E-mail: admissions@mc.edu
Web Site: http://www.mc.edu/
President/CEO: Dr. Lee G. Royce
Registrar: Carol Busbee
Admissions: Dr. Jim Turcotte
Financial Aid: Mary Givhan
Type: Comprehensive **Sex:** Coed **Affiliation:** Southern Baptist **Scores:** 100% SAT V 400+; 98% SAT M 400+; 53% ACT 18-23; 37% ACT 24-29 **% Accepted:** 57 **Admission Plans:** Early Admission; Early Decision Plan; Deferred Admission **Application Deadline:** Rolling **H.S. Requirements:** High school diploma required; GED accepted **Costs Per Year:** Comprehensive fee: $18,182 includes full-time tuition ($11,600), mandatory fees ($688), and college room and board ($5894). Part-time tuition: $365 per credit hour. Part-time mandatory fees: $133 per term. **Scholarships:** Available **Calendar System:** Semester, Summer Session Available **Enrollment:** FT 2,211, PT 342, Grad 857 **Faculty:** FT 161, PT 147 **Student-Faculty Ratio:** 11:1 **Exams:** SAT I or ACT **% Receiving Financial Aid:** 58 **% Residing in College-Owned, -Operated, or -Affiliated Housing:** 61 **Library Holdings:** 362,296 **Regional Accreditation:** Southern Association of Colleges and Schools **Credit Hours For Degree:** 130 credit hours, Bachelors **ROTC:** Army **Professional Accreditation:** AAFCS, ABA, ACA, AALS, ACBSP, CSWE, NASM, NCATE, NLN **Intercollegiate Athletics:** Baseball M; Basketball M & W; Cross-Country Running M & W; Football M; Golf M; Soccer M & W; Softball W; Tennis M & W; Volleyball W

MISSISSIPPI DELTA COMMUNITY COLLEGE
PO Box 668
Moorhead, MS 38761-0668
Tel: (662)246-6322
Admissions: (662)246-6308
Web Site: http://www.msdelta.edu/
President/CEO: Dr. Larry G. Bailey
Registrar: Joe F. Ray, Jr.
Admissions: Joseph F. Ray, Jr.
Financial Aid: Angie Sherrer
Type: Two-Year College **Sex:** Coed **Affiliation:** Mississippi State Board for Community and Junior Colleges **Admission Plans:** Preferred Admission; Deferred Admission **Application Fee:** $0.00 **H.S. Requirements:** High school diploma required; GED accepted **Costs Per Year:** Application fee: $0. State resident tuition: $1850 full-time, $83 per semester hour part-time. Nonresident tuition: $3528 full-time. Mandatory fees: $70 full-time, $10 per semester hour part-time. College room and board: $1330. College room only: $800. **Scholarships:** Available **Calendar System:** Semester, Summer Session Available **Exams:** ACT **% Residing in College-Owned, -Operated, or -Affiliated Housing:** 25 **Library Holdings:** 33,020 **Regional Accreditation:** Southern Association of Colleges and Schools **Credit Hours For Degree:** 64 semester hours, Associates **Professional Accreditation:** ADA, JRCERT, NAACLS, NLN **Intercollegiate Athletics:** Baseball M; Basketball M & W; Football M; Golf M; Soccer M; Tennis M & W; Track and Field M

MISSISSIPPI GULF COAST COMMUNITY COLLEGE
PO Box 609
Perkinston, MS 39573-0609
Tel: (601)928-5211
Admissions: (601)928-6264
Fax: (601)928-6299
Web Site: http://www.mgccc.edu/
President/CEO: Dr. Mary Graham
Registrar: Tommie Weathers

Admissions: Michelle Sekul
Financial Aid: Sheree Bond
Type: Two-Year College **Sex:** Coed **Affiliation:** Mississippi State Board for Community and Junior Colleges **% Accepted:** 100 **Admission Plans:** Open Admission; Preferred Admission; Early Admission **Application Deadline:** Rolling **Application Fee:** $0.00 **H.S. Requirements:** High school diploma required; GED accepted **Costs Per Year:** Application fee: $0. Area resident tuition: $1522 full-time, $75 per hour part-time. Nonresident tuition: $3368 full-time, $152 per hour part-time. College room and board: $3800. **Scholarships:** Available **Calendar System:** Semester, Summer Session Available **Enrollment:** FT 5,209, PT 2,597 **Faculty:** FT 337, PT 262 **Student-Faculty Ratio:** 26:1 **% Residing in College-Owned, -Operated, or -Affiliated Housing:** 7 **Library Holdings:** 100,472 **Regional Accreditation:** Southern Association of Colleges and Schools **Credit Hours For Degree:** 64 semester hours, Associates **Professional Accreditation:** ABFSE, CARC, JRCERT, JRCEMT, NAACLS, NLN **Intercollegiate Athletics:** Baseball M; Basketball M & W; Football M; Golf M; Soccer M & W; Softball W; Tennis M & W; Track and Field M

MISSISSIPPI STATE UNIVERSITY
Mississippi State, MS 39762
Tel: (662)325-2323
Admissions: (662)325-2224
Fax: (662)325-3299
E-mail: admit@admissions.msstate.edu
Web Site: http://www.msstate.edu/
President/CEO: Dr. J. Charles Lee
Registrar: Butch Stokes
Admissions: Diane D. Wolfe
Financial Aid: Bruce Crain
Type: University **Sex:** Coed **Affiliation:** Mississippi Board of Trustees of State Institutions of Higher Learning **Scores:** 44% ACT 18-23; 35% ACT 24-29 **% Accepted:** 69 **Admission Plans:** Early Admission; Deferred Admission **Application Deadline:** August 01 **Application Fee:** $0.00 **H.S. Requirements:** High school diploma required; GED accepted **Costs Per Year:** Application fee: $0. State resident tuition: $4312 full-time, $179.75 per hour part-time. Nonresident tuition: $9772 full-time, $407.25 per hour part-time. Part-time tuition varies according to course load. College room and board: $5859. College room only: $2824. Room and board charges vary according to board plan, housing facility, and student level. **Scholarships:** Available **Calendar System:** Semester, Summer Session Available **Enrollment:** FT 11,098, PT 1,457, Grad 3,289 **Faculty:** FT 974, PT 165 **Student-Faculty Ratio:** 14:1 **Exams:** SAT I or ACT **% Receiving Financial Aid:** 53 **% Residing in College-Owned, -Operated, or -Affiliated Housing:** 21 **Library Holdings:** 2,451,640 **Regional Accreditation:** Southern Association of Colleges and Schools **Credit Hours For Degree:** 128 credit hours, Bachelors **ROTC:** Army, Air Force **Professional Accreditation:** AACSB, ABET, AAFCS, ACA, ADtA, APA, ASLA, AVMA, CORE, CSWE, FIDER, NASAD, NASM, NASPAA, NCATE, SAF **Intercollegiate Athletics:** Baseball M; Basketball M & W; Cross-Country Running M & W; Football M; Golf M & W; Soccer W; Softball W; Tennis M & W; Track and Field M & W; Volleyball W

MISSISSIPPI UNIVERSITY FOR WOMEN
1100 College St., MUW-1600
Columbus, MS 39701-9998
Tel: (662)329-4750; 877-GO 2 THE W
Admissions: (601)329-7106
Fax: (662)329-7297
E-mail: admissions@muw.edu
Web Site: http://www.muw.edu/
President/CEO: Dr. Claudia Limbert
Registrar: Cay Lollar
Admissions: Terri Heath
Financial Aid: Don Rainer
Type: Comprehensive **Sex:** Coed **Affiliation:** Mississippi Institutions of Higher Learning **Scores:** 34% ACT 18-23; 48% ACT 24-29 **Admission Plans:** Early Admission **H.S. Requirements:** High school diploma required; GED accepted **Scholarships:** Available **Calendar System:** Semester, Summer Session Available **Enrollment:** FT 1,483, PT 683, Grad 162 **Faculty:** FT 134, PT 80 **Student-Faculty Ratio:** 13:1 **Exams:** SAT I or ACT **% Receiving Financial Aid:** 49 **% Residing in College-Owned, -Operated, or -Affiliated Housing:** 21 **Library Holdings:** 426,543 **Regional Accreditation:** Southern Association of Colleges and Schools **Credit Hours For Degree:** 60 semester hours, Associates; 128 semester hours, Bachelors **ROTC:** Army, Air Force **Professional Accreditation:** ASLHA, ACBSP, NASAD, NASM, NCATE, NLN **Intercollegiate Athletics:** Basketball W; Softball W; Tennis W; Volleyball W

MISSISSIPPI VALLEY STATE UNIVERSITY
14000 Hwy. 82 West
Itta Bena, MS 38941-1400
Tel: (662)254-9041
Admissions: (662)254-3344
Fax: (662)254-7900
E-mail: nbtaylor@mvsu.edu
Web Site: http://www.mvsu.edu/
President/CEO: Dr. Lester C. Newman
Registrar: Maxcine Rush
Admissions: Nora Taylor
Financial Aid: Darrell G. Boyd
Type: Comprehensive **Sex:** Coed **Affiliation:** Mississippi Institutions of Higher Learning **Scores:** 31% ACT 18-23; 3% ACT 24-29 **% Accepted:** 25 **Admission Plans:** Deferred Admission **Application Deadline:** Rolling **Application Fee:** $0.00 **H.S. Requirements:** High school diploma required; GED accepted **Costs Per Year:** Application fee: $0. State resident tuition: $4024 full-time, $168 per semester hour part-time. Nonresident tuition: $9282 full-time, $219 per semester hour part-time. Mandatory fees: $50 full-time, $25 per term part-time. Full-time tuition and fees vary according to course load and degree level. Part-time tuition and fees vary according to course load and degree level. College room and board: $3946. College room only: $2142. Room and board charges vary according to board plan and housing facility. **Scholarships:** Available **Calendar System:** Semester, Summer Session Available **Enrollment:** FT 2,434, PT 314, Grad 417 **Faculty:** FT 117, PT 66 **Student-Faculty Ratio:** 19:1 **Exams:** SAT I or ACT **% Residing in College-Owned, -Operated, or -Affiliated Housing:** 30 **Library Holdings:** 101,109 **Regional Accreditation:** Southern Association of Colleges and Schools **Credit Hours For Degree:** 124 semester hours, Bachelors **ROTC:** Army, Air Force **Professional Accreditation:** ACBSP, CSWE, NASAD, NASM, NCATE **Intercollegiate Athletics:** Baseball M; Basketball M & W; Bowling W; Cross-Country Running M & W; Football M; Golf M; Tennis M; Track and Field M & W

NORTHEAST MISSISSIPPI COMMUNITY COLLEGE
101 Cunningham Blvd.
Booneville, MS 38829
Tel: (662)728-7751
Free: 800-555-2154
Fax: (662)728-1165
E-mail: lgibson@necc.cc.ms.us
Web Site: http://www.nemcc.edu/
President/CEO: Dr. Charles W. Chance
Registrar: Ronald Sweeney
Admissions: Robert Lynn Gibson
Type: Two-Year College **Sex:** Coed **Affiliation:** Mississippi State Board for Community and Junior Colleges **Admission Plans:** Open Admission; Early Admission **Application Fee:** $0.00 **H.S. Requirements:** High school diploma required; GED accepted **Calendar System:** Semester, Summer Session Available **Enrollment:** FT 2,777, PT 447 **Faculty:** FT 134, PT 8 **Exams:** SAT I or ACT **% Residing in College-Owned, -Operated, or -Affiliated Housing:** 25 **Library Holdings:** 29,879 **Regional Accreditation:** Southern Association of Colleges and Schools **Credit Hours For Degree:** 63 semester hours, Associates **Professional Accreditation:** AAMAE, ADA, CARC, JRCERT, NAACLS, NLN **Intercollegiate Athletics:** Baseball M; Basketball M & W; Football M; Golf M; Softball W; Tennis M & W

NORTHWEST MISSISSIPPI COMMUNITY COLLEGE
4975 Hwy. 51 North
Senatobia, MS 38668-1701
Tel: (662)562-3200
Admissions: (662)562-3222
Fax: (662)562-3911
Web Site: http://www.northwestms.edu/
President/CEO: Dr. David M. Haraway
Registrar: Dr. Gary Lee Spears
Admissions: Deanna Ferguson
Financial Aid: Joe Boyles
Type: Two-Year College **Sex:** Coed **Affiliation:** Mississippi State Board for Community and Junior Colleges **Admission Plans:** Open Admission; Early Admission; Deferred Admission **Application Fee:** $0.00 **H.S. Require-**

ments: High school diploma required; GED accepted **Scholarships:** Available **Calendar System:** Semester, Summer Session Available **Student-Faculty Ratio:** 20:1 **Exams:** ACT **Library Holdings:** 38,000 **Regional Accreditation:** Southern Association of Colleges and Schools **Credit Hours For Degree:** 66 semester hours, Associates **ROTC:** Air Force **Professional Accreditation:** ABFSE, CARC, NLN **Intercollegiate Athletics:** Baseball M; Basketball M & W; Equestrian Sports M & W; Football M; Golf M; Softball W; Tennis M & W

PEARL RIVER COMMUNITY COLLEGE
101 Hwy. 11 North
Poplarville, MS 39470
Tel: (601)403-1000
Admissions: (601)795-6801
Fax: (601)403-1135
E-mail: dford@prcc.cc.ms.us
Web Site: http://www.prcc.edu/
President/CEO: Dr. William A. Lewis
Registrar: Dow Ford
Admissions: J. Dow Ford
Financial Aid: Peggy Shoemake
Type: Two-Year College **Sex:** Coed **Affiliation:** Mississippi State Board for Community and Junior Colleges **Admission Plans:** Open Admission; Preferred Admission; Early Admission; Deferred Admission **Application Fee:** $0.00 **H.S. Requirements:** High school diploma required; GED accepted **Scholarships:** Available **Calendar System:** Semester, Summer Session Available **Faculty:** FT 160, PT 65 **Exams:** ACT **% Residing in College-Owned, -Operated, or -Affiliated Housing:** 20 **Library Holdings:** 40,000 **Regional Accreditation:** Southern Association of Colleges and Schools **Credit Hours For Degree:** 64 semester hours, Associates **Professional Accreditation:** ARCEST, ADA, AOTA, APTA, CARC, JRCERT, NAACLS, NLN **Intercollegiate Athletics:** Baseball M; Basketball M & W; Football M; Golf M & W; Soccer M & W; Softball W; Tennis M & W

RUST COLLEGE
150 Rust Ave.
Holly Springs, MS 38635-2328
Tel: (662)252-8000; 888-886-8492
Admissions: (601)252-8000
Fax: (662)252-6107
E-mail: jmcdonald@rustcollege.edu
Web Site: http://www.rustcollege.edu/
President/CEO: Dr. David L. Beckley
Registrar: Clarence Smith
Admissions: Johnny McDonald
Financial Aid: Helen Street
Type: Four-Year College **Sex:** Coed **Affiliation:** United Methodist **Scores:** 25% ACT 18-23; 1% ACT 24-29 **% Accepted:** 39 **Admission Plans:** Deferred Admission **Application Deadline:** July 15 **Application Fee:** $10.00 **H.S. Requirements:** High school diploma required; GED accepted **Costs Per Year:** Application fee: $10. Comprehensive fee: $8950 includes full-time tuition ($6200) and college room and board ($2750). College room only: $1212. Part-time tuition: $267 per credit hour. Part-time tuition varies according to class time and course load. **Scholarships:** Available **Calendar System:** Semester, Summer Session Available **Enrollment:** FT 839, PT 162 **Faculty:** FT 45, PT 5 **Student-Faculty Ratio:** 15:1 **Exams:** ACT **% Receiving Financial Aid:** 96 **% Residing in College-Owned, -Operated, or -Affiliated Housing:** 65 **Library Holdings:** 123,055 **Regional Accreditation:** Southern Association of Colleges and Schools **Credit Hours For Degree:** 66 credits, Associates; 124 credits, Bachelors **ROTC:** Army **Professional Accreditation:** CSWE **Intercollegiate Athletics:** Baseball M; Basketball M & W; Cheerleading M & W; Cross-Country Running M & W; Tennis M & W; Track and Field M & W

SOUTHEASTERN BAPTIST COLLEGE
4229 Hwy. 15 North
Laurel, MS 39440-1096
Tel: (601)426-6346
President/CEO: Dr. Jentry Bond
Registrar: Dr. Medrick Savell
Admissions: Dr. Eric Parker
Financial Aid: Br. James Salisbury
Type: Four-Year College **Sex:** Coed **Affiliation:** Baptist **% Accepted:** 100 **Admission Plans:** Open Admission; Early Admission; Deferred Admission **Application Deadline:** Rolling **Application Fee:** $25.00 **H.S. Requirements:** High school diploma required; GED accepted **Costs Per Year:** Application fee: $25. Tuition: $140 per semester hour part-time. **Calendar System:** Semester, Summer Session Available **Faculty:** FT 9 **% Residing in College-Owned, -Operated, or -Affiliated Housing:** 31 **Library Holdings:** 24,119 **Credit Hours For Degree:** 66 semester hours, Associates; 129 semester hours, Bachelors **Professional Accreditation:** AABC

SOUTHWEST MISSISSIPPI COMMUNITY COLLEGE
College Dr.
Summit, MS 39666
Tel: (601)276-2000
Admissions: (601)276-2001
Fax: (601)276-3888
E-mail: mattc@smcc.edu
Web Site: http://www.smcc.cc.ms.us/
President/CEO: Dr. Horace C. Holmes
Registrar: Glenn Shoemake
Admissions: Matthew Calhoun
Financial Aid: Oliver W. Young
Type: Two-Year College **Sex:** Coed **Affiliation:** Mississippi State Board for Community and Junior Colleges **Scores:** 41.4% ACT 18-23; 5.3% ACT 24-29 **Admission Plans:** Open Admission **Application Deadline:** August 01 **Application Fee:** $0.00 **H.S. Requirements:** High school diploma required; GED accepted **Costs Per Year:** Application fee: $0. State resident tuition: $1700 full-time, $75 per hour part-time. Nonresident tuition: $3900 full-time, $170 per hour part-time. Mandatory fees: $100 full-time, $50 per term part-time. College room and board: $2180. **Scholarships:** Available **Calendar System:** Semester, Summer Session Available **Enrollment:** FT 1,176, PT 718 **Faculty:** FT 82, PT 12 **Student-Faculty Ratio:** 25:1 **% Residing in College-Owned, -Operated, or -Affiliated Housing:** 35 **Library Holdings:** 34,000 **Regional Accreditation:** Southern Association of Colleges and Schools **Credit Hours For Degree:** 64 semester hours, Associates **Professional Accreditation:** NLN **Intercollegiate Athletics:** Baseball M; Basketball M & W; Football M; Golf M; Softball W; Tennis M & W

TOUGALOO COLLEGE
500 West County Line Rd.
Tougaloo, MS 39174
Tel: (601)977-7700; 888-42GALOO
Admissions: (601)977-7765
Fax: (601)977-7739
Web Site: http://www.tougaloo.edu/
President/CEO: Dr. Beverly W. Hogan
Registrar: Carolyn L. Evans
Admissions: Juno Jacobs
Financial Aid: Inez Morris
Type: Four-Year College **Sex:** Coed **Affiliation:** United Church of Christ **Scores:** 50% ACT 18-23; 8% ACT 24-29 **Admission Plans:** Early Admission **Application Fee:** $5.00 **H.S. Requirements:** High school diploma required; GED accepted **Costs Per Year:** Application fee: $5. Comprehensive fee: $15,497 includes full-time tuition ($8800), mandatory fees ($477), and college room and board ($6220). College room only: $4400. Part-time tuition: $367 per credit hour. **Scholarships:** Available **Calendar System:** Semester, Summer Session Not available **Enrollment:** FT 883, PT 57 **Faculty:** FT 70, PT 33 **Student-Faculty Ratio:** 18:1 **Exams:** SAT I or ACT **Library Holdings:** 137,000 **Regional Accreditation:** Southern Association of Colleges and Schools **Credit Hours For Degree:** 64 hours, Associates; 124 hours, Bachelors **ROTC:** Army **Intercollegiate Athletics:** Basketball M & W; Cross-Country Running M & W; Golf M; Softball W

UNIVERSITY OF MISSISSIPPI
University, MS 38677
Tel: (662)915-7211
Admissions: (662)915-7226
Fax: (662)915-5869
E-mail: admissions@olemiss.edu
Web Site: http://www.olemiss.edu/
President/CEO: Dr. Robert C. Khayat
Registrar: Dr. Charlotte Fant
Admissions: Dr. Charlotte Fant
Financial Aid: Laura Diven-Brown
Type: University **Sex:** Coed **Affiliation:** Mississippi Institutions of Higher Learning **Scores:** 97% SAT V 400+; 98% SAT M 400+; 51% ACT 18-23; 37% ACT 24-29 **% Accepted:** 73 **Admission Plans:** Early Admission **Application Deadline:** July 20 **Application Fee:** $25.00 **H.S. Requirements:**

High school diploma required; GED accepted **Costs Per Year:** Application fee: $25, $40 for nonresidents. State resident tuition: $4320 full-time, $180 per credit part-time. Nonresident tuition: $9744 full-time, $406 per credit part-time. College room and board: $5762. College room only: $2972. Room and board charges vary according to board plan and housing facility. **Scholarships:** Available **Calendar System:** Semester, Summer Session Available **Enrollment:** FT 11,143, PT 1,054, Grad 1,976 **Faculty:** FT 622 **Student-Faculty Ratio:** 19:1 **Exams:** SAT I or ACT **% Receiving Financial Aid:** 40 **% Residing in College-Owned, -Operated, or -Affiliated Housing:** 33 **Library Holdings:** 1,338,778 **Regional Accreditation:** Southern Association of Colleges and Schools **Credit Hours For Degree:** 126 semester hours, Bachelors **ROTC:** Army, Air Force **Professional Accreditation:** AACSB, ABET, ACEJMC, AAFCS, ABA, ACPhE, ACA, APA, ASLHA, AALS, CSWE, NASAD, NASM, NCATE, NRPA **Intercollegiate Athletics:** Baseball M; Basketball M & W; Cheerleading M & W; Cross-Country Running M & W; Fencing M & W; Football M; Golf M & W; Lacrosse M; Riflery W; Rugby M; Soccer M & W; Softball W; Tennis M & W; Track and Field M & W; Volleyball M & W

UNIVERSITY OF MISSISSIPPI MEDICAL CENTER

2500 North State St.
Jackson, MS 39216-4505
Tel: (601)984-1000
Admissions: (601)984-1080
Fax: (601)984-1080
Web Site: http://umc.edu/
President/CEO: Dr. Daniel W. Jones
Registrar: Barbara M. Westerfield
Admissions: Barbara Westerfield
Financial Aid: Stacey Carter
Type: Two-Year Upper Division **Sex:** Coed **Affiliation:** University of Mississippi **Admission Plans:** Preferred Admission **Application Fee:** $10.00 **H.S. Requirements:** High school diploma required; GED accepted **Costs Per Year:** Application fee: $10. State resident tuition: $3519 full-time, $141 per credit part-time. Nonresident tuition: $7195 full-time, $294 per credit part-time. Full-time tuition varies according to program. Part-time tuition varies according to course load and program. College room only: $3354. Room charges vary according to housing facility. **Scholarships:** Available **Calendar System:** Semester, Summer Session Not available **Enrollment:** FT 452, PT 71, Grad 457 **Faculty:** FT 683, PT 161 **Student-Faculty Ratio:** 2:1 **% Receiving Financial Aid:** 41 **Library Holdings:** 310,016 **Regional Accreditation:** Southern Association of Colleges and Schools **Credit Hours For Degree:** 133 semester hours, Bachelors **Professional Accreditation:** AACN, ADA, AHIMA, AOTA, APTA, APA, ASC, LCMEAMA, NAACLS, NLN

UNIVERSITY OF SOUTHERN MISSISSIPPI

118 College Dr.
Hattiesburg, MS 39406-0001
Tel: (601)266-7011
Admissions: (601)266-5000
E-mail: kristi.motter@usm.edu
Web Site: http://www.usm.edu/
President/CEO: Dr. Shelby F. Thames
Registrar: Gregory W. Pierce
Admissions: Kristi Motter
Financial Aid: Dr. Kristi L. Motter
Type: University **Sex:** Coed **Scores:** 97% SAT V 400+; 98% SAT M 400+; 61% ACT 18-23; 22% ACT 24-29 **% Accepted:** 61 **Admission Plans:** Early Admission; Deferred Admission **Application Deadline:** Rolling **Application Fee:** $0.00 **H.S. Requirements:** High school diploma required; GED not accepted **Costs Per Year:** Application fee: $0. State resident tuition: $4312 full-time, $180 per credit hour part-time. Nonresident tuition: $9742 full-time, $407 per credit hour part-time. Mandatory fees: $30 full-time. College room and board: $5800. College room only: $2620. **Scholarships:** Available **Calendar System:** Semester, Summer Session Available **Enrollment:** FT 10,727, PT 1,741, Grad 2,562 **Faculty:** FT 713, PT 133 **Student-Faculty Ratio:** 18:1 **Exams:** SAT I or ACT **% Receiving Financial Aid:** 64 **% Residing in College-Owned, -Operated, or -Affiliated Housing:** 31 **Library Holdings:** 1,366,192 **Regional Accreditation:** Southern Association of Colleges and Schools **Credit Hours For Degree:** 128 semester hours, Bachelors **ROTC:** Army, Air Force **Professional Accreditation:** AACSB, ABET, ACEJMC, AAMFT, AACN, AAFCS, ACCE, ACA, ADtA, ALA, APA, ASLHA, CAEPK, CEPH, CSWE, FIDER, JRCEPAT, NAACLS, NASAD, NASD NASM, NAST, NCATE, NLN, NRPA **Intercollegiate Athletics:** Baseball M; Basketball M & W; Cross-Country Running M & W; Football M; Golf M & W; Tennis M & W; Track and Field M & W; Volleyball W

VIRGINIA COLLEGE AT JACKSON

5360 I-55 North
Jackson, MS 39211
Tel: (601)977-0960
Fax: (601)956-4325
Web Site: http://www.vc.edu/
Admissions: Bill Milstead
Type: Two-Year College **Sex:** Coed **Application Fee:** $100.00 **Scholarships:** Available **Calendar System:** Quarter **Student-Faculty Ratio:** 11:1 **Exams:** Other **Professional Accreditation:** ACICS

WESLEY COLLEGE

PO Box 1070
Florence, MS 39073-1070
Tel: (601)845-2265
Free: 800-748-9972
Fax: (601)845-2266
E-mail: admissions@wesleycollege.edu
Web Site: http://www.wesleycollege.com/
President/CEO: Lance Sherer
Registrar: Beverly A. Porter
Admissions: Charity Nielsen
Financial Aid: William Devore
Type: Four-Year College **Sex:** Coed **Affiliation:** Congregational Methodist **Scores:** 22% ACT 18-23; 33% ACT 24-29 **% Accepted:** 100 **Admission Plans:** Open Admission **Application Deadline:** August 01 **Application Fee:** $20.00 **H.S. Requirements:** High school diploma required; GED accepted **Costs Per Year:** Application fee: $20. Comprehensive fee: $10,980 includes full-time tuition ($6900), mandatory fees ($700), and college room and board ($3380). Part-time tuition: $230 per credit hour. **Scholarships:** Available **Calendar System:** Semester, Summer Session Not available **Enrollment:** FT 60, PT 20 **Faculty:** FT 8, PT 10 **Student-Faculty Ratio:** 6:1 **Exams:** SAT I or ACT **% Receiving Financial Aid:** 75 **% Residing in College-Owned, -Operated, or -Affiliated Housing:** 69 **Library Holdings:** 25,000 **Credit Hours For Degree:** 128 semester hours, Bachelors **Professional Accreditation:** AABC **Intercollegiate Athletics:** Basketball M

WILLIAM CAREY COLLEGE

498 Tuscan Ave.
Hattiesburg, MS 39401-5499
Tel: (601)318-6051
Fax: (601)318-6454
E-mail: admiss@mail.wmcarey.edu
Web Site: http://www.wmcarey.edu/
President/CEO: Dr. Larry Kennedy
Registrar: Cathy van Devender
Admissions: William N. Curry
Financial Aid: William Curry
Type: Comprehensive **Sex:** Coed **Affiliation:** Southern Baptist **Scores:** 100% SAT V 400+; 100% SAT M 400+; 64% ACT 18-23; 27% ACT 24-29 **Admission Plans:** Early Admission; Deferred Admission **Application Fee:** $20.00 **H.S. Requirements:** High school diploma required; GED accepted **Costs Per Year:** Application fee: $20. Comprehensive fee: $11,880 includes full-time tuition ($8100), mandatory fees ($315), and college room and board ($3465). College room only: $1305. Full-time tuition and fees vary according to degree level and location. Room and board charges vary according to board plan, housing facility, and location. Part-time tuition: $270 per hour. Part-time mandatory fees: $105 per term. Part-time tuition and fees vary according to degree level and location. **Scholarships:** Available **Calendar System:** Trimester, Summer Session Available **Enrollment:** FT 1,576, PT 277, Grad 905 **Faculty:** FT 93, PT 92 **Student-Faculty Ratio:** 19:1 **Exams:** SAT I or ACT **% Receiving Financial Aid:** 96 **% Residing in College-Owned, -Operated, or -Affiliated Housing:** 23 **Library Holdings:** 98,139 **Regional Accreditation:** Southern Association of Colleges and Schools **Credit Hours For Degree:** 128 credit hours, Bachelors **ROTC:** Army, Air Force **Professional Accreditation:** NASM, NLN **Intercollegiate Athletics:** Baseball M; Basketball M & W; Cheerleading M & W; Golf M; Soccer M & W; Softball W

ALLIED COLLEGE
13723 Riverport Dr., Ste. 103
Maryland Heights, MO 63043
Tel: (314)739-4450
Fax: (314)739-5133
Web Site: http://www.hightechinstitute.edu/
President/CEO: Larkin Hicks
Admissions: Larkin Hicks
Type: Two-Year College **Sex:** Coed **Professional Accreditation:** ABHES

AVIATION INSTITUTE OF MAINTENANCE-KANSAS CITY
3130 Terrace St.
Kansas City, MO 64111
Tel: (816)753-9920; 877-538-5627
Fax: (816)753-9941
E-mail: directoramk@aviationmaintenance.edu
Web Site: http://www.aviationmaintenance.edu/aviation-kansascity.asp
Admissions: Vickie Winfrey
Type: Two-Year College **Calendar System:** Quarter

AVILA UNIVERSITY
11901 Wornall Rd.
Kansas City, MO 64145-1698
Tel: (816)942-8400
Free: 800-GO-AVILA
Admissions: (816)501-3773
Fax: (816)942-3362
E-mail: paige.illum@avila.edu
Web Site: http://www.avila.edu/
President/CEO: Thomas F. Gordon, JD,LLM
Admissions: Paige Illum
Financial Aid: Angie Comstock
Type: Comprehensive **Sex:** Coed **Affiliation:** Roman Catholic **Scores:** 95% SAT V 400+; 94% SAT M 400+; 59% ACT 18-23; 21% ACT 24-29 **% Accepted:** 56 **Admission Plans:** Early Admission **Application Deadline:** Rolling **Application Fee:** $0.00 **H.S. Requirements:** High school diploma required; GED accepted **Costs Per Year:** Application fee: $0. Comprehensive fee: $22,100 includes full-time tuition ($16,300), mandatory fees ($400), and college room and board ($5400). Full-time tuition and fees vary according to course load. Room and board charges vary according to board plan and housing facility. Part-time tuition: $365 per credit hour. Part-time mandatory fees: $13 per credit hour. Part-time tuition and fees vary according to course load. Tuition guaranteed not to increase for student's term of enrollment. **Scholarships:** Available **Calendar System:** Semester, Summer Session Available **Enrollment:** FT 910, PT 304, Grad 483 **Faculty:** FT 64, PT 135 **Student-Faculty Ratio:** 12:1 **Exams:** SAT I or ACT **% Receiving Financial Aid:** 33 **% Residing in College-Owned, -Operated, or -Affiliated Housing:** 17 **Library Holdings:** 80,865 **Regional Accreditation:** North Central Association of Colleges and Schools **Credit Hours For Degree:** 128 credit hours, Bachelors **ROTC:** Army **Professional Accreditation:** AACN, CSWE, JRCERT **Intercollegiate Athletics:** Baseball M; Basketball M & W; Cheerleading W; Football M; Golf W; Soccer M & W; Softball W; Volleyball W

BAPTIST BIBLE COLLEGE
628 East Kearney
Springfield, MO 65803-3498
Tel: (417)268-6000
Fax: (417)831-8029
Web Site: http://www.baptist.edu/index.htm
President/CEO: Dr. Michael A. Randall
Registrar: Dr. Joe Gleason
Admissions: Dr. Joseph Gleason
Financial Aid: Larry Stonebraker
Type: Comprehensive **Sex:** Coed **Affiliation:** Baptist **Admission Plans:** Open Admission; Preferred Admission; Early Admission; Deferred Admission **Application Fee:** $40.00 **H.S. Requirements:** High school diploma required; GED accepted **Costs Per Year:** Application fee: $40. Comprehensive fee: $18,300 includes full-time tuition ($13,000) and college room and board ($5300). **Scholarships:** Available **Calendar System:** Semester, Summer Session Available **Enrollment:** , Grad 70 **Faculty:** FT 27, PT 10 **% Residing in College-Owned, -Operated, or -Affiliated Housing:** 61 **Library Holdings:** 36,844 **Regional Accreditation:** North Central Association of Colleges and Schools **Credit Hours For Degree:** 71 hours, Associates; 131 hours, Bachelors **ROTC:** Army **Professional Accreditation:** AABC **Intercollegiate Athletics:** Basketball M & W; Soccer M; Volleyball W

BARNES-JEWISH COLLEGE OF NURSING AND ALLIED HEALTH
306 South Kingshighway Blvd.
St. Louis, MO 63110-1091
Tel: (314)454-7055
Admissions: (314)454-7538
Fax: (314)454-5239
E-mail: cal7374@bjcmail.carenet.org
Web Site: http://www.barnesjewishcollege.edu/
President/CEO: Dr. Roger Lanier
Registrar: Beth Wade
Admissions: Christie Schneider
Type: Comprehensive **Sex:** Coed **Scores:** 74% ACT 18-23; 26% ACT 24-29 **Application Fee:** $25.00 **H.S. Requirements:** High school diploma required; GED accepted **Scholarships:** Available **Calendar System:** Semester, Summer Session Available **Enrollment:** FT 200, PT 486, Grad 95 **Faculty:** FT 33, PT 10 **Student-Faculty Ratio:** 10:1 **Exams:** SAT I or ACT **% Receiving Financial Aid:** 50 **% Residing in College-Owned, -Operated, or -Affiliated Housing:** 1 **Library Holdings:** 3,765 **Regional Accreditation:** North Central Association of Colleges and Schools **Credit Hours For Degree:** 66 credit hours, Associates; 121 credit hours, Bachelors **Professional Accreditation:** AACN, ADtA, ASC, JRCERT, NAACLS, NLN

BLUE RIVER COMMUNITY COLLEGE
20301 East 78 Hwy.
Independence, MO 64057
Tel: (816)655-6000
Admissions: (816)655-6118
Fax: (816)655-6014
Web Site: http://www.mcckc.edu
President/CEO: Malcolm Wilson
Admissions: Jon Burke
Type: Two-Year College **Sex:** Coed **Affiliation:** Metropolitan Community Colleges System **% Accepted:** 100 **Admission Plans:** Open Admission; Early Admission; Deferred Admission **Application Deadline:** Rolling **Application Fee:** $0.00 **H.S. Requirements:** High school diploma required; GED accepted **Costs Per Year:** Application fee: $0. Area resident tuition:

$2190 full-time, $73 per hour part-time. State resident tuition: $3990 full-time, $133 per hour part-time. Nonresident tuition: $5400 full-time, $180 per hour part-time. Mandatory fees: $150 full-time, $5 per hour part-time. **Scholarships:** Available **Calendar System:** Semester, Summer Session Available **Enrollment:** FT 1,053, PT 1,609 **Faculty:** FT 31, PT 273 **Student-Faculty Ratio:** 13:1 **Library Holdings:** 10,312 **Regional Accreditation:** North Central Association of Colleges and Schools **Credit Hours For Degree:** 62 credit hours, Associates

CALVARY BIBLE COLLEGE AND THEOLOGICAL SEMINARY
15800 Calvary Rd.
Kansas City, MO 64147-1341
Tel: (816)322-0110
Free: 800-326-3960
Web Site: http://www.calvary.edu/
President/CEO: Dr. Elwood Chipchase
Admissions: Rev. Robert Reinsch
Financial Aid: Rachel Russiaky
Type: Comprehensive **Sex:** Coed **Affiliation:** nondenominational **Scores:** 100% SAT V 400+; 100% SAT M 400+; 54.8% ACT 18-23; 25.8% ACT 24-29 **% Accepted:** 98 **Admission Plans:** Early Admission; Deferred Admission **Application Deadline:** July 15 **Application Fee:** $25.00 **H.S. Requirements:** High school diploma required; GED accepted **Costs Per Year:** Application fee: $25. Comprehensive fee: $10,996 includes full-time tuition ($6720), mandatory fees ($576), and college room and board ($3700). College room only: $1750. Part-time tuition: $240 per credit hour. Part-time mandatory fees: $19 per credit. **Scholarships:** Available **Calendar System:** Semester, Summer Session Available **Enrollment:** FT 230, PT 58, Grad 44 **Faculty:** FT 12, PT 23 **Student-Faculty Ratio:** 12:1 **Exams:** SAT I or ACT **% Receiving Financial Aid:** 77 **Library Holdings:** 56,087 **Regional Accreditation:** North Central Association of Colleges and Schools **Credit Hours For Degree:** 64 semester hours, Associates; 131 semester hours, Bachelors **Professional Accreditation:** AABC **Intercollegiate Athletics:** Basketball M & W; Cheerleading W; Soccer M; Volleyball W

CENTRAL BIBLE COLLEGE
3000 North Grant Ave.
Springfield, MO 65803-1096
Tel: (417)833-2551
Free: 800-831-4222
Fax: (417)833-5141
Web Site: http://www.cbcag.edu/
President/CEO: Rev. M. Wayne Benson
Registrar: William P. Davis
Admissions: Eunice A. Bruegman
Financial Aid: Rev. Rick Woolverton
Type: Four-Year College **Sex:** Coed **Affiliation:** Assemblies of God **Scores:** 83% SAT V 400+; 83% SAT M 400+; 47% ACT 18-23; 26% ACT 24-29 **Admission Plans:** Preferred Admission; Early Admission; Deferred Admission **Application Fee:** $25.00 **H.S. Requirements:** High school diploma required; GED accepted **Scholarships:** Available **Calendar System:** Semester, Summer Session Available **Enrollment:** FT 742, PT 75 **Faculty:** FT 40, PT 26 **Student-Faculty Ratio:** 18:1 **Exams:** SAT I or ACT **% Receiving Financial Aid:** 69 **% Residing in College-Owned, -Operated, or -Affiliated Housing:** 65 **Library Holdings:** 107,023 **Credit Hours For Degree:** 64 semester hours, Associates; 126 semester hours, Bachelors **Professional Accreditation:** AABC **Intercollegiate Athletics:** Basketball M & W; Soccer M; Volleyball W

CENTRAL CHRISTIAN COLLEGE OF THE BIBLE
911 Urbandale Dr. East
Moberly, MO 65270-1997
Tel: (660)263-3900
Fax: (660)263-3936
Web Site: http://www.cccb.edu/
President/CEO: Dr. Russell N. James, III
Registrar: Eric Stevens
Admissions: Jason Rodenbeck
Financial Aid: Rhonda Dunham
Type: Four-Year College **Sex:** Coed **Affiliation:** Christian Churches and Churches of Christ **Admission Plans:** Preferred Admission; Early Admission; Deferred Admission **Application Deadline:** Rolling **Application Fee:** $25.00 **H.S. Requirements:** High school diploma required; GED accepted **Costs Per Year:** Application fee: $25. **Scholarships:** Available **Calendar System:** Semester, Summer Session Not available **Enrollment:** FT 523, PT 8 **Faculty:** FT 16, PT 14 **Student-Faculty Ratio:** 31:1 **Exams:** SAT I or ACT **% Receiving Financial Aid:** 74 **% Residing in College-Owned, -Operated, or -Affiliated Housing:** 75 **Library Holdings:** 35,000 **Credit Hours For Degree:** 64 credits, Associates; 134 credits, Bachelors **Professional Accreditation:** AABC **Intercollegiate Athletics:** Basketball M & W; Golf M & W; Tennis M & W; Volleyball W

CENTRAL METHODIST UNIVERSITY
411 Central Methodist Square
Fayette, MO 65248-1198
Tel: (660)248-3391
Admissions: (660)248-6247
Fax: (660)248-2287
E-mail: admissions@cmc.edu
Web Site: http://www.centralmethodist.edu/
President/CEO: Dr. Marianne Inman
Registrar: Kathryn Winegard
Admissions: Edward J. Lamm
Financial Aid: Linda Mackey
Type: Comprehensive **Sex:** Coed **Affiliation:** Methodist **Scores:** 100% SAT V 400+; 100% SAT M 400+; 63.98% ACT 18-23; 29.57% ACT 24-29 **Admission Plans:** Deferred Admission **Application Fee:** $20.00 **H.S. Requirements:** High school diploma required; GED accepted **Costs Per Year:** Application fee: $20. Comprehensive fee: $20,560 includes full-time tuition ($14,490), mandatory fees ($710), and college room and board ($5360). College room only: $2640. Room and board charges vary according to board plan and housing facility. Part-time tuition: $140 per credit hour. Part-time tuition varies according to course load. **Scholarships:** Available **Calendar System:** Semester, Summer Session Available **Enrollment:** FT 751, PT 30 **Faculty:** FT 54, PT 9 **Student-Faculty Ratio:** 14:1 **Exams:** ACT, SAT I or ACT **% Receiving Financial Aid:** 80 **% Residing in College-Owned, -Operated, or -Affiliated Housing:** 71 **Library Holdings:** 97,793 **Regional Accreditation:** North Central Association of Colleges and Schools **Credit Hours For Degree:** 62 credit hours, Associates; 124 credit hours, Bachelors **ROTC:** Army, Air Force **Professional Accreditation:** JRCEPAT, NASM **Intercollegiate Athletics:** Baseball M; Basketball M & W; Cross-Country Running M & W; Football M; Soccer M & W; Softball W; Track and Field M & W; Volleyball W

CENTRAL MISSOURI STATE UNIVERSITY
PO Box 800
Warrensburg, MO 64093
Tel: (660)543-4111
Admissions: (660)543-4290
Fax: (660)543-8517
E-mail: admit@cmsuvmb.cmsu.edu
Web Site: http://www.cmsu.edu/
President/CEO: Dr. Bobby Patton
Registrar: Robert G. Rhodes
Admissions: Dr. Matt Melvin
Financial Aid: J. Phillip Shreves
Type: Comprehensive **Sex:** Coed **Scores:** 63% ACT 18-23; 27% ACT 24-29 **% Accepted:** 85 **Admission Plans:** Deferred Admission **Application Deadline:** Rolling **Application Fee:** $30.00 **H.S. Requirements:** High school diploma required; GED accepted **Costs Per Year:** Application fee: $30. State resident tuition: $5835 full-time. Nonresident tuition: $11,250 full-time. College room and board: $5109. College room only: $3406. **Scholarships:** Available **Calendar System:** Semester, Summer Session Available **Enrollment:** FT 7,168, PT 1,649, Grad 1,787 **Faculty:** FT 439, PT 266 **Student-Faculty Ratio:** 16:1 **Exams:** ACT **% Receiving Financial Aid:** 64 **% Residing in College-Owned, -Operated, or -Affiliated Housing:** 34 **Library Holdings:** 1,257,260 **Regional Accreditation:** North Central Association of Colleges and Schools **Credit Hours For Degree:** 60 credit hours, Associates; 124 credit hours, Bachelors **ROTC:** Army, Air Force **Professional Accreditation:** AACSB, ABET, AACN, AAFCS, ACCE, ASLHA, CAA, CSWE, NAIT, NASAD, NASM, NCATE, NLN **Intercollegiate Athletics:** Baseball M; Basketball M & W; Bowling M & W; Cross-Country Running M & W; Football M; Golf M; Rugby M & W; Soccer M & W; Softball W; Track and Field M & W; Volleyball W; Wrestling M

CHAMBERLAIN COLLEGE OF NURSING
6150 Oakland Ave.
St. Louis, MO 63139-3215
Tel: (314)768-3044
Free: 800-942-4310

Admissions: (314)768-3179
Fax: (314)768-5673
Web Site: http://www.deaconess.edu/
President/CEO: Carmel White
Registrar: Carrie Nelson
Admissions: Lisa Mancini
Financial Aid: Michelle Mohn
Type: Four-Year College **Sex:** Coed **Affiliation:** Tenet Healthcare Corporation **Scores:** 67% ACT 18-23; 33% ACT 24-29 **Admission Plans:** Deferred Admission **Application Fee:** $50.00 **H.S. Requirements:** High school diploma required; GED accepted **Scholarships:** Available **Calendar System:** Semester, Summer Session Available **Enrollment:** FT 137, PT 187 **Faculty:** FT 11, PT 3 **Student-Faculty Ratio:** 12:1 **Exams:** ACT **% Receiving Financial Aid:** 78 **% Residing in College-Owned, -Operated, or -Affiliated Housing:** 21 **Library Holdings:** 8,700 **Regional Accreditation:** North Central Association of Colleges and Schools **Credit Hours For Degree:** 68 credits, Associates; 128 credits, Bachelors **ROTC:** Army **Professional Accreditation:** NLN

CLEVELAND CHIROPRACTIC COLLEGE-KANSAS CITY CAMPUS
6401 Rockhill Rd.
Kansas City, MO 64131-1181
Tel: (816)501-0100
Free: 800-467-2252
Fax: (816)361-0272
E-mail: mdenton@cleveland.edu
Web Site: http://www.cleveland.edu/
President/CEO: Dr. Carl S. Cleveland, III
Registrar: Nancy Eastman
Admissions: Melissa Denton
Financial Aid: Mindy Beckley
Type: Two-Year Upper Division **Sex:** Coed **Admission Plans:** Open Admission; Deferred Admission **Application Fee:** $35.00 **H.S. Requirements:** High school diploma required; GED accepted **Calendar System:** Trimester, Summer Session Available **Enrollment:** FT 61, PT 10 **Faculty:** FT 45 **Student-Faculty Ratio:** 15:1 **Library Holdings:** 14,000 **Regional Accreditation:** North Central Association of Colleges and Schools **Credit Hours For Degree:** 123 credits, Bachelors **Professional Accreditation:** CCE

COLLEGE OF THE OZARKS
PO Box 17
Point Lookout, MO 65726
Tel: (417)334-6411
Free: 800-222-0525
Fax: (417)335-2618
E-mail: admiss4@cofo.edu
Web Site: http://www.cofo.edu/
President/CEO: Dr. Jerry C. Davis
Registrar: Fran Forman
Admissions: Marci Linson
Financial Aid: Kyla McCarty
Type: Four-Year College **Sex:** Coed **Affiliation:** Presbyterian **Scores:** 63% ACT 18-23; 24% ACT 24-29 **% Accepted:** 10 **Admission Plans:** Preferred Admission **Application Deadline:** February 15 **Application Fee:** $0.00 **H.S. Requirements:** High school diploma required; GED accepted **Costs Per Year:** Application fee: $0. Comprehensive fee: $4380 includes full-time tuition ($0), mandatory fees ($280), and college room and board ($4100). College room only: $2000. Part-time tuition: $295 per credit hour. Part-time mandatory fees: $140 per term. **Scholarships:** Available **Calendar System:** Semester, Summer Session Not available **Enrollment:** FT 1,311, PT 22 **Faculty:** FT 74, PT 32 **Student-Faculty Ratio:** 16:1 **Exams:** ACT **% Receiving Financial Aid:** 90 **% Residing in College-Owned, -Operated, or -Affiliated Housing:** 84 **Library Holdings:** 119,765 **Regional Accreditation:** North Central Association of Colleges and Schools **Credit Hours For Degree:** 125 semester hours, Bachelors **ROTC:** Army **Intercollegiate Athletics:** Baseball M; Basketball M & W; Cheerleading M & W; Volleyball W

COLUMBIA COLLEGE
1001 Rogers St.
Columbia, MO 65216-0002
Tel: (573)875-8700
Free: 800-231-2391
Admissions: (573)875-7352
Fax: (573)875-7506
E-mail: admissions@ccis.edu
Web Site: http://www.ccis.edu/
President/CEO: Dr. Gerald T. Brouder
Registrar: Sue Koopmans
Admissions: Regina Morin
Financial Aid: Sharon Abernathy
Type: Comprehensive **Sex:** Coed **Affiliation:** Christian Church (Disciples of Christ) **Scores:** 100% SAT V 400+; 86% SAT M 400+; 59% ACT 18-23; 26% ACT 24-29 **% Accepted:** 62 **Admission Plans:** Early Admission; Deferred Admission **Application Deadline:** Rolling **Application Fee:** $25.00 **H.S. Requirements:** High school diploma required; GED accepted **Costs Per Year:** Application fee: $25. Comprehehsive fee: $17,006 includes full-time tuition ($11,995) and college room and board ($5011). College room only: $3152. Full-time tuition varies according to class time and course load. Room and board charges vary according to board plan. Part-time tuition: $257 per credit hour. Part-time tuition varies according to class time, course load, and location. **Scholarships:** Available **Calendar System:** Semester, Summer Session Available **Enrollment:** FT 757, PT 252, Grad 140 **Faculty:** FT 56, PT 26 **Student-Faculty Ratio:** 13:1 **Exams:** SAT I or ACT **% Receiving Financial Aid:** 59 **% Residing in College-Owned, -Operated, or -Affiliated Housing:** 36 **Library Holdings:** 62,265 **Regional Accreditation:** North Central Association of Colleges and Schools **Credit Hours For Degree:** 60 semester hours, Associates; 120 semester hours, Bachelors **ROTC:** Army, Air Force **Professional Accreditation:** CSWE, NLN **Intercollegiate Athletics:** Basketball M & W; Cheerleading W; Soccer M; Softball W; Volleyball W

CONCEPTION SEMINARY COLLEGE
PO Box 502
Conception, MO 64433-0502
Tel: (660)944-3105
Admissions: (660)944-2886
Fax: (660)944-2829
Web Site: http://www.conceptionabbey.org/
President/CEO: Rev. Benedict Neenan, OSB
Registrar: Velda Mattson
Admissions: Vincent Casper
Financial Aid: Br. Justin Hernandez, OSB
Type: Four-Year College **Sex:** Men **Affiliation:** Roman Catholic **Scores:** 59% ACT 18-23; 18% ACT 24-29 **Admission Plans:** Preferred Admission **Application Fee:** $0.00 **H.S. Requirements:** High school diploma required; GED accepted **Costs Per Year:** Application fee: $0. Comprehensive fee: $19,498 includes full-time tuition ($12,118), mandatory fees ($180), and college room and board ($7200). College room only: $3046. Part-time tuition: $150 per credit. **Scholarships:** Available **Calendar System:** Semester, Summer Session Not available **Enrollment:** FT 90, PT 10 **Faculty:** FT 24, PT 2 **Student-Faculty Ratio:** 4:1 **Exams:** ACT **% Receiving Financial Aid:** 47 **% Residing in College-Owned, -Operated, or -Affiliated Housing:** 100 **Library Holdings:** 115,000 **Regional Accreditation:** North Central Association of Colleges and Schools **Credit Hours For Degree:** 126 credits, Bachelors

CONCORDE CAREER INSTITUTE
3239 Broadway
Kansas City, MO 64111-2407
Tel: (816)531-5223
Fax: (816)756-3231
Web Site: http://www.concordecareercolleges.com/ **Type:** Two-Year College **Sex:** Coed **Professional Accreditation:** ACCSCT, ADA, CARC

COTTEY COLLEGE
1000 West Austin
Nevada, MO 64772
Tel: (417)667-8181; 888-526-8839
Fax: (417)667-8103
E-mail: enrollmgt@cottey.edu
Web Site: http://www.cottey.edu/
President/CEO: Dr. Helen R. Washburn
Registrar: Janie Bossert
Admissions: Marjorie J. Cooke
Financial Aid: Sherry Pennington
Type: Two-Year College **Sex:** Women **Scores:** 94% SAT V 400+; 76% SAT M 400+; 49% ACT 18-23; 41% ACT 24-29 **% Accepted:** 36 **Admission Plans:** Early Admission; Deferred Admission **Application Deadline:** Rolling **Application Fee:** $20.00 **H.S. Requirements:** High school diploma

required; GED accepted **Costs Per Year:** Application fee: $20. Comprehensive fee: $17,510 includes full-time tuition ($11,600), mandatory fees ($710), and college room and board ($5200). **Scholarships:** Available **Calendar System:** Semester, Summer Session Not available **Faculty:** FT 35, PT 2 **Student-Faculty Ratio:** 10:1 **Exams:** SAT I or ACT **% Residing in College-Owned, -Operated, or -Affiliated Housing:** 98 **Library Holdings:** 54,200 **Regional Accreditation:** North Central Association of Colleges and Schools **Credit Hours For Degree:** 62 credit hours, Associates **Professional Accreditation:** NASM **Intercollegiate Athletics:** Basketball W; Volleyball W

COX COLLEGE OF NURSING AND HEALTH SCIENCES
1423 North Jefferson
Springfield, MO 65802
Tel: (417)269-3401
Admissions: (417)269-3038
Web Site: http://www.coxcollege.edu/
President/CEO: DeLois P. Weekes
Registrar: Jean Summers
Admissions: Stacy Danaher
Financial Aid: Robin Asher
Type: Four-Year College **Sex:** Coed **Affiliation:** Cox Health Systems **Admission Plans:** Early Decision Plan **Application Deadline:** February 01 **Application Fee:** $30.00 **H.S. Requirements:** High school diploma required; GED accepted **Costs Per Year:** Application fee: $30. Tuition: $9240 full-time, $308 per credit hour part-time. Mandatory fees: $1050 full-time, $35 per credit hour part-time. Full-time tuition and fees vary according to course load and program. Part-time tuition and fees vary according to course load and program. College room only: $2000. **Scholarships:** Available **Calendar System:** Semester, Summer Session Available **Enrollment:** FT 279, PT 313 **Faculty:** FT 21, PT 26 **Student-Faculty Ratio:** 13:1 **Exams:** SAT I or ACT **% Residing in College-Owned, -Operated, or -Affiliated Housing:** 15 **Regional Accreditation:** North Central Association of Colleges and Schools **Credit Hours For Degree:** 66 credit hours, Associates; 122 credit hours, Bachelors **Professional Accreditation:** AACN, NLN

CROWDER COLLEGE
601 Laclede Ave.
Neosho, MO 64850-9160
Tel: (417)451-3223; (866)238-7788
Fax: (417)451-4280
Web Site: http://www.crowder.edu/
President/CEO: Dr. Steven M. Gates
Registrar: Sonya Pearson
Admissions: Dr. Sonya Pearson
Financial Aid: Michelle Paul
Type: Two-Year College **Sex:** Coed **Affiliation:** Missouri Coordinating Board for Higher Education **% Accepted:** 100 **Admission Plans:** Open Admission **Application Deadline:** Rolling **Application Fee:** $25.00 **H.S. Requirements:** High school diploma required; GED accepted **Costs Per Year:** Application fee: $25. Area resident tuition: $1860 full-time. State resident tuition: $2640 full-time. Nonresident tuition: $3450 full-time. Mandatory fees: $360 full-time. College room and board: $3870. **Scholarships:** Available **Calendar System:** Semester, Summer Session Available **Enrollment:** FT 1,319, PT 1,296 **Faculty:** FT 64, PT 155 **Student-Faculty Ratio:** 19:1 **% Residing in College-Owned, -Operated, or -Affiliated Housing:** 10 **Library Holdings:** 37,452 **Regional Accreditation:** North Central Association of Colleges and Schools **Credit Hours For Degree:** 60 semester hours, Associates **Professional Accreditation:** NAIT **Intercollegiate Athletics:** Baseball M; Basketball W

CULVER-STOCKTON COLLEGE
1 College Hill
Canton, MO 63435-1299
Tel: (573)288-6000
Free: 800-537-1883
Fax: (573)288-6617
E-mail: bsmith@culver.edu
Web Site: http://www.culver.edu/
President/CEO: Dr. William L. Fox
Registrar: Marjorie Ellison
Admissions: Betty Smith
Financial Aid: Tina Wiseman
Type: Four-Year College **Sex:** Coed **Affiliation:** Christian Church (Disciples of Christ) **Scores:** 67% ACT 18-23; 25% ACT 24-29 **% Accepted:** 76 **Admission Plans:** Deferred Admission **Application Fee:** $25.00 **H.S. Requirements:** High school diploma required; GED accepted **Costs Per Year:** Application fee: $25. Comprehensive fee: $21,796 includes full-time tuition ($15,250) and college room and board ($6546). College room only: $3030. Part-time tuition: $400 per credit hour. Part-time mandatory fees: $10 per credit hour. **Scholarships:** Available **Calendar System:** Semester, Summer Session Available **Enrollment:** FT 766, PT 74 **Faculty:** FT 44, PT 45 **Student-Faculty Ratio:** 13:1 **Exams:** SAT I or ACT **% Receiving Financial Aid:** 89 **% Residing in College-Owned, -Operated, or -Affiliated Housing:** 71 **Library Holdings:** 155,487 **Regional Accreditation:** North Central Association of Colleges and Schools **Credit Hours For Degree:** 124 hours, Bachelors **Professional Accreditation:** NASM, NLN **Intercollegiate Athletics:** Baseball M; Basketball M & W; Cheerleading M & W; Football M; Golf M & W; Soccer M & W; Softball W; Volleyball W

DEVRY UNIVERSITY (KANSAS CITY)
City Center Square
1100 Main St., Ste. 118
Kansas City, MO 64105-2112
Tel: (816)221-1300
Fax: (816)474-0318
Web Site: http://www.devry.edu/ **Type:** Comprehensive **Sex:** Coed **Costs Per Year:** One-time mandatory fee: $40. Tuition: $11,790 full-time, $440 per credit part-time. Mandatory fees: $60 full-time, $30 per year part-time. **Calendar System:** Semester **Regional Accreditation:** North Central Association of Colleges and Schools

DEVRY UNIVERSITY (KANSAS CITY)
11224 Holmes Rd.
Kansas City, MO 64131-3698
Tel: (816)941-0430
Free: 800-821-3766
Fax: (816)941-0896
Web Site: http://www.devry.edu/
President/CEO: C. Robert Levalley
Registrar: Melissa Knudsen
Type: Four-Year College **Sex:** Coed **Affiliation:** DeVry University **Admission Plans:** Deferred Admission **Application Deadline:** Rolling **Application Fee:** $50.00 **H.S. Requirements:** High school diploma required; GED accepted **Costs Per Year:** Application fee: $50. One-time mandatory fee: $40. Tuition: $11,790 full-time, $440 per credit part-time. Mandatory fees: $270 full-time, $160 per year part-time. Full-time tuition and fees vary according to course load. Part-time tuition and fees vary according to course load. **Scholarships:** Available **Calendar System:** Semester, Summer Session Available **Enrollment:** FT 809, PT 292, Grad 132 **Faculty:** FT 49, PT 39 **Student-Faculty Ratio:** 16:1 **% Receiving Financial Aid:** 73 **Library Holdings:** 15,000 **Regional Accreditation:** North Central Association of Colleges and Schools **Credit Hours For Degree:** 67 credit hours, Associates; 122 credit hours, Bachelors **Professional Accreditation:** ABET

DEVRY UNIVERSITY (ST. LOUIS)
1801 Park 270 Dr., Ste. 260
St. Louis, MO 63146-4020
Tel: (314)542-4222
Fax: (314)542-4004
Web Site: http://www.devry.edu/ **Type:** Comprehensive **Sex:** Coed **Costs Per Year:** One-time mandatory fee: $40. Tuition: $11,790 full-time, $440 per credit part-time. Mandatory fees: $60 full-time, $30 per year part-time. Full-time tuition and fees vary according to course load. Part-time tuition and fees vary according to course load. **Calendar System:** Semester **Regional Accreditation:** North Central Association of Colleges and Schools

DRURY UNIVERSITY
900 North Benton Ave.
Springfield, MO 65802-3791
Tel: (417)873-7879
Free: 800-922-2274
Admissions: (417)873-7205
Fax: (417)873-7529
E-mail: druryad@drury.edu
Web Site: http://www.drury.edu/
President/CEO: Dr. John E. Moore, Jr.
Registrar: Gale Boutwell
Admissions: Chip Parker

Financial Aid: Annette Avery
Type: Comprehensive **Sex:** Coed **Scores:** 98.3% SAT V 400+; 98.3% SAT M 400+; 30.4% ACT 18-23; 51.4% ACT 24-29 **% Accepted:** 78 **Admission Plans:** Deferred Admission **Application Deadline:** March 15 **Application Fee:** $25.00 **H.S. Requirements:** High school diploma required; GED accepted **Costs Per Year:** Application fee: $25. Comprehensive fee: $21,302 includes full-time tuition ($15,173), mandatory fees ($339), and college room and board ($5790). Part-time tuition: $500 per semester hour. **Scholarships:** Available **Calendar System:** Semester, Summer Session Available **Enrollment:** FT 1,541, PT 39, Grad 381 **Faculty:** FT 123, PT 62 **Student-Faculty Ratio:** 13:1 **Exams:** SAT I or ACT **% Receiving Financial Aid:** 90 **% Residing in College-Owned, -Operated, or -Affiliated Housing:** 50 **Library Holdings:** 177,794 **Regional Accreditation:** North Central Association of Colleges and Schools **Credit Hours For Degree:** 124 semester hours, Bachelors **ROTC:** Army **Professional Accreditation:** ACBSP, NASM, NCATE **Intercollegiate Athletics:** Baseball M; Basketball M; Cross-Country Running M & W; Golf M & W; Soccer M & W; Swimming and Diving M & W; Tennis M & W; Volleyball W

EAST CENTRAL COLLEGE
1964 Prairie Dell Rd.
Union, MO 63084
Tel: (636)583-5193
Admissions: (636)583-5195
Fax: (636)583-1897
Web Site: http://www.eastcentral.edu/
President/CEO: Dr. Karen Herzog
Admissions: Karen Wieda
Financial Aid: Todd Martin
Type: Two-Year College **Sex:** Coed **Affiliation:** Missouri Coordinating Board for Higher Education **Admission Plans:** Open Admission; Preferred Admission; Early Admission; Deferred Admission **Application Deadline:** Rolling **Application Fee:** $0.00 **H.S. Requirements:** High school diploma required; GED accepted **Costs Per Year:** Application fee: $0. Area resident tuition: $1464 full-time, $61 per credit hour part-time. State resident tuition: $2088 full-time, $87 per credit hour part-time. Nonresident tuition: $3144 full-time, $131 per credit hour part-time. Mandatory fees: $240 full-time, $10 per credit hour part-time. **Scholarships:** Available **Calendar System:** Semester, Summer Session Available **Enrollment:** FT 1,447, PT 2,039 **Faculty:** FT 55, PT 134 **Student-Faculty Ratio:** 21:1 **Library Holdings:** 38,863 **Regional Accreditation:** North Central Association of Colleges and Schools **Credit Hours For Degree:** 64 semester hours, Associates **Intercollegiate Athletics:** Soccer M; Softball W

EVANGEL UNIVERSITY
1111 North Glenstone
Springfield, MO 65802-2191
Tel: (417)865-2811
Fax: (417)865-9599
E-mail: admissions@evangel.edu
Web Site: http://www.evangel.edu/
President/CEO: Dr. Robert H. Spence
Registrar: David I. Schoolfield
Admissions: Charity Waltner
Financial Aid: Kathy White
Type: Comprehensive **Sex:** Coed **Affiliation:** Assemblies of God **Scores:** 50% ACT 18-23; 37% ACT 24-29 **% Accepted:** 96 **Admission Plans:** Deferred Admission **Application Deadline:** August 01 **Application Fee:** $25.00 **H.S. Requirements:** High school diploma required; GED accepted **Costs Per Year:** Application fee: $25. Comprehensive fee: $17,370 includes full-time tuition ($12,040), mandatory fees ($710), and college room and board ($4620). College room only: $2270. Full-time tuition and fees vary according to course load. Room and board charges vary according to board plan. Part-time tuition: $469 per credit hour. Part-time mandatory fees: $235 per term. **Scholarships:** Available **Calendar System:** Semester, Summer Session Available **Enrollment:** FT 1,646, PT 75, Grad 80 **Faculty:** FT 96, PT 62 **Student-Faculty Ratio:** 18:1 **Exams:** SAT I or ACT **% Receiving Financial Aid:** 73 **% Residing in College-Owned, -Operated, or -Affiliated Housing:** 82 **Library Holdings:** 100,691 **Regional Accreditation:** North Central Association of Colleges and Schools **Credit Hours For Degree:** 60 credit hours, Associates; 124 credit hours, Bachelors **ROTC:** Army **Professional Accreditation:** CSWE, NASM, NCATE **Intercollegiate Athletics:** Baseball M; Basketball M & W; Cross-Country Running M & W; Football M; Golf M & W; Softball W; Tennis M & W; Track and Field M & W; Volleyball W

FONTBONNE UNIVERSITY
6800 Wydown Blvd.
St. Louis, MO 63105-3098
Tel: (314)862-3456
Admissions: (314)889-1400
Fax: (314)719-8021
E-mail: pmusen@fontbonne.edu
Web Site: http://www.fontbonne.edu/
President/CEO: Dr. Dennis C. Golden
Registrar: Mazie Moore
Admissions: Peggy Musen
Financial Aid: Nicole K. Moore
Type: Comprehensive **Sex:** Coed **Affiliation:** Roman Catholic **Scores:** 31% ACT 18-23; 26% ACT 24-29 **% Accepted:** 66 **Admission Plans:** Early Admission; Deferred Admission **Application Deadline:** August 01 **Application Fee:** $25.00 **H.S. Requirements:** High school diploma required; GED accepted **Costs Per Year:** Application fee: $25. Comprehensive fee: $24,428 includes full-time tuition ($17,120), mandatory fees ($320), and college room and board ($6988). Part-time tuition: $465 per credit hour. Part-time mandatory fees: $16 per credit hour. **Scholarships:** Available **Calendar System:** Semester, Summer Session Available **Enrollment:** FT 1,547, PT 531, Grad 758 **Faculty:** FT 72, PT 300 **Student-Faculty Ratio:** 13:1 **Exams:** SAT I or ACT **% Residing in College-Owned, -Operated, or -Affiliated Housing:** 19 **Library Holdings:** 52,980 **Regional Accreditation:** North Central Association of Colleges and Schools **Credit Hours For Degree:** 128 credits, Bachelors **ROTC:** Army **Professional Accreditation:** AAFCS, ASLHA, ACBSP, NCATE **Intercollegiate Athletics:** Baseball M; Basketball M & W; Bowling W; Cheerleading W; Cross-Country Running M & W; Golf M & W; Soccer M & W; Softball W; Tennis M & W; Volleyball W

GLOBAL UNIVERSITY OF THE ASSEMBLIES OF GOD
1211 South Glenstone Ave.
Springfield, MO 65804
Tel: (417)862-9533
Free: 800-443-1083
Fax: (417)862-5318
E-mail: jdorn@globaluniversity.edu
Web Site: http://www.globaluniversity.edu/
President/CEO: Dr. Ronald Iwasko
Registrar: Lynne Kroh
Admissions: Jessica Dorn
Type: Comprehensive **Sex:** Coed **Affiliation:** Assemblies of God **Admission Plans:** Open Admission **Application Deadline:** Rolling **Application Fee:** $35.00 **H.S. Requirements:** High school diploma required; GED accepted **Costs Per Year:** Application fee: $35. Tuition: $2160 full-time, $90 per credit hour part-time. Part-time tuition varies according to class time. **Calendar System:** Continuous, Summer Session Not available **Enrollment:** FT 1,770, PT 3,272, Grad 255 **Faculty:** FT 57, PT 561 **Student-Faculty Ratio:** 11:1 **Credit Hours For Degree:** 64 credits, Associates; 128 credits, Bachelors **Professional Accreditation:** DETC

GRANTHAM UNIVERSITY
7200 NW 86th St., Ste. M
Kansas City, MO 64153
Free: 800-955-2527
Fax: (816)595-5757
E-mail: admissions@grantham.edu
Web Site: http://www.grantham.edu/
President/CEO: Roy Winter
Registrar: Gina Tyrney
Admissions: DeAnn Wandler
Type: Comprehensive **Sex:** Coed **Admission Plans:** Open Admission **Application Deadline:** Rolling **Application Fee:** $0.00 **H.S. Requirements:** High school diploma required; GED accepted **Costs Per Year:** Application fee: $0. Tuition: $6978 full-time, $335 per credit hour part-time. **Calendar System:** Continuous **Credit Hours For Degree:** 60 credits, Associates; 125 credits, Bachelors **Professional Accreditation:** DETC

HANNIBAL-LAGRANGE COLLEGE
2800 Palmyra Rd.
Hannibal, MO 63401-1999
Tel: (573)221-3675
Free: 800-HLG-1119
Admissions: (573)221-3113
Fax: (573)221-6594

E-mail: admissio@hlg.edu
Web Site: http://www.hlg.edu/
President/CEO: Dr. Woodrow Burt
Registrar: Darla Thomason
Admissions: Raymond Carty
Financial Aid: Amy Blackwell
Type: Four-Year College **Sex:** Coed **Affiliation:** Southern Baptist **Scores:** 57% ACT 18-23; 31% ACT 24-29 **% Accepted:** 96 **Admission Plans:** Early Admission; Deferred Admission **Application Deadline:** Rolling **Application Fee:** $25.00 **H.S. Requirements:** High school diploma required; GED accepted **Costs Per Year:** Application fee: $25. Comprehensive fee: $16,390 includes full-time tuition ($11,420), mandatory fees ($360), and college room and board ($4610). Full-time tuition and fees vary according to course load. Room and board charges vary according to board plan and housing facility. Part-time tuition: $380 per hour. Part-time mandatory fees: $90 per term. Part-time tuition and fees vary according to course load. **Scholarships:** Available **Calendar System:** Semester, Summer Session Available **Enrollment:** FT 873, PT 184 **Faculty:** FT 65, PT 29 **Student-Faculty Ratio:** 12:1 **Exams:** SAT I or ACT **% Receiving Financial Aid:** 74 **% Residing in College-Owned, -Operated, or -Affiliated Housing:** 50 **Library Holdings:** 71,680 **Regional Accreditation:** North Central Association of Colleges and Schools **Credit Hours For Degree:** 64 credit hours, Associates; 124 credit hours, Bachelors **Professional Accreditation:** CARC, NLN **Intercollegiate Athletics:** Baseball M; Basketball M & W; Cheerleading M & W; Cross-Country Running M & W; Golf M; Soccer M & W; Softball W; Volleyball W

HARRIS-STOWE STATE UNIVERSITY
3026 Laclede Ave.
St. Louis, MO 63103-2136
Tel: (314)340-3366
Admissions: (314)340-3301
Fax: (314)340-3322
Web Site: http://www.hssu.edu/
President/CEO: Dr. Henry Givens, Jr.
Registrar: Carnell Jones
Admissions: LaShanda Boone
Financial Aid: Sandra Call
Type: Four-Year College **Sex:** Coed **Affiliation:** Missouri Coordinating Board for Higher Education **Admission Plans:** Open Admission; Early Admission; Deferred Admission **Application Deadline:** Rolling **Application Fee:** $15.00 **H.S. Requirements:** High school diploma required; GED accepted **Costs Per Year:** Application fee: $15. State resident tuition: $4650 full-time, $145 per hour part-time. Nonresident tuition: $8570 full-time, $285.65 per hour part-time. Mandatory fees: $150 full-time, $150 per term part-time. College room only: $5400. **Scholarships:** Available **Calendar System:** Semester, Summer Session Available **Enrollment:** FT 970, PT 692 **Faculty:** FT 47, PT 86 **Student-Faculty Ratio:** 16:1 **Exams:** SAT I or ACT **% Receiving Financial Aid:** 88 **Library Holdings:** 60,000 **Regional Accreditation:** North Central Association of Colleges and Schools **Credit Hours For Degree:** 120 credit hours, Bachelors **ROTC:** Air Force **Professional Accreditation:** ACBSP, NCATE **Intercollegiate Athletics:** Baseball M; Basketball M & W; Cheerleading M & W; Soccer M & W; Softball W; Tennis M & W; Track and Field W; Volleyball W

HERITAGE COLLEGE
534 East 99th St.
Kansas City, MO 64131-4203
Tel: (816)942-5474
Fax: (816)942-5405
Web Site: http://www.heritage-education.com/
President/CEO: Larry Cartmill
Type: Two-Year College **Sex:** Coed **Professional Accreditation:** ACCSCT

HICKEY COLLEGE
940 West Port Plaza, Ste. 101
St. Louis, MO 63146
Tel: (314)434-2212
Free: 800-777-1544
Fax: (314)434-1974
Web Site: http://www.hickeycollege.edu/
President/CEO: Christopher A. Gearin
Admissions: Michelle Hayes
Type: Two-Year College **Sex:** Coed **Application Deadline:** Rolling **Application Fee:** $50.00 **H.S. Requirements:** High school diploma required; GED accepted **Calendar System:** Semester **Enrollment:** FT 500, PT 110 **Faculty:** FT 12, PT 6 **Student-Faculty Ratio:** 38:1 **Professional Accreditation:** ACICS

HIGH-TECH INSTITUTE
9001 State Line Rd.
Kansas City, MO 64114
Tel: (602)279-9700
Web Site: http://www.high-techinstitute.com/
President/CEO: Rich Craven
Type: Two-Year College **Sex:** Coed **Calendar System:** Semester **Professional Accreditation:** ACCSCT

IHM HEALTH STUDIES CENTER
2500 Abbott Place
St. Louis, MO 63143-2636
Tel: (314)768-1234
Fax: (314)768-1595
E-mail: meyer@abbottems.org
Web Site: http://www.ihmhealthstudies.com/
President/CEO: Taz A. Meyer
Admissions: Taz A. Meyer
Type: Two-Year College **Sex:** Coed **Calendar System:** Trimester **Enrollment:** FT 72, PT 64 **Faculty:** FT 4, PT 3

ITT TECHNICAL INSTITUTE (ARNOLD)
1930 Meyer Drury Dr.
Arnold, MO 63010
Tel: (636)464-6600; 888-488-1082
Web Site: http://www.itt-tech.edu/
President/CEO: Paula Jerden
Admissions: David Heckeler
Type: Two-Year College **Sex:** Coed **Affiliation:** ITT Educational Services, Inc **Admission Plans:** Deferred Admission **Application Deadline:** Rolling **Application Fee:** $100.00 **H.S. Requirements:** High school diploma required; GED accepted **Costs Per Year:** Application fee: $100. **Scholarships:** Available **Calendar System:** Quarter, Summer Session Not available **Exams:** Other **Credit Hours For Degree:** 96 credit hours, Associates; 180 credit hours, Bachelors **Professional Accreditation:** ACICS

ITT TECHNICAL INSTITUTE (EARTH CITY)
13505 Lakefront Dr.
Earth City, MO 63045-1412
Tel: (314)298-7800
Free: 800-235-5488
Fax: (314)298-0559
Web Site: http://www.itt-tech.edu/
President/CEO: Karen Finkenkeller
Registrar: Carolyn Carter
Admissions: Karen Finkenkeller
Financial Aid: Cheryl Pace
Type: Two-Year College **Sex:** Coed **Affiliation:** ITT Educational Services, Inc **Admission Plans:** Deferred Admission **Application Deadline:** Rolling **Application Fee:** $100.00 **H.S. Requirements:** High school diploma required; GED accepted **Costs Per Year:** Application fee: $100. **Scholarships:** Available **Calendar System:** Quarter, Summer Session Not available **Exams:** Other **Credit Hours For Degree:** 96 credit hours, Associates; 180 credit hours, Bachelors **Professional Accreditation:** ACICS

ITT TECHNICAL INSTITUTE (KANSAS CITY)
1740 West 92nd St., Ste. 10
Kansas City, MO 64114
; 877-488-1442
Admissions: (816)276-1400
Web Site: http://www.itt-tech.edu/
Admissions: Eddie Colon
Type: Two-Year College **Sex:** Coed **Application Deadline:** Rolling **Application Fee:** $100.00 **Costs Per Year:** Application fee: $100. **Calendar System:** Quarter **Exams:** Other

JEFFERSON COLLEGE
1000 Viking Dr.
Hillsboro, MO 63050-2441
Tel: (636)797-3000
Fax: (636)789-4012

Web Site: http://www.jeffco.edu/
President/CEO: Bill McKenna
Registrar: Connie Kuchar
Admissions: Amy Martin-Small
Financial Aid: Amy Martin-Small
Type: Two-Year College **Sex:** Coed **Affiliation:** Missouri Coordinating Board for Higher Education **Scores:** 53% ACT 18-23; 19% ACT 24-29 **Admission Plans:** Open Admission; Early Admission **Application Fee:** $20.00 **H.S. Requirements:** High school diploma required; GED accepted **Scholarships:** Available **Calendar System:** Semester, Summer Session Available **Enrollment:** FT 2,176, PT 1,889 **Faculty:** FT 86, PT 132 **Student-Faculty Ratio:** 18:1 **Exams:** ACT, Other **% Residing in College-Owned, -Operated, or -Affiliated Housing:** 15 **Library Holdings:** 70,402 **Regional Accreditation:** North Central Association of Colleges and Schools **Credit Hours For Degree:** 62 semester hours, Associates **Intercollegiate Athletics:** Baseball M; Basketball W; Volleyball W

KANSAS CITY ART INSTITUTE
4415 Warwick Blvd.
Kansas City, MO 64111-1874
Tel: (816)472-4852
Free: 800-522-5224
Admissions: (816)474-5224
Fax: (816)531-6296
E-mail: admiss@kcai.edu
Web Site: http://www.kcai.edu/
President/CEO: Kathleen Collins
Registrar: Ida Sohm
Admissions: Larry Stone
Financial Aid: Christal Williams
Type: Four-Year College **Sex:** Coed **Scores:** 93% SAT V 400+; 88% SAT M 400+; 30% ACT 18-23; 52% ACT 24-29 **% Accepted:** 74 **Admission Plans:** Deferred Admission **Application Deadline:** Rolling **Application Fee:** $35.00 **H.S. Requirements:** High school diploma required; GED accepted **Costs Per Year:** Application fee: $35. Comprehensive fee: $29,542 includes full-time tuition ($21,446), mandatory fees ($946), and college room and board ($7150). Full-time tuition and fees vary according to program. Room and board charges vary according to board plan and housing facility. Part-time tuition: $850 per credit hour. Part-time mandatory fees: $46 per credit hour. Part-time tuition and fees vary according to program. **Scholarships:** Available **Calendar System:** Semester, Summer Session Available **Enrollment:** FT 576, PT 12 **Faculty:** FT 46, PT 48 **Student-Faculty Ratio:** 12:1 **Exams:** SAT I or ACT **% Receiving Financial Aid:** 79 **% Residing in College-Owned, -Operated, or -Affiliated Housing:** 25 **Library Holdings:** 32,235 **Regional Accreditation:** North Central Association of Colleges and Schools **Credit Hours For Degree:** 129 credit hours, Bachelors **Professional Accreditation:** NASAD

KANSAS CITY COLLEGE
402 East Bannister Rd., Ste. A
Kansas City, MO 64131
Tel: (816)444-2232; 877-582-3963
Fax: (816)444-3142
Web Site: http://www.metropolitancollege.edu/
Admissions: Rosemary Velez
Type: Four-Year College **Sex:** Coed **Application Fee:** $50.00 **Scholarships:** Available **Calendar System:** Trimester **Faculty:** FT 2, PT 13 **Student-Faculty Ratio:** 19:1 **Exams:** ACT **% Receiving Financial Aid:** 79 **Professional Accreditation:** ACCSCT

LINCOLN UNIVERSITY
820 Chestnut St.
Jefferson City, MO 65102
Tel: (573)681-5000
Free: 800-521-5052
Admissions: (573)681-5599
Fax: (573)681-6074
E-mail: enroll@lincolnu.edu
Web Site: http://www.lincolnu.edu/
President/CEO: Dr. David B. Henson
Registrar: Debra Cooper
Admissions: Craig Galbreath
Financial Aid: Alfred Robinson
Type: Comprehensive **Sex:** Coed **Affiliation:** Missouri Coordinating Board for Higher Education **Scores:** 34.14% ACT 18-23; 4.29% ACT 24-29 **% Accepted:** 94 **Admission Plans:** Open Admission; Early Admission; Deferred Admission **Application Deadline:** July 15 **Application Fee:** $17.00 **H.S. Requirements:** High school diploma required; GED accepted **Costs Per Year:** Application fee: $17. State resident tuition: $4412 full-time, $147.08 per credit hour part-time. Nonresident tuition: $8059 full-time, $268.62 per credit hour part-time. Mandatory fees: $190 full-time, $5 per credit hour part-time, $20 per term part-time. College room and board: $3790. College room only: $1850. **Scholarships:** Available **Calendar System:** Semester, Summer Session Available **Enrollment:** FT 2,017, PT 936, Grad 227 **Faculty:** FT 127, PT 47 **Student-Faculty Ratio:** 17:1 **% Receiving Financial Aid:** 70 **% Residing in College-Owned, -Operated, or -Affiliated Housing:** 28 **Library Holdings:** 187,956 **Regional Accreditation:** North Central Association of Colleges and Schools **Credit Hours For Degree:** 62 credit hours, Associates; 121 credit hours, Bachelors **ROTC:** Army **Professional Accreditation:** ACBSP, NASM, NCATE, NLN **Intercollegiate Athletics:** Baseball M; Basketball M & W; Cross-Country Running W; Football M; Golf M; Softball W; Tennis W; Track and Field M & W

LINDENWOOD UNIVERSITY
209 South Kingshighway
St. Charles, MO 63301-1695
Tel: (636)949-2000
Admissions: (636)949-4993
Fax: (636)949-4910
E-mail: sguffey@lindenwood.edu
Web Site: http://www.lindenwood.edu/
President/CEO: Dr. Dennis Spellmann
Registrar: Mary Ann Townsend
Admissions: Sheryl Guffey
Type: Comprehensive **Sex:** Coed **Affiliation:** Presbyterian **Scores:** 68% ACT 18-23; 27% ACT 24-29 **% Accepted:** 43 **Admission Plans:** Early Admission; Deferred Admission **Application Deadline:** Rolling **Application Fee:** $30.00 **H.S. Requirements:** High school diploma required; GED accepted **Costs Per Year:** Application fee: $30. Comprehensive fee: $18,240 includes full-time tuition ($12,000), mandatory fees ($240), and college room and board ($6000). College room only: $3000. Part-time tuition: $330 per credit hour. **Scholarships:** Available **Calendar System:** 4-1-4, Summer Session Available **Enrollment:** FT 5,092, PT 646, Grad 3,338 **Faculty:** FT 208, PT 400 **Student-Faculty Ratio:** 15:1 **Exams:** SAT I or ACT **% Residing in College-Owned, -Operated, or -Affiliated Housing:** 76 **Library Holdings:** 122,461 **Regional Accreditation:** North Central Association of Colleges and Schools **Credit Hours For Degree:** 128 credit hours, Bachelors **ROTC:** Army, Air Force **Intercollegiate Athletics:** Baseball M; Basketball M & W; Bowling M & W; Cheerleading M & W; Cross-Country Running M & W; Field Hockey W; Football M; Golf M & W; Ice Hockey M & W; Lacrosse M & W; Riflery M & W; Soccer M & W; Softball W; Swimming and Diving M & W; Tennis M & W; Track and Field M & W; Volleyball M & W; Water Polo M & W; Wrestling M

LINN STATE TECHNICAL COLLEGE
One Technology Dr.
Linn, MO 65051-9606
Tel: (573)897-5000
Free: 800-743-TECH
Admissions: (573)897-5196
Web Site: http://www.linnstate.edu/
President/CEO: Dr. Donald Claycomb
Admissions: Becky Dunn
Type: Two-Year College **Sex:** Coed **Scores:** 50.26% ACT 18-23; 12.82% ACT 24-29 **% Accepted:** 61 **Application Fee:** $0.00 **H.S. Requirements:** High school diploma required; GED accepted **Costs Per Year:** Application fee: $0. State resident tuition: $4080 full-time, $136 per credit part-time. Nonresident tuition: $8160 full-time, $272 per credit part-time. Mandatory fees: $630 full-time, $21 per credit part-time. College room and board: $1870. College room only: $1445. **Scholarships:** Available **Calendar System:** Semester, Summer Session Available **Enrollment:** FT 785, PT 93 **Faculty:** FT 75, PT 11 **Student-Faculty Ratio:** 10:1 **Exams:** ACT, Other **% Residing in College-Owned, -Operated, or -Affiliated Housing:** 15 **Library Holdings:** 13,774 **Regional Accreditation:** North Central Association of Colleges and Schools **Credit Hours For Degree:** 64 credit hours, Associates **ROTC:** Army **Professional Accreditation:** NAIT **Intercollegiate**

Athletics: Archery M & W; Basketball M & W; Bowling M & W; Softball M & W; Table Tennis M & W; Volleyball M & W

LOGAN UNIVERSITY-COLLEGE OF CHIROPRACTIC
1851 Schoettler Rd., Box 1065
Chesterfield, MO 63006-1065
Tel: (636)227-2100
Free: 800-533-9210
Fax: (636)227-9338
E-mail: loganadm@logan.edu
Web Site: http://www.logan.edu/
President/CEO: Dr. George A. Goodman
Registrar: Alva Rozar
Admissions: Dr. Patrick Browne
Financial Aid: Linda Haman
Type: Two-Year Upper Division **Sex:** Coed **% Accepted:** 96 **Admission Plans:** Deferred Admission **Application Fee:** $50.00 **H.S. Requirements:** High school diploma required; GED accepted **Costs Per Year:** Application fee: $50. Tuition: $3420 full-time, $95 per credit hour part-time. Mandatory fees: $330 full-time, $110 per term part-time. **Scholarships:** Available **Calendar System:** Trimester, Summer Session Not available **Enrollment:** FT 76, PT 35 **Faculty:** FT 41, PT 46 **Student-Faculty Ratio:** 12:1 **% Receiving Financial Aid:** 95 **Library Holdings:** 10,777 **Regional Accreditation:** North Central Association of Colleges and Schools **Credit Hours For Degree:** 133 credit hours, Bachelors **Professional Accreditation:** CCE

LONGVIEW COMMUNITY COLLEGE
500 Southwest Longview Rd.
Lee's Summit, MO 64081-2105
Tel: (816)672-2000
Admissions: (816)672-2249
Web Site: http://www.mcckc.edu
President/CEO: Dr. Fred L. Grogan
Registrar: Kathy Hale
Admissions: Janet Cline
Financial Aid: Lisa Fannan
Type: Two-Year College **Sex:** Coed **Affiliation:** Metropolitan Community Colleges System **% Accepted:** 100 **Admission Plans:** Open Admission; Early Admission; Deferred Admission **Application Deadline:** Rolling **Application Fee:** $0.00 **H.S. Requirements:** High school diploma required; GED accepted **Costs Per Year:** Application fee: $0. Area resident tuition: $2190 full-time, $73 per hour part-time. State resident tuition: $3990 full-time, $133 per hour part-time. Nonresident tuition: $5400 full-time, $180 per hour part-time. Mandatory fees: $150 full-time. **Scholarships:** Available **Calendar System:** Semester, Summer Session Available **Enrollment:** FT 2,419, PT 3,248 **Faculty:** FT 83, PT 297 **Student-Faculty Ratio:** 19:1 **Library Holdings:** 56,266 **Regional Accreditation:** North Central Association of Colleges and Schools **Credit Hours For Degree:** 62 credit hours, Associates **Intercollegiate Athletics:** Baseball M; Cross-Country Running W; Volleyball W

MAPLE WOODS COMMUNITY COLLEGE
2601 Northeast Barry Rd.
Kansas City, MO 64156-1299
Tel: (816)437-3000
Admissions: (816)437-3108
Web Site: http://www.mcckc.edu
President/CEO: Dr. Merna S. Saliman
Registrar: Dawn K. Hatterman
Admissions: Marilyn Donatello
Financial Aid: Hula Howard
Type: Two-Year College **Sex:** Coed **Affiliation:** Metropolitan Community Colleges System **% Accepted:** 100 **Admission Plans:** Open Admission; Early Admission; Deferred Admission **Application Deadline:** Rolling **Application Fee:** $0.00 **H.S. Requirements:** High school diploma required; GED accepted **Costs Per Year:** Application fee: $0. Area resident tuition: $2190 full-time, $73 per hour part-time. State resident tuition: $3990 full-time, $133 per hour part-time. Nonresident tuition: $5400 full-time, $180 per hour part-time. Mandatory fees: $150 full-time, $5 per hour part-time. **Scholarships:** Available **Calendar System:** Semester, Summer Session Available **Enrollment:** FT 1,817, PT 2,625 **Faculty:** FT 53, PT 293 **Student-Faculty Ratio:** 18:1 **Library Holdings:** 32,906 **Regional Accreditation:** North Central Association of Colleges and Schools **Credit Hours For Degree:** 62 credit hours, Associates **Intercollegiate Athletics:** Baseball M; Softball W

MARYVILLE UNIVERSITY OF SAINT LOUIS
13550 Conway Rd.
St. Louis, MO 63141-7299
Tel: (314)529-9300
Free: 800-627-9855
Admissions: (314)529-9350
Fax: (314)529-9927
E-mail: admissions@maryville.edu
Web Site: http://www.maryville.edu/
President/CEO: Dr. Keith Lovin
Registrar: Michelle Ziolkowski
Admissions: Dr. Beth Triplett
Financial Aid: Martha Harbaugh
Type: Comprehensive **Sex:** Coed **Scores:** 50% ACT 18-23; 44% ACT 24-29 **% Accepted:** 73 **Admission Plans:** Early Admission; Deferred Admission **Application Deadline:** August 15 **Application Fee:** $25.00 **H.S. Requirements:** High school diploma required; GED accepted **Costs Per Year:** Application fee: $25. Comprehensive fee: $24,670 includes full-time tuition ($17,000), mandatory fees ($320), and college room and board ($7350). College room only: $6425. Full-time tuition and fees vary according to course load. Room and board charges vary according to housing facility. Part-time tuition: $510 per credit hour. Part-time mandatory fees: $80 per term. Part-time tuition and fees vary according to class time. **Scholarships:** Available **Calendar System:** Semester, Summer Session Available **Enrollment:** FT 1,610, PT 1,049, Grad 564 **Faculty:** FT 99, PT 244 **Student-Faculty Ratio:** 13:1 **Exams:** SAT I or ACT **% Receiving Financial Aid:** 72 **% Residing in College-Owned, -Operated, or -Affiliated Housing:** 32 **Library Holdings:** 209,418 **Regional Accreditation:** North Central Association of Colleges and Schools **Credit Hours For Degree:** 128 credit hours, Bachelors **ROTC:** Army **Professional Accreditation:** AACN, AOTA, APTA, ACBSP, CORE, FIDER, NASAD, NASM, NCATE, NLN **Intercollegiate Athletics:** Baseball M; Basketball M & W; Cross-Country Running M & W; Golf M & W; Soccer M & W; Softball W; Tennis M & W; Track and Field M & W; Volleyball W

MESSENGER COLLEGE
PO Box 4050
Joplin, MO 64803
Tel: (417)624-7070
Fax: (417)624-5070
E-mail: tstump@messengercollege.edu
Web Site: http://www.messengercollege.edu/
President/CEO: Dr. Larry Hunt
Admissions: Ron Cannon
Financial Aid: Sheri Shackelford
Type: Four-Year College **Sex:** Coed **Affiliation:** Pentecostal **Scores:** 36% ACT 18-23; 21% ACT 24-29 **Application Fee:** $35.00 **H.S. Requirements:** High school diploma required; GED accepted **Costs Per Year:** Application fee: $35. Comprehensive fee: $8910 includes full-time tuition ($4950), mandatory fees ($460), and college room and board ($3500). Room and board charges vary according to housing facility. Part-time tuition: $165 per credit hour. **Scholarships:** Available **Calendar System:** Semester, Summer Session Not available **Enrollment:** FT 84, PT 16 **Faculty:** FT 4, PT 10 **Student-Faculty Ratio:** 8:1 **Exams:** SAT I or ACT **% Receiving Financial Aid:** 91 **Library Holdings:** 28,874 **Credit Hours For Degree:** 64 credits, Associates; 128 credits, Bachelors **Professional Accreditation:** TACCS **Intercollegiate Athletics:** Basketball M & W; Volleyball W

METRO BUSINESS COLLEGE (CAPE GIRARDEAU)
1732 North Kingshighway
Cape Girardeau, MO 63701
Tel: (573)334-9181
Fax: (573)334-0617
Web Site: http://www.metrobusinesscollege.edu/
President/CEO: George Holske
Admissions: Kyla Evans
Financial Aid: Janie McIntyre
Type: Two-Year College **Sex:** Coed **Scholarships:** Available **Calendar System:** Quarter **Enrollment:** FT 110, PT 8 **Faculty:** FT 9, PT 2 **Professional Accreditation:** ACICS

METRO BUSINESS COLLEGE (JEFFERSON CITY)
1407 Southwest Blvd.
Jefferson City, MO 65109
Tel: (573)635-6600

Free: 800-467-0786
Fax: (573)635-6999
E-mail: cheri@metrobusinesscollege.edu
Web Site: http://www.metrobusinesscollege.edu/
President/CEO: Cherie Chockley
Admissions: Cheri Chockley
Type: Two-Year College **Sex:** Coed **% Accepted:** 75 **Application Deadline:** Rolling **Application Fee:** $25.00 **Costs Per Year:** Application fee: $25. Tuition: $8385 full-time. Mandatory fees: $125 full-time. **Calendar System:** Quarter **Enrollment:** FT 140, PT 15 **Faculty:** FT 8, PT 3 **Student-Faculty Ratio:** 14:1 **Exams:** Other **Professional Accreditation:** ACICS

METRO BUSINESS COLLEGE (ROLLA)
1202 East State Route 72
Rolla, MO 65401
Tel: (573)364-8464
Free: 800-467-0785
Admissions: (314)364-8464
Fax: (573)364-8077
E-mail: cbarker@metrobusinesscollege.edu
Web Site: http://www.metrobusinesscollege.edu/
President/CEO: Christie Barker
Admissions: Cristie Barker
Type: Two-Year College **Sex:** Coed **Calendar System:** Quarter **Professional Accreditation:** ACICS

METROPOLITAN COMMUNITY COLLEGE-BUSINESS & TECHNOLOGY COLLEGE
1775 Universal Ave.
Kansas City, MO 64120
Tel: (816)482-5210
Free: 800-841-7158
Web Site: http://www.mcckc.edu
President/CEO: Al Toonis
Admissions: Debbie Goodall
Type: Two-Year College **Sex:** Coed **Affiliation:** Metropolitan Community Colleges **% Accepted:** 100 **Costs Per Year:** Area resident tuition: $2190 full-time, $730 per hour part-time. State resident tuition: $3990 full-time, $133 per hour part-time. Nonresident tuition: $5400 full-time, $180 per hour part-time. Mandatory fees: $150 full-time, $5 per hour part-time. **Calendar System:** Semester **Enrollment:** FT 118, PT 484 **Faculty:** FT 10, PT 37 **Student-Faculty Ratio:** 13:1 **Regional Accreditation:** North Central Association of Colleges and Schools

MIDWEST INSTITUTE (EARTH CITY)
4260 Shoreline Dr.
Earth City, MO 63045
Tel: (314)344-3334
Fax: (314)344-0495
Web Site: http://www.midwestinstitute.com/ **Type:** Two-Year College **Sex:** Coed **Professional Accreditation:** ABHES

MIDWEST INSTITUTE (KIRKWOOD)
10910 Manchester Rd.
Kirkwood, MO 63122
Tel: (314)965-8363
Fax: (314)965-1558
Web Site: http://www.midwestinstitute.com/
President/CEO: Christine Sheffler
Type: Two-Year College **Sex:** Coed

MINERAL AREA COLLEGE
PO Box 1000
Park Hills, MO 63601-1000
Tel: (573)431-4593
Admissions: (573)518-2206
E-mail: jsheets@mineralarea.edu
Web Site: http://www.mineralarea.edu/
President/CEO: Dr. Terry L. Barnes
Registrar: Linda Huffman
Admissions: Julie Sheets
Financial Aid: Denise Sebastian
Type: Two-Year College **Sex:** Coed **Affiliation:** Missouri Coordinating Board for Higher Education **Scores:** 57% ACT 18-23; 12% ACT 24-29 **Admission Plans:** Open Admission; Early Admission **Application Fee:** $15.00 **H.S. Requirements:** High school diploma or equivalent not required. For allied health programs, law enforcement programs: High school diploma required; GED accepted **Costs Per Year:** Application fee: $15. Area resident tuition: $2160 full-time, $72 per credit hour part-time. State resident tuition: $2880 full-time, $96 per credit hour part-time. Nonresident tuition: $3540 full-time, $118 per credit hour part-time. College room only: $2475. **Scholarships:** Available **Calendar System:** Semester, Summer Session Available **Enrollment:** FT 1,605, PT 1,215 **Faculty:** FT 52, PT 186 **Student-Faculty Ratio:** 18:1 **Exams:** ACT, Other **Library Holdings:** 32,228 **Regional Accreditation:** North Central Association of Colleges and Schools **Credit Hours For Degree:** 62 credit hours, Associates **Intercollegiate Athletics:** Baseball M; Basketball M & W; Volleyball W

MISSOURI BAPTIST UNIVERSITY
One College Park Dr.
St. Louis, MO 63141-8660
Tel: (314)434-1115; 877-434-1115
Admissions: (314)392-2291
Fax: (314)434-7596
E-mail: admissions@mobap.edu
Web Site: http://www.mobap.edu/
President/CEO: Dr. R. Alton Lacey
Registrar: Heather Matlock
Admissions: Terry Dale Cruse
Financial Aid: Robert Miller
Type: Comprehensive **Sex:** Coed **Affiliation:** Southern Baptist **Scores:** 47% ACT 18-23; 19% ACT 24-29 **% Accepted:** 52 **Application Deadline:** Rolling **Application Fee:** $25.00 **H.S. Requirements:** High school diploma required; GED accepted **Costs Per Year:** Application fee: $25. Comprehensive fee: $19,640 includes full-time tuition ($13,230), mandatory fees ($610), and college room and board ($5800). Full-time tuition and fees vary according to course load, degree level, and location. Room and board charges vary according to housing facility. Part-time tuition: $460 per credit. Part-time mandatory fees: $30 per credit. Part-time tuition and fees vary according to course load, degree level, and location. **Scholarships:** Available **Calendar System:** Semester, Summer Session Available **Enrollment:** FT 1,202, PT 2,283, Grad 975 **Faculty:** FT 58, PT 133 **Student-Faculty Ratio:** 15:1 **Exams:** SAT I or ACT **% Receiving Financial Aid:** 93 **% Residing in College-Owned, -Operated, or -Affiliated Housing:** 17 **Library Holdings:** 91,115 **Regional Accreditation:** North Central Association of Colleges and Schools **Credit Hours For Degree:** 64 credit hours, Associates; 128 credit hours, Bachelors **ROTC:** Army **Professional Accreditation:** NASM **Intercollegiate Athletics:** Baseball M; Basketball M & W; Bowling M & W; Cross-Country Running M & W; Golf M & W; Lacrosse W; Soccer M & W; Softball W; Tennis W; Track and Field M & W; Ultimate Frisbee M & W; Volleyball M & W; Wrestling M

MISSOURI COLLEGE
10121 Manchester Rd.
St. Louis, MO 63122-1583
Tel: (314)821-7700
Web Site: http://www.mocollege.com/
President/CEO: Michael VanderVelde
Registrar: Dawn Krenning
Admissions: Doug Brinker
Financial Aid: Leslie Harmon
Type: Two-Year College **Sex:** Coed **Admission Plans:** Open Admission **Application Fee:** $35.00 **H.S. Requirements:** High school diploma required; GED accepted **Scholarships:** Available **Enrollment:** FT 560 **Faculty:** FT 35, PT 19 **Student-Faculty Ratio:** 20:1 **Professional Accreditation:** ACCSCT, ADA

MISSOURI SOUTHERN STATE UNIVERSITY
3950 East Newman Rd.
Joplin, MO 64801-1595
Tel: (417)625-9300; (866)818-MSSU
Admissions: (417)625-9537
Fax: (417)659-4429
E-mail: admissions@mssu.edu
Web Site: http://www.mssu.edu/
President/CEO: Dr. Julio Leon
Registrar: Sandra Gieson
Admissions: Derek Skaggs
Financial Aid: James Gilbert

Type: Four-Year College **Sex:** Coed **Scores:** 53% ACT 18-23; 30% ACT 24-29 **% Accepted:** 99 **Admission Plans:** Deferred Admission **Application Deadline:** August 01 **Application Fee:** $15.00 **H.S. Requirements:** High school diploma required; GED accepted **Costs Per Year:** Application fee: $15. State resident tuition: $3750 full-time, $125 per credit part-time. Nonresident tuition: $7500 full-time, $250 per credit part-time. Mandatory fees: $166 full-time, $83 per term part-time. Full-time tuition and fees vary according to course load. College room and board: $4480. Room and board charges vary according to board plan and housing facility. **Scholarships:** Available **Calendar System:** Semester, Summer Session Available **Enrollment:** FT 3,849, PT 1,624 **Faculty:** FT 206, PT 102 **Student-Faculty Ratio:** 18:1 **Exams:** ACT, Other, SAT I or ACT **% Receiving Financial Aid:** 79 **% Residing in College-Owned, -Operated, or -Affiliated Housing:** 10 **Regional Accreditation:** North Central Association of Colleges and Schools **Credit Hours For Degree:** 64 credits, Associates; 124 credits, Bachelors **Professional Accreditation:** ABET, ADA, ACBSP, CARC, JRCERT, NCATE, NLN **Intercollegiate Athletics:** Baseball M; Basketball M & W; Cross-Country Running M & W; Football M; Golf M; Soccer M & W; Softball W; Tennis W; Track and Field M & W; Volleyball W

MISSOURI STATE UNIVERSITY
901 South National
Springfield, MO 65804-0094
Tel: (417)836-5000
Free: 800-492-7900
Admissions: (417)836-5521
Fax: (417)836-6334
E-mail: smsuinfo@vma.smsu.edu
Web Site: http://www.missouristate.edu/
President/CEO: Dr. John H. Keiser
Registrar: Kim Bell
Admissions: Don Simpson
Financial Aid: Billie Jo Hamilton
Type: Comprehensive **Sex:** Coed **Scores:** 51.1% ACT 18-23; 39.5% ACT 24-29 **% Accepted:** 77 **Application Deadline:** July 20 **Application Fee:** $30.00 **H.S. Requirements:** High school diploma required; GED accepted **Costs Per Year:** Application fee: $30. State resident tuition: $4920 full-time, $164 per credit hour part-time. Nonresident tuition: $9840 full-time, $328 per credit hour part-time. Mandatory fees: $534 full-time. College room and board: $5294. College room only: $3462. **Scholarships:** Available **Calendar System:** Semester, Summer Session Available **Enrollment:** FT 12,630, PT 3,527, Grad 2,771 **Faculty:** FT 728, PT 299 **Student-Faculty Ratio:** 18:1 **Exams:** SAT I or ACT **% Receiving Financial Aid:** 60 **% Residing in College-Owned, -Operated, or -Affiliated Housing:** 24 **Library Holdings:** 1,699,860 **Regional Accreditation:** North Central Association of Colleges and Schools **Credit Hours For Degree:** 125 credit hours, Bachelors **ROTC:** Army **Professional Accreditation:** AACSB, ABET, AACN, AAFCS, AANA, APTA, ASLHA, CSWE, JRCEPAT, NAIT, NASM, NASPAA, NAST, NCATE, NLN, NRPA **Intercollegiate Athletics:** Baseball M; Basketball M & W; Bowling M & W; Cross-Country Running M & W; Equestrian Sports M & W; Field Hockey W; Football M; Golf M & W; Ice Hockey M; Lacrosse M; Racquetball M & W; Riflery M & W; Soccer M & W; Softball W; Swimming and Diving M & W; Tennis M & W; Track and Field M & W; Ultimate Frisbee M & W; Volleyball M & W; Wrestling M

MISSOURI STATE UNIVERSITY-WEST PLAINS
128 Garfield
West Plains, MO 65775
Tel: (417)255-7255
Admissions: (417)255-7955
E-mail: melissajett@missouristate.edu
Web Site: http://www.wp.missouristate.edu/
President/CEO: Kent Thomas
Admissions: Melissa Jett
Type: Two-Year College **Sex:** Coed **Affiliation:** Missouri State University **% Accepted:** 100 **Admission Plans:** Open Admission **Application Deadline:** Rolling **Application Fee:** $15.00 **H.S. Requirements:** High school diploma required; GED accepted **Costs Per Year:** Application fee: $15. State resident tuition: $102 per credit hour part-time. Nonresident tuition: $204 per credit hour part-time. Mandatory fees: $77 per term part-time. College room and board: $4586. **Scholarships:** Available **Calendar System:** Semester, Summer Session Available **Enrollment:** FT 886, PT 789 **Faculty:** FT 29, PT 88 **Student-Faculty Ratio:** 17:1 **% Residing in College-Owned, -Operated, or -Affiliated Housing:** 6 **Library Holdings:** 21,210 **Regional Accreditation:** North Central Association of Colleges and Schools **Credit Hours For Degree:** 62 credit hours, Associates **Intercollegiate Athletics:** Basketball M; Volleyball W

MISSOURI TECH
1167 Corporate Lake Dr.
St. Louis, MO 63132-1716
Tel: (314)569-3600
Fax: (314)569-1167
Web Site: http://www.motech.edu/
President/CEO: Paul Dodge
Registrar: Cindy Sinnott
Admissions: Bob Honaker
Financial Aid: Terry Todd
Type: Four-Year College **Sex:** Coed **Scores:** 61.5% ACT 18-23; 23.1% ACT 24-29 **H.S. Requirements:** High school diploma required; GED accepted **Scholarships:** Available **Calendar System:** Semester, Summer Session Available **Enrollment:** FT 44, PT 157 **Faculty:** FT 7, PT 4 **Student-Faculty Ratio:** 10:1 **Exams:** ACT **% Residing in College-Owned, -Operated, or -Affiliated Housing:** 6 **Credit Hours For Degree:** 94 credit hours, Associates; 172 credit hours, Bachelors **Professional Accreditation:** ACCSCT

MISSOURI VALLEY COLLEGE
500 East College
Marshall, MO 65340-3197
Tel: (660)831-4000
Admissions: (660)831-4157
Fax: (660)831-4039
Web Site: http://www.moval.edu/
President/CEO: Dr. Chadwick B. Freeman
Registrar: Marsha Lashley
Admissions: Jamie L. Gold-Naylor
Financial Aid: Chad B. Freeman
Type: Four-Year College **Sex:** Coed **Affiliation:** Presbyterian Church **Scores:** 82% SAT V 400+; 89% SAT M 400+; 63% ACT 18-23; 13% ACT 24-29 **Admission Plans:** Early Admission; Deferred Admission **Application Fee:** $15.00 **H.S. Requirements:** High school diploma required; GED accepted **Costs Per Year:** Application fee: $15. Comprehensive fee: $20,250 includes full-time tuition ($14,500) and college room and board ($5750). **Scholarships:** Available **Calendar System:** Semester, Summer Session Available **Enrollment:** FT 1,377, PT 246 **Faculty:** FT 66, PT 47 **Student-Faculty Ratio:** 18:1 **Exams:** SAT I or ACT **% Receiving Financial Aid:** 100 **% Residing in College-Owned, -Operated, or -Affiliated Housing:** 73 **Library Holdings:** 61,907 **Regional Accreditation:** North Central Association of Colleges and Schools **Credit Hours For Degree:** 64 credit hours, Associates; 128 credit hours, Bachelors **ROTC:** Army **Intercollegiate Athletics:** Baseball M; Basketball M & W; Cheerleading M & W; Cross-Country Running M & W; Football M; Golf M & W; Soccer M & W; Softball W; Tennis M & W; Track and Field M & W; Volleyball M & W; Wrestling M & W

MISSOURI WESTERN STATE UNIVERSITY
4525 Downs Dr.
St. Joseph, MO 64507-2294
Tel: (816)271-4200
Free: 800-662-7041
Admissions: (816)271-4267
Fax: (816)271-5833
E-mail: admission@missouriwestern.edu
Web Site: http://www.missouriwestern.edu/
President/CEO: Dr. James Scanlon
Registrar: Dr. Gene Eulinger
Admissions: Howard McCauley
Financial Aid: Angie Beam
Type: Four-Year College **Sex:** Coed **Scores:** 46% ACT 18-23; 16% ACT 24-29 **% Accepted:** 100 **Admission Plans:** Open Admission; Early Admission **Application Deadline:** June 01 **Application Fee:** $15.00 **H.S. Requirements:** High school diploma required; GED accepted **Costs Per Year:** Application fee: $15. State resident tuition: $4380 full-time, $146 per credit part-time. Nonresident tuition: $8010 full-time, $267 per credit part-time. Mandatory fees: $398 full-time, $12 per credit part-time, $35. College room and board: $4756. Room and board charges vary according to board plan and housing facility. **Scholarships:** Available **Calendar System:** Semester, Summer Session Available **Enrollment:** FT 3,800, PT 1,448 **Faculty:** FT 180, PT 133 **Student-Faculty Ratio:** 19:1 **% Residing in College-Owned, -Operated, or -Affiliated Housing:** 28 **Library Holdings:** 147,509 **Regional Accreditation:** North Central Association of Colleges and

Schools **Credit Hours For Degree:** 62 credit hours, Associates; 124 credit hours, Bachelors **ROTC:** Army **Professional Accreditation:** ABET, AACN, AHIMA, APTA, CSWE, NASM, NCATE, NLN **Intercollegiate Athletics:** Baseball M; Basketball M & W; Football M; Golf M & W; Soccer W; Softball W; Tennis W; Volleyball W

MOBERLY AREA COMMUNITY COLLEGE
101 College Ave.
Moberly, MO 65270-1304
Tel: (660)263-4110
Free: 800-622-2070
Fax: (660)263-6252
Web Site: http://www.macc.edu/
President/CEO: Dr. Evelyn E. Jorgenson
Registrar: Lynn Walker
Admissions: Dr. James Grant
Financial Aid: Amy Hager
Type: Two-Year College **Sex:** Coed **Scores:** 56% ACT 18-23; 12% ACT 24-29 **Admission Plans:** Open Admission **Application Deadline:** Rolling **Application Fee:** $0.00 **H.S. Requirements:** High school diploma required; GED accepted **Costs Per Year:** Application fee: $0. Area resident tuition: $1740 full-time, $58 per credit hour part-time. State resident tuition: $2550 full-time, $85 per credit hour part-time. Nonresident tuition: $3960 full-time, $132 per credit hour part-time. Mandatory fees: $300 full-time, $10 per credit hour part-time. College room only: $1800. **Scholarships:** Available **Calendar System:** Semester, Summer Session Available **Enrollment:** FT 1,818, PT 2,017 **Faculty:** FT 66, PT 191 **Student-Faculty Ratio:** 20:1 **Exams:** ACT, Other **% Residing in College-Owned, -Operated, or -Affiliated Housing:** 1 **Library Holdings:** 23,027 **Regional Accreditation:** North Central Association of Colleges and Schools **Credit Hours For Degree:** 64 credit hours, Associates **Professional Accreditation:** NAIT **Intercollegiate Athletics:** Basketball M & W; Cheerleading M & W

NATIONAL AMERICAN UNIVERSITY
4200 Blue Ridge Blvd.
Kansas City, MO 64133-1612
Tel: (816)353-4554
Fax: (816)353-1176
E-mail: jjoy@national.edu
Web Site: http://www.national.edu/
President/CEO: Cassandra Alexander
Admissions: Cassandra Alexander
Financial Aid: Mary Anderson
Type: Four-Year College **Sex:** Coed **Affiliation:** National College **Admission Plans:** Open Admission; Early Admission; Deferred Admission **Application Fee:** $25.00 **H.S. Requirements:** High school diploma required; GED accepted **Scholarships:** Available **Calendar System:** Quarter, Summer Session Available **Faculty:** FT 3, PT 29 **Student-Faculty Ratio:** 12:1 **Library Holdings:** 1,500 **Regional Accreditation:** North Central Association of Colleges and Schools **Credit Hours For Degree:** 98 credits, Associates; 194 credits, Bachelors

NORTH CENTRAL MISSOURI COLLEGE
1301 Main St.
Trenton, MO 64683-1824
Tel: (660)359-3948
Free: 800-880-6180
E-mail: bbirdsong@mail.ncmissouri.edu
Web Site: http://www.ncmissouri.edu/
President/CEO: Dr. James Gardner
Registrar: Linda Brown
Admissions: Blaire Birdsong
Financial Aid: John Brandt
Type: Two-Year College **Sex:** Coed **% Accepted:** 58 **Admission Plans:** Open Admission **Application Deadline:** Rolling **Application Fee:** $0.00 **H.S. Requirements:** High school diploma required; GED accepted **Costs Per Year:** Application fee: $0. Area resident tuition: $1680 full-time, $56 per credit part-time. State resident tuition: $2550 full-time, $85 per credit part-time. Nonresident tuition: $3570 full-time, $119 per credit part-time. Mandatory fees: $450 full-time, $15 per credit part-time. Full-time tuition and fees vary according to course load and location. Part-time tuition and fees vary according to location. College room and board: $4149. Room and board charges vary according to board plan. **Scholarships:** Available **Calendar System:** Semester, Summer Session Available **Enrollment:** FT 702, PT 640 **Faculty:** FT 29, PT 79 **Student-Faculty Ratio:** 17:1 **% Residing in College-Owned, -Operated, or -Affiliated Housing:** 9 **Library Holdings:** 20,627 **Regional Accreditation:** North Central Association of Colleges and Schools **Credit Hours For Degree:** 60 credit hours, Associates **Intercollegiate Athletics:** Baseball M; Basketball M & W; Softball W

NORTHWEST MISSOURI STATE UNIVERSITY
800 University Dr.
Maryville, MO 64468-6001
Tel: (660)562-1212
Free: 800-633-1175
Admissions: (660)562-1587
Fax: (660)562-1121
E-mail: admissions@acad.nwmissouri.edu
Web Site: http://www.nwmissouri.edu/
President/CEO: Dr. Dean L. Hubbard
Registrar: Linda Girard
Admissions: Beverly Schenkel
Financial Aid: Del Morley
Type: Comprehensive **Sex:** Coed **Affiliation:** Missouri Coordinating Board for Higher Education **Scores:** 91.43% SAT V 400+; 85.7% SAT M 400+; 59.04% ACT 18-23; 29.48% ACT 24-29 **% Accepted:** 45 **Admission Plans:** Preferred Admission; Deferred Admission **Application Deadline:** Rolling **Application Fee:** $25.00 **H.S. Requirements:** High school diploma required; GED accepted **Costs Per Year:** Application fee: $25. State resident tuition: $5535 full-time, $172.50 per credit hour part-time. Nonresident tuition: $9540 full-time, $306 per credit hour part-time. Mandatory fees: $465 full-time, $12 per credit hour part-time, $105 per term part-time. Full-time tuition and fees vary according to course load. Part-time tuition and fees vary according to course load. College room and board: $5492. Room and board charges vary according to board plan. **Scholarships:** Available **Calendar System:** Trimester, Summer Session Available **Enrollment:** FT 4,719, PT 642, Grad 888 **Faculty:** FT 243, PT 16 **Student-Faculty Ratio:** 24:1 **Exams:** SAT I or ACT **% Receiving Financial Aid:** 49 **% Residing in College-Owned, -Operated, or -Affiliated Housing:** 49 **Library Holdings:** 326,919 **Regional Accreditation:** North Central Association of Colleges and Schools **Credit Hours For Degree:** 124 semester hours, Bachelors **ROTC:** Army **Professional Accreditation:** AAFCS, ACBSP, NASM, NCATE **Intercollegiate Athletics:** Baseball M; Basketball M & W; Cheerleading M & W; Cross-Country Running M & W; Football M; Golf M; Soccer W; Softball W; Tennis M & W; Track and Field M & W; Volleyball W

OZARK CHRISTIAN COLLEGE
1111 North Main St.
Joplin, MO 64801-4804
Tel: (417)624-2518
Free: 800-299-4622
Fax: (417)624-0090
Web Site: http://www.occ.edu/
President/CEO: Kenneth Idleman
Registrar: Jennifer McMillin
Admissions: Troy B. Nelson
Type: Four-Year College **Sex:** Coed **Affiliation:** Christian **Admission Plans:** Open Admission **Application Fee:** $30.00 **H.S. Requirements:** High school diploma required; GED accepted **Scholarships:** Available **Calendar System:** Semester, Summer Session Available **Enrollment:** FT 680, PT 119 **Faculty:** FT 30, PT 30 **Student-Faculty Ratio:** 19:1 **Exams:** SAT I or ACT **% Residing in College-Owned, -Operated, or -Affiliated Housing:** 63 **Library Holdings:** 59,808 **Credit Hours For Degree:** 96 credits, Associates; 128 credits, Bachelors **Professional Accreditation:** AABC **Intercollegiate Athletics:** Basketball M & W; Cheerleading M & W; Soccer M; Volleyball W

OZARKS TECHNICAL COMMUNITY COLLEGE
PO Box 5958
Springfield, MO 65801
Tel: (417)895-7000
Admissions: (417)895-7136
Fax: (417)895-7161
Web Site: http://www.otc.edu/
President/CEO: Dr. Norman K. Myers
Registrar: Delvan Mitchell
Admissions: Jeff Jochems
Financial Aid: Jeff Ford

Type: Two-Year College **Sex:** Coed **Affiliation:** Missouri Coordinating Board for Higher Education **Admission Plans:** Open Admission; Early Admission **Application Fee:** $0.00 **H.S. Requirements:** High school diploma required; GED accepted **Scholarships:** Available **Calendar System:** Semester, Summer Session Available **Enrollment:** FT 4,232, PT 4,256 **Faculty:** FT 127, PT 266 **Exams:** Other **Library Holdings:** 6,000 **Regional Accreditation:** North Central Association of Colleges and Schools **Credit Hours For Degree:** 62 credit hours, Associates **Professional Accreditation:** ADA, AHIMA, AOTA, APTA, CARC, NAIT

PARK UNIVERSITY
8700 NW River Park Dr.
Parkville, MO 64152-3795
Tel: (816)741-2000
Free: 800-745-7275
Admissions: (816)584-6728
Fax: (816)741-4462
Web Site: http://www.park.edu/
President/CEO: Dr. Beverley Byers-Pevitts
Registrar: Eileen West
Admissions: Cathy Colapietro
Financial Aid: Cathy Colopietro
Type: Comprehensive **Sex:** Coed **Scores:** 50% ACT 18-23; 22% ACT 24-29 **% Accepted:** 74 **Admission Plans:** Early Admission; Deferred Admission **Application Deadline:** August 01 **Application Fee:** $25.00 **H.S. Requirements:** High school diploma required; GED accepted **Costs Per Year:** Application fee: $25. Comprehensive fee: $11,956 includes full-time tuition ($6776) and college room and board ($5180). Part-time tuition: $242 per credit hour. **Scholarships:** Available **Calendar System:** Semester, Summer Session Available **Enrollment:** FT 1,002, PT 11,686, Grad 565 **Faculty:** FT 97, PT 792 **Student-Faculty Ratio:** 13:1 **Exams:** SAT I or ACT **% Receiving Financial Aid:** 46 **% Residing in College-Owned, -Operated, or -Affiliated Housing:** 1 **Library Holdings:** 150,503 **Regional Accreditation:** North Central Association of Colleges and Schools **Credit Hours For Degree:** 60 credit hours, Associates; 120 credit hours, Bachelors **ROTC:** Army **Professional Accreditation:** JRCEPAT, NLN **Intercollegiate Athletics:** Baseball M; Basketball M & W; Cross-Country Running M & W; Golf W; Soccer M & W; Softball W; Track and Field M & W; Volleyball M & W

PATRICIA STEVENS COLLEGE
330 North Fourth St., Ste. 306
St. Louis, MO 63102
Tel: (314)421-0949
Free: 800-871-0949
Fax: (314)421-0304
Web Site: http://www.patriciastevenscollege.edu/
President/CEO: Cynthia A. Musterman, JD
Registrar: Ruth Ann Holtmann
Admissions: John Willmon
Financial Aid: Gregory M. Elsenrath
Type: Two-Year College **Sex:** Coed **Admission Plans:** Deferred Admission **Application Fee:** $15.00 **H.S. Requirements:** High school diploma required; GED accepted **Scholarships:** Available **Calendar System:** Quarter, Summer Session Available **Enrollment:** FT 114, PT 98 **Faculty:** FT 5, PT 27 **Student-Faculty Ratio:** 9:1 **Credit Hours For Degree:** 122 quarter hours, Associates **Professional Accreditation:** ACICS

PENN VALLEY COMMUNITY COLLEGE
3201 Southwest Trafficway
Kansas City, MO 64111
Tel: (816)759-4000
Admissions: (816)759-4101
Web Site: http://www.mcckc.edu
President/CEO: Dr. Jackie Snyder
Registrar: Carroll O'Neal
Admissions: Lisa Minis
Financial Aid: Rossann Downing
Type: Two-Year College **Sex:** Coed **Affiliation:** Metropolitan Community Colleges System **% Accepted:** 100 **Admission Plans:** Open Admission; Early Admission **Application Deadline:** Rolling **Application Fee:** $0.00 **H.S. Requirements:** High school diploma required; GED accepted **Costs Per Year:** Application fee: $0. Area resident tuition: $2190 full-time, $73 per hour part-time. State resident tuition: $3990 full-time, $133 per hour part-time. Nonresident tuition: $5400 full-time, $180 per hour part-time. Mandatory fees: $150 full-time, $5 per hour part-time. **Scholarships:** Available **Calendar System:** Semester, Summer Session Available **Enrollment:** FT 1,457, PT 3,170 **Faculty:** FT 101, PT 336 **Student-Faculty Ratio:** 12:1 **Library Holdings:** 91,428 **Regional Accreditation:** North Central Association of Colleges and Schools **Credit Hours For Degree:** 62 credit hours, Associates **Professional Accreditation:** ADA, AHIMA, AOTA, APTA, JRCERT, NLN **Intercollegiate Athletics:** Basketball M & W

PINNACLE CAREER INSTITUTE
15329 Kensington Ave.
Kansas City, MO 64147-1212
Tel: (816)331-5700
Web Site: http://www.pcitraining.edu/
President/CEO: Dennis Townsend
Registrar: Debbie Fajen
Admissions: Ruth Matous
Financial Aid: Sharon Baldwin
Type: Two-Year College **Sex:** Coed **Application Fee:** $0.00 **Scholarships:** Available **Enrollment:** FT 170 **Faculty:** FT 12, PT 11 **Professional Accreditation:** ACCSCT

RANKEN TECHNICAL COLLEGE
4431 Finney Ave.
St. Louis, MO 63113
Tel: (314)371-0233; (866)4RA-NKEN
Fax: (314)371-0241
Web Site: http://www.ranken.edu/
President/CEO: Ben H. Ernst
Registrar: Carol Winkler
Admissions: Elizabeth Keserauskis
Financial Aid: Michelle Williams
Type: Two-Year College **Sex:** Coed **Application Fee:** $95.00 **H.S. Requirements:** High school diploma required; GED accepted **Costs Per Year:** Application fee: $95. Tuition: $10,000 full-time, $725 per term part-time. Mandatory fees: $140 full-time, $95 per term part-time. **Scholarships:** Available **Calendar System:** Semester, Summer Session Available **Enrollment:** FT 743, PT 680 **Faculty:** FT 59, PT 8 **Student-Faculty Ratio:** 15:1 **Exams:** SAT I or ACT **% Residing in College-Owned, -Operated, or -Affiliated Housing:** 0 **Library Holdings:** 11,000 **Regional Accreditation:** North Central Association of Colleges and Schools **Credit Hours For Degree:** 96 semester hours, Associates; 136 semester hours, Bachelors

RESEARCH COLLEGE OF NURSING
2252 East Meyer Blvd.
Kansas City, MO 64132
Tel: (816)995-2800
Free: 800-842-6776
Admissions: (816)276-4733
Fax: (816)276-3526
E-mail: leslie.mendenhall@researchcollege.edu
Web Site: http://www.researchcollege.edu/
President/CEO: Dr. Nancy O. DeBasio
Admissions: Leslie A. Mendenhall
Financial Aid: Stacie Withers
Type: Comprehensive **Sex:** Coed **Affiliation:** Rockhurst University **Scores:** 15% ACT 18-23; 50% ACT 24-29 **Admission Plans:** Deferred Admission **Application Fee:** $25.00 **H.S. Requirements:** High school diploma required; GED accepted **Costs Per Year:** Application fee: $25. Comprehensive fee: $25,640 includes full-time tuition ($18,900), mandatory fees ($640), and college room and board ($6100). College room only: $3100. Full-time tuition and fees vary according to program. Room and board charges vary according to board plan, housing facility, and location. Part-time tuition: $630 per credit hour. Part-time tuition varies according to class time and program. **Scholarships:** Available **Calendar System:** Semester, Summer Session Available **Enrollment:** FT 184, PT 3, Grad 26 **Faculty:** FT 25, PT 10 **Student-Faculty Ratio:** 7:1 **Exams:** SAT I or ACT **% Receiving Financial Aid:** 55 **Library Holdings:** 150,000 **Regional Accreditation:** North Central Association of Colleges and Schools **Credit Hours For Degree:** 128 credit hours, Bachelors **ROTC:** Army **Professional Accreditation:** AACN, NLN **Intercollegiate Athletics:** Baseball M; Basketball M & W; Golf M & W; Soccer M & W; Tennis M & W; Volleyball W

ROCKHURST UNIVERSITY
1100 Rockhurst Rd.
Kansas City, MO 64110-2561
Tel: (816)501-4000

Free: 800-842-6776
Admissions: (816)501-4100
Fax: (816)501-4241
E-mail: admission@rockhurst.edu
Web Site: http://www.rockhurst.edu/
President/CEO: Rev. Edward Kinerk, SJ
Registrar: Minda Thrower
Admissions: Phillip Gebauer
Financial Aid: Clara Boren
Type: Comprehensive **Sex:** Coed **Affiliation:** Roman Catholic (Jesuit) **Scores:** 98% SAT V 400+; 98% SAT M 400+; 38% ACT 18-23; 45% ACT 24-29 **% Accepted:** 74 **Admission Plans:** Deferred Admission **Application Deadline:** June 30 **Application Fee:** $25.00 **H.S. Requirements:** High school diploma required; GED accepted **Costs Per Year:** Application fee: $25. One-time mandatory fee: $60. Comprehensive fee: $25,110 includes full-time tuition ($18,500), mandatory fees ($710), and college room and board ($5900). Full-time tuition and fees vary according to class time and course load. Room and board charges vary according to board plan and housing facility. Part-time tuition: $630 per semester hour. Part-time mandatory fees: $25 per term. Part-time tuition and fees vary according to class time and course load. **Scholarships:** Available **Calendar System:** Semester, Summer Session Available **Enrollment:** FT 1,261, PT 830, Grad 853 **Faculty:** FT 127, PT 90 **Student-Faculty Ratio:** 10:1 **Exams:** SAT I or ACT **% Receiving Financial Aid:** 78 **% Residing in College-Owned, -Operated, or -Affiliated Housing:** 49 **Library Holdings:** 597,800 **Regional Accreditation:** North Central Association of Colleges and Schools **Credit Hours For Degree:** 128 semester hours, Bachelors **ROTC:** Army **Professional Accreditation:** AOTA, APTA, ASLHA, NLN, TEAC **Intercollegiate Athletics:** Baseball M; Basketball M & W; Golf M & W; Soccer M & W; Softball W; Tennis M & W; Volleyball W

SAINT CHARLES COMMUNITY COLLEGE
4601 Mid Rivers Mall Dr.
St. Peters, MO 63376-0975
Tel: (636)922-8000
Admissions: (636)922-8229
Fax: (636)922-8236
E-mail: regist@stchas.edu
Web Site: http://www.stchas.edu/
President/CEO: Dr. John M. McGuire
Registrar: Kathy A. Brockgreitens
Admissions: Kathy Brockgreitens-Gober
Financial Aid: Karen Vossenkemper
Type: Two-Year College **Sex:** Coed **Affiliation:** Missouri Coordinating Board for Higher Education **% Accepted:** 100 **Admission Plans:** Open Admission; Early Admission; Deferred Admission **Application Deadline:** Rolling **Application Fee:** $0.00 **H.S. Requirements:** High school diploma required; GED accepted **Costs Per Year:** Application fee: $0. Area resident tuition: $2280 full-time. State resident tuition: $3360 full-time. Nonresident tuition: $4980 full-time. **Scholarships:** Available **Calendar System:** Semester, Summer Session Available **Enrollment:** FT 3,378, PT 3,492 **Faculty:** FT 81, PT 348 **Student-Faculty Ratio:** 21:1 **Library Holdings:** 54,110 **Regional Accreditation:** North Central Association of Colleges and Schools **Credit Hours For Degree:** 64 semester hours, Associates **Professional Accreditation:** AHIMA, AOTA, NLN **Intercollegiate Athletics:** Baseball M; Softball W

ST. LOUIS CHRISTIAN COLLEGE
1360 Grandview Dr.
Florissant, MO 63033-6499
Tel: (314)837-6777
Free: 800-887-SLCC
Fax: (314)837-8291
Web Site: http://www.slcconline.edu/
President/CEO: Dr. Kenneth L. Beck
Registrar: Richard Fordyce
Admissions: Richard Fordyce
Financial Aid: Cathi Wilhoit
Type: Four-Year College **Sex:** Coed **Affiliation:** Christian **Scores:** 45% ACT 18-23; 45% ACT 24-29 **Admission Plans:** Early Admission **Application Fee:** $0.00 **H.S. Requirements:** High school diploma required; GED accepted **Costs Per Year:** Application fee: $0. Comprehensive fee: $13,450 includes full-time tuition ($8000), mandatory fees ($450), and college room and board ($5000). Room and board charges vary according to housing facility. Part-time tuition: $250 per credit. Part-time mandatory fees: $450 per semester hour. **Scholarships:** Available **Calendar System:** Semester, Summer Session Not available **Enrollment:** FT 143, PT 70 **Faculty:** FT 9, PT 24 **Student-Faculty Ratio:** 12:1 **Exams:** ACT **% Receiving Financial Aid:** 75 **% Residing in College-Owned, -Operated, or -Affiliated Housing:** 38 **Library Holdings:** 39,728 **Credit Hours For Degree:** 65 credit hours, Associates; 131 credit hours, Bachelors **Professional Accreditation:** AABC **Intercollegiate Athletics:** Baseball M; Basketball M; Volleyball W

ST. LOUIS COLLEGE OF HEALTH CAREERS
909 South Taylor Ave.
St. Louis, MO 63110-1511
Web Site: http://www.slchc.com/ **Type:** Two-Year College **Sex:** Coed

ST. LOUIS COLLEGE OF PHARMACY
4588 Parkview Place
St. Louis, MO 63110-1088
Tel: (314)367-8700
Admissions: (314)446-8313
Fax: (314)367-2784
E-mail: pbryant@stlcop.edu
Web Site: http://www.stlcop.edu/
President/CEO: Dr. Thomas F. Patton
Admissions: Penny Myers Bryant
Financial Aid: Dave Rice
Type: Comprehensive **Sex:** Coed **% Accepted:** 35 **Application Deadline:** February 01 **Application Fee:** $50.00 **H.S. Requirements:** High school diploma required; GED accepted **Costs Per Year:** Application fee: $50. Comprehensive fee: $26,690 includes full-time tuition ($18,900), mandatory fees ($280), and college room and board ($7510). Part-time tuition: $810 per credit. **Scholarships:** Available **Calendar System:** Semester, Summer Session Available **Faculty:** FT 60, PT 45 **Student-Faculty Ratio:** 15:1 **Exams:** SAT I or ACT **% Receiving Financial Aid:** 71 **% Residing in College-Owned, -Operated, or -Affiliated Housing:** 40 **Library Holdings:** 68,187 **Regional Accreditation:** North Central Association of Colleges and Schools **ROTC:** Army, Air Force **Professional Accreditation:** ACPhE **Intercollegiate Athletics:** Basketball M & W; Cross-Country Running M & W; Volleyball W

ST. LOUIS COMMUNITY COLLEGE AT FLORISSANT VALLEY
3400 Pershall Rd.
St. Louis, MO 63135-1499
Tel: (314)513-4200
Admissions: (314)595-4258
Fax: (314)513-2224
Web Site: http://www.stlcc.edu/
President/CEO: Marcia Pfeiffer
Registrar: Brenda Davenport
Admissions: Laura Sternman
Financial Aid: Khaneetah Cunningham
Type: Two-Year College **Sex:** Coed **Affiliation:** St. Louis Community College System **Admission Plans:** Open Admission; Early Admission **Application Deadline:** August 19 **Application Fee:** $0.00 **H.S. Requirements:** High school diploma required; GED accepted **Costs Per Year:** Application fee: $0. Area resident tuition: $78 per credit hour part-time. State resident tuition: $103 per credit hour part-time. Nonresident tuition: $138 per credit hour part-time. **Scholarships:** Available **Calendar System:** Semester, Summer Session Available **Library Holdings:** 90,021 **Regional Accreditation:** North Central Association of Colleges and Schools **Credit Hours For Degree:** 64 credit hours, Associates **ROTC:** Army **Professional Accreditation:** NASAD, NLN **Intercollegiate Athletics:** Baseball M; Basketball M & W; Cross-Country Running M & W; Soccer M & W; Softball W; Track and Field M & W; Volleyball W

ST. LOUIS COMMUNITY COLLEGE AT FOREST PARK
5600 Oakland Ave.
St. Louis, MO 63110-1316
Tel: (314)644-9100
Admissions: (314)644-9131
E-mail: bdevoti@stlcc.edu
Web Site: http://www.stlcc.edu/
President/CEO: Dr. Patricia W. Nichols
Registrar: Herv Gross
Admissions: Bart S. Devoti
Financial Aid: Paulette Johnson

Type: Two-Year College **Sex:** Coed **Affiliation:** St. Louis Community College System **Admission Plans:** Open Admission; Preferred Admission; Early Admission **Application Fee:** $0.00 **H.S. Requirements:** High school diploma required; GED accepted **Calendar System:** Semester, Summer Session Available **Faculty:** FT 114, PT 200 **Student-Faculty Ratio:** 19:1 **Library Holdings:** 72,713 **Regional Accreditation:** North Central Association of Colleges and Schools **Credit Hours For Degree:** 64 credit hours, Associates **Professional Accreditation:** ABFSE, ADA, CARC, JRCERT, NAACLS, NLN **Intercollegiate Athletics:** Baseball W; Basketball M & W; Soccer M; Volleyball W

ST. LOUIS COMMUNITY COLLEGE AT MERAMEC
11333 Big Bend Blvd.
Kirkwood, MO 63122-5720
Tel: (314)984-7500
Admissions: (314)984-7609
Fax: (314)984-7117
Web Site: http://www.stlcc.edu/
President/CEO: Dr. E. Lynn Suydam
Registrar: Jill Guyton
Admissions: Jean Campbell
Financial Aid: Helen Nauman
Type: Two-Year College **Sex:** Coed **Affiliation:** St. Louis Community College System **Admission Plans:** Open Admission; Early Admission; Deferred Admission **Application Fee:** $0.00 **H.S. Requirements:** High school diploma required; GED accepted **Scholarships:** Available **Calendar System:** Semester, Summer Session Available **Faculty:** FT 185, PT 385 **Exams:** Other **Library Holdings:** 58,911 **Regional Accreditation:** North Central Association of Colleges and Schools **Credit Hours For Degree:** 64 credit hours, Associates **ROTC:** Army, Air Force **Professional Accreditation:** AOTA, APTA, NASAD, NLN **Intercollegiate Athletics:** Baseball M; Basketball M; Soccer M & W; Softball W; Volleyball W; Wrestling M

SAINT LOUIS UNIVERSITY
221 North Grand Blvd.
St. Louis, MO 63103-2097
Tel: (314)977-2222
Free: 800-758-3678
Admissions: (314)977-3415
Fax: (314)977-7136
E-mail: admitme@sluvca.slu.edu
Web Site: http://www.slu.edu
President/CEO: Rev. Lawrence Biondi, SJ
Registrar: John-Herbert Jaffry
Admissions: Kalith Smith
Financial Aid: Sandra J. Pritt
Type: University **Sex:** Coed **Affiliation:** Roman Catholic (Jesuit) **Scores:** 99.34% SAT V 400+; 98.7% SAT M 400+; 23.76% ACT 18-23; 52.92% ACT 24-29 **% Accepted:** 78 **Admission Plans:** Deferred Admission **Application Deadline:** Rolling **Application Fee:** $25.00 **H.S. Requirements:** High school diploma required; GED accepted **Costs Per Year:** Application fee: $25. Comprehensive fee: $34,678 includes full-time tuition ($26,250), mandatory fees ($198), and college room and board ($8230). College room only: $4700. **Scholarships:** Available **Calendar System:** Semester, Summer Session Available **Enrollment:** FT 6,817, PT 604, Grad 2,895 **Faculty:** FT 616, PT 478 **Student-Faculty Ratio:** 12:1 **Exams:** SAT I or ACT **% Receiving Financial Aid:** 60 **% Residing in College-Owned, -Operated, or -Affiliated Housing:** 52 **Library Holdings:** 1,878,213 **Regional Accreditation:** North Central Association of Colleges and Schools **Credit Hours For Degree:** 120 credit hours, Bachelors **ROTC:** Army, Air Force **Professional Accreditation:** AACSB, ABET, ACEHSA, AACN, ABA, ADtA, AHIMA, AOTA, APTA, APA, ASLHA, ACIPE, AALS, CAA, CEPH, CSWE, JRCNMT, LCMEAMA, NAACLS, NASPAA NCATE, NLN **Intercollegiate Athletics:** Baseball M; Basketball M & W; Crew M & W; Cross-Country Running M & W; Fencing M & W; Field Hockey W; Golf M; Ice Hockey M; Lacrosse M & W; Rugby M; Soccer M & W; Softball W; Swimming and Diving M & W; Tennis M & W; Ultimate Frisbee M & W; Volleyball M & W

SAINT LUKE'S COLLEGE
4426 Wornall Rd.
Kansas City, MO 64111
Tel: (816)932-2233
Admissions: (816)932-2073
E-mail: mjthomas@saint-lukes.org
Web Site: http://www.saintlukescollege.edu/
President/CEO: Dr. Helen A. Jepson
Registrar: M. J. Thomas
Admissions: Christina Wood
Financial Aid: Jeff Gannon
Type: Two-Year Upper Division **Sex:** Coed **Affiliation:** Episcopal; Saint Luke's Hospital **Admission Plans:** Early Admission; Early Decision Plan **Application Fee:** $20.00 **H.S. Requirements:** High school diploma required; GED accepted **Costs Per Year:** Application fee: $20. Tuition: $8850 full-time, $295 per credit part-time. Mandatory fees: $620 full-time, $180 per term part-time. **Scholarships:** Available **Calendar System:** Semester, Summer Session Available **Enrollment:** FT 96, PT 13 **Faculty:** FT 16, PT 0 **Student-Faculty Ratio:** 7:1 **% Receiving Financial Aid:** 81 **Regional Accreditation:** North Central Association of Colleges and Schools **Credit Hours For Degree:** 124 credit hours, Bachelors **Professional Accreditation:** AACN

SANFORD-BROWN COLLEGE (FENTON)
1203 Smizer Mill Rd.
Fenton, MO 63026
Tel: (636)349-4900
Free: 800-456-7222
Fax: (636)349-9170
Web Site: http://www.sanford-brown.edu/
President/CEO: James Howard
Admissions: Judy Wilga
Type: Two-Year College **Sex:** Coed **Affiliation:** Education Management Corporation **Admission Plans:** Open Admission; Deferred Admission **Application Fee:** $25.00 **H.S. Requirements:** High school diploma required; GED accepted **Scholarships:** Available **Calendar System:** Quarter **Enrollment:** FT 394, PT 46 **Faculty:** FT 13, PT 15 **Student-Faculty Ratio:** 9:1 **Exams:** Other **Credit Hours For Degree:** 91 credits, Associates **Professional Accreditation:** ACICS, CARC, JRCERT **Intercollegiate Athletics:** Basketball M

SANFORD-BROWN COLLEGE (HAZELWOOD)
75 Village Square
Hazelwood, MO 63042
Tel: (314)731-1101
Admissions: (314)731-5200
Web Site: http://www.sanford-brown.edu/
President/CEO: Melissa Uding
Registrar: Brenda Lincoln
Admissions: Sherri Bremer
Type: Two-Year College **Sex:** Coed **Admission Plans:** Deferred Admission **H.S. Requirements:** High school diploma required; GED accepted **Scholarships:** Available **Calendar System:** Quarter **Credit Hours For Degree:** 91 credits, Associates **Professional Accreditation:** ABHES, ACICS **Intercollegiate Athletics:** Basketball M

SANFORD-BROWN COLLEGE (NORTH KANSAS CITY)
520 East 19th Ave.
North Kansas City, MO 64116
Tel: (816)472-7400
Free: 800-456-7222
Admissions: (816)472-0275
Fax: (816)472-0688
E-mail: edward.beauchamp@wix.net
Web Site: http://www.sanford-brown.edu/
President/CEO: Dennis L. Townsend
Registrar: Tommy Box
Admissions: Edward A. Beauchamp
Financial Aid: Karva Waller
Type: Two-Year College **Sex:** Coed **Admission Plans:** Deferred Admission **H.S. Requirements:** High school diploma required; GED accepted **Calendar System:** Quarter **Credit Hours For Degree:** 92 quarter hours, Associates **Professional Accreditation:** ABHES, ACICS, JRCERT

SANFORD-BROWN COLLEGE (ST. CHARLES)
3555 Franks Dr.
St. Charles, MO 63301
Tel: (314)949-2620
Admissions: (636)949-2620
E-mail: karl.peterson@wix.net
Web Site: http://www.sanford-brown.edu/

President/CEO: James Caldwell
Admissions: Karl J. Petersen
Financial Aid: Tony Merritt
Type: Two-Year College **Sex:** Coed **Admission Plans:** Deferred Admission **Application Fee:** $100.00 **H.S. Requirements:** High school diploma required; GED accepted **Calendar System:** Quarter, Summer Session Available **Faculty:** FT 18, PT 7 **Exams:** Other **% Residing in College-Owned, -Operated, or -Affiliated Housing:** 5 **Library Holdings:** 1,350 **Credit Hours For Degree:** 91 credits, Associates **Professional Accreditation:** ACICS **Intercollegiate Athletics:** Basketball M

SOUTHEAST MISSOURI HOSPITAL COLLEGE OF NURSING AND HEALTH SCIENCES
1819 Broadway
Cape Girardeau, MO 63701
Tel: (573)334-6825
Fax: (573)339-7805
E-mail: tbuttry@sehosp.org
Web Site: http://www.southeastmissourihospital.com/college/
President/CEO: Tonya Buttry
Admissions: Tonya L. Buttry
Type: Two-Year College **Sex:** Coed **Calendar System:** Miscellaneous **Regional Accreditation:** North Central Association of Colleges and Schools

SOUTHEAST MISSOURI STATE UNIVERSITY
One University Plaza
Cape Girardeau, MO 63701-4799
Tel: (573)651-2000
Admissions: (573)651-2590
E-mail: _dbelow@semo.edu
Web Site: http://www.semo.edu/
President/CEO: Dr. Kenneth W. Dobbins
Registrar: Sandra Hinkle
Admissions: Dr. Deborah Below
Financial Aid: Karen Walker
Type: Comprehensive **Sex:** Coed **Affiliation:** Missouri Coordinating Board for Higher Education **Scores:** 61% ACT 18-23; 29% ACT 24-29 **% Accepted:** 89 **Admission Plans:** Deferred Admission **Application Fee:** $20.00 **H.S. Requirements:** High school diploma required; GED accepted **Costs Per Year:** Application fee: $20. State resident tuition: $4764 full-time, $158.80 per credit hour part-time. Nonresident tuition: $8619 full-time, $287.30 per credit hour part-time. Mandatory fees: $381 full-time, $12.70 per credit hour part-time. Full-time tuition and fees vary according to course load and location. Part-time tuition and fees vary according to course load and location. College room and board: $5351. College room only: $3270. Room and board charges vary according to board plan and housing facility. **Scholarships:** Available **Calendar System:** Semester, Summer Session Available **Enrollment:** FT 6,796, PT 2,172, Grad 1,324 **Faculty:** FT 400, PT 208 **Student-Faculty Ratio:** 17:1 **Exams:** ACT **% Receiving Financial Aid:** 52 **% Residing in College-Owned, -Operated, or -Affiliated Housing:** 28 **Library Holdings:** 411,992 **Regional Accreditation:** North Central Association of Colleges and Schools **Credit Hours For Degree:** 64 credit hours, Associates; 124 credit hours, Bachelors **ROTC:** Air Force **Professional Accreditation:** AACSB, ABET, AACN, ACA, ADtA, ASLHA, CSWE, JRCEPAT, NAIT, NASM, NCATE, NRPA **Intercollegiate Athletics:** Baseball M; Basketball M & W; Cheerleading M & W; Cross-Country Running M & W; Football M; Golf M; Gymnastics W; Soccer W; Softball W; Tennis W; Track and Field M & W; Volleyball W

SOUTHWEST BAPTIST UNIVERSITY
1600 University Ave.
Bolivar, MO 65613-2597
Tel: (417)326-5281
Free: 800-526-5859
Admissions: (417)328-1817
Fax: (417)328-1514
E-mail: dcrowder@sbuniv.edu
Web Site: http://www.sbuniv.edu/
President/CEO: Dr. C. Pat Taylor
Registrar: John Credille
Admissions: Darren Crowder
Financial Aid: Brad Gamble
Type: Comprehensive **Sex:** Coed **Affiliation:** Southern Baptist **Scores:** 98% SAT V 400+; 94% SAT M 400+; 45% ACT 18-23; 37% ACT 24-29 **% Accepted:** 85 **Application Deadline:** Rolling **Application Fee:** $30.00 **H.S. Requirements:** High school diploma required; GED accepted **Costs Per Year:** Application fee: $30. Comprehensive fee: $18,300 includes full-time tuition ($13,300), mandatory fees ($800), and college room and board ($4200). College room only: $2200. Part-time tuition: $530 per hour. **Scholarships:** Available **Calendar System:** 4-1-4, Summer Session Available **Enrollment:** FT 1,778, PT 923, Grad 739 **Faculty:** FT 105, PT 141 **Student-Faculty Ratio:** 15:1 **Exams:** SAT I or ACT **% Receiving Financial Aid:** 69 **% Residing in College-Owned, -Operated, or -Affiliated Housing:** 64 **Library Holdings:** 193,821 **Regional Accreditation:** North Central Association of Colleges and Schools **Credit Hours For Degree:** 64 credit hours, Associates; 128 credit hours, Bachelors **ROTC:** Army **Professional Accreditation:** APTA, ACBSP, NASM, NLN **Intercollegiate Athletics:** Baseball M; Basketball M & W; Cheerleading M & W; Cross-Country Running M & W; Football M; Golf M; Soccer M & W; Softball W; Tennis M & W; Track and Field M & W; Volleyball W

SPRINGFIELD COLLEGE
1010 West Sunshine
Springfield, MO 65807-2488
Tel: (417)864-7220
Free: 800-475-2669
Fax: (417)865-5697
E-mail: gterrebr@cci.edu
Web Site: http://www.Springfield-college.com/
President/CEO: Gerald F. Terrebrood
Registrar: Steve Marshall
Admissions: Gerald F. Terrebrood
Type: Two-Year College **Sex:** Coed **Affiliation:** Corinthian Colleges, Inc **Admission Plans:** Open Admission; Deferred Admission **Application Fee:** $25.00 **H.S. Requirements:** High school diploma required; GED accepted **Scholarships:** Available **Calendar System:** Quarter, Summer Session Available **Faculty:** FT 9, PT 3 **Exams:** Other **Library Holdings:** 3,000 **Credit Hours For Degree:** 96 credits, Associates **Professional Accreditation:** ACICS, AAMAE

STATE FAIR COMMUNITY COLLEGE
3201 West 16th St.
Sedalia, MO 65301-2199
Tel: (660)530-5800; 877-311-SFCC
Fax: (660)530-5820
Web Site: http://www.sfcc.cc.mo.us/
President/CEO: Toni Walter
Registrar: Ron Gerstbauer
Admissions: Sharon Peacock
Financial Aid: Sylvia Deitrick
Type: Two-Year College **Sex:** Coed **Affiliation:** Missouri Coordinating Board for Higher Education **Admission Plans:** Open Admission; Early Admission **Application Fee:** $0.00 **H.S. Requirements:** High school diploma required; GED accepted **Scholarships:** Available **Calendar System:** Semester, Summer Session Available **Enrollment:** FT 1,690, PT 1,701 **Faculty:** FT 76, PT 137 **Student-Faculty Ratio:** 17:1 **Exams:** ACT, Other **Library Holdings:** 36,000 **Regional Accreditation:** North Central Association of Colleges and Schools **Credit Hours For Degree:** 64 semester hours, Associates **Professional Accreditation:** ADA, NAIT **Intercollegiate Athletics:** Basketball M & W; Soccer M; Volleyball W

STEPHENS COLLEGE
1200 East Broadway
Columbia, MO 65215-0002
Tel: (573)442-2211
Free: 800-876-7207
Admissions: (573)876-7207
Fax: (573)876-7237
E-mail: apply@stephens.edu
Web Site: http://www.stephens.edu/
President/CEO: Dr. Wendy B. Libby
Registrar: Marlene Geddes
Admissions: David Adams
Financial Aid: Rachel Touchatt
Type: Comprehensive **Scores:** 100% SAT V 400+; 100% SAT M 400+; 42% ACT 18-23; 51% ACT 24-29 **% Accepted:** 77 **Admission Plans:** Early Admission; Deferred Admission **Application Deadline:** August 01 **Application Fee:** $25.00 **H.S. Requirements:** High school diploma required; GED accepted **Costs Per Year:** Application fee: $25. Comprehensive fee: $28,475 includes full-time tuition ($20,500) and college room and board

($7975). College room only: $4760. Part-time tuition: $220 per hour. **Scholarships:** Available **Calendar System:** Semester, Summer Session Not available **Enrollment:** FT 574, PT 180, Grad 70 **Faculty:** FT 41, PT 50 **Student-Faculty Ratio:** 12:1 **Exams:** SAT I or ACT **% Receiving Financial Aid:** 73 **% Residing in College-Owned, -Operated, or -Affiliated Housing:** 70 **Library Holdings:** 121,084 **Regional Accreditation:** North Central Association of Colleges and Schools **Credit Hours For Degree:** 20 courses, Associates; 40 courses, Bachelors **ROTC:** Army, Air Force **Professional Accreditation:** AHIMA **Intercollegiate Athletics:** Basketball W; Soccer W; Swimming and Diving W; Tennis W; Volleyball W

THREE RIVERS COMMUNITY COLLEGE
2080 Three Rivers Blvd.
Poplar Bluff, MO 63901-2393
Tel: (573)840-9600; 877-TRY-TRCC
Admissions: (573)840-9675
Web Site: http://www.trcc.edu/
President/CEO: Dr. John F. Cooper
Registrar: Cindy Clark
Admissions: Marcia Fields
Financial Aid: Pauletta Burns
Type: Two-Year College **Sex:** Coed **Affiliation:** Missouri Coordinating Board for Higher Education **Scores:** 53% ACT 18-23; 15% ACT 24-29 **% Accepted:** 100 **Admission Plans:** Open Admission; Early Admission **Application Fee:** $20.00 **H.S. Requirements:** High school diploma required; GED accepted **Costs Per Year:** Application fee: $20. Area resident tuition: $1830 full-time, $61 per credit hour part-time. State resident tuition: $2940 full-time, $98 per credit hour part-time. Nonresident tuition: $3660 full-time, $122 per credit hour part-time. Mandatory fees: $375 full-time, $8.50 per credit hour part-time. College room only: $3114. **Scholarships:** Available **Calendar System:** Semester, Summer Session Available **Enrollment:** FT 1,622, PT 1,313 **Faculty:** FT 58, PT 102 **Student-Faculty Ratio:** 22:1 **% Residing in College-Owned, -Operated, or -Affiliated Housing:** 10 **Library Holdings:** 36,960 **Regional Accreditation:** North Central Association of Colleges and Schools **Credit Hours For Degree:** 64 credits, Associates **Professional Accreditation:** ACBSP, NAACLS, NLN **Intercollegiate Athletics:** Baseball M; Basketball M & W; Cheerleading M & W; Softball W; Volleyball W

TRUMAN STATE UNIVERSITY
100 East Normal St.
Kirksville, MO 63501-4221
Tel: (660)785-4000
Admissions: (660)785-4114
Fax: (660)785-7456
E-mail: admissions@truman.edu
Web Site: http://www.truman.edu/
President/CEO: Dr. Barbara Dixon
Registrar: Kay Anderson
Admissions: John Fraire
Financial Aid: Melinda Wood
Type: Comprehensive **Sex:** Coed **Scores:** 100% SAT V 400+; 100% SAT M 400+; 13% ACT 18-23; 58% ACT 24-29 **% Accepted:** 83 **Admission Plans:** Preferred Admission; Early Admission; Early Action; Deferred Admission **Application Deadline:** March 01 **Application Fee:** $0.00 **H.S. Requirements:** High school diploma required; GED accepted **Costs Per Year:** Application fee: $0. One-time mandatory fee: $150. State resident tuition: $5740 full-time, $239 per credit hour part-time. Nonresident tuition: $9920 full-time, $413 per credit hour part-time. Mandatory fees: $72 full-time. Part-time tuition varies according to course load. College room and board: $5380. Room and board charges vary according to housing facility. **Scholarships:** Available **Calendar System:** Semester, Summer Session Available **Enrollment:** FT 5,460, PT 111, Grad 232 **Faculty:** FT 353, PT 25 **Student-Faculty Ratio:** 15:1 **Exams:** ACT, SAT I or ACT **% Receiving Financial Aid:** 48 **% Residing in College-Owned, -Operated, or -Affiliated Housing:** 48 **Library Holdings:** 492,916 **Regional Accreditation:** North Central Association of Colleges and Schools **Credit Hours For Degree:** 124 credits, Bachelors **ROTC:** Army **Professional Accreditation:** AACSB, AACN, ACA, ASLHA, JRCEPAT, NASM, NCATE, NLN **Intercollegiate Athletics:** Baseball M; Basketball M & W; Cheerleading M & W; Cross-Country Running M & W; Equestrian Sports M & W; Football M; Golf M & W; Lacrosse M & W; Rugby M & W; Soccer M & W; Softball W; Swimming and Diving M & W; Tennis M & W; Track and Field M & W; Volleyball M & W; Wrestling M

UNIVERSITY OF MISSOURI-COLUMBIA
Columbia, MO 65211
Tel: (573)882-2121
Admissions: (573)882-7786
Fax: (573)882-7887
E-mail: mu4u@missouri.edu
Web Site: http://www.missouri.edu/
President/CEO: Dr. Brady Deaton
Registrar: Brenda Selman
Admissions: Barbara Rupp
Financial Aid: Joseph Camille
Type: University **Sex:** Coed **Affiliation:** University of Missouri System **Scores:** 99% SAT V 400+; 99% SAT M 400+; 33% ACT 18-23; 50% ACT 24-29 **% Accepted:** 83 **Admission Plans:** Deferred Admission **Application Deadline:** Rolling **Application Fee:** $35.00 **H.S. Requirements:** High school diploma required; GED accepted **Costs Per Year:** Application fee: $35. State resident tuition: $6495 full-time, $216.50 per credit hour part-time. Nonresident tuition: $16,272 full-time, $542.40 per credit hour part-time. Mandatory fees: $1250 full-time, $32.07 per credit hour part-time. Full-time tuition and fees vary according to course load, program, and reciprocity agreements. Part-time tuition and fees vary according to course load, program, and reciprocity agreements. College room and board: $6245. Room and board charges vary according to board plan and housing facility. **Scholarships:** Available **Calendar System:** Semester, Summer Session Available **Enrollment:** FT 19,979, PT 1,396, Grad 5,527 **Faculty:** FT 1,066, PT 83 **Student-Faculty Ratio:** 18:1 **Exams:** ACT, Other, SAT I or ACT **% Receiving Financial Aid:** 42 **% Residing in College-Owned, -Operated, or -Affiliated Housing:** 39 **Library Holdings:** 3,205,927 **Regional Accreditation:** North Central Association of Colleges and Schools **ROTC:** Army, Navy, Air Force **Professional Accreditation:** AACSB, ABET, ACEHSA, ACEJMC, AACN, AAFCS, ABA, ADtA, ALA, AOTA, APTA, APA, ASLHA, AVMA, AALS, CARC, CORE, CSWE, FIDER, JRCERT JRCNMT, LCMEAMA, NASM, NASPAA, NCATE, NRPA, SAF **Intercollegiate Athletics:** Baseball M; Basketball M & W; Cross-Country Running M & W; Football M; Golf M & W; Gymnastics W; Soccer W; Softball W; Swimming and Diving M & W; Tennis W; Track and Field M & W; Volleyball W; Wrestling M

UNIVERSITY OF MISSOURI-KANSAS CITY
5100 Rockhill Rd.
Kansas City, MO 64110-2499
Tel: (816)235-1000
Free: 800-775-8652
Admissions: (816)235-1111
Fax: (816)235-1717
E-mail: admit@umkc.edu
Web Site: http://www.umkc.edu/
President/CEO: Dr. Martha W. Gilliland
Registrar: Wilson Berry
Admissions: Jennifer DeHaemers
Financial Aid: Jan Brandow
Type: University **Sex:** Coed **Affiliation:** University of Missouri System **Scores:** 96.5% SAT V 400+; 94.8% SAT M 400+; 38.9% ACT 18-23; 40.3% ACT 24-29 **% Accepted:** 75 **Admission Plans:** Deferred Admission **Application Deadline:** Rolling **Application Fee:** $35.00 **H.S. Requirements:** High school diploma required; GED accepted **Costs Per Year:** Application fee: $35. State resident tuition: $6819 full-time, $227.30 per credit hour part-time. Nonresident tuition: $17,085 full-time, $569.50 per credit hour part-time. **Scholarships:** Available **Calendar System:** Semester, Summer Session Available **Enrollment:** FT 5,676, PT 3,815, Grad 3,296 **Faculty:** FT 641, PT 414 **Student-Faculty Ratio:** 11:1 **Exams:** SAT I or ACT **% Receiving Financial Aid:** 64 **% Residing in College-Owned, -Operated, or -Affiliated Housing:** 13 **Library Holdings:** 1,265,118 **Regional Accreditation:** North Central Association of Colleges and Schools **Credit Hours For Degree:** 120 credit hours, Bachelors **ROTC:** Army, Air Force **Professional Accreditation:** AACSB, AACN, AANA, ABA, ACPhE, ADA, APA, AALS, CSWE, LCMEAMA, NASM, NASPAA, NAST, NCATE **Intercollegiate Athletics:** Basketball M & W; Cheerleading W; Cross-Country Running M & W; Golf M & W; Riflery M & W; Soccer M; Softball W; Tennis M & W; Track and Field M & W; Volleyball W

UNIVERSITY OF MISSOURI-ROLLA
1870 Miner Circle
Rolla, MO 65409-0910
Tel: (573)341-4111
Free: 800-522-0938
Admissions: (573)341-4164
E-mail: umrolla@umr.edu
Web Site: http://www.umr.edu/

President/CEO: Dr. Gary Thomas
Registrar: Laura K. Stoll
Admissions: Lynn Stichnote
Financial Aid: Robert Whites
Type: University **Sex:** Coed **Affiliation:** University of Missouri System **Scores:** 15% ACT 18-23; 53% ACT 24-29 **Admission Plans:** Early Admission; Deferred Admission **Application Fee:** $35.00 **H.S. Requirements:** High school diploma required; GED accepted **Costs Per Year:** Application fee: $35. State resident tuition: $6451 full-time, $216.50 per credit hour part-time. Nonresident tuition: $15,576 full-time, $542.40 per credit hour part-time. Mandatory fees: $1041 full-time. Full-time tuition and fees vary according to course load, degree level, and program. Part-time tuition varies according to course load, degree level, and program. College room and board: $5840. College room only: $3570. Room and board charges vary according to board plan, housing facility, and location. **Scholarships:** Available **Calendar System:** Semester, Summer Session Available **Enrollment:** FT 3,747, PT 374, Grad 1,286 **Faculty:** FT 304, PT 88 **Student-Faculty Ratio:** 14:1 **Exams:** SAT I or ACT **% Receiving Financial Aid:** 53 **% Residing in College-Owned, -Operated, or -Affiliated Housing:** 56 **Library Holdings:** 255,768 **Regional Accreditation:** North Central Association of Colleges and Schools **Credit Hours For Degree:** 120 credit hours, Bachelors **ROTC:** Army, Navy, Air Force **Professional Accreditation:** ABET **Intercollegiate Athletics:** Baseball M; Basketball M & W; Cross-Country Running M & W; Football M; Soccer M & W; Softball W; Swimming and Diving M; Track and Field M & W

UNIVERSITY OF MISSOURI-ST. LOUIS
One University Blvd.
St. Louis, MO 63121
Tel: (314)516-5000
Admissions: (314)516-5451
Fax: (314)516-5310
E-mail: kundelj@umsl.edu
Web Site: http://www.umsl.edu/
President/CEO: Dr. Thomas F. George
Registrar: Linda C. Silman
Admissions: John A. Kundel
Financial Aid: Dr. Anthony C. Georges
Type: University **Sex:** Coed **Affiliation:** University of Missouri System **Scores:** 92% SAT V 400+; 94% SAT M 400+; 50.2% ACT 18-23; 39.3% ACT 24-29 **% Accepted:** 52 **Admission Plans:** Deferred Admission **Application Deadline:** Rolling **Application Fee:** $35.00 **H.S. Requirements:** High school diploma required; GED accepted **Costs Per Year:** Application fee: $35. State resident tuition: $6495 full-time, $216.50 per credit hour part-time. Nonresident tuition: $16,272 full-time, $542.40 per credit hour part-time. Mandatory fees: $1123 full-time, $43.20 per credit hour part-time. Full-time tuition and fees vary according to course load, program, and reciprocity agreements. Part-time tuition and fees vary according to course load, program, and reciprocity agreements. College room and board: $6428. College room only: $4561. Room and board charges vary according to board plan and housing facility. **Scholarships:** Available **Calendar System:** Semester, Summer Session Available **Enrollment:** FT 5,887, PT 6,732, Grad 2,778 **Faculty:** FT 371, PT 322 **Student-Faculty Ratio:** 19:1 **Exams:** SAT I or ACT **% Receiving Financial Aid:** 53 **% Residing in College-Owned, -Operated, or -Affiliated Housing:** 8 **Library Holdings:** 1,100,000 **Regional Accreditation:** North Central Association of Colleges and Schools **Credit Hours For Degree:** 120 credit hours, Bachelors **ROTC:** Army, Air Force **Professional Accreditation:** AACSB, ABET, AACN, ACA, AOA, APA, CSWE, NASM, NASPAA, NCATE **Intercollegiate Athletics:** Baseball M; Basketball M & W; Golf M & W; Ice Hockey M; Soccer M & W; Softball W; Tennis M & W; Volleyball W

UNIVERSITY OF PHOENIX-KANSAS CITY CAMPUS
901 East 104th St., Ste. 301
Kansas City, MO 64131-4517
Tel: (816)943-9600
Free: 800-228-7240
Admissions: (480)557-1712
Fax: (816)943-6675
Web Site: http://www.phoenix.edu/
President/CEO: Jerrad Tausz
Admissions: Nina Omelchanko
Type: Comprehensive **Sex:** Coed **Admission Plans:** Open Admission; Deferred Admission **Application Deadline:** Rolling **Application Fee:** $110.00 **H.S. Requirements:** High school diploma required; GED accepted **Costs Per Year:** Application fee: $110. Tuition: $11,145 full-time, $371.50 per credit part-time. Mandatory fees: $560 full-time. **Scholarships:** Available **Calendar System:** Continuous, Summer Session Not available **Enrollment:** FT 1,020, Grad 277 **Faculty:** FT 8, PT 119 **Student-Faculty Ratio:** 8:1 **Library Holdings:** 444 **Regional Accreditation:** North Central Association of Colleges and Schools **Credit Hours For Degree:** 60 credits, Associates; 120 credits, Bachelors

UNIVERSITY OF PHOENIX-ST. LOUIS CAMPUS
Riverport Lakes West
13801 Riverport Dr., Ste. 102
St. Louis, MO 63043-4828
Tel: (314)298-9755
Free: 800-228-7240
Admissions: (480)557-1712
Fax: (314)291-2901
Web Site: http://www.phoenix.edu/
President/CEO: Anne Gillespie
Admissions: Nina Omelchanko
Type: Comprehensive **Sex:** Coed **Admission Plans:** Open Admission; Deferred Admission **Application Deadline:** Rolling **Application Fee:** $110.00 **H.S. Requirements:** High school diploma required; GED accepted **Costs Per Year:** Application fee: $110. Tuition: $11,550 full-time, $385 per credit part-time. Mandatory fees: $560 full-time, $70 per course part-time. **Scholarships:** Available **Calendar System:** Continuous, Summer Session Not available **Enrollment:** FT 869, Grad 157 **Faculty:** FT 12, PT 155 **Student-Faculty Ratio:** 6:1 **Library Holdings:** 444 **Regional Accreditation:** North Central Association of Colleges and Schools **Credit Hours For Degree:** 60 credits, Associates; 120 credits, Bachelors

UNIVERSITY OF PHOENIX-SPRINGFIELD CAMPUS
1260 E. Kingsley St.
Springfield, MO 65804-7211
Free: 800-228-7240
Admissions: (480)557-1712
Web Site: http://www.phoenix.edu/
Admissions: Nina Omelchanko
Type: Comprehensive **Sex:** Coed **Admission Plans:** Open Admission; Deferred Admission **Application Deadline:** Rolling **Application Fee:** $110.00 **H.S. Requirements:** High school diploma required; GED accepted **Costs Per Year:** Application fee: $110. Tuition: $9450 full-time, $315 per credit part-time. Mandatory fees: $560 full-time, $70 per course part-time. **Scholarships:** Available **Enrollment:** FT 220, Grad 39 **Faculty:** FT 3, PT 32 **Student-Faculty Ratio:** 4:1 **Library Holdings:** 444 **Credit Hours For Degree:** 60 credits, Associates; 120 credits, Bachelors

VATTEROTT COLLEGE (KANSAS CITY)
8955 East 38th Terrace
Kansas City, MO 64129
Tel: (816)861-1000
Free: 800-466-3997
Fax: (816)861-1400
Web Site: http://www.vatterott-college.com/
President/CEO: Mark DeFusco
Type: Two-Year College **Sex:** Coed **Calendar System:** Semester **Professional Accreditation:** ACCSCT

VATTEROTT COLLEGE (O'FALLON)
927 East Terra Ln.
O'Fallon, MO 63366
Tel: (636)978-7488
Fax: (636)978-5121
Web Site: http://www.vatterott-college.com/ **Type:** Two-Year College **Sex:** Coed

VATTEROTT COLLEGE (ST. ANN)
3925 Industrial Dr.
St. Ann, MO 63074-1807
Tel: (314)428-5900
Free: 800-345-6018
Web Site: http://www.vatterott-college.edu/
President/CEO: John Vatterott
Registrar: Jessica Marie Brown
Admissions: Shari H. Cobb

Financial Aid: Felicia Franklin
Type: Two-Year College **Sex:** Coed **H.S. Requirements:** High school diploma required; GED accepted **Scholarships:** Available **Calendar System:** Continuous, Summer Session Not available **Enrollment:** FT 580 **Faculty:** FT 24 **Student-Faculty Ratio:** 25:1 **Credit Hours For Degree:** 72 credit hours, Associates **Professional Accreditation:** ACCSCT

VATTEROTT COLLEGE (ST. JOSEPH)
3131 Frederick Ave.
St. Joseph, MO 64506
Tel: (816)364-5399
Free: 800-282-5327
Fax: (816)364-1593
Web Site: http://www.vatterott-college.com/
President/CEO: Wayne Major
Admissions: Sandra Wisdom
Type: Two-Year College **Sex:** Coed **Costs Per Year:** Tuition guaranteed not to increase for student's term of enrollment. **Calendar System:** Semester **Faculty:** FT 18, PT 1 **Professional Accreditation:** ACCSCT

VATTEROTT COLLEGE (ST. LOUIS)
12970 Maurer Industrial Dr.
St. Louis, MO 63127
Tel: (314)843-4200
Fax: (314)843-1709
Web Site: http://www.vatterott-college.edu/
Admissions: Michelle Tinsley
Type: Two-Year College **Sex:** Coed **Calendar System:** Semester **Professional Accreditation:** ACCSCT

VATTEROTT COLLEGE (SPRINGFIELD)
1258 East Trafficway St.
Springfield, MO 65802
Tel: (417)831-8116
Free: 800-766-5829
Fax: (417)831-5099
Web Site: http://www.vatterott-college.edu/
President/CEO: Tilley Cheryl
Admissions: Jennifer Danzer
Type: Two-Year College **Sex:** Coed **Affiliation:** Vatterott College **H.S. Requirements:** High school diploma required; GED accepted **Costs Per Year:** Tuition: $8800 full-time. Mandatory fees: $900 full-time. Full-time tuition and fees vary according to degree level and program. Tuition guaranteed not to increase for student's term of enrollment. **Calendar System:** Quarter **Faculty:** FT 15, PT 4 **Credit Hours For Degree:** 108 quarter credit hours, Associates **Professional Accreditation:** ACCSCT

WASHINGTON UNIVERSITY IN ST. LOUIS
1 Brookings Dr.
St. Louis, MO 63130-4899
Tel: (314)935-5000
Free: 800-638-0700
Admissions: (314)935-6000
Fax: (314)935-4290
E-mail: admission@wustl.edu
Web Site: http://www.wustl.edu
President/CEO: Dr. Mark S. Wrighton
Registrar: Sue Hosack
Admissions: Nanette Tarbouni
Financial Aid: William H. Witbrodt
Type: University **Sex:** Coed **Scores:** 100% SAT V 400+; 100% SAT M 400+; 19% ACT 24-29 **% Accepted:** 19 **Admission Plans:** Early Admission; Early Decision Plan; Deferred Admission **Application Deadline:** January 15 **Application Fee:** $55.00 **H.S. Requirements:** High school diploma or equivalent not required **Costs Per Year:** Application fee: $55. Comprehensive fee: $44,240 includes full-time tuition ($32,800), mandatory fees ($988), and college room and board ($10,452). College room only: $6402. **Scholarships:** Available **Calendar System:** Semester, Summer Session Available **Enrollment:** FT 6,169, PT 1,297, Grad 4,701 **Faculty:** FT 850, PT 231 **Student-Faculty Ratio:** 7:1 **Exams:** SAT I or ACT **% Receiving Financial Aid:** 43 **% Residing in College-Owned, -Operated, or -Affiliated Housing:** 75 **Library Holdings:** 1,612,711 **Regional Accreditation:** North Central Association of Colleges and Schools **Credit Hours For Degree:** 120 semester hours, Bachelors **ROTC:** Army, Air Force **Professional Accreditation:** AACSB, ABET, ACEHSA, ABA, AOTA, APTA, APA, ASLHA, ACIPE, AALS, CSWE, LCMEAMA, NASAD, NCATE **Intercollegiate Athletics:** Baseball M; Basketball M & W; Crew M & W; Cross-Country Running M & W; Equestrian Sports M & W; Fencing M & W; Field Hockey W; Football M; Golf M & W; Gymnastics M & W; Ice Hockey M; Lacrosse M & W; Rugby M & W; Sailing M & W; Soccer M & W; Softball W; Swimming and Diving M & W; Table Tennis M & W; Tennis M & W; Track and Field M & W; Ultimate Frisbee M & W; Volleyball M & W; Water Polo M & W

WEBSTER UNIVERSITY
470 East Lockwood Ave.
St. Louis, MO 63119-3194
Tel: (314)968-6900
Free: 800-75-ENROL
Admissions: (314)968-6991
Fax: (314)968-7115
E-mail: admit@webster.edu
Web Site: http://www.webster.edu/
President/CEO: Dr. Richard S. Meyers
Registrar: Donald Morris
Admissions: Niel DeVasto
Financial Aid: Sharen Lowney
Type: Comprehensive **Sex:** Coed **Scores:** 47% ACT 18-23; 41% ACT 24-29 **% Accepted:** 55 **Admission Plans:** Early Admission; Deferred Admission **Application Deadline:** June 01 **Application Fee:** $25.00 **H.S. Requirements:** High school diploma required; GED accepted **Costs Per Year:** Application fee: $25. Comprehensive fee: $23,947 includes full-time tuition ($17,210) and college room and board ($6737). College room only: $3586. Full-time tuition varies according to program. Room and board charges vary according to board plan and housing facility. Part-time tuition: $445 per credit hour. Part-time tuition varies according to location. **Scholarships:** Available **Calendar System:** Semester, Summer Session Available **Enrollment:** FT 2,558, PT 965, Grad 3,804 **Faculty:** FT 172, PT 635 **Student-Faculty Ratio:** 12:1 **Exams:** SAT I or ACT **% Receiving Financial Aid:** 68 **% Residing in College-Owned, -Operated, or -Affiliated Housing:** 27 **Library Holdings:** 271,047 **Regional Accreditation:** North Central Association of Colleges and Schools **Credit Hours For Degree:** 128 credit hours, Bachelors **ROTC:** Army, Air Force **Professional Accreditation:** AANA, NASM, NCATE, NLN **Intercollegiate Athletics:** Baseball M; Basketball M & W; Cross-Country Running W; Golf M; Soccer M & W; Softball W; Swimming and Diving M & W; Tennis M & W; Volleyball W

WENTWORTH MILITARY ACADEMY AND JUNIOR COLLEGE
1880 Washington Ave.
Lexington, MO 64067
Tel: (660)259-2221
Fax: (660)259-2677
E-mail: rhamilton@wma1880.org
Web Site: http://www.wma1880.org/
President/CEO: Maj. Gen. John H. Little
Registrar: Jeanette Long
Admissions: Dr. Roger Hamilton
Financial Aid: Pam Fuenfhausen
Type: Two-Year College **Sex:** Coed **Scores:** 80% SAT V 400+; 93% SAT M 400+ **% Accepted:** 100 **Application Deadline:** September 11 **Application Fee:** $100.00 **H.S. Requirements:** High school diploma required; GED accepted **Costs Per Year:** Application fee: $100. One-time mandatory fee: $25. Tuition: $3480 full-time, $145 per hour part-time. **Scholarships:** Available **Calendar System:** Semester, Summer Session Available **Enrollment:** FT 234, PT 327 **Faculty:** FT 19, PT 44 **Student-Faculty Ratio:** 10:1 **Exams:** SAT I or ACT **Library Holdings:** 18,890 **Regional Accreditation:** North Central Association of Colleges and Schools **Credit Hours For Degree:** 64 semester hours, Associates **ROTC:** Army **Intercollegiate Athletics:** Cross-Country Running M; Track and Field M & W; Wrestling M

WESTMINSTER COLLEGE
501 Westminster Ave.
Fulton, MO 65251-1299
Tel: (573)642-3361
Free: 800-475-3361
Admissions: (573)592-5251
Fax: (573)592-5227
E-mail: admissions@westminster-mo.edu
Web Site: http://www.westminster-mo.edu/
President/CEO: Dr. Fletcher Lamkin

Registrar: Phyllis Masek
Admissions: Dr. Patrick Kirby
Financial Aid: Aimee Bristow
Type: Four-Year College **Sex:** Coed **Affiliation:** Presbyterian Church **Scores:** 90% SAT V 400+; 96% SAT M 400+; 38% ACT 18-23; 54% ACT 24-29 **% Accepted:** 79 **Admission Plans:** Early Admission; Deferred Admission **Application Fee:** $0.00 **H.S. Requirements:** High school diploma required; GED accepted **Costs Per Year:** Application fee: $0. Comprehensive fee: $21,170 includes full-time tuition ($14,600), mandatory fees ($430), and college room and board ($6140). College room only: $3170. Part-time tuition: $750 per credit hour. **Scholarships:** Available **Calendar System:** Semester, Summer Session Available **Enrollment:** FT 896, PT 22 **Faculty:** FT 55, PT 24 **Student-Faculty Ratio:** 14:1 **Exams:** SAT I or ACT **% Receiving Financial Aid:** 58 **% Residing in College-Owned, -Operated, or -Affiliated Housing:** 80 **Library Holdings:** 114,402 **Regional Accreditation:** North Central Association of Colleges and Schools **Credit Hours For Degree:** 122 credit hours, Bachelors **ROTC:** Army, Air Force **Intercollegiate Athletics:** Baseball M; Basketball M & W; Football M; Golf M & W; Soccer M & W; Softball W; Tennis M & W; Volleyball W

WILLIAM JEWELL COLLEGE
500 College Hill
Liberty, MO 64068-1843
Tel: (816)781-7700; 888-2JEWELL
Fax: (816)415-5027
E-mail: admission@william.jewell.edu
Web Site: http://www.jewell.edu/
President/CEO: Dr. David L. Sallee
Admissions: Chad Jolly
Financial Aid: Sue Armstrong
Type: Four-Year College **Sex:** Coed **Affiliation:** Baptist **Scores:** 97% SAT V 400+; 94% SAT M 400+; 31% ACT 18-23; 55% ACT 24-29 **% Accepted:** 64 **Admission Plans:** Early Action; Deferred Admission **Application Deadline:** August 15 **Application Fee:** $25.00 **H.S. Requirements:** High school diploma required; GED accepted **Costs Per Year:** Application fee: $25. Comprehensive fee: $25,660 includes full-time tuition ($20,150) and college room and board ($5510). College room only: $2320. **Scholarships:** Available **Calendar System:** Semester, Summer Session Available **Enrollment:** FT 1,285, PT 46 **Faculty:** FT 76, PT 79 **Student-Faculty Ratio:** 13:1 **Exams:** SAT I or ACT, SAT II **% Receiving Financial Aid:** 57 **% Residing in College-Owned, -Operated, or -Affiliated Housing:** 62 **Library Holdings:** 260,119 **Regional Accreditation:** North Central Association of Colleges and Schools **Credit Hours For Degree:** 124 semester hours, Bachelors **Professional Accreditation:** AACN, NASM **Intercollegiate Athletics:** Baseball M; Basketball M & W; Cheerleading M & W; Cross-Country Running M & W; Football M; Golf M & W; Soccer M & W; Softball W; Tennis M & W; Track and Field M & W; Volleyball W

WILLIAM WOODS UNIVERSITY
One University Ave.
Fulton, MO 65251-1098
Tel: (573)642-2251
Free: 800-995-3159
Admissions: (573)592-4221
Fax: (573)592-1146
E-mail: jclay@williamwoods.edu
Web Site: http://www.williamwoods.edu/
President/CEO: Dr. Jahnae Barnett
Registrar: Brenda Williamson
Admissions: Jimmy Clay
Financial Aid: Liz Bennett
Type: Comprehensive **Sex:** Coed **Affiliation:** Christian Church (Disciples of Christ) **Scores:** 88.4% SAT V 400+; 90.5% SAT M 400+; 54% ACT 18-23; 30.5% ACT 24-29 **% Accepted:** 68 **Admission Plans:** Early Admission; Deferred Admission **Application Deadline:** Rolling **Application Fee:** $25.00 **H.S. Requirements:** High school diploma required; GED accepted **Costs Per Year:** Application fee: $25. Comprehensive fee: $21,020 includes full-time tuition ($14,700), mandatory fees ($420), and college room and board ($5900). Full-time tuition and fees vary according to program. Room and board charges vary according to board plan and housing facility. Part-time tuition: $490 per credit. Part-time mandatory fees: $15 per term. Part-time tuition and fees vary according to course load and program. **Scholarships:** Available **Calendar System:** Semester, Summer Session Available **Enrollment:** FT 808, PT 365, Grad 1,874 **Faculty:** FT 50, PT 64 **Student-Faculty Ratio:** 13:1 **Exams:** SAT I or ACT **% Receiving Financial Aid:** 63 **% Residing in College-Owned, -Operated, or -Affiliated Housing:** 80 **Library Holdings:** 139,986 **Regional Accreditation:** North Central Association of Colleges and Schools **Credit Hours For Degree:** 67 credit hours, Associates; 122 credit hours, Bachelors **ROTC:** Army, Navy, Air Force **Professional Accreditation:** CSWE **Intercollegiate Athletics:** Baseball M; Basketball W; Cross-Country Running M & W; Equestrian Sports M & W; Golf M & W; Soccer M & W; Softball W; Track and Field M & W; Volleyball M & W

BLACKFEET COMMUNITY COLLEGE
PO Box 819
Browning, MT 59417-0819
Tel: (406)338-5441
Free: 800-549-7457
Admissions: (406)338-5421
Fax: (406)338-3272
Web Site: http://www.bfcc.org/
President/CEO: Terrance E. Whitright
Registrar: Deana McNabb
Admissions: Deana M. McNabb
Financial Aid: Margaret Bird
Type: Two-Year College **Sex:** Coed **Admission Plans:** Open Admission; Early Admission **Application Fee:** $20.00 **H.S. Requirements:** High school diploma required; GED accepted **Costs Per Year:** Application fee: $20. One-time mandatory fee: $20. State resident tuition: $1650 full-time, $69 per credit part-time. Nonresident tuition: $1650 full-time, $69 per credit part-time. Mandatory fees: $350 full-time, $80 per term part-time. Full-time tuition and fees vary according to course load. Part-time tuition and fees vary according to course load. **Scholarships:** Available **Calendar System:** Semester, Summer Session Not available **Enrollment:** FT 424, PT 79 **Faculty:** FT 27, PT 36 **Student-Faculty Ratio:** 12:1 **Library Holdings:** 10,000 **Credit Hours For Degree:** 60 credit hours, Associates **Professional Accreditation:** NCCU

CARROLL COLLEGE
1601 North Benton Ave.
Helena, MT 59625-0002
Tel: (406)447-4300
Free: 800-992-3648
Admissions: (406)447-4384
Fax: (406)447-4533
E-mail: enroll@carroll.edu
Web Site: http://www.carroll.edu/
President/CEO: Dr. Thomas Trebon
Registrar: Mary Pat Dutton
Admissions: Candace A. Cain
Financial Aid: Janet Riis
Type: Four-Year College **Sex:** Coed **Affiliation:** Roman Catholic **Scores:** 96% SAT V 400+; 96% SAT M 400+; 45% ACT 18-23; 47% ACT 24-29 **% Accepted:** 79 **Admission Plans:** Deferred Admission **Application Deadline:** June 01 **Application Fee:** $35.00 **H.S. Requirements:** High school diploma required; GED accepted **Costs Per Year:** Application fee: $35. Comprehensive fee: $23,484 includes full-time tuition ($16,778), mandatory fees ($300), and college room and board ($6406). College room only: $3046. Full-time tuition and fees vary according to course load. Room and board charges vary according to board plan and housing facility. Part-time tuition: $558 per credit hour. Part-time tuition varies according to course load. **Scholarships:** Available **Calendar System:** Semester, Summer Session Available **Enrollment:** FT 1,245, PT 207 **Faculty:** FT 80, PT 54 **Student-Faculty Ratio:** 13:1 **Exams:** SAT I or ACT, SAT II **% Receiving Financial Aid:** 67 **% Residing in College-Owned, -Operated, or -Affiliated Housing:** 58 **Library Holdings:** 89,003 **Credit Hours For Degree:** 60 semester hours, Associates; 122 semester hours, Bachelors **ROTC:** Army **Professional Accreditation:** ABET, AACN, NLN, NCCU **Intercollegiate Athletics:** Basketball M & W; Cheerleading M & W; Football M; Golf W; Soccer W; Swimming and Diving M & W; Volleyball W

CHIEF DULL KNIFE COLLEGE
PO Box 98
Lame Deer, MT 59043-0098
Tel: (406)477-6215
Fax: (406)477-6219
Web Site: http://www.cdkc.edu/
President/CEO: Dr. Richard E. Littlebear
Registrar: William Wertman
Admissions: William L. Wertman
Financial Aid: Donna Small
Type: Two-Year College **Sex:** Coed **Admission Plans:** Open Admission; Early Admission **Application Fee:** $0.00 **H.S. Requirements:** High school diploma required; GED accepted **Scholarships:** Available **Calendar System:** Semester, Summer Session Available **Faculty:** FT 8, PT 22 **Exams:** ACT, Other **Library Holdings:** 10,000 **Credit Hours For Degree:** 60 credit hours, Associates **Professional Accreditation:** NCCU

DAWSON COMMUNITY COLLEGE
Box 421
Glendive, MT 59330-0421
Tel: (406)377-3396
Free: 800-821-8320
Fax: (406)377-8132
Web Site: http://www.dawson.edu/
President/CEO: Dr. Terry Hetrick
Registrar: Lane Holte
Admissions: Jolene Myers
Financial Aid: Jolene Myers
Type: Two-Year College **Sex:** Coed **Affiliation:** Montana University System **Scores:** 50% ACT 18-23; 17% ACT 24-29 **Admission Plans:** Open Admission; Deferred Admission **Application Fee:** $30.00 **H.S. Requirements:** High school diploma required; GED accepted **Costs Per Year:** Application fee: $30. Area resident tuition: $1232 full-time, $44 per credit part-time. State resident tuition: $2,103 full-time, $75.10 per credit part-time. Nonresident tuition: $5,762 full-time, $205.80 per credit part-time. Mandatory fees: $1092 full-time, $39 per credit part-time. Full-time tuition and fees vary according to reciprocity agreements. Part-time tuition and fees vary according to reciprocity agreements. College room only: $1950. **Scholarships:** Available **Calendar System:** Semester, Summer Session Available **Enrollment:** FT 395, PT 144 **Faculty:** FT 21, PT 28 **Student-Faculty Ratio:** 16:1 **Exams:** ACT **% Residing in College-Owned, -Operated, or -Affiliated Housing:** 19 **Library Holdings:** 18,870 **Credit Hours For Degree:** 60 semester hours, Associates **Professional Accreditation:** NCCU **Intercollegiate Athletics:** Baseball M; Basketball M & W; Equestrian Sports M & W; Softball W

FLATHEAD VALLEY COMMUNITY COLLEGE
777 Grandview Dr.
Kalispell, MT 59901-2622
Tel: (406)756-3822
Free: 800-313-3822
Admissions: (406)756-3846
Fax: (406)756-3815
E-mail: mstoltz@fvcc.cc.mt.us

Web Site: http://www.fvcc.edu/
President/CEO: Jane A. Karas
Registrar: Sharon Hall
Admissions: Marlene C. Stoltz
Financial Aid: Bonnie Whitehouse
Type: Two-Year College **Sex:** Coed **Admission Plans:** Open Admission; Early Admission; Deferred Admission **Application Fee:** $15.00 **H.S. Requirements:** High school diploma required; GED accepted **Costs Per Year:** Application fee: $15. Area resident tuition: $1739 full-time, $62.10 per credit part-time. State resident tuition: $2856 full-time, $102 per credit part-time. Nonresident tuition: $7146 full-time, $255.20 per credit part-time. Mandatory fees: $25.75 per credit part-time, $609.50 per year part-time. Part-time tuition and fees vary according to course load. **Scholarships:** Available **Calendar System:** Semester, Summer Session Available **Enrollment:** FT 972, PT 1,128 **Faculty:** FT 40, PT 146 **Student-Faculty Ratio:** 15:1 **Library Holdings:** 19,038 **Credit Hours For Degree:** 60 semester hours, Associates **Professional Accreditation:** AAMAE, NCCU **Intercollegiate Athletics:** Cross-Country Running M & W; Soccer M & W

FORT BELKNAP COLLEGE
PO Box 159
Harlem, MT 59526-0159
Tel: (406)353-2607
Fax: (406)353-2898
Web Site: http://www.fbcc.edu/
President/CEO: Carole Falcon-Chandler
Admissions: Dixie Brockie
Financial Aid: Wayne Birdtail
Type: Two-Year College **Sex:** Coed **Admission Plans:** Open Admission; Early Admission; Deferred Admission **Application Fee:** $10.00 **H.S. Requirements:** High school diploma required; GED accepted **Scholarships:** Available **Calendar System:** Quarter, Summer Session Not available **Enrollment:** FT 117, PT 41 **Faculty:** FT 8, PT 20 **Exams:** Other **Library Holdings:** 16,000 **Credit Hours For Degree:** 92 credits, Associates **Professional Accreditation:** NCCU **Intercollegiate Athletics:** Basketball M & W; Cross-Country Running M & W; Volleyball M & W

FORT PECK COMMUNITY COLLEGE
PO Box 398
Poplar, MT 59255-0398
Tel: (406)768-5551
Admissions: (406)768-6329
Web Site: http://www.fpcc.edu/
President/CEO: Dr. James Shanley
Registrar: Terri DeLong
Admissions: Robert McAnally
Financial Aid: Haven Gorneau
Type: Two-Year College **Sex:** Coed **Admission Plans:** Open Admission; Early Admission **Application Fee:** $15.00 **Scholarships:** Available **Calendar System:** Semester, Summer Session Available **Faculty:** FT 17, PT 14 **Exams:** Other **Credit Hours For Degree:** 60 credit hours, Associates **Professional Accreditation:** NCCU

LITTLE BIG HORN COLLEGE
Box 370
Crow Agency, MT 59022-0370
Tel: (406)638-2228
Admissions: (406)638-3116
Web Site: http://www.lbhc.cc.mt.us/
President/CEO: Henry Real Bird
Registrar: Anne Bullis
Admissions: Tina Pretty On Top
Financial Aid: Berthina Deputy
Type: Two-Year College **Sex:** Coed **Admission Plans:** Open Admission **H.S. Requirements:** High school diploma or equivalent not required **Calendar System:** Quarter **Faculty:** FT 11, PT 1 **Student-Faculty Ratio:** 25:1 **Exams:** Other **Credit Hours For Degree:** 92 quarter hours, Associates **Professional Accreditation:** NCCU **Intercollegiate Athletics:** Basketball M & W

MILES COMMUNITY COLLEGE
2715 Dickinson
Miles City, MT 59301-4799
Tel: (406)874-6100
Free: 800-541-9281
Admissions: (406)874-6159
Fax: (406)874-6282
Web Site: http://www.milescc.edu/
President/CEO: Dr. Darrel L. Hammon
Registrar: Lisa Blunt
Admissions: Laura J. Pierce
Financial Aid: Jessie Dufner
Type: Two-Year College **Sex:** Coed **Affiliation:** Montana University System **Admission Plans:** Open Admission; Early Admission; Deferred Admission **Application Fee:** $40.00 **H.S. Requirements:** High school diploma required; GED accepted **Scholarships:** Available **Calendar System:** Semester, Summer Session Available **Enrollment:** FT 360, PT 114 **Faculty:** FT 27, PT 13 **Student-Faculty Ratio:** 14:1 **Exams:** SAT I or ACT **% Residing in College-Owned, -Operated, or -Affiliated Housing:** 20 **Library Holdings:** 17,563 **Credit Hours For Degree:** 62 semester hours, Associates **Professional Accreditation:** NLN, NCCU **Intercollegiate Athletics:** Basketball M & W; Golf M & W

MONTANA STATE UNIVERSITY
Bozeman, MT 59717
Tel: (406)994-0211; 888-MSU-CATS
Admissions: (406)994-2601
E-mail: zam1202@msu.oscs.montana.edu
Web Site: http://www.montana.edu/
President/CEO: Dr. Geoffrey Gamble
Registrar: Charles A. Nelson
Admissions: Charles Nelson
Financial Aid: Thomas Stump
Type: University **Sex:** Coed **Affiliation:** Montana University System **Scores:** 97% SAT V 400+; 96% SAT M 400+; 47% ACT 18-23; 38% ACT 24-29 **% Accepted:** 74 **Admission Plans:** Early Admission; Deferred Admission **Application Deadline:** Rolling **Application Fee:** $30.00 **H.S. Requirements:** High school diploma required; GED accepted **Costs Per Year:** Application fee: $30. State resident tuition: $5221 full-time, $171.10 per credit part-time. Nonresident tuition: $14,945 full-time, $572.70 per credit part-time. Full-time tuition varies according to course load. Part-time tuition varies according to course load. College room and board: $6150. Room and board charges vary according to board plan and housing facility. **Scholarships:** Available **Calendar System:** Semester, Summer Session Available **Enrollment:** FT 9,285, PT 1,557, Grad 1,324 **Faculty:** FT 553, PT 275 **Student-Faculty Ratio:** 16:1 **Exams:** SAT I or ACT **% Receiving Financial Aid:** 53 **% Residing in College-Owned, -Operated, or -Affiliated Housing:** 25 **Library Holdings:** 574,634 **Credit Hours For Degree:** 120 credits, Bachelors **ROTC:** Army, Air Force **Professional Accreditation:** AACSB, ABET, AACN, AAFCS, ACA, APA, NASAD, NASM, NCATE, NCCU **Intercollegiate Athletics:** Basketball M & W; Cheerleading M & W; Cross-Country Running M & W; Football M; Golf W; Skiing (Cross-Country) M & W; Skiing (Downhill) M & W; Tennis M & W; Track and Field M & W; Volleyball W

MONTANA STATE UNIVERSITY-BILLINGS
1500 University Dr.
Billings, MT 59101-0298
Tel: (406)657-2011
Free: 800-565-6782
Admissions: (406)657-2158
Fax: (406)657-2302
E-mail: cjohannes@msubillings.edu
Web Site: http://www.msubillings.edu/
President/CEO: Dr. Ronald P. Sexton
Registrar: Karen Everett
Admissions: Cheri Johannes
Financial Aid: Melina Hawkins
Type: Comprehensive **Sex:** Coed **Affiliation:** Montana University System **Scores:** 91% SAT V 400+; 94% SAT M 400+; 61% ACT 18-23; 22% ACT 24-29 **% Accepted:** 96 **Admission Plans:** Early Admission; Deferred Admission **Application Deadline:** July 01 **Application Fee:** $30.00 **H.S. Requirements:** High school diploma required; GED accepted **Costs Per Year:** Application fee: $30. State resident tuition: $3762 full-time, $135 per credit hour part-time. Nonresident tuition: $13,096 full-time, $364 per credit hour part-time. Mandatory fees: $1094 full-time. Full-time tuition and fees vary according to course load, degree level, and location. Part-time tuition varies according to course load, degree level, and location. College room and board: $4050. Room and board charges vary according to board plan and housing facility. **Scholarships:** Available **Calendar System:** Semester, Summer Session Available **Enrollment:** FT 3,170, PT 1,237, Grad 465

Faculty: FT 156, PT 101 **Student-Faculty Ratio:** 20:1 **Exams:** SAT I or ACT **% Receiving Financial Aid:** 67 **% Residing in College-Owned, -Operated, or -Affiliated Housing:** 10 **Library Holdings:** 488,004 **Credit Hours For Degree:** 64 credit hours, Associates; 120 credit hours, Bachelors **Professional Accreditation:** CORE, NASAD, NASM, NCATE, NCCU **Intercollegiate Athletics:** Baseball M; Basketball M & W; Cross-Country Running M & W; Golf M & W; Soccer M & W; Softball W; Tennis M & W; Volleyball W

MONTANA STATE UNIVERSITY-GREAT FALLS COLLEGE OF TECHNOLOGY
2100 16th Ave., South
Great Falls, MT 59405
Tel: (406)771-4300
Fax: (406)771-4317
E-mail: zgf2001@maia.oscs.montana.edu
Web Site: http://www.msugf.edu/
President/CEO: Dr. Mary Moe
Registrar: Carol Schopfer
Admissions: Carol Schopfer
Financial Aid: Leah J. Habel
Type: Two-Year College **Sex:** Coed **Affiliation:** Montana University System **Admission Plans:** Open Admission; Deferred Admission **Application Fee:** $30.00 **H.S. Requirements:** High school diploma required; GED accepted **Scholarships:** Available **Calendar System:** Semester, Summer Session Available **Enrollment:** FT 716, PT 747 **Faculty:** FT 40, PT 43 **Student-Faculty Ratio:** 15:1 **Exams:** Other **Library Holdings:** 4,000 **Credit Hours For Degree:** 60 credits, Associates **Professional Accreditation:** AAMAE, ADA, AHIMA, CARC, NCCU

MONTANA STATE UNIVERSITY-NORTHERN
PO Box 7751
Havre, MT 59501-7751
Tel: (406)265-3700
Admissions: (406)265-3704
Fax: (406)265-3777
Web Site: http://www.msun.edu/
President/CEO: Dr. Alex Capdeville
Registrar: Steven Jamruszka
Admissions: Rosalie Spinler
Financial Aid: Kris Dramstad
Type: Comprehensive **Sex:** Coed **Affiliation:** Montana University System **Admission Plans:** Early Admission; Deferred Admission **Application Fee:** $30.00 **H.S. Requirements:** High school diploma required; GED accepted **Scholarships:** Available **Calendar System:** Semester, Summer Session Available **Enrollment:** FT 1,060, PT 368, Grad 161 **Faculty:** FT 73, PT 30 **Student-Faculty Ratio:** 15:1 **Exams:** ACT **% Receiving Financial Aid:** 76 **Library Holdings:** 128,000 **Credit Hours For Degree:** 64 credits, Associates; 128 credits, Bachelors **Professional Accreditation:** ABET, NCATE, NLN, NCCU **Intercollegiate Athletics:** Basketball M & W; Football M; Golf W; Volleyball W; Wrestling M

MONTANA TECH OF THE UNIVERSITY OF MONTANA
1300 West Park St.
Butte, MT 59701-8997
Tel: (406)496-4101
Free: 800-445-TECH
Admissions: (406)496-4178
Fax: (406)496-4710
E-mail: tcampeau@mtech.edu
Web Site: http://www.mtech.edu/
President/CEO: Dr. W. Franklin Gilmore
Registrar: Edwin Johnson
Admissions: Tony Campeau
Financial Aid: Michael Richardson
Type: Comprehensive **Sex:** Coed **Affiliation:** Montana University System **Scores:** 93.16% SAT V 400+; 94.02% SAT M 400+; 62.5% ACT 18-23; 37.5% ACT 24-29 **% Accepted:** 98 **Admission Plans:** Open Admission; Early Admission **Application Deadline:** Rolling **Application Fee:** $30.00 **H.S. Requirements:** High school diploma required; GED accepted **Costs Per Year:** Application fee: $30. State resident tuition: $4816 full-time, $233 per credit part-time. Nonresident tuition: $13,807 full-time, $607 per credit part-time. Mandatory fees: $43 per credit part-time, $49. College room and board: $5106. College room only: $2294. **Scholarships:** Available **Calendar System:** Semester, Summer Session Available **Enrollment:** FT 1,729, PT 413, Grad 88 **Faculty:** FT 110, PT 39 **Student-Faculty Ratio:** 16:1 **Exams:** SAT I or ACT **% Receiving Financial Aid:** 63 **% Residing in College-Owned, -Operated, or -Affiliated Housing:** 15 **Library Holdings:** 165,734 **Credit Hours For Degree:** 60 credit hours, Associates; 120-136 credit hours, Bachelors **Professional Accreditation:** ABET, NCCU **Intercollegiate Athletics:** Basketball M & W; Cross-Country Running M & W; Football M; Golf M & W; Rugby M & W; Soccer M & W; Swimming and Diving M & W; Volleyball W

ROCKY MOUNTAIN COLLEGE
1511 Poly Dr.
Billings, MT 59102-1796
Tel: (406)657-1000
Free: 800-877-6259
Admissions: (406)657-1026
Fax: (406)259-9751
E-mail: admissions@rocky.edu
Web Site: http://www.rocky.edu/
President/CEO: Dr. Thomas R. Oates
Registrar: Janet Alberson
Admissions: Bonnie Knapp
Financial Aid: Lisa Browning
Type: Four-Year College **Sex:** Coed **Affiliation:** interdenominational **Scores:** 96% SAT V 400+; 94% SAT M 400+; 56% ACT 18-23; 35% ACT 24-29 **% Accepted:** 78 **Admission Plans:** Early Admission; Deferred Admission **Application Deadline:** Rolling **Application Fee:** $25.00 **H.S. Requirements:** High school diploma required; GED accepted **Costs Per Year:** Application fee: $25. Comprehensive fee: $23,013 includes full-time tuition ($16,136), mandatory fees ($253), and college room and board ($6624). College room only: $3628. Part-time tuition: $674 per credit. Part-time mandatory fees: $67 per term. **Scholarships:** Available **Calendar System:** Semester, Summer Session Available **Enrollment:** FT 895, PT 69, Grad 45 **Faculty:** FT 53, PT 60 **Student-Faculty Ratio:** 13:1 **Exams:** ACT, SAT I or ACT **% Receiving Financial Aid:** 64 **% Residing in College-Owned, -Operated, or -Affiliated Housing:** 43 **Library Holdings:** 42,674 **Credit Hours For Degree:** 62 semester hours, Associates; 124 semester hours, Bachelors **Professional Accreditation:** NCCU

SALISH KOOTENAI COLLEGE
PO Box 117
Pablo, MT 59855-0117
Tel: (406)275-4800
Admissions: (406)275-4866
Fax: (406)275-4801
Web Site: http://www.skc.edu/
President/CEO: Dr. Joseph McDonald
Registrar: Cleo Kenmille
Admissions: Jackie Moran
Financial Aid: Jeannie Burland
Type: Two-Year College **Sex:** Coed **Admission Plans:** Open Admission; Preferred Admission; Deferred Admission **H.S. Requirements:** High school diploma required; GED accepted **Scholarships:** Available **Calendar System:** Quarter, Summer Session Available **Enrollment:** FT 585, PT 503 **Faculty:** FT 45, PT 35 **Exams:** Other **Library Holdings:** 24,000 **Credit Hours For Degree:** 92 credits, Associates; 180 credits, Bachelors **Professional Accreditation:** ADA, NLN, NCCU

STONE CHILD COLLEGE
RR1, Box 1082
Box Elder, MT 59521
Tel: (406)395-4313
Fax: (406)395-4836
E-mail: uanet337@quest.ocsc.montana.edu
Web Site: http://www.montana.edu/wwwscc/
President/CEO: Steve Galbavy
Registrar: Theodore Whitford
Admissions: Ted Whitford
Financial Aid: Joe LaFronbies
Type: Two-Year College **Sex:** Coed **Admission Plans:** Open Admission **H.S. Requirements:** High school diploma required; GED accepted **Scholar-**

ships: Available **Calendar System:** Semester **Faculty:** FT 10, PT 12 **Credit Hours For Degree:** 64 semester hours, Associates **Professional Accreditation:** NCCU

UNIVERSITY OF GREAT FALLS
1301 Twentieth St. South
Great Falls, MT 59405
Tel: (406)761-8210
Free: 800-856-9544
Admissions: (406)791-5200
Fax: (406)791-5209
E-mail: enroll@ugf.edu
Web Site: http://www.ugf.edu/
President/CEO: Dr. Eugene J. McAllister
Registrar: Tracy Lampkins
Admissions: Paula Highlander
Type: Comprehensive **Sex:** Coed **Affiliation:** Roman Catholic; Providence Services **Scores:** 84% SAT V 400+; 84% SAT M 400+; 41% ACT 18-23; 22% ACT 24-29 **% Accepted:** 79 **Admission Plans:** Open Admission; Early Admission; Deferred Admission **Application Deadline:** August 01 **Application Fee:** $35.00 **H.S. Requirements:** High school diploma required; GED accepted. For home school students: High school diploma required; GED accepted **Costs Per Year:** Application fee: $35. Comprehensive fee: $20,720 includes full-time tuition ($14,600), mandatory fees ($620), and college room and board ($5500). College room only: $2400. Part-time tuition: $460 per credit. Part-time mandatory fees: $15 per credit. **Scholarships:** Available **Calendar System:** Semester, Summer Session Available **Enrollment:** FT 485, PT 188, Grad 105 **Faculty:** FT 33, PT 61 **Student-Faculty Ratio:** 11:1 **Exams:** SAT I and SAT II or ACT **% Receiving Financial Aid:** 83 **% Residing in College-Owned, -Operated, or -Affiliated Housing:** 21 **Library Holdings:** 107,541 **Credit Hours For Degree:** 64 credits, Associates; 128 credits, Bachelors **Professional Accreditation:** NCCU **Intercollegiate Athletics:** Basketball M & W; Cheerleading M & W; Cross-Country Running M & W; Golf M & W; Soccer W; Softball W; Volleyball W; Wrestling M

THE UNIVERSITY OF MONTANA-HELENA COLLEGE OF TECHNOLOGY
1115 North Roberts St.
Helena, MT 59601
Tel: (406)444-6800
Fax: (406)444-6892
Web Site: http://www.umhelena.edu/
President/CEO: Dr. Steven Hoyle
Registrar: Cris Valdez
Admissions: Vicki Cavanaugh
Financial Aid: Victoria Glass
Type: Two-Year College **Sex:** Coed **Affiliation:** Montana University System **Admission Plans:** Open Admission; Early Admission; Deferred Admission **Application Fee:** $30.00 **H.S. Requirements:** High school diploma required; GED accepted **Scholarships:** Available **Calendar System:** Semester, Summer Session Available **Faculty:** FT 50, PT 30 **Student-Faculty Ratio:** 18:1 **Exams:** Other **Library Holdings:** 2,500 **Credit Hours For Degree:** 68 credit hours, Associates **Professional Accreditation:** NCCU

THE UNIVERSITY OF MONTANA-MISSOULA
Missoula, MT 59812-0002
Tel: (406)243-0211
Free: 800-462-8636
Admissions: (406)243-2361
Fax: (406)243-5711
E-mail: admiss@umontana.edu
Web Site: http://www.umt.edu/
President/CEO: Dr. George M. Dennison
Registrar: Dr. Philip T. Bain
Admissions: Jed Liston
Financial Aid: Myron Hanson
Type: University **Sex:** Coed **Affiliation:** Montana University System **% Accepted:** 83 **Admission Plans:** Early Admission; Deferred Admission **Application Deadline:** March 01 **Application Fee:** $30.00 **H.S. Requirements:** High school diploma required; GED accepted. For home schooled applicants: High school diploma or equivalent not required **Costs Per Year:** Application fee: $30. State resident tuition: $3739 full-time, $164 per credit part-time. Nonresident tuition: $13,246 full-time, $573 per credit part-time. Mandatory fees: $1291 full-time, $40 per credit part-time. College room and board: $5860. College room only: $2660. **Scholarships:** Available **Calendar System:** Semester, Summer Session Available **Enrollment:** FT 9,620, PT 1,884, Grad 1,856 **Faculty:** FT 547, PT 187 **Student-Faculty Ratio:** 19:1 **Exams:** Other, SAT I or ACT **% Receiving Financial Aid:** 58 **% Residing in College-Owned, -Operated, or -Affiliated Housing:** 23 **Library Holdings:** 570,287 **Credit Hours For Degree:** 65 credits, Associates; 120 credits, Bachelors **ROTC:** Army **Professional Accreditation:** AACSB, ABET, ACEJMC, ABA, ACPhE, ACF, APTA, APA, AALS, CARC, CSWE, JRCEPAT, NASAD, NASM, NAST, NCATE, NRPA, NCCU, SAF **Intercollegiate Athletics:** Baseball M; Basketball M & W; Crew M & W; Cross-Country Running M & W; Equestrian Sports M & W; Fencing M & W; Field Hockey W; Football M; Golf W; Ice Hockey M & W; Lacrosse M & W; Rugby M & W; Skiing (Downhill) M & W; Soccer W; Tennis M & W; Track and Field M & W; Ultimate Frisbee M & W; Volleyball M & W

THE UNIVERSITY OF MONTANA-WESTERN
710 South Atlantic
Dillon, MT 59725-3598
Tel: (406)683-7011; (866)869-6668
Admissions: (406)683-7665
Fax: (406)683-7493
E-mail: e_murray@wmc.edu
Web Site: http://www.umwestern.edu/
President/CEO: Dr. Richard Storey
Registrar: Jason Karch
Admissions: Dr. Eric Murray
Financial Aid: Arlene Williams
Type: Four-Year College **Sex:** Coed **Affiliation:** Montana University System **Scores:** 64% SAT V 400+; 76% SAT M 400+; 61% ACT 18-23; 15% ACT 24-29 **% Accepted:** 99 **Admission Plans:** Early Admission; Deferred Admission **Application Deadline:** July 01 **Application Fee:** $30.00 **H.S. Requirements:** High school diploma required; GED accepted **Costs Per Year:** Application fee: $30. State resident tuition: $3538 full-time, $295 per credit part-time. Nonresident tuition: $12,080 full-time, $503 per credit part-time. Mandatory fees: $815 full-time. College room and board: $4920. College room only: $1970. **Scholarships:** Available **Calendar System:** Semester, Summer Session Available **Enrollment:** FT 941, PT 218 **Faculty:** FT 56, PT 16 **Student-Faculty Ratio:** 17:1 **Exams:** SAT I or ACT **% Receiving Financial Aid:** 85 **% Residing in College-Owned, -Operated, or -Affiliated Housing:** 35 **Library Holdings:** 90,431 **Credit Hours For Degree:** 64 credits, Associates; 120 credits, Bachelors **Professional Accreditation:** NCATE, NCCU **Intercollegiate Athletics:** Basketball M & W; Football M; Golf M & W; Volleyball W

BELLEVUE UNIVERSITY
1000 Galvin Rd. South
Bellevue, NE 68005-3098
Tel: (402)291-8100
Free: 800-756-7920
Admissions: (402)505-5512
Fax: (402)293-2020
E-mail: sandusky@bellevue.edu
Web Site: http://www.bellevue.edu/
President/CEO: Dr. John B. Muller
Registrar: Phillip Chapman
Admissions: Brian Sandusky
Financial Aid: Jon Dotterer
Type: Comprehensive **Sex:** Coed **Admission Plans:** Open Admission; Deferred Admission **Application Deadline:** Rolling **Application Fee:** $50.00 **H.S. Requirements:** High school diploma required; GED accepted **Costs Per Year:** Application fee: $50. Tuition: $5250 full-time, $175 per credit hour part-time. Mandatory fees: $95 full-time, $45 per term part-time. **Scholarships:** Available **Calendar System:** Semester, Summer Session Available **Enrollment:** FT 2,849, PT 1,598, Grad 1,482 **Faculty:** FT 72, PT 326 **Student-Faculty Ratio:** 15:1 **% Receiving Financial Aid:** 87 **Library Holdings:** 100,904 **Regional Accreditation:** North Central Association of Colleges and Schools **Credit Hours For Degree:** 127 credit hours, Bachelors **ROTC:** Army, Air Force **Intercollegiate Athletics:** Baseball M; Basketball M; Soccer M & W; Softball W; Volleyball W

CENTRAL COMMUNITY COLLEGE-COLUMBUS CAMPUS
4500 63rd St., PO Box 1027
Columbus, NE 68602-1027
Tel: (402)564-7132
Admissions: (402)562-1296
Fax: (402)562-1201
E-mail: myoung@cccneb.edu
Web Site: http://www.cccneb.edu/
President/CEO: Jim Fisher
Registrar: Ronda Ryan
Admissions: Mary Young
Financial Aid: Lisa Gdowski
Type: Two-Year College **Sex:** Coed **Affiliation:** Central Community College **Admission Plans:** Open Admission; Early Admission **Application Deadline:** Rolling **Application Fee:** $0.00 **H.S. Requirements:** High school diploma required; GED accepted. For nursing program: High school diploma required; GED not accepted **Costs Per Year:** Application fee: $0. State resident tuition: $1860 full-time, $62 per credit part-time. Nonresident tuition: $2790 full-time, $93 per credit part-time. Mandatory fees: $120 full-time, $4 per credit part-time. **Scholarships:** Available **Calendar System:** Semester, Summer Session Available **Enrollment:** FT 445, PT 1,554 **Faculty:** FT 38, PT 51 **Student-Faculty Ratio:** 15:1 **% Residing in College-Owned, -Operated, or -Affiliated Housing:** 17 **Library Holdings:** 22,000 **Regional Accreditation:** North Central Association of Colleges and Schools **Credit Hours For Degree:** 60 credits, Associates **Intercollegiate Athletics:** Basketball M; Volleyball W

CENTRAL COMMUNITY COLLEGE-GRAND ISLAND CAMPUS
PO Box 4903
Grand Island, NE 68802-4903
Tel: (308)398-4222
Admissions: (308)398-7406
Fax: (308)398-7398
E-mail: lkohout@cccneb.edu
Web Site: http://www.cccneb.edu/
President/CEO: Dr. Lynn C. Black
Registrar: Don Richards
Admissions: Liz Kohout
Financial Aid: Steve Millnitz
Type: Two-Year College **Sex:** Coed **Affiliation:** Central Community College **Admission Plans:** Open Admission; Early Admission **Application Deadline:** Rolling **Application Fee:** $0.00 **H.S. Requirements:** High school diploma required; GED accepted. For nursing program: High school diploma required; GED not accepted **Costs Per Year:** Application fee: $0. State resident tuition: $1860 full-time, $62 per credit part-time. Nonresident tuition: $2790 full-time, $93 per credit part-time. Mandatory fees: $120 full-time, $4 per credit part-time. **Scholarships:** Available **Calendar System:** Semester, Summer Session Available **Enrollment:** FT 399, PT 2,517 **Faculty:** FT 43, PT 69 **Student-Faculty Ratio:** 15:1 **% Residing in College-Owned, -Operated, or -Affiliated Housing:** 10 **Library Holdings:** 5,700 **Regional Accreditation:** North Central Association of Colleges and Schools **Credit Hours For Degree:** 60 credits, Associates **Professional Accreditation:** ADA, NLN

CENTRAL COMMUNITY COLLEGE-HASTINGS CAMPUS
PO Box 1024
Hastings, NE 68902-1024
Tel: (402)463-9811
Admissions: (402)461-2428
E-mail: rglenn@cccneb.edu
Web Site: http://www.cccneb.edu/
President/CEO: William Hitesman
Registrar: Don Richards
Admissions: Robert Glenn
Financial Aid: Vicki Kucera
Type: Two-Year College **Sex:** Coed **Affiliation:** Central Community College **Admission Plans:** Open Admission; Early Admission **Application Deadline:** Rolling **Application Fee:** $0.00 **H.S. Requirements:** High school diploma required; GED accepted. For nursing, dental hygiene, truck driving, medical laboratory technology programs: High school diploma required; GED not accepted **Costs Per Year:** Application fee: $0. State resident tuition: $1860 full-time, $62 per credit part-time. Nonresident tuition: $2790 full-time, $93 per credit part-time. Mandatory fees: $120 full-time, $4 per credit part-time. **Scholarships:** Available **Calendar System:** Semester, Summer Session Available **Enrollment:** FT 933, PT 1,601 **Faculty:** FT 61, PT 29 **Student-Faculty Ratio:** 15:1 **% Residing in College-Owned, -Operated, or -Affiliated Housing:** 26 **Library Holdings:** 4,025 **Regional Accreditation:** North Central Association of Colleges and Schools **Credit Hours For Degree:** 60 credits, Associates **Professional Accreditation:** AAMAE, ADA, AHIMA, NAACLS

CHADRON STATE COLLEGE
1000 Main St.
Chadron, NE 69337
Tel: (308)432-6000
Admissions: (308)432-6263

Fax: (308)432-6229
E-mail: admissions@csc1.csc.edu
Web Site: http://www.csc.edu/
President/CEO: Dr. Thomas L. Krepel
Registrar: Dale Williamson
Admissions: Tena Cook Gould
Financial Aid: Sherry Douglas
Type: Comprehensive **Sex:** Coed **Affiliation:** Nebraska State College System **Scores:** 53% ACT 18-23; 28% ACT 24-29 **Admission Plans:** Open Admission; Early Admission **Application Deadline:** Rolling **Application Fee:** $15.00 **H.S. Requirements:** High school diploma required; GED accepted **Costs Per Year:** Application fee: $15. State resident tuition: $2933 full-time, $97.25 per credit part-time. Nonresident tuition: $5865 full-time, $195.50 per credit part-time. Mandatory fees: $729 full-time. Full-time tuition and fees vary according to course load, location, and program. Part-time tuition varies according to course load, location, and program. College room and board: $4074. College room only: $1924. Room and board charges vary according to board plan and housing facility. **Scholarships:** Available **Calendar System:** Semester, Summer Session Available **Enrollment:** FT 1,634, PT 682, Grad 320 **Faculty:** FT 101, PT 9 **Student-Faculty Ratio:** 19:1 **% Receiving Financial Aid:** 97 **% Residing in College-Owned, -Operated, or -Affiliated Housing:** 65 **Library Holdings:** 593,140 **Regional Accreditation:** North Central Association of Colleges and Schools **Credit Hours For Degree:** 125 semester hours, Bachelors **Professional Accreditation:** AAFCS, ACBSP, CSWE, NCATE **Intercollegiate Athletics:** Basketball M & W; Equestrian Sports M & W; Football M; Golf W; Track and Field M & W; Volleyball W; Wrestling M

CLARKSON COLLEGE
101 South 42nd St.
Omaha, NE 68131-2739
Tel: (402)552-3100
Free: 800-647-5500
Fax: (402)552-6057
E-mail: admiss@clrkcol.crhsnet.edu
Web Site: http://www.clarksoncollege.edu/
President/CEO: Dr. J. W. Upright
Registrar: Michele Stirtz
Admissions: Nicole Wegenast
Financial Aid: Margie Harris
Type: Comprehensive **Sex:** Coed **Affiliation:** Nebraska Health System **Scores:** 65% ACT 18-23; 22% ACT 24-29 **Admission Plans:** Deferred Admission **Application Fee:** $15.00 **H.S. Requirements:** High school diploma required; GED accepted **Costs Per Year:** Application fee: $15. Comprehensive fee: $15,030 includes full-time tuition ($10,350), mandatory fees ($690), and college room and board ($3990). Part-time tuition: $345 per credit hour. Part-time mandatory fees: $22 per credit hour, $15 per term. **Scholarships:** Available **Calendar System:** Semester, Summer Session Available **Enrollment:** FT 260, PT 161, Grad 86 **Faculty:** FT 62, PT 2 **Student-Faculty Ratio:** 12:1 **Exams:** SAT I or ACT **% Receiving Financial Aid:** 75 **% Residing in College-Owned, -Operated, or -Affiliated Housing:** 20 **Library Holdings:** 8,807 **Regional Accreditation:** North Central Association of Colleges and Schools **Credit Hours For Degree:** 70 credits, Associates; 128 credits, Bachelors **ROTC:** Army, Air Force **Professional Accreditation:** APTA, JRCERT, NLN

COLLEGE OF SAINT MARY
1901 South 72nd St.
Omaha, NE 68124-2377
Tel: (402)399-2400
Free: 800-926-5534
Admissions: (402)399-2407
Fax: (402)399-2412
E-mail: enroll@csm.edu
Web Site: http://www.csm.edu/
President/CEO: Dr. Maryanne Stevens
Registrar: Deb Nugen
Admissions: Lori Werth
Financial Aid: Caprice Calamaio
Type: Four-Year College **Sex:** Women **Affiliation:** Roman Catholic **Scores:** 68% ACT 18-23; 13% ACT 24-29 **% Accepted:** 56 **Application Deadline:** Rolling **Application Fee:** $30.00 **H.S. Requirements:** High school diploma required; GED accepted **Costs Per Year:** Application fee: $30. Comprehensive fee: $24,010 includes full-time tuition ($17,750), mandatory fees ($360), and college room and board ($5900). Room and board charges vary according to housing facility. Part-time tuition: $550 per credit hour. Part-time mandatory fees: $12 per credit hour. Part-time tuition and fees vary according to class time. **Scholarships:** Available **Calendar System:** Semester, Summer Session Available **Enrollment:** FT 641, PT 358, Grad 16 **Faculty:** FT 54, PT 0 **Student-Faculty Ratio:** 10:1 **Exams:** SAT I or ACT **% Receiving Financial Aid:** 65 **% Residing in College-Owned, -Operated, or -Affiliated Housing:** 17 **Library Holdings:** 81,268 **Regional Accreditation:** North Central Association of Colleges and Schools **Credit Hours For Degree:** 64 credit hours, Associates; 128 credit hours, Bachelors **ROTC:** Army, Air Force **Professional Accreditation:** AHIMA, AOTA, NLN **Intercollegiate Athletics:** Basketball W; Cross-Country Running W; Soccer W; Softball W; Volleyball W

CONCORDIA UNIVERSITY
800 North Columbia Ave.
Seward, NE 68434-1599
Tel: (402)643-3651
Free: 800-535-5494
Admissions: (402)643-7233
Fax: (402)643-4073
E-mail: admiss@cune.edu
Web Site: http://www.cune.edu/
President/CEO: Rev. Brian Friedrich
Registrar: Edward Siffring
Admissions: Don Vos
Financial Aid: Gloria Hennig
Type: Comprehensive **Sex:** Coed **Affiliation:** Lutheran Church–Missouri Synod; Concordia University System **Scores:** 92.9% SAT V 400+; 95.2% SAT M 400+; 38% ACT 18-23; 43.8% ACT 24-29 **Admission Plans:** Deferred Admission **Application Fee:** $25.00 **H.S. Requirements:** High school diploma required; GED accepted **Costs Per Year:** Application fee: $25. Comprehensive fee: $22,434 includes full-time tuition ($17,724) and college room and board ($4710). Room and board charges vary according to board plan. **Scholarships:** Available **Calendar System:** Miscellaneous, Summer Session Available **Enrollment:** FT 1,122, PT 80, Grad 115 **Faculty:** FT 62, PT 58 **Student-Faculty Ratio:** 14:1 **Exams:** SAT I or ACT **% Receiving Financial Aid:** 80 **Library Holdings:** 171,688 **Regional Accreditation:** North Central Association of Colleges and Schools **Credit Hours For Degree:** 128 credit hours, Bachelors **ROTC:** Army, Air Force **Professional Accreditation:** NASM, NCATE **Intercollegiate Athletics:** Baseball M; Basketball M & W; Cross-Country Running M & W; Football M; Golf M & W; Soccer M & W; Softball W; Tennis M & W; Track and Field M & W; Volleyball W

THE CREATIVE CENTER
10850 Emmet St.
Omaha, NE 68164
Tel: (402)898-1000; 888-898-1789
Fax: (402)898-1301
Web Site: http://www.thecreativecenter.com/
President/CEO: Kent Carlson
Type: Two-Year College **Sex:** Coed **Application Fee:** $100.00 **Calendar System:** Semester **Professional Accreditation:** ACCSCT

CREIGHTON UNIVERSITY
2500 California Plaza
Omaha, NE 68178-0001
Tel: (402)280-2700
Free: 800-282-5835
Admissions: (402)280-2162
Fax: (402)280-2685
E-mail: admissions@creighton.edu
Web Site: http://www.creighton.edu/
President/CEO: Rev. John P. Schlegel, SJ
Registrar: John A. Krecek
Admissions: Don Bishop
Financial Aid: Robert D. Walker
Type: University **Sex:** Coed **Affiliation:** Roman Catholic (Jesuit) **Scores:** 100% SAT V 400+; 99% SAT M 400+; 26% ACT 18-23; 56% ACT 24-29 **% Accepted:** 87 **Admission Plans:** Deferred Admission **Application Deadline:** August 01 **Application Fee:** $40.00 **H.S. Requirements:** High school diploma required; GED accepted **Costs Per Year:** Application fee: $40. Comprehensive fee: $29,918 includes full-time tuition ($21,576), mandatory fees ($802), and college room and board ($7540). College room only: $4250. Room and board charges vary according to board plan and

housing facility. Part-time tuition: $675 per semester hour. Part-time mandatory fees: $134 per semester hour. **Scholarships:** Available **Calendar System:** Semester, Summer Session Available **Enrollment:** FT 3,731, PT 257, Grad 474 **Faculty:** FT 475, PT 174 **Student-Faculty Ratio:** 12:1 **Exams:** SAT I or ACT **% Receiving Financial Aid:** 57 **% Residing in College-Owned, -Operated, or -Affiliated Housing:** 56 **Library Holdings:** 481,848 **Regional Accreditation:** North Central Association of Colleges and Schools **Credit Hours For Degree:** 64 credits, Associates; 128 credits, Bachelors **ROTC:** Army, Air Force **Professional Accreditation:** AACSB, AACN, ABA, ACPhE, ADA, AOTA, APTA, AALS, CSWE, JRCEMT, LCMEAMA, NCATE **Intercollegiate Athletics:** Baseball M; Basketball M & W; Crew W; Cross-Country Running M & W; Golf M & W; Soccer M & W; Softball W; Tennis M & W; Volleyball W

DANA COLLEGE
2848 College Dr.
Blair, NE 68008-1099
Tel: (402)426-9000
Free: 800-444-3262
Admissions: (402)426-7220
Fax: (402)426-7386
E-mail: admissions@dana.edu
Web Site: http://www.dana.edu/
President/CEO: Dr. Myrvin Christopherson
Registrar: Melinda Stoner
Admissions: James Lynes
Financial Aid: Amy Lyons
Type: Four-Year College **Sex:** Coed **Affiliation:** Evangelical Lutheran Church in America **Scores:** 77.78% SAT V 400+; 88.89% SAT M 400+; 62.5% ACT 18-23; 29.5% ACT 24-29 **% Accepted:** 76 **Admission Plans:** Deferred Admission **Application Deadline:** Rolling **Application Fee:** $0.00 **H.S. Requirements:** High school diploma required; GED accepted **Costs Per Year:** Application fee: $0. Comprehensive fee: $22,770 includes full-time tuition ($16,850), mandatory fees ($600), and college room and board ($5320). College room only: $2060. Room and board charges vary according to board plan and housing facility. Part-time tuition: $510 per semester hour. Part-time mandatory fees: $35 per term. Part-time tuition and fees vary according to course load. **Scholarships:** Available **Calendar System:** 4-1-4, Summer Session Available **Enrollment:** FT 653, PT 23 **Faculty:** FT 42, PT 33 **Student-Faculty Ratio:** 12:1 **Exams:** ACT, SAT I or ACT **% Receiving Financial Aid:** 83 **% Residing in College-Owned, -Operated, or -Affiliated Housing:** 66 **Library Holdings:** 145,909 **Regional Accreditation:** North Central Association of Colleges and Schools **Credit Hours For Degree:** 128 semester hours, Bachelors **ROTC:** Army, Air Force **Professional Accreditation:** ACBSP, CSWE, NCATE **Intercollegiate Athletics:** Baseball M; Basketball M & W; Cross-Country Running M & W; Football M; Golf W; Soccer M & W; Softball W; Track and Field M & W; Volleyball W; Wrestling M

DOANE COLLEGE
1014 Boswell Ave.
Crete, NE 68333-2430
Tel: (402)826-2161
Free: 800-333-6263
Admissions: (402)826-8222
Fax: (402)826-8600
E-mail: admissions@doane.edu
Web Site: http://www.doane.edu/
President/CEO: Dr. Fred D. Brown
Registrar: Paula Valenta
Admissions: Kim Jacobs
Financial Aid: Janet Dodson
Type: Comprehensive **Sex:** Coed **Affiliation:** United Church of Christ **Scores:** 50.38% ACT 18-23; 35.38% ACT 24-29 **% Accepted:** 80 **Admission Plans:** Early Admission; Deferred Admission **Application Deadline:** Rolling **Application Fee:** $15.00 **H.S. Requirements:** High school diploma required; GED accepted **Costs Per Year:** Application fee: $15. Comprehensive fee: $22,458 includes full-time tuition ($17,186), mandatory fees ($350), and college room and board ($4922). College room only: $1850. Full-time tuition and fees vary according to location. Room and board charges vary according to board plan, housing facility, and location. Part-time tuition: $573 per credit hour. Part-time mandatory fees: $120 per year. Part-time tuition and fees vary according to degree level and location. **Scholarships:** Available **Calendar System:** 4-1-4, Summer Session Available **Enrollment:** FT 1,349, PT 247, Grad 798 **Faculty:** FT 77, PT 63 **Student-Faculty Ratio:** 10:1 **Exams:** SAT I or ACT **% Receiving Financial Aid:** 78 **Library Holdings:** 299,471 **Regional Accreditation:** North Central Association of Colleges and Schools **Credit Hours For Degree:** 132 credit hours, Bachelors **ROTC:** Army, Air Force **Professional Accreditation:** ACBSP, NCATE **Intercollegiate Athletics:** Baseball M; Basketball M & W; Cross-Country Running M & W; Football M; Golf M & W; Soccer M & W; Softball W; Tennis M & W; Track and Field M & W; Volleyball W

GRACE UNIVERSITY
1311 South Ninth St.
Omaha, NE 68108
Tel: (402)449-2800
Free: 800-383-1422
Admissions: (402)449-2831
Fax: (402)341-9587
E-mail: admissions@graceuniversity.edu
Web Site: http://www.graceuniversity.edu/
President/CEO: Dr. James P. Eckman
Admissions: Diane V. Lee
Financial Aid: Lydia Thompson
Type: Comprehensive **Sex:** Coed **Affiliation:** interdenominational **Admission Plans:** Early Admission; Deferred Admission **Application Fee:** $35.00 **H.S. Requirements:** High school diploma required; GED accepted **Costs Per Year:** Application fee: $35. Comprehensive fee: $17,380 includes full-time tuition ($11,700), mandatory fees ($280), and college room and board ($5400). College room only: $2400. Part-time tuition: $390 per credit hour. Part-time mandatory fees: $15 per term. **Scholarships:** Available **Calendar System:** Semester, Summer Session Available **Enrollment:** FT 375, PT 52, Grad 86 **Faculty:** FT 25, PT 25 **Student-Faculty Ratio:** 18:1 **Exams:** ACT **% Receiving Financial Aid:** 77 **% Residing in College-Owned, -Operated, or -Affiliated Housing:** 61 **Library Holdings:** 46,736 **Regional Accreditation:** North Central Association of Colleges and Schools **Credit Hours For Degree:** 64 credit hours, Associates; 128 credit hours, Bachelors **ROTC:** Army, Air Force **Professional Accreditation:** AABC **Intercollegiate Athletics:** Basketball M & W; Soccer M; Volleyball W

HAMILTON COLLEGE-LINCOLN
1821 K St., PO Box 82826
Lincoln, NE 68501-2826
Tel: (402)474-5315
Fax: (402)474-5302
E-mail: losc@ix.netcom.com
Web Site: http://www.hamiltonlincoln.com/
President/CEO: Todd J. Lardenoit
Registrar: Krystal Gabel
Admissions: Andy Bossler
Financial Aid: Jami Frazier
Type: Two-Year College **Sex:** Coed **Affiliation:** Quest Education Corporation **Admission Plans:** Open Admission; Early Admission **Application Fee:** $25.00 **H.S. Requirements:** High school diploma required; GED accepted **Scholarships:** Available **Calendar System:** Quarter, Summer Session Available **Faculty:** FT 13, PT 23 **Student-Faculty Ratio:** 19:1 **Exams:** Other **Library Holdings:** 7,500 **Credit Hours For Degree:** 112 credit hours, Associates **Professional Accreditation:** ACICS, AAMAE **Intercollegiate Athletics:** Basketball M & W; Golf M & W; Soccer M & W

HAMILTON COLLEGE-OMAHA
3350 North 90th St.
Omaha, NE 68134
Tel: (402)572-8500
Free: 800-642-1456
Fax: (402)573-1341
Web Site: http://www.hamiltonomaha.edu/
President/CEO: Ken Sigmon
Registrar: Linda Smith
Admissions: Mark Stoltenberger
Financial Aid: Sharon McDonald
Type: Two-Year College **Sex:** Coed **Affiliation:** Educational Medical, Inc **Admission Plans:** Early Admission; Deferred Admission **Application Fee:** $50.00 **H.S. Requirements:** High school diploma required; GED accepted **Calendar System:** Quarter, Summer Session Available **Enrollment:** FT 700 **Faculty:** FT 17, PT 18 **Student-Faculty Ratio:** 20:1 **Exams:** Other **Library**

Holdings: 4,800 **Credit Hours For Degree:** 113 credit hours, Associates **Professional Accreditation:** ACICS, AAMAE

HASTINGS COLLEGE
800 North Turner Ave.
Hastings, NE 68901-7696
Tel: (402)463-2402
Free: 800-532-7642
Admissions: (402)461-7320
Fax: (402)463-3002
E-mail: mmolliconi@hastings.edu
Web Site: http://www.hastings.edu/
President/CEO: Dr. Phillip L. Dudley, Jr.
Registrar: James Smith
Admissions: Mary Molliconi
Financial Aid: Ian Roberts
Type: Comprehensive **Sex:** Coed **Affiliation:** Presbyterian **Scores:** 99% SAT V 400+; 100% SAT M 400+; 38% ACT 18-23; 47% ACT 24-29 **% Accepted:** 79 **Application Deadline:** August 01 **Application Fee:** $20.00 **H.S. Requirements:** High school diploma required; GED accepted **Costs Per Year:** Application fee: $20. Comprehensive fee: $22,218 includes full-time tuition ($16,578), mandatory fees ($690), and college room and board ($4950). College room only: $2116. Full-time tuition and fees vary according to course level and program. Room and board charges vary according to board plan and housing facility. Part-time tuition: $686 per semester hour. Part-time mandatory fees: $182 per term. Part-time tuition and fees vary according to course level, course load, and program. **Scholarships:** Available **Calendar System:** 4-1-4, Summer Session Available **Enrollment:** FT 1,121, PT 23, Grad 45 **Faculty:** FT 79, PT 42 **Student-Faculty Ratio:** 12:1 **Exams:** SAT I or ACT **% Receiving Financial Aid:** 75 **% Residing in College-Owned, -Operated, or -Affiliated Housing:** 67 **Library Holdings:** 113,318 **Regional Accreditation:** North Central Association of Colleges and Schools **Credit Hours For Degree:** 127 semester hours, Bachelors **Professional Accreditation:** NASM, NCATE **Intercollegiate Athletics:** Baseball M; Basketball M & W; Cross-Country Running M & W; Football M; Golf M & W; Soccer M & W; Softball W; Tennis M & W; Track and Field M & W; Volleyball W

ITT TECHNICAL INSTITUTE
9814 M St.
Omaha, NE 68127-2056
Tel: (402)331-2900
Free: 800-677-9260
Fax: (402)331-9495
Web Site: http://www.itt-tech.edu/
President/CEO: Jerome S. Padak
Admissions: Jerome S. Padak
Type: Two-Year College **Sex:** Coed **Affiliation:** ITT Educational Services, Inc **Admission Plans:** Deferred Admission **Application Deadline:** Rolling **Application Fee:** $100.00 **H.S. Requirements:** High school diploma required; GED accepted **Costs Per Year:** Application fee: $100. **Scholarships:** Available **Calendar System:** Quarter, Summer Session Not available **Exams:** Other **Credit Hours For Degree:** 96 credit hours, Associates **Professional Accreditation:** ACICS

LITTLE PRIEST TRIBAL COLLEGE
PO Box 270
Winnebago, NE 68071
Tel: (402)878-2380
Fax: (402)878-2355
Web Site: http://www.lptc.bia.edu/
President/CEO: Louis LaRose
Admissions: Karen Kemling
Type: Two-Year College **Scholarships:** Available **Enrollment:** FT 67, PT 63 **Faculty:** FT 4, PT 12 **Student-Faculty Ratio:** 11:1 **Regional Accreditation:** North Central Association of Colleges and Schools

METROPOLITAN COMMUNITY COLLEGE
PO Box 3777
Omaha, NE 68103-0777
Tel: (402)457-2400
Free: 800-228-9553
Admissions: (402)457-2717
Fax: (402)457-2564
E-mail: bnicks@mccneb.edu
Web Site: http://www.mccneb.edu/
President/CEO: Dr. Jerry Moskus
Admissions: Becky Nicks
Financial Aid: Danni Warrick
Type: Two-Year College **Sex:** Coed **Affiliation:** Nebraska Coordinating Commission for Postsecondary Education **% Accepted:** 100 **Admission Plans:** Open Admission; Early Admission **Application Deadline:** Rolling **Application Fee:** $0.00 **H.S. Requirements:** High school diploma or equivalent not required. For allied health programs, pre-professional associate of science: High school diploma required; GED accepted **Costs Per Year:** Application fee: $0. State resident tuition: $1733 full-time, $38.50 per credit hour part-time. Nonresident tuition: $2610 full-time, $71 per credit hour part-time. Mandatory fees: $135 full-time, $3 per credit hour part-time. **Scholarships:** Available **Calendar System:** Quarter, Summer Session Available **Enrollment:** FT 4,798, PT 7,663 **Faculty:** FT 177, PT 541 **Student-Faculty Ratio:** 13:1 **Library Holdings:** 41,161 **Regional Accreditation:** North Central Association of Colleges and Schools **Credit Hours For Degree:** 96 quarter hours, Associates **ROTC:** Army **Professional Accreditation:** ACF, ADA, ACBSP, CARC, NLN

MID-PLAINS COMMUNITY COLLEGE
601 West State Farm Rd.
North Platte, NE 69101
Tel: (308)535-3600
Free: 800-658-4348
Admissions: (308)535-3610
Fax: (308)532-8590
Web Site: http://www.mpcca.cc.ne.us/
President/CEO: Michael Chipps
Registrar: Mari Jo Widger
Admissions: Brenda Costin
Financial Aid: Ted Fellers
Type: Two-Year College **Sex:** Coed **Admission Plans:** Open Admission **Application Fee:** $0.00 **H.S. Requirements:** High school diploma required; GED accepted **Calendar System:** Semester, Summer Session Available **Enrollment:** FT 1,083, PT 2,001 **Faculty:** FT 62, PT 131 **Student-Faculty Ratio:** 14:1 **Exams:** ACT, Other **% Residing in College-Owned, -Operated, or -Affiliated Housing:** 8 **Library Holdings:** 64,284 **Regional Accreditation:** North Central Association of Colleges and Schools **Credit Hours For Degree:** 60 semester hours, Associates **Professional Accreditation:** ADA, NAACLS **Intercollegiate Athletics:** Baseball M; Basketball M & W; Golf M; Softball W; Volleyball W

MIDLAND LUTHERAN COLLEGE
900 North Clarkson St.
Fremont, NE 68025-4200
Tel: (402)721-5480
Free: 800-642-8382
Admissions: (402)941-6521
Fax: (402)721-0250
E-mail: watson@mlc.edu
Web Site: http://www.mlc.edu/
President/CEO: Dr. Steven E. Titus
Registrar: Jennifer Verhein
Admissions: Doug G. Watson
Financial Aid: Michelle Reeson
Type: Four-Year College **Sex:** Coed **Affiliation:** Lutheran **% Accepted:** 86 **Admission Plans:** Early Admission **Application Deadline:** Rolling **Application Fee:** $30.00 **H.S. Requirements:** High school diploma required; GED accepted **Costs Per Year:** Application fee: $30. Comprehensive fee: $24,460 includes full-time tuition ($19,510) and college room and board ($4950). College room only: $2190. **Scholarships:** Available **Calendar System:** 4-1-4, Summer Session Available **Enrollment:** FT 888, PT 21 **Faculty:** FT 61, PT 31 **Student-Faculty Ratio:** 14:1 **Exams:** SAT I or ACT **% Receiving Financial Aid:** 84 **% Residing in College-Owned, -Operated, or -Affiliated Housing:** 62 **Library Holdings:** 110,000 **Regional Accreditation:** North Central Association of Colleges and Schools **Credit Hours For Degree:** 64 credit hours, Associates; 128 credit hours, Bachelors **Professional Accreditation:** NLN **Intercollegiate Athletics:** Baseball M;

Basketball M & W; Cross-Country Running M & W; Football M; Golf M & W; Soccer M & W; Softball W; Tennis M & W; Track and Field M & W; Volleyball W

MYOTHERAPY INSTITUTE
6020 South 58th St.
Lincoln, NE 68516
Tel: (402)421-7410
Free: 800-896-3363
Fax: (402)421-6736
E-mail: admissions@myomassage.net
Web Site: http://www.myotherapy.edu/
President/CEO: Sue Kozisek
Admissions: Gerri Allen
Type: Two-Year College **Sex:** Coed **Professional Accreditation:** ACCSCT

NEBRASKA CHRISTIAN COLLEGE
1800 Syracuse Ave.
Norfolk, NE 68701-2458
Tel: (402)379-5000
Web Site: http://www.nechristian.edu/
President/CEO: Rich Milliken
Registrar: June Pieper
Financial Aid: Chris Lahm
Type: Four-Year College **Sex:** Coed **Affiliation:** Christian Churches and Churches of Christ **Scores:** 42% ACT 18-23; 46% ACT 24-29 **Application Fee:** $25.00 **H.S. Requirements:** High school diploma required; GED accepted **Scholarships:** Available **Calendar System:** Semester, Summer Session Not available **Enrollment:** FT 152, PT 15 **Student-Faculty Ratio:** 17:1 **Exams:** ACT **% Receiving Financial Aid:** 88 **% Residing in College-Owned, -Operated, or -Affiliated Housing:** 85 **Library Holdings:** 250,000 **Credit Hours For Degree:** 64 semester hours, Associates; 130 semester hours, Bachelors **Professional Accreditation:** AABC **Intercollegiate Athletics:** Basketball M & W; Soccer M; Volleyball W

NEBRASKA COLLEGE OF TECHNICAL AGRICULTURE
RR3, Box 23A
Curtis, NE 69025-9205
Tel: (308)367-4124
Free: 800-3CU-RTIS
Fax: (308)367-5203
E-mail: gsundquist1@unl.edu
Web Site: http://www.ncta.unl.edu/
President/CEO: Gerald Sundquist
Registrar: Gerald Sundquist
Admissions: Gerald Sundquist
Financial Aid: David Jibben
Type: Two-Year College **Sex:** Coed **Affiliation:** University of Nebraska System **Admission Plans:** Open Admission; Early Admission **Application Fee:** $10.00 **H.S. Requirements:** High school diploma required; GED accepted **Costs Per Year:** Application fee: $10. State resident tuition: $3006 full-time. Nonresident tuition: $6012 full-time. Mandatory fees: $433 full-time. College room and board: $4149. College room only: $1824. **Scholarships:** Available **Calendar System:** Miscellaneous, Summer Session Not available **Faculty:** FT 17, PT 3 **Exams:** ACT **% Residing in College-Owned, -Operated, or -Affiliated Housing:** 44 **Library Holdings:** 5,500 **Regional Accreditation:** North Central Association of Colleges and Schools **Credit Hours For Degree:** 72 semester hours, Associates **Intercollegiate Athletics:** Basketball M & W

NEBRASKA INDIAN COMMUNITY COLLEGE
PO Box 428
Macy, NE 68039-0428
Tel: (402)837-5078; 888-843-6432
Admissions: (402)344-8428
Fax: (402)878-2522
Web Site: http://www.thenicc.edu/
President/CEO: Dr. Ross Primm
Registrar: Sarah Smith
Admissions: Ed Stevens
Financial Aid: Shelly Baxter
Type: Two-Year College **Sex:** Coed **Admission Plans:** Open Admission; Early Admission; Deferred Admission **Application Fee:** $10.00 **H.S. Requirements:** High school diploma required; GED accepted **Scholarships:** Available **Calendar System:** Semester, Summer Session Available **Enrollment:** FT 97, PT 93 **Faculty:** FT 6, PT 32 **Student-Faculty Ratio:** 8:1 **Regional Accreditation:** North Central Association of Colleges and Schools **Credit Hours For Degree:** 90 quarter hours, Associates

NEBRASKA METHODIST COLLEGE
720 N. 87th St.
Omaha, NE 68114
Tel: (402)354-4879
Free: 800-335-5510
Admissions: (402)354-7205
Fax: (402)354-4819
E-mail: deann.sterner@methodistcollege.edu
Web Site: http://www.methodistcollege.edu/
President/CEO: Dr. Dennis Joslin
Registrar: Lanny Morgan
Admissions: Deann Sterner
Financial Aid: Brenda Boyd
Type: Comprehensive **Sex:** Coed **Affiliation:** United Methodist Church **Scores:** 70% ACT 18-23; 20% ACT 24-29 **% Accepted:** 50 **Admission Plans:** Deferred Admission **Application Deadline:** April 01 **Application Fee:** $25.00 **H.S. Requirements:** High school diploma required; GED accepted **Costs Per Year:** Application fee: $25. Tuition: $11,340 full-time, $378 per credit hour part-time. Mandatory fees: $600 full-time, $20 per credit hour part-time. College room only: $2270. **Scholarships:** Available **Calendar System:** Semester, Summer Session Available **Enrollment:** FT 333, PT 126, Grad 65 **Faculty:** FT 33, PT 24 **Student-Faculty Ratio:** 10:1 **Exams:** SAT I or ACT **% Receiving Financial Aid:** 72 **% Residing in College-Owned, -Operated, or -Affiliated Housing:** 20 **Library Holdings:** 8,656 **Regional Accreditation:** North Central Association of Colleges and Schools **Credit Hours For Degree:** 82 credit hours, Associates; 127 credit hours, Bachelors **ROTC:** Army **Professional Accreditation:** AACN, CARC, JRCEDMS, NLN

NEBRASKA WESLEYAN UNIVERSITY
5000 Saint Paul Ave.
Lincoln, NE 68504-2796
Tel: (402)466-2371
Free: 800-541-3818
Admissions: (402)465-2218
Fax: (402)465-2179
E-mail: admissions@nebrwesleyan.edu
Web Site: http://www.nebrwesleyan.edu/
President/CEO: Dr. Jeanie Watson
Registrar: Patricia Hall
Admissions: Patty Karthauser
Financial Aid: Claire D. Fredstrom
Type: Comprehensive **Sex:** Coed **Affiliation:** United Methodist **Scores:** 47% ACT 18-23; 45% ACT 24-29 **% Accepted:** 84 **Admission Plans:** Early Admission; Early Decision Plan; Deferred Admission **Application Deadline:** August 15 **Application Fee:** $20.00 **H.S. Requirements:** High school diploma required; GED accepted **Costs Per Year:** Application fee: $20. Comprehensive fee: $23,425 includes full-time tuition ($18,100), mandatory fees ($310), and college room and board ($5015). Room and board charges vary according to board plan and housing facility. Part-time tuition: $683 per credit hour. Part-time tuition varies according to class time, course load, degree level, location, and program. **Scholarships:** Available **Calendar System:** Semester, Summer Session Available **Enrollment:** FT 1,606, PT 236, Grad 174 **Faculty:** FT 102, PT 123 **Student-Faculty Ratio:** 13:1 **Exams:** SAT I or ACT **% Receiving Financial Aid:** 68 **% Residing in College-Owned, -Operated, or -Affiliated Housing:** 54 **Library Holdings:** 178,531 **Regional Accreditation:** North Central Association of Colleges and Schools **Credit Hours For Degree:** 126 hours, Bachelors **ROTC:** Army, Air Force **Professional Accreditation:** ACBSP, NASM, NCATE, NLN **Intercollegiate Athletics:** Baseball M; Basketball M & W; Cross-Country Running M & W; Football M; Golf M & W; Soccer M & W; Softball W; Tennis M & W; Track and Field M & W; Volleyball W

NORTHEAST COMMUNITY COLLEGE
801 East Benjamin Ave, PO Box 469
Norfolk, NE 68702-0469
Tel: (402)371-2020
Admissions: (402)844-7258
Fax: (402)644-0650
Web Site: http://www.northeastcollege.com/
President/CEO: Dr. Bill R. Path

Registrar: Kathy Stover
Admissions: Maureen Baker
Financial Aid: Joan Zanders
Type: Two-Year College **Sex:** Coed **Affiliation:** Nebraska Coordinating Commission for Postsecondary Education **Admission Plans:** Open Admission; Early Admission **Application Deadline:** Rolling **Application Fee:** $0.00 **H.S. Requirements:** High school diploma required; GED accepted **Costs Per Year:** Application fee: $0. State resident tuition: $1770 full-time, $59 per credit hour part-time. Nonresident tuition: $2,212 full-time, $73.75 per credit hour part-time. Mandatory fees: $315 full-time, $10.50 per credit hour part-time. College room and board: $4586. **Scholarships:** Available **Calendar System:** Semester, Summer Session Available **Enrollment:** FT 2,127, PT 2,974 **Faculty:** FT 101, PT 236 **Student-Faculty Ratio:** 17:1 **% Residing in College-Owned, -Operated, or -Affiliated Housing:** 11 **Library Holdings:** 28,000 **Regional Accreditation:** North Central Association of Colleges and Schools **Credit Hours For Degree:** 60 semester hours, Associates **Professional Accreditation:** APTA, NLN **Intercollegiate Athletics:** Basketball M & W; Cheerleading W

PERU STATE COLLEGE
PO Box 10
Peru, NE 68421
Tel: (402)872-3815
Admissions: (402)872-2221
E-mail: mwillis@oakmail.peru.edu
Web Site: http://www.peru.edu/
President/CEO: Dr. Ben Johnson
Registrar: Dr. DiAnna Loy
Admissions: Micki Willis
Financial Aid: Diana Lind
Type: Comprehensive **Sex:** Coed **Affiliation:** Nebraska State College System **Scores:** 51% ACT 18-23; 15% ACT 24-29 **% Accepted:** 29 **Admission Plans:** Open Admission; Early Admission; Deferred Admission **Application Deadline:** Rolling **Application Fee:** $0.00 **H.S. Requirements:** High school diploma required; GED accepted **Costs Per Year:** Application fee: $0. Area resident tuition: $97.75 per credit hour part-time. State resident tuition: $2933 full-time, $195.50 per credit hour part-time. Nonresident tuition: $5865 full-time. Mandatory fees: $706 full-time. Part-time tuition varies according to course load, location, and reciprocity agreements. College room and board: $4486. Room and board charges vary according to board plan and housing facility. **Scholarships:** Available **Calendar System:** Semester, Summer Session Available **Enrollment:** FT 1,017, PT 693, Grad 249 **Faculty:** FT 40, PT 90 **Student-Faculty Ratio:** 20:1 **Exams:** SAT I or ACT **Library Holdings:** 177,373 **Regional Accreditation:** North Central Association of Colleges and Schools **Credit Hours For Degree:** 125 semester hours, Bachelors **ROTC:** Army, Air Force **Professional Accreditation:** NCATE **Intercollegiate Athletics:** Baseball M; Basketball M & W; Cross-Country Running W; Football M; Golf W; Softball W; Volleyball W

SOUTHEAST COMMUNITY COLLEGE, BEATRICE CAMPUS
4771 W. Scott Rd.
Beatrice, NE 68310-7042
Tel: (402)228-3468
Free: 800-233-5027
Fax: (402)228-2218
Web Site: http://www.southeast.edu/
President/CEO: Dr. Dennis Headrick
Registrar: Lila Thomas
Admissions: Mary Ann Harms
Type: Two-Year College **Sex:** Coed **Affiliation:** Southeast Community College System **Admission Plans:** Open Admission; Early Admission; Deferred Admission **Application Fee:** $0.00 **H.S. Requirements:** High school diploma required; GED accepted **Scholarships:** Available **Calendar System:** Semester, Summer Session Available **Faculty:** FT 65, PT 20 **Student-Faculty Ratio:** 12:1 **Exams:** Other, SAT I or ACT **% Residing in College-Owned, -Operated, or -Affiliated Housing:** 22 **Library Holdings:** 13,287 **Regional Accreditation:** North Central Association of Colleges and Schools **Credit Hours For Degree:** 60 credit hours, Associates **Professional Accreditation:** ACBSP, NLN **Intercollegiate Athletics:** Basketball M & W; Golf M; Volleyball W

SOUTHEAST COMMUNITY COLLEGE, LINCOLN CAMPUS
8800 O St.
Lincoln, NE 68520-1299
Tel: (402)471-3333
Free: 800-642-4075
Admissions: (402)437-2619
Web Site: http://www.southeast.edu/
President/CEO: Jeanette Volker
Registrar: Robin Moore
Admissions: David Sonenberg
Financial Aid: David Sonenberg
Type: Two-Year College **Sex:** Coed **Affiliation:** Southeast Community College System **Admission Plans:** Open Admission; Early Admission; Deferred Admission **Application Fee:** $0.00 **H.S. Requirements:** High school diploma required; GED accepted **Costs Per Year:** Application fee: $0. State resident tuition: $1755 full-time, $39 per quarter hour part-time. Nonresident tuition: $2138 full-time, $47.50 per quarter hour part-time. Mandatory fees: $45 full-time, $1 per quarter hour part-time. Full-time tuition and fees vary according to course load. Part-time tuition and fees vary according to course load. **Scholarships:** Available **Calendar System:** Quarter, Summer Session Available **Enrollment:** FT 4,095, PT 3,822 **Faculty:** FT 138, PT 410 **Student-Faculty Ratio:** 15:1 **Exams:** SAT I or ACT **Library Holdings:** 14,081 **Regional Accreditation:** North Central Association of Colleges and Schools **Credit Hours For Degree:** 90 quarter credits, Associates **Professional Accreditation:** ARCEST, ACF, ADA, ACBSP, CARC, JRCERT, NAACLS, NLN

SOUTHEAST COMMUNITY COLLEGE, MILFORD CAMPUS
600 State St.
Milford, NE 68405-8498
Tel: (402)761-2131
Free: 800-933-7223
Web Site: http://www.southeast.edu/
President/CEO: Larry Shaw
Registrar: Donna Havener
Admissions: Larry E. Meyer
Financial Aid: Merlyn Williams
Type: Two-Year College **Sex:** Coed **Affiliation:** Southeast Community College System **Admission Plans:** Open Admission **H.S. Requirements:** High school diploma required; GED accepted **Scholarships:** Available **Calendar System:** Quarter, Summer Session Not available **Enrollment:** FT 890, PT 32 **Faculty:** FT 86, PT 3 **Student-Faculty Ratio:** 20:1 **Exams:** ACT, SAT I **% Residing in College-Owned, -Operated, or -Affiliated Housing:** 33 **Library Holdings:** 10,000 **Regional Accreditation:** North Central Association of Colleges and Schools **Credit Hours For Degree:** 108 credits, Associates **Professional Accreditation:** ACBSP

UNION COLLEGE
3800 South 48th St.
Lincoln, NE 68506-4300
Tel: (402)486-2600
Free: 800-228-4600
Admissions: (402)486-2504
Fax: (402)486-2895
E-mail: ucenroll@ucollege.edu
Web Site: http://www.ucollege.edu/
President/CEO: Dr. David Smith
Registrar: Osa Berg
Admissions: Robert Weaver
Financial Aid: Jack Burdick
Type: Comprehensive **Sex:** Coed **Affiliation:** Seventh-day Adventist **Scores:** 50.32% ACT 18-23; 33.55% ACT 24-29 **% Accepted:** 43 **Application Deadline:** Rolling **Application Fee:** $0.00 **H.S. Requirements:** High school diploma required; GED accepted **Costs Per Year:** Application fee: $0. Comprehensive fee: $19,448 includes full-time tuition ($14,790), mandatory fees ($440), and college room and board ($4218). College room only: $2898. Part-time tuition: $625 per semester hour. **Scholarships:** Available **Calendar System:** Semester, Summer Session Available **Enrollment:** FT 757, PT 128, Grad 45 **Faculty:** FT 57, PT 41 **Student-Faculty Ratio:** 13:1 **Exams:** ACT **% Receiving Financial Aid:** 61 **% Residing in College-Owned, -Operated, or -Affiliated Housing:** 13 **Library Holdings:** 147,813 **Regional Accreditation:** North Central Association of Colleges and Schools **Credit Hours For Degree:** 64 semester hours, Associates; 128 semester hours, Bachelors **Professional Accreditation:** AACN, NCATE **Intercollegiate Athletics:** Basketball M & W; Volleyball W

UNIVERSITY OF NEBRASKA AT KEARNEY
905 West 25th St.
Kearney, NE 68849-0001

Tel: (308)865-8441
Free: 800-532-7639
Admissions: (308)865-8702
Fax: (308)865-8987
E-mail: admissionsug@plattc.unk.edu
Web Site: http://www.unk.edu/
President/CEO: Douglas Kristensen
Registrar: Kim Schipporeit
Admissions: Disty Newton
Financial Aid: Mary Sommers
Type: Comprehensive **Sex:** Coed **Affiliation:** University of Nebraska System **Scores:** 84% SAT V 400+; 83% SAT M 400+; 55% ACT 18-23; 30% ACT 24-29 **% Accepted:** 84 **Application Deadline:** Rolling **Application Fee:** $45.00 **H.S. Requirements:** High school diploma required; GED accepted **Costs Per Year:** Application fee: $45. State resident tuition: $3668 full-time, $122.25 per hour part-time. Nonresident tuition: $7508 full-time, $250.25 per hour part-time. Mandatory fees: $825 full-time, $16.25 per hour part-time. Full-time tuition and fees vary according to course load and degree level. Part-time tuition and fees vary according to course load and degree level. College room and board: $5326. Room and board charges vary according to board plan and housing facility. **Scholarships:** Available **Calendar System:** Semester, Summer Session Available **Enrollment:** FT 4,895, PT 486, Grad 1,064 **Faculty:** FT 306, PT 74 **Student-Faculty Ratio:** 17:1 **Exams:** SAT I and SAT II or ACT **% Receiving Financial Aid:** 59 **% Residing in College-Owned, -Operated, or -Affiliated Housing:** 33 **Library Holdings:** 320,915 **Regional Accreditation:** North Central Association of Colleges and Schools **Credit Hours For Degree:** 125 semester hours, Bachelors **Professional Accreditation:** AAFCS, ACA, ASLHA, CSWE, JRCEPAT, NAIT, NASM, NCATE **Intercollegiate Athletics:** Baseball M; Basketball M & W; Cross-Country Running M & W; Football M; Golf M & W; Softball W; Swimming and Diving W; Tennis M & W; Track and Field M & W; Volleyball W; Wrestling M

UNIVERSITY OF NEBRASKA-LINCOLN
14th and R Sts.
Lincoln, NE 68588
Tel: (402)472-7211
Free: 800-742-8800
Admissions: (402)472-2030
Fax: (402)472-0670
E-mail: admissions@unc.edu
Web Site: http://www.unl.edu/
President/CEO: Harvey Perlman
Registrar: Dr. Earl W. Hawkey
Admissions: Alan Cerveny
Financial Aid: Craig Munier
Type: University **Sex:** Coed **Affiliation:** University of Nebraska System **Scores:** 97% SAT V 400+; 98% SAT M 400+; 38% ACT 18-23; 43% ACT 24-29 **% Accepted:** 75 **Application Deadline:** May 01 **Application Fee:** $45.00 **H.S. Requirements:** High school diploma required; GED accepted **Costs Per Year:** Application fee: $45. State resident tuition: $4530 full-time, $151 per credit hour part-time. Nonresident tuition: $13,440 full-time, $448 per credit hour part-time. Mandatory fees: $1010 full-time, $8.50 per credit hour part-time, $202.10 per term part-time. Full-time tuition and fees vary according to course load. Part-time tuition and fees vary according to course load. College room and board: $6008. College room only: $3239. Room and board charges vary according to board plan and housing facility. **Scholarships:** Available **Calendar System:** Semester, Summer Session Available **Enrollment:** FT 15,768, PT 1,269, Grad 4,241 **Faculty:** FT 1,048, PT 10 **Student-Faculty Ratio:** 19:1 **Exams:** ACT, SAT I and SAT II or ACT **% Receiving Financial Aid:** 46 **% Residing in College-Owned, -Operated, or -Affiliated Housing:** 24 **Library Holdings:** 3,317,154 **Regional Accreditation:** North Central Association of Colleges and Schools **Credit Hours For Degree:** 71 credit hours, Associates; 125 credit hours, Bachelors **ROTC:** Army, Navy, Air Force **Professional Accreditation:** AACSB, ABET, ACEJMC, AAMFT, AAFCS, ABA, ACCE, ADA, ADtA, ACSP, APA, ASLHA, AALS, FIDER, NASAD, NASM, NAST, NCATE **Intercollegiate Athletics:** Baseball M; Basketball M & W; Bowling M; Crew M & W; Cross-Country Running M & W; Fencing M & W; Football M; Golf M & W; Gymnastics M & W; Riflery W; Soccer W; Softball W; Swimming and Diving W; Tennis M & W; Track and Field M & W; Volleyball W; Wrestling M

UNIVERSITY OF NEBRASKA MEDICAL CENTER
Nebraska Medical Center
Omaha, NE 68198
Tel: (402)559-4000
Free: 800-626-8431
Admissions: (402)559-6409
Fax: (402)559-6796
Web Site: http://www.unmc.edu/
President/CEO: Dr. Harold M. Maurer
Registrar: Judith D. Walker
Admissions: Judith Walker
Financial Aid: Judith Walker
Type: Two-Year Upper Division **Sex:** Coed **Affiliation:** University of Nebraska System **Admission Plans:** Preferred Admission **Application Fee:** $45.00 **H.S. Requirements:** High school diploma required; GED accepted **Costs Per Year:** Application fee: $45. State resident tuition: $6685 full-time, $191 per credit hour part-time. Nonresident tuition: $16,591 full-time, $559.75 per credit hour part-time. Mandatory fees: $733 full-time. Full-time tuition and fees vary according to course level, course load, and program. Part-time tuition varies according to program. **Scholarships:** Available **Calendar System:** Semester, Summer Session Available **Enrollment:** FT 779, PT 72, Grad 1,225 **Faculty:** FT 783, PT 224 **% Receiving Financial Aid:** 70 **Library Holdings:** 241,551 **Regional Accreditation:** North Central Association of Colleges and Schools **Credit Hours For Degree:** 131 semester hours, Bachelors **ROTC:** Army, Air Force **Professional Accreditation:** ACPE, AACN, ACPhE, ADA, ADtA, APTA, CEPH, JRCEDMS, JRCERT, JRCNMT, LCMEAMA, NAACLS

UNIVERSITY OF NEBRASKA AT OMAHA
6001 Dodge St.
Omaha, NE 68182
Tel: (402)554-2200
Admissions: (402)554-2416
Fax: (402)554-3472
E-mail: jadams@mail.unomaha.edu
Web Site: http://www.unomaha.edu/
President/CEO: Nancy Belck
Registrar: Dr. Wade Robinson
Admissions: Jolene Adams
Financial Aid: Randy Sell
Type: University **Sex:** Coed **Affiliation:** University of Nebraska System **Scores:** 95.7% SAT V 400+; 94.2% SAT M 400+; 53.7% ACT 18-23; 32.3% ACT 24-29 **% Accepted:** 89 **Admission Plans:** Deferred Admission **Application Deadline:** August 01 **Application Fee:** $45.00 **H.S. Requirements:** High school diploma required; GED accepted **Costs Per Year:** Application fee: $45. State resident tuition: $4133 full-time, $137.75 per semester hour part-time. Nonresident tuition: $12,180 full-time, $406 per semester hour part-time. Mandatory fees: $692 full-time, $19.55 per semester hour part-time, $81.50 per term part-time. Full-time tuition and fees vary according to course load and student level. Part-time tuition and fees vary according to course load and student level. College room and board: $6140. College room only: $3690. Room and board charges vary according to board plan. **Scholarships:** Available **Calendar System:** Semester, Summer Session Available **Enrollment:** FT 8,532, PT 2,797, Grad 2,764 **Faculty:** FT 482, PT 360 **Student-Faculty Ratio:** 18:1 **Exams:** SAT I or ACT **% Receiving Financial Aid:** 44 **% Residing in College-Owned, -Operated, or -Affiliated Housing:** 9 **Library Holdings:** 700,000 **Regional Accreditation:** North Central Association of Colleges and Schools **Credit Hours For Degree:** 125 semester hours, Bachelors **ROTC:** Army, Air Force **Professional Accreditation:** AACSB, ABET, ACA, ASLHA, CAA, CEPH, CSWE, JRCEPAT, NASAD, NASM, NASPAA, NCATE **Intercollegiate Athletics:** Baseball M; Basketball M & W; Cross-Country Running W; Football M; Golf W; Ice Hockey M; Soccer W; Softball W; Swimming and Diving W; Tennis W; Volleyball W; Wrestling M

VATTEROTT COLLEGE (OMAHA)
225 North 80th St.
Omaha, NE 68114
Tel: (402)392-1300
Fax: (402)392-2828
Web Site: http://www.vatterott-college.edu/
President/CEO: John Vatterott, Sr.
Registrar: Kathy Gilfillan
Admissions: Dr. James G. Hadley
Financial Aid: Bradley Dolittle
Type: Two-Year College **Sex:** Coed **Admission Plans:** Early Admission; Deferred Admission **Application Fee:** $0.00 **H.S. Requirements:** High school diploma required; GED accepted **Scholarships:** Available **Calendar**

System: Semester, Summer Session Available **Faculty:** FT 20, PT 1 **Student-Faculty Ratio:** 14:1 **Exams:** Other, SAT I or ACT **Library Holdings:** 1,900 **Credit Hours For Degree:** 100 quarter hours, Associates **Professional Accreditation:** ABHES, ACCSCT, ADA

VATTEROTT COLLEGE (OMAHA-SPRING VALLEY)
11818 I St.
Omaha, NE 68137
Tel: (402)891-9411
Fax: (402)891-9413
Web Site: http://www.vatterott-college.edu/
President/CEO: Scott Broady
Type: Two-Year College **Sex:** Coed **Calendar System:** Semester **Professional Accreditation:** ACCSCT

WAYNE STATE COLLEGE
1111 Main St.
Wayne, NE 68787
Tel: (402)375-7000
Admissions: (402)375-7234
Fax: (402)375-7204
E-mail: admit1@wsc.edu
Web Site: http://www.wsc.edu/
President/CEO: Dr. Richard Collings
Registrar: Lynette Lentz
Admissions: R. Lincoln Morris
Financial Aid: Kyle Rose
Type: Comprehensive **Sex:** Coed **Affiliation:** Nebraska State College System **Scores:** 50% ACT 18-23; 30% ACT 24-29 **% Accepted:** 100 **Admission Plans:** Open Admission; Deferred Admission **Application Deadline:** Rolling **Application Fee:** $30.00 **H.S. Requirements:** High school diploma required; GED accepted **Costs Per Year:** Application fee: $30. State resident tuition: $2933 full-time, $97.75 per credit hour part-time. Nonresident tuition: $5865 full-time, $195.50 per credit hour part-time. Mandatory fees: $870 full-time, $34.75 per credit hour part-time. Full-time tuition and fees vary according to course level and course load. Part-time tuition and fees vary according to course level and course load. College room and board: $4300. College room only: $2080. Room and board charges vary according to board plan and housing facility. **Scholarships:** Available **Calendar System:** Semester, Summer Session Available **Enrollment:** FT 2,483, PT 223, Grad 616 **Faculty:** FT 126, PT 79 **Student-Faculty Ratio:** 18:1 **% Receiving Financial Aid:** 62 **% Residing in College-Owned, -Operated, or -Affiliated Housing:** 42 **Library Holdings:** 147,205 **Regional Accreditation:** North Central Association of Colleges and Schools **Credit Hours For Degree:** 125 semester hours, Bachelors **ROTC:** Army **Professional Accreditation:** AAFCS, NCATE **Intercollegiate Athletics:** Baseball M; Basketball M & W; Cross-Country Running M & W; Football M; Golf M & W; Rugby M & W; Soccer M & W; Softball W; Track and Field M & W; Volleyball W

WESTERN NEBRASKA COMMUNITY COLLEGE
371 College Dr.
Sidney, NE 69162
Tel: (308)254-5450
Free: 800-348-4435
Admissions: (308)635-6015
Fax: (308)254-7444
E-mail: rhovey@wncc.net
Web Site: http://www.wncc.net/
President/CEO: Deanna Trowbridge
Registrar: Roger Hovey
Admissions: Troy Archuleta
Financial Aid: Penny James
Type: Two-Year College **Sex:** Coed **Affiliation:** Western Community College Area System **Admission Plans:** Open Admission **Application Fee:** $0.00 **H.S. Requirements:** High school diploma required; GED accepted **Scholarships:** Available **Calendar System:** Semester, Summer Session Available **Faculty:** FT 66, PT 292 **Student-Faculty Ratio:** 15:1 **Exams:** Other, SAT I and SAT II or ACT **% Residing in College-Owned, -Operated, or -Affiliated Housing:** 5 **Library Holdings:** 34,539 **Regional Accreditation:** North Central Association of Colleges and Schools **Credit Hours For Degree:** 60 semester hours, Associates **Professional Accreditation:** AHIMA **Intercollegiate Athletics:** Baseball M; Basketball M & W; Soccer M & W; Softball W; Volleyball W

YORK COLLEGE
1125 East 8th St.
York, NE 68467
Tel: (402)363-5600
Free: 800-950-9675
Admissions: (402)363-5608
Fax: (402)363-5666
E-mail: tjmartin@york.edu
Web Site: http://www.york.edu/
President/CEO: Dr. Wayne Baker
Admissions: Tod Martin
Type: Four-Year College **Sex:** Coed **Affiliation:** Church of Christ **Scores:** 100% SAT V 400+; 83% SAT M 400+; 57% ACT 18-23; 28% ACT 24-29 **% Accepted:** 99 **Admission Plans;** Early Admission; Deferred Admission **Application Deadline:** Rolling **Application Fee:** $20.00 **H.S. Requirements:** High school diploma required; GED accepted **Costs Per Year:** Application fee: $20. Comprehensive fee: $16,330 includes full-time tuition ($11,400), mandatory fees ($1030), and college room and board ($3900). Full-time tuition and fees vary according to course load. Room and board charges vary according to board plan and housing facility. Part-time tuition: $355 per credit hour. Part-time mandatory fees: $177 per credit hour. Part-time tuition and fees vary according to course load. **Scholarships:** Available **Calendar System:** Semester, Summer Session Available **Enrollment:** FT 412, PT 38 **Faculty:** FT 33, PT 25 **Student-Faculty Ratio:** 10:1 **Exams:** SAT I or ACT **% Receiving Financial Aid:** 81 **% Residing in College-Owned, -Operated, or -Affiliated Housing:** 60 **Library Holdings:** 106,994 **Regional Accreditation:** North Central Association of Colleges and Schools **Credit Hours For Degree:** 64 credit hours, Associates; 128 credit hours, Bachelors **ROTC:** Army, Navy, Air Force **Intercollegiate Athletics:** Baseball M; Basketball M & W; Cross-Country Running M & W; Golf M & W; Soccer M & W; Softball W; Track and Field M & W; Volleyball W; Wrestling M

THE ART INSTITUTE OF LAS VEGAS
2350 Corporate Circle Dr.
Henderson, NV 89074
Tel: (702)369-9944
Fax: (702)992-8558
E-mail: snoel@aii.edu
Web Site: http://www.ailv.artinstitutes.edu/
President/CEO: Steven E. Brooks
Admissions: Suzanne Noel
Type: Four-Year College **Sex:** Coed **Affiliation:** Education Management Corporation **Scores:** 100% SAT V 400+; 100% SAT M 400+; 80% ACT 18-23; 20% ACT 24-29 **Admission Plans:** Open Admission **Application Deadline:** Rolling **Application Fee:** $50.00 **H.S. Requirements:** High school diploma required; GED accepted **Costs Per Year:** Application fee: $50. Tuition: $16,740 full-time, $372 per credit part-time. Mandatory fees: $1000 full-time. College room only: $4725. **Calendar System:** Quarter, Summer Session Not available **Enrollment:** FT 951, PT 95 **Faculty:** FT 27, PT 52 **Student-Faculty Ratio:** 19:1 **Exams:** SAT I and SAT II or ACT **% Residing in College-Owned, -Operated, or -Affiliated Housing:** 7 **Credit Hours For Degree:** 112 credits, Associates; 192 credits, Bachelors **Professional Accreditation:** ACCSCT

CAREER COLLEGE OF NORTHERN NEVADA
1195-A Corporate Blvd.
Reno, NV 89502
Tel: (775)856-2266
E-mail: lgoldhammer@ccnn4u.com
Web Site: http://www.ccnn.edu/
President/CEO: Larry F. Clark
Registrar: Arline Cochran
Admissions: Laura Goldhammer
Financial Aid: Craig Coziahr
Type: Two-Year College **Sex:** Coed **% Accepted:** 100 **Admission Plans:** Open Admission **Application Deadline:** Rolling **Application Fee:** $25.00 **H.S. Requirements:** High school diploma required; GED accepted **Costs Per Year:** Application fee: $25. Tuition: $175 per credit hour part-time. **Scholarships:** Available **Calendar System:** Quarter, Summer Session Available **Enrollment:** FT 283 **Faculty:** FT 11, PT 12 **Student-Faculty Ratio:** 20:1 **Library Holdings:** 380 **Credit Hours For Degree:** 99.5 units, Associates **Professional Accreditation:** ACCSCT

COMMUNITY COLLEGE OF SOUTHERN NEVADA
3200 East Cheyenne Ave.
North Las Vegas, NV 89030-4296
Tel: (702)651-4000
Free: 800-492-5728
Admissions: (702)651-4060
Fax: (702)643-6243
E-mail: stops@ccmail.ccsn.nevada.edu
Web Site: http://www.ccsn.nevada.edu/
President/CEO: Paul Gianini
Registrar: Arlie Stops
Admissions: Arlie J. Stops
Financial Aid: Arlie Stops
Type: Two-Year College **Sex:** Coed **Affiliation:** University and Community College System of Nevada **Admission Plans:** Open Admission; Early Admission **Application Fee:** $5.00 **H.S. Requirements:** High school diploma or equivalent not required. For allied health programs: High school diploma required; GED accepted **Costs Per Year:** Application fee: $5. State resident tuition: $1523 full-time, $50.75 per credit part-time. Nonresident tuition: $6557 full-time, $106.75 per credit part-time. Mandatory fees: $120 full-time, $4 per credit part-time. **Scholarships:** Available **Calendar System:** Semester, Summer Session Available **Enrollment:** FT 7,850, PT 26,354 **Faculty:** FT 390, PT 1,890 **Library Holdings:** 100,000 **Credit Hours For Degree:** 60 credit hours, Associates **ROTC:** Army **Professional Accreditation:** ACF, ADA, AHIMA, AOTA, APTA, COptA, CARC, JRCEDMS, NAACLS, NLN, NCCU **Intercollegiate Athletics:** Baseball M

DEEP SPRINGS COLLEGE
HC 72, Box 45001
Dyer, NV 89010-9803
Tel: (760)872-2000
E-mail: apcom@deepsprings.edu
Web Site: http://www.deepsprings.edu/
President/CEO: Dr. F. Ross Peterson
Admissions: Dr. F. Ross Peterson
Type: Two-Year College **Sex:** Men **Scores:** 100% SAT V 400+; 100% SAT M 400+ **% Accepted:** 8 **Application Deadline:** November 15 **Application Fee:** $0.00 **H.S. Requirements:** High school diploma required; GED not accepted **Calendar System:** Miscellaneous, Summer Session Available **Enrollment:** FT 27 **Faculty:** FT 5, PT 4 **Student-Faculty Ratio:** 3:1 **Exams:** SAT I and SAT II or ACT **% Residing in College-Owned, -Operated, or -Affiliated Housing:** 100 **Library Holdings:** 20,000 **Regional Accreditation:** Western Association of Schools and Colleges **Credit Hours For Degree:** 60 hours, Associates

DEVRY UNIVERSITY
2490 Paseo Verde Parkway, Ste. 150
Henderson, NV 89074-7120
Tel: (702)933-9700; (866)783-3879
Fax: (702)933-9717
Web Site: http://www.devry.edu/ **Type:** Comprehensive **Sex:** Coed **Affiliation:** DeVry University **Admission Plans:** Deferred Admission **Application Deadline:** Rolling **Application Fee:** $50.00 **H.S. Requirements:** High school diploma required; GED accepted **Costs Per Year:** Application fee: $50. One-time mandatory fee: $40. Tuition: $11,790 full-time, $440 per credit part-time. Mandatory fees: $270 full-time, $30 per year part-time. **Calendar System:** Semester, Summer Session Available **Enrollment:** FT 55, PT 34, Grad 33 **Faculty:** PT 31 **Student-Faculty Ratio:** 7:1 **Regional Accreditation:** North Central Association of Colleges and Schools

GREAT BASIN COLLEGE
1500 College Parkway
Elko, NV 89801-3348
Tel: (775)738-8493
Admissions: (775)753-2271
E-mail: bjulie@gbcnv.edu
Web Site: http://www.gbcnv.edu/
President/CEO: Dr. Paul T. Killpatrick
Admissions: Julie Byrnes

Financial Aid: Joan Williams
Type: Two-Year College **Sex:** Coed **Affiliation:** University and Community College System of Nevada **Admission Plans:** Open Admission; Early Admission; Deferred Admission **Application Deadline:** Rolling **Application Fee:** $5.00 **H.S. Requirements:** High school diploma or equivalent not required. For nursing program: High school diploma required; GED accepted **Costs Per Year:** Application fee: $5. State resident tuition: $1575 full-time, $52.50 per credit part-time. Nonresident tuition: $4962 full-time, $110.25 per credit part-time. College room and board: $4520. College room only: $1900. **Scholarships:** Available **Calendar System:** Semester, Summer Session Available **Enrollment:** FT 853, PT 2,242 **Faculty:** FT 59, PT 172 **Student-Faculty Ratio:** 13:1 **Library Holdings:** 27,521 **Credit Hours For Degree:** 60 semester hours, Associates **Professional Accreditation:** NLN, NCCU

HERITAGE COLLEGE
3305 Spring Mountain Rd., Ste. 7
Las Vegas, NV 89102
Tel: (702)368-2338
Fax: (702)638-3853
Web Site: http://www.heritagecollege.com/
President/CEO: Brian Lahargoue
Type: Two-Year College **Professional Accreditation:** ACCSCT

HIGH-TECH INSTITUTE
2320 South Rancho Dr.
Las Vegas, NV 89102
Tel: (702)385-6700
Free: 800-987-0110
Fax: (702)388-4463
E-mail: ajhollander@hightechinstitute.com
Web Site: http://www.high-techinstitute.com/
President/CEO: Alvin Hollander
Admissions: Alvin J. Hollander
Type: Two-Year College **Sex:** Coed **Calendar System:** Semester **Professional Accreditation:** ACCSCT

ITT TECHNICAL INSTITUTE
168 Gibson Rd.
Henderson, NV 89014
Tel: (702)558-5404
Web Site: http://www.itt-tech.edu/
President/CEO: Donn Nimmer
Admissions: Peter Linzmaier
Type: Two-Year College **Sex:** Coed **Affiliation:** ITT Educational Services, Inc **Admission Plans:** Deferred Admission **Application Deadline:** Rolling **Application Fee:** $100.00 **H.S. Requirements:** High school diploma required; GED accepted **Costs Per Year:** Application fee: $100. **Scholarships:** Available **Exams:** Other **Credit Hours For Degree:** 96 credit hours, Associates; 180 credit hours, Bachelors **Professional Accreditation:** ACICS

LAS VEGAS COLLEGE
4100 West Flamingo Rd., Ste. 2100
Las Vegas, NV 89103-3926
Tel: (702)368-6200
Free: 800-903-3101
Fax: (702)368-6464
Web Site: http://www.lasvegas-college.com/
President/CEO: Deborah L. Adams
Admissions: Bill Hall
Financial Aid: Michael Holmes
Type: Two-Year College **Sex:** Coed **Affiliation:** Corinthian Colleges, Inc **Admission Plans:** Open Admission **H.S. Requirements:** High school diploma required; GED accepted **Scholarships:** Available **Calendar System:** Quarter, Summer Session Not available **Enrollment:** FT 412, PT 239 **Exams:** Other **Credit Hours For Degree:** 94 units, Associates **Professional Accreditation:** ACICS

LE CORDON BLEU COLLEGE OF CULINARY ARTS, LAS VEGAS
1451 Center Crossing Rd.
Las Vegas, NV 89144
Tel: (702)365-7690
Fax: (702)365-7911
Web Site: http://www.vegasculinary.com/
President/CEO: Jennifer White
Type: Two-Year College **Sex:** Coed **Professional Accreditation:** ACCSCT

MORRISON UNIVERSITY
10315 Professional Circle
Reno, NV 89521
Tel: (775)850-0700
Free: 800-369-6144
Fax: (775)850-0711
E-mail: richard.farmer@morrison.edu
Web Site: http://www.morrison.neumont.edu/
President/CEO: Scott McKinley
Registrar: Gerre Young
Admissions: Dr. Richard Carl Farmer
Financial Aid: Kim Droniak
Type: Comprehensive **Sex:** Coed **Admission Plans:** Open Admission; Early Admission; Deferred Admission **Application Fee:** $25.00 **H.S. Requirements:** High school diploma required; GED accepted **Costs Per Year:** Application fee: $25. Tuition: $12,000 full-time. **Scholarships:** Available **Calendar System:** Miscellaneous, Summer Session Available **Enrollment:** FT 110, Grad 20 **Faculty:** FT 15, PT 10 **Library Holdings:** 6,000 **Credit Hours For Degree:** 90 credits, Associates; 180 credits, Bachelors **Professional Accreditation:** ACICS

NEVADA STATE COLLEGE AT HENDERSON
1125 Nevada State Dr.
Henderson, NV 89015
Tel: (702)992-2000
Fax: (702)992-2226
Web Site: http://www.nsc.nevada.edu/
President/CEO: Kerry D. Romesburg
Admissions: Christina F. Twelves
Type: Four-Year College **Sex:** Coed **Affiliation:** Nevada System of Higher Education **Application Fee:** $30.00 **Calendar System:** Semester **Enrollment:** FT 248, PT 287 **Faculty:** FT 15, PT 73 **Student-Faculty Ratio:** 9:1 **Exams:** SAT I or ACT **Professional Accreditation:** NCCU

PIMA MEDICAL INSTITUTE
3333 East Flamingo Rd.
Las Vegas, NV 89121
Tel: (702)458-9650
Free: 800-477-PIMA
Web Site: http://www.pmi.edu
Admissions: Babbette Burcaw
Type: Two-Year College **Sex:** Coed **Affiliation:** Vocational Training Institutes, Inc **H.S. Requirements:** High school diploma required; GED accepted. For some certificate programs: High school diploma or equivalent not required **Calendar System:** Miscellaneous, Summer Session Not available **Faculty:** FT 7, PT 5 **Student-Faculty Ratio:** 20:1 **Exams:** Other **Professional Accreditation:** ABHES

SIERRA NEVADA COLLEGE
999 Tahoe Blvd.
Incline Village, NV 89451
Tel: (775)831-1314
Admissions: (775)831-7799
Fax: (775)831-1347
E-mail: admissions@sierranevada.edu
Web Site: http://www.sierranevada.edu/
President/CEO: Dr. James L. Ash, Jr.
Registrar: Pam Emmerich
Admissions: Dr. Thad Anglin
Financial Aid: Dorothy Caruso
Type: Comprehensive **Sex:** Coed **Scores:** 98% SAT V 400+; 97% SAT M 400+ **Admission Plans:** Early Admission; Deferred Admission **Application Fee:** $0.00 **H.S. Requirements:** High school diploma required; GED accepted **Scholarships:** Available **Calendar System:** Semester, Summer Session Available **Enrollment:** FT 302, Grad 190 **Faculty:** FT 19, PT 56 **Student-Faculty Ratio:** 8:1 **Exams:** SAT I and SAT II or ACT **% Receiving Financial Aid:** 70 **% Residing in College-Owned, -Operated, or -Affiliated Housing:** 45 **Library Holdings:** 18,500 **Credit Hours For**

Degree: 120 semester hours, Bachelors **ROTC:** Army **Professional Accreditation:** NCCU **Intercollegiate Athletics:** Equestrian Sports M & W; Skiing (Downhill) M & W

TRUCKEE MEADOWS COMMUNITY COLLEGE
7000 Dandini Blvd.
Reno, NV 89512-3901
Tel: (775)673-7000
Admissions: (775)674-7623
Fax: (775)673-7028
E-mail: dharbeck@tmcc.edu
Web Site: http://www.tmcc.edu/
President/CEO: Dr. Philip M. Ringle
Registrar: Dave Harbeck
Admissions: Dave Harbeck
Financial Aid: Mona Buckheart
Type: Two-Year College **Sex:** Coed **Affiliation:** University and Community College System of Nevada **Admission Plans:** Open Admission; Early Admission; Deferred Admission **Application Fee:** $10.00 **H.S. Requirements:** High school diploma or equivalent not required. For applicants under 18, allied health programs: High school diploma required; GED accepted **Costs Per Year:** Application fee: $10. State resident tuition: $0 full-time. Nonresident tuition: $4915 full-time, $55.75 per credit part-time. Mandatory fees: $1314 full-time, $54.75 per credit part-time. **Scholarships:** Available **Calendar System:** Semester, Summer Session Available **Enrollment:** FT 1,963, PT 7,734 **Faculty:** FT 142, PT 338 **Student-Faculty Ratio:** 31:1 **Exams:** SAT I or ACT **Library Holdings:** 42,110 **Credit Hours For Degree:** 60 credits, Associates **ROTC:** Army **Professional Accreditation:** ACF, ADA, JRCERT, NLN, NCCU

UNIVERSITY OF NEVADA, LAS VEGAS
4505 Maryland Parkway
Las Vegas, NV 89154-9900
Tel: (702)895-3011
Admissions: (702)895-5292
Fax: (702)895-1118
E-mail: stephanie.brown@unlv.edu
Web Site: http://www.unlv.edu/
President/CEO: Dr. Carol Harter
Registrar: Judy Belanger
Admissions: Dr. Stephanie G. Brown
Financial Aid: Judy Belanger
Type: University **Sex:** Coed **Affiliation:** University and Community College System of Nevada **Scores:** 89.8% SAT V 400+; 91.7% SAT M 400+; 56.4% ACT 18-23; 22.5% ACT 24-29 **% Accepted:** 81 **Admission Plans:** Deferred Admission **Application Deadline:** February 01 **Application Fee:** $60.00 **H.S. Requirements:** High school diploma required; GED accepted **Costs Per Year:** Application fee: $60. State resident tuition: $3278 full-time, $105.25 per credit hour part-time. Nonresident tuition: $13,189 full-time, $225 per credit hour part-time. Mandatory fees: $540 full-time. College room and board: $8326. College room only: $5278. **Scholarships:** Available **Calendar System:** Semester, Summer Session Available **Enrollment:** FT 15,570, PT 6,213, Grad 4,857 **Faculty:** FT 810, PT 732 **Student-Faculty Ratio:** 20:1 **Exams:** SAT I or ACT **% Receiving Financial Aid:** 42 **% Residing in College-Owned, -Operated, or -Affiliated Housing:** 4 **Library Holdings:** 1,034,288 **Credit Hours For Degree:** 124 credit hours, Bachelors **Professional Accreditation:** AACSB, ABET, ABA, ACCE, ACA, ADA, APTA, ASLA, AALS, CSWE, FIDER, JRCEPAT, JRCNMT, NAACLS, NASAD, NASM, NASPAA, NAST, NCATE, NLN NCCU **Intercollegiate Athletics:** Baseball M; Basketball M & W; Cheerleading M & W; Cross-Country Running W; Equestrian Sports W; Football M; Golf M; Soccer M & W; Softball W; Swimming and Diving M & W; Tennis M & W; Track and Field W; Volleyball W

UNIVERSITY OF NEVADA, RENO
Reno, NV 89557
Tel: (775)784-1110; (866)263-8232
Admissions: (775)784-4700
E-mail: unrug@unr.edu
Web Site: http://www.unr.edu/
President/CEO: Dr. John M. Lilley
Admissions: Dr. Melissa N. Choroszy
Financial Aid: Dr. Melisa Choroszy
Type: University **Sex:** Coed **Affiliation:** University and Community College System of Nevada **Scores:** 95% SAT V 400+; 96% SAT M 400+; 54% ACT 18-23; 33% ACT 24-29 **% Accepted:** 86 **Admission Plans:** Early Action; Deferred Admission **Application Deadline:** Rolling **Application Fee:** $60.00 **H.S. Requirements:** High school diploma required; GED not accepted **Costs Per Year:** Application fee: $60. State resident tuition: $3060 full-time, $102 per credit part-time. Nonresident tuition: $11,735 full-time, $209.75 per credit part-time. Mandatory fees: $210 full-time. Full-time tuition and fees vary according to course load. Part-time tuition varies according to course load. College room and board: $7785. College room only: $4190. Room and board charges vary according to board plan and housing facility. **Scholarships:** Available **Calendar System:** Semester, Summer Session Available **Enrollment:** FT 10,257, PT 2,680, Grad 3,184 **Faculty:** FT 489, PT 471 **Student-Faculty Ratio:** 20:1 **% Receiving Financial Aid:** 32 **% Residing in College-Owned, -Operated, or -Affiliated Housing:** 14 **Library Holdings:** 1,128,954 **Credit Hours For Degree:** 124 credits, Bachelors **ROTC:** Army **Professional Accreditation:** AACSB, ABET, ACEJMC, AACN, ACA, ADtA, APA, ASLHA, CSWE, LCMEAMA, NASM, NCATE, NCCU **Intercollegiate Athletics:** Baseball M; Basketball M & W; Cheerleading M & W; Cross-Country Running W; Football M; Golf M & W; Riflery M & W; Skiing (Cross-Country) M & W; Skiing (Downhill) M & W; Soccer W; Softball W; Swimming and Diving W; Tennis M & W; Track and Field W; Volleyball W

UNIVERSITY OF PHOENIX-NEVADA CAMPUS
7455 Washington Ave., Ste. 317
Las Vegas, NV 89128
Tel: (702)638-7279
Free: 800-228-7240
Admissions: (480)557-1712
Fax: (702)638-8035
Web Site: http://www.phoenix.edu/
President/CEO: Steve Soukup
Admissions: Nina Omelchanko
Type: Comprehensive **Sex:** Coed **Admission Plans:** Open Admission; Deferred Admission **Application Deadline:** Rolling **Application Fee:** $110.00 **H.S. Requirements:** High school diploma required; GED accepted **Costs Per Year:** Application fee: $110. Tuition: $9750 full-time, $325 per credit part-time. Mandatory fees: $560 full-time, $70 per course part-time. **Scholarships:** Available **Calendar System:** Continuous, Summer Session Not available **Enrollment:** FT 2,976, Grad 1,262 **Faculty:** FT 7, PT 310 **Student-Faculty Ratio:** 8:1 **Library Holdings:** 444 **Regional Accreditation:** North Central Association of Colleges and Schools **Credit Hours For Degree:** 60 credits, Associates; 120 credits, Bachelors

WESTERN NEVADA COMMUNITY COLLEGE
2201 West College Parkway
Carson City, NV 89703-7316
Tel: (775)445-3000
Admissions: (775)445-3271
Fax: (775)887-3141
E-mail: hull@wncc.edu
Web Site: http://www.wncc.edu/
President/CEO: Dr. Carol Lucey
Registrar: Daniel Navarett
Admissions: Dianne Hilliard
Financial Aid: Lori Tinde
Type: Two-Year College **Sex:** Coed **Affiliation:** University and Community College System of Nevada **% Accepted:** 100 **Admission Plans:** Open Admission; Early Admission **Application Deadline:** Rolling **Application Fee:** $15.00 **H.S. Requirements:** High school diploma required; GED accepted **Costs Per Year:** Application fee: $15. Area resident tuition: $52.50 per credit part-time. State resident tuition: $1575 full-time, $88 per credit part-time. Nonresident tuition: $6695 full-time, $114.25 per credit part-time. Mandatory fees: $120 full-time, $4 per credit part-time. **Scholarships:** Available **Calendar System:** Semester, Summer Session Available **Enrollment:** FT 954, PT 3,953 **Faculty:** FT 79, PT 295 **Student-Faculty Ratio:** 15:1 **Library Holdings:** 42,500 **Credit Hours For Degree:** 60 credits, Associates **Professional Accreditation:** NLN, NCCU **Intercollegiate Athletics:** Baseball M; Equestrian Sports M & W; Soccer W

CHESTER COLLEGE OF NEW ENGLAND
40 Chester St.
Chester, NH 03036-4331
Tel: (603)887-4401
Free: 800-974-6372
Admissions: (603)887-7400
E-mail: svogell@chestercollege.edu
Web Site: http://www.chestercollege.edu/
President/CEO: Dr. William A. Nevious
Registrar: Margaret Pagliuca
Admissions: Sarah Vogell
Financial Aid: Jay Walker
Type: Four-Year College **Sex:** Coed **Scores:** 90.9% SAT V 400+; 81.7% SAT M 400+; 65% ACT 18-23 **% Accepted:** 57 **Admission Plans:** Deferred Admission **Application Deadline:** Rolling **Application Fee:** $35.00 **H.S. Requirements:** High school diploma required; GED accepted **Costs Per Year:** Application fee: $35. Comprehensive fee: $22,565 includes full-time tuition ($14,700), mandatory fees ($265), and college room and board ($7600). Part-time tuition: $465 per credit. Part-time mandatory fees: $500 per year. **Scholarships:** Available **Calendar System:** Semester, Summer Session Available **Faculty:** FT 12, PT 21 **Student-Faculty Ratio:** 10:1 **% Receiving Financial Aid:** 78 **% Residing in College-Owned, -Operated, or -Affiliated Housing:** 52 **Library Holdings:** 27,000 **Regional Accreditation:** New England Association of Schools and Colleges **Credit Hours For Degree:** 60 credits, Associates; 120 credits, Bachelors

COLBY-SAWYER COLLEGE
541 Main St.
New London, NH 03257-7835
Tel: (603)526-3000
Free: 800-272-1015
Admissions: (603)526-3700
Fax: (603)526-3452
E-mail: csadmiss@colby-sawyer.edu
Web Site: http://www.colby-sawyer.edu/
President/CEO: Dr. Anne Ponder
Registrar: Carole H. Parsons
Admissions: Joseph Chillo
Financial Aid: Angela Dostie
Type: Four-Year College **Sex:** Coed **Scores:** 96% SAT V 400+; 100% SAT M 400+; 61% ACT 18-23; 25% ACT 24-29 **% Accepted:** 90 **Admission Plans:** Early Admission; Early Action; Deferred Admission **Application Deadline:** April 01 **Application Fee:** $45.00 **H.S. Requirements:** High school diploma required; GED accepted **Costs Per Year:** Application fee: $45. Comprehensive fee: $36,250 includes full-time tuition ($26,350) and college room and board ($9900). College room only: $5600. Part-time tuition: $880 per credit hour. **Scholarships:** Available **Calendar System:** Semester, Summer Session Not available **Enrollment:** FT 954, PT 17 **Faculty:** FT 57, PT 68 **Student-Faculty Ratio:** 11:1 **Exams:** SAT I or ACT **% Receiving Financial Aid:** 81 **% Residing in College-Owned, -Operated, or -Affiliated Housing:** 87 **Library Holdings:** 90,055 **Regional Accreditation:** New England Association of Schools and Colleges **Credit Hours For Degree:** 60 credit hours, Associates; 120 credit hours, Bachelors **ROTC:** Army, Air Force **Professional Accreditation:** AACN, JRCEPAT **Intercollegiate Athletics:** Baseball M; Basketball M & W; Cross-Country Running M & W; Equestrian Sports M & W; Field Hockey W; Ice Hockey M & W; Lacrosse M & W; Rugby M & W; Skiing (Cross-Country) M & W; Skiing (Downhill) M & W; Soccer M & W; Softball W; Swimming and Diving M & W; Tennis M & W; Track and Field M & W; Volleyball W

DANIEL WEBSTER COLLEGE
20 University Dr.
Nashua, NH 03063-1300
Tel: (603)577-6000
Free: 800-325-6876
Admissions: (603)577-6604
Fax: (603)577-6001
E-mail: thatcher@dwc.edu
Web Site: http://www.dwc.edu/
President/CEO: Hannah M. McCarthy
Registrar: Eileen Hocking
Admissions: Sean J. Ryan
Financial Aid: Mary Ellen Severance
Type: Four-Year College **Sex:** Coed **Scores:** 98% SAT V 400+; 99% SAT M 400+; 46.7% ACT 18-23; 40% ACT 24-29 **Admission Plans:** Early Admission; Deferred Admission **Application Fee:** $35.00 **H.S. Requirements:** High school diploma required; GED accepted **Costs Per Year:** Application fee: $35. Comprehensive fee: $31,405 includes full-time tuition ($22,130), mandatory fees ($825), and college room and board ($8450). **Scholarships:** Available **Calendar System:** Semester, Summer Session Available **Enrollment:** FT 823, PT 227, Grad 59 **Faculty:** FT 34, PT 27 **Student-Faculty Ratio:** 13:1 **Exams:** SAT I or ACT **% Receiving Financial Aid:** 96 **% Residing in College-Owned, -Operated, or -Affiliated Housing:** 80 **Library Holdings:** 34,195 **Regional Accreditation:** New England Association of Schools and Colleges **Credit Hours For Degree:** 60 credits, Associates; 120 credits, Bachelors **ROTC:** Army, Air Force **Professional Accreditation:** CAA **Intercollegiate Athletics:** Baseball M; Basketball M & W; Cross-Country Running M & W; Ice Hockey M & W; Lacrosse M; Soccer M & W; Softball W; Volleyball W

DARTMOUTH COLLEGE
Hanover, NH 03755
Tel: (603)646-1110
Admissions: (603)646-2875
Fax: (603)646-1216
E-mail: admissions.office@dartmouth.edu
Web Site: http://www.dartmouth.edu/
President/CEO: Dr. James Wright
Registrar: Polly Griffin
Admissions: Karl M. Furstenberg
Financial Aid: Virginia S. Hazen
Type: University **Sex:** Coed **Scores:** 100% SAT V 400+; 100% SAT M 400+ **% Accepted:** 17 **Admission Plans:** Early Admission; Early Decision Plan; Deferred Admission **Application Deadline:** January 01 **Application Fee:** $70.00 **H.S. Requirements:** High school diploma or equivalent not required **Costs Per Year:** Application fee: $70. Comprehensive fee: $41,436 includes full-time tuition ($31,770), mandatory fees ($276), and college room and board ($9390). College room only: $5640. Room and board charges vary according to board plan. **Scholarships:** Available **Calendar System:** Quarter, Summer Session Available **Enrollment:** FT 4,050, PT 60, Grad 1,374 **Faculty:** FT 493, PT 140 **Student-Faculty Ratio:** 8:1 **Exams:** SAT I and SAT II or ACT **% Receiving Financial Aid:** 51 **% Residing in College-**

Owned, -Operated, or -Affiliated Housing: 82 **Regional Accreditation:** New England Association of Schools and Colleges **Credit Hours For Degree:** 35 courses, Bachelors **ROTC:** Army **Professional Accreditation:** AACSB, ABET, APA, CEPH, LCMEAMA, NAST **Intercollegiate Athletics:** Badminton M & W; Baseball M; Basketball M & W; Cheerleading M & W; Crew M & W; Cross-Country Running M & W; Equestrian Sports M & W; Fencing M & W; Field Hockey W; Football M; Golf M & W; Gymnastics M & W; Ice Hockey M & W; Lacrosse M & W; Rugby M & W; Sailing M & W; Skiing (Cross-Country) M & W; Skiing (Downhill) M & W; Soccer M & W; Softball W; Squash M & W; Swimming and Diving M & W; Table Tennis M & W; Tennis M & W; Track and Field M & W; Ultimate Frisbee M & W; Volleyball M & W; Water Polo M & W; Wrestling M

FRANKLIN PIERCE COLLEGE
20 College Rd., PO Box 60
Rindge, NH 03461-0060
Tel: (603)899-4000
Free: 800-437-0048
Admissions: (603)899-4050
Fax: (603)899-4372
E-mail: admissions@rindge.fpc.edu
Web Site: http://www.fpc.edu/
President/CEO: Dr. George J. Hagerty
Registrar: Susan Chamberlin, PhD
Admissions: Lucy C. Shonk
Financial Aid: JoEllen Soucier
Type: Comprehensive **Sex:** Coed **Scores:** 95% SAT V 400+; 94% SAT M 400+ **% Accepted:** 74 **Admission Plans:** Early Admission; Deferred Admission **Application Deadline:** Rolling **Application Fee:** $0.00 **H.S. Requirements:** High school diploma required; GED accepted. For early entrance program: High school diploma or equivalent not required **Costs Per Year:** Application fee: $0. Comprehensive fee: $33,500 includes full-time tuition ($24,300), mandatory fees ($1000), and college room and board ($8200). College room only: $4600. Part-time tuition: $810 per credit. **Scholarships:** Available **Calendar System:** Semester, Summer Session Available **Enrollment:** FT 1,596, PT 39 **Faculty:** FT 74, PT 76 **Student-Faculty Ratio:** 16:1 **Exams:** SAT I or ACT **% Receiving Financial Aid:** 74 **% Residing in College-Owned, -Operated, or -Affiliated Housing:** 87 **Library Holdings:** 110,210 **Regional Accreditation:** New England Association of Schools and Colleges **Credit Hours For Degree:** 120 credits, Bachelors **ROTC:** Army, Air Force **Professional Accreditation:** APTA **Intercollegiate Athletics:** Baseball M; Basketball M & W; Crew M & W; Cross-Country Running M & W; Field Hockey W; Golf M & W; Ice Hockey M; Lacrosse M & W; Soccer M & W; Softball W; Tennis M & W; Volleyball W

GRANITE STATE COLLEGE
125 North State St.
Concord, NH 03301
Tel: (603)228-3000
Fax: (603)229-0964
Web Site: http://www.granite.edu/
President/CEO: Dr. Karol A. LaCroix
Registrar: Ruth Nawn
Admissions: Teresa McDonnell
Financial Aid: Juanita Plourde
Type: Four-Year College **Sex:** Coed **Affiliation:** University System of New Hampshire **Application Fee:** $45.00 **H.S. Requirements:** High school diploma required; GED accepted **Calendar System:** Semester, Summer Session Available **Faculty:** PT 223 **Student-Faculty Ratio:** 10:1 **Regional Accreditation:** New England Association of Schools and Colleges **Credit Hours For Degree:** 64 semester hours, Associates; 124 semester hours, Bachelors

HESSER COLLEGE
3 Sundial Ave.
Manchester, NH 03103-7245
Tel: (603)668-6660
Free: 800-526-9231
Web Site: http://www.hesser.edu/
President/CEO: Robert Moon
Registrar: Elaine Minnehan-Caron
Admissions: Julie English
Financial Aid: Debra LeDuke
Type: Two-Year College **Sex:** Coed **Affiliation:** Quest Education Corporation **Admission Plans:** Deferred Admission **Application Fee:** $10.00 **H.S. Requirements:** High school diploma required; GED accepted **Costs Per Year:** Application fee: $10. Comprehensive fee: $18,940 includes full-time tuition ($11,340), mandatory fees ($1000), and college room and board ($6600). College room only: $3600. Part-time tuition: $410 per credit. **Scholarships:** Available **Calendar System:** Semester, Summer Session Available **Enrollment:** FT 2,104, PT 1,294 **Faculty:** FT 38, PT 177 **Exams:** SAT I **% Residing in College-Owned, -Operated, or -Affiliated Housing:** 50 **Library Holdings:** 38,000 **Regional Accreditation:** New England Association of Schools and Colleges **Credit Hours For Degree:** 60 credits, Associates; 120 credits, Bachelors **Professional Accreditation:** AAMAE, APTA **Intercollegiate Athletics:** Basketball M & W; Soccer M & W; Volleyball M & W

KEENE STATE COLLEGE
229 Main St.
Keene, NH 03435
Tel: (603)352-1909
Free: 800-572-1909
Admissions: (603)358-2273
Fax: (603)358-2767
E-mail: admissions@keene.edu
Web Site: http://www.keene.edu/
President/CEO: Dr. Stanley J. Yarosewick
Registrar: Tom Richard
Admissions: Margaret Richmond
Financial Aid: Patricia Blodgett
Type: Comprehensive **Sex:** Coed **Affiliation:** University System of New Hampshire **Scores:** 95.4% SAT V 400+; 94.3% SAT M 400+ **% Accepted:** 76 **Admission Plans:** Deferred Admission **Application Deadline:** April 01 **Application Fee:** $35.00 **H.S. Requirements:** High school diploma required; GED accepted **Costs Per Year:** Application fee: $35. State resident tuition: $5780 full-time, $241 per credit part-time. Nonresident tuition: $13,050 full-time, $544 per credit part-time. Mandatory fees: $2038 full-time, $77 per credit part-time. Part-time tuition and fees vary according to course load and degree level. College room and board: $7027. College room only: $4700. Room and board charges vary according to board plan and housing facility. **Scholarships:** Available **Calendar System:** Semester, Summer Session Available **Enrollment:** FT 4,170, PT 559, Grad 117 **Faculty:** FT 187, PT 222 **Student-Faculty Ratio:** 17:1 **Exams:** SAT I or ACT **% Receiving Financial Aid:** 53 **% Residing in College-Owned, -Operated, or -Affiliated Housing:** 56 **Regional Accreditation:** New England Association of Schools and Colleges **Credit Hours For Degree:** 60 credits, Associates; 120 credits, Bachelors **ROTC:** Air Force **Professional Accreditation:** ADtA, JRCEPAT, NASM, NCATE **Intercollegiate Athletics:** Baseball M; Basketball M & W; Cross-Country Running M & W; Field Hockey W; Lacrosse M & W; Rugby M & W; Skiing (Downhill) M & W; Soccer M & W; Softball W; Swimming and Diving M & W; Track and Field M & W; Volleyball W

MAGDALEN COLLEGE
511 Kearsarge Mountain Rd.
Warner, NH 03278
Tel: (603)456-2656; 877-498-1723
Fax: (603)456-2660
E-mail: jfout@magdalen.edu
Web Site: http://www.magdalen.edu/
President/CEO: Jeffrey J. Karls
Admissions: Justin Fout
Type: Four-Year College **Sex:** Coed **Affiliation:** Roman Catholic **Scores:** 94% SAT V 400+; 87% SAT M 400+; 62% ACT 18-23; 38% ACT 24-29 **% Accepted:** 78 **Admission Plans:** Early Admission; Early Decision Plan **Application Deadline:** May 01 **Application Fee:** $35.00 **H.S. Requirements:** High school diploma required; GED accepted **Costs Per Year:** Application fee: $35. Comprehensive fee: $17,250 includes full-time tuition ($10,750) and college room and board ($6500). **Scholarships:** Available **Calendar System:** Semester, Summer Session Not available **Enrollment:** FT 72, PT 1 **Faculty:** FT 7, PT 2 **Student-Faculty Ratio:** 8:1 **Exams:** SAT I or ACT **% Receiving Financial Aid:** 59 **% Residing in College-Owned, -Operated, or -Affiliated Housing:** 100 **Library Holdings:** 26,000 **Credit Hours For Degree:** 60 credit hours, Associates; 120 credit hours, Bachelors **Professional Accreditation:** AALE

MCINTOSH COLLEGE
23 Cataract Ave.
Dover, NH 03820-3990

Tel: (603)742-1234
Free: 800-McINTOSH
Fax: (603)742-7292
Web Site: http://www.mcintoshcollege.edu/
President/CEO: Robert Saiz
Admissions: Jody LaBrie
Financial Aid: Eeva Deshon
Type: Two-Year College **Sex:** Coed **Admission Plans:** Open Admission; Early Admission; Deferred Admission **Application Fee:** $15.00 **H.S. Requirements:** High school diploma required; GED accepted **Costs Per Year:** Application fee: $15. Comprehensive fee: $25,085 includes full-time tuition ($15,600), mandatory fees ($125), and college room and board ($9360). Part-time tuition: $443 per credit. Tuition guaranteed not to increase for student's term of enrollment. **Scholarships:** Available **Calendar System:** Trimester, Summer Session Available **Faculty:** FT 42, PT 58 **Student-Faculty Ratio:** 25:1 **% Residing in College-Owned, -Operated, or -Affiliated Housing:** 25 **Library Holdings:** 11,000 **Regional Accreditation:** New England Association of Schools and Colleges **Credit Hours For Degree:** 66 credits, Associates

NEW ENGLAND COLLEGE
7 Main St.
Henniker, NH 03242-3293
Tel: (603)428-2211
Free: 800-521-7642
Admissions: (603)428-2223
E-mail: admission@nec.edu
Web Site: http://www.nec.edu/
President/CEO: Dr. Ellen S. Hurwitz
Registrar: Frank Hall
Admissions: Paul Miller
Financial Aid: Ray Nault
Type: Comprehensive **Sex:** Coed **Scores:** 76% SAT V 400+; 70% SAT M 400+; 31% ACT 18-23; 15% ACT 24-29 **% Accepted:** 83 **Admission Plans:** Deferred Admission **Application Deadline:** Rolling **Application Fee:** $30.00 **H.S. Requirements:** High school diploma required; GED accepted **Costs Per Year:** Application fee: $30. Comprehensive fee: $31,466 includes full-time tuition ($22,366), mandatory fees ($644), and college room and board ($8456). College room only: $4398. Full-time tuition and fees vary according to class time, course load, degree level, location, and program. Room and board charges vary according to board plan and housing facility. Part-time tuition: $1065 per credit. Part-time mandatory fees: $198 per term. Part-time tuition and fees vary according to class time, course load, degree level, location, and program. **Scholarships:** Available **Calendar System:** Semester, Summer Session Available **Enrollment:** FT 972, PT 69, Grad 339 **Faculty:** FT 57, PT 95 **Student-Faculty Ratio:** 11:1 **% Receiving Financial Aid:** 74 **% Residing in College-Owned, -Operated, or -Affiliated Housing:** 68 **Library Holdings:** 100,000 **Regional Accreditation:** New England Association of Schools and Colleges **Credit Hours For Degree:** 30 credits, Associates; 40 credits, Bachelors **ROTC:** Army, Air Force **Intercollegiate Athletics:** Baseball M; Basketball M & W; Cross-Country Running M & W; Field Hockey W; Ice Hockey M & W; Lacrosse M & W; Skiing (Downhill) M & W; Soccer M & W; Softball W

NEW HAMPSHIRE COMMUNITY TECHNICAL COLLEGE, BERLIN/ LACONIA
2020 Riverside Dr.
Berlin, NH 03570-3717
Tel: (603)752-1113
Free: 800-445-4525
Web Site: http://www.berlin.nhctc.edu/
President/CEO: Katharine Eneguess
Registrar: Marie Bly
Admissions: Martha P. Laflamme
Financial Aid: Jacqueline Catello
Type: Two-Year College **Sex:** Coed **Affiliation:** New Hampshire Community Technical College System **Application Fee:** $10.00 **H.S. Requirements:** High school diploma required; GED accepted **Costs Per Year:** Application fee: $10. State resident tuition: $164 per credit part-time. Nonresident tuition: $376 per credit part-time. Mandatory fees: $4 per credit part-time. **Scholarships:** Available **Calendar System:** Semester, Summer Session Available **Enrollment:** FT 708, PT 1,372 **Faculty:** FT 33, PT 72 **Exams:** Other **Library Holdings:** 10,000 **Regional Accreditation:** New England Association of Schools and Colleges **Credit Hours For Degree:** 64 credits, Associates **Intercollegiate Athletics:** Basketball M & W; Ice Hockey M & W; Soccer M & W

NEW HAMPSHIRE COMMUNITY TECHNICAL COLLEGE, MANCHESTER/STRATHAM
1066 Front St.
Manchester, NH 03102-8518
Tel: (603)668-6706
E-mail: ntravers@nhctc.edu
Web Site: http://www.manchester.nhctc.edu/
President/CEO: Thomas Wisbey
Registrar: Evelyn R. Perron
Admissions: Dr. Nancy L. Travers
Financial Aid: Pamela Boyer
Type: Two-Year College **Sex:** Coed **Affiliation:** New Hampshire Community Technical College System **% Accepted:** 90 **Admission Plans:** Early Admission; Deferred Admission **Application Deadline:** Rolling **Application Fee:** $10.00 **H.S. Requirements:** High school diploma required; GED accepted **Costs Per Year:** Application fee: $10. Area resident tuition: $3936 full-time, $164 per credit part-time. State resident tuition: $5904 full-time, $246 per credit part-time. Nonresident tuition: $9024 full-time, $376 per credit part-time. Mandatory fees: $5 per credit part-time. **Scholarships:** Available **Calendar System:** Semester, Summer Session Available **Faculty:** FT 47, PT 143 **Student-Faculty Ratio:** 14:1 **Library Holdings:** 18,000 **Regional Accreditation:** New England Association of Schools and Colleges **Credit Hours For Degree:** 64 credit hours, Associates **Professional Accreditation:** ARCEST, AAMAE, ACBSP, NLN **Intercollegiate Athletics:** Baseball W; Basketball M; Skiing (Downhill) M & W; Soccer M & W; Volleyball M & W

NEW HAMPSHIRE COMMUNITY TECHNICAL COLLEGE, NASHUA/ CLAREMONT
505 Amherst St.
Nashua, NH 03063-1026
Tel: (603)882-6923
Fax: (603)882-8690
E-mail: nashua@nhctc.edu
Web Site: http://www.ncctc.edu/
President/CEO: Lucille Jordan
Registrar: Judith French
Admissions: Patricia Goodman
Financial Aid: Julie Burns
Type: Two-Year College **Sex:** Coed **Affiliation:** New Hampshire Community Technical College System **Admission Plans:** Deferred Admission **Application Deadline:** Rolling **Application Fee:** $10.00 **H.S. Requirements:** High school diploma required; GED accepted **Costs Per Year:** Application fee: $10. State resident tuition: $5248 full-time, $164 per credit part-time. Nonresident tuition: $12,032 full-time, $376 per credit part-time. Mandatory fees: $512 full-time, $16 per credit part-time. **Scholarships:** Available **Calendar System:** Semester, Summer Session Available **Faculty:** FT 42, PT 66 **Student-Faculty Ratio:** 9:1 **Library Holdings:** 22,000 **Regional Accreditation:** New England Association of Schools and Colleges **Credit Hours For Degree:** 64 credits, Associates **Professional Accreditation:** ABET, AHIMA, AOTA, CARC, NAACLS, NLN **Intercollegiate Athletics:** Soccer M & W

NEW HAMPSHIRE INSTITUTE OF ART
148 Concord St.
Manchester, NH 03104-4158
Tel: (603)623-0313
Admissions: (866)241-4918
Fax: (603)641-1832
E-mail: lsullivan@nhia.edu
Web Site: http://www.nhia.edu/
President/CEO: Roger Williams
Registrar: Laura Cleaves
Admissions: Liam Sullivan
Financial Aid: Linda LaVallee
Type: Four-Year College **Sex:** Coed **Admission Plans:** Open Admission **Application Fee:** $25.00 **H.S. Requirements:** High school diploma required; GED accepted **Costs Per Year:** Application fee: $25. Tuition: $10,950 full-time, $365 per credit part-time. Mandatory fees: $1130 full-time, $466 per year part-time. College room only: $5700. Room charges vary according to housing facility. **Scholarships:** Available **Calendar System:** Semester, Summer Session Available **Enrollment:** FT 135, PT 45 **Faculty:**

FT 5, PT 40 **Student-Faculty Ratio:** 15:1 **Exams:** SAT I or ACT **Library Holdings:** 5,000 **Credit Hours For Degree:** 120 credits, Bachelors **Professional Accreditation:** NASAD

NEW HAMPSHIRE TECHNICAL INSTITUTE
11 Institute Dr.
Concord, NH 03301-7412
Tel: (603)271-6484
Free: 800-247-0179
Admissions: (603)271-7131
Fax: (603)271-7734
Web Site: http://www.nhti.edu/
President/CEO: Dr. William Simonton, Jr.
Registrar: Pamela M. Halen-Smith
Admissions: Francis P. Meyer
Financial Aid: Paula Marsh
Type: Two-Year College **Sex:** Coed **Affiliation:** New Hampshire Community Technical College System **% Accepted:** 73 **Admission Plans:** Preferred Admission **Application Deadline:** Rolling **Application Fee:** $10.00 **H.S. Requirements:** High school diploma required; GED accepted **Costs Per Year:** Application fee: $10. State resident tuition: $4920 full-time, $164 per credit part-time. Nonresident tuition: $11,280 full-time, $376 per credit part-time. Mandatory fees: $480 full-time, $16 per credit part-time. College room and board: $6110. College room only: $4150. **Scholarships:** Available **Calendar System:** Semester, Summer Session Available **Enrollment:** FT 1,523, PT 2,127 **Faculty:** FT 97, PT 49 **Student-Faculty Ratio:** 12:1 **Exams:** Other, SAT I or ACT **% Residing in College-Owned, -Operated, or -Affiliated Housing:** 23 **Library Holdings:** 32,000 **Regional Accreditation:** New England Association of Schools and Colleges **Credit Hours For Degree:** 64 credit hours, Associates **Professional Accreditation:** ABET, ADA, JRCERT, JRCEMT, NLN **Intercollegiate Athletics:** Baseball M; Basketball M & W; Soccer M & W; Softball W; Volleyball M & W

PLYMOUTH STATE UNIVERSITY
17 High St.
Plymouth, NH 03264-1595
Tel: (603)535-5000
Free: 800-842-6900
Fax: (603)535-2714
E-mail: plymouthadmit@plymouth.edu
Web Site: http://www.plymouth.edu/
President/CEO: Dr. Donald P. Wharton
Registrar: Matthew Burkhart
Admissions: Eugene Fahey
Financial Aid: June Schlabach
Type: Comprehensive **Sex:** Coed **Affiliation:** University System of New Hampshire **Scores:** 89% SAT V 400+; 89% SAT M 400+; 52% ACT 18-23; 14% ACT 24-29 **% Accepted:** 77 **Admission Plans:** Deferred Admission **Application Deadline:** April 01 **Application Fee:** $35.00 **H.S. Requirements:** High school diploma required; GED accepted **Costs Per Year:** Application fee: $35. State resident tuition: $5410 full-time, $226 per credit hour part-time. Nonresident tuition: $12,250 full-time, $510 per credit hour part-time. Mandatory fees: $1618 full-time, $74 per credit hour part-time. Full-time tuition and fees vary according to reciprocity agreements. Part-time tuition and fees vary according to course load and reciprocity agreements. College room and board: $6780. College room only: $4650. Room and board charges vary according to board plan and housing facility. **Scholarships:** Available **Calendar System:** Semester, Summer Session Available **Enrollment:** FT 3,956, PT 236, Grad 1,072 **Faculty:** FT 175, PT 277 **Student-Faculty Ratio:** 17:1 **Exams:** SAT I or ACT **% Receiving Financial Aid:** 52 **% Residing in College-Owned, -Operated, or -Affiliated Housing:** 53 **Library Holdings:** 306,314 **Regional Accreditation:** New England Association of Schools and Colleges **Credit Hours For Degree:** 122 semester credit hours, Bachelors **ROTC:** Army, Air Force **Professional Accreditation:** ACBSP, CSWE, JRCEPAT, NCATE **Intercollegiate Athletics:** Baseball M; Basketball M & W; Cheerleading M & W; Field Hockey W; Football M; Ice Hockey M & W; Lacrosse M & W; Skiing (Downhill) M & W; Soccer M & W; Softball W; Swimming and Diving W; Tennis W; Volleyball M & W; Wrestling M

RIVIER COLLEGE
420 Main St.
Nashua, NH 03060-5086
Tel: (603)888-1311
Free: 800-44RIVIER
Admissions: (603)897-8502
Fax: (603)891-1799
E-mail: rivadmit@rivier.edu
Web Site: http://www.rivier.edu/
President/CEO: William Farrell, PhD
Registrar: Louise Monast
Admissions: Kevin Gately
Financial Aid: Valerie Patnaude
Type: Comprehensive **Sex:** Coed **Affiliation:** Roman Catholic **Scores:** 91% SAT V 400+; 89% SAT M 400+ **% Accepted:** 72 **Admission Plans:** Early Action; Deferred Admission **Application Deadline:** Rolling **Application Fee:** $25.00 **H.S. Requirements:** High school diploma required; GED accepted **Costs Per Year:** Application fee: $25. Comprehensive fee: $28,144 includes full-time tuition ($19,980), mandatory fees ($600), and college room and board ($7564). Room and board charges vary according to board plan and housing facility. Part-time tuition: $666 per credit. Part-time tuition varies according to class time. **Scholarships:** Available **Calendar System:** Semester, Summer Session Not available **Enrollment:** FT 845, PT 543, Grad 735 **Faculty:** FT 71, PT 109 **Student-Faculty Ratio:** 9:1 **Exams:** Other, SAT I or ACT **% Receiving Financial Aid:** 92 **% Residing in College-Owned, -Operated, or -Affiliated Housing:** 46 **Library Holdings:** 92,000 **Regional Accreditation:** New England Association of Schools and Colleges **Credit Hours For Degree:** 60 credits, Associates; 120 credits, Bachelors **ROTC:** Air Force **Professional Accreditation:** NLN **Intercollegiate Athletics:** Baseball M; Basketball M & W; Cheerleading M & W; Cross-Country Running M & W; Golf M & W; Soccer M & W; Softball W; Volleyball M & W

SAINT ANSELM COLLEGE
100 Saint Anselm Dr.
Manchester, NH 03102-1310
Tel: (603)641-7000; 888-4ANSELM
Admissions: (603)641-7500
Fax: (603)641-7550
E-mail: admission@anselm.edu
Web Site: http://www.anselm.edu/
President/CEO: Rev. Jonathan DeFelice, OSB
Registrar: Mary Anne Ericson
Admissions: Nancy Davis Griffin
Financial Aid: Elizabeth Keuffel
Type: Four-Year College **Sex:** Coed **Affiliation:** Roman Catholic **Scores:** 100% SAT V 400+; 100% SAT M 400+; 46% ACT 18-23; 45% ACT 24-29 **% Accepted:** 73 **Admission Plans:** Early Admission; Early Decision Plan; Deferred Admission **Application Deadline:** Rolling **Application Fee:** $55.00 **H.S. Requirements:** High school diploma required; GED accepted **Costs Per Year:** Application fee: $55. Comprehensive fee: $33,730 includes full-time tuition ($23,990), mandatory fees ($670), and college room and board ($9070). Part-time tuition: $2400 per course. **Scholarships:** Available **Calendar System:** Semester, Summer Session Available **Enrollment:** FT 1,937, PT 49 **Faculty:** FT 131, PT 46 **Student-Faculty Ratio:** 13:1 **Exams:** SAT I or ACT **% Receiving Financial Aid:** 72 **% Residing in College-Owned, -Operated, or -Affiliated Housing:** 95 **Library Holdings:** 222,000 **Regional Accreditation:** New England Association of Schools and Colleges **Credit Hours For Degree:** 40 courses, Bachelors **ROTC:** Army, Air Force **Professional Accreditation:** AACN **Intercollegiate Athletics:** Baseball M; Basketball M & W; Cheerleading W; Field Hockey W; Football M; Golf M; Ice Hockey M; Lacrosse M & W; Skiing (Downhill) M & W; Soccer M & W; Softball W; Tennis M & W; Volleyball W

SOUTHERN NEW HAMPSHIRE UNIVERSITY
2500 North River Rd.
Manchester, NH 03106-1045
Tel: (603)668-2211
Free: 800-642-4968
Admissions: (603)645-9611
Fax: (603)645-9693
E-mail: admission@nhc.edu
Web Site: http://www.snhu.edu/
President/CEO: Dr. Paul J. LeBlanc
Registrar: Dr. Richard Ouellette
Admissions: Steve Soba
Financial Aid: Dr. Scott J. Kalicki
Type: Comprehensive **Sex:** Coed **Scores:** 92% SAT V 400+; 91% SAT M 400+ **% Accepted:** 74 **Admission Plans:** Early Action; Deferred Admission **Application Deadline:** Rolling **Application Fee:** $35.00 **H.S. Require-**

ments: High school diploma required; GED accepted **Costs Per Year:** Application fee: $35. Comprehensive fee: $30,194 includes full-time tuition ($21,384), mandatory fees ($330), and college room and board ($8480). College room only: $6080. Part-time tuition: $891 per credit. **Scholarships:** Available **Calendar System:** Semester, Summer Session Available **Enrollment:** FT 1,784, PT 60, Grad 2,043 **Faculty:** FT 114, PT 275 **Student-Faculty Ratio:** 14:1 **Exams:** SAT I or ACT **% Receiving Financial Aid:** 70 **% Residing in College-Owned, -Operated, or -Affiliated Housing:** 78 **Library Holdings:** 89,338 **Regional Accreditation:** New England Association of Schools and Colleges **Credit Hours For Degree:** 60 credits, Associates; 120 credits, Bachelors **ROTC:** Army, Air Force **Professional Accreditation:** ACF, ACBSP **Intercollegiate Athletics:** Baseball M; Basketball M & W; Cheerleading M & W; Cross-Country Running M & W; Golf M; Ice Hockey M; Lacrosse M & W; Soccer M & W; Softball W; Tennis M & W; Volleyball W

THOMAS MORE COLLEGE OF LIBERAL ARTS
6 Manchester St.
Merrimack, NH 03054-4818
Tel: (603)880-8308
Free: 800-880-8308
Fax: (603)880-9280
Web Site: http://www.thomasmorecollege.edu/
President/CEO: Dr. Peter V. Sampo
Registrar: Brian Shea
Admissions: Joanne Geiger
Financial Aid: Joanne Geiger
Type: Four-Year College **Sex:** Coed **Affiliation:** Roman Catholic Church **Scores:** 100% SAT V 400+; 100% SAT M 400+; 75% ACT 24-29 **Admission Plans:** Early Admission; Deferred Admission **Application Fee:** $0.00 **H.S. Requirements:** High school diploma required; GED accepted **Costs Per Year:** Application fee: $0. Comprehensive fee: $18,650 includes full-time tuition ($10,600), mandatory fees ($50), and college room and board ($8000). Part-time tuition: $175 per credit hour. **Scholarships:** Available **Calendar System:** Semester, Summer Session Not available **Enrollment:** FT 86 **Faculty:** FT 6, PT 1 **Student-Faculty Ratio:** 17:1 **Exams:** SAT I or ACT **% Receiving Financial Aid:** 40 **% Residing in College-Owned, -Operated, or -Affiliated Housing:** 97 **Library Holdings:** 45,000 **Regional Accreditation:** New England Association of Schools and Colleges **Credit Hours For Degree:** 120 credits, Bachelors **Professional Accreditation:** AALE

UNIVERSITY OF NEW HAMPSHIRE
Durham, NH 03824
Tel: (603)862-1234
Admissions: (603)862-1360
E-mail: admissions@unh.edu
Web Site: http://www.unh.edu/
President/CEO: Dr. Ann Weaver Hart
Registrar: Kathryn P. Forbes
Admissions: Robert McGann
Financial Aid: Susan K. Allen
Type: University **Sex:** Coed **Affiliation:** University System of New Hampshire **Scores:** 99% SAT V 400+; 99% SAT M 400+ **% Accepted:** 72 **Admission Plans:** Preferred Admission; Early Action; Deferred Admission **Application Deadline:** February 01 **Application Fee:** $45.00 **H.S. Requirements:** High school diploma required; GED accepted **Costs Per Year:** Application fee: $45. State resident tuition: $8240 full-time. Nonresident tuition: $20,690 full-time. Mandatory fees: $2161 full-time. College room and board: $7584. College room only: $4606. **Scholarships:** Available **Calendar System:** Semester, Summer Session Available **Enrollment:** FT 10,911, PT 618, Grad 3,035 **Faculty:** FT 694, PT 268 **Student-Faculty Ratio:** 16:1 **Exams:** SAT I or ACT **% Receiving Financial Aid:** 58 **% Residing in College-Owned, -Operated, or -Affiliated Housing:** 56 **Library Holdings:** 1,771,477 **Regional Accreditation:** New England Association of Schools and Colleges **Credit Hours For Degree:** 64 credits, Associates; 128 credits, Bachelors **ROTC:** Army, Air Force **Professional Accreditation:** AACSB, ABET, AAMFT, AACN, ADtA, AOTA, APA, ASLHA, CSWE, JRCEPAT, NAACLS, NASM, NRPA, SAF **Intercollegiate Athletics:** Archery M & W; Badminton M & W; Baseball M; Basketball M & W; Crew M & W; Cross-Country Running M & W; Fencing M & W; Field Hockey W; Football M; Golf M; Gymnastics W; Ice Hockey M & W; Lacrosse M & W; Rugby M & W; Sailing M & W; Skiing (Cross-Country) M & W; Skiing (Downhill) M & W; Soccer M & W; Softball W; Swimming and Diving M & W; Tennis M & W; Track and Field M & W; Volleyball M & W; Wrestling M

UNIVERSITY OF NEW HAMPSHIRE AT MANCHESTER
400 Commercial St.
Manchester, NH 03101-1113
Tel: (603)641-4321
Admissions: (603)641-4150
Fax: (603)641-4125
Web Site: http://www.unhm.unh.edu/
President/CEO: Dr. Robert Jolley
Registrar: Stacey Silva
Admissions: Miho Bean
Financial Aid: Jodi Abad
Type: Comprehensive **Sex:** Coed **Affiliation:** University System of New Hampshire **Scores:** 96% SAT V 400+; 96% SAT M 400+ **% Accepted:** 63 **Admission Plans:** Deferred Admission **Application Deadline:** June 15 **Application Fee:** $35.00 **H.S. Requirements:** High school diploma required; GED accepted **Costs Per Year:** Application fee: $35. State resident tuition: $6960 full-time, $290 per credit part-time. Nonresident tuition: $17,610 full-time, $734 per credit part-time. Mandatory fees: $203 full-time. Full-time tuition and fees vary according to course load and program. Part-time tuition varies according to course load and program. **Scholarships:** Available **Calendar System:** Semester, Summer Session Available **Enrollment:** FT 561, PT 437, Grad 167 **Faculty:** FT 33, PT 58 **Student-Faculty Ratio:** 12:1 **Exams:** SAT I **% Receiving Financial Aid:** 43 **Library Holdings:** 32,261 **Regional Accreditation:** New England Association of Schools and Colleges **Credit Hours For Degree:** 64 credits, Associates; 128 credits, Bachelors **ROTC:** Army, Air Force

ASSUMPTION COLLEGE FOR SISTERS
350 Bernardsville Rd.
Mendham, NJ 07945-0800
Tel: (973)543-6528
Fax: (973)543-9459
Web Site: http://www.acscollegeforsisters.org/
President/CEO: Sr. Mary Joseph Schultz, SCC
Registrar: Sr. Catherine Kemper, SCC
Admissions: Sr. Gerardine Tantsits
Financial Aid: Sr. Catherine Kemper, SCC
Type: Two-Year College **Sex:** Women **Affiliation:** Roman Catholic **Scores:** 100% SAT V 400+; 100% SAT M 400+ **% Accepted:** 100 **Application Fee:** $0.00 **H.S. Requirements:** High school diploma required; GED accepted **Costs Per Year:** Application fee: $0. Tuition: $3300 full-time, $100 per credit part-time. Mandatory fees: $50 full-time. **Scholarships:** Available **Calendar System:** Semester, Summer Session Available **Enrollment:** FT 30, PT 7 **Faculty:** FT 1, PT 16 **Student-Faculty Ratio:** 5:1 **Library Holdings:** 25,000 **Regional Accreditation:** Middle State Association of Colleges and Schools **Credit Hours For Degree:** 66 credits, Associates

ATLANTIC CAPE COMMUNITY COLLEGE
5100 Black Horse Pike
Mays Landing, NJ 08330-2699
Tel: (609)625-1111
Free: 800-645-CHIEF
Admissions: (609)343-5500
Fax: (609)343-4921
E-mail: accadmit@atlantic.edu
Web Site: http://www.atlantic.edu/
President/CEO: Dr. John May
Registrar: Heather Peterson
Admissions: Regina Skinner
Financial Aid: Linda DeSantis
Type: Two-Year College **Sex:** Coed **Admission Plans:** Open Admission; Early Admission; Deferred Admission **Application Deadline:** July 01 **Application Fee:** $35.00 **H.S. Requirements:** High school diploma or equivalent not required **Costs Per Year:** Application fee: $35. Area resident tuition: $2370 full-time, $79 per credit part-time. State resident tuition: $4740 full-time, $158 per credit part-time. Nonresident tuition: $9480 full-time, $316 per credit part-time. Mandatory fees: $550 full-time, $18 per credit part-time, $2.50 per term part-time. **Scholarships:** Available **Calendar System:** Semester, Summer Session Available **Enrollment:** FT 3,074, PT 3,771 **Faculty:** FT 86, PT 292 **Student-Faculty Ratio:** 24:1 **Library Holdings:** 78,000 **Regional Accreditation:** Middle State Association of Colleges and Schools **Credit Hours For Degree:** 64 credits, Associates **Professional Accreditation:** AOTA, APTA, NLN **Intercollegiate Athletics:** Archery M & W; Basketball M

BERGEN COMMUNITY COLLEGE
400 Paramus Rd.
Paramus, NJ 07652-1595
Tel: (201)447-7100
Fax: (201)444-7036
Web Site: http://www.bergen.edu/
President/CEO: Dr. Judith K. Winn
Registrar: Lamont Pride
Financial Aid: Joseph Roberto
Type: Two-Year College **Sex:** Coed **Admission Plans:** Open Admission; Preferred Admission **H.S. Requirements:** High school diploma required; GED accepted **Costs Per Year:** Area resident tuition: $2249 full-time, $93.70 per credit part-time. State resident tuition: $4632 full-time, $193 per credit part-time. Nonresident tuition: $4872 full-time, $203 per credit part-time. Mandatory fees: $568 full-time, $23 per credit part-time, $8 per term part-time. **Scholarships:** Available **Calendar System:** Semester, Summer Session Available **Enrollment:** FT 7,486, PT 7,326 **Faculty:** FT 297, PT 459 **Student-Faculty Ratio:** 22:1 **Regional Accreditation:** Middle State Association of Colleges and Schools **Credit Hours For Degree:** 64 credits, Associates **Professional Accreditation:** AAMAE, ADA, APTA, CARC, JRCEDMS, JRCERT, NAACLS, NLN **Intercollegiate Athletics:** Baseball M; Basketball M & W; Cross-Country Running M & W; Golf M; Soccer M & W; Softball W; Tennis M & W; Track and Field M & W; Volleyball W; Wrestling M

BERKELEY COLLEGE
44 Rifle Camp Rd.
West Paterson, NJ 07424-3353
Tel: (973)278-5400
Free: 800-446-5400
Fax: (973)278-2242
Web Site: http://www.berkeleycollege.edu/
President/CEO: Dr. Mildred Garcia
Registrar: Gail Okun
Admissions: Christine G. Richard
Financial Aid: Marilyn Stamas
Type: Two-Year College **Sex:** Coed **% Accepted:** 84 **Admission Plans:** Deferred Admission **Application Deadline:** Rolling **Application Fee:** $50.00 **H.S. Requirements:** High school diploma required; GED accepted **Costs Per Year:** Application fee: $50. Comprehensive fee: $26,700 includes full-time tuition ($16,950), mandatory fees ($750), and college room and board ($9000). **Scholarships:** Available **Calendar System:** Quarter, Summer Session Available **Enrollment:** FT 2,040, PT 382 **Faculty:** FT 51, PT 93 **Student-Faculty Ratio:** 22:1 **Exams:** SAT I or ACT **% Residing in College-Owned, -Operated, or -Affiliated Housing:** 1 **Library Holdings:** 49,584 **Regional Accreditation:** Middle State Association of Colleges and Schools **Credit Hours For Degree:** 90 quarter hours, Associates; 180 quarter hours, Bachelors **Professional Accreditation:** ACBSP

BETH MEDRASH GOVOHA
617 Sixth St.
Lakewood, NJ 08701-2797
Tel: (732)367-1060
Admissions: (908)367-1060
President/CEO: Rabbi A. Malkiel Kotler
Registrar: Rabbi Jacob Bursztyn
Admissions: Rabbi Yehuda Jacobs
Type: Two-Year Upper Division **Sex:** Men **Affiliation:** Jewish **H.S. Requirements:** High school diploma required; GED accepted **Calendar System:** Semester **Credit Hours For Degree:** 150 credits, Bachelors **Professional Accreditation:** AARTS

BLOOMFIELD COLLEGE
467 Franklin St.
Bloomfield, NJ 07003-9981

Tel: (973)748-9000
Free: 800-848-4555
Fax: (973)748-0916
Web Site: http://www.bloomfield.edu/
President/CEO: Richard Levao
Registrar: Annette Raymond
Admissions: Lourdes de Delgado
Financial Aid: Nalini Gadhia
Type: Four-Year College **Sex:** Coed **Affiliation:** Presbyterian Church (U.S. A.) **Scores:** 69% SAT V 400+; 72% SAT M 400+ **% Accepted:** 47 **Admission Plans:** Early Admission; Early Action; Deferred Admission **Application Deadline:** July 01 **Application Fee:** $35.00 **H.S. Requirements:** High school diploma required; GED accepted **Costs Per Year:** Application fee: $35. Comprehensive fee: $22,500 includes full-time tuition ($14,850), mandatory fees ($250), and college room and board ($7400). College room only: $3700. Part-time tuition: $1495 per course. Part-time mandatory fees: $30 per term. Part-time tuition and fees vary according to course load. **Scholarships:** Available **Calendar System:** Semester, Summer Session Available **Enrollment:** FT 1,721, PT 491 **Faculty:** FT 62, PT 220 **Student-Faculty Ratio:** 14:1 **Exams:** SAT I or ACT **% Receiving Financial Aid:** 86 **% Residing in College-Owned, -Operated, or -Affiliated Housing:** 15 **Library Holdings:** 64,700 **Regional Accreditation:** Middle State Association of Colleges and Schools **Credit Hours For Degree:** 33 courses, Bachelors **ROTC:** Army **Professional Accreditation:** AACN **Intercollegiate Athletics:** Baseball M; Basketball M & W; Cross-Country Running M; Soccer M & W; Softball W; Volleyball W

BROOKDALE COMMUNITY COLLEGE

765 Newman Springs Rd.
Lincroft, NJ 07738-1597
Tel: (732)842-1900
Admissions: (732)224-2268
Fax: (732)576-1643
Web Site: http://www.brookdalecc.edu/
President/CEO: Dr. Peter F. Burnham
Registrar: Kim Toomey
Admissions: Kim Toomey
Financial Aid: Michael Bennett
Type: Two-Year College **Sex:** Coed **Affiliation:** New Jersey Commission on Higher Education **Admission Plans:** Open Admission; Preferred Admission; Early Admission; Deferred Admission **Application Fee:** $25.00 **H.S. Requirements:** High school diploma required; GED accepted **Costs Per Year:** Application fee: $25. Area resident tuition: $2202 full-time, $91.75 per credit part-time. State resident tuition: $4404 full-time, $183.50 per credit part-time. Nonresident tuition: $5400 full-time, $225 per credit part-time. Mandatory fees: $462 full-time, $19.25 per credit part-time. **Scholarships:** Available **Calendar System:** Semester, Summer Session Available **Enrollment:** FT 6,588, PT 6,136 **Faculty:** FT 222, PT 491 **Student-Faculty Ratio:** 22:1 **Exams:** Other **Library Holdings:** 150,000 **Regional Accreditation:** Middle State Association of Colleges and Schools **Credit Hours For Degree:** 60 credits, Associates **ROTC:** Army, Air Force **Professional Accreditation:** CARC, JRCERT, NLN **Intercollegiate Athletics:** Baseball M; Basketball M & W; Cross-Country Running M & W; Golf M; Soccer M & W; Softball W; Tennis M & W

BURLINGTON COUNTY COLLEGE

Route 530
Pemberton, NJ 08068-1599
Tel: (609)894-9311
Fax: (609)894-0183
Web Site: http://www.bcc.edu/
President/CEO: Dr. Robert Messina
Admissions: Elva DeJesus-Lopez
Financial Aid: Christopher Pesotski
Type: Two-Year College **Sex:** Coed **Affiliation:** New Jersey Commission on Higher Education **Admission Plans:** Open Admission; Early Admission; Deferred Admission **Application Fee:** $20.00 **H.S. Requirements:** High school diploma required; GED accepted **Scholarships:** Available **Calendar System:** Semester, Summer Session Available **Enrollment:** FT 3,411, PT 4,108 **Faculty:** FT 66, PT 357 **Student-Faculty Ratio:** 27:1 **Exams:** Other **Library Holdings:** 92,400 **Regional Accreditation:** Middle State Association of Colleges and Schools **Credit Hours For Degree:** 64 credit hours, Associates **Professional Accreditation:** ABET, AHIMA, NLN **Intercollegiate Athletics:** Baseball M; Basketball M & W; Golf M; Soccer M & W; Softball W

CALDWELL COLLEGE

9 Ryerson Ave.
Caldwell, NJ 07006-6195
Tel: (973)618-3000; 888-864-9516
Admissions: (973)618-3226
Web Site: http://www.caldwell.edu/
President/CEO: Sr. Patrice Werner, OP
Registrar: Sr. Judith Rudolph, OP
Admissions: Kathryn Reilly
Financial Aid: Lissa Anderson
Type: Comprehensive **Sex:** Coed **Affiliation:** Roman Catholic **Scores:** 82% SAT V 400+; 80% SAT M 400+ **% Accepted:** 78 **Admission Plans:** Early Admission; Early Action; Deferred Admission **Application Deadline:** March 15 **Application Fee:** $40.00 **H.S. Requirements:** High school diploma required; GED accepted **Costs Per Year:** Application fee: $40. Comprehensive fee: $26,650 includes full-time tuition ($18,700), mandatory fees ($300), and college room and board ($7650). Room and board charges vary according to board plan and housing facility. Part-time tuition: $458 per credit. Part-time tuition varies according to course load. **Scholarships:** Available **Calendar System:** Semester, Summer Session Available **Enrollment:** FT 1,059, PT 612, Grad 558 **Faculty:** FT 83, PT 101 **Student-Faculty Ratio:** 12:1 **Exams:** SAT I or ACT **% Receiving Financial Aid:** 94 **% Residing in College-Owned, -Operated, or -Affiliated Housing:** 26 **Library Holdings:** 144,698 **Regional Accreditation:** Middle State Association of Colleges and Schools **Credit Hours For Degree:** 122 credits, Bachelors **ROTC:** Army **Professional Accreditation:** ACBSP **Intercollegiate Athletics:** Baseball M; Basketball M & W; Cross-Country Running W; Golf M; Soccer M & W; Softball W; Tennis M & W

CAMDEN COUNTY COLLEGE

PO Box 200
Blackwood, NJ 08012-0200
Tel: (856)227-7200; 888-228-2466
Web Site: http://www.camdencc.edu/
President/CEO: Dr. Phyllis Della Vecchia
Registrar: Edward Reynolds
Admissions: Jacqueline Baldwin
Financial Aid: Jacqueline Baldwin
Type: Two-Year College **Sex:** Coed **Affiliation:** New Jersey Commission on Higher Education **Admission Plans:** Open Admission; Early Admission **Application Fee:** $0.00 **H.S. Requirements:** High school diploma required; GED accepted **Costs Per Year:** Application fee: $0. Area resident tuition: $73 per credit part-time. State resident tuition: $77 per credit part-time. Mandatory fees: $13 per credit part-time. **Scholarships:** Available **Calendar System:** Semester, Summer Session Available **Faculty:** FT 132, PT 606 **Library Holdings:** 91,366 **Regional Accreditation:** Middle State Association of Colleges and Schools **Credit Hours For Degree:** 64 credits, Associates **Professional Accreditation:** ADA, COptA, NAACLS **Intercollegiate Athletics:** Baseball M; Basketball M & W; Soccer M & W; Softball W

CENTENARY COLLEGE

400 Jefferson St.
Hackettstown, NJ 07840-2100
Tel: (908)852-1400
Free: 800-236-8679
Fax: (908)852-3454
Web Site: http://www.centenarycollege.edu/
President/CEO: Dr. Kenneth L. Hoyt
Registrar: Elise Bayse
Admissions: Diane Finnan
Financial Aid: Michael Corso
Type: Comprehensive **Sex:** Coed **Affiliation:** United Methodist Church **Scores:** 72% SAT V 400+; 59% SAT M 400+; 1% ACT 18-23 **% Accepted:** 75 **Admission Plans:** Deferred Admission **Application Deadline:** Rolling **Application Fee:** $30.00 **H.S. Requirements:** High school diploma required; GED accepted **Costs Per Year:** Application fee: $30. Comprehensive fee: $28,770 includes full-time tuition ($19,840), mandatory fees ($1030), and college room and board ($7900). Full-time tuition and fees vary according to location and program. Part-time tuition: $395 per credit. Part-time mandatory fees: $10 per term. Part-time tuition and fees vary according to location and program. **Scholarships:** Available **Calendar System:** Semester, Summer Session Available **Enrollment:** FT 1,617, PT 270, Grad 585 **Faculty:** FT 63, PT 241 **Student-Faculty Ratio:** 18:1 **Exams:** SAT I or ACT **% Receiving Financial Aid:** 84 **% Residing in College-Owned, -Operated, or -Affiliated Housing:** 58 **Library Holdings:** 67,272 **Regional**

Accreditation: Middle State Association of Colleges and Schools **Credit Hours For Degree:** 64 credits, Associates; 128 credits, Bachelors **Professional Accreditation:** TEAC **Intercollegiate Athletics:** Baseball M; Basketball M & W; Cross-Country Running M & W; Equestrian Sports M & W; Golf M & W; Lacrosse M & W; Soccer M & W; Softball W; Volleyball W; Wrestling M

THE COLLEGE OF NEW JERSEY
PO Box 7718
Ewing, NJ 08628
Tel: (609)771-1855
Free: 800-624-0967
Admissions: (609)771-2131
E-mail: admiss@tcnj.edu
Web Site: http://www.tcnj.edu/
President/CEO: Dr. R. Barbara Gitenstein
Registrar: Frank Cooper
Admissions: Lisa Angeloni
Financial Aid: Kathleen Ragan
Type: Comprehensive **Sex:** Coed **Scores:** 99% SAT V 400+; 100% SAT M 400+ **% Accepted:** 45 **Admission Plans:** Early Admission; Early Decision Plan; Deferred Admission **Application Deadline:** February 15 **Application Fee:** $50.00 **H.S. Requirements:** High school diploma required; GED accepted **Costs Per Year:** Application fee: $50. State resident tuition: $7051 full-time, $249.75 per credit part-time. Nonresident tuition: $12,314 full-time, $436 per credit part-time. Mandatory fees: $2656 full-time, $93.10 per credit part-time. Part-time tuition and fees vary according to course load. College room and board: $8458. College room only: $6090. Room and board charges vary according to board plan. **Scholarships:** Available **Calendar System:** Semester, Summer Session Available **Enrollment:** FT 5,726, PT 169, Grad 873 **Faculty:** FT 341, PT 364 **Student-Faculty Ratio:** 12:1 **Exams:** SAT I or ACT **% Receiving Financial Aid:** 32 **% Residing in College-Owned, -Operated, or -Affiliated Housing:** 65 **Library Holdings:** 550,000 **Regional Accreditation:** Middle State Association of Colleges and Schools **Credit Hours For Degree:** 120 semester hours, Bachelors **ROTC:** Army, Air Force **Professional Accreditation:** AACSB, ABET, AACN, ACA, ASLHA, NASM, NCATE, NLN **Intercollegiate Athletics:** Baseball M; Basketball M & W; Cross-Country Running M & W; Field Hockey W; Football M; Golf M; Lacrosse W; Soccer M & W; Softball W; Swimming and Diving M & W; Tennis M & W; Track and Field M & W; Wrestling M

COLLEGE OF SAINT ELIZABETH
2 Convent Rd.
Morristown, NJ 07960-6989
Tel: (973)290-4000
Free: 800-210-7900
Admissions: (973)290-4700
Fax: (973)290-4710
E-mail: apply@liza.st-elizabeth.edu
Web Site: http://www.cse.edu/
President/CEO: Sr. Francis Raftery
Registrar: Dr. Carol Strobeck
Admissions: Donna Tatarka
Financial Aid: Vincent Tunstall
Type: Comprehensive **Affiliation:** Roman Catholic **Scores:** 74% SAT V 400+; 76% SAT M 400+ **% Accepted:** 79 **Admission Plans:** Early Admission; Deferred Admission **Application Deadline:** August 15 **Application Fee:** $35.00 **H.S. Requirements:** High school diploma required; GED accepted **Costs Per Year:** Application fee: $35. Comprehensive fee: $28,715 includes full-time tuition ($18,640), mandatory fees ($1100), and college room and board ($8975). Full-time tuition and fees vary according to program. Part-time tuition: $587 per credit. Part-time mandatory fees: $170. Part-time tuition and fees vary according to course load, location, and program. **Scholarships:** Available **Calendar System:** Semester, Summer Session Available **Enrollment:** FT 671, PT 534, Grad 653 **Faculty:** FT 65, PT 113 **Student-Faculty Ratio:** 10:1 **Exams:** SAT I or ACT **% Receiving Financial Aid:** 75 **% Residing in College-Owned, -Operated, or -Affiliated Housing:** 68 **Library Holdings:** 110,230 **Regional Accreditation:** Middle State Association of Colleges and Schools **Credit Hours For Degree:** 128 semester hours, Bachelors **Professional Accreditation:** AAFCS, ADtA, NLN **Intercollegiate Athletics:** Basketball W; Equestrian Sports W; Soccer W; Softball W; Swimming and Diving W; Tennis W; Volleyball W

COUNTY COLLEGE OF MORRIS
214 Center Grove Rd.
Randolph, NJ 07869-2086
Tel: (973)328-5000; 888-226-8001
Admissions: (973)328-5100
Fax: (973)328-1282
E-mail: admiss@ccm.edu
Web Site: http://www.ccm.edu/
President/CEO: Dr. Edward J. Yaw
Registrar: Kathy Verba
Admissions: Jessica Chambers
Type: Two-Year College **Sex:** Coed **Affiliation:** New Jersey Commission on Higher Education **Scores:** 77% SAT V 400+; 80% SAT M 400+ **Admission Plans:** Open Admission; Early Admission **Application Fee:** $25.00 **H.S. Requirements:** High school diploma or equivalent not required **Scholarships:** Available **Calendar System:** Semester, Summer Session Available **Faculty:** FT 174, PT 323 **Student-Faculty Ratio:** 17:1 **Exams:** Other, SAT I or ACT **Library Holdings:** 102,550 **Regional Accreditation:** Middle State Association of Colleges and Schools **Credit Hours For Degree:** 62 credits, Associates **Professional Accreditation:** ABET, ACBSP, JRCERT, NLN **Intercollegiate Athletics:** Baseball M; Basketball M & W; Golf M & W; Ice Hockey M; Soccer M; Softball W; Tennis M & W

CUMBERLAND COUNTY COLLEGE
PO Box 1500, College Dr.
Vineland, NJ 08362-1500
Tel: (856)691-8600
Fax: (856)691-6157
Web Site: http://www.cccnj.edu/
President/CEO: Dr. Kenneth L. Ender
Registrar: Maud Fried-Goodnight
Admissions: Maud Fried-Goodnight
Financial Aid: Kimberly Mitchell
Type: Two-Year College **Sex:** Coed **Affiliation:** New Jersey Commission on Higher Education **Admission Plans:** Open Admission; Early Admission; Deferred Admission **Application Fee:** $25.00 **H.S. Requirements:** High school diploma required; GED accepted **Costs Per Year:** Application fee: $25. Area resident tuition: $1848 full-time, $77 per credit part-time. State resident tuition: $3696 full-time, $154 per credit part-time. Nonresident tuition: $7392 full-time, $308 per credit part-time. Mandatory fees: $600 full-time, $25 per credit part-time. **Scholarships:** Available **Calendar System:** Semester, Summer Session Available **Enrollment:** FT 1,639, PT 1,537 **Faculty:** FT 43, PT 184 **Student-Faculty Ratio:** 19:1 **Library Holdings:** 51,000 **Regional Accreditation:** Middle State Association of Colleges and Schools **Credit Hours For Degree:** 64 credits, Associates **Professional Accreditation:** JRCERT, NLN **Intercollegiate Athletics:** Baseball M; Basketball M & W; Softball W; Track and Field M

DEVRY UNIVERSITY
630 US Hwy. 1
North Brunswick, NJ 08902-3362
Tel: (732)435-4880; (866)338-7934
Web Site: http://www.devry.edu/
President/CEO: Harold Y. McCulloch
Financial Aid: Albert Cama
Type: Four-Year College **Sex:** Coed **Affiliation:** DeVry University **Admission Plans:** Deferred Admission **Application Deadline:** Rolling **Application Fee:** $50.00 **H.S. Requirements:** High school diploma required; GED accepted **Costs Per Year:** Application fee: $50. One-time mandatory fee: $40. Tuition: $11,890 full-time, $505 per credit part-time. Mandatory fees: $270 full-time, $160 per year part-time. Full-time tuition and fees vary according to course load. Part-time tuition and fees vary according to course load. **Scholarships:** Available **Calendar System:** Semester, Summer Session Available **Enrollment:** FT 1,154, PT 349 **Faculty:** FT 52, PT 102 **Student-Faculty Ratio:** 15:1 **% Receiving Financial Aid:** 63 **Library Holdings:** 32,109 **Regional Accreditation:** North Central Association of Colleges and Schools **Credit Hours For Degree:** 65 credit hours, Associates; 126 credit hours, Bachelors **Professional Accreditation:** ABET

DREW UNIVERSITY
36 Madison Ave.
Madison, NJ 07940-1493

Tel: (973)408-3000
Admissions: (973)408-3739
Fax: (973)408-3939
E-mail: cadm@drew.edu
Web Site: http://www.drew.edu/
President/CEO: Thomas H. Kean
Registrar: Horace Tate
Admissions: Mary Beth Carey
Type: University **Sex:** Coed **Affiliation:** United Methodist Church **Scores:** 100% SAT V 400+; 100% SAT M 400+; 20% ACT 18-23; 69% ACT 24-29 **% Accepted:** 77 **Admission Plans:** Early Admission; Early Decision Plan; Deferred Admission **Application Deadline:** February 15 **Application Fee:** $50.00 **H.S. Requirements:** High school diploma or equivalent not required **Costs Per Year:** Application fee: $50. Comprehensive fee: $39,698 includes full-time tuition ($30,740), mandatory fees ($546), and college room and board ($8412). College room only: $5438. Full-time tuition and fees vary according to course load. Room and board charges vary according to board plan and housing facility. Part-time tuition: $1280 per credit. Part-time mandatory fees: $22.75 per credit, $273. Part-time tuition and fees vary according to course load. **Scholarships:** Available **Calendar System:** Semester, Summer Session Available **Enrollment:** FT 1,561, PT 52, Grad 786 **Faculty:** FT 148, PT 85 **Student-Faculty Ratio:** 11:1 **% Receiving Financial Aid:** 50 **% Residing in College-Owned, -Operated, or -Affiliated Housing:** 88 **Library Holdings:** 499,758 **Regional Accreditation:** Middle State Association of Colleges and Schools **Credit Hours For Degree:** 128 credits, Bachelors **ROTC:** Army, Air Force **Professional Accreditation:** ACIPE, ATS **Intercollegiate Athletics:** Baseball M; Basketball M & W; Cross-Country Running M & W; Equestrian Sports M & W; Fencing M & W; Field Hockey W; Lacrosse M & W; Rugby M & W; Soccer M & W; Softball W; Swimming and Diving M & W; Tennis M & W

ESSEX COUNTY COLLEGE
303 University Ave.
Newark, NJ 07102-1798
Tel: (973)877-3000
Admissions: (973)877-3119
Fax: (973)623-6449
Web Site: http://www.essex.edu/
President/CEO: Dr. Zachary Yamba
Registrar: Zee Kassa
Admissions: Marva Mack
Financial Aid: Mildred Cofer
Type: Two-Year College **Sex:** Coed **Affiliation:** New Jersey Commission on Higher Education **% Accepted:** 100 **Admission Plans:** Open Admission; Deferred Admission **Application Deadline:** August 15 **Application Fee:** $25.00 **H.S. Requirements:** High school diploma or equivalent not required **Costs Per Year:** Application fee: $25. Area resident tuition: $2318 full-time, $77.25 per credit hour part-time. State resident tuition: $4635 full-time, $154.50 per credit hour part-time. Mandatory fees: $650 full-time, $26 per credit hour part-time. **Scholarships:** Available **Calendar System:** Semester, Summer Session Available **Enrollment:** FT 5,683, PT 4,752 **Faculty:** FT 162, PT 430 **Student-Faculty Ratio:** 28:1 **Library Holdings:** 91,000 **Regional Accreditation:** Middle State Association of Colleges and Schools **Credit Hours For Degree:** 63 credit hours, Associates **ROTC:** Army **Professional Accreditation:** APTA, COptA, JRCERT, NLN **Intercollegiate Athletics:** Basketball M & W; Cross-Country Running M & W; Soccer M; Track and Field M & W

FAIRLEIGH DICKINSON UNIVERSITY, COLLEGE AT FLORHAM
285 Madison Ave.
Madison, NJ 07940-1099
Tel: (973)443-8500
Free: 800-338-8803
Admissions: (201)692-7304
Web Site: http://www.fdu.edu/
President/CEO: J. Michael Adams
Registrar: Carol Creekmore
Admissions: Bernetta Millonde
Financial Aid: Margaret McGrail
Type: Comprehensive **Sex:** Coed **Scores:** 97.5% SAT V 400+; 96.5% SAT M 400+ **% Accepted:** 72 **Admission Plans:** Deferred Admission **Application Fee:** $40.00 **H.S. Requirements:** High school diploma required; GED accepted **Costs Per Year:** Application fee: $40. Comprehensive fee: $33,932 includes full-time tuition ($24,364), mandatory fees ($540), and college room and board ($9028). College room only: $5404. Room and board charges vary according to board plan and housing facility. Part-time tuition: $725 per credit. Part-time mandatory fees: $130 per term. Part-time tuition and fees vary according to course load. **Scholarships:** Available **Calendar System:** Semester, Summer Session Available **Enrollment:** FT 2,300, PT 295, Grad 886 **Faculty:** FT 113, PT 196 **Student-Faculty Ratio:** 16:1 **Exams:** SAT I and SAT II or ACT **% Receiving Financial Aid:** 69 **% Residing in College-Owned, -Operated, or -Affiliated Housing:** 56 **Regional Accreditation:** Middle State Association of Colleges and Schools **Credit Hours For Degree:** 78 credits, Associates; 128 credits, Bachelors **ROTC:** Army **Professional Accreditation:** AACSB **Intercollegiate Athletics:** Baseball M; Basketball M & W; Cross-Country Running M & W; Field Hockey W; Football M; Golf M; Lacrosse M & W; Soccer M & W; Softball W; Swimming and Diving M & W; Tennis M & W; Volleyball W

FAIRLEIGH DICKINSON UNIVERSITY, METROPOLITAN CAMPUS
1000 River Rd.
Teaneck, NJ 07666-1914
Tel: (201)692-2000
Free: 800-338-8803
Admissions: (201)692-7304
Web Site: http://www.fdu.edu/
President/CEO: Dr. J. Michael Adams
Admissions: Bernetta Millonde
Financial Aid: Margaret McGrail
Type: Comprehensive **Sex:** Coed **Scores:** 93.7% SAT V 400+; 94.5% SAT M 400+ **% Accepted:** 65 **Admission Plans:** Early Admission; Deferred Admission **Application Fee:** $40.00 **H.S. Requirements:** High school diploma required; GED accepted **Costs Per Year:** Application fee: $40. Comprehensive fee: $32,646 includes full-time tuition ($22,604), mandatory fees ($540), and college room and board ($9502). College room only: $5878. Room and board charges vary according to board plan and housing facility. Part-time tuition: $725 per credit. Part-time mandatory fees: $130 per term. Part-time tuition and fees vary according to course load. **Scholarships:** Available **Calendar System:** Semester, Summer Session Available **Enrollment:** FT 1,833, PT 3,611, Grad 2,493 **Faculty:** FT 182, PT 379 **Student-Faculty Ratio:** 15:1 **Exams:** SAT I and SAT II or ACT **% Receiving Financial Aid:** 71 **% Residing in College-Owned, -Operated, or -Affiliated Housing:** 26 **Regional Accreditation:** Middle State Association of Colleges and Schools **Credit Hours For Degree:** 72 credits, Associates; 128 credits, Bachelors **ROTC:** Army **Professional Accreditation:** AACSB, ABET, AACN, APA **Intercollegiate Athletics:** Baseball M; Basketball M & W; Bowling W; Cross-Country Running M & W; Fencing W; Golf M; Soccer M & W; Softball W; Tennis M & W; Track and Field M & W; Volleyball W

FELICIAN COLLEGE
262 South Main St.
Lodi, NJ 07644-2117
Tel: (201)559-6000
Admissions: (201)559-6187
Fax: (973)778-4111
E-mail: admissions@inet.felician.edu
Web Site: http://www.felician.edu/
President/CEO: Sr. Theresa Martin
Registrar: June Finn
Admissions: Cara McCloud
Type: Comprehensive **Sex:** Coed **Affiliation:** Roman Catholic **% Accepted:** 87 **Application Deadline:** Rolling **Application Fee:** $30.00 **H.S. Requirements:** High school diploma required; GED accepted. For nursing, elementary education programs: High school diploma required; GED not accepted **Costs Per Year:** Application fee: $30. Comprehensive fee: $26,150 includes full-time tuition ($17,300), mandatory fees ($900), and college room and board ($7950). Part-time tuition: $575 per credit. **Scholarships:** Available **Calendar System:** Semester, Summer Session Available **Enrollment:** FT 1,157, PT 393, Grad 256 **Faculty:** FT 83, PT 65 **Student-Faculty Ratio:** 13:1 **Exams:** ACT, SAT I or ACT, SAT II **% Receiving Financial Aid:** 76 **Library Holdings:** 101,040 **Regional Accreditation:** Middle State Association of Colleges and Schools **Credit Hours For Degree:** 68 semester hours, Associates; 120 semester hours, Bachelors **Professional Accreditation:** AACN, NAACLS, NLN **Intercollegiate Athletics:** Baseball M; Basketball M & W; Cross-Country Running M & W; Soccer M & W; Softball W; Track and Field M & W

GEORGIAN COURT UNIVERSITY
900 Lakewood Ave.
Lakewood, NJ 08701-2697

Tel: (732)987-2760
Free: 800-458-8422
Admissions: (732)364-2202
Fax: (732)987-2000
E-mail: admissions@georgian.edu
Web Site: http://www.georgian.edu/
President/CEO: Sr. Rosemary Jeffries, PhD
Registrar: Jill Riley
Admissions: Kathie DeBona
Financial Aid: Carol Strauss
Type: Comprehensive **Affiliation:** Roman Catholic **Scores:** 86% SAT V 400+; 82% SAT M 400+ **% Accepted:** 75 **Admission Plans:** Early Action **Application Deadline:** August 01 **Application Fee:** $40.00 **H.S. Requirements:** High school diploma required; GED accepted **Costs Per Year:** Application fee: $40. Comprehensive fee: $26,700 includes full-time tuition ($18,380), mandatory fees ($720), and college room and board ($7600). Full-time tuition and fees vary according to program. Room and board charges vary according to board plan. Part-time tuition: $495 per credit. Part-time mandatory fees: $180 per term. Part-time tuition and fees vary according to course load and program. **Scholarships:** Available **Calendar System:** Semester, Summer Session Available **Enrollment:** FT 1,345, PT 654, Grad 1,154 **Faculty:** FT 110, PT 188 **Student-Faculty Ratio:** 13:1 **Exams:** SAT I or ACT **% Receiving Financial Aid:** 80 **% Residing in College-Owned, -Operated, or -Affiliated Housing:** 15 **Library Holdings:** 145,413 **Regional Accreditation:** Middle State Association of Colleges and Schools **Credit Hours For Degree:** 132 credits, Bachelors **Professional Accreditation:** ACBSP, CSWE **Intercollegiate Athletics:** Basketball W; Cross-Country Running W; Soccer W; Softball W; Tennis W; Volleyball W

GIBBS COLLEGE (LIVINGSTON)
630 West Mount Pleasant Ave.
Livingston, NJ 07039
Tel: (973)369-1360
Web Site: http://www.gibbsmontclair.com **Type:** Two-Year College **Sex:** Coed

GIBBS COLLEGE (MONTCLAIR)
33 Plymouth St.
Montclair, NJ 07042-2699
Tel: (973)744-2010
Admissions: (201)744-2010
E-mail: mgreco@njgibbscollege.net
Web Site: http://www.njgibbscollege.net/
President/CEO: Mary-Jo Greco
Admissions: Mary-Jo Greco
Financial Aid: Jeanie Winstrom
Type: Two-Year College **Sex:** Coed **Application Fee:** $25.00 **H.S. Requirements:** High school diploma required; GED accepted **Scholarships:** Available **Calendar System:** Quarter **Faculty:** FT 14, PT 6 **Exams:** Other **Credit Hours For Degree:** 72 credit hours, Associates **Professional Accreditation:** ACICS

GLOUCESTER COUNTY COLLEGE
1400 Tanyard Rd.
Sewell, NJ 08080
Tel: (856)468-5000
Admissions: (856)415-2209
Fax: (856)468-8498
Web Site: http://www.gccnj.edu/
President/CEO: William F. Anderson
Registrar: Kim Momballou
Admissions: David Schleicher
Financial Aid: Jeffrey Williams
Type: Two-Year College **Sex:** Coed **Affiliation:** New Jersey Commission on Higher Education **Admission Plans:** Open Admission; Deferred Admission **Application Fee:** $10.00 **H.S. Requirements:** High school diploma required; GED accepted. For those granted qualified admission: High school diploma or equivalent not required **Scholarships:** Available **Calendar System:** Semester, Summer Session Available **Enrollment:** FT 2,950, PT 2,660 **Faculty:** FT 59, PT 167 **Student-Faculty Ratio:** 33:1 **Exams:** SAT I or ACT **Library Holdings:** 55,710 **Regional Accreditation:** Middle State Association of Colleges and Schools **Credit Hours For Degree:** 63 credit hours, Associates **Professional Accreditation:** CARC, JRCEDMS, JRCNMT, NLN **Intercollegiate Athletics:** Baseball M; Basketball M & W; Cross-Country Running M & W; Soccer M & W; Softball W; Tennis M & W; Track and Field M & W; Wrestling M

HUDSON COUNTY COMMUNITY COLLEGE
25 Journal Square
Jersey City, NJ 07306
Tel: (201)656-2020
Admissions: (201)714-2115
Fax: (201)714-2136
Web Site: http://www.hccc.edu/
President/CEO: Dr. Glen Gabert
Registrar: Pinhas Friedenberg
Admissions: Robert Martin
Financial Aid: Pamela Norris-Littles
Type: Two-Year College **Sex:** Coed **Affiliation:** New Jersey Commission on Higher Education **Admission Plans:** Open Admission; Preferred Admission **Application Fee:** $15.00 **H.S. Requirements:** High school diploma or equivalent not required. For applicants under 18: High school diploma required; GED accepted **Scholarships:** Available **Calendar System:** Semester, Summer Session Available **Enrollment:** FT 4,277, PT 2,212 **Faculty:** FT 85, PT 289 **Exams:** Other **Library Holdings:** 32,000 **Regional Accreditation:** Middle State Association of Colleges and Schools **Credit Hours For Degree:** 66 credits, Associates **Professional Accreditation:** ABET, AAMAE, ACF, AHIMA

KEAN UNIVERSITY
1000 Morris Ave.
Union, NJ 07083
Tel: (908)737-KEAN
Admissions: (908)737-7100
Fax: (908)737-3415
E-mail: admitme@kean.edu
Web Site: http://www.kean.edu/
President/CEO: Dr. Dawood Farahi
Registrar: Carol Gubernat
Admissions: Audley Bridges
Financial Aid: Sandra Bembry
Type: Comprehensive **Sex:** Coed **Affiliation:** New Jersey State College System **Scores:** 86% SAT V 400+; 88% SAT M 400+ **% Accepted:** 71 **Application Deadline:** May 31 **Application Fee:** $50.00 **H.S. Requirements:** High school diploma required; GED accepted **Costs Per Year:** Application fee: $50. State resident tuition: $4898 full-time, $163.25 per credit part-time. Nonresident tuition: $7530 full-time, $251 per credit part-time. Mandatory fees: $2609 full-time, $87.70 per credit part-time. Part-time tuition and fees vary according to course load. College room and board: $8374. College room only: $5892. Room and board charges vary according to board plan and housing facility. **Scholarships:** Available **Calendar System:** Semester, Summer Session Available **Enrollment:** FT 7,591, PT 2,444, Grad 2,923 **Faculty:** FT 382, PT 778 **Student-Faculty Ratio:** 15:1 **Exams:** SAT I or ACT **% Receiving Financial Aid:** 53 **% Residing in College-Owned, -Operated, or -Affiliated Housing:** 12 **Library Holdings:** 280,000 **Regional Accreditation:** Middle State Association of Colleges and Schools **Credit Hours For Degree:** 124 semester hours, Bachelors **ROTC:** Army, Air Force **Professional Accreditation:** AHIMA, AOTA, ASLHA, CSWE, FIDER, JRCEPAT, NAIT, NASAD, NASM, NASPAA, NAST, NCATE, NLN **Intercollegiate Athletics:** Baseball M; Basketball M & W; Cheerleading M & W; Cross-Country Running M & W; Field Hockey W; Football M; Lacrosse M & W; Soccer M & W; Softball W; Tennis W; Track and Field M & W; Volleyball W

MERCER COUNTY COMMUNITY COLLEGE
1200 Old Trenton Rd., PO Box B
Trenton, NJ 08690-1004
Tel: (609)586-4800
Free: 800-392-MCCC
Fax: (609)586-6944
Web Site: http://www.mccc.edu/
President/CEO: Robert R. Rose,, PhD
Registrar: Donald Beach
Financial Aid: Reginald Page
Type: Two-Year College **Sex:** Coed **% Accepted:** 100 **Admission Plans:** Open Admission; Preferred Admission; Deferred Admission **Application Deadline:** Rolling **Application Fee:** $0.00 **H.S. Requirements:** High school diploma or equivalent not required **Costs Per Year:** Application fee: $0. Area resident tuition: $2940 full-time, $98 per credit part-time. State resident tuition: $3945 full-time, $131.50 per credit part-time. Nonresident tuition: $6045 full-time, $201.50 per credit part-time. Mandatory fees: $495 full-time, $16.50 per credit part-time. **Scholarships:** Available **Calendar System:**

Semester, Summer Session Available **Enrollment:** FT 3,404, PT 5,524 **Faculty:** FT 137, PT 392 **Student-Faculty Ratio:** 20:1 **Library Holdings:** 57,317 **Regional Accreditation:** Middle State Association of Colleges and Schools **Credit Hours For Degree:** 60 credits, Associates **ROTC:** Army, Air Force **Professional Accreditation:** ABFSE, APTA, CAA, JRCERT, NAACLS, NLN **Intercollegiate Athletics:** Baseball M; Basketball M & W; Golf M & W; Soccer M & W; Softball W; Tennis M & W; Track and Field M & W

MIDDLESEX COUNTY COLLEGE

2600 Woodbridge Ave., PO Box 3050
Edison, NJ 08818-3050
Tel: (732)548-6000
Admissions: (732)906-4243
Web Site: http://www.middlesexcc.edu/
President/CEO: Dr. John Bakum
Registrar: Edwin Griffith
Admissions: Peter W. Rice
Financial Aid: Gail Scott-Bey

Type: Two-Year College **Sex:** Coed **% Accepted:** 69 **Admission Plans:** Open Admission; Preferred Admission; Early Admission; Deferred Admission **Application Deadline:** Rolling **Application Fee:** $25.00 **H.S. Requirements:** High school diploma required; GED accepted **Costs Per Year:** Application fee: $25. Area resident tuition: $1,957 full-time, $81.55 per credit part-time. State resident tuition: $4,526 full-time, $188.60 per credit part-time. Mandatory fees: $612 full-time, $25.50 per credit part-time. **Scholarships:** Available **Calendar System:** Semester, Summer Session Available **Faculty:** FT 206, PT 346 **Student-Faculty Ratio:** 21:1 **Exams:** Other **Library Holdings:** 85,160 **Regional Accreditation:** Middle State Association of Colleges and Schools **Credit Hours For Degree:** 64 credits, Associates **ROTC:** Army **Professional Accreditation:** ABET, ADA, JRCERT, NAACLS, NLN **Intercollegiate Athletics:** Baseball M; Basketball M & W; Cross-Country Running M & W; Field Hockey W; Golf M & W; Soccer M & W; Softball W; Tennis M & W; Track and Field M & W; Wrestling M

MONMOUTH UNIVERSITY

400 Cedar Ave.
West Long Branch, NJ 07764-1898
Tel: (732)571-3400
Free: 800-543-9671
Admissions: (732)571-3456
Fax: (732)263-5166
E-mail: admission@monmouth.edu
Web Site: http://www.monmouth.edu/
President/CEO: Paul G. Guffney, II
Registrar: Susan O'Keefe
Admissions: Lauren Cifelli
Financial Aid: Claire Alasio

Type: Comprehensive **Sex:** Coed **Scores:** 99% SAT V 400+; 100% SAT M 400+; 58% ACT 18-23; 38% ACT 24-29 **% Accepted:** 69 **Admission Plans:** Early Admission; Early Action; Early Decision Plan; Deferred Admission **Application Deadline:** March 01 **Application Fee:** $35.00 **H.S. Requirements:** High school diploma required; GED accepted **Costs Per Year:** Application fee: $35. Comprehensive fee: $28,956 includes full-time tuition ($20,066), mandatory fees ($620), and college room and board ($8270). College room only: $4440. Room and board charges vary according to board plan and housing facility. Part-time tuition: $581 per credit hour. Part-time mandatory fees: $155 per term. **Scholarships:** Available **Calendar System:** Semester, Summer Session Available **Enrollment:** FT 4,116, PT 439, Grad 1,795 **Faculty:** FT 246, PT 267 **Student-Faculty Ratio:** 15:1 **Exams:** SAT I or ACT **% Receiving Financial Aid:** 64 **% Residing in College-Owned, -Operated, or -Affiliated Housing:** 43 **Library Holdings:** 260,400 **Regional Accreditation:** Middle State Association of Colleges and Schools **Credit Hours For Degree:** 63 credits, Associates; 128 credits, Bachelors **ROTC:** Air Force **Professional Accreditation:** AACSB, AACN, CSWE **Intercollegiate Athletics:** Baseball M; Basketball M & W; Cross-Country Running M & W; Field Hockey W; Football M; Golf M & W; Ice Hockey M; Lacrosse W; Soccer M & W; Softball W; Tennis M & W; Track and Field M & W

MONTCLAIR STATE UNIVERSITY

1 Normal Ave.
Montclair, NJ 07043-1624
Tel: (973)655-4000
Free: 800-331-9205
Admissions: (973)655-5116
Fax: (973)893-5455
E-mail: msuadm@saturn.montclair.edu
Web Site: http://www.montclair.edu/
President/CEO: Dr. Susan A. Cole
Registrar: Denise M. DeBlasio
Admissions: Dennis Craig
Financial Aid: Frank A. Cuozzo

Type: Comprehensive **Sex:** Coed **Scores:** 95.9% SAT V 400+; 97% SAT M 400+ **% Accepted:** 54 **Admission Plans:** Deferred Admission **Application Deadline:** March 01 **Application Fee:** $55.00 **H.S. Requirements:** High school diploma required; GED accepted **Costs Per Year:** Application fee: $55. State resident tuition: $5581 full-time, $186.04 per credit part-time. Nonresident tuition: $10,029 full-time, $334.22 per credit part-time. Mandatory fees: $2128 full-time, $69.61 per credit part-time, $20 per term part-time. College room and board: $8618. College room only: $5768. Room and board charges vary according to board plan and housing facility. **Scholarships:** Available **Calendar System:** Semester, Summer Session Available **Enrollment:** FT 9,909, PT 2,265, Grad 3,889 **Faculty:** FT 477, PT 695 **Student-Faculty Ratio:** 17:1 **Exams:** SAT I or ACT **% Receiving Financial Aid:** 47 **% Residing in College-Owned, -Operated, or -Affiliated Housing:** 27 **Library Holdings:** 426,583 **Regional Accreditation:** Middle State Association of Colleges and Schools **Credit Hours For Degree:** 120 semester hours, Bachelors **ROTC:** Air Force **Professional Accreditation:** AACSB, ABET, AAFCS, ADtA, ASLHA, NASAD, NASD, NASM, NAST, NCATE, NRPA **Intercollegiate Athletics:** Baseball M; Basketball M & W; Field Hockey W; Football M; Golf M & W; Lacrosse W; Soccer M & W; Softball W; Swimming and Diving M & W; Tennis M; Track and Field M & W; Volleyball W

NEW JERSEY CITY UNIVERSITY

2039 Kennedy Blvd.
Jersey City, NJ 07305-1597
Tel: (201)200-2000; 888-441-NJCU
Admissions: (201)200-3234
Fax: (201)200-2044
E-mail: admissions@jcs1.jcstate.edu
Web Site: http://www.njcu.edu/
President/CEO: Dr. Carlos Hernandez
Registrar: Miriam Hernandez-Laria
Admissions: Jason Hand
Financial Aid: Carmen Panlilio

Type: Comprehensive **Sex:** Coed **Scores:** 79% SAT V 400+; 84% SAT M 400+ **% Accepted:** 54 **Admission Plans:** Deferred Admission **Application Deadline:** April 01 **Application Fee:** $35.00 **H.S. Requirements:** High school diploma required; GED accepted **Costs Per Year:** Application fee: $35. State resident tuition: $5190 full-time, $173 per credit hour part-time. Nonresident tuition: $10,230 full-time, $341 per credit hour part-time. Mandatory fees: $1850 full-time, $59.95 per credit part-time. College room and board: $7306. College room only: $4630. **Scholarships:** Available **Calendar System:** Semester, Summer Session Available **Enrollment:** FT 4,192, PT 1,812, Grad 2,460 **Faculty:** FT 251, PT 273 **Student-Faculty Ratio:** 16:1 **Exams:** SAT I or ACT **% Receiving Financial Aid:** 73 **% Residing in College-Owned, -Operated, or -Affiliated Housing:** 4 **Library Holdings:** 212,786 **Regional Accreditation:** Middle State Association of Colleges and Schools **Credit Hours For Degree:** 128 credits, Bachelors **Professional Accreditation:** ACBSP, NASAD, NASM, NCATE, NLN **Intercollegiate Athletics:** Baseball M; Basketball M & W; Bowling W; Cross-Country Running W; Soccer M & W; Softball W; Track and Field M & W; Volleyball M & W

NEW JERSEY INSTITUTE OF TECHNOLOGY

University Heights
Newark, NJ 07102
Tel: (973)596-3000
Free: 800-925-NJIT
Admissions: (973)596-3300
Fax: (973)802-1854
E-mail: admissions@njit.edu
Web Site: http://www.njit.edu/
President/CEO: Dr. Robert A. Altenkirch
Registrar: Joseph F. Thompson
Admissions: William Anderson
Financial Aid: Kathy Bialk

Type: University **Sex:** Coed **Scores:** 97% SAT V 400+; 89% SAT M 400+ **% Accepted:** 71 **Admission Plans:** Preferred Admission; Early Admission;

Early Decision Plan; Deferred Admission **Application Deadline:** April 01 **Application Fee:** $50.00 **H.S. Requirements:** High school diploma required; GED accepted **Costs Per Year:** Application fee: $50. State resident tuition: $8472 full-time, $321 per credit part-time. Nonresident tuition: $14,676 full-time, $628 per credit part-time. Mandatory fees: $1350 full-time, $64 per credit part-time, $102 per term part-time. Full-time tuition and fees vary according to course load and degree level. Part-time tuition and fees vary according to course load and degree level. College room and board: $8572. College room only: $5974. Room and board charges vary according to board plan and housing facility. **Scholarships:** Available **Calendar System:** Semester, Summer Session Available **Enrollment:** FT 4,082, PT 1,181, Grad 2,795 **Faculty:** FT 416, PT 238 **Student-Faculty Ratio:** 13:1 **Exams:** SAT I or ACT, SAT II **% Receiving Financial Aid:** 58 **% Residing in College-Owned, -Operated, or -Affiliated Housing:** 28 **Library Holdings:** 160,000 **Regional Accreditation:** Middle State Association of Colleges and Schools **Credit Hours For Degree:** 124 credits, Bachelors **ROTC:** Air Force **Professional Accreditation:** AACSB, ABET, CEPH **Intercollegiate Athletics:** Baseball M; Basketball M & W; Cross-Country Running M & W; Fencing M; Golf M; Soccer M; Softball W; Swimming and Diving W; Tennis M & W; Track and Field W; Volleyball M & W

OCEAN COUNTY COLLEGE
College Dr., PO Box 2001
Toms River, NJ 08754-2001
Tel: (732)255-0400
Admissions: (732)255-0304
Web Site: http://www.ocean.edu/
President/CEO: Dr. Jon H. Larson
Registrar: Mary Fennessy
Admissions: Mary Fennessy
Financial Aid: Susan Barschow
Type: Two-Year College **Sex:** Coed **Affiliation:** New Jersey Commission on Higher Education **Admission Plans:** Open Admission; Preferred Admission; Early Admission; Deferred Admission **Application Deadline:** Rolling **Application Fee:** $15.00 **H.S. Requirements:** High school diploma or equivalent not required. For nursing program: High school diploma required; GED accepted **Costs Per Year:** Application fee: $15. Area resident tuition: $2460 full-time, $82 per credit part-time. State resident tuition: $3360 full-time, $112 per credit part-time. Nonresident tuition: $5520 full-time, $184 per credit part-time. Mandatory fees: $720 full-time, $24. **Scholarships:** Available **Calendar System:** Semester, Summer Session Available **Enrollment:** FT 4,023, PT 4,426 **Faculty:** FT 119, PT 291 **Library Holdings:** 74,215 **Regional Accreditation:** Middle State Association of Colleges and Schools **Credit Hours For Degree:** 64 semester hours, Associates **Professional Accreditation:** NLN **Intercollegiate Athletics:** Baseball M; Basketball M & W; Golf M & W; Soccer M & W; Softball W; Swimming and Diving M & W; Tennis M & W

PASSAIC COUNTY COMMUNITY COLLEGE
One College Blvd.
Paterson, NJ 07505-1179
Tel: (973)684-6800
Admissions: (973)684-6304
Web Site: http://www.pccc.cc.nj.us/
President/CEO: Dr. Steven M. Rose
Registrar: Victoria Orellano
Admissions: Patrick Noonan
Financial Aid: Sheila Attias
Type: Two-Year College **Sex:** Coed **Admission Plans:** Open Admission; Preferred Admission; Early Admission; Deferred Admission **H.S. Requirements:** High school diploma or equivalent not required **Scholarships:** Available **Calendar System:** Semester, Summer Session Available **Faculty:** FT 78, PT 279 **Exams:** Other **Library Holdings:** 90,000 **Regional Accreditation:** Middle State Association of Colleges and Schools **Credit Hours For Degree:** 64 credits, Associates **ROTC:** Army **Professional Accreditation:** AHIMA, CARC, JRCERT, NLN **Intercollegiate Athletics:** Basketball M & W; Soccer M; Volleyball W

PRINCETON UNIVERSITY
Princeton, NJ 08544-1019
Tel: (609)258-3000
Admissions: (609)258-3062
Web Site: http://www.princeton.edu/
President/CEO: Dr. Shirley M. Tilghman
Registrar: Joseph Greenberg
Admissions: Janet Rapelye
Financial Aid: Don M. Betterton
Type: University **Sex:** Coed **Scores:** 100% SAT V 400+; 100% SAT M 400+ **% Accepted:** 11 **Admission Plans:** Early Decision Plan; Deferred Admission **Application Deadline:** January 01 **Application Fee:** $65.00 **H.S. Requirements:** High school diploma required; GED not accepted **Costs Per Year:** Application fee: $65. Comprehensive fee: $42,200 includes full-time tuition ($33,000) and college room and board ($9200). College room only: $4885. **Scholarships:** Available **Calendar System:** Semester, Summer Session Not available **Enrollment:** FT 4,719, PT 187, Grad 2,010 **Faculty:** FT 809, PT 251 **Student-Faculty Ratio:** 5:1 **Exams:** SAT I and SAT II or ACT **% Receiving Financial Aid:** 51 **% Residing in College-Owned, -Operated, or -Affiliated Housing:** 98 **Library Holdings:** 6,968,555 **Regional Accreditation:** Middle State Association of Colleges and Schools **Credit Hours For Degree:** 31 courses, Bachelors **ROTC:** Army, Air Force **Professional Accreditation:** ABET **Intercollegiate Athletics:** Baseball M; Basketball M & W; Crew M & W; Cross-Country Running M & W; Fencing M & W; Field Hockey W; Football M; Golf M & W; Ice Hockey M & W; Lacrosse M & W; Soccer M & W; Softball W; Squash M & W; Swimming and Diving M & W; Tennis M & W; Track and Field M & W; Volleyball M & W; Water Polo M & W; Wrestling M

RABBI JACOB JOSEPH SCHOOL
One Plainfield Ave
Edison, NJ 08817
Tel: (908)985-6533 **Type:** Four-Year College **Affiliation:** Jewish **Professional Accreditation:** AARTS

RABBINICAL COLLEGE OF AMERICA
226 Sussex Ave., PO Box 1996
Morristown, NJ 07962-1996
Tel: (973)267-9404
Fax: (973)267-5208
President/CEO: Rabbi Moshe Herson
Registrar: Rabbi Israel Teitelbaum
Admissions: Rabbi Israel Teitelbaum
Financial Aid: Rabbi Israel Teitelbaum
Type: Four-Year College **Sex:** Men **Affiliation:** Jewish **H.S. Requirements:** High school diploma required; GED accepted **Calendar System:** Semester, Summer Session Available **Faculty:** FT 13 **Library Holdings:** 10,000 **Credit Hours For Degree:** 120 credits, Bachelors **Professional Accreditation:** AARTS

RAMAPO COLLEGE OF NEW JERSEY
505 Ramapo Valley Rd.
Mahwah, NJ 07430-1680
Tel: (201)684-7500
Admissions: (201)684-7300
Fax: (201)684-7508
E-mail: admissions@ramapo.edu
Web Site: http://www.ramapo.edu/
President/CEO: Dr. W. Sanborn Pfeiffer
Registrar: Cynthia Brennan
Admissions: Nancy Jaeger
Financial Aid: Mark Singer
Type: Comprehensive **Sex:** Coed **Affiliation:** New Jersey State College System **Scores:** 99.8% SAT V 400+; 100% SAT M 400+ **% Accepted:** 41 **Admission Plans:** Early Admission; Early Action; Deferred Admission **Application Deadline:** March 01 **Application Fee:** $55.00 **H.S. Requirements:** High school diploma required; GED accepted **Costs Per Year:** Application fee: $55. State resident tuition: $6091 full-time, $190.35 per credit part-time. Nonresident tuition: $11,008 full-time, $344 per credit part-time. Mandatory fees: $2701 full-time, $84.40 per credit part-time. College room and board: $9464. College room only: $6840. **Scholarships:** Available **Calendar System:** Semester, Summer Session Available **Enrollment:** FT 4,254, PT 979, Grad 305 **Faculty:** FT 187, PT 246 **Student-Faculty Ratio:** 16:1 **Exams:** ACT, SAT I **% Receiving Financial Aid:** 47 **% Residing in College-Owned, -Operated, or -Affiliated Housing:** 51 **Library Holdings:** 172,639 **Regional Accreditation:** Middle State Association of Colleges and Schools **Credit Hours For Degree:** 128 credits, Bachelors **ROTC:** Air Force **Professional Accreditation:** CSWE **Intercollegiate Athletics:** Baseball M;

Basketball M & W; Cheerleading W; Cross-Country Running M & W; Field Hockey W; Soccer M & W; Softball W; Tennis M & W; Track and Field M & W; Volleyball M & W

RARITAN VALLEY COMMUNITY COLLEGE
PO Box 3300
Somerville, NJ 08876-1265
Tel: (908)526-1200
Fax: (908)704-3442
E-mail: momalley@raritanval.edu
Web Site: http://www.raritanval.edu/
President/CEO: Dr. G. Jeremiah Ryan
Registrar: Richard Cole
Admissions: Mary O'Malley
Financial Aid: Audrey Loera
Type: Two-Year College **Sex:** Coed **% Accepted:** 68 **Admission Plans:** Open Admission; Early Admission **Application Deadline:** Rolling **Application Fee:** $25.00 **H.S. Requirements:** High school diploma required; GED accepted **Costs Per Year:** Application fee: $25. State resident tuition: $2430 full-time, $81 per credit part-time. Nonresident tuition: $2430 full-time, $81 per credit part-time. Mandatory fees: $850 full-time, $23 per credit part-time, $80 per term part-time. **Scholarships:** Available **Calendar System:** Semester, Summer Session Available **Enrollment:** FT 2,575, PT 3,676 **Faculty:** FT 101, PT 300 **Student-Faculty Ratio:** 19:1 **Library Holdings:** 82,942 **Regional Accreditation:** Middle State Association of Colleges and Schools **Credit Hours For Degree:** 60 credits, Associates **ROTC:** Army, Air Force **Professional Accreditation:** COptA, NLN **Intercollegiate Athletics:** Baseball M; Basketball M; Softball W

THE RICHARD STOCKTON COLLEGE OF NEW JERSEY
PO Box 195, Jimmie Leeds Rd.
Pomona, NJ 08240-0195
Tel: (609)652-1776
Admissions: (609)652-4261
Fax: (609)748-5541
E-mail: admissions@pollux.stockton.edu
Web Site: http://www.stockton.edu/
President/CEO: Dr. Herman Saatkamp
Registrar: Joseph Losasso
Admissions: Salvatore Catalfamo
Financial Aid: Jeanne S. Lewis
Type: Comprehensive **Sex:** Coed **Affiliation:** New Jersey State College System **Scores:** 99% SAT V 400+; 99% SAT M 400+ **% Accepted:** 52 **Admission Plans:** Early Admission; Early Action **Application Deadline:** May 01 **Application Fee:** $50.00 **H.S. Requirements:** High school diploma required; GED accepted **Costs Per Year:** Application fee: $50. State resident tuition: $5498 full-time, $171.82 per credit part-time. Nonresident tuition: $8896 full-time, $278 per credit part-time. Mandatory fees: $2896 full-time, $90.50 per credit part-time. College room and board: $7902. College room only: $5370. Room and board charges vary according to board plan and housing facility. **Scholarships:** Available **Calendar System:** Semester, Summer Session Available **Enrollment:** FT 5,650, PT 920, Grad 464 **Faculty:** FT 242, PT 184 **Student-Faculty Ratio:** 19:1 **Exams:** SAT I or ACT **% Receiving Financial Aid:** 52 **% Residing in College-Owned, -Operated, or -Affiliated Housing:** 38 **Library Holdings:** 258,822 **Regional Accreditation:** Middle State Association of Colleges and Schools **Credit Hours For Degree:** 128 credit hours, Bachelors **Professional Accreditation:** AACN, AOTA, APTA, CSWE, NLN **Intercollegiate Athletics:** Baseball M; Basketball M & W; Cheerleading M & W; Crew W; Cross-Country Running M & W; Field Hockey W; Lacrosse M; Soccer M & W; Softball W; Tennis W; Track and Field M & W; Volleyball W

RIDER UNIVERSITY
2083 Lawrenceville Rd.
Lawrenceville, NJ 08648-3001
Tel: (609)896-5000
Free: 800-257-9026
Admissions: (609)895-5768
Fax: (609)895-6645
E-mail: admissions@rider.edu
Web Site: http://www.rider.edu/
President/CEO: Dr. Mordechai Rozanski
Registrar: Susan A. Stefanick
Admissions: Susan C. Christian
Financial Aid: James O'Hara
Type: Comprehensive **Sex:** Coed **Scores:** 97.74% SAT V 400+; 98.6% SAT M 400+ **% Accepted:** 81 **Admission Plans:** Early Admission; Early Action; Deferred Admission **Application Deadline:** Rolling **Application Fee:** $45.00 **H.S. Requirements:** High school diploma required; GED accepted **Costs Per Year:** Application fee: $45. Comprehensive fee: $32,310 includes full-time tuition ($22,910), mandatory fees ($560), and college room and board ($8840). College room only: $4940. Part-time tuition: $432 per credit. Part-time mandatory fees: $35 per course. **Scholarships:** Available **Calendar System:** Semester, Summer Session Available **Enrollment:** FT 3,611, PT 764, Grad 1,177 **Faculty:** FT 234, PT 267 **Student-Faculty Ratio:** 13:1 **Exams:** SAT I or ACT **% Receiving Financial Aid:** 67 **% Residing in College-Owned, -Operated, or -Affiliated Housing:** 56 **Library Holdings:** 404,353 **Regional Accreditation:** Middle State Association of Colleges and Schools **Credit Hours For Degree:** 60 semester hours, Associates; 120 semester hours, Bachelors **ROTC:** Army **Professional Accreditation:** AACSB, ACA, NASM, NCATE **Intercollegiate Athletics:** Baseball M; Basketball M & W; Cheerleading M & W; Cross-Country Running M & W; Field Hockey W; Golf M; Soccer M & W; Softball W; Swimming and Diving M & W; Tennis M & W; Track and Field M & W; Volleyball W; Wrestling M

ROWAN UNIVERSITY
201 Mullica Hill Rd.
Glassboro, NJ 08028-1701
Tel: (856)256-4500
Admissions: (856)256-4200
E-mail: admissions@rowan.edu
Web Site: http://www.rowan.edu/
President/CEO: Dr. Donald Farish
Registrar: Edwin Eigenbrot, Jr.
Admissions: Marvin Sills
Financial Aid: Luis A. Taverez
Type: Comprehensive **Sex:** Coed **Affiliation:** New Jersey State College System **Scores:** 94.02% SAT V 400+; 95.88% SAT M 400+ **% Accepted:** 47 **Admission Plans:** Deferred Admission **Application Deadline:** March 15 **Application Fee:** $50.00 **H.S. Requirements:** High school diploma required; GED accepted **Costs Per Year:** Application fee: $50. State resident tuition: $6294 full-time, $262 per credit hour part-time. Nonresident tuition: $12,588 full-time, $524 per credit hour part-time. Mandatory fees: $2313 full-time, $107.20 per credit hour part-time. Full-time tuition and fees vary according to degree level. Part-time tuition and fees vary according to degree level. College room and board: $8242. Room and board charges vary according to board plan and housing facility. **Scholarships:** Available **Calendar System:** Semester, Summer Session Available **Enrollment:** FT 7,283, PT 1,201, Grad 1,278 **Faculty:** FT 436, PT 450 **Student-Faculty Ratio:** 14:1 **Exams:** SAT I or ACT **% Receiving Financial Aid:** 83 **% Residing in College-Owned, -Operated, or -Affiliated Housing:** 36 **Library Holdings:** 316,500 **Regional Accreditation:** Middle State Association of Colleges and Schools **Credit Hours For Degree:** 120 credits, Bachelors **ROTC:** Army **Professional Accreditation:** AACSB, ABET, JRCEPAT, NASAD, NASM, NAST, NCATE **Intercollegiate Athletics:** Baseball M; Basketball M & W; Cross-Country Running M & W; Field Hockey W; Football M; Lacrosse W; Soccer M & W; Softball W; Swimming and Diving M & W; Tennis M & W; Track and Field M & W; Volleyball W

RUTGERS, THE STATE UNIVERSITY OF NEW JERSEY, CAMDEN
311 North Fifth St.
Camden, NJ 08102-1401
Tel: (856)225-1766
Admissions: (732)932-4636
Web Site: http://camden-www.rutgers.edu/
President/CEO: Roger J. Dennis
Registrar: Terry L. Richartz
Admissions: Diane Williams Harris
Financial Aid: Richard Woodland
Type: University **Sex:** Coed **Affiliation:** Rutgers, The State University of New Jersey **Scores:** 100% SAT V 400+; 100% SAT M 400+ **% Accepted:** 53 **Admission Plans:** Preferred Admission; Early Admission **Application Deadline:** Rolling **Application Fee:** $50.00 **H.S. Requirements:** High school diploma required; GED accepted **Costs Per Year:** Application fee: $50. State resident tuition: $7336 full-time, $236.50 per credit hour part-time. Nonresident tuition: $14,934 full-time, $484.05 per credit hour part-time. Mandatory fees: $1692 full-time. College room and board: $8088. College room only: $5778. **Scholarships:** Available **Calendar System:** Semester, Summer Session Available **Enrollment:** FT 2,949, PT 897, Grad 688

Faculty: FT 229, PT 172 **Student-Faculty Ratio:** 11:1 **Exams:** SAT I or ACT **% Receiving Financial Aid:** 62 **% Residing in College-Owned, -Operated, or -Affiliated Housing:** 13 **Library Holdings:** 714,447 **Regional Accreditation:** Middle State Association of Colleges and Schools **Credit Hours For Degree:** 120 credit hours, Bachelors **ROTC:** Army, Air Force **Professional Accreditation:** AACSB, AACN, ABA, APTA, AALS, CSWE, NASPAA

RUTGERS, THE STATE UNIVERSITY OF NEW JERSEY, NEW BRUNSWICK/PISCATAWAY

New Brunswick, NJ 08901-1281
Tel: (732)932-4636
Web Site: http://www.rutgers.edu/
President/CEO: Dr. Richard L. McCormick
Registrar: Kenneth J. Iuso
Admissions: Diane Williams Harris
Financial Aid: Jean Rash
Type: University **Sex:** Coed **Affiliation:** Rutgers, The State University of New Jersey **Scores:** 99.8% SAT V 400+; 99.9% SAT M 400+ **% Accepted:** 61 **Admission Plans:** Preferred Admission; Early Admission **Application Deadline:** Rolling **Application Fee:** $50.00 **H.S. Requirements:** High school diploma required; GED accepted **Costs Per Year:** Application fee: $50. State resident tuition: $7336 full-time, $236.50 per credit hour part-time. Nonresident tuition: $14,934 full-time, $484 per credit hour part-time. Mandatory fees: $1885 full-time. Part-time tuition varies according to course level. College room and board: $8838. College room only: $5378. Room and board charges vary according to board plan and housing facility. **Scholarships:** Available **Calendar System:** Semester **Enrollment:** FT 24,361, PT 2,352, Grad 7,369 **Faculty:** FT 1,535, PT 689 **Student-Faculty Ratio:** 14:1 **Exams:** SAT I or ACT **% Receiving Financial Aid:** 50 **% Residing in College-Owned, -Operated, or -Affiliated Housing:** 46 **Library Holdings:** 4,737,147 **Regional Accreditation:** Middle State Association of Colleges and Schools **Credit Hours For Degree:** 120 credit hours, Bachelors **ROTC:** Army, Air Force **Professional Accreditation:** ABET, ACPhE, ACSP, ALA, APA, ASLA, CSWE, NASD, NASM **Intercollegiate Athletics:** Baseball M; Basketball M & W; Crew M & W; Cross-Country Running M & W; Fencing M & W; Football M; Golf M & W; Gymnastics W; Lacrosse M & W; Soccer M & W; Softball W; Swimming and Diving M & W; Tennis M & W; Track and Field M & W; Volleyball W; Wrestling M

RUTGERS, THE STATE UNIVERSITY OF NEW JERSEY, NEWARK

Newark, NJ 07102
Tel: (973)353-1766
Admissions: (732)932-4636
Fax: (973)353-1048
Web Site: http://www.newark.rutgers.edu/
President/CEO: Dr. Steven J. Diner
Registrar: Dr. Miguel Estremera
Admissions: Diane William Harris
Financial Aid: Melvin Brown
Type: University **Sex:** Coed **Affiliation:** Rutgers, The State University of New Jersey **Scores:** 99.8% SAT V 400+; 99.8% SAT M 400+ **% Accepted:** 47 **Admission Plans:** Preferred Admission; Early Admission **Application Deadline:** Rolling **Application Fee:** $50.00 **H.S. Requirements:** High school diploma required; GED accepted **Costs Per Year:** Application fee: $50. State resident tuition: $7336 full-time, $236.50 per credit hour part-time. Nonresident tuition: $14,934 full-time, $484.05 per credit hour part-time. Mandatory fees: $1476 full-time. College room and board: $8984. College room only: $5654. Room and board charges vary according to board plan and housing facility. **Scholarships:** Available **Calendar System:** Semester, Summer Session Available **Enrollment:** FT 4,911, PT 1,602, Grad 2,929 **Faculty:** FT 422, PT 231 **Student-Faculty Ratio:** 11:1 **Exams:** SAT I or ACT **% Receiving Financial Aid:** 64 **% Residing in College-Owned, -Operated, or -Affiliated Housing:** 15 **Library Holdings:** 941,103 **Regional Accreditation:** Middle State Association of Colleges and Schools **Credit Hours For Degree:** 124 credit hours, Bachelors **ROTC:** Army, Air Force **Professional Accreditation:** AACSB, AACN, ABA, AALS, CSWE, NASPAA, NLN

SAINT PETER'S COLLEGE

2641 Kennedy Blvd.
Jersey City, NJ 07306-5997
Tel: (201)915-9000; 888-SPC-9933
Admissions: (201)915-9495
Fax: (201)432-5860
E-mail: admissions@spcvxa.spc.edu
Web Site: http://www.spc.edu/
President/CEO: Dr. James N. Loughran, SJ
Registrar: Susan E. Nelson
Admissions: Joe Giglio
Financial Aid: Rebecca S. Royal
Type: Comprehensive **Sex:** Coed **Affiliation:** Roman Catholic (Jesuit) **Scores:** 90.1% SAT V 400+; 90.5% SAT M 400+ **Admission Plans:** Early Admission; Deferred Admission **Application Fee:** $40.00 **H.S. Requirements:** High school diploma required; GED accepted **Scholarships:** Available **Calendar System:** Semester, Summer Session Available **Faculty:** FT 118 **Student-Faculty Ratio:** 16:1 **Exams:** SAT I or ACT **% Receiving Financial Aid:** 82 **% Residing in College-Owned, -Operated, or -Affiliated Housing:** 27 **Library Holdings:** 178,587 **Regional Accreditation:** Middle State Association of Colleges and Schools **Credit Hours For Degree:** 69 credits, Associates; 129 credits, Bachelors **ROTC:** Army, Air Force **Professional Accreditation:** AACN, NLN **Intercollegiate Athletics:** Baseball M; Basketball M & W; Bowling M & W; Cross-Country Running M & W; Football M; Golf M; Soccer M & W; Softball W; Swimming and Diving M & W; Tennis M & W; Track and Field M & W; Volleyball W

SALEM COMMUNITY COLLEGE

460 Hollywood Ave.
Carneys Point, NJ 08069-2799
Tel: (856)299-2100
Admissions: (856)351-2707
Fax: (856)299-9193
Web Site: http://www.salemcc.org/
President/CEO: Dr. Peter B. Contini
Admissions: Dr. Reva Curry
Financial Aid: Suzanne Campo
Type: Two-Year College **Sex:** Coed **Affiliation:** New Jersey Commission on Higher Education **Admission Plans:** Open Admission; Early Admission; Deferred Admission **Application Deadline:** Rolling **Application Fee:** $25.00 **H.S. Requirements:** High school diploma required; GED accepted **Costs Per Year:** Application fee: $25. Area resident tuition: $2385 full-time, $79.50 per credit part-time. State resident tuition: $2685 full-time, $89.50 per credit part-time. Nonresident tuition: $2685 full-time, $89.50 per credit part-time. Mandatory fees: $920 full-time, $29 per credit part-time, $25 per term part-time. Full-time tuition and fees vary according to course load. Part-time tuition and fees vary according to course load. **Scholarships:** Available **Calendar System:** Semester, Summer Session Available **Enrollment:** FT 598, PT 653 **Faculty:** FT 22, PT 44 **Student-Faculty Ratio:** 19:1 **Library Holdings:** 28,951 **Regional Accreditation:** Middle State Association of Colleges and Schools **Credit Hours For Degree:** 64 credits, Associates **Intercollegiate Athletics:** Baseball M; Basketball M & W; Softball W; Tennis M & W

SETON HALL UNIVERSITY

400 South Orange Ave.
South Orange, NJ 07079-2697
Tel: (973)761-9000
Free: 800-THE HALL
Admissions: (973)761-9688
Fax: (973)761-9452
E-mail: terrybry@shu.edu
Web Site: http://www.shu.edu/
President/CEO: Msgr. Robert Sheeran
Registrar: Mary Ellen Farrel
Admissions: Dr. Bryan Terry
Financial Aid: Karen Struthers
Type: University **Sex:** Coed **Affiliation:** Roman Catholic **Scores:** 99% SAT V 400+; 99% SAT M 400+ **% Accepted:** 84 **Admission Plans:** Deferred Admission **Application Deadline:** March 01 **Application Fee:** $55.00 **H.S. Requirements:** High school diploma required; GED accepted **Costs Per Year:** Application fee: $55. Comprehensive fee: $35,186 includes full-time tuition ($22,770), mandatory fees ($1950), and college room and board ($10,466). College room only: $6664. Part-time tuition: $759 per credit. Part-time mandatory fees: $185 per term. **Scholarships:** Available **Calendar System:** Semester, Summer Session Available **Enrollment:** FT 4,801, PT 534, Grad 3,063 **Faculty:** FT 441, PT 485 **Student-Faculty Ratio:** 14:1 **Exams:** SAT I or ACT **% Receiving Financial Aid:** 62 **% Residing in College-Owned, -Operated, or -Affiliated Housing:** 45 **Library Holdings:** 506,042 **Regional Accreditation:** Middle State Association of Colleges and Schools **Credit Hours For Degree:** 130 credits, Bachelors **ROTC:** Army, Air

Force **Professional Accreditation:** AACSB, AAMFT, AACN, ABA, AOTA, APTA, APA, ASLHA, ACIPE, AALS, ATS, CSWE, NASPAA, NCATE, NLN **Intercollegiate Athletics:** Baseball M; Basketball M & W; Cross-Country Running M & W; Golf M; Ice Hockey M; Rugby M; Soccer M & W; Softball W; Swimming and Diving M & W; Tennis W; Track and Field M & W; Volleyball M & W

SOMERSET CHRISTIAN COLLEGE
10 Liberty Square
PO Box 9035
Zarephath, NJ 08890-9035
Tel: (732)356-1595
Free: 800-234-9305
Fax: (732)356-4846
Web Site: http://www.somerset.edu/
Admissions: Cheryl L. Burdick
Type: Two-Year College **Sex:** Coed **Admission Plans:** Deferred Admission **Application Fee:** $20.00 **H.S. Requirements:** High school diploma required; GED accepted **Calendar System:** Semester **Enrollment:** FT 11, PT 131 **Faculty:** FT 3, PT 6 **Student-Faculty Ratio:** 10:1 **Exams:** SAT I or ACT **Library Holdings:** 60,000 **Credit Hours For Degree:** 62 credits, Associates **Professional Accreditation:** AABC

STEVENS INSTITUTE OF TECHNOLOGY
Castle Point on Hudson
Hoboken, NJ 07030
Tel: (201)216-5000
Free: 800-458-5323
Admissions: (201)216-5194
Fax: (201)216-8348
E-mail: admissions@stevens.edu
Web Site: http://www.stevens.edu/
President/CEO: Dr. Harold J. Raveche
Admissions: Maureen P. Weatherall
Financial Aid: David Sheridan
Type: University **Sex:** Coed **Scores:** 99% SAT V 400+; 100% SAT M 400+ **% Accepted:** 47 **Admission Plans:** Early Admission; Early Decision Plan; Deferred Admission **Application Deadline:** February 15 **Application Fee:** $55.00 **H.S. Requirements:** High school diploma required; GED not accepted **Costs Per Year:** Application fee: $55. Comprehensive fee: $41,335 includes full-time tuition ($30,240), mandatory fees ($1595), and college room and board ($9500). College room only: $4800. Full-time tuition and fees vary according to student level. Room and board charges vary according to board plan and housing facility. Part-time tuition: $1008 per credit. Part-time mandatory fees: $528 per term. **Scholarships:** Available **Calendar System:** Semester, Summer Session Available **Enrollment:** FT 1,788, PT 1, Grad 2,900 **Faculty:** FT 210, PT 121 **Student-Faculty Ratio:** 7:1 **Exams:** SAT I or ACT, SAT II **% Receiving Financial Aid:** 68 **% Residing in College-Owned, -Operated, or -Affiliated Housing:** 80 **Library Holdings:** 115,234 **Regional Accreditation:** Middle State Association of Colleges and Schools **Credit Hours For Degree:** 136 credits, Bachelors **ROTC:** Army, Air Force **Professional Accreditation:** ABET **Intercollegiate Athletics:** Baseball M; Basketball M & W; Cross-Country Running M & W; Equestrian Sports W; Fencing M & W; Field Hockey W; Lacrosse M & W; Soccer M & W; Swimming and Diving M & W; Tennis M & W; Track and Field M & W; Volleyball M & W; Wrestling M

SUSSEX COUNTY COMMUNITY COLLEGE
1 College Hill
Newton, NJ 07860
Tel: (973)300-2100
Admissions: (973)300-2219
Web Site: http://www.sussex.edu/
President/CEO: Dr. Bradley Gottfried
Registrar: Patricia Bice
Admissions: James Donohue
Financial Aid: James Pegg
Type: Two-Year College **Sex:** Coed **Affiliation:** New Jersey Commission on Higher Education **% Accepted:** 100 **Admission Plans:** Open Admission **Application Deadline:** Rolling **Application Fee:** $15.00 **H.S. Requirements:** High school diploma or equivalent not required **Costs Per Year:** Application fee: $15. Area resident tuition: $2310 full-time, $77 per credit part-time. State resident tuition: $4620 full-time, $154 per credit part-time. Nonresident tuition: $4620 full-time, $154 per credit part-time. Mandatory fees: $510 full-time, $13 per credit part-time, $15 per term part-time. **Scholarships:** Available **Calendar System:** Semester, Summer Session Available **Enrollment:** FT 1,706, PT 1,755 **Faculty:** FT 41, PT 192 **Student-Faculty Ratio:** 22:1 **Library Holdings:** 34,346 **Regional Accreditation:** Middle State Association of Colleges and Schools **Credit Hours For Degree:** 60 credits, Associates **Intercollegiate Athletics:** Baseball M; Basketball M; Soccer M & W; Softball W

TALMUDICAL ACADEMY OF NEW JERSEY
Route 524
Adelphia, NJ 07710
Tel: (732)431-1600
Admissions: (201)431-1600
President/CEO: Yeruchim Shain
Admissions: Rabbi G. Finkel
Financial Aid: Neal Gottlieb
Type: Comprehensive **Sex:** Men **Affiliation:** Jewish **H.S. Requirements:** High school diploma required; GED accepted **Calendar System:** Semester **Professional Accreditation:** AARTS

THOMAS EDISON STATE COLLEGE
101 West State St.
Trenton, NJ 08608-1176
Tel: (609)984-1100; 888-442-8372
Fax: (609)292-9000
E-mail: admissions@tesc.edu
Web Site: http://www.tesc.edu/
President/CEO: Dr. George A. Pruitt
Registrar: Sharon Smith
Admissions: Renee San Giacomo
Financial Aid: James Owens
Type: Comprehensive **Sex:** Coed **Admission Plans:** Open Admission **Application Fee:** $75.00 **H.S. Requirements:** High school diploma required; GED accepted **Costs Per Year:** Application fee: $75. State resident tuition: $3780 per year part-time. Nonresident tuition: $5400 per year part-time. **Scholarships:** Available **Calendar System:** Continuous, Summer Session Available **Enrollment:** , PT 10,904, Grad 320 **Regional Accreditation:** Middle State Association of Colleges and Schools **Credit Hours For Degree:** 60 credits, Associates; 120 credits, Bachelors **Professional Accreditation:** NLN

UNION COUNTY COLLEGE
1033 Springfield Ave.
Cranford, NJ 07016-1599
Tel: (908)709-7000
Admissions: (908)709-7127
Fax: (908)709-0527
Web Site: http://www.ucc.edu/
President/CEO: Dr. Thomas H. Brown
Registrar: Joann Davis
Admissions: Jo Ann Davis-Wayne
Financial Aid: Elizabeth Riquez
Type: Two-Year College **Sex:** Coed **Affiliation:** New Jersey Commission on Higher Education **% Accepted:** 98 **Admission Plans:** Open Admission; Early Admission; Deferred Admission **Application Deadline:** Rolling **Application Fee:** $30.00 **H.S. Requirements:** High school diploma required; GED accepted **Costs Per Year:** Application fee: $30. Area resident tuition: $2460 full-time, $82 per credit part-time. State resident tuition: $4920 full-time, $164 per credit part-time. Mandatory fees: $780 full-time. **Scholarships:** Available **Calendar System:** Semester, Summer Session Available **Enrollment:** FT 5,327, PT 5,649 **Faculty:** FT 184, PT 259 **Student-Faculty Ratio:** 25:1 **Library Holdings:** 135,783 **Regional Accreditation:** Middle State Association of Colleges and Schools **Credit Hours For Degree:** 62 credits, Associates **ROTC:** Air Force **Professional Accreditation:** APTA, CARC, NLN **Intercollegiate Athletics:** Baseball M; Basketball M & W; Golf M & W; Soccer M; Volleyball W

WARREN COUNTY COMMUNITY COLLEGE
475 Route 57 West
Washington, NJ 07882-4343
Tel: (908)689-1090
Admissions: (908)835-2300
Web Site: http://www.warren.edu/
President/CEO: Dr. Vincent De Sanctis
Registrar: Lyn Williams

Admissions: Peggy Heim
Financial Aid: Anna Reese
Type: Two-Year College **Sex:** Coed **Affiliation:** New Jersey Commission on Higher Education **Admission Plans:** Open Admission; Early Admission; Deferred Admission **Application Fee:** $15.00 **H.S. Requirements:** High school diploma or equivalent not required **Scholarships:** Available **Calendar System:** Semester, Summer Session Available **Enrollment:** FT 347, PT 358 **Faculty:** FT 17, PT 66 **Student-Faculty Ratio:** 13:1 **Exams:** Other **Library Holdings:** 23,143 **Regional Accreditation:** Middle State Association of Colleges and Schools **Credit Hours For Degree:** 64 credits, Associates

WESTMINSTER CHOIR COLLEGE OF RIDER UNIVERSITY
101 Walnut Ln.
Princeton, NJ 08540-3899
Tel: (609)921-7100
Free: 800-96-CHOIR
Admissions: (609)921-9100
Fax: (609)921-2538
E-mail: wccadmission@rider.edu
Web Site: http://westminster.rider.edu/
Admissions: Katherine Shields
Type: Comprehensive **Sex:** Coed **Affiliation:** Rider University **Scores:** 94% SAT V 400+; 94% SAT M 400+ **% Accepted:** 76 **Admission Plans:** Deferred Admission **Application Deadline:** Rolling **Application Fee:** $45.00 **H.S. Requirements:** High school diploma required; GED accepted **Costs Per Year:** Application fee: $45. One-time mandatory fee: $560. Comprehensive fee: $32,670 includes full-time tuition ($22,910), mandatory fees ($560), and college room and board ($9200). College room only: $4380. Room and board charges vary according to board plan. Part-time tuition: $870 per credit. Part-time mandatory fees: $35 per course. Part-time tuition and fees vary according to course load and program. **Scholarships:** Available **Calendar System:** Semester, Summer Session Available **Enrollment:** FT 323, PT 10, Grad 119 **Faculty:** FT 35, PT 66 **Student-Faculty Ratio:** 7:1 **Exams:** SAT I or ACT **% Receiving Financial Aid:** 67 **% Residing in College-Owned, -Operated, or -Affiliated Housing:** 58 **Library Holdings:** 55,000 **Regional Accreditation:** Middle State Association of Colleges and Schools **Credit Hours For Degree:** 124 credits, Bachelors **ROTC:** Army **Professional Accreditation:** NASM

WILLIAM PATERSON UNIVERSITY OF NEW JERSEY
300 Pompton Rd.
Wayne, NJ 07470-8420
Tel: (973)720-2000
Admissions: (973)720-2906
Fax: (973)720-2910
E-mail: mccoyj@wpunj.edu
Web Site: http://ww2.wpunj.edu/
President/CEO: Dr. Arnold Speert
Registrar: Mark Evangelista
Admissions: Jonathan McCoy
Financial Aid: Robert Baumel
Type: Comprehensive **Sex:** Coed **Affiliation:** New Jersey State College System **Scores:** 92.4% SAT V 400+; 95.21% SAT M 400+ **% Accepted:** 67 **Admission Plans:** Early Action; Deferred Admission **Application Deadline:** May 01 **Application Fee:** $50.00 **H.S. Requirements:** High school diploma required; GED accepted **Costs Per Year:** Application fee: $50. State resident tuition: $5358 full-time, $172.16 per credit part-time. Nonresident tuition: $10,474 full-time, $339.16 per credit part-time. Mandatory fees: $3382 full-time, $108.84 per credit part-time. College room and board: $9070. College room only: $6040. Room and board charges vary according to board plan and housing facility. **Scholarships:** Available **Calendar System:** Semester, Summer Session Available **Enrollment:** FT 7,472, PT 1,638, Grad 1,860 **Faculty:** FT 372, PT 699 **Student-Faculty Ratio:** 15:1 **Exams:** SAT I or ACT **% Receiving Financial Aid:** 41 **% Residing in College-Owned, -Operated, or -Affiliated Housing:** 24 **Library Holdings:** 305,155 **Regional Accreditation:** Middle State Association of Colleges and Schools **Credit Hours For Degree:** 128 credits, Bachelors **ROTC:** Air Force **Professional Accreditation:** AACSB, AACN, ACA, ASLHA, JRCEPAT, NASM, NCATE **Intercollegiate Athletics:** Baseball M; Basketball M & W; Bowling M & W; Cheerleading M & W; Cross-Country Running M & W; Fencing M & W; Field Hockey W; Football M; Golf M; Ice Hockey M; Skiing (Downhill) M & W; Soccer M & W; Softball W; Swimming and Diving M & W; Track and Field M & W; Volleyball W

THE ART CENTER DESIGN COLLEGE
5000 Marble NE
Albuquerque, NM 87110
Tel: (505)254-7575
Free: 800-825-8753
Admissions: (520)325-0123
Fax: (505)254-4754
Web Site: http://www.theartcenter.edu/
President/CEO: Gayle Anderson
Registrar: Amy Woods
Admissions: Colleen Gimbel-Froebe
Financial Aid: Margarita Carey
Type: Two-Year College **Sex:** Coed **Application Fee:** $25.00 **H.S. Requirements:** High school diploma required; GED accepted. For non-degree programs: High school diploma or equivalent not required **Calendar System:** Quarter **Exams:** Other **Credit Hours For Degree:** 156 quarter hours, Associates **Professional Accreditation:** ACCSCT

CENTRAL NEW MEXICO COMMUNITY COLLEGE
525 Buena Vista, SE
Albuquerque, NM 87106-4096
Tel: (505)224-3000
Fax: (505)224-4740
Web Site: http://www.tvi.cc.nm.us/
President/CEO: Michael J. Glennon
Registrar: Jane Campbell
Admissions: Jane Campbell
Financial Aid: Lee Carillo
Type: Two-Year College **Sex:** Coed **% Accepted:** 100 **Admission Plans:** Open Admission; Early Admission **Application Deadline:** Rolling **Application Fee:** $0.00 **H.S. Requirements:** High school diploma or equivalent not required **Costs Per Year:** Application fee: $0. Area resident tuition: $1,490 full-time, $41.40 per credit hour part-time. State resident tuition: $1,796 full-time, $49.90 per credit hour part-time. Nonresident tuition: $7,945 full-time, $220.70 per credit hour part-time. Mandatory fees: $90 full-time, $30 per term part-time. **Scholarships:** Available **Calendar System:** Trimester, Summer Session Available **Enrollment:** FT 6,925, PT 16,182 **Faculty:** FT 331, PT 754 **Student-Faculty Ratio:** 21:1 **Regional Accreditation:** North Central Association of Colleges and Schools **Credit Hours For Degree:** 64 credit hours, Associates **ROTC:** Air Force **Professional Accreditation:** ABET, ACCE, ACF, ADA, ACBSP, CARC, NAACLS, NLN

CLOVIS COMMUNITY COLLEGE
417 Schepps Blvd.
Clovis, NM 88101-8381
Tel: (505)769-2811
Admissions: (505)769-4021
E-mail: yosic.corrie@clovis.edu
Web Site: http://www.clovis.edu/
President/CEO: Dr. Beverlee McClure
Registrar: Rosie Corrie
Admissions: Rosie Corrie
Financial Aid: April Chavez
Type: Two-Year College **Sex:** Coed **% Accepted:** 100 **Admission Plans:** Open Admission **Application Fee:** $0.00 **H.S. Requirements:** High school diploma required; GED accepted **Costs Per Year:** Application fee: $0. Area resident tuition: $736 full-time, $29 per credit hour part-time. State resident tuition: $784 full-time, $31 per credit hour part-time. Nonresident tuition: $1480 full-time, $60 per credit hour part-time. Mandatory fees: $36 full-time, $3 per credit part-time, $20 per term part-time. **Scholarships:** Available **Calendar System:** Semester, Summer Session Available **Enrollment:** FT 688, PT 3,249 **Faculty:** FT 50, PT 134 **Student-Faculty Ratio:** 15:1 **Library Holdings:** 52,000 **Regional Accreditation:** North Central Association of Colleges and Schools **Credit Hours For Degree:** 64 credit hours, Associates **Professional Accreditation:** JRCERT, NLN

COLLEGE OF SANTA FE
1600 Saint Michael's Dr.
Santa Fe, NM 87505-7634
Tel: (505)473-6011
Free: 800-456-2673
Admissions: (505)473-6133
Fax: (505)473-6127
E-mail: admissions@csf.edu
Web Site: http://www.csf.edu
President/CEO: Dr. Linda N. Hanson
Registrar: Mary Angell
Admissions: Jeff Miller
Financial Aid: Patty Hoban
Type: Comprehensive **Sex:** Coed **Scores:** 98% SAT V 400+; 97% SAT M 400+; 42% ACT 18-23; 38% ACT 24-29 **% Accepted:** 73 **Admission Plans:** Early Admission; Early Decision Plan; Deferred Admission **Application Deadline:** Rolling **Application Fee:** $35.00 **H.S. Requirements:** High school diploma required; GED accepted **Costs Per Year:** Application fee: $35. Comprehensive fee: $28,978 includes full-time tuition ($21,530), mandatory fees ($746), and college room and board ($6702). College room only: $3204. Room and board charges vary according to board plan and housing facility. Part-time tuition: $720 per credit hour. Part-time mandatory fees: $16 per credit hour. **Scholarships:** Available **Calendar System:** Semester, Summer Session Available **Enrollment:** FT 640, PT 702, Grad 319 **Faculty:** FT 76, PT 199 **Student-Faculty Ratio:** 7:1 **Exams:** SAT I or ACT **% Receiving Financial Aid:** 67 **% Residing in College-Owned, -Operated, or -Affiliated Housing:** 62 **Regional Accreditation:** North Central Association of Colleges and Schools **Credit Hours For Degree:** 64 semester hours, Associates; 128 semester hours, Bachelors **ROTC:** Air Force **Intercollegiate Athletics:** Tennis M & W

COLLEGE OF THE SOUTHWEST
6610 Lovington Hwy.
Hobbs, NM 88240-9129
Tel: (505)392-6561
Free: 800-530-4400
Admissions: (505)392-6563
Web Site: http://www.csw.edu/
President/CEO: Dr. Gary A. Dill
Registrar: Glenna M. Ohaver
Admissions: Karen Workentin
Financial Aid: David Arnold
Type: Comprehensive **Sex:** Coed **Scores:** 82% SAT V 400+; 91% SAT M 400+; 53% ACT 18-23; 8% ACT 24-29 **Admission Plans:** Early Admission; Deferred Admission **Application Fee:** $25.00 **H.S. Requirements:** High school diploma required; GED accepted **Costs Per Year:** Application fee:

$25. Comprehensive fee: $14,300 includes full-time tuition ($9300) and college room and board ($5000). Full-time tuition varies according to course load. Room and board charges vary according to housing facility. Part-time tuition: $310 per semester hour. Part-time tuition varies according to course load. **Scholarships:** Available **Calendar System:** Semester, Summer Session Available **Enrollment:** FT 427, PT 181, Grad 133 **Faculty:** FT 29, PT 61 **Student-Faculty Ratio:** 12:1 **Exams:** SAT I or ACT **% Receiving Financial Aid:** 81 **% Residing in College-Owned, -Operated, or -Affiliated Housing:** 23 **Library Holdings:** 76,217 **Regional Accreditation:** North Central Association of Colleges and Schools **Credit Hours For Degree:** 128 semester hours, Bachelors **Intercollegiate Athletics:** Baseball M; Cross-Country Running M & W; Golf M & W; Soccer M & W; Softball W; Track and Field M & W; Volleyball W

CROWNPOINT INSTITUTE OF TECHNOLOGY
PO Box 849
Crownpoint, NM 87313
Tel: (505)786-4100
Fax: (505)786-5644
Web Site: http://crownpointtech.org/
President/CEO: James M. Tutt
Type: Two-Year College **Sex:** Coed **Calendar System:** Semester **Regional Accreditation:** North Central Association of Colleges and Schools

DOÑA ANA BRANCH COMMUNITY COLLEGE
MSC-3DA, Box 30001
3400 South Espina St.
Las Cruces, NM 88003-8001
Tel: (505)527-7500
Fax: (505)527-7515
Web Site: http://dabcc-www.nmsu.edu/
President/CEO: Dr. Margie C. Huerta
Admissions: Valerie Pickett
Financial Aid: Gladys Chairez
Type: Two-Year College **Sex:** Coed **Affiliation:** New Mexico State University System **Scores:** 34% ACT 18-23; 2% ACT 24-29 **Admission Plans:** Open Admission; Deferred Admission **Application Fee:** $15.00 **H.S. Requirements:** High school diploma required; GED accepted **Costs Per Year:** Application fee: $15. Area resident tuition: $1080 full-time, $45 per credit part-time. State resident tuition: $1320 full-time, $55 per credit part-time. Nonresident tuition: $3240 full-time, $135 per credit part-time. **Scholarships:** Available **Calendar System:** Semester, Summer Session Available **Enrollment:** FT 3,596, PT 2,751 **Faculty:** FT 92, PT 304 **Student-Faculty Ratio:** 30:1 **Exams:** Other **Library Holdings:** 17,140 **Regional Accreditation:** North Central Association of Colleges and Schools **Credit Hours For Degree:** 66 credits, Associates **ROTC:** Army, Air Force **Professional Accreditation:** ADA, ACBSP, CARC, JRCERT, JRCEMT, NLN

EASTERN NEW MEXICO UNIVERSITY
1200 West University
Portales, NM 88130
Tel: (505)562-1011
Free: 800-367-3668
Admissions: (505)562-2178
Fax: (505)562-2118
E-mail: donna.kittrell@enmu.edu
Web Site: http://www.enmu.edu/
President/CEO: Dr. Steven Gamble
Registrar: Betty Crane
Admissions: Donna Kittrell
Financial Aid: Joyce Eldridge
Type: Comprehensive **Sex:** Coed **Affiliation:** Eastern New Mexico University System **Scores:** 75.8% SAT V 400+; 77.9% SAT M 400+; 51.4% ACT 18-23; 12.21% ACT 24-29 **% Accepted:** 65 **Admission Plans:** Early Admission; Deferred Admission **Application Deadline:** Rolling **Application Fee:** $0.00 **H.S. Requirements:** High school diploma required; GED accepted **Costs Per Year:** Application fee: $0. State resident tuition: $1992 full-time, $83 per credit hour part-time. Nonresident tuition: $7548 full-time, $314.50 per credit hour part-time. Mandatory fees: $792 full-time, $33 per credit hour part-time. College room and board: $4480. College room only: $2090. Room and board charges vary according to housing facility. **Scholarships:** Available **Calendar System:** Semester, Summer Session Available **Enrollment:** FT 2,510, PT 781, Grad 742 **Faculty:** FT 149, PT 114 **Student-Faculty Ratio:** 17:1 **Exams:** SAT I or ACT **% Residing in College-Owned, -Operated, or -Affiliated Housing:** 28 **Library Holdings:** 305,108 **Regional Accreditation:** North Central Association of Colleges and Schools **Credit Hours For Degree:** 64 credit hours, Associates; 128 credit hours, Bachelors **Professional Accreditation:** AAFCS, ASLHA, ACBSP, NASM, NCATE, NLN **Intercollegiate Athletics:** Baseball M; Basketball M & W; Cross-Country Running M & W; Football M; Soccer W; Softball W; Tennis W; Track and Field M & W; Volleyball W

EASTERN NEW MEXICO UNIVERSITY-ROSWELL
PO Box 6000
Roswell, NM 88202-6000
Tel: (505)624-7000
Admissions: (505)624-7145
Fax: (505)624-7119
Web Site: http://www.enmu.edu/
President/CEO: Dr. Judith Armstrong
Registrar: Ida M. Stover
Admissions: Ida M. Stover
Financial Aid: Jessie Hall
Type: Two-Year College **Sex:** Coed **Affiliation:** Eastern New Mexico University System **Admission Plans:** Open Admission; Early Admission **Application Fee:** $0.00 **H.S. Requirements:** High school diploma required; GED accepted **Scholarships:** Available **Calendar System:** Semester, Summer Session Available **Faculty:** FT 63, PT 207 **Student-Faculty Ratio:** 16:1 **Exams:** ACT **% Residing in College-Owned, -Operated, or -Affiliated Housing:** 5 **Regional Accreditation:** North Central Association of Colleges and Schools **Credit Hours For Degree:** 64 credit hours, Associates **ROTC:** Army, Navy, Air Force **Professional Accreditation:** AAMAE, AOTA, CARC, JRCEMT, NLN

INSTITUTE OF AMERICAN INDIAN ARTS
83 Avan Nu Po Rd.
Santa Fe, NM 87508
Tel: (505)424-2300
Admissions: (505)424-2328
Fax: (505)424-0505
Web Site: http://www.iaia.edu/
President/CEO: Della Warrior
Registrar: Charlotte Tenorio
Admissions: Myra Garro
Financial Aid: Danny Suazo
Type: Two-Year College **Sex:** Coed **Admission Plans:** Deferred Admission **Application Fee:** $0.00 **H.S. Requirements:** High school diploma required; GED accepted **Costs Per Year:** Application fee: $0. State resident tuition: $2400 full-time, $100 per credit hour part-time. Nonresident tuition: $2400 full-time, $100 per credit hour part-time. Mandatory fees: $200 full-time, $20 per term part-time. College room and board: $4648. College room only: $2212. Room and board charges vary according to housing facility. **Scholarships:** Available **Calendar System:** Semester, Summer Session Not available **Enrollment:** FT 156, PT 27 **Faculty:** FT 13, PT 20 **Student-Faculty Ratio:** 13:1 **Exams:** ACT **Library Holdings:** 15,200 **Regional Accreditation:** North Central Association of Colleges and Schools **Credit Hours For Degree:** 65 credits, Associates **Professional Accreditation:** NASAD

INTERNATIONAL INSTITUTE OF THE AMERICAS
4201 Central Ave. NW, Ste. J
Albuquerque, NM 87105-1649
Tel: (505)880-2877; 888-660-2428
Fax: (505)352-0199
E-mail: esigman@iia.edu
Web Site: http://www.aibtonline.com/
President/CEO: Rick Rickel
Admissions: Ed Sigman
Type: Two-Year College **Sex:** Coed **Application Deadline:** Rolling **Costs Per Year:** One-time mandatory fee: $200. Tuition: $9850 full-time. Mandatory fees: $350 full-time. **Calendar System:** Continuous **Enrollment:** FT 232 **Faculty:** FT 13, PT 6 **Student-Faculty Ratio:** 15:1 **Professional Accreditation:** ACICS

ITT TECHNICAL INSTITUTE
5100 Masthead, NE
Albuquerque, NM 87109-4366
Tel: (505)828-1114
Fax: (505)828-1849
Web Site: http://www.itt-tech.edu/

President/CEO: Marianne Rittner
Admissions: Marianne Rittner-Holmes
Financial Aid: Eulalia Chavez
Type: Two-Year College **Sex:** Coed **Affiliation:** ITT Educational Services, Inc **Admission Plans:** Deferred Admission **Application Deadline:** Rolling **Application Fee:** $100.00 **H.S. Requirements:** High school diploma required; GED accepted **Costs Per Year:** Application fee: $100. **Scholarships:** Available **Calendar System:** Quarter, Summer Session Not available **Exams:** Other **Credit Hours For Degree:** 96 credit hours, Associates; 180 credit hours, Bachelors **Professional Accreditation:** ACICS

LUNA COMMUNITY COLLEGE
PO Box 1510
Las Vegas, NM 87701
Tel: (505)454-2500
Free: 800-588-7232
Admissions: (505)454-2020
E-mail: hgriego@luna.cc.nm.us
Web Site: http://www.luna.cc.nm.us/
President/CEO: Leroy Sanchez
Registrar: Johnathan Ortiz
Admissions: Henrietta Griego
Financial Aid: Regina Madrid
Type: Two-Year College **Sex:** Coed **Admission Plans:** Open Admission **H.S. Requirements:** High school diploma required; GED accepted **Costs Per Year:** Area resident tuition: $600 full-time, $25 per credit hour part-time. State resident tuition: $888 full-time, $37 per credit hour part-time. Nonresident tuition: $1824 full-time, $76 per credit hour part-time. Mandatory fees: $44 full-time, $22 per term part-time. Full-time tuition and fees vary according to course load, program, and reciprocity agreements. Part-time tuition and fees vary according to course load, program, and reciprocity agreements. **Scholarships:** Available **Calendar System:** Semester **Enrollment:** FT 502, PT 1,539 **Faculty:** FT 33, PT 88 **Student-Faculty Ratio:** 13:1 **Library Holdings:** 37,343 **Regional Accreditation:** North Central Association of Colleges and Schools **Credit Hours For Degree:** 66 credit hours, Associates

MESALANDS COMMUNITY COLLEGE
911 South Tenth St.
Tucumcari, NM 88401
Tel: (505)461-4413
Fax: (505)461-1901
Web Site: http://www.mesalands.edu/
President/CEO: Phillip O. Barry
Admissions: Ken Brashear
Type: Two-Year College **Sex:** Coed **Costs Per Year:** State resident tuition: $1050 full-time, $37 per credit hour part-time. Nonresident tuition: $1890 full-time, $66 per credit hour part-time. Mandatory fees: $284 full-time, $7 per credit hour part-time, $27 per term part-time. **Calendar System:** Semester **Faculty:** FT 12, PT 15 **Student-Faculty Ratio:** 10:1 **Exams:** Other **Regional Accreditation:** North Central Association of Colleges and Schools

METROPOLITAN COLLEGE OF COURT REPORTING
8100 Mountain Rd. NE, Ste. 200
Albuquerque, NM 87110-4129
Tel: (505)888-3400
Fax: (505)254-3738
Web Site: http://www.metropolitancollege.edu/
Financial Aid: Misty Cordova
Type: Four-Year College **Sex:** Coed **Scholarships:** Available **Calendar System:** Trimester **Faculty:** FT 3, PT 15 **Professional Accreditation:** ACCSCT

NATIONAL AMERICAN UNIVERSITY (ALBUQUERQUE)
4775 Indian School, NE, Ste. 200
Albuquerque, NM 87110
Tel: (505)265-7517
Free: 800-843-8892
Fax: (505)265-7542
Web Site: http://www.national.edu/
President/CEO: Lisa Knigge
Registrar: Mary Borella
Admissions: Nancy Pointer
Financial Aid: Brenda Graves
Type: Four-Year College **Sex:** Coed **Admission Plans:** Open Admission **Application Fee:** $25.00 **H.S. Requirements:** High school diploma required; GED accepted **Costs Per Year:** Application fee: $25. Tuition: $11,280 full-time, $235 per quarter hour part-time. Mandatory fees: $420 full-time. Full-time tuition and fees vary according to course load and program. Part-time tuition varies according to course load and program. **Scholarships:** Available **Calendar System:** Quarter, Summer Session Available **Enrollment:** FT 218, PT 301 **Faculty:** PT 56 **Student-Faculty Ratio:** 11:1 **Regional Accreditation:** North Central Association of Colleges and Schools **Credit Hours For Degree:** 192 credits, Bachelors

NATIONAL AMERICAN UNIVERSITY (RIO RANCHO)
1601 Rio Rancho
Ste. 200
Rio Rancho, NM 87124
Tel: (505)891-1111
Web Site: http://www.national.edu/ **Type:** Two-Year College **Sex:** Coed

NATIONAL COLLEGE OF MIDWIFERY
209 State Rd. 240
Taos, NM 87571
Tel: (505)758-8914
Fax: (505)758-0302
Web Site: http://www.midwiferycollege.org/
President/CEO: Elizabeth Gilmore
Admissions: Beth Enson
Type: Comprehensive **Sex:** Women **Calendar System:** Trimester **Enrollment:** FT 30, PT 27, Grad 2 **Faculty:** FT 31, PT 0 **Student-Faculty Ratio:** 2:1 **Professional Accreditation:** MEAC

NEW MEXICO HIGHLANDS UNIVERSITY
PO Box 9000
Las Vegas, NM 87701
Tel: (505)454-3000
Free: 800-338-6648
Admissions: (505)454-3405
Fax: (505)454-3311
E-mail: johncoca@nmhu.edu
Web Site: http://www.nmhu.edu/
President/CEO: Manny M. Aragon
Registrar: John Coca
Admissions: John Coca
Financial Aid: Eileen Sedillo
Type: Comprehensive **Sex:** Coed **Scores:** 59% SAT V 400+; 76% SAT M 400+; 44% ACT 18-23; 7% ACT 24-29 **% Accepted:** 69 **Admission Plans:** Early Admission; Deferred Admission **Application Deadline:** Rolling **Application Fee:** $15.00 **H.S. Requirements:** High school diploma required; GED accepted **Costs Per Year:** Application fee: $15. State resident tuition: $2280 full-time, $95 per credit hour part-time. Nonresident tuition: $3420 full-time, $95 per credit hour part-time. Mandatory fees: $20 full-time. Full-time tuition and fees vary according to course load and location. Part-time tuition varies according to course load and location. College room and board: $3992. College room only: $2056. Room and board charges vary according to board plan and housing facility. **Scholarships:** Available **Calendar System:** Semester, Summer Session Available **Enrollment:** FT 1,245, PT 741, Grad 1,764 **Faculty:** FT 73, PT 36 **Student-Faculty Ratio:** 25:1 **% Receiving Financial Aid:** 66 **% Residing in College-Owned, -Operated, or -Affiliated Housing:** 10 **Library Holdings:** 386,489 **Regional Accreditation:** North Central Association of Colleges and Schools **Credit Hours For Degree:** 64 semester hours, Associates; 128 semester hours, Bachelors **Professional Accreditation:** ACBSP, CSWE, NCATE **Intercollegiate Athletics:** Baseball M; Basketball M & W; Cross-Country Running M & W; Football M; Soccer W; Softball W; Track and Field M & W; Volleyball W

NEW MEXICO INSTITUTE OF MINING AND TECHNOLOGY
801 Leroy Place
Socorro, NM 87801
Tel: (505)835-5011
Free: 800-428-TECH
Admissions: (505)835-5424
Fax: (505)835-5989
E-mail: admission@admin.nmt.edu
Web Site: http://www.nmt.edu/
President/CEO: Dr. Daniel H. Lopez

Registrar: Luz Diaz Barreras
Admissions: Mike Kloeppel
Financial Aid: Annette Kaus
Type: University **Sex:** Coed **Scores:** 99% SAT V 400+; 99% SAT M 400+; 22% ACT 18-23; 60% ACT 24-29 **% Accepted:** 81 **Admission Plans:** Deferred Admission **Application Deadline:** August 01 **Application Fee:** $15.00 **H.S. Requirements:** High school diploma required; GED accepted **Costs Per Year:** Application fee: $15. State resident tuition: $3156 full-time, $131.48 per hour part-time. Nonresident tuition: $9975 full-time, $415.63 per hour part-time. Mandatory fees: $448 full-time. Part-time tuition varies according to course load. College room and board: $4866. College room only: $2116. Room and board charges vary according to board plan and housing facility. **Scholarships:** Available **Calendar System:** Semester, Summer Session Available **Enrollment:** FT 1,125, PT 263, Grad 503 **Faculty:** FT 125, PT 22 **Student-Faculty Ratio:** 11:1 **Exams:** ACT, SAT I or ACT **% Receiving Financial Aid:** 40 **% Residing in College-Owned, -Operated, or -Affiliated Housing:** 49 **Library Holdings:** 321,829 **Regional Accreditation:** North Central Association of Colleges and Schools **Credit Hours For Degree:** 65 credit hours, Associates; 130 credit hours, Bachelors **Professional Accreditation:** ABET **Intercollegiate Athletics:** Golf M & W; Rugby M & W; Soccer M & W

NEW MEXICO JUNIOR COLLEGE
5317 Lovington Hwy.
Hobbs, NM 88240-9123
Tel: (505)392-4510
Admissions: (505)392-5092
Fax: (505)392-2527
Web Site: http://www.nmjc.edu/
President/CEO: Dr. Steve McCleery
Registrar: Robert Bensing
Admissions: Robert Bensing
Financial Aid: Linda Neel
Type: Two-Year College **Sex:** Coed **Affiliation:** New Mexico Commission on Higher Education **Admission Plans:** Open Admission; Early Admission; Deferred Admission **Application Fee:** $0.00 **H.S. Requirements:** High school diploma or equivalent not required. For automotive technology, medical laboratory technology, nursing programs: High school diploma required; GED accepted **Scholarships:** Available **Calendar System:** Semester, Summer Session Available **Faculty:** FT 65, PT 55 **Student-Faculty Ratio:** 19:1 **Exams:** ACT **% Residing in College-Owned, -Operated, or -Affiliated Housing:** 15 **Library Holdings:** 118,500 **Regional Accreditation:** North Central Association of Colleges and Schools **Credit Hours For Degree:** 64 semester hours, Associates **Professional Accreditation:** NLN **Intercollegiate Athletics:** Baseball M; Basketball M & W; Golf M

NEW MEXICO MILITARY INSTITUTE
101 West College Blvd.
Roswell, NM 88201-5173
Tel: (505)622-6250
Free: 800-421-5376
Admissions: (505)624-8050
Fax: (505)624-8067
E-mail: admissions@nmmi.edu
Web Site: http://www.nmmi.edu/
President/CEO: Rear Adm. David Ellison
Registrar: Maj. Edwin G. Preble
Admissions: Lt. Col. Steven D. Klein
Financial Aid: Maj. Sonja Rodriguez
Type: Two-Year College **Sex:** Coed **Affiliation:** New Mexico Commission on Higher Education **Scores:** 68% ACT 18-23; 20% ACT 24-29 **% Accepted:** 62 **Admission Plans:** Preferred Admission; Early Admission; Deferred Admission **Application Deadline:** August 01 **Application Fee:** $60.00 **H.S. Requirements:** High school diploma required; GED accepted **Costs Per Year:** Application fee: $60. State resident tuition: $1304 full-time. Nonresident tuition: $4258 full-time. Mandatory fees: $1558 full-time. College room and board: $3645. **Scholarships:** Available **Calendar System:** Semester, Summer Session Available **Enrollment:** FT 455 **Faculty:** FT 69, PT 0 **Student-Faculty Ratio:** 7:1 **Exams:** SAT I or ACT **% Residing in College-Owned, -Operated, or -Affiliated Housing:** 100 **Library Holdings:** 65,000 **Regional Accreditation:** North Central Association of Colleges and Schools **Credit Hours For Degree:** 68 hours, Associates **ROTC:** Army **Intercollegiate Athletics:** Baseball M; Basketball M; Fencing M & W; Football M; Golf M; Riflery M & W; Tennis M & W; Track and Field M; Volleyball W

NEW MEXICO STATE UNIVERSITY
PO Box 30001
Las Cruces, NM 88003-8001
Tel: (505)646-0111
Free: 800-662-6678
Admissions: (505)646-3121
Fax: (505)646-6330
E-mail: admssions@nmsu.edu
Web Site: http://www.nmsu.edu/
President/CEO: Dr. Michael Martin
Registrar: Michael R. Zimmerman
Admissions: Angela Mora-Riley
Financial Aid: Cydney Conway
Type: University **Sex:** Coed **Affiliation:** New Mexico State University System **Scores:** 53% ACT 18-23; 22% ACT 24-29 **% Accepted:** 81 **Admission Plans:** Early Admission; Deferred Admission **Application Deadline:** August 19 **Application Fee:** $15.00 **H.S. Requirements:** High school diploma required; GED accepted **Costs Per Year:** Application fee: $15. State resident tuition: $2868 full-time, $163.25 per credit part-time. Nonresident tuition: $12,156 full-time, $550.25 per credit part-time. Mandatory fees: $1050 full-time. College room and board: $5332. College room only: $3072. Room and board charges vary according to board plan and gender. **Scholarships:** Available **Calendar System:** Semester, Summer Session Available **Enrollment:** FT 10,238, PT 2,418, Grad 3,416 **Faculty:** FT 667, PT 166 **Student-Faculty Ratio:** 19:1 **Exams:** SAT I or ACT **% Receiving Financial Aid:** 57 **% Residing in College-Owned, -Operated, or -Affiliated Housing:** 16 **Library Holdings:** 1,642,678 **Regional Accreditation:** North Central Association of Colleges and Schools **Credit Hours For Degree:** 66 credits, Associates; 128 credits, Bachelors **ROTC:** Army, Air Force **Professional Accreditation:** AACSB, ABET, ACEJMC, AACN, AAFCS, ACA, APA, ASLHA, CEPH, CSWE, JRCEPAT, NASM, NASPAA, NCATE **Intercollegiate Athletics:** Baseball M; Basketball M & W; Cross-Country Running M & W; Equestrian Sports M & W; Football M; Golf M & W; Softball W; Swimming and Diving W; Tennis M & W; Track and Field W; Volleyball W

NEW MEXICO STATE UNIVERSITY-ALAMOGORDO
2400 North Scenic Dr.
Alamogordo, NM 88311-0477
Tel: (505)439-3600
Admissions: (505)439-3700
E-mail: advisor@nmsua.nmsu.edu
Web Site: http://alamo.nmsu.edu/
President/CEO: Dr. Rodger Bates
Admissions: Kathy Fuller
Financial Aid: Sharon Fischer
Type: Two-Year College **Sex:** Coed **Affiliation:** New Mexico State University System **% Accepted:** 100 **Admission Plans:** Open Admission; Early Admission; Deferred Admission **Application Deadline:** Rolling **Application Fee:** $15.00 **H.S. Requirements:** High school diploma required; GED accepted **Costs Per Year:** Application fee: $15. Area resident tuition: $1248 full-time, $52 per credit hour part-time. State resident tuition: $1416 full-time, $59 per credit hour part-time. Nonresident tuition: $3960 full-time, $165 per credit hour part-time. Mandatory fees: $48 full-time, $2 per credit hour part-time. **Scholarships:** Available **Calendar System:** Semester, Summer Session Available **Enrollment:** FT 714, PT 1,201 **Faculty:** FT 53, PT 45 **Student-Faculty Ratio:** 14:1 **Library Holdings:** 39,000 **Regional Accreditation:** North Central Association of Colleges and Schools **Credit Hours For Degree:** 66 credits, Associates **Professional Accreditation:** NAACLS, NLN

NEW MEXICO STATE UNIVERSITY-CARLSBAD
1500 University Dr.
Carlsbad, NM 88220-3509
Tel: (505)234-9200
Admissions: (505)234-9220
Fax: (505)885-4951
Web Site: http://www.cavern.nmsu.edu/
President/CEO: Dr. Melvin M. Vuk
Registrar: Everal Shannon
Admissions: Michael J. Cleary
Financial Aid: Judi Sears
Type: Two-Year College **Sex:** Coed **Affiliation:** New Mexico State University System **Admission Plans:** Open Admission; Early Admission; Deferred Admission **Application Fee:** $15.00 **H.S. Requirements:** High school diploma required; GED accepted **Scholarships:** Available **Calendar**

System: Semester, Summer Session Available **Faculty:** FT 24, PT 49 **Student-Faculty Ratio:** 23:1 **Exams:** ACT **Regional Accreditation:** North Central Association of Colleges and Schools **Credit Hours For Degree:** 66 credit hours, Associates **Professional Accreditation:** NLN

NEW MEXICO STATE UNIVERSITY-GRANTS
1500 3rd St.
Grants, NM 87020-2025
Tel: (505)287-7981
Web Site: http://grants.nmsu.edu/
President/CEO: Dr. Martin Parks
Registrar: Irene Lutz
Admissions: Irene Lutz
Financial Aid: Irene Lutz
Type: Two-Year College **Sex:** Coed **Affiliation:** New Mexico State University System **Admission Plans:** Open Admission; Early Admission **Application Fee:** $15.00 **H.S. Requirements:** High school diploma required; GED accepted **Scholarships:** Available **Calendar System:** Semester, Summer Session Available **Enrollment:** FT 233, PT 403 **Faculty:** FT 12, PT 45 **Exams:** Other **Library Holdings:** 30,000 **Regional Accreditation:** North Central Association of Colleges and Schools **Credit Hours For Degree:** 66 credits, Associates

NORTHERN NEW MEXICO COMMUNITY COLLEGE
921 Paseo de Oñate
Espanola, NM 87532
Tel: (505)747-2100
Admissions: (505)747-2193
Web Site: http://www.nnmcc.edu/
President/CEO: Dr. Sigfredo Maestas
Registrar: Michael Costello
Admissions: Mike L. Costello
Financial Aid: Alfredo Montoya
Type: Two-Year College **Sex:** Coed **Affiliation:** New Mexico Commission on Higher Education **Admission Plans:** Open Admission; Early Admission; Deferred Admission **Application Fee:** $0.00 **H.S. Requirements:** High school diploma required; GED accepted **Scholarships:** Available **Calendar System:** Semester, Summer Session Available **Faculty:** FT 45, PT 208 **% Residing in College-Owned, -Operated, or -Affiliated Housing:** 1 **Library Holdings:** 18,065 **Regional Accreditation:** North Central Association of Colleges and Schools **Credit Hours For Degree:** 64 credits, Associates **Professional Accreditation:** ACBSP, JRCERT

PIMA MEDICAL INSTITUTE
2201 San Pedro NE, Bldg. 3, Ste. 100
Albuquerque, NM 87110
Tel: (505)881-1234; 888-898-9048
Fax: (505)884-8371
Web Site: http://www.pmi.edu
President/CEO: Popie White
Registrar: Betty Hoover
Admissions: Martha Garcia
Financial Aid: Teresa Lambert
Type: Two-Year College **Sex:** Coed **Affiliation:** Vocational Training Institutes, Inc **% Accepted:** 66 **Admission Plans:** Early Admission **Application Fee:** $0.00 **H.S. Requirements:** High school diploma required; GED accepted **Costs Per Year:** Application fee: $0. **Scholarships:** Available **Calendar System:** Miscellaneous, Summer Session Not available **Enrollment:** FT 420 **Student-Faculty Ratio:** 20:1 **Exams:** Other **Credit Hours For Degree:** 88.5 credits, Associates **Professional Accreditation:** ABHES, JRCERT

ST. JOHN'S COLLEGE
1160 Camino Cruz Blanca
Santa Fe, NM 87505-4599
Tel: (505)984-6000
Free: 800-331-5232
Admissions: (505)984-6060
E-mail: admissions@sjcsf.edu
Web Site: http://www.stjohnscollege.edu/
President/CEO: Christopher B. Nelson
Registrar: Marline Marquez Scally
Admissions: Larry Clendenin
Financial Aid: Michael Rodriguez
Type: Comprehensive **Sex:** Coed **Affiliation:** St. John's College (MD) **Scores:** 100% SAT V 400+; 100% SAT M 400+; 3% ACT 18-23; 59% ACT 24-29 **% Accepted:** 83 **Admission Plans:** Early Admission; Deferred Admission **Application Deadline:** Rolling **Application Fee:** $0.00 **H.S. Requirements:** High school diploma required; GED accepted **Costs Per Year:** Application fee: $0. Comprehensive fee: $42,776 includes full-time tuition ($34,306), mandatory fees ($200), and college room and board ($8270). College room only: $3938. Part-time tuition: $1009 per unit. **Scholarships:** Available **Calendar System:** Semester, Summer Session Available **Enrollment:** FT 431, PT 4, Grad 98 **Faculty:** FT 68, PT 3 **Student-Faculty Ratio:** 6:1 **Exams:** SAT I or ACT **% Receiving Financial Aid:** 73 **% Residing in College-Owned, -Operated, or -Affiliated Housing:** 75 **Library Holdings:** 65,000 **Regional Accreditation:** North Central Association of Colleges and Schools **Credit Hours For Degree:** 132 credits, Bachelors **Intercollegiate Athletics:** Fencing M & W; Soccer M & W

SAN JUAN COLLEGE
4601 College Blvd.
Farmington, NM 87402-4699
Tel: (505)326-3311
Admissions: (505)566-3300
Fax: (505)599-3385
E-mail: florezr@sanjuancollege.edu
Web Site: http://www.sanjuancollege.edu/
President/CEO: Dr. Carol J. Spencer
Registrar: Dr. Cheryl Drangmeistar
Admissions: Rus Florez
Financial Aid: Roger Evans
Type: Two-Year College **Sex:** Coed **Affiliation:** New Mexico Commission on Higher Education **% Accepted:** 100 **Admission Plans:** Open Admission; Early Admission; Deferred Admission **Application Deadline:** Rolling **Application Fee:** $0.00 **H.S. Requirements:** High school diploma required; GED accepted **Costs Per Year:** Application fee: $0. State resident tuition: $720 full-time, $30 per credit hour part-time. Nonresident tuition: $960 full-time, $40 per credit hour part-time. **Scholarships:** Available **Calendar System:** Semester, Summer Session Available **Enrollment:** FT 2,606, PT 2,458 **Faculty:** FT 96, PT 224 **Student-Faculty Ratio:** 19:1 **Library Holdings:** 81,116 **Regional Accreditation:** North Central Association of Colleges and Schools **Credit Hours For Degree:** 64 credits, Associates **Professional Accreditation:** ABET, ADA, AHIMA, APTA, ACBSP, NLN

SANTA FE COMMUNITY COLLEGE
6401 Richards Ave.
Santa Fe, NM 87508-4887
Tel: (505)428-1000
Admissions: (505)428-1261
Fax: (505)428-1237
E-mail: atupler@sfccnm.edu
Web Site: http://www.sfccnm.edu/
President/CEO: James N. McLaughlin
Registrar: Barbara Tucci
Admissions: Anna Tupler
Financial Aid: Willie Bachicha
Type: Two-Year College **Sex:** Coed **Admission Plans:** Open Admission; Early Admission; Deferred Admission **Application Fee:** $0.00 **H.S. Requirements:** High school diploma required; GED accepted **Scholarships:** Available **Calendar System:** Semester, Summer Session Available **Enrollment:** FT 915, PT 4,537 **Faculty:** FT 56, PT 247 **Student-Faculty Ratio:** 18:1 **Library Holdings:** 38,226 **Regional Accreditation:** North Central Association of Colleges and Schools **Credit Hours For Degree:** 64 credits, Associates **Professional Accreditation:** ADA, NLN

SOUTHWESTERN INDIAN POLYTECHNIC INSTITUTE
9169 Coors, NW, Box 10146
Albuquerque, NM 87184-0146
Tel: (505)346-2347
Admissions: (505)346-2362
Fax: (505)346-2343
E-mail: mgarro@sipi.bia.edu
Web Site: http://www.sipi.bia.edu/
President/CEO: Dr. Carolyn Elgin
Registrar: Frank Kekahbah
Admissions: Myra Garro
Financial Aid: Marilyn Pargas

Type: Two-Year College **Sex:** Coed **Admission Plans:** Open Admission; Preferred Admission **Application Fee:** $0.00 **H.S. Requirements:** High school diploma required; GED accepted **Scholarships:** Available **Calendar System:** Trimester, Summer Session Available **Student-Faculty Ratio:** 15:1 **Exams:** Other **Library Holdings:** 26,000 **Regional Accreditation:** North Central Association of Colleges and Schools **Credit Hours For Degree:** 59 credit hours, Associates **Professional Accreditation:** COptA **Intercollegiate Athletics:** Cross-Country Running M & W

UNIVERSITY OF NEW MEXICO
Albuquerque, NM 87131-2039
Tel: (505)277-0111
Admissions: (505)277-2446
Fax: (505)277-6686
E-mail: apply@unm.edu
Web Site: http://www.unm.edu/
President/CEO: Louis E. Caldera
Registrar: Kathleen Sena
Admissions: Terry Babbitt
Financial Aid: Ron Martinez
Type: University **Sex:** Coed **Scores:** 93.6% SAT V 400+; 92.7% SAT M 400+; 53.9% ACT 18-23; 28.5% ACT 24-29 **% Accepted:** 74 **Admission Plans:** Early Admission; Deferred Admission **Application Deadline:** June 15 **Application Fee:** $20.00 **H.S. Requirements:** High school diploma required; GED accepted **Costs Per Year:** Application fee: $20. Area resident tuition: $171.20 per credit hour part-time. State resident tuition: $4108 full-time. Nonresident tuition: $13,438 full-time. Part-time tuition varies according to course load. College room and board: $6518. College room only: $3818. Room and board charges vary according to board plan and housing facility. **Scholarships:** Available **Calendar System:** Semester, Summer Session Available **Enrollment:** FT 14,839, PT 3,886, Grad 6,429 **Faculty:** FT 885, PT 526 **Student-Faculty Ratio:** 19:1 **Exams:** SAT I or ACT **% Receiving Financial Aid:** 48 **% Residing in College-Owned, -Operated, or -Affiliated Housing:** 11 **Library Holdings:** 2,730,993 **Regional Accreditation:** North Central Association of Colleges and Schools **Credit Hours For Degree:** 60 semester hours, Associates; 128 semester hours, Bachelors **ROTC:** Army, Navy, Air Force **Professional Accreditation:** AACSB, ABET, AACN, AAFCS, ABA, ACNM, ACCE, ACPhE, ACA, ADA, ADtA, ACSP, AOTA, APTA, APA, ASLA, ASLHA, AALS, CEPH, JRCEMT JRCEPAT, LCMEAMA, NAACLS, NASD, NASM, NASPAA, NAST, NCATE **Intercollegiate Athletics:** Baseball M; Basketball M & W; Cross-Country Running M & W; Football M; Golf M & W; Skiing (Cross-Country) M & W; Skiing (Downhill) M & W; Soccer M & W; Softball W; Swimming and Diving W; Tennis M & W; Track and Field M & W; Volleyball W

UNIVERSITY OF NEW MEXICO-GALLUP
200 College Rd.
Gallup, NM 87301-5603
Tel: (505)863-7500
Admissions: (505)863-7576
Fax: (505)863-7532
Web Site: http://www.gallup.unm.edu/
President/CEO: Beth Miller
Registrar: Tom Ray
Admissions: Pearl A. Morris
Type: Two-Year College **Sex:** Coed **Affiliation:** New Mexico Commission on Higher Education **Admission Plans:** Open Admission; Early Admission **Application Fee:** $15.00 **H.S. Requirements:** High school diploma required; GED accepted **Scholarships:** Available **Calendar System:** Semester, Summer Session Available **Faculty:** FT 75, PT 84 **Student-Faculty Ratio:** 25:1 **Exams:** ACT, SAT I **Library Holdings:** 36,172 **Regional Accreditation:** North Central Association of Colleges and Schools **Credit Hours For Degree:** 60 credit hours, Associates; 136 credit hours, Bachelors **Professional Accreditation:** ADA, AHIMA, NAACLS, NLN

UNIVERSITY OF NEW MEXICO-LOS ALAMOS BRANCH
4000 University Dr.
Los Alamos, NM 87544-2233
Tel: (505)662-5919
Admissions: (505)661-4692
E-mail: aapodaca@la.unm.edu
Web Site: http://www.la.unm.edu/
President/CEO: Dr. Carlos B. Ramirez
Registrar: Maisie Tuyillo
Admissions: Anna Mae Apodaca
Financial Aid: Yohanna Wiuff
Type: Two-Year College **Sex:** Coed **Affiliation:** New Mexico Commission on Higher Education **Admission Plans:** Open Admission; Early Admission; Deferred Admission **Application Fee:** $15.00 **H.S. Requirements:** High school diploma required; GED accepted **Scholarships:** Available **Calendar System:** Semester, Summer Session Available **Faculty:** FT 0, PT 96 **Exams:** SAT I or ACT **Library Holdings:** 10,000 **Regional Accreditation:** North Central Association of Colleges and Schools **Credit Hours For Degree:** 64 semester hours, Associates

UNIVERSITY OF NEW MEXICO-TAOS
115 Civic Plaza Dr.
Taos, NM 87571
Tel: (505)758-7667
Web Site: http://taos.unm.edu/
President/CEO: Dr. Alicia F. Chavez
Type: Two-Year College **Sex:** Coed **Calendar System:** Semester **Regional Accreditation:** North Central Association of Colleges and Schools

UNIVERSITY OF NEW MEXICO-VALENCIA CAMPUS
280 La Entrada
Los Lunas, NM 87031-7633
Tel: (505)925-8500
Admissions: (505)925-8580
Fax: (505)925-8563
Web Site: http://www.unm.edu/~unmvc/
President/CEO: Dr. Alice V. Letteney
Registrar: Lucy Sanchez
Admissions: Lucy Sanchez
Financial Aid: Ray Rondeau
Type: Two-Year College **Sex:** Coed **Affiliation:** New Mexico Commission on Higher Education **Admission Plans:** Open Admission; Early Admission; Deferred Admission **Application Fee:** $15.00 **H.S. Requirements:** High school diploma required; GED accepted **Scholarships:** Available **Calendar System:** Semester, Summer Session Available **Faculty:** FT 19, PT 74 **Exams:** Other, SAT I or ACT **Library Holdings:** 9,500 **Regional Accreditation:** North Central Association of Colleges and Schools **Credit Hours For Degree:** 60 credit hours, Associates

UNIVERSITY OF PHOENIX-NEW MEXICO CAMPUS
7471 Pan American Freeway NE
Albuquerque, NM 87109-4645
Tel: (505)821-4800
Free: 800-228-7240
Admissions: (480)557-1712
Web Site: http://www.phoenix.edu/
President/CEO: Randy Lichtenfeld
Admissions: Nina Omelchanko
Type: Comprehensive **Sex:** Coed **Admission Plans:** Open Admission; Deferred Admission **Application Deadline:** Rolling **Application Fee:** $110.00 **H.S. Requirements:** High school diploma required; GED accepted **Costs Per Year:** Application fee: $110. Tuition: $9390 full-time, $313 per credit part-time. Mandatory fees: $560 full-time, $70 per course part-time. **Scholarships:** Available **Calendar System:** Continuous, Summer Session Not available **Enrollment:** FT 3,669, Grad 1,055 **Faculty:** FT 17, PT 431 **Student-Faculty Ratio:** 11:1 **Library Holdings:** 444 **Regional Accreditation:** North Central Association of Colleges and Schools **Credit Hours For Degree:** 60 credits, Associates; 120 credits, Bachelors **Professional Accreditation:** NLN

WESTERN NEW MEXICO UNIVERSITY
PO Box 680
Silver City, NM 88062-0680
Tel: (505)538-6336
Admissions: (505)538-6106
Fax: (505)538-6155
Web Site: http://www.wnmu.edu/
President/CEO: Dr. John E. Counts
Registrar: Betsy Miller
Admissions: Michael Aleckson
Financial Aid: Charles Kelly
Type: Comprehensive **Sex:** Coed **Scores:** 43% ACT 18-23; 5% ACT 24-29 **Admission Plans:** Open Admission; Early Admission; Deferred Admission **Application Fee:** $10.00 **H.S. Requirements:** High school diploma required; GED accepted **Costs Per Year:** Application fee: $10. State

resident tuition: $2733 full-time, $95 per credit part-time. Nonresident tuition: $10,293 full-time. Mandatory fees: $85 full-time, $42.50 per term part-time. **Scholarships:** Available **Calendar System:** Semester, Summer Session Available **Faculty:** FT 90, PT 55 **Student-Faculty Ratio:** 17:1 **Exams:** ACT, Other **% Receiving Financial Aid:** 77 **Library Holdings:** 245,146 **Regional Accreditation:** North Central Association of Colleges and Schools **Credit Hours For Degree:** 64 credit hours, Associates; 128 credit hours, Bachelors **Professional Accreditation:** AOTA, ACBSP, CSWE, NCATE, NLN **Intercollegiate Athletics:** Basketball M & W; Cheerleading M & W; Football M; Golf M & W; Rock Climbing M & W; Softball W; Tennis M & W; Volleyball W

ADELPHI UNIVERSITY
One South Ave.
PO Box 701
Garden City, NY 11530-0701
Tel: (516)877-3000
Free: 800-ADE-LPHI
Admissions: (516)877-3050
Fax: (516)877-3039
E-mail: admissions@adelphi.edu
Web Site: http://www.adelphi.edu/
President/CEO: Robert A. Scott
Registrar: Ellen Deluna
Admissions: Christine Murphy
Type: University **Sex:** Coed **Scores:** 99.9% SAT V 400+; 99.9% SAT M 400+; 51.6% ACT 18-23; 40.6% ACT 24-29 **% Accepted:** 68 **Admission Plans:** Early Admission; Early Action; Deferred Admission **Application Deadline:** Rolling **Application Fee:** $35.00 **H.S. Requirements:** High school diploma required; GED accepted. For for adult students in the ABLE program: High school diploma or equivalent not required **Costs Per Year:** Application fee: $35. Comprehensive fee: $28,910 includes full-time tuition ($18,620), mandatory fees ($1100), and college room and board ($9190). College room only: $5990. Full-time tuition and fees vary according to course level, location, and program. Room and board charges vary according to board plan and housing facility. Part-time tuition: $600 per credit. Part-time mandatory fees: $550 per year. Part-time tuition and fees vary according to course level, location, and program. **Scholarships:** Available **Calendar System:** Semester, Summer Session Available **Enrollment:** FT 3,961, PT 797, Grad 3,140 **Faculty:** FT 257, PT 600 **Student-Faculty Ratio:** 11:1 **Exams:** SAT I or ACT **% Receiving Financial Aid:** 66 **% Residing in College-Owned, -Operated, or -Affiliated Housing:** 24 **Library Holdings:** 631,023 **Regional Accreditation:** Middle State Association of Colleges and Schools **Credit Hours For Degree:** 120 credits, Bachelors **ROTC:** Army, Air Force **Professional Accreditation:** AACN, APA, ASLHA, CSWE, NCATE, NLN **Intercollegiate Athletics:** Baseball M; Basketball M & W; Cross-Country Running M & W; Golf M; Lacrosse M & W; Soccer M & W; Softball W; Swimming and Diving M & W; Tennis M & W; Track and Field M & W; Volleyball W

ADIRONDACK COMMUNITY COLLEGE
640 Bay Rd.
Queensbury, NY 12804
Tel: (518)743-2200
Admissions: (518)743-2264
Fax: (518)745-1433
Web Site: http://www.sunyacc.edu/
President/CEO: Dr. Marshall Bishop
Registrar: Jeanne F. Charpentier
Admissions: Sarah Jane Linehan
Financial Aid: Maureen Reilly
Type: Two-Year College **Sex:** Coed **Affiliation:** State University of New York System **Admission Plans:** Open Admission; Early Admission; Deferred Admission **Application Fee:** $30.00 **H.S. Requirements:** High school diploma required; GED accepted **Scholarships:** Available **Calendar System:** Semester, Summer Session Available **Faculty:** FT 100, PT 144 **Student-Faculty Ratio:** 20:1 **Library Holdings:** 65,000 **Regional Accreditation:** Middle State Association of Colleges and Schools **Credit Hours For Degree:** 64 credit hours, Associates **Professional Accreditation:** AHIMA, NLN **Intercollegiate Athletics:** Baseball M; Basketball M & W; Bowling M & W; Golf M; Skiing (Cross-Country) M & W; Skiing (Downhill) M & W; Soccer M & W; Softball W; Tennis M & W; Volleyball W

ALBANY COLLEGE OF PHARMACY OF UNION UNIVERSITY
106 New Scotland Ave.
Albany, NY 12208-3425
Tel: (518)445-7200; 888-203-8010
Admissions: (518)445-7221
Fax: (518)445-7202
E-mail: connorsc@acp.edu
Web Site: http://www.acp.edu/
President/CEO: Dr. James J. Gozzo
Registrar: Janis Fisher
Admissions: Carly Connors
Financial Aid: Tiffany Gutierrez
Type: Comprehensive **Sex:** Coed **Affiliation:** Part of Union University (Albany Law School, Albany Medical College, Union College, NY) **Scores:** 100% SAT V 400+; 100% SAT M 400+; 24% ACT 18-23; 66% ACT 24-29 **% Accepted:** 58 **Admission Plans:** Early Decision Plan **Application Deadline:** February 01 **Application Fee:** $75.00 **H.S. Requirements:** High school diploma required; GED accepted **Costs Per Year:** Application fee: $75. Comprehensive fee: $24,870 includes full-time tuition ($18,300), mandatory fees ($470), and college room and board ($6100). Room and board charges vary according to board plan and housing facility. Part-time tuition: $610 per credit. **Scholarships:** Available **Calendar System:** Semester, Summer Session Available **Enrollment:** FT 856 **Faculty:** FT 63, PT 6 **Student-Faculty Ratio:** 14:1 **Exams:** SAT I or ACT **% Receiving Financial Aid:** 85 **% Residing in College-Owned, -Operated, or -Affiliated Housing:** 30 **Library Holdings:** 16,124 **Regional Accreditation:** Middle State Association of Colleges and Schools **Credit Hours For Degree:** 131 semester hours, Bachelors **ROTC:** Army, Air Force **Professional Accreditation:** ACPhE, ASC **Intercollegiate Athletics:** Basketball M & W; Soccer M & W

ALFRED UNIVERSITY
One Saxon Dr.
Alfred, NY 14802-1205
Tel: (607)871-2111
Free: 800-541-9229
Admissions: (607)871-2115
Fax: (607)871-2198
E-mail: spencer@alfred.edu
Web Site: http://www.alfred.edu/
President/CEO: Dr. Charles Edmondson
Registrar: Lawrence Casey
Admissions: Jeremy Spencer
Financial Aid: Earl E. Pierce, Jr.
Type: University **Sex:** Coed **Scores:** 99% SAT V 400+; 99% SAT M 400+; 48% ACT 18-23; 45% ACT 24-29 **% Accepted:** 77 **Admission Plans:** Early Admission; Early Decision Plan; Deferred Admission **Application Deadline:** February 01 **Application Fee:** $40.00 **H.S. Requirements:** High school diploma required; GED accepted **Costs Per Year:** Application fee: $40. Comprehensive fee: $30,706 includes full-time tuition ($20,150), mandatory fees ($810), and college room and board ($9746). College room only:

$5076. Full-time tuition and fees vary according to student level. Room and board charges vary according to board plan and housing facility. Part-time tuition: $658 per credit hour. Part-time tuition varies according to course load. **Scholarships:** Available **Calendar System:** Semester, Summer Session Available **Enrollment:** FT 1,863, PT 98, Grad 274 **Faculty:** FT 165, PT 40 **Student-Faculty Ratio:** 12:1 **Exams:** SAT I or ACT **% Receiving Financial Aid:** 82 **% Residing in College-Owned, -Operated, or -Affiliated Housing:** 67 **Library Holdings:** 288,137 **Regional Accreditation:** Middle State Association of Colleges and Schools **Credit Hours For Degree:** 124 credits, Bachelors **ROTC:** Army **Professional Accreditation:** AACSB, ABET, APA, NASAD **Intercollegiate Athletics:** Basketball M & W; Cross-Country Running M & W; Equestrian Sports M & W; Football M; Lacrosse M & W; Skiing (Cross-Country) M & W; Skiing (Downhill) M & W; Soccer M & W; Softball W; Swimming and Diving M & W; Tennis M & W; Track and Field M & W; Volleyball W

AMERICAN ACADEMY OF DRAMATIC ARTS

120 Madison Ave.
New York, NY 10016-7004
Tel: (212)686-9244
Free: 800-463-8990
Web Site: http://www.aada.org/
President/CEO: Roger Croucher
Registrar: Gary Glazer
Admissions: Karen Higginbotham
Financial Aid: Roberto Lopez
Type: Two-Year College **Sex:** Coed **% Accepted:** 38 **Admission Plans:** Deferred Admission **Application Deadline:** Rolling **Application Fee:** $50.00 **H.S. Requirements:** High school diploma required; GED accepted **Costs Per Year:** Application fee: $50. Tuition: $16,900 full-time. Mandatory fees: $500 full-time. **Scholarships:** Available **Calendar System:** Continuous, Summer Session Not available **Enrollment:** FT 220 **Faculty:** FT 7, PT 19 **Student-Faculty Ratio:** 16:1 **Library Holdings:** 7,467 **Regional Accreditation:** Middle State Association of Colleges and Schools **Credit Hours For Degree:** 70 units, Associates **Professional Accreditation:** NAST, NYSBR

AMERICAN ACADEMY MCALLISTER INSTITUTE OF FUNERAL SERVICE

450 West 56th St.
New York, NY 10019-3602
Tel: (212)757-1190
Admissions: (212)220-4275
Fax: (212)765-5923
Web Site: http://www.a-a-m-i.org/
President/CEO: Meg Dunn
Registrar: Kerrian Williams
Admissions: Norman Provost
Financial Aid: Theresa Powell
Type: Two-Year College **Sex:** Coed **Admission Plans:** Open Admission; Early Admission; Deferred Admission **Application Fee:** $35.00 **H.S. Requirements:** High school diploma required; GED accepted **Scholarships:** Available **Calendar System:** Semester, Summer Session Not available **Enrollment:** FT 130 **Faculty:** FT 2, PT 18 **Student-Faculty Ratio:** 25:1 **Library Holdings:** 1,672 **Credit Hours For Degree:** 74 credits, Associates **Professional Accreditation:** ABFSE

THE ART INSTITUTE OF NEW YORK CITY

75 Varick St., 16th Floor
New York, NY 10013
Tel: (212)226-5500
Free: 800-654-2433
Fax: (212)226-5644
Web Site: http://www.ainyc.aii.edu/
President/CEO: Michael R. Iannacone
Registrar: Charles Evans
Admissions: Lauren Malone
Financial Aid: Georgia Mattinson
Type: Two-Year College **Sex:** Coed **Affiliation:** Education Management Corporation **Admission Plans:** Open Admission **Application Deadline:** Rolling **Application Fee:** $50.00 **H.S. Requirements:** High school diploma required; GED accepted **Costs Per Year:** Application fee: $50. Tuition: $431 per credit part-time. Part-time tuition varies according to course load and degree level. Contact school directly as tuition and fees vary according to program. Tuition guaranteed not to increase for student's term of enrollment. **Scholarships:** Available **Calendar System:** Quarter, Summer Session Available **Faculty:** FT 79, PT 19 **Student-Faculty Ratio:** 16:1 **Credit Hours For Degree:** 90 credits, Associates **Professional Accreditation:** ACICS, ACF

ASA INSTITUTE, THE COLLEGE OF ADVANCED TECHNOLOGY

151 Lawrence St., 2nd Floor
Brooklyn, NY 11201
Tel: (718)522-9073
Admissions: (718)534-0773
Fax: (718)834-0835
E-mail: alice_perez@asa-institute.com
Web Site: http://www.asa-institute.com/
President/CEO: Alex Shchegol
Admissions: Alice Perez
Type: Two-Year College **Sex:** Coed **Calendar System:** Semester **Professional Accreditation:** ACICS, AAMAE

BARD COLLEGE

PO Box 5000
Annandale-on-Hudson, NY 12504
Tel: (845)758-6822
Admissions: (845)758-7472
E-mail: admission@bard.edu
Web Site: http://www.bard.edu/
President/CEO: Dr. Leon Botstein
Registrar: Peter Gadsby
Admissions: Mary Inga Backlund
Financial Aid: Denise Ackerman
Type: Comprehensive **Sex:** Coed **Scores:** 100% SAT V 400+; 100% SAT M 400+ **% Accepted:** 32 **Admission Plans:** Early Admission; Early Action; Deferred Admission **Application Deadline:** January 15 **Application Fee:** $50.00 **H.S. Requirements:** High school diploma required; GED accepted **Costs Per Year:** Application fee: $50. Comprehensive fee: $43,930 includes full-time tuition ($34,080) and college room and board ($9850). College room only: $4950. Part-time tuition: $1066 per credit. Part-time mandatory fees: $351 per term. **Scholarships:** Available **Calendar System:** Semester, Summer Session Not available **Enrollment:** FT 1,521, PT 64, Grad 273 **Faculty:** FT 130, PT 100 **Student-Faculty Ratio:** 9:1 **% Receiving Financial Aid:** 59 **% Residing in College-Owned, -Operated, or -Affiliated Housing:** 80 **Library Holdings:** 350,000 **Regional Accreditation:** Middle State Association of Colleges and Schools **Credit Hours For Degree:** 60 credits, Associates; 124 credits, Bachelors **Intercollegiate Athletics:** Basketball M & W; Cross-Country Running M & W; Soccer M & W; Squash M; Tennis M & W; Volleyball M & W

BARNARD COLLEGE

3009 Broadway
New York, NY 10027-6598
Tel: (212)854-5262
Admissions: (212)854-2014
Fax: (212)854-6220
E-mail: admissions@barnard.edu
Web Site: http://www.barnard.edu/
President/CEO: Dr. Judith R. Shapiro
Registrar: Constance A. Brown
Admissions: Jennifer Gill Fondiller
Financial Aid: Susan Lee
Type: Four-Year College **Sex:** Women **Affiliation:** Columbia University **Scores:** 100% SAT V 400+; 100% SAT M 400+; 9% ACT 18-23; 56% ACT 24-29 **% Accepted:** 27 **Admission Plans:** Early Admission; Early Decision Plan; Deferred Admission **Application Deadline:** January 01 **Application Fee:** $45.00 **H.S. Requirements:** High school diploma or equivalent not required **Costs Per Year:** Application fee: $45. Comprehensive fee: $41,802 includes full-time tuition ($29,364), mandatory fees ($1312), and college room and board ($11,126). College room only: $6764. Room and board charges vary according to board plan and housing facility. Part-time tuition: $980 per credit. **Scholarships:** Available **Calendar System:** Semester, Summer Session Not available **Enrollment:** FT 2,296, PT 60 **Faculty:** FT 193, PT 126 **Student-Faculty Ratio:** 10:1 **Exams:** SAT I and SAT II or ACT **% Receiving Financial Aid:** 43 **% Residing in College-Owned, -Operated, or -Affiliated Housing:** 90 **Library Holdings:** 204,906 **Regional Accreditation:** Middle State Association of Colleges and Schools **Credit Hours For Degree:** 122 credits, Bachelors **Professional Accreditation:** NASD **Intercollegiate Athletics:** Archery W; Basketball W; Crew W; Cross-Country Running W; Equestrian Sports W; Fencing W; Field Hockey W; Golf

W; Ice Hockey W; Lacrosse W; Rugby W; Sailing W; Skiing (Downhill) W; Soccer W; Softball W; Squash W; Swimming and Diving W; Tennis W; Track and Field W; Volleyball W

BEIS MEDRASH HEICHAL DOVID
257 Beach 17th St.
Far Rockaway, NY 11691
Tel: (718)868-2300
Fax: (718)868-0517 **Type:** Four-Year College **Professional Accreditation:** AARTS

BERKELEY COLLEGE-NEW YORK CITY CAMPUS
3 East 43rd St.
New York, NY 10017-4604
Tel: (212)986-4343
Free: 800-446-5400
Fax: (212)697-3371
Web Site: http://www.berkeleycollege.edu/
President/CEO: Dr. Mildred Garcia
Registrar: Kristin Rowe
Admissions: Christine G. Richard
Financial Aid: Janet Solomon
Type: Two-Year College **Sex:** Coed **% Accepted:** 73 **Admission Plans:** Deferred Admission **Application Deadline:** Rolling **Application Fee:** $50.00 **H.S. Requirements:** High school diploma required; GED accepted **Costs Per Year:** Application fee: $50. Tuition: $16,950 full-time. Mandatory fees: $750 full-time. **Scholarships:** Available **Calendar System:** Quarter, Summer Session Available **Enrollment:** FT 2,138, PT 183 **Faculty:** FT 40, PT 100 **Student-Faculty Ratio:** 26:1 **Exams:** SAT I or ACT **Library Holdings:** 13,164 **Regional Accreditation:** Middle State Association of Colleges and Schools **Credit Hours For Degree:** 90 quarter hour, Associates; 180 quarter hour, Bachelors

BERKELEY COLLEGE-WESTCHESTER CAMPUS
99 Church St.
White Plains, NY 10601
Tel: (914)694-1122
Free: 800-446-5400
Fax: (914)694-5832
Web Site: http://www.berkeleycollege.edu/
President/CEO: Dr. Mildred Garcia
Registrar: Tia DeLouise
Admissions: Christine G. Richard
Financial Aid: Marilyn Stamas
Type: Two-Year College **Sex:** Coed **Admission Plans:** Deferred Admission **Application Deadline:** Rolling **Application Fee:** $50.00 **H.S. Requirements:** High school diploma required; GED accepted **Costs Per Year:** Application fee: $50. Comprehensive fee: $26,700 includes full-time tuition ($16,950), mandatory fees ($750), and college room and board ($9000). **Scholarships:** Available **Calendar System:** Quarter, Summer Session Available **Enrollment:** FT 564, PT 46 **Faculty:** FT 17, PT 25 **Student-Faculty Ratio:** 22:1 **Exams:** SAT I or ACT **% Residing in College-Owned, -Operated, or -Affiliated Housing:** 10 **Library Holdings:** 9,526 **Regional Accreditation:** Middle State Association of Colleges and Schools **Credit Hours For Degree:** 90 quarter hours, Associates; 180 quarter hours, Bachelors

BERNARD M. BARUCH COLLEGE OF THE CITY UNIVERSITY OF NEW YORK
1 Bernard Baruch Way
New York, NY 10010-5585
Tel: (646)312-1000
Admissions: (212)312-1400
E-mail: udgbb@cunyvm.edu
Web Site: http://www.baruch.cuny.edu/
President/CEO: Dr. Kathleen Waldron
Registrar: Thomas McCarthy
Admissions: James F. Murphy
Financial Aid: James Murphy
Type: Comprehensive **Sex:** Coed **Affiliation:** City University of New York System **% Accepted:** 33 **Admission Plans:** Early Admission; Early Action; Early Decision Plan **Application Deadline:** February 01 **Application Fee:** $65.00 **H.S. Requirements:** High school diploma required; GED accepted **Costs Per Year:** Application fee: $65. State resident tuition: $4000 full-time, $170 per credit part-time. Nonresident tuition: $8640 full-time, $360 per credit part-time. Mandatory fees: $320 full-time, $80 per term part-time. **Scholarships:** Available **Calendar System:** Semester, Summer Session Available **Enrollment:** FT 9,753, PT 3,091, Grad 2,912 **Faculty:** FT 473, PT 452 **Student-Faculty Ratio:** 20:1 **Exams:** SAT I or ACT **% Receiving Financial Aid:** 82 **Library Holdings:** 297,959 **Regional Accreditation:** Middle State Association of Colleges and Schools **Credit Hours For Degree:** 124 credits, Bachelors **Professional Accreditation:** AACSB, ACEHSA, NASPAA **Intercollegiate Athletics:** Archery M & W; Baseball M; Basketball M & W; Cheerleading W; Cross-Country Running W; Soccer M; Softball W; Swimming and Diving M & W; Tennis M & W; Volleyball M & W; Water Polo M & W

BETH HAMEDRASH SHAAREI YOSHER INSTITUTE
4102-10 Sixteenth Ave.
Brooklyn, NY 11204
Tel: (718)854-2290
President/CEO: Rabbi Yosef Rosenblum
Registrar: Rabbi Nusyn Erlich
Admissions: Menachem Steinberg
Financial Aid: Rabbi Menachem Steinberg
Type: Comprehensive **Sex:** Men **Affiliation:** Jewish **H.S. Requirements:** High school diploma required; GED accepted **Calendar System:** Semester **Professional Accreditation:** AARTS

BETH HATALMUD RABBINICAL COLLEGE
2127 Eighty-second St.
Brooklyn, NY 11214
Tel: (718)259-2525
President/CEO: Rabbi I. Perkowsky
Admissions: Rabbi Osina
Type: Comprehensive **Sex:** Men **Affiliation:** Jewish **H.S. Requirements:** High school diploma required; GED accepted **Calendar System:** Semester **Professional Accreditation:** AARTS

BORICUA COLLEGE
3755 Broadway
New York, NY 10032-1560
Tel: (212)694-1000
Web Site: http://www.boricuacollege.edu/
President/CEO: Dr. Victor G. Alicea
Registrar: Dr. Mercedes Alicea
Admissions: Dr. Mercedes Alicea
Financial Aid: Rosalia Cruz
Type: Comprehensive **Sex:** Coed **Admission Plans:** Deferred Admission **Application Fee:** $25.00 **H.S. Requirements:** High school diploma required; GED accepted **Costs Per Year:** Application fee: $25. Tuition: $9000 full-time. Mandatory fees: $50 full-time. **Scholarships:** Available **Calendar System:** Miscellaneous, Summer Session Available **Faculty:** FT 51, PT 65 **Student-Faculty Ratio:** 20:1 **Exams:** Other **Library Holdings:** 112,600 **Regional Accreditation:** Middle State Association of Colleges and Schools **Credit Hours For Degree:** 60 credits, Associates; 124 credits, Bachelors

BOROUGH OF MANHATTAN COMMUNITY COLLEGE OF THE CITY UNIVERSITY OF NEW YORK
199 Chambers St.
New York, NY 10007-1097
Tel: (212)346-8000
Admissions: (212)220-1265
Fax: (212)346-8816
Web Site: http://www.bmcc.cuny.edu/
President/CEO: Dr. Antonio Perez
Registrar: Gregory Wist
Admissions: Eugenio Barrios
Financial Aid: Howard Entin
Type: Two-Year College **Sex:** Coed **Affiliation:** City University of New York System **Scores:** 47% SAT V 400+; 48% SAT M 400+ **% Accepted:** 89 **Admission Plans:** Open Admission; Preferred Admission; Deferred Admission **Application Deadline:** Rolling **Application Fee:** $65.00 **H.S. Requirements:** High school diploma required; GED accepted. For applicants 21 or over who are on the 24 College Credit Plan: High school diploma or equivalent not required **Costs Per Year:** Application fee: $65. State resident tuition: $2800 full-time, $120 per credit hour part-time. Nonresident tuition: $4560 full-time, $190 per credit hour part-time. Mandatory fees: $268 full-time. **Scholarships:** Available **Calendar System:** Semester, Summer Ses-

sion Available **Enrollment:** FT 10,809, PT 7,967 **Faculty:** FT 378, PT 697 **Student-Faculty Ratio:** 22:1 **Library Holdings:** 101,869 **Regional Accreditation:** Middle State Association of Colleges and Schools **Credit Hours For Degree:** 60 credits, Associates **Professional Accreditation:** AHIMA, CARC, JRCEMT, NLN **Intercollegiate Athletics:** Baseball M; Basketball M & W; Soccer M

BRAMSON ORT COLLEGE
69-30 Austin St.
Forest Hills, NY 11375-4239
Tel: (718)261-5800
Web Site: http://www.bramsonort.edu/
President/CEO: Dr. Alan Stein
Registrar: Mitra Soleymani
Admissions: Rita Baskin
Financial Aid: Angelina Marra
Type: Two-Year College **Sex:** Coed **Admission Plans:** Open Admission; Early Admission; Deferred Admission **Application Fee:** $50.00 **H.S. Requirements:** High school diploma required; GED accepted **Scholarships:** Available **Calendar System:** Semester, Summer Session Available **Faculty:** FT 32, PT 48 **Library Holdings:** 8,000 **Credit Hours For Degree:** 62 credits, Associates **Professional Accreditation:** NYSBR

BRIARCLIFFE COLLEGE
1055 Stewart Ave.
Bethpage, NY 11714
Tel: (516)918-3600
Admissions: (516)918-3705
Fax: (516)470-6020
E-mail: donohuet@bcl.org
Web Site: http://www.briarcliffe.edu/
President/CEO: Neal Raisman, PhD
Registrar: Francine Byrnes
Admissions: Theresa Donohue
Financial Aid: Roseangela Dempster
Type: Four-Year College **Sex:** Coed **Affiliation:** Career Education Corporation **Admission Plans:** Deferred Admission **Application Deadline:** Rolling **Application Fee:** $35.00 **H.S. Requirements:** High school diploma required; GED accepted **Costs Per Year:** Application fee: $35. Comprehensive fee: $23,730 includes full-time tuition ($14,592), mandatory fees ($1200), and college room and board ($7938). Part-time tuition: $608 per credit. **Scholarships:** Available **Calendar System:** Semester, Summer Session Available **Enrollment:** FT 2,373, PT 636 **Faculty:** FT 61, PT 128 **Student-Faculty Ratio:** 16:1 **% Residing in College-Owned, -Operated, or -Affiliated Housing:** 4 **Library Holdings:** 11,834 **Regional Accreditation:** Middle State Association of Colleges and Schools **Credit Hours For Degree:** 60 credits, Associates; 120 credits, Bachelors **Intercollegiate Athletics:** Baseball M; Bowling M & W; Lacrosse M; Soccer W; Softball W; Track and Field M & W

BRONX COMMUNITY COLLEGE OF THE CITY UNIVERSITY OF NEW YORK
University Ave. & West 181st St.
Bronx, NY 10453
Tel: (718)289-5100
Admissions: (718)289-5888
Web Site: http://www.bcc.cuny.edu/
President/CEO: Dr. Carolyn Grubbs Williams
Admissions: Alba Cancetty
Financial Aid: Orlando Lopez
Type: Two-Year College **Sex:** Coed **Affiliation:** City University of New York System **% Accepted:** 98 **Admission Plans:** Open Admission **Application Deadline:** July 01 **Application Fee:** $65.00 **H.S. Requirements:** High school diploma required; GED accepted **Costs Per Year:** Application fee: $65. State resident tuition: $2800 full-time, $120 per credit part-time. Nonresident tuition: $4560 full-time, $190 per credit part-time. Mandatory fees: $284 full-time, $90 per term part-time. **Calendar System:** Semester, Summer Session Available **Enrollment:** FT 5,088, PT 3,382 **Faculty:** FT 265, PT 282 **Student-Faculty Ratio:** 15:1 **Library Holdings:** 75,000 **Regional Accreditation:** Middle State Association of Colleges and Schools **Credit Hours For Degree:** 60 credits, Associates **Professional Accreditation:** ABET, ACBSP, JRCERT, JRCNMT, NLN **Intercollegiate Athletics:** Basketball M & W; Soccer M; Tennis M & W; Track and Field M & W; Volleyball W; Wrestling M

BROOKLYN COLLEGE OF THE CITY UNIVERSITY OF NEW YORK
2900 Bedford Ave.
Brooklyn, NY 11210-2889
Tel: (718)951-5000
Admissions: (718)951-5001
E-mail: admissions@brooklyn.cuny.edu
Web Site: http://www.brooklyn.cuny.edu/
President/CEO: Dr. Christoph M. Kimmich
Registrar: Joan Antonicelli
Admissions: Marianne Booufall-Tynan
Financial Aid: Sherwood Johnson
Type: Comprehensive **Sex:** Coed **Affiliation:** City University of New York System **Scores:** 90% SAT V 400+; 97% SAT M 400+ **% Accepted:** 33 **Admission Plans:** Early Admission; Deferred Admission **Application Deadline:** Rolling **Application Fee:** $65.00 **H.S. Requirements:** High school diploma required; GED accepted **Costs Per Year:** Application fee: $65. State resident tuition: $4000 full-time, $170 per credit part-time. Nonresident tuition: $8640 full-time, $360 per credit part-time. Mandatory fees: $375 full-time, $139.05 per term part-time. **Scholarships:** Available **Calendar System:** Semester, Summer Session Available **Enrollment:** FT 8,109, PT 3,255, Grad 3,917 **Faculty:** FT 517, PT 586 **Student-Faculty Ratio:** 15:1 **Exams:** SAT I or ACT, SAT II **% Receiving Financial Aid:** 77 **Library Holdings:** 1,305,602 **Regional Accreditation:** Middle State Association of Colleges and Schools **Credit Hours For Degree:** 120 credits, Bachelors **Professional Accreditation:** ADtA, ASLHA, CEPH, NCATE **Intercollegiate Athletics:** Basketball M & W; Cross-Country Running M & W; Soccer M; Softball W; Swimming and Diving M & W; Tennis M & W; Track and Field M & W; Volleyball M & W

BROOME COMMUNITY COLLEGE
PO Box 1017
Binghamton, NY 13902-1017
Tel: (607)778-5000
Admissions: (607)778-5001
Web Site: http://www.sunybroome.edu/
President/CEO: Dr. Laurence D. Spraggs
Registrar: Wilbert E. Corprew
Admissions: Anthony Fiorelli
Financial Aid: Doug Lukasik
Type: Two-Year College **Sex:** Coed **Affiliation:** State University of New York System **% Accepted:** 52 **Admission Plans:** Open Admission; Preferred Admission; Early Admission **Application Deadline:** Rolling **Application Fee:** $0.00 **H.S. Requirements:** High school diploma required; GED accepted **Costs Per Year:** Application fee: $0. One-time mandatory fee: $45. State resident tuition: $2814 full-time, $118 per credit hour part-time. Nonresident tuition: $5628 full-time, $236 per credit hour part-time. Mandatory fees: $267 full-time, $5 per credit hour part-time, $29 per term part-time. Full-time tuition and fees vary according to course load and location. Part-time tuition and fees vary according to course load and location. **Scholarships:** Available **Calendar System:** Semester, Summer Session Available **Enrollment:** FT 3,946, PT 2,285 **Faculty:** FT 145, PT 254 **Student-Faculty Ratio:** 21:1 **Library Holdings:** 60,518 **Regional Accreditation:** Middle State Association of Colleges and Schools **Credit Hours For Degree:** 62 credit hours, Associates **Professional Accreditation:** ABET, AAMAE, ADA, AHIMA, APTA, JRCERT, NAACLS, NLN **Intercollegiate Athletics:** Baseball M; Basketball M & W; Cross-Country Running M & W; Golf M; Ice Hockey M; Lacrosse M; Soccer M & W; Softball W; Tennis M & W; Volleyball W

BRYANT AND STRATTON COLLEGE (ALBANY)
1259 Central Ave.
Albany, NY 12205-5230
Tel: (518)437-1802
Fax: (518)437-1048
Web Site: http://www.bryantstratton.edu/
President/CEO: Michael Gutierrez
Admissions: Robert Ferrell
Financial Aid: Steve Kudzin
Type: Two-Year College **Sex:** Coed **Affiliation:** Bryant and Stratton College, Inc **Admission Plans:** Deferred Admission **Application Deadline:** Rolling **H.S. Requirements:** High school diploma required; GED accepted. For applicants 19 or over who meet entrance testing requirements: High school

diploma or equivalent not required **Costs Per Year:** Tuition: $18,675 full-time, $415 per credit hour part-time. Mandatory fees: $25 full-time. Full-time tuition and fees vary according to course load. Part-time tuition varies according to course load. **Scholarships:** Available **Calendar System:** Semester, Summer Session Available **Enrollment:** FT 354, PT 116 **Faculty:** FT 12, PT 33 **Exams:** Other, SAT I or ACT **Library Holdings:** 3,500 **Regional Accreditation:** Middle State Association of Colleges and Schools **Credit Hours For Degree:** 60 credit hours, Associates **Professional Accreditation:** AAMAE, NYSBR

BRYANT AND STRATTON COLLEGE, AMHERST CAMPUS
Audubon Business Center, 40 Hazelwood Dr.
Amherst, NY 14228
Tel: (716)691-0012
Fax: (716)691-6716
E-mail: mzachary@bryantstratton.edu
Web Site: http://www.bryantstratton.edu/
President/CEO: John Staschak
Registrar: Dorothy M. Attard
Admissions: Mary Zachary
Financial Aid: Robert Kociecki
Type: Two-Year College **Sex:** Coed **Affiliation:** Bryant and Stratton College **% Accepted:** 79 **Admission Plans:** Deferred Admission **Application Deadline:** Rolling **H.S. Requirements:** High school diploma or equivalent not required **Costs Per Year:** Tuition: $18,675 full-time, $415 per credit hour part-time. Mandatory fees: $25 full-time. Full-time tuition and fees vary according to class time and course load. Part-time tuition varies according to class time and course load. **Scholarships:** Available **Calendar System:** Trimester, Summer Session Available **Enrollment:** FT 240, PT 163 **Faculty:** FT 8, PT 27 **Exams:** Other, SAT I or ACT **Library Holdings:** 4,500 **Regional Accreditation:** Middle State Association of Colleges and Schools **Credit Hours For Degree:** 60 credits, Associates; 120 credits, Bachelors **Professional Accreditation:** NYSBR

BRYANT AND STRATTON COLLEGE, BUFFALO CAMPUS
465 Main St.
Ste. 400
Buffalo, NY 14203
Tel: (716)884-9120
Web Site: http://www.bryantstratton.edu/
President/CEO: John Staschak
Registrar: Dorothy Attard
Admissions: Phil Strubel
Financial Aid: Luanne Brown
Type: Two-Year College **Sex:** Coed **Affiliation:** Bryant and Stratton College **% Accepted:** 75 **Admission Plans:** Deferred Admission **Application Deadline:** Rolling **H.S. Requirements:** High school diploma or equivalent not required **Costs Per Year:** Tuition: $18,675 full-time, $415 per credit hour part-time. Mandatory fees: $25 full-time. Full-time tuition and fees vary according to class time and course load. Part-time tuition varies according to course load. **Scholarships:** Available **Calendar System:** Trimester, Summer Session Available **Enrollment:** FT 495, PT 108 **Faculty:** FT 10, PT 42 **Exams:** Other, SAT I or ACT **Library Holdings:** 30,000 **Regional Accreditation:** Middle State Association of Colleges and Schools **Credit Hours For Degree:** 60 credits, Associates **Professional Accreditation:** AAMAE, NYSBR

BRYANT AND STRATTON COLLEGE, LACKAWANNA CAMPUS
1214 Abbott Rd.
Lackawanna, NY 14218-1989
Tel: (716)821-9331
Admissions: (716)677-9500
E-mail: prkehr@bryantstratton.edu
Web Site: http://www.bryantstratton.edu/
President/CEO: John Staschak
Registrar: Dorothy Attard
Admissions: Paul Kehr
Financial Aid: Carrie McCooey
Type: Two-Year College **Sex:** Coed **Affiliation:** Bryant and Stratton College **% Accepted:** 73 **Admission Plans:** Deferred Admission **Application Deadline:** Rolling **H.S. Requirements:** High school diploma or equivalent not required **Costs Per Year:** Tuition: $18,675 full-time, $415 per credit hour part-time. Mandatory fees: $25 full-time. Full-time tuition and fees vary according to course load. Part-time tuition varies according to course load. **Scholarships:** Available **Calendar System:** Trimester, Summer Session Available **Enrollment:** FT 189, PT 80 **Faculty:** FT 7, PT 26 **Exams:** Other, SAT I or ACT **Library Holdings:** 1,402 **Regional Accreditation:** Middle State Association of Colleges and Schools **Credit Hours For Degree:** 60 credits, Associates **Professional Accreditation:** NYSBR

BRYANT AND STRATTON COLLEGE, NORTH CAMPUS
8687 Carling Rd.
Liverpool, NY 13090-1315
Tel: (315)652-6500
Web Site: http://www.bryantstratton.edu/
President/CEO: Susan Cumoletti
Admissions: Susan Cumoletti
Type: Two-Year College **Sex:** Coed **Affiliation:** Bryant and Stratton Business Institute, Inc **Admission Plans:** Deferred Admission **Application Fee:** $25.00 **H.S. Requirements:** High school diploma required; GED accepted. For applicants 19 or older who meet entrance-testing requirements: High school diploma or equivalent not required **Scholarships:** Available **Calendar System:** Semester, Summer Session Available **Enrollment:** FT 324, PT 33 **Faculty:** FT 7, PT 24 **Student-Faculty Ratio:** 14:1 **Exams:** Other **Library Holdings:** 1,936 **Regional Accreditation:** Middle State Association of Colleges and Schools **Credit Hours For Degree:** 64 semester hours, Associates **Professional Accreditation:** NYSBR **Intercollegiate Athletics:** Soccer M & W

BRYANT AND STRATTON COLLEGE (ROCHESTER-GREECE CAMPUS)
150 Bellwood Dr.
Rochester, NY 14606
Tel: (585)720-0660
Fax: (585)720-9226
Web Site: http://www.bryantstratton.edu/
President/CEO: Anne L. Loria
Admissions: Maria Scalise
Type: Two-Year College **Sex:** Coed **Affiliation:** Bryant and Stratton College **Admission Plans:** Deferred Admission **Application Deadline:** Rolling **H.S. Requirements:** High school diploma required; GED accepted, For applicants 19 or older who meet entrance testing requirements: High school diploma or equivalent not required **Costs Per Year:** Tuition: $18,675 full-time, $415 per credit hour part-time. Mandatory fees: $25 full-time. **Scholarships:** Available **Calendar System:** Semester, Summer Session Available **Enrollment:** FT 152, PT 42 **Faculty:** FT 2, PT 29 **Exams:** Other, SAT I or ACT **Library Holdings:** 250 **Regional Accreditation:** Middle State Association of Colleges and Schools **Credit Hours For Degree:** 60 semester hours, Associates **Professional Accreditation:** AAMAE, NYSBR

BRYANT AND STRATTON COLLEGE (ROCHESTER-HENRIETTA CAMPUS)
1225 Jefferson Rd.
Rochester, NY 14623-3136
Tel: (585)292-5627
Fax: (585)292-6015
Web Site: http://www.bryantstratton.edu/
President/CEO: Anne Loria
Admissions: Maria Scalise
Financial Aid: Margaret Modzel
Type: Two-Year College **Sex:** Coed **Affiliation:** Bryant and Stratton College **Admission Plans:** Deferred Admission **Application Deadline:** Rolling **H.S. Requirements:** High school diploma required; GED accepted. For applicants 19 or older who meet entrance testing requirements: High school diploma or equivalent not required **Costs Per Year:** Tuition: $18,675 full-time, $415 per credit hour part-time. Mandatory fees: $25 full-time. **Scholarships:** Available **Calendar System:** Semester, Summer Session Available **Enrollment:** FT 238, PT 59 **Faculty:** FT 16, PT 43 **Student-Faculty Ratio:** 10:1 **Exams:** Other, SAT I or ACT **Library Holdings:** 250 **Regional Accreditation:** Middle State Association of Colleges and Schools **Credit Hours For Degree:** 60 semester hours, Associates **Professional Accreditation:** AAMAE, NYSBR

BRYANT AND STRATTON COLLEGE (SYRACUSE)
953 James St.
Syracuse, NY 13203-2502
Tel: (315)472-6603
Fax: (315)474-4383
Web Site: http://www.bryantstratton.edu/

President/CEO: Michael Sattler
Admissions: Dawn Rajkowski
Financial Aid: Mary Clifton
Type: Two-Year College **Sex:** Coed **Affiliation:** Bryant and Stratton Business Institute, Inc **Application Deadline:** Rolling **H.S. Requirements:** High school diploma required; GED accepted. For applicants 19 or older who meet entrance testing requirements: High school diploma or equivalent not required **Costs Per Year:** Tuition: $18,675 full-time, $415 per credit hour part-time. Mandatory fees: $25 full-time. **Scholarships:** Available **Calendar System:** Semester, Summer Session Available **Enrollment:** FT 494, PT 142 **Faculty:** FT 15, PT 36 **Exams:** Other, SAT I or ACT **% Residing in College-Owned, -Operated, or -Affiliated Housing:** 26 **Library Holdings:** 1,325 **Regional Accreditation:** Middle State Association of Colleges and Schools **Credit Hours For Degree:** 68 semester hours, Associates **Professional Accreditation:** AAMAE, NYSBR **Intercollegiate Athletics:** Soccer M & W

BUFFALO STATE COLLEGE, STATE UNIVERSITY OF NEW YORK

1300 Elmwood Ave.
Buffalo, NY 14222-1095
Tel: (716)878-4000
Admissions: (716)878-5519
Fax: (716)878-6100
E-mail: admissions@buffalostate.edu
Web Site: http://www.buffalostate.edu/
President/CEO: Dr. Muriel A. Howard
Registrar: Mark Bausili
Admissions: Lesa Loritts
Financial Aid: Kent McGowan
Type: Comprehensive **Sex:** Coed **Scores:** 95.8% SAT V 400+; 97.7% SAT M 400+ **% Accepted:** 44 **Admission Plans:** Early Admission; Early Decision Plan; Deferred Admission **Application Deadline:** Rolling **Application Fee:** $30.00 **H.S. Requirements:** High school diploma required; GED accepted **Costs Per Year:** Application fee: $30. State resident tuition: $4350 full-time, $181 per semester hour part-time. Nonresident tuition: $10,610 full-time, $442 per semester hour part-time. Mandatory fees: $881 full-time, $36.60 per credit hour part-time. College room and board: $6672. College room only: $4136. Room and board charges vary according to board plan, housing facility, and student level. **Scholarships:** Available **Calendar System:** Semester, Summer Session Available **Enrollment:** FT 7,818, PT 1,192, Grad 2,046 **Faculty:** FT 393, PT 322 **Student-Faculty Ratio:** 17:1 **Exams:** SAT I and SAT II or ACT **% Receiving Financial Aid:** 67 **% Residing in College-Owned, -Operated, or -Affiliated Housing:** 21 **Library Holdings:** 489,069 **Regional Accreditation:** Middle State Association of Colleges and Schools **Credit Hours For Degree:** 123 semester hours, Bachelors **ROTC:** Army **Professional Accreditation:** ABET, ADtA, ASLHA, CSWE, FIDER, NCATE **Intercollegiate Athletics:** Baseball M; Basketball M & W; Bowling M & W; Cross-Country Running M & W; Fencing M; Football M; Ice Hockey M & W; Lacrosse M & W; Rugby M; Skiing (Cross-Country) M & W; Skiing (Downhill) M & W; Soccer M & W; Softball W; Swimming and Diving M & W; Tennis W; Track and Field M & W; Volleyball M & W

BUSINESS INFORMATICS CENTER, INC.

134 South Central Ave.
Valley Stream, NY 11580-5431
Tel: (516)561-0050
Fax: (516)561-0074
President/CEO: Joseph Brown
Type: Two-Year College **Sex:** Coed **Professional Accreditation:** ACCSCT

CANISIUS COLLEGE

2001 Main St.
Buffalo, NY 14208-1098
Tel: (716)883-7000
Free: 800-843-1517
Admissions: (716)888-2200
Fax: (716)888-2377
E-mail: inquiry@gort.canisius.edu
Web Site: http://www.canisius.edu/
President/CEO: Rev. Vincent M. Cooke, SJ
Registrar: Blair Foster
Admissions: Ann Marie Moscovic
Financial Aid: Curtis C. Gaume
Type: Comprehensive **Sex:** Coed **Affiliation:** Roman Catholic (Jesuit) **Scores:** 99.71% SAT V 400+; 99.57% SAT M 400+; 49.6% ACT 18-23; 40.48% ACT 24-29 **% Accepted:** 72 **Admission Plans:** Early Admission; Deferred Admission **Application Deadline:** May 01 **Application Fee:** $40.00 **H.S. Requirements:** High school diploma required; GED accepted **Costs Per Year:** Application fee: $40. Comprehensive fee: $32,257 includes full-time tuition ($22,370), mandatory fees ($927), and college room and board ($8960). College room only: $5250. Room and board charges vary according to board plan, housing facility, and student level. Part-time tuition: $638 per credit hour. Part-time mandatory fees: $20.50 per credit, $18 per term. **Scholarships:** Available **Calendar System:** Semester, Summer Session Available **Enrollment:** FT 3,310, PT 281, Grad 1,388 **Faculty:** FT 215, PT 316 **Student-Faculty Ratio:** 13:1 **Exams:** SAT I or ACT **% Receiving Financial Aid:** 76 **% Residing in College-Owned, -Operated, or -Affiliated Housing:** 41 **Library Holdings:** 328,278 **Regional Accreditation:** Middle State Association of Colleges and Schools **Credit Hours For Degree:** 120 credit hours, Bachelors **ROTC:** Army **Professional Accreditation:** AACSB, JRCEPAT, NCATE **Intercollegiate Athletics:** Baseball M; Basketball M & W; Cross-Country Running M & W; Golf M; Ice Hockey M; Lacrosse M & W; Rugby M; Soccer M & W; Softball W; Swimming and Diving M & W; Volleyball M & W

CAYUGA COUNTY COMMUNITY COLLEGE

197 Franklin St.
Auburn, NY 13021-3099
Tel: (315)255-1743
Web Site: http://www.cayuga-cc.edu/
President/CEO: Dr. Dennis Golladay
Registrar: Linda E. Szczepanski
Admissions: Bruce M. Blodgett
Financial Aid: Judith G. Miladin
Type: Two-Year College **Sex:** Coed **Affiliation:** State University of New York System **Scores:** 75% SAT V 400+; 87% SAT M 400+ **Admission Plans:** Open Admission; Deferred Admission **Application Fee:** $0.00 **H.S. Requirements:** High school diploma required; GED accepted. For applicants 19 or over: High school diploma or equivalent not required **Costs Per Year:** Application fee: $0. State resident tuition: $2900 full-time, $105 per credit part-time. Nonresident tuition: $5800 full-time, $210 per credit part-time. Mandatory fees: $311 full-time, $12 per credit part-time, $2 per term part-time. Full-time tuition and fees vary according to class time, course load, and program. Part-time tuition and fees vary according to class time, course load, and program. **Scholarships:** Available **Calendar System:** Semester, Summer Session Available **Enrollment:** FT 2,220, PT 1,676 **Faculty:** FT 44, PT 111 **Exams:** Other, SAT I or ACT **Library Holdings:** 82,205 **Regional Accreditation:** Middle State Association of Colleges and Schools **Credit Hours For Degree:** 60 credit hours, Associates **Professional Accreditation:** NLN **Intercollegiate Athletics:** Basketball M & W; Cross-Country Running M & W; Lacrosse M & W; Soccer M & W

CAZENOVIA COLLEGE

22 Sullivan St.
Cazenovia, NY 13035-1084
Tel: (315)655-7000
Free: 800-654-3210
Admissions: (315)655-7208
Fax: (315)655-2190
E-mail: rcroot@cazenovia.edu
Web Site: http://www.cazenovia.edu/
President/CEO: Dr. Mark John Tierno
Registrar: Jane Incitti
Admissions: Robert A. Croot
Financial Aid: Robert A. Croot
Type: Four-Year College **Sex:** Coed **Scores:** 91.6% SAT V 400+; 87.4% SAT M 400+; 60% ACT 18-23; 15.8% ACT 24-29 **% Accepted:** 82 **Admission Plans:** Early Admission; Deferred Admission **Application Deadline:** Rolling **Application Fee:** $30.00 **H.S. Requirements:** High school diploma required; GED accepted **Costs Per Year:** Application fee: $30. Comprehensive fee: $26,450 includes full-time tuition ($18,940) and college room and board ($7510). College room only: $4200. Full-time tuition varies according to course load. Room and board charges vary according to board plan. Part-time tuition: $400 per credit. Part-time mandatory fees: $100. Part-time tuition and fees vary according to class time and course load. **Scholarships:** Available **Calendar System:** Semester, Summer Session Available **Enrollment:** FT 812, PT 312 **Faculty:** FT 49, PT 90 **Student-Faculty Ratio:** 14:1 **Exams:** SAT I and SAT II or ACT **% Receiving Financial Aid:** 81 **% Residing in College-Owned, -Operated, or -Affiliated Housing:** 81 **Library Holdings:** 79,920 **Regional Accreditation:** Middle State Association of Colleges and Schools **Credit Hours For Degree:** 60 credits, Associates; 120

credits, Bachelors **ROTC:** Army, Air Force **Intercollegiate Athletics:** Basketball M & W; Cheerleading M & W; Crew M & W; Cross-Country Running M; Equestrian Sports M & W; Golf M; Lacrosse M & W; Soccer M & W; Softball W; Volleyball W

CENTRAL YESHIVA TOMCHEI TMIMIM-LUBAVITCH
841-853 Ocean Parkway
Brooklyn, NY 11230
Tel: (718)434-0784
Admissions: (718)859-7600
President/CEO: Rabbi David Raskin
Registrar: Rabbi Joseph Wilmowsky
Admissions: Moses Gluckowsky
Financial Aid: Rabbi Moshe M. Gluckowsky
Type: Comprehensive **Sex:** Men **Affiliation:** Jewish **H.S. Requirements:** High school diploma required; GED accepted **Calendar System:** Semester **Professional Accreditation:** AARTS

CITY COLLEGE OF THE CITY UNIVERSITY OF NEW YORK
138th St. and Convent Ave.
New York, NY 10031-9198
Tel: (212)650-7000
Admissions: (212)650-6977
Fax: (212)650-6417
E-mail: admissions@ccny.cuny.edu
Web Site: http://www.ccny.cuny.edu/
President/CEO: Dr. Gregory H. Williams
Registrar: Celia Lloyd
Admissions: Celia Lloyd
Financial Aid: Thelma Mason
Type: University **Sex:** Coed **Affiliation:** City University of New York System **Scores:** 82.4% SAT V 400+; 92.7% SAT M 400+ **% Accepted:** 37 **Admission Plans:** Early Admission; Deferred Admission **Application Deadline:** March 01 **Application Fee:** $65.00 **H.S. Requirements:** High school diploma required; GED accepted **Costs Per Year:** Application fee: $65. State resident tuition: $4080 full-time, $170 per credit part-time. Nonresident tuition: $8640 full-time, $360 per credit part-time. Full-time tuition varies according to class time and program. Part-time tuition varies according to class time, course load, and program. **Scholarships:** Available **Calendar System:** Semester, Summer Session Available **Enrollment:** FT 6,740, PT 2,754, Grad 2,946 **Faculty:** FT 534, PT 588 **Student-Faculty Ratio:** 11:1 **Exams:** SAT I or ACT **% Receiving Financial Aid:** 77 **Library Holdings:** 1,418,230 **Regional Accreditation:** Middle State Association of Colleges and Schools **Credit Hours For Degree:** 120 credits, Bachelors **ROTC:** Army, Air Force **Professional Accreditation:** ABET, APA, ASLA, NCATE **Intercollegiate Athletics:** Baseball M; Basketball M & W; Cross-Country Running M & W; Fencing W; Lacrosse M; Soccer M; Softball W; Tennis M & W; Track and Field M & W; Volleyball W

CLARKSON UNIVERSITY
Potsdam, NY 13699
Tel: (315)268-6400
Free: 800-527-6577
Admissions: (315)268-6463
Fax: (315)268-7647
E-mail: admission@clarkson.edu
Web Site: http://www.clarkson.edu/
President/CEO: Dr. Anthony G. Collins
Registrar: Lynn C. Brown
Admissions: Brian Grant
Financial Aid: Nicole M. Ashley
Type: University **Sex:** Coed **Scores:** 100% SAT V 400+; 100% SAT M 400+; 34% ACT 18-23; 56% ACT 24-29 **% Accepted:** 86 **Admission Plans:** Early Admission; Early Decision Plan; Deferred Admission **Application Deadline:** March 15 **Application Fee:** $50.00 **H.S. Requirements:** High school diploma required; GED accepted **Costs Per Year:** Application fee: $50. Comprehensive fee: $34,930 includes full-time tuition ($25,185), mandatory fees ($400), and college room and board ($9345). College room only: $4896. Full-time tuition and fees vary according to course load. Room and board charges vary according to housing facility. Part-time tuition: $840 per credit. Part-time tuition varies according to course load. **Scholarships:** Available **Calendar System:** Semester, Summer Session Available **Enrollment:** FT 2,633, PT 15, Grad 397 **Faculty:** FT 170, PT 22 **Student-Faculty Ratio:** 17:1 **Exams:** SAT I or ACT, SAT II **% Receiving Financial Aid:** 75 **% Residing in College-Owned, -Operated, or -Affiliated Housing:** 83 **Library Holdings:** 257,958 **Regional Accreditation:** Middle State Association of Colleges and Schools **Credit Hours For Degree:** 120 credit hours, Bachelors **ROTC:** Army, Air Force **Professional Accreditation:** AACSB, ABET, APTA **Intercollegiate Athletics:** Baseball M; Basketball M & W; Bowling M & W; Cross-Country Running M & W; Golf M; Ice Hockey M & W; Lacrosse M & W; Skiing (Cross-Country) M & W; Skiing (Downhill) M & W; Soccer M & W; Swimming and Diving M & W; Tennis M & W; Volleyball M & W

CLINTON COMMUNITY COLLEGE
136 Clinton Point Dr.
Plattsburgh, NY 12901-9573
Tel: (518)562-4200
Free: 800-552-1160
Admissions: (518)562-4170
Fax: (518)562-8621
Web Site: http://clintoncc.suny.edu/
President/CEO: Agnes Pearl
Registrar: Cheryl Stein
Admissions: Karen L. Burnam
Financial Aid: Karen Burnam
Type: Two-Year College **Sex:** Coed **Affiliation:** State University of New York System **Admission Plans:** Open Admission; Preferred Admission; Deferred Admission **Application Fee:** $0.00 **H.S. Requirements:** High school diploma required; GED accepted **Costs Per Year:** Application fee: $0. State resident tuition: $3020 full-time, $125 per credit hour part-time. Nonresident tuition: $7550 full-time, $312 per credit hour part-time. Mandatory fees: $166 full-time, $5 per credit hour part-time. College room and board: $6340. College room only: $3800. **Scholarships:** Available **Calendar System:** Semester, Summer Session Available **Enrollment:** FT 1,259, PT 933 **Faculty:** FT 49, PT 93 **Student-Faculty Ratio:** 18:1 **Exams:** SAT I or ACT **% Residing in College-Owned, -Operated, or -Affiliated Housing:** 6 **Library Holdings:** 33,862 **Regional Accreditation:** Middle State Association of Colleges and Schools **Credit Hours For Degree:** 60 credits, Associates **Professional Accreditation:** NAACLS, NLN **Intercollegiate Athletics:** Baseball M; Basketball M & W; Soccer M & W; Softball W

COCHRAN SCHOOL OF NURSING
967 North Broadway
Yonkers, NY 10701
Tel: (914)964-4283
Admissions: (914)964-4296
Web Site: http://www.riversidehealth.org/
President/CEO: James Foy
Registrar: Sandra Sclafani
Admissions: Sandra Sclafani
Financial Aid: Geraldine Owens
Type: Two-Year College **Sex:** Coed **Scores:** 100% SAT V 400+; 100% SAT M 400+ **Admission Plans:** Deferred Admission **Application Fee:** $25.00 **H.S. Requirements:** High school diploma required; GED accepted **Scholarships:** Available **Calendar System:** Semester, Summer Session Not available **Enrollment:** FT 101, PT 56 **Faculty:** FT 16, PT 18 **Student-Faculty Ratio:** 5:1 **Exams:** Other, SAT I **Library Holdings:** 4,314 **Credit Hours For Degree:** 72 credits, Associates **Professional Accreditation:** NYSBR

COLGATE UNIVERSITY
13 Oak Dr.
Hamilton, NY 13346-1386
Tel: (315)228-1000
Admissions: (315)228-7401
Fax: (315)228-7798
E-mail: admission@mail.colgate.edu
Web Site: http://www.colgate.edu/
President/CEO: Dr. Rebecca S. Chopp
Registrar: Gretchen Herringer
Admissions: Gary L. Ross
Financial Aid: Marcelle M. Tyburski
Type: Comprehensive **Sex:** Coed **Scores:** 100% SAT V 400+; 100% SAT M 400+; 3% ACT 18-23; 27% ACT 24-29 **% Accepted:** 27 **Admission Plans:** Early Decision Plan; Deferred Admission **Application Deadline:** January 15 **Application Fee:** $55.00 **H.S. Requirements:** High school diploma required; GED accepted **Costs Per Year:** Application fee: $55. Comprehensive fee: $41,170 includes full-time tuition ($32,885), mandatory fees ($220), and college room and board ($8065). College room only: $3895. Full-time tuition and fees vary according to course load. Room and board charges

vary according to board plan and housing facility. Part-time tuition: $4111 per course. Part-time tuition varies according to course load. **Scholarships:** Available **Calendar System:** Semester, Summer Session Not available **Enrollment:** FT 2,747, PT 24, Grad 8 **Faculty:** FT 245, PT 70 **Student-Faculty Ratio:** 10:1 **Exams:** SAT I or ACT **% Receiving Financial Aid:** 44 **% Residing in College-Owned, -Operated, or -Affiliated Housing:** 90 **Library Holdings:** 1,167,084 **Regional Accreditation:** Middle State Association of Colleges and Schools **Credit Hours For Degree:** 32 courses, Bachelors **ROTC:** Army **Intercollegiate Athletics:** Baseball M; Basketball M & W; Cheerleading M & W; Crew M & W; Cross-Country Running M & W; Equestrian Sports M & W; Fencing M & W; Field Hockey W; Football M; Golf M & W; Ice Hockey M & W; Lacrosse M & W; Rugby M & W; Sailing M & W; Skiing (Downhill) M & W; Soccer M & W; Softball W; Squash M & W; Swimming and Diving M & W; Table Tennis M & W; Tennis M & W; Track and Field M & W; Volleyball M & W; Water Polo M & W; Wrestling M & W

COLLEGE OF MOUNT SAINT VINCENT
6301 Riverdale Ave.
Riverdale, NY 10471-1093
Tel: (718)405-3200
Free: 800-665-CMSV
Admissions: (718)405-3268
Fax: (718)549-7945
E-mail: tim.nash@mountsaintvincent.edu
Web Site: http://www.mountsaintvincent.edu/
President/CEO: Dr. Charles L. Flynn, Jr.
Registrar: Jeanette Pichardo
Admissions: Timothy Nash
Financial Aid: Monica Simotas
Type: Comprehensive **Sex:** Coed **Affiliation:** Manhattan College **Scores:** 95% SAT V 400+; 96% SAT M 400+ **% Accepted:** 69 **Admission Plans:** Early Admission; Early Decision Plan; Deferred Admission **Application Deadline:** Rolling **Application Fee:** $35.00 **H.S. Requirements:** High school diploma required; GED accepted **Costs Per Year:** Application fee: $35. Comprehensive fee: $30,050 includes full-time tuition ($21,000), mandatory fees ($550), and college room and board ($8500). Part-time tuition: $685 per credit. Part-time mandatory fees: $75 per term. **Scholarships:** Available **Calendar System:** Semester, Summer Session Available **Enrollment:** FT 1,249, PT 278, Grad 328 **Faculty:** FT 77, PT 84 **Student-Faculty Ratio:** 14:1 **Exams:** SAT I or ACT **% Receiving Financial Aid:** 71 **% Residing in College-Owned, -Operated, or -Affiliated Housing:** 46 **Library Holdings:** 160,696 **Regional Accreditation:** Middle State Association of Colleges and Schools **Credit Hours For Degree:** 62 credits, Associates; 121 credits, Bachelors **ROTC:** Army, Air Force **Professional Accreditation:** AACN, ACBSP **Intercollegiate Athletics:** Baseball M; Basketball M & W; Cheerleading W; Cross-Country Running M & W; Lacrosse M & W; Soccer M & W; Softball W; Swimming and Diving W; Tennis M & W; Track and Field W; Volleyball M & W

THE COLLEGE OF NEW ROCHELLE
29 Castle Place
New Rochelle, NY 10805-2308
Tel: (914)654-5000
Free: 800-933-5923
Admissions: (914)654-5452
Fax: (914)654-5554
Web Site: http://cnr.edu/
President/CEO: Dr. Stephen J. Sweeny
Admissions: Stephanie Decker
Financial Aid: Robin Marshall
Type: Comprehensive **Sex:** Coed **Scores:** 100% SAT V 400+; 95% SAT M 400+ **% Accepted:** 50 **Admission Plans:** Early Admission; Early Decision Plan; Deferred Admission **Application Deadline:** Rolling **Application Fee:** $20.00 **H.S. Requirements:** High school diploma required; GED accepted **Costs Per Year:** Application fee: $20. Comprehensive fee: $28,476 includes full-time tuition ($20,246), mandatory fees ($350), and college room and board ($7880). Full-time tuition and fees vary according to course load and program. Room and board charges vary according to housing facility. Part-time tuition: $682 per credit. Part-time mandatory fees: $60 per term. Part-time tuition and fees vary according to course load. **Scholarships:** Available **Calendar System:** Semester, Summer Session Available **Enrollment:** FT 710, PT 396, Grad 1,200 **Faculty:** FT 85, PT 134 **Student-Faculty Ratio:** 8:1 **Exams:** SAT I or ACT **% Receiving Financial Aid:** 98 **% Residing in College-Owned, -Operated, or -Affiliated Housing:** 37 **Library Holdings:** 220,000 **Regional Accreditation:** Middle State Association of Colleges and Schools **Credit Hours For Degree:** 120 credits, Bachelors **Professional Accreditation:** AACN, CSWE, NLN **Intercollegiate Athletics:** Basketball W; Cross-Country Running W; Softball W; Swimming and Diving W; Tennis W; Volleyball W

THE COLLEGE OF SAINT ROSE
432 Western Ave.
Albany, NY 12203-1419
Tel: (518)454-5111
Free: 800-637-8556
Admissions: (518)454-5150
Fax: (518)451-2013
E-mail: admit@strose.edu
Web Site: http://www.strose.edu/
President/CEO: Dr. R. Mark Sullivan
Registrar: Judith Kelly
Admissions: Mary Grondahl
Financial Aid: James Vallee
Type: Comprehensive **Sex:** Coed **Scores:** 100% SAT V 400+; 100% SAT M 400+; 60% ACT 18-23; 32% ACT 24-29 **% Accepted:** 71 **Admission Plans:** Early Admission; Deferred Admission **Application Deadline:** February 01 **Application Fee:** $35.00 **H.S. Requirements:** High school diploma required; GED accepted **Costs Per Year:** Application fee: $35. Comprehensive fee: $25,770 includes full-time tuition ($17,368), mandatory fees ($586), and college room and board ($7816). College room only: $3684. Full-time tuition and fees vary according to course load and program. Room and board charges vary according to board plan. Part-time tuition: $578 per credit hour. Part-time tuition varies according to class time. **Scholarships:** Available **Calendar System:** Semester, Summer Session Available **Enrollment:** FT 2,795, PT 283, Grad 2,071 **Faculty:** FT 175, PT 306 **Student-Faculty Ratio:** 15:1 **Exams:** SAT I or ACT **% Receiving Financial Aid:** 77 **% Residing in College-Owned, -Operated, or -Affiliated Housing:** 30 **Library Holdings:** 205,938 **Regional Accreditation:** Middle State Association of Colleges and Schools **Credit Hours For Degree:** 122 credit hours, Bachelors **Professional Accreditation:** ASLHA, ACBSP, CSWE, NASAD, NASM, NCATE **Intercollegiate Athletics:** Baseball M; Basketball M & W; Cross-Country Running M & W; Soccer M & W; Softball W; Swimming and Diving M & W; Volleyball W

COLLEGE OF STATEN ISLAND OF THE CITY UNIVERSITY OF NEW YORK
2800 Victory Blvd.
Staten Island, NY 10314-6600
Tel: (718)982-2000
Admissions: (718)982-2011
Fax: (718)982-2500
E-mail: admissions@mail.cuny.csi.edu
Web Site: http://www.csi.cuny.edu/
President/CEO: Dr. Marlene Springer
Registrar: Alan Hoffner
Admissions: Mary-Beth Riley
Financial Aid: Sherman Whipkey
Type: Comprehensive **Sex:** Coed **Affiliation:** City University of New York System **Scores:** 91.6% SAT V 400+; 97.06% SAT M 400+ **% Accepted:** 99 **Admission Plans:** Open Admission; Early Admission; Deferred Admission **Application Deadline:** Rolling **Application Fee:** $65.00 **H.S. Requirements:** High school diploma required; GED accepted **Costs Per Year:** Application fee: $65. State resident tuition: $4000 full-time, $250 per credit part-time. Nonresident tuition: $8640 full-time, $530 per credit part-time. Mandatory fees: $328 full-time, $90.35 per term part-time. Full-time tuition and fees vary according to course load. Part-time tuition and fees vary according to course load. **Scholarships:** Available **Calendar System:** Semester, Summer Session Available **Enrollment:** FT 7,293, PT 3,627, Grad 1,163 **Faculty:** FT 330, PT 512 **Student-Faculty Ratio:** 17:1 **Exams:** SAT II **% Receiving Financial Aid:** 52 **Library Holdings:** 220,025 **Regional Accreditation:** Middle State Association of Colleges and Schools **Credit Hours For Degree:** 60 credits, Associates; 120 credits, Bachelors **Professional Accreditation:** ABET, APTA, NCATE, NLN **Intercollegiate Athletics:** Baseball M; Basketball M & W; Soccer M & W; Softball W; Swimming and Diving M & W; Tennis M & W; Volleyball W

THE COLLEGE OF WESTCHESTER
325 Central Ave., PO Box 710
White Plains, NY 10602
Tel: (914)948-4442

Free: 800-333-4924
Fax: (914)948-5441
Web Site: http://www.cw.edu/
President/CEO: Nancy Poli
Registrar: Julie Schuler
Admissions: Dale T. Smith
Financial Aid: Marie Bonafonte
Type: Two-Year College **Sex:** Coed **Admission Plans:** Deferred Admission **Application Deadline:** Rolling **Application Fee:** $40.00 **H.S. Requirements:** High school diploma required; GED accepted **Costs Per Year:** Application fee: $40. Tuition: $18,315 full-time, $385 per credit part-time. Mandatory fees: $795 full-time, $200 per term part-time. **Scholarships:** Available **Calendar System:** Quarter, Summer Session Available **Enrollment:** FT 829, PT 210 **Faculty:** FT 25, PT 57 **Student-Faculty Ratio:** 15:1 **Exams:** SAT I **Regional Accreditation:** Middle State Association of Colleges and Schools **Credit Hours For Degree:** 60 credits, Associates

COLUMBIA COLLEGE
116th St. and Broadway
New York, NY 10027
Tel: (212)854-1754
Admissions: (212)854-2522
Fax: (212)854-1209
E-mail: ugrad-admiss@columbia.edu
Web Site: http://www.college.columbia.edu/
President/CEO: Dr. Austin E. Quigley
Registrar: John Lenzi
Admissions: Jessica Marinaccio
Financial Aid: Constantino Colombo
Type: Four-Year College **Sex:** Coed **Affiliation:** Columbia University **Scores:** 100% SAT V 400+; 100% SAT M 400+; 5.17% ACT 18-23; 39.35% ACT 24-29 **% Accepted:** 11 **Admission Plans:** Early Admission; Early Decision Plan; Deferred Admission **Application Deadline:** January 02 **Application Fee:** $65.00 **H.S. Requirements:** High school diploma required; GED accepted **Costs Per Year:** Application fee: $65. Comprehensive fee: $42,584 includes full-time tuition ($31,924), mandatory fees ($1322), and college room and board ($9338). College room only: $5448. **Scholarships:** Available **Calendar System:** Semester, Summer Session Available **Enrollment:** FT 4,225 **Faculty:** FT 727, PT 0 **Student-Faculty Ratio:** 6:1 **Exams:** SAT I and SAT II or ACT **% Receiving Financial Aid:** 47 **% Residing in College-Owned, -Operated, or -Affiliated Housing:** 96 **Library Holdings:** 7,200,000 **Regional Accreditation:** Middle State Association of Colleges and Schools **Credit Hours For Degree:** 124 credits, Bachelors **ROTC:** Army, Navy, Air Force **Professional Accreditation:** ADA **Intercollegiate Athletics:** Archery M & W; Badminton M & W; Baseball M; Basketball M & W; Crew M & W; Cross-Country Running M & W; Fencing M & W; Field Hockey W; Football M; Golf M; Ice Hockey M; Lacrosse M & W; Racquetball M & W; Riflery M & W; Rugby M & W; Skiing (Cross-Country) M & W; Skiing (Downhill) M & W; Soccer M & W; Softball W; Squash M & W; Swimming and Diving M & W; Table Tennis M & W; Tennis M & W; Track and Field M & W; Ultimate Frisbee M & W; Volleyball M & W; Water Polo M & W; Wrestling M

COLUMBIA-GREENE COMMUNITY COLLEGE
4400 Route 23
Hudson, NY 12534-0327
Tel: (518)828-4181
Fax: (518)828-8543
E-mail: hallenbeck@sunycgcc.edu
Web Site: http://www.sunycgcc.edu/
President/CEO: James Campion
Registrar: Patricia Hallenbeck
Admissions: Patricia Hallenbeck
Financial Aid: Earl Tretheway
Type: Two-Year College **Sex:** Coed **Affiliation:** State University of New York System **Admission Plans:** Open Admission; Preferred Admission; Early Admission; Deferred Admission **Application Fee:** $30.00 **H.S. Requirements:** High school diploma or equivalent not required **Scholarships:** Available **Calendar System:** Semester, Summer Session Available **Enrollment:** FT 938, PT 777 **Faculty:** FT 48, PT 59 **Student-Faculty Ratio:** 18:1 **Exams:** Other, SAT I or ACT **Library Holdings:** 52,484 **Regional Accreditation:** Middle State Association of Colleges and Schools **Credit Hours For Degree:** 62 credits, Associates **Professional Accreditation:** NLN **Intercollegiate Athletics:** Baseball M; Basketball M; Soccer M & W; Softball W

COLUMBIA UNIVERSITY, SCHOOL OF GENERAL STUDIES
2970 Broadway
New York, NY 10027-6939
Tel: (212)854-2772
Free: 800-895-1169
E-mail: gs-admit@columbia.edu
Web Site: http://www.gs.columbia.edu/
President/CEO: Dr. Peter Joseph Awn
Admissions: Curtis M. Rodgers
Financial Aid: Skip Bailey
Type: Four-Year College **Sex:** Coed **Affiliation:** Columbia University **% Accepted:** 48 **Admission Plans:** Deferred Admission **Application Deadline:** July 01 **Application Fee:** $65.00 **H.S. Requirements:** High school diploma required; GED accepted **Costs Per Year:** Application fee: $65. Comprehensive fee: $40,716 includes full-time tuition ($30,900), mandatory fees ($1276), and college room and board ($8540). College room only: $5450. Full-time tuition and fees vary according to course load. Room and board charges vary according to housing facility. Part-time tuition: $1030 per credit. Part-time tuition varies according to course load. **Scholarships:** Available **Calendar System:** Semester, Summer Session Available **Enrollment:** FT 647, PT 499 **Faculty:** FT 727, PT 0 **Student-Faculty Ratio:** 7:1 **Exams:** Other, SAT I or ACT, SAT II **Library Holdings:** 5,600,000 **Regional Accreditation:** Middle State Association of Colleges and Schools **Credit Hours For Degree:** 124 credits, Bachelors **Intercollegiate Athletics:** Baseball M; Basketball M & W; Crew M & W; Cross-Country Running M & W; Fencing M & W; Field Hockey W; Football M; Golf M; Gymnastics W; Soccer M & W; Swimming and Diving M & W; Tennis M & W; Track and Field M & W; Volleyball W; Wrestling M

COLUMBIA UNIVERSITY, THE FU FOUNDATION SCHOOL OF ENGINEERING AND APPLIED SCIENCE
500 West 120th St.
New York, NY 10027
Tel: (212)854-1754
Admissions: (212)854-2522
Fax: (212)854-1209
E-mail: ugrad-admiss@columbia.edu
Web Site: http://www.engineering.columbia.edu/
President/CEO: Dr. Zvi Galil
Admissions: Jessica Marinaccio
Financial Aid: David Charlow
Type: University **Sex:** Coed **Affiliation:** Columbia University **Scores:** 100% SAT V 400+; 100% SAT M 400+; 19.45% ACT 24-29 **% Accepted:** 45 **Admission Plans:** Early Admission; Early Decision Plan; Deferred Admission **Application Deadline:** January 02 **Application Fee:** $65.00 **H.S. Requirements:** High school diploma required; GED accepted **Costs Per Year:** Application fee: $65. Comprehensive fee: $42,584 includes full-time tuition ($31,924), mandatory fees ($1322), and college room and board ($9338). College room only: $5448. Room and board charges vary according to board plan. **Scholarships:** Available **Calendar System:** Semester, Summer Session Available **Enrollment:** FT 1,436 **Faculty:** FT 137, PT 0 **Student-Faculty Ratio:** 10:1 **Exams:** SAT I and SAT II or ACT **% Receiving Financial Aid:** 57 **% Residing in College-Owned, -Operated, or -Affiliated Housing:** 99 **Library Holdings:** 7,200,000 **Regional Accreditation:** Middle State Association of Colleges and Schools **Credit Hours For Degree:** 128 credits, Bachelors **ROTC:** Army, Navy, Air Force **Professional Accreditation:** ABET **Intercollegiate Athletics:** Archery M & W; Badminton M & W; Baseball M; Basketball M & W; Crew M & W; Cross-Country Running M & W; Fencing M & W; Field Hockey W; Football M; Golf M; Ice Hockey M; Lacrosse M & W; Riflery M & W; Rugby M & W; Skiing (Cross-Country) M & W; Skiing (Downhill) M & W; Soccer M & W; Softball W; Squash M & W; Swimming and Diving M & W; Table Tennis M & W; Tennis M & W; Track and Field M & W; Volleyball M & W; Water Polo M & W; Wrestling M

CONCORDIA COLLEGE
171 White Plains Rd.
Bronxville, NY 10708-1998
Tel: (914)337-9300
Free: 800-YES-COLLEGE
Fax: (914)395-4500

E-mail: djh@concordia-ny.edu
Web Site: http://www.concordia-ny.edu/
President/CEO: Dr. Viji D. George
Registrar: Mark Blanco
Admissions: Donna J. Hoyt
Financial Aid: Kenneth Fick
Type: Four-Year College **Sex:** Coed **Affiliation:** Lutheran; Concordia University System **Scores:** 85% SAT V 400+; 81% SAT M 400+; 55% ACT 18-23 **% Accepted:** 66 **Admission Plans:** Early Admission; Early Action; Deferred Admission **Application Deadline:** March 15 **Application Fee:** $40.00 **H.S. Requirements:** High school diploma required; GED accepted **Costs Per Year:** Application fee: $40. Comprehensive fee: $28,640 includes full-time tuition ($19,800), mandatory fees ($900), and college room and board ($7940). College room only: $4400. Room and board charges vary according to board plan. Part-time tuition: $528 per credit hour. Part-time tuition varies according to course load. **Scholarships:** Available **Calendar System:** Semester, Summer Session Not available **Enrollment:** FT 592, PT 57 **Faculty:** FT 25, PT 49 **Student-Faculty Ratio:** 16:1 **Exams:** SAT I or ACT **% Residing in College-Owned, -Operated, or -Affiliated Housing:** 68 **Library Holdings:** 71,500 **Regional Accreditation:** Middle State Association of Colleges and Schools **Credit Hours For Degree:** 62 credit hours, Associates; 122 credit hours, Bachelors **Professional Accreditation:** CSWE **Intercollegiate Athletics:** Baseball M; Basketball M & W; Cross-Country Running M & W; Soccer M & W; Softball W; Tennis M & W; Volleyball W

COOPER UNION FOR THE ADVANCEMENT OF SCIENCE AND ART
30 Cooper Square
New York, NY 10003-7120
Tel: (212)353-4100
Admissions: (212)353-4120
Fax: (212)353-4343
E-mail: admissions@cooper.edu
Web Site: http://www.cooper.edu/
President/CEO: Dr. George Campbell
Registrar: Richard Bory
Admissions: Mitchell L. Lipton
Financial Aid: Mary Ruokonen
Type: Four-Year College **Sex:** Coed **Scores:** 100% SAT V 400+; 99% SAT M 400+ **% Accepted:** 13 **Admission Plans:** Early Admission; Early Decision Plan; Deferred Admission **Application Deadline:** January 01 **Application Fee:** $50.00 **H.S. Requirements:** High school diploma required; GED accepted **Costs Per Year:** Application fee: $50. One-time mandatory fee: $150. Comprehensive fee: $14,860 includes full-time tuition ($0), mandatory fees ($1500), and college room and board ($13,360). College room only: $9360. **Scholarships:** Available **Calendar System:** Semester, Summer Session Available **Enrollment:** FT 943, PT 6, Grad 54 **Faculty:** FT 52, PT 163 **Student-Faculty Ratio:** 7:1 **Exams:** SAT I or ACT, SAT II **% Receiving Financial Aid:** 33 **% Residing in College-Owned, -Operated, or -Affiliated Housing:** 19 **Library Holdings:** 97,000 **Regional Accreditation:** Middle State Association of Colleges and Schools **Credit Hours For Degree:** 128 credits, Bachelors **Professional Accreditation:** ABET, NASAD **Intercollegiate Athletics:** Basketball M; Soccer M; Table Tennis M & W; Tennis M & W; Volleyball M & W

CORNELL UNIVERSITY
Ithaca, NY 14853-0001
Tel: (607)255-2000
Admissions: (607)255-3316
Fax: (607)255-0659
E-mail: admissions_mailbox@cornell.edu
Web Site: http://5976
President/CEO: Hunter R. Rawlings, III
Registrar: David S. Yeh
Admissions: Doris Davis
Financial Aid: Donald A. Saleh
Type: University **Sex:** Coed **Scores:** 100% SAT V 400+; 100% SAT M 400+; 4% ACT 18-23; 38% ACT 24-29 **% Accepted:** 27 **Admission Plans:** Preferred Admission; Early Admission; Early Decision Plan; Deferred Admission **Application Deadline:** January 01 **Application Fee:** $65.00 **H.S. Requirements:** High school diploma or equivalent not required **Costs Per Year:** Application fee: $65. Comprehensive fee: $41,717 includes full-time tuition ($31,300), mandatory fees ($167), and college room and board ($10,250). College room only: $6080. Room and board charges vary according to board plan and housing facility. **Scholarships:** Available **Calendar System:** Semester, Summer Session Available **Enrollment:** FT 13,515, Grad 5,028 **Faculty:** FT 1,675, PT 169 **Student-Faculty Ratio:** 9:1 **Exams:** SAT I and SAT II or ACT, SAT II **% Receiving Financial Aid:** 47 **% Residing in College-Owned, -Operated, or -Affiliated Housing:** 44 **Library Holdings:** 7,200,000 **Regional Accreditation:** Middle State Association of Colleges and Schools **Credit Hours For Degree:** 120 credit hours, Bachelors **ROTC:** Army, Air Force **Professional Accreditation:** AACSB, ABET, ACEHSA, AAFCS, ABA, ADtA, ACSP, ASLA, AVMA, AALS, FIDER **Intercollegiate Athletics:** Baseball M; Basketball M & W; Crew M & W; Cross-Country Running M & W; Equestrian Sports W; Fencing W; Field Hockey W; Football M; Golf M; Gymnastics W; Ice Hockey M & W; Lacrosse M & W; Soccer M & W; Softball W; Squash M & W; Swimming and Diving M & W; Tennis M & W; Track and Field M & W; Volleyball W; Wrestling M

CORNING COMMUNITY COLLEGE
One Academic Dr.
Corning, NY 14830-3297
Tel: (607)962-9011
Admissions: (607)962-9427
Fax: (607)962-9456
E-mail: admissions@corning-cc.edu
Web Site: http://www.corning-cc.edu/
President/CEO: Dr. Floyd F. Amann
Registrar: Donna Hastings
Admissions: Karen McCarthy
Financial Aid: Donna Hastings
Type: Two-Year College **Sex:** Coed **Affiliation:** State University of New York System **% Accepted:** 98 **Admission Plans:** Open Admission; Preferred Admission; Early Admission **Application Deadline:** Rolling **Application Fee:** $25.00 **H.S. Requirements:** High school diploma required; GED accepted. For some adult applicants: High school diploma or equivalent not required **Costs Per Year:** Application fee: $25. State resident tuition: $3100 full-time, $128 per credit part-time. Nonresident tuition: $6200 full-time, $258 per credit part-time. **Scholarships:** Available **Calendar System:** Semester, Summer Session Available **Enrollment:** FT 2,638, PT 2,672 **Faculty:** FT 98, PT 160 **Student-Faculty Ratio:** 18:1 **Library Holdings:** 71,233 **Regional Accreditation:** Middle State Association of Colleges and Schools **Credit Hours For Degree:** 62 credit hours, Associates **ROTC:** Army, Navy, Air Force **Professional Accreditation:** NLN **Intercollegiate Athletics:** Basketball M & W; Cheerleading W; Soccer M & W; Softball W; Volleyball W

CROUSE HOSPITAL SCHOOL OF NURSING
736 Irving Ave.
Syracuse, NY 13210
Tel: (315)470-7481
Web Site: http://www.crouse.org/nursing/
Registrar: Tina Peers
Admissions: Karen Van Sise
Financial Aid: Peter Bullock
Type: Two-Year College **Sex:** Coed **Admission Plans:** Deferred Admission **Application Fee:** $30.00 **H.S. Requirements:** High school diploma required; GED accepted **Costs Per Year:** Application fee: $30. Tuition: $7352 full-time, $225 per credit hour part-time. Mandatory fees: $360 full-time, $130 per term part-time. College room only: $1750. **Scholarships:** Available **Calendar System:** Semester **Enrollment:** FT 140, PT 112 **Faculty:** FT 16, PT 9 **Student-Faculty Ratio:** 9:1 **Exams:** SAT I or ACT **% Residing in College-Owned, -Operated, or -Affiliated Housing:** 14 **Professional Accreditation:** NYSBR

THE CULINARY INSTITUTE OF AMERICA
1946 Campus Dr.
Hyde Park, NY 12538-1499
Tel: (845)452-9600
Free: 800-CULINARY
Fax: (845)452-8629
Web Site: http://www.ciachef.edu/
President/CEO: L. Timothy Ryan
Admissions: Drusilla Blackman
Financial Aid: Dorothy Lancella
Type: Four-Year College **Sex:** Coed **Scores:** 84.43% SAT V 400+; 87.7% SAT M 400+; 51% ACT 18-23; 31% ACT 24-29 **% Accepted:** 69 **Admission Plans:** Open Admission; Preferred Admission; Deferred Admission **Application Deadline:** Rolling **Application Fee:** $30.00 **H.S. Requirements:** High school diploma required; GED accepted **Costs Per Year:** Application fee: $30. Comprehensive fee: $26,980 includes full-time tuition ($19,180),

mandatory fees ($980), and college room and board ($6820). Full-time tuition and fees vary according to degree level. Room and board charges vary according to housing facility. **Scholarships:** Available **Calendar System:** Semester, Summer Session Not available **Enrollment:** FT 2,713 **Faculty:** FT 120, PT 28 **Student-Faculty Ratio:** 18:1 **Exams:** SAT I or ACT **% Receiving Financial Aid:** 84 **% Residing in College-Owned, -Operated, or -Affiliated Housing:** 70 **Library Holdings:** 69,000 **Regional Accreditation:** Middle State Association of Colleges and Schools **Credit Hours For Degree:** 69 credits, Associates; 132 credits, Bachelors **Professional Accreditation:** ACCSCT **Intercollegiate Athletics:** Ice Hockey M; Soccer M

DAEMEN COLLEGE
4380 Main St.
Amherst, NY 14226-3592
Tel: (716)839-3600
Free: 800-462-7652
Admissions: (716)839-8225
Fax: (716)839-8516
E-mail: dshaffne@daemen.edu
Web Site: http://www.daemen.edu/
President/CEO: Dr. Martin J. Anisman
Registrar: Paulette A. Anzelone
Admissions: Donna L. Shaffner
Financial Aid: Jeffrey Pagano
Type: Comprehensive **Sex:** Coed **Scores:** 88% SAT V 400+; 89% SAT M 400+; 52% ACT 18-23; 29% ACT 24-29 **% Accepted:** 79 **Admission Plans:** Early Admission; Early Action; Deferred Admission **Application Deadline:** Rolling **Application Fee:** $25.00 **H.S. Requirements:** High school diploma required; GED accepted **Costs Per Year:** Application fee: $25. Comprehensive fee: $24,580 includes full-time tuition ($16,350), mandatory fees ($450), and college room and board ($7780). Room and board charges vary according to board plan and housing facility. Part-time tuition: $545 per credit. Part-time mandatory fees: $4 per credit, $68 per term. Part-time tuition and fees vary according to course load. **Scholarships:** Available **Calendar System:** Semester, Summer Session Available **Enrollment:** FT 1,271, PT 332, Grad 668 **Faculty:** FT 80, PT 179 **Student-Faculty Ratio:** 13:1 **Exams:** SAT I or ACT **% Receiving Financial Aid:** 85 **% Residing in College-Owned, -Operated, or -Affiliated Housing:** 42 **Library Holdings:** 127,232 **Regional Accreditation:** Middle State Association of Colleges and Schools **Credit Hours For Degree:** 120 credits, Bachelors **ROTC:** Army **Professional Accreditation:** APTA, CSWE, NLN **Intercollegiate Athletics:** Basketball M & W; Cross-Country Running M & W; Golf M; Rugby M; Soccer M & W; Volleyball W

DARKEI NOAM RABBINICAL COLLEGE
2822 Ave. J
Brooklyn, NY 11210
Tel: (718)338-6464
President/CEO: Chaim Scharf
Registrar: Shlomoh Kupetz
Admissions: Rabbi Pinchas Horowitz
Financial Aid: Rivke Horowitz
Type: Comprehensive **Sex:** Men **Affiliation:** Jewish **Calendar System:** Semester **Faculty:** FT 3, PT 1 **Library Holdings:** 53,000 **Credit Hours For Degree:** 75 credits, Bachelors **Professional Accreditation:** AARTS

DAVIS COLLEGE
400 Riverside Dr.
Johnson City, NY 13790
Tel: (607)729-1581
Free: 800-331-4137
Fax: (607)729-2962
E-mail: admissions@davisny.edu
Web Site: http://www.davisny.edu/
President/CEO: Dr. George Miller, III
Admissions: Brian J. Murphy
Financial Aid: Jim Devine
Type: Four-Year College **Sex:** Coed **Affiliation:** nondenominational **Scores:** 36% ACT 18-23; 21% ACT 24-29 **% Accepted:** 68 **Admission Plans:** Deferred Admission **Application Deadline:** Rolling **Application Fee:** $25.00 **H.S. Requirements:** High school diploma required; GED accepted **Costs Per Year:** Application fee: $25. Comprehensive fee: $15,240 includes full-time tuition ($9440), mandatory fees ($700), and college room and board ($5100). Part-time tuition: $325 per credit. Part-time mandatory fees: $175 per term. **Scholarships:** Available **Calendar System:** Semester, Summer Session Available **Enrollment:** FT 255 **Faculty:** FT 7, PT 17 **Student-Faculty Ratio:** 17:1 **Exams:** ACT, SAT I or ACT **% Receiving Financial Aid:** 62 **% Residing in College-Owned, -Operated, or -Affiliated Housing:** 61 **Library Holdings:** 77,000 **Regional Accreditation:** Middle State Association of Colleges and Schools **Credit Hours For Degree:** 66 credits, Associates; 130 credits, Bachelors **Professional Accreditation:** AABC **Intercollegiate Athletics:** Basketball M & W; Soccer M; Volleyball W

DEVRY INSTITUTE OF TECHNOLOGY
30-20 Thomson Ave.
Long Island City, NY 11101
Tel: (718)472-2728; (866)338-7934
Web Site: http://www.devry.edu/
President/CEO: Diane Engelhardt
Financial Aid: Elviria Senese
Type: Four-Year College **Sex:** Coed **Affiliation:** DeVry University **Admission Plans:** Deferred Admission **Application Deadline:** Rolling **Application Fee:** $50.00 **H.S. Requirements:** High school diploma required; GED accepted **Costs Per Year:** Application fee: $50. One-time mandatory fee: $40. Tuition: $13,060 full-time, $475 per credit part-time. Mandatory fees: $270 full-time, $160 per year part-time. **Scholarships:** Available **Calendar System:** Semester, Summer Session Available **Enrollment:** FT 937, PT 333, Grad 106 **Faculty:** FT 47, PT 42 **Student-Faculty Ratio:** 18:1 **% Receiving Financial Aid:** 76 **Library Holdings:** 14,078 **Regional Accreditation:** North Central Association of Colleges and Schools **Credit Hours For Degree:** 67 credit hours, Associates; 128 credit hours, Bachelors **Professional Accreditation:** ABET

DOMINICAN COLLEGE
470 Western Hwy.
Orangeburg, NY 10962-1210
Tel: (845)359-7800; (866)432-4636
Admissions: (845)359-3533
Fax: (845)359-2313
E-mail: joyce.elbe@dc.edu
Web Site: http://www.dc.edu/
President/CEO: Sr. Mary Eileen O'Brien
Registrar: Sr. Madeleine McGill
Admissions: Joyce Elbe
Financial Aid: Eileen Felske
Type: Comprehensive **Sex:** Coed **Scores:** 77% SAT V 400+; 77% SAT M 400+ **% Accepted:** 83 **Admission Plans:** Deferred Admission **Application Deadline:** Rolling **Application Fee:** $35.00 **H.S. Requirements:** High school diploma required; GED accepted **Costs Per Year:** Application fee: $35. Comprehensive fee: $26,630 includes full-time tuition ($17,240), mandatory fees ($670), and college room and board ($8720). Part-time tuition: $515 per credit. Part-time mandatory fees: $160 per term. **Scholarships:** Available **Calendar System:** Semester, Summer Session Available **Enrollment:** FT 1,071, PT 338, Grad 121 **Faculty:** FT 51, PT 112 **Student-Faculty Ratio:** 14:1 **Exams:** SAT I or ACT **% Receiving Financial Aid:** 77 **% Residing in College-Owned, -Operated, or -Affiliated Housing:** 20 **Library Holdings:** 103,350 **Regional Accreditation:** Middle State Association of Colleges and Schools **Credit Hours For Degree:** 60 credits, Associates; 120 credits, Bachelors **Professional Accreditation:** AACN, AOTA, APTA, CSWE, TEAC **Intercollegiate Athletics:** Baseball M; Basketball M & W; Cross-Country Running M & W; Golf M; Lacrosse M; Soccer M & W; Softball W; Volleyball W

DOROTHEA HOPFER SCHOOL OF NURSING AT THE MOUNT VERNON HOSPITAL
53 Valentine St.
Mount Vernon, NY 10550
Tel: (914)664-8000
Fax: (914)665-7047
Web Site: http://www.ssmc.org/
President/CEO: George Haskins
Financial Aid: Cheryl Giannoni
Type: Two-Year College **Professional Accreditation:** NYSBR

DOWLING COLLEGE
Idle Hour Blvd.
Oakdale, NY 11769-1999
Tel: (631)244-3000
Free: 800-DOW-LING
Admissions: (631)244-3030

Fax: (631)563-3827
E-mail: admissions@dowling.edu
Web Site: http://www.dowling.edu/
President/CEO: Dr. Albert E. Donor
Registrar: Diane Kazanecki-Kempter
Admissions: Frank Pizzardi
Financial Aid: Diane Beltrani
Type: Comprehensive **Sex:** Coed **Scores:** 79% SAT V 400+; 82% SAT M 400+ **% Accepted:** 87 **Admission Plans:** Deferred Admission **Application Deadline:** Rolling **Application Fee:** $25.00 **H.S. Requirements:** High school diploma required; GED accepted **Costs Per Year:** Application fee: $25. Tuition: $12,960 full-time, $540 per credit hour part-time. Mandatory fees: $840 full-time, $137.50 per term part-time. Part-time tuition and fees vary according to course load and degree level. College room only: $5748. Room charges vary according to housing facility and location. **Scholarships:** Available **Calendar System:** Semester, Summer Session Available **Enrollment:** FT 2,298, PT 1,329, Grad 2,752 **Faculty:** FT 124, PT 376 **Student-Faculty Ratio:** 17:1 **Exams:** SAT I and SAT II **% Receiving Financial Aid:** 65 **% Residing in College-Owned, -Operated, or -Affiliated Housing:** 17 **Library Holdings:** 118,830 **Regional Accreditation:** Middle State Association of Colleges and Schools **Credit Hours For Degree:** 122 credit hours, Bachelors **ROTC:** Air Force **Professional Accreditation:** NCATE **Intercollegiate Athletics:** Baseball M; Basketball M & W; Crew M & W; Equestrian Sports W; Lacrosse M; Soccer M; Softball W; Tennis M & W; Volleyball W

DUTCHESS COMMUNITY COLLEGE
53 Pendell Rd.
Poughkeepsie, NY 12601-1595
Tel: (845)431-8000
Admissions: (845)431-8010
E-mail: banner@sunydutchess.edu
Web Site: http://www.sunydutchess.edu/
President/CEO: Dr. D. David Conklin
Registrar: Deborah Weibman
Admissions: Rita Banner
Financial Aid: Susan Mead
Type: Two-Year College **Sex:** Coed **Affiliation:** State University of New York System **Admission Plans:** Open Admission; Preferred Admission; Early Admission; Deferred Admission **H.S. Requirements:** High school diploma required; GED accepted **Costs Per Year:** State resident tuition: $2600 full-time, $105 per credit part-time. Nonresident tuition: $5200 full-time, $210 per credit part-time. Mandatory fees: $387 full-time, $8 per credit part-time, $24.75 per term part-time. **Scholarships:** Available **Calendar System:** Semester, Summer Session Available **Library Holdings:** 103,272 **Regional Accreditation:** Middle State Association of Colleges and Schools **Credit Hours For Degree:** 64 credits, Associates **Professional Accreditation:** NAACLS, NLN **Intercollegiate Athletics:** Baseball M; Basketball M & W; Bowling M & W; Golf M; Soccer M & W; Softball W; Tennis M & W; Volleyball W

D'YOUVILLE COLLEGE
320 Porter Ave.
Buffalo, NY 14201-1084
Tel: (716)829-8000
Free: 800-777-3921
Admissions: (716)829-7600
Fax: (716)829-7790
Web Site: http://www.dyc.edu/
President/CEO: Sr. Denise A. Roche, PhD
Registrar: Dr. W. Barry Smith
Admissions: Ron Dannecker
Financial Aid: Lorraine A. Metz
Type: Comprehensive **Sex:** Coed **Scores:** 86.2% SAT V 400+; 90.2% SAT M 400+; 55% ACT 18-23; 29% ACT 24-29 **% Accepted:** 73 **Admission Plans:** Deferred Admission **Application Deadline:** Rolling **Application Fee:** $25.00 **H.S. Requirements:** High school diploma required; GED accepted **Costs Per Year:** Application fee: $25. Comprehensive fee: $23,600 includes full-time tuition ($15,600), mandatory fees ($200), and college room and board ($7800). College room only: $6400. Full-time tuition and fees vary according to course level, degree level, and program. Room and board charges vary according to board plan and housing facility. Part-time tuition: $455 per credit. Part-time mandatory fees: $100 per term. Part-time tuition and fees vary according to course load. Tuition guaranteed not to increase for student's term of enrollment. **Scholarships:** Available **Calendar System:** Semester, Summer Session Available **Enrollment:** FT 1,220, PT 262, Grad 1,407 **Faculty:** FT 110, PT 106 **Student-Faculty Ratio:** 14:1 **Exams:** SAT I or ACT **% Receiving Financial Aid:** 93 **% Residing in College-Owned, -Operated, or -Affiliated Housing:** 20 **Library Holdings:** 122,057 **Regional Accreditation:** Middle State Association of Colleges and Schools **Credit Hours For Degree:** 120 credit hours, Bachelors **ROTC:** Army **Professional Accreditation:** AACN, ADtA, AOTA, APTA **Intercollegiate Athletics:** Baseball M; Basketball M & W; Cross-Country Running W; Golf M & W; Soccer M & W; Softball W; Volleyball M & W

ELLIS HOSPITAL SCHOOL OF NURSING
1101 Nott St.
Schenectady, NY 12308
Tel: (518)243-4471
Web Site: http://www.ehson.org/
President/CEO: Mary Lee Pollard
Admissions: Mary Lee Pollard
Type: Two-Year College **Sex:** Coed **Scholarships:** Available **Enrollment:** FT 35, PT 34 **Faculty:** FT 9, PT 0 **Student-Faculty Ratio:** 8:1 **Exams:** SAT I **Professional Accreditation:** NYSBR

ELMIRA BUSINESS INSTITUTE
303 North Main St.
Elmira, NY 14901
Tel: (607)733-7177
Free: 800-843-1812
Fax: (607)733-7178
Web Site: http://www.ebi-college.com/
President/CEO: Brad C. Phillips
Registrar: Lisa Roan
Admissions: Lisa Roan
Financial Aid: Kathleen Hamilton
Type: Two-Year College **Sex:** Coed **Admission Plans:** Open Admission **Application Deadline:** Rolling **Application Fee:** $0.00 **H.S. Requirements:** High school diploma required; GED accepted **Scholarships:** Available **Calendar System:** Semester, Summer Session Not available **Enrollment:** FT 283, PT 78 **Faculty:** FT 7, PT 27 **Library Holdings:** 800 **Credit Hours For Degree:** 61 credits, Associates **Professional Accreditation:** ACICS

ELMIRA COLLEGE
One Park Place
Elmira, NY 14901
Tel: (607)735-1800
Free: 800-935-6472
Admissions: (607)735-1724
Fax: (607)735-1718
E-mail: gfallis@elmira.edu
Web Site: http://www.elmira.edu/
President/CEO: Dr. Thomas K. Meier
Registrar: Michael L. Halperin
Admissions: Gary G. Fallis
Financial Aid: Dean Kathleen L. Cohen
Type: Four-Year College **Sex:** Coed **Scores:** 100% SAT V 400+; 100% SAT M 400+; 39% ACT 18-23; 57% ACT 24-29 **% Accepted:** 64 **Admission Plans:** Early Admission; Early Decision Plan; Deferred Admission **Application Deadline:** April 15 **Application Fee:** $50.00 **H.S. Requirements:** High school diploma required; GED accepted **Costs Per Year:** Application fee: $50. Comprehensive fee: $39,150 includes full-time tuition ($29,000), mandatory fees ($1050), and college room and board ($9100). Part-time tuition: $270 per credit. **Scholarships:** Available **Calendar System:** Miscellaneous, Summer Session Available **Enrollment:** FT 1,175, PT 309, Grad 369 **Faculty:** FT 82, PT 17 **Student-Faculty Ratio:** 12:1 **Exams:** SAT I or ACT **% Receiving Financial Aid:** 78 **% Residing in College-Owned, -Operated, or -Affiliated Housing:** 95 **Library Holdings:** 391,038 **Regional Accreditation:** Middle State Association of Colleges and Schools **Credit Hours For Degree:** 120 credits, Bachelors **ROTC:** Army, Air Force **Professional Accreditation:** NLN **Intercollegiate Athletics:** Basketball M & W; Cheerleading W; Field Hockey W; Golf M & W; Ice Hockey M & W; Lacrosse M & W; Soccer M & W; Softball W; Tennis M & W; Volleyball W

ERIE COMMUNITY COLLEGE
121 Ellicott St.
Buffalo, NY 14203-2698
Tel: (716)851-1001
Admissions: (716)851-1588

Fax: (716)842-1972
Web Site: http://www.ecc.edu/
President/CEO: William Mariani
Registrar: Susan I. Duke
Admissions: Petrina Hill-Cheatom
Financial Aid: Charlotte Coston
Type: Two-Year College **Sex:** Coed **Affiliation:** State University of New York System **Scores:** 60.88% SAT V 400+; 66.84% SAT M 400+ **% Accepted:** 76 **Admission Plans:** Open Admission **Application Deadline:** Rolling **Application Fee:** $0.00 **H.S. Requirements:** High school diploma required; GED accepted **Costs Per Year:** Application fee: $0. Area resident tuition: $2900 full-time, $121 per credit hour part-time. State resident tuition: $5800 full-time, $242 per credit hour part-time. Nonresident tuition: $5800 full-time, $242 per credit hour part-time. Mandatory fees: $320 full-time, $5 per credit hour part-time, $30 per term part-time. **Scholarships:** Available **Calendar System:** Semester, Summer Session Available **Enrollment:** FT 2,188, PT 761 **Faculty:** FT 345, PT 938 **Student-Faculty Ratio:** 17:1 **Library Holdings:** 24,927 **Regional Accreditation:** Middle State Association of Colleges and Schools **Credit Hours For Degree:** 60 credit hours, Associates **ROTC:** Army **Professional Accreditation:** ABET, AAMAE, ACBSP, COptA, JRCERT, NLN **Intercollegiate Athletics:** Baseball M; Basketball M & W; Bowling M & W; Cheerleading W; Cross-Country Running M & W; Football M; Golf M & W; Ice Hockey M; Lacrosse W; Soccer M & W; Softball W; Swimming and Diving M & W; Track and Field M & W; Volleyball W

ERIE COMMUNITY COLLEGE, NORTH CAMPUS
6205 Main St.
Williamsville, NY 14221-7095
Tel: (716)851-1002
Admissions: (716)851-1588
Fax: (716)634-3802
Web Site: http://www.ecc.edu
President/CEO: William Mariani
Registrar: Paul LaManna
Admissions: Petrina Hill-Cheatom
Financial Aid: Scott Weltjen
Type: Two-Year College **Sex:** Coed **Affiliation:** State University of New York System **Scores:** 77.4% SAT V 400+; 80.5% SAT M 400+ **% Accepted:** 91 **Admission Plans:** Open Admission **Application Deadline:** Rolling **H.S. Requirements:** High school diploma required; GED accepted **Costs Per Year:** Area resident tuition: $2900 full-time, $121 per credit hour part-time. State resident tuition: $5800 full-time, $242 per credit hour part-time. Nonresident tuition: $5800 full-time, $242 per credit hour part-time. Mandatory fees: $320 full-time, $5 per credit hour part-time, $30 per term part-time. **Scholarships:** Available **Calendar System:** Semester, Summer Session Available **Enrollment:** FT 3,779, PT 1,862 **Faculty:** FT 345, PT 938 **Student-Faculty Ratio:** 17:1 **Library Holdings:** 71,220 **Regional Accreditation:** Middle State Association of Colleges and Schools **Credit Hours For Degree:** 60 credit hours, Associates **ROTC:** Army **Professional Accreditation:** ADA, AHIMA, AOTA, CARC, NAACLS, NLN **Intercollegiate Athletics:** Baseball M; Basketball M & W; Bowling M & W; Cheerleading W; Cross-Country Running M & W; Football M; Golf M & W; Ice Hockey M; Lacrosse W; Soccer M & W; Softball W; Swimming and Diving M & W; Track and Field M & W; Volleyball W

ERIE COMMUNITY COLLEGE, SOUTH CAMPUS
4041 Southwestern Blvd.
Orchard Park, NY 14127-2199
Tel: (716)851-1003
Admissions: (716)851-1588
Fax: (716)648-9953
Web Site: http://www.ecc.edu/
President/CEO: William Mariani
Registrar: Samuel Palumbo
Admissions: Petrina Hill-Cheatom
Financial Aid: Bernice Anson
Type: Two-Year College **Sex:** Coed **Affiliation:** State University of New York System **Scores:** 80.4% SAT V 400+; 82.57% SAT M 400+ **% Accepted:** 89 **Admission Plans:** Open Admission **Application Deadline:** Rolling **H.S. Requirements:** High school diploma required; GED accepted **Costs Per Year:** Area resident tuition: $2900 full-time, $121 per credit hour part-time. State resident tuition: $5800 full-time, $242 per credit hour part-time. Nonresident tuition: $5800 full-time, $242 per credit hour part-time. Mandatory fees: $320 full-time, $5 per credit hour part-time, $30 per term part-time. **Scholarships:** Available **Calendar System:** Semester, Summer Session Available **Enrollment:** FT 2,521, PT 1,546 **Faculty:** FT 345, PT 938 **Student-Faculty Ratio:** 17:1 **Library Holdings:** 57,029 **Regional Accreditation:** Middle State Association of Colleges and Schools **Credit Hours For Degree:** 60 credit hours, Associates **ROTC:** Army **Professional Accreditation:** ADA **Intercollegiate Athletics:** Baseball M; Basketball M & W; Bowling M & W; Cheerleading W; Cross-Country Running M & W; Football M; Golf M & W; Ice Hockey M; Lacrosse W; Soccer M & W; Softball W; Swimming and Diving M & W; Track and Field M & W; Volleyball W

EUGENE LANG COLLEGE THE NEW SCHOOL FOR LIBERAL ARTS
65 West 11th St.
New York, NY 10011-8601
Tel: (212)229-5600; 877-528-3321
Admissions: (212)229-5665
Fax: (212)229-5355
E-mail: lang@newschool.edu
Web Site: http://www.lang.edu/
President/CEO: Dr. Beatrice Banu
Admissions: Nicole Curvin
Type: Four-Year College **Sex:** Coed **Affiliation:** New School University **Scores:** 99.52% SAT V 400+; 97.14% SAT M 400+ **% Accepted:** 61 **Admission Plans:** Early Admission; Early Decision Plan; Deferred Admission **Application Deadline:** February 01 **Application Fee:** $40.00 **H.S. Requirements:** High school diploma required; GED accepted **Costs Per Year:** Application fee: $40. Comprehensive fee: $38,860 includes full-time tuition ($26,540), mandatory fees ($570), and college room and board ($11,750). College room only: $8750. Full-time tuition and fees vary according to program. Room and board charges vary according to board plan and housing facility. Part-time tuition: $976 per credit. Part-time tuition varies according to course load, program, and reciprocity agreements. **Scholarships:** Available **Calendar System:** Semester, Summer Session Available **Enrollment:** FT 939, PT 46 **Faculty:** FT 44, PT 72 **Student-Faculty Ratio:** 14:1 **Exams:** SAT I or ACT **% Receiving Financial Aid:** 68 **% Residing in College-Owned, -Operated, or -Affiliated Housing:** 34 **Library Holdings:** 4,137,530 **Regional Accreditation:** Middle State Association of Colleges and Schools **Credit Hours For Degree:** 120 credits, Bachelors

EUGENIO MARÍA DE HOSTOS COMMUNITY COLLEGE OF THE CITY UNIVERSITY OF NEW YORK
500 Grand Concourse
Bronx, NY 10451
Tel: (718)518-4444
Admissions: (718)518-4406
Fax: (718)518-4256
Web Site: http://www.hostos.cuny.edu/
President/CEO: Dr. Dolores M. Fernandez
Registrar: Nelida Pastoriza
Admissions: Roland Velez
Financial Aid: Joseph R. Alicea
Type: Two-Year College **Sex:** Coed **Affiliation:** City University of New York System **Admission Plans:** Open Admission **Application Fee:** $65.00 **H.S. Requirements:** High school diploma required; GED accepted **Costs Per Year:** Application fee: $65. State resident tuition: $2500 full-time, $105 per credit part-time. Nonresident tuition: $3076 full-time, $130 per credit part-time. **Scholarships:** Available **Calendar System:** Semester, Summer Session Available **Enrollment:** FT 2,917, PT 1,423 **Faculty:** FT 166, PT 163 **Student-Faculty Ratio:** 14:1 **Exams:** ACT, Other, SAT I, SAT II **Library Holdings:** 56,100 **Regional Accreditation:** Middle State Association of Colleges and Schools **Credit Hours For Degree:** 60 credits, Associates **Professional Accreditation:** ADA, JRCERT **Intercollegiate Athletics:** Baseball M; Basketball M & W; Volleyball W

EXCELSIOR COLLEGE
7 Columbia Circle
Albany, NY 12203-5159
Tel: (518)464-8500; 888-647-2388
Fax: (518)464-8777
E-mail: info@excelsior.edu
Web Site: http://www.excelsior.edu/
President/CEO: C. Wayne Williams
Registrar: Lori Morano
Admissions: Chari Leader
Financial Aid: Donna Cooper
Type: Comprehensive **Sex:** Coed **Admission Plans:** Open Admission **Application Deadline:** Rolling **Application Fee:** $65.00 **H.S. Requirements:**

High school diploma or equivalent not required **Costs Per Year:** Application fee: $65. Tuition: $250 per credit hour part-time. Mandatory fees: $515 per year part-time. **Scholarships:** Available **Calendar System:** Continuous **Enrollment:** , PT 27,844, Grad 620 **Regional Accreditation:** Middle State Association of Colleges and Schools **Credit Hours For Degree:** 60 credits, Associates; 120 credits, Bachelors **Professional Accreditation:** ABET, NLN

FARMINGDALE STATE UNIVERSITY OF NEW YORK
Route 110, 2350 Broadhollow Rd.
Farmingdale, NY 11735
Tel: (631)420-2000; 877-4-FARMINGDALE
Admissions: (631)420-2457
Fax: (631)420-2633
Web Site: http://www.farmingdale.edu/
President/CEO: Dr. Jonathan C. Gibralter
Registrar: Cindy McCue
Admissions: Jim Hall
Financial Aid: Catherine Malnichuck
Type: Four-Year College **Sex:** Coed **Affiliation:** State University of New York System **Scores:** 90% SAT V 400+; 93% SAT M 400+ **% Accepted:** 61 **Admission Plans:** Early Admission **Application Deadline:** Rolling **Application Fee:** $40.00 **H.S. Requirements:** High school diploma required; GED accepted **Costs Per Year:** Application fee: $40. State resident tuition: $4350 full-time, $181 per credit part-time. Nonresident tuition: $10,610 full-time, $442 per credit part-time. Mandatory fees: $907 full-time, $30.85 per credit part-time. College room and board: $9660. College room only: $5670. Room and board charges vary according to board plan. **Scholarships:** Available **Calendar System:** Semester, Summer Session Available **Enrollment:** FT 4,020, PT 2,441 **Faculty:** FT 153, PT 306 **Student-Faculty Ratio:** 19:1 **Exams:** SAT I or ACT **% Receiving Financial Aid:** 44 **% Residing in College-Owned, -Operated, or -Affiliated Housing:** 10 **Library Holdings:** 125,000 **Regional Accreditation:** Middle State Association of Colleges and Schools **Credit Hours For Degree:** 60 credits, Associates; 122 credits, Bachelors **ROTC:** Army, Air Force **Professional Accreditation:** ABET, ADA, NAACLS, NLN **Intercollegiate Athletics:** Baseball M; Basketball M & W; Cross-Country Running M & W; Golf M; Lacrosse M; Soccer M & W; Softball W; Track and Field M & W; Volleyball W

FASHION INSTITUTE OF TECHNOLOGY
Seventh Ave. at 27th St.
New York, NY 10001-5992
Tel: (212)217-7999
Free: 800-GOT-OFIT
Admissions: (212)217-7675
Fax: (212)217-7481
Web Site: http://www.fitnyc.edu/
President/CEO: Dr. Joyce F. Brown
Registrar: Young-Ja Kim
Admissions: Dolores Lombardi
Financial Aid: Mina Friedmann
Type: Comprehensive **Sex:** Coed **Affiliation:** State University of New York System **% Accepted:** 41 **Admission Plans:** Early Action; Deferred Admission **Application Deadline:** February 15 **Application Fee:** $40.00 **H.S. Requirements:** High school diploma required; GED accepted **Costs Per Year:** Application fee: $40. State resident tuition: $4350 full-time, $181 per credit part-time. Nonresident tuition: $10,610 full-time, $442 per credit part-time. Mandatory fees: $420 full-time, $30 per term part-time. College room and board: $8409. College room only: $7519. **Scholarships:** Available **Calendar System:** 4-1-4, Summer Session Available **Enrollment:** FT 6,661, PT 3,538, Grad 182 **Faculty:** FT 210, PT 708 **Student-Faculty Ratio:** 17:1 **% Receiving Financial Aid:** 28 **% Residing in College-Owned, -Operated, or -Affiliated Housing:** 16 **Library Holdings:** 176,987 **Regional Accreditation:** Middle State Association of Colleges and Schools **Credit Hours For Degree:** 70 credits, Associates; 133 credits, Bachelors **Professional Accreditation:** FIDER, NASAD **Intercollegiate Athletics:** Basketball M & W; Bowling M & W; Tennis M & W; Volleyball W

FINGER LAKES COMMUNITY COLLEGE
4355 Lakeshore Dr.
Canandaigua, NY 14424-8395
Tel: (585)394-3500
Fax: (585)394-5005
E-mail: admissions@flcc.edu
Web Site: http://www.flcc.edu/
President/CEO: Dr. Daniel T. Hayes
Registrar: JoAnn Wheeler
Admissions: Bonnie B. Ritts
Financial Aid: Nancy Van Zetta
Type: Two-Year College **Sex:** Coed **Affiliation:** State University of New York System **Admission Plans:** Open Admission; Preferred Admission; Early Admission; Deferred Admission **Application Deadline:** Rolling **Application Fee:** $0.00 **H.S. Requirements:** High school diploma required; GED accepted **Costs Per Year:** Application fee: $0. State resident tuition: $2900 full-time, $117 per credit hour part-time. Nonresident tuition: $5800 full-time, $234 per credit hour part-time. Mandatory fees: $260 full-time, $7 per credit hour part-time. **Scholarships:** Available **Calendar System:** Semester, Summer Session Available **Enrollment:** FT 2,599, PT 2,311 **Faculty:** FT 109, PT 171 **Student-Faculty Ratio:** 20:1 **Library Holdings:** 73,305 **Regional Accreditation:** Middle State Association of Colleges and Schools **Credit Hours For Degree:** 64 credit hours, Associates **ROTC:** Army **Professional Accreditation:** NLN **Intercollegiate Athletics:** Baseball M; Basketball M & W; Cross-Country Running M & W; Lacrosse M & W; Soccer M & W; Softball W

FIORELLO H. LAGUARDIA COMMUNITY COLLEGE OF THE CITY UNIVERSITY OF NEW YORK
31-10 Thomson Ave.
Long Island City, NY 11101-3071
Tel: (718)482-7200
Admissions: (718)482-5114
Fax: (718)482-5599
E-mail: lavorad@lagcc.cuny.edu
Web Site: http://www.lagcc.cuny.edu/
President/CEO: Dr. Gail O. Mellow
Registrar: Olga Vega
Admissions: LaVora Desvigne
Financial Aid: Gail Baksh-Jarrett
Type: Two-Year College **Sex:** Coed **Affiliation:** City University of New York System **% Accepted:** 100 **Admission Plans:** Open Admission; Early Admission; Deferred Admission **Application Deadline:** Rolling **Application Fee:** $65.00 **H.S. Requirements:** High school diploma required; GED accepted **Costs Per Year:** Application fee: $65. Area resident tuition: $3072 full-time, $120 per credit part-time. State resident tuition: $5700 full-time, $190 per credit hour part-time. Nonresident tuition: $5700 full-time, $190 per credit hour part-time. Mandatory fees: $272 full-time. **Scholarships:** Available **Calendar System:** Miscellaneous, Summer Session Not available **Enrollment:** FT 7,453, PT 6,036 **Faculty:** FT 270, PT 503 **Student-Faculty Ratio:** 21:1 **Library Holdings:** 121,631 **Regional Accreditation:** Middle State Association of Colleges and Schools **Credit Hours For Degree:** 60 units, Associates **Professional Accreditation:** AOTA, APTA, NLN

FIVE TOWNS COLLEGE
305 North Service Rd.
Dix Hills, NY 11746-6055
Tel: (631)424-7000
Fax: (631)656-2172
Web Site: http://www.fivetowns.edu/
President/CEO: Dr. Stanley G. Cohen
Registrar: Riva Meyer
Admissions: Jerry Cohen
Financial Aid: Mary Venezia
Type: Comprehensive **Sex:** Coed **Scores:** 96% SAT V 400+; 94% SAT M 400+; 79% ACT 18-23 **% Accepted:** 77 **Admission Plans:** Early Admission; Deferred Admission **Application Deadline:** Rolling **Application Fee:** $35.00 **H.S. Requirements:** High school diploma required; GED accepted **Costs Per Year:** Application fee: $35. Comprehensive fee: $24,350 includes full-time tuition ($14,100) and college room and board ($10,250). Room and board charges vary according to board plan and location. Part-time tuition: $585 per credit. **Scholarships:** Available **Calendar System:** Semester, Summer Session Available **Enrollment:** FT 1,042, PT 46, Grad 74 **Faculty:** FT 45, PT 64 **Student-Faculty Ratio:** 13:1 **% Receiving Financial Aid:** 58 **% Residing in College-Owned, -Operated, or -Affiliated Housing:** 10 **Library Holdings:** 35,000 **Regional Accreditation:** Middle State Association of Colleges and Schools **Credit Hours For Degree:** 60 credits, Associates; 120 credits, Bachelors **Professional Accreditation:** NCATE

FORDHAM UNIVERSITY
441 East Fordham Rd.
Bronx, NY 10458
Tel: (718)817-1000

Free: 800-FOR-DHAM
Admissions: (718)817-4000
Fax: (718)367-9404
E-mail: ad_buckley@lars.fordham.edu
Web Site: http://www.fordham.edu/
President/CEO: Rev. Joseph M. McShane, SJ
Registrar: Stephen J. Bordas
Admissions: John W. Buckley
Financial Aid: Angela VanDekker
Type: University **Sex:** Coed **Affiliation:** Roman Catholic (Jesuit) **Scores:** 99.5% SAT V 400+; 99.6% SAT M 400+; 22% ACT 18-23; 65.1% ACT 24-29 **% Accepted:** 50 **Admission Plans:** Early Admission; Early Action; Deferred Admission **Application Deadline:** January 15 **Application Fee:** $50.00 **H.S. Requirements:** High school diploma required; GED accepted **Costs Per Year:** Application fee: $50. Comprehensive fee: $38,620 includes full-time tuition ($27,725) and college room and board ($10,895). College room only: $7260. **Scholarships:** Available **Calendar System:** Semester, Summer Session Available **Enrollment:** FT 6,887, PT 641, Grad 5,580 **Faculty:** FT 645, PT 681 **Student-Faculty Ratio:** 11:1 **Exams:** SAT I or ACT, SAT II **% Receiving Financial Aid:** 65 **% Residing in College-Owned, -Operated, or -Affiliated Housing:** 60 **Library Holdings:** 2,483,307 **Regional Accreditation:** Middle State Association of Colleges and Schools **Credit Hours For Degree:** 124 credits, Bachelors **ROTC:** Army, Navy, Air Force **Professional Accreditation:** AACSB, ABA, APA, AALS, CSWE, NASD, NCATE **Intercollegiate Athletics:** Baseball M; Basketball M & W; Cheerleading M & W; Crew M & W; Cross-Country Running M & W; Football M; Golf M; Ice Hockey M; Lacrosse M & W; Rugby M & W; Sailing M & W; Soccer M & W; Softball W; Squash M; Swimming and Diving M & W; Tennis M & W; Track and Field M & W; Ultimate Frisbee M & W; Volleyball W; Water Polo M

FULTON-MONTGOMERY COMMUNITY COLLEGE
2805 State Hwy. 67
Johnstown, NY 12095-3790
Tel: (518)762-4651
Fax: (518)762-6518
E-mail: jkelley@fmcc.suny.edu
Web Site: http://www.fmcc.suny.edu/
President/CEO: Dr. Barry M. Weinberg
Registrar: Susan Christiano
Admissions: Jane Kelley
Financial Aid: Rebecca Swart
Type: Two-Year College **Sex:** Coed **Affiliation:** State University of New York System **Admission Plans:** Open Admission; Early Admission; Deferred Admission **Application Fee:** $0.00 **H.S. Requirements:** High school diploma or equivalent not required. For nursing program, radiologic technology: High school diploma required; GED not accepted **Costs Per Year:** Application fee: $0. State resident tuition: $2925 full-time, $122 per credit hour part-time. Nonresident tuition: $5850 full-time, $244 per credit hour part-time. Mandatory fees: $205 full-time, $2 per credit hour part-time, $38 per term part-time. Part-time tuition and fees vary according to course load. **Scholarships:** Available **Calendar System:** Semester, Summer Session Available **Enrollment:** FT 1,404, PT 667 **Faculty:** FT 52, PT 76 **Student-Faculty Ratio:** 21:1 **Library Holdings:** 51,517 **Regional Accreditation:** Middle State Association of Colleges and Schools **Credit Hours For Degree:** 62 credits, Associates **Intercollegiate Athletics:** Baseball M; Basketball M & W; Soccer M & W; Softball W; Volleyball W

GAMLA COLLEGE
1213 Elm Ave.
Brooklyn, NY 11230
Tel: (718)339-4747
Fax: (718)998-5766 **Type:** Two-Year College **Sex:** Coed **Calendar System:** Semester **Professional Accreditation:** NYSBR

GENESEE COMMUNITY COLLEGE
1 College Rd.
Batavia, NY 14020-9704
Tel: (585)343-0055
Free: 800-CALL GCC
Fax: (585)345-4541
Web Site: http://www.genesee.edu/
President/CEO: Dr. Stuart Steiner
Registrar: Sharon Myers
Admissions: Tanya Lane-Martin
Financial Aid: Joseph Bailey
Type: Two-Year College **Sex:** Coed **Affiliation:** State University of New York System **% Accepted:** 100 **Admission Plans:** Open Admission; Preferred Admission **Application Deadline:** Rolling **Application Fee:** $0.00 **H.S. Requirements:** High school diploma required; GED accepted **Costs Per Year:** Application fee: $0. State resident tuition: $3200 full-time. Nonresident tuition: $3600 full-time. Mandatory fees: $290 full-time. College room only: $4250. **Scholarships:** Available **Calendar System:** Semester, Summer Session Available **Enrollment:** FT 3,113, PT 3,377 **Faculty:** FT 74, PT 238 **Student-Faculty Ratio:** 20:1 **Library Holdings:** 78,273 **Regional Accreditation:** Middle State Association of Colleges and Schools **Credit Hours For Degree:** 62 credit hours, Associates **ROTC:** Army **Professional Accreditation:** AOTA, APTA, CARC, NLN **Intercollegiate Athletics:** Baseball M; Basketball M & W; Cross-Country Running M & W; Soccer M & W; Softball W; Swimming and Diving M & W; Volleyball M & W

GLOBE INSTITUTE OF TECHNOLOGY
291 Broadway, Second Floor
New York, NY 10007
Tel: (212)349-4330; 877-394-5623
Fax: (212)227-5920
E-mail: admissions@globe.edu
Web Site: http://www.globe.edu/
President/CEO: Oleg Rabinovich
Registrar: Vivian Pagan
Admissions: Tanya Garelik
Financial Aid: Marcus Browne
Type: Four-Year College **Sex:** Coed **% Accepted:** 82 **Admission Plans:** Open Admission **Application Fee:** $50.00 **H.S. Requirements:** High school diploma required; GED accepted **Costs Per Year:** Application fee: $50. Tuition: $8950 full-time, $370 per credit part-time. Mandatory fees: $136 full-time, $136 per year part-time. College room only: $3600. **Scholarships:** Available **Calendar System:** Semester **Enrollment:** FT 1,655, PT 16 **Faculty:** FT 28, PT 85 **Student-Faculty Ratio:** 15:1 **Exams:** SAT I or ACT **Library Holdings:** 6,678 **Regional Accreditation:** Middle State Association of Colleges and Schools **Credit Hours For Degree:** 60 credits, Associates; 120 credits, Bachelors **Professional Accreditation:** ACICS, NYSBR **Intercollegiate Athletics:** Baseball M; Basketball M & W; Bowling M & W; Cross-Country Running M & W; Soccer M; Track and Field M & W; Volleyball W

HAMILTON COLLEGE
198 College Hill Rd.
Clinton, NY 13323-1296
Tel: (315)859-4011
Free: 800-843-2655
Admissions: (315)859-4421
Fax: (315)859-4124
E-mail: admission@hamilton.edu
Web Site: http://www.hamilton.edu/
President/CEO: Dr. Joan Hinde Stewart
Registrar: Kristin Friedel
Admissions: Monica Inzer
Financial Aid: Lora Schilder
Type: Four-Year College **Sex:** Coed **Scores:** 100% SAT V 400+; 100% SAT M 400+ **% Accepted:** 36 **Admission Plans:** Early Admission; Early Decision Plan; Deferred Admission **Application Deadline:** January 01 **Application Fee:** $50.00 **H.S. Requirements:** High school diploma or equivalent not required **Costs Per Year:** Application fee: $50. Comprehensive fee: $41,660 includes full-time tuition ($33,150), mandatory fees ($200), and college room and board ($8310). College room only: $4460. Room and board charges vary according to board plan. **Scholarships:** Available **Calendar System:** Semester, Summer Session Not available **Enrollment:** FT 1,800, PT 12 **Faculty:** FT 173, PT 32 **Student-Faculty Ratio:** 10:1 **% Receiving Financial Aid:** 55 **% Residing in College-Owned, -Operated, or -Affiliated Housing:** 98 **Library Holdings:** 538,377 **Regional Accreditation:** Middle State Association of Colleges and Schools **Credit Hours For Degree:** 32 courses, Bachelors **ROTC:** Army, Air Force **Intercollegiate Athletics:** Baseball M; Basketball M & W; Crew W; Cross-Country Running M & W; Fencing M & W; Field Hockey W; Football M; Golf M & W; Ice Hockey M & W; Lacrosse M & W; Rugby M & W; Sailing M & W; Skiing (Downhill) M & W; Soccer M & W; Softball W; Squash M & W; Swimming and Diving M & W; Tennis M & W; Track and Field M & W; Ultimate Frisbee M & W; Volleyball M & W; Water Polo M & W

HARTWICK COLLEGE
One Hartwick Dr.
Oneonta, NY 13820-4020
Tel: (607)431-4200; 888-HARTWICK
Admissions: (607)431-4150
Fax: (607)431-4138
E-mail: admissions@hartwick.edu
Web Site: http://www.hartwick.edu/
President/CEO: Richard P. Miller
Registrar: Dr. Gerald Hunsberger
Admissions: Patricia Maben
Financial Aid: Kathleen Ryan-O'Neill
Type: Four-Year College **Sex:** Coed **Scores:** 99.3% SAT V 400+; 100% SAT M 400+ **% Accepted:** 87 **Admission Plans:** Early Admission; Early Action; Early Decision Plan; Deferred Admission **Application Deadline:** February 15 **Application Fee:** $35.00 **H.S. Requirements:** High school diploma required; GED accepted **Costs Per Year:** Application fee: $35. Comprehensive fee: $34,490 includes full-time tuition ($26,480), mandatory fees ($530), and college room and board ($7480). College room only: $3940. Room and board charges vary according to board plan and housing facility. Part-time tuition: $883 per hour. **Scholarships:** Available **Calendar System:** 4-1-4, Summer Session Not available **Enrollment:** FT 1,405, PT 58 **Faculty:** FT 109, PT 61 **Student-Faculty Ratio:** 11:1 **Exams:** SAT I or ACT **% Receiving Financial Aid:** 71 **% Residing in College-Owned, -Operated, or -Affiliated Housing:** 86 **Library Holdings:** 353,776 **Regional Accreditation:** Middle State Association of Colleges and Schools **Credit Hours For Degree:** 36 courses, Bachelors **ROTC:** Army, Air Force **Professional Accreditation:** AACN, NASAD, NASM, NLN **Intercollegiate Athletics:** Baseball M; Basketball M & W; Cross-Country Running M & W; Equestrian Sports W; Field Hockey W; Football M; Golf M & W; Ice Hockey M; Lacrosse M & W; Rugby M; Soccer M & W; Softball W; Swimming and Diving M & W; Tennis M & W; Track and Field M & W; Volleyball W; Water Polo M & W

HELENE FULD COLLEGE OF NURSING OF NORTH GENERAL HOSPITAL
1879 Madison Ave.
New York, NY 10035-2709
Tel: (212)423-1000
Web Site: http://www.helenefuld.edu/
President/CEO: Dr. Margaret Wines, RN
Registrar: Gladys Pineda
Admissions: Sandra Senior
Financial Aid: Sandra Senior
Type: Two-Year College **Sex:** Coed **Admission Plans:** Preferred Admission; Deferred Admission **Application Fee:** $50.00 **H.S. Requirements:** High school diploma required; GED accepted **Scholarships:** Available **Calendar System:** Quarter, Summer Session Available **Faculty:** FT 10, PT 16 **Student-Faculty Ratio:** 13:1 **Exams:** Other **Library Holdings:** 6,200 **Regional Accreditation:** Middle State Association of Colleges and Schools **Credit Hours For Degree:** 70 credits, Associates **Professional Accreditation:** NLN

HERKIMER COUNTY COMMUNITY COLLEGE
Reservoir Rd.
Herkimer, NY 13350
Tel: (315)866-0300
Fax: (315)866-7253
Web Site: http://www.herkimer.edu
President/CEO: Dr. Ronald F. Williams
Registrar: Barbara Bouchard
Admissions: Scott J. Hughes
Type: Two-Year College **Sex:** Coed **Affiliation:** State University of New York System **Scores:** 77.3% SAT V 400+; 76.2% SAT M 400+ **Admission Plans:** Open Admission; Preferred Admission; Early Admission **Application Fee:** $0.00 **H.S. Requirements:** High school diploma required; GED accepted **Scholarships:** Available **Calendar System:** Semester, Summer Session Available **Faculty:** FT 79, PT 49 **Student-Faculty Ratio:** 22:1 **Exams:** SAT I or ACT **% Residing in College-Owned, -Operated, or -Affiliated Housing:** 25 **Library Holdings:** 70,000 **Regional Accreditation:** Middle State Association of Colleges and Schools **Credit Hours For Degree:** 63 credit hours, Associates **Professional Accreditation:** AOTA, APTA **Intercollegiate Athletics:** Baseball M; Basketball M & W; Cross-Country Running M & W; Lacrosse M & W; Soccer M & W; Softball W; Swimming and Diving M & W; Tennis M & W; Track and Field M & W; Volleyball W

HILBERT COLLEGE
5200 South Park Ave.
Hamburg, NY 14075-1597
Tel: (716)649-7900
Fax: (716)649-0702
Web Site: http://www.hilbert.edu/
President/CEO: Sr. Edmunette Paczesny
Registrar: Georgina Adamchick
Financial Aid: Beverly Chudy
Type: Four-Year College **Sex:** Coed **Scores:** 75% SAT V 400+; 80% SAT M 400+; 63% ACT 18-23; 11% ACT 24-29 **% Accepted:** 94 **Admission Plans:** Early Admission; Deferred Admission **Application Deadline:** September 01 **Application Fee:** $20.00 **H.S. Requirements:** High school diploma required; GED accepted **Costs Per Year:** Application fee: $20. Comprehensive fee: $20,480 includes full-time tuition ($14,300), mandatory fees ($600), and college room and board ($5580). College room only: $2400. Full-time tuition and fees vary according to course load. Room and board charges vary according to board plan and housing facility. Part-time tuition: $332 per credit hour. Part-time mandatory fees: $13 per credit hour, $55 per term. Part-time tuition and fees vary according to course load. **Scholarships:** Available **Calendar System:** Semester, Summer Session Available **Enrollment:** FT 723, PT 386 **Faculty:** FT 43, PT 58 **Student-Faculty Ratio:** 16:1 **Exams:** SAT I or ACT **% Receiving Financial Aid:** 87 **% Residing in College-Owned, -Operated, or -Affiliated Housing:** 10 **Library Holdings:** 41,322 **Regional Accreditation:** Middle State Association of Colleges and Schools **Credit Hours For Degree:** 60 credit hours, Associates; 120 credit hours, Bachelors **Intercollegiate Athletics:** Baseball M; Basketball M & W; Cross-Country Running M & W; Golf M & W; Soccer M & W; Softball W; Volleyball M & W

HOBART AND WILLIAM SMITH COLLEGES
Geneva, NY 14456-3397
Tel: (315)781-3000
Free: 800-245-0100
Admissions: (315)781-3472
Fax: (315)781-5471
Web Site: http://www.hws.edu/
President/CEO: Mark D. Gearan
Registrar: Peter Sarratori
Admissions: Don W. Emmons
Financial Aid: Samantha Veeder
Type: Four-Year College **Sex:** Coed **Scores:** 100% SAT V 400+; 100% SAT M 400+ **% Accepted:** 65 **Admission Plans:** Early Admission; Early Decision Plan; Deferred Admission **Application Deadline:** February 01 **Application Fee:** $45.00 **H.S. Requirements:** High school diploma required; GED accepted **Costs Per Year:** Application fee: $45. Comprehensive fee: $41,123 includes full-time tuition ($31,850), mandatory fees ($887), and college room and board ($8386). Room and board charges vary according to board plan. **Scholarships:** Available **Calendar System:** Semester, Summer Session Not available **Enrollment:** FT 1,865, PT 3, Grad 15 **Faculty:** FT 156, PT 29 **Student-Faculty Ratio:** 11:1 **Exams:** SAT I or ACT, SAT II **% Receiving Financial Aid:** 61 **% Residing in College-Owned, -Operated, or -Affiliated Housing:** 92 **Library Holdings:** 380,419 **Regional Accreditation:** Middle State Association of Colleges and Schools **Credit Hours For Degree:** 32 courses, Bachelors **Intercollegiate Athletics:** Basketball M & W; Crew M & W; Cross-Country Running M & W; Field Hockey W; Football M; Golf M & W; Ice Hockey M & W; Lacrosse M & W; Rugby M & W; Sailing M & W; Skiing (Downhill) M & W; Soccer M & W; Squash M & W; Swimming and Diving W; Tennis M & W

HOFSTRA UNIVERSITY
100 Hofstra University
Hempstead, NY 11549
Tel: (516)463-6600
Free: 800-HOF-STRA
Admissions: (516)463-6700
Fax: (516)560-7660
E-mail: admitme@hofstra.edu
Web Site: http://www.hofstra.edu/
President/CEO: Stuart Rabinowitz, JD
Registrar: Scott Singhel
Admissions: Jessica Eads
Financial Aid: Janice M. Contino
Type: University **Sex:** Coed **Scores:** 99% SAT V 400+; 99% SAT M 400+; 48% ACT 18-23; 42% ACT 24-29 **% Accepted:** 62 **Admission Plans:** Early

Admission; Early Action; Deferred Admission **Application Deadline:** Rolling **Application Fee:** $50.00 **H.S. Requirements:** High school diploma required; GED accepted **Costs Per Year:** Application fee: $50. Comprehensive fee: $30,830 includes full-time tuition ($20,500), mandatory fees ($1030), and college room and board ($9300). College room only: $6200. Full-time tuition and fees vary according to course load and program. Room and board charges vary according to board plan and housing facility. Part-time tuition: $670 per semester hour. Part-time mandatory fees: $155 per term. Part-time tuition and fees vary according to course load and program. **Scholarships:** Available **Calendar System:** 4-1-4, Summer Session Available **Enrollment:** FT 8,031, PT 853, Grad 2,966 **Faculty:** FT 527, PT 719 **Student-Faculty Ratio:** 14:1 **Exams:** SAT I or ACT, SAT II **% Receiving Financial Aid:** 59 **% Residing in College-Owned, -Operated, or -Affiliated Housing:** 44 **Library Holdings:** 1,200,000 **Regional Accreditation:** Middle State Association of Colleges and Schools **Credit Hours For Degree:** 124 semester hours, Bachelors **ROTC:** Army **Professional Accreditation:** AACSB, ABET, ACEJMC, ABA, APA, ASLHA, AALS, CORE, JRCEPAT, NCATE **Intercollegiate Athletics:** Baseball M; Basketball M & W; Cross-Country Running M & W; Field Hockey W; Football M; Golf M & W; Lacrosse M & W; Soccer M & W; Softball W; Tennis M & W; Volleyball W; Wrestling M

HOLY TRINITY ORTHODOX SEMINARY
PO Box 36
Jordanville, NY 13361
Tel: (315)858-0945
Fax: (315)858-0945
Web Site: http://www.hts.edu/
President/CEO: Rt. Rev. Archbishop Laurus
Registrar: Rev. Hieromonk Theophylact
Admissions: Very Rev. Archimandrite Luke
Type: Five-Year College **Sex:** Men **Affiliation:** Russian Orthodox **% Accepted:** 80 **Application Deadline:** May 01 **Application Fee:** $0.00 **H.S. Requirements:** High school diploma required; GED accepted **Costs Per Year:** Application fee: $0. Comprehensive fee: $5525 includes full-time tuition ($3000), mandatory fees ($25), and college room and board ($2500). Part-time tuition: $300 per course. **Calendar System:** Semester, Summer Session Not available **Enrollment:** FT 20, PT 6 **Faculty:** FT 7, PT 9 **Student-Faculty Ratio:** 2:1 **% Residing in College-Owned, -Operated, or -Affiliated Housing:** 100 **Library Holdings:** 25,000 **Credit Hours For Degree:** 162 credit hours, Bachelors **Professional Accreditation:** NYSBR

HOUGHTON COLLEGE
One Willard Ave.
Houghton, NY 14744
Tel: (585)567-9200
Free: 800-777-2556
Admissions: (585)567-9353
Fax: (585)567-9522
E-mail: admissions@houghton.edu
Web Site: http://www.houghton.edu/
President/CEO: Dr. Daniel R. Chamberlain
Registrar: Margery Avery
Admissions: Tim Fuller
Financial Aid: Troy Martin
Type: Comprehensive **Sex:** Coed **Affiliation:** Wesleyan **Scores:** 99% SAT V 400+; 98% SAT M 400+; 28% ACT 18-23; 54% ACT 24-29 **% Accepted:** 77 **Admission Plans:** Preferred Admission; Deferred Admission **Application Deadline:** Rolling **Application Fee:** $40.00 **H.S. Requirements:** High school diploma required; GED accepted **Costs Per Year:** Application fee: $40. Comprehensive fee: $25,980 includes full-time tuition ($19,420) and college room and board ($6560). Full-time tuition varies according to class time, program, and reciprocity agreements. Room and board charges vary according to board plan and housing facility. Part-time tuition: $812 per hour. **Scholarships:** Available **Calendar System:** Semester, Summer Session Available **Enrollment:** FT 1,337, PT 61, Grad 13 **Faculty:** FT 88, PT 15 **Student-Faculty Ratio:** 13:1 **Exams:** SAT I or ACT **% Receiving Financial Aid:** 76 **% Residing in College-Owned, -Operated, or -Affiliated Housing:** 82 **Library Holdings:** 242,866 **Regional Accreditation:** Middle State Association of Colleges and Schools **Credit Hours For Degree:** 63 credit hours, Associates; 125 credit hours, Bachelors **ROTC:** Army **Professional Accreditation:** NASM **Intercollegiate Athletics:** Basketball M & W; Cheerleading M & W; Cross-Country Running M & W; Field Hockey W; Soccer M & W; Track and Field M & W; Volleyball W

HUDSON VALLEY COMMUNITY COLLEGE
80 Vandenburgh Ave.
Troy, NY 12180-6096
Tel: (518)629-4822
Admissions: (518)629-4603
Web Site: http://www.hvcc.edu/
President/CEO: John L. Buono
Registrar: Kathleen Petley
Admissions: MaryClaire Bauer
Financial Aid: Lisa Van Wie
Type: Two-Year College **Sex:** Coed **Affiliation:** State University of New York System **% Accepted:** 90 **Admission Plans:** Open Admission; Early Admission; Deferred Admission **Application Deadline:** Rolling **Application Fee:** $30.00 **H.S. Requirements:** High school diploma required; GED accepted **Costs Per Year:** Application fee: $30. State resident tuition: $2700 full-time, $112 per credit hour part-time. Nonresident tuition: $8100 full-time, $336 per credit hour part-time. Mandatory fees: $480 full-time, $14 per credit hour part-time. **Scholarships:** Available **Calendar System:** Semester, Summer Session Available **Faculty:** FT 215, PT 359 **Student-Faculty Ratio:** 19:1 **Library Holdings:** 148,189 **Regional Accreditation:** Middle State Association of Colleges and Schools **Credit Hours For Degree:** 60 credits, Associates **ROTC:** Army, Air Force **Professional Accreditation:** ABET, ABFSE, ACCE, ADA, CARC, JRCERT, JRCEMT, NLN **Intercollegiate Athletics:** Basketball M & W; Bowling M & W; Cross-Country Running M & W; Football M; Golf M & W; Lacrosse M; Soccer M; Tennis M & W; Track and Field M & W; Volleyball W

HUNTER COLLEGE OF THE CITY UNIVERSITY OF NEW YORK
695 Park Ave.
New York, NY 10021-5085
Tel: (212)772-4000
Admissions: (212)772-4490
Web Site: http://www.hunter.cuny.edu/
President/CEO: Jennifer Raab
Registrar: Yechiel J. Rosenrauch
Admissions: William Zlata
Financial Aid: Kevin McGowan
Type: Comprehensive **Sex:** Coed **Affiliation:** City University of New York System **Scores:** 96.2% SAT V 400+; 98.8% SAT M 400+ **% Accepted:** 35 **Admission Plans:** Early Admission **Application Deadline:** March 15 **Application Fee:** $65.00 **H.S. Requirements:** High school diploma required; GED accepted **Costs Per Year:** Application fee: $65. State resident tuition: $4000 full-time, $170 per credit part-time. Nonresident tuition: $10,800 full-time, $360 per credit part-time. Mandatory fees: $349 full-time, $107 per term part-time. College room only: $3478. **Scholarships:** Available **Calendar System:** Semester, Summer Session Available **Enrollment:** FT 10,406, PT 5,225, Grad 5,212 **Faculty:** FT 633, PT 802 **Student-Faculty Ratio:** 14:1 **Exams:** SAT I or ACT **% Residing in College-Owned, -Operated, or -Affiliated Housing:** 1 **Library Holdings:** 789,718 **Regional Accreditation:** Middle State Association of Colleges and Schools **Credit Hours For Degree:** 120 credits, Bachelors **Professional Accreditation:** ABET, AACN, ADtA, ACSP, APTA, ASLHA, CEPH, CORE, CSWE, NCATE **Intercollegiate Athletics:** Basketball M & W; Cross-Country Running M & W; Fencing M & W; Gymnastics W; Soccer M; Swimming and Diving W; Tennis M & W; Track and Field M & W; Volleyball M & W; Wrestling M

INSTITUTE OF DESIGN AND CONSTRUCTION
141 Willoughby St.
Brooklyn, NY 11201-5317
Tel: (718)855-3661
Fax: (718)852-5889
Web Site: http://www.idcbrooklyn.org/
President/CEO: Vincent C. Battista
Admissions: Kevin Giannetti
Financial Aid: John Anselmo
Type: Two-Year College **Sex:** Coed **Application Fee:** $30.00 **H.S. Requirements:** High school diploma required; GED accepted **Scholarships:** Avail-

able **Calendar System:** Semester, Summer Session Available **Faculty:** FT 0, PT 32 **Credit Hours For Degree:** 72 credits, Associates **Professional Accreditation:** NYSBR

INTERBORO INSTITUTE
450 West 56th St.
New York, NY 10019-3602
Tel: (212)399-0093
Admissions: (212)399-0091
Fax: (212)765-5772
E-mail: ryan@interboro.com
Web Site: http://www.interboro.com/
President/CEO: Stephen H. Adolphus
Registrar: Geraldine Klass
Admissions: Jeffrey S. Bolding
Financial Aid: Minerva Vasquez
Type: Two-Year College **Sex:** Coed **Admission Plans:** Open Admission; Deferred Admission **Application Fee:** $35.00 **H.S. Requirements:** High school diploma or equivalent not required **Scholarships:** Available **Calendar System:** Semester, Summer Session Available **Enrollment:** FT 1,891 **Faculty:** FT 29, PT 63 **Student-Faculty Ratio:** 36:1 **Exams:** Other **Library Holdings:** 5,986 **Credit Hours For Degree:** 60 credit hours, Associates **Professional Accreditation:** COptA, NYSBR

IONA COLLEGE
715 North Ave.
New Rochelle, NY 10801-1890
Tel: (914)633-2000
Admissions: (914)633-2502
Fax: (914)633-2096
E-mail: TWeede@iona.edu
Web Site: http://www.iona.edu/
President/CEO: James A. Liguori, CFC
Registrar: Isabel Cavanagh
Admissions: Thomas Weede
Financial Aid: Mary Grant
Type: Comprehensive **Sex:** Coed **Affiliation:** Roman Catholic Church **Scores:** 99% SAT V 400+; 99% SAT M 400+; 46% ACT 18-23; 54% ACT 24-29 **% Accepted:** 67 **Admission Plans:** Early Admission; Early Action; Deferred Admission **Application Deadline:** February 15 **Application Fee:** $50.00 **H.S. Requirements:** High school diploma required; GED accepted **Costs Per Year:** Application fee: $50. Comprehensive fee: $30,878 includes full-time tuition ($20,110), mandatory fees ($870), and college room and board ($9898). Full-time tuition and fees vary according to class time. Room and board charges vary according to housing facility. Part-time tuition: $667 per credit. Part-time mandatory fees: $370 per term. Part-time tuition and fees vary according to class time and course load. **Scholarships:** Available **Calendar System:** Semester, Summer Session Available **Enrollment:** FT 3,122, PT 243, Grad 819 **Faculty:** FT 176, PT 197 **Student-Faculty Ratio:** 15:1 **Exams:** SAT I or ACT, SAT II **% Receiving Financial Aid:** 75 **% Residing in College-Owned, -Operated, or -Affiliated Housing:** 30 **Library Holdings:** 269,933 **Regional Accreditation:** Middle State Association of Colleges and Schools **Credit Hours For Degree:** 120 credits, Bachelors **ROTC:** Army **Professional Accreditation:** AACSB, ACEJMC, AAMFT, CSWE, NCATE **Intercollegiate Athletics:** Baseball M; Basketball M & W; Crew M & W; Cross-Country Running M & W; Football M; Golf M; Lacrosse W; Rugby M & W; Soccer M & W; Softball W; Swimming and Diving M & W; Track and Field M & W; Volleyball W; Water Polo M & W

ISLAND DRAFTING AND TECHNICAL INSTITUTE
128 Broadway
Amityville, NY 11701
Tel: (631)691-8733
Fax: (631)691-8738
E-mail: info@idti.edu
Web Site: http://www.idti.edu/
President/CEO: James G. DiLiberto
Registrar: Susan Carlson
Admissions: Steven Rothenberg
Financial Aid: Daniel Greener
Type: Two-Year College **Sex:** Coed **% Accepted:** 100 **Admission Plans:** Open Admission; Early Admission **H.S. Requirements:** High school diploma required; GED accepted **Costs Per Year:** Tuition: $11,850 full-time, $395 per credit part-time. Mandatory fees: $350 full-time. **Scholarships:** Available **Calendar System:** Semester, Summer Session Available **Enrollment:** FT 185 **Faculty:** FT 5, PT 20 **Student-Faculty Ratio:** 15:1 **Professional Accreditation:** ACCSCT

ITHACA COLLEGE
100 Job Hall
Ithaca, NY 14850-7020
Tel: (607)274-3011
Free: 800-429-4274
Admissions: (607)274-3124
Fax: (607)274-1900
E-mail: admission@ithaca.edu
Web Site: http://www.ithaca.edu/
President/CEO: Dr. Peggy R. Williams
Registrar: Christopher B. Knauer
Admissions: Paula J. Mitchell
Financial Aid: Larry R. Chambers
Type: Comprehensive **Sex:** Coed **Scores:** 99.6% SAT V 400+; 99.9% SAT M 400+ **% Accepted:** 76 **Admission Plans:** Early Admission; Early Decision Plan; Deferred Admission **Application Deadline:** February 01 **Application Fee:** $55.00 **H.S. Requirements:** High school diploma required; GED accepted **Costs Per Year:** Application fee: $55. Comprehensive fee: $35,144 includes full-time tuition ($25,194) and college room and board ($9950). College room only: $5120. Part-time tuition: $840 per credit hour. **Scholarships:** Available **Calendar System:** Semester, Summer Session Available **Enrollment:** FT 5,961, PT 137, Grad 314 **Faculty:** FT 442, PT 214 **Student-Faculty Ratio:** 12:1 **Exams:** SAT I or ACT **% Receiving Financial Aid:** 70 **% Residing in College-Owned, -Operated, or -Affiliated Housing:** 70 **Library Holdings:** 376,000 **Regional Accreditation:** Middle State Association of Colleges and Schools **Credit Hours For Degree:** 120 credit hours, Bachelors **ROTC:** Army, Air Force **Professional Accreditation:** AACSB, AOTA, APTA, ASLHA, JRCEPAT, NASM, NAST, NRPA **Intercollegiate Athletics:** Baseball M; Basketball M & W; Crew M & W; Cross-Country Running M & W; Field Hockey W; Football M; Gymnastics W; Lacrosse M & W; Soccer M & W; Softball W; Swimming and Diving M & W; Tennis M & W; Track and Field M & W; Volleyball W; Wrestling M

ITT TECHNICAL INSTITUTE (ALBANY)
13 Airline Dr.
Albany, NY 12205
Tel: (518)452-9300
Web Site: http://www.itt-tech.edu/
President/CEO: Christopher Chang
Admissions: Christopher Chang
Type: Two-Year College **Sex:** Coed **Affiliation:** ITT Educational Services, Inc **Admission Plans:** Deferred Admission **Application Deadline:** Rolling **Application Fee:** $100.00 **H.S. Requirements:** High school diploma required; GED accepted **Costs Per Year:** Application fee: $100. **Scholarships:** Available **Calendar System:** Quarter, Summer Session Not available **Exams:** Other **Credit Hours For Degree:** 96 credit hours, Associates **Professional Accreditation:** ACICS

ITT TECHNICAL INSTITUTE (GETZVILLE)
2295 Millersport Hwy.
PO Box 327
Getzville, NY 14068
Tel: (716)689-2200
Web Site: http://www.itt-tech.edu/
President/CEO: Lester Burgess
Admissions: Lester Burgess
Type: Two-Year College **Sex:** Coed **Affiliation:** ITT Educational Services, Inc **Admission Plans:** Deferred Admission **Application Deadline:** Rolling **Application Fee:** $100.00 **H.S. Requirements:** High school diploma required; GED accepted **Costs Per Year:** Application fee: $100. **Scholarships:** Available **Exams:** Other **Credit Hours For Degree:** 96 credit hours, Associates **Professional Accreditation:** ACICS

ITT TECHNICAL INSTITUTE (LIVERPOOL)
235 Greenfield Parkway
Liverpool, NY 13088
Tel: (315)461-8000
Web Site: http://www.itt-tech.edu/
President/CEO: Cheryl Anderson-Nickeson
Admissions: Laura F. Carroll
Type: Two-Year College **Sex:** Coed **Affiliation:** ITT Educational Services, Inc **Admission Plans:** Deferred Admission **Application Deadline:** Rolling

Application Fee: $100.00 **H.S. Requirements:** High school diploma required; GED accepted **Costs Per Year:** Application fee: $100. **Scholarships:** Available **Calendar System:** Semester, Summer Session Not available **Exams:** Other **Credit Hours For Degree:** 96 credit hours, Associates **Professional Accreditation:** ACICS

JAMESTOWN BUSINESS COLLEGE
7 Fairmount Ave., Box 429
Jamestown, NY 14702-0429
Tel: (716)664-5100
Fax: (716)664-3144
E-mail: jbc@epix.net
Web Site: http://www.jbcny.org/
President/CEO: Tyler Swanson
Admissions: Brenda Salemme
Financial Aid: Diane Sturzenbecker
Type: Two-Year College **Sex:** Coed **Application Fee:** $25.00 **H.S. Requirements:** High school diploma required; GED accepted **Costs Per Year:** Application fee: $25. Tuition: $8400 full-time, $233 per credit hour part-time. Mandatory fees: $450 full-time, $75 per term part-time. **Scholarships:** Available **Calendar System:** Quarter, Summer Session Available **Enrollment:** FT 327 **Faculty:** FT 7, PT 13 **Student-Faculty Ratio:** 24:1 **Library Holdings:** 279,270 **Regional Accreditation:** Middle State Association of Colleges and Schools **Credit Hours For Degree:** 90 quarter hours, Associates

JAMESTOWN COMMUNITY COLLEGE
525 Falconer St.
Jamestown, NY 14701-1999
Tel: (716)665-5220
Web Site: http://www.sunyjcc.edu/
President/CEO: Dr. Gregory T. DeCinque
Registrar: Kreig Elicker
Admissions: Wendy Present
Financial Aid: Laurie Vorp
Type: Two-Year College **Sex:** Coed **Affiliation:** State University of New York System **% Accepted:** 82 **Admission Plans:** Open Admission; Preferred Admission; Deferred Admission **Application Deadline:** Rolling **Application Fee:** $40.00 **H.S. Requirements:** High school diploma required; GED accepted **Costs Per Year:** Application fee: $40. State resident tuition: $3150 full-time, $132 per credit hour part-time. Nonresident tuition: $6300 full-time, $238 per credit hour part-time. Mandatory fees: $530 full-time, $16.75 per credit hour part-time. Full-time tuition and fees vary according to program. **Scholarships:** Available **Calendar System:** Semester, Summer Session Available **Enrollment:** FT 2,460, PT 1,212 **Faculty:** FT 83, PT 262 **Student-Faculty Ratio:** 18:1 **Library Holdings:** 66,808 **Regional Accreditation:** Middle State Association of Colleges and Schools **Credit Hours For Degree:** 60 semester hours, Associates **Professional Accreditation:** AOTA, NLN **Intercollegiate Athletics:** Baseball M; Basketball M & W; Golf M; Soccer M & W; Softball W; Swimming and Diving M & W; Volleyball W; Wrestling M

JEFFERSON COMMUNITY COLLEGE
1220 Coffeen St.
Watertown, NY 13601
Tel: (315)786-2200
Admissions: (315)786-2277
Fax: (315)786-0158
E-mail: admissions@sunyjefferson.edu
Web Site: http://www.sunyjefferson.edu/
President/CEO: Dr. Joseph B. Olson
Registrar: Natalie Spooner
Admissions: Rosanne N. Weir
Financial Aid: Betsy S. Penrose
Type: Two-Year College **Sex:** Coed **Affiliation:** State University of New York System **Admission Plans:** Preferred Admission; Early Admission; Deferred Admission **Application Deadline:** September 06 **Application Fee:** $0.00 **H.S. Requirements:** High school diploma required; GED accepted **Costs Per Year:** Application fee: $0. State resident tuition: $3294 full-time, $122 per credit hour part-time. Nonresident tuition: $4724 full-time, $182 per credit hour part-time. Mandatory fees: $366 full-time, $13 per credit hour part-time, $21. **Scholarships:** Available **Calendar System:** Semester, Summer Session Available **Enrollment:** FT 1,822, PT 1,723 **Faculty:** FT 78, PT 110 **Student-Faculty Ratio:** 20:1 **Exams:** SAT I or ACT **Library Holdings:** 62,503 **Regional Accreditation:** Middle State Association of Colleges and Schools **Credit Hours For Degree:** 62 credit hours, Associates **Professional Accreditation:** NLN **Intercollegiate Athletics:** Baseball M; Basketball M & W; Golf M & W; Lacrosse M & W; Soccer M & W; Softball W; Tennis W; Volleyball W

THE JEWISH THEOLOGICAL SEMINARY
3080 Broadway
New York, NY 10027-4649
Tel: (212)678-8000
Fax: (212)678-8947
Web Site: http://www.jtsa.edu/
President/CEO: Dr. Ismar Schorsch
Registrar: Linda Levine
Financial Aid: Linda Levine
Type: University **Sex:** Coed **Affiliation:** Jewish **Scores:** 100% SAT V 400+; 100% SAT M 400+; 14% ACT 18-23; 57% ACT 24-29 **Admission Plans:** Early Admission; Early Decision Plan; Deferred Admission **Application Fee:** $65.00 **H.S. Requirements:** High school diploma required; GED accepted **Scholarships:** Available **Calendar System:** Semester, Summer Session Available **Faculty:** FT 62, PT 62 **Student-Faculty Ratio:** 5:1 **Exams:** SAT I and SAT II or ACT **% Receiving Financial Aid:** 51 **% Residing in College-Owned, -Operated, or -Affiliated Housing:** 77 **Library Holdings:** 380,000 **Regional Accreditation:** Middle State Association of Colleges and Schools **Credit Hours For Degree:** 156 credits (96 in residence, 60 elsewhere), Bachelors **Professional Accreditation:** ACIPE

JOHN JAY COLLEGE OF CRIMINAL JUSTICE OF THE CITY UNIVERSITY OF NEW YORK
899 Tenth Ave.
New York, NY 10019-1093
Tel: (212)237-8000; 877-JOHNJAY
Admissions: (212)237-8878
Web Site: http://www.jjay.cuny.edu/
President/CEO: Jeremy Travis
Registrar: Dr. Richard Saulnier
Admissions: Richard Saulnier, PhD
Financial Aid: Arnold Osansky
Type: Comprehensive **Sex:** Coed **Affiliation:** City University of New York System **Admission Plans:** Open Admission; Early Admission; Deferred Admission **Application Fee:** $50.00 **H.S. Requirements:** High school diploma required; GED accepted **Costs Per Year:** Application fee: $50. State resident tuition: $4000 full-time, $170 per credit part-time. Nonresident tuition: $8640 full-time, $360 per credit part-time. Mandatory fees: $259 full-time, $82.35 per term part-time. Full-time tuition and fees vary according to course level and course load. Part-time tuition and fees vary according to course level and course load. **Scholarships:** Available **Calendar System:** Semester, Summer Session Available **Enrollment:** FT 12,276, Grad 1,775 **Faculty:** FT 338, PT 575 **Student-Faculty Ratio:** 20:1 **Exams:** SAT I or ACT **Library Holdings:** 310,000 **Regional Accreditation:** Middle State Association of Colleges and Schools **Credit Hours For Degree:** 60 credits, Associates; 120 credits, Bachelors **ROTC:** Air Force **Professional Accreditation:** NASPAA **Intercollegiate Athletics:** Baseball M; Basketball M & W; Cross-Country Running M & W; Soccer M & W; Softball M & W; Tennis M & W; Volleyball W

THE JUILLIARD SCHOOL
60 Lincoln Center Plaza
New York, NY 10023-6588
Tel: (212)799-5000
Fax: (212)724-0263
Web Site: http://www.juilliard.edu/
President/CEO: Dr. Joseph W. Polisi
Registrar: Elizabeth Brummett
Admissions: Lee Cioppa
Financial Aid: Joan D. Warren
Type: Comprehensive **Sex:** Coed **% Accepted:** 5 **Application Deadline:** December 01 **Application Fee:** $100.00 **H.S. Requirements:** High school diploma required; GED accepted **Costs Per Year:** Application fee: $100. Comprehensive fee: $34,500 includes full-time tuition ($24,330), mandatory fees ($600), and college room and board ($9570). Room and board charges vary according to housing facility. **Scholarships:** Available **Calendar System:** Semester, Summer Session Not available **Enrollment:** FT 478, PT 3, Grad 327 **Faculty:** FT 114, PT 152 **% Receiving Financial Aid:** 77 **% Residing in College-Owned, -Operated, or -Affiliated Housing:** 60 **Library Holdings:** 80,793 **Regional Accreditation:** Middle State Association of Colleges and Schools **Credit Hours For Degree:** 140 credits, Bachelors

KATHARINE GIBBS SCHOOL (MELVILLE)
320 South Service Rd.
Melville, NY 11747-3785
Tel: (631)370-3300
Admissions: (631)370-3307
Fax: (631)293-1276
Web Site: http://www.gibbsmelville.com/
President/CEO: Diane Engelhardt
Registrar: Kim Pandolfi
Admissions: Cynthia Gamache
Financial Aid: Mary Erickson
Type: Two-Year College **Sex:** Coed **Affiliation:** Career Education Corporation **Admission Plans:** Deferred Admission **Application Fee:** $50.00 **H.S. Requirements:** High school diploma required; GED accepted **Scholarships:** Available **Calendar System:** Quarter, Summer Session Not available **Faculty:** FT 21, PT 37 **Student-Faculty Ratio:** 24:1 **Exams:** Other, SAT I **Credit Hours For Degree:** 91 credits, Associates **ROTC:** Army **Professional Accreditation:** ACICS

KATHARINE GIBBS SCHOOL (NEW YORK)
200 Park Ave.
New York, NY 10166-0005
Tel: (212)867-9300
Web Site: http://www.katharinegibbs.com/
President/CEO: Patricia A. Martin
Registrar: Evelyn Humphreys
Admissions: Pat Martin
Financial Aid: Crystal Pierce
Type: Two-Year College **Sex:** Coed **Affiliation:** Career Education Corporation **Admission Plans:** Deferred Admission **Application Fee:** $50.00 **H.S. Requirements:** High school diploma required; GED accepted **Scholarships:** Available **Calendar System:** Quarter, Summer Session Not available **Enrollment:** FT 2,717 **Faculty:** FT 70, PT 48 **Student-Faculty Ratio:** 20:1 **Exams:** Other, SAT I **Credit Hours For Degree:** 90 credits, Associates **Professional Accreditation:** ACICS

KEHILATH YAKOV RABBINICAL SEMINARY
206 Wilson St.
Brooklyn, NY 11211-7207
Tel: (718)963-1212
Fax: (718)387-8586
President/CEO: Sandor Schwartz
Registrar: Joseph Gold
Admissions: Rabbi Zalman Gombo
Financial Aid: Joseph Weber
Type: Comprehensive **Sex:** Men **Affiliation:** Jewish **Calendar System:** Semester **Professional Accreditation:** AARTS

KEUKA COLLEGE
Keuka Park, NY 14478-0098
Tel: (315)279-5000
Free: 800-33-KEUKA
Admissions: (315)279-5262
Fax: (315)279-5216
E-mail: admissions@mail.keuka.edu
Web Site: http://www.keuka.edu/
President/CEO: Dr. Joseph G. Burke
Registrar: Linda B. Fleischman
Admissions: Dr. Carolanne Marquis
Financial Aid: Jennifer Bates
Type: Comprehensive **Sex:** Coed **Affiliation:** American Baptist Churches in the U.S.A. **Scores:** 85.5% SAT V 400+; 92% SAT M 400+; 40% ACT 18-23; 20% ACT 24-29 **% Accepted:** 81 **Admission Plans:** Early Admission; Deferred Admission **Application Deadline:** Rolling **Application Fee:** $30.00 **H.S. Requirements:** High school diploma required; GED accepted **Costs Per Year:** Application fee: $30. Comprehensive fee: $25,850 includes full-time tuition ($17,800), mandatory fees ($270), and college room and board ($7780). College room only: $3790. Full-time tuition and fees vary according to program. Room and board charges vary according to board plan and housing facility. Part-time tuition: $595 per credit hour. Part-time tuition varies according to program. **Scholarships:** Available **Calendar System:** 4-1-4, Summer Session Available **Enrollment:** FT 1,115, PT 153, Grad 100 **Faculty:** FT 57, PT 42 **Student-Faculty Ratio:** 14:1 **Exams:** SAT I or ACT **% Receiving Financial Aid:** 93 **% Residing in College-Owned, -Operated, or -Affiliated Housing:** 68 **Library Holdings:** 117,192 **Regional Accreditation:** Middle State Association of Colleges and Schools **Credit Hours For Degree:** 120 credit hours, Bachelors **Professional Accreditation:** AOTA, CSWE, NLN **Intercollegiate Athletics:** Baseball M; Basketball M & W; Cross-Country Running M & W; Lacrosse M; Soccer M & W; Softball W; Swimming and Diving W; Volleyball W

THE KING'S COLLEGE
350 Fifth Ave.
15th Floor Empire State Bldg.
New York, NY 10118
Tel: (212)659-7200; 888-969-7200
E-mail: bbell@tkc.edu
Web Site: http://www.tkc.edu/
President/CEO: J. Stanley Oakes
Admissions: Brian T. Bell
Type: Four-Year College **Sex:** Coed **Scores:** 100% SAT V 400+; 100% SAT M 400+; 29% ACT 18-23; 65% ACT 24-29 **% Accepted:** 57 **Admission Plans:** Early Action; Deferred Admission **Application Deadline:** February 01 **Application Fee:** $30.00 **H.S. Requirements:** High school diploma required; GED accepted **Costs Per Year:** Application fee: $30. Tuition: $18,590 full-time, $775 per credit part-time. Mandatory fees: $350 full-time, $175 per term part-time. College room only: $7980. **Calendar System:** Semester, Summer Session Available **Enrollment:** FT 217, PT 23 **Faculty:** FT 12, PT 11 **Student-Faculty Ratio:** 14:1 **Exams:** SAT I or ACT **% Residing in College-Owned, -Operated, or -Affiliated Housing:** 55 **Library Holdings:** 12,000 **Credit Hours For Degree:** 60 credits, Associates; 120 credits, Bachelors **Professional Accreditation:** NYSBR

KINGSBOROUGH COMMUNITY COLLEGE OF THE CITY UNIVERSITY OF NEW YORK
2001 Oriental Blvd, Manhattan Beach
Brooklyn, NY 11235
Tel: (718)368-5000
Admissions: (718)368-6800
Web Site: http://www.kbcc.cuny.edu/
President/CEO: Dr. Fred B. Malamet
Registrar: Sonia Saladuchin
Admissions: Rosalie Fayad
Financial Aid: Wayne Harewood
Type: Two-Year College **Sex:** Coed **Affiliation:** City University of New York System **Scores:** 45.3% SAT V 400+; 54.1% SAT M 400+ **Admission Plans:** Open Admission **Application Deadline:** August 23 **Application Fee:** $60.00 **H.S. Requirements:** High school diploma required; GED accepted **Costs Per Year:** Application fee: $60. State resident tuition: $2800 full-time, $120 per credit part-time. Nonresident tuition: $4560 full-time, $190 per credit part-time. Mandatory fees: $300 full-time, $79.50 per term part-time. **Scholarships:** Available **Calendar System:** Semester, Summer Session Available **Enrollment:** FT 7,968, PT 7,297 **Faculty:** FT 284, PT 387 **Student-Faculty Ratio:** 25:1 **Library Holdings:** 185,912 **Regional Accreditation:** Middle State Association of Colleges and Schools **Credit Hours For Degree:** 60 credits, Associates **Professional Accreditation:** APTA, NLN **Intercollegiate Athletics:** Baseball M; Basketball M & W; Soccer M; Softball W; Tennis M & W; Track and Field M & W; Volleyball W

KOL YAAKOV TORAH CENTER
29 West Maple Ave.
Monsey, NY 10952-2954
Tel: (914)425-3863
Web Site: http://horizons.edu/
President/CEO: James Lavin
Registrar: Rabbi Leib Shear
Financial Aid: Rabbi Leib Shear
Type: Comprehensive **Sex:** Men **Affiliation:** Jewish **Admission Plans:** Early Admission **H.S. Requirements:** High school diploma or equivalent not required **Calendar System:** Semester, Summer Session Available **Faculty:** FT 2, PT 10 **Library Holdings:** 2,000 **Credit Hours For Degree:** 130 credits, Bachelors **Professional Accreditation:** AARTS

LABORATORY INSTITUTE OF MERCHANDISING
12 East 53rd St.
New York, NY 10022-5268
Tel: (212)752-1530
Free: 800-677-1323
Fax: (212)832-6708

E-mail: khamill@limcollege.edu
Web Site: http://www.limcollege.edu/
President/CEO: Elizabeth S. Marcuse
Registrar: Angela Alexander
Admissions: Kristina Gibson
Financial Aid: Christopher Barto
Type: Four-Year College **Sex:** Coed **Scores:** 85% SAT V 400+; 78% SAT M 400+; 70% ACT 18-23 **% Accepted:** 66 **Admission Plans:** Deferred Admission **Application Deadline:** Rolling **Application Fee:** $40.00 **H.S. Requirements:** High school diploma required; GED accepted **Costs Per Year:** Application fee: $40. Comprehensive fee: $30,700 includes full-time tuition ($17,250), mandatory fees ($450), and college room and board ($13,000). Part-time tuition: $545 per credit. Part-time mandatory fees: $112.50 per term. **Scholarships:** Available **Calendar System:** Semester, Summer Session Available **Enrollment:** FT 776, PT 16 **Faculty:** FT 14, PT 76 **Student-Faculty Ratio:** 19:1 **Exams:** SAT I or ACT **% Receiving Financial Aid:** 95 **% Residing in College-Owned, -Operated, or -Affiliated Housing:** 14 **Library Holdings:** 10,300 **Regional Accreditation:** Middle State Association of Colleges and Schools **Credit Hours For Degree:** 64 credits, Associates; 126 credits, Bachelors

LE MOYNE COLLEGE
1419 Salt Springs Rd.
Syracuse, NY 13214
Tel: (315)445-4100
Free: 800-333-4733
Admissions: (315)445-4707
Fax: (315)445-4711
E-mail: admission@lemoyne.edu
Web Site: http://www.lemoyne.edu/
President/CEO: Rev. Charles J. Beirne, SJ
Registrar: Mary Chandler
Admissions: Dennis R. DePerro
Financial Aid: William C. Cheetham
Type: Comprehensive **Sex:** Coed **Affiliation:** Roman Catholic (Jesuit) **Scores:** 100% SAT V 400+; 100% SAT M 400+; 48% ACT 18-23; 45% ACT 24-29 **% Accepted:** 72 **Admission Plans:** Early Admission; Early Decision Plan; Deferred Admission **Application Deadline:** February 01 **Application Fee:** $35.00 **H.S. Requirements:** High school diploma required; GED accepted **Costs Per Year:** Application fee: $35. Comprehensive fee: $29,570 includes full-time tuition ($20,770), mandatory fees ($510), and college room and board ($8290). College room only: $5240. Room and board charges vary according to board plan and housing facility. Part-time tuition: $441 per credit hour. Part-time tuition varies according to class time. **Scholarships:** Available **Calendar System:** Semester, Summer Session Available **Enrollment:** FT 2,318, PT 471, Grad 791 **Faculty:** FT 154, PT 170 **Student-Faculty Ratio:** 13:1 **Exams:** SAT I or ACT **% Receiving Financial Aid:** 83 **% Residing in College-Owned, -Operated, or -Affiliated Housing:** 60 **Library Holdings:** 256,565 **Regional Accreditation:** Middle State Association of Colleges and Schools **Credit Hours For Degree:** 120 credit hours, Bachelors **ROTC:** Army, Air Force **Intercollegiate Athletics:** Baseball M; Basketball M & W; Cross-Country Running M & W; Golf M; Lacrosse M & W; Soccer M & W; Softball W; Swimming and Diving M & W; Tennis M & W; Volleyball W

LEHMAN COLLEGE OF THE CITY UNIVERSITY OF NEW YORK
250 Bedford Park Blvd. West
Bronx, NY 10468-1589
Tel: (718)960-8000; 877-Lehman1
Admissions: (718)960-8706
Fax: (718)960-8712
Web Site: http://www.lehman.cuny.edu/
President/CEO: Dr. Ricardo R. Fernandez
Registrar: Lenore Schultz
Admissions: Clarence A. Wilkes
Financial Aid: David Martinez
Type: Comprehensive **Sex:** Coed **Affiliation:** City University of New York System **Scores:** 69% SAT V 400+; 73% SAT M 400+ **% Accepted:** 35 **Admission Plans:** Deferred Admission **Application Deadline:** Rolling **Application Fee:** $50.00 **H.S. Requirements:** High school diploma required; GED accepted **Costs Per Year:** Application fee: $50. State resident tuition: $4000 full-time, $170 per credit part-time. Nonresident tuition: $10,800 full-time, $360 per credit part-time. Mandatory fees: $288 full-time. **Scholarships:** Available **Calendar System:** Semester, Summer Session Available **Enrollment:** FT 5,119, PT 3,323, Grad 2,173 **Exams:** SAT I or ACT **% Receiving Financial Aid:** 83 **Library Holdings:** 541,944 **Regional Accreditation:** Middle State Association of Colleges and Schools **Credit Hours For Degree:** 120 credits, Bachelors **ROTC:** Army **Professional Accreditation:** AACN, ADtA, ASLHA, CSWE, NCATE, NLN **Intercollegiate Athletics:** Baseball M; Basketball M & W; Cross-Country Running M & W; Soccer M; Softball W; Swimming and Diving M & W; Tennis M & W; Track and Field M & W; Volleyball M & W; Water Polo M; Wrestling M

LONG ISLAND BUSINESS INSTITUTE
6500 Jericho Turnpike
Commack, NY 11725
Tel: (631)499-7100
Fax: (631)499-7114
E-mail: rnazar@libi.edu
Web Site: http://www.libi.edu/commack/index.html
President/CEO: Dr. Philip Stander
Admissions: Robert Nazar
Financial Aid: Patricia Ensley
Type: Two-Year College **Sex:** Coed **% Accepted:** 100 **Admission Plans:** Open Admission **Application Deadline:** Rolling **Application Fee:** $50.00 **H.S. Requirements:** High school diploma required; GED accepted **Costs Per Year:** Application fee: $50. Tuition: $8500 full-time, $325 per credit part-time. Mandatory fees: $400 full-time, $50 per year part-time. Full-time tuition and fees vary according to course load and program. Part-time tuition and fees vary according to course load and program. **Calendar System:** Trimester, Summer Session Available **Enrollment:** FT 676, PT 214 **Faculty:** FT 24, PT 73 **Student-Faculty Ratio:** 15:1 **Library Holdings:** 1,484 **Credit Hours For Degree:** 63 credits, Associates **Professional Accreditation:** ACICS

LONG ISLAND COLLEGE HOSPITAL SCHOOL OF NURSING
340 Ct. St.
Brooklyn, NY 11231
Tel: (718)780-1953
Admissions: (718)780-1898
Fax: (718)780-1936
Web Site: http://www.futurenurselich.org/
President/CEO: Dr. Stephen Holzemer
Registrar: Peggy Rafferty, Jr.
Admissions: Marina Karpovitch
Financial Aid: Tara Wagner
Type: Two-Year College **Sex:** Coed **% Accepted:** 3 **Application Deadline:** April 28 **Application Fee:** $50.00 **H.S. Requirements:** High school diploma required; GED accepted **Costs Per Year:** Application fee: $50. Tuition: $23,025 full-time. Mandatory fees: $370 full-time. **Scholarships:** Available **Calendar System:** Semester, Summer Session Available **Enrollment:** FT 73, PT 74 **Faculty:** FT 6, PT 6 **Student-Faculty Ratio:** 12:1 **Library Holdings:** 16,000 **Credit Hours For Degree:** 67 credits, Associates **Professional Accreditation:** NLN

LONG ISLAND UNIVERSITY, BRENTWOOD CAMPUS
100 Second Ave.
Brentwood, NY 11717
Tel: (631)273-5112
Fax: (631)952-0809
Web Site: http://www.liu.edu/
Admissions: John P. Metcalfe
Type: Two-Year Upper Division **Sex:** Coed **Affiliation:** Long Island University **Costs Per Year:** Tuition: $651 per credit part-time. **Scholarships:** Available **Calendar System:** Semester, Summer Session Available **Enrollment:** FT 17, PT 45, Grad 1,053 **Faculty:** FT 20, PT 90 **Student-Faculty Ratio:** 7:1 **Library Holdings:** 55,000 **Regional Accreditation:** Middle State Association of Colleges and Schools **Credit Hours For Degree:** 128 credits, Bachelors

LONG ISLAND UNIVERSITY, BROOKLYN CAMPUS
One University Plaza
Brooklyn, NY 11201-8423
Tel: (718)488-1000
Free: 800-LIU-PLAN
Admissions: (718)488-1011
E-mail: adm_sunday@eagle.liunet.edu
Web Site: http://www.liu.edu/
President/CEO: Dr. David J. Steinberg

Registrar: Thomas Castiglione
Admissions: Kristin Cohen
Financial Aid: Rose Iannicelli
Type: University **Sex:** Coed **Affiliation:** Long Island University **% Accepted:** 61 **Admission Plans:** Deferred Admission **Application Deadline:** Rolling **Application Fee:** $30.00 **H.S. Requirements:** High school diploma required; GED accepted **Costs Per Year:** Application fee: $30. Comprehensive fee: $32,138 includes full-time tuition ($23,188), mandatory fees ($1140), and college room and board ($7810). College room only: $4640. Full-time tuition and fees vary according to program. Room and board charges vary according to board plan and housing facility. Part-time tuition: $689 per credit. Part-time mandatory fees: $590 per year. Part-time tuition and fees vary according to course load and program. **Scholarships:** Available **Calendar System:** Semester, Summer Session Available **Enrollment:** FT 4,412, PT 919, Grad 2,409 **Faculty:** FT 259, PT 695 **Student-Faculty Ratio:** 13:1 **Exams:** SAT I or ACT **% Receiving Financial Aid:** 84 **Regional Accreditation:** Middle State Association of Colleges and Schools **Credit Hours For Degree:** 64 credits, Associates; 128 credits, Bachelors **Professional Accreditation:** AACN, ACPhE, AOTA, APTA, APA, ASLHA, CARC, CSWE, NASPAA, TEAC **Intercollegiate Athletics:** Baseball M; Basketball M & W; Golf M & W; Lacrosse W; Soccer M & W; Softball W; Tennis W; Track and Field M & W; Volleyball W

LONG ISLAND UNIVERSITY, C.W. POST CAMPUS
720 Northern Blvd.
Brookville, NY 11548-1300
Tel: (516)299-2000
Free: 800-LIU-PLAN
Admissions: (516)299-2900
Web Site: http://www.liu.edu/
President/CEO: Dr. David J. Steinberg
Registrar: Chester N. Barkan
Admissions: Gary Bergman
Financial Aid: Nigel Edwards
Type: Comprehensive **Sex:** Coed **Affiliation:** Long Island University **Scores:** 93% SAT V 400+; 91.1% SAT M 400+; 45.8% ACT 18-23; 23.3% ACT 24-29 **% Accepted:** 78 **Admission Plans:** Deferred Admission **Application Deadline:** Rolling **Application Fee:** $30.00 **H.S. Requirements:** High school diploma required; GED accepted **Costs Per Year:** Application fee: $30. Comprehensive fee: $31,930 includes full-time tuition ($22,100), mandatory fees ($1130), and college room and board ($8700). College room only: $5730. Full-time tuition and fees vary according to program. Room and board charges vary according to board plan and housing facility. Part-time tuition: $689 per credit. Part-time mandatory fees: $7 per credit, $420 per year. Part-time tuition and fees vary according to course load and program. **Scholarships:** Available **Calendar System:** Semester, Summer Session Available **Enrollment:** FT 4,476, PT 693, Grad 3,303 **Faculty:** FT 355, PT 810 **Student-Faculty Ratio:** 10:1 **Exams:** SAT I or ACT **% Receiving Financial Aid:** 73 **% Residing in College-Owned, -Operated, or -Affiliated Housing:** 30 **Regional Accreditation:** Middle State Association of Colleges and Schools **Credit Hours For Degree:** 64 credits, Associates; 129 credits, Bachelors **ROTC:** Army, Air Force **Professional Accreditation:** AACSB, AACN, ADtA, AHIMA, ALA, APA, ASLHA, CSWE, JRCERT, NAACLS, NASPAA, NLN **Intercollegiate Athletics:** Baseball M; Basketball M & W; Crew M & W; Cross-Country Running M & W; Equestrian Sports M & W; Field Hockey W; Football M; Lacrosse M & W; Soccer M & W; Softball W; Swimming and Diving W; Tennis W; Track and Field M & W; Volleyball W

LONG ISLAND UNIVERSITY, FRIENDS WORLD PROGRAM
239 Montauk Hwy.
Southampton, NY 11968
Tel: (631)287-8474
Free: 800-287-8093
Admissions: (631)287-8465
Fax: (631)287-8463
E-mail: fw@southampton.liunet.edu
Web Site: http://www.southampton.liu.edu/fw/
President/CEO: Robert F.X. Sillerman
Registrar: Mary Hevi
Admissions: Joyce Tuttle
Financial Aid: Susan Taylor
Type: Four-Year College **Sex:** Coed **Affiliation:** Long Island University **Admission Plans:** Open Admission; Early Admission; Deferred Admission **Application Fee:** $30.00 **H.S. Requirements:** High school diploma required; GED accepted **Costs Per Year:** Application fee: $30. Comprehensive fee: $34,100 includes full-time tuition ($22,100), mandatory fees ($6000), and college room and board ($6000). Full-time tuition and fees vary according to location. Room and board charges vary according to location. Part-time tuition: $659 per credit. **Calendar System:** Semester, Summer Session Not available **Enrollment:** FT 189, PT 6 **Student-Faculty Ratio:** 10:1 **% Residing in College-Owned, -Operated, or -Affiliated Housing:** 20 **Library Holdings:** 115,380 **Regional Accreditation:** Middle State Association of Colleges and Schools **Credit Hours For Degree:** 120 credits, Bachelors

MACHZIKEI HADATH RABBINICAL COLLEGE
5407 Sixteenth Ave.
Brooklyn, NY 11204-1805
Tel: (718)854-8777
President/CEO: Avi Klein
Admissions: Rabbi Abraham M. Lezerowitz
Type: Comprehensive **Sex:** Men **Affiliation:** Jewish **H.S. Requirements:** High school diploma required; GED not accepted **Calendar System:** Semester **Library Holdings:** 20,000 **Credit Hours For Degree:** 120 credits, Bachelors **Professional Accreditation:** AARTS

MANHATTAN COLLEGE
Manhattan College Parkway
Riverdale, NY 10471
Tel: (718)862-8000
Admissions: (718)862-7200
Fax: (718)862-8019
E-mail: admit@manhattan.edu
Web Site: http://www.manhattan.edu/
President/CEO: Br. Thomas J. Scanlan
Registrar: Brigid McCausland
Admissions: William J. Bisset, Jr.
Financial Aid: Edward J. Keough
Type: Comprehensive **Sex:** Coed **Affiliation:** Roman Catholic Church **Scores:** 99% SAT V 400+; 99% SAT M 400+ **% Accepted:** 57 **Admission Plans:** Early Admission; Early Decision Plan; Deferred Admission **Application Deadline:** April 15 **Application Fee:** $50.00 **H.S. Requirements:** High school diploma required; GED accepted **Costs Per Year:** Application fee: $50. Comprehensive fee: $29,675 includes full-time tuition ($20,350) and college room and board ($9325). **Scholarships:** Available **Calendar System:** Semester, Summer Session Available **Enrollment:** FT 2,879, PT 147, Grad 399 **Faculty:** FT 172, PT 160 **Student-Faculty Ratio:** 14:1 **Exams:** SAT I or ACT **% Receiving Financial Aid:** 61 **% Residing in College-Owned, -Operated, or -Affiliated Housing:** 54 **Library Holdings:** 211,376 **Regional Accreditation:** Middle State Association of Colleges and Schools **Credit Hours For Degree:** 128 credit hours, Bachelors **ROTC:** Army, Air Force **Professional Accreditation:** AACSB, ABET **Intercollegiate Athletics:** Baseball M; Basketball M & W; Cheerleading M & W; Crew M & W; Cross-Country Running M & W; Golf M; Lacrosse M & W; Rugby M; Soccer M & W; Softball W; Swimming and Diving W; Tennis M & W; Track and Field M & W; Volleyball M & W

MANHATTAN SCHOOL OF MUSIC
120 Claremont Ave.
New York, NY 10027-4698
Tel: (212)749-2802
Fax: (212)749-5471
E-mail: admission@msmnyc.edu
Web Site: http://www.msmnyc.edu/
President/CEO: Robert Sirota
Admissions: Amy Anderson
Financial Aid: Amy A. Anderson
Type: Comprehensive **Sex:** Coed **% Accepted:** 33 **Admission Plans:** Deferred Admission **Application Deadline:** December 01 **Application Fee:** $100.00 **H.S. Requirements:** High school diploma required; GED accepted. For those granted qualified admission: High school diploma or equivalent not required **Costs Per Year:** Application fee: $100. Comprehensive fee: $42,760 includes full-time tuition ($27,400), mandatory fees ($2560), and college room and board ($12,800). College room only: $8400. Part-time tuition: $1200 per credit. **Scholarships:** Available **Calendar System:** Semester, Summer Session Not available **Enrollment:** FT 408, PT 8, Grad 475 **Faculty:** FT 73, PT 292 **Student-Faculty Ratio:** 5:1 **Exams:** SAT I or ACT **% Receiving Financial Aid:** 70 **% Residing in College-Owned, -Operated, or -Affiliated Housing:** 57 **Library Holdings:** 107,000 **Regional Accreditation:** Middle State Association of Colleges and Schools

Credit Hours For Degree: 120 credits, Bachelors

MANHATTANVILLE COLLEGE

2900 Purchase St.
Purchase, NY 10577-2132
Tel: (914)694-2200
Free: 800-328-4553
Admissions: (914)323-5124
Fax: (914)694-1732
E-mail: admission@mville.edu
Web Site: http://www.manhattanville.edu/
President/CEO: Richard A. Berman
Registrar: Denise Carson
Admissions: Jose Flores
Financial Aid: Maria Barlaam

Type: Comprehensive **Sex:** Coed **% Accepted:** 60 **Admission Plans:** Early Admission; Early Decision Plan; Deferred Admission **Application Deadline:** March 01 **Application Fee:** $55.00 **H.S. Requirements:** High school diploma required; GED accepted **Costs Per Year:** Application fee: $55. Comprehensive fee: $39,550 includes full-time tuition ($26,920), mandatory fees ($1080), and college room and board ($11,550). College room only: $6860. Part-time tuition: $620 per credit. Part-time mandatory fees: $40. **Scholarships:** Available **Calendar System:** Semester, Summer Session Available **Enrollment:** FT 1,651, PT 130, Grad 1,025 **Faculty:** FT 90, PT 208 **Student-Faculty Ratio:** 11:1 **Exams:** ACT, SAT I or ACT, SAT I and SAT II **% Receiving Financial Aid:** 67 **% Residing in College-Owned, -Operated, or -Affiliated Housing:** 68 **Library Holdings:** 292,846 **Regional Accreditation:** Middle State Association of Colleges and Schools **Credit Hours For Degree:** 120 credits, Bachelors **Professional Accreditation:** NCATE **Intercollegiate Athletics:** Baseball M; Basketball M & W; Field Hockey W; Golf M; Ice Hockey M & W; Lacrosse M & W; Soccer M & W; Softball W; Swimming and Diving W; Tennis M & W; Volleyball W

MANNES COLLEGE THE NEW SCHOOL FOR MUSIC

150 West 85th St.
New York, NY 10024-4402
Tel: (212)580-0210
Free: 800-292-3040
Fax: (212)580-1738
Web Site: http://www.newschool.mannes.edu/
President/CEO: Dr. Joel Lester
Registrar: Joan Morgan
Admissions: Allison Scola
Financial Aid: Eileen F. Doyle

Type: Comprehensive **Sex:** Coed **Affiliation:** New School University **% Accepted:** 29 **Admission Plans:** Deferred Admission **Application Deadline:** December 01 **Application Fee:** $100.00 **H.S. Requirements:** High school diploma required; GED accepted **Costs Per Year:** Application fee: $100. Comprehensive fee: $37,880 includes full-time tuition ($25,560), mandatory fees ($570), and college room and board ($11,750). College room only: $8750. Full-time tuition and fees vary according to degree level and program. Room and board charges vary according to board plan. Part-time tuition: $842 per credit. **Scholarships:** Available **Calendar System:** Semester, Summer Session Available **Enrollment:** FT 188, PT 20, Grad 158 **Faculty:** FT 5, PT 251 **Student-Faculty Ratio:** 4:1 **% Receiving Financial Aid:** 35 **% Residing in College-Owned, -Operated, or -Affiliated Housing:** 13 **Library Holdings:** 4,137,530 **Regional Accreditation:** Middle State Association of Colleges and Schools **Credit Hours For Degree:** 128 credits, Bachelors

MARIA COLLEGE

700 New Scotland Ave.
Albany, NY 12208-1798
Tel: (518)438-3111
Web Site: http://www.mariacollege.edu/
President/CEO: Sr. Laureen Fitzgerald
Registrar: Dr. Kenneth Clough
Admissions: Laurie A. Gilmore
Financial Aid: Dr. Kenneth Clough

Type: Two-Year College **Sex:** Coed **% Accepted:** 72 **Admission Plans:** Early Admission **Application Deadline:** August 25 **Application Fee:** $35.00 **H.S. Requirements:** High school diploma required; GED accepted **Costs Per Year:** Application fee: $35. Tuition: $7800 full-time, $285 per credit part-time. Mandatory fees: $200 full-time. **Scholarships:** Available **Calendar System:** Semester, Summer Session Available **Enrollment:** FT 277, PT 511 **Faculty:** FT 29, PT 36 **Student-Faculty Ratio:** 10:1 **Exams:** SAT I or ACT **Library Holdings:** 56,746 **Regional Accreditation:** Middle State Association of Colleges and Schools **Credit Hours For Degree:** 64 credits, Associates **ROTC:** Air Force **Professional Accreditation:** AOTA, NLN

MARIST COLLEGE

3399 North Rd.
Poughkeepsie, NY 12601-1387
Tel: (845)575-3000
Free: 800-436-5483
Admissions: (845)575-3226
Fax: (845)471-6213
E-mail: admissions@marist.edu
Web Site: http://www.marist.edu/
President/CEO: Dr. Dennis J. Murray
Registrar: Judith Ivankovic
Admissions: Sean Kaylor
Financial Aid: Joseph Weglarz

Type: Comprehensive **Sex:** Coed **Scores:** 100% SAT V 400+; 100% SAT M 400+; 21% ACT 18-23; 66% ACT 24-29 **% Accepted:** 50 **Admission Plans:** Early Admission; Early Action; Deferred Admission **Application Deadline:** February 15 **Application Fee:** $40.00 **H.S. Requirements:** High school diploma required; GED accepted **Costs Per Year:** Application fee: $40. Comprehensive fee: $30,566 includes full-time tuition ($20,712), mandatory fees ($490), and college room and board ($9364). College room only: $5964. Part-time tuition: $475 per credit. Part-time mandatory fees: $65 per term. **Scholarships:** Available **Calendar System:** Semester, Summer Session Available **Enrollment:** FT 4,413, PT 483, Grad 848 **Faculty:** FT 201, PT 395 **Student-Faculty Ratio:** 15:1 **Exams:** SAT I or ACT **% Receiving Financial Aid:** 61 **% Residing in College-Owned, -Operated, or -Affiliated Housing:** 75 **Library Holdings:** 176,347 **Regional Accreditation:** Middle State Association of Colleges and Schools **Credit Hours For Degree:** 120 credits, Bachelors **ROTC:** Army **Professional Accreditation:** AACSB, CSWE, NAACLS **Intercollegiate Athletics:** Baseball M; Basketball M & W; Bowling M & W; Cheerleading M & W; Crew M & W; Cross-Country Running M & W; Equestrian Sports M & W; Fencing M & W; Ice Hockey M; Lacrosse M & W; Rugby M & W; Skiing (Downhill) M & W; Soccer M & W; Softball W; Swimming and Diving M & W; Tennis M & W; Track and Field M & W; Volleyball M & W; Water Polo W

MARYMOUNT MANHATTAN COLLEGE

221 East 71st St.
New York, NY 10021-4597
Tel: (212)517-0400
Free: 800-MARYMOUNT
Admissions: (212)517-0430
E-mail: admissions@mmm.edu
Web Site: http://www.mmm.edu/
President/CEO: Dr. Judson R. Shaver
Registrar: Dean Luz Torres
Admissions: James Rogers
Financial Aid: Maria DeInnocentiis

Type: Four-Year College **Sex:** Coed **Scores:** 100% SAT V 400+; 98% SAT M 400+; 40% ACT 18-23; 50% ACT 24-29 **% Accepted:** 77 **Admission Plans:** Early Decision Plan; Deferred Admission **Application Deadline:** Rolling **Application Fee:** $60.00 **H.S. Requirements:** High school diploma required; GED accepted **Costs Per Year:** Application fee: $60. Comprehensive fee: $31,728 includes full-time tuition ($18,748), mandatory fees ($890), and college room and board ($12,090). College room only: $10,090. Part-time tuition: $590 per credit. Part-time mandatory fees: $393 per term. **Scholarships:** Available **Calendar System:** Semester, Summer Session Available **Enrollment:** FT 1,603, PT 404 **Faculty:** FT 85, PT 230 **Student-Faculty Ratio:** 11:1 **Exams:** SAT I or ACT **% Receiving Financial Aid:** 63 **% Residing in College-Owned, -Operated, or -Affiliated Housing:** 21 **Library Holdings:** 102,000 **Regional Accreditation:** Middle State Association of Colleges and Schools **Credit Hours For Degree:** 120 credits, Bachelors

MEDAILLE COLLEGE

18 Agassiz Circle
Buffalo, NY 14214-2695
Tel: (716)884-3281
Fax: (716)884-0291
E-mail: gflorczak@medaille.edu
Web Site: http://www.medaille.edu/

President/CEO: Joseph W. Bascuas, PhD
Registrar: Kathleen Lazar
Admissions: Greg Florczak
Financial Aid: Rachel Barker
Type: Comprehensive **Sex:** Coed **Scores:** 98% SAT V 400+; 98% SAT M 400+ **% Accepted:** 73 **Admission Plans:** Early Admission; Deferred Admission **Application Deadline:** August 01 **Application Fee:** $25.00 **H.S. Requirements:** High school diploma or equivalent not required **Costs Per Year:** Application fee: $25. Comprehensive fee: $22,460 includes full-time tuition ($15,030) and college room and board ($7430). Full-time tuition varies according to location. Room and board charges vary according to housing facility. Part-time tuition: $532 per credit hour. Part-time tuition varies according to course load. **Scholarships:** Available **Calendar System:** Semester, Summer Session Available **Enrollment:** FT 1,580, PT 197, Grad 1,241 **Faculty:** FT 91, PT 221 **Student-Faculty Ratio:** 17:1 **Exams:** SAT I or ACT, SAT I **% Receiving Financial Aid:** 82 **% Residing in College-Owned, -Operated, or -Affiliated Housing:** 21 **Library Holdings:** 56,854 **Regional Accreditation:** Middle State Association of Colleges and Schools **Credit Hours For Degree:** 60 credit hours, Associates; 120 credit hours, Bachelors **ROTC:** Army **Intercollegiate Athletics:** Baseball M; Basketball M & W; Cheerleading M & W; Cross-Country Running W; Lacrosse M & W; Soccer M & W; Softball W; Volleyball M & W

MEDGAR EVERS COLLEGE OF THE CITY UNIVERSITY OF NEW YORK

1650 Bedford St.
Brooklyn, NY 11225-2298
Tel: (718)270-4900
Admissions: (718)270-6025
Web Site: http://www.mec.cuny.edu/
President/CEO: Dr. Edison O. Jackson
Registrar: Hayden Edwards
Admissions: Warren Heusner
Financial Aid: Louise Martin
Type: Four-Year College **Sex:** Coed **Affiliation:** City University of New York System **Scores:** 42.6% SAT V 400+; 45.5% SAT M 400+ **% Accepted:** 96 **Admission Plans:** Open Admission; Preferred Admission; Deferred Admission **Application Deadline:** Rolling **Application Fee:** $60.00 **H.S. Requirements:** High school diploma required; GED accepted **Costs Per Year:** Application fee: $60. State resident tuition: $4000 full-time, $170 per credit part-time. Nonresident tuition: $8640 full-time, $360 per credit part-time. Mandatory fees: $230 full-time, $78.35 per term part-time. **Scholarships:** Available **Calendar System:** Semester, Summer Session Available **Enrollment:** FT 3,134, PT 2,078 **Faculty:** FT 150, PT 189 **Student-Faculty Ratio:** 15:1 **Exams:** SAT I and SAT II or ACT **% Receiving Financial Aid:** 76 **Library Holdings:** 111,000 **Regional Accreditation:** Middle State Association of Colleges and Schools **Credit Hours For Degree:** 64 credits, Associates; 120 credits, Bachelors **Professional Accreditation:** ACBSP, NLN **Intercollegiate Athletics:** Basketball M; Cross-Country Running M & W; Soccer M; Track and Field M & W; Volleyball W

MEMORIAL HOSPITAL SCHOOL OF NURSING

600 Northern Blvd.
Albany, NY 12204
Tel: (518)471-3260
Fax: (518)447-3559
Web Site: http://www.nehealth.com/html/NEH_Schools.asp?L1=6&L2=31
President/CEO: Mary H. Martin
Type: Two-Year College **Sex:** Coed **Calendar System:** Semester **Professional Accreditation:** NYSBR

MERCY COLLEGE

555 Broadway
Dobbs Ferry, NY 10522-1189
Tel: (914)693-4500
Free: 800-MERCY-NY
Admissions: 800-MERCY-GO
Fax: (914)674-7382
E-mail: admissions@mercy.edu
Web Site: http://www.mercy.edu/
President/CEO: Dr. Lucie Lapovsky
Registrar: Debra Kenney
Admissions: Kathleen Jackson
Financial Aid: Neal Harris
Type: Comprehensive **Sex:** Coed **% Accepted:** 42 **Admission Plans:** Open Admission; Early Admission; Deferred Admission **Application Deadline:** Rolling **Application Fee:** $37.00 **H.S. Requirements:** High school diploma required; GED accepted. For adults: High school diploma or equivalent not required **Costs Per Year:** Application fee: $37. Comprehensive fee: $21,248 includes full-time tuition ($12,370), mandatory fees ($200), and college room and board ($8678). Part-time tuition: $520 per credit. Part-time mandatory fees: $100 per term. **Scholarships:** Available **Calendar System:** Semester, Summer Session Available **Enrollment:** FT 3,694, PT 1,942, Grad 3,903 **Faculty:** FT 175, PT 655 **Student-Faculty Ratio:** 17:1 **Exams:** SAT I **Library Holdings:** 322,610 **Regional Accreditation:** Middle State Association of Colleges and Schools **Credit Hours For Degree:** 60 credits, Associates; 120 credits, Bachelors **ROTC:** Air Force **Professional Accreditation:** AACN, AOTA, APTA, ASLHA, NACSCAO, CSWE **Intercollegiate Athletics:** Baseball M; Basketball M & W; Cross-Country Running M & W; Equestrian Sports M & W; Golf M; Soccer M & W; Softball W; Tennis M; Volleyball W

MESIVTA OF EASTERN PARKWAY RABBINICAL SEMINARY

510 Dahill Rd.
Brooklyn, NY 11218-5559
Tel: (718)438-1002
President/CEO: Joseph Epstein
Registrar: Sheila H. Saslow
Admissions: Rabbi Joseph Halberstadt
Financial Aid: Ira Lieberman
Type: Comprehensive **Sex:** Men **Affiliation:** Jewish **Calendar System:** Semester, Summer Session Not available **Library Holdings:** 7,500 **Professional Accreditation:** AARTS

MESIVTA TIFERETH JERUSALEM OF AMERICA

145 East Broadway
New York, NY 10002-6301
Tel: (212)964-2830
President/CEO: Stanley Bronfeld
Registrar: Rabbi Dickstein
Admissions: Rabbi Fishellis
Type: Comprehensive **Sex:** Men **Affiliation:** Jewish **Calendar System:** Semester **Professional Accreditation:** AARTS

MESIVTA TORAH VODAATH RABBINICAL SEMINARY

425 East Ninth St.
Brooklyn, NY 11218-5299
Tel: (718)941-8000
Fax: (718)941-8032
President/CEO: Rabbi Aharon Brown
Registrar: Rabbi Aharon Brown
Admissions: Rabbi Issac Braun
Financial Aid: Kayla Goldring
Type: Comprehensive **Sex:** Men **Affiliation:** Jewish **Admission Plans:** Preferred Admission; Early Admission; Deferred Admission **H.S. Requirements:** High school diploma required; GED accepted **Calendar System:** Semester, Summer Session Available **Library Holdings:** 40,000 **Credit Hours For Degree:** 128 credits, Bachelors **Professional Accreditation:** AARTS

METROPOLITAN COLLEGE OF NEW YORK

75 Varick St.
New York, NY 10013-1919
Tel: (212)343-1234
Fax: (212)343-8470
Web Site: http://www.metropolitan.edu/
President/CEO: Stephen Greenwald
Registrar: Anita O'Brien
Admissions: Fuquan Jackson
Financial Aid: Douglas Bucher
Type: Comprehensive **Sex:** Coed **% Accepted:** 98 **Admission Plans:** Deferred Admission **Application Deadline:** August 15 **Application Fee:** $30.00 **H.S. Requirements:** High school diploma required; GED accepted **Costs Per Year:** Application fee: $30. Tuition: $14,240 full-time, $505 per credit part-time. Mandatory fees: $300 full-time. Full-time tuition and fees vary according to degree level and program. Part-time tuition varies according to degree level and program. Tuition guaranteed not to increase for student's term of enrollment. **Scholarships:** Available **Calendar System:** Miscellaneous, Summer Session Available **Enrollment:** FT 1,119, PT 72, Grad 364 **Faculty:** FT 38, PT 259 **Student-Faculty Ratio:** 16:1 **Exams:**

Other, SAT I or ACT, SAT I **% Receiving Financial Aid:** 83 **Library Holdings:** 26,800 **Regional Accreditation:** Middle State Association of Colleges and Schools **Credit Hours For Degree:** 64 credits, Associates; 128 credits, Bachelors

MILDRED ELLEY
800 New Louden Rd.
Latham, NY 12110
Tel: (518)786-0855
Free: 800-622-6327
Admissions: (518)786-3171
Web Site: http://www.mildred-elley.edu/
President/CEO: Faith Ann Takes
Registrar: Irene Farrigan
Admissions: Michael Cahalan
Financial Aid: Joseph Moltzen
Type: Two-Year College **Scholarships:** Available **Enrollment:** FT 394 **Faculty:** FT 14, PT 17 **Student-Faculty Ratio:** 20:1 **Exams:** Other **Professional Accreditation:** ACICS

MIRRER YESHIVA
1795 Ocean Parkway
Brooklyn, NY 11223-2010
Tel: (718)645-0536
President/CEO: Rabbi Moses Kalmanowitz
Registrar: Vevorah Bernbaum
Financial Aid: Rachael Bernbaum
Type: Comprehensive **Sex:** Men **Affiliation:** Jewish **H.S. Requirements:** High school diploma or equivalent not required **Calendar System:** Semester **Professional Accreditation:** AARTS

MOHAWK VALLEY COMMUNITY COLLEGE
1101 Sherman Dr.
Utica, NY 13501-5394
Tel: (315)792-5400
Admissions: (315)792-5354
Fax: (315)792-5527
E-mail: dkennelty@mvcc.edu
Web Site: http://www.mvcc.edu/
President/CEO: Dr. Michael I. Schafer
Registrar: Rosemary Spetka
Admissions: Denis J. Kennelty
Financial Aid: Annette Broski
Type: Two-Year College **Sex:** Coed **Affiliation:** State University of New York System **% Accepted:** 90 **Admission Plans:** Open Admission; Early Admission; Early Decision Plan; Deferred Admission **Application Deadline:** Rolling **Application Fee:** $0.00 **H.S. Requirements:** High school diploma required; GED accepted **Costs Per Year:** Application fee: $0. State resident tuition: $2950 full-time, $115 per credit hour part-time. Nonresident tuition: $5900 full-time, $230 per credit hour part-time. Mandatory fees: $344 full-time, $1 per credit hour part-time, $35 per term part-time. College room and board: $6260. College room only: $3530. **Scholarships:** Available **Calendar System:** Semester, Summer Session Available **Enrollment:** FT 3,779, PT 2,205 **Faculty:** FT 136, PT 160 **Student-Faculty Ratio:** 24:1 **% Residing in College-Owned, -Operated, or -Affiliated Housing:** 6 **Library Holdings:** 91,000 **Regional Accreditation:** Middle State Association of Colleges and Schools **Credit Hours For Degree:** 62 credits, Associates **ROTC:** Army **Professional Accreditation:** ABET, AHIMA, CARC, NLN **Intercollegiate Athletics:** Baseball M; Basketball M & W; Bowling M & W; Cross-Country Running M & W; Golf M & W; Ice Hockey M; Lacrosse M; Soccer M & W; Softball W; Tennis M & W; Track and Field M & W; Volleyball W

MOLLOY COLLEGE
1000 Hempstead Ave.
Rockville Centre, NY 11571-5002
Tel: (516)678-5000; 888-4MOLLOY
Web Site: http://www.molloy.edu/
President/CEO: Dr. Drew Bogner
Registrar: Sue Fortman
Admissions: Marguerite Lane
Financial Aid: Ana Lockward
Type: Comprehensive **Sex:** Coed **Scores:** 97% SAT V 400+; 98% SAT M 400+ **% Accepted:** 65 **Admission Plans:** Early Admission; Early Decision Plan; Deferred Admission **Application Deadline:** Rolling **Application Fee:** $30.00 **H.S. Requirements:** High school diploma required; GED accepted **Costs Per Year:** Application fee: $30. Tuition: $15,760 full-time, $525 per credit part-time. Mandatory fees: $700 full-time. **Scholarships:** Available **Calendar System:** 4-1-4, Summer Session Available **Enrollment:** FT 1,875, PT 857, Grad 853 **Faculty:** FT 147, PT 328 **Student-Faculty Ratio:** 10:1 **Exams:** SAT I or ACT **% Receiving Financial Aid:** 81 **Library Holdings:** 135,000 **Regional Accreditation:** Middle State Association of Colleges and Schools **Credit Hours For Degree:** 64 credits, Associates; 128 credits, Bachelors **ROTC:** Army, Navy, Air Force **Professional Accreditation:** AACN, AHIMA, CARC, CSWE, JRCNMT **Intercollegiate Athletics:** Baseball M; Basketball M & W; Cross-Country Running M & W; Equestrian Sports M & W; Lacrosse M & W; Soccer M & W; Softball W; Tennis W; Volleyball W

MONROE COLLEGE (BRONX)
Monroe College Way
Bronx, NY 10468-5407
Tel: (718)933-6700
Free: 800-55MONROE
Web Site: http://www.monroecollege.edu/
President/CEO: Stephen J. Jerome
Registrar: Edward Schneiderman
Admissions: Brad Allison
Financial Aid: Howard Leslie
Type: Comprehensive **Sex:** Coed **% Accepted:** 61 **Admission Plans:** Early Admission; Deferred Admission **Application Deadline:** August 26 **Application Fee:** $35.00 **H.S. Requirements:** High school diploma or equivalent not required **Costs Per Year:** Application fee: $35. Comprehensive fee: $16,660 includes full-time tuition ($9160), mandatory fees ($600), and college room and board ($6900). Part-time tuition: $382 per credit hour. Part-time mandatory fees: $150 per term. **Scholarships:** Available **Calendar System:** Trimester, Summer Session Available **Enrollment:** FT 3,637, PT 648 **Faculty:** FT 57, PT 180 **Student-Faculty Ratio:** 21:1 **% Receiving Financial Aid:** 87 **% Residing in College-Owned, -Operated, or -Affiliated Housing:** 1 **Library Holdings:** 28,000 **Regional Accreditation:** Middle State Association of Colleges and Schools **Credit Hours For Degree:** 20 courses, Associates; 40 courses, Bachelors **Professional Accreditation:** AHIMA **Intercollegiate Athletics:** Baseball M; Basketball M & W; Soccer M; Softball W; Volleyball W

MONROE COLLEGE (NEW ROCHELLE)
434 Main St.
New Rochelle, NY 10801-6410
Tel: (914)632-5400
Free: 800-55MONROE
Admissions: (914)654-3200
Fax: (914)632-5462
Web Site: http://www.monroecollege.edu/
President/CEO: Marc M. Jerome
Admissions: Emerson Phillips
Financial Aid: Ramon Verdego, Jr.
Type: Four-Year College **Sex:** Coed **% Accepted:** 60 **Admission Plans:** Early Admission; Deferred Admission **Application Deadline:** August 26 **Application Fee:** $35.00 **H.S. Requirements:** High school diploma or equivalent not required. For criminal justice and medical assisting: High school diploma required; GED accepted **Costs Per Year:** Application fee: $35. Comprehensive fee: $16,660 includes full-time tuition ($9160), mandatory fees ($600), and college room and board ($6900). Room and board charges vary according to board plan. Part-time tuition: $382 per credit. Part-time mandatory fees: $150 per term. **Scholarships:** Available **Calendar System:** Trimester, Summer Session Available **Enrollment:** FT 1,574, PT 207 **Faculty:** FT 17, PT 55 **Student-Faculty Ratio:** 20:1 **% Residing in College-Owned, -Operated, or -Affiliated Housing:** 20 **Library Holdings:** 8,400 **Credit Hours For Degree:** 20 courses, Associates; 40 courses, Bachelors **Intercollegiate Athletics:** Baseball M; Basketball M & W; Soccer M; Softball W; Volleyball W

MONROE COMMUNITY COLLEGE
1000 East Henrietta Rd.
Rochester, NY 14623-5780
Tel: (585)292-2000
Fax: (585)427-2749
Web Site: http://www.monroecc.edu/
President/CEO: R. Thomas Flynn
Registrar: Elizabeth Ripton

Admissions: Anthony Felicetti
Financial Aid: Jerome S. St. Croix
Type: Two-Year College **Sex:** Coed **Affiliation:** State University of New York System **Admission Plans:** Open Admission; Preferred Admission; Early Admission **Application Fee:** $20.00 **H.S. Requirements:** High school diploma required; GED accepted **Scholarships:** Available **Calendar System:** Semester, Summer Session Available **Enrollment:** FT 9,398, PT 7,198 **Faculty:** FT 303, PT 889 **Student-Faculty Ratio:** 20:1 **Library Holdings:** 110,748 **Regional Accreditation:** Middle State Association of Colleges and Schools **Credit Hours For Degree:** 62 credits, Associates **ROTC:** Army, Air Force **Professional Accreditation:** ABET, ADA, AHIMA, JRCERT, JRCEMT, NLN **Intercollegiate Athletics:** Baseball M; Basketball M & W; Golf M; Ice Hockey M; Lacrosse M; Soccer M & W; Softball W; Swimming and Diving M & W; Tennis M & W; Volleyball W

MOUNT SAINT MARY COLLEGE
330 Powell Ave.
Newburgh, NY 12550-3494
Tel: (845)561-0800; 888-937-6762
Admissions: (845)569-3248
Fax: (845)562-6762
E-mail: ogrady@msmc.edu
Web Site: http://www.msmc.edu/
President/CEO: Sr. Ann Sakac
Registrar: Patty Kobes
Admissions: J. Randall Ognibene
Financial Aid: Susan Twomey
Type: Comprehensive **Sex:** Coed **Scores:** 90% SAT V 400+; 92% SAT M 400+; 69% ACT 18-23; 8% ACT 24-29 **% Accepted:** 79 **Admission Plans:** Deferred Admission **Application Deadline:** Rolling **Application Fee:** $35.00 **H.S. Requirements:** High school diploma required; GED accepted **Costs Per Year:** Application fee: $35. Comprehensive fee: $25,250 includes full-time tuition ($16,410), mandatory fees ($520), and college room and board ($8320). College room only: $4680. Full-time tuition and fees vary according to degree level. Room and board charges vary according to board plan, housing facility, and student level. Part-time tuition: $547 per credit hour. Part-time mandatory fees: $35 per term. Part-time tuition and fees vary according to degree level. **Scholarships:** Available **Calendar System:** Semester, Summer Session Available **Enrollment:** FT 1,615, PT 424, Grad 535 **Faculty:** FT 71, PT 150 **Student-Faculty Ratio:** 17:1 **Exams:** SAT I or ACT **% Receiving Financial Aid:** 73 **% Residing in College-Owned, -Operated, or -Affiliated Housing:** 41 **Library Holdings:** 113,676 **Regional Accreditation:** Middle State Association of Colleges and Schools **Credit Hours For Degree:** 120 credit hours, Bachelors **ROTC:** Army **Professional Accreditation:** AACN, NCATE **Intercollegiate Athletics:** Baseball M; Basketball M & W; Soccer M & W; Softball W; Swimming and Diving M & W; Tennis M & W; Volleyball W

NASSAU COMMUNITY COLLEGE
1 Education Dr.
Garden City, NY 11530-6793
Tel: (516)572-7500
Admissions: (516)572-7345
Web Site: http://www.ncc.edu/
President/CEO: Dr. Sean A. Fanelli
Registrar: Barry S. Fischler
Admissions: Craig Wright
Financial Aid: Dr. Evangeline Manjares
Type: Two-Year College **Sex:** Coed **Affiliation:** State University of New York System **% Accepted:** 92 **Admission Plans:** Deferred Admission **Application Deadline:** August 01 **Application Fee:** $30.00 **H.S. Requirements:** High school diploma required; GED accepted. For applicants 18 or over who have been out of high school over 1 year: High school diploma or equivalent not required **Costs Per Year:** Application fee: $30. State resident tuition: $3310 full-time, $138 per credit part-time. Nonresident tuition: $6620 full-time, $276 per credit part-time. Mandatory fees: $242 full-time. **Scholarships:** Available **Calendar System:** Semester, Summer Session Available **Enrollment:** FT 13,528, PT 7,451 **Faculty:** FT 457, PT 1,114 **Student-Faculty Ratio:** 18:1 **Exams:** SAT I or ACT **Library Holdings:** 171,938 **Regional Accreditation:** Middle State Association of Colleges and Schools **Credit Hours For Degree:** 64 credits, Associates **ROTC:** Army **Professional Accreditation:** ABET, ARCEST, ABFSE, APTA, CARC, JRCERT, NASM, NLN **Intercollegiate Athletics:** Baseball M; Basketball M & W; Bowling M & W; Cheerleading W; Cross-Country Running M & W; Equestrian Sports M & W; Football M; Golf M & W; Lacrosse M; Soccer M & W; Softball W; Tennis M & W; Track and Field M & W; Volleyball M & W; Wrestling M

NAZARETH COLLEGE OF ROCHESTER
4245 East Ave.
Rochester, NY 14618-3790
Tel: (585)389-2525
Admissions: (585)389-2860
Fax: (585)389-2826
E-mail: tkdarin@naz.edu
Web Site: http://www.naz.edu/
President/CEO: Dr. Robert A. Miller
Registrar: Nancy C. Grear
Admissions: Thomas K. DaRin
Financial Aid: Dr. Bruce Woolley
Type: Comprehensive **Sex:** Coed **Scores:** 99.3% SAT V 400+; 99.7% SAT M 400+; 38% ACT 18-23; 55.9% ACT 24-29 **% Accepted:** 79 **Admission Plans:** Early Admission; Early Action; Early Decision Plan; Deferred Admission **Application Deadline:** February 15 **Application Fee:** $40.00 **H.S. Requirements:** High school diploma required; GED accepted **Costs Per Year:** Application fee: $40. Comprehensive fee: $28,234 includes full-time tuition ($19,214), mandatory fees ($660), and college room and board ($8360). College room only: $4680. Room and board charges vary according to board plan and housing facility. Part-time tuition: $460 per credit hour. **Scholarships:** Available **Calendar System:** Semester, Summer Session Available **Enrollment:** FT 1,864, PT 193, Grad 1,063 **Faculty:** FT 135, PT 166 **Student-Faculty Ratio:** 13:1 **Exams:** SAT I or ACT **% Receiving Financial Aid:** 78 **% Residing in College-Owned, -Operated, or -Affiliated Housing:** 57 **Library Holdings:** 162,593 **Regional Accreditation:** Middle State Association of Colleges and Schools **Credit Hours For Degree:** 120 credit hours, Bachelors **ROTC:** Army, Air Force **Professional Accreditation:** AACN, APTA, ASLHA, CSWE, NASM **Intercollegiate Athletics:** Basketball M & W; Cheerleading W; Cross-Country Running M & W; Equestrian Sports M & W; Field Hockey W; Golf M & W; Lacrosse M & W; Soccer M & W; Softball W; Swimming and Diving M & W; Tennis M & W; Track and Field M & W; Volleyball M & W

THE NEW SCHOOL FOR GENERAL STUDIES
66 West 12th St.
New York, NY 10011-8603
Tel: (212)229-5600
Free: 800-862-5039
Admissions: (212)229-5630
Fax: (212)645-0661
E-mail: admissions@dialnsa.edu
Web Site: http://www.nsu.newschool.edu/
President/CEO: Dr. Ann-Louise Shapiro
Registrar: William Kimmel
Admissions: Gerianne Brusati
Financial Aid: Eileen Doyle
Type: Two-Year Upper Division **Sex:** Coed **Affiliation:** New School University **% Accepted:** 85 **Admission Plans:** Deferred Admission **Application Fee:** $40.00 **H.S. Requirements:** High school diploma required; GED accepted **Costs Per Year:** Application fee: $40. Comprehensive fee: $30,128 includes full-time tuition ($17,808), mandatory fees ($570), and college room and board ($11,750). College room only: $8750. Room and board charges vary according to board plan. Part-time tuition: $742 per credit. **Scholarships:** Available **Calendar System:** Semester, Summer Session Available **Enrollment:** FT 376, PT 337, Grad 937 **Faculty:** FT 36, PT 470 **Library Holdings:** 368,890 **Regional Accreditation:** Middle State Association of Colleges and Schools **Credit Hours For Degree:** 120 credits, Bachelors

THE NEW SCHOOL FOR JAZZ AND CONTEMPORARY MUSIC
55 West 13th St., 5th Floor
New York, NY 10011
Tel: (212)229-5896
Web Site: http://www.jazz.newschool.edu **Type:** Four-Year College **Sex:** Coed **Costs Per Year:** Comprehensive fee: $38,600 includes full-time tuition ($27,600) and college room and board ($11,000). Part-time tuition: $900 per credit. **Calendar System:** Semester

NEW YORK CAREER INSTITUTE
11 Park Place- 4th Floor
New York, NY 10007

Tel: (212)962-0002
Fax: (212)385-7574
E-mail: cmcmahon@nyci.com
Web Site: http://www.nyci.com/
President/CEO: Ivan Londa
Admissions: Cindy McMahon
Financial Aid: Melvin Eisner
Type: Two-Year College **Sex:** Coed **Application Fee:** $25.00 **H.S. Requirements:** High school diploma required; GED accepted **Costs Per Year:** Application fee: $25. Tuition: $9600 full-time, $300 per credit part-time. Mandatory fees: $35 full-time, $35 per term part-time. Full-time tuition and fees vary according to class time, course load, and degree level. Part-time tuition and fees vary according to class time, course load, and degree level. **Scholarships:** Available **Calendar System:** Trimester, Summer Session Available **Enrollment:** FT 618, PT 98 **Faculty:** FT 4, PT 24 **Library Holdings:** 5,010 **Credit Hours For Degree:** 60 credits, Associates **Professional Accreditation:** NYSBR

NEW YORK CITY COLLEGE OF TECHNOLOGY OF THE CITY UNIVERSITY OF NEW YORK

300 Jay St.
Brooklyn, NY 11201-2983
Tel: (718)260-5000
Admissions: (718)260-5500
Fax: (718)260-5198
Web Site: http://www.citytech.cuny.edu/
President/CEO: Dr. Fred Beaufait
Registrar: Jerry Berrol
Admissions: Joseph Lento
Financial Aid: Lamont Pittman
Type: Two-Year College **Sex:** Coed **Affiliation:** City University of New York System **Scores:** 81.6% SAT V 400+; 89.5% SAT M 400+ **Admission Plans:** Open Admission **Application Fee:** $40.00 **H.S. Requirements:** High school diploma required; GED accepted **Scholarships:** Available **Calendar System:** Semester, Summer Session Available **Enrollment:** FT 7,053, PT 4,327 **Faculty:** FT 297, PT 586 **Student-Faculty Ratio:** 18:1 **Library Holdings:** 177,569 **Regional Accreditation:** Middle State Association of Colleges and Schools **Credit Hours For Degree:** 60 credits, Associates; 120 credits, Bachelors **ROTC:** Air Force **Professional Accreditation:** ABET, ADA, COptA, JRCERT, NLN **Intercollegiate Athletics:** Basketball M & W; Cross-Country Running M & W; Soccer M; Track and Field M & W; Volleyball M & W

NEW YORK COLLEGE OF HEALTH PROFESSIONS

6801 Jericho Turnpike
Syosset, NY 11791-4413
Tel: (516)364-0808
Free: 800-922-7337
Fax: (516)364-0989
E-mail: rdodas@nycollege.edu
Web Site: http://www.nycollege.edu/
President/CEO: Lisa Pamintuan
Registrar: Denise Stendardo
Admissions: Mary Rodas
Financial Aid: Nanci Raines
Type: Two-Year College **Sex:** Coed **Admission Plans:** Deferred Admission **Application Fee:** $85.00 **H.S. Requirements:** High school diploma required; GED accepted **Costs Per Year:** Application fee: $85. Tuition: $9900 full-time, $275 per credit part-time. **Scholarships:** Available **Calendar System:** Trimester, Summer Session Available **Faculty:** FT 15, PT 80 **Library Holdings:** 4,600 **Credit Hours For Degree:** 72 credits, Associates **Professional Accreditation:** NACSCAO

NEW YORK INSTITUTE OF TECHNOLOGY

PO Box 8000
Old Westbury, NY 11568-8000
Tel: (516)686-7516
Free: 800-345-NYIT
Admissions: (516)686-7871
Fax: (516)686-7613
E-mail: admissions@aol.nuit.edu
Web Site: http://www.nyit.edu/
President/CEO: Dr. Edward Guiliano
Registrar: Guy Hildebrandt
Admissions: Steve Kerge
Financial Aid: Robbie de Leur
Type: University **Sex:** Coed **Scores:** 100% SAT V 400+; 100% SAT M 400+; 52% ACT 18-23; 28% ACT 24-29 **% Accepted:** 67 **Admission Plans:** Deferred Admission **Application Deadline:** Rolling **Application Fee:** $50.00 **H.S. Requirements:** High school diploma required; GED accepted **Costs Per Year:** Application fee: $50. Comprehensive fee: $30,040 includes full-time tuition ($18,696), mandatory fees ($540), and college room and board ($10,804). College room only: $5600. Full-time tuition and fees vary according to course load and program. Room and board charges vary according to board plan, housing facility, and location. Part-time tuition: $630 per credit. Part-time mandatory fees: $230 per term. Part-time tuition and fees vary according to course load. **Scholarships:** Available **Calendar System:** Semester, Summer Session Available **Enrollment:** FT 4,163, PT 2,323, Grad 3,468 **Faculty:** FT 217, PT 458 **Student-Faculty Ratio:** 16:1 **Exams:** SAT I or ACT **% Receiving Financial Aid:** 74 **% Residing in College-Owned, -Operated, or -Affiliated Housing:** 9 **Library Holdings:** 208,620 **Regional Accreditation:** Middle State Association of Colleges and Schools **Credit Hours For Degree:** 68 credits, Associates; 120 credits, Bachelors **ROTC:** Army, Air Force **Professional Accreditation:** ABET, ACF, ADtA, AOTA, AOsA, APTA, FIDER, NCATE **Intercollegiate Athletics:** Baseball M; Basketball M & W; Cross-Country Running M & W; Lacrosse M; Soccer M & W; Softball W; Track and Field M & W; Volleyball W

NEW YORK SCHOOL OF INTERIOR DESIGN

170 East 70th St.
New York, NY 10021-5110
Tel: (212)472-1500
Free: 800-336-9743
Fax: (212)472-1867
E-mail: david@nysid.edu
Web Site: http://www.nysid.edu/
President/CEO: Inge Heckel
Registrar: Jeffrey A. Namian
Admissions: David T. Sprouls
Financial Aid: Nina Bunchuk
Type: Comprehensive **Sex:** Coed **Scores:** 100% SAT V 400+; 100% SAT M 400+ **% Accepted:** 37 **Admission Plans:** Deferred Admission **Application Deadline:** March 01 **Application Fee:** $50.00 **H.S. Requirements:** High school diploma required; GED accepted **Costs Per Year:** Application fee: $50. Tuition: $18,600 full-time, $620 per credit part-time. Mandatory fees: $220 full-time, $110 per term part-time. **Scholarships:** Available **Calendar System:** Semester, Summer Session Available **Enrollment:** FT 168, PT 556, Grad 15 **Faculty:** FT 2, PT 77 **Student-Faculty Ratio:** 10:1 **Exams:** SAT I or ACT **% Receiving Financial Aid:** 40 **Library Holdings:** 12,000 **Credit Hours For Degree:** 66 credits, Associates; 132 credits, Bachelors **Professional Accreditation:** FIDER, NASAD

NEW YORK UNIVERSITY

70 Washington Square South
New York, NY 10012-1019
Tel: (212)998-1212
Admissions: (212)998-4500
Fax: (212)995-4902
E-mail: nyuadmit@uccvm.nyu.edu
Web Site: http://www.nyu.edu/
President/CEO: Dr. John E. Sexton
Registrar: Yechiel Rosenrauch
Admissions: Barbara Hall
Financial Aid: Antonio Del Bono, Jr.
Type: University **Sex:** Coed **Scores:** 100% SAT V 400+; 100% SAT M 400+; 50% ACT 24-29 **% Accepted:** 37 **Admission Plans:** Early Decision Plan; Deferred Admission **Application Deadline:** January 15 **Application Fee:** $65.00 **H.S. Requirements:** High school diploma required; GED accepted **Costs Per Year:** Application fee: $65. Comprehensive fee: $43,170 includes full-time tuition ($29,890), mandatory fees ($1800), and college room and board ($11,480). Full-time tuition and fees vary according to program. Room and board charges vary according to board plan and housing facility. Part-time tuition: $881 per credit. Part-time mandatory fees: $53 per credit, $267 per term. Part-time tuition and fees vary according to program. **Scholarships:** Available **Calendar System:** Semester, Summer Session Available **Enrollment:** FT 18,981, PT 1,585, Grad 16,047 **Faculty:** FT 1,952, PT 2,121 **Student-Faculty Ratio:** 11:1 **Exams:** SAT I or ACT, SAT II **% Receiving Financial Aid:** 54 **% Residing in College-Owned, -Operated, or -Affiliated Housing:** 54 **Library Holdings:** 5,235,527

Regional Accreditation: Middle State Association of Colleges and Schools **Credit Hours For Degree:** 60 credits, Associates; 128 credits, Bachelors **Professional Accreditation:** AACSB, ACEHSA, ACEJMC, ABA, ACNM, ADA, ADtA, ACSP, AOTA, APTA, APA, ASLHA, ACIPE, AALS, CEPH, CORE, CSWE, JRCEDMS, LCMEAMA, MACTE NASPAA, NLN **Intercollegiate Athletics:** Baseball M & W; Basketball M & W; Cheerleading M & W; Crew M & W; Cross-Country Running M & W; Equestrian Sports W; Fencing M & W; Golf M; Ice Hockey M; Lacrosse M & W; Soccer M & W; Softball W; Swimming and Diving M & W; Tennis M & W; Track and Field M & W; Ultimate Frisbee M & W; Volleyball M & W; Wrestling M

NIAGARA COUNTY COMMUNITY COLLEGE

3111 Saunders Settlement Rd.
Sanborn, NY 14132-9460
Tel: (716)614-6222
Admissions: (716)614-6201
Fax: (716)731-4053
E-mail: saunders@niagaracc.suny.edu
Web Site: http://www.niagaracc.suny.edu/
President/CEO: Dr. James Klyczek
Registrar: Julie Speer
Admissions: Kathy Saunders

Type: Two-Year College **Sex:** Coed **Affiliation:** State University of New York System **% Accepted:** 100 **Admission Plans:** Open Admission; Early Admission **Application Fee:** $0.00 **H.S. Requirements:** High school diploma required; GED accepted **Costs Per Year:** Application fee: $0. State resident tuition: $3096 full-time, $129 per credit hour part-time. Nonresident tuition: $4644 full-time, $194 per credit hour part-time. Mandatory fees: $300 full-time, $62 per term part-time. Full-time tuition and fees vary according to program. Part-time tuition and fees vary according to program. **Scholarships:** Available **Calendar System:** Semester, Summer Session Available **Enrollment:** FT 3,605, PT 1,967 **Faculty:** FT 126, PT 162 **Student-Faculty Ratio:** 17:1 **Library Holdings:** 93,055 **Regional Accreditation:** Middle State Association of Colleges and Schools **Credit Hours For Degree:** 62 credit hours, Associates **ROTC:** Army **Professional Accreditation:** ARCEST, AAMAE, APTA, JRCEET, JRCERT, NLN **Intercollegiate Athletics:** Baseball M; Basketball M & W; Golf M & W; Soccer M & W; Softball W; Volleyball W; Wrestling M

NIAGARA UNIVERSITY

Niagara University, NY 14109
Tel: (716)285-1212
Free: 800-462-2111
Admissions: (716)286-8700
Fax: (716)286-8355
E-mail: admissions@niagara.edu
Web Site: http://www.niagara.edu/
President/CEO: Rev. Joseph L. Levesque, CM
Admissions: Mike Konopski
Financial Aid: Maureen Salfi

Type: Comprehensive **Sex:** Coed **Affiliation:** Roman Catholic Church **Scores:** 97.9% SAT V 400+; 96.5% SAT M 400+; 60% ACT 18-23; 26% ACT 24-29 **% Accepted:** 79 **Admission Plans:** Early Admission; Deferred Admission **Application Deadline:** August 01 **Application Fee:** $30.00 **H.S. Requirements:** High school diploma required; GED accepted **Costs Per Year:** Application fee: $30. Comprehensive fee: $28,250 includes full-time tuition ($19,000), mandatory fees ($800), and college room and board ($8450). Part-time tuition: $635 per credit hour. Part-time mandatory fees: $20 per term. **Scholarships:** Available **Calendar System:** Semester, Summer Session Available **Enrollment:** FT 2,816, PT 126, Grad 911 **Faculty:** FT 137, PT 197 **Student-Faculty Ratio:** 17:1 **Exams:** SAT I or ACT **% Receiving Financial Aid:** 75 **% Residing in College-Owned, -Operated, or -Affiliated Housing:** 55 **Library Holdings:** 279,793 **Regional Accreditation:** Middle State Association of Colleges and Schools **Credit Hours For Degree:** 60 credit hours, Associates; 120 credit hours, Bachelors **ROTC:** Army **Professional Accreditation:** AACSB, CSWE, NCATE **Intercollegiate Athletics:** Baseball M; Basketball M & W; Cross-Country Running M & W; Golf M; Ice Hockey M & W; Lacrosse M & W; Soccer M & W; Softball W; Swimming and Diving M & W; Tennis M & W; Volleyball W

NORTH COUNTRY COMMUNITY COLLEGE

23 Santanoni Ave., PO Box 89
Saranac Lake, NY 12983-0089
Tel: (518)891-2915; 888-TRY-NCCC
Fax: (518)891-2915
Web Site: http://www.nccc.edu/
President/CEO: Dr. Gail Rogers Rice
Registrar: Sandra Baker
Admissions: Edwin Trathen
Financial Aid: Edwin Trathen

Type: Two-Year College **Sex:** Coed **Affiliation:** State University of New York System **Scores:** 77.91% SAT V 400+; 79.07% SAT M 400+; 42.86% ACT 18-23; 14.28% ACT 24-29 **% Accepted:** 94 **Admission Plans:** Open Admission; Preferred Admission; Early Admission; Early Decision Plan; Deferred Admission **Application Deadline:** Rolling **Application Fee:** $0.00 **H.S. Requirements:** High school diploma required; GED accepted **Costs Per Year:** Application fee: $0. State resident tuition: $3250 full-time, $160 per credit hour part-time. Nonresident tuition: $8000 full-time, $375 per credit hour part-time. Mandatory fees: $730 full-time, $37.50 per credit hour part-time, $225 per term part-time. College room and board: $8150. College room only: $4750. **Scholarships:** Available **Calendar System:** Semester, Summer Session Available **Enrollment:** FT 999, PT 606 **Faculty:** FT 46, PT 105 **Student-Faculty Ratio:** 17:1 **Exams:** SAT I or ACT **% Residing in College-Owned, -Operated, or -Affiliated Housing:** 7 **Library Holdings:** 58,556 **Regional Accreditation:** Middle State Association of Colleges and Schools **Credit Hours For Degree:** 62 semester hours, Associates **Professional Accreditation:** JRCERT **Intercollegiate Athletics:** Basketball M & W; Ice Hockey M; Soccer M & W; Softball W; Volleyball W

NYACK COLLEGE

One South Blvd.
Nyack, NY 10960-3698
Tel: (845)358-1710
Free: 800-33-NYACK
Fax: (845)358-3047
Web Site: http://www.nyack.edu
President/CEO: Dr. David E. Schroeder
Registrar: Sue K. Ho
Admissions: Bethany Ilsley
Financial Aid: Andres Valenzuela

Type: Comprehensive **Sex:** Coed **Affiliation:** The Christian and Missionary Alliance **Scores:** 80.8% SAT V 400+; 79.8% SAT M 400+; 53.6% ACT 18-23; 17.9% ACT 24-29 **Admission Plans:** Early Admission; Deferred Admission **Application Deadline:** Rolling **Application Fee:** $25.00 **H.S. Requirements:** High school diploma required; GED accepted. For home schooled applicants - transcripts of courses taken: High school diploma or equivalent not required **Costs Per Year:** Application fee: $25. Comprehensive fee: $23,000 includes full-time tuition ($15,400) and college room and board ($7600). Part-time tuition: $600 per credit. **Scholarships:** Available **Calendar System:** Semester, Summer Session Available **Enrollment:** FT 1,703, PT 327, Grad 616 **Faculty:** FT 107, PT 181 **Exams:** SAT I or ACT **% Receiving Financial Aid:** 83 **% Residing in College-Owned, -Operated, or -Affiliated Housing:** 33 **Library Holdings:** 127,271 **Regional Accreditation:** Middle State Association of Colleges and Schools **Credit Hours For Degree:** 63 credit hours, Associates; 126 credit hours, Bachelors **Professional Accreditation:** NASM **Intercollegiate Athletics:** Baseball M; Basketball M & W; Cheerleading M & W; Cross-Country Running M & W; Golf M; Soccer M & W; Softball W; Volleyball W

OHR HAMEIR THEOLOGICAL SEMINARY

Furnace Woods Rd.
Peekskill, NY 10566
Tel: (914)736-1500
President/CEO: Rabbi Ely Kanarek
Registrar: Kanarek
Admissions: Rabbi M. Z. Weisverg
Financial Aid: Gwartzman

Type: Comprehensive **Sex:** Men **Affiliation:** Jewish **H.S. Requirements:** High school diploma required; GED accepted **Calendar System:** Semester **Professional Accreditation:** AARTS

OHR SOMAYACH/JOSEPH TANENBAUM EDUCATIONAL CENTER

PO Box 334, 244 Route 306
Monsey, NY 10952-0334
Tel: (914)425-1370
Web Site: http://www.ohrsomayach.edu/
President/CEO: Rabbi Yisroel Rokowsky
Registrar: Miriam Grossman
Admissions: Rabbi Avrohom Braun

Financial Aid: Rabbi Yisroel Rokowsky
Type: Five-Year College **Sex:** Men **Affiliation:** Jewish **Admission Plans:** Early Admission **H.S. Requirements:** High school diploma required; GED accepted. For those who demonstrate ability to benefit from program: High school diploma or equivalent not required **Calendar System:** Semester, Summer Session Available **Enrollment:** FT 98 **Faculty:** FT 8, PT 10 **Library Holdings:** 2,300 **Credit Hours For Degree:** 132 credit hours, Bachelors **Professional Accreditation:** AARTS

OLEAN BUSINESS INSTITUTE
301 North Union St.
Olean, NY 14760-2691
Tel: (716)372-7978
Fax: (716)372-2120
Web Site: http://www.obi.edu/
President/CEO: Patrick McCarthy
Admissions: Lori Kincaid
Financial Aid: Valerie Goodwin
Type: Two-Year College **Sex:** Coed **Application Fee:** $25.00 **H.S. Requirements:** High school diploma required; GED accepted **Scholarships:** Available **Calendar System:** Semester, Summer Session Available **Faculty:** FT 10, PT 8 **Library Holdings:** 1,800 **Credit Hours For Degree:** 68 credit hours, Associates **Professional Accreditation:** ACICS

ONONDAGA COMMUNITY COLLEGE
4941 Onondaga Rd.
Syracuse, NY 13215-2099
Tel: (315)498-2622
Admissions: (315)498-2201
Fax: (315)469-2107
Web Site: http://www.sunyocc.edu/
President/CEO: Dr. Debbie L. Sydow
Registrar: Nancy Speck
Admissions: Monty R. Flynn
Financial Aid: Lorna Roberts
Type: Two-Year College **Sex:** Coed **Affiliation:** State University of New York System **Admission Plans:** Open Admission; Preferred Admission; Early Admission; Deferred Admission **Application Fee:** $30.00 **H.S. Requirements:** High school diploma required; GED accepted. For those who demonstrate ability to benefit from program: High school diploma or equivalent not required **Scholarships:** Available **Calendar System:** Semester, Summer Session Available **Faculty:** FT 162, PT 295 **Student-Faculty Ratio:** 16:1 **Exams:** SAT I and SAT II or ACT **Library Holdings:** 96,611 **Regional Accreditation:** Middle State Association of Colleges and Schools **Credit Hours For Degree:** 62 credits, Associates **ROTC:** Army, Air Force **Professional Accreditation:** ABET, ADA, AHIMA, APTA, CARC, NLN **Intercollegiate Athletics:** Baseball M; Basketball M & W; Lacrosse M; Soccer M; Softball W; Tennis M & W; Volleyball W

ORANGE COUNTY COMMUNITY COLLEGE
115 South St.
Middletown, NY 10940-6437
Tel: (845)344-6222
Admissions: (845)341-4030
Fax: (845)343-1228
Web Site: http://www.orange.cc.ny.us/
President/CEO: Dr. William Richards
Registrar: Neil Foley
Admissions: Margot St. Lawrence
Financial Aid: Sue Sheehan
Type: Two-Year College **Sex:** Coed **Affiliation:** State University of New York System **% Accepted:** 100 **Admission Plans:** Open Admission; Preferred Admission; Early Admission; Deferred Admission **Application Deadline:** August 01 **Application Fee:** $30.00 **H.S. Requirements:** High school diploma required; GED accepted. For 24 credit hour guideline program: High school diploma or equivalent not required **Costs Per Year:** Application fee: $30. State resident tuition: $3000 full-time, $125 per credit part-time. Nonresident tuition: $6000 full-time, $250 per credit part-time. Mandatory fees: $350 full-time. **Scholarships:** Available **Calendar System:** Semester, Summer Session Available **Enrollment:** FT 3,344, PT 3,097 **Faculty:** FT 137, PT 245 **Student-Faculty Ratio:** 16:1 **Library Holdings:** 101,342 **Regional Accreditation:** Middle State Association of Colleges and Schools **Credit Hours For Degree:** 62 credits, Associates **Professional Accreditation:** ADA, AOTA, APTA, ACBSP, NAACLS, NLN **Intercollegiate Athletics:** Baseball M; Basketball M & W; Golf M & W; Soccer M & W; Softball W; Tennis M & W; Volleyball W

PACE UNIVERSITY
One Pace Plaza
New York, NY 10038
Tel: (212)346-1200
Free: 800-874-7223
Admissions: (212)346-1781
Fax: (212)346-1040
E-mail: infoctr@pace.edu
Web Site: http://www.pace.edu/
President/CEO: Dr. David A. Caputo
Registrar: Lisa Kyer
Admissions: Dr. William N. Black
Financial Aid: Suzanne Tang
Type: University **Sex:** Coed **Scores:** 98% SAT V 400+; 99% SAT M 400+; 55% ACT 18-23; 37% ACT 24-29 **% Accepted:** 73 **Admission Plans:** Early Action; Deferred Admission **Application Deadline:** March 01 **Application Fee:** $45.00 **H.S. Requirements:** High school diploma required; GED accepted **Costs Per Year:** Application fee: $45. Comprehensive fee: $34,328 includes full-time tuition ($24,756), mandatory fees ($632), and college room and board ($8940). Full-time tuition and fees vary according to student level. Room and board charges vary according to board plan and housing facility. Part-time tuition: $710 per credit. Part-time mandatory fees: $240 per term. Part-time tuition and fees vary according to course load. Tuition guaranteed not to increase for student's term of enrollment. **Scholarships:** Available **Calendar System:** Semester, Summer Session Available **Enrollment:** FT 6,879, PT 2,049, Grad 4,471 **Faculty:** FT 478, PT 760 **Student-Faculty Ratio:** 15:1 **Exams:** SAT I or ACT **% Receiving Financial Aid:** 84 **% Residing in College-Owned, -Operated, or -Affiliated Housing:** 34 **Library Holdings:** 813,997 **Regional Accreditation:** Middle State Association of Colleges and Schools **Credit Hours For Degree:** 64 credits, Associates; 128 credits, Bachelors **ROTC:** Army **Professional Accreditation:** AACSB, ABET, AACN, ABA, APA, AALS, NCATE **Intercollegiate Athletics:** Baseball M; Basketball M & W; Cross-Country Running M & W; Equestrian Sports M & W; Football M; Golf M & W; Lacrosse M; Soccer W; Softball W; Swimming and Diving M & W; Tennis M & W; Track and Field M & W; Volleyball W

PARSONS THE NEW SCHOOL FOR DESIGN
66 Fifth Ave.
New York, NY 10011-8878
Tel: (212)229-8900; 877-528-3321
Fax: (212)229-8975
Web Site: http://www.parsons.newschool.edu/
President/CEO: Paul Goldberger
Type: Comprehensive **Sex:** Coed **Affiliation:** New School University **Scores:** 90.31% SAT V 400+; 96.88% SAT M 400+ **% Accepted:** 47 **Admission Plans:** Early Admission **Application Deadline:** March 01 **Application Fee:** $50.00 **H.S. Requirements:** High school diploma required; GED accepted **Costs Per Year:** Application fee: $50. Comprehensive fee: $40,930 includes full-time tuition ($28,560), mandatory fees ($620), and college room and board ($11,750). College room only: $8750. Room and board charges vary according to board plan and housing facility. Part-time tuition: $974 per credit. **Scholarships:** Available **Calendar System:** Semester, Summer Session Available **Enrollment:** FT 2,861, PT 211, Grad 430 **Faculty:** FT 72, PT 879 **Student-Faculty Ratio:** 8:1 **Exams:** SAT I or ACT **% Receiving Financial Aid:** 66 **% Residing in College-Owned, -Operated, or -Affiliated Housing:** 21 **Library Holdings:** 4,137,530 **Regional Accreditation:** Middle State Association of Colleges and Schools **Credit Hours For Degree:** 65 credits, Associates; 134 credits, Bachelors **Professional Accreditation:** NASAD

PAUL SMITH'S COLLEGE OF ARTS AND SCIENCES
PO Box 265
Paul Smiths, NY 12970-0265
Tel: (518)327-6000
Free: 800-421-2605
Admissions: (518)327-6227
Fax: (518)327-6060
Web Site: http://www.paulsmiths.edu/
President/CEO: Dr. John W. Mills
Registrar: Gary V. Morrison
Admissions: Melik Khoury
Financial Aid: June Peoples
Type: Four-Year College **Sex:** Coed **Scores:** 86% SAT V 400+; 84% SAT M 400+; 42% ACT 18-23; 22% ACT 24-29 **% Accepted:** 83 **Admission Plans:** Early Admission; Deferred Admission **Application Deadline:** Rolling **Ap-**

plication Fee: $30.00 **H.S. Requirements:** High school diploma required; GED accepted **Costs Per Year:** Application fee: $30. Comprehensive fee: $25,590 includes full-time tuition ($16,910), mandatory fees ($1260), and college room and board ($7420). College room only: $3710. Part-time tuition: $450 per credit hour. **Scholarships:** Available **Calendar System:** Semester, Summer Session Available **Enrollment:** FT 821, PT 25 **Faculty:** FT 55, PT 30 **Student-Faculty Ratio:** 14:1 **Exams:** SAT I or ACT **% Receiving Financial Aid:** 91 **% Residing in College-Owned, -Operated, or -Affiliated Housing:** 95 **Library Holdings:** 56,000 **Regional Accreditation:** Middle State Association of Colleges and Schools **Credit Hours For Degree:** 60 credit hours, Associates; 120 credit hours, Bachelors **Professional Accreditation:** ABET, ACF **Intercollegiate Athletics:** Basketball M & W; Cross-Country Running M & W; Soccer M & W; Volleyball W

PHILLIPS BETH ISRAEL SCHOOL OF NURSING
310 East 22nd St., 9th Floor
New York, NY 10010-5702
Tel: (212)614-6110
Admissions: (212)614-6176
Fax: (212)614-6109
E-mail: bstern@bethisraelny.org
Web Site: http://www.futurenursebi.org
President/CEO: Dr. Janet Mackin, EdD,RN
Registrar: Bernice Pass-Stern
Admissions: Bernice Pass-Stern
Financial Aid: Eli Moinester
Type: Two-Year College **Sex:** Coed **Scores:** 100% SAT V 400+; 100% SAT M 400+ **% Accepted:** 12 **Admission Plans:** Deferred Admission **Application Deadline:** April 01 **Application Fee:** $50.00 **H.S. Requirements:** High school diploma required; GED accepted **Costs Per Year:** Application fee: $50. Tuition: $12,300 full-time, $300 per credit part-time. Mandatory fees: $2180 full-time. **Scholarships:** Available **Calendar System:** Semester, Summer Session Not available **Faculty:** FT 10, PT 8 **Student-Faculty Ratio:** 9:1 **Exams:** Other, SAT I **Credit Hours For Degree:** 68 credits, Associates **Professional Accreditation:** NLN

PLAZA COLLEGE
7409 37th Ave.
Jackson Heights, NY 11372-6300
Tel: (718)779-1430
Fax: (718)779-1456
Web Site: http://www.plazacollege.edu/
President/CEO: Charles E. Callahan, Sr.
Registrar: Dr. Edward Dee
Admissions: Charles E. Callahan, III
Financial Aid: Peggy Chung
Type: Two-Year College **Sex:** Coed **Application Fee:** $25.00 **H.S. Requirements:** High school diploma required; GED accepted. For adult education program: High school diploma or equivalent not required **Scholarships:** Available **Calendar System:** Quarter, Summer Session Available **Exams:** SAT I and SAT II or ACT **Regional Accreditation:** Middle State Association of Colleges and Schools **Credit Hours For Degree:** 90 credits, Associates

POLYTECHNIC UNIVERSITY, BROOKLYN CAMPUS
Six Metrotech Center
Brooklyn, NY 11201-2990
Tel: (718)260-3600
Free: 800-POLYTECH
Admissions: (718)260-5938
Fax: (718)260-3136
E-mail: uadmit@poly.edu
Web Site: http://www.poly.edu/
President/CEO: Dr. David C. Chang
Registrar: Robert Pergolis
Admissions: Kathleen Davis
Financial Aid: Veronica Lukas
Type: University **Sex:** Coed **Scores:** 98% SAT V 400+; 100% SAT M 400+ **% Accepted:** 69 **Admission Plans:** Deferred Admission **Application Deadline:** February 01 **Application Fee:** $60.00 **H.S. Requirements:** High school diploma required; GED accepted **Costs Per Year:** Application fee: $60. Comprehensive fee: $37,150 includes full-time tuition ($27,640), mandatory fees ($1010), and college room and board ($8500). College room only: $6500. Full-time tuition and fees vary according to course load. Room and board charges vary according to housing facility. Part-time tuition: $880 per credit. Part-time mandatory fees: $320 per term. Part-time tuition and fees vary according to course load. **Scholarships:** Available **Calendar System:** Semester, Summer Session Available **Enrollment:** FT 1,451, PT 68, Grad 1,282 **Faculty:** FT 126, PT 140 **Student-Faculty Ratio:** 13:1 **Exams:** SAT I or ACT, SAT II **% Receiving Financial Aid:** 82 **% Residing in College-Owned, -Operated, or -Affiliated Housing:** 13 **Library Holdings:** 150,000 **Regional Accreditation:** Middle State Association of Colleges and Schools **Credit Hours For Degree:** 124 credits, Bachelors **ROTC:** Air Force **Professional Accreditation:** ABET **Intercollegiate Athletics:** Baseball M; Basketball M & W; Cross-Country Running M & W; Soccer M & W; Softball W; Tennis M & W; Track and Field M & W; Volleyball M & W

PRATT INSTITUTE
200 Willoughby Ave.
Brooklyn, NY 11205-3899
Tel: (718)636-3600
Free: 800-331-0834
Admissions: (718)636-3669
Fax: (718)636-3670
E-mail: jaaron@pratt.edu
Web Site: http://www.pratt.edu/
President/CEO: Dr. Thomas F. Schutte
Registrar: Pat Ciavarelli
Admissions: Judy Aaron
Financial Aid: Karen Price-Scott
Type: Comprehensive **Sex:** Coed **Scores:** 99% SAT V 400+; 100% SAT M 400+; 46% ACT 18-23; 39% ACT 24-29 **% Accepted:** 50 **Admission Plans:** Early Decision Plan **Application Deadline:** February 01 **Application Fee:** $40.00 **H.S. Requirements:** High school diploma required; GED not accepted. For HEOP program accepts GED: High school diploma required; GED accepted **Costs Per Year:** Application fee: $40. Comprehensive fee: $38,082 includes full-time tuition ($28,100), mandatory fees ($1130), and college room and board ($8852). College room only: $5552. Part-time tuition: $910 per credit. Part-time mandatory fees: $303 per term. **Scholarships:** Available **Calendar System:** Semester, Summer Session Available **Enrollment:** FT 2,898, PT 149, Grad 1,541 **Faculty:** FT 121, PT 776 **Student-Faculty Ratio:** 11:1 **Exams:** SAT I or ACT **% Receiving Financial Aid:** 78 **% Residing in College-Owned, -Operated, or -Affiliated Housing:** 55 **Library Holdings:** 172,000 **Regional Accreditation:** Middle State Association of Colleges and Schools **Credit Hours For Degree:** 66 credits, Associates; 132 credits, Bachelors **ROTC:** Army **Professional Accreditation:** ACSP, ALA, FIDER, NASAD **Intercollegiate Athletics:** Basketball M; Cross-Country Running M & W; Soccer M & W; Tennis M & W; Track and Field M & W; Volleyball W

PURCHASE COLLEGE, STATE UNIVERSITY OF NEW YORK
735 Anderson Hill Rd.
Purchase, NY 10577-1400
Tel: (914)251-6000
Admissions: (914)251-6300
E-mail: admissn@brick.purchase.edu
Web Site: http://www.purchase.edu/
President/CEO: Thomas Schwarz
Registrar: Patricia Bice
Admissions: Barbara Gianoplus
Financial Aid: Emilie Devine
Type: Comprehensive **Sex:** Coed **Affiliation:** State University of New York System **Scores:** 97% SAT V 400+; 97% SAT M 400+; 52% ACT 18-23; 34% ACT 24-29 **% Accepted:** 31 **Admission Plans:** Early Admission; Early Decision Plan; Deferred Admission **Application Deadline:** June 01 **Application Fee:** $40.00 **H.S. Requirements:** High school diploma required; GED accepted **Costs Per Year:** Application fee: $40. State resident tuition: $4350 full-time, $181 per credit part-time. Nonresident tuition: $10,610 full-time, $442 per credit part-time. Mandatory fees: $1258 full-time, $.85 per credit part-time, $48.08 per term part-time. College room and board: $8466. College room only: $5378. **Scholarships:** Available **Calendar System:** Semester, Summer Session Available **Enrollment:** FT 3,231, PT 457, Grad 138 **Faculty:** FT 143, PT 197 **Student-Faculty Ratio:** 11:1 **Exams:** SAT I or ACT **% Receiving Financial Aid:** 48 **% Residing in College-Owned, -Operated, or -Affiliated Housing:** 64 **Library Holdings:** 281,686 **Regional Accreditation:** Middle State Association of Colleges and Schools **Credit Hours For Degree:** 120 credits, Bachelors **Professional Accredita-**

tion: NASAD, NASM **Intercollegiate Athletics:** Baseball M & W; Basketball M & W; Cross-Country Running M & W; Soccer M & W; Softball M & W; Volleyball M & W

QUEENS COLLEGE OF THE CITY UNIVERSITY OF NEW YORK
65-30 Kissena Blvd.
Flushing, NY 11367-1597
Tel: (718)997-5000
Admissions: (718)997-5600
Fax: (718)997-5617
E-mail: admissions@qc.edu
Web Site: http://www.qc.edu/
President/CEO: Dr. James L. Muyskens
Registrar: Ray Rivera
Admissions: Vincent Angrisani
Financial Aid: Rena Smith-Kiawu
Type: Comprehensive **Sex:** Coed **Affiliation:** City University of New York System **Scores:** 90.9% SAT V 400+; 98.5% SAT M 400+ **% Accepted:** 43 **Admission Plans:** Deferred Admission **Application Deadline:** January 01 **Application Fee:** $65.00 **H.S. Requirements:** High school diploma required; GED accepted **Costs Per Year:** Application fee: $65. State resident tuition: $4000 full-time, $170 per credit part-time. Nonresident tuition: $10,800 full-time, $360 per credit part-time. Mandatory fees: $377 full-time, $120.10 per term part-time. **Scholarships:** Available **Calendar System:** Semester, Summer Session Available **Enrollment:** FT 8,816, PT 4,202, Grad 4,620 **Faculty:** FT 575, PT 696 **Student-Faculty Ratio:** 16:1 **Exams:** SAT I or ACT, SAT II **% Receiving Financial Aid:** 49 **Library Holdings:** 985,550 **Regional Accreditation:** Middle State Association of Colleges and Schools **Credit Hours For Degree:** 120 credits, Bachelors **ROTC:** Army, Navy **Professional Accreditation:** AAFCS, ADtA, ALA, ASLHA, NCATE **Intercollegiate Athletics:** Baseball M; Basketball M & W; Fencing W; Golf M; Soccer W; Softball M; Swimming and Diving M & W; Tennis M & W; Volleyball M & W; Water Polo M & W

QUEENSBOROUGH COMMUNITY COLLEGE OF THE CITY UNIVERSITY OF NEW YORK
222-05 56th Ave.
Bayside, NY 11364
Tel: (718)631-6262
Admissions: (718)631-6044
Fax: (718)281-5189
Web Site: http://www.qcc.cuny.edu/
President/CEO: Dr. Eduardo Martí
Registrar: Ann Tullio
Admissions: Winston Yarde
Financial Aid: Dr. Mary White
Type: Two-Year College **Sex:** Coed **Affiliation:** City University of New York System **Scores:** 33.3% SAT V 400+; 47.6% SAT M 400+ **Admission Plans:** Open Admission; Deferred Admission **Application Fee:** $40.00 **H.S. Requirements:** High school diploma required; GED accepted **Costs Per Year:** Application fee: $40. Area resident tuition: $2800 full-time. State resident tuition: $4560 full-time, $120 per credit part-time. Nonresident tuition: $4560 full-time, $190 per credit part-time. Mandatory fees: $266 full-time, $70 per term part-time. Full-time tuition and fees vary according to course load. Part-time tuition and fees vary according to course load. **Scholarships:** Available **Calendar System:** Semester, Summer Session Available **Enrollment:** FT 6,195, PT 6,603 **Faculty:** FT 291, PT 517 **Student-Faculty Ratio:** 21:1 **Exams:** Other **Library Holdings:** 140,000 **Regional Accreditation:** Middle State Association of Colleges and Schools **Credit Hours For Degree:** 60 credits, Associates **ROTC:** Army **Professional Accreditation:** ABET, ACBSP, NLN **Intercollegiate Athletics:** Baseball M; Basketball M & W; Cross-Country Running M & W; Soccer M; Softball W; Tennis M & W; Track and Field M & W; Volleyball M & W

RABBINICAL ACADEMY MESIVTA RABBI CHAIM BERLIN
1605 Coney Island Ave.
Brooklyn, NY 11230-4715
Tel: (718)377-0777
President/CEO: Rabbi Aaron Schechter
Admissions: Mayer Weinberger
Type: Comprehensive **Sex:** Men **Affiliation:** Jewish **Calendar System:** Semester **Credit Hours For Degree:** 150 credits, Bachelors **Professional Accreditation:** AARTS

RABBINICAL COLLEGE BETH SHRAGA
28 Saddle River Rd.
Monsey, NY 10952-3035
Tel: (914)356-1980
President/CEO: Rabbi Sidney Schiff
Admissions: Rabbi Schiff
Type: Comprehensive **Sex:** Men **Affiliation:** Jewish **Calendar System:** Semester **Professional Accreditation:** AARTS

RABBINICAL COLLEGE BOBOVER YESHIVA B'NEI ZION
1577 Forty-eighth St.
Brooklyn, NY 11219
Tel: (718)438-2018
President/CEO: Rabbi N. Halberstam
Registrar: J. Landau
Admissions: Israel Licht
Financial Aid: Moshe Dembitzer
Type: Comprehensive **Sex:** Men **Affiliation:** Jewish **Calendar System:** Semester **Professional Accreditation:** AARTS

RABBINICAL COLLEGE CH'SAN SOFER
1876 Fiftieth St.
Brooklyn, NY 11204
Tel: (718)236-1171
President/CEO: Rabbi Ehrenfeld
Type: Comprehensive **Sex:** Men **Affiliation:** Jewish **Calendar System:** Semester **Professional Accreditation:** AARTS

RABBINICAL COLLEGE OF LONG ISLAND
201 Magnolia Blvd.
Long Beach, NY 11561-3305
Tel: (516)431-7414
President/CEO: Rabbi Y. Feigelstock
Registrar: Hellman
Type: Comprehensive **Sex:** Men **Affiliation:** Jewish **H.S. Requirements:** High school diploma required; GED accepted **Calendar System:** Semester **Professional Accreditation:** AARTS

RABBINICAL COLLEGE OF OHR SHIMON YISROEL
215-217 Hewes St.
Brooklyn, NY 11211
Tel: (718)855-4092 **Type:** Four-Year College **Affiliation:** Jewish **Professional Accreditation:** AARTS

RABBINICAL SEMINARY ADAS YEREIM
185 Wilson St.
Brooklyn, NY 11211-7206
Tel: (718)388-1751
Admissions: Hersch Greenschweig
Type: Four-Year College **Sex:** Men **Calendar System:** Semester **Professional Accreditation:** AARTS

RABBINICAL SEMINARY OF AMERICA
76-01 147th St.
Flushing, NY 11367
Tel: (718)268-4700
President/CEO: Rabbi A. H. Leibowitz
Registrar: Rabbi Abraham Semmel
Admissions: Rabbi Abraham Semmel
Financial Aid: Debbie Mittel
Type: Comprehensive **Sex:** Men **Affiliation:** Jewish **Admission Plans:** Early Admission **Application Fee:** $0.00 **H.S. Requirements:** High school diploma required; GED accepted **Calendar System:** Semester **% Residing in College-Owned, -Operated, or -Affiliated Housing:** 90 **Library Holdings:** 30,000 **Credit Hours For Degree:** 150 credits, Bachelors **Professional Accreditation:** AARTS

RABBINICAL SEMINARY M'KOR CHAIM
1571 Fifty-fifth St.
Brooklyn, NY 11219

Tel: (718)851-0183
President/CEO: Rabbi B. Paler
Registrar: Rabbi Davidowitz
Admissions: Rabbi Benjamin Paler
Financial Aid: Rabbi Davidowitz
Type: Comprehensive **Sex:** Men **Affiliation:** Jewish **Calendar System:** Semester **Professional Accreditation:** AARTS

RENSSELAER POLYTECHNIC INSTITUTE
110 8th St.
Troy, NY 12180-3590
Tel: (518)276-6000
Free: 800-448-6562
Admissions: (518)276-6216
Fax: (518)276-4072
E-mail: admissions@rpi.edu
Web Site: http://www.rpi.edu/
President/CEO: Dr. Shirley Ann Jackson
Registrar: Sharon Kunkel
Admissions: Karen Long
Financial Aid: James Stevenson
Type: University **Sex:** Coed **Scores:** 100% SAT V 400+; 100% SAT M 400+; 22% ACT 18-23; 67% ACT 24-29 **% Accepted:** 78 **Admission Plans:** Early Admission; Early Decision Plan; Deferred Admission **Application Deadline:** January 01 **Application Fee:** $70.00 **H.S. Requirements:** High school diploma required; GED accepted **Costs Per Year:** Application fee: $70. Comprehensive fee: $41,288 includes full-time tuition ($31,000), mandatory fees ($857), and college room and board ($9431). College room only: $5290. Room and board charges vary according to board plan and location. Part-time tuition: $969 per credit hour. **Scholarships:** Available **Calendar System:** Semester, Summer Session Available **Enrollment:** FT 4,926, PT 25, Grad 2,290 **Faculty:** FT 400, PT 81 **Student-Faculty Ratio:** 14:1 **Exams:** Other, SAT I or ACT, SAT I and SAT II or ACT **% Receiving Financial Aid:** 70 **% Residing in College-Owned, -Operated, or -Affiliated Housing:** 55 **Library Holdings:** 309,171 **Regional Accreditation:** Middle State Association of Colleges and Schools **Credit Hours For Degree:** 124 credit hours, Bachelors **ROTC:** Army, Navy, Air Force **Professional Accreditation:** AACSB, ABET **Intercollegiate Athletics:** Archery M & W; Badminton M & W; Baseball M; Basketball M & W; Cheerleading M & W; Crew M & W; Cross-Country Running M & W; Equestrian Sports M & W; Fencing M & W; Field Hockey W; Football M; Golf M; Gymnastics M & W; Ice Hockey M & W; Lacrosse M & W; Racquetball M & W; Riflery M & W; Rugby M & W; Sailing M & W; Skiing (Cross-Country) M & W; Skiing (Downhill) M & W; Soccer M & W; Softball W; Squash M & W; Swimming and Diving M & W; Table Tennis M & W; Tennis M & W; Track and Field M & W; Volleyball M & W; Water Polo M & W; Weight Lifting M & W

ROBERTS WESLEYAN COLLEGE
2301 Westside Dr.
Rochester, NY 14624-1997
Tel: (585)594-6000
Free: 800-777-4RWC
Admissions: (585)594-6400
Fax: (585)594-6371
E-mail: admissions@roberts.edu
Web Site: http://www.roberts.edu/
President/CEO: Dr. John A. Martin
Registrar: Lesa Kohr
Admissions: Linda Kurtz Hoffman
Financial Aid: Stephen Field
Type: Comprehensive **Sex:** Coed **Affiliation:** Free Methodist Church of North America **Scores:** 96% SAT V 400+; 98% SAT M 400+; 49% ACT 18-23; 40% ACT 24-29 **% Accepted:** 82 **Admission Plans:** Early Admission; Deferred Admission **Application Deadline:** February 01 **Application Fee:** $35.00 **H.S. Requirements:** High school diploma required; GED accepted **Costs Per Year:** Application fee: $35. Comprehensive fee: $27,734 includes full-time tuition ($19,264), mandatory fees ($1022), and college room and board ($7448). College room only: $5280. Part-time tuition: $422 per credit. **Scholarships:** Available **Calendar System:** Semester, Summer Session Available **Enrollment:** FT 1,265, PT 143, Grad 540 **Faculty:** FT 98, PT 19 **Student-Faculty Ratio:** 13:1 **Exams:** SAT I or ACT **% Receiving Financial Aid:** 86 **% Residing in College-Owned, -Operated, or -Affiliated Housing:** 69 **Library Holdings:** 123,434 **Regional Accreditation:** Middle State Association of Colleges and Schools **Credit Hours For Degree:** 62 semester hours, Associates; 124 semester hours, Bachelors **ROTC:** Army, Air Force **Professional Accreditation:** CSWE, NASAD, NASM, NLN **Intercollegiate Athletics:** Basketball M & W; Cross-Country Running M & W; Golf M & W; Soccer M & W; Tennis M & W; Track and Field M & W; Volleyball W

ROCHESTER BUSINESS INSTITUTE
1630 Portland Ave.
Rochester, NY 14621
Tel: (716)266-0430
Admissions: (585)266-0430
Fax: (716)266-8243
Web Site: http://www.rochester-institute.com/
President/CEO: Carl Silvio
Registrar: Barbara Omeluch
Admissions: Deanna Pfluke
Type: Two-Year College **Sex:** Coed **Affiliation:** Corinthian Colleges, Inc **Admission Plans:** Early Admission; Deferred Admission **Application Fee:** $0.00 **H.S. Requirements:** High school diploma required; GED accepted **Scholarships:** Available **Calendar System:** Quarter, Summer Session Available **Enrollment:** FT 1,032, PT 191 **Faculty:** FT 12, PT 51 **Student-Faculty Ratio:** 18:1 **Exams:** Other **Library Holdings:** 7,500 **Credit Hours For Degree:** 96 quarter hours, Associates **Professional Accreditation:** ACICS

ROCHESTER INSTITUTE OF TECHNOLOGY
One Lomb Memorial Dr.
Rochester, NY 14623-5603
Tel: (585)475-2411
Admissions: (585)475-6631
Fax: (585)475-7424
E-mail: admissions@rit.edu
Web Site: http://www.rit.edu/
President/CEO: Dr. Albert J. Simone
Registrar: Joseph LoFredo
Admissions: Dr. Daniel Shelley
Financial Aid: Verna Hazen
Type: Comprehensive **Sex:** Coed **Scores:** 99% SAT V 400+; 100% SAT M 400+; 28% ACT 18-23; 54% ACT 24-29 **% Accepted:** 69 **Admission Plans:** Early Admission; Early Decision Plan; Deferred Admission **Application Deadline:** March 15 **Application Fee:** $50.00 **H.S. Requirements:** High school diploma required; GED accepted **Costs Per Year:** Application fee: $50. Comprehensive fee: $32,070 includes full-time tuition ($23,247), mandatory fees ($372), and college room and board ($8451). College room only: $4863. Full-time tuition and fees vary according to course load, program, and student level. Room and board charges vary according to board plan and housing facility. Part-time tuition: $518 per credit hour. Part-time mandatory fees: $31 per term. Part-time tuition and fees vary according to class time, course load, program, and student level. **Scholarships:** Available **Calendar System:** Quarter, Summer Session Available **Enrollment:** FT 11,440, PT 1,493, Grad 2,267 **Faculty:** FT 798, PT 406 **Student-Faculty Ratio:** 14:1 **Exams:** SAT I or ACT **% Receiving Financial Aid:** 61 **% Residing in College-Owned, -Operated, or -Affiliated Housing:** 60 **Library Holdings:** 408,000 **Regional Accreditation:** Middle State Association of Colleges and Schools **Credit Hours For Degree:** 90 credit hours, Associates; 180 credit hours, Bachelors **ROTC:** Army, Navy, Air Force **Professional Accreditation:** AACSB, ABET, CSWE, FIDER, JRCEDMS, JRCNMT, NASAD **Intercollegiate Athletics:** Baseball M; Basketball M & W; Bowling M & W; Cheerleading M & W; Crew M & W; Cross-Country Running M & W; Equestrian Sports M & W; Fencing M & W; Field Hockey W; Ice Hockey M & W; Lacrosse M & W; Rugby M & W; Skiing (Downhill) M & W; Soccer M & W; Softball W; Swimming and Diving M & W; Tennis M & W; Track and Field M & W; Ultimate Frisbee M & W; Volleyball M & W; Water Polo M & W; Wrestling M

ROCKLAND COMMUNITY COLLEGE
145 College Rd.
Suffern, NY 10901-3699
Tel: (914)574-4000
Free: 800-722-7666
Fax: (914)574-4433
Web Site: http://www.sunyrockland.edu/
President/CEO: Dr. Cliff L. Wood
Registrar: Karen Gualtieri
Financial Aid: Marvin Oppenheim

Type: Two-Year College **Sex:** Coed **Affiliation:** State University of New York System **Admission Plans:** Open Admission; Early Admission; Deferred Admission **Application Fee:** $25.00 **H.S. Requirements:** High school diploma or equivalent not required **Scholarships:** Available **Calendar System:** Semester, Summer Session Available **Enrollment:** FT 3,697, PT 2,852 **Faculty:** FT 126, PT 451 **Student-Faculty Ratio:** 17:1 **Exams:** SAT I or ACT **Library Holdings:** 122,194 **Regional Accreditation:** Middle State Association of Colleges and Schools **Credit Hours For Degree:** 60 credits, Associates **ROTC:** Navy, Air Force **Professional Accreditation:** AHIMA, AOTA, NLN **Intercollegiate Athletics:** Baseball M; Basketball M & W; Bowling M & W; Golf M; Soccer M & W; Softball W; Tennis M & W; Volleyball W

RUSSELL SAGE COLLEGE
45 Ferry St.
Troy, NY 12180-4115
Tel: (518)244-2000; 888-VERY SAGE
Admissions: (518)244-2018
Fax: (518)244-6880
E-mail: rscadmin@sage.edu
Web Site: http://www.sage.edu/rsc/index.php
Admissions: Beth Robertson
Type: Four-Year College **Sex:** Women **Affiliation:** The Sage Colleges **Scores:** 96.7% SAT V 400+; 97.7% SAT M 400+; 52.6% ACT 18-23; 26.3% ACT 24-29 **% Accepted:** 81 **Admission Plans:** Early Admission; Early Decision Plan; Deferred Admission **Application Deadline:** Rolling **Application Fee:** $30.00 **H.S. Requirements:** High school diploma required; GED accepted **Costs Per Year:** Application fee: $30. Comprehensive fee: $31,060 includes full-time tuition ($22,650), mandatory fees ($870), and college room and board ($7540). College room only: $3650. Part-time tuition: $755 per credit hour. **Scholarships:** Available **Calendar System:** Semester, Summer Session Available **Enrollment:** FT 759, PT 79 **Faculty:** FT 61, PT 34 **Student-Faculty Ratio:** 12:1 **Exams:** SAT I or ACT **% Receiving Financial Aid:** 86 **% Residing in College-Owned, -Operated, or -Affiliated Housing:** 47 **Library Holdings:** 337,694 **Regional Accreditation:** Middle State Association of Colleges and Schools **Credit Hours For Degree:** 120 credits, Bachelors **ROTC:** Army, Air Force **Professional Accreditation:** AOTA, NASAD, NCATE, NLN **Intercollegiate Athletics:** Basketball W; Soccer W; Softball W; Tennis W; Volleyball W

SAGE COLLEGE OF ALBANY
140 New Scotland Ave.
Albany, NY 12208-3425
Tel: (518)292-1730; 888-VERY-SAGE
Fax: (518)292-1912
E-mail: scaadm@sage.edu
Web Site: http://www.sage.edu/sca/index.php
Admissions: Elizabeth Robertson
Type: Four-Year College **Sex:** Coed **Affiliation:** The Sage Colleges **Scores:** 97% SAT V 400+; 95% SAT M 400+; 59% ACT 18-23; 17% ACT 24-29 **% Accepted:** 28 **Admission Plans:** Deferred Admission **Application Deadline:** Rolling **Application Fee:** $30.00 **H.S. Requirements:** High school diploma required; GED accepted **Costs Per Year:** Application fee: $30. Comprehensive fee: $24,410 includes full-time tuition ($16,000), mandatory fees ($870), and college room and board ($7540). College room only: $3890. Part-time tuition: $535 per credit hour. **Scholarships:** Available **Calendar System:** Semester, Summer Session Available **Enrollment:** FT 620, PT 411 **Faculty:** FT 37, PT 51 **Student-Faculty Ratio:** 12:1 **Exams:** SAT I or ACT **% Receiving Financial Aid:** 87 **% Residing in College-Owned, -Operated, or -Affiliated Housing:** 29 **Library Holdings:** 337,694 **Regional Accreditation:** Middle State Association of Colleges and Schools **Credit Hours For Degree:** 60 credits, Associates; 120 credits, Bachelors **Professional Accreditation:** NASAD

ST. BONAVENTURE UNIVERSITY
Route 417
St. Bonaventure, NY 14778-2284
Tel: (716)375-2000
Free: 800-462-5050
Admissions: (716)375-2400
Fax: (716)375-2005
E-mail: jdirisio@sbu.edu
Web Site: http://www.sbu.edu/
President/CEO: Sr. Margaret Carney, OSF
Registrar: Heather L. Jackson
Admissions: James M. DiRisio
Financial Aid: Elisabeth Rankin
Type: Comprehensive **Sex:** Coed **Affiliation:** Roman Catholic Church **Scores:** 98% SAT V 400+; 97% SAT M 400+; 59% ACT 18-23; 22% ACT 24-29 **% Accepted:** 86 **Admission Plans:** Early Admission; Deferred Admission **Application Deadline:** April 15 **Application Fee:** $30.00 **H.S. Requirements:** High school diploma required; GED accepted **Costs Per Year:** Application fee: $30. One-time mandatory fee: $325. Comprehensive fee: $30,275 includes full-time tuition ($21,650), mandatory fees ($865), and college room and board ($7760). College room only: $3960. Part-time tuition: $650 per credit hour. **Scholarships:** Available **Calendar System:** Semester, Summer Session Available **Enrollment:** FT 2,026, PT 115, Grad 473 **Faculty:** FT 153, PT 54 **Student-Faculty Ratio:** 16:1 **Exams:** SAT I or ACT, SAT II **% Receiving Financial Aid:** 71 **% Residing in College-Owned, -Operated, or -Affiliated Housing:** 77 **Library Holdings:** 287,622 **Regional Accreditation:** Middle State Association of Colleges and Schools **Credit Hours For Degree:** 120 credit hours, Bachelors **ROTC:** Army **Professional Accreditation:** AACSB, NCATE **Intercollegiate Athletics:** Baseball M; Basketball M & W; Cheerleading M & W; Cross-Country Running M & W; Field Hockey W; Golf M; Lacrosse M & W; Rugby M & W; Soccer M & W; Softball W; Swimming and Diving M & W; Tennis M & W; Volleyball M & W

ST. ELIZABETH COLLEGE OF NURSING
2215 Genesee St.
Utica, NY 13501
Tel: (315)798-8253
E-mail: mmonahan@stemc.org
Web Site: http://www.stemc.org/
President/CEO: Sr. Marianne Monahan
Admissions: Sr. Marianne Monahan
Type: Two-Year College **Sex:** Coed **Calendar System:** Semester **Regional Accreditation:** Middle State Association of Colleges and Schools

ST. FRANCIS COLLEGE
180 Remsen St.
Brooklyn Heights, NY 11201-4398
Tel: (718)522-2300
Admissions: (718)489-5200
Fax: (718)522-1274
Web Site: http://www.stfranciscollege.edu/
President/CEO: Dr. Frank J. Macchianola
Registrar: Adam Stone
Admissions: Br. George Larkin, OSF
Financial Aid: Arlene Scotto
Type: Four-Year College **Sex:** Coed **Affiliation:** Roman Catholic **Scores:** 79% SAT V 400+; 79% SAT M 400+ **% Accepted:** 92 **Admission Plans:** Deferred Admission **Application Deadline:** Rolling **Application Fee:** $35.00 **H.S. Requirements:** High school diploma required; GED accepted **Costs Per Year:** Application fee: $35. Comprehensive fee: $20,710 includes full-time tuition ($12,450), mandatory fees ($260), and college room and board ($8000). College room only: $6500. Full-time tuition and fees vary according to course level, course load, degree level, program, and student level. Part-time tuition: $440 per credit. Part-time mandatory fees: $70 per term. Part-time tuition and fees vary according to course level, course load, degree level, program, and student level. **Scholarships:** Available **Calendar System:** Semester, Summer Session Available **Enrollment:** FT 2,019, PT 317 **Faculty:** FT 71, PT 143 **Student-Faculty Ratio:** 18:1 **Exams:** SAT I **% Receiving Financial Aid:** 64 **Library Holdings:** 120,000 **Regional Accreditation:** Middle State Association of Colleges and Schools **Credit Hours For Degree:** 64 credits, Associates; 128 credits, Bachelors **Intercollegiate Athletics:** Baseball M; Basketball M & W; Cross-Country Running M & W; Soccer M; Softball W; Swimming and Diving M & W; Tennis M & W; Track and Field M & W; Volleyball W; Water Polo M & W

ST. JOHN FISHER COLLEGE
3690 East Ave.
Rochester, NY 14618-3597
Tel: (585)385-8000
Free: 800-444-4640
Admissions: (585)385-8064
Fax: (585)385-8129
E-mail: admissions@fisher.sjfc.edu
Web Site: http://www.sjfc.edu/

President/CEO: Dr. Donald Bain
Registrar: Julia Thomas
Admissions: Gerard J. Rooney
Financial Aid: Angela Monnat
Type: Comprehensive **Sex:** Coed **Affiliation:** Roman Catholic Church **Scores:** 97.7% SAT V 400+; 98.7% SAT M 400+; 51.6% ACT 18-23; 45.2% ACT 24-29 **% Accepted:** 65 **Admission Plans:** Early Admission; Early Decision Plan; Deferred Admission **Application Deadline:** Rolling **Application Fee:** $30.00 **H.S. Requirements:** High school diploma required; GED not accepted. For HEOP admission: High school diploma required; GED accepted **Costs Per Year:** Application fee: $30. Comprehensive fee: $27,860 includes full-time tuition ($19,300), mandatory fees ($260), and college room and board ($8300). College room only: $5400. Room and board charges vary according to board plan. Part-time tuition: $525 per credit hour. Part-time mandatory fees: $25 per term. Part-time tuition and fees vary according to course load. **Scholarships:** Available **Calendar System:** Semester, Summer Session Available **Enrollment:** FT 2,448, PT 248, Grad 832 **Faculty:** FT 152, PT 153 **Student-Faculty Ratio:** 14:1 **Exams:** SAT I or ACT **% Receiving Financial Aid:** 81 **% Residing in College-Owned, -Operated, or -Affiliated Housing:** 58 **Library Holdings:** 190,903 **Regional Accreditation:** Middle State Association of Colleges and Schools **Credit Hours For Degree:** 120 credit hours, Bachelors **ROTC:** Army, Navy, Air Force **Professional Accreditation:** AACSB, AACN, NCATE **Intercollegiate Athletics:** Baseball M; Basketball M & W; Cheerleading W; Football M; Golf M; Lacrosse M & W; Soccer M & W; Softball W; Tennis M & W; Volleyball W

ST. JOHN'S UNIVERSITY
8000 Utopia Parkway
Queens, NY 11439
Tel: (718)990-6161; 888-9ST JOHNS
Admissions: (718)990-2000
E-mail: admissions@stjohns.edu
Web Site: http://www.stjohns.edu/
President/CEO: Rev. Donald J. Harrington, CM
Registrar: Joseph Capobianco
Admissions: Matthew Whelan
Financial Aid: Jorge Rodriguez
Type: University **Sex:** Coed **Affiliation:** Roman Catholic Church **Scores:** 96% SAT V 400+; 96.8% SAT M 400+ **% Accepted:** 63 **Admission Plans:** Deferred Admission **Application Deadline:** Rolling **Application Fee:** $30.00 **H.S. Requirements:** High school diploma required; GED accepted **Costs Per Year:** Application fee: $30. Comprehensive fee: $36,440 includes full-time tuition ($24,400), mandatory fees ($570), and college room and board ($11,470). College room only: $7200. Part-time tuition: $813 per credit. Part-time mandatory fees: $205 per term. **Scholarships:** Available **Calendar System:** Semester, Summer Session Available **Enrollment:** FT 11,855, PT 3,237, Grad 3,846 **Faculty:** FT 599, PT 829 **Student-Faculty Ratio:** 18:1 **Exams:** SAT I or ACT, SAT I and SAT II, SAT I **% Receiving Financial Aid:** 81 **% Residing in College-Owned, -Operated, or -Affiliated Housing:** 17 **Library Holdings:** 14,452,250 **Regional Accreditation:** Middle State Association of Colleges and Schools **Credit Hours For Degree:** 60 credits, Associates; 126 credits, Bachelors **ROTC:** Army **Professional Accreditation:** AACSB, ABA, ACPhE, ACA, ALA, APA, ASLHA, ACIPE, AALS, CORE **Intercollegiate Athletics:** Baseball M; Basketball M & W; Cross-Country Running W; Fencing M & W; Golf M & W; Lacrosse M; Soccer M & W; Softball W; Tennis M & W; Track and Field W; Volleyball W

ST. JOSEPH'S COLLEGE, NEW YORK
245 Clinton Ave.
Brooklyn, NY 11205-3688
Tel: (718)636-6800
Admissions: (718)636-6868
Fax: (718)636-7242
Web Site: http://www.sjcny.edu/
President/CEO: Sr. Elizabeth A. Hill
Registrar: Barbara Janusz
Admissions: Theresa LaRocca-Meyer
Financial Aid: Carol Sullivan
Type: Comprehensive **Sex:** Coed **Scores:** 98% SAT V 400+; 99% SAT M 400+ **% Accepted:** 80 **Admission Plans:** Early Admission; Deferred Admission **Application Deadline:** August 15 **Application Fee:** $25.00 **H.S. Requirements:** High school diploma required; GED accepted **Costs Per Year:** Application fee: $25. Tuition: $11,854 full-time, $382 per credit part-time. Mandatory fees: $382 full-time, $13 per credit part-time, $30 per term part-time. **Scholarships:** Available **Calendar System:** Semester, Summer Session Available **Enrollment:** FT 708, PT 414, Grad 196 **Faculty:** FT 52, PT 85 **Student-Faculty Ratio:** 17:1 **Exams:** SAT I or ACT **% Receiving Financial Aid:** 60 **Library Holdings:** 100,000 **Regional Accreditation:** Middle State Association of Colleges and Schools **Credit Hours For Degree:** 128 credits, Bachelors **Professional Accreditation:** NLN **Intercollegiate Athletics:** Basketball M & W; Cross-Country Running M & W; Softball W; Volleyball M & W

ST. JOSEPH'S COLLEGE, SUFFOLK CAMPUS
155 West Roe Blvd.
Patchogue, NY 11772-2399
Tel: (631)447-3200
Admissions: (631)447-3219
Fax: (631)447-1734
Web Site: http://www.sjcny.edu/
President/CEO: Sr. Elizabeth A. Hill
Registrar: Geraldine Rothaug
Admissions: Gigi Lamens
Type: Comprehensive **Sex:** Coed **Affiliation:** St. Joseph's College, Brooklyn Campus **Scores:** 99% SAT V 400+; 98% SAT M 400+; 88% ACT 18-23; 6% ACT 24-29 **% Accepted:** 86 **Admission Plans:** Early Admission; Deferred Admission **Application Deadline:** Rolling **Application Fee:** $25.00 **H.S. Requirements:** High school diploma required; GED accepted **Costs Per Year:** Application fee: $25. Tuition: $12,424 full-time, $402 per credit part-time. Mandatory fees: $342 full-time, $13 per credit part-time, $207 per term part-time. Part-time tuition and fees vary according to course load. **Scholarships:** Available **Calendar System:** 4-1-4, Summer Session Available **Enrollment:** FT 2,929, PT 932, Grad 285 **Faculty:** FT 120, PT 264 **Student-Faculty Ratio:** 17:1 **Exams:** SAT I or ACT **% Receiving Financial Aid:** 79 **Library Holdings:** 82,600 **Regional Accreditation:** Middle State Association of Colleges and Schools **Credit Hours For Degree:** 128 credits, Bachelors **ROTC:** Army, Air Force **Intercollegiate Athletics:** Baseball M; Basketball M & W; Cross-Country Running M & W; Equestrian Sports M & W; Golf M; Soccer M & W; Softball W; Swimming and Diving W; Tennis M & W; Volleyball W

SAINT JOSEPH'S HOSPITAL HEALTH CENTER SCHOOL OF NURSING
206 Prospect Ave.
Syracuse, NY 13203
Tel: (315)448-5040
Fax: (315)448-5745
Web Site: http://www.sjhsyr.org/nursing/
President/CEO: Marianne Markowitz, RN
Admissions: JoAnne Kiggins
Type: Two-Year College **Sex:** Coed **Scores:** 100% SAT V 400+; 100% SAT M 400+; 99% ACT 18-23; 1% ACT 24-29 **% Accepted:** 55 **Admission Plans:** Deferred Admission **Application Fee:** $30.00 **H.S. Requirements:** High school diploma required; GED accepted **Costs Per Year:** Application fee: $30. Tuition: $8735 full-time. Mandatory fees: $1900 full-time. College room only: $3400. **Scholarships:** Available **Calendar System:** Semester **Faculty:** FT 16, PT 13 **Student-Faculty Ratio:** 9:1 **Exams:** SAT I or ACT **% Residing in College-Owned, -Operated, or -Affiliated Housing:** 25 **Library Holdings:** 4,500 **Credit Hours For Degree:** 66 credit hours, Associates

ST. LAWRENCE UNIVERSITY
Canton, NY 13617-1455
Tel: (315)229-5011
Free: 800-285-1856
Admissions: (315)229-5261
Fax: (315)229-5502
E-mail: admiss@music.stlawu.edu
Web Site: http://www.stlawu.edu/
President/CEO: Dr. Daniel F. Sullivan
Registrar: Carolyn Fillippi
Admissions: Terry Cowdrey
Financial Aid: Patricia Farmer
Type: Comprehensive **Sex:** Coed **Scores:** 99.3% SAT V 400+; 99.6% SAT M 400+ **% Accepted:** 59 **Admission Plans:** Early Decision Plan; Deferred Admission **Application Deadline:** February 15 **Application Fee:** $50.00 **H.S. Requirements:** High school diploma required; GED accepted **Costs Per Year:** Application fee: $50. Comprehensive fee: $40,330 includes full-time tuition ($31,935), mandatory fees ($215), and college room and board ($8180). College room only: $4400. Room and board charges vary accord-

ing to board plan. Part-time tuition: $3990 per course. **Scholarships:** Available **Calendar System:** Semester, Summer Session Available **Enrollment:** FT 2,111, PT 20, Grad 133 **Faculty:** FT 167, PT 23 **Student-Faculty Ratio:** 11:1 **% Receiving Financial Aid:** 66 **% Residing in College-Owned, -Operated, or -Affiliated Housing:** 96 **Library Holdings:** 555,364 **Regional Accreditation:** Middle State Association of Colleges and Schools **Credit Hours For Degree:** 33.5 units, Bachelors **ROTC:** Army, Air Force **Intercollegiate Athletics:** Baseball M; Basketball M & W; Crew M & W; Cross-Country Running M & W; Equestrian Sports M & W; Field Hockey W; Football M; Golf M & W; Ice Hockey M & W; Lacrosse M & W; Skiing (Cross-Country) M & W; Skiing (Downhill) M & W; Soccer M & W; Softball W; Squash M & W; Swimming and Diving M & W; Tennis M & W; Track and Field M & W; Volleyball W

ST. THOMAS AQUINAS COLLEGE
125 Route 340
Sparkill, NY 10976
Tel: (845)398-4000
Free: 800-999-STAC
Admissions: (845)398-4100
E-mail: vcrapanz@stac.edu
Web Site: http://www.stac.edu/
President/CEO: Dr. Margaret M. Fitzpatrick, SC
Registrar: Mildred Alexiou
Admissions: Vincent Crapanzano
Financial Aid: Anna Chrissotimos
Type: Comprehensive **Sex:** Coed **Scores:** 88% SAT V 400+; 87% SAT M 400+; 49% ACT 18-23; 16% ACT 24-29 **% Accepted:** 76 **Admission Plans:** Early Action; Deferred Admission **Application Deadline:** Rolling **Application Fee:** $30.00 **H.S. Requirements:** High school diploma required; GED accepted **Costs Per Year:** Application fee: $30. Comprehensive fee: $25,450 includes full-time tuition ($16,200), mandatory fees ($400), and college room and board ($8850). College room only: $4780. Part-time tuition: $540 per credit. Part-time mandatory fees: $100 per term. **Scholarships:** Available **Calendar System:** Semester, Summer Session Available **Enrollment:** FT 1,328, PT 658, Grad 208 **Faculty:** FT 61, PT 78 **Student-Faculty Ratio:** 16:1 **Exams:** SAT I or ACT **Library Holdings:** 96,444 **Regional Accreditation:** Middle State Association of Colleges and Schools **Credit Hours For Degree:** 120 credits, Bachelors **Professional Accreditation:** NCATE **Intercollegiate Athletics:** Baseball M; Basketball M & W; Cross-Country Running M & W; Golf M & W; Lacrosse W; Soccer M & W; Softball W; Volleyball W

SAINT VINCENT CATHOLIC MEDICAL CENTERS SCHOOL OF NURSING
175-05 Horace Harding Expressway
Fresh Meadows, NY 11365
Tel: (718)357-0500
Fax: (718)357-4683
Web Site: http://www.svcmcny.org/
President/CEO: Genevieve M. Jensen, RN
Registrar: Lorraine Sumner
Admissions: Nancy Wolinski
Financial Aid: Lorraine Sumner
Type: Two-Year College **Sex:** Coed **Admission Plans:** Deferred Admission **Application Fee:** $20.00 **H.S. Requirements:** High school diploma required; GED accepted **Scholarships:** Available **Calendar System:** Semester, Summer Session Not available **Enrollment:** FT 30, PT 63 **Faculty:** FT 10, PT 3 **Student-Faculty Ratio:** 10:1 **Exams:** Other **Library Holdings:** 2,326 **Credit Hours For Degree:** 64 credits, Associates

SAMARITAN HOSPITAL SCHOOL OF NURSING
2215 Burdett Ave.
Troy, NY 12180
Tel: (518)271-3285
Admissions: (518)271-3734
Fax: (518)271-3303
E-mail: deBlois@nehealth.com
Web Site: http://www.nehealth.com/
President/CEO: Theresa Pepe
Admissions: Jennifer DeBlois
Type: Two-Year College **Scholarships:** Available **Faculty:** FT 5, PT 4

SARAH LAWRENCE COLLEGE
1 Mead Way
Bronxville, NY 10708-5999
Tel: (914)337-0700
Free: 800-888-2858
Admissions: (914)395-2510
Fax: (914)395-2668
E-mail: slcadmit@mail.slc.edu
Web Site: http://www.sarahlawrence.edu/
President/CEO: Dr. Michele Tolela Myers
Registrar: Daniel Licht
Admissions: Thyra L. Briggs
Financial Aid: Heather McDonnell
Type: Comprehensive **Sex:** Coed **% Accepted:** 45 **Admission Plans:** Early Admission; Early Decision Plan; Deferred Admission **Application Deadline:** January 01 **Application Fee:** $60.00 **H.S. Requirements:** High school diploma or equivalent not required **Costs Per Year:** Application fee: $60. Comprehensive fee: $45,506 includes full-time tuition ($33,270), mandatory fees ($772), and college room and board ($11,464). College room only: $7600. Full-time tuition and fees vary according to course load. Room and board charges vary according to board plan. Part-time tuition: $1109 per credit. Part-time mandatory fees: $386 per term. Part-time tuition and fees vary according to course load. **Scholarships:** Available **Calendar System:** Semester, Summer Session Not available **Enrollment:** FT 1,266, PT 73, Grad 323 **Faculty:** FT 188, PT 34 **Student-Faculty Ratio:** 6:1 **% Receiving Financial Aid:** 50 **% Residing in College-Owned, -Operated, or -Affiliated Housing:** 86 **Library Holdings:** 193,581 **Regional Accreditation:** Middle State Association of Colleges and Schools **Credit Hours For Degree:** 120 credits, Bachelors **Intercollegiate Athletics:** Basketball M; Crew M & W; Equestrian Sports M & W; Softball W; Swimming and Diving W; Volleyball W

SCHENECTADY COUNTY COMMUNITY COLLEGE
78 Washington Ave.
Schenectady, NY 12305-2294
Tel: (518)381-1200
Admissions: (518)381-1370
Web Site: http://www.sunysccc.edu/
President/CEO: Gabriel J. Basil
Registrar: Yomika S. Bennett
Admissions: David Sampson
Financial Aid: Cynthia Russell
Type: Two-Year College **Sex:** Coed **Affiliation:** State University of New York System **Admission Plans:** Open Admission; Preferred Admission; Early Admission; Deferred Admission **Application Fee:** $0.00 **H.S. Requirements:** High school diploma required; GED accepted **Scholarships:** Available **Calendar System:** Semester, Summer Session Available **Enrollment:** FT 2,052, PT 2,088 **Faculty:** FT 65, PT 140 **Student-Faculty Ratio:** 22:1 **Exams:** SAT I or ACT **Library Holdings:** 85,000 **Regional Accreditation:** Middle State Association of Colleges and Schools **Credit Hours For Degree:** 60 credit hours, Associates **Professional Accreditation:** ACF, ACBSP, NASM **Intercollegiate Athletics:** Baseball M; Basketball M & W; Bowling M & W; Softball W

SCHOOL OF VISUAL ARTS
209 East 23rd St.
New York, NY 10010-3994
Tel: (212)592-2000
Free: 800-436-4204
Admissions: (212)592-2100
Fax: (212)592-2116
E-mail: jvega@sva.edu
Web Site: http://www.schoolofvisualarts.edu/
President/CEO: David Rhodes
Registrar: Jon Todd
Admissions: Javier Vega
Financial Aid: Javier Vega
Type: Comprehensive **Sex:** Coed **Scores:** 94% SAT V 400+; 93% SAT M 400+; 53% ACT 18-23; 32% ACT 24-29 **% Accepted:** 70 **Admission Plans:** Early Decision Plan; Deferred Admission **Application Deadline:** Rolling **Application Fee:** $50.00 **H.S. Requirements:** High school diploma required; GED accepted **Costs Per Year:** Application fee: $50. Comprehensive fee: $32,580 includes full-time tuition ($20,080), mandatory fees ($1000), and college room and board ($11,500). College room only: $9000. Full-time tuition and fees vary according to program. Room and board charges vary according to board plan, gender, housing facility, and location. Part-time tuition: $670 per credit. **Scholarships:** Available **Calendar System:** Semester, Summer Session Available **Enrollment:** FT 2,923, PT 240, Grad

412 **Faculty:** FT 120, PT 640 **Exams:** SAT I or ACT **% Receiving Financial Aid:** 55 **% Residing in College-Owned, -Operated, or -Affiliated Housing:** 27 **Library Holdings:** 71,490 **Regional Accreditation:** Middle State Association of Colleges and Schools **Credit Hours For Degree:** 120 credits, Bachelors **Professional Accreditation:** FIDER, NASAD

SH'OR YOSHUV RABBINICAL COLLEGE
1 Cedarlawn Ave.
Lawrence, NY 11559-1714
Tel: (718)327-2048
Admissions: (718)327-7244
Web Site: http://www.shoryoshuv.org/
President/CEO: Herschel Leiner
Registrar: Rabbi Y. Kurland
Admissions: Rabbi Avrohom Halpern
Financial Aid: Rabbi Y. Kurland
Type: Comprehensive **Sex:** Men **Affiliation:** Jewish **Admission Plans:** Open Admission **H.S. Requirements:** High school diploma or equivalent not required **Calendar System:** Semester, Summer Session Available **Exams:** SAT I **Library Holdings:** 20,000 **Professional Accreditation:** AARTS

SIENA COLLEGE
515 Loudon Rd.
Loudonville, NY 12211-1462
Tel: (518)783-2300; 888-AT-SIENA
Admissions: (518)783-2423
Fax: (518)783-4293
E-mail: admit@siena.edu
Web Site: http://www.siena.edu/
President/CEO: Fr. Kevin Mackin, OFM
Registrar: James Serbalik
Admissions: Heather Renault
Financial Aid: Mary Lawyer
Type: Four-Year College **Sex:** Coed **Affiliation:** Roman Catholic **Scores:** 100% SAT V 400+; 100% SAT M 400+; 33.3% ACT 18-23; 64.8% ACT 24-29 **% Accepted:** 61 **Admission Plans:** Early Admission; Early Action; Early Decision Plan; Deferred Admission **Application Deadline:** March 01 **Application Fee:** $50.00 **H.S. Requirements:** High school diploma required; GED accepted **Costs Per Year:** Application fee: $50. Comprehensive fee: $30,000 includes full-time tuition ($21,285), mandatory fees ($240), and college room and board ($8475). College room only: $5280. Part-time tuition: $410 per credit hour. Part-time mandatory fees: $50 per term. **Scholarships:** Available **Calendar System:** Semester, Summer Session Available **Enrollment:** FT 3,056, PT 280 **Faculty:** FT 180, PT 132 **Student-Faculty Ratio:** 14:1 **Exams:** SAT I or ACT **% Receiving Financial Aid:** 67 **% Residing in College-Owned, -Operated, or -Affiliated Housing:** 69 **Library Holdings:** 326,332 **Regional Accreditation:** Middle State Association of Colleges and Schools **Credit Hours For Degree:** 120 credit hours, Bachelors **ROTC:** Army, Air Force **Professional Accreditation:** CSWE **Intercollegiate Athletics:** Baseball M; Basketball M & W; Cheerleading W; Crew M & W; Cross-Country Running M & W; Equestrian Sports M & W; Field Hockey W; Golf M & W; Ice Hockey M; Lacrosse M & W; Rugby M & W; Soccer M & W; Softball W; Swimming and Diving W; Tennis M & W; Track and Field M & W; Volleyball M & W; Water Polo W

SIMMONS INSTITUTE OF FUNERAL SERVICE
1828 South Ave.
Syracuse, NY 13207
Tel: (315)475-5142
Free: 800-727-3536
Fax: (315)477-3817
Web Site: http://www.simmonsinstitute.com/
President/CEO: Maurice C. Wightman
Admissions: Vera Wightman
Financial Aid: Joseph Grossman
Type: Two-Year College **Sex:** Coed **Admission Plans:** Open Admission **Application Fee:** $50.00 **H.S. Requirements:** High school diploma required; GED accepted **Scholarships:** Available **Calendar System:** Semester **Enrollment:** FT 37, PT 23 **Faculty:** FT 1, PT 8 **Library Holdings:** 1,326 **Credit Hours For Degree:** 64 semester hours, Associates **Professional Accreditation:** ABFSE

SKIDMORE COLLEGE
815 North Broadway
Saratoga Springs, NY 12866-1632
Tel: (518)580-5000
Free: 800-867-6007
Admissions: (518)580-5570
Fax: (518)581-7462
E-mail: admissions@scott.skidmore.edu
Web Site: http://www.skidmore.edu/
President/CEO: Philip A. Glotzbach
Registrar: Ann L. Henderson
Admissions: Mary Lou W. Bates
Financial Aid: Robert D. Shorb
Type: Comprehensive **Sex:** Coed **Scores:** 99.4% SAT V 400+; 99.9% SAT M 400+; 12.7% ACT 18-23; 75.4% ACT 24-29 **% Accepted:** 44 **Admission Plans:** Early Admission; Early Decision Plan; Deferred Admission **Application Deadline:** January 15 **Application Fee:** $60.00 **H.S. Requirements:** High school diploma required; GED accepted **Costs Per Year:** Application fee: $60. Comprehensive fee: $41,779 includes full-time tuition ($32,340), mandatory fees ($319), and college room and board ($9120). College room only: $5100. Full-time tuition and fees vary according to course load. Room and board charges vary according to board plan and housing facility. Part-time tuition: $1080 per credit hour. Part-time mandatory fees: $25 per term. Part-time tuition and fees vary according to course load. **Scholarships:** Available **Calendar System:** Semester, Summer Session Available **Enrollment:** FT 2,524, PT 249, Grad 55 **Faculty:** FT 228, PT 93 **Student-Faculty Ratio:** 9:1 **Exams:** SAT I or ACT, SAT II **% Receiving Financial Aid:** 42 **% Residing in College-Owned, -Operated, or -Affiliated Housing:** 76 **Library Holdings:** 352,802 **Regional Accreditation:** Middle State Association of Colleges and Schools **Credit Hours For Degree:** 120 semester hours, Bachelors **ROTC:** Army, Air Force **Professional Accreditation:** CSWE, NASAD **Intercollegiate Athletics:** Baseball M; Basketball M & W; Crew M & W; Equestrian Sports M & W; Field Hockey W; Golf M; Ice Hockey M & W; Lacrosse M & W; Skiing (Downhill) M & W; Soccer M & W; Softball W; Swimming and Diving M & W; Tennis M & W; Volleyball W

STATE UNIVERSITY OF NEW YORK AT BINGHAMTON
PO Box 6000
Binghamton, NY 13902-6000
Tel: (607)777-2000
Admissions: (607)777-2171
E-mail: admit@binghamton.edu
Web Site: http://www.binghamton.edu/
President/CEO: Dr. Lois B. DeFleur
Registrar: Jennifer Schorr
Admissions: Cheryl S. Brown
Financial Aid: Dennis Chavez
Type: University **Sex:** Coed **Affiliation:** State University of New York System **Scores:** 100% SAT V 400+; 100% SAT M 400+; 21% ACT 18-23; 67% ACT 24-29 **% Accepted:** 43 **Admission Plans:** Early Admission; Early Action; Deferred Admission **Application Deadline:** Rolling **Application Fee:** $40.00 **H.S. Requirements:** High school diploma required; GED accepted **Costs Per Year:** Application fee: $40. State resident tuition: $4350 full-time, $181 per credit hour part-time. Nonresident tuition: $10,610 full-time, $442 per credit hour part-time. Mandatory fees: $1488 full-time, $133.15 per credit hour part-time. College room and board: $8150. College room only: $4970. Room and board charges vary according to board plan and housing facility. **Scholarships:** Available **Calendar System:** Semester, Summer Session Available **Enrollment:** FT 10,734, PT 440, Grad 2,844 **Faculty:** FT 537, PT 232 **Student-Faculty Ratio:** 21:1 **Exams:** SAT I or ACT **% Receiving Financial Aid:** 46 **% Residing in College-Owned, -Operated, or -Affiliated Housing:** 58 **Library Holdings:** 1,855,600 **Regional Accreditation:** Middle State Association of Colleges and Schools **Credit Hours For Degree:** 120 credits, Bachelors **ROTC:** Air Force **Professional Accreditation:** AACSB, ABET, AACN, APA, NASM, TEAC **Intercollegiate Athletics:** Badminton M & W; Baseball M; Basketball M & W; Bowling M & W; Crew M & W; Cross-Country Running M & W; Equestrian Sports M & W; Fencing M & W; Golf M; Ice Hockey M; Lacrosse M & W; Racquetball M & W; Rugby M & W; Skiing (Downhill) M & W; Soccer M & W; Softball W; Swimming and Diving M & W; Table Tennis M & W; Tennis M & W; Track and Field M & W; Volleyball M & W; Wrestling M

STATE UNIVERSITY OF NEW YORK AT BUFFALO
Capen Hall
Buffalo, NY 14260
Tel: (716)645-2000; 888-UB-ADMIT
Admissions: (716)645-6900
Fax: (716)645-6411

E-mail: ub-admissions@buffalo.edu
Web Site: http://www.buffalo.edu/
President/CEO: John B. Simpson, PhD
Registrar: Lisa R.B. Cino
Admissions: Patricia Armstrong
Financial Aid: Patrick Lyons
Type: University **Sex:** Coed **Affiliation:** State University of New York System **Scores:** 98% SAT V 400+; 100% SAT M 400+; 40% ACT 18-23; 49% ACT 24-29 **% Accepted:** 57 **Admission Plans:** Early Admission; Early Decision Plan **Application Fee:** $40.00 **H.S. Requirements:** High school diploma required; GED accepted **Costs Per Year:** Application fee: $40. State resident tuition: $4350 full-time, $181 per credit hour part-time. Nonresident tuition: $10,610 full-time, $442 per credit hour part-time. Mandatory fees: $1718 full-time, $76 per credit hour part-time. Part-time tuition and fees vary according to course load. College room and board: $7626. College room only: $4636. Room and board charges vary according to board plan and housing facility. **Scholarships:** Available **Calendar System:** Semester, Summer Session Available **Enrollment:** FT 16,911, PT 1,254, Grad 7,058 **Faculty:** FT 1,159, PT 589 **Student-Faculty Ratio:** 15:1 **Exams:** SAT I or ACT **% Receiving Financial Aid:** 50 **% Residing in College-Owned, -Operated, or -Affiliated Housing:** 38 **Library Holdings:** 3,360,036 **Regional Accreditation:** Middle State Association of Colleges and Schools **Credit Hours For Degree:** 120 credit hours, Bachelors **ROTC:** Army **Professional Accreditation:** AACSB, ABET, AACN, AANA, ABA, ACPhE, ADA, ADtA, ACSP, ALA, AOTA, APTA, APA, ASLHA, AALS, CORE, CSWE, JRCNMT, LCMEAMA, NAACLS NAIT, NASAD **Intercollegiate Athletics:** Baseball M; Basketball M & W; Crew W; Cross-Country Running M & W; Football M; Soccer M & W; Softball W; Swimming and Diving M & W; Tennis M & W; Track and Field M & W; Volleyball W; Wrestling M

STATE UNIVERSITY OF NEW YORK COLLEGE OF AGRICULTURE AND TECHNOLOGY AT COBLESKILL

Cobleskill, NY 12043
Tel: (518)255-5011
Free: 800-295-8988
Fax: (518)255-5333
Web Site: http://www.cobleskill.edu/
President/CEO: Dr. Thomas J. Haas
Registrar: Deirdre Dibble
Financial Aid: Richard Young
Type: Four-Year College **Sex:** Coed **Affiliation:** State University of New York System **Scores:** 82% SAT V 400+; 82% SAT M 400+; 49% ACT 18-23; 2% ACT 24-29 **% Accepted:** 74 **Admission Plans:** Early Admission; Deferred Admission **Application Deadline:** Rolling **Application Fee:** $40.00 **H.S. Requirements:** High school diploma required; GED accepted. For home schooled students: High school diploma or equivalent not required **Costs Per Year:** Application fee: $40. State resident tuition: $4350 full-time, $181 per credit hour part-time. Nonresident tuition: $7210 full-time, $300 per credit hour part-time. Mandatory fees: $995 full-time, $59.12 per credit hour part-time. Full-time tuition and fees vary according to course level and degree level. Part-time tuition and fees vary according to course level and degree level. College room and board: $7270. College room only: $4300. Room and board charges vary according to board plan and housing facility. **Scholarships:** Available **Calendar System:** Semester, Summer Session Available **Enrollment:** FT 2,372, PT 110 **Faculty:** FT 105, PT 44 **Student-Faculty Ratio:** 21:1 **Exams:** SAT I or ACT **% Receiving Financial Aid:** 68 **% Residing in College-Owned, -Operated, or -Affiliated Housing:** 62 **Library Holdings:** 76,919 **Regional Accreditation:** Middle State Association of Colleges and Schools **Credit Hours For Degree:** 66 credit hours, Associates; 126 credit hours, Bachelors **Professional Accreditation:** ACF, NAACLS **Intercollegiate Athletics:** Baseball M; Basketball M & W; Cross-Country Running M & W; Golf M & W; Lacrosse M; Soccer M & W; Softball W; Swimming and Diving M & W; Tennis M & W; Track and Field M & W; Volleyball W; Wrestling M

STATE UNIVERSITY OF NEW YORK COLLEGE OF AGRICULTURE AND TECHNOLOGY AT MORRISVILLE

PO Box 901
Morrisville, NY 13408-0901
Tel: (315)684-6000
Admissions: (315)684-6046
Fax: (315)684-6116
Web Site: http://www.morrisville.edu/
President/CEO: Dr. Ray Cross
Registrar: Marian Whitney
Admissions: Timothy Williams
Financial Aid: Thomas David
Type: Two-Year College **Sex:** Coed **Affiliation:** State University of New York System **Scores:** 73.6% SAT V 400+; 80% SAT M 400+ **Admission Plans:** Early Admission; Deferred Admission **Application Fee:** $40.00 **H.S. Requirements:** High school diploma required; GED accepted **Scholarships:** Available **Calendar System:** Semester, Summer Session Available **Enrollment:** FT 2,820, PT 449 **Faculty:** FT 128, PT 118 **Student-Faculty Ratio:** 19:1 **Exams:** SAT I and SAT II or ACT, SAT I **% Residing in College-Owned, -Operated, or -Affiliated Housing:** 60 **Library Holdings:** 99,258 **Regional Accreditation:** Middle State Association of Colleges and Schools **Credit Hours For Degree:** 64 credits, Associates; 128 credits, Bachelors **ROTC:** Army **Professional Accreditation:** ABET, ACBSP, NLN **Intercollegiate Athletics:** Baseball M; Basketball M & W; Cross-Country Running M & W; Equestrian Sports M & W; Field Hockey W; Football M; Ice Hockey M; Lacrosse M & W; Skiing (Downhill) M & W; Soccer M & W; Softball W; Swimming and Diving M & W; Tennis W; Track and Field M & W; Volleyball W; Wrestling M

STATE UNIVERSITY OF NEW YORK COLLEGE AT BROCKPORT

350 New Campus Dr.
Brockport, NY 14420-2997
Tel: (585)395-2211
Admissions: (585)395-2751
Fax: (585)395-5452
E-mail: admit@brockport.edu
Web Site: http://www.brockport.edu/
President/CEO: Dr. John B. Clark
Admissions: Bernard S. Valento
Financial Aid: J. Scott Atkinson
Type: Comprehensive **Sex:** Coed **Affiliation:** State University of New York System **Scores:** 98.67% SAT V 400+; 97.94% SAT M 400+; 55.5% ACT 18-23; 40.1% ACT 24-29 **% Accepted:** 46 **Admission Plans:** Preferred Admission; Deferred Admission **Application Deadline:** Rolling **Application Fee:** $40.00 **H.S. Requirements:** High school diploma required; GED accepted **Costs Per Year:** Application fee: $40. State resident tuition: $181 per credit part-time. Nonresident tuition: $429 per credit part-time. **Scholarships:** Available **Calendar System:** Semester, Summer Session Available **Enrollment:** FT 6,178, PT 787, Grad 1,519 **Faculty:** FT 320, PT 295 **Student-Faculty Ratio:** 19:1 **Exams:** SAT I or ACT **% Receiving Financial Aid:** 69 **% Residing in College-Owned, -Operated, or -Affiliated Housing:** 35 **Library Holdings:** 584,687 **Regional Accreditation:** Middle State Association of Colleges and Schools **Credit Hours For Degree:** 120 credit hours, Bachelors **ROTC:** Army, Navy, Air Force **Professional Accreditation:** AACSB, ABET, AACN, ACA, CSWE, JRCEPAT, NASD, NASPAA, NCATE, NRPA **Intercollegiate Athletics:** Baseball M; Basketball M & W; Cross-Country Running M & W; Field Hockey W; Football M; Gymnastics W; Ice Hockey M; Lacrosse M & W; Soccer M & W; Softball W; Swimming and Diving M & W; Tennis W; Track and Field M & W; Volleyball W; Wrestling M

STATE UNIVERSITY OF NEW YORK COLLEGE AT CORTLAND

PO Box 2000
Cortland, NY 13045
Tel: (607)753-2011
Admissions: (607)753-4711
Fax: (607)753-5999
E-mail: admissions@cortland.edu
Web Site: http://www.cortland.edu/
President/CEO: Dr. Erik J. Bitterbaum
Registrar: Donna Margine
Admissions: Mark Yacavone
Financial Aid: David Canaski
Type: Comprehensive **Sex:** Coed **Affiliation:** State University of New York System **Scores:** 100% SAT V 400+; 99% SAT M 400+ **% Accepted:** 48 **Admission Plans:** Early Admission; Early Decision Plan; Deferred Admission **Application Deadline:** Rolling **Application Fee:** $40.00 **H.S. Requirements:** High school diploma required; GED accepted **Costs Per Year:** Application fee: $40. State resident tuition: $4350 full-time, $181 per credit hour part-time. Nonresident tuition: $10,610 full-time, $442 per credit hour part-time. College room and board: $7850. College room only: $4460. **Scholarships:** Available **Calendar System:** Semester, Summer Session Available **Enrollment:** FT 5,731, PT 256, Grad 1,273 **Faculty:** FT 334, PT 221 **Student-Faculty Ratio:** 16:1 **Exams:** SAT I or ACT **% Receiving Financial Aid:** 63 **% Residing in College-Owned, -Operated, or -Affiliated Housing:** 50 **Library Holdings:** 82,257 **Regional Accreditation:** Middle State

Association of Colleges and Schools **Credit Hours For Degree:** 124 credits, Bachelors **ROTC:** Army, Air Force **Professional Accreditation:** JRCEPAT, NCATE, NRPA **Intercollegiate Athletics:** Baseball M; Basketball M & W; Cross-Country Running M & W; Field Hockey W; Football M & W; Golf W; Gymnastics W; Ice Hockey M & W; Lacrosse M & W; Racquetball M & W; Rugby M & W; Soccer M & W; Softball W; Swimming and Diving M & W; Tennis W; Track and Field M & W; Volleyball M & W; Wrestling M

STATE UNIVERSITY OF NEW YORK COLLEGE OF ENVIRONMENTAL SCIENCE AND FORESTRY

1 Forestry Dr.
Syracuse, NY 13210-2779
Tel: (315)470-6500
Free: 800-777-7373
Admissions: (315)470-6600
Fax: (315)470-6933
E-mail: esfinfo@lmailbox.syr.edu
Web Site: http://www.esf.edu/
President/CEO: Dr. Cornelius B. Murphy, Jr.
Registrar: Raymond Blaskiewicz
Admissions: Susan Sanford
Financial Aid: John E. View

Type: University **Sex:** Coed **Affiliation:** State University of New York System **Scores:** 99% SAT V 400+; 100% SAT M 400+; 30% ACT 18-23; 53% ACT 24-29 **% Accepted:** 66 **Admission Plans:** Early Admission; Early Action; Deferred Admission **Application Deadline:** Rolling **Application Fee:** $40.00 **H.S. Requirements:** High school diploma required; GED accepted **Costs Per Year:** Application fee: $40. State resident tuition: $4350 full-time, $181 per credit hour part-time. Nonresident tuition: $10,610 full-time, $442 per credit hour part-time. Mandatory fees: $682 full-time, $32.85 per credit hour part-time, $19.10 per year part-time. College room and board: $10,180. College room only: $5090. **Scholarships:** Available **Calendar System:** Semester, Summer Session Not available **Enrollment:** FT 1,348, PT 44, Grad 542 **Faculty:** FT 128, PT 17 **Student-Faculty Ratio:** 12:1 **Exams:** SAT I or ACT **% Receiving Financial Aid:** 88 **% Residing in College-Owned, -Operated, or -Affiliated Housing:** 40 **Library Holdings:** 137,367 **Regional Accreditation:** Middle State Association of Colleges and Schools **Credit Hours For Degree:** 75 credit hours, Associates; 121 credit hours, Bachelors **ROTC:** Army, Air Force **Professional Accreditation:** ABET, ASLA, SAF

STATE UNIVERSITY OF NEW YORK COLLEGE OF ENVIRONMENTAL SCIENCE & FORESTRY, RANGER SCHOOL

PO Box 48, 257 Ranger School Rd.
Wanakena, NY 13695
Tel: (315)848-2566
Free: 800-777-7373
Admissions: (315)470-6600
Fax: (315)470-6933
E-mail: esfinfo@esf.edu
Web Site: http://www.esf.edu/
President/CEO: Christopher L. Westbrook
Admissions: Susan H. Sanford

Type: Two-Year College **Sex:** Coed **Affiliation:** State University of New York System **% Accepted:** 76 **Admission Plans:** Deferred Admission **Application Deadline:** Rolling **Application Fee:** $40.00 **H.S. Requirements:** High school diploma required; GED not accepted **Costs Per Year:** Application fee: $40. State resident tuition: $4350 full-time, $181 per credit hour part-time. Nonresident tuition: $10,610 full-time, $442 per credit hour part-time. Mandatory fees: $527. College room and board: $8400. College room only: $2450. **Scholarships:** Available **Calendar System:** Semester, Summer Session Not available **Enrollment:** FT 43 **Faculty:** FT 5, PT 0 **Student-Faculty Ratio:** 8:1 **Exams:** SAT I or ACT **% Residing in College-Owned, -Operated, or -Affiliated Housing:** 100 **Library Holdings:** 5,000 **Regional Accreditation:** Middle State Association of Colleges and Schools **Credit Hours For Degree:** 75 credit hours, Associates **Professional Accreditation:** ABET, SAF

STATE UNIVERSITY OF NEW YORK COLLEGE AT GENESEO

1 College Circle
Geneseo, NY 14454-1401
Tel: (585)245-5211; (866)245-5211
Admissions: (585)245-5571
Fax: (585)245-5005
E-mail: admissions@geneseo.edu
Web Site: http://www.geneseo.edu/
President/CEO: Dr. Christopher Dahl
Registrar: Denise Sullivan
Admissions: Kris Shay
Financial Aid: Archie Cureton

Type: Comprehensive **Sex:** Coed **Affiliation:** State University of New York System **Scores:** 100% SAT V 400+; 100% SAT M 400+; 6% ACT 18-23; 81% ACT 24-29 **% Accepted:** 41 **Admission Plans:** Early Admission; Early Decision Plan; Deferred Admission **Application Deadline:** January 15 **Application Fee:** $40.00 **H.S. Requirements:** High school diploma required; GED accepted **Costs Per Year:** Application fee: $40. State resident tuition: $4350 full-time, $181 per credit hour part-time. Nonresident tuition: $10,610 full-time, $442 per credit hour part-time. Mandatory fees: $1170 full-time, $48.55 per credit hour part-time. College room and board: $7390. **Scholarships:** Available **Calendar System:** Semester, Summer Session Available **Enrollment:** FT 5,174, PT 132, Grad 178 **Faculty:** FT 242, PT 88 **Student-Faculty Ratio:** 19:1 **Exams:** SAT I or ACT **% Receiving Financial Aid:** 47 **% Residing in College-Owned, -Operated, or -Affiliated Housing:** 55 **Library Holdings:** 576,700 **Regional Accreditation:** Middle State Association of Colleges and Schools **Credit Hours For Degree:** 120 semester hours, Bachelors **ROTC:** Army, Air Force **Professional Accreditation:** AACSB, ASLHA, NCATE **Intercollegiate Athletics:** Basketball M & W; Crew M & W; Cross-Country Running M & W; Equestrian Sports M & W; Field Hockey W; Ice Hockey M; Lacrosse M & W; Racquetball M & W; Rugby M & W; Sailing M & W; Soccer M & W; Softball W; Squash M & W; Swimming and Diving M & W; Tennis W; Track and Field M & W; Ultimate Frisbee M & W; Volleyball M & W

STATE UNIVERSITY OF NEW YORK COLLEGE AT OLD WESTBURY

PO Box 210
Old Westbury, NY 11568-0210
Tel: (516)876-3000
Admissions: (516)876-3073
Fax: (516)876-3307
Web Site: http://www.oldwestbury.edu/
President/CEO: Dr. Calvin O. Butts, III
Registrar: Patricia Smith
Admissions: Mary Bell
Financial Aid: Delores James

Type: Comprehensive **Sex:** Coed **Affiliation:** State University of New York System **Scores:** 96% SAT V 400+; 96% SAT M 400+; 53% ACT 18-23; 13% ACT 24-29 **% Accepted:** 59 **Admission Plans:** Early Admission; Early Decision Plan; Deferred Admission **Application Deadline:** Rolling **Application Fee:** $40.00 **H.S. Requirements:** High school diploma required; GED accepted **Costs Per Year:** Application fee: $40. State resident tuition: $4350 full-time, $181 per credit part-time. Nonresident tuition: $10,610 full-time, $442 per credit part-time. Mandatory fees: $722 full-time. College room and board: $8083. College room only: $5793. **Scholarships:** Available **Calendar System:** Semester, Summer Session Available **Enrollment:** FT 2,717, PT 656, Grad 25 **Faculty:** FT 129, PT 124 **Student-Faculty Ratio:** 17:1 **Exams:** SAT I or ACT **% Residing in College-Owned, -Operated, or -Affiliated Housing:** 25 **Library Holdings:** 196,000 **Regional Accreditation:** Middle State Association of Colleges and Schools **Credit Hours For Degree:** 120 credits, Bachelors **ROTC:** Army, Air Force **Intercollegiate Athletics:** Baseball M; Basketball M & W; Cross-Country Running M & W; Soccer M; Softball W; Swimming and Diving M & W; Volleyball W

STATE UNIVERSITY OF NEW YORK COLLEGE AT ONEONTA

Ravine Parkway
Oneonta, NY 13820-4015
Tel: (607)436-3500
Free: 800-SUNY-123
Admissions: (607)436-2524
Fax: (607)436-3074
Web Site: http://www.oneonta.edu/
President/CEO: Dr. Alan B. Donovan
Registrar: Bill Grau
Admissions: Karen A. Brown
Financial Aid: Bill Goodhue

Type: Comprehensive **Sex:** Coed **Affiliation:** State University of New York System **Scores:** 100% SAT V 400+; 100% SAT M 400+; 57% ACT 18-23; 38% ACT 24-29 **% Accepted:** 45 **Admission Plans:** Early Admission; Early Action; Deferred Admission **Application Deadline:** Rolling **Application Fee:** $40.00 **H.S. Requirements:** High school diploma required; GED accepted **Costs Per Year:** Application fee: $40. State resident tuition: $4350 full-time,

$181 per semester hour part-time. Nonresident tuition: $10,610 full-time, $442 per semester hour part-time. Mandatory fees: $1017 full-time, $34.35 per semester hour part-time. College room and board: $7538. College room only: $4378. **Scholarships:** Available **Calendar System:** Semester, Summer Session Available **Enrollment:** FT 5,488, PT 161, Grad 211 **Faculty:** FT 252, PT 215 **Student-Faculty Ratio:** 17:1 **Exams:** SAT I or ACT **% Receiving Financial Aid:** 57 **% Residing in College-Owned, -Operated, or -Affiliated Housing:** 57 **Library Holdings:** 552,389 **Regional Accreditation:** Middle State Association of Colleges and Schools **Credit Hours For Degree:** 122 semester hours, Bachelors **Professional Accreditation:** AAFCS, ADtA, NCATE **Intercollegiate Athletics:** Baseball M; Basketball M & W; Cheerleading W; Cross-Country Running M & W; Field Hockey W; Ice Hockey M; Lacrosse M & W; Rugby M & W; Soccer M & W; Softball W; Swimming and Diving M & W; Tennis M & W; Track and Field M & W; Volleyball M & W; Wrestling M

STATE UNIVERSITY OF NEW YORK COLLEGE AT POTSDAM

44 Pierrepont Ave.
Potsdam, NY 13676
Tel: (315)267-2000; 877-POTSDAM
Admissions: (315)267-2180
Fax: (315)267-2163
E-mail: admissions@potsdam.edu
Web Site: http://www.potsdam.edu/
President/CEO: Dr. John A. Fallon, III
Registrar: Dr. Ramona Ralston
Admissions: Thomas Nesbitt
Financial Aid: Susan Aldrich
Type: Comprehensive **Sex:** Coed **Affiliation:** State University of New York System **Scores:** 98.3% SAT V 400+; 97.2% SAT M 400+; 49.5% ACT 18-23; 33.7% ACT 24-29 **% Accepted:** 73 **Admission Plans:** Early Admission; Deferred Admission **Application Deadline:** Rolling **Application Fee:** $40.00 **H.S. Requirements:** High school diploma required; GED accepted **Costs Per Year:** Application fee: $40. State resident tuition: $4350 full-time, $181 per credit hour part-time. Nonresident tuition: $10,610 full-time, $442 per credit hour part-time. Mandatory fees: $939 full-time, $43.95 per credit hour part-time. College room and board: $7670. College room only: $4420. Room and board charges vary according to board plan and housing facility. **Scholarships:** Available **Calendar System:** Semester, Summer Session Available **Enrollment:** FT 3,465, PT 154, Grad 710 **Faculty:** FT 256, PT 110 **Student-Faculty Ratio:** 14:1 **Exams:** SAT I or ACT **% Receiving Financial Aid:** 66 **% Residing in College-Owned, -Operated, or -Affiliated Housing:** 52 **Library Holdings:** 408,755 **Regional Accreditation:** Middle State Association of Colleges and Schools **Credit Hours For Degree:** 120 credit hours, Bachelors **ROTC:** Army, Air Force **Professional Accreditation:** NASM, NCATE **Intercollegiate Athletics:** Basketball M & W; Cross-Country Running M & W; Equestrian Sports W; Golf M; Ice Hockey M; Lacrosse M & W; Rugby W; Soccer M & W; Softball W; Swimming and Diving M & W; Tennis W; Track and Field M & W; Volleyball W

STATE UNIVERSITY OF NEW YORK COLLEGE OF TECHNOLOGY AT ALFRED

Alfred, NY 14802
Tel: (607)587-4111
Free: 800-4-ALFRED
Admissions: (607)587-4215
Fax: (607)587-4299
E-mail: admissions@alfredstate.edu
Web Site: http://www.alfredstate.edu/
President/CEO: Uma G. Gupta
Registrar: Nancy B. Shearer
Admissions: Deborah Goodrich
Financial Aid: Valerie Nixon
Type: Two-Year College **Sex:** Coed **Affiliation:** State University of New York System **% Accepted:** 65 **Admission Plans:** Deferred Admission **Application Deadline:** Rolling **Application Fee:** $40.00 **H.S. Requirements:** High school diploma required; GED accepted **Costs Per Year:** Application fee: $40. State resident tuition: $4350 full-time. Nonresident tuition: $7210 full-time. College room and board: $6700. College room only: $3770. **Scholarships:** Available **Calendar System:** Semester, Summer Session Available **Faculty:** FT 148, PT 43 **Student-Faculty Ratio:** 20:1 **Exams:** SAT I or ACT **% Residing in College-Owned, -Operated, or -Affiliated Housing:** 70 **Library Holdings:** 71,243 **Regional Accreditation:** Middle State Association of Colleges and Schools **Credit Hours For Degree:** 60 credit hours, Associates; 120 credit hours, Bachelors **ROTC:** Army **Professional Accreditation:** ABET, ACCE, AHIMA, NLN **Intercollegiate Athletics:** Baseball M; Basketball M & W; Cheerleading M & W; Cross-Country Running M & W; Football M; Lacrosse M; Soccer M & W; Softball W; Swimming and Diving M & W; Track and Field M & W; Volleyball W; Wrestling M

STATE UNIVERSITY OF NEW YORK COLLEGE OF TECHNOLOGY AT CANTON

Cornell Dr.
Canton, NY 13617
Tel: (315)386-7011
Free: 800-388-7123
Admissions: (315)386-7123
Fax: (315)386-7930
Web Site: http://www.canton.edu/
President/CEO: Dr. Joseph L. Kennedy
Registrar: Barbara Porter
Admissions: Jodi L. Revill
Financial Aid: Kerrie Cooper
Type: Two-Year College **Sex:** Coed **Affiliation:** State University of New York System **Admission Plans:** Early Admission; Deferred Admission **Application Fee:** $40.00 **H.S. Requirements:** High school diploma required; GED accepted **Costs Per Year:** Application fee: $40. One-time mandatory fee: $20. State resident tuition: $4350 full-time, $181 per credit hour part-time. Nonresident tuition: $10,610 full-time, $442 per credit hour part-time. Mandatory fees: $1065 full-time, $39.30 per credit hour part-time, $5. Full-time tuition and fees vary according to degree level, location, and program. Part-time tuition and fees vary according to degree level, location, and program. College room and board: $7350. College room only: $4220. Room and board charges vary according to housing facility. **Scholarships:** Available **Calendar System:** Semester, Summer Session Available **Enrollment:** FT 2,055, PT 463 **Faculty:** FT 81, PT 50 **Student-Faculty Ratio:** 23:1 **% Residing in College-Owned, -Operated, or -Affiliated Housing:** 48 **Library Holdings:** 64,912 **Regional Accreditation:** Middle State Association of Colleges and Schools **Credit Hours For Degree:** 60 credit hours, Associates; 123 credit hours, Bachelors **ROTC:** Army, Air Force **Professional Accreditation:** ABET, ABFSE, AOTA, APTA, NLN **Intercollegiate Athletics:** Baseball M; Basketball M & W; Ice Hockey M; Lacrosse M & W; Soccer M & W; Softball W; Volleyball W

STATE UNIVERSITY OF NEW YORK COLLEGE OF TECHNOLOGY AT DELHI

Main St.
Delhi, NY 13753
Tel: (607)746-4000
Free: 800-96-DELHI
Fax: (607)746-4104
Web Site: http://www.delhi.edu/
President/CEO: Dr. Candace Vancko
Registrar: Dr. Jacqueline Andrews
Admissions: Larry Barrett
Financial Aid: Lorraine Horner
Type: Two-Year College **Sex:** Coed **Affiliation:** State University of New York System **% Accepted:** 61 **Admission Plans:** Early Admission; Deferred Admission **Application Deadline:** Rolling **Application Fee:** $30.00 **H.S. Requirements:** High school diploma required; GED accepted. For vocational programs: High school diploma or equivalent not required **Costs Per Year:** Application fee: $30. State resident tuition: $4350 full-time, $181 per credit hour part-time. Nonresident tuition: $7210 full-time, $300 per credit hour part-time. Mandatory fees: $1248 full-time, $42 per credit hour part-time, $5 per term part-time. College room and board: $7880. **Scholarships:** Available **Calendar System:** Semester, Summer Session Available **Enrollment:** FT 2,206, PT 351 **Faculty:** FT 97, PT 33 **Student-Faculty Ratio:** 17:1 **% Residing in College-Owned, -Operated, or -Affiliated Housing:** 61 **Library Holdings:** 47,909 **Regional Accreditation:** Middle State Association of Colleges and Schools **Credit Hours For Degree:** 60 credit hours, Associates; 126 credit hours, Bachelors **Professional Accreditation:** ACCE, NLN **Intercollegiate Athletics:** Basketball M & W; Cross-Country Running M & W; Golf M & W; Lacrosse M; Soccer M & W; Softball W; Swimming and Diving M & W; Tennis M & W; Track and Field M & W; Volleyball W; Wrestling M

STATE UNIVERSITY OF NEW YORK DOWNSTATE MEDICAL CENTER

450 Clarkson Ave.
Brooklyn, NY 11203-2098

Tel: (718)270-1000
Fax: (718)270-7592
Web Site: http://www.downstate.edu/
President/CEO: Dr. John C. La Rosa
Registrar: Sophie Christoforou
Financial Aid: Julia Clayton
Type: Two-Year Upper Division **Sex:** Coed **Affiliation:** State University of New York System **Admission Plans:** Preferred Admission **Application Fee:** $30.00 **H.S. Requirements:** High school diploma required; GED accepted **Costs Per Year:** Application fee: $30. State resident tuition: $4350 full-time, $181 per credit part-time. Nonresident tuition: $10,610 full-time, $442 per credit part-time. College room and board: $11,774. **Scholarships:** Available **Calendar System:** Semester, Summer Session Available **Enrollment:** FT 203, PT 142, Grad 450 **% Receiving Financial Aid:** 60 **Library Holdings:** 357,209 **Regional Accreditation:** Middle State Association of Colleges and Schools **Credit Hours For Degree:** 125 credits, Bachelors **Professional Accreditation:** AACN, AANA, ACNM, AOTA, APTA, JRCEDMS, LCMEAMA, NLN

STATE UNIVERSITY OF NEW YORK EMPIRE STATE COLLEGE
1 Union Ave.
Saratoga Springs, NY 12866-4391
Tel: (518)587-2100
Free: 800-847-3000
Fax: (518)587-2100
E-mail: jennifer.riley@esc.edu
Web Site: http://www.esc.edu/
President/CEO: Dr. Joseph Moore
Registrar: Mary Edinburgh
Admissions: Jennifer Riley
Financial Aid: Eileen Corrigan
Type: Comprehensive **Sex:** Coed **Affiliation:** State University of New York System **% Accepted:** 81 **Admission Plans:** Early Admission **Application Deadline:** Rolling **Application Fee:** $0.00 **H.S. Requirements:** High school diploma required; GED accepted **Costs Per Year:** Application fee: $0. One-time mandatory fee: $300. State resident tuition: $4350 full-time, $181 per credit part-time. Nonresident tuition: $10,610 full-time, $442 per credit part-time. Mandatory fees: $225 full-time, $7.10 per credit part-time, $75 per term part-time. **Calendar System:** Continuous **Enrollment:** FT 3,189, PT 6,333, Grad 474 **Faculty:** FT 154, PT 921 **Student-Faculty Ratio:** 11:1 **Library Holdings:** 11,000 **Regional Accreditation:** Middle State Association of Colleges and Schools **Credit Hours For Degree:** 64 credits, Associates; 128 credits, Bachelors

STATE UNIVERSITY OF NEW YORK, FREDONIA
Fredonia, NY 14063-1136
Tel: (716)673-3111
Free: 800-252-1212
Admissions: (716)673-3251
Fax: (716)673-3249
E-mail: admissions.office@fredonia.edu
Web Site: http://www.fredonia.edu/
President/CEO: Dr. Dennis L. Hefner
Registrar: Nancy M. Bowser
Admissions: Michael Bleecher
Financial Aid: Daniel Tramuta
Type: Comprehensive **Sex:** Coed **Affiliation:** State University of New York System **Scores:** 100% SAT V 400+; 100% SAT M 400+; 48% ACT 18-23; 44% ACT 24-29 **% Accepted:** 55 **Admission Plans:** Early Admission; Early Decision Plan; Deferred Admission **Application Deadline:** Rolling **Application Fee:** $40.00 **H.S. Requirements:** High school diploma required; GED accepted **Costs Per Year:** Application fee: $40. State resident tuition: $4350 full-time, $181 per credit hour part-time. Nonresident tuition: $10,610 full-time, $442 per credit hour part-time. Mandatory fees: $1091 full-time, $43.15 per credit hour part-time. College room and board: $6940. College room only: $4350. Room and board charges vary according to board plan and housing facility. **Scholarships:** Available **Calendar System:** Semester, Summer Session Available **Enrollment:** FT 4,843, PT 200, Grad 389 **Faculty:** FT 245, PT 160 **Student-Faculty Ratio:** 18:1 **Exams:** SAT I or ACT **% Receiving Financial Aid:** 61 **% Residing in College-Owned, -Operated, or -Affiliated Housing:** 53 **Library Holdings:** 396,000 **Regional Accreditation:** Middle State Association of Colleges and Schools **Credit Hours For Degree:** 120 credit hours, Bachelors **Professional Accreditation:** ASLHA, CSWE, NASM, NAST, NCATE **Intercollegiate Athletics:** Baseball M; Basketball M & W; Cheerleading M & W; Cross-Country Running M & W; Field Hockey M & W; Ice Hockey M; Lacrosse W; Soccer M & W; Softball W; Swimming and Diving M & W; Tennis M & W; Track and Field M & W; Volleyball M & W

STATE UNIVERSITY OF NEW YORK INSTITUTE OF TECHNOLOGY
PO Box 3050
Utica, NY 13504-3050
Tel: (315)792-7100
Free: 800-SUN-YTEC
Admissions: (315)792-7500
Fax: (315)792-7837
E-mail: admissions@sunyit.edu
Web Site: http://www.sunyit.edu/
President/CEO: Dr. Peter Spina
Registrar: Diane Palen
Admissions: Marybeth Lyons
Financial Aid: Stewart Richards
Type: Comprehensive **Sex:** Coed **Affiliation:** State University of New York System **Scores:** 99.5% SAT V 400+; 100% SAT M 400+; 50% ACT 18-23; 50% ACT 24-29 **% Accepted:** 42 **Admission Plans:** Deferred Admission **Application Deadline:** Rolling **Application Fee:** $40.00 **H.S. Requirements:** High school diploma or equivalent not required **Costs Per Year:** Application fee: $40. State resident tuition: $4350 full-time, $181 per credit hour part-time. Nonresident tuition: $10,610 full-time, $442 per credit hour part-time. Mandatory fees: $935 full-time, $36.70 per credit hour part-time. College room and board: $7290. **Scholarships:** Available **Calendar System:** Semester, Summer Session Available **Enrollment:** FT 1,241, PT 778, Grad 571 **Faculty:** FT 95, PT 67 **Student-Faculty Ratio:** 17:1 **% Receiving Financial Aid:** 67 **% Residing in College-Owned, -Operated, or -Affiliated Housing:** 18 **Library Holdings:** 193,682 **Regional Accreditation:** Middle State Association of Colleges and Schools **Credit Hours For Degree:** 124 semester hours, Bachelors **ROTC:** Army, Air Force **Professional Accreditation:** ABET, AACN, AHIMA, NLN **Intercollegiate Athletics:** Baseball M; Basketball M & W; Bowling M & W; Cross-Country Running W; Golf M & W; Lacrosse M; Soccer M & W; Softball W; Volleyball W

STATE UNIVERSITY OF NEW YORK MARITIME COLLEGE
6 Pennyfield Ave.
Throggs Neck, NY 10465-4198
Tel: (718)409-7200
Free: 800-642-1874
Admissions: (718)409-7220
Fax: (718)409-7392
E-mail: dwhitman@sunymaritime.edu
Web Site: http://www.sunymaritime.edu/
President/CEO: Vice Adm. John R. Ryan
Registrar: Carol Roth
Admissions: Deirdre Whitman
Financial Aid: Paul Bamonte
Type: Comprehensive **Sex:** Coed **Affiliation:** State University of New York System **Scores:** 100% SAT V 400+; 100% SAT M 400+; 40% ACT 18-23; 40% ACT 24-29 **% Accepted:** 70 **Admission Plans:** Early Admission; Early Decision Plan; Deferred Admission **Application Deadline:** Rolling **Application Fee:** $40.00 **H.S. Requirements:** High school diploma required; GED accepted **Costs Per Year:** Application fee: $40. State resident tuition: $4350 full-time, $181 per credit part-time. Nonresident tuition: $10,610 full-time, $442 per credit part-time. Mandatory fees: $3055 full-time, $27.53 per credit part-time. Full-time tuition and fees vary according to reciprocity agreements. Part-time tuition and fees vary according to reciprocity agreements. College room and board: $8000. College room only: $4900. Room and board charges vary according to board plan and housing facility. **Scholarships:** Available **Calendar System:** Semester, Summer Session Available **Enrollment:** FT 1,107, PT 43, Grad 144 **Faculty:** FT 60, PT 15 **Student-Faculty Ratio:** 17:1 **Exams:** SAT I or ACT, SAT II **% Residing in College-Owned, -Operated, or -Affiliated Housing:** 98 **Library Holdings:** 69,637 **Regional Accreditation:** Middle State Association of Colleges and Schools **Credit Hours For Degree:** 80 credits, Associates; 156 credits, Bachelors **ROTC:** Navy, Air Force **Professional Accreditation:** ABET **Intercollegiate Athletics:** Baseball M; Basketball M & W; Crew M & W; Cross-Country Running M & W; Ice Hockey M; Lacrosse M; Riflery M & W; Sailing M & W; Soccer M; Softball W; Swimming and Diving M & W; Tennis M & W; Volleyball W; Wrestling M

STATE UNIVERSITY OF NEW YORK AT NEW PALTZ
75 South Manheim Blvd.
New Paltz, NY 12561

Tel: (845)257-2121
Admissions: (845)257-3210
Fax: (845)257-3209
E-mail: eatond@newpaltz.edu
Web Site: http://www.newpaltz.edu/
President/CEO: Steven Poskanzer
Registrar: Debra Miller
Admissions: L. Eaton
Financial Aid: Daniel Sistarenick
Type: Comprehensive **Sex:** Coed **Affiliation:** State University of New York System **Scores:** 97% SAT V 400+; 98% SAT M 400+ **% Accepted:** 44 **Admission Plans:** Early Admission; Early Action; Deferred Admission **Application Deadline:** April 01 **Application Fee:** $40.00 **H.S. Requirements:** High school diploma required; GED accepted **Costs Per Year:** Application fee: $40. State resident tuition: $4350 full-time, $181 per credit part-time. Nonresident tuition: $10,610 full-time, $442 per credit part-time. Mandatory fees: $1010 full-time, $28.60 per credit part-time, $160 per term part-time. College room and board: $7230. College room only: $4500. **Scholarships:** Available **Calendar System:** Semester, Summer Session Available **Enrollment:** FT 5,715, PT 706, Grad 1,404 **Faculty:** FT 294, PT 412 **Student-Faculty Ratio:** 16:1 **Exams:** SAT I or ACT **% Receiving Financial Aid:** 55 **% Residing in College-Owned, -Operated, or -Affiliated Housing:** 52 **Library Holdings:** 525,296 **Regional Accreditation:** Middle State Association of Colleges and Schools **Credit Hours For Degree:** 120 credits, Bachelors **Professional Accreditation:** ABET, AACN, ASLHA, NASAD, NASM, NAST, NCATE **Intercollegiate Athletics:** Baseball M; Basketball M & W; Cross-Country Running M & W; Equestrian Sports W; Field Hockey W; Ice Hockey M; Lacrosse M; Rugby M & W; Soccer M & W; Softball W; Swimming and Diving M & W; Tennis W; Volleyball M & W

STATE UNIVERSITY OF NEW YORK AT OSWEGO

7060 Route 104
Oswego, NY 13126
Tel: (315)312-2500
Admissions: (315)312-2250
Fax: (315)312-5799
E-mail: admiss@oswego.edu
Web Site: http://www.oswego.edu/
President/CEO: Dr. Deborah F. Stanley
Registrar: Andrew Westfall
Admissions: Dr. Joseph Grant
Financial Aid: Mark Humbert
Type: Comprehensive **Sex:** Coed **Affiliation:** State University of New York System **Scores:** 100% SAT V 400+; 100% SAT M 400+; 64% ACT 18-23; 34% ACT 24-29 **% Accepted:** 56 **Admission Plans:** Early Admission; Early Decision Plan; Deferred Admission **Application Deadline:** Rolling **Application Fee:** $40.00 **H.S. Requirements:** High school diploma required; GED accepted **Costs Per Year:** Application fee: $40. State resident tuition: $4350 full-time, $181 per credit hour part-time. Nonresident tuition: $10,610 full-time, $442 per credit hour part-time. Mandatory fees: $972 full-time, $30.18 per credit hour part-time. Part-time tuition and fees vary according to class time, course load, and location. College room and board: $8340. College room only: $5090. Room and board charges vary according to board plan and housing facility. **Scholarships:** Available **Calendar System:** Semester, Summer Session Available **Enrollment:** FT 6,620, PT 518, Grad 1,144 **Faculty:** FT 317, PT 194 **Student-Faculty Ratio:** 18:1 **Exams:** SAT I or ACT **% Receiving Financial Aid:** 66 **% Residing in College-Owned, -Operated, or -Affiliated Housing:** 57 **Library Holdings:** 477,930 **Regional Accreditation:** Middle State Association of Colleges and Schools **Credit Hours For Degree:** 122 credit hours, Bachelors **ROTC:** Army **Professional Accreditation:** AACSB, NASM, NCATE **Intercollegiate Athletics:** Baseball M; Basketball M & W; Crew M & W; Cross-Country Running M & W; Field Hockey W; Golf M; Ice Hockey M; Lacrosse M & W; Soccer M & W; Softball W; Swimming and Diving M & W; Tennis M & W; Track and Field M & W; Volleyball W; Wrestling M

STATE UNIVERSITY OF NEW YORK AT PLATTSBURGH

101 Broad Steet
Plattsburgh, NY 12901-2681
Tel: (518)564-2000
Admissions: (518)564-2040
Fax: (518)564-2045
E-mail: admissions@plattsburgh.edu
Web Site: http://www.plattsburgh.edu/
President/CEO: Dr. John Ettling
Registrar: Susan Steele
Admissions: Richard Higgins
Financial Aid: Todd Moravec
Type: Comprehensive **Sex:** Coed **Affiliation:** State University of New York System **Scores:** 94.5% SAT V 400+; 95.3% SAT M 400+; 63.9% ACT 18-23; 28.4% ACT 24-29 **% Accepted:** 62 **Admission Plans:** Early Admission; Early Decision Plan; Deferred Admission **Application Deadline:** August 01 **Application Fee:** $40.00 **H.S. Requirements:** High school diploma required; GED accepted **Costs Per Year:** Application fee: $40. State resident tuition: $4350 full-time, $181 per credit hour part-time. Nonresident tuition: $10,610 full-time, $442 per credit hour part-time. Mandatory fees: $946 full-time, $39 per credit hour part-time. College room and board: $7066. College room only: $4400. **Scholarships:** Available **Calendar System:** Semester, Summer Session Available **Enrollment:** FT 5,024, PT 370, Grad 650 **Faculty:** FT 252, PT 203 **Student-Faculty Ratio:** 17:1 **Exams:** SAT I or ACT **% Receiving Financial Aid:** 58 **% Residing in College-Owned, -Operated, or -Affiliated Housing:** 48 **Library Holdings:** 378,020 **Regional Accreditation:** Middle State Association of Colleges and Schools **Credit Hours For Degree:** 120 credit hours, Bachelors **Professional Accreditation:** AACSB, AACN, ACA, ASLHA, CSWE, NLN **Intercollegiate Athletics:** Baseball M; Basketball M & W; Cross-Country Running M & W; Golf M & W; Ice Hockey M & W; Lacrosse M; Soccer M & W; Softball W; Swimming and Diving M & W; Tennis W; Track and Field M & W; Volleyball W

STATE UNIVERSITY OF NEW YORK UPSTATE MEDICAL UNIVERSITY

750 East Adams St.
Syracuse, NY 13210-2334
Tel: (315)464-5540
Free: 800-736-2171
Admissions: (315)464-4816
Fax: (315)464-8823
Web Site: http://www.upstate.edu/
President/CEO: Dr. Gregory L. Eastwood
Registrar: Jennifer Martin Tse
Admissions: Gregory Keating
Financial Aid: Irvin W. Bodofsky
Type: Two-Year Upper Division **Sex:** Coed **Affiliation:** State University of New York System **% Accepted:** 40 **Admission Plans:** Preferred Admission; Early Admission; Deferred Admission **Application Fee:** $40.00 **H.S. Requirements:** High school diploma required; GED accepted **Costs Per Year:** Application fee: $40. State resident tuition: $8700 full-time, $181 per credit part-time. Nonresident tuition: $21,200 full-time, $422 per credit part-time. Mandatory fees: $466 full-time. College room only: $3585. **Scholarships:** Available **Calendar System:** Semester, Summer Session Available **Enrollment:** FT 150, PT 93, Grad 377 **Faculty:** FT 477, PT 209 **Student-Faculty Ratio:** 2:1 **% Receiving Financial Aid:** 65 **% Residing in College-Owned, -Operated, or -Affiliated Housing:** 50 **Library Holdings:** 132,500 **Regional Accreditation:** Middle State Association of Colleges and Schools **Credit Hours For Degree:** 120 credits, Bachelors **Professional Accreditation:** ACPE, AACN, APTA, APA, ASC, CARC, JRCERT, LCMEAMA, NAACLS, NLN

STONY BROOK UNIVERSITY, STATE UNIVERSITY OF NEW YORK

Nicolls Rd.
Stony Brook, NY 11794
Tel: (631)632-6000
Free: 800-872-7869
Admissions: (631)632-6868
E-mail: admiss@mail.upsa.sunysb.edu
Web Site: http://www.sunysb.edu/
President/CEO: Dr. Shirley Strum Kenny
Registrar: Beverly Rivera
Admissions: Judith Burke-Berhanan
Financial Aid: Dr. Ana Maria Torres
Type: University **Sex:** Coed **Affiliation:** State University of New York System **Scores:** 100% SAT V 400+; 100% SAT M 400+ **% Accepted:** 51 **Admission Plans:** Early Action; Deferred Admission **Application Deadline:** March 01 **Application Fee:** $40.00 **H.S. Requirements:** High school diploma required; GED accepted **Costs Per Year:** Application fee: $40. State resident tuition: $4350 full-time, $181 per credit part-time. Nonresident tuition: $10,610 full-time, $442 per credit part-time. Mandatory fees: $1225 full-time, $59.30 per credit part-time. College room and board: $8050. Room and board charges vary according to board plan and housing facility.

Scholarships: Available **Calendar System:** Semester, Summer Session Available **Enrollment:** FT 13,180, PT 1,107, Grad 7,123 **Faculty:** FT 909, PT 480 **Student-Faculty Ratio:** 16:1 **Exams:** SAT I or ACT, SAT II **% Receiving Financial Aid:** 59 **% Residing in College-Owned, -Operated, or -Affiliated Housing:** 63 **Library Holdings:** 2,191,704 **Regional Accreditation:** Middle State Association of Colleges and Schools **Credit Hours For Degree:** 120 credits, Bachelors **ROTC:** Army, Air Force **Professional Accreditation:** ABET, AACN, ACNM, ADA, ADtA, AOTA, APTA, APA, ASC, CARC, CSWE, LCMEAMA, NAACLS, NCATE **Intercollegiate Athletics:** Baseball M; Basketball M & W; Cross-Country Running M & W; Football M; Lacrosse M & W; Soccer M & W; Softball W; Swimming and Diving M & W; Tennis M & W; Track and Field M & W; Volleyball W

SUFFOLK COUNTY COMMUNITY COLLEGE
533 College Rd.
Selden, NY 11784-2899
Tel: (631)451-4110
Web Site: http://www.sunysuffolk.edu/
President/CEO: Dr. Shirley Robinson Pippins
Registrar: Anna Flak
Financial Aid: Nancy Dunnagan
Type: Two-Year College **Sex:** Coed **Affiliation:** State University of New York System **Scores:** 77% SAT V 400+; 80% SAT M 400+; 26.11% ACT 18-23; 4.08% ACT 24-29 **Admission Plans:** Open Admission; Preferred Admission; Deferred Admission **Application Fee:** $30.00 **H.S. Requirements:** High school diploma required; GED accepted. For applicants with extenuating circumstances: High school diploma or equivalent not required **Scholarships:** Available **Calendar System:** Semester, Summer Session Available **Enrollment:** FT 10,860, PT 9,420 **Faculty:** FT 308, PT 854 **Student-Faculty Ratio:** 18:1 **Exams:** SAT I or ACT **Regional Accreditation:** Middle State Association of Colleges and Schools **Credit Hours For Degree:** 66 credits, Associates **ROTC:** Army **Professional Accreditation:** AAMAE, AHIMA, AOTA, APTA, NLN **Intercollegiate Athletics:** Baseball M; Basketball M & W; Cross-Country Running M & W; Golf M & W; Gymnastics M & W; Lacrosse M; Sailing M & W; Soccer M; Softball W; Tennis M & W; Volleyball W

SULLIVAN COUNTY COMMUNITY COLLEGE
112 College Rd.
Loch Sheldrake, NY 12759
Tel: (845)434-5750
Admissions: (914)434-5750
Fax: (845)434-4806
E-mail: sarir@sullivan.suny.edu
Web Site: http://www.sullivan.suny.edu/
President/CEO: Dr. Mamie Howard Golladay
Registrar: Ray Sheenan
Admissions: Sari Rosenheck
Financial Aid: James Winderl
Type: Two-Year College **Sex:** Coed **Affiliation:** State University of New York System **% Accepted:** 71 **Admission Plans:** Open Admission; Early Admission; Deferred Admission **Application Deadline:** Rolling **Application Fee:** $0.00 **H.S. Requirements:** High school diploma required; GED accepted **Costs Per Year:** Application fee: $0. State resident tuition: $3200 full-time, $125 per credit part-time. Nonresident tuition: $6400 full-time, $160 per credit part-time. Mandatory fees: $306 full-time, $12 per credit part-time. College room and board: $6500. College room only: $4080. **Scholarships:** Available **Calendar System:** 4-1-4, Summer Session Available **Enrollment:** FT 1,067, PT 617 **Faculty:** FT 49, PT 65 **Student-Faculty Ratio:** 18:1 **Library Holdings:** 65,699 **Regional Accreditation:** Middle State Association of Colleges and Schools **Credit Hours For Degree:** 63 credits, Associates **Professional Accreditation:** ACF, ACBSP, NLN **Intercollegiate Athletics:** Basketball M & W; Cheerleading W; Cross-Country Running M & W; Golf M; Softball W; Volleyball W

SWEDISH INSTITUTE, COLLEGE OF HEALTH SCIENCES
226 West 26th St.
New York, NY 10001-6700
Tel: (212)924-5900
Fax: (212)924-7600
E-mail: leslie@swedishinstitute.org
Web Site: http://www.swedishinstitute.org/
President/CEO: Paula J. Eckardt
Admissions: Leslie Kielson
Type: Comprehensive **Sex:** Coed **Calendar System:** Trimester **Professional Accreditation:** ACCSCT, NACSCAO

SYRACUSE UNIVERSITY
Syracuse, NY 13244
Tel: (315)443-1870
Admissions: (315)443-3611
E-mail: orange@syr.edu
Web Site: http://www.syracuse.edu/
President/CEO: Nancy Cantor
Registrar: Maureen Breed
Admissions: Susan E. Donovan
Financial Aid: Susan Donovan
Type: University **Sex:** Coed **Scores:** 100% SAT V 400+; 100% SAT M 400+ **% Accepted:** 65 **Admission Plans:** Early Admission; Early Decision Plan; Deferred Admission **Application Deadline:** January 01 **Application Fee:** $60.00 **H.S. Requirements:** High school diploma required; GED accepted **Costs Per Year:** Application fee: $60. Comprehensive fee: $38,655 includes full-time tuition ($27,210), mandatory fees ($1075), and college room and board ($10,370). College room only: $5620. Room and board charges vary according to board plan and housing facility. Part-time tuition: $1120 per credit hour. **Scholarships:** Available **Calendar System:** Semester, Summer Session Available **Enrollment:** FT 11,374, PT 67, Grad 5,071 **Faculty:** FT 865, PT 526 **Student-Faculty Ratio:** 12:1 **Exams:** SAT I or ACT **% Receiving Financial Aid:** 58 **% Residing in College-Owned, -Operated, or -Affiliated Housing:** 73 **Library Holdings:** 3,115,566 **Regional Accreditation:** Middle State Association of Colleges and Schools **Credit Hours For Degree:** 120 credit hours, Bachelors **ROTC:** Army, Air Force **Professional Accreditation:** AACSB, ABET, ACEJMC, AAMFT, ABA, ACA, ADtA, ALA, APA, ASLHA, AALS, CORE, CSWE, FIDER, NASAD, NASM, NASPAA, NCATE, NLN **Intercollegiate Athletics:** Archery M & W; Badminton M & W; Baseball M; Basketball M & W; Bowling M & W; Cheerleading M & W; Crew M & W; Cross-Country Running M & W; Equestrian Sports M & W; Fencing M & W; Field Hockey W; Football M; Gymnastics M & W; Ice Hockey M & W; Lacrosse M & W; Racquetball M & W; Riflery M & W; Rugby M & W; Sailing M & W; Skiing (Downhill) M & W; Soccer M & W; Softball M & W; Squash M & W; Swimming and Diving M & W; Table Tennis M & W; Tennis M & W; Track and Field M & W; Volleyball M & W; Water Polo M & W; Weight Lifting M & W

TALMUDICAL INSTITUTE OF UPSTATE NEW YORK
769 Park Ave.
Rochester, NY 14607-3046
Tel: (716)473-2810
Fax: (716)442-0417
Web Site: http://www.tiuny.org/
President/CEO: Rabbi M. Davidowitz
Registrar: Rabbi B. Davidowitz
Financial Aid: I. Rocklin
Type: Five-Year College **Sex:** Men **Affiliation:** Jewish **Admission Plans:** Open Admission; Early Admission **Application Fee:** $0.00 **H.S. Requirements:** High school diploma required; GED accepted **Scholarships:** Available **Calendar System:** Semester **Enrollment:** FT 22, Grad 8 **Faculty:** FT 3, PT 0 **Library Holdings:** 3,000 **Credit Hours For Degree:** 150 credits, Bachelors **Professional Accreditation:** AARTS

TALMUDICAL SEMINARY OHOLEI TORAH
667 Eastern Parkway
Brooklyn, NY 11213-3310
Tel: (718)774-5050
Admissions: (718)363-2034
President/CEO: J. Rosenfeld
Registrar: E. Piekarski
Admissions: Rabbi E. Piekarski
Financial Aid: S. Rosenseld
Type: Four-Year College **Sex:** Men **Admission Plans:** Deferred Admission **H.S. Requirements:** High school diploma required; GED accepted **Calendar System:** Semester, Summer Session Not available **Credit Hours For Degree:** 128 credits, Bachelors **Professional Accreditation:** AARTS

TAYLOR BUSINESS INSTITUTE
269 West 40th St.
New York, NY 10018
Tel: (212)643-2020
Admissions: (212)302-4000

President/CEO: Patricia Martin
Registrar: Anna Maria Camada
Admissions: Jim Morrisey
Financial Aid: Lydia Henry-Manrow
Type: Two-Year College **Sex:** Coed **Affiliation:** Phillips Colleges, Inc **Admission Plans:** Deferred Admission **Application Fee:** $0.00 **H.S. Requirements:** High school diploma required; GED accepted **Calendar System:** Quarter, Summer Session Available **Faculty:** FT 11, PT 8 **Exams:** Other **Library Holdings:** 2,873 **Credit Hours For Degree:** 97 credits, Associates **Professional Accreditation:** ACICS

TCI-THE COLLEGE OF TECHNOLOGY
320 West 31st St.
New York, NY 10001-2705
Tel: (212)594-4000
Fax: (212)629-3937
E-mail: admissions@tciedu.com
Web Site: http://www.tciedu.com/
President/CEO: Karen Romaine
Registrar: Michael Bautista
Admissions: Sandra Germer
Financial Aid: Debra Bouabidi
Type: Two-Year College **Sex:** Coed **Admission Plans:** Deferred Admission **H.S. Requirements:** High school diploma required; GED accepted **Scholarships:** Available **Calendar System:** Semester, Summer Session Available **Faculty:** FT 88, PT 120 **Student-Faculty Ratio:** 30:1 **Library Holdings:** 8,000 **Regional Accreditation:** Middle State Association of Colleges and Schools **Credit Hours For Degree:** 65 credits, Associates **Professional Accreditation:** ABET, NYSBR **Intercollegiate Athletics:** Basketball M; Volleyball W

TOMPKINS CORTLAND COMMUNITY COLLEGE
170 North St., PO Box 139
Dryden, NY 13053-0139
Tel: (607)844-8211
Admissions: (607)844-8222
Fax: (607)844-6538
Web Site: http://www.sunytccc.edu/
President/CEO: Dr. Carl Haynes
Registrar: Judith Longo
Admissions: Sandy Drumluk
Financial Aid: Michael McGraw
Type: Two-Year College **Sex:** Coed **Affiliation:** State University of New York System **Scores:** 81.5% SAT V 400+; 83% SAT M 400+; 57.1% ACT 18-23; 3.6% ACT 24-29 **Admission Plans:** Open Admission; Early Admission; Deferred Admission **Application Deadline:** Rolling **Application Fee:** $15.00 **H.S. Requirements:** High school diploma or equivalent not required. For nursing, engineering science, computer science programs: High school diploma required; GED not accepted **Costs Per Year:** Application fee: $15. State resident tuition: $3200 full-time, $124 per credit part-time. Nonresident tuition: $6700 full-time, $250 per credit part-time. Mandatory fees: $553 full-time, $15 per credit part-time. College room only: $5400. **Scholarships:** Available **Calendar System:** Semester, Summer Session Available **Enrollment:** FT 2,146, PT 1,028 **Faculty:** FT 69, PT 210 **Student-Faculty Ratio:** 18:1 **% Residing in College-Owned, -Operated, or -Affiliated Housing:** 4 **Library Holdings:** 50,630 **Regional Accreditation:** Middle State Association of Colleges and Schools **Credit Hours For Degree:** 62 credits, Associates **ROTC:** Army **Professional Accreditation:** NLN **Intercollegiate Athletics:** Basketball M & W; Cheerleading M & W; Golf M & W; Soccer M & W; Softball W; Volleyball W

TORAH TEMIMAH TALMUDICAL SEMINARY
507 Ocean Parkway
Brooklyn, NY 11218-5913
Tel: (718)853-8500
President/CEO: Rabbi Leopold Margulies
Admissions: Rabbi I. Hisiger
Financial Aid: Rabbi Israel Kleinman
Type: Four-Year College **Sex:** Men **Affiliation:** Jewish **Calendar System:** Semester **Professional Accreditation:** AARTS

TOURO COLLEGE
27-33 West 23rd St.
New York, NY 10010
Tel: (212)463-0400
Fax: (212)779-2344
Web Site: http://www.touro.edu/
President/CEO: Dr. Bernard Lander
Registrar: Richard Cohen
Admissions: Andre Baron
Financial Aid: Carol Rosenbaum
Type: Comprehensive **Sex:** Coed **Scores:** 99% SAT V 400+; 96% SAT M 400+; 55% ACT 18-23; 17% ACT 24-29 **Admission Plans:** Open Admission; Early Admission; Deferred Admission **Application Fee:** $50.00 **H.S. Requirements:** High school diploma required; GED accepted **Scholarships:** Available **Calendar System:** Semester, Summer Session Available **Enrollment:** FT 6,513, PT 880, Grad 2,934 **Faculty:** FT 264, PT 735 **Student-Faculty Ratio:** 16:1 **Exams:** SAT I or ACT **% Receiving Financial Aid:** 100 **Library Holdings:** 302,700 **Regional Accreditation:** Middle State Association of Colleges and Schools **Credit Hours For Degree:** 60 credits, Associates; 120 credits, Bachelors **Professional Accreditation:** ABA, AOTA, APTA, ASLHA, AALS

TROCAIRE COLLEGE
360 Choate Ave.
Buffalo, NY 14220-2094
Tel: (716)826-1200
Fax: (716)826-4704
Web Site: http://www.trocaire.edu/
President/CEO: Dr. Paul B. Hurley, Jr.
Admissions: Claudia M. Lesinski
Financial Aid: Janet McGrath
Type: Two-Year College **Sex:** Coed **Scores:** 88% SAT V 400+; 76% SAT M 400+; 67% ACT 18-23 **Admission Plans:** Deferred Admission **Application Fee:** $25.00 **H.S. Requirements:** High school diploma required; GED accepted **Scholarships:** Available **Calendar System:** Semester, Summer Session Available **Faculty:** FT 38, PT 75 **Student-Faculty Ratio:** 15:1 **Exams:** SAT I or ACT **Library Holdings:** 15,403 **Regional Accreditation:** Middle State Association of Colleges and Schools **Credit Hours For Degree:** 60 credit hours, Associates **Professional Accreditation:** ARCEST, AAMAE, AHIMA, JRCERT, NLN

ULSTER COUNTY COMMUNITY COLLEGE
Cottekill Rd.
Stone Ridge, NY 12484
Tel: (914)687-5000
Free: 800-724-0833
Admissions: (914)687-5027
Web Site: http://www.sunyulster.edu/
President/CEO: Dr. Donald C. Katt
Registrar: Mary Cotton-Miller
Admissions: Ann Marrott
Financial Aid: Mim Brown
Type: Two-Year College **Sex:** Coed **Affiliation:** State University of New York System **Admission Plans:** Open Admission; Early Admission; Deferred Admission **Application Fee:** $0.00 **H.S. Requirements:** High school diploma required; GED accepted **Scholarships:** Available **Calendar System:** Semester, Summer Session Available **Faculty:** FT 64, PT 131 **Student-Faculty Ratio:** 15:1 **Exams:** Other **Library Holdings:** 70,758 **Regional Accreditation:** Middle State Association of Colleges and Schools **Credit Hours For Degree:** 62 credit hours, Associates **Professional Accreditation:** NLN **Intercollegiate Athletics:** Baseball M; Basketball M & W; Golf M & W; Soccer M; Softball W; Tennis M & W; Volleyball W

UNION COLLEGE
807 Union St.
Schenectady, NY 12308-2311
Tel: (518)388-6000
Admissions: (518)388-6112
Fax: (518)388-6986
E-mail: admissions@union.edu
Web Site: http://www.union.edu/
President/CEO: Dr. Roger H. Hull
Registrar: Penelope S. Adey
Admissions: Daniel Lundquist
Financial Aid: Beth A. Post
Type: Four-Year College **Sex:** Coed **Scores:** 99.7% SAT V 400+; 100% SAT M 400+; 13.4% ACT 18-23; 68.7% ACT 24-29 **% Accepted:** 47 **Admission Plans:** Early Admission; Early Decision Plan; Deferred Admission **Application Deadline:** January 15 **Application Fee:** $50.00 **H.S. Require-**

ments: High school diploma required; GED not accepted **Costs Per Year:** Application fee: $50. Comprehensive fee: $41,595. **Scholarships:** Available **Calendar System:** Trimester, Summer Session Available **Enrollment:** FT 2,209, PT 43 **Faculty:** FT 182, PT 27 **Student-Faculty Ratio:** 11:1 **Exams:** Other, SAT I or ACT, SAT II **% Receiving Financial Aid:** 48 **% Residing in College-Owned, -Operated, or -Affiliated Housing:** 88 **Library Holdings:** 571,508 **Regional Accreditation:** Middle State Association of Colleges and Schools **Credit Hours For Degree:** 36 courses, Bachelors **ROTC:** Army, Air Force **Professional Accreditation:** ABET **Intercollegiate Athletics:** Baseball M; Basketball M & W; Crew M & W; Cross-Country Running M & W; Fencing M & W; Field Hockey W; Football M; Golf M & W; Ice Hockey M & W; Lacrosse M & W; Rugby M & W; Skiing (Downhill) M & W; Soccer M & W; Softball W; Swimming and Diving M & W; Tennis M & W; Track and Field M & W; Ultimate Frisbee M & W; Volleyball W; Water Polo M & W

UNITED STATES MERCHANT MARINE ACADEMY
300 Steamboat Rd.
Kings Point, NY 11024-1699
Tel: (516)773-5000; (866)546-4778
Admissions: (516)773-5391
Fax: (516)773-5390
Web Site: http://www.usmma.edu/
President/CEO: Vice Adm. Joseph D. Stewart
Registrar: Dr. Howard English
Admissions: Capt. Robert Johnson
Financial Aid: Sdenka Rios
Type: Four-Year College **Sex:** Coed **Scores:** 100% SAT V 400+; 100% SAT M 400+ **% Accepted:** 16 **Admission Plans:** Early Decision Plan **Application Deadline:** March 01 **Application Fee:** $0.00 **H.S. Requirements:** High school diploma required; GED accepted **Costs Per Year:** Application fee: $0. **Calendar System:** Trimester, Summer Session Not available **Enrollment:** FT 1,007 **Faculty:** FT 85, PT 10 **Student-Faculty Ratio:** 11:1 **Exams:** SAT I or ACT **% Residing in College-Owned, -Operated, or -Affiliated Housing:** 100 **Library Holdings:** 185,000 **Regional Accreditation:** Middle State Association of Colleges and Schools **Credit Hours For Degree:** 216 quarter hours, Bachelors **Professional Accreditation:** ABET **Intercollegiate Athletics:** Baseball M; Basketball M & W; Crew M & W; Cross-Country Running M & W; Football M; Golf M & W; Lacrosse M; Rugby M; Sailing M & W; Soccer M; Softball W; Swimming and Diving M & W; Tennis M & W; Track and Field M & W; Volleyball W; Wrestling M

UNITED STATES MILITARY ACADEMY
600 Thayer Rd.
West Point, NY 10996
Tel: (845)938-4011
Admissions: (845)938-4041
Fax: (845)938-3021
E-mail: 8dad@sunams.usma.army.mil
Web Site: http://www.usma.edu/
President/CEO: Lt. Gen. William L. Lennox
Registrar: Dr. Kent A. Laudeman
Admissions: Col. Michael C. Jones
Financial Aid: Col. Michael Jones
Type: Four-Year College **Sex:** Coed **Scores:** 100% SAT V 400+; 100% SAT M 400+; 3% ACT 18-23; 63% ACT 24-29 **% Accepted:** 14 **Application Deadline:** February 28 **Application Fee:** $0.00 **H.S. Requirements:** High school diploma required; GED accepted **Costs Per Year:** Application fee: $0. **Calendar System:** Semester, Summer Session Available **Enrollment:** FT 4,231 **Faculty:** FT 604, PT 0 **Student-Faculty Ratio:** 7:1 **Exams:** SAT I or ACT **% Residing in College-Owned, -Operated, or -Affiliated Housing:** 100 **Library Holdings:** 457,340 **Regional Accreditation:** Middle State Association of Colleges and Schools **Credit Hours For Degree:** 40 courses, Bachelors **Professional Accreditation:** ABET **Intercollegiate Athletics:** Baseball M; Basketball M & W; Bowling M & W; Crew M & W; Cross-Country Running M & W; Equestrian Sports M & W; Fencing M & W; Football M; Golf M; Gymnastics M; Ice Hockey M; Lacrosse M & W; Racquetball M & W; Riflery M & W; Rugby M; Sailing M & W; Skiing (Cross-Country) M & W; Skiing (Downhill) M & W; Soccer M & W; Softball W; Squash M & W; Swimming and Diving M & W; Tennis M & W; Track and Field M & W; Volleyball M & W; Water Polo M; Weight Lifting M & W; Wrestling M

UNITED TALMUDICAL SEMINARY
82 Lee Ave.
Brooklyn, NY 11211-7900
Tel: (718)963-9260
Registrar: Moses Greenfeld
Financial Aid: Jacob Kohn
Type: Comprehensive **Sex:** Men **Affiliation:** Jewish **H.S. Requirements:** High school diploma required; GED accepted **Calendar System:** Semester **Professional Accreditation:** AARTS

UNIVERSITY AT ALBANY, STATE UNIVERSITY OF NEW YORK
1400 Washington Ave.
Albany, NY 12222-0001
Tel: (518)442-3300
Admissions: (518)442-5435
E-mail: ugadmissions@albany.edu
Web Site: http://www.albany.edu/
President/CEO: Vice Adm. John R. Ryan
Registrar: Robert Gibson
Admissions: Robert Andrea
Financial Aid: Dennis Tillman
Type: University **Sex:** Coed **Affiliation:** State University of New York System **Scores:** 100% SAT V 400+; 100% SAT M 400+ **% Accepted:** 63 **Admission Plans:** Early Admission; Early Action; Deferred Admission **Application Deadline:** March 01 **Application Fee:** $40.00 **H.S. Requirements:** High school diploma required; GED accepted **Costs Per Year:** Application fee: $40. State resident tuition: $4350 full-time, $181 per credit part-time. Nonresident tuition: $10,610 full-time, $442 per credit part-time. Mandatory fees: $1537 full-time. Part-time tuition varies according to course load. College room and board: $8050. College room only: $4834. Room and board charges vary according to board plan and housing facility. **Scholarships:** Available **Calendar System:** Semester, Summer Session Available **Enrollment:** FT 11,211, PT 802, Grad 5,027 **Faculty:** FT 631, PT 530 **Student-Faculty Ratio:** 19:1 **Exams:** SAT I or ACT **% Receiving Financial Aid:** 54 **% Residing in College-Owned, -Operated, or -Affiliated Housing:** 58 **Library Holdings:** 2,064,576 **Regional Accreditation:** Middle State Association of Colleges and Schools **Credit Hours For Degree:** 120 credits, Bachelors **ROTC:** Army, Air Force **Professional Accreditation:** AACSB, ACSP, ALA, APA, CEPH, CORE, CSWE, NASPAA **Intercollegiate Athletics:** Baseball M; Basketball M & W; Crew M & W; Cross-Country Running M & W; Field Hockey W; Football M; Golf W; Lacrosse M & W; Rugby M & W; Soccer M & W; Softball W; Tennis W; Track and Field M & W; Volleyball W

UNIVERSITY OF ROCHESTER
Wilson Blvd.
Rochester, NY 14627-0250
Tel: (585)275-2121; 888-822-2256
Admissions: (585)275-3221
Fax: (585)273-1118
E-mail: admit@admissions.rochester.edu
Web Site: http://www.rochester.edu/
President/CEO: Thomas H. Jackson
Registrar: Nancy Speck
Admissions: Jonathan Burdick
Type: University **Sex:** Coed **Scores:** 99% SAT V 400+; 100% SAT M 400+; 9% ACT 18-23; 58% ACT 24-29 **% Accepted:** 48 **Admission Plans:** Early Admission; Early Decision Plan; Deferred Admission **Application Deadline:** January 15 **Application Fee:** $50.00 **H.S. Requirements:** High school diploma required; GED accepted **Costs Per Year:** Application fee: $50. Comprehensive fee: $41,485 includes full-time tuition ($30,540), mandatory fees ($757), and college room and board ($10,188). College room only: $5710. Room and board charges vary according to board plan. Part-time tuition: $534 per credit hour. Part-time tuition varies according to course load. **Scholarships:** Available **Calendar System:** Semester, Summer Session Available **Enrollment:** FT 4,435, PT 261, Grad 3,480 **Faculty:** FT 505, PT 263 **Exams:** SAT I or ACT, SAT II **% Receiving Financial Aid:** 56 **% Residing in College-Owned, -Operated, or -Affiliated Housing:** 87 **Library Holdings:** 2,992,204 **Regional Accreditation:** Middle State Association of Colleges and Schools **Credit Hours For Degree:** 128 credit hours, Bachelors **ROTC:** Navy, Air Force **Professional Accreditation:** AACSB, ABET, AAMFT, ACA, APA, ACIPE, CEPH, LCMEAMA, NASM, NCATE, NLN **Intercollegiate Athletics:** Baseball M; Basketball M & W; Crew M & W; Cross-Country Running M & W; Equestrian Sports M & W; Field Hockey W; Football M; Golf M; Ice Hockey M & W; Lacrosse M & W; Rugby M & W; Skiing (Downhill) M & W; Soccer M & W; Softball W; Squash

M; Swimming and Diving M & W; Tennis M & W; Track and Field M & W; Ultimate Frisbee M & W; Volleyball M & W

U.T.A. MESIVTA OF KIRYAS JOEL
33 Forest Rd., Ste. 101
Monroe, NY 10950
Tel: (845)873-9901
Fax: (845)782-3620 **Type:** Four-Year College **Affiliation:** Jewish **Professional Accreditation:** AARTS

UTICA COLLEGE
1600 Burrstone Rd.
Utica, NY 13502-4892
Tel: (315)792-3111
Free: 800-782-8884
Admissions: (315)792-3006
Fax: (315)792-3003
Web Site: http://www.utica.edu/
President/CEO: Dr. Todd S. Hutton
Registrar: Dominic Passalacqua
Admissions: Patrick Quinn
Financial Aid: Elizabeth C. Wilson
Type: Comprehensive **Sex:** Coed **Scores:** 85% SAT V 400+; 88% SAT M 400+; 56% ACT 18-23; 24% ACT 24-29 **% Accepted:** 79 **Admission Plans:** Early Admission; Deferred Admission **Application Deadline:** Rolling **Application Fee:** $40.00 **H.S. Requirements:** High school diploma required; GED accepted **Costs Per Year:** Application fee: $40. Comprehensive fee: $31,396 includes full-time tuition ($22,030), mandatory fees ($310), and college room and board ($9056). College room only: $4750. Full-time tuition and fees vary according to class time and course load. Room and board charges vary according to board plan and housing facility. Part-time tuition: $750 per credit hour. Part-time mandatory fees: $50 per term. Part-time tuition and fees vary according to class time and course load. **Scholarships:** Available **Calendar System:** Semester, Summer Session Available **Enrollment:** FT 2,030, PT 383, Grad 427 **Faculty:** FT 119, PT 167 **Student-Faculty Ratio:** 17:1 **Exams:** SAT I or ACT **% Receiving Financial Aid:** 90 **% Residing in College-Owned, -Operated, or -Affiliated Housing:** 48 **Library Holdings:** 183,559 **Regional Accreditation:** Middle State Association of Colleges and Schools **Credit Hours For Degree:** 120 credit hours, Bachelors **ROTC:** Army, Air Force **Professional Accreditation:** AOTA, APTA, NLN **Intercollegiate Athletics:** Baseball M; Basketball M & W; Field Hockey W; Football M; Golf M & W; Ice Hockey M & W; Lacrosse M & W; Soccer M & W; Softball W; Swimming and Diving M & W; Tennis M & W; Volleyball W; Water Polo W

UTICA SCHOOL OF COMMERCE
201 Bleecker St.
Utica, NY 13501-2280
Tel: (315)733-2307
Free: 800-321-4USC
Admissions: (315)733-2300
Fax: (315)733-9281
Web Site: http://www.uscny.edu/
President/CEO: Philip M. Williams
Admissions: Chris Tacea
Financial Aid: Fred Zuccala
Type: Two-Year College **Sex:** Coed **Admission Plans:** Open Admission; Early Admission; Deferred Admission **Application Fee:** $20.00 **H.S. Requirements:** High school diploma required; GED accepted **Scholarships:** Available **Calendar System:** Quarter, Summer Session Available **Student-Faculty Ratio:** 15:1 **Library Holdings:** 2,000 **Credit Hours For Degree:** 90 quarter hours, Associates **Professional Accreditation:** NYSBR

VASSAR COLLEGE
124 Raymond Ave.
Poughkeepsie, NY 12604
Tel: (845)437-7000
Free: 800-827-7270
Admissions: (845)437-7300
Fax: (845)437-7063
E-mail: admissions@vassar.edu
Web Site: http://www.vassar.edu/
President/CEO: Dr. Frances D. Fergusson
Registrar: Daniel J. Giannini
Admissions: Dr. David M. Borus
Financial Aid: Michael Fraher
Type: Four-Year College **Sex:** Coed **Scores:** 100% SAT V 400+; 100% SAT M 400+ **% Accepted:** 29 **Admission Plans:** Early Decision Plan; Deferred Admission **Application Deadline:** January 01 **Application Fee:** $60.00 **H.S. Requirements:** High school diploma required; GED accepted **Costs Per Year:** Application fee: $60. Comprehensive fee: $41,700 includes full-time tuition ($33,310), mandatory fees ($490), and college room and board ($7900). College room only: $4190. Room and board charges vary according to board plan and housing facility. Part-time tuition: $3920 per course. Part-time mandatory fees: $240 per year. Part-time tuition and fees vary according to course load. **Scholarships:** Available **Calendar System:** Semester, Summer Session Not available **Enrollment:** FT 2,326, PT 52 **Faculty:** FT 277, PT 29 **Student-Faculty Ratio:** 8:1 **Exams:** SAT I and SAT II or ACT **% Receiving Financial Aid:** 54 **% Residing in College-Owned, -Operated, or -Affiliated Housing:** 95 **Library Holdings:** 878,177 **Regional Accreditation:** Middle State Association of Colleges and Schools **Credit Hours For Degree:** 34 units, Bachelors **Intercollegiate Athletics:** Baseball M; Basketball M & W; Crew M & W; Cross-Country Running M & W; Fencing M & W; Field Hockey W; Golf W; Lacrosse M & W; Rugby M & W; Soccer M & W; Squash M & W; Swimming and Diving M & W; Tennis M & W; Track and Field M & W; Ultimate Frisbee M & W; Volleyball M & W

VAUGHN COLLEGE OF AERONAUTICS AND TECHNOLOGY
8601 23rd Ave.
Flushing, NY 11369-1037
Tel: (718)429-6600
Fax: (718)429-0256
E-mail: pro@aero.edu
Web Site: http://www.vaughn.edu/
President/CEO: Dr. John C. Fitzpatrick
Registrar: Regina Chan
Admissions: Sharon DeVivo
Financial Aid: Clevelette Short
Type: Four-Year College **Sex:** Coed **Scores:** 88% SAT V 400+; 91% SAT M 400+ **% Accepted:** 95 **Admission Plans:** Open Admission; Deferred Admission **Application Deadline:** Rolling **Application Fee:** $45.00 **H.S. Requirements:** High school diploma required; GED accepted **Costs Per Year:** Application fee: $45. Tuition: $13,400 full-time, $450 per credit part-time. Mandatory fees: $280 full-time. Full-time tuition and fees vary according to course load, degree level, and program. **Scholarships:** Available **Calendar System:** Semester, Summer Session Available **Enrollment:** FT 842, PT 284 **Faculty:** FT 43, PT 70 **Student-Faculty Ratio:** 11:1 **Exams:** SAT I or ACT **% Receiving Financial Aid:** 92 **Library Holdings:** 62,000 **Regional Accreditation:** Middle State Association of Colleges and Schools **Credit Hours For Degree:** 68 credits, Associates; 126 credits, Bachelors **ROTC:** Army, Air Force **Professional Accreditation:** ABET

VILLA MARIA COLLEGE OF BUFFALO
240 Pine Ridge Rd.
Buffalo, NY 14225-3999
Tel: (716)896-0700
Fax: (716)896-0705
Web Site: http://www.villa.edu/
President/CEO: Sr. Marcella Marie Garus
Registrar: Sr. M. Mark Janik
Admissions: Kevin Donovan
Financial Aid: Diane Kasprzak
Type: Two-Year College **Sex:** Coed **Affiliation:** Roman Catholic Church **Scores:** 64% SAT V 400+; 60% SAT M 400+; 50% ACT 18-23 **% Accepted:** 78 **Admission Plans:** Deferred Admission **Application Deadline:** Rolling **H.S. Requirements:** High school diploma required; GED accepted **Costs Per Year:** Tuition: $11,280 full-time, $420 per credit hour part-time. Mandatory fees: $430 full-time. **Scholarships:** Available **Calendar System:** Semester, Summer Session Available **Enrollment:** FT 396, PT 106 **Faculty:** FT 26, PT 46 **Student-Faculty Ratio:** 11:1 **Library Holdings:** 37,000 **Regional Accreditation:** Middle State Association of Colleges and Schools **Credit Hours For Degree:** 61 credits, Associates **Professional Accreditation:** APTA

WAGNER COLLEGE
1 Campus Rd.
Staten Island, NY 10301-4495
Tel: (718)390-3100
Free: 800-221-1010

Admissions: (718)390-3411
Fax: (718)390-3105
E-mail: adm@wagner.edu
Web Site: http://www.wagner.edu/
President/CEO: Dr. Richard Guarasci
Registrar: Dr. Donald Stearns
Admissions: Angelo Araimo
Financial Aid: Theresa Weimer
Type: Comprehensive **Sex:** Coed **Scores:** 99% SAT V 400+; 99% SAT M 400+; 12% ACT 18-23; 81% ACT 24-29 **% Accepted:** 61 **Admission Plans:** Early Admission; Early Decision Plan; Deferred Admission **Application Deadline:** February 15 **Application Fee:** $50.00 **H.S. Requirements:** High school diploma required; GED accepted **Costs Per Year:** Application fee: $50. Comprehensive fee: $33,300 includes full-time tuition ($25,350) and college room and board ($7950). Part-time tuition: $845 per credit hour. **Scholarships:** Available **Calendar System:** Semester, Summer Session Available **Enrollment:** FT 1,892, PT 70, Grad 325 **Faculty:** FT 99, PT 130 **Student-Faculty Ratio:** 15:1 **Exams:** SAT I or ACT **% Receiving Financial Aid:** 63 **% Residing in College-Owned, -Operated, or -Affiliated Housing:** 70 **Library Holdings:** 310,000 **Regional Accreditation:** Middle State Association of Colleges and Schools **Credit Hours For Degree:** 36 units, Bachelors **Professional Accreditation:** ACBSP, NCATE, NLN **Intercollegiate Athletics:** Baseball M; Basketball M & W; Cross-Country Running M & W; Football M; Golf M & W; Ice Hockey M; Lacrosse M & W; Soccer W; Softball W; Swimming and Diving W; Tennis M & W; Track and Field M & W; Volleyball W; Water Polo W; Wrestling M

WEBB INSTITUTE
Crescent Beach Rd.
Glen Cove, NY 11542-1398
Tel: (516)671-2213
Fax: (516)674-9838
E-mail: admissions@webb-institute.edu
Web Site: http://www.webb-institute.edu/
President/CEO: Ronald K. Kiss
Registrar: William G. Murray
Admissions: Stephen Ostendorff
Financial Aid: William G. Murray
Type: Four-Year College **Sex:** Coed **Scores:** 100% SAT V 400+; 100% SAT M 400+ **% Accepted:** 30 **Admission Plans:** Early Decision Plan **Application Deadline:** February 15 **Application Fee:** $25.00 **H.S. Requirements:** High school diploma required; GED not accepted **Costs Per Year:** Application fee: $25. Comprehensive fee: $8340 includes full-time tuition ($0) and college room and board ($8340). **Scholarships:** Available **Calendar System:** Semester, Summer Session Not available **Enrollment:** FT 80 **Faculty:** FT 8, PT 7 **Student-Faculty Ratio:** 8:1 **Exams:** Other, SAT I, SAT II **% Receiving Financial Aid:** 11 **% Residing in College-Owned, -Operated, or -Affiliated Housing:** 100 **Library Holdings:** 53,319 **Regional Accreditation:** Middle State Association of Colleges and Schools **Credit Hours For Degree:** 146 credits, Bachelors **Professional Accreditation:** ABET **Intercollegiate Athletics:** Basketball M & W; Cross-Country Running M & W; Sailing M & W; Soccer M & W; Tennis M & W; Volleyball M & W

WELLS COLLEGE
170 Main St.
Aurora, NY 13026
Tel: (315)364-3266
Free: 800-952-9355
Admissions: (315)364-3264
Fax: (315)364-3227
E-mail: admissions@wells.edu
Web Site: http://www.wells.edu/
President/CEO: Lisa Marsh Ryerson
Registrar: Karla Leybold-Taylor
Admissions: Susan Raith Sloan
Financial Aid: Cathleen Bellomo
Type: Four-Year College **Sex:** Coed **Scores:** 99% SAT V 400+; 98% SAT M 400+; 29% ACT 18-23; 55% ACT 24-29 **% Accepted:** 65 **Admission Plans:** Early Admission; Early Action; Early Decision Plan; Deferred Admission **Application Deadline:** March 01 **Application Fee:** $40.00 **H.S. Requirements:** High school diploma required; GED accepted **Costs Per Year:** Application fee: $40. Comprehensive fee: $24,180 includes full-time tuition ($15,580), mandatory fees ($1100), and college room and board ($7500). College room only: $3750. **Scholarships:** Available **Calendar System:** Semester, Summer Session Not available **Enrollment:** FT 405, PT 12 **Faculty:** FT 49, PT 18 **Student-Faculty Ratio:** 8:1 **Exams:** SAT I or ACT **% Receiving Financial Aid:** 74 **% Residing in College-Owned, -Operated, or -Affiliated Housing:** 80 **Library Holdings:** 253,458 **Regional Accreditation:** Middle State Association of Colleges and Schools **Credit Hours For Degree:** 120 credits, Bachelors **ROTC:** Air Force **Intercollegiate Athletics:** Cross-Country Running M & W; Field Hockey W; Lacrosse W; Soccer M & W; Softball W; Swimming and Diving W; Tennis W

WESTCHESTER COMMUNITY COLLEGE
75 Grasslands Rd.
Valhalla, NY 10595-1698
Tel: (914)785-6600
Admissions: (914)606-6735
Web Site: http://www.sunywcc.edu/
President/CEO: Dr. Joseph N. Hankin
Registrar: Susan S. Stanton
Admissions: Terre Wisell
Financial Aid: Vernon Huff
Type: Two-Year College **Sex:** Coed **Affiliation:** State University of New York System **Admission Plans:** Open Admission; Early Admission **Application Deadline:** Rolling **Application Fee:** $25.00 **H.S. Requirements:** High school diploma required; GED accepted **Costs Per Year:** Application fee: $25. State resident tuition: $3350 full-time, $140 per credit part-time. Nonresident tuition: $8376 full-time, $350 per credit part-time. **Scholarships:** Available **Calendar System:** Semester, Summer Session Available **Faculty:** FT 156 **Student-Faculty Ratio:** 16:1 **Library Holdings:** 96,419 **Regional Accreditation:** Middle State Association of Colleges and Schools **Credit Hours For Degree:** 64 credits, Associates **Professional Accreditation:** CARC, JRCERT **Intercollegiate Athletics:** Baseball M; Basketball M & W; Bowling M & W; Golf M; Soccer M; Softball W; Volleyball W

WOOD TOBE-COBURN SCHOOL
8 East 40th St.
New York, NY 10016
Tel: (212)686-9040
Fax: (212)686-9171
Web Site: http://www.woodtobecoburn.com/
President/CEO: Sandra Gruninger
Registrar: Susan Cohan
Admissions: Sandra L. Andujar
Financial Aid: Linda Walters
Type: Two-Year College **Sex:** Coed **Affiliation:** Bradford Schools, Inc **% Accepted:** 86 **Application Deadline:** Rolling **Application Fee:** $50.00 **H.S. Requirements:** High school diploma required; GED accepted **Costs Per Year:** Application fee: $50. Tuition: $14,400 full-time. **Scholarships:** Available **Calendar System:** Semester, Summer Session Available **Enrollment:** FT 269 **Faculty:** FT 5, PT 16 **Student-Faculty Ratio:** 27:1 **Library Holdings:** 698 **Credit Hours For Degree:** 60 credits, Associates **Professional Accreditation:** NYSBR

YESHIVA AND KOLLEL HARBOTZAS TORAH
1049 East 15th St.
Brooklyn, NY 11230
Tel: (718)692-0208 **Type:** Four-Year College **Affiliation:** Jewish **Professional Accreditation:** AARTS

YESHIVA DERECH CHAIM
1573 39th St.
Brooklyn, NY 11218
Tel: (718)438-3070
Admissions: (718)438-5476
President/CEO: Rabbi Rennert
Registrar: Rabbi Rennert
Admissions: Y. Borchardt
Financial Aid: Borchardt
Type: Comprehensive **Sex:** Men **Affiliation:** Jewish **H.S. Requirements:** High school diploma required; GED not accepted **Calendar System:** Semester **Professional Accreditation:** AARTS

YESHIVA D'MONSEY RABBINICAL COLLEGE
2 Roman Blvd.
Monsey, NY 10952
Tel: (914)352-5852

Fax: (914)362-3453 **Type:** Four-Year College **Affiliation:** Jewish **Professional Accreditation:** AARTS

YESHIVA GEDOLAH IMREI YOSEF D'SPINKA
1466 56th St.
Brooklyn, NY 11219
Tel: (718)851-8721 **Type:** Four-Year College **Affiliation:** Jewish **Professional Accreditation:** AARTS

YESHIVA KARLIN STOLIN RABBINICAL INSTITUTE
1818 Fifty-fourth St.
Brooklyn, NY 11204
Tel: (718)232-7800
Fax: (718)331-4833
President/CEO: Rabbi R. Meyer Pilchick
Admissions: Aryeh L. Wolpin
Financial Aid: Daniel Ross
Type: Comprehensive **Sex:** Men **Affiliation:** Jewish **Admission Plans:** Preferred Admission **H.S. Requirements:** High school diploma required; GED accepted **Scholarships:** Available **Calendar System:** Semester, Summer Session Not available **Enrollment:** FT 38, Grad 15 **Faculty:** FT 4, PT 3 **Library Holdings:** 6,000 **Credit Hours For Degree:** 130 credits, Bachelors **Professional Accreditation:** AARTS

YESHIVA AND KOLEL BAIS MEDRASH ELYON
73 Main St.
Monsey, NY 10952
Tel: (845)356-7064 **Type:** Four-Year College **Affiliation:** Jewish **Professional Accreditation:** AARTS

YESHIVA OF NITRA RABBINICAL COLLEGE
Pines Bridge Rd.
Mount Kisco, NY 10549
Tel: (718)384-5460
President/CEO: Alexander Fischer
Registrar: Rabbi Sandor Sable
Admissions: Ernest Schwartz
Financial Aid: Miram Schwartz
Type: Comprehensive **Sex:** Men **Affiliation:** Jewish **H.S. Requirements:** High school diploma required; GED accepted **Calendar System:** Semester **Professional Accreditation:** AARTS

YESHIVA SHAAR HATORAH TALMUDIC RESEARCH INSTITUTE
117-06 84th Ave.
Kew Gardens, NY 11418-1469
Tel: (718)846-1940
President/CEO: Rabbi Yoel Yankelewitz
Registrar: Rabbi Kalman Epstein
Admissions: Rabbi Kalman Epstein
Financial Aid: Rabbi Sholom Spitz
Type: Comprehensive **Sex:** Men **Affiliation:** Jewish **Calendar System:** Semester **Professional Accreditation:** AARTS

YESHIVA SHAAREI TORAH OF ROCKLAND
91 West Carlton Rd.
Suffern, NY 10901
Tel: (845)352-3431 **Type:** Four-Year College **Affiliation:** Jewish **Professional Accreditation:** AARTS

YESHIVA OF THE TELSHE ALUMNI
4904 Independence Ave.
Riverdale, NY 10471
Tel: (718)601-3523 **Type:** Four-Year College **Affiliation:** Jewish **Professional Accreditation:** AARTS

YESHIVA UNIVERSITY
500 West 185th St.
New York, NY 10033-3201
Tel: (212)960-5400
Admissions: (212)960-5277
Fax: (212)960-0086
Web Site: http://www.yu.edu/
President/CEO: Richard M. Joel
Registrar: Dr. Lea Honigwachs
Admissions: Michael Kranzler
Financial Aid: Robert Friedman
Type: University **Sex:** Coed **Admission Plans:** Early Admission; Deferred Admission **Application Fee:** $40.00 **H.S. Requirements:** High school diploma required; GED not accepted **Scholarships:** Available **Calendar System:** Semester, Summer Session Available **Enrollment:** FT 2,778, PT 41, Grad 1,514 **Faculty:** FT 235 **Exams:** SAT I or ACT, SAT II **% Receiving Financial Aid:** 41 **Library Holdings:** 995,312 **Regional Accreditation:** Middle State Association of Colleges and Schools **Credit Hours For Degree:** 128 credits, Bachelors **Professional Accreditation:** ABA, APA, AALS, CSWE, LCMEAMA **Intercollegiate Athletics:** Basketball M & W; Cross-Country Running M; Fencing M; Tennis M & W; Volleyball M; Wrestling M

YESHIVAS NOVOMINSK
1569 47th St.
Brooklyn, NY 11219
Tel: (718)438-2727 **Type:** Four-Year College **Affiliation:** Jewish **Professional Accreditation:** AARTS

YESHIVAT MIKDASH MELECH
1326 Ocean Parkway
Brooklyn, NY 11230-5601
Tel: (718)339-1090
President/CEO: Rabbi Haim Denolel
Registrar: Rabbi Aron Furst
Admissions: Rabbi S. Churba
Financial Aid: Rabbi Samuel Ani
Type: Four-Year College **Sex:** Men **Affiliation:** Jewish **Calendar System:** Continuous **Faculty:** FT 4, PT 5 **Professional Accreditation:** AARTS

YESHIVATH VIZNITZ
Phyllis Terrace, PO Box 446
Monsey, NY 10952
Tel: (914)356-1010
President/CEO: Gershon Meiman
Registrar: Rabbi Joseph Viznitzer
Admissions: Rabbi Bernard Rosenfeld
Financial Aid: Rabbi Bernard Rosenfeld
Type: Comprehensive **Sex:** Men **Affiliation:** Jewish **Calendar System:** Semester **Professional Accreditation:** AARTS

YESHIVATH ZICHRON MOSHE
Laurel Park Rd.
South Fallsburg, NY 12779
Tel: (914)434-5240
President/CEO: Rabbi Tzviabba Gorelieck
Registrar: Rabbi Ely Goldschmidt
Admissions: Rabbi Abba Gorelick
Financial Aid: Miryom Miller
Type: Comprehensive **Sex:** Men **Affiliation:** Jewish **Calendar System:** Semester **Professional Accreditation:** AARTS

YORK COLLEGE OF THE CITY UNIVERSITY OF NEW YORK
94-20 Guy R Brewer Blvd.
Jamaica, NY 11451-0001
Tel: (718)262-2000
Admissions: (718)262-2188
E-mail: warmsley@york.cuny.edu
Web Site: http://www.york.cuny.edu/
President/CEO: Dr. Robert L. Hampton
Registrar: Sharon Davidson
Admissions: Diane Warmsley
Type: Four-Year College **Sex:** Coed **Affiliation:** City University of New York System **Scores:** 58.15% SAT V 400+; 65.11% SAT M 400+ **% Accepted:** 46 **Admission Plans:** Deferred Admission **Application Deadline:** Rolling **Application Fee:** $65.00 **H.S. Requirements:** High school diploma required; GED accepted **Costs Per Year:** Application fee: $65. State resident tuition: $4000 full-time. Nonresident tuition: $8640 full-time. **Scholarships:** Available **Calendar System:** Semester, Summer Session Available **Enrollment:** FT 3,879, PT 2,021 **Faculty:** FT 180, PT 290 **Student-Faculty Ratio:** 15:1 **Exams:** SAT I or ACT **% Receiving Financial Aid:** 69 **Library Holdings:** 179,022 **Regional Accreditation:** Middle State Association of Colleges and Schools **Credit Hours For Degree:** 120 credits, Bachelors **ROTC:** Army, Air Force **Professional Accreditation:** AOTA, CSWE, NLN **Intercollegiate Athletics:** Baseball M & W; Basketball M & W;

Cross-Country Running M & W; Soccer M; Softball W; Swimming and Diving M & W; Tennis M; Track and Field M & W; Volleyball M & W

ALAMANCE COMMUNITY COLLEGE
PO Box 8000
Graham, NC 27253-8000
Tel: (336)578-2002
Fax: (336)578-1987
Web Site: http://www.alamance.cc.nc.us/
President/CEO: Dr. Martin H. Nadelman
Registrar: Suzanne Lucier
Admissions: Suzanne Lucier
Financial Aid: Elizabeth Solazzo
Type: Two-Year College **Sex:** Coed **Affiliation:** North Carolina Community College System **% Accepted:** 100 **Admission Plans:** Open Admission; Deferred Admission **Application Deadline:** Rolling **Application Fee:** $0.00 **H.S. Requirements:** High school diploma required; GED accepted **Costs Per Year:** Application fee: $0. State resident tuition: $1264 full-time, $39.50 per credit hour part-time. Nonresident tuition: $7024 full-time, $219.50 per credit hour part-time. Mandatory fees: $30 full-time, $5 per term part-time. **Scholarships:** Available **Calendar System:** Semester, Summer Session Available **Enrollment:** FT 1,770, PT 2,515 **Faculty:** FT 99, PT 139 **Student-Faculty Ratio:** 16:1 **Library Holdings:** 22,114 **Regional Accreditation:** Southern Association of Colleges and Schools **Credit Hours For Degree:** 64 semester hours, Associates **Professional Accreditation:** ADA, NAACLS

APEX SCHOOL OF THEOLOGY
5104 Revere Rd.
Durham, NC 27713
Tel: (919)572-1625
Fax: (919)572-1762
E-mail: info@apexsot.edu
Web Site: http://www.apexsot.org/
President/CEO: Dr. Joesph E. Perkins
Admissions: Dr. Joseph E. Perkins
Type: Comprehensive **Sex:** Coed **Affiliation:** interdenominational **% Accepted:** 75 **Admission Plans:** Open Admission **Application Fee:** $0.00 **H.S. Requirements:** High school diploma required; GED accepted **Costs Per Year:** Application fee: $0. Tuition: $325 per course part-time. **Calendar System:** Semester **Enrollment:** FT 10, PT 26, Grad 8 **Faculty:** FT 3, PT 12 **Student-Faculty Ratio:** 2:1 **Professional Accreditation:** TACCS

APPALACHIAN STATE UNIVERSITY
Boone, NC 28608
Tel: (828)262-2000
Admissions: (828)262-2120
Fax: (828)262-3296
E-mail: admissions@conrad.appstate.edu
Web Site: http://www.appstate.edu/
President/CEO: Dr. Kenneth Peacock
Registrar: Don Rankins
Admissions: Paul Hiatt
Financial Aid: Esther Captain
Type: Comprehensive **Sex:** Coed **Affiliation:** University of North Carolina System **Scores:** 99.25% SAT V 400+; 99.3% SAT M 400+; 53.85% ACT 18-23; 36.17% ACT 24-29 **% Accepted:** 69 **Admission Plans:** Early Admission; Deferred Admission **Application Deadline:** Rolling **Application Fee:** $45.00 **H.S. Requirements:** High school diploma required; GED accepted **Costs Per Year:** Application fee: $45. State resident tuition: $2221 full-time, $80 per credit hour part-time. Nonresident tuition: $11,963 full-time, $425 per credit hour part-time. Mandatory fees: $1697 full-time. College room and board: $4960. College room only: $3100. **Scholarships:** Available **Calendar System:** Semester, Summer Session Available **Enrollment:** FT 12,043, PT 943, Grad 1,667 **Faculty:** FT 703, PT 295 **Student-Faculty Ratio:** 17:1 **Exams:** SAT I or ACT **% Receiving Financial Aid:** 32 **% Residing in College-Owned, -Operated, or -Affiliated Housing:** 42 **Library Holdings:** 904,597 **Regional Accreditation:** Southern Association of Colleges and Schools **Credit Hours For Degree:** 122 semester hours, Bachelors **ROTC:** Army **Professional Accreditation:** AACSB, ABET, AAMFT, AAFCS, ACA, ADtA, APA, ASLHA, CSWE, JRCEPAT, NASAD, NASM, NASPAA, NAST, NCATE, NRPA **Intercollegiate Athletics:** Baseball M; Basketball M & W; Cross-Country Running M & W; Field Hockey W; Football M; Golf M & W; Soccer M & W; Tennis M & W; Track and Field M & W; Volleyball W; Wrestling M

THE ART INSTITUTE OF CHARLOTTE
2110 Water Ridge Parkway
Charlotte, NC 28217
Tel: (704)357-8020
Fax: (704)357-1133
E-mail: guinane@aii.edu
Web Site: http://www.aich.artinstitutes.edu/
President/CEO: Elizabeth Guinan
Admissions: Gil Cendejas
Type: Two-Year College **Sex:** Coed **Affiliation:** Education Management Corporation **Admission Plans:** Deferred Admission **Application Deadline:** Rolling **Application Fee:** $50.00 **H.S. Requirements:** High school diploma required; GED accepted **Costs Per Year:** Application fee: $50. Tuition: $23,232 full-time, $363 per credit part-time. Mandatory fees: $200 full-time. College room only: $5580. **Calendar System:** Quarter, Summer Session Available **Enrollment:** FT 564, PT 255 **Faculty:** FT 21, PT 31 **Student-Faculty Ratio:** 19:1 **Exams:** SAT I or ACT **% Residing in College-Owned, -Operated, or -Affiliated Housing:** 26 **Library Holdings:** 15,000 **Credit Hours For Degree:** 112 quarter hours, Associates; 188 quarter hours, Bachelors **Professional Accreditation:** ACICS

ASHEVILLE-BUNCOMBE TECHNICAL COMMUNITY COLLEGE
340 Victoria Rd.
Asheville, NC 28801-4897
Tel: (828)254-1921
Fax: (828)251-6355
E-mail: lbush@abtech.edu
Web Site: http://www.abtech.edu/
President/CEO: K. Ray Bailey
Registrar: Scott Douglas
Admissions: Lisa Bush
Financial Aid: Lynn Deyton
Type: Two-Year College **Sex:** Coed **Affiliation:** North Carolina Community College System **Admission Plans:** Open Admission; Deferred Admission **Application Fee:** $0.00 **H.S. Requirements:** High school diploma required; GED accepted **Costs Per Year:** Application fee: $0. State resident tuition: $1216 full-time, $38 per credit hour part-time. Nonresident tuition: $6752 full-time, $211 per credit hour part-time. Mandatory fees: $28 full-time, $11 per term part-time. **Scholarships:** Available **Calendar System:** Semester, Summer Session Available **Enrollment:** FT 2,042, PT 3,585 **Faculty:** FT 120, PT

464 **Student-Faculty Ratio:** 17:1 **Exams:** Other **Library Holdings:** 37,439 **Regional Accreditation:** Southern Association of Colleges and Schools **Credit Hours For Degree:** 64 semester hours, Associates **Professional Accreditation:** ADA, JRCERT, NAACLS

BARBER-SCOTIA COLLEGE
145 Cabarrus Ave., West
Concord, NC 28025-5187
Tel: (704)789-2900
Free: 800-610-0778
Admissions: (704)789-2902
Fax: (704)784-3817
Web Site: http://www.b-sc.edu/
President/CEO: Dr. Gloria Bromell-Tinubu
Registrar: Emma Witherspoon
Admissions: Edward Alexander
Financial Aid: Raymond Robinson
Type: Four-Year College **Sex:** Coed **Affiliation:** Presbyterian Church (U.S. A.) **Admission Plans:** Early Admission **Application Fee:** $15.00 **H.S. Requirements:** High school diploma required; GED accepted **Scholarships:** Available **Calendar System:** Semester, Summer Session Available **Enrollment:** FT 737, PT 5 **Faculty:** FT 34, PT 8 **Student-Faculty Ratio:** 19:1 **Exams:** SAT I or ACT **% Residing in College-Owned, -Operated, or -Affiliated Housing:** 90 **Library Holdings:** 24,270 **Regional Accreditation:** Southern Association of Colleges and Schools **Credit Hours For Degree:** 125 semester hours, Bachelors **ROTC:** Army, Air Force **Intercollegiate Athletics:** Basketball M & W; Cross-Country Running M & W; Softball W; Tennis M; Track and Field M & W; Volleyball W

BARTON COLLEGE
PO Box 5000
Wilson, NC 27893-7000
Tel: (252)399-6300
Free: 800-345-4973
Admissions: (252)399-6314
Fax: (252)237-4957
E-mail: adenton@barton.edu
Web Site: http://www.barton.edu/
President/CEO: Dr. Norval C. Kneten
Registrar: Sheila Milne
Admissions: Amy Denton
Financial Aid: Bettie Westbrook
Type: Four-Year College **Sex:** Coed **Affiliation:** Christian Church (Disciples of Christ) **Scores:** 88.2% SAT V 400+; 90.6% SAT M 400+ **% Accepted:** 70 **Admission Plans:** Deferred Admission **Application Deadline:** Rolling **Application Fee:** $25.00 **H.S. Requirements:** High school diploma required; GED accepted **Costs Per Year:** Application fee: $25. Comprehensive fee: $22,470 includes full-time tuition ($15,390), mandatory fees ($1280), and college room and board ($5800). College room only: $2774. Full-time tuition and fees vary according to course load and program. Room and board charges vary according to housing facility. Part-time tuition: $654 per credit hour. Part-time tuition varies according to course load and program. **Scholarships:** Available **Calendar System:** 4-1-4, Summer Session Available **Enrollment:** FT 917, PT 272 **Faculty:** FT 79, PT 32 **Student-Faculty Ratio:** 13:1 **Exams:** SAT I or ACT **% Receiving Financial Aid:** 71 **% Residing in College-Owned, -Operated, or -Affiliated Housing:** 39 **Library Holdings:** 169,836 **Regional Accreditation:** Southern Association of Colleges and Schools **Credit Hours For Degree:** 126 semester hours, Bachelors **Professional Accreditation:** CSWE, NCATE, NLN **Intercollegiate Athletics:** Baseball M; Basketball M & W; Cross-Country Running M & W; Golf M; Soccer M & W; Softball W; Tennis M & W; Volleyball W

BEAUFORT COUNTY COMMUNITY COLLEGE
PO Box 1069
Washington, NC 27889-1069
Tel: (252)946-6194
Admissions: (252)940-6233
Fax: (252)946-0271
Web Site: http://www.beaufortccc.edu/
President/CEO: Dr. David McLawhorn
Registrar: Doris King
Admissions: Gary Burbage
Financial Aid: Harold Smith
Type: Two-Year College **Sex:** Coed **Affiliation:** North Carolina Community College System **Admission Plans:** Open Admission **Application Deadline:** August 18 **Application Fee:** $0.00 **H.S. Requirements:** High school diploma required; GED accepted **Costs Per Year:** Application fee: $0. State resident tuition: $1264 full-time. Nonresident tuition: $7024 full-time. Mandatory fees: $64 full-time. **Scholarships:** Available **Calendar System:** Semester, Summer Session Available **Enrollment:** FT 733, PT 691 **Faculty:** FT 159, PT 163 **Exams:** Other, SAT I and SAT II or ACT **Library Holdings:** 25,734 **Regional Accreditation:** Southern Association of Colleges and Schools **Credit Hours For Degree:** 65 semester hours, Associates **Professional Accreditation:** NAACLS

BELMONT ABBEY COLLEGE
100 Belmont-Mt. Holly Rd.
Belmont, NC 28012-1802
Tel: (704)825-6700; 888-BAC-0110
Admissions: (704)825-6884
Fax: (704)825-6670
Web Site: http://www.belmontabbeycollege.edu/
President/CEO: Bill Thierfelder
Registrar: Heather Metress
Admissions: Michael Poll
Financial Aid: Lawton Blandford
Type: Four-Year College **Sex:** Coed **Affiliation:** Roman Catholic **Scores:** 93% SAT V 400+; 92% SAT M 400+; 58% ACT 18-23; 17% ACT 24-29 **Admission Plans:** Deferred Admission **Application Fee:** $35.00 **H.S. Requirements:** High school diploma required; GED accepted **Costs Per Year:** Application fee: $35. One-time mandatory fee: $672. Comprehensive fee: $25,310 includes full-time tuition ($15,910), mandatory fees ($814), and college room and board ($8586). College room only: $4829. Full-time tuition and fees vary according to class time, course level, course load, location, program, reciprocity agreements, and student level. Room and board charges vary according to board plan, housing facility, location, and student level. Part-time tuition: $499 per credit. Part-time mandatory fees: $201 per hour. Part-time tuition and fees vary according to class time, course level, course load, location, reciprocity agreements, and student level. **Scholarships:** Available **Calendar System:** Semester, Summer Session Available **Enrollment:** FT 712, PT 88 **Faculty:** FT 41, PT 40 **Student-Faculty Ratio:** 15:1 **Exams:** SAT I or ACT **% Receiving Financial Aid:** 65 **% Residing in College-Owned, -Operated, or -Affiliated Housing:** 48 **Library Holdings:** 110,050 **Regional Accreditation:** Southern Association of Colleges and Schools **Credit Hours For Degree:** 120 credit hours, Bachelors **ROTC:** Army, Air Force **Professional Accreditation:** NCATE **Intercollegiate Athletics:** Baseball M; Basketball M & W; Cheerleading M & W; Cross-Country Running M & W; Golf M & W; Lacrosse M & W; Soccer M & W; Softball W; Tennis M & W; Volleyball W; Wrestling M

BENNETT COLLEGE FOR WOMEN
900 East Washington St.
Greensboro, NC 27401-3239
Tel: (336)273-4431
Admissions: (336)517-8624
Web Site: http://www.bennett.edu/
President/CEO: Dr. Johnnetta B. Cole
Registrar: Dr. Carl Manuel
Admissions: Ulisa Bowles
Financial Aid: Stephanie Lynch
Type: Four-Year College **Sex:** Women **Affiliation:** United Methodist **Scores:** 62% SAT V 400+; 55% SAT M 400+; 26% ACT 18-23; 1% ACT 24-29 **% Accepted:** 57 **Admission Plans:** Deferred Admission **Application Deadline:** Rolling **Application Fee:** $30.00 **H.S. Requirements:** High school diploma required; GED accepted **Costs Per Year:** Application fee: $30. Comprehensive fee: $19,089 includes full-time tuition ($11,509), mandatory fees ($1730), and college room and board ($5850). College room only: $2937. Part-time tuition: $479 per credit hour. Part-time mandatory fees: $718 per term. **Scholarships:** Available **Calendar System:** Semester, Summer Session Available **Enrollment:** FT 566, PT 6 **Faculty:** FT 49, PT 18 **Student-Faculty Ratio:** 10:1 **Exams:** SAT I or ACT **% Receiving Financial Aid:** 85 **% Residing in College-Owned, -Operated, or -Affiliated Housing:** 75 **Library Holdings:** 119,191 **Regional Accreditation:** Southern Association of Colleges and Schools **Credit Hours For Degree:** 124 semester hours, Bachelors **ROTC:** Army, Air Force **Professional Accreditation:** CSWE, NCATE **Intercollegiate Athletics:** Basketball W; Cross-Country Running W; Softball W; Tennis W; Track and Field W; Volleyball W

BLADEN COMMUNITY COLLEGE
PO Box 266
Dublin, NC 28332-0266

Tel: (910)879-5500
Admissions: (910)879-5574
Fax: (910)879-5508
Web Site: http://www.bladen.cc.nc.us/
President/CEO: Dr. Darrell Page
Registrar: Barry Priest
Admissions: Jeff Kornegay
Financial Aid: Marva Dinkins
Type: Two-Year College **Sex:** Coed **Affiliation:** North Carolina Community College System **Admission Plans:** Open Admission; Deferred Admission **Application Deadline:** August 01 **Application Fee:** $0.00 **H.S. Requirements:** High school diploma required; GED accepted **Costs Per Year:** Application fee: $0. State resident tuition: $1264 full-time, $39.50 per hour part-time. Nonresident tuition: $7024 full-time, $219.50 per hour part-time. Mandatory fees: $66 full-time, $25.75 per term part-time. **Scholarships:** Available **Calendar System:** Semester, Summer Session Available **Enrollment:** FT 838, PT 569 **Faculty:** FT 32, PT 53 **Exams:** Other **Library Holdings:** 19,881 **Regional Accreditation:** Southern Association of Colleges and Schools **Credit Hours For Degree:** 64 semester hours, Associates

BLUE RIDGE COMMUNITY COLLEGE
180 West Campus Dr.
Flat Rock, NC 28731-4728
Tel: (828)694-1700
Admissions: (828)694-1801
Fax: (828)694-1690
E-mail: frankb@blueridge.edu
Web Site: http://www.blueridge.edu/
President/CEO: Dr. David W. Sink, Jr.
Registrar: Kirsten Bunch
Admissions: Frank Byrd
Financial Aid: Wanda Bodenhammer
Type: Two-Year College **Sex:** Coed **Affiliation:** North Carolina Community College System **Admission Plans:** Open Admission; Early Admission **Application Fee:** $0.00 **H.S. Requirements:** High school diploma required; GED accepted **Scholarships:** Available **Calendar System:** Semester, Summer Session Available **Enrollment:** FT 787, PT 1,172 **Faculty:** FT 75, PT 227 **Student-Faculty Ratio:** 14:1 **Library Holdings:** 47,655 **Regional Accreditation:** Southern Association of Colleges and Schools **Credit Hours For Degree:** 64 credit hours, Associates **Intercollegiate Athletics:** Baseball M

BREVARD COLLEGE
400 North Broad St.
Brevard, NC 28712-3306
Tel: (828)883-8292
Free: 800-527-9090
Admissions: (828)884-8300
Fax: (828)884-3790
E-mail: admissions@brevard.edu
Web Site: http://www.brevard.edu/
President/CEO: Dr. Drew L. Van Horn
Registrar: Adelaide H. Kersh
Admissions: Joretta Nelson
Financial Aid: Lisanne J. Masterson
Type: Four-Year College **Sex:** Coed **Affiliation:** United Methodist **Scores:** 90% SAT V 400+; 91% SAT M 400+; 59% ACT 18-23; 11% ACT 24-29 **% Accepted:** 74 **Admission Plans:** Deferred Admission **Application Deadline:** Rolling **Application Fee:** $30.00 **H.S. Requirements:** High school diploma required; GED accepted **Costs Per Year:** Application fee: $30. Comprehensive fee: $21,970 includes full-time tuition ($15,620), mandatory fees ($370), and college room and board ($5980). Full-time tuition and fees vary according to course load. Room and board charges vary according to board plan and housing facility. Part-time tuition: $620 per credit hour. Part-time mandatory fees: $20 per term. Part-time tuition and fees vary according to course load. **Scholarships:** Available **Calendar System:** Semester, Summer Session Not available **Enrollment:** FT 572, PT 25 **Faculty:** FT 56, PT 28 **Student-Faculty Ratio:** 9:1 **Exams:** SAT I or ACT **% Receiving Financial Aid:** 62 **% Residing in College-Owned, -Operated, or -Affiliated Housing:** 70 **Library Holdings:** 57,281 **Regional Accreditation:** Southern Association of Colleges and Schools **Credit Hours For Degree:** 124 semester hours, Bachelors **Professional Accreditation:** NASM **Intercollegiate Athletics:** Baseball M; Basketball M & W; Cheerleading M & W; Cross-Country Running M & W; Football M; Golf M; Soccer M & W; Softball W; Tennis M & W; Track and Field M & W; Volleyball W

BRUNSWICK COMMUNITY COLLEGE
PO Box 30
Supply, NC 28462-0030
Tel: (910)755-7300
Free: 800-754-1050
Admissions: (910)755-7321
Fax: (910)754-9609
Web Site: http://www.brunswick.cc.nc.us/
President/CEO: Dr. W. Michael Reaves
Registrar: Lynn Morgan
Admissions: Matlynn Bryant Yeoman
Financial Aid: Paula Almond
Type: Two-Year College **Sex:** Coed **Affiliation:** North Carolina Community College System **Admission Plans:** Open Admission **Application Fee:** $0.00 **H.S. Requirements:** High school diploma required; GED accepted **Costs Per Year:** Application fee: $0. State resident tuition: $1185 full-time, $39.50 per semester hour part-time. Nonresident tuition: $6585 full-time, $219.50 per semester hour part-time. Mandatory fees: $73 full-time, $37 per term part-time. Part-time tuition and fees vary according to course load. **Scholarships:** Available **Calendar System:** Semester, Summer Session Available **Enrollment:** FT 493, PT 510 **Faculty:** FT 29, PT 80 **Student-Faculty Ratio:** 12:1 **Exams:** Other **Library Holdings:** 20,032 **Regional Accreditation:** Southern Association of Colleges and Schools **Credit Hours For Degree:** 64 semester hours, Associates **Professional Accreditation:** AHIMA **Intercollegiate Athletics:** Basketball M & W; Golf M; Softball W

CABARRUS COLLEGE OF HEALTH SCIENCES
401 Medical Park Dr.
Concord, NC 28025
Tel: (704)783-1555
Admissions: (704)783-1616
Fax: (704)783-1764
Web Site: http://www.cabarruscollege.edu/
President/CEO: Anita A. Brown, RN
Registrar: Bob Davis
Admissions: Mark Ellison
Financial Aid: Valarie Richard
Type: Four-Year College **Sex:** Coed **Scores:** 94% SAT V 400+; 88% SAT M 400+; 75% ACT 18-23 **% Accepted:** 69 **Application Deadline:** March 01 **Application Fee:** $35.00 **H.S. Requirements:** High school diploma required; GED accepted **Costs Per Year:** Application fee: $35. Tuition: $7300 full-time, $230 per hour part-time. **Scholarships:** Available **Calendar System:** Semester, Summer Session Not available **Enrollment:** FT 207, PT 101 **Faculty:** FT 24, PT 26 **Student-Faculty Ratio:** 7:1 **Exams:** Other, SAT I or ACT **Library Holdings:** 7,676 **Regional Accreditation:** Southern Association of Colleges and Schools **Credit Hours For Degree:** 61 semester hours, Associates; 120 semester hours, Bachelors **Professional Accreditation:** ARCEST, AACN, AOTA, NLN

CALDWELL COMMUNITY COLLEGE AND TECHNICAL INSTITUTE
2855 Hickory Blvd.
Hudson, NC 28638-2397
Tel: (828)726-2200
Admissions: (828)726-2703
Fax: (828)726-2490
E-mail: cwoodard@cccti.edu
Web Site: http://www.cccti.edu/
President/CEO: Dr. Kenneth A. Boham
Registrar: Johnna Coffey
Admissions: Carolyn Woodard
Financial Aid: Dianne Henderson
Type: Two-Year College **Sex:** Coed **Affiliation:** North Carolina Community College System **% Accepted:** 100 **Admission Plans:** Open Admission; Early Admission **Application Deadline:** Rolling **Application Fee:** $0.00 **H.S. Requirements:** High school diploma required; GED accepted **Costs Per Year:** Application fee: $0. State resident tuition: $1185 full-time, $39.50 per credit hour part-time. Nonresident tuition: $6585 full-time, $219.50 per credit hour part-time. Mandatory fees: $4. **Scholarships:** Available **Calendar System:** Semester, Summer Session Available **Enrollment:** FT 1,281, PT 2,463 **Faculty:** FT 119, PT 288 **Library Holdings:** 50,770 **Regional Accreditation:** Southern Association of Colleges and Schools **Credit Hours For Degree:** 65 semester hours, Associates **Professional Ac-**

creditation: JRCEDMS, JRCERT, JRCNMT **Intercollegiate Athletics:** Basketball M & W; Golf M; Volleyball W

CAMPBELL UNIVERSITY
PO Box 97
Buies Creek, NC 27506
Tel: (910)893-1200
Free: 800-334-4111
Admissions: (910)893-1291
Fax: (910)893-1288
E-mail: kerner@mailcenter.campbell.edu
Web Site: http://www.campbell.edu/
President/CEO: Dr. Jerry M. Wallace
Registrar: David McGirt
Admissions: Herbert V. Kerner Jr.
Financial Aid: Nancy Beasley
Type: University **Sex:** Coed **Affiliation:** North Carolina Baptist State Convention **Scores:** 95% SAT V 400+; 97% SAT M 400+ **% Accepted:** 61 **Admission Plans:** Early Admission; Deferred Admission **Application Deadline:** Rolling **Application Fee:** $35.00 **H.S. Requirements:** High school diploma required; GED accepted **Costs Per Year:** Application fee: $35. Comprehensive fee: $22,835 includes full-time tuition ($17,027) and college room and board ($5808). **Scholarships:** Available **Calendar System:** Semester, Summer Session Available **Enrollment:** FT 2,566, PT 126, Grad 691 **Faculty:** FT 188, PT 148 **Student-Faculty Ratio:** 12:1 **Exams:** SAT I or ACT **% Receiving Financial Aid:** 57 **% Residing in College-Owned, -Operated, or -Affiliated Housing:** 50 **Library Holdings:** 218,000 **Regional Accreditation:** Southern Association of Colleges and Schools **Credit Hours For Degree:** 64 semester hours, Associates; 128 semester hours, Bachelors **ROTC:** Army **Professional Accreditation:** ABA, ACPhE, ATS, CSWE, JRCEPAT, NCATE **Intercollegiate Athletics:** Baseball M; Basketball M & W; Cheerleading W; Cross-Country Running M & W; Golf M & W; Soccer M & W; Softball W; Swimming and Diving W; Tennis M & W; Track and Field M & W; Volleyball W; Wrestling M

CAPE FEAR COMMUNITY COLLEGE
411 North Front St.
Wilmington, NC 28401-3993
Tel: (910)362-7000
Admissions: (910)362-7054
E-mail: lkasyan@cfcc.edu
Web Site: http://www.cfcc.edu/
President/CEO: Dr. Eric B. McKeithan
Registrar: Phil Farinholt
Admissions: Linda Kasyan
Financial Aid: Linda Smiley
Type: Two-Year College **Sex:** Coed **Affiliation:** North Carolina Community College System **Admission Plans:** Open Admission; Early Admission; Deferred Admission **Application Deadline:** August 19 **Application Fee:** $0.00 **H.S. Requirements:** High school diploma required; GED accepted. For vocational programs: High school diploma or equivalent not required **Costs Per Year:** Application fee: $0. State resident tuition: $1264 full-time, $39.50 per credit part-time. Nonresident tuition: $7024 full-time, $219.50 per credit part-time. Mandatory fees: $70 full-time, $7 per credit part-time. Full-time tuition and fees vary according to course load. Part-time tuition and fees vary according to course load. **Scholarships:** Available **Calendar System:** Semester, Summer Session Not available **Enrollment:** FT 3,160, PT 4,341 **Faculty:** FT 225, PT 249 **Student-Faculty Ratio:** 13:1 **Library Holdings:** 47,761 **Regional Accreditation:** Southern Association of Colleges and Schools **Credit Hours For Degree:** 64 semester hours, Associates **Professional Accreditation:** ADA, AOTA, NLN **Intercollegiate Athletics:** Basketball M; Cheerleading M & W; Golf M; Softball M & W; Tennis M & W; Volleyball M & W

CAROLINAS COLLEGE OF HEALTH SCIENCES
PO Box 32861, 1200 Blythe Blvd.
Charlotte, NC 28232-2861
Tel: (704)355-5043
Fax: (704)355-5967
Web Site: http://www.carolinascollege.edu/
President/CEO: Ellen Sheppard
Registrar: Rhoda Gallo
Admissions: Kim Wagner
Financial Aid: Kim Bradshaw
Type: Two-Year College **Sex:** Coed **Affiliation:** Carolinas Healthcare System **Scores:** 93% SAT V 400+; 93% SAT M 400+; 50% ACT 18-23; 13% ACT 24-29 **Admission Plans:** Preferred Admission **Application Fee:** $35.00 **H.S. Requirements:** High school diploma required; GED accepted **Costs Per Year:** Application fee: $35. Tuition: $6145 full-time, $175 per credit part-time. Mandatory fees: $250 full-time. Full-time tuition and fees vary according to course load and program. Part-time tuition varies according to course load and program. **Scholarships:** Available **Calendar System:** Semester, Summer Session Not available **Enrollment:** FT 146, PT 312 **Faculty:** FT 30, PT 21 **Student-Faculty Ratio:** 7:1 **Exams:** SAT I or ACT **% Residing in College-Owned, -Operated, or -Affiliated Housing:** 5 **Library Holdings:** 9,810 **Regional Accreditation:** Southern Association of Colleges and Schools **Credit Hours For Degree:** 56 credit hours, Associates **Professional Accreditation:** NAACLS, NLN

CARTERET COMMUNITY COLLEGE
3505 Arendell St.
Morehead City, NC 28557-2989
Tel: (252)222-6000
Admissions: (252)222-6153
Fax: (252)222-6274
Web Site: http://www.carteret.edu/
President/CEO: Dr. Joseph T. Barwick
Registrar: Rick Hill
Admissions: Rick Hill
Financial Aid: Rick Hill
Type: Two-Year College **Sex:** Coed **Affiliation:** North Carolina Community College System **Admission Plans:** Open Admission; Early Admission **Application Deadline:** Rolling **Application Fee:** $0.00 **H.S. Requirements:** High school diploma required; GED accepted **Costs Per Year:** Application fee: $0. State resident tuition: $1,314 full-time, $55.75 per credit hour part-time. Nonresident tuition: $7,074 full-time, $235.75 per credit hour part-time. Mandatory fees: $66 full-time, $15.25 per term part-time. **Scholarships:** Available **Calendar System:** Semester, Summer Session Available **Enrollment:** FT 639, PT 1,020 **Faculty:** FT 44, PT 71 **Library Holdings:** 22,000 **Regional Accreditation:** Southern Association of Colleges and Schools **Credit Hours For Degree:** 65 semester hours, Associates **Professional Accreditation:** CARC, JRCERT **Intercollegiate Athletics:** Softball M & W; Volleyball M & W

CATAWBA COLLEGE
2300 West Innes St.
Salisbury, NC 28144-2488
Tel: (704)637-4111
Free: 800-CAT-AWBA
E-mail: admissions@catawba.edu
Web Site: http://www.catawba.edu/
President/CEO: Dr. Robert E. Knott
Registrar: Carol Gamble
Admissions: Dr. Russell Watjen
Financial Aid: Melanie C. McCulloh
Type: Comprehensive **Sex:** Coed **Affiliation:** United Church of Christ **Scores:** 99% SAT V 400+; 99% SAT M 400+; 44% ACT 18-23; 35% ACT 24-29 **% Accepted:** 68 **Admission Plans:** Early Admission; Deferred Admission **Application Deadline:** Rolling **Application Fee:** $25.00 **H.S. Requirements:** High school diploma required; GED accepted **Costs Per Year:** Application fee: $25. Comprehensive fee: $25,000 includes full-time tuition ($18,750) and college room and board ($6250). Full-time tuition varies according to class time. Part-time tuition: $500 per semester hour. Part-time tuition varies according to class time, course load, and degree level. **Scholarships:** Available **Calendar System:** Semester, Summer Session Available **Enrollment:** FT 1,222, PT 34, Grad 32 **Faculty:** FT 72, PT 26 **Student-Faculty Ratio:** 15:1 **Exams:** SAT I or ACT **% Receiving Financial Aid:** 66 **% Residing in College-Owned, -Operated, or -Affiliated Housing:** 67 **Library Holdings:** 112,447 **Regional Accreditation:** Southern Association of Colleges and Schools **Credit Hours For Degree:** 124 semester hours, Bachelors **ROTC:** Army **Professional Accreditation:** JRCEPAT, NCATE **Intercollegiate Athletics:** Baseball M; Basketball M & W; Cross-Country Running M & W; Field Hockey W; Football M; Golf M; Lacrosse M; Soccer M & W; Softball W; Swimming and Diving W; Tennis M & W; Volleyball W

CATAWBA VALLEY COMMUNITY COLLEGE
2550 Hwy. 70 SE
Hickory, NC 28602-9699

Tel: (828)327-7000
Fax: (828)327-7000
Web Site: http://www.cvcc.cc.nc.us/
President/CEO: Dr. Cuyler A. Dunbar
Admissions: Caroline Farmer
Financial Aid: Deborah Barger
Type: Two-Year College **Sex:** Coed **Affiliation:** North Carolina Community College System **Admission Plans:** Open Admission; Early Admission; Deferred Admission **Application Fee:** $0.00 **H.S. Requirements:** High school diploma required; GED accepted. For some vocational programs: High school diploma or equivalent not required **Scholarships:** Available **Calendar System:** Semester, Summer Session Available **Enrollment:** FT 1,524, PT 2,419 **Faculty:** FT 101, PT 342 **Student-Faculty Ratio:** 11:1 **Exams:** Other **Library Holdings:** 46,000 **Regional Accreditation:** Southern Association of Colleges and Schools **Credit Hours For Degree:** 65 semester hours, Associates **Professional Accreditation:** ADA, AHIMA, ACBSP, CARC, JRCEMT, NLN **Intercollegiate Athletics:** Golf M; Volleyball W

CENTRAL CAROLINA COMMUNITY COLLEGE
1105 Kelly Dr.
Sanford, NC 27330-9000
Tel: (919)775-5401
Fax: (919)775-1221
Web Site: http://www.cccc.edu/
President/CEO: Dr. Marvin R. Joyner
Registrar: Katie Campbell
Admissions: Ken R. Hoyle, Jr.
Financial Aid: Jackie Thomas
Type: Two-Year College **Sex:** Coed **Affiliation:** North Carolina Community College System **Scores:** 75% SAT V 400+; 75% SAT M 400+; 25% ACT 18-23 **Admission Plans:** Open Admission; Preferred Admission; Early Admission; Deferred Admission **Application Fee:** $0.00 **H.S. Requirements:** High school diploma required; GED accepted **Scholarships:** Available **Calendar System:** Semester, Summer Session Available **Enrollment:** FT 1,845, PT 3,012 **Faculty:** FT 156, PT 269 **Student-Faculty Ratio:** 8:1 **Exams:** Other, SAT I or ACT **Library Holdings:** 50,479 **Regional Accreditation:** Southern Association of Colleges and Schools **Credit Hours For Degree:** 64 semester hours, Associates **Intercollegiate Athletics:** Basketball M & W; Golf M & W; Softball W; Volleyball W

CENTRAL PIEDMONT COMMUNITY COLLEGE
PO Box 35009
Charlotte, NC 28235-5009
Tel: (704)330-2722
Admissions: (704)330-6784
Web Site: http://www.cpcc.edu/
President/CEO: Dr. P. Anthony Zeiss
Registrar: Linda McComb
Admissions: Linda McComb
Financial Aid: Don Woodside
Type: Two-Year College **Sex:** Coed **Affiliation:** North Carolina Community College System **% Accepted:** 100 **Admission Plans:** Open Admission **Application Deadline:** Rolling **Application Fee:** $0.00 **H.S. Requirements:** High school diploma required; GED accepted. For welding program: High school diploma or equivalent not required **Costs Per Year:** Application fee: $0. State resident tuition: $1264 full-time, $39.50 per semester hour part-time. Nonresident tuition: $7024 full-time, $219.50 per semester hour part-time. Mandatory fees: $170 full-time, $56 per term part-time. **Scholarships:** Available **Calendar System:** Semester, Summer Session Available **Enrollment:** FT 6,115, PT 10,516 **Faculty:** FT 309, PT 1,725 **Student-Faculty Ratio:** 16:1 **Library Holdings:** 102,649 **Regional Accreditation:** Southern Association of Colleges and Schools **Credit Hours For Degree:** 64 semester hours, Associates **Professional Accreditation:** ABET, AAMAE, ADA, AHIMA, APTA, CARC, NAACLS

CHOWAN UNIVERSITY
200 Jones Dr.
Murfreesboro, NC 27855
Tel: (252)398-6500
Free: 800-488-4101
Admissions: (252)398-6314
Fax: (252)398-1190
E-mail: admissions@chowan.edu
Web Site: http://www.chowan.edu
President/CEO: Dr. M. Christopher White
Registrar: Lloyd Lee Wilson
Admissions: Jonathan Wirt
Financial Aid: Stephanie Harrell
Type: Four-Year College **Sex:** Coed **Affiliation:** Baptist **Scores:** 67% SAT V 400+; 67% SAT M 400+; 33% ACT 18-23; 1% ACT 24-29 **Admission Plans:** Early Admission; Deferred Admission **Application Fee:** $20.00 **H.S. Requirements:** High school diploma required; GED accepted **Costs Per Year:** Application fee: $20. Comprehensive fee: $21,350 includes full-time tuition ($14,600), mandatory fees ($150), and college room and board ($6600). College room only: $3100. Room and board charges vary according to board plan. Part-time tuition: $230 per hour. Part-time tuition varies according to course load. **Scholarships:** Available **Calendar System:** Semester, Summer Session Available **Enrollment:** FT 800 **Faculty:** FT 49, PT 30 **Student-Faculty Ratio:** 12:1 **Exams:** SAT I or ACT **% Receiving Financial Aid:** 87 **% Residing in College-Owned, -Operated, or -Affiliated Housing:** 79 **Library Holdings:** 93,676 **Regional Accreditation:** Southern Association of Colleges and Schools **Credit Hours For Degree:** 61 semester hours, Associates; 120 semester hours, Bachelors **Professional Accreditation:** NASM, NCATE **Intercollegiate Athletics:** Baseball M; Basketball M & W; Cheerleading M & W; Cross-Country Running W; Football M; Golf M; Soccer M & W; Softball W; Tennis M & W; Volleyball W

CLEVELAND COMMUNITY COLLEGE
137 South Post Rd.
Shelby, NC 28152
Tel: (704)484-4000
Admissions: (704)484-4073
Web Site: http://www.clevelandcommunitycollege.edu/
President/CEO: Dr. L. Steve Thornburg
Registrar: Shaunda Leonhardt
Admissions: Alan Price
Financial Aid: Andy Gardner
Type: Two-Year College **Sex:** Coed **Affiliation:** North Carolina Community College System **% Accepted:** 100 **Admission Plans:** Open Admission; Deferred Admission **Application Deadline:** Rolling **Application Fee:** $0.00 **H.S. Requirements:** High school diploma required; GED accepted **Costs Per Year:** Application fee: $0. State resident tuition: $1264 full-time, $39.50 per credit hour part-time. Nonresident tuition: $7024 full-time, $219.50 per credit hour part-time. Mandatory fees: $38 full-time. Full-time tuition and fees vary according to course load. Part-time tuition varies according to course load. **Scholarships:** Available **Calendar System:** Semester, Summer Session Available **Enrollment:** FT 1,241, PT 1,806 **Faculty:** FT 67, PT 176 **Library Holdings:** 34,000 **Regional Accreditation:** Southern Association of Colleges and Schools **Credit Hours For Degree:** 64 semester hours, Associates **Professional Accreditation:** JRCERT

COASTAL CAROLINA COMMUNITY COLLEGE
444 Western Blvd.
Jacksonville, NC 28546-6899
Tel: (910)455-1221
Admissions: (910)938-6254
Fax: (910)455-2767
E-mail: herringd@coastal.cc.nc.us
Web Site: http://www.coastalcarolina.edu/
President/CEO: Dr. Ronald K. Lingle, Jr.
Admissions: Don Herring
Financial Aid: John Kopka
Type: Two-Year College **Sex:** Coed **Affiliation:** North Carolina Community College System **% Accepted:** 78 **Admission Plans:** Open Admission; Deferred Admission **Application Deadline:** Rolling **Application Fee:** $0.00 **H.S. Requirements:** High school diploma required; GED accepted **Costs Per Year:** Application fee: $0. State resident tuition: $1264 full-time, $39.50 per credit hour part-time. Nonresident tuition: $7024 full-time, $219.50 per credit hour part-time. Mandatory fees: $30 full-time, $5 per term part-time. **Scholarships:** Available **Calendar System:** Semester, Summer Session Available **Enrollment:** FT 2,072, PT 2,039 **Faculty:** FT 132, PT 129 **Student-Faculty Ratio:** 16:1 **Library Holdings:** 44,062 **Regional Accreditation:** Southern Association of Colleges and Schools **Credit Hours For Degree:** 64 semester hours, Associates **Professional Accreditation:** ARCEST, ADA, NAACLS

COLLEGE OF THE ALBEMARLE
PO Box 2327
Elizabeth City, NC 27906-2327

Tel: (252)335-0821
Fax: (252)335-2011
Web Site: http://www.albemarle.edu/
President/CEO: Lynne M. Bunch
Registrar: Mary Louise Brown
Admissions: Kenny Krentz
Financial Aid: Angela Godfrey-Dawson
Type: Two-Year College **Sex:** Coed **Affiliation:** North Carolina Community College System **Scores:** 52% SAT V 400+; 64% SAT M 400+ **Admission Plans:** Open Admission; Early Admission; Deferred Admission **Application Deadline:** Rolling **Application Fee:** $0.00 **H.S. Requirements:** High school diploma required; GED accepted **Costs Per Year:** Application fee: $0. State resident tuition: $1264 full-time, $39.50 per credit hour part-time. Nonresident tuition: $7024 full-time, $219.50 per credit hour part-time. **Scholarships:** Available **Calendar System:** Semester, Summer Session Available **Enrollment:** FT 854, PT 1,217 **Faculty:** FT 60, PT 62 **Library Holdings:** 48,400 **Regional Accreditation:** Southern Association of Colleges and Schools **Credit Hours For Degree:** 65 semester hours, Associates **Professional Accreditation:** NLN **Intercollegiate Athletics:** Soccer M

CRAVEN COMMUNITY COLLEGE
800 College Ct.
New Bern, NC 28562-4984
Tel: (252)638-4131
Admissions: (252)638-7220
Fax: (252)638-4649
Web Site: http://www.craven.cc.nc.us/
President/CEO: Dr. Robert Scott Ralls
Admissions: John Fonville
Financial Aid: Kathy Banks
Type: Two-Year College **Sex:** Coed **Affiliation:** North Carolina Community College System **Admission Plans:** Open Admission **Application Fee:** $0.00 **H.S. Requirements:** High school diploma required; GED accepted **Scholarships:** Available **Calendar System:** Semester, Summer Session Available **Faculty:** FT 63, PT 103 **Student-Faculty Ratio:** 14:1 **Exams:** SAT I or ACT **Library Holdings:** 21,000 **Regional Accreditation:** Southern Association of Colleges and Schools **Credit Hours For Degree:** 64 semester hours, Associates **Intercollegiate Athletics:** Basketball M; Softball M & W

DAVIDSON COLLEGE
Davidson, NC 28035
Tel: (704)894-2000
Free: 800-768-0380
Admissions: (704)894-2230
Fax: (704)894-2016
E-mail: admission@davidson.edu
Web Site: http://www.davidson.edu/
President/CEO: Robert F. Vagt
Registrar: Dr. Hansford M. Epes, Jr.
Admissions: Christopher J. Gruber
Financial Aid: Kathleen Stevenson-McNeely
Type: Four-Year College **Sex:** Coed **Affiliation:** Presbyterian **Scores:** 100% SAT V 400+; 100% SAT M 400+; 4% ACT 18-23; 46% ACT 24-29 **% Accepted:** 27 **Admission Plans:** Early Admission; Early Decision Plan; Deferred Admission **Application Deadline:** January 02 **Application Fee:** $50.00 **H.S. Requirements:** High school diploma required; GED not accepted **Costs Per Year:** Application fee: $50. Comprehensive fee: $36,825 includes full-time tuition ($28,667) and college room and board ($8158). College room only: $4308. **Scholarships:** Available **Calendar System:** Semester, Summer Session Not available **Enrollment:** FT 1,683 **Faculty:** FT 159, PT 8 **Student-Faculty Ratio:** 10:1 **Exams:** SAT I or ACT, SAT II **% Receiving Financial Aid:** 35 **% Residing in College-Owned, -Operated, or -Affiliated Housing:** 91 **Library Holdings:** 422,035 **Regional Accreditation:** Southern Association of Colleges and Schools **Credit Hours For Degree:** 32 courses, Bachelors **ROTC:** Army, Air Force **Professional Accreditation:** NCATE **Intercollegiate Athletics:** Baseball M; Basketball M & W; Crew M & W; Cross-Country Running M & W; Fencing M & W; Field Hockey W; Football M; Golf M; Lacrosse W; Rugby M; Sailing M & W; Soccer M & W; Swimming and Diving M & W; Tennis M & W; Track and Field M & W; Ultimate Frisbee M & W; Volleyball W; Weight Lifting M & W; Wrestling M

DAVIDSON COUNTY COMMUNITY COLLEGE
PO Box 1287
Lexington, NC 27293-1287
Tel: (336)249-8186
Fax: (336)249-0379
E-mail: cottrell.judy@davidson.cc.nc.us
Web Site: http://www.davidson.cc.nc.us/
President/CEO: Dr. Mary E. Rittling
Registrar: Sara B. Dodd
Admissions: Rick Travis
Financial Aid: Anita Pennix
Type: Two-Year College **Sex:** Coed **Affiliation:** North Carolina Community College System **Admission Plans:** Open Admission; Early Admission; Deferred Admission **Application Fee:** $0.00 **H.S. Requirements:** High school diploma or equivalent not required **Costs Per Year:** Application fee: $0. State resident tuition: $1140 full-time, $38 per credit hour part-time. Nonresident tuition: $6330 full-time, $211 per credit hour part-time. Mandatory fees: $1088 full-time, $27.25 per term part-time. **Scholarships:** Available **Calendar System:** Semester, Summer Session Available **Enrollment:** FT 829, PT 1,474 **Faculty:** FT 72, PT 140 **Student-Faculty Ratio:** 11:1 **Exams:** Other **Library Holdings:** 56,445 **Regional Accreditation:** Southern Association of Colleges and Schools **Credit Hours For Degree:** 64 semester hours, Associates **Professional Accreditation:** ABET, AHIMA, NAACLS, NLN

DEVRY UNIVERSITY
4521 Sharon Rd., Ste. 145
Charlotte, NC 28211-3627
Tel: (704)362-2345; (866)923-3879
Fax: (704)362-2668
Web Site: http://www.devry.edu/ **Type:** Comprehensive **Sex:** Coed **Affiliation:** DeVry University **Admission Plans:** Deferred Admission **Application Deadline:** Rolling **Application Fee:** $50.00 **H.S. Requirements:** High school diploma required; GED accepted **Costs Per Year:** Application fee: $50. One-time mandatory fee: $40. Tuition: $11,790 full-time, $440 per credit part-time. Mandatory fees: $30 full-time, $30 per year part-time. Full-time tuition and fees vary according to course load. Part-time tuition and fees vary according to course load. **Calendar System:** Semester, Summer Session Available **Enrollment:** FT 32, PT 35, Grad 99 **Faculty:** FT 4, PT 11 **Student-Faculty Ratio:** 6:1 **Regional Accreditation:** North Central Association of Colleges and Schools **Credit Hours For Degree:** 122 credits, Bachelors

DUKE UNIVERSITY
Durham, NC 27708-0586
Tel: (919)684-8111
Admissions: (919)684-3214
Fax: (919)681-8941
E-mail: askduke@admiss.duke.edu
Web Site: http://www.duke.edu/
President/CEO: Dr. Richard H. Brodhead
Registrar: Bruce Cunningham
Admissions: Christoph Guttentag
Financial Aid: Jim Belvin, Jr.
Type: University **Sex:** Coed **Affiliation:** United Methodist Church **Scores:** 100% SAT V 400+; 100% SAT M 400+; 3% ACT 18-23; 35% ACT 24-29 **% Accepted:** 22 **Admission Plans:** Preferred Admission; Early Admission; Early Decision Plan; Deferred Admission **Application Deadline:** January 02 **Application Fee:** $70.00 **H.S. Requirements:** High school diploma required; GED not accepted **Costs Per Year:** Application fee: $70. Comprehensive fee: $43,115 includes full-time tuition ($32,845), mandatory fees ($1118), and college room and board ($9152). College room only: $4950. **Scholarships:** Available **Calendar System:** Semester, Summer Session Available **Enrollment:** FT 6,470, PT 64, Grad 5,699 **Faculty:** FT 964 **Student-Faculty Ratio:** 8:1 **Exams:** SAT I or ACT **% Receiving Financial Aid:** 40 **% Residing in College-Owned, -Operated, or -Affiliated Housing:** 82 **Library Holdings:** 5,496,408 **Regional Accreditation:** Southern Association of Colleges and Schools **Credit Hours For Degree:** 34 courses, Bachelors **ROTC:** Army, Air Force **Professional Accreditation:** AACSB, ABET, ACEHSA, AACN, AANA, ABA, APTA, APA, ACIPE, AALS, ATS, LCMEAMA, NCATE, NLN, SAF **Intercollegiate Athletics:** Badminton M & W; Baseball M; Basketball M & W; Crew M & W; Cross-Country Running M & W; Equestrian Sports M & W; Fencing M & W; Field Hockey M & W; Football M & W; Golf M & W; Ice Hockey M & W; Lacrosse M & W; Racquetball M & W; Rugby M & W; Sailing M & W; Skiing (Cross-Country) M & W; Skiing (Downhill) M & W; Soccer M & W; Softball M & W;

Squash M & W; Swimming and Diving M & W; Table Tennis M & W; Tennis M & W; Track and Field M & W; Ultimate Frisbee M & W; Volleyball M & W; Water Polo M & W; Wrestling M

DURHAM TECHNICAL COMMUNITY COLLEGE
1637 Lawson St.
Durham, NC 27703-5023
Tel: (919)686-3300
Admissions: (919)686-3619
Web Site: http://www.durhamtech.edu/
President/CEO: Dr. Phail Wynn, Jr.
Registrar: Julia Teasley
Admissions: Penny Augustine
Financial Aid: Kay Burruss
Type: Two-Year College **Sex:** Coed **Affiliation:** North Carolina Community College System **Admission Plans:** Open Admission; Deferred Admission **Application Fee:** $0.00 **H.S. Requirements:** High school diploma required; GED accepted **Scholarships:** Available **Calendar System:** Semester, Summer Session Available **Enrollment:** FT 1,464, PT 4,178 **Faculty:** FT 118, PT 359 **Student-Faculty Ratio:** 16:1 **Exams:** Other **Library Holdings:** 36,388 **Regional Accreditation:** Southern Association of Colleges and Schools **Credit Hours For Degree:** 64 credit hours, Associates **Professional Accreditation:** ADA, AOTA, COptA, CARC

EAST CAROLINA UNIVERSITY
East 5th St.
Greenville, NC 27858-4353
Tel: (252)328-6131
Admissions: (252)328-6640
Fax: (252)328-6495
Web Site: http://www.ecu.edu/
President/CEO: Dr. Steven C. Ballard
Registrar: Angela Anderson
Admissions: Dr. Thomas E. Powell
Financial Aid: Charles Hawkins
Type: University **Sex:** Coed **Affiliation:** The University of North Carolina **Scores:** 97% SAT V 400+; 98% SAT M 400+; 65% ACT 18-23; 14% ACT 24-29 **% Accepted:** 74 **Admission Plans:** Preferred Admission; Early Admission; Deferred Admission **Application Deadline:** March 15 **Application Fee:** $50.00 **H.S. Requirements:** High school diploma required; GED accepted **Costs Per Year:** Application fee: $50. State resident tuition: $2135 full-time. Nonresident tuition: $12,649 full-time. Mandatory fees: $1492 full-time. College room and board: $6840. College room only: $3790. Room and board charges vary according to board plan and housing facility. **Scholarships:** Available **Calendar System:** Semester, Summer Session Available **Enrollment:** FT 15,832, PT 1,896, Grad 5,150 **Faculty:** FT 1,096, PT 196 **Student-Faculty Ratio:** 16:1 **Exams:** SAT I or ACT **% Receiving Financial Aid:** 28 **% Residing in College-Owned, -Operated, or -Affiliated Housing:** 28 **Library Holdings:** 4,213,205 **Regional Accreditation:** Southern Association of Colleges and Schools **Credit Hours For Degree:** 120 semester hours, Bachelors **ROTC:** Army, Air Force **Professional Accreditation:** AACSB, AAMFT, AAFCS, AANA, ACNM, ACCE, ADtA, AHIMA, ACSP, AOTA, APTA, ASLHA, CORE, CSWE, FIDER, JRCEPAT, LCMEAMA, NAACLS, NAIT, NASAD NASM, NASPAA, NCATE, NLN, NRPA **Intercollegiate Athletics:** Baseball M; Basketball M & W; Cross-Country Running M & W; Football M; Golf M & W; Soccer M & W; Softball W; Swimming and Diving M & W; Tennis M & W; Track and Field M & W; Volleyball W

ECPI TECHNICAL COLLEGE
4101 Doie Cope Rd.
Raleigh, NC 27613-7387
Tel: (919)571-0057
Free: 800-986-1200
Fax: (919)571-0780
E-mail: swells@ecpi.edu
Web Site: http://www.ecpi.net/
President/CEO: Richard Wechner
Admissions: Susan Wells
Type: Two-Year College **Sex:** Coed **Application Deadline:** Rolling **H.S. Requirements:** High school diploma required; GED accepted **Costs Per Year:** Tuition: $9750 full-time. **Calendar System:** Trimester, Summer Session Not available **Student-Faculty Ratio:** 13:1 **Exams:** SAT I or ACT, SAT I, SAT II **Credit Hours For Degree:** 65 credits, Associates **Professional Accreditation:** ACCSCT

EDGECOMBE COMMUNITY COLLEGE
2009 West Wilson St.
Tarboro, NC 27886-9399
Tel: (252)823-5166
Fax: (252)823-6817
Web Site: http://www.edgecombe.edu/
President/CEO: Dr. Hartwell H. Fuller, Jr.
Registrar: Catherine Dupree
Admissions: Thomas B. Anderson
Financial Aid: Carolyn Knight
Type: Two-Year College **Sex:** Coed **Affiliation:** North Carolina Community College System **Admission Plans:** Open Admission **Application Fee:** $0.00 **H.S. Requirements:** High school diploma required; GED accepted **Costs Per Year:** Application fee: $0. State resident tuition: $1264 full-time, $39.50 per credit part-time. Nonresident tuition: $7024 full-time, $219.50 per credit part-time. Mandatory fees: $72 full-time, $2.75 per credit part-time. **Scholarships:** Available **Calendar System:** Semester, Summer Session Available **Enrollment:** FT 947, PT 1,606 **Faculty:** FT 81, PT 69 **Student-Faculty Ratio:** 16:1 **Exams:** Other, SAT I or ACT **Library Holdings:** 42,460 **Regional Accreditation:** Southern Association of Colleges and Schools **Credit Hours For Degree:** 64 semester hours, Associates **Professional Accreditation:** AHIMA, CARC, JRCERT

ELIZABETH CITY STATE UNIVERSITY
1704 Weeksville Rd.
Elizabeth City, NC 27909-7806
Tel: (252)335-3400
Free: 800-347-3278
Admissions: (252)335-3305
Fax: (252)335-3731
Web Site: http://www.ecsu.edu/
President/CEO: Dr. Mickey L. Burnim
Registrar: Vincent L. Beamon
Admissions: Grady Deese
Financial Aid: Andre Farley
Type: Comprehensive **Sex:** Coed **Affiliation:** University of North Carolina System **Scores:** 59% SAT V 400+; 66% SAT M 400+; 26% ACT 18-23; 1% ACT 24-29 **Admission Plans:** Preferred Admission; Deferred Admission **Application Fee:** $30.00 **H.S. Requirements:** High school diploma required; GED accepted **Costs Per Year:** Application fee: $30. State resident tuition: $1399 full-time. Nonresident tuition: $9738 full-time. Mandatory fees: $1824 full-time. College room and board: $4709. College room only: $2867. **Scholarships:** Available **Calendar System:** Semester, Summer Session Available **Enrollment:** FT 2,118, PT 319, Grad 33 **Faculty:** FT 128, PT 88 **Student-Faculty Ratio:** 14:1 **Exams:** SAT I or ACT **% Receiving Financial Aid:** 98 **% Residing in College-Owned, -Operated, or -Affiliated Housing:** 49 **Library Holdings:** 193,880 **Regional Accreditation:** Southern Association of Colleges and Schools **Credit Hours For Degree:** 124 semester hours, Bachelors **ROTC:** Army **Professional Accreditation:** NAIT, NCATE **Intercollegiate Athletics:** Basketball M & W; Football M; Tennis M & W; Track and Field M & W; Volleyball M & W

ELON UNIVERSITY
2700 Campus Box
Elon, NC 27244-2010
Tel: (336)278-2000
Free: 800-334-8448
Admissions: (336)278-3566
Fax: (336)538-3986
E-mail: admissions@elon.edu
Web Site: http://www.elon.edu/
President/CEO: Dr. Leo M. Lambert
Registrar: Mark R. Albertson
Admissions: Susan C. Klopman
Financial Aid: Pat Murphy
Type: Comprehensive **Sex:** Coed **Affiliation:** United Church of Christ **Scores:** 100% SAT V 400+; 100% SAT M 400+; 21% ACT 18-23; 68% ACT 24-29 **% Accepted:** 41 **Admission Plans:** Early Admission; Early Action; Early Decision Plan; Deferred Admission **Application Deadline:** January 10 **Application Fee:** $40.00 **H.S. Requirements:** High school diploma required; GED accepted **Costs Per Year:** Application fee: $40. Comprehen-

sive fee: $25,371 includes full-time tuition ($18,699), mandatory fees ($250), and college room and board ($6422). Room and board charges vary according to board plan and housing facility. Part-time tuition: $588 per hour. Part-time mandatory fees: $125 per term. Part-time tuition and fees vary according to course load. **Scholarships:** Available **Calendar System:** 4-1-4, Summer Session Available **Enrollment:** FT 4,607, PT 95, Grad 254 **Faculty:** FT 279, PT 91 **Student-Faculty Ratio:** 15:1 **Exams:** SAT I or ACT **% Receiving Financial Aid:** 34 **% Residing in College-Owned, -Operated, or -Affiliated Housing:** 59 **Library Holdings:** 240,058 **Regional Accreditation:** Southern Association of Colleges and Schools **Credit Hours For Degree:** 132 semester hours, Bachelors **ROTC:** Army, Air Force **Professional Accreditation:** AACSB, APTA, JRCEPAT, NCATE **Intercollegiate Athletics:** Baseball M; Basketball M & W; Cheerleading M & W; Cross-Country Running M & W; Football M; Golf M & W; Lacrosse M & W; Rugby M; Soccer M & W; Softball W; Swimming and Diving M & W; Tennis M & W; Track and Field W; Volleyball W

FAYETTEVILLE STATE UNIVERSITY

1200 Murchison Rd.
Fayetteville, NC 28301-4298
Tel: (910)672-1111
Free: 800-222-2594
Admissions: (910)486-1371
Fax: (910)672-1769
E-mail: rshabazz@uncfsu.edu
Web Site: http://www.uncfsu.edu/
President/CEO: Dr. T.J. Bryan
Registrar: Ivan Walker
Admissions: Roxie Shabazz
Financial Aid: Lois L. McKoy

Type: Comprehensive **Sex:** Coed **Affiliation:** University of North Carolina System **% Accepted:** 80 **Admission Plans:** Early Admission; Early Action; Early Decision Plan; Deferred Admission **Application Deadline:** July 01 **Application Fee:** $25.00 **H.S. Requirements:** High school diploma required; GED accepted **Costs Per Year:** Application fee: $25. State resident tuition: $1746 full-time. Nonresident tuition: $11,482 full-time. Mandatory fees: $1459 full-time. College room and board: $4570. College room only: $2570. **Scholarships:** Available **Calendar System:** Semester, Summer Session Available **Enrollment:** FT 4,119, PT 910, Grad 1,043 **Faculty:** FT 200, PT 74 **Student-Faculty Ratio:** 22:1 **Exams:** SAT I or ACT **% Receiving Financial Aid:** 71 **Library Holdings:** 311,016 **Regional Accreditation:** Southern Association of Colleges and Schools **Credit Hours For Degree:** 60 credit hours, Associates; 120 credit hours, Bachelors **ROTC:** Army, Air Force **Professional Accreditation:** AACN, CSWE, NCATE **Intercollegiate Athletics:** Basketball M & W; Bowling M & W; Cheerleading M & W; Cross-Country Running M & W; Football M; Golf M & W; Tennis M & W; Track and Field M & W; Volleyball W

FAYETTEVILLE TECHNICAL COMMUNITY COLLEGE

PO Box 35236
Fayetteville, NC 28303-0236
Tel: (910)678-8400
Admissions: (910)678-8274
Fax: (910)678-8407
E-mail: kelleyj@faytechcc.edu
Web Site: http://www.faytechcc.edu/
President/CEO: Dr. Larry B. Norris
Registrar: Sheila B. Locklear
Admissions: James Kelley
Financial Aid: Constance Wells

Type: Two-Year College **Sex:** Coed **Affiliation:** North Carolina Community College System **% Accepted:** 100 **Admission Plans:** Open Admission; Deferred Admission **Application Deadline:** Rolling **Application Fee:** $0.00 **H.S. Requirements:** High school diploma required; GED accepted **Costs Per Year:** Application fee: $0. State resident tuition: $1264 full-time, $39.50 per credit hour part-time. Nonresident tuition: $7024 full-time, $219.50 per credit hour part-time. Mandatory fees: $30 full-time, $30 per term part-time. **Scholarships:** Available **Calendar System:** Semester, Summer Session Available **Enrollment:** FT 3,048, PT 6,902 **Faculty:** FT 298, PT 565 **Student-Faculty Ratio:** 29:1 **Library Holdings:** 61,580 **Regional Accreditation:** Southern Association of Colleges and Schools **Credit Hours For Degree:** 65 semester hours, Associates **Professional Accreditation:** ABET, ABFSE, ADA, APTA, CARC, JRCERT, NLN

FORSYTH TECHNICAL COMMUNITY COLLEGE

2100 Silas Creek Parkway
Winston-Salem, NC 27103-5197
Tel: (336)723-0371
Admissions: (336)734-7331
Fax: (336)761-2098
Web Site: http://www.forsythtech.edu/
President/CEO: Dr. Gary M. Green
Registrar: Dr. J. Bruce Shepherd
Admissions: Patrice Mitchell
Financial Aid: Regina D. Draughn

Type: Two-Year College **Sex:** Coed **Affiliation:** North Carolina Community College System **% Accepted:** 100 **Admission Plans:** Open Admission **Application Deadline:** August 25 **H.S. Requirements:** High school diploma required; GED accepted **Costs Per Year:** State resident tuition: $948 full-time, $39.50 per credit hour part-time. Nonresident tuition: $5268 full-time, $219.50 per credit hour part-time. Mandatory fees: $35 full-time, $24 per term part-time. **Scholarships:** Available **Calendar System:** Semester, Summer Session Available **Enrollment:** FT 2,509, PT 4,469 **Faculty:** FT 175, PT 311 **Student-Faculty Ratio:** 14:1 **Exams:** Other, SAT I or ACT **Library Holdings:** 41,606 **Regional Accreditation:** Southern Association of Colleges and Schools **Professional Accreditation:** ABET, AAMAE, ADA, CARC, JRCEDMS, JRCERT, JRCNMT

GARDNER-WEBB UNIVERSITY

PO Box 997
Boiling Springs, NC 28017
Tel: (704)406-2361
Free: 800-253-6472
Admissions: (704)406-4491
Fax: (704)434-4488
E-mail: admissions@gardner-webb.edu
Web Site: http://www.gardner-webb.edu/
President/CEO: Dr. Frank R. Campbell
Registrar: Stephen Sain
Admissions: Nathan Alexander
Financial Aid: Steven C. Varley

Type: Comprehensive **Sex:** Coed **Affiliation:** Baptist **Scores:** 92% SAT V 400+; 92% SAT M 400+; 62% ACT 18-23; 20% ACT 24-29 **% Accepted:** 72 **Admission Plans:** Early Admission; Deferred Admission **Application Deadline:** Rolling **Application Fee:** $40.00 **H.S. Requirements:** High school diploma required; GED accepted **Costs Per Year:** Application fee: $40. Comprehensive fee: $21,850 includes full-time tuition ($15,960), mandatory fees ($350), and college room and board ($5540). College room only: $2840. Room and board charges vary according to board plan and housing facility. Part-time tuition: $295 per credit hour. Part-time tuition varies according to course load. **Scholarships:** Available **Calendar System:** Semester, Summer Session Available **Enrollment:** FT 2,222, PT 404, Grad 991 **Faculty:** FT 133, PT 188 **Student-Faculty Ratio:** 15:1 **Exams:** SAT I or ACT **% Receiving Financial Aid:** 67 **% Residing in College-Owned, -Operated, or -Affiliated Housing:** 71 **Library Holdings:** 230,000 **Regional Accreditation:** Southern Association of Colleges and Schools **Credit Hours For Degree:** 64 semester hours, Associates; 128 semester hours, Bachelors **ROTC:** Army **Professional Accreditation:** ACIPE, ACBSP, ATS, NASM, NCATE, NLN **Intercollegiate Athletics:** Baseball M; Basketball M & W; Cheerleading M & W; Cross-Country Running M & W; Football M; Golf M & W; Soccer M & W; Softball W; Swimming and Diving W; Tennis M & W; Track and Field M & W; Volleyball W; Wrestling M

GASTON COLLEGE

201 Hwy. 321 South
Dallas, NC 28034-1499
Tel: (704)922-6200
Admissions: (704)922-6219
Web Site: http://www.gaston.edu/
President/CEO: Dr. Patricia Skinner
Registrar: Lynn Preston
Admissions: Michelle Wray
Financial Aid: Peggy Oates

Type: Two-Year College **Sex:** Coed **Affiliation:** North Carolina Community College System **Admission Plans:** Open Admission **Application Deadline:** Rolling **Application Fee:** $0.00 **H.S. Requirements:** High school diploma required; GED accepted. For vocational programs: High school diploma or equivalent not required **Costs Per Year:** Application fee: $0. State resident tuition: $1264 full-time, $39.50 per credit hour part-time. Nonresident tuition: $7024 full-time, $219.50 per credit hour part-time. Mandatory fees: $80 full-time, $2.50 per credit hour part-time, $12 per term part-time. **Scholarships:** Available **Calendar System:** Semester, Summer Session Available **Enrollment:** FT 2,449, PT 2,599 **Faculty:** FT 119, PT 238 **Student-Faculty Ratio:** 18:1 **Library Holdings:** 49,434 **Regional Accreditation:** Southern Association of Colleges and Schools **Credit Hours For Degree:** 64 semester hours, Associates **Professional Accreditation:** ABET, AAMAE

GREENSBORO COLLEGE
815 West Market St.
Greensboro, NC 27401-1875
Tel: (336)272-7102
Free: 800-346-8226
Fax: (336)271-6634
E-mail: admissions@gborocollege.edu
Web Site: http://www.gborocollege.edu/
President/CEO: Dr. Craven E. Williams
Admissions: Timothy L. Jackson
Financial Aid: Ron Elmore
Type: Comprehensive **Sex:** Coed **Affiliation:** United Methodist **Scores:** 92% SAT V 400+; 91% SAT M 400+; 55% ACT 18-23; 24% ACT 24-29 **Admission Plans:** Early Admission; Early Action; Deferred Admission **Application Fee:** $35.00 **H.S. Requirements:** High school diploma required; GED accepted **Costs Per Year:** Application fee: $35. Comprehensive fee: $25,040 includes full-time tuition ($17,850), mandatory fees ($270), and college room and board ($6920). Full-time tuition and fees vary according to course load. Room and board charges vary according to board plan and housing facility. Part-time tuition: $480 per hour. Part-time tuition varies according to course load. **Scholarships:** Available **Calendar System:** Semester, Summer Session Available **Enrollment:** FT 923, PT 242, Grad 61 **Faculty:** FT 61, PT 64 **Student-Faculty Ratio:** 13:1 **Exams:** SAT I or ACT **% Receiving Financial Aid:** 64 **% Residing in College-Owned, -Operated, or -Affiliated Housing:** 48 **Library Holdings:** 108,350 **Regional Accreditation:** Southern Association of Colleges and Schools **Credit Hours For Degree:** 124 semester hours, Bachelors **ROTC:** Army, Air Force **Professional Accreditation:** NASM, NCATE **Intercollegiate Athletics:** Baseball M; Basketball M & W; Cheerleading M & W; Cross-Country Running M & W; Football M; Golf M; Lacrosse M & W; Soccer M & W; Softball W; Swimming and Diving W; Tennis M & W; Volleyball W

GUILFORD COLLEGE
5800 West Friendly Ave.
Greensboro, NC 27410-4173
Tel: (336)316-2000
Free: 800-992-7759
Admissions: (336)316-2100
Fax: (336)316-2954
E-mail: admission@guilford.edu
Web Site: http://www.guilford.edu/
President/CEO: Kent J. Chabotar
Registrar: Norma Middleton
Admissions: Randy Doss
Financial Aid: Dianne H. Harrison
Type: Four-Year College **Sex:** Coed **Affiliation:** Society of Friends **Scores:** 100% SAT V 400+; 100% SAT M 400+; 40% ACT 18-23; 49% ACT 24-29 **% Accepted:** 63 **Admission Plans:** Preferred Admission; Early Admission; Early Action; Deferred Admission **Application Deadline:** February 15 **Application Fee:** $25.00 **H.S. Requirements:** High school diploma required; GED accepted **Costs Per Year:** Application fee: $25. Comprehensive fee: $29,710 includes full-time tuition ($22,690), mandatory fees ($330), and college room and board ($6690). Part-time tuition: $700 per credit hour. Part-time mandatory fees: $330 per year. **Scholarships:** Available **Calendar System:** Semester, Summer Session Available **Enrollment:** FT 2,251, PT 431 **Faculty:** FT 124, PT 78 **Student-Faculty Ratio:** 17:1 **Exams:** SAT I or ACT **% Receiving Financial Aid:** 67 **% Residing in College-Owned, -Operated, or -Affiliated Housing:** 80 **Library Holdings:** 157,054 **Regional Accreditation:** Southern Association of Colleges and Schools **Credit Hours For Degree:** 128 credits, Bachelors **Professional Accreditation:** NCATE **Intercollegiate Athletics:** Baseball M; Basketball M & W; Cross-Country Running M & W; Football M; Golf M; Lacrosse M & W; Soccer M & W; Softball W; Swimming and Diving W; Tennis M & W; Volleyball W

GUILFORD TECHNICAL COMMUNITY COLLEGE
PO Box 309
Jamestown, NC 27282-0309
Tel: (336)334-4822
Web Site: http://www.gtcc.edu/
President/CEO: Dr. Donald W. Cameron
Registrar: Dr. Brad Burch
Admissions: Jeanne Groome
Financial Aid: Lisa Koretoff
Type: Two-Year College **Sex:** Coed **Affiliation:** North Carolina Community College System **Admission Plans:** Open Admission; Early Admission; Deferred Admission **Application Fee:** $0.00 **H.S. Requirements:** High school diploma required; GED accepted **Costs Per Year:** Application fee: $0. State resident tuition: $1216 full-time. Nonresident tuition: $6752 full-time. Mandatory fees: $75 full-time. **Scholarships:** Available **Calendar System:** Semester, Summer Session Available **Enrollment:** FT 2,930, PT 5,561 **Faculty:** FT 540, PT 682 **Exams:** Other **Library Holdings:** 74,958 **Regional Accreditation:** Southern Association of Colleges and Schools **Credit Hours For Degree:** 64 semester hours, Associates **ROTC:** Army, Air Force **Professional Accreditation:** AAMAE, ACF, ADA, APTA

HALIFAX COMMUNITY COLLEGE
PO Drawer 809
Weldon, NC 27890-0809
Tel: (252)536-4221
Admissions: (252)536-7220
Fax: (252)536-4144
Web Site: http://www.hcc.cc.nc.us/
President/CEO: Dr. Ted H. Gasper, Jr.
Registrar: Karen Wright
Admissions: Scottie Dickens
Financial Aid: Tara Keeten
Type: Two-Year College **Sex:** Coed **Affiliation:** North Carolina Community College System **Admission Plans:** Open Admission; Deferred Admission **Application Fee:** $0.00 **H.S. Requirements:** High school diploma required; GED accepted **Costs Per Year:** Application fee: $0. State resident tuition: $1216 full-time, $38 per credit part-time. Nonresident tuition: $6752 full-time, $211 per credit part-time. Mandatory fees: $80 full-time, $5 per credit part-time. **Scholarships:** Available **Calendar System:** Semester, Summer Session Available **Faculty:** FT 65, PT 82 **Library Holdings:** 26,527 **Regional Accreditation:** Southern Association of Colleges and Schools **Credit Hours For Degree:** 65 semester hours, Associates **Professional Accreditation:** ADA, NAACLS

HAYWOOD COMMUNITY COLLEGE
185 Freedlander Dr.
Clyde, NC 28721-9453
Tel: (828)627-2821
Admissions: (828)627-4505
Fax: (828)627-4513
Web Site: http://www.haywood.edu/
President/CEO: Dr. Nathan L. Hodges
Registrar: Jennifer Chandler
Admissions: Debbie Rowland
Financial Aid: Kathy Lovedahl
Type: Two-Year College **Sex:** Coed **Affiliation:** North Carolina Community College System **Admission Plans:** Open Admission **Application Fee:** $0.00 **H.S. Requirements:** High school diploma required; GED accepted **Costs Per Year:** Application fee: $0. State resident tuition: $1216 full-time, $38 per credit hour part-time. Nonresident tuition: $6752 full-time, $211 per credit hour part-time. Mandatory fees: $49 full-time, $13 per term part-time. **Scholarships:** Available **Calendar System:** Semester, Summer Session Not available **Enrollment:** FT 876, PT 1,112 **Faculty:** FT 67, PT 56 **Student-Faculty Ratio:** 12:1 **Exams:** Other **Library Holdings:** 26,788 **Regional Accreditation:** Southern Association of Colleges and Schools **Credit Hours For Degree:** 65 semester hours, Associates **Professional Accreditation:** AAMAE

HERITAGE BIBLE COLLEGE
PO Box 1628
Dunn, NC 28335-1628
Tel: (910)892-3178

Free: 800-297-6351
Fax: (910)892-1809
Web Site: http://www.heritagebiblecollege.org/
President/CEO: Dr. Dwarka Ramphal
Registrar: Rev. Dale Wallace
Admissions: Zhenya Ramphal
Financial Aid: Vickie Williford
Type: Four-Year College **Sex:** Coed **Affiliation:** Pentecostal Free Will Baptist **% Accepted:** 100 **Admission Plans:** Open Admission **Application Deadline:** Rolling **Application Fee:** $25.00 **H.S. Requirements:** High school diploma required; GED accepted **Costs Per Year:** Application fee: $25. Comprehensive fee: $6600 includes full-time tuition ($3600), mandatory fees ($600), and college room and board ($2400). College room only: $1440. Part-time tuition: $150 per credit. **Scholarships:** Available **Calendar System:** Semester, Summer Session Available **Enrollment:** FT 84, PT 32 **Faculty:** FT 4, PT 14 **Student-Faculty Ratio:** 17:1 **% Receiving Financial Aid:** 100 **% Residing in College-Owned, -Operated, or -Affiliated Housing:** 2 **Library Holdings:** 20,585 **Credit Hours For Degree:** 66 credit hours, Associates; 129 credit hours, Bachelors **Professional Accreditation:** AABC, TACCS

HIGH POINT UNIVERSITY

University Station, Montlieu Ave.
High Point, NC 27262-3598
Tel: (336)841-9000
Free: 800-345-6993
Admissions: (336)841-9216
Fax: (336)841-5123
E-mail: admiss@highpoint.edu
Web Site: http://www.highpoint.edu/
President/CEO: Dr. Jacob C. Martinson
Registrar: Diana L. Estey
Admissions: Jessie McIlrath-Carter
Financial Aid: Dana D. Kelly
Type: Comprehensive **Sex:** Coed **Affiliation:** United Methodist **Scores:** 96% SAT V 400+; 94% SAT M 400+; 57% ACT 18-23; 28% ACT 24-29 **% Accepted:** 67 **Admission Plans:** Deferred Admission **Application Deadline:** August 15 **Application Fee:** $25.00 **H.S. Requirements:** High school diploma required; GED accepted **Costs Per Year:** Application fee: $25. Comprehensive fee: $26,000 includes full-time tuition ($16,760), mandatory fees ($1650), and college room and board ($7590). College room only: $3400. Part-time tuition: $263 per credit hour. **Scholarships:** Available **Calendar System:** Semester, Summer Session Available **Enrollment:** FT 2,325, PT 199, Grad 236 **Faculty:** FT 122, PT 105 **Student-Faculty Ratio:** 15:1 **Exams:** SAT I or ACT, SAT II **% Receiving Financial Aid:** 76 **% Residing in College-Owned, -Operated, or -Affiliated Housing:** 60 **Library Holdings:** 205,000 **Regional Accreditation:** Southern Association of Colleges and Schools **Credit Hours For Degree:** 124 semester hours, Bachelors **ROTC:** Army, Air Force **Professional Accreditation:** ACBSP, JRCEPAT, NCATE **Intercollegiate Athletics:** Baseball M; Basketball M & W; Cross-Country Running M & W; Golf M; Soccer M & W; Tennis M & W; Track and Field M & W; Volleyball W

ISOTHERMAL COMMUNITY COLLEGE

PO Box 804
Spindale, NC 28160-0804
Tel: (828)286-3636
Fax: (828)286-8109
Web Site: http://www.isothermal.edu/
President/CEO: Dr. Willard L. Lewis
Registrar: Kelly Metcalf
Admissions: Maggie Killoran
Financial Aid: Jeff Boyle
Type: Two-Year College **Sex:** Coed **Affiliation:** North Carolina Community College System **Admission Plans:** Open Admission; Early Admission; Deferred Admission **H.S. Requirements:** High school diploma required; GED accepted **Scholarships:** Available **Calendar System:** Semester, Summer Session Available **Enrollment:** FT 988, PT 1,017 **Faculty:** FT 60, PT 54 **Student-Faculty Ratio:** 17:1 **Exams:** Other **Library Holdings:** 35,200 **Regional Accreditation:** Southern Association of Colleges and Schools **Credit Hours For Degree:** 64 semester hours, Associates

JAMES SPRUNT COMMUNITY COLLEGE

PO Box 398
Kenansville, NC 28349-0398
Tel: (910)296-2400
Admissions: (910)296-2500
Fax: (910)296-1222
Web Site: http://www.sprunt.com/
President/CEO: Dr. Mary T. Wood
Registrar: Rita B. Brown
Admissions: Lea Grady
Financial Aid: Connie Taylor
Type: Two-Year College **Sex:** Coed **Affiliation:** North Carolina Community College System **% Accepted:** 83 **Admission Plans:** Open Admission; Early Admission; Deferred Admission **Application Deadline:** Rolling **Application Fee:** $0.00 **H.S. Requirements:** High school diploma required; GED accepted **Costs Per Year:** Application fee: $0. State resident tuition: $1264 full-time, $40 per semester hour part-time. Nonresident tuition: $7024 full-time, $220 per semester hour part-time. Mandatory fees: $70 full-time, $70 per term part-time. **Scholarships:** Available **Calendar System:** Semester, Summer Session Available **Enrollment:** FT 643, PT 727 **Faculty:** FT 60, PT 69 **Student-Faculty Ratio:** 21:1 **Library Holdings:** 23,497 **Regional Accreditation:** Southern Association of Colleges and Schools **Credit Hours For Degree:** 64 semester hours, Associates **Professional Accreditation:** AAMAE **Intercollegiate Athletics:** Softball W; Volleyball M & W

JOHN WESLEY COLLEGE

2314 North Centennial St.
High Point, NC 27265-3197
Tel: (336)889-2262
E-mail: admissions@johnwesley.edu
Web Site: http://www.johnwesley.edu/
President/CEO: Dr. Brian C. Donley
Registrar: Denise Matthews
Admissions: Greg Workman
Financial Aid: Shirley Carter
Type: Four-Year College **Sex:** Coed **Affiliation:** interdenominational **% Accepted:** 52 **Admission Plans:** Early Admission; Deferred Admission **Application Deadline:** August 01 **Application Fee:** $35.00 **H.S. Requirements:** High school diploma required; GED accepted **Costs Per Year:** Application fee: $35. Tuition: $8512 full-time, $392 per semester hour part-time. Mandatory fees: $646 full-time, $323 per term part-time. Full-time tuition and fees vary according to course load. Part-time tuition and fees vary according to course load. College room only: $1990. Room charges vary according to housing facility. **Scholarships:** Available **Calendar System:** Semester, Summer Session Available **Enrollment:** FT 84, PT 46 **Faculty:** FT 10, PT 11 **Student-Faculty Ratio:** 12:1 **% Receiving Financial Aid:** 79 **% Residing in College-Owned, -Operated, or -Affiliated Housing:** 14 **Library Holdings:** 43,305 **Credit Hours For Degree:** 66 semester hours, Associates; 128 semester hours, Bachelors **Professional Accreditation:** AABC

JOHNSON C. SMITH UNIVERSITY

100 Beatties Ford Rd.
Charlotte, NC 28216-5398
Tel: (704)378-1000
Free: 800-782-7303
Admissions: (704)378-1010
E-mail: admissions@jcsu.edu
Web Site: http://www.jcsu.edu/
President/CEO: Dr. Dorothy Cowser Yancy
Registrar: Moses Jones
Admissions: Jocelyn Biggs
Financial Aid: Cynthia Anderson
Type: Four-Year College **Sex:** Coed **Scores:** 82% SAT V 400+; 80% SAT M 400+; 25% ACT 18-23 **% Accepted:** 37 **Admission Plans:** Early Admission; Deferred Admission **Application Fee:** $25.00 **H.S. Requirements:** High school diploma required; GED accepted **Costs Per Year:** Application fee: $25. Comprehensive fee: $19,962 includes full-time tuition ($12,120), mandatory fees ($2279), and college room and board ($5563). College room only: $3201. Full-time tuition and fees vary according to course load. Room and board charges vary according to board plan and housing facility. Part-time tuition: $361 per credit hour. Part-time mandatory fees: $240 per term. Part-time tuition and fees vary according to course load. **Scholarships:** Available **Calendar System:** Semester, Summer Session Available **Enrollment:** FT 1,340, PT 64 **Faculty:** FT 90, PT 31 **Student-Faculty Ratio:** 14:1 **Exams:** SAT I or ACT **% Receiving Financial Aid:** 75 **% Residing in College-Owned, -Operated, or -Affiliated Housing:** 80 **Library Holdings:** 97,340 **Regional Accreditation:** Southern Association of Colleges and

Schools **Credit Hours For Degree:** 122 semester hours, Bachelors **ROTC:** Army, Air Force **Professional Accreditation:** ACBSP, CSWE, NCATE **Intercollegiate Athletics:** Basketball M & W; Cheerleading W; Cross-Country Running M & W; Football M; Golf M; Softball W; Tennis M & W; Track and Field M & W; Volleyball W

JOHNSON & WALES UNIVERSITY
901 West Trade St., Ste. 175
Charlotte, NC 28202
Tel: (980)598-1000; (866)598-2427
E-mail: admissions.clt@jwu.edu
Web Site: http://www.jwucharlotte.org/
President/CEO: Arthur J. Gallagher
Admissions: Brian Stanley
Type: Four-Year College **Sex:** Coed **% Accepted:** 74 **Application Deadline:** Rolling **Application Fee:** $0.00 **Costs Per Year:** Application fee: $0. Comprehensive fee: $29,126 includes full-time tuition ($19,875), mandatory fees ($951), and college room and board ($8300). Part-time tuition: $368 per quarter hour. **Scholarships:** Available **Calendar System:** Quarter **Enrollment:** FT 2,150, PT 6 **Faculty:** FT 66, PT 9 **Student-Faculty Ratio:** 31:1 **Exams:** SAT I or ACT **% Receiving Financial Aid:** 82 **Regional Accreditation:** New England Association of Schools and Colleges

JOHNSTON COMMUNITY COLLEGE
PO Box 2350
Smithfield, NC 27577-2350
Tel: (919)934-3051
Admissions: (919)209-2048
Fax: (919)934-2150
Web Site: http://www.johnston.cc.nc.us/
President/CEO: Dr. Donald L. Reichard
Registrar: Deloris B. Cuddington
Admissions: Dr. Pam Harrell
Financial Aid: Dee Dee Daughtry
Type: Two-Year College **Sex:** Coed **Affiliation:** North Carolina Community College System **Admission Plans:** Open Admission **Application Deadline:** Rolling **Application Fee:** $0.00 **H.S. Requirements:** High school diploma required; GED accepted **Costs Per Year:** Application fee: $0. State resident tuition: $1264 full-time, $39.50 per credit hour part-time. Nonresident tuition: $7024 full-time, $219.50 per credit hour part-time. Mandatory fees: $70 full-time, $1 per credit hour part-time, $15 per term part-time. **Scholarships:** Available **Calendar System:** Semester, Summer Session Available **Enrollment:** FT 1,628, PT 2,467 **Faculty:** FT 122, PT 211 **Student-Faculty Ratio:** 18:1 **Library Holdings:** 31,550 **Regional Accreditation:** Southern Association of Colleges and Schools **Credit Hours For Degree:** 64 credit hours, Associates **Professional Accreditation:** JRCERT **Intercollegiate Athletics:** Golf M & W; Softball M & W; Volleyball M & W

KING'S COLLEGE
322 Lamar Ave.
Charlotte, NC 28204-2436
Tel: (704)372-0266
Free: 800-768-2255
Admissions: (704)688-3613
Fax: (704)348-2029
E-mail: brockecharlie@kingscollege.org
Web Site: http://www.kingscollege.org/
President/CEO: Barbara Rokecharlie
Admissions: Barbara Rockecharlie
Type: Two-Year College **Sex:** Coed **Costs Per Year:** Comprehensive fee: $17,920 includes full-time tuition ($11,960) and college room and board ($5960). **Calendar System:** Quarter **Professional Accreditation:** ACICS

LEES-MCRAE COLLEGE
PO Box 128
Banner Elk, NC 28604-0128
Tel: (828)898-5241
Free: 800-280-4562
Admissions: (828)898-8829
Fax: (828)898-8814
E-mail: crutchfield@lmc.edu
Web Site: http://www2.lmc.edu/
President/CEO: Dr. David Bushman
Registrar: Aaron Aure
Admissions: Walt Crutchfield
Financial Aid: Lester McKenzie
Type: Four-Year College **Sex:** Coed **Affiliation:** Presbyterian Church (U.S.A.) **Scores:** 89% SAT V 400+; 92% SAT M 400+; 55% ACT 18-23; 17% ACT 24-29 **% Accepted:** 74 **Admission Plans:** Early Admission; Deferred Admission **Application Deadline:** August 01 **Application Fee:** $25.00 **H.S. Requirements:** High school diploma required; GED accepted **Costs Per Year:** Application fee: $25. Comprehensive fee: $24,000 includes full-time tuition ($18,000) and college room and board ($6000). Part-time tuition: $500 per semester hour. **Scholarships:** Available **Calendar System:** Semester, Summer Session Available **Enrollment:** FT 866, PT 16 **Faculty:** FT 55, PT 1 **Student-Faculty Ratio:** 15:1 **Exams:** SAT I or ACT **% Receiving Financial Aid:** 58 **% Residing in College-Owned, -Operated, or -Affiliated Housing:** 70 **Library Holdings:** 88,756 **Regional Accreditation:** Southern Association of Colleges and Schools **Credit Hours For Degree:** 124 credit hours, Bachelors **ROTC:** Army **Professional Accreditation:** AACN, NCATE **Intercollegiate Athletics:** Basketball M & W; Cross-Country Running M & W; Golf M; Lacrosse M & W; Soccer M & W; Softball W; Tennis M & W; Track and Field M & W; Volleyball M & W

LENOIR COMMUNITY COLLEGE
PO Box 188
Kinston, NC 28502-0188
Tel: (252)527-6223
E-mail: tsb706@email.lenoir.cc.nc.us
Web Site: http://www.lenoircc.edu/
President/CEO: Dr. Brantley Briley
Registrar: George Vick
Admissions: Tammy Buck
Financial Aid: Mary Anne Dawson
Type: Two-Year College **Sex:** Coed **Affiliation:** North Carolina Community College System **Admission Plans:** Open Admission; Early Admission **H.S. Requirements:** High school diploma required; GED accepted **Scholarships:** Available **Calendar System:** Semester, Summer Session Available **Enrollment:** FT 1,337, PT 1,270 **Exams:** Other, SAT I or ACT **Library Holdings:** 55,053 **Regional Accreditation:** Southern Association of Colleges and Schools **Credit Hours For Degree:** 64 semester hours, Associates **Professional Accreditation:** AAMAE **Intercollegiate Athletics:** Baseball M; Basketball M; Volleyball M & W

LENOIR-RHYNE COLLEGE
625 7th Ave. NE
Hickory, NC 28603
Tel: (828)328-1741
Free: 800-277-5721
Admissions: (828)328-7300
Fax: (828)328-7338
Web Site: http://www.lrc.edu/
President/CEO: Dr. Wayne B. Powell
Registrar: Kathy Hahn
Admissions: Rachel Nichols
Financial Aid: Rachel Nichols
Type: Comprehensive **Sex:** Coed **Affiliation:** Lutheran **Scores:** 93% SAT V 400+; 91% SAT M 400+; 61% ACT 18-23; 18% ACT 24-29 **Admission Plans:** Early Action; Deferred Admission **Application Fee:** $25.00 **H.S. Requirements:** High school diploma required; GED accepted **Costs Per Year:** Application fee: $25. One-time mandatory fee: $200. Comprehensive fee: $25,600 includes full-time tuition ($18,150), mandatory fees ($770), and college room and board ($6680). Room and board charges vary according to board plan and housing facility. Part-time tuition: $455 per credit. Part-time mandatory fees: $10 per term. Part-time tuition and fees vary according to class time. **Scholarships:** Available **Calendar System:** Semester, Summer Session Available **Enrollment:** FT 1,273, PT 134, Grad 172 **Faculty:** FT 90, PT 56 **Student-Faculty Ratio:** 13:1 **Exams:** SAT I or ACT **% Receiving Financial Aid:** 81 **% Residing in College-Owned, -Operated, or -Affiliated Housing:** 60 **Library Holdings:** 275,961 **Regional Accreditation:** Southern Association of Colleges and Schools **Credit Hours For Degree:** 128 credit hours, Bachelors **ROTC:** Army **Professional Accreditation:** AOTA, ACBSP, JRCEPAT, NCATE, NLN **Intercollegiate Athletics:** Baseball M; Basketball M & W; Cross-Country Running M & W; Football M; Golf M & W; Soccer M & W; Softball W; Volleyball W

LIVINGSTONE COLLEGE
701 West Monroe St.
Salisbury, NC 28144-5298

Tel: (704)216-6000
Free: 800-835-3435
Admissions: (704)216-6005
Fax: (704)216-6217
E-mail: rburney@livingstone.edu
Web Site: http://www.livingstone.edu/
President/CEO: Dr. Algeania W. Freeman
Registrar: Mary Gibson
Admissions: Rolanda Burney
Financial Aid: Terry Jeffries
Type: Four-Year College **Sex:** Coed **Affiliation:** African Methodist Episcopal Zion Church **Scores:** 64% SAT V 400+; 42% SAT M 400+; 9% ACT 18-23 **% Accepted:** 93 **Admission Plans:** Deferred Admission **Application Deadline:** August 01 **Application Fee:** $25.00 **H.S. Requirements:** High school diploma required; GED accepted **Costs Per Year:** Application fee: $25. Comprehensive fee: $17,815 includes full-time tuition ($10,279), mandatory fees ($1895), and college room and board ($5641). College room only: $2501. Part-time tuition: $428.30 per hour. Part-time mandatory fees: $79 per hour. **Scholarships:** Available **Calendar System:** Semester, Summer Session Not available **Enrollment:** FT 863, PT 32 **Faculty:** FT 54, PT 19 **Student-Faculty Ratio:** 15:1 **Exams:** SAT I or ACT **% Residing in College-Owned, -Operated, or -Affiliated Housing:** 65 **Library Holdings:** 135,000 **Regional Accreditation:** Southern Association of Colleges and Schools **Credit Hours For Degree:** 125 semester hours, Bachelors **ROTC:** Army **Professional Accreditation:** CSWE, NCATE **Intercollegiate Athletics:** Basketball M & W; Bowling W; Cross-Country Running M & W; Football M; Softball W; Tennis W; Track and Field M & W; Volleyball W

LOUISBURG COLLEGE

501 North Main St.
Louisburg, NC 27549-2399
Tel: (919)496-2521
Free: 800-775-0208
Admissions: (919)497-3228
Fax: (919)496-1788
E-mail: admissions@earthlink.net
Web Site: http://www.louisburg.edu/
President/CEO: Dr. Reginald W. Ponder
Registrar: Martha E. Hedgepeth
Admissions: Stephanie Buchanan
Type: Two-Year College **Sex:** Coed **Affiliation:** United Methodist **Scores:** 52% SAT V 400+; 55% SAT M 400+; 50% ACT 18-23 **Admission Plans:** Deferred Admission **Application Fee:** $25.00 **H.S. Requirements:** High school diploma required; GED accepted **Scholarships:** Available **Calendar System:** Semester, Summer Session Available **Enrollment:** FT 494, PT 8 **Faculty:** FT 27, PT 19 **Student-Faculty Ratio:** 15:1 **Exams:** SAT I or ACT **% Residing in College-Owned, -Operated, or -Affiliated Housing:** 90 **Library Holdings:** 64,000 **Regional Accreditation:** Southern Association of Colleges and Schools **Credit Hours For Degree:** 64 semester hours, Associates **Intercollegiate Athletics:** Baseball M; Basketball M & W; Golf M & W; Soccer M & W; Softball W; Volleyball M & W

MARS HILL COLLEGE

PO Box 370
Mars Hill, NC 28754
Tel: (828)689-1307; (866)MHC-4-YOU
Admissions: (828)689-1201
Fax: (828)689-1474
E-mail: admissions@mhc.edu
Web Site: http://www.mhc.edu/
President/CEO: Dr. Dan G. Lunsford
Registrar: Edith Whitt
Admissions: Bob McLendon
Financial Aid: Myrtle Martin
Type: Four-Year College **Sex:** Coed **Affiliation:** Baptist **Scores:** 88% SAT V 400+; 93% SAT M 400+; 65% ACT 18-23; 29% ACT 24-29 **% Accepted:** 85 **Admission Plans:** Early Admission; Deferred Admission **Application Deadline:** Rolling **Application Fee:** $25.00 **H.S. Requirements:** High school diploma required; GED accepted **Costs Per Year:** Application fee: $25. Comprehensive fee: $24,378 includes full-time tuition ($17,950) and college room and board ($6428). College room only: $3268. Part-time tuition: $500 per credit hour. **Scholarships:** Available **Calendar System:** Semester, Summer Session Available **Enrollment:** FT 1,227, PT 151 **Faculty:** FT 75, PT 69 **Student-Faculty Ratio:** 14:1 **Exams:** SAT I or ACT **% Receiving Financial Aid:** 75 **% Residing in College-Owned, -Operated, or -Affiliated Housing:** 25 **Library Holdings:** 98,150 **Regional Accreditation:** Southern Association of Colleges and Schools **Credit Hours For Degree:** 128 credits, Bachelors **Professional Accreditation:** CSWE, JRCEPAT, NASM, NAST, NCATE **Intercollegiate Athletics:** Baseball M; Basketball M & W; Cross-Country Running M & W; Football M; Golf M & W; Lacrosse M; Soccer M & W; Softball W; Swimming and Diving W; Tennis M & W; Track and Field M & W; Volleyball W

MARTIN COMMUNITY COLLEGE

1161 Kehukee Park Rd.
Williamston, NC 27892
Tel: (252)792-1521
Fax: (252)792-0826
Web Site: http://www.martin.cc.nc.us/
President/CEO: Dr. Ann R. Britt
Registrar: Sonya Atkinson
Admissions: Sonya C. Atkinson
Financial Aid: Elvis Jones
Type: Two-Year College **Sex:** Coed **Affiliation:** North Carolina Community College System **Admission Plans:** Open Admission **Application Fee:** $0.00 **H.S. Requirements:** High school diploma required; GED accepted **Scholarships:** Available **Calendar System:** Semester, Summer Session Available **Enrollment:** FT 281, PT 553 **Faculty:** FT 28, PT 31 **Student-Faculty Ratio:** 14:1 **Exams:** Other **Library Holdings:** 36,443 **Regional Accreditation:** Southern Association of Colleges and Schools **Credit Hours For Degree:** 64 semester hours, Associates **Professional Accreditation:** AAMAE, ADA, APTA

MAYLAND COMMUNITY COLLEGE

PO Box 547
Spruce Pine, NC 28777-0547
Tel: (828)765-7351
Fax: (828)765-0728
Web Site: http://www.mayland.edu
President/CEO: Dr. Thomas E. Williams
Registrar: Brenda Ward
Admissions: Cathy Morrison
Financial Aid: Pamela Ellis
Type: Two-Year College **Sex:** Coed **Affiliation:** North Carolina Community College System **Admission Plans:** Open Admission; Deferred Admission **Application Fee:** $0.00 **H.S. Requirements:** High school diploma required; GED accepted **Scholarships:** Available **Calendar System:** Semester, Summer Session Available **Enrollment:** FT 487, PT 532 **Faculty:** FT 48, PT 84 **Student-Faculty Ratio:** 10:1 **Exams:** Other **Library Holdings:** 19,041 **Regional Accreditation:** Southern Association of Colleges and Schools **Credit Hours For Degree:** 65 credits, Associates **Intercollegiate Athletics:** Basketball M

MCDOWELL TECHNICAL COMMUNITY COLLEGE

Route 1, Box 170
Marion, NC 28752-9724
Tel: (828)652-6021
Admissions: (828)652-6024
Fax: (828)652-1014
E-mail: lisab@mail.mcdowell.cc.nc.us
Web Site: http://www.mcdowelltech.cc.nc.us/
President/CEO: Dr. Virginia R. Mitchell
Registrar: Jimmy L. Biddix
Admissions: Lisa D. Byrd
Financial Aid: Kathy J. McKinney
Type: Two-Year College **Sex:** Coed **Affiliation:** North Carolina Community College System **Admission Plans:** Open Admission; Early Admission; Deferred Admission **Application Fee:** $0.00 **H.S. Requirements:** High school diploma required; GED accepted **Scholarships:** Available **Calendar System:** Semester, Summer Session Available **Faculty:** FT 40, PT 18 **Exams:** Other **Library Holdings:** 18,055 **Regional Accreditation:** Southern Association of Colleges and Schools **Credit Hours For Degree:** 64 credit hours, Associates **Intercollegiate Athletics:** Tennis M

MEREDITH COLLEGE

3800 Hillsborough St.
Raleigh, NC 27607-5298
Tel: (919)760-8600
Free: 800-MEREDITH
Admissions: (919)760-8581

Fax: (919)829-2348
E-mail: admissions@meredith.edu
Web Site: http://www.meredith.edu/
President/CEO: Dr. Maureen A. Hartford
Registrar: Jody Hamilton-Davis
Admissions: Heidi Fletcher
Financial Aid: Patti Corjay
Type: Comprehensive **Scores:** 98.6% SAT V 400+; 98.6% SAT M 400+; 69.4% ACT 18-23; 15.3% ACT 24-29 **% Accepted:** 95 **Admission Plans:** Early Admission; Early Decision Plan; Deferred Admission **Application Deadline:** February 15 **Application Fee:** $40.00 **H.S. Requirements:** High school diploma required; GED not accepted. For if student seeking early admissions meets all high school unit/GPA requirements for admission: High school diploma or equivalent not required **Costs Per Year:** Application fee: $40. Comprehensive fee: $27,140 includes full-time tuition ($21,150), mandatory fees ($50), and college room and board ($5940). Part-time tuition: $555 per credit hour. **Scholarships:** Available **Calendar System:** Semester, Summer Session Available **Enrollment:** FT 1,645, PT 370, Grad 153 **Faculty:** FT 128, PT 122 **Student-Faculty Ratio:** 11:1 **Exams:** SAT I or ACT, SAT II **% Receiving Financial Aid:** 68 **% Residing in College-Owned, -Operated, or -Affiliated Housing:** 46 **Library Holdings:** 186,100 **Regional Accreditation:** Southern Association of Colleges and Schools **Credit Hours For Degree:** 124 semester hours, Bachelors **ROTC:** Army, Air Force **Professional Accreditation:** AAFCS, ADtA, CSWE, FIDER, NASM, NCATE **Intercollegiate Athletics:** Basketball W; Cross-Country Running W; Soccer W; Softball W; Tennis W; Volleyball W

METHODIST COLLEGE
5400 Ramsey St.
Fayetteville, NC 28311-1498
Tel: (910)630-7000
Free: 800-488-7110
Admissions: (910)630-7027
Fax: (910)630-7317
Web Site: http://www.methodist.edu/
President/CEO: Dr. M. Elton Hendricks
Registrar: Dawn Congleton
Admissions: Rick Lowe
Financial Aid: Bonnie Adamson
Type: Comprehensive **Sex:** Coed **Affiliation:** United Methodist **Scores:** 90% SAT V 400+; 92% SAT M 400+; 59% ACT 18-23; 14% ACT 24-29 **Admission Plans:** Deferred Admission **Application Fee:** $25.00 **H.S. Requirements:** High school diploma required; GED accepted **Costs Per Year:** Application fee: $25. Comprehensive fee: $24,620 includes full-time tuition ($17,580), mandatory fees ($270), and college room and board ($6770). Full-time tuition and fees vary according to class time. Room and board charges vary according to board plan and housing facility. Part-time tuition: $570 per semester hour. Part-time tuition varies according to class time. **Scholarships:** Available **Calendar System:** Semester, Summer Session Available **Enrollment:** FT 1,722, PT 473, Grad 62 **Faculty:** FT 108, PT 90 **Student-Faculty Ratio:** 15:1 **Exams:** SAT I or ACT **% Receiving Financial Aid:** 74 **% Residing in College-Owned, -Operated, or -Affiliated Housing:** 50 **Library Holdings:** 86,259 **Regional Accreditation:** Southern Association of Colleges and Schools **Credit Hours For Degree:** 62 semester hours, Associates; 124 semester hours, Bachelors **ROTC:** Army, Air Force **Professional Accreditation:** ACBSP, CSWE, JRCEPAT, NCATE **Intercollegiate Athletics:** Baseball M; Basketball M & W; Cheerleading M & W; Cross-Country Running M & W; Football M; Golf M & W; Lacrosse W; Soccer M & W; Softball W; Tennis M & W; Track and Field M & W; Volleyball W

MITCHELL COMMUNITY COLLEGE
500 West Broad
Statesville, NC 28677-5293
Tel: (704)878-3200
Admissions: (704)878-3281
Fax: (704)878-0872
Web Site: http://www.mitchell.cc.nc.us/
President/CEO: Dr. Douglas O. Eason
Registrar: Gregory Stanley
Admissions: Dan Manning
Financial Aid: Karen Krider
Type: Two-Year College **Sex:** Coed **Affiliation:** North Carolina Community College System **Admission Plans:** Open Admission **Application Fee:** $0.00 **H.S. Requirements:** High school diploma required; GED accepted **Scholarships:** Available **Calendar System:** Semester, Summer Session Available **Enrollment:** FT 993, PT 1,250 **Faculty:** FT 63, PT 77 **Student-Faculty Ratio:** 17:1 **Library Holdings:** 37,760 **Regional Accreditation:** Southern Association of Colleges and Schools **Credit Hours For Degree:** 64 semester hours, Associates **ROTC:** Army **Professional Accreditation:** AAMAE

MONTGOMERY COMMUNITY COLLEGE
1011 Page St.
Troy, NC 27371
Tel: (910)576-6222
Free: 800-839-6222
Web Site: http://www.montgomery.edu/
President/CEO: Dr. Mary Powell Kirk
Registrar: Sandra E. Smith
Admissions: Kathy W. Harris
Financial Aid: Carolyn Hager
Type: Two-Year College **Sex:** Coed **Affiliation:** North Carolina Community College System **% Accepted:** 100 **Admission Plans:** Open Admission; Preferred Admission; Early Admission; Deferred Admission **Application Deadline:** Rolling **Application Fee:** $0.00 **H.S. Requirements:** High school diploma required; GED accepted **Costs Per Year:** Application fee: $0. State resident tuition: $1264 full-time, $39.50 per semester hour part-time. Nonresident tuition: $7024 full-time, $219.50 per semester hour part-time. Mandatory fees: $57 full-time, $28.25 per term part-time. Full-time tuition and fees vary according to course load. Part-time tuition and fees vary according to course load. **Scholarships:** Available **Calendar System:** Semester, Summer Session Available **Enrollment:** FT 391, PT 459 **Faculty:** FT 31, PT 42 **Library Holdings:** 14,859 **Regional Accreditation:** Southern Association of Colleges and Schools **Credit Hours For Degree:** 64 semester hours, Associates **Professional Accreditation:** AAMAE

MONTREAT COLLEGE
PO Box 1267
Montreat, NC 28757-1267
Tel: (828)669-8012
Fax: (828)669-0120
E-mail: admissions@montreat.edu
Web Site: http://www.montreat.edu/
President/CEO: Dr. Dan W. Struble
Registrar: Keith Karriker
Admissions: Anita Darby
Financial Aid: Lisa H. Lankford
Type: Comprehensive **Sex:** Coed **Affiliation:** Presbyterian Church (U.S.A.) **Scores:** 99% SAT V 400+; 91% SAT M 400+; 54% ACT 18-23; 31% ACT 24-29 **Admission Plans:** Early Admission; Deferred Admission **Application Fee:** $15.00 **H.S. Requirements:** High school diploma required; GED accepted **Costs Per Year:** Application fee: $15. Comprehensive fee: $20,568 includes full-time tuition ($15,560) and college room and board ($5008). Part-time tuition: $480 per credit hour. **Scholarships:** Available **Calendar System:** Semester, Summer Session Not available **Enrollment:** FT 935, PT 8, Grad 92 **Faculty:** FT 31, PT 89 **Student-Faculty Ratio:** 17:1 **Exams:** SAT I or ACT **% Receiving Financial Aid:** 75 **% Residing in College-Owned, -Operated, or -Affiliated Housing:** 34 **Library Holdings:** 68,100 **Regional Accreditation:** Southern Association of Colleges and Schools **Credit Hours For Degree:** 60 semester hours, Associates; 126 semester hours, Bachelors **Professional Accreditation:** NCATE **Intercollegiate Athletics:** Baseball M; Basketball M & W; Cross-Country Running M & W; Golf M; Soccer M & W; Softball W; Tennis M & W; Volleyball W

MOUNT OLIVE COLLEGE
634 Henderson St.
Mount Olive, NC 28365
Tel: (919)658-2502
Fax: (919)658-8934
Web Site: http://www.moc.edu/
President/CEO: Dr. J. William Byrd
Registrar: David L. Bourgeois
Admissions: Tim Woodard
Financial Aid: Karen Statler
Type: Four-Year College **Sex:** Coed **Affiliation:** Free Will Baptist **Scores:** 84% SAT V 400+; 89% SAT M 400+; 50% ACT 18-23; 6% ACT 24-29 **% Accepted:** 71 **Admission Plans:** Early Admission; Deferred Admission **Application Deadline:** Rolling **Application Fee:** $20.00 **H.S. Requirements:** High school diploma required; GED accepted **Costs Per Year:** Application

fee: $20. Comprehensive fee: $17,572 includes full-time tuition ($12,620) and college room and board ($4952). College room only: $2000. Part-time tuition: $215 per credit hour. **Scholarships:** Available **Calendar System:** Miscellaneous, Summer Session Available **Enrollment:** FT 1,946, PT 884 **Faculty:** FT 73, PT 168 **Student-Faculty Ratio:** 17:1 **Exams:** SAT I or ACT, SAT I **% Receiving Financial Aid:** 49 **% Residing in College-Owned, -Operated, or -Affiliated Housing:** 13 **Library Holdings:** 65,413 **Regional Accreditation:** Southern Association of Colleges and Schools **Credit Hours For Degree:** 64 semester hours, Associates; 126 semester hours, Bachelors **Intercollegiate Athletics:** Baseball M; Basketball M & W; Cheerleading W; Cross-Country Running M & W; Golf M; Soccer M & W; Softball W; Tennis M & W; Volleyball M & W

NASH COMMUNITY COLLEGE
PO Box 7488
Rocky Mount, NC 27804-0488
Tel: (252)443-4011
Fax: (252)443-0828
Web Site: http://www.nash.cc.nc.us/
President/CEO: Dr. Katherine M. Johnson
Registrar: Kathy Adcox
Admissions: Mary Blount
Financial Aid: Tammy Lester
Type: Two-Year College **Sex:** Coed **Affiliation:** North Carolina Community College System **Admission Plans:** Open Admission; Deferred Admission **Application Fee:** $0.00 **H.S. Requirements:** High school diploma required; GED accepted **Scholarships:** Available **Calendar System:** Semester, Summer Session Available **Enrollment:** FT 904, PT 1,663 **Faculty:** FT 70, PT 50 **Student-Faculty Ratio:** 22:1 **Exams:** Other, SAT I or ACT, SAT I and SAT II or ACT **Library Holdings:** 34,000 **Regional Accreditation:** Southern Association of Colleges and Schools **Credit Hours For Degree:** 65 semester hours, Associates **Professional Accreditation:** APTA

NEW LIFE THEOLOGICAL SEMINARY
PO Box 790106
Charlotte, NC 28206-7901
Tel: (704)334-6882
Fax: (704)334-6885
Web Site: http://www.nlts.org/
President/CEO: Dr. Eddie G. Grigg
Registrar: Judith Main
Financial Aid: Judith Main
Type: Comprehensive **Sex:** Coed **Calendar System:** Quarter **Professional Accreditation:** TACCS

NORTH CAROLINA AGRICULTURAL AND TECHNICAL STATE UNIVERSITY
1601 East Market St.
Greensboro, NC 27411
Tel: (336)334-7500
Admissions: (336)334-7946
Fax: (336)334-7082
Web Site: http://www.ncat.edu/
President/CEO: Dr. James C. Renick
Registrar: Doris Graham Hunter
Admissions: Lee Young
Financial Aid: Sherri Avent
Type: University **Sex:** Coed **Affiliation:** University of North Carolina System **Scores:** 68% SAT V 400+; 73.22% SAT M 400+ **% Accepted:** 84 **Admission Plans:** Early Admission; Deferred Admission **Application Deadline:** Rolling **Application Fee:** $45.00 **H.S. Requirements:** High school diploma required; GED accepted **Costs Per Year:** Application fee: $45. State resident tuition: $1769 full-time. Nonresident tuition: $11,211 full-time. Mandatory fees: $1355 full-time. College room and board: $5254. College room only: $2954. **Scholarships:** Available **Calendar System:** Semester, Summer Session Available **Enrollment:** FT 8,856, PT 879, Grad 1,368 **Student-Faculty Ratio:** 17:1 **Exams:** SAT I or ACT **% Receiving Financial Aid:** 72 **% Residing in College-Owned, -Operated, or -Affiliated Housing:** 29 **Library Holdings:** 541,403 **Regional Accreditation:** Southern Association of Colleges and Schools **Credit Hours For Degree:** 124 semester hours, Bachelors **ROTC:** Army, Air Force **Professional Accreditation:** AACSB, ABET, AAFCS, ACCE, ACA, ASLA, CSWE, NAIT, NASM, NAST, NCATE, NLN **Intercollegiate Athletics:** Baseball M; Basketball M & W; Cross-Country Running M & W; Football M; Softball W; Swimming and Diving W; Tennis M & W; Track and Field M & W; Volleyball W

NORTH CAROLINA CENTRAL UNIVERSITY
1801 Fayetteville St.
Durham, NC 27707-3129
Tel: (919)560-6100; 877-667-7533
Admissions: (919)530-6298
Web Site: http://www.nccu.edu/
President/CEO: Dr. James Ammons
Registrar: Mildred M. Lyon
Admissions: Jocelyn L. Foy
Financial Aid: Sharon J. Oliver
Type: Comprehensive **Sex:** Coed **Affiliation:** University of North Carolina System **Scores:** 63% SAT V 400+; 68% SAT M 400+; 33% ACT 18-23; 5% ACT 24-29 **% Accepted:** 77 **Admission Plans:** Open Admission; Preferred Admission; Deferred Admission **Application Deadline:** August 01 **Application Fee:** $30.00 **H.S. Requirements:** High school diploma required; GED accepted **Costs Per Year:** Application fee: $30. State resident tuition: $1878 full-time, $235 per course part-time. Nonresident tuition: $11,622 full-time, $1453 per course part-time. Mandatory fees: $1218 full-time, $51 per course part-time. Part-time tuition and fees vary according to course load. College room and board: $4526. College room only: $2588. Room and board charges vary according to board plan and housing facility. **Scholarships:** Available **Calendar System:** Semester, Summer Session Available **Enrollment:** FT 5,005, PT 1,348, Grad 1,392 **Faculty:** FT 325, PT 235 **Student-Faculty Ratio:** 17:1 **Exams:** SAT I or ACT **% Receiving Financial Aid:** 76 **% Residing in College-Owned, -Operated, or -Affiliated Housing:** 38 **Library Holdings:** 500,712 **Regional Accreditation:** Southern Association of Colleges and Schools **Credit Hours For Degree:** 124 semester hours, Bachelors **ROTC:** Army, Air Force **Professional Accreditation:** AAFCS, ABA, ADtA, ALA, ASLHA, ACBSP, CSWE, NAST, NCATE, NLN, NRPA **Intercollegiate Athletics:** Basketball M & W; Bowling M & W; Cross-Country Running M; Football M; Golf M & W; Softball W; Tennis M & W; Track and Field M & W; Volleyball W

NORTH CAROLINA SCHOOL OF THE ARTS
1533 South Main St.
PO Box 12189
Winston-Salem, NC 27127-2188
Tel: (336)770-3399
Admissions: (336)770-3290
Fax: (336)770-3370
Web Site: http://www.ncarts.edu/
President/CEO: Wade Hobgood
Registrar: June R. Putt
Admissions: Sheeler Lawson
Financial Aid: Jane Kamiab
Type: Comprehensive **Sex:** Coed **Affiliation:** University of North Carolina System **Scores:** 94.04% SAT V 400+; 94.49% SAT M 400+ **% Accepted:** 46 **Application Deadline:** March 01 **Application Fee:** $50.00 **H.S. Requirements:** High school diploma required; GED accepted **Costs Per Year:** Application fee: $50. State resident tuition: $2755 full-time. Nonresident tuition: $14,035 full-time. Mandatory fees: $1551 full-time. Full-time tuition and fees vary according to program. College room and board: $5700. College room only: $3035. Room and board charges vary according to board plan and housing facility. **Scholarships:** Available **Calendar System:** Trimester, Summer Session Not available **Enrollment:** FT 719, PT 7, Grad 101 **Faculty:** FT 135, PT 4 **Student-Faculty Ratio:** 8:1 **Exams:** SAT I or ACT **% Receiving Financial Aid:** 57 **% Residing in College-Owned, -Operated, or -Affiliated Housing:** 55 **Library Holdings:** 87,917 **Regional Accreditation:** Southern Association of Colleges and Schools **Credit Hours For Degree:** 142 credits, Bachelors

NORTH CAROLINA STATE UNIVERSITY
Raleigh, NC 27695
Tel: (919)515-2011
Admissions: (919)515-2434
Fax: (919)515-5039
E-mail: undergrad_admissions@ncsu.edu
Web Site: http://www.ncsu.edu/
President/CEO: Dr. Robert A. Barnhardt
Registrar: Dr. Louis Hunt
Admissions: Thomas Griffin
Financial Aid: Julia Rice Mallette
Type: University **Sex:** Coed **Affiliation:** University of North Carolina System **Scores:** 100% SAT V 400+; 100% SAT M 400+; 37% ACT 18-23; 47% ACT 24-29 **% Accepted:** 66 **Admission Plans:** Preferred Admission; Early Ac-

tion; Deferred Admission **Application Deadline:** February 01 **Application Fee:** $60.00 **H.S. Requirements:** High school diploma required; GED not accepted **Costs Per Year:** Application fee: $60. State resident tuition: $3530 full-time. Nonresident tuition: $15,728 full-time. Mandatory fees: $1254 full-time. College room and board: $7040. College room only: $4288. **Scholarships:** Available **Calendar System:** Semester, Summer Session Available **Enrollment:** FT 19,226, PT 3,541, Grad 7,078 **Faculty:** FT 1,671, PT 193 **Student-Faculty Ratio:** 16:1 **Exams:** SAT I or ACT, SAT II **% Receiving Financial Aid:** 38 **% Residing in College-Owned, -Operated, or -Affiliated Housing:** 33 **Library Holdings:** 3,389,517 **Regional Accreditation:** Southern Association of Colleges and Schools **Credit Hours For Degree:** 64 credit hours, Associates; 120 credit hours, Bachelors **ROTC:** Army, Navy, Air Force **Professional Accreditation:** AACSB, ABET, ACA, APA, ASLA, AVMA, CSWE, NASAD, NASPAA, NCATE, NRPA, SAF **Intercollegiate Athletics:** Badminton M & W; Baseball M; Basketball M & W; Bowling M & W; Cheerleading M & W; Crew M & W; Cross-Country Running M & W; Equestrian Sports M & W; Fencing M & W; Field Hockey M & W; Football M; Golf M & W; Gymnastics W; Ice Hockey M & W; Lacrosse M & W; Racquetball M & W; Riflery M & W; Rugby M & W; Sailing M & W; Skiing (Downhill) M & W; Soccer M & W; Softball W; Swimming and Diving M & W; Table Tennis M & W; Tennis M & W; Track and Field M & W; Ultimate Frisbee M & W; Volleyball M & W; Water Polo M & W; Wrestling M

NORTH CAROLINA WESLEYAN COLLEGE
3400 North Wesleyan Blvd.
Rocky Mount, NC 27804-8677
Tel: (252)985-5100
Free: 800-488-6292
Fax: (252)985-5325
Web Site: http://www.ncwc.edu/
President/CEO: Dr. Ian Newbould
Registrar: Cliff Sullivan
Financial Aid: Belinda G. Faulkner
Type: Four-Year College **Sex:** Coed **Affiliation:** United Methodist Church **Scores:** 81% SAT V 400+; 83% SAT M 400+ **% Accepted:** 81 **Application Deadline:** Rolling **Application Fee:** $25.00 **H.S. Requirements:** High school diploma required; GED accepted **Costs Per Year:** Application fee: $25. Comprehensive fee: $22,670 includes full-time tuition ($16,000) and college room and board ($6670). College room only: $3000. Full-time tuition varies according to location. Room and board charges vary according to housing facility. Part-time tuition: $258 per credit hour. Part-time tuition varies according to location. **Scholarships:** Available **Calendar System:** Semester, Summer Session Available **Enrollment:** FT 1,126, PT 626 **Faculty:** FT 53, PT 111 **Student-Faculty Ratio:** 17:1 **Exams:** SAT I or ACT **% Residing in College-Owned, -Operated, or -Affiliated Housing:** 28 **Library Holdings:** 88,975 **Regional Accreditation:** Southern Association of Colleges and Schools **Credit Hours For Degree:** 124 semester hours, Bachelors **Professional Accreditation:** NCATE **Intercollegiate Athletics:** Baseball M; Basketball M & W; Golf M; Soccer M & W; Softball W; Tennis M & W; Volleyball W

PAMLICO COMMUNITY COLLEGE
PO Box 185
Grantsboro, NC 28529-0185
Tel: (252)249-1851
Fax: (252)249-2377
Web Site: http://www.pamlico.cc.nc.us/
President/CEO: Dr. F. Marion Altman
Registrar: John T. Jones
Admissions: Floyd H. Hardison
Financial Aid: John T. Jones
Type: Two-Year College **Sex:** Coed **Affiliation:** North Carolina Community College System **Admission Plans:** Open Admission; Early Admission; Deferred Admission **Application Fee:** $0.00 **H.S. Requirements:** High school diploma required; GED accepted **Scholarships:** Available **Calendar System:** Semester, Summer Session Available **Faculty:** FT 6, PT 4 **Exams:** Other **Library Holdings:** 19,500 **Regional Accreditation:** Southern Association of Colleges and Schools **Professional Accreditation:** AAMAE

PEACE COLLEGE
15 East Peace St.
Raleigh, NC 27604-1194
Tel: (919)508-2000
Free: 800-PEACE-47
Admissions: (919)508-2016
Fax: (919)508-2328
E-mail: cchurch@peace.edu
Web Site: http://www.peace.edu/
President/CEO: Laura Carpenter Bingham
Registrar: Dr. Robert Page
Admissions: Dr. Catherine Church
Financial Aid: Angela Kirkley
Type: Four-Year College **Sex:** Women **Affiliation:** Presbyterian Church (U.S.A.) **Scores:** 89% SAT V 400+; 84% SAT M 400+; 34% ACT 18-23; 11% ACT 24-29 **% Accepted:** 35 **Admission Plans:** Early Admission; Deferred Admission **Application Deadline:** Rolling **Application Fee:** $25.00 **H.S. Requirements:** High school diploma required; GED accepted **Costs Per Year:** Application fee: $25. Comprehensive fee: $26,168 includes full-time tuition ($18,906), mandatory fees ($344), and college room and board ($6918). Part-time tuition: $400 per credit hour. **Scholarships:** Available **Calendar System:** Semester, Summer Session Not available **Enrollment:** FT 668, PT 33 **Faculty:** FT 41, PT 37 **Student-Faculty Ratio:** 11:1 **Exams:** SAT I or ACT **% Receiving Financial Aid:** 70 **% Residing in College-Owned, -Operated, or -Affiliated Housing:** 82 **Library Holdings:** 51,118 **Regional Accreditation:** Southern Association of Colleges and Schools **Credit Hours For Degree:** 63 semester hours, Associates; 125 semester hours, Bachelors **ROTC:** Army, Navy, Air Force **Intercollegiate Athletics:** Basketball W; Cross-Country Running W; Soccer W; Softball W; Tennis W; Volleyball W

PFEIFFER UNIVERSITY
PO Box 960
Misenheimer, NC 28109-0960
Tel: (704)463-1360
Free: 800-338-2060
Fax: (704)463-1363
E-mail: scumming@pfeiffer.edu
Web Site: http://www.pfeiffer.edu/
President/CEO: Dr. Charles M. Ambrose
Registrar: Larry Durrett
Admissions: Steve Cumming
Financial Aid: Lois Williams
Type: Comprehensive **Sex:** Coed **Affiliation:** United Methodist **Scores:** 100% SAT V 400+; 100% SAT M 400+; 67% ACT 18-23; 14% ACT 24-29 **% Accepted:** 77 **Admission Plans:** Early Admission; Deferred Admission **Application Deadline:** Rolling **Application Fee:** $25.00 **H.S. Requirements:** High school diploma required; GED accepted **Costs Per Year:** Application fee: $25. Comprehensive fee: $21,900 includes full-time tuition ($15,590) and college room and board ($6310). College room only: $3710. Full-time tuition varies according to course load. Room and board charges vary according to housing facility. Part-time tuition: $355 per credit hour. Part-time tuition varies according to course load. **Scholarships:** Available **Calendar System:** Semester, Summer Session Available **Enrollment:** FT 1,055, PT 147, Grad 948 **Faculty:** FT 65, PT 78 **Student-Faculty Ratio:** 13:1 **Exams:** SAT I or ACT **% Residing in College-Owned, -Operated, or -Affiliated Housing:** 41 **Library Holdings:** 117,000 **Regional Accreditation:** Southern Association of Colleges and Schools **Credit Hours For Degree:** 124 semester hours, Bachelors **ROTC:** Army **Professional Accreditation:** NASM, NCATE **Intercollegiate Athletics:** Baseball M; Basketball M & W; Cheerleading M & W; Cross-Country Running M & W; Golf M & W; Lacrosse M & W; Soccer M & W; Softball W; Swimming and Diving W; Tennis M & W; Volleyball W

PIEDMONT BAPTIST COLLEGE
716 Franklin St.
Winston-Salem, NC 27101-5197
Tel: (336)725-8344
Free: 800-937-5097
Fax: (336)725-5522
Web Site: http://www.pbc.edu/
President/CEO: Dr. Charles Petitt
Registrar: Darlene Richter
Admissions: Ronnie Mathis
Financial Aid: Ronnie Mathis
Type: Comprehensive **Sex:** Coed **Affiliation:** Baptist **Scores:** 12% ACT 18-23; 1% ACT 24-29 **Admission Plans:** Open Admission; Early Admission; Early Action; Deferred Admission **Application Fee:** $50.00 **H.S. Requirements:** High school diploma required; GED accepted **Scholarships:** Available **Calendar System:** Semester, Summer Session Available **Faculty:** FT 20, PT 14 **Student-Faculty Ratio:** 11:1 **Exams:** ACT **% Residing in**

College-Owned, -Operated, or -Affiliated Housing: 32 **Library Holdings:** 50,000 **Credit Hours For Degree:** 69 credit hours, Associates; 135 credit hours, Bachelors **Professional Accreditation:** TACCS **Intercollegiate Athletics:** Baseball M; Basketball M & W; Volleyball W

PIEDMONT COMMUNITY COLLEGE
PO Box 1197
Roxboro, NC 27573-1197
Tel: (336)599-1181
Fax: (336)597-3817
Web Site: http://www.piedmont.cc.nc.us/
President/CEO: Dr. H. James Owen
Registrar: Dr. Nydia Morales
Admissions: Sheila Williamson
Financial Aid: Frances Lunsford
Type: Two-Year College **Sex:** Coed **Affiliation:** North Carolina Community College System **Admission Plans:** Open Admission; Early Admission; Deferred Admission **Application Fee:** $0.00 **H.S. Requirements:** High school diploma required; GED accepted **Scholarships:** Available **Calendar System:** Semester, Summer Session Available **Enrollment:** FT 826, PT 1,363 **Faculty:** FT 71, PT 86 **Student-Faculty Ratio:** 28:1 **Exams:** Other **Library Holdings:** 24,166 **Regional Accreditation:** Southern Association of Colleges and Schools **Credit Hours For Degree:** 74 semester hours, Associates

PITT COMMUNITY COLLEGE
Hwy. 11 South, PO Drawer 7007
Greenville, NC 27835-7007
Tel: (252)321-4200
Admissions: (252)321-4208
Fax: (252)321-4401
Web Site: http://www.pittcc.edu/
President/CEO: G. Dennis Massey
Registrar: Marietta Williams
Admissions: Kathy O. Kinlaw
Financial Aid: Lisa Reichstein
Type: Two-Year College **Sex:** Coed **Affiliation:** North Carolina Community College System **Admission Plans:** Open Admission; Deferred Admission **Application Fee:** $0.00 **H.S. Requirements:** High school diploma required; GED accepted **Scholarships:** Available **Calendar System:** Semester, Summer Session Available **Enrollment:** FT 3,200, PT 2,780 **Faculty:** FT 172, PT 156 **Student-Faculty Ratio:** 18:1 **Exams:** Other **Library Holdings:** 43,558 **Regional Accreditation:** Southern Association of Colleges and Schools **Credit Hours For Degree:** 65 semester hours, Associates **ROTC:** Army **Professional Accreditation:** AAMAE, AHIMA, AOTA, CARC, JRCEDMS, JRCERT **Intercollegiate Athletics:** Baseball M; Golf M & W; Volleyball W

QUEENS UNIVERSITY OF CHARLOTTE
1900 Selwyn Ave.
Charlotte, NC 28274-0002
Tel: (704)337-2200
Free: 800-849-0202
Admissions: (704)337-2445
Fax: (704)337-2403
E-mail: ralphb@queens.edu
Web Site: http://www.queens.edu/
President/CEO: Dr. Pamela S. Lewis
Registrar: Ruth Ann Engle
Admissions: Dr. Brian Ralph
Financial Aid: Eileen Dills
Type: Comprehensive **Sex:** Coed **Affiliation:** Presbyterian **Scores:** 98% SAT V 400+; 98% SAT M 400+; 56% ACT 18-23; 32% ACT 24-29 **% Accepted:** 67 **Admission Plans:** Deferred Admission **Application Deadline:** Rolling **Application Fee:** $40.00 **H.S. Requirements:** High school diploma required; GED accepted **Costs Per Year:** Application fee: $40. Comprehensive fee: $26,430 includes full-time tuition ($19,450) and college room and board ($6980). Part-time tuition: $290 per credit hour. **Scholarships:** Available **Calendar System:** Semester, Summer Session Available **Enrollment:** FT 1,016, PT 607, Grad 490 **Faculty:** FT 68, PT 43 **Student-Faculty Ratio:** 15:1 **Exams:** SAT I or ACT **% Receiving Financial Aid:** 55 **% Residing in College-Owned, -Operated, or -Affiliated Housing:** 75 **Library Holdings:** 126,242 **Regional Accreditation:** Southern Association of Colleges and Schools **Credit Hours For Degree:** 122 credit hours, Bachelors **ROTC:** Army, Air Force **Professional Accreditation:** AACN, ACBSP, NASM, NCATE **Intercollegiate Athletics:** Basketball M & W; Cross-Country Running M & W; Golf M & W; Lacrosse M & W; Soccer M & W; Softball W; Tennis M & W; Volleyball W

RANDOLPH COMMUNITY COLLEGE
PO Box 1009
Asheboro, NC 27204-1009
Tel: (336)633-0200
Fax: (336)629-4695
Web Site: http://www.randolph.edu/
President/CEO: Dr. Richard T. Heckman
Registrar: Carol M. Elmore
Type: Two-Year College **Sex:** Coed **Affiliation:** North Carolina Community College System **Admission Plans:** Open Admission; Deferred Admission **Application Fee:** $0.00 **H.S. Requirements:** High school diploma required; GED accepted **Scholarships:** Available **Calendar System:** Semester, Summer Session Available **Faculty:** FT 49, PT 112 **Student-Faculty Ratio:** 23:1 **Exams:** Other **Library Holdings:** 36,776 **Regional Accreditation:** Southern Association of Colleges and Schools **Credit Hours For Degree:** 64 semester hours, Associates **Professional Accreditation:** NLN

RICHMOND COMMUNITY COLLEGE
PO Box 1189
Hamlet, NC 28345-1189
Tel: (910)582-7000
Admissions: (910)582-7113
Fax: (910)582-7102
Web Site: http://www.richmondcc.edu/
President/CEO: Dr. Dianne Honeycutt
Registrar: Teri P. Jacobs
Admissions: Wanda B. Watts
Financial Aid: Beth McQueen
Type: Two-Year College **Sex:** Coed **Affiliation:** North Carolina Community College System **Admission Plans:** Open Admission; Deferred Admission **Application Deadline:** Rolling **Application Fee:** $0.00 **H.S. Requirements:** High school diploma required; GED accepted **Costs Per Year:** Application fee: $0. State resident tuition: $39.50 per credit hour part-time. Nonresident tuition: $219.50 per credit hour part-time. Mandatory fees: $12 per term part-time. **Scholarships:** Available **Calendar System:** Semester, Summer Session Available **Enrollment:** FT 691, PT 781 **Faculty:** FT 51, PT 9 **Student-Faculty Ratio:** 29:1 **Library Holdings:** 26,381 **Regional Accreditation:** Southern Association of Colleges and Schools **Credit Hours For Degree:** 64 semester hours, Associates

ROANOKE BIBLE COLLEGE
715 North Poindexter St.
Elizabeth City, NC 27909-4054
Tel: (252)334-2070
Free: 800-RBC-8980
Admissions: (252)334-2028
Fax: (252)334-2071
E-mail: jaf@roanokebible.edu
Web Site: http://www.roanokebible.edu/
President/CEO: William A. Griffin
Registrar: Joan U. Sawyer
Admissions: Julie Fields
Financial Aid: Lisa W. Pipkin
Type: Four-Year College **Sex:** Coed **Affiliation:** Christian **Scores:** 83% SAT V 400+; 84% SAT M 400+; 67% ACT 18-23 **% Accepted:** 49 **Admission Plans:** Early Admission; Deferred Admission **Application Deadline:** August 01 **Application Fee:** $25.00 **H.S. Requirements:** High school diploma required; GED accepted **Costs Per Year:** Application fee: $25. Comprehensive fee: $13,480 includes full-time tuition ($7840), mandatory fees ($680), and college room and board ($4960). College room only: $2780. Part-time tuition: $245 per credit hour. **Scholarships:** Available **Calendar System:** Semester, Summer Session Not available **Enrollment:** FT 158, PT 24 **Faculty:** FT 12, PT 15 **Student-Faculty Ratio:** 10:1 **Exams:** SAT I or ACT **% Receiving Financial Aid:** 70 **% Residing in College-Owned, -Operated, or -Affiliated Housing:** 65 **Library Holdings:** 28,552 **Regional Accreditation:** Southern Association of Colleges and Schools **Credit Hours For Degree:** 64 semester hours, Associates; 128 semester hours, Bachelors **Professional Accreditation:** AABC **Intercollegiate Athletics:** Basketball M & W; Volleyball W

ROANOKE-CHOWAN COMMUNITY COLLEGE
109 Community College Rd.
Ahoskie, NC 27910

Tel: (252)862-1200
Admissions: (252)862-1225
Fax: (252)862-1353
Web Site: http://www.roanokechowan.edu/
President/CEO: Dr. Mary C. Wyatt
Registrar: Mary Lou Byrum
Admissions: Sandra Copeland
Financial Aid: Phyllis Parker
Type: Two-Year College **Sex:** Coed **Affiliation:** North Carolina Community College System **Admission Plans:** Open Admission; Early Admission **H.S. Requirements:** High school diploma required; GED accepted **Scholarships:** Available **Calendar System:** Semester, Summer Session Available **Enrollment:** FT 491, PT 523 **Faculty:** FT 38, PT 70 **Student-Faculty Ratio:** 11:1 **Exams:** Other **Library Holdings:** 29,268 **Regional Accreditation:** Southern Association of Colleges and Schools

ROBESON COMMUNITY COLLEGE
Hwy. 301 North, PO Box 1420
Lumberton, NC 28359-1420
Tel: (910)738-7101
Admissions: (910)618-5680
Fax: (910)671-4143
Web Site: http://www.robeson.cc.nc.us/
President/CEO: Fred W. Williams, Jr.
Registrar: Georgia Moore
Admissions: Judy Revels
Financial Aid: Anna Maynor
Type: Two-Year College **Sex:** Coed **Affiliation:** North Carolina Community College System **Admission Plans:** Open Admission; Early Admission **H.S. Requirements:** High school diploma required; GED accepted **Calendar System:** Semester **Faculty:** FT 44, PT 70 **Exams:** Other **Library Holdings:** 39,000 **Regional Accreditation:** Southern Association of Colleges and Schools **Credit Hours For Degree:** 65 semester hours, Associates **Professional Accreditation:** CARC

ROCKINGHAM COMMUNITY COLLEGE
PO Box 38
Wentworth, NC 27375-0038
Tel: (336)342-4261
Web Site: http://www.rcc.cc.nc.us/
President/CEO: Dr. Robert C. Keys
Registrar: Dr. LaCheata G. Hall
Admissions: Leigh Hawkins
Financial Aid: Coe Ann Greene
Type: Two-Year College **Sex:** Coed **Affiliation:** North Carolina Community College System **Admission Plans:** Open Admission; Early Admission; Deferred Admission **Application Deadline:** Rolling **Application Fee:** $0.00 **H.S. Requirements:** High school diploma required; GED accepted **Costs Per Year:** Application fee: $0. State resident tuition: $1264 full-time, $39.50 per credit hour part-time. Nonresident tuition: $7061 full-time, $219.50 per credit hour part-time. Mandatory fees: $52 full-time. **Scholarships:** Available **Calendar System:** Semester, Summer Session Available **Enrollment:** FT 604, PT 1,432 **Faculty:** FT 66, PT 45 **Student-Faculty Ratio:** 18:1 **Library Holdings:** 43,044 **Regional Accreditation:** Southern Association of Colleges and Schools **Intercollegiate Athletics:** Baseball M; Basketball M & W; Volleyball M & W

ROWAN-CABARRUS COMMUNITY COLLEGE
PO Box 1595
Salisbury, NC 28145-1595
Tel: (704)637-0760
Fax: (704)633-6804
Web Site: http://www.rccc.cc.nc.us/
President/CEO: Dr. Richard L. Brownell
Admissions: Eddie H. Myers
Financial Aid: Lisa Ledbetter
Type: Two-Year College **Sex:** Coed **Affiliation:** North Carolina Community College System **Admission Plans:** Open Admission **Application Fee:** $0.00 **H.S. Requirements:** High school diploma required; GED accepted **Scholarships:** Available **Calendar System:** Semester, Summer Session Available **Enrollment:** FT 2,255, PT 2,945 **Faculty:** FT 120, PT 131 **Exams:** Other **Library Holdings:** 23,005 **Regional Accreditation:** Southern Association of Colleges and Schools **Credit Hours For Degree:** 64 semester hours, Associates **Professional Accreditation:** ADA, JRCERT, NLN

ST. ANDREWS PRESBYTERIAN COLLEGE
1700 Dogwood Mile
Laurinburg, NC 28352-5598
Tel: (910)277-5000
Free: 800-763-0198
Admissions: (910)277-5555
Fax: (910)277-5087
E-mail: admission@sapc.edu
Web Site: http://www.sapc.edu/
President/CEO: Dr. John Deegan, Jr.
Registrar: Deborah A. Smith
Admissions: Rev. Glenn Batten
Financial Aid: Kimberly Driggers
Type: Four-Year College **Sex:** Coed **Affiliation:** Presbyterian **Scores:** 96% SAT V 400+; 92% SAT M 400+ **% Accepted:** 76 **Admission Plans:** Early Admission; Early Decision Plan; Deferred Admission **Application Deadline:** Rolling **Application Fee:** $30.00 **H.S. Requirements:** High school diploma required; GED accepted **Costs Per Year:** Application fee: $30. Comprehensive fee: $24,756 includes full-time tuition ($17,162), mandatory fees ($900), and college room and board ($6694). College room only: $2748. Full-time tuition and fees vary according to location. Room and board charges vary according to housing facility. Part-time tuition: $410 per credit. Part-time tuition varies according to location. **Scholarships:** Available **Calendar System:** Semester, Summer Session Available **Enrollment:** FT 706, PT 75 **Faculty:** FT 44, PT 20 **Student-Faculty Ratio:** 14:1 **Exams:** SAT I or ACT **% Receiving Financial Aid:** 59 **% Residing in College-Owned, -Operated, or -Affiliated Housing:** 76 **Library Holdings:** 108,734 **Regional Accreditation:** Southern Association of Colleges and Schools **Credit Hours For Degree:** 120 credits, Bachelors **Professional Accreditation:** NCATE **Intercollegiate Athletics:** Baseball M; Basketball M & W; Cross-Country Running M & W; Equestrian Sports M & W; Golf M & W; Lacrosse M & W; Rugby M & W; Soccer M & W; Softball W; Tennis M & W; Volleyball W; Wrestling M

SAINT AUGUSTINE'S COLLEGE
1315 Oakwood Ave.
Raleigh, NC 27604-2298
Tel: (919)516-4000
Free: 800-948-1126
Admissions: (919)516-4012
Fax: (919)516-4415
Web Site: http://www.st-aug.edu/
President/CEO: Dr. Diane Broadley Suber
Registrar: Crystal Williams
Admissions: Byron Bullock
Financial Aid: Rochelle King
Type: Four-Year College **Sex:** Coed **Affiliation:** Episcopal **Scores:** 50% SAT V 400+; 49% SAT M 400+; 21% ACT 18-23; 2% ACT 24-29 **Admission Plans:** Deferred Admission **Application Fee:** $25.00 **H.S. Requirements:** High school diploma required; GED accepted **Costs Per Year:** Application fee: $25. Comprehensive fee: $17,272 includes full-time tuition ($8952), mandatory fees ($2476), and college room and board ($5844). College room only: $3322. Full-time tuition and fees vary according to course load, program, and reciprocity agreements. Room and board charges vary according to board plan, housing facility, and location. Part-time tuition: $480 per credit. Part-time mandatory fees: $103 per credit. Part-time tuition and fees vary according to course load, program, and reciprocity agreements. **Scholarships:** Available **Calendar System:** Semester, Summer Session Available **Enrollment:** FT 1,333, PT 62 **Faculty:** FT 87, PT 10 **Student-Faculty Ratio:** 13:1 **Exams:** SAT I or ACT **% Receiving Financial Aid:** 81 **% Residing in College-Owned, -Operated, or -Affiliated Housing:** 62 **Library Holdings:** 76,000 **Regional Accreditation:** Southern Association of Colleges and Schools **Credit Hours For Degree:** 124 semester hours, Bachelors **ROTC:** Army, Air Force **Professional Accreditation:** NCATE **Intercollegiate Athletics:** Baseball M; Basketball M & W; Bowling W; Cheerleading W; Cross-Country Running M & W; Football M; Golf M; Softball W; Tennis M & W; Track and Field M & W; Volleyball W

SALEM COLLEGE
PO Box 10548
Winston-Salem, NC 27108-0548
Tel: (336)721-2600

Free: 800-327-2536
Admissions: (336)721-2621
Fax: (336)724-7102
Web Site: http://www.salem.edu/
President/CEO: Dr. Julianne Still Thrift
Registrar: Joyce K. Jackson
Admissions: Dana E. Evans
Financial Aid: Julie Setzer
Type: Comprehensive **Affiliation:** Moravian **Scores:** 100% SAT V 400+; 98% SAT M 400+; 53% ACT 18-23; 41% ACT 24-29 **% Accepted:** 69 **Admission Plans:** Early Admission; Deferred Admission **Application Deadline:** Rolling **Application Fee:** $30.00 **H.S. Requirements:** High school diploma required; GED accepted **Costs Per Year:** Application fee: $30. Comprehensive fee: $26,441 includes full-time tuition ($16,975), mandatory fees ($215), and college room and board ($9251). **Scholarships:** Available **Calendar System:** 4-1-4, Summer Session Available **Enrollment:** FT 702, PT 166, Grad 241 **Faculty:** FT 57, PT 34 **Student-Faculty Ratio:** 12:1 **Exams:** SAT I or ACT **% Residing in College-Owned, -Operated, or -Affiliated Housing:** 88 **Library Holdings:** 132,510 **Regional Accreditation:** Southern Association of Colleges and Schools **Credit Hours For Degree:** 36 courses, Bachelors **ROTC:** Army **Professional Accreditation:** NASM, NCATE **Intercollegiate Athletics:** Basketball W; Cross-Country Running W; Equestrian Sports W; Field Hockey W; Soccer W; Softball W; Swimming and Diving W; Tennis W; Volleyball W

SAMPSON COMMUNITY COLLEGE
PO Box 318
Clinton, NC 28329-0318
Tel: (910)592-8081
Admissions: (910)592-8084
Fax: (910)592-8048
Web Site: http://www.sampsoncc.edu/
President/CEO: Dr. William Aiken
Registrar: Denise Rackley
Admissions: William R. Jordan
Financial Aid: Judge Tart
Type: Two-Year College **Sex:** Coed **Affiliation:** North Carolina Community College System **Admission Plans:** Open Admission; Deferred Admission **Application Fee:** $0.00 **H.S. Requirements:** High school diploma required; GED accepted **Scholarships:** Available **Calendar System:** Semester, Summer Session Available **Enrollment:** FT 679, PT 900 **Faculty:** FT 45, PT 50 **Student-Faculty Ratio:** 20:1 **Exams:** Other **Library Holdings:** 25,000 **Regional Accreditation:** Southern Association of Colleges and Schools **Credit Hours For Degree:** 65 credits, Associates

SANDHILLS COMMUNITY COLLEGE
3395 Airport Rd.
Pinehurst, NC 28374-8299
Tel: (910)692-6185
Admissions: (910)695-3735
Fax: (910)695-1823
E-mail: offuttb@sandpiper.sandhills.cc.nc.us
Web Site: http://www.sandhills.edu/
President/CEO: Dr. John Dempsey
Registrar: Libby Self
Admissions: Rosa McAllister-McRae
Financial Aid: Kellie Shoemake
Type: Two-Year College **Sex:** Coed **Affiliation:** North Carolina Community College System **Admission Plans:** Open Admission; Deferred Admission **Application Fee:** $0.00 **H.S. Requirements:** High school diploma required; GED accepted **Scholarships:** Available **Calendar System:** Semester, Summer Session Available **Faculty:** FT 111, PT 60 **Student-Faculty Ratio:** 18:1 **Exams:** Other **Library Holdings:** 76,080 **Regional Accreditation:** Southern Association of Colleges and Schools **Credit Hours For Degree:** 64 semester hours, Associates **Professional Accreditation:** CARC, JRCERT, NAACLS

SCHOOL OF COMMUNICATION ARTS
3000 Wakefield Crossing Dr.
Raleigh, NC 27614
Tel: (919)488-8500
Free: 800-288-7442
Web Site: http://www.higherdigital.com/ **Type:** Two-Year College **Sex:** Coed **Calendar System:** Quarter **Professional Accreditation:** COE

SHAW UNIVERSITY
118 East South St.
Raleigh, NC 27601-2399
Tel: (919)546-8200
Free: 800-214-6683
Admissions: (919)546-8275
Fax: (919)546-8271
E-mail: sclifton@shawu.edu
Web Site: http://www.shawuniversity.edu/
President/CEO: Dr. Clarence G. Newsome
Registrar: Gene Page
Admissions: Sandy Clifton
Financial Aid: Kamesia Ewing
Type: Comprehensive **Sex:** Coed **Affiliation:** Baptist **Scores:** 43.94% SAT V 400+; 40.65% SAT M 400+; 11.4% ACT 18-23 **% Accepted:** 65 **Admission Plans:** Early Admission; Deferred Admission **Application Deadline:** July 30 **Application Fee:** $25.00 **H.S. Requirements:** High school diploma required; GED accepted **Costs Per Year:** Application fee: $25. Comprehensive fee: $16,430 includes full-time tuition ($8280), mandatory fees ($1740), and college room and board ($6410). College room only: $3010. Part-time tuition: $345 per semester hour. Part-time mandatory fees: $29 per semester hour. **Scholarships:** Available **Calendar System:** Semester, Summer Session Available **Enrollment:** FT 2,283, PT 282, Grad 33 **Faculty:** FT 111, PT 179 **Student-Faculty Ratio:** 15:1 **Exams:** SAT I or ACT **% Receiving Financial Aid:** 94 **% Residing in College-Owned, -Operated, or -Affiliated Housing:** 39 **Library Holdings:** 154,368 **Regional Accreditation:** Southern Association of Colleges and Schools **Credit Hours For Degree:** 60 credit hours, Associates; 120 credit hours, Bachelors **ROTC:** Army, Air Force **Professional Accreditation:** ATS, CAEPK, NCATE **Intercollegiate Athletics:** Baseball M; Basketball M & W; Bowling W; Cross-Country Running M & W; Football M; Golf M; Softball W; Tennis M & W; Track and Field M & W; Volleyball W

SOUTH COLLEGE-ASHEVILLE
1567 Patton Ave.
Asheville, NC 28806
Tel: (828)252-2486
Web Site: http://www.southcollegenc.com/
President/CEO: Stephen A. South
Admissions: Michael Darnell
Financial Aid: Marty Mehringer
Type: Two-Year College **Sex:** Coed **Admission Plans:** Open Admission; Deferred Admission **Application Fee:** $40.00 **H.S. Requirements:** High school diploma required; GED accepted **Scholarships:** Available **Calendar System:** Quarter, Summer Session Available **Enrollment:** FT 88, PT 24 **Faculty:** FT 8, PT 20 **Student-Faculty Ratio:** 9:1 **Exams:** Other **Library Holdings:** 4,550 **Credit Hours For Degree:** 102 credits, Associates **Professional Accreditation:** ACICS

SOUTH PIEDMONT COMMUNITY COLLEGE
PO Box 126
Polkton, NC 28135-0126
Tel: (704)272-7635
Free: 800-766-0319
E-mail: abaucom@vnet.net
Web Site: http://www.spcc.edu/
President/CEO: Dr. John McKay
Registrar: Pat Taylor
Admissions: Jeania Martin
Financial Aid: Vicki R. Cameron
Type: Two-Year College **Sex:** Coed **Affiliation:** North Carolina Community College System **Admission Plans:** Open Admission; Early Admission; Deferred Admission **Application Fee:** $0.00 **H.S. Requirements:** High school diploma required; GED accepted **Scholarships:** Available **Calendar System:** Semester, Summer Session Available **Enrollment:** FT 746, PT 1,129 **Faculty:** FT 46, PT 100 **Student-Faculty Ratio:** 17:1 **Exams:** Other **Library Holdings:** 18,917 **Regional Accreditation:** Southern Association of Colleges and Schools **Credit Hours For Degree:** 64 semester hours, Associates **Professional Accreditation:** AAMAE, AHIMA

SOUTHEASTERN BAPTIST THEOLOGICAL SEMINARY
PO Box 1889
Wake Forest, NC 27588-1889

Tel: (919)556-3101
Free: 800-284-6317
Admissions: (919)761-2280
Web Site: http://www.sebts.edu/
President/CEO: Dr. Daniel L. Akin
Registrar: Sheldon Alexander
Admissions: Jerry Yandell
Type: Comprehensive **Sex:** Coed **Affiliation:** Southern Baptist; Southeastern Baptist Theological Seminary **Admission Plans:** Open Admission **Application Fee:** $25.00 **H.S. Requirements:** High school diploma required; GED accepted **Scholarships:** Available **Calendar System:** Semester, Summer Session Available **Enrollment:** FT 282, PT 170, Grad 544 **Faculty:** FT 59, PT 31 **Exams:** SAT I and SAT II or ACT **% Residing in College-Owned, -Operated, or -Affiliated Housing:** 30 **Library Holdings:** 167,044 **Regional Accreditation:** Southern Association of Colleges and Schools **Credit Hours For Degree:** 64 credits, Associates; 128 credits, Bachelors **Professional Accreditation:** ACIPE, ATS

SOUTHEASTERN COMMUNITY COLLEGE
PO Box 151
Whiteville, NC 28472-0151
Tel: (910)642-7141
E-mail: jfowler@sccnc.edu
Web Site: http://www.sccnc.edu/
President/CEO: Dr. Brantley Briley
Registrar: Jean D'Addario
Admissions: James Fowler
Financial Aid: Doris Caines
Type: Two-Year College **Sex:** Coed **Affiliation:** North Carolina Community College System **% Accepted:** 100 **Admission Plans:** Open Admission; Early Admission; Deferred Admission **Application Deadline:** Rolling **Application Fee:** $0.00 **H.S. Requirements:** High school diploma required; GED accepted **Costs Per Year:** Application fee: $0. State resident tuition: $948 full-time, $39.50 per credit part-time. Nonresident tuition: $5268 full-time, $219.50 per credit part-time. Mandatory fees: $64 full-time, $35 per term part-time. **Scholarships:** Available **Calendar System:** Semester, Summer Session Available **Enrollment:** FT 1,670, PT 155 **Faculty:** FT 72, PT 16 **Student-Faculty Ratio:** 20:1 **Library Holdings:** 50,297 **Regional Accreditation:** Southern Association of Colleges and Schools **Credit Hours For Degree:** 65 semester hours, Associates **Professional Accreditation:** NAACLS **Intercollegiate Athletics:** Baseball M; Softball W; Squash W; Volleyball W

SOUTHWESTERN COMMUNITY COLLEGE
447 College Dr.
Sylva, NC 28779
Tel: (828)586-4091
Fax: (828)586-4093
E-mail: pweast@southwest.cc.nc.us
Web Site: http://www.southwest.cc.nc.us/
President/CEO: Dr. Cecil Groves
Admissions: Dr. Phil Weast
Financial Aid: Melody Lawrence
Type: Two-Year College **Sex:** Coed **Affiliation:** North Carolina Community College System **Scores:** 65% SAT V 400+; 65% SAT M 400+; 20% ACT 18-23 **Admission Plans:** Open Admission; Early Admission; Deferred Admission **Application Fee:** $0.00 **H.S. Requirements:** High school diploma required; GED accepted **Scholarships:** Available **Calendar System:** Semester, Summer Session Available **Enrollment:** FT 899, PT 1,115 **Faculty:** FT 69, PT 175 **Student-Faculty Ratio:** 12:1 **Exams:** SAT I or ACT **Library Holdings:** 27,428 **Regional Accreditation:** Southern Association of Colleges and Schools **Credit Hours For Degree:** 64 semester hours, Associates **Professional Accreditation:** AHIMA, APTA, CARC, JRCEET, JRCERT, NAACLS

STANLY COMMUNITY COLLEGE
141 College Dr.
Albemarle, NC 28001-7458
Tel: (704)982-0121
Fax: (704)982-0819
E-mail: hinsonre@stanly.cc.nc.us
Web Site: http://www.stanly.edu/
President/CEO: Dr. Mike Taylor
Registrar: Dianne Burton
Admissions: Ronnie Hinson
Financial Aid: Teresa Williams
Type: Two-Year College **Sex:** Coed **Affiliation:** North Carolina Community College System **Admission Plans:** Open Admission; Early Admission; Deferred Admission **H.S. Requirements:** High school diploma required; GED accepted **Scholarships:** Available **Calendar System:** Semester, Summer Session Available **Faculty:** FT 53, PT 53 **Student-Faculty Ratio:** 9:1 **Exams:** Other, SAT I **Library Holdings:** 23,966 **Regional Accreditation:** Southern Association of Colleges and Schools **Credit Hours For Degree:** 65 semester hours, Associates **Professional Accreditation:** AAMAE, CARC

SURRY COMMUNITY COLLEGE
630 South Main St.
PO Box 304
Dobson, NC 27017-8432
Tel: (336)386-8121
Admissions: (336)386-3238
Fax: (336)386-8951
Web Site: http://www.surry.cc.nc.us/
President/CEO: Dr. G. Frank Sells
Admissions: Michael McHone
Financial Aid: Jamie P. Childress
Type: Two-Year College **Sex:** Coed **Affiliation:** North Carolina Community College System **Admission Plans:** Open Admission; Early Admission; Deferred Admission **Application Fee:** $0.00 **H.S. Requirements:** High school diploma required; GED accepted **Scholarships:** Available **Calendar System:** Semester, Summer Session Available **Faculty:** FT 150, PT 300 **Student-Faculty Ratio:** 27:1 **Exams:** Other **Library Holdings:** 47,526 **Regional Accreditation:** Southern Association of Colleges and Schools **Credit Hours For Degree:** 65 semester hours, Associates **Intercollegiate Athletics:** Baseball M; Basketball M; Volleyball W

TRI-COUNTY COMMUNITY COLLEGE
4600 East US 64
Murphy, NC 28906-7919
Tel: (828)837-6810
Fax: (828)837-3266
Web Site: http://www.tricountycc.edu
President/CEO: Dr. Norman Oglesby
Registrar: Holly Bateman
Admissions: Jason Chambers
Financial Aid: Alicia Tipton
Type: Two-Year College **Sex:** Coed **% Accepted:** 100 **Admission Plans:** Open Admission; Preferred Admission **Application Deadline:** Rolling **Application Fee:** $0.00 **H.S. Requirements:** High school diploma required; GED accepted **Costs Per Year:** Application fee: $0. State resident tuition: $970 full-time, $38 per credit hour part-time. Nonresident tuition: $5122 full-time, $211 per credit hour part-time. Mandatory fees: $60 full-time, $29.25 per term part-time. **Scholarships:** Available **Calendar System:** Semester, Summer Session Available **Enrollment:** FT 503, PT 652 **Faculty:** FT 46, PT 34 **Student-Faculty Ratio:** 21:1 **Library Holdings:** 16,224 **Regional Accreditation:** Southern Association of Colleges and Schools

THE UNIVERSITY OF NORTH CAROLINA AT ASHEVILLE
One University Heights
Asheville, NC 28804-3299
Tel: (828)251-6600
Free: 800-531-9842
Admissions: (828)251-6481
Fax: (828)251-6385
E-mail: admissions@unca.edu
Web Site: http://www.unca.edu/
President/CEO: Dr. James H. Mullen, Jr.
Registrar: Marilyn Lonon
Admissions: Scot Schaeffer
Financial Aid: Scot Schaeffer
Type: Comprehensive **Sex:** Coed **Affiliation:** University of North Carolina System **Scores:** 99.79% SAT V 400+; 99.78% SAT M 400+; 38% ACT 18-23; 51% ACT 24-29 **% Accepted:** 63 **Admission Plans:** Early Action; Deferred Admission **Application Deadline:** February 16 **Application Fee:** $50.00 **H.S. Requirements:** High school diploma required; GED not accepted **Costs Per Year:** Application fee: $50. State resident tuition: $1897 full-time. Nonresident tuition: $11,697 full-time. Mandatory fees: $1628 full-time. College room and board: $5712. College room only: $3122. Room and

board charges vary according to housing facility. **Scholarships:** Available **Calendar System:** Semester, Summer Session Available **Enrollment:** FT 2,820, PT 656, Grad 37 **Faculty:** FT 199, PT 110 **Student-Faculty Ratio:** 13:1 **Exams:** SAT I or ACT **% Receiving Financial Aid:** 42 **% Residing in College-Owned, -Operated, or -Affiliated Housing:** 39 **Library Holdings:** 254,179 **Regional Accreditation:** Southern Association of Colleges and Schools **Credit Hours For Degree:** 120 semester hours, Bachelors **Professional Accreditation:** NCATE **Intercollegiate Athletics:** Baseball M; Basketball M & W; Cheerleading M & W; Cross-Country Running M & W; Soccer M & W; Tennis M & W; Track and Field M & W; Volleyball W

THE UNIVERSITY OF NORTH CAROLINA AT CHAPEL HILL
Chapel Hill, NC 27599
Tel: (919)962-2211
Admissions: (919)966-3621
E-mail: uadm@email.unc.edu
Web Site: http://www.unc.edu/
President/CEO: Dr. James Moeser
Registrar: David C. Lanier
Admissions: Stephen Farmer
Financial Aid: Shirley Ort
Type: University **Sex:** Coed **Affiliation:** University of North Carolina System **Scores:** 99.89% SAT V 400+; 99.9% SAT M 400+; 14.19% ACT 18-23; 52.91% ACT 24-29 **% Accepted:** 36 **Admission Plans:** Preferred Admission; Early Action; Deferred Admission **Application Deadline:** January 15 **Application Fee:** $60.00 **H.S. Requirements:** High school diploma required; GED not accepted **Costs Per Year:** Application fee: $60. State resident tuition: $3205 full-time. Nonresident tuition: $17,003 full-time. Mandatory fees: $1,408 full-time. Full-time tuition and fees vary according to program. College room and board: $6516. College room only: $3630. Room and board charges vary according to board plan, housing facility, and location. **Scholarships:** Available **Calendar System:** Semester, Summer Session Available **Enrollment:** FT 15,698, PT 827, Grad 8,008 **Faculty:** FT 1,318, PT 122 **Student-Faculty Ratio:** 14:1 **Exams:** SAT I or ACT **% Receiving Financial Aid:** 33 **% Residing in College-Owned, -Operated, or -Affiliated Housing:** 42 **Library Holdings:** 5,492,451 **Regional Accreditation:** Southern Association of Colleges and Schools **Credit Hours For Degree:** 120 credit hours, Bachelors **ROTC:** Army, Navy, Air Force **Professional Accreditation:** AACSB, ABET, ACEHSA, ACEJMC, AACN, ABA, ACPhE, ACA, ADA, ADtA, ACSP, ALA, AOTA, APTA, APA, ASLHA, ACIPE, AALS, CEPH, CORE CSWE, JRCERT, JRCEPAT, LCMEAMA, NAACLS, NASPAA, NCATE, NLN, NRPA **Intercollegiate Athletics:** Baseball M & W; Basketball M & W; Crew M & W; Cross-Country Running M & W; Equestrian Sports M & W; Fencing M & W; Field Hockey W; Football M; Golf M & W; Gymnastics W; Lacrosse M & W; Racquetball M & W; Rugby M & W; Sailing M & W; Soccer M & W; Softball W; Swimming and Diving M & W; Tennis M & W; Track and Field M & W; Ultimate Frisbee M & W; Volleyball M & W; Wrestling M

THE UNIVERSITY OF NORTH CAROLINA AT CHARLOTTE
9201 University City Blvd.
Charlotte, NC 28223-0001
Tel: (704)687-2000
Admissions: (704)687-2213
Fax: (704)510-6483
E-mail: unccadm@email.uncc.edu
Web Site: http://www.uncc.edu/
President/CEO: Dr. James H. Woodward
Registrar: Richard L. Yount
Admissions: Craig Fulton
Financial Aid: Curtis R. Whalen
Type: University **Sex:** Coed **Affiliation:** University of North Carolina System **Scores:** 98% SAT V 400+; 100% SAT M 400+; 66% ACT 18-23; 25% ACT 24-29 **% Accepted:** 78 **Admission Plans:** Preferred Admission; Early Admission; Deferred Admission **Application Deadline:** July 01 **Application Fee:** $50.00 **H.S. Requirements:** High school diploma required; GED accepted **Costs Per Year:** Application fee: $50. Area resident tuition: $148 per credit hour part-time. State resident tuition: $2129 full-time, $148 per credit hour part-time. Nonresident tuition: $12,541 full-time, $582 per credit hour part-time. Mandatory fees: $1420 full-time, $59 per credit hour part-time. Full-time tuition and fees vary according to course load. Part-time tuition and fees vary according to course load. College room and board: $5550. College room only: $2840. Room and board charges vary according to board plan and housing facility. **Scholarships:** Available **Calendar System:** Semester, Summer Session Available **Enrollment:** FT 13,640, PT 2,915, Grad 4,217 **Faculty:** FT 859, PT 386 **Student-Faculty Ratio:** 14:1 **Exams:** SAT I or ACT **% Receiving Financial Aid:** 45 **% Residing in College-Owned, -Operated, or -Affiliated Housing:** 27 **Library Holdings:** 916,218 **Regional Accreditation:** Southern Association of Colleges and Schools **Credit Hours For Degree:** 120 semester hours, Bachelors **ROTC:** Army, Air Force **Professional Accreditation:** AACSB, ABET, AACN, AANA, ACA, APA, CSWE, NASPAA, NCATE **Intercollegiate Athletics:** Baseball M; Basketball M & W; Cross-Country Running M & W; Golf M; Soccer M & W; Softball W; Tennis M & W; Track and Field M & W; Volleyball W

THE UNIVERSITY OF NORTH CAROLINA AT GREENSBORO
1000 Spring Garden St.
Greensboro, NC 27412-5001
Tel: (336)334-5000
Admissions: (336)334-5243
Fax: (336)334-4180
E-mail: undergrad_admissions@uncg.edu
Web Site: http://www.uncg.edu/
President/CEO: Dr. Patricia A. Sullivan
Registrar: Ellen Robbins
Admissions: Lise Keller
Financial Aid: Deborah Tollefson
Type: University **Sex:** Coed **Affiliation:** University of North Carolina System **Scores:** 96.73% SAT V 400+; 97.62% SAT M 400+ **% Accepted:** 60 **Admission Plans:** Early Admission **Application Deadline:** March 01 **Application Fee:** $45.00 **H.S. Requirements:** High school diploma required; GED accepted **Costs Per Year:** Application fee: $45. State resident tuition: $2308 full-time. Nonresident tuition: $13,576 full-time. Mandatory fees: $1505 full-time. College room and board: $5706. College room only: $3232. **Scholarships:** Available **Calendar System:** Semester, Summer Session Available **Enrollment:** FT 10,584, PT 1,707, Grad 3,769 **Faculty:** FT 746, PT 243 **Student-Faculty Ratio:** 16:1 **Exams:** SAT I or ACT **% Receiving Financial Aid:** 65 **% Residing in College-Owned, -Operated, or -Affiliated Housing:** 34 **Library Holdings:** 844,448 **Regional Accreditation:** Southern Association of Colleges and Schools **Credit Hours For Degree:** 122 semester hours, Bachelors **ROTC:** Army, Air Force **Professional Accreditation:** AACSB, ABET, AACN, AAFCS, AANA, ACA, ADtA, ALA, APA, ASLHA, CEPH, CSWE, FIDER, NASD, NASM, NASPAA, NAST, NCATE, NLN, NRPA **Intercollegiate Athletics:** Baseball M; Basketball M & W; Cross-Country Running M & W; Golf M & W; Soccer M & W; Softball W; Tennis M & W; Volleyball W; Wrestling M

THE UNIVERSITY OF NORTH CAROLINA AT PEMBROKE
One University Dr., PO Box 1510
Pembroke, NC 28372-1510
Tel: (910)521-6000
Free: 800-949-UNCP
Admissions: (910)521-6262
Web Site: http://www.uncp.edu/
President/CEO: Dr. Allen Coats Meadors
Registrar: Sara Brackin
Admissions: Jacqueline Clark
Financial Aid: Bruce Blackmon
Type: Comprehensive **Sex:** Coed **Affiliation:** University of North Carolina System **Scores:** 81% SAT V 400+; 86% SAT M 400+; 50% ACT 18-23; 6% ACT 24-29 **% Accepted:** 86 **Admission Plans:** Early Admission; Deferred Admission **Application Deadline:** Rolling **Application Fee:** $40.00 **H.S. Requirements:** High school diploma required; GED accepted **Costs Per Year:** Application fee: $40. State resident tuition: $1689 full-time. Nonresident tuition: $11,129 full-time. Mandatory fees: $1291 full-time. Full-time tuition and fees vary according to course load and location. College room and board: $4890. College room only: $2700. Room and board charges vary according to board plan and housing facility. **Scholarships:** Available **Calendar System:** Semester, Summer Session Available **Enrollment:** FT 3,702, PT 1,361, Grad 669 **Faculty:** FT 238, PT 90 **Student-Faculty Ratio:** 16:1 **Exams:** SAT I or ACT **% Receiving Financial Aid:** 70 **% Residing in College-Owned, -Operated, or -Affiliated Housing:** 27 **Library Holdings:** 325,499 **Regional Accreditation:** Southern Association of Colleges and Schools **Credit Hours For Degree:** 120 semester hours, Bachelors **ROTC:** Army, Air Force **Professional Accreditation:** AACN, CSWE, NASM, NCATE **Intercollegiate Athletics:** Baseball M; Basketball M

& W; Cross-Country Running M & W; Golf M; Soccer M & W; Softball W; Tennis W; Track and Field M; Volleyball W; Wrestling M

THE UNIVERSITY OF NORTH CAROLINA WILMINGTON
601 South College Rd.
Wilmington, NC 28403-3297
Tel: (910)962-3000
Free: 800-228-5571
Admissions: (910)962-4198
Fax: (910)962-3038
E-mail: admissions@uncwil.edu
Web Site: http://www.uncw.edu/
President/CEO: Dr. Rosemary DePaolo
Registrar: Ronald Whittaker
Admissions: Roxie Shabazz
Financial Aid: Emily Bliss
Type: Comprehensive **Sex:** Coed **Affiliation:** University of North Carolina System **Scores:** 99% SAT V 400+; 99% SAT M 400+; 55% ACT 18-23; 38% ACT 24-29 **% Accepted:** 61 **Admission Plans:** Early Admission; Deferred Admission **Application Deadline:** February 01 **Application Fee:** $45.00 **H.S. Requirements:** High school diploma required; GED accepted **Costs Per Year:** Application fee: $45. State resident tuition: $1928 full-time. Nonresident tuition: $11,863 full-time. Mandatory fees: $1767 full-time. Full-time tuition and fees vary according to course load. College room and board: $6412. Room and board charges vary according to board plan and housing facility. **Scholarships:** Available **Calendar System:** Semester, Summer Session Available **Enrollment:** FT 9,591, PT 990, Grad 1,072 **Faculty:** FT 491, PT 285 **Student-Faculty Ratio:** 19:1 **Exams:** SAT I or ACT **% Receiving Financial Aid:** 36 **% Residing in College-Owned, -Operated, or -Affiliated Housing:** 23 **Library Holdings:** 530,368 **Regional Accreditation:** Southern Association of Colleges and Schools **Credit Hours For Degree:** 124 semester hours, Bachelors **Professional Accreditation:** AACSB, AACN, CSWE, NASM, NCATE, NLN, NRPA **Intercollegiate Athletics:** Baseball M; Basketball M & W; Cheerleading M & W; Cross-Country Running M & W; Golf M & W; Soccer M & W; Softball W; Swimming and Diving M & W; Tennis M & W; Track and Field M & W; Volleyball W

UNIVERSITY OF PHOENIX-CHARLOTTE CAMPUS
3800 Arco Corporate Dr., Ste. 100
Charlotte, NC 28273
Tel: (704)504-5409
Free: 800-228-7240
Admissions: (480)557-1712
Web Site: http://www.phoenix.edu/
Admissions: Nina Omelchanko
Type: Comprehensive **Sex:** Coed **Admission Plans:** Open Admission; Deferred Admission **Application Deadline:** Rolling **Application Fee:** $110.00 **H.S. Requirements:** High school diploma required; GED accepted **Costs Per Year:** Application fee: $110. Tuition: $10,170 full-time, $339 per credit part-time. Mandatory fees: $560 full-time, $70 per course part-time. **Scholarships:** Available **Calendar System:** Continuous, Summer Session Not available **Enrollment:** FT 854, Grad 447 **Faculty:** FT 7, PT 223 **Student-Faculty Ratio:** 10:1 **Library Holdings:** 444 **Regional Accreditation:** North Central Association of Colleges and Schools **Credit Hours For Degree:** 60 credits, Associates; 120 credits, Bachelors

UNIVERSITY OF PHOENIX-RALEIGH CAMPUS
5511 Capital Center Dr.
Raleigh, NC 27606
Free: 800-228-7240
Admissions: (480)557-1712
Web Site: http://www.phoenix.edu/
Admissions: Nina Omelchanko
Type: Comprehensive **Sex:** Coed **Admission Plans:** Open Admission; Deferred Admission **Application Deadline:** Rolling **Application Fee:** $110.00 **H.S. Requirements:** High school diploma required; GED accepted **Costs Per Year:** Application fee: $110. Tuition: $10,170 full-time, $339 per credit part-time. Mandatory fees: $560 full-time, $70 per course part-time. **Scholarships:** Available **Enrollment:** FT 134, Grad 87 **Faculty:** FT 3, PT 16 **Student-Faculty Ratio:** 5:1 **Library Holdings:** 444 **Credit Hours For Degree:** 60 credits, Associates; 120 credits, Bachelors

VANCE-GRANVILLE COMMUNITY COLLEGE
PO Box 917
Henderson, NC 27536-0917
Tel: (252)492-2061
Fax: (252)430-0460
Web Site: http://www.vgcc.cc.nc.us/
President/CEO: Robert A. Miller
Registrar: Kathy Kutl
Admissions: Gene Purvis
Financial Aid: Frank A. Clark
Type: Two-Year College **Sex:** Coed **Affiliation:** North Carolina Community College System **% Accepted:** 100 **Admission Plans:** Open Admission; Preferred Admission; Early Admission; Deferred Admission **Application Deadline:** Rolling **Application Fee:** $0.00 **H.S. Requirements:** High school diploma required; GED accepted. For vocational programs: High school diploma or equivalent not required **Costs Per Year:** Application fee: $0. State resident tuition: $948 full-time, $39.50 per credit hour part-time. Nonresident tuition: $5592 full-time, $233.50 per credit hour part-time. Mandatory fees: $38 full-time, $14 per term part-time. **Scholarships:** Available **Calendar System:** Semester, Summer Session Available **Enrollment:** FT 1,718, PT 2,339 **Faculty:** FT 141, PT 212 **Student-Faculty Ratio:** 9:1 **Library Holdings:** 38,720 **Regional Accreditation:** Southern Association of Colleges and Schools **Credit Hours For Degree:** 65 semester hours, Associates **Professional Accreditation:** JRCERT

WAKE FOREST UNIVERSITY
Reynolda Station
Winston-Salem, NC 27109
Tel: (336)758-5000
Admissions: (336)758-5201
Fax: (336)758-6074
Web Site: http://www.wfu.edu/
President/CEO: Dr. Thomas K. Hearn, Jr.
Registrar: Dot Sugden
Admissions: Martha Allman
Financial Aid: William Wells
Type: University **Sex:** Coed **Scores:** 99.91% SAT V 400+; 99.91% SAT M 400+ **% Accepted:** 39 **Admission Plans:** Early Admission; Early Decision Plan; Deferred Admission **Application Deadline:** January 15 **Application Fee:** $40.00 **H.S. Requirements:** High school diploma required; GED accepted **Costs Per Year:** Application fee: $40. Comprehensive fee: $40,940 includes full-time tuition ($32,040), mandatory fees ($100), and college room and board ($8800). College room only: $5500. Part-time tuition: $1250 per credit hour. **Scholarships:** Available **Calendar System:** Semester, Summer Session Available **Enrollment:** FT 4,138, PT 125, Grad 1,414 **Faculty:** FT 450, PT 98 **Student-Faculty Ratio:** 10:1 **Exams:** SAT I or ACT **% Receiving Financial Aid:** 35 **% Residing in College-Owned, -Operated, or -Affiliated Housing:** 78 **Library Holdings:** 923,123 **Regional Accreditation:** Southern Association of Colleges and Schools **Credit Hours For Degree:** 120 hours, Bachelors **ROTC:** Army **Professional Accreditation:** AACSB, AANA, ABA, ACA, ACIPE, AALS, ATS, LCMEAMA, NAACLS, NCATE **Intercollegiate Athletics:** Baseball M; Basketball M & W; Cross-Country Running M & W; Field Hockey W; Football M; Golf M & W; Soccer M & W; Tennis M & W; Track and Field M & W; Volleyball W

WAKE TECHNICAL COMMUNITY COLLEGE
9101 Fayetteville Rd.
Raleigh, NC 27603-5696
Tel: (919)662-3400
Admissions: (919)662-3357
Fax: (919)662-3529
Web Site: http://www.waketech.edu/
President/CEO: Dr. Stephen C. Scott
Registrar: Willa (Rita) H. Jerman
Admissions: Susan Bloomfield
Financial Aid: Laura K. Saparilas
Type: Two-Year College **Sex:** Coed **Affiliation:** North Carolina Community College System **Scores:** 76% SAT V 400+; 77.2% SAT M 400+; 45.8% ACT 18-23; 11.1% ACT 24-29 **Admission Plans:** Open Admission; Early Admission **Application Fee:** $0.00 **H.S. Requirements:** High school diploma required; GED accepted **Costs Per Year:** Application fee: $0. State resident tuition: $1264 full-time, $39.50 per credit hour part-time. Nonresident tuition: $7024 full-time, $219.50 per credit hour part-time. Mandatory fees: $52 full-time, $1 per credit hour part-time, $10 per term part-time. **Scholarships:** Available **Calendar System:** Semester, Summer Session Available **Enrollment:** FT 3,891, PT 7,481 **Faculty:** FT 271, PT 624 **Student-Faculty Ratio:** 11:1 **Exams:** Other, SAT I or ACT **Library Holdings:** 70,617 **Regional Accreditation:** Southern Association of Colleges

and Schools **Credit Hours For Degree:** 64 semester hours, Associates **Professional Accreditation:** ABET, ADA, JRCERT, NAACLS

WARREN WILSON COLLEGE
PO Box 9000
Asheville, NC 28815-9000
Tel: (828)298-3325
Free: 800-934-3536
Admissions: (828)771-2073
Fax: (828)298-1440
E-mail: admit@warren-wilson.edu
Web Site: http://www.warren-wilson.edu/
President/CEO: Dr. Douglas M. Orr, Jr.
Registrar: Christa Bridgman
Admissions: Richard Blomgren
Financial Aid: Kathy Pack
Type: Comprehensive **Sex:** Coed **Affiliation:** Presbyterian Church (U.S.A.) **Scores:** 99.5% SAT V 400+; 98.3% SAT M 400+; 11% ACT 18-23; 72% ACT 24-29 **% Accepted:** 77 **Admission Plans:** Early Admission; Early Decision Plan; Deferred Admission **Application Deadline:** March 15 **Application Fee:** $0.00 **H.S. Requirements:** High school diploma required; GED accepted **Costs Per Year:** Application fee: $0. Comprehensive fee: $26,126 includes full-time tuition ($20,126) and college room and board ($6000). **Scholarships:** Available **Calendar System:** Semester, Summer Session Not available **Enrollment:** FT 820, PT 12, Grad 69 **Faculty:** FT 62, PT 13 **Student-Faculty Ratio:** 13:1 **Exams:** SAT I or ACT **% Receiving Financial Aid:** 57 **% Residing in College-Owned, -Operated, or -Affiliated Housing:** 88 **Library Holdings:** 106,837 **Regional Accreditation:** Southern Association of Colleges and Schools **Credit Hours For Degree:** 128 semester hours, Bachelors **Professional Accreditation:** CSWE, NCATE **Intercollegiate Athletics:** Basketball M & W; Cross-Country Running M & W; Soccer M & W; Swimming and Diving M & W

WAYNE COMMUNITY COLLEGE
PO Box 8002
Goldsboro, NC 27533-8002
Tel: (919)735-5151
Fax: (919)736-3204
E-mail: msm@wayne.cc.nc.us
Web Site: http://www.waynecc.edu/
President/CEO: Dr. Edward H. Wilson, Jr.
Registrar: Susan Mooring Sasser
Admissions: Susan Mooring Sasser
Financial Aid: Yvonne Goodman
Type: Two-Year College **Sex:** Coed **Affiliation:** North Carolina Community College System **Admission Plans:** Open Admission; Deferred Admission **Application Fee:** $0.00 **H.S. Requirements:** High school diploma required; GED accepted **Scholarships:** Available **Calendar System:** Semester, Summer Session Available **Faculty:** FT 92, PT 123 **Student-Faculty Ratio:** 18:1 **Exams:** Other **Library Holdings:** 42,133 **Regional Accreditation:** Southern Association of Colleges and Schools **Credit Hours For Degree:** 64 credit hours, Associates **Professional Accreditation:** AAMAE, ADA

WESTERN CAROLINA UNIVERSITY
Cullowhee, NC 28723
Tel: (828)227-7211; 877-WCU4YOU
Admissions: (828)227-7317
E-mail: cauley@wcu.edu
Web Site: http://www.wcu.edu/
President/CEO: Dr. John W. Bardo
Registrar: Robert Gabrielsen
Admissions: Philip Cauley
Financial Aid: Nancy Dillard
Type: Comprehensive **Sex:** Coed **Affiliation:** University of North Carolina System **Scores:** 96% SAT V 400+; 98% SAT M 400+; 63% ACT 18-23; 13% ACT 24-29 **% Accepted:** 75 **Admission Plans:** Early Admission **Application Deadline:** August 01 **Application Fee:** $40.00 **H.S. Requirements:** High school diploma required; GED accepted **Costs Per Year:** Application fee: $40. State resident tuition: $278.03 per hour part-time. Nonresident tuition: $1,457.53 per hour part-time. **Scholarships:** Available **Calendar System:** Semester, Summer Session Available **Enrollment:** FT 6,015, PT 965, Grad 1,685 **Faculty:** FT 433, PT 230 **Student-Faculty Ratio:** 14:1 **Exams:** SAT I or ACT **% Receiving Financial Aid:** 47 **% Residing in College-Owned, -Operated, or -Affiliated Housing:** 50 **Library Holdings:** 694,530 **Regional Accreditation:** Southern Association of Colleges and Schools **Credit Hours For Degree:** 120 credit hours, Bachelors **Professional Accreditation:** AACSB, ABET, AACN, AAFCS, ACA, ADtA, AHIMA, APTA, ASLHA, CSWE, FIDER, JRCEMT, NAACLS, NASM, NCATE **Intercollegiate Athletics:** Baseball M; Basketball M & W; Cheerleading M & W; Cross-Country Running M & W; Football M; Golf M & W; Soccer W; Tennis W; Track and Field M & W; Volleyball W

WESTERN PIEDMONT COMMUNITY COLLEGE
1001 Burkemont Ave.
Morganton, NC 28655-4511
Tel: (828)438-6000
Admissions: (828)438-6051
Fax: (828)438-6015
E-mail: swilliams@wpcc.edu
Web Site: http://www.wpcc.edu/
President/CEO: Dr. Jim A. Richardson
Registrar: Judy Rice
Admissions: Susan Williams
Financial Aid: Keith Conley
Type: Two-Year College **Sex:** Coed **Affiliation:** North Carolina Community College System **Admission Plans:** Open Admission **H.S. Requirements:** High school diploma required; GED accepted **Scholarships:** Available **Calendar System:** Semester, Summer Session Available **Faculty:** FT 60, PT 73 **Exams:** Other **Library Holdings:** 31,195 **Regional Accreditation:** Southern Association of Colleges and Schools **Credit Hours For Degree:** 64 semester hours, Associates **Professional Accreditation:** AAMAE, ADA, NAACLS, NLN

WILKES COMMUNITY COLLEGE
1328 Collegiate Dr., PO Box 120
Wilkesboro, NC 28697
Tel: (336)838-6100
Admissions: (336)838-6141
Fax: (336)838-6277
E-mail: mac.warren@wilkescc.edu
Web Site: http://www.wilkescc.edu/
President/CEO: Dr. Gordon Burns
Registrar: Shirley G. Church
Admissions: Mac Warren
Financial Aid: Alan Whittington
Type: Two-Year College **Sex:** Coed **Affiliation:** North Carolina Community College System **% Accepted:** 100 **Admission Plans:** Open Admission; Deferred Admission **Application Deadline:** Rolling **Application Fee:** $0.00 **H.S. Requirements:** High school diploma required; GED accepted **Costs Per Year:** Application fee: $0. State resident tuition: $1264 full-time, $39.50 per credit hour part-time. Nonresident tuition: $7024 full-time, $219.50 per credit hour part-time. Mandatory fees: $58 full-time, $1.75 per credit hour part-time, $11.25 per term part-time. **Scholarships:** Available **Calendar System:** Semester, Summer Session Available **Enrollment:** FT 1,347, PT 1,270 **Faculty:** FT 73, PT 289 **Student-Faculty Ratio:** 10:1 **Library Holdings:** 56,142 **Regional Accreditation:** Southern Association of Colleges and Schools **Credit Hours For Degree:** 64 credit hours, Associates **Professional Accreditation:** ADA **Intercollegiate Athletics:** Baseball M; Basketball M & W; Volleyball W

WILSON TECHNICAL COMMUNITY COLLEGE
902 Herring Ave., PO Box 4305
Wilson, NC 27893-3310
Tel: (252)291-1195
Admissions: (252)246-1275
Fax: (252)243-7148
E-mail: dboyette@wilsontech.edu
Web Site: http://www.wilsontech.edu/
President/CEO: Dr. Stephens
Registrar: Philip Farinholt
Admissions: Donald Boyette
Financial Aid: Rex Bissette
Type: Two-Year College **Sex:** Coed **Affiliation:** North Carolina Community College System **% Accepted:** 97 **Admission Plans:** Open Admission; Deferred Admission **Application Deadline:** Rolling **Application Fee:** $0.00 **H.S. Requirements:** High school diploma required; GED accepted **Costs Per Year:** Application fee: $0. State resident tuition: $1264 full-time, $39.50 per credit hour part-time. Nonresident tuition: $7024 full-time, $219.50 per credit hour part-time. Mandatory fees: $38 full-time, $.75 per credit hour part-time, $7. **Scholarships:** Available **Calendar System:** Semester, Summer

Session Available **Enrollment:** FT 883, PT 1,042 **Faculty:** FT 54, PT 49 **Student-Faculty Ratio:** 19:1 **Library Holdings:** 38,466 **Regional Accreditation:** Southern Association of Colleges and Schools **Credit Hours For Degree:** 65 credit hours, Associates

WINGATE UNIVERSITY
PO Box 159
Wingate, NC 28174-0159
Tel: (704)233-8000
Free: 800-755-5550
E-mail: admit@wingate.edu
Web Site: http://www.wingate.edu/
President/CEO: Dr. Jerry E. McGee
Registrar: Nicci Brown
Admissions: Rhett Brown
Financial Aid: Teresa Williams
Type: Comprehensive **Sex:** Coed **Affiliation:** Baptist **Scores:** 93.7% SAT V 400+; 96.1% SAT M 400+; 54.3% ACT 18-23; 25.7% ACT 24-29 **% Accepted:** 84 **Admission Plans:** Early Admission; Early Decision Plan; Deferred Admission **Application Deadline:** Rolling **Application Fee:** $30.00 **H.S. Requirements:** High school diploma required; GED accepted. For applicants 21 or over: High school diploma required; GED accepted **Costs Per Year:** Application fee: $30. Comprehensive fee: $23,300 includes full-time tuition ($15,800), mandatory fees ($1050), and college room and board ($6450). Part-time tuition: $525 per credit hour. Part-time mandatory fees: $175 per term. **Scholarships:** Available **Calendar System:** Semester, Summer Session Available **Enrollment:** FT 1,311, PT 30, Grad 113 **Faculty:** FT 99, PT 53 **Student-Faculty Ratio:** 14:1 **Exams:** SAT I or ACT, SAT I **% Receiving Financial Aid:** 63 **% Residing in College-Owned, -Operated, or -Affiliated Housing:** 84 **Library Holdings:** 107,187 **Regional Accreditation:** Southern Association of Colleges and Schools **Credit Hours For Degree:** 125 credit hours, Bachelors **ROTC:** Army, Air Force **Professional Accreditation:** AAMAE, ACPhE, ACBSP, JRCEPAT, NASM, NCATE **Intercollegiate Athletics:** Baseball M; Basketball M & W; Cross-Country Running M & W; Football M; Golf M & W; Lacrosse M; Soccer M & W; Softball W; Swimming and Diving M & W; Tennis M & W; Volleyball W

WINSTON-SALEM BIBLE COLLEGE
4117 Northampton Dr.
PO Box 777
Winston-Salem, NC 27102-0777
Tel: (336)744-0900
Fax: (336)744-0901
Web Site: http://www.wsbc.edu/
President/CEO: Donald R. Young
Type: Four-Year College **Sex:** Coed **Affiliation:** nondenominational **Calendar System:** Semester **Professional Accreditation:** AABC

WINSTON-SALEM STATE UNIVERSITY
601 Martin Luther King Jr Dr.
Winston-Salem, NC 27110-0003
Tel: (336)750-2000
Free: 800-257-4052
Admissions: (336)750-2070
Fax: (336)750-2079
E-mail: admissions@wssu.edu
Web Site: http://www.wssu.edu/
President/CEO: Dr. Harold L. Martin, Sr.
Registrar: William E. Cain
Admissions: Dr. Maurice Allen
Financial Aid: Theodore Hindsman
Type: Comprehensive **Sex:** Coed **Affiliation:** University of North Carolina System **Scores:** 73.6% SAT V 400+; 79.3% SAT M 400+ **% Accepted:** 79 **Admission Plans:** Deferred Admission **Application Deadline:** July 15 **Application Fee:** $30.00 **H.S. Requirements:** High school diploma required; GED accepted **Costs Per Year:** Application fee: $30. State resident tuition: $1451 full-time. Nonresident tuition: $10,090 full-time. Mandatory fees: $1354 full-time. Full-time tuition and fees vary according to degree level. College room and board: $5298. College room only: $3122. Room and board charges vary according to board plan and housing facility. **Scholarships:** Available **Calendar System:** Semester, Summer Session Available **Enrollment:** FT 4,631, PT 633, Grad 302 **Faculty:** FT 208, PT 107 **Student-Faculty Ratio:** 18:1 **Exams:** SAT I or ACT **% Receiving Financial Aid:** 96 **% Residing in College-Owned, -Operated, or -Affiliated Housing:** 46 **Library Holdings:** 197,765 **Regional Accreditation:** Southern Association of Colleges and Schools **Credit Hours For Degree:** 120 semester hours, Bachelors **ROTC:** Army, Air Force **Professional Accreditation:** AACSB, ABET, AOTA, APTA, NAACLS, NASM, NCATE, NLN, NRPA **Intercollegiate Athletics:** Basketball M & W; Bowling M & W; Cheerleading M; Cross-Country Running M & W; Football M; Softball W; Tennis M & W; Volleyball W

North Dakota

AAKERS BUSINESS COLLEGE

4012 19th Ave., SW
Fargo, ND 58103
Tel: (701)277-3889
Free: 800-817-0009
Fax: (701)277-5604
E-mail: blargent@aakers-college.com
Web Site: http://www.aakers-college.com/
President/CEO: Betty Largent
Admissions: Elizabeth Largent
Financial Aid: Debora Murray
Type: Two-Year College **Sex:** Coed **Application Deadline:** October 03 **Application Fee:** $60.00 **Costs Per Year:** Application fee: $60. Tuition: $2535 full-time, $845 per course part-time. **Calendar System:** Quarter **Enrollment:** FT 320, PT 257 **Faculty:** FT 8, PT 18 **Student-Faculty Ratio:** 13:1 **Professional Accreditation:** ACICS

BISMARCK STATE COLLEGE

PO Box 5587
Bismarck, ND 58506-5587
Tel: (701)224-5400
Free: 800-445-5073
Admissions: (701)224-5426
Fax: (701)224-5643
Web Site: http://www.bismarckstate.edu/
President/CEO: Dr. Donna Thigpen
Registrar: Tom Leno
Admissions: Karla Gabriel
Financial Aid: Jeff Jacobs
Type: Two-Year College **Sex:** Coed **Affiliation:** North Dakota University System **Admission Plans:** Open Admission **Application Fee:** $35.00 **H.S. Requirements:** High school diploma required; GED accepted **Costs Per Year:** Application fee: $35. State resident tuition: $3356 full-time, $92.89 per credit hour part-time. Nonresident tuition: $8009 full-time, $248.02 per credit hour part-time. Mandatory fees: $500 full-time, $22.40 per credit hour part-time. College room and board: $4288. **Scholarships:** Available **Calendar System:** Semester, Summer Session Available **Enrollment:** FT 2,329, PT 1,212 **Faculty:** FT 107, PT 144 **Student-Faculty Ratio:** 18:1 **Exams:** SAT I or ACT **% Residing in College-Owned, -Operated, or -Affiliated Housing:** 8 **Library Holdings:** 69,142 **Regional Accreditation:** North Central Association of Colleges and Schools **Credit Hours For Degree:** 60 credits, Associates **ROTC:** Army, Air Force **Professional Accreditation:** ARCEST, JRCEMT, NAACLS **Intercollegiate Athletics:** Baseball M; Basketball M & W; Golf M & W; Tennis M & W; Volleyball W

CANKDESKA CIKANA COMMUNITY COLLEGE

PO Box 269
Fort Totten, ND 58335-0269
Tel: (701)766-4415
Admissions: (701)766-1342
Fax: (701)766-4077
Web Site: http://www.littlehoop.edu/
President/CEO: Erich Longie
Registrar: Heather Lawrence
Admissions: Ermen Brown, Jr.
Financial Aid: Clayton Blueshield
Type: Two-Year College **Sex:** Coed **Admission Plans:** Open Admission; Early Admission; Deferred Admission **H.S. Requirements:** High school diploma required; GED accepted **Calendar System:** Semester, Summer Session Available **Faculty:** FT 5, PT 10 **Student-Faculty Ratio:** 12:1 **Exams:** Other **Library Holdings:** 7,500 **Regional Accreditation:** North Central Association of Colleges and Schools **Credit Hours For Degree:** 61 credits, Associates

DICKINSON STATE UNIVERSITY

291 Campus Dr.
Dickinson, ND 58601-4896
Tel: (701)483-2507
Free: 800-279-4295
Admissions: (701)483-2331
Fax: (701)483-2006
E-mail: dsuhawk@eagle.dsu.nodak.edu
Web Site: http://www.dsu.nodak.edu/
President/CEO: Dr. Lee A. Vickers
Registrar: Marshall R. Melbye
Admissions: Marshall Melbye
Financial Aid: Sandy L. Klein
Type: Four-Year College **Sex:** Coed **Affiliation:** North Dakota University System **Scores:** 88% SAT V 400+; 100% SAT M 400+; 53% ACT 18-23; 21% ACT 24-29 **% Accepted:** 99 **Admission Plans:** Open Admission; Early Admission; Deferred Admission **Application Deadline:** Rolling **Application Fee:** $35.00 **H.S. Requirements:** High school diploma required; GED accepted **Costs Per Year:** Application fee: $35. State resident tuition: $4154 full-time. Nonresident tuition: $9712 full-time. Mandatory fees: $825 full-time. Full-time tuition and fees vary according to location, program, and reciprocity agreements. College room and board: $3694. Room and board charges vary according to board plan. **Scholarships:** Available **Calendar System:** Semester, Summer Session Available **Enrollment:** FT 1,755, PT 761 **Faculty:** FT 93, PT 112 **Student-Faculty Ratio:** 19:1 **Exams:** SAT I or ACT **% Residing in College-Owned, -Operated, or -Affiliated Housing:** 30 **Library Holdings:** 105,713 **Regional Accreditation:** North Central Association of Colleges and Schools **Credit Hours For Degree:** 64 semester hours, Associates; 128 semester hours, Bachelors **Professional Accreditation:** NCATE, NLN **Intercollegiate Athletics:** Badminton M & W; Baseball M; Basketball M & W; Cheerleading M & W; Cross-Country Running M & W; Football M; Golf M & W; Softball W; Track and Field M & W; Volleyball W; Wrestling M

FORT BERTHOLD COMMUNITY COLLEGE

PO Box 490
New Town, ND 58763-0490
Tel: (701)627-4738
Admissions: (701)627-3665
Fax: (701)627-3609
Web Site: http://www.fbcc.bia.edu/
President/CEO: Elizabeth Demaray
Registrar: Russell Mason, Jr.
Admissions: Russell Mason, Jr.
Financial Aid: Gerrianne Bird Bear
Type: Two-Year College **Sex:** Coed **Admission Plans:** Open Admission; Deferred Admission **Application Fee:** $10.00 **H.S. Requirements:** High school diploma required; GED accepted. For those who demonstrate ability

to benefit from program: High school diploma or equivalent not required **Costs Per Year:** Application fee: $10. Tuition: $2640 full-time, $110 per credit part-time. Mandatory fees: $600 full-time, $25 per term part-time. **Scholarships:** Available **Calendar System:** Semester, Summer Session Available **Faculty:** FT 12, PT 30 **Library Holdings:** 10,000 **Regional Accreditation:** North Central Association of Colleges and Schools **Credit Hours For Degree:** 64 semester hours, Associates **Intercollegiate Athletics:** Basketball M & W; Cross-Country Running M & W

JAMESTOWN COLLEGE
6000 College Ln.
Jamestown, ND 58405
Tel: (701)252-3467
Free: 800-336-2554
Fax: (701)253-4318
E-mail: admissions@jc.edu
Web Site: http://www.jc.edu/
President/CEO: Dr. Jerry Combee
Registrar: JoDee Rasmusson
Admissions: Carol Schmeichel
Financial Aid: Carol Schmeichel
Type: Four-Year College **Sex:** Coed **Affiliation:** Presbyterian **Scores:** 64% ACT 18-23; 28% ACT 24-29 **% Accepted:** 98 **Admission Plans:** Deferred Admission **Application Deadline:** Rolling **Application Fee:** $20.00 **H.S. Requirements:** High school diploma required; GED accepted. For home schooled applicants: High school diploma or equivalent not required **Costs Per Year:** Application fee: $20. Comprehensive fee: $14,890 includes full-time tuition ($10,550) and college room and board ($4340). College room only: $1850. Part-time tuition: $295 per credit. **Scholarships:** Available **Calendar System:** Semester, Summer Session Available **Enrollment:** FT 960, PT 66 **Faculty:** FT 58, PT 20 **Student-Faculty Ratio:** 15:1 **Exams:** SAT I or ACT **% Receiving Financial Aid:** 81 **% Residing in College-Owned, -Operated, or -Affiliated Housing:** 61 **Library Holdings:** 121,382 **Regional Accreditation:** North Central Association of Colleges and Schools **Credit Hours For Degree:** 128 semester hours, Bachelors **Professional Accreditation:** NLN **Intercollegiate Athletics:** Baseball M; Basketball M & W; Cross-Country Running M & W; Football M; Golf M & W; Soccer W; Softball W; Track and Field M & W; Volleyball W; Wrestling M

LAKE REGION STATE COLLEGE
1801 College Dr. North
Devils Lake, ND 58301-1598
Tel: (701)662-1600
Free: 800-443-1313
Admissions: (701)662-1513
Fax: (701)662-1570
E-mail: laurel.goulding@lrsc.nodak.edu
Web Site: http://www.lrsc.nodak.edu/
President/CEO: Dr. Sharon L. Etemad
Registrar: Judith Lee
Admissions: Laurel Goulding
Financial Aid: Katie Nettell
Type: Two-Year College **Sex:** Coed **Affiliation:** North Dakota University System **% Accepted:** 100 **Admission Plans:** Open Admission **Application Deadline:** Rolling **Application Fee:** $35.00 **H.S. Requirements:** High school diploma required; GED accepted **Costs Per Year:** Application fee: $35. State resident tuition: $2550 full-time, $133 per credit part-time. Nonresident tuition: $2550 full-time, $133 per credit part-time. Mandatory fees: $783 full-time. College room and board: $3790. **Scholarships:** Available **Calendar System:** Semester, Summer Session Available **Enrollment:** FT 409, PT 1,062 **Faculty:** FT 30, PT 76 **Student-Faculty Ratio:** 15:1 **Exams:** Other, SAT I or ACT **% Residing in College-Owned, -Operated, or -Affiliated Housing:** 30 **Library Holdings:** 42,000 **Regional Accreditation:** North Central Association of Colleges and Schools **Credit Hours For Degree:** 60 semester hours, Associates **Intercollegiate Athletics:** Basketball M & W

MAYVILLE STATE UNIVERSITY
330 3rd St., NE
Mayville, ND 58257-1299
Tel: (701)786-2301
Free: 800-437-4104
Admissions: (701)788-5222
Fax: (701)786-4748
E-mail: c_heckman@mayvillestate.edu
Web Site: http://www.mayvillestate.edu/
President/CEO: Dr. Pamela Balch
Registrar: Mary K. Iverson
Admissions: Cherine Heckman
Financial Aid: Betty Schumacher
Type: Four-Year College **Sex:** Coed **Affiliation:** North Dakota University System **Scores:** 52% ACT 18-23; 13% ACT 24-29 **% Accepted:** 68 **Admission Plans:** Open Admission; Deferred Admission **Application Deadline:** Rolling **Application Fee:** $35.00 **H.S. Requirements:** High school diploma required; GED accepted **Costs Per Year:** Application fee: $35. State resident tuition: $3300 full-time, $137.50 per credit hour part-time. Nonresident tuition: $8811 full-time, $367.14 per hour part-time. Mandatory fees: $1643 full-time, $68.45 per credit hour part-time. Full-time tuition and fees vary according to course load and reciprocity agreements. Part-time tuition and fees vary according to course load and reciprocity agreements. College room and board: $3724. College room only: $1524. Room and board charges vary according to board plan and housing facility. **Scholarships:** Available **Calendar System:** Semester, Summer Session Available **Enrollment:** FT 625, PT 287 **Faculty:** FT 37, PT 37 **Student-Faculty Ratio:** 15:1 **Exams:** SAT I or ACT **% Receiving Financial Aid:** 65 **% Residing in College-Owned, -Operated, or -Affiliated Housing:** 43 **Library Holdings:** 71,595 **Regional Accreditation:** North Central Association of Colleges and Schools **Credit Hours For Degree:** 64 semester hours, Associates; 120 semester hours, Bachelors **ROTC:** Army, Air Force **Professional Accreditation:** NCATE **Intercollegiate Athletics:** Baseball M; Basketball M & W; Football M; Soccer M & W; Softball W; Volleyball W

MEDCENTER ONE COLLEGE OF NURSING
512 North 7th St.
Bismarck, ND 58501-4494
Tel: (701)323-6271
E-mail: msmith@mohs.org
Web Site: http://medcenterone.com/college/nursing.htm
President/CEO: Dr. Karen Latham
Registrar: Janell Thomas
Admissions: Mary Smith
Financial Aid: Janell Thomas
Type: Two-Year Upper Division **Sex:** Coed **Affiliation:** Medcenter One Health Systems **Admission Plans:** Preferred Admission; Early Admission **Application Fee:** $40.00 **H.S. Requirements:** High school diploma required; GED accepted **Costs Per Year:** Application fee: $40. Tuition: $8400 full-time, $350 per credit part-time. Mandatory fees: $751 full-time, $5.25 per credit part-time, $499 per term part-time. Part-time tuition and fees vary according to course load. College room only: $1800. **Scholarships:** Available **Calendar System:** Semester, Summer Session Not available **Enrollment:** FT 86, PT 2 **Faculty:** FT 10, PT 2 **Student-Faculty Ratio:** 9:1 **% Receiving Financial Aid:** 73 **% Residing in College-Owned, -Operated, or -Affiliated Housing:** 11 **Library Holdings:** 28,470 **Regional Accreditation:** North Central Association of Colleges and Schools **Credit Hours For Degree:** 128 credits, Bachelors **Professional Accreditation:** NLN

MINOT STATE UNIVERSITY
500 University Ave. West
Minot, ND 58707-0002
Tel: (701)858-3000
Free: 800-777-0750
Admissions: (701)858-3822
Fax: (701)839-6933
E-mail: stephanie.witwer@minotstateu.edu
Web Site: http://www.minotstateu.edu/
President/CEO: Dr. David Fuller
Registrar: Lisa Johnson
Admissions: Stephanie Witwer
Financial Aid: Dale Gehring
Type: Comprehensive **Sex:** Coed **Affiliation:** North Dakota University System **Scores:** 66.3% ACT 18-23; 28.1% ACT 24-29 **% Accepted:** 85 **Admission Plans:** Deferred Admission **Application Deadline:** Rolling **Application Fee:** $35.00 **H.S. Requirements:** High school diploma required; GED accepted **Costs Per Year:** Application fee: $35. State resident tuition: $3460 full-time, $144.17 per credit hour part-time. Nonresident tuition: $9238 full-time, $384.93 per credit hour part-time. Mandatory fees: $632 full-time. Full-time tuition and fees vary according to class time, course load, location, program, and reciprocity agreements. Part-time tuition varies according to class time, location, program, and reciprocity agreements. College room and board: $4460. College room only: $2240. Room and board charges vary ac-

cording to board plan and housing facility. **Scholarships:** Available **Calendar System:** Semester, Summer Session Available **Enrollment:** FT 2,473, PT 1,074, Grad 250 **Faculty:** FT 172, PT 101 **Student-Faculty Ratio:** 15:1 **Exams:** SAT I or ACT **% Receiving Financial Aid:** 56 **% Residing in College-Owned, -Operated, or -Affiliated Housing:** 13 **Library Holdings:** 420,971 **Regional Accreditation:** North Central Association of Colleges and Schools **Credit Hours For Degree:** 128 semester hours, Bachelors **Professional Accreditation:** ASLHA, CSWE, NASM, NCATE, NLN **Intercollegiate Athletics:** Baseball M; Basketball M & W; Cheerleading W; Cross-Country Running M & W; Football M; Golf M & W; Ice Hockey M; Softball W; Track and Field M & W; Volleyball W

MINOT STATE UNIVERSITY-BOTTINEAU CAMPUS
105 Simrall Blvd.
Bottineau, ND 58318-1198
Tel: (701)228-2277
Free: 800-542-6866
Admissions: (701)228-5451
Fax: (701)228-5499
E-mail: bergpla@misu.nodak.edu
Web Site: http://www.misu-b.nodak.edu/
President/CEO: Dr. Kenneth Grosz
Registrar: Paula Berg
Admissions: Paula Berg
Financial Aid: Diane Christenson
Type: Two-Year College **Sex:** Coed **Affiliation:** North Dakota University System **Admission Plans:** Open Admission; Early Admission; Deferred Admission **Application Fee:** $35.00 **H.S. Requirements:** High school diploma required; GED accepted **Scholarships:** Available **Calendar System:** Semester, Summer Session Available **Enrollment:** FT 387, PT 233 **Faculty:** FT 26, PT 18 **Student-Faculty Ratio:** 11:1 **Exams:** SAT I or ACT **% Residing in College-Owned, -Operated, or -Affiliated Housing:** 45 **Library Holdings:** 45,000 **Regional Accreditation:** North Central Association of Colleges and Schools **Credit Hours For Degree:** 61 credits, Associates **Intercollegiate Athletics:** Baseball M; Basketball M & W; Ice Hockey M; Volleyball W

NORTH DAKOTA STATE COLLEGE OF SCIENCE
800 North Sixth St.
Wahpeton, ND 58076
Tel: (701)671-2401
Free: 800-342-4325
Admissions: (701)671-2189
Fax: (701)671-2332
Web Site: http://www.ndscs.nodak.edu/
President/CEO: Dr. Sharon Y. Hart
Admissions: Karen Reilly
Type: Two-Year College **Sex:** Coed **Affiliation:** North Dakota University System **Scores:** 48% ACT 18-23; 10% ACT 24-29 **Admission Plans:** Open Admission; Early Admission **Application Deadline:** Rolling **Application Fee:** $35.00 **H.S. Requirements:** High school diploma required; GED accepted **Costs Per Year:** Application fee: $35. State resident tuition: $3757 full-time. Nonresident tuition: $9197 full-time. College room and board: $4638. **Scholarships:** Available **Calendar System:** Semester, Summer Session Available **Enrollment:** FT 1,954, PT 514 **Faculty:** FT 127, PT 13 **Student-Faculty Ratio:** 15:1 **% Residing in College-Owned, -Operated, or -Affiliated Housing:** 56 **Library Holdings:** 124,508 **Regional Accreditation:** North Central Association of Colleges and Schools **Credit Hours For Degree:** 64 credits, Associates **Professional Accreditation:** ADA, AHIMA, AOTA, NLN **Intercollegiate Athletics:** Basketball M & W; Football M; Volleyball W

NORTH DAKOTA STATE UNIVERSITY
1301 North University Ave.
Fargo, ND 58105
Tel: (701)231-8011
Free: 800-488-NDSU
Admissions: (701)231-8643
Fax: (701)231-8802
E-mail: ndsu.admission@ndsu.edu
Web Site: http://www.ndsu.edu/
President/CEO: Dr. Joseph A. Chapman
Registrar: Dr. Catherine Wold-McCormick
Admissions: Dr. Kate Haugen
Financial Aid: James Kennedy
Type: University **Sex:** Coed **Affiliation:** North Dakota University System **Scores:** 50% ACT 18-23; 37% ACT 24-29 **% Accepted:** 84 **Application Deadline:** August 15 **Application Fee:** $35.00 **H.S. Requirements:** High school diploma required; GED accepted **Costs Per Year:** Application fee: $35. One-time mandatory fee: $45. Area resident tuition: $4360 full-time, $181.67 per credit part-time. Nonresident tuition: $11,641 full-time, $485.04 per credit part-time. Mandatory fees: $904 full-time, $37.65 per credit part-time. Full-time tuition and fees vary according to reciprocity agreements. Part-time tuition and fees vary according to course load and reciprocity agreements. College room and board: $5130. College room only: $2070. Room and board charges vary according to board plan and housing facility. **Scholarships:** Available **Calendar System:** Semester, Summer Session Available **Enrollment:** FT 9,410, PT 1,086, Grad 1,603 **Faculty:** FT 525, PT 91 **Student-Faculty Ratio:** 19:1 **Exams:** SAT I or ACT **% Receiving Financial Aid:** 59 **% Residing in College-Owned, -Operated, or -Affiliated Housing:** 28 **Library Holdings:** 303,274 **Regional Accreditation:** North Central Association of Colleges and Schools **Credit Hours For Degree:** 122 credits, Bachelors **ROTC:** Army, Air Force **Professional Accreditation:** AACSB, ABET, AAMFT, AACN, AAFCS, ACCE, ACPhE, ACA, ADtA, ASLA, CARC, FIDER, JRCEPAT, NASAD, NASM, NAST, NCATE, NLN **Intercollegiate Athletics:** Archery M & W; Baseball M; Basketball M & W; Bowling M & W; Cheerleading M & W; Cross-Country Running M & W; Football M; Golf M & W; Ice Hockey M; Riflery M & W; Rugby M & W; Soccer M & W; Softball W; Track and Field M & W; Volleyball M & W; Wrestling M

SITTING BULL COLLEGE
1341 92nd St.
Fort Yates, ND 58538-9701
Tel: (701)854-3861
Admissions: (701)854-3864
Fax: (701)854-3403
E-mail: melodys@sbcl.edu
Web Site: http://www.sittingbull.edu/
President/CEO: Dr. Ron His Horse Is Thunder
Registrar: Melody Azure
Admissions: Melody Silk
Financial Aid: Donna Seaboy
Type: Two-Year College **Sex:** Coed **Admission Plans:** Open Admission; Early Admission **H.S. Requirements:** High school diploma required; GED accepted **Scholarships:** Available **Calendar System:** Semester, Summer Session Not available **Faculty:** FT 16, PT 16 **Student-Faculty Ratio:** 6:1 **Exams:** Other **Library Holdings:** 10,000 **Regional Accreditation:** North Central Association of Colleges and Schools **Credit Hours For Degree:** 67 credit hours, Associates **Intercollegiate Athletics:** Basketball M & W

TRINITY BIBLE COLLEGE
50 South 6th Ave.
Ellendale, ND 58436-7150
Tel: (701)349-3621; 888-TBC-2DAY
Fax: (701)349-5443
Web Site: http://www.trinitybiblecollege.edu/
President/CEO: Rev. Dennis Niles
Registrar: Laura Gerling
Admissions: Rev. Steve Tvedt
Financial Aid: Don Flaherty
Type: Four-Year College **Sex:** Coed **Affiliation:** Assemblies of God **Admission Plans:** Deferred Admission **Application Fee:** $25.00 **H.S. Requirements:** High school diploma required; GED accepted **Scholarships:** Available **Calendar System:** Semester, Summer Session Available **Enrollment:** FT 272, PT 35 **Faculty:** FT 29, PT 9 **Student-Faculty Ratio:** 8:1 **Exams:** ACT, SAT I **% Receiving Financial Aid:** 96 **% Residing in College-Owned, -Operated, or -Affiliated Housing:** 69 **Library Holdings:** 67,868 **Regional Accreditation:** North Central Association of Colleges and Schools **Credit Hours For Degree:** 64 credits, Associates; 128 credits, Bachelors **Professional Accreditation:** AABC **Intercollegiate Athletics:** Baseball M; Basketball M & W; Football M; Volleyball W; Wrestling M

TURTLE MOUNTAIN COMMUNITY COLLEGE
Box 340
Belcourt, ND 58316-0340
Tel: (701)477-7862
Admissions: (701)477-5605
Fax: (701)477-7807
E-mail: jlafontaine@tm.edu

Web Site: http://www.turtle-mountain.cc.nd.us/
President/CEO: Dr. Gerald E. Monette
Registrar: Anita Parisien-Frederick
Admissions: Joni LaFontaine
Financial Aid: Wanda Laducer
Type: Two-Year College **Sex:** Coed **Admission Plans:** Open Admission; Early Admission; Deferred Admission **H.S. Requirements:** High school diploma required; GED accepted **Scholarships:** Available **Calendar System:** Semester, Summer Session Not available **Enrollment:** FT 378, PT 201 **Faculty:** FT 21, PT 21 **Exams:** ACT **Library Holdings:** 20,500 **Regional Accreditation:** North Central Association of Colleges and Schools **Credit Hours For Degree:** 62 semester hours, Associates

UNITED TRIBES TECHNICAL COLLEGE
3315 University Dr.
Bismarck, ND 58504-7596
Tel: (701)255-3285
E-mail: vgillette@uttc.edu
Web Site: http://www.uttc.edu/
President/CEO: Dr. David Gipp
Registrar: Joetta McLeod
Admissions: Vivian Gillett
Financial Aid: Robert Parisien
Type: Two-Year College **Sex:** Coed **% Accepted:** 84 **Admission Plans:** Open Admission **Application Deadline:** Rolling **Application Fee:** $0.00 **H.S. Requirements:** High school diploma required; GED accepted **Costs Per Year:** Application fee: $0. One-time mandatory fee: $100. Comprehensive fee: $6580 includes full-time tuition ($2800), mandatory fees ($780), and college room and board ($3000). Part-time tuition: $87.50 per credit. **Scholarships:** Available **Calendar System:** Semester, Summer Session Available **Enrollment:** FT 635, PT 250 **Faculty:** FT 49, PT 14 **Student-Faculty Ratio:** 8:1 **Library Holdings:** 6,000 **Regional Accreditation:** North Central Association of Colleges and Schools **Credit Hours For Degree:** 60 credit hours, Associates **Professional Accreditation:** AHIMA **Intercollegiate Athletics:** Basketball M; Cross-Country Running M & W

UNIVERSITY OF MARY
7500 University Dr.
Bismarck, ND 58504-9652
Tel: (701)255-7500
Free: 800-288-6279
Admissions: (701)355-8191
Fax: (701)255-7687
Web Site: http://www.umary.edu/
President/CEO: Sr. Thomas Welder
Registrar: Janine Thull
Admissions: Dr. Dave Hebinger
Financial Aid: Dave Hanson
Type: Comprehensive **Sex:** Coed **Affiliation:** Roman Catholic **Scores:** 58% ACT 18-23; 33% ACT 24-29 **% Accepted:** 86 **Admission Plans:** Early Admission; Deferred Admission **Application Deadline:** Rolling **Application Fee:** $25.00 **H.S. Requirements:** High school diploma required; GED accepted **Costs Per Year:** Application fee: $25. Comprehensive fee: $15,374 includes full-time tuition ($11,100), mandatory fees ($224), and college room and board ($4050). College room only: $1750. Part-time tuition: $350 per credit. Part-time mandatory fees: $7 per credit. **Scholarships:** Available **Calendar System:** Miscellaneous, Summer Session Available **Enrollment:** FT 2,044, PT 153, Grad 561 **Faculty:** FT 100, PT 249 **Student-Faculty Ratio:** 16:1 **Exams:** SAT I or ACT **% Residing in College-Owned, -Operated, or -Affiliated Housing:** 35 **Library Holdings:** 65,842 **Regional Accreditation:** North Central Association of Colleges and Schools **Credit Hours For Degree:** 64 credit hours, Associates; 128 credit hours, Bachelors **Professional Accreditation:** AACN, AOTA, APTA, CARC, CSWE, JRCEPAT, NLN **Intercollegiate Athletics:** Baseball M; Basketball M & W; Cross-Country Running M & W; Football M; Golf M & W; Soccer M & W; Softball W; Tennis M & W; Track and Field M & W; Volleyball W; Wrestling M

UNIVERSITY OF NORTH DAKOTA
Grand Forks, ND 58202
Tel: (701)777-2011
Free: 800-CALL UND
Admissions: (701)777-4463
Fax: (701)777-3650
E-mail: kenton_pauls@und.nodak.edu
Web Site: http://www.und.nodak.edu/
President/CEO: Dr. Charles Kupchella
Registrar: Dr. Nancy Krogh
Admissions: Kenton Pauls
Financial Aid: Robin Holden
Type: University **Sex:** Coed **Affiliation:** North Dakota University System **Scores:** 54% ACT 18-23; 38% ACT 24-29 **% Accepted:** 73 **Admission Plans:** Deferred Admission **Application Deadline:** July 01 **Application Fee:** $35.00 **H.S. Requirements:** High school diploma required; GED accepted **Costs Per Year:** Application fee: $35. State resident tuition: $4390 full-time. Nonresident tuition: $11,722 full-time. Mandatory fees: $937 full-time. Full-time tuition and fees vary according to degree level, program, and reciprocity agreements. College room and board: $4787. College room only: $1979. Room and board charges vary according to board plan and housing facility. **Scholarships:** Available **Calendar System:** Semester, Summer Session Available **Enrollment:** FT 9,364, PT 1,134, Grad 1,996 **Faculty:** FT 668, PT 157 **Student-Faculty Ratio:** 18:1 **Exams:** ACT, SAT I or ACT **% Receiving Financial Aid:** 54 **% Residing in College-Owned, -Operated, or -Affiliated Housing:** 31 **Library Holdings:** 925,367 **Regional Accreditation:** North Central Association of Colleges and Schools **Credit Hours For Degree:** 125 credit hours, Bachelors **ROTC:** Army, Air Force **Professional Accreditation:** AACSB, ABET, AACN, AANA, ABA, ADtA, AOTA, APTA, APA, ASC, ASLHA, AALS, CAA, CSWE, JRCEPAT, LCMEAMA, NAACLS, NAIT, NASAD, NASM NAST, NCATE **Intercollegiate Athletics:** Baseball M; Basketball M & W; Cross-Country Running M & W; Football M; Golf M & W; Ice Hockey M & W; Soccer W; Softball W; Swimming and Diving M & W; Tennis W; Track and Field M & W; Volleyball W

VALLEY CITY STATE UNIVERSITY
101 College St., SW
Valley City, ND 58072
Tel: (701)845-7990
Free: 800-532-8641
Admissions: (701)845-7204
Fax: (701)845-7245
E-mail: dan.klein@vcsu.edu
Web Site: http://www.vcsu.edu/
President/CEO: Dr. Ellen-Earle Chaffee
Admissions: Dan Klein
Financial Aid: Betty Schumacher
Type: Four-Year College **Sex:** Coed **Affiliation:** North Dakota University System **Scores:** 95% SAT V 400+; 90% SAT M 400+; 59.5% ACT 18-23; 18.4% ACT 24-29 **% Accepted:** 94 **Admission Plans:** Open Admission; Early Admission; Deferred Admission **Application Deadline:** Rolling **Application Fee:** $35.00 **H.S. Requirements:** High school diploma required; GED accepted **Costs Per Year:** Application fee: $35. State resident tuition: $3656 full-time, $114.25 per semester hour part-time. Nonresident tuition: $9761 full-time, $305.05 per semester hour part-time. Mandatory fees: $1504 full-time. College room and board: $4694. College room only: $2080. Room and board charges vary according to board plan. **Scholarships:** Available **Calendar System:** Semester, Summer Session Available **Enrollment:** FT 783, PT 230, Grad 22 **Faculty:** FT 55, PT 22 **Student-Faculty Ratio:** 18:1 **Exams:** SAT I or ACT **% Receiving Financial Aid:** 60 **% Residing in College-Owned, -Operated, or -Affiliated Housing:** 32 **Library Holdings:** 94,450 **Regional Accreditation:** North Central Association of Colleges and Schools **Credit Hours For Degree:** 128 semester hours, Bachelors **Professional Accreditation:** NASM, NCATE **Intercollegiate Athletics:** Baseball M; Basketball M & W; Football M; Softball W; Volleyball W

WILLISTON STATE COLLEGE
Box 1326
Williston, ND 58802-1326
Tel: (701)774-4200; 888-863-9455
Admissions: (701)774-4554
Fax: (701)774-4211
Web Site: http://www.wsc.nodak.edu/
President/CEO: Dr. Joseph E. McCann
Registrar: Jan Solem
Admissions: Jan Solem
Financial Aid: Lynn Hagen-Aaberg
Type: Two-Year College **Sex:** Coed **Affiliation:** North Dakota University System **% Accepted:** 98 **Admission Plans:** Open Admission **Application Deadline:** Rolling **Application Fee:** $35.00 **H.S. Requirements:** High school diploma required; GED accepted **Costs Per Year:** Application fee: $35. State resident tuition: $2073 full-time, $79.76 per credit part-time.

Nonresident tuition: $3111 full-time, $119.64 per credit part-time. Mandatory fees: $575 full-time, $22.11 per credit part-time. College room and board: $3500. College room only: $1000. **Scholarships:** Available **Calendar System:** Semester, Summer Session Available **Enrollment:** FT 557, PT 390 **Faculty:** FT 26, PT 67 **Student-Faculty Ratio:** 14:1 **% Residing in College-Owned, -Operated, or -Affiliated Housing:** 13 **Library Holdings:** 16,218 **Regional Accreditation:** North Central Association of Colleges and Schools **Credit Hours For Degree:** 62 credit hours, Associates **Professional Accreditation:** APTA **Intercollegiate Athletics:** Baseball M; Basketball M & W; Volleyball W

ACADEMY OF COURT REPORTING
2044 Euclid Ave.
Cleveland, OH 44115
Tel: (216)861-3222
Fax: (216)861-4517
E-mail: admissionaocr@hotmail.com
Web Site: http://www.acr.edu/
Admissions: Sheila Woods
Type: Two-Year College **Sex:** Coed **Faculty:** FT 20, PT 20 **Student-Faculty Ratio:** 29:1 **Professional Accreditation:** ACICS

ALLEGHENY WESLEYAN COLLEGE
2161 Woodsdale Rd.
Salem, OH 44460
Tel: (330)337-6403
Free: 800-292-3153
Fax: (330)337-6255
Web Site: http://www.awc.edu/
President/CEO: Robert E. England
Type: Four-Year College **Sex:** Coed **Calendar System:** Semester **Professional Accreditation:** AABC

ANTIOCH COLLEGE
795 Livermore St.
Yellow Springs, OH 45387-1697
Tel: (937)769-1000
Free: 800-543-9436
Admissions: (937)769-1100
Fax: (937)769-1288
E-mail: admissions@college.antioch.edu
Web Site: http://www.antioch-college.edu/
President/CEO: Dr. Joan Straumanis
Registrar: Bonnie Scranton
Admissions: Michael Thorp
Financial Aid: Larry Brickman
Type: Four-Year College **Sex:** Coed **Affiliation:** Antioch University **Scores:** 96% SAT V 400+; 96% SAT M 400+; 36% ACT 18-23; 64% ACT 24-29 **% Accepted:** 51 **Admission Plans:** Early Action; Deferred Admission **Application Deadline:** February 01 **Application Fee:** $0.00 **H.S. Requirements:** High school diploma required; GED accepted **Costs Per Year:** Application fee: $0. Comprehensive fee: $34,214 includes full-time tuition ($26,492), mandatory fees ($722), and college room and board ($7000). College room only: $3426. Part-time tuition: $435 per credit hour. **Scholarships:** Available **Calendar System:** Trimester, Summer Session Available **Enrollment:** FT 460, PT 4, Grad 6 **Faculty:** FT 51, PT 17 **Student-Faculty Ratio:** 11:1 **% Receiving Financial Aid:** 77 **% Residing in College-Owned, -Operated, or -Affiliated Housing:** 97 **Library Holdings:** 300,000 **Regional Accreditation:** North Central Association of Colleges and Schools **Credit Hours For Degree:** 107 credits and 5 semesters of cooperative education, Bachelors

ANTIOCH UNIVERSITY MCGREGOR
800 Livermore St.
Yellow Springs, OH 45387-1609
Tel: (937)769-1800; (937)769-1818
Admissions: (937)769-1823
Fax: (937)769-1805
E-mail: orobinson@mcgregor.edu
Web Site: http://www.mcgregor.edu/
President/CEO: Dr. Barbara Gellman-Danley
Registrar: Darlene Robertson
Admissions: Oscar Robinson
Financial Aid: Kathy John
Type: Two-Year Upper Division **Sex:** Coed **Affiliation:** Antioch University **Admission Plans:** Deferred Admission **Application Fee:** $45.00 **H.S. Requirements:** High school diploma required; GED accepted **Costs Per Year:** Application fee: $45. Tuition: $12,288 full-time, $256 per credit hour part-time. Mandatory fees: $225 full-time, $75 per term part-time. **Scholarships:** Available **Calendar System:** Quarter, Summer Session Available **Enrollment:** FT 57, PT 95, Grad 543 **Faculty:** FT 27, PT 63 **Student-Faculty Ratio:** 6:1 **% Receiving Financial Aid:** 43 **Library Holdings:** 285,000 **Regional Accreditation:** North Central Association of Colleges and Schools **Credit Hours For Degree:** 180 credit hours, Bachelors

ANTONELLI COLLEGE
124 East Seventh St.
Cincinnati, OH 45202-2592
Tel: (513)241-4338
Free: 800-505-4338
Fax: (513)241-9396
Web Site: http://www.antonellic.com/
President/CEO: Karen Selby
Registrar: Nancy Nolke
Admissions: Connie D. Sharp
Type: Two-Year College **Sex:** Coed **Admission Plans:** Open Admission; Early Admission; Deferred Admission **Application Fee:** $100.00 **H.S. Requirements:** High school diploma required; GED accepted **Scholarships:** Available **Calendar System:** Quarter, Summer Session Available **Enrollment:** FT 216, PT 171 **Faculty:** FT 14, PT 44 **Student-Faculty Ratio:** 10:1 **Library Holdings:** 2,000 **Credit Hours For Degree:** 95 credit hours, Associates **Professional Accreditation:** ACCSCT

ART ACADEMY OF CINCINNATI
1212 Jackson St.
Cincinnati, OH 45202
Tel: (513)562-6262
Admissions: (513)562-8744
Fax: (513)562-8778
E-mail: zumwalde@artacademy.edu
Web Site: http://www.artacademy.edu/
President/CEO: Gregory Allgire Smith
Registrar: David Johnson
Admissions: Mary Jane Zumwalde
Financial Aid: Karen Geiger
Type: Comprehensive **Sex:** Coed **Scores:** 83% SAT V 400+; 94% SAT M 400+; 57% ACT 18-23; 24% ACT 24-29 **% Accepted:** 25 **Admission Plans:** Deferred Admission **Application Deadline:** June 30 **Application Fee:** $25.00 **H.S. Requirements:** High school diploma required; GED accepted **Costs Per Year:** Application fee: $25. Tuition: $19,250 full-time, $810 per credit hour part-time. Mandatory fees: $350 full-time, $175 per term part-time. **Scholarships:** Available **Calendar System:** Semester, Summer Session Available **Enrollment:** FT 155, PT 8, Grad 1 **Faculty:** FT 16, PT 45 **Student-Faculty Ratio:** 12:1 **Exams:** SAT I or ACT **% Receiving Financial

Aid: 71 **Library Holdings:** 66,404 **Regional Accreditation:** North Central Association of Colleges and Schools **Credit Hours For Degree:** 65 credit hours, Associates; 132 credit hours, Bachelors **Professional Accreditation:** NASAD

THE ART INSTITUTE OF CINCINNATI
1171 East Kemper Rd.
Cincinnati, OH 45246
Tel: (513)751-1206
Fax: (513)751-1209
Web Site: http://www.theartinstituteofcincinnati.com/
President/CEO: Marion Allman
Admissions: Cyndi Mendell
Financial Aid: Ennis Jones
Type: Two-Year College **Sex:** Coed **Affiliation:** Education Management Corporation **Enrollment:** FT 74 **Faculty:** FT 8, PT 5 **Student-Faculty Ratio:** 9:1 **Library Holdings:** 1,500 **Credit Hours For Degree:** 120 credits, Associates **Professional Accreditation:** ACCSCT

THE ART INSTITUTE OF OHIO-CINCINNATI
1011 Glendale Milford Rd.
Cincinnati, OH 45215
Tel: (513)771-2821
Fax: 877-477-8486
E-mail: mlee@aii.edu
Web Site: http://www.aiohc.aii.edu
Admissions: Maurice Lee
Type: Two-Year College **Sex:** Coed **Affiliation:** The Art Institutes **Admission Plans:** Open Admission; Early Admission; Early Action; Early Decision Plan; Deferred Admission **Application Deadline:** Rolling **Application Fee:** $0.00 **H.S. Requirements:** High school diploma required; GED accepted **Calendar System:** Continuous, Summer Session Not available **Enrollment:** FT 229 **Faculty:** FT 2, PT 10 **Student-Faculty Ratio:** 25:1 **Library Holdings:** 7,018 **Credit Hours For Degree:** 96 quarter credits, Associates

ASHLAND UNIVERSITY
401 College Ave.
Ashland, OH 44805-3702
Tel: (419)289-4142
Free: 800-882-1548
Admissions: (419)289-5052
Fax: (419)289-5999
E-mail: auadmsn@ashland.edu
Web Site: http://www.exploreashland.com
President/CEO: Dr. G. William Benz
Registrar: Karen Little
Admissions: Thomas Mansperger
Financial Aid: Steve Howell
Type: Comprehensive **Sex:** Coed **Affiliation:** Brethren Church **Scores:** 97% SAT V 400+; 96% SAT M 400+; 56% ACT 18-23; 38% ACT 24-29 **% Accepted:** 91 **Admission Plans:** Deferred Admission **Application Deadline:** Rolling **Application Fee:** $25.00 **H.S. Requirements:** High school diploma required; GED accepted **Costs Per Year:** Application fee: $25. Comprehensive fee: $29,220 includes full-time tuition ($20,666), mandatory fees ($764), and college room and board ($7790). College room only: $4184. Part-time tuition: $635 per credit hour. **Scholarships:** Available **Calendar System:** Semester, Summer Session Available **Enrollment:** FT 2,511, PT 280, Grad 3,412 **Faculty:** FT 231, PT 362 **Student-Faculty Ratio:** 13:1 **Exams:** SAT I or ACT **% Receiving Financial Aid:** 78 **% Residing in College-Owned, -Operated, or -Affiliated Housing:** 71 **Library Holdings:** 205,200 **Regional Accreditation:** North Central Association of Colleges and Schools **Credit Hours For Degree:** 64 credit hours, Associates; 128 credit hours, Bachelors **Professional Accreditation:** AACN, AAFCS, ACBSP, ATS, CSWE, NASM, NCATE **Intercollegiate Athletics:** Baseball M; Basketball M & W; Cross-Country Running M & W; Football M; Golf M & W; Soccer M & W; Softball M & W; Swimming and Diving M & W; Tennis M & W; Track and Field M & W; Volleyball W; Wrestling M

ATS INSTITUTE OF TECHNOLOGY
230 Alpha Park
Highland Heights, OH 44143
Tel: (440)449-1700
Fax: (440)449-1389
Web Site: http://www.atsinstitute.com/
President/CEO: Helen Bykov
Type: Two-Year College **Sex:** Coed **Professional Accreditation:** ACICS

BALDWIN-WALLACE COLLEGE
275 Eastland Rd.
Berea, OH 44017-2088
Tel: (440)826-2900
Admissions: (440)826-2222
Fax: (440)826-3830
E-mail: admission@baldwinw.edu
Web Site: http://www.bw.edu/
President/CEO: Dr. Mark H. Collier
Registrar: Linda Young
Admissions: Susan Dileno
Financial Aid: Dr. George Rolleston
Type: Comprehensive **Sex:** Coed **Affiliation:** Methodist **Scores:** 97% SAT V 400+; 97% SAT M 400+; 45% ACT 18-23; 46% ACT 24-29 **% Accepted:** 79 **Admission Plans:** Deferred Admission **Application Deadline:** Rolling **Application Fee:** $25.00 **H.S. Requirements:** High school diploma required; GED accepted **Costs Per Year:** Application fee: $25. Comprehensive fee: $28,210 includes full-time tuition ($21,236) and college room and board ($6974). College room only: $3406. Part-time tuition: $674 per semester hour. **Scholarships:** Available **Calendar System:** Semester, Summer Session Available **Enrollment:** FT 2,994, PT 687, Grad 788 **Faculty:** FT 162, PT 190 **Student-Faculty Ratio:** 17:1 **Exams:** SAT I or ACT **% Receiving Financial Aid:** 77 **% Residing in College-Owned, -Operated, or -Affiliated Housing:** 58 **Library Holdings:** 200,000 **Regional Accreditation:** North Central Association of Colleges and Schools **Credit Hours For Degree:** 124 semester hours, Bachelors **ROTC:** Air Force **Professional Accreditation:** NASM, NCATE **Intercollegiate Athletics:** Baseball M; Basketball M & W; Cross-Country Running M & W; Football M; Golf M & W; Soccer M & W; Softball W; Swimming and Diving M & W; Tennis M & W; Track and Field M & W; Volleyball W; Wrestling M

BELMONT TECHNICAL COLLEGE
120 Fox Shannon Place
St. Clairsville, OH 43950-9735
Tel: (740)695-9500
Fax: (740)695-2247
E-mail: gfehr@btc.edu
Web Site: http://www.btc.edu/
President/CEO: Dr. Joseph Bukowski
Registrar: Thomas J. Tarowsky
Admissions: Gregory A. Fehr
Financial Aid: Susan Galavich
Type: Two-Year College **Sex:** Coed **Affiliation:** Ohio Board of Regents **Admission Plans:** Open Admission; Early Admission **H.S. Requirements:** High school diploma required; GED accepted **Costs Per Year:** State resident tuition: $2520 full-time, $56 per credit hour part-time. Nonresident tuition: $5220 full-time, $116 per credit hour part-time. Mandatory fees: $1050 full-time, $23 per credit hour part-time, $5 per term part-time. **Scholarships:** Available **Calendar System:** Quarter, Summer Session Available **Enrollment:** FT 1,180, PT 560 **Faculty:** FT 41, PT 60 **Exams:** Other **Library Holdings:** 5,612 **Regional Accreditation:** North Central Association of Colleges and Schools **Credit Hours For Degree:** 90 credits, Associates **Professional Accreditation:** AAMAE

BLUFFTON UNIVERSITY
1 University Dr.
Bluffton, OH 45817
Tel: (419)358-3000
Free: 800-488-3257
Admissions: (419)358-3254
Fax: (419)358-3232
E-mail: admissions@bluffton.edu
Web Site: http://www.bluffton.edu/
President/CEO: Dr. Lee Snyder
Registrar: Stephen Harnish
Admissions: Chris Jebsen
Financial Aid: Lawrence Matthews
Type: Comprehensive **Sex:** Coed **Affiliation:** Mennonite **Scores:** 91% SAT V 400+; 96% SAT M 400+; 52% ACT 18-23; 33% ACT 24-29 **% Accepted:** 71 **Admission Plans:** Deferred Admission **Application Deadline:** May 31 **Application Fee:** $20.00 **H.S. Requirements:** High school diploma required; GED accepted **Costs Per Year:** Application fee: $20. Comprehen-

sive fee: $27,652 includes full-time tuition ($20,170), mandatory fees ($400), and college room and board ($7082). College room only: $3260. Part-time tuition: $840 per credit hour. **Scholarships:** Available **Calendar System:** Semester, Summer Session Available **Enrollment:** FT 1,005, PT 74, Grad 132 **Faculty:** FT 67, PT 47 **Student-Faculty Ratio:** 14:1 **Exams:** SAT I or ACT **% Receiving Financial Aid:** 74 **% Residing in College-Owned, -Operated, or -Affiliated Housing:** 85 **Library Holdings:** 163,448 **Regional Accreditation:** North Central Association of Colleges and Schools **Credit Hours For Degree:** 124 semester hours, Bachelors **Professional Accreditation:** CSWE, NASM **Intercollegiate Athletics:** Baseball M; Basketball M & W; Cross-Country Running M & W; Football M; Soccer M & W; Softball W; Tennis M & W; Track and Field M & W; Volleyball W

BOHECKER'S BUSINESS COLLEGE
326 East Main St.
Ravenna, OH 44266
Tel: (330)297-7319
Fax: (330)297-7315
Web Site: http://www.boheckers.com/
President/CEO: Ruth Burmagin
Registrar: Sue Madick
Financial Aid: Susan Spinner
Type: Two-Year College **Sex:** Coed **Scholarships:** Available **Professional Accreditation:** ACICS

BOWLING GREEN STATE UNIVERSITY
Bowling Green, OH 43403
Tel: (419)372-2531
Admissions: (419)372-BGSU
E-mail: admissions@bgnet.bgsu.edu
Web Site: http://www.bgsu.edu/
President/CEO: Dr. Sidney A. Ribeau
Registrar: Laura Waggoner
Admissions: Gary Swegan
Financial Aid: Craig Cornell
Type: University **Sex:** Coed **Scores:** 94% SAT V 400+; 93% SAT M 400+; 60% ACT 18-23; 24% ACT 24-29 **% Accepted:** 90 **Admission Plans:** Deferred Admission **Application Deadline:** July 15 **Application Fee:** $35.00 **H.S. Requirements:** High school diploma required; GED accepted **Costs Per Year:** Application fee: $35. State resident tuition: $7314 full-time, $357 per credit hour part-time. Nonresident tuition: $14,622 full-time, $706 per credit hour part-time. Mandatory fees: $1246 full-time, $62 per credit hour part-time. Part-time tuition and fees vary according to course load. College room and board: $6434. College room only: $3934. Room and board charges vary according to board plan and housing facility. **Scholarships:** Available **Calendar System:** Semester, Summer Session Available **Enrollment:** FT 15,014, PT 1,065, Grad 2,937 **Faculty:** FT 851, PT 196 **Student-Faculty Ratio:** 19:1 **Exams:** SAT I and SAT II or ACT **% Receiving Financial Aid:** 57 **% Residing in College-Owned, -Operated, or -Affiliated Housing:** 46 **Library Holdings:** 2,468,812 **Regional Accreditation:** North Central Association of Colleges and Schools **Credit Hours For Degree:** 122 credit hours, Bachelors **ROTC:** Army, Air Force **Professional Accreditation:** AACSB, ACEJMC, AAFCS, ACCE, ADtA, APTA, APA, ASLHA, CARC, CEPH, CORE, CSWE, NAACLS, NAIT, NASAD, NASM, NAST, NCATE, NRPA **Intercollegiate Athletics:** Baseball M; Basketball M & W; Crew M; Cross-Country Running M & W; Football M; Golf M & W; Gymnastics W; Ice Hockey M; Soccer M; Softball W; Swimming and Diving M & W; Tennis M & W; Track and Field M & W; Volleyball M & W; Water Polo M & W; Weight Lifting M & W

BOWLING GREEN STATE UNIVERSITY-FIRELANDS COLLEGE
One University Dr.
Huron, OH 44839-9791
Tel: (419)433-5560
E-mail: ahazlet@bgnet.bgsu.edu
Web Site: http://www.firelands.bgsu.edu/
President/CEO: Dr. James M. Smith
Registrar: Vicki B. Hillis
Admissions: Debralee Divers
Financial Aid: Debralee Divers
Type: Two-Year College **Sex:** Coed **Affiliation:** Bowling Green State University System **Scores:** 83% SAT V 400+; 91% SAT M 400+; 61% ACT 18-23; 9% ACT 24-29 **Admission Plans:** Open Admission; Early Admission; Deferred Admission **Application Fee:** $35.00 **H.S. Requirements:** High school diploma required; GED accepted **Scholarships:** Available **Calendar System:** Semester, Summer Session Available **Enrollment:** FT 1,042, PT 876, Grad 68 **Faculty:** FT 43, PT 65 **Student-Faculty Ratio:** 19:1 **Exams:** SAT I or ACT **Library Holdings:** 41,281 **Regional Accreditation:** North Central Association of Colleges and Schools **Credit Hours For Degree:** 62 credit hours, Associates **ROTC:** Army, Air Force **Professional Accreditation:** AHIMA

BRADFORD SCHOOL
2469 Stelzer Rd.
Columbus, OH 43219
Tel: (614)416-6200
Free: 800-678-7981
Web Site: http://www.bradfordschoolcolumbus.edu/
President/CEO: Dennis Bartels
Registrar: Marie O'Donahue
Admissions: Raeann Lee
Financial Aid: Julie Harris
Type: Two-Year College **Sex:** Coed **Application Fee:** $50.00 **H.S. Requirements:** High school diploma required; GED accepted **Scholarships:** Available **Calendar System:** Semester, Summer Session Not available **Enrollment:** FT 312 **Faculty:** FT 6, PT 5 **Student-Faculty Ratio:** 25:1 **% Residing in College-Owned, -Operated, or -Affiliated Housing:** 41 **Library Holdings:** 2,000 **Professional Accreditation:** ACICS

BROWN MACKIE COLLEGE-AKRON
2791 Mogadore Rd.
Akron, OH 44312-1596
Tel: (330)733-8766
Fax: (330)733-5853
E-mail: tfoose@brownmackie.edu
Web Site: http://www.socaec.com/
President/CEO: Sandra Wilk
Registrar: Shirlene Miller
Admissions: Tanya Foose
Financial Aid: Juanita M. Smith
Type: Two-Year College **Sex:** Coed **Affiliation:** Southern Ohio College **Admission Plans:** Early Admission; Deferred Admission **Application Deadline:** Rolling **Application Fee:** $0.00 **H.S. Requirements:** High school diploma required; GED accepted **Costs Per Year:** Application fee: $0. Tuition: $179 per credit part-time. Mandatory fees: $10 per credit part-time. **Scholarships:** Available **Calendar System:** Quarter, Summer Session Available **Enrollment:** FT 521 **Faculty:** FT 7, PT 41 **Student-Faculty Ratio:** 18:1 **Library Holdings:** 3,725 **Credit Hours For Degree:** 102 quarter hours, Associates **Professional Accreditation:** ACICS, AAMAE

BROWN MACKIE COLLEGE-CINCINNATI
1011 Glendale-Milford Rd.
Cincinnati, OH 45215
Tel: (513)771-2424
Web Site: http://www.brownmackie.edu/locations.asp?locid=6
President/CEO: Danny Finuf
Registrar: Peggy Johnson
Admissions: Cherie McNeel
Financial Aid: Charlene Howard
Type: Two-Year College **Sex:** Coed **Affiliation:** American Education Centers, Inc **Admission Plans:** Open Admission; Early Admission; Deferred Admission **Application Deadline:** Rolling **Application Fee:** $20.00 **H.S. Requirements:** High school diploma required; GED accepted **Costs Per Year:** Application fee: $20. Tuition: $6444 full-time. Mandatory fees: $360 full-time. **Scholarships:** Available **Calendar System:** Quarter, Summer Session Available **Faculty:** FT 12, PT 34 **Student-Faculty Ratio:** 16:1 **Library Holdings:** 8,747 **Credit Hours For Degree:** 92 credit hours, Associates **Professional Accreditation:** ACICS, AAMAE

BROWN MACKIE COLLEGE-FINDLAY
1637 Tiffin Ave.
Findlay, OH 45840
Tel: (419)423-2211
Free: 800-842-3687
Fax: (419)423-0725
Web Site: http://www.brownmackie.edu
President/CEO: Ross Augway
Registrar: Lupe Zapien
Admissions: Angelique Walker

Financial Aid: Gena Munsey
Type: Two-Year College **Sex:** Coed **Affiliation:** Education Management Corporation **Admission Plans:** Open Admission **Application Deadline:** Rolling **Application Fee:** $0.00 **H.S. Requirements:** High school diploma required; GED accepted **Costs Per Year:** Application fee: $0. Tuition: $11,500 full-time, $250 per credit hour part-time. Mandatory fees: $460 full-time, $10 per credit hour part-time. **Scholarships:** Available **Calendar System:** Continuous, Summer Session Not available **Enrollment:** FT 459, PT 173 **Faculty:** FT 18, PT 39 **Student-Faculty Ratio:** 19:1 **Library Holdings:** 3,134 **Credit Hours For Degree:** 96 credit hours, Associates **Professional Accreditation:** ACICS

BROWN MACKIE COLLEGE-NORTH CANTON
1320 West Maple St., NW
North Canton, OH 44720-2854
Tel: (330)494-1214
E-mail: elaudermilt@brownmackie.edu
Web Site: http://www.socaec.com/
President/CEO: Peter Perkowski
Registrar: Crystal Bussell
Admissions: Greg Laudermilt
Financial Aid: Marvalene Sharp
Type: Two-Year College **Sex:** Coed **Affiliation:** Educational Management Corporation **% Accepted:** 98 **Application Deadline:** Rolling **Application Fee:** $0.00 **H.S. Requirements:** High school diploma required; GED accepted **Costs Per Year:** Application fee: $0. Tuition: $8592 full-time, $179 per credit part-time. Mandatory fees: $480 full-time, $10 per credit part-time. **Calendar System:** Quarter, Summer Session Not available **Enrollment:** FT 1,131 **Faculty:** FT 12, PT 29 **Student-Faculty Ratio:** 21:1 **Exams:** Other **Credit Hours For Degree:** 96 credit hours, Associates **Professional Accreditation:** ACICS

BRYANT AND STRATTON COLLEGE (CLEVELAND)
1700 East 13th St.
Cleveland, OH 44114-3203
Tel: (216)771-1700
Fax: (216)771-1700
E-mail: jploskonka@bryantstratton.edu
Web Site: http://www.bryantstratton.edu/
President/CEO: William B. Schatt
Registrar: Vanetta McClain
Admissions: Dr. James Ploskonka
Type: Four-Year College **Sex:** Coed **Affiliation:** Bryant and Stratton Business Institute, Inc **Admission Plans:** Deferred Admission **Application Deadline:** Rolling **H.S. Requirements:** High school diploma required; GED accepted **Costs Per Year:** Tuition: $18,675 full-time, $415 per credit hour part-time. Mandatory fees: $25 full-time. **Scholarships:** Available **Calendar System:** Semester, Summer Session Available **Enrollment:** FT 282, PT 146 **Faculty:** FT 13, PT 24 **Student-Faculty Ratio:** 10:1 **Exams:** Other, SAT I or ACT **% Receiving Financial Aid:** 87 **% Residing in College-Owned, -Operated, or -Affiliated Housing:** 10 **Library Holdings:** 4,466 **Regional Accreditation:** Middle State Association of Colleges and Schools **Credit Hours For Degree:** 64 semester credit hours, Associates; 136 semester credit hours, Bachelors

BRYANT AND STRATTON COLLEGE (PARMA)
12955 Snow Rd.
Parma, OH 44130-1013
Tel: (216)265-3151
Fax: (216)265-0325
Web Site: http://www.bryantstratton.edu/
President/CEO: Lisa Mason
Registrar: Marilyn Huber
Admissions: Lisa Mason
Type: Two-Year College **Sex:** Coed **Affiliation:** Bryant and Stratton Business Institute, Inc **Admission Plans:** Deferred Admission **Application Deadline:** Rolling **H.S. Requirements:** High school diploma required; GED accepted. For applicants 19 and older who meet entrance-testing requirements: High school diploma or equivalent not required **Costs Per Year:** Tuition: $18,675 full-time, $415 per credit hour part-time. Mandatory fees: $25 full-time. **Scholarships:** Available **Calendar System:** Semester, Summer Session Available **Enrollment:** FT 183, PT 146 **Faculty:** FT 7, PT 28 **Exams:** Other, SAT I or ACT **Library Holdings:** 1,500 **Regional Accreditation:** Middle State Association of Colleges and Schools **Credit Hours For Degree:** 68 semester hours, Associates

BRYANT AND STRATTON COLLEGE (WILLOUGHBY HILLS)
27557 Chardon Rd.
Willoughby Hills, OH 44092
Tel: (440)944-6800
Admissions: (440)444-6800
Web Site: http://www.bryantstratton.edu/
President/CEO: Dr. Ted Hansen
Admissions: William B. Schatt
Type: Two-Year College **Sex:** Coed **Affiliation:** Bryant and Stratton Business Institute, Inc **Scores:** 20% ACT 18-23 **Admission Plans:** Deferred Admission **Application Fee:** $25.00 **H.S. Requirements:** High school diploma or equivalent not required. For applicants 19 or older who meet entrance testing requirements: High school diploma or equivalent not required **Scholarships:** Available **Calendar System:** Semester, Summer Session Available **Enrollment:** FT 98, PT 74 **Faculty:** FT 3, PT 25 **Student-Faculty Ratio:** 10:1 **Exams:** Other, SAT I or ACT **Library Holdings:** 1,500 **Regional Accreditation:** Middle State Association of Colleges and Schools **Credit Hours For Degree:** 68 Semester hours, Associates **Intercollegiate Athletics:** Soccer M & W

CAPITAL UNIVERSITY
2199 East Main St.
Columbus, OH 43209-2394
Tel: (614)236-6011
Free: 800-289-6289
Admissions: (614)236-6101
Fax: (614)236-6820
E-mail: admissions@capital.edu
Web Site: http://www.capital.edu/
President/CEO: Dr. Theodore L. Fredrickson
Registrar: Amy Adams
Admissions: Kimberly V. Ebbrecht
Financial Aid: Jerry Wade
Type: Comprehensive **Sex:** Coed **Affiliation:** Evangelical Lutheran Church in America **Scores:** 97% SAT V 400+; 94% SAT M 400+; 53% ACT 18-23; 40% ACT 24-29 **% Accepted:** 78 **Admission Plans:** Early Action; Deferred Admission **Application Deadline:** April 15 **Application Fee:** $25.00 **H.S. Requirements:** High school diploma required; GED accepted **Costs Per Year:** Application fee: $25. Comprehensive fee: $30,444 includes full-time tuition ($24,100) and college room and board ($6344). Full-time tuition varies according to course load, degree level, program, and student level. Room and board charges vary according to board plan and housing facility. Part-time tuition: $756 per credit hour. Part-time tuition varies according to course load, degree level, program, and student level. **Scholarships:** Available **Calendar System:** Semester, Summer Session Available **Enrollment:** FT 2,242, PT 620, Grad 296 **Faculty:** FT 218, PT 242 **Student-Faculty Ratio:** 10:1 **Exams:** SAT I or ACT **% Receiving Financial Aid:** 81 **% Residing in College-Owned, -Operated, or -Affiliated Housing:** 36 **Library Holdings:** 187,281 **Regional Accreditation:** North Central Association of Colleges and Schools **Credit Hours For Degree:** 124 semester hours, Bachelors **ROTC:** Army, Air Force **Professional Accreditation:** AACN, ABA, AALS, ACBSP, CSWE, JRCEPAT, NASM, NCATE **Intercollegiate Athletics:** Baseball M; Basketball M & W; Cross-Country Running M & W; Football M; Golf M & W; Soccer M & W; Softball W; Tennis M & W; Track and Field M & W; Volleyball W

CASE WESTERN RESERVE UNIVERSITY
10900 Euclid Ave.
Cleveland, OH 44106
Tel: (216)368-2000
Admissions: (216)368-4450
Fax: (216)368-5111
E-mail: admission@case.edu
Web Site: http://www.case.edu/
President/CEO: Dr. Edward M. Hundert
Registrar: Amy Hammett
Admissions: Christopher Munoz
Financial Aid: Donald W. Chenelle
Type: University **Sex:** Coed **Scores:** 99.9% SAT V 400+; 100% SAT M 400+; 7.3% ACT 18-23; 42.9% ACT 24-29 **% Accepted:** 68 **Admission Plans:** Early Admission; Early Action; Deferred Admission **Application Deadline:** January 15 **Application Fee:** $35.00 **H.S. Requirements:** High school diploma required; GED accepted **Costs Per Year:** Application fee: $35. Comprehensive fee: $40,968 includes full-time tuition ($31,090), mandatory fees ($598), and college room and board ($9280). College room

only: $5440. Part-time tuition: $1296 per credit hour. **Scholarships:** Available **Calendar System:** Semester, Summer Session Available **Enrollment:** FT 3,714, PT 235, Grad 4,091 **Faculty:** FT 687, PT 166 **Student-Faculty Ratio:** 9:1 **Exams:** SAT I or ACT, SAT II **% Receiving Financial Aid:** 59 % **Residing in College-Owned, -Operated, or -Affiliated Housing:** 75 **Library Holdings:** 2,452,731 **Regional Accreditation:** North Central Association of Colleges and Schools **Credit Hours For Degree:** 120 credits, Bachelors **ROTC:** Army, Air Force **Professional Accreditation:** AACSB, ABET, ARCAA, AANA, ABA, ACNM, ADA, ADtA, APA, ASLHA, AALS, CSWE, LCMEAMA, NASM, NLN **Intercollegiate Athletics:** Archery M & W; Baseball M; Basketball M & W; Cheerleading M & W; Crew M & W; Cross-Country Running M & W; Fencing M & W; Football M; Ice Hockey M & W; Soccer M & W; Softball W; Swimming and Diving M & W; Tennis M & W; Track and Field M & W; Ultimate Frisbee M & W; Volleyball M & W; Wrestling M

CEDARVILLE UNIVERSITY
251 North Main St.
Cedarville, OH 45314-0601
Tel: (937)766-2211
Free: 800-CEDARVILLE
Admissions: (937)766-7700
Fax: (937)766-7575
E-mail: admiss@cedarville.edu
Web Site: http://www.cedarville.edu/
President/CEO: Dr. William Brown
Admissions: Roscoe Smith
Financial Aid: Fred Merritt
Type: Comprehensive **Sex:** Coed **Affiliation:** Baptist **Scores:** 100% SAT V 400+; 100% SAT M 400+; 35% ACT 18-23; 52% ACT 24-29 **% Accepted:** 83 **Admission Plans:** Early Admission; Deferred Admission **Application Deadline:** Rolling **Application Fee:** $30.00 **H.S. Requirements:** High school diploma required; GED accepted **Costs Per Year:** Application fee: $30. Comprehensive fee: $22,130 includes full-time tuition ($17,120) and college room and board ($5010). College room only: $2684. Part-time tuition: $535 per credit hour. **Scholarships:** Available **Calendar System:** Semester, Summer Session Available **Enrollment:** FT 2,930, PT 160, Grad 23 **Faculty:** FT 208, PT 51 **Student-Faculty Ratio:** 13:1 **Exams:** SAT I or ACT **% Receiving Financial Aid:** 61 **% Residing in College-Owned, -Operated, or -Affiliated Housing:** 83 **Library Holdings:** 162,195 **Regional Accreditation:** North Central Association of Colleges and Schools **Credit Hours For Degree:** 128 semester hour, Bachelors **ROTC:** Army, Air Force **Professional Accreditation:** ABET, AACN, CSWE **Intercollegiate Athletics:** Baseball M; Basketball M & W; Cross-Country Running M & W; Golf M; Soccer M & W; Softball W; Tennis M & W; Track and Field M & W; Volleyball W

CENTRAL OHIO TECHNICAL COLLEGE
1179 University Dr.
Newark, OH 43055-1767
Tel: (740)366-1351
Admissions: (740)366-9222
Fax: (740)366-5047
E-mail: lnelson@bigvax.newark.ohio-state.edu
Web Site: http://www.cotc.edu/
President/CEO: Dr. Anne C. Federlein
Registrar: Katheryn Duncan
Admissions: John K. Merrin
Financial Aid: Faith Phillips
Type: Two-Year College **Sex:** Coed **Affiliation:** Ohio Board of Regents **Admission Plans:** Open Admission; Early Admission; Deferred Admission **Application Fee:** $15.00 **H.S. Requirements:** High school diploma required; GED accepted **Scholarships:** Available **Calendar System:** Quarter, Summer Session Available **Enrollment:** FT 1,149, PT 1,443 **Faculty:** FT 50, PT 143 **Student-Faculty Ratio:** 45:1 **Exams:** Other **% Residing in College-Owned, -Operated, or -Affiliated Housing:** 1 **Library Holdings:** 45,000 **Regional Accreditation:** North Central Association of Colleges and Schools **Credit Hours For Degree:** 101 quarter hours, Associates **Professional Accreditation:** ARCEST, JRCEDMS, JRCERT, NLN **Intercollegiate Athletics:** Baseball M; Basketball M & W; Golf M & W; Soccer M; Softball W; Tennis M & W; Volleyball M & W

CENTRAL STATE UNIVERSITY
1400 Brush Row Rd.
PO Box 1004
Wilberforce, OH 45384
Tel: (937)376-6011
Admissions: (937)376-6580
Fax: (937)376-6648
E-mail: rrucker@centralstate.edu
Web Site: http://www.centralstate.edu/
President/CEO: John W. Garland
Registrar: Larry Cannon
Admissions: Robin Rucker
Financial Aid: Dr. Eric Hilton
Type: Comprehensive **Sex:** Coed **Affiliation:** Ohio Board of Regents **Scores:** 71% SAT V 400+; 60% SAT M 400+; 26% ACT 18-23; 1% ACT 24-29 **% Accepted:** 38 **Admission Plans:** Open Admission **Application Deadline:** June 15 **Application Fee:** $20.00 **H.S. Requirements:** High school diploma required; GED accepted **Costs Per Year:** Application fee: $20. State resident tuition: $2726 full-time. Nonresident tuition: $8546 full-time. Mandatory fees: $2268 full-time. Full-time tuition and fees vary according to course load. College room and board: $6982. Room and board charges vary according to board plan. **Scholarships:** Available **Calendar System:** Semester, Summer Session Available **Enrollment:** FT 1,450, PT 167, Grad 6 **Faculty:** FT 94, PT 68 **Student-Faculty Ratio:** 13:1 **Exams:** ACT, SAT I or ACT **% Residing in College-Owned, -Operated, or -Affiliated Housing:** 50 **Library Holdings:** 280,470 **Regional Accreditation:** North Central Association of Colleges and Schools **Credit Hours For Degree:** 186 quarter hours, Bachelors **ROTC:** Army **Professional Accreditation:** ABET, NASM **Intercollegiate Athletics:** Basketball M & W; Cheerleading M & W; Cross-Country Running M & W; Golf M & W; Tennis M & W; Track and Field M & W; Volleyball W

CHATFIELD COLLEGE
20918 State Route 251
St. Martin, OH 45118-9705
Tel: (513)875-3344
Fax: (513)875-3912
E-mail: ajones@chatfield.edu
Web Site: http://www.chatfield.edu/
President/CEO: Nancy Linenkugel, OSF
Registrar: Robert B. Peiffer, PhD
Admissions: Anna Jones
Financial Aid: Becky Cluxton
Type: Two-Year College **Sex:** Coed **Affiliation:** Roman Catholic Church **% Accepted:** 100 **Admission Plans:** Open Admission; Early Admission; Deferred Admission **Application Deadline:** Rolling **Application Fee:** $10.00 **H.S. Requirements:** High school diploma required; GED accepted **Costs Per Year:** Application fee: $10. Tuition: $3360 full-time, $280 per credit hour part-time. Mandatory fees: $80 full-time. **Scholarships:** Available **Calendar System:** Semester, Summer Session Available **Faculty:** FT 3, PT 40 **Student-Faculty Ratio:** 12:1 **Library Holdings:** 15,000 **Regional Accreditation:** North Central Association of Colleges and Schools **Credit Hours For Degree:** 62 semester hours, Associates

CINCINNATI CHRISTIAN UNIVERSITY
2700 Glenway Ave.
PO Box 04320
Cincinnati, OH 45204-3200
Tel: (513)244-8100
Free: 800-949-4CBC
Admissions: 800-949-4222
Fax: (513)244-8140
Web Site: http://www.ccuniversity.edu/
President/CEO: Dr. David M. Faust
Registrar: Don Thomason
Admissions: Alex Eady
Financial Aid: Carrie Derico
Type: Comprehensive **Sex:** Coed **Affiliation:** Church of Christ **Scores:** 98% SAT V 400+; 96% SAT M 400+; 45% ACT 18-23; 42% ACT 24-29 **Admission Plans:** Early Admission; Deferred Admission **Application Fee:** $35.00 **H.S. Requirements:** High school diploma required; GED accepted. For nontraditional students: High school diploma or equivalent not required **Costs Per Year:** Application fee: $35. Comprehensive fee: $15,080 includes full-time tuition ($9120), mandatory fees ($570), and college room and board ($5390). Part-time tuition: $285 per credit hour. Part-time mandatory fees: $75 per term. **Scholarships:** Available **Calendar System:** Semester, Summer Session Available **Enrollment:** FT 501, PT 125, Grad 240 **Faculty:** FT 30, PT 33 **Student-Faculty Ratio:** 16:1 **Exams:** SAT I or ACT **% Receiving**

Financial Aid: 87 **Library Holdings:** 93,000 **Regional Accreditation:** North Central Association of Colleges and Schools **Credit Hours For Degree:** 66 semester hours, Associates; 132 semester hours, Bachelors **Professional Accreditation:** AABC, ATS **Intercollegiate Athletics:** Basketball M & W; Golf M; Soccer M & W; Volleyball W

CINCINNATI COLLEGE OF MORTUARY SCIENCE
645 West North Bend Rd.
Cincinnati, OH 45224-1462
Tel: (513)761-2020
Fax: (513)761-3333
Web Site: http://www.ccms.edu/
President/CEO: Dr. Dan Flory
Registrar: Patricia Jennings
Admissions: Dr. Dan Flory
Financial Aid: Patsy Leon
Type: Two-Year College **Sex:** Coed **% Accepted:** 100 **Admission Plans:** Deferred Admission **Application Deadline:** Rolling **Application Fee:** $25.00 **H.S. Requirements:** High school diploma required; GED accepted **Costs Per Year:** Application fee: $25. Tuition: $13,500 full-time, $180 per credit hour part-time. **Scholarships:** Available **Calendar System:** Quarter, Summer Session Available **Enrollment:** FT 133 **Faculty:** FT 9, PT 5 **Student-Faculty Ratio:** 5:1 **Library Holdings:** 5,000 **Regional Accreditation:** North Central Association of Colleges and Schools **Credit Hours For Degree:** 99 quarter hours, Associates; 180 quarter hours, Bachelors **Professional Accreditation:** ABFSE

CINCINNATI STATE TECHNICAL AND COMMUNITY COLLEGE
3520 Central Parkway
Cincinnati, OH 45223-2690
Tel: (513)569-1500
Admissions: (513)569-1550
Fax: (513)569-1562
E-mail: gaby.boeckermann@cincinnatistate.edu
Web Site: http://www.cincinnatistate.edu/
President/CEO: Dr. Ronald Wright
Admissions: Gabriele Boeckermann
Financial Aid: Dawnia Reick
Type: Two-Year College **Sex:** Coed **Affiliation:** Ohio Board of Regents **Admission Plans:** Open Admission **Application Deadline:** Rolling **Application Fee:** $0.00 **H.S. Requirements:** High school diploma required; GED accepted **Costs Per Year:** Application fee: $0. State resident tuition: $4411 full-time, $80.20 per credit hour part-time. Nonresident tuition: $8822 full-time, $160.40 per credit hour part-time. Mandatory fees: $344 full-time, $6 per credit hour part-time, $31 per term part-time. **Scholarships:** Available **Calendar System:** Miscellaneous, Summer Session Available **Enrollment:** FT 3,485, PT 4,985 **Faculty:** FT 182, PT 388 **Student-Faculty Ratio:** 17:1 **Library Holdings:** 30,762 **Regional Accreditation:** North Central Association of Colleges and Schools **Credit Hours For Degree:** 102 credit hours, Associates **Professional Accreditation:** ABET, ARCEST, AAMAE, ACCE, ACF, AHIMA, AOTA, CARC, NAACLS, NLN **Intercollegiate Athletics:** Basketball M & W; Golf M & W; Soccer M & W

CIRCLEVILLE BIBLE COLLEGE
1476 Lancaster Pike, PO Box 458
Circleville, OH 43113-9487
Tel: (740)474-8896
Free: 800-701-0222
Admissions: (740)477-7741
Fax: (740)477-7755
E-mail: sfaughn@biblecollege.edu
Web Site: http://www.biblecollege.edu/
President/CEO: Dr. John W. Conley
Registrar: Shirley Pollard
Admissions: Scott Faughn
Financial Aid: Dan Starkey
Type: Four-Year College **Sex:** Coed **Affiliation:** Churches of Christ in Christian Union **Scores:** 52% ACT 18-23; 18% ACT 24-29 **Admission Plans:** Early Admission **Application Fee:** $25.00 **H.S. Requirements:** High school diploma required; GED accepted **Costs Per Year:** Application fee: $25. Comprehensive fee: $16,436 includes full-time tuition ($9596), mandatory fees ($956), and college room and board ($5884). Part-time tuition: $370 per semester hour. Part-time mandatory fees: $345 per term. **Scholarships:** Available **Calendar System:** Semester, Summer Session Available **Enrollment:** FT 284, PT 33 **Faculty:** FT 10, PT 28 **Student-Faculty Ratio:** 13:1 **Exams:** ACT, SAT I **% Receiving Financial Aid:** 94 **% Residing in College-Owned, -Operated, or -Affiliated Housing:** 55 **Library Holdings:** 37,521 **Regional Accreditation:** North Central Association of Colleges and Schools **Credit Hours For Degree:** 62 semester hours, Associates; 124 semester hours, Bachelors **Professional Accreditation:** AABC **Intercollegiate Athletics:** Baseball M; Basketball M & W; Volleyball W

CLARK STATE COMMUNITY COLLEGE
570 East Leffel Ln., PO Box 570
Springfield, OH 45501-0570
Tel: (937)325-0691
Admissions: (937)328-6027
E-mail: schaidja@clarkstate.edu
Web Site: http://www.clarkstate.edu/
President/CEO: Dr. Karen E. Rafinski
Registrar: Elizabeth Deger
Admissions: Julie Schaid
Financial Aid: Kathy A. Schuler
Type: Two-Year College **Sex:** Coed **Affiliation:** Ohio Board of Regents **% Accepted:** 100 **Admission Plans:** Open Admission; Early Admission; Deferred Admission **Application Deadline:** Rolling **Application Fee:** $15.00 **Costs Per Year:** Application fee: $15. State resident tuition: $3720 full-time, $77.50 per credit hour part-time. Nonresident tuition: $7440 full-time, $155 per credit hour part-time. Mandatory fees: $1500 full-time. **Scholarships:** Available **Calendar System:** Quarter, Summer Session Available **Enrollment:** FT 1,583, PT 1,921 **Faculty:** FT 57, PT 232 **Student-Faculty Ratio:** 16:1 **Library Holdings:** 31,988 **Regional Accreditation:** North Central Association of Colleges and Schools **Credit Hours For Degree:** 90 credit hours, Associates **ROTC:** Army **Professional Accreditation:** APTA, NAACLS, NLN **Intercollegiate Athletics:** Basketball M & W; Softball W; Volleyball W

THE CLEVELAND INSTITUTE OF ART
11141 East Blvd.
Cleveland, OH 44106-1700
Tel: (216)421-7000
Free: 800-223-4700
Admissions: (216)421-7418
Fax: (216)421-7438
E-mail: 74527.17@compuserve.com
Web Site: http://www.cia.edu/
President/CEO: David Deming
Registrar: Karen Hudy
Admissions: Catherine Redhead
Financial Aid: Michael Warinner
Type: Comprehensive **Sex:** Coed **Scores:** 98% SAT V 400+; 90% SAT M 400+; 49% ACT 18-23; 30% ACT 24-29 **Admission Plans:** Deferred Admission **Application Fee:** $30.00 **H.S. Requirements:** High school diploma required; GED accepted **Costs Per Year:** Application fee: $30. Comprehensive fee: $36,313 includes full-time tuition ($24,917), mandatory fees ($2260), and college room and board ($9136). College room only: $5480. Room and board charges vary according to board plan and housing facility. Part-time tuition: $1045 per credit. Part-time mandatory fees: $90 per credit. Part-time tuition and fees vary according to course load. **Scholarships:** Available **Calendar System:** Semester, Summer Session Not available **Enrollment:** FT 581, PT 23, Grad 5 **Faculty:** FT 47, PT 54 **Student-Faculty Ratio:** 9:1 **Exams:** SAT I or ACT **% Receiving Financial Aid:** 81 **% Residing in College-Owned, -Operated, or -Affiliated Housing:** 20 **Library Holdings:** 42,000 **Regional Accreditation:** North Central Association of Colleges and Schools **Professional Accreditation:** NASAD

CLEVELAND INSTITUTE OF ELECTRONICS
1776 East Seventeenth St.
Cleveland, OH 44114-3636
Tel: (216)781-9400
Free: 800-243-6446
Web Site: http://www.cie-wc.edu/
President/CEO: John R. Drinko
Registrar: Daniel Tuma
Financial Aid: Marites C. Capistrano
Type: Two-Year College **Sex:** Coed **Admission Plans:** Open Admission; Early Admission **Application Deadline:** Rolling **H.S. Requirements:** High school diploma required; GED accepted **Costs Per Year:** Tuition: $1770 per term part-time. **Calendar System:** Continuous, Summer Session Not available **Faculty:** FT 3, PT 3 **Library Holdings:** 5,000 **Credit Hours For**

Degree: 106 quarter hours, Associates **Professional Accreditation:** DETC

CLEVELAND INSTITUTE OF MUSIC
11021 East Blvd.
Cleveland, OH 44106-1776
Tel: (216)791-5000
Admissions: (216)795-3107
Fax: (216)791-1530
E-mail: cimadmission@po.cwru.edu
Web Site: http://www.cim.edu/
President/CEO: David Cerone
Registrar: Hallie B. Moore
Admissions: William Fay
Financial Aid: Kristine Gripp
Type: Comprehensive **Sex:** Coed **% Accepted:** 34 **Admission Plans:** Early Admission; Deferred Admission **Application Deadline:** December 01 **Application Fee:** $100.00 **H.S. Requirements:** High school diploma required; GED accepted **Costs Per Year:** Application fee: $100. Comprehensive fee: $35,596 includes full-time tuition ($25,870), mandatory fees ($1000), and college room and board ($8726). College room only: $5120. Room and board charges vary according to board plan. Part-time tuition: $1078 per credit hour. **Scholarships:** Available **Calendar System:** Semester, Summer Session Available **Enrollment:** FT 243, PT 1, Grad 165 **Faculty:** FT 33, PT 72 **Student-Faculty Ratio:** 7:1 **Exams:** SAT I or ACT, SAT I and SAT II **% Receiving Financial Aid:** 62 **% Residing in College-Owned, -Operated, or -Affiliated Housing:** 40 **Library Holdings:** 50,924 **Regional Accreditation:** North Central Association of Colleges and Schools **Credit Hours For Degree:** 124 credits, Bachelors **ROTC:** Army, Air Force **Professional Accreditation:** NASM

CLEVELAND STATE UNIVERSITY
2121 Euclid Ave.
Cleveland, OH 44115
Tel: (216)687-2000; 888-CSU-OHIO
Fax: (216)687-9366
Web Site: http://www.csuohio.edu/
President/CEO: Dr. Michael Schwartz
Registrar: Ronald Bowman
Financial Aid: Rachel M. Schmidt
Type: University **Sex:** Coed **Scores:** 78% SAT V 400+; 79% SAT M 400+; 45% ACT 18-23; 15% ACT 24-29 **% Accepted:** 80 **Admission Plans:** Open Admission; Deferred Admission **Application Deadline:** Rolling **Application Fee:** $30.00 **H.S. Requirements:** High school diploma required; GED accepted **Costs Per Year:** Application fee: $30. State resident tuition: $6792 full-time, $283 per semester hour part-time. Nonresident tuition: $9216 full-time, $384 per semester hour part-time. Full-time tuition varies according to program and student level. Part-time tuition varies according to program and student level. College room and board: $6809. College room only: $4091. Room and board charges vary according to board plan and housing facility. **Scholarships:** Available **Calendar System:** Semester, Summer Session Available **Enrollment:** FT 6,771, PT 3,182, Grad 5,019 **Faculty:** FT 575, PT 422 **Student-Faculty Ratio:** 14:1 **Exams:** SAT I or ACT **% Receiving Financial Aid:** 70 **% Residing in College-Owned, -Operated, or -Affiliated Housing:** 3 **Library Holdings:** 484,914 **Regional Accreditation:** North Central Association of Colleges and Schools **Credit Hours For Degree:** 120 semester hours, Bachelors **ROTC:** Army, Navy, Air Force **Professional Accreditation:** AACSB, ABET, ACEHSA, AACN, ABA, ACA, ACSP, AOTA, APTA, ASLHA, AALS, CEPH, CSWE, NASM, NASPAA, NCATE, NLN **Intercollegiate Athletics:** Baseball M; Basketball M & W; Cross-Country Running W; Fencing M & W; Golf M; Soccer M; Softball W; Swimming and Diving M & W; Tennis W; Track and Field W; Volleyball W; Wrestling M

COLLEGE OF ART ADVERTISING
4343 Bridgetown Rd.
Cincinnati, OH 45211-4427
Tel: (513)574-1010
Admissions: (937)294-0592
Fax: (513)574-6116
E-mail: janet.bussberg@fuse.net
Web Site: http://www.collegeofartadvertising.com/
President/CEO: Sandy Neff
Admissions: Janet Bussberg
Financial Aid: Gary Lay
Type: Two-Year College **Scholarships:** Available **Calendar System:** Quarter **Professional Accreditation:** ACCSCT

COLLEGE OF MOUNT ST. JOSEPH
5701 Delhi Rd.
Cincinnati, OH 45233-1670
Tel: (513)244-4200
Free: 800-654-9314
Admissions: (513)244-4531
Fax: (513)244-4629
E-mail: peggy_minnich@mail.msj.edu
Web Site: http://www.msj.edu/
President/CEO: Sr. Francis Marie Thrailkill, OSU
Registrar: Lew Rita Moore
Admissions: Peggy Minnich
Financial Aid: Kathryn Kelly
Type: Comprehensive **Sex:** Coed **Affiliation:** Roman Catholic **Scores:** 89% SAT V 400+; 88% SAT M 400+; 58% ACT 18-23; 23% ACT 24-29 **% Accepted:** 73 **Admission Plans:** Deferred Admission **Application Deadline:** August 15 **Application Fee:** $25.00 **H.S. Requirements:** High school diploma required; GED accepted **Costs Per Year:** Application fee: $25. Comprehensive fee: $24,860 includes full-time tuition ($18,400), mandatory fees ($390), and college room and board ($6070). College room only: $3000. Full-time tuition and fees vary according to course load, program, and reciprocity agreements. Room and board charges vary according to board plan and housing facility. Part-time tuition: $430 per semester hour. Part-time mandatory fees: $65 per term. Part-time tuition and fees vary according to course load, location, program, and reciprocity agreements. **Scholarships:** Available **Calendar System:** Semester, Summer Session Available **Enrollment:** FT 1,338, PT 597, Grad 298 **Faculty:** FT 124, PT 109 **Student-Faculty Ratio:** 11:1 **Exams:** SAT I or ACT **% Receiving Financial Aid:** 68 **% Residing in College-Owned, -Operated, or -Affiliated Housing:** 23 **Library Holdings:** 97,576 **Regional Accreditation:** North Central Association of Colleges and Schools **Credit Hours For Degree:** 64 semester hours, Associates; 128 semester hours, Bachelors **ROTC:** Army, Air Force **Professional Accreditation:** APTA, CSWE, NASM, NLN **Intercollegiate Athletics:** Baseball M; Basketball M & W; Cheerleading W; Cross-Country Running M & W; Football M; Golf M & W; Soccer M & W; Softball W; Tennis M & W; Track and Field M & W; Volleyball W; Wrestling M

THE COLLEGE OF WOOSTER
1189 Beall Ave.
Wooster, OH 44691-2363
Tel: (330)263-2000
Free: 800-877-9905
Admissions: (330)263-2270
Fax: (330)263-2621
E-mail: admissions@acs.wooster.edu
Web Site: http://www.wooster.edu/
President/CEO: Dr. R. Stanton Hales, Jr.
Registrar: Dr. Robert Blair
Admissions: Derek Guelden Zoph
Financial Aid: Dr. David Miller
Type: Four-Year College **Sex:** Coed **Affiliation:** Presbyterian Church (U.S.A.) **Scores:** 99.7% SAT V 400+; 100% SAT M 400+; 28.3% ACT 18-23; 56.4% ACT 24-29 **% Accepted:** 75 **Admission Plans:** Early Admission; Early Decision Plan; Deferred Admission **Application Deadline:** February 15 **Application Fee:** $40.00 **H.S. Requirements:** High school diploma required; GED accepted **Costs Per Year:** Application fee: $40. Comprehensive fee: $35,290 includes full-time tuition ($28,230) and college room and board ($7060). College room only: $3210. Full-time tuition varies according to course load and reciprocity agreements. **Scholarships:** Available **Calendar System:** Semester, Summer Session Available **Enrollment:** FT 1,813, PT 33 **Faculty:** FT 133, PT 58 **Student-Faculty Ratio:** 12:1 **Exams:** SAT I or ACT **% Receiving Financial Aid:** 58 **% Residing in College-Owned, -Operated, or -Affiliated Housing:** 99 **Library Holdings:** 581,518 **Regional Accreditation:** North Central Association of Colleges and Schools **Credit Hours For Degree:** 32 courses, Bachelors **Professional Accreditation:** NASM **Intercollegiate Athletics:** Badminton M & W; Baseball M; Basketball M & W; Cheerleading W; Cross-Country Running M & W; Field

Hockey W; Football M; Golf M; Lacrosse M & W; Rugby M & W; Soccer M & W; Softball W; Swimming and Diving M & W; Tennis M & W; Track and Field M & W; Volleyball M & W

COLUMBUS COLLEGE OF ART & DESIGN
107 North Ninth St.
Columbus, OH 43215-1758
Tel: (614)224-9101; 877-997-2223
Web Site: http://www.ccad.edu/
President/CEO: Dennison W. Griffith
Registrar: Yadigar Collins
Financial Aid: Anna Schofield
Type: Four-Year College **Sex:** Coed **Scores:** 94% SAT V 400+; 89% SAT M 400+; 56% ACT 18-23; 22% ACT 24-29 **% Accepted:** 72 **Admission Plans:** Deferred Admission **Application Deadline:** Rolling **Application Fee:** $25.00 **H.S. Requirements:** High school diploma required; GED accepted **Costs Per Year:** Application fee: $25. Comprehensive fee: $26,728 includes full-time tuition ($19,728), mandatory fees ($550), and college room and board ($6450). Room and board charges vary according to housing facility and student level. Part-time tuition: $822 per credit. Part-time mandatory fees: $275 per term. Part-time tuition and fees vary according to course load. **Scholarships:** Available **Calendar System:** Semester, Summer Session Available **Enrollment:** FT 1,256, PT 199 **Faculty:** FT 76, PT 105 **Student-Faculty Ratio:** 12:1 **Exams:** SAT I or ACT **% Receiving Financial Aid:** 79 **% Residing in College-Owned, -Operated, or -Affiliated Housing:** 20 **Library Holdings:** 49,330 **Regional Accreditation:** North Central Association of Colleges and Schools **Credit Hours For Degree:** 129 semester hours, Bachelors **Professional Accreditation:** FIDER, NASAD

COLUMBUS STATE COMMUNITY COLLEGE
Box 1609
Columbus, OH 43216-1609
Tel: (614)287-2400
Free: 800-621-6407
Admissions: (614)287-2669
Fax: (614)287-5117
E-mail: kconner@cscc.edu
Web Site: http://www.cscc.edu/
President/CEO: Dr. M. Valeriana Moeller
Registrar: Dr. Regina Peal
Admissions: Diane James
Financial Aid: Martin Maliwesky
Type: Two-Year College **Sex:** Coed **Affiliation:** Ohio Board of Regents **Admission Plans:** Open Admission; Early Admission; Deferred Admission **Application Fee:** $10.00 **H.S. Requirements:** High school diploma or equivalent not required. For most technology programs, gerontology, health information management, interpreting, chef's apprentice, nursing, radiology: High school diploma required; GED accepted. **Costs Per Year:** Application fee: $10. One-time mandatory fee: $35. State resident tuition: $2736 full-time, $76 per credit part-time. Nonresident tuition: $6048 full-time, $168 per credit part-time. **Scholarships:** Available **Calendar System:** Quarter, Summer Session Available **Enrollment:** FT 8,530, PT 13,342 **Faculty:** FT 263, PT 1,404 **Student-Faculty Ratio:** 19:1 **Exams:** Other **Library Holdings:** 38,192 **Regional Accreditation:** North Central Association of Colleges and Schools **Credit Hours For Degree:** 92 quarter hours, Associates **ROTC:** Army, Air Force **Professional Accreditation:** ABET, ARCEST, AAMAE, ACCE, ACF, ADA, AHIMA, ACBSP, CARC, JRCERT, JRCEMT, NAACLS, NLN **Intercollegiate Athletics:** Baseball M; Basketball M & W; Cross-Country Running M & W; Equestrian Sports M & W; Golf M; Soccer M; Softball W; Volleyball W

CUYAHOGA COMMUNITY COLLEGE
700 Carnegie Ave.
Cleveland, OH 44115-2878
Tel: (216)987-6000
Free: 800-954-8742
Admissions: (216)987-4030
Fax: (216)987-5050
Web Site: http://www.tri-c.edu/
President/CEO: Dr. Jerry Sue Thornton
Registrar: Rena Waghani-Mason
Admissions: Kevin McDaniel
Financial Aid: Rhonda McKinnon
Type: Two-Year College **Sex:** Coed **% Accepted:** 100 **Admission Plans:** Open Admission; Early Admission; Deferred Admission **Application Deadline:** Rolling **Application Fee:** $0.00 **H.S. Requirements:** High school diploma or equivalent not required **Costs Per Year:** Application fee: $0. Area resident tuition: $2416 full-time, $80.54 per credit hour part-time. State resident tuition: $3194 full-time, $106.48 per credit hour part-time. Nonresident tuition: $6541 full-time, $218.04 per credit hour part-time. **Scholarships:** Available **Calendar System:** Semester, Summer Session Available **Enrollment:** FT 10,326, PT 15,032 **Faculty:** FT 294, PT 1,210 **Student-Faculty Ratio:** 18:1 **Library Holdings:** 177,767 **Regional Accreditation:** North Central Association of Colleges and Schools **Credit Hours For Degree:** 64 credit hours, Associates **Professional Accreditation:** ARCEST, ACF, ADA, AHIMA, AOTA, APTA, ACBSP, CARC, JRCEDMS, JRCERT, JRCNMT, NLN **Intercollegiate Athletics:** Baseball M; Basketball M; Cross-Country Running M & W; Soccer M; Softball W

DAVID N. MYERS UNIVERSITY
112 Prospect Ave.
Cleveland, OH 44115
Tel: (216)696-9000
Free: 800-424-3953
Admissions: (216)523-3806
Fax: (216)523-3808
E-mail: mquinn@dnmyers.edu
Web Site: http://www.dnmyers.edu/
President/CEO: Dr. Paul Feingold
Registrar: Bobbie Lynch
Admissions: Dr. Michelita Quinn
Financial Aid: Miria Batig
Type: Comprehensive **Sex:** Coed **Admission Plans:** Early Admission; Deferred Admission **Application Fee:** $25.00 **H.S. Requirements:** High school diploma required; GED accepted **Costs Per Year:** Application fee: $25. Tuition: $9840 full-time. **Scholarships:** Available **Calendar System:** Semester, Summer Session Available **Enrollment:** FT 573, PT 523, Grad 81 **Faculty:** FT 17, PT 148 **Student-Faculty Ratio:** 12:1 **Exams:** SAT I or ACT **% Receiving Financial Aid:** 67 **Library Holdings:** 15,027 **Regional Accreditation:** North Central Association of Colleges and Schools **Credit Hours For Degree:** 60 credits, Associates; 120 credits, Bachelors

DAVIS COLLEGE
4747 Monroe St.
Toledo, OH 43623-4307
Tel: (419)473-2700
Free: 800-477-7021
Web Site: http://daviscollege.edu/
President/CEO: Diane Brunner
Registrar: Marsha Klingbeil
Admissions: Dana Stern
Financial Aid: Todd Matthews
Type: Two-Year College **Sex:** Coed **% Accepted:** 100 **Admission Plans:** Early Admission; Deferred Admission **Application Deadline:** Rolling **Application Fee:** $30.00 **H.S. Requirements:** High school diploma required; GED accepted **Costs Per Year:** Application fee: $30. Tuition: $8100 full-time, $225 per credit hour part-time. Mandatory fees: $480 full-time. **Scholarships:** Available **Calendar System:** Quarter, Summer Session Available **Enrollment:** FT 225, PT 226 **Faculty:** FT 14, PT 9 **Student-Faculty Ratio:** 14:1 **Exams:** Other **Library Holdings:** 3,207 **Regional Accreditation:** North Central Association of Colleges and Schools **Credit Hours For Degree:** 94 credit hours, Associates **Professional Accreditation:** AAMAE

DEFIANCE COLLEGE
701 North Clinton St.
Defiance, OH 43512-1610
Tel: (419)784-4010
Free: 800-520-4632
Admissions: (419)783-2361
Fax: (419)783-2468
Web Site: http://www.defiance.edu/
President/CEO: Dr. Gerald E. Wood
Registrar: Beverly J. Harrington
Admissions: William Nunn
Financial Aid: Amy Francis
Type: Comprehensive **Sex:** Coed **Affiliation:** United Church of Christ **Scores:** 92.5% SAT V 400+; 85.2% SAT M 400+; 57.4% ACT 18-23; 26.5% ACT 24-29 **% Accepted:** 72 **Admission Plans:** Deferred Admission **Application Deadline:** August 15 **Application Fee:** $25.00 **H.S. Require-**

ments: High school diploma required; GED accepted **Costs Per Year:** Application fee: $25. Comprehensive fee: $25,910 includes full-time tuition ($19,260), mandatory fees ($480), and college room and board ($6170). College room only: $3150. Part-time tuition: $325 per credit hour. Part-time mandatory fees: $65 per term. **Scholarships:** Available **Calendar System:** Semester, Summer Session Available **Enrollment:** FT 673, PT 154, Grad 103 **Faculty:** FT 38, PT 50 **Student-Faculty Ratio:** 15:1 **Exams:** SAT I or ACT **% Receiving Financial Aid:** 83 **% Residing in College-Owned, -Operated, or -Affiliated Housing:** 55 **Library Holdings:** 88,000 **Regional Accreditation:** North Central Association of Colleges and Schools **Credit Hours For Degree:** 60 semester hours, Associates; 120 semester hours, Bachelors **Professional Accreditation:** CSWE **Intercollegiate Athletics:** Baseball M; Basketball M & W; Cross-Country Running M & W; Football M; Golf M & W; Soccer M & W; Softball W; Tennis M & W; Track and Field M & W; Volleyball W

DENISON UNIVERSITY
Granville, OH 43023
Tel: (740)587-0810
Free: 800-DEN-ISON
Admissions: (740)587-6276
Fax: (740)587-6306
E-mail: admissions@denison.edu
Web Site: http://www.denison.edu/
President/CEO: Dr. Dale T. Knobel
Registrar: Larry Murdock
Admissions: Perry Robinson
Financial Aid: Nancy Hoover
Type: Four-Year College **Sex:** Coed **Scores:** 100% SAT V 400+; 100% SAT M 400+; 14% ACT 18-23; 63% ACT 24-29 **% Accepted:** 39 **Admission Plans:** Early Admission; Early Decision Plan; Deferred Admission **Application Deadline:** January 15 **Application Fee:** $40.00 **H.S. Requirements:** High school diploma required; GED accepted **Costs Per Year:** Application fee: $40. Comprehensive fee: $37,040 includes full-time tuition ($28,170), mandatory fees ($750), and college room and board ($8120). College room only: $4470. Room and board charges vary according to housing facility. Part-time tuition: $880 per semester hour. Part-time tuition varies according to course load. **Scholarships:** Available **Calendar System:** Semester, Summer Session Not available **Enrollment:** FT 2,292, PT 37 **Faculty:** FT 183, PT 15 **Student-Faculty Ratio:** 11:1 **Exams:** SAT I or ACT **% Receiving Financial Aid:** 44 **% Residing in College-Owned, -Operated, or -Affiliated Housing:** 98 **Library Holdings:** 784,189 **Regional Accreditation:** North Central Association of Colleges and Schools **Credit Hours For Degree:** 127 credit hours, Bachelors **ROTC:** Army **Intercollegiate Athletics:** Baseball M; Basketball M & W; Crew M; Cross-Country Running M & W; Equestrian Sports M & W; Field Hockey W; Football M; Golf M; Ice Hockey M; Lacrosse M & W; Riflery M & W; Rugby M & W; Sailing M & W; Skiing (Downhill) M & W; Soccer M & W; Softball W; Squash M & W; Swimming and Diving M & W; Tennis M & W; Track and Field M & W; Volleyball W

DEVRY UNIVERSITY (CLEVELAND)
200 Public Square, Ste. 150
Cleveland, OH 44114-2301
Tel: (216)781-8000
Fax: (216)781-8001
Web Site: http://www.devry.edu/ **Type:** Comprehensive **Sex:** Coed **Costs Per Year:** One-time mandatory fee: $40. Tuition: $11,790 full-time, $440 per credit part-time. Mandatory fees: $60 full-time, $30 per year part-time. Full-time tuition and fees vary according to course load. Part-time tuition and fees vary according to course load. **Calendar System:** Semester **Regional Accreditation:** North Central Association of Colleges and Schools

DEVRY UNIVERSITY (COLUMBUS)
1350 Alum Creek Dr.
Columbus, OH 43209-2705
Tel: (614)253-7291
Free: 800-426-2206
Web Site: http://www.devry.edu/
President/CEO: John Ballheim
Registrar: Robert Mitchell
Financial Aid: Jeanne Farnlacher
Type: Comprehensive **Sex:** Coed **Affiliation:** DeVry University **Admission Plans:** Deferred Admission **Application Deadline:** Rolling **Application Fee:** $50.00 **H.S. Requirements:** High school diploma required; GED accepted **Costs Per Year:** Application fee: $50. One-time mandatory fee: $40. Tuition: $11,790 full-time, $440 per credit part-time. Mandatory fees: $270 full-time, $160 per year part-time. Full-time tuition and fees vary according to course load. Part-time tuition and fees vary according to course load. **Scholarships:** Available **Calendar System:** Semester, Summer Session Available **Enrollment:** FT 1,653, PT 770, Grad 220 **Faculty:** FT 60, PT 56 **Student-Faculty Ratio:** 26:1 **% Receiving Financial Aid:** 73 **Library Holdings:** 30,000 **Regional Accreditation:** North Central Association of Colleges and Schools **Credit Hours For Degree:** 86 credit hours, Associates; 122 credit hours, Bachelors **ROTC:** Army **Professional Accreditation:** ABET

DEVRY UNIVERSITY (SEVEN HILLS)
The Genesis Bldg.
6000 Lombardo Center
Seven Hills, OH 44131-6907
Tel: (216)328-8754; (866)453-3879
Fax: (216)328-8764
Web Site: http://www.devry.edu/ **Type:** Comprehensive **Sex:** Coed **Costs Per Year:** One-time mandatory fee: $40. Tuition: $11,790 full-time, $440 per credit part-time. Mandatory fees: $60 full-time, $30 per year part-time. Full-time tuition and fees vary according to course load. Part-time tuition and fees vary according to course load. **Calendar System:** Semester **Regional Accreditation:** North Central Association of Colleges and Schools

EDISON STATE COMMUNITY COLLEGE
1973 Edison Dr.
Piqua, OH 45356-9253
Tel: (937)778-8600
Fax: (937)778-1920
E-mail: info@edison.cc.oh.us
Web Site: http://www.edisonohio.edu/
President/CEO: Dr. Kenneth A. Yowell
Registrar: Nancy Rush
Admissions: Beth Iams Culbertson
Financial Aid: Lisa Waldrop
Type: Two-Year College **Sex:** Coed **Affiliation:** Ohio Board of Regents **Admission Plans:** Open Admission; Early Admission; Deferred Admission **Application Fee:** $15.00 **H.S. Requirements:** High school diploma required; GED accepted **Calendar System:** Semester, Summer Session Available **Enrollment:** FT 1,028, PT 1,972 **Faculty:** FT 42, PT 256 **Student-Faculty Ratio:** 19:1 **Exams:** Other, SAT I or ACT **Library Holdings:** 29,851 **Regional Accreditation:** North Central Association of Colleges and Schools **Credit Hours For Degree:** 60 credit hours, Associates **ROTC:** Army, Air Force **Professional Accreditation:** NLN **Intercollegiate Athletics:** Basketball M & W; Volleyball W

ETI TECHNICAL COLLEGE OF NILES
2076 Youngstown-Warren Rd.
Niles, OH 44446-4398
Tel: (330)652-9919
Fax: (330)652-4399
Web Site: http://www.eti-college.com/
President/CEO: Renee Zuzolo
Registrar: Sherrie L. Seruga
Admissions: Diane Marstellar
Financial Aid: Kay Madigan
Type: Two-Year College **Sex:** Coed **Admission Plans:** Open Admission; Early Admission; Deferred Admission **Application Fee:** $50.00 **H.S. Requirements:** High school diploma required; GED accepted **Scholarships:** Available **Calendar System:** Semester, Summer Session Not available **Enrollment:** FT 186, PT 36 **Faculty:** FT 8, PT 6 **Student-Faculty Ratio:** 15:1 **Exams:** ACT, SAT I **Credit Hours For Degree:** 72 credits, Associates **Professional Accreditation:** ACCSCT

FRANCISCAN UNIVERSITY OF STEUBENVILLE
1235 University Blvd.
Steubenville, OH 43952-1763
Tel: (740)283-3771
Free: 800-783-6220
Admissions: (740)283-6226
Fax: (740)283-6472
E-mail: admissions@franciscan.edu
Web Site: http://www.franciscan.edu/

President/CEO: Rev. Terence Henry
Registrar: Kathryn Reehl
Admissions: Margaret Weber
Financial Aid: John Herrmann
Type: Comprehensive **Sex:** Coed **Affiliation:** Roman Catholic **Scores:** 100% SAT V 400+; 99% SAT M 400+; 38% ACT 18-23; 50% ACT 24-29 **% Accepted:** 81 **Admission Plans:** Early Admission; Deferred Admission **Application Fee:** $20.00 **H.S. Requirements:** High school diploma required; GED accepted **Costs Per Year:** Application fee: $20. Comprehensive fee: $21,950 includes full-time tuition ($16,070), mandatory fees ($380), and college room and board ($5500). Room and board charges vary according to board plan. Part-time tuition: $535 per credit. Part-time mandatory fees: $10 per credit. Part-time tuition and fees vary according to course load. **Scholarships:** Available **Calendar System:** Semester, Summer Session Available **Enrollment:** FT 1,818, PT 163, Grad 440 **Faculty:** FT 104, PT 101 **Student-Faculty Ratio:** 15:1 **Exams:** SAT I or ACT **% Receiving Financial Aid:** 67 **% Residing in College-Owned, -Operated, or -Affiliated Housing:** 56 **Library Holdings:** 231,176 **Regional Accreditation:** North Central Association of Colleges and Schools **Credit Hours For Degree:** 60 credits, Associates; 124 credits, Bachelors **Professional Accreditation:** NLN

FRANKLIN UNIVERSITY
201 South Grant Ave.
Columbus, OH 43215-5399
Tel: (614)797-4700; 877-341-6300
Fax: (614)224-8027
E-mail: info@franklin.edu
Web Site: http://www.franklin.edu/
President/CEO: Dr. Paul J. Otte
Registrar: Frank Yanchak
Admissions: Tracy Austin
Financial Aid: Lee Harrell
Type: Comprehensive **Sex:** Coed **Admission Plans:** Open Admission; Deferred Admission **Application Fee:** $0.00 **H.S. Requirements:** High school diploma required; GED accepted **Costs Per Year:** Application fee: $0. Tuition: $7320 full-time, $244 per credit hour part-time. Full-time tuition varies according to program. Part-time tuition varies according to program. **Scholarships:** Available **Calendar System:** Trimester, Summer Session Available **Enrollment:** FT 1,979, PT 3,841, Grad 1,003 **Faculty:** FT 36, PT 563 **Student-Faculty Ratio:** 19:1 **% Receiving Financial Aid:** 57 **Library Holdings:** 27,547 **Regional Accreditation:** North Central Association of Colleges and Schools **Credit Hours For Degree:** 64 credit hours, Associates; 124 credit hours, Bachelors **ROTC:** Army, Air Force

GALLIPOLIS CAREER COLLEGE
1176 Jackson Pike, Ste. 312
Gallipolis, OH 45631
Tel: (740)446-4367
Free: 800-214-0452
Admissions: (740)446-4124
Fax: (740)446-4124
E-mail: admissions@gallipaliscareercollege.com
Web Site: http://www.gallipoliscareercollege.com/
President/CEO: Robert L. Shirey
Registrar: Jack Henson
Admissions: Jack Henson
Financial Aid: Jeanette Shirey
Type: Two-Year College **Sex:** Coed **Application Deadline:** Rolling **Application Fee:** $50.00 **H.S. Requirements:** High school diploma required; GED accepted **Costs Per Year:** Application fee: $50. Tuition: $8640 full-time, $180 per credit hour part-time. Mandatory fees: $100 full-time. Tuition guaranteed not to increase for student's term of enrollment. **Calendar System:** Quarter, Summer Session Available **Enrollment:** FT 145, PT 9 **Faculty:** FT 2, PT 14 **Student-Faculty Ratio:** 22:1 **Exams:** Other **Credit Hours For Degree:** 100 quarter hours, Associates **Professional Accreditation:** ACICS

GOD'S BIBLE SCHOOL AND COLLEGE
1810 Young St.
Cincinnati, OH 45202-6838
Tel: (513)721-7944
Free: 800-486-4637
Fax: (513)721-3971
E-mail: lprofitt@gbs.edu
Web Site: http://www.gbs.edu/
President/CEO: Dr. Michael Avery
Registrar: Chris Lambeth
Admissions: Lisa Profitt
Financial Aid: Lisa Profitt
Type: Four-Year College **Sex:** Coed **Affiliation:** interdenominational **Scores:** 87.5% SAT V 400+; 75% SAT M 400+; 56.25% ACT 18-23; 25% ACT 24-29 **% Accepted:** 88 **Application Deadline:** August 18 **Application Fee:** $25.00 **H.S. Requirements:** High school diploma required; GED accepted **Costs Per Year:** Application fee: $25. Comprehensive fee: $8160 includes full-time tuition ($4200), mandatory fees ($660), and college room and board ($3300). College room only: $1350. Part-time tuition: $162 per credit hour. Part-time mandatory fees: $25 per credit hour. **Scholarships:** Available **Calendar System:** Semester, Summer Session Available **Enrollment:** FT 226, PT 45 **Faculty:** FT 12, PT 10 **Student-Faculty Ratio:** 16:1 **Exams:** SAT I or ACT, SAT I **Library Holdings:** 28,452 **Credit Hours For Degree:** 65 semester hours, Associates; 130 semester hours, Bachelors **Professional Accreditation:** AABC

HEIDELBERG COLLEGE
310 East Market St.
Tiffin, OH 44883-2462
Tel: (419)448-2000
Free: 800-434-3352
Admissions: (419)448-2330
Fax: (419)448-2334
E-mail: lsooy@heidelberg.edu
Web Site: http://www.heidelberg.edu/
President/CEO: Dr. F. Dominic Dottavio
Registrar: Dr. Pamela Faber
Admissions: Lindsay Sooy
Financial Aid: Juli Weininger
Type: Comprehensive **Sex:** Coed **Affiliation:** United Church of Christ **Scores:** 90% SAT V 400+; 90% SAT M 400+; 63% ACT 18-23; 24% ACT 24-29 **% Accepted:** 75 **Admission Plans:** Deferred Admission **Application Fee:** $25.00 **H.S. Requirements:** High school diploma required; GED accepted **Costs Per Year:** Application fee: $25. Comprehensive fee: $23,242 includes full-time tuition ($15,740), mandatory fees ($394), and college room and board ($7108). College room only: $3296. Full-time tuition and fees vary according to course load, degree level, and location. Room and board charges vary according to board plan and housing facility. Part-time tuition: $504 per semester hour. Part-time tuition varies according to degree level and location. **Scholarships:** Available **Calendar System:** Semester, Summer Session Available **Enrollment:** FT 1,179, PT 51, Grad 205 **Faculty:** FT 55, PT 85 **Student-Faculty Ratio:** 14:1 **Exams:** SAT I or ACT **% Receiving Financial Aid:** 81 **% Residing in College-Owned, -Operated, or -Affiliated Housing:** 87 **Library Holdings:** 268,702 **Regional Accreditation:** North Central Association of Colleges and Schools **Credit Hours For Degree:** 124 semester hours, Bachelors **ROTC:** Army, Air Force **Professional Accreditation:** NASM **Intercollegiate Athletics:** Baseball M; Basketball M & W; Cross-Country Running M & W; Football M; Golf M & W; Soccer M & W; Softball W; Tennis M & W; Track and Field M & W; Volleyball M & W; Wrestling M

HIRAM COLLEGE
Box 67
Hiram, OH 44234-0067
Tel: (330)569-3211
Free: 800-362-5280
Admissions: (330)569-5169
Fax: (330)569-5944
E-mail: admission@hiram.edu
Web Site: http://www.hiram.edu/
President/CEO: Thomas V. Chema
Registrar: Mary Ann Painley
Admissions: James Barrett
Financial Aid: Ann Marie Gruber
Type: Four-Year College **Sex:** Coed **Affiliation:** Christian Church (Disciples of Christ) **Scores:** 97% SAT V 400+; 98% SAT M 400+; 42% ACT 18-23; 43% ACT 24-29 **% Accepted:** 85 **Admission Plans:** Early Admission; Deferred Admission **Application Deadline:** April 01 **Application Fee:** $35.00 **H.S. Requirements:** High school diploma required; GED accepted **Costs Per Year:** Application fee: $35. Comprehensive fee: $31,790 includes full-time tuition ($23,510), mandatory fees ($670), and college room and board ($7610). College room only: $3590. Full-time tuition and fees vary according to student level. Room and board charges vary according to housing

facility. Part-time tuition: $784 per credit hour. Tuition guaranteed not to increase for student's term of enrollment. **Scholarships:** Available **Calendar System:** Semester, Summer Session Available **Enrollment:** FT 877, PT 205, Grad 29 **Faculty:** FT 64, PT 39 **Student-Faculty Ratio:** 12:1 **Exams:** SAT I or ACT **% Receiving Financial Aid:** 78 **% Residing in College-Owned, -Operated, or -Affiliated Housing:** 88 **Library Holdings:** 187,451 **Regional Accreditation:** North Central Association of Colleges and Schools **Credit Hours For Degree:** 120 credit hours, Bachelors **Professional Accreditation:** NASM **Intercollegiate Athletics:** Baseball M; Basketball M & W; Cross-Country Running M & W; Equestrian Sports M & W; Football M; Golf M & W; Rugby M & W; Sailing M & W; Soccer M & W; Softball W; Swimming and Diving M & W; Table Tennis M & W; Tennis M & W; Track and Field M & W; Volleyball W

HOCKING COLLEGE
3301 Hocking Parkway
Nelsonville, OH 45764-9588
Tel: (740)753-3591
Fax: (740)753-1452
E-mail: hull_lyn@hocking.edu
Web Site: http://www.hocking.edu/
President/CEO: Dr. John J. Light
Registrar: Alan Markovich
Admissions: Lyn Hull
Financial Aid: Roger Springer
Type: Two-Year College **Sex:** Coed **Affiliation:** Ohio Board of Regents **Admission Plans:** Open Admission **Application Fee:** $15.00 **H.S. Requirements:** High school diploma required; GED accepted **Scholarships:** Available **Calendar System:** Quarter, Summer Session Available **Faculty:** FT 182, PT 54 **Exams:** Other, SAT I or ACT **% Residing in College-Owned, -Operated, or -Affiliated Housing:** 9 **Library Holdings:** 19,663 **Regional Accreditation:** North Central Association of Colleges and Schools **Credit Hours For Degree:** 90 credit hours, Associates **ROTC:** Army **Professional Accreditation:** ABET, AAMAE, ACF, AHIMA, APTA, ACBSP, NLN

HONDROS COLLEGE
4140 Executive Parkway
Westerville, OH 43081-3855
Tel: (614)508-7277
Free: 800-783-0095
Admissions: (614)508-7244
Fax: (614)508-7279
Web Site: http://www.hondroscollege.com/
President/CEO: Neil Collins
Registrar: Kimberly Bennett
Admissions: Carol Thomas
Type: Two-Year College **Sex:** Coed **Admission Plans:** Open Admission **Calendar System:** Quarter **Professional Accreditation:** ACICS

INTERNATIONAL COLLEGE OF BROADCASTING
6 South Smithville Rd.
Dayton, OH 45431-1833
Tel: (937)258-8251
Web Site: http://www.icbcollege.com/
President/CEO: Michael LaMaster
Registrar: Vicki Chaffin
Admissions: Aan McIntosh
Financial Aid: Zena Williams
Type: Two-Year College **Sex:** Coed **Scholarships:** Available **Calendar System:** Semester **Enrollment:** FT 87 **Faculty:** FT 6, PT 6 **Student-Faculty Ratio:** 10:1 **Professional Accreditation:** ACCSCT

ITT TECHNICAL INSTITUTE (DAYTON)
3325 Stop 8 Rd.
Dayton, OH 45414-3425
Tel: (937)454-2267
Web Site: http://www.itt-tech.edu/
President/CEO: Bobby Reese
Registrar: Tracy Gardener
Admissions: Mike Shaffer
Financial Aid: Alois Johnson
Type: Two-Year College **Sex:** Coed **Affiliation:** ITT Educational Services, Inc **Admission Plans:** Deferred Admission **Application Deadline:** Rolling **Application Fee:** $100.00 **H.S. Requirements:** High school diploma required; GED accepted **Costs Per Year:** Application fee: $100. **Scholarships:** Available **Calendar System:** Quarter, Summer Session Not available **Exams:** Other **Credit Hours For Degree:** 96 credit hours, Associates **Professional Accreditation:** ACICS

ITT TECHNICAL INSTITUTE (HILLIARD)
3781 Park Mill Run Dr.
Hilliard, OH 43026
Tel: (614)771-4888; 888-483-4888
Fax: (614)921-4179
Web Site: http://www.itt-tech.edu/
President/CEO: James D. Vaas
Registrar: Jennifer Matzek
Admissions: Todd Clark
Type: Two-Year College **Sex:** Coed **Application Deadline:** Rolling **Application Fee:** $100.00 **Costs Per Year:** Application fee: $100. **Calendar System:** Quarter **Exams:** Other **Professional Accreditation:** ACICS

ITT TECHNICAL INSTITUTE (NORWOOD)
4750 Wesley Ave.
Norwood, OH 45212
Tel: (513)531-8300
Free: 800-314-8324
Web Site: http://www.itt-tech.edu/
President/CEO: Mike Thompson
Admissions: William Bradford
Type: Two-Year College **Sex:** Coed **Affiliation:** ITT Educational Services, Inc **Admission Plans:** Deferred Admission **Application Deadline:** Rolling **Application Fee:** $100.00 **H.S. Requirements:** High school diploma required; GED accepted **Costs Per Year:** Application fee: $100. **Scholarships:** Available **Calendar System:** Quarter, Summer Session Not available **Exams:** Other **Credit Hours For Degree:** 96 credit hours, Associates **Professional Accreditation:** ACICS

ITT TECHNICAL INSTITUTE (STRONGSVILLE)
14955 Sprague Rd.
Strongsville, OH 44136
Tel: (440)234-9091
Free: 800-331-1488
Web Site: http://www.itt-tech.edu/
President/CEO: Scott Behmer
Admissions: Martha Watson
Type: Two-Year College **Sex:** Coed **Affiliation:** ITT Educational Services, Inc **Admission Plans:** Deferred Admission **Application Deadline:** Rolling **Application Fee:** $100.00 **H.S. Requirements:** High school diploma required; GED accepted **Costs Per Year:** Application fee: $100. **Scholarships:** Available **Calendar System:** Quarter, Summer Session Not available **Exams:** Other **Credit Hours For Degree:** 96 credit hours, Associates **Professional Accreditation:** ACICS

ITT TECHNICAL INSTITUTE (WARRENSVILLE HEIGHTS)
4700 Richmond Rd.
Warrensville Heights, OH 44128
Tel: (216)896-6500
Free: 800-741-3494
Web Site: http://www.itt-tech.edu/
Admissions: James Unger
Type: Two-Year College **Sex:** Coed **Application Deadline:** Rolling **Application Fee:** $100.00 **Costs Per Year:** Application fee: $100. **Calendar System:** Quarter **Exams:** Other

ITT TECHNICAL INSTITUTE (YOUNGSTOWN)
1030 North Meridian Rd.
Youngstown, OH 44509-4098
Tel: (330)270-1600
Free: 800-832-5001
Fax: (330)270-8333
Web Site: http://www.itt-tech.edu/
President/CEO: Cecil W. Johnston
Registrar: Cecil Johnston
Admissions: Frank Quartini
Financial Aid: Darlene Blanche
Type: Two-Year College **Sex:** Coed **Affiliation:** ITT Educational Services, Inc **Admission Plans:** Deferred Admission **Application Deadline:** Rolling **Application Fee:** $100.00 **H.S. Requirements:** High school diploma required; GED accepted **Costs Per Year:** Application fee: $100. **Scholar-**

ships: Available **Calendar System:** Quarter, Summer Session Not available **Exams:** Other **Credit Hours For Degree:** 96 credit hours, Associates **Professional Accreditation:** ACICS

JAMES A. RHODES STATE COLLEGE
4240 Campus Dr.
Lima, OH 45804-3597
Tel: (419)995-8000
Admissions: (419)995-8050
Fax: (419)995-8098
E-mail: lingrel.s@rhodesstate.edu
Web Site: http://www.rhodesstate.edu/
President/CEO: Dr. Earl E. Keese
Registrar: Brenda Wakefield
Admissions: Scot Lingrell
Financial Aid: Dr. Scot Lingrell
Type: Two-Year College **Sex:** Coed **Admission Plans:** Open Admission; Early Admission; Deferred Admission **Application Fee:** $25.00 **H.S. Requirements:** High school diploma required; GED accepted **Scholarships:** Available **Calendar System:** Quarter, Summer Session Available **Enrollment:** FT 1,417, PT 1,425 **Faculty:** FT 57, PT 169 **Student-Faculty Ratio:** 25:1 **Exams:** ACT, Other **Library Holdings:** 80,000 **Regional Accreditation:** North Central Association of Colleges and Schools **Credit Hours For Degree:** 106 credit hours, Associates **Professional Accreditation:** ABET, AAMAE, ADA, AOTA, APTA, ACBSP, CARC, JRCERT, NLN **Intercollegiate Athletics:** Baseball M; Basketball M & W; Golf M

JEFFERSON COMMUNITY COLLEGE
4000 Sunset Blvd.
Steubenville, OH 43952-3598
Tel: (740)264-5591
Fax: (740)266-2706
Web Site: http://www.jcc.edu/
President/CEO: Dr. Laura M. Meeks
Registrar: Patty Sturch
Admissions: Chuck Mascellino
Financial Aid: Beth Sikole
Type: Two-Year College **Sex:** Coed **Affiliation:** Ohio Board of Regents **% Accepted:** 100 **Admission Plans:** Open Admission; Early Admission; Deferred Admission **Application Deadline:** August 20 **Application Fee:** $20.00 **H.S. Requirements:** High school diploma required; GED accepted **Costs Per Year:** Application fee: $20. Area resident tuition: $2550 full-time, $85 per credit part-time. State resident tuition: $2730 full-time, $91 per credit part-time. Nonresident tuition: $3450 full-time, $115 per credit part-time. Mandatory fees: $600 full-time. Full-time tuition and fees vary according to reciprocity agreements. Part-time tuition varies according to reciprocity agreements. **Scholarships:** Available **Calendar System:** Semester, Summer Session Available **Enrollment:** FT 911, PT 786 **Faculty:** FT 35, PT 89 **Student-Faculty Ratio:** 16:1 **Exams:** SAT I or ACT **Library Holdings:** 12,500 **Regional Accreditation:** North Central Association of Colleges and Schools **Credit Hours For Degree:** 60 semester hours, Associates **Professional Accreditation:** AAMAE, ADA, CARC, JRCERT, NAACLS **Intercollegiate Athletics:** Basketball M & W

JOHN CARROLL UNIVERSITY
20700 North Park Blvd.
University Heights, OH 44118-4581
Tel: (216)397-1886
Admissions: (216)397-4294
Fax: (216)397-3098
E-mail: admission@jcvaxa.jcu.edu
Web Site: http://www.jcu.edu/
President/CEO: Rev. Edward Glynn, SJ
Registrar: Kathleen DiFranco
Admissions: Thomas P. Fanning
Financial Aid: Patrick Prosser
Type: Comprehensive **Sex:** Coed **Affiliation:** Roman Catholic (Jesuit) **Scores:** 100% SAT V 400+; 99% SAT M 400+; 48% ACT 18-23; 43% ACT 24-29 **Admission Plans:** Early Admission; Deferred Admission **Application Fee:** $25.00 **H.S. Requirements:** High school diploma required; GED accepted **Costs Per Year:** Application fee: $25. Comprehensive fee: $31,156 includes full-time tuition ($23,380), mandatory fees ($250), and college room and board ($7526). Part-time tuition: $708 per credit hour. **Scholarships:** Available **Calendar System:** Semester, Summer Session Available **Enrollment:** FT 3,184, PT 166, Grad 751 **Faculty:** FT 240, PT 169 **Student-Faculty Ratio:** 15:1 **Exams:** SAT I or ACT **% Residing in College-Owned, -Operated, or -Affiliated Housing:** 57 **Library Holdings:** 620,000 **Regional Accreditation:** North Central Association of Colleges and Schools **Credit Hours For Degree:** 128 credit hours, Bachelors **ROTC:** Army **Professional Accreditation:** AACSB, ACA, NCATE **Intercollegiate Athletics:** Baseball M; Basketball M & W; Crew M & W; Cross-Country Running M & W; Football M; Golf M & W; Ice Hockey M; Lacrosse M & W; Rugby M & W; Sailing M & W; Skiing (Downhill) M & W; Soccer M & W; Softball W; Swimming and Diving M & W; Tennis M & W; Track and Field M & W; Volleyball M & W; Wrestling M

KENT STATE UNIVERSITY
PO Box 5190
Kent, OH 44242-0001
Tel: (330)672-3000
Free: 800-988-KENT
Admissions: (330)672-2444
Fax: (330)672-2499
E-mail: admissions@kent.edu
Web Site: http://www.kent.edu/
President/CEO: Dr. Carol A. Cartwright
Registrar: Roberta R. Sikula-Schwalm
Admissions: Nancy Dellavecchia
Financial Aid: Mark A. Evans
Type: University **Sex:** Coed **Affiliation:** Kent State University System **Scores:** 94.1% SAT V 400+; 93.8% SAT M 400+; 59.5% ACT 18-23; 26% ACT 24-29 **% Accepted:** 94 **Admission Plans:** Early Admission **Application Deadline:** May 01 **Application Fee:** $30.00 **H.S. Requirements:** High school diploma required; GED accepted **Costs Per Year:** Application fee: $30. State resident tuition: $7954 full-time, $363 per credit hour part-time. Nonresident tuition: $15,386 full-time, $701 per credit hour part-time. Full-time tuition varies according to course level, course load, degree level, location, program, reciprocity agreements, and student level. Part-time tuition varies according to course level, course load, degree level, location, program, reciprocity agreements, and student level. College room and board: $6640. College room only: $4040. Room and board charges vary according to board plan and housing facility. **Scholarships:** Available **Calendar System:** Semester, Summer Session Available **Enrollment:** FT 15,828, PT 2,917, Grad 4,877 **Faculty:** FT 841, PT 614 **Student-Faculty Ratio:** 19:1 **Exams:** SAT I or ACT **% Receiving Financial Aid:** 51 **% Residing in College-Owned, -Operated, or -Affiliated Housing:** 35 **Library Holdings:** 2,270,692 **Regional Accreditation:** North Central Association of Colleges and Schools **Credit Hours For Degree:** 60 semester hours, Associates; 120 semester hours, Bachelors **ROTC:** Army, Air Force **Professional Accreditation:** AACSB, ACEJMC, AACN, ACA, ADtA, ALA, APA, ASLHA, CEPH, CORE, FIDER, NASAD, NASD, NASM, NASPAA, NAST, NCATE, NRPA **Intercollegiate Athletics:** Baseball M; Basketball M & W; Cross-Country Running M & W; Field Hockey W; Football M; Golf M & W; Gymnastics W; Soccer W; Softball W; Track and Field M & W; Volleyball W; Wrestling M

KENT STATE UNIVERSITY, ASHTABULA CAMPUS
3325 West 13th St.
Ashtabula, OH 44004-2299
Tel: (440)964-3322
Admissions: (440)964-4217
Fax: (440)964-4269
E-mail: sanford@ashtabula.kent.edu
Web Site: http://www.ashtabula.kent.edu/
President/CEO: Prof. Susan Stocker
Registrar: Kelly Sanford
Admissions: Kelly Sanford
Financial Aid: Kelly Sanford
Type: Two-Year College **Sex:** Coed **Affiliation:** Kent State University System **Admission Plans:** Open Admission; Early Admission; Deferred Admission **H.S. Requirements:** High school diploma required; GED accepted **Scholarships:** Available **Calendar System:** Semester, Summer Session Available **Faculty:** FT 36, PT 44 **Exams:** SAT I or ACT **Library Holdings:** 51,884 **Regional Accreditation:** North Central Association of Colleges and Schools **Credit Hours For Degree:** 66 semester hours, Associates **ROTC:** Army **Professional Accreditation:** APTA, ACBSP, NLN

KENT STATE UNIVERSITY, EAST LIVERPOOL CAMPUS
400 East 4th St.
East Liverpool, OH 43920-3497

Tel: (330)385-3805
Admissions: (330)382-7414
Fax: (330)385-6348
E-mail: admissions@eliv.kent.edu
Web Site: http://www.kenteliv.kent.edu/
President/CEO: Dr. Jeffery L. Nolte
Admissions: Jamie Kenneally
Type: Two-Year College **Sex:** Coed **Affiliation:** Kent State University System **Admission Plans:** Open Admission; Early Admission; Deferred Admission **Application Fee:** $30.00 **H.S. Requirements:** High school diploma required; GED accepted **Scholarships:** Available **Calendar System:** Semester, Summer Session Available **Faculty:** FT 20, PT 55 **Student-Faculty Ratio:** 15:1 **Exams:** ACT **Library Holdings:** 31,320 **Regional Accreditation:** North Central Association of Colleges and Schools **Credit Hours For Degree:** 65 semester hours, Associates **ROTC:** Army, Navy, Air Force **Professional Accreditation:** AOTA, APTA, ACBSP, NLN

KENT STATE UNIVERSITY, GEAUGA CAMPUS
14111 Claridon-Troy Rd.
Burton, OH 44021-9500
Tel: (440)834-4187
Fax: (440)834-0919
E-mail: hmohan1@kent.edu
Web Site: http://www.geauga.kent.edu/
President/CEO: Dr. Chris Williams
Registrar: Dr. Henry Woudenberg
Admissions: Dr. David Mohan
Type: Two-Year College **Sex:** Coed **Affiliation:** Kent State University System **Scores:** 81% SAT V 400+; 73% SAT M 400+; 59% ACT 18-23; 8% ACT 24-29 **% Accepted:** 100 **Admission Plans:** Open Admission; Early Admission; Deferred Admission **Application Deadline:** Rolling **Application Fee:** $30.00 **H.S. Requirements:** High school diploma required; GED accepted **Costs Per Year:** Application fee: $30. State resident tuition: $4770 full-time, $217 per credit hour part-time. Nonresident tuition: $12,202 full-time, $555 per credit hour part-time. **Scholarships:** Available **Calendar System:** Semester, Summer Session Available **Enrollment:** FT 315, PT 603 **Faculty:** FT 13, PT 74 **Student-Faculty Ratio:** 14:1 **Library Holdings:** 8,300 **Regional Accreditation:** North Central Association of Colleges and Schools **Credit Hours For Degree:** 65 semester hours, Associates; 120 semester hours, Bachelors **ROTC:** Army, Air Force **Professional Accreditation:** ACBSP

KENT STATE UNIVERSITY, SALEM CAMPUS
2491 State Route 45 South
Salem, OH 44460-9412
Tel: (330)332-0361
Fax: (330)332-9256
E-mail: ask-us@salem.kent.edu
Web Site: http://www.salem.kent.edu/
President/CEO: Dr. Jeffrey L. Nolte
Admissions: Dennis L. Giacomino
Type: Two-Year College **Sex:** Coed **Affiliation:** Kent State University System **Scores:** 75% ACT 18-23; 2% ACT 24-29 **Admission Plans:** Open Admission; Early Admission; Deferred Admission **Application Fee:** $30.00 **H.S. Requirements:** High school diploma required; GED accepted **Scholarships:** Available **Calendar System:** Semester, Summer Session Available **Faculty:** FT 50, PT 56 **Student-Faculty Ratio:** 13:1 **Exams:** ACT, SAT I or ACT **Library Holdings:** 19,000 **Regional Accreditation:** North Central Association of Colleges and Schools **Credit Hours For Degree:** 65 semester hours, Associates **ROTC:** Army, Air Force **Professional Accreditation:** ACBSP, JRCERT, JRCNMT

KENT STATE UNIVERSITY, STARK CAMPUS
6000 Frank Ave., NW
Canton, OH 44720-7599
Tel: (330)499-9600
Admissions: (330)244-3259
Fax: (330)494-6121
E-mail: dspeck@stark.kent.edu
Web Site: http://www.stark.kent.edu/
President/CEO: Dr. David Baker
Registrar: Mary S. Southards
Admissions: Deborah Ann Speck
Financial Aid: Mary S. Southards
Type: Two-Year College **Sex:** Coed **Affiliation:** Kent State University System **Scores:** 5% SAT V 400+; 4% SAT M 400+; 47% ACT 18-23; 13% ACT 24-29 **Admission Plans:** Open Admission; Early Admission; Deferred Admission **Application Fee:** $30.00 **H.S. Requirements:** High school diploma required; GED accepted **Scholarships:** Available **Calendar System:** Semester, Summer Session Available **Faculty:** FT 85, PT 115 **Student-Faculty Ratio:** 19:1 **Exams:** SAT I or ACT **Library Holdings:** 72,807 **Regional Accreditation:** North Central Association of Colleges and Schools **Credit Hours For Degree:** 65 semester hours, Associates; 121 semester hours, Bachelors **ROTC:** Army, Air Force

KENT STATE UNIVERSITY, TRUMBULL CAMPUS
4314 Mahoning Ave., NW
Warren, OH 44483-1998
Tel: (330)847-0571
E-mail: info@trumbull.kent.edu
Web Site: http://www.trumbull.kent.edu/
President/CEO: Robert G. Sines
Registrar: Linda P. Petrilla
Admissions: Linda P. Petrilla
Financial Aid: Nina Conner
Type: Two-Year College **Sex:** Coed **Affiliation:** Kent State University System **Scores:** 94% SAT V 400+; 93% SAT M 400+; 59% ACT 18-23; 22% ACT 24-29 **% Accepted:** 100 **Admission Plans:** Open Admission; Early Admission; Deferred Admission **Application Deadline:** July 30 **Application Fee:** $30.00 **H.S. Requirements:** High school diploma required; GED accepted **Costs Per Year:** Application fee: $30. State resident tuition: $4770 full-time, $217 per credit hour part-time. Nonresident tuition: $12,202 full-time, $555 per credit hour part-time. **Scholarships:** Available **Calendar System:** Semester, Summer Session Available **Enrollment:** FT 893, PT 1,143 **Faculty:** FT 58, PT 66 **Student-Faculty Ratio:** 16:1 **Library Holdings:** 65,951 **Regional Accreditation:** North Central Association of Colleges and Schools **Credit Hours For Degree:** 65 credit hours, Associates **ROTC:** Army, Air Force **Professional Accreditation:** ACBSP

KENT STATE UNIVERSITY, TUSCARAWAS CAMPUS
330 University Dr., NE
New Philadelphia, OH 44663-9403
Tel: (330)339-3391
Fax: (330)339-3321
Web Site: http://www.tusc.kent.edu/
President/CEO: Dr. Gregg L. Andrews
Registrar: Agnes Swigart
Admissions: Denise L. Testa
Type: Two-Year College **Sex:** Coed **Affiliation:** Kent State University System **Scores:** 85.71% SAT V 400+; 100% SAT M 400+; 54.31% ACT 18-23; 18.54% ACT 24-29 **Admission Plans:** Open Admission; Early Admission; Deferred Admission **Application Deadline:** September 01 **Application Fee:** $30.00 **H.S. Requirements:** High school diploma required; GED accepted **Costs Per Year:** Application fee: $30. State resident tuition: $2637 full-time. Nonresident tuition: $6353 full-time. **Scholarships:** Available **Calendar System:** Semester, Summer Session Available **Enrollment:** FT 935, PT 970, Grad 44 **Faculty:** FT 48, PT 74 **Student-Faculty Ratio:** 18:1 **Exams:** SAT I and SAT II or ACT **Library Holdings:** 62,783 **Regional Accreditation:** North Central Association of Colleges and Schools **Credit Hours For Degree:** 65 semester hours, Associates **ROTC:** Army, Air Force **Professional Accreditation:** ABET, ACBSP, NLN

KENYON COLLEGE
Gambier, OH 43022-9623
Tel: (740)427-5000
Free: 800-848-2468
Admissions: (740)427-5776
Fax: (740)427-2634
E-mail: admissions@kenyon.edu
Web Site: http://www.kenyon.edu/
President/CEO: S. Georgia Nugent
Registrar: Dr. Richard L. Switzer
Admissions: Ericka Carroll
Financial Aid: Craig A. Daugherty
Type: Four-Year College **Sex:** Coed **Scores:** 100% SAT V 400+; 100% SAT M 400+; 4% ACT 18-23; 47% ACT 24-29 **% Accepted:** 36 **Admission Plans:** Early Admission; Early Decision Plan; Deferred Admission **Application Deadline:** January 15 **Application Fee:** $50.00 **H.S. Requirements:** High school diploma required; GED accepted **Costs Per Year:** Application

fee: $50. Comprehensive fee: $39,500 includes full-time tuition ($32,980), mandatory fees ($950), and college room and board ($5570). College room only: $2620. Room and board charges vary according to housing facility. Part-time tuition: $825 per credit hour. **Scholarships:** Available **Calendar System:** Semester, Summer Session Not available **Enrollment:** FT 1,640, PT 21 **Faculty:** FT 151, PT 35 **Student-Faculty Ratio:** 10:1 **Exams:** SAT I or ACT **% Receiving Financial Aid:** 43 **% Residing in College-Owned, -Operated, or -Affiliated Housing:** 98 **Library Holdings:** 826,059 **Regional Accreditation:** North Central Association of Colleges and Schools **Credit Hours For Degree:** 16 units, Bachelors **Intercollegiate Athletics:** Baseball M; Basketball M & W; Cross-Country Running M & W; Equestrian Sports M & W; Field Hockey W; Football M; Golf M; Lacrosse M & W; Rugby M & W; Soccer M & W; Softball W; Squash M & W; Swimming and Diving M & W; Tennis M & W; Track and Field M & W; Ultimate Frisbee M & W; Volleyball W

KETTERING COLLEGE OF MEDICAL ARTS
3737 Southern Blvd.
Kettering, OH 45429-1299
Tel: (937)395-8601
Free: 800-433-5262
Admissions: (937)296-7228
Fax: (937)395-8333
Web Site: http://www.kcma.edu/
President/CEO: Dr. Charles Scriven
Registrar: Robin Vanderbilt
Admissions: David Lofthouse
Financial Aid: Kim Snell
Type: Two-Year College **Sex:** Coed **Affiliation:** Seventh-day Adventist **Admission Plans:** Early Admission **Application Fee:** $25.00 **H.S. Requirements:** High school diploma required; GED accepted **Scholarships:** Available **Calendar System:** Semester, Summer Session Available **Faculty:** FT 25, PT 26 **Exams:** ACT, SAT I **% Residing in College-Owned, -Operated, or -Affiliated Housing:** 20 **Library Holdings:** 29,390 **Regional Accreditation:** North Central Association of Colleges and Schools **Credit Hours For Degree:** 64 semester hours, Associates; 126 semester hours, Bachelors **Professional Accreditation:** CARC, JRCEDMS, JRCERT, NLN

LAKE ERIE COLLEGE
391 West Washington St.
Painesville, OH 44077-3389
Tel: (440)296-1856
Free: 800-916-0904
Admissions: (440)375-7050
Fax: (440)352-3533
E-mail: jcalhoun@lec.edu
Web Site: http://www.lec.edu/
President/CEO: Dr. Harold Laydon
Registrar: Janet Stimple
Admissions: Jennifer Calhoun
Financial Aid: Patricia Canfield
Type: Comprehensive **Sex:** Coed **Scores:** 83% SAT V 400+; 89% SAT M 400+; 54% ACT 18-23; 15% ACT 24-29 **% Accepted:** 76 **Admission Plans:** Deferred Admission **Application Fee:** $25.00 **H.S. Requirements:** High school diploma required; GED accepted **Costs Per Year:** Application fee: $25. Comprehensive fee: $27,724 includes full-time tuition ($20,500), mandatory fees ($890), and college room and board ($6334). Part-time tuition: $508 per hour. Part-time mandatory fees: $26 per hour. **Scholarships:** Available **Calendar System:** Semester, Summer Session Available **Enrollment:** FT 574, PT 108, Grad 270 **Faculty:** FT 34, PT 59 **Student-Faculty Ratio:** 12:1 **Exams:** SAT I or ACT **% Residing in College-Owned, -Operated, or -Affiliated Housing:** 47 **Library Holdings:** 87,000 **Regional Accreditation:** North Central Association of Colleges and Schools **Credit Hours For Degree:** 128 semester hours, Bachelors **Intercollegiate Athletics:** Baseball M; Basketball M & W; Cross-Country Running M & W; Golf M; Soccer M & W; Softball W; Volleyball W

LAKELAND COMMUNITY COLLEGE
7700 Clocktower Dr.
Kirtland, OH 44094-5198
Tel: (440)525-7000
Admissions: (440)525-7230
Fax: (440)525-4330
Web Site: http://www.lakeland.cc.oh.us/
President/CEO: Dr. Morris W. Beverage
Registrar: Tracey L. Cooper
Admissions: Tracey Cooper
Financial Aid: Melissa Amspaugh
Type: Two-Year College **Sex:** Coed **Affiliation:** Ohio Board of Regents **Admission Plans:** Open Admission; Early Admission; Deferred Admission **Application Fee:** $15.00 **H.S. Requirements:** High school diploma required; GED accepted **Scholarships:** Available **Calendar System:** Semester, Summer Session Available **Enrollment:** FT 3,098, PT 5,537 **Faculty:** FT 118, PT 506 **Student-Faculty Ratio:** 17:1 **Exams:** Other, SAT I or ACT **Library Holdings:** 70,874 **Regional Accreditation:** North Central Association of Colleges and Schools **Credit Hours For Degree:** 64 semester hours, Associates **Professional Accreditation:** ABET, ARCEST, ADA, CARC, JCAHPO, JRCERT, NAACLS, NLN **Intercollegiate Athletics:** Baseball M; Basketball M & W; Golf M & W; Soccer M; Softball W; Volleyball W

LAURA AND ALVIN SIEGAL COLLEGE OF JUDAIC STUDIES
26500 Shaker Blvd.
Beachwood, OH 44122-7116
Tel: (216)464-4050; 888-336-2257
Fax: (216)464-5827
Web Site: http://www.siegalcollege.edu/
President/CEO: Dr. David S. Ariel
Registrar: Linda L. Rosen
Admissions: Linda L. Rosen
Financial Aid: Linda L. Rosen
Type: Comprehensive **Sex:** Coed **Admission Plans:** Open Admission; Deferred Admission **Application Fee:** $50.00 **H.S. Requirements:** High school diploma required; GED accepted **Costs Per Year:** Application fee: $50. Tuition: $15,000 full-time, $500 per credit part-time. Mandatory fees: $25 full-time. Full-time tuition and fees vary according to course load. Part-time tuition varies according to course load. **Scholarships:** Available **Calendar System:** Semester, Summer Session Available **Enrollment:** FT 2, PT 9, Grad 135 **Faculty:** FT 11, PT 31 **Student-Faculty Ratio:** 8:1 **% Receiving Financial Aid:** 100 **Library Holdings:** 28,000 **Regional Accreditation:** North Central Association of Colleges and Schools **Credit Hours For Degree:** 120 credits, Bachelors

LORAIN COUNTY COMMUNITY COLLEGE
1005 Abbe Rd., North
Elyria, OH 44035
Tel: (440)365-5222
Free: 800-995-5222
Admissions: (440)366-7566
Fax: (440)365-6519
Web Site: http://www.loraincc.edu/
President/CEO: Dr. Roy A. Church
Admissions: Dione Somervile
Financial Aid: Stephanie Sutton
Type: Two-Year College **Sex:** Coed **Affiliation:** Ohio Board of Regents **Admission Plans:** Open Admission; Early Admission; Deferred Admission **Application Fee:** $0.00 **H.S. Requirements:** High school diploma required; GED accepted **Scholarships:** Available **Calendar System:** Semester, Summer Session Available **Enrollment:** FT 3,432, PT 5,977 **Faculty:** FT 121, PT 450 **Student-Faculty Ratio:** 19:1 **Exams:** Other, SAT I or ACT **Library Holdings:** 198,984 **Regional Accreditation:** North Central Association of Colleges and Schools **Credit Hours For Degree:** 63 semester hours, Associates **Professional Accreditation:** ARCEST, AAMAE, ADA, APTA, JRCEDMS, JRCERT, NAACLS, NLN

LOURDES COLLEGE
6832 Convent Blvd.
Sylvania, OH 43560-2898
Tel: (419)885-3211
Free: 800-878-3210
Admissions: (419)885-5291
Fax: (419)882-3987
E-mail: lcadmits@lourdes.edu
Web Site: http://www.lourdes.edu/
President/CEO: Dr. Robert Helmer
Registrar: Michelle A. Rable
Admissions: Amy Mergen
Financial Aid: Gregory Guzman
Type: Comprehensive **Sex:** Coed **Affiliation:** Roman Catholic **Scores:** 100% SAT V 400+; 100% SAT M 400+; 50% ACT 18-23; 19% ACT 24-29

Admission Plans: Early Admission; Deferred Admission **Application Fee:** $25.00 **H.S. Requirements:** High school diploma required; GED accepted **Costs Per Year:** Application fee: $25. Tuition: $11,070 full-time, $369 per credit hour part-time. Mandatory fees: $1200 full-time, $40 per credit hour part-time. **Scholarships:** Available **Calendar System:** Semester, Summer Session Available **Enrollment:** FT 676, PT 714, Grad 70 **Faculty:** FT 63, PT 87 **Student-Faculty Ratio:** 10:1 **Exams:** SAT I or ACT **% Receiving Financial Aid:** 87 **Library Holdings:** 58,633 **Regional Accreditation:** North Central Association of Colleges and Schools **ROTC:** Army, Air Force **Professional Accreditation:** AACN, CSWE, NLN

MALONE COLLEGE
515 25th St., NW
Canton, OH 44709-3897
Tel: (330)471-8100
Free: 800-521-1146
Admissions: (330)471-8145
Fax: (330)454-6977
Web Site: http://www.malone.edu/
President/CEO: Dr. Ronald G. Johnson
Registrar: Gary L. Phelps
Admissions: John Chopka
Financial Aid: Michael A. Bole
Type: Comprehensive **Sex:** Coed **Affiliation:** Evangelical Friends Church–Eastern Region **Scores:** 96% SAT V 400+; 91% SAT M 400+; 54.4% ACT 18-23; 32% ACT 24-29 **% Accepted:** 81 **Admission Plans:** Early Admission; Deferred Admission **Application Deadline:** July 01 **Application Fee:** $20.00 **H.S. Requirements:** High school diploma required; GED accepted **Costs Per Year:** Application fee: $20. Comprehensive fee: $24,190 includes full-time tuition ($17,520), mandatory fees ($270), and college room and board ($6400). College room only: $3300. Part-time tuition: $330 per semester hour. Part-time mandatory fees: $67.50 per term. **Scholarships:** Available **Calendar System:** Semester, Summer Session Available **Enrollment:** FT 1,676, PT 244, Grad 357 **Faculty:** FT 104, PT 98 **Student-Faculty Ratio:** 14:1 **Exams:** SAT I or ACT **% Receiving Financial Aid:** 75 **% Residing in College-Owned, -Operated, or -Affiliated Housing:** 51 **Library Holdings:** 238,830 **Regional Accreditation:** North Central Association of Colleges and Schools **Credit Hours For Degree:** 124 credit hours, Bachelors **ROTC:** Army, Air Force **Professional Accreditation:** AACN, CSWE, NLN **Intercollegiate Athletics:** Baseball M; Basketball M & W; Cheerleading M & W; Cross-Country Running M & W; Football M; Golf M & W; Soccer M & W; Softball W; Tennis M & W; Track and Field M & W; Volleyball W

MARIETTA COLLEGE
215 Fifth St.
Marietta, OH 45750-4000
Tel: (740)376-4000
Free: 800-331-7896
Admissions: (740)376-4600
Fax: (740)376-4896
E-mail: admit@marietta.edu
Web Site: http://www.marietta.edu/
President/CEO: Dr. Jean A. Scott
Registrar: Dr. Roger H. Pitasky
Admissions: Marke Vickers
Financial Aid: James Begany
Type: Comprehensive **Sex:** Coed **Scores:** 95% SAT V 400+; 94% SAT M 400+; 51% ACT 18-23; 37% ACT 24-29 **% Accepted:** 78 **Admission Plans:** Early Admission; Deferred Admission **Application Deadline:** April 15 **Application Fee:** $25.00 **H.S. Requirements:** High school diploma required; GED accepted **Costs Per Year:** Application fee: $25. Comprehensive fee: $29,100 includes full-time tuition ($22,070), mandatory fees ($585), and college room and board ($6445). College room only: $3445. Room and board charges vary according to board plan. Part-time tuition: $735 per credit. Part-time tuition varies according to class time. **Scholarships:** Available **Calendar System:** Semester, Summer Session Available **Enrollment:** FT 1,274, PT 70, Grad 117 **Faculty:** FT 91, PT 49 **Student-Faculty Ratio:** 12:1 **Exams:** SAT I or ACT, SAT II **% Receiving Financial Aid:** 78 **% Residing in College-Owned, -Operated, or -Affiliated Housing:** 85 **Library Holdings:** 250,000 **Regional Accreditation:** North Central Association of Colleges and Schools **Credit Hours For Degree:** 61 credit hours, Associates; 120 credit hours, Bachelors **Professional Accreditation:** ABET, JRCEPAT, NCATE **Intercollegiate Athletics:** Baseball M; Basketball M & W; Cheerleading W; Crew M & W; Cross-Country Running M & W; Football M; Lacrosse M; Soccer M & W; Softball W; Tennis M & W; Track and Field M & W; Volleyball W

MARION TECHNICAL COLLEGE
1467 Mount Vernon Ave.
Marion, OH 43302-5694
Tel: (740)389-4636
Fax: (740)389-6136
E-mail: mtc@on-ramp.net
Web Site: http://www.mtc.edu/
President/CEO: Dr. John Richard Bryson
Registrar: Wendy Wiseman
Admissions: Joel O. Liles
Financial Aid: R. Andrew Harper
Type: Two-Year College **Sex:** Coed **Affiliation:** Ohio Board of Regents **Admission Plans:** Open Admission; Early Admission; Deferred Admission **Application Fee:** $20.00 **H.S. Requirements:** High school diploma or equivalent not required. For nursing, medical laboratory technology, paralegal, radiological technology, physical therapist assisting programs: High school diploma required; GED accepted. **Scholarships:** Available **Calendar System:** Quarter, Summer Session Available **Enrollment:** FT 981, PT 1,140 **Faculty:** FT 40, PT 150 **Student-Faculty Ratio:** 18:1 **Exams:** ACT **Library Holdings:** 38,000 **Regional Accreditation:** North Central Association of Colleges and Schools **Credit Hours For Degree:** 98 quarter hours, Associates **Professional Accreditation:** APTA, JRCERT, NAACLS, NLN **Intercollegiate Athletics:** Basketball M & W; Golf M & W; Volleyball W

MEDCENTRAL COLLEGE OF NURSING
335 Glessner Ave.
Mansfield, OH 44903
Tel: (419)520-2600; 877-656-4360
E-mail: charris@medcentral.edu
Web Site: http://www.medcentral.edu/
President/CEO: Dr. Richard E. Greene
Admissions: Christopher M. Harris
Type: Four-Year College **Sex:** Coed **Admission Plans:** Deferred Admission **Application Fee:** $40.00 **H.S. Requirements:** High school diploma required; GED accepted **Costs Per Year:** Application fee: $40. Tuition: $9100 full-time, $260 per credit hour part-time. Mandatory fees: $150 full-time. Full-time tuition and fees vary according to course load. Part-time tuition varies according to course load. College room only: $4200. **Calendar System:** Quarter **Enrollment:** FT 318, PT 47 **Faculty:** FT 10, PT 4 **Student-Faculty Ratio:** 15:1 **Exams:** SAT I or ACT **% Residing in College-Owned, -Operated, or -Affiliated Housing:** 18 **Regional Accreditation:** North Central Association of Colleges and Schools **Credit Hours For Degree:** 185 credits, Bachelors

MERCY COLLEGE OF NORTHWEST OHIO
2221 Madison Ave.
Toledo, OH 43624-1132
Tel: (419)251-1313; 888-80-Mercy
Fax: (419)251-4116
Web Site: http://www.mercycollege.edu/
President/CEO: Paul J. Kessler, EdD
Registrar: Heather Hoppe
Admissions: Shelly McCoy-Grissom
Type: Two-Year College **Sex:** Coed **Affiliation:** Roman Catholic Church **Scores:** 100% SAT V 400+; 69% ACT 18-23; 17% ACT 24-29 **% Accepted:** 57 **Application Deadline:** Rolling **Application Fee:** $25.00 **H.S. Requirements:** High school diploma required; GED accepted **Costs Per Year:** Application fee: $25. Tuition: $8640 full-time, $299 per credit hour part-time. Mandatory fees: $650 full-time, $5 per credit hour part-time, $650 per year part-time. **Scholarships:** Available **Calendar System:** Semester, Summer Session Available **Enrollment:** FT 397, PT 359 **Faculty:** FT 48, PT 28 **Student-Faculty Ratio:** 17:1 **Exams:** SAT I or ACT **% Residing in College-Owned, -Operated, or -Affiliated Housing:** 8 **Library Holdings:** 6,400 **Regional Accreditation:** North Central Association of Colleges and Schools **Credit Hours For Degree:** 60 semester hours, Associates; 120 semester hours, Bachelors **Professional Accreditation:** AHIMA, JRCERT, NAACLS, NLN

MIAMI-JACOBS COLLEGE
PO Box 1433
Dayton, OH 45401-1433
Tel: (937)461-5174

Fax: (937)461-3384
Web Site: http://www.miamijacobs.edu/
President/CEO: Charles G. Campbell
Registrar: Donnie Long
Admissions: Mary Percell
Type: Two-Year College **Sex:** Coed **Admission Plans:** Early Admission; Deferred Admission **Application Fee:** $50.00 **H.S. Requirements:** High school diploma required; GED accepted **Scholarships:** Available **Calendar System:** Quarter, Summer Session Available **Enrollment:** FT 317 **Faculty:** PT 38 **Student-Faculty Ratio:** 13:1 **Exams:** ACT, Other, SAT I or ACT **Credit Hours For Degree:** 91 credits, Associates **Professional Accreditation:** ACICS, AAMAE

MIAMI UNIVERSITY
Oxford, OH 45056
Tel: (513)529-1809
Admissions: (513)529-5040
Fax: (513)529-1550
E-mail: admission@muohio.edu
Web Site: http://www.muohio.edu/
President/CEO: Dr. James C. Garland
Registrar: Robert A. Kubat
Admissions: Ann Larson
Financial Aid: Chuck Knepfle
Type: University **Sex:** Coed **Affiliation:** Miami University System **Scores:** 100% SAT V 400+; 100% SAT M 400+; 16% ACT 18-23; 67% ACT 24-29 **% Accepted:** 69 **Admission Plans:** Early Action; Early Decision Plan; Deferred Admission **Application Deadline:** January 31 **Application Fee:** $45.00 **H.S. Requirements:** High school diploma required; GED accepted **Costs Per Year:** Application fee: $45. State resident tuition: $19,877 full-time. Nonresident tuition: $19,877 full-time. Mandatory fees: $1610 full-time. College room and board: $7610. College room only: $3860. Room and board charges vary according to board plan and housing facility. Ohio residents receive a minimum of $10,000 in resident scholarships. **Scholarships:** Available **Calendar System:** Semester, Summer Session Available **Enrollment:** FT 14,312, PT 331, Grad 1,695 **Faculty:** FT 842, PT 356 **Student-Faculty Ratio:** 16:1 **Exams:** SAT I or ACT **% Receiving Financial Aid:** 40 **% Residing in College-Owned, -Operated, or -Affiliated Housing:** 45 **Library Holdings:** 2,697,078 **Regional Accreditation:** North Central Association of Colleges and Schools **Credit Hours For Degree:** 128 credit hours, Bachelors **ROTC:** Army, Navy, Air Force **Professional Accreditation:** AACSB, ABET, APA, ASLHA, CSWE, FIDER, JRCEPAT, NASAD, NASM, NAST, NCATE, NLN **Intercollegiate Athletics:** Archery M & W; Baseball M; Basketball M & W; Cross-Country Running M & W; Equestrian Sports M & W; Fencing M & W; Field Hockey W; Football M; Golf M; Gymnastics M & W; Ice Hockey M; Lacrosse M; Racquetball M & W; Rugby M; Sailing M & W; Soccer M & W; Softball W; Swimming and Diving M & W; Tennis M & W; Track and Field M & W; Volleyball M & W; Wrestling M

MIAMI UNIVERSITY HAMILTON
1601 Peck Blvd.
Hamilton, OH 45011-3399
Tel: (513)785-3000
Admissions: (513)785-3111
E-mail: nelsona3@muohio.edu
Web Site: http://www.ham.muohio.edu/
President/CEO: Dr. Jack Rhodes
Registrar: Sue Wilson
Admissions: Archie Nelson
Financial Aid: Triana M. Adlon
Type: Two-Year College **Sex:** Coed **Affiliation:** Miami University System **Admission Plans:** Open Admission **Application Fee:** $25.00 **H.S. Requirements:** High school diploma required; GED accepted **Costs Per Year:** Application fee: $25. State resident tuition: $3714 full-time, $154.75 per credit part-time. Nonresident tuition: $15,246 full-time, $650 per credit part-time. Mandatory fees: $390 full-time, $14.75 per credit part-time, $18 per term part-time. **Scholarships:** Available **Calendar System:** Semester, Summer Session Available **Enrollment:** FT 2,432, PT 898, Grad 68 **Faculty:** FT 88, PT 130 **Student-Faculty Ratio:** 21:1 **Library Holdings:** 68,000 **Regional Accreditation:** North Central Association of Colleges and Schools **Credit Hours For Degree:** 64 credits, Associates; 128 credits, Bachelors **ROTC:** Navy, Air Force **Professional Accreditation:** NLN **Intercollegiate Athletics:** Baseball M; Basketball M & W; Cheerleading W; Golf M; Softball W; Tennis M & W; Volleyball W

MIAMI UNIVERSITY-MIDDLETOWN CAMPUS
4200 East University Blvd.
Middletown, OH 45042-3497
Tel: (513)727-3200
Admissions: (513)727-3346
Fax: (513)727-3223
E-mail: flynnml@muohio.edu
Web Site: http://www.mid.muohio.edu/
President/CEO: Dr. Michael P. Governanti
Registrar: David Johnson
Admissions: Mary Lou Flynn
Financial Aid: Ellen Hall
Type: Two-Year College **Sex:** Coed **Affiliation:** Miami University System **Scores:** 87% SAT V 400+; 90% SAT M 400+; 57% ACT 18-23; 15% ACT 24-29 **Admission Plans:** Open Admission; Early Admission; Deferred Admission **Application Fee:** $25.00 **H.S. Requirements:** High school diploma required; GED accepted **Scholarships:** Available **Calendar System:** Semester, Summer Session Available **Faculty:** FT 79, PT 130 **Student-Faculty Ratio:** 13:1 **Exams:** SAT I or ACT **Regional Accreditation:** North Central Association of Colleges and Schools **Credit Hours For Degree:** 64 semester hours, Associates; 128 semester hours, Bachelors **ROTC:** Air Force **Professional Accreditation:** NLN **Intercollegiate Athletics:** Baseball M; Basketball M & W; Golf M & W; Softball W; Tennis M & W; Volleyball W

MOUNT CARMEL COLLEGE OF NURSING
127 South Davis Ave.
Columbus, OH 43222
Tel: (614)234-5800
Admissions: (614)234-5144
Web Site: http://www.mccn.edu/
President/CEO: Dr. Ann E. Schiele
Registrar: Karen L. Greene
Admissions: Merchel Menefield
Financial Aid: Carol Graham
Type: Comprehensive **Sex:** Coed **Application Fee:** $30.00 **Costs Per Year:** Application fee: $30. Tuition: $15,497 full-time. Mandatory fees: $312 full-time. College room only: $1870. **Scholarships:** Available **Calendar System:** Semester **Enrollment:** FT 431, PT 119, Grad 23 **Faculty:** FT 31, PT 21 **Student-Faculty Ratio:** 13:1 **% Receiving Financial Aid:** 93 **Regional Accreditation:** North Central Association of Colleges and Schools **Professional Accreditation:** ADtA, NLN

MOUNT UNION COLLEGE
1972 Clark Ave.
Alliance, OH 44601-3993
Tel: (330)821-5320
Free: 800-992-6682
Admissions: (330)823-2590
Fax: (330)821-0425
E-mail: admission@muc.edu
Web Site: http://www.muc.edu/
President/CEO: Dr. John L. Ewing, Jr.
Registrar: Stuart Terrass
Admissions: Amy Tomko
Financial Aid: Amy Tomko
Type: Four-Year College **Sex:** Coed **Affiliation:** United Methodist **Scores:** 96% SAT V 400+; 94% SAT M 400+; 57% ACT 18-23; 31% ACT 24-29 **% Accepted:** 80 **Admission Plans:** Early Admission; Deferred Admission **Application Deadline:** Rolling **H.S. Requirements:** High school diploma required; GED accepted **Costs Per Year:** Comprehensive fee: $25,840 includes full-time tuition ($19,600), mandatory fees ($250), and college room and board ($5990). College room only: $2650. Room and board charges vary according to board plan and housing facility. Part-time tuition: $820 per semester hour. Part-time mandatory fees: $50 per term. **Scholarships:** Available **Calendar System:** Semester, Summer Session Available **Enrollment:** FT 2,021, PT 184 **Faculty:** FT 123, PT 103 **Student-Faculty Ratio:** 13:1 **Exams:** SAT I or ACT **% Receiving Financial Aid:** 79 **% Residing in College-Owned, -Operated, or -Affiliated Housing:** 67 **Library Holdings:** 244,115 **Regional Accreditation:** North Central Association of Colleges and Schools **Credit Hours For Degree:** 120 credits, Bachelors **ROTC:** Army, Air Force **Professional Accreditation:** JRCEPAT, NASM **Intercollegiate Athletics:** Baseball M; Basketball M & W; Cheerleading W; Cross-Country

Running M & W; Football M; Golf M & W; Soccer M & W; Softball W; Swimming and Diving M & W; Tennis M & W; Track and Field M & W; Volleyball W; Wrestling M

MOUNT VERNON NAZARENE UNIVERSITY
800 Martinsburg Rd.
Mount Vernon, OH 43050-9500
Tel: (740)392-6868; (866)462-6868
E-mail: admissions@mvnc.edu
Web Site: http://www.mvnu.edu/
President/CEO: Dr. E. LeBron Fairbanks
Registrar: Mel Severns
Admissions: Tim Eades
Financial Aid: Steven Tracht
Type: Comprehensive **Sex:** Coed **Affiliation:** Nazarene **Scores:** 95% SAT V 400+; 91% SAT M 400+; 55% ACT 18-23; 34% ACT 24-29 **% Accepted:** 80 **Admission Plans:** Deferred Admission **Application Deadline:** May 01 **Application Fee:** $25.00 **H.S. Requirements:** High school diploma required; GED accepted **Costs Per Year:** Application fee: $25. Comprehensive fee: $21,816 includes full-time tuition ($16,216), mandatory fees ($510), and college room and board ($5090). College room only: $2840. Part-time tuition: $585 per semester hour. Part-time mandatory fees: $18 per semester hour. **Scholarships:** Available **Calendar System:** 4-1-4, Summer Session Available **Enrollment:** FT 1,921, PT 274, Grad 354 **Faculty:** FT 88, PT 138 **Student-Faculty Ratio:** 17:1 **Exams:** SAT I or ACT **% Receiving Financial Aid:** 55 **% Residing in College-Owned, -Operated, or -Affiliated Housing:** 74 **Library Holdings:** 96,646 **Regional Accreditation:** North Central Association of Colleges and Schools **Credit Hours For Degree:** 64 credit hours, Associates; 124 credit hours, Bachelors **Professional Accreditation:** ACBSP **Intercollegiate Athletics:** Baseball M; Basketball M & W; Cross-Country Running M & W; Golf M; Soccer M & W; Softball W; Volleyball W

MUSKINGUM COLLEGE
163 Stormont St.
New Concord, OH 43762
Tel: (740)826-8211
Free: 800-752-6082
Admissions: (740)826-8137
Fax: (740)826-8404
E-mail: adminfo@muskingum.edu
Web Site: http://www.muskingum.edu/
President/CEO: Dr. Anne C. Steele
Registrar: Dan Wilson
Admissions: Jeff Zellers
Financial Aid: W. Jeff Zellers
Type: Comprehensive **Sex:** Coed **Affiliation:** Presbyterian Church (U.S.A.) **Scores:** 85% SAT V 400+; 87% SAT M 400+; 59% ACT 18-23; 24% ACT 24-29 **Admission Plans:** Early Admission; Deferred Admission **Application Fee:** $0.00 **H.S. Requirements:** High school diploma required; GED accepted **Scholarships:** Available **Calendar System:** Semester, Summer Session Available **Enrollment:** FT 1,547, PT 75, Grad 520 **Faculty:** FT 96, PT 33 **Student-Faculty Ratio:** 16:1 **Exams:** SAT I or ACT **% Receiving Financial Aid:** 77 **% Residing in College-Owned, -Operated, or -Affiliated Housing:** 88 **Library Holdings:** 233,000 **Regional Accreditation:** North Central Association of Colleges and Schools **Credit Hours For Degree:** 124 credits, Bachelors **Professional Accreditation:** NASM **Intercollegiate Athletics:** Baseball M; Basketball M & W; Cross-Country Running M & W; Football M; Golf M & W; Soccer M & W; Softball W; Tennis M & W; Track and Field M & W; Volleyball W; Wrestling M

NATIONAL INSTITUTE OF TECHNOLOGY
2545 Bailey Rd.
Cuyahoga Falls, OH 44221
Tel: (330)923-9959
Fax: (330)923-0886
Web Site: http://www.nationalinstituteoftechnology.com/ **Type:** Two-Year College **Sex:** Coed **Professional Accreditation:** ACCSCT

NORTH CENTRAL STATE COLLEGE
2441 Kenwood Circle, PO Box 698
Mansfield, OH 44901-0698
Tel: (419)755-4800
Admissions: (419)755-4813
Fax: (419)755-4750
E-mail: nfletcher@ncstatecollege.edu
Web Site: http://www.ncstatecollege.edu/
President/CEO: Dr. Ronald E. Abrams
Registrar: Mark A. Monnes
Admissions: Nikia L. Fletcher
Financial Aid: Doris Smith
Type: Two-Year College **Sex:** Coed **Affiliation:** Ohio Board of Regents **Admission Plans:** Open Admission; Early Admission; Deferred Admission **H.S. Requirements:** High school diploma required; GED accepted **Costs Per Year:** State resident tuition: $3,431 full-time, $76.25 per credit hour part-time. Nonresident tuition: $6,862 full-time, $152.50 per credit hour part-time. Mandatory fees: $245 full-time, $11.80 per credit hour part-time. Full-time tuition and fees vary according to course load. Part-time tuition and fees vary according to course load. **Scholarships:** Available **Calendar System:** Quarter, Summer Session Available **Enrollment:** FT 969, PT 2,364 **Faculty:** FT 70, PT 129 **Exams:** ACT, Other **Library Holdings:** 52,700 **Regional Accreditation:** North Central Association of Colleges and Schools **Credit Hours For Degree:** 100 quarter hours, Associates **Professional Accreditation:** APTA, ACBSP, CARC, JRCERT, NLN

NORTHWEST STATE COMMUNITY COLLEGE
22-600 State Route 34
Archbold, OH 43502-9542
Tel: (419)267-5511
Admissions: (419)267-1213
Fax: (419)267-3688
Web Site: http://www.northweststate.edu
President/CEO: Dr. Betty Young
Registrar: Denise Leu
Admissions: Jeffrey Ferezan
Financial Aid: Paul Sutcliffe
Type: Two-Year College **Sex:** Coed **Affiliation:** Ohio Board of Regents **Scores:** 53% ACT 18-23; 14% ACT 24-29 **Admission Plans:** Open Admission; Early Admission; Deferred Admission **Application Fee:** $20.00 **H.S. Requirements:** High school diploma required; GED accepted **Costs Per Year:** Application fee: $20. State resident tuition: $3660 full-time, $122 per credit part-time. Nonresident tuition: $6750 full-time, $225 per credit part-time. Mandatory fees: $180 full-time, $6 per credit part-time, $30 per term part-time. Full-time tuition and fees vary according to course load. Part-time tuition and fees vary according to course load. **Scholarships:** Available **Calendar System:** Semester, Summer Session Available **Enrollment:** FT 1,088, PT 2,057 **Faculty:** FT 45, PT 127 **Student-Faculty Ratio:** 18:1 **Library Holdings:** 15,321 **Regional Accreditation:** North Central Association of Colleges and Schools **Credit Hours For Degree:** 62 semester hours, Associates **Professional Accreditation:** ABET, ACBSP, NLN

NOTRE DAME COLLEGE
4545 College Rd.
South Euclid, OH 44121-4293
Tel: (216)381-1680
Free: 800-632-1680
Admissions: (216)373-5214
Fax: (216)381-3802
Web Site: http://www.notredamecollege.edu/
President/CEO: Dr. Andrew Roth
Registrar: Sr. Donna Paluf, SND
Admissions; David Armstrong, Esq
Financial Aid: Mary McCrystal
Type: Comprehensive **Sex:** Coed **Affiliation:** Roman Catholic **Scores:** 88% SAT V 400+; 92% SAT M 400+; 67% ACT 18-23; 10% ACT 24-29 **Admission Plans:** Deferred Admission **Application Fee:** $30.00 **H.S. Requirements:** High school diploma required; GED accepted **Costs Per Year:** Application fee: $30. Comprehensive fee: $25,868 includes full-time tuition ($18,670), mandatory fees ($550), and college room and board ($6648). College room only: $3300. Full-time tuition and fees vary according to class time, course load, and degree level. Room and board charges vary according to board plan. Part-time tuition: $405 per credit. Part-time tuition varies according to class time, course load, and degree level. **Scholarships:** Available **Calendar System:** Semester, Summer Session Available **Enrollment:** FT 505, PT 494, Grad 300 **Faculty:** FT 27, PT 60 **Student-Faculty Ratio:** 14:1 **Exams:** SAT I or ACT **% Receiving Financial Aid:** 82 **% Residing in College-Owned, -Operated, or -Affiliated Housing:** 50 **Regional Accreditation:** North Central Association of Colleges and Schools **Credit Hours For Degree:** 64 semester hours, Associates; 128 semester hours, Bachelors **Intercollegiate Athletics:** Baseball M; Basketball M & W; Cross-

Country Running M & W; Field Hockey W; Golf M & W; Soccer M & W; Softball W; Tennis M; Track and Field M & W; Volleyball W

OBERLIN COLLEGE
173 West Lorain St.
Oberlin, OH 44074
Tel: (440)775-8121
Free: 800-622-OBIE
Admissions: (440)775-8411
Fax: (440)775-8886
Web Site: http://www.oberlin.edu/
President/CEO: Dr. Nancy Schrom Dye
Registrar: Elizabeth Clerkin
Admissions: Debra Chermonte
Financial Aid: Robert Reddy
Type: Comprehensive **Sex:** Coed **Scores:** 100% SAT V 400+; 100% SAT M 400+; 13% ACT 18-23; 43% ACT 24-29 **% Accepted:** 34 **Admission Plans:** Early Admission; Early Decision Plan; Deferred Admission **Application Deadline:** January 15 **Application Fee:** $35.00 **H.S. Requirements:** High school diploma required; GED accepted **Costs Per Year:** Application fee: $35. Comprehensive fee: $40,904 includes full-time tuition ($32,524), mandatory fees ($200), and college room and board ($8180). College room only: $4300. Full-time tuition and fees vary according to course load. Room and board charges vary according to board plan and housing facility. Part-time tuition: $1350 per credit. Part-time tuition varies according to course load. **Scholarships:** Available **Calendar System:** 4-1-4, Summer Session Not available **Enrollment:** FT 2,755, PT 90, Grad 19 **Faculty:** FT 288 **Student-Faculty Ratio:** 10:1 **Exams:** SAT I or ACT, SAT II **% Receiving Financial Aid:** 60 **% Residing in College-Owned, -Operated, or -Affiliated Housing:** 73 **Library Holdings:** 1,541,260 **Regional Accreditation:** North Central Association of Colleges and Schools **Credit Hours For Degree:** 112 credit hours, Bachelors **Professional Accreditation:** NASM **Intercollegiate Athletics:** Baseball M; Basketball M & W; Cheerleading W; Cross-Country Running M & W; Equestrian Sports M & W; Fencing M & W; Field Hockey W; Football M; Golf M & W; Ice Hockey M & W; Lacrosse M & W; Rugby M & W; Soccer M & W; Softball W; Swimming and Diving M & W; Tennis M & W; Track and Field M & W; Ultimate Frisbee M & W; Volleyball M & W; Water Polo M & W

OHIO BUSINESS COLLEGE (LORAIN)
1907 North Ridge Rd.
Lorain, OH 44055
Tel: (440)277-0021; 888-514-3126
Fax: (440)277-7989
Web Site: http://www.ohiobusinesscollege.com/
Registrar: Francie Tomazin
Admissions: Jim Unger
Financial Aid: Tamara Jones
Type: Two-Year College **Sex:** Coed **Affiliation:** Tri State Educational Systems **Admission Plans:** Open Admission **Application Fee:** $25.00 **H.S. Requirements:** High school diploma required; GED accepted **Scholarships:** Available **Calendar System:** Quarter, Summer Session Available **Enrollment:** FT 232, PT 26 **Faculty:** FT 3, PT 11 **Student-Faculty Ratio:** 18:1 **Exams:** Other **Library Holdings:** 850 **Professional Accreditation:** ACICS

OHIO BUSINESS COLLEGE (SANDUSKY)
4020 Milan Rd.
Sandusky, OH 44870-5894
Tel: (419)627-8345; 888-627-8345
Fax: (419)627-1958
E-mail: sandusky@ohiobusinesscollege.edu
Web Site: http://www.ohiobusinesscollege.com/
President/CEO: Theresa Fisher
Admissions: Cecilia Blevins
Type: Two-Year College **Sex:** Coed **% Accepted:** 100 **Application Fee:** $25.00 **Costs Per Year:** Application fee: $25. Tuition: $7380 full-time. **Calendar System:** Quarter **Enrollment:** FT 157, PT 35 **Faculty:** PT 30 **Student-Faculty Ratio:** 10:1 **Professional Accreditation:** ACICS

OHIO COLLEGE OF MASSOTHERAPY
225 Heritage Woods Dr.
Akron, OH 44321
Tel: (330)665-1084
Fax: (330)665-5021
E-mail: johna@ocm.edu
Web Site: http://www.ocm.edu/
President/CEO: Jeffrey S. Morrow
Admissions: John Atkins
Type: Two-Year College **Sex:** Coed **Calendar System:** Semester **Professional Accreditation:** ACCSCT

OHIO DOMINICAN UNIVERSITY
1216 Sunbury Rd.
Columbus, OH 43219-2099
Tel: (614)253-2741
Free: 800-854-2670
Admissions: (614)251-4588
Fax: (614)252-0776
E-mail: admissions@odc.edu
Web Site: http://www.ohiodominican.edu/
President/CEO: Dr. Jack P. Calareso
Registrar: Shirley L.H. McBrayer
Admissions: David Archibald
Financial Aid: Cindy Hahn
Type: Comprehensive **Sex:** Coed **Affiliation:** Roman Catholic **Scores:** 74% ACT 18-23; 15% ACT 24-29 **% Accepted:** 72 **Admission Plans:** Deferred Admission **Application Deadline:** Rolling **Application Fee:** $25.00 **H.S. Requirements:** High school diploma required; GED accepted **Costs Per Year:** Application fee: $25. One-time mandatory fee: $125. Comprehensive fee: $25,950 includes full-time tuition ($19,400), mandatory fees ($50), and college room and board ($6500). Room and board charges vary according to board plan and housing facility. Part-time tuition: $400 per credit hour. Part-time mandatory fees: $100 per term. **Scholarships:** Available **Calendar System:** Semester, Summer Session Available **Enrollment:** FT 1,702, PT 857, Grad 383 **Faculty:** FT 66, PT 135 **Student-Faculty Ratio:** 15:1 **Exams:** SAT I or ACT **% Residing in College-Owned, -Operated, or -Affiliated Housing:** 29 **Library Holdings:** 105,722 **Regional Accreditation:** North Central Association of Colleges and Schools **Credit Hours For Degree:** 62 credit hours, Associates; 124 credit hours, Bachelors **ROTC:** Army **Intercollegiate Athletics:** Baseball M; Basketball M & W; Cheerleading M & W; Cross-Country Running M & W; Football M; Golf M & W; Soccer M & W; Softball W; Tennis M & W; Volleyball W

OHIO INSTITUTE OF PHOTOGRAPHY AND TECHNOLOGY
2029 Edgefield Rd.
Dayton, OH 45439-1917
Tel: (937)294-6155
Free: 800-932-9698
Fax: (937)294-2259
Web Site: http://www.oipt.com/
President/CEO: Robert Martin
Registrar: Nancey Springhalt
Financial Aid: Debbie Petrae
Type: Two-Year College **Sex:** Coed **Affiliation:** Kaplan Higher Education **% Accepted:** 55 **Admission Plans:** Early Admission; Deferred Admission **Application Deadline:** Rolling **Application Fee:** $100.00 **H.S. Requirements:** High school diploma required; GED accepted **Costs Per Year:** Application fee: $100. Tuition: $17,641 full-time. Mandatory fees: $1248 full-time. **Scholarships:** Available **Calendar System:** Quarter, Summer Session Available **Enrollment:** FT 740 **Faculty:** FT 21, PT 25 **Student-Faculty Ratio:** 25:1 **Library Holdings:** 640 **Credit Hours For Degree:** 96 credit hours, Associates **Professional Accreditation:** ACCSCT

OHIO NORTHERN UNIVERSITY
525 South Main
Ada, OH 45810-1599
Tel: (419)772-2000; 888-408-4ONU
Admissions: (419)772-2260
Fax: (419)772-2313
E-mail: admissions-ug@onu.edu
Web Site: http://www.onu.edu/
President/CEO: Dr. Kendall L. Baker
Registrar: Naomi Theye
Admissions: Karen Condeni
Financial Aid: Wendell Schick
Type: Comprehensive **Sex:** Coed **Affiliation:** United Methodist Church **Scores:** 98% SAT V 400+; 99% SAT M 400+; 33% ACT 18-23; 53% ACT 24-29 **% Accepted:** 88 **Admission Plans:** Deferred Admission **Application Deadline:** August 15 **Application Fee:** $30.00 **H.S. Requirements:** High

school diploma required; GED accepted **Costs Per Year:** Application fee: $30. Comprehensive fee: $35,340 includes full-time tuition ($28,050), mandatory fees ($210), and college room and board ($7080). College room only: $3540. **Scholarships:** Available **Calendar System:** Quarter, Summer Session Available **Enrollment:** FT 2,525, PT 72, Grad 1 **Faculty:** FT 205, PT 77 **Student-Faculty Ratio:** 14:1 **Exams:** SAT I or ACT **% Receiving Financial Aid:** 81 **% Residing in College-Owned, -Operated, or -Affiliated Housing:** 79 **Library Holdings:** 250,231 **Regional Accreditation:** North Central Association of Colleges and Schools **Credit Hours For Degree:** 182 credit hours, Bachelors **ROTC:** Army, Air Force **Professional Accreditation:** AACSB, ABET, ABA, ACPhE, AALS, JRCEPAT, NASM, NCATE **Intercollegiate Athletics:** Baseball M; Basketball M & W; Cross-Country Running M & W; Football M; Golf M & W; Soccer M & W; Softball W; Swimming and Diving M & W; Tennis M & W; Track and Field M & W; Volleyball W; Wrestling M

THE OHIO STATE UNIVERSITY

Enarson Hall, 154 W. 12th Ave.
Columbus, OH 43210
Tel: (614)292-6446
Admissions: (614)247-6281
Fax: (614)292-4818
Web Site: http://www.osu.edu/
President/CEO: Dr. Karen A. Holbrook
Registrar: Bradley Allan Myers
Admissions: Dr. Mabel G. Freeman
Financial Aid: Natala Kleather Hart

Type: University **Sex:** Coed **Scores:** 99% SAT V 400+; 100% SAT M 400+; 24% ACT 18-23; 60% ACT 24-29 **% Accepted:** 74 **Application Deadline:** February 01 **Application Fee:** $40.00 **H.S. Requirements:** High school diploma required; GED accepted **Costs Per Year:** Application fee: $40. State resident tuition: $7929 full-time. Nonresident tuition: $19,152 full-time. Mandatory fees: $153 full-time. Full-time tuition and fees vary according to course load, program, reciprocity agreements, and student level. College room and board: $7275. Room and board charges vary according to board plan and housing facility. **Scholarships:** Available **Calendar System:** Quarter, Summer Session Available **Enrollment:** FT 33,817, PT 3,594, Grad 9,824 **Faculty:** FT 2,872, PT 1,023 **Student-Faculty Ratio:** 13:1 **Exams:** SAT I or ACT **% Receiving Financial Aid:** 52 **% Residing in College-Owned, -Operated, or -Affiliated Housing:** 24 **Library Holdings:** 5,603,403 **Regional Accreditation:** North Central Association of Colleges and Schools **Credit Hours For Degree:** 191 quarter hours, Bachelors **ROTC:** Army, Navy, Air Force **Professional Accreditation:** AACSB, ABET, ACPE, ACEHSA, AAMFT, AACN, AAFCS, ABA, ACNM, ACPhE, ADA, ADtA, AHIMA, ACSP, AOTA, AOA, APTA, APA, ASLA, ASLHA AVMA, ACIPE, AALS, CARC, CEPH, CORE, CSWE, FIDER, LCMEAMA, NAACLS, NASAD, NASD, NASM, NASPAA, NAST, NCATE, SAF **Intercollegiate Athletics:** Baseball M; Basketball M & W; Cheerleading M & W; Cross-Country Running M & W; Fencing M & W; Field Hockey W; Football M; Golf M & W; Gymnastics M & W; Ice Hockey M & W; Lacrosse M & W; Riflery M & W; Soccer M & W; Softball W; Swimming and Diving M & W; Tennis M & W; Track and Field M & W; Volleyball M & W; Wrestling M

THE OHIO STATE UNIVERSITY AGRICULTURAL TECHNICAL INSTITUTE

1328 Dover Rd.
Wooster, OH 44691
Tel: (330)264-3911
Web Site: http://www.ati.ohio-state.edu/
President/CEO: Dr. Chris O. Igodan
Registrar: Dr. Steven Neal
Financial Aid: Barbara LaMoreaux

Type: Two-Year College **Sex:** Coed **Affiliation:** Ohio State University **Scores:** 66.6% SAT V 400+; 88.9% SAT M 400+; 46% ACT 18-23; 11% ACT 24-29 **% Accepted:** 95 **Admission Plans:** Open Admission; Early Admission **Application Deadline:** July 01 **Application Fee:** $40.00 **H.S. Requirements:** High school diploma required; GED accepted **Costs Per Year:** Application fee: $40. State resident tuition: $5478 full-time. Nonresident tuition: $16,701 full-time. Mandatory fees: $38 full-time. Full-time tuition and fees vary according to course load. College room and board: $5475. College room only: $4575. Room and board charges vary according to board plan. **Calendar System:** Quarter, Summer Session Available **Enrollment:** FT 721, PT 100 **Faculty:** FT 33, PT 37 **Student-Faculty Ratio:** 16:1 **Exams:** SAT I or ACT **% Residing in College-Owned, -Operated, or -Affiliated Housing:** 22 **Library Holdings:** 19,009 **Regional Accreditation:** North Central Association of Colleges and Schools **Credit Hours For Degree:** 100 quarter hours, Associates **ROTC:** Army, Navy, Air Force

THE OHIO STATE UNIVERSITY AT LIMA

4240 Campus Dr.
Lima, OH 45804
Tel: (419)995-8600
Admissions: (419)995-8434
Fax: (419)995-8483
E-mail: admissions@lima.ohio-state.edu
Web Site: http://www.lima.osu.edu/
President/CEO: Dr. John Snyder
Admissions: Beth Keehn
Financial Aid: Diane Douglass

Type: Comprehensive **Sex:** Coed **Affiliation:** Ohio State University **Scores:** 74% SAT V 400+; 100% SAT M 400+; 58% ACT 18-23; 24% ACT 24-29 **% Accepted:** 99 **Admission Plans:** Open Admission; Early Admission **Application Deadline:** July 01 **Application Fee:** $40.00 **H.S. Requirements:** High school diploma required; GED accepted **Costs Per Year:** Application fee: $40. State resident tuition: $5310 full-time. Nonresident tuition: $16,533 full-time. Full-time tuition varies according to course load and student level. College room and board: $6264. Room and board charges vary according to housing facility. **Calendar System:** Quarter, Summer Session Available **Enrollment:** FT 856, PT 212, Grad 77 **Faculty:** FT 38, PT 39 **Student-Faculty Ratio:** 19:1 **Exams:** SAT I or ACT **Library Holdings:** 74,619 **Regional Accreditation:** North Central Association of Colleges and Schools **Credit Hours For Degree:** 90 quarter hours, Associates; 196 quarter hours, Bachelors **ROTC:** Army, Navy, Air Force **Intercollegiate Athletics:** Basketball M & W; Golf M

THE OHIO STATE UNIVERSITY-MANSFIELD CAMPUS

1680 University Dr.
Mansfield, OH 44906-1599
Tel: (419)755-4011
Admissions: (419)755-4225
E-mail: admissions@mansfield.ohio-state.edu
Web Site: http://www.mansfield.osu.edu/
President/CEO: Dr. Evelyn B. Freeman
Admissions: Henry D. Thomas
Financial Aid: Henry D. Thomas

Type: Comprehensive **Sex:** Coed **Affiliation:** Ohio State University **Scores:** 92% SAT V 400+; 90% SAT M 400+; 58% ACT 18-23; 22% ACT 24-29 **% Accepted:** 100 **Admission Plans:** Open Admission; Early Admission **Application Deadline:** July 01 **Application Fee:** $40.00 **H.S. Requirements:** High school diploma required; GED accepted **Costs Per Year:** Application fee: $40. State resident tuition: $5310 full-time. Nonresident tuition: $16,533 full-time. Full-time tuition varies according to course load and student level. College room and board: $6264. Room and board charges vary according to housing facility. **Calendar System:** Quarter, Summer Session Available **Enrollment:** FT 1,050, PT 463, Grad 97 **Faculty:** FT 48, PT 41 **Student-Faculty Ratio:** 21:1 **Exams:** SAT I or ACT **Library Holdings:** 45,977 **Regional Accreditation:** North Central Association of Colleges and Schools **Credit Hours For Degree:** 90 quarter hours, Associates; 196 quarter hours, Bachelors **ROTC:** Army, Navy, Air Force

THE OHIO STATE UNIVERSITY AT MARION

1465 Mount Vernon Ave.
Marion, OH 43302-5695
Tel: (740)389-6786
E-mail: moreau.1@osu.edu
Web Site: http://www.marion.ohio-state.edu/
President/CEO: Dr. Gregory S. Rose
Registrar: Kimberly Ferguson
Admissions: Matthew Moreau
Financial Aid: Michael Short

Type: Comprehensive **Sex:** Coed **Affiliation:** Ohio State University **Scores:** 91% SAT V 400+; 96% SAT M 400+; 61% ACT 18-23; 19% ACT 24-29 **% Accepted:** 100 **Admission Plans:** Open Admission; Early Admission **Application Deadline:** July 01 **Application Fee:** $40.00 **H.S. Requirements:** High school diploma required; GED accepted **Costs Per Year:** Application fee: $40. State resident tuition: $5310 full-time. Nonresident tuition: $16,533 full-time. Full-time tuition varies according to course load and student level. **Calendar System:** Quarter, Summer Session Available **Enrollment:** FT 1,159, PT 247, Grad 79 **Faculty:** FT 35, PT 73 **Student-Faculty Ratio:** 22:1 **Library Holdings:** 38,858 **Regional Accreditation:** North Central Association of Colleges and Schools **Credit Hours For Degree:** 90 quarter hours, Associates; 196 quarter hours, Bachelors **ROTC:** Army, Navy, Air Force

THE OHIO STATE UNIVERSITY-NEWARK CAMPUS
1179 University Dr.
Newark, OH 43055-1797
Tel: (740)366-3321
Admissions: (614)366-9333
E-mail: vogelmeier.1@osu.edu
Web Site: http://www.newark.osu.edu/
President/CEO: Dr. Willilam MacDonald
Registrar: Kyle Morgan
Admissions: Ann Donahue
Financial Aid: Faith Phillips
Type: Comprehensive **Sex:** Coed **Affiliation:** Ohio State University **Scores:** 90% SAT V 400+; 92% SAT M 400+; 64% ACT 18-23; 17% ACT 24-29 **% Accepted:** 99 **Admission Plans:** Open Admission; Early Admission **Application Deadline:** July 01 **Application Fee:** $40.00 **H.S. Requirements:** High school diploma required; GED accepted **Costs Per Year:** Application fee: $40. State resident tuition: $5310 full-time. Nonresident tuition: $16,533 full-time. Full-time tuition varies according to course load and student level. College room and board: $6264. Room and board charges vary according to housing facility. **Calendar System:** Quarter, Summer Session Available **Enrollment:** FT 1,765, PT 323, Grad 95 **Faculty:** FT 50, PT 85 **Student-Faculty Ratio:** 25:1 **Library Holdings:** 49,232 **Regional Accreditation:** North Central Association of Colleges and Schools **Credit Hours For Degree:** 90 quarter hours, Associates; 196 quarter hours, Bachelors **ROTC:** Army, Navy, Air Force

OHIO TECHNICAL COLLEGE
1374 East 51st St.
Cleveland, OH 44103
Tel: (216)881-1700
Free: 800-322-7000
Fax: (216)881-9145
E-mail: ohioauto@aol.com
Web Site: http://www.ohiotechnicalcollege.com/
President/CEO: Marc Brenner
Admissions: Marc Brenner
Type: Two-Year College **Sex:** Coed **Professional Accreditation:** ACCSCT

OHIO UNIVERSITY
Athens, OH 45701-2979
Tel: (740)593-1000
Admissions: (740)593-4100
Fax: (740)593-4229
E-mail: uadmiss1@ohiou.edu
Web Site: http://www.ohio.edu/
President/CEO: Dr. Roderick J. McDavis
Registrar: Debra Benton
Admissions: David Garcia
Financial Aid: Sondra R. Williams
Type: University **Sex:** Coed **Affiliation:** Ohio Board of Regents **Scores:** 98% SAT V 400+; 97% SAT M 400+; 55% ACT 18-23; 36% ACT 24-29 **% Accepted:** 89 **Admission Plans:** Early Admission; Deferred Admission **Application Deadline:** February 01 **Application Fee:** $45.00 **H.S. Requirements:** High school diploma required; GED accepted **Costs Per Year:** Application fee: $45. State resident tuition: $8235 full-time, $262 per quarter hour part-time. Nonresident tuition: $17,199 full-time, $557 per quarter hour part-time. College room and board: $7686. College room only: $3855. Room and board charges vary according to board plan. **Scholarships:** Available **Calendar System:** Quarter, Summer Session Available **Enrollment:** FT 16,090, PT 1,101, Grad 2,776 **Faculty:** FT 875, PT 320 **Student-Faculty Ratio:** 18:1 **Exams:** SAT I or ACT **% Receiving Financial Aid:** 48 **% Residing in College-Owned, -Operated, or -Affiliated Housing:** 43 **Library Holdings:** 2,550,511 **Regional Accreditation:** North Central Association of Colleges and Schools **Credit Hours For Degree:** 96 quarter hours, Associates; 192 quarter hours, Bachelors **ROTC:** Army, Air Force **Professional Accreditation:** AACSB, ABET, ACEJMC, AACN, AAFCS, ACA, AOsA, APTA, APA, ASLHA, CORE, CSWE, FIDER, JRCEPAT, NASAD, NASD, NASM, NAST, NCATE, NLN NRPA **Intercollegiate Athletics:** Baseball M; Basketball M & W; Cheerleading M & W; Cross-Country Running M & W; Equestrian Sports M & W; Field Hockey W; Football M; Golf M & W; Ice Hockey M; Lacrosse M & W; Rugby M & W; Soccer M & W; Softball W; Swimming and Diving M & W; Track and Field M & W; Volleyball M & W; Water Polo M & W; Weight Lifting M; Wrestling M

OHIO UNIVERSITY-CHILLICOTHE
571 West Fifth St., PO Box 629
Chillicothe, OH 45601-0629
Tel: (740)774-7200
Fax: (740)774-7295
Web Site: http://www.ohio.edu/chillicothe/
President/CEO: Dr. Richard Bebee
Registrar: Douglas Hennig
Admissions: Doug Henning
Financial Aid: Dennis Bothel
Type: Four-Year College **Sex:** Coed **Affiliation:** Ohio Board of Regents **Admission Plans:** Open Admission; Early Admission **Application Fee:** $20.00 **H.S. Requirements:** High school diploma required; GED accepted **Costs Per Year:** Application fee: $20. State resident tuition: $115 per credit hour part-time. Nonresident tuition: $131 per credit hour part-time. Mandatory fees: $16 per credit hour part-time. **Scholarships:** Available **Calendar System:** Quarter, Summer Session Available **Faculty:** FT 41, PT 65 **Exams:** SAT I or ACT **% Receiving Financial Aid:** 72 **Library Holdings:** 47,900 **Regional Accreditation:** North Central Association of Colleges and Schools **Credit Hours For Degree:** 96 credit hours, Associates; 192 credit hours, Bachelors **ROTC:** Army, Air Force **Professional Accreditation:** NLN **Intercollegiate Athletics:** Baseball M; Basketball M & W; Golf M & W; Volleyball W

OHIO UNIVERSITY-EASTERN
45425 National Rd.
St. Clairsville, OH 43950-9724
Tel: (740)695-1720
Web Site: http://www.eastern.ohiou.edu/
President/CEO: Dr. Paul E. Bibbins, Jr.
Registrar: Kevin Chenowith
Financial Aid: Kevin Chenowith
Type: Four-Year College **Sex:** Coed **Affiliation:** Ohio Board of Regents **Admission Plans:** Open Admission; Early Admission; Deferred Admission **Application Fee:** $20.00 **H.S. Requirements:** High school diploma required; GED accepted **Costs Per Year:** Application fee: $20. Area resident tuition: $115 per credit hour part-time. Nonresident tuition: $131 per credit hour part-time. Mandatory fees: $16 per credit hour part-time. **Scholarships:** Available **Calendar System:** Quarter, Summer Session Available **Enrollment:** FT 681, PT 250, Grad 187 **Faculty:** FT 21, PT 93 **Student-Faculty Ratio:** 23:1 **Exams:** SAT I or ACT **% Receiving Financial Aid:** 65 **Library Holdings:** 50,000 **Regional Accreditation:** North Central Association of Colleges and Schools **Credit Hours For Degree:** 96 quarter hours, Associates; 192 quarter hours, Bachelors **Intercollegiate Athletics:** Basketball M & W; Volleyball W

OHIO UNIVERSITY-LANCASTER
1570 Granville Pike
Lancaster, OH 43130-1097
Tel: (740)654-6711; 888-446-4468
Fax: (740)687-9497
E-mail: shepherd@ohiou.edu
Web Site: http://www.ohiou.edu/lancaster/
President/CEO: Dr. John Furlow
Registrar: Patricia Fox
Admissions: Nathan Thomas
Financial Aid: Patricia Fox
Type: Comprehensive **Sex:** Coed **Affiliation:** Ohio Board of Regents **Scores:** 96% SAT V 400+; 93% SAT M 400+; 55% ACT 18-23; 19% ACT 24-29 **Admission Plans:** Open Admission; Early Admission; Deferred Admission **Application Fee:** $20.00 **H.S. Requirements:** High school diploma required; GED accepted **Costs Per Year:** Application fee: $20. State resident tuition: $127 per credit hour part-time. Nonresident tuition: $144 per credit hour part-time. Mandatory fees: $17 per credit hour part-time. **Scholarships:** Available **Calendar System:** Quarter, Summer Session Available **Enrollment:** FT 880, PT 737, Grad 127 **Faculty:** FT 31, PT 73 **Student-Faculty Ratio:** 30:1 **Exams:** SAT I or ACT **% Receiving Financial Aid:** 70 **Library Holdings:** 94,688 **Regional Accreditation:** North Central Association of Colleges and Schools **Credit Hours For Degree:** 96 quarter hours, Associates; 192 quarter hours, Bachelors **ROTC:** Army, Air Force **Professional Accreditation:** AAMAE **Intercollegiate Athletics:** Basketball M & W; Cheerleading W; Golf M & W; Softball W; Tennis M & W; Volleyball W

OHIO UNIVERSITY-SOUTHERN CAMPUS
1804 Liberty Ave.
Ironton, OH 45638-2214
Tel: (740)533-4600
Free: 800-626-0513
Admissions: (740)533-4612
Fax: (740)533-4632
Web Site: http://www.ohiou.edu/
President/CEO: Dr. Dan Evans
Admissions: Dr. Kim K. Lawson
Type: Comprehensive **Sex:** Coed **Affiliation:** Ohio Board of Regents **Admission Plans:** Open Admission; Early Admission; Deferred Admission **Application Fee:** $20.00 **H.S. Requirements:** High school diploma required; GED accepted **Costs Per Year:** Application fee: $20. State resident tuition: $124 per credit hour part-time. Nonresident tuition: $165 per credit hour part-time. Mandatory fees: $12 per credit hour part-time. Part-time tuition and fees vary according to student level. **Scholarships:** Available **Calendar System:** Quarter, Summer Session Available **Enrollment:** FT 1,110, PT 520, Grad 116 **Faculty:** FT 15, PT 140 **Exams:** SAT I or ACT **% Receiving Financial Aid:** 78 **Library Holdings:** 26,000 **Regional Accreditation:** North Central Association of Colleges and Schools **Credit Hours For Degree:** 96 quarter hours, Associates; 192 quarter hours, Bachelors **Intercollegiate Athletics:** Basketball M & W

OHIO UNIVERSITY-ZANESVILLE
1425 Newark Rd.
Zanesville, OH 43701-2695
Tel: (740)453-0762
Admissions: (740)588-1439
Fax: (740)453-6161
Web Site: http://www.zanesville.ohiou.edu/
President/CEO: Dr. James W. Fonseca
Registrar: Dr. Donna Clevinger
Admissions: Monica S. Jones
Financial Aid: Sharon D. Lenthe
Type: Comprehensive **Sex:** Coed **Affiliation:** Ohio Board of Regents **Scores:** 53% ACT 18-23; 21% ACT 24-29 **% Accepted:** 100 **Admission Plans:** Open Admission; Early Admission; Deferred Admission **Application Deadline:** Rolling **Application Fee:** $20.00 **H.S. Requirements:** High school diploma required; GED accepted **Costs Per Year:** Application fee: $20. State resident tuition: $4596 full-time, $144 per credit hour part-time. Nonresident tuition: $8919 full-time, $275 per credit hour part-time. Full-time tuition varies according to course level. Part-time tuition varies according to course level. **Scholarships:** Available **Calendar System:** Quarter, Summer Session Available **Enrollment:** FT 1,139, PT 710, Grad 55 **Faculty:** FT 31, PT 99 **Student-Faculty Ratio:** 23:1 **Exams:** SAT I or ACT **% Receiving Financial Aid:** 74 **Library Holdings:** 64,227 **Regional Accreditation:** North Central Association of Colleges and Schools **Credit Hours For Degree:** 96 quarter hours, Associates; 192 quarter hours, Bachelors **Professional Accreditation:** NLN **Intercollegiate Athletics:** Baseball M; Basketball M & W; Golf M & W; Softball W; Tennis M & W; Volleyball W

OHIO VALLEY COLLEGE OF TECHNOLOGY
16808 St. Clair Ave., PO Box 7000
East Liverpool, OH 43920
Tel: (330)385-1070
Web Site: http://www.ovct.edu/
President/CEO: Debra Sanford
Admissions: Scott S. Rogers
Financial Aid: Virginia Hutchinson
Type: Two-Year College **Sex:** Coed **Application Fee:** $0.00 **H.S. Requirements:** High school diploma required; GED accepted **Scholarships:** Available **Calendar System:** Semester, Summer Session Available **Enrollment:** FT 121, PT 5 **Faculty:** FT 4, PT 7 **Student-Faculty Ratio:** 18:1 **Exams:** Other **Credit Hours For Degree:** 64 credits, Associates **Professional Accreditation:** ACICS, AAMAE

OHIO WESLEYAN UNIVERSITY
61 South Sandusky St.
Delaware, OH 43015
Tel: (740)368-2000
Free: 800-922-8953
Admissions: (740)368-3025
Fax: (740)368-3314
E-mail: midrugov@owu.edu
Web Site: http://www.owu.edu/
President/CEO: Dr. Mark Huddleston
Registrar: Sally A. Sikorski
Admissions: Margaret L. Drugovich
Financial Aid: Gregory W. Matthews
Type: Four-Year College **Sex:** Coed **Affiliation:** United Methodist **Scores:** 99.42% SAT V 400+; 100% SAT M 400+; 20.76% ACT 18-23; 61.94% ACT 24-29 **% Accepted:** 75 **Admission Plans:** Early Admission; Early Action; Early Decision Plan; Deferred Admission **Application Deadline:** March 01 **Application Fee:** $35.00 **H.S. Requirements:** High school diploma required; GED accepted **Costs Per Year:** Application fee: $35. Comprehensive fee: $35,830 includes full-time tuition ($27,920), mandatory fees ($360), and college room and board ($7550). College room only: $3750. Room and board charges vary according to board plan. Part-time tuition: $3040 per course. **Scholarships:** Available **Calendar System:** Semester, Summer Session Available **Enrollment:** FT 1,941, PT 35 **Faculty:** FT 130, PT 61 **Student-Faculty Ratio:** 13:1 **Exams:** SAT I or ACT, SAT II **% Receiving Financial Aid:** 56 **% Residing in College-Owned, -Operated, or -Affiliated Housing:** 84 **Library Holdings:** 441,912 **Regional Accreditation:** North Central Association of Colleges and Schools **Credit Hours For Degree:** 34 units, Bachelors **ROTC:** Army **Professional Accreditation:** NASM **Intercollegiate Athletics:** Baseball M; Basketball M & W; Cross-Country Running M & W; Equestrian Sports M & W; Field Hockey W; Football M; Golf M; Ice Hockey M & W; Lacrosse M & W; Rugby M & W; Sailing M & W; Soccer M & W; Softball W; Swimming and Diving M & W; Tennis M & W; Track and Field M & W; Ultimate Frisbee M & W; Volleyball M & W

OTTERBEIN COLLEGE
1 Otterbein College
Westerville, OH 43081
Tel: (614)890-3000
Free: 800-488-8144
Admissions: (614)823-1500
Fax: (614)823-1200
E-mail: uotterb@otterbein.edu
Web Site: http://www.otterbein.edu/
President/CEO: Dr. C. Brent DeVore
Registrar: Donald Foster
Admissions: Dr. Cass Johnson
Financial Aid: Thomas V. Yarnell
Type: Comprehensive **Sex:** Coed **Affiliation:** United Methodist **Scores:** 95% SAT V 400+; 94% SAT M 400+; 53% ACT 18-23; 37% ACT 24-29 **% Accepted:** 77 **Admission Plans:** Deferred Admission **Application Deadline:** March 01 **Application Fee:** $25.00 **H.S. Requirements:** High school diploma required; GED accepted **Costs Per Year:** Application fee: $25. Comprehensive fee: $28,986 includes full-time tuition ($22,518) and college room and board ($6468). College room only: $2994. Full-time tuition varies according to course load and program. Room and board charges vary according to housing facility. Part-time tuition: $270 per credit hour. Part-time tuition varies according to course load and program. **Scholarships:** Available **Calendar System:** Quarter, Summer Session Available **Enrollment:** FT 2,261, PT 463, Grad 370 **Faculty:** FT 157, PT 119 **Student-Faculty Ratio:** 13:1 **Exams:** SAT I or ACT **% Residing in College-Owned, -Operated, or -Affiliated Housing:** 52 **Library Holdings:** 182,629 **Regional Accreditation:** North Central Association of Colleges and Schools **Credit Hours For Degree:** 180 credit hours, Bachelors **ROTC:** Army, Air Force **Professional Accreditation:** AACN, JRCEPAT, NASM, NAST, NCATE, NLN **Intercollegiate Athletics:** Baseball M; Basketball M & W; Cheerleading M & W; Cross-Country Running M & W; Equestrian Sports M & W; Football M; Golf M & W; Soccer M & W; Softball W; Tennis M & W; Track and Field M & W; Volleyball W

OWENS COMMUNITY COLLEGE
PO Box 10000
Toledo, OH 43699-1947
Tel: (419)661-7000
Free: 800-GO-OWENS
Admissions: (567)661-7225
E-mail: william_ivoska@owens.edu
Web Site: http://www.owens.edu/
President/CEO: Dr. Christa Adams
Registrar: Lorinda Bishop

Admissions: Dr. William Ivoska
Financial Aid: Betsy Johnson
Type: Two-Year College **Sex:** Coed **Admission Plans:** Open Admission; Early Admission **Application Deadline:** Rolling **Application Fee:** $0.00 **H.S. Requirements:** High school diploma required; GED accepted **Costs Per Year:** Application fee: $0. State resident tuition: $2784 full-time, $116 per credit part-time. Nonresident tuition: $5208 full-time, $217 per credit part-time. Mandatory fees: $400 full-time, $15 per credit part-time, $10 per term part-time. **Scholarships:** Available **Calendar System:** Semester, Summer Session Available **Enrollment:** FT 7,531, PT 12,713 **Faculty:** FT 187, PT 1,031 **Student-Faculty Ratio:** 22:1 **Library Holdings:** 78,344 **Regional Accreditation:** North Central Association of Colleges and Schools **Credit Hours For Degree:** 65 semester hours, Associates **ROTC:** Army, Air Force **Professional Accreditation:** ABET, ARCEST, ADA, AOTA, APTA, ACBSP, JRCEDMS, JRCERT, NLN **Intercollegiate Athletics:** Baseball M; Basketball M & W; Soccer M; Softball W; Volleyball W

PONTIFICAL COLLEGE JOSEPHINUM
7625 North High St.
Columbus, OH 43235-1498
Tel: (614)885-5585; 888-252-5812
E-mail: pcahall@pcj.edu
Web Site: http://www.pcj.edu/
President/CEO: Rev. Msgr. Paul J. Langsfeld
Registrar: Barbara Couts
Admissions: Perry Cahall
Financial Aid: Marky Leichtnam
Type: Comprehensive **Sex:** Coed **Affiliation:** Roman Catholic **Scores:** 25% ACT 18-23; 25% ACT 24-29 **% Accepted:** 100 **Admission Plans:** Preferred Admission; Deferred Admission **Application Deadline:** July 31 **Application Fee:** $25.00 **H.S. Requirements:** High school diploma required; GED accepted **Costs Per Year:** Application fee: $25. Comprehensive fee: $21,635 includes full-time tuition ($14,000), mandatory fees ($635), and college room and board ($7000). Part-time tuition: $565 per credit hour. **Scholarships:** Available **Calendar System:** Semester, Summer Session Not available **Enrollment:** FT 76, Grad 3 **Faculty:** FT 18, PT 19 **Student-Faculty Ratio:** 6:1 **Exams:** SAT I and SAT II or ACT **% Receiving Financial Aid:** 54 **% Residing in College-Owned, -Operated, or -Affiliated Housing:** 100 **Library Holdings:** 137,883 **Regional Accreditation:** North Central Association of Colleges and Schools **Credit Hours For Degree:** 132 credit hours, Bachelors **Professional Accreditation:** ATS

PROFESSIONAL SKILLS INSTITUTE
20 Arco Dr.
Toledo, OH 43607
Tel: (419)531-9610
Fax: (419)531-4732
Web Site: http://www.proskills.com/
President/CEO: Daniel A. Finch
Admissions: Hope Finch
Financial Aid: Julie Leslie
Type: Two-Year College **Sex:** Coed **H.S. Requirements:** High school diploma required; GED accepted **Scholarships:** Available **Calendar System:** Quarter, Summer Session Not available **Enrollment:** FT 164, PT 10 **Faculty:** FT 5, PT 4 **Student-Faculty Ratio:** 19:1 **Exams:** Other **Library Holdings:** 2,200 **Credit Hours For Degree:** 119 quarter hours, Associates **Professional Accreditation:** ABHES, APTA

RABBINICAL COLLEGE OF TELSHE
28400 Euclid Ave.
Wickliffe, OH 44092-2523
Tel: (216)943-5300 **Type:** Comprehensive **Professional Accreditation:** AARTS

REMINGTON COLLEGE-CLEVELAND CAMPUS
14445 Broadway Ave.
Cleveland, OH 44125
Tel: (216)475-7520
Fax: (216)475-6055
Web Site: http://www.remingtoncollege.edu/
President/CEO: Todd Zvaigzne
Admissions: William Cassidy
Type: Two-Year College **Sex:** Coed **Application Fee:** $50.00 **H.S. Requirements:** High school diploma required; GED accepted **Costs Per Year:** Application fee: $50. Tuition: $15,745 full-time. Full-time tuition varies according to program. **Calendar System:** Continuous **Enrollment:** FT 676 **Faculty:** FT 40, PT 25 **Student-Faculty Ratio:** 15:1 **Credit Hours For Degree:** 96 quarter credit hours, Associates **Professional Accreditation:** ACCSCT

REMINGTON COLLEGE-CLEVELAND WEST CAMPUS
26350 Brookpark Rd.
North Olmsted, OH 44070
Tel: (440)777-2560
Fax: (440)777-3238
E-mail: gary.azotea@remingtoncollege.edu
Web Site: http://www.remingtoncollege.edu/
Admissions: Gary Azotea
Type: Two-Year College **Sex:** Coed **Calendar System:** Quarter **Enrollment:** FT 399 **Faculty:** FT 11, PT 18 **Student-Faculty Ratio:** 23:1

RETS TECH CENTER
555 East Alex Bell Rd.
Centerville, OH 45459
Tel: (937)433-3410
Free: 800-837-7387
Fax: (937)435-6516
Web Site: http://www.retstechcenter.com/
President/CEO: Michael A. LeMaster
Admissions: Kenneth C. Miller
Financial Aid: Andrea Sanders
Type: Two-Year College **Sex:** Coed **Admission Plans:** Early Admission; Deferred Admission **Application Fee:** $0.00 **H.S. Requirements:** High school diploma required; GED accepted **Scholarships:** Available **Calendar System:** Semester, Summer Session Available **Enrollment:** FT 556 **Faculty:** FT 27, PT 56 **Exams:** Other **Library Holdings:** 2,200 **Credit Hours For Degree:** 63 credit hours, Associates **Professional Accreditation:** ACCSCT, AAMAE

ROSEDALE BIBLE COLLEGE
2270 Rosedale Rd.
Irwin, OH 43029-9501
Tel: (740)857-1311
Fax: (740)857-1577
E-mail: pweber@rosedale.edu
Web Site: http://www.rosedalebible.org/
President/CEO: Leon Zimmerman
Admissions: John Showalter
Type: Two-Year College **Sex:** Coed **Affiliation:** Mennonite **Calendar System:** Miscellaneous **Professional Accreditation:** AABC

SCHOOL OF ADVERTISING ART
1725 East David Rd.
Kettering, OH 45440-1612
Tel: (937)294-0592; 877-300-9866
Fax: (937)294-5869
E-mail: jayne@saacollege.com
Web Site: http://www.saacollege.com/
Admissions: Jayne Fahncke
Type: Two-Year College **Sex:** Coed **Application Deadline:** July 01 **Costs Per Year:** Tuition: $17,775 full-time. Mandatory fees: $210 full-time. **Calendar System:** Trimester **Enrollment:** FT 146 **Faculty:** FT 9, PT 11 **Student-Faculty Ratio:** 12:1 **Professional Accreditation:** ACCSCT

SHAWNEE STATE UNIVERSITY
940 Second St.
Portsmouth, OH 45662-4344
Tel: (740)354-3205
Free: 800-959-2SSU
Admissions: (740)351-3610
Fax: (740)355-2470
E-mail: admsn@shawnee.edu
Web Site: http://www.shawnee.edu/
President/CEO: Dr. Rita Rice Morris
Registrar: Dr. Stephen Midkiff
Admissions: Bob Trusz
Financial Aid: Patricia Moore
Type: Four-Year College **Sex:** Coed **Affiliation:** Ohio Board of Regents **Scores:** 55% ACT 18-23; 17% ACT 24-29 **% Accepted:** 100 **Admission Plans:** Open Admission; Deferred Admission **Application Deadline:** Rolling **Application Fee:** $0.00 **H.S. Requirements:** High school diploma required;

GED accepted **Costs Per Year:** Application fee: $0. State resident tuition: $4896 full-time, $153 per credit hour part-time. Nonresident tuition: $8784 full-time, $261 per credit hour part-time. Mandatory fees: $612 full-time, $17 per credit hour part-time. Full-time tuition and fees vary according to course load, reciprocity agreements, and student level. Part-time tuition and fees vary according to course load, reciprocity agreements, and student level. College room and board: $6729. College room only: $4281. Room and board charges vary according to board plan and housing facility. **Scholarships:** Available **Calendar System:** Quarter, Summer Session Available **Enrollment:** FT 3,197, PT 623 **Faculty:** FT 138, PT 160 **Student-Faculty Ratio:** 18:1 **Exams:** ACT **% Receiving Financial Aid:** 67 **% Residing in College-Owned, -Operated, or -Affiliated Housing:** 13 **Library Holdings:** 150,661 **Regional Accreditation:** North Central Association of Colleges and Schools **Credit Hours For Degree:** 90 quarter hours, Associates; 186 quarter hours, Bachelors **Professional Accreditation:** ADA, AOTA, APTA, ACBSP, CARC, JRCERT, NAACLS, NCATE, NLN **Intercollegiate Athletics:** Baseball M; Basketball M & W; Cross-Country Running M & W; Golf M; Soccer M & W; Softball W; Tennis W; Volleyball W

SINCLAIR COMMUNITY COLLEGE
444 West Third St.
Dayton, OH 45402-1460
Tel: (937)512-2500
Admissions: (937)512-3060
E-mail: ssmith@sinclair.edu
Web Site: http://www.sinclair.edu/
President/CEO: Dr. Steven Lee Johnson
Registrar: Raymond G. Elash
Admissions: Sara P. Smith
Financial Aid: Kathy L. Wiesenauer
Type: Two-Year College **Sex:** Coed **Affiliation:** Ohio Board of Regents **% Accepted:** 100 **Admission Plans:** Open Admission; Early Admission; Deferred Admission **Application Deadline:** Rolling **Application Fee:** $10.00 **H.S. Requirements:** High school diploma or equivalent not required. For allied health programs: High school diploma required; GED accepted **Costs Per Year:** Application fee: $10. Area resident tuition: $1910 full-time, $42.25 per credit hour part-time. State resident tuition: $3121 full-time, $69.35 per credit hour part-time. Nonresident tuition: $5940 full-time, $132 per credit hour part-time. Full-time tuition varies according to course load. Part-time tuition varies according to course load. **Scholarships:** Available **Calendar System:** Quarter, Summer Session Available **Enrollment:** FT 7,550, PT 12,013 **Faculty:** FT 466, PT 651 **Student-Faculty Ratio:** 19:1 **Library Holdings:** 147,613 **Regional Accreditation:** North Central Association of Colleges and Schools **Credit Hours For Degree:** 90 quarter hours, Associates **ROTC:** Army, Air Force **Professional Accreditation:** ABET, ARCEST, AAMAE, ACF, ADA, AHIMA, AOTA, APTA, ACBSP, CARC, JRCERT, NAIT, NASAD, NASM, NLN **Intercollegiate Athletics:** Baseball M; Basketball M & W; Golf M; Tennis M & W; Volleyball W

SOUTHEASTERN BUSINESS COLLEGE (CHILLICOTHE)
1855 Western Ave.
Chillicothe, OH 45601-1038
Tel: (740)774-6300
Fax: (740)774-2071
Web Site: http://www.careersohio.com/
President/CEO: Connie Blackburn
Admissions: Elizabeth Scott
Financial Aid: Bernard Wilson
Type: Two-Year College **Sex:** Coed **Scholarships:** Available **Calendar System:** Quarter **Faculty:** FT 3, PT 10 **Student-Faculty Ratio:** 10:1 **Professional Accreditation:** ACICS

SOUTHEASTERN BUSINESS COLLEGE (JACKSON)
504 McCarty Ln.
Jackson, OH 45640
Tel: (740)286-1554
Fax: (740)286-4476
E-mail: todd_sbc@yahoo.com
Web Site: http://www.careersohio.com/
President/CEO: Todd Riegel
Admissions: Todd A. Riegel
Type: Two-Year College **Sex:** Coed **Calendar System:** Quarter **Professional Accreditation:** ACICS

SOUTHEASTERN BUSINESS COLLEGE (LANCASTER)
1522 Sheridan Dr.
Lancaster, OH 43130-1303
Tel: (740)687-6126
Fax: (740)687-0431
E-mail: rp_sbc@yahoo.com
Web Site: http://www.careersohio.com/
President/CEO: Ray Predmore
Admissions: Ray Predmore
Type: Two-Year College **Sex:** Coed **Calendar System:** Quarter **Professional Accreditation:** ACICS

SOUTHEASTERN BUSINESS COLLEGE (NEW BOSTON)
3879 Rhodes Ave.
New Boston, OH 45662
Tel: (740)456-4124
Web Site: http://www.careersohio.com/ **Type:** Two-Year College **Sex:** Coed

SOUTHERN STATE COMMUNITY COLLEGE
100 Hobart Dr.
Hillsboro, OH 45133-9487
Tel: (937)393-3431
Fax: (937)393-9370
E-mail: wjohnson@sscc.edu
Web Site: http://www.sscc.edu/
President/CEO: Dr. Lawrence N. Dukes
Registrar: Sue Leach
Admissions: Wendy Johnson
Financial Aid: Janeen Deatley
Type: Two-Year College **Sex:** Coed **% Accepted:** 100 **Admission Plans:** Open Admission; Early Admission; Deferred Admission **Application Deadline:** Rolling **Application Fee:** $0.00 **H.S. Requirements:** High school diploma required; GED accepted. For applicants who will attend part-time: High school diploma or equivalent not required **Costs Per Year:** Application fee: $0. State resident tuition: $3213 full-time. Nonresident tuition: $6189 full-time. Full-time tuition varies according to course load. **Scholarships:** Available **Calendar System:** Quarter, Summer Session Available **Enrollment:** FT 1,297, PT 1,010 **Faculty:** FT 52, PT 82 **Student-Faculty Ratio:** 21:1 **Library Holdings:** 79,000 **Regional Accreditation:** North Central Association of Colleges and Schools **Credit Hours For Degree:** 90 quarter hours, Associates **Professional Accreditation:** AAMAE, NLN **Intercollegiate Athletics:** Baseball M; Basketball M & W; Soccer M; Softball W; Volleyball W

SOUTHWESTERN COLLEGE OF BUSINESS (CINCINNATI)
632 Vine St., Ste. 200
Cincinnati, OH 45202-4304
Tel: (513)421-3212
Web Site: http://www.swcollege.net/
President/CEO: Gary Wright
Registrar: Peter Hausman
Admissions: Betty Streber
Financial Aid: Sharon Snowden
Type: Two-Year College **Sex:** Coed **Admission Plans:** Deferred Admission **Application Fee:** $0.00 **H.S. Requirements:** High school diploma required; GED accepted **Calendar System:** Quarter, Summer Session Available **Faculty:** PT 17 **Exams:** Other **Credit Hours For Degree:** 99 credit hours, Associates **Professional Accreditation:** ACICS

SOUTHWESTERN COLLEGE OF BUSINESS (CINCINNATI)
149 Northland Blvd.
Cincinnati, OH 45246-1122
Tel: (513)874-0432
Web Site: http://www.swcollege.net/
President/CEO: Gary Wright
Registrar: Jim Potts
Admissions: Greg Petree
Type: Two-Year College **Sex:** Coed **Admission Plans:** Deferred Admission **Application Fee:** $0.00 **H.S. Requirements:** High school diploma required; GED accepted **Calendar System:** Quarter, Summer Session Available **Faculty:** FT 8, PT 11 **Exams:** Other **Credit Hours For Degree:** 96 credits,

Associates **Professional Accreditation:** ACICS

SOUTHWESTERN COLLEGE OF BUSINESS (DAYTON)
111 West First St.
Dayton, OH 45402-3003
Tel: (937)224-0061
Fax: (937)224-0065
Web Site: http://www.swcollege.net/
President/CEO: Gary Wright
Registrar: Jennifer Minge
Admissions: Kathie Day
Type: Two-Year College **Sex:** Coed **Admission Plans:** Deferred Admission **Application Fee:** $0.00 **H.S. Requirements:** High school diploma required; GED accepted **Calendar System:** Quarter, Summer Session Available **Enrollment:** FT 214 **Faculty:** FT 3, PT 14 **Student-Faculty Ratio:** 15:1 **Credit Hours For Degree:** 96 credits, Associates **Professional Accreditation:** ACICS

SOUTHWESTERN COLLEGE OF BUSINESS (FRANKLIN)
201 East Second St.
Franklin, OH 45005
Tel: (937)746-6633
Web Site: http://www.swcollege.net/
President/CEO: Gary Wright
Registrar: Gaylan Martin
Admissions: Susan Knodel
Financial Aid: Shirley Day
Type: Two-Year College **Sex:** Coed **Application Fee:** $0.00 **H.S. Requirements:** High school diploma required; GED accepted **Calendar System:** Quarter **Faculty:** FT 0, PT 19 **Credit Hours For Degree:** 99 credit hours, Associates **Professional Accreditation:** ACICS

STARK STATE COLLEGE OF TECHNOLOGY
6200 Frank Ave., NW
North Canton, OH 44720-7299
Tel: (330)494-6170
Free: 800-797-8275
Admissions: (330)966-5450
Fax: (330)497-6313
Web Site: http://www.starkstate.edu/
President/CEO: Dr. John O'Donnell
Registrar: Lisa Kasunic
Admissions: Wallace Hoffer
Financial Aid: Amy Baker
Type: Two-Year College **Sex:** Coed **Affiliation:** Ohio Board of Regents **% Accepted:** 100 **Admission Plans:** Open Admission; Early Admission; Deferred Admission **Application Deadline:** Rolling **Application Fee:** $65.00 **H.S. Requirements:** High school diploma required; GED accepted **Costs Per Year:** Application fee: $65. State resident tuition: $3810 full-time, $127 per credit hour part-time. Nonresident tuition: $5610 full-time, $187 per credit hour part-time. **Scholarships:** Available **Calendar System:** Semester, Summer Session Available **Enrollment:** FT 2,297, PT 4,560 **Faculty:** FT 285, PT 318 **Student-Faculty Ratio:** 19:1 **Library Holdings:** 70,000 **Regional Accreditation:** North Central Association of Colleges and Schools **Credit Hours For Degree:** 70 semester hours, Associates **Professional Accreditation:** ABET, AAMAE, ADA, AHIMA, AOTA, APTA, CARC, NAACLS, NLN

STAUTZENBERGER COLLEGE
5355 Southwyck Blvd.
Toledo, OH 43614
Tel: (419)866-0261
Free: 800-552-5099
Fax: (419)867-9821
E-mail: klfitzgerald@stautzenberger.com
Web Site: http://www.sctoday.com/
President/CEO: George Simon
Registrar: Patricia Pentek
Admissions: Karen Fitzgerald
Financial Aid: Mari Huffman
Type: Two-Year College **Sex:** Coed **Scholarships:** Available **Calendar System:** Quarter **Enrollment:** FT 444, PT 348 **Faculty:** FT 6, PT 41 **Student-Faculty Ratio:** 28:1 **Professional Accreditation:** ACICS, AAMAE

TECHNOLOGY EDUCATION COLLEGE
288 South Hamilton Rd.
Columbus, OH 43213-2087
Tel: (614)759-7700
Free: 800-838-3233
Admissions: (614)456-4600
Fax: (614)759-7747
E-mail: mmontgomery@teceducation.com
Web Site: http://www.teceducation.com/
President/CEO: Ron Dooley
Admissions: Michael Mongomery
Financial Aid: Patricia Shoope
Type: Two-Year College **Sex:** Coed **Scholarships:** Available **Calendar System:** Quarter **Faculty:** FT 17, PT 15 **Student-Faculty Ratio:** 12:1 **Professional Accreditation:** ACCSCT

TEMPLE BAPTIST COLLEGE
11965 Kenn Rd.
Cincinnati, OH 45240
Tel: (513)851-3800
Fax: (513)851-3800
Web Site: http://www.templebaptistcollege.com/
President/CEO: Dr. Darrell Horsley
Type: Four-Year College **Sex:** Coed **Calendar System:** Quarter **Professional Accreditation:** TACCS

TERRA STATE COMMUNITY COLLEGE
2830 Napoleon Rd.
Fremont, OH 43420-9670
Tel: (419)334-8400
Fax: (419)334-9035
E-mail: mmccue@terra.edu
Web Site: http://www.terra.edu/
President/CEO: Dr. Marsha Bordner
Registrar: Dale Stearns
Admissions: Mary McCue
Financial Aid: Dale Stearns
Type: Two-Year College **Sex:** Coed **Affiliation:** Ohio Board of Regents **Admission Plans:** Open Admission; Early Admission; Deferred Admission **Application Fee:** $15.00 **H.S. Requirements:** High school diploma required; GED accepted. For post secondary options, tech prep students: High school diploma or equivalent not required **Costs Per Year:** Application fee: $15. State resident tuition: $3278 full-time, $68.30 per credit hour part-time. Nonresident tuition: $7067 full-time, $147.23 per credit hour part-time. Mandatory fees: $334 full-time, $6.95 per credit hour part-time. Full-time tuition and fees vary according to course load. Part-time tuition and fees vary according to course load. **Scholarships:** Available **Calendar System:** Quarter, Summer Session Available **Enrollment:** FT 1,150, PT 1,484 **Faculty:** FT 42, PT 120 **Student-Faculty Ratio:** 20:1 **Exams:** Other, SAT I or ACT **Library Holdings:** 22,675 **Regional Accreditation:** North Central Association of Colleges and Schools **Credit Hours For Degree:** 90 credit hours, Associates **Intercollegiate Athletics:** Golf M; Volleyball W

TIFFIN UNIVERSITY
155 Miami St.
Tiffin, OH 44883-2161
Tel: (419)447-6442
Free: 800-968-6446
Admissions: (419)448-3368
Fax: (419)447-9605
E-mail: admiss@tiffin.edu
Web Site: http://www.tiffin.edu/
President/CEO: Dr. Paul Marion
Registrar: Alice Nichols
Admissions: Dr. Cameron Cruickshank
Financial Aid: Tera Van Doren
Type: Comprehensive **Sex:** Coed **Scores:** 68.76% SAT V 400+; 87.5% SAT M 400+; 63.6% ACT 18-23; 14.47% ACT 24-29 **% Accepted:** 73 **Admission Plans:** Deferred Admission **Application Deadline:** Rolling **Application Fee:** $20.00 **H.S. Requirements:** High school diploma required; GED accepted **Costs Per Year:** Application fee: $20. Comprehensive fee: $22,645 includes full-time tuition ($15,870) and college room and board ($6775). College room only: $3525. Part-time tuition: $529 per credit hour. **Scholarships:** Available **Calendar System:** Semester, Summer Session Available **Enrollment:** FT 1,097, PT 138, Grad 370 **Faculty:** FT 51, PT 82 **Student-Faculty Ratio:** 16:1 **Exams:** SAT I or ACT **% Residing in College-Owned, -Operated, or -Affiliated Housing:** 40 **Library Holdings:** 29,779 **Regional Accreditation:** North Central Association of Colleges and Schools **Credit**

Hours For Degree: 70 semester hours, Associates; 130 semester hours, Bachelors **ROTC:** Army, Air Force **Professional Accreditation:** ACBSP **Intercollegiate Athletics:** Baseball M; Basketball M & W; Cheerleading M & W; Cross-Country Running M & W; Football M; Golf M & W; Soccer M & W; Softball W; Tennis M & W; Track and Field M & W; Volleyball W

TRI-STATE BIBLE COLLEGE
506 Margaret St.
PO Box 445
South Point, OH 45680-8402
Tel: (740)377-2520
Fax: (740)377-0001
E-mail: tsbc@zoomnet.net
Web Site: http://www.tsbc.edu/
President/CEO: Clifford L. Marquardt, Dmin
Admissions: Dale Cook
Type: Four-Year College **Sex:** Coed **Affiliation:** nondenominational **Application Fee:** $25.00 **Calendar System:** Semester **Professional Accreditation:** AABC

TRUMBULL BUSINESS COLLEGE
3200 Ridge Rd.
Warren, OH 44484
Tel: (330)369-3200
Fax: (330)369-6792
Web Site: http://www.tbc-trumbullbusiness.com/
President/CEO: Dennis Griffith
Registrar: Teresa Shambach
Financial Aid: Florence Henning
Type: Two-Year College **Sex:** Coed **Application Fee:** $70.00 **Costs Per Year:** Application fee: $70. One-time mandatory fee: $75. Tuition: $7560 full-time, $210 per credit hour part-time. Mandatory fees: $425 full-time. Full-time tuition and fees vary according to course load and program. Part-time tuition varies according to course load and program. Tuition guaranteed not to increase for student's term of enrollment. **Scholarships:** Available **Calendar System:** Quarter **Enrollment:** FT 347, PT 64 **Faculty:** FT 9, PT 4 **Student-Faculty Ratio:** 28:1 **Professional Accreditation:** ACICS

UNION INSTITUTE & UNIVERSITY
440 East McMillan St.
Cincinnati, OH 45206-1925
Tel: (513)861-6400
Free: 800-486-3116
Fax: (513)861-0779
Web Site: http://www.tui.edu/
President/CEO: Dr. Roger H. Sublett
Registrar: Anthony Hartman
Admissions: Rick Zan
Financial Aid: Leah Stewart
Type: University **Sex:** Coed **Admission Plans:** Deferred Admission **Application Deadline:** Rolling **Application Fee:** $50.00 **H.S. Requirements:** High school diploma required; GED accepted **Costs Per Year:** Application fee: $50. Tuition: $8830 full-time, $368 per credit part-time. Mandatory fees: $80 full-time, $20 per term part-time. **Scholarships:** Available **Calendar System:** Semester, Summer Session Available **Enrollment:** FT 673, PT 449, Grad 1,257 **Faculty:** FT 52, PT 117 **Student-Faculty Ratio:** 15:1 **% Receiving Financial Aid:** 76 **Library Holdings:** 50,000 **Regional Accreditation:** North Central Association of Colleges and Schools **Credit Hours For Degree:** 120 credits, Bachelors

THE UNIVERSITY OF AKRON
302 Buchtel Common
Akron, OH 44325
Tel: (330)972-7111
Free: 800-655-4884
Admissions: (330)972-7077
Fax: (330)972-7676
E-mail: admissions@uakron.edu
Web Site: http://www.uakron.edu/
President/CEO: Dr. Luis M. Proenza
Registrar: Debra Hayes
Admissions: Diane Raybuck
Financial Aid: Douglas McNutt
Type: University **Sex:** Coed **Scores:** 87.4% SAT V 400+; 86.7% SAT M 400+; 48.1% ACT 18-23; 21% ACT 24-29 **% Accepted:** 82 **Admission Plans:** Early Admission; Early Action; Deferred Admission **Application Deadline:** August 01 **Application Fee:** $30.00 **H.S. Requirements:** High school diploma required; GED accepted **Costs Per Year:** Application fee: $30. State resident tuition: $6810 full-time, $284 per credit part-time. Nonresident tuition: $15,535 full-time, $575 per credit part-time. Mandatory fees: $1148 full-time, $47 per credit part-time. Full-time tuition and fees vary according to course load, degree level, and location. Part-time tuition and fees vary according to course load, degree level, and location. College room and board: $7208. College room only: $4494. Room and board charges vary according to board plan and housing facility. **Scholarships:** Available **Calendar System:** Semester, Summer Session Available **Enrollment:** FT 12,635, PT 4,505, Grad 3,375 **Faculty:** FT 701, PT 773 **Student-Faculty Ratio:** 18:1 **Exams:** SAT I or ACT **% Receiving Financial Aid:** 62 **% Residing in College-Owned, -Operated, or -Affiliated Housing:** 13 **Library Holdings:** 1,217,306 **Regional Accreditation:** North Central Association of Colleges and Schools **Credit Hours For Degree:** 64 credits, Associates; 128 credits, Bachelors **ROTC:** Army, Air Force **Professional Accreditation:** AACSB, ABET, ARCEST, AAMFT, AAFCS, AAMAE, AANA, ABA, ACA, ADtA, APA, ASC, ASLHA, AALS, CARC, CEPH, CSWE, FIDER, NASAD, NASD NASM, NASPAA, NCATE, NLN **Intercollegiate Athletics:** Baseball M; Basketball M & W; Cheerleading M & W; Cross-Country Running M & W; Football M; Golf M; Riflery M & W; Soccer M & W; Softball W; Swimming and Diving W; Tennis M & W; Track and Field M & W; Volleyball W

THE UNIVERSITY OF AKRON-WAYNE COLLEGE
1901 Smucker Rd.
Orrville, OH 44667-9192
Tel: (330)683-2010
Admissions: (330)684-8740
Fax: (330)684-8989
E-mail: gholly@uakron.edu
Web Site: http://www.wayne.uakron.edu/
President/CEO: Dr. John P. Kristofco
Admissions: Dr. Gordon Holly
Financial Aid: Barbara Cailler
Type: Two-Year College **Sex:** Coed **Affiliation:** The University of Akron **Scores:** 54.8% ACT 18-23; 14.6% ACT 24-29 **% Accepted:** 93 **Admission Plans:** Open Admission; Early Admission; Deferred Admission **Application Deadline:** August 30 **Application Fee:** $30.00 **H.S. Requirements:** High school diploma required; GED accepted **Costs Per Year:** Application fee: $30. State resident tuition: $4,884 full-time, $203.48 per credit hour part-time. Nonresident tuition: $13,202 full-time, $440.07 per credit hour part-time. Mandatory fees: $146 full-time, $6.07 per credit hour part-time. **Scholarships:** Available **Calendar System:** Semester, Summer Session Available **Enrollment:** FT 924, PT 813 **Faculty:** FT 27, PT 109 **Student-Faculty Ratio:** 17:1 **Exams:** Other, SAT I or ACT **Library Holdings:** 23,450 **Regional Accreditation:** North Central Association of Colleges and Schools **Credit Hours For Degree:** 64 credits, Associates **ROTC:** Army, Air Force **Professional Accreditation:** ACBSP **Intercollegiate Athletics:** Basketball M & W; Cheerleading W; Golf M; Volleyball W

UNIVERSITY OF CINCINNATI
2624 Clifton Ave.
Cincinnati, OH 45221
Tel: (513)556-6000
Admissions: (513)556-1100
E-mail: admissions@uc.edu
Web Site: http://www.uc.edu/
President/CEO: Dr. Nancy L. Zimpher
Admissions: Thomas Canepa
Financial Aid: James Williams
Type: University **Sex:** Coed **Affiliation:** University of Cincinnati System **Scores:** 97.95% SAT V 400+; 97.79% SAT M 400+; 45.85% ACT 18-23; 42.33% ACT 24-29 **% Accepted:** 76 **Admission Plans:** Preferred Admission **Application Deadline:** Rolling **Application Fee:** $40.00 **H.S. Requirements:** High school diploma required; GED not accepted **Costs Per Year:** Application fee: $40. State resident tuition: $7458 full-time, $247 per credit hour part-time. Nonresident tuition: $21,210 full-time, $629 per credit hour part-time. Mandatory fees: $1425 full-time. Full-time tuition and fees vary according to course load, degree level, location, program, and reciprocity agreements. Part-time tuition varies according to course load, degree level, location, program, and reciprocity agreements. College room and board: $7890. College room only: $4680. Room and board charges vary according to board plan and housing facility. **Scholarships:** Available **Calendar System:** Quarter, Summer Session Available **Enrollment:** FT 16,098, PT

3,414, Grad 7,402 **Faculty:** FT 1,200, PT 41 **Student-Faculty Ratio:** 14:1 **Exams:** SAT I or ACT **% Receiving Financial Aid:** 53 **% Residing in College-Owned, -Operated, or -Affiliated Housing:** 18 **Regional Accreditation:** North Central Association of Colleges and Schools **Credit Hours For Degree:** 90 credit hours, Associates; 185 credit hours, Bachelors **ROTC:** Army, Air Force **Professional Accreditation:** AACSB, ABET, AABB, AACN, AANA, ABA, ACNM, ACCE, ACPhE, ACA, ADtA, ACSP, APTA, APA, ASLHA, AALS, CSWE, FIDER, JRCEPAT, JRCNMT LCMEAMA, NAACLS, NASAD, NASD, NASM, NAST, NCATE **Intercollegiate Athletics:** Baseball M; Basketball M & W; Cheerleading M & W; Crew M & W; Cross-Country Running M & W; Football M; Golf M; Rugby M; Soccer M & W; Swimming and Diving M & W; Tennis M & W; Track and Field M & W; Volleyball W

UNIVERSITY OF CINCINNATI CLERMONT COLLEGE
4200 Clermont College Dr.
Batavia, OH 45103-1785
Tel: (513)732-5200
Admissions: (513)732-5247
Web Site: http://www.clc.uc.edu/
President/CEO: Dr. David H. Devier
Registrar: Dr. Peggy O. Chalker
Admissions: Robert W. Neel
Financial Aid: Dr. Peggy O. Chalker
Type: Two-Year College **Sex:** Coed **Affiliation:** University of Cincinnati System **Scores:** 60% SAT V 400+; 75% SAT M 400+ **Admission Plans:** Open Admission; Deferred Admission **Application Fee:** $0.00 **H.S. Requirements:** High school diploma required; GED accepted **Scholarships:** Available **Calendar System:** Quarter, Summer Session Available **Faculty:** FT 36, PT 127 **Exams:** SAT I or ACT **Library Holdings:** 19,235 **Regional Accreditation:** North Central Association of Colleges and Schools **Credit Hours For Degree:** 93 quarter hours, Associates **ROTC:** Air Force

UNIVERSITY OF CINCINNATI RAYMOND WALTERS COLLEGE
9555 Plainfield Rd.
Cincinnati, OH 45236-1007
Tel: (513)745-5600
Admissions: (513)745-5700
Fax: (513)745-5780
Web Site: http://www.rwc.uc.edu/
President/CEO: Dr. Delores Y. Straker
Registrar: Deborah Herrick
Admissions: Jenny Young
Financial Aid: Pamela D. Lineback
Type: Two-Year College **Sex:** Coed **Affiliation:** University of Cincinnati System **Scores:** 87% SAT V 400+; 82% SAT M 400+; 54% ACT 18-23; 12% ACT 24-29 **Admission Plans:** Open Admission; Deferred Admission **Application Fee:** $35.00 **H.S. Requirements:** High school diploma required; GED accepted **Costs Per Year:** Application fee: $35. State resident tuition: $4938 full-time, $142 per quarter hour part-time. Nonresident tuition: $12,801 full-time, $336 per quarter hour part-time. Mandatory fees: $222 full-time. **Scholarships:** Available **Calendar System:** Quarter, Summer Session Available **Enrollment:** FT 2,177, PT 2,244 **Faculty:** FT 117, PT 4 **Student-Faculty Ratio:** 25:1 **Library Holdings:** 48,226 **Regional Accreditation:** North Central Association of Colleges and Schools **Credit Hours For Degree:** 90 credit hours, Associates **ROTC:** Army, Air Force **Professional Accreditation:** ADA, JRCERT, NLN **Intercollegiate Athletics:** Baseball M; Basketball M & W; Crew W; Cross-Country Running M & W; Football M; Golf M; Soccer M & W; Swimming and Diving M & W; Tennis M & W; Track and Field M & W; Volleyball M & W

UNIVERSITY OF DAYTON
300 College Park
Dayton, OH 45469-1300
Tel: (937)229-1000
Free: 800-837-7433
Admissions: (937)229-4411
Fax: (937)229-4545
E-mail: admission@udayton.edu
Web Site: http://www.udayton.edu/
President/CEO: Dr. Daniel J. Curran
Registrar: Thomas J. Westendorf
Admissions: Robert Durkle
Financial Aid: Joyce J. Wilkins
Type: University **Sex:** Coed **Affiliation:** Roman Catholic **Scores:** 99.88% SAT V 400+; 99.19% SAT M 400+; 31.76% ACT 18-23; 52.86% ACT 24-29 **% Accepted:** 80 **Admission Plans:** Deferred Admission **Application Deadline:** Rolling **Application Fee:** $0.00 **H.S. Requirements:** High school diploma required; GED accepted **Costs Per Year:** Application fee: $0. Comprehensive fee: $29,626 includes full-time tuition ($22,046), mandatory fees ($800), and college room and board ($6780). College room only: $4000. Full-time tuition and fees vary according to program. Room and board charges vary according to board plan, housing facility, and student level. Part-time tuition: $708 per credit hour. Part-time mandatory fees: $25 per term. Part-time tuition and fees vary according to course load and program. **Scholarships:** Available **Calendar System:** Semester, Summer Session Available **Enrollment:** FT 6,913, PT 513, Grad 2,676 **Faculty:** FT 446, PT 450 **Student-Faculty Ratio:** 14:1 **Exams:** SAT I or ACT **% Receiving Financial Aid:** 59 **% Residing in College-Owned, -Operated, or -Affiliated Housing:** 79 **Library Holdings:** 905,924 **Regional Accreditation:** North Central Association of Colleges and Schools **Credit Hours For Degree:** 120 semester hours, Bachelors **ROTC:** Army, Air Force **Professional Accreditation:** AACSB, ABET, ABA, AALS, NASM, NCATE **Intercollegiate Athletics:** Baseball M; Basketball M & W; Crew W; Cross-Country Running M & W; Football M; Golf M & W; Soccer M & W; Softball W; Tennis M & W; Track and Field W; Volleyball W

THE UNIVERSITY OF FINDLAY
1000 North Main St.
Findlay, OH 45840-3653
Tel: (419)422-8313
Free: 800-548-0932
Admissions: (419)434-4732
Fax: (419)424-4822
Web Site: http://www.findlay.edu/
President/CEO: Dr. DeBow Freed
Registrar: Tony G. Goedde
Admissions: Randall Langston
Financial Aid: Arman J. Habegger
Type: Comprehensive **Sex:** Coed **Affiliation:** Church of God **Scores:** 100% SAT V 400+; 100% SAT M 400+; 61% ACT 18-23; 27% ACT 24-29 **% Accepted:** 70 **Admission Plans:** Deferred Admission **Application Deadline:** Rolling **Application Fee:** $0.00 **H.S. Requirements:** High school diploma required; GED accepted **Costs Per Year:** Application fee: $0. Comprehensive fee: $29,238 includes full-time tuition ($20,796), mandatory fees ($950), and college room and board ($7492). College room only: $3756. Full-time tuition and fees vary according to location and program. Room and board charges vary according to housing facility. Part-time tuition: $458 per semester hour. Part-time mandatory fees: $125 per term. Part-time tuition and fees vary according to location and program. **Scholarships:** Available **Calendar System:** Semester, Summer Session Available **Enrollment:** FT 2,648, PT 953, Grad 1,142 **Faculty:** FT 175, PT 164 **Student-Faculty Ratio:** 15:1 **Exams:** SAT I or ACT **% Receiving Financial Aid:** 71 **% Residing in College-Owned, -Operated, or -Affiliated Housing:** 41 **Library Holdings:** 132,052 **Regional Accreditation:** North Central Association of Colleges and Schools **Credit Hours For Degree:** 62 semester hours, Associates; 124 semester hours, Bachelors **ROTC:** Army, Air Force **Professional Accreditation:** AOTA, APTA, CSWE, JRCNMT, NCATE **Intercollegiate Athletics:** Baseball M; Basketball M & W; Cross-Country Running M & W; Football M; Golf M & W; Ice Hockey M & W; Soccer M & W; Softball W; Swimming and Diving M & W; Tennis M & W; Track and Field M & W; Volleyball W; Water Polo M & W; Wrestling M

UNIVERSITY OF NORTHWESTERN OHIO
1441 North Cable Rd.
Lima, OH 45805-1498
Tel: (419)227-3141
Fax: (419)229-6926
E-mail: info@nc.edu
Web Site: http://www.unoh.edu/
President/CEO: Dr. Loren R. Jarvis
Registrar: Debbie Brunk
Admissions: Rick Morrison
Financial Aid: Michael Jones
Type: Two-Year College **Sex:** Coed **% Accepted:** 98 **Admission Plans:** Open Admission; Early Admission; Deferred Admission **Application Deadline:** Rolling **Application Fee:** $50.00 **H.S. Requirements:** High school diploma required; GED accepted **Costs Per Year:** Application fee: $50. Tuition: $11,400 full-time, $190 per credit hour part-time. **Scholarships:** Available **Calendar System:** Quarter, Summer Session Available **Enrollment:** FT 2,629, PT 286 **Faculty:** FT 80, PT 27 **Student-Faculty Ratio:**

20:1 **% Residing in College-Owned, -Operated, or -Affiliated Housing:** 45 **Library Holdings:** 4,553 **Regional Accreditation:** North Central Association of Colleges and Schools **Credit Hours For Degree:** 108 credits, Associates; 180 credits, Bachelors **Professional Accreditation:** AAMAE, ACBSP

UNIVERSITY OF PHOENIX-CINCINNATI CAMPUS
9050 Centre Pointe Dr.
West Chester, OH 45069
Tel: (513)772-9600
Free: 800-228-7240
Admissions: (480)557-1712
Web Site: http://www.phoenix.edu/
Admissions: Nina Omelchanko
Type: Comprehensive **Sex:** Coed **Admission Plans:** Open Admission; Deferred Admission **Application Deadline:** Rolling **Application Fee:** $110.00 **H.S. Requirements:** High school diploma required; GED accepted **Costs Per Year:** Application fee: $110. Tuition: $11,550 full-time, $385 per credit part-time. Mandatory fees: $560 full-time, $70 per course part-time. **Scholarships:** Available **Calendar System:** Continuous, Summer Session Not available **Enrollment:** FT 407, Grad 212 **Faculty:** FT 9, PT 88 **Student-Faculty Ratio:** 6:1 **Library Holdings:** 444 **Regional Accreditation:** North Central Association of Colleges and Schools **Credit Hours For Degree:** 60 credits, Associates; 120 credits, Bachelors

UNIVERSITY OF PHOENIX-CLEVELAND CAMPUS
5005 Rockside Rd., Ste. 325
Independence, OH 44131-2194
Tel: (216)447-8807
Free: 800-228-7240
Admissions: (480)557-1712
Web Site: http://www.phoenix.edu/
Admissions: Nina Omelchanko
Type: Comprehensive **Sex:** Coed **Admission Plans:** Open Admission; Deferred Admission **Application Deadline:** Rolling **Application Fee:** $110.00 **H.S. Requirements:** High school diploma required; GED accepted **Costs Per Year:** Application fee: $110. Tuition: $11,550 full-time, $385 per credit part-time. Mandatory fees: $560 full-time, $70 per course part-time. **Scholarships:** Available **Calendar System:** Continuous, Summer Session Not available **Enrollment:** FT 675, Grad 207 **Faculty:** FT 8, PT 158 **Student-Faculty Ratio:** 5:1 **Library Holdings:** 444 **Regional Accreditation:** North Central Association of Colleges and Schools **Credit Hours For Degree:** 60 credits, Associates; 120 credits, Bachelors

UNIVERSITY OF PHOENIX-COLUMBUS OHIO CAMPUS
8425 Pulsar Place
Columbus, OH 43240
Tel: (614)433-0095
Free: 800-228-7240
Admissions: (480)557-1712
Web Site: http://www.phoenix.edu/
Admissions: Nina Omelchanko
Type: Comprehensive **Sex:** Coed **Admission Plans:** Open Admission; Deferred Admission **Application Deadline:** Rolling **Application Fee:** $110.00 **H.S. Requirements:** High school diploma required; GED accepted **Costs Per Year:** Application fee: $110. Tuition: $11,550 full-time, $385 per credit part-time. Mandatory fees: $560 full-time, $70 per course part-time. **Scholarships:** Available **Calendar System:** Continuous, Summer Session Not available **Enrollment:** FT 332, Grad 161 **Faculty:** FT 1, PT 65 **Student-Faculty Ratio:** 6:1 **Library Holdings:** 444 **Regional Accreditation:** North Central Association of Colleges and Schools **Credit Hours For Degree:** 60, Associates; 120, Bachelors

UNIVERSITY OF RIO GRANDE
218 North College Ave.
Rio Grande, OH 45674
Tel: (740)245-5353
Admissions: (740)245-7208
Fax: (740)245-9220
E-mail: gsojka@rio.edu
Web Site: http://www.rio.edu/
President/CEO: Dr. Barry M. Dorsey
Registrar: Teresa Preston
Admissions: Dr. Greg Sojka
Financial Aid: Dr. John Hill
Type: Comprehensive **Sex:** Coed **Scores:** 51% ACT 18-23; 14% ACT 24-29 **Admission Plans:** Open Admission **Application Deadline:** Rolling **Application Fee:** $25.00 **H.S. Requirements:** High school diploma required; GED accepted **Costs Per Year:** Application fee: $25. Area resident tuition: $12,540 full-time, $517 per semester hour part-time. State resident tuition: $12,750 full-time, $528 per semester hour part-time. Nonresident tuition: $13,132 full-time, $571 per semester hour part-time. Mandatory fees: $525 full-time, $13 per semester hour part-time, $91. Full-time tuition and fees vary according to course load, degree level, and program. Part-time tuition and fees vary according to course load, degree level, and program. College room and board: $6404. Room and board charges vary according to board plan. **Scholarships:** Available **Calendar System:** Semester, Summer Session Available **Enrollment:** FT 1,699, PT 442, Grad 235 **Faculty:** FT 81, PT 184 **Student-Faculty Ratio:** 18:1 **Exams:** ACT **% Receiving Financial Aid:** 72 **% Residing in College-Owned, -Operated, or -Affiliated Housing:** 25 **Library Holdings:** 96,731 **Regional Accreditation:** North Central Association of Colleges and Schools **Credit Hours For Degree:** 62 semester hours, Associates; 124 semester hours, Bachelors **ROTC:** Army **Professional Accreditation:** CSWE, NAACLS, NLN **Intercollegiate Athletics:** Baseball M; Basketball M & W; Cross-Country Running M & W; Soccer M & W; Softball W; Track and Field M & W; Volleyball W

THE UNIVERSITY OF TOLEDO
2801 West Bancroft
Toledo, OH 43606-3390
Tel: (419)530-4636
Admissions: (419)530-5737
Fax: (419)530-4940
E-mail: adm0017@uofT01.utoledo.edu
Web Site: http://www.utoledo.edu/
President/CEO: Dr. Daniel M. Johnson
Registrar: Lorinda L. Bishop
Admissions: Martino Harmon
Financial Aid: Paula Compton
Type: University **Sex:** Coed **Scores:** 91% SAT V 400+; 91% SAT M 400+; 50% ACT 18-23; 27% ACT 24-29 **Admission Plans:** Open Admission; Deferred Admission **Application Fee:** $40.00 **H.S. Requirements:** High school diploma required; GED accepted **Costs Per Year:** Application fee: $40. State resident tuition: $6430 full-time, $311 per semester hour part-time. Nonresident tuition: $15,241 full-time, $679 per semester hour part-time. Mandatory fees: $1064 full-time. Full-time tuition and fees vary according to course load, program, and reciprocity agreements. Part-time tuition varies according to course load, program, and reciprocity agreements. College room and board: $8312. Room and board charges vary according to board plan, housing facility, and location. **Scholarships:** Available **Calendar System:** Semester, Summer Session Available **Enrollment:** FT 13,146, PT 3,220, Grad 2,465 **Faculty:** FT 762, PT 519 **Student-Faculty Ratio:** 19:1 **Exams:** SAT I or ACT **% Receiving Financial Aid:** 59 **% Residing in College-Owned, -Operated, or -Affiliated Housing:** 18 **Library Holdings:** 1,800,000 **Regional Accreditation:** North Central Association of Colleges and Schools **Credit Hours For Degree:** 60 semester hours, Associates; 124 semester hours, Bachelors **ROTC:** Army, Air Force **Professional Accreditation:** AACSB, ABET, AAMAE, ABA, ACPhE, ACA, APTA, APA, ASLHA, AALS, CARC, CAEPK, CEPH, CSWE, JRCECT, JRCEPAT, NASM, NASPAA, NCATE, NLN NRPA **Intercollegiate Athletics:** Baseball M; Basketball M & W; Cross-Country Running M & W; Football M; Golf M & W; Ice Hockey M & W; Lacrosse M & W; Soccer W; Softball W; Swimming and Diving M & W; Tennis M & W; Track and Field M & W; Volleyball W

URBANA UNIVERSITY
579 College Way
Urbana, OH 43078-2091
Tel: (937)484-1400
Free: 800-7-URBANA
Admissions: (937)484-1356
Fax: (937)484-1389
Web Site: http://www.urbana.edu/
President/CEO: Dr. Robert L. Head
Registrar: Kathleen Yoder
Admissions: M. L. Smith
Financial Aid: Robin Heise
Type: Comprehensive **Sex:** Coed **Affiliation:** Church of the New Jerusalem **% Accepted:** 65 **Admission Plans:** Deferred Admission **Application Deadline:** Rolling **Application Fee:** $25.00 **H.S. Requirements:** High

school diploma required; GED accepted **Costs Per Year:** Application fee: $25. Comprehensive fee: $22,866 includes full-time tuition ($16,254) and college room and board ($6612). College room only: $2234. Part-time tuition: $337 per semester hour. **Scholarships:** Available **Calendar System:** Semester, Summer Session Available **Enrollment:** FT 904, PT 557, Grad 90 **Faculty:** FT 55, PT 65 **Student-Faculty Ratio:** 16:1 **Exams:** SAT I or ACT **% Receiving Financial Aid:** 93 **Library Holdings:** 61,600 **Regional Accreditation:** North Central Association of Colleges and Schools **Credit Hours For Degree:** 63 credit hours, Associates; 126 credit hours, Bachelors **Intercollegiate Athletics:** Baseball M; Basketball M & W; Football M; Golf M & W; Soccer M & W; Softball W; Volleyball W

URSULINE COLLEGE
2550 Lander Rd.
Pepper Pike, OH 44124-4398
Tel: (440)449-4200; 888-URSULINE
Admissions: (440)449-4203
Fax: (440)449-2235
Web Site: http://www.ursuline.edu/
President/CEO: Sr. Diana Stano, OSU
Registrar: Ann Marie Siclare
Admissions: Sarah Sundermeier
Financial Aid: Mary Lynn Perri
Type: Comprehensive **Affiliation:** Roman Catholic **Scores:** 82% SAT V 400+; 90.4% SAT M 400+; 60% ACT 18-23; 20% ACT 24-29 **% Accepted:** 65 **Admission Plans:** Early Action; Deferred Admission **Application Deadline:** Rolling **Application Fee:** $25.00 **H.S. Requirements:** High school diploma required; GED accepted **Costs Per Year:** Application fee: $25. Comprehensive fee: $25,456 includes full-time tuition ($18,900), mandatory fees ($190), and college room and board ($6366). College room only: $3252. Room and board charges vary according to board plan. Part-time tuition: $630 per credit hour. Part-time mandatory fees: $60 per term. **Scholarships:** Available **Calendar System:** Semester, Summer Session Available **Enrollment:** FT 755, PT 397, Grad 342 **Faculty:** FT 72, PT 140 **Student-Faculty Ratio:** 9:1 **Exams:** SAT I or ACT **% Receiving Financial Aid:** 78 **% Residing in College-Owned, -Operated, or -Affiliated Housing:** 14 **Library Holdings:** 108,699 **Regional Accreditation:** North Central Association of Colleges and Schools **Credit Hours For Degree:** 128 semester hours, Bachelors **Professional Accreditation:** AACN, CSWE **Intercollegiate Athletics:** Basketball W; Cross-Country Running W; Golf W; Soccer W; Softball W; Tennis W; Volleyball W

VATTEROTT COLLEGE
5025 East Royalton Rd.
Broadview Heights, OH 44147
Tel: (440)526-1660
Free: 800-864-5644
Fax: (440)526-1933
Web Site: http://www.vatterott-college.edu/
President/CEO: Vince Williamson
Admissions: Jack Chalk
Type: Two-Year College **Sex:** Coed **Calendar System:** Semester **Enrollment:** FT 143 **Professional Accreditation:** ACCSCT

VIRGINIA MARTI COLLEGE OF ART AND DESIGN
11724 Detroit Ave., PO Box 580
Lakewood, OH 44107-3002
Tel: (216)221-8584
Web Site: http://www.vmcad.edu/
President/CEO: Virginia Marti-Veith
Registrar: Deborah Marti
Admissions: Quinn Marti
Financial Aid: Jennifer Minkiewicz
Type: Two-Year College **Sex:** Coed **Admission Plans:** Early Admission; Deferred Admission **Application Fee:** $20.00 **H.S. Requirements:** High school diploma required; GED accepted **Calendar System:** Quarter, Summer Session Available **Enrollment:** FT 267 **Faculty:** FT 7, PT 44 **Student-Faculty Ratio:** 10:1 **Exams:** Other **Credit Hours For Degree:** 105 quarter hours, Associates **Professional Accreditation:** ACCSCT

WALSH UNIVERSITY
2020 East Maple St., NW
North Canton, OH 44720-3396
Tel: (330)499-7090
Free: 800-362-8846
Admissions: (330)490-7171
Fax: (330)490-7165
E-mail: admissions@walsh.edu
Web Site: http://www.walsh.edu/
President/CEO: Richard Jusseaume
Registrar: Edna McCulloh
Admissions: Brett D. Freshour
Financial Aid: Holly Van Gilder
Type: Comprehensive **Sex:** Coed **Affiliation:** Roman Catholic **Scores:** 66.2% ACT 18-23; 23.3% ACT 24-29 **% Accepted:** 80 **Admission Plans:** Early Admission; Deferred Admission **Application Deadline:** Rolling **Application Fee:** $25.00 **H.S. Requirements:** High school diploma required; GED accepted **Costs Per Year:** Application fee: $25. Comprehensive fee: $24,850 includes full-time tuition ($17,150), mandatory fees ($570), and college room and board ($7130). College room only: $4870. Part-time tuition: $570 per credit hour. Part-time mandatory fees: $19 per credit hour. **Scholarships:** Available **Calendar System:** Semester, Summer Session Available **Enrollment:** FT 1,415, PT 444, Grad 324 **Faculty:** FT 82, PT 107 **Student-Faculty Ratio:** 14:1 **Exams:** SAT I or ACT **% Receiving Financial Aid:** 76 **% Residing in College-Owned, -Operated, or -Affiliated Housing:** 50 **Library Holdings:** 136,268 **Regional Accreditation:** North Central Association of Colleges and Schools **Credit Hours For Degree:** 60 credit hours, Associates; 130 credit hours, Bachelors **Professional Accreditation:** APTA, NLN **Intercollegiate Athletics:** Baseball M; Basketball M & W; Cheerleading W; Cross-Country Running M & W; Football M; Golf M & W; Soccer M & W; Softball W; Tennis M & W; Track and Field M & W; Volleyball W

WASHINGTON STATE COMMUNITY COLLEGE
710 Colegate Dr.
Marietta, OH 45750-9225
Tel: (740)374-8716
Fax: (740)376-0257
Web Site: http://www.wscc.edu/
President/CEO: Dr. Charlotte R. Hatfield
Registrar: Michael Whitnable
Admissions: Rebecca Peroni
Financial Aid: Vickie Biddle
Type: Two-Year College **Sex:** Coed **Affiliation:** Ohio Board of Regents **Admission Plans:** Open Admission; Early Admission; Deferred Admission **H.S. Requirements:** High school diploma or equivalent not required. For medical laboratory technology, nursing programs: High school diploma required; GED accepted **Scholarships:** Available **Calendar System:** Quarter, Summer Session Available **Enrollment:** FT 1,174, PT 912 **Faculty:** FT 57, PT 87 **Student-Faculty Ratio:** 14:1 **Exams:** Other **Library Holdings:** 15,000 **Regional Accreditation:** North Central Association of Colleges and Schools **Credit Hours For Degree:** 90 credit hours, Associates **Professional Accreditation:** APTA, CARC, NAACLS

WILBERFORCE UNIVERSITY
1055 North Bickett Rd.
Wilberforce, OH 45384
Tel: (937)376-2911
Free: 800-367-8568
Admissions: (937)708-5789
Fax: (937)376-4751
E-mail: admissions@shorter.wilberforce.edu
Web Site: http://www.wilberforce.edu/
President/CEO: Rev. Dr. Floyd H. Flake
Registrar: Gail Lash
Admissions: Kenya Messer
Type: Four-Year College **Sex:** Coed **Affiliation:** African Methodist Episcopal Church **Admission Plans:** Early Admission; Deferred Admission **Application Fee:** $20.00 **H.S. Requirements:** High school diploma required; GED accepted **Costs Per Year:** Application fee: $20. Comprehensive fee: $16,100 includes full-time tuition ($9720), mandatory fees ($1060), and college room and board ($5320). Part-time tuition: $376 per credit hour. **Scholarships:** Available **Calendar System:** Semester, Summer Session Not available **Enrollment:** FT 982, PT 16 **Faculty:** FT 48, PT 28 **Student-Faculty Ratio:** 17:1 **Exams:** SAT I or ACT **% Residing in College-Owned, -Operated, or -Affiliated Housing:** 85 **Library Holdings:** 63,000 **Regional Accreditation:** North Central Association of Colleges and Schools **Credit Hours For Degree:** 128 credit hours, Bachelors **ROTC:** Army, Air Force **Intercollegiate Athletics:** Basketball M & W; Cross-Country Running M & W; Golf M & W

WILMINGTON COLLEGE
Pyle Center Box 1185
Wilmington, OH 45177
Tel: (937)382-6661
Free: 800-341-9318
Fax: (937)382-7077
E-mail: admission@wilmington.edu
Web Site: http://www.wilmington.edu/
President/CEO: Dr. Daniel DiBiasio
Registrar: Jack Campbell
Admissions: Tina Garland
Financial Aid: Cheryl LouAllen
Type: Comprehensive **Sex:** Coed **Affiliation:** Friends **Scores:** 89% SAT V 400+; 89.5% SAT M 400+; 66.9% ACT 18-23; 20.9% ACT 24-29 **% Accepted:** 98 **Admission Plans:** Deferred Admission **Application Deadline:** Rolling **H.S. Requirements:** High school diploma required; GED accepted **Costs Per Year:** Comprehensive fee: $27,016 includes full-time tuition ($19,206), mandatory fees ($756), and college room and board ($7054). College room only: $3330. Room and board charges vary according to board plan and housing facility. Part-time tuition: $785 per credit. Part-time tuition varies according to course load. **Scholarships:** Available **Calendar System:** Semester, Summer Session Available **Enrollment:** FT 1,383, PT 340, Grad 41 **Faculty:** FT 71, PT 26 **Student-Faculty Ratio:** 14:1 **Exams:** SAT I or ACT **% Receiving Financial Aid:** 86 **% Residing in College-Owned, -Operated, or -Affiliated Housing:** 62 **Library Holdings:** 103,706 **Regional Accreditation:** North Central Association of Colleges and Schools **Credit Hours For Degree:** 124 credit hours, Bachelors **Professional Accreditation:** JRCEPAT **Intercollegiate Athletics:** Baseball M; Basketball M & W; Cross-Country Running M & W; Football M; Golf M & W; Soccer M & W; Softball W; Swimming and Diving M & W; Tennis M & W; Track and Field M & W; Volleyball W; Wrestling M

WITTENBERG UNIVERSITY
PO Box 720
Springfield, OH 45501-0720
Tel: (937)327-6231
Free: 800-677-7558
Admissions: (937)327-6314
Fax: (937)327-6379
E-mail: admission@wittenberg.edu
Web Site: http://www.wittenberg.edu/
President/CEO: William H. Steinbrink
Registrar: Jack Campbell
Admissions: Kurt Schmidt
Financial Aid: Randy Green
Type: Comprehensive **Sex:** Coed **Affiliation:** Evangelical Lutheran Church **Scores:** 98% SAT V 400+; 98% SAT M 400+; 44% ACT 18-23; 44% ACT 24-29 **% Accepted:** 85 **Admission Plans:** Preferred Admission; Early Admission; Early Action; Early Decision Plan; Deferred Admission **Application Fee:** $40.00 **H.S. Requirements:** High school diploma required; GED not accepted **Costs Per Year:** Application fee: $40. Comprehensive fee: $36,778 includes full-time tuition ($29,080), mandatory fees ($200), and college room and board ($7498). College room only: $3890. Part-time tuition: $969 per credit hour. **Scholarships:** Available **Calendar System:** Semester, Summer Session Available **Enrollment:** FT 1,930, PT 148, Grad 15 **Faculty:** FT 148, PT 54 **Student-Faculty Ratio:** 12:1 **Exams:** SAT I or ACT **% Receiving Financial Aid:** 56 **% Residing in College-Owned, -Operated, or -Affiliated Housing:** 86 **Library Holdings:** 407,502 **Regional Accreditation:** North Central Association of Colleges and Schools **Credit Hours For Degree:** 130 credits, Bachelors **ROTC:** Army, Air Force **Professional Accreditation:** NASM, NCATE **Intercollegiate Athletics:** Baseball M; Basketball M & W; Cheerleading M & W; Crew M & W; Cross-Country Running M & W; Equestrian Sports W; Field Hockey W; Football M; Golf M & W; Ice Hockey M; Lacrosse M & W; Rugby M & W; Soccer M & W; Softball W; Swimming and Diving M & W; Tennis M & W; Track and Field M & W; Volleyball M & W

WRIGHT STATE UNIVERSITY
3640 Colonel Glenn Hwy.
Dayton, OH 45435
Tel: (937)775-3333
Free: 800-247-1770
Admissions: (937)775-5700
Fax: (937)775-5795
E-mail: admissions@wright.edu
Web Site: http://www.wright.edu/
President/CEO: Dr. Kim Goldenberg
Registrar: Dave Sauter
Admissions: Cathy Davis
Financial Aid: David Darr
Type: University **Sex:** Coed **Scores:** 85% SAT V 400+; 87% SAT M 400+; 54% ACT 18-23; 23% ACT 24-29 **% Accepted:** 87 **Admission Plans:** Early Admission; Deferred Admission **Application Deadline:** Rolling **Application Fee:** $30.00 **H.S. Requirements:** High school diploma required; GED accepted **Costs Per Year:** Application fee: $30. State resident tuition: $7278 full-time, $219 per hour part-time. Nonresident tuition: $14,004 full-time, $425 per hour part-time. College room and board: $7180. **Scholarships:** Available **Calendar System:** Quarter, Summer Session Available **Enrollment:** FT 10,450, PT 1,818, Grad 3,425 **Faculty:** FT 731, PT 104 **Student-Faculty Ratio:** 19:1 **Exams:** SAT I or ACT **% Residing in College-Owned, -Operated, or -Affiliated Housing:** 22 **Library Holdings:** 703,000 **Regional Accreditation:** North Central Association of Colleges and Schools **Credit Hours For Degree:** 96 credit hours, Associates; 187 credit hours, Bachelors **ROTC:** Army, Air Force **Professional Accreditation:** AACSB, ABET, AACN, ACA, APA, CORE, CSWE, JRCEPAT, LCMEAMA, NAACLS, NASM, NASPAA, NCATE, NLN **Intercollegiate Athletics:** Baseball M; Basketball M & W; Cross-Country Running M & W; Golf M; Soccer M & W; Softball W; Swimming and Diving M & W; Tennis M & W; Track and Field W; Volleyball W

WRIGHT STATE UNIVERSITY, LAKE CAMPUS
7600 State Route 703
Celina, OH 45822-2921
Tel: (419)586-0300
Admissions: (419)586-0324
Fax: (419)586-0358
Web Site: http://www.wright.edu/lake/
President/CEO: Dr. Anita Curry-Jackson
Registrar: Billie Jo Hobler
Admissions: B.J. Hobler
Financial Aid: Sandra Gilbert
Type: Two-Year College **Sex:** Coed **Affiliation:** Ohio Board of Regents **Admission Plans:** Open Admission; Early Admission; Deferred Admission **Application Fee:** $30.00 **H.S. Requirements:** High school diploma required; GED accepted **Calendar System:** Quarter, Summer Session Available **Faculty:** FT 18, PT 30 **Student-Faculty Ratio:** 15:1 **Exams:** SAT I or ACT **Library Holdings:** 26,000 **Regional Accreditation:** North Central Association of Colleges and Schools **Credit Hours For Degree:** 94 credit hours, Associates **Intercollegiate Athletics:** Basketball M & W

XAVIER UNIVERSITY
3800 Victory Parkway
Cincinnati, OH 45207
Tel: (513)745-3000
Free: 800-344-4698
Admissions: (513)745-3301
Fax: (513)745-4319
E-mail: xuadmit@admin.xu.edu
Web Site: http://www.xu.edu/
President/CEO: Rev. Michael J. Graham, SJ
Registrar: W. Allen Cole
Admissions: Marc Camille
Financial Aid: Paul Calme
Type: Comprehensive **Sex:** Coed **Affiliation:** Roman Catholic **Scores:** 100% SAT V 400+; 100% SAT M 400+; 28% ACT 18-23; 52% ACT 24-29 **% Accepted:** 66 **Admission Plans:** Early Admission; Early Action; Deferred Admission **Application Deadline:** February 01 **Application Fee:** $35.00 **H.S. Requirements:** High school diploma required; GED accepted **Costs Per Year:** Application fee: $35. Comprehensive fee: $31,070 includes full-time tuition ($21,850), mandatory fees ($580), and college room and board ($8640). College room only: $4860. Full-time tuition and fees vary according to program and student level. Room and board charges vary according to board plan and housing facility. Part-time tuition: $425 per credit hour. Part-time tuition varies according to course load. **Scholarships:** Available **Calendar System:** Semester, Summer Session Available **Enrollment:** FT 3,333, PT 546, Grad 2,786 **Faculty:** FT 294, PT 304 **Student-Faculty Ratio:** 13:1 **Exams:** SAT I or ACT **% Receiving Financial Aid:** 54 **% Residing in College-Owned, -Operated, or -Affiliated Housing:** 48 **Library Holdings:** 222,331 **Regional Accreditation:** North Central Association of Colleges and Schools **Credit Hours For Degree:** 60 semester hours, As-

sociates; 120 semester hours, Bachelors **ROTC:** Army, Air Force **Professional Accreditation:** AACSB, ACEHSA, AACN, AOTA, APA, CSWE, JRCERT, JRCEPAT, MACTE **Intercollegiate Athletics:** Baseball M; Basketball M & W; Crew M & W; Cross-Country Running M & W; Fencing M & W; Golf M & W; Lacrosse M & W; Riflery M & W; Rugby M & W; Soccer M & W; Softball W; Swimming and Diving M & W; Tennis M & W; Volleyball M & W

YOUNGSTOWN STATE UNIVERSITY
One University Plaza
Youngstown, OH 44555-0001
Tel: (330)941-3000; 877-468-6978
Admissions: (330)941-2000
Fax: (330)941-1998
E-mail: sedavis@ysu.edu
Web Site: http://www.ysu.edu/
President/CEO: Dr. David C. Sweet
Registrar: William Countryman
Admissions: Sue Davis
Financial Aid: Elaine Ruse
Type: Comprehensive **Sex:** Coed **Scores:** 84% SAT V 400+; 80% SAT M 400+; 50% ACT 18-23; 16% ACT 24-29 **% Accepted:** 99 **Admission Plans:** Open Admission; Early Admission; Early Action; Deferred Admission **Application Deadline:** August 15 **Application Fee:** $30.00 **H.S. Requirements:** High school diploma required; GED accepted **Costs Per Year:** Application fee: $30. State resident tuition: $6104 full-time, $254.33 per credit part-time. Nonresident tuition: $11,312 full-time, $471.33 per credit part-time. Mandatory fees: $229 full-time, $9.54 per credit part-time. Full-time tuition and fees vary according to course load. Part-time tuition and fees vary according to course load. College room and board: $6280. Room and board charges vary according to board plan and housing facility. **Scholarships:** Available **Calendar System:** Semester, Summer Session Available **Enrollment:** FT 9,241, PT 2,459, Grad 1,109 **Faculty:** FT 427, PT 552 **Student-Faculty Ratio:** 17:1 **Exams:** SAT I or ACT **% Residing in College-Owned, -Operated, or -Affiliated Housing:** 10 **Library Holdings:** 991,501 **Regional Accreditation:** North Central Association of Colleges and Schools **Credit Hours For Degree:** 64credits, Associates; 124 credits, Bachelors **ROTC:** Army, Air Force **Professional Accreditation:** AACSB, ABET, AAFCS, AAMAE, AANA, ACA, ADA, ADtA, APTA, CARC, CEPH, CSWE, JRCEMT, NAACLS, NASAD, NASM, NAST, NCATE, NLN **Intercollegiate Athletics:** Baseball M; Basketball M & W; Cross-Country Running M & W; Football M; Golf M & W; Soccer W; Softball W; Swimming and Diving W; Tennis M & W; Track and Field M & W; Volleyball W

ZANE STATE COLLEGE
1555 Newark Rd.
Zanesville, OH 43701-2626
Tel: (740)454-2501
Web Site: http://www.zanestate.edu/
President/CEO: Dr. Lynn H. Willett
Registrar: Tim Shepfer
Admissions: Paul Young
Financial Aid: Jennifer Clipner
Type: Two-Year College **Sex:** Coed **Admission Plans:** Open Admission; Early Admission **Application Fee:** $0.00 **H.S. Requirements:** High school diploma required; GED accepted **Scholarships:** Available **Calendar System:** Quarter, Summer Session Available **Faculty:** FT 50, PT 66 **Student-Faculty Ratio:** 18:1 **Exams:** Other, SAT I or ACT **Regional Accreditation:** North Central Association of Colleges and Schools **Credit Hours For Degree:** 110 credits, Associates **Professional Accreditation:** ABET, AAMAE, ACF, AOTA, APTA, JRCERT, NAACLS **Intercollegiate Athletics:** Baseball M & W; Basketball M & W; Golf M & W

BACONE COLLEGE
2299 Old Bacone Rd.
Muskogee, OK 74403-1597
Tel: (918)683-4581; 888-682-5514
Admissions: (918)781-7349
Fax: (918)682-5514
Web Site: http://www.bacone.edu/
President/CEO: Robert J. Duncan, Jr.
Registrar: Bill Painter
Admissions: Jerrett Phillips
Financial Aid: Shannon Panthin
Type: Four-Year College **Sex:** Coed **Affiliation:** American Baptist Churches in the U.S.A. **Scores:** 70% SAT V 400+; 70.5% SAT M 400+; 39% ACT 18-23; 5% ACT 24-29 **Admission Plans:** Early Admission; Deferred Admission **Application Fee:** $25.00 **H.S. Requirements:** High school diploma required; GED accepted **Costs Per Year:** Application fee: $25. Comprehensive fee: $14,467 includes full-time tuition ($8137), mandatory fees ($630), and college room and board ($5700). College room only: $3000. Part-time tuition: $350 per credit hour. Part-time mandatory fees: $240 per term. Part-time tuition and fees vary according to course load. **Scholarships:** Available **Calendar System:** Semester, Summer Session Available **Enrollment:** FT 697, PT 217 **Faculty:** FT 33, PT 22 **Student-Faculty Ratio:** 15:1 **Exams:** ACT, SAT I or ACT **% Residing in College-Owned, -Operated, or -Affiliated Housing:** 48 **Library Holdings:** 34,564 **Regional Accreditation:** North Central Association of Colleges and Schools **Credit Hours For Degree:** 62 semester hours, Associates; 124 semester hours, Bachelors **Professional Accreditation:** JRCERT, NLN **Intercollegiate Athletics:** Baseball M; Basketball M & W; Cheerleading M & W; Cross-Country Running M & W; Football M; Golf M & W; Soccer M & W; Softball W; Track and Field M & W; Volleyball M & W; Wrestling M

CAMERON UNIVERSITY
2800 West Gore Blvd.
Lawton, OK 73505-6377
Tel: (580)581-2200; 888-454-7600
Admissions: (580)581-2289
Fax: (580)581-5514
E-mail: admiss@cua.cameron.edu
Web Site: http://www.cameron.edu/
President/CEO: Dr. Cynthia S. Ross
Registrar: Linda Phillips
Admissions: Zoe DuRant
Financial Aid: Caryn Pacheco
Type: Comprehensive **Sex:** Coed **Affiliation:** Oklahoma State Regents for Higher Education **Scores:** 42.6% ACT 18-23; 17.2% ACT 24-29 **% Accepted:** 100 **Admission Plans:** Open Admission; Early Admission; Deferred Admission **Application Deadline:** Rolling **Application Fee:** $15.00 **H.S. Requirements:** High school diploma required; GED accepted **Costs Per Year:** Application fee: $15. State resident tuition: $3240 full-time, $108 per semester hour part-time. Nonresident tuition: $7830 full-time, $261 per semester hour part-time. Mandatory fees: $200 full-time, $100 per term part-time. Full-time tuition and fees vary according to course load. Part-time tuition and fees vary according to course load. College room and board: $3014. Room and board charges vary according to board plan. **Scholarships:** Available **Calendar System:** Semester, Summer Session Available **Enrollment:** FT 3,173, PT 2,266, Grad 434 **Faculty:** FT 180, PT 117 **Student-Faculty Ratio:** 17:1 **Exams:** SAT I or ACT **% Residing in College-Owned, -Operated, or -Affiliated Housing:** 4 **Library Holdings:** 262,835 **Regional Accreditation:** North Central Association of Colleges and Schools **Credit Hours For Degree:** 64 semester hours, Associates; 128 semester hours, Bachelors **ROTC:** Army **Professional Accreditation:** ACBSP, NASM, NCATE **Intercollegiate Athletics:** Baseball M; Basketball M & W; Cross-Country Running M; Golf M & W; Softball W; Tennis M & W; Volleyball W

CARL ALBERT STATE COLLEGE
1507 South McKenna
Poteau, OK 74953-5208
Tel: (918)647-1200
Admissions: (918)647-1301
Fax: (918)647-1306
E-mail: ddickerson@carlalbert.edu
Web Site: http://www.carlalbert.edu/
President/CEO: Dr. Joe E. White
Registrar: Dee Ann Dickerson
Admissions: Dee Ann Dickerson
Financial Aid: Robin Benson
Type: Two-Year College **Sex:** Coed **Affiliation:** Oklahoma State Regents for Higher Education **% Accepted:** 79 **Admission Plans:** Open Admission **Application Deadline:** August 13 **Application Fee:** $0.00 **H.S. Requirements:** High school diploma or equivalent not required. For nursing, physical therapy assistant programs: High school diploma required; GED accepted **Costs Per Year:** Application fee: $0. State resident tuition: $1632 full-time, $68 per credit hour part-time. Nonresident tuition: $4004 full-time, $167 per credit hour part-time. Mandatory fees: $4 full-time, $2 per term part-time. College room and board: $1520. College room only: $1000. **Scholarships:** Available **Calendar System:** Semester **Enrollment:** FT 1,484, PT 1,017 **Faculty:** FT 51, PT 103 **Student-Faculty Ratio:** 16:1 **% Residing in College-Owned, -Operated, or -Affiliated Housing:** 18 **Library Holdings:** 27,200 **Regional Accreditation:** North Central Association of Colleges and Schools **Credit Hours For Degree:** 62 credit hours, Associates **Professional Accreditation:** APTA, NLN **Intercollegiate Athletics:** Baseball M; Basketball M & W; Softball M

COMMUNITY CARE COLLEGE
4242 South Sheridan
Tulsa, OK 74145
Tel: (918)610-0027
Fax: (918)610-0029
E-mail: tknox@communitycarecollege.com
Web Site: http://www.communitycarecollege.com/
President/CEO: Teresa Knox
Admissions: Teresa Knox
Type: Two-Year College **Sex:** Coed **Affiliation:** Dental Directions, Inc. **Application Fee:** $15.00 **Costs Per Year:** Application fee: $15. Tuition: $9000 full-time. Mandatory fees: $850 full-time. **Calendar System:** Semester **Enrollment:** FT 512, PT 13 **Professional Accreditation:** ABHES

CONNORS STATE COLLEGE
Route 1 Box 1000
Warner, OK 74469-9700
Tel: (918)463-2931; (918)463-2931

Admissions: (918)463-6233
Web Site: http://www.connorsstate.edu/
President/CEO: Dr. Donnie Nero
Registrar: John Turnbull
Admissions: John A. Turnbull
Financial Aid: Wanda Fuller
Type: Two-Year College **Sex:** Coed **Affiliation:** Oklahoma State Regents for Higher Education **Admission Plans:** Open Admission; Early Admission; Deferred Admission **Application Fee:** $0.00 **H.S. Requirements:** High school diploma or equivalent not required **Scholarships:** Available **Calendar System:** Semester, Summer Session Available **Faculty:** FT 54, PT 62 **Student-Faculty Ratio:** 21:1 **Exams:** Other, SAT I or ACT **% Residing in College-Owned, -Operated, or -Affiliated Housing:** 12 **Library Holdings:** 63,728 **Regional Accreditation:** North Central Association of Colleges and Schools **Credit Hours For Degree:** 60 semester hours, Associates **Professional Accreditation:** NLN **Intercollegiate Athletics:** Baseball M; Basketball M & W; Softball W

EAST CENTRAL UNIVERSITY
1100 East 14th St.
Ada, OK 74820-6899
Tel: (580)332-8000
Admissions: (580)310-5239
Fax: (580)436-5495
E-mail: parmstro@mailclerk.ecok.edu
Web Site: http://www.ecok.edu/
President/CEO: Dr. Bill S. Cole
Registrar: Pamla Armstrong
Admissions: Pamela Armstrong
Financial Aid: Marcia Carter
Type: Comprehensive **Sex:** Coed **Affiliation:** Oklahoma State Regents for Higher Education **Scores:** 54% ACT 18-23; 22% ACT 24-29 **% Accepted:** 98 **Admission Plans:** Early Admission **Application Fee:** $20.00 **H.S. Requirements:** High school diploma required; GED accepted **Costs Per Year:** Application fee: $20. State resident tuition: $2,722 full-time, $75.11 per semester hour part-time. Nonresident tuition: $5,739 full-time, $229.55 per semester hour part-time. Mandatory fees: $844 full-time, $31.80 per semester hour part-time, $23.50 per term part-time. Full-time tuition and fees vary according to course load. Part-time tuition and fees vary according to course load. College room and board: $3000. College room only: $1070. Room and board charges vary according to board plan and housing facility. **Scholarships:** Available **Calendar System:** Semester, Summer Session Available **Enrollment:** FT 3,172, PT 631, Grad 768 **Faculty:** FT 156, PT 99 **Student-Faculty Ratio:** 20:1 **Exams:** ACT, SAT I or ACT **% Receiving Financial Aid:** 53 **Library Holdings:** 171,080 **Regional Accreditation:** North Central Association of Colleges and Schools **Credit Hours For Degree:** 124 semester hours, Bachelors **Professional Accreditation:** AHIMA, ACBSP, CORE, CSWE, NASM, NCATE, NLN **Intercollegiate Athletics:** Baseball M; Basketball M & W; Cheerleading M & W; Cross-Country Running M & W; Football M; Golf M & W; Soccer W; Softball W; Tennis M & W; Track and Field M & W

EASTERN OKLAHOMA STATE COLLEGE
1301 West Main
Wilburton, OK 74578-4999
Tel: (918)465-2361
Fax: (918)465-2431
E-mail: lmiller@eosc.edu
Web Site: http://www.eosc.edu/
President/CEO: Dr. Richard Bernard
Admissions: Leah Miller
Financial Aid: Mimi Kelley
Type: Two-Year College **Sex:** Coed **Affiliation:** Oklahoma State Regents for Higher Education **Admission Plans:** Open Admission; Early Admission; Deferred Admission **Application Fee:** $25.00 **H.S. Requirements:** High school diploma required; GED accepted. For state residents 18 or over: High school diploma or equivalent not required **Scholarships:** Available **Calendar System:** Semester, Summer Session Available **Faculty:** FT 51 **Exams:** ACT **% Residing in College-Owned, -Operated, or -Affiliated Housing:** 20 **Library Holdings:** 41,639 **Regional Accreditation:** North Central Association of Colleges and Schools **Credit Hours For Degree:** 64 semester hours, Associates **Professional Accreditation:** NLN **Intercollegiate Athletics:** Baseball M; Basketball M & W; Equestrian Sports M & W; Softball W

HERITAGE COLLEGE OF HAIR DESIGN
7100 I-35 Services Rd., Ste. 7118
Oklahoma City, OK 73149
Tel: (405)631-3399
Fax: (405)631-6711 **Type:** Two-Year College **Sex:** Coed **Professional Accreditation:** ACCSCT

HILLSDALE FREE WILL BAPTIST COLLEGE
3701 South I-35 Service Rd.
PO Box 7208
Moore, OK 73160-1208
Tel: (405)912-9000
Admissions: (405)912-9006
Fax: (405)912-9050
E-mail: gosaints@flash.net
Web Site: http://www.hc.edu/
President/CEO: Rev. Timothy W. Eaton
Registrar: Sue Chaffin
Admissions: Pamela Thompson
Financial Aid: Pam Thompson
Type: Comprehensive **Sex:** Coed **Affiliation:** Free Will Baptist **Scores:** 44.3% ACT 18-23; 10% ACT 24-29 **Admission Plans:** Early Admission; Deferred Admission **Application Fee:** $20.00 **H.S. Requirements:** High school diploma required; GED accepted **Costs Per Year:** Application fee: $20. Comprehensive fee: $12,120 includes full-time tuition ($6800), mandatory fees ($1060), and college room and board ($4260). Full-time tuition and fees vary according to course load and program. Room and board charges vary according to board plan. Part-time tuition: $260 per credit hour. Part-time mandatory fees: $15 per credit hour, $150 per term. Part-time tuition and fees vary according to program. **Scholarships:** Available **Calendar System:** Semester, Summer Session Available **Enrollment:** FT 203, PT 51, Grad 14 **Faculty:** FT 18, PT 27 **Student-Faculty Ratio:** 8:1 **Exams:** SAT I or ACT **% Residing in College-Owned, -Operated, or -Affiliated Housing:** 45 **Library Holdings:** 20,102 **Credit Hours For Degree:** 64 credit hours, Associates; 128 credit hours, Bachelors **Professional Accreditation:** TACCS **Intercollegiate Athletics:** Baseball M; Basketball M & W; Softball W

ITT TECHNICAL INSTITUTE
4943 South 78th East Ave.
Tulsa, OK.74145
Admissions: (918)619-8700
Web Site: http://www.itt-tech.edu/
Admissions: Karen Selby
Type: Two-Year College **Sex:** Coed **Application Deadline:** Rolling **Application Fee:** $100.00 **Costs Per Year:** Application fee: $100. **Calendar System:** Quarter **Exams:** Other

LANGSTON UNIVERSITY
PO Box 907
Langston, OK 73050-0907
Tel: (405)466-2231
Admissions: (405)466-2980
Fax: (405)466-3381
Web Site: http://www.lunet.edu/
President/CEO: Dr. Ernest L. Holloway
Registrar: Margie Allen Bonner
Admissions: Gayle L. Robertson
Financial Aid: Yvonne Maxwell
Type: Comprehensive **Sex:** Coed **Affiliation:** Oklahoma State Regents for Higher Education **Admission Plans:** Open Admission **H.S. Requirements:** High school diploma required; GED accepted **Scholarships:** Available **Calendar System:** Semester, Summer Session Available **Enrollment:** FT 2,230, PT 668, Grad 109 **Student-Faculty Ratio:** 30:1 **Exams:** SAT I or ACT **% Receiving Financial Aid:** 71 **Library Holdings:** 97,565 **Regional Accreditation:** North Central Association of Colleges and Schools **Credit Hours For Degree:** 62 credit hours, Associates; 124 credit hours, Bachelors **ROTC:** Army **Professional Accreditation:** ACBSP, CORE, NCATE, NLN **Intercollegiate Athletics:** Basketball M & W; Football M; Track and Field M & W

METROPOLITAN COLLEGE (OKLAHOMA CITY)
2901 North Classen Blvd., Ste. 200
Oklahoma City, OK 73106

Tel: (405)528-5000
Admissions: (405)843-1000
Fax: (405)528-0320
Web Site: http://www.metropolitancollege.edu/
Admissions: Pamela Picken
Type: Four-Year College **Sex:** Coed **Affiliation:** Wyandotte Collegiate Systems **Admission Plans:** Open Admission **Application Fee:** $50.00 **H.S. Requirements:** High school diploma required; GED accepted **Costs Per Year:** Application fee: $50. Tuition: $7710 full-time. **Calendar System:** Trimester, Summer Session Not available **Enrollment:** FT 77, PT 63 **Faculty:** FT 3, PT 15 **Exams:** Other **Credit Hours For Degree:** 69 credit hours, Associates; 126 credit hours, Bachelors **Professional Accreditation:** ACCSCT

METROPOLITAN COLLEGE (TULSA)
4528 South Sheridan Rd., Ste. 105
Tulsa, OK 74145-1011
Tel: (918)627-9300
Fax: (918)627-2122
E-mail: admissions@metropolitancollege.edu
Web Site: http://www.metropolitancollege.edu/
Admissions: Vicki Angelo
Type: Four-Year College **Sex:** Coed **Admission Plans:** Open Admission **Application Fee:** $50.00 **H.S. Requirements:** High school diploma required; GED accepted **Calendar System:** Trimester **Enrollment:** FT 223 **Faculty:** FT 4, PT 12 **Student-Faculty Ratio:** 15:1 **Exams:** Other **Credit Hours For Degree:** 63 credits, Associates; 129 credits, Bachelors **Professional Accreditation:** ACCSCT

MID-AMERICA CHRISTIAN UNIVERSITY
3500 Southwest 119th St.
Oklahoma City, OK 73170-4504
Tel: (405)691-3800
Admissions: (405)392-3241
Fax: (405)692-5165
Web Site: http://www.macu.edu/
President/CEO: Dr. John Fozard
Registrar: Debra Shoemake
Admissions: Debra Shoemake
Financial Aid: Steve Gilliland
Type: Four-Year College **Sex:** Coed **Affiliation:** Church of God **Admission Plans:** Open Admission; Early Admission **Application Fee:** $20.00 **H.S. Requirements:** High school diploma required; GED accepted **Costs Per Year:** Application fee: $20. Comprehensive fee: $14,360 includes full-time tuition ($9900) and college room and board ($4460). College room only: $2360. Full-time tuition varies according to course load. Part-time tuition: $420 per hour. Part-time tuition varies according to course load. **Scholarships:** Available **Calendar System:** Semester, Summer Session Available **Enrollment:** FT 547, PT 66 **Faculty:** FT 18, PT 28 **Student-Faculty Ratio:** 19:1 **Exams:** SAT I or ACT **% Receiving Financial Aid:** 86 **% Residing in College-Owned, -Operated, or -Affiliated Housing:** 34 **Library Holdings:** 60,000 **Regional Accreditation:** North Central Association of Colleges and Schools **Credit Hours For Degree:** 64 semester hours, Associates; 124 semester hours, Bachelors **Intercollegiate Athletics:** Baseball M; Basketball M & W; Soccer M; Softball W; Volleyball W

MURRAY STATE COLLEGE
One Murray Campus
Tishomingo, OK 73460-3130
Tel: (580)371-2371
Fax: (580)371-9844
Web Site: http://www.mscok.edu/
President/CEO: Dr. William D. Pennington
Registrar: Ann Beck
Admissions: Ann Beck
Financial Aid: Marilyn Schwarz
Type: Two-Year College **Sex:** Coed **Affiliation:** Oklahoma State Regents for Higher Education **Admission Plans:** Open Admission; Early Admission; Deferred Admission **H.S. Requirements:** High school diploma required; GED accepted **Scholarships:** Available **Calendar System:** Semester, Summer Session Available **Enrollment:** FT 1,115, PT 843 **Faculty:** FT 43, PT 30 **Student-Faculty Ratio:** 27:1 **Exams:** ACT **% Residing in College-Owned, -Operated, or -Affiliated Housing:** 6 **Library Holdings:** 20,000 **Regional Accreditation:** North Central Association of Colleges and Schools **Credit Hours For Degree:** 63 credit hours, Associates **Professional Accreditation:** APTA, NLN **Intercollegiate Athletics:** Baseball M; Basketball M & W; Softball M

NORTHEASTERN OKLAHOMA AGRICULTURAL AND MECHANICAL COLLEGE
200 I St., NE
Miami, OK 74354-6434
Tel: (918)542-8441
Admissions: (918)540-6212
Fax: (918)542-9759
Web Site: http://www.neoam.cc.ok.us/
President/CEO: Dr. Glenn E. Mayle
Registrar: Linda Oldham-Burns
Admissions: Amy Ishmael
Financial Aid: Tammy Higgins
Type: Two-Year College **Sex:** Coed **Affiliation:** Oklahoma State Regents for Higher Education **Admission Plans:** Open Admission **Application Fee:** $0.00 **H.S. Requirements:** High school diploma required; GED accepted **Scholarships:** Available **Calendar System:** Semester, Summer Session Available **Enrollment:** FT 1,473, PT 629 **Faculty:** FT 80, PT 35 **Student-Faculty Ratio:** 23:1 **Exams:** SAT I or ACT **Library Holdings:** 74,000 **Regional Accreditation:** North Central Association of Colleges and Schools **Credit Hours For Degree:** 60 credit hours, Associates **Professional Accreditation:** APTA, NAACLS, NLN **Intercollegiate Athletics:** Baseball M; Basketball M & W; Cheerleading M & W; Football M; Golf M; Softball W; Volleyball W

NORTHEASTERN STATE UNIVERSITY
600 North Grand
Tahlequah, OK 74464-2399
Tel: (918)456-5511
Fax: (918)458-2342
E-mail: nowlin@nsuok.edu
Web Site: http://www.nsuok.edu/
President/CEO: Dr. Larry Williams
Registrar: Bill Nowlin
Admissions: William E. Nowlin
Financial Aid: Teri Cochran
Type: Comprehensive **Sex:** Coed **Affiliation:** Oklahoma State Regents for Higher Education **Application Fee:** $0.00 **H.S. Requirements:** High school diploma required; GED accepted **Costs Per Year:** Application fee: $0. State resident tuition: $3300 full-time. Nonresident tuition: $8100 full-time. Full-time tuition varies according to course level, course load, and location. College room and board: $3312. Room and board charges vary according to board plan and housing facility. **Scholarships:** Available **Calendar System:** Semester, Summer Session Available **Enrollment:** FT 6,677, PT 1,866, Grad 920 **Student-Faculty Ratio:** 24:1 **Exams:** ACT **% Receiving Financial Aid:** 68 **Library Holdings:** 424,818 **Regional Accreditation:** North Central Association of Colleges and Schools **Credit Hours For Degree:** 124 semester hours, Bachelors **ROTC:** Army **Professional Accreditation:** AOA, ASLHA, ACBSP, CSWE, NASM, NCATE, NLN **Intercollegiate Athletics:** Baseball M; Basketball M & W; Cheerleading M & W; Football M; Golf M & W; Soccer M & W; Softball W; Tennis W

NORTHERN OKLAHOMA COLLEGE
1220 East Grand Ave., PO Box 310
Tonkawa, OK 74653-0310
Tel: (580)628-6200
Free: 800-429-5715
Admissions: (580)628-6221
Fax: (580)628-6209
E-mail: wwebb@north-ok.edu
Web Site: http://www.north-ok.edu/
President/CEO: Dr. Joe Kinzer
Registrar: Rick Edgington
Admissions: Wanda Webb
Financial Aid: Linda Brown
Type: Two-Year College **Sex:** Coed **Affiliation:** Oklahoma State Regents for Higher Education **Admission Plans:** Open Admission; Early Admission **Application Fee:** $25.00 **H.S. Requirements:** High school diploma required; GED accepted. For applicants 24 or over: High school diploma or equivalent not required **Scholarships:** Available **Calendar System:** Semester, Summer Session Available **Faculty:** FT 45, PT 35 **Student-Faculty Ratio:** 35:1 **Exams:** ACT **% Residing in College-Owned, -Operated, or -Affiliated Housing:** 20 **Library Holdings:** 34,458 **Regional Accreditation:** North

Central Association of Colleges and Schools **Credit Hours For Degree:** 60 credit hours, Associates **Professional Accreditation:** ACBSP, NLN **Intercollegiate Athletics:** Baseball W; Basketball M & W; Soccer M & W; Softball W; Volleyball M & W

NORTHWESTERN OKLAHOMA STATE UNIVERSITY

709 Oklahoma Blvd.
Alva, OK 73717-2799
Tel: (580)327-1700
Admissions: (580)327-8550
Fax: (580)327-1881
E-mail: smmurrow@nwosu.edu
Web Site: http://www.nwosu.edu/
President/CEO: Dr. Paul B. Beran
Registrar: Shirley Murrow
Admissions: Shirley Murrow
Financial Aid: Irala Magee

Type: Comprehensive **Sex:** Coed **Affiliation:** Oklahoma State Regents for Higher Education **Scores:** 56% ACT 18-23; 14% ACT 24-29 **% Accepted:** 99 **Admission Plans:** Early Admission **Application Deadline:** Rolling **Application Fee:** $15.00 **H.S. Requirements:** High school diploma required; GED accepted **Costs Per Year:** Application fee: $15. State resident tuition: $3270 full-time, $109 per credit hour part-time. Nonresident tuition: $8100 full-time, $270 per credit hour part-time. Full-time tuition varies according to course load, degree level, and location. Part-time tuition varies according to course load, degree level, and location. College room and board: $2980. College room only: $1000. Room and board charges vary according to board plan. **Scholarships:** Available **Calendar System:** Semester, Summer Session Available **Enrollment:** FT 1,475, PT 389, Grad 238 **Faculty:** FT 73, PT 72 **Student-Faculty Ratio:** 16:1 **Exams:** SAT I or ACT **% Receiving Financial Aid:** 57 **% Residing in College-Owned, -Operated, or -Affiliated Housing:** 20 **Library Holdings:** 344,640 **Regional Accreditation:** North Central Association of Colleges and Schools **Credit Hours For Degree:** 124 semester hours, Bachelors **Professional Accreditation:** NCATE, NLN **Intercollegiate Athletics:** Baseball M; Basketball M & W; Cheerleading M & W; Cross-Country Running M & W; Football M; Golf M & W; Soccer W; Softball W

OKLAHOMA BAPTIST UNIVERSITY

500 West University
Shawnee, OK 74804
Tel: (405)275-2850
Free: 800-654-3285
Admissions: (405)878-2033
Fax: (405)878-2046
E-mail: admissions@mail.okbu.edu
Web Site: http://www.okbu.edu/
President/CEO: Dr. Mark A. Brister
Registrar: Peggy J. Askins
Admissions: Trent Argo

Type: Four-Year College **Sex:** Coed **Affiliation:** Southern Baptist **Scores:** 100% SAT V 400+; 96% SAT M 400+; 41% ACT 18-23; 45% ACT 24-29 **Admission Plans:** Early Admission; Deferred Admission **Application Fee:** $25.00 **H.S. Requirements:** High school diploma required; GED accepted **Costs Per Year:** Application fee: $25. Comprehensive fee: $17,986 includes full-time tuition ($12,924), mandatory fees ($922), and college room and board ($4140). College room only: $1840. Full-time tuition and fees vary according to course load. Room and board charges vary according to board plan and housing facility. **Scholarships:** Available **Calendar System:** 4-1-4, Summer Session Available **Enrollment:** FT 1,511, PT 355, Grad 17 **Student-Faculty Ratio:** 15:1 **Exams:** SAT I or ACT **% Receiving Financial Aid:** 58 **% Residing in College-Owned, -Operated, or -Affiliated Housing:** 72 **Library Holdings:** 230,000 **Regional Accreditation:** North Central Association of Colleges and Schools **Credit Hours For Degree:** 128 credit hours, Bachelors **ROTC:** Air Force **Professional Accreditation:** ACBSP, NASM, NCATE, NLN **Intercollegiate Athletics:** Baseball M; Basketball M & W; Cross-Country Running M & W; Golf M & W; Softball W; Tennis M & W; Track and Field M & W

OKLAHOMA CHRISTIAN UNIVERSITY

PO Box 11000
Oklahoma City, OK 73136-1100
Tel: (405)425-5000
Admissions: (405)425-5050
Fax: (405)425-5208
Web Site: http://www.oc.edu/
President/CEO: Dr. Mike O'Neal
Registrar: Dr. Mickey Banister
Admissions: Risa Forrester
Financial Aid: Missi Bryant

Type: Comprehensive **Sex:** Coed **Affiliation:** Church of Christ **Scores:** 78.4% SAT V 400+; 92.8% SAT M 400+; 40.4% ACT 18-23; 37.3% ACT 24-29 **% Accepted:** 39 **Admission Plans:** Open Admission; Early Admission; Deferred Admission **Application Deadline:** Rolling **Application Fee:** $25.00 **H.S. Requirements:** High school diploma required; GED accepted **Costs Per Year:** Application fee: $25. Comprehensive fee: $20,416 includes full-time tuition ($13,422), mandatory fees ($1554), and college room and board ($5440). Part-time tuition: $559 per credit hour. Part-time mandatory fees: $747 per term. **Scholarships:** Available **Calendar System:** Semester, Summer Session Available **Enrollment:** FT 1,744, PT 91, Grad 220 **Faculty:** FT 85, PT 75 **Student-Faculty Ratio:** 15:1 **Exams:** SAT I or ACT **% Receiving Financial Aid:** 67 **% Residing in College-Owned, -Operated, or -Affiliated Housing:** 66 **Library Holdings:** 93,680 **Regional Accreditation:** North Central Association of Colleges and Schools **Credit Hours For Degree:** 126 semester hours, Bachelors **ROTC:** Army, Air Force **Professional Accreditation:** ABET, ACBSP, NASM, NCATE **Intercollegiate Athletics:** Basketball M & W; Cross-Country Running M & W; Golf M; Soccer M & W; Softball W; Tennis M & W; Track and Field M & W

OKLAHOMA CITY COMMUNITY COLLEGE

7777 South May Ave.
Oklahoma City, OK 73159-4419
Tel: (405)682-1611
Admissions: (405)682-7515
Web Site: http://www.okccc.edu/
President/CEO: Dr. Robert P. Todd
Registrar: Gloria Barton
Admissions: Gloria Cardenas-Barton
Financial Aid: Harold Case

Type: Two-Year College **Sex:** Coed **Affiliation:** Oklahoma State Regents for Higher Education **Scores:** 54% ACT 18-23; 16% ACT 24-29 **Admission Plans:** Open Admission; Early Admission; Deferred Admission **Application Fee:** $25.00 **H.S. Requirements:** High school diploma or equivalent not required. For applicants under 19, nursing, occupational therapy, physical therapy programs: High school diploma required; GED accepted **Scholarships:** Available **Calendar System:** Semester, Summer Session Available **Enrollment:** FT 4,863, PT 7,185 **Faculty:** FT 115, PT 403 **Student-Faculty Ratio:** 23:1 **Exams:** ACT, Other **Regional Accreditation:** North Central Association of Colleges and Schools **Credit Hours For Degree:** 60 credit hours, Associates **Professional Accreditation:** AOTA, APTA, CARC, JRCEMT, NLN

OKLAHOMA CITY UNIVERSITY

2501 North Blackwelder
Oklahoma City, OK 73106-1402
Tel: (405)521-5000
Free: 800-633-7242
Admissions: (405)208-5050
E-mail: uadmissions@okcu.edu
Web Site: http://www.okcu.edu/
President/CEO: Dr. Thomas J. McDaniel
Registrar: Charles Monnot
Admissions: Dr. Lloyd Musselman
Financial Aid: Denise Flis

Type: Comprehensive **Sex:** Coed **Affiliation:** United Methodist **Scores:** 100% SAT V 400+; 100% SAT M 400+; 41% ACT 18-23; 41% ACT 24-29 **% Accepted:** 81 **Admission Plans:** Deferred Admission **Application Deadline:** August 20 **Application Fee:** $30.00 **H.S. Requirements:** High school diploma required; GED accepted **Costs Per Year:** Application fee: $30. Comprehensive fee: $23,863 includes full-time tuition ($16,700), mandatory fees ($913), and college room and board ($6250). College room only: $3050. Full-time tuition and fees vary according to program. Room and board charges vary according to board plan and housing facility. Part-time tuition: $570 per semester hour. Part-time mandatory fees: $120 per term. Part-time tuition and fees vary according to program. **Scholarships:** Available **Calendar System:** Semester, Summer Session Available **Enrollment:** FT 1,466, PT 445, Grad 1,086 **Faculty:** FT 164, PT 121 **Student-Faculty Ratio:** 14:1 **Exams:** SAT I or ACT **% Receiving Financial Aid:** 50 **% Residing in College-Owned, -Operated, or -Affiliated Housing:** 39 **Library Holdings:** 440,374 **Regional Accreditation:** North Central Association of

Colleges and Schools **Credit Hours For Degree:** 124 semester hours, Bachelors **ROTC:** Army, Air Force **Professional Accreditation:** ABA, AALS, ACBSP, MACTE, NASM, NLN **Intercollegiate Athletics:** Baseball M; Basketball M & W; Cheerleading M & W; Crew M & W; Golf M & W; Soccer M & W; Softball W

OKLAHOMA PANHANDLE STATE UNIVERSITY

PO Box 430
Goodwell, OK 73939-0430
Tel: (580)349-2611
Free: 800-664-6778
Admissions: (580)349-1376
Fax: (580)349-2302
Web Site: http://www.opsu.edu/
President/CEO: Dr. David A. Bryant
Admissions: Bobby Jenkins
Financial Aid: Mary Ellen Riley

Type: Four-Year College **Sex:** Coed **Affiliation:** Oklahoma State Regents for Higher Education **Scores:** 56% ACT 18-23; 9% ACT 24-29 **% Accepted:** 100 **Admission Plans:** Open Admission **Application Deadline:** Rolling **Application Fee:** $0.00 **H.S. Requirements:** High school diploma required; GED accepted **Costs Per Year:** Application fee: $0. State resident tuition: $2274 full-time, $75.80 per hour part-time. Nonresident tuition: $4500 full-time, $150 per hour part-time. Mandatory fees: $1118 full-time, $34.50 per hour part-time, $62 per term part-time. Full-time tuition and fees vary according to course level and program. Part-time tuition and fees vary according to course level. College room and board: $4270. College room only: $2520. Room and board charges vary according to board plan, housing facility, and student level. **Scholarships:** Available **Calendar System:** Semester, Summer Session Available **Enrollment:** FT 920, PT 224 **Faculty:** FT 56, PT 33 **Student-Faculty Ratio:** 13:1 **Exams:** SAT I or ACT **% Residing in College-Owned, -Operated, or -Affiliated Housing:** 17 **Library Holdings:** 129,467 **Regional Accreditation:** North Central Association of Colleges and Schools **Credit Hours For Degree:** 64 credit hours, Associates; 124 credit hours, Bachelors **Professional Accreditation:** NCATE, NLN **Intercollegiate Athletics:** Baseball M; Basketball M & W; Cross-Country Running M & W; Equestrian Sports W; Football M; Golf M & W; Softball W; Volleyball W

OKLAHOMA STATE UNIVERSITY

Stillwater, OK 74078
Tel: (405)744-5000
Free: 800-852-1255
Admissions: (405)744-5358
Fax: (405)744-5285
E-mail: paul.carney@okstate.edu
Web Site: http://osu.okstate.edu/
President/CEO: Dr. David Schmidly
Registrar: Joan Payne
Admissions: Dr. Paul B. Carney
Financial Aid: Dr. Charles Bruce

Type: University **Sex:** Coed **Affiliation:** Oklahoma State University System **Scores:** 97.45% SAT V 400+; 98.44% SAT M 400+; 40.27% ACT 18-23; 45.39% ACT 24-29 **% Accepted:** 88 **Application Deadline:** Rolling **Application Fee:** $40.00 **H.S. Requirements:** High school diploma required; GED accepted **Costs Per Year:** Application fee: $40. State resident tuition: $3099 full-time, $103.30 per credit hour part-time. Nonresident tuition: $11,122 full-time, $370.75 per credit hour part-time. Mandatory fees: $1266 full-time, $42.21 per credit hour part-time. Full-time tuition and fees vary according to program and student level. Part-time tuition and fees vary according to program and student level. College room and board: $5848. College room only: $2848. Room and board charges vary according to board plan, housing facility, and location. **Scholarships:** Available **Calendar System:** Semester, Summer Session Available **Enrollment:** FT 16,731, PT 2,178, Grad 4,256 **Faculty:** FT 1,000, PT 237 **Student-Faculty Ratio:** 19:1 **Exams:** SAT I or ACT **% Receiving Financial Aid:** 51 **% Residing in College-Owned, -Operated, or -Affiliated Housing:** 40 **Library Holdings:** 2,470,138 **Regional Accreditation:** North Central Association of Colleges and Schools **Credit Hours For Degree:** 120 credit hours, Bachelors **ROTC:** Army, Air Force **Professional Accreditation:** AACSB, ABET, ACEJMC, AAMFT, ADtA, APA, ASLA, ASLHA, AVMA, FIDER, JRCEPAT, NASM, NAST, NCATE, NRPA, SAF **Intercollegiate Athletics:** Baseball M; Basketball M & W; Cross-Country Running M & W; Equestrian Sports W; Football M; Golf M & W; Soccer W; Softball W; Tennis M & W; Track and Field M & W; Wrestling M

OKLAHOMA STATE UNIVERSITY, OKLAHOMA CITY

900 North Portland
Oklahoma City, OK 73107-6120
Tel: (405)947-4421
Admissions: (405)945-3287
Fax: (405)945-3277
Web Site: http://www.osuokc.edu/
President/CEO: Dr. Jerry Carroll
Registrar: Jeanne Kubier
Admissions: Jeanne Kubier
Financial Aid: Jerry Brooks

Type: Two-Year College **Sex:** Coed **Affiliation:** Oklahoma State University **Admission Plans:** Open Admission; Early Admission **Application Fee:** $0.00 **H.S. Requirements:** High school diploma required; GED accepted **Scholarships:** Available **Calendar System:** Semester, Summer Session Available **Faculty:** FT 65, PT 185 **Student-Faculty Ratio:** 20:1 **Exams:** Other, SAT I or ACT **Library Holdings:** 11,973 **Regional Accreditation:** North Central Association of Colleges and Schools **Credit Hours For Degree:** 60 semester hours, Associates **Professional Accreditation:** NLN

OKLAHOMA STATE UNIVERSITY, OKMULGEE

1801 East Fourth St.
Okmulgee, OK 74447-3901
Tel: (918)293-4678
Free: 800-722-4471
Admissions: (918)293-5298
Web Site: http://www.osu-okmulgee.edu/
President/CEO: Dr. Robert E. Klabenes
Registrar: Cary Fox
Admissions: Kelly Hildebrant
Financial Aid: Barrett Bell

Type: Two-Year College **Sex:** Coed **Affiliation:** Oklahoma State University **Admission Plans:** Open Admission; Deferred Admission **Application Fee:** $0.00 **H.S. Requirements:** High school diploma or equivalent not required **Scholarships:** Available **Calendar System:** Trimester, Summer Session Available **Enrollment:** FT 1,717, PT 612 **Faculty:** FT 129 **Exams:** SAT I or ACT **% Residing in College-Owned, -Operated, or -Affiliated Housing:** 25 **Library Holdings:** 9,965 **Regional Accreditation:** North Central Association of Colleges and Schools **Credit Hours For Degree:** 84 credit hours, Associates

OKLAHOMA WESLEYAN UNIVERSITY

2201 Silver Lake Rd.
Bartlesville, OK 74006-6299
Tel: (918)335-6200
Admissions: (866)222-8226
Fax: (918)335-6229
E-mail: jweidman@okwu.edu
Web Site: http://www.okwu.edu/
President/CEO: Dr. Everett Piper
Registrar: Becky Tupper
Admissions: Jim Weidman
Financial Aid: Lee Kanakis

Type: Comprehensive **Sex:** Coed **Affiliation:** Wesleyan Church **Scores:** 89% SAT V 400+; 85% SAT M 400+; 60% ACT 18-23; 21% ACT 24-29 **Application Fee:** $25.00 **H.S. Requirements:** High school diploma required; GED accepted **Costs Per Year:** Application fee: $25. Comprehensive fee: $18,950 includes full-time tuition ($12,900), mandatory fees ($850), and college room and board ($5200). College room only: $2625. Full-time tuition and fees vary according to course load. Room and board charges vary according to board plan and housing facility. Part-time tuition: $475 per credit. Part-time mandatory fees: $50 per credit. **Scholarships:** Available **Calendar System:** Semester, Summer Session Available **Enrollment:** FT 864, PT 23 **Faculty:** FT 35, PT 5 **Student-Faculty Ratio:** 14:1 **Exams:** SAT I or ACT **% Receiving Financial Aid:** 84 **% Residing in College-Owned, -Operated, or -Affiliated Housing:** 70 **Library Holdings:** 124,722 **Regional Accreditation:** North Central Association of Colleges and Schools **Credit Hours For Degree:** 64 semester hours, Associates; 126 semester hours, Bachelors **Professional Accreditation:** AACN, NCATE **Intercollegiate Athletics:** Baseball M; Basketball M & W; Cheerleading W; Golf M; Soccer M & W; Softball W; Tennis M & W; Volleyball W

ORAL ROBERTS UNIVERSITY
7777 South Lewis Ave.
Tulsa, OK 74171-0001
Tel: (918)495-6161
Free: 800-678-8876
Admissions: (918)495-6529
Fax: (918)495-6222
E-mail: admissions@oru.edu
Web Site: http://www.oru.edu/
President/CEO: Dr. Richard L. Roberts
Registrar: Sheree King
Admissions: Chris Belcher
Financial Aid: Scott Carr
Type: Comprehensive **Sex:** Coed **Affiliation:** interdenominational **% Accepted:** 70 **Admission Plans:** Early Admission; Early Action; Deferred Admission **Application Deadline:** Rolling **Application Fee:** $35.00 **H.S. Requirements:** High school diploma required; GED accepted **Costs Per Year:** Application fee: $35. Comprehensive fee: $22,650 includes full-time tuition ($15,400), mandatory fees ($480), and college room and board ($6770). College room only: $3280. Room and board charges vary according to board plan and housing facility. Part-time tuition: $642 per credit hour. **Scholarships:** Available **Calendar System:** Semester, Summer Session Available **Faculty:** FT 164, PT 71 **Student-Faculty Ratio:** 16:1 **Exams:** SAT I or ACT **% Receiving Financial Aid:** 70 **% Residing in College-Owned, -Operated, or -Affiliated Housing:** 71 **Library Holdings:** 216,691 **Regional Accreditation:** North Central Association of Colleges and Schools **Credit Hours For Degree:** 128 credit hours, Bachelors **ROTC:** Air Force **Professional Accreditation:** ABET, ATS, CSWE, NASM, NCATE, NLN **Intercollegiate Athletics:** Baseball M; Basketball M & W; Cross-Country Running M & W; Golf M & W; Soccer M & W; Tennis M & W; Track and Field M & W; Volleyball W

PLATT COLLEGE (OKLAHOMA CITY)
309 South Ann Arbor Ave.
Oklahoma City, OK 73128
Tel: (405)946-7799
Fax: (405)943-2150
E-mail: janen@plattcollege.org
Web Site: http://www.plattcollege.org/
President/CEO: Jane Nowlin
Admissions: Jane Nowlin
Type: Two-Year College **Sex:** Coed **Calendar System:** Continuous **Professional Accreditation:** ACCSCT

PLATT COLLEGE (TULSA)
3801 South Sheridan Rd.
Tulsa, OK 74145
Tel: (918)663-9000
Fax: (918)622-1240
E-mail: susanr@plattcollege.org
Web Site: http://www.plattcollege.org/
President/CEO: Susan Rone
Admissions: Susan Rone
Type: Two-Year College **Sex:** Coed **Calendar System:** Continuous **Professional Accreditation:** ACCSCT

REDLANDS COMMUNITY COLLEGE
1300 South Country Club Rd.
El Reno, OK 73036-5304
Tel: (405)262-2552
Web Site: http://www.redlandscc.edu/
President/CEO: Dr. Larry F. Devane
Registrar: Dennis Harris
Financial Aid: Chris Christian
Type: Two-Year College **Sex:** Coed **Affiliation:** Oklahoma State Regents for Higher Education **Admission Plans:** Open Admission; Early Admission; Deferred Admission **Application Fee:** $0.00 **H.S. Requirements:** High school diploma required; GED accepted **Costs Per Year:** Application fee: $0. State resident tuition: $1380 full-time, $46 per credit hour part-time. Nonresident tuition: $3630 full-time, $121 per credit hour part-time. Mandatory fees: $930 full-time, $31 per credit hour part-time. Full-time tuition and fees vary according to location. Part-time tuition and fees vary according to location. **Scholarships:** Available **Calendar System:** Semester, Summer Session Available **Enrollment:** FT 583, PT 1,740 **Faculty:** FT 32, PT 93 **Student-Faculty Ratio:** 18:1 **Exams:** ACT **Library Holdings:** 14,810 **Regional Accreditation:** North Central Association of Colleges and Schools **Credit Hours For Degree:** 64 semester hours, Associates **Professional Accreditation:** NLN **Intercollegiate Athletics:** Baseball M; Basketball M & W; Volleyball W

ROGERS STATE UNIVERSITY
1701 West Will Rogers Blvd.
Claremore, OK 74017-3252
Tel: (918)343-7777
Free: 800-256-7511
Admissions: (918)343-7545
Fax: (918)343-7898
E-mail: bnoah@rsu.edu
Web Site: http://www.rsu.edu/
President/CEO: Dr. Joe Wiley
Registrar: Steve Hedges
Admissions: Becky Noah
Financial Aid: Cynthia Hoyt
Type: Four-Year College **Sex:** Coed **Affiliation:** Oklahoma State Regents for Higher Education **Scores:** 54.53% ACT 18-23; 13.22% ACT 24-29 **Admission Plans:** Open Admission **Application Fee:** $0.00 **H.S. Requirements:** High school diploma required; GED accepted **Costs Per Year:** Application fee: $0. State resident tuition: $3300 full-time, $110 per credit hour part-time. Nonresident tuition: $7860 full-time, $262 per credit hour part-time. Mandatory fees: $30 full-time, $15 per term part-time. College room and board: $6210. College room only: $4050. **Scholarships:** Available **Calendar System:** Semester, Summer Session Available **Enrollment:** FT 1,681, PT 1,619 **Faculty:** FT 88, PT 63 **Student-Faculty Ratio:** 19:1 **Exams:** ACT, Other **% Receiving Financial Aid:** 100 **% Residing in College-Owned, -Operated, or -Affiliated Housing:** 10 **Library Holdings:** 57,283 **Regional Accreditation:** North Central Association of Colleges and Schools **Credit Hours For Degree:** 60 credit hours, Associates; 120 credit hours, Bachelors **ROTC:** Air Force **Professional Accreditation:** NLN

ROSE STATE COLLEGE
6420 Southeast 15th St.
Midwest City, OK 73110-2799
Tel: (405)733-7673
Fax: (405)733-7399
E-mail: ekhutchings@ms.rose.cc.ok.us
Web Site: http://www.rose.edu/
President/CEO: Dr. James J. Cook
Registrar: Evelyn K. Hutchings
Admissions: Evelyn K. Hutchings
Financial Aid: Steve Daffen
Type: Two-Year College **Sex:** Coed **Affiliation:** Oklahoma State Regents for Higher Education **Admission Plans:** Open Admission; Early Admission; Deferred Admission **Application Fee:** $15.00 **H.S. Requirements:** High school diploma required; GED accepted **Scholarships:** Available **Calendar System:** Semester, Summer Session Available **Faculty:** FT 143, PT 269 **Exams:** Other **Library Holdings:** 90,000 **Regional Accreditation:** North Central Association of Colleges and Schools **Credit Hours For Degree:** 62 credit hours, Associates **ROTC:** Army, Air Force **Professional Accreditation:** ADA, AHIMA, CARC, JRCERT, NAACLS, NLN **Intercollegiate Athletics:** Baseball M; Basketball M & W; Soccer W

ST. GREGORY'S UNIVERSITY
1900 West MacArthur Dr.
Shawnee, OK 74804-2499
Tel: (405)878-5100; 888-STGREGS
Fax: (405)878-5198
Web Site: http://www.stgregorys.edu/
President/CEO: Fr. Lawrence Stasyszen, OSB
Registrar: Joanne Cody
Financial Aid: Jonna Raney
Type: Four-Year College **Sex:** Coed **Affiliation:** Roman Catholic **Scores:** 61% ACT 18-23; 30% ACT 24-29 **% Accepted:** 83 **Admission Plans:** Deferred Admission **Application Deadline:** Rolling **Application Fee:** $25.00 **H.S. Requirements:** High school diploma required; GED accepted **Costs Per Year:** Application fee: $25. Comprehensive fee: $19,408 includes full-time tuition ($12,922), mandatory fees ($850), and college room and board ($5636). College room only: $3200. Part-time tuition: $465 per hour. Part-time mandatory fees: $36 per hour. **Scholarships:** Available **Calendar System:** Semester, Summer Session Available **Enrollment:** FT 476, PT 392 **Faculty:** FT 31, PT 33 **Student-Faculty Ratio:** 15:1 **Exams:** SAT I or ACT

% Receiving Financial Aid: 82 **% Residing in College-Owned, -Operated, or -Affiliated Housing:** 65 **Library Holdings:** 82,715 **Regional Accreditation:** North Central Association of Colleges and Schools **Credit Hours For Degree:** 64 credit hours, Associates; 128 credit hours, Bachelors **ROTC:** Army, Air Force **Intercollegiate Athletics:** Baseball M; Basketball M & W; Cross-Country Running M & W; Golf M & W; Soccer M & W; Softball W; Track and Field M & W; Volleyball W

SEMINOLE STATE COLLEGE
PO Box 351
Seminole, OK 74818-0351
Tel: (405)382-9950
Admissions: (405)382-9272
Web Site: http://www.ssc.cc.ok.us/
President/CEO: Dr. James W. Utterback
Admissions: Chris Lindley
Financial Aid: Chris Lindley
Type: Two-Year College **Sex:** Coed **Affiliation:** Oklahoma State Regents for Higher Education **Scores:** 50% ACT 18-23; 6% ACT 24-29 **% Accepted:** 100 **Admission Plans:** Open Admission; Early Admission; Deferred Admission **Application Deadline:** Rolling **Application Fee:** $15.00 **H.S. Requirements:** High school diploma or equivalent not required. For applicants under 18, nursing, medical laboratory technology programs: High school diploma required; GED accepted **Costs Per Year:** Application fee: $15. State resident tuition: $1116 full-time, $46.50 per credit hour part-time. Nonresident tuition: $3,589 full-time, $149.55 per credit hour part-time. Mandatory fees: $719 full-time, $29.95 per credit hour part-time. College room and board: $2470. **Scholarships:** Available **Calendar System:** Semester, Summer Session Available **Enrollment:** FT 2,096, PT 488 **Faculty:** FT 48, PT 44 **% Residing in College-Owned, -Operated, or -Affiliated Housing:** 8 **Library Holdings:** 27,507 **Regional Accreditation:** North Central Association of Colleges and Schools **Credit Hours For Degree:** 62 credit hours, Associates **Professional Accreditation:** NAACLS, NLN **Intercollegiate Athletics:** Baseball M; Basketball M & W; Golf M & W; Softball W; Volleyball W

SOUTHEASTERN OKLAHOMA STATE UNIVERSITY
1405 North 4th Ave.
Durant, OK 74701-0609
Tel: (580)745-2000
Free: 800-435-1327
Admissions: (580)745-2060
Fax: (580)745-7490
E-mail: kstafford@sosu.edu
Web Site: http://www.sosu.edu/
President/CEO: Dr. Glen Johnson
Registrar: Kristie Luke
Admissions: Kyle Stafford
Financial Aid: Sherry Foster
Type: Comprehensive **Sex:** Coed **Affiliation:** Oklahoma State Regents for Higher Education **Scores:** 57% ACT 18-23; 16% ACT 24-29 **% Accepted:** 80 **Admission Plans:** Open Admission **Application Deadline:** Rolling **Application Fee:** $20.00 **H.S. Requirements:** High school diploma required; GED accepted **Costs Per Year:** Application fee: $20. State resident tuition: $2195 full-time, $73.15 per credit hour part-time. Nonresident tuition: $7016 full-time, $233.85 per credit hour part-time. Mandatory fees: $1177 full-time, $34.70 per credit part-time, $68. Full-time tuition and fees vary according to course level. Part-time tuition and fees vary according to course level and course load. College room and board: $3910. College room only: $1875. Room and board charges vary according to board plan and housing facility. **Scholarships:** Available **Calendar System:** Semester, Summer Session Available **Enrollment:** FT 2,994, PT 669, Grad 412 **Faculty:** FT 141, PT 96 **Student-Faculty Ratio:** 20:1 **Exams:** SAT I or ACT **% Receiving Financial Aid:** 67 **% Residing in College-Owned, -Operated, or -Affiliated Housing:** 20 **Library Holdings:** 187,971 **Regional Accreditation:** North Central Association of Colleges and Schools **Credit Hours For Degree:** 124 credit hours, Bachelors **Professional Accreditation:** ACBSP, NASM, NCATE **Intercollegiate Athletics:** Baseball M; Basketball M & W; Cross-Country Running W; Football M; Softball W; Tennis M & W; Volleyball W

SOUTHERN NAZARENE UNIVERSITY
6729 Northwest 39th Expressway
Bethany, OK 73008
Tel: (405)789-6400
Free: 800-648-9899
Admissions: (405)491-6324
Fax: (405)491-6381
E-mail: lhess@snu.edu
Web Site: http://www.snu.edu/
President/CEO: Dr. Loren P. Gresham
Registrar: Wes Lee
Admissions: Larry Hess
Financial Aid: Chuck Kietzman
Type: Comprehensive **Sex:** Coed **Affiliation:** Nazarene **Scores:** 45% ACT 18-23; 30% ACT 24-29 **% Accepted:** 54 **Admission Plans:** Open Admission; Deferred Admission **Application Deadline:** August 15 **Application Fee:** $25.00 **H.S. Requirements:** High school diploma required; GED accepted **Costs Per Year:** Application fee: $25. One-time mandatory fee: $350. Comprehensive fee: $20,402 includes full-time tuition ($14,400), mandatory fees ($624), and college room and board ($5378). College room only: $2458. Part-time tuition: $507 per credit hour. Part-time mandatory fees: $23 per credit hour. **Scholarships:** Available **Calendar System:** Semester, Summer Session Available **Enrollment:** FT 1,659, PT 134, Grad 425 **Faculty:** FT 69, PT 107 **Student-Faculty Ratio:** 16:1 **% Receiving Financial Aid:** 82 **% Residing in College-Owned, -Operated, or -Affiliated Housing:** 67 **Library Holdings:** 95,535 **Regional Accreditation:** North Central Association of Colleges and Schools **Credit Hours For Degree:** 62 credit hours, Associates; 124 credit hours, Bachelors **ROTC:** Army, Air Force **Professional Accreditation:** AACN, NASM, NCATE **Intercollegiate Athletics:** Baseball M; Basketball M & W; Cheerleading M & W; Cross-Country Running M & W; Football M; Golf M & W; Soccer M & W; Softball W; Tennis M & W; Track and Field M & W; Volleyball W

SOUTHWESTERN CHRISTIAN UNIVERSITY
PO Box 340
Bethany, OK 73008-0340
Tel: (405)789-7661
Web Site: http://www.swcu.edu/
President/CEO: Rev. Bob R. Ely
Registrar: Debbie Burpo
Admissions: Rev. Johnny Upton
Financial Aid: Mark Arthur
Type: Comprehensive **Sex:** Coed **Affiliation:** Pentecostal Holiness Church **Admission Plans:** Early Admission; Deferred Admission **Application Fee:** $25.00 **H.S. Requirements:** High school diploma required; GED accepted **Costs Per Year:** Application fee: $25. Comprehensive fee: $12,250 includes full-time tuition ($8250) and college room and board ($4000). Part-time tuition: $295 per credit hour. **Scholarships:** Available **Calendar System:** Semester, Summer Session Available **Enrollment:** FT 121, PT 7, Grad 71 **Faculty:** FT 5, PT 9 **Student-Faculty Ratio:** 15:1 **Exams:** ACT **% Receiving Financial Aid:** 89 **% Residing in College-Owned, -Operated, or -Affiliated Housing:** 30 **Library Holdings:** 38,900 **Regional Accreditation:** North Central Association of Colleges and Schools **Credit Hours For Degree:** 64 credits, Associates; 128 credits, Bachelors **Intercollegiate Athletics:** Basketball M; Volleyball W

SOUTHWESTERN OKLAHOMA STATE UNIVERSITY
100 Campus Dr.
Weatherford, OK 73096-3098
Tel: (580)772-6611
Admissions: (580)774-3782
Fax: (580)774-3795
Web Site: http://www.swosu.edu/
President/CEO: Dr. John Hays
Registrar: Bob Klaassen
Admissions: Todd Boyd
Financial Aid: Larry Hollingsworth
Type: Comprehensive **Sex:** Coed **Affiliation:** Southwestern Oklahoma State University **Scores:** 50% ACT 18-23; 22% ACT 24-29 **Admission Plans:** Preferred Admission; Deferred Admission **Application Fee:** $15.00 **H.S. Requirements:** High school diploma required; GED accepted **Scholarships:** Available **Calendar System:** Semester, Summer Session Available **Enrollment:** FT 3,771, PT 479, Grad 279 **Faculty:** FT 196 **Student-Faculty Ratio:** 20:1 **Exams:** ACT **% Receiving Financial Aid:** 58 **% Residing in College-Owned, -Operated, or -Affiliated Housing:** 27 **Library Holdings:** 217,051 **Regional Accreditation:** North Central Association of Colleges and Schools **Credit Hours For Degree:** 124 credit hours, Bachelors **Professional Accreditation:** ABET, ACPhE, AHIMA, APTA, ACBSP, CSWE, NASM, NCATE, NLN **Intercollegiate Athletics:** Baseball M; Basketball M & W; Cheerleading M & W; Cross-Country Running W; Equestrian Sports M & W; Football M; Golf M & W; Soccer W; Softball W

SOUTHWESTERN OKLAHOMA STATE UNIVERSITY AT SAYRE
409 East Mississippi St.
Sayre, OK 73662-1236
Tel: (580)928-5533
Web Site: http://www.swosu.edu/sayre/
President/CEO: Dr. John Hays
Registrar: Kim Seymour
Admissions: Kim Seymour
Financial Aid: T.J. Williams
Type: Two-Year College **Sex:** Coed **Affiliation:** Southwestern Oklahoma State University **Scores:** 63.29% ACT 18-23; 12.66% ACT 24-29 **% Accepted:** 100 **Admission Plans:** Open Admission; Early Admission; Deferred Admission **Application Deadline:** Rolling **Application Fee:** $15.00 **H.S. Requirements:** High school diploma required; GED accepted. For applicants 18 or over: High school diploma or equivalent not required **Costs Per Year:** Application fee: $15. State resident tuition: $3456 full-time, $108 per credit hour part-time. **Scholarships:** Available **Calendar System:** Semester, Summer Session Available **Enrollment:** FT 328, PT 221 **Faculty:** FT 12, PT 7 **Student-Faculty Ratio:** 18:1 **Exams:** ACT **Library Holdings:** 9,975 **Regional Accreditation:** North Central Association of Colleges and Schools **Credit Hours For Degree:** 64 credit hours, Associates **Professional Accreditation:** ABHES, AOTA, JRCERT

SPARTAN COLLEGE OF AERONAUTICS AND TECHNOLOGY
8820 East Pine St., PO Box 582833
Tulsa, OK 74158-2833
Tel: (918)836-6886
Web Site: http://www.spartan.edu/
President/CEO: Terrell W. Harrison
Registrar: Angie Waymire
Admissions: Mark Fowler
Financial Aid: Rick Cox
Type: Two-Year College **Sex:** Coed **Admission Plans:** Open Admission; Deferred Admission **Application Fee:** $100.00 **H.S. Requirements:** High school diploma required; GED accepted. For applicants who demonstrate ability to benefit from college: High school diploma or equivalent not required **Scholarships:** Available **Calendar System:** Miscellaneous, Summer Session Not available **Enrollment:** FT 1,500 **Faculty:** FT 120, PT 30 **Exams:** Other **Library Holdings:** 18,000 **Credit Hours For Degree:** 42 credit hours, Associates **Professional Accreditation:** ACCSCT

TULSA COMMUNITY COLLEGE
6111 East Skelly Dr.
Tulsa, OK 74135-6198
Tel: (918)595-7000
Admissions: (918)595-7811
Fax: (918)595-7910
E-mail: lbrewer@tulsacc.edu
Web Site: http://www.tulsacc.edu/
Admissions: Leanne Brewer
Financial Aid: Deborah McIntyre
Type: Two-Year College **Sex:** Coed **Affiliation:** Oklahoma State Regents for Higher Education **% Accepted:** 100 **Admission Plans:** Open Admission; Early Admission **Application Deadline:** Rolling **Application Fee:** $20.00 **H.S. Requirements:** High school diploma required; GED accepted. For adult students: High school diploma or equivalent not required **Costs Per Year:** Application fee: $20. State resident tuition: $47.80 per semester hour part-time. Nonresident tuition: $172.20 per semester hour part-time. Mandatory fees: $25 per semester hour part-time. **Scholarships:** Available **Calendar System:** Semester, Summer Session Available **Enrollment:** FT 6,162, PT 10,641 **Faculty:** FT 418, PT 867 **Student-Faculty Ratio:** 20:1 **Library Holdings:** 110,000 **Regional Accreditation:** North Central Association of Colleges and Schools **Credit Hours For Degree:** 60 credit hours, Associates **Professional Accreditation:** AAMAE, ADA, AHIMA, AOTA, APTA, CARC, JRCERT, NAACLS, NLN

TULSA WELDING SCHOOL
2545 East 11th St.
Tulsa, OK 74104-3909
Tel: (918)587-6789
Free: 800-WELD-PRO
Admissions: 800-331-2934
Fax: (918)295-6821
Web Site: http://www.weldingschool.com/
President/CEO: R. Harter
Admissions: Mike Thurber
Type: Two-Year College **Sex:** Coed **Affiliation:** Tulsa Welding School, Jacksonville Branch **Costs Per Year:** Tuition: $11,090 full-time. Mandatory fees: $1900 full-time. **Calendar System:** Continuous **Enrollment:** FT 362 **Faculty:** FT 16, PT 1 **Student-Faculty Ratio:** 16:1 **Library Holdings:** 389 **Credit Hours For Degree:** 62 credits, Associates **Professional Accreditation:** ACCSCT

UNIVERSITY OF CENTRAL OKLAHOMA
100 North University Dr.
Edmond, OK 73034-5209
Tel: (405)974-2000
Free: 800-254-4215
Admissions: (405)974-2338
Fax: (405)974-4964
Web Site: http://www.ucok.edu/
President/CEO: Dr. W. Roger Webb
Registrar: Jerry Legere
Admissions: Linda Lofton
Financial Aid: Sheila Fugett
Type: Comprehensive **Sex:** Coed **Affiliation:** Oklahoma State Regents for Higher Education **Scores:** 63% ACT 18-23; 22% ACT 24-29 **Admission Plans:** Deferred Admission **Application Deadline:** Rolling **Application Fee:** $25.00 **H.S. Requirements:** High school diploma required; GED accepted **Costs Per Year:** Application fee: $25. State resident tuition: $2811 full-time, $93.70 per semester hour part-time. Nonresident tuition: $7821 full-time, $260.70 per semester hour part-time. Mandatory fees: $807 full-time, $26.90 per semester hour part-time. Full-time tuition and fees vary according to course load, degree level, program, and student level. Part-time tuition and fees vary according to course load, degree level, program, and student level. College room and board: $4476. College room only: $2166. Room and board charges vary according to board plan and housing facility. **Scholarships:** Available **Calendar System:** Semester, Summer Session Available **Enrollment:** FT 10,512, PT 4,117, Grad 1,324 **Faculty:** FT 411, PT 401 **Student-Faculty Ratio:** 21:1 **Exams:** ACT, SAT I or ACT **% Receiving Financial Aid:** 44 **% Residing in College-Owned, -Operated, or -Affiliated Housing:** 9 **Library Holdings:** 254,478 **Regional Accreditation:** North Central Association of Colleges and Schools **Credit Hours For Degree:** 124 credit hours, Bachelors **ROTC:** Army **Professional Accreditation:** ABFSE, ADtA, ASLHA, ACBSP, FIDER, NASM, NCATE, NLN **Intercollegiate Athletics:** Baseball M; Basketball M & W; Cross-Country Running M & W; Football M; Golf M & W; Soccer W; Softball W; Tennis M & W; Volleyball W; Wrestling M

UNIVERSITY OF OKLAHOMA
660 Parrington Oval
Norman, OK 73019-0390
Tel: (405)325-0311
Free: 800-234-6868
Admissions: (405)325-4521
Fax: (405)325-7478
E-mail: admrec@ou.edu
Web Site: http://www.ou.edu/
President/CEO: David L. Boren
Registrar: Matt Hamilton
Admissions: Matt Hamilton
Financial Aid: Bradley Burnett
Type: University **Sex:** Coed **Scores:** 23% ACT 18-23; 57% ACT 24-29 **% Accepted:** 86 **Application Deadline:** April 01 **Application Fee:** $40.00 **H.S. Requirements:** High school diploma required; GED accepted **Costs Per Year:** Application fee: $40. State resident tuition: $2862 full-time, $95.40 per credit hour part-time. Nonresident tuition: $10,755 full-time, $358.50 per credit hour part-time. Mandatory fees: $1546 full-time, $44.10 per credit hour part-time, $111.50 per term part-time. Full-time tuition and fees vary according to course load, location, program, and reciprocity agreements. Part-time tuition and fees vary according to course load, location, program, and reciprocity agreements. College room and board: $6361. College room only: $3355. Room and board charges vary according to board plan and housing facility. **Scholarships:** Available **Calendar System:** Semester, Summer Session Available **Enrollment:** FT 17,716, PT 2,682, Grad 6,049 **Faculty:** FT 976, PT 228 **Student-Faculty Ratio:** 22:1 **Exams:** SAT I or ACT **% Receiving Financial Aid:** 50 **% Residing in College-Owned, -Operated, or -Affiliated Housing:** 20 **Library Holdings:** 4,264,831 **Regional Accreditation:** North Central Association of Colleges and Schools **Credit**

Hours For Degree: 124 credit hours, Bachelors **ROTC:** Army, Navy, Air Force **Professional Accreditation:** AACSB, ABET, ACEJMC, ABA, ACCE, ACSP, ALA, APA, ASLA, AALS, CSWE, FIDER, NASM, NAST, NCATE **Intercollegiate Athletics:** Baseball M; Basketball M & W; Cross-Country Running M & W; Football M; Golf M & W; Gymnastics M & W; Soccer W; Softball W; Tennis M & W; Track and Field M & W; Volleyball W; Wrestling M

UNIVERSITY OF OKLAHOMA HEALTH SCIENCES CENTER
PO Box 26901
Oklahoma City, OK 73190
Tel: (405)271-4000
Admissions: (405)271-2359
Fax: (405)271-2480
Web Site: http://www.ouhsc.edu/
President/CEO: David L. Boren
Admissions: Leslie Wilbourn
Financial Aid: Anthony Spano
Type: Two-Year Upper Division **Sex:** Coed **Affiliation:** University of Oklahoma **Admission Plans:** Preferred Admission; Deferred Admission **Application Deadline:** Rolling **Application Fee:** $40.00 **H.S. Requirements:** High school diploma required; GED accepted **Costs Per Year:** Application fee: $40. State resident tuition: $2862 full-time, $95.40 per credit hour part-time. Nonresident tuition: $10,755 full-time, $358.50 per credit hour part-time. Mandatory fees: $1382 full-time, $38.15 per credit hour part-time, $118.50 per term part-time. **Calendar System:** Semester, Summer Session Available **Enrollment:** FT 777, PT 104, Grad 645 **Faculty:** FT 273, PT 130 **Student-Faculty Ratio:** 3:1 **Library Holdings:** 300,260 **Regional Accreditation:** North Central Association of Colleges and Schools **Credit Hours For Degree:** 124 credit hours, Bachelors **ROTC:** Army, Air Force **Professional Accreditation:** ABET, ACEHSA, ACPhE, ADA, ADtA, AOTA, APTA, APA, ASLHA, ACIPE, CEPH, JRCEDMS, JRCERT, JRCNMT, LCMEAMA, NLN

UNIVERSITY OF PHOENIX-OKLAHOMA CITY CAMPUS
6501 North Broadway Extension, Ste. 100
Oklahoma City, OK 73116-8244
Tel: (405)842-8007
Free: 800-228-7240
Admissions: (480)557-1712
Web Site: http://www.phoenix.edu/
President/CEO: Wally Hedgecock
Admissions: Nina Omelchanko
Type: Comprehensive **Sex:** Coed **Admission Plans:** Open Admission; Deferred Admission **Application Deadline:** Rolling **Application Fee:** $110.00 **H.S. Requirements:** High school diploma required; GED accepted **Costs Per Year:** Application fee: $110. Tuition: $9360 full-time, $312 per credit part-time. Mandatory fees: $560 full-time, $70 per course part-time. **Scholarships:** Available **Calendar System:** Continuous, Summer Session Not available **Enrollment:** FT 876, Grad 175 **Faculty:** FT 2, PT 185 **Student-Faculty Ratio:** 6:1 **Library Holdings:** 444 **Regional Accreditation:** North Central Association of Colleges and Schools **Credit Hours For Degree:** 60 credits, Associates; 120 credits, Bachelors

UNIVERSITY OF PHOENIX-TULSA CAMPUS
10810 East 45th St., Ste. 103
Tulsa, OK 74146-3801
Tel: (918)622-4877
Free: 800-228-7240
Admissions: (480)557-1712
Web Site: http://www.phoenix.edu/
President/CEO: Lori Santiago
Admissions: Nina Omelchanko
Type: Comprehensive **Sex:** Coed **Admission Plans:** Open Admission; Deferred Admission **Application Deadline:** Rolling **Application Fee:** $110.00 **H.S. Requirements:** High school diploma required; GED accepted **Costs Per Year:** Application fee: $110. Tuition: $9360 full-time, $312 per credit part-time. Mandatory fees: $560 full-time, $70 per course part-time. **Scholarships:** Available **Calendar System:** Continuous, Summer Session Not available **Enrollment:** FT 1,114, Grad 188 **Faculty:** FT 5, PT 156 **Student-Faculty Ratio:** 8:1 **Library Holdings:** 444 **Regional Accreditation:** North Central Association of Colleges and Schools **Credit Hours For Degree:** 60 credits, Associates; 120 credits, Bachelors

UNIVERSITY OF SCIENCE AND ARTS OF OKLAHOMA
1727 West Alabama
Chickasha, OK 73018
Tel: (405)224-3140
Free: 800-933-8726
Admissions: (405)574-1204
Fax: (405)574-1220
E-mail: jwevans@usao.edu
Web Site: http://www.usao.edu/
President/CEO: Dr. John Feaver
Registrar: Joseph Evans
Admissions: Joseph Evans
Financial Aid: Nancy Moats
Type: Four-Year College **Sex:** Coed **Affiliation:** Oklahoma State Regents for Higher Education **Scores:** 54% ACT 18-23; 26% ACT 24-29 **% Accepted:** 89 **Admission Plans:** Deferred Admission **Application Deadline:** September 06 **Application Fee:** $15.00 **H.S. Requirements:** High school diploma required; GED accepted **Costs Per Year:** Application fee: $15. State resident tuition: $2490 full-time, $83 per hour part-time. Nonresident tuition: $7230 full-time, $241 per hour part-time. Mandatory fees: $990 full-time, $33 per hour part-time. College room and board: $4170. College room only: $2180. Room and board charges vary according to board plan and housing facility. **Scholarships:** Available **Calendar System:** Trimester, Summer Session Available **Enrollment:** FT 1,064, PT 366 **Faculty:** FT 48, PT 36 **Student-Faculty Ratio:** 19:1 **Exams:** Other **% Receiving Financial Aid:** 66 **% Residing in College-Owned, -Operated, or -Affiliated Housing:** 36 **Library Holdings:** 79,780 **Regional Accreditation:** North Central Association of Colleges and Schools **Credit Hours For Degree:** 124 hours, Bachelors **Professional Accreditation:** NASM, NCATE **Intercollegiate Athletics:** Baseball M; Basketball M & W; Cheerleading M & W; Soccer M & W; Softball W

UNIVERSITY OF TULSA
600 South College Ave.
Tulsa, OK 74104-3189
Tel: (918)631-2000
Free: 800-331-3050
Admissions: (918)631-2307
Fax: (918)631-2247
E-mail: admission@utulsa.edu
Web Site: http://www.utulsa.edu/
President/CEO: Dr. Steadman Upham
Registrar: Ruth V. Langston
Admissions: John Corso
Financial Aid: Vicki A. Hendrickson
Type: University **Sex:** Coed **Affiliation:** Presbyterian Church (U.S.A.) **Scores:** 98% SAT V 400+; 100% SAT M 400+; 27% ACT 18-23; 44% ACT 24-29 **% Accepted:** 75 **Admission Plans:** Early Admission; Deferred Admission **Application Deadline:** Rolling **Application Fee:** $35.00 **H.S. Requirements:** High school diploma required; GED accepted **Costs Per Year:** Application fee: $35. Comprehensive fee: $27,790 includes full-time tuition ($20,658), mandatory fees ($80), and college room and board ($7052). College room only: $3896. Part-time tuition: $741 per credit hour. Part-time mandatory fees: $3 per credit hour. **Scholarships:** Available **Calendar System:** Semester, Summer Session Available **Enrollment:** FT 2,635, PT 161, Grad 670 **Faculty:** FT 306, PT 116 **Student-Faculty Ratio:** 11:1 **Exams:** SAT I or ACT **% Receiving Financial Aid:** 50 **% Residing in College-Owned, -Operated, or -Affiliated Housing:** 64 **Library Holdings:** 940,105 **Regional Accreditation:** North Central Association of Colleges and Schools **Credit Hours For Degree:** 126 credit hours, Bachelors **ROTC:** Air Force **Professional Accreditation:** AACSB, ABET, ABA, APA, ASLHA, AALS, JRCEPAT, NASM, NCATE, NLN **Intercollegiate Athletics:** Basketball M & W; Crew W; Cross-Country Running M & W; Football M; Golf M & W; Soccer M & W; Softball W; Tennis M & W; Track and Field M & W; Volleyball W

VATTEROTT COLLEGE (OKLAHOMA CITY)
4629 Northwest 23rd St.
Oklahoma City, OK 73127
Tel: (405)945-0088; 888-948-0088
Fax: (405)945-0788
Web Site: http://www.vatterott-college.edu/
President/CEO: Robert Birkenmaier
Admissions: Mark Hybers
Type: Two-Year College **Sex:** Coed **Costs Per Year:** Tuition: $20,000 full-time. Mandatory fees: $900 full-time. Full-time tuition and fees vary according to degree level and program. Tuition guaranteed not to increase for student's term of enrollment. **Calendar System:** Semester **Enrollment:** FT

249 **Faculty:** FT 15, PT 6 **Student-Faculty Ratio:** 12:1 **Professional Accreditation:** ACCSCT

VATTEROTT COLLEGE (TULSA)
555 South Memorial Dr.
Tulsa, OK 74112
Tel: (918)835-8288; 888-857-4016
Admissions: (918)836-6656
Fax: (918)836-9698
Web Site: http://www.vatterott-college.edu/
President/CEO: Paul Shuler
Admissions: Tim Maloukis
Type: Two-Year College **Sex:** Coed **% Accepted:** 78 **Calendar System:** Semester **Enrollment:** FT 226 **Faculty:** FT 18, PT 0 **Student-Faculty Ratio:** 12:1 **Professional Accreditation:** ACCSCT

WESTERN OKLAHOMA STATE COLLEGE
2801 North Main St.
Altus, OK 73521-1397
Tel: (580)477-2000
Admissions: (580)477-7720
Fax: (580)477-7723
Web Site: http://www.wosc.edu/
President/CEO: Randy Cumby
Registrar: Dr. Larry Paxton
Admissions: Dr. Larry W. Paxton
Financial Aid: Myrna Cross
Type: Two-Year College **Sex:** Coed **Affiliation:** Oklahoma State Regents for Higher Education **% Accepted:** 100 **Admission Plans:** Open Admission; Early Admission **Application Deadline:** Rolling **Application Fee:** $15.00 **H.S. Requirements:** High school diploma required; GED accepted **Costs Per Year:** Application fee: $15. State resident tuition: $2213 full-time, $73.75 per semester hour part-time. Nonresident tuition: $5348 full-time, $178.25 per semester hour part-time. College room and board: $4400. **Scholarships:** Available **Calendar System:** Semester, Summer Session Available **Enrollment:** FT 859, PT 1,202 **Faculty:** FT 37, PT 63 **Student-Faculty Ratio:** 20:1 **Exams:** ACT **Library Holdings:** 33,000 **Regional Accreditation:** North Central Association of Colleges and Schools **Credit Hours For Degree:** 64 credits, Associates **Professional Accreditation:** JRCERT, NLN **Intercollegiate Athletics:** Baseball M; Basketball M & W; Equestrian Sports M & W; Golf M & W; Softball W

THE ART INSTITUTE OF PORTLAND
1122 NW Davis St.
Portland, OR 97209
Tel: (503)228-6528; 888-228-6528
Fax: (503)228-4227
E-mail: aipdadm@aii.edu
Web Site: http://www.aipd.artinstitutes.edu/
President/CEO: Dr. Steven Goldman
Registrar: Robert Tufts
Admissions: Lori Murray
Financial Aid: Mickey Jacobson
Type: Four-Year College **Sex:** Coed **Affiliation:** Education Management Corporation **% Accepted:** 59 **Admission Plans:** Deferred Admission **Application Deadline:** Rolling **Application Fee:** $50.00 **H.S. Requirements:** High school diploma required; GED accepted **Costs Per Year:** Application fee: $50. Tuition: $17,460 full-time. College room only: $5625. **Scholarships:** Available **Calendar System:** Quarter, Summer Session Available **Enrollment:** FT 1,078, PT 505 **Faculty:** FT 26, PT 94 **Student-Faculty Ratio:** 22:1 **% Receiving Financial Aid:** 82 **% Residing in College-Owned, -Operated, or -Affiliated Housing:** 10 **Library Holdings:** 24,231 **Credit Hours For Degree:** 105 credits, Associates; 180 credits, Bachelors **Professional Accreditation:** NCCU

BIRTHINGWAY COLLEGE OF MIDWIFERY
12113 SE Foster Rd.
Portland, OR 97299
Tel: (503)760-3131
Web Site: http://www.birthingway.edu/
President/CEO: Holly Scholles
Type: Two-Year Upper Division **Sex:** Coed **Calendar System:** Miscellaneous

BLUE MOUNTAIN COMMUNITY COLLEGE
2411 Northwest Carden Ave.
PO Box 100
Pendleton, OR 97801-1000
Tel: (541)276-1260
Admissions: (541)278-5774
Fax: (541)278-5886
Web Site: http://www.bluecc.edu/
President/CEO: Dr. Travis P. Kirkland
Registrar: Valerie Fouquette
Admissions: Valerie Fouquette
Financial Aid: Theresa Bosworth
Type: Two-Year College **Sex:** Coed **Admission Plans:** Open Admission **H.S. Requirements:** High school diploma or equivalent not required **Scholarships:** Available **Calendar System:** Quarter, Summer Session Available **Enrollment:** FT 872, PT 1,006 **Faculty:** FT 76, PT 148 **Student-Faculty Ratio:** 25:1 **Exams:** Other **Library Holdings:** 39,026 **Credit Hours For Degree:** 90 credit hours, Associates **Professional Accreditation:** ABET, ADA, NCCU **Intercollegiate Athletics:** Baseball M; Basketball M & W; Softball W; Volleyball W

CASCADE COLLEGE
9101 East Burnside St.
Portland, OR 97216-1515
Tel: (503)255-7060
Free: 800-550-7678
Admissions: (503)257-1202
E-mail: jmurphy@cascade.edu
Web Site: http://www.cascade.edu/
President/CEO: Dennis Lynn
Admissions: Jim Murphy
Type: Four-Year College **Sex:** Coed **Affiliation:** Church of Christ; Oklahoma Christian University **Scores:** 82% SAT V 400+; 80% SAT M 400+; 50% ACT 18-23; 13% ACT 24-29 **% Accepted:** 60 **Admission Plans:** Open Admission; Early Admission; Deferred Admission **Application Deadline:** Rolling **Application Fee:** $25.00 **H.S. Requirements:** High school diploma required; GED accepted **Costs Per Year:** Application fee: $25. Comprehensive fee: $18,920 includes full-time tuition ($12,200), mandatory fees ($600), and college room and board ($6120). Part-time tuition: $510 per semester hour. **Scholarships:** Available **Calendar System:** Semester, Summer Session Available **Enrollment:** FT 274, PT 18 **Faculty:** FT 13, PT 21 **Student-Faculty Ratio:** 15:1 **% Receiving Financial Aid:** 79 **% Residing in College-Owned, -Operated, or -Affiliated Housing:** 66 **Library Holdings:** 30,232 **Regional Accreditation:** North Central Association of Colleges and Schools **Credit Hours For Degree:** 126 semester hours, Bachelors **ROTC:** Army, Air Force **Intercollegiate Athletics:** Basketball M & W; Cross-Country Running M & W; Soccer M & W; Track and Field M & W; Volleyball W

CENTRAL OREGON COMMUNITY COLLEGE
2600 Northwest College Way
Bend, OR 97701-5998
Tel: (541)383-7700
Admissions: (541)383-7211
Fax: (541)383-7506
E-mail: welcome@metolius.cocc.edu
Web Site: http://www.cocc.edu/
President/CEO: Dr. James E. Middleton
Registrar: Alicia Moore
Admissions: Alicia Moore
Financial Aid: Laurie Neil
Type: Two-Year College **Sex:** Coed **Affiliation:** Oregon Community College Association **Admission Plans:** Open Admission; Preferred Admission **Application Deadline:** Rolling **Application Fee:** $25.00 **H.S. Requirements:** High school diploma or equivalent not required **Costs Per Year:** Application fee: $25. Area resident tuition: $2835 full-time, $63 per credit part-time. State resident tuition: $3870 full-time, $86 per credit part-time. Nonresident tuition: $7920 full-time, $176 per credit part-time. Mandatory fees: $114 full-time, $3.50 per credit part-time. College room and board: $6798. **Scholarships:** Available **Calendar System:** Quarter **Enrollment:** FT 1,536, PT 2,512 **Faculty:** FT 87, PT 225 **Student-Faculty Ratio:** 23:1 **Exams:** Other **% Residing in College-Owned, -Operated, or -Affiliated Housing:** 3 **Library Holdings:** 76,421 **Credit Hours For Degree:** 93 credits, Associates **Professional Accreditation:** ACF, ADA, AHIMA, NCCU

CHEMEKETA COMMUNITY COLLEGE
4000 Lancaster Dr. NE
P.O. Box 14007
Salem, OR 97309
Tel: (503)399-5000
Fax: (503)399-3918

Web Site: http://www.chemeketa.edu/
President/CEO: Dr. Gretchen S. Schuette
Registrar: Kathy Campbell
Financial Aid: Kathy Campbell
Type: Two-Year College **Sex:** Coed **Admission Plans:** Open Admission; Deferred Admission **Application Deadline:** Rolling **Application Fee:** $0.00 **H.S. Requirements:** High school diploma or equivalent not required. For nursing, fire science, allied health, emergency medical technology programs: High school diploma required; GED accepted **Costs Per Year:** Application fee: $0. State resident tuition: $2610 full-time, $58 per quarter hour part-time. Nonresident tuition: $8955 full-time, $199 per quarter hour part-time. Mandatory fees: $180 full-time, $4 per quarter hour part-time. **Scholarships:** Available **Calendar System:** Quarter, Summer Session Available **Credit Hours For Degree:** 90 credit hours, Associates **Professional Accreditation:** ADA, JRCEMT, NLN, NCCU **Intercollegiate Athletics:** Baseball M; Basketball M & W; Cross-Country Running M & W; Track and Field M & W; Volleyball W

CLACKAMAS COMMUNITY COLLEGE
19600 South Molalla Ave.
Oregon City, OR 97045-7998
Tel: (503)657-6958
Fax: (503)650-6654
Web Site: http://www.clackamas.edu/
President/CEO: Dr. Earl P. Johnson
Registrar: Diane Drebin
Admissions: Tara Sprehe
Financial Aid: Mary Jo Jackson
Type: Two-Year College **Sex:** Coed **% Accepted:** 100 **Admission Plans:** Open Admission; Early Admission **Application Deadline:** Rolling **Application Fee:** $0.00 **H.S. Requirements:** High school diploma or equivalent not required **Costs Per Year:** Application fee: $0. State resident tuition: $2520 full-time, $56 per credit hour part-time. Nonresident tuition: $8730 full-time, $194 per credit hour part-time. Mandatory fees: $180 full-time, $4 per credit hour part-time. **Scholarships:** Available **Calendar System:** Quarter, Summer Session Available **Enrollment:** FT 2,238, PT 5,091 **Faculty:** FT 158, PT 378 **Student-Faculty Ratio:** 14:1 **Library Holdings:** 41,263 **Credit Hours For Degree:** 93 credit hours, Associates **ROTC:** Air Force **Professional Accreditation:** NLN, NCCU **Intercollegiate Athletics:** Baseball M; Basketball M & W; Cross-Country Running M & W; Soccer W; Softball W; Track and Field M & W; Volleyball W; Wrestling M

CLATSOP COMMUNITY COLLEGE
1653 Jerome
Astoria, OR 97103-3698
Tel: (503)325-0910
Admissions: (503)338-2326
Fax: (503)325-5738
E-mail: klee@clatsopec.edu
Web Site: http://www.clatsopcc.edu/
President/CEO: Dr. John W. Wubben
Registrar: Roger Friesen
Admissions: Kristen Lee-Gordon
Financial Aid: Linda Gallino
Type: Two-Year College **Sex:** Coed **% Accepted:** 81 **Admission Plans:** Open Admission; Early Admission **Application Deadline:** Rolling **Application Fee:** $15.00 **H.S. Requirements:** High school diploma or equivalent not required **Costs Per Year:** Application fee: $15. State resident tuition: $2700 full-time, $60 per credit part-time. Nonresident tuition: $5400 full-time, $120 per credit part-time. **Scholarships:** Available **Calendar System:** Quarter, Summer Session Available **Enrollment:** FT 445, PT 1,379 **Faculty:** FT 40, PT 158 **Student-Faculty Ratio:** 14:1 **Library Holdings:** 48,517 **Credit Hours For Degree:** 90 credits, Associates **Professional Accreditation:** NCCU

COLUMBIA GORGE COMMUNITY COLLEGE
400 East Scenic Dr.
The Dalles, OR 97058
Tel: (541)296-6182
Admissions: (541)298-3110
Fax: (541)298-3104
E-mail: kcarter@cgcc.cc.or.us
Web Site: http://www.cgcc.cc.or.us/
President/CEO: Dr. Frank Toda
Admissions: Karen Carter
Type: Two-Year College **Sex:** Coed **Calendar System:** Quarter **Faculty:** FT 15, PT 75 **Professional Accreditation:** NCCU

CONCORDIA UNIVERSITY
2811 Northeast Holman
Portland, OR 97211-6099
Tel: (503)288-9371
Free: 800-321-9371
Admissions: (503)493-6526
Fax: (503)280-8531
Web Site: http://www.cu-portland.edu/
President/CEO: Dr. Charles E. Schlimpert
Registrar: Jim Cullen
Admissions: Bobi L. Swan
Financial Aid: Jim Cullen
Type: Comprehensive **Sex:** Coed **Affiliation:** Lutheran Church–Missouri Synod; Concordia University System **Scores:** 91.9% SAT V 400+; 92.5% SAT M 400+; 53.2% ACT 18-23; 24.1% ACT 24-29 **% Accepted:** 66 **Admission Plans:** Deferred Admission **Application Deadline:** Rolling **Application Fee:** $20.00 **H.S. Requirements:** High school diploma required; GED accepted **Costs Per Year:** Application fee: $20. Comprehensive fee: $26,000 includes full-time tuition ($19,900), mandatory fees ($200), and college room and board ($5900). College room only: $2800. Part-time tuition: $615 per credit. **Scholarships:** Available **Calendar System:** Semester, Summer Session Available **Enrollment:** FT 808, PT 198, Grad 500 **Faculty:** FT 42, PT 95 **Student-Faculty Ratio:** 17:1 **Exams:** SAT I or ACT **% Receiving Financial Aid:** 81 **% Residing in College-Owned, -Operated, or -Affiliated Housing:** 44 **Library Holdings:** 65,000 **Credit Hours For Degree:** 62 semester hours, Associates; 124 semester hours, Bachelors **ROTC:** Air Force **Professional Accreditation:** NCCU **Intercollegiate Athletics:** Baseball M; Basketball M & W; Golf M & W; Soccer M & W; Softball W; Track and Field M & W; Volleyball W

CORBAN COLLEGE
5000 Deer Park Dr., SE
Salem, OR 97301-9392
Tel: (503)581-8600
Free: 800-845-3005
Admissions: (503)375-7115
Fax: (503)585-4316
E-mail: mziesemer@corban.edu
Web Site: http://www.corban.edu/
President/CEO: Reno Hoff
Registrar: Rita Wright
Admissions: Marty Ziesemer
Financial Aid: Nathan Warthan
Type: Four-Year College **Sex:** Coed **Scores:** 98% SAT V 400+; 93% SAT M 400+; 36% ACT 18-23; 36% ACT 24-29 **% Accepted:** 83 **Admission Plans:** Early Admission **Application Deadline:** August 01 **Application Fee:** $40.00 **H.S. Requirements:** High school diploma required; GED accepted **Costs Per Year:** Application fee: $40. Comprehensive fee: $26,378 includes full-time tuition ($19,084), mandatory fees ($210), and college room and board ($7084). Part-time tuition: $795 per credit. **Scholarships:** Available **Calendar System:** Semester, Summer Session Available **Enrollment:** FT 653, PT 151, Grad 47 **Faculty:** FT 34, PT 37 **Student-Faculty Ratio:** 16:1 **Exams:** SAT I or ACT **% Receiving Financial Aid:** 86 **% Residing in College-Owned, -Operated, or -Affiliated Housing:** 55 **Library Holdings:** 98,700 **Credit Hours For Degree:** 64 credit hours, Associates; 128 credit hours, Bachelors **ROTC:** Army, Air Force **Professional Accreditation:** NCCU **Intercollegiate Athletics:** Baseball M; Basketball M & W; Cross-Country Running M & W; Golf M; Soccer M & W; Softball W; Volleyball W

DEVRY UNIVERSITY
Peterkort Center II
9755 SW Barnes Rd., Ste. 150
Portland, OR 97225-6651
Tel: (503)296-7468; (866)338-7934
Web Site: http://www.devry.edu/ **Type:** Comprehensive **Sex:** Coed **Affiliation:** DeVry University **Admission Plans:** Deferred Admission **Application Deadline:** Rolling **Application Fee:** $50.00 **Costs Per Year:** Application fee: $50. One-time mandatory fee: $40. Tuition: $11,790 full-time, $440 per credit part-time. Mandatory fees: $30 full-time, $30 per year part-time. Full-time tuition and fees vary according to course load. Part-time tuition and fees vary according to course load. **Calendar**

System: Semester, Summer Session Available **Enrollment:** FT 81, PT 50, Grad 35 **Faculty:** FT 0, PT 6 **Regional Accreditation:** North Central Association of Colleges and Schools **Credit Hours For Degree:** 122 credits, Bachelors

EASTERN OREGON UNIVERSITY
1 University Blvd.
La Grande, OR 97850-2899
Tel: (541)962-3672
Free: 800-452-3393
Admissions: (541)962-3393
Fax: (541)962-3418
E-mail: admissions@eosc.osshe.edu
Web Site: http://www.eou.edu/
President/CEO: Dr. Khosrow Fatemi
Registrar: Dea Hoffman
Admissions: Sherri Edvalson
Financial Aid: Eric Bucks
Type: Comprehensive **Sex:** Coed **Affiliation:** Oregon University System **Scores:** 87.75% SAT V 400+; 87.76% SAT M 400+; 50.65% ACT 18-23; 25.97% ACT 24-29 **% Accepted:** 73 **Admission Plans:** Preferred Admission; Early Action; Deferred Admission **Application Deadline:** September 01 **Application Fee:** $50.00 **H.S. Requirements:** High school diploma required; GED accepted **Costs Per Year:** Application fee: $50. State resident tuition: $4779 full-time. Nonresident tuition: $4779 full-time. Full-time tuition varies according to course load. College room and board: $7300. Room and board charges vary according to board plan and housing facility. **Scholarships:** Available **Calendar System:** Quarter, Summer Session Available **Enrollment:** FT 2,029, PT 1,168, Grad 336 **Faculty:** FT 97, PT 31 **Student-Faculty Ratio:** 24:1 **Exams:** SAT I or ACT **% Receiving Financial Aid:** 68 **% Residing in College-Owned, -Operated, or -Affiliated Housing:** 15 **Library Holdings:** 329,942 **Credit Hours For Degree:** 186 credit hours, Bachelors **ROTC:** Army **Professional Accreditation:** NCCU **Intercollegiate Athletics:** Baseball M; Basketball M & W; Cross-Country Running M & W; Football M; Skiing (Cross-Country) M & W; Skiing (Downhill) M & W; Soccer W; Softball W; Track and Field M & W; Volleyball M & W

EUGENE BIBLE COLLEGE
2155 Bailey Hill Rd.
Eugene, OR 97405-1194
Tel: (541)485-1780
Free: 800-322-2638
Fax: (541)343-5801
E-mail: admissions@ebc.edu
Web Site: http://www.ebc.edu/
President/CEO: David L. Cole
Registrar: Dr. James Wick
Admissions: Trent Combs
Financial Aid: Rulena Mellor
Type: Four-Year College **Sex:** Coed **Affiliation:** Open Bible Standard Churches **Scores:** 88% SAT V 400+; 96% SAT M 400+; 47% ACT 18-23; 26% ACT 24-29 **% Accepted:** 47 **Application Deadline:** September 01 **Application Fee:** $30.00 **H.S. Requirements:** High school diploma required; GED accepted **Costs Per Year:** Application fee: $30. Comprehensive fee: $12,875 includes full-time tuition ($7500), mandatory fees ($800), and college room and board ($4575). Part-time tuition: $220 per credit hour. **Scholarships:** Available **Calendar System:** Quarter, Summer Session Available **Enrollment:** FT 161, PT 42 **Faculty:** FT 14, PT 10 **Student-Faculty Ratio:** 10:1 **Exams:** SAT I or ACT **% Receiving Financial Aid:** 75 **% Residing in College-Owned, -Operated, or -Affiliated Housing:** 56 **Library Holdings:** 35,000 **Credit Hours For Degree:** 187 quarter hours, Bachelors **Professional Accreditation:** AABC **Intercollegiate Athletics:** Basketball M; Soccer M & W; Volleyball W

GEORGE FOX UNIVERSITY
414 North Meridian
Newberg, OR 97132-2697
Tel: (503)538-8383
Free: 800-765-4369
Admissions: (503)554-2240
Fax: (503)554-3830
E-mail: admissions@georgefox.edu
Web Site: http://www.georgefox.edu/
President/CEO: Dr. H. David Brandt
Registrar: Todd McCollum
Admissions: Dale Seipp
Financial Aid: Rob Clarke
Type: University **Sex:** Coed **Affiliation:** Friends **Scores:** 98% SAT V 400+; 98% SAT M 400+; 44% ACT 18-23; 44% ACT 24-29 **% Accepted:** 83 **Admission Plans:** Early Admission; Deferred Admission **Application Deadline:** February 01 **Application Fee:** $40.00 **H.S. Requirements:** High school diploma required; GED accepted **Costs Per Year:** Application fee: $40. Comprehensive fee: $29,780 includes full-time tuition ($22,250), mandatory fees ($320), and college room and board ($7210). College room only: $4050. Part-time tuition: $690 per hour. **Scholarships:** Available **Calendar System:** Semester, Summer Session Not available **Enrollment:** FT 1,541, PT 301, Grad 1,292 **Faculty:** FT 144, PT 116 **Student-Faculty Ratio:** 12:1 **Exams:** SAT I or ACT **% Receiving Financial Aid:** 81 **% Residing in College-Owned, -Operated, or -Affiliated Housing:** 59 **Library Holdings:** 123,734 **Credit Hours For Degree:** 126 semester hours, Bachelors **ROTC:** Air Force **Professional Accreditation:** APA, ACIPE, ATS, JRCEPAT, NASM, NCCU **Intercollegiate Athletics:** Baseball M; Basketball M & W; Cross-Country Running M & W; Soccer M & W; Softball W; Tennis M & W; Track and Field M & W; Volleyball W

GUTENBERG COLLEGE
1883 University St.
Eugene, OR 97403
Tel: (541)683-5141
Admissions: (541)736-9071
Fax: (541)683-6997
Web Site: http://www.gutenberg.edu/
Admissions: Terry Stollar
Type: Four-Year College **Sex:** Coed **Scores:** 100% SAT V 400+; 100% SAT M 400+; 100% ACT 18-23 **Admission Plans:** Open Admission **Application Fee:** $20.00 **H.S. Requirements:** High school diploma required; GED accepted **Costs Per Year:** Application fee: $20. Comprehensive fee: $15,075 includes full-time tuition ($9970), mandatory fees ($650), and college room and board ($4455). Full-time tuition and fees vary according to student level. Room and board charges vary according to housing facility. Part-time tuition: $350 per quarter hour. **Enrollment:** FT 38, PT 6 **Faculty:** FT 4, PT 6 **Student-Faculty Ratio:** 7:1 **Exams:** SAT I

HEALD COLLEGE-PORTLAND
625 SW Broadway, 4th Floor
Portland, OR 97205
Tel: (503)229-0492
Fax: (503)229-0498
Web Site: http://www.heald.edu/ **Type:** Two-Year College **Sex:** Coed **Admission Plans:** Open Admission; Early Admission; Deferred Admission **Application Deadline:** Rolling **Application Fee:** $40.00 **H.S. Requirements:** High school diploma required; GED accepted **Scholarships:** Available **Calendar System:** Quarter, Summer Session Available **Enrollment:** FT 149, PT 57 **Faculty:** FT 15, PT 6 **Student-Faculty Ratio:** 10:1 **Exams:** Other **Regional Accreditation:** Western Association of Schools and Colleges

ITT TECHNICAL INSTITUTE
6035 Northeast 78th Ct.
Portland, OR 97218-2854
Tel: (503)255-6500
Free: 800-234-5488
Fax: (503)255-6135
Web Site: http://www.itt-tech.edu/
President/CEO: Edward Yakimchick
Registrar: Joan Berry
Admissions: Wayne L. Matulich
Financial Aid: Suezi Lyon
Type: Two-Year College **Sex:** Coed **Affiliation:** ITT Educational Services, Inc **Admission Plans:** Deferred Admission **Application Deadline:** Rolling **Application Fee:** $100.00 **H.S. Requirements:** High school diploma required; GED accepted **Costs Per Year:** Application fee: $100. **Scholarships:** Available **Calendar System:** Quarter, Summer Session Not available **Exams:** Other **Credit Hours For Degree:** 96 credit hours, Associates; 180 credit hours, Bachelors **Professional Accreditation:** ACICS

KLAMATH COMMUNITY COLLEGE
7390 South 6th St.
Klamath Falls, OR 97603

Tel: (541)882-3521
E-mail: browng@kcc.cc.or.us
Web Site: http://www.kcc.cc.or.us/
President/CEO: Dr. Wesley Channell
Admissions: Greg Brown
Type: Two-Year College **Sex:** Coed **Calendar System:** Quarter **Professional Accreditation:** NCCU

LANE COMMUNITY COLLEGE
4000 East 30th Ave.
Eugene, OR 97405-0640
Tel: (541)747-4501
Fax: (541)744-3995
Web Site: http://www.lanecc.edu/
President/CEO: Dr. Mary Spilde
Registrar: Helen Garrett
Admissions: Helen Garrett
Financial Aid: Linda DeWitt
Type: Two-Year College **Sex:** Coed **Admission Plans:** Open Admission; Preferred Admission; Early Admission **H.S. Requirements:** High school diploma or equivalent not required. For applicants under 18 admitted with a high school release to attend credit classes: High school diploma required; GED accepted **Scholarships:** Available **Calendar System:** Quarter, Summer Session Available **Enrollment:** FT 4,565, PT 7,269 **Faculty:** FT 260, PT 325 **Student-Faculty Ratio:** 22:1 **Library Holdings:** 67,051 **Credit Hours For Degree:** 93 credit hours, Associates **Professional Accreditation:** ADA, CARC, NLN, NCCU **Intercollegiate Athletics:** Baseball M; Basketball M & W; Cross-Country Running M & W; Track and Field M & W; Volleyball W

LEWIS & CLARK COLLEGE
0615 SW Palatine Hill Rd.
Portland, OR 97219-7899
Tel: (503)768-7000
Free: 800-444-4111
Admissions: (503)768-7040
Fax: (503)768-7055
E-mail: admissions@lclark.edu
Web Site: http://www.lclark.edu/
President/CEO: Dr. Thomas Hochstettler
Admissions: Michael Sexton
Financial Aid: Glendi Gaddis
Type: Comprehensive **Sex:** Coed **Scores:** 100% SAT V 400+; 100% SAT M 400+; 7.7% ACT 18-23; 60.4% ACT 24-29 **% Accepted:** 59 **Admission Plans:** Early Admission; Early Action; Deferred Admission **Application Deadline:** February 01 **Application Fee:** $50.00 **H.S. Requirements:** High school diploma required; GED accepted **Costs Per Year:** Application fee: $50. Comprehensive fee: $35,358 includes full-time tuition ($27,494), mandatory fees ($216), and college room and board ($7648). College room only: $3974. Room and board charges vary according to board plan and housing facility. Part-time tuition: $1386 per credit hour. **Scholarships:** Available **Calendar System:** Semester, Summer Session Available **Enrollment:** FT 1,940, PT 24, Grad 722 **Faculty:** FT 205, PT 118 **Student-Faculty Ratio:** 13:1 **Exams:** Other, SAT I or ACT **% Receiving Financial Aid:** 60 **% Residing in College-Owned, -Operated, or -Affiliated Housing:** 64 **Library Holdings:** 227,609 **Credit Hours For Degree:** 128 semester hours, Bachelors **Professional Accreditation:** ABA, AALS, NCCU **Intercollegiate Athletics:** Baseball M; Basketball M & W; Crew M & W; Cross-Country Running M & W; Football M; Golf M & W; Lacrosse M & W; Soccer M & W; Softball W; Swimming and Diving M & W; Tennis M & W; Track and Field M & W; Volleyball W

LINFIELD COLLEGE
900 SE Baker St.
McMinnville, OR 97128-6894
Tel: (503)883-2200
Free: 800-640-2287
Admissions: (503)883-2213
Fax: (503)883-2472
E-mail: admission@linfield.edu
Web Site: http://www.linfield.edu/
President/CEO: Dr. Marvin C. Henberg
Registrar: Dr. Eileen L. Bourassa
Admissions: Lisa Knodle-Bragiel
Financial Aid: Dan Preston
Type: Four-Year College **Sex:** Coed **Affiliation:** American Baptist Churches in the USA **Scores:** 97.83% SAT V 400+; 98.55% SAT M 400+; 44.3% ACT 18-23; 39.24% ACT 24-29 **% Accepted:** 73 **Admission Plans:** Early Action; Deferred Admission **Application Deadline:** February 15 **Application Fee:** $40.00 **H.S. Requirements:** High school diploma required; GED accepted **Costs Per Year:** Application fee: $40. Comprehensive fee: $29,632 includes full-time tuition ($22,790), mandatory fees ($232), and college room and board ($6610). College room only: $3540. Room and board charges vary according to board plan and housing facility. Part-time tuition: $710 per credit. Part-time mandatory fees: $68 per term. Part-time tuition and fees vary according to course load. **Scholarships:** Available **Calendar System:** 4-1-4, Summer Session Available **Enrollment:** FT 1,708, PT 42 **Faculty:** FT 107, PT 57 **Student-Faculty Ratio:** 14:1 **Exams:** SAT I or ACT **% Receiving Financial Aid:** 67 **% Residing in College-Owned, -Operated, or -Affiliated Housing:** 74 **Library Holdings:** 169,087 **Credit Hours For Degree:** 125 credit hours, Bachelors **ROTC:** Air Force **Professional Accreditation:** JRCEPAT, NASM, NLN, NCCU **Intercollegiate Athletics:** Baseball M; Basketball M & W; Cross-Country Running M & W; Football M; Golf M & W; Lacrosse W; Soccer M & W; Softball W; Swimming and Diving M & W; Tennis M & W; Track and Field M & W; Volleyball W

LINN-BENTON COMMUNITY COLLEGE
6500 Southwest Pacific Blvd.
Albany, OR 97321
Tel: (541)917-4999
Admissions: (541)917-4811
Fax: (541)917-4838
Web Site: http://www.linnbenton.edu/
President/CEO: Rita Cavin, PhD
Registrar: Bruce Clemetsen
Admissions: Dr. Bruce Clemetsen
Financial Aid: Lance Popoff
Type: Two-Year College **Sex:** Coed **% Accepted:** 100 **Admission Plans:** Open Admission; Preferred Admission; Deferred Admission **Application Deadline:** Rolling **Application Fee:** $25.00 **H.S. Requirements:** High school diploma or equivalent not required. For nursing, dental assistant, public safety dispatcher, radiological technology, pharmacy technician, phlebotomy: High school diploma required; GED accepted. **Costs Per Year:** Application fee: $25. State resident tuition: $2925 full-time. Nonresident tuition: $7470 full-time. **Scholarships:** Available **Calendar System:** Quarter, Summer Session Available **Enrollment:** FT 2,839, PT 2,450 **Faculty:** FT 157, PT 327 **Library Holdings:** 42,561 **Credit Hours For Degree:** 90 quarter hours, Associates **ROTC:** Army, Air Force **Professional Accreditation:** AAMAE, ADA, NLN, NCCU **Intercollegiate Athletics:** Baseball M; Basketball M & W; Volleyball W

MARYLHURST UNIVERSITY
17600 Pacific Hwy., PO Box 261
Marylhurst, OR 97036-0261
Tel: (503)636-8141
Free: 800-634-9982
Fax: (503)636-9526
Web Site: http://www.marylhurst.edu/
President/CEO: Dr. Nancy A. Wilgenbusch
Registrar: John Rolston
Admissions: John French
Financial Aid: Marlena McKees-Flores
Type: Comprehensive **Sex:** Coed **Affiliation:** Roman Catholic **% Accepted:** 44 **Admission Plans:** Open Admission; Deferred Admission **Application Fee:** $20.00 **H.S. Requirements:** High school diploma required; GED accepted. For transfer students with at least 90 credits: High school diploma or equivalent not required **Costs Per Year:** Application fee: $20. Tuition: $13,860 full-time, $308 per quarter hour part-time. Mandatory fees: $360 full-time, $8 per quarter hour part-time. Full-time tuition and fees vary according to course load. Part-time tuition and fees vary according to course load. **Scholarships:** Available **Calendar System:** Quarter, Summer Session Available **Enrollment:** FT 238, PT 641, Grad 361 **Faculty:** FT 37, PT 172 **Student-Faculty Ratio:** 7:1 **% Receiving Financial Aid:** 88 **Credit Hours For Degree:** 180 quarter hours, Bachelors **Professional Accreditation:** NASM, NCCU

MOUNT ANGEL SEMINARY
St. Benedict, OR 97373
Tel: (503)845-3951
Web Site: http://www.mtangel.edu/Seminary/Seminary.htm

President/CEO: Rev. Patrick Brennan
Registrar: Rev. Odo Recker, OSB
Financial Aid: Dorene Preis
Type: Comprehensive **Affiliation:** Roman Catholic **Admission Plans:** Preferred Admission **Application Fee:** $25.00 **H.S. Requirements:** High school diploma required; GED accepted **Scholarships:** Available **Calendar System:** Semester, Summer Session Not available **Faculty:** FT 30, PT 23 **Exams:** SAT I **Library Holdings:** 240,000 **Credit Hours For Degree:** 124 credit hours, Bachelors **Professional Accreditation:** ACIPE, ATS, NCCU

MT. HOOD COMMUNITY COLLEGE
26000 Southeast Stark St.
Gresham, OR 97030-3300
Tel: (503)491-6422
Admissions: (503)491-7265
Fax: (503)491-7388
Web Site: http://www.mhcc.cc.or.us/
President/CEO: Dr. Robert Silverman
Registrar: Darrell Luzzo
Admissions: Dr. Craig Kolins
Financial Aid: Rod J. Boettcher
Type: Two-Year College **Sex:** Coed **Admission Plans:** Open Admission; Preferred Admission; Early Admission; Deferred Admission **Application Fee:** $0.00 **H.S. Requirements:** High school diploma or equivalent not required. For allied health, some professional-technical programs: High school diploma required; GED accepted **Scholarships:** Available **Calendar System:** Quarter, Summer Session Available **Enrollment:** FT 3,178, PT 5,593 **Faculty:** FT 173, PT 465 **Student-Faculty Ratio:** 25:1 **Exams:** Other **Library Holdings:** 64,000 **Credit Hours For Degree:** 90 credits, Associates **Professional Accreditation:** ARCEST, AAMAE, ABFSE, ADA, APTA, CARC, NLN, NCCU **Intercollegiate Athletics:** Baseball M; Basketball M & W; Cross-Country Running M & W; Softball W; Track and Field M & W; Volleyball W

MULTNOMAH BIBLE COLLEGE AND BIBLICAL SEMINARY
8435 Northeast Glisan St.
Portland, OR 97220-5898
Tel: (503)255-0332
Free: 800-275-4672
Fax: (503)254-1268
Web Site: http://www.multnomah.edu/
President/CEO: Dr. Daniel R. Lockwood
Registrar: Amy Stephens
Admissions: Amy M. Stephens
Financial Aid: David Allen
Type: Comprehensive **Sex:** Coed **Affiliation:** interdenominational **Scores:** 96.5% SAT V 400+; 92.2% SAT M 400+ **% Accepted:** 89 **Admission Plans:** Deferred Admission **Application Deadline:** July 15 **Application Fee:** $40.00 **H.S. Requirements:** High school diploma required; GED accepted **Costs Per Year:** Application fee: $40. Comprehensive fee: $16,810 includes full-time tuition ($11,750) and college room and board ($5060). Room and board charges vary according to board plan and housing facility. Part-time tuition: $486 per semester hour. Part-time tuition varies according to course load. **Scholarships:** Available **Calendar System:** Miscellaneous, Summer Session Available **Enrollment:** FT 531, PT 59, Grad 124 **Faculty:** FT 24, PT 33 **Student-Faculty Ratio:** 16:1 **Exams:** SAT I or ACT **% Receiving Financial Aid:** 86 **% Residing in College-Owned, -Operated, or -Affiliated Housing:** 50 **Library Holdings:** 84,535 **Credit Hours For Degree:** 128 semester hours, Bachelors **Professional Accreditation:** AABC, ATS, NCCU **Intercollegiate Athletics:** Basketball M; Volleyball W

NORTHWEST CHRISTIAN COLLEGE
828 East 11th Ave.
Eugene, OR 97401-3745
Tel: (541)343-1641; 877-463-6622
Admissions: (541)684-7210
Fax: (541)684-7317
E-mail: randyj@nwcc.edu
Web Site: http://www.nwcc.edu/
President/CEO: Dr. David Wilson
Registrar: Tracy Sims
Admissions: Dr. Randy Jones
Financial Aid: Jocelyn Hobbs
Type: Comprehensive **Sex:** Coed **Affiliation:** Christian **Scores:** 89% SAT V 400+; 78% SAT M 400+; 57% ACT 18-23; 22% ACT 24-29 **% Accepted:** 64 **Admission Plans:** Deferred Admission **Application Deadline:** Rolling **Application Fee:** $0.00 **H.S. Requirements:** High school diploma required; GED accepted **Costs Per Year:** Application fee: $0. Comprehensive fee: $26,314 includes full-time tuition ($19,890) and college room and board ($6424). College room only: $2800. Part-time tuition: $663 per credit. **Scholarships:** Available **Calendar System:** Quarter, Summer Session Available **Enrollment:** FT 377, PT 25, Grad 89 **Faculty:** FT 19, PT 42 **Student-Faculty Ratio:** 11:1 **Exams:** SAT I or ACT, SAT II **% Receiving Financial Aid:** 90 **Library Holdings:** 60,250 **Credit Hours For Degree:** 60 semester hours, Associates; 124 semester hours, Bachelors **ROTC:** Army **Professional Accreditation:** NCCU **Intercollegiate Athletics:** Basketball M & W; Softball W

OREGON COAST COMMUNITY COLLEGE
332 SW Coast Hwy.
Newport, OR 97365
Tel: (541)265-2283
Admissions: (541)574-7125
E-mail: k.wimer@occc.cc.or.us
Web Site: http://www.occc.cc.or.us
Admissions: Kathy Wimer
Type: Two-Year College **Sex:** Coed **% Accepted:** 100 **Admission Plans:** Open Admission **Costs Per Year:** State resident tuition: $2790 full-time, $62 per credit part-time. Nonresident tuition: $7740 full-time, $172 per credit part-time. Mandatory fees: $210 full-time, $5 per credit part-time. **Calendar System:** Quarter, Summer Session Available **Enrollment:** FT 73, PT 526 **Faculty:** FT 3, PT 42 **Student-Faculty Ratio:** 14:1 **Library Holdings:** 8,652 **Credit Hours For Degree:** 90 credits, Associates

OREGON COLLEGE OF ART & CRAFT
8245 Southwest Barnes Rd.
Portland, OR 97225
Tel: (503)297-5544
Free: 800-390-0632
Fax: (503)297-3155
E-mail: bbeach@ocac.edu
Web Site: http://www.ocac.edu/
President/CEO: Bonnie Laing-Malcolmson
Registrar: Donna Lewis
Admissions: Barry Beach
Financial Aid: Lisa Newman
Type: Four-Year College **Sex:** Coed **Scores:** 87.5% SAT V 400+; 87.5% SAT M 400+; 66% ACT 18-23; 33% ACT 24-29 **% Accepted:** 95 **Admission Plans:** Deferred Admission **Application Deadline:** Rolling **Application Fee:** $35.00 **H.S. Requirements:** High school diploma required; GED accepted **Costs Per Year:** Application fee: $35. Tuition: $16,900 full-time, $2214 per course part-time. Mandatory fees: $982 full-time, $50 per course part-time. College room only: $3600. **Scholarships:** Available **Calendar System:** Semester, Summer Session Not available **Enrollment:** FT 114, PT 39 **Faculty:** FT 9, PT 13 **Student-Faculty Ratio:** 9:1 **Exams:** ACT, SAT I **% Receiving Financial Aid:** 93 **% Residing in College-Owned, -Operated, or -Affiliated Housing:** 3 **Library Holdings:** 9,000 **Credit Hours For Degree:** 120 credits, Bachelors **Professional Accreditation:** NASAD

OREGON HEALTH & SCIENCE UNIVERSITY
3181 SW Sam Jackson Park Rd.
Portland, OR 97239-3098
Tel: (503)494-8311
Admissions: (503)494-7800
Fax: (503)494-5738
E-mail: honnellc@ohsu.edu
Web Site: http://www.ohsu.edu/
President/CEO: Dr. Peter O. Kohler
Registrar: Cherie Honnell
Admissions: Cherie Honnell
Financial Aid: Cherie Honnell
Type: Two-Year Upper Division **Sex:** Coed **Admission Plans:** Preferred Admission **Application Fee:** $125.00 **H.S. Requirements:** High school diploma required; GED accepted **Costs Per Year:** Application fee: $125. State resident tuition: $7920 full-time, $165 per credit part-time. Nonresident tuition: $18,480 full-time, $385 per credit part-time. Mandatory fees: $1193 full-time. **Scholarships:** Available **Calendar System:** Quarter, Summer Session Available **Enrollment:** FT 474, PT 175, Grad 1,126 **Faculty:** FT 503, PT 333 **% Receiving Financial Aid:** 77 **Library Holdings:** 200,771 **Credit Hours For Degree:** 186 quarter hours, Bachelors **ROTC:** Army

Professional Accreditation: AACN, ACNM, ADA, ADtA, APA, CEPH, JRCERT, LCMEAMA, NAACLS, NLN, NCCU

OREGON INSTITUTE OF TECHNOLOGY
3201 Campus Dr.
Klamath Falls, OR 97601-8801
Tel: (541)885-1000
Free: 800-343-6653
Admissions: (541)885-1150
Fax: (541)885-1115
E-mail: oit@oit.edu
Web Site: http://www.oit.edu/
President/CEO: Dr. Martha Anne Dow
Registrar: Wendy Turner
Admissions: Palmer Muntz
Financial Aid: Tracey Lehman
Type: Four-Year College **Sex:** Coed **Affiliation:** Oregon University System **Scores:** 94% SAT V 400+; 95% SAT M 400+; 56.8% ACT 18-23; 18.9% ACT 24-29 **Admission Plans:** Deferred Admission **Application Fee:** $50.00 **H.S. Requirements:** High school diploma required; GED accepted **Costs Per Year:** Application fee: $50. State resident tuition: $4101 full-time, $99 per credit part-time. Nonresident tuition: $14,310 full-time, $99 per credit part-time. Mandatory fees: $1,246 full-time. Full-time tuition and fees vary according to course load, location, and reciprocity agreements. College room and board: $6037. Room and board charges vary according to board plan. **Scholarships:** Available **Calendar System:** Quarter, Summer Session Available **Enrollment:** FT 1,985, PT 1,381, Grad 7 **Faculty:** FT 114, PT 16 **Student-Faculty Ratio:** 15:1 **Exams:** SAT I or ACT **% Receiving Financial Aid:** 85 **% Residing in College-Owned, -Operated, or -Affiliated Housing:** 15 **Library Holdings:** 90,389 **Credit Hours For Degree:** 90 credit hours, Associates; 180 credit hours, Bachelors **ROTC:** Army **Professional Accreditation:** ABET, ADA, JRCERT, NAACLS, NCCU **Intercollegiate Athletics:** Baseball M; Basketball M & W; Cross-Country Running M & W; Soccer W; Softball W; Track and Field M & W; Volleyball W

OREGON STATE UNIVERSITY
Corvallis, OR 97331
Tel: (541)737-1000
Admissions: (541)737-4411
Fax: (541)737-6157
E-mail: osuadmit@ccmail.orst.edu
Web Site: http://oregonstate.edu/
President/CEO: Dr. Edward Ray
Registrar: Barbara S. Balz
Admissions: Kate Peterson
Financial Aid: Kate L. Peterson
Type: University **Sex:** Coed **Affiliation:** Oregon University System **Scores:** 95% SAT V 400+; 96% SAT M 400+; 48% ACT 18-23; 36% ACT 24-29 **% Accepted:** 93 **Admission Plans:** Early Admission; Early Action; Deferred Admission **Application Deadline:** September 01 **Application Fee:** $50.00 **H.S. Requirements:** High school diploma required; GED accepted **Costs Per Year:** Application fee: $50. State resident tuition: $4176 full-time, $116 per credit part-time. Nonresident tuition: $16,236 full-time, $451 per credit part-time. Mandatory fees: $1,266 full-time. Part-time tuition varies according to course load. College room and board: $6930. Room and board charges vary according to board plan and housing facility. **Scholarships:** Available **Calendar System:** Quarter, Summer Session Available **Enrollment:** FT 13,862, PT 1,885, Grad 2,976 **Faculty:** FT 760, PT 455 **Student-Faculty Ratio:** 19:1 **Exams:** SAT I or ACT, SAT II **% Receiving Financial Aid:** 53 **% Residing in College-Owned, -Operated, or -Affiliated Housing:** 22 **Library Holdings:** 689,119 **Credit Hours For Degree:** 180 quarter hours, Bachelors **ROTC:** Army, Navy, Air Force **Professional Accreditation:** AACSB, ABET, AAFCS, ACCE, ACPhE, ACA, AVMA, CEPH, JRCEPAT, NCATE, NCCU, SAF **Intercollegiate Athletics:** Baseball M; Basketball M & W; Crew M & W; Football M; Golf M & W; Gymnastics W; Soccer M & W; Softball W; Swimming and Diving W; Volleyball W; Wrestling M

OREGON STATE UNIVERSITY-CASCADES
2600 NW College Way
Bend, OR 97701
Tel: (541)322-3100
Web Site: http://www.osucascades.edu **Type:** Comprehensive **Sex:** Coed **Calendar System:** Quarter

PACIFIC NORTHWEST COLLEGE OF ART
1241 NW Johnson St.
Portland, OR 97209
Tel: (503)226-4391
Admissions: (503)821-8972
Fax: (503)226-3587
E-mail: colin@pnca.edu
Web Site: http://www.pnca.edu/
President/CEO: Dr. Thomas Manley
Registrar: Jenifer DeKalb
Admissions: Rebecca Haas
Financial Aid: Jennifer Satalino
Type: Four-Year College **Sex:** Coed **Scores:** 92% SAT V 400+; 85% SAT M 400+ **% Accepted:** 72 **Admission Plans:** Deferred Admission **Application Fee:** $35.00 **H.S. Requirements:** High school diploma required; GED accepted **Costs Per Year:** Application fee: $35. Tuition: $17,480 full-time, $728 per semester hour part-time. Mandatory fees: $692 full-time, $28 per semester hour part-time. College room only: $5200. **Scholarships:** Available **Calendar System:** Semester, Summer Session Not available **Faculty:** FT 13, PT 38 **Student-Faculty Ratio:** 11:1 **% Receiving Financial Aid:** 66 **Library Holdings:** 14,650 **Credit Hours For Degree:** 120 semester hours, Bachelors **Professional Accreditation:** NASAD, NCCU

PACIFIC UNIVERSITY
2043 College Way
Forest Grove, OR 97116-1797
Tel: (503)357-6151; 877-722-8648
Admissions: (503)352-2218
Fax: (503)352-3191
E-mail: admissions@pacificu.edu
Web Site: http://www.pacificu.edu/
President/CEO: Dr. Phillip D. Creighton
Registrar: Debra Avilucea
Admissions: Karen Dunston
Financial Aid: Dala J. Ramsey
Type: Comprehensive **Sex:** Coed **Scores:** 100% SAT V 400+; 100% SAT M 400+; 39% ACT 18-23; 52% ACT 24-29 **% Accepted:** 87 **Admission Plans:** Deferred Admission **Application Deadline:** August 15 **Application Fee:** $40.00 **H.S. Requirements:** High school diploma required; GED accepted **Costs Per Year:** Application fee: $40. Comprehensive fee: $29,002 includes full-time tuition ($21,954), mandatory fees ($580), and college room and board ($6468). College room only: $3220. Part-time tuition: $916 per credit hour. **Scholarships:** Available **Calendar System:** 4-1-4, Summer Session Available **Enrollment:** FT 1,173, PT 59, Grad 579 **Faculty:** FT 82, PT 46 **Student-Faculty Ratio:** 12:1 **Exams:** SAT I or ACT **% Receiving Financial Aid:** 73 **% Residing in College-Owned, -Operated, or -Affiliated Housing:** 57 **Library Holdings:** 212,976 **Credit Hours For Degree:** 124 semester hours, Bachelors **ROTC:** Army, Air Force **Professional Accreditation:** AOTA, AOA, APTA, APA, NASM, NCCU **Intercollegiate Athletics:** Baseball M; Basketball M & W; Cheerleading M & W; Cross-Country Running M & W; Golf M & W; Lacrosse W; Soccer M & W; Softball W; Swimming and Diving M & W; Tennis M & W; Track and Field M & W; Volleyball M & W; Wrestling M & W

PIONEER PACIFIC COLLEGE
27501 Southwest Parkway Ave.
Wilsonville, OR 97070
Tel: (503)682-3903
Admissions: (503)682-1862
Fax: (503)682-1514
E-mail: jrussell@pioneerpacific.edu
Web Site: http://www.pioneerpacific.edu/
President/CEO: David J. Hallett
Registrar: Matthew Sharkey
Admissions: Joanna Russell
Financial Aid: Stacey Maurer
Type: Two-Year College **Sex:** Coed **% Accepted:** 84 **Admission Plans:** Open Admission **Application Deadline:** Rolling **Application Fee:** $50.00 **H.S. Requirements:** High school diploma required; GED accepted **Costs Per Year:** Application fee: $50. Tuition: $8280 full-time, $188 per credit hour part-time. Mandatory fees: $150 full-time. **Scholarships:** Available **Calendar System:** Continuous, Summer Session Not available **Enrollment:**

FT 1,126, PT 6 **Faculty:** FT 49, PT 70 **Student-Faculty Ratio:** 15:1 **Exams:** Other **Library Holdings:** 2,500 **Credit Hours For Degree:** 90 credit hours, Associates; 182.5 credit hours, Bachelors **Professional Accreditation:** ACICS

PORTLAND COMMUNITY COLLEGE
PO Box 19000
Portland, OR 97280-0990
Tel: (503)244-6111
Admissions: (503)977-4519
Fax: (503)452-4988
Web Site: http://www.pcc.edu/
President/CEO: Dr. Jerry Berger
Registrar: G. Frost Johnson
Admissions: Dennis Bailey-Fougnier
Financial Aid: Corbett Gottfried
Type: Two-Year College **Sex:** Coed **Admission Plans:** Open Admission **H.S. Requirements:** High school diploma or equivalent not required. For career and technical programs: High school diploma required; GED not accepted **Costs Per Year:** State resident tuition: $2880 full-time, $64 per credit part-time. Nonresident tuition: $9000 full-time, $200 per credit part-time. Mandatory fees: $240 full-time, $4.25 per credit part-time. **Scholarships:** Available **Calendar System:** Quarter, Summer Session Available **Faculty:** FT 412, PT 1,333 **Student-Faculty Ratio:** 25:1 **Library Holdings:** 91,472 **Credit Hours For Degree:** 90 credit hours, Associates **Professional Accreditation:** ADA, AHIMA, JCAHPO, JRCERT, NAACLS, NLN, NCCU **Intercollegiate Athletics:** Basketball M & W

PORTLAND STATE UNIVERSITY
PO Box 751
Portland, OR 97207-0751
Tel: (503)725-3000
Free: 800-547-8887
Admissions: (503)725-3511
Fax: (503)725-5525
E-mail: askadm@ofa.pdx.edu
Web Site: http://www.pdx.edu/
President/CEO: Dr. Daniel O. Bernstine
Admissions: Agnes A. Hoffman
Financial Aid: Gary Garoffolo
Type: University **Sex:** Coed **Affiliation:** Oregon University System **Scores:** 90.5% SAT V 400+; 94% SAT M 400+; 44% ACT 18-23; 38% ACT 24-29 **% Accepted:** 92 **Admission Plans:** Early Admission; Deferred Admission **Application Deadline:** Rolling **Application Fee:** $50.00 **H.S. Requirements:** High school diploma required; GED accepted **Costs Per Year:** Application fee: $50. State resident tuition: $3810 full-time, $93 per credit part-time. Nonresident tuition: $15,975 full-time, $93 per credit part-time. Mandatory fees: $1151 full-time, $18 per credit part-time, $48.50 per term part-time. Full-time tuition and fees vary according to program. College room and board: $8445. College room only: $6300. Room and board charges vary according to board plan and housing facility. **Scholarships:** Available **Calendar System:** Quarter, Summer Session Available **Enrollment:** FT 10,851, PT 7,120, Grad 6,149 **Faculty:** FT 737, PT 497 **Student-Faculty Ratio:** 17:1 **Exams:** SAT I or ACT **% Receiving Financial Aid:** 53 **Library Holdings:** 1,805,336 **Credit Hours For Degree:** 180 credit hours, Bachelors **ROTC:** Army, Air Force **Professional Accreditation:** AACSB, ABET, ACA, ACSP, ASLHA, CEPH, CORE, CSWE, NASAD, NASM, NASPAA, NAST, NCATE, NCCU **Intercollegiate Athletics:** Baseball M; Basketball M & W; Cross-Country Running M & W; Football M; Golf M & W; Soccer W; Softball W; Tennis M & W; Track and Field M & W; Volleyball W; Wrestling M

REED COLLEGE
3203 Southeast Woodstock Blvd.
Portland, OR 97202-8199
Tel: (503)771-1112
Free: 800-547-4750
Admissions: (503)777-7511
Fax: (503)777-7553
E-mail: admission@reed.edu
Web Site: http://www.reed.edu/
President/CEO: Colin S. Diver
Registrar: Nora McLaughlin
Admissions: Paul Marthers
Financial Aid: Leslie Limper
Type: Comprehensive **Sex:** Coed **Scores:** 100% SAT V 400+; 100% SAT M 400+; 3% ACT 18-23; 35% ACT 24-29 **% Accepted:** 45 **Admission Plans:** Early Admission; Early Decision Plan; Deferred Admission **Application Deadline:** January 15 **Application Fee:** $40.00 **H.S. Requirements:** High school diploma required; GED accepted **Costs Per Year:** Application fee: $40. Comprehensive fee: $41,106 includes full-time tuition ($32,360), mandatory fees ($230), and college room and board ($8516). College room only: $4470. Full-time tuition and fees vary according to degree level. Room and board charges vary according to board plan and housing facility. Part-time tuition: $5400 per course. Part-time tuition varies according to course level and degree level. **Scholarships:** Available **Calendar System:** Semester, Summer Session Not available **Enrollment:** FT 1,272, PT 37, Grad 31 **Faculty:** FT 116, PT 15 **Student-Faculty Ratio:** 10:1 **Exams:** SAT I or ACT, SAT II **% Receiving Financial Aid:** 52 **% Residing in College-Owned, -Operated, or -Affiliated Housing:** 65 **Library Holdings:** 528,000 **Credit Hours For Degree:** 120 semester hours, Bachelors **Professional Accreditation:** NCCU **Intercollegiate Athletics:** Basketball M; Crew M & W; Fencing M & W; Sailing M & W; Skiing (Downhill) M & W; Soccer M & W; Squash M & W; Weight Lifting M & W

ROGUE COMMUNITY COLLEGE
3345 Redwood Hwy.
Grants Pass, OR 97527-9298
Tel: (541)956-7500
Admissions: (541)956-7176
E-mail: csullivan@roguecc.edu
Web Site: http://www.roguecc.edu/
President/CEO: Richard L. Levine
Registrar: Claudia Sullivan
Admissions: Claudia Sullivan
Financial Aid: Shirlee Willis-Haslip
Type: Two-Year College **Sex:** Coed **% Accepted:** 100 **Admission Plans:** Open Admission; Preferred Admission; Early Admission **Application Deadline:** Rolling **Application Fee:** $0.00 **H.S. Requirements:** High school diploma or equivalent not required. For respiratory therapy, nursing, human services, emergency medical technology, mental health technician programs: High school diploma required; GED not accepted. **Costs Per Year:** Application fee: $0. State resident tuition: $2304 full-time, $64 per credit hour part-time. Nonresident tuition: $2772 full-time, $77 per credit hour part-time. Mandatory fees: $294 full-time, $4 per credit hour part-time. **Scholarships:** Available **Calendar System:** Quarter, Summer Session Available **Enrollment:** FT 1,341, PT 2,883 **Faculty:** FT 102, PT 397 **Student-Faculty Ratio:** 11:1 **Library Holdings:** 33,000 **Credit Hours For Degree:** 90 credits, Associates **Professional Accreditation:** CARC, NLN, NCCU

SOUTHERN OREGON UNIVERSITY
1250 Siskiyou Blvd.
Ashland, OR 97520
Tel: (541)552-7672
Admissions: (541)552-6411
Fax: (541)552-6329
E-mail: admissions@sou.edu
Web Site: http://www.sou.edu/
President/CEO: Dr. Elisabeth Zinser
Registrar: Michael Corcoran
Admissions: Mara A. Affre
Financial Aid: Peggy Nitsos
Type: Comprehensive **Sex:** Coed **Affiliation:** Oregon University System **Scores:** 93.5% SAT V 400+; 93.5% SAT M 400+; 49.61% ACT 18-23; 33.33% ACT 24-29 **% Accepted:** 80 **Admission Plans:** Early Admission; Deferred Admission **Application Deadline:** Rolling **Application Fee:** $50.00 **H.S. Requirements:** High school diploma required; GED accepted **Costs Per Year:** Application fee: $50. State resident tuition: $4986 full-time, $108 per credit part-time. Nonresident tuition: $14,691 full-time, $108 per credit part-time. Mandatory fees: $25 per credit part-time. College room and board: $6468. **Scholarships:** Available **Calendar System:** Quarter, Summer Session Available **Enrollment:** FT 3,475, PT 961, Grad 541 **Faculty:** FT 193, PT 96 **Student-Faculty Ratio:** 22:1 **Exams:** SAT I or ACT, SAT II **% Receiving Financial Aid:** 56 **% Residing in College-Owned, -Operated, or -Affiliated Housing:** 24 **Library Holdings:** 315,000 **Credit Hours For Degree:** 180 credits, Bachelors **Professional Accreditation:** NASM, NCCU **Intercollegiate Athletics:** Basketball M & W; Cross-Country Running M & W; Football M; Skiing (Downhill) M & W; Soccer W; Softball W; Tennis W;

Track and Field M & W; Volleyball W; Wrestling M

SOUTHWESTERN OREGON COMMUNITY COLLEGE
1988 Newmark Ave.
Coos Bay, OR 97420-2912
Tel: (541)888-2525
Admissions: (541)888-7611
E-mail: tnicholls@socc.edu
Web Site: http://www.socc.edu/
President/CEO: Judith M.L. Hansen, PhD
Registrar: Joanna Blount
Admissions: Tom Nicholls
Type: Two-Year College **Sex:** Coed **% Accepted:** 100 **Admission Plans:** Open Admission; Early Admission **Application Deadline:** Rolling **Application Fee:** $30.00 **H.S. Requirements:** High school diploma or equivalent not required. For nursing program: High school diploma required; GED accepted **Costs Per Year:** Application fee: $30. State resident tuition: $3330 full-time, $62 per credit part-time. Nonresident tuition: $3330 full-time, $62 per credit part-time. Mandatory fees: $330 full-time, $12 per credit part-time, $22. College room and board: $6160. **Scholarships:** Available **Calendar System:** Quarter, Summer Session Available **Enrollment:** FT 976, PT 1,004 **Faculty:** FT 66, PT 153 **Student-Faculty Ratio:** 10:1 **Library Holdings:** 40,505 **Credit Hours For Degree:** 93 credit hours, Associates **Professional Accreditation:** NCCU **Intercollegiate Athletics:** Baseball M; Basketball M & W; Cheerleading M & W; Cross-Country Running M & W; Golf M & W; Soccer M & W; Softball W; Track and Field M & W; Volleyball W; Wrestling M

TILLAMOOK BAY COMMUNITY COLLEGE
2510 First St.
Tillamook, OR 97141
Tel: (503)842-8222
Fax: (503)842-2214
E-mail: om@tillamookbay.cc
Web Site: http://www.tbcc.cc.or.us/
President/CEO: Ralph Orr
Admissions: Ralph Orr
Type: Two-Year College **Sex:** Coed **Affiliation:** Portland Community College **% Accepted:** 100 **Application Fee:** $0.00 **Costs Per Year:** Application fee: $0. State resident tuition: $2976 full-time, $62 per credit part-time. Nonresident tuition: $3936 full-time, $82 per credit part-time. Mandatory fees: $530 full-time, $33 per course part-time. **Calendar System:** Quarter **Enrollment:** FT 73, PT 226 **Faculty:** FT 6, PT 30 **Student-Faculty Ratio:** 8:1 **Professional Accreditation:** NCCU

TREASURE VALLEY COMMUNITY COLLEGE
650 College Blvd.
Ontario, OR 97914-3423
Tel: (541)889-6493
Admissions: (541)881-8822
Fax: (541)881-2721
Web Site: http://www.tvcc.cc.or.us/
President/CEO: Dr. Berton L. Glandon
Admissions: Suzanne Bergam
Financial Aid: Kathy Gibson
Type: Two-Year College **Sex:** Coed **Admission Plans:** Open Admission; Early Admission; Deferred Admission **Application Deadline:** Rolling **Application Fee:** $10.00 **H.S. Requirements:** High school diploma or equivalent not required. For nursing program: High school diploma required; GED accepted **Costs Per Year:** Application fee: $10. State resident tuition: $2970 full-time, $66 per credit hour part-time. Nonresident tuition: $3420 full-time, $76 per credit hour part-time. Mandatory fees: $455 full-time, $10 per credit hour part-time. College room and board: $4470. College room only: $1680. **Scholarships:** Available **Calendar System:** Quarter, Summer Session Available **Enrollment:** FT 1,056, PT 890 **Faculty:** FT 48, PT 92 **Student-Faculty Ratio:** 11:1 **% Residing in College-Owned, -Operated, or -Affiliated Housing:** 6 **Library Holdings:** 28,000 **Credit Hours For Degree:** 90 credits, Associates **ROTC:** Army **Professional Accreditation:** NCCU **Intercollegiate Athletics:** Baseball M; Basketball M & W; Volleyball W

UMPQUA COMMUNITY COLLEGE
PO Box 967
Roseburg, OR 97470-0226
Tel: (541)440-4600
Admissions: (541)440-4616
Fax: (541)440-4612
Web Site: http://www.umpqua.edu/
President/CEO: Dr. David N. Beyer
Registrar: David Farrington
Admissions: David Farrington
Financial Aid: Claudia Justice
Type: Two-Year College **Sex:** Coed **Admission Plans:** Open Admission; Early Admission; Deferred Admission **Application Fee:** $25.00 **H.S. Requirements:** High school diploma or equivalent not required. For nursing, emergency medical technology programs: High school diploma required; GED accepted **Scholarships:** Available **Calendar System:** Quarter, Summer Session Available **Enrollment:** FT 987, PT 1,154 **Student-Faculty Ratio:** 18:1 **Library Holdings:** 41,000 **Credit Hours For Degree:** 93 credits, Associates **Professional Accreditation:** NLN, NCCU **Intercollegiate Athletics:** Basketball M & W

UNIVERSITY OF OREGON
Eugene, OR 97403
Tel: (541)346-3111
Admissions: (541)346-3201
Fax: (541)346-5815
E-mail: diradm@uoregon.edu
Web Site: http://www.uoregon.edu/
President/CEO: Dave Frohnmayer
Registrar: Herbert R. Chereck
Admissions: Martha Pitts
Financial Aid: Elizabeth Bickford
Type: University **Sex:** Coed **Affiliation:** Oregon University System **Scores:** 97% SAT V 400+; 97% SAT M 400+ **% Accepted:** 90 **Admission Plans:** Early Admission **Application Deadline:** January 15 **Application Fee:** $50.00 **H.S. Requirements:** High school diploma required; GED accepted **Costs Per Year:** Application fee: $50. State resident tuition: $4164 full-time, $104 per credit hour part-time. Nonresident tuition: $15,996 full-time, $420 per credit hour part-time. Mandatory fees: $1449 full-time, $427 per term part-time. Full-time tuition and fees vary according to class time, course level, course load, degree level, program, and reciprocity agreements. Part-time tuition and fees vary according to class time, course level, course load, degree level, and program. College room and board: $7496. Room and board charges vary according to board plan and housing facility. **Scholarships:** Available **Calendar System:** Quarter, Summer Session Available **Enrollment:** FT 14,996, PT 1,477, Grad 3,348 **Faculty:** FT 785, PT 337 **Student-Faculty Ratio:** 18:1 **Exams:** SAT I or ACT **% Receiving Financial Aid:** 41 **% Residing in College-Owned, -Operated, or -Affiliated Housing:** 21 **Library Holdings:** 2,636,234 **Credit Hours For Degree:** 180 credit hours, Bachelors **ROTC:** Army, Air Force **Professional Accreditation:** AACSB, ACEJMC, ABA, ACSP, APA, ASLA, ASLHA, AALS, FIDER, NASAD, NASM, NASPAA, NCCU **Intercollegiate Athletics:** Badminton M & W; Baseball M; Basketball M & W; Bowling M & W; Cheerleading M & W; Crew M & W; Cross-Country Running M & W; Equestrian Sports M & W; Fencing M & W; Football M; Golf M & W; Ice Hockey M; Lacrosse M & W; Racquetball M & W; Rugby M & W; Sailing M & W; Skiing (Downhill) M & W; Soccer M & W; Softball W; Swimming and Diving M & W; Table Tennis M & W; Tennis M & W; Track and Field M & W; Ultimate Frisbee M & W; Volleyball M & W; Water Polo M & W; Wrestling M

UNIVERSITY OF PHOENIX-OREGON CAMPUS
13221 SW 68th Parkway, Ste. 500
Portland, OR 97223-8368
Tel: (503)670-0590
Free: 800-228-7240
Admissions: (480)557-1712
Fax: (503)670-0614
Web Site: http://www.phoenix.edu/
President/CEO: Pat Hardie
Admissions: Nina Omelchanko
Type: Comprehensive **Sex:** Coed **Admission Plans:** Open Admission; Deferred Admission **Application Deadline:** Rolling **Application Fee:** $110.00 **H.S. Requirements:** High school diploma required; GED accepted **Costs Per Year:** Application fee: $110. Tuition: $10,410 full-time, $347 per credit part-time. Mandatory fees: $560 full-time, $70 per course part-time. **Scholarships:** Available **Calendar System:** Continuous, Summer Session Not available **Enrollment:** FT 1,686, Grad 367 **Faculty:** FT 13, PT 270 **Student-Faculty Ratio:** 7:1 **Library Holdings:** 444 **Regional Accreditation:** North Central Association of Colleges and Schools **Credit Hours For Degree:** 60 credits, Associates; 120 credits, Bachelors

UNIVERSITY OF PORTLAND
5000 North Willamette Blvd.
Portland, OR 97203-5798
Tel: (503)943-7911; 888-627-5601
Admissions: (503)943-7147
Fax: (503)943-7399
E-mail: admissions@uofport.edu
Web Site: http://www.up.edu/
President/CEO: Rev. E. William Beauchamp, CSC
Registrar: Roberta Lindahl
Admissions: James C. Lyons
Financial Aid: Tracy Reisinger
Type: Comprehensive **Sex:** Coed **Affiliation:** Roman Catholic **Scores:** 99.7% SAT V 400+; 100% SAT M 400+ **% Accepted:** 81 **Admission Plans:** Deferred Admission **Application Deadline:** June 01 **Application Fee:** $50.00 **H.S. Requirements:** High school diploma required; GED accepted **Costs Per Year:** Application fee: $50. Comprehensive fee: $32,300 includes full-time tuition ($24,580), mandatory fees ($320), and college room and board ($7400). College room only: $3700. Full-time tuition and fees vary according to program. Room and board charges vary according to board plan and housing facility. Part-time tuition: $778 per credit hour. Part-time tuition varies according to program. **Scholarships:** Available **Calendar System:** Semester, Summer Session Available **Enrollment:** FT 2,840, PT 80, Grad 493 **Faculty:** FT 188, PT 91 **Student-Faculty Ratio:** 13:1 **Exams:** SAT I or ACT **% Receiving Financial Aid:** 51 **% Residing in College-Owned, -Operated, or -Affiliated Housing:** 54 **Library Holdings:** 350,000 **Credit Hours For Degree:** 120 semester hours, Bachelors **ROTC:** Army, Air Force **Professional Accreditation:** AACSB, ABET, AACN, NASM, NAST, NCATE, NLN, NCCU **Intercollegiate Athletics:** Baseball M; Basketball M & W; Cross-Country Running M & W; Golf M & W; Rugby M; Soccer M & W; Tennis M & W; Track and Field M & W; Volleyball W

WARNER PACIFIC COLLEGE
2219 Southeast 68th Ave.
Portland, OR 97215-4099
Tel: (503)517-1000
Free: 800-804-1510
Admissions: (503)517-1020
Fax: (503)788-7425
E-mail: admiss@warnerpacific.edu
Web Site: http://www.warnerpacific.edu/
President/CEO: Dr. Jay A. Barber, Jr.
Registrar: Victoria Cumings
Admissions: Shannon Mackey
Financial Aid: Cindy Pollard
Type: Comprehensive **Sex:** Coed **Affiliation:** Church of God **% Accepted:** 57 **Application Deadline:** Rolling **Application Fee:** $25.00 **H.S. Requirements:** High school diploma required; GED accepted **Scholarships:** Available **Calendar System:** Semester, Summer Session Available **Faculty:** FT 35, PT 0 **Student-Faculty Ratio:** 14:1 **Exams:** SAT I or ACT, SAT II **% Receiving Financial Aid:** 89 **% Residing in College-Owned, -Operated, or -Affiliated Housing:** 32 **Library Holdings:** 54,000 **Credit Hours For Degree:** 62 semester hours, Associates; 124 semester hours, Bachelors **ROTC:** Army, Air Force **Professional Accreditation:** NCCU **Intercollegiate Athletics:** Basketball M & W; Cross-Country Running M & W; Soccer M & W; Track and Field M & W; Volleyball W

WESTERN BUSINESS COLLEGE
425 Southwest Washington
Portland, OR 97204
Tel: (503)222-3225
Fax: (503)228-6926
Web Site: http://www.western-college.com/
President/CEO: Randy Rogers
Registrar: Renee Hatfield
Financial Aid: Sharon Hale
Type: Two-Year College **Sex:** Coed **Scholarships:** Available **Calendar System:** Quarter **Professional Accreditation:** ACICS

WESTERN CULINARY INSTITUTE
1235 Southwest 12th Ave., Ste. 100
Portland, OR 97201
Tel: (503)223-2245
Free: 800-666-0312
Fax: (503)223-0126
Web Site: http://www.westernculinary.com/ **Type:** Two-Year College **Sex:** Coed **Calendar System:** Continuous **Professional Accreditation:** ACCSCT, ACF

WESTERN OREGON UNIVERSITY
345 North Monmouth Ave.
Monmouth, OR 97361-1394
Tel: (503)838-8000; 877-877-1593
Admissions: (503)838-8211
Fax: (503)838-8067
E-mail: wolfgram@wou.edu
Web Site: http://www.wou.edu/
President/CEO: Dr. Philip W. Conn
Registrar: Nancy France
Admissions: Rob Findtner
Financial Aid: Donna Fossum
Type: Comprehensive **Sex:** Coed **Affiliation:** Oregon University System **Scores:** 86.6% SAT V 400+; 87% SAT M 400+; 51.2% ACT 18-23; 19% ACT 24-29 **% Accepted:** 55 **Admission Plans:** Deferred Admission **Application Deadline:** Rolling **Application Fee:** $50.00 **H.S. Requirements:** High school diploma required; GED accepted **Costs Per Year:** Application fee: $50. State resident tuition: $3240 full-time, $90 per credit part-time. Nonresident tuition: $11,685 full-time, $325 per credit part-time. Mandatory fees: $1092 full-time. College room and board: $6276. Room and board charges vary according to board plan and housing facility. **Scholarships:** Available **Calendar System:** Quarter, Summer Session Available **Enrollment:** FT 3,783, PT 478, Grad 259 **Faculty:** FT 179, PT 175 **Student-Faculty Ratio:** 17:1 **Exams:** SAT I or ACT, SAT II **% Receiving Financial Aid:** 73 **% Residing in College-Owned, -Operated, or -Affiliated Housing:** 20 **Library Holdings:** 157,186 **Credit Hours For Degree:** 93 credit hours, Associates; 180 credit hours, Bachelors **ROTC:** Army, Air Force **Professional Accreditation:** CORE, NASM, NCATE, NCCU **Intercollegiate Athletics:** Baseball M; Basketball M & W; Cross-Country Running M & W; Football M; Rugby M & W; Soccer W; Softball W; Track and Field M & W; Volleyball W

WILLAMETTE UNIVERSITY
900 State St.
Salem, OR 97301-3931
Tel: (503)370-6300; 877-542-2787
Admissions: (503)370-6303
Fax: (503)375-5363
E-mail: libarts@willamette.edu
Web Site: http://www.willamette.edu/
President/CEO: Dr. M. Lee Pelton
Registrar: Paul J. Olsen
Admissions: Dr. Robin Brown
Financial Aid: Jim Eddy
Type: Comprehensive **Sex:** Coed **Affiliation:** United Methodist **Scores:** 99% SAT V 400+; 100% SAT M 400+; 15% ACT 18-23; 66% ACT 24-29 **% Accepted:** 74 **Admission Plans:** Early Action; Deferred Admission **Application Deadline:** February 01 **Application Fee:** $50.00 **H.S. Requirements:** High school diploma required; GED accepted **Costs Per Year:** Application fee: $50. Comprehensive fee: $35,416 includes full-time tuition ($28,250), mandatory fees ($166), and college room and board ($7000). Full-time tuition and fees vary according to course load. Room and board charges vary according to board plan and housing facility. Part-time tuition: $3531 per course. Part-time tuition varies according to course load. **Scholarships:** Available **Calendar System:** Semester, Summer Session Not available **Enrollment:** FT 1,823, PT 131, Grad 241 **Faculty:** FT 184, PT 117 **Student-Faculty Ratio:** 11:1 **Exams:** SAT I or ACT **% Receiving Financial Aid:** 62 **% Residing in College-Owned, -Operated, or -Affiliated Housing:** 69 **Library Holdings:** 317,000 **Credit Hours For Degree:** 124 semester hours, Bachelors **ROTC:** Air Force **Professional Accreditation:** AACSB, ABA, AALS, NASM, NASPAA, NCCU **Intercollegiate Athletics:** Baseball M; Basketball M & W; Crew M & W; Cross-Country Running M & W; Football M; Golf M & W; Lacrosse M; Soccer M & W; Softball W; Swimming and Diving M & W; Tennis M & W; Track and Field M & W; Volleyball W

Pennsylvania

ACADEMY OF MEDICAL ARTS AND BUSINESS
2301 Academy Dr.
Harrisburg, PA 17112-1012
Tel: (717)545-4747
Fax: (717)901-9090
Web Site: http://www.acadcampus.com/
President/CEO: Gary Kay
Admissions: Gary Kay
Financial Aid: Tracy Stewart
Type: Two-Year College **Sex:** Coed **Admission Plans:** Open Admission **Application Fee:** $150.00 **H.S. Requirements:** High school diploma required; GED accepted **Costs Per Year:** Application fee: $150. Tuition: $9650 full-time. Mandatory fees: $1990 full-time. **Scholarships:** Available **Calendar System:** Continuous, Summer Session Not available **Enrollment:** FT 491 **Faculty:** FT 14, PT 13 **Student-Faculty Ratio:** 20:1 **Library Holdings:** 1,620 **Credit Hours For Degree:** 64 credit hours, Associates **Professional Accreditation:** ACCSCT

ALBRIGHT COLLEGE
13th and Bern Sts., PO Box 15234
Reading, PA 19612-5234
Tel: (610)921-2381
Free: 800-252-1856
Admissions: (610)921-7260
Fax: (610)921-7530
E-mail: albright@joe.alb.edu
Web Site: http://www.albright.edu/
President/CEO: Dr. David C. Stineback
Registrar: David C. Ballaban
Admissions: Gregory Eichhorn
Financial Aid: Maryellen Duffy
Type: Four-Year College **Sex:** Coed **Affiliation:** United Methodist Church **Scores:** 97% SAT V 400+; 95% SAT M 400+ **% Accepted:** 69 **Admission Plans:** Early Admission; Deferred Admission **Application Deadline:** Rolling **Application Fee:** $25.00 **H.S. Requirements:** High school diploma required; GED accepted **Costs Per Year:** Application fee: $25. Comprehensive fee: $33,920 includes full-time tuition ($25,232), mandatory fees ($800), and college room and board ($7888). College room only: $4490. Full-time tuition and fees vary according to program. Room and board charges vary according to board plan and housing facility. Part-time tuition: $3154 per course. Part-time tuition varies according to class time. **Scholarships:** Available **Calendar System:** 4-1-4, Summer Session Available **Enrollment:** FT 2,066, PT 46, Grad 68 **Faculty:** FT 103, PT 52 **Student-Faculty Ratio:** 14:1 **Exams:** SAT I or ACT **% Receiving Financial Aid:** 70 **% Residing in College-Owned, -Operated, or -Affiliated Housing:** 65 **Library Holdings:** 218,232 **Regional Accreditation:** Middle State Association of Colleges and Schools **Credit Hours For Degree:** 32 courses, Bachelors **Intercollegiate Athletics:** Badminton W; Baseball M; Basketball M & W; Cheerleading W; Cross-Country Running M & W; Field Hockey W; Football M; Golf M; Lacrosse M & W; Rugby M & W; Soccer M & W; Softball W; Swimming and Diving M & W; Tennis M & W; Track and Field M & W; Volleyball W; Wrestling M

ALLEGHENY COLLEGE
520 North Main St.
Meadville, PA 16335
Tel: (814)332-3100
Free: 800-521-5293
Admissions: (814)332-4351
Fax: (814)337-0431
E-mail: admissions@allegheny.edu
Web Site: http://www.allegheny.edu/
President/CEO: Dr. Richard J. Cook
Registrar: Dr. Benjamin D. Haytock
Admissions: Jennifer Winge
Financial Aid: Robin Szitas
Type: Four-Year College **Sex:** Coed **Scores:** 100% SAT V 400+; 100% SAT M 400+; 29% ACT 18-23; 59% ACT 24-29 **% Accepted:** 62 **Admission Plans:** Early Admission; Early Decision Plan; Deferred Admission **Application Deadline:** February 15 **Application Fee:** $35.00 **H.S. Requirements:** High school diploma required; GED accepted **Costs Per Year:** Application fee: $35. Comprehensive fee: $35,300 includes full-time tuition ($28,000), mandatory fees ($300), and college room and board ($7000). College room only: $3600. Part-time tuition: $1167 per credit hour. Part-time mandatory fees: $150 per term. **Scholarships:** Available **Calendar System:** Semester, Summer Session Not available **Enrollment:** FT 2,010, PT 43 **Faculty:** FT 135, PT 28 **Student-Faculty Ratio:** 14:1 **Exams:** SAT I or ACT **% Receiving Financial Aid:** 68 **% Residing in College-Owned, -Operated, or -Affiliated Housing:** 75 **Library Holdings:** 287,368 **Regional Accreditation:** Middle State Association of Colleges and Schools **Credit Hours For Degree:** 131 credit hours, Bachelors **Intercollegiate Athletics:** Baseball M; Basketball M & W; Cheerleading M & W; Cross-Country Running M & W; Equestrian Sports W; Fencing M & W; Field Hockey W; Football M; Golf M & W; Ice Hockey M; Lacrosse M & W; Rugby M & W; Skiing (Downhill) M & W; Soccer M & W; Softball W; Swimming and Diving M & W; Tennis M & W; Track and Field M & W; Ultimate Frisbee M & W; Volleyball M & W

ALLIED MEDICAL AND TECHNICAL CAREERS
166 Slocum St.
Forty Fort, PA 18704-2936
Tel: (717)288-8400
Fax: (717)287-7936
Web Site: http://www.alliedteched.com/ **Type:** Two-Year College **Sex:** Coed **Professional Accreditation:** ACCSCT

ALVERNIA COLLEGE
400 Saint Bernardine St.
Reading, PA 19607-1799
Tel: (610)796-8200
Admissions: (610)796-3005
Fax: (610)796-8336
Web Site: http://www.alvernia.edu/
President/CEO: Dr. Laurence W. Mazzeno, III
Registrar: Beth Stein
Admissions: John Diamond
Financial Aid: Lisa McMaster
Type: Comprehensive **Sex:** Coed **Affiliation:** Roman Catholic **Scores:** 88% SAT V 400+; 87% SAT M 400+; 55% ACT 18-23; 3% ACT 24-29 **% Accepted:** 76 **Admission Plans:** Deferred Admission **Application Deadline:** Rolling **Application Fee:** $25.00 **H.S. Requirements:** High school diploma required; GED accepted **Costs Per Year:** Application fee: $25. Comprehensive fee: $26,388 includes full-time tuition ($18,900), mandatory fees ($189),

and college room and board ($7299). College room only: $3477. Full-time tuition and fees vary according to class time and reciprocity agreements. Room and board charges vary according to board plan and housing facility. Part-time tuition: $555 per credit. Part-time tuition varies according to class time and course load. **Scholarships:** Available **Calendar System:** Semester, Summer Session Available **Enrollment:** FT 1,515, PT 481, Grad 739 **Faculty:** FT 74, PT 161 **Student-Faculty Ratio:** 13:1 **Exams:** SAT I or ACT **% Receiving Financial Aid:** 94 **% Residing in College-Owned, -Operated, or -Affiliated Housing:** 26 **Library Holdings:** 89,399 **Regional Accreditation:** Middle State Association of Colleges and Schools **Credit Hours For Degree:** 65 credits, Associates; 123 credits, Bachelors **ROTC:** Army **Professional Accreditation:** AACN, AOTA, ACBSP, CSWE, JRCEPAT, NLN **Intercollegiate Athletics:** Baseball M; Basketball M & W; Cross-Country Running M & W; Field Hockey W; Golf M; Lacrosse M & W; Soccer M & W; Softball W; Tennis M & W; Volleyball W

ANTONELLI INSTITUTE
300 Montgomery Ave.
Erdenheim, PA 19038
Tel: (215)836-2222
Free: 800-722-7871
Fax: (215)836-2794
Web Site: http://www.antonelli.edu/
President/CEO: Dr. Thomas D. Treacy
Admissions: Dr. Thomas D. Treacy
Financial Aid: Gene Awot
Type: Two-Year College **Sex:** Coed **% Accepted:** 65 **Admission Plans:** Open Admission; Deferred Admission **Application Deadline:** September 01 **Application Fee:** $25.00 **H.S. Requirements:** High school diploma required; GED accepted **Costs Per Year:** Application fee: $25. Tuition: $16,300 full-time, $545 per credit part-time. Mandatory fees: $25 full-time. College room only: $6200. **Scholarships:** Available **Calendar System:** Semester, Summer Session Not available **Enrollment:** FT 183, PT 6 **Faculty:** FT 14, PT 2 **Student-Faculty Ratio:** 13:1 **% Residing in College-Owned, -Operated, or -Affiliated Housing:** 40 **Library Holdings:** 4,000 **Credit Hours For Degree:** 60 credit hours, Associates **Professional Accreditation:** ACCSCT

ARCADIA UNIVERSITY
450 South Easton Rd.
Glenside, PA 19038-3295
Tel: (215)572-2900; 877-ARCADIA
Admissions: (215)572-2910
Fax: (215)572-4049
E-mail: admiss@arcadia.edu
Web Site: http://www.arcadia.edu/
President/CEO: Dr. Jerry M. Greiner
Registrar: Harold W. Stewart
Admissions: Dennis L. Nostrand
Financial Aid: Mark Lapreziosa
Type: Comprehensive **Sex:** Coed **Affiliation:** Presbyterian Church (U.S.A.) **Scores:** 99% SAT V 400+; 99% SAT M 400+; 38% ACT 18-23; 48% ACT 24-29 **% Accepted:** 79 **Admission Plans:** Early Admission; Early Decision Plan; Deferred Admission **Application Deadline:** Rolling **Application Fee:** $30.00 **H.S. Requirements:** High school diploma required; GED accepted **Costs Per Year:** Application fee: $30. Comprehensive fee: $35,650 includes full-time tuition ($25,650), mandatory fees ($340), and college room and board ($9660). Part-time tuition: $442 per credit. **Scholarships:** Available **Calendar System:** Semester, Summer Session Available **Enrollment:** FT 1,748, PT 207, Grad 1,448 **Faculty:** FT 114, PT 215 **Student-Faculty Ratio:** 12:1 **Exams:** SAT I or ACT **% Receiving Financial Aid:** 88 **% Residing in College-Owned, -Operated, or -Affiliated Housing:** 68 **Library Holdings:** 140,000 **Regional Accreditation:** Middle State Association of Colleges and Schools **Credit Hours For Degree:** 128 credits, Bachelors **ROTC:** Army **Professional Accreditation:** APTA, NASAD **Intercollegiate Athletics:** Baseball M; Basketball M & W; Cross-Country Running M & W; Equestrian Sports M & W; Field Hockey W; Golf M & W; Lacrosse W; Soccer M & W; Softball W; Swimming and Diving M & W; Tennis M & W; Volleyball W

THE ART INSTITUTE OF PHILADELPHIA
1622 Chestnut St.
Philadelphia, PA 19103-5198
Tel: (215)567-7080
Free: 800-275-2474
Admissions: (215)405-6777
E-mail: lmchugh@aii.edu
Web Site: http://www.aiph.artinstitutes.edu/
President/CEO: Frank Covaleskie
Registrar: Keith Hockenbury
Admissions: Larry McHugh
Financial Aid: Colleen Russo
Type: Two-Year College **Sex:** Coed **Affiliation:** Education Management Corporation **Scores:** 94% SAT V 400+; 94% SAT M 400+ **% Accepted:** 86 **Admission Plans:** Early Admission; Early Decision Plan; Deferred Admission **Application Deadline:** Rolling **Application Fee:** $50.00 **H.S. Requirements:** High school diploma required; GED accepted **Costs Per Year:** Application fee: $50. Tuition: $401 per quarter hour part-time. College room only: $2334. **Scholarships:** Available **Calendar System:** Quarter, Summer Session Available **Enrollment:** FT 2,427, PT 947 **Faculty:** FT 79, PT 137 **Student-Faculty Ratio:** 22:1 **% Residing in College-Owned, -Operated, or -Affiliated Housing:** 27 **Library Holdings:** 25,000 **Credit Hours For Degree:** 99 credit hours, Associates; 180 credit hours, Bachelors **Professional Accreditation:** ACICS, ACF

THE ART INSTITUTE OF PITTSBURGH
420 Blvd. of the Allies
Pittsburgh, PA 15219
Tel: (412)263-6600
Free: 800-275-2470
Fax: (412)263-6667
Web Site: http://www.aip.artinstitutes.edu/
President/CEO: George L. Pry
Registrar: Diane Carney
Admissions: Newton I. Myvett
Financial Aid: Gayle J. Knight
Type: Four-Year College **Sex:** Coed **Affiliation:** Education Management Corporation **Scores:** 87% SAT V 400+; 83% SAT M 400+; 50% ACT 18-23 **Admission Plans:** Deferred Admission **Application Fee:** $50.00 **H.S. Requirements:** High school diploma required; GED accepted **Scholarships:** Available **Calendar System:** Quarter, Summer Session Available **Enrollment:** FT 2,590, PT 2,282 **Faculty:** FT 90, PT 46 **Student-Faculty Ratio:** 20:1 **Exams:** Other, SAT I or ACT **% Residing in College-Owned, -Operated, or -Affiliated Housing:** 30 **Library Holdings:** 6,997 **Regional Accreditation:** Middle State Association of Colleges and Schools **Credit Hours For Degree:** 105 credit hours, Associates; 180 credit hours, Bachelors **Professional Accreditation:** ACICS

BAPTIST BIBLE COLLEGE OF PENNSYLVANIA
538 Venard Rd.
Clarks Summit, PA 18411-1297
Tel: (570)586-2400
Free: 800-451-7664
Fax: (570)585-9400
E-mail: gamos@bbc.edu
Web Site: http://www.bbc.edu/
President/CEO: James E. Jeffery
Registrar: Allen Dreyer
Admissions: Glenn Amos
Financial Aid: Tom Pollock
Type: Comprehensive **Sex:** Coed **Affiliation:** Baptist **Scores:** 86% SAT V 400+; 83% SAT M 400+; 41% ACT 18-23; 28% ACT 24-29 **% Accepted:** 77 **Admission Plans:** Early Admission; Deferred Admission **Application Deadline:** August 15 **Application Fee:** $30.00 **H.S. Requirements:** High school diploma required; GED accepted **Costs Per Year:** Application fee: $30. Comprehensive fee: $19,580 includes full-time tuition ($12,960), mandatory fees ($1020), and college room and board ($5600). College room only: $2500. Part-time tuition: $540 per credit. Part-time mandatory fees: $34 per credit. **Scholarships:** Available **Calendar System:** Semester, Summer Session Available **Enrollment:** FT 673, PT 26, Grad 139 **Faculty:** FT 30, PT 2 **Student-Faculty Ratio:** 22:1 **Exams:** SAT I or ACT **% Residing in College-Owned, -Operated, or -Affiliated Housing:** 80 **Library Holdings:** 104,534 **Regional Accreditation:** Middle State Association of Colleges and Schools **Credit Hours For Degree:** 64 semester hours, Associates; 124 semester hours, Bachelors **ROTC:** Army **Professional Accreditation:** AABC **Intercollegiate Athletics:** Baseball M; Basketball M & W; Cheerleading W; Cross-Country Running M & W; Golf M; Soccer M & W; Softball W; Tennis W; Track and Field M & W; Volleyball M & W; Wrestling M

BEREAN INSTITUTE
1901 West Girard Ave.
Philadelphia, PA 19130-1599

Tel: (215)763-4833
Web Site: http://www.bereaninstitute.org/
President/CEO: Dr. Norman K. Spencer
Registrar: Mamie H. Brooks
Type: Two-Year College **Sex:** Coed **Admission Plans:** Open Admission; Deferred Admission **Application Fee:** $20.00 **H.S. Requirements:** High school diploma required; GED accepted **Calendar System:** Quarter, Summer Session Not available **Enrollment:** FT 171, PT 37 **Faculty:** FT 18, PT 8 **Student-Faculty Ratio:** 15:1 **Library Holdings:** 3,500 **Credit Hours For Degree:** 1575 hours, Associates **Professional Accreditation:** ACCSCT

BERKS TECHNICAL INSTITUTE
2205 Ridgewood Rd.
Wyomissing, PA 19610-1168
Tel: (610)372-1722
Free: 800-821-4662
Fax: (610)376-4684
E-mail: jvokes@berks.edu
Web Site: http://www.berkstech.com/
President/CEO: William Klettke
Admissions: Jean Vokes
Financial Aid: Shalounda Jones
Type: Two-Year College **Sex:** Coed **Affiliation:** Fore Front Education, Inc **Scores:** 100% SAT V 400+; 100% SAT M 400+ **Admission Plans:** Early Admission **Application Fee:** $50.00 **H.S. Requirements:** High school diploma required; GED accepted **Costs Per Year:** Application fee: $50. Tuition: $23,405 full-time. Mandatory fees: $300 full-time. **Scholarships:** Available **Calendar System:** Semester, Summer Session Not available **Faculty:** FT 42, PT 11 **Student-Faculty Ratio:** 12:1 **Exams:** Other, SAT I and SAT II or ACT **Library Holdings:** 450 **Professional Accreditation:** ACCSCT, AAMAE

BIDWELL TRAINING CENTER
1815 Metropolitan St.
Pittsburgh, PA 15233-2234
Tel: (412)323-4000
Fax: (412)321-2120
Web Site: http://www.bidwell-training.org/
President/CEO: Valerie Njie
Type: Two-Year College **Sex:** Coed **Professional Accreditation:** ACCSCT

BLOOMSBURG UNIVERSITY OF PENNSYLVANIA
400 East Second St.
Bloomsburg, PA 17815-1301
Tel: (570)389-4000
Admissions: (570)389-4316
Web Site: http://www.bloomu.edu/
President/CEO: Dr. Jessica Kozloff
Admissions: Christopher Keller
Financial Aid: Thomas M. Lyons
Type: Comprehensive **Sex:** Coed **Affiliation:** Pennsylvania State System of Higher Education **Scores:** 93.8% SAT V 400+; 94.7% SAT M 400+ **% Accepted:** 68 **Admission Plans:** Preferred Admission; Early Admission; Early Decision Plan; Deferred Admission **Application Deadline:** Rolling **Application Fee:** $30.00 **H.S. Requirements:** High school diploma required; GED accepted **Costs Per Year:** Application fee: $30. State resident tuition: $4906 full-time, $204 per credit part-time. Nonresident tuition: $12,266 full-time, $511 per credit part-time. Mandatory fees: $1320 full-time, $39 per credit part-time, $61. Full-time tuition and fees vary according to course load. Part-time tuition and fees vary according to course load. College room and board: $5376. College room only: $3126. Room and board charges vary according to board plan and housing facility. **Scholarships:** Available **Calendar System:** Semester, Summer Session Available **Enrollment:** FT 7,257, PT 526, Grad 787 **Faculty:** FT 358, PT 42 **Student-Faculty Ratio:** 21:1 **Exams:** SAT I or ACT **% Receiving Financial Aid:** 78 **% Residing in College-Owned, -Operated, or -Affiliated Housing:** 42 **Library Holdings:** 408,647 **Regional Accreditation:** Middle State Association of Colleges and Schools **Credit Hours For Degree:** 60 credits, Associates; 120 credits, Bachelors **ROTC:** Army, Air Force **Professional Accreditation:** AACSB, AACN, ASLHA, CSWE, NCATE **Intercollegiate Athletics:** Baseball M; Basketball M & W; Cheerleading M & W; Cross-Country Running M & W; Equestrian Sports M & W; Field Hockey W; Football M; Lacrosse W; Soccer M & W; Softball W; Swimming and Diving M & W; Tennis M & W; Track and Field M & W; Volleyball W; Wrestling M

BRADFORD SCHOOL
707 Grant St., Gulf Tower
Pittsburgh, PA 15219
Tel: (412)391-6710
Fax: (412)471-6714
E-mail: info@bradfordpittsburgh.edu
Web Site: http://www.bradfordpittsburgh.edu/
President/CEO: Vincent Graziano
Registrar: Linda De Falle
Admissions: Vincent S. Graziano
Type: Two-Year College **Scholarships:** Available **Professional Accreditation:** ACICS

BRADLEY ACADEMY FOR THE VISUAL ARTS
1409 Williams Rd.
York, PA 17402-9012
Tel: (717)755-2300
Free: 800-864-7725
Fax: (717)840-1951
E-mail: info@bradleyacademy.net
Web Site: http://www.bradleyacademy.net/
President/CEO: Loren H. Kroh
Registrar: Roxann Harris
Admissions: James Hannigan, Jr.
Financial Aid: Francine Stefany
Type: Two-Year College **Sex:** Coed **Affiliation:** Education Management Corporation **Scores:** 85% SAT V 400+; 84% SAT M 400+ **% Accepted:** 65 **Admission Plans:** Deferred Admission **Application Deadline:** Rolling **Application Fee:** $50.00 **H.S. Requirements:** High school diploma required; GED accepted **Costs Per Year:** Application fee: $50. Tuition: $15,840 full-time, $440 per credit part-time. **Scholarships:** Available **Calendar System:** Quarter, Summer Session Available **Enrollment:** FT 552, PT 44 **Faculty:** FT 15, PT 33 **Student-Faculty Ratio:** 15:1 **Exams:** SAT I or ACT **Library Holdings:** 1,900 **Regional Accreditation:** Middle State Association of Colleges and Schools **Credit Hours For Degree:** 72 credit hours, Associates **Professional Accreditation:** ACCSCT

BRYN ATHYN COLLEGE OF THE NEW CHURCH
PO Box 717
Bryn Athyn, PA 19009-0717
Tel: (267)502-2543
Admissions: (267)502-2511
Fax: (267)502-2658
Web Site: http://www.brynathyn.edu/
President/CEO: Rev. Prescott A. Rogers
Registrar: Dr. Charles H. Ebert
Admissions: Sean Lawing
Financial Aid: W. Lesley Alden
Type: Comprehensive **Sex:** Coed **Affiliation:** Swedenborgian; The Academy of the New Church **Scores:** 98% SAT V 400+; 94% SAT M 400+; 40% ACT 18-23; 60% ACT 24-29 **% Accepted:** 96 **Admission Plans:** Deferred Admission **Application Deadline:** July 01 **Application Fee:** $30.00 **H.S. Requirements:** High school diploma required; GED accepted **Costs Per Year:** Application fee: $30. Comprehensive fee: $15,688 includes full-time tuition ($8264), mandatory fees ($1850), and college room and board ($5574). Part-time tuition: $319 per credit. Part-time mandatory fees: $70 per credit. **Scholarships:** Available **Calendar System:** Trimester, Summer Session Not available **Enrollment:** FT 134, PT 8, Grad 5 **Faculty:** FT 20, PT 29 **Student-Faculty Ratio:** 7:1 **Exams:** SAT I or ACT **% Receiving Financial Aid:** 46 **% Residing in College-Owned, -Operated, or -Affiliated Housing:** 67 **Library Holdings:** 103,911 **Regional Accreditation:** Middle State Association of Colleges and Schools **Credit Hours For Degree:** 68 credits, Associates; 136 credits, Bachelors **Intercollegiate Athletics:** Badminton M & W; Basketball M; Ice Hockey M; Lacrosse M & W; Soccer M & W; Volleyball W

BRYN MAWR COLLEGE
101 North Merion Ave.
Bryn Mawr, PA 19010-2899
Tel: (610)526-5000
Free: 800-BMC-1885
Admissions: (610)526-5152

Fax: (610)526-7471
E-mail: admissions@brynmawr.edu
Web Site: http://www.brynmawr.edu/
President/CEO: Dr. Nancy J. Vickers
Registrar: Kristen O'Beirne
Admissions: Jennifer Rickard
Financial Aid: Ethel M. Desmarais
Type: University **Scores:** 100% SAT V 400+; 100% SAT M 400+; 8% ACT 18-23; 59% ACT 24-29 **% Accepted:** 46 **Admission Plans:** Early Admission; Early Decision Plan; Deferred Admission **Application Deadline:** January 15 **Application Fee:** $50.00 **H.S. Requirements:** High school diploma required; GED accepted **Costs Per Year:** Application fee: $50. Comprehensive fee: $42,780 includes full-time tuition ($32,230) and college room and board ($10,550). College room only: $6030. Part-time tuition: $3990 per course. **Scholarships:** Available **Calendar System:** Semester, Summer Session Available **Enrollment:** FT 1,307, PT 39, Grad 453 **Faculty:** FT 150, PT 35 **Student-Faculty Ratio:** 8:1 **Exams:** SAT I and SAT II or ACT **% Receiving Financial Aid:** 54 **% Residing in College-Owned, -Operated, or -Affiliated Housing:** 97 **Library Holdings:** 1,135,493 **Regional Accreditation:** Middle State Association of Colleges and Schools **Credit Hours For Degree:** 32 courses, Bachelors **ROTC:** Air Force **Professional Accreditation:** CSWE **Intercollegiate Athletics:** Badminton W; Basketball W; Crew W; Cross-Country Running W; Field Hockey W; Lacrosse W; Rugby W; Soccer W; Swimming and Diving W; Tennis W; Track and Field W; Volleyball W

BUCKNELL UNIVERSITY
Lewisburg, PA 17837
Tel: (570)577-2000
Admissions: (570)577-1101
Fax: (570)577-3760
E-mail: admissions@bucknell.edu
Web Site: http://www.bucknell.edu/
President/CEO: Dr. Brian C. Mitchell
Registrar: Robert E. Dunkerly
Admissions: Mark D. Davies
Financial Aid: Andrea Leithner
Type: Comprehensive **Sex:** Coed **Scores:** 100% SAT V 400+; 100% SAT M 400+; 4.5% ACT 18-23; 55.5% ACT 24-29 **% Accepted:** 34 **Admission Plans:** Preferred Admission; Early Decision Plan; Deferred Admission **Application Deadline:** January 01 **Application Fee:** $60.00 **H.S. Requirements:** High school diploma required; GED accepted **Costs Per Year:** Application fee: $60. Comprehensive fee: $43,368 includes full-time tuition ($35,802), mandatory fees ($200), and college room and board ($7366). College room only: $3972. Part-time tuition: $3930 per course. **Scholarships:** Available **Calendar System:** Semester, Summer Session Available **Enrollment:** FT 3,469, PT 36, Grad 143 **Faculty:** FT 299, PT 29 **Student-Faculty Ratio:** 11:1 **Exams:** SAT I or ACT, SAT II **% Receiving Financial Aid:** 48 **% Residing in College-Owned, -Operated, or -Affiliated Housing:** 88 **Library Holdings:** 793,936 **Regional Accreditation:** Middle State Association of Colleges and Schools **Credit Hours For Degree:** 32 courses, Bachelors **ROTC:** Army **Professional Accreditation:** ABET, NASM **Intercollegiate Athletics:** Baseball M; Basketball M & W; Cheerleading M & W; Crew M & W; Cross-Country Running M & W; Equestrian Sports M & W; Field Hockey W; Football M; Golf M & W; Ice Hockey M; Lacrosse M & W; Rugby M & W; Skiing (Downhill) M & W; Soccer M & W; Softball W; Swimming and Diving M & W; Tennis M & W; Track and Field M & W; Ultimate Frisbee M & W; Volleyball M & W; Water Polo M & W; Wrestling M

BUCKS COUNTY COMMUNITY COLLEGE
275 Swamp Rd.
Newtown, PA 18940-1525
Tel: (215)968-8000
Admissions: (215)968-8123
Fax: (215)968-8110
E-mail: kulicke@bucks.edu
Web Site: http://www.bucks.edu/
President/CEO: Dr. James J. Linksz
Registrar: Elizabeth Kulick
Admissions: Elizabeth Kulick
Financial Aid: Fran McKeown
Type: Two-Year College **Sex:** Coed **% Accepted:** 99 **Admission Plans:** Open Admission; Early Admission **Application Fee:** $30.00 **H.S. Requirements:** High school diploma required; GED accepted **Costs Per Year:** Application fee: $30. Area resident tuition: $2760 full-time, $92 per credit part-time. State resident tuition: $5520 full-time, $184 per credit part-time. Nonresident tuition: $8280 full-time, $276 per credit part-time. Mandatory fees: $584 full-time. **Scholarships:** Available **Calendar System:** Semester, Summer Session Available **Enrollment:** FT 3,990, PT 5,606 **Faculty:** FT 144, PT 430 **Student-Faculty Ratio:** 23:1 **Library Holdings:** 155,779 **Regional Accreditation:** Middle State Association of Colleges and Schools **Credit Hours For Degree:** 60 credits, Associates **Professional Accreditation:** AAMAE, ACBSP, NASAD, NASM, NLN **Intercollegiate Athletics:** Baseball M; Basketball M; Equestrian Sports M & W; Golf M & W; Soccer M & W; Tennis M & W; Volleyball W

BUSINESS INSTITUTE OF PENNSYLVANIA (MEADVILLE)
628 Arch St., Ste. B105
Meadville, PA 16335
Tel: (814)724-0700
Fax: (814)724-2777
Web Site: http://www.biop.edu/
President/CEO: Patricia McMahon
Admissions: Cheryl Mever
Type: Two-Year College **Sex:** Coed **% Accepted:** 82 **Application Fee:** $50.00 **Costs Per Year:** Application fee: $50. Tuition: $7500 full-time, $250 per credit part-time. Mandatory fees: $650 full-time. **Calendar System:** Quarter **Enrollment:** FT 68 **Faculty:** FT 3, PT 3 **Student-Faculty Ratio:** 17:1 **Professional Accreditation:** ACICS

BUSINESS INSTITUTE OF PENNSYLVANIA (SHARON)
335 Boyd Dr.
Sharon, PA 16146
Tel: (724)983-0700
Free: 800-289-2069
Fax: (724)983-8355
Web Site: http://www.biop.edu/
President/CEO: Richard McMahon
Registrar: Richard McMahon
Admissions: Shannon P. McNamara
Financial Aid: Shawn O'Neill
Type: Two-Year College **Sex:** Coed **H.S. Requirements:** High school diploma required; GED accepted **Costs Per Year:** Tuition: $7500 full-time, $250 per credit part-time. Mandatory fees: $600 full-time. **Scholarships:** Available **Calendar System:** Quarter **Enrollment:** FT 98, PT 8 **Faculty:** FT 5, PT 4 **Student-Faculty Ratio:** 16:1 **Exams:** ACT **Professional Accreditation:** ACICS

BUTLER COUNTY COMMUNITY COLLEGE
College Dr., PO Box 1203
Butler, PA 16003-1203
Tel: (724)287-8711; 888-826-2829
Fax: (724)285-6047
E-mail: pattie.bajoszik@bc3.edu
Web Site: http://www.bc3.edu/
President/CEO: Dr. Cynthia E. Azari
Registrar: Ruth Scott
Admissions: Patricia Bajuszik
Financial Aid: Jean Walker
Type: Two-Year College **Sex:** Coed **Admission Plans:** Open Admission; Early Admission; Deferred Admission **Application Deadline:** August 15 **Application Fee:** $25.00 **H.S. Requirements:** High school diploma required; GED accepted **Costs Per Year:** Application fee: $25. Area resident tuition: $2130 full-time, $71 per credit part-time. State resident tuition: $4260 full-time, $142 per credit part-time. Nonresident tuition: $6390 full-time, $213 per credit part-time. Mandatory fees: $510 full-time, $17 per credit part-time. **Scholarships:** Available **Calendar System:** Semester, Summer Session Available **Enrollment:** FT 1,987, PT 1,822 **Faculty:** FT 64, PT 241 **Student-Faculty Ratio:** 20:1 **Library Holdings:** 70,000 **Regional Accreditation:** Middle State Association of Colleges and Schools **Credit Hours For Degree:** 63 credits, Associates **Professional Accreditation:** APTA, ACBSP, NAIT, NLN **Intercollegiate Athletics:** Baseball M; Basketball M; Golf M & W; Softball W; Volleyball W

CABRINI COLLEGE
610 King of Prussia Rd.
Radnor, PA 19087-3698
Tel: (610)902-8100
Free: 800-848-1003
Admissions: (610)902-8552

Fax: (610)902-8309
E-mail: admit@cabrini.edu
Web Site: http://www.cabrini.edu/
President/CEO: Dr. Antoinette Iadarola
Registrar: Phyllis Bean
Admissions: Mark Osborn
Financial Aid: Mike Colahan
Type: Comprehensive **Sex:** Coed **Affiliation:** Roman Catholic **Scores:** 96.22% SAT V 400+; 92.44% SAT M 400+ **% Accepted:** 87 **Admission Plans:** Early Admission; Deferred Admission **Application Deadline:** Rolling **Application Fee:** $35.00 **H.S. Requirements:** High school diploma required; GED accepted. For transfer students with at least 30 credits: High school diploma or equivalent not required **Costs Per Year:** Application fee: $35. Comprehensive fee: $33,340 includes full-time tuition ($23,200), mandatory fees ($800), and college room and board ($9340). Full-time tuition and fees vary according to location. Room and board charges vary according to board plan and housing facility. Part-time tuition: $395 per credit hour. Part-time mandatory fees: $45 per term. Part-time tuition and fees vary according to course load. **Scholarships:** Available **Calendar System:** Semester, Summer Session Available **Enrollment:** FT 1,550, PT 189, Grad 579 **Faculty:** FT 65, PT 172 **Student-Faculty Ratio:** 15:1 **Exams:** SAT I or ACT **% Receiving Financial Aid:** 73 **% Residing in College-Owned, -Operated, or -Affiliated Housing:** 61 **Library Holdings:** 82,865 **Regional Accreditation:** Middle State Association of Colleges and Schools **Credit Hours For Degree:** 123 credits, Bachelors **ROTC:** Army **Professional Accreditation:** CSWE **Intercollegiate Athletics:** Basketball M & W; Cross-Country Running M & W; Field Hockey W; Golf M; Lacrosse M & W; Soccer M & W; Softball W; Swimming and Diving W; Tennis M & W; Track and Field M & W; Volleyball W

CALIFORNIA UNIVERSITY OF PENNSYLVANIA
250 University Ave.
California, PA 15419-1394
Tel: (724)938-4000
Admissions: (724)938-4404
Fax: (724)938-4138
E-mail: inquiry@cup.edu
Web Site: http://www.cup.edu/
President/CEO: Dr. Angelo Armenti, Jr.
Registrar: Dr. Rose Reinhart
Admissions: William A. Edmonds
Financial Aid: Robert Thorn
Type: Comprehensive **Sex:** Coed **Affiliation:** Pennsylvania State System of Higher Education **Scores:** 93% SAT V 400+; 91% SAT M 400+ **% Accepted:** 74 **Admission Plans:** Early Admission; Deferred Admission **Application Deadline:** August 15 **Application Fee:** $25.00 **H.S. Requirements:** High school diploma required; GED accepted **Costs Per Year:** Application fee: $25. State resident tuition: $4906 full-time, $204 per credit part-time. Nonresident tuition: $7306 full-time, $307 per credit part-time. Mandatory fees: $1585 full-time, $217 per credit part-time. Full-time tuition and fees vary according to location. Part-time tuition and fees vary according to location. College room and board: $7788. College room only: $5140. Room and board charges vary according to board plan. **Scholarships:** Available **Calendar System:** Semester, Summer Session Available **Enrollment:** FT 5,273, PT 670, Grad 1,241 **Faculty:** FT 289, PT 95 **Student-Faculty Ratio:** 20:1 **Exams:** ACT, SAT I, SAT II **% Residing in College-Owned, -Operated, or -Affiliated Housing:** 25 **Library Holdings:** 437,160 **Regional Accreditation:** Middle State Association of Colleges and Schools **Credit Hours For Degree:** 60 credits, Associates; 120 credits, Bachelors **ROTC:** Army **Professional Accreditation:** AACN, APTA, ASLHA, CSWE, JRCEPAT, NCATE, NLN **Intercollegiate Athletics:** Baseball M; Basketball M & W; Cheerleading M & W; Cross-Country Running M & W; Fencing M & W; Football M; Golf M & W; Soccer M & W; Softball W; Swimming and Diving W; Tennis W; Track and Field M & W; Volleyball M & W

CAMBRIA-ROWE BUSINESS COLLEGE (INDIANA)
422 South 13th St.
Indiana, PA 15701
Tel: (724)463-0222
Fax: (724)463-7246
E-mail: rallen@crbc.net
Web Site: http://www.crbc.net/
President/CEO: Jeffrey Allen
Admissions: Amanda Artim
Type: Two-Year College **Sex:** Coed **Calendar System:** Quarter **Enrollment:** FT 111, PT 7 **Faculty:** FT 8, PT 0 **Student-Faculty Ratio:** 14:1 **Professional Accreditation:** ACICS

CAMBRIA-ROWE BUSINESS COLLEGE (JOHNSTOWN)
221 Central Ave.
Johnstown, PA 15902-2494
Tel: (814)536-5168
Fax: (814)536-5160
Web Site: http://www.crbc.net/
President/CEO: William Coward
Admissions: Amanda C. Artim
Financial Aid: Judy Miller
Type: Two-Year College **Sex:** Coed **Admission Plans:** Early Admission **Application Deadline:** Rolling **Application Fee:** $15.00 **H.S. Requirements:** High school diploma required; GED accepted **Costs Per Year:** Application fee: $15. Tuition: $15,600 full-time, $220 per credit part-time. Mandatory fees: $1875 full-time, $300 per term part-time. **Scholarships:** Available **Calendar System:** Quarter, Summer Session Available **Enrollment:** FT 230 **Faculty:** FT 11, PT 0 **Student-Faculty Ratio:** 20:1 **Credit Hours For Degree:** 90 quarter credits, Associates **Professional Accreditation:** ACICS

CAREER TRAINING ACADEMY (MONROEVILLE)
105 Mall Blvd., Ste. 300 West
Expo Mart
Monroeville, PA 15146
Tel: (412)372-3900
Fax: (412)373-4262
Web Site: http://www.careerta.com/ **Type:** Two-Year College **Sex:** Coed **Calendar System:** Quarter **Professional Accreditation:** ACCSCT, AAMAE

CAREER TRAINING ACADEMY (NEW KENSINGTON)
950 Fifth Ave.
New Kensington, PA 15068-6301
Tel: (724)337-1000
Fax: (724)335-7140
E-mail: admissions@careeta.edu
Web Site: http://www.careerta.com/
Admissions: Tyna Pitignano
Type: Two-Year College **Sex:** Coed **% Accepted:** 85 **Application Deadline:** Rolling **Application Fee:** $30.00 **Costs Per Year:** Application fee: $30. Tuition: $7000 full-time. **Calendar System:** Quarter **Enrollment:** FT 337 **Faculty:** FT 14, PT 8 **Student-Faculty Ratio:** 20:1 **Professional Accreditation:** ACCSCT, AAMAE

CAREER TRAINING ACADEMY (PITTSBURGH)
1500 Northway Mall, Ste. 200
Pittsburgh, PA 15237
Tel: (412)367-4000
Web Site: http://www.careerta.com/
President/CEO: Anna Bartolini
Type: Two-Year College **Sex:** Coed **Calendar System:** Quarter **Professional Accreditation:** ACCSCT

CARLOW UNIVERSITY
3333 Fifth Ave.
Pittsburgh, PA 15213-3165
Tel: (412)578-6005
Free: 800-333-CARLOW
Admissions: (412)578-6059
Fax: (412)578-6668
E-mail: admissions@carlow.edu
Web Site: http://www.carlow.edu/
President/CEO: Dr. Grace Ann Geibel, RSM
Registrar: Kathleen Larkin, PhD
Admissions: Christine Bell
Financial Aid: Natalie Wilson
Type: Comprehensive **Sex:** Coed **Affiliation:** Roman Catholic **Scores:** 97% SAT V 400+; 91% SAT M 400+; 55% ACT 18-23; 29% ACT 24-29 **% Accepted:** 64 **Admission Plans:** Early Admission; Early Action; Deferred Admission **Application Deadline:** April 01 **Application Fee:** $20.00 **H.S. Requirements:** High school diploma required; GED accepted **Costs Per Year:** Application fee: $20. Comprehensive fee: $25,787 includes full-time tuition ($17,760), mandatory fees ($738), and college room and board

($7289). College room only: $3720. Part-time tuition: $583 per credit. **Scholarships:** Available **Calendar System:** Semester, Summer Session Available **Enrollment:** FT 1,167, PT 456, Grad 500 **Faculty:** FT 79, PT 154 **Student-Faculty Ratio:** 12:1 **Exams:** SAT I or ACT **% Residing in College-Owned, -Operated, or -Affiliated Housing:** 21 **Library Holdings:** 81,532 **Regional Accreditation:** Middle State Association of Colleges and Schools **Credit Hours For Degree:** 120 credits, Bachelors **ROTC:** Army, Navy, Air Force **Professional Accreditation:** AACN, CSWE **Intercollegiate Athletics:** Basketball W; Crew W; Soccer W; Softball W; Tennis W; Volleyball W

CARNEGIE MELLON UNIVERSITY
5000 Forbes Ave.
Pittsburgh, PA 15213-3891
Tel: (412)268-2000
Admissions: (412)268-2082
Fax: (412)268-7838
E-mail: undergraduate-admissions@andrew.cmu.edu
Web Site: http://www.cmu.edu/
President/CEO: Dr. Jared L. Cohon
Registrar: John Papinchack
Admissions: Michael Steidel
Type: University **Sex:** Coed **Scores:** 100% SAT V 400+; 100% SAT M 400+; 4% ACT 18-23; 42% ACT 24-29 **% Accepted:** 39 **Admission Plans:** Early Admission; Early Decision Plan; Deferred Admission **Application Deadline:** January 01 **Application Fee:** $60.00 **H.S. Requirements:** High school diploma required; GED accepted **Costs Per Year:** Application fee: $60. Comprehensive fee: $43,858 includes full-time tuition ($34,180), mandatory fees ($398), and college room and board ($9280). College room only: $5440. Part-time tuition: $475 per unit. Part-time mandatory fees: $199 per term. **Scholarships:** Available **Calendar System:** Semester, Summer Session Available **Enrollment:** FT 5,384, PT 239, Grad 4,394 **Faculty:** FT 822, PT 173 **Student-Faculty Ratio:** 10:1 **Exams:** SAT I or ACT, SAT II **% Receiving Financial Aid:** 50 **% Residing in College-Owned, -Operated, or -Affiliated Housing:** 84 **Library Holdings:** 1,042,080 **Regional Accreditation:** Middle State Association of Colleges and Schools **Credit Hours For Degree:** 360 units, Bachelors **ROTC:** Army, Navy, Air Force **Professional Accreditation:** AACSB, ABET, NASAD, NASM, NASPAA **Intercollegiate Athletics:** Badminton M & W; Baseball M; Basketball M & W; Cheerleading M & W; Crew M & W; Cross-Country Running M & W; Fencing M & W; Football M; Golf M; Ice Hockey M & W; Lacrosse M & W; Rugby M & W; Soccer M & W; Softball W; Squash M & W; Swimming and Diving M & W; Tennis M & W; Track and Field M & W; Ultimate Frisbee M & W; Volleyball M & W; Water Polo M & W

CEDAR CREST COLLEGE
100 College Dr.
Allentown, PA 18104-6196
Tel: (610)437-4471
Free: 800-360-1222
Admissions: (610)740-3780
Fax: (610)606-4647
E-mail: cccadmis@cedarcrest.edu
Web Site: http://www.cedarcrest.edu/
President/CEO: Dr. Dorothy Gulbenkian Blaney
Registrar: Janet Baker
Admissions: Judith A. Neyhart
Financial Aid: Lorianne Williams
Type: Comprehensive **Sex:** Women **Affiliation:** United Church of Christ **Scores:** 98% SAT V 400+; 97% SAT M 400+; 30% ACT 18-23; 50% ACT 24-29 **Admission Plans:** Early Admission; Deferred Admission **Application Fee:** $30.00 **H.S. Requirements:** High school diploma required; GED accepted **Costs Per Year:** Application fee: $30. Comprehensive fee: $30,965 includes full-time tuition ($22,712), mandatory fees ($300), and college room and board ($7953). Full-time tuition and fees vary according to course load. Room and board charges vary according to board plan. **Scholarships:** Available **Calendar System:** Semester, Summer Session Available **Enrollment:** FT 887, PT 897, Grad 72 **Faculty:** FT 75, PT 70 **Student-Faculty Ratio:** 11:1 **Exams:** SAT I or ACT **% Receiving Financial Aid:** 88 **% Residing in College-Owned, -Operated, or -Affiliated Housing:** 80 **Library Holdings:** 133,763 **Regional Accreditation:** Middle State Association of Colleges and Schools **Credit Hours For Degree:** 69 credit hours, Associates; 120 credit hours, Bachelors **ROTC:** Army **Professional Accreditation:** CSWE, JRCNMT, NLN **Intercollegiate Athletics:** Basketball W; Cross-Country Running W; Equestrian Sports W; Field Hockey W; Lacrosse W; Soccer W; Softball W; Tennis W; Track and Field W; Volleyball W

CENTER FOR ADVANCED MANUFACTURING & TECHNOLOGY
5451 Merwin Ln.
Erie, PA 16510
Tel: (814)452-1122; 888-834-4226
Admissions: (814)897-0391
Fax: (814)452-1171
E-mail: lpeszel@gocamtech.com
Web Site: http://www.gocamtech.com/
President/CEO: Dr. Jerry B. Covert
Admissions: Lisa Peszel
Type: Two-Year College **Sex:** Coed **Calendar System:** Semester **Regional Accreditation:** Middle State Association of Colleges and Schools **Professional Accreditation:** COE

CENTRAL PENNSYLVANIA COLLEGE
College Hill & Valley Roads
Summerdale, PA 17093-0309
Tel: (717)732-0702
Free: 800-759-2727
Admissions: (717)728-2213
Fax: (717)732-5254
E-mail: admissions@centralpenn.edu
Web Site: http://www.centralpenn.edu/
President/CEO: Todd Milano
Registrar: Karen A. Weikel
Admissions: Katie Bogouic
Financial Aid: Kathy Shephard
Type: Four-Year College **Sex:** Coed **% Accepted:** 42 **Admission Plans:** Open Admission **Application Deadline:** September 20 **Application Fee:** $0.00 **H.S. Requirements:** High school diploma required; GED accepted **Costs Per Year:** Application fee: $0. Comprehensive fee: $17,670 includes full-time tuition ($10,980), mandatory fees ($630), and college room and board ($6060). College room only: $4725. Full-time tuition and fees vary according to course load and program. Room and board charges vary according to board plan and housing facility. Part-time tuition: $305 per credit hour. Part-time mandatory fees: $210 per term. Part-time tuition and fees vary according to course load and program. **Scholarships:** Available **Calendar System:** Trimester, Summer Session Available **Enrollment:** FT 701, PT 280 **Faculty:** FT 28, PT 81 **Student-Faculty Ratio:** 16:1 **% Residing in College-Owned, -Operated, or -Affiliated Housing:** 40 **Library Holdings:** 7,923 **Regional Accreditation:** Middle State Association of Colleges and Schools **Credit Hours For Degree:** 75 credits, Associates; 125 credits, Bachelors **Professional Accreditation:** AAMAE, APTA **Intercollegiate Athletics:** Basketball M & W; Bowling M & W; Golf M & W; Tennis M & W; Volleyball M & W

CHATHAM COLLEGE
Woodland Rd.
Pittsburgh, PA 15232-2826
Tel: (412)365-1100
Free: 800-837-1290
Fax: (412)365-1609
E-mail: mpoll@chatham.edu
Web Site: http://www.chatham.edu/
President/CEO: Dr. Esther L. Barazzone
Registrar: Janet Becker
Admissions: Michael Poll
Financial Aid: Jennifer A. Burns
Type: Comprehensive **Scores:** 97% SAT V 400+; 94% SAT M 400+; 33% ACT 18-23; 30% ACT 24-29 **% Accepted:** 61 **Admission Plans:** Early Admission; Deferred Admission **Application Deadline:** Rolling **Application Fee:** $35.00 **H.S. Requirements:** High school diploma required; GED accepted **Costs Per Year:** Application fee: $35. Comprehensive fee: $31,765 includes full-time tuition ($24,014), mandatory fees ($165), and college room and board ($7586). College room only: $3880. **Scholarships:** Available **Calendar System:** Miscellaneous, Summer Session Available **Enrollment:** FT 432, PT 362, Grad 646 **Faculty:** FT 70, PT 5 **Student-Faculty Ratio:** 13:1 **Exams:** SAT I or ACT **% Receiving Financial Aid:** 91 **% Residing in College-Owned, -Operated, or -Affiliated Housing:** 60 **Library Holdings:** 95,480 **Regional Accreditation:** Middle State Association of Colleges and Schools **Credit Hours For Degree:** 120 credit hours, Bachelors **ROTC:** Army, Air Force **Professional Accreditation:** AOTA, APTA, CSWE **Intercol-**

legiate Athletics: Basketball W; Crew W; Ice Hockey W; Soccer W; Softball W; Swimming and Diving W; Tennis W; Volleyball W

CHESTNUT HILL COLLEGE
9601 Germantown Ave.
Philadelphia, PA 19118-2693
Tel: (215)248-7000
Free: 800-248-0052
Admissions: (215)248-7004
Fax: (215)248-7056
E-mail: kingj@chc.edu
Web Site: http://www.chc.edu/
President/CEO: Carol Jean Vale, PhD
Registrar: Sr. Ann McAdams, SSJ
Admissions: Jodie King
Financial Aid: Jeanne Cavalieri-Grover, BS
Type: Comprehensive **Sex:** Coed **Affiliation:** Roman Catholic **Scores:** 94.5% SAT V 400+; 87% SAT M 400+; 43% ACT 18-23; 36% ACT 24-29 **% Accepted:** 73 **Admission Plans:** Open Admission; Early Admission; Deferred Admission **Application Deadline:** Rolling **Application Fee:** $35.00 **H.S. Requirements:** High school diploma required; GED accepted **Costs Per Year:** Application fee: $35. Comprehensive fee: $30,700 includes full-time tuition ($22,750) and college room and board ($7950). Part-time tuition: $500 per credit. **Scholarships:** Available **Calendar System:** Semester, Summer Session Available **Enrollment:** FT 802, PT 237, Grad 680 **Faculty:** FT 72, PT 183 **Student-Faculty Ratio:** 9:1 **Exams:** SAT I or ACT **% Receiving Financial Aid:** 79 **% Residing in College-Owned, -Operated, or -Affiliated Housing:** 67 **Library Holdings:** 128,489 **Regional Accreditation:** Middle State Association of Colleges and Schools **Credit Hours For Degree:** 60 semester hours, Associates; 120 semester hours, Bachelors **Professional Accreditation:** MACTE **Intercollegiate Athletics:** Basketball M & W; Cross-Country Running M & W; Golf M & W; Lacrosse W; Soccer M & W; Softball W; Tennis W; Volleyball W

CHEYNEY UNIVERSITY OF PENNSYLVANIA
1837 University Circle, PO Box 200
Cheyney, PA 19319-0200
Tel: (610)399-2000
Free: 800-CHE-YNEY
Admissions: (610)399-2275
Fax: (610)399-2099
E-mail: gstemley@cheyney.edu
Web Site: http://www.cheyney.edu/
President/CEO: Dr. Wallace Arnold
Registrar: Brenda Shields
Admissions: Gemma Stemley
Financial Aid: James Brown
Type: Comprehensive **Sex:** Coed **Affiliation:** Pennsylvania State System of Higher Education **Scores:** 48% SAT V 400+; 44% SAT M 400+; 19% ACT 18-23 **% Accepted:** 56 **Admission Plans:** Preferred Admission **Application Deadline:** Rolling **Application Fee:** $20.00 **H.S. Requirements:** High school diploma required; GED accepted **Costs Per Year:** Application fee: $20. State resident tuition: $4906 full-time, $204 per credit part-time. Nonresident tuition: $12,266 full-time, $511 per credit part-time. Mandatory fees: $912 full-time. Full-time tuition and fees vary according to reciprocity agreements. Part-time tuition varies according to reciprocity agreements. College room and board: $5679. College room only: $3106. Room and board charges vary according to board plan. **Scholarships:** Available **Calendar System:** 4-1-4, Summer Session Available **Enrollment:** FT 1,295, PT 106, Grad 159 **Faculty:** FT 103, PT 24 **Student-Faculty Ratio:** 14:1 **Exams:** SAT I or ACT, SAT II **% Receiving Financial Aid:** 94 **% Residing in College-Owned, -Operated, or -Affiliated Housing:** 76 **Library Holdings:** 361,539 **Regional Accreditation:** Middle State Association of Colleges and Schools **Credit Hours For Degree:** 120 credit hours, Bachelors **ROTC:** Army, Air Force **Professional Accreditation:** NCATE **Intercollegiate Athletics:** Basketball M & W; Bowling W; Cross-Country Running M & W; Football M; Track and Field M & W; Volleyball W

CHI INSTITUTE
520 St. Rd.
Southampton, PA 18966-3747
Tel: (215)357-5100
Free: 800-336-7696
Web Site: http://www.chitraining.com/
President/CEO: Dale Anspach
Admissions: Michael Herbert
Financial Aid: Nicole Gilbert
Type: Two-Year College **Sex:** Coed **Affiliation:** Quest Education **Admission Plans:** Deferred Admission **Application Fee:** $0.00 **H.S. Requirements:** High school diploma required; GED accepted **Scholarships:** Available **Calendar System:** Quarter, Summer Session Not available **Enrollment:** FT 400, PT 300 **Faculty:** FT 45, PT 20 **Student-Faculty Ratio:** 20:1 **Library Holdings:** 2,500 **Credit Hours For Degree:** 1800 hours, Associates **Professional Accreditation:** ACCSCT

CHI INSTITUTE, RETS CAMPUS
Lawrence Park Shopping Center
Rt. 320 & Lawrence Rd.
Broomall, PA 19008
Tel: (610)353-7630
Web Site: http://www.chitraining.com/
President/CEO: Robert Milot
Registrar: Barbara Ryder
Admissions: Stuart Kahn
Financial Aid: Toni Hinegardner
Type: Two-Year College **Sex:** Coed **Admission Plans:** Deferred Admission **Application Fee:** $100.00 **H.S. Requirements:** High school diploma required; GED accepted **Scholarships:** Available **Calendar System:** Quarter, Summer Session Not available **Professional Accreditation:** ACCSCT

CLARION UNIVERSITY OF PENNSYLVANIA
890 Wood St.
Clarion, PA 16214
Tel: (814)393-2000
Free: 800-672-7171
Admissions: (814)393-2306
Fax: (814)393-2030
E-mail: mdunlap@clarion.edu
Web Site: http://www.clarion.edu/
President/CEO: Dr. Joseph Grunenwald
Registrar: J. Douglas Bills
Admissions: Merrilyn Dunlap
Financial Aid: Kenneth Grugel
Type: Comprehensive **Sex:** Coed **Affiliation:** Pennsylvania State System of Higher Education **Scores:** 83% SAT V 400+; 82% SAT M 400+ **% Accepted:** 78 **Admission Plans:** Deferred Admission **Application Deadline:** Rolling **Application Fee:** $30.00 **H.S. Requirements:** High school diploma required; GED accepted **Costs Per Year:** Application fee: $30. State resident tuition: $4906 full-time, $204 per credit part-time. Nonresident tuition: $9814 full-time, $409 per credit part-time. Mandatory fees: $1561 full-time, $117 per credit part-time. College room and board: $5246. College room only: $3564. Room and board charges vary according to board plan. **Scholarships:** Available **Calendar System:** Semester, Summer Session Available **Enrollment:** FT 5,069, PT 675, Grad 594 **Faculty:** FT 254, PT 50 **Student-Faculty Ratio:** 19:1 **Exams:** SAT I or ACT **% Receiving Financial Aid:** 69 **% Residing in College-Owned, -Operated, or -Affiliated Housing:** 34 **Library Holdings:** 429,800 **Regional Accreditation:** Middle State Association of Colleges and Schools **Credit Hours For Degree:** 62 credits, Associates; 128 credits, Bachelors **Professional Accreditation:** AACSB, ALA, ASLHA, NASAD, NASM, NCATE, NLN **Intercollegiate Athletics:** Baseball M; Basketball M & W; Cross-Country Running M & W; Football M; Golf M; Softball W; Swimming and Diving M & W; Tennis W; Track and Field M & W; Volleyball W; Wrestling M

COLLEGE MISERICORDIA
301 Lake St.
Dallas, PA 18612-1098
Tel: (570)674-6400; (866)262-6363
Admissions: (570)675-4449
Fax: (570)675-2441
E-mail: jdessoye@misericordia.edu
Web Site: http://www.misericordia.edu/
President/CEO: Dr. Michael A. MacDowell
Registrar: Edward Lahart
Admissions: Jane Dessoye
Financial Aid: Jane Dessoye
Type: Comprehensive **Sex:** Coed **Affiliation:** Roman Catholic **Scores:** 94% SAT V 400+; 93% SAT M 400+; 90% ACT 18-23; 10% ACT 24-29 **% Accepted:** 81 **Admission Plans:** Early Admission; Deferred Admission **Ap-**

plication Deadline: Rolling **Application Fee:** $25.00 **H.S. Requirements:** High school diploma required; GED accepted **Costs Per Year:** Application fee: $25. Comprehensive fee: $27,950 includes full-time tuition ($18,700), mandatory fees ($1000), and college room and board ($8250). College room only: $4730. Room and board charges vary according to board plan and housing facility. Part-time tuition: $425 per credit. Part-time tuition varies according to location. **Scholarships:** Available **Calendar System:** Semester, Summer Session Available **Enrollment:** FT 1,428, PT 644, Grad 271 **Faculty:** FT 90, PT 168 **Student-Faculty Ratio:** 11:1 **Exams:** SAT I or ACT **% Receiving Financial Aid:** 81 **% Residing in College-Owned, -Operated, or -Affiliated Housing:** 39 **Library Holdings:** 90,000 **Regional Accreditation:** Middle State Association of Colleges and Schools **Credit Hours For Degree:** 120 credits, Bachelors **ROTC:** Army, Air Force **Professional Accreditation:** AACN, AOTA, APTA, ASLHA, CSWE, JRCERT, NLN **Intercollegiate Athletics:** Baseball M; Basketball M & W; Cheerleading W; Cross-Country Running M & W; Field Hockey W; Golf M; Lacrosse M & W; Soccer M & W; Softball W; Swimming and Diving M & W; Tennis W; Track and Field M & W; Volleyball W

COMMONWEALTH TECHNICAL INSTITUTE
727 Goucher St.
Johnstown, PA 15905-3092
Tel: (814)255-8200
E-mail: rhalza@state.pa.us
Web Site: http://www.hgac.org/
Admissions: Rebecca Halza
Type: Two-Year College **Sex:** Coed **% Accepted:** 89 **Admission Plans:** Open Admission; Preferred Admission **H.S. Requirements:** High school diploma required; GED accepted **Costs Per Year:** State resident tuition: $16,836 full-time, $323 per credit part-time. Mandatory fees: $75 full-time, $25 per term part-time. College room and board: $14,274. **Scholarships:** Available **Calendar System:** Trimester **Enrollment:** FT 275 **Faculty:** FT 32 **Student-Faculty Ratio:** 10:1 **Professional Accreditation:** ACCSCT

COMMUNITY COLLEGE OF ALLEGHENY COUNTY
800 Allegheny Ave.
Pittsburgh, PA 15233-1894
Tel: (412)323-2323
Web Site: http://www.ccac.edu/
President/CEO: Stewart Sutin
Registrar: Frances Dice
Type: Two-Year College **Sex:** Coed **% Accepted:** 85 **Admission Plans:** Open Admission; Deferred Admission **Application Deadline:** Rolling **Application Fee:** $0.00 **H.S. Requirements:** High school diploma or equivalent not required **Costs Per Year:** Application fee: $0. Area resident tuition: $2400 full-time, $80 per credit part-time. State resident tuition: $4800 full-time, $160 per credit part-time. Nonresident tuition: $7200 full-time, $240 per credit part-time. Mandatory fees: $295 full-time, $10.70 per credit part-time. **Scholarships:** Available **Calendar System:** Semester, Summer Session Available **Enrollment:** FT 7,580, PT 10,824 **Faculty:** FT 267, PT 1,364 **Student-Faculty Ratio:** 15:1 **Library Holdings:** 272,697 **Regional Accreditation:** Middle State Association of Colleges and Schools **Credit Hours For Degree:** 60 credits, Associates **Professional Accreditation:** ARCEST, AAMAE, AHIMA, AOTA, APTA, CARC, JRCEDMS, JRCERT, JRCNMT, NAACLS, NLN **Intercollegiate Athletics:** Baseball M; Basketball M & W; Bowling M & W; Golf M & W; Ice Hockey M; Softball W; Table Tennis M & W; Tennis M & W; Volleyball W

COMMUNITY COLLEGE OF BEAVER COUNTY
One Campus Dr.
Monaca, PA 15061-2588
Tel: (724)775-8561
Free: 800-335-0222
Fax: (724)728-7599
E-mail: mike.macon@ccbc.edu
Web Site: http://www.ccbc.edu/
President/CEO: Dr. Joe D. Forrester
Registrar: Daniel Slater
Admissions: Michael Macon
Financial Aid: Douglas Mahler
Type: Two-Year College **Sex:** Coed **Admission Plans:** Open Admission; Early Admission **Application Fee:** $25.00 **H.S. Requirements:** High school diploma or equivalent not required. For nursing, medical laboratory technology programs: High school diploma required; GED accepted **Costs Per Year:** Application fee: $25. Area resident tuition: $2400 full-time, $80 per credit part-time. State resident tuition: $4800 full-time, $160 per credit part-time. Nonresident tuition: $7200 full-time, $240 per credit part-time. Mandatory fees: $525 full-time, $17.50 per credit part-time. **Scholarships:** Available **Calendar System:** Semester, Summer Session Available **Faculty:** FT 48, PT 58 **Exams:** Other **Library Holdings:** 52,857 **Regional Accreditation:** Middle State Association of Colleges and Schools **Credit Hours For Degree:** 60 credits, Associates **Professional Accreditation:** NLN **Intercollegiate Athletics:** Baseball M; Basketball M; Softball W; Tennis M & W; Volleyball W

COMMUNITY COLLEGE OF PHILADELPHIA
1700 Spring Garden St.
Philadelphia, PA 19130-3991
Tel: (215)751-8010
Admissions: (215)751-8199
Web Site: http://www.ccp.edu/
President/CEO: Dr. Stephen M. Curtis
Registrar: Beatrice Jones
Admissions: Daivd Norris
Financial Aid: Kim Folkes
Type: Two-Year College **Sex:** Coed **Admission Plans:** Open Admission; Preferred Admission; Early Admission; Deferred Admission **Application Fee:** $20.00 **H.S. Requirements:** High school diploma required; GED accepted **Costs Per Year:** Application fee: $20. Area resident tuition: $104 per credit hour part-time. State resident tuition: $208 per credit hour part-time. Nonresident tuition: $312 per credit hour part-time. **Calendar System:** Semester, Summer Session Available **Faculty:** FT 397, PT 810 **Library Holdings:** 92,698 **Regional Accreditation:** Middle State Association of Colleges and Schools **Credit Hours For Degree:** 62 credit hours, Associates **Professional Accreditation:** AAMAE, ADA, AHIMA, CARC, JRCERT, NAACLS, NLN **Intercollegiate Athletics:** Baseball M; Basketball M & W; Cross-Country Running M & W; Soccer M; Softball W; Tennis M & W; Volleyball W

CONSOLIDATED SCHOOL OF BUSINESS (LANCASTER)
2124 Ambassador Circle
Lancaster, PA 17603
Tel: (717)394-6211
Admissions: (717)764-9550
Fax: (717)394-6213
E-mail: bobjr@csb.edu
Web Site: http://www.csb.edu/
President/CEO: Robert L. Safran, Sr.
Admissions: Robert L Safran, Jr.
Financial Aid: William Hoyt
Type: Two-Year College **Sex:** Coed **Admission Plans:** Open Admission **Application Deadline:** Rolling **Application Fee:** $25.00 **H.S. Requirements:** High school diploma required; GED accepted **Costs Per Year:** Application fee: $25. Tuition: $3500 full-time. **Scholarships:** Available **Calendar System:** Continuous, Summer Session Not available **Enrollment:** FT 173 **Faculty:** FT 17, PT 3 **Student-Faculty Ratio:** 15:1 **Credit Hours For Degree:** 72 credit hours, Associates **Professional Accreditation:** ACICS

CONSOLIDATED SCHOOL OF BUSINESS (YORK)
1605 Clugston Rd.
York, PA 17404
Tel: (717)764-9550
Free: 800-520-0691
Fax: (717)764-9469
E-mail: bobjr@csb.edu
Web Site: http://www.csb.edu/
President/CEO: Robert Safran, Sr.
Admissions: Robert L. Safran, Jr.
Type: Two-Year College **Sex:** Coed **Admission Plans:** Open Admission **Application Deadline:** Rolling **Application Fee:** $25.00 **H.S. Requirements:** High school diploma required; GED accepted **Scholarships:** Available **Calendar System:** Continuous, Summer Session Not available **Enrollment:** FT 176 **Faculty:** FT 18, PT 3 **Student-Faculty Ratio:** 15:1 **Credit Hours For Degree:** 72 credit hours, Associates **Professional Accreditation:** ACICS

THE CURTIS INSTITUTE OF MUSIC
1726 Locust St.
Philadelphia, PA 19103-6107
Tel: (215)893-5252

Admissions: (215)893-5262
Fax: (215)893-7900
Web Site: http://www.curtis.edu/
President/CEO: Gary Graffman
Registrar: Paul Bryan
Admissions: Christopher Hodges
Financial Aid: Janice Miller
Type: Comprehensive **Sex:** Coed **Scores:** 46.4% ACT 18-23; 14.5% ACT 24-29 **Admission Plans:** Early Admission **Application Fee:** $60.00 **H.S. Requirements:** High school diploma or equivalent not required **Scholarships:** Available **Calendar System:** Semester, Summer Session Not available **Enrollment:** FT 144, Grad 16 **Faculty:** PT 80 **Exams:** SAT I **% Receiving Financial Aid:** 91 **Library Holdings:** 70,000 **Regional Accreditation:** Middle State Association of Colleges and Schools **Credit Hours For Degree:** 124 semester hours, Bachelors **Professional Accreditation:** NASM

DEAN INSTITUTE OF TECHNOLOGY
1501 West Liberty Ave.
Pittsburgh, PA 15226-1103
Tel: (412)531-4433
Fax: (412)531-4435
Web Site: http://home.earthlink.net/~deantech/
President/CEO: James S. Dean
Registrar: Burt Wolfe
Admissions: Richard D. Ali
Financial Aid: June Ganser
Type: Two-Year College **Sex:** Coed **Admission Plans:** Open Admission; Early Admission; Deferred Admission **Application Fee:** $50.00 **H.S. Requirements:** High school diploma required; GED accepted **Scholarships:** Available **Calendar System:** Quarter, Summer Session Not available **Faculty:** FT 16, PT 6 **Student-Faculty Ratio:** 10:1 **Library Holdings:** 2,500 **Credit Hours For Degree:** 30 courses, Associates **Professional Accreditation:** ACCSCT

DELAWARE COUNTY COMMUNITY COLLEGE
901 South Media Line Rd.
Media, PA 19063-1094
Tel: (610)359-5000
Free: 800-543-0146
Admissions: (610)359-5333
E-mail: admiss@dccc.edu
Web Site: http://www.dccc.edu/
President/CEO: Dr. Jerome S. Parker
Registrar: Thomas W. Lugg
Admissions: Hope Lentine
Financial Aid: Raymond Toole
Type: Two-Year College **Sex:** Coed **Admission Plans:** Open Admission; Preferred Admission; Early Admission; Deferred Admission **Application Fee:** $20.00 **H.S. Requirements:** High school diploma required; GED accepted. For applicants 19 years of age and over who demonstrate equivalent life experience: High school diploma or equivalent not required **Costs Per Year:** Application fee: $20. Area resident tuition: $1968 full-time, $82 per credit part-time. State resident tuition: $3936 full-time, $164 per credit part-time. Nonresident tuition: $5904 full-time, $246 per credit part-time. Mandatory fees: $544 full-time, $21 per credit part-time, $20 per term part-time. **Scholarships:** Available **Calendar System:** Semester, Summer Session Available **Enrollment:** FT 4,263, PT 6,345 **Faculty:** FT 144, PT 521 **Student-Faculty Ratio:** 20:1 **Library Holdings:** 58,692 **Regional Accreditation:** Middle State Association of Colleges and Schools **Credit Hours For Degree:** 60 credit hours, Associates **Professional Accreditation:** ARCEST, AAMAE, CARC, NLN **Intercollegiate Athletics:** Baseball M; Basketball M & W; Golf M & W; Soccer M; Softball W; Tennis M & W; Volleyball W

DELAWARE VALLEY COLLEGE
700 East Butler Ave.
Doylestown, PA 18901-2697
Tel: (215)345-1500
Admissions: (215)489-2211
Fax: (215)345-5277
E-mail: admitme@devalcol.edu
Web Site: http://www.devalcol.edu/
President/CEO: Dr. Thomas C. Leamer
Admissions: Stephen Zenko
Financial Aid: Robert M. Sauer
Type: Comprehensive **Sex:** Coed **Scores:** 94.2% SAT V 400+; 96.5% SAT M 400+; 56.3% ACT 18-23; 37.5% ACT 24-29 **% Accepted:** 79 **Admission Plans:** Early Admission; Deferred Admission **Application Deadline:** Rolling **Application Fee:** $35.00 **H.S. Requirements:** High school diploma required; GED accepted **Costs Per Year:** Application fee: $35. Comprehensive fee: $29,944 includes full-time tuition ($20,664), mandatory fees ($1150), and college room and board ($8130). College room only: $3686. Full-time tuition and fees vary according to program. Room and board charges vary according to board plan. Part-time tuition: $560 per credit. **Scholarships:** Available **Calendar System:** Semester, Summer Session Available **Enrollment:** FT 1,600, PT 399, Grad 71 **Faculty:** FT 78, PT 114 **Student-Faculty Ratio:** 15:1 **Exams:** SAT I or ACT **% Receiving Financial Aid:** 78 **% Residing in College-Owned, -Operated, or -Affiliated Housing:** 55 **Library Holdings:** 56,347 **Regional Accreditation:** Middle State Association of Colleges and Schools **Credit Hours For Degree:** 65 credits, Associates; 126 credits, Bachelors **Intercollegiate Athletics:** Baseball M; Basketball M & W; Cheerleading W; Cross-Country Running M & W; Equestrian Sports M & W; Field Hockey W; Football M; Golf M; Soccer M & W; Softball W; Track and Field M & W; Volleyball W; Wrestling M

DESALES UNIVERSITY
2755 Station Ave.
Center Valley, PA 18034-9568
Tel: (610)282-1100
Free: 800-228-5114
Fax: (610)282-2254
E-mail: peter.rautzhan@desales.edu
Web Site: http://www.desales.edu
President/CEO: Rev. Bernard F. O'Connor
Registrar: Thomas Mantoni
Admissions: Peter Rautzhan
Financial Aid: Peter Rautzhan
Type: Comprehensive **Sex:** Coed **Affiliation:** Roman Catholic **Scores:** 99% SAT V 400+; 99% SAT M 400+; 73% ACT 18-23; 13% ACT 24-29 **% Accepted:** 79 **Admission Plans:** Early Admission; Deferred Admission **Application Deadline:** August 01 **Application Fee:** $30.00 **H.S. Requirements:** High school diploma required; GED accepted **Costs Per Year:** Application fee: $30. Comprehensive fee: $28,580 includes full-time tuition ($20,000), mandatory fees ($700), and college room and board ($7880). Full-time tuition and fees vary according to class time, course load, and degree level. Room and board charges vary according to board plan and housing facility. Part-time tuition: $830 per credit. Part-time mandatory fees: $15 per course. Part-time tuition and fees vary according to class time, course load, and degree level. **Scholarships:** Available **Calendar System:** Semester, Summer Session Available **Enrollment:** FT 1,766, PT 723, Grad 793 **Faculty:** FT 92, PT 71 **Student-Faculty Ratio:** 15:1 **Exams:** SAT I or ACT **% Receiving Financial Aid:** 55 **% Residing in College-Owned, -Operated, or -Affiliated Housing:** 72 **Library Holdings:** 138,151 **Regional Accreditation:** Middle State Association of Colleges and Schools **Credit Hours For Degree:** 40 courses, Bachelors **ROTC:** Army **Professional Accreditation:** ACBSP, NLN **Intercollegiate Athletics:** Baseball M; Basketball M & W; Cheerleading W; Cross-Country Running M & W; Equestrian Sports W; Field Hockey W; Golf M; Ice Hockey M; Lacrosse M; Soccer M & W; Softball W; Tennis M & W; Track and Field M & W; Volleyball M & W

DEVRY UNIVERSITY (CHESTERBROOK)
701 Lee Rd., Ste. 103
Chesterbrook, PA 19087-5612
Tel: (610)889-9980
Fax: (610)889-9918
Web Site: http://www.devry.edu/ **Type:** Comprehensive **Sex:** Coed **Costs Per Year:** One-time mandatory fee: $40. Tuition: $13,060 full-time, $475 per credit part-time. Mandatory fees: $60 full-time, $30 per year part-time. Full-time tuition and fees vary according to course load. Part-time tuition and fees vary according to course load. **Calendar System:** Semester **Regional Accreditation:** North Central Association of Colleges and Schools

DEVRY UNIVERSITY (FORT WASHINGTON)
1140 Virginia Dr.
Fort Washington, PA 19034

Tel: (215)591-5700; (866)338-7934
Web Site: http://www.devry.edu/
President/CEO: Barbara Hurley
Registrar: Wendy Kutchner
Financial Aid: Christal Clairborne
Type: Comprehensive **Sex:** Coed **Affiliation:** DeVry University **Admission Plans:** Deferred Admission **Application Deadline:** Rolling **Application Fee:** $50.00 **H.S. Requirements:** High school diploma required; GED accepted **Costs Per Year:** Application fee: $50. One-time mandatory fee: $40. Tuition: $13,060 full-time, $475 per credit part-time. Mandatory fees: $270 full-time, $160. Full-time tuition and fees vary according to course load. Part-time tuition and fees vary according to course load. **Scholarships:** Available **Calendar System:** Semester, Summer Session Available **Enrollment:** FT 507, PT 204, Grad 92 **Faculty:** FT 44, PT 40 **Student-Faculty Ratio:** 11:1 **% Receiving Financial Aid:** 75 **Library Holdings:** 12,755 **Regional Accreditation:** North Central Association of Colleges and Schools **Credit Hours For Degree:** 86 credit hours, Associates; 122 credit hours, Bachelors

DEVRY UNIVERSITY (PITTSBURGH)
FreeMarkets Center
210 Sixth Ave., Ste. 200
Pittsburgh, PA 15222-9123
Tel: (412)642-9072; (866)77D-EVRY
Web Site: http://www.devry.edu/ **Type:** Comprehensive **Sex:** Coed **Costs Per Year:** One-time mandatory fee: $40. Tuition: $11,890 full-time, $445 per credit part-time. Mandatory fees: $60 full-time, $30 per year part-time. Full-time tuition and fees vary according to course load. Part-time tuition and fees vary according to course load. **Calendar System:** Semester **Regional Accreditation:** North Central Association of Colleges and Schools

DICKINSON COLLEGE
PO Box 1773
Carlisle, PA 17013-2896
Tel: (717)243-5121
Free: 800-644-1773
Fax: (717)245-1442
E-mail: admit@dickinson.edu
Web Site: http://www.dickinson.edu/
President/CEO: Dr. William G. Durden
Registrar: Brenda K. Bretz
Admissions: Christopher Seth Allen
Financial Aid: Judith B. Carter
Type: Four-Year College **Sex:** Coed **Scores:** 100% SAT V 400+; 100% SAT M 400+ **% Accepted:** 49 **Admission Plans:** Early Action; Early Decision Plan; Deferred Admission **Application Deadline:** February 01 **Application Fee:** $60.00 **H.S. Requirements:** High school diploma required; GED accepted **Costs Per Year:** Application fee: $60. One-time mandatory fee: $25. Comprehensive fee: $40,170 includes full-time tuition ($31,800), mandatory fees ($320), and college room and board ($8050). College room only: $4150. Room and board charges vary according to housing facility. Part-time tuition: $3975 per course. Part-time mandatory fees: $40 per credit. **Scholarships:** Available **Calendar System:** Semester, Summer Session Available **Enrollment:** FT 2,311, PT 41 **Faculty:** FT 175, PT 34 **Student-Faculty Ratio:** 12:1 **Exams:** SAT I or ACT **% Receiving Financial Aid:** 49 **% Residing in College-Owned, -Operated, or -Affiliated Housing:** 90 **Library Holdings:** 512,232 **Regional Accreditation:** Middle State Association of Colleges and Schools **Credit Hours For Degree:** 32 courses, Bachelors **ROTC:** Army **Intercollegiate Athletics:** Baseball M; Basketball M & W; Cheerleading M & W; Crew M & W; Cross-Country Running M & W; Equestrian Sports M & W; Fencing M & W; Field Hockey W; Football M; Golf M & W; Ice Hockey M; Lacrosse M & W; Skiing (Downhill) M & W; Soccer M & W; Softball W; Squash M & W; Swimming and Diving M & W; Tennis M & W; Track and Field M & W; Ultimate Frisbee M & W; Volleyball M & W; Wrestling M

DOUGLAS EDUCATION CENTER
130 Seventh St.
Monessen, PA 15062
Tel: (724)684-3684
Fax: (724)684-7463
Web Site: http://www.douglas-school.com/
President/CEO: Jeffrey Delmbrescia
Registrar: Kevin De Imbrescia
Admissions: Linda Gambattista
Financial Aid: Jeanne Bindi
Type: Two-Year College **Sex:** Coed **H.S. Requirements:** High school diploma required; GED accepted **Scholarships:** Available **Student-Faculty Ratio:** 10:1 **Exams:** Other **Professional Accreditation:** ACICS

DREXEL UNIVERSITY
3141 Chestnut St.
Philadelphia, PA 19104-2875
Tel: (215)895-2000
Free: 800-2-DREXEL
Admissions: (215)895-2400
Fax: (215)895-5939
E-mail: undergrad-admissions@post.drexel.edu
Web Site: http://www.drexel.edu/
President/CEO: Dr. Constantine N. Papadakis
Admissions: Joan MacDonald
Financial Aid: Doug Bucher
Type: University **Sex:** Coed **Scores:** 99.5% SAT V 400+; 99.6% SAT M 400+ **% Accepted:** 82 **Admission Plans:** Deferred Admission **Application Deadline:** March 01 **Application Fee:** $50.00 **H.S. Requirements:** High school diploma required; GED accepted **Costs Per Year:** Application fee: $50. Comprehensive fee: $34,795 includes full-time tuition ($22,700), mandatory fees ($1580), and college room and board ($10,515). College room only: $6255. Full-time tuition and fees vary according to course load, program, and student level. Room and board charges vary according to board plan and housing facility. Part-time tuition: $500 per credit. Part-time mandatory fees: $100 per term. Part-time tuition and fees vary according to course load and program. **Scholarships:** Available **Calendar System:** Quarter, Summer Session Available **Enrollment:** FT 10,158, PT 2,199, Grad 5,093 **Faculty:** FT 723 **Student-Faculty Ratio:** 10:1 **Exams:** SAT I or ACT, SAT I **% Receiving Financial Aid:** 63 **% Residing in College-Owned, -Operated, or -Affiliated Housing:** 37 **Library Holdings:** 570,335 **Regional Accreditation:** Middle State Association of Colleges and Schools **Credit Hours For Degree:** 180 credit hours, Bachelors **ROTC:** Army, Air Force **Professional Accreditation:** AACSB, ABET, ACPE, AAMFT, AACN, AANA, ALA, APTA, APA, CEPH, FIDER, LCMEAMA, NASAD, NLN **Intercollegiate Athletics:** Baseball M; Basketball M & W; Crew M & W; Field Hockey W; Golf M; Lacrosse M & W; Soccer M & W; Softball W; Swimming and Diving M & W; Tennis M & W; Volleyball W; Wrestling M

DUBOIS BUSINESS COLLEGE
1 Beaver Dr.
DuBois, PA 15801-2401
Tel: (814)371-6920
E-mail: stanfordlj@dbcollege.com
Web Site: http://www.dbcollege.com/
President/CEO: Jackie Syktich
Admissions: Lisa Stanford
Financial Aid: Karen Alderton
Type: Two-Year College **Sex:** Coed **Admission Plans:** Deferred Admission **Application Fee:** $25.00 **H.S. Requirements:** High school diploma required; GED accepted **Scholarships:** Available **Calendar System:** Quarter, Summer Session Available **Faculty:** FT 14, PT 1 **Student-Faculty Ratio:** 15:1 **% Residing in College-Owned, -Operated, or -Affiliated Housing:** 7 **Library Holdings:** 2,100 **Credit Hours For Degree:** 90 credits, Associates **Professional Accreditation:** ACICS

DUFF'S BUSINESS INSTITUTE
100 Forbes Ave., Ste. 1200
Pittsburgh, PA 15222
Tel: (412)261-4520; 888-279-3314
Fax: (412)261-4546
Web Site: http://www.duffs-institute.com/
President/CEO: James Callahan
Registrar: Michael Gainey
Admissions: Lynn Fischer
Type: Two-Year College **Sex:** Coed **Affiliation:** Phillips Colleges, Inc **Admission Plans:** Deferred Admission **Application Fee:** $25.00 **H.S. Requirements:** High school diploma required; GED accepted **Scholarships:** Available **Calendar System:** Quarter, Summer Session Available **Enrollment:** FT 715, PT 536 **Faculty:** FT 13, PT 36 **Student-Faculty Ratio:**

14:1 **Exams:** Other **Library Holdings:** 7,500 **Credit Hours For Degree:** 103 credits, Associates **Professional Accreditation:** ACICS

DUQUESNE UNIVERSITY
600 Forbes Ave.
Pittsburgh, PA 15282-0001
Tel: (412)396-6000
Free: 800-456-0590
Admissions: (412)396-5000
Fax: (412)396-5779
Web Site: http://www.duq.edu/
President/CEO: Dr. Charles J. Dougherty
Registrar: Patricia Jakub
Admissions: Paul-James Cukanna
Financial Aid: Richard Esposito
Type: University **Sex:** Coed **Affiliation:** Roman Catholic **Scores:** 100% SAT V 400+; 100% SAT M 400+; 46% ACT 18-23; 44% ACT 24-29 **% Accepted:** 80 **Admission Plans:** Early Admission; Early Action; Early Decision Plan; Deferred Admission **Application Deadline:** July 01 **Application Fee:** $50.00 **H.S. Requirements:** High school diploma required; GED accepted **Costs Per Year:** Application fee: $50. Comprehensive fee: $29,534 includes full-time tuition ($19,721), mandatory fees ($1759), and college room and board ($8054). College room only: $4394. Full-time tuition and fees vary according to program. Room and board charges vary according to board plan and housing facility. Part-time tuition: $641 per credit. Part-time mandatory fees: $69 per credit. Part-time tuition and fees vary according to program. **Scholarships:** Available **Calendar System:** Semester, Summer Session Available **Enrollment:** FT 5,323, PT 327, Grad 3,090 **Faculty:** FT 429, PT 479 **Student-Faculty Ratio:** 15:1 **Exams:** SAT I or ACT **% Receiving Financial Aid:** 66 **% Residing in College-Owned, -Operated, or -Affiliated Housing:** 54 **Library Holdings:** 723,919 **Regional Accreditation:** Middle State Association of Colleges and Schools **Credit Hours For Degree:** 120 credits, Bachelors **ROTC:** Army, Navy, Air Force **Professional Accreditation:** AACSB, AACN, ABA, ACPhE, ACA, AHIMA, AOTA, APTA, APA, ASLHA, AALS, JRCEPAT, NASM, NCATE **Intercollegiate Athletics:** Baseball M; Basketball M & W; Cheerleading M & W; Crew M & W; Cross-Country Running M & W; Football M; Golf M; Ice Hockey M; Lacrosse W; Soccer M & W; Swimming and Diving M & W; Tennis M & W; Track and Field M & W; Volleyball W; Wrestling M

EAST STROUDSBURG UNIVERSITY OF PENNSYLVANIA
200 Prospect St.
East Stroudsburg, PA 18301-2999
Tel: (570)422-3211; 877-230-5547
Admissions: (570)422-3542
Fax: (570)422-3933
E-mail: jserowick@po-box.esu.edu
Web Site: http://www3.esu.edu/
President/CEO: Dr. Robert Dillman
Registrar: Georgia Prell
Admissions: Jennifer Serowick
Financial Aid: Georgia Prell
Type: Comprehensive **Sex:** Coed **Affiliation:** Pennsylvania State System of Higher Education **Scores:** 97% SAT V 400+; 96% SAT M 400+ **% Accepted:** 64 **Admission Plans:** Preferred Admission **Application Deadline:** April 01 **Application Fee:** $35.00 **H.S. Requirements:** High school diploma required; GED accepted **Costs Per Year:** Application fee: $35. Area resident tuition: $204 per credit part-time. State resident tuition: $4906 full-time, $204 per credit part-time. Nonresident tuition: $12,266 full-time, $511 per credit part-time. Mandatory fees: $1556 full-time, $55 per credit part-time. Part-time tuition and fees vary according to course load. College room and board: $4794. College room only: $3098. Room and board charges vary according to board plan and housing facility. **Scholarships:** Available **Calendar System:** Semester, Summer Session Available **Enrollment:** FT 5,056, PT 540, Grad 1,197 **Faculty:** FT 259, PT 73 **Student-Faculty Ratio:** 19:1 **Exams:** SAT I or ACT **% Receiving Financial Aid:** 64 **% Residing in College-Owned, -Operated, or -Affiliated Housing:** 44 **Library Holdings:** 449,107 **Regional Accreditation:** Middle State Association of Colleges and Schools **Credit Hours For Degree:** 60 credits, Associates; 120 credits, Bachelors **ROTC:** Army, Air Force **Professional Accreditation:** ASLHA, CEPH, JRCEPAT, NCATE, NLN, NRPA **Intercollegiate Athletics:** Baseball M; Basketball M & W; Cross-Country Running M & W; Field Hockey W; Football M; Lacrosse W; Soccer M & W; Softball W; Swimming and Diving W; Tennis M & W; Track and Field M & W; Volleyball M & W; Wrestling M

EASTERN UNIVERSITY
1300 Eagle Rd.
St. Davids, PA 19087-3696
Tel: (610)341-5800
Free: 800-452-0996
Admissions: (610)225-5005
Fax: (610)341-1723
E-mail: ugadm@eastern.edu
Web Site: http://www.eastern.edu/
President/CEO: Dr. David R. Black
Registrar: Diana S. H. Bacci
Admissions: David Urban
Type: Comprehensive **Sex:** Coed **Affiliation:** American Baptist Churches in the USA **Scores:** 99% SAT V 400+; 96% SAT M 400+; 50% ACT 18-23; 21% ACT 24-29 **Admission Plans:** Early Admission; Deferred Admission **Application Fee:** $25.00 **H.S. Requirements:** High school diploma required; GED accepted **Costs Per Year:** Application fee: $25. One-time mandatory fee: $45. Comprehensive fee: $26,670 includes full-time tuition ($18,830) and college room and board ($7840). College room only: $4280. Full-time tuition varies according to course load and program. Room and board charges vary according to board plan and housing facility. Part-time tuition: $420 per credit hour. **Scholarships:** Available **Calendar System:** Semester, Summer Session Available **Enrollment:** FT 1,946, PT 254, Grad 1,053 **Faculty:** FT 82, PT 261 **Student-Faculty Ratio:** 13:1 **Exams:** SAT I or ACT **% Receiving Financial Aid:** 69 **% Residing in College-Owned, -Operated, or -Affiliated Housing:** 74 **Library Holdings:** 143,815 **Regional Accreditation:** Middle State Association of Colleges and Schools **Credit Hours For Degree:** 60 credits, Associates; 127 credits, Bachelors **ROTC:** Army, Air Force **Professional Accreditation:** AACN, CSWE **Intercollegiate Athletics:** Baseball M; Basketball M & W; Field Hockey W; Golf M; Lacrosse M & W; Soccer M & W; Softball W; Volleyball W

EDINBORO UNIVERSITY OF PENNSYLVANIA
Edinboro, PA 16444
Tel: (814)732-2000
Free: 800-626-2203
Admissions: (814)732-2761
Fax: (814)732-2420
Web Site: http://www.edinboro.edu/
President/CEO: Dr. Frank G. Pogue, Jr.
Registrar: Timothy Pilewski
Admissions: Terrence Carlin
Financial Aid: Dorothy Body
Type: Comprehensive **Sex:** Coed **Affiliation:** Pennsylvania State System of Higher Education **Scores:** 85.4% SAT V 400+; 84% SAT M 400+; 50.62% ACT 18-23; 10.4% ACT 24-29 **% Accepted:** 82 **Admission Plans:** Deferred Admission **Application Deadline:** April 01 **Application Fee:** $30.00 **H.S. Requirements:** High school diploma required; GED accepted **Costs Per Year:** Application fee: $30. State resident tuition: $4906 full-time, $204 per credit part-time. Nonresident tuition: $9814 full-time, $409 per credit part-time. Mandatory fees: $1384 full-time, $52.32 per credit part-time. Part-time tuition and fees vary according to course load. College room and board: $5518. College room only: $3400. Room and board charges vary according to board plan. **Scholarships:** Available **Calendar System:** Semester, Summer Session Available **Enrollment:** FT 5,722, PT 801, Grad 1,168 **Faculty:** FT 363, PT 45 **Student-Faculty Ratio:** 17:1 **Exams:** ACT, SAT I or ACT, SAT I **% Receiving Financial Aid:** 77 **% Residing in College-Owned, -Operated, or -Affiliated Housing:** 27 **Library Holdings:** 501,276 **Regional Accreditation:** Middle State Association of Colleges and Schools **Credit Hours For Degree:** 60 credits, Associates; 120 credits, Bachelors **ROTC:** Army **Professional Accreditation:** AACN, ACA, ADtA, ASLHA, ACBSP, CORE, CSWE, NASM, NCATE, NLN **Intercollegiate Athletics:** Basketball M & W; Cross-Country Running M & W; Football M; Ice Hockey M; Soccer W; Softball W; Swimming and Diving M & W; Track and Field M & W; Volleyball W; Wrestling M

ELIZABETHTOWN COLLEGE
1 Alpha Dr.
Elizabethtown, PA 17022-2298
Tel: (717)361-1000
Admissions: (717)361-1400
E-mail: admissions@etown.edu

Web Site: http://www.etown.edu/
President/CEO: Dr. Theodore E. Long
Registrar: Gloria Hess
Admissions: Paul M. Cramer
Financial Aid: M. Clarke Paine
Type: Comprehensive **Sex:** Coed **Affiliation:** Church of the Brethren **Scores:** 100% SAT V 400+; 100% SAT M 400+; 49% ACT 18-23; 51% ACT 24-29 **% Accepted:** 62 **Admission Plans:** Early Admission; Deferred Admission **Application Deadline:** Rolling **Application Fee:** $30.00 **H.S. Requirements:** High school diploma required; GED accepted **Costs Per Year:** Application fee: $30. Comprehensive fee: $34,250 includes full-time tuition ($26,950) and college room and board ($7300). College room only: $3650. Part-time tuition: $660 per credit hour. **Scholarships:** Available **Calendar System:** Semester, Summer Session Available **Enrollment:** FT 1,895, PT 311, Grad 42 **Faculty:** FT 125, PT 82 **Student-Faculty Ratio:** 12:1 **Exams:** SAT I or ACT **% Receiving Financial Aid:** 71 **% Residing in College-Owned, -Operated, or -Affiliated Housing:** 85 **Library Holdings:** 190,261 **Regional Accreditation:** Middle State Association of Colleges and Schools **Credit Hours For Degree:** 125 credits, Bachelors **Professional Accreditation:** AOTA, ACBSP, CSWE, NASM **Intercollegiate Athletics:** Baseball M; Basketball M & W; Cheerleading M & W; Cross-Country Running M & W; Field Hockey W; Golf M; Lacrosse M & W; Soccer M & W; Softball W; Swimming and Diving M & W; Tennis M & W; Track and Field M & W; Volleyball M & W; Wrestling M

ERIE BUSINESS CENTER, MAIN

246 West Ninth St.
Erie, PA 16501-1392
Tel: (814)456-7504
Free: 800-352-3743
Fax: (814)456-4882
E-mail: welkera@eriebc.edu
Web Site: http://www.eriebc.edu/
President/CEO: Charles P. McGeary
Admissions: Amy Welker
Type: Two-Year College **Sex:** Coed **% Accepted:** 90 **Admission Plans:** Deferred Admission **Application Deadline:** Rolling **Application Fee:** $25.00 **H.S. Requirements:** High school diploma required; GED accepted **Costs Per Year:** Application fee: $25. Tuition: $7290 full-time, $243 per credit part-time. Mandatory fees: $850 full-time, $25 per credit part-time, $25 per term part-time. **Scholarships:** Available **Calendar System:** Trimester, Summer Session Available **Enrollment:** FT 279, PT 114 **Faculty:** FT 12, PT 34 **Student-Faculty Ratio:** 14:1 **Exams:** Other **% Residing in College-Owned, -Operated, or -Affiliated Housing:** 1 **Library Holdings:** 3,035 **Credit Hours For Degree:** 78 credits, Associates **Professional Accreditation:** ACICS

ERIE BUSINESS CENTER SOUTH

170 Cascade Galleria
New Castle, PA 16101-3950
Tel: (724)658-9066
Admissions: (724)658-3595
Fax: (724)658-3083
Web Site: http://www.eriebc.com/
President/CEO: Charles P. McGeary
Admissions: Rose Hall
Financial Aid: Rhonda Antonelli
Type: Two-Year College **Sex:** Coed **Admission Plans:** Deferred Admission **Application Fee:** $25.00 **H.S. Requirements:** High school diploma required; GED accepted **Scholarships:** Available **Calendar System:** Quarter **Enrollment:** FT 100 **Faculty:** FT 4, PT 1 **Student-Faculty Ratio:** 14:1 **Exams:** SAT I and SAT II or ACT **Library Holdings:** 1,725 **Credit Hours For Degree:** 78 credits, Associates **Professional Accreditation:** ACICS

ERIE INSTITUTE OF TECHNOLOGY

5539 Peach St.
Erie, PA 16509
Tel: (814)868-9900; (866)868-3743
Fax: (814)868-9977
Web Site: http://www.erieit.org/
President/CEO: Clinton L. Oviatt, Jr.
Admissions: Ken Haas
Financial Aid: Melissa Gabriel
Type: Two-Year College **Sex:** Coed **Application Fee:** $25.00 **H.S. Requirements:** High school diploma required; GED accepted **Scholarships:** Available **Calendar System:** Miscellaneous **Student-Faculty Ratio:** 15:1 **Professional Accreditation:** ACCSCT

FRANKLIN AND MARSHALL COLLEGE

PO Box 3003
Lancaster, PA 17604-3003
Tel: (717)291-3911
Admissions: (717)291-3953
Fax: (717)291-4389
E-mail: admission@fandm.edu
Web Site: http://www.fandm.edu/
President/CEO: John Anderson Fry
Registrar: Dr. Alan Caniglia
Admissions: Dennis Trotter
Financial Aid: Christopher Hanlon
Type: Four-Year College **Sex:** Coed **Scores:** 99.7% SAT V 400+; 100% SAT M 400+ **% Accepted:** 45 **Admission Plans:** Early Admission; Early Decision Plan; Deferred Admission **Application Deadline:** February 01 **Application Fee:** $50.00 **H.S. Requirements:** High school diploma required; GED accepted **Costs Per Year:** Application fee: $50. Comprehensive fee: $40,590 includes full-time tuition ($32,480), mandatory fees ($50), and college room and board ($8060). College room only: $5250. Full-time tuition and fees vary according to reciprocity agreements. Room and board charges vary according to board plan and housing facility. Part-time tuition: $4060 per course. Part-time tuition varies according to course load. **Scholarships:** Available **Calendar System:** Semester, Summer Session Available **Enrollment:** FT 1,982, PT 43 **Faculty:** FT 175, PT 35 **Student-Faculty Ratio:** 11:1 **Exams:** SAT I or ACT **% Receiving Financial Aid:** 48 **% Residing in College-Owned, -Operated, or -Affiliated Housing:** 66 **Library Holdings:** 479,127 **Regional Accreditation:** Middle State Association of Colleges and Schools **Credit Hours For Degree:** 32 courses, Bachelors **Intercollegiate Athletics:** Baseball M; Basketball M & W; Crew M & W; Cross-Country Running M & W; Equestrian Sports W; Field Hockey W; Football M; Golf M & W; Ice Hockey M; Lacrosse M & W; Rugby M & W; Soccer M & W; Softball W; Squash M & W; Swimming and Diving M & W; Tennis M & W; Track and Field M & W; Ultimate Frisbee M; Volleyball M & W; Wrestling M

GANNON UNIVERSITY

University Square
Erie, PA 16541-0001
Tel: (814)871-7000
Free: 800-GAN-NONU
Admissions: (814)871-7240
Fax: (814)871-5803
Web Site: http://www.gannon.edu/
President/CEO: Dr. Antoine M. Garibaldi
Registrar: Marilyn Dombrowski
Admissions: William Eilola
Financial Aid: James A. Treiber
Type: Comprehensive **Sex:** Coed **Affiliation:** Roman Catholic **Scores:** 96.5% SAT V 400+; 95.1% SAT M 400+; 54.6% ACT 18-23; 26.6% ACT 24-29 **% Accepted:** 86 **Admission Plans:** Early Admission; Deferred Admission **Application Deadline:** Rolling **Application Fee:** $25.00 **H.S. Requirements:** High school diploma required; GED accepted **Costs Per Year:** Application fee: $25. Comprehensive fee: $26,100 includes full-time tuition ($18,220), mandatory fees ($470), and college room and board ($7410). College room only: $4020. Full-time tuition and fees vary according to class time and program. Room and board charges vary according to board plan and housing facility. Part-time tuition: $565 per credit hour. Part-time mandatory fees: $15 per credit hour. Part-time tuition and fees vary according to class time and program. **Scholarships:** Available **Calendar System:** Semester, Summer Session Available **Enrollment:** FT 2,184, PT 390, Grad 1,016 **Faculty:** FT 180, PT 119 **Student-Faculty Ratio:** 11:1 **Exams:** SAT I or ACT **% Receiving Financial Aid:** 85 **% Residing in College-Owned, -Operated, or -Affiliated Housing:** 53 **Library Holdings:** 270,282 **Regional Accreditation:** Middle State Association of Colleges and Schools **Credit Hours For Degree:** 64 credits, Associates; 128 credits, Bachelors **ROTC:** Army **Professional Accreditation:** ABET, AACN, AANA, ADtA, AOTA, APTA, ACBSP, CARC, CSWE, JRCERT, NLN **Intercollegiate Athletics:** Baseball M; Basketball M & W; Cross-Country Running M & W;

Football M; Golf M & W; Lacrosse W; Soccer M & W; Softball W; Swimming and Diving M & W; Volleyball W; Water Polo M & W; Wrestling M

GENEVA COLLEGE
3200 College Ave.
Beaver Falls, PA 15010-3599
Tel: (724)846-5100
Free: 800-847-8255
Fax: (724)847-6687
Web Site: http://www.geneva.edu/
President/CEO: Dr. Kenneth A. Smith
Registrar: Andrea Korcan-Buzza
Financial Aid: Steve Bell
Type: Comprehensive **Sex:** Coed **Affiliation:** Reformed Presbyterian Church of North America **Scores:** 98% SAT V 400+; 95% SAT M 400+; 42% ACT 18-23; 44% ACT 24-29 **Admission Plans:** Early Admission; Deferred Admission **Application Fee:** $25.00 **H.S. Requirements:** High school diploma required; GED accepted **Costs Per Year:** Application fee: $25. Comprehensive fee: $24,245 includes full-time tuition ($16,910), mandatory fees ($565), and college room and board ($6770). College room only: $3530. Full-time tuition and fees vary according to course load. Room and board charges vary according to board plan and housing facility. Part-time tuition: $565 per credit. Part-time tuition varies according to course load. **Scholarships:** Available **Calendar System:** Semester, Summer Session Available **Enrollment:** FT 1,596, PT 213, Grad 332 **Faculty:** FT 82, PT 76 **Student-Faculty Ratio:** 15:1 **Exams:** SAT I and SAT II or ACT **% Receiving Financial Aid:** 83 **% Residing in College-Owned, -Operated, or -Affiliated Housing:** 69 **Library Holdings:** 163,734 **Regional Accreditation:** Middle State Association of Colleges and Schools **Credit Hours For Degree:** 63 credits, Associates; 126 credits, Bachelors **ROTC:** Army **Professional Accreditation:** ABET, ACBSP, JRCECT **Intercollegiate Athletics:** Baseball M; Basketball M & W; Cross-Country Running M & W; Football M; Soccer M & W; Softball W; Tennis W; Track and Field M & W; Volleyball M & W

GETTYSBURG COLLEGE
300 North Washington St.
Gettysburg, PA 17325-1483
Tel: (717)337-6000
Free: 800-431-0803
Admissions: (717)337-6100
Fax: (717)337-6008
E-mail: admiss@gettysburg.edu
Web Site: http://www.gettysburg.edu/
President/CEO: Dr. Katherine Haley Will
Registrar: G. Ronald Couchman
Admissions: Gail Sweezey
Financial Aid: Peter Opgenorth
Type: Four-Year College **Sex:** Coed **Affiliation:** Evangelical Lutheran Church in America **Scores:** 100% SAT V 400+; 100% SAT M 400+ **% Accepted:** 43 **Admission Plans:** Early Admission; Early Decision Plan; Deferred Admission **Application Deadline:** February 15 **Application Fee:** $45.00 **H.S. Requirements:** High school diploma required; GED accepted **Costs Per Year:** Application fee: $45. Comprehensive fee: $39,864 includes full-time tuition ($31,790), mandatory fees ($280), and college room and board ($7794). College room only: $4134. Room and board charges vary according to board plan and housing facility. Part-time tuition: $3450 per course. **Scholarships:** Available **Calendar System:** Semester, Summer Session Not available **Enrollment:** FT 2,454, PT 9 **Faculty:** FT 187, PT 87 **Student-Faculty Ratio:** 11:1 **Exams:** SAT I or ACT, SAT II **% Receiving Financial Aid:** 56 **% Residing in College-Owned, -Operated, or -Affiliated Housing:** 94 **Library Holdings:** 351,848 **Regional Accreditation:** Middle State Association of Colleges and Schools **Credit Hours For Degree:** 32 courses, Bachelors **ROTC:** Army **Intercollegiate Athletics:** Baseball M; Basketball M & W; Cheerleading M & W; Cross-Country Running M & W; Field Hockey W; Football M; Golf M & W; Lacrosse M & W; Soccer M & W; Softball W; Swimming and Diving M & W; Tennis M & W; Track and Field M & W; Volleyball W; Wrestling M

GRATZ COLLEGE
7605 Old York Rd.
Melrose Park, PA 19027
Tel: (215)635-7300
Free: 800-475-4635
Fax: (215)635-7320
E-mail: admissions@gratz.edu
Web Site: http://www.gratzcollege.edu/
President/CEO: Dr. Jonathan Rosenbaum
Registrar: Dr. Jerry Kutnick
Admissions: Dr. Jill K. Sigman
Financial Aid: Karen West
Type: Comprehensive **Sex:** Coed **Affiliation:** Jewish **% Accepted:** 71 **Admission Plans:** Open Admission; Early Admission; Deferred Admission **Application Deadline:** Rolling **Application Fee:** $50.00 **H.S. Requirements:** High school diploma required; GED accepted **Scholarships:** Available **Calendar System:** Semester, Summer Session Available **Enrollment:** FT 6, PT 10, Grad 680 **Faculty:** FT 8, PT 6 **Student-Faculty Ratio:** 12:1 **% Receiving Financial Aid:** 80 **Library Holdings:** 100,000 **Regional Accreditation:** Middle State Association of Colleges and Schools **Credit Hours For Degree:** 120 credits, Bachelors

GROVE CITY COLLEGE
100 Campus Dr.
Grove City, PA 16127-2104
Tel: (724)458-2000
Admissions: (724)458-2100
Fax: (724)458-3395
E-mail: jcmincey@gcc.edu
Web Site: http://www.gcc.edu/
President/CEO: Dr. Richard G. Jewell
Registrar: Dr. John G. Inman
Admissions: Jeffrey Mincey
Financial Aid: Patricia J. Peterson
Type: Four-Year College **Sex:** Coed **Affiliation:** Presbyterian **Scores:** 100% SAT V 400+; 100% SAT M 400+; 9% ACT 18-23; 61% ACT 24-29 **% Accepted:** 45 **Admission Plans:** Early Admission; Early Decision Plan; Deferred Admission **Application Deadline:** February 01 **Application Fee:** $50.00 **H.S. Requirements:** High school diploma required; GED accepted. For home schooled: High school diploma or equivalent not required **Costs Per Year:** Application fee: $50. Comprehensive fee: $15,984 includes full-time tuition ($10,440), mandatory fees ($200), and college room and board ($5344). Full-time tuition and fees vary according to course load. Part-time tuition: $334 per credit. **Scholarships:** Available **Calendar System:** Semester, Summer Session Available **Enrollment:** FT 2,308, PT 33 **Faculty:** FT 125, PT 59 **Student-Faculty Ratio:** 16:1 **Exams:** SAT I or ACT **% Receiving Financial Aid:** 36 **% Residing in College-Owned, -Operated, or -Affiliated Housing:** 90 **Library Holdings:** 139,000 **Regional Accreditation:** Middle State Association of Colleges and Schools **Credit Hours For Degree:** 128 credit hours, Bachelors **ROTC:** Army **Professional Accreditation:** ABET **Intercollegiate Athletics:** Baseball M; Basketball M & W; Cheerleading W; Cross-Country Running M & W; Football M; Golf M & W; Soccer M & W; Softball W; Swimming and Diving M & W; Tennis M & W; Track and Field M & W; Volleyball W; Water Polo W

GWYNEDD-MERCY COLLEGE
Sumneytown Pike
PO Box 901
Gwynedd Valley, PA 19437-0901
Tel: (215)646-7300
Fax: (215)641-5556
Web Site: http://www.gmc.edu/
President/CEO: Dr. Kathleen C. Owens
Registrar: Theresa Anderson
Admissions: James Abbuhl
Financial Aid: Sr. Barbara Kaufmann, RSM
Type: Comprehensive **Sex:** Coed **Affiliation:** Roman Catholic **Scores:** 94% SAT V 400+; 92% SAT M 400+ **% Accepted:** 65 **Admission Plans:** Early Admission; Deferred Admission **Application Deadline:** Rolling **Application Fee:** $25.00 **H.S. Requirements:** High school diploma required; GED accepted **Costs Per Year:** Application fee: $25. Comprehensive fee: $27,520 includes full-time tuition ($18,720), mandatory fees ($500), and college room and board ($8300). Part-time tuition: $415 per credit. Part-time mandatory fees: $10 per credit. **Scholarships:** Available **Calendar System:** Semester, Summer Session Available **Enrollment:** FT 1,273, PT 907, Grad 543 **Faculty:** FT 78, PT 196 **Student-Faculty Ratio:** 13:1 **Exams:** SAT I or ACT **% Receiving Financial Aid:** 71 **% Residing in College-Owned, -Operated, or -Affiliated Housing:** 20 **Library Holdings:** 99,493 **Regional Accreditation:** Middle State Association of Colleges and Schools **Credit Hours For Degree:** 62 credits, Associates; 125 credits, Bachelors **Professional Accreditation:** AHIMA, CARC, JRCECT, JRCERT, NLN **Intercollegiate**

Athletics: Basketball M & W; Field Hockey W; Lacrosse W; Soccer M; Softball W; Tennis M & W; Volleyball W

HARCUM COLLEGE
750 Montgomery Ave.
Bryn Mawr, PA 19010-3476
Tel: (610)525-4100
Free: 800-345-2600
Admissions: (610)526-6153
Fax: (610)526-6147
Web Site: http://www.harcum.edu/
President/CEO: Dr. Charles H. Trout
Registrar: Madeleine Wrightson
Admissions: Nicola Di Fronzo
Financial Aid: Mindy Henken
Type: Two-Year College **Sex:** Coed **% Accepted:** 24 **Admission Plans:** Early Admission; Deferred Admission **Application Deadline:** Rolling **Application Fee:** $25.00 **H.S. Requirements:** High school diploma required; GED accepted **Costs Per Year:** Application fee: $25. Comprehensive fee: $22,596 includes full-time tuition ($15,250), mandatory fees ($100), and college room and board ($7246). Part-time tuition: $508 per credit. **Scholarships:** Available **Calendar System:** Semester, Summer Session Available **Enrollment:** FT 385, PT 188 **Faculty:** FT 30, PT 78 **Student-Faculty Ratio:** 9:1 **Exams:** SAT I or ACT **% Residing in College-Owned, -Operated, or -Affiliated Housing:** 23 **Library Holdings:** 39,000 **Regional Accreditation:** Middle State Association of Colleges and Schools **Credit Hours For Degree:** 60 credits, Associates **Professional Accreditation:** ADA, APTA, NAACLS

HARRISBURG AREA COMMUNITY COLLEGE
1 HACC Dr.
Harrisburg, PA 17110-2999
Tel: (717)780-2300
Fax: (717)231-7674
Web Site: http://www.hacc.edu/
President/CEO: Dr. Edna V. Baehre
Registrar: Roz Ogden
Admissions: Jennifer Baker
Financial Aid: Robert Ritz
Type: Two-Year College **Sex:** Coed **% Accepted:** 98 **Admission Plans:** Open Admission; Early Admission **Application Deadline:** Rolling **Application Fee:** $30.00 **H.S. Requirements:** High school diploma or equivalent not required. For allied health programs: High school diploma required; GED accepted **Costs Per Year:** Application fee: $30. Area resident tuition: $2850 full-time, $95 per credit hour part-time. State resident tuition: $5250 full-time, $175 per credit hour part-time. Nonresident tuition: $7650 full-time, $255 per credit hour part-time. Mandatory fees: $510 full-time, $17 per credit hour part-time. **Scholarships:** Available **Calendar System:** Semester, Summer Session Available **Enrollment:** FT 6,634, PT 10,265 **Faculty:** FT 261, PT 716 **Student-Faculty Ratio:** 20:1 **Library Holdings:** 119,000 **Regional Accreditation:** Middle State Association of Colleges and Schools **Credit Hours For Degree:** 61 credit hours, Associates **ROTC:** Army **Professional Accreditation:** ADA, ACBSP, CARC, JRCEMT, NAACLS, NLN **Intercollegiate Athletics:** Basketball M & W; Soccer M & W; Swimming and Diving M & W; Tennis M & W; Volleyball M & W

HAVERFORD COLLEGE
370 Lancaster Ave.
Haverford, PA 19041-1392
Tel: (610)896-1000
Admissions: (610)896-1350
Fax: (610)896-1338
E-mail: admitme@haverford.edu
Web Site: http://www.haverford.edu/
President/CEO: Dr. Thomas Tritton
Registrar: Lee Watkins
Admissions: Jess Lord
Financial Aid: David Hoy
Type: Four-Year College **Sex:** Coed **Scores:** 100% SAT V 400+; 100% SAT M 400+ **% Accepted:** 26 **Admission Plans:** Preferred Admission; Early Admission; Early Decision Plan; Deferred Admission **Application Deadline:** January 15 **Application Fee:** $60.00 **H.S. Requirements:** High school diploma required; GED accepted **Costs Per Year:** Application fee: $60. Comprehensive fee: $41,600 includes full-time tuition ($31,466), mandatory fees ($294), and college room and board ($9840). College room only: $5540. **Scholarships:** Available **Calendar System:** Semester, Summer Session Not available **Enrollment:** FT 1,168 **Faculty:** FT 111, PT 5 **Student-Faculty Ratio:** 8:1 **Exams:** Other, SAT I or ACT **% Receiving Financial Aid:** 43 **% Residing in College-Owned, -Operated, or -Affiliated Housing:** 99 **Library Holdings:** 395,799 **Regional Accreditation:** Middle State Association of Colleges and Schools **Credit Hours For Degree:** 32 courses, Bachelors **Intercollegiate Athletics:** Baseball M; Basketball M & W; Crew M & W; Cross-Country Running M & W; Fencing M & W; Field Hockey W; Golf M & W; Lacrosse M & W; Soccer M & W; Softball W; Squash M & W; Tennis M & W; Track and Field M & W; Volleyball W; Wrestling M

HOLY FAMILY UNIVERSITY
Grant and Frankford Avenues
Philadelphia, PA 19114-2094
Tel: (215)637-7700
Free: 800-637-1191
Admissions: (215)637-3050
Fax: (215)281-1022
Web Site: http://www.holyfamily.edu/
President/CEO: Sr. Francesca Onley
Registrar: Ann Marie Vickery
Admissions: Lauren McDermott
Financial Aid: Janice Hetrick
Type: Comprehensive **Sex:** Coed **Affiliation:** Roman Catholic **Scores:** 92% SAT V 400+; 82% SAT M 400+ **Admission Plans:** Deferred Admission **Application Fee:** $25.00 **H.S. Requirements:** High school diploma required; GED accepted **Costs Per Year:** Application fee: $25. Comprehensive fee: $25,740 includes full-time tuition ($17,240), mandatory fees ($500), and college room and board ($8000). College room only: $4700. Full-time tuition and fees vary according to course load and program. Part-time tuition: $380 per credit hour. Part-time mandatory fees: $60 per term. Part-time tuition and fees vary according to program. **Scholarships:** Available **Calendar System:** Semester, Summer Session Available **Enrollment:** FT 1,086, PT 696, Grad 888 **Faculty:** FT 87, PT 171 **Student-Faculty Ratio:** 11:1 **Exams:** SAT I or ACT **Library Holdings:** 126,780 **Regional Accreditation:** Middle State Association of Colleges and Schools **Credit Hours For Degree:** 74 credits, Associates; 120 credits, Bachelors **Professional Accreditation:** JRCERT, NLN **Intercollegiate Athletics:** Basketball M & W; Cross-Country Running W; Golf M; Soccer M & W

HUSSIAN SCHOOL OF ART
1118 Market St.
Philadelphia, PA 19107-3679
Tel: (215)981-0900
Fax: (215)864-9115
E-mail: info@hussianart.edu
Web Site: http://www.hussianart.edu/
President/CEO: Ronald Dove
Registrar: Maureen Flanagan
Admissions: Lynne D. Wartman
Financial Aid: Susan Cohen
Type: Four-Year College **Sex:** Coed **% Accepted:** 94 **Admission Plans:** Deferred Admission **Application Deadline:** Rolling **Application Fee:** $25.00 **H.S. Requirements:** High school diploma required; GED accepted **Costs Per Year:** Application fee: $25. Tuition: $10,000 full-time. Mandatory fees: $465 full-time. **Scholarships:** Available **Calendar System:** Semester, Summer Session Not available **Enrollment:** FT 155 **Faculty:** FT 3, PT 23 **Student-Faculty Ratio:** 18:1 **Library Holdings:** 194,587 **Credit Hours For Degree:** 120 credits, Associates **Professional Accreditation:** ACCSCT

ICM SCHOOL OF BUSINESS & MEDICAL CAREERS
10 Wood St. at Fort Pitt Blvd.
Pittsburgh, PA 15222-1977
Tel: (412)261-2647
Free: 800-441-5222
E-mail: mrosenberg@icmschool.com
Web Site: http://www.icmschool.com/
President/CEO: Bobby L. Reese
Registrar: Carla M. Ryba
Admissions: Marcia Rosenberg
Financial Aid: Christopher Fox
Type: Two-Year College **Sex:** Coed **Application Fee:** $30.00 **H.S. Requirements:** High school diploma required; GED accepted **Costs Per Year:** Application fee: $30. Tuition: $24,400 full-time. Mandatory fees: $130 full-time.

Scholarships: Available **Calendar System:** Continuous, Summer Session Available **Enrollment:** FT 1,065, PT 30 **Faculty:** FT 32, PT 33 **Student-Faculty Ratio:** 18:1 **Exams:** Other, SAT I and SAT II or ACT **Library Holdings:** 3,100 **Credit Hours For Degree:** 1500 hours, Associates **Professional Accreditation:** ACICS, AOTA

IMMACULATA UNIVERSITY
1145 King Rd.
Immaculata, PA 19345
Tel: (610)647-4400; 877-428-6328
Fax: (610)251-1668
E-mail: admiss@immaculata.edu
Web Site: http://www.immaculata.edu/
President/CEO: Sr. R. Patricia Fadden, IHM
Registrar: Janice Bates
Admissions: Rebecca Bowlby
Financial Aid: Peter Lysionek
Type: Comprehensive **Sex:** Coed **Affiliation:** Roman Catholic **Scores:** 86.6% SAT V 400+; 93.8% SAT M 400+ **% Accepted:** 80 **Admission Plans:** Early Action; Deferred Admission **Application Deadline:** August 15 **Application Fee:** $35.00 **H.S. Requirements:** High school diploma required; GED accepted. For continuing education applicants 25 or over: High school diploma required; GED accepted **Costs Per Year:** Application fee: $35. Comprehensive fee: $29,910 includes full-time tuition ($20,575) and college room and board ($9335). College room only: $5010. Part-time tuition: $355 per credit. **Scholarships:** Available **Calendar System:** Semester, Summer Session Available **Enrollment:** FT 691, PT 2,326, Grad 1,002 **Faculty:** FT 87, PT 210 **Student-Faculty Ratio:** 12:1 **Exams:** SAT I or ACT, SAT I and SAT II or ACT **% Receiving Financial Aid:** 75 **% Residing in College-Owned, -Operated, or -Affiliated Housing:** 75 **Library Holdings:** 143,145 **Regional Accreditation:** Middle State Association of Colleges and Schools **Credit Hours For Degree:** 63 credits, Associates; 128 credits, Bachelors **Professional Accreditation:** ADtA, APA, NASM, NLN **Intercollegiate Athletics:** Basketball W; Cross-Country Running W; Field Hockey W; Lacrosse W; Soccer W; Softball W; Tennis W; Volleyball W

INDIANA UNIVERSITY OF PENNSYLVANIA
Indiana, PA 15705-1087
Tel: (724)357-2100
Free: 800-442-6830
Admissions: (724)357-2230
Fax: (724)357-2685
E-mail: admissions-inquiry@iup.edu
Web Site: http://www.iup.edu/
President/CEO: Dr. Diane L. Reinhard
Registrar: Richard DiStanislao
Admissions: Dr. Rhonda H. Luckey
Financial Aid: Christine Zuzack
Type: University **Sex:** Coed **Affiliation:** Pennsylvania State System of Higher Education **Scores:** 99% SAT V 400+; 98% SAT M 400+ **% Accepted:** 55 **Admission Plans:** Early Admission; Deferred Admission **Application Deadline:** Rolling **Application Fee:** $30.00 **H.S. Requirements:** High school diploma required; GED accepted **Costs Per Year:** Application fee: $30. State resident tuition: $4810 full-time, $204 per credit hour part-time. Nonresident tuition: $12,026 full-time, $511 per credit hour part-time. Mandatory fees: $1275 full-time, $20.40 per credit hour part-time, $167 per term part-time. Full-time tuition and fees vary according to course load, location, and reciprocity agreements. Part-time tuition and fees vary according to course load, location, and reciprocity agreements. College room and board: $4866. College room only: $2740. Room and board charges vary according to board plan, housing facility, and location. **Scholarships:** Available **Calendar System:** Semester, Summer Session Available **Enrollment:** FT 11,223, PT 824, Grad 2,034 **Faculty:** FT 639, PT 72 **Student-Faculty Ratio:** 18:1 **Exams:** SAT I or ACT **% Receiving Financial Aid:** 65 **% Residing in College-Owned, -Operated, or -Affiliated Housing:** 32 **Library Holdings:** 570,735 **Regional Accreditation:** Middle State Association of Colleges and Schools **Credit Hours For Degree:** 60 semester hours, Associates; 124 semester hours, Bachelors **ROTC:** Army **Professional Accreditation:** AACSB, ABET, AACN, AAFCS, ACF, ADtA, APA, ASLHA, CARC, JRCEPAT, NASAD, NASM, NAST, NCATE **Intercollegiate Athletics:** Baseball M; Basketball M & W; Cross-Country Running M & W; Field Hockey W; Football M; Golf M; Lacrosse W; Soccer W; Softball W; Swimming and Diving M & W; Tennis W; Track and Field M & W; Volleyball W

INFORMATION COMPUTER SYSTEMS INSTITUTE
2201 Hangar Place
Allentown, PA 18103-9504
Tel: (610)264-8029
E-mail: wbarber@ptd.net
Web Site: http://www.icsinstitute.com/
President/CEO: William H. Barber, Jr.
Admissions: Bill Barber
Type: Two-Year College **Professional Accreditation:** ACCSCT

INTERNATIONAL ACADEMY OF DESIGN & TECHNOLOGY
555 Grant St.
Pittsburgh, PA 15219
Tel: (412)391-4197
Free: 800-447-8324
Fax: (412)391-4224
Web Site: http://www.iadtpitt.com/
President/CEO: Robert H. Ley
Admissions: Debbie Love
Financial Aid: Shondra Dubrosky
Type: Two-Year College **Application Fee:** $50.00 **Calendar System:** Quarter **Enrollment:** FT 840, PT 114 **Faculty:** FT 23, PT 22 **Student-Faculty Ratio:** 15:1 **Professional Accreditation:** ACICS

JNA INSTITUTE OF CULINARY ARTS
1212 South Broad St.
Philadelphia, PA 19146
Tel: (215)468-8880
Fax: (215)468-8838
Web Site: http://www.culinaryarts.com/
President/CEO: Joseph DiGironimo
Type: Two-Year College **Sex:** Coed **Calendar System:** Continuous **Professional Accreditation:** ACCSCT

JOHNSON COLLEGE
3427 North Main Ave.
Scranton, PA 18508-1495
Tel: (570)342-6404
Free: 800-2-WE-WORK
Fax: (570)348-2181
E-mail: admit@johnson.edu
Web Site: http://www.johnson.edu/
President/CEO: Dr. Ann Pipinski
Registrar: Melissa Ide
Admissions: Melissa Ide
Financial Aid: Barbara Schmitt
Type: Two-Year College **Sex:** Coed **Scores:** 75% SAT V 400+; 70% SAT M 400+ **% Accepted:** 69 **Admission Plans:** Deferred Admission **Application Deadline:** Rolling **Application Fee:** $30.00 **H.S. Requirements:** High school diploma required; GED accepted **Costs Per Year:** Application fee: $30. Tuition: $12,267 full-time, $325 per credit part-time. Mandatory fees: $1000 full-time. College room only: $2975. **Scholarships:** Available **Calendar System:** Semester, Summer Session Available **Student-Faculty Ratio:** 17:1 **Exams:** Other, SAT I **% Residing in College-Owned, -Operated, or -Affiliated Housing:** 17 **Library Holdings:** 4,473 **Credit Hours For Degree:** 74 credits, Associates **Professional Accreditation:** ACCSCT **Intercollegiate Athletics:** Basketball M & W; Bowling M & W; Cross-Country Running M & W; Golf M & W

JUNIATA COLLEGE
1700 Moore St.
Huntingdon, PA 16652-2119
Tel: (814)641-3000; 877-JUNIATA
Admissions: (814)641-3432
Fax: (814)641-3100
Web Site: http://www.juniata.edu/
President/CEO: Dr. Thomas R. Kepple, Jr.
Registrar: Athena D. Frederick
Admissions: Michelle Bartol
Financial Aid: Randall S. Rennell
Type: Four-Year College **Sex:** Coed **Affiliation:** Church of the Brethren **Scores:** 99.7% SAT V 400+; 100% SAT M 400+ **% Accepted:** 68 **Admis-**

sion Plans: Early Admission; Early Decision Plan; Deferred Admission **Application Deadline:** March 01 **Application Fee:** $30.00 **H.S. Requirements:** High school diploma required; GED accepted **Costs Per Year:** Application fee: $30. Comprehensive fee: $35,220 includes full-time tuition ($26,900), mandatory fees ($640), and college room and board ($7680). College room only: $4030. **Scholarships:** Available **Calendar System:** Semester, Summer Session Available **Enrollment:** FT 1,389, PT 60 **Faculty:** FT 94, PT 38 **Student-Faculty Ratio:** 13:1 **Exams:** SAT I or ACT **% Receiving Financial Aid:** 76 **% Residing in College-Owned, -Operated, or -Affiliated Housing:** 84 **Library Holdings:** 275,000 **Regional Accreditation:** Middle State Association of Colleges and Schools **Credit Hours For Degree:** 120 semester hours, Bachelors **Professional Accreditation:** CSWE **Intercollegiate Athletics:** Baseball M; Basketball M & W; Cross-Country Running M & W; Equestrian Sports M & W; Field Hockey W; Football M; Golf M & W; Ice Hockey M; Lacrosse M; Rugby M & W; Soccer M & W; Softball W; Swimming and Diving W; Tennis M & W; Track and Field M & W; Ultimate Frisbee M & W; Volleyball M & W

KATHARINE GIBBS SCHOOL
2501 Monroe Blvd.
Norristown, PA 19403
Tel: (610)676-0500; (866)PAG-IBBS
Fax: (610)676-0530
E-mail: jcarretta@pagibbs.com
Web Site: http://www.pagibbs.com/
President/CEO: Joseph Carretta
Admissions: Joseph Carretta
Type: Two-Year College **Sex:** Coed **Calendar System:** Quarter **Professional Accreditation:** ACICS

KEYSTONE COLLEGE
One College Green
La Plume, PA 18440
Tel: (570)945-5141; 877-4COLLEGE
Admissions: (570)945-8112
E-mail: admissions@keystone.edu
Web Site: http://www.keystone.edu/
President/CEO: Dr. Edward G. Boehm, Jr.
Registrar: Edward D. Adams
Admissions: Sarah Keating
Financial Aid: Ginger B. Kline
Type: Two-Year College **Sex:** Coed **Scores:** 78% SAT V 400+; 63% SAT M 400+; 45% ACT 18-23 **% Accepted:** 91 **Admission Plans:** Early Admission; Deferred Admission **Application Deadline:** July 01 **Application Fee:** $25.00 **H.S. Requirements:** High school diploma required; GED accepted **Costs Per Year:** Application fee: $25. Comprehensive fee: $24,026 includes full-time tuition ($14,946), mandatory fees ($970), and college room and board ($8110). College room only: $4300. Part-time tuition: $330 per credit. Part-time mandatory fees: $110 per term. **Scholarships:** Available **Calendar System:** Semester, Summer Session Available **Enrollment:** FT 1,234, PT 404 **Faculty:** FT 62, PT 145 **Student-Faculty Ratio:** 12:1 **Exams:** SAT I or ACT **% Residing in College-Owned, -Operated, or -Affiliated Housing:** 24 **Library Holdings:** 65,000 **Regional Accreditation:** Middle State Association of Colleges and Schools **Credit Hours For Degree:** 63 credit hours, Associates; 123 credit hours, Bachelors **ROTC:** Army, Air Force **Intercollegiate Athletics:** Baseball M; Basketball M & W; Cross-Country Running M & W; Golf M; Soccer M & W; Softball W; Tennis M & W; Track and Field M & W; Volleyball W

KING'S COLLEGE
133 North River St.
Wilkes Barre, PA 18711-0801
Tel: (570)208-5900; 888-KINGSPA
Admissions: (570)208-5858
Fax: (570)208-5971
E-mail: admssions@kings.edu
Web Site: http://www.kings.edu/
President/CEO: Rev. Thomas O'Hara, CSC
Registrar: Daniel Cebrick
Admissions: Michelle Lawrence-Schmude
Financial Aid: Ellen Mcguire
Type: Comprehensive **Sex:** Coed **Affiliation:** Roman Catholic **Scores:** 97% SAT V 400+; 97% SAT M 400+ **% Accepted:** 84 **Admission Plans:** Early Admission; Deferred Admission **Application Deadline:** Rolling **Application Fee:** $30.00 **H.S. Requirements:** High school diploma required; GED accepted **Costs Per Year:** Application fee: $30. Comprehensive fee: $29,810 includes full-time tuition ($20,320), mandatory fees ($900), and college room and board ($8590). College room only: $3980. Room and board charges vary according to board plan and housing facility. Part-time tuition: $495 per credit hour. **Scholarships:** Available **Calendar System:** Semester, Summer Session Available **Enrollment:** FT 1,849, PT 261, Grad 213 **Faculty:** FT 110, PT 91 **Student-Faculty Ratio:** 14:1 **Exams:** SAT I or ACT **% Receiving Financial Aid:** 81 **% Residing in College-Owned, -Operated, or -Affiliated Housing:** 45 **Library Holdings:** 168,793 **Regional Accreditation:** Middle State Association of Colleges and Schools **Credit Hours For Degree:** 60 credit hours, Associates; 120 credit hours, Bachelors **ROTC:** Army, Air Force **Professional Accreditation:** AACSB, ACEHSA, JRCEPAT **Intercollegiate Athletics:** Baseball M; Basketball M & W; Cheerleading M & W; Cross-Country Running M & W; Field Hockey W; Football M; Golf M; Lacrosse M & W; Soccer M & W; Softball W; Swimming and Diving M & W; Tennis M & W; Volleyball W; Wrestling M

KUTZTOWN UNIVERSITY OF PENNSYLVANIA
15200 Kutztown Rd.
Kutztown, PA 19530-0730
Tel: (610)683-4000; 877-628-1915
Admissions: (610)683-4060
Fax: (610)683-1375
Web Site: http://www.kutztown.edu/
President/CEO: Dr. F. Javier Cevallos
Registrar: Laura Youtz
Admissions: Dr. William Stahler
Financial Aid: Anita Faust
Type: Comprehensive **Sex:** Coed **Affiliation:** Pennsylvania State System of Higher Education **Scores:** 96% SAT V 400+; 95% SAT M 400+ **% Accepted:** 65 **Admission Plans:** Early Admission; Deferred Admission **Application Deadline:** March 01 **Application Fee:** $35.00 **H.S. Requirements:** High school diploma required; GED accepted **Costs Per Year:** Application fee: $35. State resident tuition: $4906 full-time, $204 per credit part-time. Nonresident tuition: $12,266 full-time, $511 per credit part-time. Mandatory fees: $1519 full-time, $50.31 per credit part-time, $31 per term part-time. College room and board: $5480. College room only: $3900. **Scholarships:** Available **Calendar System:** Semester, Summer Session Available **Enrollment:** FT 7,951, PT 855, Grad 1,058 **Faculty:** FT 411, PT 50 **Student-Faculty Ratio:** 19:1 **Exams:** SAT I or ACT, SAT II **% Receiving Financial Aid:** 59 **% Residing in College-Owned, -Operated, or -Affiliated Housing:** 52 **Library Holdings:** 500,484 **Regional Accreditation:** Middle State Association of Colleges and Schools **Credit Hours For Degree:** 120 credits, Bachelors **ROTC:** Army, Air Force **Professional Accreditation:** CSWE, NASAD, NASM, NCATE, NLN **Intercollegiate Athletics:** Baseball M; Basketball M & W; Cheerleading W; Cross-Country Running M & W; Equestrian Sports M & W; Field Hockey W; Football M; Golf W; Ice Hockey M; Lacrosse M & W; Riflery M & W; Rugby M & W; Skiing (Downhill) M & W; Soccer M & W; Softball W; Swimming and Diving M & W; Tennis M & W; Track and Field M & W; Volleyball M & W; Wrestling M

LA ROCHE COLLEGE
9000 Babcock Blvd.
Pittsburgh, PA 15237-5898
Tel: (412)367-9300
Free: 800-838-4LRC
Admissions: (412)536-1198
Fax: (412)536-1075
E-mail: schaeft1@laroche.edu
Web Site: http://www.laroche.edu/
President/CEO: Sr. Candace Introcaso
Registrar: Lucille Adkins
Admissions: Thomas Schaefer
Financial Aid: John Matsko
Type: Comprehensive **Sex:** Coed **Affiliation:** Roman Catholic Church **Scores:** 83% SAT V 400+; 85% SAT M 400+; 69% ACT 18-23; 6% ACT 24-29 **% Accepted:** 65 **Admission Plans:** Early Admission; Deferred Admission **Application Deadline:** Rolling **Application Fee:** $50.00 **H.S. Requirements:** High school diploma required; GED accepted **Costs Per Year:** Application fee: $50. Comprehensive fee: $24,724 includes full-time tuition ($16,780), mandatory fees ($600), and college room and board ($7344). College room only: $4600. Full-time tuition and fees vary according to program. Part-time tuition: $512 per credit. Part-time mandatory fees: $14 per credit, $50 per term. Part-time tuition and fees vary according to program. **Scholarships:** Available **Calendar System:** Semester, Summer

Session Available **Enrollment:** FT 1,202, PT 298, Grad 207 **Faculty:** FT 62, PT 163 **Student-Faculty Ratio:** 12:1 **Exams:** SAT I or ACT **% Receiving Financial Aid:** 66 **% Residing in College-Owned, -Operated, or -Affiliated Housing:** 35 **Library Holdings:** 108,432 **Regional Accreditation:** Middle State Association of Colleges and Schools **Credit Hours For Degree:** 67 credit hours, Associates; 120 credit hours, Bachelors **ROTC:** Army, Air Force **Professional Accreditation:** AANA, ACBSP, FIDER, NASAD, NLN **Intercollegiate Athletics:** Baseball M; Basketball M & W; Cross-Country Running M & W; Golf M; Soccer M & W; Softball W; Volleyball W

LA SALLE UNIVERSITY
1900 West Olney Ave.
Philadelphia, PA 19141-1199
Tel: (215)951-1000
Free: 800-328-1910
Admissions: (215)951-1500
Fax: (215)951-1656
E-mail: admiss@lasalle.edu
Web Site: http://www.lasalle.edu/
President/CEO: Br. Michael McGinniss
Registrar: Dominic Galante
Admissions: Robert G. Voss
Financial Aid: Michael J. Payne
Type: Comprehensive **Sex:** Coed **Affiliation:** Roman Catholic **Scores:** 98% SAT V 400+; 97% SAT M 400+ **% Accepted:** 70 **Admission Plans:** Early Admission; Early Action; Deferred Admission **Application Fee:** $35.00 **H.S. Requirements:** High school diploma required; GED accepted **Costs Per Year:** Application fee: $35. Comprehensive fee: $38,110 includes full-time tuition ($27,500), mandatory fees ($310), and college room and board ($10,300). College room only: $5120. Part-time tuition: $395 per credit. **Scholarships:** Available **Calendar System:** Semester, Summer Session Available **Enrollment:** FT 3,281, PT 1,058, Grad 1,799 **Faculty:** FT 210, PT 186 **Student-Faculty Ratio:** 13:1 **Exams:** SAT I or ACT **% Receiving Financial Aid:** 74 **% Residing in College-Owned, -Operated, or -Affiliated Housing:** 62 **Library Holdings:** 400,000 **Regional Accreditation:** Middle State Association of Colleges and Schools **Credit Hours For Degree:** 60 credit hours, Associates; 120 credit hours, Bachelors **ROTC:** Army, Air Force **Professional Accreditation:** AACSB, AACN, AANA, ADtA, APA, ASLHA, CSWE, NLN **Intercollegiate Athletics:** Baseball M; Basketball M & W; Crew M & W; Cross-Country Running M & W; Field Hockey W; Football M; Golf M & W; Lacrosse W; Soccer M & W; Softball W; Swimming and Diving M & W; Tennis M & W; Track and Field M & W; Volleyball W

LACKAWANNA COLLEGE
501 Vine St.
Scranton, PA 18509
Tel: (570)961-7810
Admissions: (570)961-7852
Fax: (570)961-7858
E-mail: dudam@lackawanna.edu
Web Site: http://www.lackawanna.edu/
President/CEO: Raymond Angeli
Registrar: Joann Phillips
Admissions: Mark Duda
Financial Aid: Lucritia Hill
Type: Two-Year College **Sex:** Coed **Admission Plans:** Open Admission; Early Admission; Deferred Admission **Application Deadline:** Rolling **Application Fee:** $30.00 **H.S. Requirements:** High school diploma required; GED accepted **Costs Per Year:** Application fee: $30. Comprehensive fee: $15,770 includes full-time tuition ($9400), mandatory fees ($70), and college room and board ($6300). College room only: $4100. Full-time tuition and fees vary according to course load. Part-time tuition: $310 per credit. Part-time mandatory fees: $35 per term. Part-time tuition and fees vary according to course load. **Scholarships:** Available **Calendar System:** Semester, Summer Session Available **Enrollment:** FT 758, PT 439 **Faculty:** FT 20, PT 36 **Student-Faculty Ratio:** 13:1 **Exams:** ACT, SAT I or ACT, SAT I **% Residing in College-Owned, -Operated, or -Affiliated Housing:** 12 **Library Holdings:** 15,276 **Regional Accreditation:** Middle State Association of Colleges and Schools **Credit Hours For Degree:** 66 credits, Associates **ROTC:** Army, Air Force **Intercollegiate Athletics:** Baseball M; Basketball M & W; Football M; Golf M & W; Softball W; Volleyball W

LAFAYETTE COLLEGE
Easton, PA 18042-1798
Tel: (610)330-5000
Admissions: (610)330-5100
Fax: (610)330-5127
E-mail: rowlandc@lafayette.edu
Web Site: http://www.lafayette.edu/
President/CEO: Daniel Weiss
Registrar: Francis A. Benginia
Admissions: Carol Rowlands
Financial Aid: Arlina B. De Nardo
Type: Four-Year College **Sex:** Coed **Affiliation:** Presbyterian Church (U.S.A.) **Scores:** 100% SAT V 400+; 100% SAT M 400+; 12% ACT 18-23; 68% ACT 24-29 **% Accepted:** 37 **Admission Plans:** Early Admission; Early Decision Plan; Deferred Admission **Application Deadline:** January 01 **Application Fee:** $60.00 **H.S. Requirements:** High school diploma required; GED not accepted **Costs Per Year:** Application fee: $60. Comprehensive fee: $41,533 includes full-time tuition ($31,501), mandatory fees ($168), and college room and board ($9864). College room only: $5784. **Scholarships:** Available **Calendar System:** Semester, Summer Session Available **Enrollment:** FT 2,281, PT 65 **Faculty:** FT 195, PT 41 **Student-Faculty Ratio:** 11:1 **Exams:** SAT I and SAT II **% Receiving Financial Aid:** 55 **% Residing in College-Owned, -Operated, or -Affiliated Housing:** 98 **Library Holdings:** 530,000 **Regional Accreditation:** Middle State Association of Colleges and Schools **Credit Hours For Degree:** 120 credits, Bachelors **ROTC:** Army **Professional Accreditation:** ABET **Intercollegiate Athletics:** Baseball M; Basketball M & W; Crew M & W; Cross-Country Running M & W; Equestrian Sports M & W; Fencing M & W; Field Hockey W; Football M; Golf M; Ice Hockey M; Lacrosse M & W; Rugby M & W; Skiing (Downhill) M & W; Soccer M & W; Softball W; Squash M; Swimming and Diving M & W; Tennis M & W; Track and Field M & W; Volleyball W; Weight Lifting M & W; Wrestling M

LANCASTER BIBLE COLLEGE
901 Eden Rd., PO Box 83403
Lancaster, PA 17608-3403
Tel: (717)569-7071; (866)LBC-4YOU
Admissions: (717)560-8271
Fax: (717)560-8213
E-mail: jroper@lbc.edu
Web Site: http://www.lbc.edu/
President/CEO: Dr. Peter W. Teague
Registrar: Philip E. Dearborn
Admissions: Joanne M. Roper
Financial Aid: Karen Fox
Type: Comprehensive **Sex:** Coed **Affiliation:** nondenominational **Scores:** 98% SAT V 400+; 92% SAT M 400+; 52% ACT 18-23; 19% ACT 24-29 **% Accepted:** 57 **Admission Plans:** Early Admission; Deferred Admission **Application Deadline:** Rolling **Application Fee:** $25.00 **H.S. Requirements:** High school diploma required; GED accepted **Costs Per Year:** Application fee: $25. Comprehensive fee: $18,060 includes full-time tuition ($11,850), mandatory fees ($510), and college room and board ($5700). College room only: $2500. Part-time tuition: $417 per credit. Part-time mandatory fees: $19 per credit. **Scholarships:** Available **Calendar System:** Semester, Summer Session Available **Enrollment:** FT 589, PT 240, Grad 172 **Faculty:** FT 44, PT 42 **Student-Faculty Ratio:** 15:1 **Exams:** SAT I or ACT **% Receiving Financial Aid:** 83 **% Residing in College-Owned, -Operated, or -Affiliated Housing:** 54 **Library Holdings:** 132,599 **Regional Accreditation:** Middle State Association of Colleges and Schools **Credit Hours For Degree:** 62 credit hours, Associates; 120 credit hours, Bachelors **Professional Accreditation:** AABC **Intercollegiate Athletics:** Baseball M; Basketball M & W; Lacrosse W; Soccer M & W; Volleyball M & W

LANSDALE SCHOOL OF BUSINESS
201 Church Rd.
North Wales, PA 19454-4148
Tel: (215)699-5700
Fax: (215)699-8770
E-mail: mjohnson@lsb.edu
Web Site: http://www.lsbonline.com/
President/CEO: Marlon D. Keller

Admissions: Marianne H. Johnson
Financial Aid: Terry A. Knapp
Type: Two-Year College **Sex:** Coed **Application Fee:** $20.00 **H.S. Requirements:** High school diploma required; GED accepted **Scholarships:** Available **Calendar System:** Semester, Summer Session Available **Faculty:** FT 12, PT 25 **Library Holdings:** 2,000 **Credit Hours For Degree:** 68 credits, Associates **Professional Accreditation:** ACICS

LAUREL BUSINESS INSTITUTE
11-15 Penn St.
Uniontown, PA 15401
Tel: (724)439-4900
Fax: (724)439-3607
E-mail: ddecker@laurelbusiness.edu
Web Site: http://www.laurel.edu/
President/CEO: Nancy Decker
Registrar: Denise Robinson
Admissions: Douglas Decker
Financial Aid: Stephanie Migyanko
Type: Two-Year College **Sex:** Coed **% Accepted:** 59 **Admission Plans:** Open Admission; Deferred Admission **Application Deadline:** Rolling **Application Fee:** $55.00 **H.S. Requirements:** High school diploma required; GED accepted **Costs Per Year:** Application fee: $55. Tuition: $10,125 full-time, $215 per credit part-time. Mandatory fees: $1828 full-time, $349 per term part-time. **Scholarships:** Available **Calendar System:** Trimester **Enrollment:** FT 292, PT 5 **Faculty:** FT 16, PT 9 **Student-Faculty Ratio:** 16:1 **Exams:** Other **Professional Accreditation:** ACICS, AAMAE

LEBANON VALLEY COLLEGE
101 North College Ave.
Annville, PA 17003-1400
Tel: (717)867-6100; (866)LVC-4ADM
Admissions: (717)867-6181
Fax: (717)867-6124
E-mail: admiss@lvc.edu
Web Site: http://www.lvc.edu/
President/CEO: Dr. Stephen C. MacDonald
Registrar: Karen Best
Admissions: William J. Brown, Jr.
Financial Aid: William J. Brown, Jr.
Type: Comprehensive **Sex:** Coed **Affiliation:** United Methodist **Scores:** 98.9% SAT V 400+; 98.7% SAT M 400+ **% Accepted:** 77 **Application Deadline:** Rolling **Application Fee:** $30.00 **H.S. Requirements:** High school diploma required; GED accepted **Costs Per Year:** Application fee: $30. Comprehensive fee: $31,700 includes full-time tuition ($24,210), mandatory fees ($650), and college room and board ($6840). College room only: $3340. Room and board charges vary according to board plan and housing facility. Part-time tuition: $440 per credit. Part-time tuition varies according to class time and degree level. **Scholarships:** Available **Calendar System:** Semester, Summer Session Available **Enrollment:** FT 1,614, PT 160, Grad 141 **Faculty:** FT 100, PT 99 **Student-Faculty Ratio:** 13:1 **Exams:** SAT I or ACT **% Receiving Financial Aid:** 78 **% Residing in College-Owned, -Operated, or -Affiliated Housing:** 74 **Library Holdings:** 181,445 **Regional Accreditation:** Middle State Association of Colleges and Schools **Credit Hours For Degree:** 60 credits, Associates; 120 credits, Bachelors **ROTC:** Army **Professional Accreditation:** ACBSP, NASM **Intercollegiate Athletics:** Baseball M; Basketball M & W; Cross-Country Running M & W; Field Hockey W; Football M; Golf M; Ice Hockey M; Soccer M & W; Softball W; Swimming and Diving M & W; Tennis M & W; Track and Field M & W; Volleyball W

LEHIGH CARBON COMMUNITY COLLEGE
4525 Education Park Dr.
Schnecksville, PA 18078-2598
Tel: (610)799-2121
Admissions: (610)799-1575
Fax: (610)799-1527
E-mail: tellme@lccc.edu
Web Site: http://www.lccc.edu/
President/CEO: Donald W. Snyder
Registrar: Sandra Mosser
Admissions: Jack Mosser
Financial Aid: Marian Snyder
Type: Two-Year College **Sex:** Coed **Admission Plans:** Open Admission **Application Fee:** $25.00 **H.S. Requirements:** High school diploma or equivalent not required. For allied health, aviation, veterinary technician programs: High school diploma required; GED accepted **Costs Per Year:** Application fee: $25. Area resident tuition: $2700 full-time, $76 per credit part-time. State resident tuition: $5250 full-time, $152 per credit part-time. Nonresident tuition: $7800 full-time, $228 per credit part-time. Mandatory fees: $420 full-time, $14 per credit hour part-time. Full-time tuition and fees vary according to course load and reciprocity agreements. Part-time tuition and fees vary according to course load and reciprocity agreements. **Scholarships:** Available **Calendar System:** Semester, Summer Session Available **Enrollment:** FT 2,607, PT 4,067 **Faculty:** FT 108, PT 380 **Student-Faculty Ratio:** 14:1 **Exams:** Other **Library Holdings:** 99,734 **Regional Accreditation:** Middle State Association of Colleges and Schools **Credit Hours For Degree:** 60 credits, Associates **ROTC:** Army **Professional Accreditation:** AAMAE, AHIMA, AOTA, APTA, ACBSP, NLN **Intercollegiate Athletics:** Baseball M & W; Basketball M & W; Golf M & W; Soccer M; Softball W; Volleyball W

LEHIGH UNIVERSITY
27 Memorial Dr. West
Bethlehem, PA 18015-3094
Tel: (610)758-3000
Admissions: (610)758-3100
Fax: (610)758-4361
E-mail: admissions@lehigh.edu
Web Site: http://www.lehigh.edu/
President/CEO: Dr. Gregory C. Farrington
Registrar: Bruce S. Correll
Admissions: Eric J. Kaplan
Financial Aid: Linda F. Bell
Type: University **Sex:** Coed **Scores:** 100% SAT V 400+; 100% SAT M 400+ **% Accepted:** 41 **Admission Plans:** Early Admission; Early Decision Plan; Deferred Admission **Application Deadline:** January 01 **Application Fee:** $60.00 **H.S. Requirements:** High school diploma or equivalent not required **Costs Per Year:** Application fee: $60. Comprehensive fee: $39,980 includes full-time tuition ($31,180), mandatory fees ($240), and college room and board ($8560). College room only: $4890. Room and board charges vary according to board plan and student level. Part-time tuition: $1300 per credit. **Scholarships:** Available **Calendar System:** Semester, Summer Session Available **Enrollment:** FT 4,621, PT 58, Grad 2,069 **Faculty:** FT 434, PT 187 **Student-Faculty Ratio:** 9:1 **Exams:** SAT I or ACT **% Receiving Financial Aid:** 46 **% Residing in College-Owned, -Operated, or -Affiliated Housing:** 67 **Library Holdings:** 1,176,028 **Regional Accreditation:** Middle State Association of Colleges and Schools **Credit Hours For Degree:** 120 credit hours, Bachelors **ROTC:** Army **Professional Accreditation:** AACSB, ABET, APA, NAST **Intercollegiate Athletics:** Baseball M; Basketball M & W; Bowling M & W; Cheerleading M & W; Crew M & W; Cross-Country Running M & W; Equestrian Sports M & W; Field Hockey W; Football M & W; Golf M & W; Ice Hockey M; Lacrosse M & W; Rugby M; Skiing (Downhill) M & W; Soccer M & W; Softball W; Squash M; Swimming and Diving M & W; Tennis M & W; Track and Field M & W; Volleyball M & W; Wrestling M

LEHIGH VALLEY COLLEGE
2809 East Saucon Valley Rd.
Center Valley, PA 18034
Tel: (610)791-5100
Free: 800-227-9109
Fax: (610)791-7810
E-mail: joshua.padron@lehighvalley.edu
Web Site: http://www.lehighvalley.edu/
President/CEO: Virginia Carpenter
Registrar: Jennifer Giallonardo
Admissions: Joshua Padron
Financial Aid: Stephanie Artim-Azar
Type: Two-Year College **Sex:** Coed **Affiliation:** Career Education Corporation **% Accepted:** 25 **Admission Plans:** Open Admission; Deferred Admission **Application Deadline:** Rolling **Application Fee:** $50.00 **H.S. Requirements:** High school diploma required; GED accepted **Costs Per Year:** Application fee: $50. Tuition: $325 per credit hour part-time. Varies by program. **Scholarships:** Available **Calendar System:** Quarter, Summer

Session Not available **Faculty:** FT 40, PT 53 **Student-Faculty Ratio:** 26:1 **Exams:** Other **Credit Hours For Degree:** 90 credits, Associates **Professional Accreditation:** ACICS

LINCOLN TECHNICAL INSTITUTE (ALLENTOWN)
5151 Tilghman St.
Allentown, PA 18104-3298
Tel: (610)398-5300
Admissions: (610)398-5301
Web Site: http://www.lincolntech.com/
President/CEO: Lisa Kuntz
Registrar: Ana Maldonado
Admissions: Tony Campetti
Financial Aid: Ana Maldonado
Type: Two-Year College **Sex:** Coed **Affiliation:** Lincoln Technical Institute, Inc **Admission Plans:** Open Admission; Early Admission **Application Fee:** $100.00 **H.S. Requirements:** High school diploma required; GED accepted **Scholarships:** Available **Calendar System:** Semester, Summer Session Available **Faculty:** FT 25, PT 5 **Student-Faculty Ratio:** 20:1 **Credit Hours For Degree:** 97 credits, Associates **Professional Accreditation:** ACCSCT

LINCOLN TECHNICAL INSTITUTE (PHILADELPHIA)
9191 Torresdale Ave.
Philadelphia, PA 19136-1595
Tel: (215)335-0800
Free: 800-238-8381
Fax: (215)335-1443
E-mail: jkuntz@lincolntech.com
Web Site: http://www.lincolntech.com/
President/CEO: James Kuntz
Admissions: James Kuntz
Financial Aid: James Hinkel
Type: Two-Year College **Sex:** Coed **Affiliation:** Lincoln Technical Institute, Inc **Admission Plans:** Open Admission; Deferred Admission **Application Fee:** $25.00 **H.S. Requirements:** High school diploma required; GED accepted **Scholarships:** Available **Calendar System:** Miscellaneous, Summer Session Not available **Faculty:** FT 13, PT 6 **Credit Hours For Degree:** 76 credits, Associates **Professional Accreditation:** ACCSCT

LINCOLN UNIVERSITY
PO Box 179
Lincoln University, PA 19352
Tel: (610)932-8300
Free: 800-790-0191
E-mail: admiss@lincoln.edu
Web Site: http://www.lincoln.edu/
President/CEO: Dr. Ivory V. Nelson
Registrar: James Simington
Admissions: Michael Taylor
Financial Aid: Thelma Ross
Type: Comprehensive **Sex:** Coed **Scores:** 53% SAT V 400+; 48% SAT M 400+; 16% ACT 18-23; 6% ACT 24-29 **% Accepted:** 35 **Admission Plans:** Preferred Admission; Early Admission; Deferred Admission **Application Deadline:** Rolling **Application Fee:** $20.00 **H.S. Requirements:** High school diploma required; GED accepted **Costs Per Year:** Application fee: $20. State resident tuition: $5236 full-time, $284 per credit hour part-time. Nonresident tuition: $8912 full-time, $459 per credit hour part-time. Mandatory fees: $2382 full-time. Part-time tuition varies according to course load. College room and board: $6792. College room only: $3692. Room and board charges vary according to board plan. **Scholarships:** Available **Calendar System:** Semester, Summer Session Available **Enrollment:** FT 1,652, PT 62, Grad 564 **Faculty:** FT 93, PT 90 **Student-Faculty Ratio:** 16:1 **Exams:** SAT I or ACT **% Receiving Financial Aid:** 83 **% Residing in College-Owned, -Operated, or -Affiliated Housing:** 97 **Library Holdings:** 188,811 **Regional Accreditation:** Middle State Association of Colleges and Schools **Credit Hours For Degree:** 120 credit hours, Bachelors **ROTC:** Army, Air Force **Professional Accreditation:** NRPA **Intercollegiate Athletics:** Baseball M; Basketball M & W; Bowling M & W; Cross-Country Running M & W; Soccer M & W; Tennis M & W; Track and Field M & W; Volleyball W

LOCK HAVEN UNIVERSITY OF PENNSYLVANIA
401 N. Fairview St.
Lock Haven, PA 17745-2390
Tel: (570)893-2011
Free: 800-233-8978
Admissions: (570)893-2027
Fax: (570)893-2201
E-mail: admissions@eagle.lhup.edu
Web Site: http://www.lhup.edu/
President/CEO: Dr. Keith Miller
Registrar: Jill Reitz
Admissions: Steven Lee
Financial Aid: Dr. William A. Irwin
Type: Comprehensive **Sex:** Coed **Affiliation:** Pennsylvania State System of Higher Education **Scores:** 84.25% SAT V 400+; 84.34% SAT M 400+; 48% ACT 18-23; 11% ACT 24-29 **% Accepted:** 77 **Admission Plans:** Deferred Admission **Application Deadline:** Rolling **Application Fee:** $25.00 **H.S. Requirements:** High school diploma required; GED accepted **Costs Per Year:** Application fee: $25. State resident tuition: $4906 full-time, $204 per credit part-time. Nonresident tuition: $10,266 full-time, $428 per credit part-time. Mandatory fees: $1352 full-time, $38 per credit part-time, $98 per term part-time. Full-time tuition and fees vary according to course load and location. Part-time tuition and fees vary according to course load and location. College room and board: $5840. College room only: $3204. Room and board charges vary according to board plan and housing facility. **Scholarships:** Available **Calendar System:** Semester, Summer Session Available **Enrollment:** FT 4,556, PT 421, Grad 306 **Faculty:** FT 254, PT 19 **Student-Faculty Ratio:** 19:1 **Exams:** SAT I or ACT **% Receiving Financial Aid:** 72 **% Residing in College-Owned, -Operated, or -Affiliated Housing:** 36 **Library Holdings:** 429,941 **Regional Accreditation:** Middle State Association of Colleges and Schools **Credit Hours For Degree:** 60 semester hours, Associates; 120 semester hours, Bachelors **ROTC:** Army **Professional Accreditation:** CSWE, JRCEPAT, NCATE, NLN **Intercollegiate Athletics:** Baseball M; Basketball M & W; Cross-Country Running M & W; Field Hockey W; Football M; Lacrosse W; Soccer M & W; Softball W; Swimming and Diving W; Track and Field M & W; Volleyball W; Wrestling M

LUZERNE COUNTY COMMUNITY COLLEGE
1333 South Prospect St.
Nanticoke, PA 18634-9804
Tel: (570)740-0300
Admissions: (570)740-0342
Web Site: http://www.luzerne.edu/
President/CEO: Dr. Patricia C. Donohue
Registrar: Thomas P. Leary
Admissions: Helen Kopec
Financial Aid: Mary Kosin
Type: Two-Year College **Sex:** Coed **% Accepted:** 67 **Admission Plans:** Open Admission; Early Admission; Deferred Admission **Application Deadline:** Rolling **Application Fee:** $40.00 **H.S. Requirements:** High school diploma required; GED accepted. For those who demonstrate ability to benefit from program: High school diploma or equivalent not required **Costs Per Year:** Application fee: $40. Area resident tuition: $76 per credit part-time. State resident tuition: $152 per credit part-time. Nonresident tuition: $228 per credit part-time. Mandatory fees: $16 per credit part-time. **Scholarships:** Available **Calendar System:** Semester, Summer Session Available **Enrollment:** FT 2,940, PT 3,230 **Faculty:** FT 104, PT 371 **Student-Faculty Ratio:** 19:1 **Library Holdings:** 60,000 **Regional Accreditation:** Middle State Association of Colleges and Schools **Credit Hours For Degree:** 60 semester hours, Associates **ROTC:** Air Force **Professional Accreditation:** ARCEST, ADA, NLN **Intercollegiate Athletics:** Baseball M; Basketball M & W; Cross-Country Running M & W; Golf M & W; Soccer M & W; Softball W; Volleyball W

LYCOMING COLLEGE
700 College Place
Williamsport, PA 17701-5192
Tel: (570)321-4000
Free: 800-345-3920
Admissions: (570)321-4026
Fax: (570)321-4337
E-mail: admissions@lycoming.edu
Web Site: http://www.lycoming.edu/
President/CEO: Dr. James E. Douthat
Registrar: Rebecca Hile
Admissions: James Spencer
Financial Aid: Jamie Lowthert
Type: Four-Year College **Sex:** Coed **Affiliation:** United Methodist **Scores:** 99% SAT V 400+; 98% SAT M 400+; 52% ACT 18-23; 43% ACT 24-29 **% Accepted:** 77 **Admission Plans:** Early Admission; Deferred Admission **Ap-**

plication Deadline: June 01 **Application Fee:** $35.00 **H.S. Requirements:** High school diploma required; GED accepted **Costs Per Year:** Application fee: $35. Comprehensive fee: $30,622 includes full-time tuition ($23,680), mandatory fees ($400), and college room and board ($6542). College room only: $3356. Full-time tuition and fees vary according to course load. Room and board charges vary according to housing facility. Part-time tuition: $740 per credit hour. **Scholarships:** Available **Calendar System:** Semester, Summer Session Available **Enrollment:** FT 1,450, PT 17 **Faculty:** FT 84, PT 34 **Student-Faculty Ratio:** 14:1 **Exams:** SAT I or ACT **% Receiving Financial Aid:** 83 **% Residing in College-Owned, -Operated, or -Affiliated Housing:** 83 **Library Holdings:** 170,000 **Regional Accreditation:** Middle State Association of Colleges and Schools **Credit Hours For Degree:** 128 credits, Bachelors **ROTC:** Army **Professional Accreditation:** ACBSP **Intercollegiate Athletics:** Basketball M & W; Cheerleading M & W; Crew M & W; Cross-Country Running M & W; Equestrian Sports M & W; Football M; Golf M; Lacrosse M & W; Soccer M & W; Softball W; Swimming and Diving M & W; Tennis M & W; Ultimate Frisbee M & W; Volleyball W; Water Polo M & W; Wrestling M

MANOR COLLEGE
700 Fox Chase Rd.
Jenkintown, PA 19046
Tel: (215)885-2360
Admissions: (215)884-2216
E-mail: ftadmiss@manor.edu
Web Site: http://www.manor.edu/
President/CEO: Sr. Mary Cecilia Jurasinski, OSBM
Registrar: Richard Kukowski
Admissions: I. Jerry Czenstuch
Financial Aid: Dan Campbell
Type: Two-Year College **Sex:** Coed **Affiliation:** Byzantine Catholic **Scores:** 73% SAT V 400+; 62% SAT M 400+ **% Accepted:** 50 **Admission Plans:** Deferred Admission **Application Deadline:** Rolling **Application Fee:** $20.00 **H.S. Requirements:** High school diploma required; GED accepted **Costs Per Year:** Application fee: $20. Comprehensive fee: $16,514 includes full-time tuition ($10,868), mandatory fees ($350), and college room and board ($5296). Part-time tuition: $235 per credit hour. Part-time mandatory fees: $25 per term. **Scholarships:** Available **Calendar System:** Semester, Summer Session Available **Enrollment:** FT 433, PT 432 **Faculty:** FT 24, PT 87 **Student-Faculty Ratio:** 14:1 **Exams:** SAT I or ACT **Library Holdings:** 42,000 **Regional Accreditation:** Middle State Association of Colleges and Schools **Credit Hours For Degree:** 60 credit hours, Associates **Professional Accreditation:** ADA **Intercollegiate Athletics:** Basketball M & W; Soccer M & W; Volleyball W

MANSFIELD UNIVERSITY OF PENNSYLVANIA
Academy St.
Mansfield, PA 16933
Tel: (570)662-4000
Free: 800-577-6826
Admissions: (570)662-4813
Fax: (570)662-4121
E-mail: admissions@mnsfld.edu
Web Site: http://www.mansfield.edu/
President/CEO: Dr. John R. Halstead
Registrar: Carol Alexander
Admissions: Brian D. Barden
Financial Aid: Barbara L. Schmitt
Type: Comprehensive **Sex:** Coed **Affiliation:** Pennsylvania State System of Higher Education **Scores:** 94.3% SAT V 400+; 89% SAT M 400+ **% Accepted:** 72 **Admission Plans:** Early Admission; Deferred Admission **Application Deadline:** Rolling **Application Fee:** $25.00 **H.S. Requirements:** High school diploma required; GED accepted **Costs Per Year:** Application fee: $25. State resident tuition: $4906 full-time, $204 per credit part-time. Nonresident tuition: $12,266 full-time, $511 per credit part-time. Mandatory fees: $1502 full-time, $78 per credit part-time. Part-time tuition and fees vary according to course load. College room and board: $5868. Room and board charges vary according to board plan. **Scholarships:** Available **Calendar System:** Semester, Summer Session Available **Enrollment:** FT 2,713, PT 273, Grad 404 **Faculty:** FT 165, PT 58 **Student-Faculty Ratio:** 16:1 **Exams:** SAT I or ACT **% Receiving Financial Aid:** 74 **% Residing in College-Owned, -Operated, or -Affiliated Housing:** 50 **Library Holdings:** 246,141 **Regional Accreditation:** Middle State Association of Colleges and Schools **Credit Hours For Degree:** 61 credits, Associates; 120 credits, Bachelors **Professional Accreditation:** CARC, CSWE, JRCERT, NASM, NCATE, NLN **Intercollegiate Athletics:** Baseball M; Basketball M & W; Cross-Country Running M & W; Field Hockey W; Football M; Soccer W; Softball W; Swimming and Diving W; Track and Field M & W

MARYWOOD UNIVERSITY
2300 Adams Ave.
Scranton, PA 18509-1598
Tel: (570)348-6211
Free: 800-346-5014
Admissions: (570)348-6234
Fax: (570)961-4763
E-mail: ugadm@ac.marywood.edu
Web Site: http://www.marywood.edu/
President/CEO: Sr. Mary Reap, IHM
Registrar: Ann Boland-Chase
Admissions: Robert W. Reese
Financial Aid: Stanley F. Skrutski
Type: Comprehensive **Sex:** Coed **Affiliation:** Roman Catholic **Scores:** 98% SAT V 400+; 96% SAT M 400+; 62% ACT 18-23; 14% ACT 24-29 **Admission Plans:** Early Admission; Deferred Admission **Application Fee:** $30.00 **H.S. Requirements:** High school diploma required; GED accepted **Costs Per Year:** Application fee: $30. Comprehensive fee: $30,740 includes full-time tuition ($20,700), mandatory fees ($940), and college room and board ($9100). College room only: $5152. Room and board charges vary according to board plan and housing facility. Part-time tuition: $643 per credit. Part-time mandatory fees: $190 per term. Part-time tuition and fees vary according to course load. **Scholarships:** Available **Calendar System:** Semester, Summer Session Available **Enrollment:** FT 1,598, PT 213, Grad 1,316 **Faculty:** FT 140, PT 173 **Student-Faculty Ratio:** 12:1 **Exams:** SAT I or ACT, SAT I **% Receiving Financial Aid:** 83 **% Residing in College-Owned, -Operated, or -Affiliated Housing:** 38 **Library Holdings:** 220,205 **Regional Accreditation:** Middle State Association of Colleges and Schools **Credit Hours For Degree:** 63 credits, Associates; 126 credits, Bachelors **ROTC:** Army, Air Force **Professional Accreditation:** AAFCS, ACA, ADtA, ASLHA, ACBSP, CSWE, NASAD, NASM, NCATE, NLN **Intercollegiate Athletics:** Baseball M; Basketball M & W; Cross-Country Running M & W; Field Hockey W; Soccer M & W; Softball W; Tennis M & W; Volleyball W

MCCANN SCHOOL OF BUSINESS & TECHNOLOGY
2650 Woodglen Rd.
Pottsville, PA 17901
Tel: (570)622-7622
Fax: (570)622-7770
Web Site: http://www.mccannschool.com/
President/CEO: John E. Noone
Registrar: Bonnie Lech
Admissions: Rachel M. Schoffstall
Financial Aid: Joyce Zaleski
Type: Two-Year College **Sex:** Coed **Admission Plans:** Open Admission **Application Fee:** $40.00 **H.S. Requirements:** High school diploma required; GED accepted **Scholarships:** Available **Calendar System:** Quarter, Summer Session Available **Enrollment:** FT 540, PT 301 **Faculty:** FT 27, PT 50 **Student-Faculty Ratio:** 12:1 **Exams:** Other **Library Holdings:** 1,850 **Credit Hours For Degree:** 90 credits, Associates **Professional Accreditation:** ACICS

MEDIAN SCHOOL OF ALLIED HEALTH CAREERS
125 7th St.
Pittsburgh, PA 15222-3400
Tel: (412)391-7021
Free: 800-570-0693
Fax: (412)232-4348
Web Site: http://www.medianschool.edu/
President/CEO: Frances O. Mosle
Registrar: Mary Jo Kesman
Admissions: Kris Jackson
Financial Aid: Linda Malchano
Type: Two-Year College **Sex:** Coed **Admission Plans:** Open Admission; Deferred Admission **Application Fee:** $75.00 **H.S. Requirements:** High school diploma required; GED accepted **Scholarships:** Available **Calendar System:** Quarter, Summer Session Not available **Faculty:** FT 16, PT 7

Student-Faculty Ratio: 12:1 **Exams:** Other **Library Holdings:** 1,485 **Credit Hours For Degree:** 63 semester credits, Associates **Professional Accreditation:** ACCSCT, ADA

MERCYHURST COLLEGE
501 East 38th St.
Erie, PA 16546
Tel: (814)824-2000
Free: 800-825-1926
Admissions: (814)824-2576
Fax: (814)824-2071
Web Site: http://www.mercyhurst.edu/
President/CEO: Dr. William P. Garvey
Registrar: Sr. Patricia Whalen
Admissions: J. P. Conney
Financial Aid: James Theeuwes
Type: Comprehensive **Sex:** Coed **Affiliation:** Roman Catholic **Scores:** 100% SAT V 400+; 99% SAT M 400+; 49% ACT 18-23; 39% ACT 24-29 **% Accepted:** 78 **Admission Plans:** Open Admission; Deferred Admission **Application Deadline:** Rolling **Application Fee:** $30.00 **H.S. Requirements:** High school diploma required; GED accepted **Costs Per Year:** Application fee: $30. Comprehensive fee: $26,187 includes full-time tuition ($17,760), mandatory fees ($1353), and college room and board ($7074). College room only: $3576. Room and board charges vary according to board plan and housing facility. Part-time tuition: $592 per credit. Part-time tuition varies according to course load and location. **Scholarships:** Available **Calendar System:** Miscellaneous, Summer Session Available **Enrollment:** FT 3,378, PT 462, Grad 280 **Faculty:** FT 163, PT 85 **Student-Faculty Ratio:** 18:1 **Exams:** SAT I or ACT **% Receiving Financial Aid:** 76 **% Residing in College-Owned, -Operated, or -Affiliated Housing:** 73 **Library Holdings:** 179,680 **Regional Accreditation:** Middle State Association of Colleges and Schools **Credit Hours For Degree:** 54 credits, Bachelors **ROTC:** Army, Air Force **Professional Accreditation:** AAFCS, ADtA, APTA, CSWE, JRCEPAT, NASM, NLN **Intercollegiate Athletics:** Baseball M; Basketball M & W; Crew M & W; Cross-Country Running M & W; Field Hockey W; Football M; Golf M & W; Ice Hockey M & W; Lacrosse M & W; Soccer M & W; Softball W; Tennis M & W; Volleyball M & W; Water Polo M & W; Wrestling M

MESSIAH COLLEGE
One College Ave.
Grantham, PA 17027
Tel: (717)766-2511
Free: 800-233-4220
Admissions: (717)691-6000
Fax: (717)796-5374
E-mail: admiss@messiah.edu
Web Site: http://www.messiah.edu/
President/CEO: Dr. Kim S. Phipps
Registrar: Dr. James J. Sotherden
Admissions: Dr. William G. Strausbaugh
Financial Aid: Greg L. Gearhart
Type: Four-Year College **Sex:** Coed **Affiliation:** interdenominational **Scores:** 99.55% SAT V 400+; 99.7% SAT M 400+; 26.19% ACT 18-23; 53.17% ACT 24-29 **% Accepted:** 75 **Admission Plans:** Early Admission; Deferred Admission **Application Deadline:** Rolling **Application Fee:** $30.00 **H.S. Requirements:** High school diploma required; GED accepted **Costs Per Year:** Application fee: $30. Comprehensive fee: $28,910 includes full-time tuition ($21,420), mandatory fees ($690), and college room and board ($6800). College room only: $3540. Room and board charges vary according to board plan, housing facility, and location. Part-time tuition: $890 per credit. Part-time mandatory fees: $28 per credit. **Scholarships:** Available **Calendar System:** Semester, Summer Session Available **Enrollment:** FT 2,864, PT 52 **Faculty:** FT 170, PT 127 **Student-Faculty Ratio:** 13:1 **Exams:** SAT I or ACT **% Receiving Financial Aid:** 68 **% Residing in College-Owned, -Operated, or -Affiliated Housing:** 89 **Library Holdings:** 290,838 **Regional Accreditation:** Middle State Association of Colleges and Schools **Credit Hours For Degree:** 126 credits, Bachelors **Professional Accreditation:** ABET, AACN, JRCEPAT, NASAD, NASM **Intercollegiate Athletics:** Baseball M; Basketball M & W; Cross-Country Running M & W; Field Hockey W; Golf M; Lacrosse M & W; Soccer M & W; Softball W; Tennis M & W; Track and Field M & W; Volleyball W; Wrestling M

METROPOLITAN CAREER CENTER
100 South Broad St.
Philadelphia, PA 19110
Tel: (215)568-9215
Admissions: (215)843-6615
Fax: (215)568-3511
E-mail: khuselton@mcc-btc.org
Web Site: http://www.metropolitancareercenter.org/
President/CEO: Karen Burgess
Admissions: Ken Huselton
Type: Two-Year College **Sex:** Coed **Calendar System:** Semester **Professional Accreditation:** ACCSCT

MILLERSVILLE UNIVERSITY OF PENNSYLVANIA
PO Box 1002
Millersville, PA 17551-0302
Tel: (717)872-3011
Free: 800-MU-ADMIT
Admissions: (717)872-3371
E-mail: adm_info@mu3.millersv.edu
Web Site: http://www.millersville.edu/
President/CEO: Dr. Francine G. McNairy
Registrar: Candace A. Deen
Admissions: Douglas Zander
Financial Aid: Dwight Horsey
Type: Comprehensive **Sex:** Coed **Affiliation:** Pennsylvania State System of Higher Education **Scores:** 100% SAT V 400+; 100% SAT M 400+ **% Accepted:** 60 **Admission Plans:** Early Admission; Deferred Admission **Application Deadline:** Rolling **Application Fee:** $35.00 **H.S. Requirements:** High school diploma required; GED accepted **Costs Per Year:** Application fee: $35. State resident tuition: $4906 full-time, $204 per credit part-time. Nonresident tuition: $12,266 full-time, $511 per credit part-time. Mandatory fees: $1329 full-time, $81 per credit part-time. Part-time tuition and fees vary according to course load. College room and board: $5878. College room only: $3474. Room and board charges vary according to board plan. **Scholarships:** Available **Calendar System:** 4-1-4, Summer Session Available **Enrollment:** FT 6,378, PT 613, Grad 1,007 **Faculty:** FT 320, PT 148 **Student-Faculty Ratio:** 18:1 **Exams:** SAT I or ACT **% Receiving Financial Aid:** 52 **% Residing in College-Owned, -Operated, or -Affiliated Housing:** 37 **Library Holdings:** 503,145 **Regional Accreditation:** Middle State Association of Colleges and Schools **Credit Hours For Degree:** 60 credits, Associates; 120 credits, Bachelors **ROTC:** Army **Professional Accreditation:** ABET, ACBSP, CARC, CSWE, NAIT, NASM, NCATE, NLN **Intercollegiate Athletics:** Baseball M; Basketball M & W; Cross-Country Running M & W; Field Hockey W; Football M; Golf M; Lacrosse W; Soccer M & W; Softball W; Swimming and Diving W; Tennis M & W; Track and Field M & W; Volleyball W; Wrestling M

MONTGOMERY COUNTY COMMUNITY COLLEGE
340 DeKalb Pike
Blue Bell, PA 19422-0796
Tel: (215)641-6300
Admissions: (215)641-6551
Fax: (215)653-0585
E-mail: admrec@admin.mc3.edu
Web Site: http://www.mc3.edu
President/CEO: Dr. Karen A. Stout
Registrar: Wayne J. Ledger
Admissions: Penny Sawyer
Financial Aid: Cynthia Haney
Type: Two-Year College **Sex:** Coed **% Accepted:** 100 **Admission Plans:** Open Admission; Preferred Admission; Early Admission; Deferred Admission **Application Deadline:** May 01 **Application Fee:** $25.00 **H.S. Requirements:** High school diploma required; GED accepted. For Early Admissions Program: High school diploma or equivalent not required **Costs Per Year:** Application fee: $25. Area resident tuition: $2716 full-time, $83 per credit part-time. State resident tuition: $5348 full-time, $191 per credit part-time. Nonresident tuition: $7980 full-time, $285 per credit part-time. Mandatory fees: $14 per credit part-time. **Scholarships:** Available **Calendar System:** Semester, Summer Session Available **Enrollment:** FT 4,761, PT 6,113 **Faculty:** FT 167, PT 497 **Student-Faculty Ratio:** 23:1 **Library Holdings:** 201,174 **Regional Accreditation:** Middle State Association of Colleges and Schools **Credit Hours For Degree:** 60 credits, Associates **Professional Accreditation:** ADA, NAACLS, NLN

MOORE COLLEGE OF ART & DESIGN
20th and the Parkway
Philadelphia, PA 19103

Tel: (215)568-4515
Free: 800-523-2025
Fax: (215)568-3547
E-mail: hlee@moore.edu
Web Site: http://www.moore.edu/
President/CEO: Dr. Happy Craven Fernandez
Registrar: Dianne Runyon
Admissions: Heesung Lee
Financial Aid: Rochelle Iannuzzi
Type: Four-Year College **Sex:** Women **Scores:** 90% SAT V 400+; 85% SAT M 400+; 13% ACT 18-23; 25% ACT 24-29 **% Accepted:** 87 **Admission Plans:** Early Admission; Early Decision Plan; Deferred Admission **Application Deadline:** August 15 **Application Fee:** $40.00 **H.S. Requirements:** High school diploma required; GED accepted **Costs Per Year:** Application fee: $40. Comprehensive fee: $32,256 includes full-time tuition ($22,846), mandatory fees ($756), and college room and board ($8654). College room only: $5227. Part-time tuition: $920 per credit. Part-time mandatory fees: $189 per term. **Scholarships:** Available **Calendar System:** Semester, Summer Session Available **Enrollment:** FT 421, PT 70 **Faculty:** FT 32, PT 74 **Student-Faculty Ratio:** 8:1 **Exams:** SAT I or ACT **% Receiving Financial Aid:** 76 **% Residing in College-Owned, -Operated, or -Affiliated Housing:** 55 **Library Holdings:** 40,000 **Regional Accreditation:** Middle State Association of Colleges and Schools **Credit Hours For Degree:** 125.5 credits, Bachelors **Professional Accreditation:** FIDER, NASAD

MORAVIAN COLLEGE
1200 Main St.
Bethlehem, PA 18018-6650
Tel: (610)861-1300
Free: 800-441-3191
Admissions: (610)861-1320
Fax: (610)861-3956
E-mail: admissions@moravian.edu
Web Site: http://www.moravian.edu/
President/CEO: Dr. Ervin J. Rokke
Registrar: Mary Margaret Gross
Admissions: James P. Mackin
Financial Aid: Stephen C. Cassel
Type: Comprehensive **Sex:** Coed **Affiliation:** Moravian Church **Scores:** 100% SAT V 400+; 100% SAT M 400+ **% Accepted:** 65 **Admission Plans:** Early Admission; Early Decision Plan; Deferred Admission **Application Deadline:** February 15 **Application Fee:** $40.00 **H.S. Requirements:** High school diploma required; GED accepted **Costs Per Year:** Application fee: $40. One-time mandatory fee: $100. Comprehensive fee: $32,793 includes full-time tuition ($24,813), mandatory fees ($450), and college room and board ($7530). College room only: $4230. Room and board charges vary according to board plan and housing facility. Part-time tuition: $775 per credit. Part-time tuition varies according to class time. **Scholarships:** Available **Calendar System:** Semester, Summer Session Available **Enrollment:** FT 1,543, PT 249, Grad 188 **Faculty:** FT 118, PT 72 **Student-Faculty Ratio:** 12:1 **Exams:** SAT I or ACT **% Receiving Financial Aid:** 74 **% Residing in College-Owned, -Operated, or -Affiliated Housing:** 69 **Library Holdings:** 256,352 **Regional Accreditation:** Middle State Association of Colleges and Schools **Credit Hours For Degree:** 128 credits, Bachelors **ROTC:** Army **Professional Accreditation:** AACN, NASM **Intercollegiate Athletics:** Baseball M; Basketball M & W; Cheerleading W; Cross-Country Running M & W; Equestrian Sports W; Field Hockey W; Football M; Golf M & W; Ice Hockey M & W; Lacrosse M & W; Soccer M & W; Softball W; Tennis M & W; Track and Field M & W; Volleyball W

MOUNT ALOYSIUS COLLEGE
7373 Admiral Peary Hwy.
Cresson, PA 16630-1999
Tel: (814)886-4131; 888-823-2220
Admissions: (814)886-6383
Fax: (814)886-2978
Web Site: http://www.mtaloy.edu/
President/CEO: Sr. Mary Ann Dillon
Registrar: Carol Townsend
Admissions: Francis Crouse
Financial Aid: Stacy Schenk
Type: Comprehensive **Sex:** Coed **Affiliation:** Roman Catholic **Scores:** 85% SAT V 400+; 83% SAT M 400+; 53% ACT 18-23; 1% ACT 24-29 **% Accepted:** 77 **Admission Plans:** Early Admission; Deferred Admission **Application Deadline:** Rolling **Application Fee:** $30.00 **H.S. Requirements:** High school diploma required; GED accepted **Costs Per Year:** Application fee: $30. Comprehensive fee: $20,840 includes full-time tuition ($14,220), mandatory fees ($430), and college room and board ($6190). College room only: $3130. Full-time tuition and fees vary according to class time, course load, and program. Room and board charges vary according to board plan. Part-time tuition: $450 per credit. Part-time tuition varies according to class time, course load, and program. **Scholarships:** Available **Calendar System:** Semester, Summer Session Available **Enrollment:** FT 1,147, PT 335, Grad 57 **Faculty:** FT 62, PT 103 **Student-Faculty Ratio:** 14:1 **Exams:** SAT I or ACT **% Receiving Financial Aid:** 94 **% Residing in College-Owned, -Operated, or -Affiliated Housing:** 22 **Library Holdings:** 84,174 **Regional Accreditation:** Middle State Association of Colleges and Schools **Credit Hours For Degree:** 60 credits, Associates; 120 credits, Bachelors **Professional Accreditation:** ARCEST, AAMAE, AOTA, APTA, NLN **Intercollegiate Athletics:** Baseball M; Basketball M & W; Cross-Country Running M & W; Golf M & W; Soccer M & W; Softball W; Volleyball W

MUHLENBERG COLLEGE
2400 Chew St.
Allentown, PA 18104-5586
Tel: (484)664-3100
Admissions: (484)664-3245
Fax: (484)664-3234
E-mail: adm@muhlenberg.edu
Web Site: http://www.muhlenberg.edu/
President/CEO: Dr. Peyton Randolph Helm
Registrar: Sophia Robles
Admissions: Christopher Hooker-Haring
Financial Aid: Gregory Mitton
Type: Four-Year College **Sex:** Coed **Affiliation:** Lutheran Church **Scores:** 100% SAT V 400+; 100% SAT M 400+; 7% ACT 18-23; 63% ACT 24-29 **% Accepted:** 43 **Admission Plans:** Early Admission; Early Decision Plan; Deferred Admission **Application Deadline:** February 15 **Application Fee:** $45.00 **H.S. Requirements:** High school diploma required; GED accepted **Costs Per Year:** Application fee: $45. Comprehensive fee: $37,890 includes full-time tuition ($30,260) and college room and board ($7630). College room only: $4420. Part-time tuition: $3528 per course. **Scholarships:** Available **Calendar System:** Semester, Summer Session Available **Enrollment:** FT 2,267, PT 190 **Faculty:** FT 152, PT 104 **Student-Faculty Ratio:** 12:1 **Exams:** SAT I or ACT **% Receiving Financial Aid:** 43 **% Residing in College-Owned, -Operated, or -Affiliated Housing:** 90 **Library Holdings:** 302,946 **Regional Accreditation:** Middle State Association of Colleges and Schools **Credit Hours For Degree:** 34 courses, Bachelors **ROTC:** Army **Intercollegiate Athletics:** Baseball M; Basketball M & W; Cheerleading M & W; Cross-Country Running M & W; Field Hockey W; Football M; Golf M & W; Lacrosse M & W; Soccer M & W; Softball W; Tennis M & W; Track and Field M & W; Volleyball W; Wrestling M

NEUMANN COLLEGE
One Neumann Dr.
Aston, PA 19014-1298
Tel: (610)459-0905
Free: 800-963-8626
Admissions: (610)361-2448
E-mail: murphyjd@neumann.edu
Web Site: http://www.neumann.edu/
President/CEO: Dr. Rosalie M. Mirenda
Registrar: Larry S. Friedman
Admissions: Dennis J. Murphy
Financial Aid: Joseph Henderson
Type: Comprehensive **Sex:** Coed **Affiliation:** Roman Catholic **Scores:** 78.1% SAT V 400+; 67.1% SAT M 400+ **% Accepted:** 96 **Admission Plans:** Early Admission; Deferred Admission **Application Deadline:** April 01 **Application Fee:** $35.00 **H.S. Requirements:** High school diploma required; GED accepted **Costs Per Year:** Application fee: $35. Comprehensive fee: $25,996 includes full-time tuition ($17,300), mandatory fees ($620), and college room and board ($8076). College room only: $4796. Part-time tuition: $395 per credit. **Scholarships:** Available **Calendar System:** Semester, Summer Session Available **Enrollment:** FT 1,832, PT 481, Grad 497 **Faculty:** FT 84, PT 131 **Student-Faculty Ratio:** 16:1 **Exams:** SAT I or ACT **% Receiving Financial Aid:** 90 **% Residing in College-Owned, -Operated, or -Affiliated Housing:** 46 **Library Holdings:** 75,000 **Regional Accreditation:** Middle State Association of Colleges and Schools **Credit Hours For Degree:** 60 credits, Associates; 120 credits, Bachelors **ROTC:** Army **Professional Accreditation:** APTA, NAACLS, NLN **Intercollegiate**

Athletics: Baseball M; Basketball M & W; Field Hockey W; Golf M; Ice Hockey M & W; Lacrosse M & W; Soccer M & W; Softball W; Tennis M & W; Volleyball W

NEW CASTLE SCHOOL OF TRADES
New Castle Youngstown Rd., Route 422 RD1
Pulaski, PA 16143-9721
Tel: (724)964-8811
Free: 800-837-8299
E-mail: ncstrades@aol.com
Web Site: http://www.ncstrades.com/
President/CEO: Dr. Rex Spaulding
Admissions: Rex Spaulding
Financial Aid: Trudy Sotter
Type: Two-Year College **Sex:** Coed **Affiliation:** Educational Enterprises Incorporated **Application Fee:** $25.00 **Scholarships:** Available **Calendar System:** Quarter **Enrollment:** FT 451 **Faculty:** FT 25, PT 11 **Student-Faculty Ratio:** 18:1 **Exams:** Other **Professional Accreditation:** ACCSCT

NEWPORT BUSINESS INSTITUTE (LOWER BURRELL)
945 Greensburg Rd.
Lower Burrell, PA 15068-3929
Tel: (724)339-7542
Free: 800-752-7695
Fax: (724)339-2950
Web Site: http://www.nbi.edu
President/CEO: Bryant Mullen
Admissions: Bryant Mullen
Financial Aid: Rose Mary Leipertz
Type: Two-Year College **Sex:** Coed **% Accepted:** 100 **Admission Plans:** Open Admission; Early Admission **Application Deadline:** Rolling **Application Fee:** $25.00 **H.S. Requirements:** High school diploma required; GED accepted **Costs Per Year:** Application fee: $25. Tuition: $7800 full-time, $655 per course part-time. Mandatory fees: $1575 full-time. **Scholarships:** Available **Calendar System:** Quarter, Summer Session Not available **Enrollment:** FT 79 **Faculty:** FT 6 **Student-Faculty Ratio:** 14:1 **Library Holdings:** 962 **Credit Hours For Degree:** 90 quarter hours, Associates **Professional Accreditation:** ACICS

NEWPORT BUSINESS INSTITUTE (WILLIAMSPORT)
941 West Third St.
Williamsport, PA 17701-5855
Tel: (570)326-2869
Free: 800-962-6971
Fax: (570)326-2136
E-mail: director_NBI@suscom.net
Web Site: http://www.newportbusiness.com/
President/CEO: J. Bryant Mullen
Registrar: Susan A. Crago
Admissions: Mary Weaver
Type: Two-Year College **Sex:** Coed **% Accepted:** 100 **Admission Plans:** Deferred Admission **Application Deadline:** Rolling **Application Fee:** $25.00 **H.S. Requirements:** High school diploma required; GED accepted **Costs Per Year:** Application fee: $25. Tuition: $8850 full-time, $737.50 per course part-time. Mandatory fees: $475 full-time. **Scholarships:** Available **Calendar System:** Quarter, Summer Session Available **Enrollment:** FT 103, PT 1 **Faculty:** FT 6, PT 1 **Student-Faculty Ratio:** 15:1 **Credit Hours For Degree:** 90 quarter hours, Associates **Professional Accreditation:** ACICS

NORTH CENTRAL INDUSTRIAL TECHNICAL EDUCATION CENTER
651 Montmorenci Ave.
Ridgway, PA 15853
Tel: (814)772-1012
Free: 800-242-5872
Fax: (814)772-1554
E-mail: linzana@ncentral.com
President/CEO: Lugene Inzana
Admissions: Lugene Inzana
Type: Two-Year College **Sex:** Coed **Calendar System:** Trimester **Professional Accreditation:** ACCSCT

NORTHAMPTON COUNTY AREA COMMUNITY COLLEGE
3835 Green Pond Rd.
Bethlehem, PA 18020-7599
Tel: (610)861-5300
Admissions: (610)861-5506
E-mail: adminfo@northampton.edu
Web Site: http://www.northampton.edu/
President/CEO: Dr. Arthur L. Scott
Registrar: Carolyn H. Holmfelt
Admissions: James McCarthy
Financial Aid: Cindy King
Type: Two-Year College **Sex:** Coed **% Accepted:** 100 **Admission Plans:** Open Admission; Deferred Admission **Application Deadline:** Rolling **Application Fee:** $25.00 **H.S. Requirements:** High school diploma required; GED accepted **Costs Per Year:** Application fee: $25. Area resident tuition: $2100 full-time, $70 per credit hour part-time. State resident tuition: $4200 full-time, $140 per credit hour part-time. Nonresident tuition: $6300 full-time, $210 per credit hour part-time. Mandatory fees: $720 full-time, $24 per credit hour part-time. Full-time tuition and fees vary according to course load. Part-time tuition and fees vary according to course load. College room and board: $5944. College room only: $3434. Room and board charges vary according to board plan and housing facility. **Scholarships:** Available **Calendar System:** Semester, Summer Session Available **Enrollment:** FT 3,680, PT 5,074 **Faculty:** FT 106, PT 436 **Student-Faculty Ratio:** 21:1 **% Residing in College-Owned, -Operated, or -Affiliated Housing:** 3 **Library Holdings:** 64,758 **Regional Accreditation:** Middle State Association of Colleges and Schools **Credit Hours For Degree:** 60 credit hours, Associates **Professional Accreditation:** ABFSE, ADA, ACBSP, JRCERT, NLN **Intercollegiate Athletics:** Baseball M; Basketball M & W; Bowling M & W; Golf M & W; Ice Hockey M & W; Soccer M & W; Softball W; Tennis M & W; Volleyball M & W; Wrestling M

OAKBRIDGE ACADEMY OF ARTS
1250 Greensburg Rd.
Lower Burrell, PA 15068
Tel: (724)335-5336
Free: 800-734-5601
Fax: (724)335-3367
Web Site: http://www.akvalley.com/oakbridge/
President/CEO: Janie Gatty
Registrar: Debra Wells
Admissions: Tara Jo Pomatto
Financial Aid: Rose Leipertz
Type: Two-Year College **Sex:** Coed **Application Deadline:** August 31 **Application Fee:** $50.00 **H.S. Requirements:** High school diploma required; GED accepted **Costs Per Year:** Application fee: $50. One-time mandatory fee: $30. Tuition: $22,400 full-time, $600 per course part-time. Mandatory fees: $1750 full-time. **Scholarships:** Available **Calendar System:** Quarter **Enrollment:** FT 66 **Faculty:** FT 3, PT 2 **Student-Faculty Ratio:** 16:1 **Library Holdings:** 3,000 **Credit Hours For Degree:** 90 quarter hours, Associates **Professional Accreditation:** ACCSCT

ORLEANS TECHNICAL INSTITUTE-CENTER CITY CAMPUS
1845 Walnut St., Ste. 700
Philadelphia, PA 19103-4707
Tel: (215)854-1853
Fax: (215)854-1880
Web Site: http://www.jevs.org/schools_svs.asp
President/CEO: G. Zukerman
Registrar: Morton Levine
Admissions: Gary Bello
Financial Aid: J. Musto
Type: Two-Year College **Sex:** Coed **Admission Plans:** Open Admission **Application Fee:** $150.00 **H.S. Requirements:** High school diploma required; GED accepted **Costs Per Year:** Application fee: $150. Tuition: $10,500 full-time, $7350 per year part-time. Mandatory fees: $150 full-time. Full-time tuition and fees vary according to program. Part-time tuition varies according to program. **Scholarships:** Available **Calendar System:** Trimester, Summer Session Available **Enrollment:** FT 87, PT 48 **Faculty:** FT 3, PT 14 **Student-Faculty Ratio:** 7:1 **Exams:** Other **Library Holdings:** 625 **Credit Hours For Degree:** 82 credits, Associates **Professional Accreditation:** ACCSCT

PACE INSTITUTE
606 Ct. St.
Reading, PA 19601
Tel: (610)375-1212
Fax: (610)375-1924
Web Site: http://www.paceinstitute.com/

President/CEO: Rhonda Dersh
Admissions: Ed Levandowski
Type: Two-Year College **Sex:** Coed **Scholarships:** Available **Enrollment:** FT 201, PT 73 **Faculty:** FT 6, PT 8 **Student-Faculty Ratio:** 18:1 **Professional Accreditation:** ACICS

PEIRCE COLLEGE
1420 Pine St.
Philadelphia, PA 19102-4699
Tel: (215)545-6400; 888-467-3472
Admissions: (215)670-9236
Fax: (215)546-5996
E-mail: nmmaher@peirce.edu
Web Site: http://www.peirce.edu/
President/CEO: Dr. Arthur J. Lendo
Registrar: Nadine Maher
Admissions: Nadine Maher
Financial Aid: Lisa A. Gargiulo
Type: Four-Year College **Sex:** Coed **% Accepted:** 45 **Admission Plans:** Open Admission **Application Deadline:** Rolling **Application Fee:** $50.00 **H.S. Requirements:** High school diploma required; GED accepted **Costs Per Year:** Application fee: $50. Tuition: $11,760 full-time, $392 per credit hour part-time. Mandatory fees: $1000 full-time, $100 per course part-time. Full-time tuition and fees vary according to course load. Part-time tuition and fees vary according to course load. **Scholarships:** Available **Calendar System:** Continuous, Summer Session Available **Enrollment:** FT 825, PT 1,146 **Faculty:** FT 26, PT 115 **Student-Faculty Ratio:** 14:1 **% Receiving Financial Aid:** 70 **Library Holdings:** 30,502 **Regional Accreditation:** Middle State Association of Colleges and Schools **Credit Hours For Degree:** 61 credits, Associates; 121 credits, Bachelors **Professional Accreditation:** ACBSP

PENN COMMERCIAL BUSINESS AND TECHNICAL SCHOOL
242 Oak Spring Rd.
Washington, PA 15301
Tel: (724)222-5330
Fax: (724)222-4722
E-mail: mjoyce@penn-commercial.com
Web Site: http://www.penncommercial.net/
President/CEO: Robert S. Bazant
Registrar: Michael Joyce
Admissions: Michael John Joyce
Financial Aid: Jenny S. Slesh
Type: Two-Year College **Sex:** Coed **Admission Plans:** Open Admission; Early Admission; Deferred Admission **Application Fee:** $25.00 **H.S. Requirements:** High school diploma required; GED accepted **Scholarships:** Available **Calendar System:** Quarter, Summer Session Available **Enrollment:** FT 304 **Faculty:** FT 13, PT 17 **Student-Faculty Ratio:** 16:1 **Library Holdings:** 400 **Credit Hours For Degree:** 1500 hours, Associates **Professional Accreditation:** ACICS, AAMAE

PENN FOSTER CAREER SCHOOL
925 Oak St.
Scranton, PA 18515
Tel: (570)342-7701
Free: 800-233-4191
Web Site: http://www.pennfoster.edu/
President/CEO: David Beach
Registrar: Linda Smith
Admissions: Connie Dempsey
Type: Two-Year College **Sex:** Coed **% Accepted:** 99 **Admission Plans:** Open Admission **Application Deadline:** Rolling **H.S. Requirements:** High school diploma required; GED accepted **Costs Per Year:** Tuition: $900 per term part-time. Mandatory fees: $60 per term part-time. **Calendar System:** Semester, Summer Session Available **Faculty:** FT 17, PT 26 **Exams:** Other **Regional Accreditation:** Middle State Association of Colleges and Schools **Credit Hours For Degree:** 62 credits, Associates **Professional Accreditation:** DETC

PENNCO TECH
3815 Otter St.
Bristol, PA 19007-3696
Tel: (215)824-3200
E-mail: admissions@penncotech.com
Web Site: http://www.penncotech.com/
President/CEO: John Hobyak
Registrar: LeeAnn Dorf
Admissions: Nate R. Aldsworth
Financial Aid: Terry Carrazzino
Type: Two-Year College **Sex:** Coed **Affiliation:** Pennco Institutes, Inc **Application Fee:** $50.00 **H.S. Requirements:** High school diploma required; GED accepted. For applicants who demonstrate ability to benefit from college: High school diploma or equivalent not required **Scholarships:** Available **Calendar System:** Miscellaneous, Summer Session Not available **Faculty:** FT 20, PT 13 **Exams:** Other **Library Holdings:** 6,000 **Credit Hours For Degree:** 1560 hours, Associates **Professional Accreditation:** ACCSCT

PENNSYLVANIA COLLEGE OF ART & DESIGN
204 North Prince St., PO Box 59
Lancaster, PA 17608-0059
Tel: (717)396-7833
Fax: (717)396-1339
E-mail: smatson@pcad.edu
Web Site: http://www.pcad.edu/
President/CEO: Mary Colleen Heil
Registrar: David Hershey
Admissions: Susan Matson
Financial Aid: David Hershey
Type: Four-Year College **Sex:** Coed **% Accepted:** 63 **Admission Plans:** Open Admission; Deferred Admission **Application Deadline:** May 01 **Application Fee:** $40.00 **H.S. Requirements:** High school diploma required; GED accepted **Costs Per Year:** Application fee: $40. Tuition: $13,607 full-time, $567 per credit part-time. Mandatory fees: $450 full-time, $80 per term part-time. **Scholarships:** Available **Calendar System:** Semester, Summer Session Not available **Enrollment:** FT 203, PT 22 **Faculty:** FT 11, PT 40 **Student-Faculty Ratio:** 9:1 **Library Holdings:** 10,000 **Credit Hours For Degree:** 120 credits, Bachelors **Professional Accreditation:** NASAD

PENNSYLVANIA COLLEGE OF TECHNOLOGY
One College Ave.
Williamsport, PA 17701-5778
Tel: (570)326-3761
Admissions: (570)327-4761
Fax: (570)321-5551
E-mail: cschuman@pct.edu
Web Site: http://www.pct.edu/
President/CEO: Dr. Davie Jane Gilmour
Registrar: Dennis Dunkleberger
Admissions: Chester D. Schuman
Financial Aid: Janice A. Kuzio
Type: Four-Year College **Sex:** Coed **Affiliation:** Pennsylvania State University **% Accepted:** 97 **Admission Plans:** Open Admission; Early Admission; Deferred Admission **Application Deadline:** July 01 **Application Fee:** $50.00 **H.S. Requirements:** High school diploma required; GED accepted **Costs Per Year:** Application fee: $50. State resident tuition: $8580 full-time, $286 per credit part-time. Nonresident tuition: $11,160 full-time, $372 per credit part-time. Mandatory fees: $1500 full-time. Full-time tuition and fees vary according to course load and program. Part-time tuition varies according to course load and program. College room and board: $6900. College room only: $4200. Room and board charges vary according to board plan, housing facility, and location. **Scholarships:** Available **Calendar System:** Semester, Summer Session Available **Enrollment:** FT 5,515, PT 1,022 **Faculty:** FT 283, PT 208 **Student-Faculty Ratio:** 19:1 **Exams:** SAT I **% Residing in College-Owned, -Operated, or -Affiliated Housing:** 23 **Library Holdings:** 96,281 **Regional Accreditation:** Middle State Association of Colleges and Schools **Credit Hours For Degree:** 60 credits, Associates; 120 credits, Bachelors **ROTC:** Army **Professional Accreditation:** ABET, ACF, ADA, AOTA, JRCERT, JRCEMT, NLN **Intercollegiate Athletics:** Archery M & W; Baseball M; Basketball M & W; Bowling M & W; Cross-Country Running M & W; Golf M & W; Soccer M & W; Softball W; Tennis M & W; Volleyball M & W

PENNSYLVANIA CULINARY INSTITUTE
717 Liberty Ave.
Pittsburgh, PA 15222-3500
Tel: (412)566-2433
Free: 800-432-2433
Fax: (412)566-2434
Web Site: http://www.paculinary.com/

President/CEO: Larry Galley
Registrar: Tina McClaren
Admissions: Bob Cappel
Financial Aid: Jen Burns
Type: Two-Year College **Sex:** Coed **Application Fee:** $100.00 **H.S. Requirements:** High school diploma required; GED accepted **Costs Per Year:** Application fee: $100. Comprehensive fee: $25,570 includes full-time tuition ($18,550) and college room and board ($7020). College room only: $4450. Room and board charges vary according to board plan and housing facility. Tuition guaranteed not to increase for student's term of enrollment. **Scholarships:** Available **Calendar System:** Semester, Summer Session Not available **Enrollment:** FT 1,040 **Faculty:** FT 39, PT 0 **Student-Faculty Ratio:** 18:1 **Library Holdings:** 5,000 **Professional Accreditation:** ACCSCT, ACF

PENNSYLVANIA HIGHLAND COMMUNITY COLLEGE

PO Box 68
Johnstown, PA 15907-0068
Tel: (814)532-5300
Admissions: (814)532-5327
Web Site: http://www.pennhighlands.edu/
President/CEO: Dr. Kathleen V. Davis
Admissions: Jeff Maul
Type: Two-Year College **Sex:** Coed **Admission Plans:** Open Admission **Application Fee:** $20.00 **H.S. Requirements:** High school diploma or equivalent not required **Costs Per Year:** Application fee: $20. Area resident tuition: $1680 full-time, $70 per credit hour part-time. State resident tuition: $3360 full-time, $140 per credit hour part-time. Nonresident tuition: $5040 full-time, $210 per credit hour part-time. Mandatory fees: $390 full-time, $15 per credit hour part-time, $15 per term part-time. **Scholarships:** Available **Calendar System:** Semester **Enrollment:** FT 594, PT 733 **Faculty:** FT 25, PT 120 **Student-Faculty Ratio:** 14:1 **Regional Accreditation:** Middle State Association of Colleges and Schools **Credit Hours For Degree:** 61 credits, Associates

PENNSYLVANIA INSTITUTE OF TECHNOLOGY

800 Manchester Ave.
Media, PA 19063-4098
Tel: (610)892-1500
Free: 800-422-0025
Admissions: (610)892-1550
Fax: (610)892-1510
E-mail: info@pit.edu
Web Site: http://www.pit.edu/
President/CEO: Dr. Paul Smith
Registrar: Craig M. Jacobs
Admissions: Angela Cassetta
Financial Aid: Sandra E. Shaffer
Type: Two-Year College **Sex:** Coed **% Accepted:** 100 **Admission Plans:** Deferred Admission **Application Deadline:** September 19 **Application Fee:** $25.00 **H.S. Requirements:** High school diploma required; GED accepted **Costs Per Year:** Application fee: $25. Tuition: $9000 full-time, $300 per credit part-time. Mandatory fees: $330 full-time, $11 per credit part-time. **Scholarships:** Available **Calendar System:** Semester, Summer Session Available **Enrollment:** FT 270, PT 114 **Faculty:** FT 21, PT 26 **Student-Faculty Ratio:** 10:1 **Library Holdings:** 16,500 **Regional Accreditation:** Middle State Association of Colleges and Schools **Credit Hours For Degree:** 60 credits, Associates

THE PENNSYLVANIA STATE UNIVERSITY ABINGTON COLLEGE

1600 Woodland Rd.
Abington, PA 19001
Tel: (215)881-7300
Admissions: (814)865-5471
E-mail: admissions@psu.edu
Web Site: http://www.abington.psu.edu/
President/CEO: Dr. Karen Wiley Sandler
Registrar: Patricia A. Smith
Admissions: Randall C. Deike
Financial Aid: Christopher Walters
Type: Four-Year College **Sex:** Coed **Affiliation:** Pennsylvania State University **Scores:** 76.68% SAT V 400+; 83.89% SAT M 400+ **% Accepted:** 78 **Admission Plans:** Early Admission; Deferred Admission **Application Deadline:** Rolling **Application Fee:** $50.00 **H.S. Requirements:** High school diploma required; GED accepted **Costs Per Year:** Application fee: $50. State resident tuition: $9722 full-time, $393 per credit hour part-time. Nonresident tuition: $14,854 full-time, $619 per credit hour part-time. Mandatory fees: $468 full-time, $79 per term part-time. Full-time tuition and fees vary according to course level, location, program, and student level. Part-time tuition and fees vary according to course level, course load, location, program, and student level. **Scholarships:** Available **Calendar System:** Semester, Summer Session Available **Enrollment:** FT 2,393, PT 749 **Faculty:** FT 109, PT 98 **Student-Faculty Ratio:** 18:1 **Exams:** SAT I or ACT **% Receiving Financial Aid:** 60 **Library Holdings:** 65,866 **Regional Accreditation:** Middle State Association of Colleges and Schools **Credit Hours For Degree:** 60 credits, Associates; 120 credits, Bachelors **ROTC:** Army, Air Force **Intercollegiate Athletics:** Baseball M; Basketball M & W; Golf M; Soccer M & W; Softball W; Tennis M & W; Volleyball W

THE PENNSYLVANIA STATE UNIVERSITY ALTOONA COLLEGE

3000 Ivyside Park
Altoona, PA 16601-3760
Tel: (814)949-5000
Free: 800-848-9843
Admissions: (814)865-5471
Fax: (814)949-5011
E-mail: admissions@psu.edu
Web Site: http://www.aa.psu.edu/
President/CEO: Dr. William G. Cale, Jr.
Registrar: Margaret McNulty
Admissions: Randall C. Deike
Financial Aid: David Pearlman
Type: Four-Year College **Sex:** Coed **Affiliation:** Pennsylvania State University **Scores:** 93.51% SAT V 400+; 93.05% SAT M 400+ **% Accepted:** 80 **Admission Plans:** Early Admission; Deferred Admission **Application Deadline:** Rolling **Application Fee:** $50.00 **H.S. Requirements:** High school diploma required; GED accepted **Costs Per Year:** Application fee: $50. Area resident tuition: $423 per credit hour part-time. State resident tuition: $10,148 full-time, $423 per credit hour part-time. Nonresident tuition: $15,546 full-time, $648 per credit hour part-time. Mandatory fees: $478 full-time, $80 per term part-time. Full-time tuition and fees vary according to course level, location, program, and student level. Part-time tuition and fees vary according to course level, course load, location, program, and student level. College room and board: $6530. College room only: $3430. Room and board charges vary according to board plan and housing facility. **Scholarships:** Available **Calendar System:** Semester, Summer Session Available **Enrollment:** FT 3,338, PT 309 **Faculty:** FT 155, PT 149 **Student-Faculty Ratio:** 16:1 **Exams:** SAT I or ACT **% Receiving Financial Aid:** 67 **% Residing in College-Owned, -Operated, or -Affiliated Housing:** 24 **Library Holdings:** 70,851 **Regional Accreditation:** Middle State Association of Colleges and Schools **Credit Hours For Degree:** 60 credits, Associates; 120 credits, Bachelors **ROTC:** Army, Air Force **Professional Accreditation:** ABET **Intercollegiate Athletics:** Baseball M; Basketball M & W; Cheerleading M & W; Cross-Country Running M & W; Golf M; Ice Hockey M; Soccer M & W; Softball W; Swimming and Diving M & W; Tennis M & W; Volleyball M & W

THE PENNSYLVANIA STATE UNIVERSITY BEAVER CAMPUS OF THE COMMONWEALTH COLLEGE

100 University Dr.
Monaca, PA 15061
Tel: (724)773-3500; 877-564-6778
Admissions: (814)865-5471
Fax: (724)773-3557
E-mail: admissions@psu.edu
Web Site: http://www.br.psu.edu/
President/CEO: Dr. Gary B. Keefer
Registrar: Susan McCleary
Admissions: Randall C. Deike
Financial Aid: Gail Gray
Type: Two-Year College **Sex:** Coed **Affiliation:** Pennsylvania State University **Scores:** 87.22% SAT V 400+; 87.23% SAT M 400+ **% Accepted:** 89 **Admission Plans:** Early Admission; Deferred Admission **Application Deadline:** Rolling **Application Fee:** $50.00 **H.S. Requirements:** High school diploma required; GED accepted **Costs Per Year:** Application fee: $50. State resident tuition: $9722 full-time, $393 per credit hour part-time. Nonresident tuition: $14,854 full-time, $619 per credit hour part-time. Mandatory fees: $478 full-time. College room and board: $6530. College room only: $3430. **Scholarships:** Available **Calendar System:** Semester, Summer Session Available **Enrollment:** FT 546, PT 86, Grad 9 **Faculty:** FT

32, PT 23 **Student-Faculty Ratio:** 15:1 **Exams:** SAT I or ACT **% Residing in College-Owned, -Operated, or -Affiliated Housing:** 25 **Library Holdings:** 39,861 **Regional Accreditation:** Middle State Association of Colleges and Schools **Credit Hours For Degree:** 60 credits, Associates **Professional Accreditation:** ABET **Intercollegiate Athletics:** Baseball M; Basketball M; Softball M & W; Volleyball W

THE PENNSYLVANIA STATE UNIVERSITY BERKS CAMPUS OF THE BERKS-LEHIGH VALLEY COLLEGE
Tulpehocken Rd., PO Box 7009
Reading, PA 19610-6009
Tel: (610)396-6000
Admissions: (814)865-5471
E-mail: admissions@psu.edu
Web Site: http://www.bk.psu.edu/
President/CEO: Dr. Susan Speece
Registrar: Dr. David S. Bender
Admissions: Randall C. Deike
Financial Aid: Peter Coleman
Type: Four-Year College **Sex:** Coed **Affiliation:** Pennsylvania State University **Scores:** 88.81% SAT V 400+; 89.29% SAT M 400+ **% Accepted:** 78 **Admission Plans:** Early Admission; Deferred Admission **Application Deadline:** Rolling **Application Fee:** $50.00 **H.S. Requirements:** High school diploma required; GED accepted **Costs Per Year:** Application fee: $50. State resident tuition: $10,148 full-time, $423 per credit hour part-time. Nonresident tuition: $15,546 full-time, $648 per credit hour part-time. Mandatory fees: $478 full-time, $80 per term part-time. Full-time tuition and fees vary according to course level, course load, and student level. Part-time tuition and fees vary according to course level and student level. College room and board: $7140. College room only: $4040. Room and board charges vary according to board plan and housing facility. **Scholarships:** Available **Calendar System:** Semester, Summer Session Available **Enrollment:** FT 2,204, PT 240, Grad 44 **Faculty:** FT 101, PT 81 **Student-Faculty Ratio:** 18:1 **Exams:** SAT I or ACT **% Receiving Financial Aid:** 56 **% Residing in College-Owned, -Operated, or -Affiliated Housing:** 34 **Library Holdings:** 49,520 **Regional Accreditation:** Middle State Association of Colleges and Schools **Credit Hours For Degree:** 60 credits, Associates; 120 credits, Bachelors **Professional Accreditation:** ABET, AOTA **Intercollegiate Athletics:** Baseball M; Basketball M & W; Bowling M & W; Cheerleading M & W; Cross-Country Running M & W; Golf M; Ice Hockey M & W; Soccer M; Softball W; Tennis M & W; Volleyball M & W

THE PENNSYLVANIA STATE UNIVERSITY DELAWARE COUNTY CAMPUS OF THE COMMONWEALTH COLLEGE
25 Yearsley Mill Rd.
Media, PA 19063-5596
Tel: (610)892-1350
Admissions: (814)865-5471
E-mail: admissions@psu.edu
Web Site: http://www.de.psu.edu/
President/CEO: Dr. Edward S. J. Tomezsko
Registrar: Joyce Rigby
Admissions: Randall C. Deike
Financial Aid: Sylvia Schaffer
Type: Two-Year College **Sex:** Coed **Affiliation:** Pennsylvania State University **Scores:** 79.2% SAT V 400+; 79.2% SAT M 400+ **% Accepted:** 77 **Admission Plans:** Early Admission; Deferred Admission **Application Deadline:** Rolling **Application Fee:** $50.00 **H.S. Requirements:** High school diploma required; GED accepted **Costs Per Year:** Application fee: $50. State resident tuition: $9722 full-time, $393 per credit hour part-time. Nonresident tuition: $14,854 full-time, $619 per credit hour part-time. Mandatory fees: $478 full-time. **Scholarships:** Available **Calendar System:** Semester, Summer Session Available **Enrollment:** FT 1,356, PT 233 **Faculty:** FT 70, PT 55 **Student-Faculty Ratio:** 16:1 **Exams:** SAT I or ACT **Library Holdings:** 59,930 **Regional Accreditation:** Middle State Association of Colleges and Schools **Credit Hours For Degree:** 60 credits, Associates; 120 credits, Bachelors **ROTC:** Air Force **Intercollegiate Athletics:** Baseball M; Basketball M & W; Soccer M & W; Tennis M & W; Volleyball W

THE PENNSYLVANIA STATE UNIVERSITY DUBOIS CAMPUS OF THE COMMONWEALTH COLLEGE
College Place
DuBois, PA 15801-3199
Tel: (814)375-4700
Free: 800-346-7627
Admissions: (814)865-5471
E-mail: admissions@psu.edu
Web Site: http://www.ds.psu.edu/
President/CEO: Dr. Anita D. MacDonald
Registrar: Jeanne Hunter
Admissions: Randall C. Deike
Financial Aid: Terry Feathers
Type: Two-Year College **Sex:** Coed **Affiliation:** Pennsylvania State University **Scores:** 86% SAT V 400+; 90% SAT M 400+ **% Accepted:** 92 **Admission Plans:** Early Admission; Deferred Admission **Application Deadline:** Rolling **Application Fee:** $50.00 **H.S. Requirements:** High school diploma required; GED accepted **Costs Per Year:** Application fee: $50. State resident tuition: $9722 full-time, $393 per credit hour part-time. Nonresident tuition: $14,854 full-time, $619 per credit hour part-time. Mandatory fees: $468 full-time. **Scholarships:** Available **Calendar System:** Semester, Summer Session Available **Enrollment:** FT 595, PT 209 **Faculty:** FT 45, PT 37 **Student-Faculty Ratio:** 12:1 **Exams:** SAT I or ACT **Library Holdings:** 43,710 **Regional Accreditation:** Middle State Association of Colleges and Schools **Credit Hours For Degree:** 60 credits, Associates **Professional Accreditation:** ABET, AOTA, APTA **Intercollegiate Athletics:** Basketball M; Cross-Country Running M & W; Golf M & W; Volleyball W

THE PENNSYLVANIA STATE UNIVERSITY AT ERIE, THE BEHREND COLLEGE
5091 Station Rd.
Erie, PA 16563-0001
Tel: (814)898-6000; (866)374-3378
Admissions: (814)865-5471
E-mail: admissions@psu.edu
Web Site: http://www.pserie.psu.edu/
President/CEO: Dr. Jack D. Burke
Registrar: Dr. Mary Ellen Bayuk
Admissions: Randall C. Deike
Financial Aid: Mary-Ellen Madigan
Type: Comprehensive **Sex:** Coed **Affiliation:** Pennsylvania State University **Scores:** 97.54% SAT V 400+; 98.56% SAT M 400+ **% Accepted:** 80 **Admission Plans:** Early Admission; Deferred Admission **Application Deadline:** Rolling **Application Fee:** $50.00 **H.S. Requirements:** High school diploma required; GED accepted **Costs Per Year:** Application fee: $50. Area resident tuition: $423 per credit hour part-time. State resident tuition: $10,148 full-time, $423 per credit hour part-time. Nonresident tuition: $15,546 full-time, $648 per credit hour part-time. Mandatory fees: $478 full-time, $80 per term part-time. Full-time tuition and fees vary according to course level and student level. Part-time tuition and fees vary according to course level, course load, and student level. College room and board: $6530. College room only: $3430. Room and board charges vary according to board plan and housing facility. **Scholarships:** Available **Calendar System:** Semester, Summer Session Available **Enrollment:** FT 3,160, PT 222, Grad 160 **Faculty:** FT 200, PT 61 **Student-Faculty Ratio:** 15:1 **Exams:** SAT I or ACT **% Receiving Financial Aid:** 69 **% Residing in College-Owned, -Operated, or -Affiliated Housing:** 48 **Library Holdings:** 103,524 **Regional Accreditation:** Middle State Association of Colleges and Schools **Credit Hours For Degree:** 60 credits, Associates; 124 credits, Bachelors **ROTC:** Army **Professional Accreditation:** AACSB, ABET **Intercollegiate Athletics:** Baseball M; Basketball M & W; Cheerleading M & W; Cross-Country Running M & W; Golf M & W; Ice Hockey M; Lacrosse M; Skiing (Downhill) M & W; Soccer M & W; Softball W; Swimming and Diving M & W; Tennis M & W; Track and Field M & W; Volleyball M & W; Water Polo M & W

THE PENNSYLVANIA STATE UNIVERSITY FAYETTE CAMPUS OF THE COMMONWEALTH COLLEGE
1 University Dr., PO Box 519
Uniontown, PA 15401-0519
Tel: (724)430-4100; 877-568-4130
Admissions: (814)865-5471
Fax: (724)430-4184
E-mail: admissions@psu.edu
Web Site: http://www.fe.psu.edu/
President/CEO: Dr. Gregory W. Gray
Registrar: Germaine Fotta
Admissions: Randall C. Deike
Financial Aid: Al Thompson
Type: Two-Year College **Sex:** Coed **Affiliation:** Pennsylvania State University **Scores:** 80.13% SAT V 400+; 72.43% SAT M 400+ **% Ac-**

cepted: 86 **Admission Plans:** Early Admission; Deferred Admission **Application Deadline:** Rolling **Application Fee:** $50.00 **H.S. Requirements:** High school diploma required; GED accepted **Costs Per Year:** Application fee: $50. State resident tuition: $9722 full-time, $393 per credit hour part-time. Nonresident tuition: $14,854 full-time, $619 per credit hour part-time. Mandatory fees: $468 full-time. **Scholarships:** Available **Calendar System:** Semester, Summer Session Available **Enrollment:** FT 727, PT 268 **Faculty:** FT 50, PT 35 **Student-Faculty Ratio:** 13:1 **Exams:** SAT I or ACT **Library Holdings:** 54,610 **Regional Accreditation:** Middle State Association of Colleges and Schools **Credit Hours For Degree:** 60 credits, Associates **Professional Accreditation:** ABET **Intercollegiate Athletics:** Baseball M; Basketball M; Softball W; Volleyball W

THE PENNSYLVANIA STATE UNIVERSITY HARRISBURG CAMPUS
777 West Harrisburg Pike
Middletown, PA 17057-4898
Tel: (717)948-6000
Free: 800-222-2056
Admissions: (814)865-5471
E-mail: admissions@psu.edu
Web Site: http://www.hbg.psu.edu/
President/CEO: Dr. Madlyn Hanes
Registrar: Dr. Thomas I. Streveler
Admissions: Randall C. Deike
Financial Aid: Carolyn Julian
Type: Comprehensive **Sex:** Coed **Affiliation:** Pennsylvania State University **Scores:** 93.94% SAT V 400+; 92.92% SAT M 400+ **% Accepted:** 64 **Admission Plans:** Early Admission; Deferred Admission **Application Deadline:** Rolling **Application Fee:** $50.00 **H.S. Requirements:** High school diploma required; GED accepted **Costs Per Year:** Application fee: $50. State resident tuition: $10,148 full-time, $423 per credit hour part-time. Nonresident tuition: $15,546 full-time, $648 per credit hour part-time. Mandatory fees: $468 full-time, $79 per term part-time. Full-time tuition and fees vary according to course level, location, program, and student level. Part-time tuition and fees vary according to course level, course load, location, program, and student level. College room and board: $8030. College room only: $4930. Room and board charges vary according to board plan and housing facility. **Scholarships:** Available **Calendar System:** Semester, Summer Session Available **Enrollment:** FT 1,592, PT 476, Grad 1,668 **Faculty:** FT 169, PT 104 **Student-Faculty Ratio:** 12:1 **Exams:** SAT I or ACT **% Receiving Financial Aid:** 68 **% Residing in College-Owned, -Operated, or -Affiliated Housing:** 14 **Library Holdings:** 285,171 **Regional Accreditation:** Middle State Association of Colleges and Schools **Credit Hours For Degree:** 60 credits, Associates; 120 credits, Bachelors **ROTC:** Army **Professional Accreditation:** AACSB, ABET, NASPAA **Intercollegiate Athletics:** Baseball M; Cross-Country Running M; Soccer M; Volleyball M & W

THE PENNSYLVANIA STATE UNIVERSITY HAZLETON CAMPUS OF THE COMMONWEALTH COLLEGE
Hazleton, PA 18202-1291
Tel: (570)450-3000
Free: 800-279-8495
Admissions: (814)865-5471
E-mail: admissions@psu.edu
Web Site: http://www.hn.psu.edu/
President/CEO: Dr. John R. Madden
Registrar: Michele Jais
Admissions: Randall C. Deike
Type: Two-Year College **Sex:** Coed **Affiliation:** Pennsylvania State University **Scores:** 83.18% SAT V 400+; 88.71% SAT M 400+ **% Accepted:** 91 **Admission Plans:** Early Admission; Deferred Admission **Application Deadline:** Rolling **Application Fee:** $50.00 **H.S. Requirements:** High school diploma required; GED accepted **Costs Per Year:** Application fee: $50. State resident tuition: $9722 full-time, $393 per credit hour part-time. Nonresident tuition: $14,854 full-time, $619 per credit hour part-time. Mandatory fees: $468 full-time. College room and board: $6530. College room only: $3430. **Scholarships:** Available **Calendar System:** Semester, Summer Session Available **Enrollment:** FT 1,011, PT 54, Grad 1 **Faculty:** FT 53, PT 29 **Student-Faculty Ratio:** 16:1 **Exams:** SAT I or ACT **% Residing in College-Owned, -Operated, or -Affiliated Housing:** 43 **Library Holdings:** 83,266 **Regional Accreditation:** Middle State Association of Colleges and Schools **Credit Hours For Degree:** 60 credits, Associates **ROTC:** Army, Air Force **Professional Accreditation:** ABET, APTA, NAACLS **Intercollegiate Athletics:** Baseball M; Basketball M & W; Cheerleading M & W; Soccer M; Softball W; Tennis M & W; Volleyball M & W

THE PENNSYLVANIA STATE UNIVERSITY, LEHIGH VALLEY CAMPUS OF THE BERKS-LEHIGH VALLEY COLLEGE
8380 Mohr Ln.
Fogelsville, PA 18051-9999
Tel: (610)285-5000
Admissions: (814)865-5471
Web Site: http://www.lv.psu.edu/
President/CEO: Dr. Ann M. Williams
Registrar: Katherine Eck
Admissions: Randall C. Deike
Financial Aid: Joan Willertz
Type: Two-Year College **Sex:** Coed **Affiliation:** Pennsylvania State University **Scores:** 89.87% SAT V 400+; 91.77% SAT M 400+ **Admission Plans:** Early Admission; Deferred Admission **Application Fee:** $50.00 **H.S. Requirements:** High school diploma required; GED accepted **Costs Per Year:** Application fee: $50. State resident tuition: $9722 full-time. Nonresident tuition: $14,854 full-time. Mandatory fees: $478 full-time. Full-time tuition and fees vary according to course level. **Calendar System:** Semester, Summer Session Available **Enrollment:** FT 491, PT 153, Grad 36 **Faculty:** FT 27, PT 43 **Student-Faculty Ratio:** 13:1 **Exams:** SAT I or ACT **Library Holdings:** 36,641 **Regional Accreditation:** Middle State Association of Colleges and Schools **Credit Hours For Degree:** 60 credits, Associates; 120 credits, Bachelors **Intercollegiate Athletics:** Baseball M; Basketball M & W; Bowling M & W; Cheerleading M & W; Cross-Country Running M & W; Football M; Golf M & W; Ice Hockey M & W; Skiing (Downhill) M & W; Soccer M & W; Tennis M & W; Volleyball M & W

THE PENNSYLVANIA STATE UNIVERSITY MCKEESPORT CAMPUS OF THE COMMONWEALTH COLLEGE
4000 University Dr.
McKeesport, PA 15132-7698
Tel: (412)675-9000
Admissions: (814)865-5471
E-mail: admissions@psu.edu
Web Site: http://www.mk.psu.edu/
President/CEO: Dr. Curtiss E. Porter
Registrar: Carol Meek
Admissions: Randall C. Deike
Type: Two-Year College **Sex:** Coed **Affiliation:** Pennsylvania State University **Scores:** 89.74% SAT V 400+; 92.31% SAT M 400+ **% Accepted:** 82 **Admission Plans:** Early Admission; Deferred Admission **Application Deadline:** Rolling **Application Fee:** $50.00 **H.S. Requirements:** High school diploma required; GED accepted **Costs Per Year:** Application fee: $50. State resident tuition: $9722 full-time, $393 per credit hour part-time. Nonresident tuition: $14,854 full-time, $619 per credit hour part-time. Mandatory fees: $458 full-time. College room and board: $6530. College room only: $3430. **Scholarships:** Available **Calendar System:** Semester, Summer Session Available **Enrollment:** FT 593, PT 89 **Faculty:** FT 38, PT 34 **Student-Faculty Ratio:** 13:1 **Exams:** SAT I or ACT **% Residing in College-Owned, -Operated, or -Affiliated Housing:** 14 **Library Holdings:** 40,851 **Regional Accreditation:** Middle State Association of Colleges and Schools **Credit Hours For Degree:** 60 credits, Associates **ROTC:** Air Force **Intercollegiate Athletics:** Baseball M; Basketball M; Softball W; Volleyball W

THE PENNSYLVANIA STATE UNIVERSITY MONT ALTO CAMPUS OF THE COMMONWEALTH COLLEGE
Campus Dr.
Mont Alto, PA 17237-9703
Tel: (717)749-6000
Free: 800-392-6173
Admissions: (814)865-5471
E-mail: admissions@psu.edu
Web Site: http://www.ma.psu.edu/
President/CEO: Dr. David C. Gnage
Registrar: Linda Monn
Admissions: Randall C. Deike
Financial Aid: Darlene Gilliland
Type: Two-Year College **Sex:** Coed **Affiliation:** Pennsylvania State University **Scores:** 83.47% SAT V 400+; 86.36% SAT M 400+ **% Accepted:** 84 **Admission Plans:** Early Admission; Deferred Admission **Application Deadline:** Rolling **Application Fee:** $50.00 **H.S. Requirements:** High school diploma required; GED accepted **Costs Per Year:** Application

fee: $50. State resident tuition: $9722 full-time, $393 per credit hour part-time. Nonresident tuition: $14,854 full-time, $619 per credit hour part-time. Mandatory fees: $478 full-time. College room and board: $6530. College room only: $3430. **Scholarships:** Available **Calendar System:** Semester, Summer Session Available **Enrollment:** FT 674, PT 258 **Faculty:** FT 52, PT 39 **Student-Faculty Ratio:** 12:1 **Exams:** SAT I or ACT **% Residing in College-Owned, -Operated, or -Affiliated Housing:** 33 **Library Holdings:** 38,962 **Regional Accreditation:** Middle State Association of Colleges and Schools **Credit Hours For Degree:** 60 credits, Associates **ROTC:** Army **Professional Accreditation:** AOTA, APTA **Intercollegiate Athletics:** Basketball M & W; Cheerleading M & W; Cross-Country Running M & W; Golf M & W; Soccer M & W; Softball W; Tennis M & W; Volleyball W

THE PENNSYLVANIA STATE UNIVERSITY NEW KENSINGTON CAMPUS OF THE COMMONWEALTH COLLEGE

3550 7th St. Rd., RT 780
New Kensington, PA 15068-1798
Tel: (724)334-5466; 888-968-7297
Admissions: (814)865-5471
Fax: (724)334-6111
E-mail: admissions@psu.edu
Web Site: http://www.nk.psu.edu/
President/CEO: Dr. Carol A. Rush
Registrar: Joanne Fitzsimmons
Admissions: Randall C. Deike
Financial Aid: Carrie Guerrini

Type: Two-Year College **Sex:** Coed **Affiliation:** Pennsylvania State University **Scores:** 88.95% SAT V 400+; 85.64% SAT M 400+ **% Accepted:** 86 **Admission Plans:** Early Admission; Deferred Admission **Application Deadline:** Rolling **Application Fee:** $50.00 **H.S. Requirements:** High school diploma required; GED accepted **Costs Per Year:** Application fee: $50. State resident tuition: $9722 full-time, $393 per credit hour part-time. Nonresident tuition: $14,854 full-time, $619 per credit hour part-time. Mandatory fees: $478 full-time. **Scholarships:** Available **Calendar System:** Semester, Summer Session Available **Enrollment:** FT 628, PT 252, Grad 2 **Faculty:** FT 44, PT 44 **Student-Faculty Ratio:** 12:1 **Exams:** SAT I or ACT **Library Holdings:** 28,897 **Regional Accreditation:** Middle State Association of Colleges and Schools **Credit Hours For Degree:** 60 credits, Associates **Professional Accreditation:** ABET, JRCERT, NAACLS **Intercollegiate Athletics:** Baseball M; Basketball M & W; Cheerleading M & W; Golf M & W; Softball W; Volleyball W

THE PENNSYLVANIA STATE UNIVERSITY SCHUYLKILL CAMPUS OF THE CAPITAL COLLEGE

200 University Dr.
Schuylkill Haven, PA 17972-2208
Tel: (570)385-6000
Admissions: (814)865-5471
E-mail: admissions@psu.edu
Web Site: http://www.sl.psu.edu/
President/CEO: Dr. Sylvester Kohut, Jr.
Registrar: Stephen L. Littell
Admissions: Randall C. Deike
Financial Aid: Tammie Durham

Type: Two-Year College **Sex:** Coed **Affiliation:** Pennsylvania State University **Scores:** 74.51% SAT V 400+; 73.72% SAT M 400+ **Admission Plans:** Early Admission; Deferred Admission **Application Fee:** $50.00 **H.S. Requirements:** High school diploma required; GED accepted **Costs Per Year:** Application fee: $50. State resident tuition: $9722 full-time. Nonresident tuition: $14,854 full-time. Mandatory fees: $458 full-time. Full-time tuition and fees vary according to course level, location, program, and student level. College room and board: $7110. College room only: $3474. Room and board charges vary according to board plan and housing facility. **Scholarships:** Available **Calendar System:** Semester, Summer Session Available **Enrollment:** FT 773, PT 151, Grad 45 **Faculty:** FT 47, PT 34 **Student-Faculty Ratio:** 14:1 **Exams:** SAT I or ACT **% Residing in College-Owned, -Operated, or -Affiliated Housing:** 28 **Library Holdings:** 39,289 **Regional Accreditation:** Middle State Association of Colleges and Schools **Credit Hours For Degree:** 60 credits, Associates; 120 credits, Bachelors **Professional Accreditation:** ABET, JRCERT **Intercollegiate Athletics:** Basketball M; Cross-Country Running M & W; Golf M; Soccer M; Softball W; Volleyball W

THE PENNSYLVANIA STATE UNIVERSITY SHENANGO CAMPUS OF THE COMMONWEALTH COLLEGE

147 Shenango Ave.
Sharon, PA 16146-1537
Tel: (724)983-2814
Admissions: (814)865-5471
Fax: (724)983-2820
E-mail: admissions@psu.edu
Web Site: http://www.shenango.psu.edu/
President/CEO: Dr. Fredric M. Leeds
Registrar: Dr. Jane Williams
Admissions: Randall C. Deike

Type: Two-Year College **Sex:** Coed **Affiliation:** Pennsylvania State University **Scores:** 83.34% SAT V 400+; 76.39% SAT M 400+ **% Accepted:** 90 **Admission Plans:** Early Admission; Deferred Admission **Application Deadline:** Rolling **Application Fee:** $50.00 **H.S. Requirements:** High school diploma required; GED accepted **Costs Per Year:** Application fee: $50. State resident tuition: $9722 full-time, $393 per credit hour part-time. Nonresident tuition: $14,854 full-time, $619 per credit hour part-time. Mandatory fees: $478 full-time. **Scholarships:** Available **Calendar System:** Semester, Summer Session Available **Enrollment:** FT 508, PT 347, Grad 1 **Faculty:** FT 29, PT 42 **Student-Faculty Ratio:** 14:1 **Exams:** SAT I or ACT **Library Holdings:** 25,273 **Regional Accreditation:** Middle State Association of Colleges and Schools **Credit Hours For Degree:** 60 credits, Associates **Professional Accreditation:** ABET, APTA

THE PENNSYLVANIA STATE UNIVERSITY UNIVERSITY PARK CAMPUS

201 Old Main
University Park, PA 16802-1503
Tel: (814)865-4700
Admissions: (814)865-5471
E-mail: admissions@psu.edu
Web Site: http://www.psu.edu/
President/CEO: Dr. Graham B. Spanier
Registrar: J. James Wager
Admissions: Randall C. Deike
Financial Aid: Anna M. Griswold

Type: University **Sex:** Coed **Affiliation:** Pennsylvania State University **Scores:** 98.29% SAT V 400+; 99.31% SAT M 400+ **% Accepted:** 62 **Admission Plans:** Early Admission; Deferred Admission **Application Deadline:** Rolling **Application Fee:** $50.00 **H.S. Requirements:** High school diploma required; GED accepted **Costs Per Year:** Application fee: $50. State resident tuition: $11,024 full-time, $459 per credit hour part-time. Nonresident tuition: $21,260 full-time, $886 per credit hour part-time. Mandatory fees: $484 full-time, $180 per term part-time. College room and board: $6530. College room only: $3430. **Scholarships:** Available **Calendar System:** Semester, Summer Session Available **Enrollment:** FT 33,208, PT 1,429, Grad 6,072 **Faculty:** FT 2,233, PT 313 **Student-Faculty Ratio:** 16:1 **Exams:** SAT I or ACT **% Receiving Financial Aid:** 49 **% Residing in College-Owned, -Operated, or -Affiliated Housing:** 38 **Library Holdings:** 3,117,880 **Regional Accreditation:** Middle State Association of Colleges and Schools **Credit Hours For Degree:** 60 credits, Associates; 120 credits, Bachelors **ROTC:** Army, Navy, Air Force **Professional Accreditation:** AACSB, ABET, ACEHSA, ACEJMC, AACN, ACA, ADtA, APA, ASLA, ASLHA, CORE, JRCEPAT, NASAD, NASM, NAST, NCATE, NLN, SAF **Intercollegiate Athletics:** Archery M & W; Badminton M & W; Baseball M; Basketball M & W; Bowling M; Cheerleading M & W; Cross-Country Running M & W; Equestrian Sports M & W; Fencing M & W; Field Hockey W; Football M; Golf M & W; Gymnastics M & W; Ice Hockey M & W; Lacrosse M & W; Rugby M & W; Skiing (Downhill) M & W; Soccer M & W; Softball W; Swimming and Diving M & W; Table Tennis M; Tennis M & W; Track and Field M & W; Volleyball M & W; Water Polo M & W; Weight Lifting M & W; Wrestling M

THE PENNSYLVANIA STATE UNIVERSITY WILKES-BARRE CAMPUS OF THE COMMONWEALTH COLLEGE

PO PSU
Lehman, PA 18627-0217
Tel: (570)675-2171
Free: 800-966-6613
Admissions: (814)865-5471

E-mail: admissions@psu.edu
Web Site: http://www.wb.psu.edu/
President/CEO: Dr. Mary Hines
Registrar: Jennifer Stombaugh
Admissions: Randall C. Deike
Financial Aid: John Murphy
Type: Two-Year College **Sex:** Coed **Affiliation:** Pennsylvania State University **Scores:** 87.35% SAT V 400+; 90.5% SAT M 400+ **% Accepted:** 84 **Admission Plans:** Early Admission; Deferred Admission **Application Deadline:** Rolling **Application Fee:** $50.00 **H.S. Requirements:** High school diploma required; GED accepted **Costs Per Year:** Application fee: $50. State resident tuition: $9722 full-time, $393 per credit hour part-time. Nonresident tuition: $14,854 full-time, $619 per credit hour part-time. Mandatory fees: $478 full-time. **Scholarships:** Available **Calendar System:** Semester, Summer Session Available **Enrollment:** FT 535, PT 131, Grad 33 **Faculty:** FT 36, PT 31 **Student-Faculty Ratio:** 13:1 **Exams:** SAT I or ACT **Library Holdings:** 35,697 **Regional Accreditation:** Middle State Association of Colleges and Schools **Credit Hours For Degree:** 60 credits, Associates **ROTC:** Air Force **Professional Accreditation:** ABET **Intercollegiate Athletics:** Baseball M; Basketball M; Cross-Country Running M & W; Golf M & W; Soccer M & W; Volleyball W

THE PENNSYLVANIA STATE UNIVERSITY WORTHINGTON SCRANTON CAMPUS OF THE COMMONWEALTH COLLEGE
120 Ridge View Dr.
Dunmore, PA 18512-1699
Tel: (570)963-2500
Admissions: (814)865-5471
Fax: (570)963-2535
E-mail: admissions@psu.edu
Web Site: http://www.sn.psu.edu/
President/CEO: Dr. Mary-Beth Krogh-Jespersen
Registrar: Dr. Ralph Mastriani
Admissions: Randall C. Deike
Financial Aid: Patrick J. Rose
Type: Two-Year College **Sex:** Coed **Affiliation:** Pennsylvania State University **Scores:** 86.58% SAT V 400+; 87.88% SAT M 400+ **% Accepted:** 84 **Admission Plans:** Early Admission; Deferred Admission **Application Deadline:** Rolling **Application Fee:** $50.00 **H.S. Requirements:** High school diploma required; GED accepted **Costs Per Year:** Application fee: $50. State resident tuition: $9722 full-time, $393 per credit hour part-time. Nonresident tuition: $14,854 full-time, $619 per credit hour part-time. Mandatory fees: $458 full-time. **Scholarships:** Available **Calendar System:** Semester, Summer Session Available **Enrollment:** FT 955, PT 286, Grad 21 **Faculty:** FT 61, PT 43 **Student-Faculty Ratio:** 14:1 **Exams:** SAT I or ACT **Library Holdings:** 53,572 **Regional Accreditation:** Middle State Association of Colleges and Schools **Credit Hours For Degree:** 60 credits, Associates **ROTC:** Air Force **Professional Accreditation:** ABET **Intercollegiate Athletics:** Baseball M; Basketball M & W; Cheerleading M & W; Cross-Country Running M & W; Soccer M; Softball W; Volleyball W

THE PENNSYLVANIA STATE UNIVERSITY YORK CAMPUS OF THE COMMONWEALTH COLLEGE
1031 Edgecomb Ave.
York, PA 17403-3398
Tel: (717)771-4000
Free: 800-778-6227
Admissions: (814)865-5471
Fax: (717)771-4062
E-mail: admissions@psu.edu
Web Site: http://www.yk.psu.edu/
President/CEO: Dr. Joel M. Rodney
Registrar: Frank P. Miller
Admissions: Randall C. Deike
Type: Two-Year College **Sex:** Coed **Affiliation:** Pennsylvania State University **Scores:** 92.51% SAT V 400+; 89.87% SAT M 400+ **% Accepted:** 81 **Admission Plans:** Early Admission; Deferred Admission **Application Deadline:** Rolling **Application Fee:** $50.00 **H.S. Requirements:** High school diploma required; GED accepted **Costs Per Year:** Application fee: $50. State resident tuition: $9722 full-time, $393 per credit hour part-time. Nonresident tuition: $14,854 full-time, $619 per credit hour part-time. Mandatory fees: $458 full-time. **Scholarships:** Available **Calendar System:** Semester, Summer Session Available **Enrollment:** FT 822, PT 593, Grad 191 **Faculty:** FT 59, PT 64 **Student-Faculty Ratio:** 13:1 **Exams:** SAT I or ACT **Library Holdings:** 49,996 **Regional Accreditation:** Middle State Association of Colleges and Schools **Credit Hours For Degree:** 60 credits, Associates **Professional Accreditation:** ABET **Intercollegiate Athletics:** Basketball M & W; Cross-Country Running M & W; Soccer M; Tennis M & W; Volleyball W

PHILADELPHIA BIBLICAL UNIVERSITY
200 Manor Ave.
Langhorne, PA 19047-2990
Tel: (215)752-5800
Free: 800-366-0049
Admissions: (215)702-4550
Fax: (215)752-5812
E-mail: admissions@pcb.edu
Web Site: http://www.pbu.edu/
President/CEO: Dr. W. Sherrill Babb
Registrar: Steven Schlenker
Admissions: Lisa Fuller
Financial Aid: William Kellaris
Type: Comprehensive **Sex:** Coed **Affiliation:** nondenominational **Scores:** 97.1% SAT V 400+; 92.7% SAT M 400+; 38.1% ACT 18-23; 52.4% ACT 24-29 **% Accepted:** 94 **Admission Plans:** Early Admission; Deferred Admission **Application Deadline:** Rolling **Application Fee:** $25.00 **H.S. Requirements:** High school diploma required; GED accepted **Costs Per Year:** Application fee: $25. Comprehensive fee: $22,425 includes full-time tuition ($15,555), mandatory fees ($320), and college room and board ($6550). College room only: $3400. Part-time tuition: $469 per credit. **Scholarships:** Available **Calendar System:** Semester, Summer Session Available **Enrollment:** FT 978, PT 102, Grad 315 **Faculty:** FT 64, PT 92 **Student-Faculty Ratio:** 12:1 **Exams:** SAT I or ACT **% Receiving Financial Aid:** 71 **% Residing in College-Owned, -Operated, or -Affiliated Housing:** 52 **Library Holdings:** 96,988 **Regional Accreditation:** Middle State Association of Colleges and Schools **Credit Hours For Degree:** 60 credits, Associates; 126 credits, Bachelors **ROTC:** Air Force **Professional Accreditation:** AABC, CSWE, NASM **Intercollegiate Athletics:** Baseball M; Basketball M & W; Field Hockey W; Golf M; Soccer M & W; Softball W; Tennis M & W; Volleyball M & W

PHILADELPHIA UNIVERSITY
School House Ln. and Henry Ave.
Philadelphia, PA 19144-5497
Tel: (215)951-2700
Admissions: (215)951-2800
Fax: (215)951-2907
Web Site: http://www.philau.edu/
President/CEO: Dr. James P. Gallagher
Registrar: Paul M. Kerstetter
Admissions: Christine Greb
Financial Aid: Lisa J. Cooper
Type: Comprehensive **Sex:** Coed **Scores:** 100% SAT V 400+; 100% SAT M 400+ **% Accepted:** 64 **Admission Plans:** Deferred Admission **Application Deadline:** Rolling **Application Fee:** $35.00 **H.S. Requirements:** High school diploma required; GED accepted **Costs Per Year:** Application fee: $35. Comprehensive fee: $30,076 includes full-time tuition ($22,070), mandatory fees ($70), and college room and board ($7936). College room only: $3910. Full-time tuition and fees vary according to program. Room and board charges vary according to board plan and housing facility. Part-time tuition: $713 per credit. Part-time tuition varies according to class time and program. **Scholarships:** Available **Calendar System:** Semester, Summer Session Available **Enrollment:** FT 2,432, PT 275, Grad 486 **Faculty:** FT 104, PT 314 **Student-Faculty Ratio:** 12:1 **Exams:** SAT I or ACT **% Receiving Financial Aid:** 68 **% Residing in College-Owned, -Operated, or -Affiliated Housing:** 51 **Library Holdings:** 108,141 **Regional Accreditation:** Middle State Association of Colleges and Schools **Credit Hours For Degree:** 124 credits, Bachelors **Professional Accreditation:** ABET, ACNM, AOTA, FIDER, NASAD **Intercollegiate Athletics:** Baseball M; Basketball M & W; Field Hockey W; Golf M; Lacrosse W; Soccer M & W; Softball W; Tennis M & W; Volleyball W

PITTSBURGH INSTITUTE OF AERONAUTICS
PO Box 10897
Pittsburgh, PA 15236-0897
Tel: (412)462-9011
Free: 800-444-1440
Admissions: (412)346-2100
Fax: (412)466-0513

E-mail: admissions@piainfo.org
Web Site: http://www.pia.edu/
President/CEO: Jack Graham
Registrar: Robert F. Leonard
Admissions: Michaelene F. Kalinowski
Financial Aid: Darla Mroski
Type: Two-Year College **Sex:** Coed **Admission Plans:** Open Admission; Deferred Admission **Application Fee:** $150.00 **H.S. Requirements:** High school diploma required; GED accepted **Calendar System:** Quarter **Enrollment:** FT 571 **Faculty:** FT 31, PT 6 **Student-Faculty Ratio:** 17:1 **Library Holdings:** 15,000 **Credit Hours For Degree:** 2520 hours, Associates **Professional Accreditation:** ACCSCT

PITTSBURGH INSTITUTE OF MORTUARY SCIENCE, INCORPORATED
5808 Baum Blvd.
Pittsburgh, PA 15206-3706
Tel: (412)362-8500
Free: 800-933-5808
Fax: (412)362-1684
E-mail: pims5808@aol.com
Web Site: http://www.pims.edu/
President/CEO: Eugene C. Ogrodnik
Registrar: Karen S. Rocco
Admissions: Karen Rocco
Financial Aid: Karen S. Rocco
Type: Two-Year College **Sex:** Coed **Admission Plans:** Open Admission **Application Deadline:** Rolling **Application Fee:** $40.00 **H.S. Requirements:** High school diploma required; GED accepted **Costs Per Year:** Application fee: $40. Tuition: $8000 full-time, $240 per credit part-time. Mandatory fees: $170 full-time. **Scholarships:** Available **Calendar System:** Trimester, Summer Session Not available **Enrollment:** FT 181, PT 11 **Faculty:** FT 4, PT 12 **Student-Faculty Ratio:** 13:1 **Library Holdings:** 2,167 **Credit Hours For Degree:** 96 credits, Associates **Professional Accreditation:** ABFSE

PITTSBURGH TECHNICAL INSTITUTE
1111 McKee Rd.
Oakdale, PA 15071
Tel: (412)809-5100
Free: 800-784-9675
Fax: (412)809-5388
Web Site: http://www.pti.edu/
President/CEO: Jack McCartan
Registrar: Pat Tarvin
Admissions: Mary Lou Zook
Financial Aid: Terri Barger
Type: Two-Year College **Sex:** Coed **Calendar System:** Quarter **Regional Accreditation:** Middle State Association of Colleges and Schools

THE PJA SCHOOL
7900 West Chester Pike
Upper Darby, PA 19082-1926
Tel: (610)789-6700
Free: 800-RING-PJA
E-mail: pjaschool@dvol.com
Web Site: http://www.pjaschool.com/
President/CEO: David Hudiak
Admissions: David Hudiak
Type: Two-Year College **Sex:** Coed **Professional Accreditation:** ACCSCT

POINT PARK UNIVERSITY
201 Wood St.
Pittsburgh, PA 15222-1984
Tel: (412)391-4100
Free: 800-321-0129
Admissions: (412)392-3430
Fax: (412)391-1980
E-mail: jminford@pointpark.edu
Web Site: http://www.pointpark.edu/
President/CEO: Dr. Katherine Henderson
Registrar: Keith Paylo
Admissions: Joell Minford
Financial Aid: Sandra Cronin
Type: Comprehensive **Sex:** Coed **Scores:** 96% SAT V 400+; 91% SAT M 400+; 58% ACT 18-23; 30% ACT 24-29 **% Accepted:** 76 **Admission Plans:** Early Admission; Deferred Admission **Application Deadline:** Rolling **Application Fee:** $40.00 **H.S. Requirements:** High school diploma required; GED accepted **Costs Per Year:** Application fee: $40. Comprehensive fee: $24,160 includes full-time tuition ($16,280), mandatory fees ($460), and college room and board ($7420). College room only: $3500. Full-time tuition and fees vary according to program. Room and board charges vary according to board plan. Part-time tuition: $447 per credit. Part-time mandatory fees: $10 per credit. Part-time tuition and fees vary according to program. **Scholarships:** Available **Calendar System:** Semester, Summer Session Available **Enrollment:** FT 2,263, PT 699, Grad 445 **Faculty:** FT 87, PT 303 **Student-Faculty Ratio:** 15:1 **Exams:** SAT I or ACT **% Receiving Financial Aid:** 81 **% Residing in College-Owned, -Operated, or -Affiliated Housing:** 22 **Library Holdings:** 125,000 **Regional Accreditation:** Middle State Association of Colleges and Schools **Credit Hours For Degree:** 60 credits, Associates; 120 credits, Bachelors **ROTC:** Army, Air Force **Professional Accreditation:** ABET, NASD **Intercollegiate Athletics:** Baseball M; Basketball M & W; Cross-Country Running M & W; Soccer M; Softball W; Volleyball W

READING AREA COMMUNITY COLLEGE
PO Box 1706
Reading, PA 19603-1706
Tel: (610)372-4721
Admissions: (610)607-6224
Fax: (610)375-8255
Web Site: http://www.racc.edu/
President/CEO: Dr. Richard A. Kratz
Registrar: Benjamin Rosenberger
Admissions: David J. Adams
Financial Aid: Benjamin Rosenberger
Type: Two-Year College **Sex:** Coed **Admission Plans:** Open Admission; Early Admission; Deferred Admission **Application Fee:** $20.00 **H.S. Requirements:** High school diploma required; GED accepted **Scholarships:** Available **Calendar System:** Quarter, Summer Session Available **Enrollment:** FT 1,578, PT 2,580 **Faculty:** FT 61, PT 162 **Library Holdings:** 25,541 **Regional Accreditation:** Middle State Association of Colleges and Schools **Credit Hours For Degree:** 60 credits, Associates **Professional Accreditation:** CARC, NAACLS, NLN **Intercollegiate Athletics:** Basketball M; Soccer M; Volleyball W

THE RESTAURANT SCHOOL AT WALNUT HILL COLLEGE
4207 Walnut St.
Philadelphia, PA 19104-3518
Tel: (215)222-4200; 877-925-6884
Fax: (215)222-4219
Web Site: http://www.walnuthillcollege.edu/
President/CEO: Daniel Liberatoscioli
Admissions: Karl D. Becker
Financial Aid: Margaret McCullough
Type: Two-Year College **Sex:** Coed **Admission Plans:** Open Admission; Early Admission; Early Decision Plan; Deferred Admission **Application Fee:** $50.00 **H.S. Requirements:** High school diploma required; GED accepted **Scholarships:** Available **Calendar System:** Semester, Summer Session Not available **Faculty:** FT 21, PT 6 **Student-Faculty Ratio:** 25:1 **Exams:** SAT I or ACT **% Residing in College-Owned, -Operated, or -Affiliated Housing:** 20 **Library Holdings:** 5,000 **Professional Accreditation:** ACCSCT

ROBERT MORRIS UNIVERSITY
6001 University Blvd.
Moon Township, PA 15108-1189
Tel: (412)262-8200
Free: 800-762-0097
Admissions: (412)262-8412
Fax: (412)262-8619
E-mail: budziszewski@rmu.edu
Web Site: http://www.rmu.edu/
President/CEO: Dr. Edward A. Nicholson
Registrar: John C. Munsick
Admissions: Marianne L. Budziszewski
Financial Aid: Shari L. Payne
Type: University **Sex:** Coed **Scores:** 96.9% SAT V 400+; 96.1% SAT M 400+; 68% ACT 18-23; 22% ACT 24-29 **% Accepted:** 78 **Admission Plans:** Deferred Admission **Application Deadline:** July 01 **Application Fee:** $30.00 **H.S. Requirements:** High school diploma required; GED accepted **Costs Per Year:** Application fee: $30. Comprehensive fee: $22,822 includes

full-time tuition ($15,152) and college room and board ($7670). College room only: $4650. Room and board charges vary according to board plan and housing facility. Part-time tuition: $505 per credit. Part-time tuition varies according to course load. **Scholarships:** Available **Calendar System:** Semester, Summer Session Available **Enrollment:** FT 3,103, PT 868, Grad 1,124 **Faculty:** FT 157, PT 227 **Student-Faculty Ratio:** 16:1 **Exams:** SAT I or ACT **% Receiving Financial Aid:** 75 **% Residing in College-Owned, -Operated, or -Affiliated Housing:** 30 **Library Holdings:** 197,034 **Regional Accreditation:** Middle State Association of Colleges and Schools **Credit Hours For Degree:** 126 credits, Bachelors **ROTC:** Army, Air Force **Professional Accreditation:** ABET, JRCERT **Intercollegiate Athletics:** Baseball M; Basketball M & W; Cheerleading M & W; Crew W; Cross-Country Running M & W; Field Hockey W; Football M; Golf M & W; Ice Hockey M; Lacrosse M & W; Rugby M; Soccer M & W; Softball W; Tennis M & W; Track and Field M & W; Volleyball W

ROSEDALE TECHNICAL INSTITUTE
215 Beecham Dr.
Ste. 2
Pittsburgh, PA 15205-9791
Tel: (412)521-6200
Free: 800-521-6262
Fax: (412)521-9277
E-mail: admissions@rosedaletech.org
Web Site: http://www.rosedaletech.org/
President/CEO: Ben Wilke
Admissions: Kevin Auld
Type: Two-Year College **Sex:** Coed **% Accepted:** 65 **Calendar System:** Semester **Enrollment:** FT 200 **Faculty:** FT 14, PT 4 **Student-Faculty Ratio:** 13:1 **Professional Accreditation:** ACCSCT

ROSEMONT COLLEGE
1400 Montgomery Ave.
Rosemont, PA 19010-1699
Tel: (610)527-0200
Free: 800-331-0708
Fax: (610)527-1041
E-mail: randrews@rosemont.edu
Web Site: http://www.rosemont.edu/
President/CEO: Dr. Ann Amore
Registrar: Joseph T. Rogers
Admissions: Rennie Andrews
Financial Aid: Melissa Walsh
Type: Comprehensive **Affiliation:** Roman Catholic **Scores:** 100% SAT V 400+; 100% SAT M 400+; 100% ACT 18-23 **% Accepted:** 66 **Admission Plans:** Early Admission; Deferred Admission **Application Deadline:** Rolling **Application Fee:** $35.00 **H.S. Requirements:** High school diploma required; GED accepted **Costs Per Year:** Application fee: $35. Comprehensive fee: $29,350 includes full-time tuition ($19,450), mandatory fees ($1100), and college room and board ($8800). Room and board charges vary according to housing facility. Part-time tuition: $750 per credit. Part-time mandatory fees: $310 per term. **Scholarships:** Available **Calendar System:** Semester, Summer Session Available **Enrollment:** FT 425, PT 219, Grad 404 **Faculty:** FT 32, PT 45 **Student-Faculty Ratio:** 8:1 **Exams:** SAT I or ACT **% Receiving Financial Aid:** 77 **% Residing in College-Owned, -Operated, or -Affiliated Housing:** 70 **Library Holdings:** 161,374 **Regional Accreditation:** Middle State Association of Colleges and Schools **Credit Hours For Degree:** 128 credits, Bachelors **ROTC:** Army **Intercollegiate Athletics:** Basketball W; Field Hockey W; Softball W; Tennis W; Volleyball W

ST. CHARLES BORROMEO SEMINARY, OVERBROOK
100 East Wynnewood Rd.
Wynnewood, PA 19096
Tel: (610)667-3394
Admissions: (610)785-6271
E-mail: cas@adphila.org
Web Site: http://www.scs.edu/
President/CEO: Msgr. Michael F. Burbidge
Registrar: Lawrence A. Heyman
Admissions: Rev. Msgr. Michael Fitzgerald
Financial Aid: Mary Kay McCaughan
Type: Comprehensive **Affiliation:** Roman Catholic **Scores:** 100% SAT V 400+; 100% SAT M 400+ **% Accepted:** 100 **Admission Plans:** Deferred Admission **Application Deadline:** July 15 **Application Fee:** $0.00 **H.S. Requirements:** High school diploma required; GED accepted **Costs Per Year:** Application fee: $0. Comprehensive fee: $19,850 includes full-time tuition ($12,350) and college room and board ($7500). Part-time tuition: $150 per credit. **Scholarships:** Available **Calendar System:** Semester, Summer Session Available **Enrollment:** FT 82, PT 113, Grad 81 **Faculty:** FT 22, PT 8 **Student-Faculty Ratio:** 7:1 **Exams:** SAT I or ACT **% Residing in College-Owned, -Operated, or -Affiliated Housing:** 94 **Library Holdings:** 113,761 **Regional Accreditation:** Middle State Association of Colleges and Schools **Credit Hours For Degree:** 125 credits, Bachelors **Professional Accreditation:** ATS

SAINT FRANCIS UNIVERSITY
PO Box 600, 117 Evergreen Dr.
Loretto, PA 15940-0600
Tel: (814)472-3000
Free: 800-342-5732
Admissions: (814)472-3100
Fax: (814)472-3044
Web Site: http://www.francis.edu/
President/CEO: Gabriel Zeis
Registrar: Dr. Stephen Rombouts
Admissions: Erin McCloskey
Financial Aid: Vince Frank
Type: Comprehensive **Sex:** Coed **Affiliation:** Roman Catholic **Scores:** 92.85% SAT V 400+; 93.47% SAT M 400+; 48.57% ACT 18-23; 34.29% ACT 24-29 **% Accepted:** 91 **Admission Plans:** Deferred Admission **Application Deadline:** Rolling **Application Fee:** $30.00 **H.S. Requirements:** High school diploma required; GED accepted **Costs Per Year:** Application fee: $30. Comprehensive fee: $28,978 includes full-time tuition ($20,360), mandatory fees ($1050), and college room and board ($7568). College room only: $3672. Full-time tuition and fees vary according to course load and program. Room and board charges vary according to board plan. Part-time tuition: $636 per credit. Part-time mandatory fees: $315 per credit hour. **Scholarships:** Available **Calendar System:** Semester, Summer Session Available **Enrollment:** FT 1,255, PT 206, Grad 604 **Faculty:** FT 89, PT 75 **Student-Faculty Ratio:** 14:1 **Exams:** SAT I or ACT **% Receiving Financial Aid:** 84 **% Residing in College-Owned, -Operated, or -Affiliated Housing:** 72 **Library Holdings:** 118,333 **Regional Accreditation:** Middle State Association of Colleges and Schools **Credit Hours For Degree:** 63 credits, Associates; 128 credits, Bachelors **ROTC:** Army **Professional Accreditation:** AACN, AOTA, APTA, CSWE **Intercollegiate Athletics:** Basketball M & W; Cross-Country Running M & W; Field Hockey W; Football M; Golf M & W; Lacrosse W; Soccer M & W; Softball W; Swimming and Diving M & W; Tennis M & W; Track and Field M & W; Volleyball M & W

SAINT JOSEPH'S UNIVERSITY
5600 City Ave.
Philadelphia, PA 19131-1395
Tel: (610)660-1000
Admissions: (610)660-1300
E-mail: admit@sju.edu
Web Site: http://www.sju.edu/
President/CEO: Rev. Timothy Lannon, SJ
Registrar: Gerard Donahue
Admissions: David Conway
Financial Aid: Eileen Tucker
Type: Comprehensive **Sex:** Coed **Affiliation:** Roman Catholic (Jesuit) **Scores:** 100% SAT V 400+; 100% SAT M 400+; 36% ACT 18-23; 51% ACT 24-29 **% Accepted:** 47 **Admission Plans:** Early Action; Deferred Admission **Application Deadline:** February 01 **Application Fee:** $55.00 **H.S. Requirements:** High school diploma required; GED not accepted. For continuing education program: High school diploma required; GED accepted **Costs Per Year:** Application fee: $55. Comprehensive fee: $37,428 includes full-time tuition ($27,320), mandatory fees ($135), and college room and board ($9973). Full-time tuition and fees vary according to student level. Room and board charges vary according to board plan and housing facility. Part-time tuition: $895 per credit. **Scholarships:** Available **Calendar System:** Semester, Summer Session Available **Enrollment:** FT 4,247, PT 896, Grad 2,571 **Faculty:** FT 269, PT 329 **Student-Faculty Ratio:** 15:1 **Exams:** SAT I or ACT **% Receiving Financial Aid:** 48 **% Residing in College-Owned, -Operated, or -Affiliated Housing:** 59 **Library Holdings:** 353,101 **Regional Accreditation:** Middle State Association of Colleges and Schools **Credit Hours For Degree:** 60 credit hours, Associates; 120 credit hours, Bachelors **ROTC:** Army, Navy, Air Force **Professional Accreditation:** AACSB, AANA **Intercollegiate Athletics:** Baseball M; Basketball M & W;

Crew M & W; Cross-Country Running M & W; Field Hockey W; Golf M; Lacrosse M & W; Soccer M & W; Softball W; Tennis M & W; Track and Field M & W

SAINT VINCENT COLLEGE
300 Fraser Purchase Rd.
Latrobe, PA 15650-2690
Tel: (724)532-6600
Free: 800-782-5549
Admissions: (724)532-5089
Fax: (724)537-4554
E-mail: admission@stvincent.edu
Web Site: http://www.stvincent.edu/
President/CEO: James F. Will
Registrar: Celine Hass
Admissions: David A. Collins
Financial Aid: David Collins
Type: Comprehensive **Sex:** Coed **Affiliation:** Roman Catholic **Scores:** 97.5% SAT V 400+; 98.1% SAT M 400+; 54.5% ACT 18-23; 34.1% ACT 24-29 **% Accepted:** 73 **Admission Plans:** Early Admission; Deferred Admission **Application Deadline:** May 01 **Application Fee:** $25.00 **H.S. Requirements:** High school diploma required; GED accepted **Costs Per Year:** Application fee: $25. Comprehensive fee: $28,553 includes full-time tuition ($21,104), mandatory fees ($575), and college room and board ($6874). College room only: $3500. Room and board charges vary according to board plan and student level. Part-time tuition: $660 per credit hour. Part-time mandatory fees: $45 per term. **Scholarships:** Available **Calendar System:** Semester, Summer Session Available **Enrollment:** FT 1,471, PT 105, Grad 111 **Faculty:** FT 95, PT 72 **Student-Faculty Ratio:** 13:1 **Exams:** SAT I or ACT **% Receiving Financial Aid:** 75 **% Residing in College-Owned, -Operated, or -Affiliated Housing:** 70 **Library Holdings:** 271,481 **Regional Accreditation:** Middle State Association of Colleges and Schools **Credit Hours For Degree:** 124 credits, Bachelors **ROTC:** Air Force **Professional Accreditation:** ACBSP **Intercollegiate Athletics:** Baseball M; Basketball M & W; Cross-Country Running M & W; Equestrian Sports W; Fencing M & W; Golf M & W; Ice Hockey M; Lacrosse M & W; Soccer M & W; Softball W; Swimming and Diving M & W; Tennis M & W; Volleyball W

SCHUYLKILL INSTITUTE OF BUSINESS AND TECHNOLOGY
171 Red Horse Rd.
Pottsville, PA 17901
Tel: (570)622-4835
Fax: (570)622-4835
E-mail: sseaman@sibt.edu
Web Site: http://www.sibt.edu/
President/CEO: William Klettke
Registrar: Kimberly Shields
Admissions: Stacy Seaman
Financial Aid: Shalanda Jones
Type: Two-Year College **Sex:** Coed **Affiliation:** Fore Front Education, Inc **% Accepted:** 100 **Admission Plans:** Open Admission **Application Deadline:** October 25 **Application Fee:** $50.00 **H.S. Requirements:** High school diploma required; GED accepted **Costs Per Year:** Application fee: $50. Tuition: $10,000 full-time. Mandatory fees: $450 full-time. Full-time tuition and fees vary according to degree level and program. Tuition guaranteed not to increase for student's term of enrollment. **Scholarships:** Available **Calendar System:** Quarter, Summer Session Not available **Enrollment:** FT 136 **Faculty:** FT 15, PT 1 **Student-Faculty Ratio:** 6:1 **Library Holdings:** 920 **Credit Hours For Degree:** 81 credits, Associates **Professional Accreditation:** ACICS, AAMAE

SETON HILL UNIVERSITY
Seton Hill Dr.
Greensburg, PA 15601
Tel: (724)834-2200
Free: 800-826-6234
Admissions: (724)838-4255
Fax: (724)830-4611
E-mail: admit@setonhill.edu
Web Site: http://www.setonhill.edu/
President/CEO: Dr. JoAnne W. Boyle
Registrar: Barbara C. Hinkle
Admissions: Kimberly McCarty
Financial Aid: Maryann Dudas
Type: Comprehensive **Sex:** Coed **Affiliation:** Roman Catholic **Scores:** 98% SAT V 400+; 98% SAT M 400+; 58% ACT 18-23; 14% ACT 24-29 **% Accepted:** 70 **Admission Plans:** Early Admission; Deferred Admission **Application Deadline:** August 15 **Application Fee:** $35.00 **H.S. Requirements:** High school diploma required; GED accepted **Costs Per Year:** Application fee: $35. Comprehensive fee: $29,020 includes full-time tuition ($21,870), mandatory fees ($120), and college room and board ($7030). Room and board charges vary according to board plan and housing facility. Part-time tuition: $580 per credit. Part-time mandatory fees: $60 per term. Part-time tuition and fees vary according to course load. **Scholarships:** Available **Calendar System:** Semester, Summer Session Available **Enrollment:** FT 1,226, PT 300, Grad 337 **Faculty:** FT 68, PT 117 **Student-Faculty Ratio:** 15:1 **Exams:** SAT I or ACT **% Receiving Financial Aid:** 85 **% Residing in College-Owned, -Operated, or -Affiliated Housing:** 60 **Library Holdings:** 116,974 **Regional Accreditation:** Middle State Association of Colleges and Schools **Credit Hours For Degree:** 120 credits, Bachelors **ROTC:** Army **Professional Accreditation:** AAMFT, AAFCS, ADtA, CSWE, NASM **Intercollegiate Athletics:** Baseball M; Basketball M & W; Cross-Country Running M & W; Equestrian Sports M & W; Field Hockey W; Football M; Golf M & W; Lacrosse M & W; Soccer M & W; Softball W; Tennis M & W; Track and Field M & W; Volleyball W

SHIPPENSBURG UNIVERSITY OF PENNSYLVANIA
1871 Old Main Dr.
Shippensburg, PA 17257-2299
Tel: (717)477-7447
Admissions: (717)477-1231
Fax: (717)477-1273
E-mail: admiss@ship.edu
Web Site: http://www.ship.edu/
President/CEO: Dr. Jody Harpster
Registrar: Alana Moriarty
Admissions: Dr. Thomas Speakman
Financial Aid: Peter J. D'Annibale
Type: Comprehensive **Sex:** Coed **Affiliation:** Pennsylvania State System of Higher Education **Scores:** 95.9% SAT V 400+; 96.1% SAT M 400+; 66.7% ACT 18-23; 18.8% ACT 24-29 **% Accepted:** 66 **Admission Plans:** Early Admission; Early Action; Deferred Admission **Application Deadline:** Rolling **Application Fee:** $30.00 **H.S. Requirements:** High school diploma required; GED accepted **Costs Per Year:** Application fee: $30. State resident tuition: $4906 full-time, $204 per credit hour part-time. Nonresident tuition: $12,266 full-time, $511 per credit hour part-time. Mandatory fees: $1269 full-time, $20 per credit hour part-time, $147 per term part-time. College room and board: $5710. College room only: $3290. Room and board charges vary according to board plan and housing facility. **Scholarships:** Available **Calendar System:** Semester, Summer Session Available **Enrollment:** FT 6,175, PT 284, Grad 1,026 **Faculty:** FT 305, PT 66 **Student-Faculty Ratio:** 20:1 **Exams:** SAT I or ACT **% Receiving Financial Aid:** 46 **% Residing in College-Owned, -Operated, or -Affiliated Housing:** 34 **Library Holdings:** 447,016 **Regional Accreditation:** Middle State Association of Colleges and Schools **Credit Hours For Degree:** 120 credit hours, Bachelors **ROTC:** Army **Professional Accreditation:** AACSB, ACA, CSWE, NCATE **Intercollegiate Athletics:** Baseball M; Basketball M & W; Cross-Country Running M & W; Field Hockey W; Football M; Lacrosse W; Soccer M & W; Softball W; Swimming and Diving M & W; Tennis W; Track and Field M & W; Volleyball W; Wrestling M

SLIPPERY ROCK UNIVERSITY OF PENNSYLVANIA
1 Morrow Way
Slippery Rock, PA 16057-1383
Tel: (724)738-9000
Free: 800-SRU-9111
Fax: (724)738-2098
Web Site: http://www.sru.edu/
President/CEO: Dr. Robert M. Smith
Registrar: Eliott Baker
Financial Aid: Patricia Hladio
Type: Comprehensive **Sex:** Coed **Scores:** 96.3% SAT V 400+; 95.36% SAT M 400+; 66.9% ACT 18-23; 19.01% ACT 24-29 **% Accepted:** 41 **Admission Plans:** Preferred Admission; Deferred Admission **Application Fee:** $25.00 **H.S. Requirements:** High school diploma required; GED accepted **Costs Per Year:** Application fee: $25. State resident tuition: $4906 full-time, $204 per credit hour part-time. Nonresident tuition: $7360 full-time, $511 per credit part-time. Mandatory fees: $1369 full-time, $47 per credit part-time, $53.25 per term part-time. College room and board: $4796. College room

only: $2688. **Scholarships:** Available **Calendar System:** Semester, Summer Session Available **Enrollment:** FT 6,883, PT 531, Grad 691 **Faculty:** FT 367, PT 34 **Student-Faculty Ratio:** 19:1 **Exams:** SAT I or ACT **% Receiving Financial Aid:** 60 **% Residing in College-Owned, -Operated, or -Affiliated Housing:** 39 **Library Holdings:** 512,424 **Regional Accreditation:** Middle State Association of Colleges and Schools **Credit Hours For Degree:** 120 credits, Bachelors **ROTC:** Army **Professional Accreditation:** ACA, APTA, ACBSP, CSWE, JRCEPAT, NASD, NASM, NCATE, NLN, NRPA **Intercollegiate Athletics:** Baseball M; Basketball M & W; Cheerleading M & W; Cross-Country Running M & W; Field Hockey W; Football M; Golf M & W; Soccer M & W; Softball W; Swimming and Diving M & W; Tennis M & W; Track and Field M & W; Volleyball W; Water Polo M & W; Wrestling M

SOUTH HILLS SCHOOL OF BUSINESS & TECHNOLOGY (ALTOONA)

508 58th St.
Altoona, PA 16602
Tel: (814)944-6134
Admissions: (814)234-7755
Fax: (814)944-4684
Web Site: http://www.southhills.edu/
President/CEO: Marianne Beyer
Registrar: Heather Moyer
Admissions: Diane M. Brown
Financial Aid: Joan Grassi

Type: Two-Year College **Sex:** Coed **Admission Plans:** Open Admission **Application Fee:** $25.00 **H.S. Requirements:** High school diploma required; GED accepted **Scholarships:** Available **Calendar System:** Trimester, Summer Session Available **Enrollment:** FT 142, PT 6 **Faculty:** FT 10, PT 1 **Student-Faculty Ratio:** 13:1 **Exams:** Other **Credit Hours For Degree:** 90 credits, Associates **Professional Accreditation:** ACICS

SOUTH HILLS SCHOOL OF BUSINESS & TECHNOLOGY (STATE COLLEGE)

480 Waupelani Dr.
State College, PA 16801-4516
Tel: (814)234-7755; 888-282-7427
Fax: (814)234-0926
Web Site: http://www.southhills.edu/
President/CEO: S. Paul Mazza
Registrar: Jackie Edwards
Admissions: Diane M. Brown
Financial Aid: Harriet Arndt

Type: Two-Year College **Sex:** Coed **% Accepted:** 77 **Application Deadline:** September 02 **Application Fee:** $25.00 **H.S. Requirements:** High school diploma required; GED accepted **Costs Per Year:** Application fee: $25. Tuition: $11,637 full-time, $323 per credit part-time. Mandatory fees: $75 full-time, $25 per term part-time. **Scholarships:** Available **Calendar System:** Quarter **Enrollment:** FT 611, PT 52 **Faculty:** FT 37, PT 23 **Student-Faculty Ratio:** 15:1 **Exams:** Other **Credit Hours For Degree:** 90 credits, Associates **Professional Accreditation:** ACICS, AHIMA

SUSQUEHANNA UNIVERSITY

514 University Ave.
Selinsgrove, PA 17870
Tel: (570)374-0101
Free: 800-326-9672
Admissions: (570)372-4260
Fax: (570)372-2722
E-mail: suadmiss@susqu.edu
Web Site: http://www.susqu.edu/
President/CEO: Dr. L. Jay Lemons
Registrar: Alex G. H. Smith
Admissions: Chris Markle
Financial Aid: Helen Nunn

Type: Four-Year College **Sex:** Coed **Affiliation:** Evangelical Lutheran Church in America **Scores:** 100% SAT V 400+; 100% SAT M 400+ **% Accepted:** 81 **Admission Plans:** Early Admission; Early Decision Plan; Deferred Admission **Application Deadline:** March 01 **Application Fee:** $35.00 **H.S. Requirements:** High school diploma required; GED accepted **Costs Per Year:** Application fee: $35. Comprehensive fee: $33,465 includes full-time tuition ($26,265) and college room and board ($7200). Part-time tuition: $825 per semester hour. **Scholarships:** Available **Calendar System:** Semester, Summer Session Available **Enrollment:** FT 1,894, PT 95 **Faculty:** FT 122, PT 63 **Student-Faculty Ratio:** 13:1 **Exams:** SAT I or ACT, SAT II **% Receiving Financial Aid:** 64 **% Residing in College-Owned, -Operated, or -Affiliated Housing:** 80 **Library Holdings:** 294,337 **Regional Accreditation:** Middle State Association of Colleges and Schools **Credit Hours For Degree:** 130 semester hours, Bachelors **ROTC:** Army **Professional Accreditation:** AACSB, NASM **Intercollegiate Athletics:** Baseball M; Basketball M & W; Cheerleading M & W; Crew M & W; Cross-Country Running M & W; Equestrian Sports M & W; Field Hockey W; Football M; Golf M & W; Lacrosse M & W; Rugby M & W; Soccer M & W; Softball W; Swimming and Diving M & W; Tennis M & W; Track and Field M & W; Volleyball M & W

SWARTHMORE COLLEGE

500 College Ave.
Swarthmore, PA 19081-1397
Tel: (610)328-8000
Free: 800-667-3110
Admissions: (610)328-8300
Fax: (610)328-8673
E-mail: admissions@swarthmore.edu
Web Site: http://www.swarthmore.edu/
President/CEO: Dr. Alfred H. Bloom
Registrar: Martin O. Warner
Admissions: Jim Bock
Financial Aid: Laura Talbot

Type: Four-Year College **Sex:** Coed **Scores:** 100% SAT V 400+; 100% SAT M 400+ **% Accepted:** 22 **Admission Plans:** Early Admission; Early Decision Plan; Deferred Admission **Application Deadline:** January 02 **Application Fee:** $60.00 **H.S. Requirements:** High school diploma or equivalent not required **Costs Per Year:** Application fee: $60. Comprehensive fee: $41,280 includes full-time tuition ($31,196), mandatory fees ($320), and college room and board ($9764). College room only: $5006. Room and board charges vary according to board plan. **Scholarships:** Available **Calendar System:** Semester, Summer Session Not available **Enrollment:** FT 1,472, PT 7 **Faculty:** FT 168, PT 27 **Student-Faculty Ratio:** 8:1 **Exams:** SAT I and SAT II or ACT **% Receiving Financial Aid:** 48 **% Residing in College-Owned, -Operated, or -Affiliated Housing:** 94 **Library Holdings:** 754,499 **Regional Accreditation:** Middle State Association of Colleges and Schools **Credit Hours For Degree:** 32 courses, Bachelors **ROTC:** Army, Air Force **Professional Accreditation:** ABET **Intercollegiate Athletics:** Badminton M & W; Baseball M; Basketball M & W; Cross-Country Running M & W; Fencing M & W; Field Hockey W; Golf M; Ice Hockey M & W; Lacrosse M & W; Rugby M & W; Soccer M & W; Softball W; Squash M & W; Swimming and Diving M & W; Tennis M & W; Track and Field M & W; Ultimate Frisbee M & W; Volleyball M & W

TALMUDICAL YESHIVA OF PHILADELPHIA

6063 Drexel Rd.
Philadelphia, PA 19131-1296
Tel: (215)473-1212
Fax: (215)477-5065
President/CEO: Erwin Weinberg
Registrar: Rabbi Uri Mandelbaum
Admissions: Rabbi Elya Svei
Financial Aid: Rabbi Uri Mandelbaum

Type: Four-Year College **Sex:** Men **Affiliation:** Jewish **Admission Plans:** Early Admission; Deferred Admission **H.S. Requirements:** High school diploma required; GED accepted **Costs Per Year:** Comprehensive fee: $11,600 includes full-time tuition ($6500), mandatory fees ($100), and college room and board ($5000). **Scholarships:** Available **Calendar System:** Trimester, Summer Session Not available **Enrollment:** FT 85 **Faculty:** FT 3, PT 2 **Student-Faculty Ratio:** 23:1 **% Receiving Financial Aid:** 63 **% Residing in College-Owned, -Operated, or -Affiliated Housing:** 98 **Library Holdings:** 4,800 **Credit Hours For Degree:** 170 credit hours, Bachelors **Professional Accreditation:** AARTS

TEMPLE UNIVERSITY

1801 North Broad St.
Philadelphia, PA 19122-6096
Tel: (215)204-7000; 888-340-2222
Admissions: (215)204-8556
Fax: (215)204-5694
E-mail: tuadm@vm.temple.edu
Web Site: http://www.temple.edu/
President/CEO: Dr. David Adamany

Registrar: Jacqueline R. Resavage
Admissions: Dr. Timm Rinehart
Financial Aid: Dr. John Morris
Type: University **Sex:** Coed **Scores:** 98% SAT V 400+; 99% SAT M 400+; 62% ACT 18-23; 28% ACT 24-29 **% Accepted:** 63 **Admission Plans:** Early Admission; Deferred Admission **Application Deadline:** April 01 **Application Fee:** $35.00 **H.S. Requirements:** High school diploma required; GED accepted **Costs Per Year:** Application fee: $35. State resident tuition: $9140 full-time, $354 per credit hour part-time. Nonresident tuition: $16,736 full-time, $596 per credit hour part-time. Mandatory fees: $500 full-time, $109 per term part-time. Full-time tuition and fees vary according to course load, location, program, and reciprocity agreements. Part-time tuition and fees vary according to course load, location, program, and reciprocity agreements. College room and board: $7794. College room only: $5054. Room and board charges vary according to board plan and housing facility. **Scholarships:** Available **Calendar System:** Semester, Summer Session Available **Enrollment:** FT 20,936, PT 3,258, Grad 6,383 **Faculty:** FT 1,206, PT 1,355 **Student-Faculty Ratio:** 17:1 **Exams:** SAT I or ACT **% Receiving Financial Aid:** 71 **% Residing in College-Owned, -Operated, or -Affiliated Housing:** 26 **Library Holdings:** 3,327,935 **Regional Accreditation:** Middle State Association of Colleges and Schools **Credit Hours For Degree:** 64 semester hours, Associates; 124 semester hours, Bachelors **ROTC:** Army, Navy, Air Force **Professional Accreditation:** AACSB, ABET, ACEHSA, ACEJMC, AACN, ABA, ACPhE, ADA, AHIMA, AOTA, APTA, APMA, APA, ASLA, ASLHA, AALS, CEPH, CSWE, JRCEPAT, LCMEAMA NASAD, NASD, NASM, NAST, NCATE, NRPA **Intercollegiate Athletics:** Baseball M; Basketball M & W; Crew M & W; Fencing W; Field Hockey W; Football M; Golf M; Gymnastics M & W; Lacrosse W; Soccer M & W; Softball M & W; Tennis M; Track and Field M & W; Volleyball W

THADDEUS STEVENS COLLEGE OF TECHNOLOGY

750 East King St.
Lancaster, PA 17602-3198
Tel: (717)299-7730
Admissions: (717)299-7772
Fax: (717)391-6929
Web Site: http://www.stevenscollege.edu/
President/CEO: Dr. William E. Griscom
Registrar: Judith Leedy
Admissions: Erin Kate Nelsen
Financial Aid: Bernard McCree
Type: Two-Year College **Sex:** Coed **Admission Plans:** Preferred Admission; Deferred Admission **Application Fee:** $25.00 **H.S. Requirements:** High school diploma required; GED accepted **Scholarships:** Available **Calendar System:** Semester, Summer Session Not available **Enrollment:** FT 660 **Faculty:** FT 45, PT 3 **Student-Faculty Ratio:** 12:1 **Exams:** Other **% Residing in College-Owned, -Operated, or -Affiliated Housing:** 48 **Library Holdings:** 26,000 **Regional Accreditation:** Middle State Association of Colleges and Schools **Credit Hours For Degree:** 60 credits, Associates **Intercollegiate Athletics:** Basketball M; Cross-Country Running M; Football M; Golf M; Track and Field M; Wrestling M

THIEL COLLEGE

75 College Ave.
Greenville, PA 16125-2181
Tel: (724)589-2000
Free: 800-248-4435
Admissions: (724)589-2226
Fax: (724)589-2013
Web Site: http://www.thiel.edu/
President/CEO: Dr. Lance A. Masters
Registrar: Mark McGrath
Admissions: Gary Kelsey
Financial Aid: Cynthia Farrell
Type: Four-Year College **Sex:** Coed **Affiliation:** Evangelical Lutheran Church in America **Scores:** 85% SAT V 400+; 85% SAT M 400+; 49% ACT 18-23; 11% ACT 24-29 **% Accepted:** 75 **Admission Plans:** Early Action; Deferred Admission **Application Deadline:** June 30 **Application Fee:** $25.00 **H.S. Requirements:** High school diploma required; GED accepted **Costs Per Year:** Application fee: $25. Comprehensive fee: $24,580 includes full-time tuition ($16,200), mandatory fees ($1390), and college room and board ($6990). College room only: $3566. Full-time tuition and fees vary according to course load. Room and board charges vary according to board plan and housing facility. Part-time tuition: $400 per credit hour. Part-time mandatory fees: $21 per credit hour. Part-time tuition and fees vary according to course load. **Scholarships:** Available **Calendar System:** Semester, Summer Session Available **Enrollment:** FT 1,253, PT 67 **Faculty:** FT 61, PT 61 **Student-Faculty Ratio:** 17:1 **Exams:** SAT I or ACT **% Receiving Financial Aid:** 87 **% Residing in College-Owned, -Operated, or -Affiliated Housing:** 82 **Library Holdings:** 131,176 **Regional Accreditation:** Middle State Association of Colleges and Schools **Credit Hours For Degree:** 64 credit hours, Associates; 124 credit hours, Bachelors **Intercollegiate Athletics:** Baseball M; Basketball M & W; Cheerleading M & W; Cross-Country Running M & W; Football M; Golf M & W; Soccer M & W; Softball W; Tennis M & W; Track and Field M & W; Volleyball W; Wrestling M

THOMAS JEFFERSON UNIVERSITY

Eleventh and Walnut Sts.
Philadelphia, PA 19107
Tel: (215)955-6000; 877-533-3247
Admissions: (215)503-1040
Fax: (215)503-7241
Web Site: http://www.jefferson.edu/
President/CEO: Dr. Robert L. Barchi
Registrar: Dr. Raelynn Cooter
Admissions: Karen Jacobs
Financial Aid: Susan Batchelor
Type: University **Sex:** Coed **% Accepted:** 14 **Admission Plans:** Deferred Admission **Application Deadline:** Rolling **Application Fee:** $50.00 **H.S. Requirements:** High school diploma required; GED accepted **Costs Per Year:** Application fee: $50. Tuition: $21,975 full-time. **Scholarships:** Available **Calendar System:** Semester, Summer Session Not available **Enrollment:** FT 669, PT 319, Grad 758 **Faculty:** FT 76, PT 190 **Student-Faculty Ratio:** 10:1 **Exams:** SAT I or ACT **% Receiving Financial Aid:** 88 **% Residing in College-Owned, -Operated, or -Affiliated Housing:** 30 **Library Holdings:** 170,000 **Regional Accreditation:** Middle State Association of Colleges and Schools **Credit Hours For Degree:** 126 credits, Bachelors **ROTC:** Air Force **Professional Accreditation:** AACN, AOTA, APTA, ASC, ACIPE, JRCEDMS, JRCERT, LCMEAMA, NAACLS **Intercollegiate Athletics:** Rugby M

THOMPSON INSTITUTE

5650 Derry St.
Harrisburg, PA 17111-3518
Tel: (717)564-4112
Fax: (717)564-3779
Web Site: http://www.thompson.edu/
President/CEO: Roy M. Hawkins
Registrar: Nancy Harris
Admissions: Charles Zimmerman
Financial Aid: Sarah Brooker
Type: Two-Year College **Sex:** Coed **Affiliation:** Kaplan Higher Education Corporation **Admission Plans:** Open Admission; Deferred Admission **Application Fee:** $50.00 **H.S. Requirements:** High school diploma required; GED accepted **Costs Per Year:** Application fee: $50. Tuition: $8600 full-time. College room only: $1600. **Scholarships:** Available **Calendar System:** Quarter, Summer Session Available **Enrollment:** FT 485 **Faculty:** FT 24, PT 3 **Student-Faculty Ratio:** 25:1 **Library Holdings:** 950 **Credit Hours For Degree:** 72 credits, Associates **Professional Accreditation:** ACICS

TRI-STATE BUSINESS INSTITUTE

5757 West 26th St.
Erie, PA 16506
Tel: (814)838-7673
Fax: (814)838-8642
E-mail: geuliano@tsbi.org
Web Site: http://www.tsbi.org/
President/CEO: Guy Guyeliano
Registrar: Karen LaPaglia
Admissions: Guy M. Euliano
Financial Aid: Don Boyd
Type: Two-Year College **Professional Accreditation:** ACICS

TRIANGLE TECH, INC.-DUBOIS SCHOOL

PO Box 551
DuBois, PA 15801-0551
Tel: (814)371-2090
Free: 800-874-8324
Admissions: (412)359-1000

Fax: (814)371-9227
Web Site: http://www.triangle-tech.edu/
President/CEO: Deborah Hepburn
Admissions: John A. Mazzarese
Financial Aid: Michelle Jashinski
Type: Two-Year College **Sex:** Coed **Affiliation:** Triangle Tech, Inc **% Accepted:** 96 **Admission Plans:** Deferred Admission **Application Deadline:** Rolling **Application Fee:** $0.00 **H.S. Requirements:** High school diploma required; GED accepted **Costs Per Year:** Application fee: $0. Tuition: $11,408 full-time. **Scholarships:** Available **Calendar System:** Semester, Summer Session Not available **Enrollment:** FT 246 **Faculty:** FT 22, PT 0 **Student-Faculty Ratio:** 11:1 **Library Holdings:** 1,200 **Credit Hours For Degree:** 72 credits, Associates **Professional Accreditation:** ACCSCT

TRIANGLE TECH, INC.-ERIE SCHOOL
2000 Liberty St.
Erie, PA 16502-2594
Tel: (814)453-6016
Free: 800-TRI-TECH
Fax: (814)454-2818
Web Site: http://www.triangle-tech.com/
President/CEO: William McCollough
Admissions: John A. Mazzarese
Type: Two-Year College **Sex:** Coed **Affiliation:** Triangle Tech, Inc **Admission Plans:** Deferred Admission **Application Fee:** $0.00 **H.S. Requirements:** High school diploma required; GED accepted **Scholarships:** Available **Calendar System:** Semester **Enrollment:** FT 83 **Faculty:** FT 14 **Student-Faculty Ratio:** 12:1 **Library Holdings:** 1,000 **Credit Hours For Degree:** 72 credits, Associates **Professional Accreditation:** ACCSCT

TRIANGLE TECH, INC.-GREENSBURG SCHOOL
222 East Pittsburgh St., Ste. A
Greensburg, PA 15601-3304
Tel: (724)832-1050
Free: 800-874-8324
Admissions: (412)359-1000
Web Site: http://www.triangle-tech.com/
President/CEO: James R. Agras
Admissions: John Mazzarese
Financial Aid: Cathy Waxter
Type: Two-Year College **Sex:** Coed **Affiliation:** Triangle Tech, Inc **% Accepted:** 100 **Admission Plans:** Deferred Admission **Application Deadline:** Rolling **Application Fee:** $75.00 **H.S. Requirements:** High school diploma required; GED accepted **Costs Per Year:** Application fee: $75. Tuition: $11,408 full-time. Mandatory fees: $200 full-time. **Scholarships:** Available **Calendar System:** Semester, Summer Session Available **Enrollment:** FT 271 **Faculty:** FT 21, PT 5 **Student-Faculty Ratio:** 12:1 **Library Holdings:** 550 **Credit Hours For Degree:** 72 credits, Associates **Professional Accreditation:** ACCSCT

TRIANGLE TECH, INC.-PITTSBURGH SCHOOL
1940 Perrysville Ave.
Pittsburgh, PA 15214-3897
Tel: (412)359-1000
Free: 800-874-8324
Fax: (412)359-1012
Web Site: http://www.triangle-tech.edu/
President/CEO: Stacie Hendrickson
Admissions: John A. Mazzarese
Type: Two-Year College **Sex:** Coed **Affiliation:** Triangle Tech Group **Admission Plans:** Early Admission; Deferred Admission **H.S. Requirements:** High school diploma required; GED accepted **Costs Per Year:** Tuition: $301.78 per credit part-time. **Scholarships:** Available **Calendar System:** Semester, Summer Session Not available **Enrollment:** FT 377 **Faculty:** FT 28, PT 5 **Student-Faculty Ratio:** 10:1 **Library Holdings:** 2,000 **Credit Hours For Degree:** 72 credits, Associates **Professional Accreditation:** ACCSCT

TRIANGLE TECH, INC.-SUNBURY SCHOOL
RR No. 1, Box 51
Sunbury, PA 17801
Tel: (570)988-0700
Web Site: http://www.triangle-tech.com/ **Type:** Two-Year College **Sex:** Coed **Calendar System:** Semester **Professional Accreditation:** ACCSCT

THE UNIVERSITY OF THE ARTS
320 South Broad St.
Philadelphia, PA 19102-4944
Tel: (215)717-6000
Free: 800-616-ARTS
Admissions: (215)717-6039
Fax: (215)717-6045
E-mail: sgandy@uarts.edu
Web Site: http://www.uarts.edu/
President/CEO: Miguel Angel Corzo
Registrar: Lynn Dougherty
Admissions: Susan Gandy
Type: Comprehensive **Sex:** Coed **Scores:** 97% SAT V 400+; 89% SAT M 400+; 43% ACT 18-23; 36% ACT 24-29 **% Accepted:** 49 **Admission Plans:** Early Admission; Deferred Admission **Application Deadline:** Rolling **Application Fee:** $60.00 **H.S. Requirements:** High school diploma required; GED accepted **Costs Per Year:** Application fee: $60. Tuition: $24,730 full-time, $1070 per credit part-time. Mandatory fees: $950 full-time. College room only: $6300. **Scholarships:** Available **Calendar System:** Semester, Summer Session Not available **Enrollment:** FT 2,035, PT 44, Grad 198 **Faculty:** FT 118, PT 354 **Student-Faculty Ratio:** 9:1 **Exams:** SAT I or ACT **% Residing in College-Owned, -Operated, or -Affiliated Housing:** 36 **Library Holdings:** 123,175 **Regional Accreditation:** Middle State Association of Colleges and Schools **Credit Hours For Degree:** 123 credits, Bachelors **Professional Accreditation:** NASAD, NASM

UNIVERSITY OF PENNSYLVANIA
3451 Walnut St.
Philadelphia, PA 19104
Tel: (215)898-5000
Admissions: (215)898-7507
Web Site: http://www.upenn.edu/
President/CEO: Dr. Amy Gutmann
Registrar: Ronald Sanders
Admissions: Willis J. Stetson, Jr.
Financial Aid: William Schilling
Type: University **Sex:** Coed **Scores:** 100% SAT V 400+; 100% SAT M 400+; 3% ACT 18-23; 31% ACT 24-29 **% Accepted:** 21 **Admission Plans:** Early Admission; Early Decision Plan; Deferred Admission **Application Deadline:** January 01 **Application Fee:** $70.00 **H.S. Requirements:** High school diploma or equivalent not required **Costs Per Year:** Application fee: $70. Comprehensive fee: $41,766 includes full-time tuition ($29,030), mandatory fees ($3334), and college room and board ($9402). College room only: $5730. Room and board charges vary according to board plan and housing facility. Part-time tuition: $3708 per course. Part-time mandatory fees: $389 per course. Part-time tuition and fees vary according to course load. **Scholarships:** Available **Calendar System:** Semester, Summer Session Available **Enrollment:** FT 9,545, PT 296, Grad 6,596 **Faculty:** FT 1,388, PT 602 **Student-Faculty Ratio:** 6:1 **Exams:** SAT I and SAT II or ACT **% Receiving Financial Aid:** 45 **% Residing in College-Owned, -Operated, or -Affiliated Housing:** 64 **Library Holdings:** 5,377,472 **Regional Accreditation:** Middle State Association of Colleges and Schools **Credit Hours For Degree:** 32 courses, Bachelors **ROTC:** Army, Navy, Air Force **Professional Accreditation:** AACSB, ABET, ACEHSA, AACN, AANA, ABA, ACNM, ADA, ACSP, APA, ASLA, AVMA, ACIPE, AALS, CSWE, LCMEAMA, NLN **Intercollegiate Athletics:** Baseball M; Basketball M & W; Crew M & W; Cross-Country Running M & W; Fencing M & W; Field Hockey W; Football M; Golf M & W; Gymnastics W; Lacrosse M & W; Soccer M & W; Softball W; Squash M & W; Swimming and Diving M & W; Tennis M & W; Track and Field M & W; Volleyball W; Wrestling M

UNIVERSITY OF PHOENIX-PHILADELPHIA CAMPUS
170 South Warner Rd., Ste. 200
Wayne, PA 19087-2121
Tel: (610)989-0880
Free: 800-228-7240
Admissions: (480)557-1712
Fax: (610)989-0881
Web Site: http://www.phoenix.edu/
President/CEO: Elden Monday
Admissions: Nina Omelchanko

Type: Comprehensive **Sex:** Coed **Admission Plans:** Open Admission; Deferred Admission **Application Deadline:** Rolling **Application Fee:** $110.00 **H.S. Requirements:** High school diploma required; GED accepted **Costs Per Year:** Application fee: $110. Tuition: $13,050 full-time, $435 per credit part-time. Mandatory fees: $560 full-time, $70 per course part-time. **Scholarships:** Available **Calendar System:** Continuous, Summer Session Not available **Enrollment:** FT 1,282, Grad 412 **Faculty:** FT 13, PT 174 **Student-Faculty Ratio:** 8:1 **Library Holdings:** 444 **Regional Accreditation:** North Central Association of Colleges and Schools **Credit Hours For Degree:** 60 credits, Associates; 120 credits, Bachelors

UNIVERSITY OF PHOENIX-PITTSBURGH CAMPUS
Penn Center West Six, Ste. 100
Pittsburgh, PA 15276
Tel: (412)747-9000
Free: 800-228-7240
Admissions: (480)557-1712
Fax: (412)747-0676
Web Site: http://www.phoenix.edu/
President/CEO: David Warren
Admissions: Nina Omelchanko
Type: Comprehensive **Sex:** Coed **Admission Plans:** Open Admission; Deferred Admission **Application Deadline:** Rolling **Application Fee:** $110.00 **H.S. Requirements:** High school diploma required; GED accepted **Costs Per Year:** Application fee: $110. Tuition: $13,050 full-time, $435 per credit part-time. Mandatory fees: $560 full-time, $70 per course part-time. **Scholarships:** Available **Calendar System:** Continuous, Summer Session Not available **Enrollment:** FT 497, Grad 148 **Faculty:** FT 11, PT 106 **Student-Faculty Ratio:** 5:1 **Library Holdings:** 444 **Regional Accreditation:** North Central Association of Colleges and Schools **Credit Hours For Degree:** 60 credits, Associates; 120 credits, Bachelors

UNIVERSITY OF PITTSBURGH
4200 Fifth Ave.
Pittsburgh, PA 15260
Tel: (412)624-4141
Admissions: (412)624-7488
Fax: (412)648-8815
E-mail: oafa@pitt.edu
Web Site: http://www.pitt.edu/
President/CEO: Mark A. Nordenberg
Registrar: Samuel D. Conte
Admissions: Dr. Betsy A. Porter
Type: University **Sex:** Coed **Affiliation:** Commonwealth System of Higher Education **Scores:** 100% SAT V 400+; 100% SAT M 400+; 23% ACT 18-23; 54% ACT 24-29 **% Accepted:** 53 **Admission Plans:** Early Admission; Deferred Admission **Application Deadline:** Rolling **Application Fee:** $35.00 **H.S. Requirements:** High school diploma required; GED not accepted **Costs Per Year:** Application fee: $35. State resident tuition: $10,736 full-time, $412 per credit part-time. Nonresident tuition: $20,084 full-time, $772 per credit part-time. Mandatory fees: $700 full-time, $164 per term part-time. Full-time tuition and fees vary according to degree level and program. Part-time tuition and fees vary according to degree level and program. College room and board: $7430. College room only: $4510. Room and board charges vary according to board plan and housing facility. **Scholarships:** Available **Calendar System:** Semester, Summer Session Available **Enrollment:** FT 15,100, PT 1,924, Grad 7,718 **Exams:** SAT I or ACT **% Receiving Financial Aid:** 52 **% Residing in College-Owned, -Operated, or -Affiliated Housing:** 36 **Library Holdings:** 4,640,279 **Regional Accreditation:** Middle State Association of Colleges and Schools **Credit Hours For Degree:** 120 credits, Bachelors **ROTC:** Army, Navy, Air Force **Professional Accreditation:** AACSB, ABET, ACEHSA, AACN, AANA, ABA, ACPhE, ACA, ADA, ADtA, AHIMA, ALA, AOTA, APTA, APA, ASLHA, AALS, CEPH, CORE, CSWE JRCEMT, JRCEPAT, LCMEAMA, NASPAA, NAST **Intercollegiate Athletics:** Baseball M; Basketball M & W; Cross-Country Running M & W; Football M; Gymnastics W; Soccer M & W; Softball W; Swimming and Diving M & W; Tennis W; Track and Field M & W; Volleyball W; Wrestling M

UNIVERSITY OF PITTSBURGH AT BRADFORD
300 Campus Dr.
Bradford, PA 16701-2812
Tel: (814)362-7500
Free: 800-872-1787
Admissions: (814)362-7677
Fax: (814)362-7578
E-mail: nazemetz@upb.pitt.edu
Web Site: http://www.upb.pitt.edu/
President/CEO: Dr. Livingston Alexander
Registrar: James L. Baldwin
Admissions: Alexander Nazemetz
Financial Aid: Melissa Ibanez
Type: Four-Year College **Sex:** Coed **Affiliation:** University of Pittsburgh System **Scores:** 96.27% SAT V 400+; 93.93% SAT M 400+; 72.41% ACT 18-23; 13.79% ACT 24-29 **% Accepted:** 76 **Admission Plans:** Deferred Admission **Application Deadline:** Rolling **Application Fee:** $35.00 **H.S. Requirements:** High school diploma required; GED accepted **Costs Per Year:** Application fee: $35. State resident tuition: $9888 full-time, $380 per credit part-time. Nonresident tuition: $19,776 full-time, $760 per credit part-time. Mandatory fees: $650 full-time, $95 per term part-time. Full-time tuition and fees vary according to course load and program. Part-time tuition and fees vary according to course load and program. College room and board: $6470. Room and board charges vary according to board plan and housing facility. **Scholarships:** Available **Calendar System:** Semester, Summer Session Available **Enrollment:** FT 991, PT 310 **Faculty:** FT 65, PT 57 **Student-Faculty Ratio:** 13:1 **Exams:** SAT I or ACT **% Receiving Financial Aid:** 83 **% Residing in College-Owned, -Operated, or -Affiliated Housing:** 47 **Library Holdings:** 88,969 **Regional Accreditation:** Middle State Association of Colleges and Schools **Credit Hours For Degree:** 60 credits, Associates; 120 credits, Bachelors **ROTC:** Army **Professional Accreditation:** NLN **Intercollegiate Athletics:** Baseball M; Basketball M & W; Cross-Country Running M & W; Golf M & W; Soccer M & W; Softball W; Volleyball W

UNIVERSITY OF PITTSBURGH AT GREENSBURG
1150 Mount Pleasant Rd.
Greensburg, PA 15601-5860
Tel: (724)837-7040
Admissions: (724)836-9880
Fax: (724)836-9901
E-mail: upgadmit@pitt.edu
Web Site: http://www.upg.pitt.edu/
President/CEO: Dr. Frank A. Cassell
Registrar: Carol Calloway
Admissions: Brandi S. Darr
Financial Aid: Brandi Darr
Type: Four-Year College **Sex:** Coed **Affiliation:** University of Pittsburgh System **Scores:** 96% SAT V 400+; 95% SAT M 400+; 55% ACT 18-23; 23% ACT 24-29 **% Accepted:** 89 **Admission Plans:** Early Admission; Deferred Admission **Application Deadline:** August 01 **Application Fee:** $45.00 **H.S. Requirements:** High school diploma required; GED not accepted. For applicants 21 or over: High school diploma required; GED accepted **Costs Per Year:** Application fee: $45. State resident tuition: $9888 full-time, $380 per credit part-time. Nonresident tuition: $19,776 full-time, $760 per credit part-time. Mandatory fees: $674 full-time, $113 per term part-time. College room and board: $7210. College room only: $4910. **Scholarships:** Available **Calendar System:** Semester, Summer Session Available **Enrollment:** FT 1,641, PT 155 **Faculty:** FT 76, PT 62 **Student-Faculty Ratio:** 18:1 **Exams:** SAT I or ACT **% Receiving Financial Aid:** 77 **% Residing in College-Owned, -Operated, or -Affiliated Housing:** 35 **Library Holdings:** 75,000 **Regional Accreditation:** Middle State Association of Colleges and Schools **Credit Hours For Degree:** 120 credits, Bachelors **ROTC:** Army, Air Force **Intercollegiate Athletics:** Baseball M; Basketball M & W; Cross-Country Running M & W; Golf M & W; Soccer M & W; Softball W; Tennis M; Volleyball W

UNIVERSITY OF PITTSBURGH AT JOHNSTOWN
450 Schoolhouse Rd.
Johnstown, PA 15904-2990
Tel: (814)269-7000
Free: 800-765-4875
Admissions: (814)269-7050
Fax: (814)269-7044
E-mail: gyure@pitt.edu
Web Site: http://www.upj.pitt.edu/
President/CEO: Dr. Albert L. Etheridge
Registrar: Marilyn Alberter
Admissions: James F. Gyure
Financial Aid: Julie Salem
Type: Four-Year College **Sex:** Coed **Affiliation:** University of Pittsburgh System **Scores:** 98% SAT V 400+; 100% SAT M 400+; 73% ACT 18-23;

18% ACT 24-29 **% Accepted:** 85 **Admission Plans:** Early Admission; Deferred Admission **Application Deadline:** Rolling **Application Fee:** $35.00 **H.S. Requirements:** High school diploma required; GED accepted **Costs Per Year:** Application fee: $35. State resident tuition: $9888 full-time, $380 per credit part-time. Nonresident tuition: $19,776 full-time, $760 per credit part-time. Mandatory fees: $612 full-time, $77 per term part-time. Full-time tuition and fees vary according to program and student level. Part-time tuition and fees vary according to program and student level. College room and board: $6100. College room only: $3700. Room and board charges vary according to board plan and housing facility. **Scholarships:** Available **Calendar System:** Semester, Summer Session Available **Enrollment:** FT 2,915, PT 258 **Exams:** SAT I or ACT **% Receiving Financial Aid:** 69 **% Residing in College-Owned, -Operated, or -Affiliated Housing:** 76 **Library Holdings:** 145,507 **Regional Accreditation:** Middle State Association of Colleges and Schools **Credit Hours For Degree:** 65 credits, Associates; 120 credits, Bachelors **Professional Accreditation:** ABET, CARC **Intercollegiate Athletics:** Baseball M; Basketball M & W; Cheerleading W; Cross-Country Running W; Soccer M & W; Track and Field W; Volleyball W; Wrestling M

UNIVERSITY OF PITTSBURGH AT TITUSVILLE
PO Box 287
Titusville, PA 16354
Tel: (814)827-4400; 888-878-0462
Admissions: (814)827-4409
Fax: (814)827-4448
E-mail: uptadm@pitt.edu
Web Site: http://www.upt.pitt.edu/
President/CEO: Dr. Michael A. Worman
Registrar: Jean Spence
Admissions: John R. Mumford
Financial Aid: Melissa Burns
Type: Two-Year College **Sex:** Coed **Affiliation:** University of Pittsburgh System **Scores:** 81% SAT V 400+; 81% SAT M 400+; 23% ACT 18-23; 8% ACT 24-29 **% Accepted:** 86 **Admission Plans:** Deferred Admission **Application Deadline:** Rolling **Application Fee:** $35.00 **H.S. Requirements:** High school diploma required; GED accepted **Costs Per Year:** Application fee; $35. State resident tuition: $8710 full-time, $335 per credit part-time. Nonresident tuition: $17,610 full-time, $677 per credit part-time. Mandatory fees: $780 full-time, $93 per term part-time. Part-time tuition and fees vary according to student level. College room and board: $7234. Room and board charges vary according to board plan. **Scholarships:** Available **Calendar System:** Semester, Summer Session Available **Enrollment:** FT 413, PT 134 **Faculty:** FT 21, PT 40 **Student-Faculty Ratio:** 12:1 **Exams:** SAT I or ACT, SAT I **% Residing in College-Owned, -Operated, or -Affiliated Housing:** 48 **Library Holdings:** 49,256 **Regional Accreditation:** Middle State Association of Colleges and Schools **Credit Hours For Degree:** 60 credits, Associates **Professional Accreditation:** APTA **Intercollegiate Athletics:** Basketball M & W

UNIVERSITY OF THE SCIENCES IN PHILADELPHIA
600 South 43rd St.
Philadelphia, PA 19104-4495
Tel: (215)596-8800
Admissions: (215)596-8810
Fax: (215)895-1100
E-mail: admit@pcps.edu
Web Site: http://www.usip.edu/
President/CEO: Dr. Philip P. Gerbino
Registrar: Alan Sims
Admissions: Louis Hegyes
Financial Aid: Nicholas A. Flocco
Type: University **Sex:** Coed **Scores:** 100% SAT V 400+; 100% SAT M 400+; 33% ACT 18-23; 60% ACT 24-29 **% Accepted:** 65 **Admission Plans:** Deferred Admission **Application Deadline:** Rolling **Application Fee:** $45.00 **H.S. Requirements:** High school diploma required; GED accepted **Costs Per Year:** Application fee: $45. Comprehensive fee: $33,362 includes full-time tuition ($22,798), mandatory fees ($1184), and college room and board ($9380). College room only: $5730. Full-time tuition and fees vary according to degree level and program. Room and board charges vary according to board plan. Part-time tuition: $950 per credit. Part-time mandatory fees: $37 per credit. Part-time tuition and fees vary according to course load and degree level. **Scholarships:** Available **Calendar System:** Semester, Summer Session Available **Enrollment:** FT 1,940, PT 39, Grad 340 **Faculty:** FT 151, PT 98 **Student-Faculty Ratio:** 14:1 **Exams:** SAT I or ACT, SAT I **% Residing in College-Owned, -Operated, or -Affiliated Housing:** 29 **Library Holdings:** 87,125 **Regional Accreditation:** Middle State Association of Colleges and Schools **Credit Hours For Degree:** 120 credits, Bachelors **ROTC:** Army, Air Force **Professional Accreditation:** ACPhE, AOTA, APTA **Intercollegiate Athletics:** Baseball M; Basketball M & W; Cross-Country Running M & W; Golf M & W; Riflery M & W; Softball W; Tennis M & W; Volleyball W

THE UNIVERSITY OF SCRANTON
800 Linden St.
Scranton, PA 18510
Tel: (570)941-7400; 888-SCRANTON
Admissions: (570)941-7540
Fax: (570)941-5928
E-mail: admissions@uofs.edu
Web Site: http://www.scranton.edu/
President/CEO: Rev. Scott R. Pilarz, SJ,PhD
Registrar: Helen Stager
Admissions: Joseph Roback
Financial Aid: William R. Burke
Type: Comprehensive **Sex:** Coed **Affiliation:** Roman Catholic (Jesuit) **Scores:** 100% SAT V 400+; 99.7% SAT M 400+ **% Accepted:** 75 **Admission Plans:** Early Admission; Early Action; Deferred Admission **Application Deadline:** March 01 **Application Fee:** $40.00 **H.S. Requirements:** High school diploma required; GED accepted **Costs Per Year:** Application fee: $40. Comprehensive fee: $33,934 includes full-time tuition ($23,750), mandatory fees ($280), and college room and board ($9904). College room only: $5786. Room and board charges vary according to board plan and housing facility. Part-time tuition: $660 per credit. Part-time mandatory fees: $25 per term. **Scholarships:** Available **Calendar System:** 4-1-4, Summer Session Available **Enrollment:** FT 3,858, PT 226, Grad 1,076 **Faculty:** FT 251, PT 173 **Student-Faculty Ratio:** 12:1 **Exams:** SAT I or ACT **% Receiving Financial Aid:** 66 **% Residing in College-Owned, -Operated, or -Affiliated Housing:** 52 **Library Holdings:** 465,871 **Regional Accreditation:** Middle State Association of Colleges and Schools **Credit Hours For Degree:** 60 credit hours, Associates; 130 credit hours, Bachelors **ROTC:** Army, Air Force **Professional Accreditation:** AACSB, ABET, ACEHSA, AACN, AANA, ACA, AOTA, APTA, CORE, NCATE **Intercollegiate Athletics:** Baseball M; Basketball M & W; Bowling M & W; Crew M & W; Cross-Country Running M & W; Equestrian Sports M & W; Field Hockey W; Golf M; Ice Hockey M; Lacrosse M & W; Rugby M & W; Skiing (Downhill) M & W; Soccer M & W; Softball W; Swimming and Diving M & W; Tennis M & W; Track and Field M & W; Volleyball M & W; Wrestling M

URSINUS COLLEGE
Box 1000, Main St.
Collegeville, PA 19426-1000
Tel: (610)409-3000
Admissions: (610)409-3200
Fax: (610)489-0627
E-mail: admissions@ursinus.edu
Web Site: http://www.ursinus.edu/
President/CEO: Dr. John Strassburger
Registrar: Barbara A. Boris
Admissions: Richard G. DiFeliciantonio
Financial Aid: Suzanne Sparrow
Type: Four-Year College **Sex:** Coed **Scores:** 100% SAT V 400+; 100% SAT M 400+; 39% ACT 18-23; 44% ACT 24-29 **% Accepted:** 75 **Admission Plans:** Early Admission; Early Decision Plan; Deferred Admission **Application Deadline:** February 15 **Application Fee:** $50.00 **H.S. Requirements:** High school diploma required; GED not accepted **Costs Per Year:** Application fee: $50. Comprehensive fee: $38,950 includes full-time tuition ($31,450), mandatory fees ($150), and college room and board ($7350). Part-time tuition: $1048 per credit. **Scholarships:** Available **Calendar System:** Semester, Summer Session Not available **Enrollment:** FT 1,552, PT 19 **Faculty:** FT 115, PT 50 **Student-Faculty Ratio:** 12:1 **Exams:** SAT I or ACT, SAT II **% Receiving Financial Aid:** 83 **% Residing in College-Owned, -Operated, or -Affiliated Housing:** 91 **Library Holdings:** 200,000 **Regional Accreditation:** Middle State Association of Colleges and Schools **Credit Hours For Degree:** 128 semester hours, Bachelors **Intercollegiate Athletics:** Baseball M; Basketball M & W; Cross-Country Running M & W; Field Hockey W; Football M; Golf M & W; Gymnastics W; Lacrosse M & W;

Rugby M & W; Soccer M & W; Softball W; Swimming and Diving M & W; Tennis M & W; Track and Field M & W; Volleyball W; Wrestling M

VALLEY FORGE CHRISTIAN COLLEGE
1401 Charlestown Rd.
Phoenixville, PA 19460
Tel: (610)935-0450
Free: 800-432-8322
E-mail: admissions@vfcc.edu
Web Site: http://www.vfcc.edu/
President/CEO: Dr. Don Meyer
Registrar: Rev. James Barco
Admissions: Rev. William Chenco
Financial Aid: Evie Meyer
Type: Four-Year College **Sex:** Coed **Affiliation:** Assemblies of God **% Accepted:** 75 **Admission Plans:** Open Admission; Early Admission; Deferred Admission **Application Deadline:** August 01 **Application Fee:** $25.00 **H.S. Requirements:** High school diploma required; GED accepted **Costs Per Year:** Application fee: $25. Comprehensive fee: $17,550 includes full-time tuition ($10,750), mandatory fees ($950), and college room and board ($5850). College room only: $2650. Part-time tuition: $414 per credit. **Scholarships:** Available **Calendar System:** Semester, Summer Session Available **Enrollment:** FT 847, PT 87 **Faculty:** FT 33, PT 35 **Student-Faculty Ratio:** 20:1 **Exams:** SAT I or ACT **% Receiving Financial Aid:** 78 **% Residing in College-Owned, -Operated, or -Affiliated Housing:** 91 **Library Holdings:** 61,887 **Regional Accreditation:** Middle State Association of Colleges and Schools **Credit Hours For Degree:** 60 credit hours, Associates; 126 credit hours, Bachelors **Intercollegiate Athletics:** Baseball M; Basketball M & W; Cross-Country Running M; Soccer M; Volleyball W

VALLEY FORGE MILITARY COLLEGE
1001 Eagle Rd.
Wayne, PA 19087-3695
Tel: (610)989-1200
Free: 800-234-8362
Admissions: (610)989-1303
Fax: (610)688-1545
Web Site: http://www.vfmac.edu/
President/CEO: Rear Adm. Peter A. C. Long
Registrar: Cmdr. Tim Farrell
Admissions: Maj. Greg Potts
Financial Aid: Capt. David Smedley
Type: Two-Year College **Sex:** Coed **Scores:** 82% SAT V 400+; 83% SAT M 400+; 23% ACT 18-23; 41% ACT 24-29 **% Accepted:** 89 **Admission Plans:** Early Admission; Deferred Admission **Application Deadline:** August 02 **Application Fee:** $25.00 **H.S. Requirements:** High school diploma required; GED accepted **Costs Per Year:** Application fee: $25. Comprehensive fee: $30,977 includes full-time tuition ($19,693) and college room and board ($11,284). **Scholarships:** Available **Calendar System:** 4-1-4, Summer Session Not available **Faculty:** FT 16, PT 10 **Student-Faculty Ratio:** 10:1 **Exams:** SAT I or ACT **% Residing in College-Owned, -Operated, or -Affiliated Housing:** 100 **Library Holdings:** 75,830 **Regional Accreditation:** Middle State Association of Colleges and Schools **Credit Hours For Degree:** 60 credits, Associates **ROTC:** Army, Air Force **Intercollegiate Athletics:** Basketball M; Cross-Country Running M; Equestrian Sports M; Football M; Golf M; Lacrosse M; Riflery M; Soccer M; Tennis M; Wrestling M

VILLANOVA UNIVERSITY
800 Lancaster Ave.
Villanova, PA 19085-1699
Tel: (610)519-4500
Admissions: (610)519-4000
Fax: (610)519-6450
E-mail: gotovu@villanova.edu
Web Site: http://www.villanova.edu/
President/CEO: Rev. Edmund J. Dobbin, OSA
Registrar: Catherine Connor
Admissions: Michael Gaynor
Financial Aid: Bonnie Lee Behm
Type: Comprehensive **Sex:** Coed **Affiliation:** Roman Catholic **Scores:** 99.5% SAT V 400+; 99.94% SAT M 400+; 14.07% ACT 18-23; 61.48% ACT 24-29 **% Accepted:** 51 **Admission Plans:** Early Admission; Early Action; Deferred Admission **Application Deadline:** January 07 **Application Fee:** $70.00 **H.S. Requirements:** High school diploma required; GED accepted **Costs Per Year:** Application fee: $70. Comprehensive fee: $38,797 includes full-time tuition ($28,760), mandatory fees ($675), and college room and board ($9362). College room only: $4962. Full-time tuition and fees vary according to program and student level. Room and board charges vary according to board plan and housing facility. Part-time tuition: $624 per credit hour. Part-time mandatory fees: $280 per term. Part-time tuition and fees vary according to class time, course level, and program. **Scholarships:** Available **Calendar System:** Semester, Summer Session Available **Enrollment:** FT 6,541, PT 667, Grad 2,473 **Faculty:** FT 545, PT 353 **Student-Faculty Ratio:** 13:1 **Exams:** SAT I or ACT **% Receiving Financial Aid:** 44 **% Residing in College-Owned, -Operated, or -Affiliated Housing:** 65 **Library Holdings:** 900,248 **Regional Accreditation:** Middle State Association of Colleges and Schools **Credit Hours For Degree:** 60 credit hours, Associates; 122 credit hours, Bachelors **ROTC:** Army, Navy, Air Force **Professional Accreditation:** AACSB, ABET, AACN, AANA, ABA, AALS, NLN **Intercollegiate Athletics:** Baseball M; Basketball M & W; Cheerleading M & W; Crew M & W; Cross-Country Running M & W; Field Hockey W; Football M; Golf M; Ice Hockey M; Lacrosse M & W; Rugby M; Sailing M & W; Skiing (Downhill) M & W; Soccer M & W; Softball W; Swimming and Diving M & W; Tennis M & W; Track and Field M & W; Volleyball M & W; Water Polo M & W; Weight Lifting M & W

WASHINGTON & JEFFERSON COLLEGE
60 South Lincoln St.
Washington, PA 15301
Tel: (724)222-4400; 888-WANDJAY
Admissions: (724)223-6025
Fax: (724)223-5271
E-mail: anewell@washjeff.edu
Web Site: http://www.washjeff.edu/
President/CEO: Dr. G. Andrew Rembert
Registrar: Brent Koerber
Admissions: Alton E. Newell
Financial Aid: Michelle Vettorel
Type: Four-Year College **Sex:** Coed **Scores:** 99.7% SAT V 400+; 99.39% SAT M 400+; 33.33% ACT 18-23; 62.17% ACT 24-29 **% Accepted:** 39 **Admission Plans:** Early Admission; Early Action; Early Decision Plan; Deferred Admission **Application Deadline:** March 01 **Application Fee:** $25.00 **H.S. Requirements:** High school diploma required; GED accepted **Costs Per Year:** Application fee: $25. Comprehensive fee: $33,490 includes full-time tuition ($25,930), mandatory fees ($400), and college room and board ($7160). College room only: $4150. Room and board charges vary according to board plan and housing facility. Part-time tuition: $810 per credit hour. **Scholarships:** Available **Calendar System:** 4-1-4, Summer Session Available **Enrollment:** FT 1,400, PT 18 **Faculty:** FT 97, PT 33 **Student-Faculty Ratio:** 12:1 **Exams:** SAT I or ACT **% Receiving Financial Aid:** 73 **% Residing in College-Owned, -Operated, or -Affiliated Housing:** 80 **Library Holdings:** 157,665 **Regional Accreditation:** Middle State Association of Colleges and Schools **Credit Hours For Degree:** 34 courses, Bachelors **ROTC:** Army, Air Force **Intercollegiate Athletics:** Baseball M; Basketball M & W; Cross-Country Running M & W; Field Hockey W; Football M; Golf M & W; Ice Hockey M; Lacrosse M; Soccer M & W; Softball W; Swimming and Diving M & W; Tennis M & W; Track and Field M & W; Volleyball W; Water Polo M & W; Wrestling M

WAYNESBURG COLLEGE
51 West College St.
Waynesburg, PA 15370-1222
Tel: (724)627-8191
Free: 800-225-7393
Admissions: (724)852-3333
Fax: (724)627-8124
Web Site: http://www.waynesburg.edu/
President/CEO: Timothy R. Thyreen
Registrar: Dr. Ronald Coltrane
Admissions: Robin L. King
Financial Aid: Matthew Stokan
Type: Comprehensive **Sex:** Coed **Affiliation:** Presbyterian Church (U.S.A.) **% Accepted:** 74 **Admission Plans:** Early Admission **Application Deadline:** Rolling **Application Fee:** $20.00 **H.S. Requirements:** High school diploma required; GED accepted **Costs Per Year:** Application fee: $20. Comprehensive fee: $20,890 includes full-time tuition ($14,810) and college room and board ($6080). College room only: $3100. Full-time tuition varies according to class time. Room and board charges vary according to board plan. Part-time tuition: $620 per credit. Part-time mandatory fees: $15 per credit. Part-time tuition and fees vary according to class time, course load, and location.

Scholarships: Available **Calendar System:** Semester, Summer Session Not available **Enrollment:** FT 1,332, PT 284, Grad 543 **Faculty:** FT 62, PT 73 **Student-Faculty Ratio:** 13:1 **Exams:** SAT I or ACT **% Receiving Financial Aid:** 85 **% Residing in College-Owned, -Operated, or -Affiliated Housing:** 59 **Library Holdings:** 100,000 **Regional Accreditation:** Middle State Association of Colleges and Schools **Credit Hours For Degree:** 60 credit hours, Associates; 124 credit hours, Bachelors **ROTC:** Army **Professional Accreditation:** AACN, JRCEPAT, NLN **Intercollegiate Athletics:** Baseball M; Basketball M & W; Cross-Country Running M & W; Football M; Golf M & W; Soccer M & W; Softball W; Tennis M & W; Track and Field M & W; Volleyball W; Wrestling M

WEST CHESTER UNIVERSITY OF PENNSYLVANIA
University Ave. and High St.
West Chester, PA 19383
Tel: (610)436-1000
Admissions: (610)436-3414
E-mail: ugadmiss@wcupa.edu
Web Site: http://www.wcupa.edu/
President/CEO: Dr. Madeleine Wing Adler
Admissions: Marsha Haug
Financial Aid: Dana C. Parker
Type: Comprehensive **Sex:** Coed **Affiliation:** Pennsylvania State System of Higher Education **Scores:** 99% SAT V 400+; 98% SAT M 400+ **% Accepted:** 49 **Admission Plans:** Early Admission; Deferred Admission **Application Deadline:** Rolling **Application Fee:** $35.00 **H.S. Requirements:** High school diploma required; GED accepted **Costs Per Year:** Application fee: $35. State resident tuition: $4906 full-time, $204 per credit part-time. Nonresident tuition: $12,266 full-time, $511 per credit part-time. Mandatory fees: $1241 full-time, $47 per credit part-time. College room and board: $6208. College room only: $4140. **Scholarships:** Available **Calendar System:** Semester, Summer Session Available **Enrollment:** FT 9,788, PT 1,050, Grad 2,150 **Faculty:** FT 567, PT 230 **Student-Faculty Ratio:** 16:1 **Exams:** SAT I or ACT **% Residing in College-Owned, -Operated, or -Affiliated Housing:** 30 **Library Holdings:** 744,976 **Regional Accreditation:** Middle State Association of Colleges and Schools **Credit Hours For Degree:** 120 credits, Bachelors **ROTC:** Army, Air Force **Professional Accreditation:** AACN, ASLHA, CARC, CEPH, CSWE, JRCEPAT, NASM, NCATE, NLN **Intercollegiate Athletics:** Baseball M; Basketball M & W; Cheerleading W; Cross-Country Running M & W; Equestrian Sports M & W; Fencing M & W; Field Hockey W; Football M; Golf M; Gymnastics W; Ice Hockey M; Lacrosse W; Rugby M & W; Soccer M & W; Softball W; Swimming and Diving M & W; Tennis M & W; Track and Field M & W; Volleyball W; Water Polo M & W

WESTERN SCHOOL OF HEALTH AND BUSINESS CAREERS (MONROEVILLE)
1 Monroeville Center, Ste. 250, Route 22
3824 Northern Pike
Monroeville, PA 15146-2142
Tel: (412)373-6400
Fax: (412)373-2544
Web Site: http://www.westernschool.com/
President/CEO: Sherry Jones
Type: Two-Year College **Sex:** Coed **Calendar System:** Continuous **Professional Accreditation:** ACCSCT

WESTERN SCHOOL OF HEALTH AND BUSINESS CAREERS (PITTSBURGH)
421 Seventh Ave.
Pittsburgh, PA 15219-1907
Tel: (412)281-2600
Free: 800-333-6607
Admissions: (412)281-7083
Fax: (412)281-0319
Web Site: http://www.westernschool.com/
President/CEO: Ross Perilman
Admissions: Bruce E. Jones
Financial Aid: Eileen Randolph
Type: Two-Year College **Sex:** Coed **Scores:** 90% SAT V 400+; 76% SAT M 400+ **Admission Plans:** Early Admission; Deferred Admission **H.S. Requirements:** High school diploma required; GED accepted **Scholarships:** Available **Calendar System:** Continuous, Summer Session Not available **Faculty:** FT 21, PT 2 **Student-Faculty Ratio:** 20:1 **Exams:** SAT I or ACT, SAT II **Library Holdings:** 1,687 **Credit Hours For Degree:** 65 credits, Associates **Professional Accreditation:** ACCSCT, CARC, JRCEDMS, JRCERT

WESTMINSTER COLLEGE
319 South Market St.
New Wilmington, PA 16172-0001
Tel: (724)946-8761
Admissions: (724)946-7100
Fax: (724)946-7171
E-mail: swartzdl@westminster.edu
Web Site: http://www.westminster.edu/
President/CEO: R. Thomas Williamson
Registrar: June Garner
Admissions: Doug Swartz
Financial Aid: Robert A. Latta
Type: Comprehensive **Sex:** Coed **Affiliation:** Presbyterian Church (U.S.A.) **Scores:** 96% SAT V 400+; 99% SAT M 400+; 57% ACT 18-23; 32% ACT 24-29 **% Accepted:** 77 **Admission Plans:** Deferred Admission **Application Deadline:** May 01 **Application Fee:** $35.00 **H.S. Requirements:** High school diploma required; GED accepted **Costs Per Year:** Application fee: $35. Comprehensive fee: $31,395 includes full-time tuition ($23,220), mandatory fees ($1105), and college room and board ($7070). Part-time tuition: $730 per semester hour. **Scholarships:** Available **Calendar System:** Semester, Summer Session Available **Enrollment:** FT 1,410, PT 54, Grad 129 **Faculty:** FT 100, PT 49 **Student-Faculty Ratio:** 12:1 **Exams:** SAT I or ACT **% Receiving Financial Aid:** 78 **Library Holdings:** 283,070 **Regional Accreditation:** Middle State Association of Colleges and Schools **ROTC:** Army **Professional Accreditation:** NASM **Intercollegiate Athletics:** Baseball M; Basketball M & W; Cross-Country Running M & W; Equestrian Sports M & W; Football M; Golf M & W; Soccer M & W; Softball W; Swimming and Diving M & W; Tennis M & W; Track and Field M & W; Volleyball W

WESTMORELAND COUNTY COMMUNITY COLLEGE
400 Armbrust Rd.
Youngwood, PA 15697-1898
Tel: (724)925-4000
Admissions: (724)925-4123
Fax: (724)925-1150
E-mail: admission@wccc-pa.edu
Web Site: http://www.wccc-pa.edu/
President/CEO: Dr. Daniel C. Krezenski
Registrar: Janice T. Grabowski
Admissions: Janice T. Grabowski
Financial Aid: Gary A. Means
Type: Two-Year College **Sex:** Coed **% Accepted:** 100 **Admission Plans:** Open Admission; Early Admission **Application Deadline:** Rolling **Application Fee:** $10.00 **H.S. Requirements:** High school diploma required; GED accepted **Costs Per Year:** Application fee: $10. Area resident tuition: $68 per credit part-time. State resident tuition: $136 per credit part-time. Nonresident tuition: $204 per credit part-time. Mandatory fees: $7 per credit part-time. **Scholarships:** Available **Calendar System:** Semester, Summer Session Available **Enrollment:** FT 2,670, PT 3,463 **Faculty:** FT 76, PT 383 **Student-Faculty Ratio:** 17:1 **Library Holdings:** 34,522 **Regional Accreditation:** Middle State Association of Colleges and Schools **Credit Hours For Degree:** 60 credits, Associates **Professional Accreditation:** ACF, ADA **Intercollegiate Athletics:** Baseball M; Golf M & W; Softball W; Tennis M & W; Volleyball W

WIDENER UNIVERSITY
One University Place
Chester, PA 19013-5792
Tel: (610)499-4000; 888-WIDENER
Admissions: (610)499-4126
Fax: (610)499-4676
E-mail: admissions.office@widener.edu
Web Site: http://www.widener.edu/
President/CEO: Dr. James T. Harris, III
Registrar: Dr. Steven Foxman
Admissions: Dr. Lawrence Lesick
Financial Aid: Mary C. Reilly
Type: Comprehensive **Sex:** Coed **Scores:** 91% SAT V 400+; 91% SAT M 400+ **% Accepted:** 81 **Admission Plans:** Early Admission; Early Action; Deferred Admission **Application Deadline:** Rolling **Application Fee:** $35.00 **H.S. Requirements:** High school diploma required; GED not accepted

Costs Per Year: Application fee: $35. Comprehensive fee: $33,490 includes full-time tuition ($24,620), mandatory fees ($350), and college room and board ($8520). College room only: $3900. Full-time tuition and fees vary according to class time, course load, and program. Room and board charges vary according to board plan and housing facility. Part-time tuition: $821 per credit. Part-time mandatory fees: $65. **Scholarships:** Available **Calendar System:** Semester, Summer Session Available **Enrollment:** FT 2,375, PT 141, Grad 1,707 **Faculty:** FT 221, PT 177 **Student-Faculty Ratio:** 12:1 **Exams:** SAT I or ACT **% Receiving Financial Aid:** 81 **% Residing in College-Owned, -Operated, or -Affiliated Housing:** 61 **Library Holdings:** 238,349 **Regional Accreditation:** Middle State Association of Colleges and Schools **Credit Hours For Degree:** 119 credits, Bachelors **ROTC:** Army, Navy, Air Force **Professional Accreditation:** AACSB, ABET, ACEHSA, ABA, APTA, APA, AALS, CSWE, NLN **Intercollegiate Athletics:** Baseball M; Basketball M & W; Cheerleading W; Cross-Country Running M & W; Field Hockey W; Football M; Golf M; Lacrosse M & W; Soccer M & W; Softball W; Swimming and Diving M & W; Tennis M & W; Track and Field M & W; Volleyball W

WILKES UNIVERSITY
84 West South St.
Wilkes-Barre, PA 18766-0002
Tel: (570)408-5000
Free: 800-945-5378
Admissions: (570)408-4400
Fax: (570)408-7820
Web Site: http://www.wilkes.edu/
President/CEO: Dr. Joseph Gilmour
Registrar: Susan Hritzak
Admissions: Michael Frantz
Financial Aid: Rachael L. Lohman
Type: Comprehensive **Sex:** Coed **Scores:** 97.5% SAT V 400+; 96.8% SAT M 400+ **% Accepted:** 77 **Admission Plans:** Early Admission; Deferred Admission **Application Deadline:** Rolling **Application Fee:** $35.00 **H.S. Requirements:** High school diploma required; GED accepted **Costs Per Year:** Application fee: $35. Comprehensive fee: $30,886 includes full-time tuition ($20,592), mandatory fees ($1054), and college room and board ($9240). College room only: $5600. Room and board charges vary according to board plan and housing facility. Part-time tuition: $569 per credit. Part-time mandatory fees: $43 per credit. **Scholarships:** Available **Calendar System:** Semester, Summer Session Available **Enrollment:** FT 1,968, PT 220, Grad 2,019 **Faculty:** FT 131, PT 86 **Student-Faculty Ratio:** 15:1 **Exams:** SAT I or ACT **% Receiving Financial Aid:** 79 **% Residing in College-Owned, -Operated, or -Affiliated Housing:** 43 **Library Holdings:** 236,942 **Regional Accreditation:** Middle State Association of Colleges and Schools **Credit Hours For Degree:** 120 credits, Bachelors **ROTC:** Army, Air Force **Professional Accreditation:** ABET, AACN, ACPhE, ACBSP **Intercollegiate Athletics:** Baseball M; Basketball M & W; Field Hockey W; Football M; Golf M; Lacrosse W; Soccer M & W; Softball W; Tennis M & W; Volleyball W; Wrestling M

THE WILLIAMSON FREE SCHOOL OF MECHANICAL TRADES
106 South New Middletown Rd.
Media, PA 19063
Tel: (610)566-1776
Fax: (610)566-6502
E-mail: ebailey@williamson.edu
Web Site: http://www.williamson.edu/
President/CEO: Dr. Paul A. Reid
Registrar: Anne M. Hayes
Admissions: Edward D. Bailey
Type: Two-Year College **Sex:** Men **% Accepted:** 26 **Admission Plans:** Preferred Admission **Application Deadline:** March 15 **H.S. Requirements:** High school diploma required; GED accepted **Scholarships:** Available **Calendar System:** Semester, Summer Session Not available **Enrollment:** FT 251 **Faculty:** FT 29 **Student-Faculty Ratio:** 14:1 **Exams:** Other **% Residing in College-Owned, -Operated, or -Affiliated Housing:** 100 **Library Holdings:** 1,600 **Credit Hours For Degree:** 148 credit hours, Associates **Professional Accreditation:** ACCSCT **Intercollegiate Athletics:** Baseball M; Basketball M; Cross-Country Running M; Football M; Lacrosse M; Soccer M; Wrestling M

WILSON COLLEGE
1015 Philadelphia Ave.
Chambersburg, PA 17201-1285
Tel: (717)264-4141
Free: 800-421-8402
Admissions: (717)262-2025
Fax: (717)264-1578
E-mail: kberard@wilson.edu
Web Site: http://www.wilson.edu/
President/CEO: Dr. Lorna D. Edmundson
Registrar: Jean B. Hoover
Admissions: Kathleen H. Berard
Financial Aid: Christine Knouse
Type: Four-Year College **Sex:** Women **Affiliation:** Presbyterian Church (U.S.A.) **Scores:** 95% SAT V 400+; 92% SAT M 400+; 30% ACT 18-23; 30% ACT 24-29 **% Accepted:** 57 **Admission Plans:** Early Admission; Deferred Admission **Application Deadline:** Rolling **Application Fee:** $35.00 **H.S. Requirements:** High school diploma required; GED accepted **Costs Per Year:** Application fee: $35. Comprehensive fee: $27,660 includes full-time tuition ($19,570), mandatory fees ($480), and college room and board ($7610). College room only: $3920. Room and board charges vary according to board plan. Part-time tuition: $1960 per course. Part-time mandatory fees: $30 per course, $35 per term. Part-time tuition and fees vary according to course load. **Scholarships:** Available **Calendar System:** 4-1-4, Summer Session Available **Enrollment:** FT 348, PT 384 **Faculty:** FT 40, PT 35 **Student-Faculty Ratio:** 10:1 **Exams:** SAT I or ACT **% Receiving Financial Aid:** 73 **% Residing in College-Owned, -Operated, or -Affiliated Housing:** 32 **Library Holdings:** 172,205 **Regional Accreditation:** Middle State Association of Colleges and Schools **Credit Hours For Degree:** 18 credits, Associates; 36 credits, Bachelors **ROTC:** Army **Intercollegiate Athletics:** Basketball W; Equestrian Sports W; Field Hockey W; Gymnastics W; Soccer W; Softball W; Tennis W; Volleyball W

WINNER INSTITUTE OF ARTS & SCIENCES
One Winner Place
Transfer, PA 16154
Tel: (724)646-2433; 888-414-2433
Fax: (724)646-0218
Web Site: http://www.winner-institute.edu/
President/CEO: Ed Petrunak
Type: Two-Year College **Sex:** Coed **Calendar System:** Quarter **Professional Accreditation:** ACF

WYOTECH
500 Innovation Dr.
Blairsville, PA 15717
Tel: (724)459-9500
Free: 800-822-8253
Admissions: (724)459-3286
Fax: (724)459-6499
E-mail: whauser@wyotech.edu
Web Site: http://www.wyotech.com/
President/CEO: Guy Warpmess
Admissions: Wendy Hauser
Type: Two-Year College **Sex:** Coed **Application Fee:** $100.00 **Costs Per Year:** Application fee: $100. Tuition: $23,300 full-time. **Calendar System:** Miscellaneous **Professional Accreditation:** ACCSCT

YESHIVA BETH MOSHE
930 Hickory St., PO Box 1141
Scranton, PA 18505-2124
Tel: (717)346-1747
President/CEO: Richard Fink
Registrar: Rabbi Zwe Weiss
Admissions: Rabbi I. Bressler
Financial Aid: Rabbi Zwe Weiss
Type: Comprehensive **Sex:** Men **Affiliation:** Jewish **H.S. Requirements:** High school diploma required; GED not accepted **Calendar System:** Semester **Professional Accreditation:** AARTS

YORK COLLEGE OF PENNSYLVANIA
York, PA 17405-7199
Tel: (717)846-7788
Free: 800-455-8018
Admissions: (717)849-1600
Web Site: http://www.ycp.edu/
President/CEO: Dr. George W. Waldner

Registrar: Rebecca Link
Admissions: Nancy L. Spataro
Financial Aid: Calvin Williams
Type: Comprehensive **Sex:** Coed **Scores:** 100% SAT V 400+; 100% SAT M 400+ **% Accepted:** 75 **Admission Plans:** Early Admission; Deferred Admission **Application Deadline:** August 01 **Application Fee:** $30.00 **H.S. Requirements:** High school diploma required; GED accepted **Costs Per Year:** Application fee: $30. Comprehensive fee: $16,550 includes full-time tuition ($9350), mandatory fees ($700), and college room and board ($6500). College room only: $3625. Full-time tuition and fees vary according to course load and program. Room and board charges vary according to housing facility. Part-time tuition: $285 per credit hour. Part-time tuition varies according to course load and program. **Scholarships:** Available **Calendar System:** Semester, Summer Session Available **Enrollment:** FT 4,469, PT 701, Grad 146 **Faculty:** FT 134, PT 295 **Student-Faculty Ratio:** 21:1 **Exams:** SAT I or ACT **% Receiving Financial Aid:** 50 **% Residing in College-Owned, -Operated, or -Affiliated Housing:** 45 **Library Holdings:** 300,000 **Regional Accreditation:** Middle State Association of Colleges and Schools **Credit Hours For Degree:** 62 credit hours, Associates; 124 credit hours, Bachelors **ROTC:** Army **Professional Accreditation:** ABET, ACBSP, CARC, NLN, NRPA **Intercollegiate Athletics:** Baseball M; Basketball M & W; Cheerleading W; Cross-Country Running M & W; Field Hockey W; Golf M; Ice Hockey M; Lacrosse M & W; Soccer M & W; Softball W; Swimming and Diving M & W; Tennis M & W; Track and Field M & W; Volleyball M & W; Wrestling M

YORK TECHNICAL INSTITUTE
1405 Williams Rd.
York, PA 17402-9017
Tel: (717)757-1100
Free: 800-227-9675
Fax: (717)757-4964
Web Site: http://www.yti.edu/
President/CEO: Harold Maley
Admissions: Diane Merino
Type: Two-Year College **Sex:** Coed **Admission Plans:** Open Admission **H.S. Requirements:** High school diploma required; GED accepted **Scholarships:** Available **Calendar System:** Continuous **Enrollment:** FT 1,296 **Faculty:** FT 87 **Student-Faculty Ratio:** 25:1 **Professional Accreditation:** ACCSCT

YORKTOWNE BUSINESS INSTITUTE
West Seventh Ave.
York, PA 17404
Tel: (717)846-5000
Free: 800-840-1004
Fax: (717)848-4584
Web Site: http://www.ybi.edu/
President/CEO: Dr. James P. Murphy
Admissions: Bonnie Gillespie
Financial Aid: Deborah Bostic
Type: Two-Year College **Sex:** Coed **H.S. Requirements:** High school diploma required; GED accepted **Scholarships:** Available **Calendar System:** Semester **Faculty:** FT 18, PT 20 **Student-Faculty Ratio:** 11:1 **Credit Hours For Degree:** 75 credit hours, Associates **Professional Accreditation:** ACICS

AMERICAN UNIVERSITY OF PUERTO RICO
PO Box 2037
Bayamon, PR 00960-2037
Tel: (787)620-2040
Admissions: (787)740-6410
Fax: (787)785-7377
Web Site: http://www.aupr.edu/
President/CEO: Juan B. Nazario-Negron
Registrar: Prof. María Rodr&iguez-Paz
Admissions: Margarita Cruz
Financial Aid: Johanna Arroyo
Type: Four-Year College **Sex:** Coed **Admission Plans:** Deferred Admission **Application Fee:** $25.00 **H.S. Requirements:** High school diploma required; GED accepted **Scholarships:** Available **Calendar System:** Semester, Summer Session Available **Faculty:** FT 101, PT 120 **Exams:** Other, SAT I **% Receiving Financial Aid:** 99 **Library Holdings:** 100,000 **Regional Accreditation:** Middle State Association of Colleges and Schools **Credit Hours For Degree:** 60 credits, Associates; 133 credits, Bachelors **ROTC:** Army **Intercollegiate Athletics:** Basketball M; Cross-Country Running M & W; Swimming and Diving M & W; Tennis M & W; Track and Field M & W; Volleyball M & W

ATLANTIC COLLEGE
PO Box 3918
Guaynabo, PR 00970
Tel: (787)720-1022
Fax: (787)720-1092
Web Site: http://www.atlanticcollege-pr.com/
President/CEO: Dr. Teresa De Dios-Unanue
Admissions: Zaida Perez
Financial Aid: Janice Rivera
Type: Comprehensive **Admission Plans:** Open Admission **Application Fee:** $30.00 **H.S. Requirements:** High school diploma required; GED accepted **Scholarships:** Available **Calendar System:** Semester, Summer Session Not available **Faculty:** FT 8, PT 14 **Student-Faculty Ratio:** 19:1 **% Receiving Financial Aid:** 86 **Library Holdings:** 8,663 **Credit Hours For Degree:** 78 credits, Associates; 138 credits, Bachelors **Professional Accreditation:** ACICS

BAYAMON CENTRAL UNIVERSITY
PO Box 1725
Bayamon, PR 00960-1725
Tel: (787)786-3030
Web Site: http://www.ucb.edu.pr/
President/CEO: P. Benito Reyes Rivera, OP
Registrar: Victor Colon Rodriguez
Admissions: Christine M. Hernandez
Financial Aid: Vivian Cintron
Type: Comprehensive **Sex:** Coed **Affiliation:** Roman Catholic **Application Fee:** $15.00 **H.S. Requirements:** High school diploma required; GED accepted **Costs Per Year:** Application fee: $15. Tuition: $4080 full-time, $130 per credit part-time. Mandatory fees: $360 full-time, $180. Full-time tuition and fees vary according to course load, degree level, and program. Part-time tuition and fees vary according to course load, degree level, and program. **Scholarships:** Available **Calendar System:** Semester, Summer Session Available **Enrollment:** FT 2,205, PT 569, Grad 537 **Faculty:** FT 58, PT 160 **Student-Faculty Ratio:** 23:1 **Exams:** Other **Library Holdings:** 51,011 **Regional Accreditation:** Middle State Association of Colleges and Schools **Credit Hours For Degree:** 72 credits, Associates; 131 credits, Bachelors **ROTC:** Army, Air Force **Intercollegiate Athletics:** Basketball M & W; Cross-Country Running M & W; Softball M & W; Swimming and Diving M & W; Track and Field M & W; Volleyball M & W; Water Polo M & W

CARIBBEAN UNIVERSITY
Box 493
Bayamon, PR 00960-0493
Tel: (787)780-0070
Fax: (787)785-0101
Web Site: http://www.caribbean.edu/
President/CEO: Dr. Angel E. Juan-Ortega
Registrar: Miriam Gonzalez
Admissions: Hector Gracia
Financial Aid: Sintia Ocasio
Type: Comprehensive **Sex:** Coed **Admission Plans:** Deferred Admission **Application Fee:** $25.00 **H.S. Requirements:** High school diploma required; GED accepted **Scholarships:** Available **Calendar System:** Trimester, Summer Session Available **Faculty:** FT 44, PT 114 **Exams:** SAT I, SAT II **Library Holdings:** 17,632 **Regional Accreditation:** Middle State Association of Colleges and Schools **Credit Hours For Degree:** 79 credit hours, Associates; 140 credit hours, Bachelors **ROTC:** Army **Intercollegiate Athletics:** Basketball M; Cross-Country Running M & W; Tennis M & W; Track and Field M & W; Volleyball M & W; Weight Lifting M

CARLOS ALBIZU UNIVERSITY
151 Tanca St.
San Juan, PR 00901
Tel: (787)725-6500
Fax: (787)721-7187
Web Site: http://www.albizu.edu/
President/CEO: Dr. Salvador Santiago-Negron
Registrar: Victor Bonilla
Financial Aid: Gloria Mirabal
Type: Two-Year Upper Division **Sex:** Coed **Application Fee:** $25.00 **Calendar System:** Semester **Regional Accreditation:** Middle State Association of Colleges and Schools **Professional Accreditation:** APA

CENTRO DE ESTUDIOS MULTIDISCIPLINARIOS
Calle 13 No. 1206
Ext. San Agustin
San Juan, PR 00926
Tel: (787)765-4210
Web Site: http://www.cempr.edu/ **Type:** Two-Year College **Sex:** Coed **Application Fee:** $30.00 **Professional Accreditation:** ACCSCT

COLEGIO BIBLICO PENTECOSTAL
PO Box 901
St. Just, PR 00978-0901
Tel: (787)761-0640
Web Site: http://www.cbp.edu/
President/CEO: Dr. Ildefonso Caraballo
Registrar: Gladys Santiago

Admissions: Carolyn Figueroa
Type: Four-Year College **Sex:** Coed **Affiliation:** Pentecostal **Application Fee:** $25.00 **Calendar System:** Semester **Professional Accreditation:** AABC

COLEGIO PENTECOSTAL MIZPA
Bo Caimito Rd. 199
Apartado 20966
Rio Piedras, PR 00928-0966
Tel: (787)720-4476
Fax: (787)720-2012
President/CEO: Luis R. Cruz
Registrar: Sara Martínez
Type: Four-Year College **Affiliation:** Pentecostal Church **Admission Plans:** Open Admission **Application Fee:** $35.00 **Costs Per Year:** Application fee: $35. Comprehensive fee: $5020 includes full-time tuition ($1200), mandatory fees ($220), and college room and board ($3600). College room only: $2000. Full-time tuition and fees vary according to course level. Room and board charges vary according to board plan and housing facility. **Calendar System:** Semester **Professional Accreditation:** AABC

COLEGIO UNIVERSITARIO DE SAN JUAN
180 Jose Oliver Ave.,
Tres Monjitas Industrial Park
San Juan, PR 00918
Tel: (787)250-7111
Fax: (787)250-7395
Web Site: http://www.cunisanjuan.edu/ **Type:** Two-Year College **Sex:** Coed

COLUMBIA COLLEGE (CAGUAS)
PO Box 8517
Caguas, PR 00726
Tel: (787)743-4041
Fax: (787)744-7931
Web Site: http://www.columbiaco.edu/
President/CEO: Alex A. DeJorge
Registrar: Gladys Serrano
Admissions: Ana Rosa Burgos
Financial Aid: Virginia Guang
Type: Comprehensive **Sex:** Coed **% Accepted:** 56 **Application Deadline:** Rolling **Application Fee:** $50.00 **H.S. Requirements:** High school diploma required; GED accepted **Costs Per Year:** Application fee: $50. Tuition: $4140 full-time, $140 per unit part-time. Mandatory fees: $300 full-time, $200 per term part-time. **Calendar System:** Semester, Summer Session Not available **Enrollment:** FT 506, PT 304, Grad 49 **Faculty:** FT 15, PT 50 **Student-Faculty Ratio:** 17:1 **Library Holdings:** 10,200 **Regional Accreditation:** Middle State Association of Colleges and Schools **Credit Hours For Degree:** 71 credits, Associates; 120 credits, Bachelors **Professional Accreditation:** ACICS

COLUMBIA COLLEGE (YAUCO)
Box 3062
Yauco, PR 00698
Tel: (787)856-0945
Fax: (787)267-2335
Web Site: http://www.columbiaco.edu/
President/CEO: Alex A. De Jorge
Type: Two-Year College **Sex:** Coed **Admission Plans:** Open Admission **Application Fee:** $50.00 **Calendar System:** Semester **Professional Accreditation:** ACICS

CONSERVATORY OF MUSIC OF PUERTO RICO
350 Rafael Lamar St at FDR Ave
San Juan, PR 00918
Tel: (787)751-0160
Web Site: http://www.cmpr.edu/
President/CEO: Prof. Maria del Carmen Gil
Registrar: Eutimia Santiago
Admissions: Pilar Ruibal
Financial Aid: Jorge Medina
Type: Four-Year College **Sex:** Coed **Admission Plans:** Early Admission **Application Fee:** $25.00 **H.S. Requirements:** High school diploma required; GED accepted **Scholarships:** Available **Calendar System:** Semester, Summer Session Available **Enrollment:** FT 203, PT 63 **Faculty:** FT 36, PT 31 **Student-Faculty Ratio:** 4:1 **Exams:** SAT I, SAT II **% Receiving Financial Aid:** 53 **Library Holdings:** 24,865 **Regional Accreditation:** Middle State Association of Colleges and Schools **Credit Hours For Degree:** 142 credits, Bachelors **ROTC:** Army

ELECTRONIC DATA PROCESSING COLLEGE OF PUERTO RICO
560 Ave. Ponce de Leon
Hato Rey, PR 00919-2303
Tel: (787)765-3560
Web Site: http://www.edpcollege.edu/
President/CEO: Gladys Nieves DeBerrios
Registrar: Nydia Gutiérrez
Financial Aid: Gloria Mirabal
Type: Comprehensive **Sex:** Coed **Admission Plans:** Deferred Admission **Application Fee:** $15.00 **H.S. Requirements:** High school diploma required; GED accepted **Scholarships:** Available **Calendar System:** Semester **Faculty:** FT 18, PT 28 **Exams:** SAT I, SAT II **Library Holdings:** 10,005 **Regional Accreditation:** Middle State Association of Colleges and Schools **Credit Hours For Degree:** 74 credits, Associates; 132 credits, Bachelors **ROTC:** Army, Air Force **Professional Accreditation:** ACICS **Intercollegiate Athletics:** Basketball M & W; Cross-Country Running M & W; Gymnastics M & W; Table Tennis M & W; Tennis M & W; Track and Field M & W; Volleyball M & W; Weight Lifting M

ELECTRONIC DATA PROCESSING COLLEGE OF PUERTO RICO-SAN SEBASTIAN
Ave. Betances No. 49
San Sebastian, PR 00685
Tel: (787)896-2137
Fax: (787)896-0066
Web Site: http://www.edpcollege.edu/ **Type:** Four-Year College **Sex:** Coed **Application Fee:** $15.00 **Calendar System:** Semester **Professional Accreditation:** ACICS

ESCUELA DE ARTES PLASTICAS DE PUERTO RICO
PO Box 9021112
San Juan, PR 00902-1112
Tel: (787)725-8120
E-mail: marineslopez1974@aol.com
Web Site: http://www.eap.edu/
President/CEO: Marimar Benitez
Registrar: Ileana Meldonado
Admissions: Marin&is Lopez
Financial Aid: Marion Munoz
Type: Four-Year College **Sex:** Coed **Scores:** 86.88% SAT V 400+; 76.92% SAT M 400+ **% Accepted:** 78 **Application Deadline:** April 01 **Application Fee:** $20.00 **H.S. Requirements:** High school diploma required; GED accepted **Costs Per Year:** Application fee: $20. Area resident tuition: $75 per credit part-time. Mandatory fees: $70 per credit part-time, $212 per year part-time. **Scholarships:** Available **Calendar System:** Semester, Summer Session Available **Enrollment:** FT 368, PT 91 **Faculty:** FT 16, PT 54 **Student-Faculty Ratio:** 11:1 **% Receiving Financial Aid:** 82 **Library Holdings:** 24,582 **Regional Accreditation:** Middle State Association of Colleges and Schools **Credit Hours For Degree:** 132 credit hours, Bachelors

HUERTAS JUNIOR COLLEGE
PO Box 8429
Caguas, PR 00726
Tel: (787)743-2156
Admissions: (787)743-1242
E-mail: huertas@huertas.org
Web Site: http://www.huertasjrcollege.org/
President/CEO: Dr. Rafael Ramirez-Rivera
Registrar: Israel Lopez
Admissions: Barbara Hassim
Financial Aid: Magaly Gonzalez
Type: Two-Year College **Sex:** Coed **Admission Plans:** Open Admission; Deferred Admission **Application Fee:** $33.00 **H.S. Requirements:** High school diploma required; GED accepted **Scholarships:** Available **Calendar System:** Trimester, Summer Session Not available **Faculty:** FT 29, PT 71 **Library Holdings:** 5,524 **Regional Accreditation:** Middle State Association of Colleges and Schools **Credit Hours For Degree:** 76 credits, Associates **Professional Accreditation:** ACICS, AHIMA

HUMACAO COMMUNITY COLLEGE
PO Box 9139
Humacao, PR 00792

Tel: (787)852-1430
Admissions: (787)852-2525
Fax: (787)850-1760
President/CEO: Dr. Félix Rodriguez Matos
Registrar: Isander Velazquez
Admissions: Paula Serrano
Financial Aid: Luis R. Diaz
Type: Two-Year College **Admission Plans:** Open Admission; Early Admission **Application Fee:** $15.00 **H.S. Requirements:** High school diploma required; GED accepted **Scholarships:** Available **Calendar System:** Trimester **Professional Accreditation:** ACICS

ICPR JUNIOR COLLEGE-HATO REY CAMPUS
San Juan, PR
Web Site: http://www.icprjc.edu/ **Type:** Two-Year College **Sex:** Coed

INSTITUTO COMERCIAL DE PUERTO RICO JUNIOR COLLEGE
558 Munoz Rivera Ave., PO Box 190304
San Juan, PR 00919-0304
Tel: (787)753-6000
Fax: (787)763-7249
Web Site: http://www.icprjc.edu/
Registrar: Waveska Serrano
Admissions: Francisco Mena
Financial Aid: Palmira Arroyo
Type: Two-Year College **Sex:** Coed **Admission Plans:** Early Admission **Application Fee:** $25.00 **H.S. Requirements:** High school diploma required; GED accepted **Costs Per Year:** Application fee: $25. Comprehensive fee: $7716 includes full-time tuition ($4680), mandatory fees ($180), and college room and board ($2856). College room only: $1142. Part-time tuition: $130 per credit. **Scholarships:** Available **Calendar System:** Trimester, Summer Session Not available **Enrollment:** FT 1,086, PT 184 **Faculty:** FT 34, PT 55 **Student-Faculty Ratio:** 17:1 **Library Holdings:** 40,858 **Regional Accreditation:** Middle State Association of Colleges and Schools **Credit Hours For Degree:** 73 credits, Associates **ROTC:** Army

INTER AMERICAN UNIVERSITY OF PUERTO RICO, AGUADILLA CAMPUS
Call Box 20000
Aguadilla, PR 00605
Tel: (787)891-0925
Web Site: http://www.aguadilla.inter.edu/
President/CEO: Dr. Juan A. Aponte
Registrar: Miriam Marcial
Admissions: Doris Perez
Financial Aid: Juan Gonzalez
Type: Comprehensive **Sex:** Coed **Affiliation:** Inter American University of Puerto Rico **Admission Plans:** Early Admission **Application Deadline:** Rolling **Application Fee:** $0.00 **H.S. Requirements:** High school diploma required; GED accepted **Costs Per Year:** Application fee: $0. Tuition: $3360 full-time, $140 per credit hour part-time. Mandatory fees: $364 full-time, $144 per term part-time. **Calendar System:** Semester, Summer Session Available **Enrollment:** FT 3,465, PT 594, Grad 70 **Faculty:** FT 75, PT 179 **Student-Faculty Ratio:** 26:1 **Exams:** Other, SAT I **Library Holdings:** 56,037 **Regional Accreditation:** Middle State Association of Colleges and Schools **Credit Hours For Degree:** 55 semester hours, Associates; 129 semester hours, Bachelors **ROTC:** Army **Intercollegiate Athletics:** Baseball M; Basketball M & W; Cheerleading M & W; Cross-Country Running M & W; Soccer M; Softball M & W; Table Tennis M & W; Tennis M & W; Track and Field M & W; Volleyball M & W; Weight Lifting M & W

INTER AMERICAN UNIVERSITY OF PUERTO RICO, ARECIBO CAMPUS
PO Box 4050
Arecibo, PR 00614-4050
Tel: (787)878-5475
Fax: (787)880-1624
Web Site: http://www.arecibo.inter.edu/
President/CEO: Dr. Jean M. Gonzalez
Registrar: Carmen Rodriguez
Admissions: Provi Montalvo
Financial Aid: Ramon O. de Jesus
Type: Comprehensive **Sex:** Coed **Affiliation:** Inter American University of Puerto Rico **Admission Plans:** Early Admission; Deferred Admission **Application Fee:** $0.00 **H.S. Requirements:** High school diploma required; GED accepted **Scholarships:** Available **Calendar System:** Semester, Summer Session Available **Faculty:** FT 83, PT 151 **Student-Faculty Ratio:** 24:1 **Exams:** Other **% Receiving Financial Aid:** 91 **Library Holdings:** 68,893 **Regional Accreditation:** Middle State Association of Colleges and Schools **Credit Hours For Degree:** 60 credit hours, Associates; 124 credit hours, Bachelors **ROTC:** Army **Professional Accreditation:** AANA, CSWE **Intercollegiate Athletics:** Basketball M & W; Softball M & W; Table Tennis M & W; Tennis M & W; Track and Field M & W; Volleyball M & W

INTER AMERICAN UNIVERSITY OF PUERTO RICO, BARRANQUITAS CAMPUS
PO Box 517
Barranquitas, PR 00794
Tel: (787)857-3600
Fax: (787)857-2284
E-mail: mdiaz@br.inter.edu
Web Site: http://www.br.inter.edu/
President/CEO: Dr. Irene Fernandez
Registrar: Maribel Diaz-Peña
Admissions: Maribel Diaz-Peña
Financial Aid: Eduardo Fontanez Colon
Type: Comprehensive **Sex:** Coed **Affiliation:** Inter American University of Puerto Rico **% Accepted:** 41 **Admission Plans:** Deferred Admission **Application Deadline:** May 15 **Application Fee:** $0.00 **H.S. Requirements:** High school diploma required; GED accepted **Costs Per Year:** Application fee: $0. Comprehensive fee: $12,071 includes full-time tuition ($3920), mandatory fees ($850), and college room and board ($7301). College room only: $4978. Part-time tuition: $140 per credit. **Scholarships:** Available **Calendar System:** Semester, Summer Session Available **Enrollment:** FT 1,893, PT 419, Grad 12 **Faculty:** FT 38, PT 85 **Exams:** Other, SAT I or ACT **% Receiving Financial Aid:** 70 **Library Holdings:** 32,863 **Regional Accreditation:** Middle State Association of Colleges and Schools **Credit Hours For Degree:** 60 semester hours, Associates; 124 semester hours, Bachelors **ROTC:** Army **Intercollegiate Athletics:** Basketball M & W; Cross-Country Running M & W; Softball M & W; Table Tennis M & W; Tennis M & W; Track and Field M & W; Volleyball M & W; Weight Lifting M

INTER AMERICAN UNIVERSITY OF PUERTO RICO, BAYAMÓN CAMPUS
500 Rd. 830
Bayamon, PR 00957
Tel: (787)279-1912
Fax: (787)279-2205
E-mail: calicea@bc.inter.edu
Web Site: http://bc.inter.edu/
President/CEO: Prof. Marilina Lucca Wayland
Registrar: Eddie Ayala
Admissions: Carlos Alicea
Financial Aid: Jaime Falcon
Type: Comprehensive **Sex:** Coed **Affiliation:** Inter American University of Puerto Rico **% Accepted:** 44 **Application Deadline:** July 30 **Application Fee:** $0.00 **H.S. Requirements:** High school diploma required; GED accepted **Costs Per Year:** Application fee: $0. Tuition: $3764 full-time, $140 per credit part-time. **Calendar System:** Semester, Summer Session Available **Enrollment:** FT 4,301, PT 901, Grad 53 **Faculty:** FT 99, PT 216 **Student-Faculty Ratio:** 24:1 **Exams:** Other, SAT I **Library Holdings:** 55,695 **Regional Accreditation:** Middle State Association of Colleges and Schools **Credit Hours For Degree:** 70 semester hours, Associates; 120 semester hours, Bachelors **ROTC:** Army **Intercollegiate Athletics:** Baseball M; Basketball M & W; Cross-Country Running M & W; Softball M & W; Swimming and Diving M & W; Table Tennis M & W; Track and Field M & W; Volleyball M & W; Weight Lifting M

INTER AMERICAN UNIVERSITY OF PUERTO RICO, FAJARDO CAMPUS
Call Box 70003
Fajardo, PR 00738-7003
Tel: (787)863-2390
Admissions: (787)860-2390
E-mail: evrivera@ns.inter.edu
Web Site: http://fajardo.inter.edu/
President/CEO: Dr. Ismael Suárez
Registrar: Abigail Rivera
Admissions: Ada Caraballo

Financial Aid: Marilyn Martinez
Type: Comprehensive **Sex:** Coed **Affiliation:** Inter American University of Puerto Rico **Admission Plans:** Early Admission; Deferred Admission **H.S. Requirements:** High school diploma required; GED accepted **Calendar System:** Semester, Summer Session Available **Faculty:** FT 40, PT 78 **Exams:** Other, SAT I **Library Holdings:** 39,951 **Regional Accreditation:** Middle State Association of Colleges and Schools **Credit Hours For Degree:** 60 semester hours, Associates; 124 semester hours, Bachelors

INTER AMERICAN UNIVERSITY OF PUERTO RICO, GUAYAMA CAMPUS
Call Box 10004
Guayama, PR 00785
Tel: (787)864-2222
Web Site: http://www.guayama.inter.edu/
President/CEO: Prof. Carlos E. Colon-Ramos
Registrar: Luis A. Soto
Admissions: Laura E. Ferrer
Financial Aid: Jose A. Vechini
Type: Comprehensive **Sex:** Coed **Affiliation:** Inter American University of Puerto Rico **Application Fee:** $0.00 **H.S. Requirements:** High school diploma required; GED accepted **Scholarships:** Available **Calendar System:** Semester, Summer Session Available **Faculty:** FT 44, PT 95 **Exams:** Other, SAT I **% Receiving Financial Aid:** 51 **Library Holdings:** 21,000 **Regional Accreditation:** Middle State Association of Colleges and Schools **Credit Hours For Degree:** 60 semester hours, Associates; 120 semester hours, Bachelors **ROTC:** Army **Intercollegiate Athletics:** Baseball M; Basketball M & W; Cross-Country Running M & W; Soccer M; Softball M & W; Table Tennis M & W; Tennis M & W; Track and Field M & W; Volleyball M & W; Weight Lifting M

INTER AMERICAN UNIVERSITY OF PUERTO RICO, METROPOLITAN CAMPUS
PO Box 191293
San Juan, PR 00919-1293
Tel: (787)250-1912
Web Site: http://metro.inter.edu/
President/CEO: Generosa Vazquez
Registrar: Maria Carlo
Admissions: Lisette Rivera
Financial Aid: Raúl Rodriguez
Type: Comprehensive **Sex:** Coed **Affiliation:** Inter American University of Puerto Rico **Application Fee:** $0.00 **H.S. Requirements:** High school diploma required; GED accepted **Scholarships:** Available **Calendar System:** Semester, Summer Session Available **Faculty:** FT 245, PT 354 **Student-Faculty Ratio:** 34:1 **Exams:** SAT I **% Receiving Financial Aid:** 80 **Library Holdings:** 113,200 **Regional Accreditation:** Middle State Association of Colleges and Schools **Credit Hours For Degree:** 60 credits, Associates; 120 credits, Bachelors **ROTC:** Army, Navy, Air Force **Professional Accreditation:** ABA, CSWE, NAACLS, NLN **Intercollegiate Athletics:** Baseball M; Basketball M & W; Cross-Country Running M & W; Fencing M; Soccer M; Softball M & W; Swimming and Diving M; Table Tennis M & W; Tennis M & W; Track and Field M & W; Volleyball M & W; Weight Lifting M; Wrestling M

INTER AMERICAN UNIVERSITY OF PUERTO RICO, PONCE CAMPUS
104 Industrial Park Turpò RD 1
Mercedita, PR 00715-1602
Tel: (787)284-1912
E-mail: fldiaz@acpon1.ponce.inter.edu
Web Site: http://www.ponce.inter.edu/
President/CEO: Dr. Vilma Colon
Registrar: Maria del C. Perez
Admissions: Franco Diaz
Financial Aid: Juan Portalatin
Type: Comprehensive **Sex:** Coed **Affiliation:** Inter American University of Puerto Rico **% Accepted:** 63 **Admission Plans:** Deferred Admission **Application Deadline:** August 01 **Application Fee:** $0.00 **H.S. Requirements:** High school diploma required; GED accepted **Costs Per Year:** Application fee: $0. Tuition: $4350 full-time, $145 per credit part-time. Mandatory fees: $406 full-time, $177 per term part-time. **Calendar System:** Semester, Summer Session Available **Enrollment:** FT 4,269, PT 877, Grad 181 **Faculty:** FT 81, PT 176 **Exams:** Other, SAT I **Library Holdings:** 49,531 **Regional Accreditation:** Middle State Association of Colleges and Schools **Credit Hours For Degree:** 60 semester hours, Associates; 124 semester hours, Bachelors **Intercollegiate Athletics:** Baseball M & W; Cross-Country Running M & W; Softball M & W; Table Tennis M & W; Track and Field M & W; Volleyball M & W; Weight Lifting M & W

INTER AMERICAN UNIVERSITY OF PUERTO RICO, SAN GERMÁN CAMPUS
PO Box 5100
San German, PR 00683-5008
Tel: (787)264-1912
Fax: (787)892-6350
Web Site: http://www.sg.inter.edu/
President/CEO: Agnes Mojica
Registrar: Aida Collazo
Admissions: Mildred Camacho
Financial Aid: Maria Ines Lugo
Type: University **Sex:** Coed **Affiliation:** Inter American University of Puerto Rico **% Accepted:** 61 **Admission Plans:** Early Admission **Application Deadline:** May 13 **Application Fee:** $0.00 **H.S. Requirements:** High school diploma required; GED accepted **Costs Per Year:** Application fee: $0. Comprehensive fee: $7016 includes full-time tuition ($4200), mandatory fees ($416), and college room and board ($2400). College room only: $922. Part-time tuition: $140 per credit. Part-time mandatory fees: $208 per term. **Scholarships:** Available **Calendar System:** Semester, Summer Session Available **Enrollment:** FT 4,252, PT 620, Grad 892 **Faculty:** FT 137, PT 200 **Student-Faculty Ratio:** 26:1 **Exams:** Other **% Receiving Financial Aid:** 81 **% Residing in College-Owned, -Operated, or -Affiliated Housing:** 10 **Library Holdings:** 154,828 **Regional Accreditation:** Middle State Association of Colleges and Schools **Credit Hours For Degree:** 60 credits, Associates; 124 credits, Bachelors **ROTC:** Army, Navy, Air Force **Professional Accreditation:** AHIMA, NAACLS **Intercollegiate Athletics:** Baseball M; Basketball M & W; Cross-Country Running M & W; Soccer M; Softball M & W; Swimming and Diving M & W; Table Tennis M & W; Tennis M & W; Track and Field M & W; Volleyball M & W; Weight Lifting M

INTERNATIONAL JUNIOR COLLEGE
1254 Ave. Ponce de Leon
pda. 18 1/2
Santurce, PR 00908
Tel: (787)723-3333
Fax: (787)724-0281
Web Site: http://www.internationaljuniorcollege.com/
President/CEO: Carlos R. Montano
Registrar: Aurora Conley
Financial Aid: Joshua Aceltuno
Type: Two-Year College **Admission Plans:** Open Admission **Application Fee:** $25.00 **Scholarships:** Available **Professional Accreditation:** ACICS

NATIONAL COLLEGE
PO Box 2036
Bayamon, PR 00960
Tel: (787)780-5134
Free: 800-780-5188
Fax: (787)740-7360
E-mail: desil@nationalcollegepr.edu
Web Site: http://www.nationalcollegepr.edu/
President/CEO: Dr. Carmen Zoraida Claudio
Registrar: Glorimar Rodriguez
Admissions: Ricardo Nieves
Financial Aid: Desi Lopez
Type: Two-Year College **Application Fee:** $25.00 **Scholarships:** Available **Professional Accreditation:** ACICS

POLYTECHNIC UNIVERSITY OF PUERTO RICO
377 Ponce de Leon Ave.
Hato Rey, PR 00919
Tel: (787)754-8000
E-mail: tcardona@pupr.edu
Web Site: http://www.pupr.edu/
President/CEO: Ernesto Vazquez-Barquet
Registrar: Mayra I. Lopez
Admissions: Teresa Cardona
Financial Aid: Lydia Cruz
Type: Comprehensive **Sex:** Coed **Admission Plans:** Early Admission; Deferred Admission **Application Deadline:** August 15 **Application Fee:**

$30.00 **H.S. Requirements:** High school diploma required; GED accepted **Costs Per Year:** Application fee: $30. Tuition: $5472 full-time, $152 per credit part-time. Mandatory fees: $450 full-time, $150 per term part-time. **Scholarships:** Available **Calendar System:** Trimester, Summer Session Available **Enrollment:** FT 2,558, PT 2,512, Grad 701 **Faculty:** FT 169, PT 131 **Student-Faculty Ratio:** 19:1 **Exams:** SAT I **% Receiving Financial Aid:** 75 **Library Holdings:** 95,029 **Regional Accreditation:** Middle State Association of Colleges and Schools **Credit Hours For Degree:** 132 credit hours, Bachelors **ROTC:** Army **Professional Accreditation:** ABET **Intercollegiate Athletics:** Basketball M & W; Cross-Country Running M & W; Soccer M; Softball M & W; Table Tennis M & W; Tennis M & W; Track and Field M & W; Volleyball M & W

PONTIFICAL CATHOLIC UNIVERSITY OF PUERTO RICO
2250 Las Americas Ave., Ste. 564
Ponce, PR 00717-0777
Tel: (787)841-2000
Free: 800-981-5040
Fax: (787)840-4295
E-mail: abonilla@email.pucpr.edu
Web Site: http://www.pucpr.edu/
President/CEO: Marcelina Velez de Santiago
Registrar: Ivan Dávila
Admissions: Ana O. Bonilla
Financial Aid: Margaret D. Alustiza
Type: University **Sex:** Coed **Affiliation:** Roman Catholic **Scores:** 76% SAT V 400+; 74% SAT M 400+ **% Accepted:** 79 **Admission Plans:** Early Admission; Deferred Admission **Application Deadline:** March 15 **Application Fee:** $15.00 **H.S. Requirements:** High school diploma required; GED accepted **Costs Per Year:** Application fee: $15. Comprehensive fee: $8078 includes full-time tuition ($4480), mandatory fees ($458), and college room and board ($3140). College room only: $1100. Full-time tuition and fees vary according to course load. Part-time tuition: $140 per credit. Part-time tuition varies according to course load. **Scholarships:** Available **Calendar System:** Semester, Summer Session Available **Enrollment:** FT 4,697, PT 666, Grad 1,550 **Faculty:** FT 205, PT 147 **Student-Faculty Ratio:** 24:1 **Exams:** SAT I **% Receiving Financial Aid:** 91 **% Residing in College-Owned, -Operated, or -Affiliated Housing:** 4 **Regional Accreditation:** Middle State Association of Colleges and Schools **Credit Hours For Degree:** 67 credits, Associates; 130 credits, Bachelors **ROTC:** Army **Professional Accreditation:** ABA, ACBSP, CSWE, NAACLS, NLN **Intercollegiate Athletics:** Basketball M; Cross-Country Running M & W; Swimming and Diving M & W; Table Tennis M & W; Tennis M & W; Track and Field M & W; Volleyball M & W; Weight Lifting M & W; Wrestling M

PUERTO RICO TECHNICAL JUNIOR COLLEGE (MAYAGUEZ)
Calle Santiago R. Palmer No. 15 Est
Mayaguez, PR 00680
Tel: (787)832-2762 **Type:** Two-Year College **Sex:** Coed **Professional Accreditation:** ACCSCT

PUERTO RICO TECHNICAL JUNIOR COLLEGE (SAN JUAN)
703 Ponce De Leon Ave., Hato Rey
San Juan, PR 00917
Tel: (787)751-0133
Fax: (787)754-3431 **Type:** Two-Year College **Sex:** Coed **Admission Plans:** Open Admission **Application Fee:** $25.00 **Professional Accreditation:** ACCSCT

RAMÍREZ COLLEGE OF BUSINESS AND TECHNOLOGY
Ave. Ponce de Leon No. 70
San Juan, PR 00918
Tel: (787)763-3120
President/CEO: Rogena Kyles
Registrar: Felix Torres
Admissions: Eliecer Ayala
Financial Aid: Domingo Maldonado
Type: Two-Year College **Sex:** Coed **Admission Plans:** Open Admission **Application Fee:** $25.00 **H.S. Requirements:** High school diploma required; GED accepted **Scholarships:** Available **Calendar System:** Trimester, Summer Session Not available **Credit Hours For Degree:** 75 credits, Associates **Professional Accreditation:** ACICS

TECHNOLOGICAL COLLEGE OF SAN JUAN
180 Jose R Oliver St.
Tres Monjitas Industrial Park
San Juan, PR 00918
Tel: (787)250-7111
Fax: (787)250-7395
President/CEO: Jose A. Torres
Registrar: Julia Pisciotta
Admissions: Ruth E. Vicens
Financial Aid: Maria De Los A. Quiñonez
Type: Two-Year College **Sex:** Coed **Admission Plans:** Open Admission **Application Fee:** $15.00 **H.S. Requirements:** High school diploma required; GED accepted **Scholarships:** Available **Calendar System:** Semester, Summer Session Available **Enrollment:** FT 592, PT 185 **Faculty:** FT 40, PT 30 **Student-Faculty Ratio:** 13:1 **Exams:** Other, SAT I **Library Holdings:** 14,298 **Regional Accreditation:** Middle State Association of Colleges and Schools **Credit Hours For Degree:** 69 credits, Associates **Professional Accreditation:** NLN **Intercollegiate Athletics:** Basketball M & W; Cross-Country Running M & W; Table Tennis M & W; Tennis M & W; Track and Field M & W; Volleyball M & W; Weight Lifting M & W

UNIVERSIDAD ADVENTISTA DE LAS ANTILLAS
PO Box 118
Mayaguez, PR 00681-0118
Tel: (787)834-9595
Fax: (787)834-9597
E-mail: admissions@uaa.edu
Web Site: http://www.uaa.edu/
President/CEO: Dr. Myrna Costa
Registrar: Ana D. Torres
Admissions: Evelyn del Valle
Financial Aid: Heriberto Juarbe
Type: Comprehensive **Sex:** Coed **Affiliation:** Seventh-day Adventist **% Accepted:** 90 **Admission Plans:** Early Admission **Application Fee:** $20.00 **H.S. Requirements:** High school diploma required; GED accepted **Costs Per Year:** Application fee: $20. Comprehensive fee: $5590 includes full-time tuition ($3680), mandatory fees ($510), and college room and board ($1400). College room only: $800. Full-time tuition and fees vary according to course load. Room and board charges vary according to board plan. Part-time tuition: $130 per credit. Part-time mandatory fees: $130 per credit. Part-time tuition and fees vary according to course load. **Scholarships:** Available **Calendar System:** Semester, Summer Session Available **Enrollment:** FT 704, PT 56, Grad 71 **Faculty:** FT 42, PT 21 **Student-Faculty Ratio:** 13:1 **Exams:** Other, SAT I or ACT **% Receiving Financial Aid:** 100 **% Residing in College-Owned, -Operated, or -Affiliated Housing:** 27 **Library Holdings:** 86,465 **Regional Accreditation:** Middle State Association of Colleges and Schools **Credit Hours For Degree:** 64 credits, Associates; 128 credits, Bachelors **Professional Accreditation:** AHIMA, CARC, NLN **Intercollegiate Athletics:** Softball M

UNIVERSIDAD CENTRAL DEL CARIBE
PO Box 60-327
Bayamon, PR 00960-6032
Tel: (787)798-3001
Web Site: http://www.uccaribe.edu/
President/CEO: Dr. Nilda Candelario
Registrar: Irma I. Irizarry
Financial Aid: Vivian Cintron
Type: Two-Year College **Sex:** Coed **Application Fee:** $25.00 **Calendar System:** Semester **Regional Accreditation:** Middle State Association of Colleges and Schools **Professional Accreditation:** JRCERT, LCMEAMA

UNIVERSIDAD DEL ESTE
PO Box 2010
Carolina, PR 00983
Tel: (787)257-7373
Fax: (787)257-7373
E-mail: ue_nortiz@suagm.edu
Web Site: http://www.suagm.edu/une/
President/CEO: Alberto Maldonado Ruiz, Esq
Registrar: Nancy B. Ortiz
Admissions: Clotilde Santiago
Financial Aid: Clotilde Santiago
Type: Comprehensive **Sex:** Coed **Affiliation:** Ana G. Méndez University System **Admission Plans:** Deferred Admission **Application Fee:** $15.00 **H.S. Requirements:** High school diploma required; GED accepted **Calendar System:** Semester, Summer Session Available **Faculty:** FT 62, PT 377 **Exams:** Other **Library Holdings:** 13,856 **Regional Accreditation:**

Middle State Association of Colleges and Schools **Credit Hours For Degree:** 62 credits, Associates **Professional Accreditation:** AHIMA **Intercollegiate Athletics:** Basketball M; Track and Field M & W; Volleyball M & W

UNIVERSIDAD METROPOLITANA

Apartado 21150
San Juan, PR 00928-1150
Tel: (787)766-1717
Free: 800-747-8362
Fax: (787)759-7663
E-mail: um_frivera@suagm1.suagm.edu
Web Site: http://www.suagm.edu/umet/
President/CEO: Dr. Federico M. Matheu
Registrar: Beatriz Nieves
Admissions: Julio Rodriguez Soiza
Financial Aid: Evelyn Robledo
Type: Comprehensive **Sex:** Coed **Affiliation:** Ana G. Méndez University System **Application Fee:** $15.00 **Calendar System:** Semester, Summer Session Available **Faculty:** FT 89, PT 269 **Exams:** Other **Regional Accreditation:** Middle State Association of Colleges and Schools **Credit Hours For Degree:** 72 credits, Associates; 128 credits, Bachelors **Professional Accreditation:** NLN **Intercollegiate Athletics:** Softball M & W; Table Tennis M & W; Tennis M & W; Track and Field M & W; Volleyball M & W; Weight Lifting M & W

UNIVERSIDAD DEL TURABO

PO Box 3030
Gurabo, PR 00778-3030
Tel: (787)743-7979
E-mail: ac_msantana@suagm.edu
Web Site: http://www.suagm.edu/ut/
President/CEO: Dr. Dennis Alicea
Registrar: Maria Figueroa
Admissions: Sr. Jesus Torres
Financial Aid: Ana M. Ortega
Type: Comprehensive **Sex:** Coed **Affiliation:** Ana G. Méndez University System **Admission Plans:** Deferred Admission **Application Fee:** $15.00 **H.S. Requirements:** High school diploma required; GED accepted **Calendar System:** Semester, Summer Session Available **Faculty:** FT 103, PT 307 **Exams:** Other **Library Holdings:** 90,020 **Regional Accreditation:** Middle State Association of Colleges and Schools **Credit Hours For Degree:** 64 credits, Associates; 126 credits, Bachelors **ROTC:** Army, Air Force **Intercollegiate Athletics:** Basketball M & W; Cross-Country Running M & W; Soccer M; Tennis M; Track and Field M & W; Volleyball M & W; Weight Lifting M

UNIVERSITY COLLEGE OF CRIMINAL JUSTICE OF PUERTO RICO

HC 02 Box 12000
Gurabo, PR 00778-9601
Tel: (787)737-3351
Fax: (787)737-7619
President/CEO: Zulma Gonzalez Berrios
Type: Two-Year College **Sex:** Coed **Regional Accreditation:** Middle State Association of Colleges and Schools

UNIVERSITY OF PHOENIX-PUERTO RICO CAMPUS

B7 Tabonuco St., Ste. 700 Santander Tower
PO Box 3870
Guaynabo, PR 00968
Tel: (787)731-5400
Free: 800-228-7240
Admissions: (480)557-1712
Fax: (787)731-1510
Web Site: http://www.phoenix.edu/
President/CEO: Candida Acosta
Admissions: Beth Barilla
Type: Comprehensive **Sex:** Coed **Admission Plans:** Open Admission; Deferred Admission **Application Deadline:** Rolling **Application Fee:** $110.00 **H.S. Requirements:** High school diploma required; GED accepted **Costs Per Year:** Application fee: $110. Tuition: $5640 full-time, $188 per credit part-time. Mandatory fees: $560 full-time, $70 per course part-time. **Scholarships:** Available **Calendar System:** Continuous, Summer Session Not available **Enrollment:** FT 832, Grad 1,882 **Faculty:** FT 7, PT 102 **Student-Faculty Ratio:** 16:1 **Library Holdings:** 444 **Regional Accreditation:** North Central Association of Colleges and Schools **Credit Hours For Degree:** 60 credits, Associates; 120 credits, Bachelors

UNIVERSITY OF PUERTO RICO, AGUADILLA UNIVERSITY COLLEGE

PO Box 250-160
Aguadilla, PR 00604-0160
Tel: (787)890-2681
Web Site: http://www.uprag.edu/
President/CEO: Prof. Juana Segarra Jaramillo
Registrar: Nivia Gomez
Admissions: Melba Serrano Lugo
Financial Aid: Doris Lillian Román
Type: Four-Year College **Sex:** Coed **Affiliation:** University of Puerto Rico System **Admission Plans:** Early Admission; Deferred Admission **Application Fee:** $15.00 **H.S. Requirements:** High school diploma required; GED accepted **Calendar System:** Semester, Summer Session Available **Faculty:** FT 113, PT 20 **Exams:** Other, SAT I, SAT II **Library Holdings:** 31,420 **Regional Accreditation:** Middle State Association of Colleges and Schools **Credit Hours For Degree:** 66 credits, Associates; 129 credits, Bachelors **ROTC:** Army **Intercollegiate Athletics:** Basketball M; Cross-Country Running M & W; Softball M & W; Table Tennis M & W; Tennis M & W; Track and Field M & W; Volleyball M & W; Weight Lifting M & W

UNIVERSITY OF PUERTO RICO AT ARECIBO

PO Box 4010
Arecibo, PR 00613
Tel: (787)878-2830
Web Site: http://www.upra.edu/
President/CEO: Josefa Garcia Firpi
Registrar: Abelardo Martinez
Admissions: Delma Barrios
Financial Aid: Luis Rodriguez
Type: Four-Year College **Sex:** Coed **Affiliation:** University of Puerto Rico System **Application Fee:** $15.00 **H.S. Requirements:** High school diploma required; GED accepted **Scholarships:** Available **Calendar System:** Semester, Summer Session Available **Faculty:** FT 234, PT 40 **Student-Faculty Ratio:** 17:1 **Exams:** Other, SAT II **Library Holdings:** 65,000 **Regional Accreditation:** Middle State Association of Colleges and Schools **Credit Hours For Degree:** 68 credits, Associates; 132 credits, Bachelors **ROTC:** Army **Professional Accreditation:** NLN **Intercollegiate Athletics:** Basketball M & W; Cross-Country Running M & W; Soccer M; Softball W; Table Tennis M & W; Tennis M & W; Track and Field M & W; Volleyball M & W; Weight Lifting M & W; Wrestling M

UNIVERSITY OF PUERTO RICO AT BAYAMÓN

170 Carretera 174 Parque Industrial Minillas
Bayamon, PR 00959
Tel: (787)786-2885
E-mail: e_velez@cutb.upr.clu.edu
Web Site: http://www.uprb.edu/
President/CEO: Dr. Andrès Rodriguez Rubio
Registrar: Wanda Rivera
Admissions: Evelyn Rivera
Financial Aid: Anilda Gonzalez
Type: Four-Year College **Sex:** Coed **Affiliation:** University of Puerto Rico System **Application Fee:** $15.00 **H.S. Requirements:** High school diploma required; GED accepted **Calendar System:** Semester, Summer Session Available **Faculty:** FT 204, PT 43 **Exams:** SAT I, SAT II **Library Holdings:** 60,815 **Regional Accreditation:** Middle State Association of Colleges and Schools **Credit Hours For Degree:** 72 credits, Associates; 130 credits, Bachelors **ROTC:** Army, Air Force **Intercollegiate Athletics:** Basketball M & W; Cross-Country Running M & W; Soccer M; Swimming and Diving M & W; Tennis M & W; Track and Field M & W; Volleyball M & W; Water Polo M; Weight Lifting M; Wrestling M

UNIVERSITY OF PUERTO RICO AT CAROLINA

PO Box 4800
Carolina, PR 00984-4800
Tel: (787)257-0000
Admissions: (787)757-1485
Web Site: http://uprc.edu/
President/CEO: Dr. Victor Borrero-Aldahondo
Registrar: Gloria Rosario

Admissions: Celia Mendez
Financial Aid: Lucy Rodriguez
Type: Two-Year College **Sex:** Coed **Affiliation:** University of Puerto Rico System **Application Fee:** $15.00 **H.S. Requirements:** High school diploma required; GED accepted **Calendar System:** Quarter, Summer Session Not available **Faculty:** FT 73, PT 14 **Exams:** Other, SAT I, SAT II **Library Holdings:** 28,037 **Regional Accreditation:** Middle State Association of Colleges and Schools **Credit Hours For Degree:** 68 credits, Associates; 137 credits, Bachelors **ROTC:** Army, Air Force **Intercollegiate Athletics:** Basketball M & W; Cross-Country Running M & W; Tennis M & W; Track and Field M & W; Volleyball M & W; Weight Lifting W

UNIVERSITY OF PUERTO RICO, CAYEY UNIVERSITY COLLEGE
205 Ave. Antonio R. Barcelo
Cayey, PR 00736
Tel: (787)738-2161
Web Site: http://www.cayey.upr.edu/
President/CEO: Prof. Rafael Rivera Lehman
Registrar: Angel Matos
Admissions: Wilfredo Lopez
Financial Aid: Hector Maldonado
Type: Four-Year College **Sex:** Coed **Affiliation:** University of Puerto Rico System **Admission Plans:** Early Admission **Application Fee:** $15.00 **H.S. Requirements:** High school diploma required; GED accepted **Scholarships:** Available **Calendar System:** Semester, Summer Session Available **Enrollment:** FT 3,595, PT 392 **Faculty:** FT 180, PT 39 **Student-Faculty Ratio:** 18:1 **Exams:** Other, SAT I **% Receiving Financial Aid:** 76 **Library Holdings:** 109,776 **Regional Accreditation:** Middle State Association of Colleges and Schools **Credit Hours For Degree:** 72 credits, Associates; 128 credits, Bachelors **ROTC:** Army **Intercollegiate Athletics:** Basketball M & W; Cross-Country Running M & W; Soccer M; Softball M & W; Swimming and Diving M; Table Tennis M; Tennis M & W; Track and Field M & W; Volleyball M & W; Weight Lifting M; Wrestling M

UNIVERSITY OF PUERTO RICO AT HUMACAO
HUC Station 100, Rd. 908
Humacao, PR 00791
Tel: (787)850-0000
Admissions: (787)850-9301
Fax: (787)852-4638
E-mail: i_ferrer@cuhac.upr.clu.edu
Web Site: http://www.uprh.edu/
President/CEO: Dr. Hilda Colon Plumey
Registrar: Jorge Acevedo
Admissions: Inara Ferrer
Financial Aid: Mariolga Rotger
Type: Four-Year College **Sex:** Coed **Affiliation:** University of Puerto Rico System **Admission Plans:** Deferred Admission **Application Fee:** $15.00 **H.S. Requirements:** High school diploma required; GED accepted **Scholarships:** Available **Calendar System:** Semester, Summer Session Available **Faculty:** FT 258, PT 26 **Student-Faculty Ratio:** 15:1 **Exams:** Other, SAT I, SAT II **% Receiving Financial Aid:** 82 **Library Holdings:** 64,557 **Regional Accreditation:** Middle State Association of Colleges and Schools **Credit Hours For Degree:** 65 credits, Associates; 128 credits, Bachelors **ROTC:** Army **Professional Accreditation:** AOTA, APTA, CSWE, NLN **Intercollegiate Athletics:** Baseball M; Basketball M & W; Cross-Country Running M & W; Softball W; Swimming and Diving M & W; Tennis W; Track and Field M & W; Volleyball M & W; Wrestling M

UNIVERSITY OF PUERTO RICO, MAYAGÜ U.S. COLLEGES EZ CAMPUS
PO Box 9000
Mayaguez, PR 00681-9000
Tel: (787)832-4040
Admissions: (787)265-3811
E-mail: af_delgado@rumaxp.rum.clu.edu
Web Site: http://www.uprm.edu
President/CEO: Dr. Zulma Toro
Registrar: Briseida Melendez
Admissions: Norma Torres
Financial Aid: Salvador Cortés
Type: University **Sex:** Coed **Affiliation:** University of Puerto Rico System **Admission Plans:** Early Action **Application Fee:** $15.00 **H.S. Requirements:** High school diploma required; GED accepted **Costs Per Year:** Application fee: $15. **Scholarships:** Available **Calendar System:** Semester, Summer Session Available **Enrollment:** FT 10,010, PT 1,022, Grad 1,076 **Faculty:** FT 612, PT 38 **Student-Faculty Ratio:** 17:1 **Exams:** Other, SAT I, SAT II **% Receiving Financial Aid:** 54 **Library Holdings:** 921,392 **Regional Accreditation:** Middle State Association of Colleges and Schools **Credit Hours For Degree:** 134 credits, Bachelors **ROTC:** Army, Air Force **Professional Accreditation:** ABET, NLN **Intercollegiate Athletics:** Baseball M; Basketball M & W; Cross-Country Running M & W; Soccer M; Softball M & W; Swimming and Diving M & W; Table Tennis M & W; Tennis M & W; Track and Field M & W; Volleyball M & W; Water Polo M; Weight Lifting M; Wrestling M

UNIVERSITY OF PUERTO RICO, MEDICAL SCIENCES CAMPUS
PO Box 365067
San Juan, PR 00936-5067
Tel: (787)758-2525
Fax: (787)754-0474
E-mail: rvelez@rcm.upr.edu
Web Site: http://www.rcm.upr.edu/
President/CEO: Dr. Pedro J. Santiago Borrero
Registrar: Elizabeth Sanchez
Admissions: Rosa Velez
Financial Aid: Zoraida Figueroa
Type: Two-Year Upper Division **Sex:** Coed **Affiliation:** University of Puerto Rico System **Admission Plans:** Preferred Admission **Application Fee:** $15.00 **Scholarships:** Available **Calendar System:** Semester, Summer Session Available **Faculty:** FT 557, PT 136 **Exams:** SAT I **% Receiving Financial Aid:** 63 **Library Holdings:** 46,679 **Regional Accreditation:** Middle State Association of Colleges and Schools **Credit Hours For Degree:** 91 credits, Bachelors **Professional Accreditation:** ACEHSA, AACN, AANA, ACNM, ACPhE, ADA, ADtA, AHIMA, AOTA, APTA, ASLHA, CEPH, JRCERT, JRCNMT, LCMEAMA, NAACLS, NLN

UNIVERSITY OF PUERTO RICO AT PONCE
PO Box 7186
Ponce, PR 00732-7186
Tel: (787)844-8181
Fax: (787)844-8679
Web Site: http://upr-ponce.upr.edu/
President/CEO: Prof. Ana M. Ortiz
Registrar: Agnes Colon
Admissions: William Rodriguez Mercado
Financial Aid: Carmelo Vega
Type: Four-Year College **Sex:** Coed **Affiliation:** University of Puerto Rico System **Admission Plans:** Early Admission **Application Fee:** $15.00 **H.S. Requirements:** High school diploma required; GED accepted **Costs Per Year:** Application fee: $15. Commonwealth resident tuition: $1360 full-time, $40 per credit hour part-time. Nonresident tuition: $2400 full-time, $100 per credit hour part-time. Mandatory fees: $814 full-time. Full-time tuition and fees vary according to class time. Part-time tuition varies according to class time. **Scholarships:** Available **Calendar System:** Semester, Summer Session Available **Faculty:** FT 149, PT 52 **Student-Faculty Ratio:** 19:1 **Exams:** Other, SAT I **% Receiving Financial Aid:** 75 **Library Holdings:** 53,000 **Regional Accreditation:** Middle State Association of Colleges and Schools **Credit Hours For Degree:** 73 credits, Associates; 136 credits, Bachelors **ROTC:** Army **Professional Accreditation:** APTA **Intercollegiate Athletics:** Basketball M & W; Cross-Country Running M & W; Tennis M & W; Track and Field M & W; Volleyball M & W; Weight Lifting M & W

UNIVERSITY OF PUERTO RICO, RÍO PIEDRAS
PO Box 23300
San Juan, PR 00931-3300
Tel: (787)764-0000
Web Site: http://www.uprrp.edu/
President/CEO: Dr. Gladys Escolona de Motta
Registrar: Juan M. Aponte
Admissions: Cruz B. Valentìn
Financial Aid: Luz Santiago
Type: University **Sex:** Coed **Affiliation:** University of Puerto Rico System **Scores:** 98.8% SAT V 400+; 98.7% SAT M 400+ **Application Fee:** $15.00 **H.S. Requirements:** High school diploma required; GED accepted **Scholarships:** Available **Calendar System:** Semester, Summer Session Available **Faculty:** FT 1,420, PT 373 **Student-Faculty Ratio:** 22:1 **Exams:** Other, SAT I, SAT II **Library Holdings:** 1,804,010 **Regional Accreditation:** Middle State Association of Colleges and Schools **Credit Hours For Degree:** 120

credits, Bachelors **ROTC:** Army, Air Force **Professional Accreditation:** ABA, ACSP, ALA, AALS, CORE, CSWE, NCATE **Intercollegiate Athletics:** Basketball M & W; Cross-Country Running M & W; Soccer M; Swimming and Diving M & W; Table Tennis M & W; Tennis M & W; Track and Field M & W; Volleyball M & W; Water Polo M; Weight Lifting M

UNIVERSITY OF PUERTO RICO AT UTUADO
PO Box 2500
Utuado, PR 00641-2500
Tel: (787)894-2828
Web Site: http://upr-utuado.upr.clu.edu/
President/CEO: Prof. Luis Clos
Registrar: Norma Rivera
Financial Aid: Edgar Salva
Type: Four-Year College **Sex:** Coed **Affiliation:** University of Puerto Rico System **Admission Plans:** Early Admission; Deferred Admission **Application Fee:** $15.00 **H.S. Requirements:** High school diploma required; GED accepted **Scholarships:** Available **Calendar System:** Semester, Summer Session Available **Faculty:** FT 79, PT 27 **Student-Faculty Ratio:** 17:1 **Exams:** Other, SAT I and SAT II or ACT **Library Holdings:** 22,482 **Regional Accreditation:** Middle State Association of Colleges and Schools **Credit Hours For Degree:** 60 credits, Associates; 137 credits, Bachelors **Intercollegiate Athletics:** Basketball M & W; Cross-Country Running M & W; Softball M & W; Table Tennis M & W; Track and Field M & W; Volleyball M & W; Weight Lifting M & W

UNIVERSITY OF THE SACRED HEART
PO Box 12383
San Juan, PR 00914-0383
Tel: (787)728-1515
Web Site: http://www.sagrado.edu/
President/CEO: Dr. Jose Jaime Rivera
Registrar: Mildred Piñeiro
Admissions: Luis Heviquez
Financial Aid: Luis Aquiles
Type: Comprehensive **Sex:** Coed **Affiliation:** Roman Catholic **Admission Plans:** Early Admission **Application Fee:** $15.00 **H.S. Requirements:** High school diploma required; GED accepted **Scholarships:** Available **Calendar System:** Semester, Summer Session Available **Enrollment:** FT 3,279, PT 1,144, Grad 783 **Faculty:** FT 128, PT 215 **Student-Faculty Ratio:** 18:1 **Exams:** Other **Regional Accreditation:** Middle State Association of Colleges and Schools **Credit Hours For Degree:** 67 credits, Associates; 133 credits, Bachelors **Professional Accreditation:** CSWE, NAACLS, NLN **Intercollegiate Athletics:** Basketball M & W; Cross-Country Running M & W; Swimming and Diving M & W; Tennis M & W; Track and Field M & W; Volleyball M & W; Weight Lifting M & W

Rhode Island

BROWN UNIVERSITY
Providence, RI 02912
Tel: (401)863-1000
Admissions: (401)863-2378
Fax: (401)863-9300
E-mail: admission_undergraduate@brown.edu
Web Site: http://www.brown.edu/
President/CEO: Dr. Ruth J. Simmons
Registrar: Michael Pesta
Admissions: James Miller
Financial Aid: Michael Bartini
Type: University **Sex:** Coed **Scores:** 100% SAT V 400+; 100% SAT M 400+; 7% ACT 18-23; 38% ACT 24-29 **% Accepted:** 15 **Admission Plans:** Early Admission; Early Decision Plan; Deferred Admission **Application Deadline:** January 01 **Application Fee:** $70.00 **H.S. Requirements:** High school diploma required; GED not accepted **Costs Per Year:** Application fee: $70. Comprehensive fee: $42,020 includes full-time tuition ($32,264), mandatory fees ($960), and college room and board ($8796). College room only: $5498. Room and board charges vary according to board plan. Part-time tuition: $4033 per course. Tuition guaranteed not to increase for student's term of enrollment. **Scholarships:** Available **Calendar System:** Semester, Summer Session Available **Enrollment:** FT 5,931, PT 245, Grad 1,734 **Faculty:** FT 630, PT 258 **Student-Faculty Ratio:** 9:1 **Exams:** SAT I and SAT II or ACT **% Receiving Financial Aid:** 43 **% Residing in College-Owned, -Operated, or -Affiliated Housing:** 85 **Library Holdings:** 3,000,000 **Regional Accreditation:** New England Association of Schools and Colleges **Credit Hours For Degree:** 30 courses, Bachelors **ROTC:** Army **Professional Accreditation:** ABET, APA, CEPH, LCMEAMA **Intercollegiate Athletics:** Baseball M; Basketball M & W; Crew M & W; Cross-Country Running M & W; Equestrian Sports W; Fencing M & W; Field Hockey W; Football M; Golf M & W; Gymnastics W; Ice Hockey M & W; Lacrosse M & W; Rugby M & W; Sailing M & W; Skiing (Downhill) M & W; Soccer M & W; Softball W; Squash M & W; Swimming and Diving M & W; Tennis M & W; Track and Field M & W; Volleyball M & W; Water Polo M & W; Wrestling M

BRYANT UNIVERSITY
1150 Douglas Pike
Smithfield, RI 02917-1284
Tel: (401)232-6000
Free: 800-622-7001
Admissions: (401)232-6100
Fax: (401)232-6741
E-mail: admission@bryant.edu
Web Site: http://www.bryant.edu/
President/CEO: Ronald K. Machtley
Registrar: Susan McDonald
Admissions: Lorna J. Hunter
Financial Aid: John B. Canning
Type: Comprehensive **Sex:** Coed **Scores:** 99% SAT V 400+; 100% SAT M 400+; 50% ACT 18-23; 41% ACT 24-29 **% Accepted:** 58 **Admission Plans:** Early Admission; Early Decision Plan; Deferred Admission **Application Deadline:** February 15 **Application Fee:** $50.00 **H.S. Requirements:** High school diploma required; GED accepted **Costs Per Year:** Application fee: $50. Comprehensive fee: $34,330 includes full-time tuition ($24,762) and college room and board ($9568). College room only: $5550. Full-time tuition varies according to course load. Room and board charges vary according to board plan and housing facility. Part-time tuition: $891 per course. Part-time tuition varies according to course load. Full-time tuition includes cost of personal laptop computer. **Scholarships:** Available **Calendar System:** Semester, Summer Session Available **Enrollment:** FT 3,012, PT 191, Grad 439 **Faculty:** FT 133, PT 129 **Student-Faculty Ratio:** 16:1 **Exams:** SAT I or ACT **% Receiving Financial Aid:** 65 **% Residing in College-Owned, -Operated, or -Affiliated Housing:** 78 **Library Holdings:** 133,250 **Regional Accreditation:** New England Association of Schools and Colleges **Credit Hours For Degree:** 123 credits (exception-Applied Actuarial Mathematics is 126 credits), Bachelors **ROTC:** Army **Professional Accreditation:** AACSB **Intercollegiate Athletics:** Baseball M; Basketball M & W; Bowling M & W; Cheerleading M & W; Cross-Country Running M & W; Field Hockey W; Football M; Golf M & W; Ice Hockey M; Lacrosse M & W; Racquetball M & W; Rugby M & W; Soccer M & W; Softball W; Squash M & W; Swimming and Diving M & W; Tennis M & W; Track and Field M & W; Ultimate Frisbee M & W; Volleyball W; Wrestling M

COMMUNITY COLLEGE OF RHODE ISLAND
400 East Ave.
Warwick, RI 02886-1807
Tel: (401)825-1000
Admissions: (401)333-7302
Fax: (401)825-2418
Web Site: http://www.ccri.edu/
President/CEO: Dr. Thomas D. Sepe
Registrar: Joseph P. DiMaria
Admissions: Dr. Heather C. Smith
Financial Aid: Christine Jenkins
Type: Two-Year College **Sex:** Coed **Admission Plans:** Open Admission; Preferred Admission; Deferred Admission **Application Fee:** $20.00 **H.S. Requirements:** High school diploma required; GED accepted. For nursing, dental, allied health programs: High school diploma required; GED accepted **Costs Per Year:** Application fee: $20. State resident tuition: $2180 full-time, $102 per credit hour part-time. Nonresident tuition: $6410 full-time, $307 per credit hour part-time. Mandatory fees: $290 full-time, $8 per credit hour part-time, $32 per term part-time. Part-time tuition and fees vary according to course load. **Scholarships:** Available **Calendar System:** Semester, Summer Session Available **Enrollment:** FT 5,731, PT 10,562 **Faculty:** FT 328, PT 408 **Library Holdings:** 98,140 **Regional Accreditation:** New England Association of Schools and Colleges **Credit Hours For Degree:** 60 credits, Associates **ROTC:** Army **Professional Accreditation:** ADA, AOTA, APTA, ACBSP, CARC, JRCERT, NAACLS, NLN **Intercollegiate Athletics:** Baseball M; Basketball M & W; Cross-Country Running M & W; Golf M & W; Soccer M & W; Softball W; Tennis M & W; Track and Field M & W; Volleyball W

JOHNSON & WALES UNIVERSITY
8 Abbott Park Place
Providence, RI 02903-3703
Tel: (401)598-1000
Free: 800-342-5598
Admissions: (401)598-2310
Fax: (401)598-1835
E-mail: admissions.pvd@jwu.edu
Web Site: http://www.jwu.edu/

President/CEO: Dr. John Bowen
Registrar: Diane Riccitelli
Admissions: Maureen Dumas
Financial Aid: Lynn Robinson
Type: Comprehensive **Sex:** Coed **% Accepted:** 80 **Admission Plans:** Early Admission; Deferred Admission **Application Deadline:** Rolling **Application Fee:** $0.00 **H.S. Requirements:** High school diploma required; GED accepted **Costs Per Year:** Application fee: $0. Comprehensive fee: $28,126 includes full-time tuition ($19,875), mandatory fees ($951), and college room and board ($7300). Part-time tuition: $368 per quarter hour. **Scholarships:** Available **Calendar System:** Quarter, Summer Session Available **Enrollment:** FT 8,400, PT 937, Grad 834 **Faculty:** FT 279, PT 127 **Student-Faculty Ratio:** 27:1 **Exams:** SAT I or ACT **% Receiving Financial Aid:** 71 **Library Holdings:** 91,180 **Regional Accreditation:** New England Association of Schools and Colleges **Credit Hours For Degree:** 90 credit hours, Associates; 180 credit hours, Bachelors **Intercollegiate Athletics:** Baseball M; Basketball M & W; Cross-Country Running M & W; Equestrian Sports M & W; Golf M & W; Ice Hockey M; Sailing M & W; Soccer M & W; Softball W; Tennis M & W; Volleyball M & W; Wrestling M

NEW ENGLAND INSTITUTE OF TECHNOLOGY

2500 Post Rd.
Warwick, RI 02886-2244
Tel: (401)739-5000
E-mail: neit@ids.net
Web Site: http://www.neit.edu/
President/CEO: Dr. Richard I. Gouse
Registrar: Doreen Lasiewski
Admissions: Michael Kwiatkowski
Financial Aid: Larry Blair
Type: Two-Year College **Sex:** Coed **Admission Plans:** Open Admission; Early Admission; Deferred Admission **Application Fee:** $25.00 **H.S. Requirements:** High school diploma required; GED accepted **Scholarships:** Available **Calendar System:** Quarter, Summer Session Available **Faculty:** FT 96, PT 127 **Library Holdings:** 42,614 **Regional Accreditation:** New England Association of Schools and Colleges **Credit Hours For Degree:** 90 credits, Associates; 180 credits, Bachelors **Professional Accreditation:** ABET, ARCEST, AOTA

PROVIDENCE COLLEGE

River Ave. and Eaton St.
Providence, RI 02918
Tel: (401)865-1000
Free: 800-721-6444
Admissions: (401)865-2535
Fax: (401)865-2826
E-mail: pcadmiss@providence.edu
Web Site: http://www.providence.edu/
President/CEO: Rev. Philip A. Smith, OP
Registrar: Ann Barone
Admissions: Christopher Lydon
Financial Aid: Herbert D'Arcy
Type: Comprehensive **Sex:** Coed **Affiliation:** Roman Catholic **Scores:** 100% SAT V 400+; 100% SAT M 400+; 29% ACT 18-23; 61% ACT 24-29 **% Accepted:** 54 **Admission Plans:** Early Admission; Early Action; Deferred Admission **Application Deadline:** January 15 **Application Fee:** $55.00 **H.S. Requirements:** High school diploma required; GED not accepted **Costs Per Year:** Application fee: $55. Comprehensive fee: $34,580 includes full-time tuition ($24,800), mandatory fees ($510), and college room and board ($9270). College room only: $4970. Room and board charges vary according to board plan and housing facility. Part-time tuition: $827 per credit. **Scholarships:** Available **Calendar System:** Semester, Summer Session Available **Enrollment:** FT 3,896, PT 16, Grad 920 **Faculty:** FT 287, PT 82 **Student-Faculty Ratio:** 12:1 **Exams:** SAT I or ACT, SAT II **% Receiving Financial Aid:** 63 **% Residing in College-Owned, -Operated, or -Affiliated Housing:** 75 **Library Holdings:** 563,289 **Regional Accreditation:** New England Association of Schools and Colleges **Credit Hours For Degree:** 60 credits, Associates; 116 credits, Bachelors **ROTC:** Army **Professional Accreditation:** CSWE **Intercollegiate Athletics:** Basketball M & W; Cross-Country Running M & W; Field Hockey W; Golf M & W; Ice Hockey M & W; Lacrosse M; Racquetball M & W; Rugby M & W; Sailing M & W; Skiing (Cross-Country) M & W; Skiing (Downhill) M & W; Soccer M & W; Softball W; Swimming and Diving M & W; Tennis W; Track and Field M & W; Volleyball W

RHODE ISLAND COLLEGE

600 Mount Pleasant Ave.
Providence, RI 02908-1991
Tel: (401)456-8000
Free: 800-669-5760
Admissions: (401)456-8234
Fax: (401)456-8379
Web Site: http://www.ric.edu/
President/CEO: Dr. John Nazarian
Registrar: James Dorian
Admissions: Dr. Holly Shadoian
Financial Aid: James T. Hanbury
Type: Comprehensive **Sex:** Coed **Scores:** 87.38% SAT V 400+; 86.73% SAT M 400+ **% Accepted:** 78 **Admission Plans:** Early Admission; Deferred Admission **Application Deadline:** May 01 **Application Fee:** $50.00 **H.S. Requirements:** High school diploma required; GED accepted **Costs Per Year:** Application fee: $50. State resident tuition: $3888 full-time, $168 per credit part-time. Nonresident tuition: $11,200 full-time, $466 per credit part-time. Mandatory fees: $788 full-time, $21 per credit part-time, $60 per term part-time. Part-time tuition and fees vary according to course load. College room and board: $7010. College room only: $3740. Room and board charges vary according to board plan and housing facility. **Scholarships:** Available **Calendar System:** Semester, Summer Session Available **Enrollment:** FT 5,310, PT 2,167, Grad 1,394 **Faculty:** FT 306, PT 333 **Student-Faculty Ratio:** 16:1 **Exams:** SAT I or ACT **% Residing in College-Owned, -Operated, or -Affiliated Housing:** 12 **Library Holdings:** 639,489 **Regional Accreditation:** New England Association of Schools and Colleges **Credit Hours For Degree:** 120 semester hours, Bachelors **ROTC:** Army **Professional Accreditation:** CSWE, NASAD, NASM, NCATE, NLN **Intercollegiate Athletics:** Baseball M; Basketball M & W; Cross-Country Running M & W; Gymnastics W; Soccer M & W; Softball W; Tennis M & W; Track and Field M & W; Volleyball W; Wrestling M

RHODE ISLAND SCHOOL OF DESIGN

2 College St.
Providence, RI 02903-2784
Tel: (401)454-6100
Free: 800-364-7473
Admissions: (401)454-6307
Fax: (401)454-6309
E-mail: admissions@risd.edu
Web Site: http://www.risd.edu/
President/CEO: Roger Mandle
Registrar: Steven Berenback
Admissions: Edward Newhall
Financial Aid: Peter Riefler
Type: Comprehensive **Sex:** Coed **Scores:** 98.7% SAT V 400+; 99.4% SAT M 400+ **% Accepted:** 35 **Admission Plans:** Early Admission; Early Action; Deferred Admission **Application Deadline:** February 15 **Application Fee:** $50.00 **H.S. Requirements:** High school diploma required; GED accepted **Costs Per Year:** Application fee: $50. Comprehensive fee: $40,740 includes full-time tuition ($31,145), mandatory fees ($235), and college room and board ($9360). College room only: $5260. **Scholarships:** Available **Calendar System:** 4-1-4, Summer Session Not available **Enrollment:** FT 1,878, Grad 380 **Faculty:** FT 139, PT 355 **Student-Faculty Ratio:** 9:1 **Exams:** SAT I or ACT **% Receiving Financial Aid:** 48 **% Residing in College-Owned, -Operated, or -Affiliated Housing:** 40 **Library Holdings:** 107,436 **Regional Accreditation:** New England Association of Schools and Colleges **Credit Hours For Degree:** 126 credits, Bachelors **Professional Accreditation:** ASLA, NASAD

ROGER WILLIAMS UNIVERSITY

1 Old Ferry Rd.
Bristol, RI 02809
Tel: (401)253-1040
Free: 800-458-7144
Admissions: (401)254-3500
Fax: (401)254-3557
E-mail: admit@alpha.rwu.edu
Web Site: http://www.rwu.edu/

President/CEO: Dr. Roy J. Nirschel
Registrar: Daniel Vilenski
Admissions: Lynn Fawthrop
Financial Aid: Tracey M. DaCosta
Type: Comprehensive **Sex:** Coed **Scores:** 99.6% SAT V 400+; 99.2% SAT M 400+; 47.4% ACT 18-23; 48.7% ACT 24-29 **% Accepted:** 78 **Admission Plans:** Early Decision Plan; Deferred Admission **Application Deadline:** Rolling **Application Fee:** $50.00 **H.S. Requirements:** High school diploma required; GED accepted **Costs Per Year:** Application fee: $50. Comprehensive fee: $34,759 includes full-time tuition ($22,932), mandatory fees ($1134), and college room and board ($10,693). College room only: $5569. Part-time tuition: $956 per credit. **Scholarships:** Available **Calendar System:** Semester, Summer Session Available **Enrollment:** FT 3,741, PT 618, Grad 246 **Faculty:** FT 178, PT 220 **Student-Faculty Ratio:** 16:1 **Exams:** SAT I or ACT **% Receiving Financial Aid:** 63 **% Residing in College-Owned, -Operated, or -Affiliated Housing:** 79 **Library Holdings:** 202,495 **Regional Accreditation:** New England Association of Schools and Colleges **Credit Hours For Degree:** 60 credits, Associates; 120 credits, Bachelors **ROTC:** Army **Professional Accreditation:** ABET, ABA, ACCE **Intercollegiate Athletics:** Baseball M; Basketball M & W; Cheerleading W; Crew M & W; Cross-Country Running M & W; Equestrian Sports M & W; Lacrosse M & W; Rugby M; Sailing M & W; Soccer M & W; Softball W; Swimming and Diving M & W; Tennis M & W; Track and Field M & W; Volleyball M & W; Wrestling M

SALVE REGINA UNIVERSITY
100 Ochre Point Ave.
Newport, RI 02840-4192
Tel: (401)847-6650; 888-GO SALVE
Fax: (401)848-2823
E-mail: sruadmis@salve.edu
Web Site: http://www.salve.edu/
President/CEO: Dr. M. Therese Antone, RSM
Registrar: Dr. James Terry
Admissions: Laura McPhie Oliveira
Financial Aid: Aida Mirante
Type: Comprehensive **Sex:** Coed **Affiliation:** Roman Catholic **Scores:** 100% SAT V 400+; 100% SAT M 400+; 48% ACT 18-23; 46% ACT 24-29 **% Accepted:** 60 **Admission Plans:** Early Action; Deferred Admission **Application Deadline:** March 01 **Application Fee:** $40.00 **H.S. Requirements:** High school diploma required; GED accepted **Costs Per Year:** Application fee: $40. Comprehensive fee: $33,450 includes full-time tuition ($23,500), mandatory fees ($450), and college room and board ($9500). Room and board charges vary according to board plan. Part-time tuition: $783 per credit. Part-time mandatory fees: $40 per term. Part-time tuition and fees vary according to course load. **Scholarships:** Available **Calendar System:** Semester, Summer Session Available **Enrollment:** FT 1,987, PT 104, Grad 408 **Faculty:** FT 122, PT 118 **Student-Faculty Ratio:** 14:1 **Exams:** SAT I or ACT **% Receiving Financial Aid:** 62 **% Residing in College-Owned, -Operated, or -Affiliated Housing:** 60 **Library Holdings:** 139,161 **Regional Accreditation:** New England Association of Schools and Colleges **Credit Hours For Degree:** 64 credit hours, Associates; 128 credit hours, Bachelors **ROTC:** Army **Professional Accreditation:** CORE, CSWE, NASAD, NLN **Intercollegiate Athletics:** Baseball M; Basketball M & W; Cross-Country Running W; Equestrian Sports M & W; Field Hockey W; Football M; Golf M & W; Ice Hockey M & W; Lacrosse M & W; Rugby M; Sailing M & W; Soccer M & W; Softball W; Tennis W; Track and Field W; Volleyball W

UNIVERSITY OF RHODE ISLAND
Kingston, RI 02881
Tel: (401)874-1000
Admissions: (401)874-7100
Fax: (401)874-5523
E-mail: uriadmit@riacc.uri.edu
Web Site: http://www.uri.edu
President/CEO: Dr. Robert L. Carothers
Registrar: Harry Amaral
Admissions: David G. Taggart
Type: University **Sex:** Coed **Affiliation:** Rhode Island State System of Higher Education **Scores:** 99.4% SAT V 400+; 99.8% SAT M 400+ **% Accepted:** 77 **Admission Plans:** Preferred Admission; Early Admission; Early Action **Application Deadline:** February 01 **Application Fee:** $50.00 **H.S. Requirements:** High school diploma required; GED accepted **Costs Per Year:** Application fee: $50. State resident tuition: $5258 full-time, $219 per credit part-time. Nonresident tuition: $17,900 full-time, $746 per credit part-time. Mandatory fees: $2026 full-time, $74 per credit part-time, $48 per term part-time. Full-time tuition and fees vary according to reciprocity agreements. Part-time tuition and fees vary according to reciprocity agreements. College room and board: $8114. College room only: $4620. Room and board charges vary according to board plan and housing facility. **Scholarships:** Available **Calendar System:** Semester, Summer Session Available **Enrollment:** FT 9,766, PT 1,780, Grad 2,996 **Faculty:** FT 668, PT 23 **Student-Faculty Ratio:** 19:1 **Exams:** SAT I or ACT **% Receiving Financial Aid:** 51 **% Residing in College-Owned, -Operated, or -Affiliated Housing:** 39 **Library Holdings:** 1,205,138 **Regional Accreditation:** New England Association of Schools and Colleges **Credit Hours For Degree:** 120 credits, Bachelors **ROTC:** Army **Professional Accreditation:** AACSB, ABET, AAMFT, AACN, ACNM, ACPhE, ADtA, ACSP, ALA, APTA, APA, ASLA, ASLHA, NASM, NCATE **Intercollegiate Athletics:** Baseball M; Basketball M & W; Crew M & W; Cross-Country Running M & W; Equestrian Sports M & W; Fencing M & W; Field Hockey W; Football M; Golf M; Gymnastics W; Ice Hockey M; Lacrosse M & W; Rugby M & W; Sailing M & W; Skiing (Downhill) M & W; Soccer M & W; Softball W; Swimming and Diving M & W; Tennis M & W; Track and Field M & W; Volleyball M & W; Water Polo M

ZION BIBLE INSTITUTE
27 Middle Hwy.
Barrington, RI 02806
Tel: (401)246-0900
Free: 800-356-4014
Fax: (401)246-0906
Web Site: http://www.zbi.edu/
President/CEO: George Cope
Type: Four-Year College **Sex:** Coed **Affiliation:** Assembly of God Church **Application Fee:** $35.00 **Costs Per Year:** Application fee: $35. Comprehensive fee: $10,922 includes full-time tuition ($5842), mandatory fees ($480), and college room and board ($4600). College room only: $3200. **Calendar System:** Semester **Professional Accreditation:** AABC

AIKEN TECHNICAL COLLEGE
PO Drawer 696
Aiken, SC 29802-0696
Tel: (803)593-9231
E-mail: pridepae@atc.edu
Web Site: http://www.aik.tec.sc.us/
President/CEO: Susan A. Graham
Registrar: Dr. James Schmidt
Admissions: Evelyn Pride Patterson
Financial Aid: John Garrison
Type: Two-Year College **Sex:** Coed **Affiliation:** South Carolina State Board for Technical and Comprehensive Education **% Accepted:** 65 **Admission Plans:** Open Admission; Deferred Admission **Application Deadline:** Rolling **Application Fee:** $0.00 **H.S. Requirements:** High school diploma required; GED accepted **Costs Per Year:** Application fee: $0. Area resident tuition: $2816 full-time, $117 per credit hour part-time. State resident tuition: $3176 full-time, $132 per credit hour part-time. Nonresident tuition: $8204 full-time, $337 per credit hour part-time. Mandatory fees: $120 full-time, $4.25 per credit hour part-time, $60 per term part-time. **Scholarships:** Available **Calendar System:** Semester, Summer Session Available **Enrollment:** FT 1,397, PT 1,119 **Faculty:** FT 55, PT 109 **Library Holdings:** 32,118 **Regional Accreditation:** Southern Association of Colleges and Schools **Credit Hours For Degree:** 64 semester hours, Associates **Professional Accreditation:** ABET, ADA, ACBSP **Intercollegiate Athletics:** Basketball M

ALLEN UNIVERSITY
1530 Harden St.
Columbia, SC 29204
Tel: (803)254-4165
Admissions: (803)376-5789
Fax: (803)376-5731
Web Site: http://www.allenuniversity.edu/
President/CEO: Dr. Charles E. Young
Registrar: Nathan Vereen
Admissions: Kristy J. Sinkfield
Financial Aid: Antonia Roberts
Type: Four-Year College **Sex:** Coed **Affiliation:** African Methodist Episcopal **Admission Plans:** Open Admission **Application Fee:** $20.00 **H.S. Requirements:** High school diploma required; GED not accepted **Costs Per Year:** Application fee: $20. Comprehensive fee: $6260 includes full-time tuition ($3609), mandatory fees ($546), and college room and board ($2105). College room only: $1230. Part-time tuition: $301 per credit hour. **Scholarships:** Available **Calendar System:** Semester, Summer Session Available **Enrollment:** FT 552, PT 13 **Faculty:** FT 25, PT 14 **Student-Faculty Ratio:** 10:1 **Exams:** SAT I or ACT **% Receiving Financial Aid:** 80 **% Residing in College-Owned, -Operated, or -Affiliated Housing:** 80 **Library Holdings:** 50,000 **Regional Accreditation:** Southern Association of Colleges and Schools **Credit Hours For Degree:** 128 credit hours, Bachelors **ROTC:** Army **Intercollegiate Athletics:** Basketball M & W; Football M; Volleyball W

ANDERSON UNIVERSITY
316 Blvd.
Anderson, SC 29621-4035
Tel: (864)231-2000
Free: 800-542-3594
Admissions: (864)231-2030
Fax: (864)231-2004
E-mail: admissions@anderson-college.edu
Web Site: http://www.ac.edu/
President/CEO: Dr. Evans P. Whitaker
Registrar: Lisa Thompson
Admissions: Pam Bryant
Financial Aid: Jeff Holliday
Type: Four-Year College **Sex:** Coed **Affiliation:** Baptist **Scores:** 95.7% SAT V 400+; 96.9% SAT M 400+; 65.2% ACT 18-23; 21.4% ACT 24-29 **% Accepted:** 78 **Admission Plans:** Deferred Admission **Application Deadline:** July 01 **Application Fee:** $25.00 **H.S. Requirements:** High school diploma required; GED accepted **Costs Per Year:** Application fee: $25. Comprehensive fee: $22,950 includes full-time tuition ($15,400), mandatory fees ($1150), and college room and board ($6400). College room only: $3250. Part-time tuition: $410 per credit hour. **Scholarships:** Available **Calendar System:** Semester, Summer Session Available **Enrollment:** FT 1,277, PT 367 **Faculty:** FT 68, PT 82 **Student-Faculty Ratio:** 15:1 **Exams:** SAT I or ACT **% Receiving Financial Aid:** 86 **% Residing in College-Owned, -Operated, or -Affiliated Housing:** 50 **Library Holdings:** 69,069 **Regional Accreditation:** Southern Association of Colleges and Schools **Credit Hours For Degree:** 128 semester hours, Bachelors **ROTC:** Army, Air Force **Professional Accreditation:** NASM, NCATE **Intercollegiate Athletics:** Baseball M; Basketball M & W; Cheerleading W; Cross-Country Running M & W; Equestrian Sports M & W; Golf M & W; Soccer M & W; Softball W; Tennis M & W; Track and Field M & W; Volleyball W; Wrestling M

BENEDICT COLLEGE
1600 Harden St.
Columbia, SC 29204
Tel: (803)256-4220
Admissions: (803)253-5275
Fax: (803)253-5167
Web Site: http://www.benedict.edu/
President/CEO: Dr. David H. Swinton
Registrar: Wanda Scott-Kinney
Admissions: Gary Knight
Financial Aid: Sul M. Black
Type: Four-Year College **Sex:** Coed **Affiliation:** Baptist **Scores:** 44.31% SAT V 400+; 46.35% SAT M 400+; 11.46% ACT 18-23 **Admission Plans:** Open Admission; Early Admission; Deferred Admission **Application Fee:** $25.00 **H.S. Requirements:** High school diploma required; GED accepted **Costs Per Year:** Application fee: $25. Comprehensive fee: $18,912 includes full-time tuition ($11,574), mandatory fees ($1380), and college room and board ($5958). Part-time tuition: $388 per credit hour. Part-time mandatory fees: $45 per credit hour. **Scholarships:** Available **Calendar System:** Semester, Summer Session Available **Enrollment:** FT 2,864, PT 141 **Faculty:** FT 127, PT 41 **Student-Faculty Ratio:** 19:1 **Exams:** SAT I or ACT **% Residing in College-Owned, -Operated, or -Affiliated Housing:** 66 **Library Holdings:** 114,770 **Regional Accreditation:** Southern Association of Colleges and Schools **Credit Hours For Degree:** 125 semester hours, Bachelors **ROTC:** Army, Air Force **Professional Accreditation:** CSWE, NCATE **Intercollegiate Athletics:** Baseball M; Basketball M & W;

Cheerleading W; Cross-Country Running M & W; Football M; Golf M; Softball W; Tennis M; Track and Field M; Volleyball W

BOB JONES UNIVERSITY
1700 Wade Hampton Blvd.
Greenville, SC 29614
Tel: (803)242-5100
Free: 800-BJA-NDME
Admissions: (864)242-5100
E-mail: admissions@bju.edu
Web Site: http://www.bju.edu/
Admissions: David Christ
Type: University **Sex:** Coed **Scores:** 46% ACT 18-23; 39% ACT 24-29 **% Accepted:** 82 **Application Deadline:** August 01 **Application Fee:** $45.00 **Costs Per Year:** Application fee: $45. Comprehensive fee: $14,750 includes full-time tuition ($9180), mandatory fees ($590), and college room and board ($4980). Part-time tuition: $459 per credit hour. **Calendar System:** Semester **Enrollment:** FT 3,523, PT 52, Grad 524 **Faculty:** FT 235, PT 67 **Student-Faculty Ratio:** 15:1 **Exams:** ACT

CENTRAL CAROLINA TECHNICAL COLLEGE
506 North Guignard Dr.
Sumter, SC 29150-2499
Tel: (803)778-1961
Free: 800-221-8711
Fax: (803)773-4859
E-mail: brackenlm@cctech.edu
Web Site: http://www.cctech.edu/
President/CEO: Dr. Kay Raffield
Registrar: Mary Agnes White
Admissions: Lisa M. Bracken
Financial Aid: Bill Whitlock
Type: Two-Year College **Sex:** Coed **Affiliation:** South Carolina State Board for Technical and Comprehensive Education **Admission Plans:** Open Admission **Application Deadline:** Rolling **Application Fee:** $25.00 **H.S. Requirements:** High school diploma required; GED accepted. For nursing programs: High school diploma required; GED not accepted **Costs Per Year:** Application fee: $25. Area resident tuition: $2700 full-time, $112.50 per credit hour part-time. State resident tuition: $3168 full-time, $132.50 per credit hour part-time. Nonresident tuition: $4800 full-time, $200 per credit hour part-time. **Scholarships:** Available **Calendar System:** Semester, Summer Session Available **Enrollment:** FT 945, PT 2,299 **Faculty:** FT 82, PT 98 **Student-Faculty Ratio:** 19:1 **Library Holdings:** 20,356 **Regional Accreditation:** Southern Association of Colleges and Schools **Credit Hours For Degree:** 60 semester hours, Associates **Professional Accreditation:** ABET, ACBSP, NLN

CHARLESTON SOUTHERN UNIVERSITY
PO Box 118087
Charleston, SC 29423-8087
Tel: (843)863-7000
Free: 800-947-7474
Admissions: (843)863-7050
E-mail: enroll@csuniv.edu
Web Site: http://www.charlestonsouthern.edu/
President/CEO: Dr. Jairy C. Hunter, Jr.
Registrar: Rex Nestor
Admissions: Kathryn LaCross
Financial Aid: Cheryl Burton
Type: Comprehensive **Sex:** Coed **Affiliation:** Baptist **Scores:** 92.94% SAT V 400+; 92.37% SAT M 400+; 60.94% ACT 18-23; 14.7% ACT 24-29 **% Accepted:** 71 **Application Deadline:** Rolling **Application Fee:** $30.00 **H.S. Requirements:** High school diploma required; GED accepted **Costs Per Year:** Application fee: $30. Comprehensive fee: $23,230 includes full-time tuition ($16,780) and college room and board ($6450). Part-time tuition: $271 per credit hour. **Scholarships:** Available **Calendar System:** Miscellaneous, Summer Session Available **Enrollment:** FT 2,208, PT 374, Grad 440 **Faculty:** FT 106, PT 72 **Student-Faculty Ratio:** 18:1 **Exams:** SAT I or ACT **% Receiving Financial Aid:** 66 **% Residing in College-Owned, -Operated, or -Affiliated Housing:** 46 **Library Holdings:** 192,600 **Regional Accreditation:** Southern Association of Colleges and Schools **Credit Hours For Degree:** 62 credit hours, Associates; 125 credit hours, Bachelors **ROTC:** Air Force **Professional Accreditation:** NASM, NCATE, NLN **Intercollegiate Athletics:** Baseball M; Basketball M & W; Cheerleading M & W; Cross-Country Running M & W; Football M; Golf M & W; Soccer W; Softball W; Tennis M & W; Track and Field M & W; Volleyball W

THE CITADEL, THE MILITARY COLLEGE OF SOUTH CAROLINA
171 Moultrie St.
Charleston, SC 29409
Tel: (843)953-5000
Free: 800-868-1842
Admissions: (843)953-5230
Fax: (843)953-7084
E-mail: john.powell@citadel.edu
Web Site: http://www.citadel.edu
President/CEO: Maj. Gen. John S. Grinalds
Registrar: Maj. Sylvia Nesmith
Admissions: Lt. Col. John Powell
Financial Aid: Lt. Col. Henry M. Fuller, Jr.
Type: Comprehensive **Sex:** Coed **Scores:** 99.4% SAT V 400+; 99.8% SAT M 400+; 66.3% ACT 18-23; 27.6% ACT 24-29 **% Accepted:** 78 **Admission Plans:** Preferred Admission **Application Deadline:** Rolling **Application Fee:** $40.00 **H.S. Requirements:** High school diploma required; GED accepted **Costs Per Year:** Application fee: $40. State resident tuition: $6522 full-time, $198 per credit hour part-time. Nonresident tuition: $15,918 full-time, $397 per credit hour part-time. Mandatory fees: $998 full-time, $15 per term part-time. College room and board: $4840. **Scholarships:** Available **Calendar System:** Semester, Summer Session Available **Enrollment:** FT 2,111, PT 127, Grad 1,148 **Faculty:** FT 157, PT 75 **Student-Faculty Ratio:** 15:1 **Exams:** SAT I or ACT **% Receiving Financial Aid:** 49 **% Residing in College-Owned, -Operated, or -Affiliated Housing:** 100 **Library Holdings:** 233,745 **Regional Accreditation:** Southern Association of Colleges and Schools **ROTC:** Army, Navy, Air Force **Professional Accreditation:** AACSB, ABET, NCATE **Intercollegiate Athletics:** Baseball M; Basketball M; Crew M & W; Cross-Country Running M & W; Football M; Golf M & W; Ice Hockey M & W; Lacrosse M & W; Riflery M & W; Rugby M & W; Sailing M & W; Soccer M & W; Tennis M; Track and Field M & W; Volleyball M & W; Weight Lifting M & W; Wrestling M

CLAFLIN UNIVERSITY
400 Magnolia St.
Orangeburg, SC 29115
Tel: (803)535-5097
Admissions: (803)535-5340
Fax: (803)531-2860
E-mail: mzeigler@claflin.edu
Web Site: http://www.claflin.edu/
President/CEO: Dr. Henry N. Tisdale
Registrar: Kathryn Boyd
Admissions: Michael Zeigler
Financial Aid: Delores Cooper
Type: Comprehensive **Sex:** Coed **Affiliation:** United Methodist **Scores:** 83% SAT V 400+; 75% SAT M 400+ **% Accepted:** 40 **Admission Plans:** Deferred Admission **Application Deadline:** Rolling **Application Fee:** $20.00 **H.S. Requirements:** High school diploma required; GED accepted **Costs Per Year:** Application fee: $20. Comprehensive fee: $16,798 includes full-time tuition ($9206), mandatory fees ($1684), and college room and board ($5908). College room only: $2632. Room and board charges vary according to housing facility. Part-time tuition: $384 per credit hour. Part-time mandatory fees: $63 per credit hour. **Scholarships:** Available **Calendar System:** Semester, Summer Session Available **Enrollment:** FT 1,598, PT 80, Grad 50 **Faculty:** FT 93, PT 34 **Student-Faculty Ratio:** 14:1 **Exams:** SAT I or ACT, SAT II **% Residing in College-Owned, -Operated, or -Affiliated Housing:** 65 **Library Holdings:** 158,108 **Regional Accreditation:** Southern Association of Colleges and Schools **Credit Hours For Degree:** 124 semester hours, Bachelors **ROTC:** Army **Professional Accreditation:** ACBSP, NCATE **Intercollegiate Athletics:** Baseball M; Basketball M & W; Cross-Country Running M & W; Softball W; Tennis M & W; Track and Field M & W; Volleyball W

CLEMSON UNIVERSITY
Clemson, SC 29634
Tel: (864)656-3311
Admissions: (864)656-2287
Fax: (864)656-2464
Web Site: http://www.clemson.edu/
President/CEO: Dr. James F. Barker
Registrar: Stanley B. Smith

Admissions: Robert S. Barkley
Financial Aid: Marvin G. Carmichael
Type: University **Sex:** Coed **Scores:** 100% SAT V 400+; 100% SAT M 400+; 18% ACT 18-23; 61% ACT 24-29 **% Accepted:** 57 **Admission Plans:** Preferred Admission **Application Deadline:** May 01 **Application Fee:** $50.00 **H.S. Requirements:** High school diploma required; GED accepted **Costs Per Year:** Application fee: $50. State resident tuition: $9016 full-time, $364 per hour part-time. Nonresident tuition: $18,640 full-time, $760 per hour part-time. Full-time tuition varies according to course load and program. Part-time tuition varies according to course load and program. College room and board: $5780. College room only: $3470. Room and board charges vary according to board plan and housing facility. **Scholarships:** Available **Calendar System:** Semester, Summer Session Available **Enrollment:** FT 13,257, PT 839, Grad 3,069 **Faculty:** FT 1,015, PT 128 **Student-Faculty Ratio:** 16:1 **Exams:** SAT I or ACT **% Receiving Financial Aid:** 38 **% Residing in College-Owned, -Operated, or -Affiliated Housing:** 47 **Library Holdings:** 1,233,478 **Regional Accreditation:** Southern Association of Colleges and Schools **Credit Hours For Degree:** 128 hours, Bachelors **ROTC:** Army, Air Force **Professional Accreditation:** AACSB, ABET, ACCE, ACA, ADtA, ACSP, ASLA, NASAD, NCATE, NLN, NRPA, SAF **Intercollegiate Athletics:** Baseball M; Basketball M & W; Bowling M & W; Cheerleading M & W; Crew M & W; Cross-Country Running M & W; Equestrian Sports M & W; Fencing M & W; Field Hockey M & W; Football M; Golf M; Ice Hockey M & W; Lacrosse M & W; Riflery M & W; Rugby M & W; Sailing M & W; Soccer M & W; Softball W; Swimming and Diving M & W; Tennis M & W; Track and Field M & W; Ultimate Frisbee M & W; Volleyball M & W; Weight Lifting M & W; Wrestling M

CLINTON JUNIOR COLLEGE
PO Box 968, 1029 Crawford Rd.
Rock Hill, SC 29730
Tel: (803)327-7402
Fax: (803)327-3261
E-mail: ecopeland@clintonjrcollege.org
Web Site: http://www.clintonjuniorcollege.edu/
President/CEO: Dr. Janis Pen
Admissions: Dr. Janis Pen
Type: Two-Year College **Sex:** Coed **Affiliation:** African Methodist Episcopal Zion Church **Calendar System:** Semester **Professional Accreditation:** TACCS

COASTAL CAROLINA UNIVERSITY
PO Box 261954
Conway, SC 29528-6054
Tel: (843)347-3161
Free: 800-277-7000
Admissions: (843)349-2037
Fax: (843)349-2127
E-mail: admissions@coastal.edu
Web Site: http://www.coastal.edu/
President/CEO: Dr. Ronald R. Ingle
Registrar: Brenda Sawyer
Admissions: Dr. Judy Vogt
Financial Aid: Glenn Hanson
Type: Comprehensive **Sex:** Coed **Scores:** 99% SAT V 400+; 100% SAT M 400+; 75% ACT 18-23; 23% ACT 24-29 **% Accepted:** 74 **Admission Plans:** Preferred Admission; Deferred Admission **Application Deadline:** August 15 **Application Fee:** $45.00 **H.S. Requirements:** High school diploma required; GED accepted **Costs Per Year:** Application fee: $45. State resident tuition: $6780 full-time, $290 per credit hour part-time. Nonresident tuition: $15,020 full-time, $630 per credit hour part-time. Mandatory fees: $80 full-time. Full-time tuition and fees vary according to course load. Part-time tuition varies according to course load. College room and board: $6280. College room only: $4020. Room and board charges vary according to board plan and housing facility. **Scholarships:** Available **Calendar System:** Semester, Summer Session Available **Enrollment:** FT 5,753, PT 644, Grad 1,216 **Faculty:** FT 233, PT 181 **Student-Faculty Ratio:** 19:1 **Exams:** SAT I or ACT **% Receiving Financial Aid:** 66 **% Residing in College-Owned, -Operated, or -Affiliated Housing:** 34 **Library Holdings:** 144,361 **Regional Accreditation:** Southern Association of Colleges and Schools **Credit Hours For Degree:** 120 semester hours, Bachelors **Professional Accreditation:** AACSB, ABET, NASAD, NCATE **Intercollegiate Athletics:** Baseball M; Basketball M & W; Cheerleading M & W; Cross-Country Running M & W; Football M; Golf M & W; Soccer M & W; Softball W; Tennis M & W; Track and Field M & W; Volleyball W

COKER COLLEGE
300 East College Ave.
Hartsville, SC 29550
Tel: (843)383-8000
Free: 800-950-1908
Admissions: (843)383-8050
Fax: (843)383-8056
E-mail: admissions@coker.edu
Web Site: http://www.coker.edu/
President/CEO: Dr. B. James Dawson
Registrar: Bobb E. Riggs
Admissions: Perry Wilson
Financial Aid: Betty Williams
Type: Four-Year College **Sex:** Coed **Scores:** 91% SAT V 400+; 92% SAT M 400+; 63% ACT 18-23; 10% ACT 24-29 **% Accepted:** 66 **Admission Plans:** Deferred Admission **Application Deadline:** Rolling **Application Fee:** $15.00 **H.S. Requirements:** High school diploma required; GED accepted **Costs Per Year:** Application fee: $15. Comprehensive fee: $23,728 includes full-time tuition ($17,472), mandatory fees ($480), and college room and board ($5776). College room only: $2740. Part-time tuition: $728 per semester hour. **Scholarships:** Available **Calendar System:** Semester, Summer Session Available **Enrollment:** FT 541, PT 10 **Faculty:** FT 55, PT 10 **Student-Faculty Ratio:** 9:1 **Exams:** SAT I or ACT **% Receiving Financial Aid:** 84 **% Residing in College-Owned, -Operated, or -Affiliated Housing:** 70 **Library Holdings:** 78,706 **Regional Accreditation:** Southern Association of Colleges and Schools **Credit Hours For Degree:** 120 semester hours, Bachelors **Professional Accreditation:** NASM **Intercollegiate Athletics:** Baseball M; Basketball M & W; Cheerleading M & W; Cross-Country Running M & W; Golf M; Soccer M & W; Softball W; Tennis M & W; Volleyball W

COLLEGE OF CHARLESTON
66 George St.
Charleston, SC 29424-0001
Tel: (843)953-5507
Admissions: (843)953-5670
E-mail: admissions@cofc.edu
Web Site: http://www.cofc.edu/
President/CEO: Leo Higdon
Registrar: Pamela Anastassion
Admissions: Suzette Stille
Financial Aid: Donald Griggs
Type: Comprehensive **Sex:** Coed **Scores:** 100% SAT V 400+; 100% SAT M 400+; 48.9% ACT 18-23; 49.7% ACT 24-29 **% Accepted:** 66 **Admission Plans:** Early Admission; Early Action; Deferred Admission **Application Deadline:** April 01 **Application Fee:** $45.00 **H.S. Requirements:** High school diploma required; GED accepted **Costs Per Year:** Application fee: $45. State resident tuition: $6668 full-time, $278 per semester hour part-time. Nonresident tuition: $15,342 full-time, $639 per semester hour part-time. Part-time tuition varies according to course load. College room and board: $6948. College room only: $4768. Room and board charges vary according to board plan and housing facility. **Scholarships:** Available **Calendar System:** Semester, Summer Session Available **Enrollment:** FT 9,055, PT 823, Grad 1,454 **Faculty:** FT 515, PT 343 **Student-Faculty Ratio:** 13:1 **Exams:** SAT I or ACT **% Receiving Financial Aid:** 37 **% Residing in College-Owned, -Operated, or -Affiliated Housing:** 29 **Library Holdings:** 476,108 **Regional Accreditation:** Southern Association of Colleges and Schools **Credit Hours For Degree:** 122 semester hours, Bachelors **ROTC:** Air Force **Professional Accreditation:** AACSB, ABET, JRCEPAT, NASM, NASPAA, NCATE **Intercollegiate Athletics:** Baseball M; Basketball M & W; Cross-Country Running M & W; Equestrian Sports W; Golf M & W; Sailing M & W; Soccer M & W; Softball W; Swimming and Diving M & W; Tennis M & W; Volleyball W

COLUMBIA COLLEGE
1301 Columbia College Dr.
Columbia, SC 29203-5998
Tel: (803)786-3012
Free: 800-277-1301
Admissions: (803)786-3091
Fax: (803)786-3674
E-mail: admissions@colacoll.edu
Web Site: http://www.columbiacollegesc.edu/
President/CEO: Dr. Caroline Whitson
Admissions: Dr. Ronald G. White

Financial Aid: Anita Kaminer Elliott
Type: Comprehensive **Affiliation:** United Methodist **Scores:** 89.5% SAT V 400+; 94.23% SAT M 400+; 59.63% ACT 18-23; 22.94% ACT 24-29 **% Accepted:** 84 **Application Deadline:** August 01 **Application Fee:** $25.00 **H.S. Requirements:** High school diploma required; GED accepted **Costs Per Year:** Application fee: $25. Comprehensive fee: $25,032 includes full-time tuition ($18,864), mandatory fees ($350), and college room and board ($5818). College room only: $3034. Full-time tuition and fees vary according to class time. Room and board charges vary according to board plan and housing facility. Part-time tuition: $506 per credit hour. Part-time tuition varies according to course load. **Scholarships:** Available **Calendar System:** Semester, Summer Session Available **Enrollment:** FT 867, PT 241, Grad 385 **Faculty:** FT 82, PT 72 **Student-Faculty Ratio:** 10:1 **Exams:** SAT I or ACT **% Receiving Financial Aid:** 78 **% Residing in College-Owned, -Operated, or -Affiliated Housing:** 63 **Library Holdings:** 140,909 **Regional Accreditation:** Southern Association of Colleges and Schools **Credit Hours For Degree:** 127 credits, Bachelors **ROTC:** Army, Navy, Air Force **Professional Accreditation:** CSWE, NASAD, NASD, NASM, NCATE **Intercollegiate Athletics:** Basketball W; Soccer W; Tennis W; Volleyball W

COLUMBIA INTERNATIONAL UNIVERSITY
PO Box 3122
Columbia, SC 29230-3122
Tel: (803)754-4100
Free: 800-777-2227
Fax: (803)786-4209
E-mail: yesciu@ciu.edu
Web Site: http://www.ciu.edu/
President/CEO: Dr. George W. Murray
Registrar: Wanda Burch
Admissions: Michelle MacGregor
Financial Aid: Mary Bisesi
Type: Comprehensive **Sex:** Coed **Affiliation:** nondenominational **Scores:** 89% SAT V 400+; 96% SAT M 400+; 42% ACT 18-23; 46% ACT 24-29 **% Accepted:** 67 **Admission Plans:** Deferred Admission **Application Deadline:** Rolling **Application Fee:** $45.00 **H.S. Requirements:** High school diploma required; GED accepted **Costs Per Year:** Application fee: $45. Comprehensive fee: $20,592 includes full-time tuition ($14,880) and college room and board ($5712). Part-time tuition: $600 per semester hour. **Scholarships:** Available **Calendar System:** Semester, Summer Session Available **Enrollment:** FT 496, PT 54, Grad 327 **Faculty:** FT 23, PT 25 **Student-Faculty Ratio:** 18:1 **Exams:** SAT I or ACT **% Receiving Financial Aid:** 75 **% Residing in College-Owned, -Operated, or -Affiliated Housing:** 59 **Library Holdings:** 118,752 **Regional Accreditation:** Southern Association of Colleges and Schools **Credit Hours For Degree:** 63 semester hours, Associates; 128 semester hours, Bachelors **Professional Accreditation:** AABC, ATS

CONVERSE COLLEGE
580 East Main St.
Spartanburg, SC 29302-0006
Tel: (864)596-9000
Free: 800-766-1125
Admissions: (864)596-9040
Fax: (864)596-9158
E-mail: aaron.meis@converse.edu
Web Site: http://www.converse.edu/
President/CEO: Nancy O. Gray
Registrar: Mary Brown
Admissions: Aaron Meis
Financial Aid: Peggy Collins
Type: Comprehensive **Scores:** 97% SAT V 400+; 99% SAT M 400+; 47% ACT 18-23; 41% ACT 24-29 **% Accepted:** 84 **Admission Plans:** Early Admission; Early Action; Early Decision Plan; Deferred Admission **Application Deadline:** April 01 **Application Fee:** $40.00 **H.S. Requirements:** High school diploma required; GED accepted **Costs Per Year:** Application fee: $40. Comprehensive fee: $29,082 includes full-time tuition ($22,234) and college room and board ($6848). Part-time tuition: $720 per credit hour. Part-time mandatory fees: $20 per term. **Scholarships:** Available **Calendar System:** 4-1-4, Summer Session Available **Enrollment:** FT 648, PT 128, Grad 1,400 **Faculty:** FT 83, PT 90 **Student-Faculty Ratio:** 12:1 **Exams:** SAT I or ACT **% Receiving Financial Aid:** 71 **% Residing in College-Owned, -Operated, or -Affiliated Housing:** 90 **Library Holdings:** 129,411 **Regional Accreditation:** Southern Association of Colleges and Schools **Credit Hours For Degree:** 120 credit hours, Bachelors **ROTC:** Army **Professional Accreditation:** AAMFT, NASM **Intercollegiate Athletics:** Basketball W; Cheerleading W; Cross-Country Running W; Soccer W; Tennis W; Volleyball W

DENMARK TECHNICAL COLLEGE
Solomon Blatt Blvd., Box 327
Denmark, SC 29042-0327
Tel: (803)793-5100
Admissions: (803)793-5176
Fax: (803)793-5942
Web Site: http://www.denmarktech.edu/
President/CEO: Dr. Joann R. G. Boyd-Scotland
Admissions: Michelle McDowell
Financial Aid: Clara B. Moses
Type: Two-Year College **Sex:** Coed **Affiliation:** South Carolina State Board for Technical and Comprehensive Education **% Accepted:** 100 **Admission Plans:** Open Admission; Early Admission; Deferred Admission **Application Deadline:** Rolling **Application Fee:** $10.00 **H.S. Requirements:** High school diploma required; GED accepted **Costs Per Year:** Application fee: $10. State resident tuition: $2088 full-time, $87 per credit hour part-time. Nonresident tuition: $4176 full-time, $174 per credit hour part-time. Mandatory fees: $190 full-time, $95 per term part-time. College room and board: $3096. **Scholarships:** Available **Calendar System:** Semester, Summer Session Available **Enrollment:** FT 969, PT 439 **Faculty:** FT 30, PT 17 **Student-Faculty Ratio:** 19:1 **Exams:** Other **Library Holdings:** 15,437 **Regional Accreditation:** Southern Association of Colleges and Schools **Credit Hours For Degree:** 60 credit hours, Associates **ROTC:** Army **Professional Accreditation:** ABET, ACBSP **Intercollegiate Athletics:** Baseball M; Basketball M & W; Softball W

ERSKINE COLLEGE
2 Washington St.
PO Box 338
Due West, SC 29639
Tel: (864)379-2131
Free: 800-241-8721
Admissions: (864)379-8830
Fax: (864)379-8759
E-mail: admissions@erskine.edu
Web Site: http://www.erskine.edu/
President/CEO: Dr. John L. Carson
Registrar: Charlene Haynes
Admissions: Bart Walker
Financial Aid: Rebecca Pressley
Type: Four-Year College **Sex:** Coed **Affiliation:** Associate Reformed Presbyterian Church; Erskine Theological Seminary **Scores:** 98% SAT V 400+; 99% SAT M 400+; 45% ACT 18-23; 39% ACT 24-29 **% Accepted:** 70 **Admission Plans:** Preferred Admission **Application Deadline:** Rolling **Application Fee:** $25.00 **H.S. Requirements:** High school diploma required; GED accepted **Costs Per Year:** Application fee: $25. Comprehensive fee: $25,468 includes full-time tuition ($17,700), mandatory fees ($1342), and college room and board ($6426). Room and board charges vary according to board plan and housing facility. **Scholarships:** Available **Calendar System:** 4-1-4, Summer Session Available **Enrollment:** FT 585, PT 9, Grad 127 **Faculty:** FT 37, PT 31 **Student-Faculty Ratio:** 12:1 **Exams:** SAT I or ACT **% Receiving Financial Aid:** 81 **% Residing in College-Owned, -Operated, or -Affiliated Housing:** 88 **Library Holdings:** 233,541 **Regional Accreditation:** Southern Association of Colleges and Schools **Credit Hours For Degree:** 124 semester hours, Bachelors **Intercollegiate Athletics:** Baseball M; Basketball M & W; Cross-Country Running M & W; Equestrian Sports M & W; Soccer M & W; Softball W; Tennis M & W

FLORENCE-DARLINGTON TECHNICAL COLLEGE
2715 West Lucas St.
PO Box 100548
Florence, SC 29501-0548
Tel: (843)661-8324
Free: 800-228-5745
Admissions: (843)661-8153
Fax: (843)661-8306
E-mail: kirvenp@flo.tec.sc.us
Web Site: http://www.fdtc.edu/
President/CEO: Dr. Charles W. Gould
Registrar: Joe Onessimo, Jr.

Admissions: Kevin Qualls
Financial Aid: Joseph Durant
Type: Two-Year College **Sex:** Coed **Affiliation:** South Carolina State Board for Technical and Comprehensive Education **Admission Plans:** Open Admission; Deferred Admission **Application Fee:** $15.00 **H.S. Requirements:** High school diploma or equivalent not required. For nursing, dental services, chemical engineering technology, surgical technology, health information management, medical laboratory technology: High school diploma required; GED accepted. **Scholarships:** Available **Calendar System:** Semester, Summer Session Available **Enrollment:** FT 2,147, PT 1,894 **Faculty:** FT 110, PT 202 **Student-Faculty Ratio:** 17:1 **Exams:** Other, SAT I or ACT **Library Holdings:** 34,814 **Regional Accreditation:** Southern Association of Colleges and Schools **Credit Hours For Degree:** 61 credit hours, Associates **ROTC:** Army **Professional Accreditation:** ABET, ADA, AHIMA, ACBSP, CARC, JRCERT, NAACLS, NLN

FORREST JUNIOR COLLEGE

601 East River St.
Anderson, SC 29624
Tel: (864)225-7653
Fax: (864)261-7471
Web Site: http://www.forrestcollege.com/
President/CEO: Dr. Roger Burnett
Admissions: Janie Turmon
Financial Aid: Kathy Montgomery
Type: Two-Year College **Sex:** Coed **Admission Plans:** Deferred Admission **Application Fee:** $25.00 **H.S. Requirements:** High school diploma required; GED accepted **Costs Per Year:** Application fee: $25. Tuition: $4950 full-time, $110 per quarter hour part-time. Mandatory fees: $450 full-time, $150 per term part-time. Full-time tuition and fees vary according to course load and program. Part-time tuition and fees vary according to course load and program. **Scholarships:** Available **Calendar System:** Quarter, Summer Session Available **Enrollment:** FT 114, PT 51 **Faculty:** FT 4, PT 14 **Student-Faculty Ratio:** 16:1 **Credit Hours For Degree:** 109 quarter hours, Associates **Professional Accreditation:** ACICS

FRANCIS MARION UNIVERSITY

PO Box 100547
Florence, SC 29501-0547
Tel: (843)661-1362
Free: 800-368-7551
Admissions: (843)661-1231
Fax: (843)661-4635
Web Site: http://www.fmarion.edu/
President/CEO: Dr. Luther F. Carter
Registrar: H. Elizabeth McLean
Admissions: Cynthia Harding
Financial Aid: Kim Ellisor
Type: Comprehensive **Sex:** Coed **Scores:** 93.4% SAT V 400+; 94.3% SAT M 400+; 65% ACT 18-23; 13.2% ACT 24-29 **% Accepted:** 71 **Admission Plans:** Early Admission; Deferred Admission **Application Deadline:** Rolling **Application Fee:** $30.00 **H.S. Requirements:** High school diploma required; GED accepted **Costs Per Year:** Application fee: $30. State resident tuition: $6327 full-time, $316.35 per credit hour part-time. Nonresident tuition: $12,654 full-time, $632.70 per credit hour part-time. Mandatory fees: $185 full-time, $4.75 per credit hour part-time. College room and board: $5430. College room only: $2960. **Scholarships:** Available **Calendar System:** Semester, Summer Session Available **Enrollment:** FT 3,058, PT 442, Grad 508 **Faculty:** FT 176, PT 105 **Student-Faculty Ratio:** 17:1 **Exams:** SAT I or ACT **% Receiving Financial Aid:** 45 **% Residing in College-Owned, -Operated, or -Affiliated Housing:** 44 **Library Holdings:** 332,043 **Regional Accreditation:** Southern Association of Colleges and Schools **Credit Hours For Degree:** 120 semester hours, Bachelors **Professional Accreditation:** AACSB, NASAD, NAST, NCATE **Intercollegiate Athletics:** Baseball M; Basketball M & W; Cross-Country Running M & W; Golf M; Soccer M & W; Softball W; Tennis M & W; Track and Field M & W; Volleyball W

FURMAN UNIVERSITY

3300 Poinsett Hwy.
Greenville, SC 29613
Tel: (864)294-2000
Admissions: (864)294-2034
Fax: (864)294-3127
E-mail: admissions@furman.edu
Web Site: http://www.furman.edu/
President/CEO: Dr. David E. Shi
Registrar: Brad Barron
Admissions: David R. O'Cain
Financial Aid: Martin Carney
Type: Comprehensive **Sex:** Coed **Scores:** 100% SAT V 400+; 100% SAT M 400+; 13% ACT 18-23; 54% ACT 24-29 **% Accepted:** 53 **Admission Plans:** Preferred Admission; Early Admission; Early Decision Plan **Application Deadline:** January 15 **Application Fee:** $40.00 **H.S. Requirements:** High school diploma required; GED accepted **Costs Per Year:** Application fee: $40. Comprehensive fee: $33,264 includes full-time tuition ($25,888), mandatory fees ($464), and college room and board ($6912). College room only: $3712. Room and board charges vary according to board plan and housing facility. Part-time tuition: $809 per credit hour. Part-time tuition varies according to course load. **Scholarships:** Available **Calendar System:** Miscellaneous, Summer Session Available **Enrollment:** FT 2,699, PT 105, Grad 417 **Faculty:** FT 220, PT 52 **Student-Faculty Ratio:** 11:1 **Exams:** SAT I or ACT, SAT II **% Receiving Financial Aid:** 44 **% Residing in College-Owned, -Operated, or -Affiliated Housing:** 91 **Library Holdings:** 453,211 **Regional Accreditation:** Southern Association of Colleges and Schools **Credit Hours For Degree:** 128 credit hours, Bachelors **ROTC:** Army **Professional Accreditation:** NASM, NCATE **Intercollegiate Athletics:** Baseball M; Basketball M & W; Cheerleading M & W; Crew M & W; Cross-Country Running M & W; Fencing M & W; Football M; Golf M & W; Ice Hockey M; Lacrosse M; Rugby M & W; Soccer M & W; Softball W; Swimming and Diving M & W; Tennis M & W; Track and Field M & W; Volleyball M & W; Weight Lifting M & W

GREENVILLE TECHNICAL COLLEGE

PO Box 5616
Greenville, SC 29606-5616
Tel: (864)250-8000
Free: 800-723-0673
Admissions: (864)250-8109
Fax: (864)250-8534
Web Site: http://www.greenvilletech.com/
President/CEO: Dr. Thomas E. Barton, Jr.
Registrar: Renee Holcombe
Admissions: Martha S. White
Financial Aid: Janie Reid
Type: Two-Year College **Sex:** Coed **Affiliation:** South Carolina State Board for Technical and Comprehensive Education **Admission Plans:** Open Admission; Early Admission; Deferred Admission **Application Fee:** $25.00 **H.S. Requirements:** High school diploma required; GED accepted **Scholarships:** Available **Calendar System:** Semester, Summer Session Available **Faculty:** FT 248, PT 230 **Exams:** Other **Library Holdings:** 49,500 **Regional Accreditation:** Southern Association of Colleges and Schools **Credit Hours For Degree:** 60 semester hours, Associates **Professional Accreditation:** ABET, ACF, ADA, AHIMA, AOTA, APTA, ACBSP, CARC, JRCERT, JRCEMT, NAACLS, NLN

HORRY-GEORGETOWN TECHNICAL COLLEGE

2050 Hwy. 501, PO Box 261966
Conway, SC 29528-6066
Tel: (843)347-3186
Admissions: (843)349-5277
Fax: (843)347-4207
E-mail: george.swindoll@hgtc.edu
Web Site: http://www.hgtc.edu/
President/CEO: H. Neyle Wilson
Registrar: Mary Jo Black
Admissions: George Swindoll
Financial Aid: Susan Thompson
Type: Two-Year College **Sex:** Coed **Affiliation:** South Carolina State Board for Technical and Comprehensive Education **Admission Plans:** Open Admission; Early Admission **Application Deadline:** Rolling **Application Fee:** $25.00 **H.S. Requirements:** High school diploma or equivalent not required. For health science programs: High school diploma required; GED accepted **Costs Per Year:** Application fee: $25. Area resident tuition: $2800 full-time, $117 per credit hour part-time. State resident tuition: $3544 full-time, $148 per credit hour part-time. Nonresident tuition: $4264 full-time, $178 per credit hour part-time. Mandatory fees: $144 full-time, $1 per credit hour part-time, $35 per term part-time. **Scholarships:** Available **Calendar System:** Semester, Summer Session Available **Enrollment:** FT 2,446, PT 2,916 **Faculty:** FT 128, PT 276 **Student-Faculty Ratio:** 16:1 **Regional Ac-**

creditation: Southern Association of Colleges and Schools **Credit Hours For Degree:** 63 semester hours, Associates **Professional Accreditation:** ABET, ACF, ADA, ACBSP, JRCERT, NLN

ITT TECHNICAL INSTITUTE
6 Independence Pointe
Greenville, SC 29615
Tel: (864)288-0777
Fax: (864)297-0053
Web Site: http://www.itt-tech.edu/
President/CEO: Rod Kruse
Admissions: David Murray
Financial Aid: Andre Davis
Type: Two-Year College **Sex:** Coed **Affiliation:** ITT Educational Services, Inc **Admission Plans:** Deferred Admission **Application Deadline:** Rolling **Application Fee:** $100.00 **H.S. Requirements:** High school diploma required; GED accepted **Costs Per Year:** Application fee: $100. **Scholarships:** Available **Calendar System:** Quarter, Summer Session Not available **Exams:** Other **Credit Hours For Degree:** 96 credit hours, Associates; 180 credit hours, Bachelors **Professional Accreditation:** ACICS

LANDER UNIVERSITY
320 Stanley Ave.
Greenwood, SC 29649-2099
Tel: (864)388-8000; 888-452-6337
Admissions: (864)388-8307
Fax: (864)388-8125
E-mail: admissions@lander.edu
Web Site: http://www.lander.edu/
President/CEO: Dr. Daniel W. Ball
Registrar: R. Thomas Nelson, III
Admissions: Jonathan T. Reece
Financial Aid: Stephan Schnaiter
Type: Comprehensive **Sex:** Coed **Affiliation:** South Carolina Commission on Higher Education **Scores:** 88% SAT V 400+; 94% SAT M 400+; 51% ACT 18-23; 14% ACT 24-29 **% Accepted:** 85 **Admission Plans:** Early Admission; Deferred Admission **Application Deadline:** August 01 **Application Fee:** $35.00 **H.S. Requirements:** High school diploma required; GED accepted **Costs Per Year:** Application fee: $35. State resident tuition: $6108 full-time, $275 per semester hour part-time. Nonresident tuition: $13,528 full-time, $564 per semester hour part-time. Mandatory fees: $560 full-time. Full-time tuition and fees vary according to degree level. Part-time tuition varies according to degree level. College room and board: $5468. College room only: $3360. Room and board charges vary according to board plan and housing facility. **Scholarships:** Available **Calendar System:** Semester, Summer Session Available **Enrollment:** FT 2,373, PT 239, Grad 91 **Faculty:** FT 126, PT 64 **Student-Faculty Ratio:** 19:1 **Exams:** SAT I or ACT **% Receiving Financial Aid:** 39 **% Residing in College-Owned, -Operated, or -Affiliated Housing:** 33 **Library Holdings:** 175,366 **Regional Accreditation:** Southern Association of Colleges and Schools **Credit Hours For Degree:** 125 semester hours, Bachelors **ROTC:** Army **Professional Accreditation:** AACSB, MACTE, NASAD, NASM, NAST, NCATE, NLN **Intercollegiate Athletics:** Baseball M; Basketball M & W; Cross-Country Running W; Golf M; Soccer M & W; Softball W; Tennis M & W; Volleyball W

LIMESTONE COLLEGE
1115 College Dr.
Gaffney, SC 29340-3799
Tel: (864)489-7151
Free: 800-795-7151
Admissions: (864)488-4549
Fax: (864)487-8706
E-mail: cphenicie@limestone.edu
Web Site: http://www.limestone.edu/
President/CEO: Dr. Walt Griffin
Registrar: Brenda F. Watkins
Admissions: Chris Phenicie
Financial Aid: Summer G. Robertson
Type: Four-Year College **Sex:** Coed **Scores:** 96% SAT V 400+; 95% SAT M 400+; 54% ACT 18-23; 8% ACT 24-29 **% Accepted:** 58 **Application Deadline:** Rolling **Application Fee:** $25.00 **H.S. Requirements:** High school diploma required; GED accepted **Costs Per Year:** Application fee: $25. Comprehensive fee: $21,000 includes full-time tuition ($15,000) and college room and board ($6000). Part-time tuition: $625 per credit hour. **Scholarships:** Available **Calendar System:** Semester, Summer Session Available **Enrollment:** FT 660, PT 16 **Faculty:** FT 55, PT 32 **Student-Faculty Ratio:** 10:1 **Exams:** SAT I or ACT **% Receiving Financial Aid:** 78 **% Residing in College-Owned, -Operated, or -Affiliated Housing:** 49 **Library Holdings:** 104,582 **Regional Accreditation:** Southern Association of Colleges and Schools **Credit Hours For Degree:** 62 semester hours, Associates; 120 semester hours, Bachelors **ROTC:** Army **Professional Accreditation:** CSWE, NASM **Intercollegiate Athletics:** Baseball M; Basketball M & W; Cross-Country Running M & W; Golf M & W; Lacrosse M & W; Soccer M & W; Softball W; Swimming and Diving W; Tennis M & W; Volleyball W; Wrestling M

MEDICAL UNIVERSITY OF SOUTH CAROLINA
171 Ashley Ave.
Charleston, SC 29425-0002
Tel: (843)792-2300
Admissions: (843)792-3813
Fax: (843)792-3764
Web Site: http://www.musc.edu/
President/CEO: W. Stuart Smith
Admissions: George W. Ohlandt
Financial Aid: Pearl M. Givens
Type: Two-Year Upper Division **Sex:** Coed **Admission Plans:** Preferred Admission; Deferred Admission **Application Deadline:** February 01 **Application Fee:** $75.00 **H.S. Requirements:** High school diploma required; GED accepted **Costs Per Year:** Application fee: $75. **Scholarships:** Available **Calendar System:** Semester, Summer Session Not available **Student-Faculty Ratio:** 12:1 **Library Holdings:** 225,061 **Regional Accreditation:** Southern Association of Colleges and Schools **Credit Hours For Degree:** 128 semester hours, Bachelors **Professional Accreditation:** ACPE, ACEHSA, AACN, AANA, ACNM, ACPhE, ADA, ADtA, AOTA, APTA, APA, ASC, ASLHA, LCMEAMA, NLN

MIDLANDS TECHNICAL COLLEGE
PO Box 2408
Columbia, SC 29202-2408
Tel: (803)738-1400
Admissions: (803)738-8324
Fax: (803)738-7784
E-mail: littlejohns@midlandstech.edu
Web Site: http://www.midlandstech.edu/
President/CEO: Dr. Barry W. Russell
Registrar: Carolyn Gatlin
Admissions: Sylvia Littlejohn
Financial Aid: Margaret Hunt
Type: Two-Year College **Sex:** Coed **Affiliation:** South Carolina State Board for Technical and Comprehensive Education **% Accepted:** 69 **Admission Plans:** Open Admission; Early Admission; Deferred Admission **Application Deadline:** Rolling **H.S. Requirements:** High school diploma required; GED accepted **Costs Per Year:** Area resident tuition: $2904 full-time, $121 per credit part-time. State resident tuition: $3676 full-time, $157 per credit part-time. Nonresident tuition: $8612 full-time, $363 per credit part-time. Mandatory fees: $100 full-time, $50 per term part-time. Full-time tuition and fees vary according to class time. Part-time tuition and fees vary according to class time. **Scholarships:** Available **Calendar System:** Semester, Summer Session Available **Enrollment:** FT 4,743, PT 6,036 **Faculty:** FT 223, PT 408 **Student-Faculty Ratio:** 21:1 **Exams:** Other, SAT I or ACT **Library Holdings:** 89,618 **Regional Accreditation:** Southern Association of Colleges and Schools **Credit Hours For Degree:** 60 semester hours, Associates **Professional Accreditation:** ABET, ADA, AHIMA, APTA, ACBSP, CARC, JRCERT, NAACLS, NLN

MILLER-MOTTE TECHNICAL COLLEGE
8085 Rivers Ave., Ste. E
Charleston, SC 29418
Tel: (843)574-0101; 877-617-4740
Fax: (843)266-3434
E-mail: juliasc@miller-mott.net
Web Site: http://www.miller-motte.com/
President/CEO: Julie Corner
Admissions: Julie Corner
Type: Two-Year College **Sex:** Coed **Calendar System:** Quarter **Professional Accreditation:** ACICS

MORRIS COLLEGE
100 West College St.
Sumter, SC 29150-3599

Tel: (803)934-3200; (866)853-1345
Admissions: (803)934-3225
Fax: (803)773-3687
E-mail: dcalhoun@morris.edu
Web Site: http://www.morris.edu/
President/CEO: Dr. Luns C. Richardson
Registrar: Deborah C. Calhoun
Admissions: Deborah Calhoun
Financial Aid: Sandra Gibson
Type: Four-Year College **Sex:** Coed **Affiliation:** Baptist Educational and Missionary Convention of South Carolina **Scores:** 27% SAT V 400+; 33% SAT M 400+; 12% ACT 18-23; 1% ACT 24-29 **% Accepted:** 85 **Admission Plans:** Open Admission; Deferred Admission **Application Deadline:** Rolling **Application Fee:** $20.00 **H.S. Requirements:** High school diploma required; GED accepted **Costs Per Year:** Application fee: $20. Comprehensive fee: $12,234 includes full-time tuition ($8163), mandatory fees ($235), and college room and board ($3836). Part-time tuition: $330 per credit hour. Part-time mandatory fees: $45 per term. Part-time tuition and fees vary according to class time. **Scholarships:** Available **Calendar System:** Semester, Summer Session Available **Enrollment:** FT 844, PT 19 **Faculty:** FT 47, PT 12 **Student-Faculty Ratio:** 17:1 **Exams:** SAT I or ACT **% Receiving Financial Aid:** 96 **% Residing in College-Owned, -Operated, or -Affiliated Housing:** 72 **Library Holdings:** 102,206 **Regional Accreditation:** Southern Association of Colleges and Schools **Credit Hours For Degree:** 124 credit hours, Bachelors **ROTC:** Army **Intercollegiate Athletics:** Baseball M; Basketball M & W; Cross-Country Running M & W; Golf M; Softball W; Tennis M & W; Track and Field M & W; Volleyball W

NEWBERRY COLLEGE
2100 College St.
Newberry, SC 29108-2197
Tel: (803)276-5010
Free: 800-845-4955
Admissions: (803)321-5129
E-mail: admissions@newberry.edu
Web Site: http://www.newberry.edu/
President/CEO: Dr. Mitchell M. Zais
Registrar: Carol Bickley
Admissions: Michel Robbins
Type: Four-Year College **Sex:** Coed **Affiliation:** Evangelical Lutheran **Scores:** 93.62% SAT V 400+; 93.25% SAT M 400+; 25.31% ACT 18-23; 3.7% ACT 24-29 **% Accepted:** 59 **Admission Plans:** Early Admission; Deferred Admission **Application Deadline:** Rolling **Application Fee:** $30.00 **H.S. Requirements:** High school diploma required; GED accepted. For nontraditional students: High school diploma required; GED accepted **Costs Per Year:** Application fee: $30. Comprehensive fee: $26,511 includes full-time tuition ($18,900), mandatory fees ($731), and college room and board ($6880). College room only: $3230. Part-time tuition: $350 per hour. Part-time mandatory fees: $50 per term. **Scholarships:** Available **Calendar System:** Semester, Summer Session Available **Enrollment:** FT 841 **Faculty:** FT 50 **Student-Faculty Ratio:** 12:1 **Exams:** SAT I or ACT **% Receiving Financial Aid:** 84 **% Residing in College-Owned, -Operated, or -Affiliated Housing:** 87 **Library Holdings:** 79,899 **Regional Accreditation:** Southern Association of Colleges and Schools **Credit Hours For Degree:** 126 semester hours, Bachelors **ROTC:** Army **Professional Accreditation:** NASM, NCATE **Intercollegiate Athletics:** Baseball M; Basketball M & W; Cheerleading W; Cross-Country Running M & W; Football M; Golf M & W; Soccer M & W; Softball W; Tennis M & W; Volleyball W; Wrestling M

NORTH GREENVILLE COLLEGE
PO Box 1892
Tigerville, SC 29688-1892
Tel: (864)977-7000
Free: 800-468-6642
Admissions: (864)977-7052
Fax: (864)977-7177
E-mail: ngccwf@infoave.net
Web Site: http://www.ngc.edu/
President/CEO: Dr. James B. Epting
Registrar: Pamela Farmer
Admissions: Buddy Freeman
Financial Aid: Michael Jordan
Type: Four-Year College **Sex:** Coed **Affiliation:** Southern Baptist **Scores:** 91% SAT V 400+; 90% SAT M 400+; 57% ACT 18-23; 15% ACT 24-29 **Admission Plans:** Preferred Admission; Early Admission; Deferred Admission **Application Fee:** $25.00 **H.S. Requirements:** High school diploma required; GED accepted **Costs Per Year:** Application fee: $25. Comprehensive fee: $16,300 includes full-time tuition ($10,350) and college room and board ($5950). Part-time tuition: $200 per hour. Part-time tuition varies according to course load. **Scholarships:** Available **Calendar System:** Semester, Summer Session Available **Enrollment:** FT 1,559, PT 207 **Faculty:** FT 73, PT 59 **Student-Faculty Ratio:** 18:1 **Exams:** Other, SAT I or ACT **% Residing in College-Owned, -Operated, or -Affiliated Housing:** 66 **Library Holdings:** 49,000 **Regional Accreditation:** Southern Association of Colleges and Schools **Credit Hours For Degree:** 64 semester hours, Associates; 128 semester hours, Bachelors **ROTC:** Army **Intercollegiate Athletics:** Baseball M; Basketball M & W; Cheerleading M & W; Cross-Country Running M & W; Football M; Golf M; Soccer M & W; Softball W; Tennis M & W; Volleyball W

NORTHEASTERN TECHNICAL COLLEGE
PO Drawer 1007
Cheraw, SC 29520-1007
Tel: (843)921-6900
Admissions: (843)921-6935
Fax: (843)537-6148
E-mail: mnewton@netc.edu
Web Site: http://www.netc.edu/
President/CEO: Dr. James C. Williamson
Registrar: Catherine L. Sellers
Admissions: Mary K. Newton
Financial Aid: Sheryll N. Marshall
Type: Two-Year College **Sex:** Coed **Affiliation:** South Carolina State Board for Technical and Comprehensive Education **Admission Plans:** Open Admission; Early Admission **Application Fee:** $12.50 **H.S. Requirements:** High school diploma required; GED accepted **Costs Per Year:** Application fee: $12.50. Area resident tuition: $2496 full-time, $104 per semester hour part-time. State resident tuition: $2688 full-time, $112 per semester hour part-time. Nonresident tuition: $4080 full-time, $170 per semester hour part-time. Mandatory fees: $30 full-time, $4 per semester hour part-time. **Scholarships:** Available **Calendar System:** Semester, Summer Session Available **Faculty:** FT 28, PT 75 **Student-Faculty Ratio:** 25:1 **Exams:** SAT I **Library Holdings:** 20,502 **Regional Accreditation:** Southern Association of Colleges and Schools **Credit Hours For Degree:** 60 semester hours, Associates

ORANGEBURG-CALHOUN TECHNICAL COLLEGE
3250 St Matthews Rd., NE
Orangeburg, SC 29118-8299
Tel: (803)536-0311
Admissions: (803)535-1218
Fax: (803)535-1388
Web Site: http://www.octech.edu/
President/CEO: Dr. Anne S. Crook
Registrar: Phyllis Stoudenmire
Admissions: Bobbie Felder
Financial Aid: Chris Dooley
Type: Two-Year College **Sex:** Coed **Affiliation:** State Board for Technical and Comprehensive Education, South Carolina **Admission Plans:** Open Admission; Early Admission **Application Fee:** $15.00 **H.S. Requirements:** High school diploma required; GED accepted **Scholarships:** Available **Calendar System:** Semester, Summer Session Available **Enrollment:** FT 1,380, PT 1,111 **Faculty:** FT 78, PT 51 **Exams:** Other, SAT I and SAT II or ACT **Library Holdings:** 43,500 **Regional Accreditation:** Southern Association of Colleges and Schools **Credit Hours For Degree:** 60 semester hours, Associates **Professional Accreditation:** ABET, ACBSP, JRCERT, NAACLS, NLN

PIEDMONT TECHNICAL COLLEGE
620 North Emerald Rd.
PO Box 1467
Greenwood, SC 29648-1467
Tel: (864)941-8324
Admissions: (864)941-8603
Fax: (864)941-8555
Web Site: http://www.ptc.edu/
President/CEO: Dr. Lex D. Walters
Registrar: Katherine B. Moseley

Admissions: Steve Coleman
Financial Aid: Deborah Williams
Type: Two-Year College **Sex:** Coed **Affiliation:** South Carolina State Board for Technical and Comprehensive Education **Admission Plans:** Open Admission; Early Admission; Deferred Admission **H.S. Requirements:** High school diploma required; GED accepted **Scholarships:** Available **Calendar System:** Semester, Summer Session Available **Faculty:** FT 103, PT 130 **Student-Faculty Ratio:** 18:1 **Exams:** Other, SAT I **Library Holdings:** 27,497 **Regional Accreditation:** Southern Association of Colleges and Schools **Credit Hours For Degree:** 60 credits, Associates **Professional Accreditation:** ABET, ABFSE, ACBSP, CARC, JRCERT, NLN

PRESBYTERIAN COLLEGE
503 South Broad St.
Clinton, SC 29325
Tel: (864)833-2820
Free: 800-476-7272
Admissions: (864)833-8229
Fax: (864)833-8481
E-mail: lpatters@presby.edu
Web Site: http://www.presby.edu/
President/CEO: Dr. John V. Griffith
Registrar: Ethel W. Aldridge
Admissions: Leni Patterson
Financial Aid: Judi F. Gillespie
Type: Four-Year College **Sex:** Coed **Affiliation:** Presbyterian Church (U.S.A.) **Scores:** 100% SAT V 400+; 100% SAT M 400+; 45% ACT 18-23; 46% ACT 24-29 **% Accepted:** 76 **Admission Plans:** Early Decision Plan; Deferred Admission **Application Deadline:** April 01 **Application Fee:** $30.00 **H.S. Requirements:** High school diploma required; GED accepted **Costs Per Year:** Application fee: $30. Comprehensive fee: $30,044 includes full-time tuition ($21,222), mandatory fees ($2022), and college room and board ($6800). College room only: $3340. Full-time tuition and fees vary according to program. Room and board charges vary according to board plan and housing facility. Part-time tuition: $885 per semester hour. Part-time tuition varies according to program. **Scholarships:** Available **Calendar System:** Semester, Summer Session Available **Enrollment:** FT 1,138, PT 58 **Faculty:** FT 81, PT 29 **Student-Faculty Ratio:** 12:1 **Exams:** SAT I or ACT **% Receiving Financial Aid:** 62 **% Residing in College-Owned, -Operated, or -Affiliated Housing:** 94 **Library Holdings:** 155,830 **Regional Accreditation:** Southern Association of Colleges and Schools **Credit Hours For Degree:** 122 semester hours, Bachelors **ROTC:** Army **Professional Accreditation:** ACBSP, NCATE **Intercollegiate Athletics:** Baseball M; Basketball M & W; Cross-Country Running M & W; Football M; Golf M & W; Lacrosse M & W; Riflery M & W; Soccer M & W; Softball W; Tennis M & W; Volleyball W

SOUTH CAROLINA STATE UNIVERSITY
300 College St. Northeast
Orangeburg, SC 29117-0001
Tel: (803)536-7000
Free: 800-260-5956
Admissions: (803)536-8408
Fax: (803)536-8990
Web Site: http://www.scsu.edu/
President/CEO: Dr. Andrew Hugine, Jr.
Registrar: Annie R. Belton
Admissions: Dwight Bailey
Financial Aid: Sandra Davis
Type: Comprehensive **Sex:** Coed **Affiliation:** South Carolina Commission on Higher Education **Scores:** 64% SAT V 400+; 67% SAT M 400+; 24% ACT 18-23; 2% ACT 24-29 **Admission Plans:** Deferred Admission **Application Fee:** $25.00 **H.S. Requirements:** High school diploma required; GED accepted **Costs Per Year:** Application fee: $25. State resident tuition: $6480 full-time, $270 per credit hour part-time. Nonresident tuition: $13,288 full-time, $554 per credit hour part-time. Mandatory fees: $185 full-time. Full-time tuition and fees vary according to course load, degree level, reciprocity agreements, and student level. Part-time tuition varies according to course load, degree level, reciprocity agreements, and student level. College room and board: $6028. College room only: $3642. Room and board charges vary according to board plan and housing facility. **Scholarships:** Available **Calendar System:** Semester, Summer Session Available **Enrollment:** FT 3,345, PT 359, Grad 590 **Faculty:** FT 211, PT 56 **Student-Faculty Ratio:** 16:1 **Exams:** SAT I or ACT, SAT II **% Residing in College-Owned, -Operated, or -Affiliated Housing:** 57 **Library Holdings:** 273,264 **Regional Accreditation:** Southern Association of Colleges and Schools **Credit Hours For Degree:** 120 semester hours, Bachelors **ROTC:** Army, Air Force **Professional Accreditation:** AACSB, ABET, AAFCS, ASLHA, CORE, CSWE, NASM, NCATE **Intercollegiate Athletics:** Basketball M & W; Cross-Country Running M & W; Football M; Golf M; Softball W; Tennis M & W; Track and Field M & W; Volleyball W

SOUTH UNIVERSITY
3810 Main St.
Columbia, SC 29203-6400
Tel: (803)799-9082; (866)629-3031
Fax: (803)799-9038
Web Site: http://www.southuniversity.edu/
President/CEO: Anne F. Patton
Registrar: Brad Kauffman
Admissions: Trisha Sherwood
Financial Aid: Walt Haversat
Type: Comprehensive **Sex:** Coed **Affiliation:** South University-Savannah **Scores:** 100% SAT V 400+; 100% SAT M 400+ **% Accepted:** 69 **Admission Plans:** Deferred Admission **Application Deadline:** Rolling **Application Fee:** $25.00 **H.S. Requirements:** High school diploma required; GED accepted **Costs Per Year:** Application fee: $25. Tuition: $11,475 full-time. **Scholarships:** Available **Calendar System:** Quarter, Summer Session Available **Enrollment:** FT 289, PT 137, Grad 65 **Faculty:** FT 18, PT 22 **Student-Faculty Ratio:** 15:1 **Exams:** SAT I and SAT II or ACT **Library Holdings:** 10,765 **Credit Hours For Degree:** 92 quarter hours, Associates; 180 quarter hours, Bachelors

SOUTHERN METHODIST COLLEGE
541 Broughton Stret, PO Box 1027
Orangeburg, SC 29116-1027
Tel: (803)534-7826
Free: 800-360-1503
Web Site: http://www.smcollege.edu/
President/CEO: Daniel H. Shapley
Registrar: Glenn Blank
Admissions: Dr. Richard G. Blank
Financial Aid: Terry H. Lynch
Type: Four-Year College **Sex:** Coed **Admission Plans:** Early Admission; Early Action; Deferred Admission **Application Fee:** $25.00 **H.S. Requirements:** High school diploma required; GED accepted **Costs Per Year:** Application fee: $25. Comprehensive fee: $9400 includes full-time tuition ($4600), mandatory fees ($600), and college room and board ($4200). Full-time tuition and fees vary according to class time and course load. Room and board charges vary according to housing facility. Part-time tuition: $192 per semester hour. Part-time mandatory fees: $25 per semester hour. Part-time tuition and fees vary according to class time and course load. **Scholarships:** Available **Enrollment:** FT 61, PT 16 **Faculty:** FT 6, PT 18 **Student-Faculty Ratio:** 5:1 **Exams:** SAT I or ACT **% Receiving Financial Aid:** 89 **% Residing in College-Owned, -Operated, or -Affiliated Housing:** 19 **Library Holdings:** 21,743 **Credit Hours For Degree:** 63 credits, Associates; 124 credits, Bachelors **Professional Accreditation:** TACCS

SOUTHERN WESLEYAN UNIVERSITY
907 Wesleyan Dr., PO Box 1020
Central, SC 29630-1020
Tel: (864)644-5000
Free: 800-289-1292
Admissions: (864)644-5550
Fax: (864)644-5900
Web Site: http://www.swu.edu/
President/CEO: Dr. David J. Spittal
Registrar: Rock McCaskill
Admissions: Chad Peters
Financial Aid: Jeff Dennis
Type: Comprehensive **Sex:** Coed **Affiliation:** Wesleyan Church **Scores:** 93% SAT V 400+; 93% SAT M 400+; 47% ACT 18-23; 24% ACT 24-29 **% Accepted:** 66 **Admission Plans:** Early Admission; Deferred Admission **Application Deadline:** August 11 **Application Fee:** $25.00 **H.S. Requirements:** High school diploma required; GED accepted **Costs Per Year:** Application fee: $25. Comprehensive fee: $20,900 includes full-time tuition ($15,000), mandatory fees ($450), and college room and board ($5450). College room only: $2050. Full-time tuition and fees vary according to course load, degree level, and program. Room and board charges vary according to board plan and housing facility. Part-time tuition: $460 per credit

hour. Part-time mandatory fees: $225 per term. Part-time tuition and fees vary according to course load and degree level. **Scholarships:** Available **Calendar System:** Semester, Summer Session Available **Enrollment:** FT 1,909, PT 86, Grad 637 **Faculty:** FT 50, PT 178 **Student-Faculty Ratio:** 17:1 **Exams:** SAT I or ACT **% Receiving Financial Aid:** 42 **% Residing in College-Owned, -Operated, or -Affiliated Housing:** 16 **Library Holdings:** 88,983 **Regional Accreditation:** Southern Association of Colleges and Schools **Credit Hours For Degree:** 64 hours, Associates; 128 hours, Bachelors **ROTC:** Army, Air Force **Intercollegiate Athletics:** Baseball M; Basketball M & W; Cross-Country Running M & W; Golf M; Soccer M & W; Softball W; Volleyball W

SPARTANBURG METHODIST COLLEGE
1200 Textile Rd.
Spartanburg, SC 29301-0009
Tel: (864)587-4000
Free: 800-772-7286
Admissions: (864)587-4223
Fax: (864)587-4355
Web Site: http://www.smcsc.edu/
President/CEO: Dr. Charles Teague
Registrar: Jill Johnson
Admissions: Daniel L. Philbeck
Financial Aid: Carolyn Sparks
Type: Two-Year College **Sex:** Coed **Affiliation:** Methodist **Scores:** 100% SAT V 400+; 34% ACT 18-23; 3% ACT 24-29 **% Accepted:** 84 **Admission Plans:** Deferred Admission **Application Deadline:** Rolling **Application Fee:** $20.00 **H.S. Requirements:** High school diploma required; GED accepted **Costs Per Year:** Application fee: $20. Comprehensive fee: $15,476 includes full-time tuition ($9816), mandatory fees ($150), and college room and board ($5510). College room only: $2784. Room and board charges vary according to housing facility. Part-time tuition: $260 per credit. Part-time tuition varies according to course load. **Scholarships:** Available **Calendar System:** Semester, Summer Session Available **Enrollment:** FT 716, PT 63 **Faculty:** FT 23, PT 23 **Student-Faculty Ratio:** 23:1 **Exams:** SAT I or ACT **% Residing in College-Owned, -Operated, or -Affiliated Housing:** 75 **Library Holdings:** 75,000 **Regional Accreditation:** Southern Association of Colleges and Schools **Credit Hours For Degree:** 64 semester hours, Associates **ROTC:** Army **Intercollegiate Athletics:** Baseball M; Basketball M & W; Cheerleading M & W; Cross-Country Running M & W; Golf M & W; Soccer M & W; Softball W; Tennis M & W; Volleyball W; Wrestling M

SPARTANBURG TECHNICAL COLLEGE
PO Box 4386
Spartanburg, SC 29305-4386
Tel: (864)591-3600
Admissions: (864)592-4800
Web Site: http://www.stcsc.edu/
President/CEO: Dr. Dan Terhune
Registrar: Celcia B. Bauss
Admissions: Nancy T. Garmroth
Financial Aid: Nancy Garmroth
Type: Two-Year College **Sex:** Coed **Affiliation:** South Carolina State Board for Technical and Comprehensive Education **Admission Plans:** Open Admission; Early Admission **Application Deadline:** Rolling **Application Fee:** $0.00 **H.S. Requirements:** High school diploma required; GED accepted. For industrial technology programs: High school diploma or equivalent not required **Costs Per Year:** Application fee: $0. Area resident tuition: $3094 full-time, $127 per hour part-time. State resident tuition: $3860 full-time, $159 per hour part-time. Nonresident tuition: $5490 full-time, $228 per hour part-time. Mandatory fees: $20 full-time. **Scholarships:** Available **Calendar System:** Semester, Summer Session Available **Enrollment:** FT 2,435, PT 1,974 **Faculty:** FT 100 **Library Holdings:** 36,173 **Regional Accreditation:** Southern Association of Colleges and Schools **Credit Hours For Degree:** 60 semester hours, Associates **Professional Accreditation:** ABET, ADA, ACBSP, CARC, JRCERT, NAACLS

TECHNICAL COLLEGE OF THE LOWCOUNTRY
921 Ribaut Rd., PO Box 1288
Beaufort, SC 29901-1288
Tel: (843)525-8324
Admissions: (843)525-8307
E-mail: lbrediger@tcl.edu
Web Site: http://www.tclonline.org/
President/CEO: Dr. Anne S. McNutt
Registrar: Melanie Gallion
Admissions: Les Brediger
Financial Aid: Cleo Martin
Type: Two-Year College **Sex:** Coed **Affiliation:** South Carolina Technical and Comprehensive Education System **Admission Plans:** Open Admission; Early Admission; Deferred Admission **Application Fee:** $10.00 **H.S. Requirements:** High school diploma required; GED accepted **Scholarships:** Available **Calendar System:** Semester, Summer Session Available **Faculty:** FT 41, PT 28 **Exams:** Other, SAT I and SAT II or ACT **Library Holdings:** 25,226 **Regional Accreditation:** Southern Association of Colleges and Schools **Credit Hours For Degree:** 64 credit hours, Associates **Professional Accreditation:** ACBSP, NLN

TRI-COUNTY TECHNICAL COLLEGE
PO Box 587, 7900 Hwy. 76
Pendleton, SC 29670-0587
Tel: (864)646-8361
Admissions: (864)646-1500
E-mail: admstaff@tricty.tricounty.tec.sc.us
Web Site: http://www.tctc.edu/
President/CEO: Dr. Don C. Garrison
Registrar: Scott Harvey
Admissions: Rachel Campbell
Financial Aid: Stewart Spires
Type: Two-Year College **Sex:** Coed **Affiliation:** South Carolina State Board for Technical and Comprehensive Education **Admission Plans:** Open Admission; Early Admission **Application Fee:** $20.00 **H.S. Requirements:** High school diploma required; GED accepted. For welding, industrial mechanics programs: High school diploma or equivalent not required **Scholarships:** Available **Calendar System:** Semester, Summer Session Available **Faculty:** FT 220, PT 180 **Student-Faculty Ratio:** 25:1 **Exams:** Other, SAT I **Library Holdings:** 34,513 **Regional Accreditation:** Southern Association of Colleges and Schools **Credit Hours For Degree:** 60 credits, Associates **ROTC:** Army, Air Force **Professional Accreditation:** ABET, ADA, ACBSP, NAACLS, NLN

TRIDENT TECHNICAL COLLEGE
PO Box 118067
Charleston, SC 29423-8067
Tel: (843)574-6111
Admissions: (843)574-6483
Fax: (843)574-6109
Web Site: http://www.tridenttech.edu/
President/CEO: Dr. Mary Thornley
Registrar: Pamela Droste
Admissions: Clara Martin
Financial Aid: Cindy Seabrook
Type: Two-Year College **Sex:** Coed **Affiliation:** South Carolina State Board for Technical and Comprehensive Education **Admission Plans:** Open Admission; Early Admission **Application Deadline:** August 04 **Application Fee:** $25.00 **H.S. Requirements:** High school diploma required; GED accepted **Costs Per Year:** Application fee: $25. Area resident tuition: $2950 full-time, $120 per credit hour part-time. State resident tuition: $3276 full-time, $134 per credit hour part-time. Nonresident tuition: $5586 full-time, $230 per credit hour part-time. Mandatory fees: $50 full-time, $5 per credit hour part-time. **Scholarships:** Available **Calendar System:** Semester, Summer Session Available **Enrollment:** FT 5,270, PT 6,525 **Faculty:** FT 262, PT 375 **Student-Faculty Ratio:** 18:1 **Library Holdings:** 68,462 **Regional Accreditation:** Southern Association of Colleges and Schools **Credit Hours For Degree:** 60 credit hours, Associates **Professional Accreditation:** ABET, ACF, ADA, AOTA, APTA, ACBSP, CARC, JRCERT, NAACLS, NLN

UNIVERSITY OF SOUTH CAROLINA
Columbia, SC 29208
Tel: (803)777-7000
Admissions: (803)777-7700
E-mail: admissions-ugrad@scarolina.edu
Web Site: http://www.sc.edu/
President/CEO: Dr. Andrew A. Sorensen
Registrar: Barbara Blaney
Admissions: Scott Verzyl
Financial Aid: Dr. Ed Miller
Type: University **Sex:** Coed **Affiliation:** University of South Carolina System **Scores:** 99.54% SAT V 400+; 99.77% SAT M 400+; 36.34% ACT 18-23; 50% ACT 24-29 **% Accepted:** 68 **Application Deadline:** December 01 **Ap-**

plication Fee: $50.00 **H.S. Requirements:** High school diploma required; GED accepted **Costs Per Year:** Application fee: $50. State resident tuition: $6914 full-time, $324 per credit hour part-time. Nonresident tuition: $18,556 full-time, $844 per credit hour part-time. Full-time tuition varies according to program. College room and board: $6080. Room and board charges vary according to board plan, housing facility, and location. **Scholarships:** Available **Calendar System:** Semester, Summer Session Available **Enrollment:** FT 16,399, PT 1,963, Grad 7,263 **Faculty:** FT 1,190, PT 377 **Student-Faculty Ratio:** 18:1 **Exams:** SAT I or ACT **% Receiving Financial Aid:** 49 **% Residing in College-Owned, -Operated, or -Affiliated Housing:** 46 **Library Holdings:** 3,374,496 **Regional Accreditation:** Southern Association of Colleges and Schools **Credit Hours For Degree:** 60 credit hours, Associates; 120 credit hours, Bachelors **ROTC:** Army, Air Force **Professional Accreditation:** AACSB, ABET, ACEHSA, ACEJMC, AACN, AANA, ABA, ACPhE, ACA, ALA, APTA, APA, ASLHA, AALS, CEPH, CORE, CSWE, JRCEPAT, LCMEAMA, NASAD NASM, NASPAA, NAST, NCATE **Intercollegiate Athletics:** Baseball M; Basketball M & W; Cross-Country Running W; Equestrian Sports W; Football M; Golf M & W; Soccer M & W; Softball W; Swimming and Diving M & W; Tennis M & W; Track and Field M & W; Volleyball W

UNIVERSITY OF SOUTH CAROLINA AIKEN
471 University Parkway
Aiken, SC 29801-6309
Tel: (803)648-6851; 888-WOW-USCA
Fax: (803)641-3727
E-mail: admit@aiken.sc.edu
Web Site: http://www.usca.edu/
President/CEO: Dr. Thomas L. Hallman
Registrar: Vivan Grice
Admissions: Andrew Hendrix
Financial Aid: Glenn Shumpert
Type: Comprehensive **Sex:** Coed **Affiliation:** University of South Carolina System **Scores:** 91% SAT V 400+; 96% SAT M 400+; 73% ACT 18-23; 15% ACT 24-29 **% Accepted:** 48 **Admission Plans:** Early Admission; Deferred Admission **Application Deadline:** August 01 **Application Fee:** $35.00 **H.S. Requirements:** High school diploma required; GED accepted **Costs Per Year:** Application fee: $35. State resident tuition: $5928 full-time, $258 per semester hour part-time. Nonresident tuition: $12,070 full-time, $520 per semester hour part-time. Mandatory fees: $230 full-time, $8 per semester hour part-time, $7 per term part-time. Full-time tuition and fees vary according to reciprocity agreements. Part-time tuition and fees vary according to course load and reciprocity agreements. College room and board: $5560. College room only: $3800. Room and board charges vary according to board plan and housing facility. **Scholarships:** Available **Calendar System:** Semester, Summer Session Available **Enrollment:** FT 2,270, PT 880, Grad 153 **Faculty:** FT 147, PT 99 **Student-Faculty Ratio:** 16:1 **Exams:** SAT I or ACT **% Residing in College-Owned, -Operated, or -Affiliated Housing:** 22 **Library Holdings:** 165,459 **Regional Accreditation:** Southern Association of Colleges and Schools **Credit Hours For Degree:** 120 semester hours, Bachelors **Professional Accreditation:** AACSB, NCATE, NLN **Intercollegiate Athletics:** Baseball M; Basketball M & W; Cheerleading M & W; Cross-Country Running W; Golf M; Soccer M & W; Softball W; Tennis M & W; Volleyball W

UNIVERSITY OF SOUTH CAROLINA BEAUFORT
801 Carteret St.
Beaufort, SC 29902-4601
Tel: (843)521-4100
Web Site: http://www.sc.edu/beaufort/
President/CEO: Dr. Jane T. Upshaw
Registrar: Mary-David Fox
Financial Aid: Sally Maybin
Type: Four-Year College **Sex:** Coed **Affiliation:** University of South Carolina System **Scores:** 87% SAT V 400+; 82% SAT M 400+; 53% ACT 18-23; 42% ACT 24-29 **% Accepted:** 87 **Admission Plans:** Deferred Admission **Application Deadline:** Rolling **Application Fee:** $40.00 **H.S. Requirements:** High school diploma required; GED accepted **Costs Per Year:** Application fee: $40. State resident tuition: $4954 full-time, $207 per credit hour part-time. Nonresident tuition: $11,870 full-time, $495 per credit hour part-time. Mandatory fees: $330 full-time, $10 per credit hour part-time. College room only: $6900. **Scholarships:** Available **Calendar System:** Semester, Summer Session Available **Enrollment:** FT 676, PT 643 **Faculty:** FT 42, PT 43 **Student-Faculty Ratio:** 15:1 **Exams:** SAT I or ACT **Library Holdings:** 50,000 **Regional Accreditation:** Southern Association of Colleges and Schools **Credit Hours For Degree:** 60 semester hours, Associates; 120 semester hours, Bachelors

UNIVERSITY OF SOUTH CAROLINA LANCASTER
PO Box 889
Lancaster, SC 29721-0889
Tel: (803)313-7471
Admissions: (803)313-7000
Fax: (803)313-7106
E-mail: bparker@gwm.sc.edu
Web Site: http://usclancaster.sc.edu/
President/CEO: Dr. John Catalano
Admissions: Rebecca D. Parker
Financial Aid: Leah Sturgis
Type: Two-Year College **Sex:** Coed **Affiliation:** University of South Carolina System **Admission Plans:** Open Admission; Early Admission **Application Fee:** $40.00 **H.S. Requirements:** High school diploma required; GED accepted **Scholarships:** Available **Calendar System:** Semester, Summer Session Not available **Enrollment:** FT 459, PT 484 **Faculty:** FT 23, PT 24 **Student-Faculty Ratio:** 16:1 **Exams:** SAT I or ACT **Library Holdings:** 68,192 **Regional Accreditation:** Southern Association of Colleges and Schools **Credit Hours For Degree:** 60 semester hours, Associates **Professional Accreditation:** ACBSP, NLN

UNIVERSITY OF SOUTH CAROLINA SALKEHATCHIE
PO Box 617
Allendale, SC 29810-0617
Tel: (803)584-3446
Web Site: http://uscsalkehatchie.sc.edu/
President/CEO: Dr. Ann Carmichael
Registrar: Jane T. Brewer
Admissions: Jane T. Brewer
Financial Aid: Julie Hadwin
Type: Two-Year College **Sex:** Coed **Affiliation:** University of South Carolina System **Scores:** 7% SAT V 400+; 6% SAT M 400+ **Admission Plans:** Open Admission **H.S. Requirements:** High school diploma required; GED accepted **Scholarships:** Available **Calendar System:** Semester, Summer Session Available **Enrollment:** FT 283, PT 494 **Faculty:** FT 18, PT 20 **Exams:** SAT I or ACT **Library Holdings:** 47,877 **Regional Accreditation:** Southern Association of Colleges and Schools **Credit Hours For Degree:** 60 semester hours, Associates **ROTC:** Army, Navy, Air Force **Intercollegiate Athletics:** Baseball M; Golf M

UNIVERSITY OF SOUTH CAROLINA SUMTER
200 Miller Rd.
Sumter, SC 29150-2498
Tel: (803)775-8727
Admissions: (803)938-3882
E-mail: kbritton@uscsumter.edu
Web Site: http://www.uscsumter.edu/
President/CEO: Dr. C. Leslie Carpenter
Registrar: Flora Y. Gadson
Admissions: Keith Britton
Financial Aid: Sue Sims
Type: Two-Year College **Sex:** Coed **Affiliation:** University of South Carolina System **Scores:** 85.2% SAT V 400+; 85.2% SAT M 400+; 57.4% ACT 18-23; 3.7% ACT 24-29 **% Accepted:** 62 **Application Deadline:** August 08 **Application Fee:** $40.00 **H.S. Requirements:** High school diploma required; GED accepted **Costs Per Year:** Application fee: $40. State resident tuition: $4064 full-time, $169 per semester hour part-time. Nonresident tuition: $10,124 full-time, $422 per semester hour part-time. Mandatory fees: $260 full-time. Full-time tuition and fees vary according to degree level. **Scholarships:** Available **Calendar System:** Semester, Summer Session Available **Enrollment:** FT 580, PT 440 **Faculty:** FT 40, PT 35 **Student-Faculty Ratio:** 19:1 **Exams:** SAT I or ACT **Library Holdings:** 81,114 **Regional Accreditation:** Southern Association of Colleges and Schools **Credit Hours For Degree:** 60 semester hours, Associates **ROTC:** Army, Air Force

UNIVERSITY OF SOUTH CAROLINA UNION
PO Drawer 729
Union, SC 29379-0729
Tel: (864)427-3681
Admissions: (864)429-8728
Web Site: http://uscunion.sc.edu/

President/CEO: James W. Edwards
Registrar: Terry Young
Admissions: Terry E. Young
Financial Aid: Robert Holcombe
Type: Two-Year College **Sex:** Coed **Affiliation:** University of South Carolina System **Scores:** 75% SAT V 400+; 80% SAT M 400+ **% Accepted:** 89 **Application Deadline:** Rolling **Application Fee:** $40.00 **H.S. Requirements:** High school diploma required; GED accepted **Costs Per Year:** Application fee: $40. State resident tuition: $4064 full-time, $169 per credit hour part-time. Nonresident tuition: $10,124 full-time, $422 per credit hour part-time. Mandatory fees: $100 full-time, $10 per hour part-time. **Scholarships:** Available **Calendar System:** Semester **Enrollment:** FT 161, PT 160 **Faculty:** FT 12, PT 13 **Student-Faculty Ratio:** 14:1 **Exams:** SAT I or ACT **Regional Accreditation:** Southern Association of Colleges and Schools **Credit Hours For Degree:** 60 semester hours, Associates

UNIVERSITY OF SOUTH CAROLINA UPSTATE
800 University Way
Spartanburg, SC 29303-4999
Tel: (864)503-5000
Free: 800-277-8727
Admissions: (864)503-5280
Fax: (864)503-5201
E-mail: dstewart@uscupstate.edu
Web Site: http://www.uscupstate.edu/
President/CEO: Dr. John C. Stockwell
Registrar: Kathryn Murphy
Admissions: Donette Stewart
Financial Aid: Kim Jenerette
Type: Comprehensive **Sex:** Coed **Affiliation:** University of South Carolina System **Scores:** 94% SAT V 400+; 94% SAT M 400+; 71% ACT 18-23; 10% ACT 24-29 **% Accepted:** 33 **Admission Plans:** Deferred Admission **Application Fee:** $40.00 **H.S. Requirements:** High school diploma required; GED accepted **Costs Per Year:** Application fee: $40. State resident tuition: $6436 full-time, $282 per hour part-time. Nonresident tuition: $13,274 full-time, $583 per hour part-time. Mandatory fees: $326 full-time, $11 per hour part-time, $25 per term part-time. Full-time tuition and fees vary according to course load. Part-time tuition and fees vary according to course load. College room and board: $5160. College room only: $3200. Room and board charges vary according to board plan and housing facility. **Scholarships:** Available **Calendar System:** Semester, Summer Session Available **Enrollment:** FT 3,564, PT 845, Grad 75 **Faculty:** FT 207, PT 149 **Student-Faculty Ratio:** 15:1 **Exams:** SAT I or ACT **% Receiving Financial Aid:** 64 **% Residing in College-Owned, -Operated, or -Affiliated Housing:** 15 **Library Holdings:** 188,572 **Regional Accreditation:** Southern Association of Colleges and Schools **Credit Hours For Degree:** 71 semester hours, Associates; 120 semester hours, Bachelors **ROTC:** Army **Professional Accreditation:** AACSB, ABET, NCATE, NLN **Intercollegiate Athletics:** Baseball M; Basketball M & W; Cross-Country Running M & W; Soccer M & W; Softball W; Tennis M & W; Volleyball W

VOORHEES COLLEGE
1411 Voorhees Rd., PO Box 678
Denmark, SC 29042
Tel: (803)793-3351
Free: 800-446-6250
Admissions: (803)703-7124
Fax: (803)793-5773
Web Site: http://www.voorhees.edu/
President/CEO: Dr. Lee E. Monroe, Jr.
Registrar: Carolyn V. White
Admissions: Benjamin O. Watson
Financial Aid: Carolyn V. White
Type: Four-Year College **Sex:** Coed **Affiliation:** Episcopal **Scores:** 56% SAT V 400+; 57% SAT M 400+ **Admission Plans:** Deferred Admission **Application Fee:** $25.00 **H.S. Requirements:** High school diploma required; GED accepted **Costs Per Year:** Application fee: $25. Comprehensive fee: $11,848 includes full-time tuition ($7106), mandatory fees ($170), and college room and board ($4572). College room only: $1904. Room and board charges vary according to housing facility. Part-time tuition: $242 per semester hour. Part-time mandatory fees: $170 per term. **Scholarships:** Available **Calendar System:** Semester, Summer Session Available **Enrollment:** FT 807, PT 40 **Faculty:** FT 37, PT 27 **Student-Faculty Ratio:** 20:1 **Exams:** SAT I or ACT **% Receiving Financial Aid:** 91 **% Residing in College-Owned, -Operated, or -Affiliated Housing:** 85 **Library Holdings:** 107,260 **Regional Accreditation:** Southern Association of Colleges and Schools **Credit Hours For Degree:** 124 credit hours, Bachelors **ROTC:** Army **Professional Accreditation:** ACBSP **Intercollegiate Athletics:** Baseball M; Basketball M & W; Cross-Country Running M & W; Softball W; Track and Field M & W; Volleyball W

WILLIAMSBURG TECHNICAL COLLEGE
601 Martin Luther King, Jr Ave.
Kingstree, SC 29556-4197
Tel: (843)355-4110
Free: 800-768-2021
Fax: (843)355-4296
Web Site: http://www.wiltech.edu/
President/CEO: Dr. James C. Williamson
Registrar: Lynn Selph
Admissions: Sharon B. Hanna
Financial Aid: Joe DuRant
Type: Two-Year College **Sex:** Coed **Affiliation:** South Carolina State Board for Technical and Comprehensive Education **Admission Plans:** Open Admission; Early Admission; Deferred Admission **Application Fee:** $10.00 **H.S. Requirements:** High school diploma required; GED accepted **Scholarships:** Available **Calendar System:** Semester, Summer Session Available **Enrollment:** FT 269, PT 326 **Faculty:** FT 14, PT 34 **Student-Faculty Ratio:** 13:1 **Exams:** Other, SAT I or ACT **Library Holdings:** 25,456 **Regional Accreditation:** Southern Association of Colleges and Schools **Credit Hours For Degree:** 62 semester hours, Associates **Professional Accreditation:** ACBSP

WINTHROP UNIVERSITY
701 Oakland Ave.
Rock Hill, SC 29733
Tel: (803)323-2211
Free: 800-763-0230
Admissions: (803)323-2191
Fax: (803)323-2137
E-mail: admissions@winthrop.edu
Web Site: http://www.winthrop.edu/
President/CEO: Dr. Anthony DiGiorgio
Registrar: Timothy Drueke
Admissions: Deborah Barber
Financial Aid: Betty Whalen
Type: Comprehensive **Sex:** Coed **Affiliation:** South Carolina Commission on Higher Education **Scores:** 98.45% SAT V 400+; 98.83% SAT M 400+; 62.4% ACT 18-23; 31.82% ACT 24-29 **% Accepted:** 69 **Admission Plans:** Deferred Admission **Application Deadline:** May 01 **Application Fee:** $40.00 **H.S. Requirements:** High school diploma required; GED accepted **Costs Per Year:** Application fee: $40. State resident tuition: $8756 full-time, $364 per semester hour part-time. Nonresident tuition: $16,150 full-time, $673 per semester hour part-time. Full-time tuition varies according to degree level. Part-time tuition varies according to degree level. College room and board: $5352. College room only: $3420. Room and board charges vary according to board plan and housing facility. **Scholarships:** Available **Calendar System:** Semester, Summer Session Available **Enrollment:** FT 4,587, PT 600, Grad 1,293 **Faculty:** FT 270, PT 272 **Student-Faculty Ratio:** 14:1 **Exams:** SAT I or ACT **% Receiving Financial Aid:** 59 **% Residing in College-Owned, -Operated, or -Affiliated Housing:** 43 **Library Holdings:** 414,879 **Regional Accreditation:** Southern Association of Colleges and Schools **Credit Hours For Degree:** 124 semester hours, Bachelors **Professional Accreditation:** AACSB, ABET, ACEJMC, ACA, ADtA, CSWE, FIDER, NASAD, NASD, NASM, NAST, NCATE **Intercollegiate Athletics:** Baseball M; Basketball M & W; Cheerleading M & W; Cross-Country Running M & W; Fencing M & W; Golf M & W; Lacrosse M & W; Rugby M; Soccer M; Softball W; Tennis M & W; Track and Field M & W; Volleyball W

WOFFORD COLLEGE
429 North Church St.
Spartanburg, SC 29303-3663
Tel: (864)597-4000
Admissions: (864)597-4130
Fax: (864)597-4149
E-mail: admissions@wofford.edu
Web Site: http://www.wofford.edu/
President/CEO: Dr. Benjamin B. Dunlap

Registrar: Lucy B. Quinn
Admissions: Brand Stille
Financial Aid: Donna D. Hawkins
Type: Four-Year College **Sex:** Coed **Affiliation:** United Methodist Church **Scores:** 100% SAT V 400+; 100% SAT M 400+; 36% ACT 18-23; 54% ACT 24-29 **% Accepted:** 66 **Admission Plans:** Early Admission; Early Decision Plan; Deferred Admission **Application Deadline:** February 01 **Application Fee:** $40.00 **H.S. Requirements:** High school diploma required; GED accepted **Costs Per Year:** Application fee: $40. Comprehensive fee: $30,935 includes full-time tuition ($24,130) and college room and board ($6805). Part-time tuition: $875 per hour. **Scholarships:** Available **Calendar System:** 4-1-4, Summer Session Available **Enrollment:** FT 1,158, PT 15 **Faculty:** FT 89, PT 33 **Student-Faculty Ratio:** 12:1 **Exams:** SAT I or ACT **% Receiving Financial Aid:** 52 **% Residing in College-Owned, -Operated, or -Affiliated Housing:** 88 **Library Holdings:** 245,730 **Regional Accreditation:** Southern Association of Colleges and Schools **Credit Hours For Degree:** 124 semester hours, Bachelors **ROTC:** Army **Intercollegiate Athletics:** Baseball M; Basketball M & W; Cross-Country Running M & W; Fencing M & W; Football M; Golf M & W; Riflery M & W; Soccer M & W; Tennis M & W; Track and Field M & W; Volleyball W

YORK TECHNICAL COLLEGE
452 South Anderson Rd.
Rock Hill, SC 29730-3395
Tel: (803)327-8000
Admissions: (803)981-7021
Fax: (803)327-8059
E-mail: kaldridge@yorktech.com
Web Site: http://www.yorktech.com/
President/CEO: Dr. Dennis F. Merrell
Registrar: Kelli D. Collins
Admissions: Kenny Aldridge
Financial Aid: Regina Venson
Type: Two-Year College **Sex:** Coed **Affiliation:** South Carolina State Board for Technical and Comprehensive Education **Admission Plans:** Open Admission **Application Deadline:** Rolling **Application Fee:** $0.00 **H.S. Requirements:** High school diploma or equivalent not required. For health and human services program applicants: High school diploma required; GED accepted **Costs Per Year:** Application fee: $0. Area resident tuition: $2900 full-time, $121 per credit hour part-time. State resident tuition: $3264 full-time, $136 per credit hour part-time. Nonresident tuition: $6528 full-time, $272 per credit hour part-time. Mandatory fees: $136 full-time, $4 per credit hour part-time, $68 per term part-time. **Scholarships:** Available **Calendar System:** Semester, Summer Session Available **Enrollment:** FT 2,039, PT 2,114 **Faculty:** FT 115, PT 123 **Exams:** Other **Library Holdings:** 26,947 **Regional Accreditation:** Southern Association of Colleges and Schools **Credit Hours For Degree:** 62 semester hours, Associates **Professional Accreditation:** ABET, ADA, ACBSP, JRCERT, NAACLS, NLN

AUGUSTANA COLLEGE
2001 South Summit Ave.
Sioux Falls, SD 57197
Tel: (605)274-0770
Free: 800-727-2844
Admissions: (605)274-5516
Fax: (605)274-5518
Web Site: http://www.augie.edu/
President/CEO: Dr. Bruce R. Halverson
Registrar: Dr. Glenda Sehested
Admissions: Nancy Davidson
Financial Aid: Brenda Murtha
Type: Comprehensive **Sex:** Coed **Affiliation:** Evangelical Lutheran Church in America **Scores:** 100% SAT V 400+; 100% SAT M 400+; 43% ACT 18-23; 47% ACT 24-29 **% Accepted:** 80 **Admission Plans:** Deferred Admission **Application Deadline:** August 01 **Application Fee:** $0.00 **H.S. Requirements:** High school diploma required; GED accepted **Costs Per Year:** Application fee: $0. Comprehensive fee: $25,458 includes full-time tuition ($19,750), mandatory fees ($236), and college room and board ($5472). College room only: $2700. **Scholarships:** Available **Calendar System:** 4-1-4, Summer Session Available **Enrollment:** FT 1,621, PT 93, Grad 31 **Faculty:** FT 108, PT 72 **Student-Faculty Ratio:** 13:1 **Exams:** SAT I or ACT **% Receiving Financial Aid:** 68 **% Residing in College-Owned, -Operated, or -Affiliated Housing:** 67 **Library Holdings:** 279,918 **Regional Accreditation:** North Central Association of Colleges and Schools **Credit Hours For Degree:** 130 credits, Bachelors **Professional Accreditation:** AACN, CSWE, JRCEPAT, NASM, NCATE **Intercollegiate Athletics:** Baseball M; Basketball M & W; Cheerleading W; Cross-Country Running M & W; Football M; Golf M & W; Soccer W; Softball W; Tennis M & W; Track and Field M & W; Volleyball W; Wrestling M

BLACK HILLS STATE UNIVERSITY
1200 University St.
Spearfish, SD 57799
Tel: (605)642-6011
Free: 800-255-2478
Admissions: (605)642-6343
E-mail: jberry@mystic.bhsu.edu
Web Site: http://www.bhsu.edu/
President/CEO: Dr. Thomas O. Flickema
Registrar: April Meeker
Admissions: Steve Ochsner
Financial Aid: Deb Henriksen
Type: Comprehensive **Sex:** Coed **Affiliation:** South Dakota University System **Scores:** 58.09% ACT 18-23; 20.87% ACT 24-29 **Application Fee:** $20.00 **H.S. Requirements:** High school diploma required; GED accepted **Costs Per Year:** Application fee: $20. State resident tuition: $2444 full-time, $76.35 per credit part-time. Nonresident tuition: $7764 full-time, $242.60 per credit part-time. Mandatory fees: $2628 full-time, $82.10 per credit part-time. Full-time tuition and fees vary according to course load and reciprocity agreements. Part-time tuition and fees vary according to course load and reciprocity agreements. College room and board: $3663. College room only: $2078. Room and board charges vary according to board plan and housing facility. **Scholarships:** Available **Calendar System:** Semester, Summer Session Available **Enrollment:** FT 2,533, PT 1,120, Grad 193 **Faculty:** FT 115, PT 79 **Student-Faculty Ratio:** 21:1 **Exams:** SAT I or ACT **% Residing in College-Owned, -Operated, or -Affiliated Housing:** 20 **Library Holdings:** 310,210 **Regional Accreditation:** North Central Association of Colleges and Schools **Credit Hours For Degree:** 64 credits, Associates; 128 credits, Bachelors **ROTC:** Army **Professional Accreditation:** NASM, NCATE **Intercollegiate Athletics:** Basketball M & W; Cross-Country Running M & W; Football M; Golf W; Track and Field M & W; Volleyball W

COLORADO TECHNICAL UNIVERSITY SIOUX FALLS CAMPUS
3901 West 59th St.
Sioux Falls, SD 57108
Tel: (605)361-0200
Fax: (605)361-5954
Web Site: http://www.ctu-siouxfalls.com/
President/CEO: Dr. Vicki Strunk
Registrar: Lois Butterfield
Admissions: Catherine Taplett Allen
Type: Comprehensive **Sex:** Coed **Affiliation:** Colorado Technical University - Main Campus Colorado Springs, CO **Admission Plans:** Open Admission; Early Admission; Deferred Admission **Application Fee:** $50.00 **H.S. Requirements:** High school diploma required; GED accepted **Scholarships:** Available **Calendar System:** Quarter, Summer Session Available **Enrollment:** FT 441, PT 471, Grad 124 **Faculty:** FT 9, PT 52 **Student-Faculty Ratio:** 18:1 **Exams:** ACT **% Receiving Financial Aid:** 92 **Library Holdings:** 5,787 **Regional Accreditation:** North Central Association of Colleges and Schools **Credit Hours For Degree:** 87 credit hours, Associates; 178 credit hours, Bachelors **ROTC:** Army **Professional Accreditation:** AAMAE

DAKOTA STATE UNIVERSITY
820 North Washington
Madison, SD 57042-1799
Tel: (605)256-5111; 888-DSU-9988
Admissions: (605)256-5696
Fax: (605)256-5316
E-mail: amy.crissinger@dsu.edu
Web Site: http://www.dsu.edu/
President/CEO: Douglas Knowlton
Registrar: Sandy Anderson
Admissions: Amy Crissinger
Financial Aid: Rosie Jamison
Type: Comprehensive **Sex:** Coed **Affiliation:** South Dakota Board of Regents **Scores:** 62% ACT 18-23; 23% ACT 24-29 **% Accepted:** 97 **Admission Plans:** Deferred Admission **Application Deadline:** Rolling **Application Fee:** $20.00 **H.S. Requirements:** High school diploma required; GED accepted **Costs Per Year:** Application fee: $20. State resident tuition: $2382 full-time, $79 per credit hour part-time. Nonresident tuition: $3573 full-time, $119 per credit hour part-time. Mandatory fees: $3317 full-time, $89 per credit hour part-time. College room and board: $3927. College room only: $1924. **Scholarships:** Available **Calendar System:** Semester, Summer Session Available **Enrollment:** FT 1,162, PT 919, Grad 238 **Faculty:** FT 77, PT 31 **Student-Faculty Ratio:** 17:1 **Exams:** SAT I or ACT **% Receiving Financial Aid:** 70 **% Residing in College-Owned, -Operated, or -Affiliated Housing:** 34 **Library Holdings:** 98,156 **Regional Accreditation:** North Central Association of Colleges and Schools **Credit Hours For Degree:** 64 credit hours, Associates; 128 credit hours, Bachelors **ROTC:** Air Force **Professional Accreditation:** AHIMA, ACBSP, CARC, NCATE

Intercollegiate Athletics: Baseball M; Basketball M & W; Cheerleading M & W; Cross-Country Running M & W; Football M; Softball W; Track and Field M & W; Volleyball W

DAKOTA WESLEYAN UNIVERSITY
1200 West University Ave.
Mitchell, SD 57301-4398
Tel: (605)995-2600
Free: 800-333-8506
Admissions: (605)995-2650
Fax: (605)995-2699
E-mail: admissions@cc.dwu.edu
Web Site: http://www.dwu.edu/
President/CEO: Dr. Robert G. Duffett
Registrar: Sara Jorgensen
Admissions: Amy Novak
Financial Aid: Wilma Hjellum
Type: Comprehensive **Sex:** Coed **Affiliation:** United Methodist **Scores:** 71.11% ACT 18-23; 16.3% ACT 24-29 **% Accepted:** 72 **Application Deadline:** August 28 **Application Fee:** $25.00 **H.S. Requirements:** High school diploma required; GED accepted **Costs Per Year:** Application fee: $25. Comprehensive fee: $21,550 includes full-time tuition ($16,650) and college room and board ($4900). College room only: $2100. Part-time tuition: $350 per credit. **Scholarships:** Available **Calendar System:** Semester, Summer Session Available **Enrollment:** FT 730, PT 28, Grad 25 **Faculty:** FT 50, PT 34 **Student-Faculty Ratio:** 12:1 **Exams:** SAT I or ACT **% Receiving Financial Aid:** 99 **% Residing in College-Owned, -Operated, or -Affiliated Housing:** 43 **Library Holdings:** 63,000 **Regional Accreditation:** North Central Association of Colleges and Schools **Credit Hours For Degree:** 62 semester hours, Associates; 125 semester hours, Bachelors **Professional Accreditation:** JRCEPAT, NLN **Intercollegiate Athletics:** Baseball M; Basketball M & W; Cheerleading M & W; Cross-Country Running M & W; Football M; Golf M & W; Softball W; Track and Field M & W; Volleyball W; Wrestling M

KILIAN COMMUNITY COLLEGE
300 East 6th St.
Sioux Falls, SD 57103
Tel: (605)221-3100
Free: 800-888-1147
Fax: (605)336-2606
E-mail: amodrell@kilian.edu
Web Site: http://www.kilian.edu/
President/CEO: Dr. Robert G. Smallfoot
Registrar: Janet Garcia
Admissions: Amy Modrell
Financial Aid: Glen Poppinga
Type: Two-Year College **Sex:** Coed **% Accepted:** 100 **Admission Plans:** Open Admission; Early Admission; Deferred Admission **Application Deadline:** Rolling **Application Fee:** $25.00 **H.S. Requirements:** High school diploma required; GED accepted **Costs Per Year:** Application fee: $25. Tuition: $7020 full-time, $195 per credit hour part-time. Mandatory fees: $150 full-time, $50 per term part-time. **Scholarships:** Available **Calendar System:** Trimester, Summer Session Available **Enrollment:** FT 108, PT 430 **Faculty:** FT 7, PT 75 **Student-Faculty Ratio:** 8:1 **Library Holdings:** 78,000 **Regional Accreditation:** North Central Association of Colleges and Schools **Credit Hours For Degree:** 60 credit hours, Associates

LAKE AREA TECHNICAL INSTITUTE
230 11th St. Northeast
Watertown, SD 57201
Tel: (605)882-5284
Free: 800-657-4344
E-mail: latiinfo@lati.tec.sd.us
Web Site: http://www.lati.tec.sd.us/
President/CEO: Gary Williams
Registrar: Deb Shephard
Admissions: Debra Shephard
Financial Aid: Richard Coplan
Type: Two-Year College **Sex:** Coed **Application Fee:** $15.00 **H.S. Requirements:** High school diploma required; GED accepted **Scholarships:** Available **Calendar System:** Semester, Summer Session Not available **Student-Faculty Ratio:** 15:1 **Exams:** ACT **Library Holdings:** 5,000 **Regional Accreditation:** North Central Association of Colleges and Schools **Credit Hours For Degree:** 70 credits, Associates **Professional Accreditation:** AAMAE, ADA, AOTA, APTA, NAACLS

MITCHELL TECHNICAL INSTITUTE
821 North Capital
Mitchell, SD 57301
Tel: (605)995-3024
Free: 800-952-0042
Admissions: (605)995-3025
Fax: (605)996-3299
Web Site: http://mti.tec.sd.us/
President/CEO: Chris Paustian
Registrar: Miranda Ellefson
Admissions: Tim Edwards
Financial Aid: Grant Uecker
Type: Two-Year College **Sex:** Coed **Admission Plans:** Open Admission **Application Fee:** $25.00 **H.S. Requirements:** High school diploma required; GED accepted **Scholarships:** Available **Calendar System:** Semester, Summer Session Available **Enrollment:** FT 712, PT 120 **Faculty:** FT 54, PT 3 **Student-Faculty Ratio:** 16:1 **Exams:** ACT, Other **Regional Accreditation:** North Central Association of Colleges and Schools **Credit Hours For Degree:** 60 credits, Associates **Professional Accreditation:** AAMAE, NAACLS **Intercollegiate Athletics:** Equestrian Sports M & W

MOUNT MARTY COLLEGE
1105 West 8th St.
Yankton, SD 57078-3724
Tel: (605)668-1011
Free: 800-658-4552
Admissions: (605)668-1545
Fax: (605)668-1607
E-mail: btschumper@mtmc.edu
Web Site: http://www.mtmc.edu/
President/CEO: Dr. James T. Barry
Registrar: Sr. Erin Colgan
Admissions: Brandi Tschumper
Financial Aid: Ken Kocer
Type: Comprehensive **Sex:** Coed **Affiliation:** Roman Catholic **Scores:** 48% ACT 18-23; 32% ACT 24-29 **% Accepted:** 85 **Admission Plans:** Early Admission; Deferred Admission **Application Deadline:** Rolling **Application Fee:** $35.00 **H.S. Requirements:** High school diploma required; GED accepted **Costs Per Year:** Application fee: $35. Comprehensive fee: $20,590 includes full-time tuition ($14,050), mandatory fees ($1680), and college room and board ($4860). Full-time tuition and fees vary according to course load and location. Part-time tuition: $228 per credit hour. Part-time mandatory fees: $20 per credit hour. Part-time tuition and fees vary according to course load and location. **Scholarships:** Available **Calendar System:** Semester, Summer Session Available **Enrollment:** FT 712, PT 377, Grad 100 **Faculty:** FT 48, PT 65 **Student-Faculty Ratio:** 12:1 **Exams:** ACT, SAT I or ACT **% Receiving Financial Aid:** 88 **Library Holdings:** 76,571 **Regional Accreditation:** North Central Association of Colleges and Schools **Credit Hours For Degree:** 64 credit hours, Associates; 128 credit hours, Bachelors **ROTC:** Army **Professional Accreditation:** AANA, ADtA, NLN **Intercollegiate Athletics:** Baseball M; Basketball M & W; Cross-Country Running M & W; Soccer M & W; Softball W; Track and Field M & W; Volleyball W

NATIONAL AMERICAN UNIVERSITY (ELLSWORTH AFB)
2700 Doolittle Dr.
Ellsworth AFB, SD 57706
Tel: (605)923-5856
Web Site: http://www.national.edu/ **Type:** Two-Year College **Sex:** Coed

NATIONAL AMERICAN UNIVERSITY (RAPID CITY)
321 Kansas City St.
Rapid City, SD 57701
Tel: (605)394-4800
Free: 800-843-8892
Admissions: (605)394-4902
Fax: (605)394-4871
E-mail: abeck@national.edu
Web Site: http://www.national.edu/
President/CEO: Dr. Jerry L. Gallentine
Registrar: Tom Mahon
Admissions: Angela G. Beck, PMP

Financial Aid: Cheryl Bullinger
Type: Comprehensive **Sex:** Coed **Affiliation:** National College **% Accepted:** 100 **Admission Plans:** Open Admission; Early Admission; Deferred Admission **Application Deadline:** Rolling **Application Fee:** $25.00 **H.S. Requirements:** High school diploma required; GED accepted **Costs Per Year:** Application fee: $25. Comprehensive fee: $15,423 includes full-time tuition ($11,520), mandatory fees ($50), and college room and board ($3853). College room only: $1938. Part-time tuition: $240 per credit hour. Part-time mandatory fees: $90 per credit hour. **Scholarships:** Available **Calendar System:** Quarter, Summer Session Available **Enrollment:** FT 311, PT 152, Grad 68 **Faculty:** FT 70, PT 15 **Student-Faculty Ratio:** 26:1 **Exams:** ACT **% Residing in College-Owned, -Operated, or -Affiliated Housing:** 21 **Library Holdings:** 31,018 **Regional Accreditation:** North Central Association of Colleges and Schools **Credit Hours For Degree:** 97 credit hours, Associates; 193 credit hours, Bachelors **ROTC:** Army **Professional Accreditation:** AAMAE **Intercollegiate Athletics:** Equestrian Sports M & W; Volleyball W

NATIONAL AMERICAN UNIVERSITY-SIOUX FALLS BRANCH
2801 South Kiwanis Ave.
Ste. 100
Sioux Falls, SD 57105-4293
Tel: (605)334-5430
Free: 800-388-5430
E-mail: lhoutsma@national.edu
Web Site: http://www.national.edu/
President/CEO: Daniel Hacking
Admissions: Lisa Houtsma
Financial Aid: Rhonda Kohnen
Type: Four-Year College **Sex:** Coed **Affiliation:** National College **Admission Plans:** Open Admission; Deferred Admission **Application Fee:** $25.00 **H.S. Requirements:** High school diploma required; GED accepted **Scholarships:** Available **Calendar System:** Quarter, Summer Session Available **Faculty:** FT 0, PT 35 **Library Holdings:** 1,580 **Regional Accreditation:** North Central Association of Colleges and Schools **Credit Hours For Degree:** 91 credit hours, Associates; 184 credit hours, Bachelors

NORTHERN STATE UNIVERSITY
1200 South Jay St.
Aberdeen, SD 57401-7198
Tel: (605)626-3011
Free: 800-678-5330
Admissions: (605)626-2544
Fax: (605)626-3022
E-mail: admissionl@wolf.northern.edu
Web Site: http://www.northern.edu/
President/CEO: Dr. Partick Schloss
Registrar: Peggy Hallstrom
Admissions: Allan Vogel
Financial Aid: Sharon Kienow
Type: Comprehensive **Sex:** Coed **Affiliation:** South Dakota Board of Regents **Scores:** 57% ACT 18-23; 22% ACT 24-29 **% Accepted:** 94 **Admission Plans:** Early Admission; Deferred Admission **Application Deadline:** September 01 **Application Fee:** $15.00 **H.S. Requirements:** High school diploma required; GED accepted **Costs Per Year:** Application fee: $15. State resident tuition: $2290 full-time, $76.35 per credit hour part-time. Nonresident tuition: $7278 full-time, $242.60 per credit hour part-time. Mandatory fees: $2409 full-time, $80.30 per credit hour part-time. Full-time tuition and fees vary according to course level, course load, and reciprocity agreements. Part-time tuition and fees vary according to course level, course load, and reciprocity agreements. College room and board: $3980. College room only: $2023. Room and board charges vary according to board plan. **Scholarships:** Available **Calendar System:** Semester, Summer Session Available **Enrollment:** FT 1,595, PT 830, Grad 206 **Faculty:** FT 94, PT 0 **Student-Faculty Ratio:** 20:1 **Exams:** SAT I or ACT **% Receiving Financial Aid:** 59 **Library Holdings:** 192,007 **Regional Accreditation:** North Central Association of Colleges and Schools **Credit Hours For Degree:** 64 credit hours, Associates; 128 credit hours, Bachelors **Professional Accreditation:** NASM, NCATE **Intercollegiate Athletics:** Baseball M; Basketball M & W; Cross-Country Running M & W; Football M; Golf M & W; Soccer W; Softball W; Tennis M & W; Track and Field M & W; Volleyball W; Wrestling M

OGLALA LAKOTA COLLEGE
490 Piya Wiconi Rd.
Kyle, SD 57752-0490
Tel: (605)455-6000
Fax: (605)455-2787
Web Site: http://www.olc.edu/
President/CEO: Thomas Short Bull
Registrar: Billie Hornbeck
Financial Aid: Shirley Brewer
Type: Comprehensive **Sex:** Coed **Admission Plans:** Open Admission; Preferred Admission; Early Admission **Application Fee:** $0.00 **H.S. Requirements:** High school diploma required; GED accepted **Scholarships:** Available **Calendar System:** Semester, Summer Session Available **Library Holdings:** 15,000 **Regional Accreditation:** North Central Association of Colleges and Schools **Credit Hours For Degree:** 65 credit hours, Associates; 128 credit hours, Bachelors **Intercollegiate Athletics:** Basketball M & W; Cross-Country Running M & W

PRESENTATION COLLEGE
1500 North Main St.
Aberdeen, SD 57401-1299
Tel: (605)225-1634
Free: 800-437-6060
Admissions: (605)229-8492
Fax: (605)229-8518
E-mail: joellen.lindner@presentation.edu
Web Site: http://www.presentation.edu/
President/CEO: Dr. Lorraine M. Hale, PBVM
Registrar: Maureen Schuchardt
Admissions: Jo Ellen Lindner
Financial Aid: Valerie Weisser
Type: Four-Year College **Sex:** Coed **Affiliation:** Roman Catholic **Scores:** 55.6% ACT 18-23; 15.2% ACT 24-29 **% Accepted:** 100 **Admission Plans:** Open Admission **Application Deadline:** Rolling **Application Fee:** $0.00 **H.S. Requirements:** High school diploma required; GED accepted **Costs Per Year:** Application fee: $0. Comprehensive fee: $17,075 includes full-time tuition ($12,300) and college room and board ($4775). College room only: $3975. Part-time tuition: $450 per credit. **Scholarships:** Available **Calendar System:** Semester, Summer Session Available **Enrollment:** FT 514, PT 244 **Faculty:** FT 37, PT 50 **Student-Faculty Ratio:** 12:1 **Exams:** ACT **% Receiving Financial Aid:** 90 **% Residing in College-Owned, -Operated, or -Affiliated Housing:** 15 **Library Holdings:** 40,000 **Regional Accreditation:** North Central Association of Colleges and Schools **Credit Hours For Degree:** 60 credit hours, Associates; 120 credit hours, Bachelors **Professional Accreditation:** ARCEST, AAMAE, CSWE, JRCERT, NAACLS, NLN **Intercollegiate Athletics:** Baseball M; Basketball M & W; Cross-Country Running M & W; Golf M & W; Soccer M & W; Softball W; Volleyball W

SINTE GLESKA UNIVERSITY
150 East 2nd St.
P.O. Box 105
Rosebud, SD 57570
Tel: (605)856-8100
Fax: (605)747-2098
Web Site: http://www.sinte.edu/
President/CEO: Lionel Bordeaux
Registrar: Jack Herman
Admissions: Jack Herman
Financial Aid: William Hay
Type: Comprehensive **Sex:** Coed **Admission Plans:** Open Admission **Application Fee:** $0.00 **H.S. Requirements:** High school diploma required; GED accepted **Scholarships:** Available **Calendar System:** Semester, Summer Session Available **Library Holdings:** 25,000 **Regional Accreditation:** North Central Association of Colleges and Schools **Credit Hours For Degree:** 68 credits, Associates; 128 credits, Bachelors

SISSETON-WAHPETON COMMUNITY COLLEGE
Old Agency Box 689
Sisseton, SD 57262
Tel: (605)698-3966
Web Site: http://www.swc.tc/
President/CEO: Dr. William Harjo Bray
Registrar: Darlene Redday
Admissions: Darlene Redday
Financial Aid: Crystal Owen
Type: Two-Year College **Sex:** Coed **Admission Plans:** Open Admission; Deferred Admission **Application Fee:** $0.00 **H.S. Requirements:** High school diploma required; GED accepted **Costs Per Year:** Application fee:

$0. State resident tuition: $2880 full-time. Mandatory fees: $490 full-time. Tuition guaranteed not to increase for student's term of enrollment. **Scholarships:** Available **Calendar System:** Semester, Summer Session Available **Enrollment:** FT 147, PT 127 **Faculty:** FT 10, PT 15 **Student-Faculty Ratio:** 10:1 **Exams:** Other **Library Holdings:** 15,481 **Regional Accreditation:** North Central Association of Colleges and Schools **Credit Hours For Degree:** 64 semester hours, Associates

SOUTH DAKOTA SCHOOL OF MINES AND TECHNOLOGY
501 East Saint Joseph
Rapid City, SD 57701-3995
Tel: (605)394-2511
Free: 800-544-8162
Admissions: (605)394-2414
Fax: (605)394-2914
E-mail: admissions@sdsmt.edu
Web Site: http://www.sdsmt.edu/
President/CEO: Dr. Charles P. Ruch
Registrar: William Jones
Admissions: Julie Smoragiewicz
Financial Aid: David Martin
Type: University **Sex:** Coed **Affiliation:** South Dakota State University System **Scores:** 98% SAT V 400+; 95% SAT M 400+; 40% ACT 18-23; 47% ACT 24-29 **% Accepted:** 94 **Application Deadline:** Rolling **Application Fee:** $20.00 **H.S. Requirements:** High school diploma required; GED accepted **Costs Per Year:** Application fee: $20. State resident tuition: $2291 full-time, $76.35 per credit hour part-time. Nonresident tuition: $7278 full-time, $242.60 per credit hour part-time. Mandatory fees: $2466 full-time, $82.20 per credit hour part-time. Full-time tuition and fees vary according to course load, program, and reciprocity agreements. Part-time tuition and fees vary according to course load, program, and reciprocity agreements. College room and board: $2867. College room only: $1830. Room and board charges vary according to board plan and housing facility. **Scholarships:** Available **Calendar System:** Semester, Summer Session Available **Enrollment:** FT 1,592, PT 465, Grad 256 **Faculty:** FT 107, PT 33 **Student-Faculty Ratio:** 16:1 **Exams:** SAT I or ACT **% Receiving Financial Aid:** 53 **% Residing in College-Owned, -Operated, or -Affiliated Housing:** 32 **Library Holdings:** 273,243 **Regional Accreditation:** North Central Association of Colleges and Schools **Credit Hours For Degree:** 64 semester hours, Associates; 128 semester hours, Bachelors **ROTC:** Army **Professional Accreditation:** ABET **Intercollegiate Athletics:** Basketball M & W; Cross-Country Running M & W; Football M; Golf M & W; Tennis M; Track and Field M & W; Volleyball W

SOUTH DAKOTA STATE UNIVERSITY
PO Box 2201
Brookings, SD 57007
Tel: (605)688-4151
Free: 800-952-3541
Fax: (605)688-6384
Web Site: http://www.sdstate.edu/
President/CEO: Dr. Peggy Gordon Miller
Registrar: Dr. Rick Davis
Financial Aid: Jay Larsen
Type: University **Sex:** Coed **Scores:** 47% ACT 18-23; 42% ACT 24-29 **% Accepted:** 93 **Admission Plans:** Deferred Admission **Application Deadline:** Rolling **Application Fee:** $20.00 **H.S. Requirements:** High school diploma required; GED accepted **Costs Per Year:** Application fee: $20. State resident tuition: $2291 full-time, $76.35 per credit part-time. Nonresident tuition: $7278 full-time, $242.60 per credit part-time. Mandatory fees: $2441 full-time, $81.35 per credit part-time. Full-time tuition and fees vary according to course load, program, and reciprocity agreements. Part-time tuition and fees vary according to course load, program, and reciprocity agreements. College room and board: $4769. College room only: $2113. Room and board charges vary according to board plan and housing facility. **Scholarships:** Available **Calendar System:** Semester, Summer Session Available **Enrollment:** FT 7,749, PT 1,845, Grad 1,230 **Faculty:** FT 413, PT 171 **Student-Faculty Ratio:** 17:1 **Exams:** ACT **% Receiving Financial Aid:** 79 **% Residing in College-Owned, -Operated, or -Affiliated Housing:** 28 **Library Holdings:** 927,701 **Regional Accreditation:** North Central Association of Colleges and Schools **Credit Hours For Degree:** 64 credits, Associates; 128 credits, Bachelors **ROTC:** Army, Air Force **Professional Accreditation:** ABET, ACEJMC, AACN, AAFCS, ACPhE, ACA, JRCEPAT, NASM, NCATE **Intercollegiate Athletics:** Baseball M; Basketball M & W; Cross-Country Running M & W; Equestrian Sports W; Football M; Golf M & W; Ice Hockey M & W; Rugby M & W; Soccer M & W; Softball W; Swimming and Diving M & W; Tennis M & W; Track and Field M & W; Volleyball W; Wrestling M

SOUTHEAST TECHNICAL INSTITUTE
2320 N. Career Ave.
Sioux Falls, SD 57107-1301
Tel: (605)367-7624
E-mail: jim.rokusek@southeasttech.com
Web Site: http://www.southeasttech.com/
President/CEO: Jeff Holcomb
Registrar: Jim Rokusek
Admissions: Jim Rokusek
Type: Two-Year College **Sex:** Coed **% Accepted:** 46 **Application Deadline:** Rolling **Application Fee:** $0.00 **H.S. Requirements:** High school diploma required; GED accepted **Costs Per Year:** Application fee: $0. State resident tuition: $2112 full-time, $66 per credit part-time. Nonresident tuition: $66 per credit part-time. Mandatory fees: $1408 full-time, $44 per credit part-time. College room only: $4200. **Scholarships:** Available **Calendar System:** Semester, Summer Session Available **Faculty:** FT 83, PT 74 **Student-Faculty Ratio:** 19:1 **Exams:** ACT **% Residing in College-Owned, -Operated, or -Affiliated Housing:** 1 **Library Holdings:** 10,643 **Regional Accreditation:** North Central Association of Colleges and Schools **Credit Hours For Degree:** 60 credits, Associates **Professional Accreditation:** JRCECT, JRCNMT

UNIVERSITY OF SIOUX FALLS
1101 West 22nd St.
Sioux Falls, SD 57105-1699
Tel: (605)331-5000
Free: 800-888-1047
Admissions: (605)331-6600
Fax: (605)331-6615
E-mail: admissions@usiouxfalls.edu
Web Site: http://www.usiouxfalls.edu/
President/CEO: Dr. Mark Benedetto
Registrar: Phyllis Thompson
Admissions: Greg A. Fritz
Financial Aid: Laura Olson
Type: Comprehensive **Sex:** Coed **Affiliation:** American Baptist Churches in the USA **Scores:** 75% SAT V 400+; 75% SAT M 400+; 55% ACT 18-23; 34% ACT 24-29 **% Accepted:** 95 **Admission Plans:** Early Admission; Deferred Admission **Application Deadline:** Rolling **Application Fee:** $25.00 **H.S. Requirements:** High school diploma required; GED accepted **Costs Per Year:** Application fee: $25. Comprehensive fee: $21,920 includes full-time tuition ($16,400), mandatory fees ($320), and college room and board ($5200). College room only: $2300. Part-time tuition: $279 per semester hour. **Scholarships:** Available **Calendar System:** 4-1-4, Summer Session Available **Enrollment:** FT 1,026, PT 236, Grad 344 **Faculty:** FT 62, PT 36 **Student-Faculty Ratio:** 18:1 **Exams:** SAT I and SAT II or ACT **% Residing in College-Owned, -Operated, or -Affiliated Housing:** 28 **Library Holdings:** 85,713 **Regional Accreditation:** North Central Association of Colleges and Schools **Credit Hours For Degree:** 64 semester hours, Associates; 128 semester hours, Bachelors **Professional Accreditation:** CSWE, NCATE **Intercollegiate Athletics:** Baseball M; Basketball M & W; Cheerleading W; Cross-Country Running M & W; Football M; Golf M & W; Soccer M & W; Softball W; Tennis M & W; Track and Field M & W; Volleyball W

THE UNIVERSITY OF SOUTH DAKOTA
414 East Clark St.
Vermillion, SD 57069-2390
Tel: (605)677-5011; 877-269-6837
Admissions: (605)677-5434
Fax: (605)677-6753
E-mail: cfoster@usd.edu
Web Site: http://www.usd.edu/
President/CEO: James W. Abbott
Registrar: Carmen Howard
Admissions: Cecil Foster
Financial Aid: Julie Pier
Type: University **Sex:** Coed **Scores:** 95% SAT V 400+; 88% SAT M 400+; 53% ACT 18-23; 35% ACT 24-29 **% Accepted:** 86 **Admission Plans:** Early Admission; Deferred Admission **Application Deadline:** September 04 **Ap-**

plication Fee: $20.00 **H.S. Requirements:** High school diploma required; GED accepted **Costs Per Year:** Application fee: $20. State resident tuition: $2291 full-time, $76.35 per credit hour part-time. Nonresident tuition: $7278 full-time, $242.60 per credit hour part-time. Mandatory fees: $2538 full-time, $84.60 per credit hour part-time. Full-time tuition and fees vary according to course load and reciprocity agreements. Part-time tuition and fees vary according to course load and reciprocity agreements. College room and board: $4240. College room only: $2253. Room and board charges vary according to board plan and housing facility. **Scholarships:** Available **Calendar System:** Semester, Summer Session Available **Enrollment:** FT 4,274, PT 2,134, Grad 1,778 **Faculty:** FT 389, PT 17 **Student-Faculty Ratio:** 15:1 **Exams:** SAT I or ACT **% Receiving Financial Aid:** 60 **% Residing in College-Owned, -Operated, or -Affiliated Housing:** 31 **Library Holdings:** 335,757 **Regional Accreditation:** North Central Association of Colleges and Schools **Credit Hours For Degree:** 66 credit hours, Associates; 128 credit hours, Bachelors **ROTC:** Army **Professional Accreditation:** AACSB, ACEJMC, ABA, ACA, ADA, ADtA, AOTA, APTA, APA, ASLHA, AALS, CSWE, LCMEAMA, NASAD, NASM, NASPAA, NAST, NCATE, NLN **Intercollegiate Athletics:** Baseball M; Basketball M & W; Cross-Country Running M & W; Football M; Softball W; Swimming and Diving M & W; Tennis M & W; Track and Field M & W; Volleyball W

WESTERN DAKOTA TECHNICAL INSTITUTE
800 Mickelson Dr.
Rapid City, SD 57703
Tel: (605)394-4034
Free: 800-544-8765
Web Site: http://www.westerndakotatech.org/
President/CEO: Nancy Richter
Admissions: Janell L. Oberlander
Financial Aid: Starla Russell

Type: Two-Year College **Sex:** Coed **Admission Plans:** Open Admission **Application Fee:** $10.00 **H.S. Requirements:** High school diploma or equivalent not required **Costs Per Year:** Application fee: $10. State resident tuition: $2304 full-time, $64 per credit hour part-time. Nonresident tuition: $2304 full-time, $64 per credit hour part-time. Mandatory fees: $1688 full-time. Full-time tuition and fees vary according to program. Part-time tuition varies according to program. **Scholarships:** Available **Calendar System:** Semester, Summer Session Available **Enrollment:** FT 752, PT 305 **Faculty:** FT 58, PT 27 **Student-Faculty Ratio:** 15:1 **Exams:** ACT, Other **Library Holdings:** 10,000 **Regional Accreditation:** North Central Association of Colleges and Schools **Credit Hours For Degree:** 71 credits, Associates **Intercollegiate Athletics:** Equestrian Sports M & W

AMERICAN ACADEMY OF NUTRITION, COLLEGE OF NUTRITION
1204 -D Kenesaw, Sequoyah Hills Center
Knoxville, TN 37919-7736
Tel: (865)524-8079
Free: 800-290-4226
Fax: (865)524-8339
E-mail: aantn@aol.com
Web Site: http://www.nutritioneducation.com/
President/CEO: Christof Ballin
Admissions: Jennifer Green
Type: Two-Year College **Sex:** Coed **Admission Plans:** Open Admission; Deferred Admission **Costs Per Year:** Tuition: $3950 full-time, $150 per credit hour part-time. Mandatory fees: $200 full-time. Full-time tuition and fees vary according to program. Part-time tuition varies according to program. **Calendar System:** Continuous, Summer Session Available **Faculty:** FT 2, PT 4 **Student-Faculty Ratio:** 29:1 **Credit Hours For Degree:** 60 credit hours, Associates **Professional Accreditation:** DETC

AMERICAN BAPTIST COLLEGE OF AMERICAN BAPTIST THEOLOGICAL SEMINARY
1800 Baptist World Center Dr.
Nashville, TN 37207
Tel: (615)256-1463
E-mail: mlockhart@abcnash.edu
Web Site: http://www.abcnash.edu/
President/CEO: Dr. Forest E. Harris, Sr.
Registrar: Theresa Chandler
Admissions: Marcella Lockhart
Financial Aid: Theresa Chandler
Type: Four-Year College **Sex:** Coed **Affiliation:** Baptist **% Accepted:** 27 **Admission Plans:** Open Admission; Deferred Admission **Application Deadline:** July 12 **Application Fee:** $20.00 **H.S. Requirements:** High school diploma required; GED accepted **Costs Per Year:** Application fee: $20. Tuition: $4032 full-time, $168 per credit hour part-time. Mandatory fees: $140 full-time, $140 per term part-time. Full-time tuition and fees vary according to course load. Part-time tuition and fees vary according to course load. College room only: $1600. Room charges vary according to housing facility. **Scholarships:** Available **Calendar System:** Semester, Summer Session Available **Enrollment:** FT 64, PT 48 **Faculty:** FT 4, PT 12 **Student-Faculty Ratio:** 14:1 **% Receiving Financial Aid:** 75 **% Residing in College-Owned, -Operated, or -Affiliated Housing:** 20 **Library Holdings:** 33,383 **Credit Hours For Degree:** 68 credit hours, Associates; 128 credit hours, Bachelors **Professional Accreditation:** AABC

AQUINAS COLLEGE
4210 Harding Rd.
Nashville, TN 37205-2005
Tel: (615)297-7545
Free: 800-649-9956
Fax: (615)297-7970
Web Site: http://www.aquinas-tn.edu/
President/CEO: Thomas Aquinas Halbmaier, OP
Registrar: Sr. Mary Julius
Admissions: Diane LeJeune
Financial Aid: Zelena O'Sullivan
Type: Four-Year College **Sex:** Coed **Affiliation:** Roman Catholic; The Dominican Sisters of the Saint Cecilia Congregation **Admission Plans:** Open Admission; Deferred Admission **Application Deadline:** Rolling **Application Fee:** $25.00 **H.S. Requirements:** High school diploma required; GED accepted **Costs Per Year:** Application fee: $25. Tuition: $13,620 full-time, $454 per credit hour part-time. Mandatory fees: $425 full-time, $150 per term part-time. **Scholarships:** Available **Calendar System:** Semester, Summer Session Available **Faculty:** FT 25, PT 63 **Student-Faculty Ratio:** 14:1 **Exams:** SAT I or ACT **% Receiving Financial Aid:** 80 **Library Holdings:** 46,549 **Regional Accreditation:** Southern Association of Colleges and Schools **Credit Hours For Degree:** 64 semester hours, Associates; 126 semester hours, Bachelors **ROTC:** Army, Air Force **Professional Accreditation:** NLN

ARGOSY UNIVERSITY/NASHVILLE
341 Cool Springs Blvd., Ste. 210
Franklin, TN 37067-7226
Tel: (615)369-0616
Fax: (615)369-0601
Web Site: http://www.argosyu.edu/ **Type:** Two-Year Upper Division **Sex:** Coed **Calendar System:** Semester **Regional Accreditation:** North Central Association of Colleges and Schools

AUSTIN PEAY STATE UNIVERSITY
601 College St.
Clarksville, TN 37044-0001
Tel: (931)221-7011
Free: 800-844-2778
Admissions: (931)221-7661
Fax: (931)221-5994
E-mail: mcdonalds@apsu.edu
Web Site: http://www.apsu.edu/
President/CEO: Dr. Sherry L. Hoppe
Registrar: Sheila McCoy
Admissions: Scott McDonald
Financial Aid: Donna Price
Type: Comprehensive **Sex:** Coed **Affiliation:** Tennessee Board of Regents **Scores:** 93% SAT V 400+; 88% SAT M 400+; 64% ACT 18-23; 23% ACT 24-29 **% Accepted:** 91 **Admission Plans:** Early Admission; Deferred Admission **Application Deadline:** July 29 **Application Fee:** $15.00 **H.S. Requirements:** High school diploma required; GED accepted **Costs Per Year:** Application fee: $15. State resident tuition: $3678 full-time, $161 per credit hour part-time. Nonresident tuition: $12,990 full-time, $565 per credit hour part-time. Mandatory fees: $957 full-time, $41 per credit hour part-time, $4 per term part-time. Part-time tuition and fees vary according to location. College room and board: $4800. College room only: $2900. Room and board charges vary according to board plan and housing facility. **Scholarships:** Available **Calendar System:** Semester, Summer Session Available **Enrollment:** FT 6,348, PT 1,868, Grad 597 **Faculty:** FT 290, PT 174 **Student-Faculty Ratio:** 21:1 **Exams:** SAT I or ACT **% Receiving Financial Aid:** 70 **% Residing in College-Owned, -Operated, or -Affiliated Housing:** 15 **Library Holdings:** 400,000 **Regional Accreditation:** Southern Association of Colleges and Schools **Credit Hours For Degree:** 64 semester hours, Associates; 128 semester hours, Bachelors **ROTC:** Army **Professional Accreditation:** CSWE, NAACLS, NASAD, NASM, NCATE, NLN **Intercollegiate Athletics:** Baseball M; Basketball M & W; Cheerleading M & W; Cross-Country Running M & W; Football M; Golf M & W; Riflery W; Soccer W; Softball W; Tennis M & W; Track and Field W; Volleyball W

BAPTIST COLLEGE OF HEALTH SCIENCES
1003 Monroe Ave.
Memphis, TN 38104
Tel: (901)227-4330; (866)575-2247
Admissions: (901)572-2465
Web Site: http://www.bchs.edu/
President/CEO: Dr. Rose Temple
Admissions: Cynthia Davis
Type: Four-Year College **Sex:** Coed **Affiliation:** Southern Baptist; Baptist Memorial Health Care Corporation **Admission Plans:** Early Admission **Application Fee:** $25.00 **H.S. Requirements:** High school diploma required; GED accepted **Scholarships:** Available **Calendar System:** Semester **Faculty:** FT 49, PT 28 **Exams:** ACT, Other **% Residing in College-Owned, -Operated, or -Affiliated Housing:** 12 **Regional Accreditation:** Southern Association of Colleges and Schools **Credit Hours For Degree:** 128 credits, Bachelors **Professional Accreditation:** AACN, CARC, JRCEDMS, JRCNMT

BELMONT UNIVERSITY
1900 Belmont Blvd.
Nashville, TN 37212-3757
Tel: (615)460-6000
Free: 800-56E-NROL
Admissions: (615)460-6785
E-mail: buadmission@belmont.edu
Web Site: http://www.belmont.edu/
President/CEO: Dr. Robert C. Fisher
Registrar: Steven Reed
Admissions: Dr. Kathryn Baugher
Financial Aid: Patricia Smedley
Type: Comprehensive **Sex:** Coed **Affiliation:** Baptist **Scores:** 99.8% SAT V 400+; 100% SAT M 400+; 33.1% ACT 18-23; 54.2% ACT 24-29 **% Accepted:** 72 **Admission Plans:** Early Admission; Deferred Admission **Application Deadline:** August 01 **Application Fee:** $35.00 **H.S. Requirements:** High school diploma required; GED accepted **Costs Per Year:** Application fee: $35. Comprehensive fee: $25,910 includes full-time tuition ($16,360), mandatory fees ($900), and college room and board ($8650). College room only: $5300. Full-time tuition and fees vary according to class time and course load. Room and board charges vary according to board plan, housing facility, and location. Part-time tuition: $625 per credit hour. Part-time mandatory fees: $300 per term. Part-time tuition and fees vary according to course load. **Scholarships:** Available **Calendar System:** Semester, Summer Session Available **Enrollment:** FT 3,287, PT 358, Grad 674 **Faculty:** FT 214, PT 247 **Student-Faculty Ratio:** 13:1 **Exams:** SAT I or ACT **% Receiving Financial Aid:** 51 **% Residing in College-Owned, -Operated, or -Affiliated Housing:** 57 **Library Holdings:** 184,835 **Regional Accreditation:** Southern Association of Colleges and Schools **Credit Hours For Degree:** 128 semester hours, Bachelors **ROTC:** Army, Navy **Professional Accreditation:** AACSB, AACN, AOTA, APTA, CSWE, NASM, NCATE **Intercollegiate Athletics:** Baseball M; Basketball M & W; Cross-Country Running M & W; Golf M & W; Soccer M & W; Softball W; Tennis M & W; Track and Field M & W; Volleyball W

BETHEL COLLEGE
325 Cherry Ave.
McKenzie, TN 38201
Tel: (731)352-4000
Admissions: (731)352-4030
Fax: (731)352-4069
Web Site: http://www.bethel-college.edu/
President/CEO: Dr. Robert Prosser
Registrar: Shirley Martin
Admissions: Tina Hodges
Financial Aid: Laura Bateman
Type: Comprehensive **Sex:** Coed **Affiliation:** Cumberland Presbyterian **Scores:** 100% SAT V 400+; 100% SAT M 400+; 54% ACT 18-23; 11% ACT 24-29 **Admission Plans:** Early Admission; Deferred Admission **Application Fee:** $30.00 **H.S. Requirements:** High school diploma required; GED accepted **Scholarships:** Available **Calendar System:** Semester, Summer Session Available **Enrollment:** FT 915, PT 219, Grad 118 **Faculty:** FT 55, PT 19 **Student-Faculty Ratio:** 14:1 **Exams:** SAT I or ACT **% Residing in College-Owned, -Operated, or -Affiliated Housing:** 50 **Library Holdings:** 83,919 **Regional Accreditation:** Southern Association of Colleges and Schools **Credit Hours For Degree:** 128 semester hours, Bachelors **Intercollegiate Athletics:** Baseball M; Basketball M & W; Cheerleading M & W; Cross-Country Running M & W; Football M; Golf M & W; Soccer M & W; Softball W; Tennis M & W; Track and Field M & W; Volleyball W

BRYAN COLLEGE
PO Box 7000
Dayton, TN 37321-7000
Tel: (423)775-2041
Free: 800-277-9522
Fax: (423)775-7330
E-mail: admissions@bryan.edu
Web Site: http://www.bryan.edu/
President/CEO: Dr. Stephen D. Livesay
Registrar: Janet Piatt
Admissions: Michael Sapienza
Financial Aid: Michael Sapienza
Type: Four-Year College **Sex:** Coed **Affiliation:** interdenominational **% Accepted:** 76 **Admission Plans:** Early Admission; Deferred Admission **Application Deadline:** Rolling **Application Fee:** $30.00 **H.S. Requirements:** High school diploma required; GED accepted **Costs Per Year:** Application fee: $30. Comprehensive fee: $19,270 includes full-time tuition ($14,800) and college room and board ($4470). Part-time tuition: $625 per credit hour. **Scholarships:** Available **Calendar System:** Semester, Summer Session Available **Enrollment:** FT 757, PT 18 **Faculty:** FT 35, PT 35 **Student-Faculty Ratio:** 13:1 **Exams:** SAT I or ACT **% Receiving Financial Aid:** 75 **% Residing in College-Owned, -Operated, or -Affiliated Housing:** 74 **Library Holdings:** 98,413 **Regional Accreditation:** Southern Association of Colleges and Schools **Credit Hours For Degree:** 60 semester hours, Associates; 124 semester hours, Bachelors **Intercollegiate Athletics:** Baseball M; Basketball M & W; Cross-Country Running M & W; Soccer M & W; Tennis M & W; Volleyball W

CARSON-NEWMAN COLLEGE
1646 Russell Ave., PO Box 557
Jefferson City, TN 37760
Tel: (865)471-2000
Free: 800-678-9061
Admissions: (865)471-3223
Fax: (865)471-3502
E-mail: cnadmiss@cn.edu
Web Site: http://www.cn.edu/
President/CEO: James S. Netherton
Registrar: Edward Hart
Admissions: Tom Huebner
Financial Aid: Parker Leake
Type: Comprehensive **Sex:** Coed **Affiliation:** Southern Baptist **Scores:** 51% ACT 18-23; 28% ACT 24-29 **% Accepted:** 78 **Admission Plans:** Deferred Admission **Application Deadline:** August 01 **Application Fee:** $25.00 **H.S. Requirements:** High school diploma required; GED accepted **Costs Per Year:** Application fee: $25. Comprehensive fee: $21,260 includes full-time tuition ($15,300), mandatory fees ($760), and college room and board ($5200). College room only: $2250. Part-time tuition: $635 per semester hour. **Scholarships:** Available **Calendar System:** Semester, Summer Session Available **Enrollment:** FT 1,759, PT 92, Grad 142 **Faculty:** FT 128, PT 67 **Student-Faculty Ratio:** 13:1 **Exams:** SAT I or ACT **% Receiving Financial Aid:** 72 **% Residing in College-Owned, -Operated, or -Affiliated Housing:** 51 **Library Holdings:** 218,371 **Regional Accreditation:** Southern Association of Colleges and Schools **Credit Hours For Degree:** 128 semester hours, Bachelors **ROTC:** Army, Air Force **Professional Accreditation:** AACN, AAFCS, NASAD, NASM, NCATE, NLN **Intercollegiate Athletics:** Baseball M; Basketball M & W; Cross-Country Running M & W; Football M; Golf M; Soccer M & W; Softball W; Tennis M & W; Track and Field M & W; Volleyball W; Wrestling M

CHATTANOOGA STATE TECHNICAL COMMUNITY COLLEGE
4501 Amnicola Hwy.
Chattanooga, TN 37406-1097
Tel: (423)697-4400
Admissions: (423)697-4401
Fax: (423)697-4709
E-mail: diane.norris@chattanoogastate.edu
Web Site: http://www.chattanoogastate.edu/
President/CEO: Dr. James L. Catanzaro
Registrar: Julie Bennett
Admissions: Diane Norris

Financial Aid: Mary Knaff
Type: Two-Year College **Sex:** Coed **Affiliation:** Tennessee Board of Regents **Scores:** 49% ACT 18-23; 7% ACT 24-29 **% Accepted:** 100 **Admission Plans:** Open Admission; Early Admission; Deferred Admission **Application Deadline:** Rolling **Application Fee:** $15.00 **H.S. Requirements:** High school diploma required; GED accepted **Costs Per Year:** Application fee: $15. State resident tuition: $2142 full-time, $91 per semester hour part-time. Nonresident tuition: $8556 full-time, $369 per semester hour part-time. **Scholarships:** Available **Calendar System:** Semester, Summer Session Available **Enrollment:** FT 3,533, PT 4,303 **Faculty:** FT 201, PT 425 **Student-Faculty Ratio:** 22:1 **Library Holdings:** 73,334 **Regional Accreditation:** Southern Association of Colleges and Schools **Credit Hours For Degree:** 64 semester hours, Associates **Professional Accreditation:** ABET, ADA, AHIMA, APTA, CARC, NLN **Intercollegiate Athletics:** Baseball M; Basketball M & W; Softball W

CHRISTIAN BROTHERS UNIVERSITY
650 East Parkway South
Memphis, TN 38104-5581
Tel: (901)321-3000
Free: 800-288-7576
Admissions: (901)321-3205
Fax: (901)321-3202
E-mail: tdysart@cbu.edu
Web Site: http://www.cbu.edu/
President/CEO: Br. Stanislaus Sobczyk, FSC
Registrar: Barbara Havey
Admissions: Tracey Dysart-Ford
Financial Aid: James R. Shannon
Type: Comprehensive **Sex:** Coed **Affiliation:** Roman Catholic **Scores:** 96% SAT V 400+; 99% SAT M 400+; 47% ACT 18-23; 41% ACT 24-29 **% Accepted:** 72 **Admission Plans:** Early Admission; Deferred Admission **Application Deadline:** March 01 **Application Fee:** $25.00 **H.S. Requirements:** High school diploma required; GED accepted **Costs Per Year:** Application fee: $25. Comprehensive fee: $24,650 includes full-time tuition ($18,630), mandatory fees ($520), and college room and board ($5500). College room only: $2480. Full-time tuition and fees vary according to class time. Room and board charges vary according to board plan and housing facility. Part-time tuition: $585 per credit hour. Part-time tuition varies according to class time. **Scholarships:** Available **Calendar System:** Semester, Summer Session Available **Enrollment:** FT 1,151, PT 342, Grad 285 **Faculty:** FT 102, PT 52 **Student-Faculty Ratio:** 14:1 **Exams:** SAT I or ACT **% Receiving Financial Aid:** 68 **% Residing in College-Owned, -Operated, or -Affiliated Housing:** 31 **Library Holdings:** 92,000 **Regional Accreditation:** Southern Association of Colleges and Schools **Credit Hours For Degree:** 122 semester hours, Bachelors **ROTC:** Army, Navy, Air Force **Professional Accreditation:** ABET **Intercollegiate Athletics:** Baseball M; Basketball M & W; Cross-Country Running M & W; Golf M & W; Soccer M & W; Softball W; Tennis M & W; Volleyball W

CLEVELAND STATE COMMUNITY COLLEGE
PO Box 3570
Cleveland, TN 37320-3570
Tel: (423)472-7141
Admissions: (423)478-6212
Fax: (423)478-6255
E-mail: mburnette@clevelandstatecc.edu
Web Site: http://www.clevelandstatecc.edu/
President/CEO: Dr. Carl Hite
Registrar: Midge Burnette
Admissions: Midge Burnette
Financial Aid: Geraldine Parks
Type: Two-Year College **Sex:** Coed **Affiliation:** Tennessee Board of Regents **% Accepted:** 61 **Admission Plans:** Open Admission; Early Admission; Deferred Admission **Application Deadline:** Rolling **Application Fee:** $10.00 **H.S. Requirements:** High school diploma required; GED accepted **Costs Per Year:** Application fee: $10. State resident tuition: $2142 full-time, $91 per credit hour part-time. Nonresident tuition: $8556 full-time, $369 per credit hour part-time. Mandatory fees: $263 full-time, $28.25 per credit hour part-time. Full-time tuition and fees vary according to course load. **Scholarships:** Available **Calendar System:** Semester, Summer Session Available **Enrollment:** FT 1,586, PT 1,441 **Faculty:** FT 72, PT 118 **Student-Faculty Ratio:** 29:1 **Library Holdings:** 65,347 **Regional Accreditation:** Southern Association of Colleges and Schools **Credit Hours For Degree:** 64 semester hours, Associates **Professional Accreditation:** AAMAE, NAIT, NLN **Intercollegiate Athletics:** Baseball M; Basketball M & W; Softball W

COLUMBIA STATE COMMUNITY COLLEGE
PO Box 1315
Columbia, TN 38402-1315
Tel: (931)540-2722
Admissions: (931)540-2545
Fax: (931)540-2535
Web Site: http://www.columbiastate.edu/
President/CEO: Dr. O. Rebecca Hawkins
Registrar: Sharon Bowen
Admissions: Sharon Bowen
Financial Aid: Dr. Dan Opalewski
Type: Two-Year College **Sex:** Coed **Scores:** 100% SAT V 400+; 100% SAT M 400+; 55.3% ACT 18-23; 10.8% ACT 24-29 **Admission Plans:** Open Admission; Early Admission **Application Fee:** $10.00 **H.S. Requirements:** High school diploma required; GED accepted **Scholarships:** Available **Calendar System:** Semester, Summer Session Available **Enrollment:** FT 2,423, PT 2,190 **Faculty:** FT 98, PT 159 **Exams:** SAT I or ACT **Library Holdings:** 61,200 **Regional Accreditation:** Southern Association of Colleges and Schools **Credit Hours For Degree:** 66 semester hours, Associates **Professional Accreditation:** CARC, JRCERT, JRCEMT, NLN **Intercollegiate Athletics:** Baseball M; Basketball M & W; Softball W

CONCORDE CAREER COLLEGE
5100 Poplar Ave., Ste. 132
Memphis, TN 38137
Tel: (901)761-9494
Fax: (901)761-3293
Web Site: http://www.concordecareercolleges.com/
Financial Aid: Jeanette Garrison
Type: Two-Year College **Sex:** Coed **Professional Accreditation:** COE

CRICHTON COLLEGE
255 North Highland St.
Memphis, TN 38111
Tel: (901)320-9700
Free: 800-960-9777
Admissions: (901)320-9797
Fax: (901)320-9709
Web Site: http://www.crichton.edu/
President/CEO: Dr. Larry B. Lloyd
Registrar: Camille E. Patterson
Admissions: Carolyn Cates
Financial Aid: Dede Pirtle
Type: Four-Year College **Sex:** Coed **Affiliation:** nondenominational **Scores:** 100% SAT V 400+; 100% SAT M 400+; 56% ACT 18-23; 22% ACT 24-29 **Admission Plans:** Deferred Admission **Application Deadline:** Rolling **Application Fee:** $25.00 **H.S. Requirements:** High school diploma required; GED accepted **Costs Per Year:** Application fee: $25. Tuition: $9960 full-time, $415 per credit hour part-time. Mandatory fees: $209 full-time, $12 per credit hour part-time. Full-time tuition and fees vary according to course load and program. Part-time tuition and fees vary according to program. College room only: $3600. **Scholarships:** Available **Calendar System:** Semester, Summer Session Available **Enrollment:** FT 503, PT 469 **Faculty:** FT 34, PT 73 **Student-Faculty Ratio:** 15:1 **Exams:** SAT I or ACT **% Receiving Financial Aid:** 66 **% Residing in College-Owned, -Operated, or -Affiliated Housing:** 5 **Library Holdings:** 54,175 **Regional Accreditation:** Southern Association of Colleges and Schools **Credit Hours For Degree:** 128 semester hours, Bachelors **Intercollegiate Athletics:** Baseball M; Basketball M

CUMBERLAND UNIVERSITY
One Cumberland Square
Lebanon, TN 37087-3408
Tel: (615)444-2562
Free: 800-467-0562
Fax: (615)444-2569
E-mail: epawlawski@cumberland.edu
Web Site: http://www.cumberland.edu/
President/CEO: Dr. Harvill C. Eaton
Registrar: Regena B. Poss
Admissions: Eddie Pawlawski
Financial Aid: Larry B. Vaughan

Type: Comprehensive **Sex:** Coed **Scores:** 49% ACT 18-23; 20% ACT 24-29 **% Accepted:** 69 **Admission Plans:** Deferred Admission **Application Deadline:** Rolling **Application Fee:** $25.00 **H.S. Requirements:** High school diploma required; GED accepted **Costs Per Year:** Application fee: $25. Comprehensive fee: $18,564 includes full-time tuition ($13,344), mandatory fees ($400), and college room and board ($4820). Full-time tuition and fees vary according to course load. Room and board charges vary according to board plan and housing facility. Part-time tuition: $557 per semester hour. **Scholarships:** Available **Calendar System:** Semester, Summer Session Available **Enrollment:** FT 937, PT 146, Grad 425 **Faculty:** FT 60, PT 38 **Student-Faculty Ratio:** 15:1 **Exams:** SAT I or ACT, SAT I **% Residing in College-Owned, -Operated, or -Affiliated Housing:** 43 **Library Holdings:** 50,000 **Regional Accreditation:** Southern Association of Colleges and Schools **Credit Hours For Degree:** 64 semester hours, Associates; 120 semester hours, Bachelors **ROTC:** Army **Professional Accreditation:** ACBSP, NLN **Intercollegiate Athletics:** Baseball M; Basketball M & W; Cheerleading M & W; Cross-Country Running M & W; Football M; Golf M & W; Soccer M & W; Softball W; Tennis M & W; Volleyball W; Wrestling M

DRAUGHONS JUNIOR COLLEGE (CLARKSVILLE)
1860 Wilma Rudolph Blvd.
Clarksville, TN 37040
Tel: (931)552-7600
Fax: (931)552-3624
Web Site: http://www.draughons.edu/
President/CEO: John Hinds
Registrar: Angie Sanford
Financial Aid: Teresa Clark
Type: Two-Year College **Sex:** Coed **Admission Plans:** Open Admission **H.S. Requirements:** High school diploma required; GED accepted **Scholarships:** Available **Calendar System:** Semester **Credit Hours For Degree:** 60 semester hours, Associates **Professional Accreditation:** ACICS

DRAUGHONS JUNIOR COLLEGE (NASHVILLE)
340 Plus Park Blvd.
Nashville, TN 37217
Tel: (615)361-7555
Web Site: http://www.draughons.edu/
Registrar: Janice Darity
Financial Aid: Bob Hobart
Type: Two-Year College **Sex:** Coed **Admission Plans:** Open Admission; Deferred Admission **Application Fee:** $20.00 **H.S. Requirements:** High school diploma required; GED accepted **Scholarships:** Available **Calendar System:** Semester, Summer Session Available **Faculty:** FT 25, PT 30 **Library Holdings:** 3,250 **Credit Hours For Degree:** 60 semester hours, Associates **Professional Accreditation:** ACICS

DYERSBURG STATE COMMUNITY COLLEGE
1510 Lake Rd.
Dyersburg, TN 38024
Tel: (731)286-3200
Admissions: (731)286-3327
Fax: (731)286-3325
E-mail: gullet@dscc.edu
Web Site: http://www.dscc.edu/
President/CEO: Dr. Karen A. Bowyer
Registrar: J. Dan Gullett
Admissions: Dan J. Gullett
Financial Aid: Sandra Rockett
Type: Two-Year College **Sex:** Coed **Affiliation:** Tennessee Board of Regents **Scores:** 49.3% ACT 18-23; 5.4% ACT 24-29 **% Accepted:** 99 **Admission Plans:** Open Admission; Early Admission **Application Deadline:** Rolling **Application Fee:** $10.00 **H.S. Requirements:** High school diploma required; GED accepted. For adult students: High school diploma or equivalent not required **Costs Per Year:** Application fee: $10. State resident tuition: $2142 full-time, $91 per hour part-time. Nonresident tuition: $8556 full-time, $369 per hour part-time. Mandatory fees: $251 full-time. Part-time tuition varies according to course load. **Scholarships:** Available **Calendar System:** Semester, Summer Session Available **Enrollment:** FT 1,428, PT 1,029 **Faculty:** FT 57, PT 148 **Student-Faculty Ratio:** 24:1 **Library Holdings:** 44,033 **Regional Accreditation:** Southern Association of Colleges and Schools **Credit Hours For Degree:** 60 semester hours, Associates **Professional Accreditation:** NLN **Intercollegiate Athletics:** Baseball M; Basketball M & W; Cheerleading W; Softball W

EAST TENNESSEE STATE UNIVERSITY
807 University Parkway
Johnson City, TN 37614
Tel: (423)439-1000
Free: 800-462-3878
Admissions: (423)439-4213
Fax: (423)439-5770
E-mail: go2etsu@etsu.edu
Web Site: http://www.etsu.edu/
President/CEO: Dr. Paul E. Stanton, Jr.
Registrar: Paul Hayes
Admissions: Dr. Nancy Dishner
Financial Aid: Margaret Miller
Type: University **Sex:** Coed **Affiliation:** State University and Community College System of Tennessee, Tennessee Board of Regents **Scores:** 89.9% SAT V 400+; 93.9% SAT M 400+; 57.4% ACT 18-23; 29% ACT 24-29 **% Accepted:** 81 **Admission Plans:** Early Admission **Application Fee:** $15.00 **H.S. Requirements:** High school diploma required; GED accepted **Costs Per Year:** Application fee: $15. State resident tuition: $3678 full-time, $161 per hour part-time. Nonresident tuition: $12,990 full-time, $565 per hour part-time. Mandatory fees: $809 full-time. Full-time tuition and fees vary according to course load and program. College room and board: $4822. College room only: $2512. Room and board charges vary according to board plan and housing facility. **Scholarships:** Available **Calendar System:** Semester, Summer Session Available **Enrollment:** FT 8,183, PT 1,587, Grad 1,886 **Faculty:** FT 480, PT 309 **Student-Faculty Ratio:** 17:1 **Exams:** SAT I or ACT **% Receiving Financial Aid:** 56 **% Residing in College-Owned, -Operated, or -Affiliated Housing:** 20 **Library Holdings:** 1,073,382 **Regional Accreditation:** Southern Association of Colleges and Schools **Credit Hours For Degree:** 60 semester hours, Associates; 120 semester hours, Bachelors **ROTC:** Army **Professional Accreditation:** AACSB, ABET, ACEJMC, AAFCS, AAMAE, ACA, ADA, ADtA, APTA, ASLHA, CARC, CEPH, CSWE, JRCERT, LCMEAMA, NAACLS, NASAD, NASM, NCATE, NLN **Intercollegiate Athletics:** Baseball M; Basketball M & W; Cross-Country Running M & W; Golf M & W; Soccer W; Softball W; Tennis M & W; Track and Field M & W; Volleyball W

ELECTRONIC COMPUTER PROGRAMMING COLLEGE
3805 Brainerd Rd.
Chattanooga, TN 37411-3798
Tel: (423)624-0077
Web Site: http://www.ecpconline.com/
President/CEO: William Faour
Registrar: William Faour
Admissions: Toney McFadden
Financial Aid: Evenyn Davis
Type: Two-Year College **Scholarships:** Available **Enrollment:** FT 178 **Faculty:** FT 9, PT 4 **Student-Faculty Ratio:** 20:1 **Professional Accreditation:** ACCSCT

FISK UNIVERSITY
1000 17th Ave. North
Nashville, TN 37208-3051
Tel: (615)329-8500
Free: 800-443-FISK
Admissions: (615)329-8819
Fax: (615)329-8576
E-mail: admit@fisk.edu
Web Site: http://www.fisk.edu/
President/CEO: Dr. Hazel R. O'Leary
Registrar: Lisa Dixon
Admissions: Keith Chandler
Financial Aid: Mark Adkins
Type: Comprehensive **Sex:** Coed **Affiliation:** United Church of Christ **Scores:** 89% SAT V 400+; 83% SAT M 400+ **% Accepted:** 80 **Application Deadline:** March 01 **Application Fee:** $50.00 **H.S. Requirements:** High school diploma required; GED accepted **Costs Per Year:** Application fee: $50. Comprehensive fee: $19,910 includes full-time tuition ($12,480), mandatory fees ($700), and college room and board ($6730). College room only: $3910. Full-time tuition and fees vary according to course load. Room and board charges vary according to board plan. Part-time tuition: $520 per credit hour. Part-time tuition varies according to course load. **Scholarships:** Available **Calendar System:** Semester, Summer Session Not available **Enrollment:** FT 788, PT 46, Grad 56 **Faculty:** FT 56, PT 35 **Student-Faculty Ratio:** 13:1 **Exams:** SAT I or ACT **% Receiving Financial Aid:** 94

% Residing in College-Owned, -Operated, or -Affiliated Housing: 68 **Library Holdings:** 127,070 **Regional Accreditation:** Southern Association of Colleges and Schools **Credit Hours For Degree:** 120 credit hours, Bachelors **ROTC:** Army, Navy **Professional Accreditation:** ACBSP, NASM **Intercollegiate Athletics:** Baseball M; Basketball M & W; Cross-Country Running M & W; Tennis M & W; Track and Field M & W; Volleyball W

FOUNTAINHEAD COLLEGE OF TECHNOLOGY
3203 Tazewell Pike
Knoxville, TN 37918-2530
Tel: (865)688-9422; 888-218-7335
Fax: (865)688-2419
Web Site: http://www.fountainheadcollege.edu/
President/CEO: Richard Rackley
Registrar: Nancy Rackley
Admissions: Todd Hill
Financial Aid: Jana Deal
Type: Two-Year College **Sex:** Coed **Admission Plans:** Open Admission **Application Deadline:** Rolling **Application Fee:** $100.00 **H.S. Requirements:** High school diploma required; GED accepted **Scholarships:** Available **Calendar System:** Semester, Summer Session Available **Faculty:** FT 9, PT 1 **Student-Faculty Ratio:** 13:1 **Library Holdings:** 1,200 **Credit Hours For Degree:** 75 credits, Associates; 120 credits, Bachelors **Professional Accreditation:** ACCSCT

FREE WILL BAPTIST BIBLE COLLEGE
3606 West End Ave.
Nashville, TN 37205-2498
Tel: (615)844-5000
Free: 800-763-9222
Admissions: (615)844-1500
Fax: (615)269-6028
Web Site: http://www.fwbbc.edu/
President/CEO: Matthew Pinson
Registrar: Fred Burch
Admissions: Dr. Milton Fields
Financial Aid: Jeff Caudill
Type: Four-Year College **Sex:** Coed **Affiliation:** Free Will Baptist **Scores:** 51% ACT 18-23; 22% ACT 24-29 **% Accepted:** 67 **Admission Plans:** Open Admission; Preferred Admission; Early Admission; Deferred Admission **Application Deadline:** Rolling **Application Fee:** $35.00 **H.S. Requirements:** High school diploma required; GED accepted **Costs Per Year:** Application fee: $35. Comprehensive fee: $15,874 includes full-time tuition ($10,470), mandatory fees ($696), and college room and board ($4708). Part-time tuition: $349 per semester hour. **Scholarships:** Available **Calendar System:** Semester, Summer Session Available **Faculty:** FT 23, PT 24 **Student-Faculty Ratio:** 10:1 **Exams:** ACT **% Residing in College-Owned, -Operated, or -Affiliated Housing:** 71 **Library Holdings:** 131,200 **Regional Accreditation:** Southern Association of Colleges and Schools **Credit Hours For Degree:** 66 semester hours, Associates; 124 semester hours, Bachelors **ROTC:** Army, Air Force **Professional Accreditation:** AABC **Intercollegiate Athletics:** Basketball M & W

FREED-HARDEMAN UNIVERSITY
158 East Main St.
Henderson, TN 38340-2399
Tel: (731)989-6000
Free: 800-630-3480
Admissions: (731)989-6651
Fax: (731)989-6047
E-mail: admissions@fhu.edu
Web Site: http://www.fhu.edu/
President/CEO: Dr. Milton R. Sewell
Registrar: Larry R. Oldham
Admissions: Wayne Scott
Financial Aid: Lawrence P. Cyr
Type: Comprehensive **Sex:** Coed **Affiliation:** Church of Christ **Scores:** 53% ACT 18-23; 32% ACT 24-29 **% Accepted:** 99 **Admission Plans:** Early Admission; Deferred Admission **Application Deadline:** Rolling **Application Fee:** $0.00 **H.S. Requirements:** High school diploma required; GED accepted **Costs Per Year:** Application fee: $0. Tuition: $11,000 full-time. Mandatory fees: $2092 full-time. College room only: $3700. **Scholarships:** Available **Calendar System:** Semester, Summer Session Available **Enrollment:** FT 1,402, PT 98, Grad 530 **Faculty:** FT 106, PT 41 **Student-Faculty Ratio:** 14:1 **Exams:** SAT I or ACT **% Receiving Financial Aid:** 75 **% Residing in College-Owned, -Operated, or -Affiliated Housing:** 81 **Library Holdings:** 154,689 **Regional Accreditation:** Southern Association of Colleges and Schools **Credit Hours For Degree:** 132 semester hours, Bachelors **Professional Accreditation:** ACBSP, CSWE, NCATE **Intercollegiate Athletics:** Baseball M; Basketball M & W; Cheerleading M & W; Soccer M & W; Softball W; Tennis M & W; Volleyball W

HIGH-TECH INSTITUTE (MEMPHIS)
5865 Shelby Oaks Circle
Memphis, TN 38134
Tel: (901)387-4555
Web Site: http://www.high-techinstitute.com/
President/CEO: Larry Collins
Type: Two-Year College **Sex:** Coed **Calendar System:** Semester **Professional Accreditation:** ACCSCT

HIGH-TECH INSTITUTE (NASHVILLE)
2710 Old Lebanon Rd., Ste. 12
Nashville, TN 37214
Tel: (615)902-9705
Free: 800-987-0110
Fax: (615)902-9766
E-mail: dmartinez@hightechschools.com
Web Site: http://www.high-techinstitute.com/
President/CEO: Lisa Bacon
Admissions: David Martinez
Type: Two-Year College **Sex:** Coed **Calendar System:** Semester **Professional Accreditation:** ACCSCT

ITT TECHNICAL INSTITUTE (KNOXVILLE)
10208 Technology Dr.
Knoxville, TN 37932
Tel: (865)671-2800
Fax: (865)691-0337
Web Site: http://www.itt-tech.edu/
President/CEO: David W. Reynolds
Admissions: Dave Reynolds
Financial Aid: Kellie M. Armtrong
Type: Two-Year College **Sex:** Coed **Affiliation:** ITT Educational Services, Inc **Admission Plans:** Deferred Admission **Application Deadline:** Rolling **Application Fee:** $100.00 **H.S. Requirements:** High school diploma required; GED accepted **Costs Per Year:** Application fee: $100. **Scholarships:** Available **Calendar System:** Quarter, Summer Session Not available **Exams:** Other **Credit Hours For Degree:** 96 credit hours, Associates; 180 credit hours, Bachelors **Professional Accreditation:** ACICS

ITT TECHNICAL INSTITUTE (MEMPHIS)
1255 Lynnfield Rd., Ste. 92
Memphis, TN 38119
Tel: (901)762-0556
Admissions: (901)381-0200
Web Site: http://www.itt-tech.edu/
President/CEO: David Scarbro
Registrar: Patricia Holland
Admissions: Brenda Nash
Financial Aid: Gary Owens
Type: Two-Year College **Sex:** Coed **Affiliation:** ITT Educational Services, Inc **Admission Plans:** Deferred Admission **Application Deadline:** Rolling **Application Fee:** $100.00 **H.S. Requirements:** High school diploma required; GED accepted **Costs Per Year:** Application fee: $100. **Scholarships:** Available **Calendar System:** Quarter, Summer Session Not available **Exams:** Other **Credit Hours For Degree:** 96 credit hours, Associates; 180 credit hours, Bachelors **Professional Accreditation:** ACICS

ITT TECHNICAL INSTITUTE (NASHVILLE)
2845 Elm Hill Pike
Nashville, TN 37214-3717
Tel: (615)889-8700
Fax: (615)872-7209
Web Site: http://www.itt-tech.edu/
President/CEO: James R. Coakley
Admissions: Jim Coakley
Financial Aid: James Blackburn
Type: Two-Year College **Sex:** Coed **Affiliation:** ITT Educational Services, Inc **Admission Plans:** Deferred Admission **Application Deadline:** Rolling

Application Fee: $100.00 **H.S. Requirements:** High school diploma required; GED accepted **Costs Per Year:** Application fee: $100. **Scholarships:** Available **Calendar System:** Quarter, Summer Session Not available **Exams:** Other **Credit Hours For Degree:** 96 credit hours, Associates; 180 credit hours, Bachelors **Professional Accreditation:** ACICS

JACKSON STATE COMMUNITY COLLEGE
2046 North Parkway
Jackson, TN 38301-3797
Tel: (731)424-3520
Admissions: (731)425-2644
Fax: (731)425-2647
E-mail: mray@jscc.edu
Web Site: http://www.jscc.edu/
President/CEO: Dr. Charlie D. Roberts, Jr.
Registrar: Frances Edmonson
Admissions: Monica Ray
Financial Aid: Dewana Latimer
Type: Two-Year College **Sex:** Coed **Affiliation:** Tennessee Board of Regents **% Accepted:** 84 **Admission Plans:** Open Admission; Preferred Admission; Early Admission; Deferred Admission **Application Deadline:** August 29 **Application Fee:** $10.00 **H.S. Requirements:** High school diploma required; GED accepted **Costs Per Year:** Application fee: $10. State resident tuition: $2142 full-time, $91 per credit hour part-time. Nonresident tuition: $8556 full-time, $369 per credit hour part-time. Mandatory fees: $253 full-time, $9 per credit hour part-time, $14 per term part-time. **Scholarships:** Available **Calendar System:** Semester, Summer Session Available **Enrollment:** FT 2,048, PT 1,818 **Faculty:** FT 120, PT 96 **Student-Faculty Ratio:** 22:1 **Exams:** ACT, Other **Library Holdings:** 63,620 **Regional Accreditation:** Southern Association of Colleges and Schools **Credit Hours For Degree:** 60 semester hours, Associates **Professional Accreditation:** APTA, ACBSP, CARC, JRCERT, JRCEMT, NAACLS, NAIT, NLN **Intercollegiate Athletics:** Baseball M; Basketball M & W; Cheerleading W; Softball W

JOHN A. GUPTON COLLEGE
1616 Church St.
Nashville, TN 37203-2920
Tel: (615)327-3927
Web Site: http://www.guptoncollege.edu/
President/CEO: B. Steven Spann
Registrar: Lisa Bolin
Admissions: Lisa Bolin
Financial Aid: Alvin Oliver
Type: Two-Year College **Sex:** Coed **Admission Plans:** Deferred Admission **Application Fee:** $20.00 **H.S. Requirements:** High school diploma required; GED accepted **Scholarships:** Available **Calendar System:** Semester **Enrollment:** FT 91, PT 6 **Faculty:** FT 2, PT 16 **Student-Faculty Ratio:** 13:1 **Exams:** ACT **Library Holdings:** 4,000 **Regional Accreditation:** Southern Association of Colleges and Schools **Credit Hours For Degree:** 65 semester hours, Associates **Professional Accreditation:** ABFSE

JOHNSON BIBLE COLLEGE
7900 Johnson Dr.
Knoxville, TN 37998-1001
Tel: (865)573-4517
Free: 800-827-2122
Admissions: (865)251-2346
Fax: (865)251-2337
E-mail: twingfield@jbc.edu
Web Site: http://www.jbc.edu/
President/CEO: Dr. David L. Eubanks
Registrar: Sandra Blevins
Admissions: Tim Wingfield
Financial Aid: Janette Overton
Type: Comprehensive **Sex:** Coed **Affiliation:** Christian Churches and Churches of Christ **Scores:** 93% SAT V 400+; 93% SAT M 400+; 47% ACT 18-23; 34% ACT 24-29 **Admission Plans:** Deferred Admission **Application Fee:** $35.00 **H.S. Requirements:** High school diploma required; GED accepted **Costs Per Year:** Application fee: $35. Comprehensive fee: $10,580 includes full-time tuition ($5800), mandatory fees ($690), and college room and board ($4090). College room only: $2595. Room and board charges vary according to board plan and housing facility. Part-time tuition: $242 per semester hour. Part-time mandatory fees: $20.42 per semester hour. Part-time tuition and fees vary according to course load. **Scholarships:** Available **Calendar System:** Semester, Summer Session Available **Enrollment:** FT 728, PT 28, Grad 133 **Faculty:** FT 26, PT 32 **Student-Faculty Ratio:** 17:1 **Exams:** ACT, SAT I or ACT **% Receiving Financial Aid:** 87 **% Residing in College-Owned, -Operated, or -Affiliated Housing:** 88 **Library Holdings:** 104,808 **Regional Accreditation:** Southern Association of Colleges and Schools **Credit Hours For Degree:** 62 semester hours, Associates; 124 semester hours, Bachelors **Professional Accreditation:** AABC **Intercollegiate Athletics:** Baseball M; Basketball M & W; Cheerleading M & W; Soccer M & W; Volleyball W

KING COLLEGE
1350 King College Rd.
Bristol, TN 37620-2699
Tel: (423)968-1187
Free: 800-362-0014
Admissions: (423)652-4861
Fax: (423)968-4456
E-mail: admissions@king.edu
Web Site: http://www.king.edu/
President/CEO: Dr. Gregory D. Jordan
Registrar: Sarah Dillow
Admissions: Melinda Clark
Financial Aid: Brenda Clark
Type: Comprehensive **Sex:** Coed **Affiliation:** Presbyterian Church (U.S.A.) **Scores:** 91.4% SAT V 400+; 97.5% SAT M 400+; 60.6% ACT 18-23; 30% ACT 24-29 **% Accepted:** 95 **Admission Plans:** Early Admission; Deferred Admission **Application Deadline:** Rolling **Application Fee:** $20.00 **H.S. Requirements:** High school diploma required; GED accepted **Costs Per Year:** Application fee: $20. Comprehensive fee: $24,545 includes full-time tuition ($17,291), mandatory fees ($1054), and college room and board ($6200). College room only: $3100. Part-time tuition: $575 per credit hour. **Scholarships:** Available **Calendar System:** Semester, Summer Session Available **Enrollment:** FT 803, PT 70, Grad 97 **Faculty:** FT 50, PT 44 **Student-Faculty Ratio:** 13:1 **Exams:** SAT I or ACT **% Receiving Financial Aid:** 76 **% Residing in College-Owned, -Operated, or -Affiliated Housing:** 56 **Library Holdings:** 80,888 **Regional Accreditation:** Southern Association of Colleges and Schools **Credit Hours For Degree:** 124 semester hours, Bachelors **Professional Accreditation:** AACN **Intercollegiate Athletics:** Baseball M; Basketball M & W; Cheerleading M & W; Cross-Country Running M & W; Golf M & W; Soccer M & W; Softball M & W; Tennis M & W; Track and Field M & W; Volleyball W; Wrestling M

LAMBUTH UNIVERSITY
705 Lambuth Blvd.
Jackson, TN 38301
Tel: (731)425-2500
Free: 800-526-2884
Admissions: (731)425-3288
Fax: (731)988-4600
E-mail: burnley@lambuth.edu
Web Site: http://www.lambuth.edu/
President/CEO: Dr. R. Fred Zuker
Registrar: Nita Maxey Pearce
Admissions: Reuben Burnley
Financial Aid: Lisa Warmath
Type: Four-Year College **Sex:** Coed **Affiliation:** United Methodist **Scores:** 98% SAT V 400+; 98% SAT M 400+; 49% ACT 18-23; 42% ACT 24-29 **% Accepted:** 65 **Admission Plans:** Early Admission; Deferred Admission **Application Deadline:** Rolling **Application Fee:** $25.00 **H.S. Requirements:** High school diploma required; GED accepted **Costs Per Year:** Application fee: $25. Comprehensive fee: $23,090 includes full-time tuition ($15,980), mandatory fees ($400), and college room and board ($6710). College room only: $3195. Part-time tuition: $665 per credit hour. Part-time mandatory fees: $200 per term. **Scholarships:** Available **Calendar System:** Semester, Summer Session Available **Enrollment:** FT 766, PT 39 **Faculty:** FT 52, PT 27 **Student-Faculty Ratio:** 14:1 **Exams:** SAT I or ACT **% Receiving Financial Aid:** 69 **% Residing in College-Owned, -Operated, or -Affiliated Housing:** 59 **Library Holdings:** 272,435 **Regional Accreditation:** Southern Association of Colleges and Schools **Credit Hours For Degree:** 128 credit hours, Bachelors **Professional Accreditation:** ACBSP **Intercollegiate Athletics:** Baseball M; Basketball M & W; Cheerleading M &

W; Cross-Country Running M & W; Football M; Golf M; Soccer M & W; Softball W; Swimming and Diving M & W; Tennis M & W; Volleyball W

LANE COLLEGE
545 Ln. Ave.
Jackson, TN 38301-4598
Tel: (731)426-7500
Free: 800-960-7533
Admissions: (731)426-7533
Fax: (731)426-7559
Web Site: http://www.lanecollege.edu/
President/CEO: Dr. Wesley C. McClure
Registrar: Cynthia Murry
Admissions: E. Brown
Financial Aid: Ursula Singleton
Type: Four-Year College **Sex:** Coed **Affiliation:** Christian Methodist Episcopal Church **Scores:** 36% ACT 18-23; 2% ACT 24-29 **Admission Plans:** Early Admission; Early Decision Plan **Application Fee:** $0.00 **H.S. Requirements:** High school diploma required; GED accepted **Costs Per Year:** Application fee: $0. Comprehensive fee: $11,710 includes full-time tuition ($6576), mandatory fees ($600), and college room and board ($4534). Full-time tuition and fees vary according to course load. Part-time tuition: $292 per hour. Part-time tuition varies according to course load. **Scholarships:** Available **Calendar System:** Semester, Summer Session Available **Enrollment:** FT 1,035, PT 10 **Faculty:** FT 51, PT 1 **Student-Faculty Ratio:** 20:1 **Exams:** SAT I or ACT **% Receiving Financial Aid:** 95 **% Residing in College-Owned, -Operated, or -Affiliated Housing:** 60 **Library Holdings:** 143,940 **Regional Accreditation:** Southern Association of Colleges and Schools **Credit Hours For Degree:** 124 semester hours, Bachelors **Intercollegiate Athletics:** Baseball M; Basketball M & W; Cross-Country Running M & W; Football M; Golf M; Softball W; Tennis M & W; Track and Field M & W; Volleyball W

LEE UNIVERSITY
PO Box 3450
Cleveland, TN 37320-3450
Tel: (423)614-8000
Free: 800-533-9930
Admissions: (423)614-8500
Fax: (423)614-8533
Web Site: http://www.leeuniversity.edu/
President/CEO: Dr. Paul Conn
Registrar: Phillip M. Barber
Admissions: Phillip Cook
Financial Aid: Mike Ellis
Type: Comprehensive **Sex:** Coed **Affiliation:** Church of God **Scores:** 92.6% SAT V 400+; 90.3% SAT M 400+; 40.8% ACT 18-23; 35.7% ACT 24-29 **% Accepted:** 61 **Admission Plans:** Early Admission; Deferred Admission **Application Deadline:** September 01 **Application Fee:** $25.00 **H.S. Requirements:** High school diploma required; GED accepted **Costs Per Year:** Application fee: $25. Comprehensive fee: $14,780 includes full-time tuition ($9400), mandatory fees ($210), and college room and board ($5170). College room only: $2680. Full-time tuition and fees vary according to program. Room and board charges vary according to board plan and housing facility. Part-time tuition: $392 per credit hour. Part-time mandatory fees: $30 per term. Part-time tuition and fees vary according to program. **Scholarships:** Available **Calendar System:** Semester, Summer Session Available **Enrollment:** FT 3,316, PT 332, Grad 282 **Faculty:** FT 148, PT 164 **Student-Faculty Ratio:** 18:1 **Exams:** ACT, SAT I or ACT **% Receiving Financial Aid:** 60 **% Residing in College-Owned, -Operated, or -Affiliated Housing:** 44 **Library Holdings:** 145,435 **Regional Accreditation:** Southern Association of Colleges and Schools **Credit Hours For Degree:** 130 semester hours, Bachelors **Professional Accreditation:** NASM **Intercollegiate Athletics:** Basketball M & W; Cross-Country Running M & W; Golf M; Soccer M & W; Softball W; Tennis M & W; Volleyball W

LEMOYNE-OWEN COLLEGE
807 Walker Ave.
Memphis, TN 38126-6595
Tel: (901)774-9090
Admissions: (901)435-1550
Fax: (901)942-6272
E-mail: mark_green@loc.edu
Web Site: http://www.loc.edu/
President/CEO: James J. Wingate
Registrar: Clifford Merryman
Admissions: Mark Green
Financial Aid: Phyllis Wilson
Type: Four-Year College **Sex:** Coed **Affiliation:** United Church of Christ **Scores:** 21% ACT 18-23; 2% ACT 24-29 **% Accepted:** 38 **Admission Plans:** Open Admission **Application Deadline:** April 01 **Application Fee:** $25.00 **H.S. Requirements:** High school diploma required; GED accepted **Costs Per Year:** Application fee: $25. Comprehensive fee: $19,278 includes full-time tuition ($14,458), mandatory fees ($200), and college room and board ($4620). College room only: $2420. Room and board charges vary according to board plan. **Scholarships:** Available **Calendar System:** Semester, Summer Session Available **Enrollment:** FT 684, PT 125 **Faculty:** FT 59, PT 3 **Student-Faculty Ratio:** 14:1 **Exams:** SAT I or ACT **% Receiving Financial Aid:** 92 **% Residing in College-Owned, -Operated, or -Affiliated Housing:** 20 **Regional Accreditation:** Southern Association of Colleges and Schools **Credit Hours For Degree:** 120 credit hours, Bachelors **ROTC:** Army, Air Force **Professional Accreditation:** NCATE **Intercollegiate Athletics:** Baseball M; Basketball M & W; Cross-Country Running M; Golf M & W; Softball W; Tennis M & W; Volleyball W

LINCOLN MEMORIAL UNIVERSITY
6965 Cumberland Gap Parkway
Harrogate, TN 37752-1901
Tel: (423)869-3611
Free: 800-325-0900
Admissions: (423)869-6280
Fax: (423)869-6250
E-mail: admissions@lmunet.edu
Web Site: http://www.lmunet.edu/
President/CEO: Dr. Nancy B. Moody
Registrar: Helen Bailey
Admissions: Conrad Daniels
Financial Aid: Christy Graham
Type: Comprehensive **Sex:** Coed **Scores:** 50% ACT 18-23; 39% ACT 24-29 **% Accepted:** 37 **Application Deadline:** Rolling **Application Fee:** $25.00 **H.S. Requirements:** High school diploma required; GED accepted **Costs Per Year:** Application fee: $25. Comprehensive fee: $18,982 includes full-time tuition ($13,750) and college room and board ($5232). Part-time tuition: $573 per credit. **Scholarships:** Available **Calendar System:** Semester, Summer Session Available **Enrollment:** FT 1,012, PT 304, Grad 1,486 **Faculty:** FT 86, PT 66 **Student-Faculty Ratio:** 9:1 **Exams:** SAT I or ACT **% Receiving Financial Aid:** 63 **% Residing in College-Owned, -Operated, or -Affiliated Housing:** 32 **Library Holdings:** 145,537 **Regional Accreditation:** Southern Association of Colleges and Schools **Credit Hours For Degree:** 64 semester hours, Associates; 128 semester hours, Bachelors **Professional Accreditation:** CSWE, JRCEPAT, NAACLS, NLN **Intercollegiate Athletics:** Baseball M; Basketball M & W; Cross-Country Running M & W; Golf M & W; Soccer M & W; Softball W; Tennis M & W; Volleyball W

LIPSCOMB UNIVERSITY
3901 Granny White Pike
Nashville, TN 37204-3951
Tel: (615)269-1000; 877-582-4766
Fax: (615)269-1804
E-mail: admissions@lipscomb.edu
Web Site: http://www.lipscomb.edu/
President/CEO: Dr. Stephen Flatt
Registrar: Janet Cates
Admissions: Ricky Holaway
Financial Aid: Karita Waters
Type: Comprehensive **Sex:** Coed **Affiliation:** Church of Christ **Scores:** 98% SAT V 400+; 99% SAT M 400+; 45% ACT 18-23; 39% ACT 24-29 **% Accepted:** 76 **Admission Plans:** Early Admission **Application Deadline:** Rolling **Application Fee:** $50.00 **H.S. Requirements:** High school diploma required; GED accepted **Costs Per Year:** Application fee: $50. Comprehensive fee: $20,967 includes full-time tuition ($13,928), mandatory fees ($629), and college room and board ($6410). Full-time tuition and fees vary according to class time and degree level. Room and board charges vary according to board plan and housing facility. Part-time tuition: $525 per hour. Part-time mandatory fees: $629 per year. Part-time tuition and fees vary according to class time and degree level. **Scholarships:** Available **Calendar System:** Semester, Summer Session Available **Enrollment:** FT 2,070, PT 227, Grad 186 **Faculty:** FT 119, PT 77 **Student-Faculty Ratio:** 15:1 **Exams:** SAT I or ACT **% Receiving Financial Aid:** 52 **Library Holdings:** 202,378 **Regional**

Accreditation: Southern Association of Colleges and Schools **Credit Hours For Degree:** 132 semester hours, Bachelors **ROTC:** Army, Air Force **Professional Accreditation:** ADtA, ACBSP, ATS, CSWE, JRCEPAT, NASM, NCATE **Intercollegiate Athletics:** Baseball M; Basketball M & W; Cross-Country Running M & W; Golf M & W; Soccer M & W; Softball W; Tennis M & W; Volleyball W

MARTIN METHODIST COLLEGE
433 West Madison St.
Pulaski, TN 38478-2716
Tel: (931)363-9868
Free: 800-467-1273
Admissions: (931)363-9804
Fax: (931)363-9818
Web Site: http://www.martinmethodist.edu/
President/CEO: Dr. Ted R. Brown
Registrar: Sherry E. Yokley
Admissions: Tony Booker
Financial Aid: Ann Neville
Type: Four-Year College **Sex:** Coed **Affiliation:** United Methodist **Scores:** 63% ACT 18-23; 20% ACT 24-29 **Admission Plans:** Early Admission; Deferred Admission **Application Fee:** $25.00 **H.S. Requirements:** High school diploma required; GED accepted **Scholarships:** Available **Calendar System:** Semester, Summer Session Available **Enrollment:** FT 483, PT 231 **Faculty:** FT 33, PT 29 **Student-Faculty Ratio:** 17:1 **Exams:** SAT I or ACT **% Receiving Financial Aid:** 54 **% Residing in College-Owned, -Operated, or -Affiliated Housing:** 26 **Library Holdings:** 84,000 **Regional Accreditation:** Southern Association of Colleges and Schools **Credit Hours For Degree:** 63 hours, Associates; 120 hours, Bachelors **Intercollegiate Athletics:** Baseball M; Basketball M & W; Cheerleading W; Golf M; Soccer M & W; Softball W; Tennis M & W; Volleyball W

MARYVILLE COLLEGE
502 East Lamar Alexander Parkway
Maryville, TN 37804-5907
Tel: (865)981-8000
Free: 800-597-2687
Admissions: (865)981-8206
Fax: (865)983-0581
E-mail: admissions@maryvillecollege.edu
Web Site: http://www.maryvillecollege.edu/
President/CEO: Dr. Gerald W. Gibson
Registrar: Martha Hess
Admissions: Ned Willard
Financial Aid: Richard Brand
Type: Four-Year College **Sex:** Coed **Affiliation:** Presbyterian **Scores:** 100% SAT V 400+; 97% SAT M 400+; 46% ACT 18-23; 42% ACT 24-29 **% Accepted:** 79 **Admission Plans:** Early Admission; Early Action; Early Decision Plan; Deferred Admission **Application Deadline:** March 01 **Application Fee:** $25.00 **H.S. Requirements:** High school diploma required; GED accepted **Costs Per Year:** Application fee: $25. Comprehensive fee: $29,224 includes full-time tuition ($21,624), mandatory fees ($600), and college room and board ($7000). College room only: $3500. Full-time tuition and fees vary according to course load. Room and board charges vary according to board plan, housing facility, and location. Part-time tuition: $901 per hour. Part-time mandatory fees: $13.50 per hour. Part-time tuition and fees vary according to course load. **Scholarships:** Available **Calendar System:** 4-1-4, Summer Session Available **Enrollment:** FT 1,120, PT 26 **Faculty:** FT 73, PT 37 **Student-Faculty Ratio:** 14:1 **Exams:** SAT I or ACT **% Receiving Financial Aid:** 77 **% Residing in College-Owned, -Operated, or -Affiliated Housing:** 70 **Library Holdings:** 128,022 **Regional Accreditation:** Southern Association of Colleges and Schools **Credit Hours For Degree:** 128 semester hours, Bachelors **Professional Accreditation:** NASM **Intercollegiate Athletics:** Baseball M; Basketball M & W; Cheerleading M & W; Cross-Country Running M & W; Equestrian Sports M & W; Football M; Soccer M & W; Softball W; Tennis M & W; Volleyball W; Wrestling M

MEDVANCE INSTITUTE
1065 East 10th St.
Cookeville, TN 38501-1907
Tel: (931)526-3660
Free: 800-256-9085
Fax: (931)372-2603
Web Site: http://www.medvance.org/
President/CEO: Deborah K. Schwarzberg
Registrar: Judy Maxwell
Admissions: Sharon Mellott
Financial Aid: Cynthia Voiles
Type: Two-Year College **Sex:** Coed **H.S. Requirements:** High school diploma required; GED accepted **Scholarships:** Available **Calendar System:** Quarter, Summer Session Not available **Enrollment:** FT 231 **Faculty:** FT 8, PT 0 **Student-Faculty Ratio:** 15:1 **Exams:** Other **Credit Hours For Degree:** 96 quarter hours, Associates **Professional Accreditation:** COE, NAACLS

MEMPHIS COLLEGE OF ART
Overton Park, 1930 Poplar Ave.
Memphis, TN 38104-2764
Tel: (901)272-5100
Free: 800-727-1088
Admissions: (901)272-5153
Fax: (901)272-5104
E-mail: amoore@mca.edu
Web Site: http://www.mca.edu/
President/CEO: Jeffrey Nesin
Registrar: Sylvia Bond
Admissions: Annette Moore
Financial Aid: Cindy Stanley
Type: Comprehensive **Sex:** Coed **Scores:** 42% ACT 18-23; 28% ACT 24-29 **% Accepted:** 51 **Admission Plans:** Early Admission; Deferred Admission **Application Deadline:** Rolling **Application Fee:** $25.00 **H.S. Requirements:** High school diploma required; GED accepted **Costs Per Year:** Application fee: $25. Tuition: $17,400 full-time, $2225 per course part-time. Mandatory fees: $60 full-time. **Scholarships:** Available **Calendar System:** Semester, Summer Session Available **Enrollment:** FT 270, PT 44, Grad 12 **Faculty:** FT 21, PT 24 **Student-Faculty Ratio:** 11:1 **Exams:** SAT I or ACT **% Receiving Financial Aid:** 77 **% Residing in College-Owned, -Operated, or -Affiliated Housing:** 37 **Library Holdings:** 14,500 **Regional Accreditation:** Southern Association of Colleges and Schools **Credit Hours For Degree:** 120 credit hours, Bachelors **Professional Accreditation:** NASAD

MID-AMERICA BAPTIST THEOLOGICAL SEMINARY
PO Box 381528
Germantown, TN 38183-1528
Tel: (901)751-8453
Web Site: http://www.mabts.edu/
President/CEO: Dr. Michael Spradlin
Registrar: Louise Burnett
Admissions: Duffy Guyton
Financial Aid: Jay Jones
Type: Two-Year College **Sex:** Coed **Affiliation:** Southern Baptist **Admission Plans:** Open Admission **Application Deadline:** August 04 **Application Fee:** $25.00 **H.S. Requirements:** High school diploma required; GED accepted **Costs Per Year:** Application fee: $25. Tuition: $3600 full-time. **Scholarships:** Available **Calendar System:** Semester, Summer Session Available **Enrollment:** FT 37, PT 25, Grad 215 **Faculty:** FT 27 **Student-Faculty Ratio:** 15:1 **Library Holdings:** 119,000 **Regional Accreditation:** Southern Association of Colleges and Schools **Credit Hours For Degree:** 64 semester hours, Associates

MIDDLE TENNESSEE STATE UNIVERSITY
1301 East Main St.
Murfreesboro, TN 37132
Tel: (615)898-2300
Free: 800-433-MTSU
Admissions: (615)898-2111
E-mail: admissions@mtsu.edu
Web Site: http://www.mtsu.edu/
President/CEO: Dr. Sidney A. McPhee
Registrar: Teresa Thomas
Admissions: Lynn Palmer
Financial Aid: David L. Hutton
Type: University **Sex:** Coed **Affiliation:** Tennessee Board of Regents **Scores:** 94% SAT V 400+; 94% SAT M 400+; 62% ACT 18-23; 30% ACT 24-29 **% Accepted:** 85 **Admission Plans:** Early Admission; Deferred Admission **Application Deadline:** July 01 **Application Fee:** $25.00 **H.S. Requirements:** High school diploma required; GED accepted **Costs Per Year:** Application fee: $25. State resident tuition: $3678 full-time, $161 per semester hour part-time. Nonresident tuition: $12,990 full-time, $565 per semester hour part-time. Mandatory fees: $922 full-time. Part-time tuition

varies according to course load. College room and board: $5626. College room only: $3478. Room and board charges vary according to board plan and housing facility. **Scholarships:** Available **Calendar System:** Semester, Summer Session Available **Enrollment:** FT 17,291, PT 3,098, Grad 2,165 **Faculty:** FT 881 **Student-Faculty Ratio:** 22:1 **Exams:** SAT I or ACT **% Receiving Financial Aid:** 48 **% Residing in College-Owned, -Operated, or -Affiliated Housing:** 20 **Library Holdings:** 748,888 **Regional Accreditation:** Southern Association of Colleges and Schools **Credit Hours For Degree:** 65 semester hours, Associates; 120 semester hours, Bachelors **ROTC:** Army, Air Force **Professional Accreditation:** AACSB, ABET, ACEJMC, AACN, AAFCS, ACA, CAA, CSWE, FIDER, NAIT, NASM, NCATE, NLN, NRPA **Intercollegiate Athletics:** Baseball M; Basketball M & W; Cheerleading M & W; Cross-Country Running M & W; Equestrian Sports M & W; Football M; Golf M; Soccer W; Softball W; Tennis M & W; Track and Field M & W; Volleyball W

MILLER-MOTTE TECHNICAL COLLEGE
1820 Business Park Dr.
Clarksville, TN 37040
Tel: (931)553-0071
Admissions: 800-558-0071
Fax: (931)552-2916
E-mail: lisateague@hotmail.com
Web Site: http://www.miller-motte.com/
President/CEO: Raymond Green
Registrar: Patricia Kline
Admissions: Lisa Teague
Financial Aid: Donna A. Green
Type: Two-Year College **Sex:** Coed **Scholarships:** Available **Calendar System:** Quarter **Professional Accreditation:** ACICS, AAMAE

MILLIGAN COLLEGE
PO Box 500
Milligan College, TN 37682
Tel: (423)461-8700
Admissions: (423)461-8730
Fax: (423)461-8960
E-mail: admissions@milligan.edu
Web Site: http://www.milligan.edu/
President/CEO: Dr. Donald R. Jeanes
Registrar: Sue Skidmore
Admissions: Tracy Brinn
Financial Aid: Nancy Beverly
Type: Comprehensive **Sex:** Coed **Affiliation:** Christian **Scores:** 100% SAT V 400+; 99% SAT M 400+; 47% ACT 18-23; 45% ACT 24-29 **% Accepted:** 78 **Admission Plans:** Deferred Admission **Application Deadline:** August 01 **Application Fee:** $30.00 **H.S. Requirements:** High school diploma required; GED accepted **Costs Per Year:** Application fee: $30. Comprehensive fee: $21,990 includes full-time tuition ($16,730), mandatory fees ($510), and college room and board ($4750). College room only: $2350. Room and board charges vary according to board plan and housing facility. Part-time tuition: $290 per credit. Part-time tuition varies according to course load. **Scholarships:** Available **Calendar System:** Semester, Summer Session Available **Enrollment:** FT 730, PT 23, Grad 201 **Faculty:** FT 69, PT 39 **Student-Faculty Ratio:** 11:1 **Exams:** SAT I or ACT **% Receiving Financial Aid:** 88 **% Residing in College-Owned, -Operated, or -Affiliated Housing:** 78 **Library Holdings:** 147,491 **Regional Accreditation:** Southern Association of Colleges and Schools **Credit Hours For Degree:** 128 semester hours, Bachelors **ROTC:** Army **Professional Accreditation:** AACN, AOTA, NCATE **Intercollegiate Athletics:** Baseball M; Basketball M & W; Cross-Country Running M & W; Golf M; Soccer M & W; Softball W; Tennis M & W; Volleyball W

MOTLOW STATE COMMUNITY COLLEGE
PO Box 8500
Lynchburg, TN 37352-8500
Tel: (931)393-1500
Fax: (931)393-1681
E-mail: galsup@mscc.edu
Web Site: http://www.mscc.cc.tn.us/
President/CEO: Dr. Arthur L. Walker, Jr.
Admissions: Greer Alsup
Financial Aid: Joe Myers
Type: Two-Year College **Sex:** Coed **Affiliation:** Tennessee Board of Regents **Scores:** 80% SAT V 400+; 70% SAT M 400+; 56% ACT 18-23; 8% ACT 24-29 **Admission Plans:** Open Admission; Early Admission; Deferred Admission **Application Deadline:** August 13 **Application Fee:** $10.00 **H.S. Requirements:** High school diploma required; GED accepted **Costs Per Year:** Application fee: $10. State resident tuition: $2142 full-time, $91 per credit part-time. Nonresident tuition: $6414 full-time, $278 per credit part-time. Mandatory fees: $247 full-time, $40 per credit part-time. Full-time tuition and fees vary according to program. Part-time tuition and fees vary according to course load and program. **Scholarships:** Available **Calendar System:** Semester, Summer Session Available **Enrollment:** FT 2,015, PT 1,392 **Faculty:** FT 74, PT 133 **Student-Faculty Ratio:** 16:1 **Library Holdings:** 54,968 **Regional Accreditation:** Southern Association of Colleges and Schools **Credit Hours For Degree:** 60 semester hours, Associates **Professional Accreditation:** ACBSP, NLN **Intercollegiate Athletics:** Baseball M; Basketball M & W; Softball W

NASHVILLE AUTO DIESEL COLLEGE
1524 Gallatin Rd.
Nashville, TN 37206-3298
Tel: (615)226-3990
Free: 800-228-NADC
Fax: (615)262-8488
Web Site: http://www.nadcedu.com/
President/CEO: Jeremy D. Gibson
Registrar: Chastity Lovvorn
Admissions: Peggie Werrbach
Financial Aid: Beatrice LaChance
Type: Two-Year College **Sex:** Coed **% Accepted:** 89 **Admission Plans:** Deferred Admission **Application Deadline:** Rolling **Application Fee:** $100.00 **H.S. Requirements:** High school diploma required; GED accepted **Costs Per Year:** Application fee: $100. Tuition: $20,500 full-time. Mandatory fees: $100 full-time. **Scholarships:** Available **Calendar System:** Continuous, Summer Session Not available **Enrollment:** FT 1,306 **Faculty:** FT 73, PT 4 **Student-Faculty Ratio:** 30:1 **Exams:** SAT I or ACT **% Residing in College-Owned, -Operated, or -Affiliated Housing:** 21 **Library Holdings:** 1,309 **Professional Accreditation:** ACCSCT

NASHVILLE STATE TECHNICAL COMMUNITY COLLEGE
120 White Bridge Rd.
Nashville, TN 37209-4515
Tel: (615)353-3333
Free: 800-272-7363
Admissions: (615)353-3217
Fax: (615)353-3243
Web Site: http://www.nscc.edu/
President/CEO: Dr. George H. Van Allen
Registrar: Mira Fleischman
Admissions: Charlie McCorkle
Financial Aid: Stephen White
Type: Two-Year College **Sex:** Coed **Affiliation:** Tennessee Board of Regents **Admission Plans:** Open Admission; Preferred Admission; Deferred Admission **Application Fee:** $5.00 **H.S. Requirements:** High school diploma required; GED accepted **Costs Per Year:** Application fee: $5. State resident tuition: $2367 full-time, $91 per credit hour part-time. Nonresident tuition: $8781 full-time, $369 per credit hour part-time. Mandatory fees: $235 full-time, $10 per credit hour part-time, $5 per term part-time. Part-time tuition and fees vary according to course load. **Scholarships:** Available **Calendar System:** Semester, Summer Session Available **Enrollment:** FT 2,421, PT 4,600 **Faculty:** FT 136, PT 276 **Exams:** SAT I or ACT **Library Holdings:** 38,502 **Regional Accreditation:** Southern Association of Colleges and Schools **Credit Hours For Degree:** 64 semester hours, Associates **Professional Accreditation:** ABET, AOTA, ACBSP

NATIONAL COLLEGE OF BUSINESS & TECHNOLOGY (BRISTOL)
1328 Hwy. 11 West
Bristol, TN 37620
Tel: (423)878-4440
E-mail: adm@educorp.edu
Web Site: http://www.ncbt.edu/
President/CEO: Frank Longaker
Admissions: Angela Carrier
Financial Aid: Cheryl Wright
Type: Two-Year College **Sex:** Coed **Affiliation:** National College of Business and Technology **Admission Plans:** Open Admission **Application Fee:** $30.00 **H.S. Requirements:** High school diploma required; GED accepted **Costs Per Year:** Application fee: $30. Tuition: $6408 full-time, $178 per

credit hour part-time. Mandatory fees: $75 full-time, $15 per term part-time. **Scholarships:** Available **Calendar System:** Quarter, Summer Session Available **Faculty:** FT 7, PT 23 **Student-Faculty Ratio:** 12:1 **Credit Hours For Degree:** 96 quarter hours, Associates **Professional Accreditation:** ACICS, AAMAE

NATIONAL COLLEGE OF BUSINESS & TECHNOLOGY (KNOXVILLE)
8415 Kingston Pike
Knoxville, TN 37919
Tel: (865)539-2011
Free: 800-664-1886
Fax: (865)539-2049
E-mail: awills@ncbt.edu
Web Site: http://www.ncbt.edu/
President/CEO: Frank Alvey
Admissions: Andy W. Wills
Type: Two-Year College **Sex:** Coed **Affiliation:** National College of Business and Technology **Calendar System:** Quarter **Student-Faculty Ratio:** 12:1

NATIONAL COLLEGE OF BUSINESS & TECHNOLOGY (NASHVILLE)
Ste. 200, 5042 Linbar Dr.
Nashville, TN 37211
Tel: (615)333-3344
Free: 800-664-1886
Web Site: http://www.ncbt.edu/
President/CEO: Frank Longaker
Admissions: Robert Leonard
Financial Aid: Anna Counts
Type: Two-Year College **Sex:** Coed **Affiliation:** National College of Business and Technology **Admission Plans:** Open Admission **Application Fee:** $30.00 **H.S. Requirements:** High school diploma required; GED accepted **Costs Per Year:** Application fee: $30. Tuition: $6408 full-time, $178 per credit hour part-time. Mandatory fees: $75 full-time, $15 per term part-time. **Scholarships:** Available **Calendar System:** Quarter, Summer Session Available **Faculty:** FT 2, PT 39 **Student-Faculty Ratio:** 10:1 **Credit Hours For Degree:** 96 credit hours, Associates **Professional Accreditation:** ACICS, AAMAE

NORTH CENTRAL INSTITUTE
168 Jack Miller Blvd.
Clarksville, TN 37042
Tel: (931)431-9700
Fax: (931)431-9771
E-mail: admissions@nci.edu
Web Site: http://www.nci.edu/
President/CEO: Dr. John D. McCurdy
Admissions: Sheri Nash-Kutch
Type: Two-Year College **Sex:** Coed **% Accepted:** 100 **Admission Plans:** Open Admission; Early Admission **Application Deadline:** Rolling **Application Fee:** $35.00 **H.S. Requirements:** High school diploma required; GED accepted **Costs Per Year:** Application fee: $35. Tuition: $14,800 full-time, $60 per semester hour part-time. Mandatory fees: $800 full-time. **Scholarships:** Available **Calendar System:** Continuous, Summer Session Available **Enrollment:** FT 52, PT 78 **Faculty:** FT 6, PT 11 **Student-Faculty Ratio:** 8:1 **Library Holdings:** 200 **Credit Hours For Degree:** 62 credits, Associates **Professional Accreditation:** COE

NORTHEAST STATE TECHNICAL COMMUNITY COLLEGE
PO Box 246
Blountville, TN 37617-0246
Tel: (423)323-3191
Admissions: (423)354-2589
Fax: (423)323-0215
E-mail: phsweeney@northeaststate.edu
Web Site: http://www.northeaststate.edu/
President/CEO: Dr. William W. Locke
Registrar: Dr. Jon Pharr
Admissions: Patrick H. Sweeney
Financial Aid: Cruzita Lucero
Type: Two-Year College **Sex:** Coed **Affiliation:** Tennessee Board of Regents **Scores:** 48.6% ACT 18-23; 7.1% ACT 24-29 **% Accepted:** 100 **Admission Plans:** Open Admission; Preferred Admission **Application Deadline:** Rolling **Application Fee:** $10.00 **H.S. Requirements:** High school diploma required; GED accepted **Costs Per Year:** Application fee: $10. State resident tuition: $2404 full-time, $91 per hour part-time. Nonresident tuition: $6414 full-time, $278 per hour part-time. Mandatory fees: $262 full-time, $12 per hour part-time, $18 per term part-time. **Scholarships:** Available **Calendar System:** Semester, Summer Session Available **Enrollment:** FT 2,610, PT 2,250 **Faculty:** FT 99, PT 144 **Student-Faculty Ratio:** 22:1 **Library Holdings:** 44,997 **Regional Accreditation:** Southern Association of Colleges and Schools **Credit Hours For Degree:** 60 semester hours, Associates **Professional Accreditation:** AAMAE, ADA, ACBSP, NAACLS, NAIT

NOSSI COLLEGE OF ART
907 Two Mile Parkway, Ste. E-6
Goodlettsville, TN 37072-2319
Tel: (615)851-1088
Fax: (615)851-1087
E-mail: cyrus@nossi.com
Web Site: http://www.nossi.com/
President/CEO: Nossi Vatandoost
Registrar: Bonnie Mears
Admissions: Cyrus Vatandoost
Financial Aid: Mary Kidd
Type: Two-Year College **Sex:** Coed **H.S. Requirements:** High school diploma required; GED accepted **Scholarships:** Available **Calendar System:** Semester **Enrollment:** FT 250 **Faculty:** FT 4, PT 25 **Student-Faculty Ratio:** 17:1 **Professional Accreditation:** ACCSCT

O'MORE COLLEGE OF DESIGN
423 South Margin St.
Franklin, TN 37064-2816
Tel: (615)794-4254
Fax: (615)790-1662
Web Site: http://www.omorecollege.edu/
President/CEO: Dr. K. Mark Hilliard
Registrar: Amy Shelton
Admissions: Chris Lee
Financial Aid: Amy Shelton
Type: Four-Year College **Sex:** Coed **Admission Plans:** Deferred Admission **Application Fee:** $40.00 **H.S. Requirements:** High school diploma required; GED accepted **Scholarships:** Available **Calendar System:** Semester, Summer Session Available **Enrollment:** FT 90, PT 37 **Faculty:** FT 7, PT 47 **Student-Faculty Ratio:** 3:1 **Exams:** SAT I or ACT **Library Holdings:** 4,000 **Credit Hours For Degree:** 128 semester hours, Bachelors **Professional Accreditation:** ACCSCT, FIDER

PELLISSIPPI STATE TECHNICAL COMMUNITY COLLEGE
PO Box 22990
Knoxville, TN 37933-0990
Tel: (865)694-6400
Admissions: (865)539-7013
E-mail: latouzeau@pstcc.cc.tn.us
Web Site: http://www.pstcc.edu/
President/CEO: Dr. Allen G. Edwards
Registrar: Sheryl Burnette
Admissions: Leigh Touzeau
Financial Aid: Patricia Peace
Type: Two-Year College **Sex:** Coed **Affiliation:** Tennessee Board of Regents **Scores:** 55.4% ACT 18-23; 12.3% ACT 24-29 **Admission Plans:** Open Admission; Early Admission; Deferred Admission **Application Deadline:** Rolling **Application Fee:** $5.00 **H.S. Requirements:** High school diploma required; GED accepted. For non-degree seeking applicants 21 or over: High school diploma or equivalent not required **Costs Per Year:** Application fee: $5. Area resident tuition: $100 per credit hour part-time. State resident tuition: $1227 full-time. Nonresident tuition: $4563 full-time, $397 per credit hour part-time. Mandatory fees: $2500 full-time. **Scholarships:** Available **Calendar System:** Semester, Summer Session Available **Enrollment:** FT 3,882, PT 3,804 **Faculty:** FT 169, PT 243 **Student-Faculty Ratio:** 21:1 **Library Holdings:** 43,000 **Regional Accreditation:** Southern Association of Colleges and Schools **Credit Hours For Degree:** 64 semester hours, Associates **Professional Accreditation:** ABET, ACBSP

REMINGTON COLLEGE-MEMPHIS CAMPUS
2731 Nonconnah Blvd.
Memphis, TN 38132-2131
Tel: (901)291-4200
Admissions: (901)291-4225

Fax: (901)396-8310
E-mail: lori.may@remingtoncollege.edu
Web Site: http://www.remingtoncollege.edu/
President/CEO: Dr. Lori May
Registrar: Gloria Williams
Admissions: Dr. Lori May
Financial Aid: Lisa Wilson
Type: Two-Year College **Scholarships:** Available **Calendar System:** Quarter **Enrollment:** FT 600 **Faculty:** FT 35, PT 10 **Professional Accreditation:** ACCSCT

REMINGTON COLLEGE-NASHVILLE CAMPUS
441 Donnelson Pike, Ste. 150
Nashville, TN 37214
Tel: (615)889-5520
Fax: (615)889-5528
E-mail: frank.vivelo@remingtoncollege.edu
Web Site: http://www.remingtoncollege.edu/
President/CEO: Frank Vivelo
Admissions: Frank Vivelo
Type: Two-Year College **Sex:** Coed **Calendar System:** Quarter

RHODES COLLEGE
2000 North Parkway
Memphis, TN 38112-1690
Tel: (901)843-3000
Free: 800-844-5969
Admissions: (901)843-3700
Fax: (901)843-3719
E-mail: adminfo@rhodes.edu
Web Site: http://www.rhodes.edu/
President/CEO: Dr. William E. Troutt
Registrar: Glenn W. Munson
Admissions: David J. Wottle
Financial Aid: Forrest Stuart
Type: Comprehensive **Sex:** Coed **Affiliation:** Presbyterian **Scores:** 100% SAT V 400+; 99.72% SAT M 400+; 9.24% ACT 18-23; 63.36% ACT 24-29 **% Accepted:** 49 **Admission Plans:** Early Admission; Early Decision Plan; Deferred Admission **Application Deadline:** Rolling **Application Fee:** $45.00 **H.S. Requirements:** High school diploma required; GED accepted **Costs Per Year:** Application fee: $45. Comprehensive fee: $34,760 includes full-time tuition ($27,546), mandatory fees ($310), and college room and board ($6904). Full-time tuition and fees vary according to student level. Room and board charges vary according to board plan. Part-time tuition: $1000 per credit hour. **Scholarships:** Available **Calendar System:** Semester, Summer Session Not available **Enrollment:** FT 1,641, PT 36, Grad 15 **Faculty:** FT 141, PT 43 **Student-Faculty Ratio:** 9:1 **Exams:** SAT I or ACT **% Receiving Financial Aid:** 37 **% Residing in College-Owned, -Operated, or -Affiliated Housing:** 76 **Library Holdings:** 274,886 **Regional Accreditation:** Southern Association of Colleges and Schools **Credit Hours For Degree:** 112 credit hours, Bachelors **ROTC:** Army, Air Force **Intercollegiate Athletics:** Baseball M; Basketball M & W; Cheerleading W; Cross-Country Running M & W; Field Hockey W; Football M; Golf M & W; Lacrosse M & W; Rugby M; Soccer M & W; Softball W; Swimming and Diving M & W; Tennis M & W; Track and Field M & W; Volleyball W

ROANE STATE COMMUNITY COLLEGE
276 Patton Ln.
Harriman, TN 37748-5011
Tel: (865)354-3000
Admissions: (865)882-4523
Fax: (865)882-4562
Web Site: http://www.roanestate.edu/
President/CEO: Dr. Wade B. McCamey
Registrar: Brenda Rector
Admissions: Judith Tyl
Financial Aid: Joy Goldberg
Type: Two-Year College **Sex:** Coed **Affiliation:** Tennessee Board of Regents **Scores:** 59.5% ACT 18-23; 10.4% ACT 24-29 **% Accepted:** 100 **Admission Plans:** Open Admission; Preferred Admission; Early Admission; Deferred Admission **Application Deadline:** Rolling **Application Fee:** $10.00 **H.S. Requirements:** High school diploma required; GED accepted **Costs Per Year:** Application fee: $10. State resident tuition: $1952 full-time, $83 per semester hour part-time. Nonresident tuition: $7798 full-time, $346 per semester hour part-time. Mandatory fees: $265 full-time, $15 per semester hour part-time. Full-time tuition and fees vary according to course load and program. Part-time tuition and fees vary according to program. **Scholarships:** Available **Calendar System:** Semester, Summer Session Available **Enrollment:** FT 2,873, PT 2,282 **Faculty:** FT 130, PT 227 **Student-Faculty Ratio:** 17:1 **Library Holdings:** 66,024 **Regional Accreditation:** Southern Association of Colleges and Schools **Credit Hours For Degree:** 60 semester hours, Associates **ROTC:** Army, Air Force **Professional Accreditation:** ADA, AHIMA, AOTA, APTA, COptA, CARC, JRCERT, NLN **Intercollegiate Athletics:** Baseball M; Basketball M & W; Cheerleading W; Softball W

SEWANEE: THE UNIVERSITY OF THE SOUTH
735 University Ave.
Sewanee, TN 37383-1000
Tel: (931)598-1000
Free: 800-522-2234
Admissions: (931)598-1238
Fax: (931)598-1145
E-mail: admiss@sewanee.edu
Web Site: http://www.sewanee.edu/
President/CEO: Dr. Joel Cunningham
Registrar: Paul G. Wiley
Admissions: David Lesesne
Financial Aid: David R. Gelinas
Type: Comprehensive **Sex:** Coed **Affiliation:** Episcopal **Scores:** 100% SAT V 400+; 100% SAT M 400+; 15.52% ACT 18-23; 63.93% ACT 24-29 **% Accepted:** 67 **Admission Plans:** Early Admission; Early Decision Plan; Deferred Admission **Application Deadline:** February 01 **Application Fee:** $45.00 **H.S. Requirements:** High school diploma required; GED not accepted **Costs Per Year:** Application fee: $45. Comprehensive fee: $34,645 includes full-time tuition ($26,874), mandatory fees ($221), and college room and board ($7550). College room only: $3860. Part-time tuition: $975 per credit hour. **Scholarships:** Available **Calendar System:** Semester, Summer Session Available **Enrollment:** FT 1,410, PT 22, Grad 13 **Faculty:** FT 130, PT 44 **Student-Faculty Ratio:** 12:1 **Exams:** SAT I or ACT **% Receiving Financial Aid:** 47 **% Residing in College-Owned, -Operated, or -Affiliated Housing:** 92 **Library Holdings:** 648,459 **Regional Accreditation:** Southern Association of Colleges and Schools **Credit Hours For Degree:** 130 semester hours, Bachelors **Professional Accreditation:** ACIPE, ATS **Intercollegiate Athletics:** Baseball M; Basketball M & W; Crew M & W; Cross-Country Running M & W; Equestrian Sports M & W; Fencing M & W; Field Hockey W; Football M; Golf M & W; Lacrosse M & W; Rugby M; Soccer M & W; Softball W; Swimming and Diving M & W; Tennis M & W; Track and Field M & W; Volleyball W

SOUTH COLLEGE
720 North Fifth Ave.
Knoxville, TN 37917
Tel: (865)524-3043
Fax: (865)673-8019
Web Site: http://www.southcollegetn.edu/
President/CEO: Stephen A. South
Registrar: Kim Hatfield
Admissions: Walter Hosea
Financial Aid: Jeanne Stewart
Type: Two-Year College **Sex:** Coed **Admission Plans:** Early Admission; Deferred Admission **Application Fee:** $40.00 **H.S. Requirements:** High school diploma required; GED accepted **Scholarships:** Available **Calendar System:** Quarter, Summer Session Available **Enrollment:** FT 443 **Faculty:** FT 18, PT 50 **Student-Faculty Ratio:** 11:1 **Exams:** Other **Library Holdings:** 6,500 **Regional Accreditation:** Southern Association of Colleges and Schools **Credit Hours For Degree:** 94 quarter hours, Associates **Professional Accreditation:** AAMAE, AOTA, APTA

SOUTHEASTERN CAREER COLLEGE
2416 South 21st Ave., Ste. 300
Nashville, TN 37212
Tel: (615)269-9900
Free: 800-336-4457
Fax: (615)297-6678
Web Site: http://www.southeasterncareercollege.com/ **Type:** Two-Year College **Sex:** Coed **Professional Accreditation:** COE

SOUTHERN ADVENTIST UNIVERSITY
PO Box 370
Collegedale, TN 37315-0370

Tel: (423)236-2000
Free: 800-768-8437
Admissions: (423)236-2844
Fax: (423)236-1000
E-mail: admissions@southern.edu
Web Site: http://www.southern.edu/
President/CEO: Dr. Gordon Bietz
Registrar: Joni Zier
Admissions: Marc Grundy
Financial Aid: Marc Grundy
Type: Comprehensive **Sex:** Coed **Affiliation:** Seventh-day Adventist **Scores:** 54% ACT 18-23; 27% ACT 24-29 **% Accepted:** 69 **Admission Plans:** Deferred Admission **Application Deadline:** Rolling **Application Fee:** $25.00 **H.S. Requirements:** High school diploma required; GED accepted **Costs Per Year:** Application fee: $25. Comprehensive fee: $19,388 includes full-time tuition ($14,300), mandatory fees ($484), and college room and board ($4604). College room only: $2604. Part-time tuition: $604 per semester hour. **Scholarships:** Available **Calendar System:** Semester, Summer Session Available **Enrollment:** FT 2,083, PT 307, Grad 132 **Faculty:** FT 131, PT 86 **Student-Faculty Ratio:** 15:1 **Exams:** SAT I and SAT II or ACT **% Receiving Financial Aid:** 69 **% Residing in College-Owned, -Operated, or -Affiliated Housing:** 59 **Library Holdings:** 139,200 **Regional Accreditation:** Southern Association of Colleges and Schools **Credit Hours For Degree:** 64 semester hours, Associates; 124 semester hours, Bachelors **Professional Accreditation:** CSWE, NASM, NCATE, NLN

SOUTHWEST TENNESSEE COMMUNITY COLLEGE

PO Box 780
Memphis, TN 38101-0780
Tel: (901)333-5000; 877-717-STCC
Admissions: (901)333-4221
Fax: (901)333-4273
E-mail: bwells@southwest.tn.edu
Web Site: http://www.southwest.tn.edu/
President/CEO: Dr. Nathan Essex
Registrar: Thelma Harris
Admissions: Barbara Wells
Financial Aid: Kathryn Johnson
Type: Two-Year College **Sex:** Coed **Affiliation:** Tennessee Board of Regents **Scores:** 35% ACT 18-23; 3% ACT 24-29 **% Accepted:** 100 **Admission Plans:** Open Admission; Early Admission; Deferred Admission **Application Deadline:** September 01 **Application Fee:** $5.00 **H.S. Requirements:** High school diploma required; GED accepted **Costs Per Year:** Application fee: $5. State resident tuition: $2184 full-time, $91 per credit hour part-time. Nonresident tuition: $8856 full-time, $369 per credit hour part-time. Mandatory fees: $213 full-time, $28 per credit hour part-time. **Scholarships:** Available **Calendar System:** Semester, Summer Session Available **Enrollment:** FT 5,656, PT 5,900 **Faculty:** FT 252, PT 314 **Library Holdings:** 87,280 **Regional Accreditation:** Southern Association of Colleges and Schools **Credit Hours For Degree:** 64 semester hours, Associates **ROTC:** Army, Air Force **Professional Accreditation:** ABET, APTA, ACBSP, JRCERT, NAACLS, NLN

TENNESSEE STATE UNIVERSITY

3500 John A Merritt Blvd.
Nashville, TN 37209-1561
Tel: (615)963-5000
Admissions: (615)963-5101
Fax: (615)963-5108
E-mail: jcade@picard.tnstate.edu
Web Site: http://www.tnstate.edu/
President/CEO: Dr. James A. Hefner
Registrar: Vickie Holmes
Admissions: Dr. John Cade
Financial Aid: Mary Chambliss
Type: Comprehensive **Sex:** Coed **Affiliation:** Tennessee Board of Regents **Scores:** 80.75% SAT V 400+; 78.89% SAT M 400+; 49.7% ACT 18-23; 3.96% ACT 24-29 **% Accepted:** 36 **Admission Plans:** Preferred Admission **Application Deadline:** August 01 **Application Fee:** $15.00 **H.S. Requirements:** High school diploma required; GED accepted **Costs Per Year:** Application fee: $15. State resident tuition: $4414 full-time, $336 per hour part-time. Nonresident tuition: $13,726 full-time, $740 per hour part-time. Mandatory fees: $225 full-time. Full-time tuition and fees vary according to course load and program. Part-time tuition varies according to course load. College room and board: $4270. College room only: $2460. Room and board charges vary according to board plan and housing facility. **Scholarships:** Available **Calendar System:** Semester, Summer Session Available **Enrollment:** FT 5,873, PT 1,163, Grad 1,844 **Faculty:** FT 431, PT 173 **Student-Faculty Ratio:** 14:1 **Exams:** SAT I or ACT **% Receiving Financial Aid:** 73 **% Residing in College-Owned, -Operated, or -Affiliated Housing:** 39 **Library Holdings:** 580,650 **Regional Accreditation:** Southern Association of Colleges and Schools **Credit Hours For Degree:** 65 semester hours, Associates; 132 semester hours, Bachelors **ROTC:** Army, Navy, Air Force **Professional Accreditation:** AACSB, ABET, AAFCS, ADA, AHIMA, AOTA, APA, ASLHA, CARC, CSWE, NAACLS, NASAD, NASM, NASPAA, NCATE, NLN **Intercollegiate Athletics:** Basketball M & W; Cross-Country Running M & W; Football M; Golf M; Softball W; Tennis M & W; Track and Field M & W; Volleyball W

TENNESSEE TECHNOLOGICAL UNIVERSITY

North Dixie Ave.
Cookeville, TN 38505
Tel: (931)372-3101
Free: 800-255-8881
Admissions: (931)372-3888
Fax: (931)372-6250
E-mail: admissions@tntech.edu
Web Site: http://www.tntech.edu/
President/CEO: Dr. Robert Bell
Registrar: Yvonne Gribble
Admissions: Rebecca Tolbert
Financial Aid: Dr. Ray Holbrook
Type: University **Sex:** Coed **Affiliation:** Tennessee Board of Regents **Scores:** 96% SAT V 400+; 97% SAT M 400+; 52% ACT 18-23; 37% ACT 24-29 **% Accepted:** 75 **Admission Plans:** Preferred Admission; Early Admission; Deferred Admission **Application Deadline:** August 01 **Application Fee:** $15.00 **H.S. Requirements:** High school diploma required; GED accepted **Costs Per Year:** Application fee: $15. State resident tuition: $4660 full-time. Nonresident tuition: $14,620 full-time. College room and board: $6650. College room only: $3096. **Scholarships:** Available **Calendar System:** Semester, Summer Session Available **Enrollment:** FT 6,453, PT 802, Grad 2,058 **Faculty:** FT 380, PT 180 **Student-Faculty Ratio:** 18:1 **Exams:** ACT, SAT I or ACT **% Receiving Financial Aid:** 51 **% Residing in College-Owned, -Operated, or -Affiliated Housing:** 28 **Library Holdings:** 640,056 **Regional Accreditation:** Southern Association of Colleges and Schools **Credit Hours For Degree:** 120 semester hours, Bachelors **ROTC:** Army, Air Force **Professional Accreditation:** AACSB, ABET, AAFCS, NAIT, NASAD, NASM, NCATE, NLN **Intercollegiate Athletics:** Baseball M; Basketball M & W; Cheerleading M & W; Cross-Country Running M & W; Football M; Golf M & W; Riflery M & W; Soccer W; Softball W; Tennis M & W; Track and Field W; Volleyball W

TENNESSEE TEMPLE UNIVERSITY

1815 Union Ave.
Chattanooga, TN 37404-3587
Tel: (423)493-4100
Free: 800-553-4050
Admissions: (423)493-4371
Fax: (423)493-4497
Web Site: http://www.tntemple.edu/
President/CEO: Dr. Roger Stiles
Registrar: Richard D. Vaupel
Admissions: Chris Dooley
Financial Aid: Del Hamilton
Type: Comprehensive **Sex:** Coed **Affiliation:** Baptist **Admission Plans:** Deferred Admission **Application Fee:** $30.00 **H.S. Requirements:** High school diploma required; GED accepted **Costs Per Year:** Application fee: $30. Comprehensive fee: $13,430 includes full-time tuition ($7000), mandatory fees ($1000), and college room and board ($5430). Room and board charges vary according to board plan. Part-time tuition: $300 per semester hour. Part-time mandatory fees: $200 per term. **Scholarships:** Available **Calendar System:** Semester, Summer Session Available **Enrollment:** FT 397, PT 30 **Faculty:** FT 24, PT 23 **Student-Faculty Ratio:** 10:1 **Exams:** SAT I or ACT **% Residing in College-Owned, -Operated, or -Affiliated Housing:** 64 **Library Holdings:** 150,711 **Credit Hours For Degree:** 64

credit hours, Associates; 128 credit hours, Bachelors **Professional Accreditation:** TACCS **Intercollegiate Athletics:** Baseball M; Basketball M & W; Soccer M; Volleyball W

TENNESSEE WESLEYAN COLLEGE
PO Box 40
Athens, TN 37371-0040
Tel: (423)745-7504
Free: 800-PICK-TWC
Admissions: (423)746-5203
Fax: (423)744-9968
Web Site: http://www.twcnet.edu/
President/CEO: Dr. Floyd Falany
Registrar: Vicki Burkett
Admissions: Dr. Scott Mashburn
Type: Four-Year College **Sex:** Coed **Affiliation:** United Methodist **Scores:** 92% SAT V 400+; 92% SAT M 400+; 61% ACT 18-23; 25% ACT 24-29 **Admission Plans:** Early Admission; Deferred Admission **Application Fee:** $25.00 **H.S. Requirements:** High school diploma required; GED accepted **Costs Per Year:** Application fee: $25. Comprehensive fee: $18,650 includes full-time tuition ($13,000), mandatory fees ($550), and college room and board ($5100). Full-time tuition and fees vary according to location. Room and board charges vary according to housing facility. Part-time tuition: $375 per semester hour. Part-time mandatory fees: $180 per term. Part-time tuition and fees vary according to class time and location. **Scholarships:** Available **Calendar System:** Semester, Summer Session Available **Enrollment:** FT 687, PT 128 **Faculty:** FT 45, PT 50 **Student-Faculty Ratio:** 12:1 **Exams:** SAT I or ACT **% Receiving Financial Aid:** 80 **% Residing in College-Owned, -Operated, or -Affiliated Housing:** 27 **Library Holdings:** 79,328 **Regional Accreditation:** Southern Association of Colleges and Schools **Credit Hours For Degree:** 128 semester hours, Bachelors **Professional Accreditation:** AACN **Intercollegiate Athletics:** Baseball M; Basketball M & W; Cheerleading M & W; Cross-Country Running M & W; Golf M; Soccer M & W; Softball W; Tennis M & W; Volleyball W

TREVECCA NAZARENE UNIVERSITY
333 Murfreesboro Rd.
Nashville, TN 37210-2877
Tel: (615)248-1200; 888-210-4TNU
Admissions: (615)248-1320
Fax: (615)248-7728
E-mail: admissions_und@trevecca.edu
Web Site: http://www.trevecca.edu/
President/CEO: Dr. Millard Reed
Registrar: Rebecca Niece
Admissions: Jan R. Forman
Financial Aid: Chuck Seaman
Type: Comprehensive **Sex:** Coed **Affiliation:** Nazarene **Scores:** 93% SAT V 400+; 90% SAT M 400+; 54% ACT 18-23; 29% ACT 24-29 **% Accepted:** 69 **Admission Plans:** Early Admission; Deferred Admission **Application Deadline:** July 01 **Application Fee:** $25.00 **H.S. Requirements:** High school diploma required; GED accepted **Costs Per Year:** Application fee: $25. Comprehensive fee: $21,244 includes full-time tuition ($14,774) and college room and board ($6470). College room only: $2920. Part-time tuition: $569 per semester hour. **Scholarships:** Available **Calendar System:** Semester, Summer Session Available **Enrollment:** FT 987, PT 258, Grad 951 **Faculty:** FT 73, PT 144 **Student-Faculty Ratio:** 16:1 **Exams:** SAT I or ACT **% Receiving Financial Aid:** 63 **% Residing in College-Owned, -Operated, or -Affiliated Housing:** 57 **Library Holdings:** 106,802 **Regional Accreditation:** Southern Association of Colleges and Schools **Credit Hours For Degree:** 60 semester hours, Associates; 120 semester hours, Bachelors **ROTC:** Army **Professional Accreditation:** NASM **Intercollegiate Athletics:** Baseball M; Basketball M & W; Golf M & W; Soccer M & W; Softball W; Volleyball W

TUSCULUM COLLEGE
60 Shiloh Rd.
Greeneville, TN 37743-9997
Tel: (423)636-7300
Free: 800-729-0256
Fax: (423)638-7166
Web Site: http://www.tusculum.edu/
President/CEO: Dr. Dolphus Henry
Registrar: Nancy J. Thompson
Financial Aid: Pat Shannon
Type: Comprehensive **Sex:** Coed **Affiliation:** Presbyterian **Scores:** 88% SAT V 400+; 92% SAT M 400+; 60% ACT 18-23; 20% ACT 24-29 **% Accepted:** 67 **Admission Plans:** Early Admission; Deferred Admission **Application Deadline:** Rolling **Application Fee:** $0.00 **H.S. Requirements:** High school diploma required; GED accepted **Costs Per Year:** Application fee: $0. Comprehensive fee: $22,715 includes full-time tuition ($15,900), mandatory fees ($315), and college room and board ($6500). Part-time tuition: $695 per semester hour. **Scholarships:** Available **Calendar System:** Semester, Summer Session Available **Enrollment:** FT 2,240, PT 49, Grad 367 **Faculty:** FT 80, PT 70 **Student-Faculty Ratio:** 17:1 **Exams:** SAT I or ACT **% Receiving Financial Aid:** 68 **% Residing in College-Owned, -Operated, or -Affiliated Housing:** 65 **Library Holdings:** 49,905 **Regional Accreditation:** Southern Association of Colleges and Schools **Credit Hours For Degree:** 128 credit hours, Bachelors **Intercollegiate Athletics:** Baseball M; Basketball M & W; Cheerleading W; Cross-Country Running M & W; Football M; Golf M & W; Soccer M & W; Softball W; Tennis M & W; Volleyball W

UNION UNIVERSITY
1050 Union University Dr.
Jackson, TN 38305-3697
Tel: (731)668-1818
Free: 800-33-UNION
Admissions: (731)661-5102
Fax: (731)661-5187
E-mail: rgrimm@uu.edu
Web Site: http://www.uu.edu/
President/CEO: Dr. David S. Dockery
Registrar: Jane Betts
Admissions: Rich Grimm
Financial Aid: Bryan Nelson
Type: Comprehensive **Sex:** Coed **Affiliation:** Southern Baptist **Scores:** 97.41% SAT V 400+; 96.52% SAT M 400+; 38.02% ACT 18-23; 45.52% ACT 24-29 **% Accepted:** 86 **Admission Plans:** Early Admission; Early Action; Deferred Admission **Application Deadline:** Rolling **Application Fee:** $25.00 **H.S. Requirements:** High school diploma required; GED accepted **Costs Per Year:** Application fee: $25. Comprehensive fee: $21,920 includes full-time tuition ($15,900), mandatory fees ($550), and college room and board ($5470). College room only: $3290. Full-time tuition and fees vary according to class time, course load, location, and program. Room and board charges vary according to board plan and location. Part-time tuition: $530 per credit hour. **Scholarships:** Available **Calendar System:** 4-1-4, Summer Session Available **Enrollment:** FT 1,611, PT 475, Grad 780 **Faculty:** FT 152, PT 126 **Student-Faculty Ratio:** 12:1 **Exams:** SAT I or ACT, SAT II **% Receiving Financial Aid:** 71 **% Residing in College-Owned, -Operated, or -Affiliated Housing:** 56 **Library Holdings:** 135,877 **Regional Accreditation:** Southern Association of Colleges and Schools **Credit Hours For Degree:** 66 semester hours, Associates; 128 semester hours, Bachelors **Professional Accreditation:** AACN, CSWE, NASAD, NASM, NCATE **Intercollegiate Athletics:** Baseball M; Basketball M & W; Cheerleading W; Cross-Country Running M & W; Golf M; Soccer M & W; Softball W; Track and Field M & W; Volleyball W

UNIVERSITY OF MEMPHIS
Memphis, TN 38152
Tel: (901)678-2000
Free: 800-669-2678
Admissions: (901)678-2101
Fax: (901)678-3053
E-mail: dwallace@memphis.edu
Web Site: http://www.memphis.edu/
President/CEO: Dr. Shirley C. Raines
Registrar: Noel A. Schwartz
Admissions: David Wallace
Financial Aid: Richard Ritzman
Type: University **Sex:** Coed **Affiliation:** Tennessee Board of Regents **Scores:** 93.1% SAT V 400+; 94.2% SAT M 400+; 54.4% ACT 18-23; 24.9% ACT 24-29 **% Accepted:** 71 **Admission Plans:** Early Admission **Application Deadline:** July 01 **Application Fee:** $25.00 **H.S. Requirements:** High school diploma required; GED accepted **Costs Per Year:** Application fee: $25. State resident tuition: $4216 full-time, $178 per credit hour part-time. Nonresident tuition: $14,030 full-time, $588 per credit hour part-time. Mandatory fees: $868 full-time, $62 per credit hour part-time. Full-time tuition and fees vary according to program and reciprocity agreements. Part-time tuition

and fees vary according to course load and program. College room and board: $6069. College room only: $2950. Room and board charges vary according to housing facility. **Scholarships:** Available **Calendar System:** Semester, Summer Session Available **Enrollment:** FT 11,568, PT 4,197, Grad 4,292 **Faculty:** FT 743, PT 542 **Student-Faculty Ratio:** 17:1 **Exams:** SAT I or ACT **% Receiving Financial Aid:** 53 **% Residing in College-Owned, -Operated, or -Affiliated Housing:** 16 **Library Holdings:** 1,149,177 **Regional Accreditation:** Southern Association of Colleges and Schools **Credit Hours For Degree:** 120 semester hours, Bachelors **ROTC:** Army, Navy, Air Force **Professional Accreditation:** AACSB, ABET, ACEHSA, ACEJMC, AACN, AAFCS, ABA, ACA, ADtA, ACSP, APA, ASLHA, AALS, CORE, CSWE, FIDER, NASAD, NASM, NASPAA, NAST NCATE, NLN **Intercollegiate Athletics:** Baseball M; Basketball M & W; Cheerleading M & W; Cross-Country Running M & W; Football M; Golf M & W; Racquetball M & W; Riflery M & W; Soccer M & W; Softball W; Swimming and Diving M & W; Tennis M & W; Track and Field M & W; Volleyball W

UNIVERSITY OF PHOENIX-NASHVILLE CAMPUS

616 Marriott Dr., Ste. 150
Nashville, TN 37214
Tel: (615)872-0188
Free: 800-228-7240
Admissions: (480)557-1712
Web Site: http://www.phoenix.edu/
Admissions: Nina Omelchanko

Type: Comprehensive **Sex:** Coed **Admission Plans:** Open Admission; Deferred Admission **Application Deadline:** Rolling **Application Fee:** $110.00 **H.S. Requirements:** High school diploma required; GED accepted **Costs Per Year:** Application fee: $110. Tuition: $10,170 full-time, $339 per credit part-time. Mandatory fees: $560 full-time, $70 per course part-time. **Scholarships:** Available **Calendar System:** Continuous, Summer Session Not available **Enrollment:** FT 909, Grad 382 **Faculty:** FT 6, PT 123 **Student-Faculty Ratio:** 8:1 **Library Holdings:** 444 **Regional Accreditation:** North Central Association of Colleges and Schools **Credit Hours For Degree:** 60 credits, Associates; 120 credits, Bachelors

THE UNIVERSITY OF TENNESSEE

Knoxville, TN 37996
Tel: (865)974-1000
Admissions: (865)974-2184
Web Site: http://www.tennessee.edu/
President/CEO: John D. Petersen
Registrar: Monique Anderson
Admissions: Richard Bayer
Financial Aid: Jeff Gerkin

Type: University **Sex:** Coed **Affiliation:** University of Tennessee System **Scores:** 99% SAT V 400+; 100% SAT M 400+; 29% ACT 18-23; 56% ACT 24-29 **% Accepted:** 74 **Admission Plans:** Preferred Admission; Early Admission; Early Action; Deferred Admission **Application Deadline:** February 01 **Application Fee:** $30.00 **H.S. Requirements:** High school diploma required; GED accepted **Costs Per Year:** Application fee: $30. State resident tuition: $5290 full-time, $193 per hour part-time. Nonresident tuition: $16,360 full-time, $642 per hour part-time. Mandatory fees: $336 full-time, $30 per hour part-time. Full-time tuition and fees vary according to location and program. Part-time tuition and fees vary according to location and program. College room and board: $5560. College room only: $2890. Room and board charges vary according to board plan and housing facility. **Scholarships:** Available **Calendar System:** Semester, Summer Session Available **Enrollment:** FT 18,739, PT 1,493, Grad 8,731 **Faculty:** FT 1,356, PT 30 **Student-Faculty Ratio:** 15:1 **Exams:** SAT I or ACT **% Receiving Financial Aid:** 37 **% Residing in College-Owned, -Operated, or -Affiliated Housing:** 37 **Library Holdings:** 24,437,024 **Regional Accreditation:** Southern Association of Colleges and Schools **Credit Hours For Degree:** 120 semester hours, Bachelors **ROTC:** Army, Air Force **Professional Accreditation:** AACSB, ABET, ACEJMC, AAFCS, AANA, ABA, ACA, ADtA, ACSP, ALA, APA, ASLHA, AVMA, ACIPE, AALS, CEPH, CORE, CSWE, FIDER, JRCNMT NAACLS, NASAD, NASM, NASPAA, NCATE, NLN, NRPA, SAF **Intercollegiate Athletics:** Baseball M; Basketball M & W; Cheerleading M & W; Crew W; Cross-Country Running M & W; Football M; Golf M & W; Soccer W; Softball W; Swimming and Diving M & W; Tennis M & W; Track and Field M & W; Volleyball W

THE UNIVERSITY OF TENNESSEE AT CHATTANOOGA

615 McCallie Ave.
Chattanooga, TN 37403-2598
Tel: (423)425-4111
Admissions: (423)425-4662
Fax: (423)425-4157
Web Site: http://www.utc.edu/
President/CEO: Dr. Bill W. Stacy
Registrar: Dr. Judy Fry
Admissions: Yancy Freeman
Financial Aid: Jonathan Looney

Type: Comprehensive **Sex:** Coed **Affiliation:** University of Tennessee System **Scores:** 55% ACT 18-23; 25% ACT 24-29 **% Accepted:** 84 **Admission Plans:** Deferred Admission **Application Fee:** $25.00 **H.S. Requirements:** High school diploma required; GED accepted **Costs Per Year:** Application fee: $25. State resident tuition: $4500 full-time, $236 per hour part-time. Nonresident tuition: $14,024 full-time, $614 per hour part-time. Mandatory fees: $900 full-time. College room and board: $6238. College room only: $3790. Room and board charges vary according to housing facility. **Scholarships:** Available **Calendar System:** Semester, Summer Session Available **Enrollment:** FT 6,190, PT 1,087, Grad 1,314 **Faculty:** FT 371, PT 252 **Student-Faculty Ratio:** 16:1 **Exams:** SAT I or ACT, SAT II **% Receiving Financial Aid:** 50 **% Residing in College-Owned, -Operated, or -Affiliated Housing:** 33 **Library Holdings:** 491,179 **Regional Accreditation:** Southern Association of Colleges and Schools **Credit Hours For Degree:** 128 semester hours, Bachelors **Professional Accreditation:** AACSB, ABET, ACEJMC, AACN, AANA, ACA, APTA, CSWE, FIDER, NASAD, NASM, NASPAA, NCATE **Intercollegiate Athletics:** Basketball M & W; Crew M & W; Cross-Country Running M & W; Football M; Golf M & W; Soccer M & W; Softball W; Tennis M & W; Track and Field M & W; Volleyball W; Wrestling M

THE UNIVERSITY OF TENNESSEE AT MARTIN

University St.
Martin, TN 38238-1000
Tel: (731)881-7000
Free: 800-829-8861
Admissions: (731)881-7032
Fax: (731)881-7029
E-mail: jrayburn@utm.edu
Web Site: http://www.utm.edu/
President/CEO: Dr. Nick Dunagan
Registrar: Brandy Cartmell
Admissions: Judy Rayburn
Financial Aid: Sandy Neel

Type: Comprehensive **Sex:** Coed **Affiliation:** University of Tennessee System **Scores:** 61.31% ACT 18-23; 27.9% ACT 24-29 **% Accepted:** 78 **Admission Plans:** Deferred Admission **Application Deadline:** Rolling **Application Fee:** $25.00 **H.S. Requirements:** High school diploma required; GED accepted **Costs Per Year:** Application fee: $25. State resident tuition: $3744 full-time, $156 per credit hour part-time. Nonresident tuition: $12,798 full-time, $534 per credit hour part-time. Mandatory fees: $749 full-time, $33 per credit hour part-time. College room and board: $4220. College room only: $2000. Room and board charges vary according to board plan and housing facility. **Scholarships:** Available **Calendar System:** Semester, Summer Session Available **Enrollment:** FT 5,016, PT 926, Grad 542 **Faculty:** FT 245, PT 171 **Student-Faculty Ratio:** 19:1 **Exams:** SAT I or ACT **% Receiving Financial Aid:** 58 **% Residing in College-Owned, -Operated, or -Affiliated Housing:** 37 **Library Holdings:** 621,025 **Regional Accreditation:** Southern Association of Colleges and Schools **Credit Hours For Degree:** 120 semester hours, Bachelors **ROTC:** Army **Professional Accreditation:** AACSB, ABET, ACEJMC, AAFCS, ADtA, CSWE, NASM, NCATE, NLN **Intercollegiate Athletics:** Baseball M; Basketball M & W; Cheerleading M & W; Cross-Country Running M & W; Football M; Golf M; Riflery M & W; Soccer W; Softball W; Tennis M & W; Volleyball W

VANDERBILT UNIVERSITY

Nashville, TN 37240-1001
Tel: (615)322-7311
Free: 800-288-0432
Admissions: (615)322-2561
Fax: (615)343-7765
E-mail: admissions@vanderbilt.edu
Web Site: http://www.vanderbilt.edu/
President/CEO: Dr. E. Gordon Gee
Registrar: R. Gary Gibson

Admissions: Bill Shain
Financial Aid: Dr. David D. Mohning
Type: University **Sex:** Coed **Scores:** 100% SAT V 400+; 100% SAT M 400+; 4.5% ACT 18-23; 33% ACT 24-29 **% Accepted:** 35 **Admission Plans:** Early Admission; Early Decision Plan; Deferred Admission **Application Deadline:** January 03 **Application Fee:** $50.00 **H.S. Requirements:** High school diploma or equivalent not required **Costs Per Year:** Application fee: $50. Comprehensive fee: $41,986 includes full-time tuition ($30,920), mandatory fees ($780), and college room and board ($10,286). College room only: $6760. **Scholarships:** Available **Calendar System:** Semester, Summer Session Available **Enrollment:** FT 6,295, PT 107, Grad 3,817 **Faculty:** FT 785 **Student-Faculty Ratio:** 9:1 **Exams:** SAT I or ACT, SAT II **% Receiving Financial Aid:** 40 **% Residing in College-Owned, -Operated, or -Affiliated Housing:** 83 **Library Holdings:** 1,812,869 **Regional Accreditation:** Southern Association of Colleges and Schools **Credit Hours For Degree:** 120 semester hours, Bachelors **ROTC:** Army, Navy, Air Force **Professional Accreditation:** AACSB, ABET, ABA, ACNM, ACA, ADtA, APA, ASLHA, ACIPE, AALS, ATS, JRCNMT, LCMEAMA, NAACLS, NASM, NCATE, NLN **Intercollegiate Athletics:** Baseball M; Basketball M & W; Crew M & W; Cross-Country Running M & W; Equestrian Sports M & W; Fencing M & W; Field Hockey M & W; Football M; Golf M & W; Ice Hockey M & W; Lacrosse M & W; Rugby M & W; Sailing M & W; Soccer M & W; Squash M & W; Tennis M & W; Track and Field M & W; Volleyball M & W; Water Polo M & W; Wrestling M & W

VATTEROTT COLLEGE
6152 Macon Rd.
Memphis, TN 38134
Tel: (901)761-5730
Fax: (901)761-5730
Web Site: http://www.vatterott-college.edu/
President/CEO: Mark DeFusco
Type: Two-Year College **Sex:** Coed **Calendar System:** Semester **Professional Accreditation:** ACCSCT

VOLUNTEER STATE COMMUNITY COLLEGE
1480 Nashville Pike
Gallatin, TN 37066-3188
Tel: (615)452-8600; 888-335-8722
Fax: (615)230-3577
Web Site: http://www.volstate.edu/
President/CEO: Dr. Warren Nichols
Registrar: Janice R. Roark
Admissions: Tim Amyx
Financial Aid: Sue H. Pedigo
Type: Two-Year College **Sex:** Coed **Affiliation:** Tennessee Board of Regents **Scores:** 53.4% ACT 18-23; 8.6% ACT 24-29 **% Accepted:** 100 **Admission Plans:** Open Admission; Early Admission; Deferred Admission **Application Deadline:** September 01 **Application Fee:** $10.00 **H.S. Requirements:** High school diploma required; GED accepted **Costs Per Year:** Application fee: $10. State resident tuition: $2142 full-time, $91 per credit hour part-time. Nonresident tuition: $8556 full-time, $369 per credit hour part-time. Mandatory fees: $241 full-time, $9 per credit hour part-time, $8 per term part-time. Full-time tuition and fees vary according to course load. Part-time tuition and fees vary according to course load. **Scholarships:** Available **Calendar System:** Semester, Summer Session Available **Enrollment:** FT 3,503, PT 3,647 **Faculty:** FT 146, PT 235 **Student-Faculty Ratio:** 20:1 **Exams:** SAT I or ACT **Library Holdings:** 52,571 **Regional Accreditation:** Southern Association of Colleges and Schools **Credit Hours For Degree:** 60 semester hours, Associates **Professional Accreditation:** ADA, AHIMA, APTA, ACBSP, CARC, JRCERT, JRCEMT **Intercollegiate Athletics:** Baseball M; Basketball M & W; Softball W

WALTERS STATE COMMUNITY COLLEGE
500 South Davy Crockett Parkway
Morristown, TN 37813-6899
Tel: (423)585-2600
Admissions: (423)585-2680
E-mail: pam.goodman@ws.edu
Web Site: http://www.ws.edu/
President/CEO: Dr. Jack E. Campbell
Registrar: James Wilder
Admissions: Dr. Pamela Goodman
Financial Aid: Linda Mason
Type: Two-Year College **Sex:** Coed **Affiliation:** Tennessee Board of Regents **Scores:** 80% SAT V 400+; 80% SAT M 400+; 34% ACT 18-23; 20% ACT 24-29 **Admission Plans:** Open Admission; Early Admission **Application Fee:** $10.00 **H.S. Requirements:** High school diploma required; GED accepted **Costs Per Year:** Application fee: $10. State resident tuition: $2142 full-time, $91 per hour part-time. Nonresident tuition: $8556 full-time, $391 per hour part-time. Mandatory fees: $239 full-time, $15 per hour part-time, $7 per term part-time. **Scholarships:** Available **Calendar System:** Semester, Summer Session Available **Enrollment:** FT 3,101, PT 2,863 **Faculty:** FT 126, PT 162 **Student-Faculty Ratio:** 22:1 **Exams:** SAT I or ACT **Library Holdings:** 47,559 **Regional Accreditation:** Southern Association of Colleges and Schools **Credit Hours For Degree:** 60 semester hours, Associates **ROTC:** Army **Professional Accreditation:** ACF, APTA, ACBSP, CARC, NAIT, NLN **Intercollegiate Athletics:** Baseball M; Basketball M & W; Golf M; Softball W

WATKINS COLLEGE OF ART AND DESIGN
2298 MetroCenter Blvd.
Nashville, TN 37228
Tel: (615)383-4848
Fax: (615)383-4849
Web Site: http://www.watkins.edu/
President/CEO: Dr. Jim Brooks
Registrar: John Hinds
Admissions: Connie Baer
Financial Aid: Regina Gilbert
Type: Four-Year College **Sex:** Coed **% Accepted:** 79 **Admission Plans:** Deferred Admission **Application Deadline:** June 01 **Application Fee:** $50.00 **H.S. Requirements:** High school diploma required; GED accepted **Costs Per Year:** Application fee: $50. Tuition: $12,000 full-time, $500 per hour part-time. Mandatory fees: $720 full-time, $30 per hour part-time. College room only: $5600. **Scholarships:** Available **Calendar System:** Semester, Summer Session Available **Enrollment:** FT 214, PT 161, Grad 18 **Faculty:** FT 17, PT 48 **Student-Faculty Ratio:** 11:1 **Exams:** SAT I or ACT **% Receiving Financial Aid:** 60 **% Residing in College-Owned, -Operated, or -Affiliated Housing:** 12 **Library Holdings:** 5,000 **Credit Hours For Degree:** 84 credit hours, Associates; 120 credit hours, Bachelors **Professional Accreditation:** FIDER, NASAD

WILLIAMSON CHRISTIAN COLLEGE
200 Seaboard Ln.
Franklin, TN 37067
Tel: (615)771-7821
Fax: (615)771-7810
Web Site: http://www.williamsoncc.edu/
President/CEO: Dr. Kenneth W. Oosting
Registrar: Steven T. Smith
Admissions: Steven T. Smith
Financial Aid: Jeanie Maguire
Type: Four-Year College **Sex:** Coed **Affiliation:** interdenominational **Admission Plans:** Open Admission; Early Admission; Deferred Admission **Application Fee:** $25.00 **H.S. Requirements:** High school diploma required; GED accepted **Costs Per Year:** Application fee: $25. Tuition: $7560 full-time, $295 per credit part-time. Mandatory fees: $50 full-time, $15 per course part-time. Part-time tuition and fees vary according to course load. Tuition guaranteed not to increase for student's term of enrollment. **Scholarships:** Available **Calendar System:** Semester, Summer Session Not available **Enrollment:** FT 60, PT 10 **Faculty:** FT 4, PT 25 **Student-Faculty Ratio:** 10:1 **Exams:** ACT, SAT II **% Receiving Financial Aid:** 18 **Library Holdings:** 16,000 **Credit Hours For Degree:** 60 credits, Associates; 124 credits, Bachelors **Professional Accreditation:** AABC, TACCS

ABILENE CHRISTIAN UNIVERSITY
ACU Box 29100
Abilene, TX 79699-9100
Tel: (325)674-2000
Free: 800-460-6228
Admissions: (325)674-2765
Web Site: http://www.acu.edu/
President/CEO: Dr. Royce Money
Registrar: Danelle Brand
Admissions: Tim Johnston
Financial Aid: Gary West
Type: Comprehensive **Sex:** Coed **Affiliation:** Church of Christ **Scores:** 98% SAT V 400+; 97% SAT M 400+; 50% ACT 18-23; 36% ACT 24-29 **% Accepted:** 55 **Admission Plans:** Early Admission **Application Deadline:** August 01 **Application Fee:** $25.00 **H.S. Requirements:** High school diploma required; GED accepted **Costs Per Year:** Application fee: $25. Comprehensive fee: $20,830 includes full-time tuition ($14,610), mandatory fees ($550), and college room and board ($5670). College room only: $2750. Full-time tuition and fees vary according to course load. Room and board charges vary according to board plan and housing facility. Part-time tuition: $487 per semester hour. Part-time mandatory fees: $26.50 per semester hour, $10 per term. Part-time tuition and fees vary according to course load. **Scholarships:** Available **Calendar System:** Semester, Summer Session Available **Enrollment:** FT 3,929, PT 191, Grad 467 **Faculty:** FT 218, PT 141 **Student-Faculty Ratio:** 16:1 **Exams:** SAT I or ACT **% Receiving Financial Aid:** 61 **% Residing in College-Owned, -Operated, or -Affiliated Housing:** 42 **Library Holdings:** 490,973 **Regional Accreditation:** Southern Association of Colleges and Schools **Credit Hours For Degree:** 64 semester hours, Associates; 128 semester hours, Bachelors **Professional Accreditation:** AACSB, ACEJMC, AAMFT, AACN, AAFCS, ASLHA, ACBSP, ATS, CSWE, NASM **Intercollegiate Athletics:** Baseball M; Basketball M & W; Cross-Country Running M & W; Football M; Golf M; Soccer M & W; Softball W; Tennis M & W; Track and Field M & W; Volleyball W

THE ACADEMY OF HEALTH CARE PROFESSIONS
1900 North Loop West, Ste. 100
Houston, TX 77018
Tel: (713)862-2633
Admissions: (713)425-3111
Fax: (713)746-5466
E-mail: wfederick@academyofhealth.com
Web Site: http://www.academyofhealth.com/
President/CEO: A. John Emerald
Admissions: Wanda Federick
Type: Two-Year College **Sex:** Coed **Calendar System:** Semester **Professional Accreditation:** ABHES

ALVIN COMMUNITY COLLEGE
3110 Mustang Rd.
Alvin, TX 77511-4898
Tel: (281)756-3500
Admissions: (281)756-3531
Fax: (281)756-3854
E-mail: admiss.rec.acc@flipper.alvin.cc.tx.us
Web Site: http://www.alvincollege.edu/
President/CEO: Dr. A. Rodney Allbright
Registrar: Irene Montoya
Admissions: Stephanie Stockstill
Financial Aid: Dora Sims
Type: Two-Year College **Sex:** Coed **Admission Plans:** Open Admission **Application Fee:** $0.00 **H.S. Requirements:** High school diploma required; GED accepted **Scholarships:** Available **Calendar System:** Semester, Summer Session Available **Enrollment:** FT 1,611, PT 2,321 **Faculty:** FT 96, PT 179 **Student-Faculty Ratio:** 15:1 **Exams:** Other **Library Holdings:** 28,361 **Regional Accreditation:** Southern Association of Colleges and Schools **Credit Hours For Degree:** 62 credits, Associates **Professional Accreditation:** CARC, NLN **Intercollegiate Athletics:** Baseball M; Softball W; Volleyball W

AMARILLO COLLEGE
PO Box 447
Amarillo, TX 79178-0001
Tel: (806)371-5000
Admissions: (806)371-5024
Fax: (806)371-5370
E-mail: austin-rc@actx.edu
Web Site: http://www.actx.edu/
President/CEO: Dr. Bud Joyner
Registrar: Robert Austin
Admissions: Robert Austin
Financial Aid: Karen Mooney
Type: Two-Year College **Sex:** Coed **Admission Plans:** Open Admission; Early Admission; Deferred Admission **Application Fee:** $0.00 **H.S. Requirements:** High school diploma or equivalent not required **Costs Per Year:** Application fee: $0. Area resident tuition: $1278 full-time, $53.25 per credit part-time. State resident tuition: $1638 full-time, $68.25 per credit part-time. Nonresident tuition: $5478 full-time, $228.25 per credit part-time. **Scholarships:** Available **Calendar System:** Semester, Summer Session Available **Enrollment:** FT 3,436, PT 6,760 **Student-Faculty Ratio:** 17:1 **Exams:** Other **Library Holdings:** 75,200 **Regional Accreditation:** Southern Association of Colleges and Schools **Credit Hours For Degree:** 62 semester hours, Associates **Professional Accreditation:** ABET, ARCEST, ABFSE, ADA, AOTA, APTA, CARC, JRCERT, JRCNMT, NAACLS, NASM, NLN

AMBERTON UNIVERSITY
1700 Eastgate Dr.
Garland, TX 75041-5595
Tel: (972)279-6511
Fax: (972)279-9773
Web Site: http://www.amberton.edu/
President/CEO: Dr. Douglas W. Warner
Registrar: Dr. Algia Allen
Admissions: Dr. Algia Allen
Financial Aid: Dr. Jo Lynn Loyd
Type: Two-Year Upper Division **Sex:** Coed **Affiliation:** nondenominational **Admission Plans:** Deferred Admission **Application Fee:** $0.00 **Costs Per Year:** Application fee: $0. Tuition: $6000 full-time, $200 per hour part-time. **Calendar System:** Miscellaneous, Summer Session Available **Enrollment:** FT 126, PT 507, Grad 1,015 **Faculty:** FT 14, PT 25 **Student-Faculty Ratio:** 25:1 **Library Holdings:** 21,000 **Regional Accreditation:** Southern Association of Colleges and Schools **Credit Hours For Degree:** 126 semester hours, Bachelors

AMERICAN INTERCONTINENTAL UNIVERSITY
9999 Richmond Ave.
Houston, TX 77042
Tel: (832)242-5788
Admissions: (832)201-3600
Fax: (832)242-5775
Web Site: http://www.aiuhouston.com/
President/CEO: Jori Kadlec
Admissions: Maggie Balderas
Type: Four-Year College **Sex:** Coed **Application Deadline:** Rolling **Application Fee:** $50.00 **Costs Per Year:** Application fee: $50. Tuition: $18,420 full-time. Mandatory fees: $520 full-time. **Calendar System:** Miscellaneous **Faculty:** FT 14, PT 17 **Student-Faculty Ratio:** 11:1 **Regional Accreditation:** Southern Association of Colleges and Schools

ANGELINA COLLEGE
PO Box 1768
Lufkin, TX 75902-1768
Tel: (409)639-1301
Admissions: (936)633-5201
Fax: (409)639-4299
Web Site: http://www.angelina.cc.tx.us/
President/CEO: Larry M. Phillips, EdD
Registrar: Judith Cutting
Admissions: Dr. Patricia M. McKenzie
Financial Aid: Becky Innerarity
Type: Two-Year College **Sex:** Coed **Admission Plans:** Open Admission; Early Admission; Deferred Admission **Application Fee:** $0.00 **H.S. Requirements:** High school diploma required; GED accepted **Scholarships:** Available **Calendar System:** Semester, Summer Session Available **Exams:** Other **% Residing in College-Owned, -Operated, or -Affiliated Housing:** 1 **Library Holdings:** 37,000 **Regional Accreditation:** Southern Association of Colleges and Schools **Credit Hours For Degree:** 70 semester hours, Associates **ROTC:** Army **Professional Accreditation:** CARC, JRCERT **Intercollegiate Athletics:** Baseball M; Basketball M & W

ANGELO STATE UNIVERSITY
2601 West Ave. N
San Angelo, TX 76909
Tel: (325)942-2555
Admissions: (325)942-2185
Fax: (325)942-2038
E-mail: admissions@angelo.edu
Web Site: http://www.angelo.edu/
President/CEO: Dr. E. James Hindman
Admissions: Frederic Dietz
Financial Aid: Lyn J. Wheeler
Type: Comprehensive **Sex:** Coed **Affiliation:** Texas State University System **Scores:** 84% SAT V 400+; 84% SAT M 400+; 54% ACT 18-23; 20% ACT 24-29 **% Accepted:** 100 **Admission Plans:** Early Admission; Deferred Admission **Application Deadline:** August 01 **Application Fee:** $20.00 **H.S. Requirements:** High school diploma required; GED accepted **Costs Per Year:** Application fee: $20. State resident tuition: $3180 full-time, $156 per credit hour part-time. Nonresident tuition: $11,460 full-time, $432 per credit hour part-time. Mandatory fees: $1110 full-time. College room and board: $5314. College room only: $3147. **Scholarships:** Available **Calendar System:** Semester, Summer Session Available **Enrollment:** FT 4,840, PT 869, Grad 447 **Faculty:** FT 233, PT 117 **Student-Faculty Ratio:** 20:1 **Exams:** SAT I or ACT **% Receiving Financial Aid:** 55 **% Residing in College-Owned, -Operated, or -Affiliated Housing:** 25 **Library Holdings:** 481,826 **Regional Accreditation:** Southern Association of Colleges and Schools **Credit Hours For Degree:** 68 semester hours, Associates; 130 semester hours, Bachelors **ROTC:** Air Force **Professional Accreditation:** APTA, ACBSP, NASM, NLN **Intercollegiate Athletics:** Baseball M; Basketball M & W; Cross-Country Running M & W; Football M; Rugby M; Soccer W; Softball W; Track and Field M & W; Volleyball W

ARGOSY UNIVERSITY/DALLAS
8950 North Central Expressway
Dallas, TX 75231
Tel: (214)890-9900; (866)954-9900
Fax: (214)656-3900
Web Site: http://www.argosyu.edu/
President/CEO: Jeb Egbert
Admissions: Kara Smith
Type: Two-Year Upper Division **Sex:** Coed **Affiliation:** Argosy University System **Admission Plans:** Early Admission; Deferred Admission **Application Fee:** $50.00 **Scholarships:** Available **Calendar System:** Semester, Summer Session Available **Enrollment:** FT 18, PT 12, Grad 300 **Faculty:** FT 8, PT 3 **Student-Faculty Ratio:** 17:1 **Regional Accreditation:** North Central Association of Colleges and Schools **Credit Hours For Degree:** 120 semester hours, Bachelors

ARLINGTON BAPTIST COLLEGE
3001 West Division
Arlington, TX 76012-3425
Tel: (817)461-8741
Fax: (817)274-1138
E-mail: jhall@abconline.org
Web Site: http://www.abconline.edu/
President/CEO: Rev. David Bryant
Registrar: Jane Hall
Admissions: Janie Taylor
Financial Aid: David Clogston
Type: Four-Year College **Sex:** Coed **Affiliation:** Baptist **% Accepted:** 100 **Admission Plans:** Preferred Admission; Early Admission; Deferred Admission **Application Deadline:** Rolling **Application Fee:** $15.00 **H.S. Requirements:** High school diploma required; GED accepted **Costs Per Year:** Application fee: $15. Comprehensive fee: $9250 includes full-time tuition ($4950), mandatory fees ($500), and college room and board ($3800). Part-time tuition: $165 per hour. **Scholarships:** Available **Calendar System:** Semester, Summer Session Available **Enrollment:** FT 143, PT 38 **Faculty:** FT 7, PT 13 **Student-Faculty Ratio:** 14:1 **% Receiving Financial Aid:** 93 **% Residing in College-Owned, -Operated, or -Affiliated Housing:** 48 **Library Holdings:** 27,486 **Credit Hours For Degree:** 128 semester hours, Bachelors **Professional Accreditation:** AABC **Intercollegiate Athletics:** Baseball M; Basketball M & W; Cheerleading W; Volleyball W

THE ART INSTITUTE OF DALLAS
Two NorthPark, 8080 Park Ln., Ste. 100
Dallas, TX 75231-9959
Tel: (214)692-8080
Free: 800-275-4243
Fax: (214)750-9460
Web Site: http://www.aid.edu/
President/CEO: Paul R. McGuirk
Registrar: Mary Chris Sayer
Admissions: Chad Williams
Financial Aid: Lisa McGaha
Type: Four-Year College **Sex:** Coed **Affiliation:** Education Management Corporation **Admission Plans:** Open Admission; Deferred Admission **Application Deadline:** Rolling **Application Fee:** $50.00 **H.S. Requirements:** High school diploma required; GED accepted **Costs Per Year:** Application fee: $50. Tuition: $17,542 full-time, $390 per credit hour part-time. College room only: $4896. **Scholarships:** Available **Calendar System:** Quarter, Summer Session Available **Enrollment:** FT 997, PT 307 **Faculty:** FT 53, PT 19 **Student-Faculty Ratio:** 18:1 **% Receiving Financial Aid:** 77 **% Residing in College-Owned, -Operated, or -Affiliated Housing:** 20 **Library Holdings:** 24,000 **Regional Accreditation:** Southern Association of Colleges and Schools **Credit Hours For Degree:** 90 credit hours, Associates **Professional Accreditation:** ACF, FIDER

THE ART INSTITUTE OF HOUSTON
1900 Yorktown
Houston, TX 77056-4115
Tel: (713)623-2040
Free: 800-275-4244
Fax: (713)966-2797
E-mail: sbehrens@aii.edu
Web Site: http://www.aih.artinstitutes.edu/
President/CEO: Dr. Kim Nugent
Admissions: Susanne Behrens
Type: Four-Year College **Sex:** Coed **Affiliation:** Education Management Corporation **% Accepted:** 37 **Application Deadline:** Rolling **Application Fee:** $50.00 **H.S. Requirements:** High school diploma required; GED accepted **Costs Per Year:** Application fee: $50. Tuition: $23,580 full-time, $393 per credit part-time. College room only: $3082. **Scholarships:** Available **Calendar System:** Quarter, Summer Session Not available **Enrollment:** FT 1,066, PT 591 **Faculty:** FT 53, PT 27 **Student-Faculty Ratio:** 20:1 **Exams:** SAT I or ACT **% Residing in College-Owned, -Operated, or -Affiliated**

Housing: 15 **Library Holdings:** 10,000 **Regional Accreditation:** Southern Association of Colleges and Schools **Professional Accreditation:** ACF

ATI TECHNICAL TRAINING CENTER
6627 Maple Ave.
Dallas, TX 75235
Tel: (214)263-4284
Admissions: (214)352-2222
Fax: (214)358-7500
E-mail: bdelozier@atienterprises.edu
Web Site: http://www.aticareertraining.com/
President/CEO: Brian DeLozier
Admissions: Brian DeLozier
Type: Two-Year College **Sex:** Coed **Calendar System:** Quarter **Professional Accreditation:** ACCSCT

AUSTIN BUSINESS COLLEGE
2101 IH-35 South, Third Floor
Austin, TX 78741
Tel: (512)447-9415
Fax: (512)447-0194
E-mail: pambinns@austinbusinesscollege.org
Web Site: http://www.austinbusinesscollege.org/
President/CEO: Paul Ellis
Registrar: Carmen Garcia
Admissions: Pam Binns
Financial Aid: Ted Johnson
Type: Two-Year College **Sex:** Coed **Admission Plans:** Open Admission **H.S. Requirements:** High school diploma required; GED accepted **Scholarships:** Available **Calendar System:** Quarter **Enrollment:** FT 201, PT 51 **Faculty:** FT 25, PT 10 **Student-Faculty Ratio:** 20:1 **Exams:** Other **Library Holdings:** 1,000 **Credit Hours For Degree:** 91 quarter hours, Associates **Professional Accreditation:** ACICS

AUSTIN COLLEGE
900 North Grand Ave.
Sherman, TX 75090-4400
Tel: (903)813-2000
Free: 800-442-5363
Admissions: (903)813-3000
Fax: (903)813-3198
E-mail: admission@austincollege.edu
Web Site: http://www.austincollege.edu/
President/CEO: Dr. Oscar C. Page
Registrar: Phyllis Rieser
Admissions: Nan Davis
Financial Aid: Laurie Coulter
Type: Comprehensive **Sex:** Coed **Affiliation:** Presbyterian **Scores:** 100% SAT V 400+; 100% SAT M 400+; 26.67% ACT 18-23; 57.95% ACT 24-29 **% Accepted:** 67 **Admission Plans:** Early Admission; Early Action; Early Decision Plan; Deferred Admission **Application Deadline:** May 01 **Application Fee:** $35.00 **H.S. Requirements:** High school diploma required; GED accepted **Costs Per Year:** Application fee: $35. Comprehensive fee: $31,281 includes full-time tuition ($23,355), mandatory fees ($185), and college room and board ($7741). College room only: $3554. Part-time tuition: $3385 per course. **Scholarships:** Available **Calendar System:** 4-1-4, Summer Session Available **Enrollment:** FT 1,286, PT 12, Grad 29 **Faculty:** FT 91, PT 40 **Student-Faculty Ratio:** 12:1 **Exams:** SAT I or ACT **% Receiving Financial Aid:** 54 **% Residing in College-Owned, -Operated, or -Affiliated Housing:** 72 **Library Holdings:** 240,944 **Regional Accreditation:** Southern Association of Colleges and Schools **Credit Hours For Degree:** 34 courses, Bachelors **Intercollegiate Athletics:** Baseball M; Basketball M & W; Cheerleading M & W; Football M; Golf M; Soccer M & W; Swimming and Diving M & W; Tennis M & W; Volleyball W

AUSTIN COMMUNITY COLLEGE
5930 Middle Fiskville Rd.
Austin, TX 78752-4390
Tel: (512)223-7000
Admissions: (512)223-7766
Fax: (512)223-7665
E-mail: lkluck@austincc.edu
Web Site: http://www.austincc.edu/
President/CEO: Dr. Robert Aguero
Registrar: Linda Kluck
Admissions: Linda Kluck
Type: Two-Year College **Sex:** Coed **% Accepted:** 100 **Admission Plans:** Open Admission **Application Deadline:** Rolling **Application Fee:** $0.00 **H.S. Requirements:** High school diploma required; GED accepted **Costs Per Year:** Application fee: $0. Area resident tuition: $1170 full-time, $39 per credit hour part-time. State resident tuition: $3060 full-time, $102 per credit hour part-time. Nonresident tuition: $5670 full-time, $189 per credit hour part-time. Mandatory fees: $420 full-time, $14 per credit hour part-time. **Scholarships:** Available **Calendar System:** Semester, Summer Session Available **Enrollment:** FT 8,829, PT 23,079 **Faculty:** FT 444, PT 1,157 **Student-Faculty Ratio:** 20:1 **Library Holdings:** 115,567 **Regional Accreditation:** Southern Association of Colleges and Schools **Credit Hours For Degree:** 62 semester hours, Associates **ROTC:** Army, Air Force **Professional Accreditation:** ARCEST, ACF, ADA, AOTA, APTA, JRCEDMS, JRCERT, JRCEMT, NAACLS, NLN

AUSTIN GRADUATE SCHOOL OF THEOLOGY
1909 University Ave.
Austin, TX 78705-5610
Tel: (512)476-2772; (866)AUS-GRAD
Fax: (512)476-3919
E-mail: keason@austingrad.edu
Web Site: http://www.austingrad.edu/
President/CEO: Dr. Stanley G. Reid
Registrar: Beverly Martin
Admissions: Kirk Eason
Financial Aid: Dave Arthur
Type: Two-Year Upper Division **Sex:** Coed **Affiliation:** Church of Christ **Application Fee:** $0.00 **H.S. Requirements:** High school diploma required; GED accepted **Costs Per Year:** Application fee: $0. Tuition: $5700 full-time, $570 per course part-time. Full-time tuition varies according to course load. Part-time tuition varies according to course load. **Scholarships:** Available **Calendar System:** Semester, Summer Session Available **Enrollment:** FT 3, PT 24, Grad 34 **Faculty:** FT 4, PT 6 **Student-Faculty Ratio:** 2:1 **% Receiving Financial Aid:** 100 **Library Holdings:** 25,000 **Regional Accreditation:** Southern Association of Colleges and Schools **Credit Hours For Degree:** 120 semester hours, Bachelors

BAPTIST MISSIONARY ASSOCIATION THEOLOGICAL SEMINARY
1530 East Pine St.
Jacksonville, TX 75766-5407
Tel: (903)586-2501
Web Site: http://www.bmats.edu/
President/CEO: Dr. Charley Holmes
Registrar: Dr. Philip Attebery
Admissions: Dr. Philip Attebery
Financial Aid: Dr. Philip Attebery
Type: Comprehensive **Sex:** Coed **Affiliation:** Baptist **Admission Plans:** Open Admission **Application Fee:** $20.00 **H.S. Requirements:** High school diploma required; GED accepted. For applicants to the associate's degree program 30 or over: High school diploma or equivalent not required **Costs Per Year:** Application fee: $20. Tuition: $2880 full-time, $80 per hour part-time. Mandatory fees: $160 full-time, $40 per term part-time. College room only: $2400. **Scholarships:** Available **Calendar System:** Semester, Summer Session Available **Enrollment:** FT 14, PT 34, Grad 11 **Faculty:** FT 7, PT 2 **Student-Faculty Ratio:** 10:1 **% Receiving Financial Aid:** 67 **% Residing in College-Owned, -Operated, or -Affiliated Housing:** 36 **Library Holdings:** 63,603 **Regional Accreditation:** Southern Association of Colleges and Schools **Credit Hours For Degree:** 66 semester hours, Associates; 130 semester hours, Bachelors **Professional Accreditation:** ATS

BAPTIST UNIVERSITY OF THE AMERICAS
8019 South Pan Am Expressway
San Antonio, TX 78224-2701
Tel: (210)924-4338
Free: 800-721-1396
Fax: (210)924-2701
E-mail: mranjel@bua.edu
Web Site: http://www.bua.edu/
President/CEO: Dr. Albert Reyes
Admissions: Mary Ranjel
Financial Aid: Araceli Acosta
Type: Four-Year College **Sex:** Coed **Affiliation:** Baptist **% Accepted:** 50 **Application Deadline:** February 15 **Application Fee:** $25.00 **Costs Per**

Year: Application fee: $25. Comprehensive fee: $3037 includes full-time tuition ($1500) and college room and board ($1537). College room only: $500. Part-time tuition: $125 per hour. Part-time mandatory fees: $125 per term. **Calendar System:** Semester **Enrollment:** FT 131, PT 40 **Faculty:** FT 7, PT 9 **Student-Faculty Ratio:** 14:1 **Exams:** Other **Professional Accreditation:** AABC

BAYLOR UNIVERSITY
Waco, TX 76798
Tel: (254)710-1011
Free: 800-BAYLOR U
Admissions: (254)710-3435
E-mail: admissions_office@baylor.edu
Web Site: http://www.baylor.edu/
President/CEO: Dr. Robert B. Sloan, Jr.
Registrar: Madelyn G. Jones
Admissions: Diana M. Ramey
Financial Aid: Cliff Neel
Type: University **Sex:** Coed **Affiliation:** Baptist **Scores:** 100% SAT V 400+; 100% SAT M 400+; 38% ACT 18-23; 49% ACT 24-29 **% Accepted:** 66 **Admission Plans:** Early Admission **Application Deadline:** Rolling **Application Fee:** $50.00 **H.S. Requirements:** High school diploma required; GED accepted **Costs Per Year:** Application fee: $50. Comprehensive fee: $29,939 includes full-time tuition ($20,574), mandatory fees ($2240), and college room and board ($7125). College room only: $3600. Part-time tuition: $857 per semester hour. Part-time mandatory fees: $82 per semester hour. **Scholarships:** Available **Calendar System:** Semester, Summer Session Available **Enrollment:** FT 11,465, PT 360, Grad 1,372 **Faculty:** FT 755, PT 155 **Student-Faculty Ratio:** 16:1 **Exams:** Other, SAT I or ACT **% Receiving Financial Aid:** 51 **% Residing in College-Owned, -Operated, or -Affiliated Housing:** 34 **Library Holdings:** 2,252,780 **Regional Accreditation:** Southern Association of Colleges and Schools **Credit Hours For Degree:** 124 semester hours, Bachelors **ROTC:** Air Force **Professional Accreditation:** AACSB, ABET, ACEHSA, ACEJMC, AALE, AACN, AAFCS, ABA, ADtA, APTA, APA, ASLHA, ACIPE, AALS, ATS, CSWE, NASM, NAST, NCATE **Intercollegiate Athletics:** Badminton M & W; Baseball M; Basketball M & W; Crew M & W; Cross-Country Running M & W; Fencing M & W; Football M; Golf M & W; Ice Hockey M; Lacrosse M & W; Rugby M & W; Sailing M & W; Soccer M & W; Softball W; Tennis M & W; Track and Field M & W; Volleyball M & W; Water Polo M & W

BLINN COLLEGE
902 College Ave.
Brenham, TX 77833-4049
Tel: (979)830-4000
Admissions: (979)830-4140
Web Site: http://www.blinn.edu/
President/CEO: Dr. Donald E. Voelter
Registrar: Dr. John Harris
Admissions: Dennis K. Crowson
Financial Aid: Scot Mertz
Type: Two-Year College **Sex:** Coed **Admission Plans:** Open Admission; Early Admission; Deferred Admission **Application Fee:** $0.00 **H.S. Requirements:** High school diploma required; GED accepted **Costs Per Year:** Application fee: $0. State resident tuition: $1968 full-time, $82 per hour part-time. Nonresident tuition: $3912 full-time, $163 per hour part-time. College room and board: $3700. Room and board charges vary according to board plan, gender, and housing facility. **Scholarships:** Available **Calendar System:** Semester, Summer Session Available **Faculty:** FT 263, PT 283 **Student-Faculty Ratio:** 27:1 **Exams:** Other **% Residing in College-Owned, -Operated, or -Affiliated Housing:** 9 **Library Holdings:** 130,000 **Regional Accreditation:** Southern Association of Colleges and Schools **Credit Hours For Degree:** 63 credit hours, Associates **Professional Accreditation:** ADA, APTA, JRCERT, NLN **Intercollegiate Athletics:** Baseball M; Basketball M & W; Cheerleading M & W; Football M; Softball W; Volleyball W

BORDER INSTITUTE OF TECHNOLOGY
9611 Acer Ave.
El Paso, TX 79925-6744
Tel: (915)593-7328
Fax: (915)595-2507
Web Site: http://bitelp.edu/
President/CEO: Steve Simon
Admissions: Miguel Gamino
Financial Aid: Hector Martinez
Type: Two-Year College **Sex:** Coed **Scholarships:** Available **Calendar System:** Quarter **Faculty:** FT 20 **Student-Faculty Ratio:** 7:1 **Professional Accreditation:** ACCSCT

BRAZOSPORT COLLEGE
500 College Dr.
Lake Jackson, TX 77566-3199
Tel: (979)230-3000
Admissions: (979)230-3217
Fax: (979)230-3443
E-mail: pleyende@brazosport.edu
Web Site: http://www.brazosport.edu/
President/CEO: Dr. Millicent M. Valek
Registrar: Patricia Leyendecken
Admissions: Patricia S. Leyendecker
Financial Aid: Ann Walker
Type: Two-Year College **Sex:** Coed **Admission Plans:** Open Admission; Early Admission; Deferred Admission **Application Deadline:** August 15 **Application Fee:** $0.00 **H.S. Requirements:** High school diploma required; GED accepted **Costs Per Year:** Application fee: $0. Area resident tuition: $840 full-time, $28 per hour part-time. State resident tuition: $1470 full-time, $49 per hour part-time. Nonresident tuition: $2880 full-time, $96 per hour part-time. Mandatory fees: $300 full-time, $9 per hour part-time, $15 per term part-time. Full-time tuition and fees vary according to course load. Part-time tuition and fees vary according to course load. **Scholarships:** Available **Calendar System:** Semester, Summer Session Available **Enrollment:** FT 1,670, PT 1,833 **Faculty:** FT 72, PT 94 **Student-Faculty Ratio:** 18:1 **Exams:** Other **Library Holdings:** 85,425 **Regional Accreditation:** Southern Association of Colleges and Schools **Credit Hours For Degree:** 62 semester hours, Associates

BROOKHAVEN COLLEGE
3939 Valley View Ln.
Farmers Branch, TX 75244-4997
Tel: (972)860-4700
Admissions: (972)860-4604
Fax: (972)860-4897
Web Site: http://www.brookhavencollege.edu/
President/CEO: Dr. Alice W. Villadsen
Registrar: Barbara B. Burke
Admissions: Thoa Vo
Financial Aid: Betty Brown
Type: Two-Year College **Sex:** Coed **Affiliation:** Dallas County Community College District System **Scores:** 83% SAT V 400+; 87% SAT M 400+ **Admission Plans:** Open Admission; Early Admission; Deferred Admission **Application Fee:** $0.00 **H.S. Requirements:** High school diploma or equivalent not required **Calendar System:** Semester, Summer Session Available **Enrollment:** FT 2,472, PT 7,647 **Faculty:** FT 108, PT 386 **Exams:** Other, SAT I or ACT **Library Holdings:** 45,000 **Regional Accreditation:** Southern Association of Colleges and Schools **Credit Hours For Degree:** 60 semester hours, Associates **ROTC:** Army **Intercollegiate Athletics:** Tennis M & W; Volleyball W

BROWN MACKIE COLLEGE-DALLAS
1500 Eastgate Dr.
Garland, TX 75041
Tel: (972)279-4446; 888-699-4446
Web Site: http://www.brownmackie.edu/locations.asp?locid=5 **Type:** Two-Year College **Sex:** Coed

BROWN MACKIE COLLEGE-FORT WORTH
301 Northeast Loop 820
Hurst, TX 76053
Tel: (817)589-0505; 888-906-0505
Web Site: http://www.brownmackie.edu/locations.asp?locid=10 **Type:** Two-Year College **Sex:** Coed

CEDAR VALLEY COLLEGE
3030 North Dallas Ave.
Lancaster, TX 75134-3799
Tel: (972)860-8201
E-mail: cboswell-ward@dcccd.edu
Web Site: http://www.cedarvalleycollege.edu/cvc.htm

President/CEO: Dr. Jennifer Wimbish
Registrar: Carolyn Ward
Admissions: Carolyn Ward
Financial Aid: Frank Ellis
Type: Two-Year College **Sex:** Coed **Affiliation:** Dallas County Community College District System **% Accepted:** 100 **Admission Plans:** Open Admission; Early Admission **Application Deadline:** Rolling **Application Fee:** $0.00 **H.S. Requirements:** High school diploma required; GED accepted **Costs Per Year:** Application fee: $0. Area resident tuition: $1080 full-time, $36 per credit part-time. State resident tuition: $1980 full-time, $66 per credit part-time. Nonresident tuition: $3180 full-time, $200 per credit part-time. **Scholarships:** Available **Calendar System:** Semester, Summer Session Available **Enrollment:** FT 1,447, PT 2,843 **Faculty:** FT 64, PT 110 **Student-Faculty Ratio:** 26:1 **Exams:** Other, SAT I or ACT **Library Holdings:** 43,788 **Regional Accreditation:** Southern Association of Colleges and Schools **Credit Hours For Degree:** 61 semester hours, Associates **ROTC:** Army **Intercollegiate Athletics:** Baseball M; Basketball M; Soccer W; Volleyball W

CENTER FOR ADVANCED LEGAL STUDIES
3910 Kirby Dr., Ste. 200
Houston, TX 77098-4151
Tel: (713)529-2778
Fax: (713)523-2715
Web Site: http://www.paralegal.edu/
President/CEO: Doyle Happe
Type: Two-Year College **Professional Accreditation:** COE

CENTRAL TEXAS COLLEGE
PO Box 1800
Killeen, TX 76540-1800
Tel: (254)526-7161
Free: 800-792-3348
Admissions: (254)526-1452
Web Site: http://www.ctcd.edu/
President/CEO: Dr. James R. Anderson
Registrar: Laura Ann Forest-Griffin
Admissions: David McClure
Financial Aid: Annabelle Smith
Type: Two-Year College **Sex:** Coed **Admission Plans:** Open Admission; Early Admission; Deferred Admission **Application Fee:** $0.00 **H.S. Requirements:** High school diploma required; GED accepted **Costs Per Year:** Application fee: $0. Area resident tuition: $912 full-time, $38 per hour part-time. State resident tuition: $1104 full-time, $46 per hour part-time. Nonresident tuition: $2880 full-time, $60 per hour part-time. Mandatory fees: $390 full-time, $8 per hour part-time. Full-time tuition and fees vary according to course load and location. Part-time tuition and fees vary according to course load and location. College room and board: $2990. **Scholarships:** Available **Calendar System:** Semester, Summer Session Available **Enrollment:** FT 2,986, PT 15,365 **Faculty:** FT 222, PT 1,748 **Student-Faculty Ratio:** 40:1 **Exams:** Other, SAT I or ACT, SAT II **% Residing in College-Owned, -Operated, or -Affiliated Housing:** 1 **Library Holdings:** 80,381 **Regional Accreditation:** Southern Association of Colleges and Schools **Credit Hours For Degree:** 64 semester hours, Associates **ROTC:** Army **Professional Accreditation:** NAACLS, NLN

CISCO JUNIOR COLLEGE
101 College Heights
Cisco, TX 76437-9321
Tel: (254)442-5000
Admissions: (254)442-2567
Fax: (254)442-5100
Web Site: http://www.cisco.cc.tx.us/
President/CEO: Dr. John Muller
Registrar: Olin O. Odom, III
Admissions: Olin O. Odom, III
Financial Aid: Jerry Dodson
Type: Two-Year College **Sex:** Coed **Admission Plans:** Open Admission; Early Admission **Application Fee:** $0.00 **H.S. Requirements:** High school diploma required; GED accepted **Costs Per Year:** Application fee: $0. Area resident tuition: $1564 full-time, $111 per hour part-time. State resident tuition: $1756 full-time, $119 per hour part-time. Nonresident tuition: $2062 full-time, $272 per hour part-time. Full-time tuition varies according to course load and location. Part-time tuition varies according to course load and location. College room and board: $3100. College room only: $900. Room and board charges vary according to board plan and housing facility. **Scholarships:** Available **Calendar System:** Semester, Summer Session Available **Student-Faculty Ratio:** 18:1 **Exams:** Other, SAT I and SAT II or ACT **% Residing in College-Owned, -Operated, or -Affiliated Housing:** 12 **Library Holdings:** 34,000 **Regional Accreditation:** Southern Association of Colleges and Schools **Credit Hours For Degree:** 63 credit hours, Associates **ROTC:** Army **Professional Accreditation:** AAMAE, NLN **Intercollegiate Athletics:** Basketball M & W; Football M; Golf M; Softball W; Volleyball W

CLARENDON COLLEGE
PO Box 968
Clarendon, TX 79226-0968
Tel: (806)874-3571
Web Site: http://www.clarendoncollege.edu/
President/CEO: Dr. Myles Shelton
Registrar: Sharon Hannon
Admissions: Sharon Hannon
Financial Aid: Toni Bryant
Type: Two-Year College **Sex:** Coed **% Accepted:** 100 **Admission Plans:** Open Admission; Early Admission; Deferred Admission **Application Deadline:** Rolling **Application Fee:** $0.00 **H.S. Requirements:** High school diploma required; GED accepted **Costs Per Year:** Application fee: $0. Area resident tuition: $1140 full-time, $38 per credit hour part-time. State resident tuition: $1650 full-time, $55 per credit hour part-time. Nonresident tuition: $2100 full-time, $70 per credit hour part-time. Mandatory fees: $930 full-time, $24 per credit hour part-time, $72 per term part-time. College room and board: $3100. College room only: $1000. **Scholarships:** Available **Calendar System:** Semester, Summer Session Available **Enrollment:** FT 557, PT 566 **Faculty:** FT 30, PT 37 **Student-Faculty Ratio:** 17:1 **Library Holdings:** 22,000 **Regional Accreditation:** Southern Association of Colleges and Schools **Credit Hours For Degree:** 62 semester hours, Associates **Intercollegiate Athletics:** Baseball M; Basketball M & W; Cheerleading M & W; Softball W; Volleyball W

COASTAL BEND COLLEGE
3800 Charco Rd.
Beeville, TX 78102-2197
Tel: (361)358-2838
Admissions: (361)354-2251
Fax: (361)354-2254
Web Site: http://www.cbc.cc.tx.us/
President/CEO: Dr. John M. Brockman
Registrar: Alicia Ulloa
Admissions: Alicia Ulloa
Financial Aid: Patsy Freeman
Type: Two-Year College **Sex:** Coed **% Accepted:** 100 **Admission Plans:** Open Admission; Deferred Admission **Application Deadline:** Rolling **Application Fee:** $0.00 **H.S. Requirements:** High school diploma required; GED accepted **Costs Per Year:** Application fee: $0. **Scholarships:** Available **Calendar System:** Semester, Summer Session Available **Enrollment:** FT 1,380, PT 1,986 **Faculty:** FT 96, PT 71 **Student-Faculty Ratio:** 17:1 **% Residing in College-Owned, -Operated, or -Affiliated Housing:** 5 **Library Holdings:** 37,971 **Regional Accreditation:** Southern Association of Colleges and Schools **Credit Hours For Degree:** 62 semester hours, Associates **ROTC:** Army, Air Force **Professional Accreditation:** ADA, AHIMA

COLLEGE OF BIBLICAL STUDIES-HOUSTON
6000 Dale Carnegie Dr.
Houston, TX 77036
Tel: (713)785-5995
Admissions: (832)252-4638
Fax: (713)785-5998
E-mail: dlopez@cbshouston.edu
Web Site: http://www.cbshouston.edu/
President/CEO: Dr. William D. Boyd
Registrar: Marilynn C. Square
Admissions: Daniel Lopez
Financial Aid: Raymond Solomon
Type: Four-Year College **Sex:** Coed **Affiliation:** nondenominational **Admission Plans:** Open Admission; Preferred Admission **Application Fee:** $20.00 **H.S. Requirements:** High school diploma required; GED accepted **Costs Per Year:** Application fee: $20. One-time mandatory fee: $50. Tuition: $4250 full-time, $90 per credit part-time. Mandatory fees: $60 full-time, $6 per credit part-time, $20 per term part-time. Full-time tuition and fees vary according to course level. Part-time tuition and fees vary according to course load. Tuition

guaranteed not to increase for student's term of enrollment. **Calendar System:** Semester, Summer Session Available **Enrollment:** FT 370, PT 1,122 **Faculty:** FT 11, PT 39 **Student-Faculty Ratio:** 31:1 **Exams:** Other, SAT I and SAT II or ACT **Library Holdings:** 35,580 **Credit Hours For Degree:** 64 credits, Associates; 120 credits, Bachelors **Professional Accreditation:** AABC

COLLEGE OF THE MAINLAND
1200 Amburn Rd.
Texas City, TX 77591-2499
Tel: (409)938-1211
Fax: (409)938-1306
E-mail: kmusick@com.edu
Web Site: http://www.com.edu/
President/CEO: Dr. Homer M. Hayes
Registrar: Bill Peace
Admissions: Kelly Musick
Financial Aid: Rebecca Miles
Type: Two-Year College **Sex:** Coed **Admission Plans:** Open Admission; Early Admission; Deferred Admission **Application Deadline:** Rolling **Application Fee:** $0.00 **H.S. Requirements:** High school diploma required; GED accepted **Costs Per Year:** Application fee: $0. Area resident tuition: $863 full-time, $26 per credit part-time. State resident tuition: $1655 full-time, $59 per credit part-time. Nonresident tuition: $2423 full-time, $89 per credit part-time. Mandatory fees: $167 full-time, $10.66 per credit part-time, $64 per term part-time. **Scholarships:** Available **Calendar System:** Semester, Summer Session Available **Enrollment:** FT 1,382, PT 2,617 **Faculty:** FT 92, PT 121 **Student-Faculty Ratio:** 17:1 **Library Holdings:** 84,128 **Regional Accreditation:** Southern Association of Colleges and Schools **Credit Hours For Degree:** 62 hours, Associates **Professional Accreditation:** NLN

THE COLLEGE OF SAINT THOMAS MORE
3020 Lubbock St.
Fort Worth, TX 76109-2323
Tel: (817)923-8459
Free: 800-583-6489
Fax: (817)924-3206
E-mail: jpatrick@cstm.edu
Web Site: http://www.cstm.edu/
President/CEO: Dr. James A. Patrick
Registrar: Stephen Shivone
Admissions: Dr. James A. Patrick
Financial Aid: C. Swanson
Type: Four-Year College **Sex:** Coed **Affiliation:** Roman Catholic Church **% Accepted:** 68 **Admission Plans:** Early Admission; Deferred Admission **Application Deadline:** Rolling **Application Fee:** $35.00 **H.S. Requirements:** High school diploma required; GED accepted **Costs Per Year:** Application fee: $35. Tuition: $12,000 full-time, $2000 per course part-time. **Scholarships:** Available **Calendar System:** Semester, Summer Session Available **Enrollment:** FT 21, PT 32 **Faculty:** FT 3, PT 6 **Student-Faculty Ratio:** 4:1 **Exams:** SAT I or ACT **% Residing in College-Owned, -Operated, or -Affiliated Housing:** 51 **Library Holdings:** 12,000 **Regional Accreditation:** Southern Association of Colleges and Schools **Credit Hours For Degree:** 69 credit hours, Associates; 120 credit hours, Bachelors

COLLIN COUNTY COMMUNITY COLLEGE DISTRICT
4800 Preston Park Blvd.
Plano, TX 75093-8309
Tel: (972)758-3800
Admissions: (972)881-5174
Fax: (972)758-5468
Web Site: http://www.cccd.edu/
President/CEO: Dr. Cary A. Israel
Registrar: Stephanie Meinhardt
Admissions: Stephanie Meinhardt
Financial Aid: Debra Wilkison
Type: Two-Year College **Sex:** Coed **Admission Plans:** Open Admission **Application Deadline:** Rolling **Application Fee:** $0.00 **H.S. Requirements:** High school diploma required; GED accepted. For applicants under 18: High school diploma required; GED accepted **Costs Per Year:** Application fee: $0. Area resident tuition: $810 full-time, $27 per credit hour part-time. State resident tuition: $1020 full-time, $33 per credit hour part-time. Nonresident tuition: $2550 full-time, $80 per credit hour part-time. Mandatory fees: $306 full-time, $10 per credit hour part-time, $2 per term part-time. **Scholarships:** Available **Calendar System:** Semester, Summer Session Available **Enrollment:** FT 7,226, PT 11,231 **Faculty:** FT 252, PT 822 **Student-Faculty Ratio:** 21:1 **Exams:** Other **Library Holdings:** 129,032 **Regional Accreditation:** Southern Association of Colleges and Schools **Credit Hours For Degree:** 60 credit hours, Associates **Professional Accreditation:** ADA, CARC, NLN **Intercollegiate Athletics:** Basketball M & W; Tennis M & W; Volleyball W

COMMONWEALTH INSTITUTE OF FUNERAL SERVICE
415 Barren Springs Dr.
Houston, TX 77090
Tel: (281)873-0262
Free: 800-628-1580
Fax: (281)873-5232
Web Site: http://www.commonwealthinst.org/
President/CEO: Dr. George Poston
Registrar: Patricia Moreno
Admissions: Patricia Moreno
Financial Aid: Nancy Poston
Type: Two-Year College **Sex:** Coed **Application Fee:** $50.00 **H.S. Requirements:** High school diploma required; GED accepted **Costs Per Year:** Application fee: $50. Tuition: $9400 full-time, $13 per contact hour part-time. Mandatory fees: $100 full-time. Full-time tuition and fees vary according to course load and program. Part-time tuition varies according to course load and program. **Scholarships:** Available **Calendar System:** Quarter, Summer Session Not available **Enrollment:** FT 157, PT 7 **Faculty:** FT 4, PT 9 **Student-Faculty Ratio:** 23:1 **Exams:** Other, SAT I or ACT **Library Holdings:** 1,500 **Credit Hours For Degree:** 97 quarter hours, Associates **Professional Accreditation:** ABFSE

COMPUTER CAREER CENTER
6101 Montana Ave.
El Paso, TX 79925
Tel: (915)779-8031
Web Site: http://www.computercareercenter.com/
President/CEO: Lee Chayes
Registrar: Victor Castillo
Admissions: Sarah Hernandez
Financial Aid: Michael Reilly
Type: Two-Year College **Sex:** Coed **Admission Plans:** Open Admission **H.S. Requirements:** High school diploma required; GED accepted **Scholarships:** Available **Calendar System:** Miscellaneous **Credit Hours For Degree:** 68 units, Associates **Professional Accreditation:** COE

CONCORDIA UNIVERSITY AT AUSTIN
3400 Interstate 35 North
Austin, TX 78705-2799
Tel: (512)486-2000
Free: 800-285-4252
Fax: (512)459-8517
E-mail: kristi.kirk@concordia.edu
Web Site: http://www.concordia.edu/
President/CEO: Dr. Thomas Cedel
Registrar: Lowell Fein
Admissions: Kristi Kirk
Financial Aid: Steven Johnson
Type: Comprehensive **Sex:** Coed **Affiliation:** Lutheran Church–Missouri Synod; Concordia University System **Scores:** 94% SAT V 400+; 99% SAT M 400+; 59% ACT 18-23; 23% ACT 24-29 **% Accepted:** 73 **Admission Plans:** Early Admission; Deferred Admission **Application Deadline:** Rolling **Application Fee:** $25.00 **H.S. Requirements:** High school diploma required; GED accepted **Costs Per Year:** Application fee: $25. Comprehensive fee: $23,750 includes full-time tuition ($16,850) and college room and board ($6900). Full-time tuition varies according to course load and location. Room and board charges vary according to board plan. **Scholarships:** Available **Calendar System:** Semester, Summer Session Available **Enrollment:** FT 756, PT 373, Grad 90 **Faculty:** FT 35, PT 100 **Student-Faculty Ratio:** 13:1 **Exams:** SAT I or ACT **% Receiving Financial Aid:** 66 **% Residing in College-Owned, -Operated, or -Affiliated Housing:** 32 **Library Holdings:** 50,756 **Regional Accreditation:** Southern Association of Colleges and Schools **Credit Hours For Degree:** 64 semester hours, Associates; 128 semester hours, Bachelors **ROTC:** Army, Air Force **Intercollegiate**

Athletics: Baseball M; Basketball M & W; Cross-Country Running M & W; Golf M & W; Soccer M & W; Softball W; Tennis M & W; Volleyball W

COURT REPORTING INSTITUTE OF DALLAS
8585 North Stemmons Freeway, Ste. 200 North
Dallas, TX 75247
Tel: (214)350-9722
Free: 800-880-9722
Fax: (214)631-0143
Web Site: http://www.crid.com/
President/CEO: Eric Juhlin
Registrar: Ronda Crowder
Admissions: Debra Smith-Armstrong
Financial Aid: Linda Craft
Type: Two-Year College **Sex:** Coed **Admission Plans:** Early Decision Plan **Application Fee:** $100.00 **Scholarships:** Available **Calendar System:** Quarter **Enrollment:** FT 526 **Faculty:** FT 15, PT 15 **Student-Faculty Ratio:** 35:1 **Professional Accreditation:** ACICS

COURT REPORTING INSTITUTE OF HOUSTON
13101 Northwest Freeway, Ste. 100
Houston, TX 77040
Tel: (713)996-8300; (866)996-8300
Web Site: http://www.crid.com/ **Type:** Two-Year College **Sex:** Coed **Calendar System:** Quarter **Professional Accreditation:** ACICS

THE CRISWELL COLLEGE
4010 Gaston Ave.
Dallas, TX 75246-1537
Tel: (214)821-5433
Free: 800-899-0012
Admissions: (214)818-1305
Fax: (214)818-1310
E-mail: wdblair@criswell.edu
Web Site: http://www.criswell.edu/
President/CEO: Dr. Lamar E. Cooper, Sr.
Registrar: Myron Hardy
Admissions: W. Danny Blair
Type: Comprehensive **Sex:** Coed **Affiliation:** Southern Baptist Convention **Admission Plans:** Early Admission; Deferred Admission **Application Fee:** $30.00 **H.S. Requirements:** High school diploma required; GED accepted **Scholarships:** Available **Calendar System:** Semester, Summer Session Available **Faculty:** FT 15, PT 14 **Exams:** SAT I or ACT **% Receiving Financial Aid:** 41 **Library Holdings:** 95,000 **Regional Accreditation:** Southern Association of Colleges and Schools **Credit Hours For Degree:** 63 semester hours, Associates; 129 semester hours, Bachelors

CY-FAIR COLLEGE
14955 NW Freeway
Houston, TX 77040
Tel: (832)782-5000
Admissions: (281)290-3950
Web Site: http://www.cy-faircollege.com/
President/CEO: Diane Troyer, PhD
Admissions: Dr. Earl Campa
Type: Two-Year College **Sex:** Coed **Affiliation:** North Harris Montgomery Community Course District **Admission Plans:** Open Admission **H.S. Requirements:** High school diploma required; GED accepted **Costs Per Year:** Area resident tuition: $768 full-time, $32 per credit hour part-time. State resident tuition: $1728 full-time, $72 per credit hour part-time. Nonresident tuition: $2088 full-time, $87 per credit hour part-time. Mandatory fees: $216 full-time, $8 per credit hour part-time, $12 per term part-time. **Calendar System:** Semester, Summer Session Not available **Enrollment:** FT 1,895, PT 6,645 **Faculty:** FT 128, PT 321 **Student-Faculty Ratio:** 17:1 **Exams:** SAT I or ACT **Regional Accreditation:** Southern Association of Colleges and Schools **Credit Hours For Degree:** 60 credit hours, Associates

DALLAS BAPTIST UNIVERSITY
3000 Mountain Creek Parkway
Dallas, TX 75211-9299
Tel: (214)333-7100
Free: 800-460-1328
Admissions: (214)333-5360
Fax: (214)333-5447
E-mail: admiss@dbu.edu
Web Site: http://www.dbu.edu/
President/CEO: Dr. Gary R. Cook
Registrar: Linda Roney
Admissions: Erin Spivey
Financial Aid: Donald Zackary
Type: Comprehensive **Sex:** Coed **Affiliation:** Baptist General Convention of Texas **Scores:** 100% SAT V 400+; 100% SAT M 400+; 60% ACT 18-23; 32% ACT 24-29 **% Accepted:** 64 **Application Deadline:** Rolling **Application Fee:** $25.00 **H.S. Requirements:** High school diploma required; GED accepted **Costs Per Year:** Application fee: $25. Comprehensive fee: $17,040 includes full-time tuition ($12,270) and college room and board ($4770). College room only: $1900. Room and board charges vary according to board plan and housing facility. Part-time tuition: $409 per credit hour. **Scholarships:** Available **Calendar System:** 4-1-4, Summer Session Available **Enrollment:** FT 2,100, PT 1,467, Grad 1,421 **Faculty:** FT 100, PT 356 **Student-Faculty Ratio:** 17:1 **Exams:** SAT I or ACT **% Receiving Financial Aid:** 56 **% Residing in College-Owned, -Operated, or -Affiliated Housing:** 32 **Library Holdings:** 235,931 **Regional Accreditation:** Southern Association of Colleges and Schools **Credit Hours For Degree:** 65 credit hours, Associates; 126 credit hours, Bachelors **ROTC:** Army, Air Force **Professional Accreditation:** ACBSP, NASM **Intercollegiate Athletics:** Baseball M; Cross-Country Running M & W; Golf M & W; Soccer M & W; Tennis M & W; Track and Field M & W; Volleyball M & W

DALLAS CHRISTIAN COLLEGE
2700 Christian Parkway
Dallas, TX 75234-7299
Tel: (972)241-3371
Fax: (972)241-8021
Web Site: http://www.dallas.edu/
President/CEO: Dustin D. Rubeck
Registrar: Crystal Laidacker
Admissions: Mark Worley
Financial Aid: Jennifer Reeves
Type: Four-Year College **Sex:** Coed **Affiliation:** Christian Churches and Churches of Christ **Scores:** 75% SAT V 400+; 82% SAT M 400+; 69% ACT 18-23; 6% ACT 24-29 **Admission Plans:** Preferred Admission; Deferred Admission **Application Fee:** $30.00 **H.S. Requirements:** High school diploma required; GED accepted **Scholarships:** Available **Calendar System:** Semester, Summer Session Available **Enrollment:** FT 273, PT 93 **Faculty:** FT 7, PT 48 **Student-Faculty Ratio:** 16:1 **Exams:** SAT I or ACT **% Residing in College-Owned, -Operated, or -Affiliated Housing:** 36 **Library Holdings:** 36,616 **Credit Hours For Degree:** 130 semester hours, Bachelors **Professional Accreditation:** AABC **Intercollegiate Athletics:** Basketball M & W; Soccer M; Volleyball W

DALLAS INSTITUTE OF FUNERAL SERVICE
3909 South Buckner Blvd.
Dallas, TX 75227
Tel: (214)388-5466
Free: 800-235-5444
Fax: (214)388-0316
E-mail: difs@dallasinstitute.edu
Web Site: http://www.dallasinstitute.edu/
President/CEO: James Shoemake
Admissions: Terry Parrish
Financial Aid: Robert Clark
Type: Two-Year College **Sex:** Coed **Admission Plans:** Open Admission **Application Fee:** $50.00 **H.S. Requirements:** High school diploma required; GED accepted **Costs Per Year:** Application fee: $50. Tuition: $10,000 full-time, $200 per hour part-time. Mandatory fees: $50 full-time. **Scholarships:** Available **Calendar System:** Quarter **Enrollment:** FT 247 **Faculty:** FT 6, PT 4 **Student-Faculty Ratio:** 32:1 **Credit Hours For Degree:** 101 quarter hours, Associates **Professional Accreditation:** ABFSE

DEL MAR COLLEGE
101 Baldwin Blvd.
Corpus Christi, TX 78404-3897
Tel: (361)698-1200
Admissions: (361)698-1248
Fax: (361)698-1559
Web Site: http://www.delmar.edu/
President/CEO: Dr. Carlos A. Garcia

Registrar: Frances Jordan
Admissions: Frances P. Jordan
Financial Aid: Enrique Garcia, Jr.
Type: Two-Year College **Sex:** Coed **Admission Plans:** Open Admission; Early Admission; Deferred Admission **Application Fee:** $0.00 **H.S. Requirements:** High school diploma required; GED accepted **Scholarships:** Available **Calendar System:** Semester, Summer Session Available **Enrollment:** FT 3,819, PT 7,519 **Faculty:** FT 313, PT 384 **Student-Faculty Ratio:** 18:1 **Exams:** Other **Library Holdings:** 127,717 **Regional Accreditation:** Southern Association of Colleges and Schools **Credit Hours For Degree:** 61 semester hours, Associates **ROTC:** Army **Professional Accreditation:** ABET, ARCEST, ACF, ADA, AHIMA, AOTA, APTA, CARC, JRCEDMS, JRCERT, NAACLS, NASAD, NASM, NAST, NLN

DEVRY UNIVERSITY (HOUSTON)
11125 Equity Dr.
Houston, TX 77041
Tel: (713)850-0888; (866)338-7934
Fax: (713)850-0858
Web Site: http://www.devry.edu/
President/CEO: Marie Hallinan
Registrar: Beth Slaton
Type: Comprehensive **Sex:** Coed **Application Deadline:** Rolling **Application Fee:** $50.00 **Costs Per Year:** Application fee: $50. One-time mandatory fee: $40. Tuition: $11,790 full-time, $440 per credit part-time. Mandatory fees: $270 full-time, $160 per year part-time. Full-time tuition and fees vary according to course load. Part-time tuition and fees vary according to course load. **Calendar System:** Semester **Enrollment:** FT 379, PT 233, Grad 83 **Faculty:** FT 1, PT 96 **Student-Faculty Ratio:** 16:1 **Regional Accreditation:** North Central Association of Colleges and Schools

DEVRY UNIVERSITY (IRVING)
4800 Regent Blvd.
Irving, TX 75063-2439
Tel: (972)929-6777; (866)338-7934
Web Site: http://www.devry.edu/
President/CEO: Dr. Kathy Noble
Registrar: Rodney Phillips
Financial Aid: Nga Phan
Type: Comprehensive **Sex:** Coed **Affiliation:** DeVry University **Admission Plans:** Deferred Admission **Application Deadline:** Rolling **Application Fee:** $50.00 **H.S. Requirements:** High school diploma required; GED accepted **Costs Per Year:** Application fee: $50. One-time mandatory fee: $40. Tuition: $11,790 full-time, $440 per credit part-time. Mandatory fees: $270 full-time, $160 per year part-time. **Scholarships:** Available **Calendar System:** Semester, Summer Session Available **Enrollment:** FT 1,102, PT 498, Grad 218 **Faculty:** FT 59, PT 68 **Student-Faculty Ratio:** 17:1 **% Receiving Financial Aid:** 73 **Library Holdings:** 21,500 **Regional Accreditation:** North Central Association of Colleges and Schools **Credit Hours For Degree:** 66 credit hours, Associates; 122 credit hours, Bachelors **Professional Accreditation:** ABET

DEVRY UNIVERSITY (PLANO)
Plano Corporate Center II
2301 West Plano Parkway, Ste. 101
Plano, TX 75075-8435
Tel: (972)943-8041
Fax: (972)943-8061
Web Site: http://www.devry.edu/ **Type:** Comprehensive **Sex:** Coed **Costs Per Year:** One-time mandatory fee: $40. Tuition: $11,790 full-time, $440 per credit part-time. Mandatory fees: $60 full-time, $30 per year part-time. Full-time tuition and fees vary according to course load. Part-time tuition and fees vary according to course load. **Calendar System:** Semester **Regional Accreditation:** North Central Association of Colleges and Schools

EAST TEXAS BAPTIST UNIVERSITY
1209 North Grove
Marshall, TX 75670-1498
Tel: (903)935-7963
Free: 800-804-ETBU
Admissions: (903)923-2000
Fax: (903)938-1705
E-mail: admissions@etbu.edu
Web Site: http://www.etbu.edu/
President/CEO: Dr. Bob E. Riley
Registrar: Jeanie Pinkston
Admissions: Vince Blankenship
Financial Aid: Katherine Evans
Type: Four-Year College **Sex:** Coed **Affiliation:** Baptist **Scores:** 92% SAT V 400+; 91% SAT M 400+; 60% ACT 18-23; 23% ACT 24-29 **% Accepted:** 72 **Admission Plans:** Deferred Admission **Application Deadline:** August 17 **Application Fee:** $25.00 **H.S. Requirements:** High school diploma required; GED accepted **Costs Per Year:** Application fee: $25. Comprehensive fee: $16,713 includes full-time tuition ($12,840) and college room and board ($3873). Room and board charges vary according to board plan and housing facility. Part-time tuition: $400 per semester hour. Tuition guaranteed not to increase for student's term of enrollment. **Scholarships:** Available **Calendar System:** Miscellaneous, Summer Session Available **Enrollment:** FT 1,176, PT 150 **Faculty:** FT 66, PT 42 **Student-Faculty Ratio:** 15:1 **Exams:** SAT I or ACT **% Receiving Financial Aid:** 77 **% Residing in College-Owned, -Operated, or -Affiliated Housing:** 73 **Library Holdings:** 116,895 **Regional Accreditation:** Southern Association of Colleges and Schools **Credit Hours For Degree:** 60 semester hours, Associates; 120 semester hours, Bachelors **Professional Accreditation:** AACN, NASM **Intercollegiate Athletics:** Baseball M; Basketball M & W; Cross-Country Running M & W; Football M; Soccer M & W; Softball W; Volleyball W

EASTFIELD COLLEGE
3737 Motley Dr.
Mesquite, TX 75150-2099
Tel: (972)860-7100
Admissions: (972)860-7105
Fax: (972)860-8373
Web Site: http://www.efc.dcccd.edu/
President/CEO: Dr. Rodger A. Pool
Registrar: Charles Helton
Admissions: Glynis Miller
Financial Aid: Reva Ratten
Type: Two-Year College **Sex:** Coed **Affiliation:** Dallas County Community College District System **% Accepted:** 100 **Admission Plans:** Open Admission; Early Admission; Deferred Admission **Application Deadline:** Rolling **Application Fee:** $0.00 **H.S. Requirements:** High school diploma required; GED accepted **Costs Per Year:** Application fee: $0. Area resident tuition: $1080 full-time, $36 per credit part-time. State resident tuition: $1980 full-time, $66 per credit part-time. Nonresident tuition: $3180 full-time, $106 per credit part-time. **Scholarships:** Available **Calendar System:** Semester, Summer Session Available **Enrollment:** FT 2,322, PT 9,789 **Faculty:** FT 95, PT 401 **Student-Faculty Ratio:** 23:1 **Library Holdings:** 66,988 **Regional Accreditation:** Southern Association of Colleges and Schools **Credit Hours For Degree:** 61 credit hours, Associates **Intercollegiate Athletics:** Baseball M; Basketball M; Golf M; Soccer W; Tennis M & W; Volleyball M & W

EL CENTRO COLLEGE
801 Main St.
Dallas, TX 75202-3604
Tel: (214)860-2037
Admissions: (214)860-2618
Fax: (214)860-2335
E-mail: rcb@dcccd.edu
Web Site: http://www.ecc.dcccd.edu/
President/CEO: Dr. Wright L. Lassiter, Jr.
Registrar: Estafana Stewart
Admissions: Stevie Stewart
Financial Aid: John Wells
Type: Two-Year College **Sex:** Coed **Affiliation:** Dallas County Community College District System **% Accepted:** 100 **Admission Plans:** Open Admission; Early Admission **Application Deadline:** Rolling **Application Fee:** $0.00 **H.S. Requirements:** High school diploma required; GED accepted. For applicants 18 or over who graduated from unaccredited high schools: High school diploma or equivalent not required **Costs Per Year:** Application fee: $0. Area resident tuition: $33 per credit part-time. State resident tuition: $60 per credit part-time. Nonresident tuition: $96 per credit part-time. **Scholarships:** Available **Calendar System:** Semester, Summer Session Available **Enrollment:** FT 1,546, PT 4,543 **Faculty:** FT 110, PT 288 **Student-Faculty Ratio:** 16:1 **Library Holdings:** 72,176 **Regional Accreditation:** Southern Association of Colleges and Schools **Credit Hours For Degree:** 61 credit hours, Associates **ROTC:** Army **Professional Accreditation:** CARC, FIDER, JRCECT, JRCEDMS, JRCERT, NAACLS, NLN

EL PASO COMMUNITY COLLEGE
PO Box 20500
El Paso, TX 79998-0500
Tel: (915)831-2000
Admissions: (915)831-2580
Fax: (915)831-6145
E-mail: daryleh@epcc.edu
Web Site: http://www.epcc.edu/
President/CEO: Dr. Richard M. Rhodes
Registrar: Bonnie Casas
Admissions: Daryle Hendry
Financial Aid: Linda Hensgen
Type: Two-Year College **Sex:** Coed **Admission Plans:** Open Admission; Early Admission; Deferred Admission **Application Fee:** $10.00 **H.S. Requirements:** High school diploma required; GED accepted **Scholarships:** Available **Calendar System:** Semester, Summer Session Available **Faculty:** FT 354, PT 829 **Exams:** Other **Library Holdings:** 442,879 **Regional Accreditation:** Southern Association of Colleges and Schools **Credit Hours For Degree:** 60 credit hours, Associates **ROTC:** Army **Professional Accreditation:** ARCEST, AAMAE, ADA, AHIMA, APTA, COptA, CARC, NAACLS, NLN **Intercollegiate Athletics:** Baseball M; Softball W

EVEREST COLLEGE (ARLINGTON)
2801 East Division St., Ste. 250
Arlington, TX 76011
Tel: (817)652-7790
Fax: (817)649-6033
Web Site: http://www.everest-college.com/
President/CEO: Dick Roessler
Type: Two-Year College **Sex:** Coed **Calendar System:** Miscellaneous **Professional Accreditation:** ACICS

EVEREST COLLEGE (DALLAS)
6060 North Central Expressway, Ste. 101
Dallas, TX 75206-5209
Tel: (214)234-4850
Fax: (214)696-6208
Web Site: http://www.everest-college.com/
President/CEO: Kathy Fox
Type: Two-Year College **Sex:** Coed **Calendar System:** Miscellaneous **Professional Accreditation:** ACICS

EVEREST COLLEGE (FORT WORTH)
5237 North Riverside Dr.
Ste. G101
Fort Worth, TX 76137
Web Site: http://www.everest-college.com/ **Type:** Two-Year College **Sex:** Coed

FRANK PHILLIPS COLLEGE
Box 5118
Borger, TX 79008-5118
Tel: (806)274-5311
Free: 800-687-2056
Admissions: (806)457-4200
Fax: (806)274-6835
Web Site: http://www.fpc.cc.tx.us/
President/CEO: Dr. Herbert Swender
Registrar: Beth Raper
Admissions: Beth Raper
Financial Aid: Linda Kunce
Type: Two-Year College **Sex:** Coed **Admission Plans:** Open Admission; Early Admission; Deferred Admission **Application Fee:** $0.00 **H.S. Requirements:** High school diploma required; GED accepted **Costs Per Year:** Application fee: $0. Area resident tuition: $720 full-time, $30 per semester hour part-time. State resident tuition: $1128 full-time, $47 per semester hour part-time. Nonresident tuition: $1296 full-time, $54 per semester hour part-time. Mandatory fees: $914 full-time, $36 per semester hour part-time, $50 per term part-time. **Scholarships:** Available **Calendar System:** Semester, Summer Session Available **Faculty:** FT 28, PT 69 **Exams:** Other **Library Holdings:** 35,700 **Regional Accreditation:** Southern Association of Colleges and Schools **Credit Hours For Degree:** 64 credit hours, Associates **Intercollegiate Athletics:** Baseball M; Basketball M & W; Volleyball W

GALVESTON COLLEGE
4015 Ave. Q
Galveston, TX 77550-7496
Tel: (409)763-6551
Admissions: (409)944-1234
Fax: (409)762-9367
E-mail: blowery@gc.edu
Web Site: http://www.gc.edu/
President/CEO: Dr. Elva Concha-Allie
Registrar: Carrie Streeter
Admissions: Brian Lowery
Financial Aid: Midge Berlowe
Type: Two-Year College **Sex:** Coed **% Accepted:** 100 **Admission Plans:** Open Admission **Application Deadline:** Rolling **Application Fee:** $0.00 **H.S. Requirements:** High school diploma required; GED accepted **Costs Per Year:** Application fee: $0. State resident tuition: $900 full-time, $30 per hour part-time. Nonresident tuition: $1800 full-time, $60 per hour part-time. Mandatory fees: $430 full-time, $12 per hour part-time, $30 per term part-time. **Scholarships:** Available **Calendar System:** Semester, Summer Session Available **Enrollment:** FT 851, PT 1,379 **Faculty:** FT 54, PT 87 **Student-Faculty Ratio:** 16:1 **Library Holdings:** 45,193 **Regional Accreditation:** Southern Association of Colleges and Schools **Credit Hours For Degree:** 60 credit hours, Associates **Professional Accreditation:** JRCERT, JRCEMT, JRCNMT, NLN **Intercollegiate Athletics:** Baseball M; Softball W; Volleyball W

GRAYSON COUNTY COLLEGE
6101 Grayson Dr.
Denison, TX 75020-8299
Tel: (903)465-6030
Fax: (903)463-5284
Web Site: http://www.grayson.edu/
President/CEO: Dr. Alan Scheibmeir
Registrar: Dr. David Petrash
Admissions: Dr. David Petrash
Financial Aid: Dr. Ressie Brazzle
Type: Two-Year College **Sex:** Coed **Admission Plans:** Open Admission; Early Admission; Deferred Admission **Application Fee:** $0.00 **H.S. Requirements:** High school diploma required; GED accepted **Scholarships:** Available **Calendar System:** Semester, Summer Session Available **Enrollment:** FT 1,697, PT 1,647 **Faculty:** FT 94, PT 125 **Student-Faculty Ratio:** 16:1 **Exams:** Other, SAT I or ACT **Library Holdings:** 51,500 **Regional Accreditation:** Southern Association of Colleges and Schools **Credit Hours For Degree:** 62 semester hours, Associates **Professional Accreditation:** ADA, NAACLS, NLN **Intercollegiate Athletics:** Baseball M; Basketball M & W; Softball W

HALLMARK INSTITUTE OF AERONAUTICS
8901 Wetmore Rd.
San Antonio, TX 78216
Tel: (210)826-1000
Free: 800-683-3600
Admissions: (210)690-9000
Fax: (210)826-3707
President/CEO: Richard Fessler
Registrar: Anne Marie Moore
Admissions: David McSorley
Financial Aid: Grace Calixto
Type: Two-Year College **Sex:** Coed **Admission Plans:** Open Admission **Scholarships:** Available **Calendar System:** Continuous **Professional Accreditation:** ACCSCT

HALLMARK INSTITUTE OF TECHNOLOGY
10401 IH 10 West
San Antonio, TX 78230-1737
Tel: (210)690-9000
Free: 800-880-6600
Fax: (210)697-8225
Web Site: http://www.hallmarkinstitute.edu/
President/CEO: Joe Fisher
Registrar: Margarel Delgado
Admissions: Sonia Ross
Financial Aid: Grace Calixto
Type: Two-Year College **Sex:** Coed **H.S. Requirements:** High school diploma required; GED accepted **Scholarships:** Available **Calendar System:** Continuous **Faculty:** FT 10, PT 35 **Exams:** Other **Credit Hours For Degree:** 69 credit hours, Associates **Professional Accreditation:** ACCSCT

HARDIN-SIMMONS UNIVERSITY
2200 Hickory St.
Abilene, TX 79698-0001
Tel: (325)670-1000; 877-464-7889
Admissions: (325)670-1206
Fax: (325)677-8351
E-mail: jdsd@hsutx.edu
Web Site: http://www.hsutx.edu/
President/CEO: Dr. W. Craig Turner
Registrar: Dorothy Kiser
Admissions: Shane Davidson
Financial Aid: Jim Jones
Type: Comprehensive **Sex:** Coed **Affiliation:** Baptist **Scores:** 94% SAT V 400+; 94% SAT M 400+; 58% ACT 18-23; 28% ACT 24-29 **% Accepted:** 66 **Admission Plans:** Deferred Admission **Application Deadline:** Rolling **Application Fee:** $50.00 **H.S. Requirements:** High school diploma required; GED accepted **Costs Per Year:** Application fee: $50. Comprehensive fee: $20,206 includes full-time tuition ($14,850), mandatory fees ($776), and college room and board ($4580). College room only: $2365. Part-time tuition: $495 per semester hour. Part-time mandatory fees: $96 per term. **Scholarships:** Available **Calendar System:** Semester, Summer Session Available **Enrollment:** FT 1,779, PT 212, Grad 362 **Faculty:** FT 131, PT 48 **Student-Faculty Ratio:** 15:1 **% Receiving Financial Aid:** 69 **% Residing in College-Owned, -Operated, or -Affiliated Housing:** 44 **Library Holdings:** 226,755 **Regional Accreditation:** Southern Association of Colleges and Schools **Credit Hours For Degree:** 124 semester hours, Bachelors **Professional Accreditation:** AACN, APTA, ACBSP, ATS, CSWE, NASM **Intercollegiate Athletics:** Baseball M; Basketball M & W; Cheerleading M & W; Football M; Golf M & W; Soccer M & W; Softball W; Tennis M & W; Volleyball W

HIGH-TECH INSTITUTE
4250 North Belt Line Rd.
Irving, TX 75038
Tel: (972)871-2824
Free: 800-987-0110
E-mail: clewellen@hightechschools.com
Web Site: http://www.high-techinstitute.com/
President/CEO: Cindy Lewellen
Admissions: Cindy M. Lewellen
Type: Two-Year College **Sex:** Coed **Calendar System:** Semester **Professional Accreditation:** ACCSCT

HILL COLLEGE OF THE HILL JUNIOR COLLEGE DISTRICT
PO Box 619
Hillsboro, TX 76645-0619
Tel: (254)582-2555
E-mail: diharvey@hill-college.cc.tx.us
Web Site: http://www.hillcollege.edu/
President/CEO: Dr. W. R. Auvenshine
Admissions: Diane Harvey
Financial Aid: Nancy Holland
Type: Two-Year College **Sex:** Coed **Admission Plans:** Open Admission; Early Admission; Deferred Admission **Application Fee:** $0.00 **H.S. Requirements:** High school diploma required; GED accepted **Scholarships:** Available **Calendar System:** Semester, Summer Session Available **Enrollment:** FT 1,569, PT 1,667 **Faculty:** FT 158, PT 85 **Student-Faculty Ratio:** 25:1 **Exams:** Other, SAT I or ACT **% Residing in College-Owned, -Operated, or -Affiliated Housing:** 14 **Library Holdings:** 40,000 **Regional Accreditation:** Southern Association of Colleges and Schools **Credit Hours For Degree:** 62 credit hours, Associates **Intercollegiate Athletics:** Baseball M; Basketball M & W; Soccer W; Softball W; Volleyball W

HOUSTON BAPTIST UNIVERSITY
7502 Fondren Rd.
Houston, TX 77074-3298
Tel: (281)649-3000
Free: 800-696-3210
Fax: (281)649-3209
E-mail: unadm@hbu.edu
Web Site: http://www.hbu.edu/
President/CEO: Dr. E. Douglas Hodo
Registrar: Carolyn Albritton
Admissions: David Melton
Financial Aid: Sherry Byrd
Type: Comprehensive **Sex:** Coed **Affiliation:** Baptist **Scores:** 97% SAT V 400+; 98% SAT M 400+; 54% ACT 18-23; 35% ACT 24-29 **% Accepted:** 65 **Admission Plans:** Early Admission; Deferred Admission **Application Deadline:** Rolling **Application Fee:** $25.00 **H.S. Requirements:** High school diploma required; GED accepted **Costs Per Year:** Application fee: $25. Comprehensive fee: $21,000 includes full-time tuition ($16,500) and college room and board ($4500). College room only: $2355. Part-time tuition: $550 per semester hour. **Scholarships:** Available **Calendar System:** Quarter, Summer Session Available **Enrollment:** FT 1,653, PT 279, Grad 362 **Faculty:** FT 103, PT 66 **Student-Faculty Ratio:** 15:1 **Exams:** SAT I or ACT **% Receiving Financial Aid:** 84 **% Residing in College-Owned, -Operated, or -Affiliated Housing:** 30 **Library Holdings:** 209,366 **Regional Accreditation:** Southern Association of Colleges and Schools **Credit Hours For Degree:** 72 credit hours, Associates; 130 credit hours, Bachelors **ROTC:** Army **Professional Accreditation:** ACBSP, NLN **Intercollegiate Athletics:** Baseball M; Basketball M & W; Cheerleading M & W; Softball W; Volleyball W

HOUSTON COMMUNITY COLLEGE SYSTEM
3100 Main St.
PO Box 667517
Houston, TX 77266-7517
Tel: (713)718-2000
Admissions: (713)718-8500
Fax: (713)718-2111
Web Site: http://www.hccs.edu/
President/CEO: Dr. Bruce Leslie
Admissions: Mary Lemburg
Financial Aid: Alex Prince
Type: Two-Year College **Sex:** Coed **Admission Plans:** Open Admission **Application Deadline:** Rolling **Application Fee:** $0.00 **H.S. Requirements:** High school diploma or equivalent not required **Costs Per Year:** Application fee: $0. Area resident tuition: $1176 full-time. State resident tuition: $2472 full-time. Nonresident tuition: $2952 full-time. **Scholarships:** Available **Calendar System:** Semester, Summer Session Available **Enrollment:** FT 12,198, PT 27,318 **Faculty:** FT 814, PT 2,391 **Student-Faculty Ratio:** 20:1 **Library Holdings:** 140,674 **Regional Accreditation:** Southern Association of Colleges and Schools **Credit Hours For Degree:** 60 semester hours, Associates **ROTC:** Army **Professional Accreditation:** ABET, ADA, AHIMA, AOTA, APTA, CARC, JRCERT, JRCEMT, JRCNMT, NAACLS

HOWARD COLLEGE
1001 Birdwell Ln.
Big Spring, TX 79720
Tel: (915)264-5000; (866)HC-HAWKS
Admissions: (432)264-5105
Fax: (915)264-5082
Web Site: http://www.howardcollege.edu/
President/CEO: Dr. Cheryl T. Sparks
Registrar: Lisa Currie
Admissions: Donna Merrick
Financial Aid: Margaret Cervantes
Type: Two-Year College **Sex:** Coed **Affiliation:** Howard County Junior College District System **% Accepted:** 100 **Admission Plans:** Open Admission; Early Admission **Application Deadline:** Rolling **Application Fee:** $0.00 **H.S. Requirements:** High school diploma required; GED accepted **Costs Per Year:** Application fee: $0. Area resident tuition: $1140 full-time, $30 per credit hour part-time. State resident tuition: $1500 full-time, $40 per credit hour part-time. Nonresident tuition: $2160 full-time, $60 per credit hour part-time. Mandatory fees: $66 full-time, $50 per term part-time. Full-time tuition and fees vary according to course load, location, and program. Part-time tuition and fees vary according to course load, location, and program. College room and board: $3140. **Scholarships:** Available **Calendar System:** Semester, Summer Session Available **Enrollment:** FT 1,174, PT 1,551 **Faculty:** FT 126, PT 62 **Student-Faculty Ratio:** 11:1 **% Residing in College-Owned, -Operated, or -Affiliated Housing:** 18 **Library Holdings:** 30,921 **Regional Accreditation:** Southern Association of Colleges and Schools **Credit Hours For Degree:** 62 credit hours, Associates **Professional Accreditation:** ADA, AHIMA, NLN **Intercollegiate Athletics:** Baseball M; Basketball M & W; Cheerleading M & W; Softball W

HOWARD PAYNE UNIVERSITY
1000 Fisk St.
Brownwood, TX 76801-2715

Tel: (325)646-2502
Free: 800-880-4478
Admissions: (325)649-8027
Fax: (325)649-8905
E-mail: admissions@hputx.edu
Web Site: http://www.hputx.edu/
President/CEO: Dr. Lanny Hall
Registrar: Lana Wagner
Admissions: Cheryl Mangrum
Financial Aid: Glenda Huff
Type: Four-Year College **Sex:** Coed **Affiliation:** Baptist General Convention of Texas **Scores:** 84.3% SAT V 400+; 91.1% SAT M 400+; 51.9% ACT 18-23; 22.2% ACT 24-29 **Admission Plans:** Early Admission **Application Fee:** $25.00 **H.S. Requirements:** High school diploma required; GED accepted **Scholarships:** Available **Calendar System:** Semester, Summer Session Available **Enrollment:** FT 1,019, PT 300 **Faculty:** FT 71, PT 54 **Student-Faculty Ratio:** 13:1 **Exams:** SAT I or ACT **% Receiving Financial Aid:** 77 **% Residing in College-Owned, -Operated, or -Affiliated Housing:** 48 **Library Holdings:** 78,825 **Regional Accreditation:** Southern Association of Colleges and Schools **Credit Hours For Degree:** 64 semester hours, Associates; 128 semester hours, Bachelors **Professional Accreditation:** CSWE, NASM **Intercollegiate Athletics:** Baseball M; Basketball M & W; Cross-Country Running M & W; Football M; Softball W; Tennis M & W; Track and Field M & W; Volleyball W

HUSTON-TILLOTSON UNIVERSITY
900 Chicon St.
Austin, TX 78702-2795
Tel: (512)505-3000
Admissions: (512)505-3029
Fax: (512)505-3190
E-mail: dfprice@htu.edu
Web Site: http://www.htu.edu/
President/CEO: Dr. Larry L. Ervin
Registrar: Earnestine Strickland
Admissions: Dean Doris Price
Financial Aid: Brontè D. Jones
Type: Four-Year College **Sex:** Coed **Affiliation:** interdenominational **Scores:** 58% SAT V 400+; 54% SAT M 400+; 22% ACT 18-23; 5% ACT 24-29 **% Accepted:** 56 **Application Deadline:** March 01 **Application Fee:** $25.00 **H.S. Requirements:** High school diploma required; GED accepted **Costs Per Year:** Application fee: $25. Comprehensive fee: $14,018 includes full-time tuition ($7740), mandatory fees ($735), and college room and board ($5543). College room only: $2250. Part-time tuition: $258 per credit hour. **Scholarships:** Available **Calendar System:** Semester, Summer Session Available **Enrollment:** FT 625, PT 81 **Faculty:** FT 38, PT 27 **Student-Faculty Ratio:** 11:1 **% Receiving Financial Aid:** 88 **% Residing in College-Owned, -Operated, or -Affiliated Housing:** 42 **Library Holdings:** 88,455 **Regional Accreditation:** Southern Association of Colleges and Schools **Credit Hours For Degree:** 120 credit hours, Bachelors **ROTC:** Army, Navy **Intercollegiate Athletics:** Baseball M; Basketball M & W; Cross-Country Running W; Soccer M; Track and Field M & W; Volleyball W

ITT TECHNICAL INSTITUTE (ARLINGTON)
551 Ryan Plaza Dr.
Arlington, TX 76011
Tel: (817)794-5100
Fax: (817)275-8446
Web Site: http://www.itt-tech.edu/
President/CEO: Paulette Gallerson
Admissions: Paulette Gallerson
Financial Aid: Wilma Tippit
Type: Two-Year College **Sex:** Coed **Affiliation:** ITT Educational Services, Inc **Admission Plans:** Deferred Admission **Application Deadline:** Rolling **Application Fee:** $100.00 **H.S. Requirements:** High school diploma required; GED accepted **Costs Per Year:** Application fee: $100. **Scholarships:** Available **Calendar System:** Quarter, Summer Session Not available **Exams:** Other **Credit Hours For Degree:** 96 credit hours, Associates **Professional Accreditation:** ACICS

ITT TECHNICAL INSTITUTE (AUSTIN)
6330 East Hwy. 290, Ste. 150
Austin, TX 78723-1061
Tel: (512)467-6800
Free: 800-431-0677
Web Site: http://www.itt-tech.edu/
President/CEO: Barbara J. Anthony
Registrar: Eric Falkenbury
Admissions: Barbara Anthony
Financial Aid: Cindy Johnson
Type: Two-Year College **Sex:** Coed **Affiliation:** ITT Educational Services, Inc **Admission Plans:** Deferred Admission **Application Deadline:** Rolling **Application Fee:** $100.00 **H.S. Requirements:** High school diploma required; GED accepted **Costs Per Year:** Application fee: $100. **Scholarships:** Available **Calendar System:** Quarter, Summer Session Not available **Exams:** Other **Credit Hours For Degree:** 96 credit hours, Associates **Professional Accreditation:** ACICS

ITT TECHNICAL INSTITUTE (HOUSTON)
2222 Bay Area Blvd.
Houston, TX 77058
Tel: (281)486-2630
Web Site: http://www.itt-tech.edu/
President/CEO: Robert F. Jeffords
Registrar: Linda Womack
Admissions: Aaron Armendariz
Financial Aid: Belinda Balsano
Type: Two-Year College **Sex:** Coed **Affiliation:** ITT Educational Services, Inc **Admission Plans:** Deferred Admission **Application Deadline:** Rolling **Application Fee:** $100.00 **H.S. Requirements:** High school diploma required; GED accepted **Costs Per Year:** Application fee: $100. **Scholarships:** Available **Calendar System:** Quarter, Summer Session Not available **Exams:** Other **Credit Hours For Degree:** 96 credit hours, Associates **Professional Accreditation:** ACICS

ITT TECHNICAL INSTITUTE (HOUSTON)
2950 South Gessner
Houston, TX 77063-3751
Tel: (713)952-2294
Web Site: http://www.itt-tech.edu/
President/CEO: Robert E. Van Elsen
Admissions: Cathy Clark
Financial Aid: Mariana Canas
Type: Two-Year College **Sex:** Coed **Affiliation:** ITT Educational Services, Inc **Admission Plans:** Deferred Admission **Application Deadline:** Rolling **Application Fee:** $100.00 **H.S. Requirements:** High school diploma required; GED accepted **Costs Per Year:** Application fee: $100. **Scholarships:** Available **Calendar System:** Quarter, Summer Session Not available **Exams:** Other **Credit Hours For Degree:** 96 credit hours, Associates **Professional Accreditation:** ACICS

ITT TECHNICAL INSTITUTE (HOUSTON)
15621 Blue Ash Dr., Ste. 160
Houston, TX 77090-5821
Tel: (281)873-0512
Fax: (281)873-0518
Web Site: http://www.itt-tech.edu/
President/CEO: David D. Champlin
Registrar: Trudi White
Admissions: Tom Bonesteel
Financial Aid: Linda Trammel
Type: Two-Year College **Sex:** Coed **Affiliation:** ITT Educational Services, Inc **Admission Plans:** Deferred Admission **Application Deadline:** Rolling **Application Fee:** $100.00 **H.S. Requirements:** High school diploma required; GED accepted **Costs Per Year:** Application fee: $100. **Scholarships:** Available **Calendar System:** Quarter, Summer Session Not available **Exams:** Other **Credit Hours For Degree:** 96 credit hours, Associates **Professional Accreditation:** ACICS

ITT TECHNICAL INSTITUTE (RICHARDSON)
2101 Waterview Parkway
Richardson, TX 75080
Tel: (972)690-9100; 888-488-5761
Web Site: http://www.itt-tech.edu/
President/CEO: Maureen K. Clements
Admissions: Maureen Clements
Financial Aid: Monita Saunders
Type: Two-Year College **Sex:** Coed **Affiliation:** ITT Educational Services, Inc **Admission Plans:** Deferred Admission **Application Deadline:** Rolling **Application Fee:** $100.00 **H.S. Requirements:** High school diploma

required; GED accepted **Costs Per Year:** Application fee: $100. **Scholarships:** Available **Calendar System:** Quarter, Summer Session Not available **Exams:** Other **Credit Hours For Degree:** 96 credit hours, Associates **Professional Accreditation:** ACICS

ITT TECHNICAL INSTITUTE (SAN ANTONIO)
5700 Northwest Parkway
San Antonio, TX 78249-3303
Tel: (210)694-4612
Free: 800-880-0570
Fax: (210)694-4651
Web Site: http://www.itt-tech.edu/
President/CEO: Barry Simich
Registrar: Dan Swan
Admissions: Mark Garland
Type: Two-Year College **Sex:** Coed **Affiliation:** ITT Educational Services, Inc **Admission Plans:** Deferred Admission **Application Deadline:** Rolling **Application Fee:** $100.00 **H.S. Requirements:** High school diploma required; GED accepted **Costs Per Year:** Application fee: $100. **Scholarships:** Available **Calendar System:** Quarter, Summer Session Not available **Exams:** Other **Credit Hours For Degree:** 96 credit hours, Associates **Professional Accreditation:** ACICS

JACKSONVILLE COLLEGE
105 B J Albritton Dr.
Jacksonville, TX 75766-4759
Tel: (903)586-2518
Free: 800-256-8522
E-mail: admissions@jacksonville-college.edu
Web Site: http://www.jacksonville-college.edu/
President/CEO: Dr. Edwin Crank
Registrar: Rhonda Smith
Admissions: Melissa Walles
Financial Aid: Don Compton
Type: Two-Year College **Sex:** Coed **Affiliation:** Baptist **% Accepted:** 41 **Admission Plans:** Open Admission; Early Admission **Application Deadline:** August 15 **Application Fee:** $15.00 **H.S. Requirements:** High school diploma required; GED accepted **Costs Per Year:** Application fee: $15. Comprehensive fee: $4480 includes full-time tuition ($2800), mandatory fees ($307), and college room and board ($1373). Part-time tuition: $175 per credit hour. **Scholarships:** Available **Calendar System:** Semester, Summer Session Available **Enrollment:** FT 220, PT 80 **Faculty:** FT 10, PT 14 **Student-Faculty Ratio:** 16:1 **Exams:** ACT, Other, SAT I **% Residing in College-Owned, -Operated, or -Affiliated Housing:** 39 **Library Holdings:** 22,000 **Regional Accreditation:** Southern Association of Colleges and Schools **Credit Hours For Degree:** 64 semester hours, Associates **Intercollegiate Athletics:** Basketball M & W; Volleyball W

JARVIS CHRISTIAN COLLEGE
PO Box 1470
Hawkins, TX 75765-1470
Tel: (903)769-5700
Admissions: (903)769-5802
Fax: (903)769-4842
Web Site: http://www.jarvis.edu/
President/CEO: Dr. Sebetha Jenkins
Registrar: Autry Acrey
Admissions: Christopher Wooten
Financial Aid: Harold Abney
Type: Four-Year College **Sex:** Coed **Affiliation:** Christian Church (Disciples of Christ) **Scores:** 48.1% SAT V 400+; 40% SAT M 400+; 18% ACT 18-23 **% Accepted:** 58 **Admission Plans:** Open Admission **Application Deadline:** August 01 **Application Fee:** $25.00 **H.S. Requirements:** High school diploma required; GED accepted **Costs Per Year:** Application fee: $25. Comprehensive fee: $11,136 includes full-time tuition ($6280), mandatory fees ($700), and college room and board ($4156). College room only: $2056. Part-time tuition: $262 per hour. Part-time mandatory fees: $350 per term. **Scholarships:** Available **Calendar System:** Semester, Summer Session Available **Enrollment:** FT 559, PT 13 **Faculty:** FT 35, PT 8 **Student-Faculty Ratio:** 15:1 **Exams:** ACT, SAT I or ACT **% Residing in College-Owned, -Operated, or -Affiliated Housing:** 87 **Library Holdings:** 54,291 **Regional Accreditation:** Southern Association of Colleges and Schools **Credit Hours For Degree:** 124 semester hours, Bachelors **Professional Accreditation:** ACBSP **Intercollegiate Athletics:** Baseball M; Basketball M & W; Cheerleading W; Volleyball W

KD STUDIO
2600 Stemmons Freeway, No. 117
Dallas, TX 75207
Tel: (214)638-0484
Fax: (214)630-5140
E-mail: acting@onramp.net
Web Site: http://www.kdstudio.com/
President/CEO: Kathy Tyner
Registrar: Bitsey Kelley
Admissions: Gary Tyner
Financial Aid: Rebecca R. Harris
Type: Two-Year College **Sex:** Coed **% Accepted:** 91 **Admission Plans:** Open Admission; Deferred Admission **Application Deadline:** Rolling **Application Fee:** $100.00 **H.S. Requirements:** High school diploma required; GED accepted **Scholarships:** Available **Calendar System:** Semester, Summer Session Not available **Enrollment:** FT 152 **Faculty:** FT 23 **Student-Faculty Ratio:** 7:1 **Library Holdings:** 800 **Credit Hours For Degree:** 70 credits, Associates **Professional Accreditation:** NAST

KILGORE COLLEGE
1100 Broadway Blvd.
Kilgore, TX 75662-3299
Tel: (903)984-8531
Admissions: (903)983-8200
Fax: (903)983-8607
Web Site: http://www.kilgore.edu/
President/CEO: Dr. William M. Holda
Registrar: Phyllis Stalcup
Admissions: Phyllis Stalcup
Type: Two-Year College **Sex:** Coed **Scores:** 82% SAT V 400+; 81% SAT M 400+; 53% ACT 18-23; 17% ACT 24-29 **Admission Plans:** Open Admission; Early Admission **Application Fee:** $0.00 **H.S. Requirements:** High school diploma required; GED accepted **Costs Per Year:** Application fee: $0. Area resident tuition: $540 full-time, $18 per hour part-time. State resident tuition: $1680 full-time, $56 per hour part-time. Nonresident tuition: $2520 full-time, $84 per hour part-time. Mandatory fees: $510 full-time. College room and board: $3580. College room only: $1580. **Scholarships:** Available **Calendar System:** Semester, Summer Session Available **Enrollment:** FT 2,749, PT 2,208 **Faculty:** FT 128, PT 119 **Student-Faculty Ratio:** 19:1 **Exams:** Other, SAT I or ACT **% Residing in College-Owned, -Operated, or -Affiliated Housing:** 12 **Library Holdings:** 65,000 **Regional Accreditation:** Southern Association of Colleges and Schools **Credit Hours For Degree:** 62 credits, Associates **ROTC:** Army **Professional Accreditation:** ARCEST, AAMAE, APTA, JRCERT, NAACLS, NLN **Intercollegiate Athletics:** Basketball M & W; Cheerleading M & W; Football M

KINGWOOD COLLEGE
20000 Kingwood Dr.
Kingwood, TX 77339-3801
Tel: (281)312-1600
Admissions: (281)312-1562
Fax: (281)312-1477
Web Site: http://kcweb.nhmccd.edu/
President/CEO: Dr. Linda Stegall
Registrar: Ike Williams
Admissions: Ike Williams
Financial Aid: Carolyn Wade
Type: Two-Year College **Sex:** Coed **Affiliation:** North Harris Montgomery Community College District **% Accepted:** 100 **Admission Plans:** Open Admission; Early Admission **Application Deadline:** Rolling **Application Fee:** $0.00 **H.S. Requirements:** High school diploma required; GED accepted **Costs Per Year:** Application fee: $0. Area resident tuition: $984 full-time, $52 per credit part-time. State resident tuition: $1944 full-time, $92 per credit part-time. Nonresident tuition: $2304 full-time, $220 per credit part-time. **Scholarships:** Available **Calendar System:** Semester, Summer Session Available **Enrollment:** FT 1,308, PT 5,534 **Faculty:** FT 99, PT 288 **Student-Faculty Ratio:** 16:1 **Library Holdings:** 38,000 **Regional Accreditation:** Southern Association of Colleges and Schools **Credit Hours For Degree:** 62 credit hours, Associates **Professional Accreditation:** ADA, AOTA, CARC

LAMAR INSTITUTE OF TECHNOLOGY
PO Box 10043
Beaumont, TX 77710
Tel: (409)880-8321

Free: 800-950-8321
Admissions: (409)880-8354
E-mail: rushjc@hal.lamar.edu
Web Site: http://theinstitute.lamar.edu/
President/CEO: Dr. Robert Krienke
Admissions: James Rush
Type: Two-Year College **Sex:** Coed **Scholarships:** Available **Calendar System:** Semester **Regional Accreditation:** Southern Association of Colleges and Schools **Professional Accreditation:** ADA, AHIMA, CARC

LAMAR STATE COLLEGE-ORANGE
410 Front St.
Orange, TX 77630-5802
Tel: (409)883-7750
Admissions: (409)882-3362
Fax: (409)882-3374
Web Site: http://www.lsco.edu/
President/CEO: Dr. J. Michael Shahan
Registrar: Becky Campbell
Admissions: Kerry Olson
Financial Aid: Kerry Olson
Type: Two-Year College **Sex:** Coed **Affiliation:** The Texas State University System **% Accepted:** 70 **Admission Plans:** Open Admission; Early Admission; Deferred Admission **Application Deadline:** Rolling **Application Fee:** $0.00 **H.S. Requirements:** High school diploma required; GED accepted **Costs Per Year:** Application fee: $0. State resident tuition: $1824 full-time. Nonresident tuition: $8448 full-time. Mandatory fees: $736 full-time. **Scholarships:** Available **Calendar System:** Semester, Summer Session Available **Enrollment:** FT 920, PT 1,223 **Faculty:** FT 51, PT 47 **Student-Faculty Ratio:** 19:1 **Library Holdings:** 71,092 **Regional Accreditation:** Southern Association of Colleges and Schools **Credit Hours For Degree:** 62 credit hours, Associates **Professional Accreditation:** ADA, NAACLS

LAMAR STATE COLLEGE-PORT ARTHUR
PO Box 310
Port Arthur, TX 77641-0310
Tel: (409)983-4921
Free: 800-477-5872
Admissions: (409)984-6165
Fax: (409)984-6032
E-mail: connie.nicholas@lamarpa.edu
Web Site: http://www.lamarpa.edu/
President/CEO: Dr. Sam Monroe
Registrar: Connie Nicholas
Admissions: Connie Nicholas
Financial Aid: Diane Hargett
Type: Two-Year College **Sex:** Coed **Affiliation:** The Texas State University System **% Accepted:** 61 **Admission Plans:** Open Admission; Early Admission; Deferred Admission **Application Deadline:** Rolling **Application Fee:** $0.00 **H.S. Requirements:** High school diploma or equivalent not required **Costs Per Year:** Application fee: $0. One-time mandatory fee: $10. State resident tuition: $2340 full-time. Nonresident tuition: $10,590 full-time. Mandatory fees: $824 full-time. **Scholarships:** Available **Calendar System:** Semester, Summer Session Available **Enrollment:** FT 980, PT 1,550 **Faculty:** FT 64, PT 61 **Student-Faculty Ratio:** 13:1 **Library Holdings:** 43,726 **Regional Accreditation:** Southern Association of Colleges and Schools **Credit Hours For Degree:** 64 credit hours, Associates **ROTC:** Army **Professional Accreditation:** ARCEST, ACBSP

LAMAR UNIVERSITY
4400 Martin Luther King Parkway
Beaumont, TX 77710
Tel: (409)880-7011
Admissions: (409)880-8354
Fax: (409)880-8463
Web Site: http://www.lamar.edu/
President/CEO: Dr. James Simmons
Registrar: Keith Capps
Admissions: Jim Rush
Financial Aid: Jill Rowley
Type: University **Sex:** Coed **Affiliation:** Texas State University System **Scores:** 80% SAT V 400+; 79% SAT M 400+; 43% ACT 18-23; 10% ACT 24-29 **% Accepted:** 67 **Admission Plans:** Early Admission **Application Deadline:** August 01 **Application Fee:** $0.00 **H.S. Requirements:** High school diploma required; GED accepted **Costs Per Year:** Application fee: $0. Area resident tuition: $1262 per term part-time. State resident tuition: $2880 full-time. Nonresident tuition: $9504 full-time, $4813 per term part-time. Mandatory fees: $512 per term part-time. Part-time tuition and fees vary according to course load. College room and board: $5254. College room only: $3600. Room and board charges vary according to board plan and housing facility. **Scholarships:** Available **Calendar System:** Semester, Summer Session Available **Enrollment:** FT 6,708, PT 2,976, Grad 911 **Faculty:** FT 372, PT 170 **Student-Faculty Ratio:** 20:1 **Exams:** SAT I or ACT, SAT II **% Receiving Financial Aid:** 40 **Library Holdings:** 698,285 **Regional Accreditation:** Southern Association of Colleges and Schools **Credit Hours For Degree:** 60 semester hours, Associates; 124 semester hours, Bachelors **Professional Accreditation:** AACSB, ABET, AAFCS, ACF, ADtA, ASLHA, CSWE, JRCERT, NASM, NLN **Intercollegiate Athletics:** Baseball M; Basketball M & W; Cheerleading M & W; Cross-Country Running M & W; Football M; Golf M & W; Tennis M & W; Track and Field M & W; Volleyball W

LAREDO COMMUNITY COLLEGE
West End Washington St.
Laredo, TX 78040-4395
Tel: (956)722-0521
Admissions: (956)721-5109
Fax: (956)721-5493
Web Site: http://www.laredo.edu/
President/CEO: Dr. Ramon H. Dovalina
Registrar: Olga D. Rubio
Admissions: Diana Rubio
Financial Aid: Ricardo Moreno
Type: Two-Year College **Sex:** Coed **% Accepted:** 100 **Admission Plans:** Open Admission; Early Admission; Deferred Admission **Application Deadline:** Rolling **Application Fee:** $0.00 **Costs Per Year:** Application fee: $0. Area resident tuition: $840 full-time, $35 per credit hour part-time. State resident tuition: $1680 full-time, $70 per credit hour part-time. Nonresident tuition: $2520 full-time, $105 per credit hour part-time. Mandatory fees: $270 full-time, $24 per credit hour part-time, $28 per term part-time. College room and board: $4229. **Scholarships:** Available **Calendar System:** Semester, Summer Session Available **Enrollment:** FT 3,200, PT 5,098 **Faculty:** FT 211, PT 159 **Student-Faculty Ratio:** 18:1 **Library Holdings:** 88,006 **Regional Accreditation:** Southern Association of Colleges and Schools **Credit Hours For Degree:** 60 credit hours, Associates **Professional Accreditation:** AOTA, APTA, JRCERT, NAACLS, NLN **Intercollegiate Athletics:** Baseball M; Tennis M & W; Volleyball W

LEE COLLEGE
PO Box 818
Baytown, TX 77522-0818
Tel: (281)427-5611
Free: 800-621-8724
Admissions: (281)425-6399
Fax: (281)425-6831
E-mail: bgriffit@lee.edu
Web Site: http://www.lee.edu/
President/CEO: Dr. Martha M. Ellis
Registrar: Becki Griffith
Admissions: Becki Griffith
Financial Aid: Sharon Mullins
Type: Two-Year College **Sex:** Coed **Admission Plans:** Open Admission; Early Admission; Deferred Admission **Application Fee:** $0.00 **H.S. Requirements:** High school diploma or equivalent not required **Scholarships:** Available **Calendar System:** Semester, Summer Session Available **Enrollment:** FT 1,624, PT 4,282 **Faculty:** FT 170, PT 193 **Student-Faculty Ratio:** 16:1 **Exams:** Other **Library Holdings:** 100,000 **Regional Accreditation:** Southern Association of Colleges and Schools **Credit Hours For Degree:** 60 credit hours, Associates **ROTC:** Army **Professional Accreditation:** AHIMA, JRCEMT, NLN **Intercollegiate Athletics:** Basketball M; Tennis W; Volleyball W

LETOURNEAU UNIVERSITY
PO Box 7001
Longview, TX 75607-7001
Tel: (903)233-3000
Free: 800-759-8811
Admissions: (903)233-3400
Fax: (903)233-3411
E-mail: admissions@james.letu.edu

Web Site: http://www.letu.edu/
President/CEO: Dr. Alvin O. Austin
Registrar: Brenda S. McGhee
Admissions: James Townsend
Financial Aid: Delinda Hall
Type: Comprehensive **Sex:** Coed **Affiliation:** nondenominational **Scores:** 99.5% SAT V 400+; 97.7% SAT M 400+; 36.7% ACT 18-23; 43.3% ACT 24-29 **% Accepted:** 76 **Admission Plans:** Deferred Admission **Application Deadline:** August 01 **Application Fee:** $25.00 **H.S. Requirements:** High school diploma required; GED accepted **Costs Per Year:** Application fee: $25. Comprehensive fee: $22,176 includes full-time tuition ($15,710), mandatory fees ($180), and college room and board ($6286). Room and board charges vary according to board plan. Part-time tuition: $280 per hour. Part-time tuition varies according to course load. **Scholarships:** Available **Calendar System:** Semester, Summer Session Available **Enrollment:** FT 1,405, PT 2,201, Grad 374 **Faculty:** FT 72, PT 243 **Student-Faculty Ratio:** 14:1 **Exams:** SAT I or ACT **% Receiving Financial Aid:** 66 **% Residing in College-Owned, -Operated, or -Affiliated Housing:** 76 **Library Holdings:** 84,779 **Regional Accreditation:** Southern Association of Colleges and Schools **Credit Hours For Degree:** 63 semester hours, Associates; 124 semester hours, Bachelors **Professional Accreditation:** ABET **Intercollegiate Athletics:** Baseball M; Basketball M & W; Cross-Country Running M & W; Golf M & W; Soccer M & W; Softball W; Tennis M & W; Volleyball W

LON MORRIS COLLEGE
800 College Ave.
Jacksonville, TX 75766-2923
Tel: (903)589-4000
Free: 800-259-5753
Fax: (903)586-8562
Web Site: http://www.lonmorris.edu/
President/CEO: Dr. Clifford M. Lee
Registrar: Jennifer Baugh
Admissions: Craig Lee
Financial Aid: Kris Marquis
Type: Two-Year College **Sex:** Coed **Affiliation:** United Methodist **Scores:** 61% SAT V 400+; 66% SAT M 400+; 34% ACT 18-23; 4% ACT 24-29 **Admission Plans:** Deferred Admission **Application Fee:** $35.00 **H.S. Requirements:** High school diploma required; GED accepted **Scholarships:** Available **Calendar System:** Semester, Summer Session Available **Enrollment:** FT 394, PT 38 **Faculty:** FT 34, PT 23 **Student-Faculty Ratio:** 10:1 **Exams:** SAT I or ACT **% Residing in College-Owned, -Operated, or -Affiliated Housing:** 90 **Library Holdings:** 26,000 **Regional Accreditation:** Southern Association of Colleges and Schools **Credit Hours For Degree:** 62 credits, Associates **Intercollegiate Athletics:** Baseball M; Basketball M; Cheerleading M & W; Golf M & W; Soccer M & W; Softball W; Volleyball W

LUBBOCK CHRISTIAN UNIVERSITY
5601 19th St.
Lubbock, TX 79407-2099
Tel: (806)796-8800
Free: 800-933-7601
Admissions: (806)720-7803
Fax: (806)796-8917
E-mail: mondy.brewer@lcu.edu
Web Site: http://www.lcu.edu/
President/CEO: Dr. L. Ken Jones
Registrar: Dave Carter
Admissions: Mondy Brewer
Financial Aid: Amy Hardesty
Type: Comprehensive **Sex:** Coed **Affiliation:** Church of Christ **Scores:** 86. 96% SAT V 400+; 88.05% SAT M 400+; 50.41% ACT 18-23; 26.45% ACT 24-29 **% Accepted:** 74 **Application Deadline:** August 01 **Application Fee:** $25.00 **H.S. Requirements:** High school diploma required; GED accepted **Costs Per Year:** Application fee: $25. Comprehensive fee: $16,810 includes full-time tuition ($11,644), mandatory fees ($916), and college room and board ($4250). Full-time tuition and fees vary according to program. Room and board charges vary according to board plan and housing facility. Part-time tuition: $375 per semester hour. Part-time mandatory fees: $402 per term. Part-time tuition and fees vary according to course load and program. **Scholarships:** Available **Calendar System:** Semester, Summer Session Available **Enrollment:** FT 1,383, PT 449, Grad 215 **Faculty:** FT 81, PT 73 **Student-Faculty Ratio:** 15:1 **Exams:** SAT I or ACT **% Receiving Financial Aid:** 77 **% Residing in College-Owned, -Operated, or -Affiliated Housing:** 30 **Library Holdings:** 113,556 **Regional Accreditation:** Southern Association of Colleges and Schools **Credit Hours For Degree:** 126 semester hours, Bachelors **ROTC:** Army, Air Force **Professional Accreditation:** CSWE, NLN **Intercollegiate Athletics:** Baseball M; Basketball M & W; Cheerleading M & W; Cross-Country Running M & W; Golf M & W; Soccer M; Track and Field M & W; Volleyball W

MCLENNAN COMMUNITY COLLEGE
1400 College Dr.
Waco, TX 76708-1499
Tel: (254)299-8622
Admissions: (254)299-8689
E-mail: vjefferson@mclennan.edu
Web Site: http://www.mclennan.edu/
President/CEO: Dr. Dennis F. Michaelis
Registrar: Herman Tucker
Admissions: Vivian G. Jefferson
Financial Aid: James Kubacak
Type: Two-Year College **Sex:** Coed **Admission Plans:** Open Admission; Early Admission **H.S. Requirements:** High school diploma required; GED accepted **Costs Per Year:** Area resident tuition: $1272 full-time. State resident tuition: $1560 full-time. Nonresident tuition: $2712 full-time. Mandatory fees: $216 full-time. **Scholarships:** Available **Calendar System:** Semester, Summer Session Available **Enrollment:** FT 3,354, PT 4,208 **Exams:** Other **Library Holdings:** 93,000 **Regional Accreditation:** Southern Association of Colleges and Schools **Credit Hours For Degree:** 60 semester hours, Associates **ROTC:** Air Force **Professional Accreditation:** AHIMA, APTA, CARC, JRCERT, NAACLS, NLN **Intercollegiate Athletics:** Baseball M; Basketball M & W; Golf M & W; Softball W

MCMURRY UNIVERSITY
South 14th and Sayles
Abilene, TX 79697
Tel: (325)793-3800
Free: 800-477-0077
Admissions: (325)793-4720
Fax: (325)691-6599
E-mail: dvoskuil@mcm.edu
Web Site: http://www.mcm.edu/
President/CEO: Dr. John H. Russell
Registrar: Carolyn Calvert
Admissions: Dave Voskuil
Financial Aid: Rachel Atkins
Type: Four-Year College **Sex:** Coed **Affiliation:** United Methodist **Scores:** 83% SAT V 400+; 89% SAT M 400+; 51% ACT 18-23; 23% ACT 24-29 **% Accepted:** 86 **Admission Plans:** Deferred Admission **Application Deadline:** August 15 **Application Fee:** $20.00 **H.S. Requirements:** High school diploma required; GED accepted **Costs Per Year:** Application fee: $20. Comprehensive fee: $21,002 includes full-time tuition ($15,100), mandatory fees ($50), and college room and board ($5852). College room only: $2898. Part-time tuition: $475 per semester hour. **Scholarships:** Available **Calendar System:** Semester, Summer Session Available **Enrollment:** FT 1,187, PT 243 **Faculty:** FT 77, PT 51 **Student-Faculty Ratio:** 14:1 **Exams:** SAT I or ACT **% Receiving Financial Aid:** 80 **% Residing in College-Owned, -Operated, or -Affiliated Housing:** 51 **Library Holdings:** 153,954 **Regional Accreditation:** Southern Association of Colleges and Schools **Credit Hours For Degree:** 126 semester hours, Bachelors **ROTC:** Air Force **Professional Accreditation:** AACN **Intercollegiate Athletics:** Baseball M; Basketball M & W; Cross-Country Running M & W; Football M; Golf M & W; Soccer M & W; Swimming and Diving M & W; Tennis M & W; Track and Field M & W; Volleyball W

MIDLAND COLLEGE
3600 North Garfield
Midland, TX 79705-6399
Tel: (432)685-4500
Admissions: (432)685-5502
Fax: (432)685-4714
E-mail: twetendorf@midland.edu
Web Site: http://www.midland.edu/
President/CEO: Dr. David E. Daniel
Registrar: Phil Ebensberger
Admissions: Trey Wetendorf
Financial Aid: Latisha Williams
Type: Two-Year College **Sex:** Coed **% Accepted:** 100 **Admission Plans:** Open Admission **Application Deadline:** Rolling **Application Fee:** $0.00

H.S. Requirements: High school diploma or equivalent not required. For nursing, respiratory therapy, radiological technology programs: High school diploma required; GED accepted **Costs Per Year:** Application fee: $0. Area resident tuition: $1204 full-time, $93 per credit hour part-time. State resident tuition: $1540 full-time, $105 per credit hour part-time. Nonresident tuition: $2352 full-time, $470 per credit hour part-time. Mandatory fees: $350 full-time. College room and board: $3600. **Scholarships:** Available **Calendar System:** Semester, Summer Session Not available **Enrollment:** FT 2,027, PT 3,504 **Faculty:** FT 128, PT 141 **Student-Faculty Ratio:** 18:1 **% Residing in College-Owned, -Operated, or -Affiliated Housing:** 5 **Library Holdings:** 65,760 **Regional Accreditation:** Southern Association of Colleges and Schools **Credit Hours For Degree:** 62 semester hours, Associates; 127 semester hours, Bachelors **Professional Accreditation:** AHIMA, CARC, JRCERT, NLN **Intercollegiate Athletics:** Baseball M; Basketball M & W; Cheerleading M & W; Golf M; Softball W; Volleyball W

MIDWESTERN STATE UNIVERSITY
3410 Taft Blvd.
Wichita Falls, TX 76308
Tel: (940)397-4000
Free: 800-842-1922
Admissions: (940)397-4334
Fax: (940)397-4302
E-mail: school.relations@mwsu.edu
Web Site: http://www.mwsu.edu/
President/CEO: Dr. Jesse W. Rogers
Registrar: Darla Inglish
Admissions: Barbara Merkle
Financial Aid: Kathy Pennartz
Type: Comprehensive **Sex:** Coed **Scores:** 89.1% SAT V 400+; 90.4% SAT M 400+; 59.2% ACT 18-23; 18.2% ACT 24-29 **% Accepted:** 83 **Admission Plans:** Early Admission; Deferred Admission **Application Deadline:** August 07 **Application Fee:** $25.00 **H.S. Requirements:** High school diploma required; GED accepted **Costs Per Year:** Application fee: $25. State resident tuition: $1500 full-time, $50 per credit hour part-time. Nonresident tuition: $9750 full-time, $325 per credit hour part-time. Mandatory fees: $3066 full-time. College room and board: $5220. College room only: $2660. **Scholarships:** Available **Calendar System:** Semester, Summer Session Available **Enrollment:** FT 4,013, PT 1,531, Grad 735 **Faculty:** FT 208, PT 112 **Student-Faculty Ratio:** 20:1 **Exams:** SAT I or ACT **% Receiving Financial Aid:** 47 **% Residing in College-Owned, -Operated, or -Affiliated Housing:** 13 **Library Holdings:** 484,106 **Regional Accreditation:** Southern Association of Colleges and Schools **Credit Hours For Degree:** 64 semester hours, Associates; 124 semester hours, Bachelors **ROTC:** Air Force **Professional Accreditation:** ABET, AACN, ADA, ACBSP, CARC, CSWE, NASM, NLN **Intercollegiate Athletics:** Basketball M & W; Cheerleading M & W; Fencing M & W; Football M; Soccer M & W; Softball W; Tennis M & W; Volleyball W

MONTGOMERY COLLEGE
3200 College Park Dr.
Conroe, TX 77384
Tel: (936)273-7000
Admissions: (936)273-7236
Fax: (936)273-7234
E-mail: jade.e.borne@nhmccd.edu
Web Site: http://www.woodstock.edu/
President/CEO: Dr. Thomas E. Butler
Admissions: Jade Born
Type: Two-Year College **Sex:** Coed **Affiliation:** North Harris Montgomery Community College District **% Accepted:** 100 **Admission Plans:** Open Admission; Early Admission **Application Deadline:** Rolling **H.S. Requirements:** High school diploma required; GED accepted **Costs Per Year:** Area resident tuition: $984 full-time, $32 per credit hour part-time. State resident tuition: $1944 full-time, $72 per credit hour part-time. Nonresident tuition: $2304 full-time, $87 per credit hour part-time. Mandatory fees: $20 full-time, $8 per credit hour part-time, $12 per term part-time. **Scholarships:** Available **Calendar System:** Semester, Summer Session Available **Enrollment:** FT 2,970, PT 5,336 **Faculty:** FT 118, PT 348 **Student-Faculty Ratio:** 20:1 **Library Holdings:** 4,000 **Regional Accreditation:** Southern Association of Colleges and Schools **Credit Hours For Degree:** 62 credit hours, Associates **Professional Accreditation:** APTA

MOUNTAIN VIEW COLLEGE
4849 West Illinois Ave.
Dallas, TX 75211-6599
Tel: (214)860-8600
Admissions: (214)860-8666
Fax: (214)860-8570
E-mail: ghall@dccd.edu
Web Site: http://www.mvc.dcccd.edu/
President/CEO: Felix Zamora
Registrar: Glenda Hall
Admissions: Glenda Hall
Financial Aid: ShaDana Mingo
Type: Two-Year College **Sex:** Coed **Affiliation:** Dallas County Community College District System **Admission Plans:** Open Admission; Early Admission; Deferred Admission **Application Deadline:** Rolling **Application Fee:** $0.00 **H.S. Requirements:** High school diploma required; GED accepted **Costs Per Year:** Application fee: $0. Area resident tuition: $1008 full-time. State resident tuition: $1848 full-time. Nonresident tuition: $2968 full-time. **Scholarships:** Available **Calendar System:** Semester, Summer Session Available **Enrollment:** FT 6,496 **Faculty:** FT 80, PT 230 **Regional Accreditation:** Southern Association of Colleges and Schools **Credit Hours For Degree:** 61 credit hours, Associates **ROTC:** Army **Professional Accreditation:** AHIMA

MTI COLLEGE OF BUSINESS AND TECHNOLOGY (HOUSTON)
7277 Regency Square Blvd.
Houston, TX 77036-3163
Tel: (713)974-7181
Free: 800-344-1990
Fax: (713)974-2090
E-mail: davidw@mti.edu
Web Site: http://www.mti.com/
President/CEO: Robert Obenhaus
Registrar: Lunita Martin
Admissions: David Wood
Financial Aid: Paul Rodriguez
Type: Two-Year College **Scholarships:** Available **Calendar System:** Semester **Enrollment:** FT 718 **Faculty:** FT 31 **Student-Faculty Ratio:** 25:1 **Professional Accreditation:** ACCSCT

MTI COLLEGE OF BUSINESS AND TECHNOLOGY (HOUSTON)
11420 E. Freeway
Houston, TX 77029
Tel: (281)333-3363; 888-532-7675
Fax: (281)333-4118
E-mail: derrell@mti-tex.com
Web Site: http://www.mti.edu/
President/CEO: John Springhetti
Registrar: Karen Otero
Admissions: Derrell Beck
Financial Aid: Eunice Anthony
Type: Two-Year College **Sex:** Coed **Application Fee:** $0.00 **H.S. Requirements:** High school diploma required; GED accepted. For Certificate Programs: Must prove ability-to-benefit: High school diploma or equivalent not required **Scholarships:** Available **Calendar System:** Semester, Summer Session Not available **Enrollment:** FT 217 **Faculty:** FT 9, PT 6 **Student-Faculty Ratio:** 20:1 **Credit Hours For Degree:** 60 credit hours, Associates **Professional Accreditation:** ACCSCT

NAVARRO COLLEGE
3200 West 7th Ave.
Corsicana, TX 75110-4899
Tel: (903)874-6501
Free: 800-628-2776
Web Site: http://www.nav.cc.tx.us/
President/CEO: Dr. Richard M. Sanchez
Admissions: Judy Cutting
Financial Aid: Ed Ephlin
Type: Two-Year College **Sex:** Coed **Admission Plans:** Open Admission; Early Admission **H.S. Requirements:** High school diploma required; GED accepted **Scholarships:** Available **Calendar System:** Semester, Summer Session Available **Enrollment:** FT 2,516, PT 1,895 **Faculty:** FT 99, PT 281 **Exams:** Other, SAT I or ACT **% Residing in College-Owned, -Operated, or -Affiliated Housing:** 25 **Library Holdings:** 40,000 **Regional Accreditation:** Southern Association of Colleges and Schools **Credit Hours For Degree:** 63 semester hours, Associates **Professional Accreditation:** AOTA, NAACLS, NLN **Intercollegiate Athletics:** Baseball M; Basketball M; Football M; Golf M; Softball W; Tennis M & W; Volleyball W

NORTH CENTRAL TEXAS COLLEGE
1525 West California St.
Gainesville, TX 76240-4699
Tel: (940)668-7731
Admissions: (940)668-4222
Fax: (940)668-6049
Web Site: http://www.nctc.cc.tx.us/
President/CEO: Dr. Ronnie Glasscock
Registrar: Dr. Janie Neighbors
Admissions: Condoa Parrent
Financial Aid: Janet Dragoo
Type: Two-Year College **Sex:** Coed **Admission Plans:** Open Admission; Early Admission **H.S. Requirements:** High school diploma required; GED accepted. For some adult applicants: High school diploma or equivalent not required **Scholarships:** Available **Calendar System:** Semester, Summer Session Available **Faculty:** FT 87, PT 209 **Exams:** Other, SAT I or ACT **% Residing in College-Owned, -Operated, or -Affiliated Housing:** 2 **Library Holdings:** 44,861 **Regional Accreditation:** Southern Association of Colleges and Schools **Credit Hours For Degree:** 62 credit hours, Associates **Professional Accreditation:** NLN **Intercollegiate Athletics:** Baseball M; Equestrian Sports M & W; Tennis W; Volleyball W

NORTH HARRIS COLLEGE
2700 W. W. Thorne Dr.
Houston, TX 77073-3499
Tel: (281)618-5400
Admissions: (281)618-5794
Web Site: http://www.nhmccd.edu/
President/CEO: Dr. John E. Pickelman
Registrar: Mary Shafer
Admissions: Dr. Bennie E. Lambert
Financial Aid: Donna Smith
Type: Two-Year College **Sex:** Coed **Affiliation:** North Harris Montgomery Community College District **Admission Plans:** Open Admission; Early Admission **Application Fee:** $0.00 **H.S. Requirements:** High school diploma required; GED accepted **Scholarships:** Available **Calendar System:** Semester, Summer Session Available **Faculty:** FT 193, PT 341 **Exams:** Other, SAT I or ACT **Library Holdings:** 131,851 **Regional Accreditation:** Southern Association of Colleges and Schools **Credit Hours For Degree:** 61 credits, Associates **ROTC:** Army **Professional Accreditation:** AHIMA, MACTE, NLN

NORTH LAKE COLLEGE
5001 North MacArthur Blvd.
Irving, TX 75038-3899
Tel: (972)273-3000
Admissions: (972)273-3109
Web Site: http://www.northlakecollege.edu/
President/CEO: Dr. Herlinda Glasscock
Registrar: Steve Twenge
Admissions: Steve Twenge
Financial Aid: Paul Felix
Type: Two-Year College **Sex:** Coed **Affiliation:** Dallas County Community College District System **Admission Plans:** Open Admission; Early Admission **Application Fee:** $0.00 **H.S. Requirements:** High school diploma required; GED accepted **Scholarships:** Available **Calendar System:** Semester, Summer Session Available **Enrollment:** FT 2,925, PT 5,854 **Faculty:** FT 98, PT 439 **Student-Faculty Ratio:** 19:1 **Library Holdings:** 34,000 **Regional Accreditation:** Southern Association of Colleges and Schools **Credit Hours For Degree:** 62 semester hours, Associates **Professional Accreditation:** ACCE **Intercollegiate Athletics:** Baseball M; Basketball M; Softball W; Volleyball W

NORTHEAST TEXAS COMMUNITY COLLEGE
PO Box 1307
Mount Pleasant, TX 75456-1307
Tel: (903)572-1911
Fax: (903)572-6712
Web Site: http://www.ntcc.edu/
President/CEO: Dr. Charles B. Florio
Registrar: Mavis Brush
Admissions: Sherry Keys
Financial Aid: Pat Durst
Type: Two-Year College **Sex:** Coed **Admission Plans:** Open Admission; Early Admission **H.S. Requirements:** High school diploma required; GED accepted **Scholarships:** Available **Calendar System:** Semester, Summer Session Available **Enrollment:** FT 1,351, PT 1,161 **Faculty:** FT 51, PT 83 **Exams:** SAT I or ACT **% Residing in College-Owned, -Operated, or -Affiliated Housing:** 3 **Library Holdings:** 24,501 **Regional Accreditation:** Southern Association of Colleges and Schools **Credit Hours For Degree:** 62 credit hours, Associates **Intercollegiate Athletics:** Baseball M; Softball W

NORTHWEST VISTA COLLEGE
3535 North Ellison Dr.
San Antonio, TX 78251
Tel: (210)348-2000
Admissions: (210)348-2016
E-mail: elang@accd.edu
Web Site: http://www.accd.edu/nvc/
President/CEO: Jacqueline Claunch
Admissions: Dr. Elaine Lang
Type: Two-Year College **Sex:** Coed **Costs Per Year:** Area resident tuition: $1008 full-time. State resident tuition: $2016 full-time. Nonresident tuition: $4032 full-time. Mandatory fees: $288 full-time. **Calendar System:** Semester **Faculty:** FT 83, PT 414 **Student-Faculty Ratio:** 12:1 **Regional Accreditation:** Southern Association of Colleges and Schools

NORTHWOOD UNIVERSITY, TEXAS CAMPUS
1114 West FM 1382
Cedar Hill, TX 75104-1204
Tel: (972)291-1541
Free: 800-927-9663
Admissions: (989)837-4367
Fax: (972)291-3824
E-mail: admissions@northwood.edu
Web Site: http://www.northwood.edu/
President/CEO: Dr. Kevin G. Fegan
Registrar: Patty Shaw
Admissions: Dr. David Long
Financial Aid: Michael Rhodes
Type: Four-Year College **Sex:** Coed **Affiliation:** Northwood University (MI) **Scores:** 82% SAT V 400+; 88% SAT M 400+; 69% ACT 18-23; 13% ACT 24-29 **% Accepted:** 54 **Admission Plans:** Early Admission; Deferred Admission **Application Deadline:** Rolling **Application Fee:** $25.00 **H.S. Requirements:** High school diploma required; GED accepted **Costs Per Year:** Application fee: $25. Comprehensive fee: $22,437 includes full-time tuition ($15,216), mandatory fees ($585), and college room and board ($6636). College room only: $3567. Part-time tuition: $317 per credit hour. **Scholarships:** Available **Calendar System:** Quarter, Summer Session Available **Enrollment:** FT 815, PT 246 **Faculty:** FT 23, PT 7 **Student-Faculty Ratio:** 22:1 **Exams:** SAT I or ACT **% Receiving Financial Aid:** 71 **% Residing in College-Owned, -Operated, or -Affiliated Housing:** 28 **Library Holdings:** 12,000 **Regional Accreditation:** North Central Association of Colleges and Schools **Credit Hours For Degree:** 90 credit hours, Associates; 180 credit hours, Bachelors **Intercollegiate Athletics:** Baseball M; Cross-Country Running M & W; Golf M & W; Soccer M & W; Softball W; Track and Field M & W

ODESSA COLLEGE
201 West University Ave.
Odessa, TX 79764-7127
Tel: (432)335-6400
Admissions: (432)335-6815
Fax: (432)335-6860
E-mail: regrs@odessa.edu
Web Site: http://www.odessa.edu/
President/CEO: Dr. Vance W. Gipson
Registrar: Jeff Rhodes
Admissions: Norma Garcia
Financial Aid: Dee Nesmith
Type: Two-Year College **Sex:** Coed **Admission Plans:** Open Admission; Early Admission; Deferred Admission **Application Fee:** $0.00 **H.S. Requirements:** High school diploma required; GED accepted. For applicants with extenuating circumstances: High school diploma or equivalent not required **Costs Per Year:** Application fee: $0. Area resident tuition: $1110 full-time. State resident tuition: $1410 full-time. Nonresident tuition: $1860 full-time. Mandatory fees: $330 full-time. Full-time tuition and fees vary according to course load. College room and board: $4948. College room only: $3500. Room and board charges vary according to board plan and housing facility.

Scholarships: Available **Calendar System:** Semester, Summer Session Available **Enrollment:** FT 1,799, PT 2,770 **Faculty:** FT 119, PT 146 **Student-Faculty Ratio:** 15:1 **% Residing in College-Owned, -Operated, or -Affiliated Housing:** 3 **Library Holdings:** 79,882 **Regional Accreditation:** Southern Association of Colleges and Schools **Credit Hours For Degree:** 62 semester hours, Associates **Professional Accreditation:** ARCEST, APTA, CARC, JRCERT, NAACLS, NASM, NLN **Intercollegiate Athletics:** Baseball M; Basketball M & W; Golf M; Softball W

OUR LADY OF THE LAKE UNIVERSITY OF SAN ANTONIO
411 Southwest 24th St.
San Antonio, TX 78207-4689
Tel: (210)434-6711
Free: 800-436-6558
Fax: (210)436-0824
E-mail: boatner@lake.occusa.edu
Web Site: http://www.ollusa.edu/
President/CEO: Dr. Tessa Martinez Pollack
Registrar: Norma Anderson
Admissions: Michael Boatner
Financial Aid: Diana Perez
Type: Comprehensive **Sex:** Coed **Affiliation:** Roman Catholic **Scores:** 89% SAT V 400+; 95% SAT M 400+; 57% ACT 18-23; 9% ACT 24-29 **% Accepted:** 53 **Admission Plans:** Deferred Admission **Application Deadline:** July 15 **Application Fee:** $25.00 **H.S. Requirements:** High school diploma required; GED accepted **Costs Per Year:** Application fee: $25. Comprehensive fee: $22,928 includes full-time tuition ($17,048), mandatory fees ($498), and college room and board ($5382). College room only: $3226. Full-time tuition and fees vary according to class time and degree level. Room and board charges vary according to board plan. Part-time tuition: $553 per credit hour. Part-time mandatory fees: $12 per credit hour, $48 per term. Part-time tuition and fees vary according to class time and degree level. **Scholarships:** Available **Calendar System:** Semester, Summer Session Available **Enrollment:** FT 1,242, PT 550, Grad 1,080 **Faculty:** FT 118, PT 107 **Student-Faculty Ratio:** 13:1 **Exams:** SAT I or ACT **% Receiving Financial Aid:** 89 **% Residing in College-Owned, -Operated, or -Affiliated Housing:** 41 **Library Holdings:** 162,154 **Regional Accreditation:** Southern Association of Colleges and Schools **Credit Hours For Degree:** 128 credit hours, Bachelors **ROTC:** Army, Air Force **Professional Accreditation:** APA, ASLHA, ACBSP, CSWE

PALO ALTO COLLEGE
1400 West Villaret
San Antonio, TX 78224-2499
Tel: (210)921-5000
Admissions: (210)921-5279
Web Site: http://www.accd.edu/pac/htm/
President/CEO: Dr. Ana M. Guzman
Registrar: Leticia Sanchez-Retamozo
Admissions: Rachel Montejano
Financial Aid: Lamar Duarte
Type: Two-Year College **Sex:** Coed **Affiliation:** Alamo Community College District System **% Accepted:** 100 **Admission Plans:** Open Admission; Early Admission **Application Deadline:** Rolling **Application Fee:** $0.00 **H.S. Requirements:** High school diploma required; GED accepted **Costs Per Year:** Application fee: $0. Area resident tuition: $1546 full-time, $252 per credit hour part-time. State resident tuition: $2806 full-time, $504 per credit hour part-time. Nonresident tuition: $5318 full-time, $1008 per credit hour part-time. Mandatory fees: $280 full-time, $1 per credit hour part-time, $138 per term part-time. **Scholarships:** Available **Calendar System:** Semester, Summer Session Available **Faculty:** FT 191, PT 285 **Student-Faculty Ratio:** 17:1 **Regional Accreditation:** Southern Association of Colleges and Schools **Credit Hours For Degree:** 60 semester hours, Associates **Intercollegiate Athletics:** Cross-Country Running M & W; Swimming and Diving M & W; Track and Field M & W

PANOLA COLLEGE
1109 West Panola St.
Carthage, TX 75633-2397
Tel: (903)693-2000
Admissions: (903)693-2034
E-mail: ezoellner@panola.edu
Web Site: http://www.panola.edu/
President/CEO: Dr. Gregory Powell
Registrar: Barbara Simpson
Admissions: Dr. Erik Zoellner
Financial Aid: Tommy Young
Type: Two-Year College **Sex:** Coed **% Accepted:** 100 **Admission Plans:** Open Admission; Early Admission **Application Deadline:** Rolling **H.S. Requirements:** High school diploma required; GED accepted **Costs Per Year:** Area resident tuition: $630 full-time, $45 per semester hour part-time. State resident tuition: $1320 full-time, $68 per semester hour part-time. Nonresident tuition: $1710 full-time, $81 per semester hour part-time. Mandatory fees: $720 full-time. College room and board: $3300. **Scholarships:** Available **Calendar System:** Semester, Summer Session Available **Enrollment:** FT 946, PT 981 **Faculty:** FT 61, PT 0 **Student-Faculty Ratio:** 23:1 **% Residing in College-Owned, -Operated, or -Affiliated Housing:** 12 **Library Holdings:** 88,897 **Regional Accreditation:** Southern Association of Colleges and Schools **Credit Hours For Degree:** 60 credits, Associates **Professional Accreditation:** AHIMA, AOTA **Intercollegiate Athletics:** Baseball M; Basketball M & W; Volleyball W

PARIS JUNIOR COLLEGE
2400 Clarksville St.
Paris, TX 75460-6298
Tel: (903)785-7661
Free: 800-232-5804
Admissions: (903)782-0425
E-mail: sreece@parisjc.edu
Web Site: http://www.parisjc.edu/
President/CEO: Bobby R. Walters
Registrar: Rita Tapp
Admissions: Sheila Reece
Financial Aid: Linda Slawson
Type: Two-Year College **Sex:** Coed **% Accepted:** 100 **Admission Plans:** Open Admission; Early Admission **Application Deadline:** Rolling **Application Fee:** $0.00 **H.S. Requirements:** High school diploma required; GED accepted **Costs Per Year:** Application fee: $0. Area resident tuition: $840 full-time, $35 per hour part-time. State resident tuition: $1560 full-time, $65 per hour part-time. Nonresident tuition: $2520 full-time, $105 per hour part-time. Mandatory fees: $228 full-time. College room and board: $1882. College room only: $690. **Scholarships:** Available **Calendar System:** Semester, Summer Session Available **Enrollment:** FT 1,457, PT 2,661 **Faculty:** FT 92, PT 117 **Student-Faculty Ratio:** 24:1 **Library Holdings:** 38,150 **Regional Accreditation:** Southern Association of Colleges and Schools **Credit Hours For Degree:** 64 semester hours, Associates **Professional Accreditation:** NLN **Intercollegiate Athletics:** Basketball M & W; Golf M; Softball W; Volleyball W

PAUL QUINN COLLEGE
3837 Simpson-Stuart Rd.
Dallas, TX 75241-4331
Tel: (214)376-1000
Free: 800-237-2648
Admissions: (214)302-3575
Fax: (214)302-3559
Web Site: http://www.pqc.edu/
President/CEO: Dr. Dwight Fennell
Registrar: Beverly Smith
Admissions: Nena Taylor-Richey
Financial Aid: Nena Taylor
Type: Four-Year College **Sex:** Coed **Affiliation:** African Methodist Episcopal **Scores:** 59% SAT V 400+; 53.8% SAT M 400+; 11.9% ACT 18-23 **Application Fee:** $35.00 **H.S. Requirements:** High school diploma required; GED accepted **Scholarships:** Available **Calendar System:** Semester, Summer Session Available **Enrollment:** FT 732, PT 139 **Student-Faculty Ratio:** 22:1 **Exams:** SAT I or ACT **% Receiving Financial Aid:** 98 **% Residing in College-Owned, -Operated, or -Affiliated Housing:** 35 **Library Holdings:** 87,000 **Regional Accreditation:** Southern Association of Colleges and Schools **Credit Hours For Degree:** 124 semester hours, Bachelors **Intercollegiate Athletics:** Baseball M; Basketball M & W; Track and Field M & W

PRAIRIE VIEW A&M UNIVERSITY
PO Box 519
Prairie View, TX 77446-0519
Tel: (936)857-3311
Admissions: (936)857-2626
Fax: (936)857-2699

Web Site: http://www.pvamu.edu/
President/CEO: Dr. George C. Wright
Registrar: Christa Molloy
Admissions: Mary Gooch
Financial Aid: Advergus D. James, Jr.
Type: Comprehensive **Sex:** Coed **Affiliation:** Texas A&M University System **Scores:** 52.8% SAT V 400+; 53.8% SAT M 400+; 26.8% ACT 18-23; 2.8% ACT 24-29 **% Accepted:** 60 **Admission Plans:** Deferred Admission **Application Deadline:** June 01 **Application Fee:** $25.00 **H.S. Requirements:** High school diploma required; GED accepted **Costs Per Year:** Application fee: $25. State resident tuition: $1500 full-time, $50 per credit hour part-time. Nonresident tuition: $9780 full-time, $326 per credit hour part-time. Mandatory fees: $3406 full-time, $113.53 per credit hour part-time. Full-time tuition and fees vary according to course load and degree level. Part-time tuition and fees vary according to course load and degree level. College room and board: $6204. Room and board charges vary according to board plan and housing facility. **Scholarships:** Available **Calendar System:** Semester, Summer Session Available **Enrollment:** FT 5,151, PT 551, Grad 2,210 **Faculty:** FT 366, PT 119 **Student-Faculty Ratio:** 15:1 **Exams:** SAT I or ACT **% Receiving Financial Aid:** 91 **% Residing in College-Owned, -Operated, or -Affiliated Housing:** 52 **Library Holdings:** 347,477 **Regional Accreditation:** Southern Association of Colleges and Schools **Credit Hours For Degree:** 120 credit hours, Bachelors **ROTC:** Army, Navy **Professional Accreditation:** ABET, ADtA, CSWE, NCATE, NLN **Intercollegiate Athletics:** Baseball M; Basketball M & W; Cross-Country Running M & W; Football M; Golf M & W; Soccer W; Softball W; Tennis M & W; Track and Field M & W; Volleyball W

RANGER COLLEGE
College Circle
Ranger, TX 76470
Tel: (254)647-3234
Web Site: http://www.ranger.cc.tx.us/
President/CEO: Dr. Joe Mills
Registrar: Tammy Adams
Admissions: Jim Cockburn
Financial Aid: Sharon King
Type: Two-Year College **Sex:** Coed **Admission Plans:** Open Admission; Early Admission **H.S. Requirements:** High school diploma required; GED accepted **Scholarships:** Available **Calendar System:** Semester, Summer Session Available **Faculty:** FT 28, PT 23 **Exams:** SAT I and SAT II or ACT **% Residing in College-Owned, -Operated, or -Affiliated Housing:** 45 **Library Holdings:** 24,211 **Regional Accreditation:** Southern Association of Colleges and Schools **Credit Hours For Degree:** 62 semester hours, Associates **Intercollegiate Athletics:** Baseball M; Basketball M & W; Cross-Country Running M & W; Football M; Golf M; Softball W; Track and Field M & W

REMINGTON COLLEGE-DALLAS CAMPUS
1800 East Gate Dr.
Garland, TX 75041-5513
Tel: (972)686-7878
Fax: (972)686-5116
E-mail: skip.walls@remingtoncollege.edu
Web Site: http://www.remingtoncollege.edu/
President/CEO: Skip Walls
Registrar: Lisa Griser
Admissions: Skip Walls
Type: Two-Year College **Professional Accreditation:** ACICS

REMINGTON COLLEGE-FORT WORTH CAMPUS
300 East Loop 820
Fort Worth, TX 76112
Tel: (817)451-0017
Fax: (817)496-1257
E-mail: lynn.wey@remingtoncollege.edu
Web Site: http://www.remingtoncollege.edu/
President/CEO: Lynn Wey
Admissions: Lynn Wey
Type: Two-Year College **Sex:** Coed **Professional Accreditation:** ACCSCT

REMINGTON COLLEGE-HOUSTON CAMPUS
3110 Hayes Rd., Ste. 380
Houston, TX 77082
Tel: (281)899-1240
Fax: (281)597-8466
Web Site: http://www.remingtoncollege.edu/houston/
President/CEO: Chris Tilley
Admissions: Lance Stribling
Type: Two-Year College **Sex:** Coed **Faculty:** FT 20, PT 15 **Professional Accreditation:** ACCSCT

RICE UNIVERSITY
6100 Main St.
PO Box 1892
Houston, TX 77251-1892
Tel: (713)348-0000
Free: 800-527-OWLS
Admissions: (713)348-RICE
Fax: (713)348-5323
E-mail: admi@rice.edu
Web Site: http://www.rice.edu/
President/CEO: David W. Leebron
Registrar: Jerry Montag
Admissions: Julie M. Browning
Financial Aid: Julia Benz
Type: University **Sex:** Coed **Scores:** 99.72% SAT V 400+; 100% SAT M 400+; 6.62% ACT 18-23; 24.9% ACT 24-29 **% Accepted:** 25 **Admission Plans:** Early Admission; Early Action; Early Decision Plan; Deferred Admission **Application Deadline:** January 10 **Application Fee:** $50.00 **H.S. Requirements:** High school diploma or equivalent not required **Costs Per Year:** Application fee: $50. Comprehensive fee: $32,726 includes full-time tuition ($23,310), mandatory fees ($436), and college room and board ($8980). College room only: $5700. Full-time tuition and fees vary according to student level. Room and board charges vary according to board plan. **Scholarships:** Available **Calendar System:** Semester, Summer Session Available **Enrollment:** FT 3,057, PT 128, Grad 2,073 **Faculty:** FT 567, PT 143 **Student-Faculty Ratio:** 5:1 **Exams:** SAT I and SAT II or ACT **% Receiving Financial Aid:** 35 **% Residing in College-Owned, -Operated, or -Affiliated Housing:** 71 **Library Holdings:** 2,394,131 **Regional Accreditation:** Southern Association of Colleges and Schools **Credit Hours For Degree:** 120 semester hours, Bachelors **ROTC:** Army, Navy, Air Force **Professional Accreditation:** AACSB, ABET **Intercollegiate Athletics:** Badminton M & W; Baseball M; Basketball M & W; Cheerleading M & W; Crew M & W; Cross-Country Running M & W; Fencing M & W; Field Hockey W; Football M; Golf M; Lacrosse M & W; Rugby M & W; Sailing M & W; Soccer M & W; Softball W; Swimming and Diving W; Tennis M & W; Track and Field M & W; Ultimate Frisbee M & W; Volleyball M & W; Water Polo M & W

RICHLAND COLLEGE
12800 Abrams Rd.
Dallas, TX 75243-2199
Tel: (972)238-6106
Admissions: (972)238-6123
Fax: (972)238-6957
Web Site: http://www.rlc.dcccd.edu/
President/CEO: Dr. Stephen Mittelstet
Admissions: Donna Walker
Financial Aid: David Ximenez
Type: Two-Year College **Sex:** Coed **Affiliation:** Dallas County Community College District System **Admission Plans:** Open Admission; Early Admission **Application Fee:** $0.00 **H.S. Requirements:** High school diploma or equivalent not required **Scholarships:** Available **Calendar System:** Semester, Summer Session Available **Faculty:** FT 165, PT 500 **Exams:** SAT I or ACT **Library Holdings:** 63,000 **Regional Accreditation:** Southern Association of Colleges and Schools **Credit Hours For Degree:** 61 credits, Associates **Intercollegiate Athletics:** Baseball M; Basketball M; Soccer M & W; Volleyball W

ST. EDWARD'S UNIVERSITY
3001 South Congress Ave.
Austin, TX 78704
Tel: (512)448-8400
Free: 800-555-0164
Admissions: (512)448-8602
Fax: (512)448-8492
E-mail: seu.admit@admin.stedwards.edu
Web Site: http://www.stedwards.edu/

President/CEO: Dr. George E. Martin
Registrar: Lance R. Hayes
Admissions: Tracy Manier
Financial Aid: Doris Constantine
Type: Comprehensive **Sex:** Coed **Affiliation:** Roman Catholic **Scores:** 99.4% SAT V 400+; 99.8% SAT M 400+; 54.4% ACT 18-23; 40.8% ACT 24-29 **% Accepted:** 69 **Admission Plans:** Deferred Admission **Application Deadline:** May 01 **Application Fee:** $45.00 **H.S. Requirements:** High school diploma required; GED accepted **Costs Per Year:** Application fee: $45. Comprehensive fee: $25,700 includes full-time tuition ($18,800) and college room and board ($6900). College room only: $3900. Part-time tuition: $628 per hour. **Scholarships:** Available **Calendar System:** Semester, Summer Session Available **Enrollment:** FT 2,997, PT 967, Grad 983 **Faculty:** FT 155, PT 285 **Student-Faculty Ratio:** 14:1 **Exams:** SAT I or ACT **% Receiving Financial Aid:** 60 **% Residing in College-Owned, -Operated, or -Affiliated Housing:** 39 **Library Holdings:** 189,080 **Regional Accreditation:** Southern Association of Colleges and Schools **Credit Hours For Degree:** 120 credit hours, Bachelors **ROTC:** Army, Air Force **Professional Accreditation:** CSWE **Intercollegiate Athletics:** Baseball M; Basketball M & W; Cross-Country Running M & W; Golf M & W; Soccer M & W; Softball W; Tennis M & W; Volleyball W

ST. MARY'S UNIVERSITY OF SAN ANTONIO
1 Camino Santa Maria
San Antonio, TX 78228-8507
Tel: (210)436-3011
Free: 800-FOR-STMU
Admissions: (210)436-3126
Fax: (210)431-6742
E-mail: uadm@stmarytx.edu
Web Site: http://www.stmarytx.edu/
President/CEO: Dr. Charles L. Cotrell
Registrar: Louisa Avitua-Trevino
Admissions: Maria Ramos-Smalling
Financial Aid: David R. Krause
Type: Comprehensive **Sex:** Coed **Affiliation:** Roman Catholic **Scores:** 97% SAT V 400+; 97% SAT M 400+; 73% ACT 18-23; 24% ACT 24-29 **% Accepted:** 72 **Admission Plans:** Early Admission; Deferred Admission **Application Deadline:** Rolling **Application Fee:** $30.00 **H.S. Requirements:** High school diploma required; GED accepted **Costs Per Year:** Application fee: $30. Comprehensive fee: $26,162 includes full-time tuition ($18,274), mandatory fees ($1200), and college room and board ($6688). College room only: $3916. Full-time tuition and fees vary according to course load. Room and board charges vary according to board plan, housing facility, and student level. Part-time tuition: $548 per credit hour. Part-time mandatory fees: $250 per term. Part-time tuition and fees vary according to course load. **Scholarships:** Available **Calendar System:** Semester, Summer Session Available **Enrollment:** FT 2,185, PT 238, Grad 757 **Faculty:** FT 184, PT 149 **Student-Faculty Ratio:** 13:1 **Exams:** SAT I or ACT **% Receiving Financial Aid:** 73 **% Residing in College-Owned, -Operated, or -Affiliated Housing:** 41 **Library Holdings:** 481,137 **Regional Accreditation:** Southern Association of Colleges and Schools **Credit Hours For Degree:** 128 semester hours, Bachelors **ROTC:** Army **Professional Accreditation:** AACSB, ABET, AAMFT, ABA, ACA, AALS, NASM **Intercollegiate Athletics:** Baseball M; Basketball M & W; Golf M; Rugby M; Soccer M & W; Softball W; Tennis M & W; Volleyball W

ST. PHILIP'S COLLEGE
1801 Martin Luther King Dr.
San Antonio, TX 78203-2098
Tel: (210)531-3200
Admissions: (210)531-3290
Fax: (210)531-4831
E-mail: bcrow@accd.edu
Web Site: http://www.accd.edu/spc/
President/CEO: Dr. Angie Stokes Runnels
Admissions: Dr. Burton Crow
Financial Aid: Diego B. Bernal
Type: Two-Year College **Sex:** Coed **Affiliation:** Alamo Community College District System **Admission Plans:** Open Admission; Early Admission **Application Deadline:** Rolling **Application Fee:** $0.00 **H.S. Requirements:** High school diploma required; GED accepted **Costs Per Year:** Application fee: $0. Area resident tuition: $1200 full-time, $40 per hour part-time. State resident tuition: $2400 full-time, $80 per hour part-time. Nonresident tuition: $4800 full-time, $160 per hour part-time. Mandatory fees: $272 full-time, $136 per term part-time. **Scholarships:** Available **Calendar System:** Semester, Summer Session Available **Enrollment:** FT 4,209, PT 5,583 **Faculty:** FT 216, PT 371 **Student-Faculty Ratio:** 18:1 **Library Holdings:** 112,197 **Regional Accreditation:** Southern Association of Colleges and Schools **Credit Hours For Degree:** 60 credits, Associates **ROTC:** Army **Professional Accreditation:** ACF, AHIMA, AOTA, APTA, CARC, JRCERT, NAACLS, NLN

SAM HOUSTON STATE UNIVERSITY
Huntsville, TX 77341
Tel: (936)294-1111; (866)232-7528
Admissions: (936)294-1828
Web Site: http://www.shsu.edu/
President/CEO: Dr. James F. Gaertner
Registrar: Robert L. Dunning
Admissions: Joey Chandler
Financial Aid: Patricia Mabry
Type: University **Sex:** Coed **Affiliation:** The Texas State University System **Scores:** 96% SAT V 400+; 94% SAT M 400+; 67% ACT 18-23; 17% ACT 24-29 **Admission Plans:** Early Admission **Application Deadline:** August 01 **Application Fee:** $35.00 **H.S. Requirements:** High school diploma required; GED accepted **Costs Per Year:** Application fee: $35. State resident tuition: $3822 full-time. Nonresident tuition: $9728 full-time. Full-time tuition varies according to course load. College room and board: $5002. College room only: $2826. Room and board charges vary according to board plan and housing facility. **Scholarships:** Available **Calendar System:** Semester, Summer Session Available **Enrollment:** FT 11,120, PT 1,893, Grad 1,987 **Faculty:** FT 471, PT 210 **Student-Faculty Ratio:** 21:1 **Exams:** SAT I or ACT **% Receiving Financial Aid:** 65 **% Residing in College-Owned, -Operated, or -Affiliated Housing:** 27 **Library Holdings:** 1,202,263 **Regional Accreditation:** Southern Association of Colleges and Schools **Credit Hours For Degree:** 128 semester hours, Bachelors **ROTC:** Army **Professional Accreditation:** AACSB, AAFCS, ADtA, NASM, NCATE **Intercollegiate Athletics:** Baseball M; Basketball M & W; Cross-Country Running M & W; Equestrian Sports M & W; Football M; Golf M & W; Lacrosse M; Riflery M & W; Rugby M; Soccer M & W; Softball M & W; Tennis M & W; Track and Field M & W; Volleyball W

SAN ANTONIO COLLEGE
1300 San Pedro Ave.
San Antonio, TX 78212-4299
Tel: (210)733-2000
Free: 800-944-7575
Admissions: (210)733-2582
Fax: (210)733-2200
Web Site: http://www.accd.edu/
President/CEO: Dr. Robert E. Zeigler
Registrar: Cynthia C. Price
Admissions: Rosemarie Hoopes
Financial Aid: Richard Hernandez
Type: Two-Year College **Sex:** Coed **Affiliation:** Alamo Community College District System **Admission Plans:** Open Admission; Early Admission **Application Fee:** $0.00 **H.S. Requirements:** High school diploma required; GED accepted **Costs Per Year:** Application fee: $0. Area resident tuition: $960 full-time, $40 per semester hour part-time. State resident tuition: $1920 full-time, $80 per semester hour part-time. Nonresident tuition: $3840 full-time, $160 per semester hour part-time. Mandatory fees: $272 full-time, $136 per term part-time. **Calendar System:** Semester, Summer Session Available **Enrollment:** FT 8,587, PT 13,639 **Faculty:** FT 446, PT 590 **Student-Faculty Ratio:** 20:1 **Exams:** Other, SAT I or ACT **Library Holdings:** 233,714 **Regional Accreditation:** Southern Association of Colleges and Schools **Credit Hours For Degree:** 60 credits, Associates **ROTC:** Army, Air Force **Professional Accreditation:** AAMAE, ABFSE, ADA, NLN

SAN JACINTO COLLEGE DISTRICT
4624 Fairmont Parkway
Pasadena, TX 77504-3323
Tel: (281)998-6100
Web Site: http://www.sjcd.cc.tx.us/
President/CEO: Dr. Bill Lindemann
Financial Aid: Michael Ramsey

Type: Two-Year College **Sex:** Coed **Calendar System:** Semester **Regional Accreditation:** Southern Association of Colleges and Schools

SCHREINER UNIVERSITY
2100 Memorial Blvd.
Kerrville, TX 78028-5697
Tel: (830)896-5411
Free: 800-343-4919
Admissions: (830)792-7277
Fax: (830)792-7226
Web Site: http://www.schreiner.edu/
President/CEO: Dr. Charles Timothy (Tim) Summerlin
Registrar: Darlene Bannister
Admissions: Peg Layton
Financial Aid: Kevin Catron
Type: Comprehensive **Sex:** Coed **Affiliation:** Presbyterian **Scores:** 90.9% SAT V 400+; 90% SAT M 400+; 52.2% ACT 18-23; 29.3% ACT 24-29 **Admission Plans:** Deferred Admission **Application Fee:** $25.00 **H.S. Requirements:** High school diploma required; GED accepted **Costs Per Year:** Application fee: $25. Comprehensive fee: $22,474 includes full-time tuition ($14,742), mandatory fees ($400), and college room and board ($7332). College room only: $3900. Room and board charges vary according to board plan and housing facility. Part-time tuition: $629 per credit. **Scholarships:** Available **Calendar System:** Semester, Summer Session Available **Enrollment:** FT 717, PT 76, Grad 49 **Faculty:** FT 49, PT 33 **Student-Faculty Ratio:** 13:1 **Exams:** SAT I or ACT **% Receiving Financial Aid:** 79 **% Residing in College-Owned, -Operated, or -Affiliated Housing:** 58 **Library Holdings:** 69,873 **Regional Accreditation:** Southern Association of Colleges and Schools **Credit Hours For Degree:** 64 credit hours, Associates; 120 credit hours, Bachelors **Intercollegiate Athletics:** Baseball M; Basketball M & W; Cheerleading W; Golf M & W; Soccer M & W; Softball W; Tennis M & W; Volleyball W

SOUTH PLAINS COLLEGE
1401 South College Ave.
Levelland, TX 79336-6595
Tel: (806)894-9611
Fax: (806)897-3167
Web Site: http://www.southplainscollege.edu/
President/CEO: Dr. Gary D. McDaniel
Registrar: Teresa Salinas
Admissions: Andrea Rangel
Financial Aid: Jimmie Ann Batenhorst
Type: Two-Year College **Sex:** Coed **Admission Plans:** Open Admission; Early Admission **Application Deadline:** Rolling **Application Fee:** $0.00 **H.S. Requirements:** High school diploma required; GED accepted. For some applicants 18 or over: High school diploma or equivalent not required **Costs Per Year:** Application fee: $0. Area resident tuition: $1394 full-time, $26 per hour part-time. State resident tuition: $1922 full-time, $48 per hour part-time. Nonresident tuition: $2306 full-time, $64 per hour part-time. College room and board: $3300. **Scholarships:** Available **Calendar System:** Semester, Summer Session Available **Enrollment:** FT 4,774, PT 4,499 **Faculty:** FT 271, PT 183 **Student-Faculty Ratio:** 20:1 **Exams:** ACT, SAT II **% Residing in College-Owned, -Operated, or -Affiliated Housing:** 10 **Library Holdings:** 70,000 **Regional Accreditation:** Southern Association of Colleges and Schools **Credit Hours For Degree:** 62 semester hours, Associates **ROTC:** Army, Air Force **Professional Accreditation:** AHIMA, CARC, JRCERT, NLN **Intercollegiate Athletics:** Basketball M & W; Cross-Country Running M & W; Track and Field M & W

SOUTH TEXAS COLLEGE
3201 West Pecan
McAllen, TX 78501
Tel: (956)618-8323
Free: 800-742-7822
Admissions: (956)872-2147
Fax: (956)928-4445
E-mail: mshebbar@southtexascollege.edu
Web Site: http://www.southtexascollege.edu/
President/CEO: Dr. Shirley A. Reed
Registrar: William Serrata
Admissions: Matthew Hebbard
Type: Two-Year College **Sex:** Coed **Admission Plans:** Open Admission; Early Admission; Deferred Admission **Application Deadline:** Rolling **Application Fee:** $0.00 **H.S. Requirements:** High school diploma required; GED accepted **Costs Per Year:** Application fee: $0. One-time mandatory fee: $75. Area resident tuition: $1416 full-time, $127 per credit hour part-time. State resident tuition: $1826 full-time, $164.50 per credit hour part-time. Nonresident tuition: $4848 full-time, $202 per credit hour part-time. Mandatory fees: $400 full-time, $6 per credit hour part-time, $85 per term part-time. **Scholarships:** Available **Calendar System:** Semester, Summer Session Available **Enrollment:** FT 6,194, PT 10,031 **Faculty:** FT 354, PT 269 **Student-Faculty Ratio:** 22:1 **Exams:** Other, SAT I and SAT II or ACT **Library Holdings:** 12,611 **Regional Accreditation:** Southern Association of Colleges and Schools **Credit Hours For Degree:** 60 semester hours, Associates **ROTC:** Army **Professional Accreditation:** AHIMA, AOTA

SOUTHEASTERN CAREER INSTITUTE
5440 Harvest Hill, Ste. 200
Dallas, TX 75230-1600
Tel: (972)385-1446
Free: 800-525-1446
Fax: (972)385-0641
Web Site: http://www.southeasterncareerinstitute.com/ **Type:** Two-Year College **Sex:** Coed **Professional Accreditation:** COE

SOUTHERN METHODIST UNIVERSITY
6425 Boaz
Dallas, TX 75275
Tel: (214)768-2000
Free: 800-323-0672
Admissions: (214)768-1101
E-mail: ugadmission@smu.edu
Web Site: http://www.smu.edu/
President/CEO: Dr. R. Gerald Turner
Registrar: John A. Hall
Admissions: Ron W. Moss
Financial Aid: Marc Peterson
Type: University **Sex:** Coed **Affiliation:** United Methodist Church **Scores:** 99% SAT V 400+; 100% SAT M 400+; 23% ACT 18-23; 61% ACT 24-29 **% Accepted:** 58 **Admission Plans:** Early Admission; Early Action; Deferred Admission **Application Deadline:** January 15 **Application Fee:** $50.00 **H.S. Requirements:** High school diploma required; GED not accepted **Costs Per Year:** Application fee: $50. Comprehensive fee: $38,325 includes full-time tuition ($25,400), mandatory fees ($3230), and college room and board ($9695). College room only: $5775. Part-time tuition: $1058 per credit hour. Part-time mandatory fees: $135 per credit hour. **Scholarships:** Available **Calendar System:** Semester, Summer Session Available **Enrollment:** FT 6,126, PT 363, Grad 3,466 **Faculty:** FT 604, PT 329 **Student-Faculty Ratio:** 12:1 **Exams:** SAT I or ACT, SAT II **% Receiving Financial Aid:** 39 **% Residing in College-Owned, -Operated, or -Affiliated Housing:** 40 **Library Holdings:** 2,787,300 **Regional Accreditation:** Southern Association of Colleges and Schools **Credit Hours For Degree:** 122 credit hours, Bachelors **ROTC:** Army, Air Force **Professional Accreditation:** AACSB, ABET, ABA, ACIPE, AALS, ATS, NASD, NASM, NAST **Intercollegiate Athletics:** Baseball M; Basketball M & W; Crew M & W; Cross-Country Running M & W; Fencing M & W; Football M; Golf M & W; Ice Hockey M; Lacrosse M; Rugby M; Sailing M & W; Soccer M & W; Swimming and Diving M & W; Tennis M & W; Track and Field M & W; Volleyball W; Wrestling M

SOUTHWEST INSTITUTE OF TECHNOLOGY
5424 Hwy. 290 West, Ste. 200
Austin, TX 78735-8800
Tel: (512)892-2640
Fax: (512)892-1045
Web Site: http://www.swse.net/
President/CEO: Howard Roose
Admissions: Fredrico Garcia
Financial Aid: Lorena Villarreaz
Type: Two-Year College **Sex:** Coed **Application Fee:** $100.00 **Scholarships:** Available **Calendar System:** Continuous **Enrollment:** FT 63 **Faculty:** FT 10 **Student-Faculty Ratio:** 6:1 **Professional Accreditation:** ACCSCT

SOUTHWEST TEXAS JUNIOR COLLEGE
2401 Garner Field Rd.
Uvalde, TX 78801-6297
Tel: (830)278-4401
Web Site: http://www.swtjc.net/
President/CEO: Dr. Ismael Sosa

Registrar: Alicia Diaz
Admissions: Joe C. Barker
Financial Aid: Ismael Talavera
Type: Two-Year College **Sex:** Coed **Admission Plans:** Open Admission; Preferred Admission; Early Admission; Deferred Admission **H.S. Requirements:** High school diploma required; GED accepted **Scholarships:** Available **Calendar System:** Semester, Summer Session Available **Faculty:** FT 66, PT 100 **Exams:** Other, SAT I or ACT **% Residing in College-Owned, -Operated, or -Affiliated Housing:** 9 **Library Holdings:** 30,890 **Regional Accreditation:** Southern Association of Colleges and Schools **Credit Hours For Degree:** 62 semester hours, Associates **Intercollegiate Athletics:** Basketball M & W; Equestrian Sports M & W

SOUTHWESTERN ADVENTIST UNIVERSITY
100 Hillcrest Dr.
Keene, TX 76059
Tel: (817)645-3921
Free: 800-433-2240
Fax: (817)556-4744
E-mail: bbaldwin@swau.edu
Web Site: http://www.swau.edu/
President/CEO: Dr. Donald Sahly
Registrar: Dr. Thomas Bunch
Admissions: Brent Baldwin
Financial Aid: Patty Norwood
Type: Comprehensive **Sex:** Coed **Affiliation:** Seventh-day Adventist **Scores:** 88% SAT V 400+; 85% SAT M 400+; 63% ACT 18-23; 20% ACT 24-29 **Admission Plans:** Deferred Admission **Application Fee:** $0.00 **H.S. Requirements:** High school diploma required; GED accepted **Costs Per Year:** Application fee: $0. Comprehensive fee: $18,290 includes full-time tuition ($12,144), mandatory fees ($340), and college room and board ($5806). Full-time tuition and fees vary according to course load and program. Room and board charges vary according to board plan. Part-time mandatory fees: $170. Part-time fees vary according to course load and program. **Scholarships:** Available **Calendar System:** Semester, Summer Session Available **Enrollment:** FT 821, PT 342, Grad 28 **Faculty:** FT 50, PT 42 **Student-Faculty Ratio:** 15:1 **Exams:** SAT I or ACT **% Residing in College-Owned, -Operated, or -Affiliated Housing:** 31 **Library Holdings:** 108,481 **Regional Accreditation:** Southern Association of Colleges and Schools **Credit Hours For Degree:** 64 semester hours, Associates; 128 semester hours, Bachelors **Professional Accreditation:** CSWE, NLN **Intercollegiate Athletics:** Baseball M; Basketball M & W; Soccer M; Softball W; Volleyball M & W

SOUTHWESTERN ASSEMBLIES OF GOD UNIVERSITY
1200 Sycamore St.
Waxahachie, TX 75165-5735
Tel: (972)937-4010; 888-937-7248
Web Site: http://www.sagu.edu/
President/CEO: Rev. Kermit S. Bridges
Registrar: Greg Dufrene
Admissions: Kevin Harrison
Financial Aid: Trevor Summers
Type: Comprehensive **Sex:** Coed **Affiliation:** Assemblies of God **Scores:** 88% SAT V 400+; 88% SAT M 400+; 53% ACT 18-23; 16% ACT 24-29 **Admission Plans:** Early Admission; Deferred Admission **Application Fee:** $35.00 **H.S. Requirements:** High school diploma required; GED accepted **Scholarships:** Available **Calendar System:** Semester, Summer Session Available **Faculty:** FT 65, PT 30 **Student-Faculty Ratio:** 20:1 **Exams:** SAT I or ACT **% Receiving Financial Aid:** 70 **% Residing in College-Owned, -Operated, or -Affiliated Housing:** 55 **Library Holdings:** 110,000 **Regional Accreditation:** Southern Association of Colleges and Schools **Credit Hours For Degree:** 67 hours, Associates; 127 hours, Bachelors **ROTC:** Air Force **Professional Accreditation:** AABC **Intercollegiate Athletics:** Basketball M & W; Football M; Volleyball W

SOUTHWESTERN CHRISTIAN COLLEGE
Box 10
200 Bowser St.
Terrell, TX 75160
Tel: (972)524-3341
Admissions: (214)524-3341
Web Site: http://www.swcc.edu/
President/CEO: Dr. Jack Evans
Registrar: Zoa Ann Turner
Admissions: Thomas O. Fitzgerald, Jr.
Financial Aid: Felicia Robinson
Type: Four-Year College **Sex:** Coed **Affiliation:** Church of Christ **Admission Plans:** Open Admission; Early Admission; Deferred Admission **Application Fee:** $20.00 **H.S. Requirements:** High school diploma required; GED accepted **Scholarships:** Available **Calendar System:** Semester, Summer Session Not available **Faculty:** FT 10, PT 16 **Exams:** SAT I or ACT **% Residing in College-Owned, -Operated, or -Affiliated Housing:** 80 **Library Holdings:** 25,687 **Regional Accreditation:** Southern Association of Colleges and Schools **Credit Hours For Degree:** 62 credit hours, Associates; 124 credit hours, Bachelors **Intercollegiate Athletics:** Basketball M & W; Track and Field M & W

SOUTHWESTERN UNIVERSITY
1001 East University Ave.
Georgetown, TX 78626
Tel: (512)863-6511
Free: 800-252-3166
Admissions: (512)863-1200
Fax: (512)863-6511
E-mail: admission@southwestern.edu
Web Site: http://www.southwestern.edu/
President/CEO: Dr. Jake B. Schrum
Registrar: David H. Stones
Admissions: Tom Oliver
Financial Aid: James Gaeta
Type: Four-Year College **Sex:** Coed **Affiliation:** Methodist **Scores:** 100% SAT V 400+; 100% SAT M 400+; 21.71% ACT 18-23; 60.57% ACT 24-29 **% Accepted:** 67 **Admission Plans:** Early Decision Plan; Deferred Admission **Application Deadline:** February 15 **Application Fee:** $40.00 **H.S. Requirements:** High school diploma required; GED accepted **Costs Per Year:** Application fee: $40. Comprehensive fee: $28,447 includes full-time tuition ($21,900) and college room and board ($6547). College room only: $3143. Room and board charges vary according to board plan, housing facility, and student level. Part-time tuition: $920 per semester hour. **Scholarships:** Available **Calendar System:** Semester, Summer Session Available **Enrollment:** FT 1,286, PT 23 **Faculty:** FT 118, PT 49 **Student-Faculty Ratio:** 10:1 **Exams:** Other, SAT I and SAT II or ACT **% Receiving Financial Aid:** 48 **% Residing in College-Owned, -Operated, or -Affiliated Housing:** 83 **Library Holdings:** 323,000 **Regional Accreditation:** Southern Association of Colleges and Schools **Credit Hours For Degree:** 121 semester hours, Bachelors **Professional Accreditation:** JRCEPAT, NASM **Intercollegiate Athletics:** Baseball M; Basketball M & W; Cross-Country Running M & W; Golf M & W; Soccer M & W; Swimming and Diving M & W; Tennis M & W; Volleyball W

STEPHEN F. AUSTIN STATE UNIVERSITY
1936 North St.
Nacogdoches, TX 75962
Tel: (936)468-2011
Free: 800-731-2902
Admissions: (936)468-2504
Fax: (936)468-3849
E-mail: mbsmith@sfasu.edu
Web Site: http://www.sfasu.edu/
President/CEO: Dr. Tito Guerrero, III
Registrar: Sherry Wells
Admissions: Monique Cossich
Financial Aid: Michael O'Rear
Type: Comprehensive **Sex:** Coed **Scores:** 92.8% SAT V 400+; 92.2% SAT M 400+; 61.99% ACT 18-23; 21.47% ACT 24-29 **% Accepted:** 74 **Application Deadline:** Rolling **Application Fee:** $25.00 **H.S. Requirements:** High school diploma required; GED accepted **Costs Per Year:** Application fee: $25. State resident tuition: $4718 full-time, $126 per credit hour part-time. Nonresident tuition: $12,998 full-time, $402 per credit hour part-time. Mandatory fees: $60.50 per credit hour part-time, $9 per term part-time. Full-time tuition varies according to course load. Part-time tuition and fees vary according to course load. College room and board: $5459. Room and board charges vary according to board plan and housing facility. **Scholarships:** Available **Calendar System:** Semester, Summer Session Available **Enrollment:** FT 8,490, PT 1,316, Grad 1,629 **Faculty:** FT 434, PT 148 **Student-Faculty Ratio:** 19:1 **Exams:** SAT I or ACT **% Receiving Financial Aid:** 54 **% Residing in College-Owned, -Operated, or -Affiliated Housing:** 38 **Regional Accreditation:** Southern Association of Colleges and Schools

Credit Hours For Degree: 130 semester hours, Bachelors **ROTC:** Army **Professional Accreditation:** AACSB, ABET, AAFCS, ACA, ADtA, ASLHA, CORE, CSWE, FIDER, NASAD, NASM, NAST, NCATE, NLN, SAF **Intercollegiate Athletics:** Baseball M; Basketball M & W; Cross-Country Running M & W; Football M; Golf M; Soccer W; Softball W; Tennis W; Track and Field M & W; Volleyball W

SUL ROSS STATE UNIVERSITY
East Hwy. 90
Alpine, TX 79832
Tel: (432)837-8011; 888-722-7778
Admissions: (432)837-8050
Fax: (432)837-8334
E-mail: njenkins@sulross-.edu
Web Site: http://www.sulross.edu/
President/CEO: Dr. R. Vic Morgan
Registrar: Robert Cullins, Jr.
Admissions: Dr. Nadine Jenkins
Financial Aid: Rena Gallego
Type: Comprehensive **Sex:** Coed **Affiliation:** Texas State University System **Scores:** 67% SAT V 400+; 64% SAT M 400+; 37% ACT 18-23; 6% ACT 24-29 **Admission Plans:** Deferred Admission **Application Fee:** $25.00 **H.S. Requirements:** High school diploma required; GED accepted **Scholarships:** Available **Calendar System:** Semester, Summer Session Available **Enrollment:** FT 1,236, PT 166, Grad 552 **Faculty:** FT 88, PT 45 **Student-Faculty Ratio:** 13:1 **Exams:** SAT I or ACT **Library Holdings:** 245,567 **Regional Accreditation:** Southern Association of Colleges and Schools **Credit Hours For Degree:** 67 semester hours, Associates; 130 semester hours, Bachelors **Professional Accreditation:** ACBSP **Intercollegiate Athletics:** Baseball M; Basketball M & W; Cheerleading M & W; Cross-Country Running W; Football M; Softball W; Tennis M & W; Track and Field M & W; Volleyball W

TARLETON STATE UNIVERSITY
Box T-0001
Tarleton Station
Stephenville, TX 76402
Tel: (254)968-9000
Admissions: (254)968-9125
Fax: (254)968-9920
Web Site: http://www.tarleton.edu/
President/CEO: Dr. Dennis P. McCabe
Registrar: Kim Roberts
Admissions: Cindy Hess
Financial Aid: Betty Murray
Type: Comprehensive **Sex:** Coed **Affiliation:** Texas A&M University System **Scores:** 88% SAT V 400+; 92% SAT M 400+; 60% ACT 18-23; 16% ACT 24-29 **% Accepted:** 84 **Admission Plans:** Early Admission; Deferred Admission **Application Deadline:** April 28 **Application Fee:** $25.00 **H.S. Requirements:** High school diploma required; GED accepted **Costs Per Year:** Application fee: $25. State resident tuition: $3300 full-time, $110 per credit hour part-time. Nonresident tuition: $11,580 full-time, $386 per credit hour part-time. Mandatory fees: $870 full-time, $53 per credit hour part-time. Full-time tuition and fees vary according to course load. Part-time tuition and fees vary according to course load. College room and board: $5514. College room only: $2970. Room and board charges vary according to board plan and housing facility. **Scholarships:** Available **Calendar System:** Semester, Summer Session Available **Enrollment:** FT 6,081, PT 1,532, Grad 1,531 **Faculty:** FT 292, PT 242 **Student-Faculty Ratio:** 19:1 **Exams:** SAT I or ACT **% Receiving Financial Aid:** 67 **% Residing in College-Owned, -Operated, or -Affiliated Housing:** 19 **Library Holdings:** 320,302 **Regional Accreditation:** Southern Association of Colleges and Schools **Credit Hours For Degree:** 69 credit hours, Associates; 128 semester hours, Bachelors **ROTC:** Army **Professional Accreditation:** AACN, AAFCS, ACBSP, CSWE, NAACLS, NASM **Intercollegiate Athletics:** Baseball M; Basketball M & W; Cheerleading M & W; Cross-Country Running M & W; Football M; Golf W; Softball W; Tennis W; Track and Field M & W; Volleyball W

TARRANT COUNTY COLLEGE DISTRICT
1500 Houston St.
Fort Worth, TX 76102-6599
Tel: (817)515-5100
Admissions: (817)515-5291
Fax: (817)515-5295
Web Site: http://web.tccd.net/
President/CEO: Dr. Leonardo de la Garza
Registrar: Dr. Cathie Jackson
Admissions: Dr. Cathie Jackson
Financial Aid: Kenneth Tague
Type: Two-Year College **Sex:** Coed **% Accepted:** 100 **Admission Plans:** Open Admission; Early Admission **Application Deadline:** Rolling **Application Fee:** $0.00 **H.S. Requirements:** High school diploma or equivalent not required. For dental assisting, nursing programs: High school diploma required; GED accepted **Costs Per Year:** Application fee: $0. Area resident tuition: $1200 full-time, $50 per credit hour part-time. State resident tuition: $1512 full-time, $63 per credit hour part-time. Nonresident tuition: $3600 full-time, $150 per credit hour part-time. **Scholarships:** Available **Calendar System:** Semester, Summer Session Available **Enrollment:** FT 12,259, PT 22,633 **Faculty:** FT 519, PT 1,557 **Student-Faculty Ratio:** 19:1 **Library Holdings:** 197,352 **Regional Accreditation:** Southern Association of Colleges and Schools **Credit Hours For Degree:** 64 semester hours, Associates **ROTC:** Army, Air Force **Professional Accreditation:** ADA, AHIMA, APTA, CARC, JRCERT, NLN

TEMPLE COLLEGE
2600 South First St.
Temple, TX 76504-7435
Tel: (254)298-8282
Admissions: (254)298-8308
Web Site: http://www.templejc.edu/
President/CEO: Dr. Marc A. Nigliazzo
Registrar: Angela Balch
Admissions: Angela Balch
Financial Aid: Lanette Wigginton
Type: Two-Year College **Sex:** Coed **Admission Plans:** Open Admission; Early Admission **Application Fee:** $0.00 **H.S. Requirements:** High school diploma required; GED accepted **Costs Per Year:** Application fee: $0. Area resident tuition: $1860 full-time, $62 per hour part-time. State resident tuition: $2850 full-time, $95 per hour part-time. Nonresident tuition: $4500 full-time, $150 per hour part-time. Mandatory fees: $65 full-time. **Scholarships:** Available **Calendar System:** Semester, Summer Session Available **Enrollment:** FT 1,533, PT 2,535 **Faculty:** FT 85, PT 139 **Student-Faculty Ratio:** 18:1 **Exams:** ACT, Other **% Residing in College-Owned, -Operated, or -Affiliated Housing:** 1 **Library Holdings:** 55,536 **Regional Accreditation:** Southern Association of Colleges and Schools **Credit Hours For Degree:** 64 semester hours, Associates **Professional Accreditation:** ADA, CARC, NAACLS, NLN **Intercollegiate Athletics:** Baseball M; Basketball M & W; Softball W; Tennis M & W

TEXARKANA COLLEGE
2500 North Robison Rd.
Texarkana, TX 75599-0001
Tel: (903)838-4541
Fax: (903)832-5030
E-mail: vmiller@texarkanacollege.edu
Web Site: http://www.texarkanacollege.edu/
President/CEO: Frank Coleman
Registrar: Van Miller
Admissions: Van Miller
Financial Aid: Steve Middlebrooks
Type: Two-Year College **Sex:** Coed **Admission Plans:** Open Admission; Early Admission **Application Fee:** $0.00 **H.S. Requirements:** High school diploma required; GED accepted **Scholarships:** Available **Calendar System:** Semester, Summer Session Available **Enrollment:** FT 1,550, PT 2,345 **Faculty:** FT 84, PT 182 **Student-Faculty Ratio:** 15:1 **Exams:** Other **Library Holdings:** 46,700 **Regional Accreditation:** Southern Association of Colleges and Schools **Credit Hours For Degree:** 62 semester hours, Associates **Professional Accreditation:** NLN **Intercollegiate Athletics:** Baseball M; Softball W

TEXAS A&M INTERNATIONAL UNIVERSITY
5201 University Blvd.
Laredo, TX 78041-1900
Tel: (956)326-2001; 888-489-2648
Admissions: (956)326-2200
Fax: (956)326-2348
E-mail: adms@tamiu.edu
Web Site: http://www.tamiu.edu/

President/CEO: Dr. Ray M. Keck, III
Registrar: Barbara Lunce
Admissions: Rosa A. Espinoza
Financial Aid: Maria Laura Elizondo
Type: Comprehensive **Sex:** Coed **Affiliation:** Texas A&M University System **Scores:** 79% SAT V 400+; 81.5% SAT M 400+; 51% ACT 18-23; 6% ACT 24-29 **% Accepted:** 51 **Admission Plans:** Early Admission; Deferred Admission **Application Deadline:** July 01 **Application Fee:** $0.00 **H.S. Requirements:** High school diploma required; GED accepted **Costs Per Year:** Application fee: $0. State resident tuition: $3150 full-time. Nonresident tuition: $11,430 full-time. Mandatory fees: $1068 full-time. Full-time tuition and fees vary according to course load. College room and board: $6390. College room only: $4000. Room and board charges vary according to board plan and housing facility. **Scholarships:** Available **Calendar System:** Semester, Summer Session Available **Enrollment:** FT 2,236, PT 1,098, Grad 964 **Faculty:** FT 161, PT 112 **Student-Faculty Ratio:** 15:1 **Exams:** SAT I or ACT **% Receiving Financial Aid:** 70 **Library Holdings:** 166,951 **Regional Accreditation:** Southern Association of Colleges and Schools **Credit Hours For Degree:** 124 semester hours, Bachelors **Professional Accreditation:** AACSB, NLN **Intercollegiate Athletics:** Basketball M & W; Golf M & W; Soccer M & W; Volleyball W

TEXAS A&M UNIVERSITY
College Station, TX 77843
Tel: (979)845-3211
Admissions: (979)845-3741
E-mail: adminfo@tamu.edu
Web Site: http://www.tamu.edu/
President/CEO: Dr. Robert M. Gates
Registrar: Donald Carter
Admissions: Dr. Alice Reinarz
Financial Aid: Dr. Edward Funkhouser
Type: University **Sex:** Coed **Affiliation:** Texas A&M University System **Scores:** 100% SAT V 400+; 100% SAT M 400+; 33% ACT 18-23; 48% ACT 24-29 **% Accepted:** 70 **Admission Plans:** Preferred Admission **Application Deadline:** February 01 **Application Fee:** $50.00 **H.S. Requirements:** High school diploma required; GED accepted **Costs Per Year:** Application fee: $50. State resident tuition: $4110 full-time, $137 per semester hour part-time. Nonresident tuition: $12,390 full-time, $413 per semester hour part-time. Mandatory fees: $2289 full-time. Full-time tuition and fees vary according to course load, location, and program. College room and board: $6952. College room only: $3704. Room and board charges vary according to board plan, housing facility, and location. **Scholarships:** Available **Calendar System:** Semester, Summer Session Available **Enrollment:** FT 33,085, PT 3,283, Grad 8,028 **Faculty:** FT 1,898, PT 334 **Student-Faculty Ratio:** 20:1 **Exams:** SAT I or ACT **% Receiving Financial Aid:** 36 **% Residing in College-Owned, -Operated, or -Affiliated Housing:** 25 **Library Holdings:** 3,015,295 **Regional Accreditation:** Southern Association of Colleges and Schools **Credit Hours For Degree:** 128 semester hours, Bachelors **ROTC:** Army, Navy, Air Force **Professional Accreditation:** AACSB, ABET, ACEJMC, AAFCS, ACCE, ADtA, ACSP, APA, ASLA, AVMA, NCATE, NRPA, SAF **Intercollegiate Athletics:** Archery W; Baseball M; Basketball M & W; Cross-Country Running M & W; Equestrian Sports W; Football M; Golf M & W; Soccer W; Softball W; Swimming and Diving M & W; Tennis M & W; Track and Field M & W; Volleyball W

TEXAS A&M UNIVERSITY-COMMERCE
PO Box 3011
Commerce, TX 75429-3011
Tel: (903)886-5081
Free: 800-331-3878
Admissions: (903)886-5103
Fax: (903)886-5888
Web Site: http://www.tamu-commerce.edu/
President/CEO: Dr. Keith D. McFarland
Registrar: Paige Bussell
Admissions: Randy McDonald
Financial Aid: Smithenia Harris
Type: University **Sex:** Coed **Affiliation:** Texas A&M University System **Scores:** 87.42% SAT V 400+; 89.55% SAT M 400+; 34.93% ACT 18-23; 12.98% ACT 24-29 **Admission Plans:** Early Admission **Application Deadline:** August 11 **Application Fee:** $25.00 **H.S. Requirements:** High school diploma required; GED accepted **Costs Per Year:** Application fee: $25. State resident tuition: $3834 full-time, $278.50 per credit part-time. Nonresident tuition: $11,574 full-time, $554.50 per credit part-time. Mandatory fees: $990 full-time. Full-time tuition and fees vary according to course load. Part-time tuition varies according to course load. College room and board: $5740. Room and board charges vary according to board plan and housing facility. **Scholarships:** Available **Calendar System:** Semester, Summer Session Available **Enrollment:** FT 4,026, PT 1,245, Grad 3,516 **Faculty:** FT 295, PT 205 **Student-Faculty Ratio:** 17:1 **Exams:** SAT I or ACT **% Receiving Financial Aid:** 65 **% Residing in College-Owned, -Operated, or -Affiliated Housing:** 24 **Library Holdings:** 112,601 **Regional Accreditation:** Southern Association of Colleges and Schools **Credit Hours For Degree:** 126 semester hours, Bachelors **Professional Accreditation:** AACSB, ACA, CSWE, NAIT, NASM **Intercollegiate Athletics:** Basketball M & W; Cheerleading M & W; Cross-Country Running M & W; Football M; Golf M & W; Soccer W; Track and Field M & W; Volleyball W

TEXAS A&M UNIVERSITY-CORPUS CHRISTI
6300 Ocean Dr.
Corpus Christi, TX 78412-5503
Tel: (361)825-5700
Free: 800-482-6822
Admissions: (361)825-2414
Fax: (361)825-5810
E-mail: jmorgan@falcon.tamucc.edu
Web Site: http://www.tamucc.edu/
President/CEO: Dr. Robert R. Furgason
Admissions: Margaret Dechant
Financial Aid: Dolly Garza Zeriali
Type: Comprehensive **Sex:** Coed **Affiliation:** Texas A&M University System **Scores:** 90.2% SAT V 400+; 90.4% SAT M 400+; 65.2% ACT 18-23; 15.5% ACT 24-29 **Application Fee:** $20.00 **H.S. Requirements:** High school diploma required; GED accepted **Costs Per Year:** Application fee: $20. State resident tuition: $3348 full-time, $116 per semester hour part-time. Nonresident tuition: $11,628 full-time, $326 per semester hour part-time. Mandatory fees: $1168 full-time, $35 per semester hour part-time, $92.50. Full-time tuition and fees vary according to course load. Part-time tuition and fees vary according to course load. College room and board: $7800. College room only: $5400. Room and board charges vary according to housing facility. **Scholarships:** Available **Calendar System:** Semester, Summer Session Available **Enrollment:** FT 5,255, PT 1,326, Grad 1,646 **Faculty:** FT 254, PT 192 **Student-Faculty Ratio:** 21:1 **Exams:** SAT I or ACT **% Receiving Financial Aid:** 55 **% Residing in College-Owned, -Operated, or -Affiliated Housing:** 16 **Library Holdings:** 731,586 **Regional Accreditation:** Southern Association of Colleges and Schools **Credit Hours For Degree:** 124 semester hours, Bachelors **ROTC:** Army **Professional Accreditation:** AACSB, ABET, AACN, NAACLS, NASM **Intercollegiate Athletics:** Baseball M; Basketball M & W; Golf W; Softball W; Tennis M & W; Track and Field M & W; Volleyball W

TEXAS A&M UNIVERSITY AT GALVESTON
PO Box 1675
Galveston, TX 77553-1675
Tel: (409)740-4400; 877-322-4443
Admissions: (409)740-4414
Fax: (409)740-4709
E-mail: seaaggie@tamug.edu
Web Site: http://www.tamug.edu/
President/CEO: William C. Hearn
Registrar: Cheryl Grefenstette-Moon
Admissions: Cheryl Moon
Financial Aid: Dennis Carlton
Type: Comprehensive **Sex:** Coed **Affiliation:** Texas A&M University System **Scores:** 99% SAT V 400+; 99% SAT M 400+; 54% ACT 18-23; 37% ACT 24-29 **% Accepted:** 96 **Admission Plans:** Early Admission; Deferred Admission **Application Deadline:** Rolling **Application Fee:** $35.00 **H.S. Requirements:** High school diploma required; GED accepted **Costs Per Year:** Application fee: $35. State resident tuition: $4110 full-time, $137 per hour part-time. Nonresident tuition: $12,390 full-time, $413 per hour part-time. Mandatory fees: $1008 full-time, $504 per term part-time. Full-time tuition and fees vary according to course load and program. Part-time tuition and fees vary according to course load and program. College room and board: $4870. College room only: $1958. Room and board charges vary according to board plan and housing facility. **Scholarships:** Available **Calendar System:** Semester, Summer Session Available **Enrollment:** FT 1,488, PT 148, Grad 41 **Faculty:** FT 68, PT 102 **Student-Faculty Ratio:** 13:1 **Exams:** Other, SAT I or ACT, SAT II **% Receiving Financial Aid:** 50 **% Residing in College-Owned, -Operated, or -Affiliated Housing:** 54

Library Holdings: 56,589 **Regional Accreditation:** Southern Association of Colleges and Schools **Credit Hours For Degree:** 128 credit hours, Bachelors **ROTC:** Navy **Professional Accreditation:** ABET **Intercollegiate Athletics:** Crew M & W; Lacrosse M; Sailing M & W

TEXAS A&M UNIVERSITY-KINGSVILLE
West Santa Gertrudis
Kingsville, TX 78363
Tel: (361)593-2111
Free: 800-687-6000
Admissions: (361)593-2811
Web Site: http://www.tamuk.edu/
President/CEO: Dr. Rumaldo Juarez
Registrar: Maggie Williams
Admissions: Maggie Williams
Financial Aid: Roel Villarreal
Type: University **Sex:** Coed **Affiliation:** Texas A&M University System **Scores:** 73% SAT V 400+; 79% SAT M 400+; 44% ACT 18-23; 9% ACT 24-29 **Admission Plans:** Open Admission; Early Admission; Deferred Admission **Application Fee:** $15.00 **H.S. Requirements:** High school diploma required; GED accepted **Costs Per Year:** Application fee: $15. State resident tuition: $3060 full-time. Nonresident tuition: $11,340 full-time. Mandatory fees: $1266 full-time. **Scholarships:** Available **Calendar System:** Semester, Summer Session Available **Enrollment:** FT 3,910, PT 1,735, Grad 1,481 **Faculty:** FT 327, PT 111 **Student-Faculty Ratio:** 15:1 **Exams:** SAT I or ACT **% Receiving Financial Aid:** 92 **% Residing in College-Owned, -Operated, or -Affiliated Housing:** 30 **Library Holdings:** 358,466 **Regional Accreditation:** Southern Association of Colleges and Schools **Credit Hours For Degree:** 124 credits, Bachelors **ROTC:** Army **Professional Accreditation:** ABET, ADtA, ASLHA, ACBSP, CSWE, NAIT, NASM **Intercollegiate Athletics:** Baseball M; Basketball M & W; Cross-Country Running M & W; Equestrian Sports M & W; Football M; Riflery M & W; Softball W; Tennis M & W; Track and Field M & W; Volleyball W

TEXAS A&M UNIVERSITY SYSTEM HEALTH SCIENCE CENTER
301 Tarrow St.
7th Floor
College Station, TX 77840
Tel: (979)458-7200
Admissions: (214)828-8230
Fax: (979)458-7202
Web Site: http://www.tamhsc.edu/
President/CEO: Dr. Nancy W. Dickey
Registrar: Dana Freund
Admissions: Dr. Barbara Miller
Financial Aid: Dr. Beverly Boggs
Type: Two-Year Upper Division **Sex:** Coed **Affiliation:** Texas A&M University System Health Science Center **Application Fee:** $35.00 **Costs Per Year:** Application fee: $35. State resident tuition: $3752 full-time. Nonresident tuition: $13,342 full-time. Mandatory fees: $1,075 full-time. **Calendar System:** Semester, Summer Session Not available **Enrollment:** FT 59, Grad 113 **Faculty:** FT 137, PT 118 **Regional Accreditation:** Southern Association of Colleges and Schools **Professional Accreditation:** ADA, CEPH, LCMEAMA

TEXAS A&M UNIVERSITY-TEXARKANA
PO Box 5518
Texarkana, TX 75505-5518
Tel: (903)223-3000
Admissions: (903)223-3068
Fax: (903)832-8890
E-mail: patblack@etsu.edu
Web Site: http://www.tamut.edu/
President/CEO: Dr. Stephen R. Hensley
Registrar: Pat Black
Admissions: Patricia E. Black
Financial Aid: Marilyn Raney
Type: Two-Year Upper Division **Sex:** Coed **Affiliation:** Texas A&M University System **Admission Plans:** Open Admission **Application Fee:** $0.00 **H.S. Requirements:** High school diploma required; GED accepted **Costs Per Year:** Application fee: $0. State resident tuition: $2160 full-time, $90 per credit hour part-time. Nonresident tuition: $8784 full-time, $366 per credit hour part-time. Mandatory fees: $390 full-time, $15.75 per credit hour part-time, $6 per term part-time. Full-time tuition and fees vary according to course level, course load, and student level. Part-time tuition and fees vary according to course level, course load, and student level. **Scholarships:** Available **Calendar System:** Semester, Summer Session Available **Enrollment:** FT 385, PT 618, Grad 650 **Student-Faculty Ratio:** 14:1 **Library Holdings:** 125,991 **Regional Accreditation:** Southern Association of Colleges and Schools **Credit Hours For Degree:** 120 semester hours, Bachelors **Professional Accreditation:** AACN

TEXAS CHIROPRACTIC COLLEGE
5912 Spencer Hwy.
Pasadena, TX 77505-1699
Tel: (281)487-1170
Free: 800-468-6839
Admissions: (281)998-6017
E-mail: shughes@txchiro.edu
Web Site: http://www.txchiro.edu/
President/CEO: Dr. Richard Brassard
Registrar: Dr. Karlene Trebesiner
Admissions: Dr. Sandra Hughes
Financial Aid: Arthur Goudeau
Type: Two-Year Upper Division **Sex:** Coed **Admission Plans:** Deferred Admission **Application Fee:** $50.00 **H.S. Requirements:** High school diploma required; GED not accepted **Costs Per Year:** Application fee: $50. Tuition: $18,285 full-time, $508 per hour part-time. Mandatory fees: $315 full-time. **Scholarships:** Available **Calendar System:** Trimester **Enrollment:** FT 27, PT 26 **Faculty:** FT 28, PT 3 **Student-Faculty Ratio:** 15:1 **% Receiving Financial Aid:** 100 **Library Holdings:** 10,500 **Regional Accreditation:** Southern Association of Colleges and Schools **Credit Hours For Degree:** 146 credits, Bachelors **Professional Accreditation:** CCE

TEXAS CHRISTIAN UNIVERSITY
2800 South University Dr.
Fort Worth, TX 76129-0002
Tel: (817)257-7000
Free: 800-828-3764
Admissions: (817)257-7490
E-mail: frogmail@tcu.edu
Web Site: http://www.tcu.edu/
President/CEO: Dr. Victor Boschini
Registrar: Patrick H. Miller
Admissions: Ray Brown
Financial Aid: Michael Scott
Type: University **Sex:** Coed **Affiliation:** Christian Church (Disciples of Christ) **% Accepted:** 67 **Admission Plans:** Early Action; Deferred Admission **Application Deadline:** February 15 **Application Fee:** $40.00 **H.S. Requirements:** High school diploma required; GED not accepted **Costs Per Year:** Application fee: $40. Comprehensive fee: $28,300 includes full-time tuition ($21,280), mandatory fees ($40), and college room and board ($6980). College room only: $4180. Room and board charges vary according to board plan and housing facility. **Scholarships:** Available **Calendar System:** Semester, Summer Session Available **Enrollment:** FT 6,718, PT 453, Grad 1,258 **Faculty:** FT 465, PT 345 **Student-Faculty Ratio:** 14:1 **Exams:** SAT I or ACT **% Receiving Financial Aid:** 43 **% Residing in College-Owned, -Operated, or -Affiliated Housing:** 44 **Library Holdings:** 1,348,812 **Regional Accreditation:** Southern Association of Colleges and Schools **Credit Hours For Degree:** 124 semester hours, Bachelors **ROTC:** Army, Air Force **Professional Accreditation:** AACSB, ABET, ACEJMC, AACN, AANA, ADtA, ASLHA, ACIPE, ATS, CSWE, FIDER, JRCEPAT, NASM **Intercollegiate Athletics:** Baseball M; Basketball M & W; Cross-Country Running M & W; Football M; Golf M & W; Riflery W; Soccer M & W; Swimming and Diving M & W; Tennis M & W; Track and Field M & W; Volleyball W

TEXAS COLLEGE
2404 North Grand Ave.
PO Box 4500
Tyler, TX 75712-4500
Tel: (903)593-8311
Free: 800-306-6299
Web Site: http://www.texascollege.edu/
President/CEO: Dr. Billy C. Hawkins
Registrar: Herbert Coleman
Admissions: Anetha Francis
Financial Aid: Kathi Redricks
Type: Four-Year College **Sex:** Coed **Affiliation:** Christian Methodist Episcopal Church **Admission Plans:** Open Admission **Application Fee:** $20.00 **H.S. Requirements:** High school diploma required; GED accepted

Costs Per Year: Application fee: $20. Comprehensive fee: $12,410 includes full-time tuition ($7680) and college room and board ($4730). College room only: $3000. Part-time tuition: $320 per semester hour. **Scholarships:** Available **Calendar System:** Semester, Summer Session Available **Enrollment:** FT 694, PT 58, Grad 5 **Faculty:** FT 29, PT 22 **Student-Faculty Ratio:** 15:1 **% Receiving Financial Aid:** 92 **% Residing in College-Owned, -Operated, or -Affiliated Housing:** 75 **Library Holdings:** 73,329 **Regional Accreditation:** Southern Association of Colleges and Schools **Credit Hours For Degree:** 66 credit hours, Associates; 124 credit hours, Bachelors **Intercollegiate Athletics:** Baseball M; Basketball M & W; Football M; Soccer M & W; Softball W; Track and Field M & W; Volleyball W

TEXAS CULINARY ACADEMY
11400 Burnet Rd., Ste. 2100
Austin, TX 78758
Tel: (512)323-2511; 888-553-2433
Admissions: (512)837-2665
Fax: (512)323-2126
E-mail: ppaulette@txca.com
Web Site: http://www.txca.com/
Admissions: Paula Paulette
Type: Two-Year College **Sex:** Coed **Application Fee:** $100.00 **Scholarships:** Available **Calendar System:** Continuous **Enrollment:** FT 200 **Faculty:** FT 35, PT 6 **Student-Faculty Ratio:** 16:1 **Professional Accreditation:** COE

TEXAS LUTHERAN UNIVERSITY
1000 West Ct. St.
Seguin, TX 78155-5999
Tel: (830)372-8000
Free: 800-771-8521
Admissions: (830)372-8050
Fax: (830)372-8096
E-mail: admissions@txlutheran.edu
Web Site: http://www.tlu.edu/
President/CEO: Dr. Jon Moline
Registrar: Kristin H. Plaehn
Admissions: E. Norman Jones
Financial Aid: Debra Mattke
Type: Four-Year College **Sex:** Coed **Affiliation:** Evangelical Lutheran Church **Scores:** 96% SAT V 400+; 96% SAT M 400+; 62% ACT 18-23; 26% ACT 24-29 **% Accepted:** 72 **Admission Plans:** Deferred Admission **Application Deadline:** Rolling **Application Fee:** $25.00 **H.S. Requirements:** High school diploma required; GED accepted **Costs Per Year:** Application fee: $25. Comprehensive fee: $24,440 includes full-time tuition ($18,720), mandatory fees ($120), and college room and board ($5600). College room only: $2600. Part-time tuition: $630 per credit hour. Part-time mandatory fees: $60 per term. **Scholarships:** Available **Calendar System:** Semester, Summer Session Available **Enrollment:** FT 1,328, PT 107 **Faculty:** FT 68, PT 49 **Student-Faculty Ratio:** 16:1 **Exams:** SAT I or ACT **% Receiving Financial Aid:** 73 **% Residing in College-Owned, -Operated, or -Affiliated Housing:** 66 **Library Holdings:** 171,029 **Regional Accreditation:** Southern Association of Colleges and Schools **Credit Hours For Degree:** 124 credit hours, Bachelors **ROTC:** Army, Air Force **Professional Accreditation:** ACBSP **Intercollegiate Athletics:** Baseball M; Basketball M & W; Cross-Country Running W; Football M; Golf M & W; Soccer M & W; Softball W; Tennis M & W; Track and Field W; Volleyball W

TEXAS SOUTHERN UNIVERSITY
3100 Cleburne
Houston, TX 77004-4584
Tel: (713)313-7011
Admissions: (713)313-7472
Fax: (713)527-7842
Web Site: http://www.tsu.edu/
President/CEO: Dr. Priscilla Slade
Registrar: Norma Robinson
Admissions: Joyce Waddell
Type: University **Sex:** Coed **Affiliation:** Texas Higher Education Coordinating Board **% Accepted:** 30 **Admission Plans:** Open Admission **Application Deadline:** August 10 **Application Fee:** $42.00 **H.S. Requirements:** High school diploma required; GED accepted **Costs Per Year:** Application fee: $42. State resident tuition: $1200 full-time, $50 per hour part-time. Nonresident tuition: $7824 full-time, $326 per hour part-time. Mandatory fees: $2572 full-time, $817 per term part-time. Full-time tuition and fees vary according to course load and program. Part-time tuition and fees vary according to course load and program. College room and board: $6056. Room and board charges vary according to board plan and housing facility. **Scholarships:** Available **Calendar System:** Semester, Summer Session Available **Enrollment:** FT 7,739, PT 2,021, Grad 981 **Student-Faculty Ratio:** 25:1 **Exams:** SAT I or ACT **% Receiving Financial Aid:** 52 **% Residing in College-Owned, -Operated, or -Affiliated Housing:** 15 **Library Holdings:** 266,888 **Regional Accreditation:** Southern Association of Colleges and Schools **Credit Hours For Degree:** 124 semester hours, Bachelors **ROTC:** Army, Navy **Professional Accreditation:** AACSB, ABET, ABA, ACPhE, AHIMA, CARC, CSWE, NAACLS, NAIT **Intercollegiate Athletics:** Baseball M; Basketball M & W; Bowling W; Cross-Country Running M & W; Football M; Golf M; Soccer M & W; Softball W; Tennis M & W; Track and Field M & W; Volleyball M & W

TEXAS SOUTHMOST COLLEGE
80 Fort Brown
Brownsville, TX 78520-4991
Tel: (956)544-8200
Admissions: (956)544-8992
E-mail: rvillarreal@utb.edu
Web Site: http://www.utb.edu/
President/CEO: Dr. Juliet V. Garcia
Registrar: Ernesto Garcia
Admissions: Rene Villarreal
Financial Aid: Albert Barreda
Type: Two-Year College **Sex:** Coed **Affiliation:** University of Texas System **Admission Plans:** Open Admission; Early Admission; Deferred Admission **Application Fee:** $0.00 **H.S. Requirements:** High school diploma required; GED accepted **Calendar System:** Semester, Summer Session Available **Faculty:** FT 289, PT 248 **Student-Faculty Ratio:** 17:1 **Exams:** Other **Library Holdings:** 147,216 **Regional Accreditation:** Southern Association of Colleges and Schools **Credit Hours For Degree:** 62 credits, Associates **Professional Accreditation:** CARC, JRCERT, NAACLS, NLN **Intercollegiate Athletics:** Baseball M; Golf M & W; Volleyball W

TEXAS STATE TECHNICAL COLLEGE HARLINGEN
1902 North Loop 499
Harlingen, TX 78550-3697
Tel: (956)364-4000
Admissions: (956)364-4100
Fax: (956)364-5140
Web Site: http://www.harlingen.tstc.edu/
President/CEO: Dr. J. Gilbert Leal
Registrar: Elva Short
Admissions: Elva Short
Financial Aid: Mary Gallegos-Adams
Type: Two-Year College **Sex:** Coed **Affiliation:** Texas State Technical College System **Admission Plans:** Open Admission; Early Admission; Deferred Admission **Application Fee:** $0.00 **H.S. Requirements:** High school diploma required; GED accepted **Scholarships:** Available **Calendar System:** Semester, Summer Session Available **Enrollment:** FT 1,729, PT 2,299 **Faculty:** FT 157, PT 22 **Student-Faculty Ratio:** 17:1 **Exams:** Other, SAT I or ACT **% Residing in College-Owned, -Operated, or -Affiliated Housing:** 8 **Library Holdings:** 25,000 **Regional Accreditation:** Southern Association of Colleges and Schools **Credit Hours For Degree:** 72 semester hours, Associates **Professional Accreditation:** ADA, AHIMA

TEXAS STATE TECHNICAL COLLEGE-MARSHALL
2400 East End Blvd. S
Marshall, TX 75671
Tel: (903)935-1010
Web Site: http://www.marshall.tstc.edu **Type:** Two-Year College **Calendar System:** Semester

TEXAS STATE TECHNICAL COLLEGE WACO
3801 Campus Dr.
Waco, TX 76705-1695
Tel: (254)799-3611
Admissions: (254)867-2366
E-mail: dkhoury@tstc.edu
Web Site: http://waco.tstc.edu/
President/CEO: Elton Stuckly, Jr.
Registrar: Dawn Khoury

Admissions: Dawn Khoury
Financial Aid: Jackie Adler
Type: Two-Year College **Sex:** Coed **Affiliation:** Texas State Technical College System **% Accepted:** 100 **Admission Plans:** Open Admission; Early Admission **Application Deadline:** Rolling **Application Fee:** $0.00 **H.S. Requirements:** High school diploma required; GED accepted **Costs Per Year:** Application fee: $0. State resident tuition: $1950 full-time, $65 per credit hour part-time. Nonresident tuition: $5460 full-time, $182 per credit hour part-time. Mandatory fees: $2000 full-time, $21 per credit hour part-time. College room and board: $4100. College room only: $1860. **Scholarships:** Available **Calendar System:** Trimester, Summer Session Available **Enrollment:** FT 2,989, PT 1,463 **Faculty:** FT 243, PT 35 **Student-Faculty Ratio:** 16:1 **Exams:** Other **Library Holdings:** 60,000 **Regional Accreditation:** Southern Association of Colleges and Schools **Credit Hours For Degree:** 72 semester credits, Associates **Professional Accreditation:** ADA

TEXAS STATE TECHNICAL COLLEGE WEST TEXAS
300 College Dr.
Sweetwater, TX 79556-4108
Tel: (915)235-7300
Free: 800-592-8784
Admissions: (915)235-7374
Fax: (915)235-7359
Web Site: http://www.sweetwater.tstc.edu/
President/CEO: Homer K. Taylor
Admissions: Eileen Graham
Financial Aid: Kathleen Butler
Type: Two-Year College **Sex:** Coed **Affiliation:** Texas State Technical College System **Admission Plans:** Open Admission; Early Admission; Deferred Admission **Application Fee:** $0.00 **H.S. Requirements:** High school diploma or equivalent not required. For skill development programs: High school diploma or equivalent not required **Scholarships:** Available **Calendar System:** Semester, Summer Session Available **Faculty:** FT 107, PT 37 **Student-Faculty Ratio:** 10:1 **Exams:** Other **% Residing in College-Owned, -Operated, or -Affiliated Housing:** 29 **Library Holdings:** 12,449 **Regional Accreditation:** Southern Association of Colleges and Schools **Credit Hours For Degree:** 88 credits, Associates

TEXAS STATE UNIVERSITY-SAN MARCOS
601 University Dr.
San Marcos, TX 78666
Tel: (512)245-2111
Admissions: (512)245-2364
Fax: (512)245-8044
E-mail: admissions@txstate.edu
Web Site: http://www.txstate.edu/
President/CEO: Dr. Denise M. Trauth
Registrar: Douglas Van Den Berg
Admissions: Christie Kangas
Financial Aid: Mariko G. Gomez
Type: University **Sex:** Coed **Affiliation:** Texas State University System **Scores:** 98% SAT V 400+; 99% SAT M 400+; 55% ACT 18-23; 39% ACT 24-29 **% Accepted:** 76 **Admission Plans:** Early Admission; Deferred Admission **Application Deadline:** May 01 **Application Fee:** $40.00 **H.S. Requirements:** High school diploma required; GED accepted **Costs Per Year:** Application fee: $40. State resident tuition: $3780 full-time, $126 per semester hour part-time. Nonresident tuition: $12,060 full-time, $402 per semester hour part-time. Mandatory fees: $1472 full-time, $37 per semester hour part-time, $267 per term part-time. Full-time tuition and fees vary according to course load. Part-time tuition and fees vary according to course load. College room and board: $5610. College room only: $3524. Room and board charges vary according to board plan and housing facility. **Scholarships:** Available **Calendar System:** Semester, Summer Session Available **Enrollment:** FT 18,472, PT 4,514, Grad 4,143 **Faculty:** FT 775, PT 522 **Student-Faculty Ratio:** 24:1 **Exams:** SAT I or ACT **% Receiving Financial Aid:** 50 **% Residing in College-Owned, -Operated, or -Affiliated Housing:** 22 **Library Holdings:** 1,349,046 **Regional Accreditation:** Southern Association of Colleges and Schools **Credit Hours For Degree:** 128 semester hours, Bachelors **ROTC:** Army, Air Force **Professional Accreditation:** AACSB, ABET, ACEHSA, ACEJMC, AAFCS, ACA, ADtA, AHIMA, APTA, APA, ASLHA, CARC, CSWE, FIDER, JRCERT, JRCEPAT, NAACLS, NASM, NASPAA, NRPA **Intercollegiate Athletics:** Baseball M; Basketball M & W; Cheerleading M & W; Cross-Country Running M & W; Equestrian Sports M & W; Fencing M & W; Football M; Golf M & W; Gymnastics M & W; Lacrosse M & W; Rugby M & W; Soccer M & W; Softball M & W; Tennis M & W; Track and Field M & W; Ultimate Frisbee M & W; Volleyball W; Water Polo M & W; Weight Lifting M & W; Wrestling M & W

TEXAS TECH UNIVERSITY
Lubbock, TX 79409
Tel: (806)742-2011
Admissions: (806)742-1480
Fax: (806)742-3055
Web Site: http://www.ttu.edu/
President/CEO: Dr. David R. Smith
Registrar: Don Wickard
Admissions: Djuana D. Young
Financial Aid: Becky Wilson
Type: University **Sex:** Coed **Affiliation:** Texas Tech University System **Scores:** 100% SAT V 400+; 99% SAT M 400+; 45% ACT 18-23; 45% ACT 24-29 **% Accepted:** 71 **Admission Plans:** Early Admission **Application Deadline:** May 01 **Application Fee:** $50.00 **H.S. Requirements:** High school diploma required; GED not accepted **Costs Per Year:** Application fee: $50. State resident tuition: $3870 full-time, $129 per credit hour part-time. Nonresident tuition: $12,150 full-time, $405 per credit hour part-time. Mandatory fees: $2282 full-time, $58.75 per credit hour part-time, $291. Full-time tuition and fees vary according to course load, program, and reciprocity agreements. Part-time tuition and fees vary according to course load, program, and reciprocity agreements. College room and board: $6875. College room only: $3663. Room and board charges vary according to board plan and housing facility. **Scholarships:** Available **Calendar System:** Semester, Summer Session Available **Enrollment:** FT 20,821, PT 2,181, Grad 4,294 **Faculty:** FT 1,046, PT 77 **Student-Faculty Ratio:** 19:1 **Exams:** SAT I or ACT **% Receiving Financial Aid:** 41 **% Residing in College-Owned, -Operated, or -Affiliated Housing:** 22 **Library Holdings:** 2,386,509 **Regional Accreditation:** Southern Association of Colleges and Schools **Credit Hours For Degree:** 120 semester hours, Bachelors **ROTC:** Army, Air Force **Professional Accreditation:** AACSB, ABET, ACEHSA, ACEJMC, AAMFT, AAFCS, ABA, ACA, ADtA, APA, ASLA, ASLHA, AALS, CSWE, FIDER, JRCEMT, NASAD, NASM, NASPAA, NAST NCATE **Intercollegiate Athletics:** Baseball M; Basketball M & W; Cross-Country Running M & W; Football M; Golf M & W; Soccer W; Softball W; Tennis M & W; Track and Field M & W; Volleyball W

TEXAS WESLEYAN UNIVERSITY
1201 Wesleyan St.
Fort Worth, TX 76105-1536
Tel: (817)531-4444
Admissions: (817)531-4405
Fax: (817)531-7515
Web Site: http://www.txwesleyan.edu/
President/CEO: Dr. Harold G. Jeffcoat
Registrar: Kay Van Toorn
Admissions: Dr. Allen Henderson
Financial Aid: Dean Carpenter
Type: Comprehensive **Sex:** Coed **Affiliation:** United Methodist **Scores:** 89% SAT V 400+; 81% SAT M 400+; 57% ACT 18-23; 11% ACT 24-29 **Admission Plans:** Deferred Admission **Application Fee:** $25.00 **H.S. Requirements:** High school diploma required; GED accepted **Costs Per Year:** Application fee: $25. Comprehensive fee: $19,500 includes full-time tuition ($12,950), mandatory fees ($1050), and college room and board ($5500). College room only: $1875. Full-time tuition and fees vary according to program. Room and board charges vary according to board plan and student level. Part-time tuition: $435 per credit. Part-time mandatory fees: $50 per credit. Part-time tuition and fees vary according to program. **Scholarships:** Available **Calendar System:** Semester, Summer Session Available **Enrollment:** FT 974, PT 517, Grad 536 **Faculty:** FT 139, PT 119 **Student-Faculty Ratio:** 11:1 **Exams:** SAT I or ACT **% Receiving Financial Aid:** 82 **% Residing in College-Owned, -Operated, or -Affiliated Housing:** 10 **Library Holdings:** 192,044 **Regional Accreditation:** Southern Association of Colleges and Schools **Credit Hours For Degree:** 124 credit hours, Bachelors **ROTC:** Army, Air Force **Professional Accreditation:** AANA, ABA, NASM **Intercollegiate Athletics:** Baseball M; Basketball M & W; Golf M; Soccer M & W; Softball W; Table Tennis M; Volleyball W

TEXAS WOMAN'S UNIVERSITY
304 Administration Dr.
Denton, TX 76201
Tel: (940)898-2000; 888-948-9984
Admissions: (940)898-3040

Fax: (940)898-3198
Web Site: http://www.twu.edu/
President/CEO: Dr. Ann Stuart
Registrar: Dr. Jim Stiles
Admissions: Erma M. Nieto-Brecht
Financial Aid: Governor Jackson
Type: University **Sex:** Coed **Scores:** 89.1% SAT V 400+; 86.7% SAT M 400+; 52% ACT 18-23; 24% ACT 24-29 **% Accepted:** 64 **Admission Plans:** Early Admission; Deferred Admission **Application Deadline:** July 15 **Application Fee:** $30.00 **H.S. Requirements:** High school diploma required; GED accepted **Costs Per Year:** Application fee: $30. State resident tuition: $3690 full-time, $123 per hour part-time. Nonresident tuition: $11,970 full-time, $399 per hour part-time. Mandatory fees: $1320 full-time. College room and board: $5598. College room only: $2804. **Scholarships:** Available **Calendar System:** Semester, Summer Session Available **Enrollment:** FT 4,554, PT 1,712, Grad 5,078 **Faculty:** FT 426, PT 266 **Student-Faculty Ratio:** 15:1 **Exams:** SAT I or ACT **% Receiving Financial Aid:** 58 **% Residing in College-Owned, -Operated, or -Affiliated Housing:** 25 **Library Holdings:** 572,500 **Regional Accreditation:** Southern Association of Colleges and Schools **Credit Hours For Degree:** 124 semester hours, Bachelors **ROTC:** Army, Air Force **Professional Accreditation:** ACEHSA, AACN, AAFCS, ACA, ADA, ADtA, ALA, AOTA, APTA, APA, ASLHA, CSWE, NASD, NASM, NLN **Intercollegiate Athletics:** Basketball W; Gymnastics W; Soccer W; Softball W; Volleyball W

TOMBALL COLLEGE
30555 Tomball Parkway
Tomball, TX 77375-4036
Tel: (281)351-3300
Admissions: (281)351-3334
Fax: (281)351-3384
E-mail: tc.advisors@nhmccd.edu
Web Site: http://wwwtc.nhmccd.edu/
President/CEO: Diane K. Troyer, PhD
Admissions: Larry Rideaux
Type: Two-Year College **Sex:** Coed **Affiliation:** North Harris Montgomery Community College District **Admission Plans:** Open Admission; Early Admission **Application Fee:** $0.00 **H.S. Requirements:** High school diploma required; GED accepted **Costs Per Year:** Application fee: $0. Area resident tuition: $1080 full-time, $56 per credit hour part-time. State resident tuition: $2040 full-time, $96 per credit hour part-time. Nonresident tuition: $2400 full-time, $220 per credit hour part-time. **Scholarships:** Available **Calendar System:** Semester, Summer Session Available **Enrollment:** FT 1,463, PT 6,184 **Faculty:** FT 111, PT 247 **Student-Faculty Ratio:** 8:1 **Exams:** Other, SAT I or ACT **Library Holdings:** 24,063 **Regional Accreditation:** Southern Association of Colleges and Schools **Credit Hours For Degree:** 62 credit hours, Associates **Professional Accreditation:** AOTA

TRINITY UNIVERSITY
One Trinity Place
San Antonio, TX 78212-7200
Tel: (210)999-7011
Free: 800-TRI-NITY
Admissions: (210)999-7207
Fax: (210)999-8164
Web Site: http://www.trinity.edu/
President/CEO: Dr. John R. Brazil
Registrar: Alfred Rodriguez
Admissions: Christopher Ellertson
Financial Aid: Patricia Jost
Type: Comprehensive **Sex:** Coed **Affiliation:** Presbyterian Church **Scores:** 100% SAT V 400+; 100% SAT M 400+; 2.99% ACT 18-23; 62.28% ACT 24-29 **% Accepted:** 63 **Admission Plans:** Early Action; Early Decision Plan; Deferred Admission **Application Deadline:** February 01 **Application Fee:** $50.00 **H.S. Requirements:** High school diploma required; GED accepted **Costs Per Year:** Application fee: $50. Comprehensive fee: $30,307 includes full-time tuition ($21,432), mandatory fees ($150), and college room and board ($8725). College room only: $5815. Full-time tuition and fees vary according to course load. Room and board charges vary according to board plan. Part-time tuition: $893 per semester hour. Part-time tuition varies according to course load. **Scholarships:** Available **Calendar System:** Semester, Summer Session Available **Enrollment:** FT 2,485, PT 39, Grad 232 **Faculty:** FT 219, PT 61 **Student-Faculty Ratio:** 10:1 **Exams:** SAT I or ACT **% Receiving Financial Aid:** 41 **% Residing in College-Owned, -Operated, or -Affiliated Housing:** 77 **Library Holdings:** 917,781 **Regional Accreditation:** Southern Association of Colleges and Schools **Credit Hours For Degree:** 124 semester hours, Bachelors **ROTC:** Air Force **Professional Accreditation:** AACSB, ABET, ACEHSA, NASM, NCATE **Intercollegiate Athletics:** Baseball M; Basketball M & W; Cross-Country Running M & W; Football M; Golf M & W; Lacrosse M & W; Riflery M & W; Soccer M & W; Softball W; Swimming and Diving M & W; Tennis M & W; Track and Field M & W; Volleyball M & W

TRINITY VALLEY COMMUNITY COLLEGE
100 Cardinal Dr.
Athens, TX 75751-2765
Tel: (903)677-TVCC
Admissions: (903)675-6209
E-mail: tvccinfo@tvcc.edu
Web Site: http://www.tvcc.edu/
President/CEO: Ron Baugh
Registrar: Dr. Colette Hilliard
Admissions: Dr. Collette Hilliard
Financial Aid: Julie Lively
Type: Two-Year College **Sex:** Coed **Admission Plans:** Open Admission; Early Admission **Application Deadline:** Rolling **H.S. Requirements:** High school diploma required; GED accepted **Costs Per Year:** State resident tuition: $1200 full-time, $20 per semester hour part-time. Nonresident tuition: $3900 full-time, $65 per semester hour part-time. Mandatory fees: $900 full-time, $15 per semester hour part-time. College room and board: $3470. **Scholarships:** Available **Calendar System:** Semester, Summer Session Available **Enrollment:** FT 2,442, PT 3,379 **Faculty:** FT 124, PT 149 **Student-Faculty Ratio:** 20:1 **Library Holdings:** 54,940 **Regional Accreditation:** Southern Association of Colleges and Schools **Credit Hours For Degree:** 64 semester hours, Associates **Professional Accreditation:** ARCEST, NLN **Intercollegiate Athletics:** Basketball M & W; Cheerleading M & W; Football M

TYLER JUNIOR COLLEGE
PO Box 9020
Tyler, TX 75711-9020
Tel: (903)510-2200
Free: 800-687-5680
Admissions: (903)510-2399
Web Site: http://www.tjc.edu/
President/CEO: Dr. William R. Crowe
Registrar: William Wayne Wilmeth
Admissions: Kenneth D. Lewis
Financial Aid: Devon Wiggins
Type: Two-Year College **Sex:** Coed **Admission Plans:** Open Admission; Preferred Admission; Early Admission **Application Fee:** $0.00 **H.S. Requirements:** High school diploma required; GED accepted. For allied health programs: High school diploma required; GED not accepted **Scholarships:** Available **Calendar System:** Semester, Summer Session Available **Faculty:** FT 234, PT 222 **Student-Faculty Ratio:** 21:1 **Exams:** Other, SAT I and SAT II or ACT **% Residing in College-Owned, -Operated, or -Affiliated Housing:** 8 **Regional Accreditation:** Southern Association of Colleges and Schools **Credit Hours For Degree:** 60 semester hours, Associates **Professional Accreditation:** ARCEST, ADA, AHIMA, COptA, CARC, JRCEDMS, JRCERT, NAACLS **Intercollegiate Athletics:** Baseball M; Basketball M & W; Football M; Golf M & W; Soccer M; Tennis M & W; Volleyball W

UNIVERSAL TECHNICAL INSTITUTE
721 Lockhaven Dr.
Houston, TX 77073-5598
Tel: (281)443-6262
Web Site: http://www.uticorp.com/
President/CEO: Ken Golaszewski
Admissions: Randy Whitman
Financial Aid: Charlotte Baker
Type: Two-Year College **Enrollment:** FT 1,400 **Faculty:** FT 65, PT 0 **Professional Accreditation:** ACCSCT

UNIVERSITY OF DALLAS
1845 East Northgate Dr.
Irving, TX 75062-4736
Tel: (972)721-5000
Free: 800-628-6999

Admissions: (972)721-5266
Fax: (972)721-5017
Web Site: http://www.udallas.edu/
President/CEO: Dr. Frank Lazarus
Registrar: Janet E. Burk
Admissions: Curt Eley
Financial Aid: Laurie Rosenkratz
Type: University **Sex:** Coed **Affiliation:** Roman Catholic **Scores:** 100% SAT V 400+; 100% SAT M 400+; 25% ACT 18-23; 50% ACT 24-29 **% Accepted:** 81 **Admission Plans:** Early Admission; Early Action; Deferred Admission **Application Deadline:** August 01 **Application Fee:** $40.00 **H.S. Requirements:** High school diploma required; GED accepted **Costs Per Year:** Application fee: $40. Comprehensive fee: $29,137 includes full-time tuition ($20,780), mandatory fees ($1025), and college room and board ($7332). College room only: $4116. Part-time tuition: $900 per credit hour. Part-time mandatory fees: $1025 per year. **Scholarships:** Available **Calendar System:** Semester, Summer Session Available **Enrollment:** FT 1,070, PT 96, Grad 1,855 **Faculty:** FT 116, PT 105 **Student-Faculty Ratio:** 12:1 **Exams:** SAT I or ACT **% Receiving Financial Aid:** 65 **% Residing in College-Owned, -Operated, or -Affiliated Housing:** 61 **Library Holdings:** 223,350 **Regional Accreditation:** Southern Association of Colleges and Schools **Credit Hours For Degree:** 120 credits, Bachelors **ROTC:** Army, Air Force **Professional Accreditation:** AALE, ACBSP **Intercollegiate Athletics:** Baseball M; Basketball M & W; Cross-Country Running M & W; Golf M; Lacrosse W; Soccer M & W; Softball W; Tennis M & W; Track and Field M & W; Volleyball W

UNIVERSITY OF HOUSTON
4800 Calhoun Rd.
Houston, TX 77204
Tel: (713)743-1000
Admissions: (713)743-7542
Fax: (713)743-9633
E-mail: admissions@uh.edu
Web Site: http://www.uh.edu/
President/CEO: Dr. Jay Gogue
Registrar: Patricia M. Cavanaugh
Admissions: Susanna Finnell
Financial Aid: Robert B. Sheridan
Type: University **Sex:** Coed **Affiliation:** University of Houston System **Scores:** 94.55% SAT V 400+; 98.19% SAT M 400+; 56.16% ACT 18-23; 25.98% ACT 24-29 **% Accepted:** 80 **Admission Plans:** Early Admission; Deferred Admission **Application Deadline:** April 01 **Application Fee:** $50.00 **H.S. Requirements:** High school diploma required; GED accepted **Costs Per Year:** Application fee: $50. State resident tuition: $3920 full-time, $131 per credit hour part-time. Nonresident tuition: $12,200 full-time, $407 per credit hour part-time. Mandatory fees: $2566 full-time. Full-time tuition and fees vary according to course level, course load, degree level, location, program, reciprocity agreements, and student level. Part-time tuition varies according to course level, course load, degree level, location, program, reciprocity agreements, and student level. College room and board: $6058. College room only: $3492. Room and board charges vary according to board plan and housing facility. **Scholarships:** Available **Calendar System:** Semester, Summer Session Available **Enrollment:** FT 19,866, PT 8,320, Grad 5,240 **Faculty:** FT 1,218, PT 427 **Student-Faculty Ratio:** 21:1 **Exams:** SAT I or ACT, SAT II **% Receiving Financial Aid:** 56 **% Residing in College-Owned, -Operated, or -Affiliated Housing:** 10 **Library Holdings:** 2,231,918 **Regional Accreditation:** Southern Association of Colleges and Schools **Credit Hours For Degree:** 122 semester hours, Bachelors **ROTC:** Army, Navy **Professional Accreditation:** AACSB, ABET, ABA, ACPhE, ADtA, AOA, APA, ASLHA, AALS, CSWE, NASM, NCATE **Intercollegiate Athletics:** Baseball M; Basketball M & W; Cheerleading M & W; Cross-Country Running M & W; Football M; Golf M; Soccer W; Softball W; Swimming and Diving W; Tennis W; Track and Field M & W; Volleyball W

UNIVERSITY OF HOUSTON-CLEAR LAKE
2700 Bay Area Blvd.
Houston, TX 77058-1098
Tel: (281)283-7600
Admissions: (281)283-2518
Fax: (281)283-2530
E-mail: admissions@cl.uh.edu
Web Site: http://www.uhcl.edu/
President/CEO: Dr. William A. Staples
Registrar: Rose Sklar
Admissions: Rauchelle Jones
Financial Aid: Linda McKendree
Type: Two-Year Upper Division **Sex:** Coed **Affiliation:** University of Houston System **% Accepted:** 64 **Admission Plans:** Deferred Admission **Application Fee:** $35.00 **Costs Per Year:** Application fee: $35. State resident tuition: $2010 full-time, $120 per credit hour part-time. Nonresident tuition: $10,952 full-time, $326 per credit hour part-time. Mandatory fees: $2643 full-time, $986 per term part-time. **Scholarships:** Available **Calendar System:** Semester, Summer Session Available **Enrollment:** FT 2,096, PT 2,055, Grad 3,702 **Faculty:** FT 230, PT 294 **Student-Faculty Ratio:** 18:1 **% Receiving Financial Aid:** 11 **% Residing in College-Owned, -Operated, or -Affiliated Housing:** 3 **Library Holdings:** 650,000 **Regional Accreditation:** Southern Association of Colleges and Schools **Credit Hours For Degree:** 123 semester hours, Bachelors **Professional Accreditation:** AACSB, ABET, ACEHSA, AAMFT, NCATE

UNIVERSITY OF HOUSTON-DOWNTOWN
One Main St.
Houston, TX 77002-1001
Tel: (713)221-8000
Admissions: (713)221-5337
Fax: (713)221-8157
E-mail: uhdadmit@dt.uh.edu
Web Site: http://www.uhd.edu/
President/CEO: Dr. Max Castillo
Registrar: Penny Cureton
Admissions: Carmen Holland
Financial Aid: Latosha Jackson
Type: Comprehensive **Sex:** Coed **Affiliation:** University of Houston System **% Accepted:** 98 **Admission Plans:** Open Admission; Deferred Admission **Application Deadline:** July 01 **Application Fee:** $25.00 **H.S. Requirements:** High school diploma required; GED accepted **Costs Per Year:** Application fee: $25. State resident tuition: $3525 full-time. Nonresident tuition: $11,805 full-time. Mandatory fees: $694 full-time. **Scholarships:** Available **Calendar System:** Semester, Summer Session Available **Enrollment:** FT 5,904, PT 5,455, Grad 125 **Faculty:** FT 277, PT 296 **Student-Faculty Ratio:** 22:1 **% Receiving Financial Aid:** 44 **Regional Accreditation:** Southern Association of Colleges and Schools **Credit Hours For Degree:** 120 credit hours, Bachelors **ROTC:** Army **Professional Accreditation:** AACSB, ABET

UNIVERSITY OF HOUSTON-VICTORIA
3007 North Ben Wilson St.
Victoria, TX 77901-4450
Tel: (361)570-4848; 877-970-4848
Admissions: (361)570-4110
Fax: (361)572-9377
Web Site: http://www.vic.uh.edu/
President/CEO: Dr. Don Smith
Registrar: Trudy Wortham
Admissions: Margrete Rice
Financial Aid: Carolyn Mallory
Type: Two-Year Upper Division **Sex:** Coed **Affiliation:** University of Houston System **Application Deadline:** Rolling **Costs Per Year:** State resident tuition: $150 per semester hour part-time. Nonresident tuition: $426 per semester hour part-time. **Scholarships:** Available **Calendar System:** Semester, Summer Session Available **Enrollment:** FT 460, PT 769, Grad 1,262 **Faculty:** FT 74, PT 56 **Student-Faculty Ratio:** 16:1 **% Receiving Financial Aid:** 70 **Library Holdings:** 227,800 **Regional Accreditation:** Southern Association of Colleges and Schools **Credit Hours For Degree:** 122 semester hours, Bachelors **Professional Accreditation:** AACSB

UNIVERSITY OF THE INCARNATE WORD
4301 Broadway
San Antonio, TX 78209-6397
Tel: (210)829-6000
Free: 800-749-WORD
Admissions: (210)829-6005
Fax: (210)829-3921
E-mail: admis@uiwtx.edu
Web Site: http://www.uiw.edu/
President/CEO: Dr. Louis J. Agnese, Jr.
Registrar: Dr. Bobbye Fry
Admissions: Andrea Cyterski-Acosta

Financial Aid: Amy Carcanagnes
Type: Comprehensive **Sex:** Coed **Affiliation:** Roman Catholic **Scores:** 88% SAT V 400+; 85% SAT M 400+; 52% ACT 18-23; 14% ACT 24-29 **% Accepted:** 75 **Admission Plans:** Early Admission; Deferred Admission **Application Deadline:** Rolling **Application Fee:** $20.00 **H.S. Requirements:** High school diploma required; GED accepted **Costs Per Year:** Application fee: $20. One-time mandatory fee: $1500. Comprehensive fee: $24,747 includes full-time tuition ($17,400), mandatory fees ($872), and college room and board ($6475). College room only: $3800. Part-time tuition: $555 per semester hour. Part-time mandatory fees: $300 per term. **Scholarships:** Available **Calendar System:** Semester, Summer Session Available **Enrollment:** FT 2,597, PT 1,773, Grad 847 **Faculty:** FT 160, PT 284 **Student-Faculty Ratio:** 14:1 **Exams:** SAT I or ACT **% Receiving Financial Aid:** 75 **% Residing in College-Owned, -Operated, or -Affiliated Housing:** 20 **Library Holdings:** 257,651 **Regional Accreditation:** Southern Association of Colleges and Schools **Credit Hours For Degree:** 128 semester hours, Bachelors **ROTC:** Army, Air Force **Professional Accreditation:** AACN, ADtA, ACBSP, JRCNMT, NAST **Intercollegiate Athletics:** Baseball M; Basketball M & W; Cheerleading M & W; Cross-Country Running M & W; Golf M & W; Soccer M & W; Softball W; Swimming and Diving W; Tennis M & W; Volleyball W

UNIVERSITY OF MARY HARDIN-BAYLOR
900 College St.
Belton, TX 76513
Tel: (254)295-8642
Free: 800-727-8642
Admissions: (254)295-4520
Fax: (254)295-4535
E-mail: admissions@umhb.edu
Web Site: http://www.umhb.edu/
President/CEO: Dr. Jerry G. Bawcom
Registrar: Lillian Kroeger
Admissions: Robbin Steen
Financial Aid: Ron Brown
Type: Comprehensive **Sex:** Coed **Affiliation:** Southern Baptist **Scores:** 93% SAT V 400+; 93% SAT M 400+; 57% ACT 18-23; 37% ACT 24-29 **% Accepted:** 75 **Admission Plans:** Early Admission; Deferred Admission **Application Deadline:** Rolling **Application Fee:** $35.00 **H.S. Requirements:** High school diploma required; GED accepted **Costs Per Year:** Application fee: $35. Comprehensive fee: $19,910 includes full-time tuition ($14,250), mandatory fees ($1460), and college room and board ($4200). Part-time tuition: $475 per semester hour. Part-time mandatory fees: $47 per semester hour, $30 per term. **Scholarships:** Available **Calendar System:** Semester, Summer Session Available **Enrollment:** FT 2,270, PT 321, Grad 136 **Faculty:** FT 133, PT 94 **Student-Faculty Ratio:** 14:1 **Exams:** SAT I or ACT **% Receiving Financial Aid:** 74 **% Residing in College-Owned, -Operated, or -Affiliated Housing:** 48 **Library Holdings:** 153,120 **Regional Accreditation:** Southern Association of Colleges and Schools **Credit Hours For Degree:** 124 semester hours, Bachelors **ROTC:** Air Force **Professional Accreditation:** AACN, CSWE, NLN **Intercollegiate Athletics:** Baseball M; Basketball M & W; Football M; Golf M & W; Soccer M & W; Softball W; Tennis M & W; Volleyball W

UNIVERSITY OF NORTH TEXAS
PO Box 311277
Denton, TX 76203
Tel: (940)565-2000
Admissions: (940)565-3921
Fax: (940)565-2408
E-mail: undergrad@abn.unt.edu
Web Site: http://www.unt.edu/
President/CEO: Dr. Norval Pohl
Registrar: Lynn McCreary
Admissions: Marcilla Collinsworth
Financial Aid: Carolyn Cunningham
Type: University **Sex:** Coed **Scores:** 98% SAT V 400+; 99% SAT M 400+; 56% ACT 18-23; 37% ACT 24-29 **% Accepted:** 69 **Admission Plans:** Early Admission; Deferred Admission **Application Deadline:** June 15 **Application Fee:** $40.00 **H.S. Requirements:** High school diploma required; GED accepted **Costs Per Year:** Application fee: $40. State resident tuition: $3930 full-time, $131 per credit hour part-time. Nonresident tuition: $12,210 full-time, $407 per credit hour part-time. Mandatory fees: $1880 full-time, $488 per term part-time. Full-time tuition and fees vary according to course load. Part-time tuition and fees vary according to course load. College room and board: $5364. Room and board charges vary according to board plan and housing facility. **Scholarships:** Available **Calendar System:** Semester, Summer Session Available **Enrollment:** FT 19,830, PT 5,478, Grad 6,739 **Faculty:** FT 936, PT 477 **Student-Faculty Ratio:** 18:1 **Exams:** SAT I or ACT **% Receiving Financial Aid:** 45 **% Residing in College-Owned, -Operated, or -Affiliated Housing:** 23 **Library Holdings:** 2,072,646 **Regional Accreditation:** Southern Association of Colleges and Schools **Credit Hours For Degree:** 124 semester hours, Bachelors **ROTC:** Army, Navy **Professional Accreditation:** AACSB, ABET, ACEJMC, AAFCS, ACA, ALA, APA, ASLHA, CORE, CSWE, FIDER, NASM, NASPAA, NCATE, NRPA **Intercollegiate Athletics:** Baseball M; Basketball M & W; Bowling M & W; Cross-Country Running M & W; Fencing M & W; Football M; Golf M & W; Ice Hockey M; Lacrosse M & W; Rugby M; Sailing M & W; Soccer W; Softball W; Swimming and Diving M & W; Tennis M & W; Track and Field M & W; Ultimate Frisbee M & W; Volleyball W

UNIVERSITY OF PHOENIX-DALLAS CAMPUS
Churchill Tower
12400 Coit Rd., Ste. 100
Dallas, TX 75251
Tel: (972)385-1055
Free: 800-228-7240
Admissions: (480)557-1712
Fax: (972)385-1700
Web Site: http://www.phoenix.edu/
President/CEO: Lisa Browning
Admissions: Nina Omelchanko
Type: Comprehensive **Sex:** Coed **Admission Plans:** Open Admission; Deferred Admission **Application Deadline:** Rolling **Application Fee:** $110.00 **H.S. Requirements:** High school diploma required; GED accepted **Costs Per Year:** Application fee: $110. Tuition: $10,785 full-time, $359.50 per credit part-time. Mandatory fees: $560 full-time, $70 per course part-time. **Scholarships:** Available **Calendar System:** Continuous, Summer Session Not available **Enrollment:** FT 2,303, Grad 669 **Faculty:** FT 5, PT 238 **Student-Faculty Ratio:** 12:1 **Regional Accreditation:** North Central Association of Colleges and Schools **Credit Hours For Degree:** 60 credits, Associates; 120 credits, Bachelors

UNIVERSITY OF PHOENIX-HOUSTON CAMPUS
11451 Katy Freeway, Ste. 100
Houston, TX 77079-2004
Tel: (281)596-0363
Free: 800-228-7240
Admissions: (480)557-1712
Fax: (281)596-0336
Web Site: http://www.phoenix.edu/
President/CEO: Chad Bandy
Admissions: Nina Omelchanko
Type: Comprehensive **Sex:** Coed **Admission Plans:** Open Admission; Deferred Admission **Application Deadline:** Rolling **Application Fee:** $110.00 **H.S. Requirements:** High school diploma required; GED accepted **Costs Per Year:** Application fee: $110. Tuition: $10,785 full-time, $359.50 per credit part-time. Mandatory fees: $560 full-time, $70 per course part-time. **Scholarships:** Available **Calendar System:** Continuous, Summer Session Not available **Enrollment:** FT 3,914, Grad 894 **Faculty:** FT 7, PT 435 **Student-Faculty Ratio:** 13:1 **Regional Accreditation:** North Central Association of Colleges and Schools **Credit Hours For Degree:** 60 credits, Associates; 120 credits, Bachelors

UNIVERSITY OF ST. THOMAS
3800 Montrose Blvd.
Houston, TX 77006-4696
Tel: (713)522-7911
Free: 800-856-8565
Admissions: (713)525-3500
Fax: (713)525-3558
E-mail: admissions@basil.stthom.edu
Web Site: http://www.stthom.edu/
President/CEO: Dr. Robert Ivany
Admissions: Eduardo Prieto
Type: Comprehensive **Sex:** Coed **Affiliation:** Roman Catholic **Scores:** 98.72% SAT V 400+; 99.57% SAT M 400+; 41.86% ACT 18-23; 37.21% ACT 24-29 **% Accepted:** 92 **Admission Plans:** Deferred Admission **Application Deadline:** Rolling **Application Fee:** $35.00 **H.S. Requirements:** High school diploma required; GED accepted **Costs Per Year:** Application fee:

$35. Comprehensive fee: $23,810 includes full-time tuition ($16,950), mandatory fees ($160), and college room and board ($6700). College room only: $4000. Full-time tuition and fees vary according to course load. Room and board charges vary according to board plan and housing facility. Part-time tuition: $565 per credit hour. Part-time mandatory fees: $80 per term. Part-time tuition and fees vary according to course load. **Scholarships:** Available **Calendar System:** Semester, Summer Session Available **Enrollment:** FT 1,365, PT 519, Grad 1,806 **Faculty:** FT 121, PT 151 **Student-Faculty Ratio:** 14:1 **Exams:** SAT I or ACT **% Receiving Financial Aid:** 57 **% Residing in College-Owned, -Operated, or -Affiliated Housing:** 15 **Library Holdings:** 248,606 **Regional Accreditation:** Southern Association of Colleges and Schools **Credit Hours For Degree:** 126 credit hours, Bachelors **ROTC:** Army **Professional Accreditation:** ACIPE, ACBSP, ATS

THE UNIVERSITY OF TEXAS AT ARLINGTON
701 South Nedderman Dr.
Arlington, TX 76019
Tel: (817)272-2011
Admissions: (817)272-6287
Fax: (817)272-5656
E-mail: admissions@uta.edu
Web Site: http://www.uta.edu/
President/CEO: James Spaniolo
Registrar: Michael George
Admissions: Dr. Hans Gatterdam
Financial Aid: Karen Krause
Type: University **Sex:** Coed **Affiliation:** University of Texas System **Scores:** 92% SAT V 400+; 97% SAT M 400+; 60% ACT 18-23; 27% ACT 24-29 **% Accepted:** 79 **Admission Plans:** Early Admission; Deferred Admission **Application Deadline:** June 01 **Application Fee:** $35.00 **H.S. Requirements:** High school diploma required; GED not accepted **Costs Per Year:** Application fee: $35. State resident tuition: $3893 full-time, $134.50 per credit hour part-time. Nonresident tuition: $12,173 full-time, $410.50 per credit hour part-time. Mandatory fees: $1670 full-time, $59.58 per credit hour part-time, $102.50 per term part-time. Full-time tuition and fees vary according to course level, course load, and program. Part-time tuition and fees vary according to course level, course load, and program. College room and board: $5345. Room and board charges vary according to board plan and housing facility. **Scholarships:** Available **Calendar System:** Semester, Summer Session Available **Enrollment:** FT 13,995, PT 5,654, Grad 5,783 **Faculty:** FT 781, PT 332 **Student-Faculty Ratio:** 22:1 **Exams:** SAT I or ACT **% Receiving Financial Aid:** 52 **% Residing in College-Owned, -Operated, or -Affiliated Housing:** 14 **Library Holdings:** 1,135,943 **Regional Accreditation:** Southern Association of Colleges and Schools **Credit Hours For Degree:** 124 semester hours, Bachelors **ROTC:** Army, Air Force **Professional Accreditation:** AACSB, ABET, ACSP, ASLA, CSWE, FIDER, NASM, NASPAA, NCATE, NLN **Intercollegiate Athletics:** Baseball M; Basketball M & W; Cross-Country Running M & W; Golf M; Softball W; Tennis M & W; Track and Field M & W; Volleyball W

THE UNIVERSITY OF TEXAS AT AUSTIN
Austin, TX 78712-1111
Tel: (512)471-3434
Admissions: (512)475-7399
Fax: (512)475-7475
Web Site: http://www.utexas.edu/
President/CEO: Dr. Larry R. Faulkner
Registrar: Theodore E. Pfeifer
Admissions: Dr. Bruce Walker
Financial Aid: Lawrence W. Burt
Type: University **Sex:** Coed **Affiliation:** University of Texas System **Scores:** 98.73% SAT V 400+; 99.27% SAT M 400+; 23.81% ACT 18-23; 51.8% ACT 24-29 **% Accepted:** 51 **Admission Plans:** Preferred Admission; Deferred Admission **Application Deadline:** February 01 **Application Fee:** $60.00 **H.S. Requirements:** High school diploma required; GED accepted **Costs Per Year:** Application fee: $60. State resident tuition: $6972 full-time. Nonresident tuition: $16,310 full-time. Full-time tuition varies according to course load and program. College room and board: $7638. Room and board charges vary according to board plan, housing facility, and location. **Scholarships:** Available **Calendar System:** Semester, Summer Session Available **Enrollment:** FT 33,682, PT 3,196, Grad 11,232 **Faculty:** FT 2,482, PT 252 **Student-Faculty Ratio:** 18:1 **Exams:** SAT I or ACT, SAT II **% Receiving Financial Aid:** 52 **% Residing in College-Owned, -Operated, or -Affiliated Housing:** 18 **Regional Accreditation:** Southern Association of Colleges and Schools **Credit Hours For Degree:** 120 semester hours, Bachelors **ROTC:** Army, Navy, Air Force **Professional Accreditation:** AACSB, ABET, ACEJMC, AACN, ABA, ACPhE, ADtA, ACSP, ALA, APA, ASLHA, AALS, CORE, CSWE, FIDER, NASAD, NASD, NASM, NASPAA, NAST **Intercollegiate Athletics:** Baseball M; Basketball M & W; Crew W; Cross-Country Running M & W; Football M; Golf M & W; Soccer W; Softball W; Swimming and Diving M & W; Tennis M & W; Track and Field M & W; Volleyball W

THE UNIVERSITY OF TEXAS AT BROWNSVILLE
80 Fort Brown
Brownsville, TX 78520-4991
Tel: (956)544-8200
Admissions: (956)882-8295
Fax: (956)544-8832
E-mail: admissions@utb.edu
Web Site: http://www.utb.edu/
President/CEO: Dr. Juliet V. Garcia
Registrar: Albert Barreda
Admissions: Rene Villarreal
Financial Aid: Mavi F. Chapa
Type: Two-Year Upper Division **Sex:** Coed **Affiliation:** University of Texas System **% Accepted:** 100 **Admission Plans:** Open Admission; Early Admission **Application Deadline:** July 10 **Application Fee:** $0.00 **H.S. Requirements:** High school diploma or equivalent not required **Costs Per Year:** Application fee: $0. State resident tuition: $2256 full-time. Nonresident tuition: $8880 full-time. Mandatory fees: $943 full-time. College room only: $2300. **Scholarships:** Available **Calendar System:** Semester, Summer Session Available **Enrollment:** FT 5,560, PT 6,907, Grad 849 **Faculty:** FT 344, PT 315 **Student-Faculty Ratio:** 18:1 **% Receiving Financial Aid:** 79 **% Residing in College-Owned, -Operated, or -Affiliated Housing:** 1 **Library Holdings:** 174,660 **Regional Accreditation:** Southern Association of Colleges and Schools **Credit Hours For Degree:** 124 semester hours, Bachelors **Professional Accreditation:** JRCERT, NLN **Intercollegiate Athletics:** Baseball M; Golf M & W; Volleyball W

THE UNIVERSITY OF TEXAS AT DALLAS
PO Box 830688
Richardson, TX 75083-0688
Tel: (972)883-2111
Free: 800-889-2443
Admissions: (972)883-2270
Fax: (972)883-6803
E-mail: admissions-status@utdallas.edu
Web Site: http://www.utdallas.edu/
President/CEO: Dr. Franklyn G. Jenifer
Registrar: Karen Jarrell
Admissions: Bryan J. Bradford
Financial Aid: Maria Ramos
Type: University **Sex:** Coed **Affiliation:** University of Texas System **Scores:** 98% SAT V 400+; 100% SAT M 400+; 22% ACT 18-23; 54% ACT 24-29 **% Accepted:** 51 **Admission Plans:** Deferred Admission **Application Deadline:** July 01 **Application Fee:** $50.00 **H.S. Requirements:** High school diploma required; GED accepted. For first-year college students: High school diploma required; GED not accepted **Costs Per Year:** Application fee: $50. State resident tuition: $6831 full-time, $198 per credit part-time. Nonresident tuition: $15,111 full-time, $474 per credit part-time. Full-time tuition varies according to course load, degree level, and program. Part-time tuition varies according to course load, degree level, and program. College room and board: $6244. Room and board charges vary according to board plan and housing facility. **Scholarships:** Available **Calendar System:** Semester, Summer Session Available **Enrollment:** FT 6,613, PT 2,799, Grad 5,068 **Faculty:** FT 457, PT 239 **Student-Faculty Ratio:** 20:1 **Exams:** Other, SAT I or ACT **% Receiving Financial Aid:** 40 **% Residing in College-Owned, -Operated, or -Affiliated Housing:** 21 **Library Holdings:** 797,719 **Regional Accreditation:** Southern Association of Colleges and Schools **Credit Hours For Degree:** 120 semester hours, Bachelors **ROTC:** Army, Air Force **Professional Accreditation:** AACSB, ABET, ASLHA, NASPAA **Intercollegiate Athletics:** Baseball M; Basketball M & W; Cross-Country Running M & W; Golf M & W; Soccer M & W; Softball W; Tennis M & W; Volleyball W

THE UNIVERSITY OF TEXAS AT EL PASO
500 West University Ave.
El Paso, TX 79968-0001
Tel: (915)747-5000; 877-746-4636

Admissions: (915)747-5588
Fax: (915)747-5122
Web Site: http://www.utep.edu/
President/CEO: Dr. Diana Natalicio
Registrar: Miguel Sifuentes
Admissions: Dr. Tammie Campos-Aragon
Financial Aid: Raul H. Lerma
Type: University **Sex:** Coed **Scores:** 74.4% SAT V 400+; 79.4% SAT M 400+; 40.6% ACT 18-23; 8.2% ACT 24-29 **% Accepted:** 99 **Admission Plans:** Deferred Admission **Application Deadline:** July 31 **Application Fee:** $0.00 **H.S. Requirements:** High school diploma required; GED accepted **Costs Per Year:** Application fee: $0. State resident tuition: $3930 full-time, $131 per credit hour part-time. Nonresident tuition: $12,210 full-time. Mandatory fees: $1134 full-time. Part-time tuition varies according to course load. College room only: $4095. Room charges vary according to housing facility. **Scholarships:** Available **Calendar System:** Semester, Summer Session Available **Enrollment:** FT 10,975, PT 5,062, Grad 3,231 **Faculty:** FT 680, PT 379 **Student-Faculty Ratio:** 19:1 **Exams:** Other, SAT I or ACT **% Receiving Financial Aid:** 64 **% Residing in College-Owned, -Operated, or -Affiliated Housing:** 2 **Library Holdings:** 961,247 **Regional Accreditation:** Southern Association of Colleges and Schools **Credit Hours For Degree:** 123 semester hours, Bachelors **ROTC:** Army, Air Force **Professional Accreditation:** AACSB, ABET, AACN, ACNM, AOTA, APTA, ASLHA, CSWE, NAACLS, NASM, NASPAA **Intercollegiate Athletics:** Basketball M & W; Cross-Country Running M & W; Football M; Golf M; Riflery M & W; Tennis W; Track and Field M & W; Volleyball W

THE UNIVERSITY OF TEXAS HEALTH SCIENCE CENTER AT HOUSTON

PO Box 20036
Houston, TX 77225-0036
Tel: (713)500-3333
Admissions: (713)500-3361
Fax: (713)500-3026
E-mail: registrar@uth.tmc.edu
Web Site: http://www.uth.tmc.edu/
President/CEO: Dr. James T. Willerson
Registrar: Robert Jenkins
Admissions: Robert Jenkins
Financial Aid: Carl Gordon
Type: Two-Year Upper Division **Sex:** Coed **Affiliation:** University of Texas System **Admission Plans:** Preferred Admission **Application Fee:** $30.00 **H.S. Requirements:** High school diploma required; GED accepted **Costs Per Year:** Application fee: $30. State resident tuition: $4905 full-time, $105 per hour part-time. Nonresident tuition: $16,571 full-time, $364.50 per hour part-time. Mandatory fees: $697 full-time. Part-time tuition varies according to course load. **Scholarships:** Available **Calendar System:** Semester, Summer Session Not available **Enrollment:** FT 349, PT 32, Grad 1,932 **Faculty:** FT 1,015, PT 232 **% Receiving Financial Aid:** 57 **Library Holdings:** 339,062 **Regional Accreditation:** Southern Association of Colleges and Schools **Credit Hours For Degree:** 125 semester hours, Bachelors **ROTC:** Army **Professional Accreditation:** ABET, AACN, AANA, ADA, ADtA, APA, ASC, ACIPE, CEPH, JRCERT, LCMEAMA, NAACLS, NLN

THE UNIVERSITY OF TEXAS HEALTH SCIENCE CENTER AT SAN ANTONIO

7703 Floyd Curl Dr.
San Antonio, TX 78229-3900
Tel: (210)567-7000
Admissions: (210)567-2629
Fax: (210)567-2685
E-mail: peak@uthscsa.edu
Web Site: http://www.uthscsa.edu/
President/CEO: Dr. Francisco G. Cigarroa
Registrar: Debra Goode
Admissions: James B. Peak
Financial Aid: Robert Lawson
Type: Two-Year Upper Division **Sex:** Coed **Affiliation:** University of Texas System **Application Fee:** $50.00 **H.S. Requirements:** High school diploma required; GED accepted **Scholarships:** Available **Calendar System:** Semester, Summer Session Available **Student-Faculty Ratio:** 2:1 **Exams:** Other, SAT I or ACT **Library Holdings:** 192,576 **Regional Accreditation:** Southern Association of Colleges and Schools **Credit Hours For Degree:** 120 semester hours, Bachelors **ROTC:** Army, Air Force **Professional Accreditation:** AABB, AACN, ADA, AOTA, APTA, APA, CARC, JRCEMT, LCMEAMA, NAACLS

THE UNIVERSITY OF TEXAS MEDICAL BRANCH

301 University Blvd.
Galveston, TX 77555
Tel: (409)772-1011
Admissions: (409)772-1215
Fax: (409)772-5056
E-mail: student.admissions@utmb.edu
Web Site: http://www.utmb.edu/
President/CEO: Dr. John D. Stobo
Registrar: Vicki Brewer
Admissions: Vicki L. Brewer
Financial Aid: Ellen Gomes
Type: Two-Year Upper Division **Sex:** Coed **Affiliation:** University of Texas System **Admission Plans:** Preferred Admission **Application Fee:** $25.00 **Costs Per Year:** Application fee: $25. State resident tuition: $2160 full-time, $90 per credit hour part-time. Nonresident tuition: $8784 full-time, $366 per credit hour part-time. Mandatory fees: $530 full-time. College room only: $2322. **Scholarships:** Available **Calendar System:** Semester, Summer Session Available **Enrollment:** FT 269, PT 230, Grad 869 **Faculty:** FT 94, PT 8 **Student-Faculty Ratio:** 8:1 **Library Holdings:** 248,370 **Regional Accreditation:** Southern Association of Colleges and Schools **Credit Hours For Degree:** 120 semester hours, Bachelors **Professional Accreditation:** AACN, ACNM, AOTA, APTA, APA, CARC, CEPH, LCMEAMA, NAACLS, NLN

THE UNIVERSITY OF TEXAS-PAN AMERICAN

1201 West University Dr.
Edinburg, TX 78541-2999
Tel: (956)381-2011
Admissions: (956)381-2481
E-mail: admissions@panam.edu
Web Site: http://www.utpa.edu/
President/CEO: Dr. Miguel A. Nevarez
Registrar: David Zuniga
Admissions: Dr. Magdalena Williams
Financial Aid: Michelle Alvarado
Type: Comprehensive **Sex:** Coed **Affiliation:** University of Texas System **Scores:** 80% SAT V 400+; 83% SAT M 400+; 51% ACT 18-23; 10% ACT 24-29 **Admission Plans:** Early Admission **Application Deadline:** August 11 **Application Fee:** $0.00 **H.S. Requirements:** High school diploma required; GED accepted **Costs Per Year:** Application fee: $0. State resident tuition: $3348 full-time, $116 per semester hour part-time. Nonresident tuition: $11,598 full-time, $391 per semester hour part-time. Mandatory fees: $812 full-time, $98 per semester hour part-time. College room and board: $4333. College room only: $2406. **Scholarships:** Available **Calendar System:** Semester, Summer Session Available **Enrollment:** FT 10,617, PT 4,325, Grad 2,106 **Faculty:** FT 587, PT 119 **Student-Faculty Ratio:** 21:1 **Exams:** SAT I or ACT **% Receiving Financial Aid:** 82 **% Residing in College-Owned, -Operated, or -Affiliated Housing:** 1 **Library Holdings:** 572,162 **Regional Accreditation:** Southern Association of Colleges and Schools **Credit Hours For Degree:** 124 semester hours, Bachelors **ROTC:** Army **Professional Accreditation:** AACSB, ABET, AACN, ADtA, AOTA, ASLHA, CORE, CSWE, NAACLS, NAST **Intercollegiate Athletics:** Baseball M; Basketball M & W; Cross-Country Running M & W; Golf M & W; Tennis M & W; Track and Field M & W; Volleyball W

THE UNIVERSITY OF TEXAS OF THE PERMIAN BASIN

4901 East University Blvd.
Odessa, TX 79762-0001
Tel: (432)552-2020; (866)552-UTPB
Admissions: (432)552-2605
Fax: (432)552-2109
E-mail: gomez-v@gusher.pb.utexas.edu
Web Site: http://www.utpb.edu/
President/CEO: Dr. W. David Watts
Admissions: Vicki Gomez
Financial Aid: Robert Vasquez
Type: Comprehensive **Sex:** Coed **Affiliation:** University of Texas System **Scores:** 90% SAT V 400+; 91% SAT M 400+; 59% ACT 18-23; 17% ACT 24-29 **Admission Plans:** Deferred Admission **Application Fee:** $0.00 **H.S. Requirements:** High school diploma required; GED accepted **Scholar-**

ships: Available **Calendar System:** Semester, Summer Session Available **Enrollment:** FT 1,393, PT 619, Grad 683 **Faculty:** FT 103, PT 55 **Student-Faculty Ratio:** 18:1 **Exams:** Other, SAT I or ACT **% Receiving Financial Aid:** 67 **Library Holdings:** 257,531 **Regional Accreditation:** Southern Association of Colleges and Schools **Credit Hours For Degree:** 120 semester hours, Bachelors **Intercollegiate Athletics:** Baseball M; Basketball M & W; Cheerleading W; Soccer M & W; Softball W; Swimming and Diving M & W; Volleyball W

THE UNIVERSITY OF TEXAS AT SAN ANTONIO
6900 North Loop 1604 West
San Antonio, TX 78249-0617
Tel: (210)458-4011
Free: 800-669-0919
Admissions: (210)458-4530
Web Site: http://www.utsa.edu/
President/CEO: Dr. Ricardo Romo
Registrar: Dr. Joe DeCristoforo
Admissions: George Norton
Financial Aid: Lisa Blazer
Type: University **Sex:** Coed **Affiliation:** University of Texas System **Scores:** 93.19% SAT V 400+; 94.2% SAT M 400+; 61.16% ACT 18-23; 18.73% ACT 24-29 **% Accepted:** 99 **Application Deadline:** July 01 **Application Fee:** $30.00 **H.S. Requirements:** High school diploma required; GED accepted. For concurrent enrollment of high school students: High school diploma or equivalent not required **Costs Per Year:** Application fee: $30. State resident tuition: $3,968 full-time, $132.25 per hour part-time. Nonresident tuition: $12,248 full-time, $408.25 per hour part-time. Mandatory fees: $1890 full-time. College room and board: $7190. College room only: $4770. **Scholarships:** Available **Calendar System:** Semester, Summer Session Available **Enrollment:** FT 17,554, PT 5,877, Grad 3,906 **Faculty:** FT 860, PT 223 **Student-Faculty Ratio:** 23:1 **% Receiving Financial Aid:** 60 **Library Holdings:** 622,333 **Regional Accreditation:** Southern Association of Colleges and Schools **Credit Hours For Degree:** 120 semester hours, Bachelors **ROTC:** Army, Air Force **Professional Accreditation:** AACSB, ABET, AACN, FIDER, NASAD, NASM **Intercollegiate Athletics:** Baseball M; Basketball M & W; Cross-Country Running M & W; Golf M; Softball W; Tennis M & W; Track and Field M & W; Volleyball W

THE UNIVERSITY OF TEXAS SOUTHWESTERN MEDICAL CENTER AT DALLAS
5323 Harry Hines Blvd.
Dallas, TX 75390
Tel: (214)648-3111
Admissions: (214)648-5617
Fax: (214)648-3289
Web Site: http://www.utsouthwestern.edu/
President/CEO: Dr. Kern Wildenthal
Registrar: Charles Kettlewell
Admissions: Dr. Scott Wright
Financial Aid: Charles Kettlewell
Type: Two-Year Upper Division **Sex:** Coed **Affiliation:** University of Texas System **% Accepted:** 53 **Admission Plans:** Preferred Admission **Application Fee:** $10.00 **Costs Per Year:** Application fee: $10. State resident tuition: $2820 full-time, $48 per credit hour part-time. Nonresident tuition: $11,880 full-time, $350 per credit hour part-time. Full-time tuition varies according to course load. Part-time tuition varies according to course load. **Scholarships:** Available **Calendar System:** Semester, Summer Session Not available **Enrollment:** FT 97, PT 24, Grad 1,368 **Faculty:** FT 76, PT 27 **Library Holdings:** 257,782 **Regional Accreditation:** Southern Association of Colleges and Schools **Credit Hours For Degree:** 120 semester hours, Bachelors **Professional Accreditation:** ARCMI, ACNM, ADtA, APTA, APA, CORE, LCMEAMA, NAACLS, NANPWH, NCOPE

THE UNIVERSITY OF TEXAS AT TYLER
3900 University Blvd.
Tyler, TX 75799-0001
Tel: (903)566-7000
Admissions: (903)566-7195
Fax: (903)566-7068
Web Site: http://www.uttyler.edu/
President/CEO: Dr. Rodney Mabry
Registrar: Jim Hutto
Admissions: Jim Hutto
Financial Aid: Candice Garner
Type: Comprehensive **Sex:** Coed **Affiliation:** University of Texas System **Scores:** 98% SAT V 400+; 99% SAT M 400+; 60% ACT 18-23; 32% ACT 24-29 **% Accepted:** 75 **Admission Plans:** Deferred Admission **Application Fee:** $0.00 **H.S. Requirements:** High school diploma required; GED accepted **Costs Per Year:** Application fee: $0. State resident tuition: $3450 full-time, $115 per semester hour part-time. Nonresident tuition: $11,730 full-time, $391 per semester hour part-time. Mandatory fees: $800 full-time. Full-time tuition and fees vary according to course load and degree level. College room and board: $7010. Room and board charges vary according to housing facility. **Scholarships:** Available **Calendar System:** Semester, Summer Session Available **Enrollment:** FT 3,580, PT 1,077, Grad 1,091 **Faculty:** FT 218, PT 142 **Student-Faculty Ratio:** 17:1 **Exams:** SAT I or ACT **% Receiving Financial Aid:** 50 **% Residing in College-Owned, -Operated, or -Affiliated Housing:** 10 **Library Holdings:** 216,622 **Regional Accreditation:** Southern Association of Colleges and Schools **Credit Hours For Degree:** 124 semester hours, Bachelors **Professional Accreditation:** AACSB, ABET, AACN, NAIT, NLN **Intercollegiate Athletics:** Baseball M; Basketball M & W; Cheerleading M & W; Cross-Country Running M & W; Golf M & W; Soccer M & W; Tennis M & W; Volleyball W

VERNON COLLEGE
4400 College Dr.
Vernon, TX 76384-4092
Tel: (940)552-6291
Fax: (940)553-1753
Web Site: http://www.vernoncollege.edu/
President/CEO: Dr. Steve Thomas
Registrar: Joe Hite
Admissions: Joe Hite
Financial Aid: Melissa Elliott
Type: Two-Year College **Sex:** Coed **Admission Plans:** Open Admission; Early Admission **Application Fee:** $0.00 **H.S. Requirements:** High school diploma required; GED accepted **Scholarships:** Available **Calendar System:** Semester, Summer Session Available **Faculty:** FT 57, PT 71 **Student-Faculty Ratio:** 17:1 **Exams:** Other **Library Holdings:** 29,000 **Regional Accreditation:** Southern Association of Colleges and Schools **Credit Hours For Degree:** 60 semester hours, Associates **Professional Accreditation:** AHIMA **Intercollegiate Athletics:** Baseball M; Equestrian Sports M & W; Softball W; Volleyball W

VICTORIA COLLEGE
2200 East Red River
Victoria, TX 77901-4494
Tel: (361)573-3291
Fax: (361)572-3850
Web Site: http://www.victoriacollege.edu/
President/CEO: Dr. Jimmy Goodson
Registrar: Martha Watts
Admissions: Lavern Dentler
Financial Aid: Lauri Voss
Type: Two-Year College **Sex:** Coed **Admission Plans:** Open Admission **H.S. Requirements:** High school diploma required; GED accepted **Scholarships:** Available **Calendar System:** Semester, Summer Session Available **Exams:** Other, SAT I or ACT **Library Holdings:** 150,000 **Regional Accreditation:** Southern Association of Colleges and Schools **Credit Hours For Degree:** 62 semester hours, Associates **Professional Accreditation:** CARC, NAACLS, NLN

VIRGINIA COLLEGE AT AUSTIN
6301 East Hwy. 290
Austin, TX 78723
Tel: (512)371-3500
Fax: (512)371-3502
Web Site: http://www.vc.edu/ **Type:** Two-Year College **Sex:** Coed **Calendar System:** Quarter **Professional Accreditation:** ACICS

WADE COLLEGE
Ste. M5120, International Apparel Mart
PO Box 586343
Dallas, TX 75258-6343
Tel: (214)637-3530
Free: 800-624-4850
Fax: (214)637-0827

Web Site: http://www.wadecollege.edu/
President/CEO: Harry Davros
Admissions: Harry Davros
Type: Two-Year College **Sex:** Coed **Admission Plans:** Open Admission **Application Fee:** $0.00 **H.S. Requirements:** High school diploma required; GED accepted **Scholarships:** Available **Calendar System:** Trimester, Summer Session Available **Enrollment:** FT 177 **Faculty:** FT 4, PT 8 **Student-Faculty Ratio:** 16:1 **% Residing in College-Owned, -Operated, or -Affiliated Housing:** 45 **Library Holdings:** 7,000 **Regional Accreditation:** Southern Association of Colleges and Schools **Credit Hours For Degree:** 63 credits, Associates

WAYLAND BAPTIST UNIVERSITY
1900 West Seventh St.
Plainview, TX 79072-6998
Tel: (806)291-1000
Free: 800-588-1928
Admissions: (806)291-3500
Fax: (806)291-1960
E-mail: admityou@wbu.edu
Web Site: http://www.wbu.edu/
President/CEO: Dr. Paul Armes
Registrar: Stan DeMerritt
Admissions: Jennifer Beal
Financial Aid: Bob Womack
Type: Comprehensive **Sex:** Coed **Affiliation:** Baptist **Scores:** 87% SAT V 400+; 94% SAT M 400+; 46% ACT 18-23; 25% ACT 24-29 **% Accepted:** 65 **Application Deadline:** August 01 **Application Fee:** $35.00 **H.S. Requirements:** High school diploma required; GED accepted **Costs Per Year:** Application fee: $35. Comprehensive fee: $13,484 includes full-time tuition ($9450), mandatory fees ($450), and college room and board ($3584). College room only: $1276. Full-time tuition and fees vary according to course load and location. Room and board charges vary according to board plan and housing facility. Part-time tuition: $315 per credit hour. Part-time mandatory fees: $50 per term. Part-time tuition and fees vary according to course load and location. **Scholarships:** Available **Calendar System:** Semester, Summer Session Available **Enrollment:** FT 840, PT 164, Grad 120 **Faculty:** FT 67, PT 35 **Student-Faculty Ratio:** 12:1 **Exams:** ACT, SAT I or ACT **% Receiving Financial Aid:** 75 **% Residing in College-Owned, -Operated, or -Affiliated Housing:** 55 **Library Holdings:** 117,287 **Regional Accreditation:** Southern Association of Colleges and Schools **Credit Hours For Degree:** 60 semester hours, Associates; 124 semester hours, Bachelors **ROTC:** Army, Air Force **Professional Accreditation:** NASM **Intercollegiate Athletics:** Baseball M; Basketball M & W; Cheerleading M & W; Cross-Country Running M & W; Golf M; Track and Field M & W; Volleyball W

WEATHERFORD COLLEGE
225 College Park Ave.
Weatherford, TX 76086-5699
Tel: (817)594-5471
Free: 800-287-5471
Admissions: (817)598-6240
Fax: (817)598-6205
E-mail: durrett@wc.edu
Web Site: http://www.wc.edu/
President/CEO: Dr. Don Huff
Registrar: Arthur Stockstill
Admissions: Duane Durrett
Financial Aid: Kathy Bassham
Type: Two-Year College **Sex:** Coed **Admission Plans:** Open Admission; Early Admission **Application Deadline:** Rolling **Application Fee:** $0.00 **H.S. Requirements:** High school diploma required; GED accepted. For some adult applicants: High school diploma or equivalent not required **Costs Per Year:** Application fee: $0. Area resident tuition: $1456 full-time, $52 per hour part-time. State resident tuition: $1960 full-time, $70 per hour part-time. Nonresident tuition: $3164 full-time, $113 per hour part-time. College room and board: $6500. **Scholarships:** Available **Calendar System:** Semester, Summer Session Available **Enrollment:** FT 2,287, PT 2,265 **Faculty:** FT 95, PT 125 **Student-Faculty Ratio:** 22:1 **% Residing in College-Owned, -Operated, or -Affiliated Housing:** 7 **Library Holdings:** 59,499 **Regional Accreditation:** Southern Association of Colleges and Schools **Credit Hours For Degree:** 63 semester hours, Associates **ROTC:** Air Force **Professional Accreditation:** CARC **Intercollegiate Athletics:** Baseball M; Basketball M & W; Cheerleading W; Tennis W

WEST TEXAS A&M UNIVERSITY
2501 4th Ave.
Canyon, TX 79016-0001
Tel: (806)651-2000
Free: 800-99-WTAMU
Admissions: (806)651-2020
Fax: (806)651-2126
E-mail: admissions@mail.wtamu.edu
Web Site: http://www.wtamu.edu/
President/CEO: Dr. Russell C. Long
Registrar: Anita Loshbough
Admissions: Lila Vars
Financial Aid: James D. Reed
Type: Comprehensive **Sex:** Coed **Affiliation:** Texas A&M University System **Scores:** 90.3% SAT V 400+; 91.3% SAT M 400+; 59.4% ACT 18-23; 21.7% ACT 24-29 **% Accepted:** 73 **Application Deadline:** Rolling **Application Fee:** $25.00 **H.S. Requirements:** High school diploma required; GED accepted **Costs Per Year:** Application fee: $25. State resident tuition: $2760 full-time. Nonresident tuition: $11,040 full-time. Mandatory fees: $996 full-time. College room and board: $4916. College room only: $2300. **Scholarships:** Available **Calendar System:** Semester, Summer Session Available **Enrollment:** FT 4,461, PT 1,334, Grad 2,872 **Faculty:** FT 246, PT 75 **Student-Faculty Ratio:** 24:1 **Exams:** SAT I or ACT **% Receiving Financial Aid:** 56 **% Residing in College-Owned, -Operated, or -Affiliated Housing:** 19 **Library Holdings:** 1,081,010 **Regional Accreditation:** Southern Association of Colleges and Schools **Credit Hours For Degree:** 127 semester hours, Bachelors **Professional Accreditation:** AACN, ASLHA, ACBSP, CSWE, NASM **Intercollegiate Athletics:** Baseball M; Basketball M & W; Bowling M & W; Cross-Country Running M & W; Equestrian Sports M & W; Football M; Golf M & W; Soccer M & W; Softball W; Volleyball W

WESTERN TECHNICAL COLLEGE
1000 Texas Ave.
El Paso, TX 79901-1536
Tel: (915)532-3737
Web Site: http://www.wtc-ep.edu/
President/CEO: Randy Kuykendall
Admissions: Bill Terrell
Financial Aid: Jennifer Phillips
Type: Two-Year College **Sex:** Coed **Admission Plans:** Open Admission; Early Admission; Deferred Admission **H.S. Requirements:** High school diploma required; GED accepted **Calendar System:** Continuous **Enrollment:** FT 600, PT 225 **Faculty:** FT 98, PT 32 **Student-Faculty Ratio:** 18:1 **Professional Accreditation:** ACCSCT

WESTERN TECHNICAL INSTITUTE
9451 Diana
El Paso, TX 79930-2610
Tel: (915)566-9621
Admissions: 800-225-5984
Web Site: http://www.wti-ep.com/
President/CEO: Randy Kuykendall
Admissions: Bill Terrell
Financial Aid: Isabel Nino-Olivas
Type: Two-Year College **Scholarships:** Available **Professional Accreditation:** ACCSCT

WESTERN TEXAS COLLEGE
6200 College Ave.
Snyder, TX 79549-6105
Tel: (325)573-8511; 888-GO-TO-WTC
E-mail: jclifton@wtc.cc.tx.us
Web Site: http://www.wtc.edu/
President/CEO: Dr. Gregory Williams
Registrar: Ann Galyean
Admissions: Dr. Jim Clifton
Financial Aid: Kathy Hall
Type: Two-Year College **Sex:** Coed **Admission Plans:** Open Admission; Early Admission; Deferred Admission **H.S. Requirements:** High school diploma required; GED accepted **Scholarships:** Available **Calendar System:** Semester, Summer Session Available **Faculty:** FT 48, PT 16

Student-Faculty Ratio: 17:1 **Exams:** ACT, Other **% Residing in College-Owned, -Operated, or -Affiliated Housing:** 20 **Library Holdings:** 43,000 **Regional Accreditation:** Southern Association of Colleges and Schools **Credit Hours For Degree:** 62 semester hours, Associates **Intercollegiate Athletics:** Baseball M; Softball W

WESTWOOD COLLEGE-DALLAS
Executive Plaza I, Ste. 100
Dallas, TX 75243
Tel: (214)570-0100
Free: 800-281-2978
Admissions: 800-803-3140
Fax: (214)570-8502
Web Site: http://www.westwood.edu/
Admissions: Eric Southwell
Type: Two-Year College **Sex:** Coed **Calendar System:** Continuous **Enrollment:** FT 397, PT 7 **Professional Accreditation:** ACICS

WESTWOOD COLLEGE-FORT WORTH
1331 Airport Freeway, Ste. 402
Euless, TX 76040
Tel: (817)605-8111
Admissions: (817)685-9994
Fax: (817)605-6972
Web Site: http://www.westwood.edu/
Admissions: Lisa Hecht
Type: Two-Year College **Sex:** Coed **Scholarships:** Available **Calendar System:** Continuous **Enrollment:** FT 375, PT 97 **Professional Accreditation:** ACICS

WESTWOOD COLLEGE-HOUSTON SOUTH CAMPUS
One Arena Place, 7322 Southwest Freeway, Ste. 1900
Houston, TX 77074
Tel: (713)777-4433
Free: 800-281-2978
Fax: (713)219-2088
Web Site: http://www.westwood.edu/
President/CEO: Rick Skinner
Type: Two-Year College **Sex:** Coed **% Accepted:** 66 **Calendar System:** Continuous **Enrollment:** FT 16 **Professional Accreditation:** ACCSCT

WHARTON COUNTY JUNIOR COLLEGE
911 Boling Hwy.
Wharton, TX 77488-3298
Tel: (979)532-4560
Admissions: (979)532-6381
Web Site: http://www.wcjc.edu/
President/CEO: Betty A. McCrohan
Admissions: Albert Barnes
Financial Aid: Richard Hyde
Type: Two-Year College **Sex:** Coed **Admission Plans:** Open Admission **Application Deadline:** August 14 **Application Fee:** $10.00 **H.S. Requirements:** High school diploma required; GED accepted **Costs Per Year:** Application fee: $10. Area resident tuition: $1296 full-time, $54 per semester hour part-time. State resident tuition: $2160 full-time, $90 per semester hour part-time. Nonresident tuition: $2928 full-time, $122 per semester hour part-time. College room and board: $2500. College room only: $600. **Scholarships:** Available **Calendar System:** Semester, Summer Session Available **Faculty:** FT 136, PT 121 **Student-Faculty Ratio:** 22:1 **% Residing in College-Owned, -Operated, or -Affiliated Housing:** 5 **Library Holdings:** 51,478 **Regional Accreditation:** Southern Association of Colleges and Schools **Credit Hours For Degree:** 62 semester hours, Associates **Professional Accreditation:** ADA, AHIMA, APTA, JRCERT **Intercollegiate Athletics:** Baseball M; Volleyball W

WILEY COLLEGE
711 Wiley Ave.
Marshall, TX 75670-5199
Tel: (903)927-3300
Free: 800-658-6889
Admissions: (903)927-3356
Fax: (903)938-8100
Web Site: http://www.wileyc.edu/
President/CEO: Dr. Haywood L. Strickland
Registrar: Charles Hanks
Admissions: Lalita Estes
Financial Aid: Dr. Reginald Brazzle
Type: Four-Year College **Sex:** Coed **Affiliation:** United Methodist Church **Scores:** 41% SAT V 400+; 47.3% SAT M 400+; 10% ACT 18-23 **Admission Plans:** Early Admission; Deferred Admission **Application Fee:** $10.00 **H.S. Requirements:** High school diploma required; GED accepted **Scholarships:** Available **Calendar System:** Semester, Summer Session Available **Enrollment:** FT 648, PT 18 **Faculty:** FT 50, PT 7 **Student-Faculty Ratio:** 8:1 **Exams:** SAT I or ACT **% Receiving Financial Aid:** 92 **Library Holdings:** 24,000 **Regional Accreditation:** Southern Association of Colleges and Schools **Credit Hours For Degree:** 65 credit hours, Associates; 124 credit hours, Bachelors **Intercollegiate Athletics:** Basketball M & W; Track and Field M & W; Volleyball W

UNIVERSITY OF THE VIRGIN ISLANDS
2 John Brewers Bay
St. Thomas, VI 00802-9990
Tel: (340)776-9200
Admissions: (340)693-1224
E-mail: cooke@adminen.uvi.edu
Web Site: http://www.uvi.edu/
President/CEO: Dr. LaVerne E. Ragster
Registrar: Luther Renee
Admissions: Carolyn Cook
Financial Aid: Mavis Gilchrist
Type: Comprehensive **Sex:** Coed **Scores:** 63% SAT V 400+; 52% SAT M 400+ **% Accepted:** 72 **Admission Plans:** Early Admission; Early Action; Deferred Admission **Application Deadline:** April 30 **Application Fee:** $25.00 **H.S. Requirements:** High school diploma required; GED accepted **Costs Per Year:** Application fee: $25. Territory resident tuition: $3300 full-time, $110 per credit part-time. Nonresident tuition: $9900 full-time, $330 per credit part-time. Mandatory fees: $426 full-time, $276 per year part-time. Full-time tuition and fees vary according to course load, degree level, and program. Part-time tuition and fees vary according to course load, degree level, and program. College room and board: $7550. College room only: $1100. Room and board charges vary according to board plan and housing facility. **Scholarships:** Available **Calendar System:** Semester, Summer Session Available **Enrollment:** FT 1,227, PT 958, Grad 207 **Faculty:** FT 107, PT 152 **Student-Faculty Ratio:** 13:1 **Exams:** SAT I or ACT **% Receiving Financial Aid:** 80 **Library Holdings:** 106,361 **Regional Accreditation:** Middle State Association of Colleges and Schools **Credit Hours For Degree:** 62 semester hours, Associates; 120 semester hours, Bachelors **ROTC:** Army **Professional Accreditation:** ACBSP, NLN **Intercollegiate Athletics:** Basketball M & W; Cheerleading M & W; Cross-Country Running M & W; Tennis M & W; Track and Field M & W; Volleyball M & W

BRIGHAM YOUNG UNIVERSITY
Provo, UT 84602-1001
Tel: (801)422-1211
Admissions: (801)422-2507
Fax: (801)422-5278
E-mail: admissions@byu.edu
Web Site: http://www.byu.edu/
President/CEO: Dr. Cecil O. Samuelson
Registrar: Gene F. Priday
Admissions: Tom Gourley
Financial Aid: Paul R. Conrad
Type: University **Sex:** Coed **Affiliation:** The Church of Jesus Christ of Latter-day Saints **Scores:** 99% SAT V 400+; 100% SAT M 400+; 16% ACT 18-23; 61% ACT 24-29 **% Accepted:** 78 **Admission Plans:** Early Admission; Deferred Admission **Application Deadline:** February 15 **Application Fee:** $30.00 **H.S. Requirements:** High school diploma required; GED accepted **Costs Per Year:** Application fee: $30. Comprehensive fee: $10,906 includes full-time tuition ($5116) and college room and board ($5790). Full-time tuition varies according to reciprocity agreements. Room and board charges vary according to board plan and housing facility. **Scholarships:** Available **Calendar System:** Semester, Summer Session Available **Enrollment:** FT 27,460, PT 3,338, Grad 2,808 **Faculty:** FT 1,321, PT 441 **Student-Faculty Ratio:** 21:1 **Exams:** ACT, SAT I or ACT **% Receiving Financial Aid:** 36 **% Residing in College-Owned, -Operated, or -Affiliated Housing:** 20 **Library Holdings:** 3,539,032 **Credit Hours For Degree:** 120 credits, Bachelors **ROTC:** Army, Air Force **Professional Accreditation:** AACSB, ABET, ACEJMC, AAMFT, ABA, ACCE, ACA, ADtA, APA, ASLHA, AALS, CSWE, JRCEPAT, NAACLS, NASAD, NASD, NASM, NASPAA, NAST, NCATE NLN, NRPA, NCCU **Intercollegiate Athletics:** Baseball M; Basketball M & W; Cheerleading M & W; Cross-Country Running M & W; Football M; Golf M & W; Gymnastics W; Lacrosse M; Racquetball M & W; Rugby M; Soccer M & W; Softball W; Swimming and Diving M & W; Tennis M & W; Track and Field M & W; Volleyball M & W

CALIFORNIA COLLEGE FOR HEALTH SCIENCES
5295 South Commerce Dr.
Salt Lake City, UT 84107
Tel: 800-221-7374
Free: 800-791-7353
Fax: (801)263-0345
E-mail: admissions@cchs.edu
Web Site: http://www.cchs.edu/
President/CEO: Roy Winter
Registrar: Marita Gubbe
Admissions: Deborah Hopkins
Financial Aid: Gilda Maldonado
Type: Comprehensive **Sex:** Coed **Admission Plans:** Open Admission; Deferred Admission **Application Fee:** $100.00 **H.S. Requirements:** High school diploma required; GED accepted **Costs Per Year:** Application fee: $100. Tuition guaranteed not to increase for student's term of enrollment. **Scholarships:** Available **Calendar System:** Continuous, Summer Session Not available **Faculty:** FT 0, PT 34 **% Receiving Financial Aid:** 96 **Credit Hours For Degree:** 60 semester hours, Associates; 120 semester hours, Bachelors **Professional Accreditation:** ACCSCT, CARC, DETC

COLLEGE OF EASTERN UTAH
451 East 400 North
Price, UT 84501-2699
Tel: (435)637-2120
Admissions: (435)613-5217
Fax: (435)637-4102
E-mail: todd.olson@ceu.edu
Web Site: http://www.ceu.edu/
President/CEO: Dr. Ryan L. Thomas
Registrar: Jan Young
Admissions: Todd Olsen
Financial Aid: Bill Osborn
Type: Two-Year College **Sex:** Coed **Affiliation:** Utah System of Higher Education **Scores:** 49.1% ACT 18-23; 16.2% ACT 24-29 **% Accepted:** 100 **Admission Plans:** Open Admission; Early Admission **Application Deadline:** Rolling **Application Fee:** $25.00 **H.S. Requirements:** High school diploma required; GED accepted **Costs Per Year:** Application fee: $25. State resident tuition: $2090 full-time, $88 per credit hour part-time. Nonresident tuition: $7122 full-time, $339 per credit hour part-time. Mandatory fees: $17.08 per credit hour part-time. College room and board: $3392. **Scholarships:** Available **Calendar System:** Semester, Summer Session Available **Enrollment:** FT 1,317, PT 977 **Faculty:** FT 71, PT 118 **Student-Faculty Ratio:** 15:1 **Exams:** ACT **% Residing in College-Owned, -Operated, or -Affiliated Housing:** 15 **Library Holdings:** 44,490 **Credit Hours For Degree:** 63 credits, Associates **Professional Accreditation:** NLN, NCCU **Intercollegiate Athletics:** Baseball M; Basketball M & W; Golf M & W; Volleyball W

DIXIE STATE COLLEGE OF UTAH
225 South 700 East
St. George, UT 84770-3876
Tel: (435)652-7500; 888-GO2DIXIE
Admissions: (435)652-7704
Fax: (435)656-4005
Web Site: http://www.dixie.edu/
President/CEO: Dr. Robert Huddleston
Admissions: David Roos
Financial Aid: Peggy N. Leavitt
Type: Two-Year College **Sex:** Coed **Affiliation:** Utah System of Higher Education **Scores:** 85% SAT V 400+; 75% SAT M 400+; 55% ACT 18-23; 19% ACT 24-29 **% Accepted:** 85 **Admission Plans:** Open Admission; Early Admission; Deferred Admission **Application Deadline:** Rolling **Application Fee:** $25.00 **H.S. Requirements:** High school diploma required; GED accepted **Costs Per Year:** Application fee: $25. State resident tuition: $2100 full-time, $88 per credit part-time. Nonresident tuition: $8664 full-time, $361 per credit part-time. Mandatory fees: $392 full-time. **Scholarships:** Available **Calendar System:** Semester, Summer Session Available **Enrollment:** FT 3,395, PT 5,597 **Faculty:** FT 95, PT 258 **Student-Faculty Ratio:** 19:1 **% Residing in College-Owned, -Operated, or -Affiliated Housing:** 2 **Library Holdings:** 94,747 **Credit Hours For Degree:** 63 credits, Associates; 121 credits, Bachelors **Professional Accreditation:** ADA, JRCEMT, NCCU **Intercollegiate Athletics:** Baseball M; Basketball M & W; Football M; Golf M; Soccer W; Softball W; Volleyball W

ITT TECHNICAL INSTITUTE
920 West Levoy Dr.
Murray, UT 84123-2500
Tel: (801)263-3313
Free: 800-365-2136
Web Site: http://www.itt-tech.edu/
President/CEO: Dr. P. Michael Linzmaier
Registrar: Tonya Purdie
Admissions: Christopher J. Bowcutt
Financial Aid: Christopher J. Bowcutt
Type: Two-Year College **Sex:** Coed **Affiliation:** ITT Educational Services, Inc **Admission Plans:** Deferred Admission **Application Deadline:** Rolling **Application Fee:** $100.00 **H.S. Requirements:** High school diploma required; GED accepted **Costs Per Year:** Application fee: $100. **Scholarships:** Available **Calendar System:** Quarter, Summer Session Not available **Exams:** Other **Credit Hours For Degree:** 96 credit hours, Associates; 180 credit hours, Bachelors **Professional Accreditation:** ACICS

LDS BUSINESS COLLEGE
411 East South Temple St.
Salt Lake City, UT 84111-1392
Tel: (801)524-8100
Free: 800-999-5767
Admissions: (801)524-8144
Fax: (801)524-1900
E-mail: renae@ldsbc.edu
Web Site: http://www.ldsbc.edu/
President/CEO: Stephen K. Woodhouse
Registrar: Linda Doran
Admissions: Renae L. Richards
Financial Aid: J. Douglas Horne
Type: Two-Year College **Sex:** Coed **Affiliation:** The Church of Jesus Christ of Latter-day Saints **Admission Plans:** Open Admission; Early Admission; Deferred Admission **Application Fee:** $25.00 **H.S. Requirements:** High school diploma required; GED accepted **Costs Per Year:** Application fee: $25. Tuition: $2480 full-time. Full-time tuition varies according to course load. College room only: $2236. **Scholarships:** Available **Calendar System:** Semester, Summer Session Available **Enrollment:** FT 960, PT 322 **Faculty:** FT 14, PT 81 **Student-Faculty Ratio:** 20:1 **Exams:** ACT **% Residing in College-Owned, -Operated, or -Affiliated Housing:** 13 **Library Holdings:** 24,000 **Credit Hours For Degree:** 62 credit hours, Associates **Professional Accreditation:** AAMAE, NCCU

MIDWIVES COLLEGE OF UTAH
560 South State St., Ste. B2
Orem, UT 84058
Tel: (801)764-9068; (866)764-9068
Fax: (801)434-8704
Web Site: http://www.midwifery.edu/
Registrar: Melissa Menatti
Admissions: Jodie Fisher
Type: Comprehensive **Sex:** Women **% Accepted:** 100 **Calendar System:** Semester **Enrollment:** , PT 66, Grad 7 **Student-Faculty Ratio:** 1:1 **Professional Accreditation:** MEAC

MOUNTAIN WEST COLLEGE
3280 West 3500 South
West Valley City, UT 84119
Tel: (801)840-4800
Fax: (801)969-0828
E-mail: jasonp@cci.edu
Web Site: http://www.mwcollege.com/
President/CEO: Larry Banks
Registrar: L. Dene Samora
Admissions: Jason Peterson
Financial Aid: John Zastowney
Type: Two-Year College **Sex:** Coed **Affiliation:** Corinthian Colleges, Inc **Admission Plans:** Deferred Admission **H.S. Requirements:** High school diploma required; GED accepted **Scholarships:** Available **Calendar System:** Quarter, Summer Session Available **Faculty:** FT 12, PT 65 **Student-Faculty Ratio:** 15:1 **Exams:** Other, SAT I or ACT **Library Holdings:** 5,250 **Credit Hours For Degree:** 90 quarter hours, Associates **Professional Accreditation:** ACICS, AAMAE

NEUMONT UNIVERSITY
2755 East Cottonwood Parkway, Ste. 600
Salt Lake City, UT 84121
Tel: (801)438-1100; (866)622-3448
Admissions: (801)733-2833
Fax: (801)438-1111
E-mail: jamie.wyse@northface.edu
Web Site: http://www.neumont.edu/
President/CEO: H. Scott McKinley
Admissions: Robert Doxey
Type: Four-Year College **Sex:** Coed **Affiliation:** Morrison University **Application Fee:** $35.00 **H.S. Requirements:** High school diploma required; GED accepted **Calendar System:** Quarter **Enrollment:** FT 140 **Faculty:** FT 25, PT 5 **Student-Faculty Ratio:** 5:1 **Exams:** SAT I and SAT II or ACT **% Residing in College-Owned, -Operated, or -Affiliated Housing:** 30 **Professional Accreditation:** ACICS

PROVO COLLEGE
1450 West 820 North
Provo, UT 84601
Tel: (801)375-1861
Free: 800-748-4834
Fax: (801)375-9728
E-mail: gordonp@provocollege.org
Web Site: http://www.provocollege.com/
President/CEO: Gordon Peters
Admissions: Gordon Peters
Type: Two-Year College **Sex:** Coed **Professional Accreditation:** ACCSCT, ADA, APTA

SALT LAKE COMMUNITY COLLEGE
PO Box 30808
Salt Lake City, UT 84130-0808
Tel: (801)957-4111
Admissions: (801)957-4186
Fax: (801)957-4958
E-mail: janet.felker@slcc.edu
Web Site: http://www.slcc.edu/
President/CEO: Judd D. Morgan
Registrar: Loren Evans
Admissions: Janet Felker
Financial Aid: Cristi Easton
Type: Two-Year College **Sex:** Coed **Affiliation:** Utah System of Higher Education **% Accepted:** 100 **Admission Plans:** Open Admission; Early Admission; Deferred Admission **Application Deadline:** Rolling **Application Fee:** $35.00 **H.S. Requirements:** High school diploma or equivalent not required. For health science programs: High school diploma required; GED not accepted **Costs Per Year:** Application fee: $35. State resident tuition: $2046 full-time. Nonresident tuition: $7161 full-time. Mandatory fees: $358 full-time. **Scholarships:** Available **Calendar System:** Semester, Summer Session Available **Enrollment:** FT 8,165, PT 15,946 **Faculty:** FT 347, PT 936 **Student-Faculty Ratio:** 18:1 **Library Holdings:** 96,470 **Credit Hours For Degree:** 60 credits, Associates **ROTC:** Army, Air Force **Professional Accreditation:** ACF, ADA, AOTA, APTA, ACBSP, JRCERT, NAACLS, NLN, NCCU **Intercollegiate Athletics:** Baseball M; Basketball M & W; Cheerleading M & W; Soccer M & W; Softball W; Volleyball W

SNOW COLLEGE
150 East College Ave.
Ephraim, UT 84627-1203
Tel: (435)283-7000
Admissions: (435)283-7321
Fax: (435)283-6879
Web Site: http://www.snow.edu/
President/CEO: Dr. Michael T. Benson
Registrar: Margie Anderson
Admissions: Katie Jean Larsen
Financial Aid: Jack Dalene
Type: Two-Year College **Sex:** Coed **Affiliation:** Utah System of Higher Education **Scores:** 45% ACT 18-23; 30% ACT 24-29 **% Accepted:** 75 **Admission Plans:** Open Admission; Early Admission **Application Deadline:** June 15 **Application Fee:** $30.00 **H.S. Requirements:** High

school diploma required; GED accepted **Costs Per Year:** Application fee: $30. State resident tuition: $1784 full-time, $60 per credit hour part-time. Nonresident tuition: $7118 full-time, $237 per credit hour part-time. Mandatory fees: $380 full-time, $380 per term part-time. College room and board: $4500. **Scholarships:** Available **Calendar System:** Semester, Summer Session Available **Enrollment:** FT 2,463, PT 870 **Faculty:** FT 120, PT 133 **Student-Faculty Ratio:** 13:1 **% Residing in College-Owned, -Operated, or -Affiliated Housing:** 10 **Library Holdings:** 31,911 **Credit Hours For Degree:** 63 semester credits, Associates **Professional Accreditation:** NASM, NCCU **Intercollegiate Athletics:** Baseball M; Basketball M & W; Football M; Golf M; Softball W; Volleyball W

SOUTHERN UTAH UNIVERSITY
351 West University Blvd.
Cedar City, UT 84720-2498
Tel: (435)586-7700
Admissions: (801)586-7740
Fax: (435)586-5475
E-mail: adminfo@suu.edu
Web Site: http://www.suu.edu/
President/CEO: Dr. Steven D. Bennion
Registrar: Maxine Stolk
Admissions: Dale S. Orton
Financial Aid: Paul C. Morris
Type: Comprehensive **Sex:** Coed **Affiliation:** Utah System of Higher Education **Scores:** 89.74% SAT V 400+; 93.16% SAT M 400+; 51.42% ACT 18-23; 28.3% ACT 24-29 **% Accepted:** 80 **Admission Plans:** Early Admission; Deferred Admission **Application Deadline:** August 01 **Application Fee:** $35.00 **H.S. Requirements:** High school diploma required; GED accepted **Costs Per Year:** Application fee: $35. State resident tuition: $2834 full-time, $139 per credit hour part-time. Nonresident tuition: $9354 full-time, $461 per credit hour part-time. Mandatory fees: $524 full-time, $23 per credit hour part-time. Part-time tuition and fees vary according to course load. College room and board: $5400. College room only: $2400. Room and board charges vary according to board plan and housing facility. **Scholarships:** Available **Calendar System:** Semester, Summer Session Available **Enrollment:** FT 4,599, PT 1,866, Grad 394 **Faculty:** FT 211, PT 63 **Student-Faculty Ratio:** 23:1 **Exams:** SAT I or ACT **% Receiving Financial Aid:** 56 **% Residing in College-Owned, -Operated, or -Affiliated Housing:** 13 **Library Holdings:** 180,424 **ROTC:** Army **Professional Accreditation:** AAFCS, ACBSP, NASM, NCATE, NCCU **Intercollegiate Athletics:** Baseball M; Basketball M & W; Cross-Country Running M & W; Football M; Golf M; Gymnastics W; Softball W; Tennis W; Track and Field M & W

STEVENS-HENAGER COLLEGE
1890 West 1350 St.
Ogden, UT 84401-0251
Tel: (801)394-7791
Free: 800-371-7791
Fax: (801)393-1745
Web Site: http://www.stevenshenager.edu/
President/CEO: Vicky Dewsnup
Registrar: Jill Dewsnup
Admissions: Wynn Hurtado
Financial Aid: Lana Moon
Type: Two-Year College **Sex:** Coed **Affiliation:** CollegeAmerica, Inc **Admission Plans:** Open Admission; Early Admission; Deferred Admission **Application Fee:** $25.00 **H.S. Requirements:** High school diploma required; GED accepted **Scholarships:** Available **Calendar System:** Quarter, Summer Session Not available **Enrollment:** FT 479 **Faculty:** FT 12, PT 28 **Student-Faculty Ratio:** 17:1 **Exams:** Other, SAT I or ACT **Library Holdings:** 6,500 **Professional Accreditation:** ARCEST, AAMAE

UNIVERSITY OF PHOENIX-UTAH CAMPUS
5373 South Green St.
Salt Lake City, UT 84123-4617
Tel: (801)263-1444
Free: 800-228-7240
Admissions: (480)557-1712
Fax: (801)269-9766
Web Site: http://www.phoenix.edu/
President/CEO: Darris Howe
Admissions: Nina Omelchanko
Type: Comprehensive **Sex:** Coed **% Accepted:** 98 **Admission Plans:** Open Admission; Deferred Admission **Application Deadline:** Rolling **Application Fee:** $110.00 **H.S. Requirements:** High school diploma required; GED accepted **Costs Per Year:** Application fee: $110. Tuition: $10,020 full-time, $344 per credit part-time. Mandatory fees: $560 full-time, $70 per course part-time. **Scholarships:** Available **Calendar System:** Continuous, Summer Session Not available **Enrollment:** FT 2,663, Grad 1,472 **Faculty:** FT 8, PT 380 **Student-Faculty Ratio:** 9:1 **Library Holdings:** 444 **Regional Accreditation:** North Central Association of Colleges and Schools **Credit Hours For Degree:** 60 credits, Associates; 120 credits, Bachelors **Professional Accreditation:** ACA, NLN

UNIVERSITY OF UTAH
201 South University St.
Salt Lake City, UT 84112-1107
Tel: (801)581-7200
Free: 800-444-8638
Admissions: (801)581-7281
Fax: (801)585-3034
Web Site: http://www.utah.edu/
President/CEO: Michael K. Young, JD
Registrar: Ralph Boren
Admissions: John W. Boswell
Financial Aid: Kent D. Larson
Type: University **Sex:** Coed **Affiliation:** Utah System of Higher Education **Scores:** 95% SAT V 400+; 97% SAT M 400+; 48% ACT 18-23; 39% ACT 24-29 **% Accepted:** 85 **Application Deadline:** April 01 **Application Fee:** $35.00 **H.S. Requirements:** High school diploma required; GED accepted **Costs Per Year:** Application fee: $35. State resident tuition: $3672 full-time, $102 per credit part-time. Nonresident tuition: $12,860 full-time, $351 per credit part-time. Mandatory fees: $670 full-time. Full-time tuition and fees vary according to course level, course load, degree level, and student level. Part-time tuition varies according to course level, course load, degree level, and student level. College room and board: $5422. College room only: $2704. Room and board charges vary according to board plan and housing facility. **Scholarships:** Available **Calendar System:** Semester, Summer Session Available **Enrollment:** FT 15,551, PT 7,110, Grad 5,375 **Faculty:** FT 1,175, PT 512 **Student-Faculty Ratio:** 15:1 **Exams:** ACT, SAT I or ACT **% Receiving Financial Aid:** 41 **% Residing in College-Owned, -Operated, or -Affiliated Housing:** 7 **Library Holdings:** 2,991,692 **Credit Hours For Degree:** 122 credit hours, Bachelors **ROTC:** Army, Navy, Air Force **Professional Accreditation:** AACSB, ABET, ACEJMC, AACN, ABA, ACNM, ACPhE, ADtA, AOTA, APTA, APA, ASC, ASLHA, AALS, CEPH, CSWE, JRCEPAT, LCMEAMA, NAACLS, NASM NASPAA, NRPA, NCCU **Intercollegiate Athletics:** Baseball M; Basketball M & W; Bowling M & W; Cheerleading M & W; Cross-Country Running W; Football M; Golf M; Gymnastics W; Ice Hockey M; Racquetball M & W; Rugby M; Skiing (Cross-Country) M & W; Skiing (Downhill) M & W; Soccer M & W; Softball W; Swimming and Diving M & W; Table Tennis M & W; Tennis M & W; Track and Field W; Volleyball W

UTAH CAREER COLLEGE
1902 West 7800 South
West Jordan, UT 84088
Tel: (801)304-4224; (866)304-4224
Fax: (801)304-4229
E-mail: kcooper@utahcollege.edu
Web Site: http://www.utahcollege.edu/
President/CEO: Nathan Herrmann
Registrar: Amber East
Admissions: Karma Cooper
Financial Aid: Whitney Hannah
Type: Two-Year College **Sex:** Coed **% Accepted:** 100 **Application Deadline:** October 01 **Costs Per Year:** Tuition: $12,060 full-time, $335 per credit part-time. **Scholarships:** Available **Calendar System:** Quarter **Enrollment:** FT 152, PT 418 **Faculty:** FT 9, PT 33 **Student-Faculty Ratio:** 12:1 **Professional Accreditation:** ACCSCT, AAMAE

UTAH STATE UNIVERSITY
Old Main Hill
Logan, UT 84322
Tel: (435)797-1000
Free: 800-488-8108
Admissions: (435)797-1079
Fax: (435)797-3900
E-mail: admit@usu.edu

Web Site: http://www.usu.edu/
President/CEO: Dr. Kermit L. Hall
Registrar: Heidi Beck
Admissions: Jimmy Moore
Financial Aid: Judy Lecheminant
Type: University **Sex:** Coed **Affiliation:** Utah System of Higher Education **Scores:** 96.1% SAT V 400+; 97.7% SAT M 400+; 45.2% ACT 18-23; 43.4% ACT 24-29 **Admission Plans:** Early Admission; Deferred Admission **Application Deadline:** Rolling **Application Fee:** $40.00 **H.S. Requirements:** High school diploma required; GED accepted **Costs Per Year:** Application fee: $40. State resident tuition: $3128 full-time. Nonresident tuition: $10,072 full-time. Mandatory fees: $544 full-time. Full-time tuition and fees vary according to course load and student level. College room and board: $4330. College room only: $1550. Room and board charges vary according to board plan and housing facility. **Scholarships:** Available **Calendar System:** Semester, Summer Session Available **Enrollment:** FT 10,728, PT 2,009, Grad 1,721 **Faculty:** FT 727, PT 37 **Student-Faculty Ratio:** 19:1 **Exams:** SAT I or ACT **% Receiving Financial Aid:** 45 **Library Holdings:** 1,505,437 **Credit Hours For Degree:** 60 credit hours, Associates; 120 credit hours, Bachelors **ROTC:** Army, Air Force **Professional Accreditation:** AACSB, ABET, AAMFT, ADtA, APA, ASLA, ASLHA, CORE, CSWE, FIDER, NASM, NCATE, NRPA, NCCU, SAF **Intercollegiate Athletics:** Baseball M; Basketball M & W; Cross-Country Running M & W; Equestrian Sports M & W; Football M; Golf M; Gymnastics W; Ice Hockey M; Rugby M & W; Soccer M & W; Softball W; Tennis M & W; Track and Field M & W; Volleyball M & W

UTAH VALLEY STATE COLLEGE

800 West 1200 South St.
Orem, UT 84058-5999
Tel: (801)222-8000
Admissions: (801)863-8460
Fax: (801)225-4677
E-mail: info@uvsc.edu
Web Site: http://www.uvsc.edu/
President/CEO: William A. Sederburg
Admissions: Liz Childs
Financial Aid: Joanna McCormick
Type: Four-Year College **Sex:** Coed **Affiliation:** Utah System of Higher Education **Scores:** 89.26% SAT V 400+; 86.99% SAT M 400+; 54.24% ACT 18-23; 19.78% ACT 24-29 **% Accepted:** 100 **Admission Plans:** Open Admission; Deferred Admission **Application Deadline:** August 15 **Application Fee:** $30.00 **H.S. Requirements:** High school diploma or equivalent not required **Costs Per Year:** Application fee: $30. State resident tuition: $2580 full-time, $86 per credit part-time. Nonresident tuition: $9030 full-time, $301 per credit part-time. Mandatory fees: $442 full-time; $221 per term part-time. Part-time tuition and fees vary according to course load. **Scholarships:** Available **Calendar System:** Semester, Summer Session Available **Enrollment:** FT 11,565, PT 12,922 **Faculty:** FT 407, PT 924 **Student-Faculty Ratio:** 22:1 **Exams:** Other, SAT I or ACT **% Receiving Financial Aid:** 53 **Library Holdings:** 173,000 **Credit Hours For Degree:** 60 semester hours, Associates; 120 semester hours, Bachelors **ROTC:** Army, Air Force **Professional Accreditation:** ABET, ADA, NLN, NCCU **Intercollegiate Athletics:** Baseball M; Basketball M & W; Cross-Country Running M & W; Golf M; Soccer W; Softball W; Track and Field M & W; Volleyball W; Wrestling M

WEBER STATE UNIVERSITY

1001 University Circle
Ogden, UT 84408-1001
Tel: (801)626-6000
Free: 800-848-7770
Admissions: (801)626-6046
Fax: (801)626-6747
E-mail: ccrivera@weber.edu
Web Site: http://weber.edu/
President/CEO: Dr. Ann Millner
Registrar: Dr. L. Winslow Hurst
Admissions: Christopher Rivera
Financial Aid: Richard O. Effiong
Type: Comprehensive **Sex:** Coed **Affiliation:** Utah System of Higher Education **Scores:** 87% SAT V 400+; 84% SAT M 400+; 50% ACT 18-23; 26% ACT 24-29 **% Accepted:** 100 **Admission Plans:** Open Admission; Early Admission; Deferred Admission **Application Deadline:** August 22 **Application Fee:** $30.00 **H.S. Requirements:** High school diploma required; GED accepted **Costs Per Year:** Application fee: $30. State resident tuition: $2547 full-time. Nonresident tuition: $9008 full-time. Mandatory fees: $591 full-time. College room and board: $6500. College room only: $3300. Room and board charges vary according to board plan and housing facility. **Scholarships:** Available **Calendar System:** Semester, Summer Session Available **Enrollment:** FT 10,250, PT 7,488, Grad 404 **Faculty:** FT 465, PT 205 **Student-Faculty Ratio:** 22:1 **Exams:** SAT I or ACT **% Receiving Financial Aid:** 63 **% Residing in College-Owned, -Operated, or -Affiliated Housing:** 3 **Library Holdings:** 734,487 **Credit Hours For Degree:** 60 credit hours, Associates; 120 credit hours, Bachelors **ROTC:** Army, Navy, Air Force **Professional Accreditation:** AACSB, ABET, ADA, AHIMA, CARC, CSWE, JRCEMT, NAACLS, NASM, NCATE, NLN, NCCU **Intercollegiate Athletics:** Baseball M; Basketball M & W; Bowling M & W; Cheerleading M & W; Cross-Country Running M & W; Fencing M & W; Football M; Golf M & W; Ice Hockey M; Lacrosse M & W; Racquetball M & W; Rugby M & W; Skiing (Downhill) M & W; Soccer M & W; Softball W; Swimming and Diving M & W; Tennis M & W; Track and Field M & W; Volleyball W; Water Polo M & W

WESTERN GOVERNORS UNIVERSITY

4001 South 700 East, Ste. 700
Salt Lake City, UT 84107
Tel: (801)274-3280; 877-435-7948
Fax: (801)274-3305
Web Site: http://www.wgu.edu/
President/CEO: Robert Mendenhall
Admissions: Chris Mallett
Financial Aid: Carol Garnett
Type: Comprehensive **Sex:** Coed **Admission Plans:** Open Admission **Application Fee:** $100.00 **H.S. Requirements:** High school diploma required; GED accepted **Costs Per Year:** Application fee: $100. Tuition: $5580 full-time. Mandatory fees: $155 full-time. Full-time tuition and fees vary according to program. **Scholarships:** Available **Calendar System:** Continuous, Summer Session Not available **Enrollment:** FT 1,843, Grad 978 **Faculty:** FT 45, PT 6 **Student-Faculty Ratio:** 56:1 **% Receiving Financial Aid:** 62 **Professional Accreditation:** DETC, NCCU

WESTMINSTER COLLEGE

1840 South 1300 East
Salt Lake City, UT 84105-3697
Tel: (801)484-7651
Free: 800-748-4753
Admissions: (801)832-2200
Fax: (801)484-3252
E-mail: admission@westminstercollege.edu
Web Site: http://www.westminstercollege.edu
President/CEO: Dr. Michael Bassis
Registrar: Mindy Wennergren
Admissions: Joel Bauman
Financial Aid: Ruth Henneman
Type: Comprehensive **Sex:** Coed **Scores:** 97% SAT V 400+; 97% SAT M 400+; 46% ACT 18-23; 42% ACT 24-29 **% Accepted:** 89 **Admission Plans:** Deferred Admission **Application Deadline:** April 15 **Application Fee:** $40.00 **H.S. Requirements:** High school diploma required; GED accepted **Costs Per Year:** Application fee: $40. Comprehensive fee: $25,656 includes full-time tuition ($19,440), mandatory fees ($284), and college room and board ($5932). Full-time tuition and fees vary according to course load. Room and board charges vary according to board plan. Part-time tuition: $810 per credit hour. Part-time mandatory fees: $107 per term. **Scholarships:** Available **Calendar System:** Miscellaneous, Summer Session Available **Enrollment:** FT 1,633, PT 245, Grad 577 **Faculty:** FT 121, PT 138 **Student-Faculty Ratio:** 10:1 **Exams:** SAT I or ACT **% Receiving Financial Aid:** 70 **% Residing in College-Owned, -Operated, or -Affiliated Housing:** 26 **Library Holdings:** 119,410 **Credit Hours For Degree:** 124 semester hours, Bachelors **ROTC:** Army, Navy, Air Force **Professional Accreditation:** AACN, ACBSP, NCCU **Intercollegiate Athletics:** Basketball M & W; Golf M & W; Soccer M; Volleyball W

BENNINGTON COLLEGE
One College Dr.
Bennington, VT 05201
Tel: (802)442-5401
Free: 800-833-6845
Admissions: (802)440-4312
Fax: (802)447-4269
E-mail: admissions@bennington.edu
Web Site: http://www.bennington.edu/
President/CEO: Dr. Elizabeth Coleman
Registrar: Rosemary Odell
Admissions: Ken Himmelman
Financial Aid: Meg Woolmington
Type: Comprehensive **Sex:** Coed **Scores:** 100% SAT V 400+; 100% SAT M 400+; 12% ACT 18-23; 68% ACT 24-29 **% Accepted:** 62 **Admission Plans:** Early Admission; Early Decision Plan; Deferred Admission **Application Deadline:** January 03 **Application Fee:** $60.00 **H.S. Requirements:** High school diploma required; GED accepted **Costs Per Year:** Application fee: $60. Comprehensive fee: $41,890 includes full-time tuition ($32,700), mandatory fees ($870), and college room and board ($8320). College room only: $4460. Part-time tuition: $1050 per credit. **Scholarships:** Available **Calendar System:** Semester, Summer Session Not available **Enrollment:** FT 567, PT 4, Grad 154 **Faculty:** FT 66, PT 24 **Student-Faculty Ratio:** 7:1 **% Receiving Financial Aid:** 69 **% Residing in College-Owned, -Operated, or -Affiliated Housing:** 98 **Library Holdings:** 128,413 **Regional Accreditation:** New England Association of Schools and Colleges **Credit Hours For Degree:** 128 credits, Bachelors **Intercollegiate Athletics:** Baseball M & W; Basketball M & W; Soccer M & W; Softball M & W

BURLINGTON COLLEGE
95 North Ave.
Burlington, VT 05401-2998
Tel: (802)862-9616
Free: 800-862-9616
Fax: (802)658-0071
Web Site: http://www.burlcol.edu/
President/CEO: Mary Clancy
Registrar: Mira Shea
Admissions: Cathleen Sullivan
Financial Aid: Karen Lapan
Type: Four-Year College **Sex:** Coed **Admission Plans:** Open Admission; Deferred Admission **Application Fee:** $35.00 **H.S. Requirements:** High school diploma required; GED accepted **Costs Per Year:** Application fee: $35. Tuition: $15,600 full-time, $515 per credit hour part-time. College room only: $4500. **Scholarships:** Available **Calendar System:** Semester, Summer Session Available **Enrollment:** FT 117, PT 124 **Faculty:** PT 68 **Student-Faculty Ratio:** 8:1 **% Receiving Financial Aid:** 64 **% Residing in College-Owned, -Operated, or -Affiliated Housing:** 6 **Library Holdings:** 5,700 **Regional Accreditation:** New England Association of Schools and Colleges **Credit Hours For Degree:** 60 credits, Associates; 120 credits, Bachelors

CASTLETON STATE COLLEGE
Castleton, VT 05735
Tel: (802)468-5611
Free: 800-639-8521
Admissions: (802)468-1213
Fax: (802)468-1476
Web Site: http://www.castleton.edu/
President/CEO: David Wolk
Registrar: Lori Patten
Admissions: Maurice Ouimet
Financial Aid: Audrey Reed
Type: Comprehensive **Sex:** Coed **Affiliation:** Vermont State Colleges System **Scores:** 90% SAT V 400+; 90% SAT M 400+; 50% ACT 18-23; 20% ACT 24-29 **% Accepted:** 79 **Admission Plans:** Deferred Admission **Application Deadline:** Rolling **Application Fee:** $35.00 **H.S. Requirements:** High school diploma required; GED accepted **Costs Per Year:** Application fee: $35. One-time mandatory fee: $195. State resident tuition: $6648 full-time, $277 per credit part-time. Nonresident tuition: $14,376 full-time, $599 per credit part-time. Mandatory fees: $180 full-time. College room and board: $6942. **Scholarships:** Available **Calendar System:** Semester, Summer Session Available **Enrollment:** FT 1,684, PT 207, Grad 501 **Faculty:** FT 89, PT 112 **Student-Faculty Ratio:** 14:1 **Exams:** SAT I or ACT **% Residing in College-Owned, -Operated, or -Affiliated Housing:** 50 **Library Holdings:** 166,011 **Regional Accreditation:** New England Association of Schools and Colleges **Credit Hours For Degree:** 64 credits, Associates; 122 credits, Bachelors **ROTC:** Army **Professional Accreditation:** CSWE, JRCEPAT, NLN **Intercollegiate Athletics:** Baseball M; Basketball M & W; Cheerleading M & W; Cross-Country Running M & W; Equestrian Sports M & W; Field Hockey W; Golf M; Ice Hockey M & W; Lacrosse M & W; Rugby M & W; Skiing (Downhill) M & W; Soccer M & W; Softball W; Tennis M & W; Volleyball W

CHAMPLAIN COLLEGE
PO Box 670
Burlington, VT 05402-0670
Tel: (802)860-2700
Free: 800-570-5858
Admissions: (802)860-2727
Fax: (802)862-2772
E-mail: admission@champlain.edu
Web Site: http://www.champlain.edu/
President/CEO: Dr. Roger H. Perry
Registrar: Rebecca Peterson
Admissions: Dr. Mary Kay Kennedy
Financial Aid: David Myette
Type: Comprehensive **Sex:** Coed **% Accepted:** 64 **Application Deadline:** Rolling **Application Fee:** $40.00 **H.S. Requirements:** High school diploma required; GED accepted **Costs Per Year:** Application fee: $40. Comprehensive fee: $24,605 includes full-time tuition ($14,660), mandatory fees ($250), and college room and board ($9695). College room only: $5855. Full-time tuition and fees vary according to course load. Room and board charges vary according to board plan and housing facility. Part-time tuition: $420 per credit hour. Part-time tuition varies according to course load. **Scholarships:** Available **Calendar System:** Semester, Summer Session Available **Enrollment:** FT 1,757, PT 715, Grad 57 **Faculty:** FT 68, PT 190 **Student-Faculty Ratio:** 16:1 **Exams:** SAT I or ACT, SAT II **% Receiving Financial Aid:** 56 **% Residing in College-Owned, -Operated, or -Affiliated Housing:** 41 **Library Holdings:** 60,000 **Regional Accreditation:** New England Associa-

tion of Schools and Colleges **Credit Hours For Degree:** 60 credit hours, Associates; 120 credit hours, Bachelors **ROTC:** Army **Professional Accreditation:** CARC, JRCERT

COLLEGE OF ST. JOSEPH
71 Clement Rd.
Rutland, VT 05701-3899
Tel: (802)773-5900
Web Site: http://www.csj.edu/
President/CEO: Dr. Frank G. Miglorie, Jr.
Registrar: Patricia Miglorie
Financial Aid: Yvonne Payrits
Type: Comprehensive **Sex:** Coed **Affiliation:** Roman Catholic **Scores:** 87% SAT V 400+; 89% SAT M 400+; 100% ACT 18-23 **% Accepted:** 68 **Admission Plans:** Early Admission; Deferred Admission **Application Deadline:** Rolling **Application Fee:** $25.00 **H.S. Requirements:** High school diploma required; GED accepted **Costs Per Year:** Application fee: $25. Comprehensive fee: $22,050 includes full-time tuition ($14,650), mandatory fees ($250), and college room and board ($7150). Part-time tuition: $245 per credit. Part-time mandatory fees: $45 per term. **Scholarships:** Available **Calendar System:** Semester, Summer Session Available **Faculty:** FT 11, PT 57 **Student-Faculty Ratio:** 11:1 **Exams:** SAT I or ACT **% Receiving Financial Aid:** 91 **% Residing in College-Owned, -Operated, or -Affiliated Housing:** 31 **Library Holdings:** 75,000 **Regional Accreditation:** New England Association of Schools and Colleges **Credit Hours For Degree:** 60 credits, Associates; 127 credits, Bachelors **Intercollegiate Athletics:** Baseball M; Basketball M & W; Cross-Country Running M & W; Soccer M & W; Softball W

COMMUNITY COLLEGE OF VERMONT
PO Box 120
Waterbury, VT 05676-0120
Tel: (802)241-3535
Admissions: (802)865-4422
Web Site: http://www.ccv.edu/
President/CEO: Timothy J. Donovan
Registrar: Nancy Severance
Admissions: Susan Henry
Financial Aid: Pam Chisholm
Type: Two-Year College **Sex:** Coed **Affiliation:** Vermont State Colleges System **Admission Plans:** Open Admission **H.S. Requirements:** High school diploma required; GED accepted **Costs Per Year:** State resident tuition: $3912 full-time, $163 per credit part-time. Nonresident tuition: $7824 full-time, $326 per credit part-time. Mandatory fees: $100 full-time, $50 per term part-time. **Scholarships:** Available **Calendar System:** Semester, Summer Session Available **Faculty:** FT 0, PT 635 **Exams:** Other **Regional Accreditation:** New England Association of Schools and Colleges **Credit Hours For Degree:** 60 credits, Associates

GODDARD COLLEGE
123 Pitkin Rd.
Plainfield, VT 05667-9432
Tel: (802)454-8311
Free: 800-906-8312
Fax: (802)454-1029
Web Site: http://www.goddard.edu/
President/CEO: Dr. Mark Schulman
Registrar: Josh Castle
Admissions: Brenda Hawkins
Financial Aid: Beverly Jene
Type: Comprehensive **Sex:** Coed **% Accepted:** 92 **Admission Plans:** Deferred Admission **Application Deadline:** Rolling **Application Fee:** $40.00 **H.S. Requirements:** High school diploma required; GED accepted **Costs Per Year:** Application fee: $40. Tuition: $9806 full-time. Mandatory fees: $900 full-time. **Scholarships:** Available **Calendar System:** Semester, Summer Session Not available **Enrollment:** FT 165, Grad 395 **Faculty:** FT 2, PT 72 **Student-Faculty Ratio:** 11:1 **% Receiving Financial Aid:** 70 **Library Holdings:** 70,000 **Regional Accreditation:** New England Association of Schools and Colleges **Credit Hours For Degree:** 120 credit hours, Bachelors

GREEN MOUNTAIN COLLEGE
One College Circle
Poultney, VT 05764-1199
Tel: (802)287-8000
Free: 800-776-6675
Admissions: (802)287-8207
Fax: (802)287-8099
E-mail: admiss@greenmtn.edu
Web Site: http://www.greenmtn.edu/
President/CEO: John F. Brennan
Registrar: Aleta Holden
Admissions: Joel Wincowski
Financial Aid: Wendy Ellis
Type: Four-Year College **Sex:** Coed **Affiliation:** United Methodist Church **Scores:** 88% SAT V 400+; 78% SAT M 400+ **% Accepted:** 91 **Admission Plans:** Deferred Admission **Application Deadline:** Rolling **Application Fee:** $30.00 **H.S. Requirements:** High school diploma required; GED accepted **Costs Per Year:** Application fee: $30. Comprehensive fee: $29,894 includes full-time tuition ($21,604), mandatory fees ($600), and college room and board ($7690). College room only: $4700. Full-time tuition and fees vary according to course load. Room and board charges vary according to housing facility. Part-time tuition: $720 per credit hour. Part-time tuition varies according to course load. **Scholarships:** Available **Calendar System:** Semester, Summer Session Available **Enrollment:** FT 665, PT 31 **Faculty:** FT 41, PT 24 **Student-Faculty Ratio:** 14:1 **Exams:** SAT I or ACT **% Receiving Financial Aid:** 81 **% Residing in College-Owned, -Operated, or -Affiliated Housing:** 85 **Library Holdings:** 73,400 **Regional Accreditation:** New England Association of Schools and Colleges **Credit Hours For Degree:** 120 credits, Bachelors **Professional Accreditation:** NRPA **Intercollegiate Athletics:** Basketball M & W; Cross-Country Running M & W; Golf M; Lacrosse M; Skiing (Downhill) M & W; Soccer M & W; Softball W; Tennis M & W; Volleyball W

JOHNSON STATE COLLEGE
337 College Hill
Johnson, VT 05656-9405
Tel: (802)635-2356
Free: 800-635-2356
Admissions: (802)635-1219
Fax: (802)635-1230
E-mail: jscapply@badger.jsc.vsc.edu
Web Site: http://www.johnsonstatecollege.edu/
President/CEO: Barbara E. Murphy
Registrar: Manuela Mangiafico
Admissions: Penny P. Howrigan
Financial Aid: Penny Howrigan
Type: Comprehensive **Sex:** Coed **Affiliation:** Vermont State Colleges System **Scores:** 86% SAT V 400+; 84% SAT M 400+ **% Accepted:** 95 **Admission Plans:** Deferred Admission **Application Deadline:** Rolling **Application Fee:** $35.00 **H.S. Requirements:** High school diploma required; GED accepted **Costs Per Year:** Application fee: $35. State resident tuition: $6722 full-time, $280 per credit part-time. Nonresident tuition: $14,524 full-time, $605 per credit part-time. Mandatory fees: $184 full-time, $8 per credit part-time. College room and board: $6910. College room only: $6132. **Scholarships:** Available **Calendar System:** Semester, Summer Session Available **Enrollment:** FT 1,022, PT 544, Grad 258 **Faculty:** FT 54, PT 89 **Student-Faculty Ratio:** 17:1 **Exams:** SAT I **% Residing in College-Owned, -Operated, or -Affiliated Housing:** 57 **Library Holdings:** 100,053 **Regional Accreditation:** New England Association of Schools and Colleges **Credit Hours For Degree:** 60 credits, Associates; 120 credits, Bachelors **ROTC:** Army **Intercollegiate Athletics:** Basketball M & W; Cross-Country Running M & W; Lacrosse M; Rugby M; Soccer M & W; Softball W; Tennis M & W

LANDMARK COLLEGE
River Rd. South
Putney, VT 05346
Tel: (802)387-4767
Admissions: (802)387-6716
Fax: (802)387-4779
Web Site: http://www.landmark.edu/
President/CEO: Dr. Lynda J. Katz
Registrar: Karen Damian
Admissions: Dale Herold
Financial Aid: Catherine Mullins
Type: Two-Year College **Sex:** Coed **% Accepted:** 72 **Admission Plans:** Deferred Admission **Application Deadline:** Rolling **Application Fee:** $75.00 **H.S. Requirements:** High school diploma required; GED accepted **Costs Per Year:** Application fee: $75. One-time mandatory fee: $1850. Compre-

hensive fee: $46,470 includes full-time tuition ($38,500), mandatory fees ($770), and college room and board ($7200). College room only: $3600. **Scholarships:** Available **Calendar System:** Semester, Summer Session Available **Enrollment:** FT 233, PT 138 **Faculty:** FT 95, PT 2 **Student-Faculty Ratio:** 4:1 **Exams:** Other **% Residing in College-Owned, -Operated, or -Affiliated Housing:** 94 **Library Holdings:** 30,066 **Regional Accreditation:** New England Association of Schools and Colleges **Credit Hours For Degree:** 60 credits, Associates **Intercollegiate Athletics:** Baseball M; Basketball M & W; Cross-Country Running M & W; Rock Climbing M & W; Soccer M & W; Softball W

LYNDON STATE COLLEGE
PO Box 919
Lyndonville, VT 05851-0919
Tel: (802)626-6200
Free: 800-225-1998
Admissions: (802)626-6413
Fax: (802)626-6335
E-mail: admissions@lyndonstate.edu
Web Site: http://www.lyndonstate.edu/
President/CEO: Dr. Carol A. Moore
Registrar: Debra Hale
Admissions: Michelle McCaffrey
Financial Aid: Tanya Bradley
Type: Comprehensive **Sex:** Coed **Affiliation:** Vermont State Colleges System **Scores:** 76.79% SAT V 400+; 73.5% SAT M 400+ **% Accepted:** 94 **Admission Plans:** Early Admission; Deferred Admission **Application Deadline:** Rolling **Application Fee:** $35.00 **H.S. Requirements:** High school diploma required; GED accepted **Costs Per Year:** Application fee: $35. State resident tuition: $6312 full-time, $263 per credit hour part-time. Nonresident tuition: $13,632 full-time, $568 per credit hour part-time. Mandatory fees: $172 full-time, $8 per credit hour part-time. Full-time tuition and fees vary according to course load. Part-time tuition and fees vary according to course load. College room and board: $6674. College room only: $3974. Room and board charges vary according to board plan and housing facility. **Scholarships:** Available **Calendar System:** Semester, Summer Session Available **Enrollment:** FT 1,140, PT 133, Grad 46 **Faculty:** FT 59, PT 86 **Student-Faculty Ratio:** 21:1 **Exams:** SAT I or ACT **% Residing in College-Owned, -Operated, or -Affiliated Housing:** 50 **Library Holdings:** 109,629 **Regional Accreditation:** New England Association of Schools and Colleges **Credit Hours For Degree:** 62 credit hours, Associates; 122 credit hours, Bachelors **ROTC:** Air Force **Professional Accreditation:** NRPA **Intercollegiate Athletics:** Baseball M; Basketball M & W; Cross-Country Running M & W; Soccer M & W; Softball W; Tennis M & W; Volleyball W

MARLBORO COLLEGE
PO Box A, South Rd.
Marlboro, VT 05344
Tel: (802)257-4333
Free: 800-343-0049
Admissions: (802)258-9261
E-mail: admissions@marlboro.edu
Web Site: http://www.marlboro.edu/
President/CEO: Ellen McCulloch-Lovell
Registrar: Valerie Abrahamsen
Admissions: Alan E. Young
Financial Aid: Julie Richardson
Type: Comprehensive **Sex:** Coed **Scores:** 100% SAT V 400+; 95% SAT M 400+; 2% ACT 18-23; 13% ACT 24-29 **% Accepted:** 58 **Admission Plans:** Early Admission; Early Action; Early Decision Plan; Deferred Admission **Application Deadline:** February 15 **Application Fee:** $50.00 **H.S. Requirements:** High school diploma required; GED accepted. For home schooled applicants with curriculum documentation: High school diploma or equivalent not required **Costs Per Year:** Application fee: $50. Comprehensive fee: $35,980 includes full-time tuition ($26,940), mandatory fees ($850), and college room and board ($8190). College room only: $4540. Part-time tuition: $890 per credit. **Scholarships:** Available **Calendar System:** Semester, Summer Session Not available **Enrollment:** FT 327, PT 13, Grad 29 **Faculty:** FT 36, PT 14 **Student-Faculty Ratio:** 7:1 **Exams:** SAT I or ACT **% Receiving Financial Aid:** 75 **% Residing in College-Owned, -Operated, or -Affiliated Housing:** 82 **Library Holdings:** 65,000 **Regional Accreditation:** New England Association of Schools and Colleges **Credit Hours For Degree:** 120 credits, Bachelors **Intercollegiate Athletics:** Soccer M & W

MIDDLEBURY COLLEGE
Middlebury, VT 05753-6002
Tel: (802)443-5000
Admissions: (802)443-3000
Fax: (802)443-2056
E-mail: admissions@middlebury.edu
Web Site: http://www.middlebury.edu/
President/CEO: Dr. Ronald D. Liebowitz
Registrar: Kathryn Weiss
Admissions: Robert Clagett
Financial Aid: Robert Donaghey
Type: Comprehensive **Sex:** Coed **Scores:** 100% SAT V 400+; 100% SAT M 400+; 1% ACT 18-23; 17% ACT 24-29 **% Accepted:** 24 **Admission Plans:** Early Admission; Early Decision Plan; Deferred Admission **Application Deadline:** January 01 **Application Fee:** $55.00 **H.S. Requirements:** High school diploma or equivalent not required **Costs Per Year:** Application fee: $55. Comprehensive fee: $42,120. **Scholarships:** Available **Calendar System:** 4-1-4, Summer Session Available **Enrollment:** FT 2,420, PT 35 **Faculty:** FT 254, PT 46 **Student-Faculty Ratio:** 9:1 **Exams:** Other, SAT I and SAT II or ACT **% Receiving Financial Aid:** 43 **% Residing in College-Owned, -Operated, or -Affiliated Housing:** 97 **Library Holdings:** 853,000 **Regional Accreditation:** New England Association of Schools and Colleges **Credit Hours For Degree:** 36 courses, Bachelors **ROTC:** Army **Intercollegiate Athletics:** Baseball M; Basketball M & W; Cross-Country Running M & W; Field Hockey W; Football M; Golf M & W; Ice Hockey M & W; Lacrosse M & W; Skiing (Cross-Country) M & W; Skiing (Downhill) M & W; Soccer M & W; Softball W; Squash W; Swimming and Diving M & W; Tennis M & W; Track and Field M & W; Volleyball W

NEW ENGLAND CULINARY INSTITUTE
250 Main St.
Montpelier, VT 05602-9720
Tel: (802)223-6324; 877-223-6324
Fax: (802)223-0634
E-mail: admissions@neci.edu
Web Site: http://www.neci.edu/
President/CEO: Francis Voigt
Registrar: Susan Griswold
Admissions: Dawn Hayward
Financial Aid: Jim Hutton
Type: Two-Year College **Sex:** Coed **Admission Plans:** Early Admission; Deferred Admission **Application Fee:** $0.00 **H.S. Requirements:** High school diploma required; GED accepted **Costs Per Year:** Application fee: $0. Comprehensive fee: $28,365 includes full-time tuition ($21,500), mandatory fees ($450), and college room and board ($6415). Full-time tuition and fees vary according to degree level, program, and student level. **Scholarships:** Available **Calendar System:** Quarter, Summer Session Not available **Enrollment:** FT 606 **Faculty:** FT 68, PT 16 **Student-Faculty Ratio:** 6:1 **Exams:** SAT I **% Residing in College-Owned, -Operated, or -Affiliated Housing:** 80 **Library Holdings:** 2,400 **Credit Hours For Degree:** 60 credits, Associates; 92 credits, Bachelors **Professional Accreditation:** ACCSCT

NEW ENGLAND CULINARY INSTITUTE AT ESSEX
48 1/2 Park St.
Essex Junction, VT 05452
Tel: (802)872-3400
Admissions: (802)223-6324
E-mail: sherrigilmore@neci.edu
Web Site: http://www.neci.edu/
President/CEO: Francis Voigt
Admissions: Sherri Gilmore
Type: Two-Year College **Sex:** Coed **% Accepted:** 78 **Application Fee:** $0.00 **Costs Per Year:** Application fee: $0. Comprehensive fee: $33,830 includes full-time tuition ($23,835), mandatory fees ($3430), and college room and board ($6565). **Calendar System:** Quarter **Enrollment:** FT 501 **Faculty:** FT 65, PT 11 **Professional Accreditation:** ACCSCT

NORWICH UNIVERSITY
158 Harmon Dr.
Northfield, VT 05663
Tel: (802)485-2000

Free: 800-468-6679
Admissions: (802)485-2013
Fax: (802)485-2580
E-mail: nuadm@norwich.edu
Web Site: http://www.norwich.edu/
President/CEO: Dr. Richard Schneider
Registrar: Frances Burstein
Admissions: Karen McGrath
Type: Comprehensive **Sex:** Coed **Scores:** 90% SAT V 400+; 89% SAT M 400+ **% Accepted:** 91 **Admission Plans:** Early Admission; Early Decision Plan; Deferred Admission **Application Deadline:** Rolling **Application Fee:** $35.00 **H.S. Requirements:** High school diploma required; GED accepted **Scholarships:** Available **Calendar System:** Semester, Summer Session Available **Faculty:** FT 139, PT 133 **Student-Faculty Ratio:** 14:1 **Exams:** SAT I or ACT, SAT II **% Residing in College-Owned, -Operated, or -Affiliated Housing:** 84 **Library Holdings:** 280,000 **Regional Accreditation:** New England Association of Schools and Colleges **Credit Hours For Degree:** 120 credit hours, Bachelors **ROTC:** Army, Navy, Air Force **Professional Accreditation:** ABET, ACBSP, NLN **Intercollegiate Athletics:** Baseball M; Basketball M & W; Cross-Country Running M & W; Fencing M & W; Football M; Ice Hockey M & W; Lacrosse M & W; Riflery M & W; Rugby M & W; Sailing M & W; Skiing (Cross-Country) M & W; Skiing (Downhill) M & W; Soccer M & W; Softball W; Swimming and Diving M & W; Tennis M & W; Track and Field M & W; Volleyball M & W; Weight Lifting M & W; Wrestling M

SAINT MICHAEL'S COLLEGE
One Winooski Park
Colchester, VT 05439
Tel: (802)654-2000
Free: 800-762-8000
Admissions: (802)654-3000
Fax: (802)654-2242
E-mail: admission@smcvt.edu
Web Site: http://www.smcvt.edu/
President/CEO: Dr. Marc vanderHeyden
Registrar: John D. Sheehey
Admissions: Jerry E. Flanagan
Financial Aid: Nelberta Lunde
Type: Comprehensive **Sex:** Coed **Affiliation:** Roman Catholic **Scores:** 99% SAT V 400+; 99% SAT M 400+; 44% ACT 18-23; 47% ACT 24-29 **% Accepted:** 72 **Admission Plans:** Early Action; Deferred Admission **Application Deadline:** February 01 **Application Fee:** $45.00 **H.S. Requirements:** High school diploma required; GED accepted **Costs Per Year:** Application fee: $45. Comprehensive fee: $35,505 includes full-time tuition ($28,280), mandatory fees ($235), and college room and board ($6990). Part-time tuition: $945 per credit hour. **Scholarships:** Available **Calendar System:** Semester, Summer Session Available **Enrollment:** FT 1,945, PT 61, Grad 468 **Faculty:** FT 150, PT 67 **Student-Faculty Ratio:** 12:1 **Exams:** SAT I or ACT **% Receiving Financial Aid:** 66 **% Residing in College-Owned, -Operated, or -Affiliated Housing:** 93 **Library Holdings:** 210,811 **Regional Accreditation:** New England Association of Schools and Colleges **Credit Hours For Degree:** 124 semester hours, Bachelors **ROTC:** Army, Air Force **Intercollegiate Athletics:** Baseball M; Basketball M & W; Cheerleading M & W; Cross-Country Running M & W; Field Hockey W; Golf M; Ice Hockey M & W; Lacrosse M & W; Rugby M & W; Skiing (Cross-Country) M & W; Skiing (Downhill) M & W; Soccer M & W; Softball W; Swimming and Diving M & W; Tennis M & W; Volleyball W

SOUTHERN VERMONT COLLEGE
982 Mansion Dr.
Bennington, VT 05201-6002
Tel: (802)442-5427
Free: 800-378-2782
Admissions: (802)447-6304
Fax: (802)447-4695
E-mail: admis@svc.edu
Web Site: http://www.svc.edu/
President/CEO: Dr. Barbara P. Sirvis
Registrar: Adam Emerson
Admissions: Kathleen James
Type: Four-Year College **Sex:** Coed **Scores:** 82% SAT V 400+; 69% SAT M 400+; 61% ACT 18-23; 15% ACT 24-29 **% Accepted:** 71 **Admission Plans:** Early Admission; Deferred Admission **Application Deadline:** Rolling **Application Fee:** $30.00 **H.S. Requirements:** High school diploma required; GED accepted **Costs Per Year:** Application fee: $30. Comprehensive fee: $21,317 includes full-time tuition ($14,373) and college room and board ($6944). College room only: $3230. Part-time tuition: $399 per credit. **Scholarships:** Available **Calendar System:** Semester, Summer Session Available **Enrollment:** FT 323, PT 67 **Faculty:** FT 21, PT 24 **Student-Faculty Ratio:** 11:1 **Exams:** SAT I or ACT **% Receiving Financial Aid:** 64 **% Residing in College-Owned, -Operated, or -Affiliated Housing:** 50 **Library Holdings:** 26,000 **Regional Accreditation:** New England Association of Schools and Colleges **Credit Hours For Degree:** 60 credits, Associates; 120 credits, Bachelors **Professional Accreditation:** NLN **Intercollegiate Athletics:** Baseball M; Basketball M & W; Cross-Country Running M & W; Rugby M & W; Soccer M & W; Softball W; Track and Field M & W; Volleyball W

STERLING COLLEGE
PO Box 72
Craftsbury Common, VT 05827-0072
Tel: (802)586-7711
Free: 800-648-3591
E-mail: admissions@sterlingcollege.edu
Web Site: http://www.sterlingcollege.edu/
President/CEO: John E. Williamson
Registrar: Laurie Laggner
Admissions: Gwyn Harris
Financial Aid: Barbara Stuart
Type: Four-Year College **Sex:** Coed **Scores:** 100% SAT V 400+; 100% SAT M 400+ **% Accepted:** 65 **Admission Plans:** Deferred Admission **Application Deadline:** Rolling **Application Fee:** $35.00 **H.S. Requirements:** High school diploma required; GED accepted. For home schooled students may submit a portfolio of educational and life experiences: High school diploma or equivalent not required **Costs Per Year:** Application fee: $35. Comprehensive fee: $23,286 includes full-time tuition ($16,600), mandatory fees ($350), and college room and board ($6336). College room only: $2860. Full-time tuition and fees vary according to course load. Room and board charges vary according to board plan. Part-time tuition: $520 per credit. Part-time tuition varies according to course load. **Scholarships:** Available **Calendar System:** Semester, Summer Session Available **Enrollment:** FT 90, PT 8 **Faculty:** FT 15, PT 30 **Student-Faculty Ratio:** 4:1 **% Receiving Financial Aid:** 69 **% Residing in College-Owned, -Operated, or -Affiliated Housing:** 77 **Library Holdings:** 10,000 **Regional Accreditation:** New England Association of Schools and Colleges **Credit Hours For Degree:** 60 credits, Associates; 120 credits, Bachelors

UNIVERSITY OF VERMONT
Burlington, VT 05405
Tel: (802)656-3131
Admissions: (802)656-3370
E-mail: admissions@uvm.edu
Web Site: http://www.uvm.edu/
President/CEO: Dr. Daniel M. Fogel
Registrar: Keith P. Williams
Admissions: Donald M. Honeman
Financial Aid: Donald M. Honeman
Type: University **Sex:** Coed **Scores:** 99% SAT V 400+; 99% SAT M 400+; 35% ACT 18-23; 56% ACT 24-29 **% Accepted:** 80 **Admission Plans:** Preferred Admission; Early Action; Deferred Admission **Application Deadline:** January 15 **Application Fee:** $45.00 **H.S. Requirements:** High school diploma required; GED accepted **Costs Per Year:** Application fee: $45. State resident tuition: $9452 full-time, $394 per credit part-time. Nonresident tuition: $23,638 full-time, $985 per credit part-time. Mandatory fees: $1296 full-time. Part-time tuition varies according to course load. College room and board: $7332. College room only: $4936. Room and board charges vary according to board plan. **Scholarships:** Available **Calendar System:** Semester, Summer Session Available **Enrollment:** FT 8,652, PT 1,207, Grad 1,332 **Faculty:** FT 560, PT 163 **Student-Faculty Ratio:** 15:1 **Exams:** SAT I or ACT **% Receiving Financial Aid:** 57 **% Residing in College-Owned, -Operated, or -Affiliated Housing:** 52 **Library Holdings:** 2,410,250 **Regional Accreditation:** New England Association of Schools and Colleges **Credit Hours For Degree:** 122 credits, Bachelors **ROTC:** Army **Professional Accreditation:** AACSB, ABET, ACA, ADA, APTA, APA, ASC, ASLHA, CSWE, JRCEPAT, JRCNMT, LCMEAMA, NAACLS, NCATE, NLN, SAF **Intercollegiate Athletics:** Baseball M; Basketball M & W; Cheerleading M & W; Crew M & W; Cross-Country Running M & W; Equestrian Sports M & W; Fencing M & W; Field Hockey W; Gymnastics M & W; Ice Hockey M & W; Lacrosse M & W; Rugby M & W; Sailing M & W; Skiing (Cross-Country) M & W; Skiing (Downhill) M & W; Soccer M & W;

Softball W; Swimming and Diving W; Table Tennis M & W; Track and Field M & W; Ultimate Frisbee M & W; Volleyball M & W; Water Polo M & W

VERMONT TECHNICAL COLLEGE

PO Box 500
Randolph Center, VT 05061-0500
Tel: (802)728-1000
Free: 800-442-VTC1
Admissions: (802)728-1244
Fax: (802)728-1390
E-mail: admissions@vtc.vsc.edu
Web Site: http://www.vtc.edu/
President/CEO: Allan S. Rodgers
Registrar: Michael Dempsey
Admissions: Dwight A. Cross
Financial Aid: Catherine McCullough

Type: Four-Year College **Sex:** Coed **Affiliation:** Vermont State Colleges System **Scores:** 87% SAT V 400+; 93% SAT M 400+ **% Accepted:** 70 **Application Deadline:** Rolling **Application Fee:** $35.00 **H.S. Requirements:** High school diploma required; GED accepted **Costs Per Year:** Application fee: $35. Area resident tuition: $7680 full-time. State resident tuition: $11,544 full-time, $320 per credit part-time. Nonresident tuition: $14,640 full-time, $610 per credit part-time. Mandatory fees: $246 full-time, $50 per term part-time. Full-time tuition and fees vary according to course load and program. Part-time tuition and fees vary according to program. College room and board: $6674. College room only: $3974. Room and board charges vary according to board plan. **Scholarships:** Available **Calendar System:** Semester, Summer Session Available **Enrollment:** FT 1,033, PT 323 **Faculty:** FT 78, PT 61 **Student-Faculty Ratio:** 13:1 **Exams:** Other, SAT I or ACT, SAT I **% Receiving Financial Aid:** 77 **% Residing in College-Owned, -Operated, or -Affiliated Housing:** 66 **Library Holdings:** 59,480 **Regional Accreditation:** New England Association of Schools and Colleges **Credit Hours For Degree:** 60 credit hours, Associates; 130 credit hours, Bachelors **ROTC:** Army **Professional Accreditation:** ABET, NLN **Intercollegiate Athletics:** Baseball M; Basketball M & W; Ice Hockey M & W; Soccer M & W; Softball W; Volleyball M & W

WOODBURY COLLEGE

660 Elm St.
Montpelier, VT 05602
Tel: (802)229-0516
Fax: (802)229-2141
E-mail: admiss@woodbury-college.edu
Web Site: http://www.woodbury-college.edu/
President/CEO: Lawrence H. Mandell, Esq
Registrar: Jody Maunsell
Admissions: Kathleen Moore
Financial Aid: Marcy Spaulding

Type: Four-Year College **Sex:** Coed **Admission Plans:** Open Admission **Application Fee:** $30.00 **H.S. Requirements:** High school diploma required; GED accepted **Scholarships:** Available **Calendar System:** Trimester, Summer Session Not available **Enrollment:** FT 99, PT 39 **Faculty:** FT 15, PT 29 **Student-Faculty Ratio:** 12:1 **% Receiving Financial Aid:** 91 **Library Holdings:** 2,782 **Regional Accreditation:** New England Association of Schools and Colleges **Credit Hours For Degree:** 60 credits, Associates; 120 credits, Bachelors

ACT COLLEGE
1100 Wilson Blvd.
Arlington, VA 22209
Web Site: http://www.healthtraining.com **Type:** Two-Year College **Sex:** Coed

ADVANCED TECHNOLOGY INSTITUTE
5700 Southern Blvd.
Virginia Beach, VA 23462
Web Site: http://www.aticareers.com **Type:** Two-Year College **Sex:** Coed

ARGOSY UNIVERSITY/WASHINGTON D.C.
1550 Wilson Blvd., Ste. 600
Arlington, VA 22209
Tel: (703)526-5800; (866)703-2777
Fax: (703)243-8973
Web Site: http://www.argosyu.edu/
President/CEO: Dr. Cynthia Baum
Registrar: Ann Stapleton
Financial Aid: Liza Ziegler
Type: Two-Year Upper Division **Sex:** Coed **Affiliation:** Argosy Education Group **Application Fee:** $50.00 **Scholarships:** Available **Calendar System:** Semester **Enrollment:** FT 13 **Faculty:** FT 21 **Student-Faculty Ratio:** 7:1 **Regional Accreditation:** North Central Association of Colleges and Schools **Professional Accreditation:** APA

THE ART INSTITUTE OF WASHINGTON
1820 North Fort Meyer Dr., Ground Floor
Arlington, VA 22209
Tel: (703)358-9550; 877-303-3771
Admissions: (703)247-6857
Fax: (703)358-9759
Web Site: http://www.artinstitutes.edu/arlington/
President/CEO: James Palermo
Admissions: Sara Cruley
Type: Four-Year College **Sex:** Coed **Affiliation:** Education Management Corporation **Application Deadline:** Rolling **Application Fee:** $50.00 **H.S. Requirements:** High school diploma required; GED accepted **Costs Per Year:** Application fee: $50. Tuition: $385 per quarter hour part-time. College room only: $9500. Tuition guaranteed not to increase for student's term of enrollment. **Scholarships:** Available **Calendar System:** Quarter **Faculty:** FT 33, PT 49 **Student-Faculty Ratio:** 20:1 **Regional Accreditation:** Southern Association of Colleges and Schools

AVERETT UNIVERSITY
420 West Main St.
Danville, VA 24541-3692
Tel: (434)791-5600
Free: 800-AVE-RETT
Admissions: (434)791-7301
Fax: (434)791-5637
E-mail: ktune@averett.edu
Web Site: http://www.averett.edu/
President/CEO: Dr. Richard A. Pfau
Registrar: Dr. Larry Wilburn
Admissions: Kathie Tune
Financial Aid: Carl Bradsher
Type: Comprehensive **Sex:** Coed **Affiliation:** Baptist General Association of Virginia **Scores:** 91.36% SAT V 400+; 94.99% SAT M 400+; 56.25% ACT 18-23; 16.67% ACT 24-29 **% Accepted:** 56 **Admission Plans:** Early Admission; Deferred Admission **Application Deadline:** July 01 **Application Fee:** $0.00 **H.S. Requirements:** High school diploma required; GED accepted **Costs Per Year:** Application fee: $0. Comprehensive fee: $25,600 includes full-time tuition ($18,040), mandatory fees ($1000), and college room and board ($6560). College room only: $4800. Room and board charges vary according to board plan and housing facility. Part-time tuition: $305 per credit. Part-time mandatory fees: $250 per term. Part-time tuition and fees vary according to course load, location, and program. **Scholarships:** Available **Calendar System:** Semester, Summer Session Available **Enrollment:** FT 789, PT 43, Grad 655 **Faculty:** FT 56, PT 46 **Student-Faculty Ratio:** 13:1 **Exams:** Other, SAT I or ACT, SAT I and SAT II or ACT **% Receiving Financial Aid:** 81 **% Residing in College-Owned, -Operated, or -Affiliated Housing:** 56 **Library Holdings:** 103,193 **Regional Accreditation:** Southern Association of Colleges and Schools **Credit Hours For Degree:** 67 credit hours, Associates; 123 credit hours, Bachelors **Intercollegiate Athletics:** Baseball M; Basketball M & W; Cross-Country Running M & W; Football M; Golf M; Lacrosse W; Soccer M & W; Softball W; Tennis M & W; Volleyball W

AVIATION INSTITUTE OF MAINTENANCE-MANASSAS
9821 Godwin Dr.
Manassas, VA 20110
Tel: (703)257-5515; 877-604-2121
Fax: (703)257-5523
E-mail: directoramm@aviationmaintenance.edu
Web Site: http://www.aviationmaintenance.edu/aviation-washington-dc.asp
Admissions: Sharon Howell
Type: Two-Year College **Application Fee:** $25.00 **Costs Per Year:** Application fee: $25. **Calendar System:** Quarter

AVIATION INSTITUTE OF MAINTENANCE-VIRGINIA BEACH
1429 Miller Store Ro
Virginia Beach, VA 23455
; 888-349-5387
Admissions: (757)363-2121
E-mail: directoramn@aviationmaintenance.edu
Web Site: http://www.aviationmaintenance.edu/aviation-norfolk.asp
Admissions: Mike Huffman
Type: Two-Year College **Application Fee:** $25.00 **Costs Per Year:** Application fee: $25. Tuition: $10,260 full-time, $220 per credit hour part-time. **Calendar System:** Quarter

BETA TECH
1610 Forest Ave. - Ste214
Richmond, VA 23229
Tel: (804)673-7110 **Type:** Two-Year College

BLUE RIDGE COMMUNITY COLLEGE
PO Box 80
Weyers Cave, VA 24486-0080

Tel: (540)234-9261
Admissions: (540)453-2332
E-mail: waylandm@brcc.edu
Web Site: http://www.brcc.edu/
President/CEO: Dr. James R. Perkins
Admissions: Mary Wayland
Financial Aid: Robert Clemmer
Type: Two-Year College **Sex:** Coed **Affiliation:** Virginia Community College System **% Accepted:** 100 **Admission Plans:** Open Admission; Early Admission **Application Deadline:** Rolling **Application Fee:** $0.00 **H.S. Requirements:** High school diploma required; GED accepted **Costs Per Year:** Application fee: $0. State resident tuition: $2040 full-time, $68 per credit hour part-time. Nonresident tuition: $6420 full-time, $214 per credit hour part-time. Mandatory fees: $146 full-time, $4.85 per credit hour part-time. **Scholarships:** Available **Calendar System:** Semester, Summer Session Available **Enrollment:** FT 1,513, PT 2,291 **Faculty:** FT 60, PT 126 **Student-Faculty Ratio:** 22:1 **Library Holdings:** 59,735 **Regional Accreditation:** Southern Association of Colleges and Schools **Credit Hours For Degree:** 63 semester hours, Associates **Professional Accreditation:** NLN

BLUEFIELD COLLEGE
3000 College Dr.
Bluefield, VA 24605-1799
Tel: (276)326-3682
Free: 800-872-0175
Admissions: (276)326-4217
Fax: (276)326-4288
Web Site: http://www.bluefield.edu/
President/CEO: Dr. Daniel G. MacMillan
Registrar: Catherine L. Matherly
Admissions: Tim Havens
Financial Aid: Debra Checchio
Type: Four-Year College **Sex:** Coed **Affiliation:** Southern Baptist **Scores:** 86% SAT V 400+; 81% SAT M 400+; 66% ACT 18-23; 9% ACT 24-29 **% Accepted:** 50 **Admission Plans:** Deferred Admission **Application Deadline:** Rolling **Application Fee:** $30.00 **H.S. Requirements:** High school diploma required; GED accepted **Costs Per Year:** Application fee: $30. Comprehensive fee: $18,337 includes full-time tuition ($11,675), mandatory fees ($630), and college room and board ($6032). College room only: $2371. Part-time tuition: $382 per hour. Part-time mandatory fees: $155 per term. **Scholarships:** Available **Calendar System:** Semester, Summer Session Available **Enrollment:** FT 692, PT 84 **Faculty:** FT 30, PT 66 **Student-Faculty Ratio:** 12:1 **Exams:** SAT I or ACT **% Receiving Financial Aid:** 73 **% Residing in College-Owned, -Operated, or -Affiliated Housing:** 48 **Library Holdings:** 74,150 **Regional Accreditation:** Southern Association of Colleges and Schools **Credit Hours For Degree:** 126 semester hours, Bachelors **Intercollegiate Athletics:** Baseball M; Basketball M & W; Golf M; Soccer M & W; Softball W; Tennis M & W; Volleyball W

BRIDGEWATER COLLEGE
402 East College St.
Bridgewater, VA 22812-1599
Tel: (540)828-8000
Free: 800-759-8328
Admissions: (540)828-5375
Fax: (540)828-5481
E-mail: admissions@bridgewater.edu
Web Site: http://www.bridgewater.edu/
President/CEO: Dr. Phillip C. Stone
Registrar: Cynthia K. Howdyshell
Admissions: Linda F. Stout
Financial Aid: J. Vern Fairchilds, Jr.
Type: Four-Year College **Sex:** Coed **Affiliation:** Church of the Brethren **Scores:** 96.32% SAT V 400+; 99.21% SAT M 400+; 59.34% ACT 18-23; 19.78% ACT 24-29 **% Accepted:** 86 **Admission Plans:** Deferred Admission **Application Deadline:** Rolling **Application Fee:** $30.00 **H.S. Requirements:** High school diploma required; GED accepted **Costs Per Year:** Application fee: $30. Comprehensive fee: $29,250 includes full-time tuition ($20,190) and college room and board ($9060). College room only: $4595. Part-time tuition: $650 per credit hour. Part-time mandatory fees: $30. **Scholarships:** Available **Calendar System:** 4-1-4, Summer Session Available **Enrollment:** FT 1,495, PT 11 **Faculty:** FT 96, PT 30 **Student-Faculty Ratio:** 14:1 **Exams:** SAT I or ACT **% Receiving Financial Aid:** 68 **% Residing in College-Owned, -Operated, or -Affiliated Housing:** 83 **Library Holdings:** 138,020 **Regional Accreditation:** Southern Association of Colleges and Schools **Credit Hours For Degree:** 123 credits, Bachelors **Intercollegiate Athletics:** Baseball M; Basketball M & W; Cross-Country Running M & W; Equestrian Sports M & W; Field Hockey W; Football M; Golf M; Lacrosse W; Soccer M & W; Softball W; Tennis M & W; Track and Field M & W; Volleyball W

BRYANT AND STRATTON COLLEGE, RICHMOND
8141 Hull St. Rd.
Richmond, VA 23235-6411
Tel: (804)745-2444
Fax: (804)499-7799
E-mail: tlawson@bryanstratton.edu
Web Site: http://www.bryantstratton.edu/
President/CEO: Carl L. Newell
Registrar: Deborah Merritt
Admissions: Troy Lawson
Financial Aid: Lisa Jackson
Type: Two-Year College **Sex:** Coed **Affiliation:** Bryant and Stratton Business Institute, Inc **Admission Plans:** Deferred Admission **Application Deadline:** Rolling **H.S. Requirements:** High school diploma required; GED accepted. For applicants 19 or older who meet entrance testing requirements: High school diploma or equivalent not required **Costs Per Year:** Tuition: $18,675 full-time, $415 per credit hour part-time. Mandatory fees: $25 full-time. **Calendar System:** Semester, Summer Session Available **Enrollment:** FT 137, PT 284 **Faculty:** FT 10, PT 41 **Student-Faculty Ratio:** 10:1 **Exams:** Other, SAT I or ACT **Library Holdings:** 3,176 **Regional Accreditation:** Middle State Association of Colleges and Schools **Credit Hours For Degree:** 68 per credit, Associates

BRYANT AND STRATTON COLLEGE, VIRGINIA BEACH
301 Centre Pointe Dr.
Virginia Beach, VA 23462-4417
Tel: (757)499-7900
Fax: (757)499-7799
Web Site: http://www.bryantstratton.edu/
President/CEO: Tracy Nannery
Registrar: Sheila Koenig
Admissions: Greg Smith
Financial Aid: Anita Wyche
Type: Two-Year College **Sex:** Coed **Affiliation:** Bryant and Stratton Business Institute, Inc **Admission Plans:** Open Admission **Application Fee:** $25.00 **H.S. Requirements:** High school diploma or equivalent not required **Scholarships:** Available **Calendar System:** Semester, Summer Session Available **Enrollment:** FT 238, PT 102 **Faculty:** FT 5, PT 35 **Student-Faculty Ratio:** 10:1 **Exams:** Other **Library Holdings:** 9,646 **Regional Accreditation:** Middle State Association of Colleges and Schools **Credit Hours For Degree:** 60 credit hours, Associates; 128 credit hours, Bachelors

CENTRAL VIRGINIA COMMUNITY COLLEGE
3506 Wards Rd.
Lynchburg, VA 24502-2498
Tel: (434)832-7600
Admissions: (434)832-7630
Fax: (434)386-4700
Web Site: http://www.cvcc.vccs.edu/
President/CEO: Dr. Darrel W. Staat
Registrar: Dr. Richard A. Rainsberger
Admissions: Judy Wilhelm
Financial Aid: Robert L. Clemmer
Type: Two-Year College **Sex:** Coed **Affiliation:** Virginia Community College System **Admission Plans:** Open Admission; Early Admission; Deferred Admission **Application Fee:** $0.00 **H.S. Requirements:** High school diploma or equivalent not required. For allied health programs: High school diploma required; GED not accepted **Scholarships:** Available **Calendar System:** Semester, Summer Session Available **Faculty:** FT 57, PT 116 **Exams:** Other **Library Holdings:** 37,000 **Regional Accreditation:** Southern Association of Colleges and Schools **Credit Hours For Degree:** 62 semester hours, Associates **Professional Accreditation:** JRCERT, NAACLS

CHRISTENDOM COLLEGE
134 Christendom Dr.
Front Royal, VA 22630-5103
Tel: (540)636-2900
Free: 800-877-5456

Fax: (540)636-1655
E-mail: admissions@christendom.edu
Web Site: http://www.christendom.edu/
President/CEO: Dr. Timothy O'Donnell
Registrar: Walter Janaro
Admissions: Tom McFadden
Financial Aid: Alisa Polk
Type: Comprehensive **Sex:** Coed **Affiliation:** Roman Catholic **Scores:** 100% SAT V 400+; 100% SAT M 400+ **% Accepted:** 76 **Admission Plans:** Early Admission; Early Action **Application Deadline:** March 01 **Application Fee:** $25.00 **H.S. Requirements:** High school diploma or equivalent not required **Costs Per Year:** Application fee: $25. Comprehensive fee: $22,806 includes full-time tuition ($16,290), mandatory fees ($450), and college room and board ($6066). **Scholarships:** Available **Calendar System:** Semester, Summer Session Available **Enrollment:** FT 372, PT 7, Grad 56 **Faculty:** FT 23, PT 16 **Student-Faculty Ratio:** 12:1 **Exams:** SAT I or ACT **% Receiving Financial Aid:** 48 **% Residing in College-Owned, -Operated, or -Affiliated Housing:** 95 **Library Holdings:** 64,265 **Regional Accreditation:** Southern Association of Colleges and Schools **Credit Hours For Degree:** 84 credit hours, Associates; 126 credit hours, Bachelors **Intercollegiate Athletics:** Baseball M; Basketball M & W; Soccer M & W; Softball W; Volleyball W

CHRISTOPHER NEWPORT UNIVERSITY
1 University Place
Newport News, VA 23606-2998
Tel: (757)594-7000
Free: 800-333-4268
Admissions: (757)594-7015
Fax: (757)594-7333
E-mail: admit@cnu.edu
Web Site: http://www.cnu.edu/
President/CEO: Sen. Paul S. Trible, Jr.
Registrar: Donna A. Varner
Admissions: Patricia Cavender
Financial Aid: Mary Wiggington
Type: Comprehensive **Sex:** Coed **Scores:** 100% SAT V 400+; 100% SAT M 400+; 59% ACT 18-23; 37% ACT 24-29 **% Accepted:** 62 **Admission Plans:** Early Admission; Early Action; Deferred Admission **Application Deadline:** March 01 **Application Fee:** $35.00 **H.S. Requirements:** High school diploma required; GED accepted **Costs Per Year:** Application fee: $35. State resident tuition: $3442 full-time, $143 per credit hour part-time. Nonresident tuition: $10,464 full-time, $436 per credit hour part-time. Mandatory fees: $2384 full-time, $99. Full-time tuition and fees vary according to course load. Part-time tuition and fees vary according to course load. College room and board: $7500. Room and board charges vary according to housing facility. **Scholarships:** Available **Calendar System:** Semester, Summer Session Available **Enrollment:** FT 4,204, PT 332, Grad 163 **Faculty:** FT 218, PT 21 **Student-Faculty Ratio:** 19:1 **Exams:** SAT I or ACT **% Receiving Financial Aid:** 39 **% Residing in College-Owned, -Operated, or -Affiliated Housing:** 30 **Library Holdings:** 328,319 **Regional Accreditation:** Southern Association of Colleges and Schools **Credit Hours For Degree:** 120 semester hours, Bachelors **ROTC:** Army **Professional Accreditation:** ABET, AACN, CSWE, NASM **Intercollegiate Athletics:** Baseball M; Basketball M & W; Cross-Country Running M & W; Equestrian Sports M & W; Field Hockey W; Football M; Golf M; Lacrosse M & W; Rugby M; Sailing M & W; Soccer M & W; Softball W; Tennis M & W; Track and Field M & W; Volleyball W

THE COLLEGE OF WILLIAM AND MARY
PO Box 8795
Williamsburg, VA 23187-8795
Tel: (757)221-4000
Admissions: (757)221-4223
Fax: (757)221-1242
E-mail: admiss@facstaff.wm.edu
Web Site: http://www.wm.edu/
President/CEO: Timothy J. Sullivan
Admissions: Henry Broaddus
Financial Aid: Edward P. Irish
Type: University **Sex:** Coed **Scores:** 100% SAT V 400+; 100% SAT M 400+; 7% ACT 18-23; 43% ACT 24-29 **% Accepted:** 31 **Admission Plans:** Preferred Admission; Early Admission; Early Decision Plan; Deferred Admission **Application Deadline:** January 01 **Application Fee:** $60.00 **H.S. Requirements:** High school diploma or equivalent not required **Costs Per Year:** Application fee: $60. State resident tuition: $4730 full-time, $180 per credit hour part-time. Nonresident tuition: $20,000 full-time, $710 per credit hour part-time. Mandatory fees: $3048 full-time. Full-time tuition and fees vary according to program. Part-time tuition varies according to program. College room and board: $6417. College room only: $3856. Room and board charges vary according to board plan and housing facility. **Scholarships:** Available **Calendar System:** Semester, Summer Session Available **Enrollment:** FT 5,527, PT 67, Grad 1,334 **Faculty:** FT 596, PT 167 **Student-Faculty Ratio:** 11:1 **Exams:** SAT I or ACT, SAT II **% Receiving Financial Aid:** 27 **% Residing in College-Owned, -Operated, or -Affiliated Housing:** 75 **Library Holdings:** 2,043,345 **Regional Accreditation:** Southern Association of Colleges and Schools **Credit Hours For Degree:** 120 credit hours, Bachelors **ROTC:** Army **Professional Accreditation:** AACSB, ABA, ACA, APA, AALS, NCATE **Intercollegiate Athletics:** Baseball M; Basketball M & W; Cross-Country Running M & W; Field Hockey W; Football M; Golf M & W; Gymnastics M & W; Lacrosse W; Soccer M & W; Swimming and Diving M & W; Tennis M & W; Track and Field M & W; Volleyball W

DABNEY S. LANCASTER COMMUNITY COLLEGE
100 Dabney Dr., PO Box 1000
Clifton Forge, VA 24422
Tel: (540)863-2800
Admissions: (540)863-2815
Fax: (540)863-2915
Web Site: http://www.dl.vccs.edu/
President/CEO: Dr. Richard R. Teaff
Registrar: Heather Wood
Admissions: Dr. Mary G. Wilson
Financial Aid: Sandy Haverlack
Type: Two-Year College **Sex:** Coed **Affiliation:** Virginia Community College System **Admission Plans:** Open Admission; Early Admission; Deferred Admission **Application Deadline:** Rolling **Application Fee:** $0.00 **H.S. Requirements:** High school diploma required; GED accepted. For applicants 18 or over who demonstrate ability to benefit from a specific program: High school diploma or equivalent not required **Costs Per Year:** Application fee: $0. State resident tuition: $1740 full-time, $72.50 per credit part-time. Nonresident tuition: $5648 full-time, $235.35 per credit part-time. Mandatory fees: $157 full-time, $6.55 per credit part-time. **Scholarships:** Available **Calendar System:** Semester, Summer Session Available **Faculty:** FT 21, PT 74 **Library Holdings:** 37,716 **Regional Accreditation:** Southern Association of Colleges and Schools **Credit Hours For Degree:** 68 semester hours, Associates **Professional Accreditation:** NLN **Intercollegiate Athletics:** Basketball M

DANVILLE COMMUNITY COLLEGE
1008 South Main St.
Danville, VA 24541-4088
Tel: (434)797-2222
Free: 800-560-4291
Admissions: (434)797-8490
Fax: (434)797-8541
Web Site: http://www.dcc.vccs.edu/
President/CEO: Dr. B. Carlyle Ramsey
Admissions: Peter Castiglione
Financial Aid: Mary Gore
Type: Two-Year College **Sex:** Coed **Affiliation:** Virginia Community College System **Admission Plans:** Open Admission; Preferred Admission; Early Admission; Deferred Admission **Application Fee:** $0.00 **H.S. Requirements:** High school diploma required; GED accepted **Costs Per Year:** Application fee: $0. State resident tuition: $2150 full-time, $71.65 per credit hour part-time. Nonresident tuition: $6596 full-time, $219.85 per credit hour part-time. Mandatory fees: $111 full-time, $3.65 per credit hour part-time. **Scholarships:** Available **Calendar System:** Semester, Summer Session Available **Enrollment:** FT 1,366, PT 2,723 **Faculty:** FT 53, PT 148 **Student-Faculty Ratio:** 19:1 **Exams:** Other **Library Holdings:** 41,600 **Regional Accreditation:** Southern Association of Colleges and Schools **Credit Hours For Degree:** 62 semester hours, Associates

DEVRY UNIVERSITY (ARLINGTON)
2450 Crystal Dr.
Arlington, VA 22202
Tel: (703)414-4000; (866)563-3900
Fax: (703)414-4040
Web Site: http://www.devry.edu/

President/CEO: Loretta Franklin
Registrar: Edward Trombley
Financial Aid: Robert McDevitt
Type: Comprehensive **Sex:** Coed **Affiliation:** DeVry University **Admission Plans:** Deferred Admission **Application Deadline:** Rolling **Application Fee:** $50.00 **H.S. Requirements:** High school diploma required; GED accepted **Costs Per Year:** Application fee: $50. One-time mandatory fee: $40. Tuition: $13,060 full-time, $475 per credit part-time. Mandatory fees: $270 full-time, $160 per year part-time. Full-time tuition and fees vary according to course load. Part-time tuition and fees vary according to course load. **Scholarships:** Available **Calendar System:** Semester, Summer Session Available **Enrollment:** FT 310, PT 153, Grad 122 **Faculty:** FT 20, PT 42 **Student-Faculty Ratio:** 13:1 **% Receiving Financial Aid:** 68 **Library Holdings:** 7,800 **Regional Accreditation:** North Central Association of Colleges and Schools **Credit Hours For Degree:** 67 credit hours, Associates; 122 credit hours, Bachelors

DEVRY UNIVERSITY (MCLEAN)

1751 Pinnacle Dr., Ste. 250
McLean, VA 22102-3832
Tel: (703)556-9669
Fax: (703)556-9420
Web Site: http://www.devry.edu/ **Type:** Comprehensive **Sex:** Coed
Costs Per Year: One-time mandatory fee: $40. Tuition: $13,060 full-time, $475 per credit part-time. Mandatory fees: $60 full-time, $30 per year part-time. **Calendar System:** Semester **Regional Accreditation:** North Central Association of Colleges and Schools

EASTERN MENNONITE UNIVERSITY

1200 Park Rd.
Harrisonburg, VA 22802-2462
Tel: (540)432-4000
Free: 800-368-2665
Admissions: (540)432-4118
Fax: (540)432-4444
E-mail: admiss@emu.edu
Web Site: http://www.emu.edu/
President/CEO: Dr. Loren E, Swartzendruber
Registrar: David A. Detrow
Admissions: Stephanie C. Shafer
Financial Aid: Michele R. Hensley
Type: Comprehensive **Sex:** Coed **Affiliation:** Mennonite **Scores:** 92% SAT V 400+; 94% SAT M 400+; 38% ACT 18-23; 43% ACT 24-29 **% Accepted:** 77 **Admission Plans:** Early Admission; Deferred Admission **Application Deadline:** Rolling **Application Fee:** $25.00 **H.S. Requirements:** High school diploma required; GED accepted **Costs Per Year:** Application fee: $25. Comprehensive fee: $27,220 includes full-time tuition ($20,612), mandatory fees ($58), and college room and board ($6550). College room only: $3550. Part-time tuition: $862 per credit hour. Part-time mandatory fees: $2 per credit hour. **Scholarships:** Available **Calendar System:** Semester, Summer Session Available **Enrollment:** FT 970, PT 42, Grad 164 **Faculty:** FT 116, PT 47 **Student-Faculty Ratio:** 9:1 **Exams:** SAT I or ACT **% Receiving Financial Aid:** 72 **% Residing in College-Owned, -Operated, or -Affiliated Housing:** 66 **Library Holdings:** 163,932 **Regional Accreditation:** Southern Association of Colleges and Schools **Credit Hours For Degree:** 64 semester hours, Associates; 128 semester hours, Bachelors **Professional Accreditation:** ACA, ACIPE, ATS, CSWE, NCATE **Intercollegiate Athletics:** Baseball M; Basketball M & W; Cross-Country Running M & W; Soccer M & W; Softball W; Tennis M & W; Track and Field M & W; Volleyball M & W

EASTERN SHORE COMMUNITY COLLEGE

29300 Lankford Hwy.
Melfa, VA 23410-3000
Tel: (757)789-1789; 877-871-8455
Admissions: (757)789-1731
Fax: (757)789-1739
E-mail: eswilss@es.cc.va.us
Web Site: http://www.es.cc.va.us/
President/CEO: Dr. Richard E. Jenkins
Admissions: Faye Wilson
Financial Aid: P. Bryan Smith
Type: Two-Year College **Sex:** Coed **Affiliation:** Virginia Community College System **Admission Plans:** Open Admission; Preferred Admission **Application Fee:** $0.00 **H.S. Requirements:** High school diploma required; GED accepted **Costs Per Year:** Application fee: $0. State resident tuition: $2040 full-time, $68 per credit part-time. Nonresident tuition: $6420 full-time, $214 per credit part-time. Mandatory fees: $110 full-time, $3.65 per credit part-time. **Scholarships:** Available **Calendar System:** Semester, Summer Session Available **Enrollment:** FT 260, PT 547 **Faculty:** FT 18, PT 39 **Student-Faculty Ratio:** 13:1 **Library Holdings:** 20,479 **Regional Accreditation:** Southern Association of Colleges and Schools **Credit Hours For Degree:** 62 semester hours, Associates

ECPI COLLEGE OF TECHNOLOGY (NEWPORT NEWS)

1001 Omni Blvd., No. 100
Newport News, VA 23606
Tel: (757)838-9191
Fax: (757)827-5351
Web Site: http://www.ecpi.edu/
President/CEO: John Olsen
Registrar: Cheri Richards
Admissions: Cheryl Lokey
Financial Aid: Janet Doyan
Type: Two-Year College **Sex:** Coed **Admission Plans:** Deferred Admission **Application Fee:** $100.00 **H.S. Requirements:** High school diploma required; GED accepted **Costs Per Year:** Application fee: $100. **Scholarships:** Available **Calendar System:** Trimester, Summer Session Available **Enrollment:** FT 556 **Faculty:** FT 66, PT 64 **Student-Faculty Ratio:** 16:1 **Exams:** SAT I or ACT, SAT I, SAT II **Library Holdings:** 13,014 **Regional Accreditation:** Southern Association of Colleges and Schools **Credit Hours For Degree:** 60 semester hours, Associates

ECPI COLLEGE OF TECHNOLOGY (VIRGINIA BEACH)

5555 Greenwich Rd.
Virginia Beach, VA 23462
Tel: (757)671-7171
Free: 800-986-1200
E-mail: rballance@ecpi.edu
Web Site: http://www.ecpi.edu/
President/CEO: Mark B. Dreyfus
Admissions: Ronald Ballance
Type: Two-Year College **Sex:** Coed **% Accepted:** 69 **Admission Plans:** Deferred Admission **Application Fee:** $100.00 **H.S. Requirements:** High school diploma required; GED accepted **Costs Per Year:** Application fee: $100. Tuition: $9750 full-time. **Scholarships:** Available **Calendar System:** Trimester, Summer Session Available **Enrollment:** FT 4,312, PT 79 **Faculty:** FT 66, PT 64 **Exams:** SAT I or ACT, SAT I, SAT II **Regional Accreditation:** Southern Association of Colleges and Schools

ECPI TECHNICAL COLLEGE (GLEN ALLEN)

4305 Cox Rd.
Glen Allen, VA 23060
Tel: (804)934-0100
Free: 800-986-1200
Fax: (804)934-0054
E-mail: jpope@ecpi.edu
Web Site: http://www.ecpitech.edu/
President/CEO: Jacob Pope
Admissions: Jacob Pope
Type: Two-Year College **Sex:** Coed **% Accepted:** 82 **Application Deadline:** Rolling **Application Fee:** $100.00 **Costs Per Year:** Application fee: $100. **Calendar System:** Semester **Enrollment:** FT 473 **Student-Faculty Ratio:** 15:1 **Exams:** SAT I and SAT II or ACT, SAT I, SAT II **Professional Accreditation:** ACCSCT

ECPI TECHNICAL COLLEGE (RICHMOND)

800 Moorefield Park Dr.
Richmond, VA 23236
Tel: (804)330-5533
Free: 800-986-1200
E-mail: agerard@ecpi.edu
Web Site: http://www.ecpitech.edu/
President/CEO: Ada Gerard
Admissions: Ada Gerard
Type: Two-Year College **Sex:** Coed **% Accepted:** 75 **Admission Plans:** Deferred Admission **Application Deadline:** Rolling **Application Fee:** $100.00 **H.S. Requirements:** High school diploma required; GED accepted **Costs Per Year:** Application fee: $100. Tuition: $9750 full-time. **Scholarships:** Available **Calendar System:** Semester, Summer Session Available

Student-Faculty Ratio: 15:1 **Exams:** SAT I and SAT II or ACT, SAT I, SAT II **Library Holdings:** 3,165 **Credit Hours For Degree:** 60 semester hours, Associates **Professional Accreditation:** ACCSCT

ECPI TECHNICAL COLLEGE (ROANOKE)
5234 Airport Rd.
Roanoke, VA 24012
Tel: (540)563-8080
Free: 800-986-1200
Fax: (540)362-5400
E-mail: ehass@ecpi.edu
Web Site: http://www.ecpi.net/
President/CEO: Dr. Jerry Causey
Admissions: Elmer Haas
Type: Two-Year College **Sex:** Coed **% Accepted:** 65 **Admission Plans:** Deferred Admission **Application Deadline:** Rolling **Application Fee:** $100.00 **H.S. Requirements:** High school diploma required; GED accepted **Costs Per Year:** Application fee: $100. Tuition: $9750 full-time. **Scholarships:** Available **Calendar System:** Semester, Summer Session Available **Student-Faculty Ratio:** 15:1 **Exams:** SAT I and SAT II, SAT I, SAT II **Library Holdings:** 1,703 **Credit Hours For Degree:** 60 credit hours, Associates **Professional Accreditation:** ACCSCT

EMORY & HENRY COLLEGE
PO Box 947
Emory, VA 24327-0947
Tel: (276)944-4121
Free: 800-848-5493
Admissions: (276)944-6133
Fax: (276)944-6934
E-mail: ehadmiss@ehc.edu
Web Site: http://www.ehc.edu/
President/CEO: Dr. Thomas R. Morris
Registrar: Sherry Lyttle
Admissions: Liz Daniels
Financial Aid: Scarlett Cortner
Type: Comprehensive **Sex:** Coed **Affiliation:** United Methodist **Scores:** 99% SAT V 400+; 98% SAT M 400+; 54% ACT 18-23; 39% ACT 24-29 **% Accepted:** 76 **Admission Plans:** Early Admission; Early Decision Plan; Deferred Admission **Application Deadline:** Rolling **Application Fee:** $30.00 **H.S. Requirements:** High school diploma required; GED accepted **Costs Per Year:** Application fee: $30. Comprehensive fee: $26,570 includes full-time tuition ($19,530) and college room and board ($7040). College room only: $3500. Full-time tuition varies according to course load. Room and board charges vary according to board plan. Part-time tuition: $815 per hour. Part-time tuition varies according to course load. **Scholarships:** Available **Calendar System:** Semester, Summer Session Available **Enrollment:** FT 999, PT 28, Grad 74 **Faculty:** FT 68, PT 27 **Student-Faculty Ratio:** 13:1 **Exams:** SAT I or ACT **% Receiving Financial Aid:** 79 **% Residing in College-Owned, -Operated, or -Affiliated Housing:** 66 **Library Holdings:** 337,290 **Regional Accreditation:** Southern Association of Colleges and Schools **Credit Hours For Degree:** 116 semester hours, Bachelors **Professional Accreditation:** JRCEPAT **Intercollegiate Athletics:** Baseball M; Basketball M & W; Cross-Country Running M & W; Football M; Golf M; Soccer M & W; Softball W; Tennis M & W; Volleyball W

FERRUM COLLEGE
PO Box 1000
Ferrum, VA 24088-9001
Tel: (540)365-2121
Free: 800-868-9797
Admissions: (540)365-4290
Fax: (540)365-4266
E-mail: admissions@ferrum.edu
Web Site: http://www.ferrum.edu/
President/CEO: Dr. Jennifer L. Braaten
Registrar: Margaret M. Clark
Admissions: Gilda Q. Woods
Financial Aid: Sheila Nelson-Hensley
Type: Four-Year College **Sex:** Coed **Affiliation:** United Methodist **Scores:** 80% SAT V 400+; 76% SAT M 400+ **% Accepted:** 72 **Admission Plans:** Early Admission; Deferred Admission **Application Deadline:** Rolling **Application Fee:** $25.00 **H.S. Requirements:** High school diploma required; GED accepted **Costs Per Year:** Application fee: $25. Comprehensive fee: $24,320 includes full-time tuition ($17,990), mandatory fees ($30), and college room and board ($6300). Room and board charges vary according to housing facility. Part-time tuition: $360 per hour. Part-time tuition varies according to course load. **Scholarships:** Available **Calendar System:** Semester, Summer Session Available **Enrollment:** FT 962, PT 29 **Faculty:** FT 62, PT 18 **Student-Faculty Ratio:** 14:1 **Exams:** SAT I or ACT **% Receiving Financial Aid:** 76 **% Residing in College-Owned, -Operated, or -Affiliated Housing:** 70 **Library Holdings:** 154,370 **Regional Accreditation:** Southern Association of Colleges and Schools **Credit Hours For Degree:** 127 credit hours, Bachelors **Professional Accreditation:** CSWE, NRPA **Intercollegiate Athletics:** Baseball M; Basketball M & W; Cheerleading M & W; Cross-Country Running M & W; Equestrian Sports M & W; Football M; Golf M; Lacrosse W; Soccer M & W; Softball W; Tennis M & W; Volleyball W

GEORGE MASON UNIVERSITY
4400 University Dr.
Fairfax, VA 22030
Tel: (703)993-1000
Admissions: (703)993-2400
E-mail: admissions@gmu.edu
Web Site: http://www.gmu.edu/
President/CEO: Dr. Alan G. Merten
Registrar: Susan H. Jones
Admissions: Andrew Flagel
Financial Aid: Jevita de Freitas
Type: University **Sex:** Coed **Scores:** 98% SAT V 400+; 98% SAT M 400+; 60% ACT 18-23; 28% ACT 24-29 **% Accepted:** 69 **Admission Plans:** Early Admission; Deferred Admission **Application Deadline:** January 15 **Application Fee:** $60.00 **H.S. Requirements:** High school diploma required; GED accepted **Costs Per Year:** Application fee: $60. State resident tuition: $4356 full-time, $181.50 per credit part-time. Nonresident tuition: $15,636 full-time, $651.50 per credit part-time. Mandatory fees: $1524 full-time, $63.50 per credit part-time. Full-time tuition and fees vary according to course load. Part-time tuition and fees vary according to course load. College room and board: $6480. College room only: $3700. Room and board charges vary according to board plan and housing facility. **Scholarships:** Available **Calendar System:** Semester, Summer Session Available **Enrollment:** FT 13,578, PT 4,513, Grad 10,895 **Faculty:** FT 997, PT 958 **Student-Faculty Ratio:** 16:1 **Exams:** SAT I or ACT **% Receiving Financial Aid:** 37 **% Residing in College-Owned, -Operated, or -Affiliated Housing:** 23 **Library Holdings:** 1,460,524 **Regional Accreditation:** Southern Association of Colleges and Schools **Credit Hours For Degree:** 120 credit hours, Bachelors **ROTC:** Army, Air Force **Professional Accreditation:** AACSB, ABET, AACN, ABA, APA, AALS, CSWE, NASM, NASPAA, NCATE, NLN **Intercollegiate Athletics:** Baseball M; Basketball M & W; Cheerleading M & W; Cross-Country Running M & W; Golf M; Lacrosse W; Soccer M & W; Softball W; Swimming and Diving M & W; Tennis M & W; Track and Field M & W; Volleyball M & W; Wrestling M

GERMANNA COMMUNITY COLLEGE
2130 Germanna Hwy.
Locust Grove, VA 22508-2102
Tel: (540)727-3000
Admissions: (540)891-3016
Fax: (540)727-3207
Web Site: http://www.gcc.vccs.edu/
President/CEO: Dr. Francis S. Turnage
Registrar: Rita Dunston
Admissions: Rita Dunston
Financial Aid: Jim Brunner
Type: Two-Year College **Sex:** Coed **Affiliation:** Virginia Community College System **% Accepted:** 100 **Admission Plans:** Open Admission; Early Admission **Application Deadline:** Rolling **Application Fee:** $0.00 **H.S. Requirements:** High school diploma or equivalent not required. For nursing program: High school diploma required; GED accepted **Costs Per Year:** Application fee: $0. State resident tuition: $1632 full-time, $68 per credit part-time. Nonresident tuition: $5136 full-time, $214 per credit part-time. Mandatory fees: $118 full-time, $4.90 per credit part-time. Full-time tuition and fees vary according to course load. Part-time tuition and fees vary according to course load. **Scholarships:** Available **Calendar System:** Semester, Summer Session Available **Enrollment:** FT 1,359, PT 3,440 **Faculty:** FT 48, PT 224 **Student-Faculty Ratio:** 20:1 **Library Holdings:** 22,412 **Regional Accreditation:** Southern Association of Colleges and Schools **Credit Hours For Degree:** 61 semester hours, Associates **Professional Accreditation:** NLN

HAMPDEN-SYDNEY COLLEGE
PO Box 667
Hampden-Sydney, VA 23943
Tel: (434)223-6000
Free: 800-755-0733
Admissions: (434)223-6120
Fax: (434)223-6346
E-mail: agarland@hsc.edu
Web Site: http://www.hsc.edu/
President/CEO: Dr. Walter M. Bortz, III
Registrar: Mark Newcomb
Admissions: Anita H. Garland
Financial Aid: Keith Wellings
Type: Four-Year College **Sex:** Men **Affiliation:** Presbyterian Church (U.S. A.) **Scores:** 97% SAT V 400+; 100% SAT M 400+; 45% ACT 18-23; 47% ACT 24-29 **% Accepted:** 67 **Admission Plans:** Early Admission; Early Action; Early Decision Plan **Application Deadline:** March 01 **Application Fee:** $30.00 **H.S. Requirements:** High school diploma required; GED accepted **Costs Per Year:** Application fee: $30. Comprehensive fee: $34,295 includes full-time tuition ($25,166), mandatory fees ($1004), and college room and board ($8125). College room only: $3436. Part-time tuition: $748 per credit hour. **Scholarships:** Available **Calendar System:** Semester, Summer Session Available **Enrollment:** FT 1,060 **Faculty:** FT 91, PT 17 **Student-Faculty Ratio:** 10:1 **Exams:** SAT I or ACT, SAT II **% Receiving Financial Aid:** 47 **% Residing in College-Owned, -Operated, or -Affiliated Housing:** 93 **Library Holdings:** 219,221 **Regional Accreditation:** Southern Association of Colleges and Schools **Credit Hours For Degree:** 120 semester hours, Bachelors **ROTC:** Army **Intercollegiate Athletics:** Baseball M; Basketball M; Crew M; Cross-Country Running M; Fencing M; Football M; Golf M; Lacrosse M; Riflery M; Rugby M; Soccer M; Tennis M; Ultimate Frisbee M

HAMPTON UNIVERSITY
Hampton, VA 23668
Tel: (757)727-5000
Free: 800-624-3328
Admissions: (757)727-5328
Fax: (757)727-5084
E-mail: angela.boyd@hamptonu.edu
Web Site: http://www.hamptonu.edu/
President/CEO: Dr. William R. Harvey
Registrar: Jorsene Cooper
Admissions: Angela Boyd
Financial Aid: Cassondra Costa
Type: University **Sex:** Coed **Scores:** 100% SAT V 400+; 100% SAT M 400+; 60% ACT 18-23; 3% ACT 24-29 **% Accepted:** 77 **Admission Plans:** Early Admission; Deferred Admission **Application Deadline:** March 01 **Application Fee:** $25.00 **H.S. Requirements:** High school diploma required; GED accepted **Costs Per Year:** Application fee: $25. Comprehensive fee: $20,928 includes full-time tuition ($12,722), mandatory fees ($1460), and college room and board ($6746). College room only: $3580. Full-time tuition and fees vary according to degree level. Room and board charges vary according to board plan and housing facility. Part-time tuition: $320 per credit. **Scholarships:** Available **Calendar System:** Semester, Summer Session Available **Enrollment:** FT 4,913, PT 412, Grad 662 **Faculty:** FT 323, PT 124 **Student-Faculty Ratio:** 16:1 **Exams:** SAT I or ACT **% Receiving Financial Aid:** 67 **% Residing in College-Owned, -Operated, or -Affiliated Housing:** 59 **Library Holdings:** 336,092 **Regional Accreditation:** Southern Association of Colleges and Schools **Credit Hours For Degree:** 121 semester hours, Bachelors **ROTC:** Army, Navy **Professional Accreditation:** ABET, ACEJMC, AACN, ACPhE, APTA, ASLHA, CAA, NASM, NCATE, NLN **Intercollegiate Athletics:** Basketball M & W; Bowling W; Cross-Country Running M & W; Football M; Golf M & W; Sailing M & W; Softball W; Tennis M & W; Track and Field M & W; Volleyball W

HOLLINS UNIVERSITY
PO Box 9603
Roanoke, VA 24020-1603
Tel: (540)362-6000
Free: 800-456-9595
Admissions: (540)362-6401
Fax: (540)362-6218
E-mail: huadm@hollins.edu
Web Site: http://www.hollins.edu/
President/CEO: Dr. Lawrence Wayne Markert
Registrar: Dr. Thomas H. Mesner
Admissions: Rebecca Eckstein
Financial Aid: Rebecca Eckstein
Type: Comprehensive **Scores:** 100% SAT V 400+; 97% SAT M 400+; 37% ACT 18-23; 48% ACT 24-29 **% Accepted:** 86 **Admission Plans:** Early Admission; Early Decision Plan; Deferred Admission **Application Fee:** $35.00 **H.S. Requirements:** High school diploma required; GED accepted **Costs Per Year:** Application fee: $35. Comprehensive fee: $31,105 includes full-time tuition ($22,470), mandatory fees ($475), and college room and board ($8160). College room only: $4880. Part-time tuition: $702 per credit. **Scholarships:** Available **Calendar System:** 4-1-4, Summer Session Not available **Enrollment:** FT 790, PT 58, Grad 275 **Faculty:** FT 68, PT 41 **Student-Faculty Ratio:** 10:1 **Exams:** SAT I or ACT **% Receiving Financial Aid:** 61 **% Residing in College-Owned, -Operated, or -Affiliated Housing:** 79 **Regional Accreditation:** Southern Association of Colleges and Schools **Credit Hours For Degree:** 128 credits, Bachelors **Professional Accreditation:** TEAC **Intercollegiate Athletics:** Basketball W; Equestrian Sports W; Fencing W; Golf W; Lacrosse W; Soccer W; Swimming and Diving W; Tennis W

ITT TECHNICAL INSTITUTE (CHANTILLY)
14420 Abermarle Point Place, Ste. 100
Chantilly, VA 20151
Tel: (703)263-2541; 888-895-8324
Web Site: http://www.itt-tech.edu/
President/CEO: Peggy T. Payne
Admissions: Peggy T. Payne
Type: Two-Year College **Sex:** Coed **Affiliation:** ITT Educational Services, Inc **Admission Plans:** Deferred Admission **Application Deadline:** Rolling **Application Fee:** $100.00 **H.S. Requirements:** High school diploma required; GED accepted **Costs Per Year:** Application fee: $100. **Scholarships:** Available **Calendar System:** Quarter, Summer Session Not available **Exams:** Other **Credit Hours For Degree:** 96 credit hours, Associates **Professional Accreditation:** ACICS

ITT TECHNICAL INSTITUTE (NORFOLK)
863 Glenrock Rd., Ste. 100
Norfolk, VA 23502-3701
Tel: (757)466-1260
Web Site: http://www.itt-tech.edu/
President/CEO: Calvin E. Lawrence
Admissions: Cal Lawrence
Financial Aid: Marsha Miller
Type: Two-Year College **Sex:** Coed **Affiliation:** ITT Educational Services, Inc **Admission Plans:** Deferred Admission **Application Deadline:** Rolling **Application Fee:** $100.00 **H.S. Requirements:** High school diploma required; GED accepted **Costs Per Year:** Application fee: $100. **Scholarships:** Available **Calendar System:** Quarter, Summer Session Not available **Exams:** Other **Credit Hours For Degree:** 96 credit hours, Associates; 180 credit hours, Bachelors **Professional Accreditation:** ACICS

ITT TECHNICAL INSTITUTE (RICHMOND)
300 Gateway Centre Parkway
Richmond, VA 23235
Tel: (804)330-4992
Web Site: http://www.itt-tech.edu/
President/CEO: Jeff Sikora
Admissions: Elaine Bartoli
Type: Two-Year College **Sex:** Coed **Affiliation:** ITT Educational Services, Inc **Admission Plans:** Deferred Admission **Application Deadline:** Rolling **Application Fee:** $100.00 **H.S. Requirements:** High school diploma required; GED accepted **Costs Per Year:** Application fee: $100. **Scholarships:** Available **Calendar System:** Quarter, Summer Session Not available **Exams:** Other **Credit Hours For Degree:** 96 credit hours, Associates; 180 credit hours, Bachelors **Professional Accreditation:** ACICS

ITT TECHNICAL INSTITUTE (SPRINGFIELD)
7300 Boston Blvd.
Springfield, VA 22153
Tel: (703)440-9535; (866)817-8324
Fax: (703)440-9561
Web Site: http://www.itt-tech.edu/
President/CEO: Charles E. Boyd
Admissions: Doug Howard

Type: Two-Year College **Sex:** Coed **Affiliation:** ITT Educational Services, Inc **Admission Plans:** Deferred Admission **Application Deadline:** Rolling **Application Fee:** $100.00 **H.S. Requirements:** High school diploma required; GED accepted **Costs Per Year:** Application fee: $100. **Scholarships:** Available **Calendar System:** Quarter, Summer Session Not available **Exams:** Other **Credit Hours For Degree:** 96 credit hours, Associates **Professional Accreditation:** ACICS

J. SARGEANT REYNOLDS COMMUNITY COLLEGE
PO Box 85622
Richmond, VA 23285-5622
Tel: (804)371-3000
Admissions: (804)371-3029
Fax: (804)371-3650
E-mail: srmarss@jsr.cc.va.us
Web Site: http://www.reynolds.edu
President/CEO: Dr. Gary L. Rhodes
Registrar: Wanda Bolda
Admissions: Karen Pettis-Walden
Financial Aid: Barry Davis
Type: Two-Year College **Sex:** Coed **Affiliation:** Virginia Community College System **Admission Plans:** Open Admission **Application Fee:** $0.00 **H.S. Requirements:** High school diploma required; GED accepted **Costs Per Year:** Application fee: $0. State resident tuition: $2282 full-time, $76.05 per credit hour part-time. Nonresident tuition: $6728 full-time, $224.25 per credit hour part-time. **Scholarships:** Available **Calendar System:** Semester, Summer Session Available **Enrollment:** FT 2,871, PT 8,807 **Faculty:** FT 117, PT 450 **Student-Faculty Ratio:** 22:1 **Library Holdings:** 80,736 **Regional Accreditation:** Southern Association of Colleges and Schools **Credit Hours For Degree:** 61 credit hours, Associates **Professional Accreditation:** ADA, COptA, CARC, NAACLS, NLN

JAMES MADISON UNIVERSITY
800 South Main St.
Harrisonburg, VA 22807
Tel: (540)568-6211
Admissions: (540)568-5681
Fax: (540)568-3332
E-mail: gotojmu@jmu.edu
Web Site: http://www.jmu.edu/
President/CEO: Dr. Linwood H. Rose
Registrar: Sherry Hood
Admissions: Michael D. Walsh
Financial Aid: Lisa Tumer
Type: Comprehensive **Sex:** Coed **Scores:** 99% SAT V 400+; 99% SAT M 400+ **% Accepted:** 68 **Admission Plans:** Preferred Admission; Early Action; Deferred Admission **Application Deadline:** January 15 **Application Fee:** $40.00 **H.S. Requirements:** High school diploma required; GED accepted **Costs Per Year:** Application fee: $40. State resident tuition: $5886 full-time. Nonresident tuition: $15,322 full-time. College room and board: $6372. College room only: $3278. Room and board charges vary according to board plan and housing facility. **Scholarships:** Available **Calendar System:** Semester, Summer Session Available **Enrollment:** FT 14,885, PT 733, Grad 1,320 **Faculty:** FT 795, PT 369 **Student-Faculty Ratio:** 17:1 **Exams:** SAT I or ACT **% Receiving Financial Aid:** 30 **% Residing in College-Owned, -Operated, or -Affiliated Housing:** 39 **Regional Accreditation:** Southern Association of Colleges and Schools **Credit Hours For Degree:** 120 credit hours, Bachelors **ROTC:** Army, Air Force **Professional Accreditation:** AACSB, AACN, ACA, ADtA, AOTA, APA, ASLHA, CSWE, FIDER, JRCEPAT, NASAD, NASD, NASM, NAST, NCATE **Intercollegiate Athletics:** Archery M & W; Baseball M; Basketball M & W; Cross-Country Running M & W; Fencing W; Field Hockey W; Football M; Golf M & W; Gymnastics M & W; Lacrosse W; Soccer M & W; Softball W; Swimming and Diving M & W; Tennis M & W; Track and Field M & W; Volleyball W; Wrestling M

JEFFERSON COLLEGE OF HEALTH SCIENCES
PO Box 13186
Roanoke, VA 24031-3186
Tel: (540)985-8483; 888-985-8483
Admissions: (540)985-9083
Fax: (540)985-9773
E-mail: jmckeon@jchs.edu
Web Site: http://www.jchs.edu/
President/CEO: Dr. Harry C. Nickens
Registrar: Linda Williams
Admissions: Judith McKeon
Financial Aid: Deborah Johnson
Type: Four-Year College **Sex:** Coed **Admission Plans:** Early Decision Plan **Application Fee:** $50.00 **H.S. Requirements:** High school diploma required; GED accepted **Scholarships:** Available **Calendar System:** Semester, Summer Session Available **Enrollment:** FT 423, PT 274 **Faculty:** FT 41, PT 46 **Student-Faculty Ratio:** 11:1 **Exams:** Other, SAT I or ACT, SAT I **% Receiving Financial Aid:** 19 **% Residing in College-Owned, -Operated, or -Affiliated Housing:** 15 **Library Holdings:** 10,533 **Regional Accreditation:** Southern Association of Colleges and Schools **Credit Hours For Degree:** 70 credit hours, Associates; 124 credit hours, Bachelors **Professional Accreditation:** AACN, AOTA, APTA, CARC, JRCEMT, NLN

JOHN TYLER COMMUNITY COLLEGE
13101 Jefferson Davis Hwy.
Chester, VA 23831-5316
Tel: (804)796-4000
Admissions: (804)796-4150
Fax: (804)796-4163
Web Site: http://www.jtcc.edu/
President/CEO: Dr. Marshall W. Smith
Registrar: Joy James
Admissions: Joy James
Financial Aid: Laurie Schiavone
Type: Two-Year College **Sex:** Coed **Affiliation:** Virginia Community College System **% Accepted:** 100 **Admission Plans:** Open Admission; Preferred Admission; Early Admission; Deferred Admission **Application Deadline:** Rolling **Application Fee:** $0.00 **H.S. Requirements:** High school diploma or equivalent not required. For nursing, funeral services, physical therapist assistant programs: High school diploma required; GED accepted **Costs Per Year:** Application fee: $0. State resident tuition: $1708 full-time, $71.15 per credit part-time. Nonresident tuition: $5264 full-time, $219.35 per credit part-time. Mandatory fees: $50 full-time, $25 per term part-time. **Scholarships:** Available **Calendar System:** Semester, Summer Session Available **Enrollment:** FT 1,607, PT 4,707 **Faculty:** FT 65, PT 355 **Student-Faculty Ratio:** 27:1 **Library Holdings:** 49,393 **Regional Accreditation:** Southern Association of Colleges and Schools **Credit Hours For Degree:** 65 semester hours, Associates **ROTC:** Army **Professional Accreditation:** ABFSE, NLN

LIBERTY UNIVERSITY
1971 University Blvd.
Lynchburg, VA 24502
Tel: (434)582-2000
Free: 800-543-5317
Admissions: (434)592-3015
Fax: (434)582-2304
Web Site: http://www.liberty.edu/
President/CEO: Dr. Jerry Falwell
Registrar: Lawrence Shackleton
Admissions: Chris Johnson
Financial Aid: Rhonda Allbeck
Type: Comprehensive **Sex:** Coed **Affiliation:** nondenominational **Scores:** 89.69% SAT V 400+; 85.49% SAT M 400+; 51.14% ACT 18-23; 26.14% ACT 24-29 **% Accepted:** 67 **Admission Plans:** Early Admission; Deferred Admission **Application Deadline:** June 30 **Application Fee:** $35.00 **H.S. Requirements:** High school diploma required; GED accepted. For home schooled students-records of academic work, grades and evaluations: High school diploma or equivalent not required **Costs Per Year:** Application fee: $35. Comprehensive fee: $20,750 includes full-time tuition ($14,400), mandatory fees ($950), and college room and board ($5400). Part-time tuition: $480 per semester hour. Part-time mandatory fees: $425 per term. **Scholarships:** Available **Calendar System:** Semester, Summer Session Available **Enrollment:** FT 8,427, PT 1,548, Grad 2,121 **Faculty:** FT 336, PT 165 **Student-Faculty Ratio:** 27:1 **Exams:** SAT I or ACT **% Receiving Financial Aid:** 77 **% Residing in College-Owned, -Operated, or -Affiliated Housing:** 53 **Library Holdings:** 199,150 **Regional Accreditation:** Southern Association of Colleges and Schools **Credit Hours For Degree:** 64 semester hours, Associates; 120 semester hours, Bachelors **ROTC:** Army, Air Force **Professional Accreditation:** AACN, AAFCS, ACIPE, NCATE, NLN, TACCS **Intercollegiate Athletics:** Baseball M; Basketball M & W; Cheerleading M & W; Cross-Country Running M & W; Field Hockey W; Football M; Golf M; Ice Hockey M; Lacrosse M; Soccer M & W; Softball W; Tennis M & W; Track and Field M & W; Volleyball W

LONGWOOD UNIVERSITY
201 High St.
Farmville, VA 23909
Tel: (434)395-2000
Free: 800-281-4677
Admissions: (434)395-2060
Fax: (434)395-2332
E-mail: lcadmit@longwood.lwc.edu
Web Site: http://www.longwood.edu/
President/CEO: Dr. Patricia P. Cormier
Registrar: Alecia M. Knox
Admissions: Robert J. Chonko
Financial Aid: Michael W. Barree
Type: Comprehensive **Sex:** Coed **Affiliation:** The State Council of Higher Education for Virginia (SCHEV) **Scores:** 100% SAT V 400+; 100% SAT M 400+ **Admission Plans:** Early Admission; Early Action; Deferred Admission **Application Fee:** $40.00 **H.S. Requirements:** High school diploma required; GED accepted **Costs Per Year:** Application fee: $40. State resident tuition: $3586 full-time, $150 per credit hour part-time. Nonresident tuition: $10,270 full-time, $428 per credit hour part-time. Mandatory fees: $3434 full-time. College room and board: $5586. College room only: $3288. Room and board charges vary according to board plan. **Scholarships:** Available **Calendar System:** Semester, Summer Session Available **Enrollment:** FT 3,604, PT 135, Grad 550 **Faculty:** FT 192, PT 50 **Student-Faculty Ratio:** 20:1 **Exams:** SAT I or ACT **% Receiving Financial Aid:** 44 **% Residing in College-Owned, -Operated, or -Affiliated Housing:** 67 **Library Holdings:** 325,290 **Regional Accreditation:** Southern Association of Colleges and Schools **Credit Hours For Degree:** 120 credit hours, Bachelors **ROTC:** Army **Professional Accreditation:** AACSB, CSWE, JRCEPAT, NASM, NAST, NCATE, NRPA **Intercollegiate Athletics:** Baseball M; Basketball M & W; Cross-Country Running M & W; Equestrian Sports M & W; Field Hockey W; Golf M & W; Lacrosse W; Rugby M & W; Soccer M & W; Softball W; Swimming and Diving M & W; Tennis M & W; Track and Field M & W; Volleyball M & W; Wrestling M

LORD FAIRFAX COMMUNITY COLLEGE
173 Skirmisher Ln.
Middletown, VA 22645
Tel: (540)868-7000
Free: 800-906-5322
Admissions: (540)868-7105
Fax: (540)868-7100
Web Site: http://www.lfcc.edu/
President/CEO: Dr. John J. Sygielski
Registrar: Carroll Todd Smith
Admissions: Cynthia Bambara
Financial Aid: Barbara Ratcliff
Type: Two-Year College **Sex:** Coed **Affiliation:** Virginia Community College System **Admission Plans:** Open Admission; Early Admission **Application Deadline:** Rolling **Application Fee:** $0.00 **H.S. Requirements:** High school diploma or equivalent not required **Costs Per Year:** Application fee: $0. State resident tuition: $1740 full-time, $72.50 per credit hour part-time. Nonresident tuition: $5748 full-time, $235.35 per credit hour part-time. Mandatory fees: $117 full-time, $4.30 per credit hour part-time. **Scholarships:** Available **Calendar System:** Semester, Summer Session Available **Enrollment:** FT 1,535, PT 3,957 **Faculty:** FT 57, PT 252 **Library Holdings:** 41,000 **Regional Accreditation:** Southern Association of Colleges and Schools **Credit Hours For Degree:** 62 semester hours, Associates

LYNCHBURG COLLEGE
1501 Lakeside Dr.
Lynchburg, VA 24501-3199
Tel: (434)544-8100
Free: 800-426-8101
Admissions: (434)544-8300
Fax: (434)544-8653
E-mail: admissions@lynchburg.edu
Web Site: http://www.lynchburg.edu/
President/CEO: Kenneth R. Garren
Registrar: Jay K. Webb
Admissions: Sharon Walters-Bower
Financial Aid: Michelle G. Davis
Type: Comprehensive **Sex:** Coed **Affiliation:** Christian Church (Disciples of Christ) **Scores:** 98.3% SAT V 400+; 98.6% SAT M 400+; 68.3% ACT 18-23; 11.7% ACT 24-29 **% Accepted:** 72 **Admission Plans:** Early Admission; Early Decision Plan; Deferred Admission **Application Deadline:** Rolling **Application Fee:** $30.00 **H.S. Requirements:** High school diploma required; GED accepted **Costs Per Year:** Application fee: $30. Comprehensive fee: $30,645 includes full-time tuition ($23,700), mandatory fees ($545), and college room and board ($6400). College room only: $3200. Part-time tuition: $335 per credit hour. **Scholarships:** Available **Calendar System:** Semester, Summer Session Available **Enrollment:** FT 1,924, PT 125, Grad 379 **Faculty:** FT 142, PT 95 **Student-Faculty Ratio:** 12:1 **Exams:** SAT I or ACT **% Receiving Financial Aid:** 64 **% Residing in College-Owned, -Operated, or -Affiliated Housing:** 81 **Library Holdings:** 287,601 **Regional Accreditation:** Southern Association of Colleges and Schools **Credit Hours For Degree:** 124 semester hours, Bachelors **Professional Accreditation:** AACN, ACA, NLN **Intercollegiate Athletics:** Baseball M; Basketball M & W; Cheerleading M & W; Cross-Country Running M & W; Equestrian Sports M & W; Field Hockey W; Golf M; Lacrosse M & W; Soccer M & W; Softball W; Tennis M & W; Track and Field M & W; Volleyball W

MARY BALDWIN COLLEGE
201 East Frederick St.
Staunton, VA 24401-3610
Tel: (540)887-7000
Free: 800-468-2262
Admissions: (540)887-7019
Fax: (540)886-6634
E-mail: bbryant@mbc.edu
Web Site: http://www.mbc.edu/
President/CEO: Dr. Pamela Fox
Registrar: Dr. Lewis D. Askegaard
Admissions: Dr. Brenda Bryant
Financial Aid: Lisa Branson
Type: Comprehensive **Sex:** Coed **Scores:** 96.3% SAT V 400+; 98% SAT M 400+; 48.6% ACT 18-23; 40% ACT 24-29 **% Accepted:** 75 **Admission Plans:** Early Admission; Early Decision Plan; Deferred Admission **Application Deadline:** Rolling **Application Fee:** $35.00 **H.S. Requirements:** High school diploma required; GED accepted **Costs Per Year:** Application fee: $35. Comprehensive fee: $26,465 includes full-time tuition ($20,405), mandatory fees ($200), and college room and board ($5860). College room only: $3738. Full-time tuition and fees vary according to degree level. Room and board charges vary according to housing facility. Part-time tuition: $345 per credit hour. Part-time tuition varies according to degree level. **Scholarships:** Available **Calendar System:** Miscellaneous, Summer Session Not available **Enrollment:** FT 1,002, PT 533, Grad 205 **Faculty:** FT 76, PT 58 **Student-Faculty Ratio:** 10:1 **Exams:** SAT I or ACT **% Receiving Financial Aid:** 76 **% Residing in College-Owned, -Operated, or -Affiliated Housing:** 81 **Library Holdings:** 140,466 **Regional Accreditation:** Southern Association of Colleges and Schools **Credit Hours For Degree:** 132 semester hours, Bachelors **ROTC:** Army, Navy, Air Force **Intercollegiate Athletics:** Basketball W; Cross-Country Running W; Field Hockey W; Soccer W; Softball W; Swimming and Diving W; Tennis W; Volleyball W

MARYMOUNT UNIVERSITY
2807 North Glebe Rd.
Arlington, VA 22207-4299
Tel: (703)522-5600
Free: 800-548-7638
Admissions: (703)284-1500
Fax: (703)522-0349
E-mail: admissions@marymount.edu
Web Site: http://www.marymount.edu/
President/CEO: Dr. James Bundschuh
Admissions: Chris E. Domes
Financial Aid: Deborah Raines
Type: Comprehensive **Sex:** Coed **Affiliation:** Roman Catholic Church **Scores:** 92% SAT V 400+; 91% SAT M 400+; 57% ACT 18-23; 14% ACT 24-29 **% Accepted:** 86 **Admission Plans:** Deferred Admission **Application Deadline:** Rolling **Application Fee:** $35.00 **H.S. Requirements:** High school diploma required; GED accepted **Costs Per Year:** Application fee: $35. Comprehensive fee: $25,934 includes full-time tuition ($17,970), mandatory fees ($144), and college room and board ($7820). Part-time tuition: $582 per credit hour. Part-time mandatory fees: $6 per credit hour. **Scholarships:** Available **Calendar System:** Semester, Summer Session Available **Enrollment:** FT 1,871, PT 456, Grad 1,357 **Faculty:** FT 134, PT 218 **Student-Faculty Ratio:** 13:1 **Exams:** SAT I or ACT **% Receiving Financial Aid:** 56 **% Residing in College-Owned, -Operated, or -Affiliated Housing:** 30 **Library Holdings:** 187,097 **Regional Accredita-**

tion: Southern Association of Colleges and Schools **Credit Hours For Degree:** 64 semester hours, Associates; 120 semester hours, Bachelors **ROTC:** Army **Professional Accreditation:** ACEHSA, AACN, ACA, APTA, ACBSP, FIDER, NCATE, NLN **Intercollegiate Athletics:** Basketball M & W; Cross-Country Running M & W; Golf M; Lacrosse M & W; Soccer M & W; Swimming and Diving M & W; Volleyball W

MEDICAL CAREERS INSTITUTE (NEWPORT NEWS)
1001 Omni Blvd., Ste. 200
Newport News, VA 23606
Tel: (757)873-2423
Fax: (757)873-2472
Web Site: http://www.medicalcareersinstitute.com/ **Type:** Two-Year College **Sex:** Coed **Calendar System:** Semester **Professional Accreditation:** COE

MEDICAL CAREERS INSTITUTE (RICHMOND)
800 Moorefield Park Dr., Ste. 302
Richmond, VA 23236-3659
Tel: (804)521-0400
Fax: (804)521-0406
E-mail: dmayle@medical.edu
Web Site: http://www.medicalcareersinstitute.com/
Admissions: David K. Mayle
Type: Two-Year College **Sex:** Coed **Calendar System:** Semester **Professional Accreditation:** COE

MEDICAL CAREERS INSTITUTE (VIRGINIA BEACH)
5501 Greenwich Rd.
Virginia Beach, VA 23462
Tel: (757)497-8400
Web Site: http://www.medical.edu **Type:** Two-Year College **Sex:** Coed **Calendar System:** Semester **Professional Accreditation:** COE

MOUNTAIN EMPIRE COMMUNITY COLLEGE
PO Drawer 700
Big Stone Gap, VA 24219-0700
Tel: (540)523-2400
Admissions: (276)523-2400
Web Site: http://www.me.vccs.edu/
President/CEO: Dr. Terrance Suarez
Registrar: Perry Carroll
Admissions: Perry Carroll
Financial Aid: Perry Carroll
Type: Two-Year College **Sex:** Coed **Affiliation:** Virginia Community College System **Admission Plans:** Open Admission; Preferred Admission; Early Admission; Deferred Admission **Application Fee:** $0.00 **H.S. Requirements:** High school diploma required; GED accepted **Scholarships:** Available **Calendar System:** Semester, Summer Session Available **Enrollment:** FT 1,195, PT 1,690 **Faculty:** FT 70, PT 80 **Student-Faculty Ratio:** 18:1 **Exams:** Other **Library Holdings:** 21,600 **Regional Accreditation:** Southern Association of Colleges and Schools **Credit Hours For Degree:** 62 semester hours, Associates **Professional Accreditation:** CARC, NLN

NATIONAL COLLEGE OF BUSINESS & TECHNOLOGY (BLUEFIELD)
100 Logan St.
PO Box 629
Bluefield, VA 24605-1405
Tel: (276)326-3621
Free: 800-664-1886
Fax: (276)322-5731
Web Site: http://www.ncbt.edu/
President/CEO: Frank Longaker
Admissions: Denver Riffe
Financial Aid: Crystal Angles
Type: Two-Year College **Sex:** Coed **Affiliation:** National College of Business and Technology **Admission Plans:** Open Admission **Application Fee:** $30.00 **H.S. Requirements:** High school diploma required; GED accepted **Costs Per Year:** Application fee: $30. Tuition: $6408 full-time, $178 per credit hour part-time. Mandatory fees: $75 full-time, $15 per term part-time. Full-time tuition and fees vary according to course load. Part-time tuition and fees vary according to course load. **Scholarships:** Available **Calendar System:** Quarter, Summer Session Available **Faculty:** FT 2, PT 19 **Student-Faculty Ratio:** 10:1 **Credit Hours For Degree:** 96 quarter hours, Associates **Professional Accreditation:** ACICS, AAMAE

NATIONAL COLLEGE OF BUSINESS & TECHNOLOGY (CHARLOTTESVILLE)
1819 Emmet St.
Charlottesville, VA 22901
Tel: (434)295-0136
Free: 800-664-1886
Fax: (434)986-1344
Web Site: http://www.ncbt.edu/
President/CEO: Frank Longaker
Admissions: Adrienne D. Granitz
Financial Aid: Andrea Grooms
Type: Two-Year College **Sex:** Coed **Affiliation:** National College of Business and Technology **Admission Plans:** Open Admission **Application Fee:** $30.00 **H.S. Requirements:** High school diploma required; GED accepted **Costs Per Year:** Application fee: $30. Tuition: $6408 full-time, $178 per credit hour part-time. Mandatory fees: $75 full-time, $15 per term part-time. Full-time tuition and fees vary according to course load. Part-time tuition and fees vary according to course load. **Scholarships:** Available **Calendar System:** Quarter, Summer Session Available **Faculty:** FT 2, PT 12 **Student-Faculty Ratio:** 12:1 **Credit Hours For Degree:** 96 quarter hours, Associates **Professional Accreditation:** ACICS, AAMAE

NATIONAL COLLEGE OF BUSINESS & TECHNOLOGY (DANVILLE)
734 Main St.
Danville, VA 24541-1819
Tel: (434)793-6822
Free: 800-664-1886
Fax: (434)793-3634
Web Site: http://www.ncbt.edu/
President/CEO: Amy Bracey
Admissions: Amy Bracey
Financial Aid: Etta Wilson
Type: Two-Year College **Sex:** Coed **Affiliation:** National College of Business and Technology **Admission Plans:** Open Admission **Application Fee:** $30.00 **H.S. Requirements:** High school diploma required; GED accepted **Scholarships:** Available **Calendar System:** Quarter, Summer Session Available **Faculty:** FT 2, PT 17 **Student-Faculty Ratio:** 10:1 **Library Holdings:** 3,010 **Credit Hours For Degree:** 96 quarter hours, Associates **Professional Accreditation:** ACICS, AAMAE

NATIONAL COLLEGE OF BUSINESS & TECHNOLOGY (HARRISONBURG)
51 B Burgess Rd.
Harrisonburg, VA 22801-9709
Tel: (540)432-0943
Free: 800-664-1886
Fax: (540)986-1344
Web Site: http://www.ncbt.edu/
President/CEO: Janice Boyd
Registrar: Sumer Thompson
Admissions: Jack Evey
Financial Aid: Lou T. Olmstead
Type: Two-Year College **Sex:** Coed **Affiliation:** National College of Business and Technology **Admission Plans:** Open Admission **Application Fee:** $30.00 **H.S. Requirements:** High school diploma required; GED accepted **Costs Per Year:** Application fee: $30. Tuition: $6408 full-time, $178 per credit hour part-time. Mandatory fees: $75 full-time, $15 per term part-time. Full-time tuition and fees vary according to course load. Part-time tuition and fees vary according to course load. **Scholarships:** Available **Calendar System:** Quarter, Summer Session Available **Faculty:** FT 2, PT 18 **Student-Faculty Ratio:** 12:1 **Credit Hours For Degree:** 96 credit hours, Associates **Professional Accreditation:** ACICS, AAMAE

NATIONAL COLLEGE OF BUSINESS & TECHNOLOGY (LYNCHBURG)
104 Candlewood Ct.
Lynchburg, VA 24502-2653
Tel: (434)239-3500
Free: 800-664-1886
Fax: (434)986-1344
Web Site: http://www.ncbt.edu/
President/CEO: Frank Longaker
Admissions: Bill Baker
Financial Aid: Pamela Cotton

Type: Two-Year College **Sex:** Coed **Affiliation:** National College of Business and Technology **Admission Plans:** Open Admission **Application Fee:** $30.00 **H.S. Requirements:** High school diploma required; GED accepted **Costs Per Year:** Application fee: $30. Tuition: $6408 full-time, $178 per credit hour part-time. Mandatory fees: $75 full-time, $15 per term part-time. Full-time tuition and fees vary according to course load. Part-time tuition and fees vary according to course load. **Scholarships:** Available **Calendar System:** Quarter, Summer Session Available **Faculty:** FT 1, PT 32 **Student-Faculty Ratio:** 12:1 **Credit Hours For Degree:** 96 quarter hours, Associates **Professional Accreditation:** ACICS, AAMAE

NATIONAL COLLEGE OF BUSINESS & TECHNOLOGY (MARTINSVILLE)
10 Church St., PO Box 232
Martinsville, VA 24114
Tel: (276)632-5621
Free: 800-664-1866
Fax: (276)986-1344
Web Site: http://www.ncbt.edu/
President/CEO: Frank Longaker
Registrar: Barbara Rakes
Admissions: John Scott
Financial Aid: Pamela Cotton
Type: Two-Year College **Sex:** Coed **Affiliation:** National College of Business and Technology **Admission Plans:** Open Admission **Application Fee:** $30.00 **H.S. Requirements:** High school diploma required; GED accepted **Costs Per Year:** Application fee: $30. Tuition: $6408 full-time, $178 per credit hour part-time. Mandatory fees: $75 full-time, $15 per term part-time. **Scholarships:** Available **Calendar System:** Quarter, Summer Session Available **Faculty:** FT 2, PT 13 **Student-Faculty Ratio:** 12:1 **Credit Hours For Degree:** 96 quarter hours, Associates **Professional Accreditation:** ACICS

NATIONAL COLLEGE OF BUSINESS & TECHNOLOGY (SALEM)
1813 East Main St.
Salem, VA 24153
Tel: (540)986-1800
Free: 800-664-1886
Fax: (540)986-1344
Web Site: http://www.ncbt.edu/
President/CEO: Frank E. Longaker
Admissions: Lew Bishop
Financial Aid: Pamela Cotton
Type: Two-Year College **Sex:** Coed **Affiliation:** National College of Business and Technology **Admission Plans:** Open Admission **Application Fee:** $30.00 **H.S. Requirements:** High school diploma required; GED accepted **Costs Per Year:** Application fee: $30. Tuition: $6408 full-time, $178 per credit hour part-time. Mandatory fees: $75 full-time, $15 per term part-time. **Scholarships:** Available **Calendar System:** Quarter, Summer Session Available **Faculty:** FT 13, PT 62 **Student-Faculty Ratio:** 12:1 **Library Holdings:** 25,867 **Credit Hours For Degree:** 96 quarter hours, Associates; 180 quarter hours, Bachelors **Professional Accreditation:** ACICS, AAMAE

NEW RIVER COMMUNITY COLLEGE
PO Box 1127
Dublin, VA 24084-1127
Tel: (540)674-3600
Fax: (540)674-3644
Web Site: http://www.nr.cc.va.us/
President/CEO: Dr. Jack M. Lewis
Registrar: Margaret G. Taylor
Admissions: Margaret G. Taylor
Financial Aid: Joseph L. Sheffey
Type: Two-Year College **Sex:** Coed **Affiliation:** Virginia Community College System **Admission Plans:** Open Admission; Preferred Admission; Early Admission; Deferred Admission **Application Fee:** $0.00 **H.S. Requirements:** High school diploma or equivalent not required. For applicants under 18: High school diploma required; GED accepted **Scholarships:** Available **Calendar System:** Semester, Summer Session Available **Enrollment:** FT 2,008, PT 2,337 **Faculty:** FT 51, PT 155 **Student-Faculty Ratio:** 22:1 **Library Holdings:** 33,993 **Regional Accreditation:** Southern Association of Colleges and Schools **Credit Hours For Degree:** 62 semester hours, Associates

NORFOLK STATE UNIVERSITY
700 Park Ave.
Norfolk, VA 23504
Tel: (757)823-8600
Admissions: (757)823-8396
Fax: (757)823-9435
Web Site: http://www.nsu.edu/
President/CEO: Dr. Marie V. McDemmond
Registrar: Gary Fincher
Admissions: Michelle Marable
Financial Aid: Estherine Harding
Type: Comprehensive **Sex:** Coed **Affiliation:** State Council of Higher Education for Virginia **% Accepted:** 71 **Admission Plans:** Deferred Admission **Application Deadline:** May 31 **Application Fee:** $25.00 **H.S. Requirements:** High school diploma required; GED accepted **Costs Per Year:** Application fee: $25. State resident tuition: $4670 full-time, $204 per credit hour part-time. Nonresident tuition: $14,480 full-time, $531 per credit hour part-time. Mandatory fees: $125 per credit hour part-time. College room and board: $6474. College room only: $4110. **Scholarships:** Available **Calendar System:** Semester, Summer Session Available **Enrollment:** FT 4,420, PT 917, Grad 759 **Faculty:** FT 280, PT 106 **Student-Faculty Ratio:** 21:1 **Exams:** SAT I or ACT **% Receiving Financial Aid:** 77 **% Residing in College-Owned, -Operated, or -Affiliated Housing:** 32 **Library Holdings:** 378,323 **Regional Accreditation:** Southern Association of Colleges and Schools **Credit Hours For Degree:** 60 semester hours, Associates; 120 semester hours, Bachelors **ROTC:** Army, Navy **Professional Accreditation:** AACSB, ABET, ACEJMC, ABFSE, APA, CAEPK, CSWE, NAACLS, NAIT, NASM, NCATE, NLN **Intercollegiate Athletics:** Baseball M; Basketball M & W; Bowling W; Cross-Country Running M & W; Football M; Softball W; Tennis M & W; Track and Field M & W; Volleyball W

NORTHERN VIRGINIA COMMUNITY COLLEGE
4001 Wakefield Chapel Rd.
Annandale, VA 22003-3796
Tel: (703)323-3000
Admissions: (703)323-3195
Web Site: http://www.nv.cc.va.us/
President/CEO: Dr. Robert G. Templin
Admissions: Dr. Max L. Bassett
Financial Aid: Carol A. Mowbray
Type: Two-Year College **Sex:** Coed **Affiliation:** Virginia Community College System **Admission Plans:** Open Admission; Early Admission; Deferred Admission **Application Fee:** $0.00 **H.S. Requirements:** High school diploma required; GED accepted. For veterinary technology, dental hygiene, other health-related programs: High school diploma required; GED not accepted **Scholarships:** Available **Calendar System:** Semester, Summer Session Available **Faculty:** FT 571, PT 1,035 **Library Holdings:** 228,009 **Regional Accreditation:** Southern Association of Colleges and Schools **Credit Hours For Degree:** 60 credit hours, Associates **Professional Accreditation:** ADA, AHIMA, APTA, CARC, JRCEMT, NAACLS, NLN

OLD DOMINION UNIVERSITY
5215 Hampton Blvd.
Norfolk, VA 23529
Tel: (757)683-3000
Free: 800-348-7926
Admissions: (757)683-3648
Fax: (757)683-5357
E-mail: amcadory@odu.edu
Web Site: http://www.odu.edu/
President/CEO: Dr. Roseann Runte
Registrar: Mary Swartz
Admissions: Alice McAdory
Financial Aid: Betty Diamond
Type: University **Sex:** Coed **Scores:** 99.2% SAT V 400+; 99.1% SAT M 400+; 71% ACT 18-23; 19% ACT 24-29 **% Accepted:** 69 **Admission Plans:** Early Admission; Early Action; Deferred Admission **Application Deadline:** March 15 **Application Fee:** $40.00 **H.S. Requirements:** High school diploma required; GED accepted **Costs Per Year:** Application fee: $40. State resident tuition: $5430 full-time, $181 per credit hour part-time. Nonresident tuition: $15,394 full-time, $507 per credit hour part-time. Manda-

tory fees: $181 full-time, $39 per term part-time. College room and board: $6292. College room only: $3442. **Scholarships:** Available **Calendar System:** Semester, Summer Session Available **Enrollment:** FT 10,828, PT 4,447, Grad 5,999 **Faculty:** FT 617, PT 283 **Student-Faculty Ratio:** 17:1 **Exams:** SAT I or ACT **% Receiving Financial Aid:** 57 **% Residing in College-Owned, -Operated, or -Affiliated Housing:** 24 **Library Holdings:** 985,801 **Regional Accreditation:** Southern Association of Colleges and Schools **Credit Hours For Degree:** 120 semester hours, Bachelors **ROTC:** Army, Navy **Professional Accreditation:** AACSB, ABET, AACN, AANA, ACA, ADA, APTA, APA, ASC, ASLHA, CEPH, JCAHPO, JRCNMT, NAACLS, NASAD, NASM, NASPAA, NAST, NCATE, NRPA **Intercollegiate Athletics:** Baseball M; Basketball M & W; Cheerleading M & W; Crew M & W; Fencing M & W; Field Hockey W; Golf M & W; Ice Hockey M; Lacrosse M & W; Rugby M & W; Sailing M & W; Soccer M & W; Softball W; Swimming and Diving M & W; Tennis M & W; Volleyball M & W; Wrestling M

PARKS COLLEGE
801 North Quincy St., Ste. 501
Arlington, VA 22203
Tel: (703)248-8887
Fax: (703)351-2202
E-mail: lgreen@cci.edu
Web Site: http://www.parks-college.com/
Admissions: Lachelle Green
Type: Two-Year College **Sex:** Coed **Calendar System:** Quarter **Faculty:** FT 6, PT 28 **Professional Accreditation:** ACICS

PATRICK HENRY COLLEGE
One Patrick Henry Circle
Purcellville, VA 20132
Tel: (540)338-1776
Fax: (540)338-8707
E-mail: admissions@phc.edu
Web Site: http://www.phc.edu/
President/CEO: Michael P. Farris
Admissions: Rebekah A. Knable
Type: Four-Year College **Sex:** Coed **Affiliation:** nondenominational **Scores:** 100% SAT V 400+; 100% SAT M 400+; 62% ACT 24-29 **Application Deadline:** April 01 **Costs Per Year:** Comprehensive fee: $21,730 includes full-time tuition ($16,000) and college room and board ($5730). **Calendar System:** Semester **Enrollment:** FT 325, PT 23 **Faculty:** FT 17, PT 8 **Student-Faculty Ratio:** 16:1 **Exams:** SAT I or ACT **% Residing in College-Owned, -Operated, or -Affiliated Housing:** 94 **Regional Accreditation:** Southern Association of Colleges and Schools **Professional Accreditation:** AALE, TACCS **Intercollegiate Athletics:** Basketball M; Soccer M & W

PATRICK HENRY COMMUNITY COLLEGE
PO Box 5311
Martinsville, VA 24115-5311
Tel: (276)638-8777
Admissions: (276)656-0315
Fax: (276)656-0247
Web Site: http://www.ph.vccs.edu/
President/CEO: Dr. Max Wingett
Registrar: Nancy Riddle
Admissions: Dr. Nolan Browning
Financial Aid: Cindy Keller
Type: Two-Year College **Sex:** Coed **Affiliation:** Virginia Community College System **Admission Plans:** Open Admission; Preferred Admission; Early Admission; Deferred Admission **Application Fee:** $0.00 **H.S. Requirements:** High school diploma required; GED accepted **Costs Per Year:** Application fee: $0. State resident tuition: $1632 full-time, $68 per credit hour part-time. Nonresident tuition: $5136 full-time, $214 per credit hour part-time. Mandatory fees: $81 full-time, $3.15 per credit hour part-time, $5 per term part-time. **Scholarships:** Available **Calendar System:** Semester, Summer Session Available **Faculty:** FT 39, PT 100 **Exams:** Other **Library Holdings:** 26,160 **Regional Accreditation:** Southern Association of Colleges and Schools **Credit Hours For Degree:** 62 semester hours, Associates **Professional Accreditation:** NLN

PAUL D. CAMP COMMUNITY COLLEGE
PO Box 737, 100 North College Dr.
Franklin, VA 23851-0737
Tel: (757)569-6700
Admissions: (757)569-6725
E-mail: vccscent@pc.vccs.edu
Web Site: http://www.pc.vccs.edu/
President/CEO: Dr. Douglas W. Boyce
Admissions: Monette Williams
Financial Aid: Teresa King
Type: Two-Year College **Sex:** Coed **Affiliation:** Virginia Community College System **Scores:** 54% SAT V 400+; 54% SAT M 400+ **Admission Plans:** Open Admission; Preferred Admission; Deferred Admission **Application Fee:** $0.00 **H.S. Requirements:** High school diploma required; GED accepted **Scholarships:** Available **Calendar System:** Semester, Summer Session Available **Enrollment:** FT 391, PT 1,245 **Faculty:** FT 24, PT 50 **Student-Faculty Ratio:** 17:1 **Exams:** Other **Library Holdings:** 22,000 **Regional Accreditation:** Southern Association of Colleges and Schools **Credit Hours For Degree:** 61 semester hours, Associates **Professional Accreditation:** NLN

PIEDMONT VIRGINIA COMMUNITY COLLEGE
501 College Dr.
Charlottesville, VA 22902-7589
Tel: (434)977-3900
Admissions: (434)961-5400
Fax: (434)971-8232
Web Site: http://www.pvcc.edu/
President/CEO: Dr. Frank Friedman
Registrar: Tracey Templeton
Admissions: Mary Walsh
Financial Aid: Carol Lawson
Type: Two-Year College **Sex:** Coed **Affiliation:** Virginia Community College System **Admission Plans:** Open Admission; Early Admission **Application Deadline:** Rolling **Application Fee:** $0.00 **H.S. Requirements:** High school diploma required; GED accepted **Costs Per Year:** Application fee: $0. State resident tuition: $2175 full-time, $72.50 per credit hour part-time. Nonresident tuition: $7126 full-time, $237.55 per credit hour part-time. Mandatory fees: $159 full-time, $5.30 per credit hour part-time. **Scholarships:** Available **Calendar System:** Semester, Summer Session Available **Enrollment:** FT 1,079, PT 3,084 **Faculty:** FT 55, PT 157 **Student-Faculty Ratio:** 20:1 **Library Holdings:** 72,574 **Regional Accreditation:** Southern Association of Colleges and Schools **Credit Hours For Degree:** 67 semester hours, Associates **ROTC:** Army **Professional Accreditation:** NLN

RADFORD UNIVERSITY
PO Box 6890, RU Station
Radford, VA 24142
Tel: (540)831-5000
Free: 800-890-4265
Admissions: (540)831-5371
Fax: (540)831-5138
E-mail: dwkraus@radford.edu
Web Site: http://www.radford.edu/
President/CEO: Dr. Douglas Covington
Registrar: Heidi L. Terry
Admissions: David Kraus
Financial Aid: Barbara A. Porter
Type: Comprehensive **Sex:** Coed **Scores:** 95% SAT V 400+; 94% SAT M 400+; 66% ACT 18-23; 16% ACT 24-29 **% Accepted:** 81 **Application Deadline:** February 01 **Application Fee:** $35.00 **H.S. Requirements:** High school diploma required; GED accepted **Costs Per Year:** Application fee: $35. State resident tuition: $3235 full-time, $214 per credit hour part-time. Nonresident tuition: $10,473 full-time, $515 per credit hour part-time. Mandatory fees: $1895 full-time, $78.90 per credit hour part-time. College room and board: $6120. College room only: $3300. Room and board charges vary according to board plan and housing facility. **Scholarships:** Available **Calendar System:** Semester, Summer Session Available **Enrollment:** FT 8,028, PT 454, Grad 1,070 **Faculty:** FT 377, PT 193 **Student-Faculty Ratio:** 20:1 **Exams:** SAT I or ACT **% Receiving Financial Aid:** 39 **% Residing in College-Owned, -Operated, or -Affiliated Housing:** 39 **Library Holdings:** 395,643 **Regional Accreditation:** Southern Association of Colleges and Schools **Credit Hours For Degree:** 120 semester hours, Bachelors **ROTC:** Army, Navy **Professional Accreditation:** AACSB, ABET, AACN, ACA, ADtA, ASLHA, CSWE, NASM, NAST, NCATE, NLN, NRPA **Intercollegiate Athletics:** Baseball M; Basketball M & W; Cross-Country

Running M & W; Field Hockey W; Golf M & W; Soccer M & W; Softball W; Swimming and Diving W; Tennis M & W; Track and Field M & W; Volleyball W

RANDOLPH-MACON COLLEGE
PO Box 5005
Ashland, VA 23005-5505
Tel: (804)752-7200
Free: 800-888-1762
Admissions: (804)752-7305
Fax: (804)752-4707
E-mail: admissions@rmc.edu
Web Site: http://www.rmc.edu/
President/CEO: Dr. Roger H. Martin
Registrar: Dr. Marilyn J. Gibbs
Admissions: John C. Conkright
Financial Aid: Mary Y. Neal
Type: Four-Year College **Sex:** Coed **Affiliation:** United Methodist **Scores:** 99% SAT V 400+; 100% SAT M 400+ **% Accepted:** 79 **Admission Plans:** Early Admission; Early Decision Plan; Deferred Admission **Application Deadline:** March 01 **Application Fee:** $30.00 **H.S. Requirements:** High school diploma required; GED accepted **Costs Per Year:** Application fee: $30. Comprehensive fee: $31,250 includes full-time tuition ($23,310), mandatory fees ($635), and college room and board ($7305). College room only: $4000. Room and board charges vary according to board plan and housing facility. Part-time tuition: $863 per credit hour. **Scholarships:** Available **Calendar System:** 4-1-4, Summer Session Available **Enrollment:** FT 1,102, PT 23 **Faculty:** FT 90, PT 53 **Student-Faculty Ratio:** 10:1 **Exams:** SAT I or ACT, SAT II **% Receiving Financial Aid:** 60 **% Residing in College-Owned, -Operated, or -Affiliated Housing:** 84 **Library Holdings:** 182,368 **Regional Accreditation:** Southern Association of Colleges and Schools **Credit Hours For Degree:** 110 semester hours, Bachelors **ROTC:** Army **Intercollegiate Athletics:** Baseball M; Basketball M & W; Field Hockey W; Football M; Golf M; Lacrosse M & W; Soccer M & W; Softball W; Swimming and Diving M & W; Tennis M & W; Volleyball W

RANDOLPH-MACON WOMAN'S COLLEGE
2500 Rivermont Ave.
Lynchburg, VA 24503-1526
Tel: (434)947-8000
Free: 800-745-7692
Admissions: (434)947-8100
Fax: (434)947-8996
E-mail: admissions@rmwc.edu
Web Site: http://www.rmwc.edu/
President/CEO: Dr. Kathleen Gill Bowman
Registrar: Barbara Thrasher
Admissions: Pat LeDonne
Financial Aid: Sharon M. Wilkes
Type: Four-Year College **Sex:** Women **Affiliation:** Methodist **Scores:** 99% SAT V 400+; 99% SAT M 400+ **% Accepted:** 87 **Admission Plans:** Early Admission; Early Decision Plan; Deferred Admission **Application Deadline:** March 01 **Application Fee:** $35.00 **H.S. Requirements:** High school diploma required; GED accepted **Costs Per Year:** Application fee: $35. Comprehensive fee: $31,540 includes full-time tuition ($22,550), mandatory fees ($380), and college room and board ($8610). Part-time tuition: $940 per semester hour. Part-time mandatory fees: $45 per term. Part-time tuition and fees vary according to course load. **Scholarships:** Available **Calendar System:** Semester, Summer Session Not available **Enrollment:** FT 685, PT 27 **Faculty:** FT 72, PT 18 **Student-Faculty Ratio:** 9:1 **Exams:** SAT I or ACT **% Receiving Financial Aid:** 67 **% Residing in College-Owned, -Operated, or -Affiliated Housing:** 89 **Library Holdings:** 197,332 **Regional Accreditation:** Southern Association of Colleges and Schools **Credit Hours For Degree:** 124 semester hours, Bachelors **Intercollegiate Athletics:** Basketball W; Equestrian Sports W; Field Hockey W; Soccer W; Softball W; Swimming and Diving W; Tennis W; Volleyball W

RAPPAHANNOCK COMMUNITY COLLEGE
12745 College Dr.
Glenns, VA 23149-2616
Tel: (804)758-6700
Admissions: (804)758-6742
Fax: (804)758-3852
Web Site: http://www.rcc.vccs.edu/
President/CEO: Dr. Norman H. Scott
Registrar: Wilnet Willis
Admissions: Wilnet Willis
Financial Aid: Carolyn Ward
Type: Two-Year College **Sex:** Coed **Affiliation:** Virginia Community College System **Admission Plans:** Open Admission; Early Admission **Application Fee:** $0.00 **H.S. Requirements:** High school diploma or equivalent not required **Scholarships:** Available **Calendar System:** Semester, Summer Session Available **Exams:** Other **Library Holdings:** 46,000 **Regional Accreditation:** Southern Association of Colleges and Schools **Credit Hours For Degree:** 60 semester hours, Associates

REGENT UNIVERSITY
1000 Regent University Dr.
Virginia Beach, VA 23464-9800
Tel: (757)226-4000
Free: 800-373-5504
Admissions: (757)226-4826
E-mail: jerrfis@regent.edu
Web Site: http://www.regent.edu/
President/CEO: Dr. M.G. "Pat" Robertson
Registrar: Althea Bishard
Admissions: Jerrod Fishback
Financial Aid: Sherwin Hibbetts
Type: Comprehensive **Sex:** Coed **Application Fee:** $40.00 **Costs Per Year:** Application fee: $40. Tuition: $11,850 full-time, $375 per credit hour part-time. **Calendar System:** Trimester **Enrollment:** FT 490, PT 444, Grad 2,133 **Faculty:** FT 10, PT 89 **Student-Faculty Ratio:** 20:1 **Exams:** ACT, SAT I **Regional Accreditation:** Southern Association of Colleges and Schools **Professional Accreditation:** ABA, ACA, APA, ACIPE, ATS

RICHARD BLAND COLLEGE OF THE COLLEGE OF WILLIAM AND MARY
11301 Johnson Rd.
Petersburg, VA 23805-7100
Tel: (804)862-6100
Admissions: (804)862-6225
Fax: (804)862-6189
E-mail: admit@rbc.edu
Web Site: http://www.rbc.edu/
President/CEO: Dr. James B. McNeer
Registrar: Lois Wray
Admissions: Randy Dean
Financial Aid: Tony Jones
Type: Two-Year College **Sex:** Coed **Affiliation:** College of William and Mary **Scores:** 78.1% SAT V 400+; 77.7% SAT M 400+ **% Accepted:** 88 **Application Deadline:** August 15 **Application Fee:** $20.00 **H.S. Requirements:** High school diploma required; GED accepted **Costs Per Year:** Application fee: $20. State resident tuition: $2350 full-time, $91 per credit hour part-time. Nonresident tuition: $9608 full-time, $398 per credit hour part-time. Mandatory fees: $170 full-time, $4 per credit hour part-time. Full-time tuition and fees vary according to course load and location. Part-time tuition and fees vary according to course load and location. **Scholarships:** Available **Calendar System:** Semester, Summer Session Available **Enrollment:** FT 814, PT 623 **Faculty:** FT 32, PT 34 **Student-Faculty Ratio:** 23:1 **Exams:** Other, SAT I or ACT **Library Holdings:** 91,000 **Regional Accreditation:** Southern Association of Colleges and Schools **Credit Hours For Degree:** 63 semester hours, Associates **ROTC:** Army

ROANOKE COLLEGE
221 College Ln.
Salem, VA 24153-3794
Tel: (540)375-2500
Free: 800-388-2276
Admissions: (540)375-2270
Fax: (540)375-2267
E-mail: admissions@roanoke.edu
Web Site: http://www.roanoke.edu/
President/CEO: Dr. Sabine U. O'Hara
Registrar: Leah R. Russell
Admissions: Michael C. Maxey
Financial Aid: Thomas S. Blair, Jr.
Type: Four-Year College **Sex:** Coed **Affiliation:** Evangelical Lutheran Church in America **Scores:** 100% SAT V 400+; 99% SAT M 400+ **% Accepted:** 74 **Admission Plans:** Early Admission; Early Action; Early Decision Plan; Deferred Admission **Application Deadline:** March 15 **Application**

Fee: $30.00 **H.S. Requirements:** High school diploma required; GED accepted **Costs Per Year:** Application fee: $30. Comprehensive fee: $30,748 includes full-time tuition ($22,848), mandatory fees ($605), and college room and board ($7295). College room only: $3526. Room and board charges vary according to housing facility. Part-time tuition: $1084 per course. **Scholarships:** Available **Calendar System:** Semester, Summer Session Available **Enrollment:** FT 1,833, PT 103 **Faculty:** FT 133, PT 41 **Student-Faculty Ratio:** 14:1 **Exams:** SAT I or ACT **% Receiving Financial Aid:** 73 **% Residing in College-Owned, -Operated, or -Affiliated Housing:** 60 **Library Holdings:** 134,035 **Regional Accreditation:** Southern Association of Colleges and Schools **Credit Hours For Degree:** 33.5 courses, Bachelors **Professional Accreditation:** ACBSP, JRCEPAT **Intercollegiate Athletics:** Baseball M; Basketball M & W; Cross-Country Running M & W; Field Hockey W; Golf M & W; Ice Hockey M; Lacrosse M & W; Soccer M & W; Softball W; Tennis M & W; Track and Field M & W; Volleyball M & W

SAINT PAUL'S COLLEGE
115 College Dr.
Lawrenceville, VA 23868-1202
Tel: (434)848-3111
Free: 800-678-7071
Admissions: (434)848-6493
Fax: (434)848-0403
E-mail: rlewis@saintpauls.edu
Web Site: http://www.saintpauls.edu/
President/CEO: Dr. John K. Waddell
Registrar: Reginald B. Tucker
Admissions: Rosemary Lewis
Type: Four-Year College **Sex:** Coed **Affiliation:** Episcopal **Admission Plans:** Deferred Admission **Application Fee:** $20.00 **H.S. Requirements:** High school diploma required; GED accepted **Scholarships:** Available **Calendar System:** Semester, Summer Session Available **Faculty:** FT 33, PT 4 **Student-Faculty Ratio:** 17:1 **Exams:** SAT I or ACT **% Receiving Financial Aid:** 92 **Library Holdings:** 100,000 **Regional Accreditation:** Southern Association of Colleges and Schools **Credit Hours For Degree:** 120 credits, Bachelors **ROTC:** Army **Intercollegiate Athletics:** Baseball M; Basketball M & W; Cross-Country Running M & W; Golf M & W; Softball W; Tennis M & W; Track and Field M & W; Volleyball W

SHENANDOAH UNIVERSITY
1460 University Dr.
Winchester, VA 22601-5195
Tel: (540)665-4500
Free: 800-432-2266
Admissions: (540)665-4581
Fax: (540)665-4627
E-mail: admit@su.edu
Web Site: http://www.su.edu/
President/CEO: Dr. James A. Davis
Registrar: William Endorf
Admissions: David Anthony
Financial Aid: Nancy Bragg
Type: Comprehensive **Sex:** Coed **Affiliation:** United Methodist **Scores:** 90% SAT V 400+; 91% SAT M 400+; 43% ACT 18-23; 26% ACT 24-29 **% Accepted:** 70 **Admission Plans:** Deferred Admission **Application Deadline:** Rolling **Application Fee:** $30.00 **H.S. Requirements:** High school diploma required; GED accepted **Costs Per Year:** Application fee: $30. Comprehensive fee: $27,600 includes full-time tuition ($19,900), mandatory fees ($150), and college room and board ($7550). Full-time tuition and fees vary according to course load and program. Room and board charges vary according to board plan. Part-time tuition: $610 per credit hour. Part-time tuition varies according to course load and program. **Scholarships:** Available **Calendar System:** Semester, Summer Session Available **Enrollment:** FT 1,530, PT 76, Grad 932 **Faculty:** FT 181, PT 170 **Student-Faculty Ratio:** 9:1 **Exams:** SAT I or ACT **% Receiving Financial Aid:** 61 **% Residing in College-Owned, -Operated, or -Affiliated Housing:** 44 **Library Holdings:** 126,097 **Regional Accreditation:** Southern Association of Colleges and Schools **Credit Hours For Degree:** 60 semester hours, Associates; 120 semester hours, Bachelors **Professional Accreditation:** AACN, ACNM, ACPhE, AOTA, APTA, CARC, NASM, NLN **Intercollegiate Athletics:** Baseball M; Basketball M & W; Cross-Country Running M & W; Field Hockey W; Football M; Golf M; Lacrosse M & W; Soccer M & W; Softball W; Tennis M & W; Volleyball W

SOUTHERN VIRGINIA UNIVERSITY
One College Hill Dr.
Buena Vista, VA 24416
Tel: (540)261-8400
Free: 800-229-8420
Admissions: (540)261-2756
Fax: (540)261-8559
E-mail: tcaputo@southernvirginia.edu
Web Site: http://www.southernvirginia.edu/
President/CEO: Dr. Rodney K. Smith
Registrar: Joseph Bouchelle
Admissions: Tony Caputo
Financial Aid: Margaret Murphy
Type: Four-Year College **Sex:** Coed **Affiliation:** Latter-day Saints **Scores:** 95.6% SAT V 400+; 95.2% SAT M 400+; 46.9% ACT 18-23; 39.4% ACT 24-29 **% Accepted:** 41 **Application Deadline:** July 31 **Application Fee:** $35.00 **H.S. Requirements:** High school diploma required; GED accepted **Costs Per Year:** Application fee: $35. Comprehensive fee: $20,126 includes full-time tuition ($15,826) and college room and board ($4300). College room only: $2800. Part-time tuition: $525 per hour. **Scholarships:** Available **Calendar System:** Semester, Summer Session Available **Enrollment:** FT 648, PT 37 **Faculty:** FT 42, PT 19 **Student-Faculty Ratio:** 15:1 **Exams:** SAT I or ACT **% Receiving Financial Aid:** 67 **% Residing in College-Owned, -Operated, or -Affiliated Housing:** 85 **Library Holdings:** 107,630 **Credit Hours For Degree:** 93 credits, Bachelors **ROTC:** Army **Professional Accreditation:** AALE **Intercollegiate Athletics:** Baseball M; Basketball M & W; Cheerleading M & W; Cross-Country Running M & W; Football M; Golf M & W; Lacrosse M & W; Soccer M & W; Softball W; Tennis M & W; Track and Field M & W; Volleyball W; Wrestling M

SOUTHSIDE VIRGINIA COMMUNITY COLLEGE
109 Campus Dr.
Alberta, VA 23821-9719
Tel: (804)949-1000
Admissions: (434)949-1012
Fax: (804)949-7863
Web Site: http://www.sv.vccs.edu/
President/CEO: Dr. John J. Cavan
Registrar: Dr. Ronald Mattox
Admissions: Dr. Ronald E. Mattox
Financial Aid: Brent Richey
Type: Two-Year College **Sex:** Coed **Affiliation:** Virginia Community College System **Admission Plans:** Open Admission; Preferred Admission; Deferred Admission **Application Deadline:** Rolling **Application Fee:** $0.00 **H.S. Requirements:** High school diploma required; GED accepted. For applicants 18 or over who demonstrate ability to benefit from occupational program: High school diploma or equivalent not required **Costs Per Year:** Application fee: $0. State resident tuition: $2040 full-time, $68 per credit part-time. Nonresident tuition: $6420 full-time, $214 per credit part-time. Mandatory fees: $155 full-time, $5.15 per credit part-time. Full-time tuition and fees vary according to course load. Part-time tuition and fees vary according to course load. **Scholarships:** Available **Calendar System:** Semester, Summer Session Available **Enrollment:** FT 1,359, PT 3,327 **Faculty:** FT 70, PT 225 **Student-Faculty Ratio:** 17:1 **Library Holdings:** 27,691 **Regional Accreditation:** Southern Association of Colleges and Schools **Credit Hours For Degree:** 65 semester hours, Associates **ROTC:** Army

SOUTHWEST VIRGINIA COMMUNITY COLLEGE
PO Box SVCC
Richlands, VA 24641-1101
Tel: (276)964-2555
Admissions: (276)964-7300
Fax: (276)964-9307
Web Site: http://www.sw.edu/
President/CEO: Dr. Charles R. King
Registrar: Roderick B. Moore
Admissions: Jim Farris
Financial Aid: Roderick B. Moore
Type: Two-Year College **Sex:** Coed **Affiliation:** Virginia Community College System **Admission Plans:** Open Admission; Preferred Admission; Early Admission; Deferred Admission **Application Deadline:** Rolling **Application**

Fee: $0.00 **H.S. Requirements:** High school diploma required; GED accepted **Costs Per Year:** Application fee: $0. State resident tuition: $1904 full-time, $68 per credit hour part-time. Nonresident tuition: $5992 full-time, $214 per credit hour part-time. Mandatory fees: $130 full-time, $4.65 per credit hour part-time. Full-time tuition and fees vary according to course load. Part-time tuition and fees vary according to course load. **Scholarships:** Available **Calendar System:** Semester, Summer Session Available **Enrollment:** FT 1,514, PT 2,152 **Faculty:** FT 71, PT 181 **Student-Faculty Ratio:** 17:1 **Library Holdings:** 58,000 **Regional Accreditation:** Southern Association of Colleges and Schools **Credit Hours For Degree:** 65 semester hours, Associates **Professional Accreditation:** CARC, JRCERT, NLN **Intercollegiate Athletics:** Baseball M; Basketball M; Golf M; Rugby M

STRATFORD UNIVERSITY
7777 Leesburg Pike, Ste. 100 South
Falls Church, VA 22043
Tel: (703)821-8570
Free: 800-444-0804
Fax: (703)556-9892
E-mail: skamarah@stratford.edu
Web Site: http://www.stratford.edu/
Admissions: Saibatu Kamarah
Type: Comprehensive **Sex:** Coed **Admission Plans:** Early Decision Plan **Application Deadline:** July 30 **Application Fee:** $50.00 **H.S. Requirements:** High school diploma required; GED accepted **Costs Per Year:** Application fee: $50. Comprehensive fee: $15,750 includes full-time tuition ($10,260), mandatory fees ($50), and college room and board ($5440). Part-time tuition: $285 per credit hour. **Calendar System:** Quarter **Enrollment:** FT 189, PT 256, Grad 41 **Faculty:** FT 20, PT 41 **Student-Faculty Ratio:** 20:1 **Exams:** SAT I **Library Holdings:** 1,800 **Credit Hours For Degree:** 90 quarter credits, Associates; 180 quarter credits, Bachelors **Professional Accreditation:** ACICS, ACF, COE

SWEET BRIAR COLLEGE
Sweet Briar, VA 24595
Tel: (434)381-6100
Free: 800-381-6142
Admissions: (434)381-6142
Fax: (434)381-6173
E-mail: admissions@sbc.edu
Web Site: http://www.sbc.edu/
President/CEO: Dr. Elisabeth S. Muhlenfeld
Registrar: Deborah L. Powell
Admissions: Ken Huus
Financial Aid: Barbara S. Carpenter
Type: Comprehensive **Sex:** Women **Scores:** 98% SAT V 400+; 99% SAT M 400+; 36% ACT 18-23; 49% ACT 24-29 **% Accepted:** 79 **Admission Plans:** Early Admission; Early Decision Plan; Deferred Admission **Application Deadline:** February 01 **Application Fee:** $40.00 **H.S. Requirements:** High school diploma required; GED accepted **Costs Per Year:** Application fee: $40. Comprehensive fee: $32,820 includes full-time tuition ($23,340) and college room and board ($9480). College room only: $3810. Part-time tuition: $775 per credit hour. **Scholarships:** Available **Calendar System:** Semester, Summer Session Available **Enrollment:** FT 703, PT 36, Grad 13 **Faculty:** FT 64, PT 35 **Student-Faculty Ratio:** 8:1 **Exams:** SAT I or ACT, SAT II **% Receiving Financial Aid:** 64 **% Residing in College-Owned, -Operated, or -Affiliated Housing:** 90 **Library Holdings:** 255,175 **Regional Accreditation:** Southern Association of Colleges and Schools **Credit Hours For Degree:** 120 semester hours, Bachelors **Intercollegiate Athletics:** Equestrian Sports W; Fencing W; Field Hockey W; Lacrosse W; Soccer W; Softball W; Swimming and Diving W; Tennis W; Volleyball W

TESST COLLEGE OF TECHNOLOGY
6315 Bren Mar Dr.
Alexandria, VA 22312-6342
Tel: (703)354-1005
Free: 800-48-TESST
Admissions: (703)548-4800
Fax: (703)354-3661
E-mail: tesstal@erols.com
Web Site: http://www.tesst.com/
President/CEO: Sheri Delozier
Admissions: Bob Somers
Type: Two-Year College **Sex:** Coed **Calendar System:** Quarter **Professional Accreditation:** ACCSCT

THOMAS NELSON COMMUNITY COLLEGE
PO Box 9407
Hampton, VA 23670-0407
Tel: (757)825-2700
Admissions: (757)825-2800
Web Site: http://www.tncc.edu/
President/CEO: Dr. Charles A. Taylor
Admissions: Dr. Vicki Richmond
Financial Aid: Dr. Pamela Turner
Type: Two-Year College **Sex:** Coed **Affiliation:** Virginia Community College System **Admission Plans:** Open Admission; Preferred Admission; Early Admission; Deferred Admission **Application Deadline:** Rolling **Application Fee:** $0.00 **H.S. Requirements:** High school diploma or equivalent not required. For nursing program: High school diploma required; GED accepted **Costs Per Year:** Application fee: $0. State resident tuition: $2175 full-time, $72.50 per credit hour part-time. Nonresident tuition: $7061 full-time, $235.35 per credit hour part-time. Mandatory fees: $116 full-time, $3.15 per credit hour part-time, $10.50 per term part-time. **Scholarships:** Available **Calendar System:** Semester, Summer Session Available **Enrollment:** FT 2,658, PT 5,937 **Faculty:** FT 90, PT 343 **Library Holdings:** 66,281 **Regional Accreditation:** Southern Association of Colleges and Schools **Credit Hours For Degree:** 65 semester hours, Associates **Professional Accreditation:** NAACLS, NLN

TIDEWATER COMMUNITY COLLEGE
121 College Place
Norfolk, VA 23510
Tel: (757)822-1122
Admissions: (757)822-1068
Fax: (757)822-1060
Web Site: http://www.tcc.edu/
President/CEO: Dr. Deborah M. DiCroce
Admissions: Tyjaun Lee
Financial Aid: Karen Koonce
Type: Two-Year College **Sex:** Coed **Affiliation:** Virginia Community College System **Admission Plans:** Open Admission; Early Admission; Deferred Admission **Application Deadline:** Rolling **Application Fee:** $0.00 **H.S. Requirements:** High school diploma or equivalent not required. For nursing, allied health programs: High school diploma required; GED not accepted **Costs Per Year:** Application fee: $0. State resident tuition: $1944 full-time, $72.50 per credit part-time. Nonresident tuition: $5,905 full-time, $246.05 per credit part-time. Mandatory fees: $8.50 per credit part-time. **Scholarships:** Available **Calendar System:** Semester, Summer Session Available **Enrollment:** FT 7,850, PT 15,868 **Faculty:** FT 265, PT 1,057 **Student-Faculty Ratio:** 15:1 **Library Holdings:** 147,126 **Regional Accreditation:** Southern Association of Colleges and Schools **Credit Hours For Degree:** 65 semester hours, Associates **Professional Accreditation:** AHIMA, AOTA, CARC, JRCERT, JRCEMT, MACTE, NLN

TIDEWATER TECH
2697 Dean Dr., Ste. 100
Virginia Beach, VA 23452
Tel: (757)340-2121
Fax: (757)340-9704
Web Site: http://www.tidetech.com/
President/CEO: Chantrell Guilford
Type: Two-Year College **Sex:** Coed **Professional Accreditation:** ACCSCT

UNIVERSITY OF MANAGEMENT AND TECHNOLOGY
1901 North Fort Myers Dr.
Arlington, VA 22209
Tel: (703)516-0035
Fax: (703)516-0985
Web Site: http://www.umtweb.edu/
President/CEO: Dr. Yanping Chen
Admissions: Dr. C. Eric Kirkland
Type: Comprehensive **Sex:** Coed **Costs Per Year:** Tuition: $10,800 full-time, $390 per credit hour part-time. Mandatory fees: $90 full-time, $30 per term part-time. Tuition guaranteed not to increase for student's term of enrollment. **Calendar System:** Continuous **Faculty:** FT 0, PT 0 **Student-Faculty Ratio:** 0:1 **Professional Accreditation:** DETC

UNIVERSITY OF MARY WASHINGTON
1301 College Ave.
Fredericksburg, VA 22401-5358

Tel: (540)654-1000
Free: 800-468-5614
Admissions: (540)654-2000
Fax: (540)654-1073
E-mail: admit@umw.edu
Web Site: http://www.umw.edu/
President/CEO: Dr. William M. Anderson, Jr.
Registrar: Judy Ginter
Admissions: Dr. Martin Wilder
Financial Aid: Debra J. Harber
Type: Comprehensive **Sex:** Coed **% Accepted:** 64 **Admission Plans:** Preferred Admission; Deferred Admission **Application Deadline:** February 01 **Application Fee:** $45.00 **H.S. Requirements:** High school diploma required; GED accepted **Costs Per Year:** Application fee: $45. State resident tuition: $5634 full-time, $199 per credit part-time. Nonresident tuition: $14,776 full-time, $579 per credit part-time. Part-time tuition varies according to course load. College room and board: $6002. College room only: $3484. Room and board charges vary according to board plan and housing facility. **Scholarships:** Available **Calendar System:** Semester, Summer Session Available **Enrollment:** FT 3,519, PT 566, Grad 649 **Faculty:** FT 231, PT 107 **Student-Faculty Ratio:** 17:1 **Exams:** SAT I or ACT, SAT II **% Receiving Financial Aid:** 40 **% Residing in College-Owned, -Operated, or -Affiliated Housing:** 70 **Library Holdings:** 355,478 **Regional Accreditation:** Southern Association of Colleges and Schools **Credit Hours For Degree:** 122 semester hours, Bachelors **Professional Accreditation:** NASM **Intercollegiate Athletics:** Baseball M; Basketball M & W; Cheerleading M & W; Crew M & W; Cross-Country Running M & W; Equestrian Sports M & W; Field Hockey W; Lacrosse M & W; Rugby M & W; Soccer M & W; Softball W; Swimming and Diving M & W; Tennis M & W; Track and Field M & W; Volleyball M & W

UNIVERSITY OF NORTHERN VIRGINIA
10021 Balls Ford Rd.
Manassas, VA 20109
Tel: (703)392-0771
Fax: (703)392-6368
E-mail: bfrantz@unva.edu
Web Site: http://www.unva.edu/
President/CEO: Dr. Fay R. Avery
Registrar: Kyoko Enomoto
Admissions: Robert Frantz
Type: Comprehensive **Sex:** Coed **Application Fee:** $60.00 **Calendar System:** Quarter **Professional Accreditation:** ACICS

UNIVERSITY OF PHOENIX-NORTHERN VIRGINIA CAMPUS
11730 Plaza American Dr., Ste. 2000
Reston, VA 20190
Tel: (703)435-4402
Free: 800-228-7240
Admissions: (480)557-1712
Web Site: http://www.phoenix.edu/
Admissions: Nina Omelchanko
Type: Comprehensive **Sex:** Coed **Admission Plans:** Open Admission; Deferred Admission **Application Deadline:** Rolling **Application Fee:** $110.00 **H.S. Requirements:** High school diploma required; GED accepted **Costs Per Year:** Application fee: $110. Tuition: $11,805 full-time, $393.50 per credit part-time. Mandatory fees: $560 full-time, $70 per course part-time. **Scholarships:** Available **Enrollment:** FT 1,020, Grad 357 **Faculty:** FT 5, PT 149 **Student-Faculty Ratio:** 7:1 **Library Holdings:** 444 **Credit Hours For Degree:** 60 credits, Associates; 120 credits, Bachelors

UNIVERSITY OF PHOENIX-RICHMOND CAMPUS
6802 Paragon Place, Ste. 420
Richmond, VA 23230
Tel: (804)288-3390
Free: 800-228-7240
Admissions: (480)557-1712
Web Site: http://www.phoenix.edu/
Admissions: Nina Omelchanko
Type: Comprehensive **Sex:** Coed **Admission Plans:** Open Admission; Deferred Admission **Application Deadline:** Rolling **Application Fee:** $110.00 **H.S. Requirements:** High school diploma required; GED accepted **Costs Per Year:** Application fee: $110. Tuition: $11,370 full-time, $379 per credit part-time. Mandatory fees: $560 full-time, $70 per course part-time. **Scholarships:** Available **Enrollment:** FT 301, Grad 82 **Faculty:** FT 4, PT 34 **Student-Faculty Ratio:** 7:1 **Library Holdings:** 444 **Credit Hours For Degree:** 60 credits, Associates; 120 credits, Bachelors

UNIVERSITY OF RICHMOND
28 Westhampton Way
University of Richmond, VA 23173
Tel: (804)289-8000
Free: 800-700-1662
Admissions: (804)289-8640
Fax: (804)287-6003
E-mail: admissions@richmond.edu
Web Site: http://www.richmond.edu/
President/CEO: Dr. William E. Cooper
Registrar: Susan D. Breeden
Admissions: Pamela Spence
Financial Aid: Cynthia A. Deffenbaugh
Type: Comprehensive **Sex:** Coed **Scores:** 99.9% SAT V 400+; 99.7% SAT M 400+; 14.4% ACT 18-23; 58.1% ACT 24-29 **% Accepted:** 47 **Admission Plans:** Early Admission; Early Decision Plan; Deferred Admission **Application Deadline:** January 15 **Application Fee:** $50.00 **H.S. Requirements:** High school diploma required; GED accepted **Costs Per Year:** Application fee: $50. Comprehensive fee: $42,610 includes full-time tuition ($36,550) and college room and board ($6060). College room only: $2710. Part-time tuition: $1460 per semester hour. **Scholarships:** Available **Calendar System:** Semester, Summer Session Available **Enrollment:** FT 2,881, PT 39, Grad 266 **Faculty:** FT 262, PT 58 **Student-Faculty Ratio:** 10:1 **Exams:** SAT I or ACT **% Receiving Financial Aid:** 34 **% Residing in College-Owned, -Operated, or -Affiliated Housing:** 92 **Library Holdings:** 1,098,581 **Regional Accreditation:** Southern Association of Colleges and Schools **Credit Hours For Degree:** 60 semester hours, Associates; 122 semester hours, Bachelors **ROTC:** Army **Professional Accreditation:** AACSB, ABA, AALS, NASM **Intercollegiate Athletics:** Baseball M; Basketball M & W; Cheerleading M & W; Crew M & W; Cross-Country Running M & W; Equestrian Sports W; Fencing M & W; Field Hockey W; Football M; Golf M & W; Ice Hockey M; Lacrosse M & W; Rugby M & W; Soccer M & W; Swimming and Diving M & W; Tennis M & W; Track and Field M & W; Ultimate Frisbee M & W; Volleyball M & W; Water Polo M & W; Wrestling M

UNIVERSITY OF VIRGINIA
Charlottesville, VA 22903
Tel: (434)924-0311
Admissions: (434)982-3200
Fax: (434)924-3587
E-mail: undergrad-admission@virginia.edu
Web Site: http://www.virginia.edu/
President/CEO: John T. Casteen, III
Registrar: Carol A. J. Stanley
Admissions: John A. Blackburn
Financial Aid: Yvonne B. Hubbard
Type: University **Sex:** Coed **Scores:** 100% SAT V 400+; 100% SAT M 400+; 11% ACT 18-23; 51% ACT 24-29 **% Accepted:** 38 **Admission Plans:** Preferred Admission; Early Decision Plan; Deferred Admission **Application Deadline:** January 02 **Application Fee:** $60.00 **H.S. Requirements:** High school diploma required; GED accepted **Costs Per Year:** Application fee: $60. State resident tuition: $5602 full-time. Nonresident tuition: $22,346 full-time. Mandatory fees: $1768 full-time. College room and board: $6389. College room only: $3289. Room and board charges vary according to board plan and housing facility. **Scholarships:** Available **Calendar System:** Semester, Summer Session Available **Enrollment:** FT 13,395, PT 818, Grad 7,858 **Faculty:** FT 1,193, PT 137 **Student-Faculty Ratio:** 15:1 **Exams:** Other, SAT I and SAT II or ACT **% Receiving Financial Aid:** 24 **% Residing in College-Owned, -Operated, or -Affiliated Housing:** 46 **Library Holdings:** 4,921,442 **Regional Accreditation:** Southern Association of Colleges and Schools **Credit Hours For Degree:** 120 semester hours, Bachelors **ROTC:** Army, Navy, Air Force **Professional Accreditation:** AACSB, ABET, AACN, ABA, ACA, ADtA, ACSP, APA, ASLA, ASLHA, ACIPE, AALS, LCMEAMA, NAST, NCATE, NLN, TEAC **Intercollegiate Athletics:** Baseball M; Basketball M & W; Crew W; Cross-Country Running M & W; Field Hockey W; Football M; Golf M & W; Ice Hockey M & W; Lacrosse M & W; Soccer M & W; Softball W; Swimming and Diving M & W; Tennis M & W; Track and Field M & W; Ultimate Frisbee M & W; Volleyball M & W; Wrestling M

THE UNIVERSITY OF VIRGINIA'S COLLEGE AT WISE
1 College Ave.
Wise, VA 24293

Tel: (276)328-0100; 888-282-9324
Admissions: (276)328-0322
Fax: (276)328-0251
Web Site: http://www.uvawise.edu/
President/CEO: Dr. Ernest H. Ern
Registrar: Sheila Cox Combs
Admissions: Russell Necessary
Financial Aid: Bill D. Wendle
Type: Four-Year College **Sex:** Coed **Affiliation:** University of Virginia **Scores:** 91% SAT V 400+; 87% SAT M 400+; 52% ACT 18-23; 17% ACT 24-29 **Admission Plans:** Early Admission; Early Action **Application Fee:** $25.00 **H.S. Requirements:** High school diploma required; GED accepted **Costs Per Year:** Application fee: $25. State resident tuition: $2984 full-time, $123 per semester hour part-time. Nonresident tuition: $13,062 full-time, $539 per semester hour part-time. Mandatory fees: $2097 full-time, $38 per semester hour part-time, $14.25 per term part-time. College room and board: $6200. College room only: $3488. **Scholarships:** Available **Calendar System:** Semester, Summer Session Available **Enrollment:** FT 1,432, PT 404 **Faculty:** FT 82, PT 54 **Student-Faculty Ratio:** 16:1 **Exams:** SAT I or ACT **% Receiving Financial Aid:** 70 **% Residing in College-Owned, -Operated, or -Affiliated Housing:** 30 **Library Holdings:** 95,861 **Regional Accreditation:** Southern Association of Colleges and Schools **Credit Hours For Degree:** 120 semester hours, Bachelors **Professional Accreditation:** AACN **Intercollegiate Athletics:** Baseball M; Basketball M & W; Cross-Country Running M & W; Football M; Golf M & W; Softball W; Tennis M & W; Track and Field M & W; Volleyball W

VIRGINIA COMMONWEALTH UNIVERSITY
901 West Franklin St.
Richmond, VA 23284-9005
Tel: (804)828-0100
Free: 800-841-3638
Admissions: (804)828-1222
Fax: (804)828-1899
E-mail: vcuinfo@vcu.edu
Web Site: http://www.vcu.edu/
President/CEO: Dr. Eugene P. Trani
Registrar: Anjour B. Harris
Admissions: Delores T. Taylor
Financial Aid: Susan Kadir
Type: University **Sex:** Coed **Scores:** 97% SAT V 400+; 98% SAT M 400+; 59% ACT 18-23; 22% ACT 24-29 **% Accepted:** 68 **Admission Plans:** Preferred Admission; Early Admission; Deferred Admission **Application Deadline:** February 01 **Application Fee:** $30.00 **H.S. Requirements:** High school diploma required; GED accepted **Costs Per Year:** Application fee: $30. State resident tuition: $5385 full-time, $165.40 per credit part-time. Nonresident tuition: $17,440 full-time, $668 per credit part-time. Mandatory fees: $52.05 per credit part-time. College room and board: $7042. College room only: $4102. Room and board charges vary according to board plan. **Scholarships:** Available **Calendar System:** Semester, Summer Session Available **Enrollment:** FT 16,109, PT 4,399, Grad 7,270 **Faculty:** FT 1,744, PT 1,069 **Student-Faculty Ratio:** 19:1 **Exams:** SAT I or ACT **% Receiving Financial Aid:** 47 **% Residing in College-Owned, -Operated, or -Affiliated Housing:** 22 **Library Holdings:** 1,849,037 **Regional Accreditation:** Southern Association of Colleges and Schools **Credit Hours For Degree:** 120 credits, Bachelors **ROTC:** Army **Professional Accreditation:** AACSB, ABET, ACEHSA, AANA, ACPhE, ADA, ADtA, ACSP, AOTA, APTA, APA, ACIPE, CEPH, CORE, CSWE, FIDER, JRCERT, JRCNMT, LCMEAMA, NAACLS NASAD, NASD, NASM, NASPAA, NAST, NCATE, NLN, NRPA **Intercollegiate Athletics:** Baseball M; Basketball M & W; Crew M; Cross-Country Running M & W; Field Hockey W; Golf M; Ice Hockey M; Lacrosse M & W; Rugby M & W; Soccer M & W; Swimming and Diving M & W; Tennis M & W; Track and Field M & W; Volleyball W

VIRGINIA HIGHLANDS COMMUNITY COLLEGE
PO Box 828
Abingdon, VA 24212-0828
Tel: (276)739-2400; 877-207-6115
Admissions: (276)739-2414
Fax: (276)739-2590
Web Site: http://www.vhcc.edu/
President/CEO: Dr. F. David Wilkin
Registrar: David N. Matlock
Admissions: David N. Matlock
Financial Aid: David N. Matlock
Type: Two-Year College **Sex:** Coed **Affiliation:** Virginia Community College System **Admission Plans:** Open Admission; Preferred Admission; Early Admission; Deferred Admission **H.S. Requirements:** High school diploma or equivalent not required. For nursing program: High school diploma required; GED accepted **Scholarships:** Available **Calendar System:** Semester, Summer Session Available **Faculty:** FT 43, PT 92 **Exams:** Other **Library Holdings:** 29,683 **Regional Accreditation:** Southern Association of Colleges and Schools **Credit Hours For Degree:** 65 semester hours, Associates **Professional Accreditation:** JRCERT, NLN

VIRGINIA INTERMONT COLLEGE
1013 Moore St.
Bristol, VA 24201-4298
Tel: (276)669-6101
Free: 800-451-1842
Admissions: (276)466-7856
Fax: (276)669-5763
E-mail: viadmit@vic.edu
Web Site: http://www.vic.edu/
President/CEO: Dr. Stephen Greiner
Registrar: Pam Hammond
Admissions: Roger Lowe
Financial Aid: Nancy Roberts
Type: Four-Year College **Sex:** Coed **Affiliation:** Baptist Church **Scores:** 85% SAT V 400+; 83.5% SAT M 400+; 63% ACT 18-23; 17% ACT 24-29 **% Accepted:** 63 **Admission Plans:** Early Admission; Deferred Admission **Application Deadline:** Rolling **Application Fee:** $15.00 **H.S. Requirements:** High school diploma required; GED accepted **Costs Per Year:** Application fee: $15. Comprehensive fee: $22,200 includes full-time tuition ($15,500), mandatory fees ($950), and college room and board ($5750). College room only: $2750. Full-time tuition and fees vary according to class time and program. Room and board charges vary according to housing facility. Part-time tuition: $220 per credit. Part-time mandatory fees: $50 per credit. Part-time tuition and fees vary according to class time, course level, course load, and program. **Scholarships:** Available **Calendar System:** Semester, Summer Session Available **Enrollment:** FT 986, PT 152 **Faculty:** FT 45, PT 44 **Student-Faculty Ratio:** 11:1 **Exams:** SAT I or ACT **% Receiving Financial Aid:** 75 **% Residing in College-Owned, -Operated, or -Affiliated Housing:** 56 **Library Holdings:** 93,382 **Regional Accreditation:** Southern Association of Colleges and Schools **Credit Hours For Degree:** 64 semester hours, Associates; 124 semester hours, Bachelors **Professional Accreditation:** CSWE **Intercollegiate Athletics:** Baseball M; Basketball M & W; Cross-Country Running M & W; Equestrian Sports M & W; Golf M; Soccer M & W; Softball W; Tennis M & W; Track and Field M & W; Volleyball W

VIRGINIA MILITARY INSTITUTE
Lexington, VA 24450
Tel: (540)464-7207
Free: 800-767-4207
Admissions: (540)464-7211
Fax: (540)464-7746
E-mail: admissions@vmi.edu
Web Site: http://www.vmi.edu/
President/CEO: Maj. Gen. Josiah Bunting, III
Registrar: Maj. Janet M. Battaglia
Admissions: Col. Vernon L. Beitzel
Financial Aid: Col. Timothy P. Golden
Type: Four-Year College **Sex:** Coed **Scores:** 99.4% SAT V 400+; 99.8% SAT M 400+; 38.8% ACT 18-23; 52% ACT 24-29 **Admission Plans:** Early Admission; Early Decision Plan **Application Fee:** $35.00 **H.S. Requirements:** High school diploma required; GED not accepted **Costs Per Year:** Application fee: $35. One-time mandatory fee: $1678. State resident tuition: $4382 full-time. Nonresident tuition: $18,582 full-time. Mandatory fees: $2606 full-time. College room and board: $5666. **Scholarships:** Available **Calendar System:** Semester, Summer Session Available **Enrollment:** FT 1,362 **Faculty:** FT 110, PT 41 **Student-Faculty Ratio:** 11:1 **Exams:** SAT I or ACT **% Receiving Financial Aid:** 41 **% Residing in College-Owned, -Operated, or -Affiliated Housing:** 100 **Library Holdings:** 162,053 **Regional Accreditation:** Southern Association of Colleges and Schools **Credit Hours For Degree:** 136 semester hours, Bachelors **ROTC:** Army, Navy, Air Force **Professional Accreditation:** ABET **Intercollegiate Athletics:** Baseball M; Basketball M; Cross-Country Running M & W; Fencing M & W; Football M; Golf M; Ice Hockey M; Lacrosse M; Racquetball M & W; Riflery M & W; Rugby M & W; Soccer M; Swimming and Diving M & W;

Tennis M; Track and Field M & W; Volleyball M & W; Water Polo M & W; Weight Lifting M & W; Wrestling M

VIRGINIA POLYTECHNIC INSTITUTE AND STATE UNIVERSITY
Blacksburg, VA 24061
Tel: (540)231-6000
Fax: (540)231-3242
Web Site: http://www.vt.edu/
President/CEO: Dr. Charles W. Steger
Registrar: Wanda Dean
Financial Aid: Barry W. Simmons, Sr.
Type: University **Sex:** Coed **Scores:** 100% SAT V 400+; 100% SAT M 400+; 28% ACT 18-23; 55% ACT 24-29 **% Accepted:** 70 **Admission Plans:** Early Admission; Early Decision Plan; Deferred Admission **Application Deadline:** January 15 **Application Fee:** $40.00 **H.S. Requirements:** High school diploma required; GED accepted **Costs Per Year:** Application fee: $40. State resident tuition: $4959 full-time, $206.75 per credit hour part-time. Nonresident tuition: $16,298 full-time, $679 per credit hour part-time. Mandatory fees: $1419 full-time, $169 per term part-time. College room and board: $4400. College room only: $2346. Room and board charges vary according to board plan and location. **Calendar System:** Semester, Summer Session Available **Enrollment:** FT 21,087, PT 540, Grad 5,993 **Faculty:** FT 1,304, PT 228 **Student-Faculty Ratio:** 16:1 **Exams:** SAT I or ACT **% Receiving Financial Aid:** 37 **% Residing in College-Owned, -Operated, or -Affiliated Housing:** 41 **Library Holdings:** 2,176,916 **Regional Accreditation:** Southern Association of Colleges and Schools **Credit Hours For Degree:** 72 credit hours, Associates; 126 credit hours, Bachelors **ROTC:** Army, Navy, Air Force **Professional Accreditation:** AACSB, ABET, AAMFT, AAFCS, ACCE, ACA, ADtA, ACSP, APA, ASLA, AVMA, FIDER, NASAD, NASPAA, NAST, NCATE, SAF **Intercollegiate Athletics:** Baseball M; Basketball M & W; Bowling M & W; Crew M & W; Cross-Country Running M & W; Equestrian Sports M & W; Fencing M & W; Field Hockey M & W; Football M; Golf M; Gymnastics M & W; Ice Hockey M & W; Lacrosse M & W; Rugby M & W; Skiing (Downhill) M & W; Soccer M & W; Softball W; Swimming and Diving M & W; Tennis M & W; Track and Field M & W; Ultimate Frisbee M & W; Volleyball M & W; Water Polo M & W; Weight Lifting M & W; Wrestling M

VIRGINIA STATE UNIVERSITY
1 Hayden St.
Petersburg, VA 23806-0001
Tel: (804)524-5000
Free: 800-871-7611
Admissions: (804)524-5902
Fax: (804)524-5055
E-mail: ilogan@vsu.edu
Web Site: http://www.vsu.edu/
President/CEO: Eddie N. Moore, Jr.
Registrar: Dr. Jerome Goodwin
Admissions: Irene Logan
Financial Aid: Henry DeBose
Type: Comprehensive **Sex:** Coed **Affiliation:** State Council of Higher Education for Virginia **% Accepted:** 79 **Application Deadline:** May 01 **Application Fee:** $25.00 **H.S. Requirements:** High school diploma required; GED accepted **Costs Per Year:** Application fee: $25. State resident tuition: $2317 full-time, $161 per credit part-time. Nonresident tuition: $9668 full-time, $402 per credit part-time. Mandatory fees: $2575 full-time. Full-time tuition and fees vary according to course load. Part-time tuition varies according to course load. College room and board: $6484. College room only: $3760. Room and board charges vary according to housing facility. **Scholarships:** Available **Calendar System:** Semester, Summer Session Available **Enrollment:** FT 4,060, PT 272, Grad 723 **Faculty:** FT 226, PT 101 **Student-Faculty Ratio:** 17:1 **Exams:** SAT I or ACT **% Receiving Financial Aid:** 88 **% Residing in College-Owned, -Operated, or -Affiliated Housing:** 58 **Library Holdings:** 284,213 **Regional Accreditation:** Southern Association of Colleges and Schools **Credit Hours For Degree:** 120 credit hours, Bachelors **ROTC:** Army **Professional Accreditation:** ABET, ADtA, NASAD, NASM, NCATE **Intercollegiate Athletics:** Baseball M; Basketball M & W; Bowling W; Cheerleading M & W; Cross-Country Running M & W; Football M; Golf M & W; Softball W; Tennis M & W; Track and Field M & W; Volleyball W

VIRGINIA UNION UNIVERSITY
1500 North Lombardy St.
Richmond, VA 23220-1170
Tel: (804)257-5600
Free: 800-368-3227
Admissions: (804)257-5881
Web Site: http://www.vuu.edu/
President/CEO: Dr. Belinda C. Anderson
Registrar: Sue Ellen Coleman
Admissions: Gil Powell
Financial Aid: Phenie D. Golatt
Type: Comprehensive **Sex:** Coed **Affiliation:** Baptist **Scores:** 46.93% SAT V 400+; 39.88% SAT M 400+ **% Accepted:** 58 **Admission Plans:** Early Admission; Deferred Admission **Application Deadline:** Rolling **Application Fee:** $25.00 **H.S. Requirements:** High school diploma required; GED accepted **Costs Per Year:** Application fee: $25. Comprehensive fee: $18,432 includes full-time tuition ($11,600), mandatory fees ($1170), and college room and board ($5662). College room only: $2662. Full-time tuition and fees vary according to course level and course load. Part-time tuition: $483 per credit hour. Part-time mandatory fees: $370 per term. Part-time tuition and fees vary according to course level and course load. **Scholarships:** Available **Calendar System:** Semester, Summer Session Available **Enrollment:** FT 1,309, PT 35, Grad 27 **Faculty:** FT 84, PT 56 **Student-Faculty Ratio:** 15:1 **Exams:** SAT I or ACT **% Receiving Financial Aid:** 82 **Library Holdings:** 147,611 **Regional Accreditation:** Southern Association of Colleges and Schools **Credit Hours For Degree:** 124 semester hours, Bachelors **ROTC:** Army **Professional Accreditation:** ACIPE, ACBSP, ATS, CSWE, NCATE **Intercollegiate Athletics:** Basketball M & W; Cross-Country Running M & W; Football M; Golf M; Softball W; Tennis M; Track and Field M & W; Volleyball W

VIRGINIA UNIVERSITY OF LYNCHBURG
2058 Garfield Ave.
Lynchburg, VA 24501-6417
Tel: (804)528-5276
Fax: (804)528-4257
Web Site: http://www.vulonline.org/
President/CEO: Ralph Reavis
Registrar: Kathy C. Franklin
Type: Comprehensive **Sex:** Coed **Calendar System:** Semester **Professional Accreditation:** TACCS

VIRGINIA WESLEYAN COLLEGE
1584 Wesleyan Dr.
Norfolk, VA 23502-5599
Tel: (757)455-3200
Free: 800-737-8684
Admissions: (757)455-3208
Fax: (757)461-5238
E-mail: admissions@vwc.edu
Web Site: http://www.vwc.edu/
President/CEO: Dr. William T. Greer, Jr.
Registrar: Barbara S. Adams
Admissions: Richard T. Hinshaw
Financial Aid: Eugenia F. Hickman
Type: Four-Year College **Sex:** Coed **Affiliation:** United Methodist **Scores:** 97.4% SAT V 400+; 95.2% SAT M 400+; 50% ACT 18-23; 19.7% ACT 24-29 **% Accepted:** 81 **Application Deadline:** Rolling **Application Fee:** $40.00 **H.S. Requirements:** High school diploma required; GED accepted **Costs Per Year:** Application fee: $40. Comprehensive fee: $29,986 includes full-time tuition ($22,976), mandatory fees ($160), and college room and board ($6850). Part-time tuition: $957 per semester hour. **Scholarships:** Available **Calendar System:** 4-1-4, Summer Session Available **Enrollment:** FT 1,121, PT 271 **Faculty:** FT 80, PT 58 **Student-Faculty Ratio:** 12:1 **Exams:** SAT I or ACT **% Receiving Financial Aid:** 63 **% Residing in College-Owned, -Operated, or -Affiliated Housing:** 42 **Library Holdings:** 140,400 **Regional Accreditation:** Southern Association of Colleges and Schools **Credit Hours For Degree:** 120 semester hours, Bachelors **ROTC:** Army **Professional Accreditation:** NRPA **Intercollegiate Athletics:** Baseball M; Basketball M & W; Cheerleading W; Cross-Country Running M & W; Field Hockey W; Golf M; Lacrosse M & W; Soccer M & W; Softball W; Tennis M & W; Volleyball W

VIRGINIA WESTERN COMMUNITY COLLEGE
PO Box 14007
Roanoke, VA 24038
Tel: (540)857-7311
Admissions: (540)857-7231

Fax: (540)857-7204
Web Site: http://www.virginiawestern.edu/
President/CEO: Dr. Robert H. Sandel
Registrar: Meg Carter
Admissions: Sharlona Wimmer
Financial Aid: Dr. Larry E. Ewing
Type: Two-Year College **Sex:** Coed **Affiliation:** Virginia Community College System **Admission Plans:** Open Admission; Preferred Admission; Early Admission; Deferred Admission **Application Fee:** $0.00 **H.S. Requirements:** High school diploma required; GED accepted **Scholarships:** Available **Calendar System:** Semester, Summer Session Available **Enrollment:** FT 2,128, PT 5,996 **Faculty:** FT 87, PT 319 **Student-Faculty Ratio:** 25:1 **Exams:** SAT I or ACT **Library Holdings:** 67,129 **Regional Accreditation:** Southern Association of Colleges and Schools **Credit Hours For Degree:** 60 semester hours, Associates **Professional Accreditation:** ADA, ACBSP, JRCERT, NLN

WASHINGTON AND LEE UNIVERSITY
Lexington, VA 24450-0303
Tel: (540)458-8400
Admissions: (540)458-8710
Fax: (540)463-8062
E-mail: admissions@wlu.edu
Web Site: http://www.wlu.edu/
President/CEO: Dr. Thomas G. Burish
Registrar: D. Scott Dittman
Admissions: William M. Hartog
Financial Aid: John H. DeCourcy
Type: Comprehensive **Sex:** Coed **Scores:** 100% SAT V 400+; 100% SAT M 400+; 54% ACT 24-29 **% Accepted:** 29 **Admission Plans:** Early Decision Plan; Deferred Admission **Application Deadline:** January 15 **Application Fee:** $50.00 **H.S. Requirements:** High school diploma or equivalent not required **Costs Per Year:** Application fee: $50. Comprehensive fee: $35,860 includes full-time tuition ($27,960), mandatory fees ($675), and college room and board ($7225). College room only: $3425. Room and board charges vary according to housing facility and student level. Part-time tuition: $935 per credit. **Scholarships:** Available **Calendar System:** Miscellaneous, Summer Session Not available **Enrollment:** FT 1,766, PT 4, Grad 22 **Faculty:** FT 215, PT 2 **Student-Faculty Ratio:** 10:1 **Exams:** Other, SAT I or ACT **% Receiving Financial Aid:** 33 **% Residing in College-Owned, -Operated, or -Affiliated Housing:** 61 **Library Holdings:** 907,325 **Regional Accreditation:** Southern Association of Colleges and Schools **Credit Hours For Degree:** 121 credits, Bachelors **ROTC:** Army **Professional Accreditation:** AACSB, ACEJMC, ABA, AALS **Intercollegiate Athletics:** Baseball M; Basketball M & W; Cross-Country Running M & W; Equestrian Sports M & W; Fencing M & W; Field Hockey W; Football M; Golf M; Ice Hockey M & W; Lacrosse M & W; Rugby M; Skiing (Cross-Country) M & W; Soccer M & W; Softball W; Swimming and Diving M & W; Tennis M & W; Track and Field M & W; Ultimate Frisbee M & W; Volleyball M & W; Wrestling M

WESTWOOD COLLEGE-ANNANDALE CAMPUS
7611 Little River Turnpike, 3rd Floor
Annandale, VA 22003
Tel: (703)642-3770
Free: 800-281-2978
Web Site: http://www.westwood.edu/locations/virginia-colleges/annandale-college.asp **Type:** Two-Year College **Sex:** Coed

WESTWOOD COLLEGE-ARLINGTON BALLSTON CAMPUS
1901 North Ft. Myer Dr.
Arlington, VA 22209
Tel: 800-281-2978
Admissions: 877-268-5218
E-mail: twilliams1@westwood.edu
Web Site: http://www.westwood.edu
Admissions: Tim Williams
Type: Four-Year College **Sex:** Coed **Application Fee:** $100.00 **Costs Per Year:** Application fee: $100. Tuition: $12,300 full-time, $467 per credit part-time.

WORLD COLLEGE
5193 Shore Dr., Ste. 105
Virginia Beach, VA 23455-2500
Tel: (757)464-4600
Free: 800-696-7532
Web Site: http://www.worldcollege.edu/
President/CEO: John Randall Drinko
Registrar: Michael Smith
Admissions: Scott Katzenmeyer
Type: Four-Year College **Sex:** Coed **Admission Plans:** Open Admission; Early Admission **Application Deadline:** Rolling **H.S. Requirements:** High school diploma required; GED accepted **Costs Per Year:** Tuition: $3540 per year part-time. **Calendar System:** Semester **Faculty:** FT 3, PT 2 **Credit Hours For Degree:** 139 semester hours, Bachelors **Professional Accreditation:** DETC

WYTHEVILLE COMMUNITY COLLEGE
1000 East Main St.
Wytheville, VA 24382-3308
Tel: (276)223-4700
Admissions: (276)223-4755
Fax: (276)223-4860
E-mail: wcdixxs@wcc.vccs.edu
Web Site: http://www.wcc.vccs.edu/
President/CEO: Dr. Ann E. Alexander
Registrar: Sherry K. Dix
Admissions: Sherry K. Dix
Financial Aid: Dr. Gail S. Catron
Type: Two-Year College **Sex:** Coed **Affiliation:** Virginia Community College System **Admission Plans:** Open Admission; Preferred Admission; Early Admission **Application Fee:** $0.00 **H.S. Requirements:** High school diploma or equivalent not required. For allied health programs: High school diploma required; GED accepted **Scholarships:** Available **Calendar System:** Semester, Summer Session Available **Faculty:** FT 46 **Student-Faculty Ratio:** 16:1 **Library Holdings:** 29,000 **Regional Accreditation:** Southern Association of Colleges and Schools **Credit Hours For Degree:** 62 credit hours, Associates **Professional Accreditation:** ADA, APTA, NAACLS, NLN

ANTIOCH UNIVERSITY SEATTLE
2326 Sixth Ave.
Seattle, WA 98121-1814
Tel: (206)441-5352
Web Site: http://www.antiochsea.edu/
President/CEO: Dr. James Hall
Registrar: Barbara Talmadge
Admissions: Pamela Smith Mentz
Financial Aid: Katy Gilroy
Type: Two-Year Upper Division **Sex:** Coed **Affiliation:** Antioch University **Admission Plans:** Deferred Admission **Application Fee:** $50.00 **H.S. Requirements:** High school diploma required; GED accepted **Scholarships:** Available **Calendar System:** Quarter, Summer Session Available **Faculty:** FT 8, PT 11 **Student-Faculty Ratio:** 10:1 **% Receiving Financial Aid:** 70 **Library Holdings:** 4,750 **Regional Accreditation:** North Central Association of Colleges and Schools **Credit Hours For Degree:** 180 credits, Bachelors

APOLLO COLLEGE
1101 North Francher Rd.
Spokane, WA 99212
Tel: (509)532-8888
Fax: (509)533-5983
Web Site: http://www.apollocollege.com/
President/CEO: Deanna Baker
Admissions: Deanna Baker
Type: Two-Year College **Sex:** Coed **Professional Accreditation:** ABHES, JRCERT

ARGOSY UNIVERSITY/SEATTLE
1019 Eighth Ave. North
Seattle, WA 98109
Tel: (206)283-4500; (866)283-2777
Fax: (206)283-5777
Web Site: http://www.argosyu.edu/
President/CEO: Mark Hurtubise, EdD
Type: Two-Year Upper Division **Sex:** Coed **Scholarships:** Available **Calendar System:** Semester **Enrollment:** FT 26, PT 15, Grad 252 **Faculty:** FT 1, PT 4 **% Receiving Financial Aid:** 79 **Regional Accreditation:** North Central Association of Colleges and Schools

THE ART INSTITUTE OF SEATTLE
2323 Elliott Ave.
Seattle, WA 98121-1642
Tel: (206)448-0900
Free: 800-275-2471
Fax: (206)269-0275
E-mail: adm@ais.edu
Web Site: http://www.ais.artinstitutes.edu/
President/CEO: Shelly DuBois
Registrar: Mike Reese
Admissions: Karen Shea
Type: Four-Year College **Sex:** Coed **Affiliation:** Education Management Corporation **% Accepted:** 67 **Admission Plans:** Deferred Admission **Application Deadline:** Rolling **Application Fee:** $50.00 **H.S. Requirements:** High school diploma required; GED accepted **Costs Per Year:** Application fee: $50. Tuition: $17,550 full-time, $390 per credit part-time. College room only: $6867. **Scholarships:** Available **Calendar System:** Quarter, Summer Session Available **Enrollment:** FT 1,298, PT 1,194 **Faculty:** FT 79, PT 95 **Student-Faculty Ratio:** 19:1 **Library Holdings:** 17,164 **Professional Accreditation:** ACF, NCCU

BASTYR UNIVERSITY
14500 Juanita Dr., NE
Kenmore, WA 98028-4966
Tel: (425)823-1300
Admissions: (425)602-3014
Fax: (425)823-6222
Web Site: http://www.bastyr.edu/
President/CEO: Dr. Thomas C. Shepherd
Registrar: Chris Masterson
Admissions: Susan Weider
Financial Aid: Richard A. Dent
Type: Two-Year Upper Division **Sex:** Coed **% Accepted:** 77 **Admission Plans:** Deferred Admission **Application Fee:** $60.00 **H.S. Requirements:** High school diploma required; GED accepted **Costs Per Year:** Application fee: $60. Tuition: $13,770 full-time, $306 per credit part-time. Mandatory fees: $1611 full-time. Full-time tuition and fees vary according to course load and program. Part-time tuition varies according to course load and program. College room only: $2460. Room charges vary according to housing facility. **Scholarships:** Available **Calendar System:** Quarter, Summer Session Available **Enrollment:** FT 213, PT 51, Grad 345 **Faculty:** FT 41, PT 107 **Student-Faculty Ratio:** 15:1 **% Receiving Financial Aid:** 78 **% Residing in College-Owned, -Operated, or -Affiliated Housing:** 7 **Library Holdings:** 14,000 **Credit Hours For Degree:** 180 credits, Bachelors **Professional Accreditation:** ADtA, NACSCAO, NCCU

BATES TECHNICAL COLLEGE
1101 South Yakima Ave.
Tacoma, WA 98405-4895
Tel: (253)596-1500
Admissions: (253)680-7000
Web Site: http://www.bates.ctc.edu/
Admissions: Gwen Sailer
Type: Two-Year College **Sex:** Coed **Affiliation:** Washington State Board for Community and Technical Colleges **Application Fee:** $49.00 **Scholarships:** Available **Calendar System:** Quarter **Faculty:** FT 160, PT 229 **Student-Faculty Ratio:** 18:1 **Exams:** Other **Professional Accreditation:** ADA, NCCU

BELLEVUE COMMUNITY COLLEGE
3000 Landerholm Circle, SE
Bellevue, WA 98007-6484
Tel: (425)564-1000
Admissions: (425)564-2222
Fax: (425)564-2261
Web Site: http://www.bcc.ctc.edu/
President/CEO: B. Jean Floten
Registrar: Tika Esler
Admissions: Tika Esler
Financial Aid: Sherri Ballantyne

Type: Two-Year College **Sex:** Coed **Affiliation:** Washington State Board for Community and Technical Colleges **Admission Plans:** Open Admission **Application Fee:** $0.00 **H.S. Requirements:** High school diploma or equivalent not required. For applicants under 18: High school diploma required; GED accepted **Costs Per Year:** Application fee: $0. State resident tuition: $2655 full-time, $78.80 per credit part-time. Nonresident tuition: $7863 full-time, $250.50 per credit part-time. **Scholarships:** Available **Calendar System:** Quarter, Summer Session Available **Faculty:** FT 154, PT 362 **Student-Faculty Ratio:** 36:1 **Library Holdings:** 42,000 **Credit Hours For Degree:** 90 quarter hours, Associates **Professional Accreditation:** JRCEDMS, JRCERT, NLN, NCCU **Intercollegiate Athletics:** Baseball M; Basketball M & W; Cross-Country Running M & W; Golf M; Soccer M; Softball W; Tennis M & W; Track and Field M & W; Volleyball W

BELLINGHAM TECHNICAL COLLEGE
3028 Lindbergh Ave.
Bellingham, WA 98225
Tel: (360)738-0221
Admissions: (360)738-3105
Fax: (360)676-2798
Web Site: http://www.btc.ctc.edu/
Admissions: David Klaffke
Type: Two-Year College **Admission Plans:** Open Admission; Early Admission; Deferred Admission **Application Fee:** $33.17 **H.S. Requirements:** High school diploma or equivalent not required. For dental assisting (certificate): High school diploma required; GED accepted **Scholarships:** Available **Enrollment:** FT 968, PT 3,191 **Faculty:** FT 56, PT 111 **Student-Faculty Ratio:** 20:1 **Exams:** Other **Library Holdings:** 9,537 **Credit Hours For Degree:** 1800 clock hours, Associates **Professional Accreditation:** ACF, ADA, NCCU

BIG BEND COMMUNITY COLLEGE
7662 Chanute St., NE
Moses Lake, WA 98837-3299
Tel: (509)762-5351
Admissions: (509)793-2061
Fax: (509)762-6243
E-mail: candyl@bigbend.edu
Web Site: http://www.bigbend.edu/
President/CEO: Dr. William C. Bonaudi
Registrar: Candis Lacher
Admissions: Candis Lacher
Financial Aid: Sherril Keeler
Type: Two-Year College **Sex:** Coed **% Accepted:** 100 **Admission Plans:** Open Admission; Early Admission; Deferred Admission **Application Deadline:** Rolling **Application Fee:** $30.00 **H.S. Requirements:** High school diploma or equivalent not required. For aviation, nursing programs: High school diploma required; GED accepted **Costs Per Year:** Application fee: $30. State resident tuition: $2586 full-time, $77.30 per credit part-time. Nonresident tuition: $2986 full-time, $90.50 per credit part-time. College room and board: $5200. **Scholarships:** Available **Calendar System:** Quarter, Summer Session Available **Enrollment:** FT 1,194, PT 606 **Faculty:** FT 54, PT 78 **Student-Faculty Ratio:** 20:1 **% Residing in College-Owned, -Operated, or -Affiliated Housing:** 5 **Library Holdings:** 41,900 **Credit Hours For Degree:** 90 credit hours, Associates **Professional Accreditation:** NCCU **Intercollegiate Athletics:** Baseball M; Basketball M & W; Softball W; Volleyball W

CASCADIA COMMUNITY COLLEGE
19017 120th Ave., NE, Ste. 102
Bothell, WA 98011
Tel: (425)398-5400
Admissions: (425)352-8000
Fax: (425)398-5730
Web Site: http://www.cascadia.ctc.edu/
President/CEO: Victoria Richart
Admissions: Marla Coan
Type: Two-Year College **Sex:** Coed **Admission Plans:** Open Admission **H.S. Requirements:** High school diploma or equivalent not required **Costs Per Year:** State resident tuition: $2230 full-time, $74 per credit part-time. Nonresident tuition: $7738 full-time, $258 per credit part-time. Mandatory fees: $75 full-time, $4 per credit part-time. **Calendar System:** Quarter **Enrollment:** FT 952, PT 937 **Faculty:** FT 21, PT 80 **Student-Faculty Ratio:** 26:1 **Library Holdings:** 67,943 **Credit Hours For Degree:** 90 credits, Associates **Professional Accreditation:** NCCU

CENTRAL WASHINGTON UNIVERSITY
400 East University Way
Ellensburg, WA 98926
Tel: (509)963-1111; (866)298-4968
Admissions: (509)963-1211
Fax: (509)963-3022
E-mail: cwuadmis@cwu.edu
Web Site: http://www.cwu.edu/
President/CEO: Dr. Jerilyn McIntyre
Registrar: Carolyn L. Wells
Admissions: Lisa Garcia-Hanson
Financial Aid: Agnes Canedo
Type: Comprehensive **Sex:** Coed **Scores:** 92.5% SAT V 400+; 91.7% SAT M 400+; 55% ACT 18-23; 23.9% ACT 24-29 **% Accepted:** 76 **Application Deadline:** April 01 **Application Fee:** $50.00 **H.S. Requirements:** High school diploma required; GED accepted **Costs Per Year:** Application fee: $50. State resident tuition: $4182 full-time. Nonresident tuition: $12,477 full-time. Mandatory fees: $624 full-time. College room and board: $6924. **Scholarships:** Available **Calendar System:** Quarter, Summer Session Available **Enrollment:** FT 8,530, PT 1,087, Grad 573 **Faculty:** FT 364, PT 171 **Student-Faculty Ratio:** 22:1 **Exams:** SAT I or ACT **% Receiving Financial Aid:** 50 **% Residing in College-Owned, -Operated, or -Affiliated Housing:** 34 **Library Holdings:** 434,424 **Credit Hours For Degree:** 180 credits, Bachelors **ROTC:** Army, Air Force **Professional Accreditation:** ABET, ACCE, ADtA, JRCEMT, NASM, NCATE, NCCU **Intercollegiate Athletics:** Baseball M; Basketball M & W; Bowling M & W; Cheerleading M & W; Cross-Country Running M & W; Fencing M & W; Football M; Golf M & W; Ice Hockey M & W; Rugby M & W; Soccer M & W; Softball W; Track and Field M & W; Volleyball W; Water Polo M & W

CENTRALIA COLLEGE
600 West Locust
Centralia, WA 98531-4099
Tel: (360)736-9391
E-mail: scopeland@centralia.edu
Web Site: http://www.centralia.ctc.edu/
President/CEO: Dr. James M. Walton
Registrar: Dr. Michael Grubiak
Admissions: Scott A. Copeland
Financial Aid: Tracy Smothers
Type: Two-Year College **Sex:** Coed **Affiliation:** Washington State Board for Community and Technical Colleges **% Accepted:** 96 **Admission Plans:** Open Admission **Application Deadline:** Rolling **Application Fee:** $0.00 **H.S. Requirements:** High school diploma required; GED accepted **Costs Per Year:** Application fee: $0. State resident tuition: $2586 full-time, $74 per credit part-time. Nonresident tuition: $2946 full-time, $86 per credit part-time. Mandatory fees: $274 full-time, $8 per credit part-time, $5 per term part-time. **Scholarships:** Available **Calendar System:** Quarter, Summer Session Available **Enrollment:** FT 1,860, PT 1,967 **Faculty:** FT 58, PT 182 **Student-Faculty Ratio:** 24:1 **Library Holdings:** 38,000 **Credit Hours For Degree:** 93 credits, Associates **Professional Accreditation:** NCCU **Intercollegiate Athletics:** Baseball M; Basketball M & W; Golf W; Softball W; Volleyball W

CITY UNIVERSITY
11900 NE First St.
Bellevue, WA 98005
Tel: (425)637-1010; 888-42-CITYU
Admissions: 800-426-5596
Fax: (425)277-2437
E-mail: info@cityu.edu
Web Site: http://www.cityu.edu/
President/CEO: Dr. W. Michael Easton
Registrar: Mary Belknap
Admissions: Melissa Mecham
Financial Aid: Jean L. Roberts
Type: Comprehensive **Sex:** Coed **Admission Plans:** Open Admission; Deferred Admission **Application Deadline:** Rolling **Application Fee:** $80.00 **H.S. Requirements:** High school diploma required; GED accepted **Costs Per Year:** Application fee: $80. Tuition: $8040 full-time, $268 per credit hour part-time. Mandatory fees: $120 full-time, $40 per term part-time. **Scholarships:** Available **Calendar System:** Quarter, Summer Session Available **Enrollment:** FT 1,007, PT 787, Grad 2,226 **Faculty:** FT 52, PT 1,189 **Student-Faculty Ratio:** 7:1 **% Receiving Financial Aid:** 25 **Library Holdings:** 32,329 **Credit Hours For Degree:** 90 credits, Associates; 180 credits, Bachelors **Professional Accreditation:** NCCU

CLARK COLLEGE
1800 East McLoughlin Blvd.
Vancouver, WA 98663-3598
Tel: (360)992-2000
Admissions: (360)992-2308
Web Site: http://www.clark.edu/
President/CEO: Dr. Wayne Branch
Registrar: Lorraine Seiffert
Admissions: Sheryl Anderson
Financial Aid: Nancy Heidrick
Type: Two-Year College **Sex:** Coed **Affiliation:** Washington State Board for Community and Technical Colleges **% Accepted:** 100 **Admission Plans:** Open Admission; Early Admission; Deferred Admission **Application Deadline:** August 03 **Application Fee:** $0.00 **H.S. Requirements:** High school diploma or equivalent not required **Costs Per Year:** Application fee: $0. State resident tuition: $2704 full-time, $78 per credit hour part-time. Nonresident tuition: $3093 full-time, $91 per credit hour part-time. Full-time tuition varies according to course load and reciprocity agreements. Part-time tuition varies according to course load and reciprocity agreements. **Scholarships:** Available **Calendar System:** Quarter, Summer Session Available **Enrollment:** FT 4,255, PT 5,565 **Faculty:** FT 193, PT 383 **Student-Faculty Ratio:** 23:1 **Library Holdings:** 63,525 **Credit Hours For Degree:** 90 quarter hours, Associates **ROTC:** Army, Air Force **Professional Accreditation:** AAMAE, ADA, NLN, NCCU **Intercollegiate Athletics:** Basketball M & W; Cross-Country Running M & W; Fencing M & W; Soccer M & W; Softball W; Track and Field M & W; Volleyball W

CLOVER PARK TECHNICAL COLLEGE
4500 Steilacoom Blvd., SW
Lakewood, WA 98499
Tel: (253)589-5678
Admissions: (253)589-5570
Web Site: http://www.cptc.edu/
Admissions: Judy Richardson
Type: Two-Year College **Sex:** Coed **Affiliation:** Washington State Community and Technical College System **Admission Plans:** Open Admission **Application Fee:** $36.00 **H.S. Requirements:** High school diploma required; GED accepted **Costs Per Year:** Application fee: $36. State resident tuition: $2529 full-time, $51 per credit hour part-time. Mandatory fees: $579 full-time. **Scholarships:** Available **Enrollment:** FT 1,848, PT 6,640 **Faculty:** FT 111, PT 188 **Student-Faculty Ratio:** 22:1 **Exams:** Other **Library Holdings:** 11,219 **Professional Accreditation:** ADA, NAACLS, NCCU

COLUMBIA BASIN COLLEGE
2600 North 20th Ave.
Pasco, WA 99301-3397
Tel: (509)547-0511
Fax: (509)546-0401
Web Site: http://www.columbiabasin.edu
President/CEO: Dr. Lee R. Thornton
Registrar: Pat Campbell
Admissions: Patricia A. Campbell
Financial Aid: Cecilia Ratliff
Type: Two-Year College **Sex:** Coed **Affiliation:** Washington State Board for Community and Technical Colleges **Admission Plans:** Open Admission **H.S. Requirements:** High school diploma required; GED accepted **Scholarships:** Available **Calendar System:** Quarter, Summer Session Available **Enrollment:** FT 2,425, PT 3,412 **Faculty:** FT 114, PT 495 **Student-Faculty Ratio:** 10:1 **Exams:** Other **Library Holdings:** 54,331 **Credit Hours For Degree:** 90 quarter hours, Associates **Professional Accreditation:** ADA, JRCEMT, NLN, NCCU **Intercollegiate Athletics:** Baseball M; Basketball M & W; Golf M & W; Soccer M & W; Volleyball W

CORNISH COLLEGE OF THE ARTS
1000 Lenora St.
Seattle, WA 98121
Tel: (206)726-5151
Free: 800-726-ARTS
Admissions: (206)726-5018
Fax: (206)720-1011
E-mail: epedersen@comish.edu
Web Site: http://www.cornish.edu/
President/CEO: Sergei Tschernisch
Registrar: Adrienne Bolyard
Admissions: Eric R. Pedersen
Type: Four-Year College **Sex:** Coed **% Accepted:** 51 **Admission Plans:** Deferred Admission **Application Deadline:** August 15 **Application Fee:** $35.00 **H.S. Requirements:** High school diploma required; GED accepted **Costs Per Year:** Application fee: $35. Tuition: $21,200 full-time, $875 per credit part-time. Mandatory fees: $300 full-time. **Scholarships:** Available **Calendar System:** Semester, Summer Session Available **Enrollment:** FT 739, PT 29 **Faculty:** FT 54, PT 92 **Student-Faculty Ratio:** 8:1 **% Receiving Financial Aid:** 61 **Library Holdings:** 12,000 **Credit Hours For Degree:** 130 credits, Bachelors **Professional Accreditation:** NASAD, NCCU

CROWN COLLEGE
8739 South Hosmer
Tacoma, WA 98444-1836
Tel: (253)531-3123; 888-689-3688
Fax: (253)531-3521
Web Site: http://www.crowncollege.edu/
President/CEO: John M. Wabel
Financial Aid: Deborah Halasz
Type: Two-Year College **Sex:** Coed **Affiliation:** Killebrew Dalton, Inc **Application Fee:** $135.00 **H.S. Requirements:** High school diploma required; GED accepted **Costs Per Year:** Application fee: $135. Tuition: $7500 full-time. Mandatory fees: $385 full-time. **Scholarships:** Available **Calendar System:** Continuous, Summer Session Not available **Faculty:** FT 7, PT 16 **Student-Faculty Ratio:** 20:1 **Library Holdings:** 9,500 **Credit Hours For Degree:** 66 semester hours, Associates; 121 semester hours, Bachelors **Professional Accreditation:** ACCSCT

DEVRY UNIVERSITY (BELLEVUE)
500 108th Ave. NE, Ste. 320
Bellevue, WA 98004-5519
Tel: (425)455-2242
Fax: (425)455-2322
Web Site: http://www.devry.edu/ **Type:** Comprehensive **Sex:** Coed **Costs Per Year:** One-time mandatory fee: $40. Tuition: $13,060 full-time, $475 per credit part-time. Mandatory fees: $60 full-time, $30 per year part-time. Full-time tuition and fees vary according to course load. Part-time tuition and fees vary according to course load. **Calendar System:** Semester **Regional Accreditation:** North Central Association of Colleges and Schools

DEVRY UNIVERSITY (FEDERAL WAY)
3600 South 344th Way
Federal Way, WA 98001
Tel: (253)943-2800; (866)338-7934
Web Site: http://www.devry.edu/
President/CEO: Reed Hackett
Registrar: Katrina Orchard
Financial Aid: Diane Rooney
Type: Comprehensive **Sex:** Coed **Affiliation:** DeVry University **Admission Plans:** Deferred Admission **Application Deadline:** Rolling **Application Fee:** $50.00 **H.S. Requirements:** High school diploma required; GED accepted **Costs Per Year:** Application fee: $50. One-time mandatory fee: $40. Tuition: $13,060 full-time, $475 per credit part-time. Mandatory fees: $270 full-time, $160 per year part-time. Full-time tuition and fees vary according to course load. Part-time tuition and fees vary according to course load. **Scholarships:** Available **Calendar System:** Semester, Summer Session Available **Enrollment:** FT 549, PT 225, Grad 103 **Faculty:** FT 32, PT 18 **Student-Faculty Ratio:** 18:1 **% Receiving Financial Aid:** 80 **Library Holdings:** 6,021 **Regional Accreditation:** North Central Association of Colleges and Schools **Credit Hours For Degree:** 67 credit hours, Associates; 122 credit hours, Bachelors

DIGIPEN INSTITUTE OF TECHNOLOGY
5001 150th Ave., NE
Redmond, WA 98052
Tel: (425)558-0299
Fax: (425)558-0299
Web Site: http://www.digipen.edu/
President/CEO: Claude Comair
Type: Two-Year College **Sex:** Coed **Application Fee:** $75.00 **Costs Per Year:** Application fee: $75. One-time mandatory fee: $150. Tuition: $15,200 full-time, $380 per credit part-time. Mandatory fees: $160 full-time, $80. **Calendar System:** Semester **Enrollment:** FT 617, PT 40, Grad 20 **Student-**

Faculty Ratio: 13:1 **Exams:** SAT I or ACT **Professional Accreditation:** ACCSCT

EASTERN WASHINGTON UNIVERSITY

526 5th St.
Cheney, WA 99004-2431
Tel: (509)359-6200
Admissions: (509)359-6582
Fax: (509)359-4330
E-mail: admissions@ewu.edu
Web Site: http://www.ewu.edu/
President/CEO: Dr. Stephen Jordan
Registrar: Debra Fockler
Admissions: Shannon Carr
Financial Aid: Bruce Defrates

Type: Comprehensive **Sex:** Coed **Scores:** 89% SAT V 400+; 91% SAT M 400+; 52% ACT 18-23; 25% ACT 24-29 **% Accepted:** 83 **Admission Plans:** Early Admission; Deferred Admission **Application Deadline:** September 15 **Application Fee:** $50.00 **H.S. Requirements:** High school diploma required; GED accepted. For Running Start program accepts high school students concurrently: High school diploma or equivalent not required **Costs Per Year:** Application fee: $50. State resident tuition: $4044 full-time, $135 per credit part-time. Nonresident tuition: $17,756 full-time, $444 per credit part-time. Mandatory fees: $237 full-time, $79 per term part-time. Full-time tuition and fees vary according to course load. Part-time tuition and fees vary according to course load. College room and board: $5733. Room and board charges vary according to board plan and housing facility. **Scholarships:** Available **Calendar System:** Quarter, Summer Session Available **Enrollment:** FT 8,174, PT 1,429, Grad 1,305 **Faculty:** FT 411, PT 164 **Student-Faculty Ratio:** 21:1 **Exams:** SAT I or ACT **% Receiving Financial Aid:** 61 **% Residing in College-Owned, -Operated, or -Affiliated Housing:** 20 **Library Holdings:** 852,186 **Credit Hours For Degree:** 180 quarter hours, Bachelors **ROTC:** Army **Professional Accreditation:** AACSB, ABET, AACN, ACA, ADA, ACSP, AOTA, APTA, ASLHA, CSWE, NASM, NCATE, NLN, NRPA, NCCU **Intercollegiate Athletics:** Badminton M; Baseball M; Basketball M & W; Cross-Country Running M & W; Football M; Golf M & W; Ice Hockey M; Soccer W; Tennis M & W; Track and Field M & W; Volleyball W

EDMONDS COMMUNITY COLLEGE

20000 68th Ave. West
Lynnwood, WA 98036-5999
Tel: (425)640-1500
Admissions: (425)640-1401
Fax: (425)640-1159
E-mail: raeellen.reas@edcc.edu
Web Site: http://www.edcc.edu/
President/CEO: Dr. Jack Oharah
Admissions: Rae Ellen Reas
Financial Aid: Ted Malone

Type: Two-Year College **Sex:** Coed **Affiliation:** Washington State Board for Community and Technical Colleges **% Accepted:** 100 **Admission Plans:** Open Admission; Early Admission; Deferred Admission **Application Deadline:** Rolling **Application Fee:** $17.00 **H.S. Requirements:** High school diploma or equivalent not required **Costs Per Year:** Application fee: $17. State resident tuition: $2436 full-time, $71.80 per credit hour part-time. Nonresident tuition: $7610 full-time, $251 per credit hour part-time. Mandatory fees: $166 full-time, $4.25 per credit hour part-time. Full-time tuition and fees vary according to course load. Part-time tuition and fees vary according to course load. College room only: $4500. **Scholarships:** Available **Calendar System:** Quarter, Summer Session Available **Enrollment:** FT 3,398, PT 4,183 **Faculty:** FT 128, PT 300 **Student-Faculty Ratio:** 21:1 **Library Holdings:** 47,947 **Credit Hours For Degree:** 90 credits, Associates **Professional Accreditation:** NCCU **Intercollegiate Athletics:** Baseball M; Basketball M & W; Golf M & W; Soccer M & W; Softball W; Volleyball W

EVERETT COMMUNITY COLLEGE

2000 Tower St.
Everett, WA 98201-1327
Tel: (425)388-9100
Admissions: (425)388-9204
Fax: (425)388-9173
Web Site: http://www.evcc.ctc.edu/
President/CEO: Charles N. Earl
Admissions: Christine Kerlin
Financial Aid: Christina Castorena

Type: Two-Year College **Sex:** Coed **Affiliation:** Washington State Board for Community and Technical Colleges **Admission Plans:** Open Admission; Early Admission; Deferred Admission **Application Fee:** $0.00 **H.S. Requirements:** High school diploma or equivalent not required. For cosmetology, nursing, criminal justice, and fire science: High school diploma required; GED accepted **Costs Per Year:** Application fee: $0. State resident tuition: $2313 full-time, $69.35 per credit part-time. Nonresident tuition: $7521 full-time, $241.05 per credit part-time. Full-time tuition varies according to course load. Part-time tuition varies according to course load. **Scholarships:** Available **Calendar System:** Quarter, Summer Session Available **Enrollment:** FT 3,262, PT 3,926 **Faculty:** FT 130, PT 233 **Student-Faculty Ratio:** 20:1 **Exams:** Other **Library Holdings:** 49,600 **Credit Hours For Degree:** 90 quarter hours, Associates **Professional Accreditation:** NLN, NCCU **Intercollegiate Athletics:** Baseball M; Basketball M & W; Cross-Country Running M & W; Soccer M & W; Softball W; Volleyball W

THE EVERGREEN STATE COLLEGE

2700 Evergreen Parkway, NW
Olympia, WA 98505
Tel: (360)867-6000
Admissions: (360)867-6170
Fax: (360)867-6577
E-mail: admissions@evergreen.edu
Web Site: http://www.evergreen.edu/
President/CEO: Dr. Thomas L. Purce
Registrar: Andrea Coker-Anderson
Admissions: Doug P. Scrima
Financial Aid: Brian Shirley

Type: Comprehensive **Sex:** Coed **Affiliation:** Washington State Public Institution **Scores:** 98% SAT V 400+; 94% SAT M 400+; 37% ACT 18-23; 48% ACT 24-29 **% Accepted:** 97 **Admission Plans:** Preferred Admission; Early Admission **Application Deadline:** Rolling **Application Fee:** $50.00 **H.S. Requirements:** High school diploma required; GED accepted **Costs Per Year:** Application fee: $50. State resident tuition: $4128 full-time, $137.60 per quarter hour part-time. Nonresident tuition: $14,538 full-time, $484.60 per quarter hour part-time. Mandatory fees: $209 full-time, $2.05 per quarter hour part-time, $41 per term part-time. Full-time tuition and fees vary according to course load and degree level. Part-time tuition and fees vary according to course load and degree level. College room and board: $6924. College room only: $4482. Room and board charges vary according to board plan, housing facility, and student level. **Scholarships:** Available **Calendar System:** Quarter, Summer Session Available **Enrollment:** FT 3,655, PT 516, Grad 299 **Faculty:** FT 158, PT 63 **Student-Faculty Ratio:** 21:1 **Exams:** SAT I or ACT **% Receiving Financial Aid:** 58 **% Residing in College-Owned, -Operated, or -Affiliated Housing:** 21 **Library Holdings:** 476,500 **Credit Hours For Degree:** 180 quarter hours, Bachelors **Professional Accreditation:** NCCU **Intercollegiate Athletics:** Basketball M & W; Cross-Country Running M & W; Lacrosse M & W; Rugby W; Soccer M & W; Track and Field M & W; Volleyball W

GONZAGA UNIVERSITY

502 East Boone Ave.
Spokane, WA 99258
Tel: (509)328-4220
Free: 800-322-2584
Admissions: (509)323-6591
Fax: (509)324-5780
E-mail: admissions@gonzaga.edu
Web Site: http://www.gonzaga.edu/
President/CEO: Rev. Robert Spitzer, SJ
Registrar: Jolanta Kozyra
Admissions: Julie McCulloh
Financial Aid: Dr. Thayne McCulloh

Type: Comprehensive **Sex:** Coed **Affiliation:** Roman Catholic **Scores:** 100% SAT V 400+; 99.46% SAT M 400+; 28.16% ACT 18-23; 57.87% ACT 24-29 **% Accepted:** 73 **Admission Plans:** Early Action; Deferred Admission **Application Deadline:** February 01 **Application Fee:** $45.00 **H.S. Requirements:** High school diploma required; GED not accepted **Costs Per Year:** Application fee: $45. Comprehensive fee: $30,278 includes full-time tuition ($23,140), mandatory fees ($438), and college room and board ($6700). College room only: $3400. Room and board charges vary according to board plan and housing facility. Part-time tuition: $670 per credit. Part-time mandatory fees: $45 per term. **Scholarships:** Available **Calendar System:**

Semester, Summer Session Available **Enrollment:** FT 3,986, PT 166, Grad 1,648 **Faculty:** FT 325, PT 10 **Student-Faculty Ratio:** 12:1 **Exams:** SAT I or ACT **% Receiving Financial Aid:** 62 **% Residing in College-Owned, -Operated, or -Affiliated Housing:** 56 **Library Holdings:** 228,622 **Credit Hours For Degree:** 128 credit hours, Bachelors **ROTC:** Army **Professional Accreditation:** AACSB, ABET, AAMFT, AACN, AANA, ABA, ACIPE, AALS, ATS, NCATE, NCCU **Intercollegiate Athletics:** Baseball M; Basketball M & W; Crew M & W; Cross-Country Running M & W; Golf M & W; Skiing (Cross-Country) M & W; Skiing (Downhill) M & W; Soccer M & W; Tennis M & W; Track and Field M & W; Volleyball W

GRAYS HARBOR COLLEGE

1620 Edward P Smith Dr.
Aberdeen, WA 98520-7599
Tel: (360)532-9020
Admissions: (360)538-4030
Fax: (360)538-4293
Web Site: http://www.ghc.ctc.edu/
President/CEO: Dr. Edward Brewster
Registrar: Nancy De Verse
Admissions: Nancy DeVerse
Financial Aid: Nadine Hibbs

Type: Two-Year College **Sex:** Coed **Affiliation:** Washington State Board for Community and Technical Colleges **Admission Plans:** Open Admission; Early Admission **Application Fee:** $0.00 **H.S. Requirements:** High school diploma required; GED accepted **Scholarships:** Available **Calendar System:** Quarter, Summer Session Available **Enrollment:** FT 1,156, PT 1,025 **Faculty:** FT 57, PT 89 **Student-Faculty Ratio:** 16:1 **Exams:** Other **Library Holdings:** 39,220 **Credit Hours For Degree:** 93 credits, Associates **Professional Accreditation:** NLN, NCCU **Intercollegiate Athletics:** Baseball M; Basketball M & W; Golf M & W; Softball W; Volleyball W

GREEN RIVER COMMUNITY COLLEGE

12401 Southeast 320th St.
Auburn, WA 98092-3699
Tel: (253)833-9111
Fax: (253)288-3454
Web Site: http://www.greenriver.edu/
President/CEO: Richard A. Rutkowski
Registrar: Denise Bennatts
Admissions: Denise Bennatts
Financial Aid: Mary Edington

Type: Two-Year College **Sex:** Coed **Affiliation:** Washington State Board for Community and Technical Colleges **Admission Plans:** Open Admission; Early Admission; Deferred Admission **Application Fee:** $0.00 **H.S. Requirements:** High school diploma required; GED accepted. For nursing, physical therapy, occupational therapy, waste water technology programs: High school diploma required; GED not accepted **Scholarships:** Available **Calendar System:** Quarter, Summer Session Available **Enrollment:** FT 3,883, PT 2,738 **Faculty:** FT 117, PT 160 **Student-Faculty Ratio:** 22:1 **Exams:** Other **Library Holdings:** 32,500 **Credit Hours For Degree:** 90 quarter hours, Associates **Professional Accreditation:** AOTA, NCCU **Intercollegiate Athletics:** Baseball M; Basketball M & W; Golf M & W; Soccer M & W; Softball W; Tennis M & W; Volleyball W

HENRY COGSWELL COLLEGE

3002 Colby Ave.
Everett, WA 98201
Tel: (425)258-3351; (866)411-4221
E-mail: jbuckman@henrycogswell.edu
Web Site: http://www.henrycogswell.edu/
President/CEO: Homer Garcia, PhD
Registrar: Susan Baxter
Admissions: Jane Buckman
Financial Aid: Dawn Gerak

Type: Four-Year College **Sex:** Coed **Affiliation:** Foundation for Educational Achievement **Scores:** 100% SAT V 400+; 100% SAT M 400+; 100% ACT 18-23 **% Accepted:** 84 **Admission Plans:** Deferred Admission **Application Deadline:** Rolling **Application Fee:** $50.00 **H.S. Requirements:** High school diploma required; GED accepted **Costs Per Year:** Application fee: $50. Tuition: $17,520 full-time, $730 per credit part-time. **Scholarships:** Available **Calendar System:** Trimester, Summer Session Available **Enrollment:** FT 118, PT 82 **Faculty:** FT 14, PT 18 **Student-Faculty Ratio:** 7:1 **Exams:** SAT I or ACT **% Receiving Financial Aid:** 57 **Library Holdings:** 12,100 **Credit Hours For Degree:** 120 credits, Bachelors **Professional Accreditation:** ABET, NCCU

HERITAGE UNIVERSITY

3240 Fort Rd.
Toppenish, WA 98948-9599
Tel: (509)865-8500
Admissions: (509)865-8508
Fax: (509)865-4469
E-mail: garcia_l@heritage.edu
Web Site: http://www.heritage.edu/
President/CEO: Kathleen Ross
Registrar: Margo Perrotti
Admissions: Leticia Garcia
Financial Aid: Laura Pendleton

Type: Comprehensive **Sex:** Coed **% Accepted:** 60 **Admission Plans:** Open Admission; Early Admission; Early Decision Plan; Deferred Admission **Application Deadline:** Rolling **Application Fee:** $0.00 **H.S. Requirements:** High school diploma required; GED accepted **Costs Per Year:** Application fee: $0. Tuition: $9600 full-time, $320 per credit hour part-time. Mandatory fees: $45 full-time. **Scholarships:** Available **Calendar System:** Semester, Summer Session Available **Enrollment:** FT 568, PT 238, Grad 505 **Faculty:** FT 47, PT 140 **Student-Faculty Ratio:** 11:1 **Exams:** SAT I or ACT **% Receiving Financial Aid:** 54 **Library Holdings:** 47,500 **Credit Hours For Degree:** 60 semester hours, Associates; 126 semester hours, Bachelors **Professional Accreditation:** CSWE, NCCU

HIGHLINE COMMUNITY COLLEGE

2400 S. 240th St.
PO Box 98000
Des Moines, WA 98198-9800
Tel: (206)878-3710
Fax: (206)870-3782
Web Site: http://www.highline.edu/
President/CEO: Dr. Priscilla J. Bell
Registrar: Becky Riverman
Admissions: Debbie Faison
Financial Aid: Steve Seeman

Type: Two-Year College **Sex:** Coed **Affiliation:** Washington State Board for Community and Technical Colleges **% Accepted:** 100 **Admission Plans:** Open Admission **Application Deadline:** Rolling **Application Fee:** $21.15 **H.S. Requirements:** High school diploma or equivalent not required. For nursing, allied health programs: High school diploma required; GED accepted **Costs Per Year:** Application fee: $21.15. State resident tuition: $2445 full-time, $71.80 per credit part-time. Nonresident tuition: $2835 full-time, $85 per credit part-time. Mandatory fees: $75 full-time, $2.50 per credit part-time. **Scholarships:** Available **Calendar System:** Quarter, Summer Session Available **Enrollment:** FT 3,229, PT 3,143 **Faculty:** FT 140, PT 216 **Exams:** Other **Library Holdings:** 57,678 **Credit Hours For Degree:** 90 quarter hours, Associates **ROTC:** Army, Air Force **Professional Accreditation:** AAMAE, CARC, NLN, NCCU **Intercollegiate Athletics:** Basketball M & W; Cross-Country Running M & W; Soccer M & W; Softball W; Track and Field M & W; Volleyball W; Wrestling M

ITT TECHNICAL INSTITUTE (BOTHELL)

2525 223rd St., SE, Canyon Park East
Bothell, WA 98021
Tel: (425)485-0303
Admissions: (425)583-0200
Web Site: http://www.itt-tech.edu/
President/CEO: Mike Milford
Admissions: Dr. Dean C. Kempter
Financial Aid: Nicole Fisher

Type: Two-Year College **Sex:** Coed **Affiliation:** ITT Educational Services, Inc **Admission Plans:** Deferred Admission **Application Deadline:** Rolling **Application Fee:** $100.00 **H.S. Requirements:** High school diploma required; GED accepted **Costs Per Year:** Application fee: $100. **Scholarships:** Available **Calendar System:** Quarter, Summer Session Not available **Exams:** Other **Credit Hours For Degree:** 96 credit hours, Associates; 180 credit hours, Bachelors **Professional Accreditation:** ACICS

ITT TECHNICAL INSTITUTE (SEATTLE)

12720 Gateway Dr., Ste. 100
Seattle, WA 98168-3333
Tel: (206)244-3300
Free: 800-422-2029
Web Site: http://www.itt-tech.edu/
President/CEO: Dean Dalby

Registrar: Christina Dalton
Admissions: Kathleen A. Masiker
Financial Aid: Vu Ngyengun
Type: Two-Year College **Sex:** Coed **Affiliation:** ITT Educational Services, Inc **Admission Plans:** Deferred Admission **Application Deadline:** Rolling **Application Fee:** $100.00 **H.S. Requirements:** High school diploma required; GED accepted **Costs Per Year:** Application fee: $100. **Scholarships:** Available **Calendar System:** Quarter, Summer Session Not available **Exams:** Other **Credit Hours For Degree:** 96 credit hours, Associates; 180 credit hours, Bachelors **Professional Accreditation:** ACICS

ITT TECHNICAL INSTITUTE (SPOKANE)
1050 North Argonne Rd.
Spokane, WA 99212-2682
Tel: (509)926-2900
Free: 800-777-8324
Web Site: http://www.itt-tech.edu/
President/CEO: F. William King
Admissions: Bill King
Financial Aid: Helen Horton
Type: Two-Year College **Sex:** Coed **Affiliation:** ITT Educational Services, Inc **Admission Plans:** Deferred Admission **Application Deadline:** Rolling **Application Fee:** $100.00 **H.S. Requirements:** High school diploma required; GED accepted **Costs Per Year:** Application fee: $100. **Scholarships:** Available **Calendar System:** Quarter, Summer Session Not available **Exams:** Other **Credit Hours For Degree:** 96 credit hours, Associates; 180 credit hours, Bachelors **Professional Accreditation:** ACICS

LAKE WASHINGTON TECHNICAL COLLEGE
11605 132nd Ave. NE
Kirkland, WA 98034-8506
Tel: (425)739-8100
Admissions: (425)739-8233
Web Site: http://www.lwtc.ctc.edu/
President/CEO: Dr. Michael Metke
Admissions: Jim West
Financial Aid: Bill Chaney
Type: Two-Year College **Sex:** Coed **Affiliation:** Washington State Board for Community and Technical Colleges **Admission Plans:** Open Admission; Early Admission **Application Fee:** $0.00 **H.S. Requirements:** High school diploma or equivalent not required. For nursing, dental hygiene, medical assistant, dental assistant programs: High school diploma required; GED accepted **Scholarships:** Available **Calendar System:** Quarter, Summer Session Available **Enrollment:** FT 2,020, PT 2,840 **Faculty:** FT 60, PT 161 **Student-Faculty Ratio:** 8:1 **Exams:** Other **Library Holdings:** 18,300 **Credit Hours For Degree:** 90 credits, Associates **Professional Accreditation:** AAMAE, ACF, ADA, NCCU

LOWER COLUMBIA COLLEGE
PO Box 3010
Longview, WA 98632-0310
Tel: (360)442-2000
Admissions: (360)442-2300
Fax: (360)442-2109
E-mail: mharding@lcc.ctc.edu
Web Site: http://www.lcc.ctc.edu/
President/CEO: Dr. James L. McLaughlin
Registrar: Mary Harding
Admissions: Mary Harding
Financial Aid: James Gorman
Type: Two-Year College **Sex:** Coed **Affiliation:** Washington State Board for Community and Technical Colleges **% Accepted:** 100 **Admission Plans:** Open Admission; Early Admission; Deferred Admission **Application Deadline:** Rolling **Application Fee:** $12.50 **H.S. Requirements:** High school diploma or equivalent not required **Costs Per Year:** Application fee: $12.50. State resident tuition: $2465 full-time, $77.65 per credit part-time. Nonresident tuition: $3161 full-time, $83.40 per credit part-time. Mandatory fees: $6.10 per credit part-time. **Scholarships:** Available **Calendar System:** Quarter, Summer Session Available **Enrollment:** FT 1,755, PT 1,318 **Faculty:** FT 76, PT 79 **Student-Faculty Ratio:** 21:1 **Library Holdings:** 41,991 **Credit Hours For Degree:** 90 credits, Associates **Professional Accreditation:** AAMAE, NLN, NCCU **Intercollegiate Athletics:** Baseball M; Basketball M & W; Soccer M & W; Softball W; Volleyball W

NORTH SEATTLE COMMUNITY COLLEGE
9600 College Way North
Seattle, WA 98103-3599
Tel: (206)527-3600
Admissions: (206)527-3663
Fax: (206)527-3635
Web Site: http://www.northseattle.edu/
President/CEO: Dr. Ronald H. LaFayette
Registrar: Marci Myer
Admissions: Betsy Abts
Type: Two-Year College **Sex:** Coed **Affiliation:** Seattle Community College District System **% Accepted:** 100 **Admission Plans:** Open Admission; Early Admission; Deferred Admission **Application Deadline:** Rolling **Application Fee:** $0.00 **H.S. Requirements:** High school diploma or equivalent not required **Costs Per Year:** Application fee: $0. State resident tuition: $3213 full-time, $71.40 per credit part-time. Nonresident tuition: $10,940 full-time, $243.10 per credit part-time. Mandatory fees: $346 full-time, $115.20 per term part-time. Full-time tuition and fees vary according to course load. Part-time tuition and fees vary according to course load. **Scholarships:** Available **Calendar System:** Quarter, Summer Session Available **Enrollment:** FT 2,833, PT 3,126 **Faculty:** FT 102, PT 196 **Student-Faculty Ratio:** 23:1 **Library Holdings:** 52,496 **Credit Hours For Degree:** 90 credits, Associates **ROTC:** Army **Professional Accreditation:** AAMAE, ACF, NCCU **Intercollegiate Athletics:** Basketball M & W

NORTHWEST AVIATION COLLEGE
506 23rd, NE
Auburn, WA 98002
Tel: (253)854-4960
Fax: (253)931-0768
E-mail: spratt@afsnac.com
Web Site: http://www.afsnac.com/
President/CEO: Jamelle R. Garcia
Admissions: Shawn Pratt
Financial Aid: Linda Esekesen
Type: Two-Year College **Sex:** Coed **Application Fee:** $50.00 **H.S. Requirements:** High school diploma required; GED accepted **Scholarships:** Available **Calendar System:** Quarter, Summer Session Available **Credit Hours For Degree:** 90 quarter hours, Associates **Professional Accreditation:** ACCSCT

NORTHWEST COLLEGE OF ART
16464 State Hwy. 305
Poulsbo, WA 98370
Tel: (360)779-9993
Free: 800-769-ARTS
Fax: (360)779-9933
Web Site: http://www.nca.edu/
President/CEO: Craig Freeman
Registrar: J. Kempf
Admissions: Craig Freeman
Financial Aid: K. Perigard
Type: Four-Year College **Sex:** Coed **Admission Plans:** Deferred Admission **Application Fee:** $50.00 **H.S. Requirements:** High school diploma required; GED accepted **Costs Per Year:** Application fee: $50. Tuition: $14,300 full-time, $625 per credit part-time. Mandatory fees: $100 full-time. Part-time tuition varies according to course load. Tuition guaranteed not to increase for student's term of enrollment. **Scholarships:** Available **Calendar System:** Semester, Summer Session Available **Credit Hours For Degree:** 120 credits, Bachelors **Professional Accreditation:** ACCSCT

NORTHWEST INDIAN COLLEGE
2522 Kwina Rd.
Bellingham, WA 98226
Tel: (360)676-2772
Fax: (360)738-0136
E-mail: lignacio@nwic.edu
Web Site: http://www.nwic.edu/
President/CEO: Barbara Roberts
Registrar: David Oreiro
Admissions: Leilani Ignacio

Financial Aid: Angela Jefferson
Type: Two-Year College **Sex:** Coed **Admission Plans:** Open Admission; Preferred Admission **Application Fee:** $25.00 **Costs Per Year:** Application fee: $25. State resident tuition: $2646 full-time, $73.50 per credit part-time. Nonresident tuition: $7182 full-time, $199.50 per credit part-time. **Scholarships:** Available **Calendar System:** Quarter, Summer Session Available **Faculty:** FT 23, PT 40 **Credit Hours For Degree:** 92 credits, Associates **Professional Accreditation:** NCCU **Intercollegiate Athletics:** Basketball M & W

NORTHWEST SCHOOL OF WOODEN BOATBUILDING
251 Otto St.
Port Townsend, WA 98368
Tel: (360)385-4948
Fax: (360)385-5089
E-mail: info@nwboatschool.org
Web Site: http://www.nwboatschool.org/
President/CEO: Bill Curry
Admissions: Gretchen Siegfried
Type: Two-Year College **Sex:** Coed **Calendar System:** Semester **Professional Accreditation:** ACCSCT

NORTHWEST UNIVERSITY
5520 108th Ave. NE
Kirkland, WA 98033
Tel: (425)822-8266
Free: 800-669-3781
Admissions: (425)889-5209
Fax: (425)425-0148
E-mail: admissions@northwestu.edu
Web Site: http://www.northwestu.edu/
President/CEO: Dr. Don Argue
Registrar: Jim Jessup
Admissions: Myles Corrigan
Financial Aid: Lana Walter
Type: Comprehensive **Sex:** Coed **Affiliation:** Assemblies of God **Scores:** 95.75% SAT V 400+; 89.25% SAT M 400+; 52% ACT 18-23; 20% ACT 24-29 **% Accepted:** 83 **Admission Plans:** Early Decision Plan; Deferred Admission **Application Deadline:** August 01 **Application Fee:** $30.00 **H.S. Requirements:** High school diploma required; GED accepted **Costs Per Year:** Application fee: $30. Comprehensive fee: $24,594 includes full-time tuition ($17,920), mandatory fees ($224), and college room and board ($6450). Part-time tuition: $750 per credit. Part-time mandatory fees: $224 per year. **Scholarships:** Available **Calendar System:** Semester, Summer Session Available **Enrollment:** FT 1,051, PT 102, Grad 107 **Faculty:** FT 52, PT 42 **Student-Faculty Ratio:** 17:1 **Exams:** SAT I or ACT **% Receiving Financial Aid:** 73 **% Residing in College-Owned, -Operated, or -Affiliated Housing:** 61 **Library Holdings:** 141,427 **Credit Hours For Degree:** 62 credit hours, Associates; 125 credit hours, Bachelors **ROTC:** Army **Professional Accreditation:** AACN, NCCU **Intercollegiate Athletics:** Basketball M & W; Cross-Country Running M & W; Soccer M; Track and Field M & W; Volleyball W

OLYMPIC COLLEGE
1600 Chester Ave.
Bremerton, WA 98337-1699
Tel: (360)792-6050
Free: 800-259-6718
Admissions: (360)475-7126
Fax: (360)792-2135
E-mail: gstamm@ctc.edu
Web Site: http://www.oc.ctc.edu/~oc/
President/CEO: Dr. David C. Mitchell
Registrar: Dianna L. Larsen
Admissions: Gerry Stamm
Financial Aid: Nicholas Rengler
Type: Two-Year College **Sex:** Coed **Affiliation:** Washington State Board for Community and Technical Colleges **% Accepted:** 100 **Admission Plans:** Open Admission; Early Admission **Application Deadline:** Rolling **Application Fee:** $0.00 **H.S. Requirements:** High school diploma or equivalent not required. For nursing program, medical office assistant program: High school diploma required; GED accepted **Costs Per Year:** Application fee: $0. State resident tuition: $71.80 per credit part-time. Nonresident tuition: $115.90 per credit part-time. Mandatory fees: $60 per term part-time. **Scholarships:** Available **Calendar System:** Quarter, Summer Session Available **Enrollment:** FT 3,253, PT 3,137 **Faculty:** FT 97, PT 210 **Student-Faculty Ratio:** 25:1 **Library Holdings:** 51,443 **Credit Hours For Degree:** 90 credits, Associates **Professional Accreditation:** NLN, NCCU **Intercollegiate Athletics:** Baseball M; Basketball M & W; Golf M & W; Softball W; Volleyball W

PACIFIC LUTHERAN UNIVERSITY
Tacoma, WA 98447
Tel: (253)531-6900
Free: 800-274-6758
Admissions: (253)535-7151
Fax: (253)536-5136
E-mail: admissions@plu.edu
Web Site: http://www.plu.edu/
President/CEO: Dr. Loren J. Anderson
Registrar: Angela Bixby
Admissions: Dr. Laura Majovski
Financial Aid: Kay Soltis
Type: Comprehensive **Sex:** Coed **Affiliation:** Evangelical Lutheran Church in America **Scores:** 98% SAT V 400+; 99% SAT M 400+; 42% ACT 18-23; 40% ACT 24-29 **% Accepted:** 76 **Admission Plans:** Early Admission; Deferred Admission **Application Deadline:** Rolling **Application Fee:** $40.00 **H.S. Requirements:** High school diploma required; GED accepted **Costs Per Year:** Application fee: $40. Comprehensive fee: $28,805 includes full-time tuition ($22,040) and college room and board ($6765). College room only: $3330. Full-time tuition varies according to course load. Room and board charges vary according to board plan and housing facility. Part-time tuition: $687 per semester hour. Part-time tuition varies according to course load. **Scholarships:** Available **Calendar System:** 4-1-4, Summer Session Available **Enrollment:** FT 3,171, PT 198, Grad 311 **Faculty:** FT 236, PT 24 **Student-Faculty Ratio:** 15:1 **Exams:** SAT I or ACT **% Receiving Financial Aid:** 67 **% Residing in College-Owned, -Operated, or -Affiliated Housing:** 51 **Library Holdings:** 340,842 **Credit Hours For Degree:** 128 semester hours, Bachelors **ROTC:** Army **Professional Accreditation:** AACSB, ABET, AAMFT, AACN, CSWE, NASM, NCATE, NLN, NCCU **Intercollegiate Athletics:** Baseball M; Basketball M & W; Cheerleading M & W; Crew M & W; Cross-Country Running M & W; Football M; Golf M & W; Lacrosse M & W; Rugby M; Soccer M & W; Softball W; Swimming and Diving M & W; Tennis M & W; Track and Field M & W; Ultimate Frisbee M & W; Volleyball M & W

PENINSULA COLLEGE
1502 East Lauridsen Blvd.
Port Angeles, WA 98362-2779
Tel: (360)452-9277
Admissions: (360)417-6225
Fax: (360)457-8100
E-mail: jackh@pcadmin.ctc.edu
Web Site: http://www.pc.ctc.edu/
President/CEO: Dr. Thomas A. Keegan
Registrar: Jack Huls
Admissions: Jack Huls
Financial Aid: Cheryl Reid
Type: Two-Year College **Sex:** Coed **% Accepted:** 100 **Admission Plans:** Open Admission; Deferred Admission **Application Deadline:** Rolling **Application Fee:** $0.00 **H.S. Requirements:** High school diploma or equivalent not required **Costs Per Year:** Application fee: $0. State resident tuition: $3325 full-time, $74.70 per credit part-time. Nonresident tuition: $3715 full-time, $87.90 per credit part-time. Mandatory fees: $135 full-time, $2.90 per credit part-time, $13.25 per term part-time. **Scholarships:** Available **Calendar System:** Quarter, Summer Session Available **Enrollment:** FT 1,412, PT 2,844 **Faculty:** FT 64, PT 127 **Student-Faculty Ratio:** 19:1 **Library Holdings:** 33,736 **Credit Hours For Degree:** 90 credits, Associates **Professional Accreditation:** NCCU **Intercollegiate Athletics:** Basketball M & W; Soccer M; Softball W

PIERCE COLLEGE
1601 39th Ave. SE
Puyallup, WA 98374-2222
Tel: (253)840-8400
Admissions: (253)964-6686
Fax: (253)840-8423
Web Site: http://www.pierce.ctc.edu/
President/CEO: Dr. Michele Johnson
Admissions: Cindy Burbank

Financial Aid: Robert Walker
Type: Two-Year College **Sex:** Coed **Affiliation:** Washington State Board for Community and Technical Colleges **Admission Plans:** Open Admission; Early Admission **Application Fee:** $0.00 **H.S. Requirements:** High school diploma or equivalent not required. For international students, veterinary technology, dental hygiene programs: High school diploma required; GED accepted **Costs Per Year:** Application fee: $0. Tuition: $392 per credit hour part-time. Mandatory fees: $1000 full-time, $100 per course part-time. Full-time fees vary according to course load. Part-time tuition and fees vary according to course load. Nonresident tuition: $11,760 full-time. Mandatory fees: $1000 full-time, $100 per course part-time. Full-time tuition and fees vary according to course load. Part-time fees vary according to course load. **Scholarships:** Available **Calendar System:** Quarter, Summer Session Available **Faculty:** FT 240, PT 350 **Exams:** Other **Library Holdings:** 55,000 **Credit Hours For Degree:** 90 quarter hours, Associates **ROTC:** Army **Professional Accreditation:** ADA, NCCU **Intercollegiate Athletics:** Baseball M; Basketball M & W; Soccer M; Softball W; Volleyball W

PIMA MEDICAL INSTITUTE
1627 Eastlake Ave., East
Seattle, WA 98102
Tel: (206)322-6100; 888-898-9048
Fax: (206)324-1985
Web Site: http://www.pmi.edu
President/CEO: Janice Stiewing
Admissions: Rebecca Lombardo
Financial Aid: Brenda Moore
Type: Two-Year College **Sex:** Coed **Affiliation:** Vocational Training Institutes, Inc **Scholarships:** Available **Calendar System:** Miscellaneous **Enrollment:** FT 289 **Student-Faculty Ratio:** 10:1 **Exams:** Other **Professional Accreditation:** ABHES, JRCERT

PUGET SOUND CHRISTIAN COLLEGE
1618 Hewitt Ave., PO Box 13108
Everett, WA 98201
Tel: (425)257-3090; 888-775-8699
Admissions: (425)775-8686
Fax: (425)258-1488
Web Site: http://www.pscc.edu/
President/CEO: Dr. Randy Bridges
Registrar: Gillian Heine
Admissions: Jean Olsen
Financial Aid: Kim Bobbitt
Type: Four-Year College **Sex:** Coed **Affiliation:** Christian **Scores:** 100% SAT V 400+; 93% SAT M 400+ **Admission Plans:** Preferred Admission; Deferred Admission **Application Fee:** $50.00 **H.S. Requirements:** High school diploma required; GED accepted **Scholarships:** Available **Calendar System:** Semester, Summer Session Available **Enrollment:** FT 191, PT 36 **Faculty:** FT 10, PT 18 **Exams:** SAT I and SAT II or ACT **% Residing in College-Owned, -Operated, or -Affiliated Housing:** 34 **Library Holdings:** 37,500 **Credit Hours For Degree:** 64 semester hours, Associates; 128 semester hours, Bachelors **Professional Accreditation:** AABC **Intercollegiate Athletics:** Basketball M & W; Volleyball W

RENTON TECHNICAL COLLEGE
3000 NE Fourth St.
Renton, WA 98056-4195
Tel: (425)235-2352
Admissions: (425)235-2463
Fax: (425)235-7832
Web Site: http://www.rtc.edu/
President/CEO: Dr. Donald Bressler
Registrar: Cheri R. Danielson
Admissions: Jon Pozega
Financial Aid: Janet A. Riebe
Type: Two-Year College **Sex:** Coed **Affiliation:** Washington State Board for Community and Technical Colleges **Admission Plans:** Open Admission; Early Admission **Application Fee:** $25.00 **H.S. Requirements:** High school diploma or equivalent not required **Scholarships:** Available **Calendar System:** Quarter, Summer Session Available **Enrollment:** FT 4,019, PT 5,282 **Faculty:** FT 84, PT 198 **Student-Faculty Ratio:** 15:1 **Exams:** Other **Library Holdings:** 12,876 **Credit Hours For Degree:** 100 quarter hours, Associates **Professional Accreditation:** ARCEST, ACF, ADA, NCCU

SAINT MARTIN'S UNIVERSITY
5300 Pacific Ave., SE
Lacey, WA 98503-1297
Tel: (360)491-4700
Free: 800-368-8803
Admissions: (360)438-4590
Fax: (360)459-4124
E-mail: admissions@stmartin.edu
Web Site: http://www.stmartin.edu/
President/CEO: Dr. David Spangler
Registrar: Mary Law
Admissions: Todd Abbott
Financial Aid: Rebecca Wonderly
Type: Comprehensive **Sex:** Coed **Affiliation:** Roman Catholic **Scores:** 94% SAT V 400+; 91% SAT M 400+; 55% ACT 18-23; 17% ACT 24-29 **% Accepted:** 73 **Application Fee:** $35.00 **H.S. Requirements:** High school diploma required; GED accepted **Costs Per Year:** Application fee: $35. Comprehensive fee: $27,365 includes full-time tuition ($20,675), mandatory fees ($290), and college room and board ($6400). College room only: $3000. Part-time tuition: $689 per credit. Part-time mandatory fees: $145 per term. **Scholarships:** Available **Calendar System:** Semester, Summer Session Available **Enrollment:** FT 936, PT 244, Grad 229 **Faculty:** FT 66, PT 96 **Student-Faculty Ratio:** 11:1 **Exams:** SAT I or ACT **% Receiving Financial Aid:** 86 **% Residing in College-Owned, -Operated, or -Affiliated Housing:** 29 **Library Holdings:** 86,461 **Credit Hours For Degree:** 64 credits, Associates; 128 credits, Bachelors **ROTC:** Army **Professional Accreditation:** ABET, NCCU **Intercollegiate Athletics:** Baseball M; Basketball M & W; Cross-Country Running M & W; Golf M & W; Softball W; Track and Field M & W; Volleyball W

SEATTLE CENTRAL COMMUNITY COLLEGE
1701 Broadway
Seattle, WA 98122-2400
Tel: (206)587-3800
Admissions: (206)587-3898
Web Site: http://www.seattlecentral.edu/
President/CEO: Dr. Mildred Ollee
Registrar: Liz Baldizan
Admissions: Dr. Terri Hackett
Financial Aid: Cheryl Reid
Type: Two-Year College **Sex:** Coed **Affiliation:** Seattle Community College District System **Admission Plans:** Open Admission **Application Deadline:** Rolling **H.S. Requirements:** High school diploma or equivalent not required. For health programs: High school diploma required; GED accepted **Scholarships:** Available **Calendar System:** Quarter, Summer Session Available **Faculty:** FT 156, PT 282 **Library Holdings:** 56,338 **Credit Hours For Degree:** 90 credits, Associates **ROTC:** Army, Navy, Air Force **Professional Accreditation:** ACF, COptA, CARC, NLN, NCCU

SEATTLE PACIFIC UNIVERSITY
3307 Third Ave. West
Seattle, WA 98119-1997
Tel: (206)281-2000
Free: 800-366-3344
Admissions: (206)281-2517
E-mail: admissions@spu.edu
Web Site: http://www.spu.edu/
President/CEO: Dr. Philip W. Eaton
Registrar: Ruth Adams
Admissions: Jennifer Feddern Kenney
Financial Aid: Jordan Grant
Type: Comprehensive **Sex:** Coed **Affiliation:** Free Methodist **Scores:** 99.39% SAT V 400+; 99.54% SAT M 400+; 37.65% ACT 18-23; 47.84% ACT 24-29 **% Accepted:** 85 **Admission Plans:** Early Admission; Early Action; Deferred Admission **Application Deadline:** March 01 **Application Fee:** $45.00 **H.S. Requirements:** High school diploma required; GED accepted **Costs Per Year:** Application fee: $45. Comprehensive fee: $29,355 includes full-time tuition ($21,447), mandatory fees ($336), and college room and board ($7572). College room only: $4071. Room and board charges vary according to board plan and housing facility. Part-time tuition: $596 per credit. Part-time tuition varies according to course load. **Scholarships:** Available **Calendar System:** Quarter, Summer Session Available **Enroll-**

ment: FT 2,880, PT 142, Grad 851 **Faculty:** FT 181, PT 152 **Student-Faculty Ratio:** 14:1 **Exams:** SAT I or ACT, SAT I **% Receiving Financial Aid:** 61 **% Residing in College-Owned, -Operated, or -Affiliated Housing:** 58 **Library Holdings:** 191,807 **Credit Hours For Degree:** 180 credits, Bachelors **ROTC:** Army, Navy, Air Force **Professional Accreditation:** AACSB, ABET, AAMFT, AACN, AAFCS, NASM, NCATE, NCCU **Intercollegiate Athletics:** Basketball M & W; Crew M & W; Cross-Country Running M & W; Gymnastics W; Soccer M & W; Track and Field M & W; Volleyball W

SEATTLE UNIVERSITY
902 12th Ave., PO Box 222000
Seattle, WA 98122-1090
Tel: (206)296-6000
Free: 800-426-7123
Admissions: (206)296-2000
Fax: (206)296-5656
E-mail: admissions@seattleu.edu
Web Site: http://www.seattleu.edu/
President/CEO: Rev. Stephen V. Sundborg, SJ
Registrar: Georgia McRae
Admissions: Michael K. McKeon
Financial Aid: Jim White
Type: Comprehensive **Sex:** Coed **Affiliation:** Roman Catholic **Scores:** 99.5% SAT V 400+; 100% SAT M 400+; 34.9% ACT 18-23; 55.5% ACT 24-29 **% Accepted:** 68 **Admission Plans:** Early Admission; Deferred Admission **Application Deadline:** Rolling **Application Fee:** $45.00 **H.S. Requirements:** High school diploma required; GED accepted **Costs Per Year:** Application fee: $45. Comprehensive fee: $30,063 includes full-time tuition ($22,905) and college room and board ($7158). College room only: $4653. Full-time tuition varies according to course load. Room and board charges vary according to board plan. Part-time tuition: $509 per credit. Part-time tuition varies according to course load. **Scholarships:** Available **Calendar System:** Quarter, Summer Session Available **Enrollment:** FT 3,877, PT 305, Grad 1,744 **Faculty:** FT 387, PT 195 **Student-Faculty Ratio:** 13:1 **Exams:** SAT I or ACT **% Receiving Financial Aid:** 67 **% Residing in College-Owned, -Operated, or -Affiliated Housing:** 38 **Library Holdings:** 141,478 **Credit Hours For Degree:** 180 credit hours, Bachelors **ROTC:** Army, Air Force **Professional Accreditation:** AACSB, ABET, AACN, ABA, AALS, ATS, JRCEDMS, NASPAA, NCATE, NLN, NCCU **Intercollegiate Athletics:** Archery M & W; Baseball M & W; Basketball M & W; Cheerleading M & W; Crew M & W; Cross-Country Running M & W; Golf M & W; Riflery M & W; Skiing (Downhill) M & W; Soccer M & W; Softball W; Swimming and Diving M & W; Track and Field M & W; Volleyball M & W; Water Polo M & W

SHORELINE COMMUNITY COLLEGE
16101 Greenwood Ave. North
Shoreline, WA 98133-5696
Tel: (206)546-4101
Admissions: (206)546-4581
Fax: (206)546-4599
Web Site: http://www.shore.ctc.edu/
President/CEO: Dr. Holly Moore
Registrar: Robin Young
Admissions: Robin Young
Financial Aid: Ted Haase
Type: Two-Year College **Sex:** Coed **Affiliation:** Washington State Board for Community and Technical Colleges **Admission Plans:** Open Admission; Early Admission **H.S. Requirements:** High school diploma or equivalent not required **Scholarships:** Available **Calendar System:** Quarter, Summer Session Available **Faculty:** FT 155, PT 260 **Student-Faculty Ratio:** 21:1 **Exams:** Other, SAT I or ACT **Library Holdings:** 79,554 **Credit Hours For Degree:** 90 credits, Associates **Professional Accreditation:** ADA, AHIMA, NAACLS, NLN, NCCU **Intercollegiate Athletics:** Archery M & W; Baseball M; Basketball M & W; Cross-Country Running M & W; Soccer M & W; Softball W; Tennis M & W; Volleyball W

SKAGIT VALLEY COLLEGE
2405 College Way
Mount Vernon, WA 98273-5899
Tel: (360)416-7600
Fax: (360)416-7890
Web Site: http://www.skagit.edu/
President/CEO: Dr. Gary Tollefson
Registrar: Linda Woiwod
Admissions: Linda Woiwod
Financial Aid: Steve Epperson
Type: Two-Year College **Sex:** Coed **Affiliation:** Washington State Board for Community and Technical Colleges **Admission Plans:** Open Admission; Deferred Admission **Application Fee:** $0.00 **H.S. Requirements:** High school diploma or equivalent not required **Scholarships:** Available **Calendar System:** Quarter, Summer Session Available **Student-Faculty Ratio:** 22:1 **% Residing in College-Owned, -Operated, or -Affiliated Housing:** 1 **Library Holdings:** 78,631 **Credit Hours For Degree:** 90 credits, Associates **Professional Accreditation:** ACF, NLN, NCCU **Intercollegiate Athletics:** Baseball M; Basketball M & W; Cross-Country Running M & W; Golf M & W; Soccer M & W; Softball W; Tennis M & W; Volleyball W

SOUTH PUGET SOUND COMMUNITY COLLEGE
2011 Mottman Rd., SW
Olympia, WA 98512-6292
Tel: (360)754-7711
Fax: (360)664-9407
Web Site: http://www.spscc.ctc.edu/
President/CEO: Dr. Kenneth J. Minnaert
Registrar: Neena M. Stoskopf
Admissions: Jerry Haynes
Financial Aid: Carla Idohl-Corwin
Type: Two-Year College **Sex:** Coed **Affiliation:** Washington State Board for Community and Technical Colleges **Admission Plans:** Open Admission; Early Admission; Deferred Admission **Application Fee:** $15.00 **H.S. Requirements:** High school diploma or equivalent not required. For nursing program: High school diploma required; GED accepted **Scholarships:** Available **Calendar System:** Quarter, Summer Session Available **Enrollment:** FT 2,495, PT 3,856 **Faculty:** FT 91, PT 110 **Student-Faculty Ratio:** 20:1 **Exams:** Other, SAT I or ACT **Library Holdings:** 30,000 **Credit Hours For Degree:** 90 credits, Associates **ROTC:** Army **Professional Accreditation:** AAMAE, ACF, ADA, NLN, NCCU **Intercollegiate Athletics:** Basketball M & W; Soccer M; Softball W

SOUTH SEATTLE COMMUNITY COLLEGE
6000 16th Ave., SW
Seattle, WA 98106-1499
Tel: (206)764-5300
Admissions: (206)764-5378
E-mail: kimmanderb@sccd.ctc.edu
Web Site: http://www.sccd.ctc.edu/
President/CEO: Dr. Jill Wakefield
Registrar: Kim Manderbach
Admissions: Kim Manderbach
Financial Aid: Lorraine Odom
Type: Two-Year College **Sex:** Coed **Affiliation:** Seattle Community College District System **Admission Plans:** Open Admission; Early Admission **Application Fee:** $0.00 **H.S. Requirements:** High school diploma or equivalent not required **Scholarships:** Available **Calendar System:** Quarter, Summer Session Available **Faculty:** FT 75, PT 210 **Exams:** Other **Library Holdings:** 34,000 **Credit Hours For Degree:** 90 credits, Associates **Professional Accreditation:** ACF, NCCU

SPOKANE COMMUNITY COLLEGE
1810 North Greene St.
Spokane, WA 99217-5399
Tel: (509)533-7000
Admissions: (509)533-7075
Fax: (509)533-8839
E-mail: jdunlap@scc.spokane.edu
Web Site: http://www.scc.spokane.edu/
President/CEO: Steve Hanson
Registrar: Vicki Bolks
Admissions: Joe Dunlap
Financial Aid: Patrick Erickson
Type: Two-Year College **Sex:** Coed **Affiliation:** Washington State Board for Community and Technical Colleges **Admission Plans:** Open Admission; Early Admission; Deferred Admission **Application Deadline:** Rolling **Application Fee:** $15.00 **H.S. Requirements:** High school diploma required; GED accepted **Costs Per Year:** Application fee: $15. Tuition: $71.60 per credit part-time. Area resident tuition: $813 full-time. Nonresident tuition: $1392 full-time, $133.75 per credit part-time. **Scholarships:** Available **Calendar System:** Quarter, Summer Session Available **Enrollment:** FT 5,223, PT 929 **Faculty:** FT 192, PT 168 **Student-Faculty Ratio:** 20:1

Library Holdings: 38,967 **Credit Hours For Degree:** 90 credits, Associates **ROTC:** Army **Professional Accreditation:** ARCEST, AAMAE, ACF, ADA, AHIMA, AOA, CARC, JRCECT, NLN, NCCU **Intercollegiate Athletics:** Baseball M; Basketball M & W; Cross-Country Running M & W; Soccer M & W; Softball W; Tennis M & W; Track and Field M & W; Volleyball W

SPOKANE FALLS COMMUNITY COLLEGE
3410 West Fort George Wright Dr.
Spokane, WA 99224-5288
Tel: (509)533-3500; 888-509-7944
Admissions: (509)533-3682
Fax: (509)533-3433
Web Site: http://www.sfcc.spokane.cc.wa.us/
President/CEO: Dr. Mark Palek
Registrar: Steve Bays
Admissions: Carol Green
Financial Aid: Karen Driscoll
Type: Two-Year College **Sex:** Coed **Affiliation:** State Board for Washington Community and Technical Colleges **Admission Plans:** Open Admission; Early Admission; Deferred Admission **Application Deadline:** Rolling **Application Fee:** $15.00 **H.S. Requirements:** High school diploma required; GED accepted **Costs Per Year:** Application fee: $15. Area resident tuition: $813 full-time, $71.60 per credit part-time. Nonresident tuition: $1392 full-time, $133.75 per credit part-time. **Scholarships:** Available **Calendar System:** Quarter, Summer Session Available **Enrollment:** FT 3,934, PT 1,715 **Faculty:** FT 170, PT 422 **Student-Faculty Ratio:** 22:1 **Library Holdings:** 58,000 **Credit Hours For Degree:** 90 credits, Associates **ROTC:** Army **Professional Accreditation:** APTA, NCCU **Intercollegiate Athletics:** Baseball M; Basketball M & W; Cross-Country Running M & W; Soccer M & W; Softball W; Tennis M & W; Track and Field M & W; Volleyball W

TACOMA COMMUNITY COLLEGE
6501 South 19th St.
Tacoma, WA 98466
Tel: (253)566-5000
Admissions: (253)566-5116
Fax: (253)566-5376
E-mail: ahayward@tcc.ctc.edu
Web Site: http://www.tacomacc.edu/
President/CEO: Dr. Pamela J. Transue
Admissions: Dr. April Retherford
Type: Two-Year College **Sex:** Coed **Affiliation:** Washington State Board for Community and Technical Colleges **Admission Plans:** Open Admission; Early Admission **Application Fee:** $0.00 **H.S. Requirements:** High school diploma or equivalent not required. For allied health, law enforcement, nursing programs: High school diploma required; GED accepted **Costs Per Year:** Application fee: $0. State resident tuition: $2,542 full-time. Nonresident tuition: $2,932 full-time. Mandatory fees: $68 full-time. **Scholarships:** Available **Calendar System:** Quarter, Summer Session Available **Faculty:** FT 105, PT 229 **Student-Faculty Ratio:** 27:1 **Exams:** Other **Library Holdings:** 90,192 **Credit Hours For Degree:** 90 credits, Associates **ROTC:** Army **Professional Accreditation:** AHIMA, CARC, JRCERT, JRCEMT, NLN, NCCU **Intercollegiate Athletics:** Baseball M; Basketball M & W; Golf M & W; Soccer M & W; Volleyball W

TRINITY LUTHERAN COLLEGE
4221 228th Ave., SE
Issaquah, WA 98029-9299
Tel: (425)392-0400
Free: 800-843-5659
Admissions: (425)961-5516
Fax: (425)392-0404
E-mail: admissn@lbi.edu
Web Site: http://www.tlc.edu/
President/CEO: Dr. John M. Stamm
Registrar: Sara Kim
Admissions: Sigrid Olsen
Financial Aid: Susan Dalgleish
Type: Four-Year College **Sex:** Coed **Affiliation:** Lutheran **Scores:** 67% SAT V 400+; 73% SAT M 400+; 50% ACT 18-23; 36% ACT 24-29 **Admission Plans:** Early Admission; Deferred Admission **Application Fee:** $30.00 **H.S. Requirements:** High school diploma required; GED accepted **Costs Per Year:** Application fee: $30. Comprehensive fee: $30,307 includes full-time tuition ($21,432), mandatory fees ($150), and college room and board ($8725). College room only: $5815. Full-time tuition and fees vary according to course load. Room and board charges vary according to board plan. Part-time tuition: $893 per semester hour. Part-time tuition varies according to course load. **Scholarships:** Available **Calendar System:** Quarter, Summer Session Not available **Enrollment:** FT 115, PT 41 **Faculty:** FT 10, PT 9 **Student-Faculty Ratio:** 9:1 **Exams:** SAT I or ACT **Library Holdings:** 31,000 **Credit Hours For Degree:** 90 credits, Associates; 180 credits, Bachelors **Professional Accreditation:** NCCU

UNIVERSITY OF PHOENIX-SPOKANE CAMPUS
8775 E. Mission Ave.
Spokane Valley, WA 99212
Tel: (509)327-2443
Free: 800-228-7240
Admissions: (480)557-1712
Web Site: http://www.phoenix.edu/
Admissions: Nina Omelchanko
Type: Comprehensive **Sex:** Coed **Admission Plans:** Open Admission; Deferred Admission **Application Deadline:** Rolling **Application Fee:** $110.00 **H.S. Requirements:** High school diploma required; GED accepted **Costs Per Year:** Application fee: $110. Tuition: $9750 full-time, $325 per credit part-time. Mandatory fees: $560 full-time, $70 per course part-time. **Scholarships:** Available **Calendar System:** Continuous, Summer Session Not available **Enrollment:** FT 284, Grad 59 **Faculty:** FT 2, PT 65 **Student-Faculty Ratio:** 4:1 **Library Holdings:** 444 **Regional Accreditation:** North Central Association of Colleges and Schools **Credit Hours For Degree:** 60 credits, Associates; 120 credits, Bachelors

UNIVERSITY OF PHOENIX-WASHINGTON CAMPUS
7100 Fort Dent Way, Ste. 100
Seattle, WA 98188-7500
Tel: (206)268-5800
Free: 800-228-7240
Admissions: (480)557-1712
Fax: (206)241-8848
Web Site: http://www.phoenix.edu/
President/CEO: Renee Mona
Admissions: Nina Omelchanko
Type: Comprehensive **Sex:** Coed **Admission Plans:** Open Admission; Deferred Admission **Application Deadline:** Rolling **Application Fee:** $110.00 **H.S. Requirements:** High school diploma required; GED accepted **Costs Per Year:** Application fee: $110. Tuition: $11,055 full-time, $368.50 per credit part-time. Mandatory fees: $560 full-time, $70 per course part-time. **Scholarships:** Available **Calendar System:** Continuous, Summer Session Not available **Enrollment:** FT 1,678, Grad 494 **Faculty:** FT 16, PT 242 **Student-Faculty Ratio:** 9:1 **Library Holdings:** 444 **Regional Accreditation:** North Central Association of Colleges and Schools **Credit Hours For Degree:** 60 credits, Associates; 120 credits, Bachelors

UNIVERSITY OF PUGET SOUND
1500 North Warner St.
Tacoma, WA 98416
Tel: (253)879-3100
Free: 800-396-7191
Admissions: (253)879-3211
Fax: (253)879-3500
E-mail: admission@ups.edu
Web Site: http://www.ups.edu/
President/CEO: Dr. Ronald R. Thomas
Registrar: Dr. John M. Finney
Admissions: Dr. George Mills
Type: Comprehensive **Sex:** Coed **Scores:** 99.6% SAT V 400+; 100% SAT M 400+; 17.1% ACT 18-23; 61.6% ACT 24-29 **% Accepted:** 71 **Admission Plans:** Early Admission; Early Decision Plan; Deferred Admission **Application Deadline:** February 01 **Application Fee:** $40.00 **H.S. Requirements:** High school diploma required; GED accepted **Costs Per Year:** Application fee: $40. Comprehensive fee: $35,600 includes full-time tuition ($28,270), mandatory fees ($190), and college room and board ($7140). College room only: $3900. Full-time tuition and fees vary according to course load. Room and board charges vary according to board plan and housing facility. Part-time tuition: $3570 per unit. Part-time tuition varies according to course load. **Scholarships:** Available **Calendar System:** Semester, Summer Session Available **Enrollment:** FT 2,571, PT 33, Grad 283 **Faculty:** FT 224, PT 59 **Student-Faculty Ratio:** 11:1 **Exams:** SAT I or ACT **% Receiving Financial Aid:** 59 **% Residing in College-Owned, -Operated, or -Affiliated Housing:** 59 **Library Holdings:** 349,088 **Credit Hours For Degree:** 32 units,

Bachelors **ROTC:** Army **Professional Accreditation:** AOTA, APTA, NASM, NCATE, NCCU **Intercollegiate Athletics:** Baseball M; Basketball M & W; Cheerleading M & W; Crew M & W; Cross-Country Running M & W; Football M; Golf M & W; Lacrosse W; Rugby M & W; Skiing (Downhill) M & W; Soccer M & W; Softball W; Swimming and Diving M & W; Tennis M & W; Track and Field M & W; Volleyball W

UNIVERSITY OF WASHINGTON
Seattle, WA 98195
Tel: (206)543-2100
Admissions: (206)543-9686
Web Site: http://www.washington.edu/
President/CEO: Dr. Lee L. Huntsman
Registrar: Wilbur W. Washburn, III
Admissions: Wilbur W. Washburn, IV
Financial Aid: Eric Godfrey
Type: University **Sex:** Coed **Scores:** 98% SAT V 400+; 100% SAT M 400+; 25% ACT 18-23; 55% ACT 24-29 **% Accepted:** 67 **Admission Plans:** Preferred Admission; Early Admission **Application Deadline:** January 15 **Application Fee:** $50.00 **H.S. Requirements:** High school diploma or equivalent not required **Costs Per Year:** Application fee: $50. State resident tuition: $5532 full-time. Nonresident tuition: $19,830 full-time. **Scholarships:** Available **Calendar System:** Quarter, Summer Session Available **Enrollment:** FT 23,216, PT 4,272, Grad 9,926 **Faculty:** FT 2,879, PT 639 **Student-Faculty Ratio:** 11:1 **Exams:** SAT I or ACT **% Residing in College-Owned, -Operated, or -Affiliated Housing:** 17 **Library Holdings:** 5,820,229 **Credit Hours For Degree:** 180 credits, Bachelors **ROTC:** Army, Navy, Air Force **Professional Accreditation:** AACSB, ABET, ACEHSA, ACEJMC, AACN, ABA, ACNM, ACCE, ACPhE, ADA, ADtA, AHIMA, ACSP, ALA, AOTA, APTA, APA, ASLA, ASLHA, AALS CEPH, CSWE, LCMEAMA, NAACLS, NASM, NCOPE, NCATE, NLN, NCCU, SAF **Intercollegiate Athletics:** Baseball M; Basketball M & W; Crew M & W; Cross-Country Running M & W; Football M; Golf M & W; Gymnastics W; Soccer M & W; Softball W; Swimming and Diving M & W; Tennis M & W; Track and Field M & W; Volleyball W; Wrestling M

UNIVERSITY OF WASHINGTON, BOTHELL
18115 Campus Way NE
Bothell, WA 98011-8246
Tel: (425)352-5000
Admissions: (425)352-5305
Web Site: http://www.uwb.edu
President/CEO: Dr. Warren Buck
Admissions: Hung Dang
Type: Two-Year Upper Division **Sex:** Coed **% Accepted:** 72 **Application Fee:** $0.00 **Costs Per Year:** Application fee: $0. State resident tuition: $5496 full-time. Nonresident tuition: $19,794 full-time. **Enrollment:** FT 800, PT 515, Grad 222 **Faculty:** FT 73, PT 30 **Student-Faculty Ratio:** 14:1

UNIVERSITY OF WASHINGTON, TACOMA
1900 Commerce St.
Tacoma, WA 98402-3100
Tel: (253)692-4000
Free: 800-736-7750
Admissions: (253)692-4400
E-mail: wandaec@u.washington.edu
Web Site: http://www.tacoma.washington.edu/
President/CEO: Dr. Patricia Spakes
Admissions: Wanda Curtis
Type: Two-Year Upper Division **Sex:** Coed **Application Deadline:** January 15 **Application Fee:** $50.00 **Costs Per Year:** Application fee: $50. State resident tuition: $5532 full-time, $923 per course part-time. Nonresident tuition: $19,830 full-time, $3305 per course part-time. Mandatory fees: $90 full-time, $30 per course part-time, $30 per term part-time. College room and board: $10,125. **Calendar System:** Quarter **Enrollment:** FT 1,188, PT 530, Grad 395 **Faculty:** FT 104, PT 38 **Student-Faculty Ratio:** 16:1 **Exams:** SAT I or ACT

WALLA WALLA COLLEGE
204 South College Ave.
College Place, WA 99324-1198
Tel: (509)527-2615
Free: 800-541-8900
Admissions: (509)527-2327
Fax: (509)527-2397
E-mail: weisda@wwc.edu
Web Site: http://www.wwc.edu/
President/CEO: Dr. Jon Dybdahl
Registrar: Carolyn Denney
Admissions: Victor Brown
Financial Aid: Cassie Ragenovich
Type: Comprehensive **Sex:** Coed **Affiliation:** Seventh-day Adventist **Scores:** 93% SAT V 400+; 91.4% SAT M 400+ **% Accepted:** 28 **Admission Plans:** Deferred Admission **Application Deadline:** Rolling **Application Fee:** $40.00 **H.S. Requirements:** High school diploma required; GED accepted **Costs Per Year:** Application fee: $40. Comprehensive fee: $24,489 includes full-time tuition ($19,725), mandatory fees ($192), and college room and board ($4572). College room only: $2472. Part-time tuition: $516 per credit. **Scholarships:** Available **Calendar System:** Quarter, Summer Session Available **Enrollment:** FT 1,528, PT 142, Grad 272 **Faculty:** FT 122, PT 72 **Student-Faculty Ratio:** 12:1 **Exams:** ACT, SAT I or ACT **% Receiving Financial Aid:** 71 **% Residing in College-Owned, -Operated, or -Affiliated Housing:** 44 **Library Holdings:** 178,450 **Credit Hours For Degree:** 96 quarter hours, Associates; 192 quarter hours, Bachelors **Professional Accreditation:** ABET, ACBSP, CSWE, NASM, NLN, NCCU **Intercollegiate Athletics:** Basketball M & W; Golf M; Ice Hockey M; Soccer M; Softball W; Volleyball M & W

WALLA WALLA COMMUNITY COLLEGE
500 Tausick Way
Walla Walla, WA 99362-9267
Tel: (509)522-2500; 877-992-9292
Admissions: (509)527-4283
Fax: (509)527-3361
E-mail: admissions@mail.ww.cc.wa.us
Web Site: http://www.wwcc.edu/home/
President/CEO: Dr. Steven L. VanAusdle
Registrar: Sally Wagoner
Admissions: Sally Wagoner
Financial Aid: Terri Johnson
Type: Two-Year College **Sex:** Coed **Affiliation:** Washington State Board for Community and Technical Colleges **Admission Plans:** Open Admission **Application Fee:** $40.00 **H.S. Requirements:** High school diploma or equivalent not required. For nursing program: High school diploma required; GED accepted **Scholarships:** Available **Calendar System:** Quarter, Summer Session Available **Enrollment:** FT 2,164, PT 2,276 **Faculty:** FT 114, PT 245 **Student-Faculty Ratio:** 21:1 **Exams:** Other **Library Holdings:** 45,814 **Credit Hours For Degree:** 93 credits, Associates **Professional Accreditation:** ABET, NLN, NCCU **Intercollegiate Athletics:** Baseball M; Basketball M & W; Cross-Country Running W; Equestrian Sports M & W; Golf M & W; Soccer M & W; Softball W; Tennis M & W; Volleyball W

WASHINGTON STATE UNIVERSITY
Pullman, WA 99164
Tel: (509)335-3564; 888-468-6978
Admissions: (509)335-5586
E-mail: admiss@wsu.edu
Web Site: http://www.wsu.edu/
President/CEO: Dr. V. Lane Rawlins
Registrar: Julia Pomerenk
Admissions: Wendy Peterson
Financial Aid: Wayne Sparks
Type: University **Sex:** Coed **Scores:** 97.7% SAT V 400+; 99.4% SAT M 400+ **% Accepted:** 74 **Admission Plans:** Early Admission **Application Fee:** $50.00 **H.S. Requirements:** High school diploma required; GED accepted **Costs Per Year:** Application fee: $50. State resident tuition: $5432 full-time. Nonresident tuition: $15,072 full-time. **Scholarships:** Available **Calendar System:** Semester, Summer Session Available **Enrollment:** FT 16,786, PT 2,799, Grad 3,219 **Faculty:** FT 1,057, PT 392 **Student-Faculty Ratio:** 15:1 **Exams:** SAT I or ACT **% Receiving Financial Aid:** 51 **% Residing in College-Owned, -Operated, or -Affiliated Housing:** 37 **Library Holdings:** 2,168,735 **Credit Hours For Degree:** 120 credits, Bachelors **ROTC:** Army, Navy, Air Force **Professional Accreditation:** AACSB, ABET, AACN, ACCE, ACPhE, ADtA, APA, ASLA, ASLHA, AVMA, FIDER, JRCEPAT, NASM, NCATE, NLN, NCCU, SAF **Intercollegiate Athletics:** Baseball M; Basketball M & W; Bowling M & W; Crew M & W; Cross-Country Running M & W; Equestrian Sports M & W; Football M; Golf M & W; Ice Hockey M & W; Lacrosse M & W; Rugby M & W; Skiing (Cross-Country) M & W; Skiing (Downhill) M & W; Soccer M & W; Softball W; Swimming and Diving W; Ten-

nis W; Track and Field M & W; Volleyball M & W; Water Polo M

WENATCHEE VALLEY COLLEGE
1300 Fifth St.
Wenatchee, WA 98801-1799
Tel: (509)662-1651
Admissions: (509)682-6800
Fax: (509)664-2511
Web Site: http://wvc.ctc.edu/
President/CEO: Dr. Jack Becherer
Registrar: Marco Azurdia
Admissions: Bruce Maxwell
Financial Aid: Dr. Lee Shelley
Type: Two-Year College **Sex:** Coed **Affiliation:** Washington State Board for Community and Technical Colleges **Admission Plans:** Open Admission; Early Admission; Deferred Admission **Application Fee:** $0.00 **H.S. Requirements:** High school diploma or equivalent not required. For allied health programs: High school diploma required; GED accepted **Scholarships:** Available **Calendar System:** Quarter, Summer Session Available **Faculty:** FT 67, PT 136 **Exams:** Other **Library Holdings:** 32,000 **Credit Hours For Degree:** 90 credits, Associates **Professional Accreditation:** JRCERT, NAACLS, NLN, NCCU **Intercollegiate Athletics:** Baseball M; Basketball M & W; Soccer M & W; Softball W

WESTERN BUSINESS COLLEGE
120 Northeast 136th Ave., Ste. 130
Vancouver, WA 98684
Tel: (360)254-3282
Web Site: http://www.western-college.com/
Admissions: Maryann Green
Type: Two-Year College **Sex:** Coed **H.S. Requirements:** High school diploma required; GED accepted **Calendar System:** Quarter **Faculty:** FT 7, PT 15 **Student-Faculty Ratio:** 19:1 **Professional Accreditation:** ACICS

WESTERN WASHINGTON UNIVERSITY
516 High St.
Bellingham, WA 98225-5996
Tel: (360)650-3000
Admissions: (360)650-3440
E-mail: admit@wwu.edu
Web Site: http://www.wwu.edu/
President/CEO: Dr. Karen W. Morse
Registrar: Joseph St. Hilaire
Admissions: Karen Copetas
Financial Aid: Clara Capron
Type: Comprehensive **Sex:** Coed **Scores:** 98% SAT V 400+; 99% SAT M 400+; 43% ACT 18-23; 46% ACT 24-29 **% Accepted:** 75 **Application Deadline:** March 01 **Application Fee:** $50.00 **H.S. Requirements:** High school diploma required; GED accepted **Costs Per Year:** Application fee: $50. State resident tuition: $3673 full-time, $137 per credit part-time. Nonresident tuition: $13,623 full-time, $469 per credit part-time. Mandatory fees: $1065 full-time. Full-time tuition and fees vary according to location. Part-time tuition varies according to location. College room and board: $6524. College room only: $4209. Room and board charges vary according to board plan and housing facility. **Scholarships:** Available **Calendar System:** Quarter, Summer Session Available **Enrollment:** FT 11,943, PT 1,059, Grad 1,245 **Faculty:** FT 472, PT 156 **Student-Faculty Ratio:** 20:1 **Exams:** Other, SAT I or ACT **% Receiving Financial Aid:** 39 **% Residing in College-Owned, -Operated, or -Affiliated Housing:** 30 **Library Holdings:** 1,341,300 **Credit Hours For Degree:** 180 quarter hours, Bachelors **Professional Accreditation:** AACSB, ABET, ACA, ASLHA, CORE, NASAD, NASM, NCATE, NRPA, NCCU **Intercollegiate Athletics:** Basketball M & W; Cheerleading M & W; Crew M & W; Cross-Country Running M & W; Football M; Golf M & W; Soccer M & W; Softball W; Track and Field M & W; Volleyball W

WHATCOM COMMUNITY COLLEGE
237 West Kellogg Rd.
Bellingham, WA 98226-8003
Tel: (360)676-2170
Fax: (360)676-2171
Web Site: http://www.whatcom.ctc.edu/
President/CEO: Dr. Harold G. Heiner
Registrar: Janelle Miner
Admissions: Janelle Miner
Financial Aid: Mary Easley
Type: Two-Year College **Sex:** Coed **Affiliation:** Washington State Board for Community and Technical Colleges **Admission Plans:** Open Admission **Application Fee:** $0.00 **H.S. Requirements:** High school diploma or equivalent not required. For financial aid applicants, international students: High school diploma required; GED accepted **Costs Per Year:** Application fee: $0. State resident tuition: $2484 full-time, $73.10 per credit part-time. Nonresident tuition: $7692 full-time, $244.80 per credit part-time. Full-time tuition varies according to course load and reciprocity agreements. Part-time tuition varies according to course load and reciprocity agreements. **Scholarships:** Available **Calendar System:** Quarter, Summer Session Available **Faculty:** FT 54, PT 169 **Library Holdings:** 14,680 **Credit Hours For Degree:** 90 quarter hours, Associates **Professional Accreditation:** AAMAE, APTA, NCCU **Intercollegiate Athletics:** Basketball M & W; Cheerleading M & W; Soccer M; Volleyball W

WHITMAN COLLEGE
345 Boyer Ave.
Walla Walla, WA 99362-2083
Tel: (509)527-5111; 877-462-9448
Admissions: (509)527-5176
Fax: (509)527-4967
E-mail: admission@whitman.edu
Web Site: http://www.whitman.edu/
President/CEO: Dr. Thomas E. Cronin
Registrar: Dr. Ronald F. Urban
Admissions: Tony Cabasco
Financial Aid: Varga Fox
Type: Four-Year College **Sex:** Coed **Scores:** 100% SAT V 400+; 100% SAT M 400+; 9.3% ACT 18-23; 43% ACT 24-29 **% Accepted:** 49 **Admission Plans:** Early Decision Plan; Deferred Admission **Application Deadline:** January 15 **Application Fee:** $45.00 **H.S. Requirements:** High school diploma required; GED accepted **Costs Per Year:** Application fee: $45. Comprehensive fee: $36,110 includes full-time tuition ($28,400), mandatory fees ($240), and college room and board ($7470). College room only: $3430. Room and board charges vary according to board plan and housing facility. Part-time tuition: $1190 per credit. **Scholarships:** Available **Calendar System:** Semester, Summer Session Not available **Enrollment:** FT 1,480, PT 32 **Faculty:** FT 115, PT 72 **Student-Faculty Ratio:** 10:1 **Exams:** SAT I or ACT **% Receiving Financial Aid:** 55 **% Residing in College-Owned, -Operated, or -Affiliated Housing:** 56 **Library Holdings:** 356,731 **Credit Hours For Degree:** 124 credits, Bachelors **Professional Accreditation:** NCCU **Intercollegiate Athletics:** Baseball M; Basketball M & W; Cross-Country Running M & W; Golf M & W; Ice Hockey M; Lacrosse M & W; Rugby M & W; Skiing (Cross-Country) M & W; Skiing (Downhill) M & W; Soccer M & W; Softball M & W; Swimming and Diving M & W; Tennis M & W; Track and Field M & W; Ultimate Frisbee M & W; Volleyball M & W

WHITWORTH COLLEGE
300 West Hawthorne Rd.
Spokane, WA 99251-0001
Tel: (509)777-1000
Free: 800-533-4668
Admissions: (509)777-4348
Fax: (509)777-3773
E-mail: admissions@whitworth.edu
Web Site: http://www.whitworth.edu/
President/CEO: Dr. William P. Robinson
Registrar: Gary Whisenand
Admissions: Fred Pfursich
Financial Aid: Wendy Olson
Type: Comprehensive **Sex:** Coed **Affiliation:** Presbyterian **Scores:** 100% SAT V 400+; 100% SAT M 400+; 23% ACT 18-23; 57% ACT 24-29 **% Accepted:** 67 **Admission Plans:** Early Admission; Early Action; Deferred Admission **Application Deadline:** March 01 **Application Fee:** $0.00 **H.S. Requirements:** High school diploma required; GED accepted **Costs Per Year:** Application fee: $0. Comprehensive fee: $31,184 includes full-time tuition ($23,850), mandatory fees ($304), and college room and board ($7030). Part-time tuition: $994 per credit. **Scholarships:** Available **Calendar System:** 4-1-4, Summer Session Available **Enrollment:** FT 2,065, PT 114, Grad 262 **Faculty:** FT 120, PT 171 **Student-Faculty Ratio:** 13:1 **Exams:** SAT I or ACT **% Receiving Financial Aid:** 74 **% Residing in College-Owned, -Operated, or -Affiliated Housing:** 65 **Library Holdings:** 17,982 **Credit Hours For Degree:** 130 credits, Bachelors **ROTC:** Army

Professional Accreditation: AACN, JRCEPAT, NASM, NCATE, NLN, NCCU **Intercollegiate Athletics:** Baseball M; Basketball M & W; Cross-Country Running M & W; Football M; Golf M & W; Soccer M & W; Softball W; Swimming and Diving M & W; Tennis M & W; Track and Field M & W; Volleyball W

YAKIMA VALLEY COMMUNITY COLLEGE
PO Box 22520
Yakima, WA 98907-2520
Tel: (509)574-4600
Admissions: (509)574-6806
Fax: (509)574-6860
Web Site: http://www.yvcc.edu/
President/CEO: Dr. Linda Kaminski
Registrar: Ellie Heffernan
Admissions: Tomas Ybarra
Financial Aid: Leslie Blackaey

Type: Two-Year College **Sex:** Coed **Affiliation:** Washington State Board for Community and Technical Colleges **% Accepted:** 100 **Admission Plans:** Open Admission; Deferred Admission **Application Deadline:** September 16 **Application Fee:** $20.00 **H.S. Requirements:** High school diploma required; GED accepted. For nursing, dental hygiene, radiological technology, allied health programs: High school diploma required; GED accepted **Costs Per Year:** Application fee: $20. State resident tuition: $2550 full-time, $72 per credit part-time. Nonresident tuition: $2939 full-time. Mandatory fees: $3.50 per credit part-time. Full-time tuition varies according to course load. Part-time tuition and fees vary according to course load. College room only: $2400. **Scholarships:** Available **Calendar System:** Quarter, Summer Session Available **Enrollment:** FT 3,755, PT 2,470 **Faculty:** FT 97, PT 202 **Student-Faculty Ratio:** 20:1 **% Residing in College-Owned, -Operated, or -Affiliated Housing:** 1 **Library Holdings:** 31,716 **Credit Hours For Degree:** 90 credits, Associates **Professional Accreditation:** ADA, JRCERT, NLN, NCCU **Intercollegiate Athletics:** Baseball M; Basketball M & W; Soccer W; Softball W; Volleyball W; Wrestling M

ALDERSON-BROADDUS COLLEGE
1 College Hill Dr.
Philippi, WV 26416
Tel: (304)457-1700
Free: 800-263-1549
Fax: (304)457-6239
E-mail: admissions@ab.wvnet.edu
Web Site: http://www.ab.edu/
President/CEO: Dr. Stephen Markwood
Registrar: Saundra Hoxie
Admissions: Kimberly N. Klaus
Financial Aid: Brian Weingart
Type: Comprehensive **Sex:** Coed **Affiliation:** American Baptist Churches in the U.S.A. **Scores:** 84.61% SAT V 400+; 76.92% SAT M 400+; 55.05% ACT 18-23; 30.28% ACT 24-29 **% Accepted:** 75 **Admission Plans:** Deferred Admission **Application Deadline:** Rolling **Application Fee:** $10.00 **H.S. Requirements:** High school diploma required; GED accepted **Costs Per Year:** Application fee: $10. Comprehensive fee: $24,006 includes full-time tuition ($17,970), mandatory fees ($166), and college room and board ($5870). College room only: $2860. Full-time tuition and fees vary according to degree level. Room and board charges vary according to housing facility. Part-time tuition: $598 per credit hour. Part-time mandatory fees: $41.50 per term. Part-time tuition and fees vary according to degree level. **Scholarships:** Available **Calendar System:** Semester, Summer Session Available **Enrollment:** FT 592, PT 56, Grad 131 **Faculty:** FT 58, PT 29 **Student-Faculty Ratio:** 11:1 **Exams:** SAT I or ACT **% Receiving Financial Aid:** 90 **% Residing in College-Owned, -Operated, or -Affiliated Housing:** 41 **Library Holdings:** 100,000 **Regional Accreditation:** North Central Association of Colleges and Schools **Credit Hours For Degree:** 64 credit hours, Associates; 128 credit hours, Bachelors **Professional Accreditation:** NCATE, NLN **Intercollegiate Athletics:** Baseball M; Basketball M & W; Cross-Country Running M & W; Golf M & W; Soccer M; Softball W; Volleyball W

AMERICAN PUBLIC UNIVERSITY SYSTEM
111 West Congress St.
Charles Town, WV 25414
Tel: (304)724-6857; 877-468-6268
Admissions: (703)330-5398
Fax: (304)724-6863
Web Site: http://www.apus.edu/
President/CEO: Dr. Karen Powell
Registrar: Melanie Winter
Admissions: Lyn Geer
Financial Aid: Teresa Reed
Type: Comprehensive **Sex:** Coed **% Accepted:** 81 **Admission Plans:** Open Admission; Deferred Admission **Application Deadline:** Rolling **Application Fee:** $0.00 **H.S. Requirements:** High school diploma required; GED accepted **Costs Per Year:** Application fee: $0. One-time mandatory fee: $75. Tuition: $6000 full-time, $250 per semester hour part-time. **Calendar System:** Trimester, Summer Session Not available **Enrollment:** FT 473, PT 8,557, Grad 4,447 **Faculty:** FT 47, PT 315 **Student-Faculty Ratio:** 12:1 **Credit Hours For Degree:** 63 semester hours, Associates; 120 semester hours, Bachelors **Professional Accreditation:** DETC

APPALACHIAN BIBLE COLLEGE
PO Box ABC
Bradley, WV 25818
Tel: (304)877-6428
Free: 800-678-9ABC
Web Site: http://www.abc.edu/
President/CEO: Dr. Daniel L. Anderson
Registrar: Dr. Jerry F. Knoblet
Admissions: Angela J. Harding
Financial Aid: Shirley C. Carfrey
Type: Four-Year College **Sex:** Coed **Affiliation:** nondenominational **Application Fee:** $10.00 **H.S. Requirements:** High school diploma required; GED accepted **Costs Per Year:** Application fee: $10. Comprehensive fee: $12,808 includes full-time tuition ($7140), mandatory fees ($1268), and college room and board ($4400). Part-time tuition: $297 per credit hour. Part-time mandatory fees: $32 per credit hour. **Scholarships:** Available **Calendar System:** Semester, Summer Session Available **Enrollment:** FT 238, PT 66 **Faculty:** FT 11, PT 7 **Student-Faculty Ratio:** 17:1 **Exams:** SAT I or ACT **% Receiving Financial Aid:** 89 **Library Holdings:** 44,944 **Regional Accreditation:** North Central Association of Colleges and Schools **Credit Hours For Degree:** 63 credit hours, Associates; 126 credit hours, Bachelors **Professional Accreditation:** AABC **Intercollegiate Athletics:** Basketball M & W; Soccer M; Volleyball W

BETHANY COLLEGE
Main St.
Bethany, WV 26032
Tel: (304)829-7000
Free: 800-922-7611
Admissions: (304)829-7611
Fax: (304)829-7142
E-mail: wblair@bethanywv.edu
Web Site: http://www.bethanywv.edu/
President/CEO: G.T. "Buck" Smith
Registrar: Sandra Neel
Admissions: Wray Blair
Financial Aid: Jeffrey J. DeRubbo
Type: Four-Year College **Sex:** Coed **Affiliation:** Christian Church (Disciples of Christ) **Scores:** 87% SAT V 400+; 89% SAT M 400+; 55% ACT 18-23; 26% ACT 24-29 **% Accepted:** 75 **Admission Plans:** Deferred Admission **Application Deadline:** Rolling **Application Fee:** $25.00 **H.S. Requirements:** High school diploma required; GED accepted **Costs Per Year:** Application fee: $25. Comprehensive fee: $23,520 includes full-time tuition ($15,750) and college room and board ($7770). College room only: $4000. **Scholarships:** Available **Calendar System:** 4-1-4, Summer Session Not available **Enrollment:** FT 895, PT 7 **Faculty:** FT 63, PT 23 **Student-Faculty Ratio:** 14:1 **Exams:** SAT I or ACT **% Receiving Financial Aid:** 91 **% Residing in College-Owned, -Operated, or -Affiliated Housing:** 88 **Library Holdings:** 130,696 **Regional Accreditation:** North Central Association of Colleges and Schools **Credit Hours For Degree:** 128 semester hours, Bachelors **Professional Accreditation:** CSWE, NCATE **Intercollegiate Athletics:** Baseball M; Basketball M & W; Cheerleading M & W; Cross-Country Running M & W; Football M; Golf M & W; Ice Hockey M; Lacrosse M

& W; Rugby M; Soccer M & W; Softball W; Swimming and Diving M & W; Tennis M & W; Track and Field M & W; Volleyball W; Weight Lifting M

BLUEFIELD STATE COLLEGE
219 Rock St.
Bluefield, WV 24701-2198
Tel: (304)327-4000
Free: 800-654-7798
Admissions: (304)327-4567
Fax: (304)327-7747
E-mail: jcardwell@bscvax.wvnet.edu
Web Site: http://www.bluefieldstate.edu/
President/CEO: Dr. Albert L. Walker
Registrar: Ray Mull
Admissions: John C. Cardwell
Financial Aid: Thomas Isle
Type: Four-Year College **Sex:** Coed **Affiliation:** Higher Education Policy Commission System **Scores:** 97% SAT V 400+; 89% SAT M 400+; 51% ACT 18-23; 12% ACT 24-29 **% Accepted:** 96 **Admission Plans:** Open Admission; Deferred Admission **Application Deadline:** Rolling **Application Fee:** $0.00 **H.S. Requirements:** High school diploma required; GED accepted **Costs Per Year:** Application fee: $0. State resident tuition: $3410 full-time, $142 per credit part-time. Nonresident tuition: $7014 full-time, $292 per credit part-time. Full-time tuition varies according to degree level, program, and reciprocity agreements. Part-time tuition varies according to course load, program, and reciprocity agreements. **Scholarships:** Available **Calendar System:** Semester, Summer Session Available **Enrollment:** FT 1,400, PT 308 **Faculty:** FT 79, PT 64 **Student-Faculty Ratio:** 17:1 **Exams:** SAT I or ACT **% Receiving Financial Aid:** 64 **Library Holdings:** 76,391 **Regional Accreditation:** North Central Association of Colleges and Schools **Credit Hours For Degree:** 64 semester hours, Associates; 128 semester hours, Bachelors **Professional Accreditation:** ABET, AACN, ACBSP, JRCERT, NCATE, NLN **Intercollegiate Athletics:** Baseball M; Basketball M & W; Cheerleading W; Cross-Country Running M & W; Golf M; Softball W; Tennis M & W

COMMUNITY AND TECHNICAL COLLEGE OF SHEPHERD
400 West Stephen St.
Martinsburg, WV 25401
Tel: (304)260-4380
Fax: (304)260-4376
E-mail: lseectc@shepherd.edu
Web Site: http://www.shepherd.edu/ctcweb/
President/CEO: Dr. Peter A. Checkovich
Admissions: Leslie C. See
Type: Two-Year College **Sex:** Coed **Scores:** 100% SAT V 400+; 100% SAT M 400+; 32.88% ACT 18-23; 1.37% ACT 24-29 **% Accepted:** 100 **Application Fee:** $35.00 **Costs Per Year:** Application fee: $35. State resident tuition: $2944 full-time, $123 per credit part-time. Nonresident tuition: $8542 full-time, $355 per credit part-time. **Enrollment:** FT 427, PT 1,284 **Faculty:** FT 13, PT 57 **Student-Faculty Ratio:** 29:1 **Exams:** SAT I and SAT II or ACT

COMMUNITY & TECHNICAL COLLEGE AT WEST VIRGINIA UNIVERSITY INSTITUTE OF TECHNOLOGY
Montgomery, WV 25136
Tel: (304)442-3149; 888-554-8324
Admissions: (304)442-3167
Web Site: http://ctc.wvutech.edu/
President/CEO: Dr. Jo Harris
Admissions: Lisa Graham
Type: Two-Year College **Sex:** Coed

CONCORD UNIVERSITY
Vermillion St., PO Box 1000
Athens, WV 24712-1000
Tel: (304)384-3115; 888-384-5249
Admissions: (304)384-5248
Fax: (304)384-9044
E-mail: addsm@ccvms.wvnet.edu
Web Site: http://www.concord.edu/
President/CEO: Dr. Jerry L. Beasley
Registrar: Carolyn Cox
Admissions: Michael Curry
Financial Aid: Patricia Harmon
Type: Four-Year College **Sex:** Coed **Affiliation:** State College System of West Virginia **Scores:** 86% SAT V 400+; 81% SAT M 400+; 55% ACT 18-23; 21% ACT 24-29 **% Accepted:** 67 **Admission Plans:** Early Admission; Early Decision Plan **Application Deadline:** Rolling **Application Fee:** $0.00 **H.S. Requirements:** High school diploma required; GED accepted **Costs Per Year:** Application fee: $0. State resident tuition: $3872 full-time, $160 per credit hour part-time. Nonresident tuition: $8646 full-time, $359 per credit hour part-time. Full-time tuition varies according to course load. Part-time tuition varies according to course load. College room and board: $5796. College room only: $2966. **Scholarships:** Available **Calendar System:** Semester, Summer Session Available **Enrollment:** FT 2,444, PT 508, Grad 63 **Faculty:** FT 97, PT 88 **Student-Faculty Ratio:** 22:1 **Exams:** ACT, SAT I or ACT **% Receiving Financial Aid:** 59 **% Residing in College-Owned, -Operated, or -Affiliated Housing:** 39 **Library Holdings:** 150,151 **Regional Accreditation:** North Central Association of Colleges and Schools **Credit Hours For Degree:** 128 semester hours, Bachelors **Professional Accreditation:** CSWE, NCATE **Intercollegiate Athletics:** Baseball M; Basketball M & W; Cheerleading M & W; Cross-Country Running M & W; Football M; Golf M; Soccer W; Tennis M & W; Track and Field M & W; Volleyball W

DAVIS & ELKINS COLLEGE
100 Campus Dr.
Elkins, WV 26241-3996
Tel: (304)637-1900
Free: 800-624-3157
Admissions: (304)637-1974
Fax: (304)637-1800
E-mail: admiss@davisandelkins.edu
Web Site: http://www.davisandelkins.edu/
President/CEO: Dr. G. Thomas Mann
Registrar: Dr. Laurence B. McArthur
Admissions: Renee Heckel
Financial Aid: Susan George
Type: Four-Year College **Sex:** Coed **Affiliation:** Presbyterian **Scores:** 90% SAT V 400+; 82% SAT M 400+; 54% ACT 18-23; 17% ACT 24-29 **% Accepted:** 55 **Admission Plans:** Early Admission; Deferred Admission **Application Deadline:** Rolling **Application Fee:** $35.00 **H.S. Requirements:** High school diploma required; GED accepted **Costs Per Year:** Application fee: $35. Comprehensive fee: $22,936 includes full-time tuition ($16,312), mandatory fees ($520), and college room and board ($6104). Full-time tuition and fees vary according to course load. Room and board charges vary according to board plan. Part-time tuition: $525 per credit hour. Part-time tuition varies according to course load. **Scholarships:** Available **Calendar System:** 4-1-4, Summer Session Available **Enrollment:** FT 560, PT 64 **Faculty:** FT 44, PT 40 **Student-Faculty Ratio:** 11:1 **Exams:** SAT I or ACT **% Receiving Financial Aid:** 79 **% Residing in College-Owned, -Operated, or -Affiliated Housing:** 43 **Library Holdings:** 225,816 **Regional Accreditation:** North Central Association of Colleges and Schools **Credit Hours For Degree:** 62 credit hours, Associates; 124 credit hours, Bachelors **Professional Accreditation:** NAST, NLN **Intercollegiate Athletics:** Baseball M; Basketball M & W; Cross-Country Running M & W; Golf M; Skiing (Downhill) M & W; Soccer M & W; Softball W; Volleyball W

EASTERN WEST VIRGINIA COMMUNITY AND TECHNICAL COLLEGE
HC 65 Box 402
Moorefield, WV 26836
Tel: (304)434-8000; 877-982-2322
E-mail: sbungard@eastern.wvnet.edu
Web Site: http://www.eastern.wvnet.edu/
President/CEO: Linda S. Dunn
Admissions: Sharon Bungard
Type: Two-Year College **Sex:** Coed **% Accepted:** 100 **Costs Per Year:** State resident tuition: $1704 full-time. Nonresident tuition: $6822 full-time. **Calendar System:** Semester **Enrollment:** FT 68, PT 814 **Faculty:** FT 1, PT 40 **Student-Faculty Ratio:** 21:1 **Regional Accreditation:** North Central Association of Colleges and Schools

FAIRMONT STATE COMMUNITY & TECHNICAL COLLEGE
1201 Locust Ave.
Fairmont, WV 26554
Tel: (304)367-4892
Free: 800-641-5678
Fax: (304)367-4692

Web Site: http://www.fscwv.edu/fsctc/
President/CEO: Dr. Dan Bradley
Type: Two-Year College **Sex:** Coed **Affiliation:** Fairmont State College **Admission Plans:** Open Admission; Deferred Admission **Application Fee:** $0.00 **H.S. Requirements:** High school diploma required; GED accepted **Calendar System:** Semester, Summer Session Available **Enrollment:** FT 1,878, PT 1,477 **Faculty:** FT 42, PT 200 **Exams:** Other, SAT I or ACT **Regional Accreditation:** North Central Association of Colleges and Schools **Professional Accreditation:** ACF, AHIMA, APTA, NAACLS, NLN

FAIRMONT STATE UNIVERSITY
1201 Locust Ave.
Fairmont, WV 26554
Tel: (304)367-4000
Free: 800-641-5678
Admissions: (304)367-4702
Fax: (304)367-4789
E-mail: admit@fairmontstate.edu
Web Site: http://www.fairmontstate.edu/
President/CEO: Dr. Daniel J. Bradley
Admissions: Steve Leadman
Financial Aid: Sandra Oerly-Bennett
Type: Comprehensive **Sex:** Coed **Affiliation:** State College System of West Virginia **Scores:** 50% ACT 18-23; 6% ACT 24-29 **% Accepted:** 75 **Admission Plans:** Open Admission; Early Admission **Application Deadline:** June 15 **Application Fee:** $0.00 **H.S. Requirements:** High school diploma required; GED accepted **Costs Per Year:** Application fee: $0. State resident tuition: $4218 full-time, $155 per hour part-time. Nonresident tuition: $8808 full-time, $331 per hour part-time. Mandatory fees: $194 full-time, $177 per credit hour part-time. College room and board: $5674. College room only: $2814. **Scholarships:** Available **Calendar System:** Semester, Summer Session Available **Enrollment:** FT 5,534, PT 1,986, Grad 239 **Faculty:** FT 220, PT 315 **Student-Faculty Ratio:** 17:1 **Exams:** SAT I and SAT II or ACT **% Receiving Financial Aid:** 69 **% Residing in College-Owned, -Operated, or -Affiliated Housing:** 6 **Library Holdings:** 276,722 **Regional Accreditation:** North Central Association of Colleges and Schools **Credit Hours For Degree:** 64 credits, Associates; 128 credits, Bachelors **ROTC:** Army **Professional Accreditation:** ABET, AACN, AAFCS, NCATE **Intercollegiate Athletics:** Baseball M; Basketball M & W; Cross-Country Running M & W; Football M; Golf M & W; Softball W; Swimming and Diving M & W; Tennis M & W; Volleyball W

GLENVILLE STATE COLLEGE
200 High St.
Glenville, WV 26351-1200
Tel: (304)462-7361
Admissions: (304)462-4128
Fax: (304)462-8619
Web Site: http://www.glenville.edu/
President/CEO: Dr. Robert N. Freeman
Registrar: Dr. Marty Armentrout
Admissions: Michelle Wicks
Financial Aid: Karen Lay
Type: Four-Year College **Sex:** Coed **Affiliation:** West Virginia Higher Education Policy Commission **Scores:** 68.9% SAT V 400+; 66.6% SAT M 400+; 53.2% ACT 18-23; 11.7% ACT 24-29 **% Accepted:** 100 **Admission Plans:** Open Admission; Deferred Admission **Application Deadline:** Rolling **Application Fee:** $0.00 **H.S. Requirements:** High school diploma required; GED accepted **Costs Per Year:** Application fee: $0. State resident tuition: $3628 full-time, $151.17 per credit hour part-time. Nonresident tuition: $8640 full-time, $360 per credit hour part-time. College room and board: $5150. College room only: $2500. Room and board charges vary according to housing facility. **Scholarships:** Available **Calendar System:** Semester, Summer Session Available **Faculty:** FT 53, PT 41 **Exams:** SAT I or ACT **% Receiving Financial Aid:** 73 **% Residing in College-Owned, -Operated, or -Affiliated Housing:** 33 **Library Holdings:** 125,240 **Regional Accreditation:** North Central Association of Colleges and Schools **Credit Hours For Degree:** 64 credit hours, Associates; 128 credit hours, Bachelors **Professional Accreditation:** NCATE **Intercollegiate Athletics:** Basketball M & W; Cheerleading M & W; Cross-Country Running M & W; Football M; Golf M & W; Softball W; Track and Field M & W; Volleyball W

HUNTINGTON JUNIOR COLLEGE
900 Fifth Ave.
Huntington, WV 25701-2004
Tel: (304)697-7550
Fax: (304)697-7554
Web Site: http://www.huntingtonjuniorcollege.com/
President/CEO: Carolyn Smith
Admissions: James Garrett
Financial Aid: Darlene Cummings
Type: Two-Year College **Sex:** Coed **Admission Plans:** Open Admission **Application Fee:** $0.00 **H.S. Requirements:** High school diploma required; GED accepted **Scholarships:** Available **Calendar System:** Quarter, Summer Session Available **Student-Faculty Ratio:** 18:1 **Library Holdings:** 1,900 **Regional Accreditation:** North Central Association of Colleges and Schools **Credit Hours For Degree:** 108 credits, Associates **Professional Accreditation:** AAMAE

INTERNATIONAL ACADEMY OF DESIGN & TECHNOLOGY
2000 Green River Dr.
Fairmont, WV 26554-9790
Tel: (304)534-5677; 888-406-8324
Fax: (304)534-5669
E-mail: dhirsh@iadtwv.com
Web Site: http://iadtwv.com/
Admissions: Dennis A. Hirsh
Type: Two-Year College **Sex:** Coed **Calendar System:** Quarter **Professional Accreditation:** ACICS

MARSHALL COMMUNITY AND TECHNICAL COLLEGE
One John Marshall Dr.
Huntington, WV 25755
Tel: (304)696-6282
Admissions: (304)696-3160
Web Site: http://www.marshall.edu/ctc/
Admissions: Tammy Johnson
Type: Two-Year College **Sex:** Coed **Affiliation:** Marshall University; Community and Technical College System of West Virginia **Scores:** 72% SAT V 400+; 63% SAT M 400+; 30% ACT 18-23; 7% ACT 24-29 **% Accepted:** 100 **Admission Plans:** Open Admission; Early Admission **Application Deadline:** Rolling **Application Fee:** $25.00 **H.S. Requirements:** High school diploma required; GED accepted **Costs Per Year:** Application fee: $25. State resident tuition: $2814 full-time, $118 per credit hour part-time. Nonresident tuition: $8142 full-time, $340 per credit hour part-time. College room and board: $6272. College room only: $3496. **Calendar System:** Semester, Summer Session Available **Enrollment:** FT 1,305, PT 1,284 **Faculty:** FT 35, PT 88 **Student-Faculty Ratio:** 27:1 **Exams:** ACT, SAT I **Library Holdings:** 478,274 **Credit Hours For Degree:** 64 credits, Associates **ROTC:** Army **Professional Accreditation:** AAMAE

MARSHALL UNIVERSITY
One John Marshall Dr.
Huntington, WV 25755
Tel: (304)696-3170
Admissions: (304)696-3160
Fax: (304)696-3135
E-mail: admissions@marshall.edu
Web Site: http://www.marshall.edu/
President/CEO: Dr. Dan Angel
Registrar: Roberta Ferguson
Admissions: Barbara Tarter
Financial Aid: Jack Toney
Type: University **Sex:** Coed **Affiliation:** University System of West Virginia **Scores:** 96% SAT V 400+; 94% SAT M 400+; 62% ACT 18-23; 27% ACT 24-29 **% Accepted:** 82 **Admission Plans:** Early Admission; Deferred Admission **Application Deadline:** Rolling **Application Fee:** $25.00 **H.S. Requirements:** High school diploma required; GED accepted **Costs Per Year:** Application fee: $25. State resident tuition: $3932 full-time, $155.75 per credit hour part-time. Nonresident tuition: $10,634 full-time, $423.25 per credit hour part-time. Full-time tuition varies according to degree level, location, program, and reciprocity agreements. Part-time tuition varies according to course load, degree level, location, program, and reciprocity agreements. College room and board: $6272. College room only: $3496. Room and board charges vary according to board plan and housing facility. **Scholarships:** Available **Calendar System:** Semester, Summer Session Available **Enrollment:** FT 8,190, PT 1,651, Grad 3,934 **Faculty:** FT 469, PT 253 **Student-Faculty Ratio:** 20:1 **Exams:** SAT I or ACT **% Receiving Financial Aid:** 55 **% Residing in College-Owned, -Operated, or -Affiliated Housing:** 20 **Library Holdings:** 478,274 **Regional Accreditation:** North Central

Association of Colleges and Schools **Credit Hours For Degree:** 69 semester hours, Associates; 128 semester hours, Bachelors **ROTC:** Army **Professional Accreditation:** AACSB, ABET, ACEJMC, AAFCS, AANA, ADtA, AHIMA, APTA, ASLHA, ACBSP, CSWE, JRCEPAT, LCMEAMA, NAACLS, NASM, NCATE, NLN, NRPA **Intercollegiate Athletics:** Baseball M; Basketball M & W; Cross-Country Running M & W; Football M; Golf M & W; Lacrosse M; Rugby M & W; Soccer M & W; Softball W; Swimming and Diving W; Tennis W; Track and Field M & W; Volleyball W

MOUNTAIN STATE COLLEGE
1508 Spring St.
Parkersburg, WV 26101-3993
Tel: (304)485-5487
Free: 800-841-0201
Fax: (304)485-3524
Web Site: http://www.mountainstate.org/
President/CEO: Judith Sutton
Registrar: Nancy Hudson
Admissions: Linda Craig
Financial Aid: Faye Waggoner
Type: Two-Year College **Sex:** Coed **H.S. Requirements:** High school diploma required; GED accepted **Costs Per Year:** Tuition: $7050 full-time. Mandatory fees: $115 full-time. **Scholarships:** Available **Calendar System:** Quarter **Enrollment:** FT 166 **Faculty:** FT 7, PT 4 **Student-Faculty Ratio:** 17:1 **Exams:** Other **Professional Accreditation:** ACICS

MOUNTAIN STATE UNIVERSITY
Box 9003
Beckley, WV 25802-9003
Tel: (304)253-7351
Free: 800-766-6067
Admissions: (304)929-1358
Fax: (304)253-5072
E-mail: astone@mountainstate.edu
Web Site: http://www.mountainstate.edu/
President/CEO: Dr. Charles H. Polk
Registrar: Rebecca Hall
Admissions: Alexandria Stone
Financial Aid: Sue Pack
Type: Comprehensive **Sex:** Coed **Scores:** 100% SAT V 400+; 90% SAT M 400+; 55.1% ACT 18-23; 9.2% ACT 24-29 **% Accepted:** 100 **Admission Plans:** Open Admission; Early Admission; Deferred Admission **Application Deadline:** Rolling **Application Fee:** $25.00 **H.S. Requirements:** High school diploma required; GED accepted **Costs Per Year:** Application fee: $25. Comprehensive fee: $12,876 includes full-time tuition ($5700), mandatory fees ($1650), and college room and board ($5526). College room only: $2810. Full-time tuition and fees vary according to program. Room and board charges vary according to board plan. Part-time tuition: $190 per credit. Part-time mandatory fees: $55 per credit. Part-time tuition and fees vary according to program. **Scholarships:** Available **Calendar System:** Semester, Summer Session Available **Enrollment:** FT 2,954, PT 1,024, Grad 426 **Faculty:** FT 79, PT 237 **Student-Faculty Ratio:** 23:1 **Exams:** SAT I and SAT II or ACT **% Receiving Financial Aid:** 69 **% Residing in College-Owned, -Operated, or -Affiliated Housing:** 3 **Library Holdings:** 93,527 **Regional Accreditation:** North Central Association of Colleges and Schools **Credit Hours For Degree:** 64 semester hours, Associates; 128 semester hours, Bachelors **Professional Accreditation:** AAMAE, AANA, AOTA, APTA, CARC, CSWE, NLN **Intercollegiate Athletics:** Basketball M; Softball W; Volleyball W

NATIONAL INSTITUTE OF TECHNOLOGY
5514 Big Tyler Rd.
Cross Lanes, WV 25313-1390
Tel: (304)776-6290; 888-741-4271
Web Site: http://www.nitschools.com/
President/CEO: John Pullen
Admissions: Karen Wilkinson
Type: Two-Year College **Sex:** Coed **Affiliation:** Corinthian Schools, Inc **Admission Plans:** Deferred Admission **Application Fee:** $0.00 **H.S. Requirements:** High school diploma required; GED accepted **Scholarships:** Available **Calendar System:** Quarter, Summer Session Not available **Enrollment:** FT 520 **Faculty:** FT 15, PT 12 **Credit Hours For Degree:** 15 units, Associates **Professional Accreditation:** ACCSCT

NEW RIVER COMMUNITY AND TECHNICAL COLLEGE
167 Dye Dr.
Beckley, WV 25801
Tel: (304)255-5821
Admissions: (304)647-6564
Web Site: http://www.nrctc.org/
President/CEO: Dr. David Perkins
Admissions: Michael Palm
Type: Two-Year College **Sex:** Coed **Faculty:** FT 23

OHIO VALLEY UNIVERSITY
One Campus View Dr.
Vienna, WV 26105-8000
Tel: (304)865-6000; 877-446-8668
Admissions: (304)865-6203
Fax: (304)865-6001
E-mail: admissions@ovu.edu
Web Site: http://www.ovu.edu/
President/CEO: Dr. Robert W. Stephens
Admissions: Rob Dudley
Financial Aid: Margie Lyons
Type: Four-Year College **Sex:** Coed **Affiliation:** Church of Christ **Scores:** 93% SAT V 400+; 95% SAT M 400+; 52% ACT 18-23; 19% ACT 24-29 **% Accepted:** 48 **Admission Plans:** Early Admission; Early Action; Deferred Admission **Application Deadline:** August 15 **Application Fee:** $20.00 **H.S. Requirements:** High school diploma required; GED accepted **Costs Per Year:** Application fee: $20. Comprehensive fee: $18,972 includes full-time tuition ($11,700), mandatory fees ($1392), and college room and board ($5880). College room only: $3080. Full-time tuition and fees vary according to course load. Room and board charges vary according to board plan. Part-time tuition: $400 per credit hour. Part-time mandatory fees: $58 per credit hour. Part-time tuition and fees vary according to course load. **Scholarships:** Available **Calendar System:** Semester, Summer Session Available **Enrollment:** FT 508, PT 34 **Faculty:** FT 25, PT 35 **Student-Faculty Ratio:** 12:1 **Exams:** SAT I and SAT II or ACT **% Receiving Financial Aid:** 78 **% Residing in College-Owned, -Operated, or -Affiliated Housing:** 60 **Library Holdings:** 34,000 **Regional Accreditation:** North Central Association of Colleges and Schools **Credit Hours For Degree:** 64 semester hours, Associates; 128 semester hours, Bachelors **ROTC:** Air Force **Intercollegiate Athletics:** Baseball M; Basketball M & W; Cheerleading W; Cross-Country Running M & W; Golf M; Soccer M & W; Softball W; Volleyball W

POTOMAC STATE COLLEGE OF WEST VIRGINIA UNIVERSITY
Fort Ave.
Keyser, WV 26726-2698
Tel: (304)788-6800
Free: 800-262-7332
Admissions: (304)788-6820
Fax: (304)788-6939
Web Site: http://www.potomacstatecollege.edu/
President/CEO: Dr. Kerry S. Odell
Registrar: Beth Little
Admissions: Beth Little
Financial Aid: Beth Little
Type: Two-Year College **Sex:** Coed **Affiliation:** West Virginia Higher Education Policy Commission **Scores:** 72% SAT V 400+; 66% SAT M 400+; 50% ACT 18-23; 9% ACT 24-29 **Admission Plans:** Open Admission; Early Admission; Deferred Admission **Application Fee:** $0.00 **H.S. Requirements:** High school diploma required; GED accepted **Costs Per Year:** Application fee: $0. State resident tuition: $2328 full-time, $98 per credit hour part-time. Nonresident tuition: $7872 full-time, $329 per credit hour part-time. Part-time tuition varies according to course load. College room and board: $4914. College room only: $2340. Room and board charges vary according to board plan and location. **Scholarships:** Available **Calendar System:** Semester, Summer Session Available **Enrollment:** FT 842, PT 488 **Faculty:** FT 35, PT 60 **Student-Faculty Ratio:** 16:1 **Exams:** SAT I or ACT **% Residing in College-Owned, -Operated, or -Affiliated Housing:** 35 **Library Holdings:** 44,197 **Regional Accreditation:** North Central Association of Colleges and Schools **Credit Hours For Degree:** 64 credit hours, Associ-

ates **Intercollegiate Athletics:** Baseball M; Basketball M & W; Golf M & W; Soccer M & W; Softball W; Volleyball W

SALEM INTERNATIONAL UNIVERSITY
223 West Main St., PO Box 500
Salem, WV 26426-0500
Tel: (304)782-5011
Free: 800-283-4562
Admissions: (304)782-5336
E-mail: admissions@salemiu.edu
Web Site: http://www.salemiu.edu/
President/CEO: Dr. Richard Ferrin
Registrar: Cynthia Calise
Admissions: Thomas White
Financial Aid: Charlotte Lake
Type: Comprehensive **Sex:** Coed **Scores:** 77% SAT V 400+; 90% SAT M 400+; 53% ACT 18-23; 17% ACT 24-29 **Admission Plans:** Deferred Admission **Application Fee:** $25.00 **H.S. Requirements:** High school diploma required; GED accepted **Scholarships:** Available **Calendar System:** Miscellaneous, Summer Session Not available **Enrollment:** FT 359, PT 84, Grad 125 **Faculty:** FT 33, PT 16 **Student-Faculty Ratio:** 14:1 **Exams:** SAT I or ACT **% Receiving Financial Aid:** 38 **% Residing in College-Owned, -Operated, or -Affiliated Housing:** 64 **Library Holdings:** 179,918 **Regional Accreditation:** North Central Association of Colleges and Schools **Credit Hours For Degree:** 64 credit hours, Associates; 128 credit hours, Bachelors **Professional Accreditation:** ACBSP **Intercollegiate Athletics:** Baseball M; Basketball M & W; Cross-Country Running M & W; Equestrian Sports M & W; Golf M; Soccer M; Softball W; Swimming and Diving M & W; Tennis M & W; Volleyball W; Water Polo M & W

SHEPHERD UNIVERSITY
PO Box 3210
Shepherdstown, WV 25443-3210
Tel: (304)876-5000
Free: 800-344-5231
Admissions: (304)876-5212
Fax: (304)876-5165
E-mail: admissions@shepherd.edu
Web Site: http://www.shepherd.edu/
President/CEO: Dr. David L. Dunlop
Registrar: Tracy Seffers
Admissions: Kimberly C. Scranage
Financial Aid: Elizabeth Sturm
Type: Comprehensive **Sex:** Coed **Affiliation:** West Virginia Higher Education Policy Commission **Scores:** 95.1% SAT V 400+; 97.79% SAT M 400+; 66.37% ACT 18-23; 28.75% ACT 24-29 **% Accepted:** 93 **Admission Plans:** Early Admission; Early Action; Deferred Admission **Application Deadline:** Rolling **Application Fee:** $35.00 **H.S. Requirements:** High school diploma required; GED accepted **Costs Per Year:** Application fee: $35. State resident tuition: $4046 full-time. Nonresident tuition: $10,618 full-time. Full-time tuition varies according to degree level, program, and reciprocity agreements. College room and board: $6020. Room and board charges vary according to board plan and housing facility. **Scholarships:** Available **Calendar System:** Semester, Summer Session Available **Enrollment:** FT 2,949, PT 860, Grad 92 **Faculty:** FT 109, PT 144 **Student-Faculty Ratio:** 21:1 **Exams:** SAT I or ACT **% Receiving Financial Aid:** 48 **% Residing in College-Owned, -Operated, or -Affiliated Housing:** 25 **Library Holdings:** 183,197 **Regional Accreditation:** North Central Association of Colleges and Schools **Credit Hours For Degree:** 128 semester hours, Bachelors **Professional Accreditation:** CSWE, NASM, NCATE, NLN **Intercollegiate Athletics:** Baseball M; Basketball M & W; Football M; Golf M; Soccer M & W; Softball W; Tennis M & W; Volleyball W

SOUTHERN WEST VIRGINIA COMMUNITY AND TECHNICAL COLLEGE
Dempsey Branch Rd., PO Box 2900
Mount Gay, WV 25637-2900
Tel: (304)792-7160
Fax: (304)792-7096
E-mail: admissions@southern.wvnet.edu
Web Site: http://www.southern.wvnet.edu/
President/CEO: Joanne Tomblin
Registrar: James P. Owens
Admissions: Roy Simmons
Financial Aid: Cindy Whitlock
Type: Two-Year College **Sex:** Coed **Affiliation:** State College System of West Virginia **% Accepted:** 100 **Admission Plans:** Open Admission; Early Admission; Deferred Admission **Application Deadline:** Rolling **Application Fee:** $0.00 **H.S. Requirements:** High school diploma required; GED accepted **Costs Per Year:** Application fee: $0. State resident tuition: $1634 full-time, $68 per credit hour part-time. Nonresident tuition: $6486 full-time, $270 per credit hour part-time. **Scholarships:** Available **Calendar System:** Semester, Summer Session Available **Enrollment:** FT 1,257, PT 725 **Faculty:** FT 66, PT 100 **Student-Faculty Ratio:** 20:1 **Library Holdings:** 70,576 **Regional Accreditation:** North Central Association of Colleges and Schools **Credit Hours For Degree:** 63 semester hours, Associates **Professional Accreditation:** ARCEST, JRCERT, NAACLS, NLN

UNIVERSITY OF CHARLESTON
2300 MacCorkle Ave., SE
Charleston, WV 25304-1099
Tel: (304)357-4800
Free: 800-995-GOUC
Admissions: (304)357-4750
Fax: (304)357-4781
E-mail: admissions@ucwv.edu
Web Site: http://www.ucwv.edu/
President/CEO: Dr. Edwin H. Welch
Registrar: Alan Belcher
Admissions: Brad Parrish
Financial Aid: Janet Ruge
Type: Comprehensive **Sex:** Coed **Scores:** 89% SAT V 400+; 86% SAT M 400+; 49% ACT 18-23; 33% ACT 24-29 **% Accepted:** 96 **Admission Plans:** Early Admission; Deferred Admission **Application Deadline:** Rolling **Application Fee:** $25.00 **H.S. Requirements:** High school diploma required; GED accepted **Costs Per Year:** Application fee: $25. Comprehensive fee: $27,600 includes full-time tuition ($20,200) and college room and board ($7400). College room only: $4175. Room and board charges vary according to board plan and housing facility. Part-time tuition: $380 per credit. Part-time mandatory fees: $75 per term. Part-time tuition and fees vary according to course load and program. **Scholarships:** Available **Calendar System:** Semester, Summer Session Available **Enrollment:** FT 852, PT 135, Grad 19 **Faculty:** FT 60, PT 39 **Student-Faculty Ratio:** 13:1 **Exams:** SAT I or ACT **% Receiving Financial Aid:** 81 **% Residing in College-Owned, -Operated, or -Affiliated Housing:** 50 **Library Holdings:** 111,264 **Regional Accreditation:** North Central Association of Colleges and Schools **Credit Hours For Degree:** 60 credit hours, Associates; 120 credit hours, Bachelors **ROTC:** Army **Professional Accreditation:** CARC, JRCERT, JRCEPAT, NCATE, NLN **Intercollegiate Athletics:** Baseball M; Basketball M & W; Cheerleading W; Crew M & W; Cross-Country Running M & W; Football M; Golf M; Soccer M & W; Softball W; Swimming and Diving M & W; Tennis M & W; Track and Field M & W; Volleyball W

VALLEY COLLEGE
287 Aikens Center
Martinsburg, WV 25401
Tel: (304)263-0979
Fax: (304)263-2413
E-mail: gkennedy@vct.edu
Web Site: http://www.valleycollege.com/
President/CEO: Anne Ganse
Admissions: Gail Kennedy
Type: Two-Year College **Sex:** Coed **Costs Per Year:** Tuition: $7200 full-time, $225 per credit part-time. **Calendar System:** Continuous **Enrollment:** FT 47 **Faculty:** FT 4, PT 2 **Student-Faculty Ratio:** 14:1 **Professional Accreditation:** ACICS

WEST LIBERTY STATE COLLEGE
PO Box 295
West Liberty, WV 26074
Tel: (304)336-5000
Free: 800-732-6204
Admissions: (304)336-8076
Fax: (304)336-8285
E-mail: wladmsn1@wlsvax.wvnet.edu
Web Site: http://www.wlsc.edu/
President/CEO: Dr. Richard H. Owens
Registrar: Scott A. Cook

Admissions: Brenda M. King
Financial Aid: Scott A. Cook
Type: Four-Year College **Sex:** Coed **Affiliation:** West Virginia Higher Education Policy Commission **Scores:** 85% SAT V 400+; 75% SAT M 400+; 54% ACT 18-23; 11% ACT 24-29 **% Accepted:** 98 **Application Fee:** $0.00 **H.S. Requirements:** High school diploma required; GED accepted **Costs Per Year:** Application fee: $0. State resident tuition: $3686 full-time. Nonresident tuition: $9054 full-time. Mandatory fees: $50 full-time. College room and board: $5456. Room and board charges vary according to board plan and housing facility. **Scholarships:** Available **Calendar System:** Semester, Summer Session Available **Enrollment:** FT 1,974, PT 267, Grad 5 **Faculty:** FT 100, PT 61 **Student-Faculty Ratio:** 17:1 **Exams:** SAT I or ACT **% Receiving Financial Aid:** 67 **% Residing in College-Owned, -Operated, or -Affiliated Housing:** 45 **Library Holdings:** 194,715 **Regional Accreditation:** North Central Association of Colleges and Schools **Credit Hours For Degree:** 77 semester hours, Associates; 128 semester hours, Bachelors **Professional Accreditation:** ADA, NAACLS, NASM, NCATE, NLN **Intercollegiate Athletics:** Baseball M; Basketball M & W; Cross-Country Running M & W; Football M; Golf M & W; Softball W; Tennis M & W; Track and Field M & W; Volleyball W; Wrestling M

WEST VIRGINIA BUSINESS COLLEGE (NUTTER FORT)

116 Pennsylvania Ave.
Nutter Fort, WV 26301
Tel: (304)624-7695
Fax: (304)622-2149
Web Site: http://www.stratuswave.com/~wvbc/ **Type:** Two-Year College **Sex:** Coed **Professional Accreditation:** ACICS

WEST VIRGINIA BUSINESS COLLEGE (WHEELING)

1052 Main St.
Wheeling, WV 26003
Tel: (304)232-0361
Fax: (304)232-0363
Web Site: http://www.stratuswave.com/~wvbc/
President/CEO: Teddy Tarr
Admissions: Karen D. Shaw
Financial Aid: Brenda Mathers
Type: Two-Year College **Sex:** Coed **% Accepted:** 100 **Costs Per Year:** Tuition: $15,500 per degree program. **Scholarships:** Available **Calendar System:** Quarter **Faculty:** FT 0, PT 10 **Student-Faculty Ratio:** 6:1 **Professional Accreditation:** ACICS

WEST VIRGINIA JUNIOR COLLEGE (BRIDGEPORT)

176 Thompson Dr.
Bridgeport, WV 26330
Tel: (304)363-8824
Web Site: http://www.wvjc.com/
President/CEO: Sharon Stephens
Registrar: Delores Farend
Admissions: Rosemary Liberto
Financial Aid: Regina Murphy
Type: Two-Year College **Sex:** Coed **Admission Plans:** Open Admission; Deferred Admission **H.S. Requirements:** High school diploma required; GED accepted **Scholarships:** Available **Calendar System:** Quarter, Summer Session Available **Faculty:** FT 7, PT 0 **Library Holdings:** 550 **Credit Hours For Degree:** 98 quarter hours, Associates **Professional Accreditation:** ACICS

WEST VIRGINIA JUNIOR COLLEGE (CHARLESTON)

1000 Virginia St. East
Charleston, WV 25301-2817
Tel: (304)345-2820
Web Site: http://www.wvjc.com/
President/CEO: Thomas Crouse
Registrar: Jennifer Bias
Admissions: Thomas Crouse
Financial Aid: Bonnie Shumate
Type: Two-Year College **Sex:** Coed **Admission Plans:** Open Admission; Early Admission; Deferred Admission **H.S. Requirements:** High school diploma required; GED accepted **Calendar System:** Quarter, Summer Session Available **Library Holdings:** 1,300 **Credit Hours For Degree:** 90 quarter hours, Associates **Professional Accreditation:** ACICS

WEST VIRGINIA JUNIOR COLLEGE (MORGANTOWN)

148 Willey St.
Morgantown, WV 26505-5521
Tel: (304)296-8282
Web Site: http://www.wvjc.com/
President/CEO: Stephen A. Callen
Registrar: Patricia Callen
Admissions: Patricia A. Callen
Financial Aid: Patricia Callen
Type: Two-Year College **Sex:** Coed **Admission Plans:** Open Admission **H.S. Requirements:** High school diploma required; GED accepted **Calendar System:** Quarter **Faculty:** FT 7, PT 5 **Student-Faculty Ratio:** 14:1 **Credit Hours For Degree:** 92 quarter hours, Associates **Professional Accreditation:** ACICS

WEST VIRGINIA NORTHERN COMMUNITY COLLEGE

1704 Market St.
Wheeling, WV 26003-3699
Tel: (304)233-5900
Fax: (304)233-5900
Web Site: http://www.northern.wvnet.edu/
President/CEO: Dr. John Hunter
Admissions: Janet Fike
Financial Aid: Cindy Hudak
Type: Two-Year College **Sex:** Coed **Scores:** 77.8% SAT V 400+; 77.8% SAT M 400+; 53.4% ACT 18-23; 6.8% ACT 24-29 **% Accepted:** 53 **Admission Plans:** Open Admission; Early Admission; Deferred Admission **Application Deadline:** Rolling **H.S. Requirements:** High school diploma required; GED accepted **Costs Per Year:** State resident tuition: $1752 full-time, $73 per credit part-time. Nonresident tuition: $5592 full-time, $233 per credit part-time. Full-time tuition varies according to course load and reciprocity agreements. Part-time tuition varies according to course load and reciprocity agreements. **Scholarships:** Available **Calendar System:** Semester, Summer Session Available **Enrollment:** FT 1,421, PT 1,421 **Faculty:** FT 55, PT 95 **Student-Faculty Ratio:** 19:1 **Library Holdings:** 36,650 **Regional Accreditation:** North Central Association of Colleges and Schools **Credit Hours For Degree:** 60 credit hours, Associates **Professional Accreditation:** ARCEST, ACF, AHIMA, CARC, NAACLS, NLN

WEST VIRGINIA STATE COMMUNITY AND TECHNICAL COLLEGE

Thomas W. Cole, Jr., Complex
PO Box 1000
Institute, WV 25112
Tel: (304)766-3118
Free: 800-987-2112
Admissions: (304)766-3033
Web Site: http://fozzy.wvsc.edu/ctc/index.html
Admissions: Tyreno N. Sowell, Sr.
Type: Two-Year College **Sex:** Coed **Costs Per Year:** State resident tuition: $3222 full-time, $110 per credit hour part-time. Nonresident tuition: $7400 full-time, $294 per credit hour part-time. Full-time tuition varies according to class time, course level, and program. College room and board: $4720. College room only: $2200. Room and board charges vary according to board plan and housing facility. **Faculty:** FT 26, PT 67 **Professional Accreditation:** JRCNMT

WEST VIRGINIA STATE UNIVERSITY

Post Office Box 1000
Institute, WV 25112-1000
Tel: (304)766-3000
Free: 800-987-2112
Admissions: (304)766-3221
Fax: (304)766-4158
E-mail: sowell@wvstateu.edu
Web Site: http://www.wvstateu.edu/
President/CEO: Dr. Hazo W. Carter, Jr.
Registrar: Dr. John L. Fuller
Admissions: Tryreno Sowell, Sr.
Financial Aid: Mary E. Blizzard
Type: Comprehensive **Sex:** Coed **Affiliation:** State College System of West Virginia **% Accepted:** 50 **Admission Plans:** Early Admission **Application Deadline:** August 11 **Application Fee:** $0.00 **H.S. Requirements:** High school diploma required; GED accepted **Costs Per Year:** Application fee: $0. State resident tuition: $3528 full-time, $147 per credit hour part-time. Nonresident tuition: $8104 full-time, $338 per credit hour part-time. Full-time tuition varies according to program. Part-time tuition varies according to course load and program. College room and board: $4850. College room only: $2200. Room and board charges vary according to board plan and

housing facility. **Scholarships:** Available **Calendar System:** Semester, Summer Session Available **Enrollment:** FT 2,396, PT 1,059, Grad 36 **Faculty:** FT 120, PT 74 **Student-Faculty Ratio:** 23:1 **Exams:** SAT I or ACT, SAT I **% Residing in College-Owned, -Operated, or -Affiliated Housing:** 7 **Library Holdings:** 228,026 **Regional Accreditation:** North Central Association of Colleges and Schools **Credit Hours For Degree:** 120 semester hours, Bachelors **ROTC:** Army **Professional Accreditation:** ABET, CSWE, NCATE, NRPA **Intercollegiate Athletics:** Baseball M; Basketball M & W; Cross-Country Running M & W; Football M; Golf W; Softball W; Tennis M & W; Track and Field M & W; Volleyball W

WEST VIRGINIA UNIVERSITY
University Ave.
Morgantown, WV 26506
Tel: (304)293-0111
Free: 800-344-9881
Admissions: (304)293-2121
Fax: (304)293-3080
E-mail: wvuinfo@wvnvm.wvnet.edu
Web Site: http://www.wvu.edu/
President/CEO: David C. Hardesty, Jr.
Registrar: Steve A. Taylor
Admissions: Cheng H. Khoo
Financial Aid: Kaye C. Widney
Type: University **Sex:** Coed **Affiliation:** West Virginia Higher Education Policy Commission **Scores:** 97.2% SAT V 400+; 97.8% SAT M 400+; 49.3% ACT 18-23; 38% ACT 24-29 **% Accepted:** 92 **Admission Plans:** Preferred Admission; Early Admission; Deferred Admission **Application Deadline:** August 01 **Application Fee:** $25.00 **H.S. Requirements:** High school diploma required; GED accepted **Costs Per Year:** Application fee: $25. State resident tuition: $4164 full-time, $176 per credit hour part-time. Nonresident tuition: $12,874 full-time, $538 per credit hour part-time. Full-time tuition varies according to location, program, and reciprocity agreements. Part-time tuition varies according to course load, location, program, and reciprocity agreements. College room and board: $6342. College room only: $3348. Room and board charges vary according to board plan, housing facility, and location. **Scholarships:** Available **Calendar System:** Semester, Summer Session Available **Enrollment:** FT 18,449, PT 1,061, Grad 5,151 **Faculty:** FT 785, PT 335 **Student-Faculty Ratio:** 22:1 **Exams:** SAT I or ACT **% Receiving Financial Aid:** 50 **% Residing in College-Owned, -Operated, or -Affiliated Housing:** 26 **Library Holdings:** 1,741,627 **Regional Accreditation:** North Central Association of Colleges and Schools **Credit Hours For Degree:** 128 credit hours, Bachelors **ROTC:** Army, Air Force **Professional Accreditation:** AACSB, ABET, ACEJMC, AACN, ABA, ACPhE, ACA, ADA, ADtA, AOTA, APTA, APA, ASLA, ASLHA, ACIPE, AALS, CEPH, CORE, CSWE, FIDER JRCEPAT, LCMEAMA, NAACLS, NASAD. NASM, NASPAA, NAST, NCATE, NRPA, SAF **Intercollegiate Athletics:** Baseball M; Basketball M & W; Cheerleading M & W; Crew W; Cross-Country Running W; Football M; Gymnastics W; Riflery M & W; Soccer M & W; Swimming and Diving M & W; Tennis W; Track and Field W; Volleyball W; Wrestling M

WEST VIRGINIA UNIVERSITY INSTITUTE OF TECHNOLOGY
405 Fayette Pike
Montgomery, WV 25136
Tel: (304)442-3071; 888-554-8324
Admissions: (304)442-3167
Fax: (304)442-3097
E-mail: wvutech@wvit.wvnet.edu
Web Site: http://www.wvutech.edu/
President/CEO: Dr. Galan Janeksela
Registrar: Lisa Graham
Admissions: Lisa Graham
Financial Aid: Nina Morton
Type: Comprehensive **Sex:** Coed **Affiliation:** University System of West Virginia **Scores:** 75% SAT V 400+; 82% SAT M 400+; 55% ACT 18-23; 14% ACT 24-29 **Admission Plans:** Open Admission; Early Admission **H.S. Requirements:** High school diploma required; GED accepted **Scholarships:** Available **Calendar System:** Semester, Summer Session Available **Enrollment:** FT 1,702, PT 733, Grad 33 **Faculty:** FT 119, PT 57 **Student-Faculty Ratio:** 16:1 **Exams:** SAT I or ACT **% Receiving Financial Aid:** 54 **% Residing in College-Owned, -Operated, or -Affiliated Housing:** 26 **Library Holdings:** 166,292 **Regional Accreditation:** North Central Association of Colleges and Schools **Credit Hours For Degree:** 64 semester hours, Associates; 128 semester hours, Bachelors **ROTC:** Army **Professional Accreditation:** ABET, ADA, CARC **Intercollegiate Athletics:** Baseball M; Basketball M & W; Football M; Golf M; Softball W; Tennis M & W; Volleyball W

WEST VIRGINIA UNIVERSITY AT PARKERSBURG
300 Campus Dr.
Parkersburg, WV 26104-8647
Tel: (304)424-8000
Admissions: (304)424-8222
Web Site: http://www.wvup.edu/
President/CEO: Dr. Marie Foster Gnage
Admissions: Cecelia Malhotra
Financial Aid: August Kafer
Type: Two-Year College **Sex:** Coed **Affiliation:** West Virginia University **Scores:** 95% SAT V 400+; 80% SAT M 400+; 45% ACT 18-23; 9% ACT 24-29 **Admission Plans:** Open Admission; Early Admission; Deferred Admission **Application Fee:** $0.00 **H.S. Requirements:** High school diploma required; GED accepted **Costs Per Year:** Application fee: $0. State resident tuition: $2280 full-time, $95 per credit hour part-time. Nonresident tuition: $6024 full-time, $251 per credit hour part-time. Full-time tuition varies according to degree level and reciprocity agreements. Part-time tuition varies according to degree level and reciprocity agreements. **Calendar System:** Semester, Summer Session Available **Enrollment:** FT 2,148, PT 1,574 **Faculty:** FT 85, PT 124 **Student-Faculty Ratio:** 20:1 **Exams:** ACT **Library Holdings:** 41,300 **Regional Accreditation:** North Central Association of Colleges and Schools **Credit Hours For Degree:** 64 credit hours, Associates; 128 credit hours, Bachelors **ROTC:** Army **Professional Accreditation:** NCATE, NLN

WEST VIRGINIA WESLEYAN COLLEGE
59 College Ave.
Buckhannon, WV 26201
Tel: (304)473-8000
Free: 800-722-9933
Fax: (304)472-2571
Web Site: http://www.wvwc.edu/
President/CEO: William R. Haden
Registrar: Linda W. Winspear
Financial Aid: Robert N. Skinner
Type: Comprehensive **Sex:** Coed **Affiliation:** United Methodist Church **Scores:** 95% SAT V 400+; 93.4% SAT M 400+; 53% ACT 18-23; 39% ACT 24-29 **% Accepted:** 77 **Admission Plans:** Early Action; Early Decision Plan; Deferred Admission **Application Deadline:** July 01 **Application Fee:** $35.00 **H.S. Requirements:** High school diploma required; GED accepted **Costs Per Year:** Application fee: $35. Comprehensive fee: $26,800 includes full-time tuition ($20,250), mandatory fees ($1000), and college room and board ($5550). Full-time tuition and fees vary according to course load. Room and board charges vary according to board plan and housing facility. **Scholarships:** Available **Calendar System:** Semester, Summer Session Available **Enrollment:** FT 1,332, PT 34, Grad 42 **Faculty:** FT 80, PT 80 **Student-Faculty Ratio:** 13:1 **Exams:** SAT I or ACT, SAT II **% Receiving Financial Aid:** 74 **% Residing in College-Owned, -Operated, or -Affiliated Housing:** 80 **Library Holdings:** 91,061 **Regional Accreditation:** North Central Association of Colleges and Schools **Credit Hours For Degree:** 120 credit hours, Bachelors **Professional Accreditation:** AAFCS, JRCEPAT, NASM, NCATE, NLN **Intercollegiate Athletics:** Baseball M; Basketball M & W; Cheerleading M & W; Cross-Country Running M & W; Football M; Golf M; Lacrosse M & W; Soccer M & W; Softball W; Swimming and Diving M & W; Tennis M & W; Track and Field M & W; Volleyball W

WHEELING JESUIT UNIVERSITY
316 Washington Ave.
Wheeling, WV 26003-6295
Tel: (304)243-2000
Free: 800-624-6992
Fax: (304)243-2397
E-mail: admis@wju.edu
Web Site: http://www.wju.edu/
President/CEO: Fr. Joseph Hacala, SJ
Registrar: Chad Carter
Admissions: Carol Descak
Financial Aid: Christie Tomczyk
Type: Comprehensive **Sex:** Coed **Affiliation:** Roman Catholic (Jesuit) **Scores:** 94.3% SAT V 400+; 95% SAT M 400+; 55% ACT 18-23; 35% ACT 24-29 **Admission Plans:** Early Admission; Deferred Admission **Application Fee:** $25.00 **H.S. Requirements:** High school diploma required; GED ac-

cepted **Costs Per Year:** Application fee: $25. Comprehensive fee: $27,800 includes full-time tuition ($20,890), mandatory fees ($460), and college room and board ($6450). College room only: $3070. Full-time tuition and fees vary according to course load and program. Room and board charges vary according to board plan, gender, and housing facility. Part-time tuition: $540 per credit hour. Part-time mandatory fees: $465 per term. Part-time tuition and fees vary according to class time and program. **Scholarships:** Available **Calendar System:** Semester, Summer Session Available **Enrollment:** FT 1,049, PT 183, Grad 374 **Faculty:** FT 72, PT 2 **Student-Faculty Ratio:** 13:1 **Exams:** SAT I or ACT **% Receiving Financial Aid:** 77 **% Residing in College-Owned, -Operated, or -Affiliated Housing:** 78 **Library Holdings:** 153,590 **Regional Accreditation:** North Central Association of Colleges and Schools **Credit Hours For Degree:** 120 credit hours, Bachelors **Professional Accreditation:** AACN, APTA, ACBSP, CARC, JRCNMT **Intercollegiate Athletics:** Baseball M; Basketball M & W; Cheerleading M & W; Cross-Country Running M & W; Golf M & W; Lacrosse M; Soccer M & W; Softball W; Swimming and Diving M & W; Track and Field M & W; Volleyball W

ALVERNO COLLEGE
3400 South 43rd St., PO Box 343922
Milwaukee, WI 53234-3922
Tel: (414)382-6000
Free: 800-933-3401
Admissions: (414)382-6031
Fax: (414)382-6354
E-mail: admissions@alverno.edu
Web Site: http://www.alverno.edu/
President/CEO: Dr. Mary Meehan
Registrar: Patricia Hartmann
Admissions: Mary Kay Farrell
Financial Aid: Mark Levine
Type: Comprehensive **Affiliation:** Roman Catholic **Scores:** 56.11% ACT 18-23; 14.48% ACT 24-29 **% Accepted:** 56 **Admission Plans:** Deferred Admission **Application Deadline:** Rolling **Application Fee:** $20.00 **H.S. Requirements:** High school diploma required; GED accepted **Costs Per Year:** Application fee: $20. Comprehensive fee: $21,628 includes full-time tuition ($15,168), mandatory fees ($250), and college room and board ($6210). College room only: $2100. Full-time tuition and fees vary according to class time and program. Room and board charges vary according to board plan and housing facility. Part-time tuition: $632 per credit. Part-time mandatory fees: $125 per term. Part-time tuition and fees vary according to class time and program. **Scholarships:** Available **Calendar System:** Semester, Summer Session Available **Enrollment:** FT 1,515, PT 661, Grad 196 **Faculty:** FT 104, PT 121 **Student-Faculty Ratio:** 12:1 **Exams:** SAT I or ACT **% Residing in College-Owned, -Operated, or -Affiliated Housing:** 10 **Library Holdings:** 82,416 **Regional Accreditation:** North Central Association of Colleges and Schools **Credit Hours For Degree:** 32 units, Associates; 40 units, Bachelors **ROTC:** Army, Air Force **Professional Accreditation:** AACN, NASM, NCATE **Intercollegiate Athletics:** Basketball W; Cross-Country Running W; Soccer W; Softball W; Volleyball W

BELLIN COLLEGE OF NURSING
725 South Webster Ave, PO Box 23400
Green Bay, WI 54305-3400
Tel: (920)433-3560
Free: 800-236-8707
Admissions: (920)433-5803
Fax: (920)433-7416
Web Site: http://www.bcon.edu/
President/CEO: Dr. V. Jane Muhl
Registrar: Nancy Norman
Admissions: Dr. Penny Croghan
Financial Aid: Lena Terry
Type: Four-Year College **Sex:** Coed **Affiliation:** Bellin Health System **Scores:** 60% ACT 18-23; 37% ACT 24-29 **Application Fee:** $30.00 **H.S. Requirements:** High school diploma required; GED accepted **Costs Per Year:** Application fee: $30. Tuition: $14,500 full-time, $684 per credit part-time. Mandatory fees: $268 full-time. Full-time tuition and fees vary according to course level. Part-time tuition varies according to course load. **Scholarships:** Available **Calendar System:** Semester, Summer Session Available **Enrollment:** FT 181, PT 35, Grad 23 **Faculty:** FT 18, PT 2 **Student-Faculty Ratio:** 11:1 **Exams:** ACT **% Receiving Financial Aid:** 54 **Library Holdings:** 7,000 **Regional Accreditation:** North Central Association of Colleges and Schools **Credit Hours For Degree:** 129 credits, Bachelors **ROTC:** Army **Professional Accreditation:** AACN, NLN

BELOIT COLLEGE
700 College St.
Beloit, WI 53511-5596
Tel: (608)363-2000
Free: 800-9-BELOIT
Admissions: (608)363-2380
Fax: (608)363-2075
E-mail: admiss@beloit.edu
Web Site: http://www.beloit.edu/
President/CEO: Dr. John E. Burris
Registrar: Mary Boros-Kazai
Admissions: Nancy Monnich Benedict
Financial Aid: Jane H. Hessian
Type: Four-Year College **Sex:** Coed **Scores:** 100% SAT V 400+; 100% SAT M 400+; 14% ACT 18-23; 63% ACT 24-29 **% Accepted:** 64 **Admission Plans:** Early Admission; Early Action; Deferred Admission **Application Deadline:** January 15 **Application Fee:** $35.00 **H.S. Requirements:** High school diploma required; GED accepted **Costs Per Year:** Application fee: $35. Comprehensive fee: $32,808 includes full-time tuition ($26,664), mandatory fees ($220), and college room and board ($5924). College room only: $2890. Room and board charges vary according to board plan. Part-time tuition: $3334 per course. **Scholarships:** Available **Calendar System:** Semester, Summer Session Available **Enrollment:** FT 1,330, PT 55 **Faculty:** FT 103, PT 24 **Student-Faculty Ratio:** 11:1 **Exams:** SAT I or ACT **% Receiving Financial Aid:** 77 **% Residing in College-Owned, -Operated, or -Affiliated Housing:** 93 **Library Holdings:** 183,736 **Regional Accreditation:** North Central Association of Colleges and Schools **Credit Hours For Degree:** 31 units, Bachelors **Intercollegiate Athletics:** Baseball M; Basketball M & W; Crew M & W; Cross-Country Running M & W; Fencing M & W; Football M; Golf M & W; Ice Hockey M & W; Lacrosse M & W; Soccer M & W; Softball W; Swimming and Diving M & W; Tennis M & W; Track and Field M & W; Volleyball W

BLACKHAWK TECHNICAL COLLEGE
PO Box 5009
Janesville, WI 53547-5009
Tel: (608)758-6900
Free: 800-472-0024
Admissions: (608)757-7713
Fax: (608)757-9407
Web Site: http://www.blackhawk.edu/
President/CEO: Dr. Eric A. Larson
Registrar: Connie Richards
Admissions: Barbara Erlandson
Financial Aid: Burdette Richter
Type: Two-Year College **Sex:** Coed **Affiliation:** Wisconsin Technical College System **Admission Plans:** Open Admission; Preferred Admission **Application Fee:** $30.00 **H.S. Requirements:** High school diploma required; GED accepted **Scholarships:** Available **Calendar System:** Semester, Summer Session Available **Enrollment:** FT 1,015, PT 1,612 **Faculty:** FT 91, PT 250 **Library Holdings:** 25,000 **Regional Accreditation:** North Central Associa-

tion of Colleges and Schools **Credit Hours For Degree:** 65 credits, Associates **Professional Accreditation:** ACF, ADA, APTA, JRCERT, NLN

BRYANT AND STRATTON COLLEGE
1300 North Jackson St.
Milwaukee, WI 53202-2608
Tel: (414)276-5200
Web Site: http://www.bryantstratton.edu/
President/CEO: Peter J. Pavone
Registrar: Kate Rebholz
Admissions: Kathryn Cotey
Type: Two-Year College **Sex:** Coed **Affiliation:** Bryant and Stratton Business Institute, Inc **% Accepted:** 83 **Application Deadline:** Rolling **H.S. Requirements:** High school diploma required; GED accepted. For applicants 19 or older who meet entrance testing requirement: High school diploma or equivalent not required **Costs Per Year:** Tuition: $18,675 full-time, $415 per credit hour part-time. Mandatory fees: $25 full-time. **Scholarships:** Available **Calendar System:** Semester, Summer Session Available **Enrollment:** FT 351, PT 137 **Faculty:** FT 19, PT 83 **Student-Faculty Ratio:** 10:1 **Exams:** Other, SAT I or ACT **Regional Accreditation:** Middle State Association of Colleges and Schools **Credit Hours For Degree:** 60 semester hours, Associates; 120 semester hours, Bachelors **Professional Accreditation:** AAMAE

BRYANT AND STRATTON COLLEGE, WAUWATOSA CAMPUS
10950 W. Potter Rd.
Wauwatosa, WI 53226
Tel: (414)302-7000
Web Site: http://www.byrantstratton.edu/
Admissions: Cori Prohaska
Type: Four-Year College **Sex:** Coed **Application Deadline:** Rolling **Costs Per Year:** Tuition: $18,675 full-time, $415 per credit hour part-time. Mandatory fees: $25 full-time. **Calendar System:** Semester **Enrollment:** FT 282, PT 92 **Student-Faculty Ratio:** 10:1 **Exams:** Other, SAT I or ACT

CARDINAL STRITCH UNIVERSITY
6801 North Yates Rd.
Milwaukee, WI 53217-3985
Tel: (414)410-4000
Free: 800-347-8822
Admissions: (414)410-4040
Fax: (414)410-4239
Web Site: http://www.stritch.edu/
President/CEO: Sr. Mary Lea Schneider
Registrar: Rhonda Holland
Admissions: David Wegener
Financial Aid: John Mueller
Type: Comprehensive **Sex:** Coed **Affiliation:** Roman Catholic **Scores:** 100% SAT V 400+; 90% SAT M 400+; 54% ACT 18-23; 29.2% ACT 24-29 **Admission Plans:** Deferred Admission **Application Fee:** $25.00 **H.S. Requirements:** High school diploma required; GED accepted **Costs Per Year:** Application fee: $25. Comprehensive fee: $22,260 includes full-time tuition ($16,480), mandatory fees ($350), and college room and board ($5430). Part-time tuition: $515 per credit. Part-time mandatory fees: $125 per term. **Scholarships:** Available **Calendar System:** Semester, Summer Session Available **Enrollment:** FT 2,936, PT 315, Grad 3,534 **Faculty:** FT 106, PT 774 **Student-Faculty Ratio:** 18:1 **Exams:** ACT, SAT I or ACT **% Receiving Financial Aid:** 70 **% Residing in College-Owned, -Operated, or -Affiliated Housing:** 5 **Library Holdings:** 124,897 **Regional Accreditation:** North Central Association of Colleges and Schools **Credit Hours For Degree:** 64 credits, Associates; 128 credits, Bachelors **Professional Accreditation:** AACN, ACBSP, NCATE, NLN **Intercollegiate Athletics:** Baseball M; Basketball M & W; Cross-Country Running M & W; Soccer M & W; Softball W; Volleyball M & W

CARROLL COLLEGE
100 North East Ave.
Waukesha, WI 53186-5593
Tel: (262)547-1211
Free: 800-CAR-ROLL
Admissions: (262)524-7221
Fax: (262)524-7139
E-mail: cc.info@ccadmin.cc.edu
Web Site: http://www.cc.edu/
President/CEO: Dr. Frank Falcone
Registrar: Brian C. Boyd
Admissions: James Wiseman
Financial Aid: Dawn Thomas
Type: Comprehensive **Sex:** Coed **Affiliation:** Presbyterian **Scores:** 57% ACT 18-23; 33% ACT 24-29 **% Accepted:** 79 **Admission Plans:** Early Admission; Deferred Admission **Application Deadline:** Rolling **Application Fee:** $0.00 **H.S. Requirements:** High school diploma required; GED accepted **Costs Per Year:** Application fee: $0. Comprehensive fee: $25,980 includes full-time tuition ($19,500), mandatory fees ($410), and college room and board ($6070). College room only: $3300. Part-time tuition: $235 per credit. **Scholarships:** Available **Calendar System:** Semester, Summer Session Available **Enrollment:** FT 2,314, PT 568, Grad 241 **Faculty:** FT 103, PT 140 **Student-Faculty Ratio:** 17:1 **Exams:** SAT I and SAT II or ACT **% Receiving Financial Aid:** 75 **% Residing in College-Owned, -Operated, or -Affiliated Housing:** 54 **Library Holdings:** 200,000 **Regional Accreditation:** North Central Association of Colleges and Schools **Credit Hours For Degree:** 128 semester hours, Bachelors **ROTC:** Air Force **Professional Accreditation:** APTA **Intercollegiate Athletics:** Baseball M; Basketball M & W; Cross-Country Running M & W; Football M; Golf M & W; Soccer M & W; Softball W; Swimming and Diving M & W; Tennis M & W; Track and Field M & W; Volleyball W

CARTHAGE COLLEGE
2001 Alford Park Dr.
Kenosha, WI 53140
Tel: (262)551-8500
Free: 800-351-4058
Admissions: (262)551-5850
Fax: (262)551-5762
E-mail: admissions@carthage.edu
Web Site: http://www.carthage.edu/
President/CEO: Dr. F. Gregory Campbell
Registrar: Michele Bonn
Admissions: Brenda Poggendorf
Financial Aid: William Henderson
Type: Comprehensive **Sex:** Coed **Affiliation:** Evangelical Lutheran Church in America **% Accepted:** 76 **Admission Plans:** Early Admission; Early Action; Deferred Admission **Application Deadline:** Rolling **Application Fee:** $25.00 **H.S. Requirements:** High school diploma required; GED accepted **Costs Per Year:** Application fee: $25. Comprehensive fee: $30,450 includes full-time tuition ($23,650) and college room and board ($6800). Part-time tuition: $345 per credit hour. **Scholarships:** Available **Calendar System:** 4-1-4, Summer Session Available **Enrollment:** FT 2,145, PT 449, Grad 105 **Faculty:** FT 125, PT 85 **Student-Faculty Ratio:** 15:1 **Exams:** SAT I or ACT **% Receiving Financial Aid:** 72 **% Residing in College-Owned, -Operated, or -Affiliated Housing:** 68 **Library Holdings:** 128,551 **Regional Accreditation:** North Central Association of Colleges and Schools **Credit Hours For Degree:** 138 credit hours, Bachelors **ROTC:** Army, Air Force **Professional Accreditation:** CSWE, NASM **Intercollegiate Athletics:** Baseball M; Basketball M & W; Bowling W; Cross-Country Running M & W; Football M; Golf M & W; Ice Hockey M; Soccer M & W; Softball W; Swimming and Diving M & W; Tennis M & W; Track and Field M & W; Volleyball M & W; Water Polo W

CHIPPEWA VALLEY TECHNICAL COLLEGE
620 West Clairemont Ave.
Eau Claire, WI 54701-6162
Tel: (715)833-6200
Free: 800-547-2882
Admissions: (715)833-6245
Fax: (715)833-6470
Web Site: http://www.cvtc.edu/
President/CEO: Dr. William A. Ihlenfeldt
Registrar: Sylvia Bare
Admissions: Timothy Shepardson
Financial Aid: Mary Gorud
Type: Two-Year College **Sex:** Coed **Affiliation:** Wisconsin Technical College System **Admission Plans:** Open Admission; Early Admission; Deferred Admission **Application Fee:** $30.00 **H.S. Requirements:** High school diploma required; GED accepted **Scholarships:** Available **Calendar System:** Semester, Summer Session Available **Faculty:** FT 350, PT 50 **Student-Faculty Ratio:** 12:1 **Exams:** ACT, Other **Library Holdings:** 34,000 **Regional Accreditation:** North Central Association of Colleges and Schools **Credit Hours For Degree:** 70 credits, Associates **Professional Accredita-**

tion: AHIMA, JRCEDMS, JRCERT, NAACLS, NLN

COLLEGE OF MENOMINEE NATION
PO Box 1179
Keshena, WI 54135
Tel: (715)799-5600
Fax: (715)799-1308
Web Site: http://www.menominee.edu/
President/CEO: Dr. Verna M. Fowler
Registrar: Juanita Wilber
Admissions: Cynthia Norton
Financial Aid: Joelle Fisher
Type: Two-Year College **Sex:** Coed **Admission Plans:** Open Admission **Application Fee:** $10.00 **H.S. Requirements:** High school diploma required; GED accepted **Scholarships:** Available **Calendar System:** Semester **Enrollment:** FT 206, PT 293 **Faculty:** FT 14 **Exams:** Other **Regional Accreditation:** North Central Association of Colleges and Schools **Credit Hours For Degree:** 62 credits, Associates

COLUMBIA COLLEGE OF NURSING
2121 East Newport Ave.
Milwaukee, WI 53211-2952
Tel: (414)961-3530
Free: 800-321-6265
Admissions: (414)256-1219
Web Site: http://www.ccon.edu/
President/CEO: Katherine H. Dimmock, JD, RN
Admissions: Amy Dobson
Type: Four-Year College **Sex:** Coed **Scores:** 62% ACT 18-23; 34% ACT 24-29 **Application Fee:** $25.00 **H.S. Requirements:** High school diploma required; GED accepted **Costs Per Year:** Application fee: $25. Comprehensive fee: $21,375 includes full-time tuition ($15,975), mandatory fees ($1200), and college room and board ($4200). College room only: $3200. Room and board charges vary according to board plan, housing facility, location, and student level. Part-time tuition: $466 per credit hour. Part-time tuition varies according to program. **Scholarships:** Available **Calendar System:** Semester, Summer Session Available **Enrollment:** FT 243, PT 17 **Faculty:** FT 13, PT 5 **Student-Faculty Ratio:** 15:1 **Exams:** SAT I or ACT **% Receiving Financial Aid:** 73 **% Residing in College-Owned, -Operated, or -Affiliated Housing:** 1 **Library Holdings:** 9,060 **Regional Accreditation:** North Central Association of Colleges and Schools **Credit Hours For Degree:** 131 credits, Bachelors **Professional Accreditation:** NLN

CONCORDIA UNIVERSITY WISCONSIN
12800 North Lake Shore Dr.
Mequon, WI 53097-2402
Tel: (262)243-5700; 888-628-9472
Admissions: (262)243-4305
Fax: (262)243-4351
E-mail: kgaschk@cuw.edu
Web Site: http://www.cuw.edu/
President/CEO: Rev. Dr. Patrick T. Ferry
Registrar: Dr. Martin C. Duchow
Admissions: Kenneth Gaschk
Financial Aid: Carol Masse
Type: Comprehensive **Sex:** Coed **Affiliation:** Lutheran Church–Missouri Synod **% Accepted:** 84 **Admission Plans:** Deferred Admission **Application Deadline:** August 15 **Application Fee:** $35.00 **H.S. Requirements:** High school diploma required; GED accepted **Costs Per Year:** Application fee: $35. Comprehensive fee: $23,820 includes full-time tuition ($17,190), mandatory fees ($90), and college room and board ($6540). Full-time tuition and fees vary according to program. Room and board charges vary according to board plan. Part-time tuition: $716 per credit hour. Part-time tuition varies according to class time and program. Tuition guaranteed not to increase for student's term of enrollment. **Scholarships:** Available **Calendar System:** 4-1-4, Summer Session Available **Enrollment:** FT 2,007, PT 1,975, Grad 1,436 **Faculty:** FT 89, PT 110 **Student-Faculty Ratio:** 18:1 **Exams:** ACT **% Receiving Financial Aid:** 77 **% Residing in College-Owned, -Operated, or -Affiliated Housing:** 78 **Library Holdings:** 365,314 **Regional Accreditation:** North Central Association of Colleges and Schools **Credit Hours For Degree:** 126 credit hours, Bachelors **Professional Accreditation:** AACN, AOTA, APTA, CSWE **Intercollegiate Athletics:** Baseball M; Basketball M & W; Cross-Country Running M & W; Football M; Golf M & W; Soccer M & W; Softball W; Tennis M & W; Track and Field M & W; Volleyball W; Wrestling M

DEVRY UNIVERSITY (MILWAUKEE)
100 East Wisconsin Ave., Ste. 2550
Milwaukee, WI 53202-4107
Tel: (414)278-7677; (866)683-3879
Fax: (414)278-0137
Web Site: http://www.devry.edu/ **Type:** Comprehensive **Sex:** Coed **Affiliation:** DeVry University **Admission Plans:** Deferred Admission **Application Deadline:** Rolling **Application Fee:** $50.00 **H.S. Requirements:** High school diploma required; GED accepted **Costs Per Year:** Application fee: $50. One-time mandatory fee: $40. Tuition: $11,890 full-time, $445 per credit part-time. Mandatory fees: $30 full-time, $30 per year part-time. **Calendar System:** Semester, Summer Session Available **Enrollment:** FT 28, PT 46, Grad 142 **Faculty:** FT 1, PT 16 **Student-Faculty Ratio:** 7:1 **Regional Accreditation:** North Central Association of Colleges and Schools **Credit Hours For Degree:** 122 credits, Bachelors

DEVRY UNIVERSITY (WAUKESHA)
20935 Swenson Dr., Ste. 450
Waukesha, WI 53186-4047
Tel: (262)798-9889
Fax: (262)798-9912
Web Site: http://www.devry.edu/ **Type:** Comprehensive **Sex:** Coed **Calendar System:** Semester **Regional Accreditation:** North Central Association of Colleges and Schools

EDGEWOOD COLLEGE
1000 Edgewood College Dr.
Madison, WI 53711-1997
Tel: (608)663-4861
Free: 800-444-4861
Admissions: (608)663-2254
Fax: (608)663-3291
E-mail: admissions@edgewood.edu
Web Site: http://www.edgewood.edu/
President/CEO: Dr. Daniel Carey
Registrar: Ellen Fehring
Admissions: Scott Flanagan
Financial Aid: Scott Flanagan
Type: Comprehensive **Sex:** Coed **Affiliation:** Roman Catholic **Scores:** 63% ACT 18-23; 30% ACT 24-29 **% Accepted:** 81 **Admission Plans:** Deferred Admission **Application Deadline:** Rolling **Application Fee:** $25.00 **H.S. Requirements:** High school diploma required; GED accepted **Costs Per Year:** Application fee: $25. Comprehensive fee: $22,862 includes full-time tuition ($17,000) and college room and board ($5862). College room only: $2700. Part-time tuition: $534 per credit. **Scholarships:** Available **Calendar System:** 4-1-4, Summer Session Available **Enrollment:** FT 1,517, PT 506, Grad 623 **Faculty:** FT 86, PT 134 **Student-Faculty Ratio:** 13:1 **Exams:** SAT I or ACT **% Receiving Financial Aid:** 80 **% Residing in College-Owned, -Operated, or -Affiliated Housing:** 20 **Library Holdings:** 90,253 **Regional Accreditation:** North Central Association of Colleges and Schools **Credit Hours For Degree:** 60 credits, Associates; 120 credits, Bachelors **Professional Accreditation:** AACN, ACBSP, NCATE **Intercollegiate Athletics:** Baseball M; Basketball M & W; Cross-Country Running M & W; Golf M & W; Soccer M & W; Softball W; Tennis M & W; Volleyball W

FOX VALLEY TECHNICAL COLLEGE
1825 North Bluemound, PO Box 2277
Appleton, WI 54912-2277
Tel: (920)735-5600
Free: 800-735-3882
Admissions: (920)735-5643
Fax: (920)735-2582
Web Site: http://www.fvtc.edu/
President/CEO: Dr. David L. Buettner
Registrar: Robert Burdick
Admissions: Robert Burdick
Financial Aid: Mary Moede
Type: Two-Year College **Sex:** Coed **Affiliation:** Wisconsin Technical College System **% Accepted:** 70 **Admission Plans:** Open Admission; Early Admission; Deferred Admission **Application Deadline:** Rolling **Application Fee:** $30.00 **H.S. Requirements:** High school diploma required; GED accepted **Costs Per Year:** Application fee: $30. State resident tuition: $2610 full-time, $87 per credit part-time. Nonresident tuition: $16,089 full-time, $536.30 per credit part-time. Mandatory fees: $550 full-time. **Scholarships:** Available

Calendar System: Semester, Summer Session Available **Enrollment:** FT 1,624, PT 6,231 **Faculty:** FT 333, PT 650 **Student-Faculty Ratio:** 18:1 **Library Holdings:** 45,139 **Regional Accreditation:** North Central Association of Colleges and Schools **Credit Hours For Degree:** 64 credits, Associates **Professional Accreditation:** ACF, ADA, AOTA, NLN

GATEWAY TECHNICAL COLLEGE
3520 30th Ave.
Kenosha, WI 53144-1690
Tel: (262)564-2200
Admissions: (262)564-3224
Fax: (262)564-2201
Web Site: http://www.gtc.edu/
Registrar: Kurt Lehrmann
Admissions: Susan Roberts
Financial Aid: Zina Haywood
Type: Two-Year College **Sex:** Coed **Affiliation:** Wisconsin Technical College System **Admission Plans:** Open Admission; Early Admission; Deferred Admission **Application Fee:** $30.00 **H.S. Requirements:** High school diploma or equivalent not required. For court reporting, health occupations, law enforcement/police sciences programs: High school diploma required; GED accepted **Scholarships:** Available **Calendar System:** Semester, Summer Session Available **Enrollment:** FT 1,304, PT 5,512 **Faculty:** FT 257, PT 325 **Exams:** ACT, Other **Library Holdings:** 45,433 **Regional Accreditation:** North Central Association of Colleges and Schools **Credit Hours For Degree:** 64 credits, Associates **Professional Accreditation:** ARCEST, ADA, AHIMA, APTA, NLN

HERZING COLLEGE
5218 East Terrace Dr.
Madison, WI 53718
Tel: (608)249-6611
Free: 800-582-1227
Fax: (608)249-8593
E-mail: info@msn.herzing.edu
Web Site: http://www.herzing.edu/madison
President/CEO: Donald G. Madelung
Registrar: Derek McBeth
Admissions: Rebecca Abrams
Financial Aid: Beverly A. Faga
Type: Two-Year College **Sex:** Coed **Affiliation:** Herzing Institutes, Inc **Admission Plans:** Open Admission; Early Admission **Application Fee:** $0.00 **H.S. Requirements:** High school diploma required; GED accepted **Costs Per Year:** Application fee: $0. Tuition: $10,000 full-time, $290 per credit part-time. Mandatory fees: $25 full-time. Full-time tuition and fees vary according to course load, location, and program. Part-time tuition varies according to course load, location, and program. **Scholarships:** Available **Calendar System:** Semester **Faculty:** FT 15, PT 31 **Student-Faculty Ratio:** 13:1 **Library Holdings:** 1,500 **Regional Accreditation:** North Central Association of Colleges and Schools **Credit Hours For Degree:** 79 credits, Associates; 124 credits, Bachelors **Professional Accreditation:** ACCSCT

ITT TECHNICAL INSTITUTE (GREEN BAY)
470 Security Blvd.
Green Bay, WI 54313
Tel: (920)662-9000; 888-884-3626
Web Site: http://www.itt-tech.edu/
President/CEO: Judi Hughes
Admissions: Michael J. Kranzusch
Type: Two-Year College **Sex:** Coed **Affiliation:** ITT Educational Services, Inc **Admission Plans:** Deferred Admission **Application Deadline:** Rolling **Application Fee:** $100.00 **H.S. Requirements:** High school diploma required; GED accepted **Costs Per Year:** Application fee: $100. **Scholarships:** Available **Calendar System:** Quarter, Summer Session Not available **Exams:** Other **Credit Hours For Degree:** 96 credit hours, Associates; 180 credit hours, Bachelors **Professional Accreditation:** ACICS

ITT TECHNICAL INSTITUTE (GREENFIELD)
6300 West Layton Ave.
Greenfield, WI 53220-4612
Tel: (414)282-9494
Web Site: http://www.itt-tech.edu/
President/CEO: Jeffrey Jarmes
Registrar: Kristin Van Tassel
Admissions: Jon L. Patterson
Financial Aid: Diana Vandagrifft
Type: Two-Year College **Sex:** Coed **Affiliation:** ITT Educational Services, Inc **Admission Plans:** Deferred Admission **Application Deadline:** Rolling **Application Fee:** $100.00 **H.S. Requirements:** High school diploma required; GED accepted **Costs Per Year:** Application fee: $100. **Scholarships:** Available **Calendar System:** Quarter, Summer Session Not available **Exams:** Other **Credit Hours For Degree:** 96 credit hours, Associates; 180 credit hours, Bachelors **Professional Accreditation:** ACICS

LAC COURTE OREILLES OJIBWA COMMUNITY COLLEGE
13466 West Trepania Rd.
Hayward, WI 54843-2181
Tel: (715)634-4790; 888-526-6221
Web Site: http://www.lco-college.edu/
President/CEO: Schuyler Houser
Registrar: Annette Wiggins
Admissions: Annette Wiggins
Financial Aid: Agnes Fleming
Type: Two-Year College **Sex:** Coed **% Accepted:** 100 **Admission Plans:** Open Admission; Early Admission **Application Deadline:** Rolling **Application Fee:** $10.00 **H.S. Requirements:** High school diploma required; GED accepted. For senior citizens, those who demonstrate ability to benefit from program: High school diploma or equivalent not required **Costs Per Year:** Application fee: $10. Area resident tuition: $4050 full-time, $135 per credit part-time. Mandatory fees: $25 full-time. **Scholarships:** Available **Calendar System:** Semester, Summer Session Not available **Enrollment:** FT 294, PT 211 **Faculty:** FT 16, PT 59 **Student-Faculty Ratio:** 10:1 **Exams:** Other **Library Holdings:** 13,800 **Regional Accreditation:** North Central Association of Colleges and Schools **Credit Hours For Degree:** 64 semester hours, Associates **Professional Accreditation:** AAMAE

LAKELAND COLLEGE
PO.Box 359
Sheboygan, WI 53082-0359
Tel: (920)565-1000
Admissions: (920)565-1588
Fax: (920)565-1206
E-mail: admissions@lakeland.edu
Web Site: http://www.lakeland.edu/
President/CEO: Dr. Stephen A. Gould
Registrar: Susan Gould
Admissions: Nathan Dehne
Financial Aid: Joseph Botana
Type: Comprehensive **Sex:** Coed **Affiliation:** United Church of Christ **Scores:** 58% ACT 18-23; 18.4% ACT 24-29 **% Accepted:** 71 **Admission Plans:** Deferred Admission **Application Deadline:** September 01 **Application Fee:** $20.00 **H.S. Requirements:** High school diploma required; GED accepted **Costs Per Year:** Application fee: $20. Comprehensive fee: $22,216 includes full-time tuition ($16,080), mandatory fees ($716), and college room and board ($5420). College room only: $3882. Part-time tuition: $1608 per course. **Scholarships:** Available **Calendar System:** Miscellaneous, Summer Session Available **Enrollment:** FT 1,400, PT 1,973, Grad 648 **Faculty:** FT 54, PT 15 **Student-Faculty Ratio:** 17:1 **Exams:** SAT I or ACT **% Receiving Financial Aid:** 72 **% Residing in College-Owned, -Operated, or -Affiliated Housing:** 60 **Library Holdings:** 64,970 **Regional Accreditation:** North Central Association of Colleges and Schools **Credit Hours For Degree:** 128 credits, Bachelors **Intercollegiate Athletics:** Baseball M; Basketball M & W; Cross-Country Running M & W; Football M; Golf M & W; Soccer M & W; Softball W; Tennis M & W; Volleyball M & W; Wrestling M

LAKESHORE TECHNICAL COLLEGE
1290 North Ave.
Cleveland, WI 53015-1414
Tel: (920)693-1000; 888-GO TO LTC
Admissions: (920)693-1102
Fax: (920)693-1363
Web Site: http://www.gotoltc.com/
President/CEO: Dr. Michael Lanser
Admissions: Karla Zahn
Financial Aid: Corey Givens-Novak
Type: Two-Year College **Sex:** Coed **Affiliation:** Wisconsin Technical College System **% Accepted:** 68 **Admission Plans:** Open Admission; Early Admis-

sion; Deferred Admission **Application Deadline:** Rolling **Application Fee:** $30.00 **H.S. Requirements:** High school diploma required; GED accepted **Costs Per Year:** Application fee: $30. Area resident tuition: $2610 full-time. State resident tuition: $16,089 full-time, $87 per credit part-time. Nonresident tuition: $536.30 per credit part-time. **Scholarships:** Available **Calendar System:** Semester, Summer Session Available **Enrollment:** FT 772, PT 2,167 **Faculty:** FT 99, PT 116 **Student-Faculty Ratio:** 14:1 **Exams:** ACT, Other, SAT I or ACT **Library Holdings:** 15,749 **Regional Accreditation:** North Central Association of Colleges and Schools **Credit Hours For Degree:** 64 credits, Associates **Professional Accreditation:** ADA, JRCERT, NLN

LAWRENCE UNIVERSITY
PO Box 599
Appleton, WI 54912-0599
Tel: (920)832-7000
Free: 800-227-0982
Admissions: (920)832-6500
Fax: (920)832-6606
Web Site: http://www.lawrence.edu/
President/CEO: Dr. Jill Beck
Registrar: Anne S. Norman
Admissions: Steven T. Syverson
Financial Aid: Sara Holman
Type: Four-Year College **Sex:** Coed **Scores:** 99% SAT V 400+; 99% SAT M 400+; 13% ACT 18-23; 54% ACT 24-29 **% Accepted:** 68 **Admission Plans:** Early Admission; Early Action; Early Decision Plan; Deferred Admission **Application Deadline:** January 15 **Application Fee:** $40.00 **H.S. Requirements:** High school diploma required; GED not accepted **Costs Per Year:** Application fee: $40. Comprehensive fee: $35,979 includes full-time tuition ($29,376), mandatory fees ($222), and college room and board ($6381). College room only: $2934. **Scholarships:** Available **Calendar System:** Trimester, Summer Session Not available **Enrollment:** FT 1,383, PT 67 **Faculty:** FT 144, PT 32 **Student-Faculty Ratio:** 9:1 **Exams:** SAT I or ACT **% Receiving Financial Aid:** 61 **% Residing in College-Owned, -Operated, or -Affiliated Housing:** 98 **Library Holdings:** 389,262 **Regional Accreditation:** North Central Association of Colleges and Schools **Credit Hours For Degree:** 36 courses, Bachelors **Professional Accreditation:** NASM **Intercollegiate Athletics:** Baseball M; Basketball M & W; Crew M & W; Cross-Country Running M & W; Fencing M & W; Football M; Golf M; Ice Hockey M & W; Soccer M & W; Softball W; Swimming and Diving M & W; Tennis M & W; Track and Field M & W; Ultimate Frisbee M & W; Volleyball M & W; Wrestling M

MADISON AREA TECHNICAL COLLEGE
3550 Anderson St.
Madison, WI 53704-2599
Tel: (608)246-6100
Admissions: (608)246-6212
Web Site: http://www.matcmadison.edu/matc/
President/CEO: Dr. Beverly S. Simone
Registrar: Maureen Menendez
Admissions: Maureen Menendez
Type: Two-Year College **Sex:** Coed **Affiliation:** Wisconsin Technical College System **Admission Plans:** Open Admission; Preferred Admission; Early Admission **Application Fee:** $25.00 **H.S. Requirements:** High school diploma or equivalent not required. For health occupations programs: High school diploma required; GED accepted **Scholarships:** Available **Calendar System:** Semester, Summer Session Available **Faculty:** FT 393, PT 1,488 **Exams:** ACT **Library Holdings:** 66,000 **Regional Accreditation:** North Central Association of Colleges and Schools **Credit Hours For Degree:** 64 credits, Associates **Professional Accreditation:** ACF, ADA, AOTA, AOA, CARC, JRCERT, NAACLS, NLN **Intercollegiate Athletics:** Baseball M; Basketball M & W; Bowling M & W; Cross-Country Running M & W; Softball W; Tennis M & W; Track and Field M & W; Volleyball M & W; Wrestling M

MADISON MEDIA INSTITUTE
2702 Agriculture Dr., Ste. 1
Madison, WI 53718
Tel: (608)829-2728
Free: 800-236-4997
Admissions: (608)663-2000
Fax: (608)829-2661
E-mail: chutch@madisonmedia.com
Web Site: http://www.madisonmedia.com/
President/CEO: Chris Hutchings
Admissions: Chris K. Hutchings
Type: Two-Year College **Sex:** Coed **Application Fee:** $30.00 **Professional Accreditation:** ACCSCT

MARANATHA BAPTIST BIBLE COLLEGE
745 West Main St.
Watertown, WI 53094
Tel: (920)261-9300
Free: 800-622-2947
Admissions: (920)206-2327
Fax: (920)261-9109
E-mail: admissions@mbbc.edu
Web Site: http://www.mbbc.edu/
President/CEO: Dr. Dave Jaspers
Registrar: David Hershberger
Admissions: Dr. James H. Harrison
Financial Aid: Randy Hibbs
Type: Comprehensive **Sex:** Coed **Affiliation:** Baptist **Scores:** 51% ACT 18-23; 29% ACT 24-29 **Admission Plans:** Open Admission; Preferred Admission; Early Admission; Deferred Admission **Application Fee:** $40.00 **H.S. Requirements:** High school diploma required; GED accepted **Costs Per Year:** Application fee: $40. Comprehensive fee: $13,510 includes full-time tuition ($7680), mandatory fees ($830), and college room and board ($5000). Full-time tuition and fees vary according to course level. Part-time tuition: $240 per semester hour. Part-time tuition varies according to course level. **Scholarships:** Available **Calendar System:** Semester, Summer Session Available **Enrollment:** FT 850, Grad 54 **Faculty:** FT 66 **Student-Faculty Ratio:** 17:1 **Exams:** ACT **% Receiving Financial Aid:** 83 **% Residing in College-Owned, -Operated, or -Affiliated Housing:** 71 **Library Holdings:** 122,251 **Regional Accreditation:** North Central Association of Colleges and Schools **Credit Hours For Degree:** 64 semester hours, Associates; 128 semester hours, Bachelors **ROTC:** Air Force **Intercollegiate Athletics:** Baseball M; Basketball M & W; Cross-Country Running M & W; Football M; Soccer M & W; Softball W; Volleyball W; Wrestling M

MARIAN COLLEGE OF FOND DU LAC
45 South National Ave.
Fond du Lac, WI 54935-4699
Tel: (920)923-7600
Admissions: (920)923-7650
Fax: (920)923-8755
E-mail: admit@mariancoll.edu
Web Site: http://www.mariancollege.edu/
President/CEO: Dr. Richard I. Ridenour
Registrar: Cheryl Shell
Admissions: Eric Peterson
Financial Aid: Deborah McKinney
Type: Comprehensive **Sex:** Coed **Affiliation:** Roman Catholic **Scores:** 61% ACT 18-23; 18% ACT 24-29 **% Accepted:** 86 **Admission Plans:** Deferred Admission **Application Deadline:** Rolling **Application Fee:** $20.00 **H.S. Requirements:** High school diploma required; GED accepted **Costs Per Year:** Application fee: $20. Comprehensive fee: $21,775 includes full-time tuition ($16,380), mandatory fees ($325), and college room and board ($5070). College room only: $3350. Full-time tuition and fees vary according to class time and program. Room and board charges vary according to board plan and housing facility. Part-time tuition: $280 per credit. Part-time mandatory fees: $80 per term. Part-time tuition and fees vary according to class time, course load, and program. **Scholarships:** Available **Calendar System:** Semester, Summer Session Available **Enrollment:** FT 1,361, PT 716, Grad 898 **Faculty:** FT 78, PT 207 **Student-Faculty Ratio:** 13:1 **Exams:** SAT I or ACT **% Receiving Financial Aid:** 79 **% Residing in College-Owned, -Operated, or -Affiliated Housing:** 33 **Library Holdings:** 90,327 **Regional Accreditation:** North Central Association of Colleges and Schools **Credit Hours For Degree:** 128 credits, Bachelors **ROTC:** Army **Professional Accreditation:** AACN, CSWE, NCATE, NLN **Intercollegiate Athletics:** Baseball M; Basketball M & W; Golf M & W; Ice Hockey M; Soccer M & W; Softball W; Tennis M & W; Volleyball W

MARQUETTE UNIVERSITY
PO Box 1881
Milwaukee, WI 53201-1881
Tel: (414)288-7250
Free: 800-222-6544

Admissions: (414)288-7004
E-mail: roby.blust@marquette.edu
Web Site: http://www.marquette.edu/
President/CEO: Rev. Robert A. Wild, SJ
Registrar: Anthony D. Tortorella
Admissions: Robert Blust
Financial Aid: Daniel L. Goyette
Type: University **Sex:** Coed **Affiliation:** Roman Catholic (Jesuit) **Scores:** 99.5% SAT V 400+; 99.6% SAT M 400+; 19.9% ACT 18-23; 60.8% ACT 24-29 **% Accepted:** 70 **Admission Plans:** Early Admission; Deferred Admission **Application Deadline:** December 01 **Application Fee:** $30.00 **H.S. Requirements:** High school diploma required; GED accepted **Costs Per Year:** Application fee: $30. Comprehensive fee: $33,234 includes full-time tuition ($24,670), mandatory fees ($404), and college room and board ($8160). College room only: $5304. Part-time tuition: $725 per credit. Part-time mandatory fees: $465 per credit. **Scholarships:** Available **Calendar System:** Semester, Summer Session Available **Enrollment:** FT 7,530, PT 480, Grad 2,548 **Faculty:** FT 592, PT 454 **Student-Faculty Ratio:** 15:1 **Exams:** SAT I or ACT **% Receiving Financial Aid:** 58 **% Residing in College-Owned, -Operated, or -Affiliated Housing:** 50 **Library Holdings:** 1,120,694 **Regional Accreditation:** North Central Association of Colleges and Schools **Credit Hours For Degree:** 65 credits, Associates; 128 credits, Bachelors **ROTC:** Army, Navy, Air Force **Professional Accreditation:** AACSB, ABET, ACEJMC, AACN, ABA, ACNM, ADA, APTA, APA, ASLHA, AALS, NAACLS, NCATE, NLN **Intercollegiate Athletics:** Baseball M; Basketball M & W; Cheerleading M & W; Crew M & W; Cross-Country Running M & W; Fencing M & W; Football M; Golf M; Lacrosse M; Rugby M & W; Skiing (Downhill) M & W; Soccer M & W; Softball W; Swimming and Diving M & W; Tennis M & W; Track and Field M & W; Volleyball M & W

MID-STATE TECHNICAL COLLEGE

500 32nd St. North
Wisconsin Rapids, WI 54494-5599
Tel: (715)422-5300; 888-575-6782
Admissions: (715)422-5446
Fax: (715)422-5440
Web Site: http://www.mstc.edu/
President/CEO: Dr. John Clark
Admissions: John F. Bingham
Financial Aid: Mary Jo Green
Type: Two-Year College **Sex:** Coed **Affiliation:** Wisconsin Technical College System **Admission Plans:** Open Admission; Early Admission; Deferred Admission **Application Fee:** $25.00 **H.S. Requirements:** High school diploma required; GED accepted **Scholarships:** Available **Calendar System:** Semester, Summer Session Available **Faculty:** FT 200, PT 100 **Exams:** Other, SAT I or ACT **Library Holdings:** 20,148 **Regional Accreditation:** North Central Association of Colleges and Schools **Credit Hours For Degree:** 64 credits, Associates **Professional Accreditation:** CARC, NLN **Intercollegiate Athletics:** Basketball M & W; Bowling M & W; Golf M; Volleyball W

MILWAUKEE AREA TECHNICAL COLLEGE

700 West State St.
Milwaukee, WI 53233-1443
Tel: (414)297-6600
Admissions: (414)297-6274
Fax: (414)297-7990
Web Site: http://matc.edu
President/CEO: Dr. Darnell E. Cole
Registrar: Sarah Brown
Admissions: Robert Bullock
Financial Aid: Alfred Pinckney
Type: Two-Year College **Sex:** Coed **Affiliation:** Wisconsin Technical College System **Admission Plans:** Open Admission; Preferred Admission **Application Fee:** $30.00 **H.S. Requirements:** High school diploma required; GED accepted **Costs Per Year:** Application fee: $30. State resident tuition: $2609 full-time. Nonresident tuition: $15,503 full-time. Mandatory fees: $262 full-time, $10 per credit part-time. Full-time tuition and fees vary according to course level and program. Part-time fees vary according to course level and program. **Scholarships:** Available **Calendar System:** Semester, Summer Session Available **Faculty:** FT 597, PT 1,246 **Student-Faculty Ratio:** 16:1 **Exams:** Other **Library Holdings:** 60,847 **Regional Accreditation:** North Central Association of Colleges and Schools **Credit Hours For Degree:** 68 credits, Associates **Professional Accreditation:** ARCEST, ABFSE, ACF, ADA, AOTA, APTA, COptA, CARC, JRCECT, JRCERT, NAACLS, NLN **Intercollegiate Athletics:** Baseball M & W; Basketball M & W; Bowling M & W; Cross-Country Running M & W; Golf M & W; Soccer M; Softball M & W; Tennis M & W; Track and Field M & W; Volleyball W

MILWAUKEE INSTITUTE OF ART AND DESIGN

273 East Erie St.
Milwaukee, WI 53202-6003
Tel: (414)276-7889; 888-749-MIAD
Admissions: (414)847-3259
Fax: (414)291-8077
Web Site: http://www.miad.edu/
President/CEO: Mary Schopp
Registrar: Pauline Thomas
Admissions: Mark Fetherston
Financial Aid: Lloyd Mueller
Type: Four-Year College **Sex:** Coed **Scores:** 56% ACT 18-23; 23% ACT 24-29 **% Accepted:** 82 **Admission Plans:** Deferred Admission **Application Deadline:** Rolling **Application Fee:** $25.00 **H.S. Requirements:** High school diploma required; GED accepted **Costs Per Year:** Application fee: $25. Comprehensive fee: $30,400 includes full-time tuition ($23,100), mandatory fees ($300), and college room and board ($7000). Part-time tuition: $770 per credit hour. **Scholarships:** Available **Calendar System:** Semester, Summer Session Available **Enrollment:** FT 606, PT 39 **Faculty:** FT 34, PT 95 **Student-Faculty Ratio:** 10:1 **% Receiving Financial Aid:** 85 **% Residing in College-Owned, -Operated, or -Affiliated Housing:** 23 **Library Holdings:** 23,000 **Regional Accreditation:** North Central Association of Colleges and Schools **Credit Hours For Degree:** 123 credits, Bachelors **Professional Accreditation:** NASAD

MILWAUKEE SCHOOL OF ENGINEERING

1025 North Broadway
Milwaukee, WI 53202-3109
Tel: (414)277-7300
Free: 800-332-6763
Admissions: (414)277-6765
Fax: (414)277-7475
E-mail: explore@msoe.edu
Web Site: http://www.msoe.edu/
President/CEO: Dr. Hermann Viets
Registrar: Mary Nielsen
Admissions: Paul Borens
Financial Aid: Ben Dobner
Type: Comprehensive **Sex:** Coed **Scores:** 100% SAT V 400+; 100% SAT M 400+; 29% ACT 18-23; 58% ACT 24-29 **% Accepted:** 69 **Admission Plans:** Deferred Admission **Application Deadline:** Rolling **Application Fee:** $25.00 **H.S. Requirements:** High school diploma required; GED accepted **Costs Per Year:** Application fee: $25. Comprehensive fee: $31,149 includes full-time tuition ($24,960) and college room and board ($6189). College room only: $3969. Part-time tuition: $432 per quarter hour. **Scholarships:** Available **Calendar System:** Quarter, Summer Session Available **Enrollment:** FT 1,819, PT 273, Grad 223 **Faculty:** FT 120, PT 94 **Student-Faculty Ratio:** 12:1 **Exams:** SAT I or ACT **% Receiving Financial Aid:** 80 **% Residing in College-Owned, -Operated, or -Affiliated Housing:** 52 **Library Holdings:** 59,564 **Regional Accreditation:** North Central Association of Colleges and Schools **Credit Hours For Degree:** 205 quarter hours, Bachelors **ROTC:** Army, Navy, Air Force **Professional Accreditation:** ABET, ACPE, AACN, ACCE **Intercollegiate Athletics:** Baseball M; Basketball M & W; Cheerleading M & W; Cross-Country Running M & W; Golf M & W; Ice Hockey M; Soccer M & W; Softball W; Tennis M & W; Track and Field M & W; Volleyball M & W; Wrestling M

MORAINE PARK TECHNICAL COLLEGE

235 North National Ave, PO Box 1940
Fond du Lac, WI 54936-1940
Tel: (920)922-8611
Admissions: (920)929-2126
Fax: (920)924-2471
Web Site: http://www.morainepark.edu/
President/CEO: Dr. John J. Shanahan
Registrar: Lawrence Pasquini
Admissions: Amanda Hruska
Financial Aid: Judith Bourbonais
Type: Two-Year College **Sex:** Coed **Affiliation:** Wisconsin Technical College System **Admission Plans:** Open Admission; Deferred Admission **Application Deadline:** Rolling **Application Fee:** $30.00 **H.S. Requirements:** High

school diploma or equivalent not required **Costs Per Year:** Application fee: $30. State resident tuition: $2610 full-time, $87 per credit part-time. Nonresident tuition: $16,089 full-time, $536.30 per credit part-time. Mandatory fees: $250 full-time, $8.35 per credit part-time. **Scholarships:** Available **Calendar System:** Semester, Summer Session Available **Enrollment:** FT 1,197, PT 6,312 **Faculty:** FT 139, PT 187 **Exams:** ACT, Other **Library Holdings:** 32,166 **Regional Accreditation:** North Central Association of Colleges and Schools **Credit Hours For Degree:** 68 credits, Associates **Professional Accreditation:** ACF, AHIMA, NLN

MOUNT MARY COLLEGE
2900 North Menomonee River Parkway
Milwaukee, WI 53222-4597
Tel: (414)258-4810
Fax: (414)256-1224
E-mail: admiss@mtmary.edu
Web Site: http://www.mtmary.edu/
President/CEO: Dr. Patricia O'Donoghue
Registrar: Sr. Marie DeLourdes Larente
Admissions: Brooke Konopacki
Financial Aid: Debra Duff
Type: Comprehensive **Affiliation:** Roman Catholic **Scores:** 87.5% SAT V 400+; 100% SAT M 400+ **Admission Plans:** Deferred Admission **Application Deadline:** Rolling **Application Fee:** $25.00 **H.S. Requirements:** High school diploma required; GED accepted **Costs Per Year:** Application fee: $25. Comprehensive fee: $22,895 includes full-time tuition ($16,925), mandatory fees ($180), and college room and board ($5790). Room and board charges vary according to board plan. Part-time tuition: $466 per credit. Part-time mandatory fees: $45 per term. Part-time tuition and fees vary according to course load. **Scholarships:** Available **Calendar System:** Semester, Summer Session Available **Faculty:** FT 64, PT 134 **Student-Faculty Ratio:** 9:1 **Exams:** SAT I or ACT **% Receiving Financial Aid:** 67 **% Residing in College-Owned, -Operated, or -Affiliated Housing:** 10 **Library Holdings:** 654,128 **Regional Accreditation:** North Central Association of Colleges and Schools **Credit Hours For Degree:** 128 credits, Bachelors **ROTC:** Army **Professional Accreditation:** ADtA, AOTA, CSWE, FIDER, NLN **Intercollegiate Athletics:** Basketball W; Soccer W; Softball W; Tennis W; Volleyball W

NICOLET AREA TECHNICAL COLLEGE
Box 518
Rhinelander, WI 54501-0518
Tel: (715)365-4410
Admissions: (715)365-4451
Fax: (715)365-4445
E-mail: inquire@nicolet.tec.wi.us
Web Site: http://www.nicoletcollege.edu/
President/CEO: Dr. Adrian Lorbetske
Registrar: Ann Tegen
Admissions: Susan Kordula
Financial Aid: William Peshel
Type: Two-Year College **Sex:** Coed **Affiliation:** Wisconsin Technical College System **Admission Plans:** Open Admission; Preferred Admission; Early Admission **Application Fee:** $25.00 **H.S. Requirements:** High school diploma required; GED accepted **Costs Per Year:** Application fee: $25. State resident tuition: $3491 full-time, $109.10 per credit part-time. Nonresident tuition: $9995 full-time, $312.35 per credit part-time. Full-time tuition varies according to course level, degree level, and reciprocity agreements. Part-time tuition varies according to course level, degree level, and reciprocity agreements. **Scholarships:** Available **Calendar System:** Semester, Summer Session Available **Exams:** ACT **Library Holdings:** 38,369 **Regional Accreditation:** North Central Association of Colleges and Schools **Credit Hours For Degree:** 64 credit hours, Associates **Professional Accreditation:** NLN **Intercollegiate Athletics:** Golf M & W

NORTHCENTRAL TECHNICAL COLLEGE
1000 West Campus Dr.
Wausau, WI 54401-1899
Tel: (715)675-3331
Fax: (715)675-9776
Web Site: http://www.ntc.edu/
President/CEO: Dr. Robert Ernst
Admissions: Carolyn Michalski
Financial Aid: Glenna Ewing
Type: Two-Year College **Sex:** Coed **Affiliation:** Wisconsin Technical College System **Admission Plans:** Open Admission; Preferred Admission; Early Admission; Deferred Admission **Application Fee:** $25.00 **H.S. Requirements:** High school diploma required; GED accepted **Costs Per Year:** Application fee: $25. State resident tuition: $2415 full-time, $80.50 per credit part-time. Nonresident tuition: $15,309 full-time, $510.30 per credit part-time. Mandatory fees: $392 full-time, $8.20 per credit part-time. Full-time tuition and fees vary according to course level, course load, and program. Part-time tuition and fees vary according to course level, course load, and program. College room and board: $3952. Room and board charges vary according to board plan. **Scholarships:** Available **Calendar System:** Semester, Summer Session Available **Enrollment:** FT 1,276, PT 2,458 **Faculty:** FT 151, PT 21 **Student-Faculty Ratio:** 13:1 **Exams:** Other **Library Holdings:** 30,000 **Regional Accreditation:** North Central Association of Colleges and Schools **Credit Hours For Degree:** 64 credits, Associates **Professional Accreditation:** ADA, JRCERT, NLN

NORTHEAST WISCONSIN TECHNICAL COLLEGE
2740 W Mason St., PO Box 19042
Green Bay, WI 54307-9042
Tel: (920)498-5400
Free: 800-422-6982
Admissions: (920)498-5425
Web Site: http://www.nwtc.edu/
President/CEO: Dr. H. Jeffrey Rafn
Registrar: Mike Corcoran
Admissions: Michael Corcoran
Financial Aid: Heather Hill
Type: Two-Year College **Sex:** Coed **Affiliation:** Wisconsin Technical College System **Admission Plans:** Preferred Admission; Early Admission **Application Fee:** $30.00 **H.S. Requirements:** High school diploma required; GED accepted **Scholarships:** Available **Calendar System:** Semester, Summer Session Available **Enrollment:** FT 3,001, PT 5,759 **Faculty:** FT 256, PT 2,084 **Student-Faculty Ratio:** 39:1 **Library Holdings:** 22,250 **Regional Accreditation:** North Central Association of Colleges and Schools **Credit Hours For Degree:** 64 credits, Associates **Professional Accreditation:** ABET, ADA, AHIMA, APTA, CARC, NAACLS, NLN

NORTHLAND COLLEGE
1411 Ellis Ave.
Ashland, WI 54806-3925
Tel: (715)682-1699
Free: 800-753-1040
Admissions: (715)682-1224
Fax: (715)682-1258
E-mail: admit@wakefield.northland.edu
Web Site: http://www.northland.edu/
President/CEO: Dr. Karen Halbersleben
Registrar: Annette Nelson
Admissions: Jason Turley
Financial Aid: Tracey Staine
Type: Four-Year College **Sex:** Coed **Affiliation:** United Church of Christ **Scores:** 100% SAT V 400+; 100% SAT M 400+; 47% ACT 18-23; 46% ACT 24-29 **% Accepted:** 75 **Admission Plans:** Early Admission; Deferred Admission **Application Deadline:** May 01 **Application Fee:** $0.00 **H.S. Requirements:** High school diploma required; GED accepted **Costs Per Year:** Application fee: $0. Comprehensive fee: $26,680 includes full-time tuition ($20,188), mandatory fees ($601), and college room and board ($5891). College room only: $2384. Part-time tuition: $390 per credit. **Scholarships:** Available **Calendar System:** Miscellaneous, Summer Session Available **Enrollment:** FT 649, PT 90 **Faculty:** FT 41, PT 57 **Student-Faculty Ratio:** 13:1 **Exams:** SAT I or ACT **% Receiving Financial Aid:** 86 **% Residing in College-Owned, -Operated, or -Affiliated Housing:** 60 **Library Holdings:** 75,000 **Regional Accreditation:** North Central Association of Colleges and Schools **Credit Hours For Degree:** 124 credits, Bachelors **Intercollegiate Athletics:** Baseball M; Basketball M & W; Cross-Country Running M & W; Ice Hockey M; Soccer M & W; Softball W; Volleyball W

RIPON COLLEGE
300 Seward St., PO Box 248
Ripon, WI 54971
Tel: (920)748-8115
Free: 800-947-4766
Admissions: (920)748-8185

Fax: (920)748-7243
E-mail: adminfo@ripon.edu
Web Site: http://www.ripon.edu/
President/CEO: Dr. David C. Joyce
Admissions: Steven M. Schuetz
Financial Aid: Michele A. Wittler
Type: Four-Year College **Sex:** Coed **Scores:** 98% SAT V 400+; 97% SAT M 400+; 40% ACT 18-23; 45% ACT 24-29 **% Accepted:** 81 **Admission Plans:** Deferred Admission **Application Deadline:** Rolling **Application Fee:** $30.00 **H.S. Requirements:** High school diploma required; GED accepted **Costs Per Year:** Application fee: $30. Comprehensive fee: $28,497 includes full-time tuition ($22,162), mandatory fees ($275), and college room and board ($6060). College room only: $3030. Part-time tuition: $890 per credit. **Scholarships:** Available **Calendar System:** Semester, Summer Session Not available **Enrollment:** FT 953, PT 26 **Faculty:** FT 49, PT 38 **Student-Faculty Ratio:** 13:1 **Exams:** SAT I or ACT **% Receiving Financial Aid:** 75 **% Residing in College-Owned, -Operated, or -Affiliated Housing:** 90 **Library Holdings:** 163,615 **Regional Accreditation:** North Central Association of Colleges and Schools **Credit Hours For Degree:** 124 credits, Bachelors **ROTC:** Army **Intercollegiate Athletics:** Baseball M; Basketball M & W; Cheerleading W; Cross-Country Running M & W; Football M; Golf M & W; Ice Hockey M & W; Rugby M; Soccer M & W; Softball W; Swimming and Diving M & W; Tennis M & W; Track and Field M & W; Volleyball W; Wrestling M & W

ST. NORBERT COLLEGE
100 Grant St.
De Pere, WI 54115-2099
Tel: (920)337-3181
Free: 800-236-4878
Admissions: (920)403-3005
Fax: (920)403-4088
E-mail: admit@snc.edu
Web Site: http://www.snc.edu/
President/CEO: Dr. William J. Hynes
Registrar: Richard L. Guild
Admissions: Bridget Krage O'Connor
Financial Aid: Jeff A. Zahn
Type: Comprehensive **Sex:** Coed **Affiliation:** Roman Catholic **Scores:** 47% ACT 18-23; 44% ACT 24-29 **% Accepted:** 86 **Admission Plans:** Preferred Admission; Early Admission; Early Decision Plan; Deferred Admission **Application Deadline:** Rolling **Application Fee:** $25.00 **H.S. Requirements:** High school diploma required; GED accepted **Costs Per Year:** Application fee: $25. Comprehensive fee: $28,577 includes full-time tuition ($22,209), mandatory fees ($300), and college room and board ($6068). College room only: $3212. Full-time tuition and fees vary according to course load. Room and board charges vary according to board plan, housing facility, and student level. Part-time tuition: $694 per credit. Part-time tuition varies according to course load. **Scholarships:** Available **Calendar System:** Semester, Summer Session Available **Enrollment:** FT 1,922, PT 65, Grad 63 **Faculty:** FT 109, PT 68 **Student-Faculty Ratio:** 14:1 **Exams:** SAT I or ACT **% Receiving Financial Aid:** 65 **% Residing in College-Owned, -Operated, or -Affiliated Housing:** 75 **Library Holdings:** 217,248 **Regional Accreditation:** North Central Association of Colleges and Schools **Credit Hours For Degree:** 32 courses, Bachelors **ROTC:** Army **Intercollegiate Athletics:** Baseball M; Basketball M & W; Cross-Country Running M & W; Football M; Golf M & W; Ice Hockey M; Soccer M & W; Softball W; Swimming and Diving W; Tennis M & W; Track and Field M & W; Volleyball W

SILVER LAKE COLLEGE
2406 South Alverno Rd.
Manitowoc, WI 54220-9319
Tel: (920)684-6691
Admissions: (920)686-6208
Fax: (920)684-7082
E-mail: admslc@sl.edu
Web Site: http://www.sl.edu/
President/CEO: Dr. George Arnold
Registrar: Sr. Janice Stingle
Admissions: Jane Bishop
Type: Comprehensive **Sex:** Coed **Affiliation:** Roman Catholic **Scores:** 59% ACT 18-23; 13% ACT 24-29 **% Accepted:** 83 **Admission Plans:** Early Admission; Deferred Admission **Application Deadline:** August 31 **Application Fee:** $35.00 **H.S. Requirements:** High school diploma required; GED accepted **Costs Per Year:** Application fee: $35. Tuition: $17,108 full-time, $525 per credit part-time. College room only: $4400. **Scholarships:** Available **Calendar System:** Semester, Summer Session Available **Enrollment:** FT 214, PT 415, Grad 284 **Faculty:** FT 42, PT 126 **Student-Faculty Ratio:** 9:1 **Exams:** SAT I or ACT **% Receiving Financial Aid:** 79 **% Residing in College-Owned, -Operated, or -Affiliated Housing:** 3 **Library Holdings:** 60,466 **Regional Accreditation:** North Central Association of Colleges and Schools **Credit Hours For Degree:** 60 credits, Associates; 120 credits, Bachelors **Professional Accreditation:** NASM, NCATE **Intercollegiate Athletics:** Basketball W; Cross-Country Running M & W

SOUTHWEST WISCONSIN TECHNICAL COLLEGE
1800 Bronson Blvd.
Fennimore, WI 53809-9778
Tel: (608)822-3262
Fax: (608)822-6019
Web Site: http://www.swtc.edu/
President/CEO: Dr. Karen R. Knox
Admissions: Jeff Gilow
Financial Aid: Joy Kite
Type: Two-Year College **Sex:** Coed **Affiliation:** Wisconsin Technical College System **Admission Plans:** Open Admission; Preferred Admission; Early Admission **Application Fee:** $30.00 **H.S. Requirements:** High school diploma or equivalent not required **Scholarships:** Available **Calendar System:** Semester, Summer Session Available **Enrollment:** FT 778, PT 1,083 **Faculty:** FT 86, PT 3 **Student-Faculty Ratio:** 13:1 **Exams:** Other **% Residing in College-Owned, -Operated, or -Affiliated Housing:** 3 **Library Holdings:** 25,000 **Regional Accreditation:** North Central Association of Colleges and Schools **Credit Hours For Degree:** 64 credits, Associates **Professional Accreditation:** NLN

UNIVERSITY OF PHOENIX-WISCONSIN CAMPUS
20075 Watertower Blvd.
Brookfield, WI 53045-6608
Tel: (262)785-0608
Free: 800-228-7240
Admissions: (480)557-1712
Fax: (262)785-0608
Web Site: http://www.phoenix.edu/
President/CEO: James Chitwood
Admissions: Nina Omelchanko
Type: Comprehensive **Sex:** Coed **Admission Plans:** Open Admission; Deferred Admission **Application Deadline:** Rolling **Application Fee:** $110.00 **H.S. Requirements:** High school diploma required; GED accepted **Costs Per Year:** Application fee: $110. Tuition: $10,785 full-time, $359.50 per credit part-time. Mandatory fees: $560 full-time, $70 per course part-time. **Scholarships:** Available **Calendar System:** Continuous, Summer Session Not available **Enrollment:** FT 1,067, Grad 290 **Faculty:** FT 8, PT 209 **Student-Faculty Ratio:** 5:1 **Library Holdings:** 444 **Regional Accreditation:** North Central Association of Colleges and Schools **Credit Hours For Degree:** 60 credits, Associates; 120 credits, Bachelors

UNIVERSITY OF WISCONSIN-BARABOO/SAUK COUNTY
1006 Connie Rd.
Baraboo, WI 53913-1015
Tel: (608)356-8351
Admissions: (608)355-5255
Fax: (608)356-4074
E-mail: booinfo@uwc.edu
Web Site: http://www.baraboo.uwc.edu/
President/CEO: Michael Brophy
Admissions: Ruth Joyce
Financial Aid: Thomas Martin
Type: Two-Year College **Sex:** Coed **Affiliation:** University of Wisconsin System **Admission Plans:** Preferred Admission; Early Admission; Deferred Admission **Application Deadline:** Rolling **Application Fee:** $35.00 **H.S. Requirements:** High school diploma required; GED accepted **Costs Per Year:** Application fee: $35. State resident tuition: $4296 full-time, $180.85 per credit part-time. Nonresident tuition: $12,992 full-time, $543.35 per credit part-time. Part-time tuition varies according to course load. **Scholarships:** Available **Calendar System:** Semester, Summer Session Available **Enrollment:** FT 344, PT 204 **Faculty:** FT 17, PT 28 **Student-Faculty Ratio:** 16:1 **Exams:** ACT, SAT I or ACT **Library Holdings:** 45,000 **Regional Accreditation:** North Central Association of Colleges and Schools **Credit Hours For Degree:** 60 credits, Associates **Intercollegiate Athletics:** Basketball M; Golf

M & W; Soccer M & W; Tennis M & W; Volleyball W

UNIVERSITY OF WISCONSIN-BARRON COUNTY

1800 College Dr.
Rice Lake, WI 54868-2497
Tel: (715)234-8176
Admissions: (715)234-8024
Web Site: http://www.barron.uwc.edu/
President/CEO: Dr. Paul W. Chase
Registrar: Dale Fenton
Admissions: Dale Fenton

Type: Two-Year College **Sex:** Coed **Affiliation:** University of Wisconsin System **Admission Plans:** Deferred Admission **Application Fee:** $35.00 **H.S. Requirements:** High school diploma required; GED accepted **Costs Per Year:** Application fee: $35. State resident tuition: $3996 full-time, $165 per credit part-time. Nonresident tuition: $12,676 full-time, $528 per credit part-time. Mandatory fees: $373 full-time, $16 per credit part-time. Full-time tuition and fees vary according to reciprocity agreements. Part-time tuition and fees vary according to reciprocity agreements. **Scholarships:** Available **Calendar System:** Semester, Summer Session Available **Enrollment:** FT 308, PT 308 **Faculty:** FT 21, PT 12 **Exams:** ACT, SAT I or ACT **Library Holdings:** 39,479 **Regional Accreditation:** North Central Association of Colleges and Schools **Credit Hours For Degree:** 60 credits, Associates **Intercollegiate Athletics:** Baseball M; Basketball M & W; Golf M & W; Volleyball W

UNIVERSITY OF WISCONSIN-EAU CLAIRE

PO Box 4004
Eau Claire, WI 54702-4004
Tel: (715)836-2637
Admissions: (715)836-5415
Fax: (715)836-2380
E-mail: admissions@uwec.edu
Web Site: http://www.uwec.edu/
President/CEO: Dr. Donald J. Mash
Registrar: Sue Moore
Admissions: Kristina Anderson
Financial Aid: Kathleen Sahlhoff

Type: Comprehensive **Sex:** Coed **Affiliation:** University of Wisconsin System **Scores:** 97% SAT V 400+; 98% SAT M 400+; 42% ACT 18-23; 53% ACT 24-29 **% Accepted:** 70 **Admission Plans:** Early Admission **Application Deadline:** Rolling **Application Fee:** $35.00 **H.S. Requirements:** High school diploma required; GED accepted **Costs Per Year:** Application fee: $35. State resident tuition: $5178 full-time, $215.59 per credit part-time. Nonresident tuition: $15,224 full-time, $634.18 per credit part-time. Full-time tuition varies according to reciprocity agreements. Part-time tuition varies according to reciprocity agreements. College room and board: $4737. College room only: $2540. Room and board charges vary according to board plan. **Scholarships:** Available **Calendar System:** Semester, Summer Session Available **Enrollment:** FT 9,374, PT 689, Grad 503 **Faculty:** FT 401, PT 107 **Student-Faculty Ratio:** 20:1 **Exams:** SAT I or ACT **% Receiving Financial Aid:** 43 **% Residing in College-Owned, -Operated, or -Affiliated Housing:** 38 **Library Holdings:** 764,275 **Regional Accreditation:** North Central Association of Colleges and Schools **Credit Hours For Degree:** 60 credits, Associates; 120 credits, Bachelors **Professional Accreditation:** AACSB, ABET, ACEJMC, AACN, ASLHA, CSWE, NASM **Intercollegiate Athletics:** Basketball M & W; Cross-Country Running M & W; Football M; Golf M & W; Gymnastics W; Ice Hockey M & W; Soccer W; Softball W; Swimming and Diving M & W; Tennis M & W; Track and Field M & W; Volleyball W; Wrestling M

UNIVERSITY OF WISCONSIN-FOND DU LAC

400 University Dr.
Fond du Lac, WI 54935
Tel: (920)929-3600
Admissions: (920)929-3606
E-mail: bstrande@uwcmail.uwc.edu
Web Site: http://www.fdl.uwc.edu/
President/CEO: Daniel Blankenship
Admissions: Linda A. Reiss

Type: Two-Year College **Sex:** Coed **Affiliation:** University of Wisconsin System **Scores:** 73% ACT 18-23; 19% ACT 24-29 **Admission Plans:** Deferred Admission **Application Fee:** $35.00 **H.S. Requirements:** High school diploma required; GED accepted **Scholarships:** Available **Calendar System:** Semester, Summer Session Available **Enrollment:** FT 454, PT 262 **Faculty:** FT 20, PT 17 **Student-Faculty Ratio:** 19:1 **Exams:** ACT **Library Holdings:** 41,891 **Regional Accreditation:** North Central Association of Colleges and Schools **Credit Hours For Degree:** 60 credits, Associates **ROTC:** Army **Intercollegiate Athletics:** Basketball M & W; Golf M; Soccer M & W; Tennis M & W; Volleyball W

UNIVERSITY OF WISCONSIN-FOX VALLEY

1478 Midway Rd.
Menasha, WI 54952
Tel: (920)832-2600; 888-INFOUWC
Admissions: (920)832-2620
Fax: (920)832-2647
E-mail: foxinfo@uwc.edu
Web Site: http://www.uwfoxvalley.uwc.edu/
President/CEO: Dr. James W. Perry
Admissions: Rhonda Uschan
Financial Aid: Rhona Uschen

Type: Two-Year College **Sex:** Coed **Affiliation:** University of Wisconsin System **Admission Plans:** Early Admission **H.S. Requirements:** High school diploma required; GED accepted **Costs Per Year:** State resident tuition: $4196 full-time, $177 per credit part-time. Nonresident tuition: $12,896 full-time, $528.21 per credit part-time. Full-time tuition varies according to course load. Part-time tuition varies according to course load. **Scholarships:** Available **Calendar System:** Semester, Summer Session Available **Enrollment:** FT 912, PT 885 **Faculty:** FT 31, PT 49 **Exams:** ACT **Library Holdings:** 29,000 **Regional Accreditation:** North Central Association of Colleges and Schools **Credit Hours For Degree:** 60 credit hours, Associates **Intercollegiate Athletics:** Basketball M & W; Soccer M & W; Tennis M & W; Volleyball M & W

UNIVERSITY OF WISCONSIN-GREEN BAY

2420 Nicolet Dr.
Green Bay, WI 54311-7001
Tel: (920)465-2000; 888-367-8942
Admissions: (920)465-2111
Fax: (920)465-2032
Web Site: http://www.uwgb.edu/
President/CEO: Dr. W. Bruce Shepard
Registrar: Mike Stearney
Admissions: Pam Harvey-Jacobs
Financial Aid: Ron Ronnenberg

Type: Comprehensive **Sex:** Coed **Affiliation:** University of Wisconsin System **Scores:** 88% SAT V 400+; 100% SAT M 400+; 61% ACT 18-23; 33% ACT 24-29 **% Accepted:** 66 **Admission Plans:** Deferred Admission **Application Fee:** $35.00 **H.S. Requirements:** High school diploma required; GED accepted **Costs Per Year:** Application fee: $35. State resident tuition: $4277 full-time, $178 per credit hour part-time. Nonresident tuition: $14,323 full-time, $597 per credit hour part-time. Mandatory fees: $1148 full-time, $38 per credit hour part-time. Full-time tuition and fees vary according to reciprocity agreements. Part-time tuition and fees vary according to reciprocity agreements. College room and board: $4698. College room only: $2772. Room and board charges vary according to board plan and housing facility. **Scholarships:** Available **Calendar System:** Semester, Summer Session Available **Enrollment:** FT 4,519, PT 1,103, Grad 204 **Faculty:** FT 179, PT 100 **Student-Faculty Ratio:** 23:1 **Exams:** SAT I or ACT **% Receiving Financial Aid:** 55 **% Residing in College-Owned, -Operated, or -Affiliated Housing:** 34 **Library Holdings:** 333,482 **Regional Accreditation:** North Central Association of Colleges and Schools **Credit Hours For Degree:** 60 credits, Associates; 120 credits, Bachelors **ROTC:** Army **Professional Accreditation:** ADtA, CSWE, NASM, NLN **Intercollegiate Athletics:** Basketball M & W; Cross-Country Running M & W; Skiing (Cross-Country) M & W; Soccer M & W; Softball W; Swimming and Diving M & W; Tennis M & W; Volleyball W

UNIVERSITY OF WISCONSIN-LA CROSSE

1725 State St.
La Crosse, WI 54601-3742
Tel: (608)785-8000
Admissions: (608)785-8939
Fax: (608)785-6695
E-mail: admissions@post.uwlax.edu
Web Site: http://www.uwlax.edu
President/CEO: Dr. Douglas N. Hastad
Registrar: Diane Schumacher

Admissions: Kathryn Kiefer
Financial Aid: James Finn
Type: Comprehensive **Sex:** Coed **Affiliation:** University of Wisconsin System **Scores:** 93.6% SAT V 400+; 100% SAT M 400+ **% Accepted:** 67 **Admission Plans:** Early Admission **Application Deadline:** Rolling **Application Fee:** $35.00 **H.S. Requirements:** High school diploma required; GED accepted **Costs Per Year:** Application fee: $35. State resident tuition: $5225 full-time, $230 per credit hour part-time. Nonresident tuition: $15,271 full-time, $649 per credit hour part-time. Full-time tuition varies according to program and reciprocity agreements. Part-time tuition varies according to course load, program, and reciprocity agreements. College room and board: $4820. College room only: $2720. Room and board charges vary according to board plan. **Scholarships:** Available **Calendar System:** Semester, Summer Session Available **Enrollment:** FT 7,720, PT 413, Grad 1,264 **Faculty:** FT 339, PT 109 **Student-Faculty Ratio:** 22:1 **Exams:** ACT, SAT I or ACT **% Receiving Financial Aid:** 59 **% Residing in College-Owned, -Operated, or -Affiliated Housing:** 36 **Library Holdings:** 673,060 **Regional Accreditation:** North Central Association of Colleges and Schools **Credit Hours For Degree:** 60 credits, Associates; 120 credits, Bachelors **ROTC:** Army **Professional Accreditation:** AACSB, AANA, AOTA, APTA, CEPH, JRCERT, JRCEPAT, NAACLS, NASM, NCATE, NRPA **Intercollegiate Athletics:** Baseball M; Basketball M & W; Cross-Country Running M & W; Football M; Gymnastics W; Soccer W; Softball W; Swimming and Diving M & W; Tennis M & W; Track and Field M & W; Volleyball W; Wrestling M

UNIVERSITY OF WISCONSIN-MADISON
500 Lincoln Dr.
Madison, WI 53706-1380
Tel: (608)262-1234
Admissions: (608)262-3961
Fax: (608)262-1429
E-mail: onwisconsin@admissions.wisc.edu
Web Site: http://www.wisc.edu/
President/CEO: Dr. John Wiley
Registrar: Joanne E. Berg
Admissions: Robert Seltzer
Financial Aid: Steven Van Ess
Type: University **Sex:** Coed **Affiliation:** University of Wisconsin System **Scores:** 98% SAT V 400+; 100% SAT M 400+; 8% ACT 18-23; 64% ACT 24-29 **% Accepted:** 68 **Admission Plans:** Deferred Admission **Application Deadline:** February 01 **Application Fee:** $35.00 **H.S. Requirements:** High school diploma required; GED accepted **Costs Per Year:** Application fee: $35. State resident tuition: $6284 full-time, $264 per credit part-time. Nonresident tuition: $20,284 full-time, $847 per credit part-time. Mandatory fees: $333 full-time, $30 per credit part-time. Full-time tuition and fees vary according to degree level and reciprocity agreements. Part-time tuition and fees vary according to course load, degree level, and reciprocity agreements. College room and board: $6500. Room and board charges vary according to board plan, housing facility, and location. **Scholarships:** Available **Calendar System:** Semester, Summer Session Available **Enrollment:** FT 27,441, PT 2,665, Grad 8,841 **Faculty:** FT 2,365, PT 610 **Student-Faculty Ratio:** 13:1 **Exams:** SAT I or ACT **% Receiving Financial Aid:** 39 **% Residing in College-Owned, -Operated, or -Affiliated Housing:** 24 **Regional Accreditation:** North Central Association of Colleges and Schools **Credit Hours For Degree:** 120 semester hours, Bachelors **ROTC:** Army, Navy, Air Force **Professional Accreditation:** AACSB, ABET, ACEHSA, AACN, AAFCS, ABA, ACPhE, ADtA, ACSP, ALA, AOTA, APTA, APA, ASC, ASLA, ASLHA, AVMA, AALS, CORE, CSWE FIDER, JRCEPAT, LCMEAMA, NAACLS, NASAD, NASM, NAST, SAF **Intercollegiate Athletics:** Basketball M & W; Cheerleading M & W; Cross-Country Running M & W; Football M; Golf M & W; Ice Hockey M & W; Sailing M & W; Soccer M & W; Softball W; Swimming and Diving M & W; Tennis M & W; Track and Field M & W; Ultimate Frisbee M & W; Volleyball W; Water Polo M & W; Wrestling M

UNIVERSITY OF WISCONSIN-MANITOWOC
705 Viebahn St.
Manitowoc, WI 54220-6699
Tel: (920)683-4700
Admissions: (920)683-4708
Fax: (920)683-4776
E-mail: christopher.lewis@uwc.edu
Web Site: http://www.manitowoc.uwc.edu/
President/CEO: Dr. Glenda Gallisath
Registrar: Dr. Michael A. Herrity
Admissions: Christopher Lewis
Financial Aid: Dr. Michael A. Herrity
Type: Two-Year College **Sex:** Coed **Affiliation:** University of Wisconsin System **% Accepted:** 91 **Admission Plans:** Early Admission **Application Fee:** $35.00 **H.S. Requirements:** High school diploma required; GED accepted **Costs Per Year:** Application fee: $35. Area resident tuition: $165.71 per credit part-time. State resident tuition: $3,977 full-time, $528.21 per credit part-time. Nonresident tuition: $12,677 full-time, $528.21 per credit part-time. Mandatory fees: $211 full-time, $8.64 per credit part-time, $8.64. **Scholarships:** Available **Calendar System:** Semester, Summer Session Available **Faculty:** FT 21, PT 19 **Student-Faculty Ratio:** 24:1 **Exams:** SAT I or ACT **Library Holdings:** 25,750 **Regional Accreditation:** North Central Association of Colleges and Schools **Credit Hours For Degree:** 60 credits, Associates **Intercollegiate Athletics:** Basketball M & W; Golf M; Tennis M & W; Volleyball W

UNIVERSITY OF WISCONSIN-MARATHON COUNTY
518 South Seventh Ave.
Wausau, WI 54401-5396
Tel: (715)261-6100; 888-367-8962
Admissions: (715)261-6238
Fax: (715)261-6333
Web Site: http://www.uwmc.uwc.edu/
President/CEO: Dr. James F. Veninga
Registrar: Nolan Beck
Admissions: Dr. Nolan Beck
Financial Aid: Nolan Beck
Type: Two-Year College **Sex:** Coed **Affiliation:** University of Wisconsin System **Admission Plans:** Early Admission; Deferred Admission **Application Fee:** $35.00 **H.S. Requirements:** High school diploma required; GED accepted **Costs Per Year:** Application fee: $35. State resident tuition: $4000 full-time, $175 per credit part-time. Nonresident tuition: $13,000 full-time, $545 per credit part-time. College room and board: $3800. Room and board charges vary according to board plan. **Scholarships:** Available **Calendar System:** Semester, Summer Session Available **Enrollment:** FT 883, PT 420 **Faculty:** FT 59, PT 25 **Student-Faculty Ratio:** 24:1 **Exams:** ACT **% Residing in College-Owned, -Operated, or -Affiliated Housing:** 16 **Library Holdings:** 37,000 **Regional Accreditation:** North Central Association of Colleges and Schools **Credit Hours For Degree:** 60 credits, Associates **ROTC:** Army **Intercollegiate Athletics:** Basketball M & W; Golf M & W; Soccer M & W; Tennis M & W; Volleyball W

UNIVERSITY OF WISCONSIN-MARINETTE
750 West Bay Shore
Marinette, WI 54143-4299
Tel: (715)735-4300
Admissions: (715)735-4301
E-mail: cbailey@uwc.edu
Web Site: http://www.uwc.edu/
President/CEO: Paula Langteau
Registrar: Cindy Bailey
Admissions: Cynthia M. Bailey
Financial Aid: Cindy Bailey
Type: Two-Year College **Sex:** Coed **Affiliation:** University of Wisconsin System **Admission Plans:** Open Admission **Application Fee:** $35.00 **H.S. Requirements:** High school diploma required; GED accepted **Scholarships:** Available **Calendar System:** Semester, Summer Session Available **Enrollment:** FT 486 **Faculty:** FT 16, PT 14 **Student-Faculty Ratio:** 21:1 **Exams:** SAT I or ACT **Library Holdings:** 23,000 **Regional Accreditation:** North Central Association of Colleges and Schools **Credit Hours For Degree:** 60 credits, Associates **Intercollegiate Athletics:** Basketball M & W; Volleyball W

UNIVERSITY OF WISCONSIN-MARSHFIELD/WOOD COUNTY
2000 West 5th St.
Marshfield, WI 54449
Tel: (715)389-6500
Web Site: http://marshfield.uwc.edu/
President/CEO: Dr. Andew Keogh
Registrar: Jeff Meece
Admissions: Jeff Meece
Financial Aid: Jeff Meece
Type: Two-Year College **Sex:** Coed **Affiliation:** University of Wisconsin System **Scores:** 75% ACT 18-23; 15% ACT 24-29 **Admission Plans:** Early Admission; Deferred Admission **Application Fee:** $35.00 **H.S. Require-**

ments: High school diploma required; GED accepted **Scholarships:** Available **Calendar System:** Semester, Summer Session Available **Faculty:** FT 13, PT 23 **Student-Faculty Ratio:** 17:1 **Exams:** SAT I or ACT **Library Holdings:** 35,000 **Regional Accreditation:** North Central Association of Colleges and Schools **Credit Hours For Degree:** 60 credits, Associates **ROTC:** Army **Intercollegiate Athletics:** Basketball M & W; Golf M & W; Tennis M & W; Volleyball W

UNIVERSITY OF WISCONSIN-MILWAUKEE
PO Box 413
Milwaukee, WI 53201-0413
Tel: (414)229-1122
Admissions: (414)229-3800
Fax: (414)229-6940
E-mail: deswcb@des.uwm.edu
Web Site: http://www.uwm.edu/
President/CEO: Carlos Santiago
Admissions: Beth Weckmueller
Financial Aid: Jane Hojan-Clark
Type: University **Sex:** Coed **Affiliation:** University of Wisconsin System **Scores:** 91% SAT V 400+; 94% SAT M 400+; 58% ACT 18-23; 30% ACT 24-29 **% Accepted:** 81 **Admission Plans:** Deferred Admission **Application Deadline:** August 01 **Application Fee:** $35.00 **H.S. Requirements:** High school diploma required; GED accepted **Costs Per Year:** Application fee: $35. State resident tuition: $5494 full-time, $228.93 per credit part-time. Nonresident tuition: $18,246 full-time, $760.26 per credit part-time. Mandatory fees: $730 full-time. Full-time tuition and fees vary according to location, program, and reciprocity agreements. Part-time tuition varies according to course load, location, program, and reciprocity agreements. College room and board: $4922. College room only: $2988. Room and board charges vary according to board plan and housing facility. **Scholarships:** Available **Calendar System:** Semester, Summer Session Available **Enrollment:** FT 18,856, PT 4,060, Grad 4,586 **Exams:** Other, SAT I or ACT **% Receiving Financial Aid:** 47 **% Residing in College-Owned, -Operated, or -Affiliated Housing:** 13 **Library Holdings:** 1,449,333 **Regional Accreditation:** North Central Association of Colleges and Schools **Credit Hours For Degree:** 120 credit hours, Bachelors **ROTC:** Army, Air Force **Professional Accreditation:** AACSB, ABET, AACN, AHIMA, ACSP, ALA, AOTA, APA, ASLHA, CSWE, NAACLS, NASM **Intercollegiate Athletics:** Baseball M; Basketball M & W; Cross-Country Running M & W; Soccer M & W; Swimming and Diving M & W; Tennis M & W; Track and Field M & W; Volleyball M & W

UNIVERSITY OF WISCONSIN-OSHKOSH
800 Algoma Blvd.
Oshkosh, WI 54901
Tel: (920)424-1234
Admissions: (920)424-0202
Fax: (920)424-1098
E-mail: oshadmuw@uwosh.edu
Web Site: http://www.uwosh.edu/
President/CEO: Dr. Richard H. Wells
Registrar: Lisa M. Danielson
Admissions: Jill Endries
Financial Aid: Beatriz D. Contreras
Type: Comprehensive **Sex:** Coed **Affiliation:** University of Wisconsin System **Scores:** 62% ACT 18-23; 31% ACT 24-29 **% Accepted:** 79 **Admission Plans:** Deferred Admission **Application Deadline:** Rolling **Application Fee:** $35.00 **H.S. Requirements:** High school diploma required; GED accepted **Costs Per Year:** Application fee: $35. State resident tuition: $4,981 full-time, $209 per credit hour part-time. Nonresident tuition: $15,027 full-time, $628 per credit hour part-time. Full-time tuition varies according to reciprocity agreements. Part-time tuition varies according to reciprocity agreements. College room and board: $4884. College room only: $2784. Room and board charges vary according to board plan and housing facility. **Scholarships:** Available **Calendar System:** Semester, Summer Session Available **Enrollment:** FT 8,538, PT 1,202, Grad 1,257 **Faculty:** FT 381, PT 185 **Student-Faculty Ratio:** 20:1 **Exams:** Other, SAT I or ACT **% Receiving Financial Aid:** 60 **% Residing in College-Owned, -Operated, or -Affiliated Housing:** 34 **Library Holdings:** 446,774 **Regional Accreditation:** North Central Association of Colleges and Schools **Credit Hours For Degree:** 60 credits, Associates; 120 credits, Bachelors **ROTC:** Army **Professional Accreditation:** AACSB, ACEJMC, AACN, ACA, CSWE, NASM, NCATE **Intercollegiate Athletics:** Baseball M; Basketball M & W; Cross-Country Running M & W; Football M; Golf W; Gymnastics W; Riflery M & W; Soccer M & W; Softball W; Swimming and Diving M & W; Tennis M & W; Track and Field M & W; Volleyball W; Wrestling M

UNIVERSITY OF WISCONSIN-PARKSIDE
900 Wood Rd., Box 2000
Kenosha, WI 53141-2000
Tel: (262)595-2345
Admissions: (262)595-2784
Fax: (262)595-2630
E-mail: matthew.jensen@uwp.edu
Web Site: http://www.uwp.edu/
President/CEO: Dr. John P. Keating
Registrar: Richard Lott
Admissions: Matthew Jensen
Financial Aid: Dr. Randall McCready
Type: Comprehensive **Sex:** Coed **Affiliation:** University of Wisconsin System **Scores:** 58% ACT 18-23; 16% ACT 24-29 **% Accepted:** 92 **Admission Plans:** Deferred Admission **Application Deadline:** August 01 **Application Fee:** $35.00 **H.S. Requirements:** High school diploma required; GED accepted **Costs Per Year:** Application fee: $35. State resident tuition: $5001 full-time. Nonresident tuition: $15,047 full-time. Full-time tuition varies according to course load and reciprocity agreements. College room and board: $5500. College room only: $3250. Room and board charges vary according to board plan and housing facility. **Scholarships:** Available **Calendar System:** Semester, Summer Session Available **Enrollment:** FT 3,545, PT 1,308, Grad 91 **Faculty:** FT 181, PT 132 **Student-Faculty Ratio:** 18:1 **Exams:** SAT I or ACT **% Receiving Financial Aid:** 59 **% Residing in College-Owned, -Operated, or -Affiliated Housing:** 16 **Library Holdings:** 400,000 **Regional Accreditation:** North Central Association of Colleges and Schools **Credit Hours For Degree:** 120 credits, Bachelors **ROTC:** Army **Professional Accreditation:** AACSB **Intercollegiate Athletics:** Baseball M; Basketball M & W; Cross-Country Running M & W; Golf M; Soccer M & W; Softball W; Track and Field M & W; Volleyball W; Wrestling M

UNIVERSITY OF WISCONSIN-PLATTEVILLE
1 University Plaza
Platteville, WI 53818-3099
Tel: (608)342-1491
Free: 800-362-5515
Admissions: (608)342-1125
E-mail: admit@uwplatt.edu
Web Site: http://www.uwplatt.edu/
President/CEO: Dr. David Markee
Registrar: Edward Deneen
Admissions: Angela Udelhofen
Financial Aid: Elizabeth Tucker
Type: Comprehensive **Sex:** Coed **Affiliation:** University of Wisconsin System **Scores:** 54.4% ACT 18-23; 35.8% ACT 24-29 **% Accepted:** 85 **Admission Plans:** Preferred Admission **Application Deadline:** Rolling **Application Fee:** $35.00 **H.S. Requirements:** High school diploma required; GED accepted **Costs Per Year:** Application fee: $35. State resident tuition: $4277 full-time, $178.21 per credit part-time. Nonresident tuition: $14,323 full-time, $596.80 per credit part-time. Mandatory fees: $848 full-time, $35.17 per credit part-time, $2 per term part-time. Full-time tuition and fees vary according to course load, degree level, and reciprocity agreements. Part-time tuition and fees vary according to course load, degree level, and reciprocity agreements. College room and board: $4654. College room only: $2494. Room and board charges vary according to board plan. **Scholarships:** Available **Calendar System:** Semester, Summer Session Available **Enrollment:** FT 5,180, PT 595, Grad 656 **Faculty:** FT 249, PT 99 **Student-Faculty Ratio:** 20:1 **Exams:** SAT I or ACT **% Receiving Financial Aid:** 51 **% Residing in College-Owned, -Operated, or -Affiliated Housing:** 44 **Library Holdings:** 362,247 **Regional Accreditation:** North Central Association of Colleges and Schools **Credit Hours For Degree:** 64 credits, Associates; 120 credits, Bachelors **ROTC:** Army **Professional Accreditation:** ABET, NAIT, NASM, NCATE **Intercollegiate Athletics:** Baseball M; Basketball M & W; Bowling M & W; Cheerleading M & W; Cross-Country Running M & W; Football M; Golf W; Ice Hockey M & W; Lacrosse M & W; Rugby M & W; Soccer M & W; Softball W; Track and Field M & W; Ultimate Frisbee M & W; Volleyball M & W; Wrestling M

UNIVERSITY OF WISCONSIN-RICHLAND
1200 Hwy. 14 West
Richland Center, WI 53581
Tel: (608)647-6186

Admissions: (608)647-8422
Fax: (608)647-6225
E-mail: jpoole@uwc.edu
Web Site: http://richland.uwc.edu/
President/CEO: Dr. Deborah B. Cureton
Registrar: John Poole
Admissions: John D. Poole
Financial Aid: John Poole
Type: Two-Year College **Sex:** Coed **Affiliation:** University of Wisconsin System **Scores:** 72% ACT 18-23; 19% ACT 24-29 **Admission Plans:** Early Admission **Application Deadline:** Rolling **Application Fee:** $35.00 **H.S. Requirements:** High school diploma required; GED accepted **Costs Per Year:** Application fee: $35. State resident tuition: $4372 full-time, $182 per credit part-time. Nonresident tuition: $13,072 full-time, $545 per credit part-time. Mandatory fees: $395 full-time, $16.47 per credit part-time. College room and board: $4730. College room only: $2990. Room and board charges vary according to board plan. **Scholarships:** Available **Calendar System:** Semester, Summer Session Available **Enrollment:** FT 313, PT 151 **Faculty:** FT 13, PT 13 **Student-Faculty Ratio:** 18:1 **Exams:** ACT, SAT I or ACT **% Residing in College-Owned, -Operated, or -Affiliated Housing:** 35 **Library Holdings:** 45,000 **Regional Accreditation:** North Central Association of Colleges and Schools **Credit Hours For Degree:** 60 credits, Associates **Intercollegiate Athletics:** Basketball M & W; Volleyball W

UNIVERSITY OF WISCONSIN-RIVER FALLS
410 South Third St.
River Falls, WI 54022-5001
Tel: (715)425-3911
Admissions: (715)425-3500
Fax: (715)425-0678
Web Site: http://www.uwrf.edu/
President/CEO: Dr. Virgil C. Nylander
Registrar: Judith George
Admissions: Dr. Alan Tuchtenhagen
Financial Aid: David Woodward
Type: Comprehensive **Sex:** Coed **Affiliation:** University of Wisconsin System **Scores:** 58% ACT 18-23; 32% ACT 24-29 **Admission Plans:** Deferred Admission **Application Fee:** $35.00 **H.S. Requirements:** High school diploma required; GED accepted **Costs Per Year:** Application fee: $35. State resident tuition: $4968 full-time. Nonresident tuition: $15,014 full-time. Full-time tuition varies according to course load. **Scholarships:** Available **Calendar System:** Semester, Summer Session Available **Enrollment:** FT 5,132, PT 372, Grad 446 **Faculty:** FT 232, PT 105 **Student-Faculty Ratio:** 21:1 **Exams:** ACT **% Receiving Financial Aid:** 58 **% Residing in College-Owned, -Operated, or -Affiliated Housing:** 38 **Library Holdings:** 448,088 **Regional Accreditation:** North Central Association of Colleges and Schools **Credit Hours For Degree:** 120 semester credits, Bachelors **Professional Accreditation:** ACEJMC, ASLHA, CSWE, NASM, NCATE **Intercollegiate Athletics:** Basketball M & W; Cross-Country Running M & W; Equestrian Sports M & W; Football M; Ice Hockey M & W; Rugby M & W; Soccer M & W; Softball W; Swimming and Diving M & W; Tennis W; Track and Field M & W; Volleyball M & W; Weight Lifting M & W

UNIVERSITY OF WISCONSIN-ROCK COUNTY
2909 Kellogg Ave.
Janesville, WI 53546-5699
Tel: (608)758-6565; 888-INFO-UWC
Admissions: (608)758-6523
Fax: (608)758-6564
E-mail: gsmith@mail.uwc.edu
Web Site: http://rock.uwc.edu/
President/CEO: Dr. Jane Crisler
Registrar: Dr. Greg Smith
Admissions: Dr. Greg Smith
Type: Two-Year College **Sex:** Coed **Affiliation:** University of Wisconsin System **Admission Plans:** Deferred Admission **Application Fee:** $35.00 **H.S. Requirements:** High school diploma required; GED accepted **Scholarships:** Available **Calendar System:** Semester, Summer Session Available **Enrollment:** FT 751, PT 129 **Faculty:** FT 20, PT 24 **Student-Faculty Ratio:** 16:1 **Exams:** ACT **Library Holdings:** 79,972 **Regional Accreditation:** North Central Association of Colleges and Schools **Credit Hours For Degree:** 60 credits, Associates **Intercollegiate Athletics:** Soccer M & W; Tennis M & W; Volleyball W

UNIVERSITY OF WISCONSIN-SHEBOYGAN
One University Dr.
Sheboygan, WI 53081-4789
Tel: (920)459-6600
Admissions: (920)459-6633
Fax: (920)459-6602
Web Site: http://www.sheboygan.uwc.edu/
President/CEO: Raymond T. Hernandez
Admissions: Beth Raffaelli
Type: Two-Year College **Sex:** Coed **Affiliation:** University of Wisconsin System **Admission Plans:** Open Admission **Application Fee:** $35.00 **H.S. Requirements:** High school diploma required; GED accepted **Scholarships:** Available **Calendar System:** Semester, Summer Session Available **Faculty:** FT 23, PT 21 **Student-Faculty Ratio:** 15:1 **Exams:** ACT **Library Holdings:** 40,100 **Regional Accreditation:** North Central Association of Colleges and Schools **Credit Hours For Degree:** 60 credit hours, Associates **Intercollegiate Athletics:** Basketball M & W; Golf M & W; Tennis M & W; Volleyball W

UNIVERSITY OF WISCONSIN-STEVENS POINT
2100 Main St.
Stevens Point, WI 54481-3897
Tel: (715)346-0123
Admissions: (715)346-2441
Fax: (715)346-2561
E-mail: admiss@uwsp.edu
Web Site: http://www.uwsp.edu/
President/CEO: Dr. Linda Bunnell
Registrar: Larry Sipiorski
Admissions: Catherine Glennon
Financial Aid: Philip C. George
Type: Comprehensive **Sex:** Coed **Affiliation:** University of Wisconsin System **Scores:** 86% SAT V 400+; 95% SAT M 400+; 59% ACT 18-23; 35% ACT 24-29 **% Accepted:** 80 **Admission Plans:** Deferred Admission **Application Deadline:** Rolling **Application Fee:** $35.00 **H.S. Requirements:** High school diploma required; GED accepted **Costs Per Year:** Application fee: $35. State resident tuition: $4277 full-time, $178 per credit part-time. Nonresident tuition: $14,323 full-time, $596 per credit part-time. Mandatory fees: $785 full-time, $70 per credit part-time. Full-time tuition and fees vary according to course load and reciprocity agreements. Part-time tuition and fees vary according to course load and reciprocity agreements. College room and board: $4322. College room only: $2574. Room and board charges vary according to housing facility. **Scholarships:** Available **Calendar System:** Semester, Summer Session Available **Enrollment:** FT 7,746, PT 607, Grad 224 **Faculty:** FT 357, PT 80 **Student-Faculty Ratio:** 21:1 **Exams:** SAT I or ACT **% Receiving Financial Aid:** 49 **% Residing in College-Owned, -Operated, or -Affiliated Housing:** 36 **Regional Accreditation:** North Central Association of Colleges and Schools **Credit Hours For Degree:** 62 credits, Associates; 120 credits, Bachelors **ROTC:** Army **Professional Accreditation:** ASLHA, FIDER, NAACLS, NASAD, NASD, NASM, NAST, SAF **Intercollegiate Athletics:** Baseball M; Basketball M & W; Cross-Country Running M & W; Football M; Golf W; Ice Hockey M & W; Soccer W; Softball W; Swimming and Diving M & W; Tennis W; Track and Field M & W; Volleyball W; Wrestling M

UNIVERSITY OF WISCONSIN-STOUT
Menomonie, WI 54751
Tel: (715)232-1122
Admissions: (715)232-2639
Fax: (715)232-1667
E-mail: gilbertsc@uwstout.edu
Web Site: http://www.uwstout.edu/
President/CEO: Dr. Charles Sorensen
Registrar: Jeffrey W. Kirschling
Admissions: Cynthia Gilberts
Financial Aid: Beth Resech
Type: Comprehensive **Sex:** Coed **Affiliation:** University of Wisconsin System **Scores:** 65.3% ACT 18-23; 22.3% ACT 24-29 **% Accepted:** 81 **Application Deadline:** Rolling **Application Fee:** $35.00 **H.S. Requirements:** High school diploma required; GED accepted **Costs Per Year:** Application fee: $35. State resident tuition: $4745 full-time, $158 per credit part-time.

Nonresident tuition: $15,078 full-time, $503 per credit part-time. Mandatory fees: $1847 full-time, $62 per credit part-time. Full-time tuition and fees vary according to reciprocity agreements. Part-time tuition and fees vary according to reciprocity agreements. College room and board: $4572. College room only: $2814. Room and board charges vary according to board plan and housing facility. **Scholarships:** Available **Calendar System:** 4-1-4, Summer Session Available **Enrollment:** FT 6,605, PT 732, Grad 554 **Faculty:** FT 289, PT 105 **Student-Faculty Ratio:** 20:1 **Exams:** SAT I or ACT **% Receiving Financial Aid:** 50 **% Residing in College-Owned, -Operated, or -Affiliated Housing:** 38 **Library Holdings:** 229,986 **Regional Accreditation:** North Central Association of Colleges and Schools **Credit Hours For Degree:** 124 credits, Bachelors **Professional Accreditation:** ABET, AAMFT, ACCE, ADtA, CORE, FIDER, NAIT, NASAD, NCATE **Intercollegiate Athletics:** Baseball M; Basketball M & W; Cross-Country Running M & W; Football M; Gymnastics W; Ice Hockey M & W; Soccer M & W; Softball W; Tennis W; Track and Field M & W; Volleyball M & W

UNIVERSITY OF WISCONSIN-SUPERIOR
Belknap and Catlin
PO Box 2000
Superior, WI 54880-4500
Tel: (715)394-8101
Admissions: (715)394-8396
Fax: (715)394-8407
E-mail: admissions@uwsuper.edu
Web Site: http://www.uwsuper.edu/
President/CEO: Dr. Julius E. Erlenbach
Registrar: Barbara A. Erickson
Admissions: Jim Miller
Financial Aid: Anne Podgorak
Type: Comprehensive **Sex:** Coed **Affiliation:** University of Wisconsin System **Scores:** 100% SAT V 400+; 100% SAT M 400+; 61.12% ACT 18-23; 30.6% ACT 24-29 **% Accepted:** 74 **Admission Plans:** Early Admission; Deferred Admission **Application Deadline:** Rolling **Application Fee:** $35.00 **H.S. Requirements:** High school diploma required; GED accepted **Costs Per Year:** Application fee: $35. State resident tuition: $4,427 full-time, $184.46 per credit part-time. Nonresident tuition: $14,473 full-time, $603.05 per credit part-time. Mandatory fees: $761 full-time, $242.28 per unit part-time. College room and board: $4422. College room only: $2552. **Scholarships:** Available **Calendar System:** Semester, Summer Session Available **Enrollment:** FT 2,133, PT 450, Grad 289 **Faculty:** FT 118, PT 52 **Student-Faculty Ratio:** 17:1 **Exams:** SAT I or ACT **% Receiving Financial Aid:** 57 **% Residing in College-Owned, -Operated, or -Affiliated Housing:** 22 **Library Holdings:** 467,700 **Regional Accreditation:** North Central Association of Colleges and Schools **Credit Hours For Degree:** 64 credits, Associates; 120 credits, Bachelors **ROTC:** Air Force **Professional Accreditation:** ACA, CSWE, NASM **Intercollegiate Athletics:** Baseball M; Basketball M & W; Cheerleading M & W; Cross-Country Running M & W; Golf W; Ice Hockey M & W; Soccer M & W; Softball W; Track and Field M & W; Volleyball W

UNIVERSITY OF WISCONSIN-WASHINGTON COUNTY
400 University Dr.
West Bend, WI 53095-3699
Tel: (262)335-5200
Admissions: (262)335-5201
Fax: (262)335-5257
E-mail: www.mnelson@uwc.edu
Web Site: http://www.washington.uwc.edu/
President/CEO: Thomas Brigham
Registrar: Bridgett Golman
Admissions: Martha Nelson
Financial Aid: Bridgett Golman
Type: Two-Year College **Sex:** Coed **Affiliation:** University of Wisconsin System **Scores:** 39% ACT 18-23; 20% ACT 24-29 **% Accepted:** 67 **Admission Plans:** Deferred Admission **Application Deadline:** Rolling **Application Fee:** $35.00 **H.S. Requirements:** High school diploma required; GED accepted **Costs Per Year:** Application fee: $35. State resident tuition: $4520 full-time, $190 per credit part-time. Nonresident tuition: $11,700 full-time, $488 per credit part-time. Mandatory fees: $268 full-time, $11 per credit part-time, $132 per term part-time. **Scholarships:** Available **Calendar System:** Semester, Summer Session Available **Enrollment:** FT 663, PT 288 **Faculty:** FT 29, PT 23 **Student-Faculty Ratio:** 21:1 **Exams:** ACT, SAT I and SAT II or ACT **Library Holdings:** 46,429 **Regional Accreditation:** North Central Association of Colleges and Schools **Credit Hours For Degree:** 60 credits, Associates **Intercollegiate Athletics:** Basketball M & W; Golf M & W; Soccer M & W; Tennis M & W; Volleyball W

UNIVERSITY OF WISCONSIN-WAUKESHA
1500 University Dr.
Waukesha, WI 53188-2799
Tel: (414)521-5200
Fax: (414)521-5491
Web Site: http://www.waukesha.uwc.edu/
President/CEO: Dr. Brad Stewart
Registrar: Patricia McGregor
Financial Aid: Judy Becker
Type: Two-Year College **Sex:** Coed **Affiliation:** University of Wisconsin System **% Accepted:** 66 **Admission Plans:** Early Admission; Deferred Admission **Application Deadline:** Rolling **Application Fee:** $35.00 **H.S. Requirements:** High school diploma required; GED accepted **Costs Per Year:** Application fee: $35. State resident tuition: $4210 full-time, $177.25 per credit part-time. Nonresident tuition: $12,910 full-time, $539.75 per credit part-time. **Scholarships:** Available **Calendar System:** Semester, Summer Session Available **Enrollment:** FT 1,258, PT 806 **Faculty:** FT 37, PT 56 **Exams:** SAT I or ACT, SAT I **Library Holdings:** 41,000 **Regional Accreditation:** North Central Association of Colleges and Schools **Credit Hours For Degree:** 60 credits, Associates **Intercollegiate Athletics:** Basketball M & W; Golf M & W; Soccer M & W; Tennis M & W; Volleyball W

UNIVERSITY OF WISCONSIN-WHITEWATER
800 West Main St.
Whitewater, WI 53190-1790
Tel: (262)472-1234
Admissions: (262)472-1440
Fax: (262)472-1515
E-mail: mckellis@uww.edu
Web Site: http://www.uww.edu/
President/CEO: Jack Miller
Registrar: Daniel Edlebeck
Admissions: Stephen J. McKellips
Financial Aid: Carol A. Miller
Type: Comprehensive **Sex:** Coed **Affiliation:** University of Wisconsin System **Scores:** 56.87% ACT 18-23; 32.63% ACT 24-29 **% Accepted:** 55 **Admission Plans:** Early Admission; Deferred Admission **Application Deadline:** Rolling **Application Fee:** $35.00 **H.S. Requirements:** High school diploma required; GED accepted **Costs Per Year:** Application fee: $35. One-time mandatory fee: $100. State resident tuition: $4370 full-time, $186 per credit part-time. Nonresident tuition: $14,965 full-time, $663 per credit part-time. Mandatory fees: $710 full-time, $28.75 per credit part-time. Full-time tuition and fees vary according to degree level and reciprocity agreements. College room and board: $4210. College room only: $2460. Room and board charges vary according to board plan. **Scholarships:** Available **Calendar System:** Semester, Summer Session Available **Enrollment:** FT 8,572, PT 815, Grad 1,363 **Faculty:** FT 399, PT 98 **Student-Faculty Ratio:** 21:1 **Exams:** SAT I or ACT **% Receiving Financial Aid:** 44 **% Residing in College-Owned, -Operated, or -Affiliated Housing:** 40 **Library Holdings:** 683,564 **Regional Accreditation:** North Central Association of Colleges and Schools **Credit Hours For Degree:** 60 credits, Associates; 120 credits, Bachelors **ROTC:** Army, Air Force **Professional Accreditation:** AACSB, ACA, ASLHA, CSWE, NASM, NAST, NCATE **Intercollegiate Athletics:** Baseball M; Basketball M & W; Bowling M & W; Cheerleading M & W; Cross-Country Running M & W; Football M; Golf W; Gymnastics W; Ice Hockey M & W; Lacrosse M; Rugby M & W; Soccer M & W; Softball W; Swimming and Diving M & W; Tennis M & W; Track and Field M & W; Volleyball M & W; Weight Lifting M; Wrestling M

VITERBO UNIVERSITY
900 Viterbo Dr.
La Crosse, WI 54601-4797
Tel: (608)796-3000
Free: 800-VIT-ERBO
Admissions: (608)796-3010
Fax: (608)796-3050
E-mail: admission@viterbo.edu
Web Site: http://www.viterbo.edu/
President/CEO: Dr. William J. Medland
Registrar: Amy Gleason
Admissions: Dr. Roland Nelson

Financial Aid: Terry Norman
Type: Comprehensive **Sex:** Coed **Affiliation:** Roman Catholic **Scores:** 68.6% ACT 18-23; 21.8% ACT 24-29 **% Accepted:** 86 **Admission Plans:** Deferred Admission **Application Deadline:** Rolling **Application Fee:** $25.00 **H.S. Requirements:** High school diploma required; GED accepted **Costs Per Year:** Application fee: $25. Comprehensive fee: $23,700 includes full-time tuition ($17,640), mandatory fees ($420), and college room and board ($5640). College room only: $2430. Part-time tuition: $505 per credit. Part-time mandatory fees: $10 per credit, $30. **Scholarships:** Available **Calendar System:** Semester, Summer Session Available **Enrollment:** FT 1,429, PT 415, Grad 690 **Faculty:** FT 119, PT 105 **Student-Faculty Ratio:** 11:1 **Exams:** ACT **% Receiving Financial Aid:** 80 **% Residing in College-Owned, -Operated, or -Affiliated Housing:** 35 **Library Holdings:** 92,591 **Regional Accreditation:** North Central Association of Colleges and Schools **Credit Hours For Degree:** 62 credits, Associates; 128 credits, Bachelors **ROTC:** Army **Professional Accreditation:** AACN, ADtA, NASM, NCATE **Intercollegiate Athletics:** Baseball M; Basketball M & W; Soccer M & W; Softball W; Volleyball W

WAUKESHA COUNTY TECHNICAL COLLEGE
800 Main St.
Pewaukee, WI 53072-4601
Tel: (262)691-5566; 888-892-WCTC
Admissions: (262)691-5464
Fax: (262)691-5693
E-mail: lfrederick@wctc.edu
Web Site: http://www.wctc.edu/
President/CEO: Carol Brown
Admissions: Lesley Frederick
Financial Aid: Thomas Rabe
Type: Two-Year College **Sex:** Coed **Affiliation:** Wisconsin Technical College System **Admission Plans:** Open Admission; Early Admission **Application Deadline:** Rolling **Application Fee:** $30.00 **H.S. Requirements:** High school diploma or equivalent not required **Costs Per Year:** Application fee: $30. State resident tuition: $2610 full-time, $87 per credit part-time. Nonresident tuition: $16,089 full-time, $536 per credit part-time. **Scholarships:** Available **Calendar System:** Semester, Summer Session Available **Enrollment:** FT 1,614, PT 4,772 **Faculty:** FT 176, PT 661 **Student-Faculty Ratio:** 8:1 **Regional Accreditation:** North Central Association of Colleges and Schools **Credit Hours For Degree:** 66 credits, Associates **Professional Accreditation:** ARCEST, ACF, ADA, NLN

WESTERN TECHNICAL COLLEGE
304 6th St. North
PO Box C-908
La Crosse, WI 54602-0908
Tel: (608)785-9200
Free: 800-248-9982
Admissions: (608)785-9158
Fax: (608)785-9205
E-mail: wellsj@wwtc.edu
Web Site: http://www.wwtc.edu/
President/CEO: Dr. James Lee Rasch
Registrar: Jayne Wells
Admissions: Jane Wells
Financial Aid: Judith Erickson
Type: Two-Year College **Sex:** Coed **Affiliation:** Wisconsin Technical College System **% Accepted:** 35 **Admission Plans:** Open Admission; Early Admission **Application Deadline:** Rolling **Application Fee:** $30.00 **H.S. Requirements:** High school diploma required; GED accepted **Costs Per Year:** Application fee: $30. State resident tuition: $2610 full-time, $87 per credit part-time. Nonresident tuition: $16,089 full-time, $536.30 per credit part-time. Mandatory fees: $185 full-time, $185 per term part-time. College room only: $2312. **Scholarships:** Available **Calendar System:** Semester, Summer Session Available **Enrollment:** FT 1,910, PT 2,855 **Faculty:** FT 203, PT 685 **Student-Faculty Ratio:** 7:1 **Exams:** ACT, Other **% Residing in College-Owned, -Operated, or -Affiliated Housing:** 2 **Library Holdings:** 31,243 **Regional Accreditation:** North Central Association of Colleges and Schools **Credit Hours For Degree:** 68 credit hours, Associates **Professional Accreditation:** ADA, AHIMA, AOTA, APTA, CARC, JRCEET, JRCERT, NAACLS, NLN **Intercollegiate Athletics:** Baseball M; Basketball M & W; Volleyball W

WISCONSIN INDIANHEAD TECHNICAL COLLEGE
505 Pine Ridge Dr.
Shell Lake, WI 54871
Tel: (715)468-2815
Free: 800-243-9482
Fax: (715)468-2819
Web Site: http://www.witc.edu/
President/CEO: David Hildebrand
Admissions: Mimi Crandall
Type: Two-Year College **Sex:** Coed **Affiliation:** Wisconsin Technical College System **Application Deadline:** Rolling **Application Fee:** $35.00 **Calendar System:** Semester **Enrollment:** FT 1,561, PT 1,972 **Faculty:** FT 143, PT 193 **Student-Faculty Ratio:** 6:1 **Regional Accreditation:** North Central Association of Colleges and Schools **Professional Accreditation:** AOTA, NLN

WISCONSIN LUTHERAN COLLEGE
8800 West Bluemound Rd.
Milwaukee, WI 53226-9942
Tel: (414)443-8800; 888-WIS LUTH
Admissions: (414)443-8811
Fax: (414)443-8514
E-mail: craig_swiontek@wlc.edu
Web Site: http://www.wlc.edu/
President/CEO: Dr. Timothy J. Kriewall
Registrar: Brett Valerio
Admissions: Craig Swiontek
Financial Aid: Linda Loeffel
Type: Four-Year College **Sex:** Coed **Affiliation:** Wisconsin Evangelical Lutheran Synod **Scores:** 40% ACT 18-23; 54% ACT 24-29 **Application Fee:** $20.00 **H.S. Requirements:** High school diploma required; GED accepted **Costs Per Year:** Application fee: $20. Comprehensive fee: $23,510 includes full-time tuition ($17,340), mandatory fees ($130), and college room and board ($6040). **Scholarships:** Available **Calendar System:** Semester, Summer Session Available **Enrollment:** FT 672, PT 34 **Faculty:** FT 47, PT 41 **Student-Faculty Ratio:** 11:1 **Exams:** SAT I or ACT **% Receiving Financial Aid:** 75 **% Residing in College-Owned, -Operated, or -Affiliated Housing:** 78 **Library Holdings:** 71,731 **Regional Accreditation:** North Central Association of Colleges and Schools **Credit Hours For Degree:** 128 credits, Bachelors **ROTC:** Army, Navy, Air Force **Intercollegiate Athletics:** Baseball M; Basketball M & W; Cross-Country Running M & W; Football M; Golf M & W; Soccer M & W; Softball W; Tennis W; Track and Field M & W; Volleyball M & W

CASPER COLLEGE
125 College Dr.
Casper, WY 82601-4699
Tel: (307)268-2110
Free: 800-442-2963
Admissions: (307)268-2220
Fax: (307)268-2682
E-mail: amcnulty@caspercollege.edu
Web Site: http://www.caspercollege.edu/
President/CEO: Dr. Walter H. Nolte
Registrar: Alison McNulty
Admissions: Alison McNulty
Financial Aid: Darry Voigt
Type: Two-Year College **Sex:** Coed **Affiliation:** Wyoming Community College Commission **Scores:** 100% SAT V 400+; 90% SAT M 400+; 54% ACT 18-23; 19% ACT 24-29 **% Accepted:** 100 **Admission Plans:** Open Admission; Early Admission **Application Deadline:** August 15 **Application Fee:** $0.00 **H.S. Requirements:** High school diploma required; GED accepted **Costs Per Year:** Application fee: $0. State resident tuition: $1416 full-time, $59 per credit part-time. Nonresident tuition: $4272 full-time, $178 per credit part-time. Mandatory fees: $168 full-time, $7 per credit part-time. College room and board: $3590. **Scholarships:** Available **Calendar System:** Semester, Summer Session Available **Enrollment:** FT 1,896, PT 2,389 **Faculty:** FT 153, PT 99 **Student-Faculty Ratio:** 14:1 **% Residing in College-Owned, -Operated, or -Affiliated Housing:** 15 **Library Holdings:** 118,000 **Regional Accreditation:** North Central Association of Colleges and Schools **Credit Hours For Degree:** 64 credit hours, Associates **ROTC:** Army **Professional Accreditation:** AOTA, JRCERT, NASAD, NASM, NAST, NLN **Intercollegiate Athletics:** Basketball M & W; Cheerleading M & W; Equestrian Sports M & W; Volleyball W

CENTRAL WYOMING COLLEGE
2660 Peck Ave.
Riverton, WY 82501-2273
Tel: (307)855-2000
Free: 800-735-8418
Admissions: (307)855-2231
Fax: (307)855-2092
E-mail: tshultz@cwc.edu
Web Site: http://www.cwc.edu/
President/CEO: Dr. JoAnne McFarland
Admissions: Tami Shultz
Financial Aid: Jacquelyn Burns
Type: Two-Year College **Sex:** Coed **Affiliation:** Wyoming Community College Commission **Scores:** 88% SAT V 400+; 84% SAT M 400+; 55% ACT 18-23; 22% ACT 24-29 **% Accepted:** 100 **Admission Plans:** Open Admission; Early Admission; Deferred Admission **Application Deadline:** Rolling **Application Fee:** $0.00 **H.S. Requirements:** High school diploma required; GED accepted **Costs Per Year:** Application fee: $0. State resident tuition: $1416 full-time, $59 per credit part-time. Nonresident tuition: $4272 full-time, $178 per credit part-time. Mandatory fees: $528 full-time, $22 per credit part-time. College room and board: $3060. College room only: $1460. **Scholarships:** Available **Calendar System:** Semester, Summer Session Available **Enrollment:** FT 696, PT 941 **Faculty:** FT 41, PT 123 **Student-Faculty Ratio:** 14:1 **% Residing in College-Owned, -Operated, or -Affiliated Housing:** 9 **Library Holdings:** 78,167 **Regional Accreditation:** North Central Association of Colleges and Schools **Credit Hours For Degree:** 64 credits, Associates **Professional Accreditation:** ARCEST, NLN **Intercollegiate Athletics:** Equestrian Sports M & W

EASTERN WYOMING COLLEGE
3200 West C St.
Torrington, WY 82240-1699
Tel: (307)532-8200
Free: 800-658-3195
Admissions: (307)532-8257
Fax: (307)532-8222
E-mail: mcotant@ewc.wy.edu
Web Site: http://www.ewc.wy.edu/
President/CEO: Dr. Jack L. Bottenfield
Registrar: Marilyn J. Cotant
Admissions: Marilyn Cotant
Financial Aid: Pamela Palermo
Type: Two-Year College **Sex:** Coed **Affiliation:** Wyoming Community College Commission **Admission Plans:** Open Admission; Preferred Admission; Early Admission **Application Deadline:** Rolling **Application Fee:** $0.00 **H.S. Requirements:** High school diploma required; GED accepted **Costs Per Year:** Application fee: $0. State resident tuition: $1416 full-time, $59 per credit hour part-time. Nonresident tuition: $4272 full-time, $178 per credit hour part-time. Mandatory fees: $384 full-time, $16 per credit hour part-time. College room and board: $3220. College room only: $1364. **Scholarships:** Available **Calendar System:** Semester, Summer Session Available **Enrollment:** FT 522, PT 824 **Faculty:** FT 38, PT 67 **Student-Faculty Ratio:** 13:1 **% Residing in College-Owned, -Operated, or -Affiliated Housing:** 26 **Regional Accreditation:** North Central Association of Colleges and Schools **Credit Hours For Degree:** 64 credit hours, Associates **Intercollegiate Athletics:** Basketball M; Cheerleading M & W; Equestrian Sports M & W; Golf M; Volleyball W

LARAMIE COUNTY COMMUNITY COLLEGE
1400 East College Dr.
Cheyenne, WY 82007-3299
Tel: (307)778-5222
Admissions: (307)778-1242
Fax: (307)778-1399
Web Site: http://www.lccc.wy.edu/
President/CEO: Dr. Charles Bohlen
Registrar: Joe VonSeggern
Admissions: Donald J. VonSeggern
Financial Aid: Dennis Schroeder
Type: Two-Year College **Sex:** Coed **Affiliation:** Wyoming Community College Commission **% Accepted:** 100 **Admission Plans:** Open Admission; Early Admission **Application Deadline:** Rolling **Application Fee:** $20.00 **H.S. Requirements:** High school diploma required; GED accepted **Costs Per Year:** Application fee: $20. State resident tuition: $2004 full-time, $83.50 per credit hour part-time. Nonresident tuition: $4860 full-time, $202.50 per credit hour part-time. Mandatory fees: $24.50 per credit hour part-time. College room and board: $5024. **Scholarships:** Available **Calendar System:** Semester, Summer Session Available **Enrollment:** FT 1,704, PT 2,899 **Faculty:** FT 90, PT 187 **Student-Faculty Ratio:** 18:1 **% Residing in College-Owned, -Operated, or -Affiliated Housing:** 2 **Library Holdings:** 51,872 **Regional Accreditation:** North Central Association of Colleges and

Schools **Credit Hours For Degree:** 64 credit hours, Associates **ROTC:** Air Force **Professional Accreditation:** ADA, JRCERT, NLN **Intercollegiate Athletics:** Basketball M; Cheerleading M & W; Soccer M & W; Volleyball W

NORTHWEST COLLEGE
231 West 6th St.
Powell, WY 82435-1898
Tel: (307)754-6000
Free: 800-560-4692
Admissions: (307)754-6043
Fax: (307)754-6700
E-mail: beark@adm.nwc.whecn.edu
Web Site: http://www.northwestcollege.edu/
President/CEO: Dr. Miles LaRowe
Registrar: Linda Newell
Admissions: Brad Hammond
Financial Aid: Jennifer Almli
Type: Two-Year College **Sex:** Coed **Affiliation:** Wyoming Community College Commission **Scores:** 45% ACT 18-23; 21% ACT 24-29 **Admission Plans:** Open Admission; Early Admission; Deferred Admission **Application Fee:** $0.00 **H.S. Requirements:** High school diploma required; GED accepted **Scholarships:** Available **Calendar System:** Semester, Summer Session Available **Enrollment:** FT 1,121, PT 590 **Faculty:** FT 77, PT 77 **Student-Faculty Ratio:** 16:1 **Exams:** Other, SAT I or ACT **% Residing in College-Owned, -Operated, or -Affiliated Housing:** 46 **Library Holdings:** 55,330 **Regional Accreditation:** North Central Association of Colleges and Schools **Credit Hours For Degree:** 64 credits, Associates **Professional Accreditation:** NASM, NLN **Intercollegiate Athletics:** Basketball M & W; Equestrian Sports M & W; Riflery M & W; Volleyball W; Wrestling M

SHERIDAN COLLEGE-GILLETTE CAMPUS
300 West Sinclair St.
Gillette, WY 82718
Tel: (307)686-0254
Web Site: http://www.sheridan.edu/index_live.asp?id=2 **Type:** Two-Year College **Sex:** Coed **Calendar System:** Semester

SHERIDAN COLLEGE-SHERIDAN AND GILLETTE
PO Box 1500
Sheridan, WY 82801-1500
Tel: (307)674-6446
Free: 800-913-9139
Fax: (307)674-7205
E-mail: admissions@sheridan.edu
Web Site: http://www.sheridan.edu/
Registrar: Sandy Eisenman
Admissions: Zane Garstad
Financial Aid: Randy Thompson
Type: Two-Year College **Sex:** Coed **Affiliation:** Wyoming Community College Commission **Admission Plans:** Open Admission; Early Admission; Deferred Admission **Application Deadline:** Rolling **Application Fee:** $0.00 **H.S. Requirements:** High school diploma required; GED accepted **Costs Per Year:** Application fee: $0. State resident tuition: $1416 full-time, $59 per credit hour part-time. Nonresident tuition: $4248 full-time, $177 per credit hour part-time. Mandatory fees: $480 full-time, $20 per credit hour part-time. College room and board: $3920. **Scholarships:** Available **Calendar System:** Semester, Summer Session Available **Enrollment:** FT 1,047, PT 1,848 **Faculty:** FT 76, PT 93 **Student-Faculty Ratio:** 14:1 **% Residing in College-Owned, -Operated, or -Affiliated Housing:** 20 **Library Holdings:** 46,589 **Regional Accreditation:** North Central Association of Colleges and Schools **Credit Hours For Degree:** 64 credit hours, Associates **Professional Accreditation:** ADA, NLN **Intercollegiate Athletics:** Basketball M & W; Volleyball W

UNIVERSITY OF WYOMING
Laramie, WY 82070
Tel: (307)766-1121
Free: 800-342-5996
Admissions: (307)766-4272
Fax: (307)766-2271
E-mail: undergraduate.admissions@uwyo.edu
Web Site: http://www.uwyo.edu/
President/CEO: Dr. Philip L. Dubois
Registrar: Dr. Robert J. Hensley, Jr.
Admissions: Noah Buckley
Financial Aid: David Lee Gruen
Type: University **Sex:** Coed **Scores:** 96.3% SAT V 400+; 95.3% SAT M 400+; 48.8% ACT 18-23; 37.1% ACT 24-29 **% Accepted:** 95 **Admission Plans:** Preferred Admission; Deferred Admission **Application Deadline:** August 10 **Application Fee:** $30.00 **H.S. Requirements:** High school diploma required; GED accepted **Costs Per Year:** Application fee: $30. State resident tuition: $2760 full-time, $92 per credit hour part-time. Nonresident tuition: $9150 full-time, $305 per credit hour part-time. Mandatory fees: $666 full-time, $162 per term part-time. Full-time tuition and fees vary according to course load, location, program, and reciprocity agreements. Part-time tuition and fees vary according to course load, location, program, and reciprocity agreements. College room and board: $6240. College room only: $2709. Room and board charges vary according to board plan and housing facility. **Scholarships:** Available **Calendar System:** Semester, Summer Session Available **Enrollment:** FT 7,699, PT 1,811, Grad 3,179 **Faculty:** FT 651, PT 53 **Student-Faculty Ratio:** 15:1 **Exams:** SAT I or ACT **% Receiving Financial Aid:** 43 **% Residing in College-Owned, -Operated, or -Affiliated Housing:** 20 **Library Holdings:** 1,345,173 **Regional Accreditation:** North Central Association of Colleges and Schools **Credit Hours For Degree:** 120 semester hours, Bachelors **ROTC:** Army, Air Force **Professional Accreditation:** AACSB, ABET, AACN, AAFCS, ABA, ACPhE, ACA, APA, ASLHA, AALS, CSWE, NASM, NCATE **Intercollegiate Athletics:** Badminton M & W; Baseball M; Basketball M & W; Cheerleading M & W; Cross-Country Running M & W; Equestrian Sports M & W; Fencing M & W; Football M; Golf M & W; Ice Hockey M & W; Riflery M & W; Rugby M & W; Skiing (Downhill) M & W; Soccer M & W; Swimming and Diving M & W; Tennis W; Track and Field M & W; Ultimate Frisbee M & W; Volleyball W; Wrestling M

WESTERN WYOMING COMMUNITY COLLEGE
PO Box 428
Rock Springs, WY 82902-0428
Tel: (307)382-1600
Free: 800-226-1181
Admissions: (307)382-1647
Fax: (307)382-1636
E-mail: lwatkins@wwcc.cc.wy.us
Web Site: http://www.wwcc.wy.edu
President/CEO: Dr. Tex Boggs
Registrar: Laurie Watkins
Admissions: Laurie Watkins
Financial Aid: Stacee Hanson
Type: Two-Year College **Sex:** Coed **Scores:** 80% ACT 18-23; 10% ACT 24-29 **Admission Plans:** Open Admission; Early Admission; Deferred Admission **Application Fee:** $0.00 **H.S. Requirements:** High school diploma required; GED accepted **Costs Per Year:** Application fee: $0. State resident tuition: $1658 full-time, $70 per credit hour part-time. Nonresident tuition: $4418 full-time, $185 per credit hour part-time. Full-time tuition varies according to reciprocity agreements. Part-time tuition varies according to course load and reciprocity agreements. College room and board: $3033. College room only: $1474. Room and board charges vary according to board plan and housing facility. **Scholarships:** Available **Calendar System:** Semester, Summer Session Available **Enrollment:** FT 1,099, PT 1,555 **Faculty:** FT 65, PT 130 **Student-Faculty Ratio:** 17:1 **Exams:** Other, SAT I or ACT **% Residing in College-Owned, -Operated, or -Affiliated Housing:** 13 **Library Holdings:** 115,000 **Regional Accreditation:** North Central Association of Colleges and Schools **Credit Hours For Degree:** 64 credit hours, Associates **Professional Accreditation:** CARC, NLN **Intercollegiate Athletics:** Basketball M & W; Cheerleading M & W; Soccer M & W; Volleyball W; Wrestling M

WYOTECH
4373 North Third St.
Laramie, WY 82072-9519
Tel: (307)742-3776
Free: 800-521-7158
Web Site: http://www.wyotech.com/
President/CEO: Deborah Kirsch
Registrar: Tracy Stibitz
Admissions: Troy Chaney
Financial Aid: Byron Axlund
Type: Two-Year College **Sex:** Coed **Admission Plans:** Open Admission **Application Fee:** $100.00 **H.S. Requirements:** High school diploma required; GED accepted **Scholarships:** Available **Calendar System:** Miscellaneous

Enrollment: FT 2,011 **Faculty:** FT 107 **Student-Faculty Ratio:** 14:1 **Credit Hours For Degree:** 1500 hours, Associates **Professional Accreditation:** ACCSCT **Intercollegiate Athletics:** Basketball W; Bowling W

Canadian Colleges

ALBERTA COLLEGE OF ART & DESIGN
1407 14 Ave. NW
Calgary, AB, Canada T2N 4R3
Tel: (403)284-7600
Free: 800-251-8290
Admissions: (403)284-7689
Web Site: http://www.acad.ca/
President/CEO: Dr. Desmond Rochfort
Registrar: Susan Mackenzie
Admissions: Joy Borman
Financial Aid: Claudia Shepherd
Type: Four-Year College **Sex:** Coed **% Accepted:** 51 **Admission Plans:** Early Admission; Early Action; Early Decision Plan **Application Deadline:** April 01 **Application Fee:** $50.00 **H.S. Requirements:** High school diploma required; GED not accepted. For those granted qualified admission to Artstream program: High school diploma or equivalent not required **Costs Per Year:** Application fee: $50 Canadian dollars. Tuition, fee, and room and board charges are reported in Canadian dollars. Province resident tuition: $4,490 full-time, $575.35 per course part-time. Canadian resident tuition: $1,321 per course part-time. Mandatory fees: $674 full-time, $306.50 per year part-time. Full-time tuition and fees vary according to course load. Part-time tuition and fees vary according to course load. College room and board: $7000. College room only: $4000. International student tuition: $11,943 full-time. Room and board is available at the Southern Alberta Institute of Technology. **Scholarships:** Available **Calendar System:** Semester, Summer Session Available **Enrollment:** FT 974, PT 119 **Faculty:** FT 49, PT 65 **Student-Faculty Ratio:** 9:1 **Library Holdings:** 25,000 **Credit Hours For Degree:** 120 credits, Bachelors **Intercollegiate Athletics:** Basketball M & W; Ice Hockey M & W; Soccer M & W; Volleyball M & W

ALLIANCE UNIVERSITY COLLEGE
630, 833-4th Ave. SW
Calgary, AB, Canada T2P 3T5
Tel: (403)410-2000
Free: 800-461-1222
Web Site: http://www.auc-nuc.ca/
President/CEO: Dr. George Durance
Registrar: Barry Holtslander
Type: Comprehensive **Sex:** Coed **Affiliation:** The Christian and Missionary Alliance **Admission Plans:** Open Admission; Early Admission; Deferred Admission **Application Fee:** $50.00 **H.S. Requirements:** High school diploma required; GED accepted. For applicants 21 or over: High school diploma or equivalent not required **Scholarships:** Available **Calendar System:** Semester, Summer Session Available **Enrollment:** FT 245, PT 84 **% Residing in College-Owned, -Operated, or -Affiliated Housing:** 66 **Library Holdings:** 65,000 **Credit Hours For Degree:** 94 semester hours, Bachelors **Professional Accreditation:** AABC, ATS **Intercollegiate Athletics:** Basketball M & W; Ice Hockey M; Soccer M & W; Volleyball M & W

ATHABASCA UNIVERSITY
1 University Dr.
Athabasca, AB, Canada T9S 3A3
Tel: (780)675-6100
Free: 800-788-9041
Admissions: (780)675-6302
Fax: (780)675-6437
E-mail: reginfo@cs.athabascau.ca
Web Site: http://www.athabascau.ca/
President/CEO: Dr. Dominique Abrioux
Registrar: James D'arcy
Admissions: Gilbert Perras
Financial Aid: Joan Fraser
Type: Comprehensive **Sex:** Coed **Admission Plans:** Open Admission **Application Deadline:** Rolling **Application Fee:** $60.00 **H.S. Requirements:** High school diploma or equivalent not required **Costs Per Year:** Application fee: $60 Canadian dollars. Tuition and fee charges are reported in Canadian dollars. Area resident tuition: $418 per course part-time. Province resident tuition: $4180 full-time, $473 per course part-time. Canadian resident tuition: $4730 full-time, $696 per course part-time. International student tuition: $6960 full-time. **Scholarships:** Available **Calendar System:** Continuous, Summer Session Available **Enrollment:** , PT 30,311, Grad 3,126 **Faculty:** FT 125, PT 384 **Student-Faculty Ratio:** 0:1 **Library Holdings:** 143,000 **Regional Accreditation:** Middle State Association of Colleges and Schools **Credit Hours For Degree:** 90 credits for 3-year degrees, 120 credits for 4-year degrees, Bachelors

CONCORDIA UNIVERSITY COLLEGE OF ALBERTA
7128 Ada Blvd., NW
Edmonton, AB, Canada T5B 4E4
Tel: (780)479-8481; (866)479-5200
Admissions: (780)479-9224
Fax: (780)474-1933
Web Site: http://www.concordia.ab.ca/
President/CEO: Dr. Richard Kraemer
Registrar: Judy Kruse
Admissions: Tony Norrad
Type: Four-Year College **Sex:** Coed **Affiliation:** Lutheran **Admission Plans:** Early Admission **Application Fee:** $0.00 **H.S. Requirements:** High school diploma required; GED not accepted **Costs Per Year:** Application fee: $0 Canadian dollars, $75 Canadian dollars for nonresidents. Tuition, fee, and room and board charges are reported in Canadian dollars. Comprehensive fee: $10,588 includes full-time tuition ($5810), mandatory fees ($348), and college room and board ($4430). College room only: $2450. Full-time tuition and fees vary according to class time, course load, and program. Room and board charges vary according to board plan and student level. Part-time tuition: $726.25 per course. Part-time mandatory fees: $242.08 per credit. Part-time tuition and fees vary according to class time, course load, and program. International student tuition: $8435 full-time. **Calendar System:** Semester, Summer Session Available **Faculty:** FT 59, PT 94 **Student-Faculty Ratio:** 18:1 **% Residing in College-Owned, -Operated, or -Affiliated Housing:** 3 **Library Holdings:** 89,380 **Credit Hours For Degree:** 90 credits, Associates; 120 credits, Bachelors **Intercollegiate Athletics:** Badminton M & W; Basketball M & W; Cross-Country Running M & W; Golf M & W; Ice Hockey M; Soccer M & W; Swimming and Diving M & W

THE KING'S UNIVERSITY COLLEGE
9125 50th St.
Edmonton, AB, Canada T6B 2H3
Tel: (780)465-3500
Free: 800-661-8582
Fax: (780)465-3534

E-mail: registrar@kingsu.ca
Web Site: http://www.kingsu.ca/
President/CEO: Dr. Henk W. H. Van Andel
Registrar: Glenn Keeler
Admissions: Glenn J. Keeler
Financial Aid: Rachelle DeHaan
Type: Four-Year College **Sex:** Coed **Affiliation:** interdenominational **% Accepted:** 82 **Application Deadline:** Rolling **Application Fee:** $50.00 **H.S. Requirements:** High school diploma or equivalent not required **Costs Per Year:** Application fee: $50 Canadian dollars. Tuition, fee, and room and board charges are reported in Canadian dollars. Comprehensive fee: $12,320 includes full-time tuition ($7595), mandatory fees ($325), and college room and board ($4400). College room only: $2400. Part-time tuition: $245 per credit. Part-time mandatory fees: $81.25 per term. International student tuition: $9095 full-time. **Scholarships:** Available **Calendar System:** Miscellaneous, Summer Session Available **Enrollment:** FT 511, PT 53 **Faculty:** FT 41, PT 65 **Student-Faculty Ratio:** 9:1 **% Residing in College-Owned, -Operated, or -Affiliated Housing:** 28 **Library Holdings:** 75,295 **Credit Hours For Degree:** 93 credits, Bachelors **Intercollegiate Athletics:** Basketball M & W; Soccer M & W; Volleyball M & W

NEWMAN THEOLOGICAL COLLEGE
15611 Saint Albert Trail NW
Edmonton, AB, Canada T6V 1H3
Tel: (780)447-2993
Free: 800-386-7531
Web Site: http://www.newman.edu/
President/CEO: Rev. John (Jack) Gallagher
Registrar: Sharon Gauthier
Type: Comprehensive **Sex:** Coed **Affiliation:** Roman Catholic **Calendar System:** Semester **Professional Accreditation:** ATS

PRAIRIE BIBLE INSTITUTE
330 Sixth Ave. North, PO Box 4000
Three Hills, AB, Canada T0M 2N0
Tel: (403)443-5511
Free: 800-661-2425
Fax: (403)443-5540
Web Site: http://www.pbi.ab.ca/
President/CEO: Dr. Jon Ohlhauser
Registrar: Douglas Lewis
Admissions: Kevin Kirk
Type: Four-Year College **Sex:** Coed **Affiliation:** interdenominational **Application Fee:** $0.00 **H.S. Requirements:** High school diploma required; GED accepted **Calendar System:** Semester, Summer Session Not available **Enrollment:** FT 371, PT 86 **Faculty:** FT 31, PT 11 **Student-Faculty Ratio:** 12:1 **% Residing in College-Owned, -Operated, or -Affiliated Housing:** 78 **Library Holdings:** 60,745 **Credit Hours For Degree:** 129 credits, Bachelors **Professional Accreditation:** AABC **Intercollegiate Athletics:** Basketball M & W; Cross-Country Running M & W; Volleyball M & W

ROCKY MOUNTAIN COLLEGE
4039 Brentwood Rd., NW
Calgary, AB, Canada T2L 1L1
Tel: (403)284-5100
E-mail: enrolment@rockymountaincollege.ca
Web Site: http://www.rockymountaincollege.ca/
President/CEO: Rev. Gordon Dirks
Registrar: Gwen Nienkirchen
Admissions: Dayna Chu
Type: Four-Year College **Sex:** Coed **Affiliation:** Missionary Church **Admission Plans:** Deferred Admission **Application Fee:** $50.00 **H.S. Requirements:** High school diploma required; GED accepted **Scholarships:** Available **Calendar System:** Semester, Summer Session Available **Faculty:** FT 14, PT 13 **Student-Faculty Ratio:** 20:1 **% Residing in College-Owned, -Operated, or -Affiliated Housing:** 20 **Library Holdings:** 25,280 **Credit Hours For Degree:** 128 semester hours, Bachelors **Professional Accreditation:** AABC **Intercollegiate Athletics:** Basketball M & W; Ice Hockey M; Soccer M; Volleyball M & W

SOUTHERN ALBERTA INSTITUTE OF TECHNOLOGY
1301 16th Ave. NW
Calgary, AB, Canada T2M 0L4
Tel: (403)284-8110; 877-284-SAIT
Admissions: (403)284-7248
Fax: (403)284-7112
Web Site: http://www.sait.ca/
President/CEO: Irene Lewis
Admissions: Jennifer Bennett
Type: Four-Year College **Sex:** Coed **Application Deadline:** February 28 **Application Fee:** $25.00 **Costs Per Year:** Application fee: $25. Province resident tuition: $81.33 per credit part-time. Canadian resident tuition: $3738 full-time. Mandatory fees: $498 full-time. Full-time tuition and fees vary according to course load, degree level, and program. Part-time tuition varies according to class time. College room only: $664. International student tuition: $8306 full-time. **Calendar System:** Trimester

TAYLOR UNIVERSITY COLLEGE AND SEMINARY
11525-23 Ave.
Edmonton, AB, Canada T6J 4T3
Tel: (780)431-5200
Free: 800-567-4988
Fax: (780)436-9416
Web Site: http://www.taylor-edu.ca/
President/CEO: Dr. Marvin Dewey
Registrar: Craig Weston
Admissions: Terry Okken
Financial Aid: Terry Okken
Type: Comprehensive **Sex:** Coed **Affiliation:** North American Baptist **Admission Plans:** Deferred Admission **Application Fee:** $35.00 **H.S. Requirements:** High school diploma required; GED not accepted. For applicants 21 or over: High school diploma or equivalent not required **Calendar System:** Semester, Summer Session Not available **Enrollment:** FT 202, PT 67 **Faculty:** FT 7, PT 23 **Student-Faculty Ratio:** 16:1 **Exams:** SAT I or ACT **% Residing in College-Owned, -Operated, or -Affiliated Housing:** 55 **Library Holdings:** 50,083 **Credit Hours For Degree:** 124 credit hours, Bachelors **Professional Accreditation:** AABC, ATS **Intercollegiate Athletics:** Basketball M & W; Ice Hockey M; Volleyball M & W

UNIVERSITY OF ALBERTA
Edmonton, AB, Canada T6G 2E1
Tel: (780)492-3111
Admissions: (780)492-3113
Fax: (780)492-7172
E-mail: registrar@ualberta.ca
Web Site: http://www.ualberta.ca/
President/CEO: Roderick D. Fraser, PhD
Registrar: Carole Byrne
Admissions: Carole Byrne
Financial Aid: Ron Chilibeck
Type: University **Sex:** Coed **Admission Plans:** Preferred Admission; Deferred Admission **Application Deadline:** May 01 **Application Fee:** $100.00 **H.S. Requirements:** High school diploma or equivalent not required **Costs Per Year:** Application fee: $100 Canadian dollars. Tuition, fee, and room and board charges are reported in Canadian dollars. Province resident tuition: $479.76 per course part-time. Canadian resident tuition: $4,537 full-time, $1,509.12 per course part-time. Mandatory fees: $498 full-time, $272.20 per term part-time. College room and board: $4712. College room only: $2032. International student tuition: $15,091 full-time. **Calendar System:** Miscellaneous, Summer Session Available **Enrollment:** FT 27,145, PT 2,225, Grad 6,073 **Student-Faculty Ratio:** 21:1 **Exams:** SAT I and SAT II **% Residing in College-Owned, -Operated, or -Affiliated Housing:** 15 **Library Holdings:** 9,700,000 **Credit Hours For Degree:** 120 credits, Bachelors **Professional Accreditation:** AACSB, ADA, ALA, LCMEAMA **Intercollegiate Athletics:** Basketball M & W; Cross-Country Running M & W; Field Hockey M & W; Football M; Gymnastics M & W; Ice Hockey M & W; Rugby W; Soccer M & W; Swimming and Diving M & W; Track and Field M & W; Volleyball M & W; Wrestling M & W

UNIVERSITY OF CALGARY
2500 University Dr., NW
Calgary, AB, Canada T2N 1N4
Tel: (403)220-5110
Fax: (403)289-1253
Web Site: http://www.ucalgary.ca/
President/CEO: Dr. Harvey P. Weingarten
Registrar: David Johnston
Financial Aid: Linda Sharma
Type: University **Sex:** Coed **Admission Plans:** Early Admission **Application Fee:** $130.00 **H.S. Requirements:** High school diploma required; GED

not accepted **Costs Per Year:** Application fee: $130 Canadian dollars. Tuition and fee charges are reported in Canadian dollars. Area resident tuition: $486 per course part-time. **Calendar System:** Semester, Summer Session Available **Enrollment:** FT 19,600, PT 3,194 **Faculty:** FT 1,567, PT 800 **Student-Faculty Ratio:** 12:1 **Exams:** SAT I, SAT II **Library Holdings:** 2,429,434 **Credit Hours For Degree:** 15 full-year courses, Bachelors **Professional Accreditation:** AACSB, LCMEAMA **Intercollegiate Athletics:** Basketball M & W; Cross-Country Running M & W; Field Hockey W; Football M; Golf M & W; Ice Hockey M & W; Soccer M & W; Swimming and Diving M & W; Tennis M & W; Track and Field M & W; Volleyball M & W; Wrestling M & W

UNIVERSITY OF LETHBRIDGE
4401 University Dr.
Lethbridge, AB, Canada T1K 3M4
Tel: (403)329-2111
Admissions: (403)382-7134
E-mail: reg_admoo@hg.uleth.ca
Web Site: http://www.uleth.ca/
President/CEO: Dr. William H. Cade
Registrar: Leslie Lavers
Admissions: Peter Haney
Financial Aid: Becky Lore
Type: University **Sex:** Coed **% Accepted:** 55 **Admission Plans:** Early Admission; Early Decision Plan; Deferred Admission **Application Deadline:** June 01 **Application Fee:** $60.00 **H.S. Requirements:** High school diploma or equivalent not required. For non-Canadian students: High school diploma required; GED not accepted **Costs Per Year:** Application fee: $60. Canadian resident tuition: $4560 full-time, $456 per course part-time. Mandatory fees: $830 full-time, $97.34. College room and board: $5892. College room only: $3592. International student tuition: $9120 full-time. **Scholarships:** Available **Calendar System:** Semester, Summer Session Available **Enrollment:** FT 6,801, PT 847, Grad 338 **% Residing in College-Owned, -Operated, or -Affiliated Housing:** 10 **Library Holdings:** 539,154 **Credit Hours For Degree:** 40 semester courses, Bachelors **Intercollegiate Athletics:** Basketball M & W; Cross-Country Running M & W; Ice Hockey M & W; Soccer M & W; Swimming and Diving M & W; Track and Field M & W; Volleyball W

VANGUARD COLLEGE
11617 106 Ave., NW
Edmonton, AB, Canada T5H 0S1
Tel: (780)452-0808
Fax: (780)452-5803
Web Site: http://www.vanguardcollege.com/
President/CEO: Rev. Stephen Hertzog
Registrar: Ingrid Thompson
Admissions: Gonam Raju
Type: Four-Year College **Sex:** Coed **Affiliation:** Pentecostal Assemblies of Canada; Pentecostal Assemblies of Canada (PAOC) **Admission Plans:** Early Decision Plan **Application Fee:** $50.00 **H.S. Requirements:** High school diploma required; GED accepted **Calendar System:** Semester, Summer Session Available **Enrollment:** FT 145, PT 63 **Faculty:** FT 10, PT 25 **Student-Faculty Ratio:** 10:1 **Library Holdings:** 23,698 **Credit Hours For Degree:** 133 credits, Bachelors **Professional Accreditation:** AABC **Intercollegiate Athletics:** Ice Hockey M

BRITISH COLUMBIA INSTITUTE OF TECHNOLOGY
3700 Willingdon Ave.
Burnaby, BC, Canada V5G 3H2
Tel: (604)434-5734
Admissions: (604)432-8215
Fax: (604)278-5363
Web Site: http://www.bcit.ca/
President/CEO: Tony Knowles
Admissions: Val Karpinsky
Type: Four-Year College **Sex:** Coed **Application Fee:** $60.00 **H.S. Requirements:** High school diploma required; GED accepted **Costs Per Year:** Application fee: $60 Canadian dollars. Tuition, fee, and room only charges are reported in Canadian dollars. Province resident tuition: $4390 full-time. College room only: $3735. International student tuition: $15,071 full-time. Tuition guaranteed not to increase for student's term of enrollment. **Calendar System:** Quarter **Enrollment:** FT 7,283, PT 15,387 **Faculty:** FT 690, PT 550 **% Residing in College-Owned, -Operated, or -Affiliated Housing:** 5 **Library Holdings:** 169,404

COLUMBIA BIBLE COLLEGE
2940 Clearbrook Rd.
Abbotsford, BC, Canada V2T 2Z8
Tel: (604)853-3358
Free: 800-283-0881
Fax: (604)853-3063
E-mail: ron.penner@columbiabc.edu
Web Site: http://www.columbiabc.edu/
President/CEO: Dr. Paul Wartman
Registrar: Michael Szuk
Admissions: Dr. Ron Penner
Type: Four-Year College **Sex:** Coed **Affiliation:** Mennonite Brethren **% Accepted:** 72 **Admission Plans:** Open Admission **Application Deadline:** August 15 **Application Fee:** $50.00 **Costs Per Year:** Application fee: $50. Comprehensive fee: $12,140 includes full-time tuition ($7320) and college room and board ($4820). Full-time tuition varies according to program. Room and board charges vary according to board plan. **Scholarships:** Available **Calendar System:** Semester, Summer Session Not available **Faculty:** FT 10, PT 43 **Student-Faculty Ratio:** 21:1 **% Residing in College-Owned, -Operated, or -Affiliated Housing:** 65 **Library Holdings:** 44,000 **Credit Hours For Degree:** 126 credit hours, Bachelors **Professional Accreditation:** AABC **Intercollegiate Athletics:** Basketball M & W; Golf M & W; Soccer M & W; Volleyball M & W

KWANTLEN UNIVERSITY COLLEGE
1266 72nd Ave.
Surrey, BC, Canada V3W 2M8
Tel: (604)599-2100
Admissions: (604)599-2018
Fax: (604)555-2068
Web Site: http://www.kwantlen.ca/
President/CEO: Skip Triplett
Registrar: Jody Gordon
Admissions: Jody Gordon
Type: Four-Year College **Sex:** Coed **% Accepted:** 97 **Admission Plans:** Open Admission; Preferred Admission; Early Admission; Early Action; Early Decision Plan **Application Deadline:** June 30 **Application Fee:** $40.00 **H.S. Requirements:** High school diploma required; GED accepted **Costs Per Year:** Application fee: $40 Canadian dollars. Tuition and fee charges are reported in Canadian dollars. Province resident tuition: $3360 full-time, $112 per credit part-time. Canadian resident tuition: $3360 full-time, $112 per credit part-time. International student tuition: $11,400 full-time. **Calendar System:** Semester, Summer Session Available **Enrollment:** FT 7,291, PT 3,092 **Student-Faculty Ratio:** 35:1 **Credit Hours For Degree:** 60 credits, Associates; 120 credits, Bachelors **Professional Accreditation:** FIDER **Intercollegiate Athletics:** Baseball M & W; Basketball M & W; Golf M & W; Soccer M & W

MALASPINA UNIVERSITY-COLLEGE
900 Fifth St.
Nanaimo, BC, Canada V9R 5S5
Tel: (250)753-3245
Admissions: (250)740-6356
Web Site: http://www.mala.bc.ca/
President/CEO: Rich Johnston
Registrar: Greg Link
Admissions: Fred Jarklin
Type: Comprehensive **Sex:** Coed **Application Fee:** $30.00 **Costs Per Year:** Application fee: $30 Canadian dollars. Tuition and fee charges are reported in Canadian dollars. Area resident tuition: $3489 full-time, $116.30 per credit hour part-time. Mandatory fees: $279 full-time. **Calendar System:** Semester

OPEN LEARNING AGENCY
4355 Mathissi Place
Burnaby, BC, Canada V5G 4S8
Tel: (604)431-3000
Free: 800-663-9711
Fax: (604)431-3381
E-mail: edinfo@ola.bc.ca
Web Site: http://www.ola.ca/
President/CEO: William Harlan
Registrar: Robert Ruf
Admissions: Robert Ruff
Financial Aid: Gordon Down
Type: Four-Year College **Sex:** Coed **Affiliation:** Province of British Columbia, Canada public post-secondary system **Admission Plans:** Open Admission; Deferred Admission **H.S. Requirements:** High school diploma required; GED accepted. For required for program registration, but not for course registration: High school diploma required; GED accepted **Scholarships:** Available **Calendar System:** Continuous, Summer Session Not available **Enrollment:** , PT 13,950 **Faculty:** PT 137 **Student-Faculty Ratio:** 1:1 **Credit Hours For Degree:** 60 credit hours, Bachelors

ROYAL ROADS UNIVERSITY
2005 Sooke Rd.
Victoria, BC, Canada V9B 5Y2
Tel: (250)391-2511
Free: 800-788-8028
Admissions: (250)391-2552
Fax: (250)391-2522
Web Site: http://www.royalroads.ca/
President/CEO: Gerry Kelly
Registrar: Ann Nightingale

Admissions: Ann Nightingale
Type: Two-Year Upper Division **Sex:** Coed **Application Fee:** $50.00 **H.S. Requirements:** High school diploma or equivalent not required **Calendar System:** Continuous, Summer Session Available **Enrollment:** FT 199, PT 211, Grad 2,574 **Faculty:** FT 15, PT 115 **Student-Faculty Ratio:** 23:1 **% Residing in College-Owned, -Operated, or -Affiliated Housing:** 0 **Library Holdings:** 40,000 **Credit Hours For Degree:** 120 credits, Bachelors

SIMON FRASER UNIVERSITY
8888 University Dr.
Burnaby, BC, Canada V5A 1S6
Tel: (604)291-3111
Admissions: (604)291-3224
Fax: (604)291-4969
E-mail: undergraduate-admissions@sfu.ca
Web Site: http://www.sfu.ca/
President/CEO: Dr. Michael Stevenson
Registrar: Dr. D. Whiteley
Admissions: Nick Heath
Financial Aid: Charlotte French
Type: University **Sex:** Coed **Admission Plans:** Early Admission; Early Decision Plan **Application Deadline:** April 30 **Application Fee:** $100.00 **H.S. Requirements:** High school diploma required; GED not accepted **Costs Per Year:** Application fee: $100 Canadian dollars. Tuition and fee charges are reported in Canadian dollars. Province resident tuition: $148.10 per credit hour part-time. **Scholarships:** Available **Calendar System:** Trimester, Summer Session Available **Faculty:** FT 698 **Student-Faculty Ratio:** 25:1 **Exams:** SAT I or ACT **% Residing in College-Owned, -Operated, or -Affiliated Housing:** 4 **Library Holdings:** 1,391,540 **Credit Hours For Degree:** 120 credit hours, Bachelors **Professional Accreditation:** APA **Intercollegiate Athletics:** Basketball M & W; Cross-Country Running M & W; Field Hockey W; Football M; Golf M; Gymnastics M; Soccer M & W; Softball W; Swimming and Diving M & W; Track and Field M & W; Volleyball W; Wrestling M

SUMMIT PACIFIC COLLEGE
Box 1700
Abbotsford, BC, Canada V2S 7E7
Tel: (604)853-7491
Free: 800-976-8388
Fax: (604)853-8951
Web Site: http://www.summitpacific.ca/
President/CEO: Dr. James G. Richards
Registrar: Melody Deeley
Admissions: Melody Deeley
Financial Aid: Robert Lewis
Type: Four-Year College **Sex:** Coed **Affiliation:** Pentecostal Assemblies of Canada **Admission Plans:** Deferred Admission **H.S. Requirements:** High school diploma required; GED accepted **Calendar System:** Semester, Summer Session Available **Faculty:** FT 8, PT 6 **% Residing in College-Owned, -Operated, or -Affiliated Housing:** 68 **Library Holdings:** 35,409 **Credit Hours For Degree:** 120 credits, Bachelors **Professional Accreditation:** AABC **Intercollegiate Athletics:** Soccer M; Volleyball M & W

THOMPSON RIVERS UNIVERSITY
PO Box 3010, Station Terminal
Kamloops, BC, Canada V2C 5N3
Tel: (250)828-5000
Admissions: (250)828-5043
Fax: (250)828-5086
E-mail: admissions@tru.ca
Web Site: http://www.tru.ca
President/CEO: Dr. Roger H. Barnsley
Registrar: Dennis Mayberry
Admissions: Dennis Mayberry
Financial Aid: Garry Prevette
Type: Four-Year College **Sex:** Coed **% Accepted:** 59 **Admission Plans:** Open Admission **Application Deadline:** March 01 **Application Fee:** $25.00 **H.S. Requirements:** High school diploma required; GED accepted. For mature students: High school diploma or equivalent not required **Costs Per Year:** Application fee: $25 Canadian dollars. Tuition, fee, and room only charges are reported in Canadian dollars. Province resident tuition: $3335 full-time, $111 per credit part-time. Canadian resident tuition: $3335 full-time, $111 per credit part-time. Mandatory fees: $600 full-time. College room only: $3000. International student tuition: $12,000 full-time. **Calendar System:** Semester, Summer Session Available **Faculty:** FT 469, PT 154 **Student-Faculty Ratio:** 13:1 **% Residing in College-Owned, -Operated, or -Affiliated Housing:** 9 **Library Holdings:** 223,300 **Credit Hours For Degree:** 60 credits, Associates; 120 credits, Bachelors **Intercollegiate Athletics:** Badminton M & W; Baseball M; Basketball M & W; Soccer M & W; Volleyball M & W

TRINITY WESTERN UNIVERSITY
7600 Glover Rd.
Langley, BC, Canada V2Y 1Y1
Tel: (604)888-7511; 888-468-6898
Fax: (604)513-2061
E-mail: admissions@twu.ca
Web Site: http://www.twu.ca/
President/CEO: Dr. R. Neil Snider
Registrar: Dr. Larry Van Beek
Admissions: Sam Rehman
Financial Aid: Marty Penninga
Type: Comprehensive **Sex:** Coed **Affiliation:** Evangelical Free Church of America **Admission Plans:** Deferred Admission **Application Fee:** $40.00 **H.S. Requirements:** High school diploma required; GED accepted **Costs Per Year:** Application fee: $40 Canadian dollars. Tuition, fee, and room and board charges are reported in Canadian dollars. Comprehensive fee: $22,960 includes full-time tuition ($14,520), mandatory fees ($220), and college room and board ($8220). Full-time tuition and fees vary according to program. Room and board charges vary according to board plan, housing facility, and student level. Part-time tuition: $484 per semester hour. Part-time tuition varies according to program. **Scholarships:** Available **Calendar System:** Semester, Summer Session Available **Enrollment:** FT 768 **Faculty:** FT 77, PT 61 **Student-Faculty Ratio:** 18:1 **Exams:** SAT I or ACT **% Residing in College-Owned, -Operated, or -Affiliated Housing:** 40 **Library Holdings:** 190,565 **Credit Hours For Degree:** 122 semester hours, Bachelors **Professional Accreditation:** ACA, ATS **Intercollegiate Athletics:** Basketball M & W; Rugby M; Soccer M & W; Volleyball M & W

THE UNIVERSITY OF BRITISH COLUMBIA
2075 Wesbrook Mall
Vancouver, BC, Canada V6T 1Z1
Tel: (604)822-2211
Admissions: (604)822-3014
Fax: (604)822-3599
E-mail: registrar.admissions@ubc.ca
Web Site: http://www.ubc.ca/
President/CEO: Dr. Martha Piper
Registrar: Brian Silzer
Admissions: Rosalie Vlaar
Financial Aid: Barbara Crocker
Type: University **Sex:** Coed **% Accepted:** 57 **Admission Plans:** Early Admission **Application Deadline:** February 28 **Application Fee:** $100.00 **H.S. Requirements:** High school diploma required; GED not accepted **Scholarships:** Available **Calendar System:** Miscellaneous, Summer Session Available **Enrollment:** FT 19,961, PT 9,950, Grad 7,878 **Faculty:** FT 2,048 **Student-Faculty Ratio:** 15:1 **Exams:** SAT I and SAT II or ACT **% Residing in College-Owned, -Operated, or -Affiliated Housing:** 23 **Library Holdings:** 4,654,477 **Credit Hours For Degree:** 120 credits, Bachelors **ROTC:** Army, Air Force **Professional Accreditation:** AACSB, ACA, ADA, ACSP, ALA, APA, ASLA, LCMEAMA, NCATE **Intercollegiate Athletics:** Baseball M; Basketball M & W; Cheerleading M & W; Crew M & W; Cross-Country Running M & W; Fencing W; Field Hockey M & W; Football M; Golf M & W; Ice Hockey M & W; Rugby M & W; Skiing (Cross-Country) M & W; Skiing (Downhill) M & W; Soccer M & W; Swimming and Diving M & W; Track and Field M & W; Ultimate Frisbee M; Volleyball M & W; Water Polo M & W

UNIVERSITY COLLEGE OF THE FRASER VALLEY
33844 King Rd.
Abbotsford, BC, Canada V2S 7M8
Tel: (604)853-7441
Admissions: (604)864-4645
Fax: (604)853-9990
Web Site: http://www.ucfv.bc.ca/
President/CEO: H. A. Bassford
Admissions: Elaine Harris
Type: Comprehensive **Sex:** Coed **Affiliation:** B.C. provincial education **Admission Plans:** Open Admission; Deferred Admission **Application Fee:**

$45.00 **H.S. Requirements:** High school diploma or equivalent not required **Calendar System:** Semester, Summer Session Available **Enrollment:** FT 2,331, PT 3,656 **Faculty:** FT 268, PT 54 **Student-Faculty Ratio:** 13:1 **Credit Hours For Degree:** 60 credits, Associates; 120 credits, Bachelors **Intercollegiate Athletics:** Basketball M & W; Soccer M & W

UNIVERSITY OF NORTHERN BRITISH COLUMBIA
3333 University Way
Prince George, BC, Canada V2N 4Z9
Tel: (250)960-5555
Admissions: (250)960-6347
Fax: (250)960-5791
Web Site: http://www.unbc.ca/
President/CEO: Dr. Charles Jago
Registrar: John DeGrace
Admissions: Grant Kerr
Financial Aid: Linda Roa
Type: University **Sex:** Coed **% Accepted:** 83 **Admission Plans:** Early Admission; Early Decision Plan **Application Deadline:** March 01 **Application Fee:** $25.00 **H.S. Requirements:** High school diploma required; GED accepted **Costs Per Year:** Application fee: $25 Canadian dollars. Tuition, fee, and room only charges are reported in Canadian dollars. Area resident tuition: $4110 full-time, $137 per credit hour part-time. Mandatory fees: $648 full-time, $4.50 per credit hour part-time, $129 per term part-time. Full-time tuition and fees vary according to location and program. Part-time tuition and fees vary according to location and program. College room only: $3926. Room charges vary according to housing facility. International student tuition: $14,386 full-time. **Scholarships:** Available **Calendar System:** Semester **Enrollment:** FT 2,145, PT 942, Grad 474 **Student-Faculty Ratio:** 15:1 **% Residing in College-Owned, -Operated, or -Affiliated Housing:** 16 **Library Holdings:** 617,236 **Credit Hours For Degree:** 120 credits, Bachelors **Intercollegiate Athletics:** Basketball M & W; Skiing (Cross-Country) M & W

UNIVERSITY OF PHOENIX-VANCOUVER CAMPUS
4401 Still Creek Dr., Ste. 200
Burnaby, BC, Canada V5C 6G9
Tel: (604)205-6999
Free: 800-228-7240
Admissions: (480)557-1712
Web Site: http://www.phoenix.edu/
President/CEO: Daren Hancott
Admissions: Nina Omelchanko
Type: Comprehensive **Sex:** Coed **Admission Plans:** Open Admission; Deferred Admission **Application Deadline:** Rolling **Application Fee:** $110.00 **H.S. Requirements:** High school diploma required; GED accepted **Costs Per Year:** Application fee: $110. Tuition: $11,850 full-time, $395 per credit part-time. Mandatory fees: $560 full-time. **Calendar System:** Continuous, Summer Session Not available **Enrollment:** FT 256, Grad 389 **Faculty:** PT 6 **Student-Faculty Ratio:** 6:1 **Library Holdings:** 444 **Regional Accreditation:** North Central Association of Colleges and Schools **Credit Hours For Degree:** 60 credits, Associates; 120 credits, Bachelors

UNIVERSITY OF VICTORIA
PO Box 1700 STN CSC
Victoria, BC, Canada V8W 2Y2
Tel: (250)721-7211
Admissions: (250)721-8131
Fax: (250)721-6225
Web Site: http://www.uvic.ca/
President/CEO: Dr. David Turpin
Registrar: D. Cledwyn Thomas
Admissions: David Glen
Financial Aid: Lori L. Nolt
Type: University **Sex:** Coed **% Accepted:** 72 **Admission Plans:** Early Admission; Early Action; Deferred Admission **Application Deadline:** April 30 **Application Fee:** $100.00 **H.S. Requirements:** High school diploma required; GED accepted **Costs Per Year:** Application fee: $100 Canadian dollars. Tuition, fee, and room and board charges are reported in Canadian dollars. Province resident tuition: $3574 full-time, $294 per unit part-time. Canadian resident tuition: $952 per unit part-time. Mandatory fees: $493 full-time, $493 per year part-time. College room and board: $5009. College room only: $3014. International student tuition: $11,562 full-time. **Scholarships:** Available **Calendar System:** Miscellaneous, Summer Session Available **Enrollment:** FT 10,453, PT 5,682, Grad 2,426 **Faculty:** FT 710, PT 40 **Student-Faculty Ratio:** 25:1 **% Residing in College-Owned, -Operated, or -Affiliated Housing:** 16 **Library Holdings:** 1,800,000 **Credit Hours For Degree:** 60 units, Bachelors **Professional Accreditation:** APA **Intercollegiate Athletics:** Basketball M & W; Crew M & W; Cross-Country Running M & W; Field Hockey W; Golf M & W; Rugby M & W; Soccer M & W; Swimming and Diving M & W

BRANDON UNIVERSITY
270 18th St.
Brandon, MB, Canada R7A 6A9
Tel: (204)728-9520
Admissions: (204)727-7352
E-mail: kerr@brandonu.ca
Web Site: http://www.brandonu.ca/
President/CEO: Dr. Louis Visentin
Registrar: Darcy Bower
Admissions: Murray Kerr
Type: Comprehensive **Sex:** Coed **% Accepted:** 70 **Admission Plans:** Open Admission; Deferred Admission **Application Deadline:** Rolling **Application Fee:** $60.00 **H.S. Requirements:** High school diploma required; GED accepted **Costs Per Year:** Application fee: $60 Canadian dollars. Tuition, fee, and room and board charges are reported in Canadian dollars. Area resident tuition: $301.86 per credit part-time. Province resident tuition: $3,019 full-time, $301.68 per credit part-time. Canadian resident tuition: $3018 full-time. Mandatory fees: $345 full-time, $15.70 per credit hour part-time, $47.12. College room and board: $6270. College room only: $3614. International student tuition: $6,373 full-time. $637.26 per course for international students. **Scholarships:** Available **Calendar System:** Miscellaneous, Summer Session Available **Enrollment:** FT 2,306, PT 1,095, Grad 123 **Faculty:** FT 215, PT 13 **Student-Faculty Ratio:** 11:1 **% Residing in College-Owned, -Operated, or -Affiliated Housing:** 9 **Library Holdings:** 238,816 **Credit Hours For Degree:** 90 credit hours, Bachelors **Intercollegiate Athletics:** Basketball M & W; Volleyball M & W

CANADIAN MENNONITE UNIVERSITY
500 Shaftesbury Blvd.
Winnipeg, MB, Canada R3P 2N2
Tel: (204)487-3300; 877-231-4570
Fax: (204)487-3858
E-mail: abergen@cmu.ca
Web Site: http://www.cmu.ca/
President/CEO: Dean Peachey
Registrar: Morna Christian
Admissions: Abe Bergen
Financial Aid: Morna Christian
Type: Comprehensive **Sex:** Coed **Affiliation:** Mennonite **% Accepted:** 95 **Admission Plans:** Deferred Admission **Application Deadline:** August 28 **Application Fee:** $35.00 **H.S. Requirements:** High school diploma required; GED accepted **Costs Per Year:** Application fee: $35 Canadian dollars. Tuition, fee, and room and board charges are reported in Canadian dollars. Comprehensive fee: $9320 includes full-time tuition ($4650) and college room and board ($4670). College room only: $1612. Room and board charges vary according to board plan and housing facility. Part-time tuition: $465 per course. Part-time mandatory fees: $155 per credit hour. International student tuition: $8130 full-time. **Scholarships:** Available **Calendar System:** Semester, Summer Session Not available **Enrollment:** FT 349, PT 83, Grad 23 **Faculty:** FT 23, PT 7 **Student-Faculty Ratio:** 15:1 **% Residing in College-Owned, -Operated, or -Affiliated Housing:** 45 **Library Holdings:** 85,000 **Credit Hours For Degree:** 90 credits, Bachelors **Intercollegiate Athletics:** Basketball M & W; Ice Hockey M; Soccer M & W; Volleyball M & W

COLLÈGE UNIVERSITAIRE DE SAINT-BONIFACE
200 Ave. de la Cathèdrale
Saint-Boniface, MB, Canada R2H 0H7
Tel: (204)233-0210
Fax: (204)237-3240
Web Site: http://www.ustboniface.mb.ca/
President/CEO: Dr. Paul Ruest
Type: Comprehensive

PROVIDENCE COLLEGE AND THEOLOGICAL SEMINARY
10 College Crescent
Otterburne, MB, Canada R0A 1G0
Tel: (204)433-7488
Free: 800-668-7768
E-mail: mlittle@providence.mb.ca
Web Site: http://www.prov.ca/
President/CEO: Dr. August H. Konkel
Registrar: Mark Little
Admissions: Mark Little
Financial Aid: Mark Little
Type: Comprehensive **Sex:** Coed **Affiliation:** interdenominational **Admission Plans:** Open Admission; Deferred Admission **Application Fee:** $35.00 **H.S. Requirements:** High school diploma required; GED accepted **Costs Per Year:** Application fee: $35 Canadian dollars. Tuition, fee, and room and board charges are reported in Canadian dollars. Comprehensive fee: $10,100 includes full-time tuition ($5400), mandatory fees ($500), and college room and board ($4200). Room and board charges vary according to board plan and housing facility. Part-time tuition: $192 per credit. Part-time mandatory fees: $25 per credit hour. **Calendar System:** Semester, Summer Session Not available **Enrollment:** FT 381, PT 71 **Faculty:** FT 18, PT 32 **Student-Faculty Ratio:** 19:1 **% Residing in College-Owned, -Operated, or -Affiliated Housing:** 60 **Library Holdings:** 47,756 **Credit Hours For Degree:** 96 semester hours, Bachelors **Professional Accreditation:** AABC, ATS **Intercollegiate Athletics:** Badminton M & W; Basketball M & W; Ice Hockey M; Soccer M & W; Table Tennis M & W; Volleyball M & W

STEINBACH BIBLE COLLEGE
50 PTH 12N
Steinbach, MB, Canada R5G 1T4
Tel: (204)326-6451
Free: 800-230-8478
E-mail: thiebert@sbcollege.ca
Web Site: http://sbcollege.ca/
President/CEO: Abe Bergen
Registrar: Dr. Terry Hiebert
Admissions: Dr. Terry Hiebert
Type: Four-Year College **Sex:** Coed **Affiliation:** Mennonite **% Accepted:** 83 **Application Fee:** $35.00 **Costs Per Year:** Application fee: $35 Canadian dollars. Tuition, fee, and room and board charges are reported in Canadian dollars. Comprehensive fee: $9404 includes full-time tuition ($5376), mandatory fees ($107), and college room and board ($3921). Part-time tuition: $168 per credit hour. Part-time mandatory fees: $107 per year. **Calendar**

System: Semester **Faculty:** FT 4, PT 14 **Student-Faculty Ratio:** 13:1 **Professional Accreditation:** AABC

UNIVERSITY OF MANITOBA
Winnipeg, MB, Canada R3T 2N2
Tel: (204)474-8880
Admissions: (204)474-6382
Web Site: http://www.umanitoba.ca/
President/CEO: Dr. E. Szathmary
Registrar: Neil Marnoch
Admissions: Peter Dueck
Financial Aid: Peter Dueck
Type: University **Sex:** Coed **Admission Plans:** Preferred Admission **Application Deadline:** July 01 **Application Fee:** $35.00 **H.S. Requirements:** High school diploma required; GED not accepted. For students 21 or over: High school diploma or equivalent not required **Costs Per Year:** Application fee: $35. **Scholarships:** Available **Calendar System:** Miscellaneous, Summer Session Available **Enrollment:** FT 17,904, PT 6,363, Grad 3,332 **Library Holdings:** 1,600,000 **Credit Hours For Degree:** 90 credits, Bachelors **ROTC:** Army, Air Force **Professional Accreditation:** AACSB, ADA, APA, ASLA, FIDER, LCMEAMA **Intercollegiate Athletics:** Basketball M & W; Cross-Country Running M & W; Field Hockey M & W; Football M & W; Gymnastics M & W; Ice Hockey M & W; Swimming and Diving M & W; Track and Field M & W; Volleyball M & W

THE UNIVERSITY OF WINNIPEG
515 Portage Ave.
Winnipeg, MB, Canada R3B 2E9
Tel: (204)786-7811
Admissions: (204)786-9740
E-mail: admissions@uwinnipeg.ca
Web Site: http://www.uwinnipeg.ca/
President/CEO: Patrick Deane
Admissions: Nancy Latocki
Financial Aid: Judy A. Dyck
Type: Comprehensive **Sex:** Coed **Admission Plans:** Early Admission; Deferred Admission **Application Fee:** $35.00 **H.S. Requirements:** High school diploma required; GED not accepted. For applicants 21 or over: High school diploma required; GED accepted **Costs Per Year:** Application fee: $35 Canadian dollars. Tuition, fee, and room and board charges are reported in Canadian dollars. Canadian resident tuition: $2786 full-time. Mandatory fees: $318 full-time. Full-time tuition and fees vary according to program. College room and board: $4296. College room only: $2800. International student tuition: $5108 full-time. **Scholarships:** Available **Calendar System:** Miscellaneous, Summer Session Available **Enrollment:** FT 5,747, PT 2,650 **Student-Faculty Ratio:** 35:1 **% Residing in College-Owned, -Operated, or -Affiliated Housing:** 2 **Library Holdings:** 442,614 **Credit Hours For Degree:** 15 full-year courses, Bachelors **Professional Accreditation:** AAMFT, ATS **Intercollegiate Athletics:** Basketball M & W; Volleyball M & W

WESTERN CHRISTIAN COLLEGE
220 Whitmore Ave. West
Box 5000
Dauphin, MB, Canada R7N 2V5
Tel: (204)638-8801
Fax: (204)638-7054
Web Site: http://www.westernchristian.ca/
President/CEO: John McMillan
Type: Four-Year College **Sex:** Coed **Affiliation:** Church of Christ **Application Fee:** $50.00 **Costs Per Year:** Application fee: $50 Canadian dollars. Tuition, fee, and room and board charges are reported in Canadian dollars. **Calendar System:** Semester **Professional Accreditation:** AABC

WILLIAM AND CATHERINE BOOTH COLLEGE
447 Webb Place
Winnipeg, MB, Canada R3B 2P2
Tel: (204)947-6701
Free: 800-781-6044
Fax: (204)942-3856
Web Site: http://www.wcbc-sa.edu/
President/CEO: Dr. Jonathan Raymond
Registrar: Mary Ann Austin
Admissions: Mary Ann Austin
Type: Four-Year College **Sex:** Coed **Admission Plans:** Deferred Admission **Application Fee:** $30.00 **H.S. Requirements:** High school diploma required; GED accepted **Calendar System:** Semester, Summer Session Available **Faculty:** FT 7, PT 11 **Exams:** SAT I **Credit Hours For Degree:** 98 credit hours, Bachelors **Professional Accreditation:** AABC **Intercollegiate Athletics:** Volleyball M & W

New Brunswick

ATLANTIC BAPTIST UNIVERSITY
Box 6004
Moncton, NB, Canada E1C 9L7
Tel: (506)858-8970; 888-YOU-N-ABU
Fax: (506)858-9694
Web Site: http://www.abu.nb.ca/
President/CEO: Dr. Brian D. MacArthur
Registrar: Andrea Bishop
Admissions: Julie Hall
Type: Four-Year College **Sex:** Coed **Affiliation:** Baptist; The Council of Christian Colleges and Universities **Admission Plans:** Deferred Admission **Application Fee:** $35.00 **H.S. Requirements:** High school diploma required; GED accepted **Scholarships:** Available **Calendar System:** Semester, Summer Session Available **Faculty:** FT 24, PT 22 **Student-Faculty Ratio:** 23:1 **% Residing in College-Owned, -Operated, or -Affiliated Housing:** 22 **Library Holdings:** 57,000 **Credit Hours For Degree:** 120 credit hours, Bachelors **Intercollegiate Athletics:** Baseball M; Basketball M & W; Soccer M & W

BETHANY BIBLE COLLEGE
26 Western St.
Sussex, NB, Canada E4E 1E6
Tel: (506)432-4400; 888-432-4422
Admissions: (506)432-4422
Fax: (506)432-4425
E-mail: shanksk@bethany-ca.edu
Web Site: http://www.bethany-ca.edu/
President/CEO: Dr. David S. Medders
Registrar: Rev. Janet M. Starks
Admissions: Kathy Shanks
Financial Aid: Ruth Muscroft
Type: Four-Year College **Sex:** Coed **Affiliation:** Wesleyan Church **Scores:** 92% SAT V 400+; 68% SAT M 400+; 25% ACT 18-23; 25% ACT 24-29 **Application Deadline:** Rolling **Application Fee:** $20.00 **H.S. Requirements:** High school diploma required; GED accepted **Costs Per Year:** Application fee: $20 Canadian dollars. Tuition, fee, and room and board charges are reported in Canadian dollars. Comprehensive fee: $10,880 includes full-time tuition ($6330) and college room and board ($4550). Part-time tuition: $211 per credit hour. **Scholarships:** Available **Calendar System:** Semester, Summer Session Available **Enrollment:** FT 270, PT 19 **Faculty:** FT 12, PT 13 **Student-Faculty Ratio:** 19:1 **Exams:** SAT I or ACT **% Residing in College-Owned, -Operated, or -Affiliated Housing:** 77 **Library Holdings:** 27,319 **Credit Hours For Degree:** 134 hours, Bachelors **Professional Accreditation:** AABC **Intercollegiate Athletics:** Basketball M & W; Ice Hockey M; Soccer M & W; Softball M & W; Volleyball W

MOUNT ALLISON UNIVERSITY
65 York St.
Sackville, NB, Canada E4L 1E4
Tel: (506)364-2269
Admissions: (506)364-2166
Fax: (506)364-2272
Web Site: http://www.mta.ca/
Registrar: Chris Hunter
Admissions: Charlie Hunter
Type: Comprehensive **Sex:** Coed **% Accepted:** 61 **Admission Plans:** Deferred Admission **Application Deadline:** Rolling **Application Fee:** $50.00 **H.S. Requirements:** High school diploma required; GED accepted **Costs Per Year:** Application fee: $50 Canadian dollars. Tuition, fee, and room and board charges are reported in Canadian dollars. Province resident tuition: $6100 full-time. Mandatory fees: $242 full-time. Full-time tuition and fees vary according to course load. College room and board: $6630. College room only: $3430. Room and board charges vary according to board plan. International student tuition: $12,200 full-time. **Scholarships:** Available **Calendar System:** Miscellaneous, Summer Session Available **Enrollment:** FT 2,095, PT 267, Grad 7 **Faculty:** FT 133, PT 31 **Student-Faculty Ratio:** 15:1 **Exams:** SAT I and SAT II or ACT **% Residing in College-Owned, -Operated, or -Affiliated Housing:** 50 **Library Holdings:** 400,000 **Credit Hours For Degree:** 120 credits, Bachelors **Intercollegiate Athletics:** Basketball M & W; Football M; Ice Hockey W; Rugby M & W; Soccer M & W; Swimming and Diving M & W

ST. THOMAS UNIVERSITY
51 Dineen Dr.
Fredericton, NB, Canada E3B 5G3
Tel: (506)452-0640
Admissions: (506)452-0532
Fax: (506)450-9615
E-mail: admissions@stthomasu.ca
Web Site: http://www.stu.ca/
President/CEO: Dr. Daniel O'Brien
Registrar: Lawrence Batt
Admissions: Kathryn Monti
Type: Four-Year College **Sex:** Coed **Affiliation:** Roman Catholic **% Accepted:** 75 **Application Deadline:** March 31 **Application Fee:** $35.00 **H.S. Requirements:** High school diploma required; GED not accepted. For adult learners: High school diploma or equivalent not required **Costs Per Year:** Application fee: $35. Comprehensive fee: $10,526 includes full-time tuition ($4145), mandatory fees ($281), and college room and board ($6100). College room only: $3185. Full-time tuition and fees vary according to course load, degree level, and program. Room and board charges vary according to board plan, housing facility, and location. Part-time tuition: $467 per course. Part-time tuition varies according to course load. International student tuition: $8290 full-time. **Calendar System:** Miscellaneous, Summer Session Available **Enrollment:** FT 2,739, PT 349 **Faculty:** FT 120, PT 145 **Student-Faculty Ratio:** 17:1 **Exams:** SAT I and SAT II **% Residing in College-Owned, -Operated, or -Affiliated Housing:** 26 **Library Holdings:** 1,224,557 **Credit Hours For Degree:** 120 credit hours, Bachelors **Intercollegiate Athletics:** Basketball M & W; Ice Hockey M & W; Rugby M & W; Soccer M & W; Volleyball M & W

UNIVERSITÉ DE MONCTON
Moncton, NB, Canada E1A 3E9
Tel: (506)858-4000
Admissions: (506)858-4115
Fax: (506)858-4544
E-mail: gallanrm@umoncton.ca
Web Site: http://www.umoncton.ca/
President/CEO: Yvon Fontaine

Registrar: Suzanne LeBlanc
Admissions: Nicole Savois
Financial Aid: Louise McIntyre
Type: Comprehensive **Sex:** Coed **Admission Plans:** Deferred Admission **Application Fee:** $30.00 **H.S. Requirements:** High school diploma required; GED accepted. For education, science, engineering, nutrition, nursing, forestry programs: High school diploma required; GED not accepted **Scholarships:** Available **Calendar System:** Semester, Summer Session Available **Enrollment:** FT 4,540, PT 980 **Faculty:** FT 374, PT 113 **Student-Faculty Ratio:** 12:1 **% Residing in College-Owned, -Operated, or -Affiliated Housing:** 15 **Library Holdings:** 789,046 **Credit Hours For Degree:** 126 credits, Bachelors **Intercollegiate Athletics:** Cross-Country Running M & W; Gymnastics W; Ice Hockey M & W; Soccer M & W; Track and Field M & W; Volleyball W

UNIVERSITY OF NEW BRUNSWICK FREDERICTON
PO Box 4400
Fredericton, NB, Canada E3B 5A3
Tel: (506)453-4666
Admissions: (506)453-4865
Fax: (506)453-5016
E-mail: unbfacts@unb.ca
Web Site: http://www.unb.ca/
President/CEO: Dr. John D. McLaughlin
Registrar: David J. Hinton
Admissions: Shirley Carroll
Financial Aid: Shelley Clayton
Type: University **Sex:** Coed **% Accepted:** 79 **Admission Plans:** Early Admission; Deferred Admission **Application Deadline:** March 31 **Application Fee:** $45.00 **H.S. Requirements:** High school diploma required; GED not accepted **Costs Per Year:** Application fee: $45 Canadian dollars. Tuition, fee, and room and board charges are reported in Canadian dollars. Area resident tuition: $5008 full-time, $500 per term part-time. Mandatory fees: $613 full-time, $32 per term part-time. College room and board: $6768. Room and board charges vary according to board plan. International student tuition: $7573 full-time. **Scholarships:** Available **Calendar System:** Miscellaneous, Summer Session Available **Enrollment:** FT 7,130, PT 1,017, Grad 1,351 **Faculty:** FT 500, PT 145 **Student-Faculty Ratio:** 18:1 **Exams:** SAT I **% Residing in College-Owned, -Operated, or -Affiliated Housing:** 20 **Library Holdings:** 1,124,840 **Professional Accreditation:** APA **Intercollegiate Athletics:** Basketball M & W; Cross-Country Running M & W; Field Hockey W; Ice Hockey M & W; Soccer M & W; Swimming and Diving M & W; Volleyball M & W; Wrestling M & W

UNIVERSITY OF NEW BRUNSWICK SAINT JOHN
PO Box 5050
St. John, NB, Canada E2L 4L5
Tel: (506)648-5500
Free: 800-743-5691
Admissions: (506)648-5674
E-mail: apply@unbsj.ca
Web Site: http://www.unb.ca/
President/CEO: Dr. Kathryn Hamer
Admissions: Sue Ellis Loparco
Type: Comprehensive **Sex:** Coed **Admission Plans:** Early Admission; Deferred Admission **Application Fee:** $35.00 **H.S. Requirements:** High school diploma required; GED not accepted. For adult students: High school diploma or equivalent not required **Costs Per Year:** Application fee: $35 Canadian dollars. Tuition, fee, and room and board charges are reported in Canadian dollars. Province resident tuition: $5008 full-time. Mandatory fees: $365 full-time, $535. College room and board: $5180. Room and board charges vary according to board plan and housing facility. International student tuition: $5130 full-time. **Scholarships:** Available **Calendar System:** Miscellaneous, Summer Session Available **Enrollment:** FT 2,258, PT 482, Grad 51 **Faculty:** FT 128 **Student-Faculty Ratio:** 10:1 **Exams:** SAT I **% Residing in College-Owned, -Operated, or -Affiliated Housing:** 5 **Library Holdings:** 155,500 **Credit Hours For Degree:** 120 credits, Bachelors **Intercollegiate Athletics:** Badminton M & W; Basketball M & W; Crew M & W; Cross-Country Running M & W; Fencing M & W; Ice Hockey M & W; Rugby M & W; Soccer M & W; Volleyball M & W

Nova Scotia

ACADIA UNIVERSITY
Wolfville, NS, Canada B4P 2R6
Tel: (902)542-2201
Admissions: (902)585-1016
Fax: (902)585-1081
E-mail: admissions@acadiau.ca
Web Site: http://www.acadiau.ca/
President/CEO: Dr. Gail Dinter-Gottlieb
Registrar: Rosemary Jotcham
Admissions: Anne Scott
Type: Comprehensive **Sex:** Coed **% Accepted:** 52 **Admission Plans:** Deferred Admission **Application Deadline:** July 01 **Application Fee:** $25.00 **H.S. Requirements:** High school diploma required; GED not accepted. For adult students: High school diploma required; GED accepted **Costs Per Year:** Application fee: $25. Canadian resident tuition: $6353 full-time, $719 per course part-time. Mandatory fees: $150 full-time, $4 per course part-time. College room and board: $5363. College room only: $2818. Room and board charges vary according to board plan and housing facility. International student tuition: $11,647 full-time. **Scholarships:** Available **Calendar System:** Miscellaneous, Summer Session Available **Enrollment:** FT 3,446, PT 113, Grad 297 **Faculty:** FT 200, PT 108 **Student-Faculty Ratio:** 12:1 **Exams:** SAT I, SAT II **% Residing in College-Owned, -Operated, or -Affiliated Housing:** 40 **Library Holdings:** 923,042 **Credit Hours For Degree:** 120 credit hours, Bachelors **Professional Accreditation:** ATS **Intercollegiate Athletics:** Baseball M; Basketball M & W; Bowling M; Cheerleading M; Cross-Country Running M & W; Football M; Ice Hockey M & W; Rugby M & W; Soccer M & W; Track and Field M & W; Volleyball W

CAPE BRETON UNIVERSITY
Box 5300
1250 Grand Lake Rd.
Sydney, NS, Canada B1P 6L2
Tel: (902)539-5300; 888-959-9995
Admissions: (902)563-1198
Fax: (902)562-0119
E-mail: arlene_mullan@capebretonu.ca
Web Site: http://www.capebretonu.ca/
President/CEO: H. John Harker
Registrar: Alexis Manley
Admissions: Arlene Mullan
Financial Aid: Alexis Manley
Type: Comprehensive **Sex:** Coed **% Accepted:** 96 **Application Deadline:** August 01 **Application Fee:** $35.00 **H.S. Requirements:** High school diploma required; GED not accepted. For applicants 20 or over and out of high school at least 2 years: High school diploma or equivalent not required **Costs Per Year:** Application fee: $35. Canadian resident tuition: $5450 full-time. Mandatory fees: $98 full-time. College room only: $2760. International student tuition: $10,095 full-time. **Calendar System:** Miscellaneous, Summer Session Available **Faculty:** FT 172, PT 53 **Student-Faculty Ratio:** 16:1 **% Residing in College-Owned, -Operated, or -Affiliated Housing:** 5 **Library Holdings:** 451,271 **Credit Hours For Degree:** 90 credits, Bachelors **Intercollegiate Athletics:** Basketball M & W; Soccer M & W; Volleyball W

DALHOUSIE UNIVERSITY
Halifax, NS, Canada B3H 4R2
Tel: (902)494-2211
Admissions: (902)494-2148
Fax: (902)494-1630
E-mail: admissions@dal.ca
Web Site: http://www.dal.ca/
President/CEO: Dr. Tom Traves
Registrar: Deanne Dennison
Admissions: Terry Gallivan
Type: University **Sex:** Coed **Scores:** 97% SAT V 400+; 99% SAT M 400+ **% Accepted:** 85 **Admission Plans:** Early Decision Plan; Deferred Admission **Application Deadline:** June 01 **Application Fee:** $45.00 **H.S. Requirements:** High school diploma required; GED not accepted **Costs Per Year:** Application fee: $45 Canadian dollars. Tuition, fee, and room and

board charges are reported in Canadian dollars. Comprehensive fee: $13,952 includes full-time tuition ($5820), mandatory fees ($632), and college room and board ($7500). International student tuition: $11,460 full-time. **Scholarships:** Available **Calendar System:** Semester, Summer Session Available **Enrollment:** FT 9,326, PT 1,314, Grad 3,688 **Student-Faculty Ratio:** 14:1 **Exams:** SAT I **% Residing in College-Owned, -Operated, or -Affiliated Housing:** 14 **Library Holdings:** 1,700,000 **Credit Hours For Degree:** 15 courses, Bachelors **Professional Accreditation:** AACSB, ACEHSA, ADA, ALA, APA, LCMEAMA **Intercollegiate Athletics:** Basketball M & W; Cross-Country Running M & W; Field Hockey W; Ice Hockey M & W; Soccer M & W; Swimming and Diving M & W; Track and Field M & W; Volleyball M & W

MOUNT SAINT VINCENT UNIVERSITY
166 Bedford Hwy.
Halifax, NS, Canada B3M 2J6
Tel: (902)457-6788
Admissions: (902)457-6117
Fax: (902)457-6455
E-mail: karl.turner@msvu.ca
Web Site: http://www.msvu.ca/
President/CEO: Dr. Sheila Brown
Registrar: Lynne Theriault
Admissions: Karl Turner
Financial Aid: Frances Cody
Type: Comprehensive **Sex:** Coed **% Accepted:** 74 **Admission Plans:** Deferred Admission **Application Deadline:** March 15 **Application Fee:** $30.00 **H.S. Requirements:** High school diploma required; GED not accepted. For students out of high school 3 years or more: High school diploma required; GED accepted **Costs Per Year:** Application fee: $30 Canadian dollars. Tuition, fee, and room and board charges are reported in Canadian dollars. Province resident tuition: $1068 per unit part-time. Canadian resident tuition: $5340 full-time, $1068 per unit part-time. Mandatory fees: $584 full-time, $47.84 per unit part-time, $10 per year part-time. Full-time tuition and fees vary according to course level, course load, degree level, location, program, reciprocity agreements, and student level. Part-time tuition and fees vary according to course level, course load, degree level, location, program, reciprocity agreements, and student level. College room and board: $6340. College room only: $4220. Room and board charges vary according to board plan and housing facility. International student tuition: $10,265 full-time. **Scholarships:** Available **Calendar System:** Miscellaneous, Summer Session Available **Enrollment:** FT 2,244, PT 1,134, Grad 1,007 **Faculty:** FT 157, PT 122 **Student-Faculty Ratio:** 16:1 **Exams:** SAT I and SAT II or ACT **% Residing in College-Owned, -Operated, or -Affiliated Housing:** 6 **Library Holdings:** 207,140 **Credit Hours For Degree:** 15 full-year courses, Bachelors **Intercollegiate Athletics:** Badminton M & W; Basketball M & W; Soccer M & W; Volleyball W

NOVA SCOTIA AGRICULTURAL COLLEGE
PO Box 550
Truro, NS, Canada B2N 5E3
Tel: (902)893-6600; 888-700-6722
Admissions: (902)893-6722
E-mail: wpaquet@nsac.ca
Web Site: http://www.nsac.ns.ca/
President/CEO: Dr. Garth Coffin
Registrar: Lynn Sibley
Admissions: Wayne Paquet
Financial Aid: J. M. Smith
Type: Comprehensive **Sex:** Coed **% Accepted:** 82 **Application Deadline:** August 01 **Application Fee:** $25.00 **H.S. Requirements:** High school diploma required; GED accepted **Costs Per Year:** Application fee: $25 Canadian dollars. Tuition, fee, and room and board charges are reported in Canadian dollars. Province resident tuition: $5290 full-time, $529 per course part-time. Mandatory fees: $394 full-time, $46 per course part-time. College room and board: $5634. International student tuition: $10,580 full-time. **Scholarships:** Available **Calendar System:** Semester, Summer Session Not available **Faculty:** FT 60, PT 14 **Student-Faculty Ratio:** 9:1 **Library Holdings:** 23,000 **Credit Hours For Degree:** 40 courses, Bachelors **Intercollegiate Athletics:** Badminton M & W; Basketball M & W; Rugby M & W; Soccer M & W; Volleyball M & W

NSCAD UNIVERSITY
5163 Duke St.
Halifax, NS, Canada B3J 3J6
Tel: (902)422-7381
Admissions: (902)494-8129
Fax: (902)425-2420
E-mail: tbailey@nscad.ca
Web Site: http://www.nscad.ca/
President/CEO: Paul Geenhalgh
Registrar: Jane Harmon
Admissions: Terry Bailey
Financial Aid: Bernadette Kehoe
Type: Comprehensive **Sex:** Coed **Admission Plans:** Deferred Admission **Application Deadline:** May 15 **Application Fee:** $35.00 **H.S. Requirements:** High school diploma required; GED accepted **Costs Per Year:** Application fee: $35. Province resident tuition: $5501 full-time, $230 per credit part-time. Canadian resident tuition: $5501 full-time, $230 per credit part-time. Mandatory fees: $32.51 per term part-time. College room and board: $8022. International student tuition: $12,125 full-time. **Scholarships:** Available **Calendar System:** Semester, Summer Session Available **Enrollment:** FT 813, PT 179, Grad 19 **Faculty:** FT 53, PT 60 **Student-Faculty Ratio:** 10:1 **Library Holdings:** 32,000 **Credit Hours For Degree:** 120 credits, Bachelors

ST. FRANCIS XAVIER UNIVERSITY
Box 5000
Antigonish, NS, Canada B2G 2W5
Tel: (902)863-3300; 877-867-STFX
Admissions: (902)867-2219
Fax: (902)867-2329
E-mail: mbarry@stfx.ca
Web Site: http://www.stfx.ca/
President/CEO: Dr. Sean E. Riley
Registrar: Janet Stark
Admissions: Mairead Barry
Financial Aid: Laura Cull
Type: Comprehensive **Sex:** Coed **Affiliation:** Roman Catholic **% Accepted:** 42 **Admission Plans:** Early Decision Plan **Application Deadline:** Rolling **Application Fee:** $40.00 **H.S. Requirements:** High school diploma required; GED accepted **Costs Per Year:** Application fee: $40 Canadian dollars. Tuition, fee, and room and board charges are reported in Canadian dollars. Comprehensive fee: $13,615 includes full-time tuition ($5975), mandatory fees ($1145), and college room and board ($6495). International student tuition: $10,875 full-time. **Scholarships:** Available **Calendar System:** Miscellaneous, Summer Session Available **Enrollment:** FT 3,838, PT 657, Grad 474 **Faculty:** FT 222, PT 43 **Student-Faculty Ratio:** 16:1 **Exams:** SAT I or ACT, SAT II **% Residing in College-Owned, -Operated, or -Affiliated Housing:** 42 **Library Holdings:** 632,575 **Credit Hours For Degree:** 120 credits, Bachelors **Intercollegiate Athletics:** Basketball M & W; Cheerleading M & W; Cross-Country Running M & W; Football M; Ice Hockey M & W; Lacrosse M; Rugby M & W; Soccer M; Tennis M & W; Volleyball W

SAINT MARY'S UNIVERSITY
Halifax, NS, Canada B3H 3C3
Tel: (902)420-5400
Admissions: (902)420-5415
Fax: (902)496-8100
E-mail: greg.ferguson@smu.ca
Web Site: http://www.stmarys.ca/
President/CEO: Dr. J. Colin Dodds
Registrar: E. A. Chard
Admissions: Greg Ferguson
Financial Aid: Michelle Fougere
Type: Comprehensive **Sex:** Coed **Admission Plans:** Early Action **Application Fee:** $35.00 **H.S. Requirements:** High school diploma required; GED accepted **Scholarships:** Available **Calendar System:** Semester, Summer Session Available **Enrollment:** FT 5,660, PT 1,762, Grad 482 **Faculty:** FT 211, PT 217 **Student-Faculty Ratio:** 24:1 **% Residing in College-Owned, -Operated, or -Affiliated Housing:** 15 **Library Holdings:** 366,267 **Credit Hours For Degree:** 15 courses, Bachelors **Professional Accreditation:** AACSB **Intercollegiate Athletics:** Basketball M & W; Cross-Country Running M & W; Field Hockey W; Football M; Ice Hockey M & W; Rugby W; Soccer M & W; Track and Field M & W; Volleyball W

UNIVERSITÉ SAINTE-ANNE
Church Point, NS, Canada B0W 1M0
Tel: (902)769-2114

Fax: (902)769-2930
E-mail: admission@ustanne.ednet.ns.ca
Web Site: http://www.usainteanne.ca/
President/CEO: Dr. Andre Roberge
Registrar: Dr. Gerald C. Boudreau
Admissions: Murielle Comeau
Financial Aid: Dr. Sylvestre Muise
Type: Four-Year College **Sex:** Coed **Application Fee:** $30.00 **H.S. Requirements:** High school diploma required; GED not accepted. For applicants 22 or over: High school diploma or equivalent not required **Calendar System:** Semester, Summer Session Available **Faculty:** FT 33, PT 8 **% Residing in College-Owned, -Operated, or -Affiliated Housing:** 60 **Library Holdings:** 84,000 **Credit Hours For Degree:** 90 credits, Bachelors **Intercollegiate Athletics:** Badminton M & W; Volleyball M & W

UNIVERSITY OF KING'S COLLEGE
6350 Coburg Rd.
Halifax, NS, Canada B3H 2A1
Tel: (902)422-1271
Fax: (902)423-3357
E-mail: admissions@ukings.ns.ca
Web Site: http://www.ukings.ns.ca/
President/CEO: Dr. William Barker
Registrar: Elizabeth Yeo
Admissions: Elizabeth Yeo
Financial Aid: Elizabeth Yeo
Type: Four-Year College **Sex:** Coed **Affiliation:** Dalhousie University **% Accepted:** 74 **Application Deadline:** March 01 **Application Fee:** $45.00 **H.S. Requirements:** High school diploma required; GED not accepted. For applicants 23 or over and out of high school at least 4 years: High school diploma or equivalent not required **Costs Per Year:** Application fee: $45. Province resident tuition: $5820 full-time, $194 per credit hour part-time. Canadian resident tuition: $5820 full-time. Mandatory fees: $836 full-time, $810 per term part-time. Full-time tuition and fees vary according to course load and program. Part-time tuition and fees vary according to course load and program. College room and board: $7580. Room and board charges vary according to housing facility. International student tuition: $11,460 full-time. **Calendar System:** Miscellaneous, Summer Session Available **Enrollment:** FT 1,119, PT 30 **Faculty:** FT 47, PT 0 **Exams:** SAT I **% Residing in College-Owned, -Operated, or -Affiliated Housing:** 26 **Library Holdings:** 80,000 **Credit Hours For Degree:** 15 courses, Bachelors **Intercollegiate Athletics:** Badminton M & W; Basketball M & W; Rugby M & W; Soccer M & W; Volleyball M & W

Prince Edward Island

UNIVERSITY OF PRINCE EDWARD ISLAND
550 University Ave.
Charlottetown, PE, Canada C1A 4P3
Tel: (902)566-0439
Admissions: (902)566-0361
Fax: (902)566-0795
Web Site: http://www.upei.ca/
President/CEO: Prof. Wade MacLauchlan
Registrar: Alan Buchanan
Admissions: Alan Buchanan
Financial Aid: Philip Hooper
Type: Comprehensive **Sex:** Coed **% Accepted:** 67 **Admission Plans:** Early Admission **Application Deadline:** August 15 **Application Fee:** $50.00 **H.S. Requirements:** High school diploma required; GED not accepted. For students 22 or over and out of high school at least 2 years: High school diploma or equivalent not required **Costs Per Year:** Application fee: $50 Canadian dollars. Tuition, fee, and room and board charges are reported in Canadian dollars. Province resident tuition: $4620 full-time. Mandatory fees: $1060 full-time. Full-time tuition and fees vary according to course load and degree level. College room and board: $7490. College room only: $4300. Room and board charges vary according to board plan and housing facility. International student tuition: $8430 full-time. **Scholarships:** Available **Calendar System:** Miscellaneous, Summer Session Available **Enrollment:** FT 2,912, PT 476, Grad 141 **Faculty:** FT 208 **Student-Faculty Ratio:** 16:1 **% Residing in College-Owned, -Operated, or -Affiliated Housing:** 10 **Library Holdings:** 394,000 **Credit Hours For Degree:** 120 semester hours, Bachelors **Professional Accreditation:** AVMA **Intercollegiate Athletics:** Basketball M & W; Field Hockey W; Golf M; Ice Hockey M & W; Rugby M & W; Soccer M & W; Volleyball W

MEMORIAL UNIVERSITY OF NEWFOUNDLAND
Elizabeth Ave.
St. John's, NL, Canada A1C 5S7
Tel: (709)737-8000
Admissions: (709)737-3705
Fax: (709)737-4569
E-mail: mabbott@morgan.ucs.mun.ca
Web Site: http://www.mun.ca/
President/CEO: Dr. Axel Meisen
Admissions: Marian Abbott
Financial Aid: Dr. Lilly J. Walker
Type: University **Sex:** Coed **% Accepted:** 78 **Admission Plans:** Early Admission; Early Decision Plan; Deferred Admission **Application Deadline:** Rolling **Application Fee:** $40.00 **H.S. Requirements:** High school diploma required; GED not accepted. For mature students (over 21 years), senior citizens: High school diploma or equivalent not required **Costs Per Year:** Application fee: $40 Canadian dollars. Tuition, fee, and room and board charges are reported in Canadian dollars. Province resident tuition: $2550 full-time, $85 per credit hour part-time. Mandatory fees: $464 full-time. College room and board: $4878. College room only: $1820. International student tuition: $8800 full-time. **Calendar System:** Trimester, Summer Session Available **Enrollment:** FT 12,685, PT 2,247, Grad 2,395 **Faculty:** FT 1,081, PT 27 **Student-Faculty Ratio:** 14:1 **% Residing in College-Owned, -Operated, or -Affiliated Housing:** 10 **Library Holdings:** 1,701,350 **Credit Hours For Degree:** 120 credit hours, Bachelors **Professional Accreditation:** AACSB, LCMEAMA **Intercollegiate Athletics:** Basketball M & W; Cross-Country Running M & W; Soccer M & W; Swimming and Diving M & W; Volleyball M & W; Wrestling M & W

BROCK UNIVERSITY
500 Glenridge Ave.
St. Catharines, ON, Canada L2S 3A1
Tel: (905)688-5550
Fax: (905)988-5488
E-mail: mlea@brocku.ca
Web Site: http://www.brocku.ca/
President/CEO: Dr. David Atkinson
Registrar: Barb Anderson
Admissions: Michelle Lea
Financial Aid: Kim Meade
Type: University **Sex:** Coed **% Accepted:** 63 **Application Deadline:** April 01 **Application Fee:** $115.00 **H.S. Requirements:** High school diploma required; GED not accepted. For United States visa students: High school diploma required; GED accepted **Costs Per Year:** Application fee: $115 Canadian dollars. Tuition, fee, and room and board charges are reported in Canadian dollars. Canadian resident tuition: $4483 full-time, $896.53 per credit part-time. Mandatory fees: $528 full-time. College room and board: $7040. College room only: $3445. International student tuition: $11,378 full-time. **Scholarships:** Available **Calendar System:** Miscellaneous, Summer Session Available **Faculty:** FT 545, PT 0 **Student-Faculty Ratio:** 30:1 **% Residing in College-Owned, -Operated, or -Affiliated Housing:** 16 **Library Holdings:** 1,631,750 **Credit Hours For Degree:** 15 courses, Bachelors **Professional Accreditation:** AACSB **Intercollegiate Athletics:** Badminton M & W; Baseball M; Basketball M & W; Cheerleading M & W; Crew M & W; Cross-Country Running M & W; Fencing M & W; Field Hockey W; Golf M; Ice Hockey M & W; Lacrosse M & W; Rugby M & W; Soccer M & W; Squash M; Swimming and Diving M & W; Tennis M; Volleyball W; Wrestling M & W

CARLETON UNIVERSITY
1125 Colonel By Dr.
Ottawa, ON, Canada K1S 5B6
Tel: (613)520-7400
Admissions: (613)520-3710
Fax: (613)520-7455
E-mail: liaison@admissions.carleton.ca
Web Site: http://www.carleton.ca/
President/CEO: Dr. Richard Van Loon
Admissions: Janice O'Farrell
Financial Aid: Janice O'Farrell
Type: University **Sex:** Coed **% Accepted:** 73 **Admission Plans:** Deferred Admission **Application Deadline:** June 01 **Application Fee:** $85.00 **H.S. Requirements:** High school diploma required; GED not accepted **Costs Per Year:** Application fee: $85 Canadian dollars. Tuition, fee, and room and board charges are reported in Canadian dollars. Area resident tuition: $4691 full-time, $893 per credit part-time. Canadian resident tuition: $3031 per credit part-time. Mandatory fees: $74 per credit part-time. Full-time tuition varies according to course load, program, and reciprocity agreements. Part-time tuition and fees vary according to course load, program, and reciprocity agreements. College room and board: $7561. College room only: $5248. Room and board charges vary according to board plan and housing facility. International student tuition: $12,426 full-time. **Calendar System:** Miscellaneous, Summer Session Available **Enrollment:** FT 16,509, PT 4,237, Grad 2,937 **Faculty:** FT 783, PT 8 **Student-Faculty Ratio:** 26:1 **Exams:** SAT I and SAT II or ACT, SAT I **% Residing in College-Owned, -Operated, or -Affiliated Housing:** 15 **Library Holdings:** 1,941,340 **Credit Hours For Degree:** 15 full-year courses, Bachelors **Intercollegiate Athletics:** Basketball M & W; Crew M & W; Fencing M & W; Field Hockey W; Football M; Golf M; Ice Hockey M & W; Lacrosse M; Rugby M & W; Skiing (Cross-Country) M & W; Soccer M & W; Swimming and Diving M & W; Volleyball W; Water Polo M & W

COLLÈGE DOMINICAIN DE PHILOSOPHIE ET DE THOLOGIEÉ
96, Ave. Empress
Ottawa, ON, Canada K1R 7G3
Tel: (613)233-5696
E-mail: registraire@collegedominicain.ca
Web Site: http://www.collegedominicain.ca/
President/CEO: Dr. Michel Gourgues, OP
Registrar: Fr. Jacques Lison, OP
Admissions: Fr. Herve Tremblay, OJ
Financial Aid: Jean-Jacques Robillard, OP
Type: Comprehensive **Sex:** Coed **Affiliation:** Roman Catholic **Application Deadline:** July 15 **Application Fee:** $30.00 **H.S. Requirements:** High school diploma or equivalent not required **Costs Per Year:** Application fee: $30 Canadian dollars. Tuition, fee, and room and board charges are reported in Canadian dollars. Comprehensive fee: $8300 includes full-time tuition ($2900) and college room and board ($5400). Part-time tuition: $120 per credit. **Calendar System:** Semester, Summer Session Available **Faculty:** FT 24, PT 16 **Library Holdings:** 125,000 **Credit Hours For Degree:** 90 credits, Bachelors

EMMANUEL BIBLE COLLEGE
100 Fergus Ave.
Kitchener, ON, Canada N2A 2H2
Tel: (519)894-8900
Fax: (519)894-9430
Web Site: http://www.ebcollege.on.ca/
President/CEO: Dr. Derrick Mueller
Registrar: Chureb Kowtecky
Admissions: Chureb Kowtecky
Type: Four-Year College **Sex:** Coed **Affiliation:** Missionary Church **Admission Plans:** Deferred Admission **H.S. Requirements:** High school diploma required; GED accepted **Scholarships:** Available **Calendar System:** Semester, Summer Session Available **Faculty:** FT 9, PT 7 **Library Holdings:** 19,250 **Credit Hours For Degree:** 96 semester hours, Bachelors **Professional Accreditation:** AABC **Intercollegiate Athletics:** Badminton M & W; Basketball M & W; Ice Hockey M; Volleyball M & W

HERITAGE BAPTIST COLLEGE AND HERITAGE THEOLOGICAL SEMINARY
175 Holiday Inn Dr.
Cambridge, ON, Canada N3C 3T2
Tel: (519)651-2869
E-mail: registrar@heritagecollege.net
Web Site: http://www.heritage-theo.edu/
President/CEO: Rev. Marvin R. Brubacher
Registrar: Marylou Burkard
Admissions: Marylou Burkard
Type: Comprehensive **Sex:** Coed **Affiliation:** Baptist **% Accepted:** 5 **Admission Plans:** Open Admission; Deferred Admission **Application**

Deadline: December 01 **Application Fee:** $100.00 **H.S. Requirements:** High school diploma required; GED accepted **Costs Per Year:** Application fee: $100. Comprehensive fee: $34,500 includes full-time tuition ($24,330), mandatory fees ($600), and college room and board ($9570). **Scholarships:** Available **Calendar System:** Miscellaneous, Summer Session Available **Enrollment:** FT 478, Grad 327 **Faculty:** FT 114, PT 152 **Library Holdings:** 40,430 **Credit Hours For Degree:** 100 credit hours, Bachelors **Professional Accreditation:** AABC, ATS **Intercollegiate Athletics:** Basketball M & W; Volleyball M & W

LAKEHEAD UNIVERSITY
955 Oliver Rd.
Thunder Bay, ON, Canada P7B 5E1
Tel: (807)343-8110
Admissions: (807)343-8500
Fax: (807)343-8156
E-mail: admissions@lakeheadu.ca
Web Site: http://www.lakeheadu.ca/
President/CEO: Dr. Frederick F. Gilbert
Registrar: Pentti A. Paularinne
Admissions: John D. Smith
Type: Comprehensive **Sex:** Coed **% Accepted:** 73 **Admission Plans:** Early Admission **Application Deadline:** September 19 **Application Fee:** $105.00 **H.S. Requirements:** High school diploma required; GED not accepted **Costs Per Year:** Application fee: $105. Province resident tuition: $828 per course part-time. Canadian resident tuition: $4140 full-time. Mandatory fees: $531 full-time, $81.35 per course part-time. College room and board: $6569. College room only: $4980. International student tuition: $10,000 full-time. **Calendar System:** Miscellaneous, Summer Session Available **Enrollment:** FT 5,703, PT 1,312, Grad 543 **Faculty:** FT 285 **Student-Faculty Ratio:** 27:1 **Exams:** SAT I or ACT **% Residing in College-Owned, -Operated, or -Affiliated Housing:** 22 **Library Holdings:** 780,974 **Credit Hours For Degree:** 15 courses, Bachelors **Professional Accreditation:** LCMEAMA **Intercollegiate Athletics:** Basketball M & W; Cheerleading W; Crew M & W; Cross-Country Running M & W; Ice Hockey M; Rugby M & W; Skiing (Cross-Country) M & W; Soccer M & W; Track and Field M & W; Volleyball M & W; Weight Lifting M; Wrestling M & W

LAURENTIAN UNIVERSITY
935 Ramsey Lake Rd.
Sudbury, ON, Canada P3E 2C6
Tel: (705)675-1151
Fax: (705)675-4840
E-mail: sjunkin@admin.laurentian.ca
Web Site: http://www.laurentian.ca/
President/CEO: Dr. Kenneth-Roy Bonin
Registrar: Ron Smith
Admissions: Ron Smith
Financial Aid: Suzanne Brunette
Type: Comprehensive **Sex:** Coed **Admission Plans:** Early Admission **Application Deadline:** February 01 **Application Fee:** $50.00 **H.S. Requirements:** High school diploma required; GED not accepted **Costs Per Year:** Application fee: $50 Canadian dollars. Tuition, fee, and room only charges are reported in Canadian dollars. Tuition: $4184 full-time, $836.80 per course part-time. Mandatory fees: $332 full-time, $24.80 per term part-time. College room only: $2950. International student tuition: $10,087 full-time. **Scholarships:** Available **Calendar System:** Miscellaneous, Summer Session Available **Library Holdings:** 696,838 **Credit Hours For Degree:** 90 credits, Bachelors **Professional Accreditation:** LCMEAMA **Intercollegiate Athletics:** Basketball M & W; Cross-Country Running M & W; Field Hockey W; Ice Hockey M & W; Skiing (Cross-Country) M & W; Skiing (Downhill) M & W; Soccer M; Swimming and Diving M & W; Track and Field M & W; Volleyball M

MASTER'S COLLEGE AND SEMINARY
3080 Yonge St., Ste. 3040
Toronto, ON, Canada M4N 3N1
Tel: (416)482-2224
Free: 800-295-6368
Fax: (416)482-7004
E-mail: merv.anthony@mcs.edu
Web Site: http://www.mcs.edu/
President/CEO: Dr. Evon Horton
Registrar: Merv Anthony
Admissions: Rev. Merv Anthony
Type: Four-Year College **Sex:** Coed **Affiliation:** Pentecostal **% Accepted:** 65 **Admission Plans:** Deferred Admission **Application Deadline:** August 31 **Application Fee:** $75.00 **H.S. Requirements:** High school diploma required; GED accepted **Costs Per Year:** Application fee: $75 Canadian dollars. Tuition and fee charges are reported in Canadian dollars. Tuition: $5600 full-time, $175 per credit hour part-time. Full-time tuition varies according to course load. Part-time tuition varies according to course load. **Scholarships:** Available **Calendar System:** Semester, Summer Session Available **Faculty:** FT 5, PT 36 **Student-Faculty Ratio:** 11:1 **Library Holdings:** 46,438 **Credit Hours For Degree:** 130 credit hours, Bachelors **Professional Accreditation:** AABC **Intercollegiate Athletics:** Basketball W; Volleyball W

MCMASTER UNIVERSITY
1280 Main St. West
Hamilton, ON, Canada L8S 4M2
Tel: (905)525-9140
Fax: (905)527-1105
E-mail: macadmit@mcmaster.ca
Web Site: http://www.mcmaster.ca/
President/CEO: Dr. Peter George
Registrar: T. Sykes
Admissions: Lynn Giordano
Financial Aid: E. Seymour
Type: University **Sex:** Coed **Admission Plans:** Early Action **Application Fee:** $95.00 **H.S. Requirements:** High school diploma required; GED not accepted **Scholarships:** Available **Calendar System:** Miscellaneous, Summer Session Available **Enrollment:** FT 17,033, PT 3,050 **Faculty:** FT 1,159, PT 11 **% Residing in College-Owned, -Operated, or -Affiliated Housing:** 23 **Library Holdings:** 1,730,582 **Credit Hours For Degree:** 90 units for bachelor degree; 120 units for honors degree, Bachelors **Professional Accreditation:** ATS, LCMEAMA, NCATE **Intercollegiate Athletics:** Badminton M & W; Baseball M; Basketball M & W; Cross-Country Running M & W; Fencing M & W; Football M; Golf M & W; Lacrosse M & W; Rugby M & W; Soccer M & W; Squash M & W; Swimming and Diving M & W; Tennis M & W; Track and Field M & W; Volleyball M & W; Water Polo M & W; Wrestling M & W

NER ISRAEL YESHIVA COLLEGE OF TORONTO
8950 Bathurst St.
Thornhill, ON, Canada L4J 8A7
Tel: (905)731-1224
President/CEO: Sandy Hofstedter
Admissions: Rabbi Y. Kravetz
Financial Aid: Rabbi Moshe Friedman
Type: Comprehensive **Sex:** Men **Affiliation:** Jewish **Calendar System:** Miscellaneous, Summer Session Available **Library Holdings:** 3,000 **Professional Accreditation:** AARTS

NIPISSING UNIVERSITY
100 College Dr., Box 5002
North Bay, ON, Canada P1B 8L7
Tel: (705)474-3461
Fax: (705)474-1947
Web Site: http://www.nipissingu.ca/
President/CEO: David B. Liddle
Registrar: Heather Brown
Admissions: Andrea Robinson
Financial Aid: Ken McLellan
Type: Comprehensive **Sex:** Coed **Admission Plans:** Early Admission **Application Fee:** $40.00 **H.S. Requirements:** High school diploma required; GED not accepted **Calendar System:** Semester, Summer Session Available **Enrollment:** FT 2,201, PT 628, Grad 1,084 **Faculty:** FT 130, PT 64 **Student-Faculty Ratio:** 18:1 **% Residing in College-Owned, -Operated, or -Affiliated Housing:** 22 **Library Holdings:** 180,397 **Credit Hours For Degree:** 90 credits, Bachelors **Intercollegiate Athletics:** Soccer M & W; Volleyball M & W

QUEEN'S UNIVERSITY AT KINGSTON
Kingston, ON, Canada K7L 3N6
Tel: (613)533-2000
Admissions: (613)533-2218
Fax: (613)533-6300
Web Site: http://www.queensu.ca/

President/CEO: Dr. Karen R. Hitchcock
Admissions: Inara Metcalfe
Financial Aid: Teresa Alm
Type: University **Sex:** Coed **Scores:** 96% SAT V 400+; 99% SAT M 400+ **Admission Plans:** Deferred Admission **Application Deadline:** February 25 **Application Fee:** $90.00 **H.S. Requirements:** High school diploma required; GED not accepted **Costs Per Year:** Application fee: $90. Canadian resident tuition: $838 per credit part-time. **Scholarships:** Available **Calendar System:** Miscellaneous, Summer Session Available **Enrollment:** FT 13,291, PT 3,147, Grad 3,099 **Faculty:** FT 1,049, PT 1,210 **Student-Faculty Ratio:** 12:1 **Exams:** SAT I or ACT **% Residing in College-Owned, -Operated, or -Affiliated Housing:** 30 **Library Holdings:** 3,509,317 **Credit Hours For Degree:** 15 credits, Bachelors **Professional Accreditation:** AACSB, APA, ATS, LCMEAMA **Intercollegiate Athletics:** Baseball M; Basketball M & W; Cheerleading M & W; Crew M & W; Cross-Country Running M & W; Fencing M & W; Field Hockey W; Football M; Golf M; Gymnastics M & W; Ice Hockey M & W; Lacrosse M & W; Rugby M & W; Sailing M & W; Skiing (Cross-Country) M & W; Skiing (Downhill) M & W; Soccer M & W; Squash M & W; Swimming and Diving M & W; Table Tennis M & W; Tennis M & W; Track and Field M & W; Volleyball M & W; Water Polo M & W; Wrestling M & W

REDEEMER UNIVERSITY COLLEGE
777 Garner Rd. East
Ancaster, ON, Canada L9K 1J4
Tel: (905)648-2131
Fax: (905)648-2134
E-mail: adm@redeemer.on.ca
Web Site: http://www.redeemer.on.ca/
President/CEO: Dr. Justin Cooper
Registrar: Richard Wikkerink
Admissions: Marian Ryks-Szelekovszky
Financial Aid: Don Russell
Type: Four-Year College **Sex:** Coed **Affiliation:** interdenominational **Scores:** 36% ACT 18-23; 64% ACT 24-29 **% Accepted:** 81 **Admission Plans:** Preferred Admission; Deferred Admission **Application Deadline:** May 31 **Application Fee:** $35.00 **H.S. Requirements:** High school diploma required; GED accepted. For adult students: High school diploma or equivalent not required **Costs Per Year:** Application fee: $35. Comprehensive fee: $16,591 includes full-time tuition ($11,082), mandatory fees ($393), and college room and board ($5116). Part-time tuition: $1110 per course. Part-time mandatory fees: $39 per course. **Scholarships:** Available **Calendar System:** Semester, Summer Session Available **Enrollment:** FT 775, PT 74 **Faculty:** FT 44, PT 28 **Student-Faculty Ratio:** 17:1 **Exams:** SAT I or ACT **% Residing in College-Owned, -Operated, or -Affiliated Housing:** 56 **Library Holdings:** 117,404 **Credit Hours For Degree:** 40 courses, Bachelors **Intercollegiate Athletics:** Basketball M & W; Cross-Country Running M & W; Soccer M & W; Volleyball M & W

ROYAL MILITARY COLLEGE OF CANADA
PO Box 17000, Station Forces
Kingston, ON, Canada K7K 7B4
Tel: (613)541-6000
Fax: (613)542-3565
Web Site: http://www.rmc.ca/
President/CEO: Brig. Gen. J. M.J. Leclerc
Registrar: Cmdr. D. A. Wilson
Admissions: J. Ross McKenzie
Financial Aid: Lillian Leroux
Type: Comprehensive **Sex:** Coed **Admission Plans:** Open Admission **Application Fee:** $0.00 **H.S. Requirements:** High school diploma required; GED not accepted **Calendar System:** Miscellaneous, Summer Session Not available **Library Holdings:** 300,000 **Credit Hours For Degree:** 22.5 credits, Bachelors **Intercollegiate Athletics:** Badminton M & W; Basketball M; Cross-Country Running M & W; Fencing M & W; Ice Hockey M; Riflery M & W; Rugby M & W; Soccer M & W; Swimming and Diving M & W; Volleyball M & W

RYERSON UNIVERSITY
350 Victoria St.
Toronto, ON, Canada M5B 2K3
Tel: (416)979-5000
E-mail: chack@ryerson.ca
Web Site: http://www.ryerson.ca/
President/CEO: Dr. Claude Lajeunesse
Registrar: Keith Alnwick
Admissions: Charmaine Hack
Type: Comprehensive **Sex:** Coed **Application Deadline:** March 01 **Application Fee:** $95.00 **H.S. Requirements:** High school diploma required; GED not accepted **Costs Per Year:** Application fee: $95 Canadian dollars. Tuition, fee, and room and board charges are reported in Canadian dollars. Area resident tuition: $426 per unit part-time. Province resident tuition: $4184 full-time. Mandatory fees: $527 full-time, $19 per unit part-time. Full-time tuition and fees vary according to course load, degree level, and program. Part-time tuition and fees vary according to course load, degree level, and program. College room and board: $7257. Room and board charges vary according to board plan and housing facility. International student tuition: $12,924 full-time. **Scholarships:** Available **Calendar System:** Miscellaneous, Summer Session Available **Enrollment:** FT 13,795, PT 13,626, Grad 630 **Faculty:** FT 594, PT 185 **Student-Faculty Ratio:** 20:1 **Exams:** SAT I and SAT II **% Residing in College-Owned, -Operated, or -Affiliated Housing:** 6 **Library Holdings:** 606,603 **Professional Accreditation:** FIDER **Intercollegiate Athletics:** Badminton M & W; Basketball M & W; Fencing M & W; Ice Hockey M; Soccer M & W; Squash M & W; Swimming and Diving M & W; Volleyball M & W

SAINT PAUL UNIVERSITY
223 Main St.
Ottawa, ON, Canada K1S 1C4
Tel: (613)236-1393
Fax: (613)782-3033
Web Site: http://ustpaul.ca/
President/CEO: Dr. Dale M. Schlitt, OMI
Registrar: Claudette Dube-Socque
Admissions: Claudette Dube-Socque
Financial Aid: Colin Levangie
Type: University **Sex:** Coed **Affiliation:** University of Ottawa **Admission Plans:** Deferred Admission **Application Fee:** $35.00 **H.S. Requirements:** High school diploma required; GED not accepted **Calendar System:** Miscellaneous, Summer Session Available **Enrollment:** FT 147, PT 298, Grad 312 **Faculty:** FT 64, PT 137 **Exams:** SAT I **Library Holdings:** 400,000 **Credit Hours For Degree:** 90 credits, Bachelors

TRENT UNIVERSITY
1600 West Bank Dr.
Peterborough, ON, Canada K9J 7B8
Tel: (705)748-1011
Fax: (705)748-1629
E-mail: liaison@trentu.ca
Web Site: http://www.trentu.ca/
President/CEO: Prof. Bonnie M. Patterson
Registrar: Susan Salusbury
Admissions: Susan Salusbury
Financial Aid: Joyce Sutton
Type: University **Sex:** Coed **Admission Plans:** Deferred Admission **Application Deadline:** June 01 **Application Fee:** $95.00 **H.S. Requirements:** High school diploma required; GED accepted **Costs Per Year:** Application fee: $95. Area resident tuition: $4184 full-time. College room and board: $7300. International student tuition: $10,725 full-time. **Calendar System:** Miscellaneous, Summer Session Available **Enrollment:** FT 6,588, PT 1,334, Grad 248 **Faculty:** FT 288, PT 157 **Student-Faculty Ratio:** 20:1 **Exams:** SAT I or ACT **Library Holdings:** 579,557 **Credit Hours For Degree:** 15 courses, Bachelors **Intercollegiate Athletics:** Basketball M & W; Crew M & W; Cross-Country Running M & W; Fencing M & W; Field Hockey W; Golf M & W; Rugby M & W; Skiing (Cross-Country) M & W; Soccer M & W; Squash M & W; Swimming and Diving M & W; Volleyball M & W

TYNDALE UNIVERSITY COLLEGE & SEMINARY
25 Ballyconnor Ct.
Toronto, ON, Canada M2M 4B3
Tel: (416)226-6380
Fax: (416)226-4210
E-mail: admissions@obcots.on.ca
Web Site: http://www.tyndale.ca/
President/CEO: Dr. Brian C. Stiller
Registrar: Gladys Chan
Admissions: Gladys Chan
Type: Comprehensive **Sex:** Coed **Affiliation:** interdenominational **Admission Plans:** Deferred Admission **Application Fee:** $50.00 **H.S. Requirements:** High school diploma required; GED accepted. For mature student

category: High school diploma or equivalent not required **Costs Per Year:** Application fee: $50 Canadian dollars. Tuition, fee, and room and board charges are reported in Canadian dollars. Comprehensive fee: $13,650 includes full-time tuition ($8910) and college room and board ($4740). Full-time tuition varies according to course load. Part-time tuition: $268 per credit hour. Part-time tuition varies according to course load. **Scholarships:** Available **Calendar System:** Semester, Summer Session Available **Enrollment:** FT 348, PT 131, Grad 504 **Faculty:** FT 23, PT 25 **Student-Faculty Ratio:** 10:1 **% Residing in College-Owned, -Operated, or -Affiliated Housing:** 30 **Library Holdings:** 65,013 **Credit Hours For Degree:** 90 credit hours, Bachelors **Professional Accreditation:** AABC, ATS **Intercollegiate Athletics:** Basketball M & W; Ice Hockey M; Volleyball M & W

UNIVERSITY OF GUELPH
Guelph, ON, Canada N1G 2W1
Tel: (519)824-4120
E-mail: internat@registrar.uoguelph.ca
Web Site: http://www.uoguelph.ca/
President/CEO: Dr. Alastair Summerlee
Registrar: Ray Darling
Admissions: Ray Darling
Financial Aid: Peter Landoni
Type: University **Sex:** Coed **% Accepted:** 73 **Admission Plans:** Early Admission **Application Deadline:** March 01 **Application Fee:** $105.00 **H.S. Requirements:** High school diploma required; GED not accepted **Costs Per Year:** Application fee: $105. Province resident tuition: $4184 full-time. Canadian resident tuition: $418 per course part-time. Mandatory fees: $1,074 full-time, $16.96 per course part-time, $389.30 per term part-time. Full-time tuition and fees vary according to program. Part-time tuition and fees vary according to course load. College room and board: $7380. College room only: $3930. Room and board charges vary according to board plan and housing facility. International student tuition: $9730 full-time. **Scholarships:** Available **Calendar System:** Trimester, Summer Session Available **Enrollment:** FT 15,103, PT 1,458, Grad 2,055 **Faculty:** FT 830 **Student-Faculty Ratio:** 22:1 **Exams:** SAT I or ACT **% Residing in College-Owned, -Operated, or -Affiliated Housing:** 38 **Library Holdings:** 2,099,889 **Credit Hours For Degree:** 30 courses, Bachelors **Professional Accreditation:** AAMFT, ASLA, AVMA **Intercollegiate Athletics:** Baseball M; Basketball M & W; Crew M & W; Cross-Country Running M & W; Field Hockey W; Football M; Golf M & W; Ice Hockey M & W; Lacrosse M & W; Rugby M & W; Skiing (Cross-Country) M & W; Soccer M & W; Swimming and Diving M & W; Track and Field M & W; Volleyball M & W; Wrestling M & W

UNIVERSITY OF OTTAWA
550 Cumberland St.
Ottawa, ON, Canada K1N 6N5
Tel: (613)562-5700
Admissions: (613)562-5800
E-mail: liaison@uottawa.ca
Web Site: http://www.uottawa.ca/
President/CEO: Dr. Gilles G. Patry
Admissions: Michèle Dextras
Financial Aid: Lucie Laniel
Type: University **Sex:** Coed **% Accepted:** 62 **Admission Plans:** Early Admission **Application Deadline:** June 01 **Application Fee:** $165.00 **H.S. Requirements:** High school diploma required; GED not accepted. For adult applicants to arts and social science programs: High school diploma or equivalent not required **Costs Per Year:** Application fee: $165. Canadian resident tuition: $4163 full-time, $165 per credit part-time. Mandatory fees: $441 full-time, $92 per term part-time. Full-time tuition and fees vary according to program. Part-time tuition and fees vary according to program. College room and board: $5990. College room only: $3740. Room and board charges vary according to board plan and housing facility. **Scholarships:** Available **Calendar System:** Semester, Summer Session Available **Enrollment:** FT 24,040, PT 5,527, Grad 4,009 **Faculty:** FT 1,057, PT 816 **Student-Faculty Ratio:** 24:1 **Library Holdings:** 2,600,000 **Credit Hours For Degree:** 90 credits, Bachelors **Professional Accreditation:** AACSB, ACEHSA, APA, LCMEAMA, NRPA **Intercollegiate Athletics:** Basketball M & W; Cross-Country Running M & W; Fencing M & W; Football M; Ice Hockey M & W; Rugby W; Soccer W; Swimming and Diving M & W; Track and Field M & W; Volleyball W

UNIVERSITY OF TORONTO
Toronto, ON, Canada M5S 1A1
Tel: (416)978-2011
Admissions: (416)978-2190
E-mail: ask@adm.utoronto.ca
Web Site: http://www.utoronto.ca/uoft.html
President/CEO: Hon. Frank Iacobucci
Registrar: Karel Swift
Admissions: Karel Swift
Financial Aid: Karel Swift
Type: University **Sex:** Coed **% Accepted:** 65 **Admission Plans:** Preferred Admission; Deferred Admission **Application Deadline:** March 01 **Application Fee:** $43.00 **H.S. Requirements:** High school diploma required; GED not accepted **Costs Per Year:** Application fee: $43 Canadian dollars. Tuition, fee, and room and board charges are reported in Canadian dollars. Province resident tuition: $850 per course part-time. Canadian resident tuition: $4250 full-time, $2800 per course part-time. Mandatory fees: $800 full-time. Full-time tuition and fees vary according to program. Part-time tuition varies according to course load. College room and board: $8000. College room only: $4500. Room and board charges vary according to board plan, housing facility, and location. International student tuition: $14,000 full-time. **Calendar System:** Miscellaneous, Summer Session Available **Enrollment:** FT 39,400, PT 6,114, Grad 12,474 **Faculty:** FT 2,787, PT 362 **Student-Faculty Ratio:** 26:1 **Exams:** SAT I and SAT II or ACT **% Residing in College-Owned, -Operated, or -Affiliated Housing:** 15 **Library Holdings:** 10,306,621 **Credit Hours For Degree:** 15 courses, Bachelors **Professional Accreditation:** AACSB, ARCMI, ACEHSA, ADA, ALA, APTA, APA, ASLA, ATS, LCMEAMA **Intercollegiate Athletics:** Archery M & W; Badminton M & W; Basketball M & W; Crew M; Cross-Country Running M & W; Fencing M & W; Field Hockey W; Football M; Golf M; Gymnastics M & W; Ice Hockey M & W; Rugby M; Skiing (Cross-Country) M & W; Skiing (Downhill) M & W; Soccer M & W; Squash M & W; Swimming and Diving M & W; Tennis M & W; Track and Field M & W; Volleyball M & W; Wrestling M

UNIVERSITY OF WATERLOO
200 University Ave. West
Waterloo, ON, Canada N2L 3G1
Tel: (519)888-4567
Fax: (519)746-2882
E-mail: registrar@nhladm.uwaterloo.ca
Web Site: http://www.uwaterloo.ca/
President/CEO: Prof. David Johnston
Registrar: K. A. Lavigne
Admissions: Nancy Weiner
Financial Aid: M. Jones
Type: University **Sex:** Coed **% Accepted:** 66 **Admission Plans:** Early Admission; Deferred Admission **Application Deadline:** March 31 **Application Fee:** $115.00 **H.S. Requirements:** High school diploma required; GED not accepted **Costs Per Year:** Application fee: $115 Canadian dollars. Tuition, fee, and room and board charges are reported in Canadian dollars. Province resident tuition: $4362 full-time. Canadian resident tuition: $4362 full-time. College room and board: $7500. College room only: $4000. International student tuition: $16,092 full-time. **Scholarships:** Available **Calendar System:** Trimester, Summer Session Available **Enrollment:** FT 21,024, PT 2,011, Grad 2,865 **Faculty:** FT 941, PT 636 **Student-Faculty Ratio:** 16:1 **Exams:** Other, SAT I or ACT, SAT II **% Residing in College-Owned, -Operated, or -Affiliated Housing:** 28 **Library Holdings:** 3,800,000 **Credit Hours For Degree:** 30 term courses, Bachelors **Professional Accreditation:** AOA, APA **Intercollegiate Athletics:** Badminton M & W; Baseball M; Basketball M & W; Cheerleading M & W; Cross-Country Running M & W; Field Hockey W; Football M; Golf M & W; Ice Hockey M & W; Rugby M & W; Skiing (Cross-Country) M & W; Soccer M & W; Squash M; Swimming and Diving M & W; Tennis M & W; Track and Field M & W; Volleyball M & W

THE UNIVERSITY OF WESTERN ONTARIO
London, ON, Canada N6A 5B8
Tel: (519)661-2111
Admissions: (519)661-2116
E-mail: reguwo@uwoadmin.uwo.ca
Web Site: http://www.uwo.ca/
President/CEO: Dr. P. Davenport
Registrar: Dr. R. Harris
Admissions: Lori Gribbon
Financial Aid: Glen Tigert
Type: University **Sex:** Coed **% Accepted:** 59 **Admission Plans:** Deferred Admission **Application Deadline:** June 01 **Application Fee:** $100.00 **H.S. Requirements:** High school diploma required; GED not accepted **Costs Per**

Year: Application fee: $100. Province resident tuition: $828 per course part-time. Canadian resident tuition: $4140 full-time, $2500 per course part-time. Mandatory fees: $863 full-time, $130.53 per course part-time. Full-time tuition and fees vary according to program. Part-time tuition and fees vary according to course load and program. College room and board: $6582. College room only: $4505. Room and board charges vary according to board plan and housing facility. International student tuition: $12,500 full-time. **Scholarships:** Available **Calendar System:** Miscellaneous, Summer Session Available **Enrollment:** FT 22,616, PT 2,671, Grad 4,019 **Faculty:** FT 1,249, PT 1,200 **Student-Faculty Ratio:** 12:1 **Exams:** SAT I **% Residing in College-Owned, -Operated, or -Affiliated Housing:** 13 **Library Holdings:** 3,056,875 **Credit Hours For Degree:** 15 courses, Bachelors **Professional Accreditation:** ADA, ALA, APA, ATS, LCMEAMA **Intercollegiate Athletics:** Badminton M & W; Baseball M; Basketball M & W; Cheerleading M & W; Crew M & W; Cross-Country Running M & W; Fencing M & W; Field Hockey W; Football M; Golf M & W; Ice Hockey M & W; Lacrosse W; Rugby M & W; Skiing (Cross-Country) M & W; Soccer M & W; Squash M & W; Swimming and Diving M & W; Tennis M & W; Track and Field M & W; Volleyball M & W; Water Polo M; Wrestling M & W

UNIVERSITY OF WINDSOR
401 Sunset Ave.
Windsor, ON, Canada N9B 3P4
Tel: (519)253-3000
Fax: (519)973-7050
E-mail: liaison@uwindsor.ca
Web Site: http://www.uwindsor.ca/
President/CEO: Dr. Ross Paul
Registrar: Dr. Clayton Smith
Admissions: Charlene Yates
Financial Aid: Aase Houser
Type: University **Sex:** Coed **% Accepted:** 64 **Admission Plans:** Early Admission **Application Deadline:** Rolling **Application Fee:** $60.00 **H.S. Requirements:** High school diploma required; GED accepted **Costs Per Year:** Application fee: $60 Canadian dollars. Tuition, fee, and room and board charges are reported in Canadian dollars. Area resident tuition: $4990 full-time. Province resident tuition: $504 per course part-time. Canadian resident tuition: $1549 per course part-time. College room and board: $7124. International student tuition: $12,232 full-time. **Scholarships:** Available **Calendar System:** Semester, Summer Session Available **Enrollment:** FT 10,959, PT 3,205, Grad 1,280 **Faculty:** FT 524, PT 220 **Student-Faculty Ratio:** 24:1 **Exams:** SAT I **% Residing in College-Owned, -Operated, or -Affiliated Housing:** 13 **Library Holdings:** 2,776,724 **Credit Hours For Degree:** 30 courses, Bachelors **Professional Accreditation:** APA **Intercollegiate Athletics:** Basketball M & W; Cheerleading M & W; Cross-Country Running M & W; Football M; Golf M & W; Ice Hockey M & W; Rugby M & W; Soccer M & W; Softball W; Track and Field M & W; Volleyball M & W

WILFRID LAURIER UNIVERSITY
75 University Ave. West
Waterloo, ON, Canada N2L 3C5
Tel: (519)884-1970
Admissions: (519)884-0710
Fax: (519)884-8826
E-mail: admissions@wlu.ca
Web Site: http://www.wlu.ca/
President/CEO: Dr. Robert G. Rosehart
Registrar: Christine Hickson
Admissions: Gail Forsyth
Financial Aid: Pauline Wong
Type: Comprehensive **Sex:** Coed **Application Fee:** $85.00 **H.S. Requirements:** High school diploma required; GED not accepted **Calendar System:** Miscellaneous, Summer Session Available **Enrollment:** FT 9,569, PT 1,684, Grad 1,043 **Faculty:** FT 329, PT 395 **Student-Faculty Ratio:** 23:1 **Exams:** SAT I **Library Holdings:** 580,000 **Credit Hours For Degree:** 15 courses, Bachelors **Professional Accreditation:** AACSB, ATS **Intercollegiate Athletics:** Basketball M & W; Cross-Country Running M; Football M; Golf M; Ice Hockey M & W; Rugby M; Soccer M & W; Swimming and Diving M & W; Tennis W; Volleyball M & W

YORK UNIVERSITY
4700 Keele St.
Toronto, ON, Canada M3J 1P3
Tel: (416)736-2100
Admissions: (416)736-5000
Fax: (416)736-5741
E-mail: intlenq@yorku.ca
Web Site: http://www.yorku.ca/
President/CEO: Dr. Lorna R. Marsden, PhD
Admissions: Monique Chan
Financial Aid: Mary Scheepers
Type: University **Sex:** Coed **Scores:** 100% ACT 24-29 **Admission Plans:** Preferred Admission; Early Admission; Early Action; Deferred Admission **Application Deadline:** February 01 **Application Fee:** $90.00 **H.S. Requirements:** High school diploma required; GED not accepted. For adult students: High school diploma, or equivalent not required **Costs Per Year:** Application fee: $90. Comprehensive fee: $10,981 includes full-time tuition ($4862) and college room and board ($6119). College room only: $3719. Full-time tuition varies according to course load, degree level, and program. Room and board charges vary according to board plan and housing facility. International student tuition: $14,862 full-time. **Scholarships:** Available **Calendar System:** Semester, Summer Session Available **Enrollment:** FT 37,178, PT 7,496, Grad 4,822 **Student-Faculty Ratio:** 23:1 **Exams:** SAT I or ACT **% Residing in College-Owned, -Operated, or -Affiliated Housing:** 6 **Library Holdings:** 6,100,000 **Credit Hours For Degree:** 15 courses, Bachelors **Professional Accreditation:** APA **Intercollegiate Athletics:** Badminton M & W; Basketball M & W; Cross-Country Running M & W; Fencing M & W; Field Hockey W; Football M; Golf M; Ice Hockey M & W; Lacrosse W; Rugby M & W; Soccer M & W; Swimming and Diving M & W; Tennis M & W; Track and Field M & W; Volleyball M & W; Water Polo M & W

BISHOP'S UNIVERSITY
Lennoxville, QC, Canada J1M 1Z7
Tel: (819)822-9600; 877-822-8200
Fax: (819)822-9661
E-mail: liaison@ubishops.ca
Web Site: http://www.ubishops.ca/
President/CEO: J. M. Hodder
Registrar: Ann Montgomery
Admissions: Damien Roy
Type: Comprehensive **Sex:** Coed **Scores:** 96% SAT V 400+; 100% SAT M 400+; 25% ACT 18-23; 50% ACT 24-29 **% Accepted:** 85 **Application Deadline:** March 01 **Application Fee:** $55.00 **H.S. Requirements:** High school diploma required; GED not accepted. For some adult students: High school diploma or equivalent not required **Costs Per Year:** Application fee: $55. Province resident tuition: $1668 full-time, $55.61 per credit part-time. Canadian resident tuition: $4518 full-time, $150.60 per credit part-time. Mandatory fees: $840 full-time. College room and board: $5320. College room only: $4440. International student tuition: $10,068 full-time. **Scholarships:** Available **Calendar System:** Miscellaneous, Summer Session Available **Faculty:** FT 123, PT 54 **Student-Faculty Ratio:** 17:1 **Exams:** SAT I or ACT, SAT II **% Residing in College-Owned, -Operated, or -Affiliated Housing:** 31 **Library Holdings:** 447,086 **Credit Hours For Degree:** 93 credits, Bachelors **Intercollegiate Athletics:** Basketball M & W; Field Hockey W; Football M; Golf M; Ice Hockey W; Lacrosse M & W; Rugby M & W; Skiing (Downhill) M & W; Soccer W; Volleyball W

CONCORDIA UNIVERSITY
1455 de Maisonneuve Blvd. West
Montréal, QC, Canada H3G 1M8
Tel: (514)848-2424
Fax: (514)848-2621
Web Site: http://www.concordia.ca/
President/CEO: Dr. Frederick H. Lowy
Registrar: Linda Healey
Admissions: Sophie Fontaine
Financial Aid: Roger Cote
Type: University **Sex:** Coed **Affiliation:** Province of Quebec University System **% Accepted:** 65 **Admission Plans:** Preferred Admission **Application Deadline:** March 01 **Application Fee:** $50.00 **H.S. Requirements:** High school diploma required; GED not accepted. For applicants 21 or over and out of high school at least 2 years: High school diploma or equivalent not required **Costs Per Year:** Application fee: $50 Canadian dollars. Tuition, fee, and room and board charges are reported in Canadian dollars. Province resident tuition: $1668 full-time, $55.61 per credit part-time. Canadian resident tuition: $4651 full-time, $155.03 per credit part-time. Mandatory fees: $979 full-time, $177.96 per term part-time. Full-time tuition and fees vary according to program. Part-time tuition and fees vary according to program. College room and board: $6905. Room and board charges vary according to housing facility. International student tuition: $11,238 full-time. **Scholarships:** Available **Calendar System:** Trimester, Summer Session Available **Enrollment:** FT 16,850, PT 9,398, Grad 4,794 **Faculty:** FT 831, PT 934 **Student-Faculty Ratio:** 35:1 **% Residing in College-Owned, -Operated, or -Affiliated Housing:** 1 **Library Holdings:** 3,000,000 **Credit Hours For Degree:** 90 credits, Bachelors **Professional Accreditation:** AACSB, APA **Intercollegiate Athletics:** Baseball M; Basketball M & W; Football M; Ice Hockey M & W; Rugby M & W; Soccer M & W; Wrestling M & W

HEC MONTREAL
3000, chemin de la Côte-Sainte-Catherine
Montréal, QC, Canada H3T 2A7
Tel: (514)340-6000
Admissions: (514)340-6991
Fax: (514)340-5640
Web Site: http://www.hec.ca/
President/CEO: Dr. Jean-Marie Toulouse
Registrar: Manon Vaillant
Admissions: Brigitte Lauzon
Type: Comprehensive **Sex:** Coed **Affiliation:** Université de Montréal **% Accepted:** 72 **Admission Plans:** Deferred Admission **Application Deadline:** March 01 **Application Fee:** $60.00 **H.S. Requirements:** High school diploma required; GED not accepted **Costs Per Year:** Application fee: $60 Canadian dollars. Tuition, fee, and room only charges are reported in Canadian dollars. Province resident tuition: $1,668 full-time, $55.61 per credit part-time. Canadian resident tuition: $4,651 full-time, $155.03 per credit part-time. Mandatory fees: $622 full-time, $16.63 per credit part-time, $58.70 per term part-time. College room only: $2,927. International student tuition: $11,238 full-time. Nonresident alien program tuitions range from $9468 to $11240. **Calendar System:** Trimester, Summer Session Available **Enrollment:** FT 4,574, PT 4,563, Grad 2,647 **Faculty:** FT 251, PT 360 **Student-Faculty Ratio:** 21:1 **Library Holdings:** 345,143 **Credit Hours For Degree:** 90 credits, Bachelors **Professional Accreditation:** AACSB

MCGILL UNIVERSITY
845 Sherbrooke St. West
Montréal, QC, Canada H3A 2T5
Tel: (514)398-4455
Admissions: (514)398-4193
Fax: (514)398-4193
E-mail: admissions@mcgill.ca
Web Site: http://www.mcgill.ca/
President/CEO: Dr. Bernard Shapiro
Registrar: Sophie Marcoux
Admissions: Kim Bartlett
Financial Aid: Judy Stymest
Type: University **Sex:** Coed **Scores:** 100% SAT V 400+; 99.7% SAT M 400+; 2.13% ACT 18-23; 51.06% ACT 24-29 **% Accepted:** 56 **Admission Plans:** Deferred Admission **Application Deadline:** January 16 **Application Fee:** $60.00 **H.S. Requirements:** High school diploma required; GED not accepted **Costs Per Year:** Application fee: $60. Province resident tuition: $55.61 per credit part-time. Canadian resident tuition: $163.79 per credit part-time. **Calendar System:** Semester, Summer Session Available **Enrollment:** FT 17,972, PT 3,363, Grad 7,546 **Faculty:** FT 1,597, PT 805 **Student-Faculty Ratio:** 16:1 **Exams:** SAT I and SAT II **% Residing in College-Owned, -Operated, or -Affiliated Housing:** 10 **Library Holdings:** 4,184,776 **Credit Hours For Degree:** 120 credits, Bachelors **Professional Accreditation:** ADA, ALA, APA, ATS, LCMEAMA **Intercollegiate Athletics:** Badminton M & W; Baseball M; Basketball M & W; Cheerleading M & W; Crew M & W; Cross-Country Running M & W; Fencing M & W; Field Hockey W; Football M; Golf M & W; Ice Hockey M & W; Lacrosse M & W; Rugby M

& W; Sailing M & W; Skiing (Cross-Country) M & W; Skiing (Downhill) M & W; Soccer M & W; Squash M & W; Swimming and Diving M & W; Tennis M & W; Track and Field M & W; Ultimate Frisbee M & W; Volleyball M & W; Wrestling M & W

TÉLÉ-UNIVERSITÉ
455, rue de l'Église
C.P. 4800, succ. Terminus
Québec, QC, Canada G1K 9H5
Tel: (418)657-2262
Fax: (418)657-2094
E-mail: info@teluq.uquebec.ca
Web Site: http://www.teluq.uquebec.ca/
President/CEO: Anne Marrec
Registrar: Louise Bertrand
Admissions: Louise Bertraud
Type: Comprehensive **Sex:** Coed **Affiliation:** Université du Québec **Admission Plans:** Open Admission **Application Fee:** $30.00 **H.S. Requirements:** High school diploma required; GED not accepted **Calendar System:** Trimester, Summer Session Available **Faculty:** FT 36, PT 0 **Library Holdings:** 12,567 **Credit Hours For Degree:** 90 credits, Bachelors

UNIVERSITÉ LAVAL
C.P. 2208, succursale Terminus
Québec, QC, Canada G1K 7P4
Tel: (418)656-3333; 877-785-2825
Admissions: (418)656-3080
Fax: (418)656-2809
E-mail: info@dap.ulaval.ca
Web Site: http://www.ulaval.ca/
President/CEO: Michel Pigeon
Registrar: Danielle Fleury
Admissions: Danielle Fleury
Financial Aid: Jacques Beaulieu
Type: University **Sex:** Coed **% Accepted:** 66 **Application Deadline:** March 01 **Application Fee:** $30.00 **H.S. Requirements:** High school diploma required; GED accepted **Costs Per Year:** Application fee: $30 Canadian dollars. Tuition, fee, and room and board charges are reported in Canadian dollars. Area resident tuition: $2076 full-time. Province resident tuition: $4809 full-time. Canadian resident tuition: $10,176 full-time. Mandatory fees: $900 full-time. College room and board: $9000. College room only: $3000. **Calendar System:** Trimester, Summer Session Available **Enrollment:** FT 19,954, PT 8,356, Grad 10,124 **Faculty:** FT 1,380, PT 76 **Student-Faculty Ratio:** 7:1 **% Residing in College-Owned, -Operated, or -Affiliated Housing:** 7 **Library Holdings:** 3,000,000 **Credit Hours For Degree:** 90 credits, Bachelors **Professional Accreditation:** AACSB, ADA, LCMEAMA **Intercollegiate Athletics:** Badminton M & W; Baseball M; Basketball M & W; Cross-Country Running M & W; Football M; Golf M & W; Gymnastics M & W; Skiing (Downhill) M & W; Soccer M & W; Swimming and Diving M & W; Track and Field M & W; Volleyball M & W

UNIVERSITÉ DE MONTRÉAL
CP 6128, Succursale Centre-ville
Montréal, QC, Canada H3C 3J7
Tel: (514)343-6111
Admissions: (514)343-7076
Fax: (514)343-5788
E-mail: pierre.chenard@umontreal.ca
Web Site: http://www.umontreal.ca/
President/CEO: Robert Lacroix
Registrar: Fernand Boucher
Admissions: Pierre Chenard
Type: University **Sex:** Coed **Affiliation:** L'Ecole Polytechnique de Montrèal, HEC Montrèal **Application Deadline:** March 01 **Application Fee:** $30.00 **Costs Per Year:** Application fee: $30 Canadian dollars. Tuition and fee charges are reported in Canadian dollars. Tuition: $55.61 per unit part-time. Canadian resident tuition: $335.61 per unit part-time. **Scholarships:** Available **Calendar System:** Trimester, Summer Session Available **Enrollment:** FT 26,757, PT 14,605, Grad 13,788 **Credit Hours For Degree:** 90 credits, Bachelors **Professional Accreditation:** ACEHSA, ADA, ACSP, ALA, AOA, ASLA, AVMA, LCMEAMA **Intercollegiate Athletics:** Badminton M & W; Skiing (Downhill) M & W; Soccer M & W; Swimming and Diving M & W; Volleyball M & W

UNIVERSITÉ DU QUÉBEC EN ABITIBI-TÉMISCAMINGUE
445 Blvd. de l'Université
Rouyn-Noranda, QC, Canada J9X 5E4
Tel: (819)762-0971
Fax: (819)797-4727
Web Site: http://www.uqat.ca/
President/CEO: Jules Arsenault
Registrar: Denis Veret
Admissions: Denis Verret
Financial Aid: Norman Murphy
Type: Comprehensive **Sex:** Coed **Affiliation:** Université du Québec **Admission Plans:** Open Admission **Application Fee:** $30.00 **H.S. Requirements:** High school diploma required; GED not accepted **Calendar System:** Trimester, Summer Session Available **Faculty:** FT 71, PT 88 **Library Holdings:** 135,882 **Credit Hours For Degree:** 90 credits, Bachelors

UNIVERSITÉ DU QUÉBEC ÀCHICOUTIMI
555, Blvd. de L'Université
Chicoutimi, QC, Canada G7H 2B1
Tel: (418)545-5011
Admissions: (418)545-5005
Fax: (418)545-5012
E-mail: czoccast@uqac.uquebec.ca
Web Site: http://www.uqac.uquebec.ca/
President/CEO: Michel Belley
Admissions: Dr. Andre Dorion
Financial Aid: Renaud Theriault
Type: University **Sex:** Coed **Affiliation:** Université du Québec **Admission Plans:** Open Admission **H.S. Requirements:** High school diploma required; GED not accepted **Scholarships:** Available **Calendar System:** Trimester, Summer Session Available **Faculty:** FT 221, PT 173 **Library Holdings:** 689,214 **Credit Hours For Degree:** 90 credits, Bachelors **Intercollegiate Athletics:** Badminton M & W; Cross-Country Running M & W; Soccer W; Volleyball M & W

UNIVERSITE DU QUEBEC, ECOLE DE TECHNOLOGIE SUPERIEURE
1100, rue Notre Dame Ouest
Montréal, QC, Canada H3C 1K3
Tel: (514)396-8800
Admissions: (514)396-8885
Fax: (514)289-8950
E-mail: admission@ets.mtl.ca
Web Site: http://www.etsmtl.ca/
President/CEO: Dr. Yves Beauchamp
Registrar: Francine Gamache
Admissions: Francine Gamache
Type: Comprehensive **Sex:** Coed **Affiliation:** Universite du Quebec **Admission Plans:** Open Admission **Application Fee:** $30.00 **H.S. Requirements:** High school diploma required; GED not accepted **Scholarships:** Available **Calendar System:** Trimester, Summer Session Available **Enrollment:** FT 2,763, PT 1,091, Grad 408 **Faculty:** FT 119, PT 162 **Library Holdings:** 44,195 **Credit Hours For Degree:** 114 credits, Bachelors **Intercollegiate Athletics:** Rugby M

UNIVERSITÉ DU QUÉBEC ÀMONTRÉAL
CP 8888, Succursale Centre-ville
Montréal, QC, Canada H3C 3P8
Tel: (514)987-3000
Admissions: (514)987-7740
Fax: (514)987-7728
E-mail: admission@uqam.ca
Web Site: http://www.uqam.ca/
President/CEO: Roch Denis
Registrar: Dr. Ygal Leibu
Admissions: Ygal Leibu
Financial Aid: Ruth Bourassa
Type: University **Sex:** Coed **Affiliation:** Université du Québec **Admission Plans:** Open Admission **H.S. Requirements:** High school diploma required; GED not accepted **Calendar System:** Trimester, Summer Session Available **Faculty:** FT 993, PT 2,011 **Library Holdings:** 2,300,000 **Credit Hours For Degree:** 90 credits, Bachelors

UNIVERSITÉ DU QUÉBEC EN OUTAOUAIS

Case Postale 1250, Succursale Hull
Gatineau, QC, Canada J8X 3X7
Tel: (819)595-3900
Free: 800-567-1283
E-mail: luc.maurice@uqo.ca
Web Site: http://www.uqo.ca/
President/CEO: Dr. Francis R. Whyte
Registrar: Richard Bérubé
Admissions: Luc Maurice
Type: University **Sex:** Coed **Affiliation:** Université du Québec **Admission Plans:** Open Admission **Application Deadline:** March 01 **Application Fee:** $30.00 **H.S. Requirements:** High school diploma required; GED not accepted **Costs Per Year:** Application fee: $30. Tuition: $194.34 per credit part-time. Mandatory fees: $2099 full-time. International student tuition: $10,463 full-time. Area resident tuition: $2099 full-time. Canadian resident tuition: $474.34 per credit part-time. Mandatory fees: $2099 full-time. International student tuition: $10,463 full-time. **Calendar System:** Trimester, Summer Session Available **Library Holdings:** 230,910 **Credit Hours For Degree:** 90 credits, Bachelors

UNIVERSITÉ DU QUÉBEC ÀRIMOUSKI

300, Allee des Ursulines, CP 3300
Rimouski, QC, Canada G5L 3A1
Tel: (418)723-1986
Admissions: (418)724-1432
Fax: (418)724-1525
E-mail: raymond_cote@uqar.uquebec.ca
Web Site: http://www.uqar.qc.ca/
President/CEO: Michel Ringuet
Registrar: Raymond Cote
Admissions: Raymond Cote
Type: Comprehensive **Sex:** Coed **Affiliation:** Université du Québec **Admission Plans:** Open Admission **H.S. Requirements:** High school diploma required; GED not accepted **Calendar System:** Trimester, Summer Session Available **Faculty:** FT 168, PT 156 **Library Holdings:** 263,142 **Credit Hours For Degree:** 90 credits, Bachelors **Intercollegiate Athletics:** Badminton M & W; Cross-Country Running M & W; Skiing (Downhill) M & W

UNIVERSITÉ DU QUÉBEC ÀTROIS-RIVIÈRES

3351 blvd des Forges, Case post 500
Trois-Rivières, QC, Canada G9A 5H7
Tel: (819)376-5011
Free: 800-365-0922
Admissions: (819)376-5045
Fax: (819)376-5210
Web Site: http://www.uqtr.ca/
President/CEO: Claire V. de la Durantaye
Registrar: Denis De Carufel
Admissions: Denis De Carufel
Financial Aid: Marc-Andre Hainse
Type: University **Sex:** Coed **Affiliation:** Université du Québec **Admission Plans:** Open Admission **Application Fee:** $30.00 **H.S. Requirements:** High school diploma required; GED not accepted **Calendar System:** Trimester, Summer Session Available **Faculty:** FT 317, PT 413 **Library Holdings:** 464,338 **Credit Hours For Degree:** 90 credits, Bachelors **Intercollegiate Athletics:** Badminton M & W; Cross-Country Running M; Ice Hockey M & W; Soccer M & W; Swimming and Diving M & W; Track and Field M & W

UNIVERSITÉ DE SHERBROOKE

Sherbrooke, QC, Canada J1K 2R1
Tel: (819)821-8000
Admissions: (819)821-7685
Fax: (819)821-7966
E-mail: information@usherbrooke.ca
Web Site: http://www.usherbrooke.ca/
President/CEO: Bruno Marie Bechard
Registrar: France Myette
Admissions: France Myette
Financial Aid: Lise Grenier
Type: University **Sex:** Coed **% Accepted:** 74 **Admission Plans:** Preferred Admission; Early Admission **Application Deadline:** March 01 **Application Fee:** $50.00 **H.S. Requirements:** High school diploma required; GED not accepted **Costs Per Year:** Application fee: $50. Comprehensive fee: $8508 includes full-time tuition ($4650), mandatory fees ($362), and college room and board ($3496). College room only: $1760. Part-time tuition: $155.03 per credit. Part-time mandatory fees: $10.74 per credit, $30 per term. International student tuition: $9768 full-time. **Scholarships:** Available **Calendar System:** Miscellaneous, Summer Session Available **Enrollment:** FT 9,974, PT 3,867, Grad 7,314 **Faculty:** FT 1,014, PT 1,823 **Library Holdings:** 1,200,000 **Credit Hours For Degree:** 90 credits, Bachelors **Professional Accreditation:** LCMEAMA **Intercollegiate Athletics:** Badminton M & W; Football M; Soccer M & W; Swimming and Diving M & W; Track and Field M & W; Volleyball M & W

BRIERCREST COLLEGE
510 College Dr.
Caronport, SK, Canada S0H 0S0
Tel: (306)756-3200
Fax: (306)756-5500
Web Site: http://www.briercrest.ca/
President/CEO: Dr. Dwayne Uglem
Admissions: Mike Benallick
Financial Aid: Joan Ballantyne
Type: Four-Year College **Sex:** Coed **Affiliation:** interdenominational; Briercrest Family of Schools **% Accepted:** 59 **Admission Plans:** Open Admission; Preferred Admission; Early Admission; Deferred Admission **Application Deadline:** August 15 **Application Fee:** $35.00 **H.S. Requirements:** High school diploma required; GED accepted **Costs Per Year:** Application fee: $35. Comprehensive fee: $11,886 includes full-time tuition ($7086) and college room and board ($4800). College room only: $2719. **Scholarships:** Available **Calendar System:** Semester, Summer Session Available **Enrollment:** FT 629, PT 96 **Faculty:** FT 22, PT 34 **Student-Faculty Ratio:** 16:1 **% Residing in College-Owned, -Operated, or -Affiliated Housing:** 75 **Library Holdings:** 76,000 **Credit Hours For Degree:** 126 semester hours, Bachelors **Professional Accreditation:** AABC **Intercollegiate Athletics:** Basketball M & W; Ice Hockey M; Soccer M & W; Volleyball M & W

CENTRAL PENTECOSTAL COLLEGE
1303 Jackson Ave.
Saskatoon, SK, Canada S7H 2M9
Tel: (306)374-6655
Fax: (306)373-6968
E-mail: admissions@cpc-paoc.edu
Web Site: http://www.cpc-paoc.edu/
President/CEO: Dr. D. Munk
Registrar: Angie Hume
Admissions: Dr. David Munk
Type: Four-Year College **Sex:** Coed **Affiliation:** Pentecostal Assemblies of Canada; University of Saskatchewan **% Accepted:** 96 **Admission Plans:** Deferred Admission **Application Deadline:** September 15 **Application Fee:** $45.00 **H.S. Requirements:** High school diploma required; GED accepted **Costs Per Year:** Application fee: $45 Canadian dollars. Tuition, fee, and room and board charges are reported in Canadian dollars. Comprehensive fee: $9279 includes full-time tuition ($4864), mandatory fees ($415), and college room and board ($4000). Part-time tuition: $152 per credit hour. **Scholarships:** Available **Calendar System:** Semester, Summer Session Not available **Enrollment:** FT 50, PT 11 **Faculty:** FT 4, PT 6 **Student-Faculty Ratio:** 14:1 **% Residing in College-Owned, -Operated, or -Affiliated Housing:** 27 **Library Holdings:** 18,204 **Credit Hours For Degree:** 128 semester hours, Bachelors **Professional Accreditation:** AABC

COLLEGE OF EMMANUEL AND ST. CHAD
1337 College Dr.
Saskatoon, SK, Canada S7N 0W6
Tel: (306)975-3753
Admissions: (306)975-1558
Fax: (306)934-2683
Web Site: http://www.usask.ca/stu/emmanuel/
President/CEO: Walter Deller
Registrar: Dr. Beverly Cushman
Admissions: Colleen Walker
Type: Comprehensive **Sex:** Coed **Affiliation:** Episcopal **Admission Plans:** Open Admission; Preferred Admission **Application Deadline:** June 30 **Application Fee:** $50.00 **Costs Per Year:** Application fee: $50. Tuition: $4750 full-time, $475 per course part-time. Mandatory fees: $515 full-time. Full-time tuition and fees vary according to course level and course load. Part-time tuition varies according to course level and course load. **Calendar System:** Miscellaneous, Summer Session Available **Enrollment:** , Grad 23 **Faculty:** FT 3, PT 0 **Student-Faculty Ratio:** 8:1 **Library Holdings:** 15,000 **Credit Hours For Degree:** 32 courses, Bachelors

UNIVERSITY OF REGINA
3737 Wascana Parkway
Regina, SK, Canada S4S 0A2
Tel: (306)585-4111
Free: 800-664-4756
Admissions: (306)585-5166
Fax: (306)585-5203
E-mail: admissions.office@uregina.ca
Web Site: http://www.uregina.ca/
President/CEO: Dr. David Barnard
Admissions: Susan Husum
Type: University **Sex:** Coed **% Accepted:** 91 **Admission Plans:** Preferred Admission; Early Admission; Early Action; Deferred Admission **Application Deadline:** July 01 **Application Fee:** $60.00 **H.S. Requirements:** High school diploma required; GED not accepted. For Mature Admission (over age 21).: High school diploma or equivalent not required **Costs Per Year:** Application fee: $60 Canadian dollars. Tuition, fee, and room and board charges are reported in Canadian dollars. Province resident tuition: $136 per credit hour part-time. Canadian resident tuition: $4551 full-time, $136 per credit hour part-time. Mandatory fees: $412 full-time, $92 per term part-time. Full-time tuition and fees vary according to course load and program. Part-time tuition and fees vary according to course load and program. College room and board: $5767. College room only: $3960. Room and board charges vary according to board plan and housing facility. International student tuition: $8627 full-time. **Scholarships:** Available **Calendar System:** Semester, Summer Session Available **Enrollment:** FT 7,232, PT 4,041, Grad 1,397 **Faculty:** FT 424, PT 1 **Student-Faculty Ratio:** 22:1 **Exams:** SAT I or ACT **Library Holdings:** 1,471,017 **Credit Hours For Degree:** 120 credit hours, Bachelors **Intercollegiate Athletics:** Basketball M & W; Cross-Country Running M & W; Football M; Ice Hockey M & W; Soccer W; Swimming and Diving M & W; Track and Field M & W; Volleyball M & W; Wrestling M & W

UNIVERSITY OF SASKATCHEWAN
105 Administration Place
Saskatoon, SK, Canada S7N 5A2
Tel: (306)966-4343
Fax: (306)966-7026
Web Site: http://www.usask.ca/
President/CEO: R. Peter MacKinnon
Financial Aid: Kelly McInnes
Type: University **Sex:** Coed **% Accepted:** 81 **Admission Plans:** Preferred Admission; Early Admission; Early Action **Application Deadline:** May 01

Application Fee: $75.00 **H.S. Requirements:** High school diploma required; GED not accepted. For adult students: High school diploma or equivalent not required **Costs Per Year:** Application fee: $75 Canadian dollars. Tuition, fee, and room and board charges are reported in Canadian dollars. Area resident tuition: $4560 full-time, $152 per credit part-time. Province resident tuition: $395 per credit part-time. Mandatory fees: $448 full-time, $114 per year part-time. Full-time tuition and fees vary according to course load, degree level, location, and program. Part-time tuition and fees vary according to course load, degree level, location, and program. College room and board: $4894. College room only: $2226. Room and board charges vary according to board plan, housing facility, and location. International student tuition: $11,850 full-time. **Scholarships:** Available **Calendar System:** Miscellaneous, Summer Session Available **Library Holdings:** 1,789,000 **Credit Hours For Degree:** 120 credit units, Bachelors **Professional Accreditation:** ADA, APA, AVMA, LCMEAMA **Intercollegiate Athletics:** Basketball M & W; Cross-Country Running M & W; Football M; Ice Hockey M & W; Soccer M & W; Track and Field M & W; Volleyball M & W; Wrestling M & W

Index of Intercollegiate Athletics

Archery

Atlantic Cape Community College *New Jersey* M & W
Barnard College *New York* W
Bernard M. Baruch College of the City University of New York *New York* M & W
California State University, Long Beach *California* M & W
Case Western Reserve University *Ohio* M & W
City College of San Francisco *California* W
Columbia College *New York* M & W
Columbia University, The Fu Foundation School of Engineering and Applied Science *New York* M & W
Diné College *Arizona* M & W
James Madison University *Virginia* M & W
Linn State Technical College *Missouri* M & W
Miami University *Ohio* M & W
North Dakota State University *North Dakota* M & W
Pennsylvania College of Technology *Pennsylvania* M & W
The Pennsylvania State University University Park Campus *Pennsylvania* M & W
Rensselaer Polytechnic Institute *New York* M & W
Seattle University *Washington* M & W
Shoreline Community College *Washington* M & W
Syracuse University *New York* M & W
Texas A&M University *Texas* W
The University of Alabama in Huntsville *Alabama* M & W
University of New Hampshire *New Hampshire* M & W
University of Toronto *Ontario* M & W

Badminton

Albright College *Pennsylvania* W
Bates College *Maine* M & W
Baylor University *Texas* M & W
Boston University *Massachusetts* M & W
Brock University *Ontario* M & W
Bryn Athyn College of the New Church *Pennsylvania* M & W
Bryn Mawr College *Pennsylvania* W
California State University, Chico *California* M & W
California State University, Dominguez Hills *California* M & W
California State University, Long Beach *California* M & W
Carleton College *Minnesota* M & W
Carnegie Mellon University *Pennsylvania* M & W
Claremont McKenna College *California* M & W
Colby College *Maine* M & W
The College of Wooster *Ohio* M & W
Columbia College *New York* M & W
Columbia University, The Fu Foundation School of Engineering and Applied Science *New York* M & W
Concordia University College of Alberta *Alberta* M & W
Dartmouth College *New Hampshire* M & W
Dickinson State University *North Dakota* M & W
Duke University *North Carolina* M & W
Eastern Washington University *Washington* M
Emmanuel Bible College *Ontario* M & W
Emory University *Georgia* M & W
Long Beach City College *California* M & W
McGill University *Quebec* M & W
McMaster University *Ontario* M & W
Mission College *California* M & W
Mount Saint Vincent University *Nova Scotia* M & W
Mt. San Antonio College *California* W
North Carolina State University *North Carolina* M & W
Nova Scotia Agricultural College *Nova Scotia* M & W
The Pennsylvania State University University Park Campus *Pennsylvania* M & W
Providence College and Theological Seminary *Manitoba* M & W
Rensselaer Polytechnic Institute *New York* M & W
Rice University *Texas* M & W
Royal Military College of Canada *Ontario* M & W
Ryerson University *Ontario* M & W
San Jose State University *California* M & W
State University of New York at Binghamton *New York* M & W
Swarthmore College *Pennsylvania* M & W
Syracuse University *New York* M & W
Thompson Rivers University *British Columbia* M & W
Université Laval *Quebec* M & W
Université de Montréal *Quebec* M & W
Université du Québec àChicoutimi *Quebec* M & W
Université du Québec àRimouski *Quebec* M & W
Université du Québec àTrois-Rivières *Quebec* M & W
Université Sainte-Anne *Nova Scotia* M & W
Université de Sherbrooke *Quebec* M & W
The University of Alabama in Huntsville *Alabama* M & W
University of California, Irvine *California* M & W
University of Hartford *Connecticut* M & W
University of King's College *Nova Scotia* M & W
University of Miami *Florida* M & W
University of New Brunswick Saint John *New Brunswick* M & W
University of New Hampshire *New Hampshire* M & W
University of Oregon *Oregon* M & W
University of Toronto *Ontario* M & W
University of Waterloo *Ontario* M & W
The University of Western Ontario *Ontario* M & W
University of Wyoming *Wyoming* M & W
York University *Ontario* M & W

Baseball

Abilene Christian University *Texas* M
Abraham Baldwin Agricultural College *Georgia* M
Acadia University *Nova Scotia* M
Adelphi University *New York* M
Adirondack Community College *New York* M
Adrian College *Michigan* M
Alabama Agricultural and Mechanical University *Alabama* M
Alabama Southern Community College *Alabama* M
Alabama State University *Alabama* M
Albany State University *Georgia* M
Albertson College of Idaho *Idaho* M
Albertus Magnus College *Connecticut* M
Albion College *Michigan* M
Albright College *Pennsylvania* M
Alcorn State University *Mississippi* M
Alderson-Broaddus College *West Virginia* M
Alice Lloyd College *Kentucky* M
Allan Hancock College *California* M
Allegany College of Maryland *Maryland* M
Allegheny College *Pennsylvania* M
Allen County Community College *Kansas* M
Alma College *Michigan* M
Alvernia College *Pennsylvania* M
Alvin Community College *Texas* M
American International College *Massachusetts* M
Amherst College *Massachusetts* M
Ancilla College *Indiana* M
Anderson University *South Carolina* M
Anderson University *Indiana* M
Andrew College *Georgia* M
Angelina College *Texas* M
Angelo State University *Texas* M
Anna Maria College *Massachusetts* M
Anne Arundel Community College *Maryland* M
Anoka-Ramsey Community College *Minnesota* M
Anoka-Ramsey Community College, Cambridge Campus *Minnesota* M
Antelope Valley College *California* M
Appalachian State University *North Carolina* M
Aquinas College *Michigan* M
Arcadia University *Pennsylvania* M
Arizona State University *Arizona* M
Arizona Western College *Arizona* M
Arkansas State University *Arkansas* M
Arkansas Tech University *Arkansas* M
Arlington Baptist College *Texas* M
Armstrong Atlantic State University *Georgia* M
Ashford University *Iowa* M
Ashland University *Ohio* M
Assumption College *Massachusetts* M
Atlanta Christian College *Georgia* M
Atlantic Baptist University *New Brunswick* M
Auburn University *Alabama* M
Auburn University Montgomery *Alabama* M
Augsburg College *Minnesota* M
Augusta State University *Georgia* M
Augustana College *South Dakota* M
Augustana College *Illinois* M
Aurora University *Illinois* M
Austin College *Texas* M
Austin Peay State University *Tennessee* M
Averett University *Virginia* M
Avila University *Missouri* M
Azusa Pacific University *California* M
Babson College *Massachusetts* M
Bacone College *Oklahoma* M
Baker University *Kansas* M

M = Men; W = Women

M = Men; W = Women

M = Men; W = Women

Hamline University *Minnesota* M
Hampden-Sydney College *Virginia* M
Hannibal-LaGrange College *Missouri* M
Hanover College *Indiana* M
Hardin-Simmons University *Texas* M
Harding University *Arkansas* M
Harford Community College *Maryland* M
Harris-Stowe State University *Missouri* M
Hartnell College *California* M
Hartwick College *New York* M
Harvard University *Massachusetts* M
Harvey Mudd College *California* M
Hastings College *Nebraska* M
Haverford College *Pennsylvania* M
Hawaii Pacific University *Hawaii* M
Heidelberg College *Ohio* M
Henderson State University *Arkansas* M
Hendrix College *Arkansas* M
Henry Ford Community College *Michigan* M
Herkimer County Community College *New York* M
Hesston College *Kansas* M
Hibbing Community College *Minnesota* M
High Point University *North Carolina* M
Highland Community College *Kansas* M & W
Highland Community College *Illinois* M & W
Hilbert College *New York* M
Hill College of the Hill Junior College District *Texas* M
Hillsborough Community College *Florida* M
Hillsdale College *Michigan* M
Hillsdale Free Will Baptist College *Oklahoma* M
Hinds Community College *Mississippi* M
Hiram College *Ohio* M
Hofstra University *New York* M
Holmes Community College *Mississippi* M
Holyoke Community College *Massachusetts* M
Hope College *Michigan* M
Houston Baptist University *Texas* M
Howard College *Texas* M
Howard Payne University *Texas* M
Howard University *District of Columbia* M & W
Huntingdon College *Alabama* M
Huntington University *Indiana* M
Husson College *Maine* M
Huston-Tillotson University *Texas* M
Hutchinson Community College and Area Vocational School *Kansas* M
Illinois Central College *Illinois* M
Illinois College *Illinois* M
Illinois Eastern Community Colleges, Lincoln Trail College *Illinois* M
Illinois Eastern Community Colleges, Olney Central College *Illinois* M
Illinois Eastern Community Colleges, Wabash Valley College *Illinois* M
Illinois Institute of Technology *Illinois* M
Illinois State University *Illinois* M
Illinois Wesleyan University *Illinois* M
Imperial Valley College *California* M
Independence Community College *Kansas* M
Indian Hills Community College *Iowa* M
Indian River Community College *Florida* M
Indiana State University *Indiana* M
Indiana Tech *Indiana* M
Indiana University Bloomington *Indiana* M
Indiana University Northwest *Indiana* M
Indiana University of Pennsylvania *Pennsylvania* M
Indiana University-Purdue University Fort Wayne *Indiana* M
Indiana University Southeast *Indiana* M
Indiana Wesleyan University *Indiana* M
Inter American University of Puerto Rico, Aguadilla Campus *Puerto Rico* M
Inter American University of Puerto Rico, Bayamón Campus *Puerto Rico* M
Inter American University of Puerto Rico, Guayama Campus *Puerto Rico* M
Inter American University of Puerto Rico, Metropolitan Campus *Puerto Rico* M
Inter American University of Puerto Rico, Ponce Campus *Puerto Rico* M & W
Inter American University of Puerto Rico, San Germán Campus *Puerto Rico* M
Iona College *New York* M
Iowa Central Community College *Iowa* M
Iowa Lakes Community College *Iowa* M
Iowa Wesleyan College *Iowa* M
Iowa Western Community College *Iowa* M
Itasca Community College *Minnesota* M
Ithaca College *New York* M
Jackson State Community College *Tennessee* M
Jackson State University *Mississippi* M
Jacksonville State University *Alabama* M
Jacksonville University *Florida* M
James A. Rhodes State College *Ohio* M
James H. Faulkner State Community College *Alabama* M
James Madison University *Virginia* M
Jamestown College *North Dakota* M
Jamestown Community College *New York* M
Jarvis Christian College *Texas* M
Jefferson College *Missouri* M
Jefferson Community College *New York* M
Jefferson State Community College *Alabama* M
John A. Logan College *Illinois* M
John Carroll University *Ohio* M
John Jay College of Criminal Justice of the City University of New York *New York* M
John Wood Community College *Illinois* M
The Johns Hopkins University *Maryland* M
Johnson Bible College *Tennessee* M
Johnson County Community College *Kansas* M
Johnson & Wales University *Rhode Island* M
Johnson & Wales University *Colorado* M
Jones County Junior College *Mississippi* M
Judson College *Illinois* M
Juniata College *Pennsylvania* M
Kalamazoo College *Michigan* M
Kalamazoo Valley Community College *Michigan* M
Kankakee Community College *Illinois* M
Kansas City Kansas Community College *Kansas* M
Kansas State University *Kansas* M
Kansas Wesleyan University *Kansas* M
Kaskaskia College *Illinois* M
Kean University *New Jersey* M
Keene State College *New Hampshire* M
Kellogg Community College *Michigan* M
Kennesaw State University *Georgia* M
Kent State University *Ohio* M
Kentucky State University *Kentucky* M
Kentucky Wesleyan College *Kentucky* M
Kenyon College *Ohio* M
Keuka College *New York* M
Keystone College *Pennsylvania* M
King College *Tennessee* M
King's College *Pennsylvania* M
Kingsborough Community College of the City University of New York *New York* M
Kirkwood Community College *Iowa* M
Kishwaukee College *Illinois* M
Knox College *Illinois* M
Kutztown University of Pennsylvania *Pennsylvania* M
Kwantlen University College *British Columbia* M & W
La Roche College *Pennsylvania* M
La Salle University *Pennsylvania* M
Labette Community College *Kansas* M
Lackawanna College *Pennsylvania* M
Lafayette College *Pennsylvania* M
LaGrange College *Georgia* M
Lake City Community College *Florida* M
Lake Erie College *Ohio* M
Lake Land College *Illinois* M
Lake Michigan College *Michigan* M
Lake-Sumter Community College *Florida* M
Lakeland College *Wisconsin* M
Lakeland Community College *Ohio* M
Lamar Community College *Colorado* M
Lamar University *Texas* M
Lambuth University *Tennessee* M
Lancaster Bible College *Pennsylvania* M
Lander University *South Carolina* M
Landmark College *Vermont* M
Lane College *Tennessee* M
Lane Community College *Oregon* M
Laney College *California* M
Laredo Community College *Texas* M
Lawrence University *Wisconsin* M
Lawson State Community College *Alabama* W
Le Moyne College *New York* M
Lebanon Valley College *Pennsylvania* M
Lehigh Carbon Community College *Pennsylvania* M & W
Lehigh University *Pennsylvania* M
Lehman College of the City University of New York *New York* M
LeMoyne-Owen College *Tennessee* M
Lenoir Community College *North Carolina* M
Lenoir-Rhyne College *North Carolina* M
LeTourneau University *Texas* M
Lewis & Clark College *Oregon* M
Lewis and Clark Community College *Illinois* M
Lewis-Clark State College *Idaho* M
Lewis University *Illinois* M
Liberty University *Virginia* M
Limestone College *South Carolina* M
Lincoln Christian College *Illinois* M
Lincoln College *Illinois* M
Lincoln College-Normal *Illinois* M
Lincoln Land Community College *Illinois* M
Lincoln Memorial University *Tennessee* M
Lincoln University *Pennsylvania* M
Lincoln University *Missouri* M
Lindenwood University *Missouri* M
Lindsey Wilson College *Kentucky* M
Linfield College *Oregon* M
Linn-Benton Community College *Oregon* M
Lipscomb University *Tennessee* M
Lock Haven University of Pennsylvania *Pennsylvania* M
Lon Morris College *Texas* M
Long Beach City College *California* M
Long Island University, Brooklyn Campus *New York* M
Long Island University, C.W. Post Campus *New York* M
Longview Community College *Missouri* M
Longwood University *Virginia* M
Loras College *Iowa* M
Los Angeles Harbor College *California* M
Los Angeles Pierce College *California* M
Los Medanos College *California* M
Louisburg College *North Carolina* M
Louisiana College *Louisiana* M
Louisiana State University and Agricultural and Mechanical College *Louisiana* M
Louisiana State University at Eunice *Louisiana* M
Louisiana State University in Shreveport *Louisiana* M
Louisiana Tech University *Louisiana* M
Lower Columbia College *Washington* M
Loyola Marymount University *California* M
Loyola University New Orleans *Louisiana* M
Lubbock Christian University *Texas* M
Lurleen B. Wallace Community College *Alabama* M
Luther College *Iowa* M
Luzerne County Community College *Pennsylvania* M
Lynchburg College *Virginia* M
Lyndon State College *Vermont* M
Lynn University *Florida* M
Lyon College *Arkansas* M
Macalester College *Minnesota* M
MacMurray College *Illinois* M
Macomb Community College *Michigan* M
Madison Area Technical College *Wisconsin* M
Madonna University *Michigan* M
Malone College *Ohio* M
Manatee Community College *Florida* M
Manchester College *Indiana* M
Manchester Community College *Connecticut* M
Manhattan Christian College *Kansas* M
Manhattan College *New York* M
Manhattanville College *New York* M
Mansfield University of Pennsylvania *Pennsylvania* M
Maple Woods Community College *Missouri* M
Maranatha Baptist Bible College *Wisconsin* M
Marian College *Indiana* M
Marian College of Fond du Lac *Wisconsin* M
Marietta College *Ohio* M

M = Men; W = Women

M = Men; W = Women

Palm Beach Atlantic University *Florida* M
Palm Beach Community College *Florida* M
Panola College *Texas* M
Park University *Missouri* M
Parkland College *Illinois* M
Pasadena City College *California* M
Pasco-Hernando Community College *Florida* M
Paul Quinn College *Texas* M
Pearl River Community College *Mississippi* M
Pennsylvania College of Technology *Pennsylvania* M
The Pennsylvania State University Abington College *Pennsylvania* M
The Pennsylvania State University Altoona College *Pennsylvania* M
The Pennsylvania State University Beaver Campus of the Commonwealth College *Pennsylvania* M
The Pennsylvania State University Berks Campus of the Berks-Lehigh Valley College *Pennsylvania* M
The Pennsylvania State University Delaware County Campus of the Commonwealth College *Pennsylvania* M
The Pennsylvania State University at Erie, The Behrend College *Pennsylvania* M
The Pennsylvania State University Fayette Campus of the Commonwealth College *Pennsylvania* M
The Pennsylvania State University Harrisburg Campus *Pennsylvania* M
The Pennsylvania State University Hazleton Campus of the Commonwealth College *Pennsylvania* M
The Pennsylvania State University, Lehigh Valley Campus of the Berks-Lehigh Valley College *Pennsylvania* M
The Pennsylvania State University McKeesport Campus of the Commonwealth College *Pennsylvania* M
The Pennsylvania State University New Kensington Campus of the Commonwealth College *Pennsylvania* M
The Pennsylvania State University University Park Campus *Pennsylvania* M
The Pennsylvania State University Wilkes-Barre Campus of the Commonwealth College *Pennsylvania* M
The Pennsylvania State University Worthington Scranton Campus of the Commonwealth College *Pennsylvania* M
Pensacola Junior College *Florida* M
Pepperdine University *California* M
Peru State College *Nebraska* M
Pfeiffer University *North Carolina* M
Philadelphia Biblical University *Pennsylvania* M
Philadelphia University *Pennsylvania* M
Phoenix College *Arizona* M
Piedmont Baptist College *North Carolina* M
Piedmont College *Georgia* M
Pierce College *Washington* M
Pikeville College *Kentucky* M
Pillsbury Baptist Bible College *Minnesota* M
Pima Community College *Arizona* M
Pitt Community College *North Carolina* M
Pittsburg State University *Kansas* M
Pitzer College *California* M
Plymouth State University *New Hampshire* M
Point Loma Nazarene University *California* M
Point Park University *Pennsylvania* M
Polk Community College *Florida* M
Polytechnic University, Brooklyn Campus *New York* M
Pomona College *California* M
Porterville College *California* M
Portland State University *Oregon* M
Post University *Connecticut* M
Potomac State College of West Virginia University *West Virginia* M
Prairie State College *Illinois* M
Prairie View A&M University *Texas* M
Pratt Community College *Kansas* M
Presbyterian College *South Carolina* M
Presentation College *South Dakota* M
Prince George's Community College *Maryland* M
Princeton University *New Jersey* M
Principia College *Illinois* M
Purchase College, State University of New York *New York* M & W
Purdue University *Indiana* M
Queens College of the City University of New York *New York* M
Queen's University at Kingston *Ontario* M
Queensborough Community College of the City University of New York *New York* M
Quincy University *Illinois* M
Quinnipiac University *Connecticut* M
Quinsigamond Community College *Massachusetts* M
Radford University *Virginia* M
Ramapo College of New Jersey *New Jersey* M
Randolph-Macon College *Virginia* M
Ranger College *Texas* M
Raritan Valley Community College *New Jersey* M
Redlands Community College *Oklahoma* M
Reedley College *California* M
Regis University *Colorado* M
Reinhardt College *Georgia* M
Rend Lake College *Illinois* M
Rensselaer Polytechnic Institute *New York* M
Research College of Nursing *Missouri* M
Rhode Island College *Rhode Island* M
Rhodes College *Tennessee* M
Rice University *Texas* M
The Richard Stockton College of New Jersey *New Jersey* M
Richland College *Texas* M
Rider University *New Jersey* M
Ridgewater College *Minnesota* M
Rio Hondo College *California* M
Ripon College *Wisconsin* M
Riverland Community College *Minnesota* M
Riverside Community College District *California* M
Rivier College *New Hampshire* M
Roane State Community College *Tennessee* M
Roanoke College *Virginia* M
Robert Morris College *Illinois* M
Robert Morris University *Pennsylvania* M
Rochester College *Michigan* M
Rochester Community and Technical College *Minnesota* M
Rochester Institute of Technology *New York* M
Rock Valley College *Illinois* M
Rockford College *Illinois* M
Rockhurst University *Missouri* M
Rockingham Community College *North Carolina* M
Rockland Community College *New York* M
Roger Williams University *Rhode Island* M
Rollins College *Florida* M
Rose-Hulman Institute of Technology *Indiana* M
Rose State College *Oklahoma* M
Rowan University *New Jersey* M
Roxbury Community College *Massachusetts* M
Rust College *Mississippi* M
Rutgers, The State University of New Jersey, New Brunswick/Piscataway *New Jersey* M
Sacramento City College *California* M
Sacred Heart University *Connecticut* M
Saddleback College *California* M
Saginaw Valley State University *Michigan* M
St. Ambrose University *Iowa* M
St. Andrews Presbyterian College *North Carolina* M
Saint Anselm College *New Hampshire* M
Saint Augustine's College *North Carolina* M
St. Bonaventure University *New York* M
St. Catharine College *Kentucky* M & W
Saint Charles Community College *Missouri* M
St. Clair County Community College *Michigan* M
St. Cloud State University *Minnesota* M
St. Cloud Technical College *Minnesota* M
St. Edward's University *Texas* M
St. Francis College *New York* M
St. Gregory's University *Oklahoma* M
St. John Fisher College *New York* M
St. Johns River Community College *Florida* M
St. John's University *New York* M
Saint John's University *Minnesota* M
Saint Joseph's College *Indiana* M
Saint Joseph's College of Maine *Maine* M
St. Joseph's College, Suffolk Campus *New York* M
Saint Joseph's University *Pennsylvania* M
St. Lawrence University *New York* M
Saint Leo University *Florida* M
St. Louis Christian College *Missouri* M
St. Louis Community College at Florissant Valley *Missouri* M
St. Louis Community College at Forest Park *Missouri* W
St. Louis Community College at Meramec *Missouri* M
Saint Louis University *Missouri* M
Saint Martin's University *Washington* M
Saint Mary's College of California *California* M
St. Mary's College of Maryland *Maryland* M
Saint Mary's University of Minnesota *Minnesota* M
St. Mary's University of San Antonio *Texas* M
Saint Michael's College *Vermont* M
St. Norbert College *Wisconsin* M
St. Olaf College *Minnesota* M
Saint Paul's College *Virginia* M
Saint Peter's College *New Jersey* M
St. Petersburg College *Florida* M
St. Thomas Aquinas College *New York* M
St. Thomas University *Florida* M
Saint Vincent College *Pennsylvania* M
Saint Xavier University *Illinois* M
Salem Community College *New Jersey* M
Salem International University *West Virginia* M
Salem State College *Massachusetts* M
Salisbury University *Maryland* M
Salt Lake Community College *Utah* M
Salve Regina University *Rhode Island* M
Sam Houston State University *Texas* M
Samford University *Alabama* M
San Diego City College *California* M
San Diego Mesa College *California* M
San Diego State University *California* M
San Francisco State University *California* M & W
San Joaquin Delta College *California* M
San Jose City College *California* M
San Jose State University *California* M
Santa Ana College *California* M
Santa Barbara City College *California* M
Santa Clara University *California* M
Santa Fe Community College *Florida* M
Santa Rosa Junior College *California* M
Sauk Valley Community College *Illinois* M
Savannah College of Art and Design *Georgia* M
Savannah State University *Georgia* M
Schenectady County Community College *New York* M
Schreiner University *Texas* M
Scottsdale Community College *Arizona* M
Seattle University *Washington* M & W
Seminole Community College *Florida* M
Seminole State College *Oklahoma* M
Seton Hall University *New Jersey* M
Seton Hill University *Pennsylvania* M
Sewanee: The University of the South *Tennessee* M
Seward County Community College *Kansas* M
Shasta College *California* M
Shaw University *North Carolina* M
Shawnee Community College *Illinois* M
Shawnee State University *Ohio* M
Shelton State Community College *Alabama* M
Shenandoah University *Virginia* M
Shepherd University *West Virginia* M
Shippensburg University of Pennsylvania *Pennsylvania* M
Shoreline Community College *Washington* M
Shorter College *Georgia* M
Siena College *New York* M
Siena Heights University *Michigan* M
Sierra College *California* M
Simpson College *Iowa* M
Simpson University *California* M
Sinclair Community College *Ohio* M
Skagit Valley College *Washington* M
Skidmore College *New York* M
Skyline College *California* M
Slippery Rock University of Pennsylvania *Pennsylvania* M
Snead State Community College *Alabama* M
Snow College *Utah* M
Solano Community College *California* M

M = Men; W = Women

Sonoma State University *California* M
South Dakota State University *South Dakota* M
South Florida Community College *Florida* M
South Georgia College *Georgia* M
South Mountain Community College *Arizona* M
South Suburban College *Illinois* M
Southeast Missouri State University *Missouri* M
Southeastern Community College *North Carolina* M
Southeastern Community College, North Campus *Iowa* M
Southeastern Illinois College *Illinois* M
Southeastern Louisiana University *Louisiana* M
Southeastern Oklahoma State University *Oklahoma* M
Southeastern University *Florida* M
Southern Arkansas University-Magnolia *Arkansas* M
Southern Connecticut State University *Connecticut* M
Southern Illinois University Carbondale *Illinois* M
Southern Illinois University Edwardsville *Illinois* M
Southern Maine Community College *Maine* M
Southern Methodist University *Texas* M
Southern Nazarene University *Oklahoma* M
Southern New Hampshire University *New Hampshire* M
Southern Polytechnic State University *Georgia* M
Southern State Community College *Ohio* M
Southern Union State Community College *Alabama* M
Southern University and Agricultural and Mechanical College *Louisiana* M
Southern Utah University *Utah* M
Southern Vermont College *Vermont* M
Southern Virginia University *Virginia* M
Southern Wesleyan University *South Carolina* M
Southwest Baptist University *Missouri* M
Southwest Minnesota State University *Minnesota* M
Southwest Mississippi Community College *Mississippi* M
Southwest Virginia Community College *Virginia* M
Southwestern Adventist University *Texas* M
Southwestern College *California* M
Southwestern Community College *Iowa* M
Southwestern Illinois College *Illinois* M
Southwestern Oklahoma State University *Oklahoma* M
Southwestern Oregon Community College *Oregon* M
Southwestern University *Texas* M
Spalding University *Kentucky* M
Spartanburg Methodist College *South Carolina* M
Spokane Community College *Washington* M
Spokane Falls Community College *Washington* M
Spoon River College *Illinois* M
Spring Arbor University *Michigan* M
Spring Hill College *Alabama* M
Springfield College *Massachusetts* M
Springfield College in Illinois *Illinois* M
Stanford University *California* M
State University of New York at Binghamton *New York* M
State University of New York at Buffalo *New York* M
State University of New York College of Agriculture and Technology at Cobleskill *New York* M
State University of New York College of Agriculture and Technology at Morrisville *New York* M
State University of New York College at Brockport *New York* M
State University of New York College at Cortland *New York* M
State University of New York College at Old Westbury *New York* M
State University of New York College at Oneonta *New York* M
State University of New York College of Technology at Alfred *New York* M
State University of New York College of Technology at Canton *New York* M
State University of New York, Fredonia *New York* M
State University of New York Institute of Technology *New York* M
State University of New York Maritime College *New York* M
State University of New York at New Paltz *New York* M
State University of New York at Oswego *New York* M
State University of New York at Plattsburgh *New York* M
Stephen F. Austin State University *Texas* M
Sterling College *Kansas* M
Stetson University *Florida* M
Stevens Institute of Technology *New Jersey* M
Stonehill College *Massachusetts* M
Stony Brook University, State University of New York *New York* M
Suffolk County Community College *New York* M
Suffolk University *Massachusetts* M
Sul Ross State University *Texas* M
Surry Community College *North Carolina* M
Susquehanna University *Pennsylvania* M
Sussex County Community College *New Jersey* M
Swarthmore College *Pennsylvania* M
Syracuse University *New York* M
Tabor College *Kansas* M
Tacoma Community College *Washington* M
Taft College *California* M
Tallahassee Community College *Florida* M
Tarleton State University *Texas* M
Taylor University *Indiana* M
Temple College *Texas* M
Temple University *Pennsylvania* M
Tennessee Technological University *Tennessee* M
Tennessee Temple University *Tennessee* M
Tennessee Wesleyan College *Tennessee* M
Texarkana College *Texas* M
Texas A&M University *Texas* M
Texas A&M University-Corpus Christi *Texas* M
Texas A&M University-Kingsville *Texas* M
Texas Christian University *Texas* M
Texas College *Texas* M
Texas Lutheran University *Texas* M
Texas Southern University *Texas* M
Texas Southmost College *Texas* M
Texas State University-San Marcos *Texas* M
Texas Tech University *Texas* M
Texas Wesleyan University *Texas* M
Thiel College *Pennsylvania* M
Thomas College *Maine* M
Thomas More College *Kentucky* M
Thomas University *Georgia* M
Thompson Rivers University *British Columbia* M
Three Rivers Community College *Missouri* M
Tiffin University *Ohio* M
Toccoa Falls College *Georgia* M
Towson University *Maryland* M
Transylvania University *Kentucky* M
Treasure Valley Community College *Oregon* M
Trevecca Nazarene University *Tennessee* M
Tri-State University *Indiana* M
Trinidad State Junior College *Colorado* M
Trinity Bible College *North Dakota* M
Trinity Christian College *Illinois* M
Trinity College *Connecticut* M
Trinity International University *Illinois* M
Trinity University *Texas* M
Triton College *Illinois* M
Troy University *Alabama* M
Truett-McConnell College *Georgia* M
Truman State University *Missouri* M
Tufts University *Massachusetts* M
Tulane University *Louisiana* M
Tusculum College *Tennessee* M
Tuskegee University *Alabama* M
Tyler Junior College *Texas* M
Ulster County Community College *New York* M
Union College *New York* M
Union College *Kentucky* M
Union County College *New Jersey* M
Union University *Tennessee* M
United States Air Force Academy *Colorado* M
United States Coast Guard Academy *Connecticut* M
United States Merchant Marine Academy *New York* M
United States Military Academy *New York* M
United States Naval Academy *Maryland* M
Université Laval *Quebec* M
The University of Akron *Ohio* M
The University of Alabama *Alabama* M
The University of Alabama at Birmingham *Alabama* M
The University of Alabama in Huntsville *Alabama* M
University at Albany, State University of New York *New York* M
The University of Arizona *Arizona* M
University of Arkansas *Arkansas* M
University of Arkansas at Fort Smith *Arkansas* M
University of Arkansas at Little Rock *Arkansas* M
University of Arkansas at Monticello *Arkansas* M
University of Arkansas at Pine Bluff *Arkansas* M
University of Bridgeport *Connecticut* M
The University of British Columbia *British Columbia* M
University of California, Berkeley *California* M
University of California, Davis *California* M
University of California, Irvine *California* M
University of California, Los Angeles *California* M
University of California, Riverside *California* M
University of California, San Diego *California* M
University of California, Santa Barbara *California* M
University of Central Arkansas *Arkansas* M
University of Central Florida *Florida* M
University of Central Oklahoma *Oklahoma* M
University of Charleston *West Virginia* M
University of Chicago *Illinois* M
University of Cincinnati *Ohio* M
University of Cincinnati Raymond Walters College *Ohio* M
University of Colorado at Boulder *Colorado* M
University of Colorado at Colorado Springs *Colorado* M
University of Connecticut *Connecticut* M
University of the Cumberlands *Kentucky* M
University of Dallas *Texas* M
University of Dayton *Ohio* M
University of Delaware *Delaware* M
University of Detroit Mercy *Michigan* M
University of Dubuque *Iowa* M
University of Evansville *Indiana* M
The University of Findlay *Ohio* M
University of Florida *Florida* M
University of Georgia *Georgia* M
University of Guelph *Ontario* M
University of Hartford *Connecticut* M
University of Hawaii at Hilo *Hawaii* M
University of Hawaii at Manoa *Hawaii* M
University of Houston *Texas* M
University of Idaho *Idaho* M
University of Illinois at Chicago *Illinois* M
University of Illinois at Urbana-Champaign *Illinois* M
University of the Incarnate Word *Texas* M
University of Indianapolis *Indiana* M
The University of Iowa *Iowa* M
University of Kansas *Kansas* M
University of Kentucky *Kentucky* M
University of La Verne *California* M
University of Louisiana at Lafayette *Louisiana* M
University of Louisiana at Monroe *Louisiana* M
University of Louisville *Kentucky* M
University of Maine *Maine* M
University of Maine at Farmington *Maine* M
University of Maine at Presque Isle *Maine* M
University of Mary *North Dakota* M
University of Mary Hardin-Baylor *Texas* M
University of Mary Washington *Virginia* M
University of Maryland, Baltimore County *Maryland* M
University of Maryland, College Park *Maryland* M
University of Maryland Eastern Shore *Maryland* M
University of Massachusetts Amherst *Massachusetts* M
University of Massachusetts Boston *Massachusetts* M
University of Massachusetts Dartmouth *Massachusetts* M
University of Memphis *Tennessee* M
University of Miami *Florida* M
University of Michigan *Michigan* M
University of Minnesota, Crookston *Minnesota* M
University of Minnesota, Duluth *Minnesota* M
University of Minnesota, Morris *Minnesota* M

M = Men; W = Women

M = Men; W = Women

Basketball

M = Men; W = Women

M = Men; W = Women

M = Men; W = Women

Gordon College *Massachusetts* M & W
Goshen College *Indiana* M & W
Goucher College *Maryland* M & W
Grace Bible College *Michigan* M & W
Grace College *Indiana* M & W
Grace University *Nebraska* M & W
Graceland University *Iowa* M & W
Grambling State University *Louisiana* M & W
Grand Canyon University *Arizona* M & W
Grand Rapids Community College *Michigan* M & W
Grand Valley State University *Michigan* M & W
Grand View College *Iowa* M & W
Grays Harbor College *Washington* M & W
Grayson County College *Texas* M & W
Great Lakes Christian College *Michigan* M & W
Green Mountain College *Vermont* M & W
Green River Community College *Washington* M & W
Greensboro College *North Carolina* M & W
Greenville College *Illinois* M & W
Grinnell College *Iowa* M & W
Grossmont College *California* M & W
Grove City College *Pennsylvania* M & W
Guilford College *North Carolina* M & W
Gulf Coast Community College *Florida* M & W
Gustavus Adolphus College *Minnesota* M & W
Gwynedd-Mercy College *Pennsylvania* M & W
Hagerstown Community College *Maryland* M & W
Hamilton College *New York* M & W
Hamilton College-Lincoln *Nebraska* M & W
Hamline University *Minnesota* M & W
Hampden-Sydney College *Virginia* M
Hampshire College *Massachusetts* M & W
Hampton University *Virginia* M & W
Hannibal-LaGrange College *Missouri* M & W
Hanover College *Indiana* M & W
Hardin-Simmons University *Texas* M & W
Harding University *Arkansas* M & W
Harford Community College *Maryland* M & W
Harris-Stowe State University *Missouri* M & W
Harrisburg Area Community College *Pennsylvania* M & W
Hartnell College *California* M & W
Hartwick College *New York* M & W
Harvard University *Massachusetts* M & W
Harvey Mudd College *California* M & W
Haskell Indian Nations University *Kansas* M & W
Hastings College *Nebraska* M & W
Haverford College *Pennsylvania* M & W
Hawaii Pacific University *Hawaii* M
Heidelberg College *Ohio* M & W
Henderson State University *Arkansas* M & W
Hendrix College *Arkansas* M & W
Henry Ford Community College *Michigan* M & W
Heritage Baptist College and Heritage Theological Seminary *Ontario* M & W
Herkimer County Community College *New York* M & W
Hesser College *New Hampshire* M & W
Hesston College *Kansas* M & W
Hibbing Community College *Minnesota* M & W
High Point University *North Carolina* M & W
Highland Community College *Kansas* M & W
Highland Community College *Illinois* M & W
Highline Community College *Washington* M & W
Hilbert College *New York* M & W
Hill College of the Hill Junior College District *Texas* M & W
Hillsborough Community College *Florida* M & W
Hillsdale College *Michigan* M & W
Hillsdale Free Will Baptist College *Oklahoma* M & W
Hinds Community College *Mississippi* M & W
Hiram College *Ohio* M & W
Hobart and William Smith Colleges *New York* M & W
Hofstra University *New York* M & W
Hollins University *Virginia* W
Holmes Community College *Mississippi* M & W
Holy Cross College *Indiana* M
Holy Family University *Pennsylvania* M & W
Holy Names University *California* M & W
Holyoke Community College *Massachusetts* M & W
Hood College *Maryland* M & W
Hope College *Michigan* M & W
Hope International University *California* M & W
Houghton College *New York* M & W
Houston Baptist University *Texas* M & W
Howard College *Texas* M & W
Howard Community College *Maryland* M & W
Howard Payne University *Texas* M & W
Howard University *District of Columbia* M & W
Hudson Valley Community College *New York* M & W
Humboldt State University *California* M & W
Hunter College of the City University of New York *New York* M & W
Huntingdon College *Alabama* M & W
Huntington University *Indiana* M & W
Husson College *Maine* M & W
Huston-Tillotson University *Texas* M & W
Hutchinson Community College and Area Vocational School *Kansas* M & W
Idaho State University *Idaho* M & W
Illinois Central College *Illinois* M & W
Illinois Eastern Community Colleges, Lincoln Trail College *Illinois* M & W
Illinois Eastern Community Colleges, Olney Central College *Illinois* M & W
Illinois Eastern Community Colleges, Wabash Valley College *Illinois* M & W
Illinois Institute of Technology *Illinois* M & W
Illinois State University *Illinois* M & W
Illinois Valley Community College *Illinois* M & W
Illinois Wesleyan University *Illinois* M & W
Immaculata University *Pennsylvania* W
Imperial Valley College *California* M & W
Independence Community College *Kansas* M & W
Indian Hills Community College *Iowa* M
Indian River Community College *Florida* M & W
Indiana State University *Indiana* M & W
Indiana Tech *Indiana* M & W
Indiana University Bloomington *Indiana* M & W
Indiana University Northwest *Indiana* M
Indiana University of Pennsylvania *Pennsylvania* M & W
Indiana University-Purdue University Fort Wayne *Indiana* M & W
Indiana University-Purdue University Indianapolis *Indiana* M & W
Indiana University South Bend *Indiana* M & W
Indiana University Southeast *Indiana* M & W
Indiana Wesleyan University *Indiana* M & W
Inter American University of Puerto Rico, Aguadilla Campus *Puerto Rico* M & W
Inter American University of Puerto Rico, Arecibo Campus *Puerto Rico* M & W
Inter American University of Puerto Rico, Barranquitas Campus *Puerto Rico* M & W
Inter American University of Puerto Rico, Bayamón Campus *Puerto Rico* M & W
Inter American University of Puerto Rico, Guayama Campus *Puerto Rico* M & W
Inter American University of Puerto Rico, Metropolitan Campus *Puerto Rico* M & W
Inter American University of Puerto Rico, San Germán Campus *Puerto Rico* M & W
Iona College *New York* M & W
Iowa Central Community College *Iowa* M & W
Iowa Lakes Community College *Iowa* M & W
Iowa State University of Science and Technology *Iowa* M & W
Iowa Wesleyan College *Iowa* M & W
Iowa Western Community College *Iowa* M & W
Irvine Valley College *California* M & W
Itasca Community College *Minnesota* M & W
Itawamba Community College *Mississippi* M & W
Ithaca College *New York* M & W
Jackson State Community College *Tennessee* M & W
Jackson State University *Mississippi* M & W
Jacksonville College *Texas* M & W
Jacksonville State University *Alabama* M & W
Jacksonville University *Florida* M & W
James A. Rhodes State College *Ohio* M & W
James H. Faulkner State Community College *Alabama* M & W
James Madison University *Virginia* M & W
Jamestown College *North Dakota* M & W
Jamestown Community College *New York* M & W
Jarvis Christian College *Texas* M & W
Jefferson College *Missouri* W
Jefferson Community College *Ohio* M & W
Jefferson Community College *New York* M & W
John A. Logan College *Illinois* M & W
John Brown University *Arkansas* M & W
John Carroll University *Ohio* M & W
John Jay College of Criminal Justice of the City University of New York *New York* M & W
John Wood Community College *Illinois* M & W
The Johns Hopkins University *Maryland* M & W
Johnson Bible College *Tennessee* M & W
Johnson C. Smith University *North Carolina* M & W
Johnson College *Pennsylvania* M & W
Johnson County Community College *Kansas* M & W
Johnson State College *Vermont* M & W
Johnson & Wales University *Rhode Island* M & W
Johnson & Wales University *Colorado* M & W
Joliet Junior College *Illinois* M & W
Jones County Junior College *Mississippi* M & W
Judson College *Illinois* M & W
Judson College *Alabama* W
Juniata College *Pennsylvania* M & W
Kalamazoo College *Michigan* M & W
Kalamazoo Valley Community College *Michigan* M & W
Kankakee Community College *Illinois* M & W
Kansas City Kansas Community College *Kansas* M & W
Kansas State University *Kansas* M & W
Kansas Wesleyan University *Kansas* M & W
Kaskaskia College *Illinois* M & W
Kean University *New Jersey* M & W
Keene State College *New Hampshire* M & W
Kellogg Community College *Michigan* M & W
Kennesaw State University *Georgia* M & W
Kent State University *Ohio* M & W
Kentucky Christian University *Kentucky* M & W
Kentucky State University *Kentucky* M & W
Kentucky Wesleyan College *Kentucky* M & W
Kenyon College *Ohio* M & W
Keuka College *New York* M & W
Keystone College *Pennsylvania* M & W
Kilgore College *Texas* M & W
King College *Tennessee* M & W
King's College *Pennsylvania* M & W
The King's University College *Alberta* M & W
Kingsborough Community College of the City University of New York *New York* M & W
Kirkwood Community College *Iowa* M & W
Kishwaukee College *Illinois* M & W
Knox College *Illinois* M & W
Kutztown University of Pennsylvania *Pennsylvania* M & W
Kwantlen University College *British Columbia* M & W
La Roche College *Pennsylvania* M & W
La Salle University *Pennsylvania* M & W
La Sierra University *California* M & W
Labette Community College *Kansas* M & W
Lackawanna College *Pennsylvania* M & W
Lafayette College *Pennsylvania* M & W
LaGrange College *Georgia* M & W
Lake Erie College *Ohio* M & W
Lake Forest College *Illinois* M & W
Lake Land College *Illinois* M & W
Lake Michigan College *Michigan* M & W
Lake Region State College *North Dakota* M & W
Lake Superior State University *Michigan* M & W
Lakehead University *Ontario* M & W
Lakeland College *Wisconsin* M & W
Lakeland Community College *Ohio* M & W
Lamar Community College *Colorado* M
Lamar University *Texas* M & W
Lambuth University *Tennessee* M & W
Lancaster Bible College *Pennsylvania* M & W
Lander University *South Carolina* M & W
Landmark College *Vermont* M & W
Lane College *Tennessee* M & W
Lane Community College *Oregon* M & W
Langston University *Oklahoma* M & W
Lansing Community College *Michigan* M & W

M = Men; W = Women

M = Men; W = Women

Moraine Valley Community College *Illinois* M & W
Moravian College *Pennsylvania* M & W
Morehead State University *Kentucky* M & W
Morehouse College *Georgia* M
Morgan State University *Maryland* M & W
Morningside College *Iowa* M & W
Morris College *South Carolina* M & W
Morton College *Illinois* M & W
Motlow State Community College *Tennessee* M & W
Mott Community College *Michigan* M & W
Mount Allison University *New Brunswick* M & W
Mount Aloysius College *Pennsylvania* M & W
Mount Holyoke College *Massachusetts* W
Mt. Hood Community College *Oregon* M & W
Mount Ida College *Massachusetts* M & W
Mount Marty College *South Dakota* M & W
Mount Mary College *Wisconsin* W
Mount Mercy College *Iowa* M & W
Mount Olive College *North Carolina* M & W
Mount Saint Mary College *New York* M & W
Mount St. Mary's University *Maryland* M & W
Mount Saint Vincent University *Nova Scotia* M & W
Mt. San Antonio College *California* M & W
Mt. San Jacinto College *California* M & W
Mount Union College *Ohio* M & W
Mount Vernon Nazarene University *Ohio* M & W
Mountain State University *West Virginia* M
Muhlenberg College *Pennsylvania* M & W
Multnomah Bible College and Biblical Seminary *Oregon* M
Murray State College *Oklahoma* M & W
Murray State University *Kentucky* M & W
Muskegon Community College *Michigan* M & W
Muskingum College *Ohio* M & W
Napa Valley College *California* M & W
Nassau Community College *New York* M & W
Navarro College *Texas* M
Nazareth College of Rochester *New York* M & W
Nebraska Christian College *Nebraska* M & W
Nebraska College of Technical Agriculture *Nebraska* M & W
Nebraska Wesleyan University *Nebraska* M & W
Neosho County Community College *Kansas* M & W
Neumann College *Pennsylvania* M & W
New England College *New Hampshire* M & W
New Hampshire Community Technical College, Berlin/Laconia *New Hampshire* M & W
New Hampshire Community Technical College, Manchester/Stratham *New Hampshire* M
New Hampshire Technical Institute *New Hampshire* M & W
New Jersey City University *New Jersey* M & W
New Jersey Institute of Technology *New Jersey* M & W
New Mexico Highlands University *New Mexico* M & W
New Mexico Junior College *New Mexico* M & W
New Mexico Military Institute *New Mexico* M
New Mexico State University *New Mexico* M & W
New York City College of Technology of the City University of New York *New York* M & W
New York Institute of Technology *New York* M & W
New York University *New York* M & W
Newberry College *South Carolina* M & W
Newbury College *Massachusetts* M & W
Newman University *Kansas* M & W
Niagara County Community College *New York* M & W
Niagara University *New York* M & W
Nicholls State University *Louisiana* M & W
Nichols College *Massachusetts* M & W
Norfolk State University *Virginia* M & W
North Arkansas College *Arkansas* M & W
North Carolina Agricultural and Technical State University *North Carolina* M & W
North Carolina Central University *North Carolina* M & W
North Carolina State University *North Carolina* M & W
North Carolina Wesleyan College *North Carolina* M & W
North Central College *Illinois* M & W
North Central Missouri College *Missouri* M & W
North Central University *Minnesota* M & W
North Country Community College *New York* M & W
North Dakota State College of Science *North Dakota* M & W
North Dakota State University *North Dakota* M & W
North Florida Community College *Florida* W
North Georgia College & State University *Georgia* M & W
North Greenville College *South Carolina* M & W
North Idaho College *Idaho* M & W
North Iowa Area Community College *Iowa* M & W
North Lake College *Texas* M
North Park University *Illinois* M & W
North Seattle Community College *Washington* M & W
Northampton County Area Community College *Pennsylvania* M & W
Northeast Community College *Nebraska* M & W
Northeast Mississippi Community College *Mississippi* M & W
Northeastern Junior College *Colorado* M & W
Northeastern Oklahoma Agricultural and Mechanical College *Oklahoma* M & W
Northeastern State University *Oklahoma* M & W
Northeastern University *Massachusetts* M & W
Northern Arizona University *Arizona* M & W
Northern Essex Community College *Massachusetts* M & W
Northern Illinois University *Illinois* M & W
Northern Kentucky University *Kentucky* M & W
Northern Maine Community College *Maine* M & W
Northern Michigan University *Michigan* M & W
Northern Oklahoma College *Oklahoma* M & W
Northern State University *South Dakota* M & W
Northland College *Wisconsin* M & W
Northland Community and Technical College-Thief River Falls *Minnesota* M & W
Northwest Christian College *Oregon* M & W
Northwest College *Wyoming* M & W
Northwest Indian College *Washington* M & W
Northwest Mississippi Community College *Mississippi* M & W
Northwest Missouri State University *Missouri* M & W
Northwest Nazarene University *Idaho* M & W
Northwest-Shoals Community College *Alabama* M & W
Northwest University *Washington* M & W
Northwestern College *Minnesota* M & W
Northwestern College *Iowa* M & W
Northwestern Oklahoma State University *Oklahoma* M & W
Northwestern State University of Louisiana *Louisiana* M & W
Northwestern University *Illinois* M & W
Northwood University *Michigan* M & W
Northwood University, Florida Campus *Florida* M & W
Norwich University *Vermont* M & W
Notre Dame College *Ohio* M & W
Notre Dame de Namur University *California* M & W
Nova Scotia Agricultural College *Nova Scotia* M & W
Nova Southeastern University *Florida* M & W
Nyack College *New York* M & W
Oak Hills Christian College *Minnesota* M & W
Oakland City University *Indiana* M & W
Oakland Community College *Michigan* M & W
Oakland University *Michigan* M & W
Oakton Community College *Illinois* M & W
Oberlin College *Ohio* M & W
Occidental College *California* M & W
Ocean County College *New Jersey* M & W
Odessa College *Texas* M & W
Oglala Lakota College *South Dakota* M & W
Oglethorpe University *Georgia* M & W
Ohio Dominican University *Ohio* M & W
Ohio Northern University *Ohio* M & W
The Ohio State University *Ohio* M & W
The Ohio State University at Lima *Ohio* M & W
Ohio University *Ohio* M & W
Ohio University-Chillicothe *Ohio* M & W
Ohio University-Eastern *Ohio* M & W
Ohio University-Lancaster *Ohio* M & W
Ohio University-Southern Campus *Ohio* M & W
Ohio University-Zanesville *Ohio* M & W
Ohio Valley University *West Virginia* M & W
Ohio Wesleyan University *Ohio* M & W
Ohlone College *California* M & W
Okaloosa-Walton College *Florida* M & W
Oklahoma Baptist University *Oklahoma* M & W
Oklahoma Christian University *Oklahoma* M & W
Oklahoma City University *Oklahoma* M & W
Oklahoma Panhandle State University *Oklahoma* M & W
Oklahoma State University *Oklahoma* M & W
Oklahoma Wesleyan University *Oklahoma* M & W
Old Dominion University *Virginia* M & W
Olivet College *Michigan* M & W
Olivet Nazarene University *Illinois* M & W
Olympic College *Washington* M & W
Onondaga Community College *New York* M & W
Oral Roberts University *Oklahoma* M & W
Orange Coast College *California* M & W
Orange County Community College *New York* M & W
Oregon Institute of Technology *Oregon* M & W
Oregon State University *Oregon* M & W
Otero Junior College *Colorado* M & W
Ottawa University *Kansas* M & W
Otterbein College *Ohio* M & W
Ouachita Baptist University *Arkansas* M & W
Owens Community College *Ohio* M & W
Oxnard College *California* M & W
Ozark Christian College *Missouri* M & W
Pace University *New York* M & W
Pacific Lutheran University *Washington* M & W
Pacific Union College *California* M & W
Pacific University *Oregon* M & W
Paine College *Georgia* M & W
Palm Beach Atlantic University *Florida* M & W
Palm Beach Community College *Florida* M & W
Palomar College *California* M & W
Panola College *Texas* M & W
Paris Junior College *Texas* M & W
Park University *Missouri* M & W
Parkland College *Illinois* M & W
Pasadena City College *California* M & W
Pasco-Hernando Community College *Florida* M
Passaic County Community College *New Jersey* M & W
Patrick Henry College *Virginia* M
Patten University *California* M & W
Paul Quinn College *Texas* M & W
Paul Smith's College of Arts and Sciences *New York* M & W
Peace College *North Carolina* W
Pearl River Community College *Mississippi* M & W
Peninsula College *Washington* M & W
Penn Valley Community College *Missouri* M & W
Pennsylvania College of Technology *Pennsylvania* M & W
The Pennsylvania State University Abington College *Pennsylvania* M & W
The Pennsylvania State University Altoona College *Pennsylvania* M & W
The Pennsylvania State University Beaver Campus of the Commonwealth College *Pennsylvania* M
The Pennsylvania State University Berks Campus of the Berks-Lehigh Valley College *Pennsylvania* M & W
The Pennsylvania State University Delaware County Campus of the Commonwealth College *Pennsylvania* M & W
The Pennsylvania State University DuBois Campus of the Commonwealth College *Pennsylvania* M
The Pennsylvania State University at Erie, The Behrend College *Pennsylvania* M & W
The Pennsylvania State University Fayette Campus of the Commonwealth College *Pennsylvania* M
The Pennsylvania State University Hazleton Campus of the Commonwealth College *Pennsylvania* M & W
The Pennsylvania State University, Lehigh Valley Campus of the Berks-Lehigh Valley College *Pennsylvania* M & W
The Pennsylvania State University McKeesport Campus of the Commonwealth College *Pennsylvania* M

M = Men; W = Women

M = Men; W = Women

Seward County Community College *Kansas* M & W
Shasta College *California* M & W
Shaw University *North Carolina* M & W
Shawnee Community College *Illinois* M & W
Shawnee State University *Ohio* M & W
Shelton State Community College *Alabama* M & W
Shenandoah University *Virginia* M & W
Shepherd University *West Virginia* M & W
Sheridan College-Sheridan and Gillette *Wyoming* M & W
Shippensburg University of Pennsylvania *Pennsylvania* M & W
Shoreline Community College *Washington* M & W
Shorter College *Georgia* M & W
Siena College *New York* M & W
Siena Heights University *Michigan* M & W
Sierra College *California* M & W
Silver Lake College *Wisconsin* W
Simmons College *Massachusetts* W
Simon Fraser University *British Columbia* M & W
Simon's Rock College of Bard *Massachusetts* M & W
Simpson College *Iowa* M & W
Simpson University *California* M & W
Sinclair Community College *Ohio* M & W
Sitting Bull College *North Dakota* M & W
Skagit Valley College *Washington* M & W
Skidmore College *New York* M & W
Skyline College *California* M
Slippery Rock University of Pennsylvania *Pennsylvania* M & W
Smith College *Massachusetts* W
Snead State Community College *Alabama* M & W
Snow College *Utah* M & W
Solano Community College *California* M & W
Sonoma State University *California* M & W
South Carolina State University *South Carolina* M & W
South Dakota School of Mines and Technology *South Dakota* M & W
South Dakota State University *South Dakota* M & W
South Georgia Technical College *Georgia* M & W
South Mountain Community College *Arizona* M & W
South Plains College *Texas* M & W
South Puget Sound Community College *Washington* M & W
South Suburban College *Illinois* M & W
Southeast Community College, Beatrice Campus *Nebraska* M & W
Southeast Missouri State University *Missouri* M & W
Southeastern Community College, North Campus *Iowa* M
Southeastern Illinois College *Illinois* M & W
Southeastern Louisiana University *Louisiana* M & W
Southeastern Oklahoma State University *Oklahoma* M & W
Southeastern University *Florida* M & W
Southern Arkansas University-Magnolia *Arkansas* M & W
Southern Connecticut State University *Connecticut* M & W
Southern Illinois University Carbondale *Illinois* M & W
Southern Illinois University Edwardsville *Illinois* M & W
Southern Maine Community College *Maine* M
Southern Methodist University *Texas* M & W
Southern Nazarene University *Oklahoma* M & W
Southern New Hampshire University *New Hampshire* M & W
Southern Oregon University *Oregon* M & W
Southern Polytechnic State University *Georgia* M & W
Southern State Community College *Ohio* M & W
Southern Union State Community College *Alabama* M & W
Southern University and Agricultural and Mechanical College *Louisiana* M & W
Southern University at New Orleans *Louisiana* M
Southern University at Shreveport *Louisiana* M & W
Southern Utah University *Utah* M & W
Southern Vermont College *Vermont* M & W
Southern Virginia University *Virginia* M & W
Southern Wesleyan University *South Carolina* M & W
Southwest Baptist University *Missouri* M & W
Southwest Minnesota State University *Minnesota* M & W
Southwest Mississippi Community College *Mississippi* M & W
Southwest Texas Junior College *Texas* M & W
Southwest Virginia Community College *Virginia* M
Southwestern Adventist University *Texas* M & W
Southwestern Assemblies of God University *Texas* M & W
Southwestern Christian College *Texas* M & W
Southwestern Christian University *Oklahoma* M
Southwestern College *Kansas* M & W
Southwestern College *California* M & W
Southwestern College *Arizona* M & W
Southwestern Community College *Iowa* M & W
Southwestern Illinois College *Illinois* M & W
Southwestern Oklahoma State University *Oklahoma* M & W
Southwestern Oregon Community College *Oregon* M & W
Southwestern University *Texas* M & W
Spalding University *Kentucky* M & W
Spartanburg Methodist College *South Carolina* M & W
Spelman College *Georgia* W
Spokane Community College *Washington* M & W
Spokane Falls Community College *Washington* M & W
Spoon River College *Illinois* M & W
Spring Arbor University *Michigan* M & W
Spring Hill College *Alabama* M & W
Springfield College *Massachusetts* M & W
Springfield Technical Community College *Massachusetts* M & W
Stanford University *California* M & W
State Fair Community College *Missouri* M & W
State University of New York at Binghamton *New York* M & W
State University of New York at Buffalo *New York* M & W
State University of New York College of Agriculture and Technology at Cobleskill *New York* M & W
State University of New York College of Agriculture and Technology at Morrisville *New York* M & W
State University of New York College at Brockport *New York* M & W
State University of New York College at Cortland *New York* M & W
State University of New York College at Geneseo *New York* M & W
State University of New York College at Old Westbury *New York* M & W
State University of New York College at Oneonta *New York* M & W
State University of New York College at Potsdam *New York* M & W
State University of New York College of Technology at Alfred *New York* M & W
State University of New York College of Technology at Canton *New York* M & W
State University of New York College of Technology at Delhi *New York* M & W
State University of New York, Fredonia *New York* M & W
State University of New York Institute of Technology *New York* M & W
State University of New York Maritime College *New York* M & W
State University of New York at New Paltz *New York* M & W
State University of New York at Oswego *New York* M & W
State University of New York at Plattsburgh *New York* M & W
Stephen F. Austin State University *Texas* M & W
Stephens College *Missouri* W
Sterling College *Kansas* M & W
Stetson University *Florida* M & W
Stevens Institute of Technology *New Jersey* M & W
Stillman College *Alabama* M & W
Stonehill College *Massachusetts* M & W
Stony Brook University, State University of New York *New York* M & W
Suffolk County Community College *New York* M & W
Suffolk University *Massachusetts* M & W
Sul Ross State University *Texas* M & W
Sullivan County Community College *New York* M & W
Surry Community College *North Carolina* M
Susquehanna University *Pennsylvania* M & W
Sussex County Community College *New Jersey* M
Swarthmore College *Pennsylvania* M & W
Syracuse University *New York* M & W
Tabor College *Kansas* M & W
Tacoma Community College *Washington* M & W
Taft College *California* W
Tallahassee Community College *Florida* M & W
Tarleton State University *Texas* M & W
Taylor University *Indiana* M & W
Taylor University College and Seminary *Alberta* M & W
Taylor University Fort Wayne *Indiana* M & W
TCI-The College of Technology *New York* M
Technological College of San Juan *Puerto Rico* M & W
Temple College *Texas* M & W
Temple University *Pennsylvania* M & W
Tennessee State University *Tennessee* M & W
Tennessee Technological University *Tennessee* M & W
Tennessee Temple University *Tennessee* M & W
Tennessee Wesleyan College *Tennessee* M & W
Texas A&M International University *Texas* M & W
Texas A&M University *Texas* M & W
Texas A&M University-Commerce *Texas* M & W
Texas A&M University-Corpus Christi *Texas* M & W
Texas A&M University-Kingsville *Texas* M & W
Texas Christian University *Texas* M & W
Texas College *Texas* M & W
Texas Lutheran University *Texas* M & W
Texas Southern University *Texas* M & W
Texas State University-San Marcos *Texas* M & W
Texas Tech University *Texas* M & W
Texas Wesleyan University *Texas* M & W
Texas Woman's University *Texas* W
Thaddeus Stevens College of Technology *Pennsylvania* M
Thiel College *Pennsylvania* M & W
Thomas College *Maine* M & W
Thomas More College *Kentucky* M & W
Thompson Rivers University *British Columbia* M & W
Three Rivers Community College *Missouri* M & W
Tiffin University *Ohio* M & W
Toccoa Falls College *Georgia* M & W
Tompkins Cortland Community College *New York* M & W
Tougaloo College *Mississippi* M & W
Towson University *Maryland* M & W
Transylvania University *Kentucky* M & W
Treasure Valley Community College *Oregon* M & W
Trent University *Ontario* M & W
Trevecca Nazarene University *Tennessee* M & W
Tri-State University *Indiana* M & W
Trinidad State Junior College *Colorado* M
Trinity Baptist College *Florida* M & W
Trinity Bible College *North Dakota* M & W
Trinity Christian College *Illinois* M & W
Trinity College *Connecticut* M & W
Trinity International University *Illinois* M & W
Trinity University *Texas* M & W
Trinity Valley Community College *Texas* M & W
Trinity (Washington) University *District of Columbia* W
Trinity Western University *British Columbia* M & W
Triton College *Illinois* M & W
Troy University *Alabama* M & W
Truett-McConnell College *Georgia* M & W
Truman State University *Missouri* M & W
Tufts University *Massachusetts* M & W
Tulane University *Louisiana* M & W
Tusculum College *Tennessee* M & W
Tuskegee University *Alabama* M & W
Tyler Junior College *Texas* M & W

M = Men; W = Women

M = Men; W = Women

The University of South Dakota *South Dakota* M & W
University of South Florida *Florida* M & W
University of Southern California *California* M & W
University of Southern Indiana *Indiana* M & W
University of Southern Maine *Maine* M & W
University of Southern Mississippi *Mississippi* M & W
The University of Tampa *Florida* M & W
The University of Tennessee *Tennessee* M & W
The University of Tennessee at Chattanooga *Tennessee* M & W
The University of Tennessee at Martin *Tennessee* M & W
The University of Texas at Arlington *Texas* M & W
The University of Texas at Austin *Texas* M & W
The University of Texas at Dallas *Texas* M & W
The University of Texas at El Paso *Texas* M & W
The University of Texas-Pan American *Texas* M & W
The University of Texas of the Permian Basin *Texas* M & W
The University of Texas at San Antonio *Texas* M & W
The University of Texas at Tyler *Texas* M & W
The University of Toledo *Ohio* M & W
University of Toronto *Ontario* M & W
University of Tulsa *Oklahoma* M & W
University of Utah *Utah* M & W
University of Vermont *Vermont* M & W
University of Victoria *British Columbia* M & W
University of the Virgin Islands *United States Virgin Islands* M & W
University of Virginia *Virginia* M & W
The University of Virginia's College at Wise *Virginia* M & W
University of Washington *Washington* M & W
University of Waterloo *Ontario* M & W
The University of West Alabama *Alabama* M & W
University of West Florida *Florida* M & W
University of West Georgia *Georgia* M & W
The University of Western Ontario *Ontario* M & W
University of Windsor *Ontario* M & W
The University of Winnipeg *Manitoba* M & W
University of Wisconsin-Baraboo/Sauk County *Wisconsin* M
University of Wisconsin-Barron County *Wisconsin* M & W
University of Wisconsin-Eau Claire *Wisconsin* M & W
University of Wisconsin-Fond du Lac *Wisconsin* M & W
University of Wisconsin-Fox Valley *Wisconsin* M & W
University of Wisconsin-Green Bay *Wisconsin* M & W
University of Wisconsin-La Crosse *Wisconsin* M & W
University of Wisconsin-Madison *Wisconsin* M & W
University of Wisconsin-Manitowoc *Wisconsin* M & W
University of Wisconsin-Marathon County *Wisconsin* M & W
University of Wisconsin-Marinette *Wisconsin* M & W
University of Wisconsin-Marshfield/Wood County *Wisconsin* M & W
University of Wisconsin-Milwaukee *Wisconsin* M & W
University of Wisconsin-Oshkosh *Wisconsin* M & W
University of Wisconsin-Parkside *Wisconsin* M & W
University of Wisconsin-Platteville *Wisconsin* M & W
University of Wisconsin-Richland *Wisconsin* M & W
University of Wisconsin-River Falls *Wisconsin* M & W
University of Wisconsin-Sheboygan *Wisconsin* M & W
University of Wisconsin-Stevens Point *Wisconsin* M & W
University of Wisconsin-Stout *Wisconsin* M & W
University of Wisconsin-Superior *Wisconsin* M & W
University of Wisconsin-Washington County *Wisconsin* M & W
University of Wisconsin-Waukesha *Wisconsin* M & W
University of Wisconsin-Whitewater *Wisconsin* M & W
University of Wyoming *Wyoming* M & W
Upper Iowa University *Iowa* M & W
Urbana University *Ohio* M & W
Ursinus College *Pennsylvania* M & W
Ursuline College *Ohio* W
Utah State University *Utah* M & W
Utah Valley State College *Utah* M & W
Utica College *New York* M & W
Valdosta State University *Georgia* M & W
Valley City State University *North Dakota* M & W
Valley Forge Christian College *Pennsylvania* M & W
Valley Forge Military College *Pennsylvania* M
Valparaiso University *Indiana* M & W
Vanderbilt University *Tennessee* M & W
Vanguard University of Southern California *California* M & W
Vassar College *New York* M & W
Vennard College *Iowa* M & W
Ventura College *California* M & W
Vermilion Community College *Minnesota* M & W
Vermont Technical College *Vermont* M & W
Victor Valley College *California* M & W
Villa Julie College *Maryland* M & W
Villanova University *Pennsylvania* M & W
Vincennes University *Indiana* M & W
Virginia Commonwealth University *Virginia* M & W
Virginia Intermont College *Virginia* M & W
Virginia Military Institute *Virginia* M
Virginia Polytechnic Institute and State University *Virginia* M & W
Virginia State University *Virginia* M & W
Virginia Union University *Virginia* M & W
Virginia Wesleyan College *Virginia* M & W
Viterbo University *Wisconsin* M & W
Volunteer State Community College *Tennessee* M & W
Voorhees College *South Carolina* M & W
Wabash College *Indiana* M
Wagner College *New York* M & W
Wake Forest University *North Carolina* M & W
Waldorf College *Iowa* M & W
Walla Walla College *Washington* M & W
Walla Walla Community College *Washington* M & W
Wallace State Community College *Alabama* M & W
Walsh University *Ohio* M & W
Walters State Community College *Tennessee* M & W
Warner Pacific College *Oregon* M & W
Warner Southern College *Florida* M & W
Warren Wilson College *North Carolina* M & W
Wartburg College *Iowa* M & W
Washburn University *Kansas* M & W
Washington Bible College *Maryland* M & W
Washington College *Maryland* M & W
Washington & Jefferson College *Pennsylvania* M & W
Washington and Lee University *Virginia* M & W
Washington State University *Washington* M & W
Washington University in St. Louis *Missouri* M & W
Waubonsee Community College *Illinois* M & W
Wayland Baptist University *Texas* M & W
Wayne County Community College District *Michigan* M & W
Wayne State College *Nebraska* M & W
Wayne State University *Michigan* M & W
Waynesburg College *Pennsylvania* M & W
Weatherford College *Texas* M & W
Webb Institute *New York* M & W
Webber International University *Florida* M & W
Weber State University *Utah* M & W
Webster University *Missouri* M & W
Wellesley College *Massachusetts* W
Wenatchee Valley College *Washington* M & W
Wentworth Institute of Technology *Massachusetts* M & W
Wesley College *Mississippi* M
Wesley College *Delaware* M & W
Wesleyan College *Georgia* W
Wesleyan University *Connecticut* M & W
West Chester University of Pennsylvania *Pennsylvania* M & W
West Hills Community College *California* M
West Liberty State College *West Virginia* M & W
West Los Angeles College *California* M
West Texas A&M University *Texas* M & W
West Valley College *California* M & W
West Virginia State University *West Virginia* M & W
West Virginia University *West Virginia* M & W
West Virginia University Institute of Technology *West Virginia* M & W
West Virginia Wesleyan College *West Virginia* M & W
Westchester Community College *New York* M & W
Western Carolina University *North Carolina* M & W
Western Connecticut State University *Connecticut* M & W
Western Illinois University *Illinois* M & W
Western Kentucky University *Kentucky* M & W
Western Michigan University *Michigan* M & W
Western Nebraska Community College *Nebraska* M & W
Western New England College *Massachusetts* M & W
Western New Mexico University *New Mexico* M & W
Western Oklahoma State College *Oklahoma* M & W
Western Oregon University *Oregon* M & W
Western State College of Colorado *Colorado* M & W
Western Technical College *Wisconsin* M & W
Western Washington University *Washington* M & W
Western Wyoming Community College *Wyoming* M & W
Westfield State College *Massachusetts* M & W
Westminster College *Utah* M & W
Westminster College *Pennsylvania* M & W
Westminster College *Missouri* M & W
Westmont College *California* M & W
Whatcom Community College *Washington* M & W
Wheaton College *Massachusetts* M & W
Wheaton College *Illinois* M & W
Wheeling Jesuit University *West Virginia* M & W
Wheelock College *Massachusetts* W
Whitman College *Washington* M & W
Whittier College *California* M & W
Whitworth College *Washington* M & W
Wichita State University *Kansas* M & W
Widener University *Pennsylvania* M & W
Wilberforce University *Ohio* M & W
Wiley College *Texas* M & W
Wilfrid Laurier University *Ontario* M & W
Wilkes Community College *North Carolina* M & W
Wilkes University *Pennsylvania* M & W
Willamette University *Oregon* M & W
William Carey College *Mississippi* M & W
William Jessup University *California* M & W
William Jewell College *Missouri* M & W
William Paterson University of New Jersey *New Jersey* M & W
William Penn University *Iowa* M & W
William Rainey Harper College *Illinois* M & W
William Woods University *Missouri* W
Williams Baptist College *Arkansas* M & W
Williams College *Massachusetts* M & W
The Williamson Free School of Mechanical Trades *Pennsylvania* M
Williston State College *North Dakota* M & W
Wilmington College *Ohio* M & W
Wilmington College *Delaware* M & W
Wilson College *Pennsylvania* W
Wingate University *North Carolina* M & W
Winona State University *Minnesota* M & W
Winston-Salem State University *North Carolina* M & W
Winthrop University *South Carolina* M & W
Wisconsin Lutheran College *Wisconsin* M & W
Wittenberg University *Ohio* M & W
Wofford College *South Carolina* M & W
Worcester Polytechnic Institute *Massachusetts* M & W
Worcester State College *Massachusetts* M & W
Wright State University *Ohio* M & W
Wright State University, Lake Campus *Ohio* M & W
WyoTech *Wyoming* W
Xavier University *Ohio* M & W
Xavier University of Louisiana *Louisiana* M & W
Yakima Valley Community College *Washington* M & W

M = Men; W = Women

Yale University *Connecticut* M & W
Yavapai College *Arizona* M & W
Yeshiva University *New York* M & W
York College *Nebraska* M & W
York College of the City University of New York *New York* M & W
York College of Pennsylvania *Pennsylvania* M & W
York University *Ontario* M & W
Youngstown State University *Ohio* M & W
Yuba College *California* M & W
Zane State College *Ohio* M & W

Bowling

Acadia University *Nova Scotia* M
Adirondack Community College *New York* M & W
Alabama State University *Alabama* W
Arkansas State University *Arkansas* W
Bethune-Cookman College *Florida* W
Bowie State University *Maryland* W
Briarcliffe College *New York* M & W
Bryant University *Rhode Island* M & W
Buffalo State College, State University of New York *New York* M & W
California State University, Chico *California* M & W
California State University, Fullerton *California* M & W
California State University, Long Beach *California* M & W
California State University, Sacramento *California* M & W
Carthage College *Wisconsin* W
Central Missouri State University *Missouri* M & W
Central Pennsylvania College *Pennsylvania* M & W
Central Washington University *Washington* M & W
Cheyney University of Pennsylvania *Pennsylvania* W
Clarkson University *New York* M & W
Clemson University *South Carolina* M & W
College of Alameda *California* M & W
Community College of Allegheny County *Pennsylvania* M & W
Coppin State University *Maryland* M & W
Delaware State University *Delaware* W
Dutchess Community College *New York* M & W
Emory University *Georgia* M & W
Erie Community College *New York* M & W
Erie Community College, North Campus *New York* M & W
Erie Community College, South Campus *New York* M & W
Fairleigh Dickinson University, Metropolitan Campus *New Jersey* W
Fashion Institute of Technology *New York* M & W
Fayetteville State University *North Carolina* M & W
Florida State University *Florida* M & W
Fontbonne University *Missouri* W
Georgia Southern University *Georgia* M & W
Globe Institute of Technology *New York* M & W
Grambling State University *Louisiana* W
Hampton University *Virginia* W
Howard University *District of Columbia* W
Hudson Valley Community College *New York* M & W
Jackson State University *Mississippi* W
Johnson College *Pennsylvania* M & W
Lehigh University *Pennsylvania* M & W
Lincoln University *Pennsylvania* M & W
Lindenwood University *Missouri* M & W
Lindsey Wilson College *Kentucky* M & W
Linn State Technical College *Missouri* M & W
Livingstone College *North Carolina* W
Loyola University New Orleans *Louisiana* M & W
Madison Area Technical College *Wisconsin* M & W
Marist College *New York* M & W
McKendree College *Illinois* M & W
Merced College *California* M & W
Mid-State Technical College *Wisconsin* M & W
Milwaukee Area Technical College *Wisconsin* M & W
Mississippi Valley State University *Mississippi* W
Missouri Baptist University *Missouri* M & W
Missouri State University *Missouri* M & W
Mohawk Valley Community College *New York* M & W
Morehead State University *Kentucky* M & W
Morgan State University *Maryland* W
Murray State University *Kentucky* M & W
Nassau Community College *New York* M & W
New Jersey City University *New Jersey* W
Newman University *Kansas* M & W
Norfolk State University *Virginia* W
North Carolina Central University *North Carolina* M & W
North Carolina State University *North Carolina* M & W
North Dakota State University *North Dakota* M & W
Northampton County Area Community College *Pennsylvania* M & W
Orange Coast College *California* M & W
Pennsylvania College of Technology *Pennsylvania* M & W
The Pennsylvania State University Berks Campus of the Berks-Lehigh Valley College *Pennsylvania* M & W
The Pennsylvania State University, Lehigh Valley Campus of the Berks-Lehigh Valley College *Pennsylvania* M & W
The Pennsylvania State University University Park Campus *Pennsylvania* M
Pikeville College *Kentucky* M & W
Prince George's Community College *Maryland* M & W
Robert Morris College *Illinois* M
Rochester Institute of Technology *New York* M & W
Rockland Community College *New York* M & W
Sacred Heart University *Connecticut* M & W
Saginaw Valley State University *Michigan* M
Saint Augustine's College *North Carolina* W
St. Cloud State University *Minnesota* M & W
Saint Peter's College *New Jersey* M & W
San Jose State University *California* M & W
Schenectady County Community College *New York* M & W
Shaw University *North Carolina* W
Southern University and Agricultural and Mechanical College *Louisiana* W
State University of New York at Binghamton *New York* M & W
State University of New York Institute of Technology *New York* M & W
Syracuse University *New York* M & W
Texas Southern University *Texas* W
United States Coast Guard Academy *Connecticut* M & W
United States Military Academy *New York* M & W
The University of Alabama in Huntsville *Alabama* M & W
University of California, Santa Barbara *California* M & W
University of Colorado at Boulder *Colorado* M & W
University of Delaware *Delaware* M & W
University of Maryland, Baltimore County *Maryland* M & W
University of Minnesota, Duluth *Minnesota* M & W
University of Nebraska-Lincoln *Nebraska* M
University of North Texas *Texas* M & W
University of Oregon *Oregon* M & W
The University of Scranton *Pennsylvania* M & W
University of Utah *Utah* M & W
University of Wisconsin-Platteville *Wisconsin* M & W
University of Wisconsin-Whitewater *Wisconsin* M & W
Vincennes University *Indiana* M & W
Virginia Polytechnic Institute and State University *Virginia* M & W
Virginia State University *Virginia* W
Washington State University *Washington* M & W
Weber State University *Utah* M & W
West Texas A&M University *Texas* M & W
Westchester Community College *New York* M & W
Western New England College *Massachusetts* M & W
Wichita State University *Kansas* M & W
William Paterson University of New Jersey *New Jersey* M & W
Winona State University *Minnesota* M & W
Winston-Salem State University *North Carolina* M & W
WyoTech *Wyoming* W

Cheerleading

Acadia University *Nova Scotia* M
Albion College *Michigan* M & W
Albright College *Pennsylvania* W
Alice Lloyd College *Kentucky* M & W
Allegheny College *Pennsylvania* M & W
Anderson University *South Carolina* W
Anna Maria College *Massachusetts* W
Arkansas Tech University *Arkansas* M & W
Arlington Baptist College *Texas* W
Atlanta Metropolitan College *Georgia* M & W
Augustana College *South Dakota* W
Augustana College *Illinois* M & W
Austin College *Texas* M & W
Austin Peay State University *Tennessee* M & W
Avila University *Missouri* W
Babson College *Massachusetts* W
Bacone College *Oklahoma* M & W
Baker University *Kansas* M & W
Baptist Bible College of Pennsylvania *Pennsylvania* W
Barclay College *Kansas* M & W
Barton County Community College *Kansas* M & W
Becker College *Massachusetts* M & W
Belmont Abbey College *North Carolina* M & W
Benedict College *South Carolina* W
Benedictine College *Kansas* M & W
Bernard M. Baruch College of the City University of New York *New York* W
Berry College *Georgia* M & W
Bethany College *West Virginia* M & W
Bethel College *Tennessee* M & W
Bethel College *Indiana* M & W
Bethel University *Minnesota* W
Blackburn College *Illinois* M & W
Blinn College *Texas* M & W
Bloomsburg University of Pennsylvania *Pennsylvania* M & W
Bluefield State College *West Virginia* W
Boston University *Massachusetts* M & W
Bradley University *Illinois* M & W
Brevard College *North Carolina* M & W
Brewton-Parker College *Georgia* M & W
Brigham Young University *Utah* M & W
Brock University *Ontario* M & W
Bryant University *Rhode Island* M & W
Bucknell University *Pennsylvania* M & W
California Lutheran University *California* M & W
California State University, Chico *California* M & W
California State University, Sacramento *California* M & W
California University of Pennsylvania *Pennsylvania* M & W
Calumet College of Saint Joseph *Indiana* W
Calvary Bible College and Theological Seminary *Missouri* W
Campbell University *North Carolina* W
Campbellsville University *Kentucky* M & W
Cape Fear Community College *North Carolina* M & W
Carnegie Mellon University *Pennsylvania* M & W
Carroll College *Montana* M & W
Case Western Reserve University *Ohio* M & W
Casper College *Wyoming* M & W
Castleton State College *Vermont* M & W
Cazenovia College *New York* M & W
Cecil Community College *Maryland* W
Central Christian College of Kansas *Kansas* M & W
Central State University *Ohio* M & W
Central Washington University *Washington* M & W
Centre College *Kentucky* W
Charleston Southern University *South Carolina* M & W
Chowan University *North Carolina* M & W
Claremont McKenna College *California* M & W
Clarendon College *Texas* M & W
Clark Atlanta University *Georgia* W
Clayton State University *Georgia* W
Clemson University *South Carolina* M & W
Clinton Community College *Iowa* M & W
Coastal Carolina University *South Carolina* M & W
Coe College *Iowa* W

M = Men; W = Women

Coker College *South Carolina* M & W
Colby Community College *Kansas* W
Colgate University *New York* M & W
College of DuPage *Illinois* M & W
College Misericordia *Pennsylvania* W
College of Mount St. Joseph *Ohio* W
College of Mount Saint Vincent *New York* W
College of the Ozarks *Missouri* M & W
College of Southern Idaho *Idaho* M & W
The College of Wooster *Ohio* W
Columbia College *Missouri* W
Concord University *West Virginia* M & W
Concordia College *Minnesota* W
Concordia College *Alabama* W
Concordia University *Illinois* M & W
Converse College *South Carolina* W
Corning Community College *New York* W
Culver-Stockton College *Missouri* M & W
Cumberland University *Tennessee* M & W
Dakota State University *South Dakota* M & W
Dakota Wesleyan University *South Dakota* M & W
Dartmouth College *New Hampshire* M & W
Delaware Valley College *Pennsylvania* W
Delta State University *Mississippi* M & W
DePauw University *Indiana* M & W
DeSales University *Pennsylvania* W
Dickinson College *Pennsylvania* M & W
Dickinson State University *North Dakota* M & W
Dominican University of California *California* W
Drake University *Iowa* M & W
Duquesne University *Pennsylvania* M & W
Dyersburg State Community College *Tennessee* W
Earlham College *Indiana* M & W
East Central University *Oklahoma* M & W
East Mississippi Community College *Mississippi* W
Eastern Connecticut State University *Connecticut* W
Eastern Kentucky University *Kentucky* M & W
Eastern Wyoming College *Wyoming* M & W
Elizabethtown College *Pennsylvania* M & W
Elmira College *New York* W
Elon University *North Carolina* M & W
Embry-Riddle Aeronautical University *Florida* M & W
Emporia State University *Kansas* M & W
Enterprise-Ozark Community College *Alabama* M & W
Erie Community College *New York* W
Erie Community College, North Campus *New York* W
Erie Community College, South Campus *New York* W
Fairfield University *Connecticut* M & W
Fayetteville State University *North Carolina* M & W
Ferris State University *Michigan* M & W
Ferrum College *Virginia* M & W
Florida Atlantic University *Florida* W
Florida Gulf Coast University *Florida* W
Florida State University *Florida* M & W
Fontbonne University *Missouri* W
Fordham University *New York* M & W
Fort Lewis College *Colorado* M & W
Freed-Hardeman University *Tennessee* M & W
Furman University *South Carolina* M & W
Garden City Community College *Kansas* M & W
Gardner-Webb University *North Carolina* M & W
George Mason University *Virginia* M & W
Georgetown College *Kentucky* W
Georgia Southern University *Georgia* M & W
Gettysburg College *Pennsylvania* M & W
Glenville State College *West Virginia* M & W
Gogebic Community College *Michigan* M & W
Gordon College *Massachusetts* M & W
Grace College *Indiana* M & W
Grand Valley State University *Michigan* M & W
Greensboro College *North Carolina* M & W
Grove City College *Pennsylvania* W
Gulf Coast Community College *Florida* M & W
Hannibal-LaGrange College *Missouri* M & W
Hardin-Simmons University *Texas* M & W
Harding University *Arkansas* M & W
Harris-Stowe State University *Missouri* M & W
Haskell Indian Nations University *Kansas* M & W
Hawaii Pacific University *Hawaii* M & W
Hope College *Michigan* M & W
Hope International University *California* M & W
Houghton College *New York* M & W
Houston Baptist University *Texas* M & W
Howard College *Texas* M & W
Hutchinson Community College and Area Vocational School *Kansas* M & W
Illinois College *Illinois* W
Illinois Wesleyan University *Illinois* M & W
Independence Community College *Kansas* M & W
Indiana Tech *Indiana* M & W
Indiana Wesleyan University *Indiana* M & W
Inter American University of Puerto Rico, Aguadilla Campus *Puerto Rico* M & W
Jackson State Community College *Tennessee* W
Jarvis Christian College *Texas* W
Johnson Bible College *Tennessee* M & W
Johnson C. Smith University *North Carolina* W
Johnson & Wales University *Colorado* M & W
Kansas Wesleyan University *Kansas* M & W
Kaskaskia College *Illinois* M & W
Kean University *New Jersey* M & W
Kennesaw State University *Georgia* W
Kentucky Wesleyan College *Kentucky* M & W
Kilgore College *Texas* M & W
King College *Tennessee* M & W
King's College *Pennsylvania* M & W
Kutztown University of Pennsylvania *Pennsylvania* W
Labette Community College *Kansas* W
Lake Forest College *Illinois* M & W
Lake Land College *Illinois* W
Lakehead University *Ontario* W
Lamar University *Texas* M & W
Lambuth University *Tennessee* M & W
Laramie County Community College *Wyoming* M & W
Lehigh University *Pennsylvania* M & W
Lewis University *Illinois* M & W
Liberty University *Virginia* M & W
Lincoln Christian College *Illinois* M & W
Lindenwood University *Missouri* M & W
Lindsey Wilson College *Kentucky* M & W
Lon Morris College *Texas* M & W
Louisiana College *Louisiana* M & W
Louisiana State University and Agricultural and Mechanical College *Louisiana* M & W
Loyola University New Orleans *Louisiana* M & W
Lubbock Christian University *Texas* M & W
Lycoming College *Pennsylvania* M & W
Lynchburg College *Virginia* M & W
MacMurray College *Illinois* M & W
Malone College *Ohio* M & W
Manchester College *Indiana* M & W
Manhattan College *New York* M & W
Marian College *Indiana* M & W
Marietta College *Ohio* W
Marist College *New York* M & W
Marquette University *Wisconsin* M & W
Marshalltown Community College *Iowa* M & W
Martin Methodist College *Tennessee* W
Maryville College *Tennessee* M & W
Massachusetts Institute of Technology *Massachusetts* M & W
McGill University *Quebec* M & W
McKendree College *Illinois* M & W
Medaille College *New York* M & W
Methodist College *North Carolina* M & W
Metropolitan State College of Denver *Colorado* M & W
Miami University Hamilton *Ohio* W
Michigan State University *Michigan* M & W
MidAmerica Nazarene University *Kansas* M & W
Middle Tennessee State University *Tennessee* M & W
Midland College *Texas* M & W
Midwestern State University *Texas* M & W
Miles College *Alabama* W
Millsaps College *Mississippi* M & W
Milwaukee School of Engineering *Wisconsin* M & W
Minnesota State University Mankato *Minnesota* M & W
Minot State University *North Dakota* W
Missouri Valley College *Missouri* M & W
Mitchell College *Connecticut* M & W
Moberly Area Community College *Missouri* M & W
Monmouth College *Illinois* M & W
Montana State University *Montana* M & W
Moravian College *Pennsylvania* W
Morgan State University *Maryland* W
Mount Mercy College *Iowa* W
Mount Olive College *North Carolina* W
Mount Union College *Ohio* W
Muhlenberg College *Pennsylvania* M & W
Murray State University *Kentucky* M & W
Nassau Community College *New York* W
Nazareth College of Rochester *New York* W
New York University *New York* M & W
Newberry College *South Carolina* W
Newman University *Kansas* M & W
Nichols College *Massachusetts* M & W
North Carolina State University *North Carolina* M & W
North Central College *Illinois* W
North Dakota State University *North Dakota* M & W
North Georgia College & State University *Georgia* W
North Greenville College *South Carolina* M & W
North Idaho College *Idaho* M & W
Northeast Community College *Nebraska* W
Northeastern Oklahoma Agricultural and Mechanical College *Oklahoma* M & W
Northeastern State University *Oklahoma* M & W
Northern Kentucky University *Kentucky* M & W
Northern Michigan University *Michigan* M & W
Northwest Missouri State University *Missouri* M & W
Northwest-Shoals Community College *Alabama* M & W
Northwestern College *Minnesota* W
Northwestern Oklahoma State University *Oklahoma* M & W
Northwestern University *Illinois* M & W
Northwood University *Michigan* M & W
Nova Southeastern University *Florida* W
Nyack College *New York* M & W
Oberlin College *Ohio* W
Occidental College *California* W
Ohio Dominican University *Ohio* M & W
The Ohio State University *Ohio* M & W
Ohio University *Ohio* M & W
Ohio University-Lancaster *Ohio* W
Ohio Valley University *West Virginia* W
Oklahoma City University *Oklahoma* M & W
Oklahoma Wesleyan University *Oklahoma* W
Old Dominion University *Virginia* M & W
Olivet Nazarene University *Illinois* M & W
Otterbein College *Ohio* M & W
Ozark Christian College *Missouri* M & W
Pacific Lutheran University *Washington* M & W
Pacific University *Oregon* M & W
The Pennsylvania State University Altoona College *Pennsylvania* M & W
The Pennsylvania State University Berks Campus of the Berks-Lehigh Valley College *Pennsylvania* M & W
The Pennsylvania State University at Erie, The Behrend College *Pennsylvania* M & W
The Pennsylvania State University Hazleton Campus of the Commonwealth College *Pennsylvania* M & W
The Pennsylvania State University, Lehigh Valley Campus of the Berks-Lehigh Valley College *Pennsylvania* M & W
The Pennsylvania State University Mont Alto Campus of the Commonwealth College *Pennsylvania* M & W
The Pennsylvania State University New Kensington Campus of the Commonwealth College *Pennsylvania* M & W
The Pennsylvania State University University Park Campus *Pennsylvania* M & W
The Pennsylvania State University Worthington Scranton Campus of the Commonwealth College *Pennsylvania* M & W
Pepperdine University *California* M & W
Pfeiffer University *North Carolina* M & W
Pikeville College *Kentucky* M & W
Pima Community College *Arizona* W
Plymouth State University *New Hampshire* M & W
Pratt Community College *Kansas* W

M = Men; W = Women

Purdue University North Central *Indiana* M & W
Queen's University at Kingston *Ontario* M & W
Ramapo College of New Jersey *New Jersey* W
Rensselaer Polytechnic Institute *New York* M & W
Rhodes College *Tennessee* W
Rice University *Texas* M & W
The Richard Stockton College of New Jersey *New Jersey* M & W
Rider University *New Jersey* M & W
Ripon College *Wisconsin* W
Rivier College *New Hampshire* M & W
Roane State Community College *Tennessee* W
Robert Morris University *Pennsylvania* M & W
Rochester Institute of Technology *New York* M & W
Roger Williams University *Rhode Island* W
Rollins College *Florida* M & W
Rose-Hulman Institute of Technology *Indiana* M & W
Rust College *Mississippi* M & W
Sacred Heart University *Connecticut* W
Saginaw Valley State University *Michigan* M & W
St. Ambrose University *Iowa* W
Saint Anselm College *New Hampshire* W
Saint Augustine's College *North Carolina* W
St. Bonaventure University *New York* M & W
St. Cloud State University *Minnesota* M & W
St. Francis Xavier University *Nova Scotia* M & W
St. John Fisher College *New York* W
Saint Joseph's College *Indiana* M & W
Saint Joseph's College of Maine *Maine* M & W
Saint Michael's College *Vermont* M & W
Salt Lake Community College *Utah* M & W
San Jose State University *California* M & W
Savannah College of Art and Design *Georgia* W
Schreiner University *Texas* W
Seattle University *Washington* M & W
Shelton State Community College *Alabama* M & W
Shorter College *Georgia* M & W
Siena College *New York* W
Simon's Rock College of Bard *Massachusetts* M & W
Simpson College *Iowa* M & W
Simpson University *California* W
Slippery Rock University of Pennsylvania *Pennsylvania* M & W
Southeast Missouri State University *Missouri* M & W
Southeastern Louisiana University *Louisiana* M & W
Southern Illinois University Carbondale *Illinois* M & W
Southern Nazarene University *Oklahoma* M & W
Southern New Hampshire University *New Hampshire* M & W
Southern Virginia University *Virginia* M & W
Southwest Baptist University *Missouri* M & W
Southwestern College *Kansas* M & W
Southwestern Oklahoma State University *Oklahoma* M & W
Southwestern Oregon Community College *Oregon* M & W
Spartanburg Methodist College *South Carolina* M & W
State University of New York College at Oneonta *New York* W
State University of New York College of Technology at Alfred *New York* M & W
State University of New York, Fredonia *New York* M & W
Sterling College *Kansas* W
Stonehill College *Massachusetts* M & W
Sul Ross State University *Texas* M & W
Sullivan County Community College *New York* W
Susquehanna University *Pennsylvania* M & W
Syracuse University *New York* M & W
Tabor College *Kansas* M & W
Tarleton State University *Texas* M & W
Taylor University Fort Wayne *Indiana* M & W
Tennessee Technological University *Tennessee* M & W
Tennessee Wesleyan College *Tennessee* M & W
Texas A&M University-Commerce *Texas* M & W
Texas State University-San Marcos *Texas* M & W
Thiel College *Pennsylvania* M & W
Three Rivers Community College *Missouri* M & W
Tiffin University *Ohio* M & W
Tompkins Cortland Community College *New York* M & W
Towson University *Maryland* M & W
Transylvania University *Kentucky* M & W
Trinity Valley Community College *Texas* M & W
Truman State University *Missouri* M & W
Tusculum College *Tennessee* W
Union College *Kentucky* M & W
Union University *Tennessee* W
United States Air Force Academy *Colorado* M & W
United States Naval Academy *Maryland* M & W
The University of Akron *Ohio* M & W
The University of Akron-Wayne College *Ohio* W
The University of Alabama *Alabama* M & W
The University of Alabama in Huntsville *Alabama* M & W
The University of British Columbia *British Columbia* M & W
University of California, San Diego *California* M & W
University of Central Arkansas *Arkansas* M & W
University of Central Florida *Florida* M & W
University of Charleston *West Virginia* W
University of Cincinnati *Ohio* M & W
University of the Cumberlands *Kentucky* M & W
University of Delaware *Delaware* M & W
University of Georgia *Georgia* M & W
University of Great Falls *Montana* M & W
University of Houston *Texas* M & W
University of Illinois at Urbana-Champaign *Illinois* M & W
University of the Incarnate Word *Texas* M & W
University of Louisiana at Monroe *Louisiana* M & W
University of Louisville *Kentucky* M & W
University of Mary Washington *Virginia* M & W
University of Maryland, College Park *Maryland* W
University of Maryland Eastern Shore *Maryland* M & W
University of Massachusetts Amherst *Massachusetts* M & W
University of Massachusetts Dartmouth *Massachusetts* W
University of Memphis *Tennessee* M & W
University of Miami *Florida* M & W
University of Minnesota, Duluth *Minnesota* W
University of Mississippi *Mississippi* M & W
University of Missouri-Kansas City *Missouri* W
University of Nevada, Las Vegas *Nevada* M & W
University of Nevada, Reno *Nevada* M & W
University of New Haven *Connecticut* M & W
The University of North Carolina at Asheville *North Carolina* M & W
The University of North Carolina Wilmington *North Carolina* M & W
University of North Florida *Florida* M & W
University of Oregon *Oregon* M & W
University of the Ozarks *Arkansas* M & W
University of Pittsburgh at Johnstown *Pennsylvania* W
University of Puget Sound *Washington* M & W
University of Richmond *Virginia* M & W
University of Saint Francis *Indiana* M & W
University of St. Francis *Illinois* W
University of Science and Arts of Oklahoma *Oklahoma* M & W
University of Sioux Falls *South Dakota* W
University of South Carolina Aiken *South Carolina* M & W
University of Southern Indiana *Indiana* M & W
University of Southern Maine *Maine* M & W
The University of Tennessee *Tennessee* M & W
The University of Tennessee at Martin *Tennessee* M & W
The University of Texas of the Permian Basin *Texas* W
The University of Texas at Tyler *Texas* M & W
University of Utah *Utah* M & W
University of Vermont *Vermont* M & W
University of the Virgin Islands *United States Virgin Islands* M & W
University of Waterloo *Ontario* M & W
University of West Georgia *Georgia* M & W
The University of Western Ontario *Ontario* M & W
University of Windsor *Ontario* M & W
University of Wisconsin-Madison *Wisconsin* M & W
University of Wisconsin-Platteville *Wisconsin* M & W
University of Wisconsin-Superior *Wisconsin* M & W
University of Wisconsin-Whitewater *Wisconsin* M & W
University of Wyoming *Wyoming* M & W
Villa Julie College *Maryland* M & W
Villanova University *Pennsylvania* M & W
Vincennes University *Indiana* M & W
Virginia State University *Virginia* M & W
Virginia Wesleyan College *Virginia* W
Walsh University *Ohio* W
Warner Southern College *Florida* M & W
Wartburg College *Iowa* W
Washburn University *Kansas* M & W
Wayland Baptist University *Texas* M & W
Weatherford College *Texas* W
Weber State University *Utah* M & W
West Chester University of Pennsylvania *Pennsylvania* W
West Virginia University *West Virginia* M & W
West Virginia Wesleyan College *West Virginia* M & W
Western Carolina University *North Carolina* M & W
Western Kentucky University *Kentucky* M & W
Western New Mexico University *New Mexico* M & W
Western State College of Colorado *Colorado* W
Western Washington University *Washington* M & W
Western Wyoming Community College *Wyoming* M & W
Westfield State College *Massachusetts* M & W
Whatcom Community College *Washington* M & W
Wheaton College *Illinois* W
Wheeling Jesuit University *West Virginia* M & W
Wichita State University *Kansas* M & W
Widener University *Pennsylvania* W
William Carey College *Mississippi* M & W
William Jewell College *Missouri* M & W
William Paterson University of New Jersey *New Jersey* M & W
William Penn University *Iowa* M & W
Winston-Salem State University *North Carolina* M
Winthrop University *South Carolina* M & W
Wittenberg University *Ohio* M & W
Worcester State College *Massachusetts* M & W
York College of Pennsylvania *Pennsylvania* W

Crew

Amherst College *Massachusetts* M & W
The Art Institute of Boston at Lesley University *Massachusetts* W
Assumption College *Massachusetts* M & W
Barnard College *New York* W
Barry University *Florida* W
Bates College *Maine* M & W
Baylor University *Texas* M & W
Beloit College *Wisconsin* M & W
Berry College *Georgia* M & W
Boston College *Massachusetts* M & W
Boston University *Massachusetts* M & W
Bowdoin College *Maine* M & W
Bowling Green State University *Ohio* M
Brandeis University *Massachusetts* M
Brenau University *Georgia* W
Brock University *Ontario* M & W
Brown University *Rhode Island* M & W
Bryn Mawr College *Pennsylvania* W
Bucknell University *Pennsylvania* M & W
Butler University *Indiana* M & W
California Maritime Academy *California* M & W
California State University, Long Beach *California* M & W
California State University, Sacramento *California* M & W
Carleton College *Minnesota* M & W
Carleton University *Ontario* M & W
Carlow University *Pennsylvania* W
Carnegie Mellon University *Pennsylvania* M & W
Case Western Reserve University *Ohio* M & W
Cazenovia College *New York* M & W
Centenary College of Louisiana *Louisiana* M & W
Chapman University *California* W
Chatham College *Pennsylvania* W
The Citadel, The Military College of South Carolina *South Carolina* M & W

M = Men; W = Women

Clark University *Massachusetts* M & W
Clemson University *South Carolina* M & W
Colby College *Maine* M & W
Colgate University *New York* M & W
College of the Holy Cross *Massachusetts* M & W
College of Saint Benedict *Minnesota* W
Columbia College *New York* M & W
Columbia University, School of General Studies *New York* M & W
Columbia University, The Fu Foundation School of Engineering and Applied Science *New York* M & W
Connecticut College *Connecticut* M & W
Cornell University *New York* M & W
Creighton University *Nebraska* W
Dartmouth College *New Hampshire* M & W
Davidson College *North Carolina* M & W
Denison University *Ohio* M
DePauw University *Indiana* M & W
Dickinson College *Pennsylvania* M & W
Dowling College *New York* M & W
Drake University *Iowa* W
Drexel University *Pennsylvania* M & W
Duke University *North Carolina* M & W
Duquesne University *Pennsylvania* M & W
Eastern Michigan University *Michigan* W
Emory University *Georgia* M & W
Fairfield University *Connecticut* M & W
Florida Institute of Technology *Florida* M & W
Fordham University *New York* M & W
Franklin and Marshall College *Pennsylvania* M & W
Franklin Pierce College *New Hampshire* M & W
Furman University *South Carolina* M & W
The George Washington University *District of Columbia* M & W
Georgetown University *District of Columbia* M & W
Gonzaga University *Washington* M & W
Grand Valley State University *Michigan* M & W
Hamilton College *New York* W
Hampden-Sydney College *Virginia* M
Harvard University *Massachusetts* M & W
Haverford College *Pennsylvania* M & W
Hobart and William Smith Colleges *New York* M & W
Holy Cross College *Indiana* M & W
Humboldt State University *California* M & W
Huntingdon College *Alabama* M & W
Indiana University Bloomington *Indiana* W
Iona College *New York* M & W
Ithaca College *New York* M & W
Jacksonville University *Florida* M & W
John Carroll University *Ohio* M & W
The Johns Hopkins University *Maryland* M & W
Kansas State University *Kansas* W
La Salle University *Pennsylvania* M & W
Lafayette College *Pennsylvania* M & W
Lakehead University *Ontario* M & W
Lawrence University *Wisconsin* M & W
Lehigh University *Pennsylvania* M & W
Lesley University *Massachusetts* M & W
Lewis & Clark College *Oregon* M & W
Long Island University, C.W. Post Campus *New York* M & W
Loyola College in Maryland *Maryland* M & W
Loyola Marymount University *California* M & W
Loyola University New Orleans *Louisiana* M & W
Lycoming College *Pennsylvania* M & W
Macalester College *Minnesota* M & W
Manhattan College *New York* M & W
Marietta College *Ohio* M & W
Marist College *New York* M & W
Marquette University *Wisconsin* M & W
Massachusetts Institute of Technology *Massachusetts* M & W
Massachusetts Maritime Academy *Massachusetts* M & W
McGill University *Quebec* M & W
Mercyhurst College *Pennsylvania* M & W
Michigan State University *Michigan* W
Mills College *California* W
Mount Holyoke College *Massachusetts* W
Murray State University *Kentucky* M & W
New York University *New York* M & W
North Carolina State University *North Carolina* M & W
Northeastern University *Massachusetts* M & W
Northern Michigan University *Michigan* M & W
Nova Southeastern University *Florida* W
Occidental College *California* W
Oklahoma City University *Oklahoma* M & W
Old Dominion University *Virginia* M & W
Orange Coast College *California* M & W
Oregon State University *Oregon* M & W
Pacific Lutheran University *Washington* M & W
Pepperdine University *California* M & W
Princeton University *New Jersey* M & W
Queen's University at Kingston *Ontario* M & W
Reed College *Oregon* M & W
Rensselaer Polytechnic Institute *New York* M & W
Rice University *Texas* M & W
The Richard Stockton College of New Jersey *New Jersey* W
Robert Morris University *Pennsylvania* W
Rochester Institute of Technology *New York* M & W
Roger Williams University *Rhode Island* M & W
Rollins College *Florida* M & W
Rutgers, The State University of New Jersey, New Brunswick/Piscataway *New Jersey* M & W
Sacred Heart University *Connecticut* W
St. Cloud State University *Minnesota* M & W
St. John's College *Maryland* M & W
Saint John's University *Minnesota* M
Saint Joseph's University *Pennsylvania* M & W
St. Lawrence University *New York* M & W
Saint Leo University *Florida* M & W
Saint Louis University *Missouri* M & W
Saint Mary's College *Indiana* W
Saint Mary's College of California *California* M & W
St. Mary's College of Maryland *Maryland* M & W
Santa Clara University *California* M & W
Sarah Lawrence College *New York* M & W
Savannah College of Art and Design *Georgia* M & W
Seattle Pacific University *Washington* M & W
Seattle University *Washington* M & W
Sewanee: The University of the South *Tennessee* M & W
Siena College *New York* M & W
Simmons College *Massachusetts* W
Skidmore College *New York* M & W
Smith College *Massachusetts* W
Southern Methodist University *Texas* M & W
Stanford University *California* M & W
State University of New York at Binghamton *New York* M & W
State University of New York at Buffalo *New York* W
State University of New York College at Geneseo *New York* M & W
State University of New York Maritime College *New York* M & W
State University of New York at Oswego *New York* M & W
Stetson University *Florida* M & W
Susquehanna University *Pennsylvania* M & W
Syracuse University *New York* M & W
Temple University *Pennsylvania* M & W
Texas A&M University at Galveston *Texas* M & W
Trent University *Ontario* M & W
Trinity College *Connecticut* M & W
Tufts University *Massachusetts* M & W
Tulane University *Louisiana* M & W
Union College *New York* M & W
United States Coast Guard Academy *Connecticut* M & W
United States Merchant Marine Academy *New York* M & W
United States Military Academy *New York* M & W
United States Naval Academy *Maryland* M & W
The University of Alabama *Alabama* W
The University of Alabama in Huntsville *Alabama* M & W
University at Albany, State University of New York *New York* M & W
The University of British Columbia *British Columbia* M & W
University of California, Berkeley *California* M & W
University of California, Irvine *California* M & W
University of California, Los Angeles *California* W
University of California, San Diego *California* M & W
University of California, Santa Barbara *California* M & W
University of Central Florida *Florida* W
University of Charleston *West Virginia* M & W
University of Cincinnati *Ohio* M & W
University of Cincinnati Raymond Walters College *Ohio* W
University of Colorado at Boulder *Colorado* M & W
University of Connecticut *Connecticut* W
University of Dayton *Ohio* W
University of Delaware *Delaware* M & W
University of Guelph *Ontario* M & W
The University of Iowa *Iowa* M & W
University of Kansas *Kansas* M & W
University of Louisville *Kentucky* W
University of Mary Washington *Virginia* M & W
University of Maryland, Baltimore County *Maryland* M & W
University of Massachusetts Amherst *Massachusetts* W
University of Massachusetts Lowell *Massachusetts* M & W
University of Miami *Florida* W
University of Michigan *Michigan* W
The University of Montana-Missoula *Montana* M & W
University of Nebraska-Lincoln *Nebraska* M & W
University of New Brunswick Saint John *New Brunswick* M & W
University of New Hampshire *New Hampshire* M & W
The University of North Carolina at Chapel Hill *North Carolina* M & W
University of Notre Dame *Indiana* W
University of Oregon *Oregon* M & W
University of Pennsylvania *Pennsylvania* M & W
University of Puget Sound *Washington* M & W
University of Rhode Island *Rhode Island* M & W
University of Richmond *Virginia* M & W
University of Rochester *New York* M & W
University of St. Thomas *Minnesota* M & W
University of San Diego *California* M & W
The University of Scranton *Pennsylvania* M & W
University of Southern California *California* W
The University of Tampa *Florida* M & W
The University of Tennessee *Tennessee* W
The University of Tennessee at Chattanooga *Tennessee* M & W
The University of Texas at Austin *Texas* W
University of Toronto *Ontario* M
University of Tulsa *Oklahoma* W
University of Vermont *Vermont* M & W
University of Victoria *British Columbia* M & W
University of Virginia *Virginia* W
University of Washington *Washington* M & W
The University of Western Ontario *Ontario* M & W
Vanderbilt University *Tennessee* M & W
Vassar College *New York* M & W
Villanova University *Pennsylvania* M & W
Virginia Commonwealth University *Virginia* M
Virginia Polytechnic Institute and State University *Virginia* M & W
Wabash College *Indiana* M
Washburn University *Kansas* M & W
Washington College *Maryland* M & W
Washington State University *Washington* M & W
Washington University in St. Louis *Missouri* M & W
Wellesley College *Massachusetts* W
Wesleyan University *Connecticut* M & W
West Virginia University *West Virginia* W
Western Washington University *Washington* M & W
Wheaton College *Illinois* M & W
Wichita State University *Kansas* M & W
Willamette University *Oregon* M & W
Williams College *Massachusetts* M & W
Wittenberg University *Ohio* M & W
Worcester Polytechnic Institute *Massachusetts* M & W
Worcester State College *Massachusetts* M & W
Xavier University *Ohio* M & W

M = Men; W = Women

Yale University *Connecticut* M & W

Cross-Country Running

Abilene Christian University *Texas* M & W
Acadia University *Nova Scotia* M & W
Adams State College *Colorado* M & W
Adelphi University *New York* M & W
Adrian College *Michigan* M & W
Agnes Scott College *Georgia* W
Alabama Agricultural and Mechanical University *Alabama* M & W
Alabama State University *Alabama* M & W
Albany State University *Georgia* M & W
Albertus Magnus College *Connecticut* M & W
Albion College *Michigan* M & W
Albright College *Pennsylvania* M & W
Alcorn State University *Mississippi* M & W
Alderson-Broaddus College *West Virginia* M & W
Alfred University *New York* M & W
Allan Hancock College *California* M & W
Allegheny College *Pennsylvania* M & W
Allen County Community College *Kansas* M & W
Alliant International University *California* M & W
Alma College *Michigan* M & W
Alvernia College *Pennsylvania* M & W
Alverno College *Wisconsin* W
American River College *California* M & W
American University *District of Columbia* M & W
American University of Puerto Rico *Puerto Rico* M & W
Amherst College *Massachusetts* M & W
Anderson University *South Carolina* M & W
Anderson University *Indiana* M & W
Angelo State University *Texas* M & W
Anna Maria College *Massachusetts* M & W
Anne Arundel Community College *Maryland* M & W
Antelope Valley College *California* M & W
Appalachian State University *North Carolina* M & W
Aquinas College *Michigan* M & W
Arcadia University *Pennsylvania* M & W
Arizona State University *Arizona* M & W
Arkansas State University *Arkansas* M & W
Arkansas Tech University *Arkansas* W
Asbury College *Kentucky* M & W
Ashford University *Iowa* M & W
Ashland University *Ohio* M & W
Assumption College *Massachusetts* M & W
Auburn University *Alabama* M & W
Augsburg College *Minnesota* M & W
Augusta State University *Georgia* M & W
Augustana College *South Dakota* M & W
Augustana College *Illinois* M & W
Austin Peay State University *Tennessee* M & W
Averett University *Virginia* M & W
Azusa Pacific University *California* M & W
Babson College *Massachusetts* M & W
Bacone College *Oklahoma* M & W
Baker University *Kansas* M & W
Bakersfield College *California* M & W
Baldwin-Wallace College *Ohio* M & W
Ball State University *Indiana* M & W
Baltimore City Community College *Maryland* M & W
Baptist Bible College of Pennsylvania *Pennsylvania* M & W
Barber-Scotia College *North Carolina* M & W
Bard College *New York* M & W
Barnard College *New York* W
Barton College *North Carolina* M & W
Barton County Community College *Kansas* M & W
Bates College *Maine* M & W
Bay Path College *Massachusetts* W
Bayamon Central University *Puerto Rico* M & W
Baylor University *Texas* M & W
Becker College *Massachusetts* M & W
Belhaven College *Mississippi* M & W
Bellarmine University *Kentucky* M & W
Bellevue Community College *Washington* M & W
Belmont Abbey College *North Carolina* M & W
Belmont University *Tennessee* M & W
Beloit College *Wisconsin* M & W
Bemidji State University *Minnesota* W
Benedict College *South Carolina* M & W
Benedictine College *Kansas* M & W
Benedictine University *Illinois* M & W
Bennett College For Women *North Carolina* W
Bentley College *Massachusetts* M & W
Berea College *Kentucky* M & W
Bergen Community College *New Jersey* M & W
Bernard M. Baruch College of the City University of New York *New York* W
Berry College *Georgia* M & W
Bethany College *West Virginia* M & W
Bethany College *Kansas* M & W
Bethel College *Tennessee* M & W
Bethel College *Kansas* M & W
Bethel College *Indiana* M & W
Bethel University *Minnesota* M & W
Bethune-Cookman College *Florida* M & W
Biola University *California* M & W
Birmingham-Southern College *Alabama* M & W
Black Hills State University *South Dakota* M & W
Blackburn College *Illinois* M & W
Bloomfield College *New Jersey* M
Bloomsburg University of Pennsylvania *Pennsylvania* M & W
Bluefield State College *West Virginia* M & W
Bluffton University *Ohio* M & W
Boise State University *Idaho* M & W
Boston College *Massachusetts* M & W
Boston University *Massachusetts* M & W
Bowdoin College *Maine* M & W
Bowie State University *Maryland* M & W
Bowling Green State University *Ohio* M & W
Bradley University *Illinois* M & W
Brandeis University *Massachusetts* M & W
Brenau University *Georgia* W
Brevard College *North Carolina* M & W
Briar Cliff University *Iowa* M & W
Bridgewater College *Virginia* M & W
Bridgewater State College *Massachusetts* M & W
Brigham Young University *Utah* M & W
Brigham Young University-Hawaii *Hawaii* M & W
Brock University *Ontario* M & W
Brookdale Community College *New Jersey* M & W
Brooklyn College of the City University of New York *New York* M & W
Broome Community College *New York* M & W
Brown University *Rhode Island* M & W
Bryan College *Tennessee* M & W
Bryant University *Rhode Island* M & W
Bryn Mawr College *Pennsylvania* W
Bucknell University *Pennsylvania* M & W
Buena Vista University *Iowa* M & W
Buffalo State College, State University of New York *New York* M & W
Butler Community College *Kansas* M & W
Butler University *Indiana* M & W
Butte College *California* M & W
Cabrillo College *California* M & W
Cabrini College *Pennsylvania* M & W
Caldwell College *New Jersey* W
California Institute of Technology *California* M & W
California Lutheran University *California* M & W
California Polytechnic State University, San Luis Obispo *California* M & W
California State Polytechnic University, Pomona *California* M & W
California State University, Chico *California* M & W
California State University, East Bay *California* M & W
California State University, Fresno *California* M & W
California State University, Fullerton *California* M & W
California State University, Long Beach *California* M & W
California State University, Los Angeles *California* W
California State University, Monterey Bay *California* M & W
California State University, Northridge *California* M & W
California State University, Sacramento *California* M & W
California State University, San Marcos *California* M & W
California State University, Stanislaus *California* M & W
California University of Pennsylvania *Pennsylvania* M & W
Calumet College of Saint Joseph *Indiana* M & W
Calvin College *Michigan* M & W
Cameron University *Oklahoma* M
Campbell University *North Carolina* M & W
Campbellsville University *Kentucky* M & W
Canisius College *New York* M & W
Capital University *Ohio* M & W
Cardinal Stritch University *Wisconsin* M & W
Caribbean University *Puerto Rico* M & W
Carleton College *Minnesota* M & W
Carnegie Mellon University *Pennsylvania* M & W
Carroll College *Wisconsin* M & W
Carson-Newman College *Tennessee* M & W
Carthage College *Wisconsin* M & W
Cascade College *Oregon* M & W
Case Western Reserve University *Ohio* M & W
Castleton State College *Vermont* M & W
Catawba College *North Carolina* M & W
The Catholic University of America *District of Columbia* M & W
Cayuga County Community College *New York* M & W
Cazenovia College *New York* M
Cedar Crest College *Pennsylvania* W
Cedarville University *Ohio* M & W
Centenary College *New Jersey* M & W
Centenary College of Louisiana *Louisiana* M & W
Central Arizona College *Arizona* M & W
Central Christian College of Kansas *Kansas* M & W
Central College *Iowa* M & W
Central Connecticut State University *Connecticut* M & W
Central Methodist University *Missouri* M & W
Central Michigan University *Michigan* M & W
Central Missouri State University *Missouri* M & W
Central State University *Ohio* M & W
Central Washington University *Washington* M & W
Centre College *Kentucky* M & W
Cerritos College *California* M & W
Chabot College *California* M & W
Chaminade University of Honolulu *Hawaii* M & W
Chapman University *California* M & W
Charleston Southern University *South Carolina* M & W
Chemeketa Community College *Oregon* M & W
Chestnut Hill College *Pennsylvania* M & W
Cheyney University of Pennsylvania *Pennsylvania* M & W
Chicago State University *Illinois* M & W
Chowan University *North Carolina* W
Christian Brothers University *Tennessee* M & W
Christopher Newport University *Virginia* M & W
The Citadel, The Military College of South Carolina *South Carolina* M & W
Citrus College *California* M & W
City College of the City University of New York *New York* M & W
City College of San Francisco *California* M & W
City Colleges of Chicago, Malcolm X College *Illinois* M
Clackamas Community College *Oregon* M & W
Claflin University *South Carolina* M & W
Claremont McKenna College *California* M & W
Clarion University of Pennsylvania *Pennsylvania* M & W
Clark Atlanta University *Georgia* M & W
Clark College *Washington* M & W
Clark University *Massachusetts* M & W
Clarke College *Iowa* M & W
Clarkson University *New York* M & W
Clayton State University *Georgia* M & W
Clemson University *South Carolina* M & W
Cleveland State University *Ohio* W
Cloud County Community College *Kansas* M & W
Coastal Carolina University *South Carolina* M & W
Coe College *Iowa* M & W
Coffeyville Community College *Kansas* M & W
Coker College *South Carolina* M & W
Colby College *Maine* M & W
Colby Community College *Kansas* M & W
Colby-Sawyer College *New Hampshire* M & W
Colgate University *New York* M & W
College of the Canyons *California* M & W
College of Charleston *South Carolina* M & W

M = Men; W = Women

College of the Desert *California* M & W
College of DuPage *Illinois* M & W
College of the Holy Cross *Massachusetts* M & W
College of Lake County *Illinois* M & W
College of Marin *California* M & W
College Misericordia *Pennsylvania* M & W
College of Mount St. Joseph *Ohio* M & W
College of Mount Saint Vincent *New York* M & W
The College of New Jersey *New Jersey* M & W
The College of New Rochelle *New York* W
College of the Redwoods *California* M & W
College of Saint Benedict *Minnesota* W
College of St. Catherine *Minnesota* W
College of St. Joseph *Vermont* M & W
College of Saint Mary *Nebraska* W
The College of Saint Rose *New York* M & W
The College of St. Scholastica *Minnesota* M & W
College of San Mateo *California* M & W
College of the Sequoias *California* M & W
College of the Siskiyous *California* M & W
College of the Southwest *New Mexico* M & W
The College of William and Mary *Virginia* M & W
The College of Wooster *Ohio* M & W
Colorado Christian University *Colorado* M & W
The Colorado College *Colorado* M & W
Colorado Northwestern Community College *Colorado* W
Colorado School of Mines *Colorado* M & W
Colorado State University *Colorado* M & W
Colorado State University-Pueblo *Colorado* W
Columbia College *New York* M & W
Columbia College *California* M & W
Columbia Union College *Maryland* M & W
Columbia University, School of General Studies *New York* M & W
Columbia University, The Fu Foundation School of Engineering and Applied Science *New York* M & W
Columbus State Community College *Ohio* M & W
Columbus State University *Georgia* M & W
Community College of Philadelphia *Pennsylvania* M & W
Community College of Rhode Island *Rhode Island* M & W
Compton Community College *California* M & W
Concord University *West Virginia* M & W
Concordia College *New York* M & W
Concordia College *Minnesota* M & W
Concordia University *Nebraska* M & W
Concordia University *Michigan* M & W
Concordia University *Illinois* M & W
Concordia University *California* M & W
Concordia University at Austin *Texas* M & W
Concordia University College of Alberta *Alberta* M & W
Concordia University, St. Paul *Minnesota* M & W
Concordia University Wisconsin *Wisconsin* M & W
Connecticut College *Connecticut* M & W
Contra Costa College *California* M & W
Converse College *South Carolina* W
Coppin State University *Maryland* M & W
Corban College *Oregon* M & W
Cornell College *Iowa* M & W
Cornell University *New York* M & W
Cornerstone University *Michigan* M & W
Covenant College *Georgia* M & W
Creighton University *Nebraska* M & W
Crown College *Minnesota* M & W
Cuesta College *California* M & W
Cumberland University *Tennessee* M & W
Curry College *Massachusetts* W
Cuyahoga Community College *Ohio* M & W
Cuyamaca College *California* M & W
Daemen College *New York* M & W
Dakota State University *South Dakota* M & W
Dakota Wesleyan University *South Dakota* M & W
Dalhousie University *Nova Scotia* M & W
Dallas Baptist University *Texas* M & W
Dana College *Nebraska* M & W
Daniel Webster College *New Hampshire* M & W
Danville Area Community College *Illinois* M
Dartmouth College *New Hampshire* M & W
Davidson College *North Carolina* M & W
Davis & Elkins College *West Virginia* M & W
De Anza College *California* M & W
Defiance College *Ohio* M & W
Delaware State University *Delaware* M & W
Delaware Valley College *Pennsylvania* M & W
Delta State University *Mississippi* W
Denison University *Ohio* M & W
DePaul University *Illinois* M & W
DePauw University *Indiana* M & W
DeSales University *Pennsylvania* M & W
Diablo Valley College *California* M & W
Dickinson College *Pennsylvania* M & W
Dickinson State University *North Dakota* M & W
Dillard University *Louisiana* M & W
Diné College *Arizona* M & W
Doane College *Nebraska* M & W
Dodge City Community College *Kansas* M & W
Dominican College *New York* M & W
Dominican University *Illinois* M & W
Dordt College *Iowa* M & W
Drake University *Iowa* M & W
Drew University *New Jersey* M & W
Drury University *Missouri* M & W
Duke University *North Carolina* M & W
Duquesne University *Pennsylvania* M & W
D'Youville College *New York* W
Earlham College *Indiana* M & W
East Carolina University *North Carolina* M & W
East Central University *Oklahoma* M & W
East Stroudsburg University of Pennsylvania *Pennsylvania* M & W
East Tennessee State University *Tennessee* M & W
East Texas Baptist University *Texas* M & W
Eastern Connecticut State University *Connecticut* M & W
Eastern Illinois University *Illinois* M & W
Eastern Kentucky University *Kentucky* M & W
Eastern Mennonite University *Virginia* M & W
Eastern Michigan University *Michigan* M & W
Eastern Nazarene College *Massachusetts* M & W
Eastern New Mexico University *New Mexico* M & W
Eastern Oregon University *Oregon* M & W
Eastern Washington University *Washington* M & W
Eckerd College *Florida* W
Edgewood College *Wisconsin* M & W
Edinboro University of Pennsylvania *Pennsylvania* M & W
El Camino College *California* M & W
Electronic Data Processing College of Puerto Rico *Puerto Rico* M & W
Elgin Community College *Illinois* M & W
Elizabethtown College *Pennsylvania* M & W
Elmhurst College *Illinois* M & W
Elms College *Massachusetts* M & W
Elon University *North Carolina* M & W
Embry-Riddle Aeronautical University *Florida* M & W
Emerson College *Massachusetts* M & W
Emmanuel College *Massachusetts* M & W
Emory & Henry College *Virginia* M & W
Emory University *Georgia* M & W
Emporia State University *Kansas* M & W
Endicott College *Massachusetts* M & W
Erie Community College *New York* M & W
Erie Community College, North Campus *New York* M & W
Erie Community College, South Campus *New York* M & W
Erskine College *South Carolina* M & W
Essex County College *New Jersey* M & W
Evangel University *Missouri* M & W
Everett Community College *Washington* M & W
The Evergreen State College *Washington* M & W
Fairfield University *Connecticut* M & W
Fairleigh Dickinson University, College at Florham *New Jersey* M & W
Fairleigh Dickinson University, Metropolitan Campus *New Jersey* M & W
Fairmont State University *West Virginia* M & W
Farmingdale State University of New York *New York* M & W
Faulkner University *Alabama* M & W
Fayetteville State University *North Carolina* M & W
Felician College *New Jersey* M & W
Ferris State University *Michigan* M & W
Ferrum College *Virginia* M & W
Finger Lakes Community College *New York* M & W
Finlandia University *Michigan* M & W
Fisk University *Tennessee* M & W
Fitchburg State College *Massachusetts* M & W
Flagler College *Florida* M & W
Flathead Valley Community College *Montana* M & W
Florida Agricultural and Mechanical University *Florida* M & W
Florida Atlantic University *Florida* M & W
Florida Gulf Coast University *Florida* M & W
Florida Institute of Technology *Florida* M & W
Florida International University *Florida* M & W
Florida Memorial College *Florida* M & W
Florida Southern College *Florida* M & W
Florida State University *Florida* M & W
Fontbonne University *Missouri* M & W
Fordham University *New York* M & W
Fort Belknap College *Montana* M & W
Fort Berthold Community College *North Dakota* M & W
Fort Hays State University *Kansas* M & W
Fort Lewis College *Colorado* M & W
Framingham State College *Massachusetts* M & W
Francis Marion University *South Carolina* M & W
Franklin College *Indiana* M & W
Franklin and Marshall College *Pennsylvania* M & W
Franklin Pierce College *New Hampshire* M & W
Fresno City College *California* M & W
Fresno Pacific University *California* M & W
Friends University *Kansas* M & W
Frostburg State University *Maryland* M & W
Fullerton College *California* M & W
Furman University *South Carolina* M & W
Gadsden State Community College *Alabama* W
Gallaudet University *District of Columbia* M & W
Gannon University *Pennsylvania* M & W
Garden City Community College *Kansas* M & W
Gardner-Webb University *North Carolina* M & W
GateWay Community College *Arizona* M & W
Genesee Community College *New York* M & W
Geneva College *Pennsylvania* M & W
George Fox University *Oregon* M & W
George Mason University *Virginia* M & W
The George Washington University *District of Columbia* M & W
Georgetown College *Kentucky* M & W
Georgetown University *District of Columbia* M & W
Georgia College & State University *Georgia* M & W
Georgia Institute of Technology *Georgia* M & W
Georgia Southern University *Georgia* W
Georgia State University *Georgia* M & W
Georgian Court University *New Jersey* W
Gettysburg College *Pennsylvania* M & W
Glendale Community College *California* M & W
Glendale Community College *Arizona* M & W
Glenville State College *West Virginia* M & W
Globe Institute of Technology *New York* M & W
Gloucester County College *New Jersey* M & W
Golden West College *California* M & W
Gonzaga University *Washington* M & W
Gordon College *Massachusetts* M & W
Goshen College *Indiana* M & W
Goucher College *Maryland* M & W
Grace College *Indiana* M & W
Graceland University *Iowa* M & W
Grambling State University *Louisiana* M & W
Grand Valley State University *Michigan* M & W
Grand View College *Iowa* M & W
Green Mountain College *Vermont* M & W
Greensboro College *North Carolina* M & W
Greenville College *Illinois* M & W
Grinnell College *Iowa* M & W
Grossmont College *California* M
Grove City College *Pennsylvania* M & W
Guilford College *North Carolina* M & W
Gustavus Adolphus College *Minnesota* M & W
Hagerstown Community College *Maryland* M & W
Hamilton College *New York* M & W
Hamline University *Minnesota* M & W
Hampden-Sydney College *Virginia* M
Hampton University *Virginia* M & W
Hannibal-LaGrange College *Missouri* M & W
Hanover College *Indiana* M & W

M = Men; W = Women

Harding University *Arkansas* M & W
Hartnell College *California* M & W
Hartwick College *New York* M & W
Harvard University *Massachusetts* M & W
Harvey Mudd College *California* M & W
Haskell Indian Nations University *Kansas* M & W
Hastings College *Nebraska* M & W
Haverford College *Pennsylvania* M & W
Hawaii Pacific University *Hawaii* M & W
Heidelberg College *Ohio* M & W
Henderson State University *Arkansas* W
Hendrix College *Arkansas* M & W
Herkimer County Community College *New York* M & W
High Point University *North Carolina* M & W
Highland Community College *Kansas* M & W
Highline Community College *Washington* M & W
Hilbert College *New York* M & W
Hinds Community College *Mississippi* M
Hiram College *Ohio* M & W
Hobart and William Smith Colleges *New York* M & W
Hofstra University *New York* M & W
Holy Cross College *Indiana* M & W
Holy Family University *Pennsylvania* W
Holy Names University *California* M & W
Hood College *Maryland* M & W
Hope College *Michigan* M & W
Houghton College *New York* M & W
Howard Community College *Maryland* M & W
Howard Payne University *Texas* M & W
Howard University *District of Columbia* M & W
Hudson Valley Community College *New York* M & W
Humboldt State University *California* M & W
Hunter College of the City University of New York *New York* M & W
Huntingdon College *Alabama* M & W
Huntington University *Indiana* M & W
Huston-Tillotson University *Texas* W
Hutchinson Community College and Area Vocational School *Kansas* M & W
Idaho State University *Idaho* M & W
Illinois College *Illinois* M & W
Illinois Institute of Technology *Illinois* M & W
Illinois State University *Illinois* M & W
Illinois Wesleyan University *Illinois* M & W
Immaculata University *Pennsylvania* W
Indiana State University *Indiana* M & W
Indiana University Bloomington *Indiana* M & W
Indiana University of Pennsylvania *Pennsylvania* M & W
Indiana University-Purdue University Fort Wayne *Indiana* M & W
Indiana University-Purdue University Indianapolis *Indiana* M & W
Indiana Wesleyan University *Indiana* M & W
Inter American University of Puerto Rico, Aguadilla Campus *Puerto Rico* M & W
Inter American University of Puerto Rico, Barranquitas Campus *Puerto Rico* M & W
Inter American University of Puerto Rico, Bayamón Campus *Puerto Rico* M & W
Inter American University of Puerto Rico, Guayama Campus *Puerto Rico* M & W
Inter American University of Puerto Rico, Metropolitan Campus *Puerto Rico* M & W
Inter American University of Puerto Rico, Ponce Campus *Puerto Rico* M & W
Inter American University of Puerto Rico, San Germán Campus *Puerto Rico* M & W
Iona College *New York* M & W
Iowa Central Community College *Iowa* M & W
Iowa Lakes Community College *Iowa* M & W
Iowa State University of Science and Technology *Iowa* M & W
Irvine Valley College *California* M & W
Ithaca College *New York* M & W
Jackson State University *Mississippi* M & W
Jacksonville State University *Alabama* M & W
Jacksonville University *Florida* M & W
James Madison University *Virginia* M & W
Jamestown College *North Dakota* M & W
John Carroll University *Ohio* M & W
John Jay College of Criminal Justice of the City University of New York *New York* M & W
The Johns Hopkins University *Maryland* M & W
Johnson C. Smith University *North Carolina* M & W
Johnson College *Pennsylvania* M & W
Johnson County Community College *Kansas* M & W
Johnson State College *Vermont* M & W
Johnson & Wales University *Rhode Island* M & W
Judson College *Illinois* M & W
Juniata College *Pennsylvania* M & W
Kalamazoo College *Michigan* M & W
Kansas City Kansas Community College *Kansas* M & W
Kansas State University *Kansas* M & W
Kansas Wesleyan University *Kansas* M & W
Kean University *New Jersey* M & W
Keene State College *New Hampshire* M & W
Kennesaw State University *Georgia* M & W
Kent State University *Ohio* M & W
Kentucky Christian University *Kentucky* M & W
Kentucky State University *Kentucky* M & W
Kenyon College *Ohio* M & W
Keuka College *New York* M & W
Keystone College *Pennsylvania* M & W
King College *Tennessee* M & W
King's College *Pennsylvania* M & W
Knox College *Illinois* M & W
Kutztown University of Pennsylvania *Pennsylvania* M & W
La Roche College *Pennsylvania* M & W
La Salle University *Pennsylvania* M & W
Lafayette College *Pennsylvania* M & W
LaGrange College *Georgia* M & W
Lake Erie College *Ohio* M & W
Lake Forest College *Illinois* M & W
Lake Superior State University *Michigan* M & W
Lakehead University *Ontario* M & W
Lakeland College *Wisconsin* M & W
Lamar Community College *Colorado* W
Lamar University *Texas* M & W
Lambuth University *Tennessee* M & W
Lander University *South Carolina* W
Landmark College *Vermont* M & W
Lane College *Tennessee* M & W
Lane Community College *Oregon* M & W
Lansing Community College *Michigan* M & W
Las Positas College *California* M & W
Lasell College *Massachusetts* M & W
Lassen Community College District *California* M & W
Laurentian University *Ontario* M & W
Lawrence University *Wisconsin* M & W
Lawson State Community College *Alabama* M
Le Moyne College *New York* M & W
Lebanon Valley College *Pennsylvania* M & W
Lee University *Tennessee* M & W
Lees-McRae College *North Carolina* M & W
Lehigh University *Pennsylvania* M & W
Lehman College of the City University of New York *New York* M & W
LeMoyne-Owen College *Tennessee* M
Lenoir-Rhyne College *North Carolina* M & W
LeTourneau University *Texas* M & W
Lewis & Clark College *Oregon* M & W
Lewis-Clark State College *Idaho* M & W
Lewis University *Illinois* M & W
Liberty University *Virginia* M & W
Limestone College *South Carolina* M & W
Lincoln Christian College *Illinois* M & W
Lincoln Memorial University *Tennessee* M & W
Lincoln University *Pennsylvania* M & W
Lincoln University *Missouri* W
Lindenwood University *Missouri* M & W
Lindsey Wilson College *Kentucky* M & W
Linfield College *Oregon* M & W
Lipscomb University *Tennessee* M & W
Livingstone College *North Carolina* M & W
Lock Haven University of Pennsylvania *Pennsylvania* M & W
Long Beach City College *California* M & W
Long Island University, C.W. Post Campus *New York* M & W
Longview Community College *Missouri* W
Longwood University *Virginia* M & W
Loras College *Iowa* M & W
Los Angeles City College *California* M
Los Angeles Southwest College *California* M & W
Los Angeles Trade-Technical College *California* M & W
Los Angeles Valley College *California* M & W
Louisiana College *Louisiana* W
Louisiana State University and Agricultural and Mechanical College *Louisiana* M & W
Louisiana Tech University *Louisiana* M & W
Loyola College in Maryland *Maryland* M & W
Loyola Marymount University *California* M & W
Loyola University Chicago *Illinois* M & W
Loyola University New Orleans *Louisiana* M & W
Lubbock Christian University *Texas* M & W
Lurleen B. Wallace Community College *Alabama* M & W
Luther College *Iowa* M & W
Luzerne County Community College *Pennsylvania* M & W
Lycoming College *Pennsylvania* M & W
Lynchburg College *Virginia* M & W
Lyndon State College *Vermont* M & W
Lynn University *Florida* M & W
Lyon College *Arkansas* M & W
Macalester College *Minnesota* M & W
MacMurray College *Illinois* M & W
Macomb Community College *Michigan* M & W
Madison Area Technical College *Wisconsin* M & W
Madonna University *Michigan* M & W
Maine Maritime Academy *Maine* M & W
Malone College *Ohio* M & W
Manchester College *Indiana* M & W
Manhattan College *New York* M & W
Mansfield University of Pennsylvania *Pennsylvania* M & W
Maranatha Baptist Bible College *Wisconsin* M & W
Marian College *Indiana* M & W
Marietta College *Ohio* M & W
Marist College *New York* M & W
Marquette University *Wisconsin* M & W
Mars Hill College *North Carolina* M & W
Marshall University *West Virginia* M & W
Martin Luther College *Minnesota* M & W
Mary Baldwin College *Virginia* W
Marymount University *Virginia* M & W
Maryville College *Tennessee* M & W
Maryville University of Saint Louis *Missouri* M & W
Marywood University *Pennsylvania* M & W
Massachusetts Bay Community College *Massachusetts* M & W
Massachusetts College of Liberal Arts *Massachusetts* M & W
Massachusetts Institute of Technology *Massachusetts* M & W
Massachusetts Maritime Academy *Massachusetts* M & W
The Master's College and Seminary *California* M & W
McDaniel College *Maryland* M & W
McGill University *Quebec* M & W
McKendree College *Illinois* M & W
McMaster University *Ontario* M & W
McMurry University *Texas* M & W
McNeese State University *Louisiana* M & W
McPherson College *Kansas* M & W
Medaille College *New York* W
Medgar Evers College of the City University of New York *New York* M & W
Memorial University of Newfoundland *Newfoundland and Labrador* M & W
Menlo College *California* M & W
Merced College *California* M
Mercer University *Georgia* M & W
Mercy College *New York* M & W
Mercyhurst College *Pennsylvania* M & W
Meredith College *North Carolina* W
Meridian Community College *Mississippi* M & W
Merrimack College *Massachusetts* M & W
Merritt College *California* M
Mesa Community College *Arizona* M
Mesa State College *Colorado* W
Messiah College *Pennsylvania* M & W
Methodist College *North Carolina* M & W

M = Men; W = Women

Miami University *Ohio* M & W
Michigan State University *Michigan* M & W
Michigan Technological University *Michigan* M & W
Mid-Continent University *Kentucky* M & W
MidAmerica Nazarene University *Kansas* M & W
Middle Tennessee State University *Tennessee* M & W
Middlebury College *Vermont* M & W
Middlesex County College *New Jersey* M & W
Midland Lutheran College *Nebraska* M & W
Miles College *Alabama* M
Millersville University of Pennsylvania *Pennsylvania* M & W
Milligan College *Tennessee* M & W
Millikin University *Illinois* M & W
Mills College *California* W
Millsaps College *Mississippi* M & W
Milwaukee Area Technical College *Wisconsin* M & W
Milwaukee School of Engineering *Wisconsin* M & W
Minnesota State University Mankato *Minnesota* M & W
Minnesota State University Moorhead *Minnesota* M & W
Minot State University *North Dakota* M & W
MiraCosta College *California* M & W
Mississippi College *Mississippi* M & W
Mississippi State University *Mississippi* M & W
Mississippi Valley State University *Mississippi* M & W
Missouri Baptist University *Missouri* M & W
Missouri Southern State University *Missouri* M & W
Missouri State University *Missouri* M & W
Missouri Valley College *Missouri* M & W
Mitchell College *Connecticut* M & W
Modesto Junior College *California* M & W
Mohawk Valley Community College *New York* M & W
Molloy College *New York* M & W
Monmouth College *Illinois* M & W
Monmouth University *New Jersey* M & W
Montana State University *Montana* M & W
Montana State University-Billings *Montana* M & W
Montana Tech of The University of Montana *Montana* M & W
Monterey Peninsula College *California* M & W
Montgomery College *Maryland* M & W
Montreat College *North Carolina* M & W
Moorpark College *California* M & W
Moraine Valley Community College *Illinois* M & W
Moravian College *Pennsylvania* M & W
Morehead State University *Kentucky* M & W
Morehouse College *Georgia* M
Morgan State University *Maryland* M & W
Morningside College *Iowa* M & W
Morris College *South Carolina* M & W
Morton College *Illinois* M & W
Mott Community College *Michigan* M & W
Mount Aloysius College *Pennsylvania* M & W
Mount Holyoke College *Massachusetts* W
Mt. Hood Community College *Oregon* M & W
Mount Ida College *Massachusetts* W
Mount Marty College *South Dakota* M & W
Mount Mercy College *Iowa* M & W
Mount Olive College *North Carolina* M & W
Mount St. Mary's University *Maryland* M & W
Mt. San Antonio College *California* M & W
Mount Union College *Ohio* M & W
Mount Vernon Nazarene University *Ohio* M & W
Muhlenberg College *Pennsylvania* M & W
Murray State University *Kentucky* M & W
Muskingum College *Ohio* M & W
Napa Valley College *California* M & W
Nassau Community College *New York* M & W
Nazareth College of Rochester *New York* M & W
Nebraska Wesleyan University *Nebraska* M & W
Neosho County Community College *Kansas* M & W
New England College *New Hampshire* M & W
New Jersey City University *New Jersey* W
New Jersey Institute of Technology *New Jersey* M & W
New Mexico Highlands University *New Mexico* M & W
New Mexico State University *New Mexico* M & W
New York City College of Technology of the City University of New York *New York* M & W
New York Institute of Technology *New York* M & W
New York University *New York* M & W
Newberry College *South Carolina* M & W
Newbury College *Massachusetts* M & W
Newman University *Kansas* M & W
Niagara University *New York* M & W
Nicholls State University *Louisiana* M & W
Norfolk State University *Virginia* M & W
North Carolina Agricultural and Technical State University *North Carolina* M & W
North Carolina Central University *North Carolina* M
North Carolina State University *North Carolina* M & W
North Central College *Illinois* M & W
North Central University *Minnesota* M & W
North Dakota State University *North Dakota* M & W
North Georgia College & State University *Georgia* M & W
North Greenville College *South Carolina* M & W
North Iowa Area Community College *Iowa* W
North Park University *Illinois* M & W
Northeastern University *Massachusetts* M & W
Northern Arizona University *Arizona* M & W
Northern Essex Community College *Massachusetts* M & W
Northern Illinois University *Illinois* W
Northern Kentucky University *Kentucky* M & W
Northern Maine Community College *Maine* M & W
Northern Michigan University *Michigan* W
Northern State University *South Dakota* M & W
Northland College *Wisconsin* M & W
Northwest Missouri State University *Missouri* M & W
Northwest Nazarene University *Idaho* M & W
Northwest-Shoals Community College *Alabama* M
Northwest University *Washington* M & W
Northwestern College *Minnesota* M & W
Northwestern College *Iowa* M & W
Northwestern Oklahoma State University *Oklahoma* M & W
Northwestern State University of Louisiana *Louisiana* M & W
Northwestern University *Illinois* W
Northwood University *Michigan* M & W
Northwood University, Texas Campus *Texas* M & W
Norwich University *Vermont* M & W
Notre Dame College *Ohio* M & W
Notre Dame de Namur University *California* M & W
Nova Southeastern University *Florida* M & W
Nyack College *New York* M & W
Oakland City University *Indiana* M & W
Oakland Community College *Michigan* M & W
Oakland University *Michigan* M & W
Oakton Community College *Illinois* M & W
Oberlin College *Ohio* M & W
Occidental College *California* M & W
Oglala Lakota College *South Dakota* M & W
Oglethorpe University *Georgia* M & W
Ohio Dominican University *Ohio* M & W
Ohio Northern University *Ohio* M & W
The Ohio State University *Ohio* M & W
Ohio University *Ohio* M & W
Ohio Valley University *West Virginia* M & W
Ohio Wesleyan University *Ohio* M & W
Oklahoma Baptist University *Oklahoma* M & W
Oklahoma Christian University *Oklahoma* M & W
Oklahoma Panhandle State University *Oklahoma* M & W
Oklahoma State University *Oklahoma* M & W
Olivet College *Michigan* M & W
Olivet Nazarene University *Illinois* M & W
Oral Roberts University *Oklahoma* M & W
Orange Coast College *California* M & W
Oregon Institute of Technology *Oregon* M & W
Ottawa University *Kansas* M & W
Otterbein College *Ohio* M & W
Ouachita Baptist University *Arkansas* W
Oxnard College *California* M & W
Pace University *New York* M & W
Pacific Lutheran University *Washington* M & W
Pacific Union College *California* M & W
Pacific University *Oregon* M & W
Paine College *Georgia* M & W
Palm Beach Atlantic University *Florida* M & W
Palo Alto College *Texas* M & W
Paradise Valley Community College *Arizona* M & W
Park University *Missouri* M & W
Pasadena City College *California* M & W
Patten University *California* M & W
Paul Smith's College of Arts and Sciences *New York* M & W
Peace College *North Carolina* W
Pennsylvania College of Technology *Pennsylvania* M & W
The Pennsylvania State University Altoona College *Pennsylvania* M & W
The Pennsylvania State University Berks Campus of the Berks-Lehigh Valley College *Pennsylvania* M & W
The Pennsylvania State University DuBois Campus of the Commonwealth College *Pennsylvania* M & W
The Pennsylvania State University at Erie, The Behrend College *Pennsylvania* M & W
The Pennsylvania State University Harrisburg Campus *Pennsylvania* M
The Pennsylvania State University, Lehigh Valley Campus of the Berks-Lehigh Valley College *Pennsylvania* M & W
The Pennsylvania State University Mont Alto Campus of the Commonwealth College *Pennsylvania* M & W
The Pennsylvania State University Schuylkill Campus of the Capital College *Pennsylvania* M & W
The Pennsylvania State University University Park Campus *Pennsylvania* M & W
The Pennsylvania State University Wilkes-Barre Campus of the Commonwealth College *Pennsylvania* M & W
The Pennsylvania State University Worthington Scranton Campus of the Commonwealth College *Pennsylvania* M & W
The Pennsylvania State University York Campus of the Commonwealth College *Pennsylvania* M & W
Pepperdine University *California* M & W
Peru State College *Nebraska* W
Pfeiffer University *North Carolina* M & W
Phoenix College *Arizona* M & W
Piedmont College *Georgia* M & W
Pikeville College *Kentucky* M & W
Pima Community College *Arizona* M & W
Pine Manor College *Massachusetts* W
Pittsburg State University *Kansas* M & W
Pitzer College *California* M & W
Point Loma Nazarene University *California* M & W
Point Park University *Pennsylvania* M & W
Polytechnic University, Brooklyn Campus *New York* M & W
Polytechnic University of Puerto Rico *Puerto Rico* M & W
Pomona College *California* M & W
Pontifical Catholic University of Puerto Rico *Puerto Rico* M & W
Portland State University *Oregon* M & W
Post University *Connecticut* M & W
Prairie Bible Institute *Alberta* M & W
Prairie View A&M University *Texas* M & W
Pratt Community College *Kansas* M & W
Pratt Institute *New York* M & W
Presbyterian College *South Carolina* M & W
Presentation College *South Dakota* M & W
Princeton University *New Jersey* M & W
Principia College *Illinois* M & W
Providence College *Rhode Island* M & W
Purchase College, State University of New York *New York* M & W
Purdue University *Indiana* M & W
Queens University of Charlotte *North Carolina* M & W
Queen's University at Kingston *Ontario* M & W
Queensborough Community College of the City University of New York *New York* M & W
Quinnipiac University *Connecticut* M & W
Radford University *Virginia* M & W
Ramapo College of New Jersey *New Jersey* M & W
Ranger College *Texas* M & W

M = Men; W = Women

Redeemer University College *Ontario* M & W
Regis College *Massachusetts* W
Reinhardt College *Georgia* M & W
Rend Lake College *Illinois* M
Rensselaer Polytechnic Institute *New York* M & W
Rhode Island College *Rhode Island* M & W
Rhodes College *Tennessee* M & W
Rice University *Texas* M & W
The Richard Stockton College of New Jersey *New Jersey* M & W
Rider University *New Jersey* M & W
Rio Hondo College *California* M & W
Ripon College *Wisconsin* M & W
Riverside Community College District *California* M & W
Rivier College *New Hampshire* M & W
Roanoke College *Virginia* M & W
Robert Morris College *Illinois* M & W
Robert Morris University *Pennsylvania* M & W
Roberts Wesleyan College *New York* M & W
Rochester Institute of Technology *New York* M & W
Roger Williams University *Rhode Island* M & W
Rollins College *Florida* M & W
Rose-Hulman Institute of Technology *Indiana* M & W
Rowan University *New Jersey* M & W
Royal Military College of Canada *Ontario* M & W
Rust College *Mississippi* M & W
Rutgers, The State University of New Jersey, New Brunswick/Piscataway *New Jersey* M & W
Sacramento City College *California* M & W
Sacred Heart University *Connecticut* M & W
Saddleback College *California* M & W
Saginaw Valley State University *Michigan* M & W
St. Ambrose University *Iowa* M & W
St. Andrews Presbyterian College *North Carolina* M & W
Saint Augustine's College *North Carolina* M & W
St. Bonaventure University *New York* M & W
St. Cloud State University *Minnesota* M & W
St. Edward's University *Texas* M & W
St. Francis College *New York* M & W
Saint Francis University *Pennsylvania* M & W
St. Francis Xavier University *Nova Scotia* M & W
St. Gregory's University *Oklahoma* M & W
St. John's University *New York* W
Saint John's University *Minnesota* M
Saint Joseph College *Connecticut* W
Saint Joseph's College *Indiana* M & W
Saint Joseph's College of Maine *Maine* M & W
St. Joseph's College, New York *New York* M & W
St. Joseph's College, Suffolk Campus *New York* M & W
Saint Joseph's University *Pennsylvania* M & W
St. Lawrence University *New York* M & W
Saint Leo University *Florida* M & W
St. Louis College of Pharmacy *Missouri* M & W
St. Louis Community College at Florissant Valley *Missouri* M & W
Saint Louis University *Missouri* M & W
Saint Martin's University *Washington* M & W
Saint Mary's College *Indiana* W
Saint Mary's College of California *California* M & W
Saint Mary's University *Nova Scotia* M & W
Saint Mary's University of Minnesota *Minnesota* M & W
Saint Michael's College *Vermont* M & W
St. Norbert College *Wisconsin* M & W
St. Olaf College *Minnesota* M & W
Saint Paul's College *Virginia* M & W
Saint Peter's College *New Jersey* M & W
St. Thomas Aquinas College *New York* M & W
St. Thomas University *Florida* M & W
Saint Vincent College *Pennsylvania* M & W
Saint Xavier University *Illinois* W
Salem College *North Carolina* W
Salem International University *West Virginia* M & W
Salem State College *Massachusetts* M & W
Salisbury University *Maryland* M & W
Salve Regina University *Rhode Island* W
Sam Houston State University *Texas* M & W
Samford University *Alabama* M & W
San Bernardino Valley College *California* M & W
San Diego Christian College *California* M & W
San Diego City College *California* M & W
San Diego Mesa College *California* M & W
San Diego State University *California* W
San Francisco State University *California* M & W
San Joaquin Delta College *California* M & W
San Jose City College *California* M & W
San Jose State University *California* M & W
Santa Ana College *California* M & W
Santa Barbara City College *California* M & W
Santa Clara University *California* M & W
Santa Monica College *California* M & W
Santa Rosa Junior College *California* M & W
Sauk Valley Community College *Illinois* M & W
Savannah College of Art and Design *Georgia* M & W
Savannah State University *Georgia* W
Schoolcraft College *Michigan* W
Scottsdale Community College *Arizona* M & W
Scripps College *California* W
Seattle Pacific University *Washington* M & W
Seattle University *Washington* M & W
Seton Hall University *New Jersey* M & W
Seton Hill University *Pennsylvania* M & W
Sewanee: The University of the South *Tennessee* M & W
Shasta College *California* M & W
Shaw University *North Carolina* M & W
Shawnee State University *Ohio* M & W
Shenandoah University *Virginia* M & W
Shippensburg University of Pennsylvania *Pennsylvania* M & W
Shoreline Community College *Washington* M & W
Shorter College *Georgia* M & W
Siena College *New York* M & W
Siena Heights University *Michigan* M & W
Sierra College *California* M & W
Silver Lake College *Wisconsin* M & W
Simon Fraser University *British Columbia* M & W
Simon's Rock College of Bard *Massachusetts* M & W
Simpson College *Iowa* M & W
Simpson University *California* M & W
Skagit Valley College *Washington* M & W
Skyline College *California* M & W
Slippery Rock University of Pennsylvania *Pennsylvania* M & W
Smith College *Massachusetts* W
Soka University of America *California* M & W
Sonoma State University *California* W
South Carolina State University *South Carolina* M & W
South Dakota School of Mines and Technology *South Dakota* M & W
South Dakota State University *South Dakota* M & W
South Mountain Community College *Arizona* M & W
South Plains College *Texas* M & W
South Suburban College *Illinois* M & W
Southeast Missouri State University *Missouri* M & W
Southeastern Louisiana University *Louisiana* M & W
Southeastern Oklahoma State University *Oklahoma* W
Southern Arkansas University-Magnolia *Arkansas* M & W
Southern Connecticut State University *Connecticut* M & W
Southern Illinois University Carbondale *Illinois* M & W
Southern Illinois University Edwardsville *Illinois* M & W
Southern Methodist University *Texas* M & W
Southern Nazarene University *Oklahoma* M & W
Southern New Hampshire University *New Hampshire* M & W
Southern Oregon University *Oregon* M & W
Southern Union State Community College *Alabama* M & W
Southern University and Agricultural and Mechanical College *Louisiana* M
Southern University at New Orleans *Louisiana* M & W
Southern Utah University *Utah* M & W
Southern Vermont College *Vermont* M & W
Southern Virginia University *Virginia* M & W
Southern Wesleyan University *South Carolina* M & W
Southwest Baptist University *Missouri* M & W
Southwestern College *Kansas* M & W
Southwestern College *California* M & W
Southwestern Indian Polytechnic Institute *New Mexico* M & W
Southwestern Oklahoma State University *Oklahoma* W
Southwestern Oregon Community College *Oregon* M & W
Southwestern University *Texas* M & W
Spartanburg Methodist College *South Carolina* M & W
Spelman College *Georgia* W
Spokane Community College *Washington* M & W
Spokane Falls Community College *Washington* M & W
Spring Arbor University *Michigan* M & W
Spring Hill College *Alabama* M & W
Springfield College *Massachusetts* M & W
Stanford University *California* M & W
State University of New York at Binghamton *New York* M & W
State University of New York at Buffalo *New York* M & W
State University of New York College of Agriculture and Technology at Cobleskill *New York* M & W
State University of New York College of Agriculture and Technology at Morrisville *New York* M & W
State University of New York College at Brockport *New York* M & W
State University of New York College at Cortland *New York* M & W
State University of New York College at Geneseo *New York* M & W
State University of New York College at Old Westbury *New York* M & W
State University of New York College at Oneonta *New York* M & W
State University of New York College at Potsdam *New York* M & W
State University of New York College of Technology at Alfred *New York* M & W
State University of New York College of Technology at Delhi *New York* M & W
State University of New York, Fredonia *New York* M & W
State University of New York Institute of Technology *New York* W
State University of New York Maritime College *New York* M & W
State University of New York at New Paltz *New York* M & W
State University of New York at Oswego *New York* M & W
State University of New York at Plattsburgh *New York* M & W
Stephen F. Austin State University *Texas* M & W
Sterling College *Kansas* M & W
Stetson University *Florida* M & W
Stevens Institute of Technology *New Jersey* M & W
Stillman College *Alabama* M
Stonehill College *Massachusetts* M & W
Stony Brook University, State University of New York *New York* M & W
Suffolk County Community College *New York* M & W
Suffolk University *Massachusetts* M & W
Sul Ross State University *Texas* W
Sullivan County Community College *New York* M & W
Susquehanna University *Pennsylvania* M & W
Swarthmore College *Pennsylvania* M & W
Syracuse University *New York* M & W
Tabor College *Kansas* M & W
Tarleton State University *Texas* M & W
Taylor University *Indiana* M & W
Technological College of San Juan *Puerto Rico* M & W
Tennessee State University *Tennessee* M & W
Tennessee Technological University *Tennessee* M & W
Tennessee Wesleyan College *Tennessee* M & W
Texas A&M University *Texas* M & W
Texas A&M University-Commerce *Texas* M & W

M = Men; W = Women

Texas A&M University-Kingsville *Texas* M & W
Texas Christian University *Texas* M & W
Texas Lutheran University *Texas* W
Texas Southern University *Texas* M & W
Texas State University-San Marcos *Texas* M & W
Texas Tech University *Texas* M & W
Thaddeus Stevens College of Technology *Pennsylvania* M
Thiel College *Pennsylvania* M & W
Tiffin University *Ohio* M & W
Toccoa Falls College *Georgia* M & W
Tougaloo College *Mississippi* M & W
Towson University *Maryland* M & W
Transylvania University *Kentucky* M & W
Trent University *Ontario* M & W
Tri-State University *Indiana* M & W
Trinity Christian College *Illinois* M & W
Trinity College *Connecticut* M & W
Trinity University *Texas* M & W
Troy University *Alabama* M & W
Truett-McConnell College *Georgia* M & W
Truman State University *Missouri* M & W
Tufts University *Massachusetts* M & W
Tulane University *Louisiana* M & W
Tusculum College *Tennessee* M & W
Tuskegee University *Alabama* M & W
Union College *New York* M & W
Union College *Kentucky* M & W
Union University *Tennessee* M & W
United States Air Force Academy *Colorado* M & W
United States Coast Guard Academy *Connecticut* M & W
United States Merchant Marine Academy *New York* M & W
United States Military Academy *New York* M & W
United States Naval Academy *Maryland* M & W
United Tribes Technical College *North Dakota* M & W
Unity College *Maine* M & W
Universidad del Turabo *Puerto Rico* M & W
Université Laval *Quebec* M & W
Université de Moncton *New Brunswick* M & W
Université du Québec àChicoutimi *Quebec* M & W
Université du Québec àRimouski *Quebec* M & W
Université du Québec àTrois-Rivières *Quebec* M
The University of Akron *Ohio* M & W
The University of Alabama *Alabama* M & W
The University of Alabama at Birmingham *Alabama* W
The University of Alabama in Huntsville *Alabama* M & W
University of Alaska Anchorage *Alaska* M
University of Alaska Fairbanks *Alaska* M & W
University at Albany, State University of New York *New York* M & W
University of Alberta *Alberta* M & W
The University of Arizona *Arizona* M & W
University of Arkansas *Arkansas* M & W
University of Arkansas at Little Rock *Arkansas* M & W
University of Arkansas at Monticello *Arkansas* W
University of Arkansas at Pine Bluff *Arkansas* W
University of Bridgeport *Connecticut* M & W
The University of British Columbia *British Columbia* M & W
University of Calgary *Alberta* M & W
University of California, Berkeley *California* M & W
University of California, Davis *California* M & W
University of California, Irvine *California* M & W
University of California, Los Angeles *California* M & W
University of California, Riverside *California* M & W
University of California, San Diego *California* M & W
University of California, Santa Barbara *California* M & W
University of California, Santa Cruz *California* M & W
University of Central Arkansas *Arkansas* W
University of Central Florida *Florida* M & W
University of Central Oklahoma *Oklahoma* M & W
University of Charleston *West Virginia* M & W
University of Chicago *Illinois* M & W
University of Cincinnati *Ohio* M & W
University of Cincinnati Raymond Walters College *Ohio* M & W
University of Colorado at Boulder *Colorado* M & W
University of Colorado at Colorado Springs *Colorado* M & W
University of Connecticut *Connecticut* M & W
University of the Cumberlands *Kentucky* M & W
University of Dallas *Texas* M & W
University of Dayton *Ohio* M & W
University of Delaware *Delaware* M & W
University of Detroit Mercy *Michigan* M & W
University of Dubuque *Iowa* M & W
University of Evansville *Indiana* M & W
The University of Findlay *Ohio* M & W
University of Florida *Florida* M & W
University of Georgia *Georgia* M & W
University of Great Falls *Montana* M & W
University of Guelph *Ontario* M & W
University of Hartford *Connecticut* M & W
University of Hawaii at Hilo *Hawaii* M & W
University of Hawaii at Manoa *Hawaii* W
University of Houston *Texas* M & W
University of Idaho *Idaho* M & W
University of Illinois at Chicago *Illinois* M & W
University of Illinois at Urbana-Champaign *Illinois* M & W
University of the Incarnate Word *Texas* M & W
University of Indianapolis *Indiana* M & W
The University of Iowa *Iowa* M & W
University of Kansas *Kansas* M & W
University of Kentucky *Kentucky* M & W
University of La Verne *California* M & W
University of Lethbridge *Alberta* M & W
University of Louisiana at Lafayette *Louisiana* M & W
University of Louisiana at Monroe *Louisiana* M & W
University of Louisville *Kentucky* M & W
University of Maine *Maine* M & W
University of Maine at Farmington *Maine* M & W
University of Maine at Fort Kent *Maine* M & W
University of Maine at Machias *Maine* M & W
University of Maine at Presque Isle *Maine* M & W
University of Manitoba *Manitoba* M & W
University of Mary *North Dakota* M & W
University of Mary Washington *Virginia* M & W
University of Maryland, Baltimore County *Maryland* M & W
University of Maryland, College Park *Maryland* M & W
University of Maryland Eastern Shore *Maryland* M & W
University of Massachusetts Amherst *Massachusetts* M & W
University of Massachusetts Boston *Massachusetts* M & W
University of Massachusetts Dartmouth *Massachusetts* M & W
University of Massachusetts Lowell *Massachusetts* M & W
University of Memphis *Tennessee* M & W
University of Miami *Florida* M & W
University of Michigan *Michigan* M & W
University of Minnesota, Crookston *Minnesota* W
University of Minnesota, Duluth *Minnesota* M & W
University of Minnesota, Morris *Minnesota* W
University of Minnesota, Twin Cities Campus *Minnesota* M & W
University of Mississippi *Mississippi* M & W
University of Missouri-Columbia *Missouri* M & W
University of Missouri-Kansas City *Missouri* M & W
University of Missouri-Rolla *Missouri* M & W
University of Mobile *Alabama* M & W
The University of Montana-Missoula *Montana* M & W
University of Nebraska at Kearney *Nebraska* M & W
University of Nebraska-Lincoln *Nebraska* M & W
University of Nebraska at Omaha *Nebraska* W
University of Nevada, Las Vegas *Nevada* W
University of Nevada, Reno *Nevada* W
University of New Brunswick Fredericton *New Brunswick* M & W
University of New Brunswick Saint John *New Brunswick* M & W
University of New England *Maine* M & W
University of New Hampshire *New Hampshire* M & W
University of New Haven *Connecticut* M & W
University of New Mexico *New Mexico* M & W
University of New Orleans *Louisiana* M & W
University of North Alabama *Alabama* M & W
The University of North Carolina at Asheville *North Carolina* M & W
The University of North Carolina at Chapel Hill *North Carolina* M & W
The University of North Carolina at Charlotte *North Carolina* M & W
The University of North Carolina at Greensboro *North Carolina* M & W
The University of North Carolina at Pembroke *North Carolina* M & W
The University of North Carolina Wilmington *North Carolina* M & W
University of North Dakota *North Dakota* M & W
University of North Florida *Florida* M & W
University of North Texas *Texas* M & W
University of Northern Colorado *Colorado* W
University of Northern Iowa *Iowa* M & W
University of Notre Dame *Indiana* M & W
University of Oklahoma *Oklahoma* M & W
University of Oregon *Oregon* M & W
University of Ottawa *Ontario* M & W
University of the Ozarks *Arkansas* M & W
University of the Pacific *California* W
University of Pennsylvania *Pennsylvania* M & W
University of Pittsburgh *Pennsylvania* M & W
University of Pittsburgh at Bradford *Pennsylvania* M & W
University of Pittsburgh at Greensburg *Pennsylvania* M & W
University of Pittsburgh at Johnstown *Pennsylvania* W
University of Portland *Oregon* M & W
University of Puerto Rico, Aguadilla University College *Puerto Rico* M & W
University of Puerto Rico at Arecibo *Puerto Rico* M & W
University of Puerto Rico at Bayamón *Puerto Rico* M & W
University of Puerto Rico at Carolina *Puerto Rico* M & W
University of Puerto Rico, Cayey University College *Puerto Rico* M & W
University of Puerto Rico at Humacao *Puerto Rico* M & W
University of Puerto Rico, Mayagüez Campus *Puerto Rico* M & W
University of Puerto Rico at Ponce *Puerto Rico* M & W
University of Puerto Rico, Río Piedras *Puerto Rico* M & W
University of Puerto Rico at Utuado *Puerto Rico* M & W
University of Puget Sound *Washington* M & W
University of Redlands *California* M & W
University of Regina *Saskatchewan* M & W
University of Rhode Island *Rhode Island* M & W
University of Richmond *Virginia* M & W
University of Rio Grande *Ohio* M & W
University of Rochester *New York* M & W
University of the Sacred Heart *Puerto Rico* M & W
University of Saint Francis *Indiana* M & W
University of St. Francis *Illinois* W
University of St. Thomas *Minnesota* M & W
University of San Diego *California* M & W
University of San Francisco *California* M & W
University of Saskatchewan *Saskatchewan* M & W
University of the Sciences in Philadelphia *Pennsylvania* M & W
The University of Scranton *Pennsylvania* M & W
University of Sioux Falls *South Dakota* M & W
University of South Alabama *Alabama* M & W
University of South Carolina *South Carolina* W
University of South Carolina Aiken *South Carolina* W
University of South Carolina Upstate *South Carolina* M & W
The University of South Dakota *South Dakota* M & W

M = Men; W = Women

M = Men; W = Women

Equestrian Sports

Hartwick College *New York* W
Hillsdale College *Michigan* W
Hiram College *Ohio* M & W
Hollins University *Virginia* W
Hood College *Maryland* M & W
Johnson & Wales University *Rhode Island* M & W
Judson College *Alabama* W
Juniata College *Pennsylvania* M & W
Kenyon College *Ohio* M & W
Kutztown University of Pennsylvania *Pennsylvania* M & W
Lafayette College *Pennsylvania* M & W
Lamar Community College *Colorado* M & W
Lawson State Community College *Alabama* M
Lehigh University *Pennsylvania* M & W
Long Island University, C.W. Post Campus *New York* M & W
Longwood University *Virginia* M & W
Lycoming College *Pennsylvania* M & W
Lynchburg College *Virginia* M & W
Marist College *New York* M & W
Maryville College *Tennessee* M & W
Merced College *California* M & W
Mercy College *New York* M & W
Miami University *Ohio* M & W
Michigan State University *Michigan* M & W
Middle Tennessee State University *Tennessee* M & W
Midway College *Kentucky* W
Missouri State University *Missouri* M & W
Mitchell Technical Institute *South Dakota* M & W
Molloy College *New York* M & W
Moravian College *Pennsylvania* W
Morehead State University *Kentucky* M & W
Mount Holyoke College *Massachusetts* W
Mount Ida College *Massachusetts* W
Mount St. Mary's University *Maryland* M & W
Murray State University *Kentucky* M & W
Nassau Community College *New York* M & W
National American University (Rapid City) *South Dakota* M & W
Nazareth College of Rochester *New York* M & W
New Mexico State University *New Mexico* M & W
New York University *New York* W
North Carolina State University *North Carolina* M & W
North Central Texas College *Texas* M & W
North Georgia College & State University *Georgia* M & W
Northeastern Junior College *Colorado* M & W
Northern Michigan University *Michigan* M & W
Northwest College *Wyoming* M & W
Northwest Mississippi Community College *Mississippi* M & W
Oberlin College *Ohio* M & W
Ohio University *Ohio* M & W
Ohio Wesleyan University *Ohio* M & W
Oklahoma Panhandle State University *Oklahoma* W
Oklahoma State University *Oklahoma* W
Otterbein College *Ohio* M & W
Pace University *New York* M & W
The Pennsylvania State University University Park Campus *Pennsylvania* M & W
Post University *Connecticut* M & W
Randolph-Macon Woman's College *Virginia* W
Rensselaer Polytechnic Institute *New York* M & W
Rochester Institute of Technology *New York* M & W
Roger Williams University *Rhode Island* M & W
Sacred Heart University *Connecticut* W
St. Andrews Presbyterian College *North Carolina* M & W
St. Cloud State University *Minnesota* M & W
St. Joseph's College, Suffolk Campus *New York* M & W
St. Lawrence University *New York* M & W
Saint Mary-of-the-Woods College *Indiana* W
Saint Mary's College *Indiana* W
Saint Vincent College *Pennsylvania* W
Salem College *North Carolina* W
Salem International University *West Virginia* M & W
Salve Regina University *Rhode Island* M & W
Sam Houston State University *Texas* M & W
Sarah Lawrence College *New York* M & W
Savannah College of Art and Design *Georgia* M & W
Seton Hill University *Pennsylvania* M & W
Sewanee: The University of the South *Tennessee* M & W
Siena College *New York* M & W
Sierra Nevada College *Nevada* M & W
Skidmore College *New York* M & W
Smith College *Massachusetts* W
South Dakota State University *South Dakota* W
Southwest Texas Junior College *Texas* M & W
Southwestern Oklahoma State University *Oklahoma* M & W
Stanford University *California* M & W
State University of New York at Binghamton *New York* M & W
State University of New York College of Agriculture and Technology at Morrisville *New York* M & W
State University of New York College at Geneseo *New York* M & W
State University of New York College at Potsdam *New York* W
State University of New York at New Paltz *New York* W
Stevens Institute of Technology *New Jersey* W
Stonehill College *Massachusetts* W
Susquehanna University *Pennsylvania* M & W
Sweet Briar College *Virginia* W
Syracuse University *New York* M & W
Taylor University *Indiana* M & W
Texas A&M University *Texas* W
Texas A&M University-Kingsville *Texas* M & W
Texas State University-San Marcos *Texas* M & W
Trinity College *Connecticut* M & W
Truman State University *Missouri* M & W
United States Military Academy *New York* M & W
University of California, Santa Barbara *California* M & W
University of California, Santa Cruz *California* M & W
University of Colorado at Boulder *Colorado* M & W
University of Delaware *Delaware* M & W
University of Georgia *Georgia* M & W
University of Mary Washington *Virginia* M & W
University of Massachusetts Dartmouth *Massachusetts* M & W
The University of Montana-Missoula *Montana* M & W
University of Nevada, Las Vegas *Nevada* W
The University of North Carolina at Chapel Hill *North Carolina* M & W
University of Oregon *Oregon* M & W
University of Rhode Island *Rhode Island* M & W
University of Richmond *Virginia* W
University of Rochester *New York* M & W
University of San Diego *California* W
The University of Scranton *Pennsylvania* M & W
University of South Carolina *South Carolina* W
University of Vermont *Vermont* M & W
University of Wisconsin-River Falls *Wisconsin* M & W
University of Wyoming *Wyoming* M & W
Utah State University *Utah* M & W
Valley Forge Military College *Pennsylvania* M
Vanderbilt University *Tennessee* M & W
Vernon College *Texas* M & W
Virginia Intermont College *Virginia* M & W
Virginia Polytechnic Institute and State University *Virginia* M & W
Walla Walla Community College *Washington* M & W
Washington College *Maryland* M & W
Washington and Lee University *Virginia* M & W
Washington State University *Washington* M & W
Washington University in St. Louis *Missouri* M & W
Wesleyan College *Georgia* W
Wesleyan University *Connecticut* M & W
West Chester University of Pennsylvania *Pennsylvania* M & W
West Hills Community College *California* M & W
West Texas A&M University *Texas* M & W
Western Dakota Technical Institute *South Dakota* M & W
Western Nevada Community College *Nevada* M & W
Western Oklahoma State College *Oklahoma* M & W
Westminster College *Pennsylvania* M & W
William Woods University *Missouri* M & W
Williams College *Massachusetts* M & W
Wilson College *Pennsylvania* W
Wittenberg University *Ohio* W
Worcester State College *Massachusetts* M & W

Fencing

Allegheny College *Pennsylvania* M & W
Amherst College *Massachusetts* M & W
Barnard College *New York* W
Bates College *Maine* M & W
Baylor University *Texas* M & W
Beloit College *Wisconsin* M & W
Boston College *Massachusetts* M & W
Boston University *Massachusetts* M & W
Bradley University *Illinois* M & W
Brandeis University *Massachusetts* M & W
Brock University *Ontario* M & W
Brown University *Rhode Island* M & W
Buffalo State College, State University of New York *New York* M
California Institute of Technology *California* M & W
California State University, Fullerton *California* M & W
California State University, Long Beach *California* M & W
California University of Pennsylvania *Pennsylvania* M & W
Carleton College *Minnesota* M & W
Carleton University *Ontario* M & W
Carnegie Mellon University *Pennsylvania* M & W
Case Western Reserve University *Ohio* M & W
Central Connecticut State University *Connecticut* M & W
Central Washington University *Washington* M & W
City College of the City University of New York *New York* W
City College of San Francisco *California* W
Clark College *Washington* M & W
Clemson University *South Carolina* M & W
Cleveland State University *Ohio* M & W
Colby College *Maine* M & W
Colgate University *New York* M & W
Columbia College *New York* M & W
Columbia University, School of General Studies *New York* M & W
Columbia University, The Fu Foundation School of Engineering and Applied Science *New York* M & W
Cornell University *New York* W
Dartmouth College *New Hampshire* M & W
Davidson College *North Carolina* M & W
Dickinson College *Pennsylvania* M & W
Drew University *New Jersey* M & W
Duke University *North Carolina* M & W
Emory University *Georgia* M & W
Fairleigh Dickinson University, Metropolitan Campus *New Jersey* W
Fort Lewis College *Colorado* M & W
Furman University *South Carolina* M & W
Georgia College & State University *Georgia* M & W
Georgia Southern University *Georgia* M & W
Hamilton College *New York* M & W
Hampden-Sydney College *Virginia* M
Hampshire College *Massachusetts* M & W
Harvard University *Massachusetts* M & W
Haverford College *Pennsylvania* M & W
Hollins University *Virginia* W
Hunter College of the City University of New York *New York* M & W
Inter American University of Puerto Rico, Metropolitan Campus *Puerto Rico* M
James Madison University *Virginia* W
The Johns Hopkins University *Maryland* M & W
Lafayette College *Pennsylvania* M & W
Lake Forest College *Illinois* M & W
Lawrence University *Wisconsin* M & W
Los Angeles Valley College *California* M & W
Macalester College *Minnesota* M & W
Marist College *New York* M & W
Marquette University *Wisconsin* M & W

M = Men; W = Women

Field Hockey

M = Men; W = Women

Lindenwood University *Missouri* W
Lock Haven University of Pennsylvania *Pennsylvania* W
Long Island University, C.W. Post Campus *New York* W
Longwood University *Virginia* W
Lynchburg College *Virginia* W
Manhattanville College *New York* W
Mansfield University of Pennsylvania *Pennsylvania* W
Mary Baldwin College *Virginia* W
Marywood University *Pennsylvania* W
Massachusetts Institute of Technology *Massachusetts* W
McDaniel College *Maryland* W
McGill University *Quebec* W
Mercyhurst College *Pennsylvania* W
Merrimack College *Massachusetts* W
Messiah College *Pennsylvania* W
Miami University *Ohio* W
Michigan State University *Michigan* W
Middlebury College *Vermont* W
Middlesex County College *New Jersey* W
Millersville University of Pennsylvania *Pennsylvania* W
Missouri State University *Missouri* W
Monmouth University *New Jersey* W
Montclair State University *New Jersey* W
Moravian College *Pennsylvania* W
Mount Holyoke College *Massachusetts* W
Muhlenberg College *Pennsylvania* W
Nazareth College of Rochester *New York* W
Neumann College *Pennsylvania* W
New England College *New Hampshire* W
Nichols College *Massachusetts* W
North Carolina State University *North Carolina* M & W
Northeastern University *Massachusetts* W
Northwestern University *Illinois* W
Notre Dame College *Ohio* W
Oberlin College *Ohio* W
The Ohio State University *Ohio* W
Ohio University *Ohio* W
Ohio Wesleyan University *Ohio* W
Old Dominion University *Virginia* W
The Pennsylvania State University University Park Campus *Pennsylvania* W
Pepperdine University *California* W
Philadelphia Biblical University *Pennsylvania* W
Philadelphia University *Pennsylvania* W
Plymouth State University *New Hampshire* W
Princeton University *New Jersey* W
Providence College *Rhode Island* W
Queen's University at Kingston *Ontario* W
Quinnipiac University *Connecticut* W
Radford University *Virginia* W
Ramapo College of New Jersey *New Jersey* W
Randolph-Macon College *Virginia* W
Randolph-Macon Woman's College *Virginia* W
Regis College *Massachusetts* W
Rensselaer Polytechnic Institute *New York* W
Rhodes College *Tennessee* W
Rice University *Texas* W
The Richard Stockton College of New Jersey *New Jersey* W
Rider University *New Jersey* W
Roanoke College *Virginia* W
Robert Morris University *Pennsylvania* W
Rochester Institute of Technology *New York* W
Rosemont College *Pennsylvania* W
Rowan University *New Jersey* W
Sacred Heart University *Connecticut* W
Saint Anselm College *New Hampshire* W
St. Bonaventure University *New York* W
Saint Francis University *Pennsylvania* W
Saint Joseph's College of Maine *Maine* W
Saint Joseph's University *Pennsylvania* W
St. Lawrence University *New York* W
Saint Louis University *Missouri* W
Saint Mary's College *Indiana* W
St. Mary's College of Maryland *Maryland* W
Saint Mary's University *Nova Scotia* W
Saint Michael's College *Vermont* W
Salem College *North Carolina* W
Salem State College *Massachusetts* W
Salisbury University *Maryland* W
Salve Regina University *Rhode Island* W
Seton Hill University *Pennsylvania* W
Sewanee: The University of the South *Tennessee* W
Shenandoah University *Virginia* W
Shippensburg University of Pennsylvania *Pennsylvania* W
Siena College *New York* W
Simmons College *Massachusetts* W
Simon Fraser University *British Columbia* W
Skidmore College *New York* W
Slippery Rock University of Pennsylvania *Pennsylvania* W
Smith College *Massachusetts* W
Southern Connecticut State University *Connecticut* W
Springfield College *Massachusetts* W
Stanford University *California* M & W
State University of New York College of Agriculture and Technology at Morrisville *New York* W
State University of New York College at Brockport *New York* W
State University of New York College at Cortland *New York* W
State University of New York College at Geneseo *New York* W
State University of New York College at Oneonta *New York* W
State University of New York, Fredonia *New York* M & W
State University of New York at New Paltz *New York* W
State University of New York at Oswego *New York* W
Stevens Institute of Technology *New Jersey* W
Stonehill College *Massachusetts* W
Susquehanna University *Pennsylvania* W
Swarthmore College *Pennsylvania* W
Sweet Briar College *Virginia* W
Syracuse University *New York* W
Temple University *Pennsylvania* W
Thomas College *Maine* W
Towson University *Maryland* W
Transylvania University *Kentucky* W
Trent University *Ontario* W
Trinity College *Connecticut* W
Trinity (Washington) University *District of Columbia* W
Tufts University *Massachusetts* W
Union College *New York* W
University at Albany, State University of New York *New York* W
University of Alberta *Alberta* M & W
The University of British Columbia *British Columbia* M & W
University of Calgary *Alberta* W
University of California, Berkeley *California* W
University of California, Santa Barbara *California* W
University of Colorado at Boulder *Colorado* M & W
University of Connecticut *Connecticut* W
University of Delaware *Delaware* W
University of Guelph *Ontario* W
The University of Iowa *Iowa* W
University of Louisville *Kentucky* W
University of Maine *Maine* W
University of Maine at Farmington *Maine* W
University of Manitoba *Manitoba* M & W
University of Mary Washington *Virginia* W
University of Maryland, Baltimore County *Maryland* W
University of Maryland, College Park *Maryland* W
University of Massachusetts Amherst *Massachusetts* W
University of Massachusetts Dartmouth *Massachusetts* W
University of Massachusetts Lowell *Massachusetts* W
University of Michigan *Michigan* W
The University of Montana-Missoula *Montana* W
University of New Brunswick Fredericton *New Brunswick* W
University of New England *Maine* W
University of New Hampshire *New Hampshire* W
The University of North Carolina at Chapel Hill *North Carolina* W
University of the Pacific *California* W
University of Pennsylvania *Pennsylvania* W
University of Prince Edward Island *Prince Edward Island* W
University of Rhode Island *Rhode Island* W
University of Richmond *Virginia* W
University of Rochester *New York* W
The University of Scranton *Pennsylvania* W
University of Southern Maine *Maine* W
University of Toronto *Ontario* W
University of Vermont *Vermont* W
University of Victoria *British Columbia* W
University of Virginia *Virginia* W
University of Waterloo *Ontario* W
The University of Western Ontario *Ontario* W
Ursinus College *Pennsylvania* W
Utica College *New York* W
Vanderbilt University *Tennessee* M & W
Vassar College *New York* W
Villa Julie College *Maryland* W
Villanova University *Pennsylvania* W
Virginia Commonwealth University *Virginia* W
Virginia Polytechnic Institute and State University *Virginia* M & W
Virginia Wesleyan College *Virginia* W
Wake Forest University *North Carolina* W
Washington College *Maryland* W
Washington & Jefferson College *Pennsylvania* W
Washington and Lee University *Virginia* W
Washington University in St. Louis *Missouri* W
Wellesley College *Massachusetts* W
Wells College *New York* W
Wesley College *Delaware* W
Wesleyan University *Connecticut* W
West Chester University of Pennsylvania *Pennsylvania* W
Western New England College *Massachusetts* W
Westfield State College *Massachusetts* W
Wheaton College *Massachusetts* W
Wheelock College *Massachusetts* W
Widener University *Pennsylvania* W
Wilkes University *Pennsylvania* W
William Paterson University of New Jersey *New Jersey* W
Williams College *Massachusetts* W
Wilson College *Pennsylvania* W
Wittenberg University *Ohio* W
Worcester Polytechnic Institute *Massachusetts* W
Worcester State College *Massachusetts* W
Yale University *Connecticut* W
York College of Pennsylvania *Pennsylvania* W
York University *Ontario* W

Football

Abilene Christian University *Texas* M
Acadia University *Nova Scotia* M
Adams State College *Colorado* M
Adrian College *Michigan* M
Alabama Agricultural and Mechanical University *Alabama* M
Alabama State University *Alabama* M
Albany State University *Georgia* M
Albion College *Michigan* M
Albright College *Pennsylvania* M
Alcorn State University *Mississippi* M
Alfred University *New York* M
Allan Hancock College *California* M
Allegheny College *Pennsylvania* M
Allen University *South Carolina* M
Alma College *Michigan* M
American International College *Massachusetts* M
American River College *California* M
Amherst College *Massachusetts* M
Anderson University *Indiana* M
Angelo State University *Texas* M
Antelope Valley College *California* M
Appalachian State University *North Carolina* M
Arizona State University *Arizona* M
Arizona Western College *Arizona* M
Arkansas State University *Arkansas* M
Arkansas Tech University *Arkansas* M
Ashland University *Ohio* M

M = Men; W = Women

Assumption College *Massachusetts* M
Auburn University *Alabama* M
Augsburg College *Minnesota* M
Augustana College *South Dakota* M
Augustana College *Illinois* M
Aurora University *Illinois* M
Austin College *Texas* M
Austin Peay State University *Tennessee* M
Averett University *Virginia* M
Avila University *Missouri* M
Azusa Pacific University *California* M
Bacone College *Oklahoma* M
Baker University *Kansas* M
Bakersfield College *California* M
Baldwin-Wallace College *Ohio* M
Ball State University *Indiana* M
Bates College *Maine* M
Baylor University *Texas* M
Becker College *Massachusetts* M
Belhaven College *Mississippi* M
Beloit College *Wisconsin* M
Bemidji State University *Minnesota* M
Benedict College *South Carolina* M
Benedictine College *Kansas* M
Benedictine University *Illinois* M
Bentley College *Massachusetts* M
Bethany College *West Virginia* M
Bethany College *Kansas* M
Bethel College *Tennessee* M
Bethel College *Kansas* M
Bethel University *Minnesota* M
Bethune-Cookman College *Florida* M
Bishop's University *Quebec* M
Black Hills State University *South Dakota* M
Blackburn College *Illinois* M
Blessing-Rieman College of Nursing *Illinois* M
Blinn College *Texas* M
Bloomsburg University of Pennsylvania *Pennsylvania* M
Bluffton University *Ohio* M
Boise State University *Idaho* M
Boston College *Massachusetts* M
Bowdoin College *Maine* M
Bowie State University *Maryland* M
Bowling Green State University *Ohio* M
Brevard College *North Carolina* M
Briar Cliff University *Iowa* M
Bridgewater College *Virginia* M
Bridgewater State College *Massachusetts* M
Brigham Young University *Utah* M
Brown University *Rhode Island* M
Bryant University *Rhode Island* M
Bucknell University *Pennsylvania* M
Buena Vista University *Iowa* M
Buffalo State College, State University of New York *New York* M
Butler Community College *Kansas* M
Butler University *Indiana* M
Butte College *California* M
Cabrillo College *California* M
California Lutheran University *California* M
California Polytechnic State University, San Luis Obispo *California* M
California State University, Fresno *California* M
California State University, Northridge *California* M
California State University, Sacramento *California* M
California University of Pennsylvania *Pennsylvania* M
Campbellsville University *Kentucky* M
Capital University *Ohio* M
Carleton College *Minnesota* M
Carleton University *Ontario* M
Carnegie Mellon University *Pennsylvania* M
Carroll College *Wisconsin* M
Carroll College *Montana* M
Carson-Newman College *Tennessee* M
Carthage College *Wisconsin* M
Case Western Reserve University *Ohio* M
Catawba College *North Carolina* M
The Catholic University of America *District of Columbia* M
Central College *Iowa* M
Central Connecticut State University *Connecticut* M
Central Lakes College *Minnesota* M
Central Methodist University *Missouri* M
Central Michigan University *Michigan* M
Central Missouri State University *Missouri* M
Central Washington University *Washington* M
Centre College *Kentucky* M
Cerritos College *California* M
Chabot College *California* M
Chadron State College *Nebraska* M
Chaffey College *California* M
Chapman University *California* M
Charleston Southern University *South Carolina* M
Cheyney University of Pennsylvania *Pennsylvania* M
Chowan University *North Carolina* M
Christopher Newport University *Virginia* M
Cisco Junior College *Texas* M
The Citadel, The Military College of South Carolina *South Carolina* M
Citrus College *California* M
City College of San Francisco *California* M
Claremont McKenna College *California* M
Clarion University of Pennsylvania *Pennsylvania* M
Clark Atlanta University *Georgia* M
Clemson University *South Carolina* M
Coahoma Community College *Mississippi* M
Coastal Carolina University *South Carolina* M
Coe College *Iowa* M
Coffeyville Community College *Kansas* M
Colby College *Maine* M
Colgate University *New York* M
College of the Canyons *California* M
College of the Desert *California* M
College of DuPage *Illinois* M
College of the Holy Cross *Massachusetts* M
College of Marin *California* M & W
College of Mount St. Joseph *Ohio* M
The College of New Jersey *New Jersey* M
College of the Redwoods *California* M
College of San Mateo *California* M
College of the Sequoias *California* M
College of the Siskiyous *California* M
The College of William and Mary *Virginia* M
The College of Wooster *Ohio* M
The Colorado College *Colorado* M
Colorado School of Mines *Colorado* M
Colorado State University *Colorado* M
Columbia College *New York* M
Columbia University, School of General Studies *New York* M
Columbia University, The Fu Foundation School of Engineering and Applied Science *New York* M
Compton Community College *California* M
Concord University *West Virginia* M
Concordia College *Minnesota* M
Concordia University *Quebec* M
Concordia University *Nebraska* M
Concordia University *Illinois* M
Concordia University, St. Paul *Minnesota* M
Concordia University Wisconsin *Wisconsin* M
Contra Costa College *California* M
Copiah-Lincoln Community College *Mississippi* M
Cornell College *Iowa* M
Cornell University *New York* M
Crown College *Minnesota* M
Culver-Stockton College *Missouri* M
Cumberland University *Tennessee* M
Curry College *Massachusetts* M
Dakota State University *South Dakota* M
Dakota Wesleyan University *South Dakota* M
Dana College *Nebraska* M
Dartmouth College *New Hampshire* M
Davidson College *North Carolina* M
De Anza College *California* M
Dean College *Massachusetts* M
Defiance College *Ohio* M
Delaware State University *Delaware* M
Delaware Valley College *Pennsylvania* M
Delta State University *Mississippi* M
Denison University *Ohio* M
DePauw University *Indiana* M
Diablo Valley College *California* M
Dickinson College *Pennsylvania* M
Dickinson State University *North Dakota* M
Dixie State College of Utah *Utah* M
Doane College *Nebraska* M
Dodge City Community College *Kansas* M
Drake University *Iowa* M
Duke University *North Carolina* M & W
Duquesne University *Pennsylvania* M
Earlham College *Indiana* M
East Carolina University *North Carolina* M
East Central Community College *Mississippi* M
East Central University *Oklahoma* M
East Los Angeles College *California* M
East Mississippi Community College *Mississippi* M
East Stroudsburg University of Pennsylvania *Pennsylvania* M
East Texas Baptist University *Texas* M
Eastern Arizona College *Arizona* M
Eastern Illinois University *Illinois* M
Eastern Kentucky University *Kentucky* M
Eastern Michigan University *Michigan* M
Eastern New Mexico University *New Mexico* M
Eastern Oregon University *Oregon* M
Eastern Washington University *Washington* M
Edinboro University of Pennsylvania *Pennsylvania* M
El Camino College *California* M
Elizabeth City State University *North Carolina* M
Ellsworth Community College *Iowa* M
Elmhurst College *Illinois* M
Elon University *North Carolina* M
Emory & Henry College *Virginia* M
Emporia State University *Kansas* M
Endicott College *Massachusetts* M
Erie Community College *New York* M
Erie Community College, North Campus *New York* M
Erie Community College, South Campus *New York* M
Eureka College *Illinois* M
Evangel University *Missouri* M
Fairleigh Dickinson University, College at Florham *New Jersey* M
Fairmont State University *West Virginia* M
Fayetteville State University *North Carolina* M
Feather River College *California* M
Ferris State University *Michigan* M
Ferrum College *Virginia* M
Fitchburg State College *Massachusetts* M
Florida Agricultural and Mechanical University *Florida* M
Florida Atlantic University *Florida* M
Florida International University *Florida* M
Florida State University *Florida* M
Foothill College *California* M
Fordham University *New York* M
Fort Hays State University *Kansas* M
Fort Lewis College *Colorado* M
Fort Scott Community College *Kansas* M
Fort Valley State University *Georgia* M
Framingham State College *Massachusetts* M
Franklin College *Indiana* M
Franklin and Marshall College *Pennsylvania* M
Fresno City College *California* M
Friends University *Kansas* M
Frostburg State University *Maryland* M
Fullerton College *California* M
Furman University *South Carolina* M
Gallaudet University *District of Columbia* M
Gannon University *Pennsylvania* M
Garden City Community College *Kansas* M
Gardner-Webb University *North Carolina* M
Gavilan College *California* M
Geneva College *Pennsylvania* M
Georgetown College *Kentucky* M
Georgetown University *District of Columbia* M
Georgia Institute of Technology *Georgia* M
Georgia Military College *Georgia* M
Georgia Southern University *Georgia* M
Gettysburg College *Pennsylvania* M
Glendale Community College *California* M
Glendale Community College *Arizona* M
Glenville State College *West Virginia* M
Golden West College *California* M
Graceland University *Iowa* M
Grambling State University *Louisiana* M
Grand Rapids Community College *Michigan* M

M = Men; W = Women

Grand Valley State University *Michigan* M
Greensboro College *North Carolina* M
Greenville College *Illinois* M
Grinnell College *Iowa* M
Grossmont College *California* M
Grove City College *Pennsylvania* M
Guilford College *North Carolina* M
Gustavus Adolphus College *Minnesota* M
Hamilton College *New York* M
Hamline University *Minnesota* M
Hampden-Sydney College *Virginia* M
Hampton University *Virginia* M
Hanover College *Indiana* M
Hardin-Simmons University *Texas* M
Harding University *Arkansas* M
Hartnell College *California* M
Hartwick College *New York* M
Harvard University *Massachusetts* M
Harvey Mudd College *California* M
Haskell Indian Nations University *Kansas* M
Hastings College *Nebraska* M
Heidelberg College *Ohio* M
Henderson State University *Arkansas* M
Hibbing Community College *Minnesota* M
Highland Community College *Kansas* M
Hillsdale College *Michigan* M
Hinds Community College *Mississippi* M
Hiram College *Ohio* M
Hobart and William Smith Colleges *New York* M
Hofstra University *New York* M
Holmes Community College *Mississippi* M
Hope College *Michigan* M
Howard Payne University *Texas* M
Howard University *District of Columbia* M
Hudson Valley Community College *New York* M
Humboldt State University *California* M
Huntingdon College *Alabama* M
Husson College *Maine* M
Hutchinson Community College and Area Vocational School *Kansas* M
Idaho State University *Idaho* M
Illinois College *Illinois* M
Illinois State University *Illinois* M
Illinois Wesleyan University *Illinois* M
Independence Community College *Kansas* M
Indiana State University *Indiana* M
Indiana University Bloomington *Indiana* M
Indiana University of Pennsylvania *Pennsylvania* M
Iona College *New York* M
Iowa Central Community College *Iowa* M
Iowa State University of Science and Technology *Iowa* M
Iowa Wesleyan College *Iowa* M
Itasca Community College *Minnesota* M
Itawamba Community College *Mississippi* M
Ithaca College *New York* M
Jackson State University *Mississippi* M
Jacksonville State University *Alabama* M
Jacksonville University *Florida* M
James Madison University *Virginia* M
Jamestown College *North Dakota* M
John Carroll University *Ohio* M
The Johns Hopkins University *Maryland* M
Johnson C. Smith University *North Carolina* M
Joliet Junior College *Illinois* M
Jones County Junior College *Mississippi* M
Juniata College *Pennsylvania* M
Kalamazoo College *Michigan* M
Kansas State University *Kansas* M
Kansas Wesleyan University *Kansas* M
Kean University *New Jersey* M
Kent State University *Ohio* M
Kentucky State University *Kentucky* M
Kentucky Wesleyan College *Kentucky* M
Kenyon College *Ohio* M
Kilgore College *Texas* M
King's College *Pennsylvania* M
Knox College *Illinois* M
Kutztown University of Pennsylvania *Pennsylvania* M
La Salle University *Pennsylvania* M
Lackawanna College *Pennsylvania* M
Lafayette College *Pennsylvania* M
Lake Forest College *Illinois* M
Lakeland College *Wisconsin* M
Lamar University *Texas* M
Lambuth University *Tennessee* M
Lane College *Tennessee* M
Laney College *California* M
Langston University *Oklahoma* M
Lawrence University *Wisconsin* M
Lebanon Valley College *Pennsylvania* M
Lehigh University *Pennsylvania* M & W
Lenoir-Rhyne College *North Carolina* M
Lewis & Clark College *Oregon* M
Liberty University *Virginia* M
Lincoln University *Missouri* M
Lindenwood University *Missouri* M
Linfield College *Oregon* M
Livingstone College *North Carolina* M
Lock Haven University of Pennsylvania *Pennsylvania* M
Long Beach City College *California* M
Long Island University, C.W. Post Campus *New York* M
Loras College *Iowa* M
Los Angeles City College *California* M
Los Angeles Harbor College *California* M
Los Angeles Pierce College *California* M
Los Angeles Southwest College *California* M
Los Angeles Valley College *California* M
Los Medanos College *California* M
Louisiana College *Louisiana* M
Louisiana State University and Agricultural and Mechanical College *Louisiana* M
Louisiana Tech University *Louisiana* M
Luther College *Iowa* M
Lycoming College *Pennsylvania* M
Macalester College *Minnesota* M
MacMurray College *Illinois* M
Maine Maritime Academy *Maine* M
Malone College *Ohio* M
Manchester College *Indiana* M
Mansfield University of Pennsylvania *Pennsylvania* M
Maranatha Baptist Bible College *Wisconsin* M
Marietta College *Ohio* M
Marquette University *Wisconsin* M
Mars Hill College *North Carolina* M
Marshall University *West Virginia* M
Martin Luther College *Minnesota* M
Maryville College *Tennessee* M
Massachusetts Institute of Technology *Massachusetts* M
Massachusetts Maritime Academy *Massachusetts* M
Mayville State University *North Dakota* M
McDaniel College *Maryland* M
McGill University *Quebec* M
McKendree College *Illinois* M
McMaster University *Ontario* M
McMurry University *Texas* M
McNeese State University *Louisiana* M
McPherson College *Kansas* M
Mendocino College *California* M
Menlo College *California* M
Merced College *California* M
Mercyhurst College *Pennsylvania* M
Merrimack College *Massachusetts* M
Mesa Community College *Arizona* M
Mesa State College *Colorado* M
Mesabi Range Community and Technical College *Minnesota* M
Methodist College *North Carolina* M
Miami University *Ohio* M
Michigan State University *Michigan* M
Michigan Technological University *Michigan* M
MidAmerica Nazarene University *Kansas* M
Middle Tennessee State University *Tennessee* M
Middlebury College *Vermont* M
Midland Lutheran College *Nebraska* M
Midwestern State University *Texas* M
Miles College *Alabama* M
Millersville University of Pennsylvania *Pennsylvania* M
Millikin University *Illinois* M
Millsaps College *Mississippi* M
Minnesota State Community and Technical College-Fergus Falls *Minnesota* M
Minnesota State University Mankato *Minnesota* M
Minnesota State University Moorhead *Minnesota* M
Minnesota West Community and Technical College *Minnesota* M
Minot State University *North Dakota* M
Mississippi College *Mississippi* M
Mississippi Delta Community College *Mississippi* M
Mississippi Gulf Coast Community College *Mississippi* M
Mississippi State University *Mississippi* M
Mississippi Valley State University *Mississippi* M
Missouri Southern State University *Missouri* M
Missouri State University *Missouri* M
Missouri Valley College *Missouri* M
Missouri Western State University *Missouri* M
Modesto Junior College *California* M
Monmouth College *Illinois* M
Monmouth University *New Jersey* M
Montana State University *Montana* M
Montana State University-Northern *Montana* M
Montana Tech of The University of Montana *Montana* M
Montclair State University *New Jersey* M
Monterey Peninsula College *California* M
Moorpark College *California* M
Moravian College *Pennsylvania* M
Morehead State University *Kentucky* M
Morehouse College *Georgia* M
Morgan State University *Maryland* M
Morningside College *Iowa* M
Mount Allison University *New Brunswick* M
Mount Ida College *Massachusetts* M
Mt. San Antonio College *California* M
Mt. San Jacinto College *California* M
Mount Union College *Ohio* M
Muhlenberg College *Pennsylvania* M
Murray State University *Kentucky* M
Muskingum College *Ohio* M
Nassau Community College *New York* M
Navarro College *Texas* M
Nebraska Wesleyan University *Nebraska* M
New Mexico Highlands University *New Mexico* M
New Mexico Military Institute *New Mexico* M
New Mexico State University *New Mexico* M
Newberry College *South Carolina* M
Nicholls State University *Louisiana* M
Nichols College *Massachusetts* M
Norfolk State University *Virginia* M
North Carolina Agricultural and Technical State University *North Carolina* M
North Carolina Central University *North Carolina* M
North Carolina State University *North Carolina* M
North Central College *Illinois* M
North Dakota State College of Science *North Dakota* M
North Dakota State University *North Dakota* M
North Greenville College *South Carolina* M
North Iowa Area Community College *Iowa* M
North Park University *Illinois* M
Northeast Mississippi Community College *Mississippi* M
Northeastern Oklahoma Agricultural and Mechanical College *Oklahoma* M
Northeastern State University *Oklahoma* M
Northeastern University *Massachusetts* M
Northern Arizona University *Arizona* M
Northern Illinois University *Illinois* M
Northern Michigan University *Michigan* M
Northern State University *South Dakota* M
Northland Community and Technical College-Thief River Falls *Minnesota* M
Northwest Mississippi Community College *Mississippi* M
Northwest Missouri State University *Missouri* M
Northwestern College *Minnesota* M
Northwestern College *Iowa* M
Northwestern Oklahoma State University *Oklahoma* M
Northwestern State University of Louisiana *Louisiana* M
Northwestern University *Illinois* M
Northwood University *Michigan* M
Norwich University *Vermont* M
Oberlin College *Ohio* M

M = Men; W = Women

Occidental College *California* M
Ohio Dominican University *Ohio* M
Ohio Northern University *Ohio* M
The Ohio State University *Ohio* M
Ohio University *Ohio* M
Ohio Wesleyan University *Ohio* M
Oklahoma Panhandle State University *Oklahoma* M
Oklahoma State University *Oklahoma* M
Olivet College *Michigan* M
Olivet Nazarene University *Illinois* M
Orange Coast College *California* M
Oregon State University *Oregon* M
Ottawa University *Kansas* M
Otterbein College *Ohio* M
Ouachita Baptist University *Arkansas* M
Pace University *New York* M
Pacific Lutheran University *Washington* M
Palomar College *California* M
Pasadena City College *California* M
Pearl River Community College *Mississippi* M
The Pennsylvania State University, Lehigh Valley Campus of the Berks-Lehigh Valley College *Pennsylvania* M
The Pennsylvania State University University Park Campus *Pennsylvania* M
Peru State College *Nebraska* M
Phoenix College *Arizona* M
Pikeville College *Kentucky* M
Pima Community College *Arizona* M
Pittsburg State University *Kansas* M
Pitzer College *California* M
Plymouth State University *New Hampshire* M
Pomona College *California* M
Portland State University *Oregon* M
Prairie State College *Illinois* M
Prairie View A&M University *Texas* M
Presbyterian College *South Carolina* M
Princeton University *New Jersey* M
Principia College *Illinois* M
Purdue University *Indiana* M
Queen's University at Kingston *Ontario* M
Quincy University *Illinois* M
Randolph-Macon College *Virginia* M
Ranger College *Texas* M
Reedley College *California* M
Rensselaer Polytechnic Institute *New York* M
Rhodes College *Tennessee* M
Rice University *Texas* M
Ridgewater College *Minnesota* M
Ripon College *Wisconsin* M
Riverside Community College District *California* M
Robert Morris University *Pennsylvania* M
Rochester Community and Technical College *Minnesota* M
Rock Valley College *Illinois* M
Rockford College *Illinois* M
Rose-Hulman Institute of Technology *Indiana* M
Rowan University *New Jersey* M
Rutgers, The State University of New Jersey, New Brunswick/Piscataway *New Jersey* M
Sacramento City College *California* M
Sacred Heart University *Connecticut* M
Saddleback College *California* M
Saginaw Valley State University *Michigan* M
St. Ambrose University *Iowa* M
Saint Anselm College *New Hampshire* M
Saint Augustine's College *North Carolina* M
St. Cloud State University *Minnesota* M
Saint Francis University *Pennsylvania* M
St. Francis Xavier University *Nova Scotia* M
St. John Fisher College *New York* M
Saint John's University *Minnesota* M
Saint Joseph's College *Indiana* M
St. Lawrence University *New York* M
Saint Mary's University *Nova Scotia* M
St. Norbert College *Wisconsin* M
St. Olaf College *Minnesota* M
Saint Peter's College *New Jersey* M
Saint Xavier University *Illinois* M
Salisbury University *Maryland* M
Salve Regina University *Rhode Island* M
Sam Houston State University *Texas* M
Samford University *Alabama* M
San Bernardino Valley College *California* M
San Diego City College *California* M
San Diego Mesa College *California* M
San Diego State University *California* M
San Joaquin Delta College *California* M
San Jose City College *California* M
San Jose State University *California* M
Santa Ana College *California* M
Santa Barbara City College *California* M
Santa Monica College *California* M
Santa Rosa Junior College *California* M
Savannah State University *Georgia* M
Scottsdale Community College *Arizona* M
Seton Hill University *Pennsylvania* M
Sewanee: The University of the South *Tennessee* M
Shasta College *California* M
Shaw University *North Carolina* M
Shenandoah University *Virginia* M
Shepherd University *West Virginia* M
Shippensburg University of Pennsylvania *Pennsylvania* M
Sierra College *California* M
Simon Fraser University *British Columbia* M
Simpson College *Iowa* M
Slippery Rock University of Pennsylvania *Pennsylvania* M
Snow College *Utah* M
Solano Community College *California* M
South Carolina State University *South Carolina* M
South Dakota School of Mines and Technology *South Dakota* M
South Dakota State University *South Dakota* M
Southeast Missouri State University *Missouri* M
Southeastern Louisiana University *Louisiana* M
Southeastern Oklahoma State University *Oklahoma* M
Southern Arkansas University-Magnolia *Arkansas* M
Southern Connecticut State University *Connecticut* M
Southern Illinois University Carbondale *Illinois* M
Southern Methodist University *Texas* M
Southern Nazarene University *Oklahoma* M
Southern Oregon University *Oregon* M
Southern University and Agricultural and Mechanical College *Louisiana* M
Southern Utah University *Utah* M
Southern Virginia University *Virginia* M
Southwest Baptist University *Missouri* M
Southwest Minnesota State University *Minnesota* M
Southwest Mississippi Community College *Mississippi* M
Southwestern Assemblies of God University *Texas* M
Southwestern College *Kansas* M
Southwestern College *California* M
Southwestern Oklahoma State University *Oklahoma* M
Springfield College *Massachusetts* M
Stanford University *California* M
State University of New York at Buffalo *New York* M
State University of New York College of Agriculture and Technology at Morrisville *New York* M
State University of New York College at Brockport *New York* M
State University of New York College at Cortland *New York* M & W
State University of New York College of Technology at Alfred *New York* M
Stephen F. Austin State University *Texas* M
Sterling College *Kansas* M
Stillman College *Alabama* M
Stonehill College *Massachusetts* M
Stony Brook University, State University of New York *New York* M
Sul Ross State University *Texas* M
Susquehanna University *Pennsylvania* M
Syracuse University *New York* M
Tabor College *Kansas* M
Tarleton State University *Texas* M
Taylor University *Indiana* M
Temple University *Pennsylvania* M
Tennessee State University *Tennessee* M
Tennessee Technological University *Tennessee* M
Texas A&M University *Texas* M
Texas A&M University-Commerce *Texas* M
Texas A&M University-Kingsville *Texas* M
Texas Christian University *Texas* M
Texas College *Texas* M
Texas Lutheran University *Texas* M
Texas Southern University *Texas* M
Texas State University-San Marcos *Texas* M
Texas Tech University *Texas* M
Thaddeus Stevens College of Technology *Pennsylvania* M
Thiel College *Pennsylvania* M
Thomas More College *Kentucky* M
Tiffin University *Ohio* M
Towson University *Maryland* M
Tri-State University *Indiana* M
Trinity Bible College *North Dakota* M
Trinity College *Connecticut* M
Trinity International University *Illinois* M
Trinity University *Texas* M
Trinity Valley Community College *Texas* M
Troy University *Alabama* M
Truman State University *Missouri* M
Tufts University *Massachusetts* M
Tulane University *Louisiana* M
Tusculum College *Tennessee* M
Tuskegee University *Alabama* M
Tyler Junior College *Texas* M
Union College *New York* M
Union College *Kentucky* M
United States Air Force Academy *Colorado* M
United States Coast Guard Academy *Connecticut* M
United States Merchant Marine Academy *New York* M
United States Military Academy *New York* M
United States Naval Academy *Maryland* M
Université Laval *Quebec* M
Université de Sherbrooke *Quebec* M
The University of Akron *Ohio* M
The University of Alabama *Alabama* M
The University of Alabama at Birmingham *Alabama* M
University at Albany, State University of New York *New York* M
University of Alberta *Alberta* M
The University of Arizona *Arizona* M
University of Arkansas *Arkansas* M
University of Arkansas at Monticello *Arkansas* M
University of Arkansas at Pine Bluff *Arkansas* M
The University of British Columbia *British Columbia* M
University of Calgary *Alberta* M
University of California, Berkeley *California* M
University of California, Davis *California* M
University of California, Los Angeles *California* M
University of Central Arkansas *Arkansas* M
University of Central Florida *Florida* M
University of Central Oklahoma *Oklahoma* M
University of Charleston *West Virginia* M
University of Chicago *Illinois* M
University of Cincinnati *Ohio* M
University of Cincinnati Raymond Walters College *Ohio* M
University of Colorado at Boulder *Colorado* M
University of Connecticut *Connecticut* M
University of the Cumberlands *Kentucky* M
University of Dayton *Ohio* M
University of Delaware *Delaware* M
University of Dubuque *Iowa* M
The University of Findlay *Ohio* M
University of Florida *Florida* M
University of Georgia *Georgia* M
University of Guam *Guam* M
University of Guelph *Ontario* M
University of Hawaii at Manoa *Hawaii* M
University of Houston *Texas* M
University of Idaho *Idaho* M
University of Illinois at Urbana-Champaign *Illinois* M
University of Indianapolis *Indiana* M
The University of Iowa *Iowa* M
University of Kansas *Kansas* M
University of Kentucky *Kentucky* M
University of La Verne *California* M
University of Louisiana at Lafayette *Louisiana* M
University of Louisiana at Monroe *Louisiana* M
University of Louisville *Kentucky* M

M = Men; W = Women

University of Maine *Maine* M
University of Manitoba *Manitoba* M & W
University of Mary *North Dakota* M
University of Mary Hardin-Baylor *Texas* M
University of Maryland, College Park *Maryland* M
University of Massachusetts Amherst *Massachusetts* M
University of Massachusetts Dartmouth *Massachusetts* M
University of Massachusetts Lowell *Massachusetts* M
University of Memphis *Tennessee* M
University of Miami *Florida* M
University of Michigan *Michigan* M
University of Minnesota, Crookston *Minnesota* M
University of Minnesota, Duluth *Minnesota* M
University of Minnesota, Morris *Minnesota* M
University of Minnesota, Twin Cities Campus *Minnesota* M
University of Mississippi *Mississippi* M
University of Missouri-Columbia *Missouri* M
University of Missouri-Rolla *Missouri* M
The University of Montana-Missoula *Montana* M
The University of Montana-Western *Montana* M
University of Nebraska at Kearney *Nebraska* M
University of Nebraska-Lincoln *Nebraska* M
University of Nebraska at Omaha *Nebraska* M
University of Nevada, Las Vegas *Nevada* M
University of Nevada, Reno *Nevada* M
University of New Hampshire *New Hampshire* M
University of New Mexico *New Mexico* M
University of North Alabama *Alabama* M
The University of North Carolina at Chapel Hill *North Carolina* M
University of North Dakota *North Dakota* M
University of North Texas *Texas* M
University of Northern Colorado *Colorado* M
University of Northern Iowa *Iowa* M
University of Notre Dame *Indiana* M
University of Oklahoma *Oklahoma* M
University of Oregon *Oregon* M
University of Ottawa *Ontario* M
University of Pennsylvania *Pennsylvania* M
University of Pittsburgh *Pennsylvania* M
University of Puget Sound *Washington* M
University of Redlands *California* M
University of Regina *Saskatchewan* M
University of Rhode Island *Rhode Island* M
University of Richmond *Virginia* M
University of Rochester *New York* M
University of Saint Francis *Indiana* M
University of St. Francis *Illinois* M
University of Saint Mary *Kansas* M
University of St. Thomas *Minnesota* M
University of San Diego *California* M
University of Saskatchewan *Saskatchewan* M
University of Sioux Falls *South Dakota* M
University of South Alabama *Alabama* M
University of South Carolina *South Carolina* M
The University of South Dakota *South Dakota* M
University of South Florida *Florida* M
University of Southern California *California* M
University of Southern Mississippi *Mississippi* M
The University of Tennessee *Tennessee* M
The University of Tennessee at Chattanooga *Tennessee* M
The University of Tennessee at Martin *Tennessee* M
The University of Texas at Austin *Texas* M
The University of Texas at El Paso *Texas* M
The University of Toledo *Ohio* M
University of Toronto *Ontario* M
University of Tulsa *Oklahoma* M
University of Utah *Utah* M
University of Virginia *Virginia* M
The University of Virginia's College at Wise *Virginia* M
University of Washington *Washington* M
University of Waterloo *Ontario* M
The University of West Alabama *Alabama* M
University of West Georgia *Georgia* M
The University of Western Ontario *Ontario* M
University of Windsor *Ontario* M
University of Wisconsin-Eau Claire *Wisconsin* M
University of Wisconsin-La Crosse *Wisconsin* M
University of Wisconsin-Madison *Wisconsin* M
University of Wisconsin-Oshkosh *Wisconsin* M
University of Wisconsin-Platteville *Wisconsin* M
University of Wisconsin-River Falls *Wisconsin* M
University of Wisconsin-Stevens Point *Wisconsin* M
University of Wisconsin-Stout *Wisconsin* M
University of Wisconsin-Whitewater *Wisconsin* M
University of Wyoming *Wyoming* M
Upper Iowa University *Iowa* M
Urbana University *Ohio* M
Ursinus College *Pennsylvania* M
Utah State University *Utah* M
Utica College *New York* M
Valdosta State University *Georgia* M
Valley City State University *North Dakota* M
Valley Forge Military College *Pennsylvania* M
Valparaiso University *Indiana* M
Vanderbilt University *Tennessee* M
Ventura College *California* M
Vermilion Community College *Minnesota* M
Victor Valley College *California* M
Villanova University *Pennsylvania* M
Virginia Military Institute *Virginia* M
Virginia Polytechnic Institute and State University *Virginia* M
Virginia State University *Virginia* M
Virginia Union University *Virginia* M
Wabash College *Indiana* M
Wagner College *New York* M
Wake Forest University *North Carolina* M
Waldorf College *Iowa* M
Walsh University *Ohio* M
Wartburg College *Iowa* M
Washburn University *Kansas* M
Washington & Jefferson College *Pennsylvania* M
Washington and Lee University *Virginia* M
Washington State University *Washington* M
Washington University in St. Louis *Missouri* M
Wayne State College *Nebraska* M
Wayne State University *Michigan* M
Waynesburg College *Pennsylvania* M
Webber International University *Florida* M
Weber State University *Utah* M
Wesley College *Delaware* M
Wesleyan University *Connecticut* M
West Chester University of Pennsylvania *Pennsylvania* M
West Hills Community College *California* M
West Liberty State College *West Virginia* M
West Los Angeles College *California* M
West Texas A&M University *Texas* M
West Valley College *California* M
West Virginia State University *West Virginia* M
West Virginia University *West Virginia* M
West Virginia University Institute of Technology *West Virginia* M
West Virginia Wesleyan College *West Virginia* M
Western Carolina University *North Carolina* M
Western Connecticut State University *Connecticut* M
Western Illinois University *Illinois* M
Western Kentucky University *Kentucky* M
Western Michigan University *Michigan* M
Western New England College *Massachusetts* M
Western New Mexico University *New Mexico* M
Western Oregon University *Oregon* M
Western State College of Colorado *Colorado* M
Western Washington University *Washington* M
Westfield State College *Massachusetts* M
Westminster College *Pennsylvania* M
Westminster College *Missouri* M
Wheaton College *Illinois* M
Whittier College *California* M
Whitworth College *Washington* M
Widener University *Pennsylvania* M
Wilfrid Laurier University *Ontario* M
Wilkes University *Pennsylvania* M
Willamette University *Oregon* M
William Jewell College *Missouri* M
William Paterson University of New Jersey *New Jersey* M
William Penn University *Iowa* M
William Rainey Harper College *Illinois* M
Williams College *Massachusetts* M
The Williamson Free School of Mechanical Trades *Pennsylvania* M
Wilmington College *Ohio* M
Wingate University *North Carolina* M
Winona State University *Minnesota* M
Winston-Salem State University *North Carolina* M
Wisconsin Lutheran College *Wisconsin* M
Wittenberg University *Ohio* M
Wofford College *South Carolina* M
Worcester Polytechnic Institute *Massachusetts* M
Worcester State College *Massachusetts* M
Yale University *Connecticut* M
York University *Ontario* M
Youngstown State University *Ohio* M
Yuba College *California* M

Golf

Abilene Christian University *Texas* M
Abraham Baldwin Agricultural College *Georgia* M
Adams State College *Colorado* M
Adelphi University *New York* M
Adirondack Community College *New York* M
Adrian College *Michigan* M & W
Alabama Agricultural and Mechanical University *Alabama* M
Alabama State University *Alabama* M
Albertson College of Idaho *Idaho* M & W
Albion College *Michigan* M & W
Albright College *Pennsylvania* M
Alcorn State University *Mississippi* M & W
Alderson-Broaddus College *West Virginia* M & W
Alice Lloyd College *Kentucky* M & W
Allan Hancock College *California* M
Allegheny College *Pennsylvania* M & W
Allen County Community College *Kansas* M
Alma College *Michigan* M & W
Alpena Community College *Michigan* M
Alvernia College *Pennsylvania* M
American International College *Massachusetts* M
American River College *California* M & W
American University *District of Columbia* M
Amherst College *Massachusetts* M & W
Anderson University *South Carolina* M & W
Anderson University *Indiana* M & W
Andrew College *Georgia* M
Anna Maria College *Massachusetts* M & W
Anne Arundel Community College *Maryland* M
Appalachian State University *North Carolina* M & W
Aquinas College *Michigan* M & W
Arcadia University *Pennsylvania* M & W
Arizona State University *Arizona* M & W
Arkansas State University *Arkansas* M & W
Arkansas Tech University *Arkansas* M
Armstrong Atlantic State University *Georgia* M
Ashford University *Iowa* M & W
Ashland University *Ohio* M & W
Assumption College *Massachusetts* M
Atlanta Christian College *Georgia* M
Auburn University *Alabama* M & W
Augsburg College *Minnesota* M & W
Augustana College *South Dakota* M & W
Augustana College *Illinois* M & W
Aurora University *Illinois* M
Austin College *Texas* M
Austin Peay State University *Tennessee* M & W
Averett University *Virginia* M
Avila University *Missouri* W
Azusa Pacific University *California* M
Babson College *Massachusetts* M
Bacone College *Oklahoma* M & W
Baker University *Kansas* M & W
Bakersfield College *California* M
Baldwin-Wallace College *Ohio* M & W
Ball State University *Indiana* M
Baptist Bible College of Pennsylvania *Pennsylvania* M
Barnard College *New York* W
Barry University *Florida* M & W
Barton College *North Carolina* M
Barton County Community College *Kansas* M
Bates College *Maine* M & W
Baylor University *Texas* M & W
Becker College *Massachusetts* M
Belhaven College *Mississippi* M & W

M = Men; W = Women

Bellarmine University *Kentucky* M & W
Bellevue Community College *Washington* M
Belmont Abbey College *North Carolina* M & W
Belmont University *Tennessee* M & W
Beloit College *Wisconsin* M & W
Bemidji State University *Minnesota* M & W
Benedict College *South Carolina* M
Benedictine College *Kansas* M & W
Benedictine University *Illinois* M
Bentley College *Massachusetts* W
Berea College *Kentucky* M
Bergen Community College *New Jersey* M
Berry College *Georgia* M & W
Bethany College *West Virginia* M & W
Bethany College *Kansas* M
Bethany Lutheran College *Minnesota* M
Bethany University *California* M & W
Bethel College *Tennessee* M & W
Bethel College *Kansas* M & W
Bethel College *Indiana* M & W
Bethel University *Minnesota* M
Bethune-Cookman College *Florida* M & W
Birmingham-Southern College *Alabama* M & W
Bishop's University *Quebec* M
Bismarck State College *North Dakota* M & W
Black Hawk College *Illinois* M
Black Hills State University *South Dakota* W
Blackburn College *Illinois* M & W
Bluefield College *Virginia* M
Bluefield State College *West Virginia* M
Boise State University *Idaho* M & W
Boston College *Massachusetts* M & W
Boston University *Massachusetts* M & W
Bowdoin College *Maine* M & W
Bowling Green State University *Ohio* M & W
Bradley University *Illinois* M & W
Brandeis University *Massachusetts* M
Brescia University *Kentucky* M & W
Brevard College *North Carolina* M
Brevard Community College *Florida* M
Briar Cliff University *Iowa* M & W
Bridgewater College *Virginia* M
Brigham Young University *Utah* M & W
Brock University *Ontario* M
Brookdale Community College *New Jersey* M
Broome Community College *New York* M
Brown University *Rhode Island* M & W
Brunswick Community College *North Carolina* M
Bryant University *Rhode Island* M & W
Bucknell University *Pennsylvania* M & W
Bucks County Community College *Pennsylvania* M & W
Buena Vista University *Iowa* M & W
Bunker Hill Community College *Massachusetts* M & W
Burlington County College *New Jersey* M
Butler County Community College *Pennsylvania* M & W
Butler University *Indiana* M & W
Butte College *California* M & W
Cabrillo College *California* M & W
Cabrini College *Pennsylvania* M
Caldwell College *New Jersey* M
Caldwell Community College and Technical Institute *North Carolina* M
California Baptist University *California* W
California Institute of Technology *California* M
California Lutheran University *California* M
California Maritime Academy *California* M & W
California Polytechnic State University, San Luis Obispo *California* M
California State University, Bakersfield *California* M
California State University, Chico *California* M & W
California State University, Fresno *California* M
California State University, Long Beach *California* M & W
California State University, Monterey Bay *California* M & W
California State University, Northridge *California* M
California State University, Sacramento *California* M & W
California State University, San Bernardino *California* M

California State University, San Marcos *California* M & W
California State University, Stanislaus *California* M
California University of Pennsylvania *Pennsylvania* M & W
Calumet College of Saint Joseph *Indiana* M & W
Calvin College *Michigan* M & W
Cameron University *Oklahoma* M & W
Campbell University *North Carolina* M & W
Campbellsville University *Kentucky* M & W
Canisius College *New York* M
Cape Fear Community College *North Carolina* M
Capital University *Ohio* M & W
Carleton College *Minnesota* M & W
Carleton University *Ontario* M
Carnegie Mellon University *Pennsylvania* M
Carroll College *Wisconsin* M & W
Carroll College *Montana* W
Carson-Newman College *Tennessee* M
Carthage College *Wisconsin* M & W
Castleton State College *Vermont* M
Catawba College *North Carolina* M
Catawba Valley Community College *North Carolina* M
Cazenovia College *New York* M
Cedarville University *Ohio* M
Centenary College *New Jersey* M & W
Centenary College of Louisiana *Louisiana* M & W
Central Alabama Community College *Alabama* M
Central Arizona College *Arizona* M
Central Carolina Community College *North Carolina* M & W
Central Christian College of the Bible *Missouri* M & W
Central Christian College of Kansas *Kansas* M & W
Central College *Iowa* M & W
Central Connecticut State University *Connecticut* M & W
Central Lakes College *Minnesota* M & W
Central Missouri State University *Missouri* M
Central Ohio Technical College *Ohio* M & W
Central Pennsylvania College *Pennsylvania* M & W
Central State University *Ohio* M & W
Central Washington University *Washington* M & W
Centralia College *Washington* W
Centre College *Kentucky* M & W
Century College *Minnesota* M & W
Cerritos College *California* M
Chabot College *California* M
Chadron State College *Nebraska* W
Chaminade University of Honolulu *Hawaii* M & W
Chapman University *California* M & W
Charleston Southern University *South Carolina* M & W
Chestnut Hill College *Pennsylvania* M & W
Chicago State University *Illinois* M & W
Chowan University *North Carolina* M
Christian Brothers University *Tennessee* M & W
Christopher Newport University *Virginia* M
Cincinnati Christian University *Ohio* M
Cincinnati State Technical and Community College *Ohio* M & W
Cisco Junior College *Texas* M
The Citadel, The Military College of South Carolina *South Carolina* M & W
Citrus College *California* M & W
City College of San Francisco *California* M
Claremont McKenna College *California* M
Clarion University of Pennsylvania *Pennsylvania* M
Clark Atlanta University *Georgia* M
Clarke College *Iowa* M & W
Clarkson University *New York* M
Clayton State University *Georgia* M
Clearwater Christian College *Florida* M & W
Clemson University *South Carolina* M
Cleveland State University *Ohio* M
Coastal Carolina University *South Carolina* M & W
Coe College *Iowa* M & W
Coffeyville Community College *Kansas* M
Coker College *South Carolina* M
Colby College *Maine* M & W
Colby Community College *Kansas* M & W
Colgate University *New York* M & W
College of the Canyons *California* M

College of Charleston *South Carolina* M & W
College of the Desert *California* M & W
College of DuPage *Illinois* M
College of Eastern Utah *Utah* M & W
College of the Holy Cross *Massachusetts* M & W
College of Lake County *Illinois* M
College of Marin *California* M & W
College Misericordia *Pennsylvania* M
College of Mount St. Joseph *Ohio* M & W
The College of New Jersey *New Jersey* M
College of the Redwoods *California* M
College of Saint Benedict *Minnesota* W
College of San Mateo *California* M
College of the Sequoias *California* M
College of Southern Maryland *Maryland* M & W
College of the Southwest *New Mexico* M & W
The College of William and Mary *Virginia* M & W
The College of Wooster *Ohio* M
Colorado Christian University *Colorado* M
Colorado School of Mines *Colorado* M
Colorado State University *Colorado* M & W
Colorado State University-Pueblo *Colorado* M & W
Columbia Basin College *Washington* M & W
Columbia Bible College *British Columbia* M & W
Columbia College *New York* M
Columbia University, School of General Studies *New York* M
Columbia University, The Fu Foundation School of Engineering and Applied Science *New York* M
Columbus State Community College *Ohio* M
Columbus State University *Georgia* M
Community College of Allegheny County *Pennsylvania* M & W
Community College of Rhode Island *Rhode Island* M & W
Compton Community College *California* M
Concord University *West Virginia* M
Concordia College *Minnesota* M & W
Concordia University *Oregon* M & W
Concordia University *Nebraska* M & W
Concordia University *Michigan* M & W
Concordia University *Illinois* M
Concordia University at Austin *Texas* M & W
Concordia University College of Alberta *Alberta* M & W
Concordia University, St. Paul *Minnesota* W
Concordia University Wisconsin *Wisconsin* M & W
Copiah-Lincoln Community College *Mississippi* M & W
Corban College *Oregon* M
Cornell College *Iowa* M & W
Cornell University *New York* M
Cornerstone University *Michigan* M
County College of Morris *New Jersey* M & W
Covenant College *Georgia* M
Cowley County Community College and Area Vocational-Technical School *Kansas* M
Creighton University *Nebraska* M & W
Crossroads College *Minnesota* M & W
Crown College *Minnesota* M & W
Culver-Stockton College *Missouri* M & W
Cumberland University *Tennessee* M & W
Cypress College *California* M & W
Daemen College *New York* M
Dakota Wesleyan University *South Dakota* M & W
Dallas Baptist University *Texas* M & W
Dalton State College *Georgia* W
Dana College *Nebraska* W
Dartmouth College *New Hampshire* M & W
Darton College *Georgia* M
Davidson College *North Carolina* M
Davis & Elkins College *West Virginia* M
De Anza College *California* M & W
Dean College *Massachusetts* M
Defiance College *Ohio* M & W
Delaware County Community College *Pennsylvania* M & W
Delaware Valley College *Pennsylvania* M
Delta College *Michigan* M
Delta State University *Mississippi* M
Denison University *Ohio* M
DePaul University *Illinois* M & W
DePauw University *Indiana* M & W
Des Moines Area Community College *Iowa* M & W

M = Men; W = Women

M = Men; W = Women

Lambuth University *Tennessee* M
Lander University *South Carolina* M
Lane College *Tennessee* M
Laney College *California* M
Lansing Community College *Michigan* M
Lassen Community College District *California* M & W
Lawrence University *Wisconsin* M
Le Moyne College *New York* M
Lebanon Valley College *Pennsylvania* M
Lee University *Tennessee* M
Lees-McRae College *North Carolina* M
Lehigh Carbon Community College *Pennsylvania* M & W
Lehigh University *Pennsylvania* M & W
LeMoyne-Owen College *Tennessee* M & W
Lenoir-Rhyne College *North Carolina* M & W
LeTourneau University *Texas* M & W
Lewis & Clark College *Oregon* M & W
Lewis and Clark Community College *Illinois* M
Lewis-Clark State College *Idaho* M & W
Lewis University *Illinois* M & W
Liberty University *Virginia* M
Limestone College *South Carolina* M & W
Lincoln Christian College *Illinois* M & W
Lincoln College *Illinois* M & W
Lincoln College-Normal *Illinois* M & W
Lincoln Memorial University *Tennessee* M & W
Lincoln University *Missouri* M
Lindenwood University *Missouri* M & W
Lindsey Wilson College *Kentucky* M & W
Linfield College *Oregon* M & W
Lipscomb University *Tennessee* M & W
Lon Morris College *Texas* M & W
Long Beach City College *California* M & W
Long Island University, Brooklyn Campus *New York* M & W
Longwood University *Virginia* M & W
Loras College *Iowa* M & W
Los Angeles Harbor College *California* M
Louisburg College *North Carolina* M & W
Louisiana College *Louisiana* M
Louisiana State University and Agricultural and Mechanical College *Louisiana* M & W
Louisiana Tech University *Louisiana* M
Loyola College in Maryland *Maryland* M
Loyola Marymount University *California* M
Loyola University Chicago *Illinois* M & W
Loyola University New Orleans *Louisiana* M & W
Lubbock Christian University *Texas* M & W
Luther College *Iowa* M & W
Luzerne County Community College *Pennsylvania* M & W
Lycoming College *Pennsylvania* M
Lynchburg College *Virginia* M
Lynn University *Florida* M & W
Lyon College *Arkansas* M & W
Macalester College *Minnesota* M & W
MacMurray College *Illinois* M & W
Madonna University *Michigan* M & W
Maharishi University of Management *Iowa* M & W
Malone College *Ohio* M & W
Manchester College *Indiana* M & W
Manhattan College *New York* M
Manhattanville College *New York* M
Marian College *Indiana* M & W
Marian College of Fond du Lac *Wisconsin* M & W
Marion Military Institute *Alabama* M & W
Marion Technical College *Ohio* M & W
Marquette University *Wisconsin* M
Mars Hill College *North Carolina* M & W
Marshall University *West Virginia* M & W
Marshalltown Community College *Iowa* M & W
Martin Luther College *Minnesota* M
Martin Methodist College *Tennessee* M
Marymount College, Palos Verdes, California *California* M & W
Marymount University *Virginia* M
Maryville University of Saint Louis *Missouri* M & W
Massachusetts Bay Community College *Massachusetts* M & W
Massachusetts College of Liberal Arts *Massachusetts* M
Massachusetts Institute of Technology *Massachusetts* M
The Master's College and Seminary *California* M
McDaniel College *Maryland* M & W
McGill University *Quebec* M & W
McKendree College *Illinois* M & W
McLennan Community College *Texas* M & W
McMaster University *Ontario* M & W
McMurry University *Texas* M & W
McNeese State University *Louisiana* M & W
Mendocino College *California* M
Menlo College *California* M & W
Merced College *California* M & W
Mercer County Community College *New Jersey* M & W
Mercer University *Georgia* M & W
Mercy College *New York* M
Mercyhurst College *Pennsylvania* M & W
Meridian Community College *Mississippi* M
Mesa Community College *Arizona* M & W
Mesa State College *Colorado* W
Messiah College *Pennsylvania* M
Methodist College *North Carolina* M & W
Miami University *Ohio* M
Miami University Hamilton *Ohio* M
Miami University-Middletown Campus *Ohio* M & W
Michigan State University *Michigan* M & W
Mid-Plains Community College *Nebraska* M
Mid-State Technical College *Wisconsin* M
Middle Tennessee State University *Tennessee* M
Middlebury College *Vermont* M & W
Middlesex County College *New Jersey* M & W
Midland College *Texas* M
Midland Lutheran College *Nebraska* M & W
Miles Community College *Montana* M & W
Millersville University of Pennsylvania *Pennsylvania* M
Milligan College *Tennessee* M
Millikin University *Illinois* M & W
Millsaps College *Mississippi* M & W
Milwaukee Area Technical College *Wisconsin* M & W
Milwaukee School of Engineering *Wisconsin* M & W
Minneapolis Community and Technical College *Minnesota* M & W
Minnesota State Community and Technical College-Fergus Falls *Minnesota* M & W
Minnesota State University Mankato *Minnesota* M & W
Minnesota State University Moorhead *Minnesota* M & W
Minnesota West Community and Technical College *Minnesota* M & W
Minot State University *North Dakota* M & W
Mississippi College *Mississippi* M
Mississippi Delta Community College *Mississippi* M
Mississippi Gulf Coast Community College *Mississippi* M
Mississippi State University *Mississippi* M & W
Mississippi Valley State University *Mississippi* M
Missouri Baptist University *Missouri* M & W
Missouri Southern State University *Missouri* M
Missouri State University *Missouri* M & W
Missouri Valley College *Missouri* M & W
Missouri Western State University *Missouri* M & W
Mitchell College *Connecticut* M
Modesto Junior College *California* M
Mohawk Valley Community College *New York* M & W
Monmouth College *Illinois* M & W
Monmouth University *New Jersey* M & W
Monroe Community College *New York* M
Montana State University *Montana* W
Montana State University-Billings *Montana* M & W
Montana State University-Northern *Montana* W
Montana Tech of The University of Montana *Montana* M & W
Montclair State University *New Jersey* M & W
Monterey Peninsula College *California* M & W
Montgomery College *Maryland* M
Montreat College *North Carolina* M
Moorpark College *California* M & W
Moraine Valley Community College *Illinois* M
Moravian College *Pennsylvania* M & W
Morehead State University *Kentucky* M
Morningside College *Iowa* M & W
Morris College *South Carolina* M
Mott Community College *Michigan* M
Mount Aloysius College *Pennsylvania* M & W
Mount Holyoke College *Massachusetts* W
Mount Mercy College *Iowa* M & W
Mount Olive College *North Carolina* M
Mount St. Mary's University *Maryland* M & W
Mt. San Antonio College *California* M & W
Mt. San Jacinto College *California* M
Mount Union College *Ohio* M & W
Mount Vernon Nazarene University *Ohio* M
Muhlenberg College *Pennsylvania* M & W
Murray State University *Kentucky* M & W
Muskegon Community College *Michigan* M & W
Muskingum College *Ohio* M & W
Nassau Community College *New York* M & W
Navarro College *Texas* M
Nazareth College of Rochester *New York* M & W
Nebraska Wesleyan University *Nebraska* M & W
Neumann College *Pennsylvania* M
New Jersey Institute of Technology *New Jersey* M
New Mexico Institute of Mining and Technology *New Mexico* M & W
New Mexico Junior College *New Mexico* M
New Mexico Military Institute *New Mexico* M
New Mexico State University *New Mexico* M & W
New York University *New York* M
Newberry College *South Carolina* M & W
Newbury College *Massachusetts* M & W
Newman University *Kansas* M & W
Niagara County Community College *New York* M & W
Niagara University *New York* M
Nicholls State University *Louisiana* M & W
Nichols College *Massachusetts* M & W
Nicolet Area Technical College *Wisconsin* M & W
North Carolina Central University *North Carolina* M & W
North Carolina State University *North Carolina* M & W
North Carolina Wesleyan College *North Carolina* M
North Central College *Illinois* M & W
North Dakota State University *North Dakota* M & W
North Greenville College *South Carolina* M
North Iowa Area Community College *Iowa* M & W
North Park University *Illinois* M
Northampton County Area Community College *Pennsylvania* M & W
Northeast Mississippi Community College *Mississippi* M
Northeastern Oklahoma Agricultural and Mechanical College *Oklahoma* M
Northeastern State University *Oklahoma* M & W
Northern Arizona University *Arizona* W
Northern Illinois University *Illinois* M & W
Northern Kentucky University *Kentucky* M & W
Northern Maine Community College *Maine* M & W
Northern Michigan University *Michigan* M
Northern State University *South Dakota* M & W
Northland Community and Technical College-Thief River Falls *Minnesota* M & W
Northwest Mississippi Community College *Mississippi* M
Northwest Missouri State University *Missouri* M
Northwest Nazarene University *Idaho* M
Northwest-Shoals Community College *Alabama* M
Northwestern College *Minnesota* M
Northwestern College *Iowa* M & W
Northwestern Oklahoma State University *Oklahoma* M & W
Northwestern University *Illinois* M & W
Northwood University *Michigan* M & W
Northwood University, Florida Campus *Florida* M & W
Northwood University, Texas Campus *Texas* M & W
Notre Dame College *Ohio* M & W
Notre Dame de Namur University *California* M & W
Nova Southeastern University *Florida* M & W
Nyack College *New York* M
Oakland City University *Indiana* M & W
Oakland Community College *Michigan* M
Oakland University *Michigan* M & W

M = Men; W = Women

Oakton Community College *Illinois* M
Oberlin College *Ohio* M & W
Occidental College *California* M & W
Ocean County College *New Jersey* M & W
Odessa College *Texas* M
Oglethorpe University *Georgia* M & W
Ohio Dominican University *Ohio* M & W
Ohio Northern University *Ohio* M & W
The Ohio State University *Ohio* M & W
The Ohio State University at Lima *Ohio* M
Ohio University *Ohio* M & W
Ohio University-Chillicothe *Ohio* M & W
Ohio University-Lancaster *Ohio* M & W
Ohio University-Zanesville *Ohio* M & W
Ohio Valley University *West Virginia* M
Ohio Wesleyan University *Ohio* M
Oklahoma Baptist University *Oklahoma* M & W
Oklahoma Christian University *Oklahoma* M
Oklahoma City University *Oklahoma* M & W
Oklahoma Panhandle State University *Oklahoma* M & W
Oklahoma State University *Oklahoma* M & W
Oklahoma Wesleyan University *Oklahoma* M
Old Dominion University *Virginia* M & W
Olivet College *Michigan* M & W
Olivet Nazarene University *Illinois* M
Olympic College *Washington* M & W
Oral Roberts University *Oklahoma* M & W
Orange Coast College *California* M & W
Orange County Community College *New York* M & W
Oregon State University *Oregon* M & W
Otero Junior College *Colorado* M & W
Ottawa University *Kansas* M
Otterbein College *Ohio* M & W
Ouachita Baptist University *Arkansas* M
Pace University *New York* M & W
Pacific Lutheran University *Washington* M & W
Pacific University *Oregon* M & W
Paine College *Georgia* M
Palm Beach Atlantic University *Florida* M
Paradise Valley Community College *Arizona* M & W
Paris Junior College *Texas* M
Park University *Missouri* W
Parkland College *Illinois* M
Patten University *California* M
Pearl River Community College *Mississippi* M & W
Pennsylvania College of Technology *Pennsylvania* M & W
The Pennsylvania State University Abington College *Pennsylvania* M
The Pennsylvania State University Altoona College *Pennsylvania* M
The Pennsylvania State University Berks Campus of the Berks-Lehigh Valley College *Pennsylvania* M
The Pennsylvania State University DuBois Campus of the Commonwealth College *Pennsylvania* M & W
The Pennsylvania State University at Erie, The Behrend College *Pennsylvania* M & W
The Pennsylvania State University, Lehigh Valley Campus of the Berks-Lehigh Valley College *Pennsylvania* M & W
The Pennsylvania State University Mont Alto Campus of the Commonwealth College *Pennsylvania* M & W
The Pennsylvania State University New Kensington Campus of the Commonwealth College *Pennsylvania* M & W
The Pennsylvania State University Schuylkill Campus of the Capital College *Pennsylvania* M
The Pennsylvania State University University Park Campus *Pennsylvania* M & W
The Pennsylvania State University Wilkes-Barre Campus of the Commonwealth College *Pennsylvania* M & W
Pepperdine University *California* M & W
Peru State College *Nebraska* W
Pfeiffer University *North Carolina* M & W
Philadelphia Biblical University *Pennsylvania* M
Philadelphia University *Pennsylvania* M
Phoenix College *Arizona* M & W
Piedmont College *Georgia* M & W
Pikeville College *Kentucky* M & W
Pillsbury Baptist Bible College *Minnesota* M & W
Pima Community College *Arizona* M & W
Pitt Community College *North Carolina* M & W
Pittsburg State University *Kansas* M
Pitzer College *California* M
Point Loma Nazarene University *California* M
Pomona College *California* M & W
Portland State University *Oregon* M & W
Post University *Connecticut* M
Potomac State College of West Virginia University *West Virginia* M & W
Prairie State College *Illinois* M & W
Prairie View A&M University *Texas* M & W
Pratt Community College *Kansas* M & W
Presbyterian College *South Carolina* M & W
Presentation College *South Dakota* M & W
Prince George's Community College *Maryland* M
Princeton University *New Jersey* M & W
Principia College *Illinois* M
Providence College *Rhode Island* M & W
Purdue University *Indiana* M & W
Queens College of the City University of New York *New York* M
Queens University of Charlotte *North Carolina* M & W
Queen's University at Kingston *Ontario* M
Quincy University *Illinois* M & W
Quinnipiac University *Connecticut* M
Radford University *Virginia* M & W
Randolph-Macon College *Virginia* M
Ranger College *Texas* M
Reedley College *California* M
Regis University *Colorado* M & W
Reinhardt College *Georgia* M
Rend Lake College *Illinois* M & W
Rensselaer Polytechnic Institute *New York* M
Research College of Nursing *Missouri* M & W
Rhodes College *Tennessee* M & W
Rice University *Texas* M
Rider University *New Jersey* M
Ripon College *Wisconsin* M & W
Riverland Community College *Minnesota* M & W
Riverside Community College District *California* M
Rivier College *New Hampshire* M & W
Roanoke College *Virginia* M & W
Robert Morris College *Illinois* M & W
Robert Morris University *Pennsylvania* M & W
Roberts Wesleyan College *New York* M & W
Rochester Community and Technical College *Minnesota* M & W
Rock Valley College *Illinois* M
Rockford College *Illinois* M
Rockhurst University *Missouri* M & W
Rockland Community College *New York* M
Rollins College *Florida* M & W
Rose-Hulman Institute of Technology *Indiana* M & W
Rutgers, The State University of New Jersey, New Brunswick/Piscataway *New Jersey* M & W
Sacramento City College *California* M & W
Sacred Heart University *Connecticut* M & W
Saddleback College *California* M & W
Saginaw Valley State University *Michigan* M
St. Ambrose University *Iowa* M & W
St. Andrews Presbyterian College *North Carolina* M & W
Saint Anselm College *New Hampshire* M
Saint Augustine's College *North Carolina* M
St. Bonaventure University *New York* M
St. Clair County Community College *Michigan* M
St. Cloud State University *Minnesota* M & W
St. Edward's University *Texas* M & W
Saint Francis University *Pennsylvania* M & W
St. Gregory's University *Oklahoma* M & W
St. John Fisher College *New York* M
St. John's University *New York* M & W
Saint John's University *Minnesota* M
Saint Joseph's College *Indiana* M & W
Saint Joseph's College of Maine *Maine* M
St. Joseph's College, Suffolk Campus *New York* M
Saint Joseph's University *Pennsylvania* M
St. Lawrence University *New York* M & W
Saint Leo University *Florida* M & W
Saint Louis University *Missouri* M
Saint Martin's University *Washington* M & W
Saint Mary's College of California *California* M
St. Mary's College of Maryland *Maryland* M & W
Saint Mary's University of Minnesota *Minnesota* M & W
St. Mary's University of San Antonio *Texas* M
Saint Michael's College *Vermont* M
St. Norbert College *Wisconsin* M & W
St. Olaf College *Minnesota* M & W
Saint Paul's College *Virginia* M & W
Saint Peter's College *New Jersey* M
St. Thomas Aquinas College *New York* M & W
St. Thomas University *Florida* M & W
Saint Vincent College *Pennsylvania* M & W
Saint Xavier University *Illinois* M
Salem International University *West Virginia* M
Salem State College *Massachusetts* M
Salve Regina University *Rhode Island* M & W
Sam Houston State University *Texas* M & W
Samford University *Alabama* M & W
San Bernardino Valley College *California* M
San Diego City College *California* M & W
San Diego State University *California* M & W
San Joaquin Delta College *California* M & W
San Jose City College *California* M
San Jose State University *California* M & W
Santa Ana College *California* M
Santa Barbara City College *California* M & W
Santa Clara University *California* M & W
Santa Rosa Junior College *California* M
Savannah College of Art and Design *Georgia* M & W
Schoolcraft College *Michigan* M & W
Schreiner University *Texas* M & W
Scott Community College *Iowa* M & W
Scottsdale Community College *Arizona* M & W
Scripps College *California* W
Seattle University *Washington* M & W
Seminole State College *Oklahoma* M & W
Seton Hall University *New Jersey* M
Seton Hill University *Pennsylvania* M & W
Sewanee: The University of the South *Tennessee* M & W
Shasta College *California* M & W
Shaw University *North Carolina* M
Shawnee State University *Ohio* M
Shenandoah University *Virginia* M
Shepherd University *West Virginia* M
Shorter College *Georgia* M & W
Siena College *New York* M & W
Siena Heights University *Michigan* M
Sierra College *California* M & W
Simon Fraser University *British Columbia* M
Simpson College *Iowa* M & W
Sinclair Community College *Ohio* M
Skagit Valley College *Washington* M & W
Skidmore College *New York* M
Slippery Rock University of Pennsylvania *Pennsylvania* M & W
Snow College *Utah* M
Sonoma State University *California* M
South Carolina State University *South Carolina* M
South Dakota School of Mines and Technology *South Dakota* M & W
South Dakota State University *South Dakota* M & W
Southeast Community College, Beatrice Campus *Nebraska* M
Southeast Missouri State University *Missouri* M
Southeastern Louisiana University *Louisiana* M
Southeastern University *Florida* M
Southern Arkansas University-Magnolia *Arkansas* M
Southern Connecticut State University *Connecticut* M
Southern Illinois University Carbondale *Illinois* M & W
Southern Illinois University Edwardsville *Illinois* M & W
Southern Maine Community College *Maine* M & W
Southern Methodist University *Texas* M & W
Southern Nazarene University *Oklahoma* M & W
Southern New Hampshire University *New Hampshire* M
Southern University and Agricultural and Mechanical College *Louisiana* M & W
Southern Utah University *Utah* M

M = Men; W = Women

M = Men; W = Women

University of the Sciences in Philadelphia *Pennsylvania* M & W
The University of Scranton *Pennsylvania* M
University of Sioux Falls *South Dakota* M & W
University of South Alabama *Alabama* M & W
University of South Carolina *South Carolina* M & W
University of South Carolina Aiken *South Carolina* M
University of South Carolina Salkehatchie *South Carolina* M
University of South Florida *Florida* M & W
University of Southern California *California* M & W
University of Southern Indiana *Indiana* M & W
University of Southern Maine *Maine* M & W
University of Southern Mississippi *Mississippi* M & W
The University of Tampa *Florida* M
The University of Tennessee *Tennessee* M & W
The University of Tennessee at Chattanooga *Tennessee* M & W
The University of Tennessee at Martin *Tennessee* M
The University of Texas at Arlington *Texas* M
The University of Texas at Austin *Texas* M & W
The University of Texas at Brownsville *Texas* M & W
The University of Texas at Dallas *Texas* M & W
The University of Texas at El Paso *Texas* M
The University of Texas-Pan American *Texas* M & W
The University of Texas at San Antonio *Texas* M
The University of Texas at Tyler *Texas* M & W
The University of Toledo *Ohio* M & W
University of Toronto *Ontario* M
University of Tulsa *Oklahoma* M & W
University of Utah *Utah* M
University of Victoria *British Columbia* M & W
University of Virginia *Virginia* M & W
The University of Virginia's College at Wise *Virginia* M & W
University of Washington *Washington* M & W
University of Waterloo *Ontario* M & W
University of West Florida *Florida* M
University of West Georgia *Georgia* M & W
The University of Western Ontario *Ontario* M & W
University of Windsor *Ontario* M & W
University of Wisconsin-Baraboo/Sauk County *Wisconsin* M & W
University of Wisconsin-Barron County *Wisconsin* M & W
University of Wisconsin-Eau Claire *Wisconsin* M & W
University of Wisconsin-Fond du Lac *Wisconsin* M
University of Wisconsin-Madison *Wisconsin* M & W
University of Wisconsin-Manitowoc *Wisconsin* M
University of Wisconsin-Marathon County *Wisconsin* M & W
University of Wisconsin-Marshfield/Wood County *Wisconsin* M & W
University of Wisconsin-Oshkosh *Wisconsin* W
University of Wisconsin-Parkside *Wisconsin* M
University of Wisconsin-Platteville *Wisconsin* W
University of Wisconsin-Sheboygan *Wisconsin* M & W
University of Wisconsin-Stevens Point *Wisconsin* W
University of Wisconsin-Superior *Wisconsin* W
University of Wisconsin-Washington County *Wisconsin* M & W
University of Wisconsin-Waukesha *Wisconsin* M & W
University of Wisconsin-Whitewater *Wisconsin* W
University of Wyoming *Wyoming* M & W
Upper Iowa University *Iowa* M & W
Urbana University *Ohio* M & W
Ursinus College *Pennsylvania* M & W
Ursuline College *Ohio* W
Utah State University *Utah* M
Utah Valley State College *Utah* M
Utica College *New York* M & W
Valdosta State University *Georgia* M
Valley Forge Military College *Pennsylvania* M
Vanderbilt University *Tennessee* M & W
Vassar College *New York* W
Ventura College *California* M
Victor Valley College *California* M
Villa Julie College *Maryland* M & W
Villanova University *Pennsylvania* M
Vincennes University *Indiana* M
Virginia Commonwealth University *Virginia* M
Virginia Intermont College *Virginia* M
Virginia Military Institute *Virginia* M
Virginia Polytechnic Institute and State University *Virginia* M
Virginia State University *Virginia* M & W
Virginia Union University *Virginia* M
Virginia Wesleyan College *Virginia* M
Wabash College *Indiana* M
Wagner College *New York* M & W
Wake Forest University *North Carolina* M & W
Waldorf College *Iowa* M & W
Walla Walla College *Washington* M
Walla Walla Community College *Washington* M & W
Wallace State Community College *Alabama* M
Walsh University *Ohio* M & W
Walters State Community College *Tennessee* M
Warner Southern College *Florida* M & W
Wartburg College *Iowa* M & W
Washburn University *Kansas* M
Washington & Jefferson College *Pennsylvania* M & W
Washington and Lee University *Virginia* M
Washington State University *Washington* M & W
Washington University in St. Louis *Missouri* M & W
Waubonsee Community College *Illinois* M
Wayland Baptist University *Texas* M
Wayne County Community College District *Michigan* M & W
Wayne State College *Nebraska* M & W
Wayne State University *Michigan* M
Waynesburg College *Pennsylvania* M & W
Webber International University *Florida* M & W
Weber State University *Utah* M & W
Webster University *Missouri* M
Wellesley College *Massachusetts* W
Wentworth Institute of Technology *Massachusetts* M & W
Wesley College *Delaware* M & W
Wesleyan University *Connecticut* M
West Chester University of Pennsylvania *Pennsylvania* M
West Liberty State College *West Virginia* M & W
West Los Angeles College *California* M
West Texas A&M University *Texas* M & W
West Valley College *California* M
West Virginia State University *West Virginia* W
West Virginia University Institute of Technology *West Virginia* M
West Virginia Wesleyan College *West Virginia* M
Westchester Community College *New York* M
Western Carolina University *North Carolina* M & W
Western Illinois University *Illinois* M & W
Western Kentucky University *Kentucky* M & W
Western Michigan University *Michigan* W
Western New England College *Massachusetts* M
Western New Mexico University *New Mexico* M & W
Western Oklahoma State College *Oklahoma* M & W
Western Washington University *Washington* M & W
Westminster College *Utah* M & W
Westminster College *Pennsylvania* M & W
Westminster College *Missouri* M & W
Westmoreland County Community College *Pennsylvania* M & W
Wheaton College *Illinois* M & W
Wheeling Jesuit University *West Virginia* M & W
Whitman College *Washington* M & W
Whittier College *California* M
Whitworth College *Washington* M & W
Wichita State University *Kansas* M & W
Widener University *Pennsylvania* M
Wilberforce University *Ohio* M & W
Wilfrid Laurier University *Ontario* M
Wilkes University *Pennsylvania* M
Willamette University *Oregon* M & W
William Carey College *Mississippi* M
William Jewell College *Missouri* M & W
William Paterson University of New Jersey *New Jersey* M
William Penn University *Iowa* M
William Woods University *Missouri* M & W
Williams Baptist College *Arkansas* M
Williams College *Massachusetts* M & W
Wilmington College *Ohio* M & W
Wingate University *North Carolina* M & W
Winona State University *Minnesota* M & W
Winthrop University *South Carolina* M & W
Wisconsin Lutheran College *Wisconsin* M & W
Wittenberg University *Ohio* M & W
Wofford College *South Carolina* M & W
Worcester State College *Massachusetts* M
Wright State University *Ohio* M
Xavier University *Ohio* M & W
Yale University *Connecticut* M & W
York College *Nebraska* M & W
York College of Pennsylvania *Pennsylvania* M
York University *Ontario* M
Youngstown State University *Ohio* M & W
Zane State College *Ohio* M & W

Gymnastics

Arizona State University *Arizona* W
Auburn University *Alabama* W
Ball State University *Indiana* W
Boise State University *Idaho* W
Boston University *Massachusetts* M & W
Bowling Green State University *Ohio* W
Brigham Young University *Utah* W
Brown University *Rhode Island* W
California Polytechnic State University, San Luis Obispo *California* W
California State University, Fullerton *California* W
California State University, Sacramento *California* W
Carleton College *Minnesota* W
Centenary College of Louisiana *Louisiana* W
Central Michigan University *Michigan* W
City College of San Francisco *California* W
The College of William and Mary *Virginia* M & W
Columbia University, School of General Studies *New York* W
Cornell University *New York* W
Dartmouth College *New Hampshire* M & W
Eastern Michigan University *Michigan* W
El Camino College *California* W
Electronic Data Processing College of Puerto Rico *Puerto Rico* M & W
Emory University *Georgia* M & W
The George Washington University *District of Columbia* W
Gustavus Adolphus College *Minnesota* W
Hamline University *Minnesota* W
Hunter College of the City University of New York *New York* W
Illinois State University *Illinois* W
Iowa State University of Science and Technology *Iowa* W
Ithaca College *New York* W
James Madison University *Virginia* M & W
Kent State University *Ohio* W
Los Angeles City College *California* M
Los Angeles Valley College *California* M & W
Louisiana State University and Agricultural and Mechanical College *Louisiana* W
Massachusetts Institute of Technology *Massachusetts* M & W
Merritt College *California* M & W
Miami University *Ohio* M & W
Michigan State University *Michigan* W
Modesto Junior College *California* W
North Carolina State University *North Carolina* W
Northern Illinois University *Illinois* W
The Ohio State University *Ohio* M & W
Oregon State University *Oregon* W
The Pennsylvania State University University Park Campus *Pennsylvania* M & W
Queen's University at Kingston *Ontario* M & W
Rensselaer Polytechnic Institute *New York* M & W
Rhode Island College *Rhode Island* W
Rutgers, The State University of New Jersey, New Brunswick/Piscataway *New Jersey* W
Saint Mary's College *Indiana* W
San Jose State University *California* W
Seattle Pacific University *Washington* W
Simon Fraser University *British Columbia* M
Southeast Missouri State University *Missouri* W
Southern Connecticut State University *Connecticut* M & W

M = Men; W = Women

Southern Utah University *Utah* W
Springfield College *Massachusetts* M & W
Stanford University *California* M & W
State University of New York College at Brockport *New York* W
State University of New York College at Cortland *New York* W
Suffolk County Community College *New York* M & W
Syracuse University *New York* M & W
Temple University *Pennsylvania* M & W
Texas State University-San Marcos *Texas* M & W
Texas Woman's University *Texas* W
Towson University *Maryland* W
Tulane University *Louisiana* M & W
United States Air Force Academy *Colorado* M & W
United States Military Academy *New York* M
United States Naval Academy *Maryland* M & W
Université Laval *Quebec* M & W
Université de Moncton *New Brunswick* W
The University of Alabama *Alabama* W
University of Alaska Anchorage *Alaska* W
University of Alberta *Alberta* M & W
The University of Arizona *Arizona* W
University of Arkansas *Arkansas* W
University of Bridgeport *Connecticut* W
University of California, Berkeley *California* M & W
University of California, Davis *California* W
University of California, Los Angeles *California* W
University of California, Santa Barbara *California* M & W
University of Denver *Colorado* W
University of Florida *Florida* W
University of Georgia *Georgia* W
University of Illinois at Chicago *Illinois* M & W
University of Illinois at Urbana-Champaign *Illinois* M & W
The University of Iowa *Iowa* M & W
University of Kentucky *Kentucky* W
University of Manitoba *Manitoba* M & W
University of Maryland, College Park *Maryland* W
University of Michigan *Michigan* M & W
University of Minnesota, Twin Cities Campus *Minnesota* M & W
University of Missouri-Columbia *Missouri* W
University of Nebraska-Lincoln *Nebraska* M & W
University of New Hampshire *New Hampshire* W
The University of North Carolina at Chapel Hill *North Carolina* W
University of Oklahoma *Oklahoma* M & W
University of Pennsylvania *Pennsylvania* W
University of Pittsburgh *Pennsylvania* W
University of Rhode Island *Rhode Island* W
University of Toronto *Ontario* M & W
University of Utah *Utah* W
University of Vermont *Vermont* M & W
University of Washington *Washington* W
University of Wisconsin-Eau Claire *Wisconsin* W
University of Wisconsin-La Crosse *Wisconsin* W
University of Wisconsin-Oshkosh *Wisconsin* W
University of Wisconsin-Stout *Wisconsin* W
University of Wisconsin-Whitewater *Wisconsin* W
Ursinus College *Pennsylvania* W
Utah State University *Utah* W
Virginia Polytechnic Institute and State University *Virginia* M & W
Washington University in St. Louis *Missouri* M & W
West Chester University of Pennsylvania *Pennsylvania* W
West Virginia University *West Virginia* W
Western Michigan University *Michigan* W
Wilson College *Pennsylvania* W
Winona State University *Minnesota* W
Yale University *Connecticut* W

Ice Hockey

Acadia University *Nova Scotia* M & W
Alberta College of Art & Design *Alberta* M & W
Allegheny College *Pennsylvania* M
Alliance University College *Alberta* M
American International College *Massachusetts* M
Amherst College *Massachusetts* M & W
Assumption College *Massachusetts* M
Augsburg College *Minnesota* M & W
Babson College *Massachusetts* M & W
Ball State University *Indiana* M
Barnard College *New York* W
Bates College *Maine* M & W
Baylor University *Texas* M
Becker College *Massachusetts* M & W
Beloit College *Wisconsin* M & W
Bemidji State University *Minnesota* M & W
Bentley College *Massachusetts* M
Bethany Bible College *New Brunswick* M
Bethany College *West Virginia* M
Bethel University *Minnesota* M & W
Bishop's University *Quebec* W
Boston College *Massachusetts* M & W
Boston University *Massachusetts* M & W
Bowdoin College *Maine* M & W
Bowling Green State University *Ohio* M
Bradley University *Illinois* M
Briercrest College *Saskatchewan* M
Brock University *Ontario* M & W
Broome Community College *New York* M
Brown University *Rhode Island* M & W
Bryant University *Rhode Island* M
Bryn Athyn College of the New Church *Pennsylvania* M
Bucknell University *Pennsylvania* M
Buffalo State College, State University of New York *New York* M & W
Butler University *Indiana* M
California Institute of Technology *California* M
California State University, Sacramento *California* M
Calvin College *Michigan* M
Canadian Mennonite University *Manitoba* M
Canisius College *New York* M
Carleton College *Minnesota* M & W
Carleton University *Ontario* M & W
Carnegie Mellon University *Pennsylvania* M & W
Carthage College *Wisconsin* M
Case Western Reserve University *Ohio* M & W
Castleton State College *Vermont* M & W
Central Washington University *Washington* M & W
Chatham College *Pennsylvania* W
The Citadel, The Military College of South Carolina *South Carolina* M & W
Clarkson University *New York* M & W
Clemson University *South Carolina* M & W
Colby College *Maine* M & W
Colby-Sawyer College *New Hampshire* M & W
Colgate University *New York* M & W
College of the Holy Cross *Massachusetts* M & W
College of Saint Benedict *Minnesota* W
College of St. Catherine *Minnesota* W
The College of St. Scholastica *Minnesota* M
The Colorado College *Colorado* M & W
Columbia College *New York* M
Columbia University, The Fu Foundation School of Engineering and Applied Science *New York* M
Community College of Allegheny County *Pennsylvania* M
Concordia College *Minnesota* M & W
Concordia University *Quebec* M & W
Concordia University College of Alberta *Alberta* M
Connecticut College *Connecticut* M & W
Cornell University *New York* M & W
County College of Morris *New Jersey* M
The Culinary Institute of America *New York* M
Curry College *Massachusetts* M
Dalhousie University *Nova Scotia* M & W
Daniel Webster College *New Hampshire* M & W
Dartmouth College *New Hampshire* M & W
Denison University *Ohio* M
DeSales University *Pennsylvania* M
Dickinson College *Pennsylvania* M
Dordt College *Iowa* M
Duke University *North Carolina* M & W
Duquesne University *Pennsylvania* M
Eastern Washington University *Washington* M
Edinboro University of Pennsylvania *Pennsylvania* M
Elmira College *New York* M & W
Emmanuel Bible College *Ontario* M
Erie Community College *New York* M
Erie Community College, North Campus *New York* M
Erie Community College, South Campus *New York* M
Ferris State University *Michigan* M
Finlandia University *Michigan* M & W
Fitchburg State College *Massachusetts* M
Fordham University *New York* M
Fort Lewis College *Colorado* M & W
Framingham State College *Massachusetts* M
Franklin and Marshall College *Pennsylvania* M
Franklin Pierce College *New Hampshire* M
Furman University *South Carolina* M
Georgetown University *District of Columbia* M
Georgia Institute of Technology *Georgia* M
Grand Valley State University *Michigan* M
Gustavus Adolphus College *Minnesota* M & W
Hamilton College *New York* M & W
Hamline University *Minnesota* M & W
Hartwick College *New York* M
Harvard University *Massachusetts* M & W
Hillsdale College *Michigan* M
Hobart and William Smith Colleges *New York* M & W
Hope College *Michigan* M
John Carroll University *Ohio* M
Johnson & Wales University *Rhode Island* M
Juniata College *Pennsylvania* M
Kettering University *Michigan* M
Kutztown University of Pennsylvania *Pennsylvania* M
Lafayette College *Pennsylvania* M
Lake Forest College *Illinois* M & W
Lake Superior State University *Michigan* M
Lakehead University *Ontario* M
Laurentian University *Ontario* M & W
Lawrence University *Wisconsin* M & W
Lebanon Valley College *Pennsylvania* M
Lehigh University *Pennsylvania* M
Liberty University *Virginia* M
Lindenwood University *Missouri* M & W
Loras College *Iowa* M
Macalester College *Minnesota* M & W
Manhattanville College *New York* M & W
Marian College of Fond du Lac *Wisconsin* M
Marist College *New York* M
Massachusetts College of Liberal Arts *Massachusetts* M & W
Massachusetts Institute of Technology *Massachusetts* M & W
McGill University *Quebec* M & W
McKendree College *Illinois* M
Mercyhurst College *Pennsylvania* M & W
Merrimack College *Massachusetts* M
Miami University *Ohio* M
Michigan State University *Michigan* M & W
Michigan Technological University *Michigan* M & W
Middlebury College *Vermont* M & W
Milwaukee School of Engineering *Wisconsin* M
Minnesota State University Mankato *Minnesota* M & W
Minot State University *North Dakota* M
Minot State University-Bottineau Campus *North Dakota* M
Missouri State University *Missouri* M
Mohawk Valley Community College *New York* M
Monmouth University *New Jersey* M
Monroe Community College *New York* M
Moravian College *Pennsylvania* M & W
Mount Allison University *New Brunswick* W
Mount St. Mary's University *Maryland* M
Neumann College *Pennsylvania* M & W
New England College *New Hampshire* M & W
New Hampshire Community Technical College, Berlin/Laconia *New Hampshire* M & W
New York University *New York* M
Niagara University *New York* M & W
Nichols College *Massachusetts* M
North Carolina State University *North Carolina* M & W
North Country Community College *New York* M
North Dakota State University *North Dakota* M
Northampton County Area Community College *Pennsylvania* M & W
Northeastern University *Massachusetts* M & W
Northern Maine Community College *Maine* M & W

M = Men; W = Women

Northern Michigan University *Michigan* M & W
Northland College *Wisconsin* M
Northwestern College *Minnesota* M
Norwich University *Vermont* M & W
Oak Hills Christian College *Minnesota* M
Oakland University *Michigan* M & W
Oberlin College *Ohio* M & W
The Ohio State University *Ohio* M & W
Ohio University *Ohio* M
Ohio Wesleyan University *Ohio* M & W
Old Dominion University *Virginia* M
The Pennsylvania State University Altoona College *Pennsylvania* M
The Pennsylvania State University Berks Campus of the Berks-Lehigh Valley College *Pennsylvania* M & W
The Pennsylvania State University at Erie, The Behrend College *Pennsylvania* M
The Pennsylvania State University, Lehigh Valley Campus of the Berks-Lehigh Valley College *Pennsylvania* M & W
The Pennsylvania State University University Park Campus *Pennsylvania* M & W
Plymouth State University *New Hampshire* M & W
Princeton University *New Jersey* M & W
Providence College *Rhode Island* M & W
Providence College and Theological Seminary *Manitoba* M
Queen's University at Kingston *Ontario* M & W
Quinnipiac University *Connecticut* M & W
Rensselaer Polytechnic Institute *New York* M & W
Ripon College *Wisconsin* M & W
Roanoke College *Virginia* M
Robert Morris University *Pennsylvania* M
Rochester Institute of Technology *New York* M & W
Rocky Mountain College *Alberta* M
Royal Military College of Canada *Ontario* M
Ryerson University *Ontario* M
Sacred Heart University *Connecticut* M & W
Saint Anselm College *New Hampshire* M
St. Cloud State University *Minnesota* M & W
St. Francis Xavier University *Nova Scotia* M & W
Saint John's University *Minnesota* M
Saint Joseph's College of Maine *Maine* M & W
St. Lawrence University *New York* M & W
Saint Louis University *Missouri* M
Saint Mary's University *Nova Scotia* M & W
Saint Mary's University of Minnesota *Minnesota* M & W
Saint Michael's College *Vermont* M & W
St. Norbert College *Wisconsin* M
St. Olaf College *Minnesota* M & W
St. Thomas University *New Brunswick* M & W
Saint Vincent College *Pennsylvania* M
Salem State College *Massachusetts* M
Salve Regina University *Rhode Island* M & W
San Jose State University *California* M & W
Santa Rosa Junior College *California* M
Seton Hall University *New Jersey* M
Siena College *New York* M
Skidmore College *New York* M & W
South Dakota State University *South Dakota* M & W
Southern Methodist University *Texas* M
Southern New Hampshire University *New Hampshire* M
Stanford University *California* M
State University of New York at Binghamton *New York* M
State University of New York College of Agriculture and Technology at Morrisville *New York* M
State University of New York College at Brockport *New York* M
State University of New York College at Cortland *New York* M & W
State University of New York College at Geneseo *New York* M
State University of New York College at Oneonta *New York* M
State University of New York College at Potsdam *New York* M
State University of New York College of Technology at Canton *New York* M
State University of New York, Fredonia *New York* M
State University of New York Maritime College *New York* M
State University of New York at New Paltz *New York* M
State University of New York at Oswego *New York* M
State University of New York at Plattsburgh *New York* M & W
Stonehill College *Massachusetts* M
Suffolk University *Massachusetts* M
Swarthmore College *Pennsylvania* M & W
Syracuse University *New York* M & W
Taylor University College and Seminary *Alberta* M
Trinity College *Connecticut* M & W
Tufts University *Massachusetts* M
Tulane University *Louisiana* M & W
Tyndale University College & Seminary *Ontario* M
Union College *New York* M & W
United States Air Force Academy *Colorado* M
United States Coast Guard Academy *Connecticut* M
United States Military Academy *New York* M
United States Naval Academy *Maryland* M
Université de Moncton *New Brunswick* M & W
Université du Québec àTrois-Rivières *Quebec* M & W
The University of Alabama in Huntsville *Alabama* M
University of Alaska Anchorage *Alaska* M
University of Alaska Fairbanks *Alaska* M
University of Alberta *Alberta* M & W
The University of Arizona *Arizona* M
The University of British Columbia *British Columbia* M & W
University of Calgary *Alberta* M & W
University of Colorado at Boulder *Colorado* M & W
University of Connecticut *Connecticut* M & W
University of Delaware *Delaware* M
University of Denver *Colorado* M
The University of Findlay *Ohio* M & W
University of Guelph *Ontario* M & W
University of Idaho *Idaho* M
The University of Iowa *Iowa* M
University of Lethbridge *Alberta* M & W
University of Maine *Maine* M & W
University of Maine at Farmington *Maine* M
University of Manitoba *Manitoba* M & W
University of Maryland, Baltimore County *Maryland* M
University of Massachusetts Amherst *Massachusetts* M
University of Massachusetts Boston *Massachusetts* M
University of Massachusetts Dartmouth *Massachusetts* M
University of Massachusetts Lowell *Massachusetts* M
University of Michigan *Michigan* M
University of Michigan-Dearborn *Michigan* M
University of Minnesota, Crookston *Minnesota* M
University of Minnesota, Duluth *Minnesota* M & W
University of Minnesota, Twin Cities Campus *Minnesota* M & W
University of Missouri-St. Louis *Missouri* M
The University of Montana-Missoula *Montana* M & W
University of Nebraska at Omaha *Nebraska* M
University of New Brunswick Fredericton *New Brunswick* M & W
University of New Brunswick Saint John *New Brunswick* M & W
University of New Hampshire *New Hampshire* M & W
University of North Dakota *North Dakota* M & W
University of North Texas *Texas* M
University of Notre Dame *Indiana* M
University of Oregon *Oregon* M
University of Ottawa *Ontario* M & W
University of Prince Edward Island *Prince Edward Island* M & W
University of Regina *Saskatchewan* M & W
University of Rhode Island *Rhode Island* M
University of Richmond *Virginia* M
University of Rochester *New York* M & W
University of St. Thomas *Minnesota* M & W
University of San Diego *California* M
University of Saskatchewan *Saskatchewan* M & W
The University of Scranton *Pennsylvania* M
University of Southern Indiana *Indiana* M
University of Southern Maine *Maine* M & W
The University of Toledo *Ohio* M & W
University of Toronto *Ontario* M & W
University of Utah *Utah* M
University of Vermont *Vermont* M & W
University of Virginia *Virginia* M & W
University of Waterloo *Ontario* M & W
The University of Western Ontario *Ontario* M & W
University of Windsor *Ontario* M & W
University of Wisconsin-Eau Claire *Wisconsin* M & W
University of Wisconsin-Madison *Wisconsin* M & W
University of Wisconsin-Platteville *Wisconsin* M & W
University of Wisconsin-River Falls *Wisconsin* M & W
University of Wisconsin-Stevens Point *Wisconsin* M & W
University of Wisconsin-Stout *Wisconsin* M & W
University of Wisconsin-Superior *Wisconsin* M & W
University of Wisconsin-Whitewater *Wisconsin* M & W
University of Wyoming *Wyoming* M & W
Utah State University *Utah* M
Utica College *New York* M & W
Vanderbilt University *Tennessee* M & W
Vanguard College *Alberta* M
Vermont Technical College *Vermont* M & W
Villanova University *Pennsylvania* M
Virginia Commonwealth University *Virginia* M
Virginia Military Institute *Virginia* M
Virginia Polytechnic Institute and State University *Virginia* M & W
Wagner College *New York* M
Walla Walla College *Washington* M
Washington College *Maryland* M
Washington & Jefferson College *Pennsylvania* M
Washington and Lee University *Virginia* M & W
Washington State University *Washington* M & W
Washington University in St. Louis *Missouri* M
Wayne State University *Michigan* M & W
Weber State University *Utah* M
Wentworth Institute of Technology *Massachusetts* M
Wesleyan University *Connecticut* M & W
West Chester University of Pennsylvania *Pennsylvania* M
Western Michigan University *Michigan* M
Western New England College *Massachusetts* M
Western State College of Colorado *Colorado* M
Wheaton College *Illinois* M
Whitman College *Washington* M
Wichita State University *Kansas* M & W
Wilfrid Laurier University *Ontario* M & W
William Paterson University of New Jersey *New Jersey* M
Williams College *Massachusetts* M & W
Winona State University *Minnesota* M
Wittenberg University *Ohio* M
Worcester State College *Massachusetts* M
Yale University *Connecticut* M & W
York College of Pennsylvania *Pennsylvania* M
York University *Ontario* M & W

Lacrosse

Adelphi University *New York* M & W
Albright College *Pennsylvania* M & W
Alfred University *New York* M & W
Allegheny College *Pennsylvania* M & W
Alvernia College *Pennsylvania* M & W
American International College *Massachusetts* M & W
American University *District of Columbia* W
Amherst College *Massachusetts* M & W
Anne Arundel Community College *Maryland* M
Arcadia University *Pennsylvania* W
Assumption College *Massachusetts* M & W
Augustana College *Illinois* M
Averett University *Virginia* W
Babson College *Massachusetts* M & W
Barnard College *New York* W
Bates College *Maine* M & W
Baylor University *Texas* M & W

M = Men; W = Women

Becker College *Massachusetts* M
Bellarmine University *Kentucky* M
Belmont Abbey College *North Carolina* M & W
Beloit College *Wisconsin* M & W
Bentley College *Massachusetts* M & W
Berry College *Georgia* M & W
Bethany College *West Virginia* M & W
Bishop's University *Quebec* M & W
Bloomsburg University of Pennsylvania *Pennsylvania* W
Boston College *Massachusetts* M & W
Boston University *Massachusetts* M & W
Bowdoin College *Maine* M & W
Brandeis University *Massachusetts* M & W
Briarcliffe College *New York* M
Bridgewater College *Virginia* W
Bridgewater State College *Massachusetts* M & W
Brigham Young University *Utah* M
Brock University *Ontario* M & W
Broome Community College *New York* M
Brown University *Rhode Island* M & W
Bryant University *Rhode Island* M & W
Bryn Athyn College of the New Church *Pennsylvania* M & W
Bryn Mawr College *Pennsylvania* W
Bucknell University *Pennsylvania* M & W
Buffalo State College, State University of New York *New York* M & W
Butler University *Indiana* M
Cabrini College *Pennsylvania* M & W
California State University, Chico *California* M & W
California State University, Sacramento *California* M & W
Calvin College *Michigan* M & W
Canisius College *New York* M & W
Carleton College *Minnesota* M & W
Carleton University *Ontario* M
Carnegie Mellon University *Pennsylvania* M & W
Castleton State College *Vermont* M & W
Catawba College *North Carolina* M
The Catholic University of America *District of Columbia* M & W
Cayuga County Community College *New York* M & W
Cazenovia College *New York* M & W
Cedar Crest College *Pennsylvania* W
Centenary College *New Jersey* M & W
Central Connecticut State University *Connecticut* M & W
Chestnut Hill College *Pennsylvania* W
Christopher Newport University *Virginia* M & W
The Citadel, The Military College of South Carolina *South Carolina* M & W
City College of the City University of New York *New York* M
Claremont McKenna College *California* M & W
Clark University *Massachusetts* M
Clarkson University *New York* M & W
Clemson University *South Carolina* M & W
Colby College *Maine* M & W
Colby-Sawyer College *New Hampshire* M & W
Colgate University *New York* M & W
College of the Holy Cross *Massachusetts* M & W
College Misericordia *Pennsylvania* M & W
College of Mount Saint Vincent *New York* M & W
The College of New Jersey *New Jersey* W
College of Notre Dame of Maryland *Maryland* W
College of Saint Benedict *Minnesota* W
The College of William and Mary *Virginia* W
The College of Wooster *Ohio* M & W
The Colorado College *Colorado* M & W
Columbia College *New York* M & W
Columbia University, The Fu Foundation School of Engineering and Applied Science *New York* M & W
Connecticut College *Connecticut* M & W
Cornell University *New York* M & W
Curry College *Massachusetts* M & W
Daniel Webster College *New Hampshire* M
Dartmouth College *New Hampshire* M & W
Davidson College *North Carolina* W
Dean College *Massachusetts* M & W
Denison University *Ohio* M & W
DeSales University *Pennsylvania* M
Dickinson College *Pennsylvania* M & W
Dominican College *New York* M
Dordt College *Iowa* M
Dowling College *New York* M
Drew University *New Jersey* M & W
Drexel University *Pennsylvania* M & W
Duke University *North Carolina* M & W
Duquesne University *Pennsylvania* W
Earlham College *Indiana* M & W
East Stroudsburg University of Pennsylvania *Pennsylvania* W
Eastern Connecticut State University *Connecticut* M & W
Eastern Nazarene College *Massachusetts* M
Eastern University *Pennsylvania* M & W
Elizabethtown College *Pennsylvania* M & W
Elmira College *New York* M & W
Elms College *Massachusetts* W
Elon University *North Carolina* M & W
Emerson College *Massachusetts* M & W
Emory University *Georgia* M & W
Endicott College *Massachusetts* M & W
Erie Community College *New York* W
Erie Community College, North Campus *New York* W
Erie Community College, South Campus *New York* W
The Evergreen State College *Washington* M & W
Fairfield University *Connecticut* M & W
Fairleigh Dickinson University, College at Florham *New Jersey* M & W
Farmingdale State University of New York *New York* M
Ferrum College *Virginia* W
Finger Lakes Community College *New York* M & W
Flagler College *Florida* M
Fordham University *New York* M & W
Fort Lewis College *Colorado* M
Framingham State College *Massachusetts* W
Franklin and Marshall College *Pennsylvania* M & W
Franklin Pierce College *New Hampshire* M & W
Frostburg State University *Maryland* W
Furman University *South Carolina* M
Gannon University *Pennsylvania* W
George Mason University *Virginia* W
Georgetown University *District of Columbia* M & W
Georgia Institute of Technology *Georgia* M & W
Georgia Southern University *Georgia* M
Gettysburg College *Pennsylvania* M & W
Gordon College *Massachusetts* M & W
Goucher College *Maryland* M & W
Green Mountain College *Vermont* M
Greensboro College *North Carolina* M & W
Guilford College *North Carolina* M & W
Gustavus Adolphus College *Minnesota* M
Gwynedd-Mercy College *Pennsylvania* W
Hamilton College *New York* M & W
Hampden-Sydney College *Virginia* M
Harding University *Arkansas* M
Harford Community College *Maryland* M & W
Hartwick College *New York* M & W
Harvard University *Massachusetts* M & W
Harvey Mudd College *California* W
Haverford College *Pennsylvania* M & W
Herkimer County Community College *New York* M & W
Hillsdale College *Michigan* M
Hobart and William Smith Colleges *New York* M & W
Hofstra University *New York* M & W
Hollins University *Virginia* W
Holy Cross College *Indiana* M
Hood College *Maryland* M & W
Hope College *Michigan* M
Howard Community College *Maryland* M
Howard University *District of Columbia* W
Hudson Valley Community College *New York* M
Humboldt State University *California* M & W
Illinois Wesleyan University *Illinois* M
Immaculata University *Pennsylvania* W
Indiana University of Pennsylvania *Pennsylvania* W
Iona College *New York* W
Ithaca College *New York* M & W
James Madison University *Virginia* W
Jefferson Community College *New York* M & W
John Carroll University *Ohio* M & W
The Johns Hopkins University *Maryland* M & W
Johnson State College *Vermont* M
Juniata College *Pennsylvania* M
Kean University *New Jersey* M & W
Keene State College *New Hampshire* M & W
Kenyon College *Ohio* M & W
Kettering University *Michigan* M
Keuka College *New York* M
King's College *Pennsylvania* M & W
Kutztown University of Pennsylvania *Pennsylvania* M & W
La Salle University *Pennsylvania* W
Lafayette College *Pennsylvania* M & W
Lake Forest College *Illinois* M & W
Lancaster Bible College *Pennsylvania* W
Lasell College *Massachusetts* M & W
Le Moyne College *New York* M & W
Lees-McRae College *North Carolina* M & W
Lehigh University *Pennsylvania* M & W
Lewis & Clark College *Oregon* M & W
Liberty University *Virginia* M
Limestone College *South Carolina* M & W
Lindenwood University *Missouri* M & W
Linfield College *Oregon* W
Lock Haven University of Pennsylvania *Pennsylvania* W
Long Island University, Brooklyn Campus *New York* W
Long Island University, C.W. Post Campus *New York* M & W
Longwood University *Virginia* W
Loyola College in Maryland *Maryland* M & W
Loyola Marymount University *California* M & W
Lycoming College *Pennsylvania* M & W
Lynchburg College *Virginia* M & W
Maine Maritime Academy *Maine* M
Manhattan College *New York* M & W
Manhattanville College *New York* M & W
Marietta College *Ohio* M
Marist College *New York* M & W
Marquette University *Wisconsin* M
Mars Hill College *North Carolina* M
Marshall University *West Virginia* M
Marymount University *Virginia* M & W
Massachusetts Institute of Technology *Massachusetts* M & W
Massachusetts Maritime Academy *Massachusetts* M
McDaniel College *Maryland* M & W
McGill University *Quebec* M & W
McMaster University *Ontario* M & W
Medaille College *New York* M & W
Mercyhurst College *Pennsylvania* M & W
Merrimack College *Massachusetts* M & W
Messiah College *Pennsylvania* M & W
Methodist College *North Carolina* W
Miami University *Ohio* M
Michigan State University *Michigan* M
Middlebury College *Vermont* M & W
Millersville University of Pennsylvania *Pennsylvania* W
Missouri Baptist University *Missouri* W
Missouri State University *Missouri* M
Mitchell College *Connecticut* M
Mohawk Valley Community College *New York* M
Molloy College *New York* M & W
Monmouth University *New Jersey* W
Monroe Community College *New York* M
Montclair State University *New Jersey* W
Moravian College *Pennsylvania* M & W
Mount Holyoke College *Massachusetts* W
Mount Ida College *Massachusetts* M
Mount St. Mary's University *Maryland* M & W
Muhlenberg College *Pennsylvania* M & W
Nassau Community College *New York* M
Nazareth College of Rochester *New York* M & W
Neumann College *Pennsylvania* M & W
New England College *New Hampshire* M & W
New York Institute of Technology *New York* M
New York University *New York* M & W
Newman University *Kansas* M
Niagara University *New York* M & W
Nichols College *Massachusetts* M & W

M = Men; W = Women

North Carolina State University *North Carolina* M & W
Northern Michigan University *Michigan* M
Northwestern University *Illinois* W
Norwich University *Vermont* M
Notre Dame de Namur University *California* M
Oberlin College *Ohio* M & W
Occidental College *California* M & W
The Ohio State University *Ohio* M & W
Ohio University *Ohio* M & W
Ohio Wesleyan University *Ohio* M & W
Old Dominion University *Virginia* M & W
Onondaga Community College *New York* M
Pace University *New York* M
Pacific Lutheran University *Washington* M & W
Pacific University *Oregon* W
The Pennsylvania State University at Erie, The Behrend College *Pennsylvania* M
The Pennsylvania State University University Park Campus *Pennsylvania* M & W
Pepperdine University *California* M
Pfeiffer University *North Carolina* M & W
Philadelphia University *Pennsylvania* W
Pine Manor College *Massachusetts* W
Plymouth State University *New Hampshire* M & W
Presbyterian College *South Carolina* M & W
Princeton University *New Jersey* M & W
Providence College *Rhode Island* M
Queens University of Charlotte *North Carolina* M & W
Queen's University at Kingston *Ontario* M & W
Quinnipiac University *Connecticut* M & W
Randolph-Macon College *Virginia* M & W
Regis College *Massachusetts* W
Regis University *Colorado* W
Rensselaer Polytechnic Institute *New York* M & W
Rhodes College *Tennessee* M & W
Rice University *Texas* M & W
The Richard Stockton College of New Jersey *New Jersey* M
Roanoke College *Virginia* M & W
Robert Morris University *Pennsylvania* M & W
Rochester Institute of Technology *New York* M & W
Roger Williams University *Rhode Island* M & W
Rowan University *New Jersey* W
Rutgers, The State University of New Jersey, New Brunswick/Piscataway *New Jersey* M & W
Sacred Heart University *Connecticut* M & W
Saginaw Valley State University *Michigan* W
St. Andrews Presbyterian College *North Carolina* M & W
Saint Anselm College *New Hampshire* M & W
St. Bonaventure University *New York* M & W
Saint Francis University *Pennsylvania* W
St. Francis Xavier University *Nova Scotia* M
St. John Fisher College *New York* M & W
St. John's University *New York* M
Saint John's University *Minnesota* M
Saint Joseph College *Connecticut* W
Saint Joseph's University *Pennsylvania* M & W
St. Lawrence University *New York* M & W
Saint Leo University *Florida* M
Saint Louis University *Missouri* M & W
Saint Mary's College of California *California* M & W
St. Mary's College of Maryland *Maryland* M & W
Saint Michael's College *Vermont* M & W
St. Thomas Aquinas College *New York* W
Saint Vincent College *Pennsylvania* M & W
Salisbury University *Maryland* M & W
Salve Regina University *Rhode Island* M & W
Sam Houston State University *Texas* M
Santa Clara University *California* M & W
Scripps College *California* W
Seton Hill University *Pennsylvania* M & W
Sewanee: The University of the South *Tennessee* M & W
Shenandoah University *Virginia* M & W
Shippensburg University of Pennsylvania *Pennsylvania* W
Siena College *New York* M & W
Skidmore College *New York* M & W
Smith College *Massachusetts* W
Southern Methodist University *Texas* M
Southern New Hampshire University *New Hampshire* M & W
Southern Virginia University *Virginia* M & W
Springfield College *Massachusetts* M & W
Stanford University *California* M & W
State University of New York at Binghamton *New York* M & W
State University of New York College of Agriculture and Technology at Cobleskill *New York* M
State University of New York College of Agriculture and Technology at Morrisville *New York* M & W
State University of New York College at Brockport *New York* M & W
State University of New York College at Cortland *New York* M & W
State University of New York College at Geneseo *New York* M & W
State University of New York College at Oneonta *New York* M & W
State University of New York College at Potsdam *New York* M & W
State University of New York College of Technology at Alfred *New York* M
State University of New York College of Technology at Canton *New York* M & W
State University of New York College of Technology at Delhi *New York* M
State University of New York, Fredonia *New York* W
State University of New York Institute of Technology *New York* M
State University of New York Maritime College *New York* M
State University of New York at New Paltz *New York* M
State University of New York at Oswego *New York* M & W
State University of New York at Plattsburgh *New York* M
Stevens Institute of Technology *New Jersey* M & W
Stonehill College *Massachusetts* M & W
Stony Brook University, State University of New York *New York* M & W
Suffolk County Community College *New York* M
Susquehanna University *Pennsylvania* M & W
Swarthmore College *Pennsylvania* M & W
Sweet Briar College *Virginia* W
Syracuse University *New York* M & W
Taylor University *Indiana* M & W
Temple University *Pennsylvania* W
Texas A&M University at Galveston *Texas* M
Texas State University-San Marcos *Texas* M & W
Thomas College *Maine* M & W
Towson University *Maryland* M & W
Trinity College *Connecticut* M & W
Trinity University *Texas* M & W
Trinity (Washington) University *District of Columbia* W
Truman State University *Missouri* M & W
Tufts University *Massachusetts* M & W
Tulane University *Louisiana* M & W
Union College *New York* M & W
United States Air Force Academy *Colorado* M
United States Coast Guard Academy *Connecticut* M & W
United States Merchant Marine Academy *New York* M
United States Military Academy *New York* M & W
United States Naval Academy *Maryland* M & W
University at Albany, State University of New York *New York* M & W
The University of Arizona *Arizona* M & W
University of California, Berkeley *California* W
University of California, Davis *California* M & W
University of California, Irvine *California* M & W
University of California, Santa Barbara *California* M & W
University of California, Santa Cruz *California* M & W
University of Colorado at Boulder *Colorado* M & W
University of Connecticut *Connecticut* W
University of Dallas *Texas* W
University of Delaware *Delaware* M & W
University of Denver *Colorado* M & W
University of Guelph *Ontario* M & W
University of Hartford *Connecticut* M
The University of Iowa *Iowa* M & W
University of Maine at Farmington *Maine* M
University of Maine at Machias *Maine* M & W
University of Mary Washington *Virginia* M & W
University of Maryland, Baltimore County *Maryland* M & W
University of Maryland, College Park *Maryland* M & W
University of Massachusetts Amherst *Massachusetts* M & W
University of Massachusetts Boston *Massachusetts* M
University of Massachusetts Dartmouth *Massachusetts* M & W
University of Minnesota, Duluth *Minnesota* M & W
University of Mississippi *Mississippi* M
The University of Montana-Missoula *Montana* M & W
University of New England *Maine* M & W
University of New Hampshire *New Hampshire* M & W
University of New Haven *Connecticut* W
The University of North Carolina at Chapel Hill *North Carolina* M & W
University of North Texas *Texas* M & W
University of Northern Colorado *Colorado* M
University of Notre Dame *Indiana* M & W
University of Oregon *Oregon* M & W
University of Pennsylvania *Pennsylvania* M & W
University of Puget Sound *Washington* W
University of Redlands *California* W
University of Rhode Island *Rhode Island* M & W
University of Richmond *Virginia* M & W
University of Rochester *New York* M & W
University of St. Thomas *Minnesota* M & W
University of San Diego *California* M & W
The University of Scranton *Pennsylvania* M & W
University of Southern Maine *Maine* M & W
The University of Toledo *Ohio* M & W
University of Vermont *Vermont* M & W
University of Virginia *Virginia* M & W
The University of Western Ontario *Ontario* W
University of Wisconsin-Platteville *Wisconsin* M & W
University of Wisconsin-Whitewater *Wisconsin* M
Ursinus College *Pennsylvania* M & W
Utica College *New York* M & W
Valley Forge Military College *Pennsylvania* M
Vanderbilt University *Tennessee* M & W
Vassar College *New York* M & W
Villa Julie College *Maryland* M & W
Villanova University *Pennsylvania* M & W
Virginia Commonwealth University *Virginia* M & W
Virginia Military Institute *Virginia* M
Virginia Polytechnic Institute and State University *Virginia* M & W
Virginia Wesleyan College *Virginia* M & W
Wabash College *Indiana* M
Wagner College *New York* M & W
Washington College *Maryland* M & W
Washington & Jefferson College *Pennsylvania* M
Washington and Lee University *Virginia* M & W
Washington State University *Washington* M & W
Washington University in St. Louis *Missouri* M & W
Weber State University *Utah* M & W
Wellesley College *Massachusetts* W
Wells College *New York* W
Wentworth Institute of Technology *Massachusetts* M
Wesley College *Delaware* M & W
Wesleyan University *Connecticut* M & W
West Chester University of Pennsylvania *Pennsylvania* W
West Virginia Wesleyan College *West Virginia* M & W
Western Connecticut State University *Connecticut* W
Western New England College *Massachusetts* M & W
Western State College of Colorado *Colorado* M & W
Westmont College *California* W
Wheaton College *Massachusetts* W
Wheaton College *Illinois* M & W
Wheeling Jesuit University *West Virginia* M
Whitman College *Washington* M & W

M = Men; W = Women

Whittier College *California* M & W
Widener University *Pennsylvania* M & W
Wilkes University *Pennsylvania* W
Willamette University *Oregon* M
Williams College *Massachusetts* M & W
The Williamson Free School of Mechanical Trades *Pennsylvania* M
Wingate University *North Carolina* M
Winthrop University *South Carolina* M & W
Wittenberg University *Ohio* M & W
Worcester State College *Massachusetts* W
Xavier University *Ohio* M & W
Yale University *Connecticut* M & W
York College of Pennsylvania *Pennsylvania* M & W
York University *Ontario* W

Racquetball

Brigham Young University *Utah* M & W
Bryant University *Rhode Island* M & W
California State University, Sacramento *California* M & W
Columbia College *New York* M & W
Duke University *North Carolina* M & W
Emory University *Georgia* M & W
Miami University *Ohio* M & W
Michigan Technological University *Michigan* M & W
Missouri State University *Missouri* M & W
Nichols College *Massachusetts* M & W
North Carolina State University *North Carolina* M & W
Providence College *Rhode Island* M & W
Rensselaer Polytechnic Institute *New York* M & W
Simon's Rock College of Bard *Massachusetts* M & W
Stanford University *California* M & W
State University of New York at Binghamton *New York* M & W
State University of New York College at Cortland *New York* M & W
State University of New York College at Geneseo *New York* M & W
Syracuse University *New York* M & W
United States Military Academy *New York* M & W
University of California, Irvine *California* M & W
University of Colorado at Boulder *Colorado* M & W
University of Hartford *Connecticut* M & W
University of Memphis *Tennessee* M & W
University of Miami *Florida* M & W
The University of North Carolina at Chapel Hill *North Carolina* M & W
University of Oregon *Oregon* M & W
University of Utah *Utah* M & W
Virginia Military Institute *Virginia* M & W
Weber State University *Utah* M & W
Wichita State University *Kansas* M & W

Riflery

Austin Peay State University *Tennessee* W
Birmingham-Southern College *Alabama* W
The Citadel, The Military College of South Carolina *South Carolina* M & W
Clemson University *South Carolina* M & W
College of Saint Benedict *Minnesota* W
Columbia College *New York* M & W
Columbia University, The Fu Foundation School of Engineering and Applied Science *New York* M & W
Denison University *Ohio* M & W
Georgia Military College *Georgia* M & W
Hampden-Sydney College *Virginia* M
Hillsdale College *Michigan* M & W
Jacksonville State University *Alabama* M & W
Kutztown University of Pennsylvania *Pennsylvania* M & W
Lassen Community College District *California* M & W
Lindenwood University *Missouri* M & W
Massachusetts Institute of Technology *Massachusetts* M & W
Massachusetts Maritime Academy *Massachusetts* M & W
McNeese State University *Louisiana* M & W
Mercer University *Georgia* M & W
Michigan Technological University *Michigan* M & W
Missouri State University *Missouri* M & W
Morehead State University *Kentucky* M & W
Murray State University *Kentucky* M & W
New Mexico Military Institute *New Mexico* M & W
North Carolina State University *North Carolina* M & W
North Dakota State University *North Dakota* M & W
North Georgia College & State University *Georgia* M & W
Northwest College *Wyoming* M & W
Norwich University *Vermont* M & W
The Ohio State University *Ohio* M & W
Presbyterian College *South Carolina* M & W
Rensselaer Polytechnic Institute *New York* M & W
Rose-Hulman Institute of Technology *Indiana* M & W
Royal Military College of Canada *Ontario* M & W
Saint John's University *Minnesota* M
Sam Houston State University *Texas* M & W
Seattle University *Washington* M & W
State University of New York Maritime College *New York* M & W
Syracuse University *New York* M & W
Tennessee Technological University *Tennessee* M & W
Texas A&M University-Kingsville *Texas* M & W
Texas Christian University *Texas* W
Trinity College *Connecticut* M & W
Trinity University *Texas* M & W
Tuskegee University *Alabama* M & W
United States Air Force Academy *Colorado* M & W
United States Coast Guard Academy *Connecticut* M & W
United States Military Academy *New York* M & W
United States Naval Academy *Maryland* M & W
The University of Akron *Ohio* M & W
The University of Alabama at Birmingham *Alabama* M & W
University of Alaska Fairbanks *Alaska* M & W
University of Alaska Southeast *Alaska* M & W
University of Idaho *Idaho* M & W
University of Kentucky *Kentucky* M & W
University of Memphis *Tennessee* M & W
University of Mississippi *Mississippi* W
University of Missouri-Kansas City *Missouri* M & W
University of Nebraska-Lincoln *Nebraska* W
University of Nevada, Reno *Nevada* M & W
University of San Francisco *California* M & W
University of the Sciences in Philadelphia *Pennsylvania* M & W
The University of Tennessee at Martin *Tennessee* M & W
The University of Texas at El Paso *Texas* M & W
University of Wisconsin-Oshkosh *Wisconsin* M & W
University of Wyoming *Wyoming* M & W
Valley Forge Military College *Pennsylvania* M
Virginia Military Institute *Virginia* M & W
Wentworth Institute of Technology *Massachusetts* M & W
West Virginia University *West Virginia* M & W
Western Kentucky University *Kentucky* M & W
Wofford College *South Carolina* M & W
Xavier University *Ohio* M & W

Rock Climbing

California State University, Chico *California* M & W
Fort Lewis College *Colorado* M & W
Landmark College *Vermont* M & W
Western New Mexico University *New Mexico* M & W

Rugby

Acadia University *Nova Scotia* M & W
Albright College *Pennsylvania* M & W
Allegheny College *Pennsylvania* M & W
Amherst College *Massachusetts* M & W
Angelo State University *Texas* M
Babson College *Massachusetts* M & W
Ball State University *Indiana* M & W
Barnard College *New York* W
Bates College *Maine* M & W
Baylor University *Texas* M & W
Bethany College *West Virginia* M
Bishop's University *Quebec* M & W
Boston College *Massachusetts* M & W
Boston University *Massachusetts* M & W
Bowdoin College *Maine* M & W
Brandeis University *Massachusetts* M & W
Brigham Young University *Utah* M
Brock University *Ontario* M & W
Brown University *Rhode Island* M & W
Bryant University *Rhode Island* M & W
Bryn Mawr College *Pennsylvania* W
Bucknell University *Pennsylvania* M & W
Buffalo State College, State University of New York *New York* M
Butler University *Indiana* M
California Institute of Technology *California* M
California Maritime Academy *California* M
California State University, Chico *California* M & W
California State University, Fullerton *California* M
California State University, Long Beach *California* M
California State University, Sacramento *California* M
Canisius College *New York* M
Carleton College *Minnesota* M & W
Carleton University *Ontario* M & W
Carnegie Mellon University *Pennsylvania* M & W
Castleton State College *Vermont* M & W
Central Missouri State University *Missouri* M & W
Central Washington University *Washington* M & W
Christopher Newport University *Virginia* M
The Citadel, The Military College of South Carolina *South Carolina* M & W
Claremont McKenna College *California* M & W
Clemson University *South Carolina* M & W
Colby College *Maine* M & W
Colby-Sawyer College *New Hampshire* M & W
Colgate University *New York* M & W
College of Saint Benedict *Minnesota* W
The College of Wooster *Ohio* M & W
The Colorado College *Colorado* M & W
Columbia College *New York* M & W
Columbia University, The Fu Foundation School of Engineering and Applied Science *New York* M & W
Concordia University *Quebec* M & W
Connecticut College *Connecticut* W
Coppin State University *Maryland* M
Daemen College *New York* M
Dartmouth College *New Hampshire* M & W
Davidson College *North Carolina* M
Denison University *Ohio* M & W
DePauw University *Indiana* M
Drew University *New Jersey* M & W
Duke University *North Carolina* M & W
Earlham College *Indiana* M & W
Eastern Illinois University *Illinois* M & W
Elon University *North Carolina* M
Emory University *Georgia* M
The Evergreen State College *Washington* W
Florida State University *Florida* M & W
Fordham University *New York* M & W
Franklin and Marshall College *Pennsylvania* M & W
Furman University *South Carolina* M & W
Georgetown University *District of Columbia* M & W
Georgia Institute of Technology *Georgia* M
Georgia Southern University *Georgia* M & W
Grand Valley State University *Michigan* M & W
Gustavus Adolphus College *Minnesota* M & W
Hamilton College *New York* M & W
Hampden-Sydney College *Virginia* M
Hartwick College *New York* M
Hendrix College *Arkansas* M
Hiram College *Ohio* M & W
Hobart and William Smith Colleges *New York* M & W
Humboldt State University *California* M & W
Iona College *New York* M & W
John Carroll University *Ohio* M & W
Johnson State College *Vermont* M
Juniata College *Pennsylvania* M & W
Keene State College *New Hampshire* M & W
Kenyon College *Ohio* M & W
Kutztown University of Pennsylvania *Pennsylvania* M & W
Lafayette College *Pennsylvania* M & W
Lake Forest College *Illinois* M & W
Lakehead University *Ontario* M & W
Lehigh University *Pennsylvania* M
Longwood University *Virginia* M & W

M = Men; W = Women

Loras College *Iowa* M
Loyola Marymount University *California* M
Loyola University New Orleans *Louisiana* M
Macalester College *Minnesota* M & W
Manhattan College *New York* M
Marist College *New York* M & W
Marquette University *Wisconsin* M & W
Marshall University *West Virginia* M & W
McGill University *Quebec* M & W
McMaster University *Ontario* M & W
Miami University *Ohio* M
Michigan State University *Michigan* M & W
Montana Tech of The University of Montana *Montana* M & W
Mount Allison University *New Brunswick* M & W
Mount St. Mary's University *Maryland* M & W
New Mexico Institute of Mining and Technology *New Mexico* M & W
Nichols College *Massachusetts* M & W
North Carolina State University *North Carolina* M & W
North Dakota State University *North Dakota* M & W
Northern Michigan University *Michigan* M & W
Norwich University *Vermont* M & W
Nova Scotia Agricultural College *Nova Scotia* M & W
Oberlin College *Ohio* M & W
Occidental College *California* M & W
Ohio University *Ohio* M & W
Ohio Wesleyan University *Ohio* M & W
Old Dominion University *Virginia* M & W
Pacific Lutheran University *Washington* M
The Pennsylvania State University University Park Campus *Pennsylvania* M & W
Pepperdine University *California* M
Providence College *Rhode Island* M & W
Queen's University at Kingston *Ontario* M & W
Rensselaer Polytechnic Institute *New York* M & W
Rhodes College *Tennessee* M
Rice University *Texas* M & W
Ripon College *Wisconsin* M
Robert Morris University *Pennsylvania* M
Rochester Institute of Technology *New York* M & W
Roger Williams University *Rhode Island* M
Royal Military College of Canada *Ontario* M & W
St. Andrews Presbyterian College *North Carolina* M & W
St. Bonaventure University *New York* M & W
St. Cloud State University *Minnesota* M & W
St. Francis Xavier University *Nova Scotia* M & W
Saint John's University *Minnesota* M
Saint Louis University *Missouri* M
Saint Mary's College of California *California* M & W
St. Mary's College of Maryland *Maryland* M & W
Saint Mary's University *Nova Scotia* W
St. Mary's University of San Antonio *Texas* M
Saint Michael's College *Vermont* M & W
St. Thomas University *New Brunswick* M & W
Salve Regina University *Rhode Island* M
Sam Houston State University *Texas* M
San Jose State University *California* M
Santa Clara University *California* M & W
Santa Rosa Junior College *California* M
Scripps College *California* W
Seton Hall University *New Jersey* M
Sewanee: The University of the South *Tennessee* M
Siena College *New York* M & W
South Dakota State University *South Dakota* M & W
Southern Methodist University *Texas* M
Southern Vermont College *Vermont* M & W
Southwest Virginia Community College *Virginia* M
Stanford University *California* M & W
State University of New York at Binghamton *New York* M & W
State University of New York College at Cortland *New York* M & W
State University of New York College at Geneseo *New York* M & W
State University of New York College at Oneonta *New York* M & W
State University of New York College at Potsdam *New York* W
State University of New York at New Paltz *New York* M & W
Stonehill College *Massachusetts* M & W
Susquehanna University *Pennsylvania* M & W
Swarthmore College *Pennsylvania* M & W
Syracuse University *New York* M & W
Tabor College *Kansas* M
Texas State University-San Marcos *Texas* M & W
Thomas Jefferson University *Pennsylvania* M
Trent University *Ontario* M & W
Trinity College *Connecticut* M & W
Trinity Western University *British Columbia* M
Truman State University *Missouri* M & W
Tulane University *Louisiana* M
Union College *New York* M & W
United States Air Force Academy *Colorado* W
United States Coast Guard Academy *Connecticut* M & W
United States Merchant Marine Academy *New York* M
United States Military Academy *New York* M
United States Naval Academy *Maryland* M & W
Universite du Quebec, Ecole de technologie superieure *Quebec* M
University at Albany, State University of New York *New York* M & W
University of Alberta *Alberta* W
The University of Arizona *Arizona* M & W
The University of British Columbia *British Columbia* M & W
University of California, Berkeley *California* M
University of California, Irvine *California* M
University of California, Santa Barbara *California* M
University of California, Santa Cruz *California* M & W
University of Cincinnati *Ohio* M
University of Colorado at Boulder *Colorado* M & W
University of Delaware *Delaware* W
University of Guelph *Ontario* M & W
University of Hartford *Connecticut* M & W
University of Hawaii at Manoa *Hawaii* M
University of Idaho *Idaho* M & W
The University of Iowa *Iowa* M & W
University of Kansas *Kansas* M & W
University of King's College *Nova Scotia* M & W
University of Mary Washington *Virginia* M & W
University of Maryland, Baltimore County *Maryland* M & W
University of Minnesota, Duluth *Minnesota* M & W
University of Mississippi *Mississippi* M
The University of Montana-Missoula *Montana* M & W
University of New Brunswick Saint John *New Brunswick* M & W
University of New Hampshire *New Hampshire* M & W
The University of North Carolina at Chapel Hill *North Carolina* M & W
University of North Texas *Texas* M
University of Northern Colorado *Colorado* M & W
University of Oregon *Oregon* M & W
University of Ottawa *Ontario* W
University of Portland *Oregon* M
University of Prince Edward Island *Prince Edward Island* M & W
University of Puget Sound *Washington* M & W
University of Rhode Island *Rhode Island* M & W
University of Richmond *Virginia* M & W
University of Rochester *New York* M & W
University of San Diego *California* M
The University of Scranton *Pennsylvania* M & W
University of Southern Indiana *Indiana* M
University of Toronto *Ontario* M
University of Utah *Utah* M
University of Vermont *Vermont* M & W
University of Victoria *British Columbia* M & W
University of Waterloo *Ontario* M & W
The University of Western Ontario *Ontario* M & W
University of Windsor *Ontario* M & W
University of Wisconsin-Platteville *Wisconsin* M & W
University of Wisconsin-River Falls *Wisconsin* M & W
University of Wisconsin-Whitewater *Wisconsin* M & W
University of Wyoming *Wyoming* M & W
Ursinus College *Pennsylvania* M & W
Utah State University *Utah* M & W
Vanderbilt University *Tennessee* M & W
Vassar College *New York* M & W
Villanova University *Pennsylvania* M
Virginia Commonwealth University *Virginia* M & W
Virginia Military Institute *Virginia* M & W
Virginia Polytechnic Institute and State University *Virginia* M & W
Wabash College *Indiana* M
Washington College *Maryland* M & W
Washington and Lee University *Virginia* M
Washington State University *Washington* M & W
Washington University in St. Louis *Missouri* M & W
Wayne State College *Nebraska* M & W
Weber State University *Utah* M & W
Wellesley College *Massachusetts* W
Wentworth Institute of Technology *Massachusetts* M
Wesleyan University *Connecticut* M & W
West Chester University of Pennsylvania *Pennsylvania* M & W
Western Oregon University *Oregon* M & W
Western State College of Colorado *Colorado* M & W
Westmont College *California* M
Whitman College *Washington* M & W
Wichita State University *Kansas* M
Wilfrid Laurier University *Ontario* M
Williams College *Massachusetts* M & W
Winona State University *Minnesota* M & W
Winthrop University *South Carolina* M
Wittenberg University *Ohio* M & W
Xavier University *Ohio* M & W
York University *Ontario* M & W

Sailing

Amherst College *Massachusetts* M & W
Ball State University *Indiana* M & W
Barnard College *New York* W
Bates College *Maine* M & W
Baylor University *Texas* M & W
Boston College *Massachusetts* M & W
Boston University *Massachusetts* M & W
Bowdoin College *Maine* M & W
Brandeis University *Massachusetts* M & W
Brown University *Rhode Island* M & W
California Maritime Academy *California* M & W
California State University, Long Beach *California* M & W
Carleton College *Minnesota* M & W
Christopher Newport University *Virginia* M & W
The Citadel, The Military College of South Carolina *South Carolina* M & W
Clemson University *South Carolina* M & W
Colby College *Maine* M & W
Colgate University *New York* M & W
College of Charleston *South Carolina* M & W
Connecticut College *Connecticut* M & W
Dartmouth College *New Hampshire* M & W
Davidson College *North Carolina* M & W
Denison University *Ohio* M & W
Duke University *North Carolina* M & W
Eckerd College *Florida* M & W
Emory University *Georgia* M & W
Fordham University *New York* M & W
Georgetown University *District of Columbia* M & W
Grand Valley State University *Michigan* M & W
Hamilton College *New York* M & W
Hampton University *Virginia* M & W
Harvard University *Massachusetts* M & W
Hiram College *Ohio* M & W
Hobart and William Smith Colleges *New York* M & W
Huntingdon College *Alabama* M & W
John Carroll University *Ohio* M & W
Johnson & Wales University *Rhode Island* M & W
Lake Forest College *Illinois* M & W
Maine Maritime Academy *Maine* M & W
Massachusetts Institute of Technology *Massachusetts* M & W
Massachusetts Maritime Academy *Massachusetts* M & W
McGill University *Quebec* M & W
Miami University *Ohio* M & W
Michigan State University *Michigan* M & W
Mitchell College *Connecticut* M & W

M = Men; W = Women

North Carolina State University *North Carolina* M & W
Norwich University *Vermont* M & W
Ohio Wesleyan University *Ohio* M & W
Old Dominion University *Virginia* M & W
Pepperdine University *California* M & W
Providence College *Rhode Island* M & W
Queen's University at Kingston *Ontario* M & W
Reed College *Oregon* M & W
Rensselaer Polytechnic Institute *New York* M & W
Rice University *Texas* M & W
Roger Williams University *Rhode Island* M & W
Rollins College *Florida* M & W
Saint Mary's College *Indiana* W
St. Mary's College of Maryland *Maryland* M & W
Salve Regina University *Rhode Island* M & W
San Jose State University *California* M & W
Savannah College of Art and Design *Georgia* M & W
Simmons College *Massachusetts* W
Southern Methodist University *Texas* M & W
Stanford University *California* M & W
State University of New York College at Geneseo *New York* M & W
State University of New York Maritime College *New York* M & W
Suffolk County Community College *New York* M & W
Syracuse University *New York* M & W
Texas A&M University at Galveston *Texas* M & W
Trinity College *Connecticut* M & W
Tufts University *Massachusetts* M & W
Tulane University *Louisiana* M & W
United States Coast Guard Academy *Connecticut* M & W
United States Merchant Marine Academy *New York* M & W
United States Military Academy *New York* M & W
United States Naval Academy *Maryland* M & W
University of California, Irvine *California* M & W
University of California, Santa Barbara *California* M & W
University of California, Santa Cruz *California* M & W
University of Delaware *Delaware* M & W
University of Hawaii at Manoa *Hawaii* M & W
The University of Iowa *Iowa* M & W
University of Maryland, Baltimore County *Maryland* M & W
University of New Hampshire *New Hampshire* M & W
The University of North Carolina at Chapel Hill *North Carolina* M & W
University of North Texas *Texas* M & W
University of Oregon *Oregon* M & W
University of Rhode Island *Rhode Island* M & W
University of Southern Maine *Maine* M & W
University of Vermont *Vermont* M & W
University of Wisconsin-Madison *Wisconsin* M & W
Vanderbilt University *Tennessee* M & W
Villanova University *Pennsylvania* M & W
Wabash College *Indiana* M
Washington College *Maryland* M & W
Washington University in St. Louis *Missouri* M & W
Webb Institute *New York* M & W
Wellesley College *Massachusetts* W
Wesleyan University *Connecticut* M & W
Williams College *Massachusetts* M & W

Skiing (Cross-Country)

Adirondack Community College *New York* M & W
Albertson College of Idaho *Idaho* M & W
Alfred University *New York* M & W
Bates College *Maine* M & W
Bowdoin College *Maine* M & W
Buffalo State College, State University of New York *New York* M & W
Carleton College *Minnesota* M & W
Carleton University *Ontario* M & W
Clarkson University *New York* M & W
Colby College *Maine* M & W
Colby-Sawyer College *New Hampshire* M & W
College of Saint Benedict *Minnesota* W
Columbia College *New York* M & W
Columbia University, The Fu Foundation School of Engineering and Applied Science *New York* M & W
Concordia College *Minnesota* M & W
Connecticut College *Connecticut* M & W
Dartmouth College *New Hampshire* M & W
Duke University *North Carolina* M & W
Eastern Oregon University *Oregon* M & W
Finlandia University *Michigan* M & W
Fort Lewis College *Colorado* M & W
Gonzaga University *Washington* M & W
Gustavus Adolphus College *Minnesota* M & W
Harvard University *Massachusetts* M & W
Lake Tahoe Community College *California* M & W
Lakehead University *Ontario* M & W
Laurentian University *Ontario* M & W
Macalester College *Minnesota* M & W
Massachusetts Institute of Technology *Massachusetts* M & W
McGill University *Quebec* M & W
Michigan State University *Michigan* M & W
Michigan Technological University *Michigan* M & W
Middlebury College *Vermont* M & W
Montana State University *Montana* M & W
Northern Michigan University *Michigan* M & W
Norwich University *Vermont* M & W
Providence College *Rhode Island* M & W
Queen's University at Kingston *Ontario* M & W
Rensselaer Polytechnic Institute *New York* M & W
St. Cloud State University *Minnesota* M & W
Saint John's University *Minnesota* M
St. Lawrence University *New York* M & W
Saint Michael's College *Vermont* M & W
St. Olaf College *Minnesota* M & W
Sierra College *California* M & W
Stanford University *California* M & W
Trent University *Ontario* M & W
United States Air Force Academy *Colorado* M & W
United States Military Academy *New York* M & W
University of Alaska Anchorage *Alaska* M & W
University of Alaska Fairbanks *Alaska* M & W
The University of British Columbia *British Columbia* M & W
University of Colorado at Boulder *Colorado* M & W
University of Denver *Colorado* M & W
University of Guelph *Ontario* M & W
University of Idaho *Idaho* M & W
University of Maine at Fort Kent *Maine* M & W
University of Nevada, Reno *Nevada* M & W
University of New Hampshire *New Hampshire* M & W
University of New Mexico *New Mexico* M & W
University of Northern British Columbia *British Columbia* M & W
University of Toronto *Ontario* M & W
University of Utah *Utah* M & W
University of Vermont *Vermont* M & W
University of Waterloo *Ontario* M & W
The University of Western Ontario *Ontario* M & W
University of Wisconsin-Green Bay *Wisconsin* M & W
Washington and Lee University *Virginia* M & W
Washington State University *Washington* M & W
Western State College of Colorado *Colorado* M & W
Whitman College *Washington* M & W
Williams College *Massachusetts* M & W

Skiing (Downhill)

Adirondack Community College *New York* M & W
Albertson College of Idaho *Idaho* M & W
Alfred University *New York* M & W
Allegheny College *Pennsylvania* M & W
Amherst College *Massachusetts* M & W
Babson College *Massachusetts* M & W
Barnard College *New York* W
Bates College *Maine* M & W
Bishop's University *Quebec* M & W
Boise State University *Idaho* W
Boston College *Massachusetts* M & W
Boston University *Massachusetts* M & W
Brandeis University *Massachusetts* M & W
Brown University *Rhode Island* M & W
Bucknell University *Pennsylvania* M & W
Buffalo State College, State University of New York *New York* M & W
California State University, Long Beach *California* M & W
California State University, Sacramento *California* M & W
Carleton College *Minnesota* M & W
Castleton State College *Vermont* M & W
Claremont McKenna College *California* M & W
Clarkson University *New York* M & W
Colby College *Maine* M & W
Colby-Sawyer College *New Hampshire* M & W
Colgate University *New York* M & W
The Colorado College *Colorado* M & W
Colorado Mountain College, Alpine Campus *Colorado* M & W
Colorado School of Mines *Colorado* M
Columbia College *New York* M & W
Columbia University, The Fu Foundation School of Engineering and Applied Science *New York* M & W
Connecticut College *Connecticut* M & W
Dartmouth College *New Hampshire* M & W
Davis & Elkins College *West Virginia* M & W
Denison University *Ohio* M & W
Dickinson College *Pennsylvania* M & W
Duke University *North Carolina* M & W
Eastern Oregon University *Oregon* M & W
Fort Lewis College *Colorado* M & W
Garrett College *Maryland* M & W
Gonzaga University *Washington* M & W
Grand Valley State University *Michigan* M & W
Green Mountain College *Vermont* M & W
Hamilton College *New York* M & W
Harvard University *Massachusetts* M & W
Hobart and William Smith Colleges *New York* M & W
Holyoke Community College *Massachusetts* M & W
Idaho State University *Idaho* M & W
John Carroll University *Ohio* M & W
Keene State College *New Hampshire* M & W
Kutztown University of Pennsylvania *Pennsylvania* M & W
Lafayette College *Pennsylvania* M & W
Laurentian University *Ontario* M & W
Lehigh University *Pennsylvania* M & W
Loras College *Iowa* M
Marist College *New York* M & W
Marquette University *Wisconsin* M & W
Massachusetts Institute of Technology *Massachusetts* M & W
McGill University *Quebec* M & W
Michigan State University *Michigan* M
Michigan Technological University *Michigan* M & W
Middlebury College *Vermont* M & W
Montana State University *Montana* M & W
New England College *New Hampshire* M & W
New Hampshire Community Technical College, Manchester/Stratham *New Hampshire* M & W
Nichols College *Massachusetts* M
North Carolina State University *North Carolina* M & W
Northern Michigan University *Michigan* M & W
Norwich University *Vermont* M & W
The Pennsylvania State University at Erie, The Behrend College *Pennsylvania* M & W
The Pennsylvania State University, Lehigh Valley Campus of the Berks-Lehigh Valley College *Pennsylvania* M & W
The Pennsylvania State University University Park Campus *Pennsylvania* M & W
Plymouth State University *New Hampshire* M & W
Providence College *Rhode Island* M & W
Queen's University at Kingston *Ontario* M & W
Reed College *Oregon* M & W
Rensselaer Polytechnic Institute *New York* M & W
Rochester Institute of Technology *New York* M & W
Saint Anselm College *New Hampshire* M & W
St. Cloud State University *Minnesota* M & W
St. Lawrence University *New York* M & W
Saint Mary's College *Indiana* W
Saint Michael's College *Vermont* M & W
St. Olaf College *Minnesota* M & W
Scripps College *California* W

M = Men; W = Women

Seattle University *Washington* M & W
Sierra College *California* M & W
Sierra Nevada College *Nevada* M & W
Skidmore College *New York* M & W
Smith College *Massachusetts* W
Southern Oregon University *Oregon* M & W
Stanford University *California* M & W
State University of New York at Binghamton *New York* M & W
State University of New York College of Agriculture and Technology at Morrisville *New York* M & W
Syracuse University *New York* M & W
Trinity College *Connecticut* M & W
Union College *New York* M & W
United States Air Force Academy *Colorado* M & W
United States Military Academy *New York* M & W
United States Naval Academy *Maryland* M & W
Université Laval *Quebec* M & W
Université de Montréal *Quebec* M & W
Université du Québec àRimouski *Quebec* M & W
University of Alaska Anchorage *Alaska* M & W
The University of British Columbia *British Columbia* M & W
University of California, Santa Barbara *California* M & W
University of Colorado at Boulder *Colorado* M & W
University of Denver *Colorado* M & W
University of Idaho *Idaho* M & W
University of Maine at Fort Kent *Maine* M & W
University of Maryland, Baltimore County *Maryland* M & W
University of Massachusetts Amherst *Massachusetts* M & W
University of Minnesota, Duluth *Minnesota* M & W
The University of Montana-Missoula *Montana* M & W
University of Nevada, Reno *Nevada* M & W
University of New Hampshire *New Hampshire* M & W
University of New Mexico *New Mexico* M & W
University of Oregon *Oregon* M & W
University of Puget Sound *Washington* M & W
University of Rhode Island *Rhode Island* M & W
University of Rochester *New York* M & W
University of St. Thomas *Minnesota* M & W
The University of Scranton *Pennsylvania* M & W
University of Toronto *Ontario* M & W
University of Utah *Utah* M & W
University of Vermont *Vermont* M & W
University of Wyoming *Wyoming* M & W
Villanova University *Pennsylvania* M & W
Virginia Polytechnic Institute and State University *Virginia* M & W
Washington State University *Washington* M & W
Weber State University *Utah* M & W
Wellesley College *Massachusetts* W
Wesleyan University *Connecticut* M & W
Western State College of Colorado *Colorado* M & W
Whitman College *Washington* M & W
William Paterson University of New Jersey *New Jersey* M & W
Williams College *Massachusetts* M & W
Winona State University *Minnesota* M & W

Soccer

Abilene Christian University *Texas* M & W
Abraham Baldwin Agricultural College *Georgia* W
Acadia University *Nova Scotia* M & W
Adelphi University *New York* M & W
Adirondack Community College *New York* M & W
Adrian College *Michigan* M & W
Agnes Scott College *Georgia* W
Alabama Agricultural and Mechanical University *Alabama* M
Albany College of Pharmacy of Union University *New York* M & W
Alberta College of Art & Design *Alberta* M & W
Albertson College of Idaho *Idaho* M & W
Albertus Magnus College *Connecticut* M & W
Albion College *Michigan* M & W
Albright College *Pennsylvania* M & W
Alcorn State University *Mississippi* W
Alderson-Broaddus College *West Virginia* M
Alfred University *New York* M & W
Allan Hancock College *California* M & W
Allegany College of Maryland *Maryland* M & W
Allegheny College *Pennsylvania* M & W
Allen County Community College *Kansas* M & W
Alliance University College *Alberta* M & W
Alliant International University *California* M & W
Alma College *Michigan* M & W
Alvernia College *Pennsylvania* M & W
Alverno College *Wisconsin* W
American International College *Massachusetts* M & W
American River College *California* M & W
American University *District of Columbia* M & W
Amherst College *Massachusetts* M & W
Anderson University *South Carolina* M & W
Anderson University *Indiana* M & W
Andrew College *Georgia* M & W
Angelo State University *Texas* W
Anna Maria College *Massachusetts* M & W
Anne Arundel Community College *Maryland* M & W
Antelope Valley College *California* W
Appalachian Bible College *West Virginia* M
Appalachian State University *North Carolina* M & W
Aquinas College *Michigan* M & W
Arcadia University *Pennsylvania* M & W
Arizona State University *Arizona* W
Arizona Western College *Arizona* M
Arkansas State University *Arkansas* W
The Art Institute of Boston at Lesley University *Massachusetts* M & W
Asbury College *Kentucky* M & W
Ashford University *Iowa* M & W
Ashland University *Ohio* M & W
Assumption College *Massachusetts* M & W
Atlanta Christian College *Georgia* M & W
Atlantic Baptist University *New Brunswick* M & W
Auburn University *Alabama* W
Auburn University Montgomery *Alabama* M & W
Augsburg College *Minnesota* M & W
Augustana College *South Dakota* W
Augustana College *Illinois* M & W
Aurora University *Illinois* M & W
Austin College *Texas* M & W
Austin Peay State University *Tennessee* W
Averett University *Virginia* M & W
Avila University *Missouri* M & W
Azusa Pacific University *California* M & W
Babson College *Massachusetts* M & W
Bacone College *Oklahoma* M & W
Baker University *Kansas* M & W
Bakersfield College *California* W
Baldwin-Wallace College *Ohio* M & W
Ball State University *Indiana* M & W
Baptist Bible College *Missouri* M
Baptist Bible College of Pennsylvania *Pennsylvania* M & W
Barclay College *Kansas* M
Bard College *New York* M & W
Barnard College *New York* W
Barry University *Florida* M & W
Barton College *North Carolina* M & W
Barton County Community College *Kansas* M & W
Bates College *Maine* M & W
Bay Path College *Massachusetts* W
Baylor University *Texas* M & W
Becker College *Massachusetts* M & W
Belhaven College *Mississippi* M & W
Bellarmine University *Kentucky* M & W
Bellevue Community College *Washington* M
Bellevue University *Nebraska* M & W
Belmont Abbey College *North Carolina* M & W
Belmont University *Tennessee* M & W
Beloit College *Wisconsin* M & W
Bemidji State University *Minnesota* W
Benedictine College *Kansas* M & W
Benedictine University *Illinois* M & W
Bennington College *Vermont* M & W
Bentley College *Massachusetts* M & W
Berea College *Kentucky* M & W
Bergen Community College *New Jersey* M & W
Bernard M. Baruch College of the City University of New York *New York* M
Berry College *Georgia* M & W
Bethany Bible College *New Brunswick* M & W
Bethany College *West Virginia* M & W
Bethany College *Kansas* M & W
Bethany Lutheran College *Minnesota* M & W
Bethany University *California* M & W
Bethel College *Tennessee* M & W
Bethel College *Kansas* M & W
Bethel College *Indiana* M & W
Bethel University *Minnesota* M & W
Biola University *California* M & W
Birmingham-Southern College *Alabama* M & W
Bishop's University *Quebec* W
Blackburn College *Illinois* M & W
Blessing-Rieman College of Nursing *Illinois* M & W
Bloomfield College *New Jersey* M & W
Bloomsburg University of Pennsylvania *Pennsylvania* M & W
Bluefield College *Virginia* M & W
Bluffton University *Ohio* M & W
Boise State University *Idaho* W
Borough of Manhattan Community College of the City University of New York *New York* M
Bossier Parish Community College *Louisiana* M
Boston College *Massachusetts* M & W
Boston University *Massachusetts* M & W
Bowdoin College *Maine* M & W
Bowling Green State University *Ohio* M
Bradley University *Illinois* M & W
Brandeis University *Massachusetts* W
Brenau University *Georgia* W
Brescia University *Kentucky* M & W
Brevard College *North Carolina* M & W
Brewton-Parker College *Georgia* M & W
Briar Cliff University *Iowa* M & W
Briarcliffe College *New York* W
Bridgewater College *Virginia* M & W
Bridgewater State College *Massachusetts* M & W
Briercrest College *Saskatchewan* M & W
Brigham Young University *Utah* M & W
Brock University *Ontario* M & W
Bronx Community College of the City University of New York *New York* M
Brookdale Community College *New Jersey* M & W
Brooklyn College of the City University of New York *New York* M
Broome Community College *New York* M & W
Broward Community College *Florida* W
Brown University *Rhode Island* M & W
Bryan College *Tennessee* M & W
Bryant and Stratton College, North Campus *New York* M & W
Bryant and Stratton College (Syracuse) *New York* M & W
Bryant and Stratton College (Willoughby Hills) *Ohio* M & W
Bryant University *Rhode Island* M & W
Bryn Athyn College of the New Church *Pennsylvania* M & W
Bryn Mawr College *Pennsylvania* W
Bucknell University *Pennsylvania* M & W
Bucks County Community College *Pennsylvania* M & W
Buena Vista University *Iowa* M & W
Buffalo State College, State University of New York *New York* M & W
Bunker Hill Community College *Massachusetts* M & W
Burlington County College *New Jersey* M & W
Butler Community College *Kansas* W
Butler University *Indiana* M & W
Butte College *California* W
Cabrillo College *California* M & W
Cabrini College *Pennsylvania* M & W
Caldwell College *New Jersey* M & W
California Baptist University *California* M & W
California Institute of Technology *California* M & W
California Lutheran University *California* M & W
California Maritime Academy *California* M
California Polytechnic State University, San Luis Obispo *California* M & W
California State Polytechnic University, Pomona *California* M & W
California State University, Bakersfield *California* M
California State University, Chico *California* M & W

M = Men; W = Women

California State University, Dominguez Hills *California* M & W
California State University, East Bay *California* M & W
California State University, Fresno *California* M & W
California State University, Fullerton *California* M & W
California State University, Long Beach *California* M & W
California State University, Los Angeles *California* M & W
California State University, Monterey Bay *California* M & W
California State University, Northridge *California* M
California State University, Sacramento *California* M & W
California State University, San Bernardino *California* M & W
California State University, Stanislaus *California* M & W
California University of Pennsylvania *Pennsylvania* M & W
Calumet College of Saint Joseph *Indiana* M & W
Calvary Bible College and Theological Seminary *Missouri* M
Calvin College *Michigan* M & W
Camden County College *New Jersey* M & W
Campbell University *North Carolina* M & W
Campbellsville University *Kentucky* M & W
Canadian Mennonite University *Manitoba* M & W
Canisius College *New York* M & W
Cape Breton University *Nova Scotia* M & W
Capital University *Ohio* M & W
Cardinal Stritch University *Wisconsin* M & W
Carleton College *Minnesota* M & W
Carleton University *Ontario* M & W
Carlow University *Pennsylvania* W
Carnegie Mellon University *Pennsylvania* M & W
Carroll College *Wisconsin* M & W
Carroll College *Montana* W
Carson-Newman College *Tennessee* M & W
Carthage College *Wisconsin* M & W
Cascade College *Oregon* M & W
Case Western Reserve University *Ohio* M & W
Castleton State College *Vermont* M & W
Catawba College *North Carolina* M & W
The Catholic University of America *District of Columbia* M & W
Cayuga County Community College *New York* M & W
Cazenovia College *New York* M & W
Cedar Crest College *Pennsylvania* W
Cedar Valley College *Texas* W
Cedarville University *Ohio* M & W
Centenary College *New Jersey* M & W
Centenary College of Louisiana *Louisiana* M & W
Central Bible College *Missouri* M
Central Christian College of Kansas *Kansas* M & W
Central College *Iowa* M & W
Central Connecticut State University *Connecticut* M & W
Central Lakes College *Minnesota* M & W
Central Maine Community College *Maine* M & W
Central Methodist University *Missouri* M & W
Central Michigan University *Michigan* W
Central Missouri State University *Missouri* M & W
Central Ohio Technical College *Ohio* M
Central Washington University *Washington* M & W
Centre College *Kentucky* M & W
Cerritos College *California* M
Chabot College *California* M & W
Chaffey College *California* M & W
Chapman University *California* M & W
Charleston Southern University *South Carolina* W
Chatham College *Pennsylvania* W
Chesapeake College *Maryland* M & W
Chestnut Hill College *Pennsylvania* M & W
Chowan University *North Carolina* M & W
Christendom College *Virginia* M & W
Christian Brothers University *Tennessee* M & W
Christopher Newport University *Virginia* M & W
Cincinnati Christian University *Ohio* M & W
Cincinnati State Technical and Community College *Ohio* M & W
The Citadel, The Military College of South Carolina *South Carolina* M & W
Citrus College *California* M & W
City College of the City University of New York *New York* M
City College of San Francisco *California* M
City Colleges of Chicago, Kennedy-King College *Illinois* M
Clackamas Community College *Oregon* W
Claremont McKenna College *California* M & W
Clark College *Washington* M & W
Clark University *Massachusetts* M & W
Clarke College *Iowa* M & W
Clarkson University *New York* M & W
Clayton State University *Georgia* M & W
Clearwater Christian College *Florida* M
Clemson University *South Carolina* M & W
Cleveland State University *Ohio* M
Clinton Community College *New York* M & W
Clinton Community College *Iowa* M & W
Cloud County Community College *Kansas* M & W
Coastal Carolina University *South Carolina* M & W
Cochise College (Douglas) *Arizona* W
Cochise College (Sierra Vista) *Arizona* W
Coe College *Iowa* M & W
Coker College *South Carolina* M & W
Colby College *Maine* M & W
Colby-Sawyer College *New Hampshire* M & W
Colgate University *New York* M & W
College of the Atlantic *Maine* M & W
College of the Canyons *California* W
College of Charleston *South Carolina* M & W
College of the Desert *California* M
College of DuPage *Illinois* M & W
College of the Holy Cross *Massachusetts* M & W
College of Lake County *Illinois* M & W
College of Marin *California* M & W
College Misericordia *Pennsylvania* M & W
College of Mount St. Joseph *Ohio* M & W
College of Mount Saint Vincent *New York* M & W
The College of New Jersey *New Jersey* M & W
College of Notre Dame of Maryland *Maryland* W
College of the Redwoods *California* W
College of Saint Benedict *Minnesota* W
College of St. Catherine *Minnesota* W
College of Saint Elizabeth *New Jersey* W
College of St. Joseph *Vermont* M & W
College of Saint Mary *Nebraska* W
The College of Saint Rose *New York* M & W
The College of St. Scholastica *Minnesota* M & W
College of San Mateo *California* W
College of the Sequoias *California* W
College of Southern Maryland *Maryland* M & W
College of the Southwest *New Mexico* M & W
College of Staten Island of the City University of New York *New York* M & W
College of The Albemarle *North Carolina* M
The College of William and Mary *Virginia* M & W
The College of Wooster *Ohio* M & W
Colorado Christian University *Colorado* M & W
The Colorado College *Colorado* M & W
Colorado Mountain College *Colorado* M & W
Colorado School of Mines *Colorado* M
Colorado State University-Pueblo *Colorado* M & W
Columbia Basin College *Washington* M & W
Columbia Bible College *British Columbia* M & W
Columbia College *South Carolina* W
Columbia College *New York* M & W
Columbia College *Missouri* M
Columbia-Greene Community College *New York* M & W
Columbia Union College *Maryland* M & W
Columbia University, School of General Studies *New York* M & W
Columbia University, The Fu Foundation School of Engineering and Applied Science *New York* M & W
Columbus State Community College *Ohio* M
Columbus State University *Georgia* W
Community College of Philadelphia *Pennsylvania* M
Community College of Rhode Island *Rhode Island* M & W
Concord University *West Virginia* W
Concordia College *New York* M & W
Concordia College *Minnesota* M & W
Concordia College *Alabama* M
Concordia University *Quebec* M & W
Concordia University *Oregon* M & W
Concordia University *Nebraska* M & W
Concordia University *Michigan* M & W
Concordia University *Illinois* M & W
Concordia University *California* M & W
Concordia University at Austin *Texas* M & W
Concordia University College of Alberta *Alberta* M & W
Concordia University, St. Paul *Minnesota* M & W
Concordia University Wisconsin *Wisconsin* M & W
Connecticut College *Connecticut* M & W
Converse College *South Carolina* W
Cooper Union for the Advancement of Science and Art *New York* M
Corban College *Oregon* M & W
Cornell College *Iowa* M & W
Cornell University *New York* M & W
Cornerstone University *Michigan* M & W
Corning Community College *New York* M & W
Cosumnes River College (Sacramento) *California* M & W
County College of Morris *New Jersey* M
Covenant College *Georgia* M & W
Creighton University *Nebraska* M & W
Crown College *Minnesota* M & W
Cuesta College *California* W
The Culinary Institute of America *New York* M
Culver-Stockton College *Missouri* M & W
Cumberland University *Tennessee* M & W
Curry College *Massachusetts* M & W
Cuyahoga Community College *Ohio* M
Cuyamaca College *California* M & W
Cypress College *California* M & W
Daemen College *New York* M & W
Dakota County Technical College *Minnesota* M & W
Dalhousie University *Nova Scotia* M & W
Dallas Baptist University *Texas* M & W
Dallas Christian College *Texas* M
Dana College *Nebraska* M & W
Daniel Webster College *New Hampshire* M & W
Dartmouth College *New Hampshire* M & W
Darton College *Georgia* M & W
Davidson College *North Carolina* M & W
Davis College *New York* M
Davis & Elkins College *West Virginia* M & W
De Anza College *California* M & W
Dean College *Massachusetts* M & W
Defiance College *Ohio* M & W
Delaware County Community College *Pennsylvania* M
Delaware Technical & Community College, Stanton/Wilmington Campus *Delaware* M
Delaware Valley College *Pennsylvania* M & W
Delta College *Michigan* M
Denison University *Ohio* M & W
DePaul University *Illinois* M & W
DePauw University *Indiana* M & W
DeSales University *Pennsylvania* M & W
Diablo Valley College *California* W
Dickinson College *Pennsylvania* M & W
Dixie State College of Utah *Utah* W
Doane College *Nebraska* M & W
Dominican College *New York* M & W
Dominican University *Illinois* M & W
Dominican University of California *California* M & W
Dordt College *Iowa* M & W
Dowling College *New York* M
Drake University *Iowa* M & W
Drew University *New Jersey* M & W
Drexel University *Pennsylvania* M & W
Drury University *Missouri* M & W
Duke University *North Carolina* M & W
Duquesne University *Pennsylvania* M & W
Dutchess Community College *New York* M & W
D'Youville College *New York* M & W
Earlham College *Indiana* M & W
East Carolina University *North Carolina* M & W
East Central College *Missouri* M
East Central University *Oklahoma* W
East Los Angeles College *California* M

M = Men; W = Women

M = Men; W = Women

Jones County Junior College *Mississippi* M & W
Judson College *Illinois* M & W
Juniata College *Pennsylvania* M & W
Kalamazoo College *Michigan* M & W
Kansas City Kansas Community College *Kansas* M
Kansas Wesleyan University *Kansas* M & W
Kean University *New Jersey* M & W
Keene State College *New Hampshire* M & W
Kellogg Community College *Michigan* M
Kent State University *Ohio* W
Kentucky Christian University *Kentucky* M & W
Kentucky Wesleyan College *Kentucky* M & W
Kenyon College *Ohio* M & W
Kettering University *Michigan* M
Keuka College *New York* M & W
Keystone College *Pennsylvania* M & W
King College *Tennessee* M & W
King's College *Pennsylvania* M & W
The King's University College *Alberta* M & W
Kingsborough Community College of the City University of New York *New York* M
Kirkwood Community College *Iowa* M & W
Kishwaukee College *Illinois* M
Knox College *Illinois* M & W
Kutztown University of Pennsylvania *Pennsylvania* M & W
Kwantlen University College *British Columbia* M & W
La Roche College *Pennsylvania* M & W
La Salle University *Pennsylvania* M & W
La Sierra University *California* M
Lafayette College *Pennsylvania* M & W
LaGrange College *Georgia* M & W
Lake Erie College *Ohio* M & W
Lake Forest College *Illinois* M & W
Lakehead University *Ontario* M & W
Lakeland College *Wisconsin* M & W
Lakeland Community College *Ohio* M
Lambuth University *Tennessee* M & W
Lancaster Bible College *Pennsylvania* M & W
Lander University *South Carolina* M & W
Landmark College *Vermont* M & W
Laramie County Community College *Wyoming* M & W
Las Positas College *California* M & W
Lasell College *Massachusetts* M & W
Laurentian University *Ontario* M
Lawrence University *Wisconsin* M & W
Le Moyne College *New York* M & W
Lebanon Valley College *Pennsylvania* M & W
Lee University *Tennessee* M & W
Lees-McRae College *North Carolina* M & W
Lehigh Carbon Community College *Pennsylvania* M
Lehigh University *Pennsylvania* M & W
Lehman College of the City University of New York *New York* M
Lenoir-Rhyne College *North Carolina* M & W
Lesley University *Massachusetts* M & W
LeTourneau University *Texas* M & W
Lewis & Clark College *Oregon* M & W
Lewis and Clark Community College *Illinois* M & W
Lewis University *Illinois* M & W
Liberty University *Virginia* M & W
Limestone College *South Carolina* M & W
Lincoln Christian College *Illinois* M & W
Lincoln College *Illinois* M & W
Lincoln College-Normal *Illinois* M & W
Lincoln Land Community College *Illinois* M
Lincoln Memorial University *Tennessee* M & W
Lincoln University *Pennsylvania* M & W
Lindenwood University *Missouri* M & W
Lindsey Wilson College *Kentucky* M & W
Linfield College *Oregon* M & W
Lipscomb University *Tennessee* M & W
Lock Haven University of Pennsylvania *Pennsylvania* M & W
Lon Morris College *Texas* M & W
Long Beach City College *California* M & W
Long Island University, Brooklyn Campus *New York* M & W
Long Island University, C.W. Post Campus *New York* M & W
Longwood University *Virginia* M & W
Loras College *Iowa* M & W
Los Angeles Harbor College *California* M
Los Medanos College *California* M
Louisburg College *North Carolina* M & W
Louisiana College *Louisiana* M & W
Louisiana State University and Agricultural and Mechanical College *Louisiana* W
Lower Columbia College *Washington* M & W
Loyola College in Maryland *Maryland* M & W
Loyola Marymount University *California* M & W
Loyola University Chicago *Illinois* M & W
Loyola University New Orleans *Louisiana* M & W
Lubbock Christian University *Texas* M
Luther College *Iowa* M & W
Luzerne County Community College *Pennsylvania* M & W
Lycoming College *Pennsylvania* M & W
Lynchburg College *Virginia* M & W
Lyndon State College *Vermont* M & W
Lynn University *Florida* M & W
Lyon College *Arkansas* M & W
Macalester College *Minnesota* M & W
MacMurray College *Illinois* M & W
Macomb Community College *Michigan* M
Madonna University *Michigan* M & W
Maharishi University of Management *Iowa* M & W
Maine Maritime Academy *Maine* M & W
Malone College *Ohio* M & W
Manchester College *Indiana* M & W
Manchester Community College *Connecticut* M & W
Manhattan Christian College *Kansas* M & W
Manhattan College *New York* M & W
Manhattanville College *New York* M & W
Manor College *Pennsylvania* M & W
Mansfield University of Pennsylvania *Pennsylvania* W
Maranatha Baptist Bible College *Wisconsin* M & W
Marian College *Indiana* M & W
Marian College of Fond du Lac *Wisconsin* M & W
Marietta College *Ohio* M & W
Marion Military Institute *Alabama* M & W
Marist College *New York* M & W
Marlboro College *Vermont* M & W
Marquette University *Wisconsin* M & W
Mars Hill College *North Carolina* M & W
Marshall University *West Virginia* M & W
Marshalltown Community College *Iowa* M & W
Martin Luther College *Minnesota* M & W
Martin Methodist College *Tennessee* M & W
Mary Baldwin College *Virginia* W
Marymount University *Virginia* M & W
Maryville College *Tennessee* M & W
Maryville University of Saint Louis *Missouri* M & W
Marywood University *Pennsylvania* M & W
Massachusetts Bay Community College *Massachusetts* M & W
Massachusetts College of Liberal Arts *Massachusetts* M & W
Massachusetts Institute of Technology *Massachusetts* M & W
Massachusetts Maritime Academy *Massachusetts* M
Massasoit Community College *Massachusetts* M & W
The Master's College and Seminary *California* M & W
Mayville State University *North Dakota* M & W
McDaniel College *Maryland* M & W
McGill University *Quebec* M & W
McHenry County College *Illinois* M
McKendree College *Illinois* M & W
McMaster University *Ontario* M & W
McMurry University *Texas* M & W
McNeese State University *Louisiana* W
Medaille College *New York* M & W
Medgar Evers College of the City University of New York *New York* M
Memorial University of Newfoundland *Newfoundland and Labrador* M & W
Menlo College *California* M & W
Merced College *California* M
Mercer County Community College *New Jersey* M & W
Mercer University *Georgia* M & W
Mercy College *New York* M & W
Mercyhurst College *Pennsylvania* M & W
Meredith College *North Carolina* W
Meridian Community College *Mississippi* M
Merrimack College *Massachusetts* M & W
Merritt College *California* M
Mesa Community College *Arizona* M & W
Mesa State College *Colorado* W
Messiah College *Pennsylvania* M & W
Methodist College *North Carolina* M & W
Metropolitan State College of Denver *Colorado* M & W
Miami University *Ohio* M & W
Michigan State University *Michigan* M & W
Michigan Technological University *Michigan* M & W
Mid-America Christian University *Oklahoma* M
Mid-Continent University *Kentucky* M
MidAmerica Nazarene University *Kansas* M & W
Middle Georgia College *Georgia* M & W
Middle Tennessee State University *Tennessee* W
Middlebury College *Vermont* M & W
Middlesex County College *New Jersey* M & W
Midland Lutheran College *Nebraska* M & W
Midway College *Kentucky* W
Midwestern State University *Texas* M & W
Millersville University of Pennsylvania *Pennsylvania* M & W
Milligan College *Tennessee* M & W
Millikin University *Illinois* M & W
Mills College *California* W
Millsaps College *Mississippi* M & W
Milwaukee Area Technical College *Wisconsin* M
Milwaukee School of Engineering *Wisconsin* M & W
Minnesota State University Mankato *Minnesota* W
Minnesota State University Moorhead *Minnesota* W
MiraCosta College *California* W
Mission College *California* M & W
Mississippi College *Mississippi* M & W
Mississippi Delta Community College *Mississippi* M
Mississippi Gulf Coast Community College *Mississippi* M & W
Mississippi State University *Mississippi* W
Missouri Baptist University *Missouri* M & W
Missouri Southern State University *Missouri* M & W
Missouri State University *Missouri* M & W
Missouri Valley College *Missouri* M & W
Missouri Western State University *Missouri* W
Mitchell College *Connecticut* M & W
Modesto Junior College *California* M & W
Mohawk Valley Community College *New York* M & W
Molloy College *New York* M & W
Monmouth College *Illinois* M & W
Monmouth University *New Jersey* M & W
Monroe College (Bronx) *New York* M
Monroe College (New Rochelle) *New York* M
Monroe Community College *New York* M & W
Montana State University-Billings *Montana* M & W
Montana Tech of The University of Montana *Montana* M & W
Montclair State University *New Jersey* M & W
Montgomery College *Maryland* M & W
Montreat College *North Carolina* M & W
Moody Bible Institute *Illinois* M
Moorpark College *California* M & W
Moraine Valley Community College *Illinois* M & W
Moravian College *Pennsylvania* M & W
Morehead State University *Kentucky* W
Morningside College *Iowa* M & W
Morton College *Illinois* M
Mount Allison University *New Brunswick* M & W
Mount Aloysius College *Pennsylvania* M & W
Mount Holyoke College *Massachusetts* W
Mount Ida College *Massachusetts* M & W
Mount Marty College *South Dakota* M & W
Mount Mary College *Wisconsin* W
Mount Mercy College *Iowa* M & W
Mount Olive College *North Carolina* M & W
Mount Saint Mary College *New York* M & W
Mount St. Mary's University *Maryland* M & W
Mount Saint Vincent University *Nova Scotia* M & W
Mt. San Antonio College *California* M & W
Mt. San Jacinto College *California* W
Mount Union College *Ohio* M & W
Mount Vernon Nazarene University *Ohio* M & W
Muhlenberg College *Pennsylvania* M & W

M = Men; W = Women

Murray State University *Kentucky* W
Muskingum College *Ohio* M & W
Napa Valley College *California* M
Nassau Community College *New York* M & W
Nazareth College of Rochester *New York* M & W
Nebraska Christian College *Nebraska* M
Nebraska Wesleyan University *Nebraska* M & W
Neumann College *Pennsylvania* M & W
New England College *New Hampshire* M & W
New Hampshire Community Technical College, Berlin/Laconia *New Hampshire* M & W
New Hampshire Community Technical College, Manchester/Stratham *New Hampshire* M & W
New Hampshire Community Technical College, Nashua/Claremont *New Hampshire* M & W
New Hampshire Technical Institute *New Hampshire* M & W
New Jersey City University *New Jersey* M & W
New Jersey Institute of Technology *New Jersey* M
New Mexico Highlands University *New Mexico* W
New Mexico Institute of Mining and Technology *New Mexico* M & W
New York City College of Technology of the City University of New York *New York* M
New York Institute of Technology *New York* M & W
New York University *New York* M & W
Newberry College *South Carolina* M & W
Newbury College *Massachusetts* M
Newman University *Kansas* M & W
Niagara County Community College *New York* M & W
Niagara University *New York* M & W
Nicholls State University *Louisiana* W
Nichols College *Massachusetts* M & W
Nipissing University *Ontario* M & W
North Carolina State University *North Carolina* M & W
North Carolina Wesleyan College *North Carolina* M & W
North Central College *Illinois* M & W
North Central University *Minnesota* M & W
North Country Community College *New York* M & W
North Dakota State University *North Dakota* M & W
North Georgia College & State University *Georgia* M & W
North Greenville College *South Carolina* M & W
North Idaho College *Idaho* M & W
North Iowa Area Community College *Iowa* M & W
North Park University *Illinois* M & W
Northampton County Area Community College *Pennsylvania* M & W
Northeastern State University *Oklahoma* M & W
Northeastern University *Massachusetts* M & W
Northern Arizona University *Arizona* W
Northern Illinois University *Illinois* M & W
Northern Kentucky University *Kentucky* M & W
Northern Maine Community College *Maine* M & W
Northern Michigan University *Michigan* W
Northern Oklahoma College *Oklahoma* M & W
Northern State University *South Dakota* W
Northland College *Wisconsin* M & W
Northwest Missouri State University *Missouri* W
Northwest Nazarene University *Idaho* W
Northwest University *Washington* M
Northwestern College *Minnesota* M & W
Northwestern College *Iowa* M & W
Northwestern Oklahoma State University *Oklahoma* W
Northwestern State University of Louisiana *Louisiana* W
Northwestern University *Illinois* M & W
Northwood University *Michigan* M & W
Northwood University, Florida Campus *Florida* M & W
Northwood University, Texas Campus *Texas* M & W
Norwich University *Vermont* M & W
Notre Dame College *Ohio* M & W
Notre Dame de Namur University *California* M & W
Nova Scotia Agricultural College *Nova Scotia* M & W
Nova Southeastern University *Florida* M & W
Nyack College *New York* M & W
Oakland City University *Indiana* M & W
Oakland Community College *Michigan* M
Oakland University *Michigan* M & W
Oakton Community College *Illinois* M & W
Oberlin College *Ohio* M & W
Occidental College *California* M & W
Ocean County College *New Jersey* M & W
Oglethorpe University *Georgia* M & W
Ohio Dominican University *Ohio* M & W
Ohio Northern University *Ohio* M & W
The Ohio State University *Ohio* M & W
Ohio University *Ohio* M & W
Ohio Valley University *West Virginia* M & W
Ohio Wesleyan University *Ohio* M & W
Ohlone College *California* M & W
Oklahoma Christian University *Oklahoma* M & W
Oklahoma City University *Oklahoma* M & W
Oklahoma State University *Oklahoma* W
Oklahoma Wesleyan University *Oklahoma* M & W
Old Dominion University *Virginia* M & W
Olivet College *Michigan* M & W
Olivet Nazarene University *Illinois* M & W
Onondaga Community College *New York* M
Oral Roberts University *Oklahoma* M & W
Orange Coast College *California* M & W
Orange County Community College *New York* M & W
Oregon Institute of Technology *Oregon* W
Oregon State University *Oregon* M & W
Ottawa University *Kansas* M & W
Otterbein College *Ohio* M & W
Ouachita Baptist University *Arkansas* M & W
Owens Community College *Ohio* M
Oxnard College *California* M & W
Ozark Christian College *Missouri* M
Pace University *New York* W
Pacific Lutheran University *Washington* M & W
Pacific University *Oregon* M & W
Palm Beach Atlantic University *Florida* M & W
Palomar College *California* M
Paradise Valley Community College *Arizona* M & W
Park University *Missouri* M & W
Parkland College *Illinois* M & W
Pasadena City College *California* M & W
Passaic County Community College *New Jersey* M
Patrick Henry College *Virginia* M & W
Patten University *California* M & W
Paul Smith's College of Arts and Sciences *New York* M & W
Peace College *North Carolina* W
Pearl River Community College *Mississippi* M & W
Peninsula College *Washington* M
Pennsylvania College of Technology *Pennsylvania* M & W
The Pennsylvania State University Abington College *Pennsylvania* M & W
The Pennsylvania State University Altoona College *Pennsylvania* M & W
The Pennsylvania State University Berks Campus of the Berks-Lehigh Valley College *Pennsylvania* M
The Pennsylvania State University Delaware County Campus of the Commonwealth College *Pennsylvania* M & W
The Pennsylvania State University at Erie, The Behrend College *Pennsylvania* M & W
The Pennsylvania State University Harrisburg Campus *Pennsylvania* M
The Pennsylvania State University Hazleton Campus of the Commonwealth College *Pennsylvania* M
The Pennsylvania State University, Lehigh Valley Campus of the Berks-Lehigh Valley College *Pennsylvania* M & W
The Pennsylvania State University Mont Alto Campus of the Commonwealth College *Pennsylvania* M & W
The Pennsylvania State University Schuylkill Campus of the Capital College *Pennsylvania* M
The Pennsylvania State University University Park Campus *Pennsylvania* M & W
The Pennsylvania State University Wilkes-Barre Campus of the Commonwealth College *Pennsylvania* M & W
The Pennsylvania State University Worthington Scranton Campus of the Commonwealth College *Pennsylvania* M
The Pennsylvania State University York Campus of the Commonwealth College *Pennsylvania* M
Pepperdine University *California* M & W
Pfeiffer University *North Carolina* M & W
Philadelphia Biblical University *Pennsylvania* M & W
Philadelphia University *Pennsylvania* M & W
Phoenix College *Arizona* M & W
Piedmont College *Georgia* M & W
Pierce College *Washington* M
Pikes Peak Community College *Colorado* M
Pikeville College *Kentucky* M & W
Pillsbury Baptist Bible College *Minnesota* M
Pima Community College *Arizona* M & W
Pine Manor College *Massachusetts* W
Pitzer College *California* M & W
Plymouth State University *New Hampshire* M & W
Point Loma Nazarene University *California* M & W
Point Park University *Pennsylvania* M & W
Polk Community College *Florida* W
Polytechnic University, Brooklyn Campus *New York* M & W
Polytechnic University of Puerto Rico *Puerto Rico* M
Pomona College *California* M & W
Porterville College *California* M & W
Portland State University *Oregon* W
Post University *Connecticut* M & W
Potomac State College of West Virginia University *West Virginia* M & W
Prairie State College *Illinois* M & W
Prairie View A&M University *Texas* W
Pratt Institute *New York* M & W
Presbyterian College *South Carolina* M & W
Presentation College *South Dakota* M & W
Prince George's Community College *Maryland* M & W
Princeton University *New Jersey* M & W
Principia College *Illinois* M & W
Providence College *Rhode Island* M & W
Providence College and Theological Seminary *Manitoba* M & W
Purchase College, State University of New York *New York* M & W
Purdue University *Indiana* W
Queens College of the City University of New York *New York* W
Queens University of Charlotte *North Carolina* M & W
Queen's University at Kingston *Ontario* M & W
Queensborough Community College of the City University of New York *New York* M
Quincy University *Illinois* M & W
Quinnipiac University *Connecticut* M & W
Radford University *Virginia* M & W
Ramapo College of New Jersey *New Jersey* M & W
Randolph-Macon College *Virginia* M & W
Randolph-Macon Woman's College *Virginia* W
Reading Area Community College *Pennsylvania* M
Redeemer University College *Ontario* M & W
Reed College *Oregon* M & W
Regis College *Massachusetts* W
Regis University *Colorado* M & W
Reinhardt College *Georgia* M & W
Rensselaer Polytechnic Institute *New York* M & W
Research College of Nursing *Missouri* M & W
Rhode Island College *Rhode Island* M & W
Rhodes College *Tennessee* M & W
Rice University *Texas* M & W
The Richard Stockton College of New Jersey *New Jersey* M & W
Richland College *Texas* M & W
Rider University *New Jersey* M & W
Ripon College *Wisconsin* M & W
Riverside Community College District *California* M & W
Rivier College *New Hampshire* M & W
Roanoke College *Virginia* M & W
Robert Morris College *Illinois* M & W
Robert Morris University *Pennsylvania* M & W
Roberts Wesleyan College *New York* M & W
Rochester College *Michigan* M & W
Rochester Community and Technical College *Minnesota* W
Rochester Institute of Technology *New York* M & W
Rockford College *Illinois* M & W

M = Men; W = Women

Rockhurst University *Missouri* M & W
Rockland Community College *New York* M & W
Rocky Mountain College *Alberta* M
Roger Williams University *Rhode Island* M & W
Rollins College *Florida* M & W
Rose-Hulman Institute of Technology *Indiana* M & W
Rose State College *Oklahoma* W
Rowan University *New Jersey* M & W
Roxbury Community College *Massachusetts* M & W
Royal Military College of Canada *Ontario* M & W
Russell Sage College *New York* W
Rutgers, The State University of New Jersey, New Brunswick/Piscataway *New Jersey* M & W
Ryerson University *Ontario* M & W
Sacramento City College *California* W
Sacred Heart University *Connecticut* M & W
Saginaw Valley State University *Michigan* M & W
St. Ambrose University *Iowa* M & W
St. Andrews Presbyterian College *North Carolina* M & W
Saint Anselm College *New Hampshire* M & W
St. Bonaventure University *New York* M & W
St. Cloud State University *Minnesota* M & W
St. Edward's University *Texas* M & W
St. Francis College *New York* M
Saint Francis University *Pennsylvania* M & W
St. Francis Xavier University *Nova Scotia* M
St. Gregory's University *Oklahoma* M & W
St. John Fisher College *New York* M & W
St. John's College *New Mexico* M & W
St. John's University *New York* M & W
Saint John's University *Minnesota* M
Saint Joseph College *Connecticut* W
Saint Joseph's College *Indiana* M & W
Saint Joseph's College of Maine *Maine* M & W
St. Joseph's College, Suffolk Campus *New York* M & W
Saint Joseph's University *Pennsylvania* M & W
St. Lawrence University *New York* M & W
Saint Leo University *Florida* M & W
St. Louis Community College at Florissant Valley *Missouri* M & W
St. Louis Community College at Forest Park *Missouri* M
St. Louis Community College at Meramec *Missouri* M & W
Saint Louis University *Missouri* M & W
Saint Mary-of-the-Woods College *Indiana* W
Saint Mary's College *Indiana* W
Saint Mary's College of California *California* M & W
St. Mary's College of Maryland *Maryland* M & W
Saint Mary's University *Nova Scotia* M & W
Saint Mary's University of Minnesota *Minnesota* M & W
St. Mary's University of San Antonio *Texas* M & W
Saint Michael's College *Vermont* M & W
St. Norbert College *Wisconsin* M & W
St. Olaf College *Minnesota* M & W
Saint Peter's College *New Jersey* M & W
St. Thomas Aquinas College *New York* M & W
St. Thomas University *New Brunswick* M & W
St. Thomas University *Florida* M & W
Saint Vincent College *Pennsylvania* M & W
Saint Xavier University *Illinois* M & W
Salem College *North Carolina* W
Salem International University *West Virginia* M
Salem State College *Massachusetts* M & W
Salisbury University *Maryland* M & W
Salt Lake Community College *Utah* M & W
Salve Regina University *Rhode Island* M & W
Sam Houston State University *Texas* M & W
Samford University *Alabama* M & W
San Bernardino Valley College *California* M & W
San Diego Christian College *California* M & W
San Diego City College *California* M & W
San Diego Mesa College *California* M & W
San Diego State University *California* M & W
San Francisco State University *California* M & W
San Joaquin Delta College *California* M & W
San Jose State University *California* M & W
Santa Ana College *California* M
Santa Barbara City College *California* M & W
Santa Clara University *California* M & W
Santa Monica College *California* W
Santa Rosa Junior College *California* M & W
Savannah College of Art and Design *Georgia* M & W
Schoolcraft College *Michigan* M & W
Schreiner University *Texas* M & W
Scott Community College *Iowa* M & W
Scottsdale Community College *Arizona* M & W
Scripps College *California* W
Seattle Pacific University *Washington* M & W
Seattle University *Washington* M & W
Seton Hall University *New Jersey* M & W
Seton Hill University *Pennsylvania* M & W
Sewanee: The University of the South *Tennessee* M & W
Shasta College *California* M & W
Shawnee State University *Ohio* M & W
Shelton State Community College *Alabama* W
Shenandoah University *Virginia* M & W
Shepherd University *West Virginia* M & W
Shippensburg University of Pennsylvania *Pennsylvania* M & W
Shoreline Community College *Washington* M & W
Shorter College *Georgia* M & W
Siena College *New York* M & W
Siena Heights University *Michigan* M & W
Simmons College *Massachusetts* W
Simon Fraser University *British Columbia* M & W
Simon's Rock College of Bard *Massachusetts* M & W
Simpson College *Iowa* M & W
Simpson University *California* M & W
Skagit Valley College *Washington* M & W
Skidmore College *New York* M & W
Skyline College *California* M
Slippery Rock University of Pennsylvania *Pennsylvania* M & W
Smith College *Massachusetts* W
Sonoma State University *California* M & W
South Dakota State University *South Dakota* M & W
South Georgia College *Georgia* M
South Mountain Community College *Arizona* M
South Puget Sound Community College *Washington* M
Southeast Missouri State University *Missouri* W
Southeastern Louisiana University *Louisiana* W
Southeastern University *Florida* M & W
Southern Connecticut State University *Connecticut* M & W
Southern Illinois University Edwardsville *Illinois* M & W
Southern Maine Community College *Maine* M & W
Southern Methodist University *Texas* M & W
Southern Nazarene University *Oklahoma* M & W
Southern New Hampshire University *New Hampshire* M & W
Southern Oregon University *Oregon* W
Southern Polytechnic State University *Georgia* M
Southern State Community College *Ohio* M
Southern Vermont College *Vermont* M & W
Southern Virginia University *Virginia* M & W
Southern Wesleyan University *South Carolina* M & W
Southwest Baptist University *Missouri* M & W
Southwest Minnesota State University *Minnesota* W
Southwestern Adventist University *Texas* M
Southwestern College *Kansas* M & W
Southwestern College *California* M
Southwestern Illinois College *Illinois* M
Southwestern Oklahoma State University *Oklahoma* W
Southwestern Oregon Community College *Oregon* M & W
Southwestern University *Texas* M & W
Spalding University *Kentucky* M & W
Spartanburg Methodist College *South Carolina* M & W
Spelman College *Georgia* W
Spokane Community College *Washington* M & W
Spokane Falls Community College *Washington* M & W
Spring Arbor University *Michigan* M & W
Spring Hill College *Alabama* M & W
Springfield College *Massachusetts* M & W
Springfield College in Illinois *Illinois* M & W
Springfield Technical Community College *Massachusetts* M & W
Stanford University *California* M & W
State Fair Community College *Missouri* M
State University of New York at Binghamton *New York* M & W
State University of New York at Buffalo *New York* M & W
State University of New York College of Agriculture and Technology at Cobleskill *New York* M & W
State University of New York College of Agriculture and Technology at Morrisville *New York* M & W
State University of New York College at Brockport *New York* M & W
State University of New York College at Cortland *New York* M & W
State University of New York College at Geneseo *New York* M & W
State University of New York College at Old Westbury *New York* M
State University of New York College at Oneonta *New York* M & W
State University of New York College at Potsdam *New York* M & W
State University of New York College of Technology at Alfred *New York* M & W
State University of New York College of Technology at Canton *New York* M & W
State University of New York College of Technology at Delhi *New York* M & W
State University of New York, Fredonia *New York* M & W
State University of New York Institute of Technology *New York* M & W
State University of New York Maritime College *New York* M
State University of New York at New Paltz *New York* M & W
State University of New York at Oswego *New York* M & W
State University of New York at Plattsburgh *New York* M & W
Stephen F. Austin State University *Texas* W
Stephens College *Missouri* W
Sterling College *Kansas* M & W
Stetson University *Florida* M & W
Stevens Institute of Technology *New Jersey* M & W
Stonehill College *Massachusetts* M & W
Stony Brook University, State University of New York *New York* M & W
Suffolk County Community College *New York* M
Suffolk University *Massachusetts* M
Summit Pacific College *British Columbia* M
Susquehanna University *Pennsylvania* M & W
Sussex County Community College *New Jersey* M & W
Swarthmore College *Pennsylvania* M & W
Sweet Briar College *Virginia* W
Syracuse University *New York* M & W
Tabor College *Kansas* M & W
Tacoma Community College *Washington* M & W
Taft College *California* M
Taylor University *Indiana* M & W
Taylor University Fort Wayne *Indiana* M
Temple University *Pennsylvania* M & W
Tennessee Technological University *Tennessee* W
Tennessee Temple University *Tennessee* M
Tennessee Wesleyan College *Tennessee* M & W
Texas A&M International University *Texas* M & W
Texas A&M University *Texas* W
Texas A&M University-Commerce *Texas* W
Texas Christian University *Texas* M & W
Texas College *Texas* M & W
Texas Lutheran University *Texas* M & W
Texas Southern University *Texas* M & W
Texas State University-San Marcos *Texas* M & W
Texas Tech University *Texas* W
Texas Wesleyan University *Texas* M & W
Texas Woman's University *Texas* W
Thiel College *Pennsylvania* M & W
Thomas College *Maine* M & W
Thomas More College *Kentucky* M & W
Thomas University *Georgia* M & W

M = Men; W = Women

Thompson Rivers University *British Columbia* M & W
Tiffin University *Ohio* M & W
Toccoa Falls College *Georgia* M & W
Tompkins Cortland Community College *New York* M & W
Towson University *Maryland* M & W
Transylvania University *Kentucky* M & W
Trent University *Ontario* M & W
Trevecca Nazarene University *Tennessee* M & W
Tri-State University *Indiana* M & W
Trinity Christian College *Illinois* M & W
Trinity College *Connecticut* M & W
Trinity International University *Illinois* M & W
Trinity University *Texas* M & W
Trinity (Washington) University *District of Columbia* W
Trinity Western University *British Columbia* M & W
Triton College *Illinois* M
Troy University *Alabama* W
Truett-McConnell College *Georgia* M & W
Truman State University *Missouri* M & W
Tufts University *Massachusetts* M & W
Tulane University *Louisiana* M & W
Tusculum College *Tennessee* M & W
Tuskegee University *Alabama* M
Tyler Junior College *Texas* M
Ulster County Community College *New York* M
Union College *New York* M & W
Union College *Kentucky* M & W
Union County College *New Jersey* M
Union University *Tennessee* M & W
United States Air Force Academy *Colorado* M & W
United States Coast Guard Academy *Connecticut* M & W
United States Merchant Marine Academy *New York* M
United States Military Academy *New York* M & W
United States Naval Academy *Maryland* M & W
Unity College *Maine* M
Universidad del Turabo *Puerto Rico* M
Université Laval *Quebec* M & W
Université de Moncton *New Brunswick* M & W
Université de Montréal *Quebec* M & W
Université du Québec àChicoutimi *Quebec* W
Université du Québec àTrois-Rivières *Quebec* M & W
Université de Sherbrooke *Quebec* M & W
The University of Akron *Ohio* M & W
The University of Alabama *Alabama* W
The University of Alabama at Birmingham *Alabama* M & W
The University of Alabama in Huntsville *Alabama* M & W
University at Albany, State University of New York *New York* M & W
University of Alberta *Alberta* M & W
The University of Arizona *Arizona* M & W
University of Arkansas *Arkansas* W
University of Arkansas at Little Rock *Arkansas* W
University of Bridgeport *Connecticut* M & W
The University of British Columbia *British Columbia* M & W
University of Calgary *Alberta* M & W
University of California, Berkeley *California* M & W
University of California, Davis *California* M & W
University of California, Irvine *California* M & W
University of California, Los Angeles *California* M & W
University of California, San Diego *California* M & W
University of California, Santa Barbara *California* M & W
University of California, Santa Cruz *California* M & W
University of Central Arkansas *Arkansas* M & W
University of Central Florida *Florida* M & W
University of Central Oklahoma *Oklahoma* W
University of Charleston *West Virginia* M & W
University of Chicago *Illinois* M & W
University of Cincinnati *Ohio* M & W
University of Cincinnati Raymond Walters College *Ohio* M & W
University College of the Fraser Valley *British Columbia* M & W
University of Colorado at Boulder *Colorado* M & W
University of Colorado at Colorado Springs *Colorado* M & W
University of Connecticut *Connecticut* M & W
University of the Cumberlands *Kentucky* M & W
University of Dallas *Texas* M & W
University of Dayton *Ohio* M & W
University of Delaware *Delaware* M & W
University of Denver *Colorado* M & W
University of Detroit Mercy *Michigan* M & W
University of the District of Columbia *District of Columbia* M
University of Dubuque *Iowa* M & W
University of Evansville *Indiana* M & W
The University of Findlay *Ohio* M & W
University of Florida *Florida* W
University of Georgia *Georgia* M & W
University of Great Falls *Montana* W
University of Guam *Guam* M
University of Guelph *Ontario* M & W
University of Hartford *Connecticut* M & W
University of Hawaii at Manoa *Hawaii* W
University of Houston *Texas* W
University of Idaho *Idaho* M & W
University of Illinois at Chicago *Illinois* M
University of Illinois at Springfield *Illinois* M
University of Illinois at Urbana-Champaign *Illinois* W
University of the Incarnate Word *Texas* M & W
University of Indianapolis *Indiana* M & W
The University of Iowa *Iowa* M & W
University of Kansas *Kansas* W
University of Kentucky *Kentucky* M & W
University of King's College *Nova Scotia* M & W
University of La Verne *California* M & W
University of Lethbridge *Alberta* M & W
University of Louisiana at Lafayette *Louisiana* W
University of Louisiana at Monroe *Louisiana* W
University of Louisville *Kentucky* M & W
University of Maine *Maine* M & W
The University of Maine at Augusta *Maine* W
University of Maine at Farmington *Maine* M & W
University of Maine at Fort Kent *Maine* M & W
University of Maine at Machias *Maine* M & W
University of Maine at Presque Isle *Maine* M & W
University of Mary *North Dakota* M & W
University of Mary Hardin-Baylor *Texas* M & W
University of Mary Washington *Virginia* M & W
University of Maryland, Baltimore County *Maryland* M & W
University of Maryland, College Park *Maryland* M & W
University of Massachusetts Amherst *Massachusetts* M & W
University of Massachusetts Boston *Massachusetts* M & W
University of Massachusetts Dartmouth *Massachusetts* M & W
University of Massachusetts Lowell *Massachusetts* M
University of Memphis *Tennessee* M & W
University of Miami *Florida* W
University of Michigan *Michigan* M & W
University of Minnesota, Crookston *Minnesota* W
University of Minnesota, Duluth *Minnesota* M & W
University of Minnesota, Morris *Minnesota* W
University of Minnesota, Twin Cities Campus *Minnesota* W
University of Mississippi *Mississippi* M & W
University of Missouri-Columbia *Missouri* W
University of Missouri-Kansas City *Missouri* M
University of Missouri-Rolla *Missouri* M & W
University of Missouri-St. Louis *Missouri* M & W
University of Mobile *Alabama* M & W
The University of Montana-Missoula *Montana* W
University of Montevallo *Alabama* M & W
University of Nebraska-Lincoln *Nebraska* W
University of Nebraska at Omaha *Nebraska* W
University of Nevada, Las Vegas *Nevada* M & W
University of Nevada, Reno *Nevada* W
University of New Brunswick Fredericton *New Brunswick* M & W
University of New Brunswick Saint John *New Brunswick* M & W
University of New England *Maine* M & W
University of New Hampshire *New Hampshire* M & W
University of New Haven *Connecticut* M & W
University of New Mexico *New Mexico* M & W
University of North Alabama *Alabama* W
The University of North Carolina at Asheville *North Carolina* M & W
The University of North Carolina at Chapel Hill *North Carolina* M & W
The University of North Carolina at Charlotte *North Carolina* M & W
The University of North Carolina at Greensboro *North Carolina* M & W
The University of North Carolina at Pembroke *North Carolina* M & W
The University of North Carolina Wilmington *North Carolina* M & W
University of North Dakota *North Dakota* W
University of North Florida *Florida* M & W
University of North Texas *Texas* W
University of Northern Colorado *Colorado* M & W
University of Northern Iowa *Iowa* W
University of Notre Dame *Indiana* M & W
University of Oklahoma *Oklahoma* W
University of Oregon *Oregon* M & W
University of Ottawa *Ontario* W
University of the Ozarks *Arkansas* M & W
University of the Pacific *California* W
University of Pennsylvania *Pennsylvania* M & W
University of Pittsburgh *Pennsylvania* M & W
University of Pittsburgh at Bradford *Pennsylvania* M & W
University of Pittsburgh at Greensburg *Pennsylvania* M & W
University of Pittsburgh at Johnstown *Pennsylvania* M & W
University of Portland *Oregon* M & W
University of Prince Edward Island *Prince Edward Island* M & W
University of Puerto Rico at Arecibo *Puerto Rico* M
University of Puerto Rico at Bayamón *Puerto Rico* M
University of Puerto Rico, Cayey University College *Puerto Rico* M
University of Puerto Rico, Mayagüez Campus *Puerto Rico* M
University of Puerto Rico, Río Piedras *Puerto Rico* M
University of Puget Sound *Washington* M & W
University of Redlands *California* M & W
University of Regina *Saskatchewan* W
University of Rhode Island *Rhode Island* M & W
University of Richmond *Virginia* M & W
University of Rio Grande *Ohio* M & W
University of Rochester *New York* M & W
University of Saint Francis *Indiana* M & W
University of St. Francis *Illinois* M & W
University of Saint Mary *Kansas* M & W
University of St. Thomas *Minnesota* M & W
University of San Diego *California* M & W
University of San Francisco *California* M & W
University of Saskatchewan *Saskatchewan* M & W
University of Science and Arts of Oklahoma *Oklahoma* M & W
The University of Scranton *Pennsylvania* M & W
University of Sioux Falls *South Dakota* M & W
University of South Alabama *Alabama* W
University of South Carolina *South Carolina* M & W
University of South Carolina Aiken *South Carolina* M & W
University of South Carolina Upstate *South Carolina* M & W
University of South Florida *Florida* M & W
University of Southern California *California* W
University of Southern Indiana *Indiana* M & W
University of Southern Maine *Maine* M & W
The University of Tampa *Florida* M & W
The University of Tennessee *Tennessee* W
The University of Tennessee at Chattanooga *Tennessee* M & W
The University of Tennessee at Martin *Tennessee* W
The University of Texas at Austin *Texas* W
The University of Texas at Dallas *Texas* M & W

M = Men; W = Women

Softball

M = Men; W = Women

Bakersfield College *California* W
Baldwin-Wallace College *Ohio* W
Ball State University *Indiana* W
Baptist Bible College of Pennsylvania *Pennsylvania* W
Barber-Scotia College *North Carolina* W
Barnard College *New York* W
Barry University *Florida* W
Barton College *North Carolina* W
Barton County Community College *Kansas* W
Bates College *Maine* W
Bay Path College *Massachusetts* W
Bayamon Central University *Puerto Rico* M & W
Baylor University *Texas* W
Becker College *Massachusetts* W
Belhaven College *Mississippi* W
Bellarmine University *Kentucky* W
Bellevue Community College *Washington* W
Bellevue University *Nebraska* W
Belmont Abbey College *North Carolina* W
Belmont University *Tennessee* W
Beloit College *Wisconsin* W
Bemidji State University *Minnesota* W
Benedict College *South Carolina* W
Benedictine College *Kansas* W
Benedictine University *Illinois* W
Bennett College For Women *North Carolina* W
Bennington College *Vermont* M & W
Bentley College *Massachusetts* W
Berea College *Kentucky* W
Bergen Community College *New Jersey* W
Bernard M. Baruch College of the City University of New York *New York* W
Bethany Bible College *New Brunswick* M & W
Bethany College *West Virginia* W
Bethany College *Kansas* W
Bethany Lutheran College *Minnesota* W
Bethany University *California* W
Bethel College *Tennessee* W
Bethel College *Indiana* W
Bethel University *Minnesota* W
Bethune-Cookman College *Florida* W
Bevill State Community College *Alabama* W
Big Bend Community College *Washington* W
Biola University *California* W
Birmingham-Southern College *Alabama* W
Bishop State Community College *Alabama* W
Black Hawk College *Illinois* W
Blackburn College *Illinois* W
Blinn College *Texas* W
Bloomfield College *New Jersey* W
Bloomsburg University of Pennsylvania *Pennsylvania* W
Blue Mountain Community College *Oregon* W
Bluefield College *Virginia* W
Bluefield State College *West Virginia* W
Bluffton University *Ohio* W
Bossier Parish Community College *Louisiana* W
Boston College *Massachusetts* W
Boston University *Massachusetts* W
Bowdoin College *Maine* W
Bowie State University *Maryland* W
Bowling Green State University *Ohio* W
Bradley University *Illinois* W
Brandeis University *Massachusetts* W
Brenau University *Georgia* W
Brescia University *Kentucky* W
Brevard College *North Carolina* W
Brevard Community College *Florida* W
Brewton-Parker College *Georgia* W
Briar Cliff University *Iowa* W
Briarcliffe College *New York* W
Bridgewater College *Virginia* W
Bridgewater State College *Massachusetts* W
Brigham Young University *Utah* W
Brigham Young University-Hawaii *Hawaii* W
Brookdale Community College *New Jersey* W
Brooklyn College of the City University of New York *New York* W
Broome Community College *New York* W
Broward Community College *Florida* W
Brown Mackie College-Salina *Kansas* W
Brown University *Rhode Island* W
Brunswick Community College *North Carolina* W
Bryant University *Rhode Island* W
Bucknell University *Pennsylvania* W
Buena Vista University *Iowa* W
Buffalo State College, State University of New York *New York* W
Bunker Hill Community College *Massachusetts* W
Burlington County College *New Jersey* W
Butler Community College *Kansas* W
Butler County Community College *Pennsylvania* W
Butler University *Indiana* W
Butte College *California* W
Cabrillo College *California* W
Cabrini College *Pennsylvania* W
Caldwell College *New Jersey* W
California Baptist University *California* W
California Lutheran University *California* W
California Polytechnic State University, San Luis Obispo *California* W
California State University, Bakersfield *California* W
California State University, Chico *California* W
California State University, East Bay *California* W
California State University, Fresno *California* W
California State University, Fullerton *California* W
California State University, Long Beach *California* W
California State University, Northridge *California* W
California State University, Sacramento *California* W
California State University, San Bernardino *California* W
California State University, Stanislaus *California* W
California University of Pennsylvania *Pennsylvania* W
Calumet College of Saint Joseph *Indiana* W
Calvin College *Michigan* W
Camden County College *New Jersey* W
Cameron University *Oklahoma* W
Campbell University *North Carolina* W
Campbellsville University *Kentucky* W
Canisius College *New York* W
Cape Fear Community College *North Carolina* M & W
Capital University *Ohio* W
Cardinal Stritch University *Wisconsin* W
Carl Albert State College *Oklahoma* M
Carleton College *Minnesota* W
Carlow University *Pennsylvania* W
Carnegie Mellon University *Pennsylvania* W
Carroll College *Wisconsin* W
Carson-Newman College *Tennessee* W
Carteret Community College *North Carolina* M & W
Carthage College *Wisconsin* W
Case Western Reserve University *Ohio* W
Castleton State College *Vermont* W
Catawba College *North Carolina* W
The Catholic University of America *District of Columbia* W
Cazenovia College *New York* W
Cecil Community College *Maryland* W
Cedar Crest College *Pennsylvania* W
Cedarville University *Ohio* W
Centenary College *New Jersey* W
Centenary College of Louisiana *Louisiana* W
Central Alabama Community College *Alabama* W
Central Arizona College *Arizona* W
Central Baptist College *Arkansas* W
Central Carolina Community College *North Carolina* W
Central Christian College of Kansas *Kansas* W
Central College *Iowa* W
Central Connecticut State University *Connecticut* W
Central Florida Community College *Florida* W
Central Lakes College *Minnesota* W
Central Maine Community College *Maine* W
Central Methodist University *Missouri* W
Central Michigan University *Michigan* W
Central Missouri State University *Missouri* W
Central Ohio Technical College *Ohio* W
Central Washington University *Washington* W
Centralia College *Washington* W
Centre College *Kentucky* W
Cerritos College *California* W
Chabot College *California* W
Chaffey College *California* W
Chaminade University of Honolulu *Hawaii* W
Chapman University *California* W
Charleston Southern University *South Carolina* W
Chatham College *Pennsylvania* W
Chattahoochee Valley Community College *Alabama* W
Chattanooga State Technical Community College *Tennessee* W
Chesapeake College *Maryland* W
Chestnut Hill College *Pennsylvania* W
Chipola College *Florida* W
Chowan University *North Carolina* W
Christendom College *Virginia* W
Christian Brothers University *Tennessee* W
Christopher Newport University *Virginia* W
Cisco Junior College *Texas* W
Citrus College *California* W
City College of the City University of New York *New York* W
Clackamas Community College *Oregon* W
Claflin University *South Carolina* W
Claremont McKenna College *California* W
Clarendon College *Texas* W
Clarion University of Pennsylvania *Pennsylvania* W
Clark Atlanta University *Georgia* W
Clark College *Washington* W
Clark State Community College *Ohio* W
Clark University *Massachusetts* W
Clarke College *Iowa* W
Clearwater Christian College *Florida* W
Clemson University *South Carolina* W
Cleveland State Community College *Tennessee* W
Cleveland State University *Ohio* W
Clinton Community College *New York* W
Clinton Community College *Iowa* W
Cloud County Community College *Kansas* W
Coastal Carolina University *South Carolina* W
Coastal Georgia Community College *Georgia* W
Coe College *Iowa* W
Coffeyville Community College *Kansas* W
Coker College *South Carolina* W
Colby College *Maine* W
Colby Community College *Kansas* W
Colby-Sawyer College *New Hampshire* W
Colgate University *New York* W
College of the Canyons *California* W
College of Charleston *South Carolina* W
College of the Desert *California* W
College of DuPage *Illinois* W
College of the Holy Cross *Massachusetts* W
College of Lake County *Illinois* W
College Misericordia *Pennsylvania* W
College of Mount St. Joseph *Ohio* W
College of Mount Saint Vincent *New York* W
The College of New Jersey *New Jersey* W
The College of New Rochelle *New York* W
College of the Redwoods *California* W
College of Saint Benedict *Minnesota* W
College of St. Catherine *Minnesota* W
College of Saint Elizabeth *New Jersey* W
College of St. Joseph *Vermont* W
College of Saint Mary *Nebraska* W
The College of Saint Rose *New York* W
The College of St. Scholastica *Minnesota* W
College of the Sequoias *California* W
College of the Siskiyous *California* W
College of Southern Maryland *Maryland* W
College of the Southwest *New Mexico* W
College of Staten Island of the City University of New York *New York* W
The College of Wooster *Ohio* W
The Colorado College *Colorado* W
Colorado Northwestern Community College *Colorado* W
Colorado School of Mines *Colorado* W
Colorado State University *Colorado* W
Colorado State University-Pueblo *Colorado* W
Columbia College *New York* W
Columbia College *Missouri* W
Columbia-Greene Community College *New York* W
Columbia State Community College *Tennessee* W
Columbia Union College *Maryland* W
Columbia University, The Fu Foundation School of Engineering and Applied Science *New York* W
Columbus State Community College *Ohio* W
Columbus State University *Georgia* W

M = Men; W = Women

Community College of Allegheny County *Pennsylvania* W
Community College of Beaver County *Pennsylvania* W
Community College of Philadelphia *Pennsylvania* W
Community College of Rhode Island *Rhode Island* W
Concordia College *New York* W
Concordia College *Minnesota* W
Concordia College *Alabama* W
Concordia University *Oregon* W
Concordia University *Nebraska* W
Concordia University *Michigan* W
Concordia University *Illinois* W
Concordia University *California* W
Concordia University at Austin *Texas* W
Concordia University, St. Paul *Minnesota* W
Concordia University Wisconsin *Wisconsin* W
Connors State College *Oklahoma* W
Contra Costa College *California* W
Copiah-Lincoln Community College *Mississippi* W
Coppin State University *Maryland* W
Corban College *Oregon* W
Cornell College *Iowa* W
Cornell University *New York* W
Cornerstone University *Michigan* W
Corning Community College *New York* W
Cosumnes River College (Sacramento) *California* W
County College of Morris *New Jersey* W
Covenant College *Georgia* W
Cowley County Community College and Area Vocational-Technical School *Kansas* W
Craven Community College *North Carolina* M & W
Creighton University *Nebraska* W
Crossroads College *Minnesota* W
Crown College *Minnesota* W
Cuesta College *California* W
Culver-Stockton College *Missouri* W
Cumberland County College *New Jersey* W
Cumberland University *Tennessee* W
Curry College *Massachusetts* W
Cuyahoga Community College *Ohio* W
Cypress College *California* W
Dakota State University *South Dakota* W
Dakota Wesleyan University *South Dakota* W
Dalton State College *Georgia* M & W
Dana College *Nebraska* W
Daniel Webster College *New Hampshire* W
Danville Area Community College *Illinois* W
Dartmouth College *New Hampshire* W
Darton College *Georgia* W
Davis & Elkins College *West Virginia* W
Dawson Community College *Montana* W
Daytona Beach Community College *Florida* W
De Anza College *California* W
Dean College *Massachusetts* W
Defiance College *Ohio* W
Delaware County Community College *Pennsylvania* W
Delaware State University *Delaware* W
Delaware Technical & Community College, Jack F. Owens Campus *Delaware* W
Delaware Technical & Community College, Stanton/Wilmington Campus *Delaware* W
Delaware Valley College *Pennsylvania* W
Delta College *Michigan* W
Delta State University *Mississippi* W
Denison University *Ohio* W
Denmark Technical College *South Carolina* W
DePaul University *Illinois* W
DePauw University *Indiana* W
Des Moines Area Community College *Iowa* W
DeSales University *Pennsylvania* W
Diablo Valley College *California* W
Dickinson College *Pennsylvania* W
Dickinson State University *North Dakota* W
Dixie State College of Utah *Utah* W
Doane College *Nebraska* W
Dodge City Community College *Kansas* W
Dominican College *New York* W
Dominican University *Illinois* W
Dominican University of California *California* W
Dordt College *Iowa* W
Dowling College *New York* W
Drake University *Iowa* W
Drew University *New Jersey* W
Drexel University *Pennsylvania* W
Duke University *North Carolina* M & W
Dutchess Community College *New York* W
Dyersburg State Community College *Tennessee* W
D'Youville College *New York* W
East Carolina University *North Carolina* W
East Central College *Missouri* W
East Central Community College *Mississippi* W
East Central University *Oklahoma* W
East Los Angeles College *California* W
East Mississippi Community College *Mississippi* W
East Stroudsburg University of Pennsylvania *Pennsylvania* W
East Tennessee State University *Tennessee* W
East Texas Baptist University *Texas* W
Eastern Arizona College *Arizona* W
Eastern Connecticut State University *Connecticut* W
Eastern Illinois University *Illinois* W
Eastern Kentucky University *Kentucky* W
Eastern Mennonite University *Virginia* W
Eastern Michigan University *Michigan* W
Eastern Nazarene College *Massachusetts* W
Eastern New Mexico University *New Mexico* W
Eastern Oklahoma State College *Oklahoma* W
Eastern Oregon University *Oregon* W
Eastern University *Pennsylvania* W
Eckerd College *Florida* W
Edgewood College *Wisconsin* W
Edinboro University of Pennsylvania *Pennsylvania* W
Edmonds Community College *Washington* W
El Paso Community College *Texas* W
Elgin Community College *Illinois* W
Elizabethtown College *Pennsylvania* W
Ellsworth Community College *Iowa* W
Elmhurst College *Illinois* W
Elmira College *New York* W
Elms College *Massachusetts* W
Elon University *North Carolina* W
Emerson College *Massachusetts* W
Emmanuel College *Massachusetts* W
Emmanuel College *Georgia* W
Emory & Henry College *Virginia* W
Emory University *Georgia* W
Emporia State University *Kansas* W
Endicott College *Massachusetts* W
Enterprise-Ozark Community College *Alabama* W
Erie Community College *New York* W
Erie Community College, North Campus *New York* W
Erie Community College, South Campus *New York* W
Erskine College *South Carolina* W
Eureka College *Illinois* W
Evangel University *Missouri* W
Everett Community College *Washington* W
Fairfield University *Connecticut* W
Fairleigh Dickinson University, College at Florham *New Jersey* W
Fairleigh Dickinson University, Metropolitan Campus *New Jersey* W
Fairmont State University *West Virginia* W
Farmingdale State University of New York *New York* W
Faulkner University *Alabama* W
Feather River College *California* W
Felician College *New Jersey* W
Ferris State University *Michigan* W
Ferrum College *Virginia* W
Finger Lakes Community College *New York* W
Finlandia University *Michigan* W
Fisher College *Massachusetts* W
Fitchburg State College *Massachusetts* W
Florida Agricultural and Mechanical University *Florida* W
Florida Atlantic University *Florida* W
Florida Community College at Jacksonville *Florida* W
Florida Gulf Coast University *Florida* W
Florida Institute of Technology *Florida* W
Florida International University *Florida* W
Florida Southern College *Florida* W
Florida State University *Florida* W
Fontbonne University *Missouri* W
Foothill College *California* W
Fordham University *New York* W
Fort Hays State University *Kansas* W
Fort Lewis College *Colorado* W
Fort Scott Community College *Kansas* W
Framingham State College *Massachusetts* W
Francis Marion University *South Carolina* W
Franklin College *Indiana* W
Franklin and Marshall College *Pennsylvania* W
Franklin Pierce College *New Hampshire* W
Frederick Community College *Maryland* W
Freed-Hardeman University *Tennessee* W
Fresno City College *California* W
Friends University *Kansas* W
Frostburg State University *Maryland* W
Fulton-Montgomery Community College *New York* W
Furman University *South Carolina* W
Gadsden State Community College *Alabama* W
Gallaudet University *District of Columbia* W
Galveston College *Texas* W
Gannon University *Pennsylvania* W
Garden City Community College *Kansas* W
Gardner-Webb University *North Carolina* W
Gateway Community College *Connecticut* W
Gavilan College *California* W
Genesee Community College *New York* W
Geneva College *Pennsylvania* W
George Corley Wallace State Community College *Alabama* W
George Fox University *Oregon* W
George Mason University *Virginia* W
Georgetown College *Kentucky* W
Georgetown University *District of Columbia* W
Georgia College & State University *Georgia* W
Georgia Institute of Technology *Georgia* W
Georgia Perimeter College *Georgia* W
Georgia Southern University *Georgia* W
Georgia Southwestern State University *Georgia* W
Georgia State University *Georgia* W
Georgian Court University *New Jersey* W
Gettysburg College *Pennsylvania* W
Glen Oaks Community College *Michigan* W
Glendale Community College *California* W
Glendale Community College *Arizona* W
Glenville State College *West Virginia* W
Gloucester County College *New Jersey* W
Golden West College *California* W
Goldey-Beacom College *Delaware* W
Gordon College *Massachusetts* W
Gordon College *Georgia* W
Goshen College *Indiana* W
Grace College *Indiana* W
Graceland University *Iowa* W
Grand Rapids Community College *Michigan* W
Grand Valley State University *Michigan* W
Grand View College *Iowa* W
Grays Harbor College *Washington* W
Grayson County College *Texas* W
Green Mountain College *Vermont* W
Green River Community College *Washington* W
Greensboro College *North Carolina* W
Greenville College *Illinois* W
Grinnell College *Iowa* W
Grossmont College *California* W
Grove City College *Pennsylvania* W
Guilford College *North Carolina* W
Gulf Coast Community College *Florida* W
Gustavus Adolphus College *Minnesota* W
Gwynedd-Mercy College *Pennsylvania* W
Hagerstown Community College *Maryland* W
Hamilton College *New York* W
Hamline University *Minnesota* W
Hampton University *Virginia* W
Hannibal-LaGrange College *Missouri* W
Hanover College *Indiana* W
Hardin-Simmons University *Texas* W
Harford Community College *Maryland* W
Harris-Stowe State University *Missouri* W
Hartnell College *California* W
Hartwick College *New York* W
Harvard University *Massachusetts* W

M = Men; W = Women

Harvey Mudd College *California* W
Haskell Indian Nations University *Kansas* W
Hastings College *Nebraska* W
Haverford College *Pennsylvania* W
Hawaii Pacific University *Hawaii* W
Heidelberg College *Ohio* W
Henderson State University *Arkansas* W
Hendrix College *Arkansas* W
Henry Ford Community College *Michigan* W
Herkimer County Community College *New York* W
Hesston College *Kansas* W
Hibbing Community College *Minnesota* W
Highland Community College *Illinois* W
Highline Community College *Washington* W
Hilbert College *New York* W
Hill College of the Hill Junior College District *Texas* W
Hillsborough Community College *Florida* W
Hillsdale College *Michigan* W
Hillsdale Free Will Baptist College *Oklahoma* W
Hinds Community College *Mississippi* W
Hiram College *Ohio* W
Hofstra University *New York* W
Holmes Community College *Mississippi* W
Holyoke Community College *Massachusetts* W
Hood College *Maryland* W
Hope College *Michigan* W
Hope International University *California* W
Houston Baptist University *Texas* W
Howard College *Texas* W
Howard Payne University *Texas* W
Humboldt State University *California* W
Huntingdon College *Alabama* W
Huntington University *Indiana* W
Husson College *Maine* W
Hutchinson Community College and Area Vocational School *Kansas* W
Illinois Central College *Illinois* W
Illinois College *Illinois* W
Illinois Eastern Community Colleges, Lincoln Trail College *Illinois* W
Illinois Eastern Community Colleges, Olney Central College *Illinois* W
Illinois Eastern Community Colleges, Wabash Valley College *Illinois* W
Illinois State University *Illinois* W
Illinois Wesleyan University *Illinois* W
Immaculata University *Pennsylvania* W
Imperial Valley College *California* W
Independence Community College *Kansas* W
Indian Hills Community College *Iowa* W
Indian River Community College *Florida* W
Indiana State University *Indiana* W
Indiana Tech *Indiana* W
Indiana University Bloomington *Indiana* W
Indiana University Northwest *Indiana* W
Indiana University of Pennsylvania *Pennsylvania* W
Indiana University-Purdue University Fort Wayne *Indiana* W
Indiana University-Purdue University Indianapolis *Indiana* W
Indiana Wesleyan University *Indiana* W
Inter American University of Puerto Rico, Aguadilla Campus *Puerto Rico* M & W
Inter American University of Puerto Rico, Arecibo Campus *Puerto Rico* M & W
Inter American University of Puerto Rico, Barranquitas Campus *Puerto Rico* M & W
Inter American University of Puerto Rico, Bayamón Campus *Puerto Rico* M & W
Inter American University of Puerto Rico, Guayama Campus *Puerto Rico* M & W
Inter American University of Puerto Rico, Metropolitan Campus *Puerto Rico* M & W
Inter American University of Puerto Rico, Ponce Campus *Puerto Rico* M & W
Inter American University of Puerto Rico, San Germán Campus *Puerto Rico* M & W
Iona College *New York* W
Iowa Central Community College *Iowa* W
Iowa Lakes Community College *Iowa* W
Iowa State University of Science and Technology *Iowa* W
Iowa Wesleyan College *Iowa* W
Iowa Western Community College *Iowa* W
Itasca Community College *Minnesota* W
Ithaca College *New York* W
Jackson State Community College *Tennessee* W
Jackson State University *Mississippi* W
Jacksonville State University *Alabama* W
Jacksonville University *Florida* W
James H. Faulkner State Community College *Alabama* W
James Madison University *Virginia* W
James Sprunt Community College *North Carolina* W
Jamestown College *North Dakota* W
Jamestown Community College *New York* W
Jefferson Community College *New York* W
Jefferson State Community College *Alabama* W
John A. Logan College *Illinois* W
John Carroll University *Ohio* W
John Jay College of Criminal Justice of the City University of New York *New York* M & W
John Wood Community College *Illinois* W
Johnson C. Smith University *North Carolina* W
Johnson County Community College *Kansas* W
Johnson State College *Vermont* W
Johnson & Wales University *Rhode Island* W
Johnston Community College *North Carolina* M & W
Joliet Junior College *Illinois* W
Jones County Junior College *Mississippi* W
Judson College *Illinois* W
Judson College *Alabama* W
Juniata College *Pennsylvania* W
Kalamazoo College *Michigan* W
Kalamazoo Valley Community College *Michigan* W
Kankakee Community College *Illinois* W
Kansas City Kansas Community College *Kansas* W
Kansas Wesleyan University *Kansas* W
Kaskaskia College *Illinois* W
Kean University *New Jersey* W
Keene State College *New Hampshire* W
Kellogg Community College *Michigan* W
Kennesaw State University *Georgia* W
Kent State University *Ohio* W
Kentucky State University *Kentucky* W
Kentucky Wesleyan College *Kentucky* W
Kenyon College *Ohio* W
Keuka College *New York* W
Keystone College *Pennsylvania* W
King College *Tennessee* M & W
King's College *Pennsylvania* W
Kingsborough Community College of the City University of New York *New York* W
Kirkwood Community College *Iowa* W
Kishwaukee College *Illinois* W
Knox College *Illinois* W
Kutztown University of Pennsylvania *Pennsylvania* W
La Roche College *Pennsylvania* W
La Salle University *Pennsylvania* W
Labette Community College *Kansas* W
Lackawanna College *Pennsylvania* W
Lafayette College *Pennsylvania* W
LaGrange College *Georgia* W
Lake City Community College *Florida* W
Lake Erie College *Ohio* W
Lake Forest College *Illinois* W
Lake Land College *Illinois* W
Lake Michigan College *Michigan* W
Lake-Sumter Community College *Florida* W
Lake Superior State University *Michigan* W
Lakeland College *Wisconsin* W
Lakeland Community College *Ohio* W
Lamar Community College *Colorado* W
Lambuth University *Tennessee* W
Lander University *South Carolina* W
Landmark College *Vermont* W
Lane College *Tennessee* W
Laney College *California* W
Lasell College *Massachusetts* W
Lassen Community College District *California* W
Lawrence University *Wisconsin* W
Le Moyne College *New York* W
Lebanon Valley College *Pennsylvania* W
Lee University *Tennessee* W
Lees-McRae College *North Carolina* W
Lehigh Carbon Community College *Pennsylvania* W
Lehigh University *Pennsylvania* W
Lehman College of the City University of New York *New York* W
LeMoyne-Owen College *Tennessee* W
Lenoir-Rhyne College *North Carolina* W
Lesley University *Massachusetts* W
LeTourneau University *Texas* W
Lewis & Clark College *Oregon* W
Lewis and Clark Community College *Illinois* W
Lewis University *Illinois* W
Liberty University *Virginia* W
Limestone College *South Carolina* W
Lincoln Christian College *Illinois* M & W
Lincoln College *Illinois* W
Lincoln College-Normal *Illinois* W
Lincoln Land Community College *Illinois* W
Lincoln Memorial University *Tennessee* W
Lincoln University *Missouri* W
Lindenwood University *Missouri* W
Lindsey Wilson College *Kentucky* W
Linfield College *Oregon* W
Linn State Technical College *Missouri* M & W
Lipscomb University *Tennessee* W
Livingstone College *North Carolina* W
Lock Haven University of Pennsylvania *Pennsylvania* W
Lon Morris College *Texas* W
Long Beach City College *California* W
Long Island University, Brooklyn Campus *New York* W
Long Island University, C.W. Post Campus *New York* W
Longwood University *Virginia* W
Loras College *Iowa* W
Los Angeles Pierce College *California* W
Los Medanos College *California* W
Louisburg College *North Carolina* W
Louisiana College *Louisiana* W
Louisiana State University and Agricultural and Mechanical College *Louisiana* W
Louisiana Tech University *Louisiana* W
Lower Columbia College *Washington* W
Loyola University Chicago *Illinois* W
Lurleen B. Wallace Community College *Alabama* W
Luther College *Iowa* W
Luzerne County Community College *Pennsylvania* W
Lycoming College *Pennsylvania* W
Lynchburg College *Virginia* W
Lyndon State College *Vermont* W
Lynn University *Florida* W
Macalester College *Minnesota* W
MacMurray College *Illinois* W
Macomb Community College *Michigan* W
Madison Area Technical College *Wisconsin* W
Madonna University *Michigan* W
Maine Maritime Academy *Maine* W
Malone College *Ohio* W
Manatee Community College *Florida* W
Manchester College *Indiana* W
Manchester Community College *Connecticut* W
Manhattan College *New York* W
Manhattanville College *New York* W
Mansfield University of Pennsylvania *Pennsylvania* W
Maple Woods Community College *Missouri* W
Maranatha Baptist Bible College *Wisconsin* W
Marian College *Indiana* W
Marian College of Fond du Lac *Wisconsin* W
Marietta College *Ohio* W
Marist College *New York* W
Marquette University *Wisconsin* W
Mars Hill College *North Carolina* W
Marshall University *West Virginia* W
Marshalltown Community College *Iowa* W
Martin Luther College *Minnesota* W
Martin Methodist College *Tennessee* W
Mary Baldwin College *Virginia* W
Maryville College *Tennessee* W
Maryville University of Saint Louis *Missouri* W
Marywood University *Pennsylvania* W
Massachusetts Bay Community College *Massachusetts* W

M = Men; W = Women

Massachusetts College of Liberal Arts *Massachusetts* W
Massachusetts Institute of Technology *Massachusetts* W
Massachusetts Maritime Academy *Massachusetts* W
Massasoit Community College *Massachusetts* W
The Master's College and Seminary *California* W
Mayville State University *North Dakota* W
McDaniel College *Maryland* W
McHenry County College *Illinois* W
McKendree College *Illinois* W
McLennan Community College *Texas* W
McNeese State University *Louisiana* W
McPherson College *Kansas* W
Medaille College *New York* W
Menlo College *California* W
Merced College *California* W
Mercer County Community College *New Jersey* W
Mercer University *Georgia* W
Mercy College *New York* W
Mercyhurst College *Pennsylvania* W
Meredith College *North Carolina* W
Meridian Community College *Mississippi* W
Merrimack College *Massachusetts* W
Mesa Community College *Arizona* W
Mesa State College *Colorado* W
Mesabi Range Community and Technical College *Minnesota* W
Messiah College *Pennsylvania* W
Methodist College *North Carolina* W
Miami Dade College *Florida* W
Miami University *Ohio* W
Miami University Hamilton *Ohio* W
Miami University-Middletown Campus *Ohio* W
Michigan State University *Michigan* W
Mid-America Christian University *Oklahoma* W
Mid-America College of Funeral Service *Indiana* M & W
Mid-Continent University *Kentucky* W
Mid-Plains Community College *Nebraska* W
MidAmerica Nazarene University *Kansas* W
Middle Georgia College *Georgia* W
Middle Tennessee State University *Tennessee* W
Middlebury College *Vermont* W
Middlesex County College *New Jersey* W
Midland College *Texas* W
Midland Lutheran College *Nebraska* W
Midway College *Kentucky* W
Midwestern State University *Texas* W
Miles College *Alabama* W
Millersville University of Pennsylvania *Pennsylvania* W
Milligan College *Tennessee* W
Millikin University *Illinois* W
Millsaps College *Mississippi* W
Milwaukee Area Technical College *Wisconsin* M & W
Milwaukee School of Engineering *Wisconsin* W
Minnesota State Community and Technical College-Fergus Falls *Minnesota* W
Minnesota State University Mankato *Minnesota* W
Minnesota State University Moorhead *Minnesota* W
Minnesota West Community and Technical College *Minnesota* W
Minot State University *North Dakota* W
Mission College *California* W
Mississippi College *Mississippi* W
Mississippi Gulf Coast Community College *Mississippi* W
Mississippi State University *Mississippi* W
Mississippi University for Women *Mississippi* W
Missouri Baptist University *Missouri* W
Missouri Southern State University *Missouri* W
Missouri State University *Missouri* W
Missouri Valley College *Missouri* W
Missouri Western State University *Missouri* W
Mitchell College *Connecticut* W
Modesto Junior College *California* W
Mohawk Valley Community College *New York* W
Molloy College *New York* W
Monmouth College *Illinois* W
Monmouth University *New Jersey* W
Monroe College (Bronx) *New York* W
Monroe College (New Rochelle) *New York* W
Monroe Community College *New York* W
Montana State University-Billings *Montana* W
Montclair State University *New Jersey* W
Monterey Peninsula College *California* W
Montreat College *North Carolina* W
Moorpark College *California* W
Moraine Valley Community College *Illinois* W
Moravian College *Pennsylvania* W
Morehead State University *Kentucky* W
Morgan State University *Maryland* W
Morningside College *Iowa* W
Morris College *South Carolina* W
Morton College *Illinois* W
Motlow State Community College *Tennessee* W
Mott Community College *Michigan* W
Mount Aloysius College *Pennsylvania* W
Mount Holyoke College *Massachusetts* W
Mt. Hood Community College *Oregon* W
Mount Ida College *Massachusetts* W
Mount Marty College *South Dakota* W
Mount Mary College *Wisconsin* W
Mount Mercy College *Iowa* W
Mount Olive College *North Carolina* W
Mount Saint Mary College *New York* W
Mount St. Mary's University *Maryland* W
Mt. San Antonio College *California* W
Mount Union College *Ohio* W
Mount Vernon Nazarene University *Ohio* W
Mountain State University *West Virginia* W
Muhlenberg College *Pennsylvania* W
Murray State College *Oklahoma* M
Muscatine Community College *Iowa* W
Muskegon Community College *Michigan* W
Muskingum College *Ohio* W
Napa Valley College *California* W
Nassau Community College *New York* W
Navarro College *Texas* W
Nazareth College of Rochester *New York* W
Nebraska Wesleyan University *Nebraska* W
Neosho County Community College *Kansas* W
Neumann College *Pennsylvania* W
New England College *New Hampshire* W
New Hampshire Technical Institute *New Hampshire* W
New Jersey City University *New Jersey* W
New Jersey Institute of Technology *New Jersey* W
New Mexico Highlands University *New Mexico* W
New Mexico State University *New Mexico* W
New York Institute of Technology *New York* W
New York University *New York* W
Newberry College *South Carolina* W
Newbury College *Massachusetts* W
Newman University *Kansas* W
Niagara County Community College *New York* W
Niagara University *New York* W
Nicholls State University *Louisiana* W
Nichols College *Massachusetts* W
Norfolk State University *Virginia* W
North Arkansas College *Arkansas* W
North Carolina Agricultural and Technical State University *North Carolina* W
North Carolina Central University *North Carolina* W
North Carolina State University *North Carolina* W
North Carolina Wesleyan College *North Carolina* W
North Central College *Illinois* W
North Central Missouri College *Missouri* W
North Country Community College *New York* W
North Dakota State University *North Dakota* W
North Florida Community College *Florida* W
North Georgia College & State University *Georgia* W
North Greenville College *South Carolina* W
North Idaho College *Idaho* W
North Iowa Area Community College *Iowa* W
North Lake College *Texas* W
North Park University *Illinois* W
Northampton County Area Community College *Pennsylvania* W
Northeast Mississippi Community College *Mississippi* W
Northeast Texas Community College *Texas* W
Northeastern Junior College *Colorado* W
Northeastern Oklahoma Agricultural and Mechanical College *Oklahoma* W
Northeastern State University *Oklahoma* W
Northern Illinois University *Illinois* W
Northern Kentucky University *Kentucky* W
Northern Michigan University *Michigan* W
Northern Oklahoma College *Oklahoma* W
Northern State University *South Dakota* W
Northland College *Wisconsin* W
Northland Community and Technical College-Thief River Falls *Minnesota* W
Northwest Christian College *Oregon* W
Northwest Mississippi Community College *Mississippi* W
Northwest Missouri State University *Missouri* W
Northwest Nazarene University *Idaho* W
Northwest-Shoals Community College *Alabama* W
Northwestern College *Minnesota* W
Northwestern College *Iowa* W
Northwestern Oklahoma State University *Oklahoma* W
Northwestern State University of Louisiana *Louisiana* W
Northwestern University *Illinois* W
Northwood University *Michigan* W
Northwood University, Florida Campus *Florida* W
Northwood University, Texas Campus *Texas* W
Norwich University *Vermont* W
Notre Dame College *Ohio* W
Notre Dame de Namur University *California* W
Nova Southeastern University *Florida* W
Nyack College *New York* W
Oakland City University *Indiana* W
Oakland Community College *Michigan* W
Oakland University *Michigan* W
Oakton Community College *Illinois* W
Oberlin College *Ohio* W
Occidental College *California* W
Ocean County College *New Jersey* W
Odessa College *Texas* W
Ohio Dominican University *Ohio* W
Ohio Northern University *Ohio* W
The Ohio State University *Ohio* W
Ohio University *Ohio* W
Ohio University-Lancaster *Ohio* W
Ohio University-Zanesville *Ohio* W
Ohio Valley University *West Virginia* W
Ohio Wesleyan University *Ohio* W
Ohlone College *California* W
Okaloosa-Walton College *Florida* W
Oklahoma Baptist University *Oklahoma* W
Oklahoma Christian University *Oklahoma* W
Oklahoma City University *Oklahoma* W
Oklahoma Panhandle State University *Oklahoma* W
Oklahoma State University *Oklahoma* W
Oklahoma Wesleyan University *Oklahoma* W
Old Dominion University *Virginia* W
Olivet College *Michigan* W
Olivet Nazarene University *Illinois* W
Olympic College *Washington* W
Onondaga Community College *New York* W
Orange Coast College *California* W
Orange County Community College *New York* W
Oregon Institute of Technology *Oregon* W
Oregon State University *Oregon* W
Otero Junior College *Colorado* W
Ottawa University *Kansas* W
Otterbein College *Ohio* W
Ouachita Baptist University *Arkansas* W
Owens Community College *Ohio* W
Pace University *New York* W
Pacific Lutheran University *Washington* W
Pacific University *Oregon* W
Paine College *Georgia* W
Palm Beach Atlantic University *Florida* W
Palm Beach Community College *Florida* W
Paradise Valley Community College *Arizona* W
Paris Junior College *Texas* W
Park University *Missouri* W
Parkland College *Illinois* W
Pasadena City College *California* W
Pasco-Hernando Community College *Florida* W
Patten University *California* W
Peace College *North Carolina* W

M = Men; W = Women

M = Men; W = Women

Southeastern Community College, North Campus *Iowa* W
Southeastern Illinois College *Illinois* W
Southeastern Louisiana University *Louisiana* W
Southeastern Oklahoma State University *Oklahoma* W
Southern Arkansas University-Magnolia *Arkansas* W
Southern Connecticut State University *Connecticut* W
Southern Illinois University Carbondale *Illinois* W
Southern Illinois University Edwardsville *Illinois* W
Southern Maine Community College *Maine* W
Southern Nazarene University *Oklahoma* W
Southern New Hampshire University *New Hampshire* W
Southern Oregon University *Oregon* W
Southern State Community College *Ohio* W
Southern Union State Community College *Alabama* W
Southern University and Agricultural and Mechanical College *Louisiana* W
Southern Utah University *Utah* W
Southern Vermont College *Vermont* W
Southern Virginia University *Virginia* W
Southern Wesleyan University *South Carolina* W
Southwest Baptist University *Missouri* W
Southwest Minnesota State University *Minnesota* W
Southwest Mississippi Community College *Mississippi* W
Southwestern Adventist University *Texas* W
Southwestern College *Kansas* W
Southwestern College *California* W
Southwestern Community College *Iowa* W
Southwestern Illinois College *Illinois* W
Southwestern Oklahoma State University *Oklahoma* W
Southwestern Oregon Community College *Oregon* W
Spalding University *Kentucky* W
Spartanburg Methodist College *South Carolina* W
Spokane Community College *Washington* W
Spokane Falls Community College *Washington* W
Spoon River College *Illinois* W
Spring Arbor University *Michigan* W
Spring Hill College *Alabama* W
Springfield College *Massachusetts* W
Springfield College in Illinois *Illinois* W
Stanford University *California* W
State University of New York at Binghamton *New York* W
State University of New York at Buffalo *New York* W
State University of New York College of Agriculture and Technology at Cobleskill *New York* W
State University of New York College of Agriculture and Technology at Morrisville *New York* W
State University of New York College at Brockport *New York* W
State University of New York College at Cortland *New York* W
State University of New York College at Geneseo *New York* W
State University of New York College at Old Westbury *New York* W
State University of New York College at Oneonta *New York* W
State University of New York College at Potsdam *New York* W
State University of New York College of Technology at Alfred *New York* W
State University of New York College of Technology at Canton *New York* W
State University of New York College of Technology at Delhi *New York* W
State University of New York, Fredonia *New York* W
State University of New York Institute of Technology *New York* W
State University of New York Maritime College *New York* W
State University of New York at New Paltz *New York* W
State University of New York at Oswego *New York* W
State University of New York at Plattsburgh *New York* W

Stephen F. Austin State University *Texas* W
Sterling College *Kansas* W
Stetson University *Florida* W
Stonehill College *Massachusetts* W
Stony Brook University, State University of New York *New York* W
Suffolk County Community College *New York* W
Suffolk University *Massachusetts* W
Sul Ross State University *Texas* W
Sullivan County Community College *New York* W
Susquehanna University *Pennsylvania* W
Sussex County Community College *New Jersey* W
Swarthmore College *Pennsylvania* W
Sweet Briar College *Virginia* W
Syracuse University *New York* M & W
Tabor College *Kansas* W
Taft College *California* W
Tallahassee Community College *Florida* W
Tarleton State University *Texas* W
Taylor University *Indiana* W
Taylor University Fort Wayne *Indiana* W
Temple College *Texas* W
Temple University *Pennsylvania* M & W
Tennessee State University *Tennessee* W
Tennessee Technological University *Tennessee* W
Tennessee Wesleyan College *Tennessee* W
Texarkana College *Texas* W
Texas A&M University *Texas* W
Texas A&M University-Corpus Christi *Texas* W
Texas A&M University-Kingsville *Texas* W
Texas College *Texas* W
Texas Lutheran University *Texas* W
Texas Southern University *Texas* W
Texas State University-San Marcos *Texas* M & W
Texas Tech University *Texas* W
Texas Wesleyan University *Texas* W
Texas Woman's University *Texas* W
Thiel College *Pennsylvania* W
Thomas College *Maine* W
Thomas More College *Kentucky* W
Thomas University *Georgia* W
Three Rivers Community College *Missouri* W
Tiffin University *Ohio* W
Tompkins Cortland Community College *New York* W
Tougaloo College *Mississippi* W
Towson University *Maryland* W
Transylvania University *Kentucky* W
Trevecca Nazarene University *Tennessee* W
Tri-State University *Indiana* W
Trinidad State Junior College *Colorado* W
Trinity Christian College *Illinois* W
Trinity College *Connecticut* W
Trinity International University *Illinois* W
Trinity University *Texas* W
Trinity (Washington) University *District of Columbia* W
Triton College *Illinois* W
Troy University *Alabama* W
Truett-McConnell College *Georgia* W
Truman State University *Missouri* W
Tufts University *Massachusetts* W
Tusculum College *Tennessee* W
Ulster County Community College *New York* W
Union College *New York* W
Union College *Kentucky* W
Union University *Tennessee* W
United States Air Force Academy *Colorado* W
United States Coast Guard Academy *Connecticut* W
United States Merchant Marine Academy *New York* W
United States Military Academy *New York* W
United States Naval Academy *Maryland* W
Universidad Adventista de las Antillas *Puerto Rico* M
Universidad Metropolitana *Puerto Rico* M & W
The University of Akron *Ohio* W
The University of Alabama *Alabama* W
The University of Alabama at Birmingham *Alabama* W
The University of Alabama in Huntsville *Alabama* W
University at Albany, State University of New York *New York* W
The University of Arizona *Arizona* W
University of Arkansas *Arkansas* W

University of Arkansas at Monticello *Arkansas* W
University of Bridgeport *Connecticut* W
University of California, Berkeley *California* W
University of California, Davis *California* W
University of California, Irvine *California* M & W
University of California, Los Angeles *California* W
University of California, Riverside *California* W
University of California, San Diego *California* W
University of California, Santa Barbara *California* W
University of California, Santa Cruz *California* W
University of Central Arkansas *Arkansas* W
University of Central Oklahoma *Oklahoma* W
University of Charleston *West Virginia* W
University of Chicago *Illinois* W
University of Colorado at Boulder *Colorado* W
University of Colorado at Colorado Springs *Colorado* W
University of Connecticut *Connecticut* W
University of the Cumberlands *Kentucky* W
University of Dallas *Texas* W
University of Dayton *Ohio* W
University of Delaware *Delaware* W
University of Detroit Mercy *Michigan* W
University of Dubuque *Iowa* W
University of Evansville *Indiana* W
The University of Findlay *Ohio* W
University of Florida *Florida* W
University of Georgia *Georgia* W
University of Great Falls *Montana* W
University of Hartford *Connecticut* W
University of Hawaii at Hilo *Hawaii* W
University of Hawaii at Manoa *Hawaii* W
University of Houston *Texas* W
University of Illinois at Chicago *Illinois* W
University of Illinois at Springfield *Illinois* W
University of the Incarnate Word *Texas* W
University of Indianapolis *Indiana* W
The University of Iowa *Iowa* W
University of Kansas *Kansas* W
University of Kentucky *Kentucky* W
University of La Verne *California* W
University of Louisiana at Lafayette *Louisiana* W
University of Louisiana at Monroe *Louisiana* W
University of Louisville *Kentucky* W
University of Maine *Maine* W
University of Maine at Farmington *Maine* W
University of Maine at Presque Isle *Maine* W
University of Mary *North Dakota* W
University of Mary Hardin-Baylor *Texas* W
University of Mary Washington *Virginia* W
University of Maryland, Baltimore County *Maryland* W
University of Maryland, College Park *Maryland* W
University of Maryland Eastern Shore *Maryland* W
University of Massachusetts Amherst *Massachusetts* W
University of Massachusetts Boston *Massachusetts* W
University of Massachusetts Dartmouth *Massachusetts* W
University of Memphis *Tennessee* W
University of Miami *Florida* W
University of Michigan *Michigan* W
University of Minnesota, Crookston *Minnesota* W
University of Minnesota, Duluth *Minnesota* W
University of Minnesota, Morris *Minnesota* W
University of Minnesota, Twin Cities Campus *Minnesota* W
University of Mississippi *Mississippi* W
University of Missouri-Columbia *Missouri* W
University of Missouri-Kansas City *Missouri* W
University of Missouri-Rolla *Missouri* W
University of Missouri-St. Louis *Missouri* W
University of Mobile *Alabama* W
University of Nebraska at Kearney *Nebraska* W
University of Nebraska-Lincoln *Nebraska* W
University of Nebraska at Omaha *Nebraska* W
University of Nevada, Las Vegas *Nevada* W
University of Nevada, Reno *Nevada* W
University of New England *Maine* W
University of New Hampshire *New Hampshire* W
University of New Haven *Connecticut* W
University of New Mexico *New Mexico* W
University of North Alabama *Alabama* W

M = Men; W = Women

The University of North Carolina at Chapel Hill *North Carolina* W
The University of North Carolina at Charlotte *North Carolina* W
The University of North Carolina at Greensboro *North Carolina* W
The University of North Carolina at Pembroke *North Carolina* W
The University of North Carolina Wilmington *North Carolina* W
University of North Dakota *North Dakota* W
University of North Florida *Florida* W
University of North Texas *Texas* W
University of Northern Colorado *Colorado* W
University of Northern Iowa *Iowa* W
University of Notre Dame *Indiana* W
University of Oklahoma *Oklahoma* W
University of Oregon *Oregon* W
University of the Ozarks *Arkansas* W
University of the Pacific *California* W
University of Pennsylvania *Pennsylvania* W
University of Pittsburgh *Pennsylvania* W
University of Pittsburgh at Bradford *Pennsylvania* W
University of Pittsburgh at Greensburg *Pennsylvania* W
University of Puerto Rico, Aguadilla University College *Puerto Rico* M & W
University of Puerto Rico at Arecibo *Puerto Rico* W
University of Puerto Rico, Cayey University College *Puerto Rico* M & W
University of Puerto Rico at Humacao *Puerto Rico* W
University of Puerto Rico, Mayagüez Campus *Puerto Rico* M & W
University of Puerto Rico at Utuado *Puerto Rico* M & W
University of Puget Sound *Washington* W
University of Redlands *California* W
University of Rhode Island *Rhode Island* W
University of Rio Grande *Ohio* W
University of Rochester *New York* W
University of Saint Francis *Indiana* W
University of St. Francis *Illinois* W
University of Saint Mary *Kansas* W
University of St. Thomas *Minnesota* W
University of San Diego *California* W
University of San Francisco *California* M & W
University of Science and Arts of Oklahoma *Oklahoma* W
University of the Sciences in Philadelphia *Pennsylvania* W
The University of Scranton *Pennsylvania* W
University of Sioux Falls *South Dakota* W
University of South Carolina *South Carolina* W
University of South Carolina Aiken *South Carolina* W
University of South Carolina Upstate *South Carolina* W
The University of South Dakota *South Dakota* W
University of South Florida *Florida* W
University of Southern Indiana *Indiana* W
University of Southern Maine *Maine* W
The University of Tampa *Florida* W
The University of Tennessee *Tennessee* W
The University of Tennessee at Chattanooga *Tennessee* W
The University of Tennessee at Martin *Tennessee* W
The University of Texas at Arlington *Texas* W
The University of Texas at Austin *Texas* W
The University of Texas at Dallas *Texas* W
The University of Texas of the Permian Basin *Texas* W
The University of Texas at San Antonio *Texas* W
The University of Toledo *Ohio* W
University of Tulsa *Oklahoma* W
University of Utah *Utah* W
University of Vermont *Vermont* W
University of Virginia *Virginia* W
The University of Virginia's College at Wise *Virginia* W
University of Washington *Washington* W
The University of West Alabama *Alabama* W
University of West Florida *Florida* W
University of West Georgia *Georgia* W
University of Windsor *Ontario* W
University of Wisconsin-Eau Claire *Wisconsin* W
University of Wisconsin-Green Bay *Wisconsin* W
University of Wisconsin-La Crosse *Wisconsin* W
University of Wisconsin-Madison *Wisconsin* W
University of Wisconsin-Oshkosh *Wisconsin* W
University of Wisconsin-Parkside *Wisconsin* W
University of Wisconsin-Platteville *Wisconsin* W
University of Wisconsin-River Falls *Wisconsin* W
University of Wisconsin-Stevens Point *Wisconsin* W
University of Wisconsin-Stout *Wisconsin* W
University of Wisconsin-Superior *Wisconsin* W
University of Wisconsin-Whitewater *Wisconsin* W
Upper Iowa University *Iowa* W
Urbana University *Ohio* W
Ursinus College *Pennsylvania* W
Ursuline College *Ohio* W
Utah State University *Utah* W
Utah Valley State College *Utah* W
Utica College *New York* W
Valdosta State University *Georgia* W
Valley City State University *North Dakota* W
Valparaiso University *Indiana* W
Vanguard University of Southern California *California* W
Ventura College *California* W
Vermilion Community College *Minnesota* W
Vermont Technical College *Vermont* W
Vernon College *Texas* W
Victor Valley College *California* W
Villa Julie College *Maryland* W
Villanova University *Pennsylvania* W
Virginia Intermont College *Virginia* W
Virginia Polytechnic Institute and State University *Virginia* W
Virginia State University *Virginia* W
Virginia Union University *Virginia* W
Virginia Wesleyan College *Virginia* W
Viterbo University *Wisconsin* W
Volunteer State Community College *Tennessee* W
Voorhees College *South Carolina* W
Wagner College *New York* W
Waldorf College *Iowa* W
Walla Walla College *Washington* W
Walla Walla Community College *Washington* W
Wallace State Community College *Alabama* W
Walsh University *Ohio* W
Walters State Community College *Tennessee* W
Warner Southern College *Florida* W
Wartburg College *Iowa* W
Washburn University *Kansas* W
Washington College *Maryland* W
Washington & Jefferson College *Pennsylvania* W
Washington and Lee University *Virginia* W
Washington State University *Washington* W
Washington University in St. Louis *Missouri* W
Waubonsee Community College *Illinois* W
Wayne State College *Nebraska* W
Wayne State University *Michigan* W
Waynesburg College *Pennsylvania* W
Webber International University *Florida* W
Weber State University *Utah* W
Webster University *Missouri* W
Wellesley College *Massachusetts* W
Wells College *New York* W
Wenatchee Valley College *Washington* W
Wentworth Institute of Technology *Massachusetts* W
Wesley College *Delaware* W
Wesleyan College *Georgia* W
Wesleyan University *Connecticut* W
West Chester University of Pennsylvania *Pennsylvania* W
West Hills Community College *California* W
West Liberty State College *West Virginia* W
West Texas A&M University *Texas* W
West Virginia State University *West Virginia* W
West Virginia University Institute of Technology *West Virginia* W
West Virginia Wesleyan College *West Virginia* W
Westchester Community College *New York* W
Western Connecticut State University *Connecticut* W
Western Illinois University *Illinois* W
Western Kentucky University *Kentucky* W
Western Michigan University *Michigan* W
Western Nebraska Community College *Nebraska* W
Western New England College *Massachusetts* W
Western New Mexico University *New Mexico* W
Western Oklahoma State College *Oklahoma* W
Western Oregon University *Oregon* W
Western Texas College *Texas* W
Western Washington University *Washington* W
Westfield State College *Massachusetts* W
Westminster College *Pennsylvania* W
Westminster College *Missouri* W
Westmoreland County Community College *Pennsylvania* W
Wheaton College *Massachusetts* W
Wheaton College *Illinois* W
Wheeling Jesuit University *West Virginia* W
Wheelock College *Massachusetts* W
Whitman College *Washington* M & W
Whittier College *California* W
Whitworth College *Washington* W
Wichita State University *Kansas* W
Widener University *Pennsylvania* W
Wilkes University *Pennsylvania* W
Willamette University *Oregon* W
William Carey College *Mississippi* W
William Jewell College *Missouri* W
William Paterson University of New Jersey *New Jersey* W
William Penn University *Iowa* W
William Rainey Harper College *Illinois* W
William Woods University *Missouri* W
Williams Baptist College *Arkansas* W
Williams College *Massachusetts* W
Wilmington College *Ohio* W
Wilmington College *Delaware* W
Wilson College *Pennsylvania* W
Wingate University *North Carolina* W
Winona State University *Minnesota* W
Winston-Salem State University *North Carolina* W
Winthrop University *South Carolina* W
Wisconsin Lutheran College *Wisconsin* W
Wittenberg University *Ohio* W
Worcester Polytechnic Institute *Massachusetts* W
Worcester State College *Massachusetts* W
Wright State University *Ohio* W
Xavier University *Ohio* W
Yakima Valley Community College *Washington* W
Yale University *Connecticut* W
York College *Nebraska* W
York College of the City University of New York *New York* W
York College of Pennsylvania *Pennsylvania* W
Young Harris College *Georgia* W
Youngstown State University *Ohio* W
Yuba College *California* W

Squash

Amherst College *Massachusetts* M & W
Bard College *New York* M
Barnard College *New York* W
Bates College *Maine* M & W
Bowdoin College *Maine* M & W
Brandeis University *Massachusetts* M
Brock University *Ontario* M
Brown University *Rhode Island* M & W
Bryant University *Rhode Island* M & W
Carnegie Mellon University *Pennsylvania* M & W
Colby College *Maine* M & W
Colgate University *New York* M & W
Columbia College *New York* M & W
Columbia University, The Fu Foundation School of Engineering and Applied Science *New York* M & W
Connecticut College *Connecticut* M & W
Cornell University *New York* M & W
Dartmouth College *New Hampshire* M & W
Denison University *Ohio* M & W
Dickinson College *Pennsylvania* M & W
Duke University *North Carolina* M & W
Fordham University *New York* M
Franklin and Marshall College *Pennsylvania* M & W
Hamilton College *New York* M & W
Harvard University *Massachusetts* M & W
Haverford College *Pennsylvania* M & W

M = Men; W = Women

Hobart and William Smith Colleges *New York* M & W
Kenyon College *Ohio* M & W
Lafayette College *Pennsylvania* M
Lehigh University *Pennsylvania* M
Massachusetts Institute of Technology *Massachusetts* M
McGill University *Quebec* M & W
McMaster University *Ontario* M & W
Michigan Technological University *Michigan* M & W
Middlebury College *Vermont* W
Mount Holyoke College *Massachusetts* W
Princeton University *New Jersey* M & W
Queen's University at Kingston *Ontario* M & W
Reed College *Oregon* M & W
Rensselaer Polytechnic Institute *New York* M & W
Ryerson University *Ontario* M & W
St. Lawrence University *New York* M & W
Smith College *Massachusetts* W
Southeastern Community College *North Carolina* W
Stanford University *California* M & W
State University of New York College at Geneseo *New York* M & W
Swarthmore College *Pennsylvania* M & W
Syracuse University *New York* M & W
Trent University *Ontario* M & W
Trinity College *Connecticut* M & W
Tufts University *Massachusetts* M & W
United States Military Academy *New York* M & W
United States Naval Academy *Maryland* M
University of Colorado at Boulder *Colorado* M & W
University of Hartford *Connecticut* M & W
University of Miami *Florida* M & W
University of Pennsylvania *Pennsylvania* M & W
University of Rochester *New York* M
University of Toronto *Ontario* M & W
University of Waterloo *Ontario* M
The University of Western Ontario *Ontario* M & W
Vanderbilt University *Tennessee* M & W
Vassar College *New York* M & W
Wellesley College *Massachusetts* W
Wesleyan University *Connecticut* M & W
Williams College *Massachusetts* M & W
Yale University *Connecticut* M & W

Swimming and Diving

Adelphi University *New York* M & W
Agnes Scott College *Georgia* W
Albion College *Michigan* M & W
Albright College *Pennsylvania* M & W
Alfred University *New York* M & W
Allegheny College *Pennsylvania* M & W
Alma College *Michigan* M & W
American River College *California* M & W
American University *District of Columbia* M & W
American University of Puerto Rico *Puerto Rico* M & W
Amherst College *Massachusetts* M & W
Arcadia University *Pennsylvania* M & W
Arizona State University *Arizona* M & W
Asbury College *Kentucky* M & W
Ashland University *Ohio* M & W
Auburn University *Alabama* M & W
Augustana College *Illinois* M & W
Austin College *Texas* M & W
Babson College *Massachusetts* M & W
Baldwin-Wallace College *Ohio* M & W
Ball State University *Indiana* M & W
Barnard College *New York* W
Bates College *Maine* M & W
Bayamon Central University *Puerto Rico* M & W
Beloit College *Wisconsin* M & W
Benedictine University *Illinois* M & W
Bentley College *Massachusetts* M & W
Berea College *Kentucky* M & W
Bernard M. Baruch College of the City University of New York *New York* M & W
Bethany College *West Virginia* M & W
Biola University *California* M & W
Bloomsburg University of Pennsylvania *Pennsylvania* M & W
Boston College *Massachusetts* M & W
Boston University *Massachusetts* M & W
Bowdoin College *Maine* M & W
Bowling Green State University *Ohio* M & W
Brandeis University *Massachusetts* M & W
Bridgewater State College *Massachusetts* M & W
Brigham Young University *Utah* M & W
Brock University *Ontario* M & W
Brooklyn College of the City University of New York *New York* M & W
Broward Community College *Florida* M & W
Brown University *Rhode Island* M & W
Bryant University *Rhode Island* M & W
Bryn Mawr College *Pennsylvania* W
Bucknell University *Pennsylvania* M & W
Buffalo State College, State University of New York *New York* M & W
Butler University *Indiana* M & W
Cabrillo College *California* M & W
Cabrini College *Pennsylvania* W
California Baptist University *California* M & W
California Institute of Technology *California* M & W
California Lutheran University *California* M & W
California Polytechnic State University, San Luis Obispo *California* M & W
California State University, Bakersfield *California* M & W
California State University, East Bay *California* W
California State University, Fresno *California* W
California State University, Northridge *California* M & W
California State University, San Bernardino *California* M & W
California University of Pennsylvania *Pennsylvania* W
Calvin College *Michigan* M & W
Campbell University *North Carolina* W
Canisius College *New York* M & W
Carleton College *Minnesota* M & W
Carleton University *Ontario* M & W
Carnegie Mellon University *Pennsylvania* M & W
Carroll College *Wisconsin* M & W
Carroll College *Montana* M & W
Carthage College *Wisconsin* M & W
Case Western Reserve University *Ohio* M & W
Catawba College *North Carolina* W
The Catholic University of America *District of Columbia* M & W
Centenary College of Louisiana *Louisiana* M & W
Central Connecticut State University *Connecticut* W
Centre College *Kentucky* M & W
Cerritos College *California* M & W
Chabot College *California* M & W
Chaffey College *California* M & W
Chapman University *California* M & W
Chatham College *Pennsylvania* W
Citrus College *California* M & W
City College of San Francisco *California* M
Claremont McKenna College *California* M & W
Clarion University of Pennsylvania *Pennsylvania* M & W
Clark University *Massachusetts* M & W
Clarkson University *New York* M & W
Clemson University *South Carolina* M & W
Cleveland State University *Ohio* M & W
Coe College *Iowa* M & W
Colby College *Maine* M & W
Colby-Sawyer College *New Hampshire* M & W
Colgate University *New York* M & W
College of the Canyons *California* M & W
College of Charleston *South Carolina* M & W
College of DuPage *Illinois* M & W
College of the Holy Cross *Massachusetts* M & W
College of Marin *California* M & W
College Misericordia *Pennsylvania* M & W
College of Mount Saint Vincent *New York* W
The College of New Jersey *New Jersey* M & W
The College of New Rochelle *New York* W
College of Notre Dame of Maryland *Maryland* W
College of Saint Benedict *Minnesota* W
College of St. Catherine *Minnesota* W
College of Saint Elizabeth *New Jersey* W
The College of Saint Rose *New York* M & W
College of the Sequoias *California* M & W
College of Staten Island of the City University of New York *New York* M & W
The College of William and Mary *Virginia* M & W
The College of Wooster *Ohio* M & W
The Colorado College *Colorado* M & W
Colorado School of Mines *Colorado* M & W
Colorado State University *Colorado* W
Columbia College *New York* M & W
Columbia University, School of General Studies *New York* M & W
Columbia University, The Fu Foundation School of Engineering and Applied Science *New York* M & W
Concordia College *Minnesota* W
Concordia University College of Alberta *Alberta* M & W
Connecticut College *Connecticut* M & W
Cornell University *New York* M & W
Cosumnes River College (Sacramento) *California* M & W
Cuesta College *California* M & W
Cypress College *California* M & W
Dalhousie University *Nova Scotia* M & W
Dartmouth College *New Hampshire* M & W
Darton College *Georgia* M & W
Davidson College *North Carolina* M & W
De Anza College *California* M & W
Delta State University *Mississippi* M & W
Denison University *Ohio* M & W
DePauw University *Indiana* M & W
Diablo Valley College *California* M & W
Dickinson College *Pennsylvania* M & W
Drew University *New Jersey* M & W
Drexel University *Pennsylvania* M & W
Drury University *Missouri* M & W
Duke University *North Carolina* M & W
Duquesne University *Pennsylvania* M & W
East Carolina University *North Carolina* M & W
East Los Angeles College *California* W
East Stroudsburg University of Pennsylvania *Pennsylvania* W
Eastern Connecticut State University *Connecticut* W
Eastern Illinois University *Illinois* M & W
Eastern Michigan University *Michigan* M & W
Eckerd College *Florida* M & W
Edinboro University of Pennsylvania *Pennsylvania* M & W
El Camino College *California* M & W
Elizabethtown College *Pennsylvania* M & W
Elms College *Massachusetts* M & W
Elon University *North Carolina* M & W
Emory University *Georgia* M & W
Erie Community College *New York* M & W
Erie Community College, North Campus *New York* M & W
Erie Community College, South Campus *New York* M & W
Eureka College *Illinois* M & W
Fairfield University *Connecticut* M & W
Fairleigh Dickinson University, College at Florham *New Jersey* M & W
Fairmont State University *West Virginia* M & W
Florida Agricultural and Mechanical University *Florida* M & W
Florida Atlantic University *Florida* M & W
Florida Southern College *Florida* M & W
Florida State University *Florida* M & W
Foothill College *California* M & W
Fordham University *New York* M & W
Franklin and Marshall College *Pennsylvania* M & W
Frostburg State University *Maryland* M & W
Fullerton College *California* M & W
Furman University *South Carolina* M & W
Gallaudet University *District of Columbia* M & W
Gannon University *Pennsylvania* M & W
Gardner-Webb University *North Carolina* W
Genesee Community College *New York* M & W
George Mason University *Virginia* M & W
The George Washington University *District of Columbia* M & W
Georgetown University *District of Columbia* M & W
Georgia Institute of Technology *Georgia* M & W
Georgia Southern University *Georgia* W
Gettysburg College *Pennsylvania* M & W
Golden West College *California* M & W
Gordon College *Massachusetts* M & W
Goucher College *Maryland* M & W

M = Men; W = Women.

M = Men; W = Women

San Diego State University *California* W
San Francisco State University *California* M & W
San Joaquin Delta College *California* M & W
San Jose State University *California* W
Santa Ana College *California* M
Santa Monica College *California* M & W
Santa Rosa Junior College *California* M & W
Sarah Lawrence College *New York* W
Savannah College of Art and Design *Georgia* M & W
Scripps College *California* W
Seattle University *Washington* M & W
Seton Hall University *New Jersey* M & W
Sewanee: The University of the South *Tennessee* M & W
Shasta College *California* M & W
Shippensburg University of Pennsylvania *Pennsylvania* M & W
Siena College *New York* W
Sierra College *California* M & W
Simmons College *Massachusetts* W
Simon Fraser University *British Columbia* M & W
Simon's Rock College of Bard *Massachusetts* M & W
Simpson College *Iowa* M & W
Skidmore College *New York* M & W
Slippery Rock University of Pennsylvania *Pennsylvania* M & W
Smith College *Massachusetts* W
Soka University of America *California* M & W
Solano Community College *California* M & W
South Dakota State University *South Dakota* M & W
Southern Connecticut State University *Connecticut* M & W
Southern Illinois University Carbondale *Illinois* M & W
Southern Methodist University *Texas* M & W
Southwestern College *California* M & W
Southwestern University *Texas* M & W
Spring Hill College *Alabama* M & W
Springfield College *Massachusetts* M & W
Stanford University *California* M & W
State University of New York at Binghamton *New York* M & W
State University of New York at Buffalo *New York* M & W
State University of New York College of Agriculture and Technology at Cobleskill *New York* M & W
State University of New York College of Agriculture and Technology at Morrisville *New York* M & W
State University of New York College at Brockport *New York* M & W
State University of New York College at Cortland *New York* M & W
State University of New York College at Geneseo *New York* M & W
State University of New York College at Old Westbury *New York* M & W
State University of New York College at Oneonta *New York* M & W
State University of New York College at Potsdam *New York* M & W
State University of New York College of Technology at Alfred *New York* M & W
State University of New York College of Technology at Delhi *New York* M & W
State University of New York, Fredonia *New York* M & W
State University of New York Maritime College *New York* M & W
State University of New York at New Paltz *New York* M & W
State University of New York at Oswego *New York* M & W
State University of New York at Plattsburgh *New York* M & W
Stephens College *Missouri* W
Stevens Institute of Technology *New Jersey* M & W
Stony Brook University, State University of New York *New York* M & W
Susquehanna University *Pennsylvania* M & W
Swarthmore College *Pennsylvania* M & W
Sweet Briar College *Virginia* W
Syracuse University *New York* M & W
Texas A&M University *Texas* M & W
Texas Christian University *Texas* M & W
Towson University *Maryland* M & W
Transylvania University *Kentucky* M & W
Trent University *Ontario* M & W
Trinity College *Connecticut* M & W
Trinity University *Texas* M & W
Trinity (Washington) University *District of Columbia* W
Triton College *Illinois* W
Truman State University *Missouri* M & W
Tufts University *Massachusetts* M & W
Tulane University *Louisiana* M & W
Union College *New York* M & W
Union College *Kentucky* M & W
United States Air Force Academy *Colorado* M & W
United States Coast Guard Academy *Connecticut* M & W
United States Merchant Marine Academy *New York* M & W
United States Military Academy *New York* M & W
United States Naval Academy *Maryland* M & W
Université Laval *Quebec* M & W
Université de Montréal *Quebec* M & W
Université du Québec àTrois-Rivières *Quebec* M & W
Université de Sherbrooke *Quebec* M & W
The University of Akron *Ohio* W
The University of Alabama *Alabama* M & W
The University of Alabama at Birmingham *Alabama* W
University of Alaska Anchorage *Alaska* M
University of Alaska Fairbanks *Alaska* W
University of Alberta *Alberta* M & W
The University of Arizona *Arizona* M & W
University of Arkansas *Arkansas* W
University of Arkansas at Little Rock *Arkansas* W
University of Bridgeport *Connecticut* W
The University of British Columbia *British Columbia* M & W
University of Calgary *Alberta* M & W
University of California, Berkeley *California* M & W
University of California, Davis *California* M & W
University of California, Irvine *California* M & W
University of California, Los Angeles *California* W
University of California, San Diego *California* M & W
University of California, Santa Barbara *California* M & W
University of California, Santa Cruz *California* M & W
University of Charleston *West Virginia* M & W
University of Chicago *Illinois* M & W
University of Cincinnati *Ohio* M & W
University of Cincinnati Raymond Walters College *Ohio* M & W
University of Colorado at Boulder *Colorado* M & W
University of Connecticut *Connecticut* M & W
University of the Cumberlands *Kentucky* M & W
University of Delaware *Delaware* M & W
University of Denver *Colorado* M & W
University of Evansville *Indiana* M & W
The University of Findlay *Ohio* M & W
University of Florida *Florida* M & W
University of Georgia *Georgia* M & W
University of Guelph *Ontario* M & W
University of Hawaii at Manoa *Hawaii* M & W
University of Houston *Texas* W
University of Illinois at Chicago *Illinois* M & W
University of Illinois at Urbana-Champaign *Illinois* W
University of the Incarnate Word *Texas* W
University of Indianapolis *Indiana* M & W
The University of Iowa *Iowa* M & W
University of Kansas *Kansas* W
University of Kentucky *Kentucky* M & W
University of La Verne *California* M & W
University of Lethbridge *Alberta* M & W
University of Louisiana at Monroe *Louisiana* M & W
University of Louisville *Kentucky* M & W
University of Maine *Maine* M & W
University of Manitoba *Manitoba* M & W
University of Mary Washington *Virginia* M & W
University of Maryland, Baltimore County *Maryland* M & W
University of Maryland, College Park *Maryland* M & W
University of Massachusetts Amherst *Massachusetts* M & W
University of Massachusetts Dartmouth *Massachusetts* M & W
University of Massachusetts Lowell *Massachusetts* M
University of Memphis *Tennessee* M & W
University of Miami *Florida* W
University of Michigan *Michigan* M & W
University of Minnesota, Morris *Minnesota* W
University of Minnesota, Twin Cities Campus *Minnesota* M & W
University of Missouri-Columbia *Missouri* M & W
University of Missouri-Rolla *Missouri* M
University of Nebraska at Kearney *Nebraska* W
University of Nebraska-Lincoln *Nebraska* W
University of Nebraska at Omaha *Nebraska* W
University of Nevada, Las Vegas *Nevada* M & W
University of Nevada, Reno *Nevada* W
University of New Brunswick Fredericton *New Brunswick* M & W
University of New England *Maine* W
University of New Hampshire *New Hampshire* M & W
University of New Mexico *New Mexico* W
The University of North Carolina at Chapel Hill *North Carolina* M & W
The University of North Carolina Wilmington *North Carolina* M & W
University of North Dakota *North Dakota* M & W
University of North Florida *Florida* W
University of North Texas *Texas* M & W
University of Northern Colorado *Colorado* W
University of Northern Iowa *Iowa* W
University of Notre Dame *Indiana* M & W
University of Oregon *Oregon* M & W
University of Ottawa *Ontario* M & W
University of the Pacific *California* M & W
University of Pennsylvania *Pennsylvania* M & W
University of Pittsburgh *Pennsylvania* M & W
University of Puerto Rico at Bayamón *Puerto Rico* M & W
University of Puerto Rico, Cayey University College *Puerto Rico* M
University of Puerto Rico at Humacao *Puerto Rico* M & W
University of Puerto Rico, Mayagüez Campus *Puerto Rico* M & W
University of Puerto Rico, Río Piedras *Puerto Rico* M & W
University of Puget Sound *Washington* M & W
University of Redlands *California* M & W
University of Regina *Saskatchewan* M & W
University of Rhode Island *Rhode Island* M & W
University of Richmond *Virginia* M & W
University of Rochester *New York* M & W
University of the Sacred Heart *Puerto Rico* M & W
University of St. Thomas *Minnesota* M & W
University of San Diego *California* W
The University of Scranton *Pennsylvania* M & W
University of South Carolina *South Carolina* M & W
The University of South Dakota *South Dakota* M & W
University of Southern California *California* M & W
The University of Tampa *Florida* M & W
The University of Tennessee *Tennessee* M & W
The University of Texas at Austin *Texas* M & W
The University of Texas of the Permian Basin *Texas* M & W
The University of Toledo *Ohio* M & W
University of Toronto *Ontario* M & W
University of Utah *Utah* M & W
University of Vermont *Vermont* W
University of Victoria *British Columbia* M & W
University of Virginia *Virginia* M & W
University of Washington *Washington* M & W
University of Waterloo *Ontario* M & W
The University of Western Ontario *Ontario* M & W
University of Wisconsin-Eau Claire *Wisconsin* M & W
University of Wisconsin-Green Bay *Wisconsin* M & W

M = Men; W = Women

University of Wisconsin-La Crosse *Wisconsin* M & W
University of Wisconsin-Madison *Wisconsin* M & W
University of Wisconsin-Milwaukee *Wisconsin* M & W
University of Wisconsin-Oshkosh *Wisconsin* M & W
University of Wisconsin-River Falls *Wisconsin* M & W
University of Wisconsin-Stevens Point *Wisconsin* M & W
University of Wisconsin-Whitewater *Wisconsin* M & W
University of Wyoming *Wyoming* M & W
Ursinus College *Pennsylvania* M & W
Utica College *New York* M & W
Valparaiso University *Indiana* M & W
Vassar College *New York* M & W
Ventura College *California* M & W
Villanova University *Pennsylvania* M & W
Vincennes University *Indiana* M & W
Virginia Commonwealth University *Virginia* M & W
Virginia Military Institute *Virginia* M & W
Virginia Polytechnic Institute and State University *Virginia* M & W
Wabash College *Indiana* M
Wagner College *New York* W
Warren Wilson College *North Carolina* M & W
Washington College *Maryland* M & W
Washington & Jefferson College *Pennsylvania* M & W
Washington and Lee University *Virginia* M & W
Washington State University *Washington* W
Washington University in St. Louis *Missouri* M & W
Wayne State University *Michigan* M & W
Weber State University *Utah* M & W
Webster University *Missouri* M & W
Wellesley College *Massachusetts* W
Wells College *New York* W
Wesleyan University *Connecticut* M & W
West Chester University of Pennsylvania *Pennsylvania* M & W
West Valley College *California* M & W
West Virginia University *West Virginia* M & W
West Virginia Wesleyan College *West Virginia* M & W
Western Connecticut State University *Connecticut* W
Western Illinois University *Illinois* M & W
Western Kentucky University *Kentucky* M & W
Western New England College *Massachusetts* W
Westfield State College *Massachusetts* W
Westminster College *Pennsylvania* M & W
Wheaton College *Massachusetts* M & W
Wheaton College *Illinois* M & W
Wheeling Jesuit University *West Virginia* M & W
Wheelock College *Massachusetts* W
Whitman College *Washington* M & W
Whittier College *California* M & W
Whitworth College *Washington* M & W
Wichita State University *Kansas* M & W
Widener University *Pennsylvania* M & W
Wilfrid Laurier University *Ontario* M & W
Willamette University *Oregon* M & W
William Paterson University of New Jersey *New Jersey* M & W
Williams College *Massachusetts* M & W
Wilmington College *Ohio* M & W
Wingate University *North Carolina* M & W
Wittenberg University *Ohio* M & W
Worcester Polytechnic Institute *Massachusetts* M & W
Wright State University *Ohio* M & W
Xavier University *Ohio* M & W
Yale University *Connecticut* M & W
York College of the City University of New York *New York* M & W
York College of Pennsylvania *Pennsylvania* M & W
York University *Ontario* M & W
Youngstown State University *Ohio* W

Table Tennis

Bradley University *Illinois* M & W
California State University, Long Beach *California* M
Colgate University *New York* M & W
Columbia College *New York* M & W
Columbia University, The Fu Foundation School of Engineering and Applied Science *New York* M & W
Community College of Allegheny County *Pennsylvania* M & W
Cooper Union for the Advancement of Science and Art *New York* M & W
Dalton State College *Georgia* M & W
Dartmouth College *New Hampshire* M & W
Duke University *North Carolina* M & W
Electronic Data Processing College of Puerto Rico *Puerto Rico* M & W
Emory University *Georgia* M & W
Florida State University *Florida* M & W
Hiram College *Ohio* M & W
Inter American University of Puerto Rico, Aguadilla Campus *Puerto Rico* M & W
Inter American University of Puerto Rico, Arecibo Campus *Puerto Rico* M & W
Inter American University of Puerto Rico, Barranquitas Campus *Puerto Rico* M & W
Inter American University of Puerto Rico, Bayamón Campus *Puerto Rico* M & W
Inter American University of Puerto Rico, Guayama Campus *Puerto Rico* M & W
Inter American University of Puerto Rico, Metropolitan Campus *Puerto Rico* M & W
Inter American University of Puerto Rico, Ponce Campus *Puerto Rico* M & W
Inter American University of Puerto Rico, San Germán Campus *Puerto Rico* M & W
Linn State Technical College *Missouri* M & W
Michigan Technological University *Michigan* M & W
North Carolina State University *North Carolina* M & W
Northwestern Polytechnic University *California* M
The Pennsylvania State University University Park Campus *Pennsylvania* M
Polytechnic University of Puerto Rico *Puerto Rico* M & W
Pontifical Catholic University of Puerto Rico *Puerto Rico* M & W
Providence College and Theological Seminary *Manitoba* M & W
Queen's University at Kingston *Ontario* M & W
Rensselaer Polytechnic Institute *New York* M & W
State University of New York at Binghamton *New York* M & W
Syracuse University *New York* M & W
Talladega College *Alabama* M & W
Technological College of San Juan *Puerto Rico* M & W
Texas Wesleyan University *Texas* M
Universidad Metropolitana *Puerto Rico* M & W
University of California, Irvine *California* M & W
University of California, Santa Cruz *California* M & W
The University of Iowa *Iowa* M & W
University of Oregon *Oregon* M & W
University of Puerto Rico, Aguadilla University College *Puerto Rico* M & W
University of Puerto Rico at Arecibo *Puerto Rico* M & W
University of Puerto Rico, Cayey University College *Puerto Rico* M
University of Puerto Rico, Mayagüez Campus *Puerto Rico* M & W
University of Puerto Rico, Río Piedras *Puerto Rico* M & W
University of Puerto Rico at Utuado *Puerto Rico* M & W
University of Utah *Utah* M & W
University of Vermont *Vermont* M & W
Washington College *Maryland* M & W
Washington University in St. Louis *Missouri* M & W
Yale University *Connecticut* M

Tennis

Abilene Christian University *Texas* M & W
Abraham Baldwin Agricultural College *Georgia* M & W
Adelphi University *New York* M & W
Adirondack Community College *New York* M & W
Adrian College *Michigan* M & W
Agnes Scott College *Georgia* W
Alabama Agricultural and Mechanical University *Alabama* M & W
Alabama State University *Alabama* M & W
Albany State University *Georgia* M
Albertson College of Idaho *Idaho* M & W
Albertus Magnus College *Connecticut* M & W
Albion College *Michigan* M & W
Albright College *Pennsylvania* M & W
Alcorn State University *Mississippi* M & W
Alfred University *New York* M & W
Alice Lloyd College *Kentucky* M & W
Allan Hancock College *California* M & W
Allegany College of Maryland *Maryland* M & W
Allegheny College *Pennsylvania* M & W
Alliant International University *California* M & W
Alma College *Michigan* M & W
Alvernia College *Pennsylvania* M & W
American International College *Massachusetts* M & W
American River College *California* M & W
American University *District of Columbia* M & W
American University of Puerto Rico *Puerto Rico* M & W
Amherst College *Massachusetts* M & W
Anderson University *South Carolina* M & W
Anderson University *Indiana* M & W
Antelope Valley College *California* W
Appalachian State University *North Carolina* M & W
Aquinas College *Michigan* M & W
Arcadia University *Pennsylvania* M & W
Arizona State University *Arizona* M & W
Arkansas State University *Arkansas* W
Arkansas Tech University *Arkansas* W
Armstrong Atlantic State University *Georgia* M & W
Asbury College *Kentucky* M & W
Ashland University *Ohio* M & W
Assumption College *Massachusetts* M & W
Auburn University *Alabama* M & W
Auburn University Montgomery *Alabama* M & W
Augusta State University *Georgia* M & W
Augustana College *South Dakota* M & W
Augustana College *Illinois* M & W
Aurora University *Illinois* M & W
Austin College *Texas* M & W
Austin Peay State University *Tennessee* M & W
Averett University *Virginia* M & W
Azusa Pacific University *California* M
Babson College *Massachusetts* M & W
Baker University *Kansas* M & W
Bakersfield College *California* M & W
Baldwin-Wallace College *Ohio* M & W
Ball State University *Indiana* M & W
Baptist Bible College of Pennsylvania *Pennsylvania* W
Barber-Scotia College *North Carolina* M
Barclay College *Kansas* M & W
Bard College *New York* M & W
Barnard College *New York* W
Barry University *Florida* M & W
Barton College *North Carolina* M & W
Barton County Community College *Kansas* M & W
Bates College *Maine* M & W
Bay Path College *Massachusetts* W
Baylor University *Texas* M & W
Becker College *Massachusetts* M & W
Belhaven College *Mississippi* M & W
Bellarmine University *Kentucky* M & W
Bellevue Community College *Washington* M & W
Belmont Abbey College *North Carolina* M & W
Belmont University *Tennessee* M & W
Beloit College *Wisconsin* M & W
Bemidji State University *Minnesota* W
Benedict College *South Carolina* M
Benedictine College *Kansas* M & W
Benedictine University *Illinois* W
Bennett College For Women *North Carolina* W
Bentley College *Massachusetts* M & W
Berea College *Kentucky* M & W
Bergen Community College *New Jersey* M & W
Bernard M. Baruch College of the City University of New York *New York* M & W
Berry College *Georgia* M & W

M = Men; W = Women

Bethany College *West Virginia* M & W
Bethany College *Kansas* M & W
Bethany Lutheran College *Minnesota* M & W
Bethel College *Tennessee* M & W
Bethel College *Kansas* M & W
Bethel College *Indiana* M & W
Bethel University *Minnesota* M & W
Bethune-Cookman College *Florida* M & W
Biola University *California* W
Birmingham-Southern College *Alabama* M & W
Bismarck State College *North Dakota* M & W
Blackburn College *Illinois* W
Bloomsburg University of Pennsylvania *Pennsylvania* M & W
Blue Mountain College *Mississippi* W
Bluefield College *Virginia* M & W
Bluefield State College *West Virginia* M & W
Bluffton University *Ohio* M & W
Boise State University *Idaho* M & W
Boston College *Massachusetts* M & W
Boston University *Massachusetts* M & W
Bowdoin College *Maine* M & W
Bowie State University *Maryland* W
Bowling Green State University *Ohio* M & W
Bradley University *Illinois* M & W
Brandeis University *Massachusetts* M & W
Brenau University *Georgia* W
Brescia University *Kentucky* W
Brevard College *North Carolina* M & W
Briar Cliff University *Iowa* W
Bridgewater College *Virginia* M & W
Bridgewater State College *Massachusetts* M & W
Brigham Young University *Utah* M & W
Brigham Young University-Hawaii *Hawaii* M & W
Brock University *Ontario* M
Bronx Community College of the City University of New York *New York* M & W
Brookdale Community College *New Jersey* M & W
Brookhaven College *Texas* M & W
Brooklyn College of the City University of New York *New York* M & W
Broome Community College *New York* M & W
Broward Community College *Florida* W
Brown University *Rhode Island* M & W
Bryan College *Tennessee* M & W
Bryant University *Rhode Island* M & W
Bryn Mawr College *Pennsylvania* W
Bucknell University *Pennsylvania* M & W
Bucks County Community College *Pennsylvania* M & W
Buena Vista University *Iowa* M & W
Buffalo State College, State University of New York *New York* W
Butler Community College *Kansas* M & W
Butler University *Indiana* M & W
Butte College *California* M & W
Cabrillo College *California* M & W
Cabrini College *Pennsylvania* M & W
Caldwell College *New Jersey* M & W
California Baptist University *California* W
California Institute of Technology *California* M & W
California Lutheran University *California* M & W
California Polytechnic State University, San Luis Obispo *California* M & W
California State Polytechnic University, Pomona *California* M & W
California State University, Bakersfield *California* W
California State University, Fresno *California* M & W
California State University, Fullerton *California* W
California State University, Long Beach *California* W
California State University, Los Angeles *California* W
California State University, Northridge *California* W
California State University, Sacramento *California* M & W
California University of Pennsylvania *Pennsylvania* W
Calvin College *Michigan* M & W
Cameron University *Oklahoma* M & W
Campbell University *North Carolina* M & W
Campbellsville University *Kentucky* M & W
Cape Fear Community College *North Carolina* M & W
Capital University *Ohio* M & W
Caribbean University *Puerto Rico* M & W

Carleton College *Minnesota* M & W
Carlow University *Pennsylvania* W
Carnegie Mellon University *Pennsylvania* M & W
Carroll College *Wisconsin* M & W
Carson-Newman College *Tennessee* M & W
Carthage College *Wisconsin* M & W
Case Western Reserve University *Ohio* M & W
Castleton State College *Vermont* M & W
Catawba College *North Carolina* M & W
The Catholic University of America *District of Columbia* M & W
Cedar Crest College *Pennsylvania* W
Cedarville University *Ohio* M & W
Centenary College of Louisiana *Louisiana* M & W
Central Alabama Community College *Alabama* M & W
Central Christian College of the Bible *Missouri* M & W
Central Christian College of Kansas *Kansas* M & W
Central College *Iowa* M & W
Central Florida Community College *Florida* W
Central Ohio Technical College *Ohio* M & W
Central Pennsylvania College *Pennsylvania* M & W
Central State University *Ohio* M & W
Centre College *Kentucky* M & W
Cerritos College *California* M & W
Chabot College *California* M & W
Chaffey College *California* M & W
Chaminade University of Honolulu *Hawaii* M & W
Chapman University *California* M & W
Charleston Southern University *South Carolina* M & W
Chatham College *Pennsylvania* W
Chesapeake College *Maryland* M & W
Chestnut Hill College *Pennsylvania* W
Chicago State University *Illinois* M & W
Chowan University *North Carolina* M & W
Christian Brothers University *Tennessee* M & W
Christopher Newport University *Virginia* M & W
The Citadel, The Military College of South Carolina *South Carolina* M
Citrus College *California* M & W
City College of the City University of New York *New York* M & W
City College of San Francisco *California* M & W
City Colleges of Chicago, Harry S. Truman College *Illinois* M & W
Claflin University *South Carolina* M & W
Claremont McKenna College *California* M & W
Clarion University of Pennsylvania *Pennsylvania* W
Clark Atlanta University *Georgia* M & W
Clark University *Massachusetts* M & W
Clarke College *Iowa* M & W
Clarkson University *New York* M & W
Clayton State University *Georgia* W
Clemson University *South Carolina* M & W
Cleveland State University *Ohio* W
Cloud County Community College *Kansas* M & W
Coastal Carolina University *South Carolina* M & W
Coe College *Iowa* M & W
Coker College *South Carolina* M & W
Colby College *Maine* M & W
Colby-Sawyer College *New Hampshire* M & W
Colgate University *New York* M & W
College of Charleston *South Carolina* M & W
College of the Desert *California* M & W
College of DuPage *Illinois* M & W
College of the Holy Cross *Massachusetts* M & W
College of Lake County *Illinois* M & W
College of Marin *California* M & W
College Misericordia *Pennsylvania* W
College of Mount St. Joseph *Ohio* M & W
College of Mount Saint Vincent *New York* M & W
The College of New Jersey *New Jersey* M & W
The College of New Rochelle *New York* W
College of Notre Dame of Maryland *Maryland* W
College of Saint Benedict *Minnesota* W
College of St. Catherine *Minnesota* W
College of Saint Elizabeth *New Jersey* W
The College of St. Scholastica *Minnesota* M & W
College of San Mateo *California* W
College of Santa Fe *New Mexico* M & W
College of the Sequoias *California* M & W
College of Southern Maryland *Maryland* M & W

College of Staten Island of the City University of New York *New York* M & W
The College of William and Mary *Virginia* M & W
The College of Wooster *Ohio* M & W
Collin County Community College District *Texas* M & W
Colorado Christian University *Colorado* M & W
The Colorado College *Colorado* M & W
Colorado School of Mines *Colorado* M & W
Colorado State University *Colorado* W
Colorado State University-Pueblo *Colorado* M & W
Columbia College *South Carolina* W
Columbia College *New York* M & W
Columbia College *California* M & W
Columbia University, School of General Studies *New York* M & W
Columbia University, The Fu Foundation School of Engineering and Applied Science *New York* M & W
Columbus State University *Georgia* M & W
Community College of Allegheny County *Pennsylvania* M & W
Community College of Beaver County *Pennsylvania* M & W
Community College of Philadelphia *Pennsylvania* M & W
Community College of Rhode Island *Rhode Island* M & W
Concord University *West Virginia* M & W
Concordia College *New York* M & W
Concordia College *Minnesota* M & W
Concordia University *Nebraska* M & W
Concordia University *Illinois* M & W
Concordia University at Austin *Texas* M & W
Concordia University Wisconsin *Wisconsin* M & W
Connecticut College *Connecticut* M & W
Converse College *South Carolina* W
Cooper Union for the Advancement of Science and Art *New York* M & W
Copiah-Lincoln Community College *Mississippi* M & W
Coppin State University *Maryland* M & W
Cornell College *Iowa* M & W
Cornell University *New York* M & W
Cosumnes River College (Sacramento) *California* M & W
County College of Morris *New Jersey* M & W
Covenant College *Georgia* M & W
Cowley County Community College and Area Vocational-Technical School *Kansas* M & W
Creighton University *Nebraska* M & W
Crossroads College *Minnesota* M & W
Cuesta College *California* W
Cumberland University *Tennessee* M & W
Curry College *Massachusetts* M & W
Cuyamaca College *California* W
Cypress College *California* M & W
Dallas Baptist University *Texas* M & W
Dalton State College *Georgia* M & W
Dartmouth College *New Hampshire* M & W
Davidson College *North Carolina* M & W
De Anza College *California* M & W
Defiance College *Ohio* M & W
Delaware County Community College *Pennsylvania* M & W
Delaware State University *Delaware* M & W
Delaware Technical & Community College, Stanton/Wilmington Campus *Delaware* M & W
Delta State University *Mississippi* M & W
Denison University *Ohio* M & W
DePaul University *Illinois* M & W
DePauw University *Indiana* M & W
DeSales University *Pennsylvania* M & W
Diablo Valley College *California* M & W
Dickinson College *Pennsylvania* M & W
Dillard University *Louisiana* M & W
Doane College *Nebraska* M & W
Dominican University *Illinois* M & W
Dominican University of California *California* M & W
Dordt College *Iowa* M & W
Dowling College *New York* M & W
Drake University *Iowa* M & W
Drew University *New Jersey* M & W
Drexel University *Pennsylvania* M & W

M = Men; W = Women

Drury University *Missouri* M & W
Duke University *North Carolina* M & W
Duquesne University *Pennsylvania* M & W
Dutchess Community College *New York* M & W
Earlham College *Indiana* M & W
East Carolina University *North Carolina* M & W
East Central Community College *Mississippi* M & W
East Central University *Oklahoma* M & W
East Stroudsburg University of Pennsylvania *Pennsylvania* M & W
East Tennessee State University *Tennessee* M & W
Eastern Illinois University *Illinois* M & W
Eastern Kentucky University *Kentucky* M & W
Eastern Mennonite University *Virginia* M & W
Eastern Michigan University *Michigan* W
Eastern Nazarene College *Massachusetts* M & W
Eastern New Mexico University *New Mexico* W
Eastern Washington University *Washington* M & W
Eastfield College *Texas* M & W
Eckerd College *Florida* M & W
Edgewood College *Wisconsin* M & W
Edward Waters College *Florida* M & W
El Camino College *California* M & W
Electronic Data Processing College of Puerto Rico *Puerto Rico* M & W
Elgin Community College *Illinois* W
Elizabeth City State University *North Carolina* M & W
Elizabethtown College *Pennsylvania* M & W
Elmhurst College *Illinois* M & W
Elmira College *New York* M & W
Elon University *North Carolina* M & W
Embry-Riddle Aeronautical University *Florida* M & W
Emerson College *Massachusetts* M & W
Emmanuel College *Massachusetts* W
Emmanuel College *Georgia* M & W
Emory & Henry College *Virginia* M & W
Emory University *Georgia* M & W
Emory University, Oxford College *Georgia* M & W
Emporia State University *Kansas* M & W
Endicott College *Massachusetts* M & W
Erskine College *South Carolina* M & W
Eureka College *Illinois* M & W
Evangel University *Missouri* M & W
Fairfield University *Connecticut* M & W
Fairleigh Dickinson University, College at Florham *New Jersey* M & W
Fairleigh Dickinson University, Metropolitan Campus *New Jersey* M & W
Fairmont State University *West Virginia* M & W
Fashion Institute of Technology *New York* M & W
Fayetteville State University *North Carolina* M & W
Ferris State University *Michigan* M & W
Ferrum College *Virginia* M & W
Fisk University *Tennessee* M & W
Flagler College *Florida* M & W
Florida Agricultural and Mechanical University *Florida* M & W
Florida Atlantic University *Florida* M & W
Florida Community College at Jacksonville *Florida* W
Florida Gulf Coast University *Florida* M & W
Florida Institute of Technology *Florida* M & W
Florida International University *Florida* W
Florida Southern College *Florida* M & W
Florida State University *Florida* M & W
Fontbonne University *Missouri* M & W
Foothill College *California* M
Fordham University *New York* M & W
Fort Hays State University *Kansas* W
Fort Valley State University *Georgia* M & W
Francis Marion University *South Carolina* M & W
Franklin College *Indiana* M & W
Franklin and Marshall College *Pennsylvania* M & W
Franklin Pierce College *New Hampshire* M & W
Freed-Hardeman University *Tennessee* M & W
Fresno City College *California* M & W
Fresno Pacific University *California* M & W
Friends University *Kansas* M & W
Frostburg State University *Maryland* M & W
Fullerton College *California* M & W
Furman University *South Carolina* M & W
Gadsden State Community College *Alabama* M
Gallaudet University *District of Columbia* M
Gardner-Webb University *North Carolina* M & W
GateWay Community College *Arizona* M & W
Gavilan College *California* M
Geneva College *Pennsylvania* W
George C. Wallace Community College *Alabama* M & W
George Corley Wallace State Community College *Alabama* M & W
George Fox University *Oregon* M & W
George Mason University *Virginia* M & W
The George Washington University *District of Columbia* M & W
Georgetown College *Kentucky* M & W
Georgetown University *District of Columbia* M & W
Georgia College & State University *Georgia* M & W
Georgia Institute of Technology *Georgia* M & W
Georgia Perimeter College *Georgia* M & W
Georgia Southern University *Georgia* M & W
Georgia Southwestern State University *Georgia* M & W
Georgia State University *Georgia* M & W
Georgian Court University *New Jersey* W
Gettysburg College *Pennsylvania* M & W
Glen Oaks Community College *Michigan* W
Glendale Community College *California* M & W
Glendale Community College *Arizona* M & W
Gloucester County College *New Jersey* M & W
Golden West College *California* M & W
Goldey-Beacom College *Delaware* M & W
Gonzaga University *Washington* M & W
Gordon College *Massachusetts* M & W
Gordon College *Georgia* W
Goshen College *Indiana* M & W
Goucher College *Maryland* M & W
Grace College *Indiana* M & W
Graceland University *Iowa* M & W
Grambling State University *Louisiana* M & W
Grand Canyon University *Arizona* W
Grand Rapids Community College *Michigan* M & W
Grand Valley State University *Michigan* M & W
Green Mountain College *Vermont* M & W
Green River Community College *Washington* M & W
Greensboro College *North Carolina* M & W
Greenville College *Illinois* M & W
Grinnell College *Iowa* M & W
Grossmont College *California* M & W
Grove City College *Pennsylvania* M & W
Guilford College *North Carolina* M & W
Gustavus Adolphus College *Minnesota* M & W
Gwynedd-Mercy College *Pennsylvania* M & W
Hamilton College *New York* M & W
Hamline University *Minnesota* M & W
Hampden-Sydney College *Virginia* M
Hampton University *Virginia* M & W
Hanover College *Indiana* M & W
Hardin-Simmons University *Texas* M & W
Harding University *Arkansas* M & W
Harford Community College *Maryland* M & W
Harris-Stowe State University *Missouri* M & W
Harrisburg Area Community College *Pennsylvania* M & W
Hartnell College *California* M & W
Hartwick College *New York* M & W
Harvard University *Massachusetts* M & W
Harvey Mudd College *California* M & W
Hastings College *Nebraska* M & W
Haverford College *Pennsylvania* M & W
Hawaii Pacific University *Hawaii* M & W
Heidelberg College *Ohio* M & W
Henderson State University *Arkansas* M & W
Hendrix College *Arkansas* M & W
Henry Ford Community College *Michigan* W
Herkimer County Community College *New York* M & W
Hesston College *Kansas* M & W
High Point University *North Carolina* M & W
Hillsborough Community College *Florida* W
Hinds Community College *Mississippi* M & W
Hiram College *Ohio* M & W
Hobart and William Smith Colleges *New York* M & W
Hofstra University *New York* M & W
Hollins University *Virginia* W
Holmes Community College *Mississippi* M & W
Holyoke Community College *Massachusetts* M & W
Hood College *Maryland* M & W
Hope College *Michigan* M & W
Hope International University *California* M & W
Howard Community College *Maryland* M & W
Howard Payne University *Texas* M & W
Howard University *District of Columbia* M & W
Hudson Valley Community College *New York* M & W
Hunter College of the City University of New York *New York* M & W
Huntingdon College *Alabama* W
Huntington University *Indiana* M & W
Hutchinson Community College and Area Vocational School *Kansas* M & W
Idaho State University *Idaho* M & W
Illinois College *Illinois* M & W
Illinois Eastern Community Colleges, Wabash Valley College *Illinois* M
Illinois State University *Illinois* M & W
Illinois Valley Community College *Illinois* M & W
Illinois Wesleyan University *Illinois* M & W
Immaculata University *Pennsylvania* W
Imperial Valley College *California* M & W
Independence Community College *Kansas* M & W
Indiana State University *Indiana* M & W
Indiana University Bloomington *Indiana* M & W
Indiana University of Pennsylvania *Pennsylvania* W
Indiana University-Purdue University Fort Wayne *Indiana* M & W
Indiana University-Purdue University Indianapolis *Indiana* M & W
Indiana University Southeast *Indiana* M & W
Indiana Wesleyan University *Indiana* M & W
Inter American University of Puerto Rico, Aguadilla Campus *Puerto Rico* M & W
Inter American University of Puerto Rico, Arecibo Campus *Puerto Rico* M & W
Inter American University of Puerto Rico, Barranquitas Campus *Puerto Rico* M & W
Inter American University of Puerto Rico, Guayama Campus *Puerto Rico* M & W
Inter American University of Puerto Rico, Metropolitan Campus *Puerto Rico* M & W
Inter American University of Puerto Rico, San Germán Campus *Puerto Rico* M & W
Iowa State University of Science and Technology *Iowa* W
Irvine Valley College *California* M & W
Itawamba Community College *Mississippi* M & W
Ithaca College *New York* M & W
Jackson State University *Mississippi* M & W
Jacksonville State University *Alabama* M & W
Jacksonville University *Florida* M & W
James H. Faulkner State Community College *Alabama* M & W
James Madison University *Virginia* M & W
Jefferson Community College *New York* W
John Brown University *Arkansas* M & W
John Carroll University *Ohio* M & W
John Jay College of Criminal Justice of the City University of New York *New York* M & W
The Johns Hopkins University *Maryland* M & W
Johnson C. Smith University *North Carolina* M & W
Johnson County Community College *Kansas* M & W
Johnson State College *Vermont* M & W
Johnson & Wales University *Rhode Island* M & W
Johnson & Wales University *Colorado* M & W
Joliet Junior College *Illinois* M & W
Jones County Junior College *Mississippi* M & W
Judson College *Illinois* M & W
Judson College *Alabama* W
Juniata College *Pennsylvania* M & W
Kalamazoo College *Michigan* M & W
Kalamazoo Valley Community College *Michigan* M & W
Kansas State University *Kansas* W
Kansas Wesleyan University *Kansas* M & W
Kean University *New Jersey* W
Kennesaw State University *Georgia* W
Kentucky State University *Kentucky* M & W
Kentucky Wesleyan College *Kentucky* W
Kenyon College *Ohio* M & W

M = Men; W = Women

Keystone College *Pennsylvania* M & W
King College *Tennessee* M & W
King's College *Pennsylvania* M & W
Kingsborough Community College of the City University of New York *New York* M & W
Kishwaukee College *Illinois* W
Knox College *Illinois* M & W
Kutztown University of Pennsylvania *Pennsylvania* M & W
La Salle University *Pennsylvania* M & W
Labette Community College *Kansas* W
Lafayette College *Pennsylvania* M & W
LaGrange College *Georgia* M & W
Lake Forest College *Illinois* M & W
Lake Land College *Illinois* M & W
Lake Superior State University *Michigan* M & W
Lakeland College *Wisconsin* M & W
Lamar University *Texas* M & W
Lambuth University *Tennessee* M & W
Lander University *South Carolina* M & W
Lane College *Tennessee* M & W
Laredo Community College *Texas* M & W
Lawrence University *Wisconsin* M & W
Le Moyne College *New York* M & W
Lebanon Valley College *Pennsylvania* M & W
Lee College *Texas* W
Lee University *Tennessee* M & W
Lees-McRae College *North Carolina* M & W
Lehigh University *Pennsylvania* M & W
Lehman College of the City University of New York *New York* M & W
LeMoyne-Owen College *Tennessee* M & W
LeTourneau University *Texas* M & W
Lewis & Clark College *Oregon* M & W
Lewis and Clark Community College *Illinois* M & W
Lewis-Clark State College *Idaho* M & W
Lewis University *Illinois* M & W
Liberty University *Virginia* M & W
Limestone College *South Carolina* M & W
Lincoln College *Illinois* M & W
Lincoln Memorial University *Tennessee* M & W
Lincoln University *Pennsylvania* M & W
Lincoln University *Missouri* W
Lindenwood University *Missouri* M & W
Lindsey Wilson College *Kentucky* M & W
Linfield College *Oregon* M & W
Lipscomb University *Tennessee* M & W
Livingstone College *North Carolina* W
Long Beach City College *California* M & W
Long Island University, Brooklyn Campus *New York* W
Long Island University, C.W. Post Campus *New York* W
Longwood University *Virginia* M & W
Loras College *Iowa* M & W
Los Angeles Harbor College *California* W
Los Angeles Pierce College *California* M & W
Los Angeles Trade-Technical College *California* M
Los Angeles Valley College *California* M & W
Louisiana College *Louisiana* W
Louisiana State University and Agricultural and Mechanical College *Louisiana* M & W
Louisiana Tech University *Louisiana* W
Loyola College in Maryland *Maryland* M & W
Loyola Marymount University *California* M & W
Loyola University New Orleans *Louisiana* M & W
Luther College *Iowa* M & W
Lycoming College *Pennsylvania* M & W
Lynchburg College *Virginia* M & W
Lyndon State College *Vermont* M & W
Lynn University *Florida* M & W
Lyon College *Arkansas* M & W
Macalester College *Minnesota* M & W
MacMurray College *Illinois* M & W
Madison Area Technical College *Wisconsin* M & W
Malone College *Ohio* M & W
Manchester College *Indiana* M & W
Manhattan College *New York* M & W
Manhattanville College *New York* M & W
Marian College *Indiana* M & W
Marian College of Fond du Lac *Wisconsin* M & W
Marietta College *Ohio* M & W
Marion Military Institute *Alabama* M & W
Marist College *New York* M & W
Marquette University *Wisconsin* M & W
Mars Hill College *North Carolina* M & W
Marshall University *West Virginia* W
Martin Luther College *Minnesota* M & W
Martin Methodist College *Tennessee* M & W
Mary Baldwin College *Virginia* W
Marymount College, Palos Verdes, California *California* M & W
Maryville College *Tennessee* M & W
Maryville University of Saint Louis *Missouri* M & W
Marywood University *Pennsylvania* M & W
Massachusetts Bay Community College *Massachusetts* M & W
Massachusetts College of Liberal Arts *Massachusetts* W
Massachusetts Institute of Technology *Massachusetts* M & W
McDaniel College *Maryland* M & W
McDowell Technical Community College *North Carolina* M
McGill University *Quebec* M & W
McHenry County College *Illinois* M & W
McKendree College *Illinois* M & W
McMaster University *Ontario* M & W
McMurry University *Texas* M & W
McNeese State University *Louisiana* W
Merced College *California* M & W
Mercer County Community College *New Jersey* M & W
Mercer University *Georgia* M & W
Mercy College *New York* M
Mercyhurst College *Pennsylvania* M & W
Meredith College *North Carolina* W
Meridian Community College *Mississippi* M & W
Merrimack College *Massachusetts* M & W
Merritt College *California* M & W
Mesa Community College *Arizona* M & W
Mesa State College *Colorado* M & W
Messiah College *Pennsylvania* M & W
Methodist College *North Carolina* M & W
Metropolitan State College of Denver *Colorado* M & W
Miami University *Ohio* M & W
Miami University Hamilton *Ohio* M & W
Miami University-Middletown Campus *Ohio* M & W
Michigan State University *Michigan* M & W
Michigan Technological University *Michigan* M & W
Middle Tennessee State University *Tennessee* M & W
Middlebury College *Vermont* M & W
Middlesex County College *New Jersey* M & W
Midland Lutheran College *Nebraska* M & W
Midway College *Kentucky* W
Midwestern State University *Texas* M & W
Millersville University of Pennsylvania *Pennsylvania* M & W
Milligan College *Tennessee* M & W
Millikin University *Illinois* W
Mills College *California* W
Millsaps College *Mississippi* M & W
Milwaukee Area Technical College *Wisconsin* M & W
Milwaukee School of Engineering *Wisconsin* M & W
Minnesota State University Mankato *Minnesota* M & W
Minnesota State University Moorhead *Minnesota* W
Mission College *California* M & W
Mississippi College *Mississippi* M & W
Mississippi Delta Community College *Mississippi* M & W
Mississippi Gulf Coast Community College *Mississippi* M & W
Mississippi State University *Mississippi* M & W
Mississippi University for Women *Mississippi* W
Mississippi Valley State University *Mississippi* M
Missouri Baptist University *Missouri* W
Missouri Southern State University *Missouri* W
Missouri State University *Missouri* M & W
Missouri Valley College *Missouri* M & W
Missouri Western State University *Missouri* W
Modesto Junior College *California* M & W
Mohawk Valley Community College *New York* M & W
Molloy College *New York* W
Monmouth College *Illinois* M & W
Monmouth University *New Jersey* M & W
Monroe Community College *New York* M & W
Montana State University *Montana* M & W
Montana State University-Billings *Montana* M & W
Montclair State University *New Jersey* M
Monterey Peninsula College *California* M & W
Montgomery College *Maryland* M & W
Montreat College *North Carolina* M & W
Moraine Valley Community College *Illinois* M & W
Moravian College *Pennsylvania* M & W
Morehead State University *Kentucky* M & W
Morehouse College *Georgia* M
Morgan State University *Maryland* M & W
Morningside College *Iowa* M & W
Morris College *South Carolina* M & W
Mount Holyoke College *Massachusetts* W
Mount Mary College *Wisconsin* W
Mount Olive College *North Carolina* M & W
Mount Saint Mary College *New York* M & W
Mount St. Mary's University *Maryland* M & W
Mt. San Antonio College *California* M & W
Mt. San Jacinto College *California* M & W
Mount Union College *Ohio* M & W
Muhlenberg College *Pennsylvania* M & W
Murray State University *Kentucky* M & W
Muskegon Community College *Michigan* M & W
Muskingum College *Ohio* M & W
Napa Valley College *California* M & W
Nassau Community College *New York* M & W
Navarro College *Texas* M & W
Nazareth College of Rochester *New York* M & W
Nebraska Wesleyan University *Nebraska* M & W
Neumann College *Pennsylvania* M & W
New Jersey Institute of Technology *New Jersey* M & W
New Mexico Military Institute *New Mexico* M & W
New Mexico State University *New Mexico* M & W
New York University *New York* M & W
Newberry College *South Carolina* M & W
Newbury College *Massachusetts* M & W
Newman University *Kansas* M & W
Niagara University *New York* M & W
Nicholls State University *Louisiana* M & W
Nichols College *Massachusetts* M & W
Norfolk State University *Virginia* M & W
North Carolina Agricultural and Technical State University *North Carolina* M & W
North Carolina Central University *North Carolina* M & W
North Carolina State University *North Carolina* M & W
North Carolina Wesleyan College *North Carolina* M & W
North Central College *Illinois* M & W
North Central Texas College *Texas* W
North Georgia College & State University *Georgia* M & W
North Greenville College *South Carolina* M & W
North Park University *Illinois* W
Northampton County Area Community College *Pennsylvania* M & W
Northeast Mississippi Community College *Mississippi* M & W
Northeastern State University *Oklahoma* W
Northeastern University *Massachusetts* M
Northern Arizona University *Arizona* M & W
Northern Illinois University *Illinois* M & W
Northern Kentucky University *Kentucky* M & W
Northern State University *South Dakota* M & W
Northwest Mississippi Community College *Mississippi* M & W
Northwest Missouri State University *Missouri* M & W
Northwest-Shoals Community College *Alabama* W
Northwestern College *Minnesota* M & W
Northwestern State University of Louisiana *Louisiana* W
Northwestern University *Illinois* M & W
Northwood University *Michigan* M & W
Northwood University, Florida Campus *Florida* M & W
Norwich University *Vermont* M & W
Notre Dame College *Ohio* M
Nova Southeastern University *Florida* W

M = Men; W = Women

Oakland City University *Indiana* M & W
Oakland Community College *Michigan* W
Oakland University *Michigan* W
Oakton Community College *Illinois* M & W
Oberlin College *Ohio* M & W
Occidental College *California* M & W
Ocean County College *New Jersey* M & W
Oglethorpe University *Georgia* M & W
Ohio Dominican University *Ohio* M & W
Ohio Northern University *Ohio* M & W
The Ohio State University *Ohio* M & W
Ohio University-Lancaster *Ohio* M & W
Ohio University-Zanesville *Ohio* M & W
Ohio Wesleyan University *Ohio* M & W
Oklahoma Baptist University *Oklahoma* M & W
Oklahoma Christian University *Oklahoma* M & W
Oklahoma State University *Oklahoma* M & W
Oklahoma Wesleyan University *Oklahoma* M & W
Old Dominion University *Virginia* M & W
Olivet College *Michigan* M & W
Olivet Nazarene University *Illinois* M & W
Onondaga Community College *New York* M & W
Oral Roberts University *Oklahoma* M & W
Orange Coast College *California* M & W
Orange County Community College *New York* M & W
Otterbein College *Ohio* M & W
Ouachita Baptist University *Arkansas* M & W
Pace University *New York* M & W
Pacific Lutheran University *Washington* M & W
Pacific University *Oregon* M & W
Palm Beach Atlantic University *Florida* M & W
Palomar College *California* M & W
Paradise Valley Community College *Arizona* M & W
Pasadena City College *California* M & W
Pasco-Hernando Community College *Florida* W
Peace College *North Carolina* W
Pearl River Community College *Mississippi* M & W
Pennsylvania College of Technology *Pennsylvania* M & W
The Pennsylvania State University Abington College *Pennsylvania* M & W
The Pennsylvania State University Altoona College *Pennsylvania* M & W
The Pennsylvania State University Berks Campus of the Berks-Lehigh Valley College *Pennsylvania* M & W
The Pennsylvania State University Delaware County Campus of the Commonwealth College *Pennsylvania* M & W
The Pennsylvania State University at Erie, The Behrend College *Pennsylvania* M & W
The Pennsylvania State University Hazleton Campus of the Commonwealth College *Pennsylvania* M & W
The Pennsylvania State University, Lehigh Valley Campus of the Berks-Lehigh Valley College *Pennsylvania* M & W
The Pennsylvania State University Mont Alto Campus of the Commonwealth College *Pennsylvania* M & W
The Pennsylvania State University University Park Campus *Pennsylvania* M & W
The Pennsylvania State University York Campus of the Commonwealth College *Pennsylvania* M & W
Pepperdine University *California* M & W
Pfeiffer University *North Carolina* M & W
Philadelphia Biblical University *Pennsylvania* M & W
Philadelphia University *Pennsylvania* M & W
Phoenix College *Arizona* M & W
Piedmont College *Georgia* M & W
Pikeville College *Kentucky* M & W
Pima Community College *Arizona* M & W
Pine Manor College *Massachusetts* W
Pitzer College *California* M & W
Plymouth State University *New Hampshire* W
Point Loma Nazarene University *California* M & W
Polytechnic University, Brooklyn Campus *New York* M & W
Polytechnic University of Puerto Rico *Puerto Rico* M & W
Pomona College *California* M & W
Pontifical Catholic University of Puerto Rico *Puerto Rico* M & W

M = Men; W = Women

Porterville College *California* M & W
Portland State University *Oregon* M & W
Prairie State College *Illinois* W
Prairie View A&M University *Texas* M & W
Pratt Institute *New York* M & W
Presbyterian College *South Carolina* M & W
Prince George's Community College *Maryland* M & W
Princeton University *New Jersey* M & W
Principia College *Illinois* M & W
Providence College *Rhode Island* W
Purdue University *Indiana* M & W
Queens College of the City University of New York *New York* M & W
Queens University of Charlotte *North Carolina* M & W
Queen's University at Kingston *Ontario* M & W
Queensborough Community College of the City University of New York *New York* M & W
Quincy University *Illinois* M & W
Quinnipiac University *Connecticut* M & W
Radford University *Virginia* M & W
Ramapo College of New Jersey *New Jersey* M & W
Randolph-Macon College *Virginia* M & W
Randolph-Macon Woman's College *Virginia* W
Reedley College *California* M & W
Regis College *Massachusetts* W
Reinhardt College *Georgia* M & W
Rend Lake College *Illinois* W
Rensselaer Polytechnic Institute *New York* M & W
Research College of Nursing *Missouri* M & W
Rhode Island College *Rhode Island* M & W
Rhodes College *Tennessee* M & W
Rice University *Texas* M & W
The Richard Stockton College of New Jersey *New Jersey* W
Rider University *New Jersey* M & W
Ridgewater College *Minnesota* M & W
Rio Hondo College *California* M & W
Ripon College *Wisconsin* M & W
Riverside Community College District *California* M & W
Roanoke College *Virginia* M & W
Robert Morris College *Illinois* W
Robert Morris University *Pennsylvania* M & W
Roberts Wesleyan College *New York* M & W
Rochester Institute of Technology *New York* M & W
Rock Valley College *Illinois* M & W
Rockford College *Illinois* M & W
Rockhurst University *Missouri* M & W
Rockland Community College *New York* M & W
Roger Williams University *Rhode Island* M & W
Rollins College *Florida* M & W
Rose-Hulman Institute of Technology *Indiana* M & W
Rosemont College *Pennsylvania* W
Rowan University *New Jersey* M & W
Roxbury Community College *Massachusetts* M & W
Russell Sage College *New York* W
Rust College *Mississippi* M & W
Rutgers, The State University of New Jersey, New Brunswick/Piscataway *New Jersey* M & W
Sacramento City College *California* M & W
Sacred Heart University *Connecticut* M & W
Saddleback College *California* M & W
Saginaw Valley State University *Michigan* W
St. Ambrose University *Iowa* M & W
St. Andrews Presbyterian College *North Carolina* M & W
Saint Anselm College *New Hampshire* M & W
Saint Augustine's College *North Carolina* M & W
St. Bonaventure University *New York* M & W
St. Cloud State University *Minnesota* M & W
St. Edward's University *Texas* M & W
St. Francis College *New York* M & W
Saint Francis University *Pennsylvania* M & W
St. Francis Xavier University *Nova Scotia* M & W
St. John Fisher College *New York* M & W
St. John's University *New York* M & W
Saint John's University *Minnesota* M
Saint Joseph College *Connecticut* W
Saint Joseph's College *Indiana* M & W
St. Joseph's College, Suffolk Campus *New York* M & W
Saint Joseph's University *Pennsylvania* M & W

St. Lawrence University *New York* M & W
Saint Leo University *Florida* M & W
Saint Louis University *Missouri* M & W
Saint Mary's College *Indiana* W
Saint Mary's College of California *California* M & W
St. Mary's College of Maryland *Maryland* M & W
Saint Mary's University of Minnesota *Minnesota* M & W
St. Mary's University of San Antonio *Texas* M & W
Saint Michael's College *Vermont* M & W
St. Norbert College *Wisconsin* M & W
St. Olaf College *Minnesota* M & W
Saint Paul's College *Virginia* M & W
Saint Peter's College *New Jersey* M & W
St. Thomas University *Florida* M & W
Saint Vincent College *Pennsylvania* M & W
Salem College *North Carolina* W
Salem Community College *New Jersey* M & W
Salem International University *West Virginia* M & W
Salem State College *Massachusetts* M & W
Salisbury University *Maryland* M & W
Salve Regina University *Rhode Island* W
Sam Houston State University *Texas* M & W
Samford University *Alabama* M & W
San Bernardino Valley College *California* M & W
San Diego City College *California* M & W
San Diego Mesa College *California* M & W
San Diego State University *California* M & W
San Joaquin Delta College *California* M & W
San Jose State University *California* W
Santa Ana College *California* M & W
Santa Barbara City College *California* M & W
Santa Clara University *California* M & W
Santa Monica College *California* W
Santa Rosa Junior College *California* M & W
Sauk Valley Community College *Illinois* M & W
Savannah College of Art and Design *Georgia* M & W
Savannah State University *Georgia* W
Schreiner University *Texas* M & W
Scottsdale Community College *Arizona* M & W
Scripps College *California* W
Seton Hall University *New Jersey* W
Seton Hill University *Pennsylvania* M & W
Sewanee: The University of the South *Tennessee* M & W
Seward County Community College *Kansas* M & W
Shasta College *California* M & W
Shaw University *North Carolina* M & W
Shawnee Community College *Illinois* M
Shawnee State University *Ohio* W
Shenandoah University *Virginia* M & W
Shepherd University *West Virginia* M & W
Shippensburg University of Pennsylvania *Pennsylvania* W
Shoreline Community College *Washington* M & W
Shorter College *Georgia* M & W
Siena College *New York* M & W
Sierra College *California* M & W
Simmons College *Massachusetts* W
Simpson College *Iowa* M & W
Sinclair Community College *Ohio* M & W
Skagit Valley College *Washington* M & W
Skidmore College *New York* M & W
Slippery Rock University of Pennsylvania *Pennsylvania* M & W
Smith College *Massachusetts* W
Snead State Community College *Alabama* W
Sonoma State University *California* M & W
South Carolina State University *South Carolina* M & W
South Dakota School of Mines and Technology *South Dakota* M
South Dakota State University *South Dakota* M & W
South Florida Community College *Florida* W
South Mountain Community College *Arizona* M & W
Southeast Missouri State University *Missouri* W
Southeastern Louisiana University *Louisiana* M & W
Southeastern Oklahoma State University *Oklahoma* M & W
Southern Arkansas University-Magnolia *Arkansas* W
Southern Illinois University Carbondale *Illinois* M & W

Southern Illinois University Edwardsville *Illinois* M & W
Southern Methodist University *Texas* M & W
Southern Nazarene University *Oklahoma* M & W
Southern New Hampshire University *New Hampshire* M & W
Southern Oregon University *Oregon* W
Southern University and Agricultural and Mechanical College *Louisiana* M & W
Southern Utah University *Utah* W
Southern Virginia University *Virginia* M & W
Southwest Baptist University *Missouri* M & W
Southwest Minnesota State University *Minnesota* W
Southwest Mississippi Community College *Mississippi* M & W
Southwestern College *Kansas* M & W
Southwestern College *California* M & W
Southwestern Illinois College *Illinois* M & W
Southwestern University *Texas* M & W
Spartanburg Methodist College *South Carolina* M & W
Spelman College *Georgia* W
Spokane Community College *Washington* M & W
Spokane Falls Community College *Washington* M & W
Spring Arbor University *Michigan* M & W
Spring Hill College *Alabama* M & W
Springfield College *Massachusetts* M & W
Springfield Technical Community College *Massachusetts* M & W
Stanford University *California* M & W
State University of New York at Binghamton *New York* M & W
State University of New York at Buffalo *New York* M & W
State University of New York College of Agriculture and Technology at Cobleskill *New York* M & W
State University of New York College of Agriculture and Technology at Morrisville *New York* W
State University of New York College at Brockport *New York* W
State University of New York College at Cortland *New York* W
State University of New York College at Geneseo *New York* W
State University of New York College at Oneonta *New York* M & W
State University of New York College at Potsdam *New York* W
State University of New York College of Technology at Delhi *New York* M & W
State University of New York, Fredonia *New York* M & W
State University of New York Maritime College *New York* M & W
State University of New York at New Paltz *New York* W
State University of New York at Oswego *New York* M & W
State University of New York at Plattsburgh *New York* W
Stephen F. Austin State University *Texas* W
Stephens College *Missouri* W
Stetson University *Florida* M & W
Stevens Institute of Technology *New Jersey* M & W
Stillman College *Alabama* M & W
Stonehill College *Massachusetts* M & W
Stony Brook University, State University of New York *New York* M & W
Suffolk County Community College *New York* M & W
Suffolk University *Massachusetts* M & W
Sul Ross State University *Texas* M & W
Susquehanna University *Pennsylvania* M & W
Swarthmore College *Pennsylvania* M & W
Sweet Briar College *Virginia* W
Syracuse University *New York* M & W
Tabor College *Kansas* M & W
Talladega College *Alabama* M & W
Tarleton State University *Texas* W
Taylor University *Indiana* M & W
Technological College of San Juan *Puerto Rico* M & W
Temple College *Texas* M & W
Temple University *Pennsylvania* M
Tennessee State University *Tennessee* M & W
Tennessee Technological University *Tennessee* M & W
Tennessee Wesleyan College *Tennessee* M & W
Texas A&M University *Texas* M & W
Texas A&M University-Corpus Christi *Texas* M & W
Texas A&M University-Kingsville *Texas* M & W
Texas Christian University *Texas* M & W
Texas Lutheran University *Texas* M & W
Texas Southern University *Texas* M & W
Texas State University-San Marcos *Texas* M & W
Texas Tech University *Texas* M & W
Thiel College *Pennsylvania* M & W
Thomas College *Maine* M
Thomas More College *Kentucky* M & W
Tiffin University *Ohio* M & W
Towson University *Maryland* M & W
Transylvania University *Kentucky* M & W
Tri-State University *Indiana* M & W
Trinity College *Connecticut* M & W
Trinity University *Texas* M & W
Trinity (Washington) University *District of Columbia* W
Troy University *Alabama* M & W
Truman State University *Missouri* M & W
Tufts University *Massachusetts* M & W
Tulane University *Louisiana* M & W
Tusculum College *Tennessee* M & W
Tuskegee University *Alabama* M & W
Tyler Junior College *Texas* M & W
Ulster County Community College *New York* M & W
Union College *New York* M & W
Union College *Kentucky* M & W
United States Air Force Academy *Colorado* M & W
United States Coast Guard Academy *Connecticut* M & W
United States Merchant Marine Academy *New York* M & W
United States Military Academy *New York* M & W
United States Naval Academy *Maryland* M & W
Universidad Metropolitana *Puerto Rico* M & W
Universidad del Turabo *Puerto Rico* M
The University of Akron *Ohio* M & W
The University of Alabama *Alabama* M & W
The University of Alabama at Birmingham *Alabama* M & W
The University of Alabama in Huntsville *Alabama* M & W
University at Albany, State University of New York *New York* W
The University of Arizona *Arizona* M & W
University of Arkansas *Arkansas* M & W
University of Arkansas at Little Rock *Arkansas* M & W
University of Arkansas at Monticello *Arkansas* W
University of Calgary *Alberta* M & W
University of California, Berkeley *California* M & W
University of California, Davis *California* M & W
University of California, Irvine *California* M & W
University of California, Los Angeles *California* M & W
University of California, Riverside *California* M & W
University of California, San Diego *California* M & W
University of California, Santa Barbara *California* M & W
University of California, Santa Cruz *California* M & W
University of Central Arkansas *Arkansas* W
University of Central Florida *Florida* M & W
University of Central Oklahoma *Oklahoma* M & W
University of Charleston *West Virginia* M & W
University of Chicago *Illinois* M & W
University of Cincinnati *Ohio* M & W
University of Cincinnati Raymond Walters College *Ohio* M & W
University of Colorado at Boulder *Colorado* M & W
University of Colorado at Colorado Springs *Colorado* M & W
University of Connecticut *Connecticut* M & W
University of the Cumberlands *Kentucky* M & W
University of Dallas *Texas* M & W
University of Dayton *Ohio* M & W
University of Delaware *Delaware* M & W
University of Denver *Colorado* M & W
University of Detroit Mercy *Michigan* W
University of the District of Columbia *District of Columbia* M & W
University of Dubuque *Iowa* M & W
University of Evansville *Indiana* W
The University of Findlay *Ohio* M & W
University of Florida *Florida* M & W
University of Georgia *Georgia* M & W
University of Hartford *Connecticut* M & W
University of Hawaii at Hilo *Hawaii* M & W
University of Hawaii at Manoa *Hawaii* M & W
University of Houston *Texas* W
University of Idaho *Idaho* M & W
University of Illinois at Chicago *Illinois* M & W
University of Illinois at Springfield *Illinois* M & W
University of Illinois at Urbana-Champaign *Illinois* M & W
University of the Incarnate Word *Texas* M & W
University of Indianapolis *Indiana* M & W
The University of Iowa *Iowa* M & W
University of Kansas *Kansas* W
University of Kentucky *Kentucky* M & W
University of La Verne *California* M & W
University of Louisiana at Lafayette *Louisiana* M & W
University of Louisiana at Monroe *Louisiana* M & W
University of Louisville *Kentucky* M & W
University of Mary *North Dakota* M & W
University of Mary Hardin-Baylor *Texas* M & W
University of Mary Washington *Virginia* M & W
University of Maryland, Baltimore County *Maryland* M & W
University of Maryland, College Park *Maryland* M & W
University of Maryland Eastern Shore *Maryland* M & W
University of Massachusetts Amherst *Massachusetts* M
University of Massachusetts Boston *Massachusetts* M & W
University of Massachusetts Dartmouth *Massachusetts* M & W
University of Massachusetts Lowell *Massachusetts* M & W
University of Memphis *Tennessee* M & W
University of Miami *Florida* M & W
University of Michigan *Michigan* M & W
University of Minnesota, Crookston *Minnesota* W
University of Minnesota, Duluth *Minnesota* M & W
University of Minnesota, Morris *Minnesota* M & W
University of Minnesota, Twin Cities Campus *Minnesota* M & W
University of Mississippi *Mississippi* M & W
University of Missouri-Columbia *Missouri* W
University of Missouri-Kansas City *Missouri* M & W
University of Missouri-St. Louis *Missouri* M & W
University of Mobile *Alabama* W
The University of Montana-Missoula *Montana* M & W
University of Montevallo *Alabama* W
University of Nebraska at Kearney *Nebraska* M & W
University of Nebraska-Lincoln *Nebraska* M & W
University of Nebraska at Omaha *Nebraska* W
University of Nevada, Las Vegas *Nevada* M & W
University of Nevada, Reno *Nevada* M & W
University of New Hampshire *New Hampshire* M & W
University of New Haven *Connecticut* W
University of New Mexico *New Mexico* M & W
University of New Orleans *Louisiana* M & W
University of North Alabama *Alabama* M & W
The University of North Carolina at Asheville *North Carolina* M & W
The University of North Carolina at Chapel Hill *North Carolina* M & W
The University of North Carolina at Charlotte *North Carolina* M & W
The University of North Carolina at Greensboro *North Carolina* M & W
The University of North Carolina at Pembroke *North Carolina* W
The University of North Carolina Wilmington *North Carolina* M & W

M = Men; W = Women

University of North Dakota *North Dakota* W
University of North Florida *Florida* M & W
University of North Texas *Texas* M & W
University of Northern Colorado *Colorado* M & W
University of Northern Iowa *Iowa* M & W
University of Notre Dame *Indiana* M & W
University of Oklahoma *Oklahoma* M & W
University of Oregon *Oregon* M & W
University of the Ozarks *Arkansas* M & W
University of the Pacific *California* M & W
University of Pennsylvania *Pennsylvania* M & W
University of Pittsburgh *Pennsylvania* W
University of Pittsburgh at Greensburg *Pennsylvania* M
University of Portland *Oregon* M & W
University of Puerto Rico, Aguadilla University College *Puerto Rico* M & W
University of Puerto Rico at Arecibo *Puerto Rico* M & W
University of Puerto Rico at Bayamón *Puerto Rico* M & W
University of Puerto Rico at Carolina *Puerto Rico* M & W
University of Puerto Rico, Cayey University College *Puerto Rico* M & W
University of Puerto Rico at Humacao *Puerto Rico* W
University of Puerto Rico, Mayagüez Campus *Puerto Rico* M & W
University of Puerto Rico at Ponce *Puerto Rico* M & W
University of Puerto Rico, Río Piedras *Puerto Rico* M & W
University of Puget Sound *Washington* M & W
University of Redlands *California* M & W
University of Rhode Island *Rhode Island* M & W
University of Richmond *Virginia* M & W
University of Rochester *New York* M & W
University of the Sacred Heart *Puerto Rico* M & W
University of Saint Francis *Indiana* M & W
University of St. Francis *Illinois* M & W
University of St. Thomas *Minnesota* M & W
University of San Diego *California* M & W
University of San Francisco *California* M & W
University of the Sciences in Philadelphia *Pennsylvania* M & W
The University of Scranton *Pennsylvania* M & W
University of Sioux Falls *South Dakota* M & W
University of South Alabama *Alabama* M & W
University of South Carolina *South Carolina* M & W
University of South Carolina Aiken *South Carolina* M & W
University of South Carolina Upstate *South Carolina* M & W
The University of South Dakota *South Dakota* M & W
University of South Florida *Florida* M & W
University of Southern California *California* M & W
University of Southern Indiana *Indiana* M & W
University of Southern Maine *Maine* M & W
University of Southern Mississippi *Mississippi* M & W
The University of Tampa *Florida* W
The University of Tennessee *Tennessee* M & W
The University of Tennessee at Chattanooga *Tennessee* M & W
The University of Tennessee at Martin *Tennessee* M & W
The University of Texas at Arlington *Texas* M & W
The University of Texas at Austin *Texas* M & W
The University of Texas at Dallas *Texas* M & W
The University of Texas at El Paso *Texas* W
The University of Texas-Pan American *Texas* M & W
The University of Texas at San Antonio *Texas* M & W
The University of Texas at Tyler *Texas* M & W
The University of Toledo *Ohio* M & W
University of Toronto *Ontario* M & W
University of Tulsa *Oklahoma* M & W
University of Utah *Utah* M & W
University of the Virgin Islands *United States Virgin Islands* M & W
University of Virginia *Virginia* M & W
The University of Virginia's College at Wise *Virginia* M & W
University of Washington *Washington* M & W
University of Waterloo *Ontario* M & W
University of West Florida *Florida* M & W
The University of Western Ontario *Ontario* M & W
University of Wisconsin-Baraboo/Sauk County *Wisconsin* M & W
University of Wisconsin-Eau Claire *Wisconsin* M & W
University of Wisconsin-Fond du Lac *Wisconsin* M & W
University of Wisconsin-Fox Valley *Wisconsin* M & W
University of Wisconsin-Green Bay *Wisconsin* M & W
University of Wisconsin-La Crosse *Wisconsin* M & W
University of Wisconsin-Madison *Wisconsin* M & W
University of Wisconsin-Manitowoc *Wisconsin* M & W
University of Wisconsin-Marathon County *Wisconsin* M & W
University of Wisconsin-Marshfield/Wood County *Wisconsin* M & W
University of Wisconsin-Milwaukee *Wisconsin* M & W
University of Wisconsin-Oshkosh *Wisconsin* M & W
University of Wisconsin-River Falls *Wisconsin* W
University of Wisconsin-Rock County *Wisconsin* M & W
University of Wisconsin-Sheboygan *Wisconsin* M & W
University of Wisconsin-Stevens Point *Wisconsin* W
University of Wisconsin-Stout *Wisconsin* W
University of Wisconsin-Washington County *Wisconsin* M & W
University of Wisconsin-Waukesha *Wisconsin* M & W
University of Wisconsin-Whitewater *Wisconsin* M & W
University of Wyoming *Wyoming* W
Upper Iowa University *Iowa* M & W
Ursinus College *Pennsylvania* M & W
Ursuline College *Ohio* W
Utah State University *Utah* M & W
Utica College *New York* M & W
Valdosta State University *Georgia* M & W
Valley Forge Military College *Pennsylvania* M
Valparaiso University *Indiana* M & W
Vanderbilt University *Tennessee* M & W
Vanguard University of Southern California *California* M & W
Vassar College *New York* M & W
Ventura College *California* M & W
Victor Valley College *California* M & W
Villa Julie College *Maryland* M & W
Villanova University *Pennsylvania* M & W
Vincennes University *Indiana* M
Virginia Commonwealth University *Virginia* M & W
Virginia Intermont College *Virginia* M & W
Virginia Military Institute *Virginia* M
Virginia Polytechnic Institute and State University *Virginia* M & W
Virginia State University *Virginia* M & W
Virginia Union University *Virginia* M
Virginia Wesleyan College *Virginia* M & W
Wabash College *Indiana* M
Wagner College *New York* M & W
Wake Forest University *North Carolina* M & W
Walla Walla Community College *Washington* M & W
Wallace State Community College *Alabama* M & W
Walsh University *Ohio* M & W
Warner Southern College *Florida* M & W
Wartburg College *Iowa* M & W
Washburn University *Kansas* M & W
Washington College *Maryland* M & W
Washington & Jefferson College *Pennsylvania* M & W
Washington and Lee University *Virginia* M & W
Washington State University *Washington* W
Washington University in St. Louis *Missouri* M & W
Waubonsee Community College *Illinois* M & W
Wayne State University *Michigan* M & W
Waynesburg College *Pennsylvania* M & W
Weatherford College *Texas* W
Webb Institute *New York* M & W
Webber International University *Florida* M & W
Weber State University *Utah* M & W
Webster University *Missouri* M & W
Wellesley College *Massachusetts* W
Wells College *New York* W
Wentworth Institute of Technology *Massachusetts* M & W
Wesley College *Delaware* M & W
Wesleyan College *Georgia* W
Wesleyan University *Connecticut* M & W
West Chester University of Pennsylvania *Pennsylvania* M & W
West Hills Community College *California* W
West Liberty State College *West Virginia* M & W
West Valley College *California* M & W
West Virginia State University *West Virginia* M & W
West Virginia University *West Virginia* W
West Virginia University Institute of Technology *West Virginia* M & W
West Virginia Wesleyan College *West Virginia* M & W
Western Carolina University *North Carolina* W
Western Connecticut State University *Connecticut* M & W
Western Illinois University *Illinois* M & W
Western Kentucky University *Kentucky* M & W
Western Michigan University *Michigan* M & W
Western New England College *Massachusetts* M & W
Western New Mexico University *New Mexico* M & W
Westminster College *Pennsylvania* M & W
Westminster College *Missouri* M & W
Westmont College *California* M & W
Westmoreland County Community College *Pennsylvania* M & W
Wheaton College *Massachusetts* M & W
Wheaton College *Illinois* M & W
Whitman College *Washington* M & W
Whittier College *California* M & W
Whitworth College *Washington* M & W
Wichita State University *Kansas* M & W
Widener University *Pennsylvania* M & W
Wilfrid Laurier University *Ontario* W
Wilkes University *Pennsylvania* M & W
Willamette University *Oregon* M & W
William Jewell College *Missouri* M & W
Williams College *Massachusetts* M & W
Wilmington College *Ohio* M & W
Wilson College *Pennsylvania* W
Wingate University *North Carolina* M & W
Winona State University *Minnesota* M & W
Winston-Salem State University *North Carolina* M & W
Winthrop University *South Carolina* M & W
Wisconsin Lutheran College *Wisconsin* W
Wittenberg University *Ohio* M & W
Wofford College *South Carolina* M & W
Worcester State College *Massachusetts* M & W
Wright State University *Ohio* M & W
Xavier University *Ohio* M & W
Xavier University of Louisiana *Louisiana* M & W
Yale University *Connecticut* M & W
Yeshiva University *New York* M & W
York College of the City University of New York *New York* M
York College of Pennsylvania *Pennsylvania* M & W
York University *Ontario* M & W
Young Harris College *Georgia* W
Youngstown State University *Ohio* M & W
Yuba College *California* M & W

Track and Field

Abilene Christian University *Texas* M & W
Acadia University *Nova Scotia* M & W
Adams State College *Colorado* M & W
Adelphi University *New York* M & W
Adrian College *Michigan* M & W
Alabama Agricultural and Mechanical University *Alabama* M & W
Alabama State University *Alabama* M & W
Albany State University *Georgia* M & W

M = Men; W = Women

Albion College *Michigan* M & W
Albright College *Pennsylvania* M & W
Alcorn State University *Mississippi* M & W
Alfred University *New York* M & W
Allan Hancock College *California* M & W
Allegheny College *Pennsylvania* M & W
Allen County Community College *Kansas* M & W
Alliant International University *California* M & W
Alma College *Michigan* M & W
American River College *California* M & W
American University *District of Columbia* M & W
American University of Puerto Rico *Puerto Rico* M & W
Amherst College *Massachusetts* M & W
Anderson University *South Carolina* M & W
Anderson University *Indiana* M & W
Angelo State University *Texas* M & W
Antelope Valley College *California* M & W
Appalachian State University *North Carolina* M & W
Aquinas College *Michigan* M & W
Arizona State University *Arizona* M & W
Arkansas State University *Arkansas* M & W
Ashford University *Iowa* M & W
Ashland University *Ohio* M & W
Assumption College *Massachusetts* M & W
Auburn University *Alabama* M & W
Augsburg College *Minnesota* M & W
Augustana College *South Dakota* M & W
Augustana College *Illinois* M & W
Austin Peay State University *Tennessee* W
Azusa Pacific University *California* M & W
Babson College *Massachusetts* M & W
Bacone College *Oklahoma* M & W
Baker University *Kansas* M & W
Bakersfield College *California* M & W
Baldwin-Wallace College *Ohio* M & W
Ball State University *Indiana* M & W
Baltimore City Community College *Maryland* M & W
Baptist Bible College of Pennsylvania *Pennsylvania* M & W
Barber-Scotia College *North Carolina* M & W
Barnard College *New York* W
Barton County Community College *Kansas* M & W
Bates College *Maine* M & W
Bayamon Central University *Puerto Rico* M & W
Baylor University *Texas* M & W
Bellarmine University *Kentucky* M & W
Bellevue Community College *Washington* M & W
Belmont University *Tennessee* M & W
Beloit College *Wisconsin* M & W
Bemidji State University *Minnesota* M & W
Benedict College *South Carolina* M
Benedictine College *Kansas* M & W
Benedictine University *Illinois* M & W
Bennett College For Women *North Carolina* W
Bentley College *Massachusetts* M & W
Berea College *Kentucky* M & W
Bergen Community College *New Jersey* M & W
Berry College *Georgia* M & W
Bethany College *West Virginia* M & W
Bethany College *Kansas* M & W
Bethel College *Tennessee* M & W
Bethel College *Kansas* M & W
Bethel College *Indiana* M & W
Bethel University *Minnesota* M & W
Bethune-Cookman College *Florida* M & W
Biola University *California* M & W
Black Hills State University *South Dakota* M & W
Bloomsburg University of Pennsylvania *Pennsylvania* M & W
Bluffton University *Ohio* M & W
Boise State University *Idaho* M & W
Boston College *Massachusetts* M & W
Boston University *Massachusetts* M & W
Bowdoin College *Maine* M & W
Bowie State University *Maryland* M & W
Bowling Green State University *Ohio* M & W
Bradley University *Illinois* W
Brandeis University *Massachusetts* M & W
Brevard College *North Carolina* M & W
Briar Cliff University *Iowa* M & W
Briarcliffe College *New York* M & W
Bridgewater College *Virginia* M & W
Bridgewater State College *Massachusetts* M & W
Brigham Young University *Utah* M & W
Bronx Community College of the City University of New York *New York* M & W
Brooklyn College of the City University of New York *New York* M & W
Brown University *Rhode Island* M & W
Bryant University *Rhode Island* M & W
Bryn Mawr College *Pennsylvania* W
Bucknell University *Pennsylvania* M & W
Buena Vista University *Iowa* M & W
Buffalo State College, State University of New York *New York* M & W
Butler Community College *Kansas* M & W
Butler University *Indiana* M & W
Butte College *California* M & W
Cabrillo College *California* M & W
Cabrini College *Pennsylvania* M & W
California Institute of Technology *California* M & W
California Lutheran University *California* M & W
California Polytechnic State University, San Luis Obispo *California* M & W
California State Polytechnic University, Pomona *California* M & W
California State University, Bakersfield *California* M & W
California State University, Chico *California* M & W
California State University, Fresno *California* M & W
California State University, Fullerton *California* M & W
California State University, Long Beach *California* M & W
California State University, Los Angeles *California* M & W
California State University, Northridge *California* M & W
California State University, Sacramento *California* M & W
California State University, San Marcos *California* M & W
California State University, Stanislaus *California* M & W
California University of Pennsylvania *Pennsylvania* M & W
Calvin College *Michigan* M & W
Campbell University *North Carolina* M & W
Campbellsville University *Kentucky* M & W
Capital University *Ohio* M & W
Caribbean University *Puerto Rico* M & W
Carleton College *Minnesota* M & W
Carnegie Mellon University *Pennsylvania* M & W
Carroll College *Wisconsin* M & W
Carson-Newman College *Tennessee* M & W
Carthage College *Wisconsin* M & W
Cascade College *Oregon* M & W
Case Western Reserve University *Ohio* M & W
The Catholic University of America *District of Columbia* M & W
Cedar Crest College *Pennsylvania* W
Cedarville University *Ohio* M & W
Central Arizona College *Arizona* M & W
Central College *Iowa* M & W
Central Connecticut State University *Connecticut* M & W
Central Methodist University *Missouri* M & W
Central Michigan University *Michigan* M & W
Central Missouri State University *Missouri* M & W
Central State University *Ohio* M & W
Central Washington University *Washington* M & W
Centre College *Kentucky* M & W
Cerritos College *California* M & W
Chabot College *California* M & W
Chadron State College *Nebraska* M & W
Chaffey College *California* M & W
Chapman University *California* W
Charleston Southern University *South Carolina* M & W
Chemeketa Community College *Oregon* M & W
Cheyney University of Pennsylvania *Pennsylvania* M & W
Chicago State University *Illinois* M & W
Christopher Newport University *Virginia* M & W
The Citadel, The Military College of South Carolina *South Carolina* M & W
Citrus College *California* M & W
City College of the City University of New York *New York* M & W
City College of San Francisco *California* M & W
City Colleges of Chicago, Kennedy-King College *Illinois* M & W
Clackamas Community College *Oregon* M & W
Claflin University *South Carolina* M & W
Claremont McKenna College *California* M & W
Clarion University of Pennsylvania *Pennsylvania* M & W
Clark Atlanta University *Georgia* M & W
Clark College *Washington* M & W
Clayton State University *Georgia* M & W
Clemson University *South Carolina* M & W
Cleveland State University *Ohio* W
Cloud County Community College *Kansas* M & W
Coastal Carolina University *South Carolina* M & W
Coe College *Iowa* M & W
Coffeyville Community College *Kansas* M & W
Colby College *Maine* M & W
Colby Community College *Kansas* M & W
Colby-Sawyer College *New Hampshire* M & W
Colgate University *New York* M & W
College of the Canyons *California* M & W
College of the Desert *California* M & W
College of DuPage *Illinois* M & W
College of the Holy Cross *Massachusetts* M & W
College of Marin *California* M & W
College Misericordia *Pennsylvania* M & W
College of Mount St. Joseph *Ohio* M & W
College of Mount Saint Vincent *New York* W
The College of New Jersey *New Jersey* M & W
College of the Redwoods *California* M & W
College of Saint Benedict *Minnesota* W
College of St. Catherine *Minnesota* W
The College of St. Scholastica *Minnesota* M & W
College of San Mateo *California* M & W
College of the Sequoias *California* M & W
College of the Siskiyous *California* M & W
College of the Southwest *New Mexico* M & W
The College of William and Mary *Virginia* M & W
The College of Wooster *Ohio* M & W
The Colorado College *Colorado* M & W
Colorado School of Mines *Colorado* M & W
Colorado State University *Colorado* M & W
Columbia College *New York* M & W
Columbia Union College *Maryland* M & W
Columbia University, School of General Studies *New York* M & W
Columbia University, The Fu Foundation School of Engineering and Applied Science *New York* M & W
Community College of Rhode Island *Rhode Island* M & W
Compton Community College *California* M & W
Concord University *West Virginia* M & W
Concordia College *Minnesota* M & W
Concordia University *Oregon* M & W
Concordia University *Nebraska* M & W
Concordia University *Illinois* M & W
Concordia University *California* M & W
Concordia University, St. Paul *Minnesota* M & W
Concordia University Wisconsin *Wisconsin* M & W
Connecticut College *Connecticut* M & W
Contra Costa College *California* M & W
Copiah-Lincoln Community College *Mississippi* M
Coppin State University *Maryland* M & W
Cornell College *Iowa* M & W
Cornell University *New York* M & W
Cornerstone University *Michigan* M & W
Cosumnes River College (Sacramento) *California* M & W
Cuesta College *California* M & W
Cumberland County College *New Jersey* M
Cuyamaca College *California* M & W
Dakota State University *South Dakota* M & W
Dakota Wesleyan University *South Dakota* M & W
Dalhousie University *Nova Scotia* M & W
Dallas Baptist University *Texas* M & W
Dana College *Nebraska* M & W
Danville Area Community College *Illinois* M & W
Dartmouth College *New Hampshire* M & W
Davidson College *North Carolina* M & W
De Anza College *California* M & W

M = Men; W = Women

Defiance College *Ohio* M & W
Delaware State University *Delaware* M & W
Delaware Valley College *Pennsylvania* M & W
Delgado Community College *Louisiana* W
Denison University *Ohio* M & W
DePaul University *Illinois* M & W
DePauw University *Indiana* M & W
DeSales University *Pennsylvania* M & W
Diablo Valley College *California* M & W
Dickinson College *Pennsylvania* M & W
Dickinson State University *North Dakota* M & W
Doane College *Nebraska* M & W
Dordt College *Iowa* M & W
Drake University *Iowa* M & W
Duke University *North Carolina* M & W
Duquesne University *Pennsylvania* M & W
Earlham College *Indiana* M & W
East Carolina University *North Carolina* M & W
East Central University *Oklahoma* M & W
East Los Angeles College *California* M & W
East Stroudsburg University of Pennsylvania *Pennsylvania* M & W
East Tennessee State University *Tennessee* M & W
Eastern Connecticut State University *Connecticut* M & W
Eastern Illinois University *Illinois* M & W
Eastern Kentucky University *Kentucky* M & W
Eastern Mennonite University *Virginia* M & W
Eastern Michigan University *Michigan* M & W
Eastern New Mexico University *New Mexico* M & W
Eastern Oregon University *Oregon* M & W
Eastern Washington University *Washington* M & W
Edinboro University of Pennsylvania *Pennsylvania* M & W
Edward Waters College *Florida* M & W
El Camino College *California* M & W
Electronic Data Processing College of Puerto Rico *Puerto Rico* M & W
Elizabeth City State University *North Carolina* M & W
Elizabethtown College *Pennsylvania* M & W
Elmhurst College *Illinois* M & W
Elon University *North Carolina* W
Emmanuel College *Massachusetts* M & W
Emory University *Georgia* M & W
Emporia State University *Kansas* M & W
Erie Community College *New York* M & W
Erie Community College, North Campus *New York* M & W
Erie Community College, South Campus *New York* M & W
Essex County College *New Jersey* M & W
Evangel University *Missouri* M & W
The Evergreen State College *Washington* M & W
Fairleigh Dickinson University, Metropolitan Campus *New Jersey* M & W
Farmingdale State University of New York *New York* M & W
Fayetteville State University *North Carolina* M & W
Felician College *New Jersey* M & W
Ferris State University *Michigan* M & W
Fisk University *Tennessee* M & W
Fitchburg State College *Massachusetts* M & W
Florida Agricultural and Mechanical University *Florida* M & W
Florida Atlantic University *Florida* W
Florida International University *Florida* M & W
Florida Memorial College *Florida* M & W
Florida State University *Florida* M & W
Fordham University *New York* M & W
Fort Hays State University *Kansas* M & W
Fort Lewis College *Colorado* M & W
Fort Valley State University *Georgia* M & W
Francis Marion University *South Carolina* M & W
Franklin College *Indiana* M & W
Franklin and Marshall College *Pennsylvania* M & W
Fresno City College *California* M & W
Fresno Pacific University *California* M & W
Friends University *Kansas* M & W
Frostburg State University *Maryland* M & W
Fullerton College *California* M & W
Furman University *South Carolina* M & W
Gallaudet University *District of Columbia* M & W
Garden City Community College *Kansas* M & W
Gardner-Webb University *North Carolina* M & W
Geneva College *Pennsylvania* M & W
George Fox University *Oregon* M & W
George Mason University *Virginia* M & W
Georgetown College *Kentucky* M & W
Georgetown University *District of Columbia* M & W
Georgia Institute of Technology *Georgia* M & W
Georgia Southern University *Georgia* W
Georgia State University *Georgia* M & W
Gettysburg College *Pennsylvania* M & W
Glendale Community College *California* M & W
Glendale Community College *Arizona* M & W
Glenville State College *West Virginia* M & W
Globe Institute of Technology *New York* M & W
Gloucester County College *New Jersey* M & W
Golden West College *California* M & W
Gonzaga University *Washington* M & W
Goshen College *Indiana* M & W
Goucher College *Maryland* M & W
Grace College *Indiana* M & W
Graceland University *Iowa* M & W
Grambling State University *Louisiana* M & W
Grand Rapids Community College *Michigan* M
Grand Valley State University *Michigan* M & W
Grand View College *Iowa* M & W
Greenville College *Illinois* M & W
Grinnell College *Iowa* M & W
Grossmont College *California* M
Grove City College *Pennsylvania* M & W
Gustavus Adolphus College *Minnesota* M & W
Hagerstown Community College *Maryland* M & W
Hamilton College *New York* M & W
Hamline University *Minnesota* M & W
Hampton University *Virginia* M & W
Hanover College *Indiana* M & W
Harding University *Arkansas* M & W
Harris-Stowe State University *Missouri* W
Hartnell College *California* M & W
Hartwick College *New York* M & W
Harvard University *Massachusetts* M & W
Harvey Mudd College *California* M & W
Haskell Indian Nations University *Kansas* M & W
Hastings College *Nebraska* M & W
Haverford College *Pennsylvania* M & W
Heidelberg College *Ohio* M & W
Hendrix College *Arkansas* M & W
Henry Ford Community College *Michigan* M
Herkimer County Community College *New York* M & W
High Point University *North Carolina* M & W
Highland Community College *Kansas* M & W
Highline Community College *Washington* M & W
Hillsdale College *Michigan* M & W
Hinds Community College *Mississippi* M
Hiram College *Ohio* M & W
Hood College *Maryland* M & W
Hope College *Michigan* M & W
Houghton College *New York* M & W
Howard Community College *Maryland* M & W
Howard Payne University *Texas* M & W
Howard University *District of Columbia* M & W
Hudson Valley Community College *New York* M & W
Humboldt State University *California* M & W
Hunter College of the City University of New York *New York* M & W
Huntington University *Indiana* M & W
Huston-Tillotson University *Texas* M & W
Hutchinson Community College and Area Vocational School *Kansas* M & W
Idaho State University *Idaho* M & W
Illinois College *Illinois* M & W
Illinois State University *Illinois* M & W
Illinois Wesleyan University *Illinois* M & W
Independence Community College *Kansas* M & W
Indiana State University *Indiana* M & W
Indiana University Bloomington *Indiana* M & W
Indiana University of Pennsylvania *Pennsylvania* M & W
Indiana University-Purdue University Fort Wayne *Indiana* W
Indiana Wesleyan University *Indiana* M & W
Inter American University of Puerto Rico, Aguadilla Campus *Puerto Rico* M & W
Inter American University of Puerto Rico, Arecibo Campus *Puerto Rico* M & W
Inter American University of Puerto Rico, Barranquitas Campus *Puerto Rico* M & W
Inter American University of Puerto Rico, Bayamón Campus *Puerto Rico* M & W
Inter American University of Puerto Rico, Guayama Campus *Puerto Rico* M & W
Inter American University of Puerto Rico, Metropolitan Campus *Puerto Rico* M & W
Inter American University of Puerto Rico, Ponce Campus *Puerto Rico* M & W
Inter American University of Puerto Rico, San Germán Campus *Puerto Rico* M & W
Iona College *New York* M & W
Iowa State University of Science and Technology *Iowa* M & W
Iowa Wesleyan College *Iowa* M & W
Itawamba Community College *Mississippi* M
Ithaca College *New York* M & W
Jackson State University *Mississippi* M & W
Jacksonville University *Florida* W
James Madison University *Virginia* M & W
Jamestown College *North Dakota* M & W
John Carroll University *Ohio* M & W
The Johns Hopkins University *Maryland* M & W
Johnson C. Smith University *North Carolina* M & W
Johnson County Community College *Kansas* M & W
Jones County Junior College *Mississippi* M
Juniata College *Pennsylvania* M & W
Kansas City Kansas Community College *Kansas* M & W
Kansas State University *Kansas* M & W
Kansas Wesleyan University *Kansas* M & W
Kean University *New Jersey* M & W
Keene State College *New Hampshire* M & W
Kent State University *Ohio* M & W
Kentucky State University *Kentucky* M & W
Kenyon College *Ohio* M & W
Keystone College *Pennsylvania* M & W
King College *Tennessee* M & W
Kingsborough Community College of the City University of New York *New York* M & W
Knox College *Illinois* M & W
Kutztown University of Pennsylvania *Pennsylvania* M & W
La Salle University *Pennsylvania* M & W
Lafayette College *Pennsylvania* M & W
Lake Forest College *Illinois* M & W
Lake Superior State University *Michigan* M & W
Lakehead University *Ontario* M & W
Lamar University *Texas* M & W
Lane College *Tennessee* M & W
Lane Community College *Oregon* M & W
Langston University *Oklahoma* M & W
Lansing Community College *Michigan* M & W
Lassen Community College District *California* M & W
Laurentian University *Ontario* M & W
Lawrence University *Wisconsin* M & W
Lebanon Valley College *Pennsylvania* M & W
Lees-McRae College *North Carolina* M & W
Lehigh University *Pennsylvania* M & W
Lehman College of the City University of New York *New York* M & W
Lewis & Clark College *Oregon* M & W
Lewis University *Illinois* M & W
Liberty University *Virginia* M & W
Lincoln University *Pennsylvania* M & W
Lincoln University *Missouri* M & W
Lindenwood University *Missouri* M & W
Lindsey Wilson College *Kentucky* M & W
Linfield College *Oregon* M & W
Livingstone College *North Carolina* M & W
Lock Haven University of Pennsylvania *Pennsylvania* M & W
Long Beach City College *California* M & W
Long Island University, Brooklyn Campus *New York* M & W
Long Island University, C.W. Post Campus *New York* M & W
Longwood University *Virginia* M & W
Loras College *Iowa* M & W
Los Angeles City College *California* M & W

M = Men; W = Women

M = Men; W = Women

Saint Mary's University *Nova Scotia* M & W
Saint Mary's University of Minnesota *Minnesota* M & W
St. Norbert College *Wisconsin* M & W
St. Olaf College *Minnesota* M & W
Saint Paul's College *Virginia* M & W
Saint Peter's College *New Jersey* M & W
Salem State College *Massachusetts* M & W
Salisbury University *Maryland* M & W
Salve Regina University *Rhode Island* W
Sam Houston State University *Texas* M & W
Samford University *Alabama* M & W
San Bernardino Valley College *California* M & W
San Diego City College *California* M & W
San Diego Mesa College *California* M & W
San Diego State University *California* W
San Francisco State University *California* M & W
San Joaquin Delta College *California* M & W
San Jose City College *California* M & W
Santa Ana College *California* M & W
Santa Barbara City College *California* M & W
Santa Clara University *California* M & W
Santa Monica College *California* M & W
Santa Rosa Junior College *California* M & W
Savannah State University *Georgia* M & W
Scottsdale Community College *Arizona* M & W
Scripps College *California* W
Seattle Pacific University *Washington* M & W
Seattle University *Washington* M & W
Seton Hall University *New Jersey* M & W
Seton Hill University *Pennsylvania* M & W
Sewanee: The University of the South *Tennessee* M & W
Shasta College *California* M & W
Shaw University *North Carolina* M & W
Shippensburg University of Pennsylvania *Pennsylvania* M & W
Shorter College *Georgia* M & W
Siena College *New York* M & W
Siena Heights University *Michigan* M & W
Sierra College *California* M & W
Simmons College *Massachusetts* W
Simon Fraser University *British Columbia* M & W
Simpson College *Iowa* M & W
Skyline College *California* M & W
Slippery Rock University of Pennsylvania *Pennsylvania* M & W
Smith College *Massachusetts* W
Soka University of America *California* M & W
Sonoma State University *California* W
South Carolina State University *South Carolina* M & W
South Dakota School of Mines and Technology *South Dakota* M & W
South Dakota State University *South Dakota* M & W
South Mountain Community College *Arizona* M & W
South Plains College *Texas* M & W
Southeast Missouri State University *Missouri* M & W
Southeastern Louisiana University *Louisiana* M & W
Southern Arkansas University-Magnolia *Arkansas* M & W
Southern Connecticut State University *Connecticut* M & W
Southern Illinois University Carbondale *Illinois* M & W
Southern Illinois University Edwardsville *Illinois* M & W
Southern Methodist University *Texas* M & W
Southern Nazarene University *Oklahoma* M & W
Southern Oregon University *Oregon* M & W
Southern University and Agricultural and Mechanical College *Louisiana* M & W
Southern University at New Orleans *Louisiana* M & W
Southern Utah University *Utah* M & W
Southern Vermont College *Vermont* M & W
Southern Virginia University *Virginia* M & W
Southwest Baptist University *Missouri* M & W
Southwestern Christian College *Texas* M & W
Southwestern College *Kansas* M & W
Southwestern College *California* M & W
Southwestern Oregon Community College *Oregon* M & W
Spelman College *Georgia* W
Spokane Community College *Washington* M & W
Spokane Falls Community College *Washington* M & W
Spoon River College *Illinois* M & W
Spring Arbor University *Michigan* M & W
Springfield College *Massachusetts* M & W
Stanford University *California* M & W
State University of New York at Binghamton *New York* M & W
State University of New York at Buffalo *New York* M & W
State University of New York College of Agriculture and Technology at Cobleskill *New York* M & W
State University of New York College of Agriculture and Technology at Morrisville *New York* M & W
State University of New York College at Brockport *New York* M & W
State University of New York College at Cortland *New York* M & W
State University of New York College at Geneseo *New York* M & W
State University of New York College at Oneonta *New York* M & W
State University of New York College at Potsdam *New York* M & W
State University of New York College of Technology at Alfred *New York* M & W
State University of New York College of Technology at Delhi *New York* M & W
State University of New York, Fredonia *New York* M & W
State University of New York at Oswego *New York* M & W
State University of New York at Plattsburgh *New York* M & W
Stephen F. Austin State University *Texas* M & W
Sterling College *Kansas* M & W
Stevens Institute of Technology *New Jersey* M & W
Stillman College *Alabama* M & W
Stonehill College *Massachusetts* M & W
Stony Brook University, State University of New York *New York* M & W
Sul Ross State University *Texas* M & W
Susquehanna University *Pennsylvania* M & W
Swarthmore College *Pennsylvania* M & W
Syracuse University *New York* M & W
Tabor College *Kansas* M & W
Tarleton State University *Texas* M & W
Taylor University *Indiana* M & W
Technological College of San Juan *Puerto Rico* M & W
Temple University *Pennsylvania* M & W
Tennessee State University *Tennessee* M & W
Tennessee Technological University *Tennessee* W
Texas A&M University *Texas* M & W
Texas A&M University-Commerce *Texas* M & W
Texas A&M University-Corpus Christi *Texas* M & W
Texas A&M University-Kingsville *Texas* M & W
Texas Christian University *Texas* M & W
Texas College *Texas* M & W
Texas Lutheran University *Texas* W
Texas Southern University *Texas* M & W
Texas State University-San Marcos *Texas* M & W
Texas Tech University *Texas* M & W
Thaddeus Stevens College of Technology *Pennsylvania* M
Thiel College *Pennsylvania* M & W
Tiffin University *Ohio* M & W
Towson University *Maryland* M & W
Tri-State University *Indiana* M & W
Trinity Baptist College *Florida* M
Trinity Christian College *Illinois* M & W
Trinity College *Connecticut* M & W
Trinity International University *Illinois* M & W
Trinity University *Texas* M & W
Troy University *Alabama* M
Truman State University *Missouri* M & W
Tufts University *Massachusetts* M & W
Tulane University *Louisiana* M & W
Tuskegee University *Alabama* M & W
Union College *New York* M & W
Union College *Kentucky* M & W
Union University *Tennessee* M & W
United States Air Force Academy *Colorado* M & W
United States Coast Guard Academy *Connecticut* M & W
United States Merchant Marine Academy *New York* M & W
United States Military Academy *New York* M & W
United States Naval Academy *Maryland* M & W
Universidad del Este *Puerto Rico* M & W
Universidad Metropolitana *Puerto Rico* M & W
Universidad del Turabo *Puerto Rico* M & W
Université Laval *Quebec* M & W
Université de Moncton *New Brunswick* M & W
Université du Québec àTrois-Rivières *Quebec* M & W
Université de Sherbrooke *Quebec* M & W
The University of Akron *Ohio* M & W
The University of Alabama *Alabama* M & W
The University of Alabama at Birmingham *Alabama* W
The University of Alabama in Huntsville *Alabama* M & W
University at Albany, State University of New York *New York* M & W
University of Alberta *Alberta* M & W
The University of Arizona *Arizona* M & W
University of Arkansas *Arkansas* M & W
University of Arkansas at Little Rock *Arkansas* M & W
University of Arkansas at Pine Bluff *Arkansas* M & W
The University of British Columbia *British Columbia* M & W
University of Calgary *Alberta* M & W
University of California, Berkeley *California* M
University of California, Davis *California* M & W
University of California, Irvine *California* M & W
University of California, Los Angeles *California* M & W
University of California, Riverside *California* M & W
University of California, San Diego *California* M & W
University of California, Santa Barbara *California* M & W
University of California, Santa Cruz *California* M & W
University of Central Arkansas *Arkansas* W
University of Central Florida *Florida* W
University of Charleston *West Virginia* M & W
University of Chicago *Illinois* M & W
University of Cincinnati *Ohio* M & W
University of Cincinnati Raymond Walters College *Ohio* M & W
University of Colorado at Boulder *Colorado* M & W
University of Colorado at Colorado Springs *Colorado* M & W
University of Connecticut *Connecticut* M & W
University of the Cumberlands *Kentucky* M & W
University of Dallas *Texas* M & W
University of Dayton *Ohio* W
University of Delaware *Delaware* M & W
University of Detroit Mercy *Michigan* M & W
University of the District of Columbia *District of Columbia* M & W
University of Dubuque *Iowa* M & W
The University of Findlay *Ohio* M & W
University of Florida *Florida* M & W
University of Georgia *Georgia* M & W
University of Guelph *Ontario* M & W
University of Hartford *Connecticut* M & W
University of Hawaii at Manoa *Hawaii* W
University of Houston *Texas* M & W
University of Idaho *Idaho* M & W
University of Illinois at Chicago *Illinois* M & W
University of Illinois at Urbana-Champaign *Illinois* M & W
University of Indianapolis *Indiana* M & W
The University of Iowa *Iowa* M & W
University of Kansas *Kansas* M & W
University of Kentucky *Kentucky* M & W
University of La Verne *California* M & W
University of Lethbridge *Alberta* M & W
University of Louisiana at Lafayette *Louisiana* M & W
University of Louisiana at Monroe *Louisiana* M & W
University of Louisville *Kentucky* M & W
University of Maine *Maine* M & W

M = Men; W = Women

University of Manitoba *Manitoba* M & W
University of Mary *North Dakota* M & W
University of Mary Washington *Virginia* M & W
University of Maryland, Baltimore County *Maryland* M & W
University of Maryland, College Park *Maryland* M & W
University of Maryland Eastern Shore *Maryland* M & W
University of Massachusetts Amherst *Massachusetts* M & W
University of Massachusetts Boston *Massachusetts* M & W
University of Massachusetts Dartmouth *Massachusetts* M & W
University of Massachusetts Lowell *Massachusetts* M & W
University of Memphis *Tennessee* M & W
University of Miami *Florida* M & W
University of Michigan *Michigan* M & W
University of Minnesota, Duluth *Minnesota* M & W
University of Minnesota, Morris *Minnesota* M & W
University of Minnesota, Twin Cities Campus *Minnesota* M & W
University of Mississippi *Mississippi* M & W
University of Missouri-Columbia *Missouri* M & W
University of Missouri-Kansas City *Missouri* M & W
University of Missouri-Rolla *Missouri* M & W
University of Mobile *Alabama* M & W
The University of Montana-Missoula *Montana* M & W
University of Nebraska at Kearney *Nebraska* M & W
University of Nebraska-Lincoln *Nebraska* M & W
University of Nevada, Las Vegas *Nevada* W
University of Nevada, Reno *Nevada* W
University of New Hampshire *New Hampshire* M & W
University of New Haven *Connecticut* M & W
University of New Mexico *New Mexico* M & W
University of New Orleans *Louisiana* M & W
The University of North Carolina at Asheville *North Carolina* M & W
The University of North Carolina at Chapel Hill *North Carolina* M & W
The University of North Carolina at Charlotte *North Carolina* M & W
The University of North Carolina at Pembroke *North Carolina* M
The University of North Carolina Wilmington *North Carolina* M & W
University of North Dakota *North Dakota* M & W
University of North Florida *Florida* M & W
University of North Texas *Texas* M & W
University of Northern Colorado *Colorado* M & W
University of Northern Iowa *Iowa* M & W
University of Notre Dame *Indiana* M & W
University of Oklahoma *Oklahoma* M & W
University of Oregon *Oregon* M & W
University of Ottawa *Ontario* M & W
University of Pennsylvania *Pennsylvania* M & W
University of Pittsburgh *Pennsylvania* M & W
University of Pittsburgh at Johnstown *Pennsylvania* W
University of Portland *Oregon* M & W
University of Puerto Rico, Aguadilla University College *Puerto Rico* M & W
University of Puerto Rico at Arecibo *Puerto Rico* M & W
University of Puerto Rico at Bayamón *Puerto Rico* M & W
University of Puerto Rico at Carolina *Puerto Rico* M & W
University of Puerto Rico, Cayey University College *Puerto Rico* M & W
University of Puerto Rico at Humacao *Puerto Rico* M & W
University of Puerto Rico, Mayagüez Campus *Puerto Rico* M & W
University of Puerto Rico at Ponce *Puerto Rico* M & W
University of Puerto Rico, Río Piedras *Puerto Rico* M & W
University of Puerto Rico at Utuado *Puerto Rico* M & W
University of Puget Sound *Washington* M & W
University of Redlands *California* M & W
University of Regina *Saskatchewan* M & W
University of Rhode Island *Rhode Island* M & W
University of Richmond *Virginia* M & W
University of Rio Grande *Ohio* M & W
University of Rochester *New York* M & W
University of the Sacred Heart *Puerto Rico* M & W
University of Saint Francis *Indiana* M & W
University of St. Francis *Illinois* W
University of St. Thomas *Minnesota* M & W
University of San Francisco *California* W
University of Saskatchewan *Saskatchewan* M & W
The University of Scranton *Pennsylvania* M & W
University of Sioux Falls *South Dakota* M & W
University of South Alabama *Alabama* M & W
University of South Carolina *South Carolina* M & W
The University of South Dakota *South Dakota* M & W
University of South Florida *Florida* M & W
University of Southern California *California* M & W
University of Southern Maine *Maine* M & W
University of Southern Mississippi *Mississippi* M & W
The University of Tennessee *Tennessee* M & W
The University of Tennessee at Chattanooga *Tennessee* M & W
The University of Texas at Arlington *Texas* M & W
The University of Texas at Austin *Texas* M & W
The University of Texas at El Paso *Texas* M & W
The University of Texas-Pan American *Texas* M & W
The University of Texas at San Antonio *Texas* M & W
The University of Toledo *Ohio* M & W
University of Toronto *Ontario* M & W
University of Tulsa *Oklahoma* M & W
University of Utah *Utah* W
University of Vermont *Vermont* M & W
University of the Virgin Islands *United States Virgin Islands* M & W
University of Virginia *Virginia* M & W
The University of Virginia's College at Wise *Virginia* M & W
University of Washington *Washington* M & W
University of Waterloo *Ontario* M & W
University of West Florida *Florida* W
The University of Western Ontario *Ontario* M & W
University of Windsor *Ontario* M & W
University of Wisconsin-Eau Claire *Wisconsin* M & W
University of Wisconsin-La Crosse *Wisconsin* M & W
University of Wisconsin-Madison *Wisconsin* M & W
University of Wisconsin-Milwaukee *Wisconsin* M & W
University of Wisconsin-Oshkosh *Wisconsin* M & W
University of Wisconsin-Parkside *Wisconsin* M & W
University of Wisconsin-Platteville *Wisconsin* M & W
University of Wisconsin-River Falls *Wisconsin* M & W
University of Wisconsin-Stevens Point *Wisconsin* M & W
University of Wisconsin-Stout *Wisconsin* M & W
University of Wisconsin-Superior *Wisconsin* M & W
University of Wisconsin-Whitewater *Wisconsin* M & W
University of Wyoming *Wyoming* M & W
Upper Iowa University *Iowa* M & W
Ursinus College *Pennsylvania* M & W
Utah State University *Utah* M & W
Utah Valley State College *Utah* M & W
Valparaiso University *Indiana* M & W
Vanderbilt University *Tennessee* M & W
Vanguard University of Southern California *California* M & W
Vassar College *New York* M & W
Ventura College *California* M & W
Victor Valley College *California* M & W
Villa Julie College *Maryland* M & W
Villanova University *Pennsylvania* M & W
Vincennes University *Indiana* M & W
Virginia Commonwealth University *Virginia* M & W
Virginia Intermont College *Virginia* M & W
Virginia Military Institute *Virginia* M & W
Virginia Polytechnic Institute and State University *Virginia* M & W
Virginia State University *Virginia* M & W
Virginia Union University *Virginia* M & W
Voorhees College *South Carolina* M & W
Wabash College *Indiana* M
Wagner College *New York* M & W
Wake Forest University *North Carolina* M & W
Wallace State Community College *Alabama* M & W
Walsh University *Ohio* M & W
Warner Pacific College *Oregon* M & W
Warner Southern College *Florida* M & W
Wartburg College *Iowa* M & W
Washington & Jefferson College *Pennsylvania* M & W
Washington and Lee University *Virginia* M & W
Washington State University *Washington* M & W
Washington University in St. Louis *Missouri* M & W
Wayland Baptist University *Texas* M & W
Wayne State College *Nebraska* M & W
Waynesburg College *Pennsylvania* M & W
Webber International University *Florida* M & W
Weber State University *Utah* M & W
Wellesley College *Massachusetts* W
Wentworth Military Academy and Junior College *Missouri* M & W
Wesleyan University *Connecticut* M & W
West Chester University of Pennsylvania *Pennsylvania* M & W
West Liberty State College *West Virginia* M & W
West Los Angeles College *California* M & W
West Valley College *California* M
West Virginia State University *West Virginia* M & W
West Virginia University *West Virginia* W
West Virginia Wesleyan College *West Virginia* M & W
Western Carolina University *North Carolina* M & W
Western Illinois University *Illinois* M & W
Western Kentucky University *Kentucky* M & W
Western Michigan University *Michigan* W
Western Oregon University *Oregon* M & W
Western State College of Colorado *Colorado* M & W
Western Washington University *Washington* M & W
Westfield State College *Massachusetts* M & W
Westminster College *Pennsylvania* M & W
Westmont College *California* M & W
Wheaton College *Massachusetts* M & W
Wheaton College *Illinois* M & W
Wheeling Jesuit University *West Virginia* M & W
Whitman College *Washington* M & W
Whittier College *California* M & W
Whitworth College *Washington* M & W
Wichita State University *Kansas* M & W
Widener University *Pennsylvania* M & W
Wiley College *Texas* M & W
Willamette University *Oregon* M & W
William Jewell College *Missouri* M & W
William Paterson University of New Jersey *New Jersey* M & W
William Penn University *Iowa* M & W
William Rainey Harper College *Illinois* M & W
William Woods University *Missouri* M & W
Williams College *Massachusetts* M & W
Wilmington College *Ohio* M & W
Winona State University *Minnesota* W
Winthrop University *South Carolina* M & W
Wisconsin Lutheran College *Wisconsin* M & W
Wittenberg University *Ohio* M & W
Wofford College *South Carolina* M & W
Worcester Polytechnic Institute *Massachusetts* M & W
Worcester State College *Massachusetts* M & W
Wright State University *Ohio* W
Yale University *Connecticut* M & W
York College *Nebraska* M & W
York College of the City University of New York *New York* M & W
York College of Pennsylvania *Pennsylvania* M & W
York University *Ontario* M & W
Youngstown State University *Ohio* M & W

M = Men; W = Women

Yuba College *California* M & W

Ultimate Frisbee

Allegheny College *Pennsylvania* M & W
Amherst College *Massachusetts* M & W
Augustana College *Illinois* M & W
Bates College *Maine* M & W
Boston University *Massachusetts* M & W
Bowdoin College *Maine* M & W
Bryant University *Rhode Island* M & W
Bucknell University *Pennsylvania* M & W
California State University, Chico *California* M & W
Carleton College *Minnesota* M & W
Carnegie Mellon University *Pennsylvania* M & W
Case Western Reserve University *Ohio* M & W
Clemson University *South Carolina* M & W
Colby College *Maine* M & W
College of Saint Benedict *Minnesota* W
The Colorado College *Colorado* M & W
Columbia College *New York* M & W
Connecticut College *Connecticut* M & W
Dartmouth College *New Hampshire* M & W
Davidson College *North Carolina* M & W
Dickinson College *Pennsylvania* M & W
Duke University *North Carolina* M & W
Earlham College *Indiana* M & W
Emory University *Georgia* M & W
Fordham University *New York* M & W
Fort Lewis College *Colorado* M & W
Franklin and Marshall College *Pennsylvania* M
Georgetown University *District of Columbia* M & W
Georgia Southern University *Georgia* M & W
Gustavus Adolphus College *Minnesota* M & W
Hamilton College *New York* M & W
Hampden-Sydney College *Virginia* M
Harding University *Arkansas* M & W
Illinois Wesleyan University *Illinois* M & W
Juniata College *Pennsylvania* M & W
Kenyon College *Ohio* M & W
Lake Forest College *Illinois* M & W
Lawrence University *Wisconsin* M & W
Loyola University New Orleans *Louisiana* M & W
Lycoming College *Pennsylvania* M & W
Macalester College *Minnesota* W
McGill University *Quebec* M & W
Missouri Baptist University *Missouri* M & W
Missouri State University *Missouri* M & W
New York University *New York* M & W
North Carolina State University *North Carolina* M & W
Oberlin College *Ohio* M & W
Occidental College *California* M & W
Ohio Wesleyan University *Ohio* M & W
Pacific Lutheran University *Washington* M & W
Pomona College *California* M & W
Rice University *Texas* M & W
Rochester Institute of Technology *New York* M & W
St. Cloud State University *Minnesota* M & W
Saint John's University *Minnesota* M
Saint Louis University *Missouri* M & W
Saint Mary's College *Indiana* W
St. Mary's College of Maryland *Maryland* M & W
Stanford University *California* M & W
State University of New York College at Geneseo *New York* M & W
Stonehill College *Massachusetts* M & W
Swarthmore College *Pennsylvania* M & W
Texas State University-San Marcos *Texas* M & W
Trinity College *Connecticut* M & W
Union College *New York* M & W
The University of British Columbia *British Columbia* M
University of California, Santa Barbara *California* M & W
University of California, Santa Cruz *California* M & W
University of Colorado at Boulder *Colorado* M & W
The University of Iowa *Iowa* M & W
University of Maryland, Baltimore County *Maryland* M & W
The University of Montana-Missoula *Montana* M & W
The University of North Carolina at Chapel Hill *North Carolina* M & W
University of North Texas *Texas* M & W
University of Oregon *Oregon* M & W
University of Richmond *Virginia* M & W
University of Rochester *New York* M & W
University of Southern Indiana *Indiana* M & W
University of Vermont *Vermont* M & W
University of Virginia *Virginia* M & W
University of Wisconsin-Madison *Wisconsin* M & W
University of Wisconsin-Platteville *Wisconsin* M & W
University of Wyoming *Wyoming* M & W
Vassar College *New York* M & W
Virginia Polytechnic Institute and State University *Virginia* M & W
Washington College *Maryland* M & W
Washington and Lee University *Virginia* M & W
Washington University in St. Louis *Missouri* M & W
Wellesley College *Massachusetts* W
Whitman College *Washington* M & W

Volleyball

Abilene Christian University *Texas* W
Acadia University *Nova Scotia* W
Adams State College *Colorado* W
Adelphi University *New York* W
Adirondack Community College *New York* W
Adrian College *Michigan* W
Agnes Scott College *Georgia* W
Alabama Agricultural and Mechanical University *Alabama* W
Alabama State University *Alabama* W
Albany State University *Georgia* W
Alberta College of Art & Design *Alberta* M & W
Albertson College of Idaho *Idaho* W
Albertus Magnus College *Connecticut* W
Albion College *Michigan* M & W
Albright College *Pennsylvania* W
Alcorn State University *Mississippi* W
Alderson-Broaddus College *West Virginia* W
Alexandria Technical College *Minnesota* W
Alfred University *New York* W
Allan Hancock College *California* W
Allegany College of Maryland *Maryland* W
Allegheny College *Pennsylvania* M & W
Allen County Community College *Kansas* W
Allen University *South Carolina* W
Alliance University College *Alberta* M & W
Alliant International University *California* W
Alma College *Michigan* W
Alpena Community College *Michigan* W
Alvernia College *Pennsylvania* W
Alverno College *Wisconsin* W
Alvin Community College *Texas* W
American International College *Massachusetts* W
American River College *California* M & W
American University *District of Columbia* W
American University of Puerto Rico *Puerto Rico* M & W
Amherst College *Massachusetts* M & W
Ancilla College *Indiana* W
Anderson University *South Carolina* W
Anderson University *Indiana* W
Angelo State University *Texas* W
Anna Maria College *Massachusetts* W
Anne Arundel Community College *Maryland* W
Anoka-Ramsey Community College *Minnesota* W
Anoka-Ramsey Community College, Cambridge Campus *Minnesota* W
Antelope Valley College *California* W
Appalachian Bible College *West Virginia* W
Appalachian State University *North Carolina* W
Aquinas College *Michigan* W
Arcadia University *Pennsylvania* W
Arizona State University *Arizona* W
Arizona Western College *Arizona* W
Arkansas Baptist College *Arkansas* M & W
Arkansas State University *Arkansas* W
Arkansas Tech University *Arkansas* W
Arlington Baptist College *Texas* W
Armstrong Atlantic State University *Georgia* W
The Art Institute of Boston at Lesley University *Massachusetts* M & W
Asbury College *Kentucky* W
Ashford University *Iowa* W
Ashland University *Ohio* W
Assumption College *Massachusetts* W
Atlanta Christian College *Georgia* W
Auburn University *Alabama* W
Augsburg College *Minnesota* W
Augusta State University *Georgia* W
Augustana College *South Dakota* W
Augustana College *Illinois* M & W
Aurora University *Illinois* W
Austin College *Texas* W
Austin Peay State University *Tennessee* W
Averett University *Virginia* W
Avila University *Missouri* W
Azusa Pacific University *California* M & W
Babson College *Massachusetts* W
Bacone College *Oklahoma* M & W
Baker University *Kansas* W
Bakersfield College *California* W
Baldwin-Wallace College *Ohio* W
Ball State University *Indiana* M & W
Baptist Bible College *Missouri* W
Baptist Bible College of Pennsylvania *Pennsylvania* M & W
Barber-Scotia College *North Carolina* W
Barclay College *Kansas* W
Bard College *New York* M & W
Barnard College *New York* W
Barry University *Florida* W
Barstow College *California* W
Barton College *North Carolina* W
Barton County Community College *Kansas* W
Bates College *Maine* M & W
Bay Path College *Massachusetts* W
Bayamon Central University *Puerto Rico* M & W
Baylor University *Texas* M & W
Becker College *Massachusetts* W
Belhaven College *Mississippi* W
Bellarmine University *Kentucky* W
Bellevue Community College *Washington* W
Bellevue University *Nebraska* W
Belmont Abbey College *North Carolina* W
Belmont University *Tennessee* W
Beloit College *Wisconsin* W
Bemidji State University *Minnesota* W
Benedict College *South Carolina* W
Benedictine College *Kansas* W
Benedictine University *Illinois* W
Bennett College For Women *North Carolina* W
Bentley College *Massachusetts* W
Berea College *Kentucky* W
Bergen Community College *New Jersey* W
Bernard M. Baruch College of the City University of New York *New York* M & W
Berry College *Georgia* W
Bethany Bible College *New Brunswick* W
Bethany College *West Virginia* W
Bethany College *Kansas* W
Bethany Lutheran College *Minnesota* W
Bethany University *California* M & W
Bethel College *Tennessee* W
Bethel College *Kansas* W
Bethel College *Indiana* W
Bethel University *Minnesota* M & W
Bethune-Cookman College *Florida* W
Bevill State Community College *Alabama* W
Big Bend Community College *Washington* W
Biola University *California* W
Birmingham-Southern College *Alabama* W
Bishop's University *Quebec* W
Bismarck State College *North Dakota* W
Black Hawk College *Illinois* W
Black Hills State University *South Dakota* W
Blackburn College *Illinois* W
Blessing-Rieman College of Nursing *Illinois* M & W
Blinn College *Texas* W
Bloomfield College *New Jersey* W
Bloomsburg University of Pennsylvania *Pennsylvania* W
Blue Mountain Community College *Oregon* W
Bluefield College *Virginia* W
Bluffton University *Ohio* W
Boise State University *Idaho* W
Boston College *Massachusetts* W
Boston University *Massachusetts* M & W
Bowdoin College *Maine* W

M = Men; W = Women

M = Men; W = Women

M = Men; W = Women

Harrisburg Area Community College *Pennsylvania* M & W
Hartnell College *California* W
Hartwick College *New York* W
Harvard University *Massachusetts* M & W
Harvey Mudd College *California* W
Haskell Indian Nations University *Kansas* W
Hastings College *Nebraska* W
Haverford College *Pennsylvania* W
Hawaii Pacific University *Hawaii* W
Heidelberg College *Ohio* M & W
Henderson State University *Arkansas* W
Hendrix College *Arkansas* W
Henry Ford Community College *Michigan* W
Heritage Baptist College and Heritage Theological Seminary *Ontario* M & W
Herkimer County Community College *New York* W
Hesser College *New Hampshire* M & W
Hesston College *Kansas* W
Hibbing Community College *Minnesota* W
High Point University *North Carolina* W
Highland Community College *Kansas* W
Highland Community College *Illinois* W
Highline Community College *Washington* W
Hilbert College *New York* M & W
Hill College of the Hill Junior College District *Texas* W
Hillsborough Community College *Florida* W
Hillsdale College *Michigan* W
Hiram College *Ohio* W
Hofstra University *New York* W
Holy Names University *California* M & W
Holyoke Community College *Massachusetts* W
Hood College *Maryland* W
Hope College *Michigan* W
Hope International University *California* M & W
Houghton College *New York* W
Houston Baptist University *Texas* W
Howard Community College *Maryland* W
Howard Payne University *Texas* W
Howard University *District of Columbia* W
Hudson Valley Community College *New York* W
Humboldt State University *California* M & W
Hunter College of the City University of New York *New York* M & W
Huntingdon College *Alabama* W
Huntington University *Indiana* W
Husson College *Maine* W
Huston-Tillotson University *Texas* W
Hutchinson Community College and Area Vocational School *Kansas* W
Idaho State University *Idaho* W
Illinois Central College *Illinois* W
Illinois College *Illinois* W
Illinois Eastern Community Colleges, Lincoln Trail College *Illinois* W
Illinois Eastern Community Colleges, Olney Central College *Illinois* W
Illinois Eastern Community Colleges, Wabash Valley College *Illinois* W
Illinois Institute of Technology *Illinois* W
Illinois State University *Illinois* W
Illinois Wesleyan University *Illinois* M & W
Immaculata University *Pennsylvania* W
Independence Community College *Kansas* W
Indian Hills Community College *Iowa* W
Indian River Community College *Florida* W
Indiana State University *Indiana* W
Indiana Tech *Indiana* W
Indiana University Bloomington *Indiana* W
Indiana University Northwest *Indiana* W
Indiana University of Pennsylvania *Pennsylvania* W
Indiana University-Purdue University Fort Wayne *Indiana* M & W
Indiana University-Purdue University Indianapolis *Indiana* W
Indiana University Southeast *Indiana* W
Indiana Wesleyan University *Indiana* W
Inter American University of Puerto Rico, Aguadilla Campus *Puerto Rico* M & W
Inter American University of Puerto Rico, Arecibo Campus *Puerto Rico* M & W
Inter American University of Puerto Rico, Barranquitas Campus *Puerto Rico* M & W
Inter American University of Puerto Rico, Bayamón Campus *Puerto Rico* M & W
Inter American University of Puerto Rico, Guayama Campus *Puerto Rico* M & W
Inter American University of Puerto Rico, Metropolitan Campus *Puerto Rico* M & W
Inter American University of Puerto Rico, Ponce Campus *Puerto Rico* M & W
Inter American University of Puerto Rico, San Germán Campus *Puerto Rico* M & W
Iona College *New York* W
Iowa Central Community College *Iowa* W
Iowa Lakes Community College *Iowa* W
Iowa State University of Science and Technology *Iowa* W
Iowa Wesleyan College *Iowa* W
Iowa Western Community College *Iowa* W
Irvine Valley College *California* M
Itasca Community College *Minnesota* W
Ithaca College *New York* W
Jackson State University *Mississippi* W
Jacksonville College *Texas* W
Jacksonville State University *Alabama* W
Jacksonville University *Florida* W
James H. Faulkner State Community College *Alabama* W
James Madison University *Virginia* W
James Sprunt Community College *North Carolina* M & W
Jamestown College *North Dakota* W
Jamestown Community College *New York* W
Jarvis Christian College *Texas* W
Jefferson College *Missouri* W
Jefferson Community College *New York* W
John A. Logan College *Illinois* W
John Brown University *Arkansas* W
John Carroll University *Ohio* M & W
John Jay College of Criminal Justice of the City University of New York *New York* W
John Wood Community College *Illinois* W
The Johns Hopkins University *Maryland* W
Johnson Bible College *Tennessee* W
Johnson C. Smith University *North Carolina* W
Johnson County Community College *Kansas* W
Johnson & Wales University *Rhode Island* M & W
Johnston Community College *North Carolina* M & W
Joliet Junior College *Illinois* W
Judson College *Illinois* W
Judson College *Alabama* W
Juniata College *Pennsylvania* M & W
Kalamazoo College *Michigan* W
Kalamazoo Valley Community College *Michigan* W
Kankakee Community College *Illinois* W
Kansas City Kansas Community College *Kansas* W
Kansas State University *Kansas* W
Kansas Wesleyan University *Kansas* W
Kaskaskia College *Illinois* W
Kean University *New Jersey* W
Keene State College *New Hampshire* W
Kellogg Community College *Michigan* W
Kent State University *Ohio* W
Kentucky Christian University *Kentucky* W
Kentucky State University *Kentucky* W
Kentucky Wesleyan College *Kentucky* W
Kenyon College *Ohio* W
Kettering University *Michigan* M
Keuka College *New York* W
Keystone College *Pennsylvania* W
King College *Tennessee* W
King's College *Pennsylvania* W
The King's University College *Alberta* M & W
Kingsborough Community College of the City University of New York *New York* W
Kirkwood Community College *Iowa* W
Kishwaukee College *Illinois* W
Knox College *Illinois* W
Kutztown University of Pennsylvania *Pennsylvania* M & W
La Roche College *Pennsylvania* W
La Salle University *Pennsylvania* W
La Sierra University *California* M & W
Labette Community College *Kansas* W
Lackawanna College *Pennsylvania* W
Lafayette College *Pennsylvania* W
LaGrange College *Georgia* W
Lake Erie College *Ohio* W
Lake Forest College *Illinois* M & W
Lake Land College *Illinois* W
Lake Michigan College *Michigan* W
Lake-Sumter Community College *Florida* W
Lake Superior State University *Michigan* W
Lake Tahoe Community College *California* W
Lakehead University *Ontario* M & W
Lakeland College *Wisconsin* M & W
Lakeland Community College *Ohio* W
Lamar Community College *Colorado* W
Lamar University *Texas* W
Lambuth University *Tennessee* W
Lancaster Bible College *Pennsylvania* M & W
Lander University *South Carolina* W
Lane College *Tennessee* W
Lane Community College *Oregon* W
Laney College *California* W
Lansing Community College *Michigan* W
Laramie County Community College *Wyoming* W
Laredo Community College *Texas* W
Lasell College *Massachusetts* M & W
Lassen Community College District *California* W
Laurentian University *Ontario* M
Lawrence University *Wisconsin* M & W
Lawson State Community College *Alabama* W
Le Moyne College *New York* W
Lebanon Valley College *Pennsylvania* W
Lee College *Texas* W
Lee University *Tennessee* W
Lees-McRae College *North Carolina* M & W
Lehigh Carbon Community College *Pennsylvania* W
Lehigh University *Pennsylvania* M & W
Lehman College of the City University of New York *New York* M & W
LeMoyne-Owen College *Tennessee* W
Lenoir Community College *North Carolina* M & W
Lenoir-Rhyne College *North Carolina* W
Lesley University *Massachusetts* M & W
LeTourneau University *Texas* W
Lewis & Clark College *Oregon* W
Lewis and Clark Community College *Illinois* W
Lewis-Clark State College *Idaho* W
Lewis University *Illinois* M & W
Liberty University *Virginia* W
Life Pacific College *California* W
Limestone College *South Carolina* W
Lincoln Christian College *Illinois* W
Lincoln College *Illinois* W
Lincoln College-Normal *Illinois* W
Lincoln Land Community College *Illinois* W
Lincoln Memorial University *Tennessee* W
Lincoln University *Pennsylvania* W
Lindenwood University *Missouri* M & W
Lindsey Wilson College *Kentucky* W
Linfield College *Oregon* W
Linn-Benton Community College *Oregon* W
Linn State Technical College *Missouri* M & W
Lipscomb University *Tennessee* W
Livingstone College *North Carolina* W
Lock Haven University of Pennsylvania *Pennsylvania* W
Lon Morris College *Texas* W
Long Beach City College *California* M & W
Long Island University, Brooklyn Campus *New York* W
Long Island University, C.W. Post Campus *New York* W
Longview Community College *Missouri* W
Longwood University *Virginia* M & W
Loras College *Iowa* M & W
Los Angeles City College *California* M & W
Los Angeles Harbor College *California* W
Los Angeles Pierce College *California* M & W
Los Angeles Valley College *California* M & W
Los Medanos College *California* W
Louisburg College *North Carolina* M & W
Louisiana State University and Agricultural and Mechanical College *Louisiana* W
Louisiana Tech University *Louisiana* W
Lower Columbia College *Washington* W
Loyola College in Maryland *Maryland* W
Loyola Marymount University *California* M & W

M = Men; W = Women

Loyola University Chicago *Illinois* M & W
Loyola University New Orleans *Louisiana* W
Lubbock Christian University *Texas* W
Luther College *Iowa* W
Luzerne County Community College *Pennsylvania* W
Lycoming College *Pennsylvania* W
Lynchburg College *Virginia* W
Lyndon State College *Vermont* W
Lynn University *Florida* W
Lyon College *Arkansas* W
Macalester College *Minnesota* M & W
MacMurray College *Illinois* W
Macomb Community College *Michigan* W
Madison Area Technical College *Wisconsin* M & W
Madonna University *Michigan* W
Maine Maritime Academy *Maine* W
Malone College *Ohio* W
Manatee Community College *Florida* W
Manchester College *Indiana* W
Manhattan Christian College *Kansas* W
Manhattan College *New York* M & W
Manhattanville College *New York* W
Manor College *Pennsylvania* W
Maranatha Baptist Bible College *Wisconsin* W
Marian College *Indiana* W
Marian College of Fond du Lac *Wisconsin* W
Marietta College *Ohio* W
Marion Technical College *Ohio* W
Marist College *New York* M & W
Marquette University *Wisconsin* M & W
Mars Hill College *North Carolina* W
Marshall University *West Virginia* W
Marshalltown Community College *Iowa* W
Martin Luther College *Minnesota* W
Martin Methodist College *Tennessee* W
Mary Baldwin College *Virginia* W
Marymount University *Virginia* W
Maryville College *Tennessee* W
Maryville University of Saint Louis *Missouri* W
Marywood University *Pennsylvania* W
Massachusetts Bay Community College *Massachusetts* W
Massachusetts Institute of Technology *Massachusetts* M & W
Massachusetts Maritime Academy *Massachusetts* W
Master's College and Seminary *Ontario* W
The Master's College and Seminary *California* W
Mayville State University *North Dakota* W
McDaniel College *Maryland* W
McGill University *Quebec* M & W
McHenry County College *Illinois* W
McKendree College *Illinois* W
McMaster University *Ontario* M & W
McMurry University *Texas* W
McNeese State University *Louisiana* W
McPherson College *Kansas* W
Medaille College *New York* M & W
Medgar Evers College of the City University of New York *New York* W
Memorial University of Newfoundland *Newfoundland and Labrador* M & W
Mendocino College *California* W
Menlo College *California* W
Merced College *California* W
Mercer University *Georgia* W
Mercy College *New York* W
Mercyhurst College *Pennsylvania* M & W
Meredith College *North Carolina* W
Merrimack College *Massachusetts* M & W
Mesa Community College *Arizona* W
Mesa State College *Colorado* W
Mesabi Range Community and Technical College *Minnesota* W
Messenger College *Missouri* W
Messiah College *Pennsylvania* W
Methodist College *North Carolina* W
Metropolitan State College of Denver *Colorado* W
Miami Dade College *Florida* W
Miami University *Ohio* M & W
Miami University Hamilton *Ohio* W
Miami University-Middletown Campus *Ohio* W
Michigan State University *Michigan* M & W
Michigan Technological University *Michigan* W
Mid-America Christian University *Oklahoma* W
Mid-Continent University *Kentucky* W
Mid-Plains Community College *Nebraska* W
Mid-State Technical College *Wisconsin* W
MidAmerica Nazarene University *Kansas* W
Middle Tennessee State University *Tennessee* W
Middlebury College *Vermont* W
Midland College *Texas* W
Midland Lutheran College *Nebraska* W
Midwestern State University *Texas* W
Millersville University of Pennsylvania *Pennsylvania* W
Milligan College *Tennessee* W
Millikin University *Illinois* W
Mills College *California* W
Millsaps College *Mississippi* W
Milwaukee Area Technical College *Wisconsin* W
Milwaukee School of Engineering *Wisconsin* M & W
Mineral Area College *Missouri* W
Minnesota State Community and Technical College-Fergus Falls *Minnesota* W
Minnesota State University Mankato *Minnesota* W
Minnesota State University Moorhead *Minnesota* W
Minnesota West Community and Technical College *Minnesota* W
Minot State University *North Dakota* W
Minot State University-Bottineau Campus *North Dakota* W
Mississippi College *Mississippi* W
Mississippi State University *Mississippi* W
Mississippi University for Women *Mississippi* W
Missouri Baptist University *Missouri* M & W
Missouri Southern State University *Missouri* W
Missouri State University *Missouri* M & W
Missouri State University-West Plains *Missouri* W
Missouri Valley College *Missouri* M & W
Missouri Western State University *Missouri* W
Mitchell College *Connecticut* W
Modesto Junior College *California* W
Mohawk Valley Community College *New York* W
Molloy College *New York* W
Monmouth College *Illinois* W
Monroe College (Bronx) *New York* W
Monroe College (New Rochelle) *New York* W
Monroe Community College *New York* W
Montana State University *Montana* W
Montana State University-Billings *Montana* W
Montana State University-Northern *Montana* W
Montana Tech of The University of Montana *Montana* W
Montclair State University *New Jersey* W
Monterey Peninsula College *California* W
Montgomery College *Maryland* W
Montreat College *North Carolina* W
Moody Bible Institute *Illinois* M & W
Moorpark College *California* M & W
Moraine Valley Community College *Illinois* W
Moravian College *Pennsylvania* W
Morehead State University *Kentucky* W
Morgan State University *Maryland* W
Morningside College *Iowa* W
Morris College *South Carolina* W
Morton College *Illinois* W
Mott Community College *Michigan* W
Mount Aloysius College *Pennsylvania* W
Mount Holyoke College *Massachusetts* W
Mt. Hood Community College *Oregon* W
Mount Ida College *Massachusetts* M & W
Mount Marty College *South Dakota* W
Mount Mary College *Wisconsin* W
Mount Mercy College *Iowa* W
Mount Olive College *North Carolina* M & W
Mount Saint Mary College *New York* W
Mount Saint Vincent University *Nova Scotia* W
Mt. San Antonio College *California* M & W
Mt. San Jacinto College *California* W
Mount Union College *Ohio* W
Mount Vernon Nazarene University *Ohio* W
Mountain State University *West Virginia* W
Muhlenberg College *Pennsylvania* W
Multnomah Bible College and Biblical Seminary *Oregon* W
Murray State University *Kentucky* W
Muskegon Community College *Michigan* W
Muskingum College *Ohio* W
Napa Valley College *California* W
Nassau Community College *New York* M & W
National American University (Rapid City) *South Dakota* W
Navarro College *Texas* W
Nazareth College of Rochester *New York* M & W
Nebraska Christian College *Nebraska* W
Nebraska Wesleyan University *Nebraska* W
Neosho County Community College *Kansas* W
Neumann College *Pennsylvania* W
New Hampshire Community Technical College, Manchester/Stratham *New Hampshire* M & W
New Hampshire Technical Institute *New Hampshire* M & W
New Jersey City University *New Jersey* M & W
New Jersey Institute of Technology *New Jersey* M & W
New Mexico Highlands University *New Mexico* W
New Mexico Military Institute *New Mexico* W
New Mexico State University *New Mexico* W
New York City College of Technology of the City University of New York *New York* M & W
New York Institute of Technology *New York* W
New York University *New York* M & W
Newberry College *South Carolina* W
Newbury College *Massachusetts* M & W
Newman University *Kansas* M & W
Niagara County Community College *New York* W
Niagara University *New York* W
Nicholls State University *Louisiana* W
Nichols College *Massachusetts* W
Nipissing University *Ontario* M & W
Norfolk State University *Virginia* W
North Carolina Agricultural and Technical State University *North Carolina* W
North Carolina Central University *North Carolina* W
North Carolina State University *North Carolina* M & W
North Carolina Wesleyan College *North Carolina* W
North Central College *Illinois* W
North Central Texas College *Texas* W
North Central University *Minnesota* W
North Country Community College *New York* W
North Dakota State College of Science *North Dakota* W
North Dakota State University *North Dakota* M & W
North Greenville College *South Carolina* W
North Idaho College *Idaho* W
North Iowa Area Community College *Iowa* W
North Lake College *Texas* W
North Park University *Illinois* M & W
Northampton County Area Community College *Pennsylvania* M & W
Northeastern Junior College *Colorado* W
Northeastern Oklahoma Agricultural and Mechanical College *Oklahoma* W
Northeastern University *Massachusetts* W
Northern Arizona University *Arizona* W
Northern Essex Community College *Massachusetts* M & W
Northern Illinois University *Illinois* W
Northern Kentucky University *Kentucky* W
Northern Michigan University *Michigan* W
Northern Oklahoma College *Oklahoma* M & W
Northern State University *South Dakota* W
Northland College *Wisconsin* W
Northland Community and Technical College-Thief River Falls *Minnesota* W
Northwest College *Wyoming* W
Northwest Missouri State University *Missouri* W
Northwest Nazarene University *Idaho* M & W
Northwest-Shoals Community College *Alabama* W
Northwest University *Washington* W
Northwestern College *Minnesota* W
Northwestern College *Iowa* W
Northwestern State University of Louisiana *Louisiana* W
Northwestern University *Illinois* W
Northwood University *Michigan* W
Northwood University, Florida Campus *Florida* W
Norwich University *Vermont* M & W
Notre Dame College *Ohio* W

M = Men; W = Women

Notre Dame de Namur University *California* W
Nova Scotia Agricultural College *Nova Scotia* M & W
Nova Southeastern University *Florida* W
Nyack College *New York* W
Oak Hills Christian College *Minnesota* W
Oakland City University *Indiana* W
Oakland Community College *Michigan* W
Oakland University *Michigan* W
Oakton Community College *Illinois* W
Oberlin College *Ohio* M & W
Occidental College *California* M & W
Oglethorpe University *Georgia* W
Ohio Dominican University *Ohio* W
Ohio Northern University *Ohio* W
The Ohio State University *Ohio* M & W
Ohio University *Ohio* M & W
Ohio University-Chillicothe *Ohio* W
Ohio University-Eastern *Ohio* W
Ohio University-Lancaster *Ohio* W
Ohio University-Zanesville *Ohio* W
Ohio Valley University *West Virginia* W
Ohio Wesleyan University *Ohio* M & W
Ohlone College *California* M & W
Oklahoma Panhandle State University *Oklahoma* W
Oklahoma Wesleyan University *Oklahoma* W
Old Dominion University *Virginia* M & W
Olivet College *Michigan* W
Olivet Nazarene University *Illinois* W
Olympic College *Washington* W
Onondaga Community College *New York* W
Oral Roberts University *Oklahoma* W
Orange Coast College *California* M & W
Orange County Community College *New York* W
Oregon Institute of Technology *Oregon* W
Oregon State University *Oregon* W
Otero Junior College *Colorado* W
Ottawa University *Kansas* W
Otterbein College *Ohio* W
Ouachita Baptist University *Arkansas* W
Owens Community College *Ohio* W
Oxnard College *California* W
Ozark Christian College *Missouri* W
Pace University *New York* W
Pacific Lutheran University *Washington* M & W
Pacific Union College *California* M & W
Pacific University *Oregon* M & W
Paine College *Georgia* W
Palm Beach Atlantic University *Florida* M & W
Palm Beach Community College *Florida* M & W
Palomar College *California* W
Panola College *Texas* W
Paris Junior College *Texas* W
Park University *Missouri* M & W
Parkland College *Illinois* W
Pasadena City College *California* W
Pasco-Hernando Community College *Florida* W
Passaic County Community College *New Jersey* W
Paul Smith's College of Arts and Sciences *New York* W
Peace College *North Carolina* W
Pennsylvania College of Technology *Pennsylvania* M & W
The Pennsylvania State University Abington College *Pennsylvania* W
The Pennsylvania State University Altoona College *Pennsylvania* M & W
The Pennsylvania State University Beaver Campus of the Commonwealth College *Pennsylvania* W
The Pennsylvania State University Berks Campus of the Berks-Lehigh Valley College *Pennsylvania* M & W
The Pennsylvania State University Delaware County Campus of the Commonwealth College *Pennsylvania* W
The Pennsylvania State University DuBois Campus of the Commonwealth College *Pennsylvania* W
The Pennsylvania State University at Erie, The Behrend College *Pennsylvania* M & W
The Pennsylvania State University Fayette Campus of the Commonwealth College *Pennsylvania* W
The Pennsylvania State University Harrisburg Campus *Pennsylvania* M & W
The Pennsylvania State University Hazleton Campus of the Commonwealth College *Pennsylvania* M & W
The Pennsylvania State University, Lehigh Valley Campus of the Berks-Lehigh Valley College *Pennsylvania* M & W
The Pennsylvania State University McKeesport Campus of the Commonwealth College *Pennsylvania* W
The Pennsylvania State University Mont Alto Campus of the Commonwealth College *Pennsylvania* W
The Pennsylvania State University New Kensington Campus of the Commonwealth College *Pennsylvania* W
The Pennsylvania State University Schuylkill Campus of the Capital College *Pennsylvania* W
The Pennsylvania State University University Park Campus *Pennsylvania* M & W
The Pennsylvania State University Wilkes-Barre Campus of the Commonwealth College *Pennsylvania* W
The Pennsylvania State University Worthington Scranton Campus of the Commonwealth College *Pennsylvania* W
The Pennsylvania State University York Campus of the Commonwealth College *Pennsylvania* W
Pepperdine University *California* M & W
Peru State College *Nebraska* W
Pfeiffer University *North Carolina* W
Philadelphia Biblical University *Pennsylvania* M & W
Philadelphia University *Pennsylvania* W
Philander Smith College *Arkansas* W
Phoenix College *Arizona* W
Piedmont Baptist College *North Carolina* W
Piedmont College *Georgia* W
Pierce College *Washington* W
Pikes Peak Community College *Colorado* W
Pikeville College *Kentucky* W
Pillsbury Baptist Bible College *Minnesota* W
Pima Community College *Arizona* W
Pine Manor College *Massachusetts* W
Pitt Community College *North Carolina* W
Pittsburg State University *Kansas* W
Pitzer College *California* W
Plymouth State University *New Hampshire* M & W
Point Loma Nazarene University *California* W
Point Park University *Pennsylvania* W
Polk Community College *Florida* W
Polytechnic University, Brooklyn Campus *New York* M & W
Polytechnic University of Puerto Rico *Puerto Rico* M & W
Pomona College *California* W
Pontifical Catholic University of Puerto Rico *Puerto Rico* M & W
Porterville College *California* W
Portland State University *Oregon* W
Post University *Connecticut* W
Potomac State College of West Virginia University *West Virginia* W
Prairie Bible Institute *Alberta* M & W
Prairie View A&M University *Texas* W
Pratt Community College *Kansas* W
Pratt Institute *New York* W
Presbyterian College *South Carolina* W
Presentation College *South Dakota* W
Prince George's Community College *Maryland* W
Princeton University *New Jersey* M & W
Principia College *Illinois* W
Providence College *Rhode Island* W
Providence College and Theological Seminary *Manitoba* M & W
Puget Sound Christian College *Washington* W
Purchase College, State University of New York *New York* M & W
Purdue University *Indiana* W
Queens College of the City University of New York *New York* M & W
Queens University of Charlotte *North Carolina* W
Queen's University at Kingston *Ontario* M & W
Queensborough Community College of the City University of New York *New York* M & W
Quincy University *Illinois* M & W
Quinnipiac University *Connecticut* W
Radford University *Virginia* W
Rainy River Community College *Minnesota* W
Ramapo College of New Jersey *New Jersey* M & W
Randolph-Macon College *Virginia* W
Randolph-Macon Woman's College *Virginia* W
Reading Area Community College *Pennsylvania* W
Redeemer University College *Ontario* M & W
Redlands Community College *Oklahoma* W
Reedley College *California* W
Regis College *Massachusetts* W
Regis University *Colorado* W
Rend Lake College *Illinois* W
Rensselaer Polytechnic Institute *New York* M & W
Research College of Nursing *Missouri* W
Rhode Island College *Rhode Island* W
Rhodes College *Tennessee* W
Rice University *Texas* M & W
The Richard Stockton College of New Jersey *New Jersey* W
Richland College *Texas* W
Rider University *New Jersey* W
Ridgewater College *Minnesota* W
Rio Hondo College *California* W
Ripon College *Wisconsin* W
Riverland Community College *Minnesota* W
Riverside Community College District *California* W
Rivier College *New Hampshire* M & W
Roanoke Bible College *North Carolina* W
Roanoke College *Virginia* M & W
Robert Morris College *Illinois* W
Robert Morris University *Pennsylvania* W
Roberts Wesleyan College *New York* W
Rochester College *Michigan* W
Rochester Community and Technical College *Minnesota* W
Rochester Institute of Technology *New York* M & W
Rock Valley College *Illinois* W
Rockford College *Illinois* M & W
Rockhurst University *Missouri* W
Rockingham Community College *North Carolina* M & W
Rockland Community College *New York* W
Rocky Mountain College *Alberta* M & W
Roger Williams University *Rhode Island* M & W
Rollins College *Florida* W
Rose-Hulman Institute of Technology *Indiana* W
Rosemont College *Pennsylvania* W
Rowan University *New Jersey* W
Royal Military College of Canada *Ontario* M & W
Russell Sage College *New York* W
Rutgers, The State University of New Jersey, New Brunswick/Piscataway *New Jersey* W
Ryerson University *Ontario* M & W
Sacramento City College *California* W
Sacred Heart University *Connecticut* M & W
Saddleback College *California* W
Saginaw Valley State University *Michigan* W
St. Ambrose University *Iowa* M & W
St. Andrews Presbyterian College *North Carolina* W
Saint Anselm College *New Hampshire* W
Saint Augustine's College *North Carolina* W
St. Bonaventure University *New York* M & W
St. Clair County Community College *Michigan* W
St. Cloud State University *Minnesota* M & W
St. Cloud Technical College *Minnesota* W
St. Edward's University *Texas* W
St. Francis College *New York* W
Saint Francis University *Pennsylvania* M & W
St. Francis Xavier University *Nova Scotia* W
St. Gregory's University *Oklahoma* W
St. John Fisher College *New York* W
St. Johns River Community College *Florida* W
St. John's University *New York* W
Saint John's University *Minnesota* M
Saint Joseph College *Connecticut* W
Saint Joseph's College *Indiana* W
Saint Joseph's College of Maine *Maine* W
St. Joseph's College, New York *New York* M & W
St. Joseph's College, Suffolk Campus *New York* W
St. Lawrence University *New York* W
Saint Leo University *Florida* W
St. Louis Christian College *Missouri* W
St. Louis College of Pharmacy *Missouri* W

M = Men; W = Women

St. Louis Community College at Florissant Valley *Missouri* W
St. Louis Community College at Forest Park *Missouri* W
St. Louis Community College at Meramec *Missouri* W
Saint Louis University *Missouri* M & W
Saint Martin's University *Washington* W
Saint Mary's College *Indiana* W
Saint Mary's College of California *California* M & W
St. Mary's College of Maryland *Maryland* M & W
Saint Mary's University *Nova Scotia* W
Saint Mary's University of Minnesota *Minnesota* W
St. Mary's University of San Antonio *Texas* W
Saint Michael's College *Vermont* W
St. Norbert College *Wisconsin* W
St. Olaf College *Minnesota* W
Saint Paul's College *Virginia* W
Saint Peter's College *New Jersey* W
St. Petersburg College *Florida* W
St. Thomas Aquinas College *New York* W
St. Thomas University *New Brunswick* M & W
St. Thomas University *Florida* W
Saint Vincent College *Pennsylvania* W
Saint Xavier University *Illinois* W
Salem College *North Carolina* W
Salem International University *West Virginia* W
Salem State College *Massachusetts* W
Salisbury University *Maryland* W
Salt Lake Community College *Utah* W
Salve Regina University *Rhode Island* W
Sam Houston State University *Texas* W
Samford University *Alabama* W
San Bernardino Valley College *California* W
San Diego Christian College *California* W
San Diego City College *California* M & W
San Diego Mesa College *California* M & W
San Diego State University *California* M & W
San Francisco State University *California* W
San Joaquin Delta College *California* W
San Jose City College *California* W
San Jose State University *California* M & W
Santa Ana College *California* W
Santa Barbara City College *California* M & W
Santa Clara University *California* M & W
Santa Monica College *California* M & W
Santa Rosa Junior College *California* W
Sarah Lawrence College *New York* W
Savannah College of Art and Design *Georgia* W
Savannah State University *Georgia* W
Schoolcraft College *Michigan* W
Schreiner University *Texas* W
Scottsdale Community College *Arizona* W
Scripps College *California* W
Seattle Pacific University *Washington* W
Seattle University *Washington* M & W
Seminole State College *Oklahoma* W
Seton Hall University *New Jersey* M & W
Seton Hill University *Pennsylvania* W
Sewanee: The University of the South *Tennessee* W
Seward County Community College *Kansas* W
Shasta College *California* W
Shaw University *North Carolina* W
Shawnee Community College *Illinois* W
Shawnee State University *Ohio* W
Shenandoah University *Virginia* W
Shepherd University *West Virginia* W
Sheridan College-Sheridan and Gillette *Wyoming* W
Shippensburg University of Pennsylvania *Pennsylvania* W
Shoreline Community College *Washington* W
Shorter College *Georgia* W
Siena College *New York* M & W
Siena Heights University *Michigan* W
Sierra College *California* W
Simmons College *Massachusetts* W
Simon Fraser University *British Columbia* W
Simpson College *Iowa* W
Simpson University *California* W
Sinclair Community College *Ohio* W
Skagit Valley College *Washington* W
Skidmore College *New York* W
Skyline College *California* W
Slippery Rock University of Pennsylvania *Pennsylvania* W
Smith College *Massachusetts* W
Snow College *Utah* W
Solano Community College *California* W
Sonoma State University *California* W
South Carolina State University *South Carolina* W
South Dakota School of Mines and Technology *South Dakota* W
South Dakota State University *South Dakota* W
South Florida Community College *Florida* W
South Mountain Community College *Arizona* W
South Suburban College *Illinois* W
Southeast Community College, Beatrice Campus *Nebraska* W
Southeast Missouri State University *Missouri* W
Southeastern Community College *North Carolina* W
Southeastern Community College, North Campus *Iowa* W
Southeastern Louisiana University *Louisiana* W
Southeastern Oklahoma State University *Oklahoma* W
Southeastern University *Florida* W
Southern Arkansas University-Magnolia *Arkansas* W
Southern Connecticut State University *Connecticut* W
Southern Illinois University Carbondale *Illinois* W
Southern Illinois University Edwardsville *Illinois* W
Southern Maine Community College *Maine* M & W
Southern Methodist University *Texas* W
Southern Nazarene University *Oklahoma* W
Southern New Hampshire University *New Hampshire* W
Southern Oregon University *Oregon* W
Southern State Community College *Ohio* W
Southern Union State Community College *Alabama* W
Southern University and Agricultural and Mechanical College *Louisiana* W
Southern Vermont College *Vermont* W
Southern Virginia University *Virginia* W
Southern Wesleyan University *South Carolina* W
Southwest Baptist University *Missouri* W
Southwest Minnesota State University *Minnesota* W
Southwestern Adventist University *Texas* M & W
Southwestern Assemblies of God University *Texas* W
Southwestern Christian University *Oklahoma* W
Southwestern College *Kansas* W
Southwestern College *Arizona* W
Southwestern Community College *Iowa* W
Southwestern Illinois College *Illinois* W
Southwestern Oregon Community College *Oregon* W
Southwestern University *Texas* W
Spalding University *Kentucky* W
Spartanburg Methodist College *South Carolina* W
Spelman College *Georgia* W
Spokane Community College *Washington* W
Spokane Falls Community College *Washington* W
Spoon River College *Illinois* W
Spring Arbor University *Michigan* W
Spring Hill College *Alabama* W
Springfield College *Massachusetts* M & W
Springfield College in Illinois *Illinois* W
Stanford University *California* M & W
State Fair Community College *Missouri* W
State University of New York at Binghamton *New York* M & W
State University of New York at Buffalo *New York* W
State University of New York College of Agriculture and Technology at Cobleskill *New York* W
State University of New York College of Agriculture and Technology at Morrisville *New York* W
State University of New York College at Brockport *New York* W
State University of New York College at Cortland *New York* M & W
State University of New York College at Geneseo *New York* M & W
State University of New York College at Old Westbury *New York* W
State University of New York College at Oneonta *New York* M & W
State University of New York College at Potsdam *New York* W
State University of New York College of Technology at Alfred *New York* W
State University of New York College of Technology at Canton *New York* W
State University of New York College of Technology at Delhi *New York* W
State University of New York, Fredonia *New York* M & W
State University of New York Institute of Technology *New York* W
State University of New York Maritime College *New York* W
State University of New York at New Paltz *New York* M & W
State University of New York at Oswego *New York* W
State University of New York at Plattsburgh *New York* W
Stephen F. Austin State University *Texas* W
Stephens College *Missouri* W
Sterling College *Kansas* W
Stetson University *Florida* W
Stevens Institute of Technology *New Jersey* M & W
Stillman College *Alabama* W
Stonehill College *Massachusetts* M & W
Stony Brook University, State University of New York *New York* W
Suffolk County Community College *New York* W
Suffolk University *Massachusetts* W
Sul Ross State University *Texas* W
Sullivan County Community College *New York* W
Summit Pacific College *British Columbia* M & W
Surry Community College *North Carolina* W
Susquehanna University *Pennsylvania* M & W
Swarthmore College *Pennsylvania* M & W
Sweet Briar College *Virginia* W
Syracuse University *New York* M & W
Tabor College *Kansas* W
Tacoma Community College *Washington* W
Taft College *California* W
Tarleton State University *Texas* W
Taylor University *Indiana* M & W
Taylor University College and Seminary *Alberta* M & W
Taylor University Fort Wayne *Indiana* W
TCI-The College of Technology *New York* W
Technological College of San Juan *Puerto Rico* M & W
Temple University *Pennsylvania* W
Tennessee State University *Tennessee* W
Tennessee Technological University *Tennessee* W
Tennessee Temple University *Tennessee* W
Tennessee Wesleyan College *Tennessee* W
Terra State Community College *Ohio* W
Texas A&M International University *Texas* W
Texas A&M University *Texas* W
Texas A&M University-Commerce *Texas* W
Texas A&M University-Corpus Christi *Texas* W
Texas A&M University-Kingsville *Texas* W
Texas Christian University *Texas* W
Texas College *Texas* W
Texas Lutheran University *Texas* W
Texas Southern University *Texas* M & W
Texas Southmost College *Texas* W
Texas State University-San Marcos *Texas* W
Texas Tech University *Texas* W
Texas Wesleyan University *Texas* W
Texas Woman's University *Texas* W
Thiel College *Pennsylvania* W
Thomas College *Maine* W
Thomas More College *Kentucky* W
Thompson Rivers University *British Columbia* M & W
Three Rivers Community College *Missouri* W
Tiffin University *Ohio* W
Toccoa Falls College *Georgia* W
Tompkins Cortland Community College *New York* W
Towson University *Maryland* M & W
Transylvania University *Kentucky* W
Treasure Valley Community College *Oregon* W
Trent University *Ontario* M & W
Trevecca Nazarene University *Tennessee* W

M = Men; W = Women

Tri-State University *Indiana* W
Trinidad State Junior College *Colorado* W
Trinity Bible College *North Dakota* W
Trinity Christian College *Illinois* W
Trinity College *Connecticut* M & W
Trinity International University *Illinois* W
Trinity University *Texas* M & W
Trinity (Washington) University *District of Columbia* W
Trinity Western University *British Columbia* M & W
Triton College *Illinois* W
Troy University *Alabama* W
Truman State University *Missouri* M & W
Tufts University *Massachusetts* W
Tulane University *Louisiana* M & W
Tusculum College *Tennessee* W
Tuskegee University *Alabama* W
Tyler Junior College *Texas* W
Tyndale University College & Seminary *Ontario* M & W
Ulster County Community College *New York* W
Union College *New York* W
Union College *Nebraska* W
Union College *Kentucky* W
Union County College *New Jersey* W
Union University *Tennessee* W
United States Air Force Academy *Colorado* W
United States Coast Guard Academy *Connecticut* W
United States Merchant Marine Academy *New York* W
United States Military Academy *New York* M & W
United States Naval Academy *Maryland* M & W
Unity College *Maine* W
Universidad del Este *Puerto Rico* M & W
Universidad Metropolitana *Puerto Rico* M & W
Universidad del Turabo *Puerto Rico* M & W
Université Laval *Quebec* M & W
Université de Moncton *New Brunswick* W
Université de Montréal *Quebec* M & W
Université du Québec àChicoutimi *Quebec* M & W
Université Sainte-Anne *Nova Scotia* M & W
Université de Sherbrooke *Quebec* M & W
The University of Akron *Ohio* W
The University of Akron-Wayne College *Ohio* W
The University of Alabama *Alabama* W
The University of Alabama at Birmingham *Alabama* W
The University of Alabama in Huntsville *Alabama* W
University of Alaska Anchorage *Alaska* W
University of Alaska Fairbanks *Alaska* W
University at Albany, State University of New York *New York* W
University of Alberta *Alberta* M & W
The University of Arizona *Arizona* M & W
University of Arkansas *Arkansas* W
University of Arkansas at Fort Smith *Arkansas* W
University of Arkansas at Little Rock *Arkansas* W
University of Arkansas at Pine Bluff *Arkansas* W
University of Bridgeport *Connecticut* W
The University of British Columbia *British Columbia* M & W
University of Calgary *Alberta* M & W
University of California, Berkeley *California* W
University of California, Davis *California* M & W
University of California, Irvine *California* M & W
University of California, Los Angeles *California* M & W
University of California, Riverside *California* W
University of California, San Diego *California* M & W
University of California, Santa Barbara *California* M & W
University of California, Santa Cruz *California* M & W
University of Central Arkansas *Arkansas* W
University of Central Florida *Florida* W
University of Central Oklahoma *Oklahoma* W
University of Charleston *West Virginia* W
University of Chicago *Illinois* W
University of Cincinnati *Ohio* W
University of Cincinnati Raymond Walters College *Ohio* M & W
University of Colorado at Boulder *Colorado* M & W
University of Colorado at Colorado Springs *Colorado* M & W
University of Connecticut *Connecticut* W
University of the Cumberlands *Kentucky* W
University of Dallas *Texas* W
University of Dayton *Ohio* W
University of Delaware *Delaware* W
University of Denver *Colorado* M & W
University of the District of Columbia *District of Columbia* W
University of Dubuque *Iowa* W
University of Evansville *Indiana* W
The University of Findlay *Ohio* W
University of Florida *Florida* W
University of Georgia *Georgia* M & W
University of Great Falls *Montana* W
University of Guam *Guam* M & W
University of Guelph *Ontario* M & W
University of Hartford *Connecticut* M & W
University of Hawaii at Hilo *Hawaii* W
University of Hawaii at Manoa *Hawaii* M & W
University of Houston *Texas* W
University of Idaho *Idaho* W
University of Illinois at Chicago *Illinois* W
University of Illinois at Springfield *Illinois* W
University of Illinois at Urbana-Champaign *Illinois* W
University of the Incarnate Word *Texas* W
University of Indianapolis *Indiana* W
The University of Iowa *Iowa* M & W
University of Kansas *Kansas* W
University of Kentucky *Kentucky* W
University of King's College *Nova Scotia* M & W
University of La Verne *California* W
University of Lethbridge *Alberta* W
University of Louisiana at Lafayette *Louisiana* W
University of Louisiana at Monroe *Louisiana* W
University of Louisville *Kentucky* W
University of Maine *Maine* W
University of Maine at Farmington *Maine* W
University of Maine at Machias *Maine* W
University of Maine at Presque Isle *Maine* W
University of Manitoba *Manitoba* M & W
University of Mary *North Dakota* W
University of Mary Hardin-Baylor *Texas* W
University of Mary Washington *Virginia* M & W
University of Maryland, Baltimore County *Maryland* M & W
University of Maryland, College Park *Maryland* W
University of Maryland Eastern Shore *Maryland* W
University of Massachusetts Amherst *Massachusetts* W
University of Massachusetts Boston *Massachusetts* W
University of Massachusetts Dartmouth *Massachusetts* W
University of Massachusetts Lowell *Massachusetts* W
University of Memphis *Tennessee* W
University of Miami *Florida* M & W
University of Michigan *Michigan* W
University of Michigan-Dearborn *Michigan* W
University of Minnesota, Crookston *Minnesota* W
University of Minnesota, Duluth *Minnesota* M & W
University of Minnesota, Morris *Minnesota* W
University of Minnesota, Twin Cities Campus *Minnesota* W
University of Mississippi *Mississippi* M & W
University of Missouri-Columbia *Missouri* W
University of Missouri-Kansas City *Missouri* W
University of Missouri-St. Louis *Missouri* W
The University of Montana-Missoula *Montana* M & W
The University of Montana-Western *Montana* W
University of Montevallo *Alabama* W
University of Nebraska at Kearney *Nebraska* W
University of Nebraska-Lincoln *Nebraska* W
University of Nebraska at Omaha *Nebraska* W
University of Nevada, Las Vegas *Nevada* W
University of Nevada, Reno *Nevada* W
University of New Brunswick Fredericton *New Brunswick* M & W
University of New Brunswick Saint John *New Brunswick* M & W
University of New England *Maine* W
University of New Hampshire *New Hampshire* M & W
University of New Haven *Connecticut* M & W
University of New Mexico *New Mexico* W
University of New Orleans *Louisiana* W
University of North Alabama *Alabama* W
The University of North Carolina at Asheville *North Carolina* W
The University of North Carolina at Chapel Hill *North Carolina* M & W
The University of North Carolina at Charlotte *North Carolina* W
The University of North Carolina at Greensboro *North Carolina* W
The University of North Carolina at Pembroke *North Carolina* W
The University of North Carolina Wilmington *North Carolina* W
University of North Dakota *North Dakota* W
University of North Florida *Florida* W
University of North Texas *Texas* W
University of Northern Colorado *Colorado* W
University of Northern Iowa *Iowa* W
University of Notre Dame *Indiana* W
University of Oklahoma *Oklahoma* W
University of Oregon *Oregon* M & W
University of Ottawa *Ontario* W
University of the Pacific *California* M & W
University of Pennsylvania *Pennsylvania* W
University of Pittsburgh *Pennsylvania* W
University of Pittsburgh at Bradford *Pennsylvania* W
University of Pittsburgh at Greensburg *Pennsylvania* W
University of Pittsburgh at Johnstown *Pennsylvania* W
University of Portland *Oregon* W
University of Prince Edward Island *Prince Edward Island* W
University of Puerto Rico, Aguadilla University College *Puerto Rico* M & W
University of Puerto Rico at Arecibo *Puerto Rico* M & W
University of Puerto Rico at Bayamón *Puerto Rico* M & W
University of Puerto Rico at Carolina *Puerto Rico* M & W
University of Puerto Rico, Cayey University College *Puerto Rico* M & W
University of Puerto Rico at Humacao *Puerto Rico* M & W
University of Puerto Rico, Mayagüez Campus *Puerto Rico* M & W
University of Puerto Rico at Ponce *Puerto Rico* M & W
University of Puerto Rico, Río Piedras *Puerto Rico* M & W
University of Puerto Rico at Utuado *Puerto Rico* M & W
University of Puget Sound *Washington* W
University of Redlands *California* W
University of Regina *Saskatchewan* M & W
University of Rhode Island *Rhode Island* M & W
University of Richmond *Virginia* M & W
University of Rio Grande *Ohio* W
University of Rochester *New York* M & W
University of the Sacred Heart *Puerto Rico* M & W
University of Saint Francis *Indiana* W
University of St. Francis *Illinois* W
University of Saint Mary *Kansas* W
University of St. Thomas *Minnesota* W
University of San Diego *California* M & W
University of San Francisco *California* M & W
University of Saskatchewan *Saskatchewan* M & W
University of the Sciences in Philadelphia *Pennsylvania* W
The University of Scranton *Pennsylvania* M & W
University of Sioux Falls *South Dakota* W
University of South Alabama *Alabama* W
University of South Carolina *South Carolina* W
University of South Carolina Aiken *South Carolina* W
University of South Carolina Upstate *South Carolina* W
The University of South Dakota *South Dakota* W
University of South Florida *Florida* W
University of Southern California *California* M & W

M = Men; W = Women

University of Southern Indiana *Indiana* W
University of Southern Maine *Maine* W
University of Southern Mississippi *Mississippi* W
The University of Tampa *Florida* W
The University of Tennessee *Tennessee* W
The University of Tennessee at Chattanooga *Tennessee* W
The University of Tennessee at Martin *Tennessee* W
The University of Texas at Arlington *Texas* W
The University of Texas at Austin *Texas* W
The University of Texas at Brownsville *Texas* W
The University of Texas at Dallas *Texas* W
The University of Texas at El Paso *Texas* W
The University of Texas-Pan American *Texas* W
The University of Texas of the Permian Basin *Texas* W
The University of Texas at San Antonio *Texas* W
The University of Texas at Tyler *Texas* W
The University of Toledo *Ohio* W
University of Toronto *Ontario* M & W
University of Tulsa *Oklahoma* W
University of Utah *Utah* W
University of Vermont *Vermont* M & W
University of the Virgin Islands *United States Virgin Islands* M & W
University of Virginia *Virginia* M & W
The University of Virginia's College at Wise *Virginia* W
University of Washington *Washington* W
University of Waterloo *Ontario* M & W
The University of West Alabama *Alabama* W
University of West Florida *Florida* W
University of West Georgia *Georgia* W
The University of Western Ontario *Ontario* M & W
University of Windsor *Ontario* M & W
The University of Winnipeg *Manitoba* M & W
University of Wisconsin-Baraboo/Sauk County *Wisconsin* W
University of Wisconsin-Barron County *Wisconsin* W
University of Wisconsin-Eau Claire *Wisconsin* W
University of Wisconsin-Fond du Lac *Wisconsin* W
University of Wisconsin-Fox Valley *Wisconsin* M & W
University of Wisconsin-Green Bay *Wisconsin* W
University of Wisconsin-La Crosse *Wisconsin* W
University of Wisconsin-Madison *Wisconsin* W
University of Wisconsin-Manitowoc *Wisconsin* W
University of Wisconsin-Marathon County *Wisconsin* W
University of Wisconsin-Marinette *Wisconsin* W
University of Wisconsin-Marshfield/Wood County *Wisconsin* W
University of Wisconsin-Milwaukee *Wisconsin* M & W
University of Wisconsin-Oshkosh *Wisconsin* W
University of Wisconsin-Parkside *Wisconsin* W
University of Wisconsin-Platteville *Wisconsin* M & W
University of Wisconsin-Richland *Wisconsin* W
University of Wisconsin-River Falls *Wisconsin* M & W
University of Wisconsin-Rock County *Wisconsin* W
University of Wisconsin-Sheboygan *Wisconsin* W
University of Wisconsin-Stevens Point *Wisconsin* W
University of Wisconsin-Stout *Wisconsin* M & W
University of Wisconsin-Superior *Wisconsin* W
University of Wisconsin-Washington County *Wisconsin* W
University of Wisconsin-Waukesha *Wisconsin* W
University of Wisconsin-Whitewater *Wisconsin* M & W
University of Wyoming *Wyoming* W
Upper Iowa University *Iowa* M & W
Urbana University *Ohio* W
Ursinus College *Pennsylvania* W
Ursuline College *Ohio* W
Utah State University *Utah* M & W
Utah Valley State College *Utah* W
Utica College *New York* W
Valdosta State University *Georgia* W
Valley City State University *North Dakota* W
Valley Forge Christian College *Pennsylvania* W
Valparaiso University *Indiana* W
Vanderbilt University *Tennessee* M & W
Vanguard University of Southern California *California* W
Vassar College *New York* M & W
Vennard College *Iowa* W
Ventura College *California* W
Vermilion Community College *Minnesota* W
Vermont Technical College *Vermont* M & W
Vernon College *Texas* W
Victor Valley College *California* W
Villa Julie College *Maryland* W
Villanova University *Pennsylvania* M & W
Vincennes University *Indiana* W
Virginia Commonwealth University *Virginia* W
Virginia Intermont College *Virginia* W
Virginia Military Institute *Virginia* M & W
Virginia Polytechnic Institute and State University *Virginia* M & W
Virginia State University *Virginia* W
Virginia Union University *Virginia* W
Virginia Wesleyan College *Virginia* W
Viterbo University *Wisconsin* W
Voorhees College *South Carolina* W
Wagner College *New York* W
Wake Forest University *North Carolina* W
Waldorf College *Iowa* W
Walla Walla College *Washington* M & W
Walla Walla Community College *Washington* W
Wallace State Community College *Alabama* W
Walsh University *Ohio* W
Warner Pacific College *Oregon* W
Warner Southern College *Florida* W
Wartburg College *Iowa* W
Washburn University *Kansas* W
Washington Bible College *Maryland* W
Washington College *Maryland* W
Washington & Jefferson College *Pennsylvania* W
Washington and Lee University *Virginia* M & W
Washington State University *Washington* M & W
Washington University in St. Louis *Missouri* M & W
Waubonsee Community College *Illinois* W
Wayland Baptist University *Texas* W
Wayne County Community College District *Michigan* W
Wayne State College *Nebraska* W
Wayne State University *Michigan* W
Waynesburg College *Pennsylvania* W
Webb Institute *New York* M & W
Webber International University *Florida* M & W
Weber State University *Utah* W
Webster University *Missouri* W
Wellesley College *Massachusetts* W
Wentworth Institute of Technology *Massachusetts* M & W
Wesleyan College *Georgia* W
Wesleyan University *Connecticut* M & W
West Chester University of Pennsylvania *Pennsylvania* W
West Hills Community College *California* W
West Liberty State College *West Virginia* W
West Los Angeles College *California* W
West Texas A&M University *Texas* W
West Valley College *California* M & W
West Virginia State University *West Virginia* W
West Virginia University *West Virginia* W
West Virginia University Institute of Technology *West Virginia* W
West Virginia Wesleyan College *West Virginia* W
Westchester Community College *New York* W
Western Carolina University *North Carolina* W
Western Connecticut State University *Connecticut* W
Western Illinois University *Illinois* W
Western Kentucky University *Kentucky* W
Western Michigan University *Michigan* W
Western Nebraska Community College *Nebraska* W
Western New England College *Massachusetts* W
Western New Mexico University *New Mexico* W
Western Oregon University *Oregon* W
Western State College of Colorado *Colorado* M & W
Western Technical College *Wisconsin* W
Western Washington University *Washington* W
Western Wyoming Community College *Wyoming* W
Westfield State College *Massachusetts* W
Westminster College *Utah* W
Westminster College *Pennsylvania* W
Westminster College *Missouri* W
Westmont College *California* M & W
Westmoreland County Community College *Pennsylvania* W
Wharton County Junior College *Texas* W
Whatcom Community College *Washington* W
Wheaton College *Massachusetts* W
Wheaton College *Illinois* M & W
Wheeling Jesuit University *West Virginia* W
Whitman College *Washington* M & W
Whittier College *California* W
Whitworth College *Washington* W
Wichita State University *Kansas* M & W
Widener University *Pennsylvania* W
Wiley College *Texas* W
Wilfrid Laurier University *Ontario* M & W
Wilkes Community College *North Carolina* W
Wilkes University *Pennsylvania* W
Willamette University *Oregon* W
William and Catherine Booth College *Manitoba* M & W
William Jessup University *California* W
William Jewell College *Missouri* W
William Paterson University of New Jersey *New Jersey* W
William Penn University *Iowa* W
William Rainey Harper College *Illinois* W
William Woods University *Missouri* M & W
Williams Baptist College *Arkansas* W
Williams College *Massachusetts* M & W
Williston State College *North Dakota* W
Wilmington College *Ohio* W
Wilmington College *Delaware* W
Wilson College *Pennsylvania* W
Wingate University *North Carolina* W
Winona State University *Minnesota* M & W
Winston-Salem State University *North Carolina* W
Winthrop University *South Carolina* W
Wisconsin Lutheran College *Wisconsin* M & W
Wittenberg University *Ohio* M & W
Wofford College *South Carolina* W
Worcester Polytechnic Institute *Massachusetts* W
Worcester State College *Massachusetts* M & W
Wright State University *Ohio* W
Xavier University *Ohio* M & W
Yakima Valley Community College *Washington* W
Yale University *Connecticut* M & W
Yavapai College *Arizona* W
Yeshiva University *New York* M
York College *Nebraska* W
York College of the City University of New York *New York* M & W
York College of Pennsylvania *Pennsylvania* M & W
York University *Ontario* M & W
Youngstown State University *Ohio* W
Yuba College *California* W

Water Polo

Amherst College *Massachusetts* M & W
Arizona State University *Arizona* W
Ball State University *Indiana* M
Bates College *Maine* M & W
Bayamon Central University *Puerto Rico* M & W
Baylor University *Texas* M & W
Bernard M. Baruch College of the City University of New York *New York* M & W
Boston College *Massachusetts* M
Boston University *Massachusetts* W
Bowdoin College *Maine* M & W
Bowling Green State University *Ohio* M & W
Bridgewater State College *Massachusetts* M & W
Brigham Young University-Hawaii *Hawaii* M
Brown University *Rhode Island* M & W
Bucknell University *Pennsylvania* M & W
Cabrillo College *California* M & W
California Baptist University *California* M & W
California Institute of Technology *California* M & W
California Lutheran University *California* M & W
California Maritime Academy *California* M & W
California State University, Bakersfield *California* W
California State University, Chico *California* M & W
California State University, East Bay *California* W

M = Men; W = Women

California State University, Long Beach *California* M & W
Carleton College *Minnesota* M & W
Carleton University *Ontario* M & W
Carnegie Mellon University *Pennsylvania* M & W
Carthage College *Wisconsin* W
Central Washington University *Washington* M & W
Cerritos College *California* M
Chaffey College *California* M & W
Chaminade University of Honolulu *Hawaii* M
Chapman University *California* M & W
Citrus College *California* M & W
City College of San Francisco *California* M
Claremont McKenna College *California* M & W
Colby College *Maine* M & W
Colgate University *New York* M & W
College of the Canyons *California* M
College of Marin *California* M & W
College of the Sequoias *California* M
The Colorado College *Colorado* M & W
Colorado State University *Colorado* W
Columbia College *New York* M & W
Columbia University, The Fu Foundation School of Engineering and Applied Science *New York* M & W
Connecticut College *Connecticut* M & W
Cosumnes River College (Sacramento) *California* M & W
Cuesta College *California* M & W
Cypress College *California* M & W
Dartmouth College *New Hampshire* M & W
De Anza College *California* M
Diablo Valley College *California* M & W
Duke University *North Carolina* M & W
El Camino College *California* M
Emory University *Georgia* M & W
Foothill College *California* M & W
Fordham University *New York* M
Fullerton College *California* M
Gannon University *Pennsylvania* M & W
The George Washington University *District of Columbia* M
Georgetown University *District of Columbia* M
Golden West College *California* M & W
Grand Valley State University *Michigan* M & W
Grossmont College *California* M & W
Grove City College *Pennsylvania* W
Hamilton College *New York* M & W
Hartnell College *California* M
Hartwick College *New York* M & W
Harvard University *Massachusetts* M & W
Harvey Mudd College *California* M & W
Illinois Wesleyan University *Illinois* M
Indiana University Bloomington *Indiana* W
Iona College *New York* M & W
The Johns Hopkins University *Maryland* M
Lake Forest College *Illinois* M & W
Lehman College of the City University of New York *New York* M
Lindenwood University *Missouri* M & W
Long Beach City College *California* M & W
Los Angeles Pierce College *California* M
Los Angeles Valley College *California* M
Loyola Marymount University *California* M & W
Lycoming College *Pennsylvania* M & W
Macalester College *Minnesota* M & W
Marist College *New York* W
Massachusetts Institute of Technology *Massachusetts* M
McMaster University *Ontario* M & W
Merced College *California* M
Mercyhurst College *Pennsylvania* M & W
Michigan State University *Michigan* M & W
Michigan Technological University *Michigan* M & W
Modesto Junior College *California* M & W
Mt. San Antonio College *California* M & W
North Carolina State University *North Carolina* M & W
Oberlin College *Ohio* M & W
Occidental College *California* M & W
Ohio University *Ohio* M & W
Ohlone College *California* M
Orange Coast College *California* M & W
Palomar College *California* M
Pasadena City College *California* M
The Pennsylvania State University at Erie, The Behrend College *Pennsylvania* M & W
The Pennsylvania State University University Park Campus *Pennsylvania* M & W
Pepperdine University *California* M & W
Pitzer College *California* M & W
Pomona College *California* M & W
Princeton University *New Jersey* M & W
Queens College of the City University of New York *New York* M & W
Queen's University at Kingston *Ontario* M & W
Rensselaer Polytechnic Institute *New York* M & W
Rice University *Texas* M & W
Rio Hondo College *California* M & W
Riverside Community College District *California* M & W
Rochester Institute of Technology *New York* M & W
Sacramento City College *California* W
Saddleback College *California* M & W
St. Francis College *New York* M & W
Saint John's University *Minnesota* M
Saint Mary's College *Indiana* W
Saint Mary's College of California *California* M & W
Salem International University *West Virginia* M & W
San Diego Mesa College *California* M & W
San Diego Miramar College *California* M & W
San Diego State University *California* W
San Joaquin Delta College *California* M & W
San Jose State University *California* W
Santa Ana College *California* M
Santa Clara University *California* M & W
Santa Monica College *California* M & W
Santa Rosa Junior College *California* M & W
Scripps College *California* W
Seattle University *Washington* M & W
Siena College *New York* W
Sierra College *California* M & W
Slippery Rock University of Pennsylvania *Pennsylvania* M & W
Soka University of America *California* M & W
Solano Community College *California* M & W
Sonoma State University *California* W
Stanford University *California* M & W
Syracuse University *New York* M & W
Texas State University-San Marcos *Texas* M & W
Trinity College *Connecticut* M & W
Tulane University *Louisiana* M & W
Union College *New York* M & W
United States Air Force Academy *Colorado* M
United States Coast Guard Academy *Connecticut* M
United States Military Academy *New York* M
United States Naval Academy *Maryland* M
The University of British Columbia *British Columbia* M & W
University of California, Davis *California* M & W
University of California, Irvine *California* M & W
University of California, Los Angeles *California* M & W
University of California, San Diego *California* M & W
University of California, Santa Barbara *California* M & W
University of California, Santa Cruz *California* M & W
University of Colorado at Boulder *Colorado* M & W
The University of Findlay *Ohio* M & W
University of Hawaii at Manoa *Hawaii* W
University of La Verne *California* M & W
University of Maryland, College Park *Maryland* W
University of Miami *Florida* M & W
University of Michigan *Michigan* W
University of Oregon *Oregon* M & W
University of the Pacific *California* M & W
University of Puerto Rico at Bayamón *Puerto Rico* M
University of Puerto Rico, Mayagüez Campus *Puerto Rico* M
University of Puerto Rico, Río Piedras *Puerto Rico* M
University of Redlands *California* M & W
University of Rhode Island *Rhode Island* M
University of Richmond *Virginia* M & W
University of Southern California *California* M & W
University of Vermont *Vermont* M & W
The University of Western Ontario *Ontario* M
University of Wisconsin-Madison *Wisconsin* M & W
Utica College *New York* W
Vanderbilt University *Tennessee* M & W
Ventura College *California* M & W
Villanova University *Pennsylvania* M & W
Virginia Military Institute *Virginia* M & W
Virginia Polytechnic Institute and State University *Virginia* M & W
Wabash College *Indiana* M
Wagner College *New York* W
Washington & Jefferson College *Pennsylvania* M & W
Washington State University *Washington* M
Washington University in St. Louis *Missouri* M & W
Weber State University *Utah* M & W
Wesleyan University *Connecticut* M
West Chester University of Pennsylvania *Pennsylvania* M & W
West Valley College *California* M
Wheaton College *Illinois* W
Whittier College *California* M & W
Williams College *Massachusetts* M & W
Worcester Polytechnic Institute *Massachusetts* M & W
York University *Ontario* M & W

Weight Lifting

Bethany College *West Virginia* M
Bowling Green State University *Ohio* M & W
Caribbean University *Puerto Rico* M
The Citadel, The Military College of South Carolina *South Carolina* M & W
Clemson University *South Carolina* M & W
Coppin State University *Maryland* M & W
Davidson College *North Carolina* M & W
Electronic Data Processing College of Puerto Rico *Puerto Rico* M
Furman University *South Carolina* M & W
Inter American University of Puerto Rico, Aguadilla Campus *Puerto Rico* M & W
Inter American University of Puerto Rico, Barranquitas Campus *Puerto Rico* M
Inter American University of Puerto Rico, Bayamón Campus *Puerto Rico* M
Inter American University of Puerto Rico, Guayama Campus *Puerto Rico* M
Inter American University of Puerto Rico, Metropolitan Campus *Puerto Rico* M
Inter American University of Puerto Rico, Ponce Campus *Puerto Rico* M & W
Inter American University of Puerto Rico, San Germán Campus *Puerto Rico* M
Iowa Lakes Community College *Iowa* M & W
Lafayette College *Pennsylvania* M & W
Lakehead University *Ontario* M
Louisiana Tech University *Louisiana* M & W
McNeese State University *Louisiana* M & W
Norwich University *Vermont* M & W
Ohio University *Ohio* M
The Pennsylvania State University University Park Campus *Pennsylvania* M & W
Pontifical Catholic University of Puerto Rico *Puerto Rico* M & W
Reed College *Oregon* M & W
Rensselaer Polytechnic Institute *New York* M & W
Syracuse University *New York* M & W
Technological College of San Juan *Puerto Rico* M & W
Texas State University-San Marcos *Texas* M & W
United States Air Force Academy *Colorado* M & W
United States Military Academy *New York* M & W
United States Naval Academy *Maryland* M & W
Universidad Metropolitana *Puerto Rico* M & W
Universidad del Turabo *Puerto Rico* M
University of California, Irvine *California* M & W
University of Minnesota, Duluth *Minnesota* M & W
University of Puerto Rico, Aguadilla University College *Puerto Rico* M & W
University of Puerto Rico at Arecibo *Puerto Rico* M & W
University of Puerto Rico at Bayamón *Puerto Rico* M
University of Puerto Rico at Carolina *Puerto Rico* W

M = Men; W = Women

University of Puerto Rico, Cayey University College *Puerto Rico* M
University of Puerto Rico, Mayagüez Campus *Puerto Rico* M
University of Puerto Rico at Ponce *Puerto Rico* M & W
University of Puerto Rico, Río Piedras *Puerto Rico* M
University of Puerto Rico at Utuado *Puerto Rico* M & W
University of the Sacred Heart *Puerto Rico* M & W
University of Wisconsin-River Falls *Wisconsin* M & W
University of Wisconsin-Whitewater *Wisconsin* M
Villanova University *Pennsylvania* M & W
Virginia Military Institute *Virginia* M & W
Virginia Polytechnic Institute and State University *Virginia* M & W

Wrestling

Adams State College *Colorado* M
Albright College *Pennsylvania* M
American International College *Massachusetts* M
American University *District of Columbia* M
Anderson University *South Carolina* M
Appalachian State University *North Carolina* M
Arizona State University *Arizona* M
Ashland University *Ohio* M
Augsburg College *Minnesota* M
Augustana College *South Dakota* M
Augustana College *Illinois* M
Bacone College *Oklahoma* M
Bakersfield College *California* M
Baldwin-Wallace College *Ohio* M
Ball State University *Indiana* M
Baptist Bible College of Pennsylvania *Pennsylvania* M
Belmont Abbey College *North Carolina* M
Bergen Community College *New Jersey* M
Bethel College *Indiana* M
Bloomsburg University of Pennsylvania *Pennsylvania* M
Boise State University *Idaho* M
Boston College *Massachusetts* M
Boston University *Massachusetts* M
Briar Cliff University *Iowa* M
Bridgewater State College *Massachusetts* M
Brock University *Ontario* M & W
Bronx Community College of the City University of New York *New York* M
Broward Community College *Florida* M
Brown University *Rhode Island* M
Bryant University *Rhode Island* M
Bucknell University *Pennsylvania* M
Buena Vista University *Iowa* M
Cabrillo College *California* M
California Polytechnic State University, San Luis Obispo *California* M
California State University, Bakersfield *California* M
California State University, Fresno *California* M
California State University, Fullerton *California* M
Campbell University *North Carolina* M
Campbellsville University *Kentucky* M
Carson-Newman College *Tennessee* M
Case Western Reserve University *Ohio* M
Centenary College *New Jersey* M
Central College *Iowa* M
Central Michigan University *Michigan* M
Central Missouri State University *Missouri* M
Cerritos College *California* M
Chabot College *California* M
Chadron State College *Nebraska* M
The Citadel, The Military College of South Carolina *South Carolina* M
City Colleges of Chicago, Harry S. Truman College *Illinois* M
City Colleges of Chicago, Kennedy-King College *Illinois* M
City Colleges of Chicago, Wilbur Wright College *Illinois* M
Clackamas Community College *Oregon* M
Clarion University of Pennsylvania *Pennsylvania* M
Clemson University *South Carolina* M
Cleveland State University *Ohio* M
Coe College *Iowa* M
Colby Community College *Kansas* M
Colgate University *New York* M & W
College of Mount St. Joseph *Ohio* M
The College of New Jersey *New Jersey* M
Colorado School of Mines *Colorado* M
Columbia College *New York* M
Columbia University, School of General Studies *New York* M
Columbia University, The Fu Foundation School of Engineering and Applied Science *New York* M
Concordia College *Minnesota* M
Concordia University *Quebec* M & W
Concordia University Wisconsin *Wisconsin* M
Coppin State University *Maryland* M
Cornell College *Iowa* M
Cornell University *New York* M
Cuesta College *California* M
Cumberland University *Tennessee* M
Cypress College *California* M
Dakota County Technical College *Minnesota* M
Dakota Wesleyan University *South Dakota* M
Dana College *Nebraska* M
Dartmouth College *New Hampshire* M
Davidson College *North Carolina* M
Delaware State University *Delaware* M
Delaware Valley College *Pennsylvania* M
Dickinson College *Pennsylvania* M
Dickinson State University *North Dakota* M
Drexel University *Pennsylvania* M
Duke University *North Carolina* M
Duquesne University *Pennsylvania* M
East Los Angeles College *California* M
East Stroudsburg University of Pennsylvania *Pennsylvania* M
Eastern Illinois University *Illinois* M
Eastern Michigan University *Michigan* M
Edinboro University of Pennsylvania *Pennsylvania* M
El Camino College *California* M
Elizabethtown College *Pennsylvania* M
Ellsworth Community College *Iowa* M
Elmhurst College *Illinois* M
Embry-Riddle Aeronautical University *Arizona* M
Emory University *Georgia* M
Florida State University *Florida* M & W
Fort Hays State University *Kansas* M
Fort Lewis College *Colorado* M & W
Franklin and Marshall College *Pennsylvania* M
Fresno City College *California* M
Gallaudet University *District of Columbia* M
Gannon University *Pennsylvania* M
Gardner-Webb University *North Carolina* M
George Mason University *Virginia* M
Georgia Institute of Technology *Georgia* M
Georgia Southern University *Georgia* M & W
Gettysburg College *Pennsylvania* M
Gloucester County College *New Jersey* M
Golden West College *California* M
Grand Rapids Community College *Michigan* M
Grand Valley State University *Michigan* M
Harvard University *Massachusetts* M
Haverford College *Pennsylvania* M
Heidelberg College *Ohio* M
Highline Community College *Washington* M
Hofstra University *New York* M
Hunter College of the City University of New York *New York* M
Illinois College *Illinois* M
Indiana University Bloomington *Indiana* M
Inter American University of Puerto Rico, Metropolitan Campus *Puerto Rico* M
Iowa Central Community College *Iowa* M
Iowa State University of Science and Technology *Iowa* M
Itasca Community College *Minnesota* M
Ithaca College *New York* M
James Madison University *Virginia* M
Jamestown College *North Dakota* M
Jamestown Community College *New York* M
John Carroll University *Ohio* M
The Johns Hopkins University *Maryland* M
Johnson & Wales University *Rhode Island* M
Kent State University *Ohio* M
King College *Tennessee* M
King's College *Pennsylvania* M
Knox College *Illinois* M
Kutztown University of Pennsylvania *Pennsylvania* M
Labette Community College *Kansas* M
Lafayette College *Pennsylvania* M
Lake Forest College *Illinois* M & W
Lakehead University *Ontario* M & W
Lakeland College *Wisconsin* M
Lassen Community College District *California* M
Lawrence University *Wisconsin* M
Lehigh University *Pennsylvania* M
Lehman College of the City University of New York *New York* M
Limestone College *South Carolina* M
Lincoln College *Illinois* M
Lincoln College-Normal *Illinois* M
Lindenwood University *Missouri* M
Lock Haven University of Pennsylvania *Pennsylvania* M
Longwood University *Virginia* M
Loras College *Iowa* M
Los Angeles Valley College *California* M
Loyola University New Orleans *Louisiana* M
Luther College *Iowa* M
Lycoming College *Pennsylvania* M
MacMurray College *Illinois* M & W
Madison Area Technical College *Wisconsin* M
Manchester College *Indiana* M
Maranatha Baptist Bible College *Wisconsin* M
Maryville College *Tennessee* M
Massachusetts Institute of Technology *Massachusetts* M
McDaniel College *Maryland* M
McGill University *Quebec* M & W
McKendree College *Illinois* M
McMaster University *Ontario* M & W
Memorial University of Newfoundland *Newfoundland and Labrador* M & W
Menlo College *California* M & W
Mercyhurst College *Pennsylvania* M
Mesa Community College *Arizona* M
Messiah College *Pennsylvania* M
Miami University *Ohio* M
Michigan State University *Michigan* M
Middlesex County College *New Jersey* M
Millersville University of Pennsylvania *Pennsylvania* M
Millikin University *Illinois* M
Milwaukee School of Engineering *Wisconsin* M
Minnesota State University Mankato *Minnesota* M
Minnesota State University Moorhead *Minnesota* M
Minnesota West Community and Technical College *Minnesota* M
Missouri Baptist University *Missouri* M
Missouri State University *Missouri* M
Missouri Valley College *Missouri* M & W
Modesto Junior College *California* M
Montana State University-Northern *Montana* M
Moorpark College *California* M
Morningside College *Iowa* M
Mt. San Antonio College *California* M
Mount Union College *Ohio* M
Muhlenberg College *Pennsylvania* M
Muskegon Community College *Michigan* M
Muskingum College *Ohio* M
Napa Valley College *California* M
Nassau Community College *New York* M
New York University *New York* M
Newberry College *South Carolina* M
Newman University *Kansas* M
Niagara County Community College *New York* M
North Carolina State University *North Carolina* M
North Central College *Illinois* M
North Dakota State University *North Dakota* M
North Idaho College *Idaho* M
Northampton County Area Community College *Pennsylvania* M
Northern Illinois University *Illinois* M
Northern State University *South Dakota* M
Northwest College *Wyoming* M
Northwestern College *Iowa* M
Northwestern University *Illinois* M

M = Men; W = Women

Norwich University *Vermont* M
Ohio Northern University *Ohio* M
The Ohio State University *Ohio* M
Ohio University *Ohio* M
Oklahoma State University *Oklahoma* M
Old Dominion University *Virginia* M
Olivet College *Michigan* M
Oregon State University *Oregon* M
Pacific University *Oregon* M & W
Palomar College *California* M
The Pennsylvania State University University Park Campus *Pennsylvania* M
Pitzer College *California* M
Plymouth State University *New Hampshire* M
Pontifical Catholic University of Puerto Rico *Puerto Rico* M
Portland State University *Oregon* M
Princeton University *New Jersey* M
Purdue University *Indiana* M
Queen's University at Kingston *Ontario* M & W
Rhode Island College *Rhode Island* M
Rider University *New Jersey* M
Ridgewater College *Minnesota* M
Rio Hondo College *California* M
Ripon College *Wisconsin* M & W
Rochester Community and Technical College *Minnesota* M
Rochester Institute of Technology *New York* M
Roger Williams University *Rhode Island* M
Rose-Hulman Institute of Technology *Indiana* M
Rutgers, The State University of New Jersey, New Brunswick/Piscataway *New Jersey* M
Sacramento City College *California* M
Sacred Heart University *Connecticut* M
St. Andrews Presbyterian College *North Carolina* M
St. Cloud State University *Minnesota* M
Saint John's University *Minnesota* M
St. Louis Community College at Meramec *Missouri* M
St. Olaf College *Minnesota* M
San Bernardino Valley College *California* M
San Francisco State University *California* M
San Joaquin Delta College *California* M
San Jose State University *California* M & W
Santa Ana College *California* M
Santa Rosa Junior College *California* M
Shippensburg University of Pennsylvania *Pennsylvania* M
Sierra College *California* M
Simon Fraser University *British Columbia* M
Simpson College *Iowa* M
Skyline College *California* M
Slippery Rock University of Pennsylvania *Pennsylvania* M
South Dakota State University *South Dakota* M
Southern Connecticut State University *Connecticut* M
Southern Illinois University Edwardsville *Illinois* M
Southern Methodist University *Texas* M
Southern Oregon University *Oregon* M
Southern Virginia University *Virginia* M
Southwest Minnesota State University *Minnesota* M
Southwestern Oregon Community College *Oregon* M
Spartanburg Methodist College *South Carolina* M
Springfield College *Massachusetts* M
Springfield Technical Community College *Massachusetts* M
Stanford University *California* M
State University of New York at Binghamton *New York* M
State University of New York at Buffalo *New York* M
State University of New York College of Agriculture and Technology at Cobleskill *New York* M
State University of New York College of Agriculture and Technology at Morrisville *New York* M
State University of New York College at Brockport *New York* M
State University of New York College at Cortland *New York* M
State University of New York College at Oneonta *New York* M
State University of New York College of Technology at Alfred *New York* M
State University of New York College of Technology at Delhi *New York* M
State University of New York Maritime College *New York* M
State University of New York at Oswego *New York* M
Stevens Institute of Technology *New Jersey* M
Texas State University-San Marcos *Texas* M & W
Thaddeus Stevens College of Technology *Pennsylvania* M
Thiel College *Pennsylvania* M
Tri-State University *Indiana* M
Trinity Bible College *North Dakota* M
Trinity College *Connecticut* M
Triton College *Illinois* M
Truman State University *Missouri* M
United States Air Force Academy *Colorado* M
United States Coast Guard Academy *Connecticut* M
United States Merchant Marine Academy *New York* M
United States Military Academy *New York* M
United States Naval Academy *Maryland* M
University of Alberta *Alberta* M & W
The University of Arizona *Arizona* M
University of Calgary *Alberta* M & W
University of California, Davis *California* M
University of Central Oklahoma *Oklahoma* M
University of Chicago *Illinois* M
University of Colorado at Boulder *Colorado* M
University of the Cumberlands *Kentucky* M & W
University of Delaware *Delaware* M
University of Dubuque *Iowa* M
The University of Findlay *Ohio* M
University of Great Falls *Montana* M
University of Guelph *Ontario* M & W
University of Illinois at Urbana-Champaign *Illinois* M
University of Indianapolis *Indiana* M
The University of Iowa *Iowa* M
University of Mary *North Dakota* M
University of Maryland, Baltimore County *Maryland* M
University of Maryland, College Park *Maryland* M
University of Maryland Eastern Shore *Maryland* M
University of Massachusetts Lowell *Massachusetts* M
University of Michigan *Michigan* M
University of Minnesota, Twin Cities Campus *Minnesota* M
University of Missouri-Columbia *Missouri* M
University of Nebraska at Kearney *Nebraska* M
University of Nebraska-Lincoln *Nebraska* M
University of Nebraska at Omaha *Nebraska* M
University of New Brunswick Fredericton *New Brunswick* M & W
University of New Hampshire *New Hampshire* M
The University of North Carolina at Chapel Hill *North Carolina* M
The University of North Carolina at Greensboro *North Carolina* M
The University of North Carolina at Pembroke *North Carolina* M
University of Northern Colorado *Colorado* M
University of Northern Iowa *Iowa* M
University of Oklahoma *Oklahoma* M
University of Oregon *Oregon* M
University of Pennsylvania *Pennsylvania* M
University of Pittsburgh *Pennsylvania* M
University of Pittsburgh at Johnstown *Pennsylvania* M
University of Puerto Rico at Arecibo *Puerto Rico* M
University of Puerto Rico at Bayamón *Puerto Rico* M
University of Puerto Rico, Cayey University College *Puerto Rico* M
University of Puerto Rico at Humacao *Puerto Rico* M
University of Puerto Rico, Mayagüez Campus *Puerto Rico* M
University of Regina *Saskatchewan* M & W
University of Richmond *Virginia* M
University of Saskatchewan *Saskatchewan* M & W
The University of Scranton *Pennsylvania* M
University of Southern Maine *Maine* M
The University of Tennessee at Chattanooga *Tennessee* M
University of Toronto *Ontario* M
University of Virginia *Virginia* M
University of Washington *Washington* M
The University of Western Ontario *Ontario* M & W
University of Wisconsin-Eau Claire *Wisconsin* M
University of Wisconsin-La Crosse *Wisconsin* M
University of Wisconsin-Madison *Wisconsin* M
University of Wisconsin-Oshkosh *Wisconsin* M
University of Wisconsin-Parkside *Wisconsin* M
University of Wisconsin-Platteville *Wisconsin* M
University of Wisconsin-Stevens Point *Wisconsin* M
University of Wisconsin-Whitewater *Wisconsin* M
University of Wyoming *Wyoming* M
Upper Iowa University *Iowa* M
Ursinus College *Pennsylvania* M
Utah Valley State College *Utah* M
Valley Forge Military College *Pennsylvania* M
Vanderbilt University *Tennessee* M & W
Victor Valley College *California* M
Virginia Military Institute *Virginia* M
Virginia Polytechnic Institute and State University *Virginia* M
Wabash College *Indiana* M
Wagner College *New York* M
Waldorf College *Iowa* M
Wartburg College *Iowa* M
Washington & Jefferson College *Pennsylvania* M
Washington and Lee University *Virginia* M
Waubonsee Community College *Illinois* M
Waynesburg College *Pennsylvania* M
Wentworth Military Academy and Junior College *Missouri* M
Wesleyan University *Connecticut* M
West Liberty State College *West Virginia* M
West Valley College *California* M
West Virginia University *West Virginia* M
Western New England College *Massachusetts* M
Western State College of Colorado *Colorado* M & W
Western Wyoming Community College *Wyoming* M
Wheaton College *Illinois* M
Wichita State University *Kansas* M
Wilkes University *Pennsylvania* M
William Penn University *Iowa* M
William Rainey Harper College *Illinois* M
Williams College *Massachusetts* M
The Williamson Free School of Mechanical Trades *Pennsylvania* M
Wilmington College *Ohio* M
Winona State University *Minnesota* M
Worcester Polytechnic Institute *Massachusetts* M
Yakima Valley Community College *Washington* M
Yeshiva University *New York* M
York College *Nebraska* M
York College of Pennsylvania *Pennsylvania* M

M = Men; W = Women

Index of Professional Accreditations

AACSB International-The Association to Advance CollegiateAACSB International-The Association to Advance Collegiate Schools of Business (AACSB)

Norfolk State University *Virginia*
North Carolina Agricultural and Technical State University *North Carolina*
North Carolina State University *North Carolina*
North Dakota State University *North Dakota*
Northeastern University *Massachusetts*
Northern Arizona University *Arizona*
Northern Illinois University *Illinois*
Northern Kentucky University *Kentucky*
Northern Michigan University *Michigan*
Northwestern State University of Louisiana *Louisiana*
Northwestern University *Illinois*
Oakland University *Michigan*
Ohio Northern University *Ohio*
The Ohio State University *Ohio*
Ohio University *Ohio*
Oklahoma State University *Oklahoma*
Old Dominion University *Virginia*
Oregon State University *Oregon*
Ouachita Baptist University *Arkansas*
Pace University *New York*
Pacific Lutheran University *Washington*
The Pennsylvania State University at Erie, The Behrend College *Pennsylvania*
The Pennsylvania State University Harrisburg Campus *Pennsylvania*
The Pennsylvania State University University Park Campus *Pennsylvania*
Pepperdine University *California*
Pittsburg State University *Kansas*
Portland State University *Oregon*
Purdue University *Indiana*
Queen's University at Kingston *Ontario*
Quinnipiac University *Connecticut*
Radford University *Virginia*
Rensselaer Polytechnic Institute *New York*
Rice University *Texas*
Rider University *New Jersey*
Rochester Institute of Technology *New York*
Rollins College *Florida*
Rowan University *New Jersey*
Rutgers, The State University of New Jersey, Camden *New Jersey*
Rutgers, The State University of New Jersey, Newark *New Jersey*
Saginaw Valley State University *Michigan*
St. Bonaventure University *New York*
St. Cloud State University *Minnesota*
St. John Fisher College *New York*
St. John's University *New York*
Saint Joseph's University *Pennsylvania*
Saint Louis University *Missouri*
Saint Mary's University *Nova Scotia*
St. Mary's University of San Antonio *Texas*
Salisbury University *Maryland*
Sam Houston State University *Texas*
Samford University *Alabama*
San Diego State University *California*
San Francisco State University *California*
San Jose State University *California*
Santa Clara University *California*
Seattle Pacific University *Washington*
Seattle University *Washington*
Seton Hall University *New Jersey*
Shippensburg University of Pennsylvania *Pennsylvania*
South Carolina State University *South Carolina*
Southeast Missouri State University *Missouri*
Southeastern Louisiana University *Louisiana*
Southern Illinois University Carbondale *Illinois*
Southern Illinois University Edwardsville *Illinois*
Southern Methodist University *Texas*
Southern University and Agricultural and Mechanical College *Louisiana*
Stanford University *California*
State University of New York at Binghamton *New York*
State University of New York at Buffalo *New York*
State University of New York College at Brockport *New York*
State University of New York College at Geneseo *New York*
State University of New York at Oswego *New York*
State University of New York at Plattsburgh *New York*
Stephen F. Austin State University *Texas*
Stetson University *Florida*
Suffolk University *Massachusetts*
Susquehanna University *Pennsylvania*
Syracuse University *New York*
Temple University *Pennsylvania*
Tennessee State University *Tennessee*
Tennessee Technological University *Tennessee*
Texas A&M International University *Texas*
Texas A&M University *Texas*
Texas A&M University-Commerce *Texas*
Texas A&M University-Corpus Christi *Texas*
Texas Christian University *Texas*
Texas Southern University *Texas*
Texas State University-San Marcos *Texas*
Texas Tech University *Texas*
Towson University *Maryland*
Trinity University *Texas*
Truman State University *Missouri*
Tulane University *Louisiana*
Tuskegee University *Alabama*
United States Air Force Academy *Colorado*
Université Laval *Quebec*
The University of Akron *Ohio*
The University of Alabama *Alabama*
The University of Alabama at Birmingham *Alabama*
The University of Alabama in Huntsville *Alabama*
University of Alaska Anchorage *Alaska*
University of Alaska Fairbanks *Alaska*
University at Albany, State University of New York *New York*
University of Alberta *Alberta*
The University of Arizona *Arizona*
University of Arkansas *Arkansas*
University of Arkansas at Little Rock *Arkansas*
University of Baltimore *Maryland*
The University of British Columbia *British Columbia*
University of Calgary *Alberta*
University of California, Berkeley *California*
University of California, Davis *California*
University of California, Irvine *California*
University of California, Los Angeles *California*
University of California, Riverside *California*
University of Central Arkansas *Arkansas*
University of Central Florida *Florida*
University of Chicago *Illinois*
University of Cincinnati *Ohio*
University of Colorado at Boulder *Colorado*
University of Colorado at Colorado Springs *Colorado*
University of Colorado at Denver and Health Sciences Center - Downtown Denver Campus *Colorado*
University of Connecticut *Connecticut*
University of Dayton *Ohio*
University of Delaware *Delaware*
University of Denver *Colorado*
University of Detroit Mercy *Michigan*
University of Florida *Florida*
University of Georgia *Georgia*
University of Hartford *Connecticut*
University of Hawaii at Manoa *Hawaii*
University of Houston *Texas*
University of Houston-Clear Lake *Texas*
University of Houston-Downtown *Texas*
University of Houston-Victoria *Texas*
University of Idaho *Idaho*
University of Illinois at Chicago *Illinois*
University of Illinois at Urbana-Champaign *Illinois*
The University of Iowa *Iowa*
University of Kansas *Kansas*
University of Kentucky *Kentucky*
University of Louisiana at Lafayette *Louisiana*
University of Louisiana at Monroe *Louisiana*
University of Louisville *Kentucky*
University of Maine *Maine*
University of Manitoba *Manitoba*
University of Maryland, College Park *Maryland*
University of Massachusetts Amherst *Massachusetts*
University of Massachusetts Boston *Massachusetts*
University of Massachusetts Dartmouth *Massachusetts*
University of Massachusetts Lowell *Massachusetts*
University of Memphis *Tennessee*
University of Miami *Florida*
University of Michigan *Michigan*
University of Michigan-Dearborn *Michigan*
University of Michigan-Flint *Michigan*
University of Minnesota, Duluth *Minnesota*
University of Minnesota, Twin Cities Campus *Minnesota*
University of Mississippi *Mississippi*
University of Missouri-Columbia *Missouri*
University of Missouri-Kansas City *Missouri*
University of Missouri-St. Louis *Missouri*
The University of Montana-Missoula *Montana*
University of Montevallo *Alabama*
University of Nebraska-Lincoln *Nebraska*
University of Nebraska at Omaha *Nebraska*
University of Nevada, Las Vegas *Nevada*
University of Nevada, Reno *Nevada*
University of New Hampshire *New Hampshire*
University of New Mexico *New Mexico*
University of New Orleans *Louisiana*
The University of North Carolina at Chapel Hill *North Carolina*
The University of North Carolina at Charlotte *North Carolina*
The University of North Carolina at Greensboro *North Carolina*
The University of North Carolina Wilmington *North Carolina*
University of North Dakota *North Dakota*
University of North Florida *Florida*
University of North Texas *Texas*
University of Northern Colorado *Colorado*
University of Northern Iowa *Iowa*
University of Notre Dame *Indiana*
University of Oklahoma *Oklahoma*
University of Oregon *Oregon*
University of Ottawa *Ontario*
University of the Pacific *California*
University of Pennsylvania *Pennsylvania*
University of Pittsburgh *Pennsylvania*
University of Portland *Oregon*
University of Rhode Island *Rhode Island*
University of Richmond *Virginia*
University of Rochester *New York*
University of San Diego *California*
University of San Francisco *California*
The University of Scranton *Pennsylvania*
University of South Alabama *Alabama*
University of South Carolina *South Carolina*
University of South Carolina Aiken *South Carolina*
University of South Carolina Upstate *South Carolina*
The University of South Dakota *South Dakota*
University of South Florida *Florida*
University of Southern California *California*
University of Southern Indiana *Indiana*
University of Southern Maine *Maine*
University of Southern Mississippi *Mississippi*
The University of Tampa *Florida*
The University of Tennessee *Tennessee*
The University of Tennessee at Chattanooga *Tennessee*
The University of Tennessee at Martin *Tennessee*
The University of Texas at Arlington *Texas*
The University of Texas at Austin *Texas*
The University of Texas at Dallas *Texas*
The University of Texas at El Paso *Texas*
The University of Texas-Pan American *Texas*
The University of Texas at San Antonio *Texas*
The University of Texas at Tyler *Texas*
The University of Toledo *Ohio*
University of Toronto *Ontario*
University of Tulsa *Oklahoma*
University of Utah *Utah*
University of Vermont *Vermont*
University of Virginia *Virginia*
University of Washington *Washington*
University of West Florida *Florida*
University of West Georgia *Georgia*
University of Wisconsin-Eau Claire *Wisconsin*
University of Wisconsin-La Crosse *Wisconsin*
University of Wisconsin-Madison *Wisconsin*
University of Wisconsin-Milwaukee *Wisconsin*
University of Wisconsin-Oshkosh *Wisconsin*
University of Wisconsin-Parkside *Wisconsin*
University of Wisconsin-Whitewater *Wisconsin*
University of Wyoming *Wyoming*
Utah State University *Utah*

Valdosta State University *Georgia*
Valparaiso University *Indiana*
Vanderbilt University *Tennessee*
Villanova University *Pennsylvania*
Virginia Commonwealth University *Virginia*
Virginia Polytechnic Institute and State University *Virginia*
Wake Forest University *North Carolina*
Washington and Lee University *Virginia*
Washington State University *Washington*
Washington University in St. Louis *Missouri*
Wayne State University *Michigan*
Weber State University *Utah*
West Virginia University *West Virginia*
Western Carolina University *North Carolina*
Western Illinois University *Illinois*
Western Kentucky University *Kentucky*
Western Michigan University *Michigan*
Western New England College *Massachusetts*
Western Washington University *Washington*
Wichita State University *Kansas*
Widener University *Pennsylvania*
Wilfrid Laurier University *Ontario*
Willamette University *Oregon*
William Paterson University of New Jersey *New Jersey*
Winston-Salem State University *North Carolina*
Winthrop University *South Carolina*
Worcester Polytechnic Institute *Massachusetts*
Wright State University *Ohio*
Xavier University *Ohio*
Yale University *Connecticut*
Youngstown State University *Ohio*

Accreditation Board for Engineering and TechnologyAccreditation Board for Engineering and Technology, Inc. (ABET)

Aiken Technical College *South Carolina*
Alabama Agricultural and Mechanical University *Alabama*
Alfred University *New York*
Amarillo College *Texas*
Appalachian State University *North Carolina*
Arizona State University *Arizona*
Arizona State University at the Polytechnic Campus *Arizona*
Arkansas State University *Arkansas*
Arkansas State University-Beebe *Arkansas*
Arkansas Tech University *Arkansas*
Armstrong Atlantic State University *Georgia*
Auburn University *Alabama*
Augusta Technical College *Georgia*
Ball State University *Indiana*
Baylor University *Texas*
Benjamin Franklin Institute of Technology *Massachusetts*
Blue Mountain Community College *Oregon*
Bluefield State College *West Virginia*
Boise State University *Idaho*
Boston University *Massachusetts*
Bowie State University *Maryland*
Bradley University *Illinois*
Brigham Young University *Utah*
Brigham Young University -Idaho *Idaho*
Bronx Community College of the City University of New York *New York*
Broome Community College *New York*
Brown University *Rhode Island*
Bucknell University *Pennsylvania*
Buffalo State College, State University of New York *New York*
Burlington County College *New Jersey*
California Institute of Technology *California*
California Maritime Academy *California*
California Polytechnic State University, San Luis Obispo *California*
California State Polytechnic University, Pomona *California*
California State University, Chico *California*
California State University, Dominguez Hills *California*
California State University, Fresno *California*
California State University, Fullerton *California*
California State University, Long Beach *California*
California State University, Los Angeles *California*
California State University, Northridge *California*
California State University, Sacramento *California*
California State University, San Bernardino *California*
Calvin College *Michigan*
Capitol College *Maryland*
Carnegie Mellon University *Pennsylvania*
Carroll College *Montana*
Case Western Reserve University *Ohio*
The Catholic University of America *District of Columbia*
Cedarville University *Ohio*
Central Carolina Technical College *South Carolina*
Central Connecticut State University *Connecticut*
Central Maine Community College *Maine*
Central Missouri State University *Missouri*
Central New Mexico Community College *New Mexico*
Central Piedmont Community College *North Carolina*
Central State University *Ohio*
Central Washington University *Washington*
Chattahoochee Technical College *Georgia*
Chattanooga State Technical Community College *Tennessee*
Christian Brothers University *Tennessee*
Christopher Newport University *Virginia*
Cincinnati State Technical and Community College *Ohio*
The Citadel, The Military College of South Carolina *South Carolina*
City College of the City University of New York *New York*
Clarkson University *New York*
Clemson University *South Carolina*
Cleveland State University *Ohio*
Coastal Carolina University *South Carolina*
College of Charleston *South Carolina*
The College of New Jersey *New Jersey*
College of Staten Island of the City University of New York *New York*
Colorado School of Mines *Colorado*
Colorado State University *Colorado*
Colorado State University-Pueblo *Colorado*
Colorado Technical University *Colorado*
Columbia University, The Fu Foundation School of Engineering and Applied Science *New York*
Columbus State Community College *Ohio*
Cooper Union for the Advancement of Science and Art *New York*
Cornell University *New York*
County College of Morris *New Jersey*
Dartmouth College *New Hampshire*
Davidson County Community College *North Carolina*
DeKalb Technical College *Georgia*
Del Mar College *Texas*
Delaware Technical & Community College, Stanton/Wilmington Campus *Delaware*
Delgado Community College *Louisiana*
Delta College *Michigan*
Denmark Technical College *South Carolina*
DeVry Institute of Technology *New York*
DeVry University *New Jersey*
DeVry University (Addison) *Illinois*
DeVry University (Alpharetta) *Georgia*
DeVry University (Chicago) *Illinois*
DeVry University (Columbus) *Ohio*
DeVry University (Decatur) *Georgia*
DeVry University (Fremont) *California*
DeVry University (Irving) *Texas*
DeVry University (Kansas City) *Missouri*
DeVry University (Long Beach) *California*
DeVry University (Phoenix) *Arizona*
DeVry University (Pomona) *California*
DeVry University (West Hills) *California*
Dordt College *Iowa*
Drexel University *Pennsylvania*
Duke University *North Carolina*
East Tennessee State University *Tennessee*
Eastern Kentucky University *Kentucky*
Eastern Washington University *Washington*
Embry-Riddle Aeronautical University *Florida*
Embry-Riddle Aeronautical University *Arizona*
Erie Community College *New York*
Excelsior College *New York*
Fairfield University *Connecticut*
Fairleigh Dickinson University, Metropolitan Campus *New Jersey*
Fairmont State University *West Virginia*
Farmingdale State University of New York *New York*
Fayetteville Technical Community College *North Carolina*
Ferris State University *Michigan*
Florence-Darlington Technical College *South Carolina*
Florida Agricultural and Mechanical University *Florida*
Florida Atlantic University *Florida*
Florida Institute of Technology *Florida*
Florida International University *Florida*
Florida State University *Florida*
Forsyth Technical Community College *North Carolina*
Fort Valley State University *Georgia*
Gannon University *Pennsylvania*
Gaston College *North Carolina*
Gateway Community College *Connecticut*
Geneva College *Pennsylvania*
George Mason University *Virginia*
The George Washington University *District of Columbia*
Georgia Institute of Technology *Georgia*
Georgia Southern University *Georgia*
Gonzaga University *Washington*
Grambling State University *Louisiana*
Grand Valley State University *Michigan*
Greenville Technical College *South Carolina*
Grove City College *Pennsylvania*
Hampton University *Virginia*
Harvard University *Massachusetts*
Harvey Mudd College *California*
Henry Cogswell College *Washington*
Hocking College *Ohio*
Hofstra University *New York*
Hope College *Michigan*
Horry-Georgetown Technical College *South Carolina*
Houston Community College System *Texas*
Howard University *District of Columbia*
Hudson County Community College *New Jersey*
Hudson Valley Community College *New York*
Humboldt State University *California*
Hunter College of the City University of New York *New York*
Idaho State University *Idaho*
Illinois Institute of Technology *Illinois*
Illinois State University *Illinois*
Indiana Tech *Indiana*
Indiana University of Pennsylvania *Pennsylvania*
Indiana University-Purdue University Fort Wayne *Indiana*
Indiana University-Purdue University Indianapolis *Indiana*
Iowa State University of Science and Technology *Iowa*
Iowa Western Community College *Iowa*
Jackson State University *Mississippi*
James A. Rhodes State College *Ohio*
John Brown University *Arkansas*
The Johns Hopkins University *Maryland*
Kansas State University *Kansas*
Kent State University, Tuscarawas Campus *Ohio*
Kettering University *Michigan*
Lafayette College *Pennsylvania*
Lake Superior State University *Michigan*
Lakeland Community College *Ohio*
Lamar University *Texas*
Lawrence Technological University *Michigan*
Lehigh University *Pennsylvania*
LeTourneau University *Texas*
Louisiana State University and Agricultural and Mechanical College *Louisiana*
Louisiana State University in Shreveport *Louisiana*
Louisiana Tech University *Louisiana*
Loyola College in Maryland *Maryland*
Loyola Marymount University *California*
Maine Maritime Academy *Maine*
Manhattan College *New York*
Marietta College *Ohio*
Marquette University *Wisconsin*
Marshall University *West Virginia*

Massachusetts Institute of Technology *Massachusetts*
McNeese State University *Louisiana*
Mercer University *Georgia*
Merrimack College *Massachusetts*
Messiah College *Pennsylvania*
Metropolitan State College of Denver *Colorado*
Miami University *Ohio*
Michigan State University *Michigan*
Michigan Technological University *Michigan*
Middle Tennessee State University *Tennessee*
Middlesex County College *New Jersey*
Midlands Technical College *South Carolina*
Midwestern State University *Texas*
Millersville University of Pennsylvania *Pennsylvania*
Milwaukee School of Engineering *Wisconsin*
Minnesota State University Mankato *Minnesota*
Mississippi State University *Mississippi*
Missouri Southern State University *Missouri*
Missouri State University *Missouri*
Missouri Western State University *Missouri*
Mohawk Valley Community College *New York*
Monroe Community College *New York*
Montana State University *Montana*
Montana State University-Northern *Montana*
Montana Tech of The University of Montana *Montana*
Montclair State University *New Jersey*
Morgan State University *Maryland*
Morrison Institute of Technology *Illinois*
Murray State University *Kentucky*
Nashville State Technical Community College *Tennessee*
Nassau Community College *New York*
Naugatuck Valley Community College *Connecticut*
New England Institute of Technology *Rhode Island*
New Hampshire Community Technical College, Nashua/Claremont *New Hampshire*
New Hampshire Technical Institute *New Hampshire*
New Jersey Institute of Technology *New Jersey*
New Mexico Institute of Mining and Technology *New Mexico*
New Mexico State University *New Mexico*
New York City College of Technology of the City University of New York *New York*
New York Institute of Technology *New York*
Nicholls State University *Louisiana*
Norfolk State University *Virginia*
North Carolina Agricultural and Technical State University *North Carolina*
North Carolina State University *North Carolina*
North Dakota State University *North Dakota*
Northeast Wisconsin Technical College *Wisconsin*
Northeastern University *Massachusetts*
Northern Arizona University *Arizona*
Northern Illinois University *Illinois*
Northern Kentucky University *Kentucky*
Northwest State Community College *Ohio*
Northwestern State University of Louisiana *Louisiana*
Northwestern University *Illinois*
Norwich University *Vermont*
Oakland University *Michigan*
Ohio Northern University *Ohio*
The Ohio State University *Ohio*
Ohio University *Ohio*
Oklahoma Christian University *Oklahoma*
Oklahoma State University *Oklahoma*
Old Dominion University *Virginia*
Olivet Nazarene University *Illinois*
Onondaga Community College *New York*
Oral Roberts University *Oklahoma*
Orangeburg-Calhoun Technical College *South Carolina*
Oregon Institute of Technology *Oregon*
Oregon State University *Oregon*
Owens Community College *Ohio*
Pace University *New York*
Pacific Lutheran University *Washington*
Paul Smith's College of Arts and Sciences *New York*
Pellissippi State Technical Community College *Tennessee*
Pennsylvania College of Technology *Pennsylvania*
The Pennsylvania State University Altoona College *Pennsylvania*
The Pennsylvania State University Beaver Campus of the Commonwealth College *Pennsylvania*
The Pennsylvania State University Berks Campus of the Berks-Lehigh Valley College *Pennsylvania*
The Pennsylvania State University DuBois Campus of the Commonwealth College *Pennsylvania*
The Pennsylvania State University at Erie, The Behrend College *Pennsylvania*
The Pennsylvania State University Fayette Campus of the Commonwealth College *Pennsylvania*
The Pennsylvania State University Harrisburg Campus *Pennsylvania*
The Pennsylvania State University Hazleton Campus of the Commonwealth College *Pennsylvania*
The Pennsylvania State University New Kensington Campus of the Commonwealth College *Pennsylvania*
The Pennsylvania State University Schuylkill Campus of the Capital College *Pennsylvania*
The Pennsylvania State University Shenango Campus of the Commonwealth College *Pennsylvania*
The Pennsylvania State University University Park Campus *Pennsylvania*
The Pennsylvania State University Wilkes-Barre Campus of the Commonwealth College *Pennsylvania*
The Pennsylvania State University Worthington Scranton Campus of the Commonwealth College *Pennsylvania*
The Pennsylvania State University York Campus of the Commonwealth College *Pennsylvania*
Philadelphia University *Pennsylvania*
Piedmont Technical College *South Carolina*
Pittsburg State University *Kansas*
Point Park University *Pennsylvania*
Polytechnic University, Brooklyn Campus *New York*
Polytechnic University of Puerto Rico *Puerto Rico*
Portland State University *Oregon*
Prairie View A&M University *Texas*
Prince George's Community College *Maryland*
Princeton University *New Jersey*
Purdue University *Indiana*
Purdue University Calumet *Indiana*
Purdue University North Central *Indiana*
Queensborough Community College of the City University of New York *New York*
Radford University *Virginia*
Rensselaer Polytechnic Institute *New York*
Rice University *Texas*
Robert Morris University *Pennsylvania*
Rochester Institute of Technology *New York*
Roger Williams University *Rhode Island*
Rose-Hulman Institute of Technology *Indiana*
Rowan University *New Jersey*
Rutgers, The State University of New Jersey, New Brunswick/Piscataway *New Jersey*
Saginaw Valley State University *Michigan*
St. Ambrose University *Iowa*
St. Cloud State University *Minnesota*
Saint Louis University *Missouri*
Saint Martin's University *Washington*
St. Mary's University of San Antonio *Texas*
San Diego State University *California*
San Francisco State University *California*
San Jose State University *California*
San Juan College *New Mexico*
Santa Clara University *California*
Savannah State University *Georgia*
Savannah Technical College *Georgia*
Seattle Pacific University *Washington*
Seattle University *Washington*
Sinclair Community College *Ohio*
South Carolina State University *South Carolina*
South Dakota School of Mines and Technology *South Dakota*
South Dakota State University *South Dakota*
Southeast Missouri State University *Missouri*
Southeastern Louisiana University *Louisiana*
Southern Connecticut State University *Connecticut*
Southern Illinois University Carbondale *Illinois*
Southern Illinois University Edwardsville *Illinois*
Southern Methodist University *Texas*
Southern Polytechnic State University *Georgia*
Southern University and Agricultural and Mechanical College *Louisiana*
Southwest Tennessee Community College *Tennessee*
Southwestern Oklahoma State University *Oklahoma*
Spartanburg Technical College *South Carolina*
Stanford University *California*
Stark State College of Technology *Ohio*
State University of New York at Binghamton *New York*
State University of New York at Buffalo *New York*
State University of New York College of Agriculture and Technology at Morrisville *New York*
State University of New York College at Brockport *New York*
State University of New York College of Environmental Science & Forestry, Ranger School *New York*
State University of New York College of Environmental Science and Forestry *New York*
State University of New York College of Technology at Alfred *New York*
State University of New York College of Technology at Canton *New York*
State University of New York Institute of Technology *New York*
State University of New York Maritime College *New York*
State University of New York at New Paltz *New York*
Stephen F. Austin State University *Texas*
Stevens Institute of Technology *New Jersey*
Stony Brook University, State University of New York *New York*
Swarthmore College *Pennsylvania*
Syracuse University *New York*
TCI-The College of Technology *New York*
Temple University *Pennsylvania*
Tennessee State University *Tennessee*
Tennessee Technological University *Tennessee*
Texas A&M University *Texas*
Texas A&M University-Corpus Christi *Texas*
Texas A&M University at Galveston *Texas*
Texas A&M University-Kingsville *Texas*
Texas Christian University *Texas*
Texas Southern University *Texas*
Texas State University-San Marcos *Texas*
Texas Tech University *Texas*
Three Rivers Community College *Connecticut*
Towson University *Maryland*
Tri-County Technical College *South Carolina*
Tri-State University *Indiana*
Trident Technical College *South Carolina*
Trinidad State Junior College *Colorado*
Trinity College *Connecticut*
Trinity University *Texas*
Tufts University *Massachusetts*
Tulane University *Louisiana*
Tuskegee University *Alabama*
Union College *New York*
United States Air Force Academy *Colorado*
United States Coast Guard Academy *Connecticut*
United States Merchant Marine Academy *New York*
United States Military Academy *New York*
United States Naval Academy *Maryland*
The University of Akron *Ohio*
The University of Alabama *Alabama*
The University of Alabama at Birmingham *Alabama*
The University of Alabama in Huntsville *Alabama*
University of Alaska Anchorage *Alaska*
University of Alaska Fairbanks *Alaska*
The University of Arizona *Arizona*
University of Arkansas *Arkansas*
University of Arkansas at Little Rock *Arkansas*
University of Bridgeport *Connecticut*
University of California, Berkeley *California*
University of California, Davis *California*
University of California, Irvine *California*
University of California, Los Angeles *California*
University of California, Riverside *California*
University of California, San Diego *California*
University of California, Santa Barbara *California*
University of California, Santa Cruz *California*
University of Central Florida *Florida*
University of Cincinnati *Ohio*
University of Colorado at Boulder *Colorado*

University of Colorado at Colorado Springs *Colorado*
University of Colorado at Denver and Health Sciences Center - Downtown Denver Campus *Colorado*
University of Connecticut *Connecticut*
University of Dayton *Ohio*
University of Delaware *Delaware*
University of Denver *Colorado*
University of Detroit Mercy *Michigan*
University of the District of Columbia *District of Columbia*
University of Evansville *Indiana*
University of Florida *Florida*
University of Georgia *Georgia*
University of Hartford *Connecticut*
University of Hawaii at Manoa *Hawaii*
University of Houston *Texas*
University of Houston-Clear Lake *Texas*
University of Houston-Downtown *Texas*
University of Idaho *Idaho*
University of Illinois at Chicago *Illinois*
University of Illinois at Urbana-Champaign *Illinois*
The University of Iowa *Iowa*
University of Kansas *Kansas*
University of Kentucky *Kentucky*
University of Louisiana at Lafayette *Louisiana*
University of Louisiana at Monroe *Louisiana*
University of Louisville *Kentucky*
University of Maine *Maine*
University of Maryland, Baltimore County *Maryland*
University of Maryland, College Park *Maryland*
University of Massachusetts Amherst *Massachusetts*
University of Massachusetts Dartmouth *Massachusetts*
University of Massachusetts Lowell *Massachusetts*
University of Memphis *Tennessee*
University of Miami *Florida*
University of Michigan *Michigan*
University of Michigan-Dearborn *Michigan*
University of Minnesota, Duluth *Minnesota*
University of Minnesota, Twin Cities Campus *Minnesota*
University of Mississippi *Mississippi*
University of Missouri-Columbia *Missouri*
University of Missouri-Rolla *Missouri*
University of Missouri-St. Louis *Missouri*
The University of Montana-Missoula *Montana*
University of Nebraska-Lincoln *Nebraska*
University of Nebraska at Omaha *Nebraska*
University of Nevada, Las Vegas *Nevada*
University of Nevada, Reno *Nevada*
University of New Hampshire *New Hampshire*
University of New Haven *Connecticut*
University of New Mexico *New Mexico*
University of New Orleans *Louisiana*
University of North Alabama *Alabama*
The University of North Carolina at Chapel Hill *North Carolina*
The University of North Carolina at Charlotte *North Carolina*
The University of North Carolina at Greensboro *North Carolina*
University of North Dakota *North Dakota*
University of North Florida *Florida*
University of North Texas *Texas*
University of Notre Dame *Indiana*
University of Oklahoma *Oklahoma*
University of Oklahoma Health Sciences Center *Oklahoma*
University of the Pacific *California*
University of Pennsylvania *Pennsylvania*
University of Pittsburgh *Pennsylvania*
University of Pittsburgh at Johnstown *Pennsylvania*
University of Portland *Oregon*
University of Puerto Rico, Mayagüez Campus *Puerto Rico*
University of Rhode Island *Rhode Island*
University of Rochester *New York*
University of St. Thomas *Minnesota*
University of San Diego *California*
The University of Scranton *Pennsylvania*
University of South Alabama *Alabama*
University of South Carolina *South Carolina*
University of South Carolina Upstate *South Carolina*
University of South Florida *Florida*
University of Southern California *California*
University of Southern Indiana *Indiana*
University of Southern Maine *Maine*
University of Southern Mississippi *Mississippi*
The University of Tennessee *Tennessee*
The University of Tennessee at Chattanooga *Tennessee*
The University of Tennessee at Martin *Tennessee*
The University of Texas at Arlington *Texas*
The University of Texas at Austin *Texas*
The University of Texas at Dallas *Texas*
The University of Texas at El Paso *Texas*
The University of Texas Health Science Center at Houston *Texas*
The University of Texas-Pan American *Texas*
The University of Texas at San Antonio *Texas*
The University of Texas at Tyler *Texas*
The University of Toledo *Ohio*
University of Tulsa *Oklahoma*
University of Utah *Utah*
University of Vermont *Vermont*
University of Virginia *Virginia*
University of Washington *Washington*
University of West Georgia *Georgia*
University of Wisconsin-Eau Claire *Wisconsin*
University of Wisconsin-Madison *Wisconsin*
University of Wisconsin-Milwaukee *Wisconsin*
University of Wisconsin-Platteville *Wisconsin*
University of Wisconsin-Stout *Wisconsin*
University of Wyoming *Wyoming*
Utah State University *Utah*
Utah Valley State College *Utah*
Valparaiso University *Indiana*
Vanderbilt University *Tennessee*
Vaughn College of Aeronautics and Technology *New York*
Vermont Technical College *Vermont*
Villanova University *Pennsylvania*
Virginia Commonwealth University *Virginia*
Virginia Military Institute *Virginia*
Virginia Polytechnic Institute and State University *Virginia*
Virginia State University *Virginia*
Wake Technical Community College *North Carolina*
Walla Walla College *Washington*
Walla Walla Community College *Washington*
Washington State University *Washington*
Washington University in St. Louis *Missouri*
Wayne State University *Michigan*
Webb Institute *New York*
Weber State University *Utah*
Wentworth Institute of Technology *Massachusetts*
West Virginia State University *West Virginia*
West Virginia University *West Virginia*
West Virginia University Institute of Technology *West Virginia*
Western Carolina University *North Carolina*
Western Kentucky University *Kentucky*
Western Michigan University *Michigan*
Western New England College *Massachusetts*
Western Washington University *Washington*
Wichita State University *Kansas*
Widener University *Pennsylvania*
Wilkes University *Pennsylvania*
Winona State University *Minnesota*
Winston-Salem State University *North Carolina*
Winthrop University *South Carolina*
Worcester Polytechnic Institute *Massachusetts*
Wright State University *Ohio*
Yale University *Connecticut*
York College of Pennsylvania *Pennsylvania*
York Technical College *South Carolina*
Youngstown State University *Ohio*
Zane State College *Ohio*

Accreditation Committee for Perfusion EducationAccreditation Committee for Perfusion Education (ACPE)

Barry University *Florida*
Drexel University *Pennsylvania*
Medical University of South Carolina *South Carolina*
Milwaukee School of Engineering *Wisconsin*
Northeastern University *Massachusetts*
The Ohio State University *Ohio*
Rush University *Illinois*
State University of New York Upstate Medical University *New York*
University of Nebraska Medical Center *Nebraska*

Accreditation Review Committee on Education forAccreditation Review Committee on Education for the Anesthesiologist Assistant (ARCAA)

Case Western Reserve University *Ohio*
Emory University *Georgia*

Accreditation Review Committee on Education inAccreditation Review Committee on Education in Surgical Technology (ARCEST)

Amarillo College *Texas*
Ashland Community and Technical College *Kentucky*
Augusta Technical College *Georgia*
Austin Community College *Texas*
Baker College of Cadillac *Michigan*
Baker College of Clinton Township *Michigan*
Baker College of Flint *Michigan*
Baker College of Jackson *Michigan*
Baker College of Muskegon *Michigan*
Baker College of Port Huron *Michigan*
Baltimore City Community College *Maryland*
Bismarck State College *North Dakota*
Bunker Hill Community College *Massachusetts*
Cabarrus College of Health Sciences *North Carolina*
Career Technical College *Louisiana*
Central Florida Institute *Florida*
Central Ohio Technical College *Ohio*
Central Wyoming College *Wyoming*
Cincinnati State Technical and Community College *Ohio*
City Colleges of Chicago, Malcolm X College *Illinois*
Coastal Carolina Community College *North Carolina*
Columbus State Community College *Ohio*
Columbus Technical College *Georgia*
Community College of Allegheny County *Pennsylvania*
Community College of Denver *Colorado*
Cuyahoga Community College *Ohio*
Del Mar College *Texas*
Delaware County Community College *Pennsylvania*
Delta College *Michigan*
East Central Community College *Mississippi*
Eastern Idaho Technical College *Idaho*
El Paso Community College *Texas*
Frederick Community College *Maryland*
Gateway Technical College *Wisconsin*
Griffin Technical College *Georgia*
Henry Ford Community College *Michigan*
Holmes Community College *Mississippi*
Itawamba Community College *Mississippi*
Ivy Tech Community College-Central Indiana *Indiana*
Ivy Tech Community College-Columbus *Indiana*
Ivy Tech Community College-East Central *Indiana*
Ivy Tech Community College-Lafayette *Indiana*
Ivy Tech Community College-Northwest *Indiana*
Ivy Tech Community College-Southwest *Indiana*
Ivy Tech Community College-Wabash Valley *Indiana*
James H. Faulkner State Community College *Alabama*
Kilgore College *Texas*
Kirkwood Community College *Iowa*
Lakeland Community College *Ohio*
Lamar State College-Port Arthur *Texas*
Loma Linda University *California*
Lorain County Community College *Ohio*
Luzerne County Community College *Pennsylvania*
Macomb Community College *Michigan*
Manchester Community College *Connecticut*
Mercy College of Health Sciences *Iowa*
Milwaukee Area Technical College *Wisconsin*
Montgomery College *Maryland*
Mount Aloysius College *Pennsylvania*
Mt. Hood Community College *Oregon*
Nassau Community College *New York*
National School of Technology, Inc. (Hialeah) *Florida*
National School of Technology, Inc. (North Miami Beach) *Florida*
New England Institute of Technology *Rhode Island*

New Hampshire Community Technical College, Manchester/Stratham *New Hampshire*
Niagara County Community College *New York*
North Arkansas College *Arkansas*
Northwest Technical College *Minnesota*
Northwestern Technical College *Georgia*
Odessa College *Texas*
Our Lady of the Lake College *Louisiana*
Owens Community College *Ohio*
Parkland College *Illinois*
Pearl River Community College *Mississippi*
Presentation College *South Dakota*
Renton Technical College *Washington*
Richland Community College *Illinois*
Rochester Community and Technical College *Minnesota*
St. Cloud Technical College *Minnesota*
San Joaquin Valley College *California*
Seward County Community College *Kansas*
Sinclair Community College *Ohio*
Skyline College *California*
Southeast Arkansas College *Arkansas*
Southeast Community College, Lincoln Campus *Nebraska*
Southern University at Shreveport *Louisiana*
Southern West Virginia Community and Technical College *West Virginia*
Southwestern College *California*
Spokane Community College *Washington*
Springfield Technical Community College *Massachusetts*
Stevens-Henager College *Utah*
Trinity Valley Community College *Texas*
Trocaire College *New York*
Tyler Junior College *Texas*
The University of Akron *Ohio*
University of Arkansas at Fort Smith *Arkansas*
University of Arkansas for Medical Sciences *Arkansas*
University of Saint Francis *Indiana*
Vincennes University *Indiana*
Waukesha County Technical College *Wisconsin*
Wayne County Community College District *Michigan*
West Virginia Northern Community College *West Virginia*
Wichita Area Technical College *Kansas*

Accreditation Review Committee for the MedicalAccreditation Review Committee for the Medical Illustrator (ARCMI)

The Johns Hopkins University *Maryland*
Medical College of Georgia *Georgia*
University of Illinois at Chicago *Illinois*
University of Michigan *Michigan*
The University of Texas Southwestern Medical Center at Dallas *Texas*
University of Toronto *Ontario*

Accrediting Association of Bible CollegesAccrediting Association of Bible Colleges (AABC)

Alaska Bible College *Alaska*
Allegheny Wesleyan College *Ohio*
Alliance University College *Alberta*
American Baptist College of American Baptist Theological Seminary *Tennessee*
Appalachian Bible College *West Virginia*
Arlington Baptist College *Texas*
Baptist Bible College *Missouri*
Baptist Bible College of Pennsylvania *Pennsylvania*
Baptist University of the Americas *Texas*
Barclay College *Kansas*
Bethany Bible College *New Brunswick*
Bethesda Christian University *California*
Beulah Heights Bible College *Georgia*
Boise Bible College *Idaho*
Briercrest College *Saskatchewan*
Calvary Bible College and Theological Seminary *Missouri*
Carver Bible College *Georgia*
Central Bible College *Missouri*
Central Christian College of the Bible *Missouri*
Central Pentecostal College *Saskatchewan*
Cincinnati Christian University *Ohio*
Circleville Bible College *Ohio*
Clear Creek Baptist Bible College *Kentucky*
Colegio Biblico Pentecostal *Puerto Rico*
Colegio Pentecostal Mizpa *Puerto Rico*
College of Biblical Studies-Houston *Texas*
Columbia Bible College *British Columbia*
Columbia International University *South Carolina*
Crossroads Bible College *Indiana*
Crossroads College *Minnesota*
Crown College *Minnesota*
Dallas Christian College *Texas*
Davis College *New York*
Emmanuel Bible College *Ontario*
Emmanuel Bible College *California*
Emmaus Bible College *Iowa*
Eugene Bible College *Oregon*
Faith Baptist Bible College and Theological Seminary *Iowa*
Florida Christian College *Florida*
Free Will Baptist Bible College *Tennessee*
God's Bible School and College *Ohio*
Grace Bible College *Michigan*
Grace University *Nebraska*
Great Lakes Christian College *Michigan*
Heritage Baptist College and Heritage Theological Seminary *Ontario*
Heritage Bible College *North Carolina*
Heritage Christian University *Alabama*
Hobe Sound Bible College *Florida*
John Wesley College *North Carolina*
Johnson Bible College *Tennessee*
Kentucky Mountain Bible College *Kentucky*
The King's College and Seminary *California*
Kuyper College *Michigan*
Lancaster Bible College *Pennsylvania*
Life Pacific College *California*
Lincoln Christian College *Illinois*
Magnolia Bible College *Mississippi*
Manhattan Christian College *Kansas*
Master's College and Seminary *Ontario*
Moody Bible Institute *Illinois*
Multnomah Bible College and Biblical Seminary *Oregon*
Nazarene Bible College *Colorado*
Nebraska Christian College *Nebraska*
Oak Hills Christian College *Minnesota*
Ozark Christian College *Missouri*
Philadelphia Biblical University *Pennsylvania*
Pillsbury Baptist Bible College *Minnesota*
Prairie Bible Institute *Alberta*
Providence College and Theological Seminary *Manitoba*
Puget Sound Christian College *Washington*
Roanoke Bible College *North Carolina*
Rocky Mountain College *Alberta*
Rosedale Bible College *Ohio*
St. Louis Christian College *Missouri*
School of Urban Missions-New Orleans *Louisiana*
Somerset Christian College *New Jersey*
Southeastern Baptist College *Mississippi*
Southeastern Bible College *Alabama*
Southwestern Assemblies of God University *Texas*
Steinbach Bible College *Manitoba*
Summit Pacific College *British Columbia*
Taylor University College and Seminary *Alberta*
Toccoa Falls College *Georgia*
Tri-State Bible College *Ohio*
Trinity Bible College *North Dakota*
Trinity College of Florida *Florida*
Tyndale University College & Seminary *Ontario*
Vanguard College *Alberta*
Vennard College *Iowa*
Washington Bible College *Maryland*
Wesley College *Mississippi*
Western Christian College *Manitoba*
William and Catherine Booth College *Manitoba*
William Jessup University *California*
Williamson Christian College *Tennessee*
Winston-Salem Bible College *North Carolina*
Zion Bible Institute *Rhode Island*

Accrediting Bureau of Health Education SchoolsAccrediting Bureau of Health Education Schools (ABHES)

The Academy of Health Care Professions *Texas*
Allied College *Missouri*
Apollo College *Washington*
Apollo College *Idaho*
Apollo College-Phoenix, Inc. *Arizona*
Apollo College-Tri-City, Inc. *Arizona*
Apollo College-Tucson, Inc. *Arizona*
Apollo College-Westside, Inc. *Arizona*
Arizona College of Allied Health *Arizona*
Bay State College *Massachusetts*
Brown Mackie College-Merrillville *Indiana*
Brown Mackie College-Michigan City *Indiana*
The Bryman School *Arizona*
Cambridge College *Colorado*
Central Florida Institute *Florida*
CollegeAmerica-Flagstaff *Arizona*
Community Care College *Oklahoma*
Davenport University (Granger) *Indiana*
Davenport University (Merrillville) *Indiana*
IntelliTec Medical Institute *Colorado*
Keiser College (Fort Lauderdale) *Florida*
Keiser College (Melbourne) *Florida*
Keiser College (Pembroke Pines) *Florida*
Keiser College (Port St. Lucie) *Florida*
Keiser College (Sarasota) *Florida*
Keiser College (Tallahassee) *Florida*
MedVance Institute *Florida*
Midwest Institute (Earth City) *Missouri*
National School of Technology, Inc. (Fort Lauderdale) *Florida*
National School of Technology, Inc. (Hialeah) *Florida*
National School of Technology, Inc. (Miami) *Florida*
National School of Technology, Inc. (North Miami Beach) *Florida*
Pima Medical Institute *Washington*
Pima Medical Institute *New Mexico*
Pima Medical Institute *Nevada*
Pima Medical Institute *Colorado*
Pima Medical Institute *California*
Pima Medical Institute (Mesa) *Arizona*
Pima Medical Institute (Tucson) *Arizona*
Professional Skills Institute *Ohio*
Sanford-Brown College (Hazelwood) *Missouri*
Sanford-Brown College (North Kansas City) *Missouri*
Sanford-Brown Institute (Jacksonville) *Florida*
Sonoma College (Petaluma) *California*
Sonoma College (San Francisco) *California*
Southwestern Oklahoma State University at Sayre *Oklahoma*
Vatterott College (Omaha) *Nebraska*

Accrediting Commission of Career Schools andAccrediting Commission of Career Schools and Colleges of Technology (ACCSCT)

Academy of Medical Arts and Business *Pennsylvania*
Allied Medical and Technical Careers *Pennsylvania*
American Academy of Art *Illinois*
American Trans Air Aviation Training Academy *Indiana*
Antonelli College *Ohio*
Antonelli College (Hattiesburg) *Mississippi*
Antonelli College (Jackson) *Mississippi*
Antonelli Institute *Pennsylvania*
Arizona Automotive Institute *Arizona*
The Art Center Design College *New Mexico*
The Art Center Design College *Arizona*
The Art Institute of California-San Diego *California*
The Art Institute of Cincinnati *Ohio*
The Art Institute of Las Vegas *Nevada*
ATI Career Training Center (Fort Lauderdale) *Florida*
ATI Career Training Center (Miami) *Florida*
ATI Career Training Center (Oakland Park) *Florida*
ATI Health Education Center *Florida*
ATI Technical Training Center *Texas*
Baton Rouge School of Computers *Louisiana*
Bel-Rea Institute of Animal Technology *Colorado*
Berean Institute *Pennsylvania*
Berks Technical Institute *Pennsylvania*
Bidwell Training Center *Pennsylvania*
Border Institute of Technology *Texas*
Boulder College of Massage Therapy *Colorado*
Bradley Academy for the Visual Arts *Pennsylvania*
Brown College *Minnesota*
Brown Mackie College-Hopkinsville *Kentucky*

Brown Mackie College-Louisville *Kentucky*
Bryman College (Ontario) *California*
The Bryman School *Arizona*
Business Informatics Center, Inc. *New York*
California College for Health Sciences *Utah*
California Culinary Academy *California*
Cambridge College *Colorado*
Career College of Northern Nevada *Nevada*
Career Training Academy (Monroeville) *Pennsylvania*
Career Training Academy (New Kensington) *Pennsylvania*
Career Training Academy (Pittsburgh) *Pennsylvania*
Central Florida College *Florida*
Centro de Estudios Multidisciplinarios *Puerto Rico*
CHI Institute *Pennsylvania*
CHI Institute, RETS Campus *Pennsylvania*
College of Art Advertising *Ohio*
CollegeAmerica-Colorado Springs *Colorado*
CollegeAmerica-Denver *Colorado*
CollegeAmerica-Flagstaff *Arizona*
CollegeAmerica-Fort Collins *Colorado*
Collins College: A School of Design and Technology *Arizona*
Colorado School of Healing Arts *Colorado*
Colorado School of Trades *Colorado*
Columbia College Hollywood *California*
Commonwealth Technical Institute *Pennsylvania*
Concorde Career Institute *Missouri*
Concorde Career Institute *California*
The Cooking and Hospitality Institute of Chicago *Illinois*
The Creative Center *Nebraska*
Crown College *Washington*
The Culinary Institute of America *New York*
Dean Institute of Technology *Pennsylvania*
Delta College of Arts and Technology *Louisiana*
Denver Automotive and Diesel College *Colorado*
Denver Career College *Colorado*
DigiPen Institute of Technology *Washington*
ECPI Technical College *North Carolina*
ECPI Technical College (Glen Allen) *Virginia*
ECPI Technical College (Richmond) *Virginia*
ECPI Technical College (Roanoke) *Virginia*
Electronic Computer Programming College *Tennessee*
Erie Institute of Technology *Pennsylvania*
ETI Technical College of Niles *Ohio*
Everglades University (Boca Raton) *Florida*
Everglades University (Sarasota) *Florida*
Florida College of Natural Health (Bradenton) *Florida*
Florida College of Natural Health (Maitland) *Florida*
Florida College of Natural Health (Miami) *Florida*
Florida College of Natural Health (Pompano Beach) *Florida*
Foundation College *California*
Fountainhead College of Technology *Tennessee*
Full Sail Real World Education *Florida*
Georgia Medical Institute-DeKalb *Georgia*
Gretna Career College *Louisiana*
Hallmark Institute of Aeronautics *Texas*
Hallmark Institute of Technology *Texas*
Hamilton Technical College *Iowa*
Heritage College *Nevada*
Heritage College *Missouri*
Heritage College *Colorado*
Heritage College of Hair Design *Oklahoma*
Herzing College *Wisconsin*
Herzing College *Minnesota*
Herzing College *Alabama*
High-Tech Institute *Texas*
High-Tech Institute *Nevada*
High-Tech Institute *Missouri*
High-Tech Institute *Minnesota*
High-Tech Institute *Georgia*
High-Tech Institute *Florida*
High-Tech Institute *California*
High-Tech Institute *Arizona*
High-Tech Institute (Memphis) *Tennessee*
High-Tech Institute (Nashville) *Tennessee*
Hussian School of Art *Pennsylvania*
The Illinois Institute of Art-Chicago *Illinois*
The Illinois Institute of Art-Schaumburg *Illinois*
Information Computer Systems Institute *Pennsylvania*
IntelliTec College (Colorado Springs) *Colorado*
IntelliTec College (Grand Junction) *Colorado*
Interior Designers Institute *California*
International College of Broadcasting *Ohio*
Island Drafting and Technical Institute *New York*
ITI Technical College *Louisiana*
JNA Institute of Culinary Arts *Pennsylvania*
Johnson College *Pennsylvania*
Kansas City College *Missouri*
Le Cordon Bleu College of Culinary Arts, Las Vegas *Nevada*
Lincoln Technical Institute *Indiana*
Lincoln Technical Institute (Allentown) *Pennsylvania*
Lincoln Technical Institute (Philadelphia) *Pennsylvania*
Long Technical College *Arizona*
Madison Media Institute *Wisconsin*
Maric College (North Hollywood) *California*
Maric College (San Diego) *California*
Median School of Allied Health Careers *Pennsylvania*
Metropolitan Career Center *Pennsylvania*
Metropolitan College of Court Reporting *New Mexico*
Metropolitan College of Court Reporting *Arizona*
Metropolitan College (Oklahoma City) *Oklahoma*
Metropolitan College (Tulsa) *Oklahoma*
Missouri College *Missouri*
Missouri Tech *Missouri*
Mt. Sierra College *California*
MTI College of Business and Technology (Houston) *Texas*
MTI College of Business and Technology (Houston) *Texas*
Myotherapy Institute *Nebraska*
Nashville Auto Diesel College *Tennessee*
National Institute of Technology *West Virginia*
National Institute of Technology *Ohio*
New Castle School of Trades *Pennsylvania*
New England Culinary Institute *Vermont*
New England Culinary Institute at Essex *Vermont*
New England School of Communications *Maine*
North Central Industrial Technical Education Center *Pennsylvania*
Northrop Rice Aviation Institute of Technology *California*
Northwest Aviation College *Washington*
Northwest College of Art *Washington*
Northwest School of Wooden Boatbuilding *Washington*
Northwest Technical Institute *Minnesota*
Northwestern Technical College *California*
Nossi College of Art *Tennessee*
Oakbridge Academy of Arts *Pennsylvania*
Ohio College of Massotherapy *Ohio*
Ohio Institute of Photography and Technology *Ohio*
Ohio Technical College *Ohio*
O'More College of Design *Tennessee*
Orleans Technical Institute-Center City Campus *Pennsylvania*
Paducah Technical College *Kentucky*
Paier College of Art, Inc. *Connecticut*
Pennco Tech *Pennsylvania*
Pennsylvania Culinary Institute *Pennsylvania*
Pima Medical Institute (Mesa) *Arizona*
Pinnacle Career Institute *Missouri*
Pittsburgh Institute of Aeronautics *Pennsylvania*
The PJA School *Pennsylvania*
Platt College *Colorado*
Platt College (Cerritos) *California*
Platt College-Los Angeles, Inc *California*
Platt College (Newport Beach) *California*
Platt College (Oklahoma City) *Oklahoma*
Platt College (Ontario) *California*
Platt College San Diego *California*
Platt College (Tulsa) *Oklahoma*
Professional Careers Institute *Indiana*
Provo College *Utah*
Puerto Rico Technical Junior College (Mayaguez) *Puerto Rico*
Puerto Rico Technical Junior College (San Juan) *Puerto Rico*
The Refrigeration School *Arizona*
Remington College-Cleveland Campus *Ohio*
Remington College-Fort Worth Campus *Texas*
Remington College-Houston Campus *Texas*
Remington College-Jacksonville Campus *Florida*
Remington College-Little Rock Campus *Arkansas*
Remington College-Memphis Campus *Tennessee*
Remington College-Mobile Campus *Alabama*
Remington College-New Orleans Campus *Louisiana*
Remington College-Pinellas Campus *Florida*
Remington College-Tampa Campus *Florida*
The Restaurant School at Walnut Hill College *Pennsylvania*
RETS Tech Center *Ohio*
Rosedale Technical Institute *Pennsylvania*
School of Advertising Art *Ohio*
Scottsdale Culinary Institute *Arizona*
Southern California Institute of Technology *California*
Southwest Institute of Healing Arts *Arizona*
Southwest Institute of Technology *Texas*
Spartan College of Aeronautics and Technology *Oklahoma*
Swedish Institute, College of Health Sciences *New York*
Technology Education College *Ohio*
TESST College of Technology *Virginia*
TESST College of Technology (Baltimore) *Maryland*
TESST College of Technology (Beltsville) *Maryland*
TESST College of Technology (Towson) *Maryland*
Tidewater Tech *Virginia*
Triangle Tech, Inc.-DuBois School *Pennsylvania*
Triangle Tech, Inc.-Erie School *Pennsylvania*
Triangle Tech, Inc.-Greensburg School *Pennsylvania*
Triangle Tech, Inc.-Pittsburgh School *Pennsylvania*
Triangle Tech, Inc.-Sunbury School *Pennsylvania*
Tulsa Welding School *Oklahoma*
Universal Technical Institute *Texas*
Universal Technical Institute *Arizona*
Utah Career College *Utah*
Vatterott College *Tennessee*
Vatterott College *Ohio*
Vatterott College *Iowa*
Vatterott College (Kansas City) *Missouri*
Vatterott College (Oklahoma City) *Oklahoma*
Vatterott College (Omaha) *Nebraska*
Vatterott College (Omaha-Spring Valley) *Nebraska*
Vatterott College (St. Ann) *Missouri*
Vatterott College (St. Joseph) *Missouri*
Vatterott College (St. Louis) *Missouri*
Vatterott College (Springfield) *Missouri*
Vatterott College (Tulsa) *Oklahoma*
Virginia Marti College of Art and Design *Ohio*
Western Career College (Emeryville) *California*
Western Career College (Fremont) *California*
Western Career College (San Jose) *California*
Western Career College (Walnut Creek) *California*
Western Culinary Institute *Oregon*
Western School of Health and Business Careers (Monroeville) *Pennsylvania*
Western School of Health and Business Careers (Pittsburgh) *Pennsylvania*
Western Technical College *Texas*
Western Technical Institute *Texas*
Westwood College-Anaheim *California*
Westwood College-Atlanta Midtown *Georgia*
Westwood College-Chicago O'Hare Airport *Illinois*
Westwood College-Denver North *Colorado*
Westwood College-Denver South *Colorado*
Westwood College-Houston South Campus *Texas*
Westwood College-Inland Empire *California*
Westwood College-Long Beach *California*
The Williamson Free School of Mechanical Trades *Pennsylvania*
WyoTech *Wyoming*
WyoTech *Pennsylvania*
WyoTech (Fremont) *California*
WyoTech (West Sacramento) *California*
York Technical Institute *Pennsylvania*

Accrediting Commission on Education for HealthAccrediting Commission on Education for Health Services Administration (ACEHSA)

Arizona State University *Arizona*
Baylor University *Texas*
Bernard M. Baruch College of the City University of New York *New York*
Boston University *Massachusetts*
California State University, Long Beach *California*
Cleveland State University *Ohio*

Cornell University *New York*
Dalhousie University *Nova Scotia*
Duke University *North Carolina*
Florida International University *Florida*
The George Washington University *District of Columbia*
Georgia State University *Georgia*
Governors State University *Illinois*
Indiana University-Purdue University Indianapolis *Indiana*
The Johns Hopkins University *Maryland*
King's College *Pennsylvania*
Marymount University *Virginia*
Medical University of South Carolina *South Carolina*
New York University *New York*
Northwestern University *Illinois*
The Ohio State University *Ohio*
The Pennsylvania State University University Park Campus *Pennsylvania*
Rush University *Illinois*
Saint Louis University *Missouri*
San Diego State University *California*
Simmons College *Massachusetts*
Temple University *Pennsylvania*
Texas State University-San Marcos *Texas*
Texas Tech University *Texas*
Texas Woman's University *Texas*
Trinity University *Texas*
Tulane University *Louisiana*
Université de Montréal *Quebec*
The University of Alabama at Birmingham *Alabama*
University of Arkansas at Little Rock *Arkansas*
University of California, Berkeley *California*
University of California, Los Angeles *California*
University of Central Florida *Florida*
University of Colorado at Denver and Health Sciences Center - Downtown Denver Campus *Colorado*
University of Florida *Florida*
University of Houston-Clear Lake *Texas*
The University of Iowa *Iowa*
University of Kansas *Kansas*
University of Kentucky *Kentucky*
University of Memphis *Tennessee*
University of Miami *Florida*
University of Michigan *Michigan*
University of Minnesota, Twin Cities Campus *Minnesota*
University of Missouri-Columbia *Missouri*
The University of North Carolina at Chapel Hill *North Carolina*
University of Oklahoma Health Sciences Center *Oklahoma*
University of Ottawa *Ontario*
University of Pennsylvania *Pennsylvania*
University of Pittsburgh *Pennsylvania*
University of Puerto Rico, Medical Sciences Campus *Puerto Rico*
University of St. Thomas *Minnesota*
The University of Scranton *Pennsylvania*
University of South Carolina *South Carolina*
University of Southern California *California*
University of Southern Maine *Maine*
University of Toronto *Ontario*
University of Washington *Washington*
University of Wisconsin-Madison *Wisconsin*
Virginia Commonwealth University *Virginia*
Washington University in St. Louis *Missouri*
Widener University *Pennsylvania*
Xavier University *Ohio*
Yale University *Connecticut*

Accrediting Council on Education in JournalismAccrediting Council on Education in Journalism and Mass Communications (ACEJMC)

Abilene Christian University *Texas*
American University *District of Columbia*
Arizona State University *Arizona*
Arkansas State University *Arkansas*
Auburn University *Alabama*
Ball State University *Indiana*
Baylor University *Texas*
Bowling Green State University *Ohio*
Brigham Young University *Utah*
California State University, Chico *California*
California State University, Fullerton *California*
California State University, Northridge *California*
Central Michigan University *Michigan*
Colorado State University *Colorado*
Drake University *Iowa*
East Tennessee State University *Tennessee*
Eastern Illinois University *Illinois*
Florida Agricultural and Mechanical University *Florida*
Florida International University *Florida*
Grambling State University *Louisiana*
Hampton University *Virginia*
Hofstra University *New York*
Howard University *District of Columbia*
Indiana University Bloomington *Indiana*
Iona College *New York*
Iowa State University of Science and Technology *Iowa*
Jackson State University *Mississippi*
Kansas State University *Kansas*
Kent State University *Ohio*
Louisiana State University and Agricultural and Mechanical College *Louisiana*
Marquette University *Wisconsin*
Marshall University *West Virginia*
Michigan State University *Michigan*
Middle Tennessee State University *Tennessee*
Murray State University *Kentucky*
New Mexico State University *New Mexico*
New York University *New York*
Nicholls State University *Louisiana*
Norfolk State University *Virginia*
Northwestern State University of Louisiana *Louisiana*
Northwestern University *Illinois*
Ohio University *Ohio*
Oklahoma State University *Oklahoma*
The Pennsylvania State University University Park Campus *Pennsylvania*
St. Cloud State University *Minnesota*
San Francisco State University *California*
San Jose State University *California*
South Dakota State University *South Dakota*
Southern Illinois University Carbondale *Illinois*
Southern University and Agricultural and Mechanical College *Louisiana*
Syracuse University *New York*
Temple University *Pennsylvania*
Texas A&M University *Texas*
Texas Christian University *Texas*
Texas State University-San Marcos *Texas*
Texas Tech University *Texas*
The University of Alabama *Alabama*
University of Alaska Anchorage *Alaska*
University of Alaska Fairbanks *Alaska*
The University of Arizona *Arizona*
University of Arkansas *Arkansas*
University of California, Berkeley *California*
University of Colorado at Boulder *Colorado*
University of Connecticut *Connecticut*
University of Florida *Florida*
University of Georgia *Georgia*
University of Hawaii at Manoa *Hawaii*
University of Illinois at Urbana-Champaign *Illinois*
The University of Iowa *Iowa*
University of Kansas *Kansas*
University of Kentucky *Kentucky*
University of Louisiana at Lafayette *Louisiana*
University of Louisiana at Monroe *Louisiana*
University of Maryland, College Park *Maryland*
University of Memphis *Tennessee*
University of Miami *Florida*
University of Minnesota, Twin Cities Campus *Minnesota*
University of Mississippi *Mississippi*
University of Missouri-Columbia *Missouri*
The University of Montana-Missoula *Montana*
University of Nebraska-Lincoln *Nebraska*
University of Nevada, Reno *Nevada*
The University of North Carolina at Chapel Hill *North Carolina*
University of North Texas *Texas*
University of Oklahoma *Oklahoma*
University of Oregon *Oregon*
University of South Carolina *South Carolina*
The University of South Dakota *South Dakota*
University of South Florida *Florida*
University of Southern California *California*
University of Southern Mississippi *Mississippi*
The University of Tennessee *Tennessee*
The University of Tennessee at Chattanooga *Tennessee*
The University of Tennessee at Martin *Tennessee*
The University of Texas at Austin *Texas*
University of Utah *Utah*
University of Washington *Washington*
University of Wisconsin-Eau Claire *Wisconsin*
University of Wisconsin-Oshkosh *Wisconsin*
University of Wisconsin-River Falls *Wisconsin*
Washington and Lee University *Virginia*
West Virginia University *West Virginia*
Western Kentucky University *Kentucky*
Winthrop University *South Carolina*

Accrediting Council for Independent Colleges andAccrediting Council for Independent Colleges and Schools (ACICS)

Aakers Business College *North Dakota*
Academy of Art University *California*
Academy College *Minnesota*
Academy of Court Reporting *Ohio*
The Art Institute of California-Los Angeles *California*
The Art Institute of California-Orange County *California*
The Art Institute of California-San Francisco *California*
The Art Institute of Charlotte *North Carolina*
The Art Institute of Colorado *Colorado*
The Art Institute of Fort Lauderdale *Florida*
The Art Institute of New York City *New York*
The Art Institute of Philadelphia *Pennsylvania*
The Art Institute of Phoenix *Arizona*
The Art Institute of Pittsburgh *Pennsylvania*
The Art Institutes International Minnesota *Minnesota*
ASA Institute, The College of Advanced Technology *New York*
Atlantic College *Puerto Rico*
ATS Institute of Technology *Ohio*
Austin Business College *Texas*
Beal College *Maine*
Beckfield College *Kentucky*
Blair College *Colorado*
Bohecker's Business College *Ohio*
Bradford School *Pennsylvania*
Bradford School *Ohio*
Brooks College (Long Beach) *California*
Brooks College (Sunnyvale) *California*
Brooks Institute of Photography *California*
Brown Mackie College-Akron *Ohio*
Brown Mackie College-Cincinnati *Ohio*
Brown Mackie College-Findlay *Ohio*
Brown Mackie College-Fort Wayne *Indiana*
Brown Mackie College-Hopkinsville *Kentucky*
Brown Mackie College-Louisville *Kentucky*
Brown Mackie College-Merrillville *Indiana*
Brown Mackie College-Michigan City *Indiana*
Brown Mackie College-North Canton *Ohio*
Brown Mackie College-Northern Kentucky *Kentucky*
Brown Mackie College-South Bend *Indiana*
Business Institute of Pennsylvania (Meadville) *Pennsylvania*
Business Institute of Pennsylvania (Sharon) *Pennsylvania*
California Design College *California*
Cambria-Rowe Business College (Indiana) *Pennsylvania*
Cambria-Rowe Business College (Johnstown) *Pennsylvania*
Camelot College *Louisiana*
Career Colleges of Chicago *Illinois*
Chaparral College *Arizona*
Charter College *Alaska*
City College (Casselberry) *Florida*
City College (Fort Lauderdale) *Florida*
City College (Gainesville) *Florida*
City College (Miami) *Florida*
Coleman College (La Mesa) *California*
Coleman College (San Marcos) *California*
College of Court Reporting *Indiana*
The College of Office Technology *Illinois*
Columbia College (Caguas) *Puerto Rico*

Newport Business Institute (Williamsport) *Pennsylvania*
Newschool of Architecture & Design *California*
Northwestern Polytechnic University *California*
Ohio Business College (Lorain) *Ohio*
Ohio Business College (Sandusky) *Ohio*
Ohio Valley College of Technology *Ohio*
Olean Business Institute *New York*
Orlando Culinary Academy *Florida*
Pace Institute *Pennsylvania*
Pacific States University *California*
Parks College *Virginia*
Parks College (Aurora) *Colorado*
Parks College (Denver) *Colorado*
Patricia Stevens College *Missouri*
Penn Commercial Business and Technical School *Pennsylvania*
Pioneer Pacific College *Oregon*
Potomac College *District of Columbia*
Prince Institute of Professional Studies *Alabama*
Professional Golfers Career College *California*
Ramírez College of Business and Technology *Puerto Rico*
Rasmussen College Eagan *Minnesota*
Rasmussen College Eden Prairie *Minnesota*
Rasmussen College Mankato *Minnesota*
Rasmussen College St. Cloud *Minnesota*
Remington College-Baton Rouge Campus *Louisiana*
Remington College-Colorado Springs Campus *Colorado*
Remington College-Dallas Campus *Texas*
Remington College-Denver Campus *Colorado*
Remington College-Honolulu Campus *Hawaii*
Remington College-Lafayette Campus *Louisiana*
Remington College-San Diego Campus *California*
Remington College-Tempe Campus *Arizona*
Rochester Business Institute *New York*
Rockford Business College *Illinois*
Sage College *California*
San Diego Golf Academy *California*
Sanford-Brown College (Fenton) *Missouri*
Sanford-Brown College (Hazelwood) *Missouri*
Sanford-Brown College (North Kansas City) *Missouri*
Sanford-Brown College (St. Charles) *Missouri*
Sanford-Brown Institute (Jacksonville) *Florida*
Sanford-Brown Institute (Tampa) *Florida*
Sawyer College (Hammond) *Indiana*
Sawyer College (Merrillville) *Indiana*
Schiller International University *Florida*
Schuylkill Institute of Business and Technology *Pennsylvania*
Silicon Valley University *California*
South Coast College *California*
South College-Asheville *North Carolina*
South Hills School of Business & Technology (Altoona) *Pennsylvania*
South Hills School of Business & Technology (State College) *Pennsylvania*
Southeastern Business College (Chillicothe) *Ohio*
Southeastern Business College (Jackson) *Ohio*
Southeastern Business College (Lancaster) *Ohio*
Southwest Florida College (Fort Myers) *Florida*
Southwestern College of Business *Kentucky*
Southwestern College of Business (Cincinnati) *Ohio*
Southwestern College of Business (Cincinnati) *Ohio*
Southwestern College of Business (Dayton) *Ohio*
Southwestern College of Business (Franklin) *Ohio*
Spencerian College *Kentucky*
Spencerian College-Lexington *Kentucky*
Springfield College *Missouri*
Stautzenberger College *Ohio*
Stratford University *Virginia*
Taylor Business Institute *New York*
Taylor Business Institute *Illinois*
Teikyo Loretto Heights University *Colorado*
Thompson Institute *Pennsylvania*
Tri-State Business Institute *Pennsylvania*
Trumbull Business College *Ohio*
University of Advancing Technology *Arizona*
University of Northern Virginia *Virginia*
Valley College *West Virginia*
VC Tech *Alabama*
Virginia College at Austin *Texas*
Virginia College at Birmingham *Alabama*
Virginia College at Huntsville *Alabama*
Virginia College at Jackson *Mississippi*
Webster College (Holiday) *Florida*
Webster College (Ocala) *Florida*
West Virginia Business College (Nutter Fort) *West Virginia*
West Virginia Business College (Wheeling) *West Virginia*
West Virginia Junior College (Bridgeport) *West Virginia*
West Virginia Junior College (Charleston) *West Virginia*
West Virginia Junior College (Morgantown) *West Virginia*
Western Business College *Washington*
Western Business College *Oregon*
Westwood College-Chicago Du Page *Illinois*
Westwood College-Chicago Loop Campus *Illinois*
Westwood College-Chicago O'Hare Airport *Illinois*
Westwood College-Chicago River Oaks *Illinois*
Westwood College-Dallas *Texas*
Westwood College-Fort Worth *Texas*
Westwood College-Los Angeles *California*
Yorktowne Business Institute *Pennsylvania*

American Academy for Liberal EducationAmerican Academy for Liberal Education (AALE)

Ave Maria College *Michigan*
Ave Maria University *Florida*
Baylor University *Texas*
Magdalen College *New Hampshire*
Michigan State University *Michigan*
Patrick Henry College *Virginia*
Soka University of America *California*
Southern Virginia University *Virginia*
Thomas Aquinas College *California*
Thomas More College of Liberal Arts *New Hampshire*
University of Dallas *Texas*

American Association of Blood BanksAmerican Association of Blood Banks (AABB)

The George Washington University *District of Columbia*
University of Cincinnati *Ohio*
University of Illinois at Chicago *Illinois*
The University of Texas Health Science Center at San Antonio *Texas*

American Association of Colleges of NursingAmerican Association of Colleges of Nursing (AACN)

Abilene Christian University *Texas*
Adelphi University *New York*
Alvernia College *Pennsylvania*
Alverno College *Wisconsin*
Arizona State University *Arizona*
Armstrong Atlantic State University *Georgia*
Ashland University *Ohio*
Auburn University Montgomery *Alabama*
Augsburg College *Minnesota*
Augustana College *South Dakota*
Aurora University *Illinois*
Avila University *Missouri*
Azusa Pacific University *California*
Baker University *Kansas*
Baptist College of Health Sciences *Tennessee*
Barnes-Jewish College of Nursing and Allied Health *Missouri*
Barry University *Florida*
Baylor University *Texas*
Bellarmine University *Kentucky*
Bellin College of Nursing *Wisconsin*
Belmont University *Tennessee*
Bemidji State University *Minnesota*
Berea College *Kentucky*
Bethel College *Kansas*
Bethel University *Minnesota*
Blessing-Rieman College of Nursing *Illinois*
Bloomfield College *New Jersey*
Bloomsburg University of Pennsylvania *Pennsylvania*
Bluefield State College *West Virginia*
Boston College *Massachusetts*
Cabarrus College of Health Sciences *North Carolina*
California State University, Bakersfield *California*
California State University, Chico *California*
California State University, Dominguez Hills *California*
California State University, Fullerton *California*
California State University, Long Beach *California*
California State University, Northridge *California*
California State University, Sacramento *California*
California State University, San Bernardino *California*
California State University, Stanislaus *California*
California University of Pennsylvania *Pennsylvania*
Capital University *Ohio*
Cardinal Stritch University *Wisconsin*
Carlow University *Pennsylvania*
Carroll College *Montana*
Carson-Newman College *Tennessee*
Cedarville University *Ohio*
Central Connecticut State University *Connecticut*
Central Missouri State University *Missouri*
Christopher Newport University *Virginia*
Clarke College *Iowa*
Cleveland State University *Ohio*
Coe College *Iowa*
Colby-Sawyer College *New Hampshire*
College Misericordia *Pennsylvania*
College of Mount Saint Vincent *New York*
The College of New Jersey *New Jersey*
The College of New Rochelle *New York*
College of Saint Benedict *Minnesota*
The College of St. Scholastica *Minnesota*
Concordia College *Minnesota*
Concordia University Wisconsin *Wisconsin*
Cox College of Nursing and Health Sciences *Missouri*
Creighton University *Nebraska*
Curry College *Massachusetts*
Delaware State University *Delaware*
Delta State University *Mississippi*
DePaul University *Illinois*
Dominican College *New York*
Dominican University of California *California*
Drexel University *Pennsylvania*
Duke University *North Carolina*
Duquesne University *Pennsylvania*
D'Youville College *New York*
East Texas Baptist University *Texas*
Eastern Kentucky University *Kentucky*
Eastern Michigan University *Michigan*
Eastern University *Pennsylvania*
Eastern Washington University *Washington*
Edgewood College *Wisconsin*
Edinboro University of Pennsylvania *Pennsylvania*
Elmhurst College *Illinois*
Elms College *Massachusetts*
Emory University *Georgia*
Fairfield University *Connecticut*
Fairleigh Dickinson University, Metropolitan Campus *New Jersey*
Fairmont State University *West Virginia*
Fayetteville State University *North Carolina*
Felician College *New Jersey*
Fitchburg State College *Massachusetts*
Florida Atlantic University *Florida*
Florida Gulf Coast University *Florida*
Florida Southern College *Florida*
Florida State University *Florida*
Fort Hays State University *Kansas*
Gannon University *Pennsylvania*
George Mason University *Virginia*
Georgetown University *District of Columbia*
Georgia Southern University *Georgia*
Georgia State University *Georgia*
Gonzaga University *Washington*
Goshen College *Indiana*
Graceland University *Iowa*
Grand Canyon University *Arizona*
Grand Valley State University *Michigan*
Grand View College *Iowa*
Gustavus Adolphus College *Minnesota*
Hampton University *Virginia*
Hardin-Simmons University *Texas*
Hartwick College *New York*
Holy Names University *California*
Humboldt State University *California*

Hunter College of the City University of New York *New York*
Husson College *Maine*
Idaho State University *Idaho*
Illinois State University *Illinois*
Illinois Wesleyan University *Illinois*
Indiana University Kokomo *Indiana*
Indiana University Northwest *Indiana*
Indiana University of Pennsylvania *Pennsylvania*
Indiana University-Purdue University Indianapolis *Indiana*
Indiana University South Bend *Indiana*
Indiana University Southeast *Indiana*
Indiana Wesleyan University *Indiana*
Jacksonville State University *Alabama*
Jacksonville University *Florida*
James Madison University *Virginia*
Jefferson College of Health Sciences *Virginia*
The Johns Hopkins University *Maryland*
Kennesaw State University *Georgia*
Kent State University *Ohio*
King College *Tennessee*
La Salle University *Pennsylvania*
Lakeview College of Nursing *Illinois*
Lees-McRae College *North Carolina*
Lehman College of the City University of New York *New York*
Lewis-Clark State College *Idaho*
Lewis University *Illinois*
Liberty University *Virginia*
Loma Linda University *California*
Long Island University, Brooklyn Campus *New York*
Long Island University, C.W. Post Campus *New York*
Louisiana College *Louisiana*
Louisiana State University Health Sciences Center *Louisiana*
Lourdes College *Ohio*
Loyola University Chicago *Illinois*
Luther College *Iowa*
Lynchburg College *Virginia*
MacMurray College *Illinois*
Malone College *Ohio*
Marian College of Fond du Lac *Wisconsin*
Marquette University *Wisconsin*
Marymount University *Virginia*
Maryville University of Saint Louis *Missouri*
McMurry University *Texas*
Medical University of South Carolina *South Carolina*
Mercer University *Georgia*
Mercy College *New York*
Mercy College of Health Sciences *Iowa*
Mesa State College *Colorado*
Messiah College *Pennsylvania*
Metropolitan State University *Minnesota*
Michigan State University *Michigan*
MidAmerica Nazarene University *Kansas*
Middle Tennessee State University *Tennessee*
Midwestern State University *Texas*
Milligan College *Tennessee*
Millikin University *Illinois*
Milwaukee School of Engineering *Wisconsin*
Minnesota State University Mankato *Minnesota*
Minnesota State University Moorhead *Minnesota*
Missouri State University *Missouri*
Missouri Western State University *Missouri*
Molloy College *New York*
Monmouth University *New Jersey*
Montana State University *Montana*
Moravian College *Pennsylvania*
Mount Mercy College *Iowa*
Mount Saint Mary College *New York*
Mount St. Mary's College *California*
Murray State University *Kentucky*
National University *California*
Nazareth College of Rochester *New York*
Nebraska Methodist College *Nebraska*
New Mexico State University *New Mexico*
Newman University *Kansas*
Nicholls State University *Louisiana*
North Dakota State University *North Dakota*
North Park University *Illinois*
Northeastern University *Massachusetts*
Northern Arizona University *Arizona*
Northern Illinois University *Illinois*
Northern Michigan University *Michigan*
Northwest Nazarene University *Idaho*
Northwest University *Washington*
Northwestern State University of Louisiana *Louisiana*
Oakland University *Michigan*
The Ohio State University *Ohio*
Ohio University *Ohio*
Oklahoma Wesleyan University *Oklahoma*
Old Dominion University *Virginia*
Olivet Nazarene University *Illinois*
Oregon Health & Science University *Oregon*
Otterbein College *Ohio*
Pace University *New York*
Pacific Lutheran University *Washington*
The Pennsylvania State University University Park Campus *Pennsylvania*
Pittsburg State University *Kansas*
Point Loma Nazarene University *California*
Purdue University *Indiana*
Queens University of Charlotte *North Carolina*
Radford University *Virginia*
Regis University *Colorado*
Research College of Nursing *Missouri*
The Richard Stockton College of New Jersey *New Jersey*
Rush University *Illinois*
Rutgers, The State University of New Jersey, Camden *New Jersey*
Rutgers, The State University of New Jersey, Newark *New Jersey*
Sacred Heart University *Connecticut*
St. Ambrose University *Iowa*
Saint Anselm College *New Hampshire*
Saint Anthony College of Nursing *Illinois*
Saint Francis University *Pennsylvania*
St. John Fisher College *New York*
Saint John's University *Minnesota*
Saint Joseph College *Connecticut*
Saint Joseph's College of Maine *Maine*
Saint Louis University *Missouri*
Saint Luke's College *Missouri*
Saint Mary's College of California *California*
St. Olaf College *Minnesota*
Saint Peter's College *New Jersey*
Saint Xavier University *Illinois*
Salem State College *Massachusetts*
Salisbury University *Maryland*
Samford University *Alabama*
Samuel Merritt College *California*
San Diego State University *California*
San Francisco State University *California*
San Jose State University *California*
Seattle Pacific University *Washington*
Seattle University *Washington*
Seton Hall University *New Jersey*
Shenandoah University *Virginia*
Simmons College *Massachusetts*
South Dakota State University *South Dakota*
Southeast Missouri State University *Missouri*
Southern Connecticut State University *Connecticut*
Southern Illinois University Edwardsville *Illinois*
Southern Nazarene University *Oklahoma*
Southern University and Agricultural and Mechanical College *Louisiana*
Southwestern College *Kansas*
Spalding University *Kentucky*
Spring Arbor University *Michigan*
Spring Hill College *Alabama*
State University of New York at Binghamton *New York*
State University of New York at Buffalo *New York*
State University of New York College at Brockport *New York*
State University of New York Downstate Medical Center *New York*
State University of New York Institute of Technology *New York*
State University of New York at New Paltz *New York*
State University of New York at Plattsburgh *New York*
State University of New York Upstate Medical University *New York*
Stony Brook University, State University of New York *New York*
Tabor College *Kansas*
Tarleton State University *Texas*
Temple University *Pennsylvania*
Tennessee Wesleyan College *Tennessee*
Texas A&M University-Corpus Christi *Texas*
Texas A&M University-Texarkana *Texas*
Texas Christian University *Texas*
Texas Woman's University *Texas*
Thomas Jefferson University *Pennsylvania*
Towson University *Maryland*
Trinity Christian College *Illinois*
Truman State University *Missouri*
Union College *Nebraska*
Union University *Tennessee*
The University of Alabama *Alabama*
The University of Alabama at Birmingham *Alabama*
The University of Alabama in Huntsville *Alabama*
The University of Arizona *Arizona*
University of Arkansas *Arkansas*
University of California, Los Angeles *California*
University of Central Arkansas *Arkansas*
University of Central Florida *Florida*
University of Cincinnati *Ohio*
University of Colorado at Colorado Springs *Colorado*
University of Florida *Florida*
University of Hawaii at Manoa *Hawaii*
University of Illinois at Chicago *Illinois*
University of the Incarnate Word *Texas*
University of Indianapolis *Indiana*
The University of Iowa *Iowa*
University of Kansas *Kansas*
University of Kentucky *Kentucky*
University of Louisiana at Monroe *Louisiana*
University of Louisville *Kentucky*
University of Maine *Maine*
University of Maine at Fort Kent *Maine*
University of Mary *North Dakota*
University of Mary Hardin-Baylor *Texas*
University of Massachusetts Amherst *Massachusetts*
University of Massachusetts Boston *Massachusetts*
University of Massachusetts Lowell *Massachusetts*
University of Memphis *Tennessee*
University of Michigan *Michigan*
University of Michigan-Flint *Michigan*
University of Minnesota, Twin Cities Campus *Minnesota*
University of Mississippi Medical Center *Mississippi*
University of Missouri-Columbia *Missouri*
University of Missouri-Kansas City *Missouri*
University of Missouri-St. Louis *Missouri*
University of Nebraska Medical Center *Nebraska*
University of Nevada, Reno *Nevada*
University of New Hampshire *New Hampshire*
University of New Mexico *New Mexico*
The University of North Carolina at Chapel Hill *North Carolina*
The University of North Carolina at Charlotte *North Carolina*
The University of North Carolina at Greensboro *North Carolina*
The University of North Carolina at Pembroke *North Carolina*
The University of North Carolina Wilmington *North Carolina*
University of North Dakota *North Dakota*
University of Northern Colorado *Colorado*
University of Pennsylvania *Pennsylvania*
University of Pittsburgh *Pennsylvania*
University of Portland *Oregon*
University of Puerto Rico, Medical Sciences Campus *Puerto Rico*
University of Rhode Island *Rhode Island*
University of Saint Francis *Indiana*
University of San Diego *California*
University of San Francisco *California*
The University of Scranton *Pennsylvania*
University of South Alabama *Alabama*
University of South Carolina *South Carolina*
University of South Florida *Florida*
University of Southern California *California*
University of Southern Indiana *Indiana*
University of Southern Mississippi *Mississippi*
The University of Tennessee at Chattanooga *Tennessee*
The University of Texas at Austin *Texas*
The University of Texas at El Paso *Texas*

The University of Texas Health Science Center at Houston *Texas*
The University of Texas Health Science Center at San Antonio *Texas*
The University of Texas Medical Branch *Texas*
The University of Texas-Pan American *Texas*
The University of Texas at San Antonio *Texas*
The University of Texas at Tyler *Texas*
University of Utah *Utah*
University of Virginia *Virginia*
The University of Virginia's College at Wise *Virginia*
University of Washington *Washington*
University of West Florida *Florida*
University of West Georgia *Georgia*
University of Wisconsin-Eau Claire *Wisconsin*
University of Wisconsin-Madison *Wisconsin*
University of Wisconsin-Milwaukee *Wisconsin*
University of Wisconsin-Oshkosh *Wisconsin*
University of Wyoming *Wyoming*
Ursuline College *Ohio*
Valdosta State University *Georgia*
Valparaiso University *Indiana*
Villanova University *Pennsylvania*
Viterbo University *Wisconsin*
Washburn University *Kansas*
Washington State University *Washington*
Wayne State University *Michigan*
Waynesburg College *Pennsylvania*
West Chester University of Pennsylvania *Pennsylvania*
West Suburban College of Nursing *Illinois*
West Texas A&M University *Texas*
West Virginia University *West Virginia*
Western Carolina University *North Carolina*
Western Connecticut State University *Connecticut*
Western Kentucky University *Kentucky*
Western Michigan University *Michigan*
Westminster College *Utah*
Wheeling Jesuit University *West Virginia*
Whitworth College *Washington*
Wichita State University *Kansas*
Wilkes University *Pennsylvania*
William Jewell College *Missouri*
William Paterson University of New Jersey *New Jersey*
Wilmington College *Delaware*
Winona State University *Minnesota*
Wright State University *Ohio*
Xavier University *Ohio*
Yale University *Connecticut*

American Association of Family and ConsumerAmerican Association of Family and Consumer Sciences (AAFCS)

Abilene Christian University *Texas*
Alabama Agricultural and Mechanical University *Alabama*
Alcorn State University *Mississippi*
Appalachian State University *North Carolina*
Ashland University *Ohio*
Auburn University *Alabama*
Ball State University *Indiana*
Baylor University *Texas*
Berea College *Kentucky*
Berry College *Georgia*
Bowling Green State University *Ohio*
Bradley University *Illinois*
California State University, Fresno *California*
California State University, Long Beach *California*
California State University, Northridge *California*
Carson-Newman College *Tennessee*
Central Missouri State University *Missouri*
Chadron State College *Nebraska*
College of Saint Elizabeth *New Jersey*
Colorado State University *Colorado*
Concordia College *Minnesota*
Cornell University *New York*
Delta State University *Mississippi*
East Carolina University *North Carolina*
East Tennessee State University *Tennessee*
Eastern Illinois University *Illinois*
Eastern Kentucky University *Kentucky*
Eastern New Mexico University *New Mexico*
Fairmont State University *West Virginia*
Florida State University *Florida*
Fontbonne University *Missouri*
Fort Valley State University *Georgia*
Framingham State College *Massachusetts*
Georgia Southern University *Georgia*
Harding University *Arkansas*
Henderson State University *Arkansas*
Illinois State University *Illinois*
Indiana State University *Indiana*
Indiana University of Pennsylvania *Pennsylvania*
Iowa State University of Science and Technology *Iowa*
Jacksonville State University *Alabama*
Kansas State University *Kansas*
Lamar University *Texas*
Liberty University *Virginia*
Louisiana State University and Agricultural and Mechanical College *Louisiana*
Louisiana Tech University *Louisiana*
Marshall University *West Virginia*
Marygrove College *Michigan*
Marywood University *Pennsylvania*
The Master's College and Seminary *California*
McNeese State University *Louisiana*
Mercyhurst College *Pennsylvania*
Meredith College *North Carolina*
Michigan State University *Michigan*
Middle Tennessee State University *Tennessee*
Mississippi College *Mississippi*
Mississippi State University *Mississippi*
Missouri State University *Missouri*
Montana State University *Montana*
Montclair State University *New Jersey*
Morehead State University *Kentucky*
Murray State University *Kentucky*
New Mexico State University *New Mexico*
Nicholls State University *Louisiana*
North Carolina Agricultural and Technical State University *North Carolina*
North Carolina Central University *North Carolina*
North Dakota State University *North Dakota*
Northern Illinois University *Illinois*
Northwest Missouri State University *Missouri*
Northwestern State University of Louisiana *Louisiana*
The Ohio State University *Ohio*
Ohio University *Ohio*
Olivet Nazarene University *Illinois*
Oregon State University *Oregon*
Ouachita Baptist University *Arkansas*
Pittsburg State University *Kansas*
Point Loma Nazarene University *California*
Purdue University *Indiana*
Queens College of the City University of New York *New York*
Saint Joseph College *Connecticut*
St. Olaf College *Minnesota*
Sam Houston State University *Texas*
Samford University *Alabama*
San Francisco State University *California*
Seattle Pacific University *Washington*
Seton Hill University *Pennsylvania*
South Carolina State University *South Carolina*
South Dakota State University *South Dakota*
Southern University and Agricultural and Mechanical College *Louisiana*
Southern Utah University *Utah*
State University of New York College at Oneonta *New York*
Stephen F. Austin State University *Texas*
Tarleton State University *Texas*
Tennessee State University *Tennessee*
Tennessee Technological University *Tennessee*
Texas A&M University *Texas*
Texas State University-San Marcos *Texas*
Texas Tech University *Texas*
Texas Woman's University *Texas*
Tuskegee University *Alabama*
The University of Akron *Ohio*
The University of Alabama *Alabama*
The University of Arizona *Arizona*
University of Arkansas *Arkansas*
University of Arkansas at Pine Bluff *Arkansas*
University of Central Arkansas *Arkansas*
University of Florida *Florida*
University of Georgia *Georgia*
University of Idaho *Idaho*
University of Kentucky *Kentucky*
University of Louisiana at Lafayette *Louisiana*
University of Louisiana at Monroe *Louisiana*
University of Maryland Eastern Shore *Maryland*
University of Massachusetts Amherst *Massachusetts*
University of Memphis *Tennessee*
University of Mississippi *Mississippi*
University of Missouri-Columbia *Missouri*
University of Montevallo *Alabama*
University of Nebraska at Kearney *Nebraska*
University of Nebraska-Lincoln *Nebraska*
University of New Mexico *New Mexico*
University of North Alabama *Alabama*
The University of North Carolina at Greensboro *North Carolina*
University of North Texas *Texas*
University of Northern Iowa *Iowa*
University of Southern Mississippi *Mississippi*
The University of Tennessee *Tennessee*
The University of Tennessee at Martin *Tennessee*
University of Wisconsin-Madison *Wisconsin*
University of Wyoming *Wyoming*
Virginia Polytechnic Institute and State University *Virginia*
Wayne State College *Nebraska*
West Virginia Wesleyan College *West Virginia*
Western Carolina University *North Carolina*
Western Illinois University *Illinois*
Western Kentucky University *Kentucky*
Western Michigan University *Michigan*
Youngstown State University *Ohio*

American Association for Marriage and FamilyAmerican Association for Marriage and Family Therapy (AAMFT)

Abilene Christian University *Texas*
Alliant International University *California*
Appalachian State University *North Carolina*
Auburn University *Alabama*
Brigham Young University *Utah*
Central Connecticut State University *Connecticut*
Colorado State University *Colorado*
Converse College *South Carolina*
Drexel University *Pennsylvania*
East Carolina University *North Carolina*
Fairfield University *Connecticut*
Florida State University *Florida*
Friends University *Kansas*
Gonzaga University *Washington*
Harding University *Arkansas*
Indiana State University *Indiana*
Iona College *New York*
Iowa State University of Science and Technology *Iowa*
Kansas State University *Kansas*
Loma Linda University *California*
Mercer University *Georgia*
Michigan State University *Michigan*
North Dakota State University *North Dakota*
Northern Illinois University *Illinois*
Northwestern University *Illinois*
Nova Southeastern University *Florida*
The Ohio State University *Ohio*
Oklahoma State University *Oklahoma*
Pacific Lutheran University *Washington*
Purdue University *Indiana*
Purdue University Calumet *Indiana*
Saint Joseph College *Connecticut*
St. Mary's University of San Antonio *Texas*
Seattle Pacific University *Washington*
Seton Hall University *New Jersey*
Seton Hill University *Pennsylvania*
Southern Connecticut State University *Connecticut*
Syracuse University *New York*
Texas Tech University *Texas*
The University of Akron *Ohio*
University of Connecticut *Connecticut*
University of Georgia *Georgia*
University of Guelph *Ontario*
University of Houston-Clear Lake *Texas*
University of Kentucky *Kentucky*
University of Louisiana at Monroe *Louisiana*
University of Louisville *Kentucky*
University of Maryland, College Park *Maryland*
University of Massachusetts Boston *Massachusetts*

University of Minnesota, Twin Cities Campus *Minnesota*
University of Nebraska-Lincoln *Nebraska*
University of New Hampshire *New Hampshire*
University of Rhode Island *Rhode Island*
University of Rochester *New York*
University of San Diego *California*
University of Southern Mississippi *Mississippi*
The University of Winnipeg *Manitoba*
University of Wisconsin-Stout *Wisconsin*
Utah State University *Utah*
Valdosta State University *Georgia*
Virginia Polytechnic Institute and State University *Virginia*

American Association of Medical Assistants' EndowmentAmerican Association of Medical Assistants' Endowment (AAMAE)

Alpena Community College *Michigan*
Arkansas Tech University *Arkansas*
ASA Institute, The College of Advanced Technology *New York*
Baker College of Auburn Hills *Michigan*
Baker College of Cadillac *Michigan*
Baker College of Clinton Township *Michigan*
Baker College of Flint *Michigan*
Baker College of Jackson *Michigan*
Baker College of Muskegon *Michigan*
Baker College of Owosso *Michigan*
Baker College of Port Huron *Michigan*
Beal College *Maine*
Belmont Technical College *Ohio*
Bergen Community College *New Jersey*
Berks Technical Institute *Pennsylvania*
Blair College *Colorado*
Bossier Parish Community College *Louisiana*
Briarwood College *Connecticut*
Broome Community College *New York*
Brown Mackie College-Akron *Ohio*
Brown Mackie College-Cincinnati *Ohio*
Brown Mackie College-South Bend *Indiana*
Bryant and Stratton College *Wisconsin*
Bryant and Stratton College (Albany) *New York*
Bryant and Stratton College, Buffalo Campus *New York*
Bryant and Stratton College (Rochester-Greece Campus) *New York*
Bryant and Stratton College (Rochester-Henrietta Campus) *New York*
Bryant and Stratton College (Syracuse) *New York*
The Bryman School *Arizona*
Bucks County Community College *Pennsylvania*
Cabrillo College *California*
Capital Community College *Connecticut*
Career Training Academy (Monroeville) *Pennsylvania*
Career Training Academy (New Kensington) *Pennsylvania*
Central Community College-Hastings Campus *Nebraska*
Central Pennsylvania College *Pennsylvania*
Central Piedmont Community College *North Carolina*
Chabot College *California*
Charles R. Drew University of Medicine and Science *California*
Cincinnati State Technical and Community College *Ohio*
Cisco Junior College *Texas*
City College of San Francisco *California*
Clark College *Washington*
Cleveland State Community College *Tennessee*
College of Southern Idaho *Idaho*
Colorado Technical University Sioux Falls Campus *South Dakota*
Columbus State Community College *Ohio*
Community College of Allegheny County *Pennsylvania*
Community College of Philadelphia *Pennsylvania*
Cosumnes River College (Sacramento) *California*
Dakota County Technical College *Minnesota*
Dalton State College *Georgia*
Davis College *Ohio*
De Anza College *California*
Delaware County Community College *Pennsylvania*
Delaware Technical & Community College, Stanton/Wilmington Campus *Delaware*
Duluth Business University *Minnesota*
East Tennessee State University *Tennessee*
Eastern Idaho Technical College *Idaho*
Eastern Kentucky University *Kentucky*
Eastern New Mexico University-Roswell *New Mexico*
El Paso Community College *Texas*
Erie Community College *New York*
Flathead Valley Community College *Montana*
Florida Metropolitan University-Brandon Campus *Florida*
Florida Metropolitan University-Lakeland Campus *Florida*
Florida Metropolitan University-Melbourne Campus *Florida*
Florida Metropolitan University-Pinellas Campus *Florida*
Florida Metropolitan University-South Orlando Campus *Florida*
Florida Metropolitan University-Tampa Campus *Florida*
Forsyth Technical Community College *North Carolina*
Gaston College *North Carolina*
George C. Wallace Community College *Alabama*
Globe College *Minnesota*
Goodwin College *Connecticut*
Guam Community College *Guam*
Guilford Technical Community College *North Carolina*
Hamilton College (Cedar Rapids) *Iowa*
Hamilton College-Lincoln *Nebraska*
Hamilton College-Omaha *Nebraska*
Haywood Community College *North Carolina*
Heald College-Honolulu *Hawaii*
Hesser College *New Hampshire*
Highline Community College *Washington*
Hinds Community College *Mississippi*
Hocking College *Ohio*
Hudson County Community College *New Jersey*
Huntington Junior College *West Virginia*
Idaho State University *Idaho*
Indian River Community College *Florida*
Indiana Business College (Evansville) *Indiana*
International Business College (Fort Wayne) *Indiana*
International College *Florida*
Iowa Lakes Community College *Iowa*
Ivy Tech Community College-Central Indiana *Indiana*
Ivy Tech Community College-Columbus *Indiana*
Ivy Tech Community College-East Central *Indiana*
Ivy Tech Community College-Kokomo *Indiana*
Ivy Tech Community College-Lafayette *Indiana*
Ivy Tech Community College-North Central *Indiana*
Ivy Tech Community College-Northeast *Indiana*
Ivy Tech Community College-Northwest *Indiana*
Ivy Tech Community College-Southern Indiana *Indiana*
Ivy Tech Community College-Southwest *Indiana*
Ivy Tech Community College-Wabash Valley *Indiana*
Ivy Tech Community College-Whitewater *Indiana*
Jackson Community College *Michigan*
James A. Rhodes State College *Ohio*
James Sprunt Community College *North Carolina*
Jefferson Community College *Ohio*
Kalamazoo Valley Community College *Michigan*
Kapiolani Community College *Hawaii*
Kaplan University *Iowa*
Keiser College (Daytona Beach) *Florida*
Kilgore College *Texas*
Kirkwood Community College *Iowa*
Kirtland Community College *Michigan*
Lac Courte Oreilles Ojibwa Community College *Wisconsin*
Lake Area Technical Institute *South Dakota*
Lake Washington Technical College *Washington*
Laurel Business Institute *Pennsylvania*
LDS Business College *Utah*
Lehigh Carbon Community College *Pennsylvania*
Lenoir Community College *North Carolina*
Linn-Benton Community College *Oregon*
Lorain County Community College *Ohio*
Lower Columbia College *Washington*
Macomb Community College *Michigan*
Marshall Community and Technical College *West Virginia*
Martin Community College *North Carolina*
Miami-Jacobs College *Ohio*
Middlesex Community College *Massachusetts*
Midstate College *Illinois*
Miller-Motte Technical College *Tennessee*
Minnesota School of Business-Richfield *Minnesota*
Minnesota West Community and Technical College *Minnesota*
Mitchell Community College *North Carolina*
Mitchell Technical Institute *South Dakota*
Modesto Junior College *California*
Montana State University-Great Falls College of Technology *Montana*
Montgomery Community College *North Carolina*
Mount Aloysius College *Pennsylvania*
Mt. Hood Community College *Oregon*
Mount Wachusett Community College *Massachusetts*
Mountain State University *West Virginia*
Mountain West College *Utah*
National American University (Rapid City) *South Dakota*
National College of Business & Technology (Bluefield) *Virginia*
National College of Business & Technology (Bristol) *Tennessee*
National College of Business & Technology (Charlottesville) *Virginia*
National College of Business & Technology (Danville) *Virginia*
National College of Business & Technology (Danville) *Kentucky*
National College of Business & Technology (Florence) *Kentucky*
National College of Business & Technology (Harrisonburg) *Virginia*
National College of Business & Technology (Lexington) *Kentucky*
National College of Business & Technology (Louisville) *Kentucky*
National College of Business & Technology (Lynchburg) *Virginia*
National College of Business & Technology (Nashville) *Tennessee*
National College of Business & Technology (Pikeville) *Kentucky*
National College of Business & Technology (Richmond) *Kentucky*
National College of Business & Technology (Salem) *Virginia*
New England Institute of Technology at Palm Beach *Florida*
New Hampshire Community Technical College, Manchester/Stratham *New Hampshire*
Niagara County Community College *New York*
North Seattle Community College *Washington*
Northeast Mississippi Community College *Mississippi*
Northeast State Technical Community College *Tennessee*
Northwest Technical College *Minnesota*
Northwestern Business College *Illinois*
Northwestern Connecticut Community College *Connecticut*
Northwestern Technical College *Georgia*
Oakland Community College *Michigan*
Ohio University-Lancaster *Ohio*
Ohio Valley College of Technology *Ohio*
Pamlico Community College *North Carolina*
Parks College (Denver) *Colorado*
Penn Commercial Business and Technical School *Pennsylvania*
Pitt Community College *North Carolina*
Presentation College *South Dakota*
Quinebaug Valley Community College *Connecticut*
Quinsigamond Community College *Massachusetts*
Red Rocks Community College *Colorado*
RETS Tech Center *Ohio*
Robert Morris College *Illinois*
Rochester Community and Technical College *Minnesota*
Rockford Business College *Illinois*
St. Vincent's College *Connecticut*
San Antonio College *Texas*

San Diego Mesa College *California*
Schuylkill Institute of Business and Technology *Pennsylvania*
Sinclair Community College *Ohio*
South College *Tennessee*
South Piedmont Community College *North Carolina*
South Puget Sound Community College *Washington*
South University *Georgia*
South University *Alabama*
South University (West Palm Beach) *Florida*
Southeastern Community College, North Campus *Iowa*
Southern State Community College *Ohio*
Southwestern Illinois College *Illinois*
Spokane Community College *Washington*
Springfield College *Missouri*
Springfield Technical Community College *Massachusetts*
Stanly Community College *North Carolina*
Stark State College of Technology *Ohio*
Stautzenberger College *Ohio*
Stevens-Henager College *Utah*
Suffolk County Community College *New York*
Sullivan University *Kentucky*
Trocaire College *New York*
Tulsa Community College *Oklahoma*
The University of Akron *Ohio*
University of Alaska Anchorage *Alaska*
University of Alaska Fairbanks *Alaska*
University of Northwestern Ohio *Ohio*
The University of Toledo *Ohio*
Utah Career College *Utah*
Wallace State Community College *Alabama*
Wayne Community College *North Carolina*
West Valley College *California*
Western Career College (Pleasant Hill) *California*
Western Career College (Sacramento) *California*
Western Career College (San Leandro) *California*
Western Piedmont Community College *North Carolina*
Westwood College-Denver North *Colorado*
Whatcom Community College *Washington*
William Rainey Harper College *Illinois*
Wingate University *North Carolina*
Youngstown State University *Ohio*
Zane State College *Ohio*

American Association of Nurse AnesthetistsAmerican Association of Nurse Anesthetists (AANA)

Arkansas State University *Arkansas*
Barry University *Florida*
Boston College *Massachusetts*
Bradley University *Illinois*
California State University, Fullerton *California*
Case Western Reserve University *Ohio*
Central Connecticut State University *Connecticut*
DePaul University *Illinois*
Drexel University *Pennsylvania*
Duke University *North Carolina*
East Carolina University *North Carolina*
Florida Gulf Coast University *Florida*
Florida International University *Florida*
Gannon University *Pennsylvania*
Georgetown University *District of Columbia*
Gonzaga University *Washington*
Inter American University of Puerto Rico, Arecibo Campus *Puerto Rico*
La Roche College *Pennsylvania*
La Salle University *Pennsylvania*
Louisiana State University Health Sciences Center *Louisiana*
Marshall University *West Virginia*
Medical College of Georgia *Georgia*
Medical University of South Carolina *South Carolina*
Midwestern University, Glendale Campus *Arizona*
Missouri State University *Missouri*
Mount Marty College *South Dakota*
Mountain State University *West Virginia*
Murray State University *Kentucky*
Newman University *Kansas*
Northeastern University *Massachusetts*
Oakland University *Michigan*
Old Dominion University *Virginia*
Rush University *Illinois*
Saint Joseph's University *Pennsylvania*
Saint Mary's University of Minnesota *Minnesota*
Samford University *Alabama*
Samuel Merritt College *California*
Southern Connecticut State University *Connecticut*
Southern Illinois University Edwardsville *Illinois*
State University of New York at Buffalo *New York*
State University of New York Downstate Medical Center *New York*
Texas Christian University *Texas*
Texas Wesleyan University *Texas*
The University of Akron *Ohio*
The University of Alabama at Birmingham *Alabama*
University of Cincinnati *Ohio*
University of Detroit Mercy *Michigan*
The University of Iowa *Iowa*
University of Kansas *Kansas*
University of Michigan-Flint *Michigan*
University of Minnesota, Twin Cities Campus *Minnesota*
University of Missouri-Kansas City *Missouri*
University of New England *Maine*
The University of North Carolina at Charlotte *North Carolina*
The University of North Carolina at Greensboro *North Carolina*
University of North Dakota *North Dakota*
University of Pennsylvania *Pennsylvania*
University of Pittsburgh *Pennsylvania*
University of Puerto Rico, Medical Sciences Campus *Puerto Rico*
The University of Scranton *Pennsylvania*
University of South Carolina *South Carolina*
University of Southern California *California*
The University of Tennessee *Tennessee*
The University of Tennessee at Chattanooga *Tennessee*
The University of Texas Health Science Center at Houston *Texas*
University of Wisconsin-La Crosse *Wisconsin*
Villanova University *Pennsylvania*
Virginia Commonwealth University *Virginia*
Wake Forest University *North Carolina*
Wayne State University *Michigan*
Webster University *Missouri*
Xavier University of Louisiana *Louisiana*
Youngstown State University *Ohio*

American Bar AssociationAmerican Bar Association (ABA)

American University *District of Columbia*
Arizona State University *Arizona*
Barry University *Florida*
Baylor University *Texas*
Boston College *Massachusetts*
Boston University *Massachusetts*
Brigham Young University *Utah*
Campbell University *North Carolina*
Capital University *Ohio*
Case Western Reserve University *Ohio*
The Catholic University of America *District of Columbia*
Chapman University *California*
Cleveland State University *Ohio*
The College of William and Mary *Virginia*
Cornell University *New York*
Creighton University *Nebraska*
DePaul University *Illinois*
Drake University *Iowa*
Duke University *North Carolina*
Duquesne University *Pennsylvania*
Emory University *Georgia*
Florida Agricultural and Mechanical University *Florida*
Florida International University *Florida*
Florida State University *Florida*
Fordham University *New York*
George Mason University *Virginia*
The George Washington University *District of Columbia*
Georgetown University *District of Columbia*
Georgia State University *Georgia*
Golden Gate University *California*
Gonzaga University *Washington*
Hamline University *Minnesota*
Harvard University *Massachusetts*
Hofstra University *New York*
Howard University *District of Columbia*
Illinois Institute of Technology *Illinois*
Inter American University of Puerto Rico, Metropolitan Campus *Puerto Rico*
Lewis & Clark College *Oregon*
Louisiana State University and Agricultural and Mechanical College *Louisiana*
Loyola Marymount University *California*
Loyola University Chicago *Illinois*
Loyola University New Orleans *Louisiana*
Marquette University *Wisconsin*
Mercer University *Georgia*
Mississippi College *Mississippi*
New York University *New York*
North Carolina Central University *North Carolina*
Northeastern University *Massachusetts*
Northern Illinois University *Illinois*
Northern Kentucky University *Kentucky*
Northwestern University *Illinois*
Nova Southeastern University *Florida*
Ohio Northern University *Ohio*
The Ohio State University *Ohio*
Oklahoma City University *Oklahoma*
Pace University *New York*
Pepperdine University *California*
Pontifical Catholic University of Puerto Rico *Puerto Rico*
Quinnipiac University *Connecticut*
Regent University *Virginia*
Roger Williams University *Rhode Island*
Rutgers, The State University of New Jersey, Camden *New Jersey*
Rutgers, The State University of New Jersey, Newark *New Jersey*
St. John's University *New York*
Saint Louis University *Missouri*
St. Mary's University of San Antonio *Texas*
St. Thomas University *Florida*
Samford University *Alabama*
Santa Clara University *California*
Seattle University *Washington*
Seton Hall University *New Jersey*
Southern Illinois University Carbondale *Illinois*
Southern Methodist University *Texas*
Southern University and Agricultural and Mechanical College *Louisiana*
Stanford University *California*
State University of New York at Buffalo *New York*
Stetson University *Florida*
Suffolk University *Massachusetts*
Syracuse University *New York*
Temple University *Pennsylvania*
Texas Southern University *Texas*
Texas Tech University *Texas*
Texas Wesleyan University *Texas*
Touro College *New York*
Tulane University *Louisiana*
The University of Akron *Ohio*
The University of Alabama *Alabama*
The University of Arizona *Arizona*
University of Arkansas *Arkansas*
University of Arkansas at Little Rock *Arkansas*
University of Baltimore *Maryland*
University of California, Berkeley *California*
University of California, Davis *California*
University of California, Los Angeles *California*
University of Chicago *Illinois*
University of Cincinnati *Ohio*
University of Colorado at Boulder *Colorado*
University of Connecticut *Connecticut*
University of Dayton *Ohio*
University of Denver *Colorado*
University of Detroit Mercy *Michigan*
University of the District of Columbia *District of Columbia*
University of Florida *Florida*
University of Georgia *Georgia*
University of Hawaii at Manoa *Hawaii*
University of Houston *Texas*
University of Idaho *Idaho*
University of Illinois at Urbana-Champaign *Illinois*
The University of Iowa *Iowa*
University of Kansas *Kansas*
University of Kentucky *Kentucky*
University of Louisville *Kentucky*
University of Memphis *Tennessee*

University of Miami *Florida*
University of Michigan *Michigan*
University of Minnesota, Twin Cities Campus *Minnesota*
University of Mississippi *Mississippi*
University of Missouri-Columbia *Missouri*
University of Missouri-Kansas City *Missouri*
The University of Montana-Missoula *Montana*
University of Nebraska-Lincoln *Nebraska*
University of Nevada, Las Vegas *Nevada*
University of New Mexico *New Mexico*
The University of North Carolina at Chapel Hill *North Carolina*
University of North Dakota *North Dakota*
University of Notre Dame *Indiana*
University of Oklahoma *Oklahoma*
University of Oregon *Oregon*
University of the Pacific *California*
University of Pennsylvania *Pennsylvania*
University of Pittsburgh *Pennsylvania*
University of Puerto Rico, Río Piedras *Puerto Rico*
University of Richmond *Virginia*
University of St. Thomas *Minnesota*
University of San Diego *California*
University of San Francisco *California*
University of South Carolina *South Carolina*
The University of South Dakota *South Dakota*
University of Southern California *California*
University of Southern Maine *Maine*
The University of Tennessee *Tennessee*
The University of Texas at Austin *Texas*
The University of Toledo *Ohio*
University of Tulsa *Oklahoma*
University of Utah *Utah*
University of Virginia *Virginia*
University of Washington *Washington*
University of Wisconsin-Madison *Wisconsin*
University of Wyoming *Wyoming*
Valparaiso University *Indiana*
Vanderbilt University *Tennessee*
Villanova University *Pennsylvania*
Wake Forest University *North Carolina*
Washburn University *Kansas*
Washington and Lee University *Virginia*
Washington University in St. Louis *Missouri*
Wayne State University *Michigan*
West Virginia University *West Virginia*
Western New England College *Massachusetts*
Whittier College *California*
Widener University *Pennsylvania*
Willamette University *Oregon*
Yale University *Connecticut*
Yeshiva University *New York*

American Board of Funeral Service EducationAmerican Board of Funeral Service Education (ABFSE)

Amarillo College *Texas*
American Academy McAllister Institute of Funeral Service *New York*
American River College *California*
Arapahoe Community College *Colorado*
Arkansas State University-Mountain Home *Arkansas*
Bishop State Community College *Alabama*
Briarwood College *Connecticut*
Carl Sandburg College *Illinois*
Cincinnati College of Mortuary Science *Ohio*
City Colleges of Chicago, Malcolm X College *Illinois*
Commonwealth Institute of Funeral Service *Texas*
The Community College of Baltimore County *Maryland*
Cypress College *California*
Dallas Institute of Funeral Service *Texas*
Delgado Community College *Louisiana*
East Mississippi Community College *Mississippi*
Fayetteville Technical Community College *North Carolina*
Florida Community College at Jacksonville *Florida*
Gupton-Jones College of Funeral Service *Georgia*
Hudson Valley Community College *New York*
Jefferson State Community College *Alabama*
John A. Gupton College *Tennessee*
John Tyler Community College *Virginia*
Kansas City Kansas Community College *Kansas*
Mercer County Community College *New Jersey*
Mesa Community College *Arizona*
Miami Dade College *Florida*
Mid-America College of Funeral Service *Indiana*
Milwaukee Area Technical College *Wisconsin*
Mississippi Gulf Coast Community College *Mississippi*
Mt. Hood Community College *Oregon*
Mount Ida College *Massachusetts*
Nassau Community College *New York*
Norfolk State University *Virginia*
Northampton County Area Community College *Pennsylvania*
Northwest Mississippi Community College *Mississippi*
Ogeechee Technical College *Georgia*
Piedmont Technical College *South Carolina*
Pittsburgh Institute of Mortuary Science, Incorporated *Pennsylvania*
St. Louis Community College at Forest Park *Missouri*
St. Petersburg College *Florida*
San Antonio College *Texas*
Simmons Institute of Funeral Service *New York*
Southern Illinois University Carbondale *Illinois*
State University of New York College of Technology at Canton *New York*
University of Arkansas Community College at Hope *Arkansas*
University of Central Oklahoma *Oklahoma*
University of the District of Columbia *District of Columbia*
University of Minnesota, Twin Cities Campus *Minnesota*
Vincennes University *Indiana*
Wayne State University *Michigan*
Worsham College of Mortuary Science *Illinois*

American College of Nurse-MidwivesAmerican College of Nurse-Midwives (ACNM)

Boston University *Massachusetts*
California State University, Fullerton *California*
Case Western Reserve University *Ohio*
Charles R. Drew University of Medicine and Science *California*
East Carolina University *North Carolina*
Emory University *Georgia*
Georgetown University *District of Columbia*
Marquette University *Wisconsin*
Medical University of South Carolina *South Carolina*
New York University *New York*
The Ohio State University *Ohio*
Oregon Health & Science University *Oregon*
Philadelphia University *Pennsylvania*
San Diego State University *California*
Shenandoah University *Virginia*
State University of New York Downstate Medical Center *New York*
Stony Brook University, State University of New York *New York*
University of Cincinnati *Ohio*
University of Florida *Florida*
University of Illinois at Chicago *Illinois*
University of Indianapolis *Indiana*
University of Kansas *Kansas*
University of Miami *Florida*
University of Michigan *Michigan*
University of Minnesota, Twin Cities Campus *Minnesota*
University of New Mexico *New Mexico*
University of Pennsylvania *Pennsylvania*
University of Puerto Rico, Medical Sciences Campus *Puerto Rico*
University of Rhode Island *Rhode Island*
The University of Texas at El Paso *Texas*
The University of Texas Medical Branch *Texas*
The University of Texas Southwestern Medical Center at Dallas *Texas*
University of Utah *Utah*
University of Washington *Washington*
Vanderbilt University *Tennessee*
Wayne State University *Michigan*
Yale University *Connecticut*

American Council for Construction EducationAmerican Council for Construction Education (ACCE)

Arizona State University *Arizona*
Auburn University *Alabama*
Boise State University *Idaho*
Bowling Green State University *Ohio*
Bradley University *Illinois*
Brigham Young University *Utah*
California Polytechnic State University, San Luis Obispo *California*
California State University, Chico *California*
California State University, Fresno *California*
California State University, Sacramento *California*
Central Connecticut State University *Connecticut*
Central Missouri State University *Missouri*
Central New Mexico Community College *New Mexico*
Central Washington University *Washington*
Cincinnati State Technical and Community College *Ohio*
Clemson University *South Carolina*
Colorado State University *Colorado*
Columbus State Community College *Ohio*
East Carolina University *North Carolina*
Eastern Kentucky University *Kentucky*
Eastern Michigan University *Michigan*
Ferris State University *Michigan*
Florida International University *Florida*
Georgia Institute of Technology *Georgia*
Georgia Southern University *Georgia*
Hudson Valley Community College *New York*
Indiana State University *Indiana*
Jefferson State Community College *Alabama*
John A. Logan College *Illinois*
John Brown University *Arkansas*
Kansas State University *Kansas*
Louisiana State University and Agricultural and Mechanical College *Louisiana*
Michigan State University *Michigan*
Milwaukee School of Engineering *Wisconsin*
Minnesota State University Moorhead *Minnesota*
North Carolina Agricultural and Technical State University *North Carolina*
North Dakota State University *North Dakota*
North Lake College *Texas*
Northern Arizona University *Arizona*
Northern Kentucky University *Kentucky*
Oregon State University *Oregon*
Purdue University *Indiana*
Roger Williams University *Rhode Island*
Santa Fe Community College *Florida*
Southern Illinois University Edwardsville *Illinois*
Southern Polytechnic State University *Georgia*
State University of New York College of Technology at Alfred *New York*
State University of New York College of Technology at Delhi *New York*
Texas A&M University *Texas*
University of Arkansas at Little Rock *Arkansas*
University of Cincinnati *Ohio*
University of Florida *Florida*
University of Louisiana at Monroe *Louisiana*
University of Maryland Eastern Shore *Maryland*
University of Nebraska-Lincoln *Nebraska*
University of Nevada, Las Vegas *Nevada*
University of New Mexico *New Mexico*
University of North Florida *Florida*
University of Oklahoma *Oklahoma*
University of Southern Mississippi *Mississippi*
University of Washington *Washington*
University of Wisconsin-Stout *Wisconsin*
Virginia Polytechnic Institute and State University *Virginia*
Washington State University *Washington*
Wentworth Institute of Technology *Massachusetts*

American Council on Pharmaceutical EducationAmerican Council on Pharmaceutical Education (ACPhE)

Albany College of Pharmacy of Union University *New York*
Auburn University *Alabama*

Butler University *Indiana*
Campbell University *North Carolina*
Creighton University *Nebraska*
Drake University *Iowa*
Duquesne University *Pennsylvania*
Ferris State University *Michigan*
Florida Agricultural and Mechanical University *Florida*
Hampton University *Virginia*
Howard University *District of Columbia*
Idaho State University *Idaho*
Loma Linda University *California*
Long Island University, Brooklyn Campus *New York*
Massachusetts College of Pharmacy and Health Sciences *Massachusetts*
Medical University of South Carolina *South Carolina*
Mercer University *Georgia*
Midwestern University, Glendale Campus *Arizona*
North Dakota State University *North Dakota*
Northeastern University *Massachusetts*
Nova Southeastern University *Florida*
Ohio Northern University *Ohio*
The Ohio State University *Ohio*
Oregon State University *Oregon*
Palm Beach Atlantic University *Florida*
Purdue University *Indiana*
Rutgers, The State University of New Jersey, New Brunswick/Piscataway *New Jersey*
St. John's University *New York*
St. Louis College of Pharmacy *Missouri*
Samford University *Alabama*
Shenandoah University *Virginia*
South Dakota State University *South Dakota*
South University *Georgia*
Southern Illinois University Edwardsville *Illinois*
Southwestern Oklahoma State University *Oklahoma*
State University of New York at Buffalo *New York*
Temple University *Pennsylvania*
Texas Southern University *Texas*
The University of Arizona *Arizona*
University of Arkansas for Medical Sciences *Arkansas*
University of California, San Diego *California*
University of Cincinnati *Ohio*
University of Connecticut *Connecticut*
University of Florida *Florida*
University of Georgia *Georgia*
University of Houston *Texas*
University of Illinois at Chicago *Illinois*
The University of Iowa *Iowa*
University of Kansas *Kansas*
University of Kentucky *Kentucky*
University of Louisiana at Monroe *Louisiana*
University of Michigan *Michigan*
University of Minnesota, Twin Cities Campus *Minnesota*
University of Mississippi *Mississippi*
University of Missouri-Kansas City *Missouri*
The University of Montana-Missoula *Montana*
University of Nebraska Medical Center *Nebraska*
University of New Mexico *New Mexico*
The University of North Carolina at Chapel Hill *North Carolina*
University of Oklahoma Health Sciences Center *Oklahoma*
University of the Pacific *California*
University of Pittsburgh *Pennsylvania*
University of Puerto Rico, Medical Sciences Campus *Puerto Rico*
University of Rhode Island *Rhode Island*
University of the Sciences in Philadelphia *Pennsylvania*
University of South Carolina *South Carolina*
University of Southern California *California*
The University of Texas at Austin *Texas*
The University of Toledo *Ohio*
University of Utah *Utah*
University of Washington *Washington*
University of Wisconsin-Madison *Wisconsin*
University of Wyoming *Wyoming*
Virginia Commonwealth University *Virginia*
Washington State University *Washington*
Wayne State University *Michigan*
West Virginia University *West Virginia*
Wilkes University *Pennsylvania*
Wingate University *North Carolina*
Xavier University of Louisiana *Louisiana*

American Counseling AssociationAmerican Counseling Association (ACA)

Adams State College *Colorado*
Andrews University *Michigan*
Appalachian State University *North Carolina*
Arizona State University *Arizona*
Arkansas State University *Arkansas*
Auburn University *Alabama*
Ball State University *Indiana*
Barry University *Florida*
Boise State University *Idaho*
Bradley University *Illinois*
Brigham Young University *Utah*
Butler University *Indiana*
California Polytechnic State University, San Luis Obispo *California*
California State University, Fresno *California*
California State University, Los Angeles *California*
California State University, Northridge *California*
Capella University *Minnesota*
Chicago State University *Illinois*
Clemson University *South Carolina*
Cleveland State University *Ohio*
The College of New Jersey *New Jersey*
The College of William and Mary *Virginia*
Colorado State University *Colorado*
Columbus State University *Georgia*
Concordia University *Illinois*
Delta State University *Mississippi*
Duquesne University *Pennsylvania*
East Tennessee State University *Tennessee*
Eastern Illinois University *Illinois*
Eastern Kentucky University *Kentucky*
Eastern Mennonite University *Virginia*
Eastern Michigan University *Michigan*
Eastern Washington University *Washington*
Edinboro University of Pennsylvania *Pennsylvania*
Emporia State University *Kansas*
Fairfield University *Connecticut*
Florida State University *Florida*
Gallaudet University *District of Columbia*
The George Washington University *District of Columbia*
Georgia State University *Georgia*
Governors State University *Illinois*
Idaho State University *Idaho*
Illinois State University *Illinois*
Indiana University Bloomington *Indiana*
Indiana Wesleyan University *Indiana*
James Madison University *Virginia*
John Carroll University *Ohio*
Kansas State University *Kansas*
Kent State University *Ohio*
Lindsey Wilson College *Kentucky*
Louisiana State University and Agricultural and Mechanical College *Louisiana*
Loyola College in Maryland *Maryland*
Loyola University New Orleans *Louisiana*
Lynchburg College *Virginia*
Marymount University *Virginia*
Marywood University *Pennsylvania*
Middle Tennessee State University *Tennessee*
Minnesota State University Mankato *Minnesota*
Minnesota State University Moorhead *Minnesota*
Mississippi College *Mississippi*
Mississippi State University *Mississippi*
Montana State University *Montana*
Murray State University *Kentucky*
New Mexico State University *New Mexico*
North Carolina Agricultural and Technical State University *North Carolina*
North Carolina State University *North Carolina*
North Dakota State University *North Dakota*
Northeastern Illinois University *Illinois*
Northern Arizona University *Arizona*
Northern Illinois University *Illinois*
Northwest Nazarene University *Idaho*
Northwestern State University of Louisiana *Louisiana*
Oakland University *Michigan*
Ohio University *Ohio*
Old Dominion University *Virginia*
Oregon State University *Oregon*
Our Lady of Holy Cross College *Louisiana*
The Pennsylvania State University University Park Campus *Pennsylvania*
Pittsburg State University *Kansas*
Portland State University *Oregon*
Purdue University *Indiana*
Radford University *Virginia*
Regent University *Virginia*
Rider University *New Jersey*
Rollins College *Florida*
Roosevelt University *Illinois*
St. Cloud State University *Minnesota*
St. John's University *New York*
St. Mary's University of San Antonio *Texas*
San Francisco State University *California*
Shippensburg University of Pennsylvania *Pennsylvania*
Slippery Rock University of Pennsylvania *Pennsylvania*
Sonoma State University *California*
South Dakota State University *South Dakota*
Southeast Missouri State University *Missouri*
Southeastern Louisiana University *Louisiana*
Southern Connecticut State University *Connecticut*
Southern Illinois University Carbondale *Illinois*
State University of New York College at Brockport *New York*
State University of New York at Plattsburgh *New York*
Stephen F. Austin State University *Texas*
Stetson University *Florida*
Syracuse University *New York*
Texas A&M University-Commerce *Texas*
Texas State University-San Marcos *Texas*
Texas Tech University *Texas*
Texas Woman's University *Texas*
Trinity Western University *British Columbia*
Troy University *Alabama*
Truman State University *Missouri*
The University of Akron *Ohio*
The University of Alabama *Alabama*
University of Arkansas *Arkansas*
The University of British Columbia *British Columbia*
University of Central Florida *Florida*
University of Cincinnati *Ohio*
University of Colorado at Colorado Springs *Colorado*
University of Colorado at Denver and Health Sciences Center - Downtown Denver Campus *Colorado*
University of Detroit Mercy *Michigan*
University of Florida *Florida*
University of Georgia *Georgia*
University of Hawaii at Manoa *Hawaii*
University of Idaho *Idaho*
University of Illinois at Springfield *Illinois*
The University of Iowa *Iowa*
University of Louisiana at Monroe *Louisiana*
University of Maryland, College Park *Maryland*
University of Memphis *Tennessee*
University of Minnesota, Duluth *Minnesota*
University of Mississippi *Mississippi*
University of Missouri-St. Louis *Missouri*
University of Montevallo *Alabama*
University of Nebraska at Kearney *Nebraska*
University of Nebraska at Omaha *Nebraska*
University of Nevada, Las Vegas *Nevada*
University of Nevada, Reno *Nevada*
University of New Mexico *New Mexico*
University of New Orleans *Louisiana*
The University of North Carolina at Chapel Hill *North Carolina*
The University of North Carolina at Charlotte *North Carolina*
The University of North Carolina at Greensboro *North Carolina*
University of North Florida *Florida*
University of North Texas *Texas*
University of Northern Colorado *Colorado*
University of Northern Iowa *Iowa*
University of Phoenix-Phoenix Campus *Arizona*
University of Phoenix-Southern Arizona Campus *Arizona*
University of Phoenix-Utah Campus *Utah*
University of Pittsburgh *Pennsylvania*
University of Rochester *New York*

The University of Scranton *Pennsylvania*
University of South Carolina *South Carolina*
The University of South Dakota *South Dakota*
University of Southern Maine *Maine*
University of Southern Mississippi *Mississippi*
The University of Tennessee *Tennessee*
The University of Tennessee at Chattanooga *Tennessee*
The University of Toledo *Ohio*
University of Vermont *Vermont*
University of Virginia *Virginia*
University of West Georgia *Georgia*
University of Wisconsin-Oshkosh *Wisconsin*
University of Wisconsin-Superior *Wisconsin*
University of Wisconsin-Whitewater *Wisconsin*
University of Wyoming *Wyoming*
Vanderbilt University *Tennessee*
Virginia Polytechnic Institute and State University *Virginia*
Wake Forest University *North Carolina*
Wayne State University *Michigan*
West Virginia University *West Virginia*
Western Carolina University *North Carolina*
Western Connecticut State University *Connecticut*
Western Illinois University *Illinois*
Western Michigan University *Michigan*
Western Washington University *Washington*
William Paterson University of New Jersey *New Jersey*
Wilmington College *Delaware*
Winona State University *Minnesota*
Winthrop University *South Carolina*
Wright State University *Ohio*
Youngstown State University *Ohio*

American Culinary Federation, Inc. American Culinary Federation, Inc. (ACF)

Anne Arundel Community College *Maryland*
The Art Institute of Atlanta *Georgia*
The Art Institute of Colorado *Colorado*
The Art Institute of Dallas *Texas*
The Art Institute of Fort Lauderdale *Florida*
The Art Institute of Houston *Texas*
The Art Institute of New York City *New York*
The Art Institute of Philadelphia *Pennsylvania*
The Art Institute of Seattle *Washington*
The Art Institutes International Minnesota *Minnesota*
Austin Community College *Texas*
Baker College of Muskegon *Michigan*
Bellingham Technical College *Washington*
Bishop State Community College *Alabama*
Blackhawk Technical College *Wisconsin*
Boise State University *Idaho*
Bossier Parish Community College *Louisiana*
California Culinary Academy *California*
Central New Mexico Community College *New Mexico*
Central Oregon Community College *Oregon*
Chattahoochee Technical College *Georgia*
Cincinnati State Technical and Community College *Ohio*
City College of San Francisco *California*
College of DuPage *Illinois*
Columbia College *California*
Columbus State Community College *Ohio*
Community College of Southern Nevada *Nevada*
The Cooking and Hospitality Institute of Chicago *Illinois*
Cuyahoga Community College *Ohio*
Del Mar College *Texas*
Delgado Community College *Louisiana*
Des Moines Area Community College *Iowa*
Diablo Valley College *California*
Elgin Community College *Illinois*
Fairmont State Community & Technical College *West Virginia*
Florida Community College at Jacksonville *Florida*
Florida Culinary Institute *Florida*
Fox Valley Technical College *Wisconsin*
Grand Rapids Community College *Michigan*
Greenville Technical College *South Carolina*
Guilford Technical Community College *North Carolina*
Gulf Coast Community College *Florida*
Hennepin Technical College *Minnesota*
Henry Ford Community College *Michigan*
Hillsborough Community College *Florida*
Hocking College *Ohio*
Horry-Georgetown Technical College *South Carolina*
Hudson County Community College *New Jersey*
Idaho State University *Idaho*
The Illinois Institute of Art-Chicago *Illinois*
Indian Hills Community College *Iowa*
Indiana University of Pennsylvania *Pennsylvania*
Iowa Western Community College *Iowa*
Ivy Tech Community College-Central Indiana *Indiana*
Ivy Tech Community College-North Central *Indiana*
Ivy Tech Community College-Northeast *Indiana*
Ivy Tech Community College-Northwest *Indiana*
James H. Faulkner State Community College *Alabama*
Jefferson Community and Technical College *Kentucky*
Jefferson State Community College *Alabama*
Johnson County Community College *Kansas*
Joliet Junior College *Illinois*
Kapiolani Community College *Hawaii*
Keiser College (Melbourne) *Florida*
Keiser College (Tallahassee) *Florida*
Kendall College *Illinois*
Kirkwood Community College *Iowa*
Lake Washington Technical College *Washington*
Lamar University *Texas*
Leeward Community College *Hawaii*
Los Angeles Trade-Technical College *California*
Macomb Community College *Michigan*
Madison Area Technical College *Wisconsin*
Manchester Community College *Connecticut*
Maui Community College *Hawaii*
Metropolitan Community College *Nebraska*
Milwaukee Area Technical College *Wisconsin*
Monroe County Community College *Michigan*
Moraine Park Technical College *Wisconsin*
New York Institute of Technology *New York*
North Seattle Community College *Washington*
Northwestern Michigan College *Michigan*
Oakland Community College *Michigan*
Orange Coast College *California*
Paul Smith's College of Arts and Sciences *New York*
Pennsylvania College of Technology *Pennsylvania*
Pennsylvania Culinary Institute *Pennsylvania*
Pensacola Junior College *Florida*
Pueblo Community College *Colorado*
Renton Technical College *Washington*
Saint Paul College-A Community & Technical College *Minnesota*
St. Philip's College *Texas*
Salt Lake Community College *Utah*
San Joaquin Delta College *California*
Santa Barbara City College *California*
Savannah Technical College *Georgia*
Schenectady County Community College *New York*
Scottsdale Culinary Institute *Arizona*
Seattle Central Community College *Washington*
Sinclair Community College *Ohio*
Skagit Valley College *Washington*
South Puget Sound Community College *Washington*
South Seattle Community College *Washington*
Southeast Community College, Lincoln Campus *Nebraska*
Southern New Hampshire University *New Hampshire*
Southwestern Illinois College *Illinois*
Spokane Community College *Washington*
State University of New York College of Agriculture and Technology at Cobleskill *New York*
Stratford University *Virginia*
Sullivan County Community College *New York*
Sullivan University *Kentucky*
Trident Technical College *South Carolina*
Truckee Meadows Community College *Nevada*
The University of Montana-Missoula *Montana*
Virginia College at Birmingham *Alabama*
Walters State Community College *Tennessee*
Washtenaw Community College *Michigan*
Waukesha County Technical College *Wisconsin*
West Virginia Northern Community College *West Virginia*
Western Culinary Institute *Oregon*
Westmoreland County Community College *Pennsylvania*
Winner Institute of Arts & Sciences *Pennsylvania*
Zane State College *Ohio*

American Dental AssociationAmerican Dental Association (ADA)

Aiken Technical College *South Carolina*
Alamance Community College *North Carolina*
Albany Technical College *Georgia*
Allegany College of Maryland *Maryland*
Amarillo College *Texas*
Apollo College *Idaho*
Armstrong Atlantic State University *Georgia*
Asheville-Buncombe Technical Community College *North Carolina*
Athens Technical College *Georgia*
Atlanta Technical College *Georgia*
Augusta Technical College *Georgia*
Austin Community College *Texas*
Baker College of Port Huron *Michigan*
Baltimore City Community College *Maryland*
Bates Technical College *Washington*
Bellingham Technical College *Washington*
Bergen Community College *New Jersey*
Big Sandy Community and Technical College *Kentucky*
Blackhawk Technical College *Wisconsin*
Blinn College *Texas*
Blue Mountain Community College *Oregon*
Boise State University *Idaho*
Boston University *Massachusetts*
Brevard Community College *Florida*
Briarwood College *Connecticut*
Bristol Community College *Massachusetts*
Broome Community College *New York*
Broward Community College *Florida*
Cabrillo College *California*
Calhoun Community College *Alabama*
Camden County College *New Jersey*
Cape Cod Community College *Massachusetts*
Cape Fear Community College *North Carolina*
Carl Sandburg College *Illinois*
Case Western Reserve University *Ohio*
Catawba Valley Community College *North Carolina*
Central Community College-Grand Island Campus *Nebraska*
Central Community College-Hastings Campus *Nebraska*
Central Georgia Technical College *Georgia*
Central Lakes College *Minnesota*
Central New Mexico Community College *New Mexico*
Central Oregon Community College *Oregon*
Central Piedmont Community College *North Carolina*
Century College *Minnesota*
Cerritos College *California*
Chabot College *California*
Chaffey College *California*
Chattanooga State Technical Community College *Tennessee*
Chemeketa Community College *Oregon*
Citrus College *California*
City College of San Francisco *California*
City Colleges of Chicago, Kennedy-King College *Illinois*
Clark College *Washington*
Clayton State University *Georgia*
Clover Park Technical College *Washington*
Coastal Bend College *Texas*
Coastal Carolina Community College *North Carolina*
College of Alameda *California*
College of DuPage *Illinois*
College of Lake County *Illinois*
College of Marin *California*
College of the Redwoods *California*
College of San Mateo *California*
Collin County Community College District *Texas*
Colorado Northwestern Community College *Colorado*
Columbia Basin College *Washington*
Columbia College *New York*
Columbus State Community College *Ohio*
Columbus Technical College *Georgia*
Community College of Denver *Colorado*

Community College of Philadelphia *Pennsylvania*
Community College of Rhode Island *Rhode Island*
Community College of Southern Nevada *Nevada*
Concorde Career Institute *Missouri*
Contra Costa College *California*
Creighton University *Nebraska*
Cuyahoga Community College *Ohio*
Cypress College *California*
Dakota County Technical College *Minnesota*
Dalhousie University *Nova Scotia*
Darton College *Georgia*
Daytona Beach Community College *Florida*
Del Mar College *Texas*
Delaware Technical & Community College, Stanton/Wilmington Campus *Delaware*
Delta College *Michigan*
Des Moines Area Community College *Iowa*
Diablo Valley College *California*
Dixie State College of Utah *Utah*
Doña Ana Branch Community College *New Mexico*
Duluth Business University *Minnesota*
Durham Technical Community College *North Carolina*
East Tennessee State University *Tennessee*
Eastern Washington University *Washington*
Edison College *Florida*
El Paso Community College *Texas*
Elgin Community College *Illinois*
Erie Community College, North Campus *New York*
Erie Community College, South Campus *New York*
Eugenio María de Hostos Community College of the City University of New York *New York*
Farmingdale State University of New York *New York*
Fayetteville Technical Community College *North Carolina*
Ferris State University *Michigan*
Flint Hills Technical College *Kansas*
Florence-Darlington Technical College *South Carolina*
Florida Community College at Jacksonville *Florida*
Foothill College *California*
Forsyth Technical Community College *North Carolina*
Fox Valley Technical College *Wisconsin*
Fresno City College *California*
Front Range Community College *Colorado*
Gainesville College *Georgia*
Gateway Technical College *Wisconsin*
Georgia Highlands College *Georgia*
Georgia Perimeter College *Georgia*
Grand Rapids Community College *Michigan*
Grayson County College *Texas*
Greenville Technical College *South Carolina*
Guilford Technical Community College *North Carolina*
Gulf Coast Community College *Florida*
Gwinnett Technical College *Georgia*
Halifax Community College *North Carolina*
Harcum College *Pennsylvania*
Harrisburg Area Community College *Pennsylvania*
Harvard University *Massachusetts*
Hawkeye Community College *Iowa*
Henderson Community College *Kentucky*
Hennepin Technical College *Minnesota*
Hibbing Community College *Minnesota*
Hillsborough Community College *Florida*
Hinds Community College *Mississippi*
Horry-Georgetown Technical College *South Carolina*
Houston Community College System *Texas*
Howard College *Texas*
Howard University *District of Columbia*
Hudson Valley Community College *New York*
Idaho State University *Idaho*
Illinois Central College *Illinois*
Illinois Valley Community College *Illinois*
Indian River Community College *Florida*
Indiana University Northwest *Indiana*
Indiana University-Purdue University Fort Wayne *Indiana*
Indiana University-Purdue University Indianapolis *Indiana*
Indiana University South Bend *Indiana*
Iowa Western Community College *Iowa*
Ivy Tech Community College-Columbus *Indiana*
Ivy Tech Community College-Lafayette *Indiana*
J. Sargeant Reynolds Community College *Virginia*
Jacksonville University *Florida*
James A. Rhodes State College *Ohio*
James H. Faulkner State Community College *Alabama*
Jefferson Community College *Ohio*
John A. Logan College *Illinois*
Johnson County Community College *Kansas*
Kalamazoo Valley Community College *Michigan*
Kaskaskia College *Illinois*
Kellogg Community College *Michigan*
Kingwood College *Texas*
Kirkwood Community College *Iowa*
Lake Area Technical Institute *South Dakota*
Lake Land College *Illinois*
Lake Michigan College *Michigan*
Lake Superior College *Minnesota*
Lake Washington Technical College *Washington*
Lakeland Community College *Ohio*
Lakeshore Technical College *Wisconsin*
Lamar Institute of Technology *Texas*
Lamar State College-Orange *Texas*
Lane Community College *Oregon*
Lanier Technical College *Georgia*
Lansing Community College *Michigan*
Laramie County Community College *Wyoming*
Lewis and Clark Community College *Illinois*
Lexington Community College *Kentucky*
Linn-Benton Community College *Oregon*
Loma Linda University *California*
Lorain County Community College *Ohio*
Los Angeles City College *California*
Louisiana State University Health Sciences Center *Louisiana*
Luzerne County Community College *Pennsylvania*
Madison Area Technical College *Wisconsin*
Manatee Community College *Florida*
Manor College *Pennsylvania*
Marquette University *Wisconsin*
Marshalltown Community College *Iowa*
Martin Community College *North Carolina*
Massachusetts College of Pharmacy and Health Sciences *Massachusetts*
Massasoit Community College *Massachusetts*
Maui Community College *Hawaii*
McGill University *Quebec*
Median School of Allied Health Careers *Pennsylvania*
Medical College of Georgia *Georgia*
Medical University of South Carolina *South Carolina*
Meridian Community College *Mississippi*
Metropolitan Community College *Nebraska*
Miami Dade College *Florida*
Mid-Plains Community College *Nebraska*
Middle Georgia Technical College *Georgia*
Middlesex Community College *Massachusetts*
Middlesex County College *New Jersey*
Midlands Technical College *South Carolina*
Midwestern State University *Texas*
Milwaukee Area Technical College *Wisconsin*
Minneapolis Community and Technical College *Minnesota*
Minnesota State University Mankato *Minnesota*
Minnesota West Community and Technical College *Minnesota*
Mississippi Delta Community College *Mississippi*
Missouri College *Missouri*
Missouri Southern State University *Missouri*
Modesto Junior College *California*
Monroe Community College *New York*
Montana State University-Great Falls College of Technology *Montana*
Monterey Peninsula College *California*
Montgomery County Community College *Pennsylvania*
Mott Community College *Michigan*
Mt. Hood Community College *Oregon*
Mount Ida College *Massachusetts*
New Hampshire Technical Institute *New Hampshire*
New York City College of Technology of the City University of New York *New York*
New York University *New York*
Normandale Community College *Minnesota*
North Dakota State College of Science *North Dakota*
Northampton County Area Community College *Pennsylvania*
Northcentral Technical College *Wisconsin*
Northeast Mississippi Community College *Mississippi*
Northeast State Technical Community College *Tennessee*
Northeast Wisconsin Technical College *Wisconsin*
Northern Arizona University *Arizona*
Northern Essex Community College *Massachusetts*
Northern Virginia Community College *Virginia*
Northwest Technical College *Minnesota*
Northwestern Michigan College *Michigan*
Nova Southeastern University *Florida*
Oakland Community College *Michigan*
Ogeechee Technical College *Georgia*
The Ohio State University *Ohio*
Okaloosa-Walton College *Florida*
Old Dominion University *Virginia*
Onondaga Community College *New York*
Orange Coast College *California*
Orange County Community College *New York*
Oregon Health & Science University *Oregon*
Oregon Institute of Technology *Oregon*
Owens Community College *Ohio*
Oxnard College *California*
Ozarks Technical Community College *Missouri*
Palm Beach Community College *Florida*
Palomar College *California*
Parkland College *Illinois*
Pasadena City College *California*
Pasco-Hernando Community College *Florida*
Pearl River Community College *Mississippi*
Penn Valley Community College *Missouri*
Pennsylvania College of Technology *Pennsylvania*
Pensacola Junior College *Florida*
Phoenix College *Arizona*
Pierce College *Washington*
Pikes Peak Community College *Colorado*
Pima Community College *Arizona*
Portland Community College *Oregon*
Prairie State College *Illinois*
Professional Careers Institute *Indiana*
Provo College *Utah*
Pueblo Community College *Colorado*
Pulaski Technical College *Arkansas*
Quinsigamond Community College *Massachusetts*
Renton Technical College *Washington*
Rio Salado College *Arizona*
Riverside Community College District *California*
Roane State Community College *Tennessee*
Rochester Community and Technical College *Minnesota*
Rock Valley College *Illinois*
Rose State College *Oklahoma*
Rowan-Cabarrus Community College *North Carolina*
Sacramento City College *California*
St. Cloud Technical College *Minnesota*
St. Louis Community College at Forest Park *Missouri*
St. Petersburg College *Florida*
Salish Kootenai College *Montana*
Salt Lake Community College *Utah*
San Antonio College *Texas*
San Diego Mesa College *California*
San Joaquin Valley College *California*
San Jose City College *California*
San Juan College *New Mexico*
Santa Fe Community College *New Mexico*
Santa Fe Community College *Florida*
Santa Rosa Junior College *California*
Savannah Technical College *Georgia*
Scott Community College *Iowa*
Shasta College *California*
Shawnee State University *Ohio*
Sheridan College-Sheridan and Gillette *Wyoming*
Shoreline Community College *Washington*
Sinclair Community College *Ohio*
South Central Technical College *Minnesota*
South Florida Community College *Florida*
South Puget Sound Community College *Washington*
Southeast Community College, Lincoln Campus *Nebraska*
Southern Illinois University Carbondale *Illinois*
Southern Illinois University Edwardsville *Illinois*
Southern University at Shreveport *Louisiana*
Southwestern College *California*
Spartanburg Technical College *South Carolina*

Spokane Community College *Washington*
Springfield Technical Community College *Massachusetts*
Stark State College of Technology *Ohio*
State Fair Community College *Missouri*
State University of New York at Buffalo *New York*
Stony Brook University, State University of New York *New York*
Taft College *California*
Tallahassee Community College *Florida*
Tarrant County College District *Texas*
Temple College *Texas*
Temple University *Pennsylvania*
Tennessee State University *Tennessee*
Texas A&M University System Health Science Center *Texas*
Texas State Technical College Harlingen *Texas*
Texas State Technical College Waco *Texas*
Texas Woman's University *Texas*
Tri-County Technical College *South Carolina*
Trident Technical College *South Carolina*
Truckee Meadows Community College *Nevada*
Tufts University *Massachusetts*
Tulsa Community College *Oklahoma*
Tunxis Community College *Connecticut*
Tyler Junior College *Texas*
Université Laval *Québec*
Université de Montréal *Quebec*
The University of Alabama at Birmingham *Alabama*
University of Alaska Anchorage *Alaska*
University of Alberta *Alberta*
University of Arkansas at Fort Smith *Arkansas*
University of Arkansas for Medical Sciences *Arkansas*
University of Bridgeport *Connecticut*
The University of British Columbia *British Columbia*
University of California, Los Angeles *California*
University of Cincinnati Raymond Walters College *Ohio*
University of Detroit Mercy *Michigan*
University of Florida *Florida*
University of Hawaii at Manoa *Hawaii*
University of Illinois at Chicago *Illinois*
The University of Iowa *Iowa*
University of Kentucky *Kentucky*
University of Louisiana at Monroe *Louisiana*
University of Louisville *Kentucky*
The University of Maine at Augusta *Maine*
University of Manitoba *Manitoba*
University of Michigan *Michigan*
University of Minnesota, Twin Cities Campus *Minnesota*
University of Mississippi Medical Center *Mississippi*
University of Missouri-Kansas City *Missouri*
University of Nebraska-Lincoln *Nebraska*
University of Nebraska Medical Center *Nebraska*
University of Nevada, Las Vegas *Nevada*
University of New England *Maine*
University of New Haven *Connecticut*
University of New Mexico *New Mexico*
University of New Mexico-Gallup *New Mexico*
The University of North Carolina at Chapel Hill *North Carolina*
University of Oklahoma Health Sciences Center *Oklahoma*
University of the Pacific *California*
University of Pennsylvania *Pennsylvania*
University of Pittsburgh *Pennsylvania*
University of Puerto Rico, Medical Sciences Campus *Puerto Rico*
University of Saskatchewan *Saskatchewan*
The University of South Dakota *South Dakota*
University of Southern California *California*
University of Southern Indiana *Indiana*
The University of Texas Health Science Center at Houston *Texas*
The University of Texas Health Science Center at San Antonio *Texas*
University of Toronto *Ontario*
University of Vermont *Vermont*
University of Washington *Washington*
The University of Western Ontario *Ontario*
Utah Valley State College *Utah*
Valdosta State University *Georgia*
Valdosta Technical College *Georgia*
Valencia Community College *Florida*
Vatterott College (Omaha) *Nebraska*
Virginia Commonwealth University *Virginia*
Virginia Western Community College *Virginia*
Volunteer State Community College *Tennessee*
Wake Technical Community College *North Carolina*
Wallace State Community College *Alabama*
Washtenaw Community College *Michigan*
Waukesha County Technical College *Wisconsin*
Wayne Community College *North Carolina*
Wayne County Community College District *Michigan*
Weber State University *Utah*
West Central Technical College *Georgia*
West Kentucky Community and Technical College *Kentucky*
West Liberty State College *West Virginia*
West Los Angeles College *California*
West Virginia University *West Virginia*
West Virginia University Institute of Technology *West Virginia*
Western Iowa Tech Community College *Iowa*
Western Kentucky University *Kentucky*
Western Piedmont Community College *North Carolina*
Western Technical College *Wisconsin*
Westmoreland County Community College *Pennsylvania*
Wharton County Junior College *Texas*
Wichita Area Technical College *Kansas*
Wichita State University *Kansas*
Wilkes Community College *North Carolina*
William Rainey Harper College *Illinois*
Wytheville Community College *Virginia*
Yakima Valley Community College *Washington*
York Technical College *South Carolina*
Youngstown State University *Ohio*

American Dietetic AssociationAmerican Dietetic Association (ADtA)

Alcorn State University *Mississippi*
Andrews University *Michigan*
Appalachian State University *North Carolina*
Arizona State University at the Polytechnic Campus *Arizona*
Ball State University *Indiana*
Barnes-Jewish College of Nursing and Allied Health *Missouri*
Bastyr University *Washington*
Baylor University *Texas*
Benedictine University *Illinois*
Boston University *Massachusetts*
Bowling Green State University *Ohio*
Brigham Young University *Utah*
Brooklyn College of the City University of New York *New York*
Buffalo State College, State University of New York *New York*
California State Polytechnic University, Pomona *California*
California State University, Chico *California*
California State University, Fresno *California*
California State University, Long Beach *California*
California State University, Los Angeles *California*
California State University, Northridge *California*
California State University, Sacramento *California*
Case Western Reserve University *Ohio*
Central Michigan University *Michigan*
Central Washington University *Washington*
Clemson University *South Carolina*
College of Saint Benedict *Minnesota*
College of Saint Elizabeth *New Jersey*
Colorado State University *Colorado*
Concordia College *Minnesota*
Cornell University *New York*
Delta State University *Mississippi*
D'Youville College *New York*
East Carolina University *North Carolina*
East Tennessee State University *Tennessee*
Eastern Illinois University *Illinois*
Eastern Kentucky University *Kentucky*
Eastern Michigan University *Michigan*
Edinboro University of Pennsylvania *Pennsylvania*
Emory University *Georgia*
Florida International University *Florida*
Florida State University *Florida*
Framingham State College *Massachusetts*
Gannon University *Pennsylvania*
Georgia State University *Georgia*
Harvard University *Massachusetts*
Howard University *District of Columbia*
Hunter College of the City University of New York *New York*
Idaho State University *Idaho*
Illinois State University *Illinois*
Immaculata University *Pennsylvania*
Indiana State University *Indiana*
Indiana University of Pennsylvania *Pennsylvania*
Indiana University-Purdue University Indianapolis *Indiana*
Iowa State University of Science and Technology *Iowa*
James Madison University *Virginia*
The Johns Hopkins University *Maryland*
Kansas State University *Kansas*
Keene State College *New Hampshire*
Kent State University *Ohio*
La Salle University *Pennsylvania*
Lamar University *Texas*
Lehman College of the City University of New York *New York*
Life University *Georgia*
Lipscomb University *Tennessee*
Loma Linda University *California*
Long Island University, C.W. Post Campus *New York*
Louisiana State University and Agricultural and Mechanical College *Louisiana*
Louisiana Tech University *Louisiana*
Loyola University Chicago *Illinois*
Marshall University *West Virginia*
Marywood University *Pennsylvania*
McNeese State University *Louisiana*
Medical University of South Carolina *South Carolina*
Mercyhurst College *Pennsylvania*
Meredith College *North Carolina*
Michigan State University *Michigan*
Mississippi State University *Mississippi*
Montclair State University *New Jersey*
Morehead State University *Kentucky*
Mount Carmel College of Nursing *Ohio*
Mount Marty College *South Dakota*
Mount Mary College *Wisconsin*
Murray State University *Kentucky*
New York Institute of Technology *New York*
New York University *New York*
Nicholls State University *Louisiana*
North Carolina Central University *North Carolina*
North Dakota State University *North Dakota*
Northern Illinois University *Illinois*
Oakwood College *Alabama*
The Ohio State University *Ohio*
Oklahoma State University *Oklahoma*
Oregon Health & Science University *Oregon*
The Pennsylvania State University University Park Campus *Pennsylvania*
Prairie View A&M University *Texas*
Purdue University *Indiana*
Queens College of the City University of New York *New York*
Radford University *Virginia*
Rush University *Illinois*
Saint Joseph College *Connecticut*
Saint Louis University *Missouri*
Sam Houston State University *Texas*
San Diego State University *California*
San Francisco State University *California*
San Jose State University *California*
Seton Hill University *Pennsylvania*
Simmons College *Massachusetts*
Southeast Missouri State University *Missouri*
Southern Illinois University Carbondale *Illinois*
Southern University and Agricultural and Mechanical College *Louisiana*
State University of New York at Buffalo *New York*
State University of New York College at Oneonta *New York*
Stephen F. Austin State University *Texas*
Stony Brook University, State University of New York *New York*
Syracuse University *New York*
Texas A&M University *Texas*
Texas A&M University-Kingsville *Texas*
Texas Christian University *Texas*

Texas State University-San Marcos *Texas*
Texas Tech University *Texas*
Texas Woman's University *Texas*
Tufts University *Massachusetts*
Tulane University *Louisiana*
The University of Akron *Ohio*
The University of Alabama *Alabama*
The University of Alabama at Birmingham *Alabama*
University of Alaska Anchorage *Alaska*
The University of Arizona *Arizona*
University of Arkansas for Medical Sciences *Arkansas*
University of California, Berkeley *California*
University of California, Davis *California*
University of California, Los Angeles *California*
University of Central Arkansas *Arkansas*
University of Central Oklahoma *Oklahoma*
University of Cincinnati *Ohio*
University of Connecticut *Connecticut*
University of Delaware *Delaware*
University of Florida *Florida*
University of Georgia *Georgia*
University of Houston *Texas*
University of Idaho *Idaho*
University of Illinois at Chicago *Illinois*
University of Illinois at Urbana-Champaign *Illinois*
University of the Incarnate Word *Texas*
The University of Iowa *Iowa*
University of Kansas *Kansas*
University of Kentucky *Kentucky*
University of Louisiana at Lafayette *Louisiana*
University of Maine *Maine*
University of Maryland, College Park *Maryland*
University of Maryland Eastern Shore *Maryland*
University of Massachusetts Amherst *Massachusetts*
University of Memphis *Tennessee*
University of Michigan *Michigan*
University of Minnesota, Twin Cities Campus *Minnesota*
University of Missouri-Columbia *Missouri*
University of Nebraska-Lincoln *Nebraska*
University of Nebraska Medical Center *Nebraska*
University of Nevada, Reno *Nevada*
University of New Hampshire *New Hampshire*
University of New Mexico *New Mexico*
The University of North Carolina at Chapel Hill *North Carolina*
The University of North Carolina at Greensboro *North Carolina*
University of North Dakota *North Dakota*
University of North Florida *Florida*
University of Northern Colorado *Colorado*
University of Oklahoma Health Sciences Center *Oklahoma*
University of Pittsburgh *Pennsylvania*
University of Puerto Rico, Medical Sciences Campus *Puerto Rico*
University of Rhode Island *Rhode Island*
The University of South Dakota *South Dakota*
University of Southern California *California*
University of Southern Mississippi *Mississippi*
The University of Tennessee *Tennessee*
The University of Tennessee at Martin *Tennessee*
The University of Texas at Austin *Texas*
The University of Texas Health Science Center at Houston *Texas*
The University of Texas-Pan American *Texas*
The University of Texas Southwestern Medical Center at Dallas *Texas*
University of Utah *Utah*
University of Virginia *Virginia*
University of Washington *Washington*
University of Wisconsin-Green Bay *Wisconsin*
University of Wisconsin-Madison *Wisconsin*
University of Wisconsin-Stout *Wisconsin*
Utah State University *Utah*
Vanderbilt University *Tennessee*
Virginia Commonwealth University *Virginia*
Virginia Polytechnic Institute and State University *Virginia*
Virginia State University *Virginia*
Viterbo University *Wisconsin*
Washington State University *Washington*
Wayne State University *Michigan*
West Virginia University *West Virginia*
Western Carolina University *North Carolina*
Western Michigan University *Michigan*
Winthrop University *South Carolina*
Yale University *Connecticut*
Youngstown State University *Ohio*

American Health Information Management AssociationAmerican Health Information Management Association (AHIMA)

Adirondack Community College *New York*
Arapahoe Community College *Colorado*
Arkansas Tech University *Arkansas*
Baker College of Clinton Township *Michigan*
Baker College of Flint *Michigan*
Baker College of Jackson *Michigan*
Baker College of Muskegon *Michigan*
Baltimore City Community College *Maryland*
Bishop State Community College *Alabama*
Boise State University *Idaho*
Borough of Manhattan Community College of the City University of New York *New York*
Bowling Green State University-Firelands College *Ohio*
Briarwood College *Connecticut*
Bristol Community College *Massachusetts*
Broome Community College *New York*
Broward Community College *Florida*
Brunswick Community College *North Carolina*
Burlington County College *New Jersey*
Catawba Valley Community College *North Carolina*
Central Community College-Hastings Campus *Nebraska*
Central Oregon Community College *Oregon*
Central Piedmont Community College *North Carolina*
Chabot College *California*
Charles R. Drew University of Medicine and Science *California*
Chattanooga State Technical Community College *Tennessee*
Chicago State University *Illinois*
Chippewa Valley Technical College *Wisconsin*
Cincinnati State Technical and Community College *Ohio*
City College of San Francisco *California*
Clark Atlanta University *Georgia*
Coastal Bend College *Texas*
College of DuPage *Illinois*
College of Lake County *Illinois*
College of St. Catherine-Minneapolis *Minnesota*
College of Saint Mary *Nebraska*
The College of St. Scholastica *Minnesota*
Columbus State Community College *Ohio*
Community College of Allegheny County *Pennsylvania*
Community College of Philadelphia *Pennsylvania*
Community College of Southern Nevada *Nevada*
Cosumnes River College (Sacramento) *California*
Cuyahoga Community College *Ohio*
Cypress College *California*
Dakota State University *South Dakota*
Darton College *Georgia*
Davidson County Community College *North Carolina*
Daytona Beach Community College *Florida*
Del Mar College *Texas*
Delgado Community College *Louisiana*
Duquesne University *Pennsylvania*
East Carolina University *North Carolina*
East Central University *Oklahoma*
East Los Angeles College *California*
Eastern Kentucky University *Kentucky*
Edgecombe Community College *North Carolina*
El Paso Community College *Texas*
Erie Community College, North Campus *New York*
Fairmont State Community & Technical College *West Virginia*
Ferris State University *Michigan*
Fisher College *Massachusetts*
Florence-Darlington Technical College *South Carolina*
Florida Agricultural and Mechanical University *Florida*
Florida Community College at Jacksonville *Florida*
Florida International University *Florida*
Fresno City College *California*
Gateway Technical College *Wisconsin*
Gogebic Community College *Michigan*
Greenville Technical College *South Carolina*
Gwynedd-Mercy College *Pennsylvania*
Hagerstown Business College *Maryland*
Henry Ford Community College *Michigan*
Hinds Community College *Mississippi*
Hocking College *Ohio*
Houston Community College System *Texas*
Howard College *Texas*
Hudson County Community College *New Jersey*
Huertas Junior College *Puerto Rico*
Hutchinson Community College and Area Vocational School *Kansas*
Idaho State University *Idaho*
Illinois State University *Illinois*
Indian Hills Community College *Iowa*
Indian River Community College *Florida*
Indiana University Northwest *Indiana*
Indiana University-Purdue University Fort Wayne *Indiana*
Indiana University-Purdue University Indianapolis *Indiana*
Inter American University of Puerto Rico, San Germán Campus *Puerto Rico*
International College *Florida*
Itawamba Community College *Mississippi*
John A. Logan College *Illinois*
Kean University *New Jersey*
Kennebec Valley Community College *Maine*
Kirkwood Community College *Iowa*
Labouré College *Massachusetts*
Lake-Sumter Community College *Florida*
Lamar Institute of Technology *Texas*
Lee College *Texas*
Lehigh Carbon Community College *Pennsylvania*
Loma Linda University *California*
Long Island University, C.W. Post Campus *New York*
Louisiana Tech University *Louisiana*
Macon State College *Georgia*
Marshall University *West Virginia*
McLennan Community College *Texas*
Medical College of Georgia *Georgia*
Mercy College of Northwest Ohio *Ohio*
Meridian Community College *Mississippi*
Miami Dade College *Florida*
Midland College *Texas*
Midlands Technical College *South Carolina*
Missouri Western State University *Missouri*
Mohawk Valley Community College *New York*
Molloy College *New York*
Monroe College (Bronx) *New York*
Monroe Community College *New York*
Montana State University-Great Falls College of Technology *Montana*
Montgomery College *Maryland*
Moraine Park Technical College *Wisconsin*
Moraine Valley Community College *Illinois*
Mountain View College *Texas*
National College of Business & Technology (Louisville) *Kentucky*
National Park Community College *Arkansas*
New Hampshire Community Technical College, Nashua/Claremont *New Hampshire*
North Dakota State College of Science *North Dakota*
North Harris College *Texas*
Northeast Iowa Community College *Iowa*
Northeast Wisconsin Technical College *Wisconsin*
Northeastern University *Massachusetts*
Northern Essex Community College *Massachusetts*
Northern Virginia Community College *Virginia*
Northwest Iowa Community College *Iowa*
Northwest Technical College *Minnesota*
Northwestern Business College *Illinois*
Oakton Community College *Illinois*
The Ohio State University *Ohio*
Onondaga Community College *New York*
Ozarks Technical Community College *Missouri*
Panola College *Texas*
Passaic County Community College *New Jersey*
Penn Valley Community College *Missouri*
Pensacola Junior College *Florida*
Phoenix College *Arizona*

Pitt Community College *North Carolina*
Polk Community College *Florida*
Portland Community College *Oregon*
Prince George's Community College *Maryland*
Rasmussen College Eagan *Minnesota*
Rasmussen College Eden Prairie *Minnesota*
Rasmussen College Mankato *Minnesota*
Rasmussen College St. Cloud *Minnesota*
Regis University *Colorado*
Rend Lake College *Illinois*
Ridgewater College *Minnesota*
Roane State Community College *Tennessee*
Rochester Community and Technical College *Minnesota*
Rockland Community College *New York*
Rose State College *Oklahoma*
Saint Charles Community College *Missouri*
Saint Louis University *Missouri*
St. Petersburg College *Florida*
St. Philip's College *Texas*
San Diego Mesa College *California*
San Juan College *New Mexico*
Santa Barbara City College *California*
Santa Fe Community College *Florida*
Schoolcraft College *Michigan*
Shawnee Community College *Illinois*
Shoreline Community College *Washington*
Sinclair Community College *Ohio*
South Hills School of Business & Technology (State College) *Pennsylvania*
South Piedmont Community College *North Carolina*
South Plains College *Texas*
South Texas College *Texas*
Southeastern Illinois College *Illinois*
Southern University at Shreveport *Louisiana*
Southwestern Community College *North Carolina*
Southwestern Illinois College *Illinois*
Southwestern Oklahoma State University *Oklahoma*
Spokane Community College *Washington*
Stark State College of Technology *Ohio*
State University of New York College of Technology at Alfred *New York*
State University of New York Institute of Technology *New York*
Stephens College *Missouri*
Suffolk County Community College *New York*
Tacoma Community College *Washington*
Tarrant County College District *Texas*
Temple University *Pennsylvania*
Tennessee State University *Tennessee*
Texas Southern University *Texas*
Texas State Technical College Harlingen *Texas*
Texas State University-San Marcos *Texas*
Tidewater Community College *Virginia*
Trocaire College *New York*
Tulsa Community College *Oklahoma*
Tyler Junior College *Texas*
United Tribes Technical College *North Dakota*
Universidad Adventista de las Antillas *Puerto Rico*
Universidad del Este *Puerto Rico*
The University of Alabama at Birmingham *Alabama*
University of Alaska Southeast, Sitka Campus *Alaska*
University of Central Florida *Florida*
University of Illinois at Chicago *Illinois*
University of Kansas *Kansas*
University of Louisiana at Lafayette *Louisiana*
University of Maine *Maine*
University of Mississippi Medical Center *Mississippi*
University of New Mexico-Gallup *New Mexico*
University of Pittsburgh *Pennsylvania*
University of Puerto Rico, Medical Sciences Campus *Puerto Rico*
University of Washington *Washington*
University of Wisconsin-Milwaukee *Wisconsin*
Vernon College *Texas*
Vincennes University *Indiana*
Volunteer State Community College *Tennessee*
Wallace State Community College *Alabama*
Washburn University *Kansas*
Weber State University *Utah*
West Virginia Northern Community College *West Virginia*
Western Carolina University *North Carolina*
Western Kentucky University *Kentucky*
Western Nebraska Community College *Nebraska*
Western Technical College *Wisconsin*
Wharton County Junior College *Texas*

American Institute of Certified Planners/Association ofAmerican Institute of Certified Planners/Association of Collegiate Schools of Planning (ACSP)

Alabama Agricultural and Mechanical University *Alabama*
Arizona State University *Arizona*
Auburn University *Alabama*
Ball State University *Indiana*
California Polytechnic State University, San Luis Obispo *California*
California State Polytechnic University, Pomona *California*
Clemson University *South Carolina*
Cleveland State University *Ohio*
Cornell University *New York*
East Carolina University *North Carolina*
Eastern Michigan University *Michigan*
Eastern Washington University *Washington*
Florida Atlantic University *Florida*
Florida State University *Florida*
Georgia Institute of Technology *Georgia*
Harvard University *Massachusetts*
Hunter College of the City University of New York *New York*
Iowa State University of Science and Technology *Iowa*
Kansas State University *Kansas*
Massachusetts Institute of Technology *Massachusetts*
Michigan State University *Michigan*
Morgan State University *Maryland*
New York University *New York*
The Ohio State University *Ohio*
Portland State University *Oregon*
Pratt Institute *New York*
Rutgers, The State University of New Jersey, New Brunswick/Piscataway *New Jersey*
San Jose State University *California*
State University of New York at Buffalo *New York*
Texas A&M University *Texas*
Tufts University *Massachusetts*
Université de Montréal *Quebec*
University at Albany, State University of New York *New York*
The University of Arizona *Arizona*
The University of British Columbia *British Columbia*
University of California, Berkeley *California*
University of California, Irvine *California*
University of California, Los Angeles *California*
University of Cincinnati *Ohio*
University of Colorado at Denver and Health Sciences Center - Downtown Denver Campus *Colorado*
University of Florida *Florida*
University of Hawaii at Manoa *Hawaii*
University of Illinois at Chicago *Illinois*
University of Illinois at Urbana-Champaign *Illinois*
The University of Iowa *Iowa*
University of Kansas *Kansas*
University of Maryland, College Park *Maryland*
University of Massachusetts Amherst *Massachusetts*
University of Memphis *Tennessee*
University of Michigan *Michigan*
University of Minnesota, Twin Cities Campus *Minnesota*
University of Nebraska-Lincoln *Nebraska*
University of New Mexico *New Mexico*
University of New Orleans *Louisiana*
The University of North Carolina at Chapel Hill *North Carolina*
University of Oklahoma *Oklahoma*
University of Oregon *Oregon*
University of Pennsylvania *Pennsylvania*
University of Puerto Rico, Río Piedras *Puerto Rico*
University of Rhode Island *Rhode Island*
University of Southern California *California*
The University of Tennessee *Tennessee*
The University of Texas at Arlington *Texas*
The University of Texas at Austin *Texas*
University of Virginia *Virginia*
University of Washington *Washington*
University of Wisconsin-Madison *Wisconsin*
University of Wisconsin-Milwaukee *Wisconsin*
Virginia Commonwealth University *Virginia*
Virginia Polytechnic Institute and State University *Virginia*
Wayne State University *Michigan*

American Library AssociationAmerican Library Association (ALA)

The Catholic University of America *District of Columbia*
Clarion University of Pennsylvania *Pennsylvania*
Clark Atlanta University *Georgia*
Dalhousie University *Nova Scotia*
Dominican University *Illinois*
Drexel University *Pennsylvania*
Emporia State University *Kansas*
Florida State University *Florida*
Indiana University Bloomington *Indiana*
Kent State University *Ohio*
Long Island University, C.W. Post Campus *New York*
Louisiana State University and Agricultural and Mechanical College *Louisiana*
McGill University *Quebec*
North Carolina Central University *North Carolina*
Pratt Institute *New York*
Queens College of the City University of New York *New York*
Rutgers, The State University of New Jersey, New Brunswick/Piscataway *New Jersey*
St. John's University *New York*
San Jose State University *California*
Simmons College *Massachusetts*
Southern Connecticut State University *Connecticut*
State University of New York at Buffalo *New York*
Syracuse University *New York*
Texas Woman's University *Texas*
Université de Montréal *Quebec*
The University of Alabama *Alabama*
University at Albany, State University of New York *New York*
University of Alberta *Alberta*
The University of Arizona *Arizona*
The University of British Columbia *British Columbia*
University of California, Los Angeles *California*
University of Denver *Colorado*
University of Hawaii at Manoa *Hawaii*
University of Illinois at Urbana-Champaign *Illinois*
The University of Iowa *Iowa*
University of Kentucky *Kentucky*
University of Maryland, College Park *Maryland*
University of Michigan *Michigan*
University of Missouri-Columbia *Missouri*
The University of North Carolina at Chapel Hill *North Carolina*
The University of North Carolina at Greensboro *North Carolina*
University of North Texas *Texas*
University of Oklahoma *Oklahoma*
University of Pittsburgh *Pennsylvania*
University of Puerto Rico, Río Piedras *Puerto Rico*
University of Rhode Island *Rhode Island*
University of South Carolina *South Carolina*
University of South Florida *Florida*
University of Southern Mississippi *Mississippi*
The University of Tennessee *Tennessee*
The University of Texas at Austin *Texas*
University of Toronto *Ontario*
University of Washington *Washington*
The University of Western Ontario *Ontario*
University of Wisconsin-Madison *Wisconsin*
University of Wisconsin-Milwaukee *Wisconsin*
Wayne State University *Michigan*

American Occupational Therapy AssociationAmerican Occupational Therapy Association (AOTA)

Alabama State University *Alabama*
Allegany College of Maryland *Maryland*
Alvernia College *Pennsylvania*
Amarillo College *Texas*
American International College *Massachusetts*
Anoka Technical College *Minnesota*
Atlantic Cape Community College *New Jersey*

Augusta Technical College *Georgia*
Austin Community College *Texas*
Baker College of Muskegon *Michigan*
Barry University *Florida*
Bay Path College *Massachusetts*
Belmont University *Tennessee*
Boston University *Massachusetts*
Brenau University *Georgia*
Briarwood College *Connecticut*
Bristol Community College *Massachusetts*
Brown Mackie College-Fort Wayne *Indiana*
Brown Mackie College-South Bend *Indiana*
Cabarrus College of Health Sciences *North Carolina*
California State University, Dominguez Hills *California*
Cape Fear Community College *North Carolina*
Casper College *Wyoming*
Chatham College *Pennsylvania*
Chicago State University *Illinois*
Cincinnati State Technical and Community College *Ohio*
City Colleges of Chicago, Wilbur Wright College *Illinois*
Cleveland State University *Ohio*
College Misericordia *Pennsylvania*
College of St. Catherine *Minnesota*
College of St. Catherine-Minneapolis *Minnesota*
College of Saint Mary *Nebraska*
The College of St. Scholastica *Minnesota*
Colorado State University *Colorado*
Community College of Allegheny County *Pennsylvania*
The Community College of Baltimore County *Maryland*
Community College of Rhode Island *Rhode Island*
Community College of Southern Nevada *Nevada*
Concordia University Wisconsin *Wisconsin*
Creighton University *Nebraska*
Cuyahoga Community College *Ohio*
Darton College *Georgia*
Daytona Beach Community College *Florida*
Del Mar College *Texas*
Delaware Technical & Community College, Jack F. Owens Campus *Delaware*
Delaware Technical & Community College, Stanton/Wilmington Campus *Delaware*
Delgado Community College *Louisiana*
Dominican College *New York*
Dominican University of California *California*
Duquesne University *Pennsylvania*
Durham Technical Community College *North Carolina*
D'Youville College *New York*
East Carolina University *North Carolina*
Eastern Kentucky University *Kentucky*
Eastern Michigan University *Michigan*
Eastern New Mexico University-Roswell *New Mexico*
Eastern Washington University *Washington*
Elizabethtown College *Pennsylvania*
Erie Community College, North Campus *New York*
Fiorello H. LaGuardia Community College of the City University of New York *New York*
Florida Agricultural and Mechanical University *Florida*
Florida Gulf Coast University *Florida*
Florida Hospital College of Health Sciences *Florida*
Florida International University *Florida*
Fox Valley Technical College *Wisconsin*
Gannon University *Pennsylvania*
Genesee Community College *New York*
Governors State University *Illinois*
Grand Rapids Community College *Michigan*
Grand Valley State University *Michigan*
Green River Community College *Washington*
Greenville Technical College *South Carolina*
Grossmont College *California*
Herkimer County Community College *New York*
Holmes Community College *Mississippi*
Housatonic Community College *Connecticut*
Houston Community College System *Texas*
Howard University *District of Columbia*
Husson College *Maine*
ICM School of Business & Medical Careers *Pennsylvania*
Idaho State University *Idaho*
Illinois Central College *Illinois*
Ithaca College *New York*
James A. Rhodes State College *Ohio*
James Madison University *Virginia*
Jamestown Community College *New York*
Jefferson College of Health Sciences *Virginia*
Jefferson Community and Technical College *Kentucky*
John A. Logan College *Illinois*
Kapiolani Community College *Hawaii*
Kean University *New Jersey*
Keiser College (Fort Lauderdale) *Florida*
Keiser College (Melbourne) *Florida*
Kennebec Valley Community College *Maine*
Kent State University, East Liverpool Campus *Ohio*
Keuka College *New York*
Kingwood College *Texas*
Kirkwood Community College *Iowa*
Lake Area Technical Institute *South Dakota*
Lake Michigan College *Michigan*
Laredo Community College *Texas*
Lehigh Carbon Community College *Pennsylvania*
Lenoir-Rhyne College *North Carolina*
Lewis and Clark Community College *Illinois*
Lincoln Land Community College *Illinois*
Loma Linda University *California*
Long Island University, Brooklyn Campus *New York*
Louisiana State University Health Sciences Center *Louisiana*
Macomb Community College *Michigan*
Madison Area Technical College *Wisconsin*
Madisonville Community College *Kentucky*
Manatee Community College *Florida*
Manchester Community College *Connecticut*
Maria College *New York*
Maryville University of Saint Louis *Missouri*
Medical College of Georgia *Georgia*
Medical University of South Carolina *South Carolina*
Mercy College *New York*
Middle Georgia College *Georgia*
Midwestern University, Glendale Campus *Arizona*
Milligan College *Tennessee*
Milwaukee Area Technical College *Wisconsin*
Mott Community College *Michigan*
Mount Aloysius College *Pennsylvania*
Mount Mary College *Wisconsin*
Mountain State University *West Virginia*
Murray State University *Kentucky*
Nashville State Technical Community College *Tennessee*
Navarro College *Texas*
New England Institute of Technology *Rhode Island*
New Hampshire Community Technical College, Nashua/Claremont *New Hampshire*
New York Institute of Technology *New York*
New York University *New York*
North Dakota State College of Science *North Dakota*
North Shore Community College *Massachusetts*
Northland Community and Technical College-East Grand Forks *Minnesota*
Northwestern Technical College *Georgia*
Nova Southeastern University *Florida*
The Ohio State University *Ohio*
Oklahoma City Community College *Oklahoma*
Orange County Community College *New York*
Owens Community College *Ohio*
Ozarks Technical Community College *Missouri*
Pacific University *Oregon*
Panola College *Texas*
Parkland College *Illinois*
Pearl River Community College *Mississippi*
Penn Valley Community College *Missouri*
Pennsylvania College of Technology *Pennsylvania*
The Pennsylvania State University Berks Campus of the Berks-Lehigh Valley College *Pennsylvania*
The Pennsylvania State University DuBois Campus of the Commonwealth College *Pennsylvania*
The Pennsylvania State University Mont Alto Campus of the Commonwealth College *Pennsylvania*
Philadelphia University *Pennsylvania*
Pitt Community College *North Carolina*
Polk Community College *Florida*
Pueblo Community College *Colorado*
Quinnipiac University *Connecticut*
Quinsigamond Community College *Massachusetts*
Rend Lake College *Illinois*
The Richard Stockton College of New Jersey *New Jersey*
Roane State Community College *Tennessee*
Rockhurst University *Missouri*
Rockland Community College *New York*
Rush University *Illinois*
Russell Sage College *New York*
Sacramento City College *California*
Sacred Heart University *Connecticut*
Saginaw Valley State University *Michigan*
St. Ambrose University *Iowa*
Saint Charles Community College *Missouri*
Saint Francis University *Pennsylvania*
St. Louis Community College at Meramec *Missouri*
Saint Louis University *Missouri*
St. Philip's College *Texas*
Salem State College *Massachusetts*
Salt Lake Community College *Utah*
Samuel Merritt College *California*
San Francisco Conservatory of Music *California*
San Jose State University *California*
Santa Ana College *California*
Seton Hall University *New Jersey*
Shawnee Community College *Illinois*
Shawnee State University *Ohio*
Shenandoah University *Virginia*
Sinclair Community College *Ohio*
South Arkansas Community College *Arkansas*
South College *Tennessee*
South Suburban College *Illinois*
South Texas College *Texas*
Southeastern Illinois College *Illinois*
Southwestern Oklahoma State University at Sayre *Oklahoma*
Spalding University *Kentucky*
Springfield College *Massachusetts*
Springfield Technical Community College *Massachusetts*
Stark State College of Technology *Ohio*
State University of New York at Buffalo *New York*
State University of New York College of Technology at Canton *New York*
State University of New York Downstate Medical Center *New York*
Stony Brook University, State University of New York *New York*
Suffolk County Community College *New York*
Temple University *Pennsylvania*
Tennessee State University *Tennessee*
Texas Woman's University *Texas*
Thomas Jefferson University *Pennsylvania*
Tidewater Community College *Virginia*
Tomball College *Texas*
Touro College *New York*
Towson University *Maryland*
Trident Technical College *South Carolina*
Tufts University *Massachusetts*
Tulsa Community College *Oklahoma*
Tuskegee University *Alabama*
The University of Alabama at Birmingham *Alabama*
University of Central Arkansas *Arkansas*
The University of Findlay *Ohio*
University of Florida *Florida*
University of Hartford *Connecticut*
University of Illinois at Chicago *Illinois*
University of Indianapolis *Indiana*
University of Kansas *Kansas*
University of Kentucky *Kentucky*
University of Louisiana at Monroe *Louisiana*
University of Mary *North Dakota*
University of Minnesota, Twin Cities Campus *Minnesota*
University of Mississippi Medical Center *Mississippi*
University of Missouri-Columbia *Missouri*
University of New England *Maine*
University of New Hampshire *New Hampshire*
University of New Mexico *New Mexico*
The University of North Carolina at Chapel Hill *North Carolina*
University of North Dakota *North Dakota*
University of Oklahoma Health Sciences Center *Oklahoma*
University of Pittsburgh *Pennsylvania*
University of Puerto Rico at Humacao *Puerto Rico*

University of Puerto Rico, Medical Sciences Campus *Puerto Rico*
University of Puget Sound *Washington*
University of Saint Francis *Indiana*
University of the Sciences in Philadelphia *Pennsylvania*
The University of Scranton *Pennsylvania*
University of South Alabama *Alabama*
The University of South Dakota *South Dakota*
University of Southern California *California*
University of Southern Indiana *Indiana*
University of Southern Maine *Maine*
The University of Texas at El Paso *Texas*
The University of Texas Health Science Center at San Antonio *Texas*
The University of Texas Medical Branch *Texas*
The University of Texas-Pan American *Texas*
University of Utah *Utah*
University of Washington *Washington*
University of Wisconsin-La Crosse *Wisconsin*
University of Wisconsin-Madison *Wisconsin*
University of Wisconsin-Milwaukee *Wisconsin*
Utica College *New York*
Virginia Commonwealth University *Virginia*
Wallace State Community College *Alabama*
Washington University in St. Louis *Missouri*
Wayne County Community College District *Michigan*
Wayne State University *Michigan*
West Virginia University *West Virginia*
Western Career College (San Leandro) *California*
Western Kentucky University *Kentucky*
Western Michigan University *Michigan*
Western New Mexico University *New Mexico*
Western Technical College *Wisconsin*
Winston-Salem State University *North Carolina*
Wisconsin Indianhead Technical College *Wisconsin*
Worcester State College *Massachusetts*
Xavier University *Ohio*
York College of the City University of New York *New York*
Zane State College *Ohio*

American Optometric AssociationAmerican Optometric Association (AOA)

Ferris State University *Michigan*
Indiana University Bloomington *Indiana*
Madison Area Technical College *Wisconsin*
Northeastern State University *Oklahoma*
Nova Southeastern University *Florida*
The Ohio State University *Ohio*
Pacific University *Oregon*
Spokane Community College *Washington*
Université de Montréal *Quebec*
The University of Alabama at Birmingham *Alabama*
University of California, Berkeley *California*
University of Houston *Texas*
University of Missouri-St. Louis *Missouri*
University of Waterloo *Ontario*

American Osteopathic AssociationAmerican Osteopathic Association (AOsA)

Michigan State University *Michigan*
Midwestern University, Glendale Campus *Arizona*
New York Institute of Technology *New York*
Nova Southeastern University *Florida*
Ohio University *Ohio*
Pikeville College *Kentucky*
University of New England *Maine*

American Physical Therapy AssociationAmerican Physical Therapy Association (APTA)

Alabama State University *Alabama*
Allegany College of Maryland *Maryland*
Amarillo College *Texas*
American International College *Massachusetts*
Andrews University *Michigan*
Angelo State University *Texas*
Anne Arundel Community College *Maryland*
Anoka-Ramsey Community College *Minnesota*
Arapahoe Community College *Colorado*
Arcadia University *Pennsylvania*
Arkansas State University *Arkansas*
Armstrong Atlantic State University *Georgia*
Athens Technical College *Georgia*
Atlantic Cape Community College *New Jersey*
Austin Community College *Texas*
Azusa Pacific University *California*
Baker College of Flint *Michigan*
Baker College of Muskegon *Michigan*
Baltimore City Community College *Maryland*
Bay State College *Massachusetts*
Baylor University *Texas*
Becker College *Massachusetts*
Bellarmine University *Kentucky*
Belmont University *Tennessee*
Bergen Community College *New Jersey*
Berkshire Community College *Massachusetts*
Bishop State Community College *Alabama*
Black Hawk College *Illinois*
Blackhawk Technical College *Wisconsin*
Blinn College *Texas*
Bossier Parish Community College *Louisiana*
Boston University *Massachusetts*
Bowling Green State University *Ohio*
Bradley University *Illinois*
Broome Community College *New York*
Broward Community College *Florida*
Brown Mackie College-South Bend *Indiana*
Butler County Community College *Pennsylvania*
California State University, Fresno *California*
California State University, Long Beach *California*
California State University, Northridge *California*
California State University, Sacramento *California*
California University of Pennsylvania *Pennsylvania*
Capital Community College *Connecticut*
Carl Albert State College *Oklahoma*
Carroll College *Wisconsin*
Carroll Community College *Maryland*
Central Florida Community College *Florida*
Central Michigan University *Michigan*
Central Pennsylvania College *Pennsylvania*
Central Piedmont Community College *North Carolina*
Cerritos College *California*
Chapman University *California*
Chatham College *Pennsylvania*
Chattanooga State Technical Community College *Tennessee*
Chesapeake College *Maryland*
Clark State Community College *Ohio*
Clarke College *Iowa*
Clarkson College *Nebraska*
Clarkson University *New York*
Cleveland State University *Ohio*
Colby Community College *Kansas*
College of DuPage *Illinois*
College Misericordia *Pennsylvania*
College of Mount St. Joseph *Ohio*
College of St. Catherine *Minnesota*
College of St. Catherine-Minneapolis *Minnesota*
The College of St. Scholastica *Minnesota*
College of Southern Maryland *Maryland*
College of Staten Island of the City University of New York *New York*
Community College of the Air Force *Alabama*
Community College of Allegheny County *Pennsylvania*
Community College of Rhode Island *Rhode Island*
Community College of Southern Nevada *Nevada*
Concordia University Wisconsin *Wisconsin*
Creighton University *Nebraska*
Cuyahoga Community College *Ohio*
Daemen College *New York*
Darton College *Georgia*
Daytona Beach Community College *Florida*
De Anza College *California*
Del Mar College *Texas*
Delaware Technical & Community College, Jack F. Owens Campus *Delaware*
Delaware Technical & Community College, Stanton/Wilmington Campus *Delaware*
Delgado Community College *Louisiana*
Delta College *Michigan*
Dominican College *New York*
Drexel University *Pennsylvania*
Duke University *North Carolina*
Duquesne University *Pennsylvania*
D'Youville College *New York*
East Carolina University *North Carolina*
East Tennessee State University *Tennessee*
Eastern Washington University *Washington*
El Paso Community College *Texas*
Elon University *North Carolina*
Emory University *Georgia*
Essex County College *New Jersey*
Fairmont State Community & Technical College *West Virginia*
Fayetteville Technical Community College *North Carolina*
Finlandia University *Michigan*
Fiorello H. LaGuardia Community College of the City University of New York *New York*
Florida Agricultural and Mechanical University *Florida*
Florida Community College at Jacksonville *Florida*
Florida Gulf Coast University *Florida*
Florida International University *Florida*
Franklin Pierce College *New Hampshire*
Gannon University *Pennsylvania*
GateWay Community College *Arizona*
Gateway Technical College *Wisconsin*
Genesee Community College *New York*
George C. Wallace Community College *Alabama*
The George Washington University *District of Columbia*
Georgia State University *Georgia*
Governors State University *Illinois*
Grand Valley State University *Michigan*
Greenville Technical College *South Carolina*
Guilford Technical Community College *North Carolina*
Gulf Coast Community College *Florida*
Gwinnett Technical College *Georgia*
Hampton University *Virginia*
Harcum College *Pennsylvania*
Hardin-Simmons University *Texas*
Hazard Community and Technical College *Kentucky*
Henry Ford Community College *Michigan*
Herkimer County Community College *New York*
Hesser College *New Hampshire*
Hinds Community College *Mississippi*
Hocking College *Ohio*
Housatonic Community College *Connecticut*
Houston Community College System *Texas*
Howard University *District of Columbia*
Hunter College of the City University of New York *New York*
Husson College *Maine*
Idaho State University *Idaho*
Illinois Central College *Illinois*
Indian Hills Community College *Iowa*
Indian River Community College *Florida*
Indiana University-Purdue University Indianapolis *Indiana*
Itawamba Community College *Mississippi*
Ithaca College *New York*
Ivy Tech Community College-East Central *Indiana*
Ivy Tech Community College-Northwest *Indiana*
Jackson State Community College *Tennessee*
James A. Rhodes State College *Ohio*
Jefferson College of Health Sciences *Virginia*
Jefferson Community and Technical College *Kentucky*
Jefferson State Community College *Alabama*
Kansas City Kansas Community College *Kansas*
Kapiolani Community College *Hawaii*
Kaskaskia College *Illinois*
Keiser College (Fort Lauderdale) *Florida*
Kellogg Community College *Michigan*
Kennebec Valley Community College *Maine*
Kent State University, Ashtabula Campus *Ohio*
Kent State University, East Liverpool Campus *Ohio*
Kilgore College *Texas*
Kingsborough Community College of the City University of New York *New York*
Kirkwood Community College *Iowa*
Lake Area Technical Institute *South Dakota*
Lake City Community College *Florida*
Lake Land College *Illinois*
Lake Superior College *Minnesota*
Laredo Community College *Texas*
Lehigh Carbon Community College *Pennsylvania*
Loma Linda University *California*
Long Island University, Brooklyn Campus *New York*

Lorain County Community College *Ohio*
Louisiana State University Health Sciences Center *Louisiana*
Louisiana State University in Shreveport *Louisiana*
Macomb Community College *Michigan*
Madisonville Community College *Kentucky*
Manatee Community College *Florida*
Manchester Community College *Connecticut*
Marion Technical College *Ohio*
Marquette University *Wisconsin*
Marshall University *West Virginia*
Martin Community College *North Carolina*
Marymount University *Virginia*
Maryville University of Saint Louis *Missouri*
Massachusetts Bay Community College *Massachusetts*
McLennan Community College *Texas*
Medical College of Georgia *Georgia*
Medical University of South Carolina *South Carolina*
Mercer County Community College *New Jersey*
Mercy College *New York*
Mercyhurst College *Pennsylvania*
Meridian Community College *Mississippi*
Miami Dade College *Florida*
Midlands Technical College *South Carolina*
Midwestern University, Glendale Campus *Arizona*
Milwaukee Area Technical College *Wisconsin*
Missouri State University *Missouri*
Missouri Western State University *Missouri*
Montgomery College *Texas*
Montgomery College *Maryland*
Morgan Community College *Colorado*
Morton College *Illinois*
Mott Community College *Michigan*
Mount Aloysius College *Pennsylvania*
Mt. Hood Community College *Oregon*
Mount St. Mary's College *California*
Mount Wachusett Community College *Massachusetts*
Mountain State University *West Virginia*
Murray State College *Oklahoma*
Nash Community College *North Carolina*
Nassau Community College *New York*
Naugatuck Valley Community College *Connecticut*
Nazareth College of Rochester *New York*
Neumann College *Pennsylvania*
New York Institute of Technology *New York*
New York University *New York*
Niagara County Community College *New York*
North Central State College *Ohio*
North Georgia College & State University *Georgia*
North Iowa Area Community College *Iowa*
North Shore Community College *Massachusetts*
Northeast Community College *Nebraska*
Northeast Wisconsin Technical College *Wisconsin*
Northeastern Oklahoma Agricultural and Mechanical College *Oklahoma*
Northeastern University *Massachusetts*
Northern Arizona University *Arizona*
Northern Illinois University *Illinois*
Northern Virginia Community College *Virginia*
Northwestern Connecticut Community College *Connecticut*
Northwestern University *Illinois*
Nova Southeastern University *Florida*
Oakland University *Michigan*
Oakton Community College *Illinois*
Odessa College *Texas*
The Ohio State University *Ohio*
Ohio University *Ohio*
Ohlone College *California*
Oklahoma City Community College *Oklahoma*
Old Dominion University *Virginia*
Onondaga Community College *New York*
Orange County Community College *New York*
Our Lady of the Lake College *Louisiana*
Owens Community College *Ohio*
Ozarks Technical Community College *Missouri*
Pacific University *Oregon*
Pearl River Community College *Mississippi*
Penn Valley Community College *Missouri*
The Pennsylvania State University DuBois Campus of the Commonwealth College *Pennsylvania*
The Pennsylvania State University Hazleton Campus of the Commonwealth College *Pennsylvania*
The Pennsylvania State University Mont Alto Campus of the Commonwealth College *Pennsylvania*
The Pennsylvania State University Shenango Campus of the Commonwealth College *Pennsylvania*
Pensacola Junior College *Florida*
Polk Community College *Florida*
Professional Skills Institute *Ohio*
Provo College *Utah*
Pueblo Community College *Colorado*
Quinnipiac University *Connecticut*
Regis University *Colorado*
The Richard Stockton College of New Jersey *New Jersey*
Roane State Community College *Tennessee*
Rockhurst University *Missouri*
Rutgers, The State University of New Jersey, Camden *New Jersey*
Sacramento City College *California*
Sacred Heart University *Connecticut*
St. Ambrose University *Iowa*
Saint Francis University *Pennsylvania*
St. Louis Community College at Meramec *Missouri*
Saint Louis University *Missouri*
St. Petersburg College *Florida*
St. Philip's College *Texas*
Salt Lake Community College *Utah*
Samuel Merritt College *California*
San Diego Mesa College *California*
San Francisco State University *California*
San Juan College *New Mexico*
Seminole Community College *Florida*
Seton Hall University *New Jersey*
Shawnee State University *Ohio*
Shenandoah University *Virginia*
Simmons College *Massachusetts*
Sinclair Community College *Ohio*
Slippery Rock University of Pennsylvania *Pennsylvania*
Somerset Community College *Kentucky*
Sonoma College (Petaluma) *California*
South Arkansas Community College *Arkansas*
South College *Tennessee*
South University *Georgia*
South University *Alabama*
South University (West Palm Beach) *Florida*
Southeast Kentucky Community and Technical College *Kentucky*
Southern Illinois University Carbondale *Illinois*
Southwest Baptist University *Missouri*
Southwest Georgia Technical College *Georgia*
Southwest Tennessee Community College *Tennessee*
Southwestern Community College *North Carolina*
Southwestern Illinois College *Illinois*
Southwestern Oklahoma State University *Oklahoma*
Spokane Falls Community College *Washington*
Springfield College *Massachusetts*
Springfield Technical Community College *Massachusetts*
Stark State College of Technology *Ohio*
State University of New York at Buffalo *New York*
State University of New York College of Technology at Canton *New York*
State University of New York Downstate Medical Center *New York*
State University of New York Upstate Medical University *New York*
Stony Brook University, State University of New York *New York*
Suffolk County Community College *New York*
Tarrant County College District *Texas*
Temple University *Pennsylvania*
Texas State University-San Marcos *Texas*
Texas Woman's University *Texas*
Thomas Jefferson University *Pennsylvania*
Touro College *New York*
Trident Technical College *South Carolina*
Tulsa Community College *Oklahoma*
Tunxis Community College *Connecticut*
Union County College *New Jersey*
The University of Alabama at Birmingham *Alabama*
University of Central Arkansas *Arkansas*
University of Central Florida *Florida*
University of Cincinnati *Ohio*
University of Connecticut *Connecticut*
University of Delaware *Delaware*
University of Evansville *Indiana*
The University of Findlay *Ohio*
University of Florida *Florida*
University of Hartford *Connecticut*
University of Illinois at Chicago *Illinois*
University of Indianapolis *Indiana*
The University of Iowa *Iowa*
University of Kansas *Kansas*
University of Kentucky *Kentucky*
University of Louisville *Kentucky*
University of Mary *North Dakota*
University of Maryland Eastern Shore *Maryland*
University of Massachusetts Lowell *Massachusetts*
University of Miami *Florida*
University of Michigan-Flint *Michigan*
University of Minnesota, Twin Cities Campus *Minnesota*
University of Mississippi Medical Center *Mississippi*
University of Missouri-Columbia *Missouri*
University of Mobile *Alabama*
The University of Montana-Missoula *Montana*
University of Nebraska Medical Center *Nebraska*
University of Nevada, Las Vegas *Nevada*
University of New England *Maine*
University of New Mexico *New Mexico*
The University of North Carolina at Chapel Hill *North Carolina*
University of North Dakota *North Dakota*
University of North Florida *Florida*
University of Oklahoma Health Sciences Center *Oklahoma*
University of the Pacific *California*
University of Pittsburgh *Pennsylvania*
University of Pittsburgh at Titusville *Pennsylvania*
University of Puerto Rico at Humacao *Puerto Rico*
University of Puerto Rico, Medical Sciences Campus *Puerto Rico*
University of Puerto Rico at Ponce *Puerto Rico*
University of Puget Sound *Washington*
University of Rhode Island *Rhode Island*
University of Saint Francis *Indiana*
University of the Sciences in Philadelphia *Pennsylvania*
The University of Scranton *Pennsylvania*
University of South Alabama *Alabama*
University of South Carolina *South Carolina*
The University of South Dakota *South Dakota*
University of South Florida *Florida*
University of Southern California *California*
The University of Tennessee at Chattanooga *Tennessee*
The University of Texas at El Paso *Texas*
The University of Texas Health Science Center at San Antonio *Texas*
The University of Texas Medical Branch *Texas*
The University of Texas Southwestern Medical Center at Dallas *Texas*
The University of Toledo *Ohio*
University of Toronto *Ontario*
University of Utah *Utah*
University of Vermont *Vermont*
University of Washington *Washington*
University of Wisconsin-La Crosse *Wisconsin*
University of Wisconsin-Madison *Wisconsin*
Utica College *New York*
Villa Maria College of Buffalo *New York*
Vincennes University *Indiana*
Virginia Commonwealth University *Virginia*
Volunteer State Community College *Tennessee*
Wallace State Community College *Alabama*
Walsh University *Ohio*
Walters State Community College *Tennessee*
Washburn University *Kansas*
Washington State Community College *Ohio*
Washington University in St. Louis *Missouri*
Wayne State University *Michigan*
West Kentucky Community and Technical College *Kentucky*
West Virginia University *West Virginia*
Western Carolina University *North Carolina*
Western Iowa Tech Community College *Iowa*
Western Technical College *Wisconsin*
Wharton County Junior College *Texas*
Whatcom Community College *Washington*

American Podiatric Medical AssociationAmerican Podiatric Medical Association (APMA)

American Psychological AssociationAmerican Psychological Association (APA)

University of Southern Mississippi *Mississippi*
The University of Tennessee *Tennessee*
The University of Texas at Austin *Texas*
The University of Texas Health Science Center at Houston *Texas*
The University of Texas Health Science Center at San Antonio *Texas*
The University of Texas Medical Branch *Texas*
The University of Texas Southwestern Medical Center at Dallas *Texas*
The University of Toledo *Ohio*
University of Toronto *Ontario*
University of Tulsa *Oklahoma*
University of Utah *Utah*
University of Vermont *Vermont*
University of Victoria *British Columbia*
University of Virginia *Virginia*
University of Washington *Washington*
University of Waterloo *Ontario*
The University of Western Ontario *Ontario*
University of Windsor *Ontario*
University of Wisconsin-Madison *Wisconsin*
University of Wisconsin-Milwaukee *Wisconsin*
University of Wyoming *Wyoming*
Utah State University *Utah*
Vanderbilt University *Tennessee*
Virginia Commonwealth University *Virginia*
Virginia Polytechnic Institute and State University *Virginia*
Washington State University *Washington*
Washington University in St. Louis *Missouri*
Wayne State University *Michigan*
West Virginia University *West Virginia*
Western Michigan University *Michigan*
Wheaton College *Illinois*
Wichita State University *Kansas*
Widener University *Pennsylvania*
Wright State University *Ohio*
Xavier University *Ohio*
Yale University *Connecticut*
Yeshiva University *New York*
York University *Ontario*

American Society of CytopathologyAmerican Society of Cytopathology (ASC)

Albany College of Pharmacy of Union University *New York*
Barnes-Jewish College of Nursing and Allied Health *Missouri*
Bellarmine University *Kentucky*
Eastern Kentucky University *Kentucky*
Indiana University-Purdue University Indianapolis *Indiana*
Loma Linda University *California*
Medical University of South Carolina *South Carolina*
Nicholls State University *Louisiana*
Oakland University *Michigan*
Old Dominion University *Virginia*
State University of New York Upstate Medical University *New York*
Stony Brook University, State University of New York *New York*
Thomas Jefferson University *Pennsylvania*
The University of Akron *Ohio*
The University of Alabama at Birmingham *Alabama*
University of Arkansas for Medical Sciences *Arkansas*
University of California, Los Angeles *California*
University of Kansas *Kansas*
University of Mississippi Medical Center *Mississippi*
University of North Dakota *North Dakota*
The University of Texas Health Science Center at Houston *Texas*
University of Utah *Utah*
University of Vermont *Vermont*
University of Wisconsin-Madison *Wisconsin*
Wayne State University *Michigan*

American Society of Landscape ArchitectsAmerican Society of Landscape Architects (ASLA)

Arizona State University *Arizona*
Auburn University *Alabama*
Ball State University *Indiana*
California Polytechnic State University, San Luis Obispo *California*
California State Polytechnic University, Pomona *California*
City College of the City University of New York *New York*
Clemson University *South Carolina*
Colorado State University *Colorado*
Cornell University *New York*
Florida International University *Florida*
Harvard University *Massachusetts*
Iowa State University of Science and Technology *Iowa*
Kansas State University *Kansas*
Louisiana State University and Agricultural and Mechanical College *Louisiana*
Michigan State University *Michigan*
Mississippi State University *Mississippi*
Morgan State University *Maryland*
North Carolina Agricultural and Technical State University *North Carolina*
North Carolina State University *North Carolina*
North Dakota State University *North Dakota*
The Ohio State University *Ohio*
Oklahoma State University *Oklahoma*
The Pennsylvania State University University Park Campus *Pennsylvania*
Purdue University *Indiana*
Rhode Island School of Design *Rhode Island*
Rutgers, The State University of New Jersey, New Brunswick/Piscataway *New Jersey*
State University of New York College of Environmental Science and Forestry *New York*
Temple University *Pennsylvania*
Texas A&M University *Texas*
Texas Tech University *Texas*
Université de Montréal *Quebec*
The University of Arizona *Arizona*
University of Arkansas *Arkansas*
The University of British Columbia *British Columbia*
University of California, Berkeley *California*
University of California, Davis *California*
University of Colorado at Denver and Health Sciences Center - Downtown Denver Campus *Colorado*
University of Connecticut *Connecticut*
University of Florida *Florida*
University of Georgia *Georgia*
University of Guelph *Ontario*
University of Idaho *Idaho*
University of Illinois at Urbana-Champaign *Illinois*
University of Kentucky *Kentucky*
University of Manitoba *Manitoba*
University of Maryland, College Park *Maryland*
University of Massachusetts Amherst *Massachusetts*
University of Michigan *Michigan*
University of Minnesota, Twin Cities Campus *Minnesota*
University of Nevada, Las Vegas *Nevada*
University of New Mexico *New Mexico*
University of Oklahoma *Oklahoma*
University of Oregon *Oregon*
University of Pennsylvania *Pennsylvania*
University of Rhode Island *Rhode Island*
The University of Texas at Arlington *Texas*
University of Toronto *Ontario*
University of Virginia *Virginia*
University of Washington *Washington*
University of Wisconsin-Madison *Wisconsin*
Utah State University *Utah*
Virginia Polytechnic Institute and State University *Virginia*
Washington State University *Washington*
West Virginia University *West Virginia*

American Speech-Language-Hearing AssociationAmerican Speech-Language-Hearing Association (ASLHA)

Abilene Christian University *Texas*
Adelphi University *New York*
Alabama Agricultural and Mechanical University *Alabama*
Appalachian State University *North Carolina*
Arizona State University *Arizona*
Arkansas State University *Arkansas*
Auburn University *Alabama*
Ball State University *Indiana*
Baylor University *Texas*
Bloomsburg University of Pennsylvania *Pennsylvania*
Boston University *Massachusetts*
Bowling Green State University *Ohio*
Brigham Young University *Utah*
Brooklyn College of the City University of New York *New York*
Buffalo State College, State University of New York *New York*
California State University, Chico *California*
California State University, East Bay *California*
California State University, Fresno *California*
California State University, Fullerton *California*
California State University, Long Beach *California*
California State University, Los Angeles *California*
California State University, Northridge *California*
California State University, Sacramento *California*
California University of Pennsylvania *Pennsylvania*
Case Western Reserve University *Ohio*
Central Michigan University *Michigan*
Central Missouri State University *Missouri*
Clarion University of Pennsylvania *Pennsylvania*
Cleveland State University *Ohio*
College Misericordia *Pennsylvania*
The College of New Jersey *New Jersey*
The College of Saint Rose *New York*
Duquesne University *Pennsylvania*
East Carolina University *North Carolina*
East Stroudsburg University of Pennsylvania *Pennsylvania*
East Tennessee State University *Tennessee*
Eastern Illinois University *Illinois*
Eastern Kentucky University *Kentucky*
Eastern Michigan University *Michigan*
Eastern New Mexico University *New Mexico*
Eastern Washington University *Washington*
Edinboro University of Pennsylvania *Pennsylvania*
Emerson College *Massachusetts*
Florida Atlantic University *Florida*
Florida International University *Florida*
Florida State University *Florida*
Fontbonne University *Missouri*
Fort Hays State University *Kansas*
Gallaudet University *District of Columbia*
The George Washington University *District of Columbia*
Georgia State University *Georgia*
Governors State University *Illinois*
Hampton University *Virginia*
Hofstra University *New York*
Howard University *District of Columbia*
Hunter College of the City University of New York *New York*
Idaho State University *Idaho*
Illinois State University *Illinois*
Indiana State University *Indiana*
Indiana University Bloomington *Indiana*
Indiana University of Pennsylvania *Pennsylvania*
Ithaca College *New York*
Jackson State University *Mississippi*
James Madison University *Virginia*
Kansas State University *Kansas*
Kean University *New Jersey*
Kent State University *Ohio*
La Salle University *Pennsylvania*
Lamar University *Texas*
Lehman College of the City University of New York *New York*
Loma Linda University *California*
Long Island University, Brooklyn Campus *New York*
Long Island University, C.W. Post Campus *New York*
Louisiana State University and Agricultural and Mechanical College *Louisiana*
Louisiana State University Health Sciences Center *Louisiana*
Louisiana Tech University *Louisiana*
Loyola College in Maryland *Maryland*
Marquette University *Wisconsin*
Marshall University *West Virginia*
Marywood University *Pennsylvania*
Medical University of South Carolina *South Carolina*

Mercy College *New York*
Miami University *Ohio*
Michigan State University *Michigan*
Minnesota State University Mankato *Minnesota*
Minnesota State University Moorhead *Minnesota*
Minot State University *North Dakota*
Mississippi University for Women *Mississippi*
Missouri State University *Missouri*
Montclair State University *New Jersey*
Murray State University *Kentucky*
Nazareth College of Rochester *New York*
New Mexico State University *New Mexico*
New York University *New York*
North Carolina Central University *North Carolina*
Northeastern State University *Oklahoma*
Northeastern University *Massachusetts*
Northern Arizona University *Arizona*
Northern Illinois University *Illinois*
Northern Michigan University *Michigan*
Northwestern University *Illinois*
Nova Southeastern University *Florida*
The Ohio State University *Ohio*
Ohio University *Ohio*
Oklahoma State University *Oklahoma*
Old Dominion University *Virginia*
Our Lady of the Lake University of San Antonio *Texas*
The Pennsylvania State University University Park Campus *Pennsylvania*
Portland State University *Oregon*
Purdue University *Indiana*
Queens College of the City University of New York *New York*
Radford University *Virginia*
Rockhurst University *Missouri*
Rush University *Illinois*
St. Cloud State University *Minnesota*
St. John's University *New York*
Saint Louis University *Missouri*
Saint Xavier University *Illinois*
San Diego State University *California*
San Francisco State University *California*
San Jose State University *California*
Seton Hall University *New Jersey*
South Carolina State University *South Carolina*
Southeast Missouri State University *Missouri*
Southeastern Louisiana University *Louisiana*
Southern Connecticut State University *Connecticut*
Southern Illinois University Carbondale *Illinois*
Southern Illinois University Edwardsville *Illinois*
Southern University and Agricultural and Mechanical College *Louisiana*
State University of New York at Buffalo *New York*
State University of New York College at Geneseo *New York*
State University of New York, Fredonia *New York*
State University of New York at New Paltz *New York*
State University of New York at Plattsburgh *New York*
Stephen F. Austin State University *Texas*
Syracuse University *New York*
Temple University *Pennsylvania*
Tennessee State University *Tennessee*
Texas A&M University-Kingsville *Texas*
Texas Christian University *Texas*
Texas State University-San Marcos *Texas*
Texas Tech University *Texas*
Texas Woman's University *Texas*
Touro College *New York*
Towson University *Maryland*
Truman State University *Missouri*
The University of Akron *Ohio*
The University of Alabama *Alabama*
The University of Arizona *Arizona*
University of Arkansas *Arkansas*
University of Arkansas at Little Rock *Arkansas*
University of California, San Diego *California*
University of Central Arkansas *Arkansas*
University of Central Florida *Florida*
University of Central Oklahoma *Oklahoma*
University of Cincinnati *Ohio*
University of Colorado at Boulder *Colorado*
University of Connecticut *Connecticut*
University of the District of Columbia *District of Columbia*
University of Florida *Florida*
University of Georgia *Georgia*
University of Hawaii at Manoa *Hawaii*
University of Houston *Texas*
University of Illinois at Urbana-Champaign *Illinois*
The University of Iowa *Iowa*
University of Kansas *Kansas*
University of Kentucky *Kentucky*
University of Louisiana at Lafayette *Louisiana*
University of Louisiana at Monroe *Louisiana*
University of Louisville *Kentucky*
University of Maine *Maine*
University of Maryland, College Park *Maryland*
University of Massachusetts Amherst *Massachusetts*
University of Memphis *Tennessee*
University of Minnesota, Duluth *Minnesota*
University of Minnesota, Twin Cities Campus *Minnesota*
University of Mississippi *Mississippi*
University of Missouri-Columbia *Missouri*
University of Montevallo *Alabama*
University of Nebraska at Kearney *Nebraska*
University of Nebraska-Lincoln *Nebraska*
University of Nebraska at Omaha *Nebraska*
University of Nevada, Reno *Nevada*
University of New Hampshire *New Hampshire*
University of New Mexico *New Mexico*
The University of North Carolina at Chapel Hill *North Carolina*
The University of North Carolina at Greensboro *North Carolina*
University of North Dakota *North Dakota*
University of North Texas *Texas*
University of Northern Colorado *Colorado*
University of Northern Iowa *Iowa*
University of Oklahoma Health Sciences Center *Oklahoma*
University of Oregon *Oregon*
University of the Pacific *California*
University of Pittsburgh *Pennsylvania*
University of Puerto Rico, Medical Sciences Campus *Puerto Rico*
University of Redlands *California*
University of Rhode Island *Rhode Island*
University of South Alabama *Alabama*
University of South Carolina *South Carolina*
The University of South Dakota *South Dakota*
University of South Florida *Florida*
University of Southern Mississippi *Mississippi*
The University of Tennessee *Tennessee*
The University of Texas at Austin *Texas*
The University of Texas at Dallas *Texas*
The University of Texas at El Paso *Texas*
The University of Texas-Pan American *Texas*
The University of Toledo *Ohio*
University of Tulsa *Oklahoma*
University of Utah *Utah*
University of Vermont *Vermont*
University of Virginia *Virginia*
University of Washington *Washington*
University of Wisconsin-Eau Claire *Wisconsin*
University of Wisconsin-Madison *Wisconsin*
University of Wisconsin-Milwaukee *Wisconsin*
University of Wisconsin-River Falls *Wisconsin*
University of Wisconsin-Stevens Point *Wisconsin*
University of Wisconsin-Whitewater *Wisconsin*
University of Wyoming *Wyoming*
Utah State University *Utah*
Valdosta State University *Georgia*
Vanderbilt University *Tennessee*
Washington State University *Washington*
Washington University in St. Louis *Missouri*
Wayne State University *Michigan*
West Chester University of Pennsylvania *Pennsylvania*
West Texas A&M University *Texas*
West Virginia University *West Virginia*
Western Carolina University *North Carolina*
Western Illinois University *Illinois*
Western Kentucky University *Kentucky*
Western Michigan University *Michigan*
Western Washington University *Washington*
Wichita State University *Kansas*
William Paterson University of New Jersey *New Jersey*
Worcester State College *Massachusetts*

American Veterinary Medical AssociationAmerican Veterinary Medical Association (AVMA)

Auburn University *Alabama*
Colorado State University *Colorado*
Cornell University *New York*
Iowa State University of Science and Technology *Iowa*
Kansas State University *Kansas*
Louisiana State University and Agricultural and Mechanical College *Louisiana*
Michigan State University *Michigan*
Mississippi State University *Mississippi*
North Carolina State University *North Carolina*
The Ohio State University *Ohio*
Oklahoma State University *Oklahoma*
Oregon State University *Oregon*
Purdue University *Indiana*
Texas A&M University *Texas*
Tufts University *Massachusetts*
Tuskegee University *Alabama*
Université de Montréal *Quebec*
University of California, Davis *California*
University of Florida *Florida*
University of Georgia *Georgia*
University of Guelph *Ontario*
University of Illinois at Urbana-Champaign *Illinois*
University of Maryland, College Park *Maryland*
University of Minnesota, Twin Cities Campus *Minnesota*
University of Missouri-Columbia *Missouri*
University of Pennsylvania *Pennsylvania*
University of Prince Edward Island *Prince Edward Island*
University of Saskatchewan *Saskatchewan*
The University of Tennessee *Tennessee*
University of Wisconsin-Madison *Wisconsin*
Virginia Polytechnic Institute and State University *Virginia*
Washington State University *Washington*

Association of Advanced Rabbinical and TalmudicAssociation of Advanced Rabbinical and Talmudic Schools (AARTS)

Beis Medrash Heichal Dovid *New York*
Beth Benjamin Academy of Connecticut *Connecticut*
Beth HaMedrash Shaarei Yosher Institute *New York*
Beth Hatalmud Rabbinical College *New York*
Beth Medrash Govoha *New Jersey*
Central Yeshiva Tomchei Tmimim-Lubavitch *New York*
Darkei Noam Rabbinical College *New York*
Kehilath Yakov Rabbinical Seminary *New York*
Kol Yaakov Torah Center *New York*
Machzikei Hadath Rabbinical College *New York*
Mesivta of Eastern Parkway Rabbinical Seminary *New York*
Mesivta Tifereth Jerusalem of America *New York*
Mesivta Torah Vodaath Rabbinical Seminary *New York*
Mirrer Yeshiva *New York*
Ner Israel Rabbinical College *Maryland*
Ner Israel Yeshiva College of Toronto *Ontario*
Ohr Hameir Theological Seminary *New York*
Ohr Somayach/Joseph Tanenbaum Educational Center *New York*
Rabbi Jacob Joseph School *New Jersey*
Rabbinical Academy Mesivta Rabbi Chaim Berlin *New York*
Rabbinical College of America *New Jersey*
Rabbinical College Beth Shraga *New York*
Rabbinical College Bobover Yeshiva B'nei Zion *New York*
Rabbinical College Ch'san Sofer *New York*
Rabbinical College of Long Island *New York*
Rabbinical College of Ohr Shimon Yisroel *New York*
Rabbinical College of Telshe *Ohio*
Rabbinical Seminary Adas Yereim *New York*
Rabbinical Seminary of America *New York*
Rabbinical Seminary M'kor Chaim *New York*
Sh'or Yoshuv Rabbinical College *New York*
Talmudic College of Florida *Florida*

Talmudical Academy of New Jersey *New Jersey*
Talmudical Institute of Upstate New York *New York*
Talmudical Seminary Oholei Torah *New York*
Talmudical Yeshiva of Philadelphia *Pennsylvania*
Telshe Yeshiva-Chicago *Illinois*
Torah Temimah Talmudical Seminary *New York*
United Talmudical Seminary *New York*
U.T.A. Mesivta of Kiryas Joel *New York*
Yeshiva And Kollel Harbotzas Torah *New York*
Yeshiva Beth Moshe *Pennsylvania*
Yeshiva College of the Nation's Capital *Maryland*
Yeshiva Derech Chaim *New York*
Yeshiva D'Monsey Rabbinical College *New York*
Yeshiva Geddolah of Greater Detroit Rabbinical College *Michigan*
Yeshiva Gedolah Imrei Yosef D'Spinka *New York*
Yeshiva Gedolah Rabbinical College *Florida*
Yeshiva Karlin Stolin Rabbinical Institute *New York*
Yeshiva and Kolel Bais Medrash Elyon *New York*
Yeshiva of Nitra Rabbinical College *New York*
Yeshiva Ohr Elchonon Chabad/West Coast Talmudical Seminary *California*
Yeshiva Shaar Hatorah Talmudic Research Institute *New York*
Yeshiva Shaarei Torah of Rockland *New York*
Yeshiva of the Telshe Alumni *New York*
Yeshiva Toras Chaim Talmudical Seminary *Colorado*
Yeshivas Novominsk *New York*
Yeshivat Mikdash Melech *New York*
Yeshivath Viznitz *New York*
Yeshivath Zichron Moshe *New York*

Association of American Law SchoolsAssociation of American Law Schools (AALS)

American University *District of Columbia*
Arizona State University *Arizona*
Baylor University *Texas*
Boston College *Massachusetts*
Boston University *Massachusetts*
Brigham Young University *Utah*
Capital University *Ohio*
Case Western Reserve University *Ohio*
The Catholic University of America *District of Columbia*
Cleveland State University *Ohio*
The College of William and Mary *Virginia*
Cornell University *New York*
Creighton University *Nebraska*
DePaul University *Illinois*
Drake University *Iowa*
Duke University *North Carolina*
Duquesne University *Pennsylvania*
Emory University *Georgia*
Florida State University *Florida*
Fordham University *New York*
George Mason University *Virginia*
The George Washington University *District of Columbia*
Georgetown University *District of Columbia*
Georgia State University *Georgia*
Golden Gate University *California*
Gonzaga University *Washington*
Hamline University *Minnesota*
Harvard University *Massachusetts*
Hofstra University *New York*
Howard University *District of Columbia*
Illinois Institute of Technology *Illinois*
Lewis & Clark College *Oregon*
Louisiana State University and Agricultural and Mechanical College *Louisiana*
Loyola Marymount University *California*
Loyola University Chicago *Illinois*
Loyola University New Orleans *Louisiana*
Marquette University *Wisconsin*
Mercer University *Georgia*
Mississippi College *Mississippi*
New York University *New York*
Northeastern University *Massachusetts*
Northern Illinois University *Illinois*
Northern Kentucky University *Kentucky*
Northwestern University *Illinois*
Nova Southeastern University *Florida*
Ohio Northern University *Ohio*
The Ohio State University *Ohio*
Oklahoma City University *Oklahoma*
Pace University *New York*
Pepperdine University *California*
Quinnipiac University *Connecticut*
Rutgers, The State University of New Jersey, Camden *New Jersey*
Rutgers, The State University of New Jersey, Newark *New Jersey*
St. John's University *New York*
Saint Louis University *Missouri*
St. Mary's University of San Antonio *Texas*
St. Thomas University *Florida*
Samford University *Alabama*
Santa Clara University *California*
Seattle University *Washington*
Seton Hall University *New Jersey*
Southern Illinois University Carbondale *Illinois*
Southern Methodist University *Texas*
Stanford University *California*
State University of New York at Buffalo *New York*
Stetson University *Florida*
Suffolk University *Massachusetts*
Syracuse University *New York*
Temple University *Pennsylvania*
Texas Tech University *Texas*
Touro College *New York*
Tulane University *Louisiana*
The University of Akron *Ohio*
The University of Alabama *Alabama*
The University of Arizona *Arizona*
University of Arkansas *Arkansas*
University of Arkansas at Little Rock *Arkansas*
University of Baltimore *Maryland*
University of California, Berkeley *California*
University of California, Davis *California*
University of California, Los Angeles *California*
University of Chicago *Illinois*
University of Cincinnati *Ohio*
University of Colorado at Boulder *Colorado*
University of Connecticut *Connecticut*
University of Dayton *Ohio*
University of Denver *Colorado*
University of Detroit Mercy *Michigan*
University of Florida *Florida*
University of Georgia *Georgia*
University of Hawaii at Manoa *Hawaii*
University of Houston *Texas*
University of Idaho *Idaho*
University of Illinois at Urbana-Champaign *Illinois*
The University of Iowa *Iowa*
University of Kansas *Kansas*
University of Kentucky *Kentucky*
University of Louisville *Kentucky*
University of Maine *Maine*
University of Memphis *Tennessee*
University of Miami *Florida*
University of Michigan *Michigan*
University of Minnesota, Twin Cities Campus *Minnesota*
University of Mississippi *Mississippi*
University of Missouri-Columbia *Missouri*
University of Missouri-Kansas City *Missouri*
The University of Montana-Missoula *Montana*
University of Nebraska-Lincoln *Nebraska*
University of Nevada, Las Vegas *Nevada*
University of New Mexico *New Mexico*
The University of North Carolina at Chapel Hill *North Carolina*
University of North Dakota *North Dakota*
University of Notre Dame *Indiana*
University of Oklahoma *Oklahoma*
University of Oregon *Oregon*
University of the Pacific *California*
University of Pennsylvania *Pennsylvania*
University of Pittsburgh *Pennsylvania*
University of Puerto Rico, Río Piedras *Puerto Rico*
University of Richmond *Virginia*
University of San Diego *California*
University of San Francisco *California*
University of South Carolina *South Carolina*
The University of South Dakota *South Dakota*
University of Southern California *California*
The University of Tennessee *Tennessee*
The University of Texas at Austin *Texas*
The University of Toledo *Ohio*
University of Tulsa *Oklahoma*
University of Utah *Utah*
University of Virginia *Virginia*
University of Washington *Washington*
University of Wisconsin-Madison *Wisconsin*
University of Wyoming *Wyoming*
Valparaiso University *Indiana*
Vanderbilt University *Tennessee*
Villanova University *Pennsylvania*
Wake Forest University *North Carolina*
Washburn University *Kansas*
Washington and Lee University *Virginia*
Washington University in St. Louis *Missouri*
Wayne State University *Michigan*
West Virginia University *West Virginia*
Western New England College *Massachusetts*
Whittier College *California*
Widener University *Pennsylvania*
Willamette University *Oregon*
Yale University *Connecticut*
Yeshiva University *New York*

Association for Clinical Pastoral Education, Inc.Association for Clinical Pastoral Education, Inc. (ACIPE)

Anderson University *Indiana*
Baylor University *Texas*
Boston University *Massachusetts*
Drew University *New Jersey*
Duke University *North Carolina*
Eastern Mennonite University *Virginia*
Emory University *Georgia*
Gardner-Webb University *North Carolina*
George Fox University *Oregon*
Georgetown University *District of Columbia*
Gonzaga University *Washington*
Harvard University *Massachusetts*
Howard University *District of Columbia*
Indiana University-Purdue University Indianapolis *Indiana*
The Jewish Theological Seminary *New York*
The Johns Hopkins University *Maryland*
Liberty University *Virginia*
Loma Linda University *California*
Loyola University Chicago *Illinois*
Mount Angel Seminary *Oregon*
New Orleans Baptist Theological Seminary *Louisiana*
New York University *New York*
The Ohio State University *Ohio*
Regent University *Virginia*
Rush University *Illinois*
Sacred Heart Major Seminary *Michigan*
St. John's University *New York*
Saint Louis University *Missouri*
Seton Hall University *New Jersey*
Sewanee: The University of the South *Tennessee*
Southeastern Baptist Theological Seminary *North Carolina*
Southern Baptist Theological Seminary *Kentucky*
Southern Methodist University *Texas*
Stanford University *California*
Texas Christian University *Texas*
Thomas Jefferson University *Pennsylvania*
The University of Alabama at Birmingham *Alabama*
University of Arkansas for Medical Sciences *Arkansas*
University of California, Davis *California*
University of California, Los Angeles *California*
University of Chicago *Illinois*
University of Dubuque *Iowa*
The University of Iowa *Iowa*
University of Kentucky *Kentucky*
University of Louisville *Kentucky*
University of Minnesota, Twin Cities Campus *Minnesota*
The University of North Carolina at Chapel Hill *North Carolina*
University of Notre Dame *Indiana*
University of Oklahoma Health Sciences Center *Oklahoma*
University of Pennsylvania *Pennsylvania*
University of Rochester *New York*
University of St. Thomas *Texas*
University of St. Thomas *Minnesota*
The University of Tennessee *Tennessee*
The University of Texas Health Science Center at Houston *Texas*

University of Virginia *Virginia*
Vanderbilt University *Tennessee*
Virginia Commonwealth University *Virginia*
Virginia Union University *Virginia*
Wake Forest University *North Carolina*
Washington University in St. Louis *Missouri*
West Virginia University *West Virginia*
Yale University *Connecticut*

Association of Collegiate Business Schools andAssociation of Collegiate Business Schools and Programs (ACBSP)

Abilene Christian University *Texas*
Aiken Technical College *South Carolina*
Alabama State University *Alabama*
Albany State University *Georgia*
Alpena Community College *Michigan*
Alvernia College *Pennsylvania*
Anderson University *Indiana*
Angelo State University *Texas*
Arkansas Northeastern College *Arkansas*
Ashland Community and Technical College *Kentucky*
Ashland University *Ohio*
Athens State University *Alabama*
Athens Technical College *Georgia*
Atlanta Metropolitan College *Georgia*
Aurora University *Illinois*
Baker University *Kansas*
Baltimore City Community College *Maryland*
Berkeley College *New Jersey*
Biola University *California*
Bishop State Community College *Alabama*
Bluefield State College *West Virginia*
Bowie State University *Maryland*
Bronx Community College of the City University of New York *New York*
Bucks County Community College *Pennsylvania*
Butler County Community College *Pennsylvania*
Caldwell College *New Jersey*
California Baptist University *California*
California State University, Dominguez Hills *California*
Cameron University *Oklahoma*
Capital University *Ohio*
Cardinal Stritch University *Wisconsin*
Catawba Valley Community College *North Carolina*
Central Carolina Technical College *South Carolina*
Central Maine Community College *Maine*
Central New Mexico Community College *New Mexico*
Chadron State College *Nebraska*
Chattahoochee Technical College *Georgia*
City Colleges of Chicago, Harold Washington College *Illinois*
City Colleges of Chicago, Wilbur Wright College *Illinois*
Claflin University *South Carolina*
College of Mount Saint Vincent *New York*
The College of Saint Rose *New York*
College of Southern Maryland *Maryland*
Columbus State Community College *Ohio*
Community College of Rhode Island *Rhode Island*
Cossatot Community College of the University of Arkansas *Arkansas*
County College of Morris *New Jersey*
Cumberland University *Tennessee*
Cuyahoga Community College *Ohio*
Dakota State University *South Dakota*
Dallas Baptist University *Texas*
Dana College *Nebraska*
Delaware Technical & Community College, Jack F. Owens Campus *Delaware*
Delaware Technical & Community College, Stanton/Wilmington Campus *Delaware*
Delaware Technical & Community College, Terry Campus *Delaware*
Delgado Community College *Louisiana*
Delta State University *Mississippi*
Denmark Technical College *South Carolina*
DeSales University *Pennsylvania*
Doane College *Nebraska*
Dominican University *Illinois*
Doña Ana Branch Community College *New Mexico*
Drury University *Missouri*
East Arkansas Community College *Arkansas*
East Central University *Oklahoma*
Eastern New Mexico University *New Mexico*
Edgewood College *Wisconsin*
Edinboro University of Pennsylvania *Pennsylvania*
Elizabethtown College *Pennsylvania*
Embry-Riddle Aeronautical University *Florida*
Embry-Riddle Aeronautical University, Extended Campus *Florida*
Erie Community College *New York*
Fisk University *Tennessee*
Florence-Darlington Technical College *South Carolina*
Florida Community College at Jacksonville *Florida*
Florida Memorial College *Florida*
Fontbonne University *Missouri*
Freed-Hardeman University *Tennessee*
Gadsden State Community College *Alabama*
Gainesville College *Georgia*
Gallaudet University *District of Columbia*
Gannon University *Pennsylvania*
Gardner-Webb University *North Carolina*
Geneva College *Pennsylvania*
Georgian Court University *New Jersey*
Goldey-Beacom College *Delaware*
Governors State University *Illinois*
Grand Canyon University *Arizona*
Greenville Technical College *South Carolina*
Hardin-Simmons University *Texas*
Harding University *Arkansas*
Harris-Stowe State University *Missouri*
Harrisburg Area Community College *Pennsylvania*
Henry Ford Community College *Michigan*
High Point University *North Carolina*
Hocking College *Ohio*
Holyoke Community College *Massachusetts*
Horry-Georgetown Technical College *South Carolina*
Houston Baptist University *Texas*
Indiana University East *Indiana*
Ivy Tech Community College-Bloomington *Indiana*
Ivy Tech Community College-Central Indiana *Indiana*
Ivy Tech Community College-Columbus *Indiana*
Ivy Tech Community College-East Central *Indiana*
Ivy Tech Community College-Kokomo *Indiana*
Ivy Tech Community College-Lafayette *Indiana*
Ivy Tech Community College-North Central *Indiana*
Ivy Tech Community College-Northeast *Indiana*
Ivy Tech Community College-Northwest *Indiana*
Ivy Tech Community College-Southeast *Indiana*
Ivy Tech Community College-Southern Indiana *Indiana*
Ivy Tech Community College-Southwest *Indiana*
Ivy Tech Community College-Wabash Valley *Indiana*
Ivy Tech Community College-Whitewater *Indiana*
Jackson Community College *Michigan*
Jackson State Community College *Tennessee*
James A. Rhodes State College *Ohio*
Jarvis Christian College *Texas*
Jefferson State Community College *Alabama*
Johnson C. Smith University *North Carolina*
Johnson County Community College *Kansas*
Joliet Junior College *Illinois*
Jones County Junior College *Mississippi*
Kansas City Kansas Community College *Kansas*
Kennebec Valley Community College *Maine*
Kent State University, Ashtabula Campus *Ohio*
Kent State University, East Liverpool Campus *Ohio*
Kent State University, Geauga Campus *Ohio*
Kent State University, Salem Campus *Ohio*
Kent State University, Trumbull Campus *Ohio*
Kent State University, Tuscarawas Campus *Ohio*
Kentucky State University *Kentucky*
Kettering University *Michigan*
La Roche College *Pennsylvania*
LaGrange College *Georgia*
Lamar State College-Port Arthur *Texas*
Lambuth University *Tennessee*
Langston University *Oklahoma*
Lawrence Technological University *Michigan*
Lawson State Community College *Alabama*
Lebanon Valley College *Pennsylvania*
Lehigh Carbon Community College *Pennsylvania*
Lenoir-Rhyne College *North Carolina*
Lincoln University *Missouri*
Lipscomb University *Tennessee*
Louisiana College *Louisiana*
Lycoming College *Pennsylvania*
Marshall University *West Virginia*
Marymount University *Virginia*
Maryville University of Saint Louis *Missouri*
Marywood University *Pennsylvania*
McHenry County College *Illinois*
Medgar Evers College of the City University of New York *New York*
Methodist College *North Carolina*
Metropolitan Community College *Nebraska*
Midlands Technical College *South Carolina*
Midwestern State University *Texas*
Millersville University of Pennsylvania *Pennsylvania*
Millikin University *Illinois*
Mississippi College *Mississippi*
Mississippi University for Women *Mississippi*
Mississippi Valley State University *Mississippi*
Missouri Southern State University *Missouri*
Morehead State University *Kentucky*
Motlow State Community College *Tennessee*
Mount Vernon Nazarene University *Ohio*
Nashville State Technical Community College *Tennessee*
National Park Community College *Arkansas*
Nebraska Wesleyan University *Nebraska*
New Hampshire Community Technical College, Manchester/Stratham *New Hampshire*
New Jersey City University *New Jersey*
New Mexico Highlands University *New Mexico*
North Carolina Central University *North Carolina*
North Central State College *Ohio*
North Georgia College & State University *Georgia*
North Hennepin Community College *Minnesota*
Northampton County Area Community College *Pennsylvania*
Northeast State Technical Community College *Tennessee*
Northeastern State University *Oklahoma*
Northern Maine Community College *Maine*
Northern New Mexico Community College *New Mexico*
Northern Oklahoma College *Oklahoma*
Northwest Missouri State University *Missouri*
Northwest Nazarene University *Idaho*
Northwest State Community College *Ohio*
Northwestern Business College *Illinois*
Northwestern College *Minnesota*
Northwestern Michigan College *Michigan*
Norwich University *Vermont*
Oakwood College *Alabama*
Oklahoma Baptist University *Oklahoma*
Oklahoma Christian University *Oklahoma*
Oklahoma City University *Oklahoma*
Orange County Community College *New York*
Orangeburg-Calhoun Technical College *South Carolina*
Our Lady of the Lake University of San Antonio *Texas*
Owens Community College *Ohio*
Paine College *Georgia*
Peirce College *Pennsylvania*
Pellissippi State Technical Community College *Tennessee*
Philander Smith College *Arkansas*
Phillips Community College of the University of Arkansas *Arkansas*
Piedmont Technical College *South Carolina*
Plymouth State University *New Hampshire*
Point Loma Nazarene University *California*
Pontifical Catholic University of Puerto Rico *Puerto Rico*
Pratt Community College *Kansas*
Presbyterian College *South Carolina*
Purdue University North Central *Indiana*
Queens University of Charlotte *North Carolina*
Queensborough Community College of the City University of New York *New York*
Reid State Technical College *Alabama*
Roanoke College *Virginia*
Roosevelt University *Illinois*
St. Ambrose University *Iowa*
Saint Vincent College *Pennsylvania*
Saint Xavier University *Illinois*
Salem International University *West Virginia*
Salt Lake Community College *Utah*

San Juan College *New Mexico*
Schenectady County Community College *New York*
Shawnee State University *Ohio*
Sinclair Community College *Ohio*
Slippery Rock University of Pennsylvania *Pennsylvania*
South Suburban College *Illinois*
Southeast Community College, Beatrice Campus *Nebraska*
Southeast Community College, Lincoln Campus *Nebraska*
Southeast Community College, Milford Campus *Nebraska*
Southeastern Oklahoma State University *Oklahoma*
Southern New Hampshire University *New Hampshire*
Southern Polytechnic State University *Georgia*
Southern Utah University *Utah*
Southwest Baptist University *Missouri*
Southwest Tennessee Community College *Tennessee*
Southwestern Illinois College *Illinois*
Southwestern Oklahoma State University *Oklahoma*
Spartanburg Technical College *South Carolina*
Spring Hill College *Alabama*
State University of New York College of Agriculture and Technology at Morrisville *New York*
Sul Ross State University *Texas*
Sullivan County Community College *New York*
Tarleton State University *Texas*
Technical College of the Lowcountry *South Carolina*
Texas A&M University-Kingsville *Texas*
Texas Lutheran University *Texas*
Three Rivers Community College *Missouri*
Three Rivers Community College *Connecticut*
Tiffin University *Ohio*
Tri-County Technical College *South Carolina*
Trident Technical College *South Carolina*
Trinity Christian College *Illinois*
Troy University *Alabama*
The University of Akron-Wayne College *Ohio*
University of Bridgeport *Connecticut*
University of Central Oklahoma *Oklahoma*
University of Dallas *Texas*
University of the District of Columbia *District of Columbia*
University of the Incarnate Word *Texas*
University of Indianapolis *Indiana*
University of Mobile *Alabama*
University of North Alabama *Alabama*
University of Northwestern Ohio *Ohio*
University of St. Thomas *Texas*
University of South Carolina Lancaster *South Carolina*
University of the Virgin Islands *United States Virgin Islands*
The University of West Alabama *Alabama*
Vincennes University *Indiana*
Virginia Union University *Virginia*
Virginia Western Community College *Virginia*
Volunteer State Community College *Tennessee*
Voorhees College *South Carolina*
Wagner College *New York*
Walla Walla College *Washington*
Walters State Community College *Tennessee*
West Texas A&M University *Texas*
Western New Mexico University *New Mexico*
Westminster College *Utah*
Wheeling Jesuit University *West Virginia*
Wilkes University *Pennsylvania*
William Rainey Harper College *Illinois*
Williamsburg Technical College *South Carolina*
Wingate University *North Carolina*
Woodbury University *California*
Xavier University of Louisiana *Louisiana*
York College of Pennsylvania *Pennsylvania*
York Technical College *South Carolina*

Association of Theological Schools in theAssociation of Theological Schools in the United States and Canada (ATS)

Abilene Christian University *Texas*
Acadia University *Nova Scotia*
Alliance University College *Alberta*
Anderson University *Indiana*
Andrews University *Michigan*
Ashland University *Ohio*
Azusa Pacific University *California*
Baptist Missionary Association Theological Seminary *Texas*
Barry University *Florida*
Baylor University *Texas*
Biola University *California*
Boston College *Massachusetts*
Boston University *Massachusetts*
Campbell University *North Carolina*
The Catholic University of America *District of Columbia*
Cincinnati Christian University *Ohio*
Columbia International University *South Carolina*
Dominican School of Philosophy and Theology *California*
Drew University *New Jersey*
Duke University *North Carolina*
Eastern Mennonite University *Virginia*
Emory University *Georgia*
Gardner-Webb University *North Carolina*
George Fox University *Oregon*
Gonzaga University *Washington*
Hardin-Simmons University *Texas*
Harvard University *Massachusetts*
Heritage Baptist College and Heritage Theological Seminary *Ontario*
Howard University *District of Columbia*
La Sierra University *California*
Lipscomb University *Tennessee*
Loyola Marymount University *California*
Loyola University Chicago *Illinois*
McGill University *Quebec*
McMaster University *Ontario*
Mercer University *Georgia*
Mount Angel Seminary *Oregon*
Mount St. Mary's University *Maryland*
Multnomah Bible College and Biblical Seminary *Oregon*
New Orleans Baptist Theological Seminary *Louisiana*
Newman Theological College *Alberta*
Oakland City University *Indiana*
Oral Roberts University *Oklahoma*
Pontifical College Josephinum *Ohio*
Providence College and Theological Seminary *Manitoba*
Queen's University at Kingston *Ontario*
Regent University *Virginia*
Sacred Heart Major Seminary *Michigan*
St. Charles Borromeo Seminary, Overbrook *Pennsylvania*
Saint John's University *Minnesota*
Samford University *Alabama*
Seattle University *Washington*
Seton Hall University *New Jersey*
Sewanee: The University of the South *Tennessee*
Shaw University *North Carolina*
Southeastern Baptist Theological Seminary *North Carolina*
Southern Baptist Theological Seminary *Kentucky*
Southern Christian University *Alabama*
Southern Methodist University *Texas*
Taylor University College and Seminary *Alberta*
Texas Christian University *Texas*
Trinity International University *Illinois*
Trinity Western University *British Columbia*
Tyndale University College & Seminary *Ontario*
University of Chicago *Illinois*
University of Dubuque *Iowa*
University of Notre Dame *Indiana*
University of St. Thomas *Texas*
University of St. Thomas *Minnesota*
University of Toronto *Ontario*
The University of Western Ontario *Ontario*
The University of Winnipeg *Manitoba*
Vanderbilt University *Tennessee*
Virginia Union University *Virginia*
Wake Forest University *North Carolina*
Wilfrid Laurier University *Ontario*
Yale University *Connecticut*

Commission on Opticianry AccreditationCommission on Opticianry Accreditation (COptA)

Camden County College *New Jersey*
Community College of Southern Nevada *Nevada*
DeKalb Technical College *Georgia*
Durham Technical Community College *North Carolina*
El Paso Community College *Texas*
Erie Community College *New York*
Essex County College *New Jersey*
Hillsborough Community College *Florida*
Holyoke Community College *Massachusetts*
Indiana University Bloomington *Indiana*
Interboro Institute *New York*
J. Sargeant Reynolds Community College *Virginia*
Miami Dade College *Florida*
Middlesex Community College *Connecticut*
Milwaukee Area Technical College *Wisconsin*
New York City College of Technology of the City University of New York *New York*
Ogeechee Technical College *Georgia*
Raritan Valley Community College *New Jersey*
Roane State Community College *Tennessee*
Seattle Central Community College *Washington*
Southwestern Indian Polytechnic Institute *New Mexico*
Tyler Junior College *Texas*

Committee on Accreditation of Education ProgramsCommittee on Accreditation of Education Programs in Kinesiotherapy (CAEPK)

California State University, Long Beach *California*
Norfolk State University *Virginia*
San Diego State University *California*
Shaw University *North Carolina*
University of Southern Mississippi *Mississippi*
The University of Toledo *Ohio*

Committee on Accreditation for Respiratory CareCommittee on Accreditation for Respiratory Care (CARC)

Allegany College of Maryland *Maryland*
Alvin Community College *Texas*
Amarillo College *Texas*
American River College *California*
Angelina College *Texas*
Apollo College-Phoenix, Inc. *Arizona*
Apollo College-Tri-City, Inc. *Arizona*
Armstrong Atlantic State University *Georgia*
Ashland Community and Technical College *Kentucky*
Athens Technical College *Georgia*
ATI Career Training Center (Miami) *Florida*
ATI Health Education Center *Florida*
Augusta Technical College *Georgia*
Baltimore City Community College *Maryland*
Baptist College of Health Sciences *Tennessee*
Bellarmine University *Kentucky*
Bergen Community College *New Jersey*
Berkshire Community College *Massachusetts*
Black River Technical College *Arkansas*
Boise State University *Idaho*
Borough of Manhattan Community College of the City University of New York *New York*
Bossier Parish Community College *Louisiana*
Bowling Green State University *Ohio*
Bowling Green Technical College *Kentucky*
Brevard Community College *Florida*
Brookdale Community College *New Jersey*
Broward Community College *Florida*
Butte College *California*
California College for Health Sciences *Utah*
Carteret Community College *North Carolina*
Catawba Valley Community College *North Carolina*
Central New Mexico Community College *New Mexico*
Central Piedmont Community College *North Carolina*
Champlain College *Vermont*

Chattanooga State Technical Community College *Tennessee*
Cincinnati State Technical and Community College *Ohio*
College of DuPage *Illinois*
College of St. Catherine-Minneapolis *Minnesota*
Collin County Community College District *Texas*
Columbia State Community College *Tennessee*
Columbia Union College *Maryland*
Columbus State Community College *Ohio*
Community College of Allegheny County *Pennsylvania*
Community College of Aurora *Colorado*
The Community College of Baltimore County *Maryland*
Community College of Philadelphia *Pennsylvania*
Community College of Rhode Island *Rhode Island*
Community College of Southern Nevada *Nevada*
Concorde Career Institute *Missouri*
Concorde Career Institute *California*
Copiah-Lincoln Community College-Natchez Campus *Mississippi*
Crafton Hills College *California*
Cuyahoga Community College *Ohio*
Dakota State University *South Dakota*
Darton College *Georgia*
Daytona Beach Community College *Florida*
Del Mar College *Texas*
Delaware County Community College *Pennsylvania*
Delaware Technical & Community College, Jack F. Owens Campus *Delaware*
Delaware Technical & Community College, Stanton/Wilmington Campus *Delaware*
Delgado Community College *Louisiana*
Delta College *Michigan*
Des Moines Area Community College *Iowa*
Doña Ana Branch Community College *New Mexico*
Durham Technical Community College *North Carolina*
East Los Angeles College *California*
East Tennessee State University *Tennessee*
Eastern New Mexico University-Roswell *New Mexico*
Edgecombe Community College *North Carolina*
Edison College *Florida*
El Camino College *California*
El Centro College *Texas*
El Paso Community College *Texas*
Erie Community College, North Campus *New York*
Fayetteville Technical Community College *North Carolina*
Ferris State University *Michigan*
Florence-Darlington Technical College *South Carolina*
Florida Agricultural and Mechanical University *Florida*
Florida Community College at Jacksonville *Florida*
Foothill College *California*
Forsyth Technical Community College *North Carolina*
Frederick Community College *Maryland*
Fresno City College *California*
Front Range Community College *Colorado*
Gannon University *Pennsylvania*
GateWay Community College *Arizona*
Genesee Community College *New York*
George C. Wallace Community College *Alabama*
Georgia State University *Georgia*
Gloucester County College *New Jersey*
Greenville Technical College *South Carolina*
Grossmont College *California*
Gulf Coast Community College *Florida*
Gwinnett Technical College *Georgia*
Gwynedd-Mercy College *Pennsylvania*
Hannibal-LaGrange College *Missouri*
Harrisburg Area Community College *Pennsylvania*
Hawkeye Community College *Iowa*
Henry Ford Community College *Michigan*
Highline Community College *Washington*
Hillsborough Community College *Florida*
Hinds Community College *Mississippi*
Houston Community College System *Texas*
Hudson Valley Community College *New York*
Illinois Central College *Illinois*
Indian River Community College *Florida*
Indiana University Northwest *Indiana*
Indiana University of Pennsylvania *Pennsylvania*
Indiana University-Purdue University Indianapolis *Indiana*
Itawamba Community College *Mississippi*
Ivy Tech Community College-Central Indiana *Indiana*
Ivy Tech Community College-Lafayette *Indiana*
Ivy Tech Community College-Northeast *Indiana*
Ivy Tech Community College-Northwest *Indiana*
J. Sargeant Reynolds Community College *Virginia*
Jackson State Community College *Tennessee*
James A. Rhodes State College *Ohio*
Jefferson College of Health Sciences *Virginia*
Jefferson Community College *Ohio*
Jefferson Community and Technical College *Kentucky*
Johnson County Community College *Kansas*
Kalamazoo Valley Community College *Michigan*
Kankakee Community College *Illinois*
Kansas City Kansas Community College *Kansas*
Kapiolani Community College *Hawaii*
Kaskaskia College *Illinois*
Kennebec Valley Community College *Maine*
Kettering College of Medical Arts *Ohio*
Kingwood College *Texas*
Kirkwood Community College *Iowa*
Labette Community College *Kansas*
Lake Superior College *Minnesota*
Lakeland Community College *Ohio*
Lamar Institute of Technology *Texas*
Lane Community College *Oregon*
Lexington Community College *Kentucky*
Lincoln Land Community College *Illinois*
Loma Linda University *California*
Long Island University, Brooklyn Campus *New York*
Long Technical College *Arizona*
Los Angeles Valley College *California*
Louisiana State University at Eunice *Louisiana*
Louisiana State University Health Sciences Center *Louisiana*
Macomb Community College *Michigan*
Macon State College *Georgia*
Madison Area Technical College *Wisconsin*
Madisonville Community College *Kentucky*
Manatee Community College *Florida*
Manchester Community College *Connecticut*
Mansfield University of Pennsylvania *Pennsylvania*
Marygrove College *Michigan*
Massachusetts Bay Community College *Massachusetts*
Massasoit Community College *Massachusetts*
Maysville Community and Technical College *Kentucky*
McLennan Community College *Texas*
Medical College of Georgia *Georgia*
Metropolitan Community College *Nebraska*
Miami Dade College *Florida*
Mid-State Technical College *Wisconsin*
Midland College *Texas*
Midlands Technical College *South Carolina*
Midwestern State University *Texas*
Millersville University of Pennsylvania *Pennsylvania*
Milwaukee Area Technical College *Wisconsin*
Mississippi Gulf Coast Community College *Mississippi*
Missouri Southern State University *Missouri*
Modesto Junior College *California*
Mohawk Valley Community College *New York*
Molloy College *New York*
Monroe County Community College *Michigan*
Montana State University-Great Falls College of Technology *Montana*
Moraine Valley Community College *Illinois*
Morehead State University *Kentucky*
Mott Community College *Michigan*
Mt. Hood Community College *Oregon*
Mt. San Antonio College *California*
Mountain Empire Community College *Virginia*
Mountain State University *West Virginia*
Muskegon Community College *Michigan*
Napa Valley College *California*
Nassau Community College *New York*
National-Louis University *Illinois*
Naugatuck Valley Community College *Connecticut*
Nebraska Methodist College *Nebraska*
New Hampshire Community Technical College, Nashua/Claremont *New Hampshire*
Newman University *Kansas*
Nicholls State University *Louisiana*
North Central State College *Ohio*
North Dakota State University *North Dakota*
North Shore Community College *Massachusetts*
Northeast Iowa Community College *Iowa*
Northeast Mississippi Community College *Mississippi*
Northeast Wisconsin Technical College *Wisconsin*
Northeastern University *Massachusetts*
Northern Essex Community College *Massachusetts*
Northern Kentucky University *Kentucky*
Northern Virginia Community College *Virginia*
NorthWest Arkansas Community College *Arkansas*
Northwest Mississippi Community College *Mississippi*
Northwest Technical College *Minnesota*
Norwalk Community College *Connecticut*
Oakland Community College *Michigan*
Odessa College *Texas*
The Ohio State University *Ohio*
Ohlone College *California*
Oklahoma City Community College *Oklahoma*
Onondaga Community College *New York*
Orange Coast College *California*
Our Lady of Holy Cross College *Louisiana*
Ozarks Technical Community College *Missouri*
Palm Beach Community College *Florida*
Parkland College *Illinois*
Passaic County Community College *New Jersey*
Pearl River Community College *Mississippi*
Pensacola Junior College *Florida*
Piedmont Technical College *South Carolina*
Pima Community College *Arizona*
Pima Medical Institute *Colorado*
Pima Medical Institute (Mesa) *Arizona*
Pima Medical Institute (Tucson) *Arizona*
Pitt Community College *North Carolina*
Prince George's Community College *Maryland*
Pueblo Community College *Colorado*
Pulaski Technical College *Arkansas*
Quinnipiac University *Connecticut*
Quinsigamond Community College *Massachusetts*
Reading Area Community College *Pennsylvania*
Roane State Community College *Tennessee*
Robeson Community College *North Carolina*
Rochester Community and Technical College *Minnesota*
Rock Valley College *Illinois*
Rogue Community College *Oregon*
Rose State College *Oklahoma*
Rowan Technical College *Kentucky*
St. Augustine College *Illinois*
St. Louis Community College at Forest Park *Missouri*
Saint Paul College-A Community & Technical College *Minnesota*
St. Petersburg College *Florida*
St. Philip's College *Texas*
Salisbury University *Maryland*
San Joaquin Valley College *California*
Sandhills Community College *North Carolina*
Sanford-Brown College (Fenton) *Missouri*
Santa Fe Community College *Florida*
Santa Monica College *California*
Seattle Central Community College *Washington*
Seminole Community College *Florida*
Seward County Community College *Kansas*
Shawnee State University *Ohio*
Shelton State Community College *Alabama*
Shenandoah University *Virginia*
Sinclair Community College *Ohio*
Skyline College *California*
South Plains College *Texas*
Southeast Community College, Lincoln Campus *Nebraska*
Southeast Kentucky Community and Technical College *Kentucky*
Southern Illinois University Carbondale *Illinois*
Southern Maine Community College *Maine*
Southern University at Shreveport *Louisiana*
Southwest Georgia Technical College *Georgia*
Southwest Virginia Community College *Virginia*
Southwestern Community College *North Carolina*

Southwestern Illinois College *Illinois*
Spartanburg Technical College *South Carolina*
Spokane Community College *Washington*
Springfield Technical Community College *Massachusetts*
Stanly Community College *North Carolina*
Stark State College of Technology *Ohio*
State University of New York Upstate Medical University *New York*
Stony Brook University, State University of New York *New York*
Tacoma Community College *Washington*
Tallahassee Community College *Florida*
Tarrant County College District *Texas*
Temple College *Texas*
Tennessee State University *Tennessee*
Texas Southern University *Texas*
Texas Southmost College *Texas*
Texas State University-San Marcos *Texas*
Tidewater Community College *Virginia*
Trident Technical College *South Carolina*
Triton College *Illinois*
Tulsa Community College *Oklahoma*
Tyler Junior College *Texas*
Union County College *New Jersey*
Universidad Adventista de las Antillas *Puerto Rico*
The University of Akron *Ohio*
The University of Alabama at Birmingham *Alabama*
University of Arkansas Community College at Hope *Arkansas*
University of Arkansas for Medical Sciences *Arkansas*
University of Central Florida *Florida*
University of Charleston *West Virginia*
University of the District of Columbia *District of Columbia*
University of Hartford *Connecticut*
University of Kansas *Kansas*
University of Mary *North Dakota*
University of Missouri-Columbia *Missouri*
The University of Montana-Missoula *Montana*
University of Pittsburgh at Johnstown *Pennsylvania*
University of South Alabama *Alabama*
University of Southern Indiana *Indiana*
The University of Texas Health Science Center at San Antonio *Texas*
The University of Texas Medical Branch *Texas*
The University of Toledo *Ohio*
Valencia Community College *Florida*
Victor Valley College *California*
Victoria College *Texas*
Vincennes University *Indiana*
Volunteer State Community College *Tennessee*
Wallace State Community College *Alabama*
Walters State Community College *Tennessee*
Washburn University *Kansas*
Washington State Community College *Ohio*
Wayne County Community College District *Michigan*
Weatherford College *Texas*
Weber State University *Utah*
West Chester University of Pennsylvania *Pennsylvania*
West Virginia Northern Community College *West Virginia*
West Virginia University Institute of Technology *West Virginia*
Westchester Community College *New York*
Western School of Health and Business Careers (Pittsburgh) *Pennsylvania*
Western Technical College *Wisconsin*
Western Wyoming Community College *Wyoming*
Wheeling Jesuit University *West Virginia*
York College of Pennsylvania *Pennsylvania*
Youngstown State University *Ohio*

Council on Aviation AccreditationCouncil on Aviation Accreditation (CAA)

Arizona State University at the Polytechnic Campus *Arizona*
Auburn University *Alabama*
Central Missouri State University *Missouri*
Daniel Webster College *New Hampshire*
Embry-Riddle Aeronautical University *Florida*
Embry-Riddle Aeronautical University *Arizona*
Florida Institute of Technology *Florida*
Hampton University *Virginia*
Louisiana Tech University *Louisiana*
Mercer County Community College *New Jersey*
Middle Tennessee State University *Tennessee*
North Shore Community College *Massachusetts*
Purdue University *Indiana*
St. Cloud State University *Minnesota*
Saint Louis University *Missouri*
University of Nebraska at Omaha *Nebraska*
University of North Dakota *North Dakota*
Western Michigan University *Michigan*

The Council on Chiropractic EducationThe Council on Chiropractic Education (CCE)

Cleveland Chiropractic College-Kansas City Campus *Missouri*
Cleveland Chiropractic College-Los Angeles Campus *California*
Life University *Georgia*
Logan University-College of Chiropractic *Missouri*
Palmer College of Chiropractic *Iowa*
Texas Chiropractic College *Texas*
University of Bridgeport *Connecticut*

Council of Colleges of Acupuncture and Oriental MedicineCouncil of Colleges of Acupuncture and Oriental Medicine (NACSCAO)

Bastyr University *Washington*
Mercy College *New York*
New York College of Health Professions *New York*
Swedish Institute, College of Health Sciences *New York*
University of Bridgeport *Connecticut*

Council on Education for Public HealthCouncil on Education for Public Health (CEPH)

Arizona State University *Arizona*
Armstrong Atlantic State University *Georgia*
Boston University *Massachusetts*
Bowling Green State University *Ohio*
Brooklyn College of the City University of New York *New York*
Brown University *Rhode Island*
California State University, Fresno *California*
California State University, Long Beach *California*
California State University, Northridge *California*
Cleveland State University *Ohio*
Dartmouth College *New Hampshire*
Drexel University *Pennsylvania*
East Stroudsburg University of Pennsylvania *Pennsylvania*
East Tennessee State University *Tennessee*
Emory University *Georgia*
Florida Agricultural and Mechanical University *Florida*
Florida International University *Florida*
The George Washington University *District of Columbia*
Harvard University *Massachusetts*
Hunter College of the City University of New York *New York*
Idaho State University *Idaho*
Indiana University Bloomington *Indiana*
Indiana University-Purdue University Indianapolis *Indiana*
The Johns Hopkins University *Maryland*
Kent State University *Ohio*
Loma Linda University *California*
Louisiana State University Health Sciences Center *Louisiana*
Morgan State University *Maryland*
New Jersey Institute of Technology *New Jersey*
New Mexico State University *New Mexico*
New York University *New York*
Northern Arizona University *Arizona*
Northern Illinois University *Illinois*
Northwestern University *Illinois*
Nova Southeastern University *Florida*
The Ohio State University *Ohio*
Old Dominion University *Virginia*
Oregon Health & Science University *Oregon*
Oregon State University *Oregon*
Portland State University *Oregon*
Saint Louis University *Missouri*
San Diego State University *California*
San Francisco State University *California*
San Jose State University *California*
Southern Connecticut State University *Connecticut*
Temple University *Pennsylvania*
Texas A&M University System Health Science Center *Texas*
Tufts University *Massachusetts*
Tulane University *Louisiana*
The University of Akron *Ohio*
The University of Alabama at Birmingham *Alabama*
University at Albany, State University of New York *New York*
The University of Arizona *Arizona*
University of Arkansas for Medical Sciences *Arkansas*
University of California, Berkeley *California*
University of California, Los Angeles *California*
University of Hawaii at Manoa *Hawaii*
University of Illinois at Chicago *Illinois*
The University of Iowa *Iowa*
University of Kansas *Kansas*
University of Maryland, College Park *Maryland*
University of Massachusetts Amherst *Massachusetts*
University of Miami *Florida*
University of Michigan *Michigan*
University of Minnesota, Twin Cities Campus *Minnesota*
University of Nebraska Medical Center *Nebraska*
University of Nebraska at Omaha *Nebraska*
University of New Mexico *New Mexico*
The University of North Carolina at Chapel Hill *North Carolina*
The University of North Carolina at Greensboro *North Carolina*
University of Northern Colorado *Colorado*
University of Oklahoma Health Sciences Center *Oklahoma*
University of Pittsburgh *Pennsylvania*
University of Puerto Rico, Medical Sciences Campus *Puerto Rico*
University of Rochester *New York*
University of South Carolina *South Carolina*
University of South Florida *Florida*
University of Southern California *California*
University of Southern Mississippi *Mississippi*
The University of Tennessee *Tennessee*
The University of Texas Health Science Center at Houston *Texas*
The University of Texas Medical Branch *Texas*
The University of Toledo *Ohio*
University of Utah *Utah*
University of Washington *Washington*
University of Wisconsin-La Crosse *Wisconsin*
Virginia Commonwealth University *Virginia*
West Chester University of Pennsylvania *Pennsylvania*
West Virginia University *West Virginia*
Western Kentucky University *Kentucky*
Wichita State University *Kansas*
Yale University *Connecticut*
Youngstown State University *Ohio*

Council on Occupational EducationCouncil on Occupational Education (COE)

Albany Technical College *Georgia*
Altamaha Technical College *Georgia*
Appalachian Technical College *Georgia*
Ashland Community and Technical College *Kentucky*
Atlanta Technical College *Georgia*
Aviation & Electronic Schools of America *California*
Big Sandy Community and Technical College *Kentucky*
Bowling Green Technical College *Kentucky*
Brown Mackie College-Atlanta *Georgia*
Cameron College *Louisiana*
Career Technical College *Louisiana*
Center for Advanced Legal Studies *Texas*
Center for Advanced Manufacturing & Technology *Pennsylvania*
Central Georgia Technical College *Georgia*

College of Business and Technology *Florida*
Computer Career Center *Texas*
ConCorde Career College *Tennessee*
Coosa Valley Technical College *Georgia*
East Central Technical College *Georgia*
Flint Hills Technical College *Kansas*
Flint River Technical College *Georgia*
Florida Culinary Institute *Florida*
Gateway Community and Technical College *Kentucky*
Georgia Aviation & Technical College *Georgia*
Griffin Technical College *Georgia*
H. Councill Trenholm State Technical College *Alabama*
Heart of Georgia Technical College *Georgia*
Interactive College of Technology *Georgia*
J. F. Drake State Technical College *Alabama*
Keiser College (Pembroke Pines) *Florida*
Keiser College (Port St. Lucie) *Florida*
Keiser College (West Palm Beach) *Florida*
Lanier Technical College *Georgia*
Medical Careers Institute (Newport News) *Virginia*
Medical Careers Institute (Richmond) *Virginia*
Medical Careers Institute (Virginia Beach) *Virginia*
MedVance Institute *Tennessee*
MedVance Institute *Louisiana*
MedVance Institute *Florida*
Metropolitan Community College *Louisiana*
Middle Georgia Technical College *Georgia*
Morrison Institute of Technology *Illinois*
Moultrie Technical College *Georgia*
New England Institute of Technology at Palm Beach *Florida*
North Central Institute *Tennessee*
North Georgia Technical College *Georgia*
North Metro Technical College *Georgia*
Northeast Kansas Technical College *Kansas*
Northwest Kansas Technical College *Kansas*
Northwestern Technical College *Georgia*
Ogeechee Technical College *Georgia*
Okefenokee Technical College *Georgia*
Owensboro Community and Technical College *Kentucky*
Reid State Technical College *Alabama*
Rowan Technical College *Kentucky*
Sandersville Technical College *Georgia*
School of Communication Arts *North Carolina*
Somerset Community College *Kentucky*
South Georgia Technical College *Georgia*
Southeastern Career College *Tennessee*
Southeastern Career Institute *Texas*
Southeastern Technical College *Georgia*
Southwest Georgia Technical College *Georgia*
Stratford University *Virginia*
Swainsboro Technical College *Georgia*
Texas Culinary Academy *Texas*
Valdosta Technical College *Georgia*
West Central Technical College *Georgia*
West Georgia Technical College *Georgia*
West Kentucky Community and Technical College *Kentucky*
Wichita Area Technical College *Kansas*

Council on Rehabilitation EducationCouncil on Rehabilitation Education (CORE)

Alabama Agricultural and Mechanical University *Alabama*
Arkansas State University *Arkansas*
Assumption College *Massachusetts*
Auburn University *Alabama*
Ball State University *Indiana*
Boston University *Massachusetts*
Bowling Green State University *Ohio*
California State University, Fresno *California*
California State University, Los Angeles *California*
California State University, Sacramento *California*
California State University, San Bernardino *California*
Coppin State University *Maryland*
Drake University *Iowa*
East Carolina University *North Carolina*
East Central University *Oklahoma*
Edinboro University of Pennsylvania *Pennsylvania*
Emporia State University *Kansas*
Florida State University *Florida*
Fort Valley State University *Georgia*
The George Washington University *District of Columbia*
Georgia State University *Georgia*
Hofstra University *New York*
Hunter College of the City University of New York *New York*
Illinois Institute of Technology *Illinois*
Jackson State University *Mississippi*
Kent State University *Ohio*
Langston University *Oklahoma*
Louisiana State University Health Sciences Center *Louisiana*
Maryville University of Saint Louis *Missouri*
Michigan State University *Michigan*
Minnesota State University Mankato *Minnesota*
Mississippi State University *Mississippi*
Montana State University-Billings *Montana*
New York University *New York*
Northeastern University *Massachusetts*
Northern Illinois University *Illinois*
The Ohio State University *Ohio*
Ohio University *Ohio*
The Pennsylvania State University University Park Campus *Pennsylvania*
Portland State University *Oregon*
St. Cloud State University *Minnesota*
St. John's University *New York*
Salve Regina University *Rhode Island*
San Diego State University *California*
San Francisco State University *California*
South Carolina State University *South Carolina*
Southern Illinois University Carbondale *Illinois*
Southern University and Agricultural and Mechanical College *Louisiana*
Springfield College *Massachusetts*
State University of New York at Buffalo *New York*
Stephen F. Austin State University *Texas*
Syracuse University *New York*
Thomas University *Georgia*
Troy University *Alabama*
The University of Alabama *Alabama*
The University of Alabama at Birmingham *Alabama*
University at Albany, State University of New York *New York*
The University of Arizona *Arizona*
University of Arkansas *Arkansas*
University of Arkansas at Little Rock *Arkansas*
University of Florida *Florida*
University of Hawaii at Manoa *Hawaii*
University of Idaho *Idaho*
University of Illinois at Urbana-Champaign *Illinois*
The University of Iowa *Iowa*
University of Kentucky *Kentucky*
University of Maryland, College Park *Maryland*
University of Maryland Eastern Shore *Maryland*
University of Massachusetts Boston *Massachusetts*
University of Memphis *Tennessee*
University of Missouri-Columbia *Missouri*
The University of North Carolina at Chapel Hill *North Carolina*
University of North Florida *Florida*
University of North Texas *Texas*
University of Northern Colorado *Colorado*
University of Pittsburgh *Pennsylvania*
University of Puerto Rico, Río Piedras *Puerto Rico*
The University of Scranton *Pennsylvania*
University of South Carolina *South Carolina*
University of South Florida *Florida*
University of Southern Maine *Maine*
The University of Tennessee *Tennessee*
The University of Texas at Austin *Texas*
The University of Texas-Pan American *Texas*
The University of Texas Southwestern Medical Center at Dallas *Texas*
University of Wisconsin-Madison *Wisconsin*
University of Wisconsin-Stout *Wisconsin*
Utah State University *Utah*
Virginia Commonwealth University *Virginia*
Wayne State University *Michigan*
West Virginia University *West Virginia*
Western Michigan University *Michigan*
Western Oregon University *Oregon*
Western Washington University *Washington*
Wright State University *Ohio*

Council on Social Work EducationCouncil on Social Work Education (CSWE)

Abilene Christian University *Texas*
Adelphi University *New York*
Alabama Agricultural and Mechanical University *Alabama*
Alabama State University *Alabama*
Albany State University *Georgia*
Alvernia College *Pennsylvania*
Anderson University *Indiana*
Andrews University *Michigan*
Anna Maria College *Massachusetts*
Appalachian State University *North Carolina*
Arizona State University *Arizona*
Arizona State University West *Arizona*
Arkansas State University *Arkansas*
Ashland University *Ohio*
Atlantic Union College *Massachusetts*
Auburn University *Alabama*
Augsburg College *Minnesota*
Augustana College *South Dakota*
Aurora University *Illinois*
Austin Peay State University *Tennessee*
Avila University *Missouri*
Azusa Pacific University *California*
Ball State University *Indiana*
Barry University *Florida*
Barton College *North Carolina*
Baylor University *Texas*
Belmont University *Tennessee*
Bemidji State University *Minnesota*
Benedict College *South Carolina*
Bennett College For Women *North Carolina*
Bethany College *West Virginia*
Bethany College *Kansas*
Bethel College *Kansas*
Bethel University *Minnesota*
Bloomsburg University of Pennsylvania *Pennsylvania*
Bluffton University *Ohio*
Boise State University *Idaho*
Boston College *Massachusetts*
Boston University *Massachusetts*
Bowie State University *Maryland*
Bowling Green State University *Ohio*
Bradley University *Illinois*
Brescia University *Kentucky*
Briar Cliff University *Iowa*
Bridgewater State College *Massachusetts*
Brigham Young University *Utah*
Brigham Young University-Hawaii *Hawaii*
Bryn Mawr College *Pennsylvania*
Buena Vista University *Iowa*
Buffalo State College, State University of New York *New York*
Cabrini College *Pennsylvania*
California State University, Bakersfield *California*
California State University, Chico *California*
California State University, Fresno *California*
California State University, Long Beach *California*
California State University, Los Angeles *California*
California State University, Northridge *California*
California State University, Sacramento *California*
California State University, San Bernardino *California*
California State University, Stanislaus *California*
California University of Pennsylvania *Pennsylvania*
Calvin College *Michigan*
Campbell University *North Carolina*
Campbellsville University *Kentucky*
Capital University *Ohio*
Carlow University *Pennsylvania*
Carthage College *Wisconsin*
Case Western Reserve University *Ohio*
Castleton State College *Vermont*
The Catholic University of America *District of Columbia*
Cedar Crest College *Pennsylvania*
Cedarville University *Ohio*
Central Connecticut State University *Connecticut*
Central Michigan University *Michigan*
Central Missouri State University *Missouri*
Chadron State College *Nebraska*

Chatham College *Pennsylvania*
Chicago State University *Illinois*
Christopher Newport University *Virginia*
Clark Atlanta University *Georgia*
Clarke College *Iowa*
Cleveland State University *Ohio*
College Misericordia *Pennsylvania*
College of Mount St. Joseph *Ohio*
The College of New Rochelle *New York*
College of Saint Benedict *Minnesota*
College of St. Catherine *Minnesota*
The College of Saint Rose *New York*
The College of St. Scholastica *Minnesota*
Colorado State University *Colorado*
Colorado State University-Pueblo *Colorado*
Columbia College *South Carolina*
Columbia College *Missouri*
Concord University *West Virginia*
Concordia College *New York*
Concordia College *Minnesota*
Concordia University Wisconsin *Wisconsin*
Coppin State University *Maryland*
Cornerstone University *Michigan*
Creighton University *Nebraska*
Daemen College *New York*
Dana College *Nebraska*
Defiance College *Ohio*
Delaware State University *Delaware*
Delta State University *Mississippi*
Dominican College *New York*
Dominican University *Illinois*
Dordt College *Iowa*
East Carolina University *North Carolina*
East Central University *Oklahoma*
East Tennessee State University *Tennessee*
Eastern Connecticut State University *Connecticut*
Eastern Kentucky University *Kentucky*
Eastern Mennonite University *Virginia*
Eastern Michigan University *Michigan*
Eastern Nazarene College *Massachusetts*
Eastern University *Pennsylvania*
Eastern Washington University *Washington*
Edinboro University of Pennsylvania *Pennsylvania*
Elizabethtown College *Pennsylvania*
Elms College *Massachusetts*
Evangel University *Missouri*
Fayetteville State University *North Carolina*
Ferris State University *Michigan*
Ferrum College *Virginia*
Florida Agricultural and Mechanical University *Florida*
Florida Atlantic University *Florida*
Florida Gulf Coast University *Florida*
Florida International University *Florida*
Florida State University *Florida*
Fordham University *New York*
Fort Hays State University *Kansas*
Freed-Hardeman University *Tennessee*
Frostburg State University *Maryland*
Gallaudet University *District of Columbia*
Gannon University *Pennsylvania*
George Mason University *Virginia*
Georgia State University *Georgia*
Georgian Court University *New Jersey*
Gordon College *Massachusetts*
Goshen College *Indiana*
Governors State University *Illinois*
Grace College *Indiana*
Grambling State University *Louisiana*
Grand Valley State University *Michigan*
Hardin-Simmons University *Texas*
Harding University *Arkansas*
Hawaii Pacific University *Hawaii*
Heritage University *Washington*
Hood College *Maryland*
Hope College *Michigan*
Howard Payne University *Texas*
Howard University *District of Columbia*
Humboldt State University *California*
Hunter College of the City University of New York *New York*
Idaho State University *Idaho*
Illinois State University *Illinois*
Indiana State University *Indiana*
Indiana University Bloomington *Indiana*
Indiana University East *Indiana*
Indiana University Northwest *Indiana*
Indiana University-Purdue University Indianapolis *Indiana*
Indiana University South Bend *Indiana*
Indiana Wesleyan University *Indiana*
Inter American University of Puerto Rico, Arecibo Campus *Puerto Rico*
Inter American University of Puerto Rico, Metropolitan Campus *Puerto Rico*
Iona College *New York*
Jackson State University *Mississippi*
Jacksonville State University *Alabama*
James Madison University *Virginia*
Johnson C. Smith University *North Carolina*
Juniata College *Pennsylvania*
Kansas State University *Kansas*
Kean University *New Jersey*
Kentucky Christian University *Kentucky*
Kentucky State University *Kentucky*
Keuka College *New York*
Kutztown University of Pennsylvania *Pennsylvania*
La Salle University *Pennsylvania*
La Sierra University *California*
Lamar University *Texas*
Lehman College of the City University of New York *New York*
Lewis-Clark State College *Idaho*
Limestone College *South Carolina*
Lincoln Memorial University *Tennessee*
Lipscomb University *Tennessee*
Livingstone College *North Carolina*
Lock Haven University of Pennsylvania *Pennsylvania*
Loma Linda University *California*
Long Island University, Brooklyn Campus *New York*
Long Island University, C.W. Post Campus *New York*
Longwood University *Virginia*
Loras College *Iowa*
Louisiana College *Louisiana*
Louisiana State University and Agricultural and Mechanical College *Louisiana*
Lourdes College *Ohio*
Loyola University Chicago *Illinois*
Lubbock Christian University *Texas*
Luther College *Iowa*
MacMurray College *Illinois*
Madonna University *Michigan*
Malone College *Ohio*
Manchester College *Indiana*
Mansfield University of Pennsylvania *Pennsylvania*
Marian College of Fond du Lac *Wisconsin*
Marist College *New York*
Mars Hill College *North Carolina*
Marshall University *West Virginia*
Marygrove College *Michigan*
Marywood University *Pennsylvania*
McDaniel College *Maryland*
Mercy College *New York*
Mercyhurst College *Pennsylvania*
Meredith College *North Carolina*
Methodist College *North Carolina*
Metropolitan State College of Denver *Colorado*
Metropolitan State University *Minnesota*
Miami University *Ohio*
Michigan State University *Michigan*
Middle Tennessee State University *Tennessee*
Midwestern State University *Texas*
Miles College *Alabama*
Millersville University of Pennsylvania *Pennsylvania*
Minnesota State University Mankato *Minnesota*
Minnesota State University Moorhead *Minnesota*
Minot State University *North Dakota*
Mississippi College *Mississippi*
Mississippi State University *Mississippi*
Mississippi Valley State University *Mississippi*
Missouri State University *Missouri*
Missouri Western State University *Missouri*
Molloy College *New York*
Monmouth University *New Jersey*
Morehead State University *Kentucky*
Morgan State University *Maryland*
Mount Mary College *Wisconsin*
Mount Mercy College *Iowa*
Mountain State University *West Virginia*
Murray State University *Kentucky*
Nazareth College of Rochester *New York*
New Mexico Highlands University *New Mexico*
New Mexico State University *New Mexico*
New York University *New York*
Newman University *Kansas*
Niagara University *New York*
Norfolk State University *Virginia*
North Carolina Agricultural and Technical State University *North Carolina*
North Carolina Central University *North Carolina*
North Carolina State University *North Carolina*
Northeastern Illinois University *Illinois*
Northeastern State University *Oklahoma*
Northern Arizona University *Arizona*
Northern Kentucky University *Kentucky*
Northern Michigan University *Michigan*
Northwest Nazarene University *Idaho*
Northwestern College *Iowa*
Northwestern State University of Louisiana *Louisiana*
Oakwood College *Alabama*
The Ohio State University *Ohio*
Ohio University *Ohio*
Olivet Nazarene University *Illinois*
Oral Roberts University *Oklahoma*
Our Lady of the Lake University of San Antonio *Texas*
Pacific Lutheran University *Washington*
Pacific Union College *California*
Philadelphia Biblical University *Pennsylvania*
Philander Smith College *Arkansas*
Pittsburg State University *Kansas*
Plymouth State University *New Hampshire*
Pontifical Catholic University of Puerto Rico *Puerto Rico*
Portland State University *Oregon*
Prairie View A&M University *Texas*
Presentation College *South Dakota*
Providence College *Rhode Island*
Radford University *Virginia*
Ramapo College of New Jersey *New Jersey*
Regis College *Massachusetts*
Rhode Island College *Rhode Island*
The Richard Stockton College of New Jersey *New Jersey*
Roberts Wesleyan College *New York*
Rochester Institute of Technology *New York*
Rust College *Mississippi*
Rutgers, The State University of New Jersey, Camden *New Jersey*
Rutgers, The State University of New Jersey, New Brunswick/Piscataway *New Jersey*
Rutgers, The State University of New Jersey, Newark *New Jersey*
Sacred Heart University *Connecticut*
Saginaw Valley State University *Michigan*
St. Ambrose University *Iowa*
St. Cloud State University *Minnesota*
St. Edward's University *Texas*
Saint Francis University *Pennsylvania*
Saint John's University *Minnesota*
Saint Joseph College *Connecticut*
Saint Leo University *Florida*
Saint Louis University *Missouri*
Saint Mary's College *Indiana*
St. Olaf College *Minnesota*
Salem State College *Massachusetts*
Salisbury University *Maryland*
Salve Regina University *Rhode Island*
San Diego State University *California*
San Francisco State University *California*
San Jose State University *California*
Savannah State University *Georgia*
Seton Hall University *New Jersey*
Seton Hill University *Pennsylvania*
Shepherd University *West Virginia*
Shippensburg University of Pennsylvania *Pennsylvania*
Siena College *New York*
Simmons College *Massachusetts*
Skidmore College *New York*
Slippery Rock University of Pennsylvania *Pennsylvania*
Smith College *Massachusetts*
South Carolina State University *South Carolina*
Southeast Missouri State University *Missouri*

Southeastern Louisiana University *Louisiana*
Southern Adventist University *Tennessee*
Southern Arkansas University-Magnolia *Arkansas*
Southern Connecticut State University *Connecticut*
Southern Illinois University Carbondale *Illinois*
Southern Illinois University Edwardsville *Illinois*
Southern University and Agricultural and Mechanical College *Louisiana*
Southern University at New Orleans *Louisiana*
Southwest Minnesota State University *Minnesota*
Southwestern Adventist University *Texas*
Southwestern Oklahoma State University *Oklahoma*
Spalding University *Kentucky*
Spring Arbor University *Michigan*
Springfield College *Massachusetts*
State University of New York at Buffalo *New York*
State University of New York College at Brockport *New York*
State University of New York, Fredonia *New York*
State University of New York at Plattsburgh *New York*
Stephen F. Austin State University *Texas*
Stony Brook University, State University of New York *New York*
Syracuse University *New York*
Talladega College *Alabama*
Tarleton State University *Texas*
Taylor University *Indiana*
Temple University *Pennsylvania*
Tennessee State University *Tennessee*
Texas A&M University-Commerce *Texas*
Texas A&M University-Kingsville *Texas*
Texas Christian University *Texas*
Texas Southern University *Texas*
Texas State University-San Marcos *Texas*
Texas Tech University *Texas*
Texas Woman's University *Texas*
Troy University *Alabama*
Tulane University *Louisiana*
Tuskegee University *Alabama*
Union University *Tennessee*
The University of Akron *Ohio*
The University of Alabama *Alabama*
The University of Alabama at Birmingham *Alabama*
University of Alaska Anchorage *Alaska*
University of Alaska Fairbanks *Alaska*
University at Albany, State University of New York *New York*
University of Arkansas *Arkansas*
University of Arkansas at Little Rock *Arkansas*
University of Arkansas at Monticello *Arkansas*
University of Arkansas at Pine Bluff *Arkansas*
University of California, Berkeley *California*
University of California, Los Angeles *California*
University of Central Florida *Florida*
University of Chicago *Illinois*
University of Cincinnati *Ohio*
University of Connecticut *Connecticut*
University of Denver *Colorado*
University of Detroit Mercy *Michigan*
University of the District of Columbia *District of Columbia*
The University of Findlay *Ohio*
University of Georgia *Georgia*
University of Guam *Guam*
University of Hawaii at Manoa *Hawaii*
University of Houston *Texas*
University of Illinois at Chicago *Illinois*
University of Illinois at Springfield *Illinois*
University of Illinois at Urbana-Champaign *Illinois*
University of Indianapolis *Indiana*
The University of Iowa *Iowa*
University of Kansas *Kansas*
University of Kentucky *Kentucky*
University of Louisiana at Monroe *Louisiana*
University of Louisville *Kentucky*
University of Maine *Maine*
University of Maine at Presque Isle *Maine*
University of Mary *North Dakota*
University of Mary Hardin-Baylor *Texas*
University of Maryland, Baltimore County *Maryland*
University of Memphis *Tennessee*
University of Michigan *Michigan*
University of Michigan-Flint *Michigan*
University of Minnesota, Duluth *Minnesota*
University of Minnesota, Twin Cities Campus *Minnesota*
University of Mississippi *Mississippi*
University of Missouri-Columbia *Missouri*
University of Missouri-Kansas City *Missouri*
University of Missouri-St. Louis *Missouri*
The University of Montana-Missoula *Montana*
University of Montevallo *Alabama*
University of Nebraska at Kearney *Nebraska*
University of Nebraska at Omaha *Nebraska*
University of Nevada, Las Vegas *Nevada*
University of Nevada, Reno *Nevada*
University of New England *Maine*
University of New Hampshire *New Hampshire*
University of North Alabama *Alabama*
The University of North Carolina at Chapel Hill *North Carolina*
The University of North Carolina at Charlotte *North Carolina*
The University of North Carolina at Greensboro *North Carolina*
The University of North Carolina at Pembroke *North Carolina*
The University of North Carolina Wilmington *North Carolina*
University of North Dakota *North Dakota*
University of North Texas *Texas*
University of Northern Iowa *Iowa*
University of Oklahoma *Oklahoma*
University of Pennsylvania *Pennsylvania*
University of Pittsburgh *Pennsylvania*
University of Puerto Rico at Humacao *Puerto Rico*
University of Puerto Rico, Río Piedras *Puerto Rico*
University of Rio Grande *Ohio*
University of the Sacred Heart *Puerto Rico*
University of Saint Francis *Indiana*
University of St. Francis *Illinois*
University of St. Thomas *Minnesota*
University of Sioux Falls *South Dakota*
University of South Carolina *South Carolina*
The University of South Dakota *South Dakota*
University of South Florida *Florida*
University of Southern California *California*
University of Southern Indiana *Indiana*
University of Southern Maine *Maine*
University of Southern Mississippi *Mississippi*
The University of Tennessee *Tennessee*
The University of Tennessee at Chattanooga *Tennessee*
The University of Tennessee at Martin *Tennessee*
The University of Texas at Arlington *Texas*
The University of Texas at Austin *Texas*
The University of Texas at El Paso *Texas*
The University of Texas-Pan American *Texas*
The University of Toledo *Ohio*
University of Utah *Utah*
University of Vermont *Vermont*
University of Washington *Washington*
University of West Florida *Florida*
University of Wisconsin-Eau Claire *Wisconsin*
University of Wisconsin-Green Bay *Wisconsin*
University of Wisconsin-Madison *Wisconsin*
University of Wisconsin-Milwaukee *Wisconsin*
University of Wisconsin-Oshkosh *Wisconsin*
University of Wisconsin-River Falls *Wisconsin*
University of Wisconsin-Superior *Wisconsin*
University of Wisconsin-Whitewater *Wisconsin*
University of Wyoming *Wyoming*
Ursuline College *Ohio*
Utah State University *Utah*
Valdosta State University *Georgia*
Valparaiso University *Indiana*
Virginia Commonwealth University *Virginia*
Virginia Intermont College *Virginia*
Virginia Union University *Virginia*
Walla Walla College *Washington*
Warren Wilson College *North Carolina*
Wartburg College *Iowa*
Washburn University *Kansas*
Washington University in St. Louis *Missouri*
Wayne State University *Michigan*
Weber State University *Utah*
West Chester University of Pennsylvania *Pennsylvania*
West Texas A&M University *Texas*
West Virginia State University *West Virginia*
West Virginia University *West Virginia*
Western Carolina University *North Carolina*
Western Connecticut State University *Connecticut*
Western Illinois University *Illinois*
Western Kentucky University *Kentucky*
Western Michigan University *Michigan*
Western New England College *Massachusetts*
Western New Mexico University *New Mexico*
Westfield State College *Massachusetts*
Wheelock College *Massachusetts*
Whittier College *California*
Wichita State University *Kansas*
Widener University *Pennsylvania*
William Woods University *Missouri*
Winona State University *Minnesota*
Winthrop University *South Carolina*
Wright State University *Ohio*
Xavier University *Ohio*
Yeshiva University *New York*
York College of the City University of New York *New York*
Youngstown State University *Ohio*

Distance Education and Training CouncilDistance Education and Training Council (DETC)

American Academy of Nutrition, College of Nutrition *Tennessee*
American College of Computer & Information Sciences *Alabama*
American Public University System *West Virginia*
Andrew Jackson University *Alabama*
Ashworth College *Georgia*
Aspen University *Colorado*
California College for Health Sciences *Utah*
California National University for Advanced Studies *California*
Cleveland Institute of Electronics *Ohio*
College of the Humanities and Sciences, Harrison Middleton University *Arizona*
Columbia Southern University *Alabama*
Global University of the Assemblies of God *Missouri*
Grantham University *Missouri*
Griggs University *Maryland*
International Import-Export Institute *Arizona*
The Paralegal Institute, Inc. *Arizona*
Penn Foster Career School *Pennsylvania*
Universidad FLET *Florida*
University of Management and Technology *Virginia*
Western Governors University *Utah*
World College *Virginia*

Foundation for Interior Design Education ResearchFoundation for Interior Design Education Research (FIDER)

Academy of Art University *California*
American InterContinental University *California*
American InterContinental University (Atlanta) *Georgia*
Arizona State University *Arizona*
The Art Center Design College *Arizona*
The Art Institute of Atlanta *Georgia*
The Art Institute of Dallas *Texas*
Auburn University *Alabama*
Boston Architectural College *Massachusetts*
Brenau University *Georgia*
Brigham Young University -Idaho *Idaho*
Buffalo State College, State University of New York *New York*
California College of the Arts *California*
California State University, Fresno *California*
California State University, Northridge *California*
California State University, Sacramento *California*
Colorado State University *Colorado*
Columbus College of Art & Design *Ohio*
Cornell University *New York*
Dakota County Technical College *Minnesota*
Design Institute of San Diego *California*
Drexel University *Pennsylvania*
East Carolina University *North Carolina*
Eastern Michigan University *Michigan*
El Centro College *Texas*
Endicott College *Massachusetts*
Fashion Institute of Technology *New York*

Index of Professional Accreditations

Florida State University *Florida*
The George Washington University *District of Columbia*
Georgia Southern University *Georgia*
Harrington College of Design *Illinois*
The Illinois Institute of Art-Chicago *Illinois*
The Illinois Institute of Art-Schaumburg *Illinois*
Illinois State University *Illinois*
Indiana University Bloomington *Indiana*
Interior Designers Institute *California*
International Academy of Design & Technology *Illinois*
International Academy of Design & Technology *Florida*
Iowa State University of Science and Technology *Iowa*
James Madison University *Virginia*
Kansas State University *Kansas*
Kean University *New Jersey*
Kent State University *Ohio*
Kwantlen University College *British Columbia*
La Roche College *Pennsylvania*
Lawrence Technological University *Michigan*
Louisiana State University and Agricultural and Mechanical College *Louisiana*
Louisiana Tech University *Louisiana*
Marymount University *Virginia*
Maryville University of Saint Louis *Missouri*
Meredith College *North Carolina*
Miami University *Ohio*
Michigan State University *Michigan*
Middle Tennessee State University *Tennessee*
Mississippi State University *Mississippi*
Moore College of Art & Design *Pennsylvania*
Mount Ida College *Massachusetts*
Mount Mary College *Wisconsin*
New York Institute of Technology *New York*
New York School of Interior Design *New York*
Newbury College *Massachusetts*
North Dakota State University *North Dakota*
The Ohio State University *Ohio*
Ohio University *Ohio*
Oklahoma State University *Oklahoma*
O'More College of Design *Tennessee*
Philadelphia University *Pennsylvania*
Pratt Institute *New York*
Purdue University *Indiana*
Ringling School of Art and Design *Florida*
Rochester Institute of Technology *New York*
Rocky Mountain College of Art & Design *Colorado*
Ryerson University *Ontario*
Samford University *Alabama*
School of Visual Arts *New York*
Southern Illinois University Carbondale *Illinois*
Stephen F. Austin State University *Texas*
Suffolk University *Massachusetts*
Syracuse University *New York*
Texas Christian University *Texas*
Texas State University-San Marcos *Texas*
Texas Tech University *Texas*
The University of Akron *Ohio*
The University of Alabama *Alabama*
University of Arkansas *Arkansas*
University of California, Berkeley *California*
University of California, Los Angeles *California*
University of Central Oklahoma *Oklahoma*
University of Cincinnati *Ohio*
University of Florida *Florida*
University of Georgia *Georgia*
University of Kentucky *Kentucky*
University of Louisiana at Lafayette *Louisiana*
University of Louisville *Kentucky*
University of Manitoba *Manitoba*
University of Memphis *Tennessee*
University of Minnesota, Twin Cities Campus *Minnesota*
University of Missouri-Columbia *Missouri*
University of Nebraska-Lincoln *Nebraska*
University of Nevada, Las Vegas *Nevada*
The University of North Carolina at Greensboro *North Carolina*
University of North Texas *Texas*
University of Oklahoma *Oklahoma*
University of Oregon *Oregon*
University of Southern Mississippi *Mississippi*
The University of Tennessee *Tennessee*
The University of Tennessee at Chattanooga *Tennessee*
The University of Texas at Arlington *Texas*
The University of Texas at Austin *Texas*
The University of Texas at San Antonio *Texas*
University of Wisconsin-Madison *Wisconsin*
University of Wisconsin-Stevens Point *Wisconsin*
University of Wisconsin-Stout *Wisconsin*
Utah State University *Utah*
Virginia Commonwealth University *Virginia*
Virginia Polytechnic Institute and State University *Virginia*
Washington State University *Washington*
Watkins College of Art and Design *Tennessee*
Wentworth Institute of Technology *Massachusetts*
West Valley College *California*
West Virginia University *West Virginia*
Western Carolina University *North Carolina*
Western Michigan University *Michigan*
Winthrop University *South Carolina*
Woodbury University *California*

Joint Commission on Allied Health PersonnelJoint Commission on Allied Health Personnel in Ophthalmology (JCAHPO)

Emory University *Georgia*
Lakeland Community College *Ohio*
Louisiana State University Health Sciences Center *Louisiana*
Old Dominion University *Virginia*
Portland Community College *Oregon*
Pueblo Community College *Colorado*
Triton College *Illinois*

Joint Review Committee on Education inJoint Review Committee on Education in Cardiovascular Technology (JRCECT)

Augusta Technical College *Georgia*
Edison College *Florida*
El Centro College *Texas*
Geneva College *Pennsylvania*
Grossmont College *California*
Gwynedd-Mercy College *Pennsylvania*
Milwaukee Area Technical College *Wisconsin*
Orange Coast College *California*
Southeast Technical Institute *South Dakota*
Spokane Community College *Washington*
The University of Toledo *Ohio*

Joint Review Committee on Education inJoint Review Committee on Education in Diagnostic Medical Sonography (JRCEDMS)

Austin Community College *Texas*
Baptist College of Health Sciences *Tennessee*
Bellevue Community College *Washington*
Bergen Community College *New Jersey*
Boise State University *Idaho*
Broward Community College *Florida*
Bunker Hill Community College *Massachusetts*
Caldwell Community College and Technical Institute *North Carolina*
Central Ohio Technical College *Ohio*
Chippewa Valley Technical College *Wisconsin*
College of St. Catherine *Minnesota*
Community College of Allegheny County *Pennsylvania*
Community College of Southern Nevada *Nevada*
Cuyahoga Community College *Ohio*
Del Mar College *Texas*
Delaware Technical & Community College, Stanton/Wilmington Campus *Delaware*
Delta College *Michigan*
El Centro College *Texas*
Florida Hospital College of Health Sciences *Florida*
Forsyth Technical Community College *North Carolina*
The George Washington University *District of Columbia*
Gloucester County College *New Jersey*
Hillsborough Community College *Florida*
Jackson Community College *Michigan*
Keiser College (Daytona Beach) *Florida*
Keiser College (Fort Lauderdale) *Florida*
Kettering College of Medical Arts *Ohio*
Lorain County Community College *Ohio*
Medical College of Georgia *Georgia*
Mercy College of Health Sciences *Iowa*
Miami Dade College *Florida*
Middlesex Community College *Massachusetts*
Nebraska Methodist College *Nebraska*
New York University *New York*
Oakland Community College *Michigan*
Orange Coast College *California*
Owens Community College *Ohio*
Pitt Community College *North Carolina*
Rochester Institute of Technology *New York*
Seattle University *Washington*
Springfield Technical Community College *Massachusetts*
State University of New York Downstate Medical Center *New York*
Thomas Jefferson University *Pennsylvania*
Triton College *Illinois*
Tyler Junior College *Texas*
University of Nebraska Medical Center *Nebraska*
University of Oklahoma Health Sciences Center *Oklahoma*
Valencia Community College *Florida*
Wallace State Community College *Alabama*
Western School of Health and Business Careers (Pittsburgh) *Pennsylvania*

Joint Review Committee on Education inJoint Review Committee on Education in Electroneurodiagnostic Technology (JRCEET)

Kirkwood Community College *Iowa*
Labouré College *Massachusetts*
Niagara County Community College *New York*
Orange Coast College *California*
Scott Community College *Iowa*
Southwestern Community College *North Carolina*
Western Technical College *Wisconsin*

Joint Review Committee on Education inJoint Review Committee on Education in Radiological Technology (JRCERT)

Aims Community College *Colorado*
Albany Technical College *Georgia*
Allegany College of Maryland *Maryland*
Allen College *Iowa*
Amarillo College *Texas*
Angelina College *Texas*
Anne Arundel Community College *Maryland*
Apollo College *Washington*
Arkansas State University *Arkansas*
Armstrong Atlantic State University *Georgia*
Asheville-Buncombe Technical Community College *North Carolina*
Athens Technical College *Georgia*
Austin Community College *Texas*
Avila University *Missouri*
Bacone College *Oklahoma*
Baker College of Jackson *Michigan*
Baker College of Owosso *Michigan*
Bakersfield College *California*
Ball State University *Indiana*
Barnes-Jewish College of Nursing and Allied Health *Missouri*
Bellevue Community College *Washington*
Bergen Community College *New Jersey*
Blackhawk Technical College *Wisconsin*
Blinn College *Texas*
Bluefield State College *West Virginia*
Boise State University *Idaho*
Brevard Community College *Florida*
Bronx Community College of the City University of New York *New York*
Brookdale Community College *New Jersey*
Broome Community College *New York*
Bunker Hill Community College *Massachusetts*
Cabrillo College *California*
Caldwell Community College and Technical Institute *North Carolina*
California State University, Long Beach *California*

California State University, Northridge *California*
Cañada College *California*
Capital Community College *Connecticut*
Carl Sandburg College *Illinois*
Carteret Community College *North Carolina*
Casper College *Wyoming*
Central Ohio Technical College *Ohio*
Central Virginia Community College *Virginia*
Chaffey College *California*
Champlain College *Vermont*
Charles R. Drew University of Medicine and Science *California*
Chesapeake College *Maryland*
Chippewa Valley Technical College *Wisconsin*
City College of San Francisco *California*
City Colleges of Chicago, Malcolm X College *Illinois*
City Colleges of Chicago, Wilbur Wright College *Illinois*
Clarkson College *Nebraska*
Cleveland Community College *North Carolina*
Clovis Community College *New Mexico*
Coastal Georgia Community College *Georgia*
College of DuPage *Illinois*
College of Lake County *Illinois*
College Misericordia *Pennsylvania*
College of St. Catherine-Minneapolis *Minnesota*
Columbia State Community College *Tennessee*
Columbus State Community College *Ohio*
Community College of Allegheny County *Pennsylvania*
The Community College of Baltimore County *Maryland*
Community College of Denver *Colorado*
Community College of Philadelphia *Pennsylvania*
Community College of Rhode Island *Rhode Island*
Copiah-Lincoln Community College *Mississippi*
County College of Morris *New Jersey*
Cumberland County College *New Jersey*
Cuyahoga Community College *Ohio*
Cypress College *California*
Del Mar College *Texas*
Delaware Technical & Community College, Jack F. Owens Campus *Delaware*
Delaware Technical & Community College, Stanton/Wilmington Campus *Delaware*
Delgado Community College *Louisiana*
Delta College *Michigan*
Doña Ana Branch Community College *New Mexico*
East Tennessee State University *Tennessee*
Eastern Maine Community College *Maine*
Edgecombe Community College *North Carolina*
Edison College *Florida*
El Camino College *California*
El Centro College *Texas*
Elizabethtown Community and Technical College *Kentucky*
Emory University *Georgia*
Erie Community College *New York*
Essex County College *New Jersey*
Eugenio María de Hostos Community College of the City University of New York *New York*
Fayetteville Technical Community College *North Carolina*
Ferris State University *Michigan*
Florence-Darlington Technical College *South Carolina*
Florida Hospital College of Health Sciences *Florida*
Foothill College *California*
Forsyth Technical Community College *North Carolina*
Fort Hays State University *Kansas*
Fresno City College *California*
Gadsden State Community College *Alabama*
Galveston College *Texas*
Gannon University *Pennsylvania*
Gateway Community College *Connecticut*
GateWay Community College *Arizona*
George C. Wallace Community College *Alabama*
Grand Rapids Community College *Michigan*
Greenville Technical College *South Carolina*
Gulf Coast Community College *Florida*
Gwinnett Technical College *Georgia*
Gwynedd-Mercy College *Pennsylvania*
Hagerstown Community College *Maryland*
Hazard Community and Technical College *Kentucky*
Hillsborough Community College *Florida*
Hinds Community College *Mississippi*
Holy Family University *Pennsylvania*
Holyoke Community College *Massachusetts*
Horry-Georgetown Technical College *South Carolina*
Houston Community College System *Texas*
Howard University *District of Columbia*
Hudson Valley Community College *New York*
Hutchinson Community College and Area Vocational School *Kansas*
Illinois Central College *Illinois*
Illinois Eastern Community Colleges, Olney Central College *Illinois*
Indian Hills Community College *Iowa*
Indian River Community College *Florida*
Indiana University Northwest *Indiana*
Indiana University-Purdue University Indianapolis *Indiana*
Indiana University South Bend *Indiana*
Iowa Central Community College *Iowa*
Itawamba Community College *Mississippi*
Ivy Tech Community College-Central Indiana *Indiana*
Ivy Tech Community College-Wabash Valley *Indiana*
Jackson State Community College *Tennessee*
James A. Rhodes State College *Ohio*
Jefferson Community College *Ohio*
Jefferson State Community College *Alabama*
Johnston Community College *North Carolina*
Jones County Junior College *Mississippi*
Kapiolani Community College *Hawaii*
Kaskaskia College *Illinois*
Keiser College (Fort Lauderdale) *Florida*
Kellogg Community College *Michigan*
Kent State University, Salem Campus *Ohio*
Kettering College of Medical Arts *Ohio*
Kilgore College *Texas*
Kishwaukee College *Illinois*
Labette Community College *Kansas*
Labouré College *Massachusetts*
Lake Michigan College *Michigan*
Lakeland Community College *Ohio*
Lakeshore Technical College *Wisconsin*
Lamar University *Texas*
Lansing Community College *Michigan*
Laramie County Community College *Wyoming*
Laredo Community College *Texas*
Lincoln Land Community College *Illinois*
Loma Linda University *California*
Long Beach City College *California*
Long Island University, C.W. Post Campus *New York*
Lorain County Community College *Ohio*
Los Angeles City College *California*
Louisiana State University at Eunice *Louisiana*
Madison Area Technical College *Wisconsin*
Manatee Community College *Florida*
Mansfield University of Pennsylvania *Pennsylvania*
Marion Technical College *Ohio*
Marygrove College *Michigan*
Massachusetts Bay Community College *Massachusetts*
Massasoit Community College *Massachusetts*
McLennan Community College *Texas*
McNeese State University *Louisiana*
Medical College of Georgia *Georgia*
Merced College *California*
Mercer County Community College *New Jersey*
Mercy College of Northwest Ohio *Ohio*
Meridian Community College *Mississippi*
Merritt College *California*
Mesa State College *Colorado*
Miami Dade College *Florida*
Mid Michigan Community College *Michigan*
Middlesex Community College *Massachusetts*
Middlesex Community College *Connecticut*
Middlesex County College *New Jersey*
Midland College *Texas*
Midlands Technical College *South Carolina*
Milwaukee Area Technical College *Wisconsin*
Mississippi Delta Community College *Mississippi*
Mississippi Gulf Coast Community College *Mississippi*
Missouri Southern State University *Missouri*
Monroe Community College *New York*
Moorpark College *California*
Moraine Valley Community College *Illinois*
Morehead State University *Kentucky*
Mt. San Antonio College *California*
Nassau Community College *New York*
National-Louis University *Illinois*
National Park Community College *Arkansas*
Naugatuck Valley Community College *Connecticut*
New Hampshire Technical Institute *New Hampshire*
New York City College of Technology of the City University of New York *New York*
Newman University *Kansas*
Niagara County Community College *New York*
North Arkansas College *Arkansas*
North Central State College *Ohio*
North Country Community College *New York*
North Shore Community College *Massachusetts*
Northampton County Area Community College *Pennsylvania*
Northcentral Technical College *Wisconsin*
Northeast Mississippi Community College *Mississippi*
Northern Essex Community College *Massachusetts*
Northern Kentucky University *Kentucky*
Northern New Mexico Community College *New Mexico*
Northwest Technical College *Minnesota*
Northwestern State University of Louisiana *Louisiana*
Oakland Community College *Michigan*
Odessa College *Texas*
Orange Coast College *California*
Orangeburg-Calhoun Technical College *South Carolina*
Oregon Health & Science University *Oregon*
Oregon Institute of Technology *Oregon*
Our Lady of the Lake College *Louisiana*
Owens Community College *Ohio*
Owensboro Community and Technical College *Kentucky*
Palm Beach Community College *Florida*
Parkland College *Illinois*
Pasadena City College *California*
Passaic County Community College *New Jersey*
Pearl River Community College *Mississippi*
Penn Valley Community College *Missouri*
Pennsylvania College of Technology *Pennsylvania*
The Pennsylvania State University New Kensington Campus of the Commonwealth College *Pennsylvania*
The Pennsylvania State University Schuylkill Campus of the Capital College *Pennsylvania*
Pensacola Junior College *Florida*
Piedmont Technical College *South Carolina*
Pima Community College *Arizona*
Pima Medical Institute *Washington*
Pima Medical Institute *New Mexico*
Pima Medical Institute *Colorado*
Pima Medical Institute (Mesa) *Arizona*
Pima Medical Institute (Tucson) *Arizona*
Pitt Community College *North Carolina*
Polk Community College *Florida*
Portland Community College *Oregon*
Presentation College *South Dakota*
Prince George's Community College *Maryland*
Quinnipiac University *Connecticut*
Quinsigamond Community College *Massachusetts*
Riverland Community College *Minnesota*
Roane State Community College *Tennessee*
Robert Morris University *Pennsylvania*
Rose State College *Oklahoma*
Rowan-Cabarrus Community College *North Carolina*
St. Louis Community College at Forest Park *Missouri*
St. Philip's College *Texas*
Salt Lake Community College *Utah*
Sandhills Community College *North Carolina*
Sanford-Brown College (Fenton) *Missouri*
Sanford-Brown College (North Kansas City) *Missouri*
Santa Barbara City College *California*
Santa Fe Community College *Florida*
Santa Rosa Junior College *California*
Sauk Valley Community College *Illinois*
Scott Community College *Iowa*
Shawnee State University *Ohio*
Sinclair Community College *Ohio*
South Arkansas Community College *Arkansas*

South Plains College *Texas*
South Suburban College *Illinois*
Southeast Arkansas College *Arkansas*
Southeast Community College, Lincoln Campus *Nebraska*
Southern Maine Community College *Maine*
Southern Union State Community College *Alabama*
Southern University at Shreveport *Louisiana*
Southern West Virginia Community and Technical College *West Virginia*
Southwest Tennessee Community College *Tennessee*
Southwest Virginia Community College *Virginia*
Southwestern Community College *North Carolina*
Southwestern Illinois College *Illinois*
Southwestern Oklahoma State University at Sayre *Oklahoma*
Spartanburg Technical College *South Carolina*
Springfield Technical Community College *Massachusetts*
State University of New York Upstate Medical University *New York*
Tacoma Community College *Washington*
Tarrant County College District *Texas*
Texas Southmost College *Texas*
Texas State University-San Marcos *Texas*
Thomas Jefferson University *Pennsylvania*
Tidewater Community College *Virginia*
Trident Technical College *South Carolina*
Triton College *Illinois*
Trocaire College *New York*
Truckee Meadows Community College *Nevada*
Tulsa Community College *Oklahoma*
Tyler Junior College *Texas*
Universidad Central del Caribe *Puerto Rico*
The University of Alabama at Birmingham *Alabama*
University of Arkansas at Fort Smith *Arkansas*
University of Arkansas for Medical Sciences *Arkansas*
University of Central Florida *Florida*
University of Charleston *West Virginia*
University of Cincinnati Raymond Walters College *Ohio*
University of the District of Columbia *District of Columbia*
University of Hartford *Connecticut*
University of Louisiana at Monroe *Louisiana*
University of Louisville *Kentucky*
University of Michigan-Flint *Michigan*
University of Missouri-Columbia *Missouri*
University of Nebraska Medical Center *Nebraska*
The University of North Carolina at Chapel Hill *North Carolina*
University of Oklahoma Health Sciences Center *Oklahoma*
University of Puerto Rico, Medical Sciences Campus *Puerto Rico*
University of Saint Francis *Indiana*
University of Southern Indiana *Indiana*
The University of Texas at Brownsville *Texas*
The University of Texas Health Science Center at Houston *Texas*
University of Wisconsin-La Crosse *Wisconsin*
Valdosta Technical College *Georgia*
Valencia Community College *Florida*
Vance-Granville Community College *North Carolina*
Virginia Commonwealth University *Virginia*
Virginia Highlands Community College *Virginia*
Virginia Western Community College *Virginia*
Volunteer State Community College *Tennessee*
Wake Technical Community College *North Carolina*
Wallace State Community College *Alabama*
Washburn University *Kansas*
Washtenaw Community College *Michigan*
Wayne State University *Michigan*
Wenatchee Valley College *Washington*
Westchester Community College *New York*
Western Oklahoma State College *Oklahoma*
Western School of Health and Business Careers (Pittsburgh) *Pennsylvania*
Western Technical College *Wisconsin*
Wharton County Junior College *Texas*
Wor-Wic Community College *Maryland*
Xavier University *Ohio*
Yakima Valley Community College *Washington*
York Technical College *South Carolina*
Yuba College *California*
Zane State College *Ohio*

Joint Review Committee on Educational ProgramsJoint Review Committee on Educational Programs in Athletic Training (JRCEPAT)

Alvernia College *Pennsylvania*
Anderson University *Indiana*
Appalachian State University *North Carolina*
Arkansas State University *Arkansas*
Augustana College *South Dakota*
Azusa Pacific University *California*
Ball State University *Indiana*
Barry University *Florida*
Bethel University *Minnesota*
Boise State University *Idaho*
Boston University *Massachusetts*
Bridgewater State College *Massachusetts*
Brigham Young University *Utah*
California State University, Fresno *California*
California State University, Fullerton *California*
California State University, Northridge *California*
California State University, Sacramento *California*
California University of Pennsylvania *Pennsylvania*
Campbell University *North Carolina*
Canisius College *New York*
Capital University *Ohio*
Castleton State College *Vermont*
Catawba College *North Carolina*
Central Connecticut State University *Connecticut*
Central Methodist University *Missouri*
Central Michigan University *Michigan*
Colby-Sawyer College *New Hampshire*
College of Charleston *South Carolina*
Dakota Wesleyan University *South Dakota*
DePauw University *Indiana*
Duquesne University *Pennsylvania*
East Carolina University *North Carolina*
East Stroudsburg University of Pennsylvania *Pennsylvania*
Eastern Illinois University *Illinois*
Eastern Kentucky University *Kentucky*
Eastern Michigan University *Michigan*
Elon University *North Carolina*
Emory & Henry College *Virginia*
Emporia State University *Kansas*
Endicott College *Massachusetts*
Florida Southern College *Florida*
Fort Lewis College *Colorado*
George Fox University *Oregon*
The George Washington University *District of Columbia*
Georgia Southern University *Georgia*
Grand Valley State University *Michigan*
Gustavus Adolphus College *Minnesota*
High Point University *North Carolina*
Hofstra University *New York*
Hope College *Michigan*
Illinois State University *Illinois*
Indiana State University *Indiana*
Indiana University Bloomington *Indiana*
Indiana University of Pennsylvania *Pennsylvania*
Iowa State University of Science and Technology *Iowa*
Ithaca College *New York*
James Madison University *Virginia*
Kansas State University *Kansas*
Kean University *New Jersey*
Keene State College *New Hampshire*
King's College *Pennsylvania*
Lasell College *Massachusetts*
Lenoir-Rhyne College *North Carolina*
Lincoln Memorial University *Tennessee*
Linfield College *Oregon*
Lipscomb University *Tennessee*
Lock Haven University of Pennsylvania *Pennsylvania*
Longwood University *Virginia*
Manchester College *Indiana*
Marietta College *Ohio*
Mars Hill College *North Carolina*
Marshall University *West Virginia*
Mercyhurst College *Pennsylvania*
Merrimack College *Massachusetts*
Messiah College *Pennsylvania*
Methodist College *North Carolina*
Miami University *Ohio*
Minnesota State University Mankato *Minnesota*
Missouri State University *Missouri*
Mount Union College *Ohio*
New Mexico State University *New Mexico*
North Dakota State University *North Dakota*
Northeastern University *Massachusetts*
Northern Illinois University *Illinois*
Ohio Northern University *Ohio*
Ohio University *Ohio*
Oklahoma State University *Oklahoma*
Oregon State University *Oregon*
Otterbein College *Ohio*
Park University *Missouri*
The Pennsylvania State University University Park Campus *Pennsylvania*
Plymouth State University *New Hampshire*
Purdue University *Indiana*
Roanoke College *Virginia*
Rowan University *New Jersey*
Sacred Heart University *Connecticut*
Salem State College *Massachusetts*
Salisbury University *Maryland*
Samford University *Alabama*
San Diego State University *California*
San Jose State University *California*
Slippery Rock University of Pennsylvania *Pennsylvania*
South Dakota State University *South Dakota*
Southeast Missouri State University *Missouri*
Southern Connecticut State University *Connecticut*
Southern Illinois University Carbondale *Illinois*
Southwestern University *Texas*
Springfield College *Massachusetts*
State University of New York College at Brockport *New York*
State University of New York College at Cortland *New York*
Stetson University *Florida*
Temple University *Pennsylvania*
Texas Christian University *Texas*
Texas State University-San Marcos *Texas*
Towson University *Maryland*
Troy University *Alabama*
Truman State University *Missouri*
The University of Alabama *Alabama*
University of Central Florida *Florida*
University of Charleston *West Virginia*
University of Cincinnati *Ohio*
University of Delaware *Delaware*
University of Florida *Florida*
University of Georgia *Georgia*
University of Illinois at Urbana-Champaign *Illinois*
University of Indianapolis *Indiana*
The University of Iowa *Iowa*
University of Mary *North Dakota*
The University of Montana-Missoula *Montana*
University of Nebraska at Kearney *Nebraska*
University of Nebraska at Omaha *Nebraska*
University of Nevada, Las Vegas *Nevada*
University of New Hampshire *New Hampshire*
University of New Mexico *New Mexico*
The University of North Carolina at Chapel Hill *North Carolina*
University of North Dakota *North Dakota*
University of North Florida *Florida*
University of Northern Colorado *Colorado*
University of Northern Iowa *Iowa*
University of Pittsburgh *Pennsylvania*
University of South Carolina *South Carolina*
University of Southern Maine *Maine*
University of Southern Mississippi *Mississippi*
The University of Toledo *Ohio*
University of Tulsa *Oklahoma*
University of Utah *Utah*
University of Vermont *Vermont*
The University of West Alabama *Alabama*
University of Wisconsin-La Crosse *Wisconsin*
University of Wisconsin-Madison *Wisconsin*
Valdosta State University *Georgia*
Vanguard University of Southern California *California*
Washington State University *Washington*
Waynesburg College *Pennsylvania*

West Chester University of Pennsylvania *Pennsylvania*
West Virginia University *West Virginia*
West Virginia Wesleyan College *West Virginia*
Western Illinois University *Illinois*
Westfield State College *Massachusetts*
Whitworth College *Washington*
William Paterson University of New Jersey *New Jersey*
Wilmington College *Ohio*
Wingate University *North Carolina*
Winona State University *Minnesota*
Wright State University *Ohio*
Xavier University *Ohio*

Joint Review Committee on Educational ProgramsJoint Review Committee on Educational Programs for the EMT-Paramedic (JRCEMT)

Austin Community College *Texas*
Bismarck State College *North Dakota*
Borough of Manhattan Community College of the City University of New York *New York*
Brevard Community College *Florida*
Broward Community College *Florida*
Capital Community College *Connecticut*
Catawba Valley Community College *North Carolina*
Central Florida Community College *Florida*
Central Washington University *Washington*
Century College *Minnesota*
Chemeketa Community College *Oregon*
Columbia Basin College *Washington*
Columbia College *California*
Columbia State Community College *Tennessee*
Columbus State Community College *Ohio*
Crafton Hills College *California*
Creighton University *Nebraska*
Daytona Beach Community College *Florida*
Delaware Technical & Community College, Terry Campus *Delaware*
Delgado Community College *Louisiana*
Dixie State College of Utah *Utah*
Doña Ana Branch Community College *New Mexico*
Eastern Kentucky University *Kentucky*
Eastern New Mexico University-Roswell *New Mexico*
Edison College *Florida*
Florida Community College at Jacksonville *Florida*
Gadsden State Community College *Alabama*
Galveston College *Texas*
George C. Wallace Community College *Alabama*
Greenville Technical College *South Carolina*
Gulf Coast Community College *Florida*
Harrisburg Area Community College *Pennsylvania*
Hillsborough Community College *Florida*
Holmes Community College *Mississippi*
Houston Community College System *Texas*
Hudson Valley Community College *New York*
Indian River Community College *Florida*
Ivy Tech Community College-Southwest *Indiana*
Jackson State Community College *Tennessee*
Jefferson College of Health Sciences *Virginia*
Johnson County Community College *Kansas*
Jones County Junior College *Mississippi*
Lake City Community College *Florida*
Lansing Community College *Michigan*
Lee College *Texas*
Lurleen B. Wallace Community College *Alabama*
Miami Dade College *Florida*
Mississippi Gulf Coast Community College *Mississippi*
Monroe Community College *New York*
New Hampshire Technical Institute *New Hampshire*
Nicholls State University *Louisiana*
Northeast Alabama Community College *Alabama*
Northern Virginia Community College *Virginia*
NorthWest Arkansas Community College *Arkansas*
Oklahoma City Community College *Oklahoma*
Palm Beach Community College *Florida*
Pasco-Hernando Community College *Florida*
Pennsylvania College of Technology *Pennsylvania*
Pensacola Junior College *Florida*
Polk Community College *Florida*
Pueblo Community College *Colorado*
St. Petersburg College *Florida*
Santa Fe Community College *Florida*
Seminole Community College *Florida*
Southern Union State Community College *Alabama*
Tacoma Community College *Washington*
Tallahassee Community College *Florida*
Texas Tech University *Texas*
Tidewater Community College *Virginia*
The University of Alabama at Birmingham *Alabama*
University of Arkansas for Medical Sciences *Arkansas*
University of Maryland, Baltimore County *Maryland*
University of New Mexico *New Mexico*
University of Pittsburgh *Pennsylvania*
University of South Alabama *Alabama*
The University of Texas Health Science Center at San Antonio *Texas*
Valencia Community College *Florida*
Volunteer State Community College *Tennessee*
Wallace State Community College *Alabama*
Weber State University *Utah*
Western Carolina University *North Carolina*
Youngstown State University *Ohio*

Joint Review Committee on Educational ProgramsJoint Review Committee on Educational Programs in Nuclear Medicine Technology (JRCNMT)

Amarillo College *Texas*
Baptist College of Health Sciences *Tennessee*
Bronx Community College of the City University of New York *New York*
Broward Community College *Florida*
Caldwell Community College and Technical Institute *North Carolina*
Cedar Crest College *Pennsylvania*
Community College of Allegheny County *Pennsylvania*
Cuyahoga Community College *Ohio*
Delaware Technical & Community College, Stanton/Wilmington Campus *Delaware*
Ferris State University *Michigan*
Florida Hospital College of Health Sciences *Florida*
Forsyth Technical Community College *North Carolina*
Galveston College *Texas*
Gateway Community College *Connecticut*
Gloucester County College *New Jersey*
Hillsborough Community College *Florida*
Houston Community College System *Texas*
Indiana University-Purdue University Indianapolis *Indiana*
Kent State University, Salem Campus *Ohio*
Massachusetts College of Pharmacy and Health Sciences *Massachusetts*
Medical College of Georgia *Georgia*
Molloy College *New York*
Old Dominion University *Virginia*
Prince George's Community College *Maryland*
Rochester Institute of Technology *New York*
Saint Louis University *Missouri*
Saint Mary's University of Minnesota *Minnesota*
Salem State College *Massachusetts*
Santa Fe Community College *Florida*
Southeast Technical Institute *South Dakota*
Springfield Technical Community College *Massachusetts*
State University of New York at Buffalo *New York*
Triton College *Illinois*
The University of Alabama at Birmingham *Alabama*
University of Arkansas for Medical Sciences *Arkansas*
University of Cincinnati *Ohio*
The University of Findlay *Ohio*
University of the Incarnate Word *Texas*
The University of Iowa *Iowa*
University of Missouri-Columbia *Missouri*
University of Nebraska Medical Center *Nebraska*
University of Nevada, Las Vegas *Nevada*
University of Oklahoma Health Sciences Center *Oklahoma*
University of Puerto Rico, Medical Sciences Campus *Puerto Rico*
The University of Tennessee *Tennessee*
University of Vermont *Vermont*
Vanderbilt University *Tennessee*
Virginia Commonwealth University *Virginia*
West Virginia State Community and Technical College *West Virginia*
Wheeling Jesuit University *West Virginia*
Worcester State College *Massachusetts*

Liaison Committee on Medical Education/American MedicalLiaison Committee on Medical Education/American Medical Association (LCMEAMA)

Boston University *Massachusetts*
Brown University *Rhode Island*
Case Western Reserve University *Ohio*
Creighton University *Nebraska*
Dalhousie University *Nova Scotia*
Dartmouth College *New Hampshire*
Drexel University *Pennsylvania*
Duke University *North Carolina*
East Carolina University *North Carolina*
East Tennessee State University *Tennessee*
Emory University *Georgia*
Florida State University *Florida*
The George Washington University *District of Columbia*
Georgetown University *District of Columbia*
Harvard University *Massachusetts*
Howard University *District of Columbia*
Indiana University-Purdue University Indianapolis *Indiana*
The Johns Hopkins University *Maryland*
Lakehead University *Ontario*
Laurentian University *Ontario*
Loma Linda University *California*
Louisiana State University Health Sciences Center *Louisiana*
Louisiana State University in Shreveport *Louisiana*
Loyola University Chicago *Illinois*
Marshall University *West Virginia*
McGill University *Quebec*
McMaster University *Ontario*
Medical College of Georgia *Georgia*
Medical University of South Carolina *South Carolina*
Memorial University of Newfoundland *Newfoundland and Labrador*
Mercer University *Georgia*
Michigan State University *Michigan*
New York University *New York*
Northwestern University *Illinois*
The Ohio State University *Ohio*
Oregon Health & Science University *Oregon*
Queen's University at Kingston *Ontario*
Rush University *Illinois*
Saint Louis University *Missouri*
Southern Illinois University Carbondale *Illinois*
Stanford University *California*
State University of New York at Buffalo *New York*
State University of New York Downstate Medical Center *New York*
State University of New York Upstate Medical University *New York*
Stony Brook University, State University of New York *New York*
Temple University *Pennsylvania*
Texas A&M University System Health Science Center *Texas*
Thomas Jefferson University *Pennsylvania*
Tufts University *Massachusetts*
Tulane University *Louisiana*
Universidad Central del Caribe *Puerto Rico*
Université Laval *Quebec*
Université de Montréal *Quebec*
Université de Sherbrooke *Quebec*
The University of Alabama at Birmingham *Alabama*
University of Alberta *Alberta*
The University of Arizona *Arizona*
University of Arkansas for Medical Sciences *Arkansas*
The University of British Columbia *British Columbia*
University of Calgary *Alberta*
University of California, Davis *California*
University of California, Irvine *California*
University of California, Los Angeles *California*
University of California, San Diego *California*
University of Chicago *Illinois*
University of Cincinnati *Ohio*
University of Florida *Florida*

University of Hawaii at Manoa *Hawaii*
University of Illinois at Chicago *Illinois*
The University of Iowa *Iowa*
University of Kansas *Kansas*
University of Kentucky *Kentucky*
University of Louisville *Kentucky*
University of Manitoba *Manitoba*
University of Miami *Florida*
University of Michigan *Michigan*
University of Minnesota, Duluth *Minnesota*
University of Minnesota, Twin Cities Campus *Minnesota*
University of Mississippi Medical Center *Mississippi*
University of Missouri-Columbia *Missouri*
University of Missouri-Kansas City *Missouri*
University of Nebraska Medical Center *Nebraska*
University of Nevada, Reno *Nevada*
University of New Mexico *New Mexico*
The University of North Carolina at Chapel Hill *North Carolina*
University of North Dakota *North Dakota*
University of Oklahoma Health Sciences Center *Oklahoma*
University of Ottawa *Ontario*
University of Pennsylvania *Pennsylvania*
University of Pittsburgh *Pennsylvania*
University of Puerto Rico, Medical Sciences Campus *Puerto Rico*
University of Rochester *New York*
University of Saskatchewan *Saskatchewan*
University of South Alabama *Alabama*
University of South Carolina *South Carolina*
The University of South Dakota *South Dakota*
University of South Florida *Florida*
University of Southern California *California*
The University of Texas Health Science Center at Houston *Texas*
The University of Texas Health Science Center at San Antonio *Texas*
The University of Texas Medical Branch *Texas*
The University of Texas Southwestern Medical Center at Dallas *Texas*
University of Toronto *Ontario*
University of Utah *Utah*
University of Vermont *Vermont*
University of Virginia *Virginia*
University of Washington *Washington*
The University of Western Ontario *Ontario*
University of Wisconsin-Madison *Wisconsin*
Vanderbilt University *Tennessee*
Virginia Commonwealth University *Virginia*
Wake Forest University *North Carolina*
Washington University in St. Louis *Missouri*
Wayne State University *Michigan*
West Virginia University *West Virginia*
Wright State University *Ohio*
Yale University *Connecticut*
Yeshiva University *New York*

Midwifery Education Accreditation CouncilMidwifery Education Accreditation Council (MEAC)

The Florida School of Midwifery *Florida*
Miami Dade College *Florida*
Midwives College of Utah *Utah*
National College of Midwifery *New Mexico*

Montessori Accreditation Council for Teacher EducationMontessori Accreditation Council for Teacher Education (MACTE)

Barry University *Florida*
Brevard Community College *Florida*
Chaminade University of Honolulu *Hawaii*
Chestnut Hill College *Pennsylvania*
Contra Costa College *California*
Fort Valley State University *Georgia*
Indiana University South Bend *Indiana*
Lander University *South Carolina*
New York University *New York*
North Harris College *Texas*
Oklahoma City University *Oklahoma*
Palm Beach Community College *Florida*
Saint Mary's College of California *California*
Three Rivers Community College *Connecticut*
Tidewater Community College *Virginia*
Xavier University *Ohio*

National Accrediting Agency for Clinical LaboratoryNational Accrediting Agency for Clinical Laboratory Sciences (NAACLS)

Alamance Community College *North Carolina*
Alexandria Technical College *Minnesota*
Allegany College of Maryland *Maryland*
Amarillo College *Texas*
Andrews University *Michigan*
Arapahoe Community College *Colorado*
Arizona State University *Arizona*
Arkansas State University *Arkansas*
Arkansas State University-Beebe *Arkansas*
Armstrong Atlantic State University *Georgia*
Asheville-Buncombe Technical Community College *North Carolina*
Auburn University Montgomery *Alabama*
Austin Community College *Texas*
Austin Peay State University *Tennessee*
Baker College of Owosso *Michigan*
Barnes-Jewish College of Nursing and Allied Health *Missouri*
Barton County Community College *Kansas*
Beaufort County Community College *North Carolina*
Bellarmine University *Kentucky*
Bergen Community College *New Jersey*
Bevill State Community College *Alabama*
Bismarck State College *North Dakota*
Bowling Green State University *Ohio*
Brevard Community College *Florida*
Brigham Young University *Utah*
Bristol Community College *Massachusetts*
Broome Community College *New York*
California State University, Dominguez Hills *California*
Camden County College *New Jersey*
Carolinas College of Health Sciences *North Carolina*
Central Community College-Hastings Campus *Nebraska*
Central Georgia Technical College *Georgia*
Central Maine Community College *Maine*
Central New Mexico Community College *New Mexico*
Central Piedmont Community College *North Carolina*
Central Texas College *Texas*
Central Virginia Community College *Virginia*
Chippewa Valley Technical College *Wisconsin*
Cincinnati State Technical and Community College *Ohio*
Clark State Community College *Ohio*
Clinton Community College *New York*
Clover Park Technical College *Washington*
Coastal Carolina Community College *North Carolina*
Coastal Georgia Community College *Georgia*
Columbus State Community College *Ohio*
Community College of Allegheny County *Pennsylvania*
Community College of Philadelphia *Pennsylvania*
Community College of Rhode Island *Rhode Island*
Community College of Southern Nevada *Nevada*
Copiah-Lincoln Community College *Mississippi*
Dalton State College *Georgia*
Darton College *Georgia*
Davidson County Community College *North Carolina*
DeKalb Technical College *Georgia*
Del Mar College *Texas*
Delaware Technical & Community College, Jack F. Owens Campus *Delaware*
Delaware Technical & Community College, Stanton/Wilmington Campus *Delaware*
Delgado Community College *Louisiana*
Des Moines Area Community College *Iowa*
Dutchess Community College *New York*
East Carolina University *North Carolina*
East Tennessee State University *Tennessee*
Eastern Kentucky University *Kentucky*
Eastern Michigan University *Michigan*
El Centro College *Texas*
El Paso Community College *Texas*
Elgin Community College *Illinois*
Erie Community College, North Campus *New York*
Fairmont State Community & Technical College *West Virginia*
Farmingdale State University of New York *New York*
Felician College *New Jersey*
Ferris State University *Michigan*
Fitchburg State College *Massachusetts*
Florence-Darlington Technical College *South Carolina*
Florida Community College at Jacksonville *Florida*
Florida Gulf Coast University *Florida*
Gadsden State Community College *Alabama*
The George Washington University *District of Columbia*
Grand Valley State University *Michigan*
Grayson County College *Texas*
Greenville Technical College *South Carolina*
Halifax Community College *North Carolina*
Harcum College *Pennsylvania*
Harford Community College *Maryland*
Harrisburg Area Community College *Pennsylvania*
Hartnell College *California*
Hawkeye Community College *Iowa*
Hazard Community and Technical College *Kentucky*
Henderson Community College *Kentucky*
Hibbing Community College *Minnesota*
Hinds Community College *Mississippi*
Housatonic Community College *Connecticut*
Houston Community College System *Texas*
Idaho State University *Idaho*
Illinois Central College *Illinois*
Illinois State University *Illinois*
Indian River Community College *Florida*
Indiana University Northwest *Indiana*
Indiana University-Purdue University Indianapolis *Indiana*
Inter American University of Puerto Rico, Metropolitan Campus *Puerto Rico*
Inter American University of Puerto Rico, San Germán Campus *Puerto Rico*
Iowa Central Community College *Iowa*
Ivy Tech Community College-North Central *Indiana*
Ivy Tech Community College-Wabash Valley *Indiana*
J. Sargeant Reynolds Community College *Virginia*
Jackson State Community College *Tennessee*
Jefferson Community College *Ohio*
Jefferson State Community College *Alabama*
John A. Logan College *Illinois*
Kankakee Community College *Illinois*
Kapiolani Community College *Hawaii*
Keiser College (Fort Lauderdale) *Florida*
Kellogg Community College *Michigan*
Kilgore College *Texas*
Lake Area Technical Institute *South Dakota*
Lake City Community College *Florida*
Lake Superior College *Minnesota*
Lakeland Community College *Ohio*
Lamar State College-Orange *Texas*
Lanier Technical College *Georgia*
Lansing Community College *Michigan*
Laredo Community College *Texas*
Lincoln Memorial University *Tennessee*
Loma Linda University *California*
Long Island University, C.W. Post Campus *New York*
Lorain County Community College *Ohio*
Louisiana State University at Alexandria *Louisiana*
Louisiana State University Health Sciences Center *Louisiana*
Madison Area Technical College *Wisconsin*
Manchester Community College *Connecticut*
Marion Technical College *Ohio*
Marist College *New York*
Marquette University *Wisconsin*
Marshall University *West Virginia*
McLennan Community College *Texas*
McNeese State University *Louisiana*
Medical College of Georgia *Georgia*
MedVance Institute *Tennessee*
MedVance Institute *Louisiana*
Mercer County Community College *New Jersey*
Mercy College of Northwest Ohio *Ohio*
Meridian Community College *Mississippi*
Miami Dade College *Florida*
Michigan State University *Michigan*
Mid-Plains Community College *Nebraska*

Middlesex County College *New Jersey*
Midlands Technical College *South Carolina*
Milwaukee Area Technical College *Wisconsin*
Minnesota State Community and Technical College-Fergus Falls *Minnesota*
Minnesota West Community and Technical College *Minnesota*
Mississippi Delta Community College *Mississippi*
Mississippi Gulf Coast Community College *Mississippi*
Mitchell Technical Institute *South Dakota*
Montgomery County Community College *Pennsylvania*
Morgan State University *Maryland*
Mt. San Antonio College *California*
National Park Community College *Arkansas*
Navarro College *Texas*
Neumann College *Pennsylvania*
New Hampshire Community Technical College, Nashua/Claremont *New Hampshire*
New Mexico State University-Alamogordo *New Mexico*
Norfolk State University *Virginia*
North Arkansas College *Arkansas*
North Georgia Technical College *Georgia*
North Hennepin Community College *Minnesota*
Northeast Mississippi Community College *Mississippi*
Northeast State Technical Community College *Tennessee*
Northeast Wisconsin Technical College *Wisconsin*
Northeastern Oklahoma Agricultural and Mechanical College *Oklahoma*
Northeastern University *Massachusetts*
Northern Illinois University *Illinois*
Northern Michigan University *Michigan*
Northern Virginia Community College *Virginia*
Northwest Technical College *Minnesota*
Oakton Community College *Illinois*
Odessa College *Texas*
The Ohio State University *Ohio*
Okefenokee Technical College *Georgia*
Old Dominion University *Virginia*
Orange County Community College *New York*
Orangeburg-Calhoun Technical College *South Carolina*
Oregon Health & Science University *Oregon*
Oregon Institute of Technology *Oregon*
Our Lady of the Lake College *Louisiana*
Pearl River Community College *Mississippi*
The Pennsylvania State University Hazleton Campus of the Commonwealth College *Pennsylvania*
The Pennsylvania State University New Kensington Campus of the Commonwealth College *Pennsylvania*
Phillips Community College of the University of Arkansas *Arkansas*
Pikeville College *Kentucky*
Pontifical Catholic University of Puerto Rico *Puerto Rico*
Portland Community College *Oregon*
Presentation College *South Dakota*
Quinnipiac University *Connecticut*
Reading Area Community College *Pennsylvania*
Rend Lake College *Illinois*
Rose State College *Oklahoma*
Rush University *Illinois*
St. Louis Community College at Forest Park *Missouri*
Saint Louis University *Missouri*
Saint Paul College-A Community & Technical College *Minnesota*
St. Petersburg College *Florida*
St. Philip's College *Texas*
Salisbury University *Maryland*
Salt Lake Community College *Utah*
San Francisco State University *California*
Sandhills Community College *North Carolina*
Seminole State College *Oklahoma*
Seward County Community College *Kansas*
Shawnee Community College *Illinois*
Shawnee State University *Ohio*
Shoreline Community College *Washington*
Somerset Community College *Kentucky*
South Arkansas Community College *Arkansas*
South Central Technical College *Minnesota*
Southeast Community College, Lincoln Campus *Nebraska*
Southeast Kentucky Community and Technical College *Kentucky*
Southeastern Community College *North Carolina*
Southeastern Illinois College *Illinois*
Southern Illinois University Carbondale *Illinois*
Southern Illinois University Edwardsville *Illinois*
Southern University at Shreveport *Louisiana*
Southern West Virginia Community and Technical College *West Virginia*
Southwest Georgia Technical College *Georgia*
Southwest Tennessee Community College *Tennessee*
Southwestern Community College *North Carolina*
Southwestern Illinois College *Illinois*
Spartanburg Technical College *South Carolina*
Springfield Technical Community College *Massachusetts*
Stark State College of Technology *Ohio*
State University of New York at Buffalo *New York*
State University of New York College of Agriculture and Technology at Cobleskill *New York*
State University of New York Upstate Medical University *New York*
Stony Brook University, State University of New York *New York*
Tarleton State University *Texas*
Temple College *Texas*
Tennessee State University *Tennessee*
Texas A&M University-Corpus Christi *Texas*
Texas Southern University *Texas*
Texas Southmost College *Texas*
Texas State University-San Marcos *Texas*
Thomas Jefferson University *Pennsylvania*
Thomas Nelson Community College *Virginia*
Three Rivers Community College *Missouri*
Tri-County Technical College *South Carolina*
Trident Technical College *South Carolina*
Tulsa Community College *Oklahoma*
Tuskegee University *Alabama*
Tyler Junior College *Texas*
The University of Alabama at Birmingham *Alabama*
University of Alaska Anchorage *Alaska*
The University of Arizona *Arizona*
University of Arkansas for Medical Sciences *Arkansas*
University of California, Davis *California*
University of California, Irvine *California*
University of Central Florida *Florida*
University of Cincinnati *Ohio*
University of Connecticut *Connecticut*
University of Delaware *Delaware*
University of Hartford *Connecticut*
University of Hawaii at Manoa *Hawaii*
University of Illinois at Springfield *Illinois*
The University of Iowa *Iowa*
University of Kansas *Kansas*
University of Kentucky *Kentucky*
The University of Maine at Augusta *Maine*
University of Maine at Presque Isle *Maine*
University of Massachusetts Dartmouth *Massachusetts*
University of Massachusetts Lowell *Massachusetts*
University of Minnesota, Twin Cities Campus *Minnesota*
University of Mississippi Medical Center *Mississippi*
University of Nebraska Medical Center *Nebraska*
University of Nevada, Las Vegas *Nevada*
University of New Hampshire *New Hampshire*
University of New Mexico *New Mexico*
University of New Mexico-Gallup *New Mexico*
The University of North Carolina at Chapel Hill *North Carolina*
University of North Dakota *North Dakota*
University of Puerto Rico, Medical Sciences Campus *Puerto Rico*
University of Rio Grande *Ohio*
University of the Sacred Heart *Puerto Rico*
University of South Alabama *Alabama*
University of Southern Mississippi *Mississippi*
The University of Tennessee *Tennessee*
The University of Texas at El Paso *Texas*
The University of Texas Health Science Center at Houston *Texas*
The University of Texas Health Science Center at San Antonio *Texas*
The University of Texas Medical Branch *Texas*
The University of Texas-Pan American *Texas*
The University of Texas Southwestern Medical Center at Dallas *Texas*
University of Utah *Utah*
University of Vermont *Vermont*
University of Washington *Washington*
University of West Florida *Florida*
University of Wisconsin-La Crosse *Wisconsin*
University of Wisconsin-Madison *Wisconsin*
University of Wisconsin-Milwaukee *Wisconsin*
University of Wisconsin-Stevens Point *Wisconsin*
Valdosta Technical College *Georgia*
Vanderbilt University *Tennessee*
Victoria College *Texas*
Villa Julie College *Maryland*
Virginia Commonwealth University *Virginia*
Wake Forest University *North Carolina*
Wake Technical Community College *North Carolina*
Wallace State Community College *Alabama*
Washington State Community College *Ohio*
Wayne State University *Michigan*
Weber State University *Utah*
Wenatchee Valley College *Washington*
West Central Technical College *Georgia*
West Liberty State College *West Virginia*
West Virginia Northern Community College *West Virginia*
West Virginia University *West Virginia*
Western Carolina University *North Carolina*
Western Piedmont Community College *North Carolina*
Western Technical College *Wisconsin*
Wichita Area Technical College *Kansas*
Wichita State University *Kansas*
Winston-Salem State University *North Carolina*
Wright State University *Ohio*
Wytheville Community College *Virginia*
York Technical College *South Carolina*
Youngstown State University *Ohio*
Zane State College *Ohio*

National Association of Industrial TechnologyNational Association of Industrial Technology (NAIT)

Alcorn State University *Mississippi*
Arizona State University at the Polytechnic Campus *Arizona*
Bowling Green State University *Ohio*
Butler County Community College *Pennsylvania*
California Polytechnic State University, San Luis Obispo *California*
California State University, Chico *California*
Central Connecticut State University *Connecticut*
Central Missouri State University *Missouri*
Cleveland State Community College *Tennessee*
College of the Redwoods *California*
Crowder College *Missouri*
Delgado Community College *Louisiana*
East Carolina University *North Carolina*
Eastern Illinois University *Illinois*
Eastern Kentucky University *Kentucky*
Eastern Michigan University *Michigan*
Elaine P. Nunez Community College *Louisiana*
Elizabeth City State University *North Carolina*
Georgia Southern University *Georgia*
Illinois State University *Illinois*
Indiana State University *Indiana*
Iowa State University of Science and Technology *Iowa*
Ivy Tech Community College-Central Indiana *Indiana*
Ivy Tech Community College-Lafayette *Indiana*
Ivy Tech Community College-Northeast *Indiana*
Ivy Tech Community College-Southern Indiana *Indiana*
Ivy Tech Community College-Southwest *Indiana*
Ivy Tech Community College-Wabash Valley *Indiana*
Ivy Tech Community College-Whitewater *Indiana*
Jackson State Community College *Tennessee*
Jackson State University *Mississippi*
Jacksonville State University *Alabama*
Kean University *New Jersey*
Linn State Technical College *Missouri*

Middle Tennessee State University *Tennessee*
Millersville University of Pennsylvania *Pennsylvania*
Minnesota State University Moorhead *Minnesota*
Missouri State University *Missouri*
Moberly Area Community College *Missouri*
Morehead State University *Kentucky*
Norfolk State University *Virginia*
North Carolina Agricultural and Technical State University *North Carolina*
Northeast State Technical Community College *Tennessee*
Northern Illinois University *Illinois*
Northern Michigan University *Michigan*
Ozarks Technical Community College *Missouri*
Purdue University *Indiana*
San Jose State University *California*
Sinclair Community College *Ohio*
Southeast Missouri State University *Missouri*
Southeastern Louisiana University *Louisiana*
Southern Illinois University Carbondale *Illinois*
Southern University at Shreveport *Louisiana*
State Fair Community College *Missouri*
State University of New York at Buffalo *New York*
Tennessee Technological University *Tennessee*
Texas A&M University-Commerce *Texas*
Texas A&M University-Kingsville *Texas*
Texas Southern University *Texas*
University of Arkansas at Pine Bluff *Arkansas*
University of Louisiana at Lafayette *Louisiana*
University of Nebraska at Kearney *Nebraska*
University of North Dakota *North Dakota*
University of Northern Iowa *Iowa*
University of Southern Maine *Maine*
The University of Texas at Tyler *Texas*
University of Wisconsin-Platteville *Wisconsin*
University of Wisconsin-Stout *Wisconsin*
Walters State Community College *Tennessee*
Western Kentucky University *Kentucky*

National Association of Nurse Practitioners inNational Association of Nurse Practitioners in Women's Health (NANPWH)

Emory University *Georgia*
The University of Texas Southwestern Medical Center at Dallas *Texas*

National Association of Schools of ArtNational Association of Schools of Art and Design (NASAD)

Academy of Art University *California*
Alfred University *New York*
Appalachian State University *North Carolina*
Arcadia University *Pennsylvania*
Arizona State University *Arizona*
Arkansas State University *Arkansas*
Art Academy of Cincinnati *Ohio*
Art Center College of Design *California*
The Art Institute of Boston at Lesley University *Massachusetts*
Auburn University *Alabama*
Augusta State University *Georgia*
Austin Peay State University *Tennessee*
Ball State University *Indiana*
Belhaven College *Mississippi*
Biola University *California*
Boise State University *Idaho*
Bowling Green State University *Ohio*
Bradley University *Illinois*
Brigham Young University *Utah*
Bucks County Community College *Pennsylvania*
California College of the Arts *California*
California Institute of the Arts *California*
California Polytechnic State University, San Luis Obispo *California*
California State Polytechnic University, Pomona *California*
California State University, Chico *California*
California State University, East Bay *California*
California State University, Fullerton *California*
California State University, Long Beach *California*
California State University, Los Angeles *California*
California State University, Northridge *California*
California State University, Sacramento *California*
California State University, San Bernardino *California*
California State University, Stanislaus *California*
Carnegie Mellon University *Pennsylvania*
Carson-Newman College *Tennessee*
Casper College *Wyoming*
Central Missouri State University *Missouri*
Clarion University of Pennsylvania *Pennsylvania*
Clemson University *South Carolina*
The Cleveland Institute of Art *Ohio*
Coastal Carolina University *South Carolina*
College for Creative Studies *Michigan*
The College of Saint Rose *New York*
Columbia College *South Carolina*
Columbus College of Art & Design *Ohio*
Columbus State University *Georgia*
Cooper Union for the Advancement of Science and Art *New York*
Corcoran College of Art and Design *District of Columbia*
Cornish College of the Arts *Washington*
Del Mar College *Texas*
Delta State University *Mississippi*
Drake University *Iowa*
Drexel University *Pennsylvania*
East Carolina University *North Carolina*
East Tennessee State University *Tennessee*
Eastern Illinois University *Illinois*
Emporia State University *Kansas*
Fashion Institute of Technology *New York*
Ferris State University *Michigan*
FIDM/The Fashion Institute of Design & Merchandising, Los Angeles Campus *California*
FIDM/The Fashion Institute of Design & Merchandising, Orange County Campus *California*
FIDM/The Fashion Institute of Design & Merchandising, San Francisco Campus *California*
FIDM/The Fashion Institute of Design & Merchandising, San Diego Campus *California*
Florida International University *Florida*
Florida State University *Florida*
Francis Marion University *South Carolina*
Georgia Southern University *Georgia*
Georgia State University *Georgia*
Grand Valley State University *Michigan*
Harrington College of Design *Illinois*
Hartwick College *New York*
Hope College *Michigan*
Howard University *District of Columbia*
Humboldt State University *California*
Illinois State University *Illinois*
Indiana State University *Indiana*
Indiana University Bloomington *Indiana*
Indiana University of Pennsylvania *Pennsylvania*
Indiana University-Purdue University Indianapolis *Indiana*
Institute of American Indian Arts *New Mexico*
Jackson State University *Mississippi*
Jacksonville State University *Alabama*
James Madison University *Virginia*
Kansas City Art Institute *Missouri*
Kansas State University *Kansas*
Kean University *New Jersey*
Kennesaw State University *Georgia*
Kent State University *Ohio*
Kutztown University of Pennsylvania *Pennsylvania*
La Roche College *Pennsylvania*
Laguna College of Art & Design *California*
Lander University *South Carolina*
Lawrence Technological University *Michigan*
Louisiana State University and Agricultural and Mechanical College *Louisiana*
Louisiana Tech University *Louisiana*
Loyola Marymount University *California*
Lyme Academy College of Fine Arts *Connecticut*
Maine College of Art *Maine*
Maryland Institute College of Art *Maryland*
Maryville University of Saint Louis *Missouri*
Marywood University *Pennsylvania*
Massachusetts College of Art *Massachusetts*
Memphis College of Art *Tennessee*
Messiah College *Pennsylvania*
Metropolitan State College of Denver *Colorado*
Miami University *Ohio*
Milwaukee Institute of Art and Design *Wisconsin*
Minneapolis College of Art and Design *Minnesota*
Minnesota State University Mankato *Minnesota*
Minnesota State University Moorhead *Minnesota*
Mississippi State University *Mississippi*
Mississippi University for Women *Mississippi*
Mississippi Valley State University *Mississippi*
Montana State University *Montana*
Montana State University-Billings *Montana*
Montclair State University *New Jersey*
Montserrat College of Art *Massachusetts*
Moore College of Art & Design *Pennsylvania*
Mount Ida College *Massachusetts*
Murray State University *Kentucky*
New Hampshire Institute of Art *New Hampshire*
New Jersey City University *New Jersey*
New World School of the Arts *Florida*
New York School of Interior Design *New York*
Nicholls State University *Louisiana*
North Carolina State University *North Carolina*
North Dakota State University *North Dakota*
Northern Illinois University *Illinois*
Northwestern State University of Louisiana *Louisiana*
The Ohio State University *Ohio*
Ohio University *Ohio*
Old Dominion University *Virginia*
Oregon College of Art & Craft *Oregon*
Otis College of Art and Design *California*
Pacific Northwest College of Art *Oregon*
Parsons The New School for Design *New York*
Pennsylvania College of Art & Design *Pennsylvania*
The Pennsylvania State University University Park Campus *Pennsylvania*
Philadelphia University *Pennsylvania*
Portland State University *Oregon*
Pratt Institute *New York*
Purchase College, State University of New York *New York*
Rhode Island College *Rhode Island*
Rhode Island School of Design *Rhode Island*
Ringling School of Art and Design *Florida*
Roberts Wesleyan College *New York*
Rochester Institute of Technology *New York*
Rocky Mountain College of Art & Design *Colorado*
Rowan University *New Jersey*
Russell Sage College *New York*
Sage College of Albany *New York*
St. Cloud State University *Minnesota*
St. Louis Community College at Florissant Valley *Missouri*
St. Louis Community College at Meramec *Missouri*
Saint Mary's College *Indiana*
Salem State College *Massachusetts*
Salve Regina University *Rhode Island*
San Diego State University *California*
San Francisco Art Institute *California*
San Francisco State University *California*
San Jose State University *California*
School of the Art Institute of Chicago *Illinois*
School of the Museum of Fine Arts, Boston *Massachusetts*
School of Visual Arts *New York*
Siena Heights University *Michigan*
Sinclair Community College *Ohio*
Skidmore College *New York*
Sonoma State University *California*
Southern Illinois University Carbondale *Illinois*
State University of New York at Buffalo *New York*
State University of New York at New Paltz *New York*
Stephen F. Austin State University *Texas*
Suffolk University *Massachusetts*
Syracuse University *New York*
Temple University *Pennsylvania*
Tennessee State University *Tennessee*
Tennessee Technological University *Tennessee*
Texas Tech University *Texas*
Union University *Tennessee*
The University of Akron *Ohio*
The University of Alabama *Alabama*
The University of Alabama at Birmingham *Alabama*
University of Alaska Anchorage *Alaska*
The University of Arizona *Arizona*
University of Arkansas at Little Rock *Arkansas*
University of Arkansas at Pine Bluff *Arkansas*
The University of the Arts *Pennsylvania*
University of Bridgeport *Connecticut*
University of Central Arkansas *Arkansas*

University of Cincinnati *Ohio*
University of Connecticut *Connecticut*
University of Denver *Colorado*
University of Florida *Florida*
University of Georgia *Georgia*
University of Hartford *Connecticut*
University of Idaho *Idaho*
University of Illinois at Chicago *Illinois*
University of Illinois at Urbana-Champaign *Illinois*
University of Kansas *Kansas*
University of Louisiana at Lafayette *Louisiana*
University of Massachusetts Dartmouth *Massachusetts*
University of Massachusetts Lowell *Massachusetts*
University of Memphis *Tennessee*
University of Michigan *Michigan*
University of Mississippi *Mississippi*
The University of Montana-Missoula *Montana*
University of Montevallo *Alabama*
University of Nebraska-Lincoln *Nebraska*
University of Nebraska at Omaha *Nebraska*
University of Nevada, Las Vegas *Nevada*
University of New Orleans *Louisiana*
University of North Alabama *Alabama*
University of North Dakota *North Dakota*
University of Northern Iowa *Iowa*
University of Notre Dame *Indiana*
University of Oregon *Oregon*
University of the Pacific *California*
University of Saint Francis *Indiana*
University of South Alabama *Alabama*
University of South Carolina *South Carolina*
The University of South Dakota *South Dakota*
University of South Florida *Florida*
University of Southern Maine *Maine*
University of Southern Mississippi *Mississippi*
The University of Tennessee *Tennessee*
The University of Tennessee at Chattanooga *Tennessee*
The University of Texas at Austin *Texas*
The University of Texas at San Antonio *Texas*
University of West Georgia *Georgia*
University of Wisconsin-Madison *Wisconsin*
University of Wisconsin-Stevens Point *Wisconsin*
University of Wisconsin-Stout *Wisconsin*
Valdosta State University *Georgia*
Vincennes University *Indiana*
Virginia Commonwealth University *Virginia*
Virginia Polytechnic Institute and State University *Virginia*
Virginia State University *Virginia*
Washburn University *Kansas*
Washington University in St. Louis *Missouri*
Watkins College of Art and Design *Tennessee*
West Virginia University *West Virginia*
Western Kentucky University *Kentucky*
Western Michigan University *Michigan*
Western Washington University *Washington*
Winthrop University *South Carolina*
Youngstown State University *Ohio*

National Association of Schools of DanceNational Association of Schools of Dance (NASD)

Barnard College *New York*
Brigham Young University *Utah*
Butler University *Indiana*
California Institute of the Arts *California*
California State University, Fullerton *California*
California State University, Long Beach *California*
Columbia College *South Carolina*
Florida State University *Florida*
Fordham University *New York*
Hope College *Michigan*
Jacksonville University *Florida*
James Madison University *Virginia*
Kent State University *Ohio*
Loyola Marymount University *California*
Montclair State University *New Jersey*
New World School of the Arts *Florida*
Oakland University *Michigan*
The Ohio State University *Ohio*
Ohio University *Ohio*
Point Park University *Pennsylvania*
Rutgers, The State University of New Jersey, New Brunswick/Piscataway *New Jersey*
St. Olaf College *Minnesota*
San Jose State University *California*
Slippery Rock University of Pennsylvania *Pennsylvania*
Southern Methodist University *Texas*
State University of New York College at Brockport *New York*
Temple University *Pennsylvania*
Texas Woman's University *Texas*
Towson University *Maryland*
The University of Akron *Ohio*
The University of Alabama *Alabama*
The University of Arizona *Arizona*
University of California, Santa Barbara *California*
University of Cincinnati *Ohio*
University of Hartford *Connecticut*
University of Illinois at Urbana-Champaign *Illinois*
University of Minnesota, Twin Cities Campus *Minnesota*
University of New Mexico *New Mexico*
The University of North Carolina at Greensboro *North Carolina*
University of Southern Mississippi *Mississippi*
The University of Texas at Austin *Texas*
University of Wisconsin-Stevens Point *Wisconsin*
Virginia Commonwealth University *Virginia*
Wayne State University *Michigan*
Western Michigan University *Michigan*
Wichita State University *Kansas*
Winthrop University *South Carolina*

National Association of Schools of MusicNational Association of Schools of Music (NASM)

Abilene Christian University *Texas*
Adams State College *Colorado*
Alabama State University *Alabama*
Albion College *Michigan*
Alcorn State University *Mississippi*
Alma College *Michigan*
Alverno College *Wisconsin*
Amarillo College *Texas*
American University *District of Columbia*
Anderson University *South Carolina*
Anderson University *Indiana*
Andrews University *Michigan*
Angelo State University *Texas*
Anna Maria College *Massachusetts*
Appalachian State University *North Carolina*
Arizona State University *Arizona*
Arkansas State University *Arkansas*
Arkansas Tech University *Arkansas*
Armstrong Atlantic State University *Georgia*
Asbury College *Kentucky*
Ashland University *Ohio*
Atlantic Union College *Massachusetts*
Auburn University *Alabama*
Augsburg College *Minnesota*
Augusta State University *Georgia*
Augustana College *South Dakota*
Augustana College *Illinois*
Austin Peay State University *Tennessee*
Baker University *Kansas*
Baldwin-Wallace College *Ohio*
Ball State University *Indiana*
The Baptist College of Florida *Florida*
Baylor University *Texas*
Belhaven College *Mississippi*
Belmont University *Tennessee*
Bemidji State University *Minnesota*
Benedictine College *Kansas*
Berry College *Georgia*
Bethany College *Kansas*
Biola University *California*
Birmingham-Southern College *Alabama*
Black Hills State University *South Dakota*
Bluffton University *Ohio*
Boise State University *Idaho*
The Boston Conservatory *Massachusetts*
Boston University *Massachusetts*
Bowling Green State University *Ohio*
Bradley University *Illinois*
Brevard College *North Carolina*
Brewton-Parker College *Georgia*
Brigham Young University *Utah*
Brigham Young University -Idaho *Idaho*
Broward Community College *Florida*
Bucknell University *Pennsylvania*
Bucks County Community College *Pennsylvania*
Butler University *Indiana*
California Baptist University *California*
California Institute of the Arts *California*
California Polytechnic State University, San Luis Obispo *California*
California State University, Chico *California*
California State University, Dominguez Hills *California*
California State University, East Bay *California*
California State University, Fresno *California*
California State University, Fullerton *California*
California State University, Long Beach *California*
California State University, Los Angeles *California*
California State University, Northridge *California*
California State University, Sacramento *California*
California State University, San Bernardino *California*
California State University, Stanislaus *California*
Calvin College *Michigan*
Cameron University *Oklahoma*
Campbellsville University *Kentucky*
Capital University *Ohio*
Carnegie Mellon University *Pennsylvania*
Carson-Newman College *Tennessee*
Carthage College *Wisconsin*
Case Western Reserve University *Ohio*
Casper College *Wyoming*
The Catholic University of America *District of Columbia*
Centenary College of Louisiana *Louisiana*
Central College *Iowa*
Central Connecticut State University *Connecticut*
Central Methodist University *Missouri*
Central Michigan University *Michigan*
Central Missouri State University *Missouri*
Central State University *Ohio*
Central Washington University *Washington*
Chapman University *California*
Charleston Southern University *South Carolina*
Chicago State University *Illinois*
Chowan University *North Carolina*
Christopher Newport University *Virginia*
Clarion University of Pennsylvania *Pennsylvania*
Clarke College *Iowa*
Cleveland Institute of Music *Ohio*
Cleveland State University *Ohio*
Coe College *Iowa*
Coker College *South Carolina*
The Colburn School Conservatory of Music *California*
College of Charleston *South Carolina*
College of Mount St. Joseph *Ohio*
The College of New Jersey *New Jersey*
College of Saint Benedict *Minnesota*
College of St. Catherine *Minnesota*
The College of Saint Rose *New York*
The College of Wooster *Ohio*
Colorado State University *Colorado*
Colorado State University-Pueblo *Colorado*
Columbia College *South Carolina*
Columbus State University *Georgia*
The Community College of Baltimore County *Maryland*
Concordia College *Minnesota*
Concordia University *Nebraska*
Concordia University *Illinois*
Converse College *South Carolina*
Cornerstone University *Michigan*
Cottey College *Missouri*
Culver-Stockton College *Missouri*
The Curtis Institute of Music *Pennsylvania*
Dallas Baptist University *Texas*
Del Mar College *Texas*
Delta State University *Mississippi*
DePaul University *Illinois*
DePauw University *Indiana*
Drake University *Iowa*
Drury University *Missouri*
Duquesne University *Pennsylvania*
East Carolina University *North Carolina*
East Central University *Oklahoma*
East Tennessee State University *Tennessee*
East Texas Baptist University *Texas*

Eastern Illinois University *Illinois*
Eastern Kentucky University *Kentucky*
Eastern Michigan University *Michigan*
Eastern New Mexico University *New Mexico*
Eastern Washington University *Washington*
Edinboro University of Pennsylvania *Pennsylvania*
Elizabethtown College *Pennsylvania*
Emory University *Georgia*
Emporia State University *Kansas*
Evangel University *Missouri*
Fisk University *Tennessee*
Florida Atlantic University *Florida*
Florida International University *Florida*
Florida State University *Florida*
Fort Hays State University *Kansas*
Fort Lewis College *Colorado*
Friends University *Kansas*
Furman University *South Carolina*
Gardner-Webb University *North Carolina*
George Fox University *Oregon*
George Mason University *Virginia*
The George Washington University *District of Columbia*
Georgia College & State University *Georgia*
Georgia Southern University *Georgia*
Georgia State University *Georgia*
Gordon College *Massachusetts*
Grace College *Indiana*
Grambling State University *Louisiana*
Grand Rapids Community College *Michigan*
Grand Valley State University *Michigan*
Greensboro College *North Carolina*
Gustavus Adolphus College *Minnesota*
Hamline University *Minnesota*
Hampton University *Virginia*
Hardin-Simmons University *Texas*
Harding University *Arkansas*
Hartwick College *New York*
Hastings College *Nebraska*
Heidelberg College *Ohio*
Henderson State University *Arkansas*
Hendrix College *Arkansas*
Hiram College *Ohio*
Holyoke Community College *Massachusetts*
Hope College *Michigan*
Houghton College *New York*
Howard Payne University *Texas*
Howard University *District of Columbia*
Humboldt State University *California*
Huntingdon College *Alabama*
Huntington University *Indiana*
Idaho State University *Idaho*
Illinois Central College *Illinois*
Illinois State University *Illinois*
Illinois Wesleyan University *Illinois*
Immaculata University *Pennsylvania*
Indiana State University *Indiana*
Indiana University Bloomington *Indiana*
Indiana University of Pennsylvania *Pennsylvania*
Indiana University-Purdue University Fort Wayne *Indiana*
Indiana Wesleyan University *Indiana*
Iowa State University of Science and Technology *Iowa*
Ithaca College *New York*
Jackson State University *Mississippi*
Jacksonville State University *Alabama*
Jacksonville University *Florida*
James Madison University *Virginia*
The Johns Hopkins University *Maryland*
Joliet Junior College *Illinois*
Judson College *Alabama*
Kansas State University *Kansas*
Kean University *New Jersey*
Keene State College *New Hampshire*
Kennesaw State University *Georgia*
Kent State University *Ohio*
Kentucky State University *Kentucky*
Kutztown University of Pennsylvania *Pennsylvania*
La Sierra University *California*
Lamar University *Texas*
Lander University *South Carolina*
Lawrence University *Wisconsin*
Lebanon Valley College *Pennsylvania*
Lee University *Tennessee*
Limestone College *South Carolina*
Lincoln University *Missouri*
Linfield College *Oregon*
Lipscomb University *Tennessee*
Longwood University *Virginia*
Louisiana State University and Agricultural and Mechanical College *Louisiana*
Louisiana Tech University *Louisiana*
Loyola Marymount University *California*
Loyola University New Orleans *Louisiana*
Luther College *Iowa*
Lynn University *Florida*
Mansfield University of Pennsylvania *Pennsylvania*
Mars Hill College *North Carolina*
Marshall University *West Virginia*
Marylhurst University *Oregon*
Maryville College *Tennessee*
Maryville University of Saint Louis *Missouri*
Marywood University *Pennsylvania*
McNally Smith College of Music *Minnesota*
McNeese State University *Louisiana*
Mercer University *Georgia*
Mercyhurst College *Pennsylvania*
Meredith College *North Carolina*
Messiah College *Pennsylvania*
Metropolitan State College of Denver *Colorado*
Miami University *Ohio*
Michigan State University *Michigan*
MidAmerica Nazarene University *Kansas*
Middle Tennessee State University *Tennessee*
Midwestern State University *Texas*
Millersville University of Pennsylvania *Pennsylvania*
Millikin University *Illinois*
Minnesota State University Mankato *Minnesota*
Minnesota State University Moorhead *Minnesota*
Minot State University *North Dakota*
Mississippi College *Mississippi*
Mississippi State University *Mississippi*
Mississippi University for Women *Mississippi*
Mississippi Valley State University *Mississippi*
Missouri Baptist University *Missouri*
Missouri State University *Missouri*
Missouri Western State University *Missouri*
Montana State University *Montana*
Montana State University-Billings *Montana*
Montclair State University *New Jersey*
Montgomery College *Maryland*
Moody Bible Institute *Illinois*
Moravian College *Pennsylvania*
Morehead State University *Kentucky*
Morgan State University *Maryland*
Morningside College *Iowa*
Mount St. Mary's College *California*
Mount Union College *Ohio*
Murray State University *Kentucky*
Musicians Institute *California*
Muskingum College *Ohio*
Nassau Community College *New York*
Nazareth College of Rochester *New York*
Nebraska Wesleyan University *Nebraska*
New England Conservatory of Music *Massachusetts*
New Jersey City University *New Jersey*
New Mexico State University *New Mexico*
New Orleans Baptist Theological Seminary *Louisiana*
New World School of the Arts *Florida*
Newberry College *South Carolina*
Nicholls State University *Louisiana*
Norfolk State University *Virginia*
Normandale Community College *Minnesota*
North Carolina Agricultural and Technical State University *North Carolina*
North Dakota State University *North Dakota*
North Park University *Illinois*
Northeastern State University *Oklahoma*
Northern Arizona University *Arizona*
Northern Illinois University *Illinois*
Northern Kentucky University *Kentucky*
Northern Michigan University *Michigan*
Northern State University *South Dakota*
Northwest College *Wyoming*
Northwest Missouri State University *Missouri*
Northwest Nazarene University *Idaho*
Northwestern College *Minnesota*
Northwestern State University of Louisiana *Louisiana*
Northwestern University *Illinois*
Notre Dame de Namur University *California*
Nyack College *New York*
Oakland University *Michigan*
Oberlin College *Ohio*
Odessa College *Texas*
Ohio Northern University *Ohio*
The Ohio State University *Ohio*
Ohio University *Ohio*
Ohio Wesleyan University *Ohio*
Oklahoma Baptist University *Oklahoma*
Oklahoma Christian University *Oklahoma*
Oklahoma City University *Oklahoma*
Oklahoma State University *Oklahoma*
Old Dominion University *Virginia*
Olivet Nazarene University *Illinois*
Oral Roberts University *Oklahoma*
Otterbein College *Ohio*
Ouachita Baptist University *Arkansas*
Pacific Lutheran University *Washington*
Pacific Union College *California*
Pacific University *Oregon*
Palm Beach Atlantic University *Florida*
Peabody Conservatory of Music of The Johns Hopkins University *Maryland*
The Pennsylvania State University University Park Campus *Pennsylvania*
Pepperdine University *California*
Pfeiffer University *North Carolina*
Philadelphia Biblical University *Pennsylvania*
Pittsburg State University *Kansas*
Point Loma Nazarene University *California*
Portland State University *Oregon*
Purchase College, State University of New York *New York*
Queens University of Charlotte *North Carolina*
Quincy University *Illinois*
Radford University *Virginia*
Rhode Island College *Rhode Island*
Rider University *New Jersey*
Roberts Wesleyan College *New York*
Rollins College *Florida*
Roosevelt University *Illinois*
Rowan University *New Jersey*
Rutgers, The State University of New Jersey, New Brunswick/Piscataway *New Jersey*
St. Cloud State University *Minnesota*
Saint John's University *Minnesota*
Saint Mary-of-the-Woods College *Indiana*
Saint Mary's College *Indiana*
St. Mary's University of San Antonio *Texas*
St. Olaf College *Minnesota*
Saint Xavier University *Illinois*
Salem College *North Carolina*
Sam Houston State University *Texas*
Samford University *Alabama*
San Francisco Conservatory of Music *California*
San Francisco State University *California*
San Jose State University *California*
Schenectady County Community College *New York*
Seattle Pacific University *Washington*
Seton Hill University *Pennsylvania*
Shenandoah University *Virginia*
Shepherd University *West Virginia*
Shorter College *Georgia*
Silver Lake College *Wisconsin*
Simpson College *Iowa*
Sinclair Community College *Ohio*
Slippery Rock University of Pennsylvania *Pennsylvania*
Snow College *Utah*
Sonoma State University *California*
South Carolina State University *South Carolina*
South Dakota State University *South Dakota*
South Suburban College *Illinois*
Southeast Missouri State University *Missouri*
Southeastern Louisiana University *Louisiana*
Southeastern Oklahoma State University *Oklahoma*
Southern Adventist University *Tennessee*
Southern Arkansas University-Magnolia *Arkansas*
Southern Baptist Theological Seminary *Kentucky*
Southern Illinois University Carbondale *Illinois*
Southern Illinois University Edwardsville *Illinois*
Southern Methodist University *Texas*
Southern Nazarene University *Oklahoma*
Southern Oregon University *Oregon*

Southern University and Agricultural and Mechanical College *Louisiana*
Southern Utah University *Utah*
Southwest Baptist University *Missouri*
Southwest Minnesota State University *Minnesota*
Southwestern College *Kansas*
Southwestern Oklahoma State University *Oklahoma*
Southwestern University *Texas*
Spelman College *Georgia*
State University of New York at Binghamton *New York*
State University of New York College at Potsdam *New York*
State University of New York, Fredonia *New York*
State University of New York at New Paltz *New York*
State University of New York at Oswego *New York*
Stephen F. Austin State University *Texas*
Stetson University *Florida*
Susquehanna University *Pennsylvania*
Syracuse University *New York*
Tabor College *Kansas*
Tarleton State University *Texas*
Taylor University *Indiana*
Temple University *Pennsylvania*
Tennessee State University *Tennessee*
Tennessee Technological University *Tennessee*
Texas A&M University-Commerce *Texas*
Texas A&M University-Corpus Christi *Texas*
Texas A&M University-Kingsville *Texas*
Texas Christian University *Texas*
Texas State University-San Marcos *Texas*
Texas Tech University *Texas*
Texas Wesleyan University *Texas*
Texas Woman's University *Texas*
Toccoa Falls College *Georgia*
Towson University *Maryland*
Trevecca Nazarene University *Tennessee*
Trinity University *Texas*
Troy University *Alabama*
Truett-McConnell College *Georgia*
Truman State University *Missouri*
Union University *Tennessee*
The University of Akron *Ohio*
The University of Alabama *Alabama*
The University of Alabama at Birmingham *Alabama*
The University of Alabama in Huntsville *Alabama*
University of Alaska Anchorage *Alaska*
University of Alaska Fairbanks *Alaska*
The University of Arizona *Arizona*
University of Arkansas *Arkansas*
University of Arkansas at Little Rock *Arkansas*
University of Arkansas at Monticello *Arkansas*
University of Arkansas at Pine Bluff *Arkansas*
The University of the Arts *Pennsylvania*
University of Central Arkansas *Arkansas*
University of Central Florida *Florida*
University of Central Oklahoma *Oklahoma*
University of Cincinnati *Ohio*
University of Colorado at Boulder *Colorado*
University of Colorado at Denver and Health Sciences Center - Downtown Denver Campus *Colorado*
University of Connecticut *Connecticut*
University of Dayton *Ohio*
University of Delaware *Delaware*
University of Denver *Colorado*
University of Evansville *Indiana*
University of Florida *Florida*
University of Georgia *Georgia*
University of Hartford *Connecticut*
University of Hawaii at Manoa *Hawaii*
University of Houston *Texas*
University of Idaho *Idaho*
University of Illinois at Urbana-Champaign *Illinois*
University of Indianapolis *Indiana*
The University of Iowa *Iowa*
University of Kansas *Kansas*
University of Kentucky *Kentucky*
University of Louisiana at Lafayette *Louisiana*
University of Louisiana at Monroe *Louisiana*
University of Louisville *Kentucky*
University of Maine *Maine*
University of Mary Washington *Virginia*
University of Maryland, College Park *Maryland*
University of Massachusetts Amherst *Massachusetts*
University of Massachusetts Lowell *Massachusetts*
University of Memphis *Tennessee*
University of Miami *Florida*
University of Michigan *Michigan*
University of Michigan-Flint *Michigan*
University of Minnesota, Duluth *Minnesota*
University of Minnesota, Twin Cities Campus *Minnesota*
University of Mississippi *Mississippi*
University of Missouri-Columbia *Missouri*
University of Missouri-Kansas City *Missouri*
University of Missouri-St. Louis *Missouri*
University of Mobile *Alabama*
The University of Montana-Missoula *Montana*
University of Montevallo *Alabama*
University of Nebraska at Kearney *Nebraska*
University of Nebraska-Lincoln *Nebraska*
University of Nebraska at Omaha *Nebraska*
University of Nevada, Las Vegas *Nevada*
University of Nevada, Reno *Nevada*
University of New Hampshire *New Hampshire*
University of New Mexico *New Mexico*
University of New Orleans *Louisiana*
University of North Alabama *Alabama*
The University of North Carolina at Greensboro *North Carolina*
The University of North Carolina at Pembroke *North Carolina*
The University of North Carolina Wilmington *North Carolina*
University of North Dakota *North Dakota*
University of North Florida *Florida*
University of North Texas *Texas*
University of Northern Colorado *Colorado*
University of Northern Iowa *Iowa*
University of Oklahoma *Oklahoma*
University of Oregon *Oregon*
University of the Pacific *California*
University of Portland *Oregon*
University of Puget Sound *Washington*
University of Redlands *California*
University of Rhode Island *Rhode Island*
University of Richmond *Virginia*
University of Rochester *New York*
University of St. Thomas *Minnesota*
University of Science and Arts of Oklahoma *Oklahoma*
University of South Alabama *Alabama*
University of South Carolina *South Carolina*
The University of South Dakota *South Dakota*
University of South Florida *Florida*
University of Southern California *California*
University of Southern Maine *Maine*
University of Southern Mississippi *Mississippi*
The University of Tampa *Florida*
The University of Tennessee *Tennessee*
The University of Tennessee at Chattanooga *Tennessee*
The University of Tennessee at Martin *Tennessee*
The University of Texas at Arlington *Texas*
The University of Texas at Austin *Texas*
The University of Texas at El Paso *Texas*
The University of Texas at San Antonio *Texas*
The University of Toledo *Ohio*
University of Tulsa *Oklahoma*
University of Utah *Utah*
University of Washington *Washington*
University of West Florida *Florida*
University of West Georgia *Georgia*
University of Wisconsin-Eau Claire *Wisconsin*
University of Wisconsin-Green Bay *Wisconsin*
University of Wisconsin-La Crosse *Wisconsin*
University of Wisconsin-Madison *Wisconsin*
University of Wisconsin-Milwaukee *Wisconsin*
University of Wisconsin-Oshkosh *Wisconsin*
University of Wisconsin-Platteville *Wisconsin*
University of Wisconsin-River Falls *Wisconsin*
University of Wisconsin-Stevens Point *Wisconsin*
University of Wisconsin-Superior *Wisconsin*
University of Wisconsin-Whitewater *Wisconsin*
University of Wyoming *Wyoming*
Utah State University *Utah*
Valdosta State University *Georgia*
Valley City State University *North Dakota*
Valparaiso University *Indiana*
Vanderbilt University *Tennessee*
VanderCook College of Music *Illinois*
Virginia Commonwealth University *Virginia*
Virginia State University *Virginia*
Viterbo University *Wisconsin*
Walla Walla College *Washington*
Wartburg College *Iowa*
Washburn University *Kansas*
Washington State University *Washington*
Wayland Baptist University *Texas*
Wayne State University *Michigan*
Weber State University *Utah*
Webster University *Missouri*
Wesleyan College *Georgia*
West Chester University of Pennsylvania *Pennsylvania*
West Liberty State College *West Virginia*
West Texas A&M University *Texas*
West Virginia University *West Virginia*
West Virginia Wesleyan College *West Virginia*
Western Carolina University *North Carolina*
Western Connecticut State University *Connecticut*
Western Illinois University *Illinois*
Western Kentucky University *Kentucky*
Western Michigan University *Michigan*
Western Oregon University *Oregon*
Western State College of Colorado *Colorado*
Western Washington University *Washington*
Westminster Choir College of Rider University *New Jersey*
Westminster College *Pennsylvania*
Wheaton College *Illinois*
Whitworth College *Washington*
Wichita State University *Kansas*
Willamette University *Oregon*
William Carey College *Mississippi*
William Jewell College *Missouri*
William Paterson University of New Jersey *New Jersey*
William Rainey Harper College *Illinois*
Wingate University *North Carolina*
Winona State University *Minnesota*
Winston-Salem State University *North Carolina*
Winthrop University *South Carolina*
Wittenberg University *Ohio*
Wright State University *Ohio*
Xavier University of Louisiana *Louisiana*
Yale University *Connecticut*
Young Harris College *Georgia*
Youngstown State University *Ohio*

National Association of Schools of PublicNational Association of Schools of Public Affairs and Administration (NASPAA)

Albany State University *Georgia*
American University *District of Columbia*
Appalachian State University *North Carolina*
Arizona State University *Arizona*
Arkansas State University *Arkansas*
Auburn University *Alabama*
Auburn University Montgomery *Alabama*
Bernard M. Baruch College of the City University of New York *New York*
Boise State University *Idaho*
Brigham Young University *Utah*
California State University, Bakersfield *California*
California State University, Chico *California*
California State University, Dominguez Hills *California*
California State University, East Bay *California*
California State University, Fresno *California*
California State University, Fullerton *California*
California State University, Long Beach *California*
California State University, Los Angeles *California*
California State University, San Bernardino *California*
California State University, Stanislaus *California*
Carnegie Mellon University *Pennsylvania*
Clark Atlanta University *Georgia*
Cleveland State University *Ohio*
College of Charleston *South Carolina*
DePaul University *Illinois*
East Carolina University *North Carolina*
Eastern Kentucky University *Kentucky*
Eastern Michigan University *Michigan*
Florida Atlantic University *Florida*

Florida International University *Florida*
Florida State University *Florida*
George Mason University *Virginia*
The George Washington University *District of Columbia*
Georgia College & State University *Georgia*
Georgia Southern University *Georgia*
Georgia State University *Georgia*
Governors State University *Illinois*
Grambling State University *Louisiana*
Grand Valley State University *Michigan*
Harvard University *Massachusetts*
Howard University *District of Columbia*
Indiana University Bloomington *Indiana*
Indiana University Northwest *Indiana*
Indiana University-Purdue University Fort Wayne *Indiana*
Indiana University-Purdue University Indianapolis *Indiana*
Indiana University South Bend *Indiana*
Iowa State University of Science and Technology *Iowa*
Jackson State University *Mississippi*
John Jay College of Criminal Justice of the City University of New York *New York*
Kansas State University *Kansas*
Kean University *New Jersey*
Kent State University *Ohio*
Kentucky State University *Kentucky*
Long Island University, Brooklyn Campus *New York*
Long Island University, C.W. Post Campus *New York*
Michigan State University *Michigan*
Mississippi State University *Mississippi*
Missouri State University *Missouri*
New Mexico State University *New Mexico*
New York University *New York*
North Carolina State University *North Carolina*
Northeastern University *Massachusetts*
Northern Illinois University *Illinois*
Oakland University *Michigan*
The Ohio State University *Ohio*
Old Dominion University *Virginia*
The Pennsylvania State University Harrisburg Campus *Pennsylvania*
Portland State University *Oregon*
Rutgers, The State University of New Jersey, Camden *New Jersey*
Rutgers, The State University of New Jersey, Newark *New Jersey*
Saint Louis University *Missouri*
San Diego State University *California*
San Francisco State University *California*
San Jose State University *California*
Savannah State University *Georgia*
Seattle University *Washington*
Seton Hall University *New Jersey*
Southern Illinois University Carbondale *Illinois*
Southern Illinois University Edwardsville *Illinois*
Southern University and Agricultural and Mechanical College *Louisiana*
State University of New York College at Brockport *New York*
Suffolk University *Massachusetts*
Syracuse University *New York*
Tennessee State University *Tennessee*
Texas State University-San Marcos *Texas*
Texas Tech University *Texas*
The University of Akron *Ohio*
The University of Alabama at Birmingham *Alabama*
University at Albany, State University of New York *New York*
The University of Arizona *Arizona*
University of Arkansas at Little Rock *Arkansas*
University of Baltimore *Maryland*
University of Central Florida *Florida*
University of Colorado at Colorado Springs *Colorado*
University of Colorado at Denver and Health Sciences Center - Downtown Denver Campus *Colorado*
University of Connecticut *Connecticut*
University of Delaware *Delaware*
University of Georgia *Georgia*
University of Illinois at Chicago *Illinois*
University of Illinois at Springfield *Illinois*
University of Kansas *Kansas*
University of Kentucky *Kentucky*
University of La Verne *California*
University of Louisville *Kentucky*
University of Maine *Maine*
University of Maryland, Baltimore County *Maryland*
University of Maryland, College Park *Maryland*
University of Memphis *Tennessee*
University of Missouri-Columbia *Missouri*
University of Missouri-Kansas City *Missouri*
University of Missouri-St. Louis *Missouri*
University of Nebraska at Omaha *Nebraska*
University of Nevada, Las Vegas *Nevada*
University of New Mexico *New Mexico*
The University of North Carolina at Chapel Hill *North Carolina*
The University of North Carolina at Charlotte *North Carolina*
The University of North Carolina at Greensboro *North Carolina*
University of North Florida *Florida*
University of North Texas *Texas*
University of Oregon *Oregon*
University of Pittsburgh *Pennsylvania*
University of South Carolina *South Carolina*
The University of South Dakota *South Dakota*
University of South Florida *Florida*
University of Southern California *California*
University of Southern Maine *Maine*
The University of Tennessee *Tennessee*
The University of Tennessee at Chattanooga *Tennessee*
The University of Texas at Arlington *Texas*
The University of Texas at Austin *Texas*
The University of Texas at Dallas *Texas*
The University of Texas at El Paso *Texas*
The University of Toledo *Ohio*
University of Utah *Utah*
University of West Florida *Florida*
University of West Georgia *Georgia*
Valdosta State University *Georgia*
Virginia Commonwealth University *Virginia*
Virginia Polytechnic Institute and State University *Virginia*
Wayne State University *Michigan*
West Virginia University *West Virginia*
Western Michigan University *Michigan*
Wichita State University *Kansas*
Willamette University *Oregon*
Wright State University *Ohio*

National Association of Schools of TheatreNational Association of Schools of Theatre (NAST)

American Academy of Dramatic Arts *New York*
American Academy of Dramatic Arts/Hollywood *California*
Appalachian State University *North Carolina*
Auburn University *Alabama*
Ball State University *Indiana*
Baylor University *Texas*
Boise State University *Idaho*
Bowling Green State University *Ohio*
Bradley University *Illinois*
Brigham Young University *Utah*
Butler University *Indiana*
California Institute of the Arts *California*
California State University, Dominguez Hills *California*
California State University, Fresno *California*
California State University, Fullerton *California*
California State University, Long Beach *California*
California State University, Northridge *California*
California State University, Sacramento *California*
California State University, San Bernardino *California*
California State University, Stanislaus *California*
Casper College *Wyoming*
College of the Holy Cross *Massachusetts*
Columbus State University *Georgia*
The Community College of Baltimore County *Maryland*
Dartmouth College *New Hampshire*
Davis & Elkins College *West Virginia*
Del Mar College *Texas*
Florida International University *Florida*
Florida State University *Florida*
Francis Marion University *South Carolina*
Grambling State University *Louisiana*
Hope College *Michigan*
Howard University *District of Columbia*
Humboldt State University *California*
Illinois State University *Illinois*
Indiana University Bloomington *Indiana*
Indiana University of Pennsylvania *Pennsylvania*
Ithaca College *New York*
Jacksonville State University *Alabama*
James Madison University *Virginia*
Kansas State University *Kansas*
KD Studio *Texas*
Kean University *New Jersey*
Kennesaw State University *Georgia*
Kent State University *Ohio*
Lander University *South Carolina*
Lehigh University *Pennsylvania*
Longwood University *Virginia*
Loyola Marymount University *California*
Loyola University Chicago *Illinois*
Mars Hill College *North Carolina*
Miami University *Ohio*
Missouri State University *Missouri*
Montclair State University *New Jersey*
New World School of the Arts *Florida*
North Carolina Agricultural and Technical State University *North Carolina*
North Carolina Central University *North Carolina*
North Dakota State University *North Dakota*
Northern Illinois University *Illinois*
Northwestern State University of Louisiana *Louisiana*
Northwestern University *Illinois*
Oakland University *Michigan*
The Ohio State University *Ohio*
Ohio University *Ohio*
Oklahoma State University *Oklahoma*
Old Dominion University *Virginia*
Otterbein College *Ohio*
The Pennsylvania State University University Park Campus *Pennsylvania*
Portland State University *Oregon*
Purdue University *Indiana*
Radford University *Virginia*
Rowan University *New Jersey*
St. Cloud State University *Minnesota*
St. Olaf College *Minnesota*
Salem State College *Massachusetts*
San Diego State University *California*
San Francisco State University *California*
San Jose State University *California*
Southern Illinois University Carbondale *Illinois*
Southern Methodist University *Texas*
State University of New York, Fredonia *New York*
State University of New York at New Paltz *New York*
Stephen F. Austin State University *Texas*
Temple University *Pennsylvania*
Texas Tech University *Texas*
Towson University *Maryland*
The University of Alabama *Alabama*
The University of Arizona *Arizona*
University of Arkansas at Little Rock *Arkansas*
University of California, Los Angeles *California*
University of Central Arkansas *Arkansas*
University of Cincinnati *Ohio*
University of Connecticut *Connecticut*
University of Florida *Florida*
University of Georgia *Georgia*
University of Illinois at Urbana-Champaign *Illinois*
University of the Incarnate Word *Texas*
The University of Iowa *Iowa*
University of Louisville *Kentucky*
University of Maryland, College Park *Maryland*
University of Memphis *Tennessee*
University of Minnesota, Twin Cities Campus *Minnesota*
University of Missouri-Kansas City *Missouri*
The University of Montana-Missoula *Montana*
University of Nebraska-Lincoln *Nebraska*
University of Nevada, Las Vegas *Nevada*
University of New Mexico *New Mexico*
University of New Orleans *Louisiana*
The University of North Carolina at Greensboro *North Carolina*

University of North Dakota *North Dakota*
University of Oklahoma *Oklahoma*
University of Pittsburgh *Pennsylvania*
University of Portland *Oregon*
University of South Carolina *South Carolina*
The University of South Dakota *South Dakota*
University of South Florida *Florida*
University of Southern Mississippi *Mississippi*
The University of Texas at Austin *Texas*
The University of Texas-Pan American *Texas*
University of Virginia *Virginia*
University of West Georgia *Georgia*
University of Wisconsin-Madison *Wisconsin*
University of Wisconsin-Stevens Point *Wisconsin*
University of Wisconsin-Whitewater *Wisconsin*
Valdosta State University *Georgia*
Vincennes University *Indiana*
Virginia Commonwealth University *Virginia*
Virginia Polytechnic Institute and State University *Virginia*
Wayne State University *Michigan*
West Virginia University *West Virginia*
Western Michigan University *Michigan*
Winona State University *Minnesota*
Winthrop University *South Carolina*
Youngstown State University *Ohio*

National Commission on Orthotic and ProstheticNational Commission on Orthotic and Prosthetic Education (NCOPE)

California State University, Dominguez Hills *California*
The University of Texas Southwestern Medical Center at Dallas *Texas*
University of Washington *Washington*

National Council for Accreditation of TeacherNational Council for Accreditation of Teacher Education (NCATE)

Adelphi University *New York*
Alabama Agricultural and Mechanical University *Alabama*
Alabama State University *Alabama*
Alaska Pacific University *Alaska*
Albany State University *Georgia*
Alcorn State University *Mississippi*
Alderson-Broaddus College *West Virginia*
Alverno College *Wisconsin*
American University *District of Columbia*
Anderson University *South Carolina*
Anderson University *Indiana*
Andrews University *Michigan*
Appalachian State University *North Carolina*
Arkansas State University *Arkansas*
Arkansas Tech University *Arkansas*
Armstrong Atlantic State University *Georgia*
Asbury College *Kentucky*
Ashland University *Ohio*
Athens State University *Alabama*
Atlanta Christian College *Georgia*
Auburn University *Alabama*
Auburn University Montgomery *Alabama*
Augsburg College *Minnesota*
Augusta State University *Georgia*
Augustana College *South Dakota*
Augustana College *Illinois*
Austin Peay State University *Tennessee*
Azusa Pacific University *California*
Baker University *Kansas*
Baldwin-Wallace College *Ohio*
Ball State University *Indiana*
Barton College *North Carolina*
Baylor University *Texas*
Bellarmine University *Kentucky*
Belmont Abbey College *North Carolina*
Belmont University *Tennessee*
Bemidji State University *Minnesota*
Benedict College *South Carolina*
Benedictine College *Kansas*
Bennett College For Women *North Carolina*
Berea College *Kentucky*
Berry College *Georgia*
Bethany College *West Virginia*
Bethany College *Kansas*
Bethel College *Indiana*
Bethune-Cookman College *Florida*
Birmingham-Southern College *Alabama*
Black Hills State University *South Dakota*
Bloomsburg University of Pennsylvania *Pennsylvania*
Bluefield State College *West Virginia*
Boise State University *Idaho*
Boston College *Massachusetts*
Bowie State University *Maryland*
Bowling Green State University *Ohio*
Bradley University *Illinois*
Brenau University *Georgia*
Bridgewater State College *Massachusetts*
Brigham Young University *Utah*
Brooklyn College of the City University of New York *New York*
Buffalo State College, State University of New York *New York*
Butler University *Indiana*
California Lutheran University *California*
California State University, Bakersfield *California*
California State University, Dominguez Hills *California*
California State University, East Bay *California*
California State University, Fresno *California*
California State University, Fullerton *California*
California State University, Long Beach *California*
California State University, Los Angeles *California*
California State University, Northridge *California*
California State University, San Bernardino *California*
California State University, San Marcos *California*
California State University, Stanislaus *California*
California University of Pennsylvania *Pennsylvania*
Calvin College *Michigan*
Cameron University *Oklahoma*
Campbell University *North Carolina*
Canisius College *New York*
Capital University *Ohio*
Cardinal Stritch University *Wisconsin*
Carson-Newman College *Tennessee*
Catawba College *North Carolina*
The Catholic University of America *District of Columbia*
Central Connecticut State University *Connecticut*
Central Michigan University *Michigan*
Central Missouri State University *Missouri*
Central Washington University *Washington*
Chadron State College *Nebraska*
Charleston Southern University *South Carolina*
Cheyney University of Pennsylvania *Pennsylvania*
Chicago State University *Illinois*
Chowan University *North Carolina*
The Citadel, The Military College of South Carolina *South Carolina*
City College of the City University of New York *New York*
Claflin University *South Carolina*
Clarion University of Pennsylvania *Pennsylvania*
Clark Atlanta University *Georgia*
Clayton State University *Georgia*
Clemson University *South Carolina*
Cleveland State University *Ohio*
Coastal Carolina University *South Carolina*
College of Charleston *South Carolina*
The College of New Jersey *New Jersey*
College of Notre Dame of Maryland *Maryland*
College of Saint Benedict *Minnesota*
The College of Saint Rose *New York*
College of Staten Island of the City University of New York *New York*
The College of William and Mary *Virginia*
Colorado State University *Colorado*
Columbia College *South Carolina*
Columbus State University *Georgia*
Concord University *West Virginia*
Concordia University *Nebraska*
Concordia University *Michigan*
Concordia University *Illinois*
Concordia University, St. Paul *Minnesota*
Coppin State University *Maryland*
Creighton University *Nebraska*
Dakota State University *South Dakota*
Dana College *Nebraska*
Davidson College *North Carolina*
Delaware State University *Delaware*
Delta State University *Mississippi*
DePaul University *Illinois*
DePauw University *Indiana*
Dickinson State University *North Dakota*
Dillard University *Louisiana*
Doane College *Nebraska*
Dowling College *New York*
Drury University *Missouri*
Duke University *North Carolina*
Duquesne University *Pennsylvania*
East Carolina University *North Carolina*
East Central University *Oklahoma*
East Stroudsburg University of Pennsylvania *Pennsylvania*
East Tennessee State University *Tennessee*
Eastern Connecticut State University *Connecticut*
Eastern Illinois University *Illinois*
Eastern Kentucky University *Kentucky*
Eastern Mennonite University *Virginia*
Eastern Michigan University *Michigan*
Eastern New Mexico University *New Mexico*
Eastern Washington University *Washington*
Edgewood College *Wisconsin*
Edinboro University of Pennsylvania *Pennsylvania*
Elizabeth City State University *North Carolina*
Elmhurst College *Illinois*
Elon University *North Carolina*
Emory University *Georgia*
Emporia State University *Kansas*
Evangel University *Missouri*
Fairmont State University *West Virginia*
Fayetteville State University *North Carolina*
Fitchburg State College *Massachusetts*
Five Towns College *New York*
Florida Agricultural and Mechanical University *Florida*
Florida Atlantic University *Florida*
Florida International University *Florida*
Florida Memorial College *Florida*
Florida State University *Florida*
Fontbonne University *Missouri*
Fordham University *New York*
Fort Hays State University *Kansas*
Fort Valley State University *Georgia*
Francis Marion University *South Carolina*
Franklin College *Indiana*
Freed-Hardeman University *Tennessee*
Friends University *Kansas*
Frostburg State University *Maryland*
Furman University *South Carolina*
Gallaudet University *District of Columbia*
Gardner-Webb University *North Carolina*
George Mason University *Virginia*
The George Washington University *District of Columbia*
Georgia College & State University *Georgia*
Georgia Southern University *Georgia*
Georgia Southwestern State University *Georgia*
Georgia State University *Georgia*
Glenville State College *West Virginia*
Gonzaga University *Washington*
Goshen College *Indiana*
Governors State University *Illinois*
Grace College *Indiana*
Graceland University *Iowa*
Grambling State University *Louisiana*
Grand Valley State University *Michigan*
Greensboro College *North Carolina*
Guilford College *North Carolina*
Gustavus Adolphus College *Minnesota*
Hamline University *Minnesota*
Hampton University *Virginia*
Hanover College *Indiana*
Harding University *Arkansas*
Harris-Stowe State University *Missouri*
Hastings College *Nebraska*
Henderson State University *Arkansas*
Hendrix College *Arkansas*
High Point University *North Carolina*
Hofstra University *New York*
Hope College *Michigan*
Howard University *District of Columbia*
Hunter College of the City University of New York *New York*

Huntington University *Indiana*
Idaho State University *Idaho*
Illinois State University *Illinois*
Indiana State University *Indiana*
Indiana University Bloomington *Indiana*
Indiana University East *Indiana*
Indiana University Kokomo *Indiana*
Indiana University Northwest *Indiana*
Indiana University of Pennsylvania *Pennsylvania*
Indiana University-Purdue University Fort Wayne *Indiana*
Indiana University South Bend *Indiana*
Indiana University Southeast *Indiana*
Indiana Wesleyan University *Indiana*
Iona College *New York*
Jackson State University *Mississippi*
Jacksonville State University *Alabama*
James Madison University *Virginia*
John Brown University *Arkansas*
John Carroll University *Ohio*
The Johns Hopkins University *Maryland*
Johnson C. Smith University *North Carolina*
Kansas State University *Kansas*
Kansas Wesleyan University *Kansas*
Kean University *New Jersey*
Keene State College *New Hampshire*
Kennesaw State University *Georgia*
Kent State University *Ohio*
Kentucky State University *Kentucky*
Kutztown University of Pennsylvania *Pennsylvania*
Lander University *South Carolina*
Langston University *Oklahoma*
Lees-McRae College *North Carolina*
Lehman College of the City University of New York *New York*
LeMoyne-Owen College *Tennessee*
Lenoir-Rhyne College *North Carolina*
Lewis University *Illinois*
Liberty University *Virginia*
Lincoln University *Missouri*
Lipscomb University *Tennessee*
Livingstone College *North Carolina*
Lock Haven University of Pennsylvania *Pennsylvania*
Longwood University *Virginia*
Louisiana State University and Agricultural and Mechanical College *Louisiana*
Louisiana State University in Shreveport *Louisiana*
Louisiana Tech University *Louisiana*
Loyola College in Maryland *Maryland*
Loyola Marymount University *California*
Loyola University Chicago *Illinois*
Loyola University New Orleans *Louisiana*
Luther College *Iowa*
Lyon College *Arkansas*
Madonna University *Michigan*
Manchester College *Indiana*
Manhattanville College *New York*
Mansfield University of Pennsylvania *Pennsylvania*
Marian College *Indiana*
Marian College of Fond du Lac *Wisconsin*
Marietta College *Ohio*
Marquette University *Wisconsin*
Mars Hill College *North Carolina*
Marshall University *West Virginia*
Marygrove College *Michigan*
Marymount University *Virginia*
Maryville University of Saint Louis *Missouri*
Marywood University *Pennsylvania*
Mayville State University *North Dakota*
McDaniel College *Maryland*
McMaster University *Ontario*
McNeese State University *Louisiana*
McPherson College *Kansas*
Meredith College *North Carolina*
Methodist College *North Carolina*
Metropolitan State College of Denver *Colorado*
Miami University *Ohio*
Middle Tennessee State University *Tennessee*
Millersville University of Pennsylvania *Pennsylvania*
Milligan College *Tennessee*
Millsaps College *Mississippi*
Minnesota State University Mankato *Minnesota*
Minnesota State University Moorhead *Minnesota*
Minot State University *North Dakota*
Mississippi College *Mississippi*
Mississippi State University *Mississippi*
Mississippi University for Women *Mississippi*
Mississippi Valley State University *Mississippi*
Missouri Southern State University *Missouri*
Missouri State University *Missouri*
Missouri Western State University *Missouri*
Montana State University *Montana*
Montana State University-Billings *Montana*
Montana State University-Northern *Montana*
Montclair State University *New Jersey*
Montreat College *North Carolina*
Morehead State University *Kentucky*
Morgan State University *Maryland*
Morningside College *Iowa*
Mount Saint Mary College *New York*
Murray State University *Kentucky*
National-Louis University *Illinois*
Nebraska Wesleyan University *Nebraska*
New Jersey City University *New Jersey*
New Mexico Highlands University *New Mexico*
New Mexico State University *New Mexico*
New York Institute of Technology *New York*
Newberry College *South Carolina*
Niagara University *New York*
Nicholls State University *Louisiana*
Norfolk State University *Virginia*
North Carolina Agricultural and Technical State University *North Carolina*
North Carolina Central University *North Carolina*
North Carolina State University *North Carolina*
North Carolina Wesleyan College *North Carolina*
North Dakota State University *North Dakota*
North Georgia College & State University *Georgia*
Northeastern Illinois University *Illinois*
Northeastern State University *Oklahoma*
Northern Illinois University *Illinois*
Northern Kentucky University *Kentucky*
Northern Michigan University *Michigan*
Northern State University *South Dakota*
Northwest Missouri State University *Missouri*
Northwest Nazarene University *Idaho*
Northwestern College *Iowa*
Northwestern Oklahoma State University *Oklahoma*
Northwestern State University of Louisiana *Louisiana*
Oakland City University *Indiana*
Oakland University *Michigan*
Oakwood College *Alabama*
Ohio Northern University *Ohio*
The Ohio State University *Ohio*
Ohio University *Ohio*
Oklahoma Baptist University *Oklahoma*
Oklahoma Christian University *Oklahoma*
Oklahoma Panhandle State University *Oklahoma*
Oklahoma State University *Oklahoma*
Oklahoma Wesleyan University *Oklahoma*
Old Dominion University *Virginia*
Olivet Nazarene University *Illinois*
Oral Roberts University *Oklahoma*
Oregon State University *Oregon*
Ottawa University *Kansas*
Otterbein College *Ohio*
Ouachita Baptist University *Arkansas*
Our Lady of Holy Cross College *Louisiana*
Pace University *New York*
Pacific Lutheran University *Washington*
The Pennsylvania State University University Park Campus *Pennsylvania*
Peru State College *Nebraska*
Pfeiffer University *North Carolina*
Philander Smith College *Arkansas*
Pittsburg State University *Kansas*
Plymouth State University *New Hampshire*
Portland State University *Oregon*
Prairie View A&M University *Texas*
Presbyterian College *South Carolina*
Purdue University *Indiana*
Purdue University Calumet *Indiana*
Queens College of the City University of New York *New York*
Queens University of Charlotte *North Carolina*
Radford University *Virginia*
Rhode Island College *Rhode Island*
Rider University *New Jersey*
Roosevelt University *Illinois*
Rowan University *New Jersey*
Russell Sage College *New York*
Saginaw Valley State University *Michigan*
St. Andrews Presbyterian College *North Carolina*
Saint Augustine's College *North Carolina*
St. Bonaventure University *New York*
St. Cloud State University *Minnesota*
St. John Fisher College *New York*
Saint John's University *Minnesota*
Saint Joseph's College *Indiana*
Saint Louis University *Missouri*
Saint Mary-of-the-Woods College *Indiana*
Saint Mary's College *Indiana*
St. Olaf College *Minnesota*
St. Thomas Aquinas College *New York*
Saint Xavier University *Illinois*
Salem College *North Carolina*
Salem State College *Massachusetts*
Salisbury University *Maryland*
Sam Houston State University *Texas*
Samford University *Alabama*
San Diego State University *California*
San Francisco State University *California*
San Jose State University *California*
Seattle Pacific University *Washington*
Seattle University *Washington*
Seton Hall University *New Jersey*
Shaw University *North Carolina*
Shawnee State University *Ohio*
Shepherd University *West Virginia*
Shippensburg University of Pennsylvania *Pennsylvania*
Silver Lake College *Wisconsin*
Slippery Rock University of Pennsylvania *Pennsylvania*
Sonoma State University *California*
South Carolina State University *South Carolina*
South Dakota State University *South Dakota*
Southeast Missouri State University *Missouri*
Southeastern Louisiana University *Louisiana*
Southeastern Oklahoma State University *Oklahoma*
Southern Adventist University *Tennessee*
Southern Arkansas University-Magnolia *Arkansas*
Southern Illinois University Carbondale *Illinois*
Southern Illinois University Edwardsville *Illinois*
Southern Nazarene University *Oklahoma*
Southern University and Agricultural and Mechanical College *Louisiana*
Southern University at New Orleans *Louisiana*
Southern Utah University *Utah*
Southwestern College *Kansas*
Southwestern Oklahoma State University *Oklahoma*
Spalding University *Kentucky*
Spelman College *Georgia*
Spring Arbor University *Michigan*
Stanford University *California*
State University of New York College at Brockport *New York*
State University of New York College at Cortland *New York*
State University of New York College at Geneseo *New York*
State University of New York College at Oneonta *New York*
State University of New York College at Potsdam *New York*
State University of New York, Fredonia *New York*
State University of New York at New Paltz *New York*
State University of New York at Oswego *New York*
Stephen F. Austin State University *Texas*
Stetson University *Florida*
Stillman College *Alabama*
Stony Brook University, State University of New York *New York*
Syracuse University *New York*
Taylor University *Indiana*
Temple University *Pennsylvania*
Tennessee State University *Tennessee*
Tennessee Technological University *Tennessee*
Texas A&M University *Texas*
Texas Tech University *Texas*
Towson University *Maryland*
Transylvania University *Kentucky*
Trinity University *Texas*
Trinity (Washington) University *District of Columbia*
Troy University *Alabama*
Truman State University *Missouri*

National League for NursingNational League for Nursing (NLN)

Gateway Technical College *Wisconsin*
Genesee Community College *New York*
George C. Wallace Community College *Alabama*
George Corley Wallace State Community College *Alabama*
George Mason University *Virginia*
Georgetown University *District of Columbia*
Georgia College & State University *Georgia*
Georgia Highlands College *Georgia*
Georgia Perimeter College *Georgia*
Georgia Southern University *Georgia*
Georgia Southwestern State University *Georgia*
Georgia State University *Georgia*
Germanna Community College *Virginia*
Glendale Community College *Arizona*
Gloucester County College *New Jersey*
Golden West College *California*
Gordon College *Georgia*
Goshen College *Indiana*
Governors State University *Illinois*
Graceland University *Iowa*
Grambling State University *Louisiana*
Grand Canyon University *Arizona*
Grand Rapids Community College *Michigan*
Grays Harbor College *Washington*
Grayson County College *Texas*
Great Basin College *Nevada*
Greenfield Community College *Massachusetts*
Greenville Technical College *South Carolina*
Grossmont College *California*
Gulf Coast Community College *Florida*
Gustavus Adolphus College *Minnesota*
Gwynedd-Mercy College *Pennsylvania*
Hampton University *Virginia*
Hannibal-LaGrange College *Missouri*
Harding University *Arkansas*
Harford Community College *Maryland*
Harrisburg Area Community College *Pennsylvania*
Hartwick College *New York*
Hawaii Community College *Hawaii*
Hawaii Pacific University *Hawaii*
Heartland Community College *Illinois*
Helene Fuld College of Nursing of North General Hospital *New York*
Henderson Community College *Kentucky*
Henderson State University *Arkansas*
Henry Ford Community College *Michigan*
Hesston College *Kansas*
Highline Community College *Washington*
Hillsborough Community College *Florida*
Hinds Community College *Mississippi*
Hocking College *Ohio*
Holmes Community College *Mississippi*
Holy Family University *Pennsylvania*
Holy Names University *California*
Holyoke Community College *Massachusetts*
Hope College *Michigan*
Hopkinsville Community College *Kentucky*
Horry-Georgetown Technical College *South Carolina*
Houston Baptist University *Texas*
Howard College *Texas*
Howard Community College *Maryland*
Howard University *District of Columbia*
Hudson Valley Community College *New York*
Husson College *Maine*
Hutchinson Community College and Area Vocational School *Kansas*
Illinois Central College *Illinois*
Illinois Eastern Community Colleges, Frontier Community College *Illinois*
Illinois Eastern Community Colleges, Lincoln Trail College *Illinois*
Illinois Eastern Community Colleges, Olney Central College *Illinois*
Illinois Eastern Community Colleges, Wabash Valley College *Illinois*
Illinois State University *Illinois*
Illinois Valley Community College *Illinois*
Immaculata University *Pennsylvania*
Indian River Community College *Florida*
Indiana State University *Indiana*
Indiana University Bloomington *Indiana*
Indiana University East *Indiana*
Indiana University Kokomo *Indiana*
Indiana University Northwest *Indiana*
Indiana University-Purdue University Fort Wayne *Indiana*
Indiana University-Purdue University Indianapolis *Indiana*
Indiana University South Bend *Indiana*
Inter American University of Puerto Rico, Metropolitan Campus *Puerto Rico*
Inver Hills Community College *Minnesota*
Iowa Central Community College *Iowa*
Iowa Wesleyan College *Iowa*
Itawamba Community College *Mississippi*
Ivy Tech Community College-Bloomington *Indiana*
Ivy Tech Community College-Central Indiana *Indiana*
Ivy Tech Community College-Lafayette *Indiana*
Ivy Tech Community College-North Central *Indiana*
Ivy Tech Community College-Southwest *Indiana*
Ivy Tech Community College-Whitewater *Indiana*
J. Sargeant Reynolds Community College *Virginia*
Jackson State Community College *Tennessee*
Jacksonville University *Florida*
James A. Rhodes State College *Ohio*
Jamestown College *North Dakota*
Jamestown Community College *New York*
Jefferson College of Health Sciences *Virginia*
Jefferson Community College *New York*
Jefferson Community and Technical College *Kentucky*
Jefferson Davis Community College *Alabama*
Jefferson State Community College *Alabama*
John Tyler Community College *Virginia*
The Johns Hopkins University *Maryland*
Johnson County Community College *Kansas*
Joliet Junior College *Illinois*
Jones County Junior College *Mississippi*
Kansas City Kansas Community College *Kansas*
Kansas Wesleyan University *Kansas*
Kapiolani Community College *Hawaii*
Kaskaskia College *Illinois*
Kauai Community College *Hawaii*
Kean University *New Jersey*
Kennebec Valley Community College *Maine*
Kennesaw State University *Georgia*
Kent State University, Ashtabula Campus *Ohio*
Kent State University, East Liverpool Campus *Ohio*
Kent State University, Tuscarawas Campus *Ohio*
Kentucky State University *Kentucky*
Kettering College of Medical Arts *Ohio*
Keuka College *New York*
Kilgore College *Texas*
Kingsborough Community College of the City University of New York *New York*
Kutztown University of Pennsylvania *Pennsylvania*
La Roche College *Pennsylvania*
La Salle University *Pennsylvania*
Labette Community College *Kansas*
Labouré College *Massachusetts*
LaGrange College *Georgia*
Lake City Community College *Florida*
Lake Land College *Illinois*
Lake Michigan College *Michigan*
Lake Superior State University *Michigan*
Lakeland Community College *Ohio*
Lakeshore Technical College *Wisconsin*
Lakeview College of Nursing *Illinois*
Lamar University *Texas*
Lander University *South Carolina*
Lane Community College *Oregon*
Langston University *Oklahoma*
Lansing Community College *Michigan*
Laramie County Community College *Wyoming*
Laredo Community College *Texas*
Lawson State Community College *Alabama*
Lee College *Texas*
Lehigh Carbon Community College *Pennsylvania*
Lehman College of the City University of New York *New York*
Lenoir-Rhyne College *North Carolina*
Lewis and Clark Community College *Illinois*
Lewis University *Illinois*
Lexington Community College *Kentucky*
Liberty University *Virginia*
Lincoln Land Community College *Illinois*
Lincoln Memorial University *Tennessee*
Lincoln University *Missouri*
Linfield College *Oregon*
Linn-Benton Community College *Oregon*
Lock Haven University of Pennsylvania *Pennsylvania*
Long Beach City College *California*
Long Island College Hospital School of Nursing *New York*
Long Island University, C.W. Post Campus *New York*
Lorain County Community College *Ohio*
Los Angeles Harbor College *California*
Los Angeles Pierce College *California*
Los Angeles Trade-Technical College *California*
Los Angeles Valley College *California*
Louisiana College *Louisiana*
Louisiana State University at Alexandria *Louisiana*
Louisiana State University at Eunice *Louisiana*
Louisiana Tech University *Louisiana*
Lourdes College *Ohio*
Lower Columbia College *Washington*
Loyola University Chicago *Illinois*
Loyola University New Orleans *Louisiana*
Lubbock Christian University *Texas*
Luzerne County Community College *Pennsylvania*
Lynchburg College *Virginia*
Macomb Community College *Michigan*
Macon State College *Georgia*
Madison Area Technical College *Wisconsin*
Madisonville Community College *Kentucky*
Madonna University *Michigan*
Malone College *Ohio*
Manatee Community College *Florida*
Manhattan Area Technical College *Kansas*
Mansfield University of Pennsylvania *Pennsylvania*
Maria College *New York*
Marian College *Indiana*
Marian College of Fond du Lac *Wisconsin*
Marion Technical College *Ohio*
Marquette University *Wisconsin*
Marshall University *West Virginia*
Marymount University *Virginia*
Maryville University of Saint Louis *Missouri*
Marywood University *Pennsylvania*
Massachusetts Bay Community College *Massachusetts*
Massachusetts College of Pharmacy and Health Sciences *Massachusetts*
Massasoit Community College *Massachusetts*
Maui Community College *Hawaii*
McKendree College *Illinois*
McLennan Community College *Texas*
McNeese State University *Louisiana*
Medcenter One College of Nursing *North Dakota*
Medgar Evers College of the City University of New York *New York*
Medical College of Georgia *Georgia*
Medical University of South Carolina *South Carolina*
Mercer County Community College *New Jersey*
Mercy College of Health Sciences *Iowa*
Mercy College of Northwest Ohio *Ohio*
Mercyhurst College *Pennsylvania*
Meridian Community College *Mississippi*
Mesa Community College *Arizona*
Metropolitan Community College *Nebraska*
Metropolitan State College of Denver *Colorado*
Metropolitan State University *Minnesota*
Miami Dade College *Florida*
Miami University *Ohio*
Miami University Hamilton *Ohio*
Miami University-Middletown Campus *Ohio*
Mid-State Technical College *Wisconsin*
MidAmerica Nazarene University *Kansas*
Middle Georgia College *Georgia*
Middle Tennessee State University *Tennessee*
Middlesex Community College *Massachusetts*
Middlesex County College *New Jersey*
Midland College *Texas*
Midland Lutheran College *Nebraska*
Midlands Technical College *South Carolina*
Midway College *Kentucky*
Midwestern State University *Texas*
Miles Community College *Montana*
Millersville University of Pennsylvania *Pennsylvania*
Millikin University *Illinois*
Milwaukee Area Technical College *Wisconsin*
Minneapolis Community and Technical College *Minnesota*

Minnesota State University Mankato *Minnesota*
Minnesota State University Moorhead *Minnesota*
Minnesota West Community and Technical College *Minnesota*
Minot State University *North Dakota*
Mississippi College *Mississippi*
Mississippi Delta Community College *Mississippi*
Mississippi Gulf Coast Community College *Mississippi*
Mississippi University for Women *Mississippi*
Missouri Southern State University *Missouri*
Missouri State University *Missouri*
Missouri Western State University *Missouri*
Mohawk Valley Community College *New York*
Monroe Community College *New York*
Monroe County Community College *Michigan*
Montana State University-Northern *Montana*
Monterey Peninsula College *California*
Montgomery County Community College *Pennsylvania*
Moorpark College *California*
Moraine Park Technical College *Wisconsin*
Moraine Valley Community College *Illinois*
Morehead State University *Kentucky*
Morningside College *Iowa*
Motlow State Community College *Tennessee*
Mott Community College *Michigan*
Mount Aloysius College *Pennsylvania*
Mount Carmel College of Nursing *Ohio*
Mt. Hood Community College *Oregon*
Mount Marty College *South Dakota*
Mount Mary College *Wisconsin*
Mount Wachusett Community College *Massachusetts*
Mountain Empire Community College *Virginia*
Mountain State University *West Virginia*
Murray State College *Oklahoma*
Murray State University *Kentucky*
Nassau Community College *New York*
National Park Community College *Arkansas*
Naugatuck Valley Community College *Connecticut*
Navarro College *Texas*
Nebraska Methodist College *Nebraska*
Nebraska Wesleyan University *Nebraska*
Neosho County Community College *Kansas*
Neumann College *Pennsylvania*
New Hampshire Community Technical College, Manchester/Stratham *New Hampshire*
New Hampshire Community Technical College, Nashua/Claremont *New Hampshire*
New Hampshire Technical Institute *New Hampshire*
New Jersey City University *New Jersey*
New Mexico Junior College *New Mexico*
New Mexico State University-Alamogordo *New Mexico*
New Mexico State University-Carlsbad *New Mexico*
New York City College of Technology of the City University of New York *New York*
New York University *New York*
Niagara County Community College *New York*
Nicholls State University *Louisiana*
Nicolet Area Technical College *Wisconsin*
Norfolk State University *Virginia*
Normandale Community College *Minnesota*
North Arkansas College *Arkansas*
North Carolina Agricultural and Technical State University *North Carolina*
North Carolina Central University *North Carolina*
North Central State College *Ohio*
North Central Texas College *Texas*
North Dakota State College of Science *North Dakota*
North Dakota State University *North Dakota*
North Georgia College & State University *Georgia*
North Harris College *Texas*
North Hennepin Community College *Minnesota*
North Idaho College *Idaho*
North Iowa Area Community College *Iowa*
North Shore Community College *Massachusetts*
Northampton County Area Community College *Pennsylvania*
Northcentral Technical College *Wisconsin*
Northeast Alabama Community College *Alabama*
Northeast Community College *Nebraska*
Northeast Mississippi Community College *Mississippi*
Northeast Wisconsin Technical College *Wisconsin*
Northeastern Oklahoma Agricultural and Mechanical College *Oklahoma*
Northeastern State University *Oklahoma*
Northeastern University *Massachusetts*
Northern Essex Community College *Massachusetts*
Northern Illinois University *Illinois*
Northern Kentucky University *Kentucky*
Northern Maine Community College *Maine*
Northern Oklahoma College *Oklahoma*
Northern Virginia Community College *Virginia*
Northwest College *Wyoming*
Northwest Mississippi Community College *Mississippi*
Northwest-Shoals Community College *Alabama*
Northwest State Community College *Ohio*
Northwestern Oklahoma State University *Oklahoma*
Northwestern State University of Louisiana *Louisiana*
Norwalk Community College *Connecticut*
Norwich University *Vermont*
Oakland Community College *Michigan*
Oakton Community College *Illinois*
Ocean County College *New Jersey*
Odessa College *Texas*
Ohio University *Ohio*
Ohio University-Chillicothe *Ohio*
Ohio University-Zanesville *Ohio*
Ohlone College *California*
Oklahoma Baptist University *Oklahoma*
Oklahoma City Community College *Oklahoma*
Oklahoma City University *Oklahoma*
Oklahoma Panhandle State University *Oklahoma*
Oklahoma State University, Oklahoma City *Oklahoma*
Olympic College *Washington*
Onondaga Community College *New York*
Oral Roberts University *Oklahoma*
Orange County Community College *New York*
Orangeburg-Calhoun Technical College *South Carolina*
Oregon Health & Science University *Oregon*
Otero Junior College *Colorado*
Otterbein College *Ohio*
Our Lady of Holy Cross College *Louisiana*
Our Lady of the Lake College *Louisiana*
Owens Community College *Ohio*
Pacific Lutheran University *Washington*
Pacific Union College *California*
Palm Beach Community College *Florida*
Palomar College *California*
Paris Junior College *Texas*
Park University *Missouri*
Parkland College *Illinois*
Pasadena City College *California*
Pasco-Hernando Community College *Florida*
Passaic County Community College *New Jersey*
Patrick Henry Community College *Virginia*
Paul D. Camp Community College *Virginia*
Pearl River Community College *Mississippi*
Penn Valley Community College *Missouri*
Pennsylvania College of Technology *Pennsylvania*
The Pennsylvania State University University Park Campus *Pennsylvania*
Phillips Beth Israel School of Nursing *New York*
Phillips Community College of the University of Arkansas *Arkansas*
Phoenix College *Arizona*
Piedmont Technical College *South Carolina*
Piedmont Virginia Community College *Virginia*
Pima Community College *Arizona*
Pittsburg State University *Kansas*
Point Loma Nazarene University *California*
Polk Community College *Florida*
Pontifical Catholic University of Puerto Rico *Puerto Rico*
Portland Community College *Oregon*
Prairie State College *Illinois*
Prairie View A&M University *Texas*
Pratt Community College *Kansas*
Presentation College *South Dakota*
Prince George's Community College *Maryland*
Pueblo Community College *Colorado*
Purdue University *Indiana*
Purdue University Calumet *Indiana*
Purdue University North Central *Indiana*
Queensborough Community College of the City University of New York *New York*
Quincy College *Massachusetts*
Quinnipiac University *Connecticut*
Quinsigamond Community College *Massachusetts*
Radford University *Virginia*
Randolph Community College *North Carolina*
Raritan Valley Community College *New Jersey*
Reading Area Community College *Pennsylvania*
Redlands Community College *Oklahoma*
Regis College *Massachusetts*
Regis University *Colorado*
Research College of Nursing *Missouri*
Rhode Island College *Rhode Island*
The Richard Stockton College of New Jersey *New Jersey*
Richland Community College *Illinois*
Ridgewater College *Minnesota*
Riverland Community College *Minnesota*
Riverside Community College District *California*
Rivier College *New Hampshire*
Roane State Community College *Tennessee*
Roberts Wesleyan College *New York*
Rochester Community and Technical College *Minnesota*
Rockford College *Illinois*
Rockhurst University *Missouri*
Rockland Community College *New York*
Rogers State University *Oklahoma*
Rogue Community College *Oregon*
Rose State College *Oklahoma*
Rowan-Cabarrus Community College *North Carolina*
Roxbury Community College *Massachusetts*
Rush University *Illinois*
Russell Sage College *New York*
Rutgers, The State University of New Jersey, Newark *New Jersey*
Sacred Heart University *Connecticut*
Saddleback College *California*
Saginaw Valley State University *Michigan*
Saint Anthony College of Nursing *Illinois*
Saint Charles Community College *Missouri*
Saint Francis Medical Center College of Nursing *Illinois*
St. John's College *Illinois*
Saint John's University *Minnesota*
Saint Joseph College *Connecticut*
St. Joseph's College, New York *New York*
St. Louis Community College at Florissant Valley *Missouri*
St. Louis Community College at Forest Park *Missouri*
St. Louis Community College at Meramec *Missouri*
Saint Louis University *Missouri*
Saint Mary's College *Indiana*
St. Olaf College *Minnesota*
Saint Paul College-A Community & Technical College *Minnesota*
Saint Peter's College *New Jersey*
St. Petersburg College *Florida*
St. Philip's College *Texas*
St. Vincent's College *Connecticut*
Saint Xavier University *Illinois*
Salem State College *Massachusetts*
Salisbury University *Maryland*
Salish Kootenai College *Montana*
Salt Lake Community College *Utah*
Salve Regina University *Rhode Island*
San Antonio College *Texas*
San Bernardino Valley College *California*
San Diego City College *California*
San Francisco State University *California*
San Joaquin Delta College *California*
San Juan College *New Mexico*
Santa Ana College *California*
Santa Barbara City College *California*
Santa Fe Community College *New Mexico*
Santa Fe Community College *Florida*
Santa Monica College *California*
Scottsdale Community College *Arizona*
Seattle Central Community College *Washington*
Seattle University *Washington*
Seminole Community College *Florida*
Seminole State College *Oklahoma*
Seton Hall University *New Jersey*
Seward County Community College *Kansas*

Shawnee State University *Ohio*
Shelton State Community College *Alabama*
Shenandoah University *Virginia*
Shepherd University *West Virginia*
Sheridan College-Sheridan and Gillette *Wyoming*
Shoreline Community College *Washington*
Simmons College *Massachusetts*
Sinclair Community College *Ohio*
Skagit Valley College *Washington*
Slippery Rock University of Pennsylvania *Pennsylvania*
Somerset Community College *Kentucky*
Sonoma State University *California*
South Georgia College *Georgia*
South Plains College *Texas*
South Puget Sound Community College *Washington*
South Suburban College *Illinois*
Southeast Arkansas College *Arkansas*
Southeast Community College, Beatrice Campus *Nebraska*
Southeast Community College, Lincoln Campus *Nebraska*
Southeast Kentucky Community and Technical College *Kentucky*
Southeastern Louisiana University *Louisiana*
Southern Adventist University *Tennessee*
Southern Arkansas University-Magnolia *Arkansas*
Southern Connecticut State University *Connecticut*
Southern Illinois University Edwardsville *Illinois*
Southern Maine Community College *Maine*
Southern State Community College *Ohio*
Southern Union State Community College *Alabama*
Southern University and Agricultural and Mechanical College *Louisiana*
Southern Vermont College *Vermont*
Southern West Virginia Community and Technical College *West Virginia*
Southwest Baptist University *Missouri*
Southwest Mississippi Community College *Mississippi*
Southwest Tennessee Community College *Tennessee*
Southwest Virginia Community College *Virginia*
Southwest Wisconsin Technical College *Wisconsin*
Southwestern Adventist University *Texas*
Southwestern College *Kansas*
Southwestern College *California*
Southwestern Illinois College *Illinois*
Southwestern Oklahoma State University *Oklahoma*
Spalding University *Kentucky*
Spokane Community College *Washington*
Springfield Technical Community College *Massachusetts*
Stark State College of Technology *Ohio*
State University of New York College of Agriculture and Technology at Morrisville *New York*
State University of New York College of Technology at Alfred *New York*
State University of New York College of Technology at Canton *New York*
State University of New York College of Technology at Delhi *New York*
State University of New York Downstate Medical Center *New York*
State University of New York Institute of Technology *New York*
State University of New York at Plattsburgh *New York*
State University of New York Upstate Medical University *New York*
Stephen F. Austin State University *Texas*
Suffolk County Community College *New York*
Sullivan County Community College *New York*
Syracuse University *New York*
Tacoma Community College *Washington*
Tarrant County College District *Texas*
Technical College of the Lowcountry *South Carolina*
Technological College of San Juan *Puerto Rico*
Temple College *Texas*
Tennessee State University *Tennessee*
Tennessee Technological University *Tennessee*
Texarkana College *Texas*
Texas A&M International University *Texas*
Texas Southmost College *Texas*
Texas Woman's University *Texas*
Thomas Edison State College *New Jersey*
Thomas More College *Kentucky*
Thomas Nelson Community College *Virginia*
Three Rivers Community College *Missouri*
Three Rivers Community College *Connecticut*
Tidewater Community College *Virginia*
Tompkins Cortland Community College *New York*
Tri-County Technical College *South Carolina*
Trident Technical College *South Carolina*
Trinity Christian College *Illinois*
Trinity Valley Community College *Texas*
Triton College *Illinois*
Trocaire College *New York*
Troy University *Alabama*
Truckee Meadows Community College *Nevada*
Truman State University *Missouri*
Tulsa Community College *Oklahoma*
Tuskegee University *Alabama*
Ulster County Community College *New York*
Umpqua Community College *Oregon*
Union County College *New Jersey*
Universidad Adventista de las Antillas *Puerto Rico*
Universidad Metropolitana *Puerto Rico*
The University of Akron *Ohio*
The University of Alabama in Huntsville *Alabama*
University of Alaska Anchorage *Alaska*
The University of Arizona *Arizona*
University of Arkansas *Arkansas*
University of Arkansas Community College at Batesville *Arkansas*
University of Arkansas at Fort Smith *Arkansas*
University of Arkansas at Little Rock *Arkansas*
University of Arkansas for Medical Sciences *Arkansas*
University of Arkansas at Monticello *Arkansas*
University of Arkansas at Pine Bluff *Arkansas*
University of California, Los Angeles *California*
University of Central Arkansas *Arkansas*
University of Central Florida *Florida*
University of Central Oklahoma *Oklahoma*
University of Charleston *West Virginia*
University of Cincinnati Raymond Walters College *Ohio*
University of Colorado at Colorado Springs *Colorado*
University of Connecticut *Connecticut*
University of Delaware *Delaware*
University of Detroit Mercy *Michigan*
University of the District of Columbia *District of Columbia*
University of Evansville *Indiana*
University of Guam *Guam*
University of Hartford *Connecticut*
University of Hawaii at Hilo *Hawaii*
University of Hawaii at Manoa *Hawaii*
University of Indianapolis *Indiana*
University of Kentucky *Kentucky*
University of Louisiana at Lafayette *Louisiana*
The University of Maine at Augusta *Maine*
University of Maine at Fort Kent *Maine*
University of Mary *North Dakota*
University of Mary Hardin-Baylor *Texas*
University of Massachusetts Dartmouth *Massachusetts*
University of Memphis *Tennessee*
University of Miami *Florida*
University of Michigan-Flint *Michigan*
University of Minnesota, Twin Cities Campus *Minnesota*
University of Mississippi Medical Center *Mississippi*
University of Mobile *Alabama*
University of Nevada, Las Vegas *Nevada*
University of New England *Maine*
University of New Mexico-Gallup *New Mexico*
University of North Alabama *Alabama*
The University of North Carolina at Chapel Hill *North Carolina*
The University of North Carolina at Greensboro *North Carolina*
The University of North Carolina Wilmington *North Carolina*
University of North Florida *Florida*
University of Northern Colorado *Colorado*
University of Oklahoma Health Sciences Center *Oklahoma*
University of Pennsylvania *Pennsylvania*
University of Phoenix-Atlanta Campus *Georgia*
University of Phoenix-Bay Area Campus *California*
University of Phoenix-Central Florida Campus *Florida*
University of Phoenix-Denver Campus *Colorado*
University of Phoenix-Hawaii Campus *Hawaii*
University of Phoenix-Louisiana Campus *Louisiana*
University of Phoenix-Metro Detroit Campus *Michigan*
University of Phoenix-New Mexico Campus *New Mexico*
University of Phoenix-North Florida Campus *Florida*
University of Phoenix Online Campus *Arizona*
University of Phoenix-Phoenix Campus *Arizona*
University of Phoenix-Sacramento Valley Campus *California*
University of Phoenix-San Diego Campus *California*
University of Phoenix-South Florida Campus *Florida*
University of Phoenix-Southern Arizona Campus *Arizona*
University of Phoenix-Southern California Campus *California*
University of Phoenix-Southern Colorado Campus *Colorado*
University of Phoenix-Utah Campus *Utah*
University of Phoenix-West Florida Campus *Florida*
University of Phoenix-West Michigan Campus *Michigan*
University of Pittsburgh at Bradford *Pennsylvania*
University of Portland *Oregon*
University of Puerto Rico at Arecibo *Puerto Rico*
University of Puerto Rico at Humacao *Puerto Rico*
University of Puerto Rico, Mayagüez Campus *Puerto Rico*
University of Puerto Rico, Medical Sciences Campus *Puerto Rico*
University of Rio Grande *Ohio*
University of Rochester *New York*
University of the Sacred Heart *Puerto Rico*
University of Saint Francis *Indiana*
University of St. Francis *Illinois*
University of San Francisco *California*
University of South Carolina Aiken *South Carolina*
University of South Carolina Lancaster *South Carolina*
University of South Carolina Upstate *South Carolina*
The University of South Dakota *South Dakota*
University of South Florida *Florida*
University of Southern Maine *Maine*
University of Southern Mississippi *Mississippi*
The University of Tampa *Florida*
The University of Tennessee *Tennessee*
The University of Tennessee at Martin *Tennessee*
The University of Texas at Arlington *Texas*
The University of Texas at Brownsville *Texas*
The University of Texas Health Science Center at Houston *Texas*
The University of Texas Medical Branch *Texas*
The University of Texas at Tyler *Texas*
The University of Toledo *Ohio*
University of Tulsa *Oklahoma*
University of Vermont *Vermont*
University of the Virgin Islands *United States Virgin Islands*
University of Virginia *Virginia*
University of Washington *Washington*
The University of West Alabama *Alabama*
University of West Florida *Florida*
University of West Georgia *Georgia*
University of Wisconsin-Green Bay *Wisconsin*
Utah Valley State College *Utah*
Utica College *New York*
Valdosta State University *Georgia*
Valencia Community College *Florida*
Vanderbilt University *Tennessee*
Vermont Technical College *Vermont*
Victoria College *Texas*
Villa Julie College *Maryland*
Villanova University *Pennsylvania*
Vincennes University *Indiana*
Virginia Commonwealth University *Virginia*
Virginia Highlands Community College *Virginia*
Virginia Western Community College *Virginia*
Wagner College *New York*
Walla Walla College *Washington*
Walla Walla Community College *Washington*
Wallace State Community College *Alabama*

Walsh University *Ohio*
Walters State Community College *Tennessee*
Washington State University *Washington*
Washtenaw Community College *Michigan*
Waukesha County Technical College *Wisconsin*
Wayne State University *Michigan*
Waynesburg College *Pennsylvania*
Weber State University *Utah*
Webster University *Missouri*
Wenatchee Valley College *Washington*
Wesley College *Delaware*
West Chester University of Pennsylvania *Pennsylvania*
West Kentucky Community and Technical College *Kentucky*
West Liberty State College *West Virginia*
West Suburban College of Nursing *Illinois*
West Virginia Northern Community College *West Virginia*
West Virginia University at Parkersburg *West Virginia*
West Virginia Wesleyan College *West Virginia*
Western Connecticut State University *Connecticut*
Western Iowa Tech Community College *Iowa*
Western Kentucky University *Kentucky*
Western Michigan University *Michigan*
Western Nevada Community College *Nevada*
Western New Mexico University *New Mexico*
Western Oklahoma State College *Oklahoma*
Western Piedmont Community College *North Carolina*
Western Technical College *Wisconsin*
Western Wyoming Community College *Wyoming*
Whitworth College *Washington*
Widener University *Pennsylvania*
William Carey College *Mississippi*
William Rainey Harper College *Illinois*
Wilmington College *Delaware*
Winona State University *Minnesota*
Winston-Salem State University *North Carolina*
Wisconsin Indianhead Technical College *Wisconsin*
Worcester State College *Massachusetts*
Wright State University *Ohio*
Wytheville Community College *Virginia*
Yakima Valley Community College *Washington*
Yale University *Connecticut*
Yavapai College *Arizona*
York College of the City University of New York *New York*
York College of Pennsylvania *Pennsylvania*
York Technical College *South Carolina*
Youngstown State University *Ohio*

National Recreation and Park AssociationNational Recreation and Park Association (NRPA)

Appalachian State University *North Carolina*
Arizona State University *Arizona*
Arizona State University West *Arizona*
Arkansas Tech University *Arkansas*
Aurora University *Illinois*
Bowling Green State University *Ohio*
Brigham Young University *Utah*
California Polytechnic State University, San Luis Obispo *California*
California State University, Chico *California*
California State University, Fresno *California*
California State University, Long Beach *California*
California State University, Northridge *California*
California State University, Sacramento *California*
Central Michigan University *Michigan*
Clemson University *South Carolina*
Colorado State University *Colorado*
East Carolina University *North Carolina*
East Stroudsburg University of Pennsylvania *Pennsylvania*
Eastern Illinois University *Illinois*
Eastern Kentucky University *Kentucky*
Eastern Michigan University *Michigan*
Eastern Washington University *Washington*
Ferris State University *Michigan*
Ferrum College *Virginia*
Florida International University *Florida*
Florida State University *Florida*
Frostburg State University *Maryland*
Gallaudet University *District of Columbia*
Georgia Southern University *Georgia*
Grambling State University *Louisiana*
Green Mountain College *Vermont*
Illinois State University *Illinois*
Indiana State University *Indiana*
Indiana University Bloomington *Indiana*
Ithaca College *New York*
Kansas State University *Kansas*
Kent State University *Ohio*
Lincoln University *Pennsylvania*
Longwood University *Virginia*
Lyndon State College *Vermont*
Marshall University *West Virginia*
Metropolitan State College of Denver *Colorado*
Michigan State University *Michigan*
Middle Tennessee State University *Tennessee*
Minnesota State University Mankato *Minnesota*
Missouri State University *Missouri*
Montclair State University *New Jersey*
North Carolina Central University *North Carolina*
North Carolina State University *North Carolina*
Northern Arizona University *Arizona*
Ohio University *Ohio*
Oklahoma State University *Oklahoma*
Old Dominion University *Virginia*
Radford University *Virginia*
San Diego State University *California*
San Francisco State University *California*
San Jose State University *California*
Slippery Rock University of Pennsylvania *Pennsylvania*
Southeast Missouri State University *Missouri*
Southern Illinois University Carbondale *Illinois*
Springfield College *Massachusetts*
State University of New York College at Brockport *New York*
State University of New York College at Cortland *New York*
Temple University *Pennsylvania*
Texas A&M University *Texas*
Texas State University-San Marcos *Texas*
University of Arkansas *Arkansas*
University of Florida *Florida*
University of Georgia *Georgia*
University of Idaho *Idaho*
University of Illinois at Urbana-Champaign *Illinois*
The University of Iowa *Iowa*
University of Maine at Machias *Maine*
University of Maine at Presque Isle *Maine*
University of Minnesota, Twin Cities Campus *Minnesota*
University of Mississippi *Mississippi*
University of Missouri-Columbia *Missouri*
The University of Montana-Missoula *Montana*
University of New Hampshire *New Hampshire*
The University of North Carolina at Chapel Hill *North Carolina*
The University of North Carolina at Greensboro *North Carolina*
The University of North Carolina Wilmington *North Carolina*
University of North Texas *Texas*
University of Northern Iowa *Iowa*
University of Ottawa *Ontario*
University of St. Francis *Illinois*
University of Southern Mississippi *Mississippi*
The University of Tennessee *Tennessee*
The University of Toledo *Ohio*
University of Utah *Utah*
University of Wisconsin-La Crosse *Wisconsin*
Utah State University *Utah*
Virginia Commonwealth University *Virginia*
Virginia Wesleyan College *Virginia*
West Virginia State University *West Virginia*
West Virginia University *West Virginia*
Western Illinois University *Illinois*
Western Kentucky University *Kentucky*
Western Washington University *Washington*
Winston-Salem State University *North Carolina*
York College of Pennsylvania *Pennsylvania*

New York State Board of RegentsNew York State Board of Regents (NYSBR)

American Academy of Dramatic Arts *New York*
Bramson ORT College *New York*
Bryant and Stratton College (Albany) *New York*
Bryant and Stratton College, Amherst Campus *New York*
Bryant and Stratton College, Buffalo Campus *New York*
Bryant and Stratton College, Lackawanna Campus *New York*
Bryant and Stratton College, North Campus *New York*
Bryant and Stratton College (Rochester-Greece Campus) *New York*
Bryant and Stratton College (Rochester-Henrietta Campus) *New York*
Bryant and Stratton College (Syracuse) *New York*
Cochran School of Nursing *New York*
Crouse Hospital School of Nursing *New York*
Dorothea Hopfer School of Nursing at The Mount Vernon Hospital *New York*
Ellis Hospital School of Nursing *New York*
Gamla College *New York*
Globe Institute of Technology *New York*
Holy Trinity Orthodox Seminary *New York*
Institute of Design and Construction *New York*
Interboro Institute *New York*
The King's College *New York*
Memorial Hospital School of Nursing *New York*
New York Career Institute *New York*
TCI-The College of Technology *New York*
Utica School of Commerce *New York*
Wood Tobe-Coburn School *New York*

Northwest Commission on Colleges and UniversitiesNorthwest Commission on Colleges and Universities (NCCU)

Alaska Pacific University *Alaska*
Albertson College of Idaho *Idaho*
The Art Institute of Portland *Oregon*
The Art Institute of Seattle *Washington*
Bastyr University *Washington*
Bates Technical College *Washington*
Bellevue Community College *Washington*
Bellingham Technical College *Washington*
Big Bend Community College *Washington*
Blackfeet Community College *Montana*
Blue Mountain Community College *Oregon*
Boise State University *Idaho*
Brigham Young University *Utah*
Brigham Young University -Idaho *Idaho*
Carroll College *Montana*
Cascadia Community College *Washington*
Central Oregon Community College *Oregon*
Central Washington University *Washington*
Centralia College *Washington*
Chemeketa Community College *Oregon*
Chief Dull Knife College *Montana*
City University *Washington*
Clackamas Community College *Oregon*
Clark College *Washington*
Clatsop Community College *Oregon*
Clover Park Technical College *Washington*
College of Eastern Utah *Utah*
College of Southern Idaho *Idaho*
Columbia Basin College *Washington*
Columbia Gorge Community College *Oregon*
Community College of Southern Nevada *Nevada*
Concordia University *Oregon*
Corban College *Oregon*
Cornish College of the Arts *Washington*
Dawson Community College *Montana*
Dixie State College of Utah *Utah*
Eastern Idaho Technical College *Idaho*
Eastern Oregon University *Oregon*
Eastern Washington University *Washington*
Edmonds Community College *Washington*
Everett Community College *Washington*
The Evergreen State College *Washington*
Flathead Valley Community College *Montana*
Fort Belknap College *Montana*
Fort Peck Community College *Montana*
George Fox University *Oregon*
Gonzaga University *Washington*
Grays Harbor College *Washington*
Great Basin College *Nevada*
Green River Community College *Washington*
Henry Cogswell College *Washington*
Heritage University *Washington*
Highline Community College *Washington*

Society of American ForestersSociety of American Foresters (SAF)

Teacher Education Accreditation CouncilTeacher Education Accreditation Council (TEAC)

Transnational Association of Christian Colleges andTransnational Association of Christian Colleges and Schools (TACCS)

Index of U.S. Colleges

Index of Canadian Colleges